SECOND EDITION

Infectious Diseases

Infectious Diseases
SECOND EDITION

Jonathan Cohen MB BS FRCP FRCPath FRCPE FMedSci
Professor of Infectious Diseases
Dean, Brighton & Sussex Medical School
University of Brighton, Falmer, UK

William G Powderly MD FRCPI
Professor of Medicine;
Director, Division of Infectious Diseases
Washington University School of Medicine
St. Louis, MO, USA

Seth F Berkley MD
President and CEO
International AIDS Vaccine Initiative
New York, NY, USA

Thierry Calandra MD PhD
Assistant Professor, Division of Infectious Diseases,
Department of Internal Medicine, CHUV
Lausanne, Switzerland

Nathan Clumeck MD
Professor of Medicine and Infectious Diseases,
Department of Infectious Diseases and Internal
Medicine
St Pierre University Hospital
Brussels, Belgium

Roger G Finch MB BS FRCP FRCPath FRCPEd FFPM
Professor of Infectious Diseases
Department of Microbiology and Infectious Diseases
Nottingham City Hospital
Nottingham, UK

Scott M Hammer MD
Chief, Division of Infectious Diseases
Department of Medicine
Columbia Presbyterian Medical Center
New York, NY, USA

Steven M Holland MD
Head, Immunopathogenesis Unit
Clinical Pathophysiology Section
Laboratory of Host Defenses
National Institute of Allergy and Infectious Disease
Bethesda, MD, USA

Timothy E Kiehn PhD
Chief, Microbiology Service
Department of Clinical Laboratories
Memorial Sloan-Kettering Cancer Center
New York, NY, USA

Keith PWJ McAdam MD FRCP
Wellcome Professor of Clinical Tropical Medicine
London School of Hygiene and Tropical Medicine
London, UK

Dennis G Maki MD
Professor of Medicine
Head, Section of Infectious Diseases
Attending Physician, Center for Trauma and Life
Support
Department of Infectious Diseases/Medicine
University of Wisconsin Hospital and Clinics
Madison, WI, USA

S Ragnar Norrby MD PhD FRCP (Edin)
Professor and Director General
The Swedish Institute for Infectious Disease Control
Solna, Sweden

Steven M Opal MD
Professor of Medicine,
Brown University School of Medicine
Infectious Disease Division
Memorial Hospital of Rhode Island
Pawtucket, RI, USA

Allan R Ronald MD FRCPC FACP
Distinguished Professor Emeritus
University of Manitoba;
Visiting Professor
Makerere University;
University of Manitoba
Winnipeg, MB, Canada

Claus O Solberg MD
Professor of Medicine and Infectious Diseases;
Chairman Medical Department Bergen
University Hospital
Haukeland Hospital
Bergen, Norway

Jan Verhoef MD PhD
Professor of Medical Microbiology
Eijkman-Winkler Institute for Microbiology
Infectious Diseases and Inflammation
Utrecht, The Netherlands

Mosby

Edinburgh London New York Oxford Philadelphia St Louis Sydney Toronto 2004

Mosby
An affiliate of Elsevier Limited

First published 1999
Second edition 2004

ISBN 0323024076 (Main edition)

ISBN 0323026079 **edition**

British Library Cataloguing in Publication Data
A catalogue record for this book is available from the British Library

Library of Congress Cataloging in Publication Data
A catalog record for this book is available from the Library of Congress

Notice
Medical knowledge is constantly changing. Standard safety precautions must be followed, but as new research and clinical experience broaden our knowledge, changes in treatment and drug therapy may become necessary or appropriate. Readers are advised to check the most current product information provided by the manufacturer of each drug to be administered to verify the recommended dose, the method and duration of administration, and contraindications. It is the responsibility of the practitioner, relying on experience and knowledge of the patient, to determine dosages and the best treatment for each individual patient. Neither the Publisher nor the editors nor contributors assume any liability for any injury and/or damage to persons or property arising from this publication.
The Publisher

Printed in Spain

The publisher's policy is to use **paper manufactured from sustainable forests**

Cover image: Immunofluorescent LM of active macrophages
© NANCY KEDERSHA/SCIENCE PHOTO LIBRARY

Commissioning Editor: Tom Hartman
Project Development Manager: Shuet-Kei Cheung
Project Manager: Susan Skinner
Illustration Manager: Mick Ruddy
Design Manager: Jayne Jones
Illustrators: Robin Dean, Richard Prime

Preface

When we sat down five years ago to plan the first edition of *Infectious Diseases* we were determined to make it make it innovative, comprehensive and accessible. It is very gratifying to record that the responses we have had from colleagues all over the world suggest that, in large part, we succeeded in those aims. Many of the ideas that we introduced have proved popular with our readers, in particular the use of full-color illustrations, the down-loadable slide picture library, the Practice Points feature of common but difficult problems, and the international scope of both the content and the authorship. It was this success, as well as the breathtaking speed with which new developments in infectious diseases were occurring, that persuaded us that a second edition could no longer be delayed.

In putting together this second edition we have looked rigorously at all parts of the book, re-structuring where necessary, adding and updating material and inviting new editors to strengthen the team. The emergence of unsuspected clinical syndromes (West Nile fever in the USA is just one example), and unwanted challenges for infectious diseases physicians (sadly, the spectre of bioterrorism has found its way on to these pages) has resulted in new chapters and new authors. But we were also keen to continue the innovative approach that we took for the first edition, and have added a substantial new element to the book, the *Infectious Diseases* website. Although this existed in a rudimentary form before, for this second edition Steven Opal has taken the lead in creating an extraordinary resource of material that will complement the book.

No project of this size and complexity can be undertaken without the help of a very large number of people. Section editors and authors have worked against a very challenging timetable to ensure that the book is as up-to-date as possible. We are also indebted to the publishers, and in particular to Shuet-Kei Cheung, who was in at the beginning of the project and worked tirelessly to see it through to production, and also to Deborah Russell and Jill Day for their contributions.

A final word of thanks must go to the Section Editors who worked on the first edition: Claude Carbon, David Durack, Don Louria, Bruce Polsky and Paul Quie, and to Donald Armstrong, whose vision contributed so much. Without their input we would never have had the opportunity to work on this second edition. We are greatly indebted to them.

Jonathan Cohen
William G Powderly

User Guide

Volumes, Sections and Color Coding

Infectious Diseases is divided into two volumes. The book is divided into eight sections, which are color-coded as follows for reference:

Volume 1

Section 1	– Introduction to Infectious Diseases
Section 2	– Syndromes by Body System
Section 3	– Special Problems in Infectious Disease Practice
Section 4	– Infections in the Immunocompromised Host

Volume 2

Section 5	– HIV and AIDS
Section 6	– Geographic and Travel Medicine
Section 7	– Anti-Infective Therapy
Section 8	– Clinical Microbiology

Practice Points

Practice Points are grouped together into Practice Point chapters. To find a Practice Point find the chapter in which it appears and turn to the first page. On this page you will find a mini-contents list for that chapter which will give you the exact page number on which the Practice Point appears. Practice Points are picked out in bold in the Contents list.

Contents

Section 3: Special Problems in Infectious Disease Practice

Jonathan Cohen, Steven M Opal

Section 4: Infections in the Immunocompromised Host

Thierry Calandra, Steven M Holland

INTRODUCTION

Volume 2

Section 5: HIV and AIDS

Nathan Clumeck, William G Powderly

PREVENTION

PATHOGENESIS

CLINICAL PRESENTATION

Section 7: Anti-Infective Therapy

Scott M Hammer, S Ragnar Norrby

Section 8: Clinical Microbiology

Timothy E Kiehn, Jan Verhoef

VIRUSES

PRIONS

BACTERIA

FUNGI

PARASITES

Contributors

Michael Adler CBE MD FRCP FFPHM
Professor of Genitourinary Medicine
Department of STDs
Royal Free and University College Medical School
London, UK

Kjell Alestig MD PhD
Professor of Infectious Diseases
Department of Infectious Diseases
Sahlgrenska University Hospital
Goteburg, Sweden

Upton Allen MBBS MS FAAP FRCPC
Associate Professor
Consultant in Infectious Diseases
Division of Infectious Diseases
Hospital for Sick Children
Toronto, ON, Canada

Gunnar I Andriesse PhD MD
Resident in Microbiology
Eijkman-Winkler Institute for Microbiology, Infectious Diseases amd Inflammation
Utrecht, The Netherlands

Wendy Armstrong MD
Associate Staff
Department of Infectious Diseases
Cleveland Clinic Foundation
Cleveland, OH, USA

Andrew W Artenstein MD FACP
Director, Center for Biodefense and Emerging Pathogens
Associate Professor of Medicine
Brown Medical School
Division of Infectious Diseases
Center for Biodefense and Emerging Pathogens
Pawtucket, RI, USA

Om P Arya MD
Emeritus Consultant Physician and Senior Research Fellow
Department of Medical Microbiology
And Genitourinary Medicine
University of Liverpool
Liverpool, UK

Edwin J Asturias MD
Research Scientist
Center for Health Studies
John Hopkins University School of Public Health
Guatemala City, Guatemala

John C Atherton MRCP
Professor of Gastroenterology
MRC Senior Clinical Fellow
Division of Gastroenterology and Institute of Infection, Immunity and Inflammation
University of Nottingham
Nottingham, UK

Hilary Babcock MD
Instructor of Medicine
Washington University School of Medicine
St Louis, MO, USA

Robin Bailey BA BM DTMH PhD FRCP
Reader in Tropical Medicine,
London School Hygiene and Tropical Medicine;
Senior Clinical Scientist,
MRC Laboratories
Banjul, The Gambia

Guy Baily MD FRCP
Consultant Physician
Department of Infection and Immunity
Barts and The London NHS Trust
London, UK

David R Baldwin MD FRCP
Consultant Respiratory Physician
Respiratory Medicine Unit
David Evans Centre
Nottingham City Hospital
Nottingham, UK

Chris Bandel MD
Research Fellow
Department of Dermatology
University of Texas Southwestern Medical School
Dallas, TX, USA

Barbara A Bannister MSc FRCP
Consultant in Infectious and Tropical Diseases
Department of Infectious and Tropical Diseases
Royal Free Hospital
London, UK

Philip S Barie MD MBA FCCM FACS
Director, Surgical Intensive Care Unit
The New York Hospital;
Associate Professor of Surgery
Cornell University
Medical College
New York Hospital
New York, NY, USA

David J Barillo MD FACS
Acting Director, US Army Burn Center
US Army Institute of Surgical Research
Houston, TX, USA

Pierre-Alexandre Bart MD
Attending Physician
Division of Allergy and Immunology
Department of Internal Medicine
CHUV
Lausanne, Switzerland

Michael Barza MD
Director of Medicine
Carney Hospital
Boston, MA, USA

Roger Bayston MMedSci PhD MSc MIBiol FRCPath
Senior Lecturer in Biomaterials-Related Infection
Biomaterials-Related Infection Group
School of Medical and Surgical Sciences,
University of Nottingham
Nottingham, UK

Nick J Beeching MA FRCP FRACP DCH DTM&H
Senior Lecturer in Infectious Diseases
Clinical Research Group
Liverpool School of Tropical Medicine
Liverpool, UK

Rodolfo E Bégué MD
Associate Professor of Pediatrics
Department of Pediatrics
Health Sciences Center
Louisiana State University
New Orleans, LA, USA

Philip Bejon BSc MBBS MRCP
Specialist Registrar in Infectious Diseases
Nuffield Department of Medicine
John Radcliffe Hospital
Oxford, UK

Constance A Benson MD
Professor of Medicine
University of Colorado Health Sciences Center
Denver, CO, USA

Elie F Berbari MD
Assistant Professor of Medicine
Division of Infectious Diseases
Department of Internal Medicine
Rochester, MN, USA

Anthony R Berendt BM BCh MRCP
Consultant Physician-in-Charge
Bone Infection Unit
Nuffield Orthopaedic Centre
Oxford, UK

Eugénie Bergogne-Bérézin MD PhD
Professor of Microbiology
University of Paris
Paris, France

Verka Beric MD
Specialist Registrar, Department of Imaging
Hammersmith Hospital
London, UK

Seth F Berkley MD
President and CEO
International AIDS Vaccine Initiative
New York, NY, USA

Madhav P Bhatta MPH
Doctoral Candidate
Department of Epidemiology
University of Alabama at Birmingham
Birmingham, AL, USA

Finn T Black MD DMSc DTM&H
Professor of Infectious Diseases and Tropical Medicine
Department of Infectious Diseases
University Hospital of Aarhus
Aårhus, Denmark

Robert Bortolussi MD FRCPC
Professor of Pediatrics, Associate Professor of Microbiology
Dalhousie University, Chief of Research
IWK Health Center
Halifax, NS, Canada

Charles AB Boucher MD PhD
Clinical Virologist
Department of Virology
Eijkman-Winkler Institute
for Microbiology, Infectious Diseases and Inflammation
Utrecht, The Netherlands

Emilio S Bouza MD PhD
Head, Clinical Microbiology and Infectious Diseases
Hospital General Universitario 'Grejorio Marañon'
Madrid, Spain

William R Bowie MD FRCPC
Professor of Medicine
Division of Infectious Diseases
The University of British Columbia
Vancouver, BC, Canada

Warwick J Britton PhD MBBS BScMed FRACP FRCP FRCPA DTM&H
Professor of Medicine
Department of Medicine
University of Sydney
Sydney, NSW, Australia

Itzhak Brook MD MSc
Professor of Pediatric Medicine
Georgetown University School of Medicine
Washington DC, USA

David Brown MBBS MSc FRCPath
Director
Enteric, Respiratory and Neurological Virus Laboratory
Specialist and Reference Microbiology Division
Health Protection Agency
London, UK

R Mark L Buller PhD
Professor of Molecular Microbiology and Immunology
Deparment. of Molecular Microbiology and Immunology
St. Louis University
St. Louis, MO, USA

Baudouin Byl MD
Hospital Epidemiologist
Hospital Epidemiology and Infection Control Unit
Universite Libre de Bruxelles - Hopital Erasme
Brussels, Belgium

Thierry Calandra MD PhD
Assistant Professor
Division of Infectious Diseases
Department of Internal Medicine
CHUV
Lausanne, Switzerland

D William Cameron MD FRCPC
Professor of Medicine
Division of Infectious Diseases
University of Ottowa at The Ottawa Hospital
Ottawa, ON, Canada

Michel Caraël PhD
Professor of Social Sciences; Chief, Evaluation,
UNAIDS
Geneva, Switzerland

Jonathan R Carapetis PhD FRACP FAFPHM MBBS BMedSc
Senior Lecturer in Paediatric Infectious Diseases
Centre for International Child Health
University of Melbourne Department of Paediatrics
Royal Children's Hospital
Parkville, Vict, Australia

Claude J Carbon MD
Professor of Internal Medicine
Hôpital Bichat
Paris, France

E Jane Carter MD
Assistant Professor of Medicine
Divisions of Infectious Disease and Pulmonary/Critical
Care, Brown University
The Miriam Hospital
Providence, RI, USA

Richard A Cash MD MPH
Senior Lecturer
Department of Population and International Health
Harvard School of Public Health
Boston, MA, USA

Richard E Chaisson MD
Professor of Medicine, Epidemiology and International Health
Centre for Tubercolosis Research
Johns Hopkins University
Baltimore, MD, USA

Trudie Chalder PhD MSc SRN RMN Dip Behav Psych
Reader in Psychology and Nursing
Academic Department of Psychological Medicine
Guy's, King's and St Thomas's School of Medicine and Institute of Psychiatry
London, UK

Stephen T Chambers MD ChB MSc FRACP
Professor of Pathology, Christchurch School of Medicine, University of Otago; Clinical Director of Infectious Diseases, Christchurch Hospital
Department of Infectious Diseases
Christchurch Hospital
Christchurch, New Zealand

Peter L Chiodini BSc MBBS PhD FRCP FRCPath
Consultant Parasitologist
Department of Clinical Parasitology
Hospital for Tropical Diseases
London, UK

Anthony C Chu FRCP
Senior Lecturer, Honorary Consultant Dermatologist
Unit of Dermatology
Hammersmith Hospital
London, UK

Ben Clark BSc MRCP(UK) DTM&H
Lecturer in Infectious Diseases and Tropical Medicine
Honorary Specialist Registrar
Department of Genomic Medicine
University of Sheffield
Sheffield, UK

Graham M Cleator Dip Bact FI Biol MSc PhD
Reader in Medical Virology
Laboratory Medicine Academic Group
Manchester Royal Infirmary
University of Manchester Clinical Sciences Building
Manchester, UK

Dennis A Clements MD MPH PhD
Professor of Pediatrics and Infectious Diseases
Duke University Medical Center
Durham, NC, USA

Nathan Clumeck MD
Professor of Medicine and Infectious Diseases
Department of Infectious Diseases and Internal Medicine
St Pierre University Hospital
Brussels, Belgium

Clay J Cockerell MD
Clinical Professor of Dermatology and Pathology
Department of Dermatology and Pathology
University of Texas South Western Medical Center
Dallas, TX, USA

Jonathan Cohen MB BS FRCP FRCPath FRCPE FMedSci
Professor of Infectious Diseases
Dean, Brighton and Sussex Medical School
University of Brighton
Falmer, UK

Myron S Cohen MD
Professor of Medicine Microbiology and Immunology
The University of North Carolina at Chapel Hill
Chapel Hill, NC, USA

John Collinge MRCP MD FRCPath
Professor of Neurology
Head of Department, Department of Neurodegenerative Diseases/
Director, MRC Prion Unit
Insitute of Neurology
University College London
London, UK

John A Collins MD
Professor of Obstetrics and Gynaecology
McMaster Univerity
Hamilton, ON, Canada

Helen L Collins PhD
Lecturer in Immunology
School of Health and Life Sciences
Kings College London
London, UK

Christopher P Conlon MA MD FRCP
Consultant Physician in Infectious Diseases
Nuffield Deparment of Medicine
John Radcliffe Hospital
Oxford, UK

G Ralph Corey MD
Professor of Infectious Diseases
Duke University Medical Center
Durham, NC, USA

Patricia Cristofaro MD
Instructor in Medicine
Department of Infectious Diseases
Miriam Hospital and Memorial Hospital
Providence, RI, USA

Christopher Crnich MD
Infectious Disease Fellow
Section of Infectious Diseases, Department of Medicine
University of Wisconsin Hospital and Clinics
Madison, WI, USA

John H Cross PhD
Professor, Tropical Public Health
Department of Preventive Medicine and Biometrics
Uniformed Services University of the Health Sciences
Bethesda, MD, USA

Natasha Crowcroft MA MSc MRCP MFPHM
Consultant Epidemiologist
Immunisation Division
Health Protection Agency
London, UK

Judith Currier MD
Associate Professor of Medicine
Center for Clinical AIDS Research and Education
David Geffen School of Medicine
University of California
Los Angeles, CA, USA

Gina Dallabetta MD
Director, Technical Support
HIV/AIDS Institute
Family Health International
Arlington, VA, USA

David AB Dance MB ChB MSc FRCPath DLSHTM ILTM
Director and Consultant Microbiologist
Plymouth Public Health Laboratory
Plymouth, UK

Jacob Dankert PhD
Professor of Medical Microbiology
Department of Medical Microbiology
University of Amsterdam
Amsterdam, The Netherlands

Debby Ben David MD
Infectious Diseases Unit
Sheba Medical Centre
Tel-Aviv University
School of Medicine
Tel-Hashomer, Israel

Robert N Davidson MD FRCP DTM&H
Consultant Physician, Hon. Senior Lecturer
Department of Infectious and Tropical Diseases
Northwick Park Hospital
Harrow, UK

Stéphane De Wit MD PhD
Senior Physician
Division of Infectious Diseases
Saint Pierre University Hospital
Brussels, Belgium

Martin Dedicoat MRCP
Research Fellow
Liverpool School of Tropical Medicine
Liverpool, UK

David T Dennis MD MPH DCMT
Medical Epidemiologist
Divison Victor- Borne Infectious Diseases
Centre for Disease Control and Prevention
Fort Collins, CO, USA

Mehmet Doganay MD
Professor in Infectious Diseases
Erciyes Universitesi
Tip Fakultesi
Kayseri, Turkey

Tom Doherty MD FRCP DTM&H
Consultant Physician
Hospital for Tropical Diseases
London, UK

Edgar Dorman MRCGP, MRCOG
Consultant Obstetrician and Gynaecologist
Homerton University Hospital
London, UK

Dominique Dormont MD
Chief of Neurovirology
Service de Neuroviorologie
Departement de Recherche Medicale
Fontenay aux Roses, France

Harminder S Dua MBBS DO DO(Lond) MS MNAMS FRCS FRCOphth MD PhD
Professor of Ophthalmology
Division of Opthalmology and Visual Sciences
Queen's Medical Centre University Hospital
Nottingham, UK

Jay S Duker MD
Director, New England Eye Center;
Director, Pediatric Retinal Referral Center
New England Eye Center
Boston, MA, USA

Herbert L DuPont MD
Chief of Medicine, St. Luke's Episcopal Hospital;
Director, Center for Infectious Diseases, University of Texas; Clinical Professor, Baylor College of Medicine and University of Texas - Houston
St Luke's Episcopal Hospital
Houston, TX, USA

Soumitra R Eachempati MD FACS
Assistant Professor of Surgery
Division of Critical Care and Trauma
Weill Medical College of Cornell University
New York, NY, USA

Charles N Edwards FRCPC FACP FACG
Associate Senior Lecturer
School of Clinical Medicine and Research
University of the West Indies
Barbados

Androulla Efstratiou PhD SRCS
Top Grade Clinical Microbiologist;
Head of WHO Collaborative for Diphtheria and Streptococcal Infections
London, UK

Martha Espinosa-Cantellano MD DSC
Associate Professor
Center for Research and Advanced Studies
CINVESTAV-IPN
Col. San Pedro Zacat
Mexico

Michael JG Farthing MD FRCP
Professor of Medicine
Faculty of Medicine
University of Glasgow
Glasgow, UK

Patricia E Fast MD PhD FAAP
Director, Medical Affairs
International AIDS Vaccine Initiative
New York, NY, USA

Florence Fenollar MD PhD
Unité des Ricksttsies
Faculté de Médecine
Marseille, France

Luis A Fernandez MD
Assistant Professor of Surgery
Department of Surgery
University of Wisconsin School of Medicine
Madison, WI, USA

Mary Lyn Field MSN FNP
Technical Officer
Family Health International
Arlington, VA, USA

Roger G Finch MB BS FRCP FRCPath FRCPEd FFPM
Professor of Infectious Diseases
Department of Microbiology and Infectious Diseases
Nottingham City Hospital
Nottingham, UK

Charles W Flexner MD
Associate Professor of Medicine
Pharmacology and
Molecular Sciences and International Health
Division of Clinical Pharmacology
Johns Hopkins University
Baltimore, MD, USA

Marco Floridia MD
Researcher
Istituto Superiore di Sanità
Rome, Italy

Ad C Fluit PhD
Associate Professor of Medical Microbiology
Eijkman-Winkler Institute
for Microbiology, Infectious Diseases and Inflammation
Utrecht, The Netherlands

Hélène Fontaine MD
Service d'Hepatologie
Hôpital Necker
Paris, France

E Lee Ford-Jones MD FRCPC
Professor of Pediatrics
Division of Infectious Diseases
The Hospital for Sick Children
Toronto, ON, Canada

Kimberley K Fox MD MPH
Chief, Field Epidemiology Unit
ESB/DSTDP/NCHSTP
National Center for HIV STD and TB Prevention
Atlanta, GA, USA

David N Fredricks MD
Assistant Professor of Medicine
University of Washington
Fred Hutchinson Cancer Research Center
Seattle, WA, USA

Jon S Friedland MA PhD FRCP FRCPE
Reader in Infectious and Tropical Diseases
Imperial College
London, UK

Thomas R Fritsche PhD, MD, ABMM
Associate Director
The Jones Group / JMI Laboratories
North Liberty, IO, USA

Kenneth L Gage PhD
Chief, Plague Section
Bacterial Zoonoses Branch
Division of Vector-Borne Infectious Diseases
Fort Collins, CO, USA

Nelson M Gantz MD FACP
Chairman, Department of Medicine
Chief Division of Infectious Diseases
Clinical Professor of Medicine
MCP Hahnemann School of Medicine
Pinnacle Health Systems
Harrisburg, PA, USA

Lynne S Garcia MS F(AAM) CLS(NCA) MT(ASCP)
Director
LSG and Associates
Santa Monica, CA, USA

David F Gardiner MD
Clinical Fellow
Division of International Medicine and Infectious Diseases
Department of Medicine
Weill Medical College of Cornell University
New York, NY, USA

Arturo S Gastañaduy MD
Assistant Professor of Clinical Pediatrics
Louisiana State University
Department of Pediatrics
LSU Health Sciences Center
New Orleans, LA, USA

José M Gatell MD PhD
Senior Consultant and Head of Infectious Diseases and AIDS Unit
Institute of Infectious Diseases and Immunology
Hospital Clinic of Barcelona
Barcelona, Spain

Dale N Gerding MD
Professor and Associate Chair
Department of Medicine
Northwestern University School of Medicine
Chicago, IL, USA

Veronique Gibbons BSc RGN
Immunisation Advice Nurse
Immunisation Division
Communicable Disease Surveillance Centre
London, UK

Stephen H Gillespie MD FRCP(Edin) FRCPath
Professor of Medical Microbiology
Department of Microbiology
University College London
London, UK

Jill Gilmour PhD
Director, Clinical Immunology
International AIDS Vaccine Initiative (IAVI)
New York, NY, USA

Pierre-Marie Girard MD PhD
Professor of Medicine
Service des Maladies Infectieuses et Tropicales
Hôpital Saint-Antoine
Paris, France

Marshall J Glesby MD PhD
Assistant Professor of Medicine and Public Health
Division of International Medicine and Infectious Disease
Department of Medicine
Weil Medical College of Cornell University
New York, NY, USA

John W Gnann Jr MD
Professor of Medicine, Pediatrics and Microbiology
Division of Infectious Diseases
University of Alabama at Birmingham and the Birmingham Veterans Administration Medical Center
Birmingham, AL, USA

Diane Goade MD
Assistant Professor Department of Medicine
The University of New Mexico School of Medicine
Albuquerque, NM, USA

Andrew F Goddard MA MD MRCP
Consultant Gastroenterologist
Derby City General Hospital
Derby, UK

Ellie JC Goldstein MD, FIDSA
Director, RM Alden Research Laboratory
Santa Monica - UCLA Medical Center;
Clinical Professor of Medicine
UCLA School of Medicine
Santa Monica, CA, USA

Bruno Gottstein PhD
Professor of Parasitology
Institute of Parasitology
Faculty of Veterinary Medicine and Faculty of Medicine
Berne, Switzerland

Ravi Gowda MBBS MRCP DTM&H DCH DRCOG MRCGP
Specialist Registrar in Infectious Diseases, Tropical Medicine and General (Internal) Medicine
Department of Infection and Tropical Medicine
Royal Hallamshire Hospital
Sheffield, UK

John M Grange MD MSc
Visiting Professor
Centre for Infectious Diseases and International Health
Royal Free and University College Medical School
London, UK

M Lindsay Grayson MD FRACP FAFPHM
Director, Infectious Diseases Department
Austin and Repatriation Medical Centre
University Of Melborne
Heidelberg, Vic, Australia

Michael DL Green MD MPH
Professor of Pediatrics and Surgery
Division of Allergy, Immunology and Infectious Diseases
Children's Hospital of Pittsburgh
Pittsburgh, PA, USA

Stephen T Green MD BSc FRCP(London) FRCP (Glasgow) DTM&H
Consultant Physician in Infectious Disease and Tropical Medicine
Department of Infection and Tropical Medicine
Royal Hallamshire Hospitals
Sheffield, UK

Aric L Gregson MD
Instructor of Medicine
Malaria Section
Division of Infectious Diseases
Center for Vaccine Development
Baltimore, MD, USA

George Griffin BSc PhD FRCP
Professor of Infectious Diseases
St. George's Hospital Medical School
London, UK

David E Griffith MD
Professor of Medicine, Center for Pulmonary Infectious Disease Control
University of Texas Health Center
Tyler, TX, USA

Andrew H Groll MD
c/o Thomas J Walsh MD
Head, Immunocompromised Host Section
Pediatric Oncology Branch
National Cancer Institute
Bethesda, MD, USA

Hans-Peter Grunert PhD
Senior Scientist
Free University of Berlin
University Hospital Benjamin Franklin
Institute of Infectious Diseases Medicine
Department of Virology
Berlin, Germany

Anur R Guhan MD MRCP
Specialist Registrar in Respiratory Medicine
Cardio-Thoracic Department
Freeman Hospital
Newcastle upon Tyne, UK

Aditya K Gupta MD FRCP(C)
Assistant Professor, Division of Dermatology
Department of Medicine
Sunnybrook Health Science Center and the University of Toronto
London, ON, Canada

Kalpana Gupta PhD
Manager, Global Surveillance and Special Projects
International AIDS Vaccine Initiative (IAVI)
New York, NY, USA

Kok-Ann Gwee MBBS MMed MRCP FAMS PhD FRCP
Associate Professor of Medicine;
Consultant Gastroenterologist
Singapore, Malaysia

Scott B Halstead MD
Adjunct Professor of Preventive Medicine
Preventive Medicine and Biometrics
Uniformed Services, University of the Health Sciences
Bethesda, MD, USA

Davidson H Hamer MD
Director, Traveler's Health Service
New England Medical Center
Assistant Professor of Medicine and Nutrition
Tufts University School of Medicine
Friedman School of Nutritional Science and Policy
Adjunct Professor of Internation Health,
Center for International Health
Boston University School of Public Health
New England Medical Center Hospital
Boston, USA

Scott M Hammer MD
Chief, Division of Infectious Diseases
Department of Medicine
Columbia Presbyterian Medical Center
New York, NY, USA

Sajeev Handa MD
Director, Academic Medical Center Internal Medicine
Inpatient Service (AMC-IMIS) Rhode Island Hospital and The Miriam Hospital
Rhode Island Hospital
Providence, RI, USA

Anthony D Harries MA MD FRCP DTM&H
Foundation Professor of Medicine,
Malawi College of Medicine
Blantyre, Malawi

Barry J Hartman MD
Clinical Professor of Medicine
Department of International Medicine and Infectious Diseases
Cornell University Medical College New York
New York, NY, USA

Peter L Havens MD, MS
Professor of Pediatrics and Epidemiology Medical
College of Wisconsin; Director Wisconsin HIV Primary Care Support Network Children's Hospital of Wisconsin
Medical College of Wisconsin
Milwaukee, WI, USA

Roderick J Hay DM FRCP FRCPath
Professor of Dermatology
Faculty of Medicine and Health Sciences
Queens University Belfast
Belfast, UK

Frederick G Hayden MD
Professor of Internal Medicine and Pathology
Department of Internal Medicine
University of Virginia
Charlottesville, VA, USA

David K Henderson MD
Deputy Director for Clinical Care
Warren G Magnuson Clinical Center
National Institutes of Health
Bethesda, MD, USA

Luke Herbert FRCOphth
Consultant and Clinical Director
Department of Ophthalmology
The Queen Elizabeth II Hospital
Welwyn Garden City, UK

David R Hill MD DTM&H
Director
National Travel Health Network and Centre
Hospital for Tropical Diseases
London, UK

Jay CD Hinton PhD
Head of Molecular Microbiology
Institute of Food Research
Norwich, UK

John David Hinze DO
Fellow in Pulmonary Critical Care Medicine
Texas A&M College of Medicine
Temple, Texas, USA

Bernard Hirschel MD
Head, Private Clinic
Division of Infectious Diseases
Hopital Cantonal Universitaire
Geneva, Switzerland

Derek Hood BSc PhD
Honorary University Lecturer and Senior Research Scientist
Department of Paediatrics and Molecular Infectious Diseases Group
Weatherall Institute of Molecular Medicine
John Radcliffe Hospital
Oxford, UK

Andy IM Hoepelman MD PhD
Professor of Medicine, Infectious Diseases Specialist, Head Division Acute Medicine and Infectious Diseases
Department of Medicine
Division of Infectious Diseases
University Medical Centre
Utrecht, The Netherlands

Steven M Holland MD
Head, Immunopathogenesis Unit
Clinical Pathophysiology Section
Laboratory of Host Defenses
National Institute of Allergy and Infectious Disease
Bethesda, MD, USA

Stig E Holm MD
Emeritus Professor of Clinical Bacteriology
Department of Clinical Microbiology
University Hospital of Umea
Umea, Sweden

Benjamin P Howden MBBS FRACP
Microbiology Registrar
Department of Microbiology
Austin and Repatriation Medical Centre
Melbourne, Vic, Australia

Robin Howe MBBS DRCPath
Consultant Senior Lecturer in Clinical Microbiology
Department of Microbiology
Southmead Hospital
Bristol, UK

James M Hughes MD
Director, National Center for Infectious Diseases
Centers for Disease Control and Prevention
Altanta, GA, USA

Vito R Iacoviello MD
Assistant Professor of Medicine, Harvard Medical School
Division of Infectious Diseases
Mount Auburn Hospital
Cambridge, MA, USA

Clark B Inderlied PhD
Professor of Clinical Pathology
University of Southern California
Childrens Hospital Los Angeles
Los Angeles, CA, USA

Michael Ison MD
Fellow, Division of Infectious Diseases and International Health
University of Virginia Health System
Charlottesville, VA, USA

Jenifer Leaf Jaeger MD MA
Director of Pediatrics and Chief of Infection Control
Bradley Hospital
East Providence, RI, USA

James R Johnson MD
Professor of Medicine University of Minnesota
Infectious Diseases
VA Medical Center
Minneapolis, MN, USA

Stuart Johnson MD
Associate Professor of Medicine
Infectious Diseases Section
Loyola University Medical Center
Maywood, IL, USA

Thomas C Jones MD FACP
Adjunct Professor of Medicine; Head, Clinical Research Consultants
Clinical Research Consultants
Basel, Switzerland

Munkolenkole C Kamenga MD MPH
Technical Officer
Family Health International
Arlington, VA , USA

Christine Katlama MD
Professor of Infectious Diseases
Service de Maladies Infectieuses
Centre Hospitalier Pitié Salpétriere
Paris, France

Stefan HE Kaufmann PhD
Professor of Immunology and Medical Microbiology
Department of Immunology
Max-Planck Institute for Infection Biology
Berlin, Germany

Powel Kazanjian MD
Director, HIV/AIDS Program
University of Michigan Medical Center
Ann Arbor, MI, USA

Patrick J Kelly
University of Zimbabwe Veterinary School
Harare, Zimbabwe

Jason S Kendler MD
Assistant Professor of Medicine
Department of International Medicine and Infectious Diseases
Cornell University Medical School New York
New York, NY, USA

Gerald T Keusch MD
Associate Director for International Research and Director, Fogarty International Center
National Institutes of Health
Bethesda, MD, USA

Ali S Khan MD
Associate Director for Medical Science
Division of Parasitic Diseases
National Center for Infectious Disease,
Centers for Disease Control and Prevention
Atlanta, GA, USA

Grace T Kho MD
Department of Laboratory Medicine
Vancouver Island Health Authority
Royal Jubilee Hospital
Victoria, BC, Canada

Timothy E Kiehn PhD
Chief, Microbial Service
Department of Clinical Laboratories
Memorial Sloan-Kettering Cancer Center
New York, NY, USA

George R Kinghorn MD FRCP
Clinical Director, Directorate of Communicable Diseases
Royal Hallamshire Hospital
Sheffield, UK

Nigar Kirmani MD
Associate Professor of Medicine
Division of Infectious Diseases
Washington University School of Medicine
St Louis, MO, USA

Paul E Klapper PhD FRCPath
Consultant Clinical Scientist and Honorary Senior Lecturer
Health Protection Agency
Leeds Laboratory
Leeds, UK

Menno Kok PhD
Senior Staff Member
Medical Faculty
Erasmus MC
Rotterdam, The Netherlands

John N Krieger MD
Professor of Urology
Department of Urology
University of Washington School of Medicine
Seattle, WA, USA

Christine J Kubin Pharm D BCPS
Clinical Pharmacy Manager
Infectious Diseases
New York-Presbyterian Hospital
New York, NY, USA

Bart-Jan Kullberg MD
Associate Professor of Medicine
Deparment of General Internal Medicine
WMC gr Radboud Nijmegen
Nijmegen, The Netherlands

Daniel R Kuritzkes MD
Director of AIDS Research
Brigham and Women's Hospital
Associate Professor of Medicine
Harvard Medical School
Partners AIDS Research Center
Cambridge, MA, USA

Alberto M La Rosa MD
Director of Clinical Trials Unit
Asociacion Civil Impacta Salud Y Educacion
Lima, Peru

David G Lalloo MBBS MD FRCP
Senior Lecturer in Clinical Tropical Medicine
Liverpool School of Tropical Medicine
Liverpool, UK

Didier M Lambert PharmD PhD
Professor of Medicinal Chemistry
Unité de Chimie Pharmaceutique et Radiopharmacie
Brussels, Belgium

Harold Lambert MD FRCP FRC Path FFPHM Hon FRCPCH
Emeritus Professor of Microbial Diseases
St George's Hospital Medical School
London, UK

Lucia Larson MD
Assistant Professor of Medicine and Obstetrics/Gynecology
Department of Medicine
Brown Medical School
Women and Infants Hospital
Providence, RI, USA

Barbara Law BSc MD FRCP
Section Head Paediatric Infectious Diseases, Professor of Medical Microbiology, Professor of Paediatrcs and Child Health
Faculty of Medicine
University of Manitoba
Winnepeg, MB, Canada

Pascal Lebray MD
Service d'Hepatologie
Hôpital Necker
Paris, France

Stephen L Leib MD
Assistant Professor, Consultant Physician
Infectious Diseases
Institute for Infectious Diseases
Bern, Switzerland

Itzchak Levi MD
Infectious Diseases Unit
Sheba Medical Center
Tel Hashomer
Ramat Gan, Israel

Alexandra M Levitt PhD
Health Scientist
Office of the Director
National Center for Infectious Diseases,
Centers for Disease Contol and Infection
Atlanta, GA, USA

Chen Liang PhD
Assistant Professor of Microbiology
McGill University AIDS Centre
Jewish General Hospital
Montreal, QC, Canada

Wei-Shen Lim MB BS MRCP DM
Consultant Physician, Respiratory Medicine Unit
City Hospital Nottingham
Nottingham, UK

Graham Lloyd PhD MSc BSc FIBMS CMS
Head of Special Pathogens Reference Unit
Health Protection Agency
Centre for Applied Microbiology and Research
Porton Down, Salisbury, UK

Franklin D Lowy MD
Professor of Medicine and Pathology
Division of Infectious Diseases
Columbia University
College of Physicians and Surgeons
New York, NY, USA

Benjamin J Luft MD
Edmund D Pellegrino Professor
Chairman, Department of Medicine
State University of New York at Stony Brook
New York, NY, USA

William A Lynn MD FRCP
Divisional Director, Medicine and A&E
Infection and Immunity Unit
Ealing Hospital
Southall, UK

Keith PWJ McAdam MD FRCP
Wellcome Professor of Clinical Tropical Medicine
London School of Hygiene and Tropical Medicine
London, UK

John T Macfarlane MA DM FRCP MRCGP
Consultant Physician
Respiratory Medicine Unit
Nottingham City Hospital
Nottingham, UK

Alasdair MacGowan BMedBiol MD FRCP(Ed) FRCPath
Professor of Clinical Microbiology and Antimicrobial Therapeutics
Department of Medical Microbiology
Bristol Centre for Antimicrobial Research and Evaluation
Bristol, UK

Andrew D Mackay MRCPath MA MRCP
Consultant Microbiologist
Greenwich District General Hospital
London, UK

Philip A Mackowiak MD
Professor of Medicine; Vice Chairman
Department of Medicine
Chief, Medical Care Clinical Center
VA Maryland Health Care System
University of Maryland School of Medicine
Baltimore, MD, USA

Kim Maeder RN MN CIC
Infection Control Program
Harbor - UCLA Medical Center
Torrance, CA, USA

Janine R Maenza MD
Clinical Assistant Professor of Medicine
Primary Infection Clinic
University of Washington
Seattle, WA, USA

Adel A F Mahmoud MD PhD
President, Merck Vaccines, Merck & Co., Inc.
Adjunct Professor of Medicine, Case Western Reserve University
Whitehouse Station, NJ, USA

Timothy Mailman MD FRCPC
Assistant Professor in Pediatrics
Dalhousie University
IWK Health Center
Halifax, NS, Canada

Janice Main FRCP (Edin & Lond)
Senior Lecturer in Infectious Diseases and Medicine
Imperial College School of Medicine
St Mary's Hospital
London, UK

Dennis G Maki MD
Professor of Medicine
Head, Section of Infectious Diseases
Attending Physician, Center for Trauma and Life Support
Department of Infectious Diseases / Medicine
University of Wisconsin Hospital and Clinics
Madison, WI, USA

Julie E Mangino MD
Associate Professor of Clinical Internal Medicine
Division of Infectious Diseases, and Medical Director, Department of Epidemiology
The Ohio State University College of Medicine
Columbus, OH, USA

Oscar Marchetti MD
Division of Infectious Diseases
Department of Internal Medicine
Centre Hospitalier Universitaire Vaudois
Lausanne, Switzerland

Per-Anders Mårdh MD PhD
Professor of Medicine
Department of Obstetrics and Gynecology
University Hospital
Lund, Sweden

Kieren A Marr MD
Assistant Professor of Medicine
University of Washington
Fred Hutchinson Cancer Research Center
Seattle, WA, USA

Pablo Martín-Rabadán MD DTM&H
Consultant Physician
Servicio de Microbiologia y Enjermedades Infecciosas
Hospital General Universitario Gregorio Maranon
Madrid, Spain

Augusto Julio Martinez MD
(Deceased)
Professor of Pathology
University of Pittsburgh School of Medicine
Pittsburgh, PA, USA

Adolfo Martínez-Palomo MD DSc
Professor of Experimental Pathology
Department of Experimental Pathology
Center for Research and Advances Studies
México DF, Mexico

Ellen M Mascini MD PhD
Medical Microbiologist
Eijkman-Winkler Center for Microbiology, Infectious Diseases and Inflammation
Utrecht, The Netherlands

Peter R Mason MRCPath
Professor of Laboratory Medicine
Biomedical Research and Training Institute
Harare, Zimbabwe

Kenneth H Mayer MD
Professor of Medicine and Community Health, Brown University;
Director of Brown University AIDS Program;
Medical Director of Research, Fonway Community Health
Infectious Diseases Division
The Miriam Hospital
Providence, RI, USA

Joseph B McCormick MD
Regional Dean and James H Steele Professor
School of Public Health
University of Texas Houston Health Science Center
Brownsville, TX, USA

Michael W McKendrick MBBS MRCP
Lead Physician
Deparment of Infection and Tropical Medicine
Central Sheffield University Hospitals Trust
Royal Hallamshire Hospital
Sheffield, UK

Barbara McKeown MRCPI FRCR
Consultant Radiologist
Department of Radiology
Peterborough District Hospital
Peterborough, UK

Albert T McManus PhD
Senior Scientist; Chief, Laboratory Division
US Army Institute of Surgical Research
Houston, TX, USA

Francis Mégraud MD
Professor of Bacteriology
Laboratoire de Bactériologie
Hôpitaux Pellegrin
Bordeaux, France

Andre Z Meheus MD PhD
Professor, Epidemiology and Social Medicine
University of Antwerp
Antwerp, Belgium

Marian G Michaels MD MPH
Associate Professor of Pediatrics and Surgery
Division of Allergy, Immunology and Infectious Diseases
Childrens Hospital of Pittsburgh
Pittsburgh, PA, USA

Dana Milatovic MD PhD
Associate Professor
Eijkman-Winkler Institute for Microbiology, Infectious Diseases and Inflammation
Utrecht, The Netherlands

Michael A Miles MSc PhD DSc FRCPath
Professor of Medical Protozoology
Department of Infectious and Tropical Diseases
London School of Hygiene and Tropical Medicine
London, UK

Alastair Miller MA MBBS FRCP FRCP(Ed) DTM&H
Consultant Physician; Honorary Senior Lecturer
Worcester Acute Hospitals Trust
Worcester Royal Infirmary
Worcester, UK

Marie-Paule Mingeot-Leclercq MSc PharmD PhD
Professor of Pharmacology and Biochemistry
Unité de Pharmacologie Cellulaire et Moléculaire
Brussels, Belgium

Thomas G Mitchell PhD
Associate Professor of Molecular Genetics and Microbiolgy
Deparment of Molecular Genetics and Microbiology
Duke University Medical Center
Durham, NC, USA

Julio SG Montaner MD FRCPC FCCP
Professor of Medicine and Chair of AIDS Research
St. Paul's Hospital/University of British Columbia
Vancouver, BC, Canada

Martin Montes MD
Fellow, Infectious Diseases
Infectious Diseases
University of Texas Houston Medical School
Houston, TX, USA

Valentina Montessori MD FRCPC
Clinical Assistant Professor
Canadian HIV Trials Network,
Division of Infectious Diseases
British Columbia Centre for Excellence in HIV/AIDS
St Paul's Hospital / University of British Columbia
Vancouver, BC, Canada

John Z Montgomerie MB, ChB, FRACD
Professor Emeritus
Department of Medicine
Keck School of Medicine,
University of Southern California
Los Angeles, CA, USA

Jose G Montoya MD
Assistant Professor of Medicine, Stanford University
School of Medicine; Co-Director, Toxoplasma Serology Laboratory
Division of Infectious Diseases and Geographic Medicine
Stanford University School of Medicine
Stanford, CA, USA

Philippe Moreillon MD PhD
Professor
Institute of Fundamental Microbiology
University of Lausanne
Lausanne, Switzerland

Peter Morgan-Capner BSc, MBBS, FRCPath, FRCP, Hon FFPHM
Honorary Professor of Clinical Virology
Department of Microbiology
Royal Preston Hospital
Preston, UK

Peter J Moss MD MRCP DTM&H
Consultant in Infectious Diseases
Castle Hill Hospital
Cottingham
East Riding, UK

Richard E Moxon MA FRCP FRCPCH, FMedSci
Head, Department of Paediatrics and Molecular Infectious Diseases Group
University of Oxford
Oxford, UK

Patricia Muñoz MD, PhD
Associate Professor
Clinical Microbiology and Infectious Diseases Deparment
Hospital General Universitario 'Gregorio Maranon'
Madrid, Spain

Maurice E Murphy MB MRCPI
Consultant/Honorary Senior Lecturer
Infection and Immunity Specialty Group
St Bartholomew's Hospital, Barts and the London NHS Trust
London, UK

Andrew R Murry MD
Clinical Assistant Professor of Medicine
The Ohio State University College of Medicine
Columbus, OH, USA

Kurt G Naber MD, PhD
Professor and Head of Urology
Department of Urology
Hospital St Elisabeth
Straubing, Germany

Stanley J Naides MD FACP
Thomas B. Hallowell Professor of Medicine; Professor of Microbiology and Immunology and Pharmacology; Chief, Division of Rheumatology Medicine
Penn State Milton S. Hershey Medical Centre
Hershey, PA, USA

W Garrett Nichols MD MSc
Associate in Clinical Research, Program in Infectious Diseases
Fred Hutchinson Cancer Research Center
Seattle, WA, USA

Lindsay E Nicolle BSc, BScMed, MD, FRCPC
Professor of Internal Medicine and Medical Microbiology
University of Manitoba
Winnipeg, MB, Canada

Charles H Nightingale PhD
Vice President for Research, Hartford Hospital
Research Professor, University of Connecticut
Hartford, CT, USA

Carl W Norden MD
Professor of Medicine
Head Division of Infectious Diseases
Cooper Hospital/University Medical Center
Camden, NJ, USA

S Ragnar Norrby MD PhD FRCP (Edin)
Professor and Director General
The Swedish Institute for Infectious Disease Control
Solna, Sweden

Luigi Notarangelo MD
Head, Department of Pediatrics
University of Brescia
Brescia, Italy

Jon S Odorico MD
Assistant Professor of Surgery
Department of Surgery
University of Wisconsin Hospital
Madison, WI, USA

Edmund L C Ong MBBS MSc FRCP FRCPI DTM&H
Consultant Physician/Senior Lecturer
Head of Department
Department of Infection and Tropical Medicine
University of Newcastle Medical School
Newcastle upon Tyne, UK

Michelle Onorato MD
Division of Infectious Diseases
The University of Texas Medical Branch
Galveston, TX, USA

Steven M Opal MD
Professor of Medicine,
Brown University
School of Medicine
Infectious Disease Division
Memorial Hospital of Rhode Island
Pawtucket, RI, USA

L Peter Ormerod BSc MBChB (Hons) MD DSc (Med) FRCP
Professor of Medicine
Chest Clinic
Blackburn Royal Infirmary
Blackburn, UK

Douglas R Osmon MD
Associate Professor of Medicine
Division of Infectious Diseases
Department of Internal Medicine
Rochester, MN, USA

Eric A Ottesen MD
Research Professor and Director
Lymphatic Filariasis Support Center
Department of International Health
Emory University
Atlanta, GA, USA

Giuseppe Pantaleo MD
Professor of Medicine
Division of Immunology and Allergy
Department of Medicine
Lausanne, Switzerland

Philippe Parola MD PhD
Faculte de Medecine
Unite Des Rickettsies
Marseille, France

Eldryd HO Parry OBE
Visiting Professor
London School Of Hygiene and Tropical Health
London, UK

Geoffrey Pasvol MA MB ChB DPhil FRCP FRCPE
Professor of Infection and Tropical Medicine
Imperial College London
Harrow, UK

Nicholas I J Paton MD, MRCP
Consultant and Head
Department of Infectious Diseases
Tan Tock Seng Hospital
Singapore, Malaysia

Andrew T Pavia MD
Professor of Pediatrics and Medicine
Chief, Division of Pediatric Infectious Diseases
Division of Pediatric Infectious Diseases
University of Utah Health Sciences Center
Salt Lake City, UT, USA

Carlos V Paya MD PhD
Professor of Medicine, Consultant in Infectious Diseases
Division of Infectious Diseases and Transplant Center
Mayo Clinic
Rochester, MN, USA

Jean-Claude Pechère MD
Professor of Genetics and Microbiology
Centre Medical Universitaire
Universite de Geneve
Geneva, Switzerland

Stephen I Pelton MD
Professor of Pediatrics
Boston University School of Medicine
The Maxwell Finland Laboratory for Infectious Diseases
Boston, MA, USA

Wallace Peters MD DSc DTM&H FRCP
Emeritus Professor of Medical Parasitology
Centre for Tropical Antiprotozoal Chemotherapy
Northwick Park Institute for Medical Research
Harrow, UK

Peter Phillips MD FRCPC
Clinical Professor of Medicine
St Paul's Hospital / University of British Columbia
Vancouver, BC, Canada

Robert Pinner MD
c/o Montse Soriano-Gabarró
Meningitis and Special Pathogens Branch
Centers for Disease Control and Prevention
Altanta, GA, USA

Peter Piot MD PhD
Executive Director, Joint United Nations Programme on HIV/AIDS
Joint United Nations Programme on HIV/AIDS
UNAIDS
Geneva, Switzerland

Stephen C Piscitelli PharmD
Director
Discovery Medicine – Antivirals
GlaxoSmithKline
Research Triangle Park, NC, USA

Didier Pittet MD MS
Professor of Medicine
Infection Control Program
University of Geneva Hospitals
Geneva, Switzerland

Stanislas Pol MD PhD
Head of the Unit
Service d'Hepatologie
Hôpital Necker
Paris, France

Richard B Pollard MD
Professor, Department of Internal Medicine
Division of Infectious and Immunologic Diseases
Sacramento, CA, USA

Bruce Polsky MD
Vice Chairman for Academic Affairs
Department of Medicine
Chief, Division of Infectious Diseases
St. Luke's-Roosevelt Hospital Center
New York, NY, USA

Klara M Posfay-Barbe MD
Visiting Instructor
Division of Allergy, Immunology and Infectious Diseases
Children's Hospital of Pittsburgh
Pittsburgh, PA, USA

Michael T Poshkus MD
Fellow in Infectious Diseases
Division of Infectious Diseases
Rhode Island Hospital
Providence, RI, USA

William G Powderly MD FRCPI
Professor of Medicine;
Director, Division of Infectious Diseases
Washington University School of Medicine
St. Louis, MO, USA

Nicholas Price BSc MRCP DTM&H
Specialist Registrar
Department of Infection and Tropical Medicine
Lister Unit
Harrow, UK

Thomas C Quinn MD MSc
Professor of Medicine
Division of Infectious Diseases
Department of Medicine
Johns Hopkins University
Baltimore, MD, USA

Richard Quintiliani MD FACP
Professor of Medicine
School of Medicine
University of Connecticut
Farmington, CT, USA

Richard Quintiliani Jr MD
Adjunct Assistant Professor
Georgetown University Medical Center
Washington DC, USA

Justin D Radolf MD
Professor of Medicine, Genetics and Development Biology
Center for Microbial Pathogenesis
University of Connecticut Health Center
Farmington, CT, USA

Daniel W Rahn MD
Professor of Medicine Vice Dean for Clinical Affairs
Medical College of Georgia
Augusta, GA, USA

Didier Raoult MD PhD
Professor
Unité des Rickettsies
Faculté de Médecine
Marseille, France

Raymund R Razonable MD
Division of Infectious Diseases and Transplant Center
Mayo Clinic
Rochester, MN, USA

Robert C Read MD FRCP
Professor in Infectious Diseases
University of Sheffield Medical School
Sheffield, UK

Gili Regev-Yochay MD
Infectious Diseases Unit
Sheba Medical Centre
Tel-Aviv University
School of Medicine
Tel-Hashomer, Israel

Peter Reiss MD PhD
Associate Professor of Medicine and Deputy Director
National AIDS Therapy Evaluation Center
Academic Medical Center
Amsterdam, The Netherlands

Pierre Reusser MD
Professor of Medicine
Basel University School of Medicine
Head, Division of Medicine
Hopital du Jura - site de Porrentruy
Porrentruy, Switzerland

Malcolm D Richardson PhD CIBiol FIBiol FRCPath
Senior Lecturer in Medical Mycology
Department of Bacteriology and Immunology
Haartman Institute
Helsinki, Finland

John Richens MA MBBS MSc FRCPE
Clinical Lecturer
Department of Sexually Transmitted Diseases
University College London
London, UK

Claudia Rodriguez MD
Fellow
Clinical Microbiology and Infectious Diseases Deparment
Hospital General Universitario 'Gregorio Maranon'
Madrid, Spain

Rodrigo LC Romulo MD
Assistant Professor
University of Santo Tomas Faculty of Medicine and Surgery
Makati City, Philippines

Allan R Ronald MD FRCPC FACP
Distinguished Professor Emeritus
University of Manitoba;
Visiting Professor
Makerere University;
University of Manitoba
Winnipeg, MB, Canada

Daniel Rosenbluth MD
Associate Professor of Medicine; Director, Adult Cystic Fibrosis Program
Washington University School of Medicine
St Louis, MO, USA

Nancy E Rosenstein MD
Medical Epidemiologist
Division of Bacterial and Mycotic Diseases
Center for Disease Control and Prevention
Atlanta, GA, USA

Sergio D Rosenzweig MD
Immunopathogenesis Unit
Clinical Pathophysiology Section
Laboratory of Host Defenses
National Institute of Allergy and Infectious Diseases
National Institutes of Health
Bethesda, MD, USA and
Servicio de Inmunologia Hospital Nacional de Pediatria "J.P. Garrahan"
Buenos Aires, Argentina

Virginia R Roth MD FRCPC
Assistant Professor of Medicine
Division of Infectious Diseases
University of Ottawa and the Ottawa General Hospital
Ottawa, ON, Canada

Maja Rozenberg-Arska MD PhD
Associate Professor
Eijkman-Winkler Institute for Microbiology, Infectious Disease and Inflammation
Utrecht, The Netherlands

Robert H Rubin MD FACP FCCP
Associate Director
Brigham Womens Hospital
Division of Infectious Diseases
Boston, MA, USA

James Rubin BSc MSc PhD
Research Associate
Department of Psychological Medicine
Guy's, King's and St Thomas's School of Medicine and Institute of Psychiatry
London, UK

Bina Rubinovitch MD
Sheba Medical Center
Tel Hashomer
Ramat Gan, Israel

Ethan Rubinstein MD LLB
Professor of Internal Medicine
Infectious Diseases Unit
Sheba Medical Centre
Tel-Aviv University
School of Medicine
Tel-Hashomer, Israel

Charles E Rupprecht VMD MS PhD
Chief, Rabies Section
Centers for Disease Control and Prevention
Atlanta, GA, USA

Greg Ryan MB FRCFC
Associate Professor
Deparment of Obstetrics and Gynecology
Division of Fetal and Maternal Medicine
Mount Sinai Hospital
Toronto, ON, Canada

Stephen D Ryder DM MRCP
Consultant Hepatologist\Physician
Queen's Medical Center
Nottingham, UK

Nasia Safdar MD
Postgraduate Trainee
Section of Infectious Diseases
Department of Medicine
University of Wisconsin Hospital and Clinics
Madison, WI, USA

Steven Safren PhD
Assistant Professor of Psychology
Harvard Medical School/Massachusetts General Hospital;
Research Scientist
Fenway Community Health
Boston, MA, USA

Pekka AI Saikku MD PhD
Professor of Medical Microbiology
Department of Medical Microbiology
University of Oulu
Oulu, Finland

Juan C Salazar MD MPH
Assistant Professor of Pediatrics
Department of Pediatrics, Division of Infectious Diseases
University of Connecticut Health Center
Children's Medical Center
Hartford, CT, USA

Michelle R Salvaggio MD
Instructor of Medicine
Division of Infectious Diseases
University of Alabama at Birmingham and the Birmingham Veterans Administration Medical Center
Birmingham, AL, USA

Hugo Sax MD
Attending Physician
Infection Control Program
University of Geneva Hospitals
Geneva, Switzerland

Franz-Josef Schmitz MD PhD
Professor of Medicine
Institute for Laboratory Medicine, Microbiology, Hygiene and Transfusion Medicine
Hospital Minden
Minden, Germany

Richard-Fabian Schumacher MD
Attendant Physician, Children's Hospital
Department of Pediatrics
University of Brescia
Brescia, Italy

Bernhard Schwartländer MD PhD
Director, Department of HIV
World Health Organization
Geneva, Switzerland

Euan M Scrimgeour MD FRACP DTM&H FAFPHM
Associate Professor in Infectious and Tropical Diseases
Department of Medicine
Sultan Qaboos University
Sultanate of Oman

Edward D Seaton MA MRCP
Clinical Research Fellow
Unit of Dermatology
Imperial College School of Medicine
London, UK

Brahm H Segal MD
Assistant Professor of Medicine, SUNY at Buffalo
Head, Division of Infectious Diseases
Roswell Park Cancer Institute
New York, NY, USA

John W Sellors MD
Senior Medical Advisor, Reproductive Health
Program for Appropriate Technology in Health
Seattle, WA, USA

Kent A Sepkowitz MD FACP
Associate Professor of Medicine
Memorial Sloan-Kettering Cancer Center
New York, NY, USA

Graham R Serjeant CMG CD MD FRCP FRCPE
Director, MRC Laboratories (Jamaica)
University of West Indies
Kingston, Jamaica

Beverly E Sha MD
Associate Professor of Medicine
Section of Infectious Diseases
Rush St Luke's Medical Center
Chicago, IL, USA

Keerti V Shah MD DrPH
Professor of Molecular Microbiology and Immunology
Department of Molecular Microbiology and Immunology
Professor of Oncology
Department of Oncology
Johns Hopkins Bloomberg School of of Public Health
Baltimore, MD, USA

Daniel S Shapiro MD
Director, Clinical Microbiology and Molecular Diagnostics Laboratory
Associate Professor of Medicine, Pathology and Laboratory Medicine.
Clinical Microbiology Laboratory
Boston Medical Center
Boston, MA, USA

Shmuel Shoham MD
c/o Thomas J Walsh MD
Head, Immunocompromised Host Section
Pediatric Oncology Branch
National Cancer Institute
Bethesda, MD, USA

Caroline Shulman MRCGP PhD
(Formerly) Clinical Senior Lecturer
Department of Infectious and Tropical Disease
London School of Hygiene and Tropical Medicine
London, UK

Rehka Sivadas MD
Fellow in Infectious Diseases
Department of Medicine
State University of New York at Stonybrook
New York, NY, USA

Mary PE Slack MA MB BChir FRCPath
Senior Lecturer in Bacteriology
John Radcliffe Hospital
Headington
Oxford, UK

Jihad Slim MD
Associate Professor
Seton Hall PG Medical School
St. Michael's Medical Center
Newark, NJ, USA

Leon Smith MD
Professor of Medicine
St Michael's Medical Centre
Newark, NJ, USA

Jack D Sobel MD
Professor of Medicine
Chief, Division of Infectious Diseases
Detroit Medical Center
Chief Division of Infectious Diseases
Department of Internal Medicine
Harper Hospital
Detroit, MI, USA

Rudolph Sobesky MD
Service d'Hepatologie
Hopital Necker
Paris, France

Claus O Solberg MD
Professor of Medicine and Infectious Diseases
Chairman Medical Department Bergen
University Hospital, Haukeland Hospital
Bergen, Norway

Joseph S Solomkin MD FACS
Professor of Surgery
Department of Surgery
University of Cincinnati College of Medicine
Cincinnati, OH, USA

Alex Soriano
Specialist, Infectious Diseases and AIDS Units
Institute of Infectious Diseases and Immunology,
Hospital Clinic of Barcelona
Barcelona, Spain

Montse Soriano-Gabarró MD MSc
Meningitis and Special Pathogens Branch
Centers for Disease Control and Prevention
Altanta, GA, USA

Lisa A Spacek MD PhD
Post Doctoral Fellow
Division of Infectious Diseases
Department of Medicine
John Hopkins University
Baltimore, MD, USA

Shiranee Sriskandan PhD FRCP MA MBBChir
Senior Lecturer in Infectious Diseases
Consultant in Infectious Diseases
Department of Infectious Diseases
Faculty of Medicine
Imperial College School of Medicine
London, UK

Samuel L Stanley Jr MD
Professor of Medicine
Department of Medicine
Division of Infectious Diseases
Washington University School of Medicine
St Louis, MO, USA

James M Steckelberg MD
Professor of Medicine
Division of Infectious Disease
Department of Internal Medicine
Rochester, MN, USA

David Stephens MD
c/o Montse Soriano-Gabarró
Meningitis and Special Pathogens Branch
Centers for Disease Control and Prevention
Altanta, GA, USA

Iain Stephenson MRCP MA (Cantab) MB BChir
Specialist Registrar
Infectious Diseases Unit
Leicester Royal Infirmary
Leicester, UK

Dennis L Stevens PhD MD
Professor of Medicine, University of Washington
School of Medicine, Seattle, WA
Chief, Infectious Diseases Section
Veterans Affairs Medical Center
Boise, ID, USA

Athena Stoupis MD
Rhode Island Hospital/Jane Brown
Providence, RI, USA

Marc J Struelens MD PhD
Professor of Medical Microbiology
Service de Microbiologie
Universite Libre de Bruxelles - Hôpital Erasme
Bruxelles, Belgium

Richard C Summerbell PhD
Senior Researcher
Centraalbureau voor Schimmelcultures
Royal Netherlands Academy of Sciences
Utrecht, The Netherlands

Sarah J Tabrizi BSc (Hons) MRCP PhD
Department of Health National Clinical Scientist and Clinical Senior Lecturer
Department of Neurodegenerative Diseases/MRC
Prion Unit
Institute of Neurology
London, UK

Marc A Tack MD
Infectious Diseases Consultant
Medical Associates of the Hudson Valley P.C.
Kingston
New York, NY, USA

Martin G Täuber MD
Professor of Medicine and Infectious Diseases
Chief, Division of Infectious Diseases
Director, Institute for Infectious Diseases
University of Berne
Berne, Switzerland

Pablo Tebas MD
Associate Professor of Medicine
Division of Infectious Disease
Washington University School of Medicine
St Louis, MO, USA

Marleen Temmerman MD PhD
Professor of Obstetrics and Gynaecology
Department of Obstetrics and Gynaecology
Ghent University
Ghent, Belgium

Steven FT Thijsen MD PhD
Attending Physician
Department of Medical Microbiology
Diakonessenhuis
Utrecht, The Netherlands

Umberto Tirelli MD
Director
Division of Medical Oncology
National Cancer Institute
Aviano, Italy

Nina E Tolkoff-Rubin MD FACP FCCP
Director of the End Stage
Renal Disease Program
and Medical Director of Transplantaion,
Chief of the Hemo- and Peritoneal Dialysis Units,
Massachusetts General Hospital;
Associate Professor of Medicine,
Harvard Medical School,
Boston, MA, USA

Gregory C Townsend MD
Assistant Professor of Medicine
Division of Infectious Diseases
University of Virginia
Charlottesville, VA, USA

Paul M Tulkens MD PhD
Professor of Pharmacology
Unite de Pharmacologie Cellulaire et Moleculaire
Universite Catholique de Louvain
Brussels, Belgium

Mark W Tyndall MD ScD FRCPC
Program Director, Epidemiology BC
Assistant Professor of Medicine
Division of Infectious Diseases
BC Centre for Excellence in HIV/AIDS
St. Paul's Hospital
University of British Colombia
Vancouver, BC, Canada

Emanuela Vaccher
Centro di Riferimento Oncologico
Aviano, Italy

Françoise van Bambeke PharmD PhD
Research Associate of the Belgian Fonds National de la Recherche Scientifique
Unité de Pharmacologie Cellulaire et Moléculaire
Brussels, Belgium

Jos W M van der Meer MD PhD FRCP
Professor of Medicine, Catholic University Nijmegen
Department of Medicine
University Medical Centre
Nijmegen, The Netherlands

Anton M van Loon PhD
Director
Department of Virology
University Medical Centre Utrecht
Utrecht, The Netherlands

Anaïs Vallet-Pichard MD
Service d'Hepatologie
Hopital Necker
Paris, France

Andrew M Veitch BSc MRCP
Research Fellow in Gastroenterology
Whipps Cross Hospital
London, UK

Stefano Vella MD
Research Director
Instituto Superiore di Sanita
Rome, Italy

Jan Verhoef MD PhD
Professor of Medical Microbiology
Eijkman-Winkler Institute for Microbiology
Infectious Diseases and Inflammation
Utrecht, The Netherlands

Sten H Vermund MD PhD
Professor of Medicine, Pediatrics, and Epidemiology and International Health
University of Alabama at Birmingham
Birmingham, AL, USA

Maarten R Visser MD PhD
Associate Professor
Eijkman-Winkler Institute for Microbiology,
Infectious Diseases and Inflammation
Utrecht, The Netherlands

Govinda S Visvesvara PhD
Research Microbiologist
Division of Parasitic Diseases
Centers for Disease Control and Prevention
Atlanta, GA, USA

Mark A Wainberg PhD
Professor of Medicine
Director McGill University AIDS Centre
McGill University AIDS Centre
Montreal, QC, Canada

Thomas J Walsh MD
Head, Immunocompromised Host Section
Pediatric Oncology Branch
National Cancer Institute
Bethesda, MD, USA

Katherine N Ward BSc MA PhD MB BChir FRCPath
Consultant Virologist/Senior Lecturer
Department of Virology
Royal Free and University College Medical School,
University College London
London, UK

David W Warnock MD PhD FRCPath
Associate Director, Division of Bacterial and Mycotic Diseases
Adjunct Professor of Microbiology and Immunology
Emory School of Medicine
National Center for Infectious Diseases
Centers for Disease Control and Prevention
Atlanta, GA, USA

Mary J Warrell MBBS MRCP FRCPath
Clinical Virologist
The Centre for Tropical Medicine
John Radcliffe Hospital
Oxford, UK

David A Warrell MA DM DSc FRCP FRCPE FMedSci
Head, Nuffield Department of Clinical Medicine
University of Oxford
The Centre for Tropical Medicine
Oxford, UK

Rainer Weber MD
Professor of Infectious Diseases
Division of Infectious Diseases and Hospital Epidemiology
Department of Internal Medicine
University Hospital
Zurich, Switzerland

Wolfgang Weidner MD
Professor and Head of Urology
Deparment of Urology
University of Giessen
Giessen
Germany

Robert A Weinstein MD
Chaiman, Infectious Diseases, Cook County Hospital;
Professor of Medicine, Rush Medical College
Division of Infectious Disease
Cook County Hospital
Chicago, IL, USA

Peter F Weller MD FACP
Professor of Medicine, Harvard Medical School
Chief, Allergy and Inflammation Divisions
Department of Medicine
Beth Israel Deaconess Medical Center
Boston, MA, USA

Simon Wessely MA BM BCh MSc MD FRCP FRCPsych FMed Sci
Professor of Epidemiological and Liaison Psychiatry
Department of Psychological Medicine
Guy's, King's and St Thomas's School of Medicine and
Institute of Psychiatry
London, UK

L Joseph Wheat MD
Director, MiraVista Diagnostics and MiraBella Technologies
MiraVista Diagnostics
Indianapolis IN, USA

Estella Whimbey MD
Associate Medical Director
University of Washington Medical Center
Seattle, WA, USA

Michael Whitby MD BS DTM&H MPH FRACP FRCPA FRC Path FAFPHM
Director, Infection Management Services
Princess Alexandra Hospital
Brisbane, Qld, Australia

Richard J Whitley MD
Loeb Eminent Scholar Chair in Pediatrics;
Professor of Pediatrics, Medicine and Microbiology
The University of Alabama at Birmingham
Birmingham, AL, USA

Hilton C Whittle FRCP FWACP F Med Sci OBE
Deputy Director and Visiting Professor,
London School Hygiene and Tropical Medicine
MRC Laboratories
Banjul, The Gambia

Rodney E Willoughby Jr MD
Director, Clinical Infectious Diseases
Johns Hopkins Hospital
Baltimore, MD, USA

Mary E Wilson MD FACP
Associate Professor of Medicine
Mount Auburn Hospital
Cambridge, MA, USA

Robert Wilson MD FRCP
Consultant Physician,
Royal Brompton Hospital;
Reader, National Heart and Lung Institute,
Imperial College of Science,
Technology and Medicine
Royal Brompton Hospital
London, UK

Richard E Winn MD
Divison Director of Pulmonary Medicine and Infectious Diseases Staff,
Scott and White Clinic;
Professor of Internal Medicine,
Texas A&M College of Medicine
Temple, TX, USA

Martin J Wiselka MD PhD FRCP
Consultant in Infectious Disease
Leicester Royal Infirmary
Leicester, UK

Martin J Wood MA FRCP FRCP(Ed)
(Deceased)
Consultant Physician
Department of Infection
Heartlands Hospital
Birmingham, UK

James R Yankaskas MD
Professor of Medicine
Cystic Fibrosis / Pulmonary Research and Treatment Center
The University of North Carolina
Chapel Hill, NC, USA

Heinz Zeichhardt PhD
Professor of Virology
Institute of Infectious Diseases Medicine
Department of Virology
Free University of Berlin
University Hospital Benjamin Franklin
Berlin, Germany

Jonathan M Zenilman MD
Professor of Medicine
Johns Hopkins University School of Medicine
Baltimore, MD, USA

George Zhanel PharmD PhD
Professor of Medical Microbiology
Faculty of Medicine
University of Manitoba
Winnipeg, MB, Canada

Stephen H Zinner MD
Charles S. Davidson Professor of Medicine,
Harvard Medical School
Chair, Department of Medicine
Mount Auburn Hospital
Cambridge, MA, USA

Arie J Zuckerman MD DSc FRCP FRCPath
Professor of Medical Microbiology
Academic Centre for Travel Medicine and Vaccines
Royal Free Hospital Medical School
London, UK

Jane N Zuckerman MBBS MD
Senior Lecturer and Honorary Consultant
Academic Centre for Travel Medicine and Vaccines
Royal Free Hospital Medical School
London, UK

Alimuddin Zumla PhD FRCP (Lon) FRCP(Edin)
Professor of Infectious Diseases and International Health
Royal Free and University College London Medical School
London, UK

SECTION

5

HIV AND AIDS

Nathan Clumeck
William G Powderly

chapter 115

Epidemiology of HIV Infection

Michel Caraël, Bernhard Schwartländer & Peter Piot

INTRODUCTION

This chapter describes the distribution and transmission patterns of HIV infection. Although the biology and modes of transmission are broadly the same in the developing and industrialized world, there are some striking differences in the epidemiology, which are due to a variety of behavioral factors and socio-economic conditions. Furthermore, the AIDS problem is overwhelmingly concentrated in developing countries, where more than 90% of all people infected with HIV live.

In less than 15 years HIV has reached the level of a pandemic and AIDS has been reported in over 190 countries.[1] It is also increasingly clear that the HIV pandemic consists of several separate epidemics, each with its own distinct characteristics. On a world scale, the epidemic has evolved predominantly into a heterosexually transmitted disease in the developing world and, increasingly, of underprivileged and marginalized populations in the industrialized world.

FREQUENCY OF HIV INFECTION AND AIDS AND DEFINITION

Shortly after the first reports of AIDS in the USA in 1981 among homosexual men and injecting drug users, it became obvious that the disease was also present in Haitians living in North America and in Africans seen in Belgium for medical care at the end of 1983.[2,3] Subsequently, surveys in Haiti and in central Africa confirmed the occurrence of several epidemic foci of HIV in these areas.[4–7]

The identification of another variant of the virus, labeled HIV-2, among West African populations and then in other African countries with a Portuguese colonial history increased further the heterogeneity of what quickly emerged as a global pandemic. The routes of transmission and risk factors of HIV-2 and HIV-1 are similar, but it has become increasingly clear that the pathogenic effect of HIV-2 is lower than that of HIV-1.[8] In the rest of this chapter, HIV refers to HIV-1.

Although there are no doubts that the HIV epidemic has spread well beyond the most pessimistic predictions, its exact magnitude is difficult to assess. This is due to the largely silent nature of this infection and to limited surveillance in many countries. In addition, diagnostic facilities for HIV infection and its associated opportunistic diseases are still limited in many clinical settings. Another longstanding obstacle has been the absence of a simple definition for AIDS. Indeed, the early definition of AIDS of the Centers for Disease Control and Prevention required expanded laboratory diagnostic capabilities. The World Health Organization (WHO) has adopted a simplified definition of AIDS in adults (1985 Bangui definition), based on the recognition of at least two major clinical signs in combination with at least one minor sign. This is straightforward to use and allows identification of AIDS cases without the need to perform expensive tests. In early 1994, taking into account better access to laboratory diagnostic methods, a positive serologic test for HIV-1 and/or HIV-2 and a broader spectrum of clinical manifestations of HIV such as tuberculosis and pneumonia were added to this definition.[9]

GLOBAL CASES: REPORTS AND ESTIMATIONS

By the end of 2001, over 2.7 million cumulative AIDS cases had been reported to the WHO. However, because of under-reporting, underdiagnosis and delays in reporting, the joint United Nations Program on HIV/AIDS (UNAIDS) and WHO estimated that a total of more than 22 million cumulative AIDS cases in adults and children may have occurred worldwide. The developing world as a whole accounted for well over 80% of all AIDS cases. According to UNAIDS nearly 2.7 million cases are pediatric AIDS cases resulting from mother-to-child HIV transmission. During 2001 alone, HIV infection and AIDS-associated illnesses killed an estimated 3 million people, including 580,000 children; this represents 25% of all deaths since the start of this global epidemic, illustrating that on, a worldwide scale, mortality from HIV infection is accelerating, notwithstanding declining mortality from HIV infection in most industrialized countries.

A more complete picture of the extent of the epidemic is given by the number of people infected with HIV (Table 115.1).[1] By conservative estimates, well over 37.2 million adults and a further 2.7 million children under 15 years have been infected with HIV since the start of the pandemic. Figure 115.1 shows the estimated regional distribution of young people aged 15–24 who have HIV infection and AIDS. More than 13 million children under 15 years of age have lost their mothers or both parents as a result of AIDS-related death.

The incidence of HIV infection in the general population is not known but there have been several cohort studies or repeated surveys of the same population in some countries. The highest HIV incidence rates – 10–15% a year – have been found among sex workers and injecting drug users in various cities around the world. Based on HIV infection trends in different parts of the world, the number of new AIDS cases is expected to continue to increase, mostly in Africa, but also in Asia and eastern Europe.

Geographic distribution of HIV infection and AIDS

North America, Europe and Australia

The cumulative total of reported AIDS cases in the USA was nearly 717,000 at the end of 1999 and it was estimated that more than 940,000 adults and children are living with HIV/AIDS. The annual incidence of AIDS and deaths among people living with AIDS declined during 1996, reflecting the beneficial impact of new available therapies. Although this trend continued through 1998, data for 1999 suggest that the number of AIDS cases and deaths might be leveling out.[10] Early in the epidemic, most infections occurred in men who have sex with men, but the incidence in this group leveled off as early as 1985–7. However, HIV prevalence levels of 7–9% are still found among young adult homosexual and bisexual men in major cities such as San Francisco and New York. The largest decline in the proportion of reported AIDS cases in the USA has occurred among homosexual and bisexual men, whereas cases reported to be acquired by heterosexual transmission have increased, with highest rates in women. Each year approximately 7000 women with HIV

GLOBAL ESTIMATES OF HIV/AIDS WORLDWIDE AT END OF 2001		
Number of people living with HIV/AIDS	Total	40 million
	Adults	37.2 million
	Women	17.6 million
	Children under 15 years	2.7 million
People newly infected with HIV in 2001	Total	5 million
	Adults	4.3 million
	Women	1.8 million
	Children under 15 years	800,000
AIDS deaths in 2001	Total	3 million
	Adults	2.4 million
	Women	1.1 million
	Children under 15 years	580,000

Table 115.1 Global estimates of HIV/AIDS worldwide at end of 2001.

infection give birth, and without prophylactic treatment 1000–2000 of their infants would be infected with HIV. The prevalence of HIV among injecting drug users has been increasing steadily as well, but with large regional differences. Since the late 1980s on the west coast of the USA, about 90% of people who have AIDS are men who have sex with men, whereas on the northeastern coast the majority of newly diagnosed people with AIDS are injecting drug users. Young adults belonging to ethnic minorities (including men who have sex with men) face considerably greater risks of infection that they did 5 years ago. African-Americans, for instance, make up only 12% of the population of the USA but constituted 47% of AIDS cases reported in 2000 (Fig. 115.2).

Canada has a cumulative number of HIV infections estimated to be around 50,000. Women now represent 24% of new HIV infections, as compared with 8.5% in 1995. The estimated number of new infections has been slowly declining and was around 2000 in 2001. There was, however, concern about recent outbreaks in the injecting drug user community in Vancouver and an incidence of 5 new infections per 100 drug injectors per year in Montreal, one of the highest rates in North America.[11]

By the end of 1999, in western Europe as a whole, AIDS incidence appeared to have decreased and this seems mainly due to a decrease in the incidence of homosexually acquired AIDS and of injecting drug use (Fig. 115.3).[12] However, in Italy, Spain and Portugal, where the majority of the cases are acquired through injecting drug use, the AIDS incidence is still high. As a consequence of this shift, there is a marked increase in the proportion of reported female cases, from 12% in 1986 to 25% in 2000. Following the introduction of highly active antiretroviral therapy (HAART), the number of reports of deaths among AIDS cases also continued to decrease, at an average annual rate of –30% between 1997 and 2000.

In countries of eastern Europe, which are experiencing profound social change, HIV epidemics are much more recent but are increasing exponentially, mainly in relation to drug use. Ukraine recently reported a rise of HIV prevalence among injecting drug users in Nikolayev from 2% to 57% in 1996 within 1 year. Although fewer than 400 HIV infections were recorded between 1987 and 1994, a total of 1500 were recorded in 1995 and close to 40,000 in 2000. The Russian Federation and eastern European countries are experiencing a similar progression, especially among injecting drug users. Furthermore, in the former Soviet Union, syphilis incidence rates doubled in 1995 compared with those in 1994 to reach close to 200/100,000 population, illustrating increased unsafe sexual behavior. A particular problem has resulted from the nosocomial epidemics in children in Romania and the Russian Federation in the late 1980s, which are the cause of HIV infection in over 50% of children who have AIDS in central and eastern Europe today. With an estimated cumulative total of more than 113,000 HIV infections, the Russian Federation and Ukraine have a similar number of HIV infections to western Europe.

YOUNG WOMEN AND MEN (AGED 15–24) ESTIMATED TO BE LIVING WITH HIV/AIDS, 2001

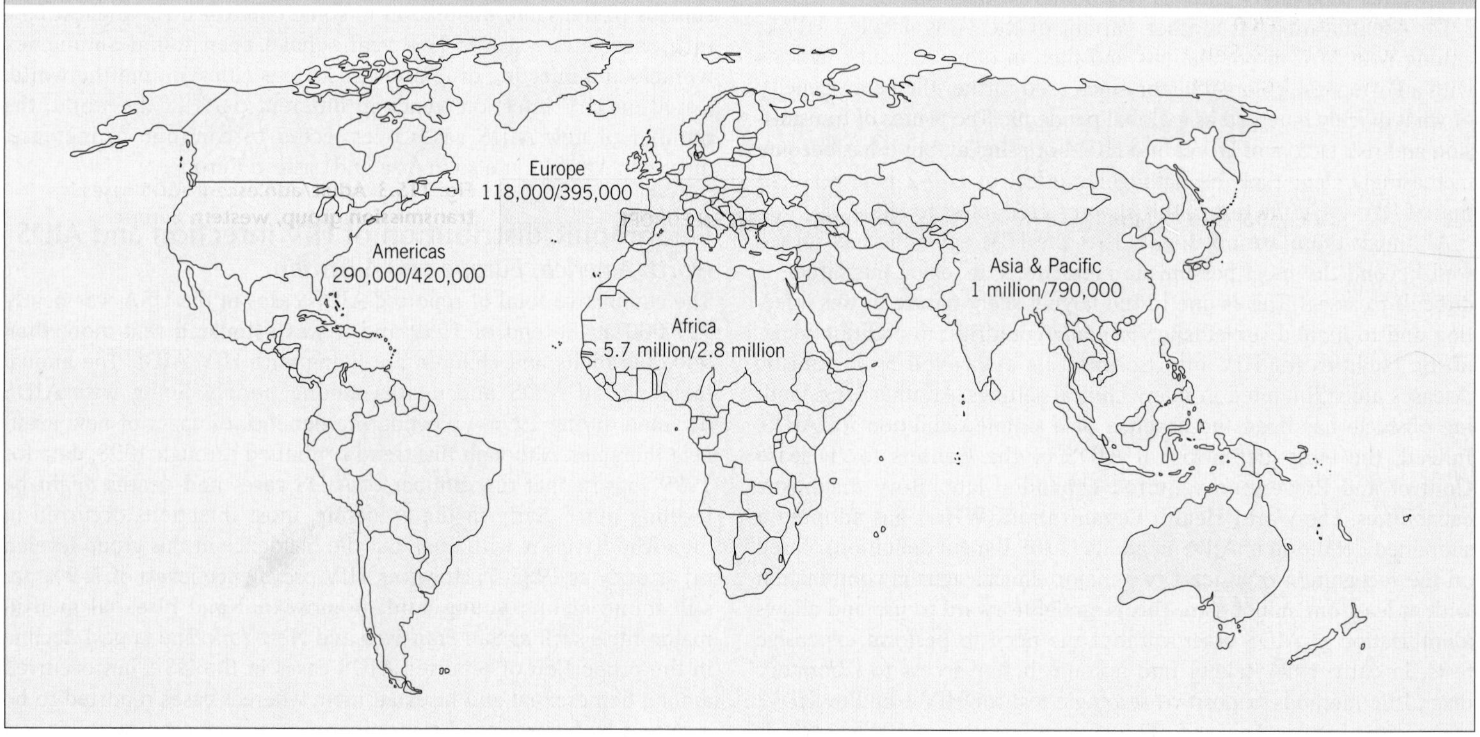

Fig. 115.1 Young women and men (aged 15–24 years) estimated to be living with HIV/AIDS, 2001. Total at end of 2001, 40 million.

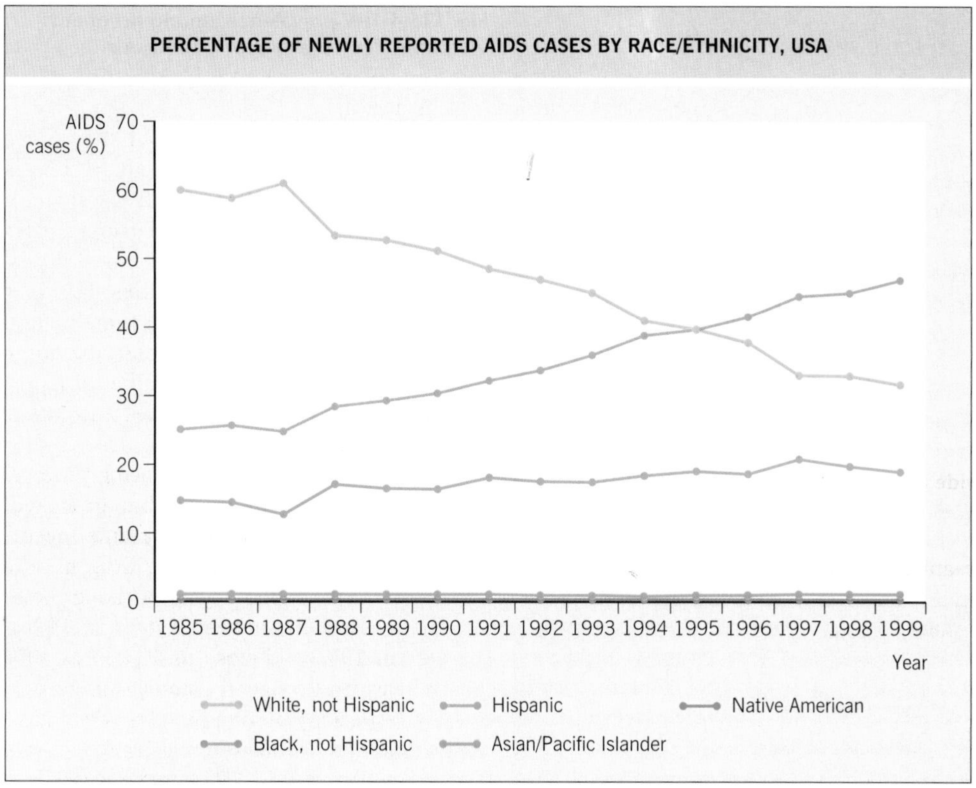

Fig. 115.2 Percentage of newly reported AIDS cases by race/ethnicity, USA.

In Australia and New Zealand, just as in several countries of northern Europe and some parts of the USA and Canada, the vast majority of HIV infections have been acquired through sexual contacts between men, but the incidence reached a peak in the mid 1980s. Programs involving community members and allowing easy access to sterile injecting equipment and methadone treatment have permitted the prevalence in injecting drug users to remain very low, at around 1% in several major cities. Heterosexual transmission is rare. There is evidence that HIV infection rates have reached a plateau in Australia and are declining in New Zealand.

Sub-Saharan Africa

In the nations of sub-Saharan Africa, prevalence rates in the general population vary from less than 1% to 20% and more. Although the epidemic was first recognized in central and east Africa, where it remains at high levels, there is also a large epidemic in west Africa within and around the Ivory Coast. According to UNAIDS, at the end of 2000, 28.1 million adults and children had HIV infection in sub-Saharan Africa, of whom 50% were female. Of the 5.1 million estimated HIV-infected children born in the world since the beginning of the pandemic, over 90% have been born in Africa. In some cities in central and southern Africa, approximately 35% of women attending antenatal clinics have HIV.[1]

The prevalence of HIV continues to increase, mainly in the southern part of Africa and in the west. In major urban areas of Botswana, HIV prevalence levels in adults had reached more than 40% by 1997. HIV prevalence in pregnant women in South Africa has also increased dramatically; for example, between 1990 and 1998 HIV

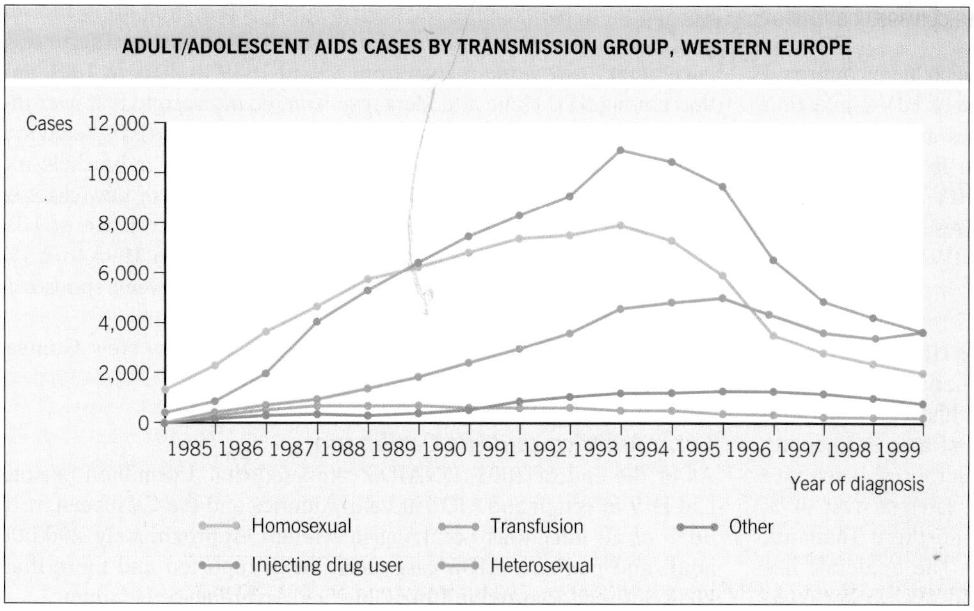

Fig. 115.3 Adult/adolescent AIDS cases by transmission group, western Europe.

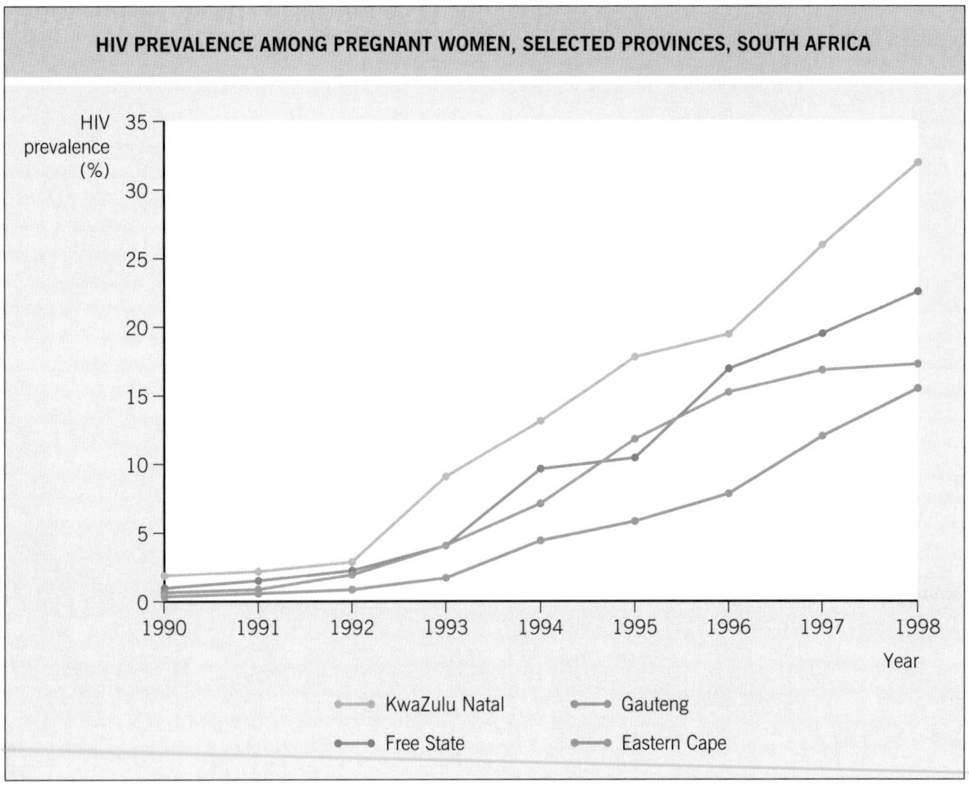

Fig. 115.4 HIV prevalence among pregnant women, selected provinces, South Africa.

prevalence in pregnant women increased from 1% to 21% in the Free State, the North Cape, Mpumalanga and the northern and north west states (Fig 115.4).

National and city-based serosurveys carried out at the end of the 1980s have given age- and sex-specific seroprevalence rates that show a similar pattern everywhere, typical of heterosexual and perinatal transmission of HIV from mother to child. Rates usually show a bimodal curve with a first peak prevalence in children under 5 years of age, then very few infections, and a second peak at 20–30 years of age, with very few infections in people over 40. In Kinshasa, Zaire, but also in east Africa, young women under 25 years of age were three to five times more frequently infected with HIV than men of the same age. In contrast, after 35 years of age this ratio reverses and more men than women are infected. An explanation for these differences is probably found in a combination of biologic factors, such as a higher biologic susceptibility to HIV infection and other sexually transmitted diseases (STDs) in young women, and cultural patterns, such as the preference of men for female partners younger than themselves.[13,14]

HIV-2 is primarily found in West Africa but has also been confirmed in other African countries. The highest prevalence of HIV-2 infection is found in Guinea Bissau, with prevalence rates as high as 9.5% among adults and an annual incidence of 0.9%. In contrast to the increasing spread of HIV-1, the prevalence of HIV-2 has remained rather stable in West Africa. This is probably the result of the higher transmissibility of HIV-1 compared with that of HIV-2.[15]

Asia and the Pacific

It is estimated that about 7.1 million people have HIV infection and AIDS in Asia and the Pacific and 90% of them live in India, Thailand and Myanmar. The spread of HIV in this region became detectable in the second half of the 1980s, at first among injecting drug users in Myanmar and Thailand. The HIV seroprevalence rate among injecting drug users varies substantially; rates of over 60% have been found in China's Yunnan Province, northern Thailand, Manipur state in India, Vietnam and Myanmar. The epidemic has quickly spread out of the injecting drug user and sex worker communities in some major cities of India and into the general population. In Mumbai, in less than 5 years (i.e. by 1996), HIV prevalence had reached 50% among sex workers, 33% in STD patients and 4.3% in pregnant women. Most HIV transmission in Asia and eastern Europe is due to the sharing of infected needles among injecting drug users (Fig. 115.5).

Estimates of the number of adults and children infected with HIV in India are close to 4 million and by the turn of the century there may have been more people in India who had AIDS than in any other country in the world. In most of Asia, heterosexual transmission is now by far the predominant mode of spread.

Surveillance data in China leads to an estimation of more than 1 million people living with HIV. Increasing evidence has emerged of serious epidemics in Henan province in central China, where many tens of thousands of rural villagers have become infected by selling their blood to collecting centers.

In Thailand, the epidemic has been particularly well studied. HIV has spread in overlapping waves through injecting drug users and sex workers, their clients and the female partners of clients. The prevalence among sex workers rose from 3% in 1989 to 30% in 1996 and that among STD clinic attenders rose from nearly zero to 9% over the same period. There is convincing evidence of a fall in risky behaviors following extensive programs to promote condom use in brothels and to discourage men from visiting them.[16] The number of new cases of STDs seen in clinics has fallen and the national prevalence of HIV among young military recruits dropped from 3.6% in 1993 to 2.5% in 1996. There are indications that transmission between spouses is now responsible for more than half of new infections.

An HIV epidemic has recently developed in Papua New Guinea, fueled mainly by heterosexual transmission.

Latin America and the Caribbean

As of the end of 2001, UNAIDS estimated that 1.4 million persons had HIV infection and AIDS in Latin America and the Caribbean, with 30% of all infections occurring in women. Approximately 200,000 adult and pediatric AIDS cases have been reported and more than 70% of these occurred in Brazil, Mexico, Argentina or Honduras.

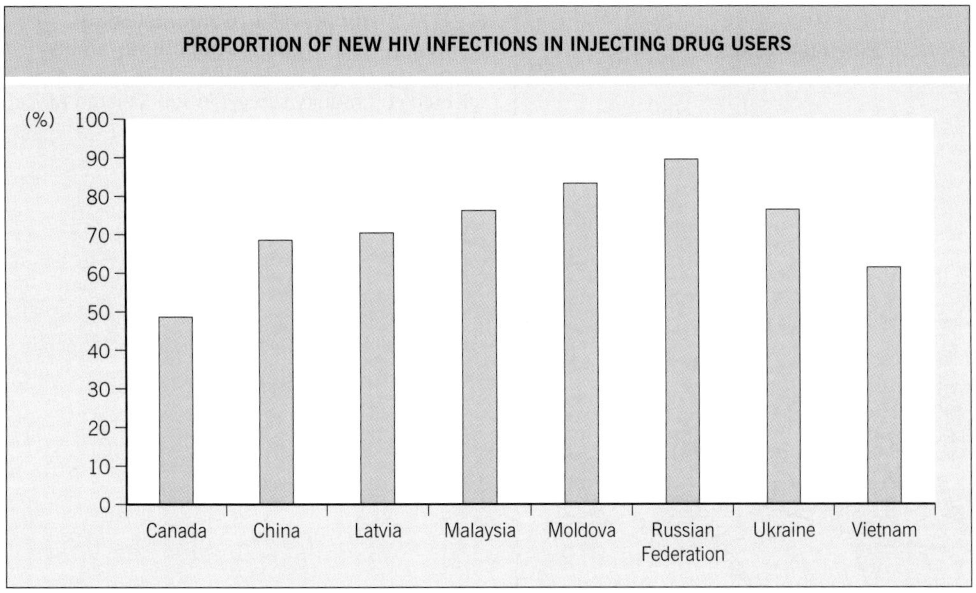

Fig. 115.5 Proportion of new HIV infections in injecting drug users.

In the early years of the HIV epidemic in Latin America, over 50% of reported infections were among homosexual and bisexual men; heterosexual transmission contributed another 25%. However, since the mid-1980s, there has been an increase in heterosexual transmission, principally among bisexual men and their female sexual partners, and among sex workers and their clients. In Brazil, for example, the proportion of reported AIDS cases attributable to heterosexual transmission increased from 3% in 1985 to 31% in 1996. In Saõ Paulo, data suggest a different pattern of HIV spread between men and women; whereas HIV prevalence among male STD clinic attenders was stable between 1993 and 1994, rates may have increased more than 5-fold among female STD clinic attenders over the same period. It was estimated in 1999 in Brazil that, in addition to the 30,900 children orphaned as a result of HIV infection and AIDS, more than 100,000 children had mothers who were currently infected with HIV (Fig. 115.6). HIV is also reported to be spreading rapidly among injecting drug users in Brazil and Argentina and presents a growing problem.

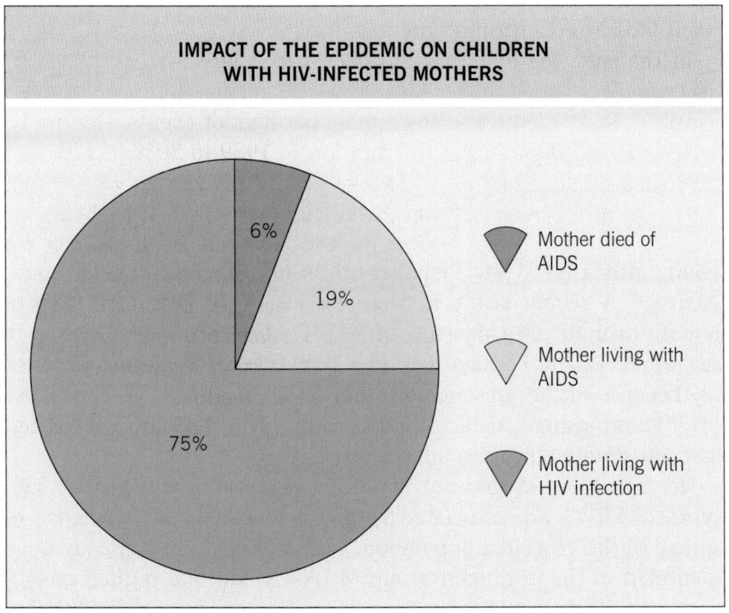

Fig. 115.6 Impact of the epidemic on children with HIV-infected mothers. Model of Global Orphan Project, data from Brazil.

Of the Central American countries, Honduras has been especially broadly affected by heterosexual transmission; nearly 60% of the AIDS cases reported in the subregion are in Honduras. In most of the Caribbean, heterosexual transmission has been the predominant mode of transmission for at least a decade. Prevalence rates among pregnant women have reached 4%, 10% and 6% in the Bahamas, Haiti and Trinidad–Tobago respectively. In contrast, infection rates remain relatively low in Jamaica but have risen in marginalized groups such as crack cocaine users and migrant laborers. In the Dominican Republic, HIV seroprevalence has reached levels of up to 11% among female sex workers, 3–4% among STD patients and 1.4% in pregnant women.

North Africa and the Middle East

By the end of 2001, approximately 440,000 persons in this region had HIV infection and AIDS, with a male:female ratio of 2.5:1. So far, the spread of the virus appears to be limited to homosexual men and injecting drug users in large cities. About 75% of the AIDS cases have been reported from Morocco, Sudan, Saudi Arabia, Tunisia and Djibouti. HIV seroprevalence levels among the general population show seropositivity far less than 1%. Djibouti seems to be the hardest hit country in the region, with prevalence levels of up to 9% in pregnant women. A rise in HIV prevalence among STD patients has recently been noticed in Sudan.

Dynamics of the HIV epidemic

Under circumstances that are not yet fully understood, epidemics may suddenly explode, with rates of infection increasing several-fold within only a few years. For example, estimation of HIV seroprevalence among injecting drug users seeking treatment in Bangkok increased from zero in 1985–6 to 16% in 1988 and 40–60% in 1992. Outside these vulnerable groups, contrasting situations have been found in the general population. Cambodia did not record its first diagnosis of HIV infection until 1991. By 1996, HIV prevalence among pregnant women was approaching 5% but was estimated to have declined to 2.3% at the end of 2000 through the implementation of 100% condom use in brothels.

In sub-Saharan Africa, most new HIV infections are now occurring among young people and particularly among young girls (Fig. 115.7). There is often a doubling of the HIV rate between the 15–19 age group and the 20–24 age group. In these relatively generalized epidemics, more women are infected with HIV than men both in their late teens and in their early 20s. The pattern is consistent

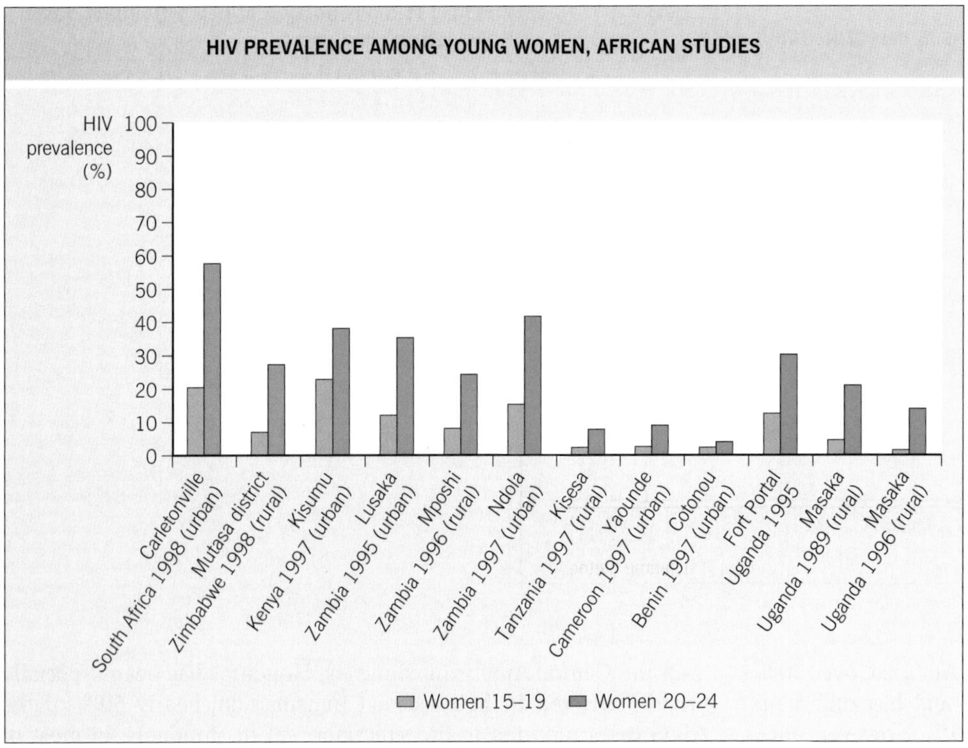

Fig. 115.7 HIV prevalence among young women, African studies. Seropositivity among women aged 15–19 years and 20–24 years in selected community surveys in sub-Saharan Africa, 1995–2000.

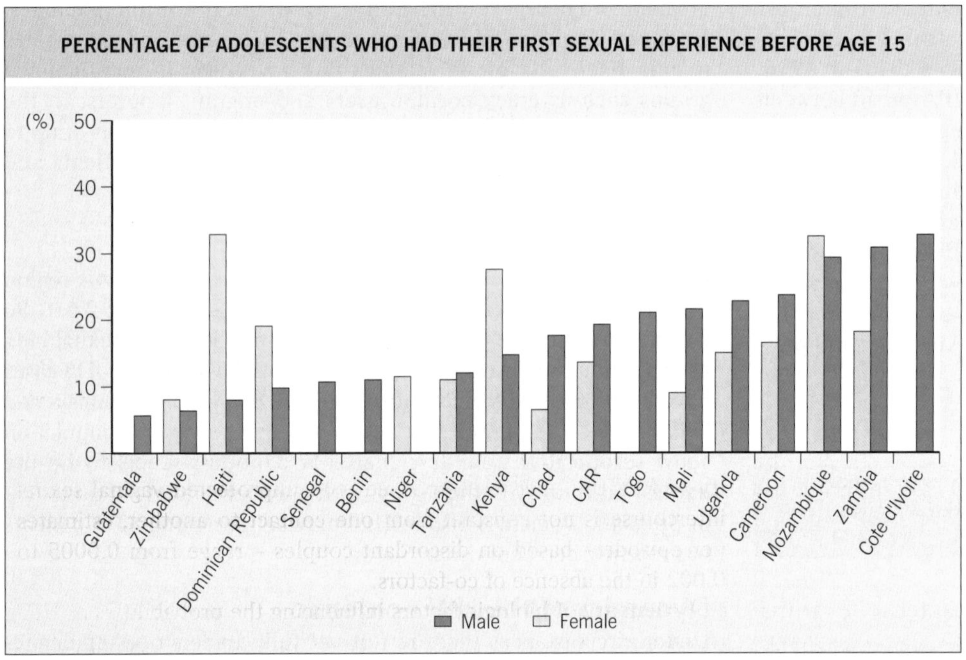

Fig. 115.8 Percentage of adolescents who had their first sexual experience before age 15 years.

regardless of the overall level of HIV prevalence, and regardless of whether the study is conducted in an urban or a rural area. On average, eight times more girls than boys are infected with HIV in their late teens, while among young people in their early 20s three times as many women are infected as men. Sexual behavior patterns and sexual networks are believed to play a critical role as well as an increased biologic susceptibility to HIV/STD associated with early age at first sexual intercourse (Fig 115.8).[17] Another factor influencing the efficiency of the transmission of HIV is the lack of male circumcision and the prevalence of other STDs in a community.

More attention is given now to the role of herpes simplex virus type 2 (HSV-2) as enhancing susceptibility to HIV per sexual act. Figure 115.9 shows the dramatic increase in HSV-2 seropositivity in young girls after a few sexual contacts in a mining town of South Africa.[18] A recent study in Thailand also found that the risk of female-to-male transmission of HIV is about 10 times higher in sex worker–client contact than in a stable sexual relationship, possibly because of the presence of other STDs, such as HSV-2, because of different sexual practices and because of new primary infections associated with a peak in infectiousness.[19,20]

The possibility should not be excluded that different genetic subtypes of HIV-1 are associated with differences in the efficiency of spread of the virus in a population. Nine subtypes have already been identified in the dominant group M (A–H) and one outlier categorized as O. However, only scarce information exists on their distribution in HIV infected populations (Fig. 115.10).[21] Prospective studies and/or repeated studies in the same populations should allow control

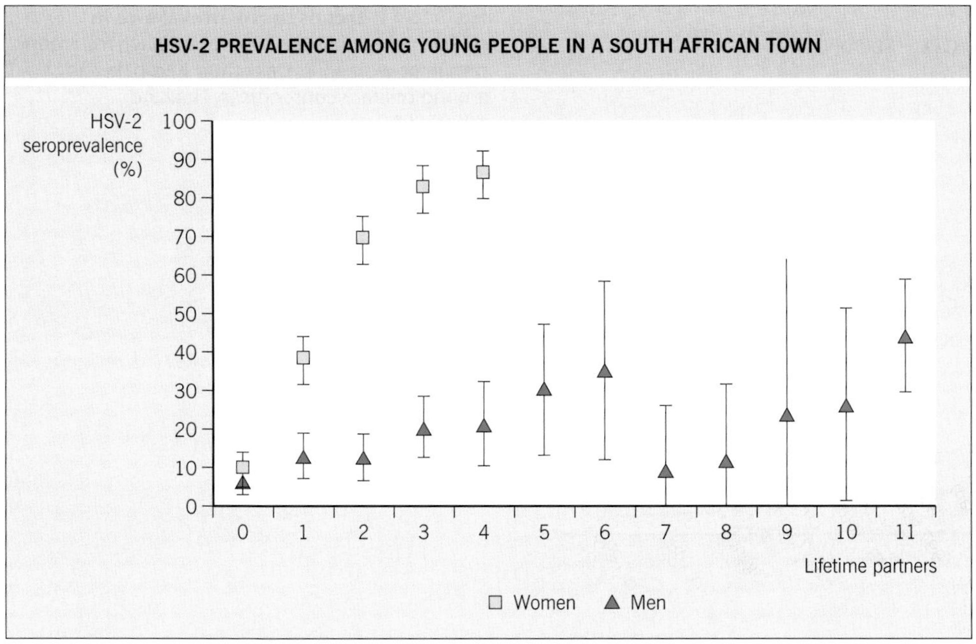

Fig. 115.9 HSV-2 among young people in a South African town. Seroprevalence among male and female adolescents aged 15–24 years by number of lifetime sexual partners.

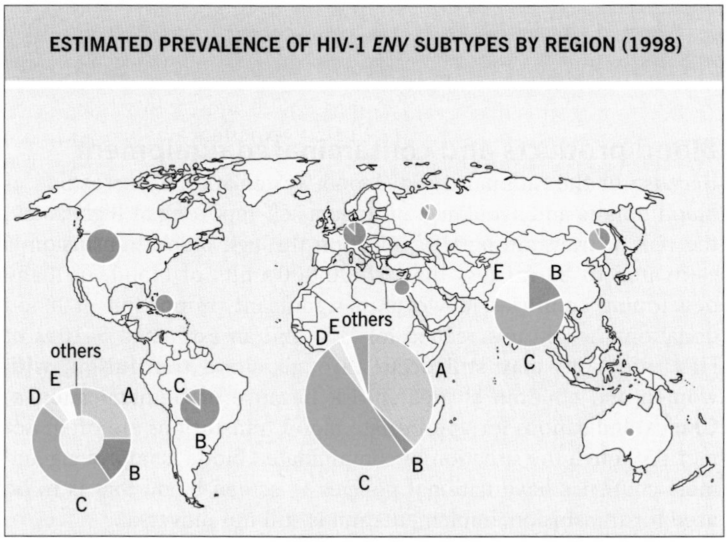

Fig. 115.10 Estimated prevalence of HIV-1 *env* subtypes by region, 1998.

for the many confounders before concluding on differences in the transmissibility of HIV subtypes.[22] The recent observation that some sex workers who had been repeatedly exposed to HIV infections remained HIV-antibody-negative raised the hypothesis that some people have a weaker susceptibility to or even immunity against the virus or specific subtypes.[23] It has been suggested that factors such as certain HLA haplotypes and, more recently, polymorphisms of the chemokine receptor gene *CKR5* may explain such resistance but there is still no conclusive evidence.

The hope that the number of new infections is decreasing comes from studies in many countries in the developed world as well as from Thailand,[16] Senegal[24] and Uganda, a country with one of the older epidemics in Africa. A study of recent trends in HIV infection in young pregnant women in urban Uganda showed a 35% decline in HIV prevalence.[25] This may be explained by a variety of factors such as increased death rates among seropositive people, saturation of the most susceptible and decreased infectiousness of people with HIV over time until the occurrence of AIDS. However, a 2-year delay in the average age at first sexual intercourse, a slight reduction in the number of casual partners and a substantially increased use of condoms are the more likely explanations of the HIV decline among youth in Uganda. Figure 115.11 shows HIV prevalence levels over time in selected sites or nationally for Thailand.

MODES OF TRANSMISSION

Sexual transmission

In contrast to the industrialized world, heterosexual intercourse accounts for more than 85% of cases of HIV infection in developing countries. Early epidemiologic studies showed that risk factors associated with HIV infection were unprotected sexual intercourse with multiple partners or an infected partner and the presence of STDs or a history of STDs.[26–30] More recent studies have highlighted sex differences in patterns of HIV transmission; for many monogamous women the main risk factor for HIV may be the heterosexual and homosexual behavior of their steady partner. Although the probability of HIV transmission associated with unprotected vaginal sexual intercourse is not constant from one contact to another, estimates per episode – based on discordant couples – range from 0.0005 to 0.002 in the absence of co-factors.

A summary of biologic factors influencing the probabilities of HIV transmission from an infected person to a susceptible individual is given in Table 115.2. The presence of STDs suggests a marked risk of concurrent HIV infection, for at least two reasons:

- the modes of transmission of HIV and other STDs are similar; and
- the role of STD-induced genital ulcers, including genital herpes, chancroid[31] and syphilis, as well as nonulcerative STD, facilitates transmission of HIV.

Studies among prostitutes in Kinshasa and Nairobi found gonorrhea, chlamydial infections and trichomoniasis to be independent risk factors for HIV acquisition, with relative risks of 2.7–3.5.[32] Lack of circumcision in males has been shown in most studies to be associated with the risk of acquiring STDs, especially genital ulcer and HIV.[33] Early diagnosis and treatment of STDs have been shown to reduce the incidence of HIV infection significantly in a controlled trial in Mwanza, Tanzania. In the intervention communities, a 42% decline in the rate of newly acquired HIV infections was observed.[34]

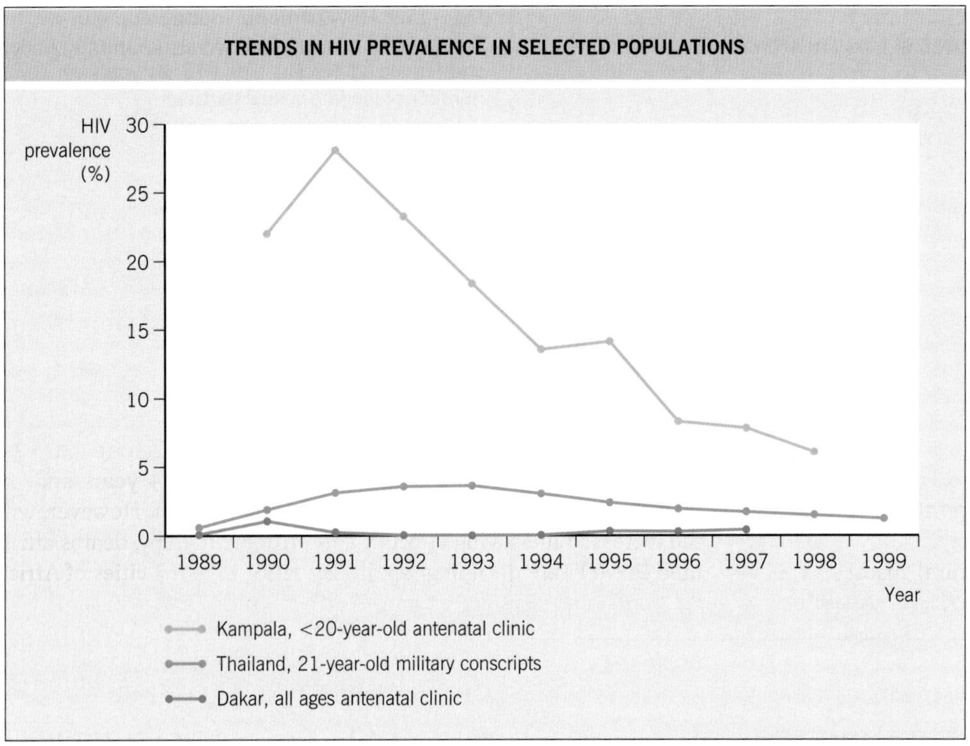

Fig. 115.11 Trends in HIV prevalence in selected populations. HIV seroprevalence among pregnant women in Dakar and Kampala and among military conscripts in Thailand, 1989–1999.

BIOLOGIC FACTORS INCREASING THE PROBABILITY OF SEXUAL TRANSMISSION OF HIV	
Confirmed	Acute primary HIV infection Advanced clinical stage of HIV Sexually transmitted diseases Anal intercourse Menstruation
	HIV-1 versus HIV-2
Under study	Lack of male circumcision Hormonal contraception Cervical ectopy Genital trauma (use of vaginal products)
	Specific HIV-1 clades

Table 115.2 Biologic factors increasing the probability of sexual transmission of HIV.

Perinatal transmission

As a result of heterosexual transmission in women, the number of infants born with HIV infection is growing dramatically. Documented rates of transmission of HIV-1 from mother to child vary from 13% to 48%. HIV-2 is apparently very rarely transmitted perinatally. Mechanisms responsible for such variations in transmission rates of HIV are not yet well understood and probably involve multiple factors such as the immunologic status and viral load of the mother, maternal vitamin A deficiency, ingestion by the newborn at the time of delivery of the mother's HIV-infected blood or amniotic fluid, and ingestion of infected breast milk.

Although the virus has been isolated in breast milk, the risk attributable to breast-feeding and the timing of transmission has not yet been fully assessed and varied from 10% to 20% among mothers with HIV infection. A review of studies estimated that the risk of postnatal HIV transmission was about 30% when mothers seroconverted during the period of breast-feeding.[35,36]

Blood products and contaminated equipment

Because of the rational use of blood, systematic HIV screening of blood donors and avoidance of donors self-reporting at higher risk, the risk of transmitting HIV infection through blood transfusion is estimated to be far less than 1/100,000 units of blood. In many developing countries, however, a significant proportion of blood donations remain unscreened for HIV and an estimated 5–10% of HIV infections may still occur through blood transfusion, with women and children at greater risk because of frequent anemia. Clinical indications for appropriate blood transfusions are often not met. Although the situation of contaminated blood is improving and most countries have national policies to screen blood that is to be used for transfusion, implementation is still not universal.

In many developing countries disposable needles and syringes are often not available and sterilization practices are not always adequate. The use of other skin piercing instruments, for instance for scarification and circumcision, also has some potential for HIV transmission. This results in potentially frequent parenteral exposure to HIV in populations where HIV prevalence is high, including among health care workers.

The probability of HIV infection due to puncture by a contaminated needle may be in the range of that estimated for a single episode of sexual intercourse with an infected partner or for a single episode of intravenous drug use with HIV-contaminated equipment (0.003–0.007). The potential for HIV transmission by unsterilized needles in medical settings is probably weak, but localized outbreaks in the Russian Federation, Romania and Libya among infants and young children have shown that it can occur in special circumstances. In Romania, over 90% of cases have occurred in children living in public institutions as a result of the re-use of contaminated and inadequately sterilized injection equipment or repeated microtransfusions of contaminated blood from one child to another.

In 2001, it became widely known that, in a number of Chinese provinces but mostly in Henan in central China, paid blood donation had caused HIV infections, with estimates ranging from below 100,000 to several hundreds of thousands. Before 1996, poor rural farmers had been selling blood and plasma to commercial blood processing companies to supplement their small income. Blood from many donors was collected and mixed. The red blood cells were separated from the pooled plasma and re-injected back into donors to reduce anemia. Infection rates between villages appear to be highly variable but might be more than 50% of the population in some villages. The risky practice of selling plasma to blood products companies has been illegal for several years now and should not be confused with blood donations for medical purposes, which are screened for HIV and other blood-borne diseases.

NATURAL HISTORY

Data from seroincident cohorts in industrialized countries suggest a median adult incubation period of about 10 years,[37] which increased to 10–12 years in the late 1990s with improvements in the use of antiviral therapy and will probably become even longer with the introduction of antiretroviral combination therapy.

Little information is available about the natural history of HIV infection in many developing countries. The literature suggests, nevertheless, that both the incubation and the symptomatic survival period may be shorter than in industrialized countries because of a combination of poor health care, the particularly high burden of other infections and faster progression to severe immunodeficiency. In African studies the reported median times to AIDS are 2–7.5 years. A recent cohort study in Uganda estimated the cumulative progression to AIDS in their incident group – 22% at 5 years – to be similar to that seen in cohorts of homosexual men.[38] Many previous studies have been of sex workers, in whom the disease may progress faster due to HIV infection with more than one HIV strain and/or immune depression linked with repeated infections by STDs.[39]

It has not been convincingly shown that other infections act as cofactors in the development of AIDS, except for tuberculosis. *Pneumocystis carinii* and Kaposi's sarcoma are less frequently associated with AIDS in developing countries than in industrialized countries.

An unanticipated consequence of the AIDS epidemic has been a dramatic rise in the incidence of tuberculosis. In sub-Saharan Africa, it is estimated that the annual incidence of tuberculosis is 15 times higher among HIV-positive people than among those who are seronegative.[40] In addition, among people who have HIV infection, tuberculosis is now the most common and deadly opportunistic infection, accounting for 40% of all adult deaths, and it is likely that it increases immunodeficiency. Many countries have seen the number of tuberculosis cases doubling or tripling over the past 5 years. This new situation poses an unprecedented challenge to tuberculosis control programs in much of the developing world.

Demographic and social impact

In cities of western Europe such as Paris and Amsterdam, and in more than 66 cities in the Americas, AIDS was at one time the leading cause of death for young men aged 25–44 years and the third most common cause of death for young women. However, with the increased life-saving effect of antiretroviral therapy, deaths attributed to AIDS are declining rapidly. By 1989, in many cities of Africa, AIDS was the leading cause of death and of years of potential life lost in men over 15 years of age, and the second most important cause, after maternal mortality, among adult women. In a rural area of Uganda, with an HIV prevalence of 8%, 50% of all adult deaths and 89% of deaths in those aged 25–34 years were attributed to HIV.[41] Countries with such high HIV prevalence are showing national increases in adult mortality of the order of 300%. Recent projections suggest that life expectancy in sub-Saharan countries most affected by HIV will have been reduced as much as 15 years by the year 2000 when compared with projections without HIV (Fig. 115.12).[42] The long-term implications of AIDS mortality on the population pyramid for Botswana are illustrated in Figure 115.13. In the absence of antiretroviral treatment for AIDS patients, it is projected that there will be more adults in their 60s and 70s in 20 years time than there will be adults in their 40s and 50s.

The HIV pandemic kills adults in their most productive years, when they are responsible for the support and care of dependants. It has been estimated that by the end of 2001 over 13 million children

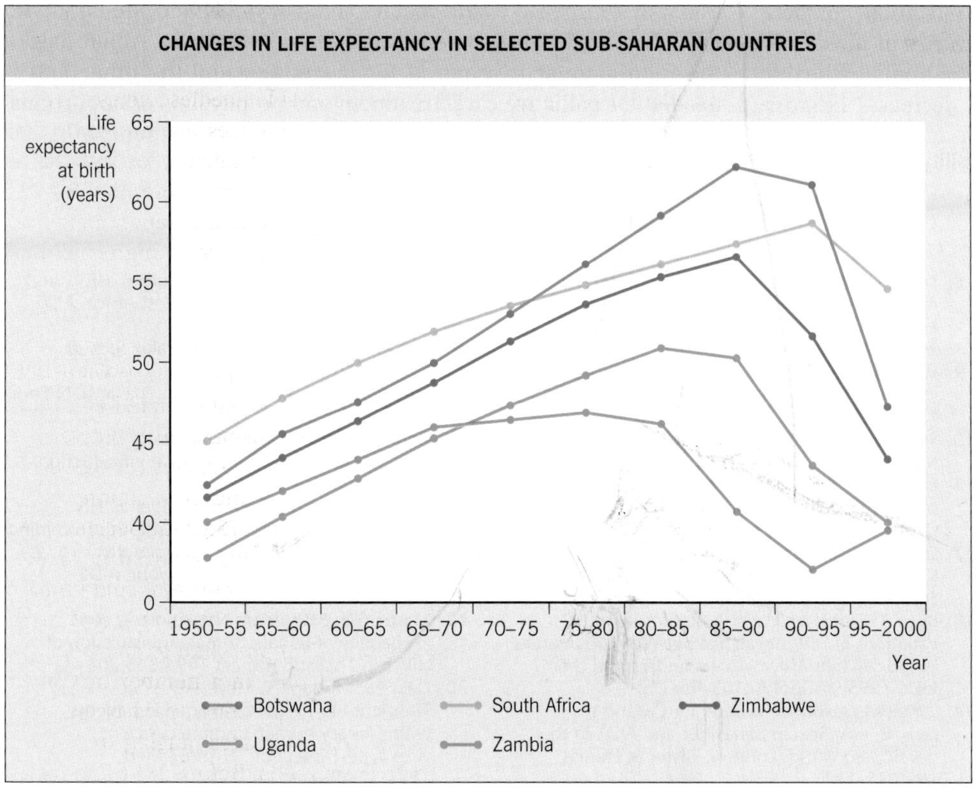

Fig. 115.12 Changes in life expectancy in selected sub-Saharan countries. Projected life expectancy at birth, 1950–2000.

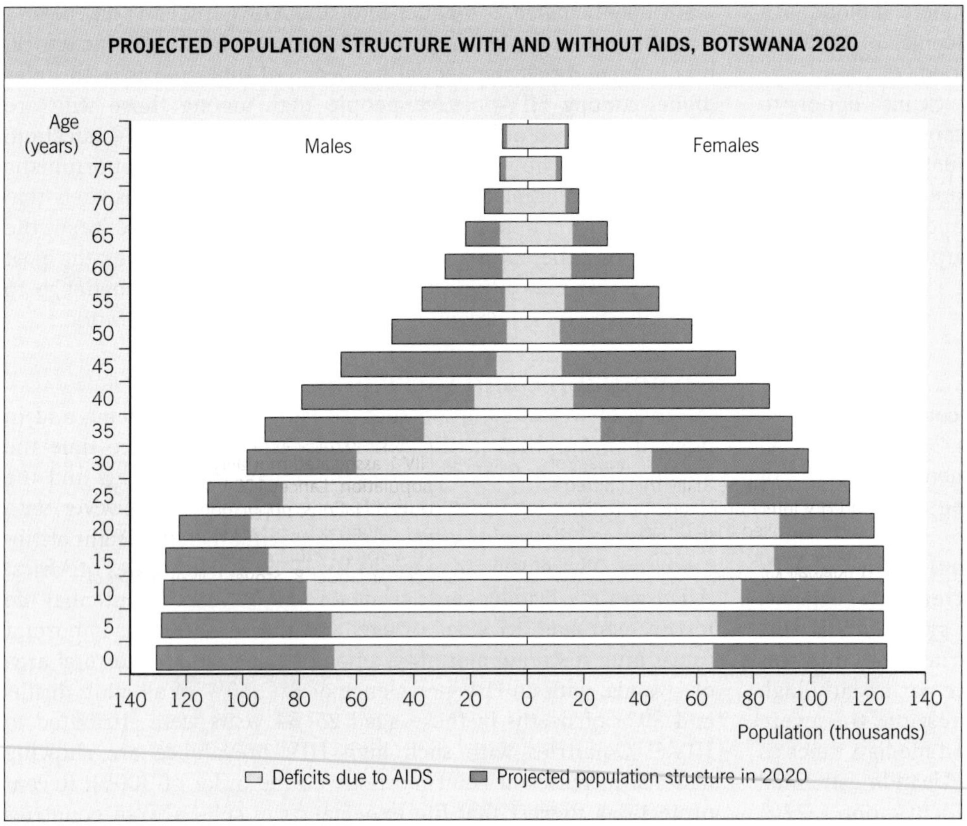

Fig. 115.13 Projected population structure with and without AIDS, Botswana, 2020.

had lost their mothers or both parents because of AIDS.[1] Such orphanhood rates may cause traditional child fostering arrangements, which are common in many cultures, to break down.

AIDS has profoundly affected the health systems in industrialized and developing countries alike. In industrialized countries, AIDS has illustrated the need to strengthen some of the weakest components of health services, such as access to appropriate care, counseling and prevention activities and participation of the sick in treatment and medical decision making. In the developing world, HIV vulnerability has been fueled by rapid urbanization, increased migration, conflicts and wars and increased inequalities. In many countries of the developing world, the economic impact of AIDS is felt not only on health care costs but also on skilled labour forces and decreases in gross domestic product, which in turn has a negative impact on many social indicators such as education and health. In cities where HIV prevalence is higher than 10%, hospital wards are overloaded with patients who have AIDS and tuberculosis and require long, repeated hospitalizations, so consuming scarce resources. At the turn of this century, AIDS is posing a threat to economic growth and development in many regions. In June 2001, government and civil society representatives met for a Special Session of the General Assembly of the United Nations to consider an expanded response to HIV/AIDS. This policy forum endorsed the results of a study estimating that, by 2005, that response would require about US$9 billion annually, with half of these resources needed in sub-Saharan Africa. About half of the total amount is required for prevention and the other half is needed for palliative care, treatment and prophylaxis of opportunistic infections, support for orphans and antiretroviral therapy.[43]

REFERENCES

1. UNAIDS/WHO. Report on the global HIV/AIDS epidemic. Geneva: UNAIDS/WHO; 2001.
2. Pitchenik AE, Fischl MA, Dickinson GM, *et al.* Opportunistic infections and Kaposi's sarcoma among Haitians: evidence of a new acquired immunodeficiency state. Ann Intern Med 1983;98:277–84.
3. Clumeck N, Sonnet J, Taelman H, *et al.* AIDS in African patients. N Engl J Med 1984;310:492–7.
4. Pape J, Liautaud B, Thomas F, *et al.* Characteristics of the acquired immunodeficiency syndrome (AIDS) in Haiti. N Engl J Med 1983;309:945–50.
5. Piot P, Quinn TC, Taelman H, *et al.* Acquired immunodeficiency syndrome in a heterosexual population in Zaire. Lancet 1984;2:65–9.
6. Van De Perre P, Rouvroy D, Lepage P, *et al.* Acquired immunodeficiency syndrome in Rwanda. Lancet 1984;2:62–5.
7. Serwadda D, Mugerwa RD, Sewankambo NK, *et al.* Slim disease: a new disease in Uganda and its association with HTLV-III infection. Lancet 1985;2:849–52.
8. Marlink R, Kanki P, Thior I, *et al.* Reduced rate of disease development after HIV-2 infection as compared to HIV-1. Science 1994;265:1587–90.
9. WHO. WHO case definition for AIDS surveillance in adults and adolescents. Wkly Epidemiol Rec 1994;69:273–5.
10. Summary of notifiable diseases, 1999. MMWR Morb Mortal Wkly Rep 2001;48,53.
11. EPI update. Bureau of HIV/AIDS and STD update series. In: Health Canada. Ottawa: Laboratory Centre for Disease Control; 2001.
12. European Centre for the Epidemiological Monitoring of AIDS. HIV/AIDS surveillance in Europe. Q Rep 2001;1–63.
13. Buve A, Caraël M, Hayes R, Robinson NJ. Variations in HIV prevalence between urban areas in sub-saharan Africa: do we understand them? AIDS 1995;9(Suppl.A):103–9.
14. Caraël M. Sexual behaviour. In: Cleland J, Ferry B, eds. Sexual behaviour and AIDS in the developing world. London: Taylor & Francis; 1995:75–123.
15. De Cock KM, Brun-Vezinet F, Soro B. HIV-1 and HIV-2 infections and AIDS in West Africa. AIDS 1991;5(Suppl.1):21–8.
16. Nelson K, Celentano D, Eiumtrakol S, *et al.* Changes in sexual behaviour and decline in HIV infection among young men in Thailand. N Engl J Med 1996;335:297–303.
17. Caraël M, Holmes KK. Dynamics of HIV epidemics in sub-Saharan Africa: introduction. AIDS 2001;15(Suppl.4):S1–4.
18. Auvert B, Ballard R, Campbell C, *et al.* HIV infection among youth in a South African mining town is associated with herpes simplex virus-2 seropositivity and sexual behaviour. AIDS 2001;15:885–98.
19. Mastro TD, Satten GA, Nopkesorn T, *et al.* Probability of female-to-male transmission of HIV-1 in Thailand. Lancet 1994;343:204–7.
20. Daar ES, Moudgil T, Meyer RD, *et al.* Transient high levels of viremia in patients with primary human immunodeficiency virus type-1 infection. N Engl J Med 1991;324:961–4.

21. Hu DJ, Dondero TJ, Rayfield MA, *et al.* The emerging genetic diversity of HIV. JAMA 1996;275:210–6.
22. Expert group of the Joint United Nations Program on HIV/AIDS. Implications of HIV variability for transmission: scientific and policy issues. AIDS 1997;11:1–15.
23. Rowland-Jones S, Sutton J, Ariyoshi K, *et al.* HIV-specific cytoxic T-cells in HIV exposed but uninfected Gambian women. Nat Med 1995;1:59–64.
24. Meda N, Ndoye I, M'Boup S, *et al.* Low and stable HIV infection rates in Senegal: natural course of the epidemic or evidence for success of prevention? AIDS 1999;13:1397–405.
25. Asiimwe-Okiror G, Opio AA, Musinguzi J, *et al.* Change in sexual behaviour and decline in HIV infection among young pregnant women in urban Uganda. AIDS 1997;11:1757–63.
26. Vandeperre Ph, Clumeck N, Caraël M, *et al.* Female prostitutes: a risk group for infection with T-cell lymphotropic virus type III. Lancet 1985;2:524–6.
27. Kreiss JK, Koech D, Plummer FA, *et al.* AIDS virus infection in Nairobi prostitutes. N Engl J Med 1986;314:414–8.
28. Piot P, Caraël M. Epidemiological and sociological aspects of HIV infection in developing countries. Br Med Bull 1988;44:68–88.
29. D'Costa LJ, Plummer FA, Bowmer I, *et al.* Prostitutes are a major reservoir for STD in Nairobi, Kenya. Sex Transm Dis 1985;12:64–7.
30. Nzila N, Laga M, Manoka AT, *et al.* HIV and other STD among female prostitutes in Kinshasa. AIDS 1991;5:715–21.
31. Cameron DW, Simonsen N, D'Costa LJ, *et al.* Female-to-male transmission of HIV-1: risk factors for seroconversion in men. Lancet 1989;2:403–8.
32. Laga M, Alary M, Nzila N, *et al.* Condom promotion, sexually transmitted diseases treatment, and declining incidence of HIV-1 infection in female Zairian sex workers. Lancet 1994;344:246–8.
33. Auvert B, Buve A, Lagarde E *et al.* Male circumcision and HIV infection in four cities in sub-Saharan Africa. AIDS 2001;15(Suppl.4):S31–40.
34. Grosskurt H, Mosha F, Todd J, *et al.* Impact of improved treatment of sexually transmitted diseases on HIV infection in rural Tanzania: randomised controlled trial. Lancet 1995;346:530–6.
35. Dunn DT, Newell ML, Ades AE, Peckham CS. Risk of HIV type 1 transmission through breastfeeding. Lancet 1992;340:585–8.
36. Van de Perre P. Breast milk transmission of HIV-1. Laboratory and clinical studies. Ann NY Acad Sci 2000;918:122–7.
37. Jaffe HW, Darrow WW, Eschenberg DF, *et al.* Acquired immunodeficiency syndrome in a cohort of homosexual men. A six-year follow-up study. Ann Intern Med 1985;103:210–4.
38. Morgan D, Maude GH, Malamba S *et al.* HIV-1 disease progression and AIDS-defining disorders in rural Uganda. Lancet 1997;350:245–250.
39. Grant A, Djomand G, De Cock KM. Natural history and spectrum of disease in adults with HIV/AIDS in Africa. AIDS 1997;11(Suppl.B):S43–54.
40. De Cock KM, Soro B, Coulibaly IM, Lucas SB. Tuberculosis and HIV infection in sub-saharan Africa. JAMA 1992;268:1581–7.
41. Mulder DW, Nunn A, Kamali A, *et al.* Two-year HIV-1 associated mortality in an Ugandan rural population. Lancet 1994;343:1021–38.
42. United Nations, population division. World population prospects: the 1996 revision. New York; 1996.
43. Schwartlander B, Stover J, Walker N *et al.* Resource needs for HIV/AIDS. Science 2001;292:2434–6.

chapter 116

Prevention of HIV Transmission Through Behavioral and Biological Interventions

Kenneth H Mayer & Steven A Safren

HIV TRANSMISSION DYNAMICS

HIV transmission is a high-consequence but low-probability event with the majority of relevant exposures not resulting in new infections.[1] There are multiple co-factors that may affect HIV transmission, which is why there is a high level of variability in estimates of the relative risk of infection for specific exposures (Table 116.1).[2,3] HIV may be transmitted as cell-free or cell-associated virus, and different factors may affect expression of virus concentrations in different body fluids (i.e. blood, semen or cervicovaginal secretions).[4–7] Although lower blood concentrations of HIV are associated with lower rates of HIV transmission,[8] antiretroviral drugs do not necessarily make HIV-infected people noninfectious or incapable of transmitting the virus. In fact, the sexual transmission of multidrug-resistant HIV has been well documented,[9,10] underscoring the need for providers to promote safer sex among their patients in their care, including those taking antiretroviral therapy.

BIOLOGIC ISSUES RELATED TO HIV TRANSMISSION

HIV is most often transmitted through intimate sexual contact by rapidly binding to cells that are present in the cervical, vaginal, penile, urethral and rectal mucosa.[11] The male foreskin contains abundant cells that can bind HIV; thus, being uncircumcised confers an additional risk for HIV seroconversion[12,13] (Table 116.2). All the specific mechanisms responsible for the sexual transmission of HIV in humans are not fully understood, since HIV can be found either as cell-free or cell-associated virus in blood and genital secretions and can bind multiple cell types.[4,14,15] The cells that can bind HIV in the genital tract include T helper lymphocytes, monocyte/macrophage cells, Langerhans cells and follicular dendritic cells. These last cells may be particularly important because of their mobility, since they can bind HIV on their surface membrane and/or internalize it and migrate via draining lymphatics to distal sites, where propagation in submucosal lymphoid tissue can occur, resulting in subsequent viral dissemination through the bloodstream.

Factors associated with increased HIV infectiousness include sexually transmitted infections[16] and noninfectious factors that can result in genital tract inflammation, recruiting more white blood cells to genital mucosal surfaces.[17] Among the sexually transmitted diseases, ulcerative sexually transmitted diseases such as syphilis, chancroid and genital herpes simplex virus infection afford additional portals of entry through mucosal ulcerations but also recruit inflammatory cells that bind and propagate HIV infection.[18] Inflammatory sexually transmitted diseases, such as gonorrhea, *Chlamydia trachomatis* infection and trichomoniasis have also been associated with increased HIV susceptibility and infectiousness, and may act either by increasing the number of white blood cells in the genital tract or by elaborating cytokines and chemokines that upregulate HIV expression and increase the viral load in the genital tract.[19,20] Other local genital factors associated with increased inflammation include douching and traumatic sexual intercourse, particularly after sexual assault.[21]

Different tissues in the genital tract have varying levels of susceptibility to being infected with HIV.[7] The vaginal epithelium is stratified and contains fewer cells with co-receptors that can bind HIV.[17] Thus, vaginal mucosa are less likely to become HIV-infected than the endocervix, which has a thinner layer, is highly vascular and contains a much higher concentration of HIV-binding cells. Any physiologic event that results in ectropion (i.e. increased exposure of the endocervix), such as the use of hormonal contraceptives or occult *C. trachomatis* infection, increases susceptibility to HIV.[22] The penile foreskin contains many cells that can readily bind and express HIV, resulting in increased HIV acquisition or transmission in uncircumcised males.[13] The oropharynx contains many fewer cells that can bind HIV, which may partially explain the relative inefficiency of oral exposure to HIV as a means of transmission.[23] Moreover, salivary secretions contain several compounds that have been found to inhibit HIV transmission in vitro, most notably secretory leukocyte protease inhibitor (SLPI).[24] However, rhesus macaques have been readily infected with simian immunodeficiency virus after oral challenge, with evidence of viral replication in tonsillar and adenoidal tissues.[25]

EPIDEMIOLOGIC ISSUES RELATED TO HIV TRANSMISSION

Because of the multiple co-factors that may alter the amount of virus in the blood and genital tract, the calculation of exact risk for infection for each type of HIV exposure is imprecise (see Tables 116.1 and 116.2). Moreover, much of the data that has been obtained to generate per-contact risks has been based on cohort studies in which individuals recollect their level of risk during preceding time intervals (often every 3–6 months). Some of the participants in these studies may be worried that they have become newly infected or their sexual behavior may have been under the influence of drugs or alcohol, affecting precise recall. Thus, although many people want to have a precise calculation of risk associated with specific practices, it is very difficult to determine with any certainty the precise likelihood of transmission for each specific act. It is important when patients ask questions about the likelihood of risk after an exposure to reassure them that a one-time exposure to HIV is unlikely to result in transmission but that the reason why the epidemic has become so widespread is because of individuals engaging in recurrent risk-taking behavior.

Having noted the limitations of how risk calculations have been obtained, certain key principles have emerged. Direct intravenous exposure to HIV (e.g. blood transfusions) is the most efficient way of transmitting the virus, while percutaneous needle sticks are much less efficient in transmitting HIV.[26] Individuals who share needles who pull back on the syringe and leave substantial blood in the syringe when passing it to their partner are more likely to transmit HIV than in a common health care setting where an occupational needle stick occurs with a solid suture needle.[27] The range of risk for individuals who share intravenous drug paraphernalia ranges from 0.6% to 3% (see Table 116.2). This range overlaps with the level of

ESTIMATES OF PER-CONTACT RISK OF HIV INFECTION	
Type of contact	**Risk**
Needle-sharing	6/1000 to 3/100
Occupational needle stick	1/300
Receptive anal	8/1000 to 3/100
Receptive vaginal	8/1000 to 2/1000
Insertive anal or vaginal	3/10,000 to 1/1000
Receptive oral	Case reports/no denominator

Table 116.1 Estimates of per-contact risk of HIV infection.

MODIFIERS OF THE EFFICIENCY OF HIV TRANSMISSION		
Modifier	**Infectiousness**	**Susceptibility**
Sexually transmitted diseases	↑	↑
Genital tract inflammation (e.g. traumatic sex, douching)	↑	↑
Circumcision	↓	↓
Cervical ectopy	?	↑
Genetics*	?	↓
HIV subtype†	↑	NA
Monocytotropic strain	↑	NA
Acute infection	↑	NA
Advanced infection	↑	NA
Antiretroviral therapy	↓?	NA

* CCR5 mutation. † Subtype A or C compared with B.

Table 116.2 Modifiers of the efficiency of HIV transmission.

risk for individuals who engage in unprotected receptive anal or vaginal intercourse.[28] One study suggested that, on average, receptive anal intercourse was more than seven times as efficient at transmitting HIV as insertive anal intercourse.[29]

For each type of exposure, many contextual variables may alter the risk of transmission. For example, variations in the prevalence of HIV in different communities may mean that a behavior carrying the same risk has a different likelihood of resulting in infection in two different communities. The amount of virus in the infected source plays a role in determining the risk of becoming HIV-infected after a contact. Co-factors, such as a source with a high plasma viral load[5,8,30] or concomitant sexually transmitted infection, can greatly increase the average per contact risk.[31,32]

In the developed world, the epidemiologic data would suggest that men are more likely to transmit HIV to their female partners. However, in several studies of HIV serodiscordant couples in sub-Saharan Africa, the rates of male-to-female and female-to-male transmission were quite similar.[8] The reasons for the difference in the efficiency of female-to-male transmission in the developing world as compared with the developed world may include the decreased prevalence of male circumcision in the places where these studies were conducted, as well as the high co-prevalence of other sexually transmitted infections. For anal intercourse, the insertive partner is less likely to acquire HIV from an infected receptive partner than vice versa; but there are sufficient cells in the distal male urethra and the foreskin, and such an abundance of HIV-infected cells and mucus secretions containing virus in infected receptive partners, that an insertive partner is still at substantial risk of acquiring HIV from unprotected intercourse.

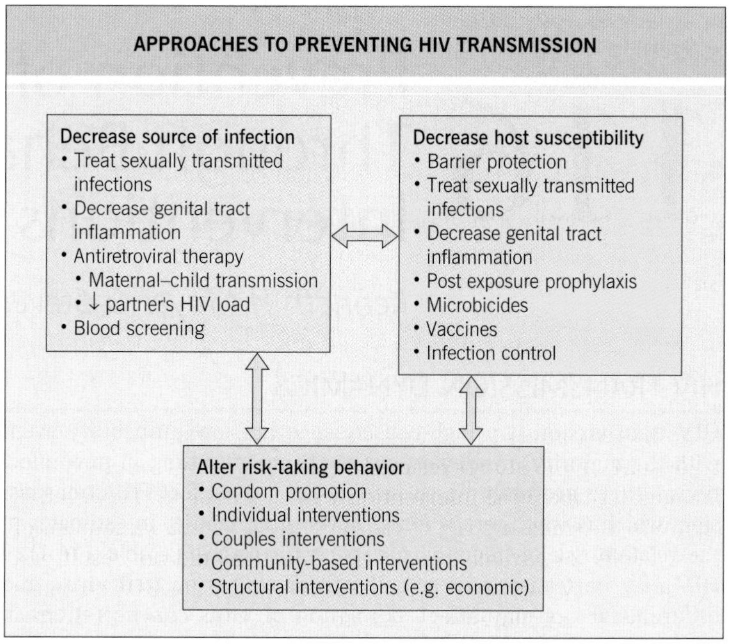

Fig. 116.1 Approaches to preventing HIV transmission.

It is clear that receptive oral intercourse, either fellatio or cunilingus, is a much less efficient way to acquire HIV, but case reports showing that oral exposure to ejaculate may result in HIV transmission have been well documented. The relative efficiency of oral exposure to HIV is below that of unprotected vaginal intercourse; thus, it may be in the realm of less than 1 per 1000 contacts. However, animal studies have demonstrated that HIV can readily be transmitted orally, since there is lymphoid tissue in the oropharynx that might acquire HIV from genital secretions. In counseling patients who have concerns about the risk of acquiring HIV through oral exposure, it is important to indicate that it is less efficient than unprotected anal or vaginal intercourse but that transmission can still occur. Thus, if an individual wants a zero-risk situation, it is preferable for them to avoid any oral exposure to semen or cervicovaginal secretions from a partner who is known to be HIV-infected or at risk. However, if oral sex is a substitute for unprotected anal or vaginal sex, the patient can be told that this is less risky. Although HIV has been found in very small concentrations in pre-ejaculatory secretions, there are no reliable case reports of HIV transmission through exposure to pre-ejaculate without semen. Thus, it is important to counsel patients that being able to negotiate with their partners about limiting exposure to semen may be a helpful means for 'harm reduction.'

PREVENTION OF HIV TRANSMISSION

HIV transmission may be decreased by biologic or behavioral means (Fig. 116.1). Treating sexually transmitted infections can decrease genital tract HIV load in co-infected patients and can decrease susceptibility in at-risk persons. Antiretroviral therapy can decrease genital as well as plasma viral load but the transmission of multidrug-resistant HIV suggests that these drugs may only have an impact on wider HIV transmission if coupled with programs that encourage safer sexual behavior and optimal drug therapy adherence. Antiretroviral drugs may be used to decrease the likelihood of maternal–child transmission or be used for postexposure prophylaxis. Other experimental approaches, such as microbicides and vaccines, will also be discussed elsewhere. However, for any biologically plausible intervention to work, attention will need to be paid to the behavioral context in which the intervention will be undertaken. For example, a biologically effective microbicide may fail if the at-risk population refrains from lubricated sex. The following section reviews interventions designed to decrease HIV through sexually transmitted infection treatment and behavioral interventions.

TREATING SEXUALLY TRANSMITTED INFECTIONS

As noted above, there are several different ways that HIV transmission may be minimized; aggressively diagnosing and treating sexually transmitted infections is biologically plausible and cheaper than chronic antiretroviral therapy. There have been several studies conducted in sub-Saharan Africa to test this hypothesis. In a study in the Mwanza district of Uganda, specific syndromic management of sexually transmitted infections in an area where the epidemic was still in its early stages (i.e. 1% of the adult population were infected at the start of the study) resulted in decreasing HIV incidence in communities where the intervention was undertaken.[33] However, in a study in the Rakai district of Tanzania, periodic mass treatment of at-risk adults for sexually transmitted infections did not result in a decrease in HIV incidence.[31] In the latter study, the HIV epidemic was already much more advanced (i.e. 16% of the adult population were infected at the start of the study) and there was a high background rate of concomitant herpes simplex infection, which was not treated in the course of the study.

Thus, the lessons from these studies are that, if one is to decrease HIV spread through treating sexually transmitted diseases, the treatment should be specifically tailored to individual patients, focusing on aggressively diagnosing sexually transmitted diseases that are common in that community. In addition, the benefit of sexually transmitted disease control will be greatest in areas of lower HIV prevalence. In communities where the epidemic is already more widespread, the likelihood of encountering a new partner who is HIV infected may be substantial, so the benefit of modifying a cofactor will be more limited.

HIV SCREENING AS A PREVENTION MODALITY

Other approaches to the prevention of HIV in the developed world are so well established that they seem routine; (i.e. the routine screening of blood).[34] The use of more sensitive antibody screening and careful donor history have resulted in enhanced safety in the blood supply, such that the transmission of HIV via infected blood in the past decade and a half is exceedingly rare. In other parts of the world where the relative cost of blood screening is high, blood supplies may not be as safe.

Another routine practice that results in the prevention of HIV transmission is the guideline that pregnant women be universally offered HIV antibody testing before delivery.[35] Although this guideline is not commonly adhered to, the rate of new perinatally transmitted infections in the USA has decreased dramatically, with fewer than 100 new infections in the past year. The reasons why any perinatal transmission has occurred recently are generally the mother's refusal to be tested because she perceives that she is not at risk or the obstetrician/gynecologist's failure to offer the test, or to spend time with the patient to discuss the reasons for her resistance to being tested. At the present time, because of the great efficacy of antiretroviral medication in decreasing mother-to-child transmission from a rate of 1 in 3 to less than 1 in 10, routine HIV screening for all pregnant woman is the standard of care.

BEHAVIORAL APPROACHES – OVERVIEW

Despite access to antiretroviral therapy, blood screening and treatment of sexually transmitted infections, the number of new HIV infections in the USA has remained at a plateau of approximately 40,000 new infections per year over most of the past decade. The decision to engage in HIV risk behavior is a complex one that may involve issues related to early life events (such as sexual abuse in childhood), low self-esteem, contextual issues in relationships, concomitant substance use and addiction to specific forms of sexual pleasure. Gender-related power dynamics (e.g. the role of women in many societies) may also limit opportunities to promote safer sex. Thus, no single behavioral approach will invariably lead to an adaptation of consistent safer sexual or drug using practices. Much like dieting, regular exercise and smoking cessation, no single program of HIV risk reduction will work for all at-risk individuals. However, several studies have now indicated that the provision of either individual counseling and/or small group sessions can be helpful in assisting at-risk individuals in moderating their risk.

Good elements of risk reduction programs include the ability of the counselor to approach the patient in a nonjudgmental manner to elicit a realistic assessment of the person's pattern of risk-taking behavior. Given the slow progress in the development of cheap, safe and effective vaccines, microbicides and other biologic approaches to the prevention of HIV transmission, the role of the primary care provider in patient education, discussion of risk-taking behavior, initiation of risk reduction counseling and triage to appropriate prevention services is an essential part of stopping further spread of the epidemic. In the next section, the elements of successful HIV risk reduction interventions are reviewed.

PSYCHOSOCIAL MODELS OF RISK BEHAVIOR UNDERLYING PREVENTION INTERVENTIONS

Knowledge is one aspect of HIV prevention but ongoing risk-taking is a function of many other complex psychosocial variables. The three most common models that have been employed to explain HIV risk-taking are the health belief model, the theory of reasoned action and social cognitive theory (i.e. self-efficacy models).[36] Health beliefs models emphasize the role of perceived benefits and barriers to condom use and perceived severity of and vulnerability to getting HIV.[37] In the theory of reasoned action, health behavior – condom use – is a function of intentions to use condoms and, in turn, intention to use condoms is a function of variables such as attitudes and norms regarding HIV and condom use.[38] Social cognitive models (i.e. self-efficacy) explain condom use as a function of an individual's knowledge about HIV, expectation about the outcomes of using condoms (i.e. pleasure reduction versus disease prevention) and self-efficacy – that the individual will be able to use a condom in different sexual situations.[39,40] These psychosocial models of HIV prophylactic behavior have been tested both cross-sectionally and longitudinally in a variety of populations and are the basis of many behavioral interventions reviewed below.

Intervention models that address information, motivation and behavioral skills[41] typically take into account models of HIV risk prevention. One is the transtheoretical model of change,[42] which posits that an intervention needs to be adaptable to an individual's current readiness to change. For example, people who are currently at a 'precontemplative' level of readiness to change do not see that their behavior as problematic and do not see a reason to change; someone at a 'contemplative' level may be ambivalent about changing and someone at a 'determination or preparation' level is ready to make a commitment. Additional levels of change include 'action', 'maintenance' and 'relapse prevention', each with different suggested strategies to assist an individual in a counseling situation. Interventions based on the transtheoretical model try to move individuals to a more serious, higher level of readiness to change than where they are initially. Accordingly, an individual at an earlier level may benefit most from information and education, whereas someone at a mid-level or higher might benefit from more intensive motivational support and skills training.

Many of the randomized controlled trials of interventions reviewed below use aspects of the transtheoretical model of behavioral change, other information–motivation–behavior skills interventions and/or variables relating to self-efficacy, health beliefs and attitudes in the risk-reduction interventions. HIV prevention studies typically collect sexual risk-taking data on HIV-negative individuals but sexually transmitted disease (STD) or HIV incidence may also be used as end points. To address the overarching public health significance of HIV, community randomized designs employ more of a wider-scale approach. These interventions are formulated to develop population-based HIV prevention approaches and compare communities that receive the intervention with another similar community that does not.

OUTCOME OF LARGE SCALE AND HIGH-IMPACT-FOR-HIV PREVENTION STUDIES IN THE USA

Trials primarily involving heterosexual individuals in STD and primary care clinics

Two different randomized controlled trials of HIV prevention interventions have examined the efficacy of risk-reduction counseling approaches in individuals at high risk for HIV infection, by studying heterosexual individuals attending STD or primary care clinics. The first study, the US National Institute of Mental Health's Multisite HIV Prevention Trial (Project Light), recruited 3,706 individuals from 37 inner-city community-based clinics in seven sites across the USA.[43] The three risk groups were:

- men presenting in an STD clinic;
- women presenting in an STD clinic; and
- women presenting in health service organizations.

All participants, at screening, reported engaging in unprotected vaginal or anal sex within 90 days. Approximately one-half were randomized to seven sessions of risk reduction counseling in a group format, and the other half to watch a 1-hour AIDS video followed by a question and answer session. Those in the intervention group reported fewer unprotected sexual acts and were more likely to use condoms consistently over the follow-up period. The intervention group also reported higher overall levels of condom use. With respect to STD infections, there were no overall differences in infection rates between intervention and control group; however, among the men who were recruited from STD clinics, there was a decreased incidence of gonorrhea.

The second large-scale study, Project RESPECT, recruited over 5,787 heterosexual HIV-negative patients who presented for care at STD clinics in across the USA.[44] Participants were randomized to a four-session ('enhanced counseling'), a two-session ('brief counseling') or a noninteractive ('didactic message') condition. The enhanced counseling was based on the theory of reasoned action and social cognitive theory, targeting variables such as self-efficacy, attitudes and perceived norms. At the various sessions, participants would set goals for a next step in risk reduction, and at the final session would interactively come up with a long-term plan. For the brief counseling, participants discussed differences between actual and perceived risk, and also worked on a next step behavioral plan. The didactic message group sought to mimic what is standard of care in most clinics. The counselor would deliver messages (noninteractively) regarding HIV prevention and the meaning of their test result. Those assigned four-session and two-session interactive interventions had fewer new HIV infections at both 6- and 12-month intervals than did those who received the noninteractive counseling. Additionally, self-reported 100% condom use was higher in both interactive counseling groups as compared with the didactic message control.

As HIV risk behavior is a necessary factor for HIV infection, the two studies taken together reveal that HIV risk reduction counseling can both increase condom use and decrease STD infections. They also provide data for the feasibility of adding risk reduction counseling to standard of care in STD and primary care clinics. However, it is not clear whether STD and primary care clinics are routinely implementing these approaches.

Trials including men who have sex with men

Individually randomized controlled trials

One of the earlier individually randomized intervention trials[45] compared an integrated cognitive-behavioral intervention to a waiting list control among 104 gay men in a metropolitan area. The integrated intervention included AIDS risk information as well as cognitive-behavioral self-management training, sexual assertion training and strategies for increasing positive social supports/relationship skills. The intervention was delivered in groups and consisted of 12 sessions. At the post-training assessment, the experimental group had fewer high-risk sexual practices and better behavioral skills for sexual coercive situations than the wait list control.

In a study of African-American men who have sex with men,[46] 318 individuals were randomized, who were recruited from bars, bathhouses, erotic bookstores, organizations for African-American men who have sex with men, street outreach and personal referrals of other participants. The study had three arms; two included cognitive-behavioral self-management training, assertion training and issues related to social identity and support. Of these two arms, one was a single session and the other was three sessions. The third arm was a wait-list control. Those in the triple session arm had strong reductions in risky behavior. Those in the single session intervention had mild improvements with respect to frequency of unprotected anal intercourse compared with the control group.

To address issues such as attrition and dissemination of interventions, a study in London[47] examined the benefits of a 1-day workshop. Participants had an acute sexually transmitted infection and reported having unprotected anal intercourse at least once over the past year at entry. Both intervention and control participants received 20 minutes of one-to-one counseling about sexual risk behavior and could be referred for clinic-based community counseling services. At 6 and 12 months, the proportions of those who had unprotected intercourse were not different between groups. Also, those in intervention were slightly (borderline statistically significant) more likely to have a new STD.

Some have erroneously concluded, on the basis of this study, that behavioral interventions for HIV prevention do not work. Subsequent criticisms of this conclusion, however, highlight the fact that the intervention was only a one-off workshop, which is unlikely, in general, to have lasting effects.[48,49] Given the complexity of the ontogeny of risk behavior, more than a single workshop would be necessary for high-risk individuals.

Community randomized controlled trials

One of the first community randomized controlled trials, the Mpowerment Project, studied a peer-outreach program for young gay men (aged 18–29 years),[50] which used a wait-list crossover design. The intervention involved peer outreach (training peers to spread prevention messages and to recruit more individuals to participate), small groups that focused on misperceptions of safer sex, eroticizing safer sex, verbal and nonverbal safer sex strategies, informal outreach and a publicity campaign. To assess outcome, a cohort of 300 individuals from two communities were surveyed. In the intervention community, the proportion of participants who reported unprotected anal intercourse with nonprimary partners decreased, as did the proportion of participants who reported unprotected anal intercourse with their boyfriends. No significant changes occurred in the comparison community.

Another large-scale community randomized trial[51] involved delivering the intervention through opinion leaders (popular individuals) from the gay community in four US states. Each state randomly had both an intervention city and comparison city. In the intervention city, popular gay men were trained to spread behavior-change messages (to change norms), and in the comparison city pamphlets were placed at gay bars. The team identified 'popular' men with the assistance of bartenders in intervention city bars. The bartenders would observe their customers and record the names of individuals who were greeted most often, greeted others and seemed well-liked. Participants then completed surveys in the bars. Across all states, 1126 men completed baseline surveys and 1010 completed follow-up surveys. At 1-year follow-up, those in the intervention cities reported a significantly greater reduction in the frequency of unprotected anal sex during the previous 2 months and a significantly greater increase in condom use for anal sex compared with comparison cities. Consistent with this finding, more condoms were taken from bars in the intervention cities than in the comparison cities.

The idea of using community opinion leaders to promote HIV prevention among heterosexuals is currently being studied in five international sites – India, Russia, Zimbabwe, China and Peru. The community randomized trials among men who have sex with men validate the utility of providing HIV prevention, on a larger scale, to communities of men who have sex with men. From a public health perspective, raising awareness and changing norms regarding HIV prophylactic behavior can influence transmission rates on the community level. Although recruiting opinion leaders and/or providing an integrated prevention program involving peers, groups, workshops and outreach can be a complex undertaking, these two studies show that such efforts can be useful approaches to curtailing HIV risk-taking, which, in turn, would curtail HIV transmission.

Prevention trials for women

Individually randomized controlled trials

Several large-scale multisite studies have investigated risk reduction counseling among low-income and/or minority women. Kelly *et al.*[52] randomized 197 high-risk women from an urban primary health clinic to a cognitive-behavioral risk reduction intervention or comparison. The intervention consisted of five sessions, including skills training in condom use, sexual assertiveness, problem-solving risk, trigger self-management and peer support for change efforts. The comparison condition received three sessions covering health topics not specifically related to AIDS. Three months later, the intervention group evidenced better sexual communication and negotiation skills (assessed by role play and self-report) and less unprotected sexual intercourse. The comparison group had no changes on these measures.

A second study of HIV risk-reduction counseling among women[53] sought to adapt models of behavioral change to social and contextual variables relevant to 128 economically disadvantaged African American women between the ages of 18 and 29 years. Accordingly, the intervention used the theory of gender and power as a guide and was social skills based. It included the following components delivered in five 2-hour long sessions: ethnic and gender pride, risk reduction information, sexual assertiveness and communication training, condom use skills and norms, and cognitive coping skills, including sexual self-control. At the 3-month follow-up, women in the more intensive intervention showed increased consistent condom use, sexual self-control, sexual communication and sexual assertiveness, and partner's adoption of norms supporting consistent condom use than those in the delayed educational control.

A study of 206 pregnant inner city women randomized participants to an AIDS prevention group or one of two controls.[54] The AIDS prevention intervention consisted of four sessions, each delivered in group format, and included videos as well as group activities such as role play or discussions. Sessions also included cognitive rehearsal skills for behaviors such as using a condom during sex, aversive-conditioning segments that involved imagining a scene in which women practiced an unhealthy sexual behavior, and relapse prevention. After the intervention and after 6 month follow-up, the AIDS prevention group had increases in knowledge and safer sex behaviors in comparison with the two control groups.

Because of difficulties with retention and attrition of high-risk and hard-to-reach women in HIV prevention trials, Belcher *et al.* developed and tested the utility of a single session 2-hour one-on-one intervention using motivational interviewing and information–motivation–behavioral skills training.[55] No differences in HIV knowledge resulted but the group that received skills training and motivational interviewing showed higher levels of HIV protective behaviors than the control group, including higher rates of condom use during vaginal intercourse, demonstrating the efficacy of a brief, minimal intervention.

Carey and colleagues conducted two randomized controlled trials of an HIV risk reduction intervention using information, motivation enhancement and skills training intervention for low-income, primarily African-American women.[56,57] In both studies, the intervention consisted of four 90-minute sessions that included personalized feedback about their HIV knowledge, risk perceptions and sexual behavior. It also included a motivational videotape, decisional balance motivational exercises (pros and cons of risky and safer sex) and the impact of HIV on other life issues. Finally, the intervention group worked on developing personalized plans for future behaviors, skills training and education. Women in the first study who received the intervention reported stronger intentions to practice safe sex and to communicate these intentions to partners, less unprotected intercourse and less substance use near the time of sexual activity; and these gains were maintained at the 3-month follow-up. In the second study, 102 women comprising a new sample were randomized. Overall, the results of the second study were corroborated.

Taken together, the series of randomized controlled trials of HIV prevention counseling for high-risk women demonstrate both the feasibility and the efficacy of such approaches. While many of these approaches are useful, some may be difficult to disseminate. The utility of the single-session intervention provides support for its further replication.[55] This and the others, however, require special training, and most require a significant expenditure of time by both the participants and the counselors. Future study of individually administered interventions should now focus on ways to implement and disseminate interventions in community-based settings.

Community randomized controlled trials

To attempt to address some of the limitations of clinic-based intervention approaches for women, two studies of community randomized trials have been undertaken. The first used nine low-income housing developments[56] and nine demographically matched control developments. The community-level intervention included workshops and community HIV prevention events implemented by popular opinion leaders within each community. The researchers identified opinion leaders by including questions in the baseline survey – asking each participant to name up to five women whom they liked and trusted most. The women in the housing developments (n = 690) were surveyed at baseline and 1 year later. This revealed that women in the intervention communities showed better decreases in unprotected sex (past 2 months) and frequency of unprotected acts.

A second community-based randomized control trial targeted low-income, primarily African-American women in four urban settings.[57] Four communities in metropolitan areas were selected: two public housing communities, a low-income neighborhood and a group of inner-city neighborhoods. The intervention was specifically based on the transtheoretical model of change, attempting to reach women who would be at different levels of readiness to change. The intervention consisted of distribution of HIV prevention materials, developing a peer network of community organizers and businesses, and delivering prevention messages by outreach specialists, both individually and in groups. The intervention communities evidenced increases in talking with main partners about condoms and trying to get main partners to use condoms.

Prevention interventions specific to injection drug users

A recent review of 42 studies between 1989 and 1999 suggested that the majority found that needle-exchange programs prevent HIV risk behavior and seroconversion among injection drug users.[58]

Most of the other studies of HIV prevention interventions for drug users are observational or quasi-experimental evaluation studies, which show within-participant reductions in HIV risk behavior.[59]

The SAFE study was a randomized controlled trial of 117 HIV-negative injection drug users who had reported that they had used and shared injection drugs in the previous 6 months.[60] The innovative experimental condition was to have injection drug users bring in the members of their drug network whom they had previously listed in an interview. The index participant and his or her drug network members received a manualized intervention delivered by former heroin users who had stayed in contact with active drug users in their community. The intervention consisted of six sessions that involved recognizing personal risk, committing to practicing both individual and group vigilance toward risk reduction, making plans (and discussing previous plans), assertiveness skills and role play of real-life situations that would involve risk (e.g. one member wanting to share without cleaning). The comparison group received counseling and testing. At the 18-month outcome assessment, the experimental group had significantly less needle sharing and less sharing of cookers for the prior 6 months.

Although innovative and useful, this intervention was arguably hard to deliver. Some 22% of potential index participants did not return with members of their drug network and another 36% did bring in at least one other drug network member but did not ever start the sessions.

Other studies and less extensive interventions have revealed mixed results at best. Kwiatkowski and colleagues did not find differences in high-risk behaviors among 3357 injecting drug users, not in treatment, randomized to standard or enhanced interventions.[61,62] In general, individuals in this study maintained risk behavior and the authors concluded that new and creative ways to target this population were needed. Another similar study of standard and enhanced interventions for out-of-treatment drug users found both interventions to be at least moderately effective in reducing risk but less so than with sexual risk.[63] Gibson and colleagues[64] studied 295 individuals who were in treatment for heroin detoxification. Participants were randomized to counseling or brochures. Although differences between groups did not emerge, self-reported decreases in injection-related and sexual risk behaviors were present in both groups 6 and 12 months later. However, it is notable that, in this study, participants were acutely presenting for treatment of drug abuse and may have been more motivated to change than those not already in treatment.

Among the studies of prevention interventions for injection drug users, methodologies differ and, consequently, so do the results. Sexual behavior, as shown in previous sections, is a difficult and complex behavior to change. When co-morbid with drug dependence or addiction, its complexity grows; intensive multimodal interventions currently show the most utility in this population.

SUMMARY

Behavioral interventions to decrease HIV transmission have been successful in a wide array of settings and with diverse populations. However, in most situations, interventions were needed to sustain behavior change. Moreover, there is limited experience with these interventions in parts of the world where the epidemic is spreading most rapidly and where the social construction of reality (e.g. disempowerment of women, limited health care infrastructure) may limit the effectiveness of programs developed in resource-rich settings. Clearly, additional work is needed to develop culturally specific behavioral interventions, while the development of more effective biologic prevention modalities (i.e. microbicides and vaccines) is underway.

REFERENCES

1. Anderson RM, May RM. Epidemiologic parameters of HIV transmission. Nature 1988;333:514–9.
2. Royce RA, Seny Y, Cates W, *et al.* Sexual transmission of HIV: host factors that shape the epidemic and implications for prevention. N Engl J Med 1997;269:2853–9.
3. Vernazza PL, Eron JJ. Probability of heterosexual transmission of HIV (letter). J Acquir Immune Defic Syndr 1997;14:85.
4. Fiore JR, Bjorndal IA, Peipke KA, *et al.* The biological phenotype of HIV-1 is usually retained during and after sexual transmission. Virology 1994;204:297–303.
5. Busch MP, Operkalski EA, *et al.* Factors influencing human immunodeficiency virus type 1 transmission by blood transfusion. J Infect Dis 1996;174:26–33.
6. Lu Y, Brosio P, Lafaile M, *et al.* Vaginal transmission of chimeric simian/human immunodeficiency viruses in Rhesus macaques. J Virol 1996;70:3045–50.
7. Littman DR. Chemokine receptors: keys to AIDS pathogenesis? Cell 1998;93:677–80.
8. Quinn TC, Wawer MJ, Sewan Kambo N, *et al.* Viral load and heterosexual transmission of human immunodeficiency virus type 1. Rakai Project Study Group. N Engl J Med 2000;342:921–9.
9. Little SJ, Daar ES, D'Aquila RT, *et al.* Reduced antiretroviral drug susceptibility among patients with primary HIV infection. JAMA 1999;282:1142–9.
10. Borden D, Hurley A, Zhang L, *et al.* HIV-1 drug resistance in newly infected individuals. JAMA 1999;282:1135–41.
11. Buchacz KA, Wilkinson DA, Krowka JF, *et al.* Genetic and immunological host factors associated with susceptibility of HIV-1 infection. AIDS 1998;12(Suppl.A):S87–94.
12. Lavreys L, Rakwar JP, Thompson ML, *et al.* Effect of circumcision on incidence of human immunodeficiency virus type 1 and other sexually transmitted diseases: A prospective cohort study of trucking company employees in Kenya. J Infect Dis 1999;180:330–6.
13. Moses S, Bailey RC, Ronald AR. Male circumcision: Assessment of health benefits and risks. Sex Transm Infect 1998;74:368–73.
14. Schuitemaker H, Koot M, Kootstra NA, *et al.* Biological phenotype of human immunodeficiency virus type 1 clones at different stages of infection: progression of disease is associated with a shift from monocytotropic to T-cell-tropic virus population. J Virol 1992.;66:1354–60.
15. Zhu T, Mo H, Wang N, *et al.* Genotypic and phenotypic characterizations of HIV-1 in patients with primary infection. Science 1993;261:1179–81.
16. Fleming DT, Wasserheit JN. From epidemiological synergy to public health policy and practice: the contribution of other sexually transmitted diseases to sexual transmission of HIV infection. Sex Transm Infect 1999;75:3–17.
17. Patterson BK, Landay A, Anderson J, *et al.* Repertoire of chemokine receptor expression in the female genital tract: implications for human immunodeficiency virus transmission. Am J Pathol 1998;153:481–90.
18. Wasserheit JN. HIV infection and other STDs: so close and yet so far. Sex Transm Dis 1999;26:549–50.
19. Anderson DJ, Politch JA, Tucker LD, *et al.* Quantitation of mediators of inflammation and immunity in genital tract secretions and their relevance to HIV type 1 transmission. AIDS Res Hum Retrovir 1998;14(Suppl.1):S43–9.

20. Cohen MS. Sexually transmitted diseases enhance HIV transmission: no longer a hypothesis. Lancet 1998;351(Suppl.3):5–7.
21. Vermund SH. Transmission of HIV-1 among adolescents and adults. In: DeVita VT, Hellman S, Rosenberg SA, eds. AIDS: etiology, diagnosis, treatment and preventions, 4th ed. Philadelphia: Lippincott-Raven; 1996:147–65.
22. Sinei SK, Fortney JA, Kigondu CS, *et al.* Contraceptive use and HIV infection in Kenyan family planning clinic attenders. Int J STD AIDS 1996;7:65–70.
23. Gerbert F, Herzig K, Volberding P. Counseling patients about the risk of oral sex for HIV transmission. J Gen Intern Med 1997;12:698–704.
24. Cohen MS, Anderson DJ. Genitourinary mucosal defenses. In: Holmes KK, Mardh P-A, Sparling PF, *et al.*, eds. Sexually transmitted diseases, 3rd ed. New York: McGraw-Hill; 1999:173–90.
25. Baba TW, Trichel AM, An L, *et al.* Infection and AIDS in adult macaques after nontraumatic oral exposure to cell-free SIV. Science 1996;272:1486–9.
26. Lackritz, EM, Satten GA, Aberle-Grasse J, *et al.* Estimated risk of transmission of the human immunodeficiency virus by screened blood in the United States. N Engl J Med 1995;333:1721–5.
27. Centers for Disease Control and Prevention. Management of possible sexual, injecting-drug-use, or other nonoccupational exposure to HIV, including considerations related to antiretroviral therapy. Public Health Service Statement. MMWR Morb Mortal Wkly Rep 1998;47(RR-17):1–14.
28. Padian NS, Shiboski SC, Jewell NP. The effect of number of exposures on the risk of heterosexual HIV transmission of human immunodeficiency virus. J Infect Dis 1990;161:883–7.
29. DeGruttola V, Seage GR, Mayer KH, Horsburg CR. Infectiousness of HIV between male homosexual partners. J Clin Epidemiol 1989;42:849–56.
30. Lee TH, Sakahara N, Fiebig E, *et al.* Correlation of HIV-1 RNA levels in plasma and heterosexual transmission of HIV-1 from infected transfusion recipients (letter). J Acquir Immune Defic Syndr 1996;12:427–8.
31. Wawer MJ, Sewankambo NK, Serwadda D, *et al.* Control of sexually transmitted diseases for AIDS prevention in Uganda: a randomised community trial. Rakai Project Study Group. Lancet 1999;353:525–35.
32. Cohen M, Hoffman I, Royce R, *et al.* Reduction of concentration of HIV-1 in semen after treatment of urethritis: implications for prevention of sexual transmission of HIV-1. Lancet 1997;349:1868–73.
33. Grooskurth H, Mosha F, Todd J, *et al.* Impact of improved treatment of sexually transmitted disease on HIV infection in rural Tanzania: randomized controlled trial. Lancet 1995;346:530–6.
34. Centers for Disease Control and Prevention. Guidelines for national human immunodeficiency virus case surveillance, including monitoring for human immunodeficiency virus infection and acquired immunodeficiency syndrome. MMWR Morb Mortal Wkly Rep 1999;48(RR-13):1–29.
35. Centers for Disease Control and Prevention. Revised recommendations for HIV screening of pregnant women. MMWR Morb Mortal Wkly Rep 2001;50(RR-19):63–85.
36. Aggleton, P, O'Reilly K, Slutkin G, Davies P. Risking everything? Risk behavior, behavior change, and AIDS. Science 1994;265:341–5.
37. Carmel S. The Health Belief Model in the research of AIDS-related preventive behavior. Public Health Rev 1990/91;18:73–85.
38. Fishbein M, Middlestadt S. Using the theory of reasoned action as a framework for understanding and changing AIDS-related behaviors. In: Mays V, Albee G, Schneider S, eds. Primary prevention of AIDS: psychological approaches. Newbury Park, CA: Sage; 1989:93–110.
39. Bandura A. Perceived self-efficacy in the exercise of control over AIDS infection. Evaluation Program Plan 1990;13:9–17.
40. Wulfert E, Wan CK. Safer sex intentions and condom use viewed from a health belief, reasoned action, and social cognitive perspective. J Sex Res 1995;4: 293–305.
41. Fisher JD, Fisher WA. Changing AIDS-risk behavior. Psychol Bull 1992;118:392–404.
42. Prochaska JO, Velicer WF, Rossi JS, *et al.* Stages of change and decisional balance for 12 problem behaviors. Health Psychol 1994;13:39–46.
43. National Institute of Mental Health (NIMH) Multisite HIV Prevention Trial Group. The NIMH Multisite HIV Prevention Trial: reducing sexual risk behavior. Science 1998;280:1889–94.
44. Kamb ML, Fishbein M, Douglas JM, *et al.*, and the Project Respect Study Group. Efficacy of risk-reduction counseling to prevent human immunodeficiency virus and sexually transmitted diseases – a randomized controlled trial. JAMA 1998;280:1161–7.
45. Kelly JA, St Lawrence JS, Hood HV, Brasfield TL. Behavioral intervention to reduce AIDS risk activities. J Consult Clin Psychol 1989;57:47–64.
46. Peterson JL, Coates TJ, Catania JA, *et al.* Evaluation of an HIV risk reduction intervention among African-American homosexual and bisexual men. AIDS 1996;10:319–25.
47. Imrie J, Stephenson JM, Cowan FM, *et al.* A cognitive behavioral intervention to reduce sexually transmitted infections among gay men: randomized trial. Br Med J 2001;322:1451–6.
48. Noar SM, Zimmerman RS. No doubt should be cast on efficacy of cognitive behavioral interventions (letter). Br Med J 2001;323:867.
49. Bonell C, Strange V. Social and behavioral interventions are effective in prevention HIV transmission (letter). Br Med J 2001;323: 867.
50. Kegeles SM, Hays RB, Coates T. The Mpowerment project: a community-level HIV prevention intervention for young gay men. Am J Publ Health 1996;86:1129–36.
51. Kelly JA, Murphy DA, Sikkema KJ, *et al.*, and the Community HIV Prevention Research Collaborative. Randomised, controlled, community-level HIV prevention intervention for sexual-risk behavior among homosexual men in US cities. Lancet 1997;350:1500–5.
52. Kelly JA, Murphy DA, Washington CD, *et al.* The effects of HIV/AIDS intervention groups for high-risk women in urban clinics. Am J Publ Health 1994;84:1918–22.
53. DiClimente RJ, Wingood GM. Randomized controlled trial of an HIV sexual risk reduction program for young African-American women. JAMA 1995;274:1271–6.
54. Hobfoll SE, Jackson AP, Lavin J, Britton PJ, Shepherd JB. Reducing inner-city women's AIDS risk activities: a study of single, pregnant women. Health Psychol 1994;13:397–403.
55. Belcher L, Kalichman S, Topping M, *et al.* A randomized controlled trial of a brief HIV risk reduction counseling intervention for women. J Consult Clin Psychol 1998;66:856–61.
56. Sikkema KJ, Kelly JA, Winett RA, *et al.* Outcomes of a randomized community level HIV prevention intervention for women living in 18 low-income housing developments. Am J Publ Health 2000;90:57–63.
57. Lauby JL, Smith PJ, Stark M, Person B, Adams J. A community-level HIV prevention intervention for inner-city women: results of the women and infants demonstration projects. Am J Publ Health 2000;90:216–22.
58. Gibson DR, Flynn NM, Perales D. Effectiveness of syringe exchange programs in reducing HIV risk behavior and HIV seroconversion among injecting drug users. AIDS 2001;15:1329–41.
59. Coyle S, Needle R, Normand J. Outreach-based HIV prevention for injecting drug users: a review of published outcome data. Publ Health Rep 1998;113:S19–30.
60. Latkin CA, Mandell W, Vlahov D, Oziemkowska M, Celentano DD. The long term outcome of a personal network-oriented HIV prevention intervention for injection drug users. Am J Commun Psychol 1996;24:341–64.
61. Kwiatkowski CF, Stober DR, Booth RE, Zhang Y. Predictors of increased condom use following HIV intervention with heterosexually active drug users. Drug Alcohol Depend 1999;54:57–62.
62. Booth RE, Kwiatkowski CF, Stephens RC. Effectiveness of HIV/AIDS interventions on drug use and needle risk behaviors for out of treatment injection drug users. J Psychoactive Drugs 1998;30:269–78.
63. Schilling FR, El-Bassel N, Schinke SP. Building skills of recovering women drug users to reduce heterosexual AIDS transmission. Publ Health Rep 1991;106:297–304.
64. Gibson DR, Lovelle-Drache J, Young M, Hudes ES, Sorensen JL. Effectiveness of brief counseling in reducing HIV risk behavior in injecting drug users: final results of randomized trials of counseling with and without HIV testing. AIDS Behav 1999;3:3–12.

chapter

117 Preventing Occupational Infection with HIV in the Health Care Environment

David K Henderson

This chapter addresses strategies designed to prevent the transmission of HIV in the health care setting.

EPIDEMIOLOGY

Occupational risks, including risks for physical injuries, chemical exposures and infectious diseases, have long been prevalent in the health care workplace. The introduction of HIV infection into the health care workplace in the 1980s, however, focused the attention of health care providers, perhaps for the first time, on the issue of occupational risk. Ironically, HIV infection is only one of the blood-borne pathogen-associated risks in the health care setting. Blood-borne pathogens have been identified as occupational risks for health care workers since the epidemiology and routes of transmission of hepatitis B were delineated in the 1960s. For reasons incompletely understood at present, unlike occupational hepatitis B virus infection, occupational HIV infection remains relatively uncommon. Even with broad use of the hepatitis B vaccine, occupational hepatitis B virus infections continue to occur in US health care workers.

By June 2001, the US Public Health Service's Centers for Disease Control and Prevention (CDC) had recorded only 57 instances of documented occupational HIV infections and 138 instances of probable or possible occupational HIV infections among health care workers in the USA.[1] For each of these 57 cases, the health care worker sustained an occupational exposure to HIV, had a baseline serum sample drawn and evaluated by HIV serology and then, during follow-up, developed serologic evidence consistent with HIV infection. Fewer than 50 additional cases of documented occupational infections and approximately 60 instances of 'possible or probable' occupational infections have been reported from outside the USA. For the 138 'possible or probable' occupational infections reported to the CDC, the exposed health care workers either were unaware of the occurrence of an occupational exposure, did not report the exposure and/or did not have baseline serologic studies performed to document that they were not infected prior to the occupational exposure.

A comparison of the demographics of the 'possible/probable' and definite occupational infection cases reveals substantial differences. When one compares the demographics of these categories of infection with those of all health care workers in the USA, the likelihood that some of the 'possible/probable' cases have occurred as a result of community exposures seems quite high.[2]

A number of both general and specific factors, taken together, determine an individual practitioner's risk for occupational infection with HIV. First, the prevalence of HIV infection among the population of patients served is a major determinant of the overall risk. Second, the type of practice in which the provider engages (e.g. medical, emergency room, surgical) is associated with varying levels of risk for occupational exposure to blood-borne pathogens. Third, the types and frequencies of procedures performed in the practice, as well as the conditions under which the procedures are performed (i.e. emergent versus elective), also contribute to the risk equation. The extent to which the practitioner adheres to recommended infection control procedures and practices is also likely to be a determinant of risk for exposure and infection. Finally, the individual practitioner's technique and attention to detail are also likely contributors to the risk.

Several specific factors contribute to the risk for occupational HIV infection in the health care workplace. Tables 117.1 and 117.2 list factors that have been demonstrated[3] or suggested in the literature to contribute to the risk for occupational infection with HIV.

Many of the reported cases share several features in common. Most are transcutaneous exposures and the majority of these are injection needlestick injuries. All of the clinical cases have occurred following exposure to blood or grossly blood-stained bodily fluids from HIV-infected patients. As yet, no cases have been documented following a needlestick injury with a solid surgical needle.

To attempt to identify specific factors associated with risk for occupational HIV infection, public health authorities from the USA, France and the UK conducted a retrospective case-control study, matching the known anecdotal case reports of occupational HIV infections with 'controls' from the public health surveillance studies of occupational exposures in each of these countries.[3] This study identified five specific risk factors for occupational infection; these five factors and the level of statistical significance assigned to each in the study are listed in Table 117.2. The first four of these factors very likely relate directly to the inoculum effect. That an inoculum effect is present in this setting is supported by several pieces of information:

- transfusion of a unit of blood from an HIV-infected donor is associated with virtually 100% risk for infection;[4]
- the depth of a percutaneous exposure is an independent risk factor for occupational HIV infection;[3]
- the presence of visible blood on the device producing the injury was independently associated with risk for infection;[3]
- instruments that had been placed in source-patients' vascular channels were more likely to result in occupational infection;[3] and
- the fact that all of the needlestick exposures to blood have been caused by hollow-bore needles (i.e. injection, as compared with suturing needles).

Both in the CDC study, as well as in the majority of the anecdotal case reports, the source-patients for the exposures resulting in occupational HIV infections had advanced HIV disease. This finding is likely to be a surrogate marker for either the level of circulating viremia, the level of circulating 'free' virus, or both. Finally, most occupational infections have followed parenteral (as compared with mucosal or cutaneous) occupational exposures. These latter routes of exposure are associated with lower risks for occupational infection.

Percutaneous exposure

Several longitudinal studies have attempted to determine the magnitude of risk associated with different types of occupational exposures (summarized by Ippolito *et al.*[5] and Henderson[6]. Combining

FACTORS CONTRIBUTING TO THE RISK FOR OCCUPATIONAL HIV INFECTION
Exposure factors 1. Route of exposure (e.g. percutaneous,* mucous membrane, cutaneous) 2. Inoculum size • Size of the device producing injury • For needlestick exposures, type of needle (i.e. hollow-bore* vs solid) • Extent of contamination (e.g. visible blood on device,† whether or not device had been placed in an artery or vein†) • 'Depth/severity' of exposure*† • Type of contamination (e.g. blood,* pleural fluid, etc.)
Source/'donor' factors 1. Extent of viremia (e.g. by polymerase chain reaction or branch-chain DNA assay) 2. Stage of illness (as a presumed surrogate for extent of viremia†) 3. Circulating free (as opposed to cell-associated) virus 4. Antiretroviral chemotherapy (presumably reducing level of viremia)
* Features shared by many, if not most, of the occupational infections reported in the literature † Features identified as significantly associated with risk for occupational infection in the CDC case-control study[3]

Table 117.1 Factors contributing to the risk for occupational HIV infection.

RISK FACTORS FOR OCCUPATIONAL HIV INFECTION IDENTIFIED IN A RETROSPECTIVE CASE-CONTROL STUDY
The risk for occupational HIV infection was increased when: • the occupational exposure was deep, as compared with superficial ($p<0.0001$) • blood was visible on the device causing the occupational exposure ($p=0.0014$) • the device causing the exposure had been placed in a source-patient's vein or artery ($p=0.0028$) • the source-patient died within 60 days of the exposure ($p=0.0011$) • the exposed health care worker did not take zidovudine postexposure chemoprophylaxis ($p=0.0026$)

Table 117.2 Risk factors for occupational HIV infection identified in a retrospective case-control study conducted in the USA, UK and France.[3]

OCCUPATIONAL RISKS FOR HIV INFECTION	Percutaneous exposures	Mucous membrane exposures
Number of longitudinal studies	27	21
Number of exposures	6807	2768
Number of documented infections	21	0/1*
Infection rate per exposure	0.31%	0–0.11%†

* See text for discussion
† Using the rule of three[9]

Table 117.3 Occupational risks for HIV infection.

the data from the available studies, health care workers have sustained more than 6800 percutaneous exposures to sharp devices contaminated with blood or other blood-stained body fluids from patients known to be infected with HIV. Twenty-one occupational HIV infections have been documented in these studies, resulting in a risk of transmission per injury of 0.31% (Table 117.3). Thus, one in 324 parenteral exposures in these studies resulted in occupational HIV infection.

Although such a pooled risk estimate provides the best available data concerning the magnitude of risk for occupational HIV infection, this type of analysis has substantial limitations. For example, the longitudinal studies vary somewhat in experimental design and are therefore not directly comparable. Such an analysis implicitly assumes that all parenteral occupational exposures are associated with equal risk, an assumption that does not make intuitive sense and that has apparently been shown to be flawed by the CDC's case-control study cited above.[3] Similarly, all source-patients are also not likely to present the same level of risk for occupational infection, with patients with advanced disease (and high-grade viremia) more likely to transmit than are patients early in the course of HIV infection (see Table 117.2). Because of the large number of factors that influence the risk for occupational infection, these summary data cannot address the risk associated with a specific, discrete exposure in an individual health care worker.

Mucous membrane exposure

Occupational exposures other than parenteral exposures to blood present a lower level of risk for occupational infection. Anecdotal reports document, in rare circumstances, that mucous membrane or cutaneous exposures may produce occupational infections in health care workers.[7] Certain of the longitudinal studies cited above have also addressed occupational risks associated with mucous membrane exposure to blood from HIV-infected patients. To date, with more than 2700 exposures followed prospectively, only one study has reported a seroconversion following a mucous membrane exposure.[8] Thus, as a maximum estimate, (using the 'rule of three' as an approximation for a zero numerator),[9] the pooled risk estimate for infection associated with a mucous membrane exposure is 0.11% per exposure (see Table 117.3). Again, such a pooled risk estimate provides only a framework for considering the risks associated with a discrete exposure.

Occupational exposures other than percutaneous and mucous membrane exposures

Occupational exposures other than percutaneous and mucous membrane exposures are even less likely to result in infection. Prospective studies,[10,11] which include hundreds of person-years of follow-up, have not identified a single instance of transmission of HIV. Whereas exposures to other fluids are likely to be associated with some occupational risk, this risk is below currently measurable levels.

When one evaluates the occupational exposures that have produced infection, almost all of them result from exposure to blood from HIV-infected patients. Whereas other body fluids may ultimately be shown to represent a risk for occupational infection, the major risk in the health care setting has come from occupational exposures to blood from HIV-infected patients.

PATHOGENESIS

Although the retrospective case-control study of risk factors for occupational HIV infection cited above[3] provided some insight into factors associated with risk for occupational HIV infection, the precise pathogenetic mechanisms of the occupational infection event are, as yet, poorly understood. The major risk for occupational infection is associated with percutaneous injury with a needle or other sharp device that has been used on an HIV-infected patient. The risk is associated primarily with blood exposure. Precisely how the transmission event occurs in the skin, subcutaneous tissue or underlying muscle remains unclear. Current interest in the pathogenesis of infection by this route focuses on the role of host defense and on the role of the dendritic cell.

The role of host defense in protection against occupational infection is poorly understood. Scientists working at the National Cancer Institute have demonstrated that 75% of health care workers exposed to blood from HIV-infected patients who do not become infected with HIV develop HIV-specific T-helper activity.[12] In a subsequent study these investigators demonstrated that 35% of uninfected health care workers who had sustained occupational exposure to blood from HIV-infected patients studied developed cytotoxic lymphocyte responses to HIV-related envelope antigens.[13] Among health care workers who had sustained occupational exposures to blood from patients who were not infected with HIV, none responded to HIV-associated envelope antigens. Whereas the precise role that cellular immunity plays in host defense against occupational HIV infection remains to be delineated, these data, when combined with results from animal studies, suggest that the role may be an important one. One recent case report also supports a significant role for cellular immunity in the defense against HIV infection.[14] In this case, a health care worker who sustained an HIV needlestick exposure had HIV DNA detected by nucleic acid sequence-based amplification during a course of three-drug antiretroviral postexposure chemoprophylaxis. Despite the detection of proviral DNA, this individual ultimately remained uninfected (as assessed by serial nucleic acid tests and antibody determinations). The health care worker did, however, develop a robust HIV-specific cellular immune response.

INTERVENTIONS DESIGNED TO DECREASE THE RISK FOR OCCUPATIONAL HIV INFECTION

Interventions designed to limit occupational exposures

Several approaches have been used to attempt to decrease risks for occupational exposure to (and therefore occupational infection with) blood-borne pathogens in the health care setting (Table 117.4). Such interventions can be considered as primary prevention. Major categories of intervention include:

- education,
- work practice controls (e.g. adherence to infection control procedures designed to limit risk), and
- engineered controls.

PREVENTION STRATEGIES FOR HEALTH CARE WORKERS AND INSTITUTIONS TO DECREASE RISKS FOR OCCUPATIONAL HIV INFECTION
1. Use of 'standard precautions' or other isolation procedures designed to place effective barriers between the health care worker and blood or other body fluids.
2. Educating new staff and retraining existing staff regarding occupational risks for blood-borne pathogen infection in the context of other occupational risks present and prevalent in the health care workplace; making certain staff are aware of these risks.
3. Including information about all occupational risks (including those associated with caring for patients who have blood-borne pathogen infections) in biomedical training schools' curricula.
4. Evaluating all procedures associated with occupational risk for exposure to blood-borne pathogens (particularly those presenting risks for transcutaneous exposures), with the intent of modifying the aspects of these procedures associated with risks for occupational exposures.
5. Aggressive use of newly developed engineered controls, including careful evaluation of 'safety devices' for safety, efficacy and cost-effectiveness; implementation of those devices that meet these tests.
6. Development of efficient, readily accessible, user-friendly institutional postexposure management systems, including the option for postexposure antiretroviral chemoprophylaxis for documented occupational HIV exposures.

Table 117.4 Prevention strategies for health care workers and institutions to decrease risks for occupational HIV infection.[2]

Education and use of infection control procedures

Staff should be routinely informed about all occupational risks. Since the major risk for occupational HIV infection (and for infection with other blood-borne pathogens as well) is by parenteral inoculation, some critics of the use of infection control procedures for managing all patients as if they were potentially infected with blood-borne pathogens (e.g. universal precautions, body substance isolation, standard precautions (discussed below)) have suggested that these precautions will have little impact on the number of occupational infections. However, since these and later guidelines educate staff about the careful handling of needles and sharp objects, recommend against practices associated with a high risk for parenteral exposures (e.g. needle recapping, needle bending or needle clipping) and stress appropriate disposal of needles and other sharp objects,[15,16] their implementation will probably be associated with a decreased parenteral exposure rate. Two centers have documented a significant decrease in such exposures,[17,18] one in temporal association with training in, and implementation of, universal precautions.[17] Up to one third of parenteral occupational exposures may be preventable by following guidelines designed to minimize occupational exposures.[19] The use of appropriate barriers may actually reduce occupational risk; the act of piercing a latex glove with a needle covered with blood may reduce the blood inoculum by as much as 50%.[20] Making health care workers aware of the presence of occupational risks may, in itself, result in occupational behavior modification. In a survey of certified nurse-midwives, both knowledge of the routes of transmission of blood-borne pathogens and perception of risk for occupational infection were statistically associated with the appropriate use of precautions. However, risk perception and use of precautions were more closely linked, suggesting that knowledge, in itself, may be insufficient to produce behavior modification.[21]

Employers in the USA are governed by regulations issued by the Occupational Safety and Health Administration of the US Department of Labor in 1991. One regulation mandates that employers follow certain protocols when managing health care workers who have sustained occupational exposures to blood-borne pathogens.[22] This 'final rule' has become the subject of mandatory education for health care workers at every health care institution in the USA.

Work practice controls

In 1987, the CDC issued guidelines for the management of patients infected with blood-borne pathogens that have since provided the underpinnings for all subsequent guidelines in the USA.[15] These 'universal precautions' guidelines set out clearly the principle that health care workers should treat blood and blood-stained body fluids from all patients as potentially infectious, in order to prevent the transmission of blood-borne pathogens (in particular, HIV) from patients to health care workers. More recently, the CDC has issued revised isolation guidelines, called 'standard precautions', which focus on the bidirectional spread of organisms to and from patients and health care providers.[16] All of these sets of guidelines and precautions emphasize:

- that blood and other blood-containing body fluids represent risk to health care workers, and
- that health care workers should use barriers and take precautions to prevent occupational exposures to these materials.

Use of these kinds of precautions in health care settings has resulted in decreased risk for occupational exposure to blood and, presumably, decreased risks for occupational infections with blood-borne pathogens.

Based on self-reports of occupational exposures to blood, Fahey and co-workers at the National Institutes of Health estimated that, in the year prior to training the staff in universal precautions, staff members experienced an average of 36 cutaneous exposures to blood.[23] Eighteen months after the staff were trained in universal precautions, this number decreased to 18. For all categories of employees and information analyzed, exposures to blood were reduced by approximately 50%. These results suggest that changes in behavior occurred between the two surveys, and, although a causal relationship with training cannot be proved, such a relationship can reasonably be inferred.

Compliance with these precautions has been problematic. Gerberding and co-workers identified substantial noncompliance at San Francisco General Hospital.[24] Although Fahey identified substantial improvement in her staff's compliance with universal precautions, the reduction in blood exposures was only 50% (implying that 50% of such exposures continued to occur, despite implementation of these precautions).[23]

Although data regarding procedure-specific adverse exposure rates are limited, certain procedures and devices seem intrinsically associated with increased risk for occupational exposures. To the extent that such modifications are possible, inherently risky procedures should be modified. In some instances, risk modification can be achieved by practitioners modifying the procedure themselves. In other circumstances, new devices or engineering controls (discussed below) may be needed. Some work practice interventions have been shown to reduce the risks for blood exposures. For example, the use of 'double-gloving' in surgery reduced the risk for skin exposure to blood significantly.[25,26]

Engineered controls

Whereas work practice controls can eliminate a substantial fraction of occupational exposures to blood-borne pathogens, modifying medical devices that, in their current formats, are intrinsically associated with exposure risks can reduce these risks further. Among authorities in the field, Jagger and co-workers detailed the importance of the design of medical devices in the prevention of occupational exposures to blood-borne pathogens.[27,28]

In the past several years, a number of engineered controls (i.e. presumably 'safer' devices) have been introduced. Of these new safety devices, the following have been identified in at least one published study as being associated with decreased risks for cutaneous and/or percutaneous blood exposures:

- a surgical repair assist device,
- blunt surgical needles,
- surgical finger guards and glove liners,
- phlebotomy equipment,
- needleless intravenous administration systems, and
- modified (e.g. self-capping) intravenous catheters.

Despite their implementation, some exposures will still occur. Development of a process for the systematic, objective evaluation of these devices is crucial to effective risk reduction for all health care institutions.[29]

Interventions designed to decrease the risk for occupational infection once exposure to HIV has occurred

Immediate postexposure management

Despite the emphasis on the prevention of occupational exposures, institutions should also develop strategies for managing occupational exposures effectively. Important constituents of a postexposure management program are listed in Table 117.5.

Health care workers must be educated about the importance of reporting occupational exposures. Institutional reporting procedures should be simple, straightforward and widely publicized. When an exposure occurs, first aid should be administered and the exposure site should be allowed to bleed freely. The wound should be cleansed and decontaminated as soon as patient safety permits. Wounds should be washed with soap and water and then irrigated with sterile saline, a disinfectant or other suitable solution. Mucosal exposures should be decontaminated by vigorously flushing with water. Eyes should be irrigated with clean water, saline or sterile eye irrigants.

Exposures should be reported promptly. A mechanism to facilitate reporting and provision of follow-up care should be both readily accessible and widely publicized. Reporting systems should offer access to expert consultants. Institutional occupational medical systems must protect the confidentiality of the exposed worker. If confidentiality is not preserved, institutional programs are doomed to failure.

At the time an exposure is reported, occupational medical personnel should draw baseline serologies and chemistries. For docu-

COMPONENTS OF POSTEXPOSURE MANAGEMENT PROGRAMS FOR HEALTH CARE WORKERS EXPOSED TO HIV
1. Institutions should develop thorough, thoughtful, aggressive, employee educational campaigns concerning the presence of occupational risks in the health care workplace, including the risks for blood-borne pathogen infection; these educational campaigns should emphasize risk prevalence, risk reduction strategies, the importance of reporting adverse occupational exposures and postexposure management protocols.
2. Postexposure management systems must include mechanisms to facilitate both exposure reporting and the provision of follow-up care; these systems should be readily accessible, widely publicized, convenient and user friendly; occupational medicine personnel should be instructed to provide immediate 'first aid' for staff sustaining adverse exposures to blood and body fluids.
3. Institutions should develop a system for categorizing occupational exposures that require differing management strategies and different types of follow-up; protocols should address 'source-unknown' and 'source refuses serologic testing' exposures.
4. Postexposure management protocols should include appropriate serologic testing (mindful of state and local laws regarding consent) of both the source-patient as well as the employee sustaining the occupational exposure.
5. Occupational medicine staff should be thoroughly trained in the counseling of staff sustaining occupational exposures to HIV; all exposed staff should be given appropriate counseling regarding risks for infection and prevention of secondary transmission; all staff should have access to further counseling, if needed; all exposed staff should be given access to experts in the areas of occupational risks and HIV infection.
6. Exposed employees should be counseled to return for appropriate clinical and serologic follow-up and should be instructed to return if signs and/or symptoms of the acute primary HIV infection syndrome should develop.
7. Postexposure management protocols should offer antiretroviral chemoprophylaxis, with appropriate follow-up, for health care workers sustaining occupational exposure to HIV.
8. Counseling should include attention to the known/expected toxicities of the selected regimen. Pre-emptive therapy of these symptoms/side-effects (e.g. prescriptions to treat nausea, diarrhea, etc.) may increase regimen adherence.
9. Postexposure management protocols must, at all costs, maintain the exposed health care worker's medical privacy and confidentiality.

Table 117.5 Components of postexposure management programs for health care workers exposed to HIV.

mented occupational exposures to HIV, follow-up should occur at 6 weeks, 3 months, 6 months and 1 year following exposure. The value of the 1 year follow-up visit remains somewhat controversial; however, some case reports of late seroconversion (i.e. more than 6 months following exposure) have now appeared. More aggressive diagnostic evaluation, such as the use of polymerase chain reaction analysis to detect viral or proviral nucleic acids, is ordered if the health care worker develops symptoms suggestive of acute, primary HIV infection (i.e. the seroconversion illness). Institutions must develop policies regarding the testing of source-patients and employees that are consonant with local and state laws. Occupational medicine staff should counsel the exposed health care worker about the signs and symptoms of the seroconversion illness and should instruct the employee to return for evaluation should any illness consistent with this syndrome occur.

Postexposure chemoprophylaxis with antiretroviral agents

The use of antiretroviral agents as postexposure chemoprophylaxis for occupational exposures was controversial from its inception.[30] Data accumulated over the past 10 years, however, provide a firmer foundation for postexposure chemoprophylaxis programs. Recently, several animal studies of postexposure chemoprophylaxis (most of which use substantially lower viral inocula) have been able to demonstrate efficacy. Another piece of scientific evidence that indirectly supports its use comes from the success of antiretroviral agents administered in pregnancy in reducing maternal–fetal transmission of HIV[31,32] (see Chapter 135). One of the factors identified in the collaborative retrospective case-control study as significantly associated with an increased risk for occupational HIV infection was 'not taking zidovudine chemoprophylaxis'.[3] In this study, administering zidovudine chemoprophylaxis to exposed health care workers was associated with an approximately 80% reduction in the risk for occupational infection following transcutaneous exposures to HIV.[3]

The US Public Health Service has published guidelines that recommended the use of postexposure antiretroviral chemoprophylaxis in some settings.[33] The current recommendations (summarized in Table 117.6) advocate the use of three agents (zidovudine, lamivudine and one of four additional agents (see Table 117.6)) for the most severe occupational exposures and the use of two of these agents (i.e. zidovudine plus lamivudine) or one of two other alternative two-drug regimens for lesser exposures. If the source-patient for an exposure is (or recently has been) receiving antiretroviral therapy, some authorities have recommended the use of alternative regimens comprising agents to which the source-patient's virus has not been exposed, tailoring the construction of the regimen in a fashion similar to the planning of 'salvage therapy' for active HIV infection.

This latter point underscores the importance of obtaining expert guidance from individuals knowledgeable about the use of antiretroviral agents in tailoring a regimen for a health care worker, especially in circumstances in which the source-patient is known or highly suspected to harbor a resistant virus. Clinicians who are skilled in providing care to HIV-infected patients are perhaps best situated to provide this kind of advice. If you cannot identify a local expert, the US Public Health Service sponsors a post-exposure hotline that can provide this expertise (either over the telephone (888-448-4911) or via the World Wide Web at http://pepline.ucsf.edu/pepline). Recently, the use of nevirapine has been contraindicated because of the risk of severe liver toxicity, which can include hepatic failure.[34]

Another special circumstance worthy of additional consideration relates to the administration of postexposure prophylaxis to a health care worker who is (or thinks she may be) pregnant. Because of our extremely limited experience with the use of these agents in uninfected individuals, the risks associated with administering the drugs to pregnant women are essentially undefined. The only relevant clinical experience in humans comes from the administration of the drugs to HIV-infected pregnant women, a circumstance that is not exactly consonant with the postexposure prophylaxis setting. Based on the limited clinical data, as well as several relevant animal studies, general guidelines for this situation have been developed and are summarized in Table 117.7.[33,35]

Virtually all of the marketed antiretroviral agents have potential for carcinogenicity, teratogenicity and mutagenicity. Efavirenz has been shown to be teratogenic in cynomolgus monkeys at drug levels similar to those in humans. In addition, administration of the didanosine/stavudine combination in pregnancy has been associated with cases of severe pancreatitis and severe lactic acidosis among

CURRENT US PUBLIC HEALTH SERVICE RECOMMENDATIONS FOR CHEMOPROPHYLAXIS OF OCCUPATIONAL EXPOSURES TO HIV

HIV exposures with a recognized transmission risk	'Basic regimen'	Zidovudine (ZDV) plus lamivudine (3TC)
	Alternative	Stavudine (D4T) plus lamivudine
	'Basic regimen'	Stavudine plus didanosine (ddI)†
HIV exposures for which the nature of the exposure suggests an elevated transmission risk*	'Basic regimen' plus one of the following agents	Indinavir† Nelfinavir Abacavir Efavirenz†

* Elevated risk is associated with 'larger' volume of blood and/or blood containing a high titer of HIV
† Agents not advisable for use in pregnancy and increasingly not recommended in practice

Table 117.6 Current US Public Health Service recommendations for chemoprophylaxis of occupational exposures to HIV.[33]

GENERAL PRINCIPLES FOR ADMINISTERING ANTIRETROVIRAL CHEMOPROPHYLAXIS TO PREGNANT HEALTH CARE WORKERS

1. A pregnant, exposed health care worker is the only person who can decide whether to take chemoprophylaxis, and she must be empowered to make this decision. No one should attempt to make this decision for her.
2. The practitioner providing care to a pregnant, HIV-exposed woman must provide up-to-date and accurate information about what is known (and not known) concerning:
   - the magnitude of risk for infection associated with her exposure;
   - the efficacy of postexposure prophylaxis;
   - the safety of the treatment, including the potential for harm to the health care worker and her fetus; and
   - the risk of the fetus becoming infected (and the possible interventions that could be taken to reduce this risk) should the health care worker become infected from the exposure.
3. The practitioner should select a regimen appropriate for the exposure (i.e. pregnancy per se should not dictate the regimen, but consideration should be given to agents for which an experience base exists (e.g. zidovudine and lamivudine)). Some agents/regimens (i.e. those with known toxicities in pregnancy) should be avoided whenever possible (e.g. didanosine plus stavudine; efavirenz, indinavir).
4. Pregnant workers electing to take postexposure chemoprophylaxis must be followed closely for signs of toxicity (both maternal and fetal); pregnancy represents another circumstance in which expert consultative advice is essential.

Table 117.7 General principles for administering antiretroviral chemoprophylaxis to pregnant health care workers.[33,35]

HIV-infected women, and both maternal and fetal deaths have been recorded.[36] Other issues that may be relevant to the administration of chemoprophylaxis to pregnant health care workers include data from France suggesting a risk for severe mitochondrial toxicity in uninfected infants born to mothers who had taken nucleoside analogues[37] (an experience that has not been detected in the USA) as well as the potential for hepatotoxicity and nephrolithiasis associated with indinavir use.

Despite the encouraging data concerning the use and efficacy of postexposure antiretroviral chemoprophylaxis, legitimate concern remains about the use of these agents in this setting. Antiretrovirals are not trivial agents in terms of potential toxicity. Toxicity data in healthy individuals, especially for the newer agents, are extremely limited; however, it is fair to emphasize that virtually all the studies of antiretroviral chemoprophylaxis for occupational HIV exposures in health care workers have demonstrated substantial side-effects, often limiting completion of the prescribed regimen.[38] Finally, several cases of zidovudine chemoprophylaxis failure (eight of which have direct clinical relevance) have appeared in the literature.

The US Public Health Service last revised its guidelines concerning postexposure prophylaxis in 2001[33] and intends to revise the guidelines whenever new information becomes available concerning the risks or benefits of postexposure chemoprophylaxis. In spite of these considerations, all institutions need to have a policy on postexposure prophylaxis. Offering chemoprophylaxis is seen as 'empowering' by exposed workers. Workers who have had these frightening occupational exposures appreciate the fact that their institutions are willing to offer these drugs.

REFERENCES

1. Centers for Disease Control and Prevention. Surveillance of health care workers with HIV/AIDS. http://www.cdc.gov/hiv/stats/hasr1201/tabl17.html. Accessed 3/28/02.
2. Beekmann SE, Fahey BJ, Gerberding JL, Henderson DK. Risky business: using necessarily imprecise casualty counts to estimate occupational risks for HIV-1 infection. Infect Control Hosp Epidemiol 1990;11:371–9.
3. Cardo DM, Culver DH, Ciesielski CA, *et al.* A case-control study of HIV seroconversion in health care workers after percutaneous exposure. Centers for Disease Control and Prevention Needlestick Surveillance Group. N Engl J Med 1997;337:1485–90.
4. Ward JW, Deppe DA, Samson S, Perkins H, *et al.* Human immunodeficiency virus infection from blood donors who later developed the acquired immunodeficiency syndrome. Ann Intern Med 1987;106:61–2.
5. Ippolito G, Puro V, Heptonstall J, Jagger J, De Carli G, Petrosillo N. Occupational human immunodeficiency virus infection in health care workers: worldwide cases through September 1997. Clin Infect Dis 1999;28:365–83.
6. Henderson DK. Risks for exposures to and infection with HIV among health care providers in the emergency department. Emerg Med Clin North Am 1995;13:199–211.
7. Chamberland ME, Ciesielski CA, Howard RJ, Fry DE, Bell DM. Occupational risk of infection with human immunodeficiency virus. Surg Clin North Am 1995;75:1057–70.
8. Ippolito G, Puro P, De Carli G, Italian Study Group on Occupational Risk of HIV Infection. The risk of occupational HIV infection in health care workers: Italian multicentre study. Arch Intern Med 1993;153:1451–8.
9. Hanley JA, Lippman-Hand A. If nothing goes wrong, is everything all right? Interpreting zero numerators. JAMA 1983;249:1743–5.
10. Gershon R, Vlahov D, Nelson K. The risk of transmission of HIV-1 through non-percutaneous, non-sexual modes – a review. AIDS 1990;4:645–50.
11. Friedland G. Additional evidence for lack of transmission of HIV infection by close interpersonal (casual) contact. AIDS 1990;4:639–44.
12. Clerici M, Levin JM, Kessler HA, *et al.* HIV-specific T-helper activity in seronegative health care workers exposed to contaminated blood. JAMA 1994;271:42–6.
13. Pinto LA, Sullivan J, Berzofsky JA, *et al.* ENV-specific cytotoxic T lymphocyte responses in HIV seronegative health care workers occupationally exposed to HIV-contaminated body fluids. J Clin Invest 1995;96:867–76.
14. Puro V, Calcagno G, Anselmo M, *et al.* Transient detection of plasma HIV-1 RNA during postexposure prophylaxis. Infect Control Hosp Epidemiol 2000;21:529–31.
15. Centers for Disease Control. Update: universal precautions for prevention of transmission of human immunodeficiency virus, hepatitis B virus, and other bloodborne pathogens in health-care settings. MMWR Morb Mortal Wkly Rep 1988;37:377–82, 387–8.
16. Garner JS. Guideline for isolation precautions in hospitals. The Hospital Infection Control Practices Advisory Committee. Infect Control Hosp Epidemiol 1996;17:53–80.
17. Beekmann SE, Vlahov D, Koziol DE, McShalley ED, Schmitt JM, Henderson DK. Temporal association between implementation of universal precautions and a sustained, progressive decrease in percutaneous exposures to blood. Clin Infect Dis 1994;18:562–9.
18. Haiduven DJ, DeMaio TM, Stevens DA. A five-year study of needlestick injuries: significant reduction associated with communication, education, and convenient placement of sharps containers. Infect Control Hosp Epidemiol 1992;13:265–71.
19. Marcus R, Cooperative Needlestick Surveillance Group. Surveillance of health care workers exposed to blood from patients infected with the human immunodeficiency virus. N Engl J Med 1988;319:1118–23.
20. Mast ST, Woolwine JD, Gerberding JL. Efficacy of gloves in reducing blood volumes transferred during simulated needlestick injury. J Infect Dis 1993;168:1589–92.
21. Willy ME, Dhillon G, Loewen NL, Wesley RA, Henderson DK. Adverse exposures and universal precautions practices among a group of highly exposed health professionals. Infect Control Hosp Epidemiol 1990;11:351–6.
22. Department of Labor OSHA. Occupational exposure to bloodborne pathogens; final rule. Federal Register 1991;56:64175–82.
23. Fahey BJ, Koziol DE, Banks SM, Henderson DK. Frequency of nonparenteral occupational exposures to blood and body fluids before and after universal precautions training. Am J Med 1991;90:145–53.
24. Gerberding JL, Bryant-LeBlanc CE, Nelson K, *et al.* Risk of transmitting the human immunodeficiency virus, cytomegalovirus, and hepatitis B virus to health care workers exposed to patients with AIDS and AIDS-related conditions. J Infect Dis 1987;156:1–8.
25. Gerberding JL, Littell C, Tarkington A, Brown A, Schecter WP. Risk of exposure of surgical personnel to patients' blood during surgery at San Francisco General Hospital. N Engl J Med 1990;322:1788–93.
26. Greco RJ, Garza JR. Use of double gloves to protect the surgeon from blood contact during aesthetic procedures. Aesthetic Plast Surg 1995;19:265–7.
27. Jagger J, Hunt EH, Pearson RD. Sharp object injuries in the hospital: causes and strategies for prevention. Am J Infect Control 1990;18:227–31.
28. Jagger J, Pearson RD. Universal precautions: still missing the point on needlesticks. Infect Control Hosp Epidemiol 1991;12:211–3.
29. Chiarello LA. Selection of needlestick prevention devices: a conceptual framework for approaching product evaluation. Am J Infect Control 1995;23:386–95.
30. Henderson DK, Gerberding JL. Prophylactic zidovudine after occupational exposure to the human immunodeficiency virus: an interim analysis. J Infect Dis 1989;160:321–7.
31. Connor EM, Mofenson LM. Zidovudine for the reduction of perinatal human immunodeficiency virus transmission: pediatric AIDS Clinical Trials Group Protocol 076–results and treatment recommendations. Pediatr Infect Dis J 1995;14:536–41.
32. Wade NA, Birkhead GS, Warren BL, *et al.* Abbreviated regimens of zidovudine prophylaxis and perinatal transmission of the human immunodeficiency virus. N Engl J Med 1998;339:1409–14.
33. Centers for Disease Control and Prevention. Updated US Public Health Service guidelines for the management of occupational exposures to HBV, HCV, and HIV and recommendations for postexposure prophylaxis. MMWR Morb Mortal Wkly Rep 2001;50(RR-11):1–52.
34. Centers for Disease Control and Prevention. Serious adverse events attributed to nevirapine regimens for postexposure prophylaxis after HIV exposures – worldwide, 1997–2000. MMWR Morb Mortal Wkly Rep 2001;49:1153–6.
35. Henderson DK. HIV postexposure prophylaxis in the 21st century. Emerg Infect Dis 2001;7:254–8.
36. Food and Drug Administration. Important drug warning. http//www.fda.gov/medwatch/safety/2001/safety01.htm#zerit. Accessed 3/28/02.
37. Blanche S, Tardieu M, Rustin P, *et al.* Persistent mitochondrial dysfunction and perinatal exposure to antiretroviral nucleoside analogues. Lancet 1999;354:1084–9.
38. Lee LM, Henderson DK. Tolerability of postexposure antiretroviral prophylaxis for occupational exposures to HIV. Drug Saf 2001;24:587–97.

chapter 118

HIV Vaccines: Research and Development

Patricia E Fast, Jill Gilmour & Kalpana Gupta

THE NEED FOR A VACCINE TO PREVENT HIV-1 INFECTION AND AIDS

Identification of HIV-1 as the cause of AIDS led to development of methods to diagnose the infection, quantify the virus in plasma and cells and document the evolution of the disease and treatments. Understanding the mode of transmission has led to some success in prevention, through interventions such as screening of the blood supply, drug treatment for pregnant women and promotion of barrier methods and safe sex. Despite these modest gains, the epidemic has moved with a speed that defies imagination. The hardest-hit countries, in sub-Saharan Africa, have experienced enormous losses, with up to half the young adults infected in some areas and the average lifespan decreased by as much as two decades.[1] The epidemic in Asia threatens to dwarf that in Africa. Meanwhile, in the USA, hard-won gains in education and behavioral prevention seem to be slipping away; infection rates are increasing in certain groups, particularly young gay men and minority women.[2] An effective vaccine is needed more than ever to stop the growth of this epidemic.

PROSPECTS FOR SUCCESS

HIV-1 is a formidable challenge for vaccine prevention programs, from the standpoint of science, development and eventual utilization of a safe and effective vaccine. Its immune evasion mechanisms include molecular tricks to avoid neutralization by antibody, down-regulation of immune functions, direct destruction of the CD4 T cells that support both antibody and effector T-cell responses, and a very rapid mutation rate that gives rise to virus strains lacking the antigenic markers (epitopes) to which effective immune responses are directed. Nevertheless, there is evidence that immunity can prevent establishment of infection in exposed persons. The immune responses induced by acute infection clearly establish some control of HIV-1 replication. Vaccine-induced immunity could more frequently prevent or more effectively control virus replication. Limiting virus replication could, in turn, delay disease onset and reduce transmission of HIV-1 to sexual partners, infants or other contacts. Even a modest reduction in the susceptibility to infection or likelihood of transmission could have a significant impact on the HIV-1 pandemic.[3] A reduced replication rate might also diminish the ability of HIV-1 to develop mutations leading to drug resistance or escape from immune responses.

Three types of evidence suggest that vaccines will be effective in preventing HIV-1 infection and/or AIDS (Table 118.1). First, chronic infection with HIV-1 occurs after only a small fraction of all exposures, suggesting that a modest immune defense might be effective.[5] This reasoning is supported by the apparent resistance to infection of some persons who are repeatedly exposed to HIV-1.[6] Cell-mediated immune responses in exposed but uninfected individuals are thought to be induced by autologous infected cells, suggesting that, prior to the establishment of a chronic HIV-1 infection, there may be a brief phase in which the infection can be aborted, perhaps by immune destruction of the infected cells.[7] Second, the natural history of HIV-1 infection shows that, after an initial phase of rapid viral

EVIDENCE THAT AN HIV-1 VACCINE IS POSSIBLE			
Setting	**Type of evidence**	**Conclusion**	**Strength of evidence***
Human epidemiology	Studies of adults repeatedly exposed to HIV-1 by sex or injections and infants exposed during birth or nursing	Infection occurs infrequently after exposure; risk depends on quantity of virus	+++
	T-cell responses reported in some exposed but uninfected persons	T-cell responses are induced by exposure to HIV-1 (abortive infection?)	+
Natural history of HIV-1 infection in humans (and related viruses in animal models)	Virus concentration in blood is very high during acute infection, then drops as T-cell responses appear	T-cell responses induced by infection partially control viral replication, usually for years	+++
	Virus concentration in blood increases late in infection when T-cell levels are very low	T-cell responses control viral replication	+++
	Prompt postexposure drug treatment can prevent or abort infection	A small number of infected cells can be destroyed (by immune mechanisms)	++
Studies of active and passive immunization in animal models	Passive antibody transfer or monoclonal antibody infusion	Antibodies prevent infection (probably by neutralizing the virus)	++
	Vaccination with antigens inducing CD8 T cells or depletion of CD8 T cells in infected animals	T-cell responses limit viral replication after challenge	+++
		T-cell responses slow progression to disease	+++

* Evidence is strong when most or all of several studies lead to the same conclusion; evidence is weaker when there are few or conflicting studies. The evidence has recently been reviewed.[4]

Table 118.1 Evidence that an HIV-1 vaccine is possible.

replication, immune responses may control HIV-1 replication and slow its pathogenic effects for many years.[8,9] Third, nonhuman primate models (e.g. SIV in macaques or the man-made chimeric SHIV in macaques) show that some vaccines given prior to challenge can prevent infection or slow viral replication and disease progression,[10–13] an effect dependent at least in part on CD8 effector cells.[14,15] Likewise, antibodies that are able to neutralize HIV-1 or SHIV can prevent infection in animal models.[16–19] Immunization that induces mucosal responses is particularly effective against mucosal challenges.[20]

SCIENTIFIC BASIS FOR HIV VACCINE DEVELOPMENT

Immune targets in the HIV infection process

The HIV-1 replication cycle begins with the envelope protein binding to receptors on the host cell surface (CD4, a chemokine receptor molecule, or both) and fusing with the cell membrane, resulting in virus entry and introduction of the viral genetic material into the host cell nucleus. DNA transcribed from viral RNA integrates into the host genome and directs synthesis of viral RNA and proteins, which assemble to form progeny viral particles that bud from the surface of the infected cell. Shortly after infection of a cell, peptides derived from virus proteins (envelope, gag, polymerase and regulatory proteins) are displayed on the surface of the cell, in association with HLA molecules. These can activate T cells and serve as their targets. Some cells, however, can harbor HIV-1 without being 'visible' to T cells.[21] In the first days after infection, HIV-1 and related viruses rapidly spread from the portal of entry, usually at a mucosal surface, to blood, secondary lymphoid organs and lymphoid cells in tissues such as the gut.[22,23]

Vaccines against other viral diseases may allow asymptomatic infection but prevent disease. Once it is established, HIV-1 infection may not be eradicable. The ideal HIV-1 vaccine will prevent the establishment of infection by inducing antibodies that neutralize HIV-1 virus by binding to envelope protein or by inducing effector T cells that can inhibit virus replication and eliminate the first few cells to become infected. Even if infection is not prevented, priming the immune response could lead to more rapid immune control of virus replication and delayed onset of disease. Immune responses that occur at mucosal sites may play a particularly important role, as most HIV-1 exposure occurs through mucosal routes and the gut lymphoid tissue is an important site for HIV-1 replication regardless of route of infection.[24] As in other viral diseases, it is likely that all components of the immune system will need to work synergistically: the nonadaptive component that offers initial protection and provides the impetus for adaptive responses,[25,26] antigen-presenting cells of several types, B cells that make antibodies and a multiplicity of T cells, including effectors, that secrete antiviral cytokines and kill virus-infected cells or helpers that simply control the activities of effector T and B cells, and memory cells for each adaptive component will likely be involved in reducing the number of infectious virions, limiting viral replication and eliminating infected cells.[27]

Neutralizing antibodies

Neutralizing antibodies can block the virus from binding to the host cell membrane, thus interfering with envelope–receptor complex formation, and/or with membrane fusion. As a result, the virus cannot enter the cell and replicate.

Neutralizing antibodies are directed against either linear or conformational epitopes (antigenic portions) of the folded viral envelope glycoprotein. Several features of HIV-1 envelope (conformational flexibility, a complex and labile structure, the presence of variable loops and glycosylation of some antigenic regions) contribute to mechanisms by which HIV-1 can avoid inducing neutralizing antibodies or withstand their effects.[28] In addition, after infection, new HIV-1 'escape mutants' emerge that are no longer susceptible to neutralization by the host's antibodies.[29,30]

Nevertheless, it is clear that neutralizing antibodies can be protective if they are present prior to infection. Neutralization of HIV-1 by passively infused antibodies protects chimpanzees[31] or SCID-hu mice (which lack their own immune system and have a transplanted human system[18,32]) against infection with HIV-1, and monkeys from infection by the man-made chimeric viruses with the envelope of HIV-1 and other genes derived from the SIV.[19,33]

When antibodies from individuals chronically infected with HIV-1 are tested for neutralization, the response is often weak. However, broadly cross-reactive neutralizing antibodies can be made by at least some humans; a few human monoclonal antibodies (mAbs) have been developed that efficiently neutralize a range of primary HIV-1 isolates.[34–36] Unfortunately, no vaccine has been identified that will induce high titers of broadly cross-reactive and durable neutralizing antibodies against strains of HIV-1 recently isolated from human peripheral blood mononuclear cells (PBMCs), often called primary isolates. This standard may be too stringent (it is not necessarily met by all successful vaccines against other viruses); only analysis of the immune responses from one or more efficacious vaccines will resolve the issue. Rational design approaches focusing on structure–function analyses of envelope–antibody binding, further elucidation of the structure of envelope, and library screening for identification of possible immunogens are currently under investigation and may lead to novel strategies for inducing broadly cross-reactive neutralizing antibodies.

Cell-mediated immunity

T cells may protect against HIV-1 infection by killing infected cells (cytotoxic lymphocytes (CTLs)), by producing soluble antiviral substances such as interferon-γ or other inflammatory mediators or by 'helping' or amplifying the cytotoxic or antibody responses. T cells bearing the CD8 marker on their surface are effectors (cytotoxic or secrete cytokines), while T cells with CD4 on their surface frequently regulate antibody or cell-mediated responses or may have cytolytic activity. CD8 cells are thought to be most important in controlling virus infections, because they recognize peptides from endogenously produced antigens, such as those found on the surface of virus-infected cells.

T-cell responses are directed against HIV-1 proteins, regardless of their function (structural, enzymatic or regulatory).[37] Thus, T cells have a wider variety of targets and some of the targets are constrained in their genetic variability by the need to preserve functional structures. They can react with a variety of HIV-1 isolates, either because the epitopes are conserved between various strains of HIV-1 or because of immunologic cross-reactivity between similar epitopes.[38,39] Nevertheless, T-cell epitopes may vary and when the predominant response to retrovirus infection is limited to one or a few specificities, viruses bearing a changed epitope may escape from immune control and cause disease progression.[40,41] Additionally, due to its high mutation rate, HIV-1 may tend to evolve by losing epitopes to which a specific population responds well,[42] or it might lose epitopes contained in an initially effective vaccine.

Evaluation of vaccine-induced immune responses

Vaccine trials require robust, sensitive and reproducible methods to measure vaccine-induced immune responses. Most of the existing licensed vaccines were developed empirically with little knowledge of what immune responses mediate protection, in an era when only antibody responses could be measured accurately. It is likely that the

CHARACTERISTICS OF HIV-1 NEUTRALIZATION ASSAYS	
Virus type	Strains adapted to long-term culture in T cells or recently isolated 'primary isolates' or genetically engineered viruses with HIV-1 envelope, some containing a reporter gene
Target cells	PBMCs stimulated with a mitogen to induce cell division, cell lines expressing appropriate cell surface markers (HIV-1 receptor and coreceptor) or genetically engineered cell lines containing a reporter gene
Indicator system	Cell death or cytopathic effect, viral protein production, molecular reporter gene (e.g. green fluorescent protein, luciferase, β-galactosidase). Some are highly reproducible and capable of high throughput automation
Number of replication cycles	Single or multiple (affects assay duration and variability)

Table 118.2 Characteristics of HIV-1 neutralization assays.

arms of the immune response work synergistically and with the non-adaptive innate immune system. However, the practical reality of vaccine development necessitates selection of one immune response as an indicator of vaccine potency. Manufacturers require highly reproducible and rapid potency assays. This immune response will be used to compare vaccine approaches, to decide which candidate vaccines progress to further testing, and eventually to monitor lot-to-lot consistency in a licensed vaccine or allow modifications in the vaccine without repeating full-scale, placebo-controlled efficacy trials. The ideal assay would be based on protective mechanisms (still unproven) and validated to meet the requirements of good laboratory practices.[43]

Antibody assays

Antibody assays measure binding to viral proteins or neutralization. Binding antibodies are detected by standard enzyme-linked immunosorbent assay (ELISA) colorimetry, Western blot or real-time binding assays.[44] Neutralization, though more difficult to measure, is thought to be more relevant to protection. Antibodies may neutralize HIV by binding to a specific neutralizing epitope[45] or by coating virions and interfering with viral envelope–host cell membrane fusion.[46]

Neutralization measures the reduction of infectivity of cell-free virus particles. Infection of cells by HIV-1 is measured in the presence and absence of serum or other fluids. Neutralizing activity often appears to be very weak, even in the serum of chronically infected individuals. However, the choice of HIV-1 strain(s) used in the neutralization assay will influence the measurements. It appears that most antibodies against HIV-1 have a very narrow spectrum of activity while HIV-1 can vary enormously, even within one infected person. Many methods have been developed for assessing neutralizing antibodies (Table 118.2). Conventional neutralizing assays mimic in vivo neutralization of HIV-1, using stimulated PBMCs as targets and measuring cell death[47–49] or the inhibition of viral protein production.[50] Newer assays may rely on viruses or cell lines that are genetically engineered to contain reporter genes[51] as a surrogate for productive infection, or on flow cytometry[52] to measure infection in individual cells. These assays must take into account the two different types of receptors utilized by HIV-1: CD4 and chemokine receptors. HIV-1 strains adapted to growth in cell lines are often much easier to neutralize than primary isolates.[53]

Assays of cell-mediated immunity

For all assays of cell-mediated immunity (Table 118.3), isolated mononuclear cells or whole-blood specimens are stimulated with antigens that may consist of proteins, peptides or virus-infected cells. The specimen is usually peripheral blood, although T cells can be cloned from secretions or tissue biopsies.[54] T cells are stimulated by peptides associated with HLA molecules on the surface of antigen-presenting cells such as dendritic cells.[55] The classic measurements of responses, killing of virus-infected or peptide-coated target cells (predominantly CD8 cells) and antigen-induced lymphocyte proliferation (CD4), are difficult to apply, especially in resource-poor settings. Assays that measure production of cytokines or chemokines (e.g. IFN-γ, IL-2, TNF-α, MIP-1β) by individual PBMCs in response to antigen or peptide are now widely used (Fig. 118.1). ELIspot enumerates individual cells that secrete particular cytokines, thus revealing the capabilities of the responding cells. Even more informative is intracellular cytokine flow cytometry, which identifies both the cytokine being produced and immune markers on the surface of a cell, such as CD4 or CD8, and molecules indicating activation or propensity to migrate to certain tissues. These assays are simpler, more robust and more informative and they can be validated to meet the requirements of good laboratory practices.[43] Assays on fresh blood, while more technically challenging, are more sensitive and reliable. Artificial fluorescent molecules that mimic antigens and bind to T-cell receptors can also be used (tetramer assay), but this assay is technically much more difficult because of genetic restrictions on T-cell receptor binding to epitopes.[56]

CLINICAL TRIALS

The process

Clinical trials for preventive HIV-1 vaccines are complex. Like all clinical studies, they must comply with ethical principles, applicable laws and good laboratory practices.[43] Volunteers must fully

CHARACTERISTICS OF ASSAYS OF T-CELL RESPONSES TO HIV-1 ANTIGENS					
	Chromium release	**Proliferation**	**ELISPOT**	**Intracellular CFC**	**Tetramer**
Measures	Cell killing	Cell division	Cytokine release	Cytokine production	MHC–peptide complex binding
Enumeration	Semi-quantitative	Semi-quantitative	Enumerates single cells	Enumerates single cells	Enumerates single cells
Cells	PBMCs expanded for 2 weeks in vitro	Separated PBMCs expanded in vitro for 4–7 days	Separated PBMCs, 1–2 day stimulation	Whole blood assay (6h stimulation)	Whole blood simple stain (2h)
Sensitivity (approximate)	1 in 1000	1 in 10,000	1 in 10–50,000	1 in 10–50,000	1 in 10–50,000
Read-out	Total cell killing	Total DNA synthesis	Cytokine-producing cells (or CD8 subset)	Multi-parametric	Multi-parametric

Table 118.3 Characteristics of assays of T-cell responses to HIV-1 antigens.

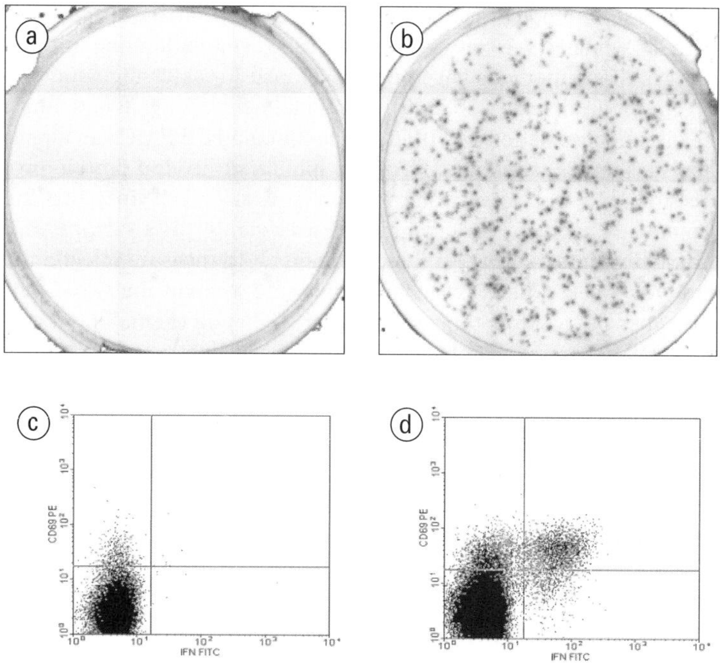

Fig. 118.1 Two newer methods for studying responses to HIV vaccines. (a) and (b) are representative negative and positive wells (respectively) from an interferon-γ (IFN-γ) ELISPOT assay. Mononuclear cells are separated from blood, placed in wells coated with antibody against IFN-γ, and stimulated overnight with (b) or without (a) peptides from the antigen of interest. On stimulation, antigen-specific T cells release IFN-γ; the captured IFN-γ is stained using a second antibody with an enzymatic tag to develop a color change, much like a conventional ELISA test. A colored spot appears for each cell producing IFN-γ. The lower panels are representative of the result from a cytokine flow cytometry (CFC) assay. Whole blood from an HIV$^+$ patient is cultured without (c) or with (d) peptides from the HIV *gag* gene in the presence of an inhibitor of Golgi secretion. Newly synthesized cytokine within the cells, in addition to cell surface markers, are then stained using fluorescently labeled antibodies and analyzed on a fluorescence activated cell sorter (FACS). The cells in (c) and (d) have been labeled for CD3 (general T-cell marker), CD4 (helper class of T cells) and CD69 (activation marker); they are also permeabilized and stained to reveal intracellular IFN-γ. The cells staining for CD3 but not CD4 (i.e. CD8 or effector T cells) were selected using automated software. The upper right quadrant indicates which of the CD8 cells are newly activated (CD69 positive) and producing IFN-γ.

understand the trial, including the rationale for use of a placebo and the process of randomization.

Risk for HIV-1 infection can be reduced by behavior change. It is critical that volunteers understand the need to protect themselves against HIV-1 infection by standard methods (limiting partners, barriers and avoiding contaminated needles) and that they have the knowledge and means to do so; they need to know that an untested HIV-1 vaccine candidate is not a 'magic bullet'. Trial organizers must educate, counsel and provide protective devices such as condoms or clean needles and syringes to the extent that it is feasible and legally permissible. It is necessary to estimate the incidence of HIV-1 infection in the presence of such interventions in order to determine accurately the sample size for efficacy trials. Research suggests that, in US trials, risk-taking by volunteers has not increased during the trials.[57] This may differ depending on the social circumstances and education of volunteers. Many persons at risk from HIV-1 lack power over their own risks; they may be at risk, for example, through a spouse's risky behavior. These people are the most in need of an effective vaccine.

Certain vaccine candidates may induce antibodies that render a standard diagnostic HIV-1 test positive, even in the absence of HIV-1 infection, and each trial must offer accurate diagnostic testing for trial participants. Stigmatization or discrimination could occur as a result of false-positive testing or, more likely, simply based on trial participation.[58,59]

Early trials (phase 1) enroll healthy volunteers who are usually not at high risk for HIV-1 infection, as indicated by a screening interview. Risk can change and occasionally such volunteers do encounter HIV-1 in the community and become infected. The clinical course of these infections has been scrutinized and it appears to be no different from acute HIV-1 infection in nonvaccinated individuals,[60] but the number of cases is small. Later stage (phase 2) trials and efficacy trials (phase 3) enroll participants at higher risk of HIV-1 infection, either through sexual contact or injection drug use. Infants at risk of infection through breast-feeding (after initial protection by perinatal drug therapy) are also at risk for infection and early-stage trials have shown that certain vaccine candidates are safe in neonates.[61]

The end points for clinical trials could include prevention of infection or, if infection occurs, modification of viral replication. Slower viral replication would be expected to result in slower disease progression and less risk of transmission to others. Data are insufficient to detect an effect of vaccination on disease progression at this time.[60] Nonhuman primate studies support both possible outcomes and a useful vaccine will likely have both effects.

Progress to date

Several HIV-1 vaccines have recently entered trials or are expected to do so soon.[62] A number of vaccines have been tested and, lacking credible immunogenicity data, abandoned. Table 118.4 shows the status of HIV-1 clinical trials at the time of writing, but the reader is encouraged to seek more current information through websites or newsletters (www.iavi.org/trialsdb; www.vrc.org; www.hvtn.org; http://www.iavi.org/iavireport/; and others).

One vaccine design, bivalent recombinant gp120 (envelope) protein adjuvanted with alum, has entered two phase 3 trials. One efficacy trial which enrolled primarily men who have sex with men, testing a bivalent vaccine in which both components are based on HIV-1 of the B subtype has failed to show overall efficacy in preventing HIV-1 infection (www.vaxgen.com). Post hoc analyses showed the possibility of benefit in certain subgroups, blacks and Asians. However, the numbers were too few to be conclusive and further studies will be needed. A trial in Thailand with an analogous vaccine containing one component derived from B subtype and one derived from E subtype is also underway, enrolling injection drug users. These vaccines induce antibodies that neutralize 'laboratory-adapted' HIV-1 strains but not freshly isolated HIV-1. A novel approach will be required to induce antibodies that can neutralize primary isolates.

A third efficacy trial is planned for Thailand, enrolling heterosexual men and women; this trial will combine a vaccine designed to induce cell-mediated immunity (primarily mediated by CD8 T cells). The vaccine, designed to induce cell-mediated immunity, is recombinant canarypox containing genes that encode HIV-1 envelope, gag and protease, based on the B and E subtypes. The canarypox is an attenuated form of a virus that infects birds but not mammals. The virus enters mammalian cells, uncoats and releases its genetic material, which then directs the synthesis of endogenous antigens but does not replicate. This induces CD8 T cells that release antiviral substances such as interferon-γ and/or kill HIV-infected host cells and CD4 (helper) T cells. In the Thai efficacy trial, the canarypox recombinant will be combined with gp120, in a 'prime-boost' regimen designed to induce both T-cell and antibody responses.[63]

Several novel vaccine candidates are now in clinical trials. Most of these are designed to induce CD8 T cells and some may induce antibodies as well. Recently, lipopeptides have been tested in healthy volunteers;[64] these antigens are more effectively presented than the nonlipidated peptide vaccines tested some years ago.[65]

PREVENTIVE HIV-1 VACCINES CURRENTLY IN CLINICAL TRIALS (2003)					
Vaccine type		***Gene(s)*/protein(s)**	**Phase**	**HIV subtype**	**Countries**
Protein	Recombinant protein(s)*	gp120	3	B	North America, Netherlands†
			3	B+E	Thailand
		tat/nef + gp120	1	B	USA
		tat	1§	B	Italy
Peptide	Lipopeptides‡	gag, nef, pol	1	B	France
Nucleic acid	DNA	*gag*	1	B	USA
	DNA	*gag plus epitopes from other genes*	1	A	UK, Kenya Uganda
	DNA	*envelope, gag, nef*	1	B	USA
	DNA	*gag, rt, envelope, tat, rev, vpu*	1	B	USA
	DNA	*nef*	1	B	Finland
	DNA	*gag, pol, envelope, nef*	1	A, B, C	US
	DNA	*CTL epitopes from: gag, pol, vpr, nef, rev, envelope*	1§	SHARED	US, Botswana
	DNA	*gag, pol, nef*	1§	B, C	Europe
Virus vector	ALVAC (Canarypox)	*envelope, gag, portions of enzymes (inactivated)*	2	B	North America, Caribbean, South America
	ALVAC (Canarypox)	*envelope, gag, portions of enzymes (inactivated)*	2	B+E	Thailand
	ALVAC plus gp 120	*Envelope, gag, portions of enzymes (inactivated)*	3§	B+E	Thailand
	Modified Vaccinia Ankara¶	*gag plus epitopes from other genes*	1	A	UK, Kenya, Uganda
	Adenovirus¶	*gag*	1	B	USA
	VEE	*gag*	1§	C	USA, South Africa

* gp160 and p24 (gag component) have also been tested.
† Preliminary analysis available.
‡ Peptides without the lipid component have also been tested.
§ Scheduled for 2003
¶ Both recombinant MVA and recombinant adenovirus have been used as a 'boost' subsequent to 'priming' with the corresponding DNA vaccine.

Table 118.4 Preventive HIV-1 vaccines currently in clinical trials (2003).

DNA vaccines are directly injected into skin or muscle or applied topically. When taken up by host cells, the plasmids direct the synthesis of vaccine antigens. Early trials with DNA vaccines alone showed limited immunogenicity.[66] Therefore, several groups are studying DNA vaccines as a 'prime' followed by recombinant viral vectors as a boost. This is a different variation of 'prime-boost', in which the initial DNA vaccination is thought to focus the immune response, primarily mediated by T cells, on the products of the HIV-1 genes rather than on the gene products encoded by the virus vector itself,[67] while the recombinant vector induces more effector cells and/or antibodies. DNA priming followed by a recombinant, replication-defective vaccinia boost (MVA) is now being tested in the UK and Kenya[68] and DNA priming followed by a recombinant, replication-defective adenovirus is being tested in the USA.[10] In these trials, the current vaccine constructs are based on the *gag* gene; the groups plan to add new HIV-1 genes to the vaccines.

Which are the most important antigen(s) or gene(s) to include in a recombinant HIV-1 vaccine? The inherent variability of the gene within HIV-1 is likely to be important (clearly, a more conserved gene will be well matched to a larger spectrum of virus strains). For vaccines intended to induce neutralizing antibodies, envelope is the critical gene. However, the selection of the 'best' envelope sequence from among the myriad isolates is difficult. Vaccines could incorporate intact envelope proteins or modified versions that lack some of the features that modify immunogenicity such as variable 'loop' segments and heavy glycosylation.[69] For vaccines designed to induce T cells, the quantity of viral protein made in an infected cell may be important and targeting genes expressed early in infection could lead to destruction of infected cells before they release new virions. Even the optimal number of genes or gene products is debated; a larger number of targets seems desirable but some viral antigens may interfere with responses to others. This debate will be resolved finally by clinical trials.

Newer vaccines, not yet in clinical trials, may utilize different viral or bacterial vaccines as vectors. These vectors each have unique virtues. Some can be grown cheaply, amplifying the HIV-1 genes they carry along with their own. Some can be administered simply, such as bacterial vaccines that are effective when given orally. They may supply the stimulus to the innate immune system that will amplify immunity or deliver the antigen to dendritic cells in lymph nodes or to mucosal lymphoid tissues.

However, vectored vaccines also have real or theoretical drawbacks. For each novel vaccine, safety must be carefully evaluated in phase 1, 2 and 3 trials and then after marketing. They may confer long-lasting immunity; however, if immunity to the vector precludes effective boosting or interferes with the use of a different vaccine employing the same vector, this may interfere with use on a worldwide, public health scale. Likewise, if naturally occurring immunity to the vector can interfere with immunization, the effects of a vaccine in different populations may be difficult to predict. These issues must be examined during vaccine development.

Older virus vaccines are almost all based on one of two designs: whole inactivated ('killed') or attenuated ('live') versions of the pathogenic virus. These have not been used in prophylactic HIV-1 vaccine trials. Whole killed HIV may be feasible, although inactivating without destroying envelope protein structure and proving that it has been entirely inactivated will be a challenge.[70] In animal studies, live attenuated SIV has proven to be an effective vaccine, but it is unsafe because of occasional reversion.[71] The seemingly insurmountable obstacle for a vaccine based on replication-competent HIV-1 is that there would be no clear way to prove its safety.[72] Such vaccines, however, may prove to be useful in experimental animal models, for understanding immunity to the retroviruses.

HIV-1 VACCINES AS THERAPY

Almost from the beginning of HIV-1 vaccine research, investigators have wondered whether an HIV-1 vaccine could improve the apparently inadequate and waning immune response of infected persons. A large, controlled trial of gp160 protein as a therapeutic vaccine showed clearly that the groups receiving vaccine and placebo had an identical clinical course.[73] Recent trials of whole killed vaccine as a therapy have failed to show convincing benefit. Measures of virus replication and perhaps clinical end points will be required in therapeutic vaccine trials. The best chance for a therapeutic vaccine would appear to be if it is given in the presence of highly active antiretroviral therapy (HAART), otherwise immune activation of HIV-1-specific CD4 cells could render them more vulnerable to infection and destruction by HIV-1. Trials are now being undertaken to suppress virus with HAART, vaccinate and then interrupt therapy.[74,75]

If vaccine therapy is successful, it will be encouraging for the field of preventive HIV-1 vaccine research, but not conclusive. If unsuccessful, it may not reflect the potential of that vaccine to prevent HIV-1 infection or AIDS if given prior to infection. After the initial days and weeks of virus replication, more cells may be infected, more genetic variation may have arisen and ineradicable reservoirs may exist in nonreplicating cells or inaccessible anatomic compartments in 'established' HIV-1 infection than the initial encounter with HIV-1.

FUTURE CHALLENGES

Conducting trials of HIV vaccines in the countries most affected by the epidemic is a challenge,[76] albeit one that has been successfully met in Thailand. When one or more HIV-1 vaccines is identified, the task will be just beginning. The next step will be ensuring access for populations where the need is the greatest. Currently, over 60 million people have become infected with HIV-1 and hundreds of millions are at risk. Many of these individuals have little access to medical care, no access to adult vaccinations and live in countries where the per capita expenditure on health care is a few dollars. Often, HIV-1 is ill understood and stigmatized. Diagnostic tests or algorithms may need to be altered. Education will be needed to convey not only the value but the anticipated limitations of the vaccines, so that other preventive strategies will be maintained. The role of community organizations in maintaining this balance will be critical (www.avac.org).

Regulatory approvals in numerous countries will be required. The issues in the USA are complex.[77] Internationally, there are greater challenges. If a vaccine has not been demonstrated to be universally effective against every HIV-1 subtype, the standard paradigm of approval in one or more industrialized countries followed years or even decades later by acceptance in and distribution to developing countries will not apply. Both the governments of countries affected by HIV-1 and the international regulatory and health authorities must plan ahead for the advent of an HIV-1 vaccine to avoid unnecessary delays.

HIV-1 vaccines might induce antibody responses that would completely prevent HIV-1 infection by strains of virus that are sufficiently well matched to the vaccine. Unfortunately, HIV-1 evolves continuously both within an individual (the source of infection) and within human populations. Therefore, a vaccinated person might be protected initially, but later encounter a virus against which he or she is not immune. Multivalent vaccines or repeated immunization with an updated vaccine may be required for continued protection. Thus, eventually, one might imagine licensure not of a specific HIV-1 vaccine but of a method for producing the vaccine and its updated versions, somewhat analogous to the annual updates of influenza vaccine.

The scientific challenges involved in discovery of a safe and effective vaccine against HIV-1, although daunting, are only the prelude. The task of developing and deploying a vaccine against HIV-1 will be enormous (i.e. gaining licensure and scaling up to produce vaccine for worldwide distribution, developing distribution methods and establishing purchase mechanisms will require an unprecedented co-operative effort by governments, international agencies, philanthropic organizations and the private sector).[78] Recent recognition of the importance of controlling HIV-1 for public health, economic and political stability has been encouraging and there has been substantial growth in academic, government, nonprofit and pharmaceutical industry vaccine research, but the fight is not over. Stopping the march of the pandemic will conserve economic and human resources needed to care for those already infected. Ending the HIV-1 epidemic is critical to allow economic development and promote political stability in the developing world and to reduce loss of life and suffering worldwide.

Acknowledgements

The illustrations in Figure 118.1 were kindly provided by Dr P. Hayes and ZellNet Consulting Inc. We wish to thank Dr P. Kahn and C. Chiaffarelli for editorial assistance.

REFERENCES

1. Marais H, Wilson A. Report on the global HIV/AIDS epidemic 2002. http://www.unaids.org/barcelona/presskit/barcelona%20report/contents.html: UNAIDS, 2002
2. Centers for Disease Control and Prevention. Number of US AIDS cases remain stable after recent declines. http://www.cdc.gov/od/oc/media/pressrel/ro20707.htm
3. Anderson RM, Swinton J, Garnett GP. Potential impact of low efficacy HIV-1 vaccines in populations with high rates of infection. Proc R Soc Lond B Biol Sci 1995;261:147–51.
4. Graham BS. Clinical trials of HIV vaccines. Annu Rev Med 2002;53:207–21.
5. Gray RH, Wawer MJ, Brookmeyer R, *et al.* Probability of HIV-1 transmission per coital act in monogamous, heterosexual, HIV-1-discordant couples in Rakai, Uganda. Lancet 2001;357:1149–53.
6. Plummer FA, Ball TB, Kimani J, Fowke KR. Resistance to HIV-1 infection among highly exposed sex workers in Nairobi: what mediates protection and why does it develop? Immunol Lett 1999;66:27–34.
7. McMichael AJ, Callan M, Appay V, Hanke T, Ogg G, Rowland-Jones S. The dynamics of the cellular immune response to HIV infection: implications for vaccination. Philos Trans R Soc Lond B Biol Sci 2000;355:1007–11.
8. Koup RA, Safrit JT, Cao Y, *et al.* Temporal association of cellular immune responses with the initial control of viremia in primary human

immunodeficiency virus type 1 syndrome. J Virol 1994;68:4650–5.
9. Borrow P, Lewicki H, Hahn BH, Shaw GM, Oldstone MB. Virus-specific CD8+ cytotoxic T-lymphocyte activity associated with control of viremia in primary human immunodeficiency virus type 1 infection. J Virol 1994;68:6103–10.
10. Amara RR, Villinger F, Altman JD, *et al.* Control of a mucosal challenge and prevention of AIDS by a multiprotein DNA/MVA vaccine. Science 2001;292:69–74.
11. Shiver JW, Fu TM, Chen L, *et al.* Replication-incompetent adenoviral vaccine vector elicits effective anti-immunodeficiency-virus immunity. Nature 2002;415:331–5.
12. Barouch DH, Fu TM, Montefiori DC, Lewis MG, Shiver JW, Letvin NL. Vaccine-elicited immune responses prevent clinical AIDS in SHIV(89.6P)-infected rhesus monkeys. Immunol Lett 2001;79:57–61.
13. Ourmanov I, Brown CR, Moss B, *et al.* Comparative efficacy of recombinant modified vaccinia virus Ankara expressing simian immunodeficiency virus (SIV) Gag-Pol and/or Env in macaques challenged with pathogenic SIV. J Virol 2000;74:2740–51.
14. Letvin NL, Schmitz JE, Jordan HL, *et al.* Cytotoxic T lymphocytes specific for the simian immunodeficiency virus. Immunol Rev 1999;170:127–34.
15. Metzner KJ, Jin X, Lee FV, *et al.* Effects of *in vivo* CD8(+) T cell depletion on virus replication in rhesus macaques immunized with a live, attenuated simian immunodeficiency virus vaccine. J Exp Med 2000;191:1921–31.
16. Shibata R, Igarashi T, Haigwood N, *et al.* Neutralizing antibody directed against the HIV-1 envelope glycoprotein can completely block HIV-1/SIV chimeric virus infections of macaque monkeys. Nat Med 1999;5:204–10.
17. Parren PW, Marx PA, Hessell AJ, *et al.* Antibody protects macaques against vaginal challenge with a pathogenic R5 simian/human immunodeficiency virus at serum levels giving complete neutralization *in vitro.* J Virol 2001;75:8340–7.
18. Gauduin MC, Parren PW, Weir R, Barbas CF, Burton DR, Koup RA. Passive immunization with a human monoclonal antibody protects hu-PBL-SCID mice against challenge by primary isolates of HIV-1. Nat Med 1997;3:1389–93.
19. Mascola JR, Lewis MG, Stiegler G, *et al.* Protection of macaques against pathogenic simian/human immunodeficiency virus 89.6PD by passive transfer of neutralizing antibodies. J Virol 1999;73:4009–18.
20. Belyakov IM, Hel Z, Kelsall B, *et al.* Mucosal AIDS vaccine reduces disease and viral load in gut reservoir and blood after mucosal infection of macaques. Nat Med 2001;7:1320–6.
21. Blankson JN, Persaud D, Siliciano RF. The challenge of viral reservoirs in HIV-1 infection. Annu Rev Med 2002;53:557–93.
22. Haase AT. The pathogenesis of sexual mucosal transmission and early stages of infection: obstacles and a narrow window of opportunity for prevention. AIDS 2001;15(Suppl.1):S10–1.
23. Zhang Z, Schuler T, Zupancic M, *et al.* Sexual transmission and propagation of SIV and HIV in resting and activated CD4+ T cells. Science 1999;286:1353–7.
24. Veazey RS, Lackner AA. The gastrointestinal tract and the pathogenesis of AIDS. AIDS 1998;12:S35–42.
25. Biron CA. Role of early cytokines, including alpha and beta interferons (IFN-alpha/beta), in innate and adaptive immune responses to viral infections. Semin Immunol 1998;10:383–90.
26. Fearon DT, Locksley RM. The instructive role of innate immunity in the acquired immune response. Science 1996;272:50–3.
27. Ho D, Huang Y. The HIV-1 vaccine race. Cell 2002;110:135–8.
28. Burton DR, Parren PW. Vaccines and the induction of functional antibodies: time to look beyond the molecules of natural infection? Nat Med 2000;6:123–5.
29. Wyatt R, Kwong PD, Desjardins E, *et al.* The antigenic structure of the HIV gp120 envelope glycoprotein. Nature 1998;393:705–11.
30. Wei X, Decker JM, Wang S, *et al.* Antibody neutralization and escape by HIV-1. Nature 2003;422:307–12.
31. Emini EA, Schleif WA, Nunberg JH, *et al.* Prevention of HIV-1 infection in chimpanzees by gp120 V3 domain- specific monoclonal antibody. Nature 1992;355:728–30.
32. Mascola JR, Snyder SW, Weislow OS, *et al.* Immunization with envelope subunit vaccine products elicits neutralizing antibodies against laboratory-adapted but not primary isolates of human immunodeficiency virus type 1. The National Institute of Allergy and Infectious Diseases AIDS Vaccine Evaluation Group. J Infect Dis 1996;173:340–8.
33. Shibata R, Igarashi T, Haigwood N, *et al.* Neutralizing antibody directed against the HIV-1 envelope glycoprotein can completely block HIV-1/SIV-1 chimeric virus infections of macacque monkeys. Nat Med 1999;5:204-10.
34. Frankel SS, Steinman RM, Michael NL, *et al.* Neutralizing monoclonal antibodies block human immunodeficiency virus type 1 infection of dendritic cells and transmission to T cells. J Virol 1998;72:9788–94.
35. Stiegler G, Kunert R, Purtscher M, *et al.* A potent cross-clade neutralizing human monoclonal antibody against a novel epitope on gp41 of human immunodeficiency virus type 1. AIDS Res Hum Retroviruses 2001;17:1757–65.
36. Sharon M, Kessler N, Levy R, Zolla-Pazner S, Görlach M, Anglister J. Alternative conformations of HIV-1 V3 loops mimic β hairpins in chemokines, suggesting a mechanism for coreceptor selectivity. Structure 2003;11:225–236.
37. Walker BD, Plata F. Cytotoxic T lymphocytes against HIV. AIDS 1990;4:177–84.
38. Rowland-Jones SL, Dong T, Dorrell L, *et al.* Broadly cross-reactive HIV-specific cytotoxic T-lymphocytes in highly-exposed persistently seronegative donors. Immunol Lett 1999;66:9–14.
39. Cao H, Mani I, Vincent R, *et al.* Cellular immunity to human immunodeficiency virus type 1 (HIV-1) clades: relevance to HIV-1 vaccine trials in Uganda. J Infect Dis 2000;182:1350–6.
40. Barouch DH, Kunstman J, Kuroda MJ, *et al.* Eventual AIDS vaccine failure in a rhesus monkey by viral escape from cytotoxic T lymphocytes. Nature 2002;415:335–9.
41. Walker BD, Goulder PJ. AIDS. Escape from the immune system. Nature 2000;407:313–4.
42. Goulder PJ, Brander C, Tang Y, *et al.* Evolution and transmission of stable CTL escape mutations in HIV infection. Nature 2001;412:334–8.
43. US Food and Drug Administration. Title 21 – food and drugs good laboratory practice. http://www.fda.com/SIGGLP204/index.html
44. VanCott TC, Loomis LD, Redfield RR, Birx DL. Real-time biospecific interaction analysis of antibody reactivity to peptides from the envelope glycoprotein, gp160, of HIV-1. J Immunol Methods 1992;146:163–76.
45. Zwick MB, Wang M, Poignard P, *et al.* Neutralization synergy of human immunodeficiency virus type 1 primary isolates by cocktails of broadly neutralizing antibodies. J Virol 2001;75:12198–208.
46. Parren PW, Wang M, Trkola A, *et al.* Antibody neutralization-resistant primary isolates of human immunodeficiency virus type 1. J Virol 1998;72:10270–4.
47. Nara PL, Hatch WC, Dunlop NM, *et al.* Simple, rapid, quantitative, syncytium-forming microassay for the detection of human immunodeficiency virus neutralizing antibody. AIDS Res Hum Retroviruses 1987;3:283–302.
48. Sawyer LS, Wrin MT, Crawford-Miksza L, *et al.* Neutralization sensitivity of human immunodeficiency virus type 1 is determined in part by the cell in which the virus is propagated. J Virol 1994;68:1342–9.
49. Wei X, Decker JM, Liu H, *et al.* Emergence of resistant human immunodeficiency virus type 1 in patients receiving fusion inhibitor (T-20) monotherapy. Antimicrob Agents Chemother 2002;46:1896–905.
50. Montefiori DC, Zhou IY, Barnes B, *et al.* Homotypic antibody responses to fresh clinical isolates of human immunodeficiency virus. Virology 1991;182:635–43.
51. Cecilia D, Kewal Ramani VN, O'Leary J, *et al.* Neutralization profiles of primary human immunodeficiency virus type 1 isolates in the context of coreceptor usage. J Virol 1998;72:6988–96.
52. Mascola JR, Louder MK, Winter C, *et al.* Human immunodeficiency virus type 1 neutralization measured by flow cytometric quantitation of single-round infection of primary human T cells. J Virol 2002;76:4810–21.
53. Moore JP, Cao Y, Qing L, *et al.* Primary isolates of human immunodeficiency virus type 1 are relatively resistant to neutralization by monoclonal antibodies to gp120, and their neutralization is not predicted by studies with monomeric gp120. J Virol 1995;69:101–9.
54. Musey L, Hu Y, Eckert L, Christensen M, Karchmer T, McElrath MJ. HIV-1 induces cytotoxic T lymphocytes in the cervix of infected women. J Exp Med 1997;185:293–303.
55. Banchereau J, Steinman RM. Dendritic cells and the control of immunity. Nature 1998;392:245–52.
56. Altman JD, Moss PA, Goulder PJ, *et al.* Phenotypic analysis of antigen-specific T lymphocytes. Science 1996;274:94–6.
57. Sheon AR. Overview: HIV vaccine feasibility studies. AIDS Res Hum Retroviruses 1994;10:S195–6.
58. Fast PE, Sawyer LA, Wescott SL. Clinical considerations in vaccine trials with special reference to candidate HIV vaccines. Pharm Biotechnol 1995;6:97–134.
59. Fast PE, Mathieson BJ, Schultz AM. Efficacy trials of AIDS vaccines: how science can inform ethics. Curr Opin Immunol 1994;6:691–7.
60. Graham BS, McElrath MJ, Connor RI, *et al.* Analysis of intercurrent human immunodeficiency virus type 1 infections in phase I and II trials of candidate AIDS vaccines. AIDS Vaccine Evaluation Group, and the Correlates of HIV Immune Protection Group. J Infect Dis 1998;177:310–9.
61. Borkowsky W, Wara D, Fenton T, *et al.* Lymphoproliferative responses to recombinant HIV-1 envelope antigens in neonates and infants receiving gp120 vaccines. AIDS Clinical Trial Group 230 Collaborators. J Infect Dis 2000;181:890–6.
62. Girard M, Mastro T, Koff W. Human immunodeficiency virus. In: Plotkin S, Orenstein W, eds. Vaccines. Philadelphia: Harcourt Brace & Company;2003.
63. Excler JL, Plotkin S. The prime-boost concept applied to HIV preventive vaccines. AIDS 1997;11:S127–37.
64. Pialoux G, Gahery-Segard H, Sermet S, *et al.* Lipopeptides induce cell-mediated anti-HIV immune responses in seronegative volunteers. AIDS 2001;15:1239–49.
65. Hosmalina A, Andrieu M, Loing E, *et al.* Lipopeptide presentation pathway in dendritic cells. Immunol Lett 2001;79:97–100.
66. Boyer JD, Cohen AD, Vogt S, *et al.* Vaccination of seronegative volunteers with a human immunodeficiency virus type 1 env/rev DNA vaccine induces antigen-specific proliferation and lymphocyte production of beta-chemokines. J Infect Dis 2000;181:476–83.
67. Hanke T, Blanchard TJ, Schneider J, *et al.* Enhancement of MHC class I-restricted peptide-specific T cell induction by a DNA prime/MVA boost vaccination regime. Vaccine 1998;16:439–45.

68. Hanke T, McMichael AJ. Design and construction of an experimental HIV-1 vaccine for a year- 2000 clinical trial in Kenya. Nat Med 2000;6:951–5.
69. Johnson WE, Morgan J, Reitter J, *et al.* A replication-competent, neutralization-sensitive variant of simian immunodeficiency virus lacking 100 amino acids of envelope. J Virol 2002;76:2075–86.
70. Stott J, Hahn BH. AIDS 1999. Vaccines and immunology: overview. AIDS 1999;13:S103–4.
71. Murphey-Corb M. Live-attenuated HIV vaccines: how safe is safe enough? Nat Med 1997;3:17–8.
72. Mills J, Desrosiers R, Rud E, Almond N. Live attenuated HIV vaccines: a proposal for further research and development. AIDS Res Hum Retroviruses 2000;16:1453–61.
73. Redfield RR, Birx DL, Ketter N, *et al.* A phase I evaluation of the safety and immunogenicity of vaccination with recombinant gp160 in patients with early human immunodeficiency virus infection. Military Medical Consortium for Applied Retroviral Research. N Engl J Med 1991;324:1677–84.
74. Schooley RT, Spino C, Kuritzkes D, *et al.* Two double-blinded, randomized, comparative trials of 4 human immunodeficiency virus type 1 (HIV-1) envelope vaccines in HIV-1-infected individuals across a spectrum of disease severity: AIDS Clinical Trials Groups 209 and 214. J Infect Dis 2000;182:1357–64.
75. Walker BD. The rationale for immunotherapy in HIV-1 infection. J Acquir Immune Defic Syndr 1994;7:S6–13.
76. Mugerwa RD, Kaleebu P, Mugyenyi P, *et al.* First trial of the HIV-1 vaccine in Africa: Ugandan experience. Br Med J 2002;324:226–9.
77. Goldenthal KL, Vaillancourt JM, Geber A, Lucey DR. Preventive HIV type 1 vaccine clinical trials: a regulatory perspective. AIDS Res Hum Retroviruses 1998;14(suppl 3):S333–40.
78. Berkley S. The need for an AIDS vaccine in Africa. In: Essex M, ed. AIDS in Africa. New York: Raven Press; 2002.

chapter 119 Practice Point

Postexposure prophylaxis for nonoccupational HIV exposure

David K Henderson

Introduction

In spite of considerable investment in education and training of the public, community exposures to HIV continue to occur commonly and frequently require clinical intervention. The introduction of postexposure chemoprophylaxis for occupational exposures to HIV in the health care workplace quickly prompted questions about the potential use of these agents for nonoccupational exposures. Several issues related to the administration of postexposure chemoprophylaxis for community exposures are distinctly different from offering these agents for occupational exposures in the health care setting. Since none of the available agents has a specific indication for use in prophylaxis, all antiretroviral chemoprophylaxis (for both occupational and nonoccupational exposures) must be considered 'off-label' use. This Practice Point reviews the immediate management of nonoccupational exposures and discusses the issues that are uniquely relevant to providing chemoprophylaxis for sexual, needle-sharing and other nonoccupational exposures.

Efficacy of postexposure chemoprophylaxis

The recent San Francisco Post Exposure Prophylaxis study demonstrated the feasibility of developing and implementing a postexposure program for managing community/nonoccupational exposures to HIV. Much of what we know about the potential for efficacy of antiretroviral postexposure chemoprophylaxis for sexual or nonoccupational exposures is derived from our experience using these agents in health care workers. Despite differences in the route of exposure (and in other variables likely to influence, at least to some extent, the specific risks for transmission), the results from animal studies, studies of vertical transmission and clinical experience to date with postexposure chemoprophylaxis for occupational exposures would seem to be directly relevant to the use of these agents for chemoprophylaxis for sexual or nonoccupational exposures.

Risk for infection associated with nonoccupational exposures to HIV

The per-exposure risk for HIV infection associated with community exposures varies significantly by the type of exposure. Considering community-based exposures, the risks associated with needle sharing in intravenous drug abuse are perhaps the greatest (Table 119.1). Whereas reasonable estimates of the risks for transmission associated with various sexual encounters have been published, these data clearly represent estimates and the precise risks for infection associated with these exposures are not known (see also Chapter 116). In addition, such estimates are useful only to understand the general risk for events of a certain type, since a variety of additional factors influence the risk associated with a single exposure (e.g. blood exposure, partner's viral burden, presence of reproductive tract infections, viral strain-specific differences in infectivity, cervical ectopy, circumcision and a variety of other factors). With these limitations in mind, estimates for the risk of transmission associated with different kinds of HIV exposures are summarized in Table 119.1.

Special problems

Chemoprophylaxis following consensual sexual exposure

Perhaps the most common circumstance for which postexposure prophylaxis is sought for community exposures to HIV is consensual sexual exposure. The details surrounding such exposures vary substantially and should be carefully considered before making the decision to initiate postexposure antiretroviral therapy. Circumstances of exposure and commitment to risk reduction/safe sex strategies should be an important determinant of the decision to administer prophylaxis. Several authorities have argued that postexposure prophylaxis is not appropriate for individuals who plan on continuing risk behavior. Conversely, offering postexposure prophylaxis to someone who is committed to risk reduction but had a temporary relapse of higher risk behavior makes implicit sense. From a practical perspective, determining an individual patient's commitment to risk reduction strategies may be extremely difficult, particularly in the context of a single patient–physician encounter. For this reason, most physicians decide to offer treatment unless they are convinced that the individual is not interested in risk reduction. Withholding treatment from someone who is uninterested in risk reduction seems cruel, but may actually be in the individual's best interest (particularly if the availability of postexposure prophylaxis is contributing to the individual's willingness to participate in risk behaviors). Offering repeated courses of prophylaxis may place the patient at increased risk and may be associated with societal risks as well (discussed below).

Rape/sexual abuse

A special set of problems arises with respect to the victims of sexual assault and/or sexual abuse. In most instances, the victim will not be aware of the HIV status of the assailant, and so these exposures represent the equivalent of 'source-unknown' exposures in the health care setting (see Chapter 117). Sexual assault, by its very nature, may be associated with increased risk for HIV transmission due to the increased likelihood of blood exposure, trauma and simultaneous exposure to other sexually transmitted diseases. In fact, several cases of HIV transmission have been directly linked to sexual assaults.

ESTIMATED HIV TRANSMISSION RISKS ASSOCIATED WITH SELECTED TYPES OF HIV EXPOSURES	
Route/type of exposure	**Risk for infection mean/range (%)**
Transfusion of contaminated blood	84–100
Intravenous drug use (needle sharing)	0.8
Receptive anal intercourse	0.3–0.8
Insertive anal intercourse	0.04–0.1*
Occupational needlestick exposure	0.28–0.33
Insertive vaginal intercourse	0.03–0.09
Receptive vaginal intercourse	0.005–0.02
Insertive oral intercourse	0.003–0.008*
Receptive oral intercourse	0.006–0.02*

* Estimates drawn from Varghese *et al.* (2002), Donegan *et al.* (1990), Henderson *et al.* (1986); Kaplan and Heimer (1994) and Royce *et al.* (1997).

Table 119.1 Estimated HIV transmission risks associated with selected types of HIV exposures.

The Centers for Disease Control and Prevention has recommended the use of antiretroviral chemoprophylaxis for rape victims, but has stopped short of recommending (either for or against) prophylaxis for consensual sexual exposures. The emotional trauma associated with a sexual assault is substantial and is compounded by the possibility of HIV transmission. For this reason, counseling must be an integral part of the postexposure management program. In many centers, follow-up for victims of sexual assault is extremely difficult, often because the victims do not give correct identification information and cannot be located for follow-up. In addition, many such victims do not return for follow-up appointments (even with prompting). Counseling of assault victims is crucial to the postexposure management process; such individuals must be made aware of the importance of follow-up, particularly if they embark on a postexposure prophylaxis regimen. Some authorities have suggested that offering postexposure prophylaxis may improve follow-up adherence.

Prophylaxis in children and adolescents who are the victims of sexual abuse

Children who are victims of sexual abuse may also be at risk for sexually transmitted diseases, including HIV infection. Experience administering antiretrovirals to healthy children is virtually nonexistent and the possibility exists that risks associated with the administration of these agents may be different, and perhaps higher, in children. Nonetheless, for documented sexual abuse exposures in children and adolescents, most authorities would recommend the administration of postexposure prophylaxis.

Parenteral exposures in the community

The most common source of parenteral exposures to HIV in the community setting is needle sharing in the process of intravenous drug use. If an individual shares needles with a partner known to be HIV infected, antiretroviral chemoprophylaxis is definitely indicated. For the more common set of circumstances (i.e. the HIV infection status of the needle-sharing partner is unknown), individualized decisions about postexposure prophylaxis should be made, based on the likelihood of HIV exposure in the community.

An unfortunately common circumstance in emergency rooms is the appearance of a child who has discovered a needle or syringe and has sustained a needlestick exposure. Quantitating the transmission risk in this setting is almost impossible, although some factors may be helpful in deciding whether to administer prophylaxis. Realistically, many such exposures present minimal risk for transmission of HIV; however, exclusion of risk may be almost impossible. The presence of blood in the syringe or on the needle would clearly identify increased risk. Each of these exposures must be assessed epidemiologically for circumstances that might be associated with increased risk and independent decisions must be made about each exposure.

Timing of prophylaxis in relationship to the exposure

Ideally, postexposure prophylaxis with antiretroviral agents should be administered as soon after an exposure as possible. In most of the more recent animal studies, if prophylaxis was begun within 24 hours of exposure the animals were protected. Clearly, delay of treatment is likely to be detrimental. In situations in which the picture of exposure is less than clear (e.g. an exposure to a source whose HIV status is uncertain), I would encourage the individual to initiate prophylaxis (to preserve the option) while the situation is being clarified. A special problem arises with respect to individuals who delay reporting of the exposure. As is the case for health care workers who, for a variety of reasons (e.g. denial, the urgencies of patient care, etc.), delay reporting infections, chemoprophylaxis should still be offered to exposed, susceptible individuals who have sustained community exposures to HIV. The practitioner should explain what is known about the importance of early administration of prophylaxis and should explain that, based on the animal models of retroviral infections, the chance for protection for individuals who delay reporting may be reduced and the risk:benefit ratio of prophylaxis may be altered. In fact, some authorities have recommended that prophylaxis should not be administered if more than 72 hours have elapsed from the time of the exposure. Nonetheless, in my view, withholding treatment in most instances is extremely difficult and I tend to err on the side of offering the treatment, despite a delay in reporting.

Postexposure management approach

As noted above, since an ongoing commitment to risk reduction by the exposed patient is an important determinant of the administration of prophylaxis, a thorough history is essential in the management of such exposures. Since these interactions often take place in a hectic emergency room, obtaining an appropriate history may be a challenge, but is essential to good management. Having trained counselors with experience in this field participate in the management (including history taking) is optimal. Important aspects of the history include (but are not limited to) the following: prior history of having taken courses of prophylaxis, prior history (especially recent history) of risk behaviors, assessment of current commitment to risk reduction, history (especially recent) of other sexually transmitted diseases, specific characteristics of the exposure for which prophylaxis is sought, and as much detailed information about the partner as can be gleaned.

Baseline laboratory studies should be obtained, including serologic testing for HIV infection. The so-called 'rapid' HIV tests are useful in that they are generally quite sensitive, but relatively nonspecific. As a screening test in the absence of risk behavior in the recent past, a negative test is quite useful. A positive test should be confirmed with traditional enzyme-linked immunosorbent assay (ELISA) testing, as well as by an additional confirmatory test, if the ELISA is positive. In addition, baseline chemistries and hematologic studies (in anticipation of prophylaxis administration) and a urinary pregnancy test for women should be undertaken, as well as microbiologic and serologic studies for other sexually transmitted diseases (e.g. gonorrhea, syphilis, chlamydia, hepatitis B and C). Depending on the patient's recent history of risk behavior, consideration should be given to assessing for circulating HIV nucleic acid using polymerase chain reaction (PCR) technology, if readily available. The HIV serologic tests should be repeated at 6 weeks, 3 months and 6 months following the exposure. If prophylaxis is administered, chemistries, including hepatic function studies, and hematologic studies should be conducted bi-weekly. Patients should be instructed to return immediately if they develop any of the signs and symptoms of the acute seroconversion illness or if any of the signs and symptoms of severe drug toxicity develop. Symptoms associated with treatment (e.g. nausea, vomiting, diarrhea, etc.) should be managed aggressively, and perhaps even pre-emptively, with medications addressing these symptoms.

Information about the source of the exposure is extremely useful. If the partner is known and can be tested, determining the partner's HIV antibody status, viral RNA, stage of illness, antiretroviral treatment history and presence of factors that may increase the risk for transmission (e.g. presence of other genitourinary infections, recent menstrual history, etc.) all can be of value. In instances in which the partner cannot be identified, the decision to offer prophylaxis should be based on the practitioner's best epidemiologic assessment of the likelihood of exposure (based on the patient's history, the prevalence of infection in the community, the type of encounter and the time from exposure to presentation), as well as the individual's commitment to risk reduction in the future.

The regimens for postexposure prophylaxis are summarized in Table 119.2. These recommendations are based on experience with these agents for occupational exposures to HIV in the health care setting. The currently recommended duration of therapy is 4 weeks; however, the choice of 4 weeks is arbitrary and based on limited clinical experience, experience with animal models of retroviral infections and in vitro studies evaluating the prevention of retroviral infection of susceptible tissue culture cells.

No discussion of postexposure management would be complete without underscoring the importance of counseling in this setting. All patients presenting with possible nonoccupational exposures to HIV should be counseled in detail regarding risk behaviors and risk reduction strategies. Counseling should also focus on the specific circumstances of the individual's exposure and should offer constructive suggestions regarding risk reduction.

Managing exposures when the source patient is or might have been taking antiretrovirals

Frequently, a source/partner for an HIV exposure has been taking antiretrovirals as therapy. If the source/partner's HIV infection is not suppressed, the individual may harbor resistant isolates. Prophylaxis should be initiated immediately and then modified if additional information becomes available.

SUGGESTED BASIC AND EXPANDED POSTEXPOSURE PROPHYLAXIS REGIMENS FOR CHEMOPROPHYLAXIS AFTER NONOCCUPATIONAL EXPOSURES TO HIV

HIV exposures with a recognized transmission risk	'Basic regimen'	Zidovudine (ZDV) plus lamivudine (3TC)
	Alternative 'basic regimens'	Stavudine (d4t) plus lamivudine
		d4t plus didanosine (ddI)†
HIV exposures for which the nature of the exposure suggests an elevated transmission risk*	'Basic regimen' plus one of the following agents	Indinavir† Nelfinavir Abacavir Efavirenz†

* Elevated risk is associated with exposures associated with increased risks for transmission (e.g. sexual assault, trauma, blood exposure, concomitant sexually transmitted disease, source patient with high circulating viral burden, etc.; see text)

† Agent(s)/regimens not advisable for use in pregnancy (see text)

Table 119.2 Suggested basic and expanded postexposure prophylaxis regimens for chemoprophylaxis after nonoccupational exposures to HIV. Modeled after CDC (2001).

Influence on risk behavior – impact on primary prevention strategies and the relationship to societal risks

One significant concern frequently expressed is that the use of antiretroviral agents for postexposure prophylaxis of nonoccupational exposures may actually increase risk behavior. Individuals may feel that they can take risks that can be abrogated by postexposure treatment and, in so doing, may ironically be putting themselves at increased risk for infection. Several studies have attempted to address this issue but failed to identify evidence that knowledge of the availability of prophylaxis was associated with increased sexual risk behavior. Conversely, the San Francisco prophylaxis study found that 12% of the individuals who participated in the trial returned for a second prophylaxis course within 6 months of the completion of the initial regimen. In spite of the 12% return rate in this study, the authors found that the majority of individuals who enrolled in the program following a sexual exposure to HIV had experienced a temporary lapse in risk reduction behavior that was not related to a consistent pattern of ongoing risk behavior.

Even authorities who are committed to working in this field have raised the concern that the availability of postexposure prophylaxis might undermine public health HIV prevention efforts. To avoid a negative public health impact, a postexposure prophylaxis program should be presented as a secondary prevention intervention, and primary prevention (i.e. avoiding unsafe behaviors, stressing condom use) should be underscored as far more effective, less toxic and less expensive interventions.

Further reading

Babl FE, Cooper ER, Damon B, Louie T, Kharasch S, Harris JA. HIV postexposure prophylaxis for children and adolescents. Am J Emerg Med 2000;18:282–7.

Bamberger JD, Waldo CR, Gerberding JL, Katz MH. Postexposure prophylaxis for human immunodeficiency virus (HIV) infection following sexual assault. Am J Med 1999;106:323–6.

Centers for Disease Control and Prevention. 1998 guidelines for treatment of sexually transmitted diseases. Centers for Disease Control and Prevention. MMWR Morb Mortal Wkly Rep 1998;47(RR-1):1–111.

Centers for Disease Control and Prevention. Updated US Public Health Service guidelines for the management of occupational exposures to HBV, HCV, and HIV and recommendations for postexposure prophylaxis. MMWR Morb Mortal Wkly Rep 2001;50(RR-11):1–52.

DeGruttola V, Seage GR 3rd, Mayer KH, Horsburgh CR Jr. Infectiousness of HIV between male homosexual partners. J Clin Epidemiol 1989;42:849–56.

Donegan E, Stuart M, Niland JC, *et al.* Infection with human immunodeficiency virus type 1 (HIV-1) among recipients of antibody-positive blood donations. Ann Intern Med 1990;113:733–9.

Henderson DK. HIV postexposure prophylaxis in the 21st century. Emerg Infect Dis 2001;7:254–8.

Henderson DK, Saah AJ, Zak BJ, *et al.* Risk of nosocomial infection with human T-cell lymphotropic virus type III/lymphadenopathy-associated virus in a large cohort of intensively exposed health care workers. Ann Intern Med 1986;104:644–7.

Kahn JO, Martin JN, Roland ME, *et al.* Feasibility of postexposure prophylaxis (PEP) against human immunodeficiency virus infection after sexual or injection drug use exposure: the San Francisco PEP Study. J Infect Dis 2001;183:707–14.

Kaplan EH, Heimer R. HIV incidence among needle exchange participants: estimates from syringe tracking and testing data. J Acquir Immune Defic Syndr 1994;7:182–9.

Katz MH, Gerberding JL. Postexposure treatment of people exposed to the human immunodeficiency virus through sexual contact or injection-drug use. N Engl J Med 1997;336:1097–100.

Katz MH, Gerberding JL. The care of persons with recent sexual exposure to HIV. Ann Intern Med 1998;128:306–12.

Lamba H, Murphy SM. Sexual assault and sexually transmitted infections: an updated review. Int J STD AIDS 2000;11:487–91.

Royce RA, Sena A, Cates W Jr, Cohen MS. Sexual transmission of HIV. N Engl J Med 1997;336:1072–8.

Varghese B, Maher JE, Peterman TA, Branson BM, Steketee RW. Reducing the risk of sexual HIV transmission: quantifying the per-act risk for HIV on the basis of choice of partner, sex act, and condom use. Sex Transm Dis 2002;29:38–43.

Waldo CR, Stall RD, Coates TJ. Is offering post-exposure prevention for sexual exposures to HIV related to sexual risk behavior in gay men? AIDS 2000;14:1035–9.

chapter 120

The Immunopathogenesis of HIV-1 Infection

Pierre-Alexandre Bart & Giuseppe Pantaleo

This chapter examines the immunologic and virologic mechanisms involved in the pathogenesis of HIV-1 infection and the interaction between the virus and the host. The recent availability of highly active antiretroviral combination therapy (HAART) has significantly influenced the natural history of the infection, delaying the progression to overt AIDS and prolonging survival. At the same time, increasing knowledge of the pathogenic mechanisms and of the limitations of HAART has made it clear that eradication of the virus with the available conventional antiviral drugs is not feasible. Recent advances in our understanding of the correlates of protective immunity have drawn attention to the development of immune-based interventions in order to achieve long-term control of HIV-1 disease.

THE NATURAL HISTORY OF HIV INFECTION

The typical course of HIV-1 infection is defined by different phases that generally occur during a period of between 8 and 12 years. Although the pattern and the course of the infection is highly variable among HIV-1-infected patients, three distinct phases can be identified (Fig. 120.1):[1]

- primary HIV-1 infection;
- chronic asymptomatic phase; and
- overt AIDS.

The three phases of the disease

Primary HIV-1 infection

Primary HIV-1 infection is a transient condition, revealed by a symptomatic illness of variable severity in 40–90% of patients, and is invariably accompanied by:

- an initial rapid rise in plasma viremia, often to levels in excess of 1,000,000 RNA copies/ml;
- a decrease in the blood $CD4^+$ T cell; and
- a large increase in the blood $CD8^+$ T cell count.

The marked decline of plasma viremia generally coincides with the resolution of the clinical syndrome.[2] The decrease in the viral load correlates with the appearance of the virus-specific immune responses (see below), particularly HIV-1-specific cytotoxic T lymphocytes (CTLs), indicating that virus-specific immune responses certainly play a crucial role in the initial downregulation of virus replication.[3–6]

The signs and symptoms of primary HIV-1 infection generally appear 2–4 weeks after virus exposure (Fig. 120.1).

The duration of the clinical syndrome ranges between a few days and more than 10 weeks but generally lasts less than 14 days. The clinical presentation of the primary HIV-1 infection may mimic acute mononucleosis (primary Epstein–Barr virus infection; see Chapter 122) as well as many other febrile acute illnesses, emphasizing the non-specific nature of these symptoms and the difficulty of obtaining an accurate early diagnosis.

Because the acute clinical syndrome associated with primary infection is not specific for HIV-1, the diagnosis is based on laboratory tests. In this regard, it is important to underscore the fact that anti-HIV-1 antibodies are usually negative during the acute phase of illness, as well as the Western blot (i.e. the laboratory assay used to confirm the diagnosis of HIV-1 infection), which evaluates the generation of specific antibodies against different HIV-1 proteins. The Western blot is considered to be positive when there are at least three specific bands and/or two bands but with antibody reactivity against HIV-1 *env* and *gag*. Early diagnosis, therefore, relies on a history of exposure, a positive p24 antigen enzyme-linked immunosorbent assay (ELISA) or the detection of plasma viral RNA (almost always more than 50,000 copies/ml of plasma).[2]

The chronic asymptomatic phase

The primary HIV-1 infection is followed by a long phase of clinical latency (median time of 10 years), during which neither signs nor symptoms of illness are present. Relatively stable levels of virus replication and of $CD4^+$ T cell counts for a variable period of time characterize this phase of infection. This 'stability' of measures of disease activity is apparent in the blood only. Virus replication and the accumulation of extracellular virus trapped in the follicular dendritic cell network are particularly active in the lymphoid tissue, where a progressive anatomic and functional deterioration occurs, impairing the ability to maintain effective specific immune responses over time.[7,8] This is reflected by the rapid increase in the levels of viremia and by a drop in $CD4^+$ T cell counts, which may suddenly speed up the transition from this phase to the advanced stage of the disease.

The advanced stage of HIV-1 disease is marked by low $CD4^+$ T cell counts (below 200 cells/μl) and by the appearance of constitutional symptoms. It may be complicated by the development of AIDS-defining opportunistic infections.[1]

Overt AIDS

Overt AIDS defines the end stage of HIV-1 infection. In the absence of antiretroviral therapy, this phase leads to death in 2–3 years. The risk for death and opportunistic infections significantly increases with $CD4^+$ T cell counts below 50 cells/μl. Fortunately, the recent advent of HAART, including at present as many as 15 antiretroviral drugs administered in different combinations, is significantly decreasing the rate of progression, morbidity and mortality of HIV-1 infection.

Clinical course of the infection

The clinical course of HIV-1 infection is variable. In the majority (60–70%) of HIV-1-infected patients, the median time between infection and development of AIDS, in the absence of therapy, is 10–11 years. These HIV-1-infected persons are defined as typical progressers (Fig. 120.2), and the clinical course of the infection that they generally experience is the one described above.

However, about 10–20% of subjects progress rapidly, developing AIDS in less than 5 years of infection, and they are therefore called rapid progressers (see Fig. 120.2). In these patients, after the primary HIV-1 infection, plasma virus levels are often higher than 10^5 copies of HIV-1 RNA/ml and, in particular, $CD4^+$ T cell counts start to

KINETICS OF VIRAL LOAD AND IMMUNE RESPONSE DURING THE PHASES OF HIV-1 INFECTION

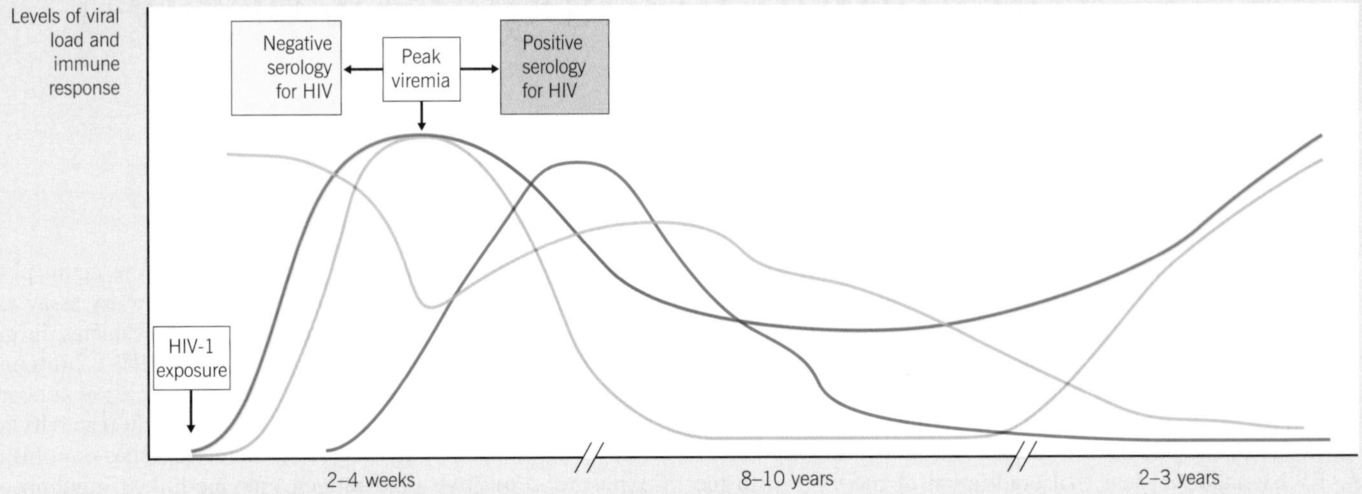

Acute clinical syndrome	
Symptoms	**% of patients**
Fever	80–90
Fatigue	70–90
Rash	40–80
Headache	32–70
Lymphadenopathy	40–70
Pharyngitis	50–70
Arthralgia	5--70
Myalgia	50–70
Night sweats	50
Gastrointestinal symptoms	30–60
Aseptic meningitis	24
Oral or genital ulcers	5–20

Phase of clinical latency

Late appearance of constitutional symptoms

Overt AIDS

Severe constitutional symptoms

Opportunistic infections

Neoplasms

— Plasma viremia

— Viral load in lymphoid tissue

— Immune response (HIV-1-specific cytotoxic lymphocytes)

— $CD4^+$ T lymphocyte count

Fig. 120.1 Kinetics of viral load and immune response during the phases of HIV-1 infection. After HIV-1 exposure, initial virus replication and spread occur in the lymphoid organs, and systemic dissemination of HIV-1 is reflected by the peak of plasma viremia. A clinical syndrome of varying severity is associated with this phase of primary HIV-1 infection in up to 70% of HIV-1-infected persons. Downregulation of viremia during the transition from the primary to the early chronic phase coincides with the appearance of HIV-1-specific cytotoxic T cells and with the progressive resolution of the clinical syndrome. The long phase of clinical latency is associated with active virus replication, particularly in the lymphoid tissue. During the clinically latent period, $CD4^+$ T cell counts slowly decrease, as does the HIV-1-specific immune response. When $CD4^+$ T cell counts decrease below H 200 cells/μl (i.e. when overt AIDS occurs), the clinical picture is characterized by severe constitutional symptoms and by the possible development of opportunistic infections and/or neoplasms.

decrease much earlier and more rapidly during the chronic asymptomatic phase, leading to the eventual development of AIDS. Furthermore, both humoral and cell-mediated HIV-1-specific immune responses are either never detected or rapidly lost after the transition from the acute to the chronic phase of infection.

At the other extreme, it is estimated that 5–15% of HIV-1-infected people will remain free of AIDS for more than 15 years; these people are termed slow progressors (see Fig. 120.2). In this situation, $CD4^+$T cell counts remain stable and they are frequently above 500 cells/μl, and plasma virus levels are usually below 10,000 HIV-1 RNA copies/ml.

Slow progressers include a further subgroup of HIV-1-infected people, so-called long-term nonprogressors (see Fig. 120.2). About 1% of HIV-1-infected subjects probably fall into this category. The definition of long-term nonprogressors should be limited to those who have had a documented infection for at least 8–10 years, are naive to antiretroviral therapy and have no signs of disease progression (e.g. constant high counts of $CD4^+$ T cells and either low (500–1000 copies of RNA/ml) or very low (<50 copies/ml) plasma virus levels).[1,9]

This wide variability of the natural course of the disease is evidence of the presence of different driving forces – genetic, immunologic and virologic factors – that determine the evolutionary pattern of HIV-1 infection in the individual patient.[10] It is therefore important, first, to identify the different determinants of the rate of disease progression and, second, to elucidate how these driving forces work together. Furthermore, the potential ability of HAART to restore some determinants of long-term control of the virus must be evaluated in depth. These arguments are discussed in detail below.

The variability of the natural course of HIV-1 infection also underlines the need for markers of disease progression (see below) that may identify as early as possible the patients who are at risk for a more rapid disease progression. This could warrant either the use of different, perhaps more aggressive, therapeutic strategies or the need to monitor these patients more closely, or both.

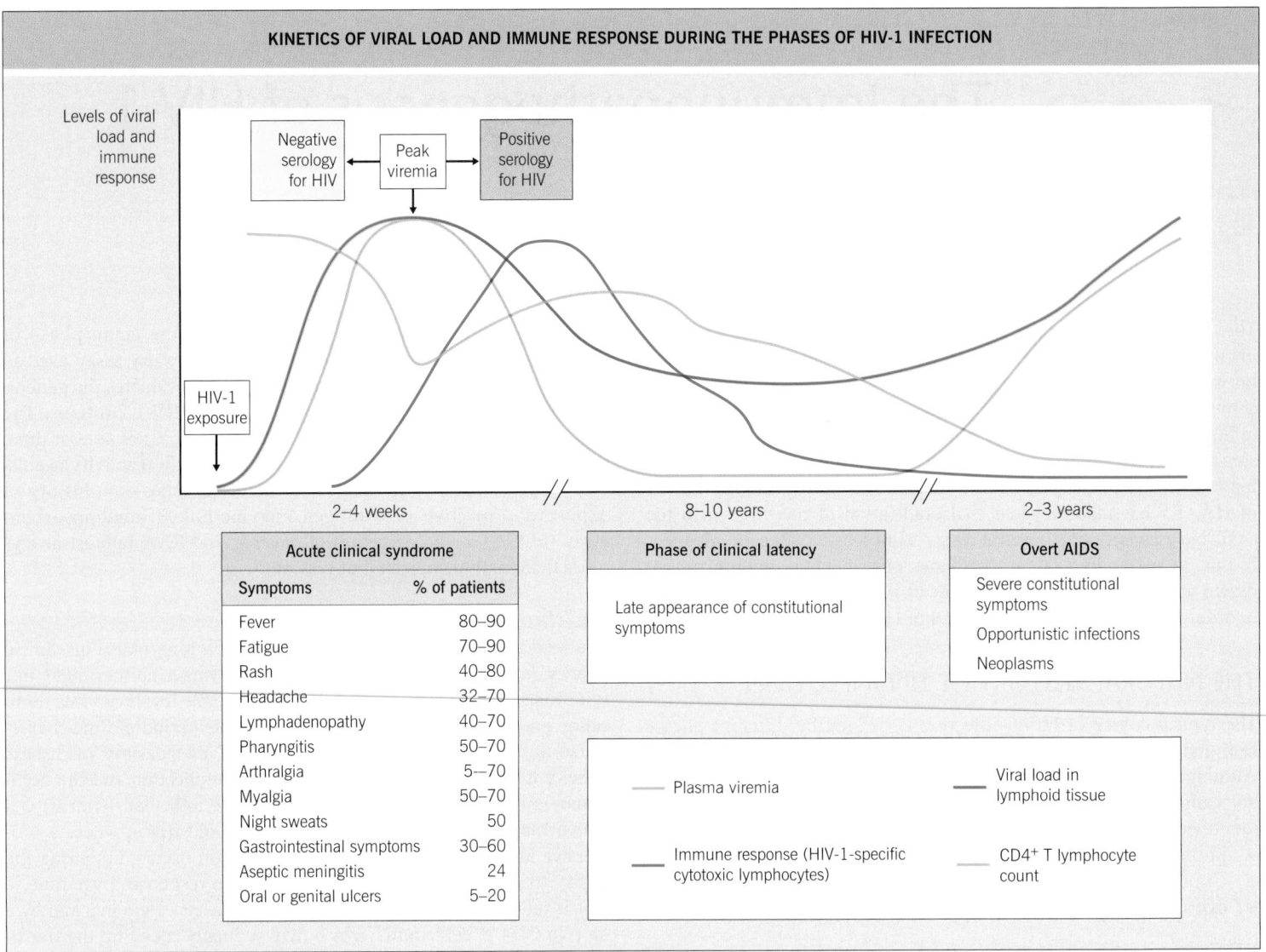

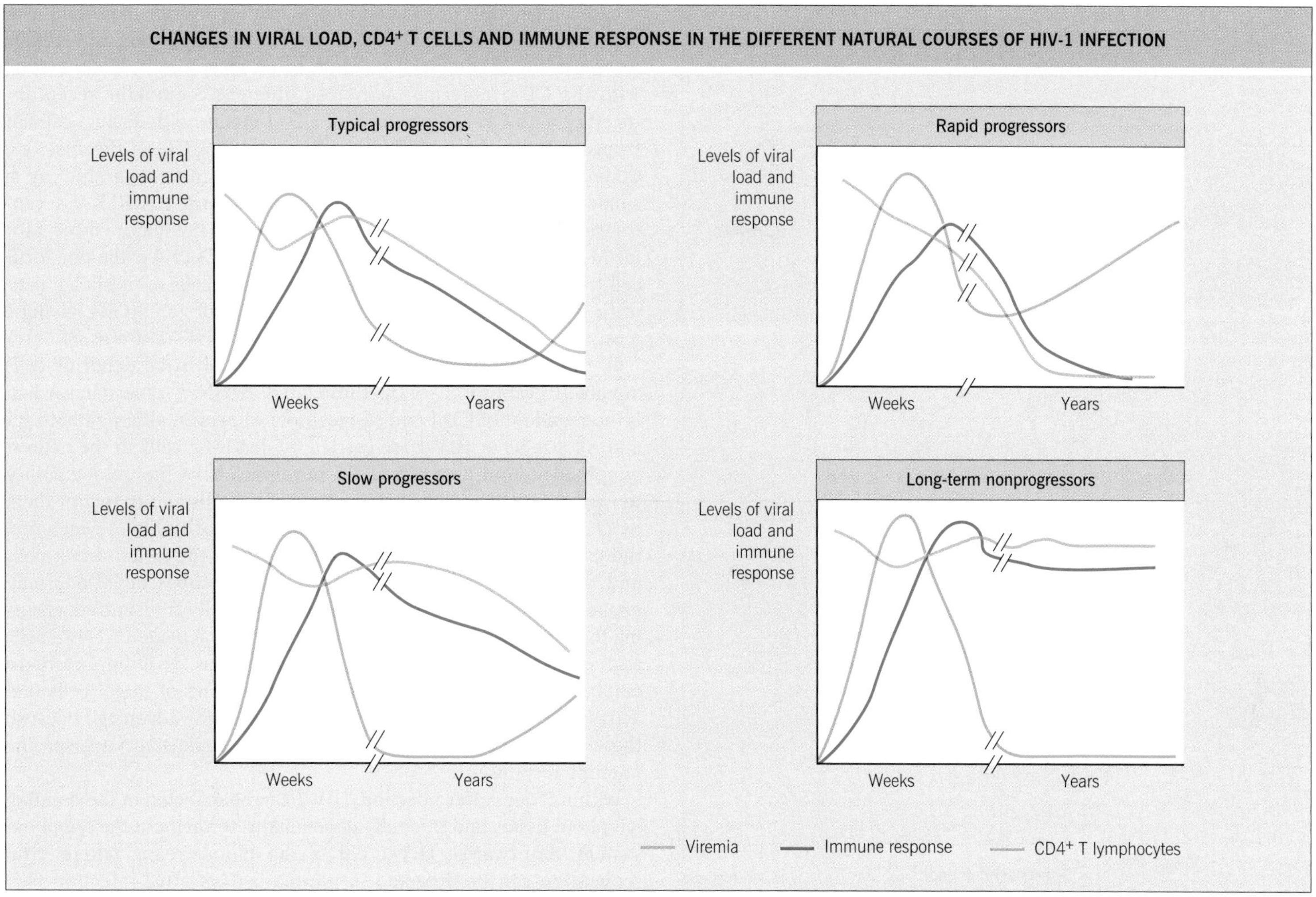

Fig. 120.2 Changes in viral load, $CD4^+$ T cells and immune response in the different natural courses of HIV-1 infection. Typical progressors represent 60–70% of the total HIV-1-infected population, rapid progressors represent 10–20%, slow progressors represent 5–15% and long-term nonprogressors represent 1%.

SEQUENCE OF PATHOGENIC EVENTS LEADING TO THE ESTABLISHMENT OF HIV-1 INFECTION

HIV-1 can be transmitted by different routes: by sexual contact, through either genital–genital or genital–oral sex; by blood–blood contamination, via either transfusion of blood and infected blood-derived products or needle sharing among injection-drug users; and by maternal–fetal transmission. The most common route of infection is sexual transmission at the genital mucosa.[11]

Early pathogenic events after entry of HIV-1 into the body

The acute intravaginal infection of rhesus monkeys with the simian immunodeficiency virus (SIV) represents a very useful model for studying the sequence of cellular events that characterize the very early steps of infection after sexual transmission. In this model, tissue dendritic cells (i.e. Langerhans cells that reside in the lamina propria subjacent to the vaginal epithelium) are the first potential target cells of HIV-1 (Fig. 120.3).[12]

The dendritic cells constitute a complex and highly developed system of antigen-presenting cells that are able to prime naive T cells. Their potent antigen-presenting ability is associated with the high expression of major histocompatibility complex (MHC) class I and class II molecules and costimulatory molecules on the cell surface. The ability of dendritic cells to attract and prime naive T cells can be explained by the expression of a type II membrane protein with an external mannose binding, C-type lectin domain, named DC-SIGN.[13,14] It has been suggested that interaction between DC-SIGN and intracellular adhesion molecule (ICAM)-3 is responsible for the initial contact between dendritic cells and resting T cells, which represents a critical step for the initiation of the T cell immune response. Furthermore, a major contribution to the ability of dendritic cells to initiate T cell immunity is also provided by the fact that dendritic cells express high levels of specific chemokines that target naive rather than memory T cells.[15] Therefore, dendritic cells play a key role, both in priming the initial virus-specific immune response and in serving as a carrier for the transport of HIV-1 to the nearest lymphoid station.

It is important, however, to mention the differences existing between the Langerhans cells (also called 'epidermal' or 'epithelial' dendritic cells) and the 'dermal' or 'subepithelial' dendritic cells.[13] Langerhans cells do not express DC-SIGN and, once they have encountered HIV-1 below the vaginal epithelium, they can either be infected or pick up HIV-1 virions. Epidermal, DC-SIGN-negative dendritic cells are thought to select for the macrophage (M)-tropic viruses that are the most frequently transmitted variants.[16,17] The M-tropic HIV-1 carried by epidermal dendritic cells can bind to additional subepithelial DC-SIGN-positive dendritic cells. DC-SIGN can capture HIV-1 on the cell surface of dendritic cells without allowing viral entry.[18] It is thought that DC-SIGN-positive dendritic cells play the major role in the delivery of virus to T cells, thus greatly amplifying HIV-1 infection.[17] Subsequently, dendritic cells migrate to the internal iliac lymph nodes, where they target the T cell areas and then present

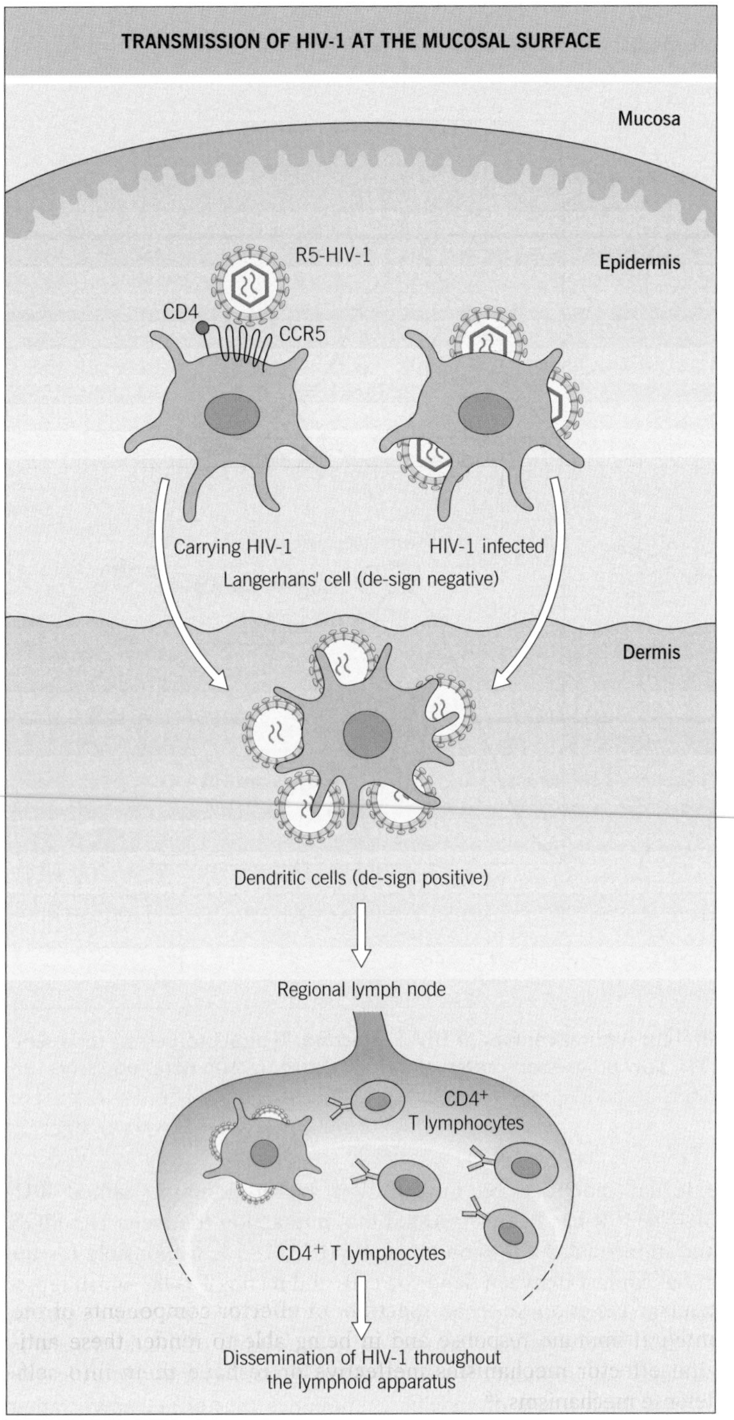

Fig. 120.3 Transmission of HIV-1 at the mucosal surface. After entry at the mucosal epithelium, Langerhans cells, also named epidermal dendritic cells, can either be infected by R5 (macrophage (M)-tropic) strains of HIV-1 or pick up HIV-1 virions. Epidermal, DC-SIGN-negative dendritic cells are thought to select for the M-tropic viruses that are the most frequently transmitted variants. The M-tropic HIV-1 carried by epidermal dendritic cells can bind to additional subepithelial DC-SIGN-positive dendritic cells. DC-SIGN can capture HIV-1 on the cell surface of dendritic cells without allowing viral entry. It is thought that DC-SIGN-positive dendritic cells play the major role in the delivery of virus to T cells, thus greatly amplifying HIV-1 infection.

the viral antigens to activated virus-specific T cells. Dendritic cells can support viral replication only in the presence of activated T cells.[15]

Recent advances in our understanding of the mechanisms that modulate the infectivity of HIV-1 can explain why 95% of viruses transmitted are M-tropic. For more than 10 years, it has been known that human CD4 is sufficient for binding HIV-1 gp120 to cells, but it is sufficient neither for fusion nor for penetration of the viral envelope into the host cell.[19–21] It is now clear that certain cell-surface receptors for chemokines function as co-receptors by co-operating with the CD4 molecule; moreover, different chemokine receptors, together with CD4, allow entry of HIV-1 strains with distinct cellular tropism. There are two classes of chemokine: CC, if the first two cysteines are adjacent; and CXC, if they are separated by a single amino acid. The CC-chemokine receptor (CCR)5, a seven-transmembrane G-protein-coupled receptor, is the major co-receptor for M-tropic or R5 strains of HIV-1, whereas CXCR4 is the one for T-cell-tropic or X4 strains of HIV-1. Langerhans cells or epithelial dendritic cells express CCR5 but they may not express CXCR4, giving a reason for the preferential transmission of R5 HIV-1 strains.[22]

To this extent, it is worth noting that subepithelial dendritic cells are able to capture the virus through DC-SIGN,[18] a mechanism that is independent of CD4 and co-receptors. However, although both R5 and X4 strains of HIV-1 are carried by dendritic cells to the nearest lymphoid station, only R5 HIV-1 envelopes have the unique ability to mediate an activation signal into $CD4^+$ T cells and to recruit them by chemotaxis.[23] Therefore, the combination of the two events (i.e. the differential expression of co-receptors on the initial target cells and the unique signaling ability of R5 envelopes of HIV-1) may explain why R5 HIV-1 variants are preferentially transmitted, ensuring the rapid recruitment of a large number of activated $CD4^+$ T cells and spread of HIV-1 in the lymphoid organs. It is important to emphasize that rapid recruitment and spreading of target cells (i.e. activated $CD4^+$ T cells) confers to HIV-1 a major advantage because these events occur before the appearance of effective virus-specific immune responses.

Within 2 days after infection, HIV-1 can be detected in the draining lymphoid tissue, and it rapidly disseminates throughout the lymphoid system. Afterwards, HIV-1 enters the bloodstream, where viral replication can be detected in plasma 5 days after infection (see Fig. 120.3). In humans, the time from mucosal infection and initial plasma viremia varies, ranging between 4 days and 11 days according to available estimates. It is of note that the risk of infection is increased by conditions that decrease the function of mucosal barriers, such as lesions caused by the presence of concomitant inflammatory or infectious diseases (e.g. cervicitis, urethritis, genital ulcers).

These same steps of infection can be described in the case of genital–oral HIV-1 transmission, because nasopharyngeal tonsils and adenoid tissue contain many cells of dendritic origin that can support viral replication more efficiently than Langerhans cells.[2]

The role of the lymph nodes in primary HIV-1 infection

The study of virologic events occurring during primary infection with either HIV-1 or SIV emphasizes the key role of lymphoid tissue in the establishment of infection. Longitudinal and cross-sectional analyses of HIV-1 or SIV distribution were performed on lymph node biopsies taken from rhesus monkeys or HIV-1-infected patients. In the SIV model of acute infection, virus can be detected in the lymph node as early as 5 days after infection. At this time, as shown by in-situ hybridization analysis for the detection of HIV-1/SIV RNA, virus is mostly present in the form of numerous individual cells expressing viral RNA, and the highest number of virus-expressing cells is observed 7 days after SIV inoculation. Interestingly, the occurrence of the peak number of virus-expressing cells in the lymph node occurs at the same time as the peak of plasma viremia, or shortly precedes it. The cross-sectional analysis of lymph nodes obtained from HIV-1-infected patients indicates that the kinetics of virus distribution in lymph nodes are consistent with those in the SIV model of acute infection. Altogether, these

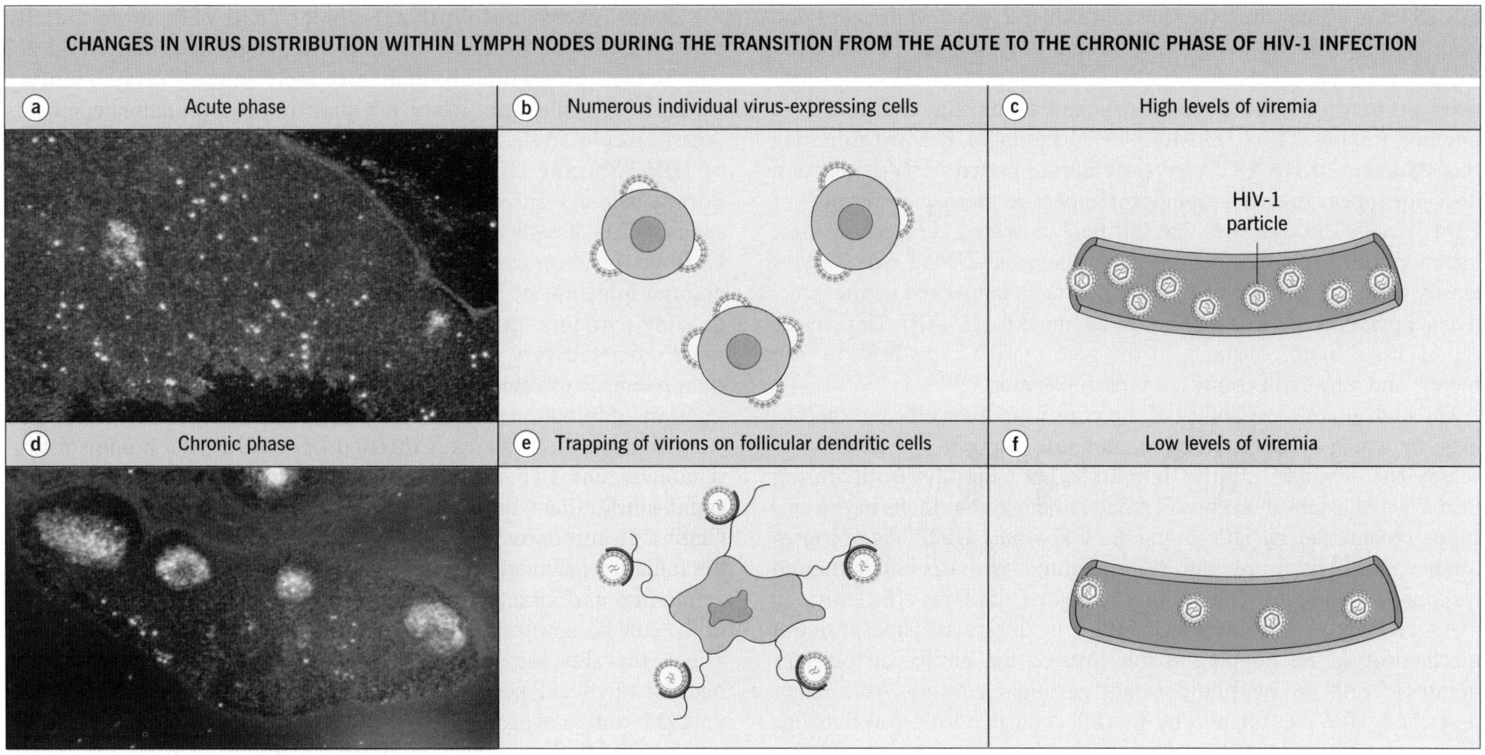

Fig. 120.4 Changes in virus distribution within lymph nodes during the transition from the acute to the chronic phase of HIV-1 infection. (a) During the initial weeks of primary HIV-1 infection, the virus is detected in lymphoid tissue as individual virus-expressing cells. This is shown by in-situ hybridization for the detection of HIV-1 RNA (white dots indicate HIV-1 RNA-positive cells). (b) Numerous individual virus-expressing cells seen in the acute phase. (c) Elevated virion levels are found in the circulation in the acute phase. (d) After transition to the chronic phase of the disease, virions trapped in the follicular dendritic cell network become the dominant form of HIV-1, as shown by in-situ hybridization for the detection of HIV-1 RNA (diffuse white areas indicate virus trapped within follicular dendritic cells). (e) Binding of virions on the extracellular surface of follicular dendritic cells in the chronic phase. (f) The number of circulating virions is dramatically reduced in the chronic phase.

findings indicate that the lymph node is the primary anatomic site of infection.[8,24]

During the transition from primary to chronic infection, a switch from individual virus-expressing cells to virus trapped by the follicular dendritic cell network of lymph node germinal centers occurs (Fig. 120.4). The trapped virus becomes the dominant form of virus present in lymph nodes, and this event is associated with a dramatic decrease in the number of individual cells expressing viral RNA.[8,24]

At least in part, this is the result of the emergence of virus-specific CTLs that can be detected very early during primary infection and may mediate the elimination of HIV-1-producing cells. Furthermore, the trapping of HIV-1 virions in the follicular dendritic cell network is itself the result of the HIV-1-specific humoral response. In fact, HIV-1 virions are complexed with immunoglobulins and complement, and the binding of these complexes on the extracellular surface of follicular dendritic cells occurs through complement receptors expressed on follicular dendritic cells. In both SIV and HIV-1 infection, the transition from primary to early chronic infection is marked by a decrease of viral RNA in plasma and the resolution of the acute clinical syndrome. Therefore, it is clear that virus-specific immune responses are not only present very early during primary infection but may also significantly affect virus distribution occurring in the early phase of both SIV and HIV-1 infection.[25]

MECHANISMS RESPONSIBLE FOR VIRUS ESCAPE FROM IMMUNE RESPONSE AND ESTABLISHMENT OF CHRONIC INFECTION

Early in primary HIV-1 infection, vigorous virus-specific immune responses can be detected, and they may contribute to both control of the initial peak of virus replication and the reduction in plasma viremia.[3–6] However, primary HIV-1 infection invariably results in the establishment of chronic disease in the host, inducing a progressive deterioration of the different components of the immune response.

HIV-1-specific immune responses lack the ability to control HIV-1 and to block the progression of the disease. Nevertheless, similar types of immune response are effective against other viruses, such as Epstein–Barr virus and cytomegalovirus (CMV). HIV-1 differs from these other viruses by being able to target very early (during the primary infection) a broad spectrum of effector components of the antiviral immune response and in being able to render these antiviral effector mechanisms ineffective or reshape them into self-defense mechanisms.[26]

Virologic mechanisms of HIV-1 escape from the immune response

HIV-1 possesses the ability to put in motion several mechanisms as the result of the interaction with the host. Some of these virologic mechanisms can be identified:

- formation of a stable pool of latently HIV-1-infected $CD4^+$ T cells containing virus that is capable of replicating;[27–31]
- the genetic variability of HIV-1;[32] and
- trapping of infectious virions on the surface of follicular dendritic cells.[33]

The rapid formation of a pool of latently HIV-1-infected $CD4^+$ T cells is a key event in the immunopathogenesis of HIV-1 infection for several reasons. First, this event occurs very early and most probably before the appearance of the host's virus-specific immune responses. Second, the pool of latently infected $CD4^+$ T cells contains replication-competent HIV-1 proviral DNA. The proviral DNA can be detected even in compliant HIV-1-infected persons who have been receiving

HAART for a long time (i.e. for more than 2 years); moreover, the virus is wild-type with respect to known drug-induced mutations in the genome. This emphasizes the fact that this pool of cells is a stable reservoir in which HIV-1 remains sheltered from the effects of host immune responses and HAART.[27–31] Furthermore, it is worth noting that initiation of HAART very early during primary HIV-1 infection does not appear to have a significant impact on the size of this pool of CD4+ T cells. This indicates that this pool is created very rapidly after infection. Third, the decay of this pool of infected CD4+ T lymphocytes is very slow, and the rate of decay is not much influenced by the effective suppression of virus replication obtained by HAART. This clearly represents a major obstacle to the goal of HIV-1 eradication (see below) and long-term control of virus replication.[29–31]

The high genetic variability of the virus is another efficient mechanism by which it escapes the host immune response.[32,34] HIV-1 possesses the intrinsic ability to mutate very rapidly. Both during primary and established chronic infection, rapid mutations in the epitopes recognized by HIV-1-specific CTLs may occur. As a consequence, both humoral and cell-mediated virus-specific immune responses quickly lose their ability to control the virus efficiently.

An additional way by which HIV-1 is able to reshape antiviral mechanisms is the trapping of the virus on the surface of follicular dendritic cells in lymphoid tissue germinal centers. As already described, HIV-1 is trapped by the follicular dendritic cell network during the transition from primary to chronic infection and this becomes the dominant form of virus in lymphoid tissue in the chronic phase. Formation of immune complexes and their attachment to the follicular dendritic cell network are physiologic mechanisms that are generally devoted to the clearance of the pathogen and to the generation and maintenance of effective immune responses. In HIV-1 infection, however, these mechanisms lead to the formation of a stable reservoir of infectious virions, representing a continuous source for the infection of CD4+ T cells, and to a chronic inflammatory reaction that ultimately results in the destruction of the lymphoid tissue.[7,8]

Immunologic mechanisms of HIV-1 escape from the immune response

In addition to the virologic mechanisms described above, through which HIV-1 escapes and reshapes the host immune response, there are some immunologic mechanisms that can be identified:

- deletion of HIV-specific CD4+ T cell clones;[35]
- deletion of HIV-specific cytotoxic CD8+ T cell clones;[36]
- generation of virus escape mutants mediated by CTLs;[26]
- egress of CTLs from lymph nodes;[37]
- impairment of the function of antigen-presenting cells;[26] and
- interference with humoral neutralizing response.[26]

In the majority of HIV-1-infected patients who have established chronic infection, HIV-1-specific CD4+ helper T cell responses cannot be detected, although it is possible to find evidence of such HIV-1-specific CD4+ T cell responses in long-term nonprogressors.[35] In contrast, HIV-1-specific effector CD4+ T cell responses are consistently detected in patients who have chronic infection.[38] The persistence of the CD4+ helper T cell response may represent one of the determinants of the course of the disease in long-term nonprogressors. In contrast, typical progressors do lose CD4+ helper T cell responses very early in the natural history of the disease (during the primary HIV-1 infection) as a result of direct or indirect virus-induced cytopathology.[35] Furthermore, initiation of HAART during chronic infection and even during early HIV-1 infection is associated with the restoration of the HIV-1-specific CD4+ helper T cell responses only in a subset (about 30–40%) of patients after prolonged treatment.[39] It is, however, possible to preserve HIV-1-specific CD4+ T cell responses if HAART is initiated at the time of the peak of plasma viral RNA (i.e. very early during primary HIV-1-infection).[35]

It is also worth noting that T helper (Th)1 cells preferentially express CCR5 on the membrane surface, suggesting that HIV-1 R5 strains may preferentially and selectively infect Th1 cells during primary HIV infection, when R5 quasispecies predominate. In this regard, recent studies have demonstrated that the initial expansion of HIV-1-specific CD4+ T cells with effector function is aborted during primary infection.[40] In contrast, the expansion of CMV-specific CD4+ T cells in patients who experienced primary HIV-1 and CMV co-infection was not suppressed. These studies indicate a preferential infection of HIV-1-specific CD4+ T cells. Furthermore, they provide evidence that HIV-1-specific CD4+ T cell clones may be rapidly deleted very early during primary HIV-1 infection and that the possibility of rescuing these responses is strictly dependent upon the time of initiation of HAART.[35,40]

Furthermore, the lack of HIV-1-specific CD4+ helper T cell responses has two other important consequences. First, it can significantly affect the induction and persistence of HIV-1-specific CD8+ CTL responses, because the latter require continuous cognate Th function provided by antigen-specific CD4+ T cells. Therefore, generation and maintenance of vigorous virus-specific responses by CTLs can be compromised over time. Second, it can considerably affect the development of HIV-1-specific antibody responses, because the development of humoral responses is strictly dependent on CD4+ antigen-specific Th cells.[26]

A rapid deletion of certain HIV-1-specific cytotoxic CD8+ T cell clones also occurs during primary HIV-1 infection, in a manner that is analogous to the HIV-1-specific responses mediated by CD4+ helper T cells.[36] These CD8+ T cell clones undergo massive clonal expansion and may be deleted by a mechanism analogous to the clonal exhaustion that is observed in mice during acute lymphocytic choriomeningitis virus infection. This clonal exhaustion of HIV-1-specific CD8+ CTLs causes the early impairment of the virus-specific responses by CTLs. The extent of this phenomenon may determine the varying ability to control virus replication efficiently and therefore it may significantly affect the rate of disease progression. In fact, it is now clear that the appearance of virus-specific responses by CTLs correlates with the decrease in plasma viremia.[6,41] Furthermore, the higher the relative frequency of HIV-1-specific CTLs, the lower the levels of circulating viral RNA, and higher levels of CTL activity correlate with slower rates of disease progression.[6,41,42] However, the clonal exhaustion of virus-specific CTLs does not necessarily result in a complete loss of HIV-1-specific CTL activity, although it does provide additional evidence of how HIV-1 is able to target and impair host immune responses early in the course of the infection.

The detection of CTL-escape variants is common during the course of chronic HIV-1 infection; they may also, however, be found during primary HIV-1 infection. This event provides further evidence of the ability of HIV-1 to reshape some antiviral mechanisms of the immune response into self-defense mechanisms. In fact, although HIV-specific CTLs contribute to the control of both plasma viremia and disease progression,[6,41,42] the pressure exerted by CTLs can, at the same time, facilitate the selection of virus mutants that are able to escape the host immune response.[26,36]

As described above, lymph nodes play a crucial role in the immunopathogenesis of HIV-1 infection. Very high levels of virus replication and spread occur in the lymph nodes during primary infection. Therefore, CTL responses specific for HIV-1 should be predominantly concentrated in the lymphoid tissue in order to achieve the most effective clearance of the virus. However, an early accumulation of HIV-1-specific CTLs in peripheral blood can be observed; CTLs therefore accumulate in a compartment where they cannot efficiently mediate their effector function (i.e. killing of productively HIV-infected cells). Egress of antigen-specific CTLs from lymphoid tissue into the circulation is likely to be a physiologic step that occurs after the generation of the immune response in order to achieve a wide distribution of antigen-specific effector cells in different anatomic sites. In HIV-1 infection, however, this phenomenon also serves to redirect virus-specific CTLs away from the primary site of virus replication and spread. The observation that the number of HIV-1-expressing cells in lymph nodes does not significantly differ between primary and early chronic infection provides further support for the hypothesis of a defective control of HIV-1 during the early phases of infection.[8]

In addition to CD4+ and CD8+ HIV-1-specific T cells, HIV-1 may interfere with the function of antigen-presenting cells. These cells play a central role in the generation of an effective host immune responses. Cells of the monocyte–macrophage line and dendritic cells can function as specialized antigen-presenting cells and induce both humoral and cell-mediated immune responses. The effect of HIV-1 on these components of the immune system is produced by a quantitative depletion through direct cytopathogenesis or by interference with the formation of MHC–antigenic peptide complexes. To this extent, the expression of MHC class I molecules on antigen-presenting cells can be downregulated by HIV-1 Nef protein, thus affecting both generation of antigen-specific immune responses and recognition of virus-infected target cells by CTLs.[43]

Humoral response against HIV-1 can be detected early during primary HIV-1 infection. This response, however, comprises low-avidity Env-specific IgG that possesses little or no neutralizing activity. Although the reasons for the delay in the appearance of the neutralizing antibody response are poorly understood, such a response is detectable only either after the transition from primary HIV-1 infection to established early chronic HIV-1 infection, or even much later. The virologic and immunologic mechanisms described above significantly affect the global host immune response, within which the CD4+ Th cell function and the interactions between T cells and B cells are profoundly altered. These events may ultimately interfere with circulating titers, avidity maturation and neutralizing activity of HIV-1-specific antibodies.

HOST AND VIROLOGIC FACTORS THAT INFLUENCE THE COURSE OF HIV-1 INFECTION

The events that result in the establishment of chronic HIV-1 infection emphasize the ability of the virus to target the host's antiviral immune response and reshape it into a self-defense mechanism. In this context, the mutual interactions between the virus and the host are major determinants of disease progression. Primary HIV-1 infection is a key phase in the immunopathogenesis of the infection, because all of the events that occur at this stage can determine both the pattern and rate of progression of the disease. In the transition from primary to early chronic HIV-1 infection, levels of plasma viral RNA tend to reach a virologic set point that is predictive of the rate of disease progression (see below).[44,45] The virologic set point varies among HIV-1-infected patients and tends to remain stable in the same person during the chronic phase. The virologic set point that a person attains is determined both by the mechanisms involved in the establishment of chronic infection and by host factors that can modulate the course of HIV-1 disease.

Several factors play an important role in modulating both the antiviral host immune response and the susceptibility to HIV-1, and these factors can thus result in a slower rate of disease progression. These factors are mainly genetic, immunologic and virologic (Table 120.1).[10,26]

Genetic host factors

Patients infected with HIV-1 who experience a nonprogressive disease are more likely to possess certain HLA class I haplotypes than other members of the general population. Clusters of haplotypes rather than a single haplotype are involved; these haplotypes are more efficient than others at binding peptides that correspond to epitopes recognized by virus-specific CTLs. This suggests that persons who have inherited these clusters of haplotypes could generate HIV-1-specific CTL responses against multiple epitopes, thus resulting in a more efficient antiviral response, as a consequence of their HLA genetic background.[42]

The recent identification and study of the function of several α- and β-chemokine receptors that can serve as HIV-1 co-receptors have provided evidence of varying chemokine receptor genetic polymorphisms that can influence susceptibility to HIV-1 infection and are associated with different rates of disease progression. Chemokines can be classified into two subfamilies, namely CXC or α-chemokines and CC or β-chemokines, both of whose receptor molecules are part of the vast and functionally diverse family of seven-transmembrane G protein-coupled receptors. CXCR4, the first identified co-receptor, mediates T-cell-tropic viral fusion and entry (X4 HIV-1 strains), but it does not function as a co-receptor for the macrophage-tropic HIV-1 envelope. The major co-receptor for macrophage-tropic HIV-1 strains is CCR5, and other CC chemokine receptors, such as CCR2b, CCR3 and CCR8, can serve as co-receptors for R5 or dual-tropic (i.e. primary HIV-1 isolates) HIV-1 strains.[46–51]

Some HIV-1-negative persons, despite being at high risk of exposure, appear to have an innate ability to 'resist' HIV-1 infection. Mapping of the CCR5 structural gene on the human chromosome 3p21 allowed the identification of a 32-base-pair deletion allele (Δ32CCR5) that encodes a truncated and nonfunctional molecule that fails to reach the cell surface. As a result, cells susceptible to HIV-1 are highly resistant to infection by R5 strains. Available prevalence estimates indicate that between 15% and 20% of Caucasians are heterozygous for the mutation, whereas 1% or fewer are homozygous.[52] The

HOST FACTORS AND VIROLOGIC FACTORS IN HIV-1 INFECTION

Genetic host factors	Immunologic host factors	Virologic factors
HLA class I haplotype	Qualitative differences in the primary immune response	Extent of HIV-1 replication
Mutations in chemokine receptor or ligand genes: Ø32 in CCR5 m303 in CCR5 V641 in CCR2b G801A in SDF	Clonal deletion of HIV-1-specific cytotoxic T cells	Viral phenotype (syncytium-inducing or non-syncytium-inducing strains of HIV-1)
	Persistence of HIV-1-specific CD4+ T cell responses	Trapping of virions in follicular dendritic cell network
Levels of β-chemokines (RANTES, MIP-1α and MIP-1β)	Chronic immune activation	Viral latency
		Size of inoculum

Table 120.1 Host factors and virologic factors in HIV-1 infection.

study of large cohorts of HIV-1-negative persons, including those who have had multiple exposures to HIV-1, and HIV-1-infected patients has provided evidence that the homozygous genotype for the mutation (i.e. Δ32CCR5–Δ32CCR5) confers high resistance to infection by HIV-1,[52] although a few HIV-1-infected patients possess the Δ32CCR5–Δ32CCR5 homozygous genotype. However, the heterozygous genotype (CCR5–Δ32CCR5) does not prevent HIV-1 from infecting susceptible cells but is significantly associated with a slower rate of disease progression in HIV-1-infected patients and is found more commonly in long-term nonprogressors.[53] In heterozygotes there is a decreased expression of the CCR5 receptor, which can be explained by a transdominant inhibition of wild-type CCR5 receptor function owing to the concomitant intracellular presence of both normal and defective gene products withheld in the endoplasmic reticulum.[54] Another mutation (m303) in the *CCR5* gene prevents the expression of the receptor on the cell surface by introducing a premature stop codon. This mutation, when in *trans* with the Δ32CCR5 defective gene, confers resistance because no expression of CCR5 receptor occurs.[55]

Furthermore, other genetic variants do not prevent infection but rather delay the progression of HIV-1 disease. However, their protective effect has not been confirmed in all studies, emphasizing the need to evaluate their role in larger cohorts. These genetic variants include a mutant CCR2b allele (V64I), which encodes a base mutation that replaces valine with isoleucine at position 64 in the transmembrane domain I of the CCR2b receptor;[56–60] and a guanosine-to-adenosine transition at position 801 (G801A) in the 3' untranslated region of the reference sequence in the gene of the stromal-derived factor (SDF)-1,[61,62] which is the ligand for CXCR4.

Epidemiologically, the inheritance of the CCR2b mutant is less beneficial than the inheritance of the Δ32CCR5 mutant in terms of reducing the risk of progression to AIDS; however, as in the case of CCR5–Δ32CCR5 heterozygosity, the V64I mutant is more commonly found in long-term nonprogressors.[58] Biologically, it is not clear how the V64I allele could interfere with the co-receptor function, because valine and isoleucine are chemically very similar. It is possible that the V64I allele is in linkage disequilibrium with other mutations,[56,57,59] as it has been described with a point mutation in the CCR5 regulatory region.[59]

As far as the SDF-1 G801A mutant allele is concerned, available data are somewhat puzzling. On the one hand, the status of homozygosity for the mutation has been associated with a lower risk of progression to AIDS.[61] A possible explanation for such a protective effect is that the presence of mutant alleles induces a higher than usual release of SDF-1, which inhibits X4 HIV-1 strains. X4 strains tend to emerge during the late phase of the disease and their appearance is generally associated with a more rapid progression. The SDF-1 at high levels could therefore interfere with the spreading of X4 HIV-1 strains, thus reducing the rate of disease progression. Homozygosity for the SDF-1 mutant has been linked to a higher risk of death, although the potential explanation is unclear.[62]

The initial studies that discovered the role of chemokine receptors as HIV-1 co-receptors originated from the observation that chemokines can potently modulate HIV-1 infectivity.[63] The β-chemokines that are 'regulated upon activation, normal T expressed and secreted' (RANTES) – macrophage inflammatory protein (MIP)-1α and MIP-1β – have been identified as major HIV-suppressive factors produced by CD8$^+$ T cells in vitro. Furthermore, endogenous levels of RANTES, MIP-1α and MIP-1β expression in CD4$^+$ T cells were much elevated in some people who remained uninfected despite multiple sexual exposures to HIV-1-infected partners.[64] The binding of one chemokine to its cognate receptor essentially mediates the downregulation of surface chemokine receptor expression. Therefore, in addition to genetic control, chemokine levels themselves may influence infectivity and disease progression. In particular, there is evidence that very high levels of RANTES, MIP-1α and MIP-1β are detectable in persons bearing the Δ32CCR5–Δ32CCR5 homozygous genotype.[64] Similarly, unusually high levels of β-chemokines have been found in people with hemophilia who have remained uninfected with HIV-1 despite repeated exposure to contaminated blood products before HIV-1 testing became available.[65] Furthermore, levels of MIP-1β (which is the only suppressive CCR5-specific chemokine) in those who have overt AIDS can be significantly lower than those in HIV-1-infected patients who have chronic disease; moreover, higher levels of MIP-1β are associated with a lower risk of disease progression.[66]

These observations suggest that suppressive β-chemokines may play a role in the control of HIV-1. Production of chemokines by effector CD4$^+$ T cells occurs at the site of virus replication, and the chemokines may protect local target cells and activated effector cells by downregulating CCR5 in an autocrine manner. The varying extents to which these mechanisms are put in motion may explain the varying levels of protection against disease progression.

In summary, host genetic factors do play a role in modulating the course of HIV-1 infection. Furthermore, the potential role of chemokines in affecting infectivity and disease progression may further widen our therapeutic options along with HAART.

Immunologic factors

Importance of HIV-1-specific CD4$^+$ T cells

CD4$^+$ T cells play a fundamental role in the generation of antigen-specific immune responses. Studies performed in mice have clearly demonstrated that stimulation and expansion of antigen-specific CD4$^+$ T cells precedes that of CD8$^+$ T cells during acute virus infection in vivo.[67] Even although CD4$^+$ T cells do not seem to be critical for the generation of the primary virus-specific CD8$^+$ T cell response, the presence of virus-specific CD4$^+$ T cells is required for the maintenance of the CD8$^+$ T cell response over time during the phase of chronic infection.[68,69]

The progressive depletion of CD4$^+$ T cells is the hallmark of HIV-1 infection.[70] However, even in the early stages of HIV-1 infection when the CD4$^+$ T cell count may still remain in the normal range, certain HIV-1-specific CD4$^+$ T cell functions, such as the ability to proliferate after stimulation with different virus protein, are already absent in the majority (80–90%) of HIV-1-infected patients.[71,72] The antigen-specific proliferation ability is also known as T helper function. Therefore, the defect of HIV-1-specific CD4$^+$ Th cells occurs very early during HIV-1 infection. Despite the lack of virus-specific CD4$^+$ helper responses, HIV-1-specific CD4$^+$ T cells have been identified even in patients who have progressive disease on the basis of their ability to secrete interferon (IFN)-γ following short (6h) stimulation with HIV-1 antigens.[38]

The discordance between the lack of HIV-1-specific CD4 proliferation and the detection of HIV-1-specific IFN-γ-secreting CD4$^+$ T cells can be explained by the stimulation of different populations of antigen-specific CD4$^+$ T cells in the two assays. Stimulation of precursors of antigen-specific memory T cells occurs in the 6 days proliferation assay while the short-term (6h) stimulation IFN-γ flow cytometry assay probably detects functionally differentiated antigen-specific T cells.

The hypothesis above is supported by a series of recent studies that have shed light on memory CD4$^+$ and CD8$^+$ T cells.[73,74] These studies have shown that different populations of memory T cells can be distinguished upon the expression of different cell surface markers such as CD45RA and the chemokine receptor CCR7. Interestingly, these different populations of memory T cells are at different stages of differentiation and have different functions. Therefore, memory CD4$^+$ T cells with the proliferation function are contained within the precursor cell populations that are at earlier stages of differentiation while memory T cells at late stages of differentiation acquire effector functions and are able to secrete proinflammatory cytokines such as IFN-γ and tumor necrosis factor α. Therefore, in HIV-1 infection there is a selective defect of HIV-1-specific CD4+ helper T cells while HIV-specific CD4+ T cells secreting IFN-γ are still present.[35,38,75]

How is it possible to explain the persistence of HIV-specific memory CD4+ T cells secreting IFN-γ in the absence of the memory cells, (e.g. T helper cells) that function as precursors? The likely explanation is that HIV-1-specific memory CD4+ T cells secreting IFN-γ belong to the population of long-lived memory T cells that may persist for several years even in the absence of the replenishment by the precursor cell populations.

CD4+ T cell responses against other viruses such as CMV are detected in most HIV-1-infected patients but they are eventually lost in the advanced stages of disease.[76] In this regard, it is important to underscore the fact that both CMV-specific memory CD4 helper and effector T cell responses are consistently detected. Therefore, the defect of virus-specific memory CD4+ T cells seems to be selective for HIV-1-specific and no for other virus-specific CD4+ helper T cell responses. This suggests that the elimination of HIV-1-specific helper T cells does not occur randomly. It is likely that already at the time of primary HIV-1 infection, when there is massive virus replication and spreading and thus high antigen levels, the pool of precursors of memory HIV-1-specific T cells is rapidly eliminated in the process of responding to the infection.

In addition to the large number of studies in the field of basic immunology and in human virus infections such as CMV and hepatitis C virus,[76–78] there are also several observations in HIV-1 infection that link the presence of optimal CD4+ T cell responses to lack of progression of HIV-1 disease and better control of virus replication. As mentioned above, a small percentage (1%) of HIV-1-infected patients (i.e. long-term nonprogressors) experience no signs of disease progression, no decline in CD4+ T cell counts and low/absent levels of virus replication, even several (10–15) years after infection. HIV-1-specific CD4+ helper and effector T cell responses are consistently found in long-term nonprogressers. Therefore, it is important to underscore that the detection of HIV-1-specific helper and effector T cell responses represents a constant feature of the effective immune response found in long-term nonprogressors.

Importance of HIV-1-specific CD8+ T cells

There are at least three major lines of evidence for the central role played by CTLs in controlling HIV-1 replication. First, primary HIV-1 infection is associated with a very potent CTL response that generally coincides with the peak in viremia and precedes the neutralizing antibody response.[3–5] This response is associated with major oligoclonal expansion of HIV-1-specific CD8+ T cells. In some patients a large percentage (up to 40%) of circulating CD8+ T cells are specific for HIV-1.[5] The advent of CTL response is temporally associated with the downregulation of viremia.[4,5] This observation indicates a role for CTLs, which are mostly contained in the T cell population characterized by the expression of the CD8 surface molecule, in the initial control of virus replication. However, direct demonstration of the important role played by CD8+ CTLs comes from the SIV monkey model of HIV-1 infection. In fact, it has been demonstrated that the depletion of CD8+ cells following infusion with a specific anti-CD8 monoclonal antibody resulted in a failure to control the early peak of viremia in the infected animals.[79] Along the same lines, the depletion of CD8+ CTLs in SIV chronically infected monkeys was associated with transient rises in the viremia levels[80] and loss of immune control occurs following the emergence of virus mutants in vivo that are not recognized by CTLs.[81–86]

Second, it has been shown that the HLA type may significantly influence the rate of HIV-1 disease progression.[87] In particular, HLA types such as HLA-B27 and HLA-B57 are associated with slow disease progression and HLA-B35 with faster disease progression. Since CTLs recognize virus peptides presented by HLA class I molecules, different HLA types may have different ability to present peptides and thus substantially influence the quality of the immune response elicited.

Third, HIV-1-specific CD8+ T cell responses have been found in virus-exposed uninfected individuals[88] and/or animals.[89,90] Therefore, the above observations, together with a large quantity of recently accumulated experimental evidence, indicate that CD8+ T cells may potentially play a major role in the control of HIV-1 replication, and the development of a preventive HIV-1 vaccine based on the induction of CD8 CTLs may potentially confer partial and/or complete control of HIV-1 infection.

However, despite all this evidence in support of the fundamental role that CD8+ T cells may exert in the control of HIV-1 replication and disease, this vigorous immune response is not able to eliminate HIV-1 at the time of primary infection and the control of HIV-1 replication after the transition to the chronic phase of infection is only partial. The partially effective control of HIV-1 replication does not fit very well with the magnitude of the HIV-1-specific immune response detected at the time of primary infection and its persistence for several years.[91] Therefore, the observations above indicate that the inability of the HIV-1-specific CD8+ T cell immune response to control virus replication cannot be explained by a defect in the magnitude of the immune response. Even although it has been shown that certain HIV-1-specific CD8+ T cell clones are rapidly deleted during primary infection,[44] this event does not seem to influence significantly the magnitude of the CD8+ T cell response.

These latter observations indicate that the detection of large frequencies of HIV-specific CTLs does not necessarily reflect the effectiveness of the immune response in the control of HIV infection. CD8+ T cells may mediate antiviral activity by the production of soluble factors such as the cytokine IFN-γ,[92–94] the chemokines MIP-1α, MIP-1β and RANTES,[95–97] and the partially characterized CD8+ T cell antiviral factor CAF,[98,99] and/or by lytic mechanisms. HIV-1-specific CTLs are able to produce the above antiviral factors. However, recent studies have strongly suggested that the HIV-1-specific CD8+ T cells present in HIV-1-infected patients may have major abnormalities at both functional and maturational levels. In this regard, it has been shown that HIV-1-specific CTLs have a selective defect in their levels of intracellular perforin that may significantly affect their lytic capacity.[100] Therefore, although HIV-1-specific CTLs have been shown to lyse HIV-1-infected CD4+ T cells following activation in vitro,[101] freshly isolated virus-specific T cells show poor lytic activity.[102,103]

Furthermore, recent studies have also demonstrated that the pool of memory T cells is composed of several populations of memory CD8+ T cells with different functional capacities and at different stages of maturation.[73,74] Studies aimed at the functional characterization of the different populations of memory HIV-1- and CMV-specific CD8+ T cells have allowed the development of a lineage differentiation pattern for memory CD8+ T cells and have demonstrated major differences within the composition of the HIV-1- and CMV-specific memory CD8+ T cell pools.[74] The HIV-1-specific memory CD8+ T cell pool is predominantly composed of pre-terminally differentiated CD8+ T cells, as compared with the CMV-specific memory CD8+ T cell pool, which is mostly composed of terminally differentiated CD8+ T cells.[74] The differences in the maturation between HIV-1-specific and CMV-specific CD8+ T cells are probably associated with a different lytic capacity, since CMV- but not HIV-1-specific CD8+ T cells have normal intracellular levels of perforin.[100] More importantly, the different composition in the pool of memory CD8+ T cells seems to translate into a different efficacy in the control of the two virus infections: effective control of CMV infection versus poor control of HIV-1 infection and progressive disease. Taken together, these observations indicate that the detection of large number of antigen-specific CD8+ T cells by tetramer staining as well as a high frequency of IFN-γ secreting cells is not necessarily an indicator of an effective immune response.

Virologic factors

As discussed above, interaction among different host factors helps to determine a certain virologic set point in each HIV-1-infected person after the transition from primary to chronic HIV-1 infection.[44,45] This set point represents the level of plasma viral RNA that accurately predicts disease progression (i.e. the level of plasma viremia that corresponds to a risk of progression to either AIDS or death). In the past, many predictors have been identified, clinical, biologic and virologic. The CD4+ T cell count is historically the most important and widely used predictor. However, the load of plasma RNA is nowadays the most accurate predictor, especially when used along with the CD4+ T cell count.[45] Therefore, the higher the plasma viral RNA load, the greater the risk of rapid progression to AIDS and death. It is worth noting that the power of association between levels of plasma HIV-1 RNA and risk of progression does not significantly vary if viremia is measured after seroconversion (i.e. knowing the date and duration of HIV-1 infection) or during the established chronic asymptomatic phase (i.e. with no available information about the duration of the infection, as is often the case in clinical settings).[44] Viral load is therefore a very powerful predictor if measured during the chronic asymptomatic phase, once the virologic set point has been reached.

However, the level of plasma viral RNA lacks accuracy and reliability as a predictor if measured during primary HIV-1 infection.[104] In this phase, rapid disease progression is predicted by:

- a retroviral syndrome lasting more than 14 days;
- the number and the intensity of clinical signs and symptoms;
- central nervous system involvement; and
- viral phenotype.

The viral phenotype is an important virologic factor that can contribute to the rate of disease progression. R5 HIV-1 strains are non-syncytium-inducing strains, whereas X4 HIV-1 strains are syncytium-inducing strains. Syncytium-inducing strains tend to emerge during the late phase of the disease and a shift in viral phenotype from non-syncytium-inducing strains to syncytium-inducing strains heralds disease progression. The viral phenotype of the non-syncytium-inducing strains is associated with prolonged AIDS-free survival and is more commonly found in long-term nonprogressors.[105]

ERADICATION OF HIV-1 INFECTION

An understanding of the immunologic and virologic events that occur during primary HIV-1 infection and that lead to the establishment of the chronic phase has been achieved. Also, the mechanisms that HIV-1 has evolved in order to escape the immune response, have been elucidated. These advances have challenged the most widely accepted theories about the feasibility of HIV eradication.

Decay of HIV-1-infected compartments after highly active antiretroviral combination therapy

The recent development of HAART has permitted the study of the decay of the different HIV-infected compartments after effective suppression of virus replication and, thus, the estimation of the turnover of both virions and cells supporting virus replication. These studies[106–108] have proposed a two-phase decay model of viral load (Fig. 120.5). By assessing the decay of plasma viral RNA after HAART, it has been estimated that about 10^{10}–10^{11} virions are pro-

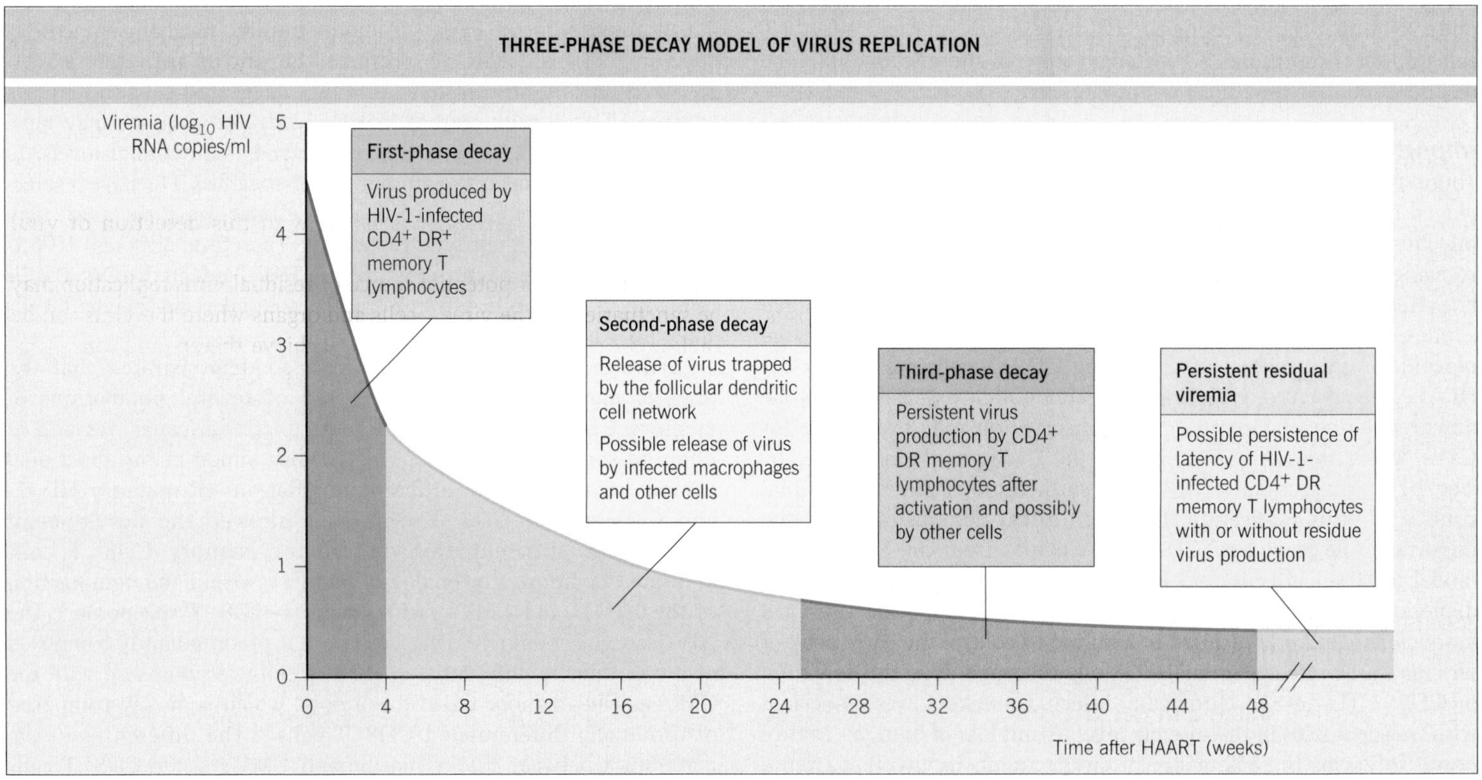

Fig. 120.5 Three-phase decay model of virus replication. Viremia below 50 HIV-1 RNA copies/ml plasma does not correspond to complete suppression of virus replication. Residual viremia (5–10 HIV-1 RNA copies/ml plasma) may still be detected 48 weeks after initiation of HAART. However, it is still unclear whether HAART induces complete suppression of virus replication and, if it does, what duration of HAART is needed to achieve this goal.

duced daily. Two factors determine the decay and the inclination of the slope of plasma viremia after HAART:

- the extent of clearance of virions, and
- the decrease in the number of cells actively producing virus as a result of the inhibition of new rounds of infection.

By means of mathematical models, it has been determined that free virions are eliminated with a half-life of 6 hours, whereas productively infected cells have a half-life of 1.6 days.[107–109] The combination of these two events explains the first rapid phase of decay of plasma viremia. The nature of this phenomenon is clarified by the mechanisms leading to productive HIV-1 infection. As discussed above, although HIV-1 can target different populations of cells – $CD4^+$ T cells, monocytes and macrophages, dendritic cells and others – virus replication is mostly supported by activated $CD4^+$ T cells with the memory phenotype. The preferential replication in $CD4^+$ T cells can be explained by the physiologic differences and by the differential anatomic distribution of the various cells targeted by HIV. No efficient virus replication can occur without activation of the target cell. Although HIV-1 is able to infect resting $CD4^+$ T cells, proviral DNA is not integrated and thus no active virus replication is achieved. The state of target cell activation is therefore a fundamental requirement for HIV-1 to replicate efficiently.

$CD4^+$ T cell activation may be caused either by antigen-specific stimulation or by the physiologic activation of the small number of cycling $CD4^+$ T cells. About 1% of $CD4^+$ and $CD8^+$ T cells are proliferating at any given time in healthy people. Monocytes, macrophages and dendritic cells turn over at a much lower rate than do T cells, and their activation is probably limited to sites of inflammation. Therefore, the activated pool of proliferating $CD4^+$ T cells can support efficient replication of HIV-1, whereas other cell types, although being susceptible to HIV-1 infection, are probably responsible for a negligible amount of virus production. In addition, cells that continuously recirculate from lymph nodes to the bloodstream are almost exclusively $CD4^+$ T cells. These observations explain not only why $CD4^+$ T cells are responsible for between 98% and 99% of the total virus produced, but also the fact that the use of HAART, which efficiently inhibits the virus so that it cannot complete its replication cycle, causes a rapid and steep decrease in the plasma viral load (first phase of decay).[108,109]

The first phase of decay of plasma viremia is then followed by a much slower reduction of the levels of HIV-1 RNA in plasma (second phase of decay). Tissue macrophages and long-lived, latently infected T cells could support the residual virus replication, havinga half-life of 1–4 weeks and 0.5–2 weeks, respectively. More likely, HIV-1 virions are released from the deposits trapped in the follicular dendritic cell network in the germinal centers of the lymphoid tissues. In support of this hypothesis, HAART efficiently depletes these deposits over a period of 6–12 months.[110] Consistently, this second phase of decay is flatter and tends to last much longer than the first one.

On the basis of this two-phase decay model, eradication of HIV-1 was hypothesized as being achievable in a relatively short time – between 2 and 3 years.[109] However, this goal could be realized only if a complete suppression of virus replication had been sustained and if there were no pool of long-lived, latently infected cells to serve as a virus reservoir.[27–31]

The results obtained from HIV-1-infected patients after long-term HAART (2–3 years of treatment) have significantly challenged these theories. In this regard, a pool of latently HIV-1-infected resting memory $CD4^+$ T cells can be detected in HIV-1-infected patients who have adhered to HAART for up to 3 years.[27–31] This pool possesses a longer half-life than the original estimate of 1–4 weeks and is composed of quiescent memory $CD4^+$ T cells. More importantly, these cells contain replication-competent proviral DNA, and after appropriate activation they are able to support efficient viral replication.

Although the estimated extent of this pool is quantitatively limited, ranging between 50,000 and 5,000,000 resting memory $CD4^+$ T cells for the whole body,[27–31] this pool of cells has been estimated to have a half-life of 3–6 months,[109] which corresponds approximately to the half-life of uninfected resting memory $CD4^+$ T cells, thus dramatically changing the estimates of the potential time required for HIV-1 eradication.

As mentioned above, this pool probably originates from productively infected cells at the time of the primary HIV-1 infection. It is noteworthy that initiation of HAART as early as 10 days after the onset of symptoms of primary HIV-1 infection does not prevent the generation of this pool, despite the successful control of plasma viremia shortly after initiation of HAART. This emphasizes the rapidity with which viral reservoirs are established after initial infection, and HAART is probably not able to interfere with this immunopathogenic process. It is, therefore, clear that this pool of cells represents a major obstacle in the attempt to eradicate HIV-1 completely in infected people.

The immunopathogenic role of long-lived resting memory $CD4^+$ T cells in HIV-1 infection may reside not only in their function as a reservoir but also in the fact that they may possess the ability to support virus production in vivo, albeit at low levels.[111] Results from several clinical trials show that viral load decreases below detectable levels (i.e. below either 400 copies or 50 copies of HIV-1 RNA/ml plasma) in the majority of HIV-1-infected persons taking HAART for over 6 months. However, the recent availability of more sensitive tests that can detect viremia down to 5 copies of HIV-1 RNA/ml plasma[112] has significantly changed the interpretation of such results, indicating that viral load below 50 copies does not necessarily correspond to complete suppression of viral replication. Between 40% and 60% of patients have levels of viremia that are lower than 50 but higher than 5 HIV-1 RNA copies/ml plasma after 36–48 weeks of HAART. This indicates that the use of ultrasensitive tests measuring plasma viremia allows both detection and quantification of residual virus production.

These observations complicate the situation, in that persistence of very low residual levels of virus replication may be another mechanism through which HIV-1 is able to maintain itself in the host by renewing the pool of cells that can serve as a reservoir. In fact, long-lived infected $CD4^+$ T cells may be responsible for supporting the residual viral replication in vivo. The rapid rebound of plasma viremia to pretherapy levels that occurs within 2–4 weeks of stopping long-term HAART is consistent with this detection of viral persistence.[111]

However, another potential source of residual virus replication may be sanctuaries for the virus – cells and organs where the virus can be sheltered or where HAART does not achieve therapeutic concentrations of drug (Table 120.2). Tissue sanctuaries for the virus include the lymphoid tissue, the mucosa-associated lymphoid tissue, the genital organs and the central nervous system, where the achievable

TISSUE AND CELLULAR SANCTUARIES FOR HIV-1	
Tissue sanctuaries	**Cellular sanctuaries**
Lymphoid organs	Resting memory $CD4^+$ T cells
Mucosal-associated lymphoid tissue	Macrophages
Central nervous system	Microglial cells
Cerebrospinal fluid	Langerhans cells
Genital organs	

Table 120.2 Tissue and cellular sanctuaries for HIV-1.

concentration of antiviral drugs, in particular of protease inhibitors, may be suboptimal. These sites may serve both as a potential source of low-level virus replication and as a reservoir of latently HIV-1-infected cells. Latently infected resting CD4+ memory T cells, macrophages, microglial cells, dendritic cells and Langerhans cells may conceivably be cellular sanctuaries for HIV-1.

It appears, then, that cells with a prolonged turnover and a decreased extent of activation, which reduces the susceptibility of HAART, and structures where the bioavailability of antiviral drugs is limited further complicate the issue of HIV-1 eradication.

These observations may indicate the existence of residual virus replication (viremia), whose decay is difficult to evaluate, based on the limited sensitivity of the available laboratory assays.[111] Furthermore, it is difficult to envisage to what extent the population of long-lived latently HIV-infected resting CD4+ T cells may affect the putative time needed to achieve eradication of HIV-1, because no conclusive data are available on the half-life of these cells. However, the time to eradicate HIV-1 has now been set up to 5–10 years, considering a half-life of 4 months for these cells and provided that effective and durable suppression of viral replication is achieved by HAART.

Production of CD4+ T cells after highly active antiretroviral combination therapy

The issue of HIV-1 eradication is also linked to the extent of immune restoration that can be achieved with the prolonged use of HAART. In this context, the study of the kinetics of proliferating CD4+ T cells carried out in both peripheral blood and lymph nodes of HIV-1-infected persons at an early stage of infection has yielded important insights into the extent of HAART-induced restoration of immunity.[113]

Estimates of the production of CD4+ T cells can be obtained by assessing the proportion of cells that are positive for the Ki67 antigen, which is a nuclear antigen associated with proliferation. Using this approach, it is possible to define three phases in the kinetics of production of CD4+ T cells after HAART. Shortly after the initiation of HAART, a rapid increase in peripheral CD4+ T cell counts can be observed, which is not associated with an increase of proliferating CD4+ T cells. The rise in the counts of CD4+ T cells may be associated with a redistribution of T cells from lymphoid compartments, and therefore this first phase may be termed the 'phase of redistribution'. After this phase, there is a progressive and significant increase in the number of proliferating CD4+ T cells. This occurs between 12 and 48 weeks of HAART. During this phase, the 'phase of production', a significant restoration in the CD4+ T cell count occurs. Interestingly, in HIV-1-infected patients who are receiving HAART and who have peripheral CD4+ T cell counts that return to normal levels and remain stable, the phase of production is replaced with a 'plateau phase', as the fraction of proliferating CD4+ T cells tends either to stabilize or to decrease after 36–48 weeks of HAART.

These observations emphasize the fact that the regenerative capacity of CD4+ T cells is present and functional during the early chronic phase of HIV-1 infection. Furthermore, the institution of HAART may play a crucial role in driving the restoration of CD4+ T cells to normal levels.

HIGHLY ACTIVE ANTIRETROVIRAL COMBINATION THERAPY COMBINED WITH IMMUNE-BASED STRATEGIES

There are some important limitations associated with the use of HAART. First, eradication of HIV-1 after HAART cannot be achieved in the originally estimated time (2–3 years) and it probably cannot be eradicated in less than 50–60 years. As discussed above, the T cell reservoir of HIV-1, which is established very early in the natural history of the disease; the residual virus production that persists despite prolonged, effective HAART; and the presence of sanctuaries for the virus constitute major obstacles for the long-term control and eradication of the virus. At the same time, these facts emphasize that simply waiting for the natural extinction of long-lived, latently infected cells may not be a good option because it is unrealistic to maintain HAART over the estimated prolonged period of time needed to achieve HIV-1 eradication.

Second, the questions of when to initiate HAART during established chronic HIV-1 infection and which drugs to use in combination as first-choice therapy are important ones, owing to the observed virologic failure that occurs in about half the HIV-infected persons who take HAART.[114–116] Virologic failure, however, is more likely in persons who have previously received suboptimal antiviral therapy, such as monotherapy or dual therapy with reverse transcriptase inhibitors; moreover, virologic failure depends on both the clinical stage of HIV-1 disease and the adherence to treatment. On the other hand, the use of HAART in antiviral-therapy-naive asymptomatic HIV-1-infected persons at an early stage of the disease (i.e. when the CD4+ T cell count is 300–400 cells/ml or more) is rarely associated with virologic failure, provided there is good adherence to therapy. Adherence is obviously related to the acceptability of antiviral combination therapy in terms of both daily number and schedule of pills and to drug toxicity. The acceptability of protease inhibitor-sparing regimens[117] is likely to be superior to that of protease inhibitor-containing regimens. However, the long-term virologic and immunologic responses to the former need to be investigated further.

Third, drug toxicity is a fundamental issue. Particular attention has recently been focused on the long-term effects of HAART on metabolism, which include glucose intolerance and altered levels of lipids and fat distribution;[118] however, from an intention-to-treat viewpoint, the benefits that HAART can provide outweigh the drug-toxicity-related risks.

Taken together, these observations emphasize that HAART used alone is unlikely to eradicate HIV-1 infection. However, HAART is undoubtedly the cornerstone of HIV-1 therapy, because it is able to induce effective and durable suppression of virus replication, to block disease progression and to provide some restoration of the immune response despite the presence of residual virus replication. Highly active antiretroviral combination therapy is at present the best available option to prepare the necessary background (i.e. the best achievable control of virus replication and the greatest possible immune restoration) for subsequent immune-based therapies aimed at long-term control or eradication of HIV-1.

There are several possible objectives of immune-based therapies to achieve both the induction of immune-mediated control of HIV-1 and the elimination of cellular sanctuaries for the virus (see Chapter 140).[111] These objectives include:

- the maintenance or enhancement of existing HIV-1-specific immune responses and the restoration or strengthening of nonspecific immune responses; therapies with interleukin-2 may be the best tool for achieving these goals, because they can improve CD4+ helper T cell function and cell-mediated immunity;
- the induction of HIV-1-specific immune responses *de novo*, using therapeutic vaccine strategies with HIV-1-specific antigens; and
- contributing to the clearance of the pool of latently HIV-1-infected cells – strategies aimed at inducing massive activation of memory CD4+ T cells are being developed because activating these cells may reactivate replication of latent HIV-1 and thus cause virus-mediated killing of the target cell, or virus eradication by HAART.

It is, however, worth noting that the accomplishment of these strategies must take into account both the time of initiation of HAART and the stage of the disease, because different immune-based therapies and the type of immune restoration vary according to these factors. Before the introduction of immune-based therapies it is necessary to suppress virus replication efficiently with HAART. Finally, the stage of HIV-1 disease may warrant different rationales of immune-based intervention.[118]

REFERENCES

1. Pantaleo G, Cohen O, Graziosi C, *et al.* Immunopathogenesis of human immunodeficiency virus infection. In: De Vita VTJ, Hellman S, Rosenberg SA, eds. AIDS. Philadelphia: Lippincott-Raven; 1997:78–88.
2. Kahn JO, Walker BD. Acute human immunodeficiency virus type I infection. N Engl J Med 1998;339:33–9.
3. Koup RA, Safrit JT, Cao Y, *et al.* Temporal association of cellular immune responses with the initial control of viremia in primary human immunodeficiency virus type 1 syndrome. J Virol 1994;68:4650–5.
4. Borrow P, Lewicki H, Hahn BH, Shaw GM, Oldstone MB. Virus-specific CD8+ cytotoxic T-lymphocyte activity associated with control of viremia in primary human immunodeficiency virus type 1 infection. J Virol 1994;68:6103–10.
5. Pantaleo G, Demarest JF, Soudeyns H, *et al.* Major expansion of CD8+ T cells with a predominant Vb usage during the primary immune response to HIV. Nature 1994;370:463–7.
6. Musey L, Hughes J, Schacker T, Shea T, Corey L, McElrath MJ. Cytotoxic-T-cell responses, viral load, and disease progression in early human immunodeficiency virus type 1. N Engl J Med 1997;337:1267–74.
7. Pantaleo G, Graziosi C, Demarest JF, *et al.* HIV infection is active and progressive in lymphoid tissue during the clinically latent stage of disease. Nature 1993;362:355–8.
8. Pantaleo G, Cohen OJ, Schacker T, *et al.* Evolutionary pattern of human immunodeficiency virus (HIV) replication and distribution in lymph nodes following primary infection: implications for antiviral therapy. Nat Med 1998;4:341–5.
9. Pantaleo G, Vaccarezza M, Graziosi C, Cohen OJ, Fauci AS. Antiviral immunity in HIV-1 infected long-term non-progressors. Semin Virol 1996;7:131–8.
10. Fauci AS. Host factors and the pathogenesis of HIV-induced disease. Nature 1996;384:529–34.
11. Royce RA, Seña A, Cates WJ, Cohen MS. Sexual transmission of HIV. N Engl J Med 1997;336:1072–8.
12. Spira AI, Marx PA, Patterson BK, *et al.* Cellular targets of infection and route of viral dissemination after an intravaginal inoculation of simian immunodeficiency virus into rhesus macaques. J Exp Med 1996;183:215–25.
13. Steinman MR. DC-SIGN: a guide to some mysteries of dendritic cells. Cell 2000;100:491–4.
14. Geijtenbeek TB, Torensma R, van Vliet SJ, *et al.* Identification of DC-SIGN, a novel dendritic cell-specific ICAM-3 receptor that supports primary immune response. Cell 2000;100:575–85.
15. Cameron P, Pope M, Granelli-Piperno A, Steinman RM. Dendritic cells and the replication of HIV-1. J Leukoc Biol 1996;59:158–71.
16. Zhu T, Mo H, Wang N, *et al.* Genotypic and phenotypic characterization of HIV-1 patients with primary infection. Science 1993;261:1179–81.
17. Zhu T, Wang N, Carr A, *et al.* Genetic characterization of human immunodeficiency virus type 1 in blood and genital secretions: evidence for viral compartmentalization and selection during sexual transmission. J Virol 1996;70:3098–107.
18. Geijtenbeek TB, Kwon DS, Torensma R, *et al.* DC-SIGN, a dendritic cell-specific HIV-1-binding protein that enhances trans-infection of T cells. Cell 2000;100:587–597.
19. Dalgleish AG, Beverley PC, Clapham PR, Crawford DH, Greaves MF, Weiss RA. The CD4 (T4) antigen is an essential component of the receptor for the AIDS retrovirus. Nature 1984;312:763–7.
20. Klatzmann D, Champagne E, Chamaret S, *et al.* T-lymphocyte T4 molecule behaves as the receptor for human retrovirus LAV. Nature 1984;312:767–8.
21. Maddon PJ, Dalgleish AG, McDougal JS, Clapham PR, Weiss RA, Axel R. The T4 gene encodes the AIDS virus receptor and is expressed in the immune system and the brain. Cell 1986;47:333–48.
22. Zaitseva M, Blauvelt A, Lee S, *et al.* Expression and function of CCR5 and CXCR4 on human Langerhans cells and macrophages: implications for HIV primary infection. Nat Med 1997;3:1369–75.
23. Weissman D, Rabin RL, Arthos J, *et al.* Macrophage-tropic HIV and SIV envelope proteins induce a signal through the CCR5 chemokine receptor. Nature 1997;389:981–5.
24. Chakrabarti L, Isola P, Cumont MC, *et al.* Early stages of simian immunodeficiency virus infection in lymph nodes. Evidence for high viral load and successive populations of target cells. Am J Pathol 1994;144:1226–37.
25. Graziosi C, Soudeyns H, Rizzardi GP, Bart PA, Chapuis A, Pantaleo G. Immunopathogenesis of HIV infection. AIDS Res Hum Retroviruses 1998;14(Suppl.):135–42.
26. Soudeyns H, Pantaleo G. The moving target. Immunol Today 1999;20:446–50.
27. Chun TW, Finzi D, Margolick J, Chadwick K, Schwartz D, Siliciano RF. In vivo fate of HIV-1-infected T cells: quantitative analysis of the transition to stable latency. Nat Med 1995;1:1284–90.
28. Chun TW, Carruth L, Finzi D, *et al.* Quantification of latent tissue reservoirs and total body viral load in HIV-1 infection. Nature 1997;387:183–8.
29. Finzi D, Hermankova M, Pierson T, *et al.* Identification of a reservoir for HIV-1 in patients on highly active antiretroviral therapy. Science 1997;278:1295–300.
30. Chun TW, Stuyver L, Mizell SB, *et al.* Presence of an inducible HIV-1 latent reservoir during highly active antiretroviral therapy. Proc Natl Acad Sci USA 1997;94:13193–7.
31. Wong JK, Hezareh M, Gunthard HF, *et al.* Recovery of replication-competent HIV despite prolonged suppression of plasma viremia. Science 1997;278:1291–5.
32. Coffin JM. HIV population dynamics in vivo: implications for genetic variation, pathogenesis, and therapy. Science 1995;267:483–9.
33. Pantaleo G, Graziosi C, Demarest JF, *et al.* Role of lymphoid organs in the pathogenesis of human immunodeficiency virus (HIV) infection. Immunol Rev 1994;140:105–30.
34. Phillips RE, Rowland-Jones S, Nixon DF, *et al.* Human immunodeficiency virus genetic variation that can escape cytotoxic T cell recognition. Nature 1991;354:453–9.
35. Rosenberg ES, Billingsley JM, Caliendo AM, *et al.* Vigorous HIV-1-specific CD4+ T cell responses associated with control of viremia. Science 1997;278:1447–50.
36. Pantaleo G, Soudeyns H, Demarest JF, *et al.* Evidence for rapid disappearance of initially expanded HIV-specific CD8+ T cell clones during primary infection. Proc Natl Acad Sci USA 1997;94:9848–53.
37. Pantaleo G, Soudeyns H, Demarest JF, *et al.* Accumulation of human immunodeficiency virus-specific cytotoxic T lymphocytes away from the predominant site of virus replication during primary infection. Eur J Immunol 1997;27:3166–73.
38. Pitcher CJ, Quittner C, Peterson DM, *et al.* HIV-1-specific CD4+ T cells are detectable in most individuals with active HIV-1 infection, but decline with prolonged viral suppression. Nat Med 1999;5:518–525.
39. Palmer BE, Boritz E, Blyveis N, Wilson CC. Discordance between frequency of human immunodeficiency virus type 1 (HIV-1)-specific gamma interferon-producing CD4(+) T cells and HIV-1-specific lymphoproliferation in HIV-1-infected subjects with active viral replication. J Virol 2002;76:5925–36.
40. Harari A, Rizzardi GP, Ellefsen K, *et al.* Analysis of HIV-1- and CMV-specific memory CD4 T cell responses during primary and chronic infection. Blood 2002;100:1381–7.
41. Ogg GS, Jin X, Bonhoeffer S, *et al.* Quantitation of HIV-1-specific cytotoxic T lymphocytes and plasma load of viral RNA. Science 1998;279:2103–6.
42. Haynes BF, Pantaleo G, Fauci AS. Toward an understanding of the correlates of protective immunity to HIV infection. Science 1996;271:324–8.
43. Collins KL, Chen BK, Kalams SA, Walker BD, Baltimore D. HIV-1 Nef protein protects infected primary cells against killing by cytotoxic T lymphocytes. Nature 1998;391:397–401.
44. Mellors JW, Rinaldo CR, Gupta P, White RM, Todd JA, Kingsley LA. Prognosis in HIV-1 infection predicted by the quantity of virus in plasma. Science 1996;272:1167–70.
45. Mellors JW, Munoz A, Giorgi JV, *et al.* Plasma viral load and CD4+ lymphocytes as prognostic markers of HIV-1 infection. Ann Intern Med 1997;126:946–54.
46. Deng H, Liu R, Ellmeier W, *et al.* Identification of a major co-receptor for primary isolates of HIV-1. Nature 1996;381:661–6.
47. Dragic T, Litwin V, Allaway GP, *et al.* HIV-1 entry into CD4+ cells is mediated by the chemokine receptor CC-CKR-5. Nature 1996;381:667–73.
48. Alkhatib G, Combadiere C, Broder CC, *et al.* CC CKR5: a RANTES, MIP-1α, MIP-1β receptor as a fusion cofactor for macrophage-tropic HIV-1. Science 1996;272:1955–8.
49. Feng Y, Broder CC, Kennedy PE, Berger EA. HIV-1 entry cofactor: functional cDNA cloning of a seven-transmembrane, G protein-coupled receptor. Science 1996;272:872–7.
50. Choe H, Farzan M, Sun Y, *et al.* The beta-chemokine receptors CCR3 and CCR5 facilitate infection by primary HIV-1 isolates. Cell 1996;85:1135–48.
51. Doranz BJ, Rucker J, Yi Y, *et al.* A dual-tropic primary HIV-1 isolate that uses fusin and the beta-chemokine receptors CKR-5, CKR-3, and CKR-2b as fusion cofactors. Cell 1996;85:1149–58.
52. Dean M, Carrington M, Winkler C, *et al.* Genetic restriction of HIV-1 infection and progression to AIDS by a deletion allele of the

CKR5 structural gene. Science 1996;273:1856–62.
53. Morawetz RA, Rizzardi GP, Glauser D, *et al.* Genetic polymorphism of CCR5 gene and HIV disease: the heterozygous (CCR5/ΔCCR5) genotype is neither essential nor sufficient for protection against disease progression. Eur J Immunol 1997;27:3223–7.
54. Garzino-Demo A, DeVico AL, Cocchi F, Gallo RC. β-chemokines and protection from HIV type 1 disease. AIDS Res Hum Retroviruses 1998;14(Suppl.):177–84.
55. Quillent C, Oberlin E, Braun J, *et al.* HIV-1-resistance phenotype conferred by combination of two separate inherited mutations of CCR5 gene. Lancet 1997;351:14–8.
56. Smith MW, Dean M, Carrington M, *et al.* Contrasting genetic influence of CCR2 and CCR5 variants on HIV-1 infection and disease progression. Science 1997;277:959–65.
57. Smith MW, Carrington M, Winkler C, *et al.* CCR2 chemokine receptor and AIDS progression. Nat Med 1997;3:1052–3.
58. Rizzardi GP, Morawetz RA, Vicenzi E, *et al.* CCR2 polymorphism and HIV disease. Nat Med 1998;4:252–3.
59. Kostrikis LG, Huang Y, Moore JP, *et al.* A chemokine receptor CCR2 allele delays HIV-1 disease progression and is associated with a CCR5 promoter mutation. Nat Med 1998;4:350–3.
60. Michael N, Louie LG, Rohrbaugh AL, *et al.* The role of CCR5 and CCR2 polymorphisms in HIV-1 transmission and disease progression. Nat Med 1997;3:1160–2.
61. Winkler C, Modi W, Smith MW, *et al.* Genetic restriction of AIDS pathogenesis by an SDF-1 chemokine gene variant. Science 1998;279:389–93.
62. Mummidi S, Ahuja SS, Gonzalez E, *et al.* Genealogy of the CCR5 locus and chemokine system gene variants associated with altered rates of HIV-1 disease progression. Nat Med 1998;4:786–93.
63. Cocchi F, DeVico AL, Garzino-Demo A, Arya SK, Gallo RC, Lusso P. Identification of RANTES, MIP-1 alpha, and MIP-1 beta as the major HIV-suppressive factors produced by CD8+ T cells. Science 1995;270:1811–5.
64. Paxton WA, Martin SR, Tse D, *et al.* Relative resistance to HIV-1 infection of CD4 lymphocytes from persons who remain uninfected despite multiple high-risk sexual exposure. Nat Med 1996;2:412–7.
65. Zagury D, Lachgar A, Chams V, *et al.* C-C chemokines, pivotal in protection against HIV type 1 infection. Proc Natl Acad Sci USA 1998;95:3857–61.
66. Ullum H, Cozzi LA, Victor J, *et al.* Production of beta-chemokines in human immunodeficiency virus (HIV) infection: evidence that high levels of macrophage inflammatory protein-1β are associated with a decreased risk of HIV disease progression. J Infect Dis 1998;177:331–6.
67. Topham DJ, Doherty PC. Longitudinal analysis of the acute Sendai Virus-specific CD4+ T cell response and memory. J Immunol 1998;160:3790–6.
68. Von Herrath MG, Yokoyama M, Dockter J, Oldstone MB, Whitton JL. CD4-deficient mice have reduced levels of memory cytotoxic T lymphocytes after immunization and show diminished resistance to subsequent virus challenge. J Virol 1996;70:1072–9.
69. Matloubian M, Concepcion RJ, Ahmed R. CD4+ T cells are required to sustain CD8+ cytotoxic T-cell responses during chronic viral infection. J Virol 1994;68:8056–63.
70. Pantaleo G, Fauci AS. New concepts in the immunopathogenesis of HIV infection. Annu Rev Immunol 1995;13:487–512.
71. Lane HC, Depper JM, Greene WC, Whalen G, Waldmann TA, Fauci AS. Qualitative analysis of immune function in patients with the acquired immunodeficiency syndrome. Evidence for a selective defect in soluble antigen recognition. N Engl J Med 1985;313:79–84.
72. Clerici M, Stocks NI, Zajac RA, *et al.* Detection of three distinct patterns of T helper cell dysfunction in asymptomatic, human immunodeficiency virus-seropositive patients. Independence of CD4+ cell numbers and clinical staging. J Clin Invest 1989;84:1892–9.
73. Sallusto F, Lenig D, Forster R, Lipp M, Lanzavecchia A. Two subsets of memory T lymphocytes with distinct homing potentials and effector functions. Nature 1999;401:708–12.
74. Champagne P, Ogg GS, King AS, *et al.* Skewed maturation of memory HIV-specific CD8 T lymphocytes. Nature 2001;410:106–11.
75. Rosenberg ES, Altfeld M, Poon SH, *et al.* Immune control of HIV-1 after early treatment of acute infection. Nature 2000;407:523–6.
76. Komanduri KV, Donahoe SM, Moretto WJ, *et al.* Direct measurement of CD4+ and CD8+ T-cell responses to CMV in HIV-1-infected subjects. Virology 2001;279:459–70.
77. Battegay M, Moskophidis D, Rahemtulla A, Hengartner H, Mak TW, Zinkernagel RM. Enhanced establishment of a virus carrier state in adult CD4+ T-cell-deficient mice. J Virol 1994;68:4700–4.
78. Lechner F, Wong DK, Dunbar PR, *et al.* Analysis of successful immune responses in persons infected with hepatitis C virus. J Exp Med 2000;191:1499–512.
79. Schmitz JE, Kuroda MJ, Santra S, *et al.* Control of viremia in simian immunodeficiency virus infection by CD8+ lymphocytes. Science 1999;283:857–60.
80. Jin X, Bauer DE, Tuttleton SE, *et al.* Dramatic rise in plasma viremia after CD8+ T cell depletion in simian immunodeficiency virus-infected macaques. J Exp Med 1999;189:991–8.
81. Koenig S, Conley AJ, Brewah YA, *et al.* Transfer of HIV-1 specific cytotoxic T lymphocytes to an AIDS patient leads to selection for mutant HIV variants and subsequent disease progression. Nat Med 1995;1:330–6.
82. Borrow P, Lewicki H, Wei X, *et al.* Antiviral pressure exerted by HIV-1-specific cytotoxic T lymphocytes (CTLs) during primary infection demonstrated by rapid selection of CTL escape virus. Nat Med 1997;3:205–11.
83. Price DA, Goulder PJ, Klenerman P, *et al.* Positive selection of HIV-1 cytotoxic T lymphocyte escape variants during primary infection. Proc Natl Acad Sci USA 1997;94:1890–5.
84. Goulder PJ, Phillips RE, Colbert RA, *et al.* Late escape from an immunodominant cytotoxic T-lymphocyte response associated with progression to AIDS. Nat Med 1997;3:212–7.
85. Kelleher AD, Long C, Holmes EC, *et al.* Clustered mutations in HIV-1 gag are consistently required for escape from HLA-B27-restricted CTL responses. J Exp Med 2001;193:375–86.
86. Soudeyns H, Paolucci S, Chappey C, *et al.* Selective pressure exerted by immunodominant HIV-1-specific cytotoxic T lymphocyte responses during primary infection drives genetic variation restricted to the cognate epitope. Eur J Immunol 1999;11:3629–35.
87. Kaslow RA, Carrington M, Apple R, *et al.* Influence of combinations of human major histocompatibility complex genes on the course of HIV-1 infection. Nat Med 1996;2:405–11.
88. Rowland-Jones SL, Dong T, Fowke KR, *et al.* Cytotoxic T cell responses to multiple conserved HIV epitopes in HIV-resistant prostitutes in Nairobi. J Clin Invest 1998;102:1758–65.
89. Lifson JD, Rossio JL, Arnaout R, *et al.* Containment of simian immunodeficiency virus infection: cellular immune responses and protection from rechallenge following transient postinoculation antiretroviral treatment. J Virol 2000;74:2584–93.
90. Putkonen P, Makitalo B, Bottiger D, Biberfeld G, Thorstensson R. Protection of human immunodeficiency virus type 2-exposed seronegative macaques from mucosal simian immunodeficiency virus transmission. J Virol 1997;71:4981–4.
91. Betts MR, Ambrozak DR, Douek DC, *et al.* Analysis of total Human Immunodeficiency Virus (HIV)-specific CD4(+) and CD8(+) T-cell responses: relationship to viral load in untreated HIV infection. J Virol 2001;75:11983–91.
92. Meylan PR, Guatelli JC, Munis JR, Richman DD, Kornbluth RS. Mechanisms for the inhibition of HIV replication by interferons-alpha, -beta, and -gamma in primary human macrophages. Virology 1993;193:138–48.
93. Emilie D, Maillot MC, Nicolas JF, Fior R, Galanaud P. Antagonistic effect of interferon-gamma on tat-induced transactivation of HIV long terminal repeat. J Biol Chem 1992;267:20565–70.
94. Bollinger RC, Quinn TC, Liu AY, *et al.* Cytokines from vaccine-induced HIV-1 specific cytotoxic T lymphocytes: effects on viral replication. AIDS Res Hum Retroviruses 1993;9:1067–77.
95. Wagner L, Yang OO, Garcia-Zepeda EA, *et al.* Chemokines are released from HIV-1-specific cytolytic T-cell granules complexed to proteoglycans. Nature 1998;391:908–11.
96. Price DA, Sewell AK, Dong T, *et al.* Antigen-specific release of β-chemokines by anti-HIV-1 cytotoxic T lymphocytes. Curr Biol 1998;8:355–8.
97. Cocchi F, DeVico AL, Garzino-Demo A, *et al.* Identification of RANTES, MIP-1, and MIP-1 as the major HIV-suppressive factors produced by CD8+ T cells. Science 1995;270:1811–5.
98. Mackewicz C, Levy JA. CD8+ cell anti-HIV activity: nonlytic suppression of virus replication. AIDS Res Hum Retroviruses 1992;8:1039–50.
99. Levy JA, Mackewicz CE, Barker E. Controlling HIV pathogenesis: the role of noncytotoxic anti-HIV response of CD8+ T cells. Immunol Today 1996;17:217–24.
100. Appay V, Nixon DF, Donahoe SM, *et al.* HIV-specific CD8+ T cells produce antiviral cytokines but are impaired in cytolytic function. J Exp Med 2000;192:63–75.
101. Yang OO, Kalams SA, Rosenzweig M, *et al.* Efficient lysis of human immunodeficiency virus type 1-infected cells by cytotoxic T lymphocytes. J Virol 1996;70:5799–806.
102. Zajac AJ, Blattman JN, Murali-Krishna K, *et al.* Viral immune evasion due to persistence of activated T cells without effector function. J Exp Med 1998;188:2205–13.
103. Kalams SA, Walker BD. The critical need for CD4 help in maintaining effective cytotoxic T lymphocyte responses. J Exp Med 1998;188:2199–204.
104. Schacker TW, Hughes JP, Shea T, Coombs RW, Corey L. Biological and virologic characteristics of primary HIV infection. Ann Intern Med 1998;128:613–20.
105. Schuitemaker H, Koot M, Kootstra NA, *et al.* Biological phenotype of human immunodeficiency virus type 1 clones at different stages of infection: progression of disease is associated with a shift from monocytotropic to T-cell-tropic virus population. J Virol 1992;66:1354–60.
106. Wei X, Ghosh SK, Taylor ME, *et al.* Viral dynamics in human immunodeficiency virus type 1 infection. Nature 1995;373:117–22.
107. Ho DD, Neumann AU, Perelson AS, Chen W, Leonard JM, Markowitz M. Rapid turnover of plasma virions and CD4 lymphocytes in HIV-1 infection. Nature 1995;373:123–6.
108. Perelson AS, Neumann AU, Markowitz M, Leonard JM, Ho DD. HIV-1 dynamics in vivo: virion clearance rate, infected cell life-span, and viral generation time. Science 1996;271:1852–6.
109. Perelson AS, Essunger P, Cao Y, *et al.* Decay characteristics of HIV-1-infected compartments during combination therapy. Nature 1997;387:188–91.

110. Cavert W, Notermans DW, Staskus K, *et al.* Kinetics of response in lymphoid tissues to antiretroviral therapy of HIV-1 infection. Science 1997;276:960–4.
111. Pantaleo G. How immune-based interventions can change HIV therapy. Nat Med 1997;3:483–6.
112. Pantaleo G, Perrin L. Can HIV be eradicated? AIDS 1998;12(Suppl.):175–80.
113. Fleury S, de Boer RJ, Rizzardi GP, *et al.* Limited $CD4^{+}$ T cell renewal in early HIV-1 infection: effect of highly active antiretroviral therapy. Nat Med 1998;4:794–801.
114. Palella FJJ, Delaney KM, Moorman AC, *et al.* Declining morbidity and mortality among patients with advanced human immunodeficiency virus infection. N Engl J Med 1998;338:853–60.
115. Kaufmann D, Pantaleo G, Sudre P, Telenti A. CD4-cell count in HIV-1 infected individuals remaining viraemic with highly active antiretroviral therapy. Lancet 1998;351:723–4.
116. Piketty C, Castiel P, Belec L, *et al.* Discrepant responses to triple combination antiretroviral therapy in advanced HIV disease. AIDS 1998;12:745–50.
117. Montaner JS, Reiss P, Cooper D, *et al.* A randomized, double-blind trial comparing combinations of nevirapine, didanosine, and zidovudine for HIV-infected patients: the INCAS Trial. JAMA 1998;279:930–7.
118. Flexner C. HIV-protease inhibitors. N Engl J Med 1998;338:1281–92.

chapter

121 Virology of HIV

Chen Liang & Mark A Wainberg

This chapter reviews the life cycle and genetic structure of HIV-1 in the context of understanding how viral and cellular regulatory factors may affect viral replication. Potential as well as current targets of antiviral chemotherapy are discussed. The synthesis of viral proteins and the manner in which viral assembly takes place is also considered.

GENERAL DESCRIPTION OF HIV-1

The virion

The HIV-1 virion forms an icosahedral sphere with projections consisting of the envelope (Env) glycoproteins gp120 and gp41. Gp120 is loosely and noncovalently associated with gp41 and the latter transverses the lipid bilayer. Figure 121.1 is a schematic representation of the mature HIV-1 virion. Under the lipid layer, the matrix (MA) protein (p17) covers the internal surface of the viral coat. The capsid (CA) protein (p24) constitutes the shell of the cone-shaped core, and the nucleocapsid (NC) protein (p7) forms part of a nucleoid structure that also consists of reverse transcriptase (RT), integrase (IN), and two copies of the single-stranded viral genomic RNA.[1]

Genomic organization of HIV-1

The HIV-1 provirus (i.e. the DNA form of the viral nucleic acid) is about 9.5kb in length and contains long terminal repeats (LTRs, 634bp) at each of the 5' and 3' ends.[2] Figure 121.2 is a schematic description of the HIV-1 genome and the known functions of its gene products. The LTRs consist of the U3, R, and U5 regions within which exist *cis*-acting elements essential for viral integration and transcription. RNA synthesis is initiated within the 5'-LTR at the junction between the U3 and R regions. HIV-1 harbors three structural genes (i.e. *gag*, *pol* and *env*) and six regulatory genes (i.e. *vif*, *vpr*, *tat*, *rev*, *vpu* and *nef*). The structural genes code for polyprotein precursors that are involved in virion construction. The open reading frames for the regulatory genes are positioned in the central portion of the genome and flank the *env* gene. The Vpr, Vif as well as Nef proteins are packaged into mature virions.[3–5]

Gag and Gag–Pol proteins

Pr55Gag and its products

The open reading frame of the *gag* gene (1536 nucleotides) is translated directly into a 55kDa Gag precursor (Pr55Gag; Fig. 121.3). This polyprotein is further cleaved by the viral protease (PR) to yield mature proteins, including MA, CA, NC and p6.[6] Although processing of Pr55 can be detected in the cytoplasm, it is generally believed that this event takes place mainly on the membrane of the host cell or inside the released viral particle. Processing of the precursor is accompanied by morphologic rearrangement of virus particles, and this can be visualized by electron microscopy. Notably, cleavage between p24 and p2 at the late stage of virus morphogenesis allows the formation of the cone-shaped core structure.[7] The final products include:

- p17 – MA protein, which comes from the N terminus of Pr55 and is myristylated at its N terminus;
- p24 – CA protein, which is derived from the central part of Pr55 and forms the cone-shaped core;
- p7 – NC protein, which is highly basic and tightly associated with viral genomic RNA;
- p6, which is part of the core structure; and
- p2 and p1 – spacer peptides, which regulate Pr55 processing.

The MA protein directs the intracellular transport and membrane association of the Gag polyprotein.[8] As part of the preintegration complex, MA is also critical for transporting the complex into the nucleus by virtue of a nuclear localization signal (NLS) at its N-terminus; this process is essential for productive infection of non-dividing cells and may be responsible for recruiting viral envelope proteins to the surface of host cells.[9]

The CA forms the core of the mature virion. It is believed that proteolytic liberation of Pro1 (i.e. the first amino acid in CA) allows the formation of a salt bridge between Pro1 and Asp51, which in turn triggers conformational rearrangement of CA and consequently the formation of the core structure.[10] CA contains a major homology region (MHR) at its C-terminus that plays crucial and yet ill-characterized roles in Gag aggregation. CA recruits the cellular factor cyclophilin A (Cyp A) into virus particles; Cyp A is needed for uncoating after virus entry into the host cells.[11]

NC serves as the interaction domain that mediates Gag–Gag interactions. This protein is highly basic and possesses two copies of zinc finger motifs (CCHC). NC binds to nucleic acid sequences and further modifies their structures to thermostable states; thus, this protein is defined as a nucleic acid chaperone. Multiple functional roles of NC protein have been identified and these are:[12]

- to stimulate reverse transcription;
- to assist in viral genomic RNA packaging; and
- to promote dimerization of viral RNA.

The protein p6 contains the late domain (P(T/S)AP) that is needed for successful budding of virus particles from the plasma membrane. p6 is also responsible for the incorporation of Vpr into virus particles.

Certain drugs have been identified that may antagonize the zinc finger regions of the NC proteins. These compounds may conceivably be tested in future clinical trials.

Pr160 and its products

The open reading frame of the *pol* gene (3045 nucleotides) is translated only as a Gag–Pol fusion protein, Pr160, by a translational frameshift mechanism as ribosomes read full-length genomic HIV-1 transcripts. In mature virions, the *gag* and *pol* gene products are found in a ratio of about 20:1 (see Fig. 121.3).[13] The Pol precursor is cleaved to produce PR (p10), RT (p66/51) and IN (p32).[14]

- PR is responsible for processing the Gag and Gag–Pol precursors – mutations in the catalytic region of PR are lethal to the virus;
- RT is responsible for catalyzing the conversion of viral RNA into DNA (reverse transcription); and
- IN plays a key role in inserting viral DNA into the host cell chromosome.

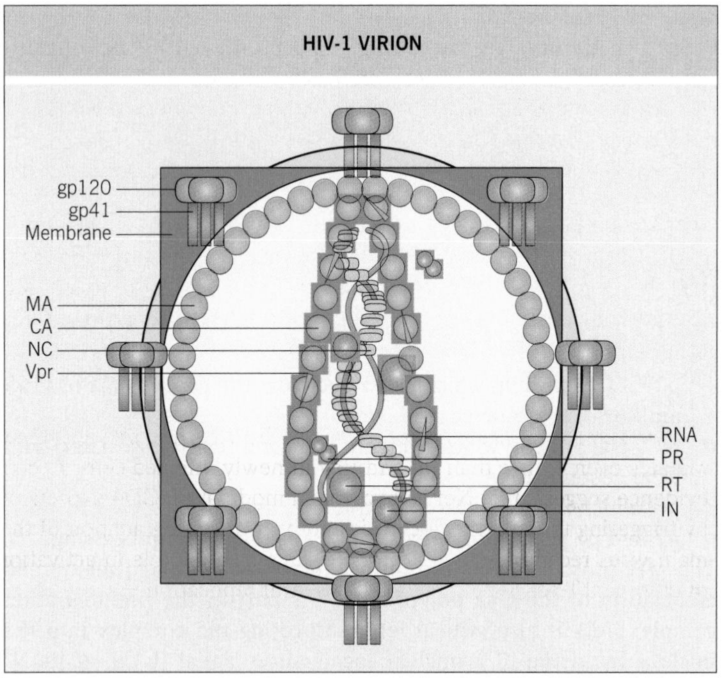

Fig. 121.1 HIV-1 virion. The glycoprotein gp120 constitutes the outer envelope of the virus and is noncovalently linked to the transmembrane protein gp41. The matrix protein (p17) bridges the envelope protein with the cone-shaped structure formed by the capsid protein (p24). The viral genomic RNA and processed nucleocapsid (NC; p7) and Pol proteins, reverse transcriptase (RT) and integrase (IN), are located inside the capsid core. PR, protease.

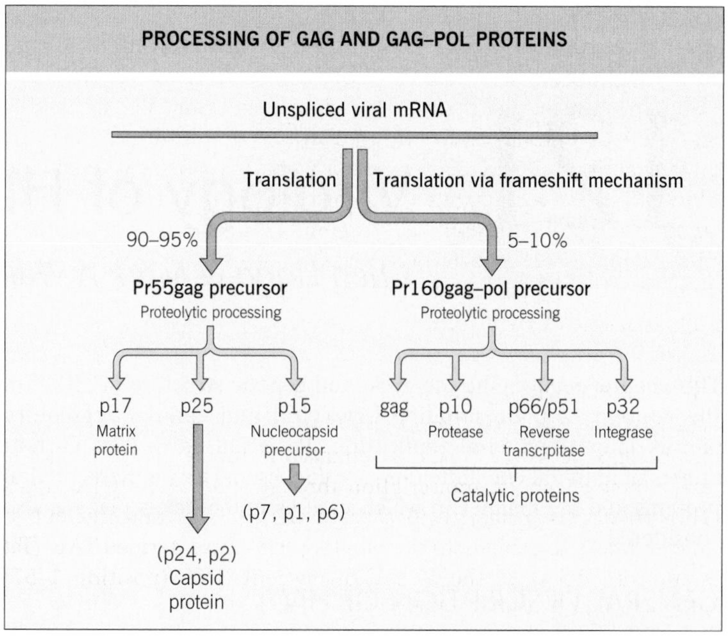

Fig. 121.3 Processing of Gag and Gag–Pol proteins. The Gag proteins are initially translated as a 55kDa polyprecursor. Proteolytic processing of Pr55Gag generates several mature products. The catalytic proteins, including reverse transcriptase (RT), integrase (IN) and protease (PR), are first produced as a Gag–Pol precursor (Pr160Gag–Pol) through a translational frameshift mechanism; Pr160Gag-Pol is then cleaved to the smaller enzymatically active subunits.

To date, viral RT and PR have been the principal targets of antiviral chemotherapy. Viral IN represents another obvious target for such efforts, and development of drugs that target IN constitutes an important area of research.

The *env* gene and its products

The *env* gene is translated into a polyprotein of 160kDa. This precursor protein is folded and further glycosylated in the endoplasmic reticulum (ER) and Golgi apparatus before being trans-

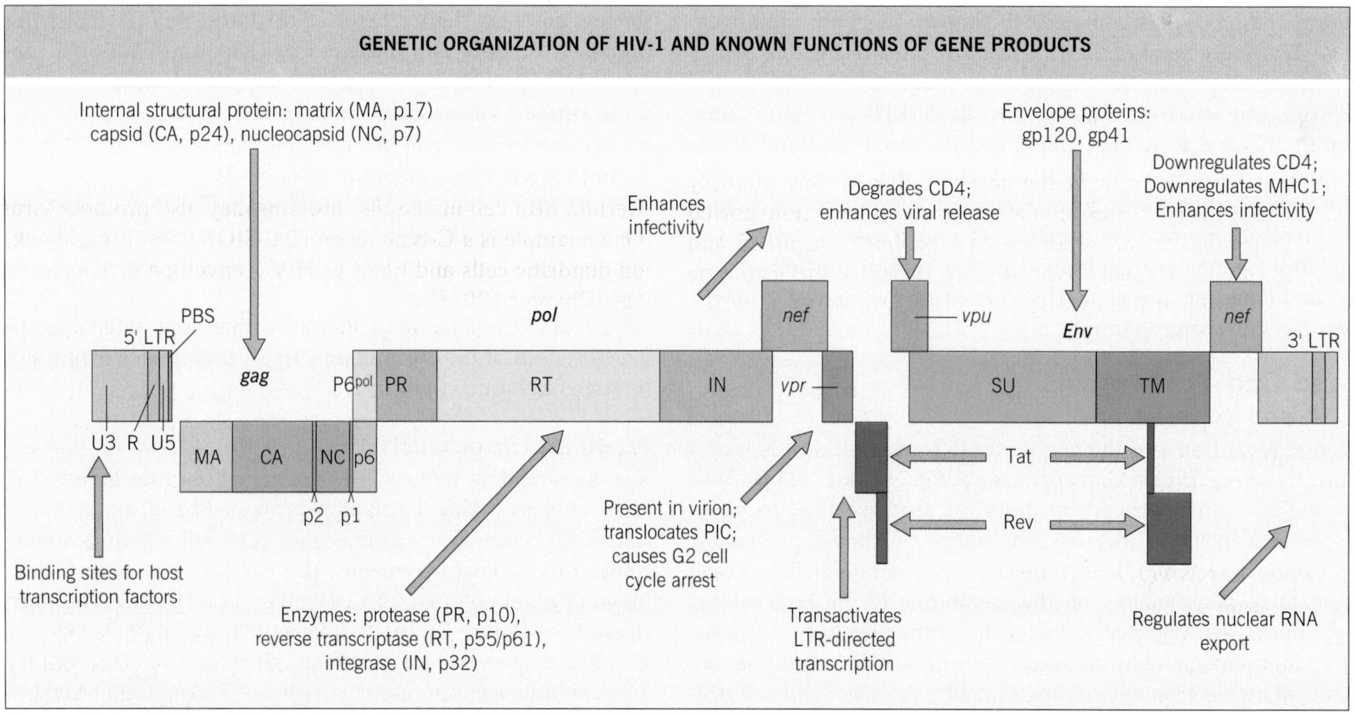

Fig. 121.2 Genetic organization of HIV-1 and known functions of gene products. The structural genes are *gag, gag–pol* and *env*. Catalytic proteins are encoded by the *pol* gene. Regulatory proteins are translated from fully spliced mRNA. Within the HIV-1 genome, there are additional open reading frames that flank the *env* gene and encode several regulatory proteins including Vif, Vpr, Tat, Rev, Vpu and Nef. LTR, long terminal repeat; PIC, pre-integration complex consisting of viral cDNA, IN, RT, Vpr, MA and NC.

ported to the plasma membrane. A signal peptide (about 30 amino acid residues) at the N terminus of gp160 is removed and a subsequent proteolytic step in the Golgi compartment, mediated by a cellular enzyme, yields the N-terminal gp120 and the C-terminal gp41.[1] Although the external viral protein gp120 plays a key role in interacting with the CD4 receptor and/or co-receptor of susceptible cells,[15] the transmembrane protein gp41 is responsible for anchoring gp120 through noncovalent interactions and mediating the fusion process between viruses and target cells. Peptide inhibitors have been developed that specifically bind to gp41 and thus block virus entry.[16]

HIV-1 regulatory proteins

Tat protein, or viral transactivator

Tat belongs to a novel class of eukaryotic regulatory proteins that exert their effects on transcription through binding to RNA motifs. This protein is primarily located in the nucleus and nucleoli of infected cells and binds to a stem–loop structure, termed TAR (Tat-associated RNA), at the 5' end of nascent RNA (position 1–57). Interaction of Tat and RNA may:

- increase the stability of the RNA polymerase to allow more efficient synthesis of full-length transcripts;
- increase the frequency of RNA initiation; and
- increase the efficiency of translation of TAR-containing RNA.

Tat plays its roles in transcription activation through recruitment of cellular factors to the transcription complex that is assembled along the LTR promoter. Tat directly interacts with cellular factor cyclin T1 and the ternary complex thus assembled, together with TAR RNA, further recruits cyclin-T-dependent kinase (CDK)9, which, in turn, phosphorylates the C-terminal domain (CTD) of RNA polymerase II.[17] Tat can also regulate HIV-1 reverse transcription.[18,19] In addition, Tat exerts a variety of effects on cell growth and proliferation and is likely to play a significant role in selective depletion of infected cells by triggering apoptosis.

Rev protein (regulator of virion protein expression)

Rev has a profound effect on the fate of primary RNA transcripts within the nucleus. Like Tat, Rev is located primarily in the nucleus and nucleoli of infected cells. The Rev protein binds to a complex stem–loop structure, the Rev-responsive region (RRE), within the HIV-1 *env* gene. The RRE is present in both full-length and singly spliced viral RNAs but is excluded by splicing from multiply spliced viral mRNAs. Consequently, in the absence of Rev, only multiply spliced RNAs, which encode regulatory proteins, are transported into the cytoplasm. In the presence of Rev, both unspliced and singly spliced viral mRNAs (for viral structural and catalytic proteins) are found in the cytoplasm. Rev shuttles between the nucleus and the cytoplasm. This activity is mediated by interactions between its nuclear export signal (NES) or NLS with cellular factors exportin-1 and importin-β, respectively.[20] Although Rev has been found to be phosphorylated on serine residues, such modification is apparently not required for viral replication. Efforts are ongoing to develop drugs that can antagonize the function of Tat and Rev.

Vif, or the virion infectivity gene

Vif is made from a singly spliced mRNA that accumulates late in infection. Although Vif is dispensable for viral replication in some immortalized cell clones, it is required in peripheral blood mononuclear cells. This suggests that it may play an important role in infected hosts.[21] Vif is associated with viral RNA and may play a role in virus assembly. Because only traces of this protein are found in virions (amounts comparable with those of Pol proteins), its effects are assumed to be indirect.

Vpu protein

Vpu is made from the same singly spliced mRNA as the envelope glycoprotein. At least two functional roles have been identified:

- downmodulation of CD4 by stimulating degradation of CD4 in the ER; and
- enhancement of virion release by a yet to be defined mechanism.

Vpr regulatory protein

Vpr is packaged into mature virus particles through interactions with p6. It appears to be important in assisting the transport of the pre-integration complex from the cytoplasm into the nucleus. Vpr is also able to arrest infected cells at the G2 phase.

Nef protein

Nef is encoded by the extreme 3' end of the viral genome and accumulates even earlier than Tat and Rev in newly infected cells. Recent evidence suggests that Nef is involved in modulating CD4 expression by triggering the rapid endocytosis and lysosomal degradation of this main virus receptor. The Nef protein plays a major role in activation of quiescent T cells and thus facilitates viral replication.[22]

HIV-1 REPLICATION CYCLE

Entry of HIV-1

A schematic description of the HIV-1 life cycle is presented in Figure 121.4. HIV-1 uses the CD4 receptor (a 58kDa transmembrane protein) to mediate initial attachment to cells through high-affinity interactions between the viral envelope glycoprotein (gp120) and a specific region of the CD4 molecule.[21] On the surface of both immature T cells and mature $CD4^+$ T helper cells, CD4 is present in abundance. It is present at lower concentrations on monocytes, macrophages and antigen-presenting dendritic cells.

A variety of co-receptors have now been identified on lymphocytes and monocytes that promote the entry of HIV-1 into target cells after the initial binding step between CD4 and viral gp120.[15] Two major co-receptors are CCR5 and CXCR4. While cells of monocyte/macrophage origin generally express only the former, many lymphocyte populations can express both types of co-receptor. These differences in co-receptor expression help to explain why:

- HIV-1 variants may be either lymphocyte-tropic or macrophage-tropic, or both; and
- some viruses may be able to cause lymphocytes to fuse together into giant cells.

Certain host cell membrane proteins may also promote virus entry. One example is a C-type lectin (DC-SIGN) that is highly expressed on dendritic cells and binds to HIV-1 envelope glycoprotein gp120 (see Chapter 120).[23]

Efforts are underway to develop compounds that antagonize the entry of HIV-1 into susceptible cells by interfering with either the CD4 receptor or the various co-receptors on cells of different origins. Cell entry probably occurs by a fusion of viral and cell membranes, mediated by the viral transmembrane protein (gp41). Following fusion, the virion is uncoated by a proteolytic event that is most probably mediated by the virion-encoded protease.

Reverse transcription

After viral entry, the viral RNA is converted into DNA, which is then integrated into host cell chromosomal DNA. Reverse transcription initiates from a cellular $tRNA^{Lys.3}$ that is bound to a viral RNA fragment termed the primer binding site (PBS). This is followed by the first strand transfer, the priming of plus-strand DNA synthesis from the polypurine tract (PPT) and the second-strand transfer. The process of reverse transcription usually occurs within 4–6 hours of infection, takes place mainly in the cytoplasm

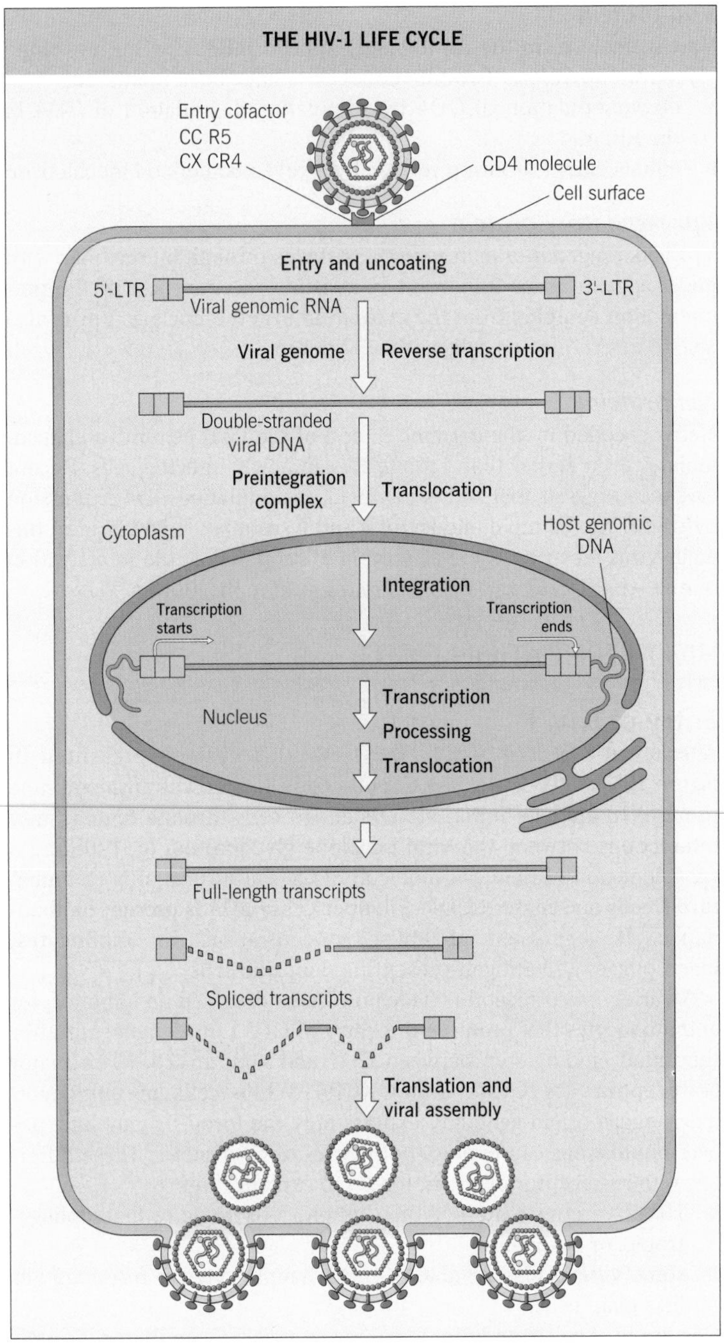

Fig. 121.4 The HIV-1 life cycle. The diagram shows the various stages involved, including entry, uncoating, reverse transcription, integration, expression of proviral genome, viral assembly and particle release.

and is catalyzed by virion-encoded RT. Reverse transcriptase has at least three enzymatic functions:

- RNA-dependent DNA polymerase activity that copies viral RNA into viral cDNA;
- DNA-dependent DNA polymerase activity that copies (–) strand viral cDNA into (+) strand viral cDNA; and
- ribonuclease H activity (RNase H) that degrades the viral RNA template during synthesis of viral cDNA.

The final products of reverse transcription are double-stranded (ds) DNA molecules that are longer at each end than the viral RNA as a result of duplication of the LTR. It is likely that cellular factors are required for the completion of reverse transcription, as most reverse transcribed products in unstimulated quiescent peripheral blood lymphocytes consist of incomplete viral DNAs.[24] The nature of the host cell factors or cellular activation pathways involved is unknown.

Integration

As stated above, reverse transcription products are mainly generated in the cytoplasm of infected cells. These dsDNAs are then transported into the nucleus of the cell, where viral DNA is integrated into host cell chromosomal DNA. The pre-integration complex of HIV-1 consists of IN, RT, MA, NC, Vpr and reverse-transcribed DNA.

The integration reaction is catalyzed by the virion-encoded IN, which is found in the viral particle. After reverse transcription of genomic viral RNA, IN remains associated with viral DNA as a high-molecular-weight nucleoprotein pre-integration complex. The IN first removes two nucleotides from the 3' end of viral DNA and then cleaves target host DNA. This is followed by insertion of viral DNA into host cell DNA. The 5' gaps flanking the provirus as well as the two nonpaired nucleotides are presumably repaired or removed by a cellular enzyme. The final products (provirus) are flanked by 5-basepair (bp) direct target duplications, which have lost 2bp from each end. Once integrated, viral DNA remains permanently associated with the host genetic material for as long as the cell is alive.

Viral gene expression

HIV-1 exploits the host cell transcription and translation machineries to generate its own gene products. The primary RNA transcripts of the provirus are made by host cell RNA polymerase II. Cellular activation and proliferation signals result in the binding of transcription factors to the LTR and lead to increased rates of initiation of transcription. Tat and Rev are two key virion-encoded proteins that positively regulate viral gene expression and replication, whereas the accessory proteins, including Nef, Vif, Vpu and Vpr, are crucial determinants of HIV virulence.[25] The primary viral RNA transcripts are either transported into the cytoplasm to direct Gag/Gag–Pol synthesis and to serve as genomic RNA for packaging or are spliced to generate around 30 different species of RNAs for the production of additional viral proteins. Host cellular ribosomes translate proviral mRNA into viral proteins in either cap-dependent or cap-independent modes. The cap-independent mechanism involves an internal ribosomal entry site (IRES) present at the 5' end of viral RNA. All viral structural proteins are made as polyproteins. Regulatory proteins are made by translation of spliced mRNA.

Packaging and assembly

Gag proteins are the driving force for virus assembly. Three functional domains have been characterized within Gag; these are the membrane binding domain (M domain), interaction domain (I domain) and late budding domain (L domain). The M domain is located at the N terminus of MA, the I domain involves NC sequences, and the L domain consists of a P(T/S)AP sequence within p6. The Gag proteins play a central role in recruiting both viral proteins and host-cell-derived elements into mature viral particles. Env proteins are recruited into virus particles through interactions between MA and gp41. Two copies of full-length viral RNA are incorporated into each virus particle through interactions of their 5' end RNA sequences with Gag precursors. The replication primer $tRNA^{Lys.3}$ is most probably selected by the viral Gag–Pol protein, together with cellular enzyme $tRNA^{Lys.3}$ synthetase.[26] The L domain recruits a cellular factor, tumor susceptibility gene (TSG)101, to the virus assembly site on the plasma membrane and facilitates the 'pinch-off' of virus particles.[27] Virus budding may require ubiqitination of Gag proteins and cellular factors involved in protein transportation. HIV-1 particles assemble at microdomains of plasma membrane that are enriched in sphingolipids and cholesterol. HIV-1 also recruits other cellular factors, such as Cyp A, Staufen, translation elongation factor 1α and actin, that may assist to assemble infectious virus particles.

THERAPEUTIC CONSIDERATIONS

As stated above, the major targets of anti-HIV chemotherapy have been the viral RT and PR enzymes. The RT of HIV-1 is responsible for copying viral RNA into DNA. However, this enzyme has a high error rate (i.e. about one mutation/virus replication event). This means that mutants are constantly being generated that have the potential for drug resistance, which may be selected under treatment. Drug resistance to HIV will occur when these mutations result in altered forms of the viral RT and PR proteins that can still function yet are no longer efficiently inhibited by antiviral nucleoside and non-nucleoside inhibitors of RT and antagonists of the HIV PR enzyme. Since HIV-1 uses cellular machineries to complete its life cycle, it follows that reasonably conserved cellular components might also be potential targets for development of anti-HIV-1 compounds. The subject of HIV drug resistance is dealt with in detail elsewhere (see Chapter 137).

REFERENCES

1. Haseltine WA. Molecular biology of HIV-1. FASEB J 1991;5:2349–60.
2. Cullen BR. Regulation of HIV-1 gene expression. FASEB J 1991;5:2361–8.
3. Cohen, EA, Dehni G, Sodroski JG, *et al.* Human immunodeficiency virus Vpr product is a virion-associated regulatory protein. J Virol 1990;64:3097–9.
4. Liu H, Wu X, Newman M, *et al.* The vif protein of human and simian immunodeficiency viruses is packaged into virions and associates with viral core structures. J Virol 1995;69:7630–8.
5. Welker R, Kottler H, Kalbiter HR, *et al.* Human immunodeficiency virus type 1 Nef is incorporated into virus particles and specifically cleaved by the viral proteinase. Virology 1996;219:228–36.
6. Kaplan AH, Swanstrom R. HIV-1 Gag proteins are processed in two cellular compartments. Proc Natl Acad Sci USA 1991;88:4528–32.
7. Weigers K, Rutter G, Kottler H, *et al.* Sequential steps in human immunodeficiency virus particle maturation revealed by alterations of individual Gag polyprotein cleavage sites. J Virol 1998;72:2846–54.
8. Gottlinger HG, Sodroski JG, Haseltine WA. Role of capsid precursor processing and myristylation in morphogenesis and infectivity of HIV-1. Proc Natl Acad Sci USA 1989;86:5781–5.
9. Bukrinsky MI, Sharova N, Dempsey M, *et al.* Active nuclear import of HIV-1 preintegration complexes. Proc Natl Acad Sci USA 1992;89:6580–4.
10. Von Schwedler UK, Stemmler TL, Klishko VY, *et al.* Proteolytic refolding of the HIV-1 capsid protein amino-terminus facilitates viral core assembly. EMBO J 1998;17:1555–68.
11. Reicin AS, Paik S, Berkowitz RD, *et al.* Linker insertions in the HIV-1 gag gene: effects on virion particle assembly, release, and infectivity. J Virol 1995;69:642–50.
12. Li X, Quan Y, Arts EJ, *et al.* HIV-1 nucleocapsid protein (NCp7) directs specific initiation of minus strand DNA synthesis by primed human tRNALys.3 in vivo. J Virol 1996;70:4996–5004.
13. Jacks T, Power MD, Masiarz FR, *et al.* Characterization of ribosomal frameshifting in HIV-1 gag–pol expression. Nature 1988;331:280–3.
14. Ratner L, Haseltine W, Patarca R, *et al.* Complete nucleotide sequence of the AIDS virus, HTLV-III. Nature 1985;313:277–84.
15. Cocchi F, DeVico AL, Garzino-Demo A, *et al.* The V3 domain of the HIV-1 gp120 envelope glycoprotein is critical for chemokine-mediated blockade of infection. Nat Med 1996;2:1244–7.
16. Sordorski JG. HIV-1 entry inhibitors in the side pocket. Cell 1999;99:243–6.
17. Wei P, Garber ME, Fang SM, *et al.* A novel CDK9-associated C-type cyclin interacts directly with HIV-1 Tat and mediates its high-affinity, loop-specific binding to TAR RNA. Cell 1998;92:451–62.
18. Harrich D, Ulich C, Garcia-Martinez LF, *et al.* Tat is required for efficient HIV-1 reverse transcription. EMBO J 1997;16:1224–35.
19. Kameoka M, Rong L, Gotte M, *et al.* Role for human immunodeficiency virus type 1 Tat protein in suppression of viral reverse transcriptase activity during late stages of viral replication. J Virol 2001;75:2675–83.
20. Pollard VW, Malim MH. The HIV-1 Rev protein. Annu Rev Microbiol 1998;52:491–532.
21. Rosenberg ZF, Fauci A. Immunopathogenesis of HIV-1 infection. FASEB J 1991;5:2382–90.
22. Schrager JA, Marsh JW. HIV-1 Nef increases T cell activation in a stimulus-dependent manner. Proc Natl Acad Sci USA 1999;96:8167–72.
23. Geijtenbeek TBH, Kwon DS, Torensma R, *et al.* DC-SIGN, a dendritic cell–specific HIV-1-binding protein that enhances trans-infection of T cells. Cell 2000;100:587–97.
24. Zack JA, Arrigo SJ, Weitsman SR, *et al.* HIV-1 entry into quiescent primary lymphocytes: molecular analysis reveals a labile, latent virus structure. Cell 1990;61:213–22.
25. Emerman M, Malim MH. HIV-1 regulatory/accessory genes: keys to unraveling viral and host cell biology. Science 1998;280:1880–4.
26. Cen S, Khorchid A, Javanbakht H, *et al.* Incorporation of lysyl-tRNA synthetase into human immunodeficiency virus type 1. J Virol 2001;75:5043–8.
27. Perez OD, Nolan GP. Resistance is futile: assimilation of cellular machinery by HIV-1. Immunity 2001;15:687–90.

chapter

122 Primary HIV Infection

Bernard Hirschel

INTRODUCTION

Although primary HIV infection (PHI) is a rarely diagnosed, self-limiting disease,[1] it is a topic of considerable interest, since the first encounter of HIV with the immune system sheds light on many aspects of pathogenesis. The severity of PHI predicts progression to immunodeficiency years later; therefore, it is reasonable to hope that treatment of PHI prevents or retards AIDS. From a public health perspective, a diagnosis of PHI is important because such patients are highly infectious;[2,3] to miss a diagnosis of PHI is to miss an opportunity for prevention.[4]

Experience shows that the diagnosis is not difficult to make; education is the key.

EPIDEMIOLOGY

Primary HIV infection is often asymptomatic but sometimes it presents with spectacular manifestations requiring hospital admission. There is a spectrum between complete absence of symptoms during the time of seroconversion and severe disease; therefore, it is not surprising that opinions vary about the percentage of patients who have symptomatic PHI. A physician's previous experience with PHI and a high index of suspicion greatly increase the number of diagnoses. Retrospective analysis from the US armed forces showed that 33% of patients suffered from an identifiable disease between their last seronegative and first seropositive serum sample. At the other extreme, in Australia,[5] 93% of seroconverting persons reported having been 'sick' compared with 40% of controls; 12% of seroconverting patients were hospitalized.

It is not known what factors determine the severity of PHI. Theoretically, the size of the inoculum, the virulence of the infecting HIV strain (including such factors as cellular tropism and cytopathogenicity), and the patient's immune status could be involved, but evidence as to whether these factors are important is lacking. One case series of transfusion-associated cases found that symptomatic PHI was more frequent among those infected by people who had late-stage disease. There is little evidence that the frequency or severity of PHI differs between transmission categories or between men and women. Symptomatic PHI can occur with HIV-2 infection and in children, although almost all cases have been reported in adults infected with HIV-1. There are theoretic reasons to believe that co-infection with other viruses, particularly from the herpes group, might enhance the proliferation of HIV, and patients who are simultaneously co-infected with cytomegalovirus have had particularly severe symptoms.

Symptoms typically start 2–4 weeks after infection, with extremes of 5 and more than 90 days. The median duration of symptoms is difficult to quantify and is between 12 and 28 days.[6] Moderate and subjective symptoms such as fatigue may persist for months, although almost all patients eventually enter an asymptomatic phase lasting years.

PATHOGENESIS AND PATHOLOGY

Because PHI most often presents as a benign self-limiting disease, pathologic information is only available from easily biopsied tissues.

The skin rash is caused by a dermal perivascular lymphohistiocytic infiltrate around vessels of the superficial dermis; the epidermis is normal. The inflammatory cells are predominantly of the $CD4^+$ phenotype, and may represent a T-cell-mediated reaction to HIV and to the p24 antigen, which can be detected in the Langerhans cells.

Lymph node biopsies reveal abundant HIV, including the envelope proteins gp120 and gp160 in dendritic reticulum cells, as well as in lymphocytes. The structure of the germinal centers is relatively normal and quite unlike the follicular hyperplasia of established HIV-1 infection, but extrafollicular B lymphocytes are reduced in number and the follicles are infiltrated by $CD8^+$ T cells.[7]

Therapy has a pronounced effect on the quantity of HIV detectable in lymph nodes. There is a lag of more than 6 months between disappearance of the virus from plasma and disappearance from lymph nodes. However, even patients who are aviremic for several months while treated for PHI and whose lymph node biopsies are apparently free from HIV relapse after discontinuing medication, emphasizing the role of a virus reservoir such as memory T cells.[8]

CLINICAL FEATURES

During PHI, HIV floods the blood,[9] the central nervous system (CNS)[10] and the lymphatic system, and invades a number of other tissues. Therefore, it is not surprising that PHI is a disease with protean manifestations. Three main presentations have been described.

Cutaneous presentation

This is characterized by a maculopapular rash, 'roseola' and mucosal ulcerations (Figs 122.1–122.4). The rash affects the face, neck and trunk more than the limbs, although the palms and soles may be involved. Individual lesions are usually less than 1cm in diameter and confluence is rare. Case reports have mentioned pustular eruptions, urticaria, erythema multiforme and, during the healing phase of PHI, alopecia and desquamation. Ulceration may occur on the genital and oral mucosa, including the esophagus, where differentiation from herpetic lesions or esophageal candidiasis is difficult.

Presentation resembling infectious mononucleosis

This is characterized by fever, pharyngitis, arthralgia, myalgia and lymphadenopathy. Although the expression 'mononucleosis-like illness' is firmly established, there are many differences from classic infectious mononucleosis, most notably the lack of prominent tonsillar involvement. In a large series (Table 122.1), only 20% of patients had a fever in combination with sore throat and enlarged cervical lymph nodes, whereas 10% did not have fever, sore throat or cervical lymphadenopathy.

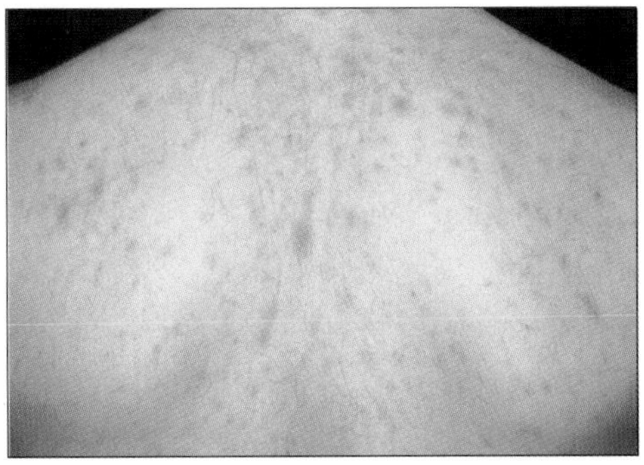

Fig. 122.1 Maculopapular rash during primary HIV infection.

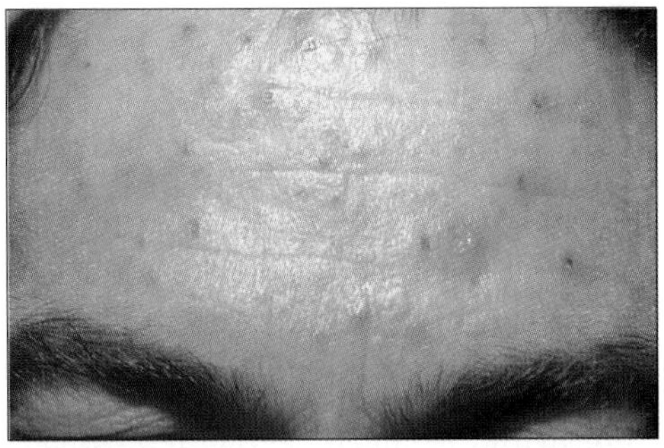

Fig. 122.2 Acneiform lesions during primary HIV infection.

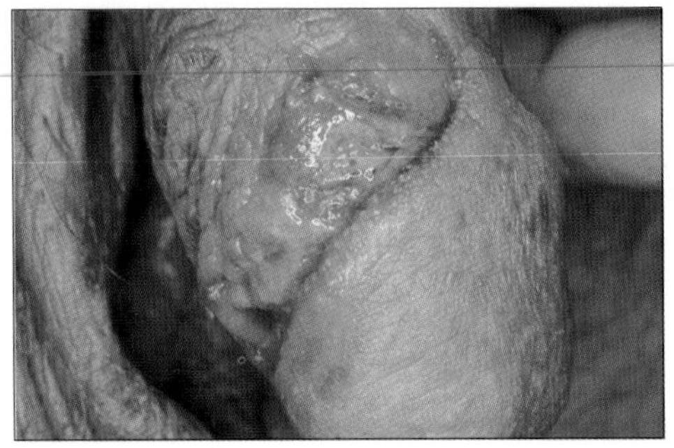

Fig. 122.3 Penile ulcer during primary HIV infection.

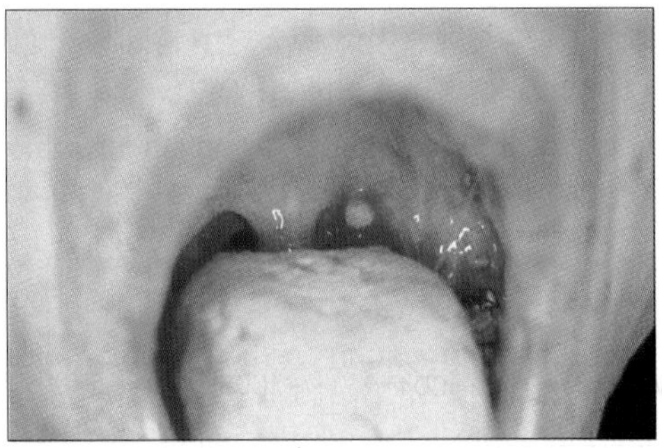

Fig. 122.4 Mucosal ulcerations during primary HIV infection.

Meningoencephalitis

Meningoencephalitis is characterized by photophobia and neck stiffness, headaches and disordered consciousness. The headache is typically retro-orbital and exacerbated by eye movements. Depression and changes in mood are frequent and may reflect underlying encephalitis.

Other symptoms

Table 122.1 shows the frequencies of signs and recorded symptoms in the medical charts of more than 200 patients from Switzerland and Australia. Digestive manifestations have not been well recognized in the past, but they are quite common. In exceptional cases, esophageal candidiasis (an AIDS-defining disease) may occur with a transient decline in CD4+ lymphocyte count.

SIGNS AND SYMPTOMS OF PRIMARY HIV INFECTION		
	Symptom/sign	**%**
Reported by more than 50%	Fever	77
	Lethargy/fatigue	66
	Rash	56
	Myalgia	55
	Headache	51
Reported by 20–50%	Pharyngitis	44
	Cervical adenopathy	39
	Arthralgia	31
	Oral ulcer	29
	Pain on swallowing	28
	Axillary adenopathy	24
	Weight loss	24
	Nausea	24
	Diarrhea	23
	Night sweats	22
	Cough	22
	Anorexia	22
Reported by 5–20%	Abdominal pain	19
	Oral candidiasis	17
	Vomiting	12
	Photophobia	12
	Meningitis	12
	Genital ulcer	7
	Tonsillitis	7
	Depression	7
	Dizziness	6

Table 122.1 Signs and symptoms of primary HIV infection. These are the signs and symptoms reported by at least 5% of patients.[1,2]

Apart from these major groups of symptoms and signs, many unusual manifestations have been described during PHI, most notably:

- neurologic syndromes such as radiculopathy, peripheral facial neuropathy and Guillain–Barré syndrome, and severe encephalitis with prolonged coma and seizures; and
- pulmonary involvement, which may be more frequent in intravenous drug users where PHI can be associated with bacterial pneumonia; severe pneumonitis leading to intubation and *Pneumocystis carinii* pneumonia[11] (with CD4+ lymphocyte counts of less than 100/mm^3) is exceptional.

Differential diagnosis

Important differential diagnoses are listed in Table 122.2; PHI must be distinguished from Epstein–Barr virus infection (infectious mononucleosis) and enterovirus meningitis, and according to the local epidemiologic context, typhoid fever, rickettsial infections and many others.

DIAGNOSIS

Seroconversion (i.e. the appearance of HIV antibodies in the serum) occurs days after the beginning of the symptoms of PHI. Therefore, the usual antibody tests for HIV are not entirely reliable; they are expected to be negative during the first few days of PHI (Fig. 122.5). Assays differ in the duration of this 'seronegative period'; with the currently used sensitive tests it is usually less than 1 week.

The p24 antigen is positive when the antibody test is still negative during PHI, and the same is true of HIV viremia. Whereas both tests can be used to screen for PHI, the p24 antigen test is considerably cheaper.[12] Viremia levels reach extremely high values, often in excess of 10^6 viral genomes/ml[13] and high titers of infectious virus have

IMPORTANT DIFFERENTIAL DIAGNOSES		
Clinical feature	**Epstein–Barr virus infection**	**HIV infection**
Onset	Gradual	Abrupt
Tonsil involvement	+++	+
Pharyngeal exudate	+++	–
Rash	Rare except in patients treated with antibiotics	Frequent
Jaundice	10%	Never
Diarrhea	Rare	25%
Clinical feature	**Syphilis**	**HIV infection**
Serology	Always positive	At first negative
Chancre: timing	Before roseola	At the same time as rash
Chancre: pain	Painless	Painful
Clinical feature	**Enterovirus meningitis**	**HIV meningitis**
Population	Young adults	Young adults
Diarrhea	Rare	23%
Season	Summer–autumn	None in particular
Duration	<8 days	Often >20 days
Encephalitis	None	Frequent
Skin lesions	Rare	Frequent
Pain on swallowing	None	Frequent

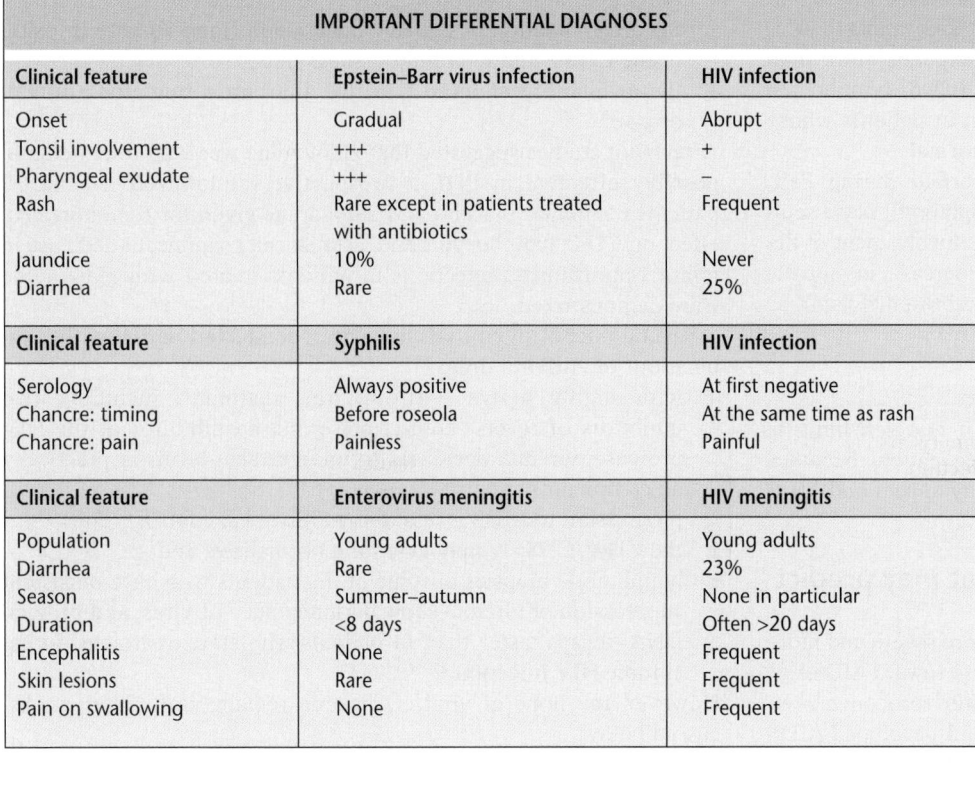

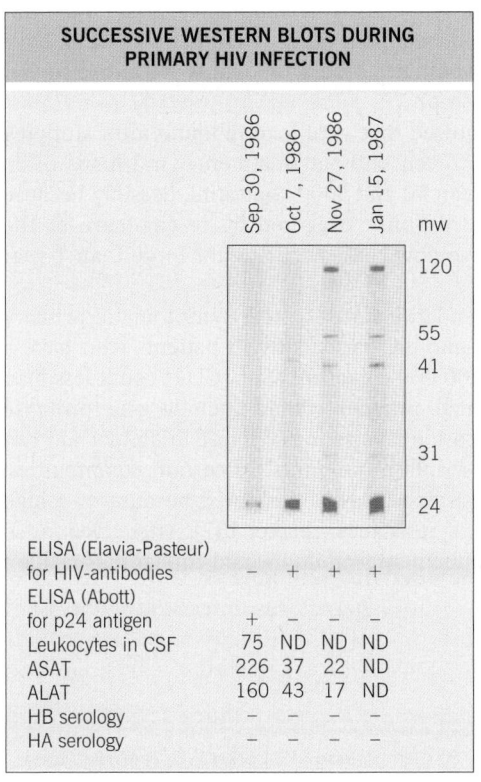

Table 122.2 Important differential diagnoses.

SUCCESSIVE WESTERN BLOTS DURING PRIMARY HIV INFECTION

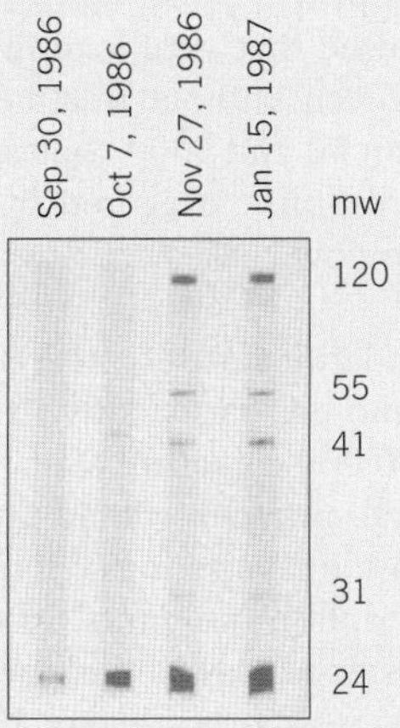

	Sep 30, 1986	Oct 7, 1986	Nov 27, 1986	Jan 15, 1987
ELISA (Elavia-Pasteur) for HIV-antibodies	–	+	+	+
ELISA (Abott) for p24 antigen	+	–	–	–
Leukocytes in CSF	75	ND	ND	ND
ASAT	226	37	22	ND
ALAT	160	43	17	ND
HB serology	–	–	–	–
HA serology	–	–	–	–

Fig. 122.5 Successive Western blots during primary HIV infection. Note that on September 30, 1986, when the patient presented with fever, rash, meningitis and subclinical hepatitis, the screening enzyme-linked immunosorbent assay (ELISA) test for HIV antibodies was negative, while the Western blot showed only a single weak band corresponding to the p24 antigen. CSF, cerebrospinal fluid; ASAT, aspartate transaminase; ALAT, alanine transaminase; H, hepatitis (A or B); ND, not done.

CHANGES IN LYMPHOCYTE SUBPOPULATIONS AND HIV VIREMIA DURING PHI

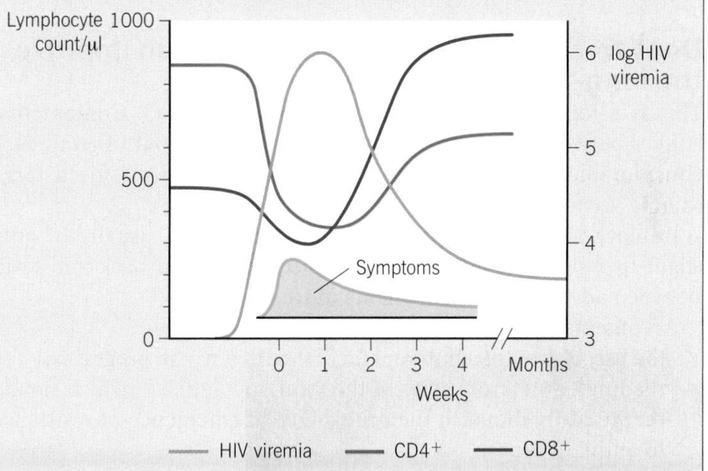

Fig. 122.6 Changes in lymphocyte subpopulations and HIV viremia during primary HIV infection.

been isolated from many tissues, including seminal fluid, corroborating the epidemiologic evidence that patients who have PHI are highly infectious. Viremia decreases rapidly – at least 100-fold within days after seroconversion – but remains detectable in more than 95% of patients. Steady-state plasma viremia levels predict progression to advanced immunodeficiency and death.[14] Levels tend to remain higher in those who have symptomatic PHI.[15]

The occurrence of HIV infection without the presence of antibodies for many months ('seronegative HIV infection') has caused much controversy, fueled by conflicting results and the extreme sensitivity of the polymerase chain reaction, which makes it vulnerable to contamination and false-positive results. Although patients with chronic seronegative infections may rarely occur, there is no evidence that these individuals are infective, and no patients with symptomatic PHI who have subsequently failed to seroconvert have been described. However, a seronegative patient who is in the process of seroconverting can transmit HIV, for instance by blood transfusion. The results of plasma viremia and p24 antigen tests as well as the clinical history and exposure must guide the interpretation of a negative serologic result.

Like viremia levels, lymphocyte subsets undergo rapid changes during PHI (Fig. 122.6). During the first 5–10 days, lymphopenia characteristically affects both $CD4^+$ and $CD8^+$ lymphocytes, with levels[11] that may be as low as those observed in AIDS. Although opportunistic infections are rare, in-vitro tests of both B and T cells show immunosuppression. Within another 2–3 weeks there is a lymphocytosis. The $CD8^+$ lymphocyte count expands more than the $CD4^+$ lymphocyte count, leading to a $CD4^+/CD8^+$ lymphocyte ratio of less than 1. This low ratio persists even in patients whose $CD4^+$ lymphocyte count subsequently rises to normal.

Many other laboratory values may be abnormal during PHI, reflecting the acute inflammatory response (e.g. high erythrocyte sedimentation rate, increase in C-reactive protein) and involvement of the bone marrow (thrombocytopenia), the liver (increase in hepatic transaminases) and the CNS (pleocytosis of the cerebrospinal fluid).

MANAGEMENT

Although PHI can be severe and prolonged, it is a self-limiting disease; the symptoms eventually abate and the patient becomes asymptomatic. Years later, immunosuppression may appear and AIDS may develop.

Features of primary HIV infection that may predict the subsequent course toward AIDS

A considerable body of evidence suggests that more severe and more prolonged PHI indicates a more unfavorable course toward AIDS.[16-18] For instance, in patients who were followed after seroconversion, 58% of those who had had symptomatic PHI had developed AIDS 7 years later compared with 28% of those who had asymptomatic PHI.[17] Another study suggested that the presence of neurologic signs at the time of PHI predicted accelerated immunosuppression,[18] although there was no specific relation to the neurologic signs of AIDS, such as AIDS-related dementia or opportunistic infections of the CNS.

Does treatment of primary HIV infection improve the long-term outcome?

This is a logical question that remains unanswered. Comparative studies between a treated group and an untreated control group face considerable practical obstacles, including the need for a large sample, extremely long follow-up and ethical issues.

Primary HIV infection is a self-limiting disease, usually of only slight or moderate severity. The balance has shifted back and forth between advocates and opponents of treatment.

Arguments in favor are:

- the association of symptomatic PHI with a worse prognosis;
- the limited heterogeneity of the viral population,[19] which should theoretically diminish the probability of emergence of resistance to antiviral drugs;
- the potential impact on infectivity and transmission;[2]
- the generalization of the HIV infection during PHI with invasion of the CNS[10] and lymphoid tissues; and
- the availability of more effective and better tolerated antiviral drugs.[20]

After pilot studies suggested that zidovudine was well tolerated and possibly effective in PHI, a prospective randomized trial in 77 patients compared placebo and zidovudine given for 6 months.[6] An effect on $CD4^+$ lymphocytes and a statistically significant decrease in minor opportunistic infections in patients treated with zidovudine were demonstrated.

Several uncontrolled trials have been conducted in PHI with combinations of antiviral drugs:

- with highly active antiretroviral treatment, including two inhibitors of reverse transcriptase and an inhibitor of the HIV protease, viremia decreases to undetectable levels in practically all compliant patients;[21,22]
- progression to AIDS is less than in historical control groups;[23]
- the $CD4^+/CD8^+$ lymphocyte ratio normalizes; and
- lymph node biopsies of some of the patients who have persistent suppression of viremia show disappearance of virus, and proviral DNA decays faster than in patients who start treatment during chronic HIV infection.[21,24]

However, the hope of viral eradication remains unfulfilled, as discussed below.

Opponents of antiviral treatment for primary HIV infection point to the lack of studies showing clinical benefits, the high incidence of side effects, expense and problems with compliance. Some 6 months or so after having started treatment during PHI, patients often have high $CD4^+$ counts and would not otherwise qualify for antiretroviral treatment. Should they stop?

A small case series showed that viral load rebound after stopping was universal. However, even without treatment, viral loads often fell again to levels between 50 and 5000 copies/ml, possibly because of a vigorous immune response triggered by re-exposure to the virus. Many patients have now ceased therapy for more than 1 year and have done well.[25]

The present recommendations are to treat symptomatic primary infection as soon as diagnosed, particularly in patients who have a viral load greater than 100,000 copies/ml and a $CD4^+$ count less than 500 cells/μl. The optimal regimen would include one protease inhibitor (or a non-nucleoside reverse transcriptase inhibitor) and two nucleoside reverse transcriptase inhibitors. In certain communities, genotypic testing for resistance may be indicated because of a high prevalence of primary drug resistance (chapter 137). After a year or so of therapy, a trial of treatment interruption would appear reasonable.

REFERENCES

1. Cooper DA, Gold J, Maclean P, *et al.* Acute AIDS retrovirus infection. Definition of a clinical illness associated with seroconversion. Lancet 1985;1:537–40.
2. Pilcher CD, Shugars DC, Fiscus SA, *et al.* HIV in body fluids during primary HIV infection: implications for pathogenesis, treatment and public health. AIDS 2001;15:837–45.
3. Yerly S, Vora S, Rizzardi P, *et al.* Acute HIV infection: impact on the spread of HIV and transmission of drug resistance. AIDS 2001;15:2287–92.
4. Jolles S, De Loës SK, Johnson MA, Janossy G. Primary HIV-1 infection: a new medical emergency? Recognition of this initial illness may permit early diagnosis and treatment. Br Med J 1996;312:1243–4.
5. Tindall B, Barker S, Donovan B, *et al.* Characterization of the acute clinical illness associated with human immunodeficiency virus infection. Arch Intern Med 1988;148:945–9.
6. Kinloch-De Loës S, Hirschel B, Hoen B, *et al.* A controlled trial of zidovudine in primary human immunodeficiency virus infection. N Engl J Med 1995;333:408–13.
7. Sinicco A, Palestro G, Caramello P, *et al.* Acute HIV-1 infection : clinical and biological study of 12 patients. J Acquir Immune Defic Syndr 1990;3:260–5.
8. Finzi D, Hermankova M, Pierson T, *et al.* Identification of a reservoir for HIV-1 in patients on highly active antiretroviral therapy. Science 1997;278:1295–300.
9. Clark SJ, Saag MS, Decker WD, *et al.* High titers of cytopathic virus in plasma of patients with symptomatic primary HIV-1 infection. N Engl J Med 1991;324:954–60.
10. Ho DD, Rota TR, Schooley RT, *et al.* Isolation of HTLV-III from cerebrospinal fluid and neural tissues of patients with neurologic syndromes related to the acquired immunodeficiency syndrome. N Engl J Med 1985;313:1493–7.
11. Vento S, Di Perri G, Garofano T, Concia E, Bassetti D. *Pneumocystis carinii* pneumonia during primary HIV-1 infection. Lancet 1993;342:24–5.
12. Daar ES, Little S, Pitt J, *et al.* Diagnosis of primary HIV-1 infection. Ann Intern Med 2001;134:25–9.

13. Baumberger C, Kinloch S, Yerly S, Hirschel B, Perrin L. High levels of ciruculating RNA in patients with symptomatic primary HIV-1 infection. AIDS 1994;7:S59–64.
14. Mellors JW, Rinaldo CR Jr, Gupta P, White RM, Todd JA, Kingsley LA. Prognosis in HIV-1 infection predicted by the quantity of virus in plasma. Science 1996;272:1167–70.
15. Henrard DR, Daar E, Farzadegan H, *et al.* Virologic and immunologic characterization of symptomatic and asymptomatic primary HIV-1 infection. J Acquir Immune Defic Syndr Hum Retrovirol 1995;9:305–10.
16. Pedersen C, Lindhardt BO, Jensen BL, *et al.* Clinical course of primary HIV infection: consequences for subsequent course of infection. Br Med J 1989;299:154–7.
17. Lindback S, Brostrom C, Karlsson A, Gaines H. Does symptomatic primary HIV-1 infection accelerate progression to CDC stage IV disease, CD4 count below 200 × 10^6/l, AIDS, and death from AIDS? Br Med J 1994;309:1535–7.
18. Boufassa F, Bachmeyer C, Carré N, *et al.* Influence of neurologic manifestations of primary human immunodeficiency virus infection on disease progression. J Infect Dis 1995;171:1190–5.
19. Antonioli IM, Baumberger C, Yerly S, Perrin L. V3 sequences in primary HIV-1 infection. AIDS 1995; 9: 11–7.
20. Ho DD. Time to hit HIV, early and hard. N Engl J Med 1995;333:450–1.
21. Yerly S, Perneger TV, Vora S, Hirschel B, Perrin L. Decay of cell-associated HIV-1 DNA correlates with residual replication in patients treated during acute HIV-1 infection. AIDS 2000;14:2805–12.
22. Smith DM, Berrey MM, Robertson M, *et al.* Virological and immunological effects of combination antiretroviral therapy with zidovudine, lamivudine, and indinavir during primary human immunodeficiency virus type 1 infection. J Infect Dis 2000;182:950–4.
23. Berrey MM, Schacker T, Collier AC, *et al.* Treatment of primary human immunodeficiency virus type 1 infection with potent antiretroviral therapy reduces frequency of rapid progression to AIDS. J Infect Dis 2001;183:1466–75.
24. Ngo GH, Deveau C, Da Silva I, *et al.* Proviral HIV-1 DNA in subjects followed since primary HIV-1 infection who suppress plasma viral load after one year of highly active antiretroviral therapy. AIDS 2001;15:665–73.
25. Rosenberg ES, Altfeld M, Poon SH, *et al.* Immune control of HIV-1 after early treatment of acute infection. Nature 2000;407:523–6.

chapter 123

Prevention of Opportunistic Infections

Nathan Clumeck & Stéphane de Wit

INTRODUCTION

One of the major clinical advances in the management of patients who have HIV infection has been the implementation in the mid-1980s of antimicrobial prophylaxis for patients with severe immune impairment. Together with the use of antiretroviral drugs, this has led to decreased morbidity and improved survival in patients with AIDS.

Such prophylaxis requires regular measurements of $CD4^+$ lymphocyte counts and compliance on the part of the patient, who must take many pills each day for the rest of his/her life. There are also issues of tolerance, drug interactions, emergence of resistance and cost.

Since the extensive use in Western countries of highly active antiretroviral therapy (HAART), a further marked decrease in the occurrence of AIDS-related opportunistic infections has been noted and the question of continuing or stopping prophylactic regimens has been raised in patients who have $CD4^+$ counts increasing beyond the critical level of 200 lymphocytes/mm^3.[1] Figure 123.1 summarizes the evolution of the incidence of most opportunistic infections among a cohort of 2000 patients followed at CHU Saint-Pierre hospital in Brussels.

Although prophylactic regimens against most of the opportunistic infections that occur in patients who have HIV infection exist, the decision to use prophylaxis should consider factors such as:

- the incidence and prevalence of specific infections in HIV infected individuals;
- the potential severity of disease in terms of morbidity and mortality;
- the level of immunosuppression at which each disease is likely to occur;
- the feasibility and efficacy of preventive measures, and in particular their impact on quality of life and survival;
- the potential for emergence of organisms resistant to the agents used for prophylaxis;
- the risk of toxicities and drug interactions with antiretrovirals and other drugs used by HIV-infected patients;
- the issue of compliance; and
- the cost-effectiveness of prophylaxis.

INCIDENCE AND PREVALENCE OF OPPORTUNISTIC INFECTIONS

There is a wide geographic variability in the epidemiology of opportunistic infections. The probability of developing a given disease depends on the risk for exposure to potential pathogens, the virulence of the pathogens and the level of immunosuppression of the patient.

In the USA and Northern Europe, *Pneumocystis carinii* pneumonia (PCP), oropharyngeal or esophageal candidiasis, cytomegalovirus disease and infections caused by *Mycobacterium avium* complex (MAC) are common. The incidence of toxoplasmosis and tuberculosis is higher in central and southern Europe and in the developing countries, depending on the prevalence of latent infection in the general population. This geographic heterogenicity has important implications for prophylaxis. In the case of low incidence, prophylactic measures should be targeted to high-risk patients such as those who have a positive antitoxoplasma serology, a positive polymerase chain reaction for cytomegalovirus or a positive cutaneous tuberculin test for tuberculosis. In addition, for tuberculosis, epidemiologic assessment of risk should be used for some high-risk populations (intravenous drug users, migrants from an endemic area).

LEVEL OF IMMUNOSUPPRESSION

Blood $CD4^+$ lymphocyte levels is the best marker for immune status. It has been clearly established that the number of circulating $CD4^+$ lymphocytes is closely correlated with the risk of developing several opportunistic infections (Fig. 123.2). Once the $CD4^+$ lymphocyte count falls below 200 cells/μl, the cumulative risk for developing an AIDS-defining opportunistic infection is 33% by year 1 and 58% by 2 years. Therefore, $CD4^+$ lymphocyte counts remain an important parameter for monitoring patients who have HIV infection because of their predictive value for both opportunistic infections and mortality.

EFFICACY OF PROPHYLACTIC MEASURES AND IMPACT ON SURVIVAL

The survival benefit of prophylaxis for opportunistic infections has been demonstrated in a number of studies, particularly in patients who have severe immunosuppression. In the early 1980s, before the widespread use of antiretroviral therapy, it was demonstrated that trimethoprim–sulfamethoxazole (TMP–SMX) use for prevention of PCP did significantly prolong survival. A similar impact has been shown with MAC prophylaxis with clarithromycin or rifabutin.

It is clear that a prophylactic regimen that prolongs survival should be used in priority to one that does not. In this setting, the use of fluconazole for prophylaxis of systemic mycoses and oral ganciclovir for cytomegalovirus disease have failed to demonstrate a clear survival benefit and are not widely recommended.

EMERGENCE OF DRUG RESISTANCE

The development of resistance to the most commonly used agents is one of the major concerns with the use of long-term antimicrobial prophylaxis in patients who have HIV infection.

Resistance or cross-resistance has become increasingly common with prophylaxis for MAC, fungal infections and PCP. The major consequence is that, when the specific drugs are needed to treat acute infections, resistance hinders their use and alternative less effective or more toxic agents are the only option.[2]

This issue was well illustrated with clarithromycin as prophylaxis for MAC. Despite receiving prophylaxis, 58% of the patients developing MAC had clarithromycin-resistant isolates.[3]

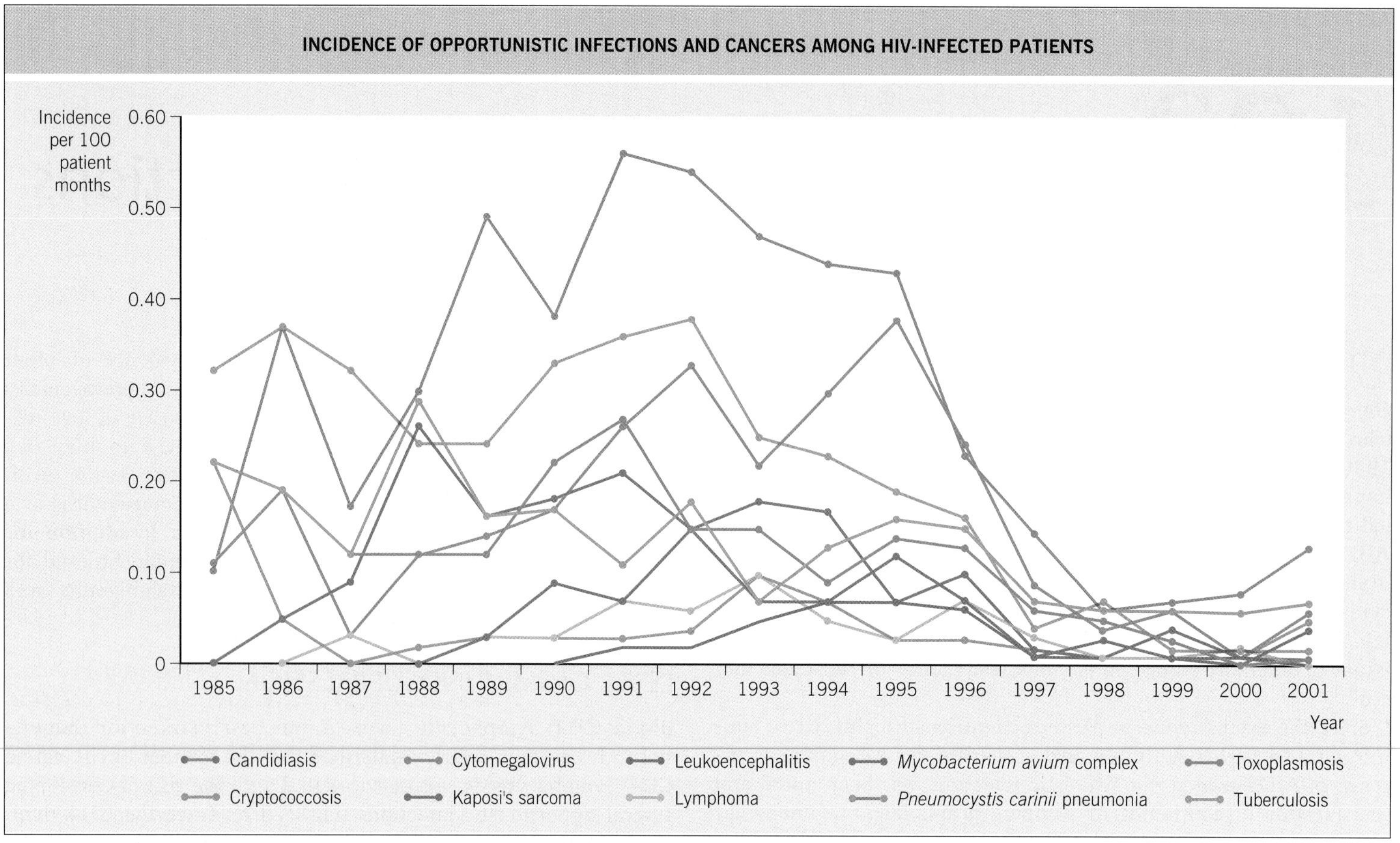

Fig. 123.1 Incidence of opportunistic infections among patients who have HIV infection. CHU Saint-Pierre, 1985–2001.

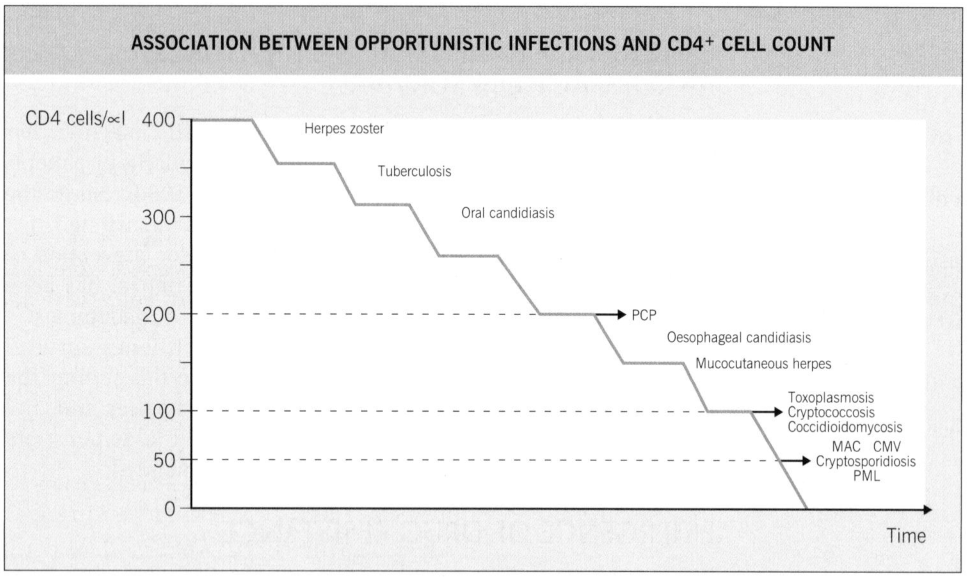

Fig. 123.2 Association between opportunistic infections and CD4⁺ cell count.

Prophylactic treatment of non-life-threatening infections, such as oral thrush with fluconazole, has probably contributed to the emergence and spreading of azole-resistant fungi.

Prophylactic regimens may also lead to the development of cross-resistance against more common pathogens. For example, rifabutin used for MAC prophylaxis may result in the emergence of rifampin-resistant strains of *M. tuberculosis*.[4] Likewise, the widespread use of broad-spectrum antibiotics, such as clarithromycin, azithromycin or TMP–SMX, may lead to the development of resistance among organisms such as pneumococci that were not the primary targets of prophylaxis. An increasing prevalence of *Streptococcus pneumoniae* resistant to TMP–SMX, for example, could decrease the effectiveness of this agent in preventing community-acquired pneumonia in advanced HIV patients and limit therapeutic options for treating common outpatient illnesses such as respiratory, skin and soft tissue infections.[2]

DRUG TOXICITY AND DRUG INTERACTIONS

Drug toxicity can be a major factor limiting the usefulness of widely used agents. The incidence of adverse drug reactions in patients who have HIV infection varies with the type of drug and dosages used, the interactions between drugs and the stage of HIV infection.[5]

HIV-related idiosyncratic factors, organ dysfunction in late stage disease and multiple drug therapy are the primary reasons for the increased risk of drug toxicities in HIV patients.

The issue of drug interactions has become particularly critical in the era of protease inhibitors. However, although the number of potential drug interactions is substantial, few require dosage modifications. Among these, clinicians should be vigilant when using concomitantly prophylaxis and treatment of mycobacterial diseases with rifamycin and macrolides and HIV protease inhibitors.

COMPLIANCE ISSUES

The use of combination therapy for prophylaxis against multiple opportunistic pathogens significantly increases the complexity of treatment of HIV patients. In particular, it may dramatically increase the number of pills that are necessary in combination antiretroviral regimens. Such increasingly complex regimens may lead to patient noncompliance and inability to tolerate other therapeutic regimens, inducing antiretrovirals.

COST-EFFECTIVENESS

To be most cost-effective prophylaxis should be directed at the most common infections in the patient population. However, an expensive prophylactic regimen may be cost-effective if it has a positive impact on quality and duration of life or if it reduces other costs. This is particularly true in severely immunocompromised HIV patients, in whom any intervention, even costly prophylaxis, that significantly reduces the incidence of hospitalization will have a favorable impact on the costs of caring. Studies have shown that prophylaxis for PCP and MAC is cost-effective, whereas prophylaxis for fungal disease and cytomegalovirus is not.[6]

DURATION OF PROPHYLAXIS AGAINST OPPORTUNISTIC INFECTIONS

Since HAART was introduced, it has become clear that prophylaxis against opportunistic infections need not necessarily be life long. As mentioned above, susceptibility to opportunistic infections can accurately be assessed by the $CD4^+$ T cell count.

It is thus logical to stop primary or secondary prophylaxis in patients whose immunity has improved as a consequence of HAART.

Data generated until now support this approach and recommendations concerning the safety of stopping primary or secondary prophylaxis can now be made for many pathogens.

By contrast, no data are available regarding the re-initiation of prophylaxis when the $CD4^+$ lymphocyte count decreases again to levels at which the risk for opportunistic infections exists. In particular, it is unknown whether it is better to use the threshold at which prophylaxis was stopped or the threshold below which initial prophylaxis is recommended.[7]

RECOMMENDATIONS FOR PROPHYLAXIS AGAINST OPPORTUNISTIC INFECTIONS

The US Public Health Services and the Infectious Diseases Society of America have established disease-specific recommendations for the prevention of opportunistic infections in individuals who have HIV infection, which were updated in November 2001. These recommendations include guidelines for preventing exposure to pathogens as well as on specific regimens for preventing initial episodes.[8]

Category I regimens are strongly recommended as standard of care. Category II should be strongly considered in eligible patients. Category III regimens are not routinely recommended but may be considered for use in selected patients (Table 123.1).

Recommendations on prophylactic regimens to prevent recurrence of opportunistic infections have also been updated (Table 123.2).

DISEASE-SPECIFIC CONSIDERATIONS

Pneumocystis carinii

Prophylaxis of PCP has been shown to be highly cost-effective.

A meta-analysis of 35 studies of PCP prophylaxis in 6583 patients showed that TMP–SMX was superior to dapsone or aerosolized pentamidine but there was no statistically significant survival advantage for TMP–SMX versus alternative agents. An advantage of TMP–SMX over alternative drugs is a significant reduction in bacterial infections. Side-effects are sufficiently severe to require discontinuation of the drug in 25–50% of TMP–SMX recipients compared to 25–40% of dapsone recipients and 2–4% of recipients of aerosolized pentamidine. There is good evidence that lower doses of TMP–SMX are better tolerated, and many advocate either the use of the lower dose regimens using one single-strength tablet daily or one double-strength tablet thrice weekly. Patients who have adverse reactions to TMP–SMX usually tolerate dapsone.

Primary and secondary prophylaxis against PCP should be discontinued in patients treated with HAART who show an increase in $CD4^+$ T cells to above $200/mm^3$ for at least 3 months. Prophylaxis should be reintroduced if the $CD4^+$ T cell count decreases to less than $200/mm^3$.[9,10]

Toxoplasma gondii

Toxoplasma seropositive patients who have a $CD4^+$ T cell count below $100/mm^3$ or who have had a previous episode of toxoplasmic encephalitis should receive prophylaxis against toxoplasmic encephalitis.

The double-strength tablet daily dose of TMP–SMX is recommended. Alternative regimens in patients who cannot tolerate TMP–SMX include dapsone–pyrimethamine or atovaquone (with or without pyrimethamine). Prophylactic monotherapy with dapsone, clindamycin, pyrimethamine, azithromycin or clarithromycin are not recommended.

Primary prophylaxis against toxoplasmic encephalitis should be discontinued in patients treated with HAART showing an increase in $CD4^+$ T cells to above $200/mm^3$ for at least 3 months. Discontinuation of prophylaxis in patients where $CD4^+$ counts have increased to 100–200 cells/mm^3 has not been carefully evaluated. No firm recommendation can be made regarding discontinuation of secondary prophylaxis, but it appears reasonable to consider discontinuation in patients who have $CD4^+$ T cells above $200/mm^3$ for at least 3 months. Prophylaxis should be reintroduced if the $CD4^+$ T cell count decreases to below 100–200/mm^3.[10,11]

Mycobacterium tuberculosis

Latent tuberculosis infection should be treated in all patients who have HIV infection and a positive tuberculin skin test, with no evidence of active tuberculosis and no history of treatment for active or latent tuberculosis.

PROPHYLAXIS OF FIRST EPISODE OF OPPORTUNISTIC INFECTIONS IN ADULTS AND ADOLESCENTS WITH HIV INFECTION			
Pathogen	**Target population**	**First-choice regimen**	**Alternative regimens**
Category I: recommended as standard of care			
Pneumocystis carinii	CD4+ lymphocyte count <200/mm³ *and/or* oropharyngeal candidiasis	TMP–SMX 1 DS q24h or 1 SS q24h	Dapsone 100mg q24h or 50mg q12h Dapsone 50mg q24h plus pyrimethamine 50mg weekly plus leucovorin 25mg weekly Dapsone 200mg weekly plus pyrimethamine 75mg weekly plus leucovorin 25mg weekly Aerosolized pentamidine 300mg monthly by nebulizer Atovaquone 1500mg q24h TMP–SMX 1 DS three times a week
Toxoplasma gondii	CD4+ lymphocyte count <100/mm³ *and* positive anti-*Toxoplasma* IgG	TMP–SMX 1 DS q24h	TMP–SMX 1 SS q24h Dapsone 50mg q24h plus pyrimethamine 50mg weekly plus leucovorin 25mg weekly Dapsone 200mg weekly plus pyrimethamine 75mg weekly plus leucovorin 25mg weekly Atovaquone 1500mg q24h
Mycobacterium tuberculosis	Positive PPD (5mm) *and/or* previous positive PPD without treatment *and/or* contact with active case (regardless of PPD result)	Isoniazid 300mg q24h plus pyridoxine 50mg q24h for 12 months *or* isoniazid 900mg and pyridoxine 50mg twice weekly with directly observed therapy for 12 months	Rifampin (rifampicin) 600mg q24h for 12 months Rifampin 600mg q24h plus pyrazinamide 20mg/kg/day for 2 months Rifampin 450–600mg twice weekly plus pyrazinamide 1500–2500mg twice weekly for 2 months *If isoniazid resistance*: rifampin 600mg q24h for 12 months or rifabutin 600mg q24h for 12 months *If multidrug resistance*: choice of drugs depends on susceptibility of isolate from source patient
Mycobacterium avium complex	CD4+ lymphocyte count <50 cells/mm³	Clarithromycin 500mg q12h *or* azithromycin 1200mg weekly	Rifabutin 300mg q24h or azithromycin 1200mg weekly plus rifabutin 300mg q24h
Varicella-zoster virus (VZV)	Exposure to chickenpox or shingles *and* no history of either or negative serology	Varicella-zoster virus Ig, 5 vials im within 96 hours of exposure (preferably within 48h)	
Category II: generally recommended			
Streptococcus pneumoniae	CD4+ lymphocyte count >200 cells/mm³	23 valent polysaccharide vaccine 0.5ml im (single dose); repeat in 5 years time	
Hepatitis B virus	All anti-HBV-negative patients	Hepatitis B vaccine 10mg im (three doses)	
Influenza virus	All patients	Inactivated trivalent Influenza vaccine 0.5ml im each year in autumn	Oseltamivir 75mg q24h (influenza A or B) Amantadine 100mg q12h Rimantadine 100mg q12h (influenza A only)
Hepatitis A virus	All anti-HAV-negative patients at increased risk (illicit drug users, men who have sex with men, hemophiliacs) or with chronic liver disease, including chronic hepatitis B or C	Hepatitis A vaccine (two doses)	
Category III: not recommended for most patients. To be considered in selected patients only			
Cytomegalovirus	CD4+ lymphocyte count < 50 cells/μl *and* positive cytomegalovirus antibodies	Oral ganciclovir 1g q8h	
Bacteria	Neutropenia	G-CSF 5–10μg/kg sc q24h for 2–4 weeks *or* GM-CSF 250μg/m² iv q24h for 2–4 weeks	
Cryptococcus neoformans	CD4+ lymphocyte count <50 cells/mm³	Fluconazole 100–200mg q24h *or* itraconazole 200mg q24h	
Histoplasmosis	CD4+ lymphocyte count <100 cells/mm³ *and* residence in endemic area	Itraconazole 200mg q24h	

Table 123.1 Prophylaxis of first episode of opportunistic infections in adults and adolescents with HIV infection. DS, double strength; G-CSF, granulocyte colony-stimulating factor; GM-CSF, granulocyte–macrophage colony-stimulating factor; PPD, purified protein derivatives; SS, single strength; TMP–SMX, trimethoprim–sulfamethoxazole. Adapted from USPHS/IDSA guidelines.[8]

PROPHYLAXIS TO PREVENT RECURRENCE OF OPPORTUNISTIC DISEASE IN ADULTS AND ADOLESCENTS WITH HIV INFECTION			
Pathogen	**Indication**	**First-choice regimen**	**Alternative regimens**
Category I: Recommended as standard of care			
Pneumocystis carinii	Previous PCP	TMP–SMX 1SS q24h *or* 1 DS q24h	Dapsone 50mg q12h or 100mg q24h Dapsone 50mg q24h plus pyrimethamine 50mg weekly *plus* leucovorin 25mg weekly Dapsone 200mg *plus* pyrimethamine 75mg *plus* leucovorin 25mg weekly Aerosolized pentamidine 300mg monthly by nebulizer Atovaquone 1500mg q24h TMP–SMX, 1 DS three times weekly
Toxoplasma gondii	Prior toxoplasmic encephalitis	Sulfadiazine 500–1000mg q6h *plus* pyrimethamine 25–50mg q24h *plus* leucovorin 10–25mg po q24h (confers protection against PCP)	Clindamycin 300–450mg q6–8h *plus* pyrimethamine 25–50mg q24h *plus* leucovorin 10–25mg q24h Atovaquone 750mg q6–12h *with or without* pyrimethamine 25mg q24h *plus* leucovorin 10mg q24h
Mycobacterium avium complex	Documented disseminated disease	Clarithromycin 500mg q12h *plus* ethambutol 15mg/kg q24h (*with or without* rifabutin 300mg q24h)	Azithromycin 500mg q24h *plus* ethambutol 15mg/kg q24h (*with or without* rifabutin 300mg q24h)
Cytomegalovirus	Previous end-organ disease	Ganciclovir 5–6mg/kg/day iv 5–7 days/week *or* 1000mg orally q8h *or* foscarnet 90–120mg/kg q24h *or* (for retinitis) ganciclovir sustained-release implant every 6–9 months *plus* ganciclovir 1.0–1.5g po q8h	Cidofovir 5mg/kg every 2 weeks (with probenecid) Fomivirsen 1 vial (330μg) injected into the vitreous, then repeated every 2–4 weeks Valganciclovir 900mg q24h
Cryptococcus neoformans	Documented disease	Fluconazole 200mg q24h	Amphotericin B 0.6–1.0mg/kg weekly Itraconazole 200mg q24h
Histoplasma capsulatum	Documented disease	Itraconazole 200mg q12h	Amphotericin B 1.0mg/kg weekly
Coccidioides immitis	Documented disease	Fluconazole 400mg q24h	Amphotericin B 1.0mg/kg weekly Itraconazole 200mg q12h
Salmonella spp. (non-*typhi*)	Bacteremia	Ciprofloxacin 500mg q12h for several months	Antibiotic chemoprophylaxis with another active agent
Category II: Recommended only if subsequent episodes are frequent or severe			
Herpes simplex virus	Frequent/severe recurrences	Aciclovir 200mg q8h *or* 400mg q12h *or* Famciclovir 250mg q12h	Valaciclovir 500mg q12h
Candida (oropharyngeal, vaginal or esophageal)	Frequent/severe recurrences	Fluconazole 100–200mg q24h	Itraconazole solution 200mg q24h

Table 123.2 Prophylaxis to prevent recurrence of opportunistic disease in adults and adolescents with HIV infection. DS, double strength; SS, single strength. Adapted from USPHS/IDSA guidelines.[8]

Regimens include:

- daily or twice weekly isoniazid (plus pyridoxine) for 9 months;
- daily rifampin or rifabutin for 4 months; and
- daily rifampin (or rifabutin) plus pyrazinamide for 2 months (although severe liver injury has been associated with this combination).

In patients whose initial skin test is negative and whose CD4+ T cell count has increased to above 200/mm^3 with HAART, a repeat tuberculin skin test should be considered.[12]

Mycobacterium avium complex

Patients who have a CD4+ T cell count below 50/mm^3 should receive clarithromycin (500mg q12h) or azithromycin (1200mg weekly). Combination with rifabutin is not recommended. Both macrolides confer protection against respiratory bacterial infections. Rifabutin is an alternative in patients who cannot tolerate macrolides.

Primary prophylaxis should be discontinued in patients treated with HAART who show an increase in CD4+ T cells to above 100/mm^3 for at least 3 months and should be reintroduced if the CD4+ T cell count decreases to less than 50–100/mm^3.[13]

Patients who have disseminated MAC should receive lifelong therapy with clarithromycin (or azithromycin) and ethambutol with or without rifabutin. It is reasonable to consider discontinuation of treatment in patients who have completed a course of at least 12 months of therapy, have no symptoms and show a CD4+ T cell count above 100/mm^3 following HAART for at least 6 months.[14]

Streptococcus pneumoniae

Patients who have a CD4+ T cell count greater than 200/mm^3 should receive a single dose of 23-valent polysaccharide pneumococcal vaccine every 5 years. If the CD4+ T cell count is below 200/mm^3, vaccination should be considered (with revaccination when the count increases to above 200/mm^3).[15]

Cryptococcosis

Primary prophylaxis should not be used routinely. Patients who have had cryptococcosis should receive lifelong suppressive treatment with fluconazole unless they have a sustained (≥ 6 months) increase in the CD4+ T cell count following HAART. Suppressive therapy should be reinitiated if the CD4+ T cell count decreases to less than 100–200/mm^3.[16]

Cytomegalovirus

Patients who have had active cytomegalovirus disease should receive lifelong maintenance therapy with any of the following regimens: parenteral or oral ganciclovir, parenteral foscarnet, combined parenteral ganciclovir and foscarnet, parenteral cidofovir or oral valganciclovir. Administration of ganciclovir via intraocular implant or repetitive intravitreous injections of fomivirsen may be used in patients who have retinitis only, and are generally combined with oral ganciclovir. Repetitive intravitreous injections of ganciclovir, foscarnet and cidofovir have been shown to be effective in uncontrolled case series.[17,18]

Discontinuation of secondary prophylaxis should be considered in patients who have received HAART and show an increase in CD4+ T cells to above 100–150/mm^3 for at least 6 months. All these patients should continue to undergo regular ophthalmologic examination. Secondary prophylaxis should be restarted when the CD4+ T cell count falls to below 100–150/mm^3.[19]

Varicella-zoster virus disease

HIV adults who have no history of chickenpox or are seronegative for varicella-zoster virus (VZV) should receive VZV immunoglobulin as soon as possible but within 96 hours after exposure to a patient who has chickenpox or shingles. The efficacy of aciclovir in this setting is unknown.

REFERENCES

1. Chaisson RE, Moore RD. Prevention of opportunistic infections in the era of improved antiretroviral therapy. J Acquir Immune Defic Syndr Hum Retrovirol 1997;16(Suppl.1):S14-22.
2. Kaplan JE, Masur H, Jaffe HW, Holmes KK. Reducing the impact of opportunistic infections in patients with HIV infection: new guidelines. JAMA 1995;274:347–8.
3. Pierce M, Crampton S, Henry D, *et al.* A randomized trial of clarithromycin as prophylaxis against disseminated *Mycobacterium avium complex* infection in patients with advanced acquired immunodeficiency syndrome. N Engl J Med 1996;335:384–91.
4. Moore RD, Fortgant I, Keruly J, Chaisson RE. Adverse events from drug therapy for Human immunodeficiency virus disease. Am J Med 1996;101:34–40.
5. Piscitelli SC, Flexner C, Minor JR, Polis MA, Masur H. Drug interactions in patients infected with Human immunodeficiency virus. Clin Infect Dis 1996;23:685–93.
6. Freedberg K, Scharfstein A, Seage G III, *et al.* The cost-effectiveness of preventing AIDS-related opportunistic infections. JAMA 1998;279:130–6.
7. Autran B, Carcelain G, Li TS, *et al.* Positive effects of combined antiretroviral therapy on CD4+ T cell homeostasis and function in advanced HIV disease. Science 1997;277:112–6.
8. USPHS/IDSA guidelines for the prevention of opportunistic infections in persons infected with human immunodeficiency virus. Washington, DC: US Public Health Service; 2001.
9. Ledergerber B, Mocroft A, Reiss P, *et al.* Discontinuation of secondary prophylaxis against *Pneumocystis carinii* pneumonia in patients with HIV infection who have a response to antiretroviral therapy. N Engl J Med 2001;344:168–74.
10. Mussini C, Pezzotti P, Govoni A, *et al.* Discontinuation of primary prophylaxis for *Pneumocystis carinii* pneumonia and toxoplasmic encephalitis in human immunodeficiency virus type I-infected patients: the changes in opportunistic prophylaxis study. J Infect Dis 2000;181:1635–42.
11. Miro JM, Podzamczer D, Pena JM, *et al.* Discontinuation of primary and secondary *Toxoplasma gondii* prophylaxis is safe in HIV-1 infected patients after immunological recovery with HAART. Final results of the GESIDA 04/98 study. In: Abstracts of the 39th Interscience Conference on Antimicrobial Agents and Chemotherapy. San Francisco, CA: American Society for Microbiology; 2000:abstract L16.
12. Centers for Disease Control and Prevention. Targeted tuberculin testing and treatment of latent tuberculosis infection. MMWR Morb Mortal Wkly Rep 2000;49(RR-6).
13. El-Sadr WM, Burman WJ, Grant LB, *et al.* Discontinuation of prophylaxis for *Mycobacterium avium* complex disease in HIV-infected patients who have a response to antiretroviral therapy. N Engl J Med 2000;342:1085–92.
14. Shafran SD, Gill MJ, Lajonde RG, *et al.* Successful discontinuation of MAC therapy following effective HAART. In: Program and abstracts of the 8th Conference on Retroviruses and Opportunistic Infections, 4–8 February 2001, Chicago, IL: abstract 547.
15. Dworkin MS, Ward JW, Hanson DL, *et al.* Pneumococcal disease among HIV-infected persons: incidence, risk factors, and impact of vaccination. Clin Infect Dis 2001;32:794–800.
16. Mussini C, Cossarizza A, Pezzotti P, *et al.* Discontinuation or continuation of maintenance therapy for cryptococcal meningitis in patients with AIDS treated with HAART. In : Program and abstracts of the 8th Conference on Retroviruses and Opportunistic Infections, 4–8 February 2001, Chicago, IL: abstract 546.
17. Martin DF, Kupperman BD, Wolitz RA, *et al.* Oral ganciclovir for patients with cytomegalovirus retinitis treated with a ganciclovir implant, N Engl J Med 1999;340:1063–70.
18. DeSmet MD, Meenken C, van den Horn GJ. Fomivirsen – a phosphorothioate oligonucleotide for the treatment of CMV retinitis. Ocular Immunol Inflamm 1999;7:189–98.
19. Jouan M, Saves H, Tubiana R, *et al.* Discontinuation of maintenance therapy for cytomegalovirus retinitis in HIV infected patients receiving highly active antiretroviral therapy. Restimop Study Team. AIDS 2001;15:23–31.

chapter

124 *Pneumocystis carinii* Pneumonia

Pierre-Marie Girard

EPIDEMIOLOGY

Historically, the occurrence of *Pneumocystis carinii* pneumonia (PCP) in American homosexuals who had no previously known immune deficiency revealed the spread of the AIDS epidemic.[1] Although the implementation of prophylaxis (see Chapter 123) and the advances in effective antiretroviral therapy have markedly decreased its incidence, PCP remains frequent, especially in patients unaware of their HIV seropositivity or who have poor access to the health care system. The use of highly active antiretroviral therapy (HAART) has decreased the incidence of PCP as compared with other pulmonary diseases such as bacterial pneumonia and non-Hodgkin's lymphoma.[2–5] Development of PCP is mainly due to reactivation of latent infection acquired during childhood or adolescence; however, genetic studies of *P. carinii* isolates suggest that some cases of PCP may be due to recent exposure to environmental strains.[6] In Africa, PCP, initially thought to be a rare complication of AIDS in this area, can actually account for as much as 30% of AIDS-defining diseases.[7,8]

The best predictor of occurrence of PCP in HIV-infected patients is the CD4+ lymphocyte blood count.[9] A significant risk of PCP exists when the CD4+ lymphocyte count is less than 200/mm^3 or 15–20% of total lymphocytes, and clinical manifestations (e.g. thrush, herpes zoster, unexplained fever, weight loss) or a history of such manifestations are correlated with increased risk, independently of the CD4+ lymphocyte count. Cytotoxic chemotherapies also increase the risk of PCP whatever the CD4+ lymphocyte count. The rate of relapse after a first episode of PCP is high (approximately 60% incidence within 1 year) when neither specific prophylaxis nor HAART is initiated.

PATHOGENESIS AND PATHOLOGY

Development of *P. carinii* is restricted to the lung tissue in more than 95% of cases. The use of aerosolized pentamidine, which has negligible extrapulmonary deposition, explains the occurrence of disseminated infections in bone marrow, spleen, liver, retina and skin.[10]

Pneumocystis carinii pneumonia is characterized by a foamy eosinophilic exudate and the 'honeycomb' appearance of the lung tissue due to mild interstitial pneumonitis with proliferation of type II pneumocytes. *Pneumocystis carinii* cysts are visualized by methenamine–silver nitrate or toluidine blue O stains in the exudate, and trophozoite forms (visualized by Giemsa stains or its derivatives) proliferate and attach to type I pneumocytes. Extensive interstitial fibrosis is the natural process of untreated infections leading to respiratory distress. Mild fibrosis also occurs under treatment.

Other less common pathologic characteristics are seen in people who have AIDS. Diffuse alveolar damage may predominate without alveolar exudate. Cystic and cavitary lesions predominating in upper lobes may also develop. Pneumothorax is a frequent complication resulting from the rupture of cysts. Noncaseating granulomatous inflammation, sometimes with calcification, is occasionally seen.

Animal experiments indicate that CD4+ lymphocytes play a critical role in the host's ability to resist and recover from *P. carinii* infection. In addition, macrophage function may be important for clearance of the micro-organisms and the macrophage mannose receptor seems important for binding and uptake of *P. carinii*. Among cytokines, tumor necrosis factor has been shown to be directly lethal to *P. carinii*.

CLINICAL FEATURES

The most common clinical presentation of PCP in AIDS is a progressive dyspnea with dry cough, fever (often mild) and weight loss. The mean duration of breathlessness is 3–4 weeks at presentation. On examination, fever and tachypnea are common, whereas lung auscultation may be normal or reveal only basal crepitations.

Chest radiography is an important step in the diagnosis procedure of lung diseases in AIDS. The chest radiograph is normal in less than 5% of cases. The most common pattern is a fine bilateral interstitial and then alveolointerstitial infiltrate progressing from the perihilar to the peripheral regions (Fig. 124.1). Without therapy, or even during the first days of treatment, the alveolar interstitial pattern worsens. In advanced cases, progressive consolidation with air bronchograms and complete opacification of the lungs may develop (Fig. 124.2).

Numerous atypical patterns of PCP may occur. They include localized infiltrates, notably of the upper lobes, in patients who fail to respond to aerosolized pentamidine prophylaxis, cavitary lesions, solitary lung nodules, spontaneous pneumothoraces and pleural effusions. Lymphadenopathies causing hilar or mediastinal enlargement are very rare and are usually linked to lymphoma and concomitant infections such as mycobacteriosis.

Parenchymal involvement is well assessed by computerized tomography (CT), which in typical cases exhibits bilateral ground-glass infiltrates that may not have been seen on chest radiography. The

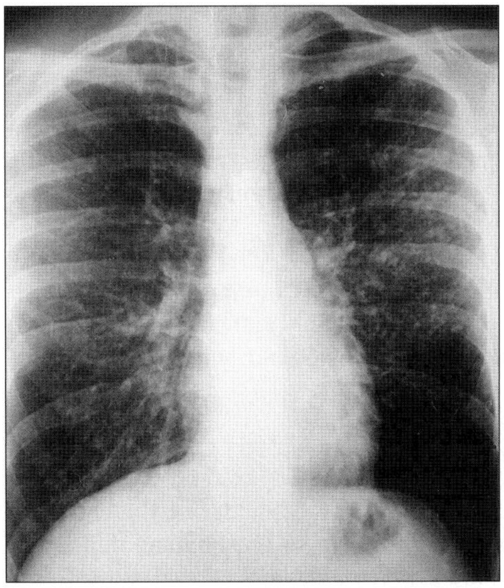

Fig. 124.1 Mild *Pneumocystis carinii* pneumonia. There are bilateral micronodular lesions.

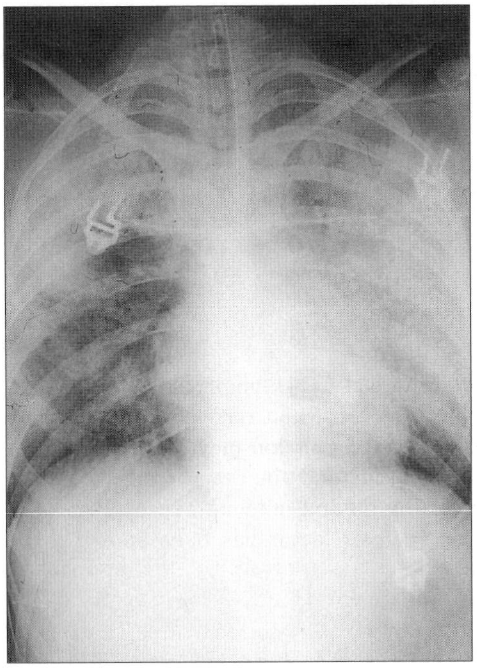

Fig. 124.2 Severe *Pneumocystis carinii* pneumonia. This shows an extensive alveolar interstitial infiltrate with consolidation of the left lung and upper right lobe. Courtesy of A Cabié.

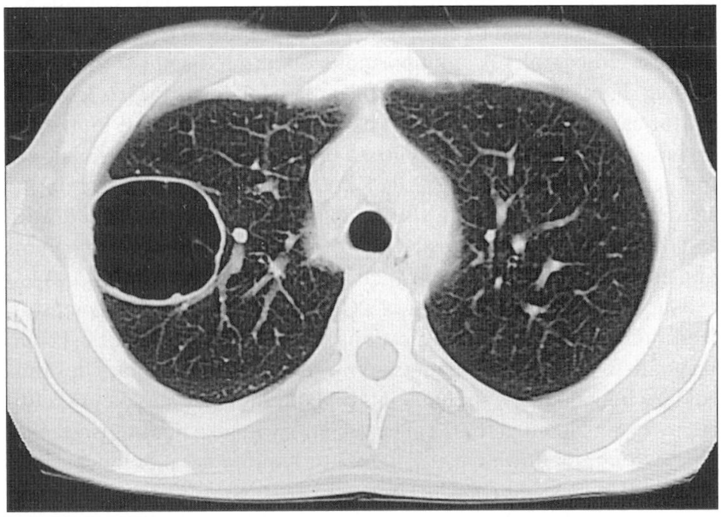

Fig. 124.3 Six weeks after treatment of moderate *Pneumocystis carinii* pneumonia. Chest CT shows large, thin-walled bullae of the right lung.

infiltrates can be dense and homogeneous or patchy in both lungs. Parenchymal destruction, from bullae (Fig. 124.3) predominating in the apices to extensive emphysematous changes, may also be seen on CT. Small pulmonary cysts with thin walls throughout the lungs are common.

In extrapulmonary *P. carinii* infections, CT or ultrasonography demonstrates multiple abscess-like lesions varying from several millimeters to a few centimeters in size, mainly in the spleen (Fig. 124.4) and sometimes in the liver. The radiologic abnormalities are not characteristic of *Pneumocystis* infection.

DIFFERENTIAL DIAGNOSIS

A wide spectrum of lung diseases may occur during the course of AIDS, especially in patients who have severe immune deficiency, which is the usual situation for developing PCP.

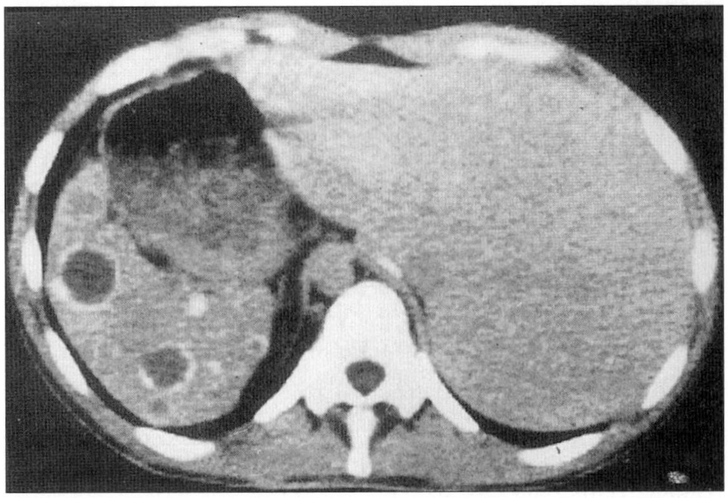

Fig. 124.4 Splenic *Pneumocystis carinii* pneumonia. Abdominal CT shows multiple ring-enhancing abscess-like round formations. Courtesy of C Bazin.

Kaposi's sarcoma is the most common lung tumor and occurs almost exclusively in homosexual men. Clinical presentation may be a progressive dyspnea and the patient is usually afebrile. Cutaneous and/or palatal Kaposi's sarcoma is frequently diagnosed before lung localization. On chest radiography or CT, nodular lesions and peribronchovascular thickening are more frequent than interstitial abnormalities. In most cases, the macroscopic appearance of the tracheobronchial tract is characteristic. Other considerations include bacterial and fungal pneumonia, and tuberculosis.

Lymphocytic interstitial pneumonia is a rare disease due to lung infiltration by $CD8^+$ lymphocytes and occurs usually in patients who have a $CD4^+$ lymphocyte count above 200/mm^3.

DIAGNOSIS

Establishing a diagnosis of PCP requires the morphologic demonstration of the micro-organism. Because the sampling procedures that combine both high sensitivity and specificity are invasive (i.e. fiberoptic bronchoscopy with bronchoalveolar lavage, or, less frequently, transbronchial biopsy), the need to make a definite diagnosis before starting anti-*Pneumocystis* therapy is still controversial. Diagnosis on pulmonary samples can be improved by the use of either monoclonal antibodies or polymerase chain reaction (PCR).

Arterial blood gases must be measured to assess the severity of the disease, but have no diagnostic value. Two functional tests that have been thoroughly evaluated – decreased diffusing capacity and increase of alveolar–arterial gradient with exercise – have yielded high sensitivity and low specificity. Increased serum lactate dehydrogenase (LDH) may confirm the lung disease in cases of subtle symptoms or radiologic abnormalities but has no specificity. The level of serum LDH and, more precisely, the slope of its decrease during the first days of treatment have prognostic value. These tests are therefore routinely included in the diagnostic algorithms used by some teams to select patients who will benefit from fiberoptic bronchoscopy. Because of their low specificity their use should not alter the time for bronchoscopy.

No specific biologic marker of *P. carinii* infection exists for individual diagnosis. Antibodies to *P. carinii* are commonly detected in the adult general population and may be less detectable in immunocompromised patients. Attempts to detect *P. carinii* antigens in serum have failed to establish a diagnosis of PCP. Even PCR detection of *P. carinii* genome in blood has been very disappointing. In fact PCR tests are sensitive enough only in the very rare cases of disseminated infection, although they may be useful for detecting *P. carinii* in lung respiratory samples (bronchoalveolar lavage, induced sputum or possibly saliva).[11]

Identification of *Pneumocystis carinii*

Methods of sampling

Sputum examination is the least invasive procedure for collecting lower respiratory specimens. Because patients who have PCP generally do not have a productive cough, an induced sputum can be obtained after aerosolization of hypertonic saline, ideally under the supervision of a physiotherapist. In routine practice, the sensitivity of the test is approximately 50–60% and is slightly improved by using an immunofluorescence technique for visualization, with monoclonal antibodies directed to the cysts.

Fiberoptic bronchoscopy with bronchoalveolar lavage is the reference routine diagnostic procedure because its sensitivity is more than 95% and its specificity is 100%. When the diagnosis can not be obtained from bronchoalveolar lavage fluid, transbronchial lung biopsy may help, although it is more invasive and is associated with a risk of bleeding and pneumothorax (5–10%). This procedure has a higher sensitivity than bronchoalveolar lavage, especially in patients receiving prophylaxis by aerosolized pentamidine.

Methods of staining

It is recommended that two stains be used to visualize both cysts (methenamine silver or toluidine blue O for the cyst wall, Wright–Giemsa for nuclei) and trophozoites (Wright–Giemsa or Diff–Quik). Immunofluorescent stains are more expensive and are mostly valuable for less-than-optimal samples such as induced sputum, where their sensitivity is superior to conventional stains. The PCR methods are of little benefit on lung samples but can increase the diagnosis rate on induced sputum.

MANAGEMENT

The measurement of arterial gas is used routinely to delineate mild ($Pa\text{O}_2$ ≥70mmHg), moderate ($Pa\text{O}_2$ 50–70mmHg) and severe ($Pa\text{O}_2$ <50mmHg) PCP. In mild PCP, outpatient management with oral therapy is often possible providing no other disease is present, there is low risk of drug malabsorption and the patient has a good understanding of the management and is aware of the potential side effects of therapy. Hospitalization is required for moderate and severe PCP to ensure careful monitoring of treatment, which will be administered intravenously, at least during the first days. Besides blood gas assessment, other factors listed in Table 124.1 are useful prognostic factors that can be taken into account for proposing hospitalization.

FACTORS ASSOCIATED WITH A POOR PROGNOSIS OF PCP	
At diagnosis	Prolonged history of respiratory symptoms
	Recurrent PCP
	Severe hypoxemia
	Marked radiographic abnormalities
	High plasma LDH level
	High plasma angiotensin-converting enzyme level
	Hypoalbuminemia
	Neutrophilia (>5%) in bronchoalveolar lavage fluid
During the course of the disease	Worsening hypoxemia
	Mechanical ventilation, especially when delayed after initiation of therapy
	Pneumothorax and multiple cavitary lesions or emphysema
	Bacterial co-infection of the respiratory tract
	Persisting high serum levels of LDH

Table 124.1 Factors associated with a poor prognosis of *Pneumocystis carinii* pneumonia.

Anti-*Pneumocystis* drugs

Therapeutic progress, although quite laborious because of the difficulty encountered with in-vitro cultivation of *P. carinii,* has been made in four main fields:

- the optimal use of old drugs such as pentamidine and trimethoprim–sulfamethoxazole (TMP–SMX) has been defined through numerous trials;
- new combinations of old drugs such as dapsone plus trimethoprim, and clindamycin plus primaquine have been evaluated;
- two innovative compounds, atovaquone and trimetrexate, have been developed and are approved for treatment of PCP; and
- the indications of adjunctive corticosteroids have been carefully defined.

Last, but not least, despite much controversy, the real benefit of mechanical ventilation for a subset of patients has now been established.[12]

Trimethoprim–sulfamethoxazole is the drug of choice for PCP whatever its severity, and no other drug or combination of drugs has demonstrated improved efficacy in control trials. The classic dose of 20mg/kg/day trimethoprim with 100mg/kg/day sulfamethoxazole in three or four divided doses can be reduced to 15mg/kg/day trimethoprim with 80mg/kg/day sulfamethoxazole without loss of efficacy. The unexpectedly high rate of TMP–SMX side effects was noticed early in patients who have AIDS; these include rash, fever, pruritus, digestive disturbances and cytopenia.[13] Most side effects occur after 7–10 days of therapy. More recently, hyperkalemia has been reported. However, many of these side effects, whose mechanisms are still poorly understood, spontaneously resolve and in these cases treatment does not need to be discontinued. Approximately 10–20% of patients will need to be switched to another treatment because of TMP–SMX intolerance. It is possible that adjunctive treatment with corticosteroids decreases the incidence of the cutaneous side effects of TMP–SMX. Monitoring blood concentrations of trimethoprim (concentration maintained below 5–8μg/ml) in order to avoid hematologic toxicity is rarely necessary except in patients who have substantially impaired renal function.

Pentamidine (3–4mg/kg/day intravenously) an aromatic diamidine endowed with antiprotozoal activity, was the first drug successfully used for therapy of PCP in patients who did not have AIDS. Trials conducted in people who have AIDS have confirmed the risk of severe side effects but have not shown activity superior to that of TMP–SMX.[14] The side effects are severe and include hypotension, hypoglycemia, pancreatitis, diabetes, *torsades de pointes* and renal insufficiency. The indications for pentamidine have narrowed with the development of alternative oral combinations for mild PCP in TMP–SMX-intolerant patients and are now restricted to patients who have severe PCP but cannot tolerate or fail to respond to TMP–SMX.

Trimethoprim plus dapsone at 20mg/kg/day and 100mg/day is an oral alternative to TMP–SMX and has appeared to be as effective as TMP–SMX in several trials of mild PCP,[15,16] although experience is limited. Side effects include rash, methemoglobinemia, hemolytic anemia and neutropenia.

Clindamycin (600–900mg/day) plus primaquine (15–30mg/day) is another oral alternative to TMP–SMX for therapy of mild PCP. These drugs have the advantage of structurally differing from sulfonamide or sulfone compounds, thus limiting the risk of cross-toxicity. This combination is as effective as the previously mentioned combinations in nonsevere PCP[16] but skin rashes, albeit often transient, and digestive complications due to clindamycin occur in 20–25% of patients.

Atovaquone (2250mg/day) is a hydroxynaphthoquinone compound initially developed for its antimalarial activity. Only an oral formulation, which must be taken with food, is available; it has a bioavailability of less than 10%. A new micronized formulation with improved bioavailability has been developed recently and offers better results.[17] Therefore, atovaquone is used as second-line therapy in patients with nonsevere PCP who are or have become intolerant to TMP–SMX and whose digestive absorption is not impaired. Administration of rifampin should be avoided.

Trimetrexate (45mg/m^2 of body surface area) is a lipophilic inhibitor of dihydrofolate reductase that is 1500 times more potent in vitro against *P. carinii* than trimethoprim. However, controlled trials have not shown it to be superior to conventional therapies such as TMP–SMX and intravenous pentamidine.[18] Serious treatment-limiting toxicity was significantly less frequent among patients receiving trimetrexate than TMP–SMX. Trimetrexate is currently used as a second-line therapy for patients requiring intravenous therapy who are refractory or fail to respond to other treatment. It must be administered with leucovorin acid (80mg/m^2 of body surface area) to prevent the development of cytopenia as a severe side effect.

Choice of therapy

The choice of therapy is guided by:
- severity of the disease (see Table 124.1);
- the likelihood of digestive drug absorption; and
- the history of drug intolerance.

The first two criteria will indicate whether an oral regimen is advisable. In case of drug intolerance, it is important to evaluate the severity of past toxicity. In practice, contraindication to reintroduction of TMP–SMX or to the use of a combination with potential cross-intolerance to sulfonamide is based on a history of anaphylaxis or exfoliative dermatitis or other life-threatening toxicity such as severe cytolytic hepatitis. Whenever possible, the first-line therapy is TMP–SMX. For cases of mild PCP and a history of nonsevere TMP–SMX intolerance, one can choose between the use of:
- TMP–SMX;
- dapsone plus trimethoprim; and
- clindamycin plus primaquine or atovaquone.

For cases of mild PCP and a high risk of severe intolerance to TMP–SMX, atovaquone is a reasonable alternative, providing its absorption will not be impaired by digestive malabsorption.

Mutations in *P. carinii* genes expressing genes targeted by current drugs (sulfonamides, sulfones and atovaquone) were reported in the late 1990s. Although several studies have reported an increasing frequency of mutations in the dihydropteroate synthase gene[19–21] and in cytochrome *b*,[22] the impact of these mutations on clinical outcome remains controversial.

In most cases, respiratory symptoms and oxygenation improve after 5–10 days. Early mild deterioration is not infrequent during the first days of treatment. Duration of treatment is classically 21 days, although a shorter duration (2 weeks) might be sufficient but has not been adequately evaluated. When TMP–SMX is initiated intravenously, it can be switched to an oral formulation after a few days. There is no need for repeat fibroscopy, and persistence of *P. carinii*, the viability of which is unknown, is common. Secondary prophylaxis is required after treatment of the attack.

Mechanical ventilation should be considered in patients who fail to improve under non-invasive oxygenation methods. The decision is taken according to the patient's wishes and general condition. Anti-*P. carinii* therapy is administered intravenously and TMP–SMX remains the drug of choice, unless there is a history of severe intolerance. In this latter case, pentamidine or trimetrexate with folinic acid rescue are the two alternatives.

In addition to anti-*P. carinii* therapy, corticosteroids are administered as soon as possible in patients who have moderate to severe disease. The use of corticosteroids is recommended in patients whose $Pa\text{O}_2$ is less than 65mmHg for improving oxygenation, reducing the risk of fibrosis, decreasing the need of mechanical ventilation and reducing the case fatality rate. The corticosteroid regimen used is as follows:
- on days 1–5, 40mg oral prednisone (prednisolone) q12h;
- on days 6–10, 40mg oral prednisone/day; and
- on days 11–21, 20mg oral prednisone/day.

When corticosteroid therapy is used one should be aware of possible reactivation of latent co-infections such as mycobacterial and herpes infections.

Management of deterioration on therapy

Patients who deteriorate under therapy need to be carefully evaluated for lung complications related to PCP and associated diseases. The value of changing the initial anti-PCP therapy for another one has not been well demonstrated, but this is common practice. Clindamycin–primaquine (the latter being not available in all countries) could be an attractive regimen in this setting, as suggested by a meta-analysis of 27 clinical trials.[23] Obviously, patients who deteriorate on oral therapy should receive intravenous therapy with either TMP–SMX, pentamidine or trimetrexate. Reasons for the deterioration are various and include:
- severe pulmonary lesions with alveolar and interstitial edema;
- pneumatoceles;
- bullae and cavities that can provoke pneumothorax; and
- emphysema.

In hypoxemic patients, cardiac failure is common and will require appropriate monitoring and treatment.

Associated diseases include bacterial pneumonia (community-acquired or, more frequently, nosocomial), fungal diseases and Kaposi's sarcoma. Repeat bronchoscopy with bronchoalveolar lavage and transbronchial biopsy should therefore be considered. Persistence of *P. carinii* is usual and does not indicate failure of anti-*P. carinii* therapy. In the past 15 years, the case fatality rate of PCP has markedly decreased and is now around 5%. This globally improved prognosis may be due to several factors:
- better awareness of the disease by physicians and patients leading to earlier diagnosis;
- aggressive therapy despite mild toxicity;
- the use of adjunctive corticosteroids; and
- better defined indications of intensive care.

REFERENCES

1. Gottlieb M, Schroff R, Shanker H, *et al.* *Pneumocystis carinii* pneumonia and mucosal candidiasis in previously healthy homosexual men. Evidence of a new acquired cellular immunodeficiency. N Engl J Med 1981;305:1425–31.
2. Wolff AJ, O'Donnell AE. Pulmonary manifestations of HIV infection in the era of highly active antiretroviral therapy. Chest 2001;120:1888–93.
3. Asch SM, Gifford AL, Bozzette SA, *et al.*. Under use of primary *Mycobacterium avium* complex and *Pneumocystis carinii* prophylaxis in the United States. J Acquir Immune Defic Syndr 2001;28:340–4.
4. Abgrall S, Matheron S, Le Moing V, Dupont C, Costagliola D. Pneumocystis carinii pneumonia recurrence in HIV patients on highly active antiretroviral therapy: secondary prophylaxis. J Acquir Immune Defic Syndr 2001;26:151–8.
5. Detels R, Tarwater P, Phair J, Margloick J, Riddler SA, Munoz A. Effectiveness of potent antiretroviral therapies on the incidence of opportunistic infection before and after AIDS diagnosis. AIDS 2001;15:347–55.
6. Beard CB, Carter JL, Keely SP *et al.* Genetic variation in Pneumocystis carinii isolates from different geographic regions: implications for transmission. Emerg Infect Dis 2000;6:265–72.

7. Mahomed AG, Murray J, Klempman S, *et al.* *Pneumocystis carinii* pneumonia in HIV infected patients from South Africa. East Afr Med J 1999;76:80–4.
8. Chokephaibulkit K, Wanachiwanawin D, Chearskul S, *et al.* *Pneumocystis carinii* severe pneumonia among human immunodeficiency virus-infected children in Thailand: the effect of primary prophylaxis strategy. Pediatr Infect Dis J 1999;18:147–52.
9. Phair J, Munoz A, Detels R, Kaslow R, Rinaldo C, Saah A. The risk of *Pneumocystis carinii* pneumonia among men infected with human immunodeficiency virus type I. N Engl J Med 1990;322:161–5.
10. Raviglione MC. Extrapulmonary pneumocystosis: the first 50 cases. Rev Infect Dis 1990;12:1127–38.
13. Kovacs JA, Hiemenz JW, Macher AM, *et al.* *Pneumocystis carinii* pneumonia: a comparison between patients with the acquired immunodeficiency syndrome and patients with other immunodeficiencies. Ann Intern Med 1984;100:663–71.
11. Lipschik GY, Gill VJ, Lundgren JD, *et al.* Improved diagnosis of *Pneumocystis carinii* infection by polymerase chain reaction on induced sputum and blood. Lancet 1992;340:203–6.
12. Wachter R, Luce J, Safrin S, *et al.* Cost and outcome of intensive care for patients with AIDS *Pneumocystis carinii* pneumonia and severe respiratory failure. JAMA 1995;273:230–5.
14. Sattler FR, Cowan R, Nielsen DM, Ruskin J. Trimethoprim–sulfamethoxazole compared with pentamidine for treatment of *Pneumocystis carinii* pneumonia in the acquired immunodeficiency syndrome: a prospective, noncrossover study. Ann Intern Med 1988;109:280–7.
15. Medina I, Mills L, Leoung G, *et al.* Oral therapy for *Pneumocystis carinii* pneumonia in the acquired immunodeficiency syndrome: a controlled trial of trimethoprim–sulfamethoxazole versus trimethoprim–dapsone. N Engl J Med 1990;323:776–82.
16. Safrin S, Finkelstein DM, Feinberg J, *et al.* Comparison of three regimens for treatment of mild to moderate *Pneumocystis carinii* pneumonia in patients with AIDS. Ann Intern Med 1996;124:792–802.
17. Rosenberg DM, McCarthy W, Slavinsky J *et al.* Atovaquone suspension for treatment of *Pneumocystis carinii* pneumonia in HIV-infected patients. AIDS 2001;15:211–4.
18. Sattler FR, Frame P, Davis R, *et al.* Comparison of trimetrexate with leucovorin versus trimethoprim–sulfamethoxazole for moderate-to-severe episodes of *Pneumocystis carinii* pneumonia in patients with AIDS: a prospective, controlled multicenter investigation of the AIDS Clinical Trials Group protocol 029/031. J Infect Dis 1994;170:165–72.
19. Helweg-Larsen J, Benfield TL, Eugen-Olsen J, Lundgren JD, Lundgren B. Effects of mutations in *Pneumocystis carinii* dihydropteroate synthase gene on outcome of AIDS-associated *P. carinii* pneumonia. Lancet 1999;354: 1318–9.
20. Navin TR, Beard CB, Huang L, *et al.* Effect of mutations in *Pneumocystis carinii* dihydropteroate synthase gene on outcome of *P. carinii* pneumonia in patients with HIV-1: a prospective study. Lancet 2001;358:545–9.
21. Dworkin MS, Hanson DL, Navin TR. Survival of patients with AIDS after diagnosis of *Pneumocystis carinii* in the United States. J Infect Dis 2001;183:1409–12.
22. Kazanjian P, Armstrong W, Hossler PA, *et al.* *Pneumocystis carinii* cytochrome *b* mutations are associated with atovaquone exposure in patients with AIDS. J Infect Dis 2001;183:819–22.
23. Smego RA, Nagar S, Maloba B, Popara M. A meta-analysis of salvage therapy for *Pneumocystis carinii* pneumonia. Arch Intern Med 2001;161:1529–33.

chapter
125 Viral Infection

Maurice E Murphy & Bruce Polsky

INTRODUCTION

Viral infections are an important cause of morbidity and mortality in patients who have HIV disease. Over the past two decades, substantial progress has been made in our understanding of the pathogenesis and natural history of viral infections in this patient population. The development of more sensitive diagnostic laboratory techniques and effective therapeutic agents has had a significant impact on the management of these conditions. The introduction of highly active antiretroviral therapy (HAART) for HIV disease has exerted a profound effect on the epidemiology, natural history, clinical manifestations and responses to treatment of opportunistic infections, including viral infections, in HIV-infected patients.[1] With recovery of immune function as a result of effective antiretroviral therapy, the incidence of opportunistic infections has fallen dramatically, chronic and refractory infections are more amenable to treatment, and lifelong treatment is no longer necessary in many instances.

Table 125.1 lists the spectrum of viral infections and associated diseases in HIV-infected people. Most clinically important viral infections in HIV disease are caused by DNA viruses, the majority belonging to the Herpesviridae family. However, improved life expectancy among HIV-infected patients has led to a change in the spectrum of infections influencing morbidity and mortality in this population. Hepatitis B and particularly hepatitis C have emerged as major contributors to morbidity and mortality in HIV-infected patients. This chapter examines the main clinical viral syndromes in HIV disease. The role of viral infections such as human herpes virus-8, Epstein–Barr virus and human papillomavirus in HIV-related neoplastic disorders is discussed elsewhere (see Chapter 130).

CYTOMEGALOVIRUS INFECTIONS

EPIDEMIOLOGY

Serologic evidence of cytomegalovirus (CMV) infection can be detected in approximately 60% of the adult population in the USA. The prevalence of infection is strongly influenced by socioeconomic status and sexual practices; up to 95% of homosexual men are seropositive for CMV.[2]

Before widespread use of HAART, the relative incidence of CMV disease had been increasing and CMV infection was the most common major opportunistic infection associated with AIDS, affecting as many as 45% of patients.[3] Retinitis is the commonest manifestation of CMV infection in patients who have HIV infection or AIDS, accounting for 85% of CMV disease, and is the leading cause of visual loss.[4] Other clinical syndromes include esophagitis, colitis, polyradiculopathy, ventriculoencephalitis, pneumonitis, adrenalitis and pancreatitis.

PATHOGENESIS AND PATHOLOGY

In patients who have AIDS, CMV disease usually results from reactivation of latent infection. Progressive loss of cell-mediated immunity in patients who have advanced HIV disease abrogates the immunologic suppression of CMV replication. Asymptomatic excretion of CMV in urine can be detected in approximately 50% of patients who have advanced HIV disease, and over half of the patients who have CMV viremia go on to develop clinical CMV disease within 8–12 months.[5,6] Cytomegalovirus end-organ disease usually occurs when the $CD4^+$ lymphocyte count falls below 50 cells/mm^3.[4,7]

Cytomegalovirus infects many cell types and tissues. Infection results in tissue necrosis and non-specific inflammation. Microscopically the hallmark of CMV infection is a large (cytomegalic) cell containing a large basophilic intranuclear 'owl's eye' and intracytoplasmic inclusion bodies.

PREVENTION

Patients who have $CD4^+$ lymphocyte counts less than 50/mm^3 should have ophthalmologic screening performed every 3–6 months. Oral ganciclovir is approved for the primary prophylaxis of CMV retinitis in patients who have $CD4^+$ lymphocyte counts below 100/mm^3. However, this approach is not universal. Results from two randomized controlled trials are conflicting,[8,9] and the cost benefits of primary CMV prophylaxis are controversial. Newer viral quantitative measures such as quantitative polymerase chain reaction (PCR) and antigenemia assays may identify those patients who would benefit from 'targeted' prophylaxis or 'pre-emptive' therapy even in the absence of end-organ disease.

Patients on HAART experiencing sustained $CD4^+$ lymphocyte counts above 100/mm^3 have a greatly reduced risk of developing CMV disease and evidence suggests that primary and secondary prophylaxis can be discontinued safely in this situation.[1,10,11] However, CMV disease can recur after virological and immunological failure of HAART if $CD4^+$ lymphocyte counts fall below 50 cells/mm^3.

CLINICAL FEATURES AND DIAGNOSIS

Cytomegalovirus retinitis

Cytomegalovirus causes a relentlessly progressive, necrotizing retinitis. Cytomegalovirus retinitis is usually unilateral in the first instance, progressing to affect the contralateral eye if untreated. Patients may be initially asymptomatic but may subsequently experience blurring of vision, floaters and painless progressive visual loss.

Diagnosis of CMV retinitis is made by systematic funduscopic examination by direct or indirect ophthalmoscopy. Characteristically, white, fluffy, or granular lesions with perivascular white exudates associated with retinal hemorrhages are seen (Fig. 125.1).

Cytomegalovirus lesions may be categorized as occurring in three arbitrarily defined anatomic zones. Retinitis located in the immediate vicinity of the macula or optic disc (zone 1) is sight-threatening and should prompt immediate initiation of treatment. Lesions outside the major vascular vessels (zones 2 and 3), commonly referred to as 'peripheral retinitis', are not immediately sight-threatening but will progress if left untreated.

Table 125.1 Viral infections and clinical syndromes in HIV-infected patients.

VIRAL INFECTIONS AND CLINICAL SYNDROMES IN HIV-INFECTED PATIENTS			
Family	Subfamily	Genus and species	Clinical syndromes
Herpesviridae (DNA)	Alphaherpesvirinae	Herpes simplex 1,2	Orolabial ulceration Anogenital ulceration Herpetic whitlow Encephalitis
		Varicella-zoster virus	Varicella Herpes zoster Disseminated VZV infection Pneumonitis Encephalitis Hepatitis Retinal necrosis
	Betaherpesvirinae	Cytomegalovirus	CMV viremia retinitis esophagitis enterocolitis pneumonitis encephalitis polyradiculopathy adrenalitis
		Human herpesvirus 6	Unknown ? Retinal disease ? Enhanced HIV replication
	Gammaherpesvirinae	Epstein–Barr virus	Oral hairy leukoplakia Lymphoma, Hodgkin's and non-Hodgkin's disease
		Human herpesvirus 8	Kaposi's sarcoma Primary effusion lymphoma Multicentric Castleman's disease
Papovaviridae (DNA)		Papillomavirus	Common and genital warts Squamous intraepithelial neoplasia Cervical carcinoma Anal carcinoma
		Polyomavirus, JC virus	Progressive multifocal leukoencephalopathy
Hepadnaviridae (DNA)		Hepatitis B virus	Hepatitis, acute and chronic cirrhosis Liver carcinoma
Parvoviridae (DNA)		Human parvovirus B19	Aplastic anemia
Poxviridae (DNA)		Molluscum contagiosum virus	Molluscum contagiosum
Flaviviridae (RNA)		Hepatitis C virus	Hepatitis, acute and chronic cirrhosis Liver carcinoma

Gastrointestinal cytomegalovirus disease

The clinical manifestations of CMV infection in the gastrointestinal tract depend largely on the site of infection. In the upper gastrointestinal tract, CMV causes discrete esophageal ulcers, diffuse esophagitis, gastritis, gastric ulcers, duodenal ulcers and enteritis. Esophageal CMV infection usually presents with painful dysphagia. Endoscopic examination frequently reveals inflammation and ulceration, and diagnosis is established by finding characteristic pathologic features on tissue biopsy; it can be confirmed by immunohistochemical or CMV DNA in-situ hybridization techniques. Cytomegalovirus enterocolitis occurs in 5–10% of patients who have AIDS.[12] Lower gastrointestinal CMV disease usually presents with abdominal pain and persistent small-volume diarrhea. Endoscopic examination of the colon reveals plaque-like pseudomembranes, multiple erosions and ulcers, although a mucosa of grossly normal appearance is seen in approximately 10% of patients.

Cytomegalovirus disease of the central nervous system

The two major CMV neurologic syndromes associated with HIV disease are CMV polyradiculopathy and CMV ventriculoencephalitis.[12,13] Polyradiculopathy is a devastating complication in patients who have advanced AIDS. Approximately 50% of patients have an associated myelitis. It is characterized by lower extremity pain, sensory deficits, weakness that can rapidly progress to flaccid paralysis, and bowel and bladder dysfunction. The most marked pathologic changes in CMV polyradiculomyelitis are found in the cauda equina and lumbosacral roots. In the appropriate clinical setting, findings on magnetic resonance imaging (MRI) of diffuse enhancement of the cauda equina and the surface of the conus strongly support the diagnosis. Cerebrospinal fluid findings include a polymorphonuclear pleocytosis, raised protein concentration and moderately low glucose concentration. Culture of cerebrospinal fluid may be nega-

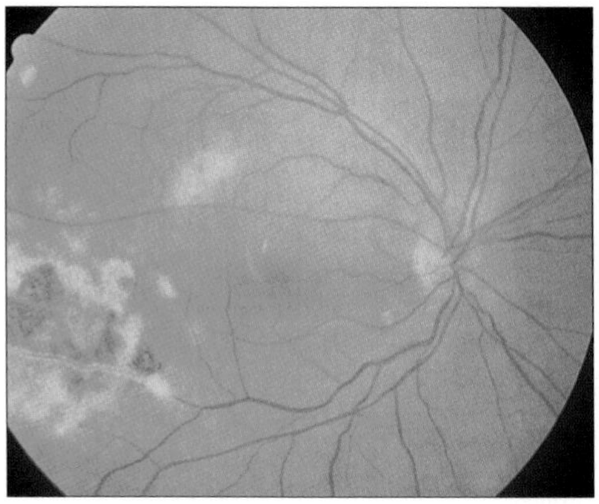

Fig. 125.1 Cytomegalovirus retinitis, with characteristic perivascular hemorrhages and exudates.

tive but CMV antigen assays and PCR for CMV DNA are more sensitive techniques.

Ventriculoencephalitis usually occurs in the setting of a diagnosis of CMV disease elsewhere. Patients present with fever, lethargy and confusion. Characteristic neurologic findings include nystagmus and cranial nerve palsies. Magnetic resonance imaging with gadolinium enhancement may demonstrate periventricular enhancement. Cytomegalovirus DNA can often be detected in cerebrospinal fluid using PCR.

Pulmonary cytomegalovirus disease

There are no particular distinguishing clinical or radiologic features to differentiate CMV pneumonitis from other causes of pneumonitis in HIV disease. Patients present with shortness of breath, dyspnea on exertion and a dry, nonproductive cough. Chest radiographs shows diffuse interstitial infiltrates, and hypoxemia is usually present. Definitive diagnosis of pulmonary CMV disease in patients who have advanced HIV disease is difficult to establish because of a high incidence of asymptomatic CMV shedding – CMV can be isolated in approximately 50% of HIV-infected patients undergoing bronchoscopic examination.[14] However, the true incidence of CMV pneumonitis is less than 10% in patients who have diagnostic bronchoscopy for evaluation of pulmonary infiltrates of unknown origin.[15]

MANAGEMENT

The therapeutic options and strategies for the treatment and prevention of CMV retinitis are outlined in Table 125.2. Similar treatment strategies are commonly employed in treating other end-organ CMV disease.[16,17] Treatment options for CMV retinitis include systemic antiviral treatment and maintenance therapy, intraocular implant devices and intraocular injections of antiviral agents. However, the optimal use, combination and timing of each treatment remains to be determined. Important factors to consider include relative efficacies, potential toxicities, the use of concurrent medications and the need for permanent vascular access.

Five antiviral drugs are currently available for the treatment of CMV retinitis:

- ganciclovir, a nucleoside analogue;
- foscarnet, a pyrophosphate analogue;
- cidofovir, a nucleotide analogue;
- valganciclovir, a prodrug of ganciclovir; and
- fomivirsen, an antisense oligonucleotide.

For systemic treatment, each agent is initially given in high doses (induction) for 2–3 weeks, depending on clinical response, followed by lower maintenance doses. In the absence of HAART-mediated immune reconstitution, most patients eventually have reactivation of CMV infection despite long-term suppressive therapy and require further or re-induction therapy.

Ganciclovir, a nucleoside analogue, is phosphorylated in CMV-infected cells by viral-encoded thymidine kinase. In its active form, it inhibits viral DNA replication. It is available as a parenteral and oral preparation.

Intravenous foscarnet is a pyrophosphate analogue that inhibits DNA polymerase without the need for prior phosphorylation. It has a broad spectrum of activity against the herpesviruses.

In 80–90% of patients, intravenous administration of ganciclovir or foscarnet q12h for 14–21 days (induction) initially halts inflammation and retinal necrosis. In the only published trial directly comparing foscarnet with ganciclovir for the treatment of CMV retinitis, efficacy was similar for both agents.[18] However, there was a significant survival benefit for patients treated with foscarnet, probably owing to the intrinsic anti-HIV activity of foscarnet. Combination therapy with ganciclovir and foscarnet has been shown to be synergistic, or at least additive in vitro, and in one trial it was found to be superior to either drug alone for treatment of recurrent CMV retinitis.[19] This may be a useful strategy in patients who have immediately sight-threatening retinitis or repeated episodes of retinitis and in patients not responding to standard therapy. Both ganciclovir and foscarnet require permanent intravenous vascular access, such as a Hickman–Broviac catheter or a Port-a-Cath catheter, for maintenance therapy.

Oral ganciclovir is licensed for maintenance therapy of patients who have CMV retinitis. However, its bioavailability is poor and time to relapse of retinitis is shorter than with intravenous maintenance therapy.[20] It may be particularly useful for patients who do not have extensive or immediately sight-threatening disease and where long-term venous access is not feasible.

Valganciclovir, recently licensed for treating CMV retinitis, is a monovalyl ester oral prodrug that is rapidly hydrolyzed to ganciclovir. The bioavailability of ganciclovir from oral valganciclovir is 60%, with equivalent blood levels to standard systemic ganciclovir, and it is as effective as intravenous ganciclovir for the management of CMV retinitis in patients who have AIDS.[21]

Intravenous cidofovir is a nucleotide analogue of cytosine with potent in-vitro and in-vivo activity against a broad spectrum of herpesviruses including CMV, herpes simplex viruses 1 and 2, varicella-zoster virus and Epstein–Barr virus.[22] Unlike ganciclovir, which requires intracellular activation by viral-encoded enzyme, conversion of cidofovir to cidofovir diphosphate is by host cellular enzymes and therefore is independent of viral replication. The diphosphate form has a long intracellular half-life and a major advantage of cidofovir is the possibility for maintenance therapy to be given as one injection every 2 weeks, thus obviating the need for an indwelling venous catheter. However, renal toxicity is high and cidofovir therapy must be closely monitored.

Because of the toxicity associated with systemic therapy for CMV retinitis, local (intraocular) therapy has been developed. Intravitreal therapy is effective in controlling retinitis and may be particularly useful as salvage therapy in patients who are no longer tolerant of systemic therapy. Intravitreal injections of ganciclovir, foscarnet and cidofovir have been used. Fomivirsen, the first of a new class of highly selective and novel therapeutics, antisense oligonucleotides, has potent anti-CMV activity, and when it is administered intravitreously it is effective for peripheral retinitis and retinitis not controlled by other anti-CMV drugs.[23,24] Another important approach has been the development of intravitreal devices or implants to deliver ganciclovir continuously over several months.[25] These provide better control of retinitis than systemic therapy and offer significant improvement in the quality of life. Specific complications include bleeding, infection, change in refraction and early retinal detachment. Although implants provide excellent local control of retinitis, the incidence of subsequent contralateral eye disease and systemic disease is high. For this reason, concomitant systemically active treatment (e.g. with oral valganciclovir) is recommended in patients who receive implants.

THERAPEUTIC REGIMENS FOR MANAGEMENT OF CMV RETINITIS IN HIV-INFECTED PATIENTS			
Drug	**Regimen**	**Adverse effects**	**Comments**
Ganciclovir (iv)	**Induction** 5mg/kg q12h × 14–21d 7.5mg/kg q12h × 14–21d for refractory disease **Maintenance** 5mg/kg q24h range 5–10mg/kg q24h	Neutropenia (15–40%) Thrombocytopenia (5–10%) Anemia (5–10%) Nausea, vomiting Confusion, headaches Seizures (rare)	Median time to progression 47–104 days Monitor hematology indices Bone marrow suppression with AZT Administer G-CSF or GM-CSF for neutropenia (ANC <500/mm^3) Drug of choice in patients with baseline renal insufficiency or taking nephrotoxic drugs Requires indwelling venous catheter
Ganciclovir (po)	**Maintenance** 1g q8h	Nausea, dyspepsia (40–50%) Diarrhea (50–60%) Neutropenia (25%) Anemia (10%) Thrombocytopenia Pancreatitis (rare)	Median time to progression 29–56 days 8–10% bioavailability ? Primary prophylaxis Less effective than maintenance iv ganciclovir Rarely used now because valganciclovir available
Ganciclovir intraocular implant	4.5mg implanted for 5–8 months	Retinal detachment (12%) Hemorrhage, infection Endophthalmitis	Median time to progression 196–226 days Contralateral eye disease in 50% and extraocular CMV disease in more than 30% at 6 months
Ganciclovir intraocular injections	400µg twice weekly	Hemorrhage, infection Retinal detachment	
Foscarnet (iv)	**Induction** 90mg/kg q12h × 14–21d **Maintenance** 90–120mg/kg q24h	Renal impairment (20–30%) Hypocalcemia, hypomagnesemia, hypokalemia, hypophosphatemia (20–30%) Nausea (25–40%) Confusion, agitation Anemia Genital ulceration	Median time to progression 53–93 days Monitor electrolytes and replete iv or oral hydration reduces adverse effects Potential survival benefit over ganciclovir Active against aciclovir-resistant herpes viruses Requires indwelling venous catheter
Foscarnet intraocular injections	2400µg twice weekly	Hemorrhage, infection Retinal detachment	
Cidofovir (iv)	**Induction** 5mg/kg weekly × 14d **Maintenance** 3–5mg/kg every 2 weeks	Proteinuria (20%), renal insufficiency Fanconi syndrome (25%) Nausea/vomiting Neutropenia	Median time to progression 64–120 days iv hydration pre- and postadministration and pre- and post-probenecid reduces renal toxicity
Valganciclovir (po)	**Induction** 900mg q12h × 21d **Maintenance** 900mg q24h	Diarrhea 19%, Neutropenia 14%	Median time to progression 160 days Prodrug of ganciclovir with 60% bioavailability of ganciclovir
Fomivirsen intravitreous injections	**Induction** 165µg once weekly × 21d **Maintenance** 165µg alternate weeks	Anterior chamber inflammation Increased intra-ocular pressure	Median time to progression 71 days Higher dose 330µg effective in relapsed disease or in infections failing to respond to alternative treatments

Table 125.2 Therapeutic regimens for management of cytomegalovirus retinitis in HIV-infected patients.

HERPES SIMPLEX VIRUS INFECTIONS

EPIDEMIOLOGY

Severe herpes simplex virus (HSV) infection was one of the initial clinical manifestations heralding the onset of the AIDS epidemic.[26] Herpes simplex virus 1 is normally acquired early in life, whereas HSV-2 is usually acquired through sexual contact, the risk of infection being correlated with the number of sexual partners.[27,28] The highest prevalence of antibodies to HSV-2 in the USA is among female commercial workers and homosexual males. In HIV-infected people, seroprevalence rates up to 77% for HSV-2 have been reported, reflecting common risk factors for transmission.[29]

PATHOGENESIS AND PATHOLOGY

After initial or primary infection, which may be asymptomatic, HSV has the capacity to establish latent infection in the dorsal root or sensory ganglia. Viral reactivation occurs intermittently and leads to a recurrence of cutaneous or mucosal lesions. Immunosuppressed patients are at greater risk of both recurrent and disseminated HSV infections. Reactivation of HSV occurs frequently in patients who have advanced HIV disease, particularly in those who have low $CD4^+$ lymphocyte counts (<100 cells/mm^3). The histopathologic characteristics of primary or recurrent HSV infection reflect virus-mediated cellular death and associated inflammatory response.

PREVENTION

Frequent or severe recurrent HSV infections can be managed with suppressive oral aciclovir, valaciclovir and famciclovir therapy. The management of recurrent aciclovir-resistant HSV infections is not well established but may require maintenance therapy with foscarnet.

CLINICAL FEATURES AND DIAGNOSIS

The hallmark of herpetic lesions is painful vesicular formation at a mucocutaneous site, progressing rapidly to ulceration with an erythematous base, followed by eventual healing and re-epithelialization. Herpes simplex virus 1 most commonly causes orolabial lesions and HSV-2 generally infects the genital and perianal regions. However, there is considerable overlap in the epidemiology and clinical features of HSV-1 and HSV-2 infections. The clinical manifestations of HSV infections in HIV disease depend on:

- the subtype of HSV;
- the site of infection; and
- the degree of underlying immunosuppression.

As patients become more immunosuppressed, infections are characterized by prolonged viral shedding, more frequent episodes, and severe and persistent clinical disease.[26,28] Diagnostic techniques available for the diagnosis of HSV infections include cytologic preparations (e.g. the Tzanck test) for multinucleated giant cells, fluorescein-conjugated monoclonal antibodies of scrapings from lesions, cell culture and PCR assays for HSV DNA.

Primary orolabial infection is more frequent in children who have AIDS, who are at risk of severe gingivostomatitis. In adults, orolabial infection is usually due to reactivation of latent infection. Recurrences may increase in frequency and severity as immunosuppression increases. Recurrent genital and perirectal ulcerative lesions are the most common manifestations of HSV infection in patients who have HIV disease and are usually due to reactivation of HSV-2. Lesions may be atypical and severe in patients who have advanced disease (Fig. 125.2). Prolonged new lesion formation, with continued tissue destruction, persistent viral shedding and severe local pain, is common.

Herpes simplex esophagitis may occur in the absence of herpetic lesions in the oropharynx and is difficult to distinguish from CMV esophagitis on clinical and radiologic grounds. Both cause retrosternal pain and dysphagia. Definitive diagnosis requires endoscopy and biopsy. Herpes encephalitis is a rare, life-threatening complication in HIV disease. It usually occurs as a complication of primary or reactivated orolabial HSV infection. Symptoms include headache, personality changes, meningismus, lethargy, confusion, focal neurologic deficits and fits. Computerized tomography (CT) scans or MRI may reveal temporal lobe abnormalities. Cerebrospinal fluid findings are usually nonspecific, with a lymphocytosis and elevated protein. Detection of HSV DNA by PCR is highly sensitive and specific for HSV encephalitis.[30]

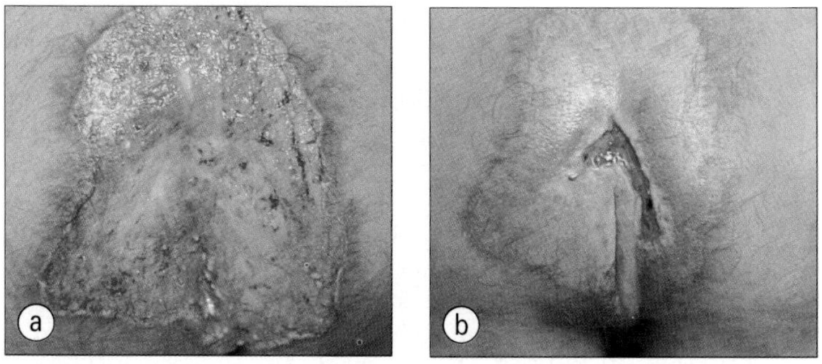

Fig. 125.2 Severe perianal aciclovir-resistant herpes simplex virus 2 infection. (a) Untreated appearance. (b) Healing and re-epithelialization after treatment with foscarnet and institution of HAART.

MANAGEMENT

For over 20 years, aciclovir has been the drug of choice for treating HSV infections. Aciclovir undergoes selective phosphorylation by virus-induced thymidine kinase in HSV-infected cells. Aciclovir monophosphate is further phosphorylated by cellular kinases to the active triphosphate form, which selectively inhibits viral DNA polymerase. Bioavailability of oral aciclovir is approximately 10–20%. The optimum route of administration, dosage and duration of therapy will depend on the site and severity of the HSV infection (Table 125.3).

Valaciclovir and famciclovir are newer, effective and convenient alternatives agents for episodic and suppressive treatment of HSV infection. Oral valaciclovir is rapidly metabolized to aciclovir by the liver achieving a bioavailability of 3–5 times that of oral aciclovir. Famciclovir is a prodrug of penciclovir, an acyclic nucleoside similar to aciclovir but with a significantly longer intracellular half-life.

Infections with HSV that are resistant to aciclovir are increasingly recognized in patients who have advanced HIV disease.[31] Most aciclovir-resistant HSV isolates are deficient in thymidine kinase activity. Persistent ulcerative HSV lesions that fail to respond to aciclovir should alert the physician to the possibility of aciclovir resistance. The degree of immunosuppression and chronicity of mucocutaneous HSV infection are the strongest independent risk factors for the development of resistance in vitro. Foscarnet, which does not require viral-mediated phosphorylation for activity, is the treatment of choice for aciclovir-resistant HSV infections in HIV disease. Topical trifluorothymidine solution and cidofovir gel have also been shown to be effective against aciclovir-resistant HSV infections.

VARICELLA-ZOSTER VIRUS INFECTIONS

EPIDEMIOLOGY

Primary varicella or chickenpox is a common childhood infection. In the USA and Europe, most adults who have HIV disease have previously been infected with varicella-zoster virus (VZV). Among

TREATMENT OF HSV AND VZV INFECTIONS IN HIV-INFECTED PATIENTS

Type of infection	Treatment
Mucocutaneous HSV infection	Aciclovir 200–400mg po 5 times/d Famciclovir 500mg po q8h Valaciclovir 500mg po q12h Aciclovir 15–30mg/kg/day iv
Disseminated/visceral HSV infection	Aciclovir 30mg/kg/day iv
Recurrent mucocutaneous HSV infection	Aciclovir 400mg po bid to q6h Valaciclovir 500mg po q12h Famciclovir 500mg bid po q12h
Aciclovir-resistant HSV infection	Foscarnet 60mg/kg q12h iv Topical trifluorothymidine 2% q8h
Primary VZV infection (varicella)	Aciclovir 800mg po 5 times/day Aciclovir 10mg/kg/q8h iv
Herpes zoster	Aciclovir 800mg po 5 times/d Aciclovir 10mg/kg/q8h iv Valaciclovir 500mg po q12h Famciclovir 500mg po q8h
Disseminated/visceral VZV infection	Aciclovir 10mg/kg/q8h iv
Aciclovir-resistant VZV infection	Foscarnet 60mg/kg q12h iv

Table 125.3 Treatment of herpes simplex virus and varicella-zoster virus infections in HIV-infected patients. Treatment for HSV and VZV is usually for 5–10 days or until resolution of symptoms.

HIV-infected children and adults, the manifestations of VZV infections include:

- uncomplicated primary varicella;
- disseminated varicella;
- localized and disseminated herpes zoster; and
- chronic varicella-zoster.

PATHOGENESIS AND PATHOLOGY

Primary VZV infection is usually acquired in susceptible hosts by contact with persons infected with chickenpox, either via the respiratory route or through contact with cutaneous lesions. It can also be acquired by contact with patients who have herpes zoster. Following initial replication, patients become viremic and develop the characteristic vesicular rash of varicella. Crops of new vesicles occur with successive episodes of viremia. Patients who have HIV disease can have prolonged viremia and an extended period of new lesion formation.

During primary infection, VZV enters cutaneous endings of sensory nerves and migrates to reach sensory nerve ganglia, where the virus establishes latency. With the waning of cellular immunity, the virus can reactivate, causing herpes zoster. The vesicular eruption of zoster typically remains confined to one dermatome or to several contiguous dermatomes, corresponding to the distribution of innervation of the affected sensory ganglion.

CLINICAL FEATURES AND DIAGNOSIS

Primary varicella zoster virus infection (Varicella)

The rash of primary VZV infection appears 10–21 days after infection. Lesions progress from small erythematous macules to papules and vesicles that ulcerate, dry and form crusts. A centripetal distribution, successive crops of lesions and lesions at all stages of development are characteristic of varicella. Owing to impaired cellular immunity, HIV-infected patients who have primary VZV are at risk of prolonged new lesion formation and are a higher risk of life-threatening visceral dissemination.

Herpes zoster

Herpes zoster may be the first indication of HIV disease and can occur at any stage of HIV infection. It usually appears as a localized or segmental painful erythematous maculopapular eruption along a single dermatome (Fig. 125.3). Lesions evolve over 1–3 days to form vesicles, pustules and crusts. In HIV-infected patients, zoster lesions may be particularly bullous, hemorrhagic or necrotic. Herpes zoster of the ophthalmic division of the trigeminal nerve can cause anterior uveitis and corneal scarring with visual loss. The diagnosis of herpes zoster is usually clinical but laboratory studies may be required for confirmation. A Tzanck preparation from scrapings of lesions can demonstrate multinucleated giant cells but is not specific for herpes zoster. Fluorescein-conjugated monoclonal antibodies confirm the presence of VZV from scrapings from the base of lesions and their presence is a more rapid and reliable test than virus culture.

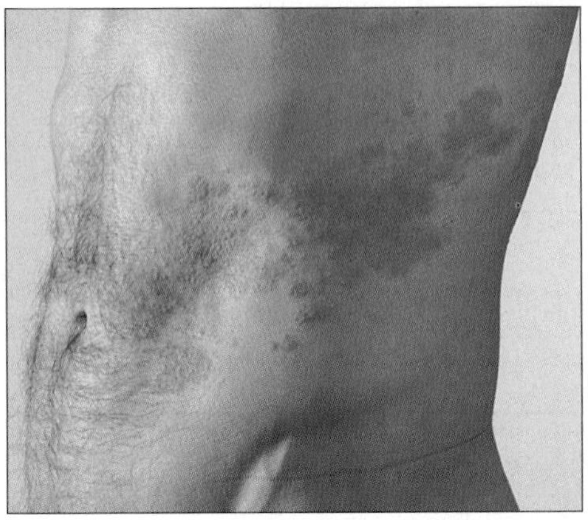

Fig. 125.3 Herpes zoster in the T10 dermatome. Courtesy of Professor Anthony J Pinching.

Patients infected with HIV are at risk of recurrent episodes of herpes zoster. A less frequent manifestation is persistent localized herpes zoster. These patients typically fail to clear lesions with aciclovir, or lesions recur rapidly after treatment is completed. Occasionally, widespread cutaneous and visceral dissemination may occur.

Visceral dissemination to the lungs, the liver and the central nervous system may cause life-threatening disease. The symptoms, signs and chest radiograph of VZV pneumonitis are non-specific. Encephalitis is a rare complication of VZV infection. Symptoms develop 1–2 weeks after the development of herpes zoster, and include headache and lethargy. Pathologically it is characterized by necrotic and demyelinating lesions, mostly in superficial white matter, the periventricular area and white–gray matter junctions. Cerebrospinal fluid findings may be non-specific, showing a mild mononuclear pleocytosis and elevated protein. Detection of VZV DNA by PCR analysis is diagnostic. Chronic disseminated herpes zoster may present as widespread erythematous ulcerative or hyperkeratotic verrucous lesions, particularly after prolonged treatment with aciclovir. Rapidly progressive herpetic retinal necrosis syndrome is a rare complication that is most often associated with VZV infection. Aggressive antiviral treatment is required to prevent loss of vision.[32]

MANAGEMENT

Primary VZV infection or herpes zoster in HIV-infected patients must be treated with specific antiviral therapy. Higher concentrations of aciclovir are required to inhibit replication of VZV than of HSV (see Table 125.3). Aciclovir significantly reduces pain and shortens the duration of viral shedding, the duration of new lesion formation, the time to crusting of lesions and the time to complete healing. High-dose oral aciclovir, 800mg five times daily, may be used for the treatment of localized herpes zoster in HIV-infected patients who do not require hospitalization. In severe or disseminated VZV infection, high-dose intravenous aciclovir (10mg/kg q8h) is indicated. Famciclovir and valaciclovir are licensed for use in non-immunocompromised patients who have herpes zoster.

Persistent disseminated VZV infection that fails to respond to aciclovir has been described in patients who have advanced HIV disease. In-vitro susceptibility studies have demonstrated isolates that are resistant to aciclovir, usually because of deficient or altered thymidine kinase activity. Intravenous foscarnet is the antiviral drug of choice for infection with aciclovir-resistant VZV.

For HIV infected patients who develop recurrent VZV lesions when aciclovir is discontinued, chronic suppressive aciclovir is indicated.

INFECTION WITH HEPATITIS C VIRUS

EPIDEMIOLOGY

With improved life expectancy among HIV-infected patients as a result of HAART, hepatitis C virus (HCV) infection is emerging as a leading cause of significant morbidity and death in this population. Because of shared risk factors, concomitant HCV and HIV infection is common. A recent study conducted in the USA estimated an overall prevalence of HCV 16% in a nationally distributed HIV cohort, rising to 73% in higher risk populations such as hemophiliacs and injection drug users.[33] There are six known genotypes of HCV. In a recent study from the USA, type 1 was the most prevalent in co-infected patients and was found in 83%. Chronic HCV infection occurs in about 85% of patients, with cirrhosis and end-stage liver failure eventually developing in approximately 20% of infected individuals in two to three decades.[34] Co-infection with HIV accelerates HCV-related liver disease, and end-stage liver disease morbidity and mortality are greater in co-infected individuals.[35] Conversely, HCV may be independently associated with an increased risk of progression to AIDS and death.[36]

CLINICAL FEATURES AND DIAGNOSIS

Most patients who have acute HCV infection are symptom free, with a minority becoming jaundiced. It is usually with the development of chronic liver disease or extrahepatic manifestations that patients develop symptoms. Virtually all patients who have chronic HCV infection develop histologic features of chronic hepatitis, with as many as 20% progressing to cirrhosis over 20 years. Hepatitis C virus infection is readily diagnosed by enzyme-linked immunosorbent assay (ELISA) with specificity ensured using a recombinant immunoblot assay (RIBA). Signal amplification assays and PCR-based assays allow qualitative and quantitative detection of HCV RNA in plasma. Liver biopsy is an important tool to determine the degree of inflammation and fibrosis.

MANAGEMENT

In recent years significant advances have been made in the management of chronic HCV infection. Treatment is recommended for patients who have elevated alanine aminotransferase (ALT) levels, detectable serum HCV RNA and moderate to severe injury on liver biopsy. Table 125.4 outlines treatment options for HCV.

In 1998, two pivotal studies established the effectiveness of combination therapy with interferon-α-2b (3MU three times weekly) and ribavirin (1000–1200mg daily) for HCV infection in HIV-negative patients.[37,38] Sustained virologic response rates were observed in 38–43% of patients at 48 weeks with improvement in liver inflammation on histologic examination. Genotypes 2 and 3 show the most favorable responses to treatment. Slow-release α-interferons, covalently bound to polyethylene glycol (PEG), a nontoxic polymer, have been developed that allow for more convenient once-weekly injections. Pegylated interferon with ribavirin is now the standard of care in treating chronic HCV infection, with overall sustained virologic response rates of 54–56%.[39,40]

Data are limited to date on treatment of HIV/HCV co-infected patients. Pegylated interferon-α-2a plus ribavirin has recently been reported to lead to significant treatment responses compared with conventional interferon-α-2a plus ribavirin in HIV/HCV co-infected patients.[41] In co-infected patients, progression of liver disease is associated with a $CD4^+$ lymphocyte count of less than 400cells/mm^3 and patients who have higher $CD4^+$ counts demonstrate greater response rates to HCV treatment.[42] Therefore, in co-infected patients treatment for HCV should be considered before significant decline in immune function occurs or, in those who have low $CD4^+$ counts, antiretroviral therapy should be a priority prior to HCV treatment.

INFECTION WITH HEPATITIS B VIRUS

EPIDEMIOLOGY

Hepatitis B virus (HBV) is a major world health problem and a common cause of cirrhosis and hepatocellular carcinoma. Because of shared risk factors, concomitant HBV and HIV infection is common, particularly in homosexual men. The outcome of acute HBV infection depends on the age of acquisition, the immune status of the host and the rate of replication of the virus. Less than 5% of adult-acquired infection progresses to chronic infection (chronic active hepatitis or asymptomatic carriers). In HIV-infected patients plasma HBV DNA levels are higher than in controls,[43] and recent data suggest that chronic HBV infection increases the risk of liver-related deaths in patients co-infected with HIV.[44]

CLINICAL FEATURES AND DIAGNOSIS

The clinical presentation of acute HBV ranges from subclinical hepatitis (70%) to icteric hepatitis (30%) with rare cases of fulminant hepatitis (0.1–0.5%). Chronic HBV ranges from the asymptomatic carrier through chronic active HBV to cirrhosis and hepatocellular carcinoma.

TREATMENT OPTIONS FOR CHRONIC HBV AND HCV INFECTION IN NON-HIV-INFECTED AND HIV-INFECTED PATIENTS

	Dosing schedule	Response/comments
Hepatitis B		
Interferon-α-2b	5MU C q24h or 10MU weekly for 4 months	HBeAg loss/seroconversion in 33%
Lamivudine	100mg po q24h for 1 year	HBeAg loss/seroconversion in 17% Prolonged use associated with genotypic-resistant variants Licensed for HIV infection at 300mg daily
Adefovir dipoxivil	10mg po q24h	Effective against lamivudine resistant HBV variants Mean drop in HBV DNA, $-4.77\log_{10}$, in HIV co-infected patients
Tenofovir	300mg po q24h	Licensed for HIV infection
Hepatitis C		
Interferon-α-2b and ribavirin	Interferon-α-2b 3MU 3 times weekly, ribavirin 1000–1200mg q24h for 6–12 months	SVR in 38–43% Higher response rates with genotypes 2 and 3
Pegylated interferon and ribavirin	Ribavirin 800–1200mg q24h; peg-IFN-α-2b (Peg-Intron) 1.5µg/kg or peg-IFN-α-2a (Pegasys) 180µg per week	SVR in 54–56% Higher response rates with genotypes 2 and 3 SVR 44% in HIV/HCV co-infected patients (Pegasys plus ribavirin)

Table 125.4 Treatment options for chronic hepatitis B virus and hepatitis C virus infection in non-HIV-infected and HIV-infected patients. SVR, sustained virologic response.

Serologic markers of HBV infection are well established. The persistence of hepatitis B surface antigen beyond 6 months suggests progression to chronic HBV infection. Hepatitis B e antigen (HBeAg) is a marker of active HBV replication and infectivity and is usually associated with active liver disease. The presence of serum HBV DNA (using signal amplification or PCR-based assays) is sensitive and specific for viral replication and is used to assess patients who have chronic HBV for treatment and to evaluate response.

MANAGEMENT

To date interferon-α, lamivudine and adefovir are the only agents approved for the treatment of chronic HBV (see Table 125.4). Viral clearance (HBeAg loss/seroconversion) occurs in 33% of those treated with interferon-α and 16–18% treated with lamivudine for 1 year.[45–47] Patients who have lower ALT levels or higher HBV DNA levels and immunosuppressed patients have a poorer response. Lamivudine profoundly suppresses viral replication and with prolonged use achieves an HBeAg seroconversion rate similar to interferon-α. It is also effective in patients not usually responsive to interferon. However, genotypic-resistant mutations emerge after 9–10 months of treatment with a frequency of 50% after 3 years. With both treatments, virologic responses are associated with biochemical and histologic improvement.

Adefovir dipivoxil, an adenine nucleotide analogue, has demonstrated encouraging preliminary results against HBV.[48] Moreover, it is active against lamivudine-resistant strains of HBV. Tenofovir, another nucleotide analogue, which is licensed to treat HIV, is being investigated for treatment of HBV and produces substantial reductions in HBV viral load in co-infected patients. Studies continue to define and refine optimal treatment regimens, and combination therapy studies with approved agents and experimental agents are now in progress.

OTHER VIRAL INFECTIONS

A variety of other viral infections and diseases occur in patients who have HIV disease (see Table 125.1). Those viruses implicated in neoplastic conditions, such as Epstein–Barr virus, human papillomavirus and human herpes virus 8, are discussed in detail in other sections (see Chapter 130). A brief summary of other viral conditions encountered in HIV-infected patients is outlined here.

PROGRESSIVE MULTIFOCAL LEUKOENCEPHALOPATHY

Progressive multifocal leukoencephalopathy (PML) is an opportunistic demyelinating infection caused by JC virus. JC virus is a ubiquitous DNA papovavirus and over 70% of adults are seropositive for it. Progressive multifocal leukoencephalopathy occurs in patients who have deficient cell-mediated immunity and is estimated to affect up to 4% of patients who have AIDS.[49] Mortality is high, and average reported survival in AIDS patients is 2–4 months. The symptoms and characteristic radiologic findings of PML are due to virus-induced lysis of oligodendrocytes, resulting in microscopic foci of myelin breakdown that coalesce to produce larger white matter lesions (Fig. 125.4). Definitive diagnosis requires tissue from brain biopsy but the identification of JC virus in the cerebrospinal fluid by PCR has a high specificity for active disease.

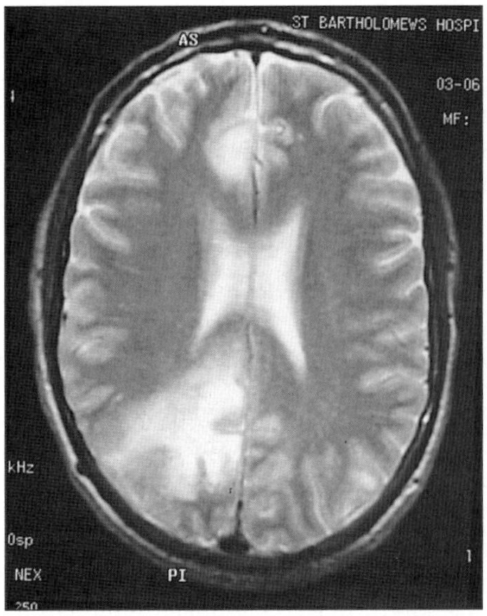

Fig. 125.4 Progressive multifocal leukoencephalopathy. MRI scan showing frontal and occipital white matter lesions. Courtesy of Dr Jane Anderson.

There is no definitive treatment for PML. Aciclovir, vidarabine and cytarabine have all been used to little effect. Cidofovir is active against polyomaviruses and several case reports have suggested therapeutic benefit in PML using dosing regimens recommended for CMV retinitis.[50] Immune reconstitution following antiretroviral therapy may influence the course of PML in HIV-infected patients, and there are several reports of regression of PML and prolonged survival in patients receiving HAART. Optimal retroviral therapy is now regarded as treatment of choice for PML.

MOLLUSCUM CONTAGIOSUM

Molluscum contagiosum is caused by a double stranded DNA virus, namely molluscum contagiosum virus (MCV). Molecular epidemiology studies have identified at least two major subtypes, MCV-1 and MCV-2. The majority of infections are caused by MCV-1. Cell-mediated immunity is important in the control of molluscum contagiosum and lesions occur in 5–18% of patients. Pathologic features consist of focal areas of hyperplastic and hypertrophied epidermis surrounding a core of keratin and epithelial debris. Ultrastructural studies have demonstrated MCV in all layers of the epidermis.

Lesions appear as small white or pink cutaneous papules. Larger lesions may be umbilicated. In HIV-infected patients, molluscum contagiosum may be extensive, large and disfiguring, and lesions are commonly localized around the head and neck.[51]

Diagnosis is usually made on the basis of the characteristic clinical features. Treatment involves direct disruption of lesions with enucleation, cauterization and cryotherapy. Treatment in HIV-infected patients is less satisfactory owing to the widespread nature of the lesions and the high rate of recurrence. Recalcitrant cases have been reported to respond to topical cidofovir cream 1–2%[52] and topical imiquimod 5% cream, an immune response modifier with antiviral properties.[53] Remission may occur after immune reconstitution with HAART.

REFERENCES

1. Sepkowitz KA. Effect of HAART on natural history of AIDS-related opportunistic disorders. Lancet 1998;351:228–30.
2. Drew WL, Mintz L, Miner RC, Sands M, Ketterer B. Prevalence of cytomegalovirus infections in homosexual men. J Infect Dis 1981;143:188–92.
3. Hoover DR, Saah AJ, Bacellar H, *et al.* Clinical manifestations of AIDS in the era of pneumocystis prophylaxis. Multicenter AIDS Cohort Study. N Engl J Med 1993;329:1922–6.
4. Gallant JE, Moore RD, Richman DD, Keruly J, Chaisson RE. Incidence and natural history of cytomegalovirus disease in patients with advanced human immunodeficiency virus treated with zidovudine. The Zidovudine Epidemiology Study Group. J Infect Dis 1992;166:1223–7.
5. Salomon D, Lacassin F, Harzic F, *et al.* Predictive value of cytomegalovirus viremia for the occurrence of CMV organ involvement in AIDS. J Med Virol 1990;32:160–3.
6. Bowen EF, Sabin CA, Wilson P, *et al.* Cytomegalovirus (CMV) viraemia detected by polymerase chain reaction identifies a group of HIV-positive patients at high risk of CMV disease. AIDS 1997;11:889–93.
7. Pertel P, Hirschtick R, Phair J, Chmiel J, Poggensee L, Murphy R. Risk of developing cytomegalovirus retinitis in persons infected with the human immunodeficiency virus. J Acquir Immune Defic Syndr 1992;5:1069–74.
8. Spector SA, McKinley GF, Lalezari JP, *et al.* Oral ganciclovir for the prevention of cytomegalovirus disease in persons with AIDS. N Engl J Med 1996;334:1491–7.
9. Brosgart CL, Louis TA, Hillman DW, *et al.* A randomized, placebo-controlled trial of the safety and efficacy of oral ganciclovir for prophylaxis of cytomegalovirus disease in HIV-infected individuals. Terry Beirn Community Programs for Clinical Research on AIDS. AIDS 1998;12:269–77.
10. Macdonald JC, Torriani FJ, Morse LS, *et al.* Lack of reactivation of cytomagalovirus (CMV) retinitis after stopping CMV maintenance therapy in AIDS patients with sustained elevations in CD4 T cells in response to highly active antiretroviral therapy. J Infect Dis 1998;177:1182–7.
11. US Public Health Service/Infectious Diseases Society of America. 2001 USPHS/IDSA guidelines for the prevention of opportunistic infections in persons infected with human immunodeficiency virus. Rockville, MD: HIV/AIDS Treatment Information Service; 2001.
12. Drew WL. Cytomegalovirus infection in patients with AIDS. Clin Infect Dis 1992;14:608–15.
13. McCutchan JA. Cytomegalovirus infections of the nervous system in patients with AIDS. Clin Infect Dis 1995;20:747–54.
14. Miles PR, Baughman RP, Linnemann CC. Cytomegalovirus in the bronchoalveolar lavage fluid of patients with AIDS. Chest 1990;97:1072–6.
15. Rodriquez-Barradas MC, Stool E, Musher DM, *et al.* Diagnosing and treating cytomegalovirus pneumonia in patients with AIDS. Clin Infect Dis 1996;23:76–81.
16. Jacoboson MA. Treatment of cytomegalovirus retinitis in patients with the acquired immunodeficiency syndrome. N Engl J Med 1997;337:105–114.
17. Whitley RJ, Jacoboson MA, Friedberg DN, *et al.* Guidelines for the treatment of cytomegalovirus diseases in patients with AIDS in the era of potent antiretroviral therapy. Arch Intern Med 1998;158:957–69.
18. Studies of Ocular Complications of AIDS Research Group, in collaboration with the AIDS Clinical Trials Group. Mortality in patients with the acquired immunodeficiency syndrome treated with either foscarnet or ganciclovir for cytomegalovirus retinitis. N Engl J Med 1992;326:213–20.
19. Studies of Ocular Complications of AIDS Research Group, in collaboration with the AIDS Clinical Trials Group. Combination foscarnet and ganciclovir therapy vs monotherapy for the treatment of relapsed cytomegalovirus retinitis in patients with AIDS. Arch Ophthalmol 1996;114:23–33.
20. Drew WL, Ives D, Lalezari JP, *et al.* Oral ganciclovir as maintenance treatment for cytomegalovirus retinitis in patients with AIDS. N Engl J Med 1995;333:615–20.
21. Martin DF, Sierra-Madero J, Walmsley S, *et al.* A controlled trial of valganciclovir as induction therapy for cytomegalovirus retinitis. N Engl J Med 2002;346:1119–1126.
22. Lalezari JP, Staag RJ, Kuppermann BD, *et al.* Intravenous cidofovir for peripheral cytomegalovirus retinitis in patients with AIDS – a randomized controlled trial. Ann Intern Med 1997;126:257–63.
23. The Vitravene Study Group. A randomized controlled clinical trial of intravitreous fomivirsen for treatment of newly diagnosed peripheral cytomegalovirus retinitis in patients with AIDS. Am J Ophthal 2002;133:467–74.
24. The Vitravene Study Group. Randomized dose-comparison studies of intravitreous fomivirsen for treatment of cytomegalovirus retinitis that has reactivated or is persistently active despite other therapies in patients with AIDS. Am J Ophthalmol 2002;475–83.
25. Musch DC, Martin DF, Gordon JF, Davis MD, Kuppermann BD, the Ganciclovir Implant Study Group. Treatment of cytomegalovirus retinitis with a sustained-release ganciclovir implant. N Engl J Med 1997;337:83–90.
26. Siegal FP, Lopez C, Hammer GS, *et al.* Severe acquired immunodeficiency in male homosexuals, manifested by chronic perianal ulcerative herpes simplex lesions. N Engl J Med 1981;305:1439–44.
27. Whitley RJ, Kimberlin DW, Roizman B. Herpes simplex viruses. Clin Infect Dis 1998;26:541–55.
28. Stewart JA, Reef SE, Pellet PE, Corey L, Whitley RJ. Herpesvirus infections in persons infected with human immunodeficiency virus. Clin Infect Dis 1995;21(Suppl.1):114–20.
29. Safrin S, Ashley R, Houlihan C, Cusick PS, Mills J. Clinical and serological features of herpes simplex virus infection in patients with AIDS. AIDS 1991;5:1107–10.
30. Cinque P, Vago L, Marenzi R, *et al.* Herpes simplex virus infections of the central nervous system in human immunodeficiency virus-infected patients: clinical management by polymerase chain reaction assay of cerebrospinal fluid. Clin Infect Dis 1998;27:303–9.
31. Erlich KS, Mills J, Chatis P, *et al.* Aciclovir-resistant herpes simplex virus infections in patients with the acquired immunodeficiency syndrome. N Engl J Med 1989;320:293–6.
32. Ormerod LD, Larkin JA, Margo CA, *et al.* Rapidly progressive herpetic retinal necrosis: a blinding disease characteristic of advanced AIDS. Clin Infect Dis 1998;26:34–45.
33. Sherman KE, Rouster SD, Chung RT, *et al.* Hepatitis C prevalence among patients infected with Human Immunodeficiency Virus: a cross-sectional analysis of the US adult AIDS Clinical Trials Group. Clin Infect Dis 2002;34:831–7.
34. Di Bisceglie AM. Hepatitis C. Lancet 1998;351:351–5.
35. Zylberberg H, Pol S. Reciprocal interactions between human immunodeficiency virus and hepatitis C virus infections. Clin Infect Dis 1996;23:1117–25.
36. Greub G, Lederberger B, Battegay M, *et al.* Clinical progression, survival, and immune recovery during antiretroviral therapy in patients with HIV-1 and hepatitis C coinfection. Lancet 2000;356:1800–5.
37. McHutchinson JG, Gordon SC, Schiff ER, *et al.* Interferon alfa-2b alone or in combination with ribavirin as initial treatment for chronic hepatitis C. N Engl J Med 1998;339:1485–92.
38. Poynard T, Marcellin P. Lee SS, *et al.* Randomised trial of interferon alfa-2b plus ribavirin for 48 weeks or 24 weeks versus interferon alfa-2b plus placebo for 48 weeks for treatment of chronic infection with hepatitis C virus. Lancet 1998;352:1426–32.
39. Manns MP, McHutchinson JG, Gordon SC, *et al.* Peginterferon alfa-2b plus ribavirin compared with interferon alfa-2b plus ribavirin for initial treatment of chronic hepatitis C: a randomised trial. Lancet 2001;358:958–65.
40. Soriano V, Sulkowski M, Bergin C, *et al.* Care of patients with chronic hepatitis C and HIV co-infection: recommendations from the HIV-HCV International Panel. AIDS 2002;16:813–28.
41. Chung R, Naderson J, Alston B, *et al.* A randomized, controlled trial of pegylated interferon alfa-2a with ribavirin vs interferon alfa-2a with ribavirin for the treatment of chronic HCV in co-infection: ACTG A5071. 9th Conference on Retroviruses and Opportunistic Infections, Seattle, February 24–28, 2002:Abstract 15.
42. Fuster D, Tural C, Tor J, *et al.* Factors associated with liver fibrosis in HIV-1 HCV co-infected patients on antiretroviral therapy. 9th Conference on Retroviruses and Opportunistic Infections, Seattle, February 24–28, 2002:Abstract 646.
43. Gilson RJ, Hawkins AE, Beecham MR, *et al.* Interactions between HIV and hepatitis B virus in homosexual men: effects on the natural history of infection. AIDS 1997;11:597–606.
44. Thio CL, Seaberg EC, Skolasky R, *et al.* Liver disease mortality in HIV-HBV co-infected persons. 9th Conference on Retroviruses and Opportunistic Infections, Seattle, February 24–28, 2002:Abstract 656.
45. Wong DK, Cheung AM, O'Rourke K, *et al.* Effect of alpha-interferon treatment in patients with Hepatitis B e antigen-positive chronic hepatitis B: a meta-analysis. Ann Intern Med 1993;119:312–23.
46. Malik A, Lee W. Chronic hepatitis B virus infection: treatment strategies for the next millennium. Ann Intern Med 2000:132;723–31.
47. Matthews GV, Nelson MR. The management of hepatitis B infection. Int J STD AIDS 2001;12:353–7.
48. Benhamou Y, Bochet M, Thibault V, *et al.* Adefovir dipivoxil 10mg suppresses HBV viral replication in HIV/HBV co-infected patients with lamivudine resistant HBV. 9th Conference on Retroviruses and Opportunistic Infections, Seattle, February 24–28, 2002:Abstract 123.
49. Greenlee JE. Progressive multifocal leukoencephalopathy – progress made and lessons relearned. N Engl J Med 1998;1378–80.
50. Segarra-Newnham M, Vodolo KM. Use of cidofovir in progressive multifocal leukoencephalopathy. Ann Pharmacother 2001;35:741–4.
51. Schwartz JJ, Myskowski PL. Molluscum contagiosum in patients with human immunodeficiency virus infection. A review of twenty-seven patients. J Am Acad Dermatol 1992;27:583–8.
52. Calista D. Topical cidofovir for severe cutaneous human papillomavirus and molluscum contagiosum infections in patients with HIV/AIDS. J Eur Acad Dermatol Venereol 2000;14:484–8.
53. Strauss RM, Doyle EL, Moshen AH, *et al.* Successful treatment of molluscum contagiosum with topical imiquimod in a severely immunocompromised HIV-positive patient. Int J STD AIDS 2001;12:264–6.

chapter

126 Fungal Infection

William G Powderly

Fungi are among the most ubiquitous pathogens seen in patients who have HIV disease but are not the most common causes of mortality. Virtually all major fungal pathogens cause disease in patients who have HIV infection.

CANDIDIASIS

EPIDEMIOLOGY

Candidal infection in AIDS is almost exclusively mucosal – systemic invasion is a rare and late event. Oropharyngeal candidiasis occurs in about three-quarters of all those who have HIV infection. In about one-third it tends to be recurrent and becomes progressively more severe with increasing immunodeficiency. Esophageal involvement occurs in 20–40% of all AIDS patients, predominantly in patients who have advanced disease and severe depletion of $CD4^+$ lymphocytes. Vulvovaginal candidiasis occurs in about 30–40% of women who have HIV infection; it appears that HIV infection per se is not an important risk factor for vaginal infection, although it may influence the severity and persistence of disease.

Most candidal disease, especially initial episodes, is associated with infection by *Candida albicans*. Recurrent disease is caused by the same strain of *Candida* in about 50% of cases; the remaining 50% are caused by new strains of *C. albicans* or new species.[1] Other species, notably *Candida glabrata, C. dubliniensis* and *C. parapsilosis*, tend to cause infection in patients who have very advanced disease and have had extensive previous exposure to antifungal agents (especially the azoles; see Chapter 237).

PATHOGENESIS AND PATHOLOGY

Most patients are readily colonized with *Candida* spp., which appears as part of the mouth flora in over 80% of people who have HIV infection. The specific local immunologic defects that predispose to disease are unknown, although it is assumed that some deficiency in T cell immunity is important because disease is clearly more common as the $CD4^+$ lymphocyte count falls. Additional defects in local oral clearance mechanisms (e.g. epithelial barriers, salivary flow, lysozyme and lactoferrin release) have been described in people who have HIV infection and may be relevant to candidiasis. In addition, non-specific factors such as dental hygiene, smoking and the use of antibacterials for prophylaxis may predispose to candidiasis.

CLINICAL FEATURES

Most patients are symptomatic and complain of some oral discomfort. The classic presentation is of creamy-white plaques on an erythematous base – the pseudomembranous form of thrush (Fig. 126.1). Other manifestations include:

- an atrophic form that presents as erythema without plaques (often associated with patchy atrophic glossitis); and

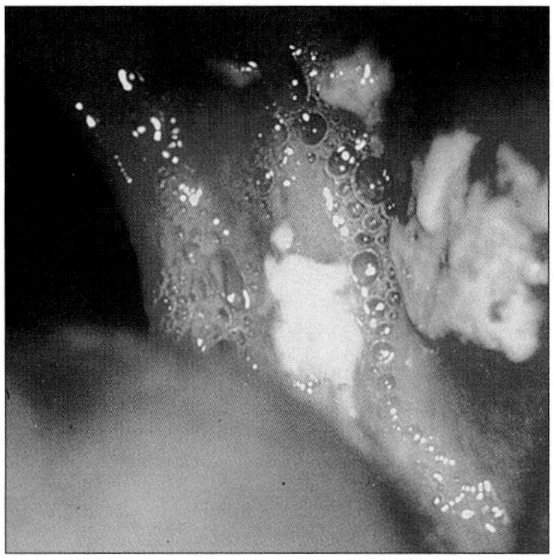

Fig. 126.1 Pseudomembranous oral candidiasis ('thrush').

- angular cheilitis, which appears as cracking, fissuring, ulceration or erythema at the corner of the mouth.

Most patients who have vaginal candidiasis present with vaginal itching, burning or pain, and usually complain of a vaginal discharge. Examination of the vaginal cavity usually reveals thrush, identical to that seen in the oropharynx.

Patients who have esophageal candidiasis develop ulcers and erosions of the esophagus and experience odynophagia or dysphagia. The combination of oral candidiasis and esophageal symptoms is both specific and sensitive in predicting esophageal involvement. Patients can be treated empirically with antifungal therapy. Endoscopy is reserved for those patients who fail to respond to evaluate for other diagnoses such as herpetic or cytomegalovirus esophagitis, idiopathic ulceration or resistant candidiasis.[2]

MANAGEMENT

The development of oral candidiasis in an HIV-positive patient should be taken as a sign of progressive immunodeficiency. Patients should have a $CD4^+$ count measured. If they are not currently receiving antiretroviral therapy, it should be initiated. If they are on antiretroviral therapy, it should be reassessed and, if necessary, changed.

A number of options – both local and systemic – are available for the treatment of oral candidiasis (Table 126.1). Initially, most patients respond well clinically to any form of antifungal therapy, although mycologic responses are less common. In general, topical therapy should be used initially and systemic therapy reserved for more difficult problems such as treatment failure or noncompliant patients. Of the local therapies, troches are generally used more effectively by patients than suspensions. Episodes of vulvovaginal candidiasis are also managed readily with topical therapy or short courses of systemic azoles. Esophageal disease requires systemic therapy. Fluconazole 200–400mg q24h orally for 2–3 weeks is probably the therapy of choice;[3] itraconazole 100–200mg q12h orally is also effective.

Relapses are common and at least one-third of patients develop recurrent mucosal candidiasis. One approach to management is to

THERAPEUTIC OPTIONS FOR ORAL OR ESOPHAGEAL CANDIDIASIS		
Agent	**Formulation**	**Dosage**
Nystatin	Oral suspension	400–600 000 units (4–6ml) q6h
	Pastille	1–2 pastilles q6h
Glotrimazole	Troche	10mg (1 troche) 5 times daily
Ketoconazole	Tablet	200mg q24h 400–600mg q24h (esophageal disease)
Fluconazole	Tablet	50–100mg q24h 200–400mg q24h (esophageal disease)
	Oral suspension	50–100mg (5–10ml) q24h
Itraconazole	Capsule	200mg q24h
	Oral suspension	100mg (10ml) q12h
Amphotericin B	Oral suspension	500mg (5ml) q6h–q8h
	Lozenge	One q6h
	Intravenous infusion	0.3–0.5mg/kg q24h

Table 126.1 Therapeutic options for oral or esophageal candidiasis. Not all formulations are widely available. Dosage is the usual dose for the typical patient – the average duration of therapy is 7–14 days and individual patients may require higher doses or more prolonged treatment.

treat each episode as it occurs. However, in many patients, recurrent symptomatic disease may be sufficiently severe to warrant considering chronic suppression. Fluconazole 100–200mg q24h has proved highly successful in suppressing recurrent oropharyngeal disease and preventing esophagitis, and a dose of 100mg per week can prevent vaginal candidiasis. The major risk of this approach is the possibility of developing azole-resistant disease.

Approximately 5–7% of patients who have advanced HIV disease (usually resistant to available antiretroviral therapy) develop candidiasis that is refractory to standard fluconazole therapy. The major risk factors are:

- advanced immunodeficiency ($CD4^+$ lymphocyte counts less than 50 cells/mm^3 and often less than 10 cells/mm^3), and
- extensive previous exposure to fluconazole.[4]

Isolates also tend to be resistant in vitro, with minimum inhibitory concentrations of more than 64mg/ml to fluconazole. The clinical expression of disease is a progressive and symptomatic infection with frequent esophagitis.

Therapy for resistant candidal infection is unsatisfactory. Improving immune function (e.g. with antiretroviral therapy) is the best strategy, but options may be limited. Higher doses of fluconazole (up to 800mg) may be effective in patients who have infection caused by organisms with intermediate susceptibility but are usually not effective for truly resistant strains. The cyclodextrin oral suspension formulation of itraconazole has been reported to be effective in about 60% of cases but the benefit is short-lived if some form of chronic maintenance therapy is not given.[5] Many patients require parenteral amphotericin B or caspofungin for symptomatic control.

CRYPTOCOCCOSIS

EPIDEMIOLOGY

Virtually all HIV-associated infection is caused by *Cryptococcus neoformans* var. *neoformans*. The organism is found worldwide as a soil organism. About 5% of patients who have advanced HIV infection in the Western world develop disseminated cryptococcosis; the disease is more prevalent in sub-Saharan Africa and southern Asia. Most cases of infection occur in patients who have very low $CD4^+$ lymphocyte counts (<50,000/ml).

PATHOGENESIS AND PATHOLOGY

It is assumed that transmission occurs via inhalation of the basidiospores or unencapsulated forms, leading to colonization of the airways and subsequent respiratory infection. The absence of an intact cell-mediated response results in ineffective ingestion and killing of the organism, leading to dissemination and an increased cryptococcal burden. The polysaccharide capsule, composed mainly of glucuronoxylomannan, is thought to be the organism's primary virulence factor. It is unclear whether cryptococcal infection in patients who have AIDS represents an acute primary infection or reactivation of previously dormant disease.

CLINICAL FEATURES

Cryptococcosis most commonly presents as a subacute meningitis or meningoencephalitis with fever, malaise and headache.[6] Symptoms are usually present for 2–4 weeks before diagnosis. Classic meningeal symptoms and signs (such as neck stiffness or photophobia) occur in about one-third of patients. Some patients may present with encephalopathic symptoms such as lethargy, altered mentation, personality changes and memory loss. Analysis of the cerebrospinal fluid (CSF) usually shows:

- mildly elevated serum protein;
- normal or slightly low glucose;
- a few lymphocytes; and
- numerous organisms.

Cryptococcal antigen is almost invariably detectable in the CSF at high titer. The CSF opening pressure is elevated in 25% of patients, and this has important prognostic and therapeutic implications.

About one-half of patients have evidence of pulmonary involvement with cough or dyspnea and abnormal chest radiograms. Although most patients who have pneumonic involvement also have disseminated infection, isolated pulmonary involvement may be one of the earliest manifestations of cryptococcal infection. Most patients who have cryptococcal meningitis have positive blood cultures. Skin involvement is common and several types of skin lesion have been described; the most common form is that resembling molluscum contagiosum (Fig. 126.2).

DIAGNOSIS

The latex agglutination test for cryptococcal polysaccharide antigen in the serum is highly sensitive and specific for diagnosing of infection with *C. neoformans,* and a positive serum cryptococcal antigen titer

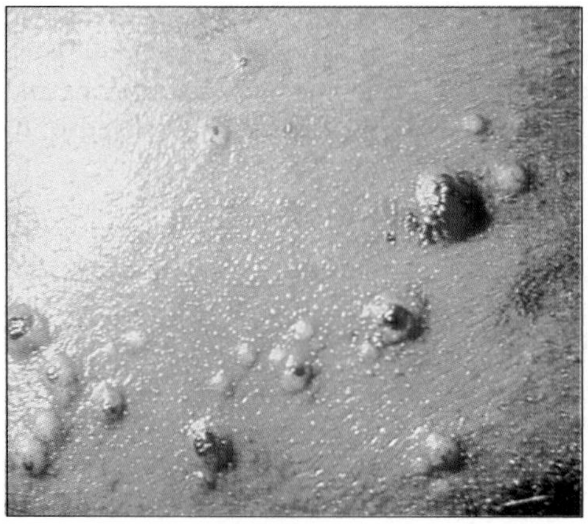

Fig. 126.2 Cutaneous cryptococcosis. This lesion is typical of the skin lesions of most endemic mycoses that occur in patients who have AIDS, and such a lesion may therefore also be seen in an AIDS patient who has disseminated histoplasmosis or penicilliosis.

of more than 1:8 is presumptive evidence of cryptococcal infection. The serum cryptococcal antigen can therefore be used as a screening test for the presence of cryptococcal infection in febrile patients who have HIV infection. The finding of a positive cryptococcal antigen titer in this setting is sufficient to warrant antifungal therapy.

MANAGEMENT

An algorithm for the treatment of cryptococcal meningitis is shown in Figure 126.3. Untreated, cryptococcal meningitis is fatal. Amphotericin B (0.7mg/kg intravenously) given for 2 weeks followed by fluconazole 400mg orally for a further 8 weeks is associated with the best outcome in prospective trials, with a mortality of less than 10% and a mycologic response of approximately 70%.[7] The addition of flucytosine 100mg/kg q24h to the amphotericin B phase does not improve immediate outcome but may decrease the risk of relapse. Initial azole therapy (itraconazole or fluconazole) is associated with a suboptimal 50% response rate. Early results with a combination of fluconazole 400–800mg q24h with flucytosine and the liposomal formulation of amphotericin B suggest that these may be options for patients who are unable to tolerate the usual formulation of amphotericin B.

Clinical deterioration may be due to cerebral edema, which may be diagnosed by a raised opening CSF pressure. Recent studies have linked elevated opening pressures (>200mmH_2O) with an increased risk of early mortality and/or blindness.[8] The opening pressure of all patients who have cryptococcal meningitis should be measured when a lumbar puncture is performed, and strong consideration should be given to reducing such pressure (by repeated lumbar puncture, a lumbar drain or a shunt) if the opening pressure is high (>200mmH_2O).

Cryptococcal meningitis requires lifelong suppressive therapy, unless there is improvement in immune function. Prospective trials have established the superiority of fluconazole 200mg q24h when compared with placebo, weekly amphotericin B or itraconazole.[9] Prospective trials have also established that fluconazole, in dosages ranging from 400mg per week to 200mg q24h, and itraconazole, 100mg q12h, are very effective in preventing invasive cryptococcal infections, especially in patients who have CD4+ lymphocyte counts below 50–100 cells/mm^3,[10] and fluconazole use has probably resulted in the reduced incidence of cryptococcosis as a complication of AIDS. Because of the relative infrequency of invasive fungal infections, antifungal prophylaxis is not associated with a survival advantage.

All patients who have cryptococcal infection should receive optimal antiretroviral therapy. An immune reconstitution syndrome has been described in some patients who initiate potent antiretroviral therapy after cryptococcal infection. Aseptic meningitis (with a prominent cellular reaction in the CSF) and lymphadenitis have been reported. Chronic suppressive therapy for cryptococcal infection may be discontinued in patients who have had at least 1 year of treatment and who have received successful antiretroviral therapy for at least 6 months. Such patients should have undetectable plasma HIV viral RNA and a rise in CD4+ lymphocyte count to at least 100 cells/mm^3.

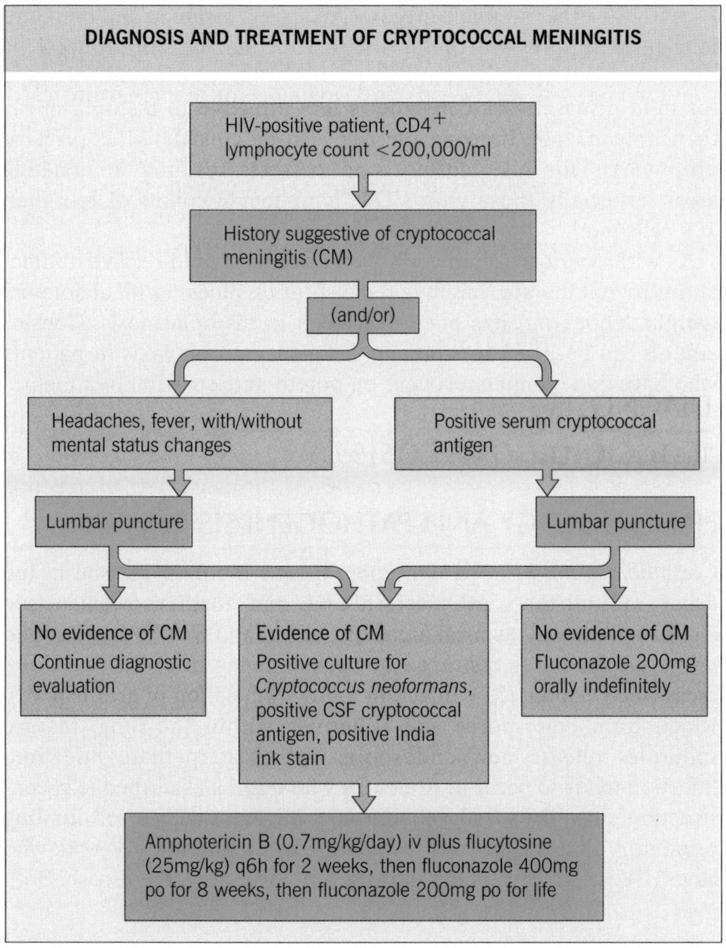

Fig. 126.3 Algorithm for the diagnosis and treatment of cryptococcal meningitis.

HISTOPLASMOSIS AND PENICILLIOSIS

EPIDEMIOLOGY AND PATHOGENESIS

Histoplasmosis is caused by the dimorphic fungus *Histoplasma capsulatum,* which is endemic in the Mississippi and Ohio river valleys of North America as well as certain parts of Central and South America and the Caribbean (Fig. 126.4). Penicilliosis is caused by the dimorphic fungus *Penicillium marneffei*, which is endemic in South East Asia (especially northern Thailand and southern China; Fig. 126.5).

The mycelial form of histoplasmosis is found in the soil and is particularly associated with bird roosts and caves. The environmental niche for *P. marneffei* is unknown, although it is also assumed to be a soil organism. Both fungi cause disseminated infection in 20–30% of patients who have AIDS in endemic areas, as well as sporadic infection among HIV-positive migrants from and visitors to endemic areas.

Infection with both fungi results when spores are inhaled into the lung and these are then converted to the pathogenic yeast form at

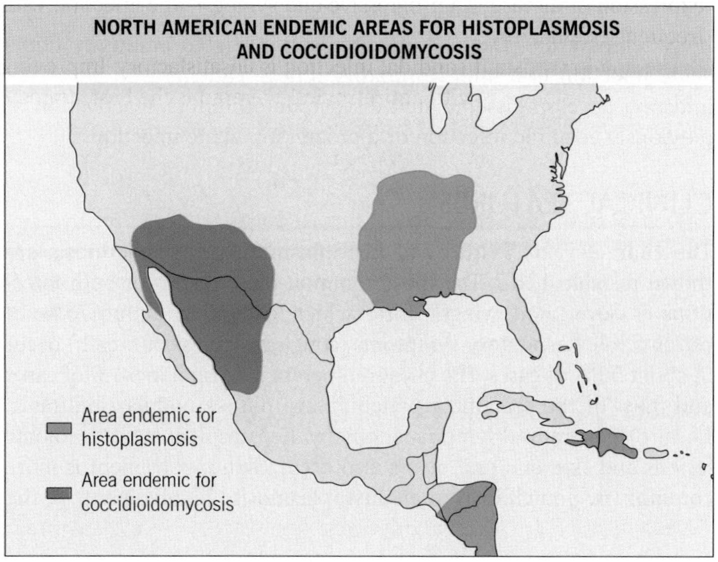

Fig. 126.4 North American Endemic areas for histoplasmosis and coccidioidomycosis.

ENDEMIC AREAS FOR PENICILLIOSIS

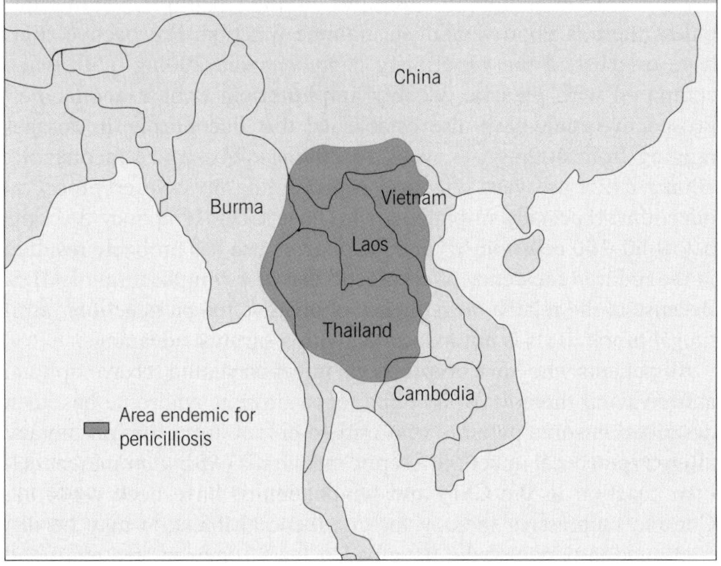

Fig. 126.5 Endemic area for penicilliosis.

CHARACTERISTICS OF HISTOPLASMOSIS AND PENICILLIOSIS		
Characteristic	**Histoplasmosis**	**Penicilliosis**
Appearance of organism on biopsy	1–5μm round to oval	1–8μm pleomorphic, elongated
Method of duplication	Budding	Fission
Clinical features (% of cases)		
Fever	95	99
Weight loss	90	75
Anemia	70	75
Pulmonary disease	50	50
Lymphadenopathy	20	40–50
Skin lesions	5–10	70
Hepatosplenomegaly	25	50

Table 126.2 Characteristics of histoplasmosis and penicilliosis.

body temperature. Usually, effective cell-mediated immunity limits acute infection to a mild respiratory illness. Patients who have HIV infection develop disseminated disease due to either reactivation of previously acquired infection or a progressive acute infection.

CLINICAL FEATURES

The characteristic features of histoplasmosis and penicilliosis are shown in Table 126.2. The most common presentation of both infections is fever and weight loss, which occurs in about 75% of patients.[11,12] Respiratory symptoms (cough, shortness of breath) occur in about 50% of cases. The chest radiogram is normal in 50% of cases and most of the remaining patients have diffuse nodular infiltrates. Local or generalized lymphadenopathy, hepatosplenomegaly, colonic lesions and skin and oral ulcers also occur. Skin involvement is more common in penicilliosis than histoplasmosis. Involvement of the gastrointestinal tract (usually as ulcers) may present with abdominal pain or gastrointestinal bleeding. Between 5% and 10% of patients have an acute septic-shock-like syndrome that includes hypotension and evidence of disseminated coagulopathy. This presentation carries a very poor prognosis. Laboratory findings may include anemia, neutropenia or thrombocytopenia (because of bone marrow involvement) and elevated hepatic enzymes.

DIAGNOSIS

The diagnosis is usually made by culture or by histopathologic examination of bone marrow aspirate or biopsy, lavage fluid or biopsy material from lung or skin lesions. A peripheral blood smear may show intracellular organisms in white cells in many patients. Blood cultures, especially when collected using the lysis centrifugation system, are positive in over 90% of patients. Anti-*H. capsulatum* antibodies are detected by immunodiffusion or complement fixation in about 70–80% and antigen detection in either urine or serum is an excellent method for diagnosing disseminated histoplasmosis. Serologic tests are not yet useful for diagnosing penicilliosis.

MANAGEMENT

The management of both infections appears to be similar. Patients should receive an initial period of treatment with amphotericin B (for 1–2 weeks) until there is clinical resolution (defervescence and improvement in skin lesions), followed by itraconazole 200mg orally q12h. A small study has suggested that initial treatment with liposomal amphotericin B (4 mg/kg q24h) was superior to amphotericin B deoxycholate for disseminated histoplasmosis suggesting this preparation should be considered for patients who have severe disease.[13] As with the other systemic mycoses, relapse is common and therefore long-term suppressive therapy with itraconazole 200mg q24h is warranted.[14,15] Itraconazole can probably be used as sole therapy for mild disease.[16] Fluconazole is less effective in histoplasmosis than itraconazole. Itraconazole can also be considered as primary prophylaxis for histoplasmosis in patients residing in endemic areas, especially those with $CD4^+$ lymphocyte counts of less than 100 cells/mm^3.

As with cryptococcal infection, all patients should receive optimal antiretroviral therapy. Immune reconstitution illness (with abdominal lymphadenopathy) has been described in histoplasmosis. Consideration can be given to stopping secondary prophylaxis in patients who have had immune recovery on potent antiretroviral treatment.

COCCIDIOIDOMYCOSIS

EPIDEMIOLOGY AND PATHOGENESIS

Coccidioides immitis is a dimorphic fungus found in the soil in the desert around the south-western USA and northern Mexico (see Fig. 126.4), as well as focal areas of Central and South America, and primary infection is restricted to persons living in or visiting those areas (see Chapter 237). Infection follows inhalation of arthrospores, which form endospores and spherules within the lung. Mature spherules release new endospores, which perpetuate infection. Infection tends to occur in situations where soil is disturbed (e.g. construction sites, dry windy conditions), but is usually a self-limiting respiratory illness controlled by cell-mediated immunity. People who have HIV infection develop more severe, disseminated disease. Both new primary infection and reactivation of previously acquired coccidioidomycosis can occur in patients who have HIV infection. Consequently, both individuals who have had previous coccidioidomycosis and those who have never been infected can develop progressive coccidioidal infections during the course of HIV infection. As with other endemic mycoses, migrants who have HIV infection and visitors to the endemic area are also at risk of infection.

CLINICAL FEATURES

Most patients, especially if their $CD4^+$ lymphocyte count is less than 250 cells/mm^3, develop pneumonia, presenting with fever, weight loss, night sweats, cough and dyspnea with symptoms lasting from several weeks to several months before diagnosis.[17] Disseminated disease occurs in at least 30%, resulting in generalized lymphadenopathy, skin nodules or ulcers, peritonitis, liver abnormalities, and bone and joint involvement. Meningeal disease, with symptoms of lethargy, fever, headache, nausea, vomiting and/or confusion, occurs in about 10% of patients. Cerebrospinal fluid analysis typically reveals a lymphocytic pleocytosis with a lymphocyte count of more than 50/ml.

DIAGNOSIS

Diagnosis is made by culturing the organism from clinical specimens or by demonstrating the typical spherule on histopathologic examination. As *C. immitis* is a highly contagious organism and can infect laboratory workers handling specimens, the clinical laboratory should be warned of the possibility of positive cultures (see Chapter 90). Blood cultures are positive in a minority of patients. Coccidioidal serology is often positive, but may be negative in up to 25% of patients who have disseminated infection. Patients who present with fever and have positive coccidioidal serology without focal lesions are presumed to have coccidioidal infection.[18]

MANAGEMENT

Amphotericin B, 0.5–1.0mg/kg q24h, is the mainstay of therapy and should be used initially in patients who have diffuse pulmonary or disseminated disease. Some experts advocate combining amphotericin B with fluconazole initially. Fluconazole, 400–800mg q24h orally, may be an alternative for patients who have mild disease. Complete eradication is unlikely and chronic suppressive therapy with either fluconazole 200–400mg q24h or itraconazole 200mg q12h is needed. Successful treatment with itraconazole or fluconazole has been reported in approximately 80% patients who have *C. immitis* meningitis.

There is no evidence that chemoprophylaxis with any of the azole antifungals can prevent coccidioidomycosis. People living in or visiting endemic areas are advised to avoid activities that would increase their exposure to disturbed soil.

ASPERGILLOSIS

EPIDEMIOLOGY

Infection with *Aspergillus* spp. is increasingly seen in patients who have advanced HIV disease. Specific risk factors that have been identified include neutropenia, use of corticosteroids and broad-spectrum antibacterial therapy and previous pneumonia, especially *Pneumocystis carinii* pneumonia. There is also some evidence that aspergillosis may be a direct effect of advanced HIV disease and may occur in the absence of other predisposing factors. Typically, patients have extremely low $CD4^+$ lymphocyte counts and a history of other AIDS-defining opportunistic infections.

CLINICAL FEATURES, DIAGNOSIS AND MANAGEMENT

Two major syndromes predominate:

- respiratory tract disease, and
- central nervous system infection.[19,20]

Patients often present with cough, shortness of breath and fever. Because aspergilli have a tendency to invade blood vessels and cause infarction, chest pain and hemoptysis are common. Nodular infiltrates, which may be localized or diffuse and commonly cavitate, are seen on chest radiography.

Diagnosis of invasive pulmonary aspergillosis may be difficult. A definitive diagnosis requires a biopsy demonstrating fungal invasion. A presumptive diagnosis of invasive aspergillosis may be made in patients who have pulmonary symptoms and new chest radiographic abnormalities and whose sputum or bronchial secretions grow aspergilli in culture. Additional respiratory syndromes of pulmonary aspergilloma and localized tracheobronchial aspergillosis have been reported occasionally in patients who have AIDS.

Patients who have central nervous system aspergillosis usually present with symptoms and signs of a mass lesion or with features of a stroke due to invasion of blood vessels. Therefore, seizures, hemiparesis and focal abnormalities are common. Computerized tomography or magnetic resonance imaging (MRI) of the head may show single or multiple lesions, usually nonenhancing, with surrounding edema. Bony invasion is common and, because the disease may have spread from involved sinuses, the sinuses may be abnormal. Patients who have fungal sinusitis usually have the classic features of sinusitis (fever, facial pain and swelling, nasal discharge and headache). Often, there is a history of previous sinus infection treated with broad-spectrum antibacterial therapy. As in other sites, aspergilli tend to invade locally. Computerized tomography of the sinuses will usually show bony erosion, and penetration into adjacent tissues such as the brain or orbit can occur.

The prognosis of aspergillosis is poor, in part because of the fungal infection itself and in part because it tends to occur in patients who have advanced AIDS and many other complications of end-stage HIV infection. There is a poorer response to therapy in patients who have AIDS than in other immunocompromised patients.[21] Therefore in most series the median time to death after a diagnosis of aspergillosis is only 2–4 months. Initial therapy should be with amphotericin B (1.0-1.5mg/kg/day of amphotericin B deoxycholate or 5-10mg/kg/day of liposomal amphotericin) or with voriconazole 200mg bid (see Chapter 208). A recent study[22] suggested voriconazole was superior to amphotericin B as initial therapy; however that study did not include many patients with AIDS.

OTHER FUNGAL INFECTIONS

The other endemic mycoses, blastomycosis and paracoccidioidomycosis, have been reported rarely in patients who have AIDS and do not appear to be major opportunists. Typically, there is disseminated disease.

There have also been case reports of disseminated sporotrichosis and localized mucormycosis in patients who have AIDS.

REFERENCES

1. Powderly WG, Robinson K, Keath EJ. Molecular epidemiology of recurrent oral candidiasis in HIV-positive patients: evidence for two patterns of recurrence. J Infect Dis 1993;168:463–6.
2. Rabeneck L, Laine L. Esophageal candidiasis in patients infected with the human immunodeficiency virus. A decision analysis to assess cost-effectiveness of alternative management strategies. Arch Intern Med 1994;154:2705–10.
3. Laine L, Dretler RH, Conteas CN, *et al.* Fluconazole compared with ketoconazole for the treatment of *Candida* esophagitis in AIDS. A randomized trial. Ann Intern Med 1992;117:655–60.
4. Fichtenbaum CJ, Koletar S, Yiannoutsos C, *et al.* Refractory mucosal Candidiasis in advanced human immunodeficiency virus infection. Clin Infect Dis 2000;30:749–56.
5. Philips P, Zemcov J, Mahmood W, Montaner JSG, Craib K, Clarke AM. Itraconazole cyclodextrin solution for fluconazole-refractory oropharyngeal candidiasis in AIDS: correlation of clinical response with in vitro susceptibility. AIDS 1996;10:1369–76.
6. Chuck SL, Sande MA. Infections with *Cryptococcus neoformans* in the acquired immunodeficiency syndrome. N Engl J Med 1989;321:794–9.
7. Van der Horst CM, Saag NS, Cloud GA, *et al.* Treatment of AIDS-associated acute cryptococcal meningitis: a four-arm, two step clinical trial. N Engl J Med 1997;337:15–21.
8. Graybill JR, Sobel J, Saag M, *et al.* Diagnosis and management of increased intracranial pressure in patients with AIDS and cryptococcal meningitis. Clin Infect Dis 2000;30:47–54.
9. Powderly WG, Saag MS, Clo ud GA, *et al.* A controlled trial of fluconazole or amphotericin B to prevent relapse of cryptococcal meningitis in patients with the acquired immunodeficiency syndrome. N Engl J Med 1992;326:793–8.
10. Powderly WG, Finkelstein D, Feinberg J, *et al.* A randomized trial comparing fluconazole with clotrimazole troches for the prevention of fungal infections in patients with advanced human immunodeficiency virus infection. N Engl J Med 1995;332:700–5.
11. Wheat LJ, Connolly-Stringfield P, Baker RL, *et al.* Disseminated histoplasmosis in the acquired immune deficiency syndrome: clinical findings, diagnosis and treatment, and review of the literature. Medicine 1990; 69:361–74.
12. Supparatpinyo K, Khamwan C, Baosoung V, Nelson KE, Sirisanthana T. Disseminated *Penicillium marneffei* infection in southeast Asia. Lancet 1994;344:110–3.
13. Johnson PC, Wheat LJ, Cloud GA, *et al.* Safety and efficacy of liposomal amphotericin B compared with conventional amphotericin B for induction therapy of histoplasmosis in patients with AIDS. Ann Intern Med 2002;137:105–9.
14. Wheat LJ, Hafner RE, Wulfsohn M, *et al.* Prevention of relapse of histoplasmosis with itraconazole in patients with the acquired immunodeficiency syndrome. Ann Intern Med 1993;118:610–6.
15. Supparatpinyo K, Perriens J, Nelson KE, Sirisanthana T. A controlled trial of itraconazole to prevent relapse of *Penicillium marneffei* infection in patients infected with the human immunodeficiency virus. N Engl J Med 1998;339:1739–43.
16. Wheat LJ, Hafner RE, Korzun A, *et al.* Itraconazole treatment of disseminated histoplasmosis in patients with the acquired immunodeficiency syndrome. Am J Med 1995;98:336–42.
17. Fish DG, Ampel NM, Galgiani JN, *et al.* Coccidioidomycosis during human immunodeficiency virus infection. A review of 77 patients. Medicine 1990;69:384–91.
18. Arguinchona HL, Ampel NM, Dols CL, Galgiani JN, Mohler MJ, Fish DG. Persistent coccidioidal seropositivity without clinical evidence of active coccidioidomycosis in patients infected with human immunodeficiency virus. Clin Infect Dis 1995;20:1281–5.
19. Lortholary O, Meyohas MC, Dupont B, *et al.* Invasive aspergillosis in patients with acquired immunodeficiency syndrome: report of 33 cases. French cooperative study group on aspergillosis in AIDS. Am J Med 1993;95:177–87.
20. Khoo SH, Denning DW. Invasive aspergillosis in patients with AIDS. Clin Infect Dis 1994;19(Suppl.1):41–8.
21. Denning D, Lee JY, Hostetler JS, *et al.* NIAID mycoses study group multicenter trial of oral itraconazole therapy for invasive aspergillosis Am J Med 1994;97:135–44.
22. Herbrecht R, Denning DW, Patterson TF, *et al.* Voriconazole versus amphotericin B for primary therapy of invasive aspergillosis. N Engl J Med 2002:347;408-15.

chapter 127

Parasitic Infections

Christine Katlama

The use of highly active antiretroviral therapies has profoundly changed the epidemiology of the clinical manifestations of HIV disease. Overall, the incidence of opportunistic infections has decreased by 50–80%; however, toxoplasmosis remains frequent, often revealing AIDS and HIV infection in untreated patients; on the other hand cryptosporidiosis and microsporidiosis, which used to be common in the course of AIDS, are occurring much less frequently in patients with improved immune status because of potent antiretroviral therapy.

TOXOPLASMA GONDII

EPIDEMIOLOGY AND PATHOGENESIS

Toxoplasmosis, caused by *Toxoplasma gondii,* an obligate intracellular protozoan, is a common opportunistic infection in patients with AIDS. It has a prevalence ranging from 10–40% in Europe, the Caribbean area and Africa, to 5–10% in USA. This is due to the different prevalence of *T. gondii* infection in the general population of these areas (e.g. 50–70% in Europe, but 10–40% in the USA).[1] The widespread use of primary prophylaxis that is active against both *Pneumocystis carinii* and *T. gondii* in patients with HIV infection has decreased the incidence of these two most common opportunistic infections. The underlying immune cellular defect in HIV infection is the major cause of the reactivation of latent *T. gondii* infection that has persisted in the central nervous system (CNS) or extraneural tissues after earlier acute infection. Toxoplasmosis usually occurs late in HIV disease, when the $CD4^+$ lymphocyte count is less than $100/mm^3$. By now, given the impact of antiretroviral therapy in western countries and the use of systematic toxoplasmosis and *P. carinii* pneumonia prophylaxis as soon as CD4 cells count are below $200/mm^3$, most of the cases of toxoplasmosis are diagnosed in patients known to have HIV infection but without any medical follow-up (see also Chapter 245).

CLINICAL FEATURES

The CNS is by far the most common site of toxoplasmosis, representing approximately 80% of cases. The next most common site is the retina (5–10%); pneumonitis and myocarditis are less common manifestations.[2] Involvement of other organs, such as the liver and bladder, is usually a histologic or autopsy finding in the context of disseminated disease.

Encephalitis

Toxoplasmic encephalitis (TE) commonly manifests as single or multiple intracerebral abscesses, with focal neurologic signs and constitutional symptoms that progress over a few days or weeks.[3–5] Fever and headaches are present in 40–70% of cases, neurologic dysfunction including confusion and lethargy in 40% of cases, focal CNS deficits in 50–60% of cases, and seizures in 30–40% of cases, which frequently are the presenting symptom of TE.

The constellation of fever, headaches, mild neurologic deficit or any unexplained neurologic symptoms should suggest the diagnosis of TE (Fig. 127.1), and prompt computerized tomography (CT) scanning or magnetic resonance imaging (MRI) should be undertaken.

Retinitis

Toxoplasmic retinitis represents the third most common opportunistic infection of the retina in AIDS. Symptoms include decreased visual acuity, defects in the visual field, 'floaters' and loss of peripheral vision. Diagnosis relies on funduscopic examination (Fig. 127.2), which typically shows a thick, dense, opaque appearance of retinal lesions with very distinct borders, and an intense vitreal inflammation. There is usually little or no hemorrhage, which is the opposite of the situation in retinitis caused by cytomegalovirus.

Pneumonitis

Toxoplasmic pneumonitis occurs generally in a context of disseminated disease and presents as a bilateral interstitial pneumonia.[6] Clinical and radiologic symptoms are non-specific; they include fever, cough, dyspnea and interstitial radiologic abnormalities. Diagnosis is made by finding *T. gondii* cysts in bronchoalveolar fluid.

DIAGNOSIS

Because it occurs in AIDS as a result of reactivation of a latent preexisting infection caused by the immune suppression induced by HIV, a diagnosis of toxoplasmic disease should be suspected in patients with:

- a low $CD4^+$ lymphocyte count, usually less than $100/mm^3$;
- specific antitoxoplasmal antibodies, indicating past infection; and
- no specific current primary prophylaxis.

In patients with HIV infection and any neurologic symptoms, CNS imaging is the most urgent diagnostic procedure (see Fig. 127.1). Magnetic resonance imaging is more sensitive than CT scanning. Toxoplasmic abscesses are typically contrast-enhancing lesions surrounded by edema; there may be a mass effect, with displacement of the ventricles. Magnetic resonance imaging may also reveal hemorrhages, which are highly suggestive of toxoplasmic necrosis.

Although no neuroradiologic findings can be considered pathognomonic for TE, some findings, such as the presence of multiple lesions, a localization of lesions in the basal ganglia or at the corticomedullary junction, the presence of edema, a mass effect and hemorrhages, may help to distinguish TE from CNS lymphoma, which is the main differential diagnosis.

Antitoxoplasmic therapy leads to a decrease in number and size of the lesions within 10–15 days, and this may confirm the diagnosis. Mild radiologic sequelae with no clinical consequences may persist at the end of therapy. In the absence of any improvement, a cerebral biopsy should be performed to exclude a lymphoma or progressive multifocal leukoencephalopathy.

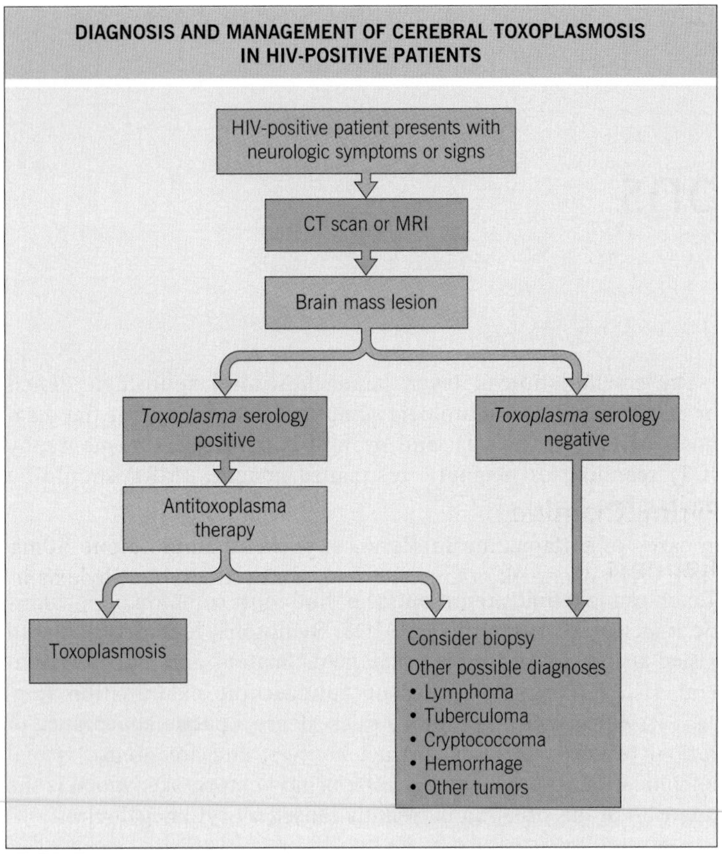

Fig. 127.1 Diagnosis and management of cerebral toxoplasmosis in HIV-positive patients.

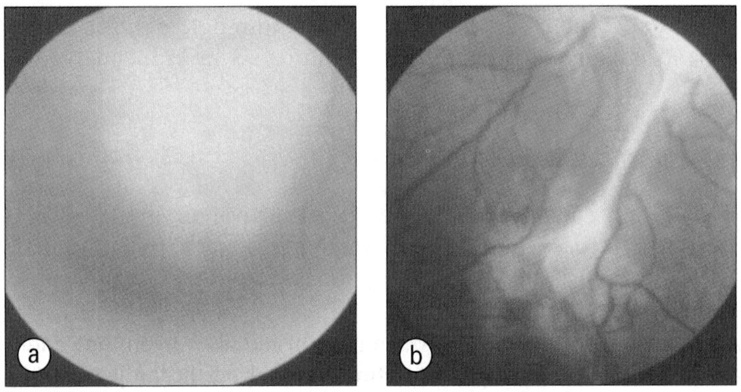

Fig. 127.2 Toxoplasmic retinitis. (a) Diagnosis from fundoscopy. (b) Evolution after antitoxoplasma therapy.

The detection of *Toxoplasma* antibodies in patients with HIV infection has no significance other than the assessment of a previous exposure to the parasite, which indicates the potential risk of reactivation in case of severe immunodepression.

In most of cases of encephalitis or retinitis, the diagnosis of toxoplasmosis is presumptive, made on clinical–radiologic criteria and confirmed by the therapeutic response.

The identification of *T. gondii* in extraneural or extraretinal tissue or body fluid gives a definitive diagnosis of toxoplasmosis if a biopsy is performed. The characteristic toxoplasmic lesions found on cerebral biopsy are necrotic abscesses surrounded by a prominent inflammatory infiltrate that contains extracellular *T. gondii* tachyzoites, edema, vasculitis and hemorrhages. Isolation of *T. gondii* from blood, cerebrospinal fluid, bronchoalveolar lavage fluid or by using polymerase chain reaction appears to be more frequent in disseminated disease than it is in localized disease.[7]

MANAGEMENT

Appropriate treatment is especially important, both because the response to therapy is the main criterion for diagnosis of TE, and because early initiation of therapy gives the best prognosis. Treatment consists of initial acute therapy over 3–6 weeks followed by lifelong maintenance therapy to prevent further reactivation (Table 127.1). Initiation of antiretroviral therapy should be preferentially delayed 3–4 weeks to avoid overlap in drug toxicities.

Sulfadiazine and pyrimethamine combination

The combination of pyrimethamine 50–75mg/day orally and sulfadiazine 4–6g/day is the first-line acute therapy.[3–5] These drugs act synergistically by blocking the folic acid pathway of tachyzoites, but have no effect on the cyst forms of the parasite. Folinic acid 25mg/day orally should be given as well to prevent hematotoxicity

Clinical improvement occurs within 5–10 days; the diagnosis of TE is confirmed by a decrease in both neuroradiologic and clinical abnormalities (Fig. 127.3). The duration of therapy is 3–6 weeks.

Fever and rash are the most common adverse events of pyrimethamine–sulfadiazine that may lead to discontinuation of therapy; they occur in 20–25% of cases. Other side-effects include hematotoxicity, crystalluria and transaminase elevation.

In the maintenance phase the recommended therapy is pyrimethamine 25mg/day orally plus sulfadiazine 2g/day orally lifelong or until a CD4 cell count of more than 200/mm^3 for more than 3 months is reached in cases of antiretroviral therapy. This combination is also effective as primary prophylaxis for *P. carinii* pneumonia.

Pyrimethamine plus clindamycin

The combination of pyrimethamine 50mg/day orally and clindamycin 2.4g/day orally or intravenously as acute therapy, followed by pyrimethamine 25mg/day orally plus clindamycin 1.2g/day orally as maintenance therapy[3,4] is considered as second-line therapy for use in cases of intolerance to sulfadiazine, because it has a higher relapse rate (15%) than pyrimethamine–sulfadiazine (3%) in maintenance therapy.[4–6] Side-effects include rash (30%) and diarrhea (20%), and there is a risk of pseudomembranous colitis induced by clindamycin.

Atovaquone

Atovaquone 750mg q6h orally, a hydroxynaphthoquinone that is a potent in-vitro inhibitor of *T. gondii* and *P. carinii*,[8–10] may be used in acute or maintenance therapy for patients who are intolerant to the standard therapies mentioned above.[11] Although there have been no comparative controlled studies, the few available data suggest that atovaquone is less effective than standard therapies, with a 25% relapse rate that might be due to wide variations in plasma concentrations of the drug between patients and within the same patient. It is recommended that atovaquone should be combined with pyrimethamine.[10]

Macrolides

Clarithromycin 2g/day orally and azithromycin 500mg/day orally have been given in combination with pyrimethamine in small, open, noncomparative pilot studies. They have been found to have an efficacy rate of 50–70%.[11] However, these drugs are not considered to be major antitoxoplasma drugs.

PREVENTION

In patients with HIV infection who have negative toxoplasma serology, prevention measures to avoid contamination should be recommended (e.g. avoiding contacts with raw meat, cooking meat properly, washing vegetables). Control serology should be performed on a regular basis to warn that contamination might have occurred.

THERAPEUTIC MANAGEMENT OF TOXOPLASMOSIS			
	Acute initial therapy	**Maintenance therapy**	**Notes**
First-choice treatment	Pyrimethamine 50mg/day plus sulfadiazine 4g/day po	Pyrimethamine 25mg/day plus sulfadiazine 2g/day po	Highest efficacy; also effective as prophylaxis for *P. carinii* pneumonia
Second-choice treatment	Pyrimethamine 50mg/day plus clindamycin 2.4g/day po or iv	Pyrimethamine 25mg/day plus clindamycin 1.2g/day po	Relapse rate is 25%; prophylaxis for *P. carinii* pneumonia should be added
Alternative treatment	Atovaquone 750mg q6h po Pyrimethamine–clarithromycin	Atovaquone 750mg q6h po	Relapse rate is 25%; also effective as prophylaxis for *P. carinii* pneumonia

Table 127.1 Therapeutic management of toxoplasmosis.

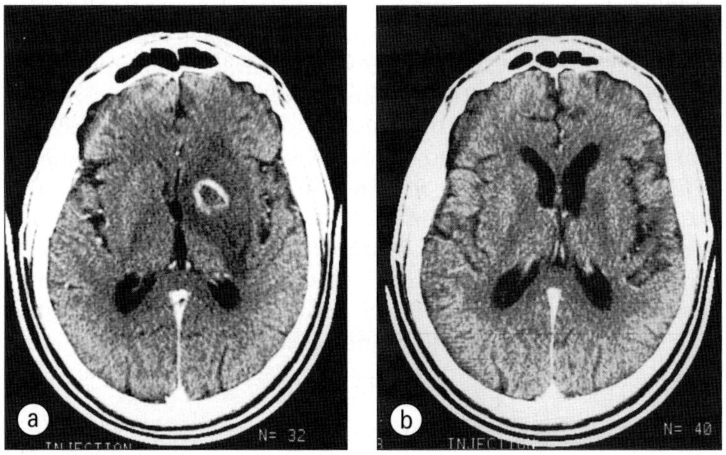

Fig. 127.3 Toxoplasmic encephalitis. (a) CT scan at diagnosis. (b) Evolution of the disease after 42 days of treatment with pyrimethamine–sulfadiazine.

Primary prophylaxis is indicated in patients at high risk of infection with *T. gondii*. High-risk patients are defined as those who have a $CD4^+$ lymphocyte count of less than 200 cells/mm^3 and positive antitoxoplasmal serology.[12] The use of drugs having activity against both *P. carinii* and *T. gondii* should be a priority.

Trimethoprim–sulfamethoxazole

Trimethoprim–sulfamethoxazole (co-trimoxazole) is effective in preventing both pneumocystosis and toxoplasmosis.[13,14] The most commonly used regimens are trimethoprim 160mg and sulfamethoxazole 800mg every day orally or every second day, or trimethoprim 80mg and sulfamethoxazole 400mg every day. Main side-effects are rash and fever (in 5–20% of cases); toxicity appears to be dose-related. The superiority of trimethoprim–sulfamethoxazole over other prophylaxis for both pneumocystosis and toxoplasmosis justifies desensitization procedures in patients with moderate intolerance to these compounds; desensitization has a 50–60% success rate.

Dapsone–pyrimethamine

Recommended regimens are dapsone 50mg/day plus pyrimethamine 50mg per week.[15] A weekly regimen with dapsone 200mg orally plus pyrimethamine 75mg orally showed similar results.[16] However, side-effects are frequent, occurring in 25–70% of patients; rash, hematotoxicity and digestive intolerance are the most common. In clinical practice, dapsone–pyrimethamine offers almost no advantages over trimethoprim–sulfamethoxazole, and cross-intolerance between these two combinations is frequent.

Pyrimethamine

In cases of sulfadiazine intolerance, pyrimethamine alone 50mg three times per week orally may be used as primary prophylaxis in combination with folinic acid 25mg three times per week.[17] Pentamidine aerosol should be added, because pyrimethamine does not provide effective prophylaxis against *P. carinii* pneumonia.

Discontinuation of prophylactic regimen

Several observational and two randomized studies[18,19] have shown that primary and secondary prophylaxis can be discontinued with minimal risk of developing TE in patients who have responded to highly active antiretroviral therapy (HAART) with an increase in $CD4^+$ T cells for at least 3 months. In case of changes in the immune state following failure or discontinuation of antiretroviral therapy that may lead to a decrease in CD4 cells, prophylaxis should be reintroduced if the $CD4^+$ T cell count decreases to less than 200 cells.

CRYPTOSPORIDIOSIS

EPIDEMIOLOGY

Cryptosporidiosis is a worldwide protozoan infection that is more prevalent in poorly developed countries. Cryptosporodiosis may affect patients with acute disease but more frequently patients with an immune deficit.[20] The prevalence of this infection in the context of HIV disease in Europe was 1–2% and in North America 3–4% before HAART, but the rate has fallen considerably given the generalized use of combined potent antiretroviral drugs in the year 2000; in Asia, Africa, and Central and South America it is 15–10%.[21,22] Human cryptosporidiosis is generally caused by *Cryptosporidium parvum*, which is transmitted primarily by the fecal–oral route through person to person transmission or indirectly; outbreaks from municipal water, person to person transmission and animal to person transmission have been described. Healthy carriers of oocysts may play a major role in transmission.

CLINICAL FEATURES AND DIAGNOSIS

Diarrhea is the main clinical symptom, ranging in severity from mild diarrhea to cholera-like, watery diarrhea. Abdominal cramps, nausea, vomiting and anorexia usually accompany the diarrhea when it is moderate or severe. Fever is uncommon and may be due to other concurrent infections. The severity of the disease is more pronounced in patients with $CD4^+$ lymphocyte counts of less than 50/mm^3. Cryptosporidiosis may involve the gallbladder, the biliary tract, the pancreatic ducts (leading to cholecystitis and pancreatitis), the bronchi and the lungs.

Diagnosis is based on the identification of the parasite in feces, in tissue specimens or in other fluids such as in bronchoalveolar lavage, using a modified acid-fast stain such as the Ziehl–Neelsen stain. Other techniques include Giemsa stain, fluorescent auramine–rhodamine, Sheather's sucrase flotation and indirect immunofluorescence.[22] Occasionally, cryptosporidiosis oocysts are associated with other pathogens, including *Entamoeba, Microsporidia* and *Giardia* spp. and cytomegalovirus.

MANAGEMENT AND PREVENTION

Treatment of cryptosporidiosis is essentially symptomatic. Efforts to find useful therapies have been impeded by the absence of an in-vitro model and the lack of a universally accepted animal model, and there is currently no agent that can reliably eradicate the organism. Among the various pharmaceutical agents that have been used, paromomycin,[23] azithromycin and nitazoxanide[24] have shown some efficacy in non-HIV related cryptosporidiasis. However, because the course of cryptosporidial disease depends mainly on immune status, the best option for therapy and prevention against chronic cryptosporidiosis is the restoration of immune function that has been observed as a consequence of potent antiretroviral therapy. Most of the devastating symptoms of cryptosporidiosis are observed in patients with severe immunosuppression and no antiviral therapy; initiation of antiretroviral therapy is the best option for treating cryptosporidiasis. This underlines clearly the role of the immune deficiency in the symptomatic disease. In the absence of specific effective treatment, the following preventive measures should be considered in patients whose $CD4^+$ lymphocyte count is less than $200/mm^3$:

- drinking boiled water or water filtered through a 1µm filter (bottled water may be an option);
- avoiding the consumption of raw fruits or vegetables that have been washed in unfiltered water; and
- avoiding contact with the feces of animals, or the wearing of gloves if such exposure cannot be avoided.

MICROSPORIDIOSIS

MICROBIOLOGY AND EPIDEMIOLOGY

Microsporidiosis is mainly seen in immunocompromised patients.[25] It is caused by an obligate intracellular protozoan parasite. Five genera have been reported in humans – *Enterocytozoon*, *Encephalitozoon* and *Septata* spp. are the most frequent; *Pleistophora* and *Nosema* spp. are uncommon. The source of human infection is unknown; contamination is thought to occur through ingestion of spores.

CLINICAL FEATURES AND DIAGNOSIS

The intestine is by far the most common site of microsporidiosis in patients with HIV infection, and 90% of cases are caused by *Enterocytozoon bieneusi*. Diarrhea of variable intensity between patients is the most frequent symptom; it may be accompanied by abdominal pain and cramps and nausea. Other localized forms of the disease include cholangitis and cholecystitis.[26] *Septata intestinalis* may cause a similar gastrointestinal syndrome or cholangitis, and it sometimes spreads to the urinary tract, when the organism may be be detectable in the urine.[27] *Nosema corneum* and *Encephalitozoon hellem* have been reported in corneal infection or keratoconjunctivitis.

Microsporidia can be identified in fluids (e.g. feces, urine, sinus mucus and bronchoalveolar lavage) using specific staining procedures such as modified trichrome, calcofluor or uvitex, and in tissue biopsies (e.g. intestinal and sinus biopsies) using staining procedures such as Giemsa, trichrome, periodic acid–Schiff or toluidine blue. Electron microscopy remains the reference diagnostic procedure that allows identification of the species of the organisms that are found (see Chapter 243).

MANAGEMENT

In a placebo controlled study, fumagillin (200mg q8h), an antiparasitic drug used in veterinary medicine, has been shown to be effective in clearing *E. bieneusi* in patients with HIV infection and chronic diarrhea related to this opportunistic infection. Bone marrow toxicity, mainly thrombocytopenia, is the principal side-effect of fumagillin.[28]

ISOSPORIASIS

Isosporiasis is a rare intestinal infection caused by *Isospora belli*. It is seen in immunocompetent patients in endemic areas – Central and South America, South East Asia and Africa – and in immunocompromised patients. Humans are the only known reservoir for *I. belli*.[29] The main route of transmission is thought to be oral absorption of food or water contaminated by *I. belli* oocysts. *Isospora belli* infection has been reported in less than 0.5% of AIDS patients in the USA, and in 15% of AIDS patients in Haiti and Africa. The generalized use of trimethoprim–sulfamethoxazole as prophylaxis against *P. carinii* pneumonia has lead to a large decrease in the prevalence of this infection in HIV-positive patients. Isosporiasis usually manifests in patients with HIV infection as chronic diarrhea that leads to malabsorption syndrome and weight loss.

Diagnosis is made by identification of *I. belli* cysts in specimens of stool; several stool samples must be examined (see Chapter 243).

Specific therapy of *I. belli* is trimethoprim–sulfamethoxazole (trimethoprim 160mg q12h, sulfamethoxazole 800mg q8h, for 10 days).[29] Long-term prophylaxis with trimethoprim–sulfamethoxazole (one double-strength tablet (trimethoprim 160mg and sulfamethoxazole 800mg) three times per week) is required to prevent relapse. Pyrimethamine (50–75mg/day) may be used in patients intolerant to sulfonamides.

LEISHMANIASIS

Visceral leishmaniasis (VL) in the course of HIV infection is mainly seen in southern Europe (Spain, Italy and the south of France) and south America (Venezuela and Brazil). It is estimated that 25–70% of adult VL cases in these areas are related to HIV infection and that 1.5–9% of AIDS patients develop newly acquired or reactivated VL. The majority of cases are due to *Leishmania infantum*. Visceral leishmaniasis usually occurs in late-stage HIV infection (when the $CD4^+$ lymphocyte count is less than $200/mm^3$), and it may be observed several years after the patient has left an endemic area.

The clinical manifestations are those of classic VL, with fever in 90% of cases. Other manifestations may include hepatomegaly and splenomegaly; digestive, pulmonary, or cutaneous disorders may be the only symptoms of VL. Biologic abnormalities include leukopenia and anemia, which may be at least partly due to the HIV infection.

Diagnosis relies on the identification of *Leishmania* spp. in a bone marrow aspirate; this test has a sensitivity of 95% for a first episode and 65% for relapses. Blood smears reveal the parasite in 50% of cases; this increases to 70% after culture of white blood cells. Serology has only limited diagnostic value, with only 35–50% positivity.

Acute therapy consists of meglumine antimoniate (20mg/kg body weight per day) for 28 days; this leads to a positive response in 80–90% of cases. Alternative drugs are pentamidine (4mg/kg/day on alternate days) for 4–12 weeks or amphotericin B (0.5–1mg/kg/day on alternate days) for 4–8 weeks.

The relapse rate is high (50% of cases relapse), justifying the need for long-term maintenance therapy. Different regimens have been suggested; pentavalent antimonials (850mg antimonials per month), pentamidine (2mg/kg every 2 weeks), or amphotericin B (1mg/kg every 2–4 weeks). In the absence of any comparative controlled trials, the best maintenance treatment remains uncertain.

REFERENCES

1. Luft BJ, Remington JS. Toxoplasmic encephalitis in AIDS. Clin Infect Dis 1992;15:211–22.
2. May T, Rabaud C, Amiel C, *et al.* Extracerebral toxoplasmosis in patients infected with HIV: a French national survey. Medicine 1994;73:306–14.
3. Katlama C, De Wit S, Guichard A, Van Pottelsberghe C, *et al.* Treatment of toxoplasmic encephalitis in AIDS: a randomized European trial comparing pyrimethamine–clindamycin to pyrimethamine–sulfadiazine. Clin Infect Dis 1996;22:268–75.
4. Dannemann B, McCutchan JA, Israelski D, *et al.* Treatment of toxoplasmic encephalitis in patients with AIDS: a randomized trial comparing pyrimethamine plus clindamycin to pyrimethamine plus sulfadiazine. Ann Intern Med 1992;116:33–43.
5. Porter S, Sande MA. Toxoplasmosis of the central nervous system in the acquired immunodeficiency syndrome. N Engl J Med 1992;327:1643–8.
6. Oksenhendler E, Cadranel J, Sarfati C, *et al.* *Toxoplasma gondii* pneumonia in patients with the AIDS. Am J Med 1990;88:18N–21N.
7. Lamoril J, Molina JM, De Gouvello A, *et al.* Detection by PCR of *Toxoplasma gondii* in blood in the diagnosis of cerebral toxoplasmosis in patients with AIDS. J Clin Pathol 1996;49:89–92.
8. Araujo F, Huskinson J, Remington JS. Remarkable in vitro and in vivo activities of the hydroxynaphtoquinone, 566C80, against tachyzoites and tissues cyst of *Toxoplasma gondii.* Antimicrob Agents Chemother 1991;35:293–9.
9. Kovacs JA. Efficacy of atovaquone in treatment of toxoplasmosis in patients with AIDS. Lancet 1992;340:637–8.
10. Katlama C, Mouthon B, Gourdon D, Lapierre D, Rousseau F, Atovaquone Study Group. Atovaquone as long-term suppressive therapy for toxoplasmic encephalitis in patients with AIDS and multiple drug intolerance. AIDS 1996;10:1107–12.
11. Fernandez-Martin J, Leport C, Morlat P, Meyohas MC, Chauvin JP, Vilde JL. Pyrimethamine–clarithromycin combination for therapy of acute *Toxoplasma* encephalitis in patients with AIDS. Antimicrob Agents Chemother 1991;10:2049–52.
12. Masur H, Kaplan JE, Holmes KK. Guidelines for preventing opportunistic infections among HIV-infected persons – 2002. Recommendations of the US Public Health Service and the infectious Diseases Society of America. Ann Intern Med 2002;137:435–77.
13. Carr A, Tindall B, Brew BJ, *et al.* Low-dose trimethroprim–sulfamethoxazole prophylaxis. Ann Intern Med 1992;117:106–11.
14. Podzcamer D, Santin M, Jimenez J, Casanova A, Bolaon F, Gudiol GRF. Thrice-weekly cotrimoxazole is better than weekly dapsone/pyrimethamine for the primary prevention of *Pneumocystis carinii* pneumonia and toxoplasmic encephalitis. Am J Med 1993;35:573–83.
15. Girard PM, Landman R, Gaudebout C, *et al.* Dapsone pyrimethamine compared with aerosolized pentamidine as primary prophylaxis against *Pneumocystis carinii* pneumonia and toxoplasmosis in HIV infection. N Engl J Med 1993;328:1514–20.
16. Opravil M, Heald A, Lazzarin A, *et al.* Combined prophylaxis of *Pneumocystis carinii* pneumonia and toxoplasmosis: prospective, randomized trial of dapsone + pyrimethamine versus aerosolized pendamidine. Clin Infect Dis 1995;20:531–41.
17. Leport C, Chene G, Morlat P, *et al.* Pyrimethamine for primary prophylaxis of toxoplasmic encephalitis in HIV patients: a double blind randomised trial. J Infect Dis 1996;172:91–7.
18. Soriano V, Dona C, Rodrigues-Rosado R, *et al.* Discontinuation of secondary prophylaxis for opportunistic infections in HIV-infected patients receiving highly active antiretroviral therapy. AIDS 2000;14:383–6.
19. Kirk O, Reiss P, Ubberti-Foppa C, *et al.* Safe interruption of maintenance therapy against previous infection with four common HIV-associated opportunistic pathogens during potent antiretroviral therapy. Ann Intern Med 2002;137:239–50.
20. Chen XM, Keithly JS, Paya CV, *et al.* Cryptosporidiosis. N Engl J Med 2002;346:1723–31.
21. Petersen C. Cryptosporidiosis in patients infected with the human immunodeficiency virus. Clin Infect Dis 1992;15:903–9.
22. Current WL, Garcia LS. Cryptosporidiosis. Clin Lab Med 1991;11:873–95
23. White AC, Chappell CL, Hayat CS, *et al.* Paromomycin for cryptosporidiosis in AIDS: a prospective, double-blind trial. J Infect Dis 1994;170:419–24.
24. Rossignol JFA, Ayoub A, Ayers MS. Treatment of diarrhea caused by *Cryptosporidium parvum*: a prospective randomized, double-blind, placebo-controlled study of nitazoxanide J Infect Dis 2001;184:103–6.
25. Bryan RT, Cali A, Owen RL, *et al.* Microsporidia: opportunistic pathogens in patients with AIDS. Prog Clin Parasitol 1991;2:1–26.
26. Pol S, Romana CA, Richard S, *et al.* Microsporidia infection in patient with the human immunodeficiency virus and unexplained cholangitis. N Engl J Med 1993;328:95–9.
27. Molina JM, Oksenhendler E, Beauvais B, *et al.* Disseminated microsporidiosis due to *Septata intestinalis* in patients with AIDS. Clinical features and response to albendazole therapy. J Infect Dis 1995;171:245–9.
28. Molina JM, Sarfati C, Tourneur M, *et al.* for the ANRS 090 Study Group. Fumagillin for treatment of intestinal microsporidiosis in immunocompromised patients: a randomized double-blind controlled trial (ANRS 090). N Engl J Med 2002;346:1963–9.
29. Pape JW, Verdier RI, Johnson WD Jr. Treatment and prophylaxis of *Isospora belli* infection in patients with the acquired immunodeficiency syndrome. N Engl J Med 1989;320:1044–7.

chapter

128 Bacterial Infections in HIV Disease

Janine R Maenza & Richard E Chaisson

Parasitic, fungal, mycobacterial and viral diseases are often viewed as the central opportunistic infections in HIV disease, because together they form the majority of AIDS-defining conditions. Bacterial infections as a group, however, are actually the most common complication of HIV disease. Patients with HIV infection are at greater risk for infections caused by common bacterial pathogens (e.g. *Streptococcus pneumoniae*, *Haemophilus influenzae*, *Salmonella* spp.) than are HIV-seronegative persons. The relevance of bacterial infections was demonstrated by the addition, in 1993, of recurrent bacterial pneumonia to the Centers for Disease Control and Prevention definition of AIDS indicator conditions.[1] This chapter reviews the underlying immunologic changes that lead to the occurrence of bacterial infections in HIV-infected patients, the epidemiology of these infections and the clinical manifestations and management of these conditions, in the developed world.

EPIDEMIOLOGY

The epidemiology of bacterial infections as complications of HIV infection has been most carefully studied for bacterial pneumonia. The increased risk of bacterial pneumonia in HIV-infected injection drug users was demonstrated in a study that found the annual risk of community-acquired pneumonia was 9.7% in HIV-infected injection drug users without AIDS, compared with 2.1% in HIV-negative injection drug users and only 0.3% in the general population.[2] In another, prospective, study of over 4000 former injection drug users the incidence of community-acquired pneumonia was again markedly higher among HIV-infected patients (90.5/1000 person-years) than among HIV-negative persons (14.2/1000 person-years; Fig. 128.1).[3]

Other studies have examined the risk of bacterial pneumonia in populations that include other exposure categories as well as injection drug use. The epidemiology of bacterial pneumonia was described in the Pulmonary Complications of HIV Infection Study.[4] In this longitudinal study, the majority of participants were homosexual or bisexual men. Again, the rate of bacterial pneumonia was significantly higher in HIV-infected patients than in HIV-negative controls (5.5/100 person-years compared with 0.9/100 person-years).[4] Tobacco smoking was also found to be associated with a significantly increased risk of bacterial pneumonia in both HIV-infected and -uninfected patients.[4]

The introduction of highly active antiretroviral therapy (HAART) in the late 1990s has influenced the incidence of HIV-associated bacterial infections. There appears to have been a decline in the incidence of community-acquired and nosocomial bacterial pneumonia after potent antiretrovirals became widely used.[5] In contrast, the proportion of hospitalizations due to bacterial infections has increased as rates of *Pneumocystis carinii* and other more opportunistic infections have declined.[6,7] Nevertheless, the increased rate of bacterial pneumonia in HIV-infected patients without AIDS, in comparison to HIV-negative persons, serves to emphasize that pyogenic bacterial infections may occur when immunity is relatively intact owing to the virulence of these organisms compared with other more opportunistic pathogens. Epidemiologic studies of other bacterial infections (e.g. bacteremia and infections caused by enteric pathogens) confirm the generally higher incidence of pyogenic infections in HIV-infected patients than in HIV-negative patients. Discussion of the increased frequency of specific diseases and the risk factors for disease development are found within the specific clinical sections of this chapter.

PATHOGENESIS AND PATHOLOGY

There are a variety of immunologic defects in HIV infection that may predispose patients to acquire bacterial infections. Among these immunologic abnormalities are deficits of mucosal immunity, cell-mediated immunity, humoral immunity and the complement system (Table 128.1).[8]

Defects of mucosal (or local) immunity are ascribed to decreased levels of IgA_2 at mucosal surfaces. It is postulated that this abnormality may increase the risk of invasive bacterial infections with *S. pneumoniae* and *Salmonella* spp. in particular.[8,9]

A reduction in the $CD4^+$ lymphocyte count and a reversal of the CD4:CD8 ratio in HIV infection is implicated as a predisposing factor for bacterial infections in several ways. $CD4^+$ lymphocytes may also be involved in cell-mediated immunity as mediators of antibody-dependent and antibody-independent killing of enteric bacterial pathogens by mononuclear cells.[10] Changes in regulatory effects secondary to decreased levels of interleukin-2 and interferon-γ production are also likely to contribute to an immunologic deficit.[11] In addition, abnormalities of $CD8^+$ lymphocyte activity may occur, leading to decreased cytotoxic function.[11]

Defects in humoral immunity are also present in HIV infection – although patients with HIV infection often have a polyclonal IgG gammopathy, the function of these antibodies is frequently abnormal and levels of specific IgG subclasses (e.g. IgG_2) may be low.[12] There is also evidence that some patients who have HIV infection have low levels of specific complement components or abnormalities of complement activation, or both.[13,14] Deficits in hepatic and splenic clearance of opsonized organisms may occur. Children in particular are at an increased risk of developing infections caused by encapsulated bacteria (e.g. *S. pneumoniae, H. influenzae*), probably because of a lack of protective antibody in the absence of previous exposure to these organisms.

Neutropenia is a common complication of advanced HIV infection itself, as well as being a toxicity of many medications used in the management of HIV-infected patients. Neutropenia (absolute neutrophil count <1000 cells/mm^3) is an independent risk factor for the development of bacterial infections in patients with advanced HIV disease, and the risk rises as the absolute neutrophil count falls.[15] Low CD4 counts have also been shown to increase the risk of infection during neutropenia.[16] It should be noted, however, that infection rates in patients with HIV infection are substantially lower than in patients with neutropenia related to cancer chemotherapy. This may be because the nadir in the absolute neutrophil count in patients with HIV infection is usually higher than that seen in cancer patients.

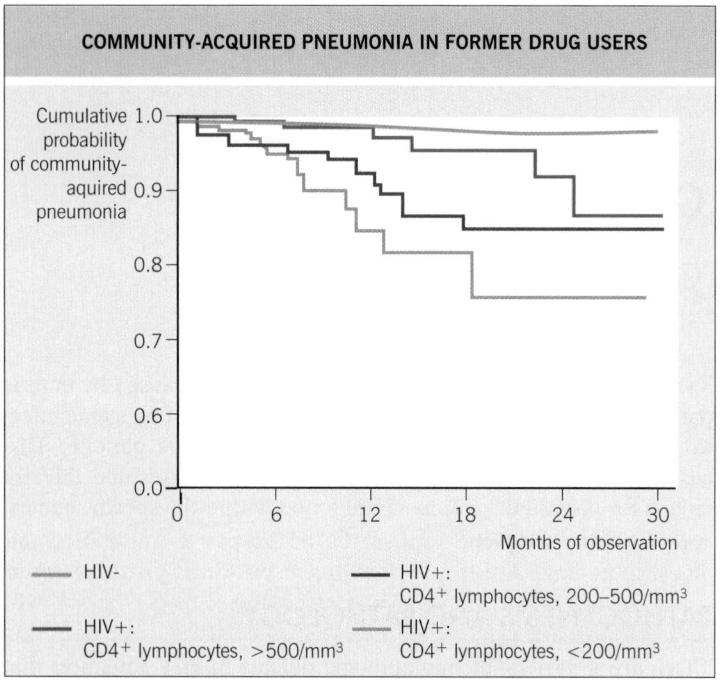

Fig. 128.1 Community–acquired pneumonia in former drug users. Kaplan–Meier estimates of the cumulative probability of community–acquired pneumonia in HIV-negative and HIV-positive former drug users. Adapted from Boschini *et al.*[3]

FACTORS ASSOCIATED WITH BACTERIAL INFECTIONS IN HIV-INFECTED PATIENTS
Defects of mucosal immunity
Decreased levels of IgA_2 at mucosal surfaces
T-lymphocyte defects
Loss of $CD4^+$ lymphocytes
Impaired cytotoxic T-lymphocyte function
Decreased production of interleukin-2 and interferon-γ
Defects of humoral immunity
Polyclonal gammopathy
Functional abnormalities of antibodies
Decreased levels of IgG subclasses
Granulocyte defects
HIV-related neutropenia
Drug-induced neutropenia
Complement defects
Low complement levels
Abnormal complement activation

Table 128.1 Factors associated with bacterial infections in HIV-infected patients.

PREVENTION

Prevention of bacterial infections may take several forms:

- avoidance of exposure,
- prophylactic antibiotics,
- vaccination,
- passive immunotherapy,
- the use of growth factors, and
- the use of HAART.

Avoidance of exposure

Measures involved in the avoidance of exposure range from avoiding the use of unsanitary water that may be associated with the transmission of enteric pathogens to the strict hygienic techniques recommended for patients with indwelling intravenous catheters. Patients should also avoid undercooked eggs and poultry and unpasteurized milk.[17]

Prophylactic antibiotics

The use of prophylactic antibiotics to prevent other opportunistic infections may have the added benefit of decreasing a patient's risk of bacterial infection. Trimethoprim–sulfamethoxazole (co-trimoxazole), a first-line agent for prophylaxis for *P. carinii*, may decrease the risk of bacterial infections as well. Studies have shown that its use is associated with a decrease in the number of confirmed episodes of bacterial pneumonia,[4] as well as bacterial infections in general.[18] Other studies, however, have failed to show a specific protective effect against pneumococcal infection;[19] this may be associated with selection of pneumococcal strains with decreased susceptibility to this agent.[20] In addition, trimethoprim–sulfamethoxazole has also been shown to be associated with a decline in the susceptibility of *S. pneumoniae* to penicillin.[21] The use of macrolide antibiotics (clarithromycin, azithromycin) as prophylaxis against the development of *Mycobacterium avium* infection has also been shown to be associated with a decreased risk of pyogenic bacterial infections.[22–24]

Thus, antibacterials being used for prophylaxis of *P. carinii*, toxoplasmosis or *M. avium* may decrease the risk of bacterial infections. Nevertheless, because of the risk of the development of resistance, antibiotics have not been recommended solely to prevent bacterial infections. Recent data from two placebo-controlled trials in Cote d'Ivoire suggest, however, that trimethoprim–sulmethoxazole prophylaxis may provide a health or survival benefit in developing countries where more costly therapies are not available.[25,26]

Vaccination

Both the pneumococcal vaccine and the *H. influenzae* type b (Hib) vaccine have been evaluated in HIV-infected patients. Antibody responses to the 23-valent pneumococcal vaccine have been shown to be more effective in patients with higher $CD4^+$ lymphocyte counts (Fig. 128.2).[20,27] There is also clinical evidence from observational studies indicating increased effectiveness when the vaccine is used earlier in the course of HIV infection (when the $CD4^+$ lympho-

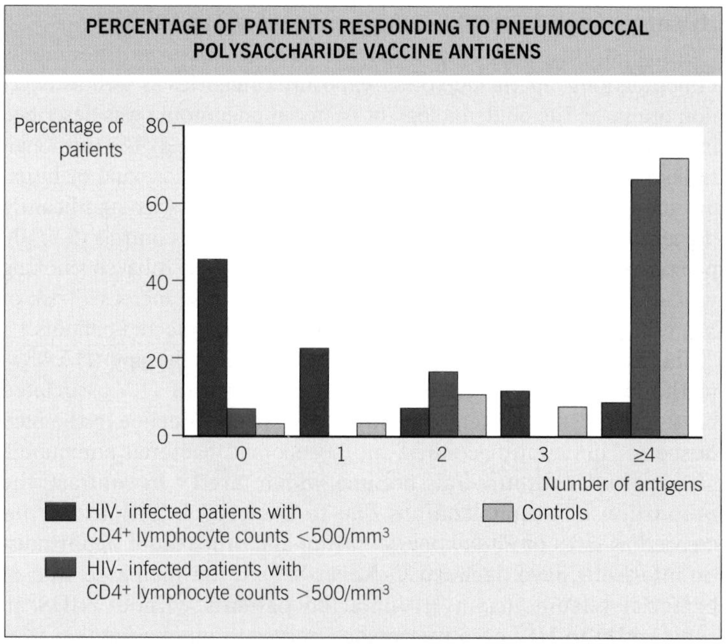

Fig. 128.2 Percentage of patients responding to pneumococcal polysaccharide vaccine antigens. Adapted from Rodriquez-Barradas *et al.*[20]

cyte count is greater than 200/mm^3).[19] In a placebo-controlled trial of pneumococcal vaccine in HIV-infected adults in Uganda, however, recipients of the 23-valent vaccine had a marginally higher rate of invasive pneumococcal infections and a significantly higher rate of all forms of pneumonia.[28] A clear rationale for why pneumococcal vaccination should increase the risk of disease is not apparent. Despite the findings of the Ugandan trial, the pneumococcal vaccine is currently recommended in the USA as a preventive measure for all patients with HIV infection and CD4$^+$ lymphocyte counts over 200/mm^3. For patients with CD4$^+$ lymphocyte counts under 200/mm^3, the vaccine is optional given the poor antibody and clinical response. Re-vaccination after 6 years is also recommended for patients with HIV infection, but a recent trial suggests that the risk of reactogenicity is considerable and the immunologic benefits may be limited.[29]

Vaccination against Hib has similarly been shown to elicit a better antibody response when used earlier in the course of disease.[30] The Hib polysaccharide vaccine is currently recommended for all children (regardless of HIV status).[31] The benefit of this vaccine in HIV-infected adults is less clear; although the incidence of *H. influenzae* is clearly increased in HIV-infected patients, the low absolute incidence of Hib infection mitigates against the routine use of the vaccine.[32]

Passive immunotherapy

Passive immunotherapy with high-dose intravenous immunoglobulin is often used to prevent recurrent bacterial infections in HIV-infected children.[33,34] One controlled trial has shown that such therapy may be effective in HIV-infected adults as well; a reduction in the frequency of serious bacterial infections and hospitalizations in patients who were treated with intravenous immunoglobulin every 21 days was demonstrated.[35]

Use of growth factors

Measures to prevent or correct neutropenia must be tailored to the underlying cause of the cytopenia (e.g. treatment of infection causing bone marrow suppression, elimination of myelopsuppressive drugs). As an adjunct to these measures, when elimination of the underlying cause is not possible, or when there is no specific discernible cause of neutropenia, the use of granulocyte colony stimulating factor (G-CSF) should be considered. The use of G-CSF in patients with an absolute neutrophil count less than 1000/mm^3 is associated with a decline in bacterial infections, decreased duration of hospitalizations and improved survival.[36–38]

Use of highly active antiretroviral therapy

As noted above, HAART has been strongly associated with a decreased incidence of bacterial infections, particularly bacterial respiratory tract infections, in patients with HIV infection. The use of HAART is generally governed by guidelines from professional and governmental groups and is based on the potency and tolerability of specific regimens, the relative risk of disease progression based on clinical status and surrogate markers, and the long-term toxicities of treatment (see Chapter 139).

CLINICAL MANIFESTATIONS AND TREATMENT

The most common clinical manifestations of bacterial infection in HIV-infected patients are skin infections, respiratory infections, sinusitis, enterocolitis and bacteremia.

Skin infections

Bacterial skin infections in HIV-infected patients may vary from impetigo to folliculitis to cutaneous abscesses; cutaneous abscesses are often associated with injection drug use as well. Recurrences may be more frequent than in the HIV-negative population, but physical findings and responsible organisms (*Staphylcoccus aureus* and *Streptococcus* spp.) are similar. Treatment involves agents with good coverage of Gram-positive organisms, such as cephalexin or dicloxacillin.

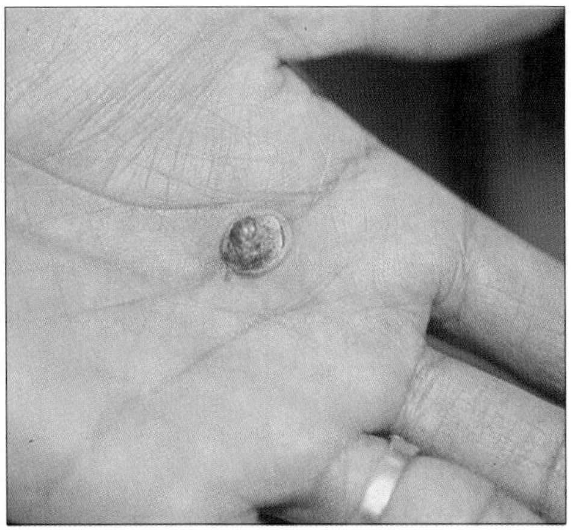

Fig. 128.3 Typical appearance of bacillary angiomatosis. Courtesy of Ciro Martins, MD.

Bacillary angiomatosis is a distinct skin infection that is specifically associated with HIV disease. The condition is caused either by *Bartonella henselae*, the organism that is also responsible for cat-scratch disease, or by *Bartonella quintana*. The clinical appearance is of very erythematous subcutaneous nodules that may occasionally resemble Kaposi's sarcoma (Fig. 128.3). Lymphadenopathy may be associated with these skin findings. Much less frequently, *B. henselae* has been identified as the cause of more deeply seated infections, including endocarditis, osteomyelitis and hepatic lesions (peliosis hepatis).[39] Diagnosis of the skin infection may be based on the characteristic appearance, but biopsy may be carried out to rule out other causes, and it is necessary to diagnose solid organ involvement. Histology shows vascular proliferation and mixed inflammatory cells. Warthin– Starry staining reveals the organism. Treatment is with a macrolide (erythromycin orally 250–500mg q6h) or a tetracycline (doxycycline orally 100mg q12h) for 1–2 months for skin disease, and longer for other sites of infection.

Sinusitis

Both acute and chronic sinusitis are common complications of HIV infection. Symptoms may include headache, fever, congestion and cough. However, many patients present with only headache or cough and without more typical symptoms of bacterial sinusitis (Table 128.2).

In one study, the organisms most commonly isolated as the cause of sinusitis were viridans streptococci, *S. pneumoniae* and *Pseudomonas aeruginosa*.[40] Other organisms that may be responsible include *H. influenzae*, other *Haemophilus* spp. and *Moraxella catarrhalis*.

The diagnosis is often made clinically, although sinus radiographs or computerized tomography (CT) scanning may be useful in demonstrating mucosal thickening, air–fluid levels or sinus opacification. Sinus CT is more sensitive for these findings than plain films.[40]

Treatment should include a decongestant in addition to antimicrobial therapy. The choice of antimicrobial is often made on empiric grounds with first-line options including amoxicillin–clavulanate, clindamycin, cefuroxime, clarithromycin or azithromycin. In patients who do not respond to such therapy, consideration should be given to sinus aspiration or the addition of antipseudomonal agents (see Chapters 32 and 229). In patients with CD4$^+$ lymphocyte counts less than 200/mm^3, response to antibiotic treatment for acute sinusitis is often incomplete, leading to chronic sinusitis.[40]

PRESENTING CLINICAL FEATURES OF SINUSITIS IN HIV-INFECTED PATIENTS

		Percentage of patients
Symptoms	Fever	93
	Headache	89
	Nasal congestion	79
	Postnasal drainage	54
	Facial pain	36
	Watery discharge	21
	Purulent discharge	14
	Fever, headache	14
	Fever, headache, congestion	68
	Fever, headache, facial pain, discharge	14
Signs	Fever – temperature over 100.4°F (38°C)	79
	Facial tenderness	50
	Nasal discharge	31
	Facial swelling	21

Table 128.2 Signs and symptoms of sinusitis in HIV-infected patients. These data relate to 72 HIV-infected patients as reported by Godofsky *et al.*[40]

RATES OF BACTERIAL PNEUMONIA IN HIV-POSITIVE AND HIV-NEGATIVE PATIENTS

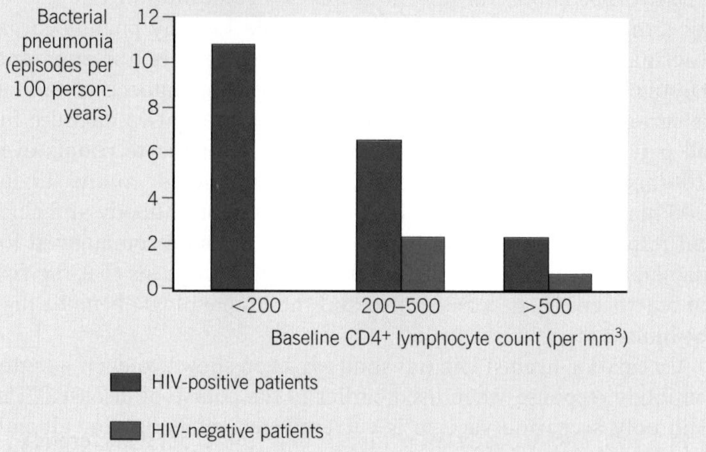

Fig. 128.4 Rates of bacterial pneumonia in in HIV-positive and HIV-negative patients. The rates are shown by baseline CD4+ lymphocyte count. Data from Hirschtick *et al.*[4]

Pneumonia

As described above, bacterial pneumonia is more common in patients with HIV infection than in HIV-seronegative comparison groups. The introduction of potent antiretroviral therapy, which has caused a decline in more opportunistic infections, has also led to bacterial pneumonia (and other bacterial infections) being responsible for proportionately more hospitalizations of HIV-infected patients.[6,7] Risk factors for the development of bacterial pneumonia have been investigated in observational studies and include lower $CD4^+$ lymphocyte counts,[3,4,41] injection drug use,[4] cigarette smoking[4] and illicit drug use.[41] In addition, risk factors for pneumococcal infection specifically include any previous history of pneumonia, low serum albumin and a lack of receipt of the pneumococcal vaccination when the patient had a $CD4^+$ lymphocyte count greater than $200/mm^3$.[19] The specific amount of risk associated with declining immunity has been described; a rate of bacterial pneumonia of 2.3/100 person-years in patients with $CD4^+$ lymphocyte counts over $500/mm^3$ was found.[4] This rate increased to 6.8/100 person-years in those with $CD4^+$ lymphocyte counts between 200 and $500/mm^3$, and 10.8/100 person-years in those with $CD4^+$ lymphocyte counts less than $200/mm^3$ (Fig. 128.4).[4]

The clinical presentation of bacterial pneumonia in HIV-infected patients is indistinguishable from that in HIV-negative patients. The history usually reveals an acute onset of symptoms, including fever, productive cough, dyspnea and pleuritic chest pain. Physical examination commonly shows localized pulmonary findings, and laboratory evaluation may show leukocytosis and hypoxemia. Typical chest radiograph findings are of focal infiltrates, although diffuse disease may be seen. Sputum Gram stain will show multiple polymorphonuclear leukocytes, and sputum cultures are usually positive. These findings differ from the classic presentation of *P. carinii* pneumonia, the most common nonbacterial cause of pneumonia in HIV-infected patients, in which the presentation is more often subacute with a nonproductive cough, a paucity of physical findings and diffuse interstitial infiltrates on chest radiograph. Nevertheless, there are frequently cases in which induced sputum examination or bronchoscopy with bronchoalveolar lavage are necessary to obtain a microbiologic diagnosis.

The pathogens most commonly responsible for bacterial pneumonia are *S. pneumoniae*, *H. influenzae* and *Haemophilus* spp. other than *H. influenzae*.[42] Other organisms that may cause disease include *M. catarrhalis*, *Klebsiella pneumoniae* and *Staphylococcus aureus*. Empiric therapy usually includes a second- or third-generation cephalosporin. If there is a lack of clinical response, other bacteria that may not respond to such treatment must be considered as possible causes (e.g. *Chlamydia pneumoniae*,[3] *Nocardia* spp.[43] and *Legionella* spp.[44]). In addition, unlike HIV-negative patients, in whom *P. aeruginosa* is usually responsible for only nosocomial infections, in HIV-infected patients *Pseudomonas* pneumonia frequently occurs as a community-acquired infection.[45,46] There are also data that suggest a shift in bacterial pathogens since the introduction of HAART. A decline in *P. aeruginosa* infections has been reported, and seems to be associated with both generally higher CD4 lymphocyte counts and a reduction in the use of trimethoprim–sulfamethoxazole prophylaxis.[47]

An unusual organism responsible for bacterial pneumonia in HIV-infected patients is *Rhodococcus equii*. This bacterium is a Gram-positive rod usually associated with infections of domestic animals.[48] In HIV-infected patients, the clinical presentation is often subacute and characterized by fever, cough, pleuritic chest pain, fatigue and weight loss.[49] Chest radiographs often show cavitating lesions.[48,50,51] Blood cultures may be more sensitive for diagnosis than sputum cultures – 83% sensitivity compared with 33% in one study.[51] Treatment is usually with vancomycin (intravenously 1g q12h) but ciprofloxacin (orally 750mg q12h) or imipenem (intravenously 500mg q6h) may also be used and duration of therapy is 2–4 weeks.

Bacteremia in the setting of pneumonia occurs more commonly in HIV-infected than in HIV-negative patients – increased rates of bacteremia with pneumococcal and *H. influenzae* pneumonia have been documented (Fig. 128.5).[52–55] Bacteremia may also occur with other pathogens responsible for pulmonary infections (e.g. *P. aeruginosa*). Mortality rates from bacterial pneumonia may also be higher in HIV-infected patients, but there are conflicting data on this topic.[56–59]

Enterocolitis

Many etiologic agents may cause diarrhea in HIV-infected patients. Among the bacterial pathogens commonly encountered are nontyphoidal *Salmonella* spp., *Shigella flexneri*, *Campylobacter jejuni* and *Clostridium difficile*. *Shigella* and *Campylobacter* infections manifest similarly – patients note severe diarrhea (which may be bloody) associated with abdominal cramping, nausea and fever.

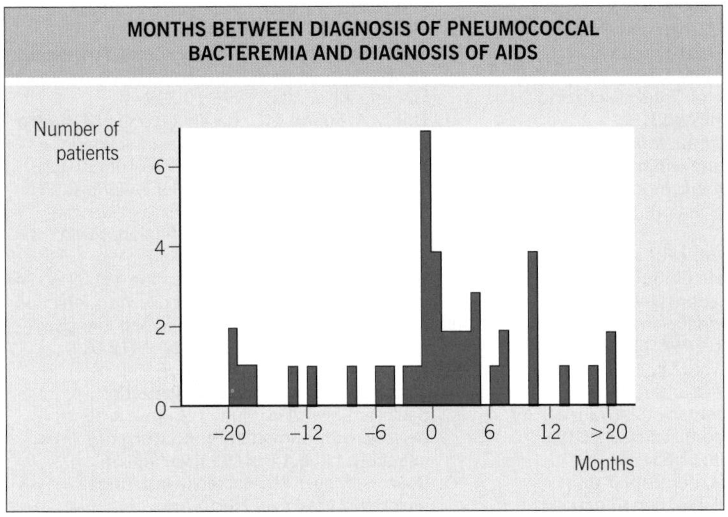

Fig. 128.5 Months between diagnosis of pneumococcal bacteremia and diagnosis of AIDS. The data relate to 37 patients as reported by Redd *et al.*[53]

Diagnosis is by stool culture. These infections may both be treated with oral quinolones (see Chapter 43).

Nontyphoidal *Salmonella* spp. infections may present either with or without diarrhea and other symptoms of colitis. In patients without gastrointestinal symptoms, the infection may manifest solely as fever without any localizing findings. The occurrence of *Salmonella* bacteremia is more common in patients with HIV infection than in HIV-seronegative groups.[60] In addition, relapses of bacteremia are common.[61] Unlike the recommendations for patients who are not immunosuppressed, even *Salmonella* infections limited to the gastrointestinal tract should be treated in HIV-infected patients. Treatment is usually with ciprofloxacin (500mg q12h for 2–4 weeks), and suppressive therapy with ciprofloxacin is often used because of the risk of relapse.

Infection due to *C. difficile* also has characteristics in HIV-infected patients that differ from those seen in the HIV-negative population. Clinical symptoms may be more severe in HIV-infected patients, and these patients are more likely to have relapses and chronic symptoms. Antibiotic use and hospitalization are associated with the development of infection, just as they are in HIV-negative patients.[62,63] *Clostridium difficile* may also occur as a community-acquired infection in HIV-infected patients.[64] Treatment is with oral metronidazole or vancomycin.

Bacteremia

As discussed above, bacteremia may frequently occur as a result of *Salmonella* spp. infections and pneumonia. Bacteremia may also be associated with soft tissue infections and urinary infections. Injection drug use is associated with the development of *S. aureus* bacteremia and endocarditis. In this setting, $CD4^+$ lymphocyte count has been shown to have an inverse correlation with mortality rate.[65] In addition, bacteremia may be a complication of the use of long-term intravenous catheters, which may be needed in the management of HIV-infected patients (e.g. for the intravenous treatment of cytomegalovirus retinitis). In one study of HIV-infected patients admitted with bacteremia, 35% had an infection associated with an intravenous catheter.[66] In this and other studies, the causative organisms most frequently isolated were *S. aureus* and coagulase-negative staphylococci.[66,67] Line infections caused by Gram-negative organisms are less frequent, but certainly not uncommon – *Escherichia coli*, *Proteus mirabilis*, *Serratia marcescens*, *P. aeruginosa*[46,67] and other Gram-negative rods have all been isolated as the cause of infections related to an intraveneous catheter. Empiric therapy of line infections while culture results are awaited should therefore involve vancomycin and an aminoglycoside (or vancomycin and a β-lactam with broad Gram-negative coverage). Removal of the intravenous line may not be necessary in treating *S. aureus* and coagulase-negative staphylococcal infections, but it is usually recommended for Gram-negative bacterial infections. Of interest, however, are data from one study indicating similar recurrence rates whether or not the catheter was removed.[66] As with other infections, the incidence of HIV-associated bacteremia declined after HAART became available. One study has shown that this decline has been associated with a reduction in the use of central venous catheters and in neutropenia.[68]

REFERENCES

1. Centers for Disease Control and Prevention. 1993 revised classification for HIV infection and expanded surveillance case definition for AIDS among adolescents and adults. MMWR Morb Mortal Wkly Rep 1992;41:1–19.
2. Selwyn PA, Feingold AR, Hartel D, *et al.* Increased risk of bacterial pneumonia in HIV-infected intravenous drug users without AIDS. AIDS 1988;2:267–72.
3. Boschini A, Smacchia C, Di Fine M, *et al.* Community-acquired pneumonia in a cohort of former injection drug users with and without human immunodeficiency virus infection: incidence, etiologies, and clinical aspects. Clin Infect Dis 1996;23:107–13.
4. Hirschtick RE, Glassroth J, Jordan MC, *et al.* Bacterial pneumonia in persons infected with the human immunodeficiency virus. N Engl J Med 1995;333:845–51.
5. De Gaetano Donati K, Bertagnolio S, Tumbarello M, *et al.* Effect of highly active antiretroviral therapy on the incidence of bacterial pneumonia in HIV-infected subjects. Int J Antimicrob Agents 2000;16:357–60.
6. Wolff AJ, O'Donnell AE. Pulmonary manifestations of HIV infection in the era of highly active antiretroviral therapy. Chest 2001;120:1888–93.
7. Segal R, Poznansky MC, Connors L, Sands K, Barlam T. Changing patterns of patients with HIV-related disease at a tertiary referral centre and its implications for physician training. Int J STD AIDS 2001;12:453–9.
8. Janoff EN, Breiman RF, Daley CL, Hopewell PC. Pneumococcal disease during HIV infection: epidemiologic, clinical, and immunologic perspectives. Ann Intern Med 1992;117:314–24.
9. Müller F, Froland SS, Hvatum M, Radl J, Brandtzaeg P. Both IgA subclasses are reduced in parotid saliva from patients with AIDS. Clin Exp Immunol 1991;83:203–9.
10. Tagliabue A, Villa L, Boraschi D, Peri G, de Gori V, Nencioni L. Natural anti-bacterial activity against *Salmonella typhi* by human T4 + lymphocytes armed with IgA antibodies. J Immunol 1985;135:4178–82.
11. Fish DN, Danziger LH. Neglected pathogens: bacterial infections in persons with human immunodeficiency virus infection. Pharmacotherapy 1993;13:415–39.
12. Müller F, Froland SS, Brandtzaeg P. Altered IgG-subclass distribution in lymph node cells and serum of adults infected with human immunodeficiency virus (HIV). Clin Exp Immunol 1989;78:153–8.
13. Bender BS, Bohnsack JF, Sourlis SH, Frank MM, Quinn TC. Demonstration of defective C3-receptor-mediated clearance by the reticuloendothelial system in patients with acquired immunodeficiency syndrome. J Clin Invest 1987;79:715–20.
14. Tausk FA, McCutchan A, Spechko P, Schreiber RD, Gigli I. Altered erythrocyte C3b receptor expression, immune complexes, and complement activation in homosexual men in varying risk groups for acquired immune deficiency syndrome. J Clin Invest 1986;78:977–82.
15. Moore RD, Keruly JC, Chaisson RE. Neutropenia and bacterial infection in acquired immunodeficiency syndrome. Arch Intern Med 1995;155:1965–70.
16. Moore DA, Benepal T, Portsmouth S, Gill J, Gazzard BG. Etiology and natural history of neutropenia in human immunodeficiency virus disease: a prospective study. Clin Infect Dis 2001;32:469–75.
17. Berger BJ, Hussain F, Roistacher K. Bacterial infections in HIV-infected patients. Infect Dis Clin North Am 1994;8:449–65.
18. Mayer HB, Rose DN, Cohen S, Gurtman AC, Cheung TW, Szabo S. The effect of *Pneumocystis carinii* pneumonia prophylaxis regimens on the

incidence of bacterial infections in HIV-infected patients. AIDS 1993;7:1687–9.
19. Gebo KA, Moore RD, Keruly JC, Chaisson RE. Risk factors for pneumococcal disease in human immunodeficiency virus-infected patients. J Infect Dis 1996;173:857–62.
20. Rodriquez-Barradas MC, Musher DM, Lahart C, *et al.* Antibody to capsular polysaccharides of *Streptococcus pneumoniae* after vaccination of human immunodeficiency virus-infected subjects with 23-valent pneumococcal vaccine. J Infect Dis 1992;165:553–6.
21. Meynard JL, Barbut F, Blum L, *et al.* Risk factors for isolation of *Streptococcus pneumoniae* with decreased susceptibility to penicillin G from patients infected with human immunodeficiency virus. Clin Infect Dis 1996;22:437–40.
22. Oldfield EC, Fessel WJ, Dunne MW, *et al.* Once weekly azithromycin therapy for the prevention of *Mycobacterium avium* complex infection in AIDS patients: a randomized, double-blind, placebo-controlled trial. Clin Infect Dis 1998;26:611–9.
23. Currier JS, Williams P, Feinberg J, Becker S, Owen S, Benson C. Impact of prophylaxis for *Mycobacterium avium* complex on bacterial infections in patients with advanced human immunodeficiency virus disease. Clin Infect Dis 2001;32:1615–22.
24. Pierce M, Cramptom S, Henry D, *et al.* A randomized trial of clarithromycin as prophylaxis against disseminated *Mycobacterium avium* complex infection in patients with advanced acquired immunodeficiency syndrome. N Engl J Med 1996;335:384–91.
25. Wiktor SZ, Sassan-Morokro M, Grant AD, *et al.* Efficacy of trimethoprim–sulfamethoxazole prophylaxis to decrease morbidity and mortality in HIV-1 infected patients with tuberculosis in Abidjan, Cote d'Ivoire: a randomised controlled trial. Lancet 1999;353:1469–75.
26. Anglaret X, Chene G, Attia A, *et al.* Early chemoprophylaxis with trimethoprim–sulfamethoxazole for HIV-1 infected adults in Abidjan, Cote d'Ivoire: a randomised trial. Lancet 1999;353:1463–8.
27. Glaser JB, Volpe S, Aguirre A, Simpkins H, Schiffman G. Zidovudine improves response to pneumococcal vaccine among persons with AIDS and AIDS-related complex. J Infect Dis 1991;164:761–4.
28. Tasker SA, Wallace MR, Rubins JB, Paxton WB, O'Brien J, Janoff EN. Reimmunization with 23-valent pneumococcal vaccine for patients infected with human immunodeficiency virus type 1: clinical, immunologic, and virologic response. Clin Infect Dis 2002;34:813–21.
29. French N, Nakiyingi J, Carpenter LM, *et al.* 23-valent pneumococcal polysaccharide vaccine in HIV-1 infected Ugandan adults: double-blind, randomised and placebo controlled trial. Lancet 2000;355:2106–11.
30. Steinhoff MC, Auerbach BS, Nelson KE, *et al.* Antibody responses to *Haemophilus influenzae* type B vaccines in men with human immunodeficiency virus infection. N Engl J Med 1991;325:1837–42.
31. Centers for Disease Control and Prevention. Recommendations for use of *Haemophilus* b vaccines and combined diphtheria, tetanus, pertussis and *Haemophilus* b vaccine. MMWR Morb Mortal Wkly Rep 1993;42(RR-13):1–15.
32. Keller DW, Breiman RF. Preventing bacterial respiratory tract infections among persons infected with human immunodeficiency virus. Clin Infect Dis 1995;21(Suppl.1):S77–83.
33. Mofenson LM, Moye J Jr, Bethel J, Hirschhorn R, Jordan C, Nugent R. Prophylactic intravenous immunoglobulin in HIV-infected children with CD4+ counts of 0.20×10^9/L or more: effect on viral, opportunistic, and bacterial infections: the National Institute of Child Health and Human Development Intravenous Immunoglobulin Clinical Trial Study Group. JAMA 1992;268:483–8.
34. The International Institute of Child Health and Human Development Intravenous Immunoglobulin Study Group. Intravenous immune globulin for the prevention of bacterial infections in children with symptomatic human immunodeficiency virus infection. N Engl J Med 1991;325:73–80.
35. Kiehl MG, Stoll R, Broder M, *et al.* A controlled trial of intravenous immune globulin for the prevention of serious infections in adults with advanced human immunodeficiency virus infection. Arch Intern Med 1996;156:2545–50.
36. Kuritzkes DR, Parenti D, Ward DJ, *et al.* Filgrastim prevents severe neutropenia and reduces infective morbidity in patients with advanced HIV infection: results of a randomized multicenter controlled trial. AIDS 1998;12:65–74.
37. Kuritzkes DR. Neutropenia, neutrophil dysfunction, and bacterial infection in patient with human immunodeficiency virus disease: the role of granulocyte colony-stimulating factor. Clin Infect Dis 2000;30:256–60.
38. Keiser P, Rademacher S, Smith JW, Skiest D, Vadde V. Granulocyte colony-stimulating factor use is associated with decreased bacteremia and increased survival in neutropenic HIV-infected patients. Am J Med 1998;104:48–55.
39. Regnery RL, Childs JE, Koehler JE. Infections associated with *Bartonella* species in persons infected with human immunodeficiency virus. Clin Infect Dis 1995;21(Suppl.1):S94–8.
40. Godofsky EW, Zinreich J, Armstong M, Leslie JM, Weikel CS. Sinusitis in HIV-infected patients: a clinical and radiographic review. Am J Med 1992;93:163–70.
41. Caiaffa WT, Vlahov D, Graham NMH, *et al.* Drug smoking, *Pneumocystis carinii* pneumonia, and immunosuppression increase risk of bacterial pneumonia in human immunodeficiency virus-seropositive injection drug users. Am J Resp Crit Care Med 1994;150:1493–8.
42. Burack JH, Hahn JA, Saint-Maurice D, Jacobson MA. Microbiology of community-acquired bacterial pneumonia in persons with and at risk for human immunodeficiency virus type 1 infection: implications for rational empiric antibiotic therapy. Arch Intern Med 1994;154:2589–96.
43. Javaly K, Horowitz HW, Wormser GP. Nocardiosis in patients with human immunodeficiency virus infection: report of 2 cases and review of the literature. Medicine 1992;71:128–38.
44. Blatt SP, Dolan MJ, Hendrix CW, Melcher GP. Legionnaires' disease in human immunodeficiency virus-infected patients: eight cases and review. Clin Infect Dis 1994;18:227–32.
45. Fichtenbaum CJ, Woeltje KF, Powderly WG. Serious *Pseudomonas aeruginosa* infections in patients infected with human immunodeficiency virus: a case–control study. Clin Infect Dis 1994;19:417–22.
46. Dropulic LK, Leslie JM, Eldred LJ, Zenilman J, Sears CL. Clinical manifestations and risk factors of *Pseudomonas aeruginosa* infection in patients with AIDS. J Infect Dis 1995;171:930–7.
47. Boumis E, Petrosillo N, Girardi E, *et al.* Changing patterns in the etiology of HIV-associated bacterial pneumonia in the era of highly active antiretroviral therapy. Eur J Clin Microbiol Infect Dis 2001;20:71–3.
48. Gallant JE, Ko AH. Cavitary pulmonary lesions in patients infected with human immunodeficiency virus. Clin Infect Dis 1996;22:671–82.
49. Verville TD, Huycke MM, Greenfield RA, Fine DP, Kuhls TL, Slater LN. *Rhodococcus equi* infections in humans: 12 cases and a review of the literature. Medicine 1994;73:119–32.
50. Sutor G-C, Fibich C, Kirschner, *et al.* Poststenotic cavitating pneumonia due to *Rhodococcus equi* in HIV infection. AIDS 1996;10:339–40.
51. Donisi A, Suardi MG, Casari S, Longo M, Cadeo GP, Carosi G. *Rhodococcus equi* infection in HIV-infected patients. AIDS 1996;10:359–62.
52. Steinhart R, Reingold AL, Taylor F, Anderson G, Wenger JD. Invasive *Haemophilus influenzae* infections in men with HIV infection. JAMA 1992;268:3350–2.
53. Redd SC, Rutherford GW III, Sande MA, *et al.* The role of human immunodeficiency virus infection in pneumococcal bacteremia in San Francisco residents. J Infect Dis 1990;162:1012–7.
54. Janoff EN, O'Brien J, Thompson P, *et al.* *Streptococcus pneumoniae* colonization, bacteremia, and immune response among persons with human immunodeficiency virus infection. J Infect Dis 1993;167:49–56.
55. Daar ES, Meyer RD. Bacterial and fungal infections. Med Clin North Am 1992;76:173–203.
56. Caiaffa WT, Graham NMH, Vlahov D. Bacterial pneumonia in adult populations with human immunodeficiency virus (HIV) infection. Am J Epidemiol 1993;138:909–22.
57. Stoneburner RL, Des Jarlais DC, Benezra D, *et al.* A larger spectrum of severe HIV-1-related disease in intravenous drug users in New York City. Science 1988;242:916–9.
58. Mientjes GH, van Ameijden EJ, van den Hoek JAR, *et al.* Increasing morbidity without rise in non-AIDS mortality among HIV-infected intravenous drug users in Amsterdam. AIDS 1992;6:207–12.
59. Perucci CA, Davoli M, Rapiti E, *et al.* Mortality of intravenous drug users in Rome: a cohort study. Am J Public Health 1991;81:1307–10.
60. Celum CL, Chaisson RE, Rutherford GW, *et al.* Incidence of salmonellosis in patients with AIDS. J Infect Dis 1987;156:998–1002.
61. Jacobs JL, Gold JWM, Murray HW, *et al.* *Salmonella* infections in patients with the acquired immunodeficiency syndrome. Ann Intern Med 1985;102:186–8.
62. Tumbarello M, Tacconelli E, Leone F, Cauda R, Ortona L. *Clostridium difficile*-associated diarrhoea in patients with human immunodeficiency virus infection: a case–control study. Eur J Gastroenterol Hepatol 1995;7:259–63.
63. Hutin Y, Molina J-M, Casin I, *et al.* Risk factors for *Clostridium difficile*-associated diarrhoea in HIV-infected patients. AIDS 1993;7:1441–7.
64. Harrison KS, Bartlett JG. *Clostridium difficile* diarrhea in AIDS patients. Program and Abstracts of the Thirty-first Interscience Conference on Antimicrobial Agents and Chemotherapy [Abstract 547]. American Society of Microbiology; 1991.
65. Pulvirenti JJ, Kerns E, Benson C, Lisowski J, Demarais P, Weinstein RA. Infective endocarditis in injection drug users: importance of human immunodeficiency virus serostatus and degree of immunosuppression. Clin Infect Dis 1996;22:40–5.
66. Fichtenbaum CJ, Dunagan WC, Powderly WG. Bacteremia in hospitalized patients infected with the human immunodeficiency virus: a case–control study of risk factors and outcome. J Acquir Immune Defic Syndr 1995;8:51–7.
67. Krumholz MM, Sande MA, Lo B. Community-acquired bacteremia in patients with acquired immunodeficiency syndrome: clinical presentation, bacteriology, and outcome. Am J Med 1989;86:776.
68. Tumbarello M, Tacconelli E, Donati KG, *et al.* HIV-associated bacteremia: how it has changed in the highly active antiretroviral therapy (HAART) era. J Acquir Immune Defic Syndr 2000;23:145–51.

chapter 129

Mycobacterial Infections in HIV-infected Patients

Alex Soriano & José M Gatell

EPIDEMIOLOGY

Mycobacterial infections are common AIDS-defining events in HIV-infected patients. *Mycobacterium tuberculosis* and *Mycobacterium avium* complex (MAC) are the most frequently found infections and have different distributions around the world. *Mycobacterium tuberculosis* has the highest incidence rate in Africa, Asia and southern Europe and MAC in the USA and northern Europe.

HIV infection, because of its immunosuppressive effect, is the most significant risk factor for the development of active tuberculosis.[1] The number of reported cases of tuberculosis increased dramatically during the 1980s and early 1990s and the World Health Organization estimated that, between the onset of the HIV pandemic and mid-1993, more than 5 million persons worldwide had been co-infected by both HIV and *M. tuberculosis*. More than 3.5 million of these are in sub-Saharan Africa (Fig. 129.1).

HIV infection has not only modified the incidence of tuberculosis during the last 15 years but has also altered the clinical presentation, with an increase in extrapulmonary forms of tuberculosis.[3] Furthermore, the mortality rate of tuberculosis before the introduction of new antiretroviral drugs was four to eight times higher in HIV-positive than in HIV-negative patients.[4] Since the introduction of highly active antiretroviral therapy (HAART) the incidence of opportunistic infections and mortality has dramatically decreased. However, the decrease in the incidence of tuberculosis is less evident (Fig. 129.2) and it is still much higher among HIV-infected patients in all strata of $CD4^+$ lymphocytes than in the general population (Fig. 129.3).

Mycobacterium avium complex is ubiquitous in the environment and has been isolated from a variety of sources around the world, including soil, natural water, municipal water systems, food, house dust and domestic and wild animals. These isolates are thought to be the source of most human infections but there is no evidence of MAC transmission from person to person. In the USA the incidence of MAC disease has been studied prospectively in a number of cohorts; the cumulative probability of disseminated disease due to MAC in subjects who have $CD4^+$ lymphocyte counts below 50 cells/mm^3 is 30%, and 20% in those who have $CD4^+$ lymphocyte counts of 50–100 cells/mm^3, while in Europe the rates are 20% and 11% respectively.[6] Furthermore, MAC was also infrequently isolated in AIDS patients from Africa. The differences in epidemiologic data between the USA and Europe or Africa have been attributed to a potential cross-immune protection between MAC and *M. tuberculosis* or MAC and bacille Calmette–Guérin (BCG) vaccine, which is much more frequently administered in Europe and Africa.

ESTIMATED GLOBAL DISTRIBUTION OF ADULTS CO-INFECTED WITH HIV AND *MYCOBACTERIUM TUBERCULOSIS*, TO MID 1993

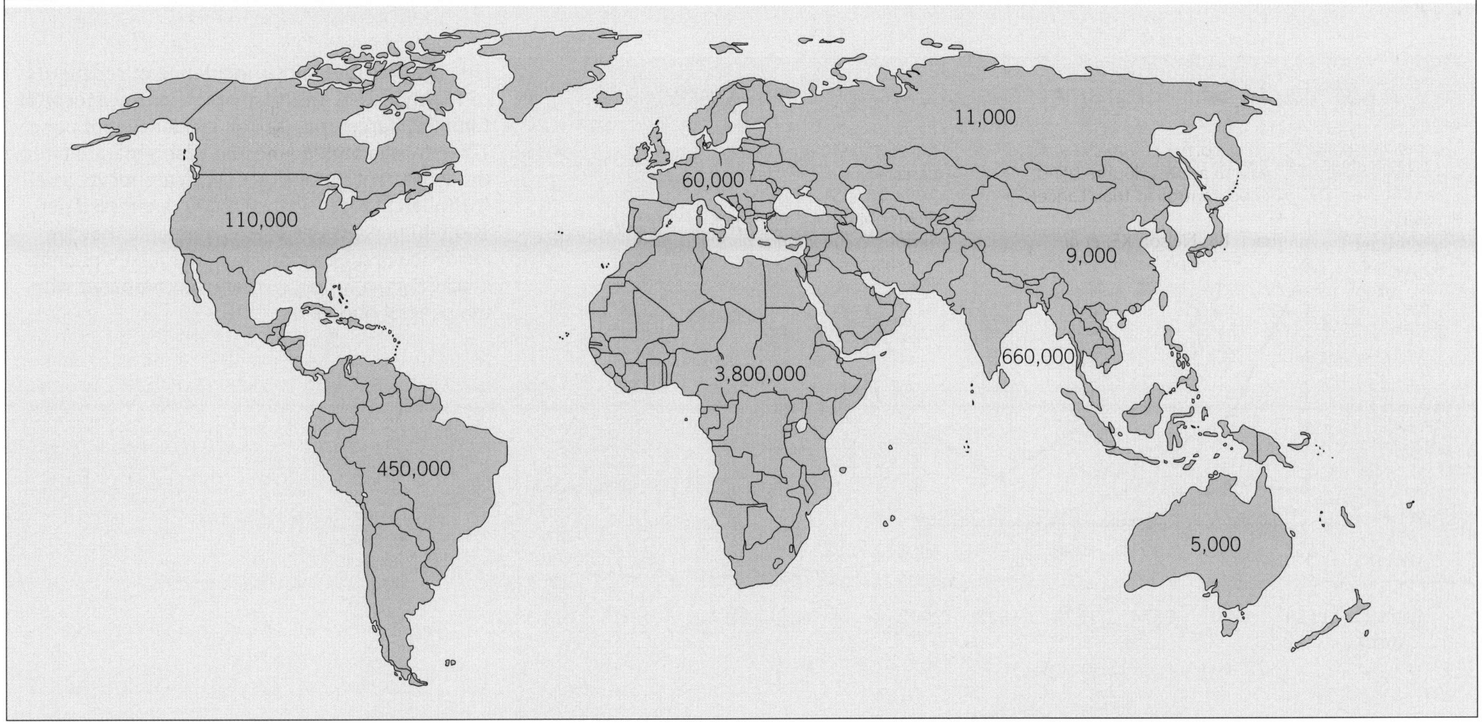

Fig. 129.1 Estimated global distribution of adults co-infected with HIV and *Mycobacterium tuberculosis*, to mid-1993. From the World Health Organization Tuberculosis Program. Redrawn with permission from Snider *et al.*[2]

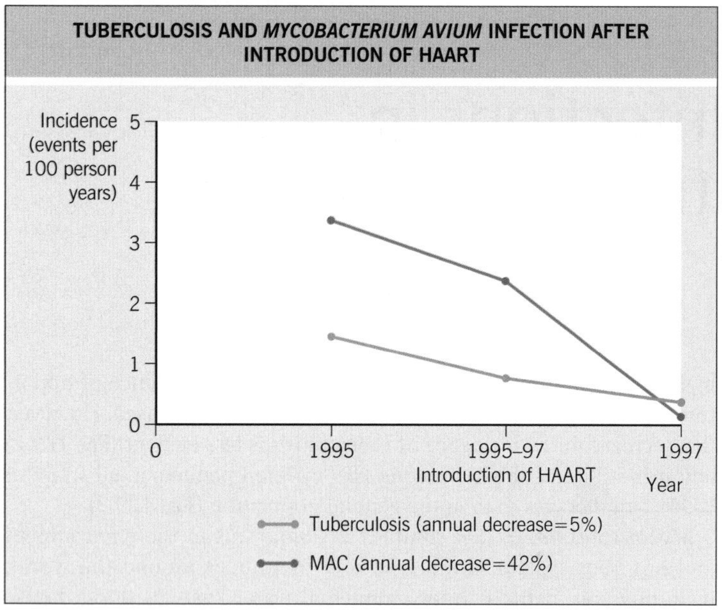

Fig. 129.2 Tuberculosis and *Mycobacterium avium* infection after introduction of highly active antiretroviral therapy. Incidence among HIV-positive patients. Between 1995 and1997 the use of HAART became general practice in Europe. Redrawn with permission from Kirk *et al.*[5]

The use of primary prophylaxis for MAC with clarithromycin, azithromycin or rifabutin and the introduction of HAART are the most likely explanations of the decreased incidence rate of MAC disease[5] (see Fig. 129.2).

PATHOGENESIS

Mycobacterium tuberculosis is acquired via inhalation. In the lung alveoli an immune response is established, mediated by a complex interaction between mononuclear phagocytes and different subsets of T cells. While the former cells act as the main effectors, the latter serve as the predominant inducers of protection. A co-ordinated communication between both cells mediated by different cytokines is essential for optimum protection, especially cytokines such as interferon (INF)-γ and tumor necrosis factor (TNF)-α. Such 'co-ordination' is best achieved in the granulomatous lesion. Frequently, if not always, full eradication of the pathogen is not achieved and the bacilli remain dormant or latent until the host defenses become impaired, as in HIV co-infected patients. This complex immune response is disrupted early in the evolution of HIV infection, which may explain why pulmonary tuberculosis is the first and most common AIDS-defining event in endemic areas. In addition, pulmonary tuberculosis develops in patients who have only mild immunosuppression in contrast to other opportunistic infections (Fig. 129.4).

The histologic patterns of tuberculosis reflect the degree of integrity of the cellular immune response of the patient. Different patterns have been identified and correlate well with the stage of HIV infection. Patients who have relatively intact cellular immunity develop a typical granulomatous response. Epithelioid macrophages and Langhans giant cells are abundant and numbers of acid-fast bacilli (AFB) are low. Patients who have moderate and advanced immunosuppression show a decrease in epithelioid macrophages, Langhans giant cells and $CD4^+$ T cells, which results in poor intracellular killing of mycobacteria. The granulomatous response is absent and there is a large number of AFB surrounded by tissue necrosis.[8]

Mycobacterium avium complex is acquired through inhalation or ingestion and adheres to specific receptors on the epithelial cells that allow the colonization and invasion of the mucosa. It gains entry to macrophages by opsonic or complement-mediated pathways. Once into the phagosome, MAC inhibits lysosome fusion, allowing their intracellular survival and replication, enhanced by co-infection with HIV.

The immune response against MAC is mediated by $CD4^+$ lymphocytes, cytotoxic lymphocyte responses and local fluxes of the growth-enhancing (i.e. interleukin (IL)-6) and growth-inhibiting cytokines (i.e. INF-γ, TNF-α, IL-12). The importance of $CD4^+$ cells is shown by the fact that the increase in $CD4^+$ T cells evoked by HAART considerably reduces the risk of disseminated MAC disease.

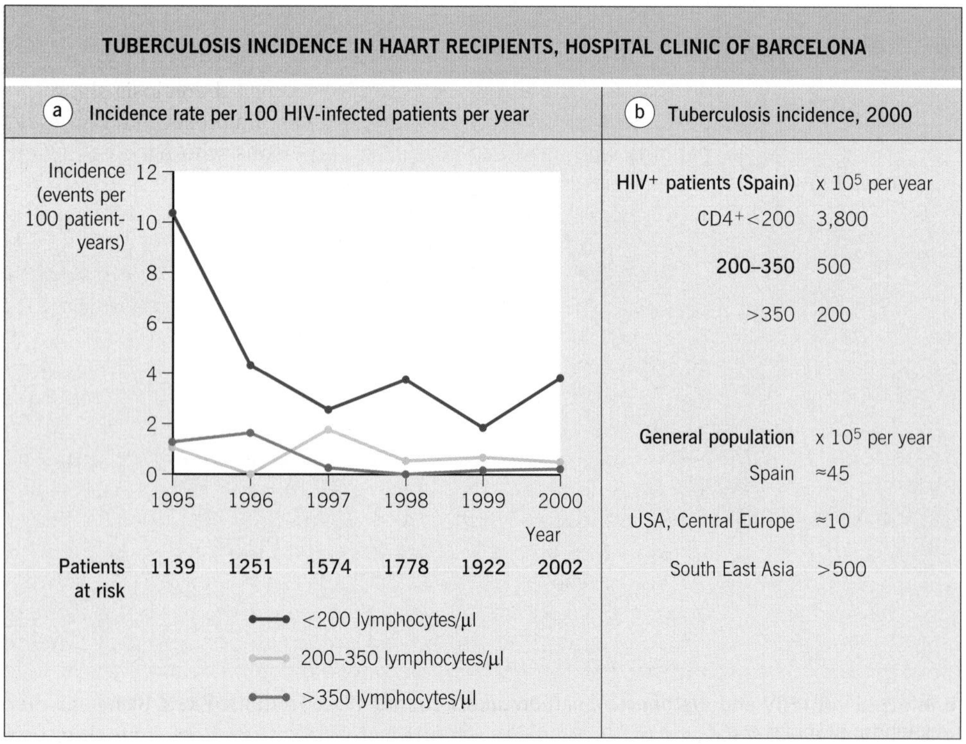

Fig. 129.3 Tuberculosis incidence in recipients of highly active antiretroviral therapy, Hospital Clinic of Barcelona. (a) The incidence rate per 100 HIV-infected patients per year, separated into three different groups by $CD4^+$ lymphocyte level. (b) Tuberculosis incidence, 2000, expressed per 100,000 persons per year. It is notable that the incidence of tuberculosis is higher in HIV patients in all $CD4^+$ lymphocyte strata, as compared with the general population.

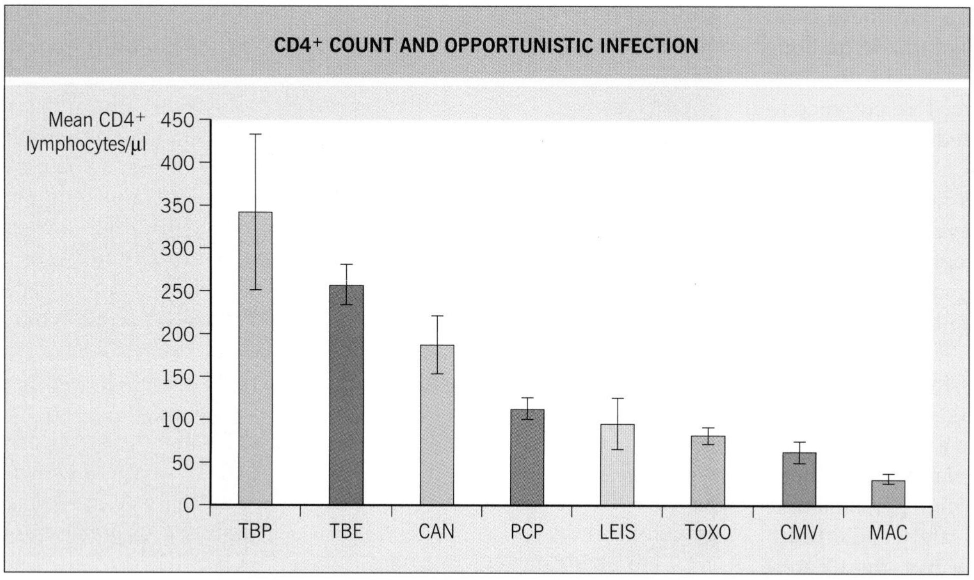

Fig. 129.4 CD4+ count and opportunistic infection. Relation between CD4+ lymphocyte count and the main opportunistic infections in HIV-infected patients. Data from Hospital Clinic AIDS unit, Barcelona. CAN, esophageal candidiasis; CMV, cytomegalovirus infection; LEIS, disseminated leishmaniasis; MAC, *Mycobacterium avium* complex infection; PCP, *Pneumocystis carinii* pneumonia; TBE, extrapulmonary tuberculosis; TBP, pulmonary tuberculosis; TOXO, central nervous system toxoplasmosis. Redrawn with permission from Miro *et al.*[7]

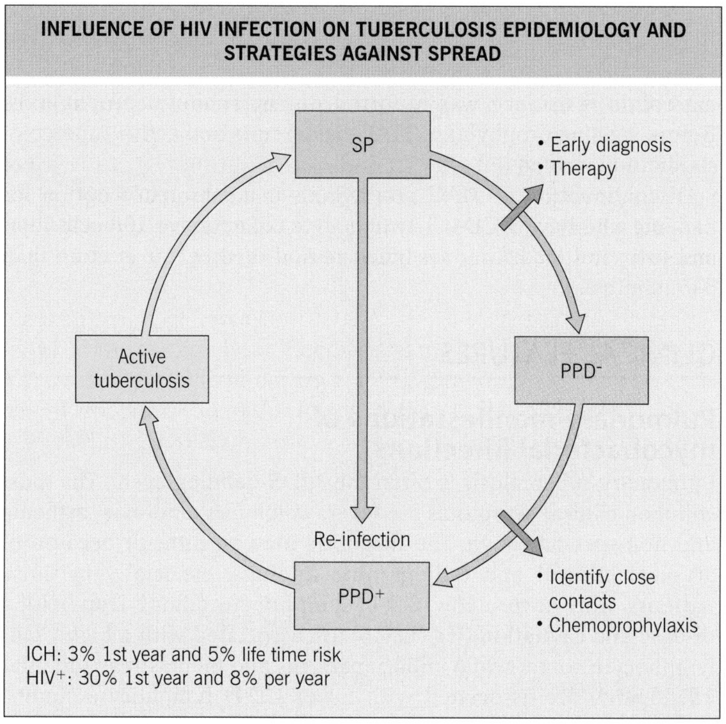

Fig. 129.5 Influence of HIV infection on tuberculosis epidemiology and strategies against spread. HIV+, HIV-infected patients; ICH, immunocompetent host; PPD, purified protein derivative; SP, smear-positive.

PREVENTION

The influence of HIV infection in the spread of tuberculosis is shown by the fact that HIV-infected patients who have latent tuberculosis (detected by a positive tuberculin skin test in immunocompetent hosts) have a substantially higher risk of developing active tuberculosis than those who are HIV-negative. Approximately 30–50% of people exposed to *M. tuberculosis* become infected. Immunocompetent people have an effective immune response that allows the successful containment of the infection and only have a 5–10% lifetime risk of developing active tuberculosis later. Conversely, 8% per year of HIV-positive intravenous drug abusers in a methadone program who had a positive tuberculin skin test developed active tuberculosis.[9] Another study demonstrated that 30% of HIV-positive patients who had a positive skin test followed up during 1 year and who did not receive prophylaxis developed active tuberculosis.[10] Therefore, in the HIV era it is very important to promote strategies to prevent the spread of tuberculosis such as investigation of the close contacts of tuberculosis patients, identification and treatment of latent tuberculosis infection, and early diagnosis and adequate therapy of active tuberculosis, including directly observed therapy when necessary (Fig. 129.5).

Vaccination with BCG has demonstrated a high protection rate against serious forms of tuberculosis in children (tuberculous meningitis and disseminated tuberculosis) but its protective efficacy against pulmonary tuberculosis shows enormous variability, ranging from 0% to over 75%. This wide range of protective efficacy is not well understood and, in countries with a low tuberculosis incidence, vaccination is not recommended so as to preserve the tuberculin skin test as a useful tool to diagnose latent tuberculosis infection.

Identification and treatment of latent tuberculosis infection

As CD4+ lymphocyte count decreases, the percentage of patients who have latent infection whose tuberculin skin test is positive decreases.[11] Therefore, screening for latent tuberculosis should be performed as soon as HIV infection is diagnosed. HIV-infected patients who have had contact with persons who have contagious tuberculosis have a higher risk of being infected and of developing active disease; therefore, they must be evaluated for tuberculosis as soon as possible after exposure. For this reason, it is necessary to establish tuberculosis screening initiatives in settings where the prevalence of HIV infection and tuberculosis is high (prisons, drug abuse treatment programs, syringe exchange programs, residences for AIDS patients and homeless shelters). Because of the complexity of problems associated with active tuberculosis in HIV-infected patients, and as a part of the efforts to control and eliminate tuberculosis, all HIV-infected persons identified as latently infected with *M. tuberculosis* should complete a full recommended course of preventive therapy. In certain outpatient and institutional settings, directly observed preventive therapy should be implemented.

The tuberculin skin test with 5TU of purified protein derivative is used to diagnose latent tuberculosis infection. A reaction size of 5mm or more of induration is considered positive in HIV-infected patients. Persons who have less than 5mm but who have a history of exposure to tuberculosis should also be considered to be infected with *M. tuberculosis*. Unfortunately, false-negative tuberculin skin test (anergy) is common in HIV-infected patients but there is no other test to identify latent tuberculosis infection. In anergic patients a course of preventive therapy with isoniazid does not reduce the incidence of tuberculosis, therefore it is not recommended. However, these patients should be tested with PPD after responding to HAART.[12]

Before starting preventive chemotherapy it is necessary to rule out active tuberculosis via medical history (fever, night sweats, cough, weigh loss or anorexia) and chest radiograph. Those patients who have clinical and/or radiologic abnormalities must collect three consecutive sputum samples for smear and culture to rule out active tuberculosis.

The therapy of choice for latent tuberculosis infection in HIV-infected patients is 9 months of daily isoniazid. It is possible to administer a 9-month regimen of isoniazid twice a week but direct observed therapy is always recommended. Recently it has been reported that 2 months of daily rifampin (rifampicin)–pyrazinamide in a cohort of HIV-infected patients is similar in safety and efficacy to a daily 12-month regimen of isoniazid.[13] However, the Centers for Disease Control and Prevention (CDC) have reported 21 non-HIV patients who developed fatal and severe liver injuries associated with a rifampin–pyrazinamide regimen for a latent tuberculosis infection and they recommend caution, especially in patients concurrently taking other medications associated with liver injury or/and alcoholism. Rifampin–pyrazinamide is not recommended for persons who have underlying liver disease or for those who have had isoniazid-associated liver injury. Therefore, close monitoring of patients receiving a rifampin–pyrazinamide regimen is necessary. Major indications are those patients likely to be infected with an isoniazid-resistant strain of tuberculosis and those who are under control only for brief periods of time (e.g. prisoners serving 2–4 months).

For patients who have pyrazinamide intolerance, a 4- to 6-month regimen of rifampin alone is recommended, although information on its effectiveness is still scarce. In addition, rifampin is contraindicated in HIV-infected patients on protease-inhibitor-containing regimens, except ritonavir, and taking non-nucleoside reverse transcriptase inhibitors, except efavirenz. Rifabutin can be used as an alternative for patients treated with indinavir, nelfinavir, amprenavir and nevirapine, adjusting the doses as described below (see Management).

Preventive treatment for patients who are likely to be infected with isoniazid–rifampin-resistant strains include the use of a combination of at least two antituberculous drugs (e.g. ethambutol, pyrazinamide or levofloxacin). The clinician should always review the drug susceptibility pattern of the *M. tuberculosis* strain isolated from the infecting source before choosing a preventive therapy regimen.

Mycobacterium avium complex prophylaxis

Prophylaxis for MAC is now recommended for all AIDS patients who have CD4+ lymphocyte counts lower than 50 cells/mm³. This recommendation is based on the high incidence of MAC bacteremia in this population, the morbidity and mortality associated with disseminated MAC and the efficacy of the available prophylactic agents. In randomized, placebo-controlled trials, 6% of patients receiving clarithromycin 500mg/day developed MAC infection versus 16% of those assigned to receive placebo,[14] representing an estimated 69% reduction in risk for disseminated infection with MAC. In a similar study design using 1200mg of azithromycin once a week, MAC bacteremia was reduced by 66%. Both regimens have proved to be superior to rifabutin for MAC prophylaxis.[15] It is of note that macrolide resistance has been identified in 29–58% of patients failing clarithromycin prophylaxis and in 16% on an azithromycin regimen. Not even one case of macrolide resistance was reported during rifabutin prophylaxis. Before starting prophylaxis, MAC bacteremia and active tuberculosis should be ruled out.

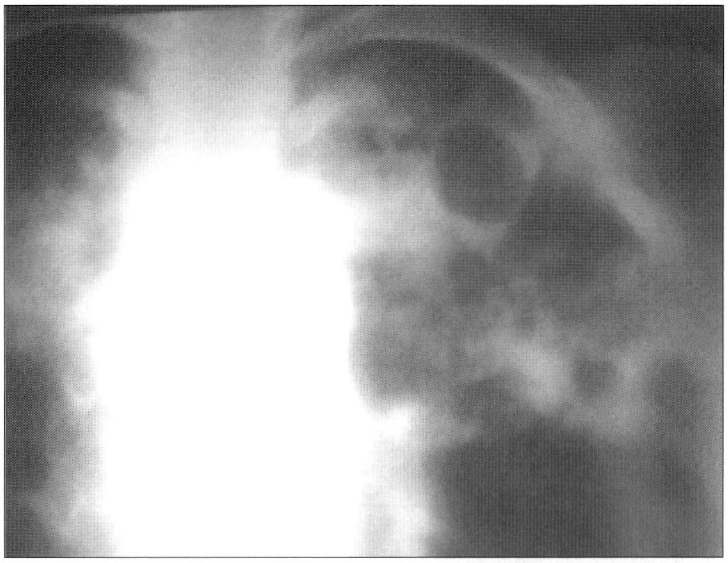

Fig. 129.6 Characteristic upper lobe cavity on chest radiograph in an HIV patient who has tuberculosis.

Discontinuation of MAC prophylaxis is a reasonable option for patients who have a CD4+ T lymphocyte count above 100 cells/mm³ and low viral load for a sustained period of time[16] (e.g. more than 3–6 months).

CLINICAL FEATURES

Pulmonary manifestations of mycobacterial infections

Pulmonary tuberculosis is often the AIDS-defining event. The most common clinical symptoms are fever, weigh loss, anorexia, asthenia and non-specific cough. The diagnosis may be difficult because of atypical clinical and radiographic findings, especially in those patients who have a low CD4+ lymphocyte count. Upper lobe disease and cavitation (Fig. 129.6) are associated with a high CD4+ lymphocyte count, while miliary patterns and mediastinal and hilar adenopathy are associated with lower CD4+ lymphocyte counts. Presence of adenopathies, pleural effusion and/or cavitation are useful to differentiate tuberculosis from *Pneumocystis carinii* pneumonia. In addition, a normal chest radiograph or diffuse infiltrates mimicking *P. carinii* pneumonia may occur. Acid-fast micro-organisms are found in the sputum smear in 40–67% of patients who have HIV-associated tuberculosis and sputum culture is usually positive in 74–95% of cases. The likelihood that a sputum sample will be smear-positive for AFB decreases with a decreasing CD4+ lymphocyte count and when the chest radiograph is normal.

Pulmonary disease associated with MAC is rare and criteria for diagnosis are not well established. Patients should have a repeatedly positive culture in sputum, an infiltrate on chest radiograph, absence of other lung pathogens and preferably biopsy specimens showing AFB in abnormal lung tissue.

The most frequent nontuberculous mycobacterium isolated from sputum in HIV-infected patients is *Mycobacterium kansasii*. Patients who have *M. kansasii* infection tend to have a low CD4+ lymphocyte count (less than 50 cells/mm³) and the clinical and radiologic manifestations are not different from tuberculosis. The isolation of *M. kansasii* from sputum is always considered diagnostic of pulmonary disease, since colonization is uncommon.

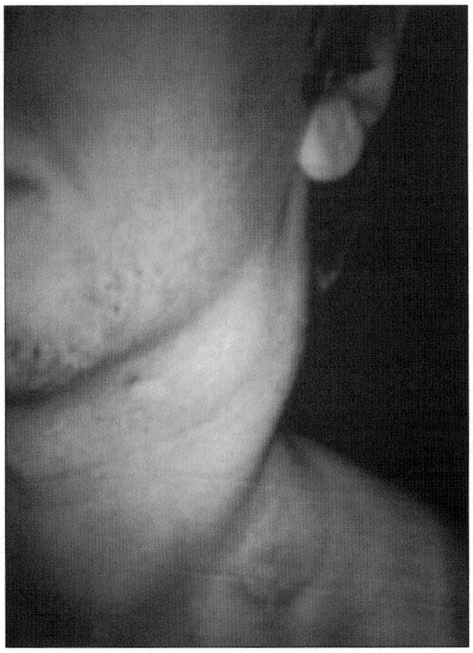

Fig. 129.7 Laterocervical adenopathy in a HIV-infected patient. The needle aspiration demonstrated abundant AFB.

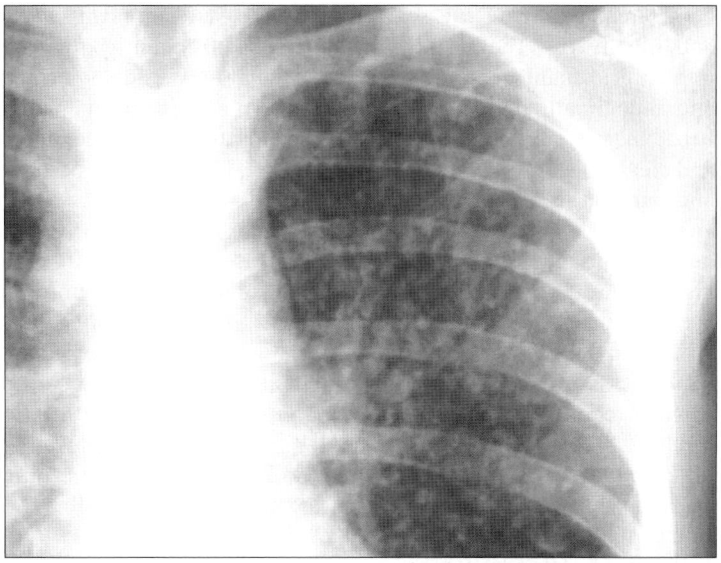

Fig. 129.9 Chest radiograph of HIV-infected patient who has miliary tuberculosis.

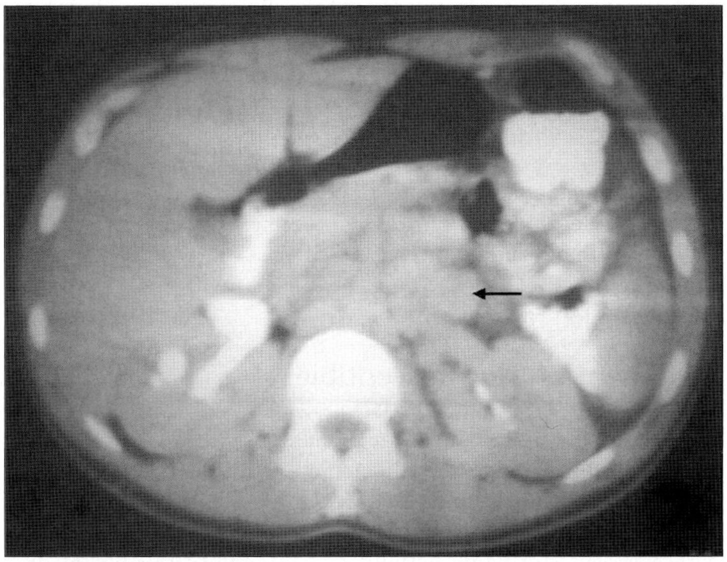

Fig. 129.8 Abdominal CT scan of an HIV-infected patient who has tuberculosis. Multiple retroperitoneal lymph nodes (arrow) are typical findings.

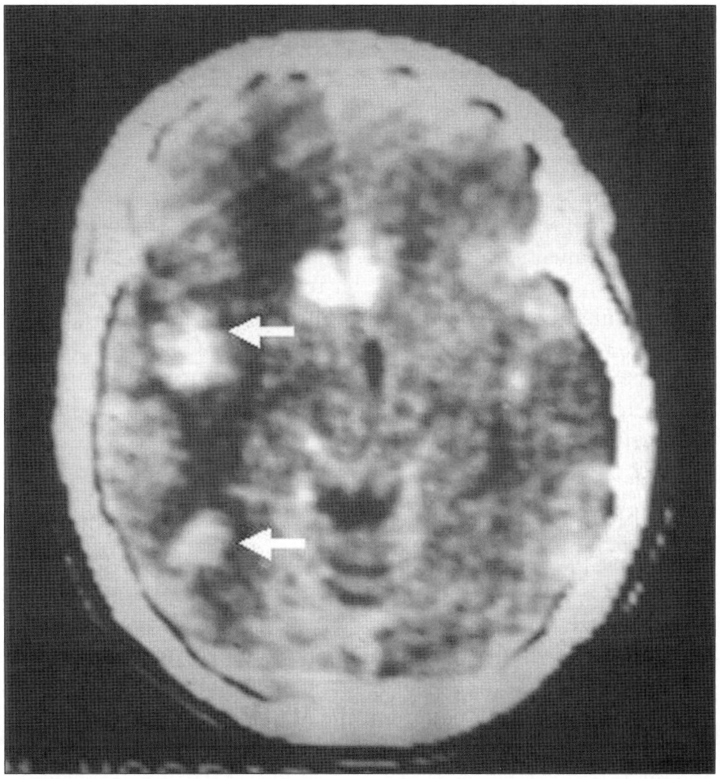

Fig. 129.10 Multiple cerebral cortical densities (tuberculomas, arrows) on CT scan of a patient who has tuberculosis of the central nervous system.

Extrapulmonary manifestations of mycobacterial diseases

As the level of immunosuppression increases in HIV-infected patients, tuberculosis involving pulmonary and extrapulmonary locations and mycobacteremia become progressively more frequent. The disseminated disease, defined as having more than one focus or progressive hematogenous disease, has been reported in 38% of cases.[17] These forms show a rapidly and progressive evolution with diffuse pulmonary infiltrates, acute respiratory failure and high mortality rate.

Lymphadenitis is the most common extrapulmonary location (Fig. 129.7). This form is generally multifocal, also invading mediastinal and mesenteric lymph nodes, associated with general major systemic symptoms such as fever or weight loss. Low-density areas in the nodes visualized in computerized tomography (CT) are very characteristic (Fig. 129.8) and the material removed by fine-needle aspiration is usually positive on acid-fast stain (AFS).

Miliary tuberculosis in AIDS can be detected in 10% of pulmonary tuberculosis and in 38% of extrapulmonary tuberculosis cases (Fig. 129.9). The presence of major constitutional symptoms is characteristic. Only 10% of cases have a positive tuberculin skin test and the sputum smear is positive in only 25%, but cultures of other tissues may be positive (e.g. bone marrow, liver or peripheral blood).

The clinical picture of central nervous system tuberculosis is not altered by HIV infection, except for a higher frequency of nodular lesions (tuberculomas), which appear on CT as avascular masses with surrounding edema (Fig. 129.10). Medical therapy without surgery is the preferred approach. Other locations of tuberculosis (pleural, skeletal, genitourinary or gastrointestinal) have a similar clinical presentation to that in immunocompetent patients.

Disseminated MAC disease is characterized by fever, night sweats and weight loss. The gastrointestinal tract is frequently involved and clinical manifestations are nausea, vomiting, watery diarrhea and abdominal pain, which can be severe. At physical examination hepatomegaly, splenomegaly and lymphadenopathy are very common, and elevations of serum alkaline phosphatase, lactate dehydrogenase and anemia are the most frequent laboratory findings. Worsening anemia and an elevated alkaline phosphatase out of proportion to hepatic transaminase elevation should increase suspicion of disseminated MAC. Other unusual manifestations of MAC disease in AIDS patients include cutaneous disease, arthritis, sinusitis, orchitis, peritonitis, chylous ascites, appendicitis, endophthalmitis, choroiditis, pancreatitis, pericarditis and meningitis.[18] Other nontuberculous mycobacterias, including *Mycobacterium genavense, M. intracellulare, M. haemophilum, M. simiae, M. xenopi, M. scrofulaceum, M. marinum* and *M. fortuitum*, have also been described as a cause of disseminated infection in HIV-infected patients.

Paradoxic reactions

Paradoxic reactions during antimycobacterial therapy have been described in up to 36% of patients who began HAART early during antimycobacterial treatment.[19] In contrast, only 7% of patients who received antimycobacterial therapy but not antiretroviral therapy had paradoxic reactions. These reactions appear after clinical improvement and are characterized by fever, worsening chest infiltrates on radiograph and peripheral, mediastinal or abdominal regrowth of lymphadenopathy. However, these manifestations are not associated with changes in *M. tuberculosis* bacteriology (e.g. no change from negative to positive culture and smear) and patients generally feel well and have no signs of toxicity. These reactions are accompanied by a substantial reduction in the HIV burden and a marked increase in reactivity on tuberculin skin testing, which suggest that they are caused by inflammation from a stronger immune response to *M. tuberculosis* or MAC after antiretroviral therapy. In general, paradoxic reactions are self-limited in 10–40 days; however, some reactions are severe and may require a short course of treatment with corticosteroids.

DIAGNOSIS

The physician should always keep in mind the possibility of mycobacterial infection in HIV-positive patients and most especially in those AIDS patients who have fever of unknown origin, any kind of infiltrates on chest radiograph, multifocal lymphadenopathies and subacute lymphocytic meningitis.

The tuberculin skin test has a high proportion of false negatives in patients who have fewer than 400 cells/mm^3 CD4$^+$ lymphocytes/l. Therefore, a rapid diagnosis of tuberculosis in AIDS patients is based on AFS of sputum (instead of normal chest radiograph), urine, bone marrow, lymph node and other samples (e.g. ascites or cerebrospinal fluid). However, AFS is positive in only 50–75% of cases. In addition, a bronchoscopy in AIDS patients yields a rapid diagnosis (based on smears and histologic features) in only one-third of cases.[20] Therefore, it is necessary to start empiric antimycobacterial therapy in patients who have suspected and/or are at risk of tuberculosis even where AFS is negative until the definitive result of the Löwenstein culture is obtained (which requires from 15 days up to 2 months). New tests for rapid identification of *M. tuberculosis* complex based on polymerase chain reaction (PCR) have sensitivity and specificity higher than 95%. Polymerase chain reaction is not necessary in HIV-infected patients who have a positive AFS in whom the clinical suspicion of tuberculosis is high. However, when the AFS is positive and the suspicion of tuberculosis is intermediate or low, a positive PCR is useful to rule out other nontuberculous mycobacterias such as MAC or *M. kansasii* and it allows the use of therapy against tuberculosis only. Positive PCR when AFS is negative avoids invasive procedures (e.g. fiberoptic bronchoscopy) and allows an early diagnosis of tuberculosis. The PCR is also useful in epidemiologic investigations, especially since one study performed in San Francisco demonstrated that patients who have smear-negative and culture-positive tuberculosis were responsible for about 17% of tuberculosis transmission.[21] Restriction fragment length polymorphism (RFLP) analysis of *M. tuberculosis* isolates allows the identification of specific strains. This test has demonstrated that recent infection appears with a similar frequency to reactivation of infections acquired in the past[22] and that exogenous re-infection occurs after curative treatment, especially in areas with a high incidence of the disease.[23] Analysis using RFLP can also be helpful to determine cross-contamination in the laboratory.

The diagnosis of disseminated disease caused by MAC requires the isolation of the organism from a sterile site. A single blood culture has a high diagnostic yield, which is 90–95% sensitive. Currently there are a variety of culture systems that are useful. Liquid media is superior to conventional culture on Löwenstein–Jensen agar slants. In the Bactec radiometric system, the blood taken from a patient is inoculated into culture media containing radiolabeled substrate that is metabolized in the presence of mycobacteria to carbon dioxide and detected by radiorespirometric methods. A growth signal can usually be detected within 8–14 days. Once sufficient growth is achieved, the diagnosis of MAC can be made in few hours with the use of DNA probes. The diagnosis can also be made by identification of MAC from other sterile sites such as bone marrow, liver or lymph node biopsy.

Although colonization can occur in AIDS patients, the isolation of MAC in respiratory or gastrointestinal tract in those patients who have CD4$^+$ lymphocyte counts below 50 cells/mm^3 represents a high risk for the development of MAC bacteremia.[24] In this case prophylaxis or treatment should be considered.

MANAGEMENT

Treatment of drug-susceptible *Mycobacterium tuberculosis*

Isoniazid is the most potent bactericidal drug and kills more than 90% of bacilli within 7 days by acting on the metabolically active ones. It is also quite effective at preventing the emergence of drug resistance. Rifampin and rifabutin are also good bactericidal drugs with a potent sterilizing activity and the ability to prevent drug resistance. Both drugs are active against dividing bacilli and those that remain inactive for long periods of time but have intermittent periods of active metabolism. Pyrazinamide is particularly effective at killing intracellular bacilli inside macrophages in an acid environment. Ethambutol and streptomycin are less potent drugs but are effective at preventing emergence of resistance to rifampin and isoniazid. A fourth drug (such as ethambutol or streptomycin) is necessary when the rate of isoniazid resistance in the community is known to be higher than 4%. These drugs can be withdrawn once test results indicate *M. tuberculosis* susceptibility to isoniazid and rifampin.

There is a debate on how long patients who have HIV disease with tuberculosis should be treated.[25] Current CDC and American Thoracic Society guidelines recommend a 6-month treatment regimen but suggest prolonged therapy (9 months or 4 months after culture conversion) for patients who have a delayed clinical and bacteriologic response to antituberculosis therapy. Therefore, sputum evaluation 2 months after initiation of treatment (induction phase) should be performed among persons infected with HIV.

The standard 6- or 9-month regimens based on rifampin or rifabutin and 9- or 12-month regimen without rifamycins are summarized in

TREATMENT REGIMENS FOR HIV-RELATED TUBERCULOSIS				
	Induction phase		Continuation phase	
	Drugs	Interval and duration*	Drugs	Interval and duration*
6–9† months rifamycin-based therapy	Isoniazid, rifampin or rifabutin, pyrazinamide, ethambutol‡	Daily for 2 months, or daily for 2 weeks and then twice a week for 6 weeks	Isoniazid, rifampin or rifabutin	Daily or twice a week for 4–7 months
Rifamycin free therapies				
12-month regimen	Isoniazid, pyrazinamide, ethambutol, streptomycin	Daily for 2 months, or daily for 2 weeks and then 2–3 times a week for 6 weeks	Isoniazid, ethambutol	Daily or 2–3 times a week for 10 months
9-month regimen§	Isoniazid, pyrazinamide, ethambutol, streptomycin	Daily for 2 months, or daily for 2 weeks and then 2–3 times a week for 6 weeks	Isoniazid, pyrazinamide, streptomycin	Daily or 2–3 times a week for 7 months

* All intermittent therapies should be directly observed. † Duration of therapy should be prolonged for patients who have delayed response to therapy (see text). ‡ Ethambutol should be stopped if *Mycobacterium tuberculosis* is susceptible to isoniazid and rifampin. § We do not recommend this regimen, since a prolonged course of streptomycin is related to severe adverse events such as tubular necrosis and renal failure, deafness due to cochlear toxicity and vertigo due to damage to vestibular organs.

Table 129.1 Treatment regimens for HIV-related tuberculosis.

Table 129.1. The selection of a regimen in HIV-infected patients depends on consideration of a number of factors including:

- the high rate of adverse reactions to antituberculosis drugs;
- the drug interactions between antituberculosis and antiviral drugs; and
- the susceptibility pattern of the strain.

Adverse reactions to many drugs occur at high frequency among persons who have HIV infection. Several studies have compared HIV-infected and HIV-uninfected patients and have shown 20–40% adverse reactions in HIV-infected patients in comparison with 3–5% in persons not infected with HIV.[3,26] The majority of adverse reactions occurred within the first 2 months after starting therapy. Rifampin adverse reactions are the most frequently observed. Generally, rifampin-free regimens are preferable, although there have been reports of successful desensitization to rifampin in HIV-uninfected persons.[27]

Drug interactions between antituberculosis drugs and antiretrovirals occur as a result of induction and inhibition of metabolic pathways. Rifamycins (rifampin and rifabutin) are potent inducers of isoenzyme CYP3A4 of the cytochrome P450 enzyme system and they lead to a reduction of the area under the curve (AUC) of those drugs metabolized by CYP3A4, such as protease inhibitors and non-nucleoside reverse transcriptase inhibitors[28] (interactions are summarized in Table 129.2). Nucleoside reverse transcriptase inhibitors are not metabolized via CYP3A4, but rifampin decreases the AUC of zidovudine by 30%. The clinical relevance of this change is unclear. Rifabutin does not alter the pharmacokinetics of nucleoside reverse transcriptase inhibitors.

Rifampin has the most potent CYP3A4 enzyme-inducing effect, with a resultant 80% decrease in the AUC of all protease inhibitors, with the exception of ritonavir, which is decreased by 35%. Therefore, the combination of rifampin with protease inhibitors is contraindicated (with the possible exception of ritonavir).

To overcome the problems associated with rifampin, the use of rifabutin has been recommended because of its lower enzyme-inducing effect. Rifabutin decreases the AUCs of indinavir and nelfinavir by 30%, amprenavir by 15% and lopinavir/ritonavir by 0%. When indinavir and rifabutin are co-administered, it is recommended that the dose of indinavir be increased to 1g q8h. Furthermore, protease inhibitors are inhibitors of CYP3A4, which can induce an increase in the plasma levels of rifabutin and thus increase its toxicity (leukopenia, uveitis and arthralgia). Therefore, it is necessary to reduce the doses of rifabutin (standard dose is 300mg q24h) to 150mg q24h when it is co-administered with indinavir, nelfinavir and amprenavir and to 150mg twice or three times weekly when administered with lopinavir/ritonavir (since ritonavir is the most potent inhibitor of CYP3A4). Rifabutin reduces the AUC of saquinavir by approximately 45%; therefore, this combination is contraindicated. Rifampin can be combined with ritonavir (at usual doses); however, the utility of this approach is limited because of the poor tolerability of full-dose ritonavir. It may be possible also to use rifampin with ritonavir 400mg and saquinavir 400mg q12h, although this combination has only been evaluated in a few patients.[29]

As in the case of protease inhibitors, rifampin induces a decrease in the AUCs of nevirapine, delavirdine and efavirenz by 37%, 96% and 25% respectively. Thus, co-administration of rifampin with delavirdine is contraindicated. It may be possible to use rifampin with nevirapine, but clinical experience is scarce. Pharmacokinetic studies have shown that levels of efavirenz at a dose of 800mg q24h plus rifampin are equal to 600mg efavirenz q24h without rifampin.[30] Rifabutin can be used with nevirapine without dosage adjustment. Data on the interaction between rifabutin 300mg and efavirenz 600mg showed no significant effect on the pharmacokinetics of efavirenz but a decrease in the AUC of rifabutin of about 30%. Therefore, it may be necessary to increase the dose of rifabutin to 450–600mg q24h without changing the dosage of efavirenz.

Taking into account this information, the most important priority for physicians managing tuberculosis in the HIV-positive patient is to treat tuberculosis, even more so in smear-positive cases. There are two well defined clinical situations: a patient who is naive to antiretroviral therapy and a patient who is already on therapy. In the former, HAART can be delayed in order to improve adherence to antituberculosis treatment and to avoid toxicity and paradoxic reactions. After 2 months of antituberculosis therapy, the recommendation for antiretroviral therapy should be determined on the basis of clinical factors, $CD4^+$ lymphocyte count, HIV viral load and patient commitment to therapy.

However, it is well known that the use of antiretroviral therapy leads to significant reductions in viral load, AIDS-defining illness and mortality, especially in those patients who have advanced HIV infection ($CD4^+$ <100 cells/mm^3). In such patients, delaying HAART is not warranted and it is recommended that HAART be

DRUG INTERACTIONS WITH RIFAMYCIN						
Antiviral drug (AVD)	Rifampin (RIF)			Rifabutin (RBT)		
	RIF's effect on AVD	AVD's effect on RIF	Comments	RBT's effect on AVD	AVD's effect on RBT	Comments
Saquinavir	80% decrease	No data	Contraindicated	45% decrease	No data	Contraindicated
Ritonavir	35% decrease	Unchanged	No dosage adjustments required; not recommended*	No data	293% increase	Not recommended†
Indinavir	89% decrease	No data	Contraindicated	34% decrease	173% increase	The dose of indinavir should be increased to 1g q8h and RBT should be decreased to 150mg daily
Nelfinavir	82% decrease	No data	Contraindicated	32% decrease	200% increase	No dosage adjustments required; RBT should be decreased to 150mg daily
Amprenavir	81% decrease	Unchanged	Contraindicated	15% decrease	200% increase	The dose of RBT should be decreased to 150mg daily
Lopinavir/ritonavir	75% decrease	No data	Contraindicated	Unchanged	290% increase	Not recommended†
Nevirapine	37–68% decrease	Unchanged	No data	16% decrease	Unchanged	No dosage adjustments required
Delavirdine	96% decrease	Unchanged	Contraindicated	80% decrease	342% increase	Contraindicated
Efavirenz	25% decrease	Unchanged	The dose of efavirenz should be increased to 800mg daily	Unchanged	32% decrease	The dose of RBT should be increased to 450–600mg daily

* Ritonavir is not well tolerated and could hinder the adherence to antituberculosis treatment.
† The association is possible using 150mg 2–3 times/week, however, it is not recommended due to the high risk of RBT toxicity (uveitis, leukopenia and arthralgia).

Table 129.2 Drug interactions with rifamycin. The effects of rifamycin administration with protease inhibitors or non-nucleoside reverse transcriptase inhibitors on the plasma levels of each drug are expressed as a percentage change in the AUC of the concomitant treatment relative to the level for a single drug treatment.

started early, at the same time as tuberculosis therapy.[31] The antiretroviral therapy we recommended is the combination of efavirenz plus two nucleoside reverse transcriptase inhibitors or, alternatively, three nucleoside reverse transcriptase inhibitors (including abacavir). Both regimens are simple, well tolerated and allow the use of a rifamycin-based regimen for tuberculosis therapy. The alternative therapy is the use of nelfinavir or indinavir plus two nucleoside reverse transcriptase inhibitors and the substitution of rifampin by rifabutin. Rifampin induction of the CYP3A system can persist for up to 2 weeks. Therefore, rifampin should be substituted by rifabutin for 2 weeks before antiretroviral therapy is initiated, with the required dosage adjustment (Fig. 129.11).

Patients already on treatment with a protease inhibitor regimen (indinavir, nelfinavir, amprenavir or lopinavir/ritonavir) and good CD4+ and viral load response who develop tuberculosis could be treated with a rifabutin-based regimen. If the protease inhibitor is saquinavir, this should be switched to an alternative protease inhibitor. Rifampin therapy is possible if the protease inhibitor is ritonavir. In the case of non-nucleoside reverse transcriptase inhibitor regimens, rifampin or rifabutin could be used with efavirenz and nevirapine with appropriate dosage adjustment, while delavirdine should be changed to efavirenz or nevirapine. In all situations it is also possible to switch therapy to a nucleoside reverse transcriptase inhibitor regimen while tuberculosis treatment is ongoing. Non-rifamycin-containing regimens are only recommended for patients who have serious adverse effects with rifamycins or who are infected with a rifamycin-resistant isolate.

Treatment of drug-resistant tuberculosis

Resistance to isoniazid alone is the most common pattern of drug resistance. If the minimum inhibitory concentration (MIC) for isoniazid is more than 1mg/L, the association of rifampin (or rifabutin), pyrazinamide and ethambutol or streptomycin for the first 2 months followed by rifampin plus ethambutol for 10 months is the regimen recommended. It is possible to include isoniazid, when the MIC for isoniazid is more than 0.1mg/L but less than 1mg/L. Monoresistance to rifampin is more common in HIV-infected patients than in immunocompetent persons.[32] It is associated with nonadherence to therapy, the use of rifabutin as prophylaxis against MAC and the presence of diarrhea. The treatment regimen should consist of an initial 2-month phase of isoniazid, pyrazinamide and ethambutol or streptomycin and a second phase of isoniazid and ethambutol for 10 months. It is possible to reduce the duration of therapy using streptomycin associated with isoniazid and pyrazinamide for 9 months, but the toxicity and route of streptomycin administration makes this regimen less appropriate. For the treatment of multidrug-resistant tuberculosis (resistant to both isoniazid and rifampin), the regimen should include four or five drugs to which the organism is susceptible (aminoglycosides, fluoroquinolones, ethionamide, cycloserine, PAS, thiacetazone or clofazimine) for at least 18–24 months.[33]

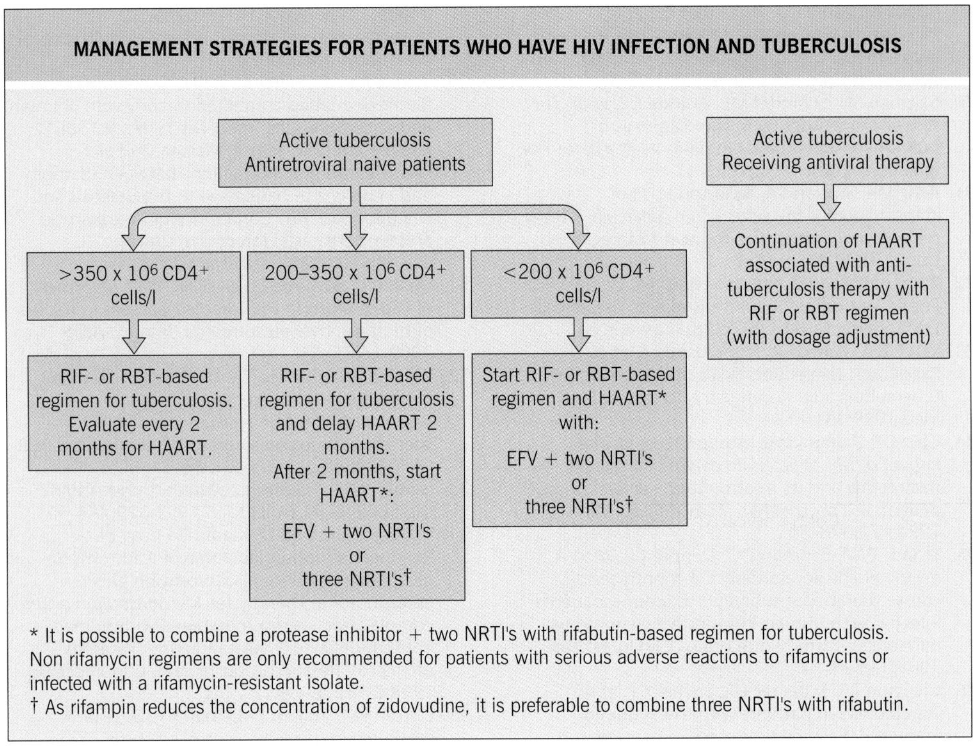
MANAGEMENT STRATEGIES FOR PATIENTS WHO HAVE HIV INFECTION AND TUBERCULOSIS
Active tuberculosis
Antiretroviral naive patients
Active tuberculosis
Receiving antiviral therapy
>350 x 10⁶ CD4+ cells/l
200–350 x 10⁶ CD4+ cells/l
<200 x 10⁶ CD4+ cells/l
Continuation of HAART associated with anti-tuberculosis therapy with RIF or RBT regimen (with dosage adjustment)
RIF- or RBT-based regimen for tuberculosis. Evaluate every 2 months for HAART.
RIF- or RBT-based regimen for tuberculosis and delay HAART 2 months. After 2 months, start HAART*: EFV + two NRTI's or three NRTI's†
Start RIF- or RBT-based regimen and HAART* with: EFV + two NRTI's or three NRTI's†
* It is possible to combine a protease inhibitor + two NRTI's with rifabutin-based regimen for tuberculosis. Non rifamycin regimens are only recommended for patients with serious adverse reactions to rifamycins or infected with a rifamycin-resistant isolate.
† As rifampin reduces the concentration of zidovudine, it is preferable to combine three NRTI's with rifabutin.

Fig. 129.11 Management strategies for patients who have HIV infection and tuberculosis. EFV, efavirenz; NRTI, nucleoside reverse transcriptase inhibitor; RBT, rifabutin; RIF, rifampin.

Therapy for *Mycobacterium avium* complex

Treatment regimens should include a macrolide (clarithromycin or azithromycin) plus ethambutol.[34] The addition of rifabutin should be considered, since triple therapy has been associated with a reduction in relapses and in the emergence of resistant strains.[35] Aminoglycosides and quinolones may be useful in macrolide-resistant cases. In the era of HAART, it is important to note that the association of clarithromycin and efavirenz is contraindicated since the AUC of clarithromycin is decreased by about 40%. In addition, ritonavir and lopinavir induce an increase of 100% in the AUC of clarithromycin; therefore, when creatinine clearance is less than 60ml/min, it is necessary to reduce the dose of clarithromycin by 50%.

In general, as with other opportunistic infections, therapy for disseminated MAC is for life. However, in situations where CD4+ T cell counts increase to more than 100×10^6 cells/l after 6–12 months of HAART, patients are at low risk of recurrence of MAC and the treatment can be stopped. Although the number of patients who have been evaluated is small, there is increasing confidence that it is possible to discontinue maintenance therapy[36] in such patients.

Treatment of other nontuberculous mycobacterias

Mycobacterium kansasii is the second most frequent cause of pulmonary and disseminated nontuberculous mycobacterial disease. The treatment consists of a daily regimen of rifampin (or rifabutin), isoniazid and ethambutol for 12–18 months. Therapy of other nontuberculous mycobacterias is briefly described. *Mycobacterium genavense* and *M. haemophilum* are resistant to isoniazid, pyrazinamide and ethambutol. *Mycobacterium genavense* may be treated with a regimen similar to MAC and *M. haemophilum* with a combination of rifampin plus another active antituberculosis drug (ciprofloxacin, doxycycline, clarithromycin or amikacin). *Mycobacterium simiae* and *M. xenopi* are susceptible to isoniazid, rifampin, ethambutol and should be treated for 12 months. *Mycobacterium scrofulaceum* therapy requires surgery and isoniazid plus rifampin for 24 months with amikacin for 2–3 months. *Mycobacterium marinum* is resistant to isoniazid and pyrazinamide. Minocycline or clarithromycin or rifampin plus ethambutol for 3 months are possible therapies. *Mycobacterium fortuitum* therapy consists of amikacin plus cefoxitin plus ciprofloxacin for 1 month followed by quinolone plus clarithromycin for 3–6 months.

REFERENCES

1. Raviglione MC, Snider DE Jr, Kochi A. Global epidemiology of tuberculosis. Morbidity and mortality of a worldwide epidemic. JAMA 1995;273:220–6.
2. Snider DE, Raviglione JM, Kochi A. Global burden of tuberculosis. Washington, DC: ASM Press; 1994.
3. Soriano E, Mallolas J, Gatell JM, *et al.* Characteristics of tuberculosis in HIV-infected patients: a case-control study. AIDS 1988;2:429–32.
4. Perriens JH, Colebunders RL, Karahunga C, *et al.* Increased mortality and tuberculosis treatment failure rate among human immunodeficiency virus (HIV) seropositive compared with HIV seronegative patients with pulmonary tuberculosis treated with 'standard' chemotherapy in Kinshasa, Zaire. Am Rev Respir Dis 1991;144:750–5.
5. Kirk O, Gatell JM, Mocroft A, *et al.* Infections with *Mycobacterium tuberculosis* and *Mycobacterium avium* among HIV-infected patients after the introduction of highly active antiretroviral therapy. EuroSIDA Study Group JD. Am J Respir Crit Care Med 2000;162:865–72.
6. Low N, Pfluger D, Egger M. Disseminated *Mycobacterium avium* complex disease in the Swiss HIV Cohort Study: increasing incidence, unchanged prognosis. AIDS 1997;11:1165–71.
7. Miro JM, Buira E, Mallolas J, *et al.* CD4+ lymphocytes and opportunistic infections and neoplasms in patients with human immunodeficiency virus. Med Clin (Barc) 1994;102:316.
8. Lucas S, Nelson AM. Pathogenesis of tuberculosis in human immunodeficiency virus-infected people. In: Bloom BR, ed. Tuberculosis: pathogenesis, protection, and control. Washington, DC: ASM Press; 1994.
9. Selwyn PA, Hartel D, Lewis VA, *et al.* A prospective study of the risk of tuberculosis among intravenous drug users with human immunodeficiency virus infection. N Engl J Med 1989;320:545–50.
10. Guelar A, Gatell JM, Verdejo J, *et al.* A prospective study of the risk of tuberculosis among HIV-infected patients. AIDS 1993;7:1345–9.
11. Johnson MP, Coberly JS, Clermont HC, *et al.* Tuberculin skin test reactivity among adults infected with human immunodeficiency virus. J Infect Dis 1992;166:194–8.
12. Gordin FM, Matts JP, Miller C, *et al.* A controlled trial of isoniazid in persons with anergy and human immunodeficiency virus infection who are at high risk for tuberculosis.

Terry Beirn Community Programs for Clinical Research on AIDS. N Engl J Med 1997;337:315–20.
13. Gordin F, Chaisson RE, Matts JP, *et al.* Rifampin and pyrazinamide vs isoniazid for prevention of tuberculosis in HIV-infected persons: an international randomized trial. Terry Beirn Community Programs for Clinical Research on AIDS, the Adult AIDS Clinical Trials Group, the Pan American Health Organization, and the Centers for Disease Control and Prevention Study Group. JAMA 2000;283:1445–50.
14. Pierce M, Crampton S, Henry D, *et al.* A randomized trial of clarithromycin as prophylaxis against disseminated *Mycobacterium avium* complex infection in patients with advanced acquired immunodeficiency syndrome. N Engl J Med 1996;335:384–91.
15. Havlir DV, Dube MP, Sattler FR, *et al.* Prophylaxis against disseminated *Mycobacterium avium* complex with weekly azithromycin, daily rifabutin, or both. California Collaborative Treatment Group. N Engl J Med 1996;335:392–8.
16. Currier JS, Williams PL, Koletar SL, *et al.* Discontinuation of *Mycobacterium avium* complex prophylaxis in patients with antiretroviral therapy-induced increases in $CD4^+$ cell count. A randomized, double-blind, placebo-controlled trial. AIDS Clinical Trials Group 362 Study Team. Ann Intern Med 2000;133:493–503.
17. Shafer RW, Kim DS, Weiss JP, Quale JM. Extrapulmonary tuberculosis in patients with human immunodeficiency virus infection. Medicine (Baltimore) 1991;70:384–97.
18. Havlir DV, Ellner JJ. *Mycobacterium avium* complex. In: Mandel GL, Bennet JE, Dolin R, eds. Principles and practice of infectious disease, 5th ed. Edinburgh: Churchill Livingstone; 2000:2616–30.
19. Narita M, Ashkin D, Hollender ES, *et al.* Paradoxical worsening of tuberculosis following antiretroviral therapy in patients with AIDS. Am J Respir Crit Care Med 1998;158:157–61.
20. Salzman SH, Schindel ML, Aranda CP, *et al.* The role of bronchoscopy in the diagnosis of pulmonary tuberculosis in patients at risk for HIV infection. Chest 1992;102:143–6.
21. Behr MA, Warren SA, Salamon H, *et al.* Transmission of *Mycobacterium tuberculosis* from patients smear-negative for acid-fast bacilli. Lancet 1999;353:444–9.
22. Barnes PF, Yang Z, Preston-Martin S, *et al.* Patterns of tuberculosis transmission in Central Los Angeles. JAMA 1997;278:1159–63.
23. Van Rie A, Warren R, Richardson M, *et al.* Exogenous reinfection as a cause of recurrent tuberculosis after curative treatment. N Engl J Med 1999;341:1174–9.
24. Chin DP, Reingold AL, Stone EN, *et al.* The impact of *Mycobacterium avium* complex bacteremia and its treatment on survival of AIDS patients – a prospective study. J Infect Dis 1994;170:578–84.
25. El Sadr WM, Perlman DC, Denning E, *et al.* A review of efficacy studies of 6-month short-course therapy for tuberculosis among patients infected with human immunodeficiency virus: differences in study outcomes. Clin Infect Dis 2001;32:623–32.
26. Chaisson RE, Schecter GF, Theuer CP, *et al.* Tuberculosis in patients with the acquired immunodeficiency syndrome. Clinical features, response to therapy, and survival. Am Rev Respir Dis 1987;136:570–4.
27. Holland CL, Malasky C, Ogunkoya A, *et al.* Rapid oral desensitization to isoniazid and rifampin. Chest 1990;98:1518–9.
28. Department of Health and Human Services and the Henry J Kaiser Family Foundation. Guidelines for the use of antiretroviral agents in HIV-infected adults and adolescents. Available at http://www.hivatis.org/guidelines/adult/text/introduction.htm/2000.
29. Veldkamp AI, Hoetelmans RM, Beijnen JH, *et al.* Ritonavir enables combined therapy with rifampin and saquinavir. Clin Infect Dis 1999;29:1586.
30. Lopez-Cortes LF, Ruiz R, Viciana P, *et al.* Pharmacokinetic interactions between rifampin and efavirenz in patients with tuberculosis and HIV infection. 8th Conference on Retroviruses and Opportunistic Infections, Chicago, IL, 4–8 February 2001: abstract 32.
31. Dean GL, Edwards SG, Ives NJ, *et al.* Treatment of tuberculosis in HIV-infected persons in the era of highly active antiretroviral therapy. AIDS 2002;16:75–83.
32. Whelen AC, Felmlee TA, Hunt JM, *et al.* Direct genotypic detection of *Mycobacterium tuberculosis* rifampin resistance in clinical specimens by using single-tube heminested PCR. J Clin Microbiol 1995;33:556–61.
33. Iseman MD. Treatment of multidrug-resistant tuberculosis. N Engl J Med 1993;329:784–91.
34. Ward TT, Rimland D, Kauffman C, *et al.* Randomized, open-label trial of azithromycin plus ethambutol vs. clarithromycin plus ethambutol as therapy for *Mycobacterium avium* complex bacteremia in patients with human immunodeficiency virus infection. Veterans Affairs HIV Research Consortium. Clin Infect Dis 1998;27:1278–85.
35. Gordin FM, Sullam PM, Shafran SD, *et al.* A randomized, placebo-controlled study of rifabutin added to a regimen of clarithromycin and ethambutol for treatment of disseminated infection with *Mycobacterium avium* complex. Clin Infect Dis 1999;28:1080–5.
36. Hadad DJ, Lewi DS, Pignatari AC, *et al.* Resolution of *Mycobacterium avium* complex bacteremia following highly active antiretroviral therapy. Clin Infect Dis 1998;26:758–9.

chapter

130 Neoplastic Disease

Umberto Tirelli & Emanuela Vaccher

INTRODUCTION

Infection with human immunodeficiency virus (HIV) is associated with an increased risk of developing cancers, particularly Kaposi's sarcoma (KS) and non-Hodgkin's lymphoma (NHL). The risk of KS and NHL is increased respectively 1000- and 100-fold among HIV-infected patients compared with the general population.[1,2]

The widespread use of highly active antiretroviral therapy (HAART) has radically changed the clinical spectrum of HIV infection in industrialized countries since the mid-1990s. Incidence rates of opportunistic infections (OIs), KS, primary central nervous system lymphoma (PCNSL) and recently systemic NHL have significantly decreased in the HAART era.[3–6] Kaposi's sarcoma, PCNSL, systemic intermediate/high-grade B-cell NHL and invasive cervical cancer have been designated as AIDS-defining illnesses, but other malignancies have been reported to be associated with HIV infection. These include Hodgkin's disease and high-grade anal epithelial lesions.[1–3,7] Possible excesses of other types of cancer, such as nonmelanomatous skin cancer, lung and testicular carcinoma and myeloma, need to be confirmed.[1–3]

This chapter focuses on the epidemiology, pathology, clinical features and treatment of the two most common malignant tumors in HIV-infected patients: KS and NHL.

KAPOSI'S SARCOMA

EPIDEMIOLOGY

The epidemiology of KS among HIV-infected individuals has dramatically changed during the second decade of the AIDS epidemic. Kaposi's sarcoma incidence rates started to decline in the late 1980s and then more remarkably with the introduction of HAART in the mid-1990s.[1–4] In a meta-analysis of data on 47,936 HIV-seropositive individuals from North America, Europe and Australia, the KS rate ratio for 1997–99 vs 1992–96 was 0.3.[3] The risk of KS among male homosexuals is greater than 100,000-fold that of persons with other HIV risk behaviors.[1]

In 1994, Chang *et al* discovered a new herpes virus, called KS-associated herpes virus or human herpes virus 8 (HHV-8), and subsequent studies showed that this was an essential causative agent for all forms of KS.[8] HHV-8 transmission correlates with a history of sexually transmitted diseases and number of male sexual partners. Co-infection with both HHV-8 and HIV increases the risk of developing KS as much as 10,000-fold as compared with HHV-8 infection alone. The 10-year probability of developing KS after co-infection with both HHV-8 and HIV approaches 50%.[8,9]

PATHOLOGY AND PATHOGENESIS

Kaposi's sarcoma is an angioproliferative disease characterized by angiogenesis, endothelial spindle cell growth (KS cells), inflammatory cell infiltration and edema. The histological cell of origin of KS spindle cells remains uncertain, but is probably a mesenchymal progenitor cell of either endothelial or monocyte-macrophage lineage.

Kaposi's sarcoma lesions arise from a contest of immune dysregulation characterized by $CD8^+$ T-cell activation and production of Th1 type cytokines (i.e. interferon-γ), interleukin (IL)-1β, IL-6 and tumor necrosis factor-α) and angiogenic factors (i.e. basic fibroblastic growth factor and vascular endothelial growth factor), that induces a generalized activation of endothelial cells leading to adhesion and tissue extravasation of lymphomonocytes, spindle cell formation and angiogenesis. These phenomena are triggered or enhanced by HHV-8 infection that, in turn, is reactivated by the same cytokines. Productively infected circulation cells are recruited into 'activated' tissue sites where HHV-8 finds an optimal environment for establishing a persistent latent infection of KS spindle cells. Although early KS is a reactive process of polyclonal nature that can regress, in time it can progress into a true sarcoma. The progression of KS appears to be due to the deregulated expression of oncogenes and oncosuppressor genes and to the long-lasting expression of the HHV-8 latency genes and is promoted by proliferative and angiogenic effects of the HIV Tat protein.[10]

CLINICAL FEATURES

Kaposi's sarcoma ranges from an indolent to an aggressive disease with significant morbidity and mortality. Typically, the disease presents with disseminated skin lesions, often with lymph node and visceral involvement such as the gastrointestinal (GI) tract and lungs. Skin lesions arise as macular or papular eruptions, which progress to nodular plaques or lesions (Fig. 130.1); any area of the skin may be involved. Nodular KS does not usually cause necrosis of overlying skin and rarely invades underlying bone structure.

Lymphedema, particularly of the face, genitalia and lower extremities, may be out of proportion to the cutaneous disease and may be related not just to lymphatic obstruction, but also to the cytokines involved in the pathogenesis of KS. Lymphadenopathic KS primarily affects peripheral lymph nodes, sometimes causing massive nodal enlargement, and it may be present in the absence of mucocutaneous disease.

Oral cavity KS occurs in approximately 35% of patients and is the initial site of disease in about 15%. Intraoral lesions most commonly affect the palate and gingiva and may interfere with nutrition and speech.

Over 50% of patients with skin disease have GI lesions. Any segment of the GI tract may be involved, although the stomach and duodenum are most commonly affected. Gastrointestinal KS is seldom symptomatic, but may cause bowel malabsorption or obstruction and, rarely, bleeding.

Pulmonary involvement is also quite common and may be life threatening. In approximately 20% of cases it may occur in the absence of skin lesions. The symptoms, including shortness of breath, fever, cough, hemoptysis and chest pain, and radiologic appearance of pulmonary KS are indistinguishable from those of the more

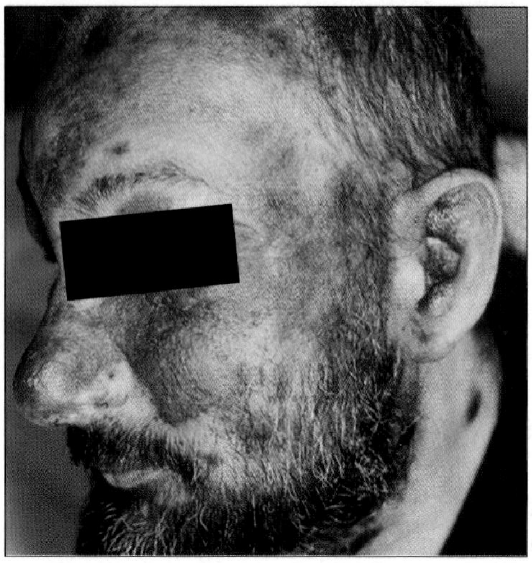

Fig. 130.1 Kaposi's sarcoma. There are large confluent hyperpigmented patch-stage lesions with lymphedema.

STAGING SYSTEM FOR HIV ASSOCIATED KAPOSI'S SARCOMA		
	Good risk	**Poor risk**
Tumor	Confined to skin and/or lymph nodes and/or minimal oral disease (confined to palate)	Tumor-associated edema or ulceration; extensive oral Kaposi's sarcoma; gastrointestinal Kaposi's sarcoma; Kaposi's sarcoma in visceral organs
Immune system	$CD4^+$ lymphocytes ≥200/μl	$CD4^+$ lymphocytes <200/μl
Systemic illness	No history of opportunistic infection or thrush; no systemic 'B' symptoms*; Karnofsky performance status	History of opportunistic infection or thrush; systemic 'B' symptoms; Karnofsky performance status <70%; other HIV-related illness

Table 130.1 Staging system for HIV-associated Kaposi's sarcoma. *Systemic 'B' symptoms are fever, night sweats and/or weight loss >10% of normal body weight. Adapted from reference.[11]

common opportunistic infections. Radiographic findings vary greatly and can include nodular, interstitial and alveolar infiltrates, pleural effusion, hilar and mediastinal adenopathy, and even an isolated pulmonary nodule. The pleural effusions of KS are typically serosanguinous in nature and are associated with KS lesions on the visceral pleura.

DIAGNOSIS

Although a presumptive diagnosis of KS can often be readily made by a trained observer, a skin biopsy can confirm the diagnosis. It is especially important to biopsy lesions that are less typical of KS because other conditions, such as bacillary angiomatosis, may be confused with KS.

Lesions in the GI tract are often recognized easily on endoscopy; however, because the lesions tend to be submucosal, biopsies may not demonstrate KS.

Bronchoscopy is the procedure of choice for pulmonary KS, but gallium–thallium scanning may also be helpful in evaluating an abnormal radiograph. Kaposi's sarcoma is usually thallium avid and gallium negative, whereas infections are usually gallium avid and thallium negative.

The AIDS Clinical Trial Group (ACTG) classification groups patients according to extent of the tumor, immune status and severity of systemic illness (Table 130.1).[11]

MANAGEMENT

Kaposi's sarcoma is a heterogeneous disease and no specific therapy is curative. Therefore, treatment needs to be individualized, based on the patient's overall clinical and immunological status.

Localized KS cutaneous lesions are treated with radiation therapy, laser therapy, cryotherapy, intralesional injections of antineoplastic drugs and alitretinoin topical gel.[12]

Prolongation of time to treatment failure as well as clinical improvement of KS disease by HAART has been reported in the literature,[12,13] and there are numerous anecdotal reports of KS regression while on HAART alone. Anti-KS activity of HAART appears to be linked to immuno-reconstitution and to a lesser extent to suppression of HIV replication. Interestingly, a recent study indicates that protease inhibitors are also potent antiangiogenic molecules in *in vitro* and *in vivo* KS models.[14]

Cytotoxic chemotherapy is indicated for patients who do not respond to HAART and for patients with life-threatening or visceral disease. A wide variety of cytotoxic drugs, including vinca alkaloids (vincristine, vinblastine), bleomycin, doxorubicin individually and in combination, have produced tumor regression in 21–59% of patients, with lower rates for monochemotherapy. Randomized trials showed that liposomal anthracyclines are superior to conventional chemotherapy (BV or ABV regimens) in terms of response rate and toxicity profiles.[15,16] Paclitaxel is the newest systemic chemotherapeutic agent approved for relapsed KS patients. Response rates range between 59% and 71% and the median duration response (10 months) is the longest of any chemotherapy trial reported thus far.[12]

New treatment modalities including al-transretinoic acid and angiostatic agents are currently under investigation.[12]

Corticosteroid therapy induces the development of KS and worsens pre-existing KS lesions.

PROGNOSIS

Prognostic factors for survival are the immune status of the patients (I) and, to a lesser extent, the initial stage (T) of the neoplasm. Median survival of patients with CD4 count ≥150/μl and early T stage disease (I_0 and T_0 according to the ACTG) is 35 months, while for patients with CD4 <150/μl (I_1) median survival is comparable for early (T_0) and advanced (T_1) T stage disease, being 13 and 12 months respectively.[12]

NON-HODGKIN'S LYMPHOMA

EPIDEMIOLOGY

The incidence of NHL among HIV-infected patients has decreased significantly since the introduction of HAART and the decline has been most pronounced for PCNSL. Systemic NHL incidence decreased less than KS and later than for the other AIDS-defining illnesses. Consequently, lymphoma has become the most common AIDS-associated cancer among patients receiving HAART. Non-Hodgkin's lymphoma constituted 16% and 8% of all AIDS-related diseased diagnosed in 1998, compared with 4% and 6% in 1994, in Western Europe and the United States, respectively.[1–6]

Risk factors for HIV-related NHL are older age, degree and duration of immunosuppression, no prior HAART use or insufficient immunologic and virologic response to combined antiretroviral therapy.[7] Moreover, the risk of KS as well as NHL is decreased for people with the CCR5 Δ32 polymorphism and NHL risk is increased with the stromal cell-derived factor 1 polymorphism.[1]

PATHOLOGIC FEATURES OF HIV-LYMPHOPROLIFERATIVE DISEASES	
Non-Hodgkin's lymphomas	
Body cavity-based lymphoma	Primary brain (immunoblastic)
Systemic Blastic cell lymphomas • large noncleaved cell (G–WF) • immunoblastic (H–WF) with or without plasma cell differentiation • small noncleaved cell (J–WF) with or without plasma cell differentiation • ?extramedullary plasmacytoma • blastic cell with 'intermediate' features	Anaplastic' cell lymphomas • anaplastic large-cell (CD30/Ki-l$^+$) Others (rare types)
Hodgkin's lymphoma	
Mixed cellularity	Lymphocyte depletion
Multicentric Castleman's disease	

Table 130.2 Pathologic features of HIV lymphoproliferative diseases. WF, Working Formulation.

Non-Hodgkin's lymphoma occurs among all population groups at risk for HIV infection, in all age groups and in different countries, with similar epidemiologic and clinicopathologic features.

HIV-related NHL are broadly divisible into three categories according to their anatomical site of origin: systemic NHL, PCNSL and body cavity-based lymphoma or primary effusion lymphoma (PEL). PELs are uncommon, accounting for approximately 3% or less of HIV-NHL. They exhibit a unique constellation of clinical, pathological and molecular characteristics and thus represent a distinct clinicopathological entity.

PATHOLOGY AND PATHOGENESIS

The pathological classification has been redefined at our institution (Table 130.2). The systemic NHLs are histologically heterogeneous, with 80–90% featuring three Working Formulation categories:

- large cell lymphoma (G group);
- large cell immunoblastic lymphoma (LCIBL, H group); and
- small noncleaved cell lymphoma (J group), the equivalent of Burkitt's-type lymphoma (BL).

Cases showing 'intermediate' histologic features may be detected and, in addition, B-cell CD30$^+$ anaplastic large cell lymphoma (ALCL), a heterogeneous group of high-grade lymphomas at the borderline between Hodgkin's disease and NHL, may be found. In contrast with the heterogeneity of systemic NHL, PCNSLs represent a more uniform group and in the vast majority of the cases share LCIBL histologic features. The PELs, typically growing as lymphomatous effusions, have morphologic and immunophenotypic characteristics similar to those of LCIBL or ALCL.

The pathogenesis of HIV-NHL is a multistep process involving factors provided by the host as well as alterations intrinsic to the tumor clone. The molecular pathways of viral infection and lesions of cancer-related genes associated with HIV-NHL vary substantially in different clinicopathological categories of the disease and highlight the marked degree of biological heterogeneity of these lymphomas.

At present, four major molecular pathways can be identified, each of which is associated with peculiar clinical features and restricted to a given NHL histological type. The first pathway associates with BL and is characterized by relatively mild immunodeficiency of the host and multiple genetic lesions of the tumor, including activation of c-*myc*, disruption of p53 and, less frequently, infection by Epstein–Barr virus (EBV). Typically, EBV-infected BL fail to express

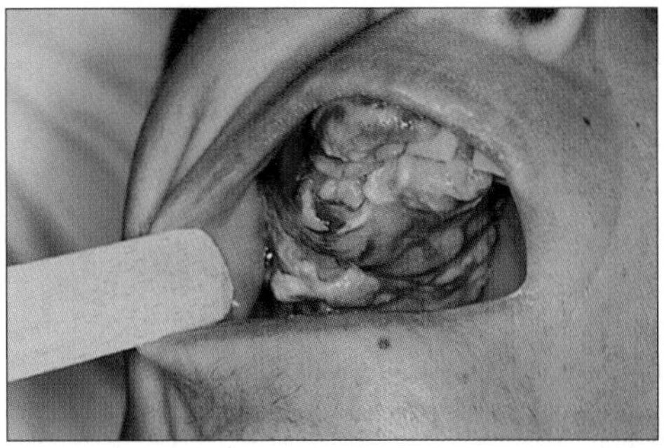

Fig. 130.2 Non-Hodgkin's lymphoma. Bulky disease in the gingiva.

the viral transforming antigens latent membrane protein 1 (LMP-1) and Epstein–Barr virus nuclear antigen 2 (EBNA-2). Histogenetic studies have shown that BL derives from germinal center (GC) cells, of which the lymphoma closely mimics the phenotype.

Two distinct pathways associate with diffuse large cell lymphoma (DLCL), a type of NHL frequently characterized by a marked disruption of immunofunction. Whereas the majority of DLCL are EBV positive, only a fraction of cases express the viral antigen LMP-1. Expression of LMP-1 and BCL-6 segregate the two pathways associated with HIV-DLCL. On the other hand, LMP-1 positive HIV-DLCL fail to express the BCL-6 protein and display features consistent with immunoblastic-plasmacytoid differentiation, suggesting a derivation from post-GC cells. However, LMP-1 negative DLCL express BCL-6 and display a large noncleaved cell morphology, suggesting an origin from the GC.

Finally, the fourth pathway associates with PEL. This rare lymphoma type consistently harbors infection by HHV-8 and frequently also by EBV. All other genetic lesions commonly detected among HIV-NHL are consistently negative in HIV-PEL. Histogenetic studies have shown that PEL reflects a post-GC stage or differentiation close to plasma cells.

The identification of the molecular and histogenetic heterogeneity of HIV-NHL is of potential clinical value, because the molecular and histogenetic features of the tumor have been shown to influence the prognosis of several B-cell disorders of immunocompetent hosts.[17]

CLINICAL FEATURES

One of the distinguishing features of NHL is the widespread extent of disease at initial presentation and the frequency of systemic 'B' symptoms, including fever, night sweats and weight loss of more than 10% of the normal body weight. At the time of diagnosis approximately 75% of patients have advanced disease with frequent involvement of extranodal sites, the most common being the central nervous system (CNS), bone marrow, GI tract and liver. Any site of the body, however, may be affected (Fig. 130.2).

Approximately 20–40% of patients have CNS meningeal infiltration at presentation, whereas 65% have brain infiltration at the time of autopsy examination. Leptomeningeal disease, identified during routine lumbar puncture as part of the initial staging evaluation, remains asymptomatic in approximately 20% of patients. Gastrointestinal tract involvement, sometimes at multiple sites, develops in 10–40% of the cases. Bulky disease can be observed in the anorectal region, particularly in homosexual men.

The PCNSL (i.e. intracranial parenchymal lymphoma limited to the CNS) is a manifestation of very advanced HIV disease. Usually the CD4$^+$ lymphocyte count at diagnosis is less than 50/μl. The lymphoma develops as single or multiple lesions in the deep regions of white matter, in the basal ganglia and in the cerebellum. The clinical presentation of PCNSL is not specific and approximately 50% of patients present with lethargy, confusion and personality change, whereas many others lack lateralizing neurologic signs.

The PEL grows exclusively or mainly within pleural, pericardial or peritoneal cavities as lymphomatous effusions, usually in the absence of a contiguous tumor mass. It usually remains strictly localized to the body cavity of origin and only infrequently spreads to local lymph nodes or distant sites.

In the setting of HIV disease, NHL can be difficult to diagnose because of its variable presentation. It can mask many conditions of both HIV disease itself and its associated opportunistic infections. For instance, systemic 'B' symptoms are frequently associated with both advanced HIV infection and opportunistic infections. These symptoms mandate a careful evaluation to exclude other causes, including the presence of *Mycobacterium avium-intracellulare*, cytomegalovirus or tuberculosis infection.

The PCNSL may be radiographically indistinguishable from cerebral toxoplasmosis or other CNS infections. It has been shown that detection of cerebrospinal fluid (CSF) EBV-DNA by polymerase chain reaction (PCR) in HIV-infected patients is reliably associated with PCNSL. By combining CSF EBV-DNA detection by PCR with ^{201}T1 single photon emission computed tomography, the presence of increased uptake and positive EBV-DNA had 100% sensitivity and 100% negative predictive value. Thus in patients with hyperactive lesions and positive EBV-DNA, brain biopsy may be avoided and patients could promptly undergo definitive therapy.[7]

DIAGNOSIS

A diagnosis of NHL should be made by histologic examination of the tissue obtained by incisional or excisional biopsy. It may be possible, however, to make an adequate diagnosis from needle aspiration cytology and this may be required if the patient's clinical condition is critical or deteriorating rapidly.

MANAGEMENT

Optimal therapy for HIV-NHL has not been defined and whether intensive or conservative chemotherapy regimens are indicated in these patients is still a matter of controversy. In fact, poor bone marrow reserve and underlying HIV immunodeficiency challenge the optimal management of systemic NHL. For PCNSL primary therapy consists of whole-brain radiation with intrathecal chemotherapy.

Therapeutic guidelines that should be considered in the management of systemic NHL are:

- first, as with other aggressive lymphomas, the use of combination chemotherapy is essential; and
- second, chemotherapy regimens must include intrathecal chemotherapy, as either a prophylactic or therapeutic modality.

Initially, intensive chemotherapy regimens have been associated with a significant risk of early death due to OIs, suggesting that less intensive treatment strategies should be explored. The use of a low-dose regimen of methotrexate-leucoverin rescue-bleomycin-doxorubicin-cyclophosphamide-vincristine and dexamethasone (m-BACOD) results in a complete response (CR) rate of 46–56%, but median survival is only 15 months for CR patients and 6.5 months for all patients. No significant differences are observed in response rate, response duration or survival when low-dose m-BACOD is randomly compared with standard-dose m-BACOD, in phase III trials. Only 27% of CR patients receiving low-dose therapy and 24% receiving standard-dose therapy survive more than 1 year.[18]

Studies conducted in the pre-HAART era demonstrated that a subset of patients with HIV-NHL is able to tolerate aggressive chemotherapy and appears to do reasonably well in terms of lymphoma-free survival.[7] The use of a continuous infusion of cyclophosphamide-doxorubicin and etoposide (CDE) plus didanosine results in a CR rate of 53% and a median survival of 18 months. However, in the pre-HAART era these encouraging results were associated with a significant and sustained reduction in the CD4 cell count and a twofold increase in the risk of OIs after chemotherapy.[19]

HIV-ASSOCIATED NON-HODGKIN'S LYMPHOMA	
Unfavorable prognostic factors for survival	
Major	CD4$^+$ lymphocyte count <100/μl* Previous AIDS diagnosis Low performance status
Minor	Bone marrow involvement Extranodal disease No response to therapy 'B' symptoms Immunoblastic lymphoma Age ≥40 years Increased lactate dehydrogenase concentration

Table 130.3 HIV-associated non-Hodgkin's lymphoma. *<200/μl in some series.

Preliminary studies show that combination therapy with cyclophosphamide-doxorubicin-vincristine and prednisone chemotherapy (CHOP) and HAART is feasible in HIV-NHL patients.[20,21] Overall response rate as well as duration response and survival may be favorably affected by the use of HAART along with chemotherapy and future trials should be designed to address this issue.

In conclusion, our recommendations are to give standard-dose chemotherapy regimens (like CHOP or CDE) to low- or good-risk category patients and conservative chemotherapy regimens (i.e. single drug or low-dose CHOP-like regimens) to high- or poor-risk patients.

PROGNOSIS

NHL is significantly associated with a worse prognosis than many other complications of AIDS. Nevertheless, some prognostic factors for survival have been identified (Table 130.3). The classic prognostic criteria of the general population (i.e. age, performance status, stage, extranodal involvement) have to be supplemented by host prognostic criteria in the HIV setting, namely low CD4$^+$ lymphocyte count (<100/μl) and a previous AIDS diagnosis, both of which reflect the underlying immunodeficiency. Patients with a low CD4$^+$ lymphocyte count and a previous AIDS diagnosis have a median survival of 3 months, whereas patients without these adverse prognostic features have a median survival of 12 months.[7]

There is some evidence from single institution cohorts that median survival of HIV-NHL patients is improving and is at least three times longer in the HAART than in the pre-HAART era.[5–6]

HUMAN PAPILLOMAVIRUS AS CAUSATIVE AGENT FOR CERVICAL/ANAL CANCER

An association between HIV infection and human papillomavirus (HPV)-related anogenital neoplasia has recently been recognized. The overall risk of all HPV-associated cancers and their in situ precursor lesions in both women and men is elevated across all HIV exposure risk categories.[1,2] Risk factors include multiple sexual partners, cigarette smoking and sexually transmitted disease, particularly HPV.

Viral sequences are found in more than 99% of cervical squamous cell carcinomas and in most anal cancers, with HPV type 16 present in 50% and types 18, 31 and 45 in another 30%. High-grade intraepithelial neoplasia precursor lesions have similarly high rates of the same HPV types. At the molecular level, HPV-associated oncogenesis appears to result from upregulated expression of viral-encoded transforming proteins, including E6 and E7. These proteins interact with and inactivate the products of host cell tumor suppressor genes, including retinoblastoma and p53. This process results in unregulated progression through the cell cycle, insufficient DNA repair and, eventually, transformation to a malignant phenotype.[22]

HIV appears to accelerate the pathogenesis of anogenital cancers at the molecular level although clinical evidence of disease progression is limited. HIV-infected lymphocytes, monocytes and macrophages can be detected in cervical and anal epithelium, and *in vitro* studies suggest the HIV-encoded Tat protein may enhance the expression of HPV E6 and E7 transforming proteins.[23]

The degree of HIV-related immunosuppression appears to be related to the occurrence and the severity of the anogenital neoplasia.

A direct effect of HAART on HPV infections and associated lesions seems unlikely.[23] Screening programs associated with local therapy of early lesions have dramatically reduced the incidence of cervical cancer among HIV-negative women and may have the potential to reduce anal cancer as well. Preventive and therapeutic approaches, i.e. HPV vaccines, need to be urgently evaluated by prospective studies in HIV-infected patients.

REFERENCES

1. Goedert JJ, Cotè TR, Virgo P, *et al.* Spectrum of AIDS-associated malignant disorders. Lancet 1998;351:1833–9.
2. Dal Maso L, Serraino D, Franceschi S. Epidemiology of AIDS-related tumors in developed and developing countries. Eur J Cancer 2001;37:1188–201.
3. International Collaboration on HIV and Cancer. Highly active antiretroviral therapy and incidence of cancer in human immunodeficiency virus-infected adults. J Natl Cancer Inst 2000;92:1823–30.
4. Grulich AE, Li Y, McDonald AM, *et al.* Decreasing rates of Kaposi's sarcoma and non-Hodgkin's lymphoma in the era of potent combination anti-retroviral therapy. AIDS 2001;15:629–33.
5. Besson C, Goubar A, Gabarre J, *et al.* Changes in AIDS-related lymphoma since the era of highly active antiretroviral therapy. Blood 2001;98:2339–44.
6. Kirk O, Pedersen C, Cozzi-Lepri A, *et al.* Non-Hodgkin's lymphoma in HIV-infected patients in the era of highly active antiretroviral therapy. Blood 2001;98:3406–12.
7. Tirelli U, Spina M, Gaidano G, *et al.* Epidemiology, biological and clinical feature of HIV-related lymphomas in the era of highly active antiretroviral therapy. AIDS 2000;14:1675–88.
8. Chang Y, Cesarman E, Pessin MS. Identification of herpesvirus-like DNA sequences in AIDS-associated Kaposi's sarcoma. Science 1994;266:1865–9.
9. Cannon M, Cesarman E. Kaposi's sarcoma-associated herpes virus and acquired immunodeficiency syndrome-related malignancy. Semin Oncol 2000;27:409–19.
10. Ensoli B, Sgadari C, Barillari G, *et al.* Biology of Kaposi's sarcoma. Eur J Cancer 2001;37:1251–69.
11. Krown SE, Metroka C, Wernz JC, *et al.* Kaposi's sarcoma in the acquired immunodeficiency syndrome: a proposal for uniform evaluation response, and staging criteria. J Clin Oncol 1989;7:1201–7.
12. Levine AM, Tulpule A. Clinical aspects and management of AIDS-related Kaposi's sarcoma. Eur J Cancer 2001;37:1288–95.
13. Lebbe C, Blum L, Pellet C, *et al.* Clinical and biological impact of antiretroviral therapy with protease inhibitors on HIV related Kaposi's sarcoma. AIDS 1998;12:F45–F49.
14. Sgadari C, Barillari G, Toschi E, *et al.* HIV protease inhibitors are potent anti-angiogenic molecules and promote regression of Kaposi's sarcoma. Nature Med 2002;8:225–32.
15. Gill PS, Wernz J, Scadden DT, *et al.* Randomised phase III trial of liposomal daunorubicin (DaunoXome) versus doxorubicin, bleomycin, vincristine (ABV) in AIDS-related Kaposi's sarcoma. J Clin Oncol 1996;14:2353–64.
16. Northfelt DW, Dezube B, Thommes JA, *et al.* Pegylated liposomial doxorubicin versus doxorubicin, bleomycin, and vincristine in the treatment of AIDS-related Kaposi's sarcoma: results of a randomized phase III clinical trial. J Clin Oncol 1998;16:2445–51.
17. Carbone A, Gloghini A, Capello D, Gaidano G. Genetic pathways and histogenetic models of AIDS-related lymphomas. Eur J Cancer 2001;37:1270–5.
18. Kaplan LD, Straus DJ, Testa MA, *et al.* Low-dose compared with standard-dose m-BACOD chemotherapy for non-Hodgkin's lymphoma associated with human immunodeficiency virus infection. N Engl J Med 1997;336:1641–8.
19. Sparano JA, Wiernik PH, Hu X, *et al.* A pilot trial of infusional cyclophosphamide, doxorubicin and etoposide plus didanosine and filgrastim in patients with HIV-associated non-Hodgkin's lymphoma. J Clin Oncol 1996;14:3026–35.
20. Vaccher E, Spina M, di Gennaro G, *et al.* Concomitant CHOP chemotherapy and highly active antiretroviral therapy (HAART) in patients with HIV-related non-Hodgkin's lymphoma. Cancer 2001;91:155–63.
21. Ratner L, Lee J, Tang, *et al.* Chemotherapy for human immunodeficiency virus-associated non-Hodgkin's lymphoma in combination with highly active antiretroviral therapy. J Clin Oncol 2001;19:2171–8.
22. Del Mistro A, Chieco Bianchi L. HPV-related neoplasias in HIV-infected individuals. Eur J Cancer 2001;37:1227–35.
23. Vernon S, Hart CE, Reeves WC, *et al.* The HIV-1 Tat protein enhances E2-dependent human papillomavirus 16 transcription. Virus Res 1993;27:133–45.

chapter 131

HIV-associated Wasting and Nutrition

Nicholas IJ Paton & George Griffin

EPIDEMIOLOGY

Before the advent of highly active antiretroviral therapy (HAART), wasting syndrome (defined as loss of more than 10% of body weight together with fever or diarrhea for more than 30 days) was present in about 10% of patients at the time of AIDS diagnosis[1] and occurred in the majority of patients at some stage before death. Although the introduction of HAART has decreased the incidence of opportunistic infections and associated wasting, wasting still remains a common problem in clinical practice.[2]

PATHOGENESIS AND PATHOLOGY

Basal metabolic rate is generally increased at all stages of HIV infection, particularly during opportunistic infections, but this is offset by reductions in physical activity and total energy requirements are therefore normal or reduced.[3] The key etiologic factor in wasting is therefore a reduction in energy intake. The numerous causes include nausea, taste disturbances, dysphagia, early satiety, depression and dementia. Profound anorexia mediated by cytokine release accompanies acute opportunistic infections and results in rapid weight loss (Fig. 131.1).

WEIGHT LOSS ASSOCIATED WITH OPPORTUNISTIC INFECTIONS

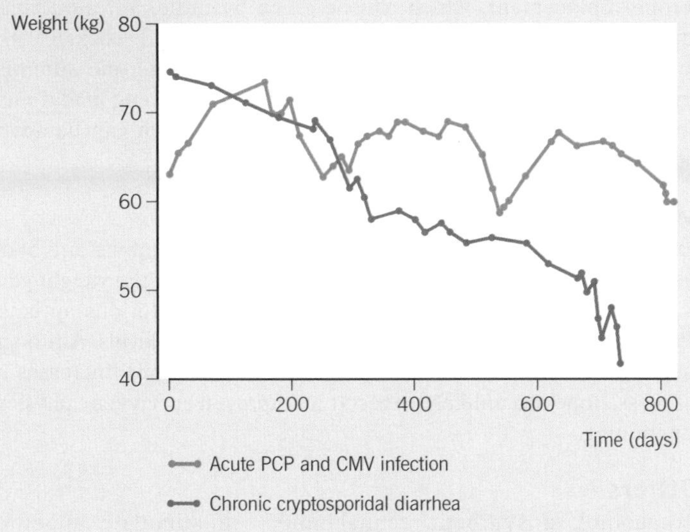

Fig. 131.1 Weight loss associated with opportunistic infections. Weight chart of one patient who had episodes of rapid weight loss and partial recovery coinciding with episodes of acute opportunistic infection – *Pneumocystis carinii* pneumonia (PCP) and cytomegalovirus (CMV) – and one patient who had chronic progressive weight loss associated with cryptosporidial diarrhea. Reproduced with permission by the American Journal of Clinical Nutrition © Am L Clin Nutr. American Society for Clinical Nutrition.

Malabsorption is common in AIDS and can be idiopathic (HIV enteropathy) or secondary to gastrointestinal pathogens, especially protozoa. Although malabsorption alone rarely leads to significant weight loss, it may exacerbate the energy intake deficit when combined with other factors. Furthermore, the associated diarrhea may cause a voluntary reduction in food intake in an attempt to minimize symptoms. Chronic gastrointestinal disease often results in a pattern of progressive weight loss (see Fig. 131.1).

HIV infection is accompanied by disturbances in intermediary metabolism, but these are not necessarily of importance in determining the quantity or quality of tissue that is lost. However, hypogonadism is common and may result in preferential lean tissue depletion.

PREVENTION

Patients should be weighed regularly on the same set of scales and the results should be displayed graphically in the medical notes. Assessment at regular intervals by a dietitian is recommended for all patients who have HIV infection. Such reviews should reinforce the need to maintain adequate energy and protein intake to prevent wasting and may correct misconceptions about what constitutes a healthy diet. Regular physical exercise should be encouraged and will assist in maintaining muscle mass.

CLINICAL FEATURES

Clinical assessment of HIV-associated wasting is directed at confirming the diagnosis of malnutrition, estimating severity and also identifying any underlying cause.

Nutritional state can be assessed in several ways. Comparison of body weight with pre-illness weight or ideal weight (determined from standard tables) is the simplest method. A reduction of 10% indicates significant wasting; a loss of over 35% is associated with a grave prognosis. Calculation of body mass index (BMI) can also be used to grade the severity of malnutrition:

$$\text{BMI} = \frac{\text{weight in kg}}{\text{height in m}^2}$$

Severity of malnutrition is graded as follows:

- grade I, <18.5kg/m²;
- grade II, <17kg/m²; and
- grade III, <16kg/m².

Grade III malnutrition is regarded as life-threatening. Measurement of mid-upper-arm circumference or estimation of body cell mass by bioelectrical impedance analysis (BIA) may be more sensitive than body weight or BMI in detecting early malnutrition and provide an additional estimate of severity in advanced wasting. Although single measurements of body weight, BMI, mid-upper-arm circumference and BIA are of some use, serial assessment gives a better indication of nutritional status and the urgency for treatment.

Complications of malnutrition include decubitus ulcers, hypothermia, amenorrhea in women and further propensity to develop infections. Patients may die from severe wasting alone without other specific complications of HIV disease.[4]

As well as confirming the presence and estimating the severity of wasting, the history and examination should be directed at identifying potential causes. Specific inquiry should be made about anorexia, taste disturbances, dysphagia, odynophagia, nausea, vomiting, abdominal pain, diarrhea and symptoms of depression. Examination may help to distinguish HIV-associated wasting from the lipodystrophy syndrome that occurs as a complication of antiretroviral therapy. Loss of fat from the face and limbs may initially suggest a diagnosis of HIV-associated wasting, but in the lipodystrophy syndrome muscle mass is preserved and truncal fat mass is usually maintained or increased, so that there is minimal change in overall body weight.

DIAGNOSIS

The purpose of laboratory investigations is to determine the cause of wasting. The choice of tests is influenced by the clinical features but investigations usually include:

- hematology – a full blood count, which may show anemia due to malabsorption;
- biochemistry – low serum albumin accompanies malnutrition and low serum testosterone indicates hypogonadism;
- microbiology – blood should be cultured and at least three stool samples should be assessed;
- virology – serial HIV viral load and $CD4^+$ lymphocyte count estimates may indicate accelerated viral replication;
- radiology – a plain chest radiogram may reveal lymphoma, tuberculosis or subclinical *Pneumocystis carinii* pneumonia, and an abdominal ultrasound may reveal lymphadenopathy (mycobacterial infection or lymphoma), hepatic lesions or abscess; and
- other investigations include an upper gastrointestinal endoscopy with small bowel biopsy or colonoscopy and biopsy.

MANAGEMENT

The aim is to increase lean body mass and so improve quality of life and physical functioning and increase survival. The initial step is to identify and remove any underlying causes for the wasting. Nausea and vomiting should be managed aggressively. Treatment and recovery from acute opportunistic infection is often accompanied by a repletion of body weight (see Fig. 131.1)[5] and lean tissue. Reduction of viral load by effective antiretroviral therapy may sometimes be followed by substantial weight gain, although lean tissue may not be restored fully. For patients who remain malnourished, dietary counseling, nutritional therapies and progressive resistance exercise should be tried in the first instance. Hypogonadal patients should have testosterone replacement. If these steps are unsuccessful, additional pharmacologic therapies may be indicated. Management should be tailored to the individual patient.

NUTRITIONAL THERAPIES AND EXERCISE

High-energy oral nutritional supplements

A valuable increase in total energy intake can be achieved by nutritional supplements, although some patients find them unpalatable or develop 'taste fatigue'.

Nasogastric feeding

Patients who have mechanical difficulties in swallowing or severe anorexia may benefit from feeding through a fine-bore nasogastric tube. This approach has the benefit of allowing nocturnal feeding. Although sometimes well tolerated for short periods of time, a nasogastric tube can be uncomfortable and distressing.

Percutaneous endoscopic gastrotomy tube feeding

Insertion of a percutaneous endoscopic gastrotomy tube is a straightforward procedure performed under local anesthetic. Percutaneous endoscopic gastrotomy feeding can produce dramatic increases in body weight in selected patients who have HIV disease, and serious complications are infrequent. However, preexisting diarrhea may be exacerbated, and therefore an initial trial of nasogastric feeding is recommended.

Total parenteral nutrition

A controlled trial in malnourished AIDS patients demonstrated that total parenteral nutrition significantly increased body weight and lean tissue when compared with dietary counseling.[6] However, it is a complex and expensive treatment that should only be considered when enteral nutrition has failed. The duration of therapy should be clearly defined at the outset because the decision to stop is often difficult.

Progressive resistance exercise

A supervised training program of progressive resistance exercise can increase lean body mass and may have other health benefits such as increasing high-density lipoprotein (HDL) cholesterol.[7]

PHARMACOLOGIC THERAPIES

Growth hormone

Recombinant human growth hormone at a dose of 0.1mg (0.3 units)/kg q24h increases lean body mass and exercise capacity in patients who have HIV-associated wasting.[8] Although effective, widespread use of growth hormone is limited by its cost. A short course of growth hormone may prevent the loss of lean tissue accompanying opportunistic infection, although further data is needed on this approach and growth hormone should not be used in critically ill HIV patients.[9]

Testosterone

Hypogonadal HIV-positive men may benefit from physiologic testosterone replacement, which can be given by either intramuscular injection (e.g. testosterone enanthate 300mg every 3 weeks)[10] or a cutaneous patch. Supraphysiologic doses of testosterone administered for a few months increase lean body mass in eugonadal men but more safety data is needed before this approach can be advocated for longer term use.[7]

Megestrol acetate

At a dose of 800mg q24h, megestrol increases food intake and body weight in patients who have HIV infection, although the weight gain is predominantly fat.[11] This drug may have a deleterious antianabolic action mediated by decreases in testosterone levels. Although megestrol may be of use for the palliation of anorexia, increases in fat mass alone are unlikely to result in improved survival or physical functioning.

Others

Dronabinol, a synthetic cannabinoid, can stimulate appetite, although sedation and psychotropic symptoms are common. Anabolic steroids that have greater anabolic activity than testosterone are potentially useful in HIV disease, although there is insufficient data from controlled clinical trials to recommend their use and there are concerns over safety (especially in patients who have concomitant hepatic disease). Thalidomide can increase body weight, although drug tolerability (rash and fever) limit its use and treatment is associated with an increase in viral load.[12]

REFERENCES

1. Nahlen BL, Chu SY, Nwanyanwu OC, *et al.* HIV wasting syndrome in the United States. AIDS 1993;7:183–8.
2. Wanke CA, Silva M, Knox T, *et al.* Weight loss and wasting remain common complications in individuals infected with human immunodeficiency virus in the era of highly active antiretroviral therapy. Clin Infect Dis 2000;31:803–5.
3. Macallan DC, Noble C, Baldwin C, *et al.* Energy expenditure and wasting in human immunodeficiency virus infection. N Engl J Med 1995;333:83–8.
4. Kotler DP, Tierney AR, Wang J, *et al.* Magnitude of body-cell-mass depletion and the timing of death from wasting in AIDS. Am J Clin Nutr 1989;50:444–7.
5. Macallan DC, Noble C, Baldwin C, *et al.* Prospective analysis of patterns of weight change in stage IV human immunodeficiency virus infection. Am J Clin Nutr 1993;58:417–24.
6. Melchior J-C, Chastang C, Gelas P, *et al.* Efficacy of 2-month total parenteral nutrition in AIDS patients: a controlled randomised prospective trial. AIDS 1996;10:379–84.
7. Grinspoon S, Corcoran C, Parlman K, *et al.* Effects of testosterone and progressive resistance training in eugonadal men with AIDS wasting. A randomised, controlled trial. Ann Intern Med 2000;133:348–355.
8. Schambelan M, Mulligan K, Grunfeld C, *et al.* Recombinant human growth hormone in patients with HIV-associated wasting. A randomised, placebo-controlled trial. Ann Intern Med 1997;125:873–82.
9. Paton NI, Newton PJ, Sharpstone DR *et al.* Short term growth hormone administration at the time of opportunistic infections in HIV-positive patients. AIDS 1999;13:1195–202.
10. Grinspoon S, Corcoran C, Askari H, *et al.* Effects of androgen administration in men with the AIDS wasting syndrome. A randomised, double-blind, placebo-controlled trial. Ann Intern Med 1998;129:18–26.
11. Oster MH, Enders SR, Samuels SJ, *et al.* Megestrol acetate in patients with AIDS and cachexia. Ann Intern Med 1994;121:400–8.
12. Kaplan G, Thomas S, Fierer DS *et al.* Thalidomide for the treatment of AIDS-associated wasting. AIDS Res Hum Retroviruses 2000;16:1345–55.

chapter 132

Dermatologic Manifestations of HIV Infection

Grace T Kho, Chris Bandel & Clay J Cockerell

INTRODUCTION

The skin is commonly affected in patients who have HIV infection and AIDS. Because it is the organ most readily evaluated by inspection it is essential that the clinicians become proficient in the recognition of skin disorders that herald the presence of HIV disease.[1] The prevalence of cutaneous involvement approaches 100% and in many cases is the motivating force that causes the patient to seek medical care.

To the alert physician, dermatologic manifestations of HIV infection may provide the initial diagnostic clues, not only of the presence of the infection per se but also in some cases the stage of involvement.[2] Early-stage disease (CD4 count 200–500/mm^3) can be associated with seborrheic dermatitis, oral hairy leukoplakia (OHL), Kaposi's Sarcoma (KS), oropharyngeal or recurrent vulvovaginal candidiasis, herpes zoster or recurrent herpes simplex virus (HSV) infection. With a CD4 count of 50–200/mm^3, bacillary angiomatosis, esophageal candidiasis, disseminated deep fungal infections, molluscum contagiosum, chronic herpetic ulcers and eosinophilic folliculitis become more prominent. With advanced HIV disease (CD4 <50/mm^3), profound immunosuppression may lead to the occurrence of several co-existing infections and neoplasms. In general, skin infections and neoplastic conditions in patients who have AIDS are aggressive and difficult to treat. Early recognition of the different skin diseases will facilitate the use of a pertinent therapeutic approach.

With the introduction of highly active antiretroviral therapy (HAART) in the mid 1990s, changes in the dermatologic manifestations paralleled the stabilization and improvement in CD4 counts.[3,4] Significant decreases in the incidence of KS, OHL, oral candidiasis, bacterial folliculitis, recurrent HSV and, to a lesser degree, seborrheic dermatitis, psoriasis, drug eruptions, dry skin and pruritus were noted. Conversely, conditions such as warts of all kinds, scabies, photosensitivity and eosinophilic folliculitis did not abate significantly and, in some cases, increased in incidence. Adverse drug reactions improved or worsened with different drugs and individuals. Some entities, such as molluscum contagiosum, became less prevalent in some series and more in others, reflecting varying influences such as immune restoration, altered cytokine patterns and improved lifestyle and increased exposure. As CD4 counts normalize with HAART therapy, many of the skin disorders affecting HIV-infected patients become similar to those seen in immunocompetent patients.

Modifying the influences of HAART therapy is the fact that fewer than 10% of the globally infected individuals have access to the therapy, which remains expensive. Resistant cases are also encountered. Thus, it behoves the clinician to remain knowledgeable about the skin conditions particular to HIV-infected patients.[5]

This chapter describes the most common dermatologic manifestations of HIV infection, including skin changes present early in infection and in advanced disease, such as neoplastic, infectious and noninfectious conditions, hair, nail and oral changes and drug reactions.

EARLY DERMATOLOGIC MANIFESTATIONS OF HIV INFECTION: ACUTE EXANTHEM OF HIV INFECTION

The acute exanthem, which is symptomatic in about 80% of patients, begins 1–5 weeks after exposure to the virus and is associated with prodromal symptoms such as lymphadenopathy, fatigue, fever and night sweats. The skin eruption consists of erythematous, round to oval macules and papules affecting the trunk, chest, back and upper back (Fig. 132.1). The syndrome generally lasts for 4–5 days and resolves with complete recovery.[6] Rarely, a severe form of acute HIV infection can evolve, characterized by recurrent viremia, rapid decline in CD4$^+$ cell numbers and an accelerated disease course. Pneumonitis, esophagitis, meningitis, abdominal pain and melena are the most common systemic manifestations and are often accompanied by urticaria, palatal ulceration, candidiasis and herpesvirus infections. The prognosis for patients who have the severe form of acute HIV infection is poorer than for those who are asymptomatic or have mild symptoms (see Chapter 122).[6]

NON-NEOPLASTIC INFECTIOUS DERMATOLOGIC CONDITIONS

Patients who have HIV infection may present with a broad array of infectious processes, some of which are characteristic of AIDS. Because of immunosuppression these infectious processes may exhibit more aggressive behavior than is usually expected in immunocompetent individuals.

Viral infections

Herpes simplex virus

Infections with HSV types 1 and 2 result in recurrent, severe painful grouped vesicles with an erythematous base localized mainly on the lips, genital and perianal areas. If untreated these lesions may enlarge and become confluent ulcerations that may persist for over 1 month, displaying slow healing and often becoming secondarily infected with bacteria. It is essential to establish the specific diagnosis by means of a biopsy and/or viral cultures. Sometimes, ulceration takes place without well-defined vesicles ever being noted.[7] While the immune system is intact, the course of the disease is similar to that in noninfected individuals. Once immunosuppression sets in, the lesions become persistent. Ulcers can expand and reach large size. Periungual infection is also a manifestation. Culture of tissue can be positive even if a swab is negative. An aggressive therapeutic approach should be used with these patients, as they may be poorly responsive to the standard treatment. Oral aciclovir in doses of up to 400mg five times a day for 10 days should be used. In severe cases hospitalization for administration of high-dose intravenous aciclovir may be required.[8] Foscarnet is recommended in patients in whom aciclovir resistance is suspected (see also Chapter 125).

Fig. 132.1 Acute exanthem of HIV infection. There is morbilliform eruption involving the trunk and extremities. The eruption is similar to a morbilliform drug eruption and to other viral exanthemata.

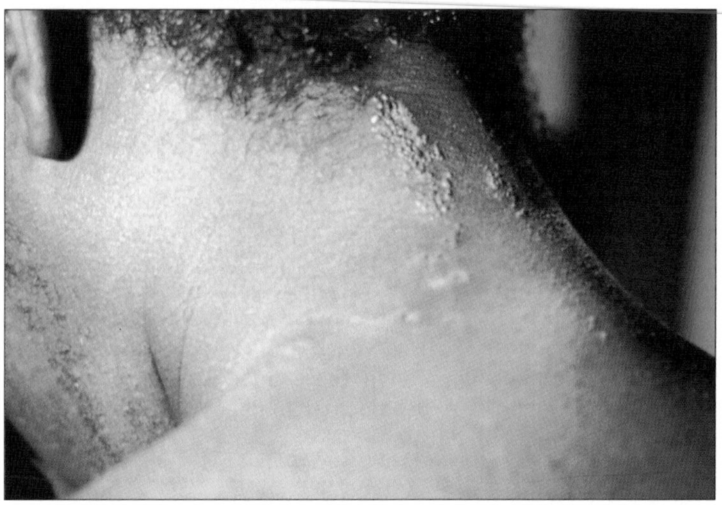

Fig. 132.2 Herpes zoster. A painful linear-zosteriform eruption of vesicles on an erythematous base is characteristic of herpes zoster. The eruption may be persistent and verrucous lesions are not uncommon.

Varicella-zoster virus

The development of recrudescent varicella-zoster virus (VZV) infection in a patient at risk of HIV infection may be a sign of the presence of HIV and should alert the clinician to screen the patient.[9] It usually occurs early in the course of the disease and precedes thrush and hairy leukoplakia by about a year. Varicella-zoster virus exists in a dormant state in a dorsal root ganglion that becomes infected during prior varicella infection. With reactivation, the virus progresses downward through the nerve tracts of a solitary dermatome, leading to the characteristic zosteriform distribution of painful tense vesicles of skin (Fig. 132.2). In individuals who have HIV infection, the infection may be recurrent, severe, with more than one dermatome involved, and may run a protracted course associated with residual postherpetic neuralgia and scarring. Disseminated herpes-zoster is not as common but may be more common in HIV-infected individuals. Chronic lesions can be verrucous or ecthymatous. Chickenpox can develop in previously unexposed individuals with HIV infection. The infection can be

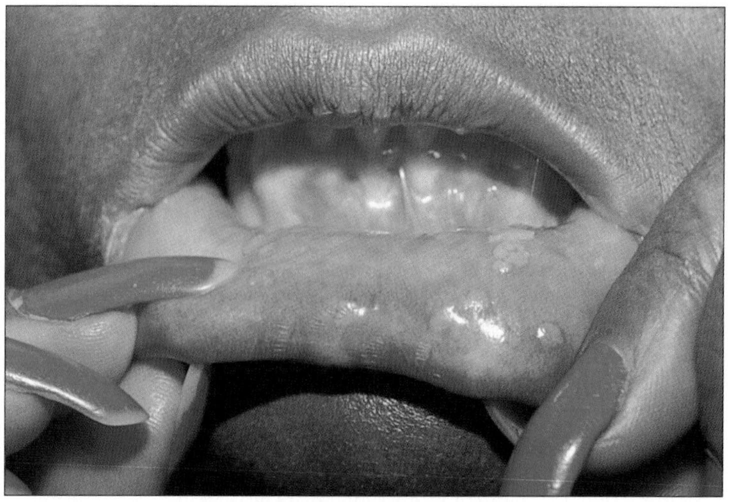

Fig. 132.3 Human papillomavirus infection. Human papillomavirus infections are common in HIV-infected patients. They may have unusual features, as demonstrated here, and may be refractory to therapy.

more severe, cause visceral disease and be fatal. Large doses of aciclovir (up to 800mg q4h) are used to treat these patients and often systemic administration is necessary.

Cytomegalovirus

Cytomegalovirus (CMV) is the most common cause of serious opportunistic viral infection in patients who have AIDS.[10] However, cutaneous involvement is rare. In the skin, CMV has different clinical manifestations, including ulcerations, keratotic verrucous lesions and palpable purpuric papules. Because the mucocutaneous lesions caused by CMV do not have specific features, tissue biopsy of the lesions, as well as immunoglobulin titers (IgG and IgM) and viral cultures, are required to define the etiologic cause. The treatment of choice for CMV infection is intravenous ganciclovir. Foscarnet should be used if ganciclovir resistance is suspected.

Epstein–Barr virus

The majority of adults harbor the Epstein–Barr virus (EBV) in the latent phase. With advanced immunodeficiency seen in HIV-infected patients, EBV replication occurs, leading to OHL or EBV-associated large cell lymphoma. Oral hairy leukoplakia manifests as single or multiple white plaques on the lateral margins of the tongue, with a verrucous surface. The presence of oral leukoplakia correlates with moderate to advanced immunodeficiency and has also been correlated with progression from HIV infection to AIDS.[11] Oral hairy leukoplakia responds well to systemically administered aciclovir, although there is prompt recurrence after treatment. Good response to topical application of podophyllin has also been reported.[12] In some patients, OHL may regress with highly active antiviral therapy alone.

Human papillomavirus

Different types of human papillomavirus (HPV) tend to cause different clinical lesions, although there is significant overlap. Infections of the skin and mucous membranes by HPV can cause widespread warts in patients who have AIDS. Types of warts observed include filiform, flat and plantar. Warts can develop in unusual locations, such as on the lips, tongue and oral mucosa (Fig. 132.3). These lesions are often treated with cryotherapy, electrocauterization or topical treatment with caustic agents such as podophyllin. However, the majority of these lesions are resistant to treatment and should be treated repeatedly. In men, HPV affects the penis, urethra, scrotum, perianal, anal and rectal mucosa in the form of condylo-

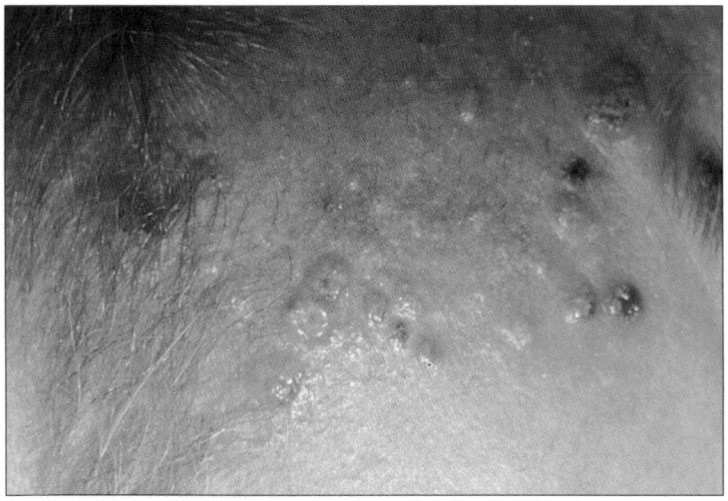

Fig. 132.4 Molluscum contagiosum. These lesions are characteristically translucent, waxy papules with central umbilication.

mata acuminata that are usually recognized as soft sessile lesions with finger-like projections. In women, the spectrum of clinical disease induced by HPV is broad with vulvar, vaginal and cervical condylomata being observed. Other clinical presentations of HPV infection include bowenoid papulosis and epidermodysplasia verruciformis. The former manifests as small, brown, flat-topped papules affecting the perianal and genital areas in both sexes, but is more common in men. The latter consists of a widespread papular eruption of pink-red, flat, wart-like lesions distributed mostly on sun-exposed areas of the skin.[13]

Infection with HPV may cause development of carcinoma, especially in HIV-infected hosts.[14] The most common of these are cervical intraepithelial neoplasia in women and squamous cell carcinoma in men. As with zoster, whenever extensive warts develop in otherwise healthy patients known to be at risk of HIV infection, the patient should be screened for the infection.

Poxvirus

The most common disease caused by poxviruses is molluscum contagiosum, which develops in 10–20% of patients who have AIDS. Molluscum contagiosum is characterized by dome-shaped umbilicated translucent 2–4mm papules that develop in any part of the body but especially the face and genital areas (Fig. 132.4). In AIDS patients these lesions are widespread and may attain immense size.[15] Most patients who have extensive molluscum contagiosum associated with HIV infection have $CD4^+$ counts well below 250 cells/ml. In immunosuppressed patients the diagnosis of molluscum contagiosum should be confirmed by histologic examination in any case that is questionable because this may simulate more serious infections such as cutaneous pneumocystosis, histoplasmosis and *Penicillium marneffei* infection and cryptococcosis. Molluscum contagiosum is treated with cryotherapy, electrodesiccation, curettage or topical application of keratolytic preparations.

Other viral infections

Several viral infections have been reported to develop with increased frequency in patients who have HIV infection. Parvovirus B19, which causes erythema infectiosum, has been reported to produce an exanthem and polyarthralgia in HIV-positive patients. Coxsackie virus and enterovirus may also lead to morbilliform or vesicular eruptions. Measles occur sporadically in nonimmune patients who have AIDS. When associated with encephalitis and pneumonitis, measles can be fatal. Treatment with intravenous ribavirin and gammaglobulin has been used successfully in some patients.

Bacterial infections

Folliculitis

Bacterial folliculitis is common in HIV-infected patients, appearing as widely distributed acneiform papules and pustules. Lesions may be pruritic and become excoriated. Most cases are caused by *Staphylococcus aureus*,[16] but other organisms such as *Staphylococcus epidermidis* and *Pseudomonas aeruginosa* may also cause folliculitis. Bacterial folliculitis in HIV-infected patients is often resistant to standard treatment and prolonged use of systemic antibiotics may be required.[17] Recurrent bacterial folliculitis may serve as a clue to screen a patient for possible HIV infection.

Impetigo, abscesses, cellulitis, lymphadenitis and necrotizing fasciitis

Impetigo, usually caused by *S. aureus*, is seen most commonly on the face, shoulders, axillary and inguinal areas. The infection begins with painful red macules that become vesicles and pustules and contain purulent fluid; these soon rupture and give rise to the characteristic honey-colored crust. Soft tissue and deep-seated bacterial infections such as cellulitis, abscesses and necrotizing fasciitis may also develop in HIV-infected patients. These manifest as diffuse, red, warm, tender areas in the skin, associated with severe toxemia. Streptococcal axillary lymphadenitis is a diffuse, painful swelling of lymph nodes in the axilla that is usually bilateral. Aggressive antibiotic treatment is recommended for these processes.

Mycobacterial infections

Mycobacteria may produce a wide variety of skin lesions in HIV-infected individuals and infection by these organisms usually signifies severe disseminated systemic infection. Active infection is caused primarily by *Mycobacterium avium-intracellulare* and *M. tuberculosis* and less commonly by *M. kansaii, M. haemophilum, M. genavense, M. marinarum* and *M. leprae*. The infection can manifest as small papules and pustules resembling folliculitis, atopic dermatitis-like eruptions, cutaneous abscesses, lymphadenitis and ulcerations. Culture and tissue biopsy are required for specific diagnosis of the infection. *Mycobacterium haemophilum*, where the only manifestation of infection may be a single or multiple skin lesions, must be cultured at room temperature and with a source of iron in the media.

Bacillary angiomatosis

Bacillary angiomatosis (BA) is a pseudoneoplastic, infectious cutaneous vascular disorder[18] caused by bacteria of the genus *Bartonella*, including *Bartonella quintana* and *Bartonella henselae*.[19] There are a number of clinical manifestations of BA. The earliest and most common lesion appears as discrete pinpoint red–purple papules similar to pyogenic granulomata. These lesions may ulcerate and become crusted (Fig. 132.5). Another variant consists of subcutaneous nodules that may extend into the underlying skeletal muscle and bone. Patients who have BA may have systemic signs and symptoms, including fever, chills, night sweats and weight loss. In advanced cases, the liver and spleen may be involved. Bacillary angiomatosis occurs primarily in the context of the advanced stage of HIV infection, but may occur in patients who have other forms of immunosuppression or in a healthy host. Because the clinical presentation of this infection can easily be confused with pyogenic granuloma, biopsy should be performed. Bacillary angiomatosis responds to treatment with macrolide antibiotics such as erythromycin, clarithromycin and azithromycin or doxycycline. Recurrence is common.

Sexually transmitted disease

The accurate diagnosis of sexually transmitted diseases (STDs) is of exceptional importance in individuals at high risk of HIV infection,

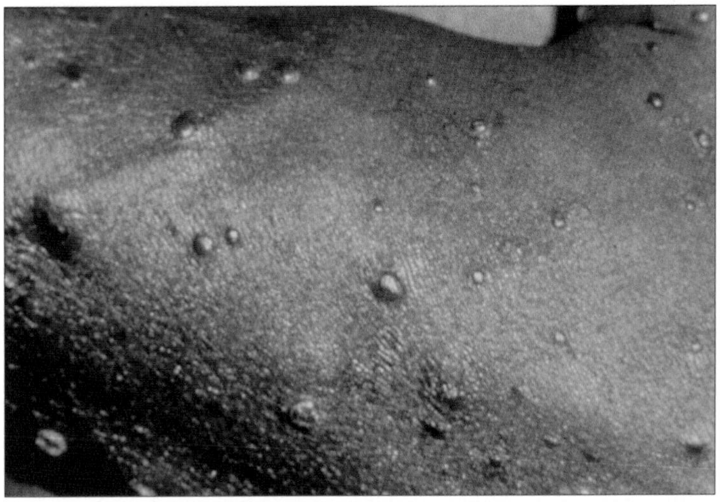

Fig. 132.5 Bacillary angiomatosis. There are elevated vascular papules of the glabrous skin. When incised, these lesions bleed profusely.

because their presence increases the risk of transmitting and acquiring HIV infection. Studies have demonstrated that, in some populations, the pattern of HIV acquisition parallels that of STD.[20]

Syphilis

A high prevalence of syphilis, active as well as latent, has been found among AIDS patients in the USA.[20] In HIV-infected patients, the primary infection with *Treponema pallidum* does not show major variations. Secondary syphilis may occur in a number of forms in patients who have HIV infection, ranging from the classic papulosquamous form with involvement of palms, soles and mucous membranes to unusual forms such as verrucous plaques, extensive oral ulcerations, keratoderma, deep cutaneous nodules and widespread gummata. The disease may progress faster from secondary to tertiary syphilis in HIV-seropositive patients than in HIV-seronegative individuals. Early central nervous system (CNS) relapse can also be more common in HIV-infected individuals. Syphilis is a strong indicator that an individual may be infected with HIV and all patients should undergo HIV serotesting. Serologic negativity may not rule out secondary syphilis in HIV-infected individuals as true negative serologic studies can be seen with both the FTA-ab and VDRL tests. Skin biopsies and demonstration of spirochetes may be necessary to establish the diagnosis.

Other sexually transmitted diseases

Although granuloma inguinale is a relatively uncommon STD in the USA and other developed countries, HIV-infected patients may develop this disease. In contrast, this condition is extremely common in Africa. It is caused by the Gram-negative rod *Calymmatobacterium granulomatis* and manifests clinically as vegetating lesions on the penis associated with pseudobuboes in the inguinal crease. Culture and skin biopsy for identification of the safety pin-shaped organisms (Donovan bodies) is required to establish the diagnosis. Lymphogranuloma venereum is uncommon in HIV-infected patients, but it manifests as generalized lymphadenopathy with vulvar or penile edema with ulcerations and erosions. Endemic in Africa, chancroid has become more common in the USA during the past few years. The causative organism is the Gram-negative coccobacillus *Haemophilus ducrei*. The disease manifests clinically as nonhealing ulcers in the genital organs and/or legs.[21]

Fungal infections

Candidiasis

Mucosal candidiasis is a very common finding in immunocompromised patients. Since the beginning of the AIDS epidemic a close

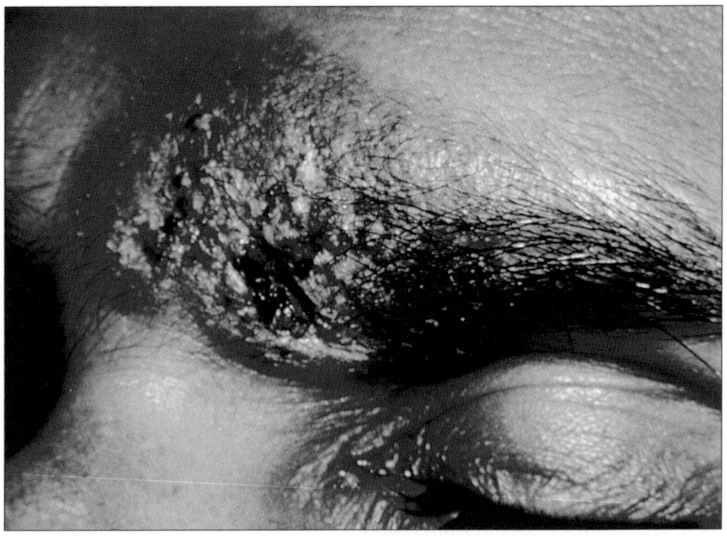

Fig. 132.6 Cutaneous histoplasmosis. These lesions are characteristically quite nondescript and may simulate other infectious disorders and verrucous neoplastic conditions.

relationship between candidiasis and AIDS has been recognized.[21] The clinical presentation is that of a whitish exudate present on the tongue or buccal mucosa that can easily be scraped away. Candidiasis may involve the esophagus and can disseminate to produce candidal septicemia, brain abscesses and meningitis. Oral candidiasis may be the initial sign of HIV infection in many individuals and has been shown to be a predictor of progression from HIV infection to AIDS. Intertrigo as well as acute and chronic paronychia simulate those seen in non-HIV-infected individuals (see Chapter 126).

Dermatophytosis

Cutaneous dermatophytosis is common in HIV infection and can be extensive and severe. Usually feet, toenails and fingernails are affected. Tinea corporis may manifest as extensive widespread involvement of the trunk and extremities. In any individual with extensive tinea corporis the possibility of underlying HIV infection should be considered.

Systemic fungal infections

The most common opportunistic fungal infections to affect the skin in HIV-seropositive patients are histoplasmosis and cryptococcosis. These occur in patients with advanced HIV disease. Cutaneous involvement may be seen with disseminated disease. Blastomycosis and sporotrichosis have also been observed in HIV-seropositive patients but rarely. Mucocutaneous lesions associated with systemic fungal infections consist of pustules, ulcers, papules and nodules (Fig. 132.6). Less often, the infection manifests as patches, plaques and mucosal ulcerations. Mucocutaneous fungal infections in general may mimic other disorders such as HSV infection, cellulitis or molluscum contagiosum infection. For this reason, when the clinical diagnosis of possible fungal infection is considered, a tissue biopsy of the lesion should be performed for histologic evaluation and microbiologic cultures (see also Chapter 126).[22]

Parasitic and ectoparasitic infections

HIV-seropositive individuals may present with a wide variety of parasitic and ectoparasitic infections, including scabies, demodicidosis, acanthamebiasis, leishmaniasis and toxoplasmosis. This group of infections manifest either as localized conditions or disseminated disease. The clinical presentation can be unusual and the use of cultures and skin biopsies is essential to render accurate diagnosis.[23]

Scabies

The causative agent of scabies is the mite *Sarcoptes scabei*. Scabies is one of the most frequent conditions encountered in HIV infection and is the most common ectoparasitic infection.[17] The clinical presentation can vary from discrete scattered pruritic papules and slight scale to a widespread papulosquamous eruption that resembles atopic dermatitis. A common clinical presentation is that of hyperkeratotic plaques present on the palms, soles, trunk and extremities. Patients complain of intense pruritus that is worse at night. Contacts are almost always infected.

Demodicidosis

The causative agent of demodicidosis is the mite *Demodex*. Demodicidosis has been reported only sporadically in patients who have AIDS. The clinical presentation is that of a persistent pruritic follicular eruption of the face, trunk and extremities.

Acanthamebiasis

Acanthamebiasis, caused by *Acanthamoeba castellani*, may be seen in AIDS patients and may have a very aggressive course because of immunosuppression. The clinical presentation is that of painful ulcerated nodules located on the trunk and extremities.

Strongyloidiasis

The helminth *Strongyloides stercoralis* can rarely cause skin disease in HIV patients. Clinically, lesions can manifest as urticaria, figurate erythema and livedo reticularis.[5]

Leishmaniasis

The skin lesions resemble those of kala-azar with scaly lichenified depigmented plaques with lichen simplex chronicus. Nonulcerated nodules on the extensor surfaces of the limbs overlying the joints have also been described. Given the prevalence of HIV infection in the Americas, the incidence of leishmaniasis in these patients is surprisingly low.

Pneumocystosis

Pneumocystis carinii may involve the skin, primarily in patients who use aerosolized pentamidine for prophylaxis of *P. carinii* pneumonia. Most common are friable reddish papules or nodules in the ear canal or nares. Small translucent molluscum contagiosum-like papules, bluish cellulitic plaques and deeply seated abscesses have also been observed.[5]

NONINFECTIOUS DERMATOSES

The noninfectious dermatoses associated with HIV infection are numerous and may occur in all stages of the disease. Although none of the disorders reported in this group has been linked directly to an infectious agent, these conditions may be in part caused by an abnormal host response to infectious agents. Noninfectious dermatoses in these patients may have atypical clinical presentations, greater severity and may fail to respond to routine treatment.[24] Because these dermatoses often have atypical presentations in these patients, biopsies and cultures are often required for diagnosis.

Acquired xerosis and ichthyosis

HIV-infected individuals commonly complain of increased dryness of skin. Typically, xerosis is most prominent on the anterior lower legs. In the winter it is more severe and may be associated with inflammation. Patients who have advanced AIDS may present with ichthyosis – dry, thick skin with plate-like scales. The severity of the ichthyosis correlates with the degree of wasting.

Seborrheic dermatitis

This is perhaps the best known dermatosis associated with HIV infection and is seen in up to 85% of all these individuals at some point during the course of the illness.[25] The etiology of seborrheic dermatitis is poorly understood but is thought to be multifactorial. Clinically, the disease is characterized by slightly indurated, diffuse or confluent pinkish-red plaques with yellowish greasy scales and crusting in typical locations, including malar and retro-auricular areas, nasolabial folds, eyebrows and scalp (Fig. 132.7). In severe cases, which are also more common in HIV-infected patients, it extends to the chest, neck and other parts of the body. Seborrheic dermatitis in patients who have HIV infection is often resistant to treatment, which should serve as a clue that a patient might be infected. With HAART therapy, the incidence of refractory cases appears to be diminishing, however.

Psoriasis

This develops in 5% of individuals with HIV infection[26] and may have a number of different manifestations. It may resemble the classic form found in immunocompetent hosts, which consists of reddish plaques with superficial gray to silver scales on the extensor surfaces and nail changes of onycholysis, pitting and subungual hyperkeratosis. Guttate psoriasis may also be seen, with or without classic psoriasis vulgaris. Severe forms may be encountered, such as erythroderma. Treatment of psoriasis in these patients may be difficult, although fortunately it is one of the inflammatory conditions that responds well to therapy, especially with systemic retinoids, either isotretinoin or etretinate. Psoriasis may undergo partial remission in response to zidovudine therapy, although recurrences are common. Other treatments that may be beneficial include topical keratolytic agents, systemic methotrexate and phototherapy.

Eosinophilic folliculitis

Eosinophilic folliculitis (EF), also known as eosinophilic pustular folliculitis, is an inflammatory process of the hair follicles, the etiology of which remains undetermined, although mites, Gram-negative bacteria and fungi have all been implicated as causative. The condition is more common in men and has a peak incidence in the third decade of life. Affected patients may develop marked eosinophilia and elevated levels of IgE. Virtually all patients who have EF have $CD4^+$ counts below 200 cells/mm^3; thus, it is an important cutaneous

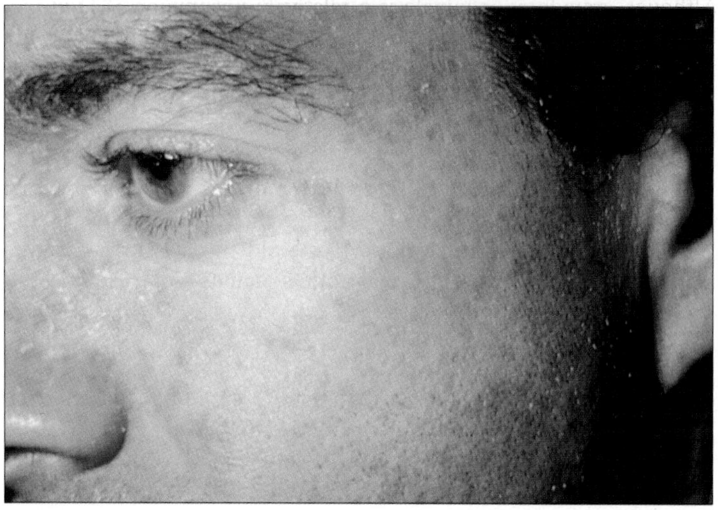

Fig. 132.7 Seborrheic dermatitis. Note the characteristic greasy scale and the erythematous plaques involving the face, especially the nasolabial folds and the eyebrows.

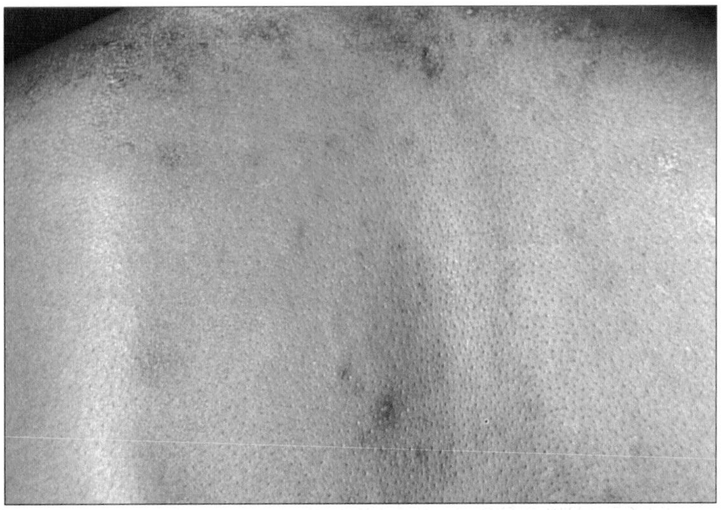

Fig. 132.8 Eosinophilic folliculitis. There are follicular papules, many of which have been excoriated, involving the upper trunk and the face. Histologically, numerous eosinophils are present within the follicular ostia.

marker of advanced HIV infection.[27] Clinically, patients develop folliculocentric pruritic urticarial papules measuring 1–4mm in diameter on the upper trunk, face, neck and proximal extremities (Fig. 132.8). There may be coalescence of papules to form plaques and virtually all cases are associated with lichenification secondary to chronic rubbing and scratching. Therapy of EF includes exposure to ultraviolet B and natural sunlight, oral metronidazole, erythromycin and isotretinoin.

Papular dermatitis of AIDS

This is a non-specific chronic papular eruption that has been reported in HIV-seropositive patients.[28] The nosology of this condition has been the subject of debate and many experts consider this to represent a form of eosinophilic folliculitis. Clinically, skin-colored papules are present on the head, neck and upper trunk, many of which may be folliculocentric. The diagnosis is made only by exclusion; thus other eruptions with similar clinical presentation should be excluded, including EF, scabies, papular mucinosis, secondary syphilis, viral exanthem and drug eruption.

Prurigo nodularis

Prurigo nodularis refers to thickened, verrucous papules and nodules and is a reaction pattern of the skin that is associated with a number of pruritic conditions. Patients who have itchy skin chronically rub and scratch, resulting in thickening with formation of typical lesions of prurigo nodularis. Although many different disorders may lead to the condition, in many patients the preceding event has long since resolved and the condition is perpetuated by the so-called itch–scratch cycle. Treatment of the disorder is based on correcting the underlying pruritus by the use of systemic and topical agents to lessen itching, such as topical corticosteroids, topical menthol- and phenol-containing lotions, topical antihistamines and systemic antipruritic agents.

Atopic dermatitis

Atopic dermatitis is seen somewhat more commonly in children who have HIV infection, having been reported in up to 20%.[29] Patients who have atopic dermatitis antedating HIV infection experience increased severity and persistence of their disease. The pathogenesis of atopic dermatitis in these patients has been associated with elevated circulating IgE antibodies to HIV and *S. aureus*. The clinical presentation is similar to that in immunocompetent hosts, with erythematous patches and plaques with fine papulovesicles associated with scaling and crusting.

Granuloma annulare

There have been a number of sporadic case reports of granuloma annulare (GA) in HIV-seropositive patients.[30] A unique feature of GA in these patients is a tendency toward widespread distribution and photoexacerbation. The clinical presentation is that of violaceous, firm papules with annular arrangement distributed on the hands, feet, arms, legs and trunk. In some patients, there may be similarity to KS. The reason for the development of GA in these patients remains unknown.

Leukocytoclastic vasculitis

Patients who have HIV disease may develop leukocytoclastic vasculitis.[31] This condition is a manifestation of immune complex-mediated disease. The clinical presentation progresses through several stages, beginning as urticarial papules or small petechiae. In most cases, characteristic palpable purpuric papules develop. Lesions are distributed on the extremities, although any body site can be affected. In HIV-infected individuals, they are more numerous and more florid than in immunocompetent hosts. The treatment of leukocytoclastic vasculitis consists primarily of identifying the underlying cause and correcting the associated abnormalities. Administration of nonsteroidal anti-inflammatory agents may be beneficial, although colchicine, dapsone or systemic corticosteroids may be required in severe cases.

NEOPLASMS

A number of different neoplastic disorders may develop in these patients as well. Lymphoreticular and vascular neoplasms are commonly observed; however, epithelial, mesenchymal and melanocytic neoplasms have been also described. Among the vascular lesions, KS is the most common neoplasm and is also a hallmark of AIDS. The development of malignant neoplasms is of great significance because they are often sources of morbidity and mortality.[14]

Kaposi's sarcoma

Kaposi's sarcoma is a vascular neoplastic disorder that is divided into classic and epidemic forms. The classic form is an uncommon disorder that was first described in 1827 and is seen mainly in elderly men of Mediterranean origin, black equatorial Africans and patients who have lymphoma or with primary or iatrogenically induced immune deficiencies. The epidemic form of KS is associated with AIDS. This was one of the first indicators of the AIDS epidemic when it was noted in approximately 50% of male homosexual patients in San Francisco.[32] The pathogenesis of the epidemic KS has recently been associated with infection by a human herpesvirus type 8 (KS-associated herpesvirus) (see Chapter 215).[33] Today, of all patients who have HIV infection, 15% develop KS during their clinical course. The clinical presentation may be that of single or multiple skin lesions and there may be mucosal, visceral and/or lymphatic involvement, particularly in the gastrointestinal tract and pulmonary parenchyma. Clinically, KS has three stages, including macule or patch, plaque and nodule (Fig. 132.9). Regressions of KS have been seen in patients treated with antiretroviral combinations including protease inhibitors.

Macule or patch

These lesions are faint pink macules or patches oriented along skin cleavage lines. Initially lesions may be innocuous in appearance and are easily overlooked, being mistaken for bruises, purpura or nevi. The correct recognition of the early lesions can be accomplished by performing biopsies for histopathologic examination.

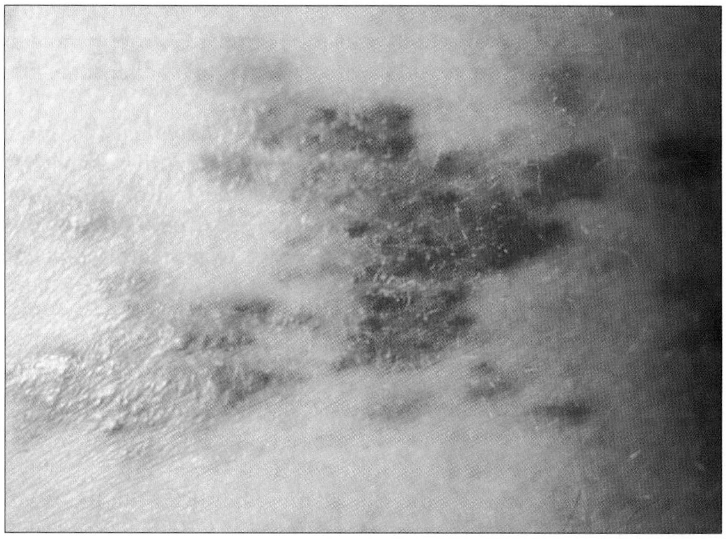

Fig. 132.9 Kaposi's sarcoma, plaque stage. There is an erythematous plaque, which is linear in shape, arranged along skin cleavage lines.

Plaque
In time lesions darken and develop into raised firm indurated plaques. The color is purple to brownish because of the presence of abundant blood vessels, extravasated erythrocytes and siderophages. In some cases, lesions may ulcerate.

Nodule
Nodular lesions are dome-shaped, elevated lesions that are usually purple. On palpation they are firm and may be ulcerated. They may simulate bacillary angiomatosis and pyogenic granulomata.

Treatment
Treatment of uncomplicated KS of the skin is performed for cosmetic purposes. Local destructive measures are generally the most effective. Liquid nitrogen cryotherapy, radiation and intralesional injections of vinblastine sulfate 2–4mg/ml and interferon-α-2b have all been used successfully. Systemic chemotherapy is effective but generally avoided as it further depresses the immune system unless the tumor has disseminated (see also Chapter 130).

Lymphomas and lymphoreticular neoplasms
A number of different lymphoreticular malignancies of both B and T cells may develop in HIV-positive patients. The majority of these are based in the lymph nodes and reticuloendothelial system, although the skin may be involved primarily or secondarily. Most are advanced at the time of diagnosis and are associated with a short medial survival time (see Chapter 130).

Non-Hodgkin's lymphoma with skin manifestations in patients who have AIDS is most commonly of B-lymphocyte origin and mostly high and intermediate grade. Cutaneous T-lymphocyte lymphoma (CTCL), Hodgkin's disease, lymphomatoid granulomatosis and adult T-lymphocyte leukemia/lymphoma also have been reported. The pathogenesis of lymphoreticular neoplasms in these patients is controversial. Chromosomal abnormalities have been encountered and a possible viral etiology has also been suggested.[34] Most cases involve visceral sites and, when the skin is affected, these are usually pink–purple papules or nodules with necrosis. Any site may be involved, including the head, neck, trunk and extremities. Deep-seated soft tissue involvement may expand superficially, forming dome-shaped nodules that often ulcerate. Hodgkin's lymphoma appears similar to non-Hodgkin's lymphoma, either as diffuse nodular lesions or as a panniculitis. CTCL may have the clinical appearance of mycosis fungoides with widespread erythematous scaly lesions distributed usually on the trunk and resembling 'eczema'. Lesions become red– brown ulcerated plaques and tumors during the more advanced stages of the disease.

The diagnosis of lymphoreticular neoplasms should be based on histopathologic examination of tissue biopsies. In many cases the use of gene rearrangement studies, flow cytometry and DNA analysis is necessary to characterize these neoplasms.

Treatment consists of the usual therapy for systemic lymphoma. CTCL may respond to psoralen and ultraviolet A therapy, total body electron beam or topical nitrogen mustard. The prognosis for HIV-positive patients who have lymphoma is poor; survival is in general between 5 and 10 months after diagnosis.

Other cancers
Several reports in the literature have described an increased incidence of intraepithelial and invasive carcinoma of the anus in patients who have AIDS-associated HPV infection. Although there are relatively few case reports, skin cancers may develop more rapidly and behave somewhat more aggressively. Among these malignancies, squamous cell carcinoma and basal cell carcinoma are the most frequently seen. Melanoma has been described, but only a few case reports have been published. There is no information on the incidence of melanomas in HIV patients compared with that in the general population.

Hair and nail changes
A number of abnormalities of hair and nails may be encountered in HIV-positive patients. Chronic inflammatory and noninflammatory alopecia has been observed. Alopecia universalis may also develop and is associated with decreased $CD4^+$ counts.[35] Other hair changes that have been observed include premature graying, thinning and diffuse hair loss. Hypertrichosis has also been associated with HIV infection; however, the cause is unknown. Nail changes, including yellow discoloration, hyperpigmentation, transverse and longitudinal ridging and decreased size or loss of the lunulae, have all been reported. Longitudinal hyperpigmentation is observed in association with treatment with zidovudine.

Oral manifestations
Oral manifestations are common in HIV disease and include novel presentations of previously known opportunistic diseases and some distinctive lesions.[36]

Oral candidiasis usually occurs when the CD4 counts are falling and may be manifest as a pseudomembranous, erythematous, hyperplastic form or as angular cheilitis (see Chapter 126).

Other opportunistic infections such as MAI, histoplasmosis and cryptococcosis may present as palatal masses or ulceration. Herpetic gingivostomatitis is more common in HIV-infected individuals and is painful and slow to heal. Herpes-zoster involving the oral cavity usually shows concurrent skin involvement. Oral HPV lesions are solitary or multiple and can be smooth-surfaced or papillomatous. The HPV types 7, 13 and 32 have been identified in these lesions.

Periodontal disease may occur in clean mouths in HIV-infected patients and present acutely with pain, rapid loss of bone and soft tissue. Response to treatment may be poor and recurrence common. Necrotizing periodontitis and linear gingival erythema are other manifestations.

Recurrent aphthous ulcers are usually idiopathic. They can be as simple as self-limited pinpoint lesions or progressively enlarging destructive lesions. There may be extensive hemorrhage and necrosis. They are frequently recurrent. Pain can be quite severe and esophageal ulceration is well described. Lesions should be cultured for HSV and a biopsy may be needed to rule out malignancy (e.g. lymphoma) or infection. Smaller ulcers may be treated with a topical corticosteroid preparation. Thalidomide, 200mg/day orally, given for 4 weeks, has been shown to be effective for larger oral and esophageal lesions.[37] It is vital that precautions are taken to avoid exposure to thalidomide during pregnancy.

Oral hairy leukoplakia and intraoral KS may be the first clue to HIV infection. Oral hairy leukoplakia presents unilaterally or bilaterally as a whitish corrugated plaque on the lateral sides of the tongue and is caused by EBV. It is seen in 20% of HIV-infected patients and is a harbinger of progression to AIDS (30% over 3 years). *Candida* is often associated with it. Biopsy shows the characteristic acanthosis, marked parakeratosis and extensive ballooning degeneration of epithelial cells. Intraoral KS may appear alone or be associated with skin or disseminated lesions. It may be flat, raised, solitary or multiple and is red–blue or purple. A biopsy may be required to distinguish it from other vascular or pigmented lesions.

Salivary gland involvement with lymphoepithelial cyst formation can lead to xerostomia and salivary gland enlargement in HIV patients. Labial salivary glands may demonstrate lymphocytic infiltrates similar to Sjögren's syndrome although the infiltrate is composed predominantly of CD8 cells.

Complications of antiretroviral agents

With the advent of more effective antiretroviral agents and the use of HAART therapy, many of the cutaneous manifestations of HIV discussed previously in this chapter occur less frequently. However, a new subset of dermatologic conditions has arisen related to the use of these drugs, namely cutaneous side-effects of antiretroviral agents. Currently there are three classes of medications used for the treatment of HIV: protease inhibitors (PI), nucleoside analogue reverse transcriptase inhibitors (NRTI) and non-nucleoside reverse transcriptase inhibitors (NNRTI).

A wide variety of side-effects occur with the potent antiretroviral therapy. Although each individual drug has its own cutaneous side-effects, therapy has been associated with lipodystrophy (LD). Lipodystrophy consists of the symmetric loss of fat from both the upper and lower extremities as well as the buttocks, causing the muscles and veins to appear more prominent, giving these patients a pseudoathletic appearance. The buccal, parotid and pre-auricular fat pads are also sites of lipoatrophy. Abnormal fat distribution may also be seen in patients with LD. Fat deposits may occur in the abdomen (crix belly), breasts, posterior neck (buffalo hump) and in the supraclavicular area. The concomitant occurrence of peripheral atrophy and abnormal fat deposition has been called the LD syndrome. Striae formation[38] and angiolipomas[39] have been reported in association with the LD syndrome. The simultaneous occurrence of lipoatrophy and fat accumulation is more common than either one occurring alone.[40] These fat abnormalities are often associated with metabolic derangements, including hypertriglyceridemia, hypercholesterolemia, insulin resistance, hyperglycemia and increased C-peptide levels (see also Chapters 139 and 141).[41–43]

Incidence of LD has been reported to be from 10% to 80%, but the largest reports put this number around 50%.[44,45] This number is difficult to establish, in part because there is no formal definition of LD and it has been measured differently in multiple studies. Signs of LD may begin as early as 2 months but no later than 1 year after initiation of combination therapy. Risk factors for the development of LD include female sex, nonintravenous drug user, increased age and longer duration of exposure to antiretroviral drugs.[46]

Although the LD syndrome has been connected to PI therapy, no known treatment for the LD syndrome exists. Metabolic abnormalities improve somewhat upon cessation of PIs or by switching to a different class of antiretrovirals, but the peripheral atrophy remains although some improvement on switching from thymidine analogues (e.g. stavudine) has been noted.[47–49]

Specific side-effects are associated with the individual PIs. Fixed drug eruptions have occurred as a result of therapy with saquinavir.[50] Indinavir has been associated with paronychia, most often seen on the great toes. Pyogenic granulomas may also occur in sulci of affected nails. Cessation of indinavir has led to partial or complete reversal of the paronychia over several weeks. Alopecia has also been caused by indinavir, usually on the lower extremities, but hair loss has also been seen in the pubic, axillary and thoracic regions as well as the scalp. Hair regrowth occurs within months of cessation of therapy. Additionally, indinavir has caused cheilitis and dry skin which, along with alopecia and paronychia, are side-effects of retinoid therapy.

Zidovudine, a NRTI, is the oldest drug approved for the treatment of HIV. Two well-known side effects of zidovudine are nail pigmentation and hypertrichosis. Nail pigmentation may occur on several[51] or all nails of the hands and feet.[52] The color of nail pigmentation ranges from yellow-brown to bluish. The discoloration may occur in longitudinal bands or transverse bands or it may affect the entire nail. Transverse bands occur presumably because zidovudine treatment was started and stopped over a short period of time in a patient who would have experienced entire nail pigmentary changes if zidovudine treatment had been prolonged. After cessation of zidovudine therapy, nail growth resumes normal coloration. Nail pigmentation may occur as a result of zidovudine stimulation or toxicity of the melanocytes in the nail matrix.

Hypertrichosis may also be seen with zidovudine. One patient who experienced nail discoloration also noticed increased length of hair on his dorsal forearm and darkening of his pubic hair.[53] HIV-induced alopecia has resolved in a female treated with zidovudine, then recurred upon cessation of therapy, and later resolved again when zidovudine was restarted.[54] Another patient complained of increased length of eyelashes after beginning treatment with zidovudine; this was the only place on the body affected.[55] A few other rare side-effects have been attributed to zidovudine therapy. An infant born to an HIV-positive mother who was perinatally exposed to zidovudine developed a severe paronychia secondary to *E. coli* and *C. albicans*.[56] The paronychia resolved after treatment with antifungal and antiseptic agents. Torres et al.[57] reported two patients who suffered from leukocytoclastic vasculitis thought to be caused by zidovudine. In both patients, the vasculitis started soon after initiation of zidovudine and resolved with withdrawal of the drug and then recurred when the patients were rechallenged with the drug. Increased sensitivity to mosquito bites has also been linked to zidovudine treatment. Within 3 months of starting zidovudine, three patients reported that following mosquito bites they experienced a heightened reaction to the bites, including immediate pruritic wheals that later developed into indurated areas and subcutaneous nodules lasting from 1 to 4 weeks. None of these patients had ever experienced this type of reaction to a mosquito bite before starting zidovudine therapy.[58]

Dideoxyinosine (DDI), a NRTI, has been reported to cause unusual side-effects in some HIV patients. One case of Ofuji papuloerythroderma, a disease in which the eruption of many confluent erythematous papules causes the appearance of erythroderma, has been reported in association with DDI use.[59] A small vessel vasculitis has been seen with DDI,[60] as has a morbilliform rash[61] (Fig. 132.10) and even the Stevens–Johnson syndrome.[62] Lamivudine, another NRTI, has also been associated with paronychia, mostly of the great toes, but also occasionally seen in fingernails.[63]

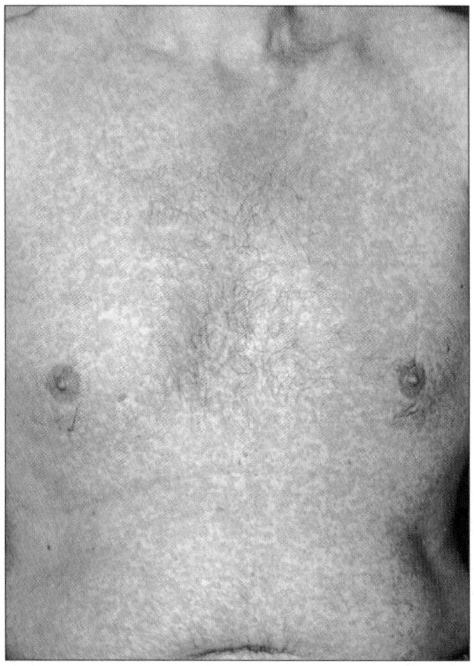

Fig. 132.10 Morbilliform drug eruption. There is a diffuse eruption of fine pink macules and papules, which have coalesced, involving the trunk and the extremities. The most common cause of these eruptions is trimethoprim–sulfamethoxazole.

A self-limited slightly pruritic maculopapular eruption has occurred within the first few days of ritonavir (PI) use. The eruption faded within days despite continued use of ritonavir. Hypersensitivity reactions have also been reported with zidovudine and nevirapine. Hypersensitivity with nevirapine is fairly common and may often be prevented by using either a gradually escalating dose or by co-administration of prednisone or an antihistamine during the initial weeks of nevirapine therapy.[64,65] Despite use of an escalating dose, the Stevens–Johnson reaction has been seen in patients on nevirapine therapy.[66] Abacavir, a NRTI, can cause a severe hypersensitivity reaction which may even be life threatening, especially if treatment is continued despite the reaction or if the patient is rechallenged with abacavir after resolution of the initial reaction.[67]

Acute generalized exanthematous pustulosis was seen in a patient on multiple antiretroviral drug therapy. Although the causative drug cannot be proven with certainty, there was a strong temporal relationship of onset and resolution of the reaction with the use of zidovudine, lamivudine and stavudine.[68]

REFERENCES

1. Cockerell CJ. Cutaneous clues to HIV infection diagnosis and treatment. Semin Dermatopathol 1994;13:275–85.
2. Johnson R. Human immunodeficiency virus disease in the era of HAART: a reevaluation of the mucocutaneous manifestations. Curr Clin Top Infect Dis 1999;19:252–86.
3. Maurer T. HIV skin complications in the age of HAART: an interview with Toby Maurer. BETA 1999;12:67–70.
4. Hengge UR, Franz B, Goos M. Decline of infectious skin manifestations in the era of highly active antiretroviral therapy. AIDS 2000;14:1069–70.
5. Aftergut K, Cockerell C. Update on the cutaneous manifestations of HIV infection. Dermatol Clin 1999;17:445–71.
6. Huselbosch HJ, Claessen FA, van Ginkel CJ, *et al.* Human immunodeficiency virus exanthem. J Am Acad Dermatol 1990;23:483–6.
7. Berger T. Dermatologic manifestations of HIV infection. In: Cohen PT, Sande MA, Volberding PA, eds. The AIDS Knowledge Base. Philadelphia: Lippincott Williams and Wilkins; 1999:425–44.
8. Friedman-Kien AE, Cockerell CJ. Management of skin infection in patients with HIV infection. In: Leoung GS, ed. Opportunistic infections in patients with acquired immunodeficiency syndrome. New York: Marcel Dekker; 1988:135–44.
9. Melbye M, Grossman RJ, Goedert J, *et al.* Risk of AIDS after herpes zoster. Lancet 1987;1:728–31.
10. Klatt EC, Shibata D. Cytomegalovirus infection in the acquired immunodeficiency syndrome. Arch Pathol Lab Med 1988;112:540–4.
11. Greenspan D, Greenspan JS, Overby G, *et al.* Risk factors from hairy leukoplakia to AIDS: a nested case control study. J Acquir Immune Defic Syndr 1991;4:652.
12. Sanchez M, Spielman T, Epstein W, Moy J. Treatment of oral leukoplakia with podophyllin. Arch Dermatol 1992;128:1659.
13. Berger TG, Sawchuk WS, Leonardi PE, *et al.* Epidermodysplasia verruciformis associated papillomavirus infection complicating human immunodeficiency virus disease. Br J Dermatol 1991;124:79–83.
14. Cockerell CJ. Mucocutaneous neoplasms in patients with human immunodeficiency virus infection. Semin Diagn Pathol 1996;13:19–39.
15. Izu R, Manzano D, Gardeazabal J, *et al.* Giant molluscum contagiosum presenting as a tumor in HIV-infected patient. Int J Dermatol 1994;33:266–7.
16. Becker BA, Frieden IJ, Odam RB, *et al.* Atypical plaque-like staphylococcal folliculitis in human immunodeficiency virus infected persons. J Am Acad Dermatol 1989;21:1024–6.
17. Cockerell CJ, Friedman-Kien AE. Skin manifestations of HIV infection. Primary Care 1989;16:621–43.
18. Cockerell CJ, LeBoit PE. Bacillary angiomatosis: a newly characterized pseudoneoplastic, infectious cutaneous vascular disorder. J Am Acad Dermatol 1990;22:501–12.
19. Cockerell CJ, Tierno PM, Friedman-Kien A, Kim KS. Clinical, histologic, microbiologic and biochemical characterization of the causative agent of bacillary (epithelioid) angiomatosis: a rickettsial illness with features of bartonellosis. J Invest Dermatol 1991;97:812–7.
20. Quinn TC, Glasser D, Cannon RO, *et al.* Human immunodeficiency virus infection among patients attending clinics for sexually transmitted diseases. N Engl J Med 1988;318:197–202.
21. Klein RS, Harris CA, Small CB, *et al.* Oral candidiasis in high-risk patients as the initial manifestation of the acquired immune deficiency syndrome. N Engl J Med 1984;311:354–7.
22. Penneys NS. Venereal disease. In: Penneys NS, ed. Skin manifestations of AIDS, 2nd ed. London: Martin Dunitz; 1995:75–83.
23. Cockerell CJ, Friedman-Kien AE. Cutaneous manifestations of HIV infection. In: Friedman-Kien AE, Cockerell CJ, eds. Color atlas of AIDS, 2nd ed. Philadelphia: WB Saunders; 1996:81–158.
24. Cockerell CJ. Noninfectious inflammatory skin disease in HIV-infected individuals. Clin Dermatol 1991;9:531–41.
25. Mathes BM, Douglas MC. Seborrheic dermatitis in patients with acquired immunodeficiency syndrome. J Am Acad Dermatol 1985;13:947–51.
26. Duvic M, Johnson TM, Rapini RP, *et al.* Acquired immunodeficiency syndrome associated psoriasis and Reiter's syndrome. Arch Dermatol 1987;123:1622–32.
27. Rosenthal D, LeBoit PE, Klumpp L, *et al.* Human immunodeficiency virus-associated eosinophilic folliculitis: a unique dermatosis associated with advanced human immunodeficiency virus infection. Arch Dermatol 1991;127:206–9.
28. Smith KJ, Skelton HG III, James WD, *et al.* Papular eruption of human immunodeficiency virus disease. Am J Dermatopathol 1991;13:445–51.
29. Ball LM, Harper JI. Atopic eczema in HIV seropositive hemophiliacs. Lancet 1987;11:627–8.
30. Bakos L, Hampe S, da Rocha JL, *et al.* Generalized granuloma annulare in a patient with acquired immunodeficiency syndrome (AIDS). J Am Acad Dermatol 1987;17:844–5.
31. Chren MM, Silverman RA, Sorensen RU, *et al.* Leukocytoclastic vasculitis in a patient infected with human immunodeficiency virus. J Am Acad Dermatol 1989;21:804–14.
32. Rutherford GW, Payne SF, Lemp GF, *et al.* The epidemiology of AIDS-related Kaposi's sarcoma in San Francisco. J Acquir Immune Defic Syndr 1990;(Suppl.1):S4–S7.
33. Schwartz RA. Kaposi's sarcoma: advance and perspective. J Am Acad Dermatol 1996;34:804–14.
34. Bernheim A, Berger R. Cytogenetic studies in Burkitt's lymphoma/leukemia in patients with acquired immunodeficiency syndrome. Cancer Genet Cytogenet 1988;32:67–74.
35. Penneys NS. Miscellaneous dermatoses. In: Penneys NS, ed. Skin manifestations of AIDS, 2nd ed. London: Martin Dunitz; 1995:171–208.
36. Greenspan D. Opportunistic infections of the mouth. In: Cohen PT, Sande MA, Volbeerding PA, eds. The AIDS Knowledge Base. Philadelphia: Lippincott Williams and Wilkins; 1999:415–424.
37. Darvay A, Acland K, Lynn W, *et al.* Striae formation in two HIV-positive persons receiving protease inhibitors. J Am Acad Dermatol 1999;41:467–9.
38. Jacobson JM, Greenspan JS, Spritzler J, *et al.* Thalidomide for the treatment of oral aphthous ulcers in patients with human immunodeficiency virus infection. National Institute of Allergy and Infectious Diseases AIDS Clinical Trials Group. N Engl J Med 1997;336:1487–93.
39. Dank JP, Cloven R. Protease inhibitor-associated angiolipomatosis. J Am Acad Dermatol 2000;42:129–31.
40. Savés M, Raffi F, Capeau J, *et al.* Factors related to lipodystrophy and metabolic alterations in patients with human immunodeficiency virus infection receiving highly active antiretroviral therapy. Clin Infect Dis 2002;34:1396–405.
41. Purnell JQ, Zambon A, Knopp RH. Effect of ritonavir on lipids and post-heparin lipase activities in normal subjects. AIDS 2000;14:51–7.

42. Mulligan K, Grunfeld C, Tai VW, *et al.* Hyperlipidemia and insulin resistance are induced by protease inhibitors independent of changes in body composition in patients with HIV infection. J Acq Immune Defic Syndr 2000;23:35–43.
43. Hadigan C, Meigs JB, Corcoran C, *et al.* Metabolic abnormalities and cardiovascular disease risk factors in adults with human immunodeficiency virus infection and lipodystrophy. Clin Infect Dis 2001;32:130–9.
44. Safrin S, Grunfeld C. Fat distribution and metabolic changes in patients with HIV infection. AIDS 1999;13:2493–505.
45. Boubaker K, Flepp M, Sudre P, *et al.* Hyperlactatermia and antiretroviral therapy: the Swiss HIV Cohort Study. Clin Infect Dis 2001;33:1931–7.
46. Martinez E, Mocroft A, Garcia-Viejo M, *et al.* Risk of lipodystrophy in HIV-1 infected patients treated with protease inhibitors: a prospective cohort study. Lancet 2001;357:592–8.
47. Carr A, Hudson J, Chuah J, *et al.* HIV protease inhibitor substitution in patients with lipodystrophy: a randomised, controlled, open-label, multicentre study. AIDS 2001;15:1811–22.
48. Domingo P, Matias-Guiu X, Pujol RM, *et al.* Switching to nevirapine decreases insulin levels but does not improve subcutaneous adipocyte apoptosis in patients with highly active antiretroviral therapy-associated lipodystrophy. J Infect Dis 2001;184:1197–201.
49. Carr A, Workman C, Smith DE, *et al.* Abacavir substitution for nucleoside analogs in patients with HIV lipoatrophy: a randomized trial. JAMA 2002;288:207–15.
50. Smith KJ, Yeager J, Skelton H. Fixed drug eruptions to human immunodeficiency virus-1 protease inhibitor. Cutis 2000;66:29–32.
51. Fisher CA, McPoland PR. Azidothymidine-induced nail pigmentation. Cutis 1989;43:552–4.
52. Furth P, Kazakis A. Nail pigmentation changes associated with azidothymidine (zidovudine). Ann Intern Med 1987;107:350.
53. Sahai J, Conway B, Cameron D, *et al.* Zidovudine-associated hypertrichosis and nail pigmentation in an HIV-infected patient. AIDS 1991;5:1395–6.
54. Vernazza PL, Galleazzi RL. HIV-associated alopecia in a woman and regrowth of hair after zidovudine therapy. V International Conference on AIDS. Montreal, 1989 (abstract MBP364).
55. Klutman NE, Hinthorn DR. Excessive growth of eyelashes in a patient with AIDS being treated with zidovudine. N Engl J Med 1991;324:1896.
56. Russo F, Collantes C, Guerrero J. Severe paronychia due to zidovudine-induced neutropenia in a neonate. J Am Acad Dermatol 1999;40:322–4.
57. Torres RA, Lin RY, Lee M, *et al.* Zidovudine-induced leukocytoclastic vasculitis. Arch Intern Med 1992;152:850–1.
58. Diven DG, Newton RC, Ramsey KM. Heightened cutaneous reactions to mosquito bites in patients with acquired immunodeficiency syndrome receiving zidovudine. Arch Intern Med 1988;148:2296.
59. Just M, Carrascosa JM, Ribera M, *et al.* Dideoxyinosine-associated Ofuji papuloerythroderma in an HIV-infected patient. Dermatology 1997;195:410–11.
60. Herranz P, Fernandez-Diaz ML, Lucas R, *et al.* Cutaneous vasculitis associated with didanosine. Lancet 1994;344:680.
61. Yarchoan R, Pluda JM, Thomas RV, *et al.* Long-term toxicity/activity profile of 2′,3′-dideoxyinosine in AIDS or AIDS-related complex. Lancet 1990;336:526–9.
62. Parneix-Spake A, Bastuji-Garin S, Levy Y, *et al.* Didanosine as probable cause of Stevens Johnson syndrome. Lancet 1992;340:857–8.
63. Zerboni R, Angius AG, Cusini M, *et al.* Lamivudine-induced paronychia. Lancet 1998;351:1256.
64. Barreiro P, Soriano V, Gonzalez-Lahoz J. Prevention of nevirapine-associated rash. Lancet 2001;357:392.
65. Barreiro P, Soriano V, Casas E, *et al.* Prevention of nevirapine-associated exanthema using slow dose escalation and/or corticosteroids. AIDS 2000;14:2153–7.
66. Metry DW, Lahart C, Farmer KL, *et al.* Stevens-Johnson syndrome caused by the antiretroviral drug nevirapine. J Am Acad Dermatol 2001;44:354–7.
67. Hewitt RG. Abacavir hypersensitivity reaction. Clin Infect Dis 2002;34:1137–42.
68. Aquilina C, Viraben R, Roueire A. Acute generalized exanthematous pustulosis: a cutaneous adverse effect due to prophylactic antiviral therapy with protease inhibitor. Arch Intern Med 1998;158:2160–1.

chapter

133 HIV/AIDS-related Problems in Developing Countries

Lisa A Spacek & Thomas C Quinn

INTRODUCTION AND EPIDEMIOLOGY

Since the beginning of the HIV epidemic, approximately 60 million people have been infected.[1] As of December 2001, an estimated 40 million people (37.2 million adults and 2.7 million children) were infected with HIV and 25 million people had died. In 2001 alone, 5 million new HIV infections occurred worldwide. In the developing world, the majority of incident cases occur in young adults. People aged 15–24 years comprise about one-third of those living with HIV/AIDS. In 2001, illnesses associated with HIV/AIDS caused the deaths of approximately 3 million people, including an estimated 580,000 children younger than 15 years. More than 95% of these infections and deaths occurred in developing countries. Accompanying the morbidity and mortality borne by those infected with HIV is the dramatic alteration of the social structure attributable to the HIV epidemic. Because of the premature death of HIV-infected parents, 13 million children have been orphaned. The number of orphaned children is forecast to more than double by 2010.[2]

The contrast between the impact of HIV/AIDS in the developed world and in the developing world is striking. Figure 133.1 illustrates the discrepancy between the annual AIDS deaths in sub-Saharan Africa versus the USA. Whereas AIDS-related mortality is declining in the USA, western Europe and Australia, it is continuing to rise rapidly in sub-Saharan Africa, South East Asia and Latin America.[3–5] One in 200 adults aged 15–49 years is infected with HIV in the USA and Europe, but 10–40% of pregnant women in some parts of sub-Saharan Africa are infected with HIV. Although antiretroviral therapy is given to pregnant women and their newborn infants in developed countries to prevent transmission, most pregnant women who have HIV infection in developing countries receive little or no antiretroviral therapy, creating an enormous discrepancy in perinatal transmission of HIV in these two regions of the world. In addition, recent surveys have demonstrated that nearly 75% of people with HIV infection are aware of their serostatus in the USA and Europe, whereas 80–90% of infected people in developing countries have never been tested for HIV and remain unaware of their infection.

Since the initial recognition of the AIDS epidemic, much has been done to respond to HIV infection by way of prevention and behavioral modification. Government-supported efforts in Thailand, including HIV and AIDS surveillance systems and programs such as the '100% condom use' campaign for commercial sex, have contributed to decreased rates of HIV and sexually transmitted diseases in military recruits.[6] Similarly, in Cambodia the prevalence of HIV among pregnant women declined by almost a third between 1997 and 2000, to 2.3%. Widespread health education, increased used of condoms and voluntary HIV counseling and testing appear to have lowered the prevalence of HIV infection in some areas of sub-Saharan Africa. In rural Uganda, the most striking decline in HIV prevalence was seen among females aged 20–24. Age-specific prevalence decreased from 20.9% in 1989–90 to 13.8% in 1996–7.

However, in the setting of this mature epidemic, declines in HIV seroprevalence have been seen in the presence of stable and high incidence.[7] Death due to HIV disease, rather than a true decrease in the incidence of HIV infection, appears to have contributed most to the reduced HIV prevalence. Figure 133.2 models the lifetime risk of AIDS death for 15-year-old boys based on current HIV prevalence in adults aged 15–49 years. The upper line, based on current HIV prevalence, is compared with the lower line, which assumes that the risk for new HIV infection at each age decreases by half over the next 15 years. This indicates that, even with successful prevention campaigns, without access to treatment the proportion of young people who will die of AIDS is very high.[8]

Despite ongoing prevention efforts, the overwhelming burden of HIV disease is borne by the developing world. The factors responsible for the discrepancies between the developed and developing world in terms of the diagnosis and care of people with HIV infection and the magnitude of the HIV pandemic are multifactorial. Limited access to care, lack of diagnostic equipment and insufficient money to support either prevention or treatment programs are primarily responsible for the continuing rise in morbidity and mortality associated with HIV infection in developing countries. Underlying high prevalence rates of HIV infection and a combination of high-risk behavior and the widespread prevalence of sexually transmitted diseases act synergistically to propel the epidemic further in many areas of the developing world. Furthermore, the coexistence of other endemic diseases that are widely prevalent in developing countries, such as tuberculosis and gastrointestinal infections, complicate the care of people with HIV infection and pose additional problems for the medical personnel caring for them. This chapter reviews some of these aspects as they relate to the care of people with HIV infection living in developing countries.

CLINICAL FEATURES

The clinical manifestations of HIV infection in developing countries are diverse and reflect the wide variety of other endemic diseases within each region.[9] More than 100 pathogens, including viruses, bacteria, fungi, protozoa, helminths and arthropods, have been identified as having caused opportunistic disease in persons with HIV infection. A relatively small number of these pathogens cause a majority of the infections, yet their impact on the health of persons with HIV infection is enormous. Although the reasons for the differences between the spectrum of opportunistic infections observed in developing countries and in developed countries are not completely understood, they are likely to include factors such as the prevalence of pathogens in the environment, social behaviors, ecologic factors that result in exposure to these pathogens, and other undefined factors.

Determining the spectrum of opportunistic infections in a given region requires surveillance systems and diagnostic services that may not be available in many developing countries. For example, oppor-

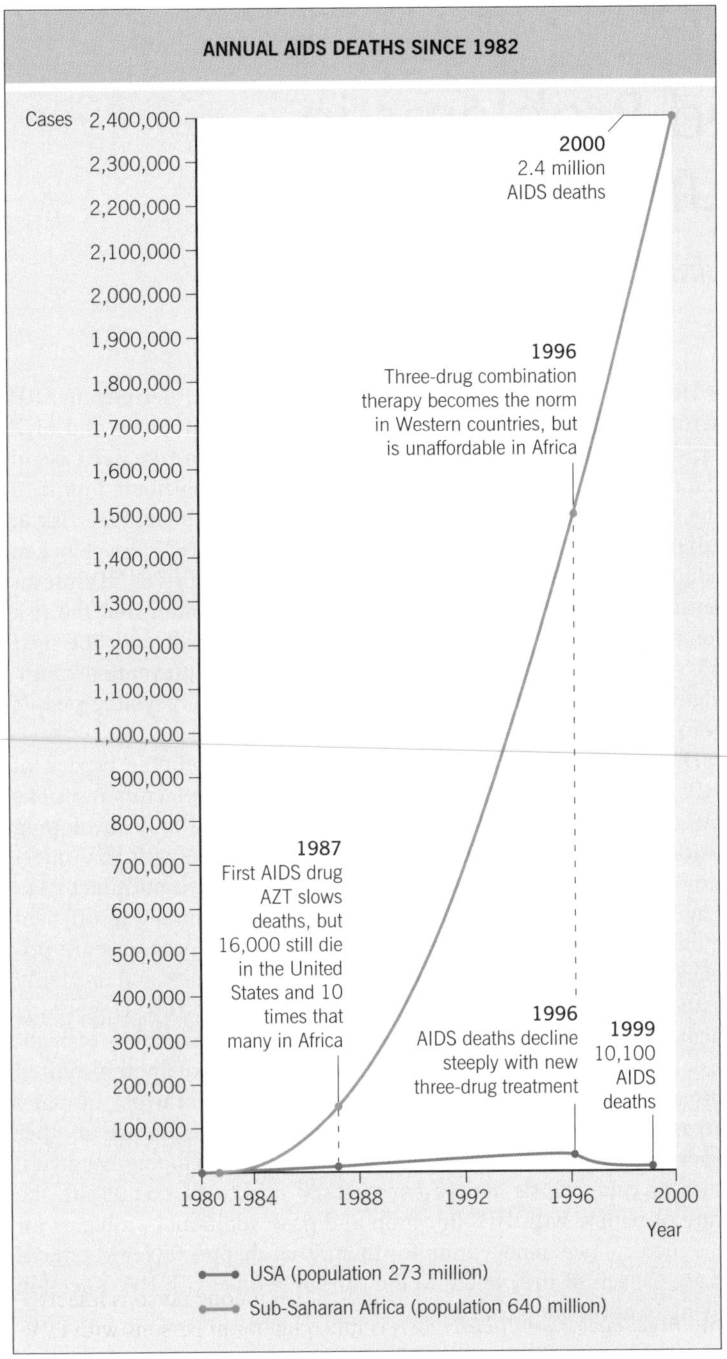

Fig. 133.1 Annual AIDS deaths since 1982. Deaths in the USA are contrasted with those in sub-Saharan Africa.

tunistic infections that can be diagnosed with reasonable accuracy by physical examination (e.g., oral candidiasis) or by inexpensive laboratory techniques (e.g., Indian ink stain of cerebrospinal fluid for *Cryptococcus neoformans*) may be documented more frequently than opportunistic infections requiring more expensive diagnostic technologies (e.g., *Pneumocystis carinii* pneumonia, disseminated *Mycobacterium avium* complex (MAC) and cytomegalovirus disease). Because most clinical studies that document opportunistic infections are conducted in urban hospitals, those infected outside of urban centers are often not included in disease surveillance efforts. Furthermore, longitudinal cohort studies are costly to maintain in resource-poor settings. Biases in diagnosing and reporting opportunistic infections may be especially important among socially disadvantaged groups with limited access to diagnostic and health care services. Finally, differences in clinical definitions may make comparisons between published reports difficult. For these reasons and for others, much less is known about the frequency of different opportunistic infections in the developing world than in industrialized countries.

Although it is clear that HIV infection has a definite impact on a wide variety of microbial agents in developing countries, less is known about the impact of these diseases on HIV infection. Although it has been shown that HIV disease progresses more rapidly in developing countries, recent studies report similar rates of HIV disease progression when compared with the epidemiology of HIV disease in developed countries prior to the introduction of highly-active antiretroviral therapy (HAART).[10] Data quantifying the median time from seroconversion to AIDS is limited. Early studies suggested that time to AIDS was much shorter in sub-Saharan Africa and South East Asia. Obstacles included pinpointing the time of seroconversion and reconciling different definitions of AIDS. Similarly, time from seroconversion to AIDS and death has been compared with that seen in the developed world early in the HIV epidemic. In a population-based study in Uganda, the median survival from AIDS to death was 9.3 months but varied according to AIDS-defining illness.[11] Median survival associated with wasting syndrome, Kaposi's sarcoma and esophageal candidiasis was less than 3.5 months, compared with survival longer than 20 months associated with cryptosporidial diarrhea, chronic herpes simplex virus (HSV) infection and extrapulmonary tuberculosis. The median $CD4^+$ lymphocyte count at the time of AIDS onset was 150 cells/mm^3. Notably, the most common opportunistic infections in resource-poor settings, including tuberculosis and endemic bacterial infections, develop at $CD4^+$ lymphocyte counts higher than 150 cells/mm^3. Without the benefit of prophylaxis against opportunistic infections and treatment with antiretroviral medications, those infected with HIV will ultimately suffer AIDS-related morbidity and death.

In addition to the clinical spectrum of disease defined by opportunistic infection, co-infection with endemic diseases and resulting immune activation may increase susceptibility to HIV infection. A person whose immune system is activated at the time of exposure to HIV may be more susceptible to infection with HIV. In this regard, the success of an aggressive sexually transmitted disease (STD) treatment program in Tanzania in decreasing the incidence of new HIV infections may be due in part to the removal of immune-activating factors. A similar community-based study conducted in Uganda and designed to evaluate the effect of STD treatment on the development of incident HIV infection found no difference.[12] The lack of a positive effect may be related to the effect of antihelminthic therapy provided to the control group. The eradication of helminths may have had an effect similar to the treatment of STDs. Furthermore, the trial did not treat for genital ulcerative disease due to HSV infection. Future clinical trials will evaluate the effect of treating genital HSV infection on HIV infection and transmission. A recent review outlines the documented associations between chronic immune activation and infections prevalent in the developing world that appear to enhance the pathogenesis of HIV.[13] Thus, both the rate of spread of the HIV epidemic as well as the clinical course in the developing world may be greatly influenced by the underlying state of heightened immune activation that exists in many people in these countries.

Tropical diseases may directly lead to an increased risk of infection with HIV. Treatment of severe anemia induced by malaria has led to HIV infection by transfusion. Female genital schistosomiasis, like other genital inflammatory conditions, may increase the efficiency of HIV transmission. Several drugs used in the treatment and prophylaxis of tropical diseases have an immunosuppressive effect and may thereby influence susceptibility to HIV. Specific interactions between HIV and infectious diseases in developing countries are listed briefly below.

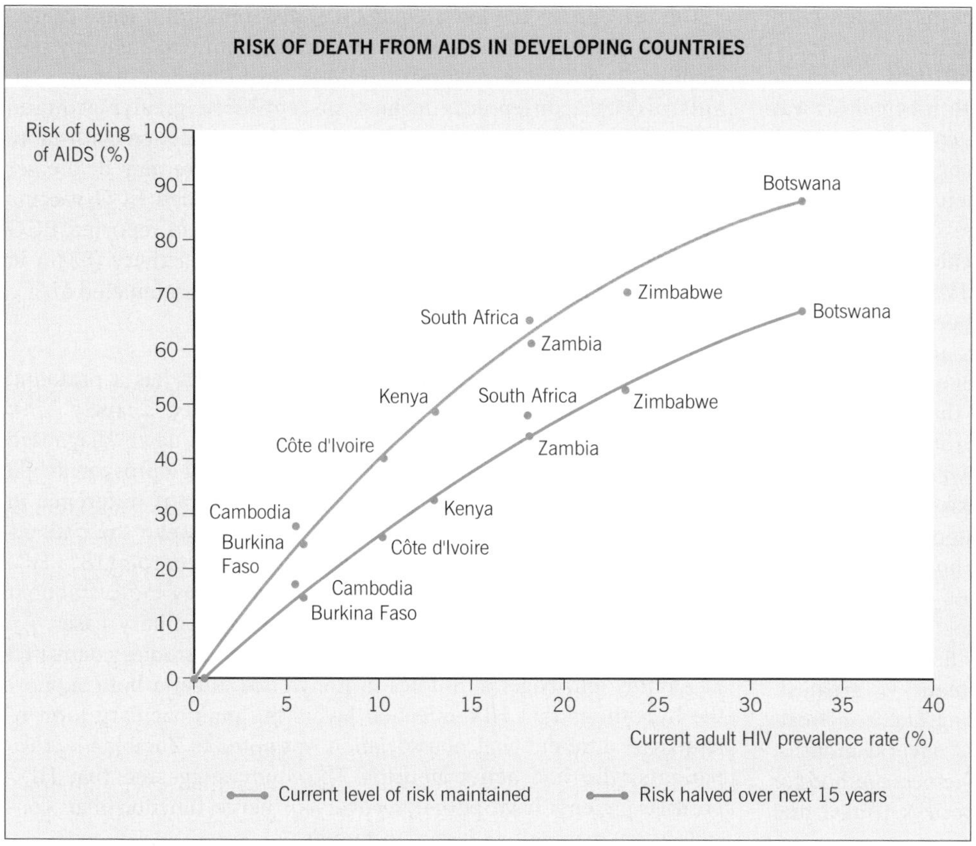

Fig. 133.2 Risk of death from AIDS in developing countries. Lifetime risk of AIDS death among 15-year-old boys, assuming unchanged or halved risk of becoming infected with HIV, in selected countries.

Mycobacterial infections

Tuberculosis

Tuberculosis is the most important severe opportunistic infection observed among patients with HIV infection in developing countries because it occurs frequently, is transmissible to both people with HIV infection and uninfected persons, can be readily treated and can be prevented. Globally, tuberculosis is the leading cause of death among people with HIV infection, accounting for a third of deaths due to AIDS. The World Health Organization (WHO) estimates that the number of people infected with the tubercle bacillus is one-third of the world population; throughout the world a new tuberculosis infection occurs every second.[14] The greatest number of tuberculosis infections occur in people living in Asia, sub-Saharan Africa and Latin America, where about half of the adult population is infected. These are the same areas in which HIV continues to increase steadily. The WHO considers HIV as the single most important factor driving the increase in tuberculosis incidence in Africa over the past 10 years.

The increase in tuberculosis attributable to HIV has resulted in increased demand for already overburdened tuberculosis programs. During the initial stages of the HIV epidemic, when incidence rates increased dramatically, tuberculosis rates increased as well. For example, in the early stage of the HIV epidemic in northern Thailand from 1989–90, HIV seroprevalence increased exponentially from 5% to 40% and there was a 5–7% increase in tuberculosis between 1990 and 1992. In developing countries where young adults have high rates of infection with both HIV and tuberculosis, the risk of co-infection is correspondingly high. Worldwide, an estimated 640,000 incident cases of tuberculosis (8%) occur in the setting of HIV infection. Although the largest group of co-infected individuals lives in India, the burden of HIV infection per capita is highest in sub-Saharan Africa, with 32% of tuberculosis cases co-infected with HIV.

Infection with HIV and tuberculosis has become a particular problem in many African countries. A recent review of major causes of HIV-related diseases identified tuberculosis as the most frequently occurring opportunistic infection in hospital and clinic patients in Côte d'Ivoire, South Africa, Kenya and Ethiopia. In the central African countries of Zimbabwe and Malawi, the annual incidence of tuberculosis doubled in the 5 years 1985–90 and 20–44% of AIDS patients developed tuberculosis during the course of their infection. In contrast, only 4% of AIDS patients in the USA have tuberculosis. In a study of tuberculosis treatment in Uganda, a high prevalence (49%) of *Mycobacterium africanum* isolates was identified in patients with HIV infection who had pulmonary tuberculosis. In Uganda, the prevalence of HIV infection among tuberculosis patients was 5.9 times greater than that among patients who had inactive tuberculosis. In Lusaka, Zambia, as many as 37% of hospitalized children who had tuberculosis were infected with HIV, compared with 11% of nontuberculosis controls. Cohort studies have also shown that the risk of developing active tuberculosis among persons infected with *Mycobacterium tuberculosis* is much higher in persons with HIV infection than in HIV-seronegative persons. For someone who is co-infected with HIV and tuberculosis, the annual risk of developing active tuberculosis ranges from 5% to 15%, whereas the lifetime risk among people who have tuberculosis in the absence of HIV infection is only 5–10%.

During the period 1997–9, the estimated number of incident cases of tuberculosis increased from 8.0 million to 8.4 million. If the present trend continues, the WHO estimates an expected 10.2 million new cases by 2005. The progressive increase is largely due to the HIV/AIDS pandemic. In patients dying with HIV disease in Abidjan, Côte d'Ivoire, tuberculosis was present in more than half of those who had AIDS and was responsible for one-third of the deaths. The importance of tuberculosis was demonstrated in an autopsy study among patients dying of pulmonary disease in Abidjan; 40% of the HIV-positive patients died of tuberculosis, compared with only 4% of the HIV-negative patients. In Mexico, disseminated tuberculosis was found at autopsy in 25% of patients who had AIDS; this compares with 6% of patients in the USA and 5% of patients in Italy. This observation is consistent with the higher incidence of pulmonary tuberculosis in Latin America than in the USA, as well as with the higher incidence of tuberculosis in the USA among foreign-born people and people of Latin American or Asian descent.

A prospective cohort study conducted in South Africa demonstrated that the increased mortality associated with tuberculosis was observed only in patients with a $CD4^+$ lymphocyte count greater than 200 cells/mm^3 and in those without AIDS at baseline.[15] The authors proposed that the immune activation due to tuberculosis increased HIV replication and accelerated HIV disease progression.

Diagnosis, treatment and prophylaxis of tuberculosis is discussed in Chapter 37. Trials of isoniazid prophylaxis of HIV-positive populations with a positive tuberculin skin test have been conducted in Mexico, Haiti, Kenya, Zambia and Uganda. Meta-analyses of these studies showed a definite reduction in the development of active tuberculosis in the treated group compared with the placebo group during a period of 2–3 years.[16,17] No significant protection could be demonstrated in the groups with skin test anergy who were included in the same trials. Thus, the benefit of prophylaxis for populations that are already anergic as a result of immunosuppression is more difficult to evaluate because they indicate either no previous exposure to tuberculosis or previous infection with loss of immunologic reactivity. As with many other diseases, the cost of medication needed to carry out effective treatment of tuberculosis is lacking in many developing countries, where the problem is greatest. Furthermore, patient compliance may be a limiting factor in treatment regimens of multiple drugs for periods of several months. Research priorities include the determination of the best method for detection of active tuberculosis in resource-poor settings, and optimum duration of preventive therapy.

In order to prevent active tuberculosis, up to 70% of the world's children are vaccinated with bacillus Calmette–Guérin (BCG). Unfortunately, the efficacy of BCG in HIV-infected populations is unclear. One study found no benefit of vaccination in HIV-seropositive children; another study found a benefit of childhood vaccination in HIV-seropositive adults and protection from disease caused by *M. tuberculosis*. Recent data suggesting a beneficial effect of early BCG vaccination on mortality from all causes in children not infected with HIV indicate that measures of benefit in HIV-seropositive people need to be broader than mere prevention of tuberculosis. The WHO recommends that BCG should be given to people who have asymptomatic HIV infection in areas with a high risk of tuberculosis infection. In areas where the risk of tuberculosis is minimal, BCG is not recommended, particularly for those who are infected with HIV. Recombinant BCG vector-based vaccines are currently being evaluated in animal models for potential use in vaccination against HIV.

Mycobacterium avium *complex*

Although MAC is very common in advanced HIV infection in the USA and Europe, it has rarely been documented in developing countries. In one study in Uganda, none of 95 blood cultures from severely ill patients who had advanced AIDS were positive for *M. avium*; neither were any of 165 mycobacterial sputum cultures from HIV-seropositive and HIV-seronegative patients at the same hospital. In Côte d'Ivoire, none of 202 blood cultures from HIV-positive adult inpatients were positive for *M. avium*, whereas 4% grew *M. tuberculosis*. Intestinal biopsies from 98 Ugandan, Zairian and Zambian patients who had chronic HIV-related enteropathy yielded histology suggestive of *M. avium* infection in only one case. Similarly, autopsies on 78 HIV-seropositive children in Côte d'Ivoire revealed no evidence of *M. avium* infection. In Kenya and Mexico, *M. avium* has been documented in 6% of patients hospitalized with late-stage HIV disease; in Brazil it has been documented in 18% of 125 hospitalized patients. A recent study conducted in South Africa demonstrated a 10% prevalence of disseminated MAC in 10% of hospitalized patients with a $CD4^+$ lymphocyte count of less than 100 cells/mm^3.[18]

The reasons for the low frequency of disseminated disease caused by MAC in the developing world are unclear, but there are many possibilities, including less exposure to MAC, exposure to different variants of MAC, differences in host susceptibility, greater acquired immunity to mycobacteria, earlier death from infection with more virulent pathogens, and diagnostic difficulties. There may be greater acquired immunity to mycobacterial disease through BCG vaccine or previous infection with *M. tuberculosis*, but the reported BCG coverage (50%) and purified protein derivative reactivity (82%) in Uganda seem unlikely to explain the lack of any disseminated MAC.

Mycobacterium leprae

To date, there is little evidence that HIV infection has a profound effect on the frequency of *M. leprae* infection (see Chapter 154). Several studies have examined serology for HIV in newly diagnosed leprosy. In one study in Uganda of 189 new cases of leprosy matched for age, sex and district of residence, no significant difference in overall rates of HIV seropositivity was found between the patients who had leprosy (12% HIV seropositive) and the controls (18% HIV seropositive). Interestingly, HIV seropositivity was more frequent among the multibacillary cases than the paucibacillary cases. An association between HIV and leprosy was seen in studies conducted in Zambia and Nigeria. Studies in Kenya and Nigeria both support the hypothesis that HIV infection favors the multibacillary form of leprosy. A different clinical association was noted in Zambian leprosy patients who had active neuritis. The study suggested that HIV-positive patients have poorer recovery of nerve function than controls after treatment with corticosteroids.

Thus, there appears to be no striking evidence that HIV infection has an adverse effect on the course of leprosy. Multibacillary disease could possibly develop under the influence of HIV infection but, because leprosy is chronic and slow in progression, it is difficult to discern the influence of HIV on leprosy directly.

Nonmycobacterial pulmonary infections

Bacterial pneumonia

Investigations of patients with HIV who have pulmonary disease demonstrate that bacterial pneumonia caused by *Streptococcus pneumoniae* and *Haemophilus influenzae* occur as frequently in developing countries as they do in the developed world. In a study in Nairobi, Kenya, 79 episodes of invasive pneumococcal disease were seen in 587 HIV-positive women, whereas there was only one episode in 132 HIV-seronegative women.[19] Serotyping revealed that most recurrent events were related to re-infection. A wide spectrum of HIV-related pneumococcal disease was seen; 56% of cases were pneumonia, 30% were sinusitis and 11% were occult bacteremia. The mean $CD4^+$ lymphocyte count was 302 cells/mm^3 at first presentation and 171 cells/mm^3 for recurrent episodes. In this study *S. pneumoniae* caused more disease at an earlier stage of HIV immunosuppression than did *M. tuberculosis*.

The importance of pneumococcal disease in the host with HIV infection cannot be underestimated. Invasive pneumococcal disease has been shown to cause significant morbidity and mortality. The use of the pneumococcal polysaccharide vaccine to prevent infection in people with HIV infection has been evaluated and generally recommended by the Centers for Disease Control and Prevention. In light of the increased prevalence of antibiotic resistance and ease of administration, this vaccine would appear to be a prudent use of resources. However, studies have shown that the polysaccharide vaccine is not beneficial in individuals with HIV infection in African populations. Conjugate pneumococcal vaccines hold greater promise to reduce the incidence of invasive pneumococcal disease. Evaluations in pediatric population are underway in South Africa and the Gambia.

Pneumocystis carinii *pneumonia*

Several opportunistic infections that are common in developed countries are rarely identified in developing countries. For example, in Abidjan, *P. carinii* pneumonia accounts for only 8% of deaths from HIV-associated pulmonary disease and only 2% of all HIV-associated deaths. A recent report from Zimbabwe demonstrated that even after selecting patients who had abnormal chest radiographs that were consistent with *P. carinii* pneumonia, tuberculosis was still a more frequent diagnosis than *P. carinii* pneumonia.

Although *P. carinii* pneumonia appears to be infrequent in Africa and Asia, it is relatively common in Latin America and Caribbean countries, with rates similar to those documented in the USA. A retrospective case series in a clinic in London, UK, found a significantly higher rate of *P. carinii* pneumonia as a presenting diagnosis in non-Africans (34%) than in Africans (17%). Prevalence rates are also low in Haiti, with a case series incidence of less than 10%. Other reported rates include 7–25% in Thailand, 20–24% in Mexico and 32–45% in Brazil.

The reasons for lower rates of *P. carinii* pneumonia in parts of the developing world are unclear. Possible explanations include less environmental exposure to *P. carinii*, exposure to different strains of *P. carinii*, differences in host susceptibility, earlier deaths in patients in the tropics who have AIDS owing to exposure to more virulent organisms, and diagnostic difficulties. When it does occur, the clinical presentation of *P. carinii* pneumonia in developing countries appears to be similar to that in industrialized countries. Frequent co-infection with tuberculosis may obscure the diagnosis. The diagnosis and treatment of *P. carinii* pneumonia are discussed in Chapter 124.

Diarrheal disease

In addition to tuberculosis, one of the more common clinical syndromes seen in persons with HIV infection in developing countries is a diarrhea–wasting syndrome frequently referred to as 'slim disease' (Chapter 131). Diarrhea lasting longer than 1 month occurs in up to 50% of patients in Africa who have AIDS, a rate that is more frequent than that observed in persons with HIV infection in industrialized countries. The diarrhea is usually intermittent and not associated with blood or mucus, and it is only rarely secretory in nature. In one-third to two-thirds of patients who have diarrhea in Uganda, Zaire and Zambia, no cause was found despite detailed examinations. In other studies, pathogens (including cryptosporidia, microsporidia, *Shigella* spp., *Salmonella* spp. and *Campylobacter* spp.) have been identified with frequencies of 7–48%.

Other diagnoses are also common among patients who have such profound wasting. In an autopsy study in Côte d'Ivoire, 44% of patients dying with HIV wasting syndrome had disseminated tuberculosis, compared with 25% without the syndrome. A chronic fever syndrome is also frequently associated with tuberculosis and nontyphoid salmonellosis. Often there is very little that can be done for patients who have this syndrome except to provide nutritional support.

Protozoan infections

Toxoplasmosis

Toxoplasma gondii is a common opportunistic infection in both developed and developing countries, and the incidence is proportional to the prevalence of latent infection in the population at risk for HIV. A higher prevalence of cerebral toxoplasmosis has been documented among Latin American patients than in the USA, which is consistent with the higher underlying prevalence of toxoplasmosis in Latin America. Although there is a suggestion that up to 50% of seropositive AIDS patients in some parts of the world may develop toxoplasmal encephalitis, its frequency in developing countries is unclear because of limited diagnostic capabilities. Autopsy series that have included examination of the brain have suggested disease prevalence rates in late-stage AIDS patients of 15% in Abidjan, 25% in Mexico City and 36% in Kampala. For more detailed information on toxoplasmosis, see Chapters 127 & 158.

Visceral leishmaniasis

The overlap of visceral leishmaniasis and AIDS is increasing because of the spread of the AIDS pandemic to rural areas and the spread of visceral leishmaniasis to suburban areas. Consequently, cases of co-infection with *Leishmania* spp. and HIV are becoming more frequent, with important clinical, diagnostic, chemotherapeutic, epidemiologic and economic implications. Co-infection with *Leishmania* spp. and HIV is now considered an 'emerging disease', especially in southern Europe, where 25–75% of adult visceral leishmaniasis cases are related to HIV infection and 1.5–9% of patients who have AIDS suffer from newly acquired or reactivated visceral leishmaniasis. The WHO reviewed 692 retrospective cases that occurred between 1985 and 1996 in southern Europe and eastern Africa.[20] Of the cases of co-infection, 90% were observed in patients with $CD4^+$ lymphocyte counts of less than 200 cells/mm^3. Bone marrow aspiration was the most frequently used technique for parasitologic diagnosis. In two-thirds of these cases, the diagnosis of HIV was made before that of leishmaniasis.

Multiple visceral locations outside of the reticuloendothelial system are frequent during co-infection; these locations include the blood, skin, gastrointestinal tract, lungs and central nervous system. Because of the high frequency of leishmaniasis in the peripheral blood of these patients, transmission via blood or needles, particularly among injecting drug users, is a major problem.

The *Leishmania* spp. frequently involved in HIV infection are those that cause visceral disease, such as *Leishmania donovani* and *L. infantum* in Asia, southern Europe and Africa, and *L. chagasi* in Latin America. Cutaneous leishmaniasis has a much wider geographic distribution than visceral disease but it is only rarely involved as a complication of HIV infection. Classic visceral leishmaniasis documented in patients with HIV infection is probably caused by reactivation of a latent infection, owing to increasing immunosuppression. In one study, the $CD4^+$ lymphocyte count was less than 200 cells/mm^3 in more than 75% of the patients with HIV infection in whom visceral leishmaniasis was diagnosed, and fewer than 5% of patients had counts of 500 cells/mm^3 or greater.

The clinical presentations of visceral leishmaniasis in HIV are quite similar to that described in HIV-negative patients; clinical features include weight loss, fever, pancytopenia and hepatosplenomegaly. Diagnosis is based on a high index of suspicion in a person who has resided in or traveled to an endemic area, and treatment is similar to that employed in patients without HIV infection who have leishmaniasis (see Chapters 127 and 172). In Ethiopia, a recent clinical trial evaluated the treatment of visceral leishmaniasis in patients with and without HIV infection. Those co-infected had a greater mortality (33.3% vs 3.6%) and relapse rate (16.7% vs 1.2%). The authors expressed the concern that HIV-positive patients with relapsing visceral leishmaniasis could serve as a reservoir of resistant organisms. Treatment guidelines support the use of two drug combination therapy.

Trypanosomiasis

Trypanosoma cruzi, the cause of Chagas' disease, infects millions of people in Latin America. Reports from Argentina, Brazil and Chile have described clinical and laboratory findings in about two dozen patients co-infected with HIV and *T. cruzi*.[21] These reports suggest that Chagas' disease may result from reactivation of latent *T. cruzi* infection and that clinical manifestations such as meningoencephalitis may be more frequent and more severe in those infected with HIV.

Activation of *T. cruzi* infection by HIV or AIDS usually presents with central nervous system manifestations, but in one review trypanosomes were demonstrated in the blood of five of six cases in whom the examination was done. In one pathologic study of 23 cases, acute myocarditis was frequently noted in those cases that were autopsied, but no information was presented as to whether clinical evidence of myocarditis was present during life.

Malaria

Multiple studies have examined the effect of HIV on the course of malaria, and in general they have found no changes in the severity, incidence or successful treatment of malaria (see Chapter 166). The failure of HIV to affect the course of malaria may be in part due to the complex immune response to malaria, which is not easily perturbed by a predominantly T-cell immunodeficiency. In one study of patients in Burkina Faso, investigators demonstrated a preservation of some components of the malaria-specific immune response in AIDS patients who were co-infected with *Plasmodium falciparum*. Similarly, studies have been unable to demonstrate a significant effect of HIV on malaria or vice versa in children, despite the fact that malarial infection is associated with increased levels of the proinflammatory cytokine tumor necrosis factor α, which would be expected to upregulate HIV replication.

Challenging the apparent lack of a significant interaction are several recent studies conducted in Uganda. A hospital-based case–control study, a rural population-based cohort study and an urban clinic-based cohort study all showed that HIV infection was associated with increased frequency and severity of clinical episodes of malaria parasitemia.[22–24] The effect increased with declining immunosuppression as indicated by decreasing $CD4^+$ lymphocyte counts. Two recent studies have shown that infant mortality is higher in babies born to mothers who are co-infected with placental malaria and HIV. It was also shown that HIV infection impairs the pregnant woman's ability to control *P. falciparum* infection. Thus, there is an interaction between HIV and malaria at the placenta. In addition, malaria can contribute to the increased spread of HIV, owing to the need for more frequent transfusions to treat the anemia of malaria.

Enteric parasitic infections

Enteric parasitic infections such as isosporiasis and cryptosporidiosis may be reported in as many as 5–10% of patients who have AIDS in the tropics, compared with 0.2% of patients who have AIDS in the USA. Reports have also shown that the risk of isosporiasis among residents of the USA with AIDS is higher among those born in Latin America and Haiti than among those born in the USA. In Zambia, evaluation of persistent diarrhea in patients with AIDS revealed cryptosporidiosis (7%), microsporidiosis (16%), isosporiasis (37%) and no etiology (40%); treatment with albendazole resulted in a complete or partial response in 60% of those shown to have enteric parasitic infection.[25]

Penicillium marneffei

A common fungal pathogen in AIDS patients in South East Asia is *Penicillium marneffei*.[26] It causes the third most common opportunistic infection in HIV disease in northern Thailand, after extrapulmonary tuberculosis and cryptococcal meningitis. *Penicillium marneffei* was first isolated in 1956 and infection was a rare event before the arrival of the AIDS pandemic in South East Asia. Since then hundreds of cases have been diagnosed, mainly in southern China, northern Thailand, Hong Kong, Vietnam, Singapore, Indonesia and Myanmar. The environmental reservoir of *P. marneffei* is unknown, but the organism has been isolated from the organs, feces and burrows of three species of bamboo rat. Exposure to soil appears to be a key factor in transmission.

Disseminated *P. marneffei* infection is characterized by fever, anemia, weight loss and papular skin lesions. Other frequent signs and symptoms include cough, generalized lymphadenopathy, hepatomegaly and diarrhea. The most common cutaneous manifestation is a generalized papular rash with a central umbilication that resembles the lesions of molluscum contagiosum. These are predominantly found on the face, scalp and upper extremities, but occur throughout the body. Chest radiographs are frequently abnormal, with diffused reticulonodular or localized alveolar infiltrates.

The mean duration of illness before presentation is 4 weeks. The incubation period of disseminated disease is unclear and the disease may be a result of reactivation of latent infection as opposed to new infection or re-infection. However, the development of clinically active disease within weeks of exposure in endemic areas, and the reports of children who have vertically transmitted HIV infection developing disease in the first months and years of life demonstrate that primary infection can quickly lead to disseminated disease. Finally, the pronounced seasonal variation in disease incidence implies an important role for exogenous re-infection and the expression of disease with *P. marneffei* in AIDS patients in endemic areas. In addition to endemic areas, travelers from regions where *P. marneffei* is not endemic have become infected with this pathogen while traveling in South East Asia. Diagnosis and treatment are discussed in Chapters 126 and 237.

Other opportunistic infections

Other opportunistic infections, which may be similar in all areas of the world, include oral and esophageal candidiasis, cryptococcosis, cytomegalovirus infection and Kaposi's sarcoma. Herpes simplex virus infection, herpes zoster and cerebral toxoplasmosis also appear to be relatively common in most areas where diagnostic equipment is readily available. It should be noted that regional variations in frequencies of these diseases do exist within developing countries. Cryptococcosis accounted for only 2% of AIDS deaths in Abidjan but is probably more common in central and southern Africa.

Mycobacterial infections apart from tuberculosis, such as *Mycobacterium kansasii*, have been long-standing health problems among miners in South Africa and may now be emerging as HIV-associated infections in those miners with HIV infection.

Endemic Kaposi's sarcoma has a striking geographic distribution, being most common in central Africa. Kaposi's sarcoma associated with HIV is likely to have a similar heterogeneous disease frequency, although the incidence of Kaposi's sarcoma has increased in all countries in which HIV disease occurs. Kaposi's sarcoma has recently been associated with a new human herpes virus, namely HHV-8, although the epidemiology of this virus and its distribution worldwide remains unknown (see Chapter 215).

HIV TESTING

Currently, HIV testing in the developing world is done mostly for purposes of surveillance. This involves very small population samples and is done anonymously. If people have little hope of treatment, they feel little incentive to be tested. In many countries there are no voluntary testing and counseling facilities because of lack of funds. In one study in South Africa, only 2% of people who were HIV-positive knew their status. In Kenya, only one of 63 randomly chosen women who tested HIV-positive was aware of her infection. In addition to cost, the fact that current testing procedures require at least two visits to a testing site further complicates access to testing. In rural South Africa, only 17% of people who asked to be tested came back for their results. Rapid test formats for HIV detection of antibody provide an alternative that has been successful in various countries, but the cost is high and the assay is not readily available in many locations. In one study of these rapid tests, however, 96% chose to know the result and were informed before leaving the clinic.

Thus, it is apparent that over 90% of people with HIV infection in the developing world do not know their HIV status. At current estimates, this suggests that there are over 27 million people in the world today who have no idea that they are infected. There are important reasons for knowing one's HIV status. The earlier people know they are infected, the greater the opportunity for them to access treatment, some forms of which are not expensive, and to apply pressure on communities and governments for improved access to care. The earlier people are aware of their infection, the better able they are to make informed and responsible decisions about childbearing and avoiding transmission to spouses or partners, and to make plans for family welfare before they become ill or die. Furthermore, the one important benefit of self-knowledge of HIV status is that it helps unmask the invisible epidemic and permits a genuine community response. If people become aware of their infection early on, while they are still relatively healthy, this gives them time and energy to support one another as well as to alert the community to the epidemic.

However, these benefits to individuals, families and communities are realistically achievable only where people feel safe in finding out whether they are infected. Efforts by governments and civil society to combat rejection and discrimination directed at people who have HIV are vital (UNAIDS).

In 1997, WHO issued guidelines for the selection and use of HIV antibody tests applicable for use in developing countries.[27] The three main objectives for HIV antibody testing are:

- screening of blood and blood products;
- unlinked and anonymous testing for the purpose of monitoring prevalence and trends of HIV infection; and
- diagnosis of HIV infection among asymptomatic people and those with clinical signs and symptoms suggestive of HIV infection.

There are three strategies recommended by the WHO. In strategy 1, all serum and plasma is tested with one enzyme-linked immunosorbent assay (ELISA) or rapid assay. Serum that is reactive is considered HIV antibody positive. This strategy can be used for screening blood donors to protect the blood supply but it should not be used for notification of the blood donor unless strategy 2 or 3 is implemented. Strategy 1 can also be used for surveillance when screening anonymous samples.

Strategy 2 includes testing serum by one ELISA or rapid assay and, if it is reactive on the first assay, it is then retested with a second ELISA or rapid assay based on a different antigen preparation or a different test principle. Concordant results after repeat testing will indicate a positive or negative result. If the results of the two assays remain discordant, the specimen is considered indeterminate. Strategy 2 is recommended for surveillance, particularly when testing populations with a low prevalence of HIV. The additional test in strategy 2 compared with strategy 1 is necessary in order not to overestimate the HIV prevalence of such regions. Strategy 2 is also recommended for notification of the blood donor, particularly in developing countries, where strategy 2 is more cost effective than strategy 3.

Strategy 3 is similar to strategy 2, except that it requires a third test if the serum is found to be reactive on the second assay. The three tests in this strategy should be based on different antigen preparations or different test principles. A specimen is considered to be antibody-positive if it is reactive on all three assays. If the serum is discordant on any of the three assays, it is considered to be indeterminate. This strategy is recommended for diagnosis and patient notification.

In the selection of HIV antibody tests for use in strategies 2 and 3, the first test should have the highest sensitivity, whereas the second and third tests should have higher specificity than the first. The number of initial discordant or indeterminate results should not exceed 5%.

An HIV test kit bulk purchase program has been established by the WHO in collaboration with UNAIDS in order to provide national AIDS control programs that use tests giving the most accurate results at the lowest possible cost.

PREVENTION OF HIV INFECTION

Although the epidemic continues to spread throughout the developing world, it is also likely that increased preventive efforts could effectively limit the magnitude of the epidemic. For example, in those countries where the epidemic is still in an expansion phase but is not yet fully visible, the public health response is likely to have a decisive influence on its course. There is every reason to believe that the course of the pandemic could still be altered profoundly by the introduction of HIV prevention strategies that are within the technical reach of all countries. Several successes in slowing the HIV pandemic have provided encouragement and further stimulus for improved programs. Aggressive treatment of STDs coupled with a program of condom distribution has already been shown to be effective in decreasing HIV incidence rates in populations at high risk for HIV in sub-Saharan Africa and Asia. Needle-exchange programs have helped to stabilize and in some cases reduce HIV incidence among intravenous drug users in selected countries. HIV incidence rates can be reduced by an estimated 50% with adequately supported prevention programs. In Asia alone this could mean the prevention of several million AIDS deaths among young adults in their most productive years.

While we await the availability of a vaccine and the effect of therapeutic interventions, a primary prevention strategy must be focused on educational efforts to influence social, cultural and behavioral factors. To control the AIDS epidemic, countries will need not only to promote individual behavior change but also to address the related problems of social disruption associated with mounting unemployment, accelerated urbanization, commercial sex, rapid decline in health services and drug abuse. Fundamental social changes, such as improving the social status of women, will be required if AIDS control efforts are to succeed. In view of the rapid pace of HIV transmission in sub-Saharan Africa and Asia, implementation of these principles of AIDS prevention and care is needed urgently.

Despite the existing economic and logistic restraints of health services in some developing countries, good care for HIV/AIDS patients is possible. The value of symptomatic treatment combined with supportive psychological, pastoral and social services has been well documented in many localities, and establishment of services is a prerequisite for the acceptance of a preventive intervention within any comprehensive control program. Policy makers should invest limited resources in improving the infrastructure of the existing health services to enable them to cope with the increasing number of cases of tuberculosis, pneumonia and other opportunistic infections.

PREVENTION OF OPPORTUNISTIC INFECTIONS

Those opportunistic infections associated with the greatest degree of morbidity and mortality, as well as available preventive and therapeutic options, include tuberculosis and bacteremia due to non-*typhi Salmonella* spp. and *S. pneumoniae*.[28] Tuberculosis and other endemic bacterial infections regularly occur in patients with HIV infection but without profound immunosuppression. Primary preventive therapy against tuberculosis provides an important first line of defense against the development of disease in earlier stages of HIV infection.

Recent studies have evaluated the role of trimethoprim-sulfamethoxazole (TMP–SMX) prophylaxis in reduction of infections other than *P. carinii* pneumonia in patients with HIV infection. A randomized trial conducted in Côte d'Ivoire showed that events leading to hospitalization or death were 43% lower in African adults with early symptomatic HIV disease treated with TMP–SMX rather than with placebo. The beneficial effect was due to activity of TMP–SMX against bacterial infections, malaria and isosporosis. A recent observational study conducted by the Centers for Disease Control illustrated that TMP–SMX prophylaxis during intervals when patients had $CD4^+$ lymphocyte counts of less than 200 cells/mm^3 was associated with significant protection from toxoplasmosis, salmonellosis, infection with *Haemophilus* spp., invasive or any staphylococcal infection, and *P. carinii* pneumonia. In South Africa, TMP–SMX reduced mortality and the incidence of severe HIV-related illness in patients with advanced immunosuppression ($CD4^+$ lymphocyte count <200 cells/mm^3 or total lymphocyte count of 1250 cells/mm^3), despite the low incidence of *P. carinii* pneumonia in this population.[29] Concerns cited as limitations to the use of TMP–SMX include an anticipated increase in antimicrobial resistance in pathogens such as nontyphoidal salmonellas and the pneumococcus. Of additional concern is the potential for cross-resistance between pyrimethamine and trimethoprim, as sulfadoxine–pyrimethamine is one of the most widely used treatments against *P. falciparum*.

HIV TREATMENT IN DEVELOPING COUNTRIES

On April 22nd 2002, the WHO announced the first treatment guidelines for children and adults infected with HIV in the developing world.[30] This action has set the stage for a tremendous increase in access to care; WHO estimated that at least 3 million people needing treatment should have access to medicines by 2005. The treatment guidelines were accompanied by the expansion of the Essential Medicines List to include antiretrovirals in addition to nevirapine and zidovudine, which were previously listed for the prevention of mother-to-child HIV transmission. The WHO report presents a standardization and simplification of HAART. However, the complexity of providing care to millions of people in resource-poor areas extends well beyond access to medications.

In order to ensure the safe and appropriate use of antiretrovirals, resources for evaluating patients prior to the initiation of therapy and monitoring for response to therapy, as well as for the development of potential side effects, must also be available. The WHO recommends initiation of therapy based on clinical staging and $CD4^+$ lymphocyte count or total lymphocyte count.

- WHO stage I includes those individuals with HIV infection who are asymptomatic or manifest persistent generalized lymphadenopathy;
- stage II includes those with weight loss (<10% of body weight), minor mucocutaneous manifestations, herpes zoster and recurrent upper respiratory tract infections;
- stage III includes those with weight loss (>10% body weight), unexplained chronic diarrhea, unexplained prolonged fever, thrush, oral hairy leukoplakia, pulmonary tuberculosis, severe bacterial infections and bedridden for less than 50% of the day during the past month; and
- stage IV includes those with clinical syndromes consistent with AIDS and/or bedridden for more than 50% of the day during the past month.

The guidelines, shown in Table 133.1, recommend starting HAART in those who have WHO stage IV disease irrespective of $CD4^+$ lymphocyte count and WHO stage I, II or III with $CD4^+$ lymphocyte count below 200 cells/mm^3 in areas where $CD4^+$ lymphocyte count is available. If $CD4^+$ lymphocyte count is unavailable, HAART is recommended in those with WHO stage II or III with total lymphocyte count below the range of 1000–1200 cells/mm^3. Assessment of HIV viral load is not considered essential for determining the need for therapy.

WHO RECOMMENDATIONS FOR STARTING HIV/AIDS THERAPY.	
If CD4 testing is available	WHO stage IV disease irrespective of $CD4^+$ lymphocyte count WHO stage I, II, III with $CD4^+$ lymphocyte counts <200 cells/mm^3
If CD4 testing unavailable	WHO stage IV disease irrespective of total lymphocyte count WHO stage II or III disease with a total lymphocyte count <1000–1200 cells/mm^3

Table 133.1 World Health Organization recommendations for starting HIV/AIDS therapy. Recommendations for initiating antiretroviral therapy in adults and adolescents with documented HIV infection.

In addition to the assessment of immunologic function as indicated by symptoms and lymphocyte count, further testing for the safe and effective use of HAART is divided into four categories listed in Table 133.2: absolute minimum tests, basic tests, desirable tests and optional tests. Absolute minimum testing includes an HIV antibody test and hemoglobin or hematocrit level. Basic testing adds white blood cell count and differential, liver enzymes, serum creatinine and/or blood urea nitrogen, serum glucose and pregnancy tests for women. Desirable tests include bilirubin, amylase, lipid levels and $CD4^+$ lymphocyte count. Testing for HIV viral load is deemed to be optional.

The guidelines are based on rigorous evaluation conducted almost exclusively in developed countries. A matter for concern is whether guidelines created for the populations of developed nations are adaptable to HIV-infected populations worldwide. Specifics regarding the presence of different HIV subtypes, endemic infections such as tuberculosis, genetic determinants and environmental factors such as nutritional status may introduce factors that alter response to treatment.

Developing nations that have successfully implemented HAART include Brazil, Thailand, Senegal and Uganda. Studies are needed to examine responses to HAART and whether changes to the guidelines would better serve populations in different regions around the world.

WHO GUIDELINES FOR LABORATORY MONITORING OF ANTIRETROVIRAL DRUG USE	
Absolute minimum tests	HIV antibody test Hemoglobin or hematocrit
Basic tests	White blood cell count and differential Alanine or aspartate aminotransferase Creatinine and/or blood urea nitrogen Serum glucose Pregnancy test for women
Desirable tests	Bilirubin amylase Serum lipids $CD4^+$ lymphocyte count
Optional test	HIV viral load

Table 133.2 World Health Organization guidelines for laboratory monitoring of antiretroviral drug use.

With initiation of HAART on a population-wide scale, continuous surveillance of drug-resistant viruses will be needed to inform treatment guidelines. A recent study conducted in Gabon demonstrated resistance to antiretroviral therapy. Of great concern is that antiviral drug resistance due to suboptimal therapies could limit the potency of available treatments. In parallel with promulgation of the guidelines, the WHO, in collaboration with the International AIDS Society, is developing a global HIV drug resistance surveillance network.

Multiple studies conducted in developed nations have proved the tremendous benefit available to people with HIV infection by the initiation of HAART. Consequently, morbidity and mortality due to HIV have declined dramatically. In developed or developing nations, HAART provides the only hope of survival for those with HIV infection who are able to adhere to daily lifelong therapy. Moreover, the availability of HAART can reinforce prevention activities by offering an incentive to seek HIV testing, preventing mother-to-child transmission and decreasing the risk of sexual transmission.

IMPACT OF HIV AND AIDS ON HEALTH CARE SYSTEMS

As the number of people with HIV infection in developing countries continues to increase, HIV/AIDS will continue to make increasing demands on the health care system at all levels. UNAIDS has estimated that, by 2005, US$9.2 billion will be needed per year to support prevention ($4.8 billion) and treatment and support interventions ($4.4 billion).[31] The allocation of funds for prevention versus care and support varies according to region, with 66% and 32% of estimated expenditure needed for care and support in sub-Saharan Africa and Asia respectively. AIDS prevention activities include teacher training and peer education, condom promotion and distribution, treatment of STDs, voluntary testing and counseling, transfusion screening and prevention of mother-to-child HIV transmission. Included in care and support activities are diagnostic testing, palliative care, opportunistic infection treatment, drug costs and monitoring for HAART, as well as orphanage care and living assistance. Mobilization of such tremendous resources will require a considerable commitment from both domestic and donor sources.

Unfortunately, these demands come at a time of great financial vulnerability for health systems and at a stage, particularly in developing countries, when a great deal of work remains to be done to increase primary health care. Primary care is intended to be the interface of contact between communities and the national health care system, bringing health care as close as possible to where people live and work. Diagnosis and treatment to relieve symptoms and to prevent and treat opportunistic infections can ease suffering and prolong the productive lives of people who have HIV, sometimes at a low cost. As the patient's immune system collapses, however, available treatments become increasingly more expensive. An analysis by the World Bank of alternative treatment and care options concludes that community-initiated care provided at home, although often shifting costs from the national taxpayer to the local community, also greatly reduces the cost of care and thereby offers hope of affordability in improving the quality of the last years of life of people who have AIDS.

The epidemic will undoubtedly increase demand for medical care and reduce its supply at a given quality and price. As the number of people who have HIV infection increases, access to medical care will become more difficult and more expensive for everyone, including people not infected with HIV, and total health expenditure per capita will rise. Governments are under pressure to increase their share of health care spending and to provide special subsidies for the treatment of HIV infection. Unfortunately, because of the scarcity of resources and the inability or unwillingness of governments to increase public health spending enough to offset these pressures, either of these policies may exacerbate the impact of the epidemic on the health care sector.

Governments should ensure that patients who have HIV infection benefit from the same access to care as other patients who have comparable illnesses and similar ability to pay. Because of discrimination, people who have HIV are frequently denied treatment or face barriers to care that others do not encounter. Governments should also provide information about the efficacy of treatments for opportunistic illnesses, HIV infection and AIDS; subsidize the treatment of STDs and contagious opportunistic infections; subsidize the screening of the blood supply; and ensure access to health care for the poorest, regardless of HIV infection status.

REFERENCES

1. Joint United Nations Program on HIV/AIDS and World Health Organization. AIDS epidemic update. Geneva: United Nations AIDS Program; 2001.
2. United Nations Special Session on HIV/AIDS. Global crisis – global action. New York: United Nations: 2001.
3. Centers for Disease Control. The global HIV and AIDS Epidemic, 2001. MMWR Morb Mortal Wkly Rep 2001;50:434–9.
4. Piot P, Bartos M, Ghys PD, *et al.* The global impact of HIV/AIDS. Nature 2001;410:968–73.
5. Joint United Nations Program on HIV/AIDS, World Health Organization and Pan American Health Organization. HIV and AIDS in the Americas: an epidemic with many faces. Rio de Janeiro: UN/WHO/PAHO; 2000.
6. Wiput R, Hanenberg R. The 100% condom program in Thailand. AIDS 1996;10:1–7.
7. Wawer MJ, Serwadda D, Gray RH, *et al.* Trends in HIV-1 prevalence may not reflect trends in incidence in mature epidemics: data from the Rakai population-based cohort, Uganda. AIDS 1997;11:1023–30.
8. Joint United Nations Program on HIV/AIDS. Report on the global HIV/AIDS epidemic. Geneva: United Nations AIDS Program; 2000.
9. Grant AD, Kaplan JE, DeCock KM. Preventing opportunistic infections among human immunodeficiency virus-infected adults in African countries. Am J Trop Med Hyg 2001;65:810–21.
10. Morgan D, Whitworth JAG. The natural history of HIV-1 infection in Africa. Nat Med 2001;7:143–5.
11. Morgan D, Malamba SS, Orem J, *et al.* Survival by AIDS defining condition in rural Uganda. Sex Transm Inf 2000;76:193–7.
12. Wawer MJ, Sewankambo NK, Serwadda D. Control of sexually transmitted diseases for AIDS prevention in Uganda: a randomised community trial. Lancet 1999;353:525–35.
13. Bentwich Z, Maartens G, Torten D, *et al.* Concurrent infections and HIV pathogenesis. AIDS 2000;14:2071–81.
14. World Health Organization. WHO report on the tuberculosis epidemic, 2001. Geneva: WHO; 2001.
15. Badri M, Ehrlich R, Wood R, *et al.* Association between tuberculosis and HIV disease progression in a high tuberculosis prevalence area. Int J Tuberc Lung Dis 2001;5:225–32.
16. Wilkinson D, Squire SB, Garner P, 1998. Effect of preventive treatment for tuberculosis in adults infected with HIV: systematic review of randomised placebo controlled trials. Br Med J 1998;317:625–9.
17. Bucher HC, Griffith LE, Guyatt GH, *et al.* Isoniazid prophylaxis for tuberculosis in HIV infection: a meta-analysis of randomised controlled trials. AIDS 1999;13:501–7.
18. Pettipher CA, Karstaedt, Hopley M. Prevalence and clinical manifestations of disseminated *Mycobacterium avium* complex infections in South Africans with acquired immunodeficiency syndrome. Clin Infect Dis 2001;33:2068–71.
19. Gilks CF, Ojoo SA, Ojoo, JC, *et al.* Invasive pneumococcal disease in a cohort of predominantly HIV-1 infected female sex-workers in Nairobi, Kenya. Lancet 1996;347:718–23.
20. World Health Organization. Leishmania/HIV co-infection: epidemiological analysis of 692 retrospective cases. Wkly Epidemiol Rec 1997;72:49–56.
21. Cahn P, Belloso WH, Murillo J, *et al.* AIDS in Latin America. Infect Dis Clin North Am 2000;14:185–209.
22. Whitworth J, Morgan D, Quiqley M, *et al.* Effect of HIV-1 and increasing immunosuppression on malaria parasitaemia and clinical episodes in adults in rural Uganda: a cohort study. Lancet 2000;356:1051–6.
23. Francesconi P, Fabiani M, Dente MG, *et al.* HIV, malaria parasites, and acute febrile episodes in Ugandan adults: a case-control study. AIDS 2001;15:2445–50.
24. French N, Nakiyingi J, Lugada E, *et al.* Increasing rates of malarial fever with deteriorating immune

status in HIV-1 infected Ugandan adults. AIDS 2001;15:899–906.
25. Zulu I, Veitch A, Sianongo S, *et al.* Albendazole chemotherapy for AIDS-related diarrhoea in Zambia—clinical, parasitological and mucosal responses. Aliment Pharmacol Ther 2002;16:595–601.
26. Marques SA, Robles AM, Tortorano AM, *et al.* Mycoses associated with AIDS in the Third World. Med Mycol 2000;38(Suppl.1):269–79.
27. World Health Organization. Revised recommendations for the selection and use of HIV antibody tests. Wkly Epidemiol Rec 1997;72:81–8.
28. Anglaret A, Dakoury-Dogbo N, Bonard D. Causes and empirical treatment of fever in HIV-infected adult outpatients, Abidjan, Côte d'Ivoire. AIDS 2002;16:909–18.
29. Badri M, Ehrlich R, Wood R, *et al.* Initiating co-trimoxazole prophylaxis in HIV-infected patients in Africa: an evaluation of the provisional WHO/UNAIDS recommendations. AIDS 2001;15:1143–8.
30. World Health Organization. Scaling up antiretroviral therapy in resource limited settings: guidelines for a public health approach. Geneva: WHO; 2002.
31. Schwartlander B, Stover J, Walker N, *et al.* Resource needs for HIV/AIDS. Science 2001;292:2434–6.

chapter 134

Pediatric HIV Infection

Peter L Havens

EPIDEMIOLOGY

The vast majority of HIV infection in children is perinatally acquired, via transmission from mother to child. HIV in children less commonly occurs from blood transfusion or receipt of blood components (e.g. during treatment of hemophilia or other coagulation disorders). Transmission may also occur by sexual exposure, either sexual abuse in younger children, or consensual sex in older adolescents and young adults.

The first cases of AIDS in children were reported in 1982. The World Health Organization (WHO) estimated that by the end of 2001, for children under 15 years of age, there were 2.7 million children living with HIV/AIDS, 800,000 new infections, and 580,000 child deaths due to HIV/AIDS in that year. Most children with HIV infection live in sub-Saharan Africa, but all regions of the world are affected (Table 134.1).[1] Reported cases of pediatric AIDS make up 1–2% of the total number AIDS cases in developed countries, but 15–20% of the total number in some developing countries.[2] At least 10.4 million children under age 15 years have lost their mother or both parents to AIDS, and this number of orphans is expected to double by 2010.[3]

Because most children who have HIV infection acquire the virus by transmission from their mother, the epidemiology of perinatally acquired HIV infection closely parallels the epidemiology of HIV infection in women (see Chapters 115 and 135). In most regions of the world, heterosexual transmission is the most common cause of HIV infection in women (see Table 134.1). The greatest growth in numbers of children with HIV infection would be expected in regions where women make up a high percentage of the case total, and where heterosexual exposure is the most common mode of HIV transmission (see Chapter 133).

Half of all new cases of HIV infection are in children and young adults under 25 years of age.[3] Since younger women often have sex with older men, and since transmission from males to females is more likely to result in HIV transmission, HIV infection is more common in female teenagers, with rates in males increasing after the teenage years. HIV infection in adolescents can be associated with heterosexual activity, injection drug use and men having sex with other men (see Chapter 115).

PATHOGENESIS AND PATHOLOGY

In the absence of intervention, the risk of HIV transmission from mother to baby is about 25%, with estimates ranging from 13 to 43% in different regions of the world.[4] While maternal, obstetric, fetal, postnatal and genetic factors may modify perinatal transmission risk (Table 134.2), maternal virus load is critical in determining the risk of perinatal HIV transmission. Maternal–fetal HLA concordance increases perinatal transmission risk,[5] while CCR5 haplotype may be permissive or protective, depending on the specific mutation.[6]

Perinatal transmission of HIV occurs in utero by the virus entering the fetal circulation from maternal blood, by exposure to infected blood or secretions during labor and delivery, or by ingestion of breast milk. Children with HIV infection can be separated into groups of 'rapid progressors' (20–25% of cases) and 'slow progressors' (75–80% of cases), based on the timing of onset of clinical symptoms of HIV disease.[7] Some rapid progressors may have acquired infection in utero, and HIV-1 has been found in villous Hofbauer cells and in fetal tissue in the first trimester of pregnancy. In-utero infection is operationally defined as detection of HIV by culture or identification of HIV genome by polymerase chain reaction (PCR) in infant blood within 48 hours of birth.[8] Peripartum infection, operationally defined in children who were not breast-fed and who have negative HIV culture or tests for HIV DNA or RNA by PCR in the first week of life, followed by positive tests from days 7–90,[8] is associated with slower disease progression. Transmission occurs in utero 26–38% of the time, and in the peripartum period 65–74% of the time.[9,10] Breast-feeding increases transmission risk by 14–16%.[11]

The immaturity of the neonatal immune response may be responsible for the more rapid progression of HIV infection in children than adults.[12] Neonatal natural killer cells have diminished antibody-mediated recognition and killing of HIV-infected cells. Neonatal T cells have diminished ability to produce cytokines. Responses of cytotoxic T cells ($CD8^+$) to HIV *gag* proteins are detected in a smaller proportion of infants (aged under 6 months) than adults.[13]

Genetic factors also play a role in the rate of disease progression in children. The CCR5Δ32 allele slows disease progression,[14] and the stromal cell derived factor 1 3'A mutation accelerates the rate of disease progression.[15]

Although the immunodeficiency of T helper ($CD4^+$) cells has great impact on the clinical manifestations of HIV infection in both adults and children, B-cell dysfunction has an important role in the clinical expression of illness in children. Hypergammaglobulinemia may precede $CD4^+$ T cell depletion in children. Many children have deficient antibody responses to vaccination, especially to polysaccharide antigens. B-cell immunodeficiency is frequently manifest in children as recurrent otitis media, sinusitis, or severe bacterial infections with *Streptococcus pneumoniae* or *Haemophilus influenzae* type b. Children also have impaired phagocytic cell oxidative capacity, which may further increase the frequency and severity of pyogenic bacterial infections.

PREVENTION

Treatment of the mother with zidovudine (ZDV) during pregnancy and labor, and treatment of the newborn for the first 6 weeks of life decreases mother to child transmission (MTCT) of HIV from 25 to 8% in the absence of breast-feeding (Table 134.3).[16] Zidovudine treatment begun before 28 weeks of gestation can interrupt in-utero transmission.[17] Other combinations of prepartum and postpartum therapy can reduce MTCT, including shorter courses of ZDV, with or without lamivudine, and a single prepartum and postpartum dose of nevirapine.[18] Treatment of the infant with ZDV within 48 hours after birth may diminish MTCT, but antiretroviral treatment efficacy is clearly better if started during pregnancy. For women being treated

HIV/AIDS IN CHILDREN UNDER 15 YEARS OF AGE AND FACTORS AFFECTING INCREASE IN HIV/AIDS IN CHILDREN BY REGION, AT YEAR END 2001					
Region	HIV/AIDS in children under 15 years of age			Factors affecting Increase in HIV/AIDS in children	
	Children living with HIV/AIDS at year end, 2001	Children newly infected with HIV in 2001	Deaths from HIV/AIDS in children during 2001	% of HIV-infected adults who are women	Main modes of transmission for persons with HIV*
Sub-Saharan Africa	2,400,000	700,000	500,000	55	Hetero
North Africa and Middle East	20,000	12,000	6000	40	Hetero, IDU
South and South East Asia	200,000	65,000	40,000	35	Hetero, IDU
East Asia and Pacific	7000	3000	1500	20	IDU, Hetero, MSM
Latin America	40,000	10,000	8000	30	MSM, IDU, Hetero
Caribbean	20,000	6000	5000	50	Hetero, MSM
Eastern Europe and Central Asia	15,000	1000	<100	20	IDU
Western Europe	4000	<500	<100	25	MSM, IDU
North America	10,000	<500	<100	20	MSM, IDU, Hetero
Australia and New Zealand	<200	<100	<100	10	MSM
Total	2,700,000	800,000	580,000	48	

* Hetero, heterosexual transmission; IDU, transmission through injecting drug use; MSM, sexual transmission among men who have sex with men

Table 134.1 HIV/AIDS in children under 15 years of age and factors affecting the increase in HIV/AIDS in children by region, at year end 2001. Adapted from World Health Organization.[1]

with three antiretroviral drugs whose viral load is below limits of quantitation on ultrasensitive assays, perinatal HIV transmission risk is less than 1%.[19] Some practitioners recommend elective cesarean section at 38 weeks be considered to reduce perinatal transmission because cesarean section performed before labor onset and before rupture of membranes reduces HIV transmission risk by 50% in women treated with ZDV alone.[20] Even for women with viral load less than 1000, antiretroviral therapy and elective cesarean delivery (before rupture of membranes and before labor onset) can reduce MTCT.[21] Cesarean delivery is not expected to further reduce the low risk of MTCT for women on triple therapy with undetectable virus load (see also Chapter 135).

Because breast-feeding increases the risk of perinatal transmission of HIV,[11] women with HIV infection should be advised not to breast-feed their infants in countries where safe alternatives to breast-feeding are readily available.[22] In developing countries, the risk of HIV infection from breast-feeding may be lower than the risk of death from other diseases that occur with high frequency in bottle-fed infants, and breast-feeding is still recommended for women in those areas, even those with HIV infection.[23]

Vaginal washes have not been successful in reducing vertical HIV transmission, and peripartum vaginal cleaning is not currently recommended for routine use. Information concerning MTCT of HIV is updated frequently by the WHO and UNAIDS, and is available at http://www.unaids.org/publications/documents/mtct/index.html. Issues of treatment of pregnant women with HIV infection are discussed more fully in Chapter 135.

CLINICAL FEATURES

The Centers for Disease Control and Prevention (CDC) classification of adolescents[24] and children who have HIV infection (Table 134.4, 134.6 and 134.7)[25] outlines clinical manifestations related either directly to HIV infection and the resulting immune response, or those related to the progressive loss of $CD4^+$ T cells and secondary (opportunistic) infections or cancers.

Compared with adults, children have more rapid disease progression, and have a different pattern of primary and secondary HIV-related manifestations (Table 134.5).[26,27] Symptoms are most common in children under age 4 years, and in those with in-utero transmission, high virus load and rapid disease progression.[28] Growth delay (failure to thrive) and abnormalities of the central nervous system (CNS) with microcephaly and developmental delay are the most important primary manifestations of HIV infection in children. Cardiomyopathy, nephropathy and possibly enteropathy also represent complications primarily related to HIV infection, whereas swollen parotid glands, lymphoid interstitial pneumonitis, hepatomegaly, splenomegaly and lymphadenopathy may result from the immune response to HIV infection. Important opportunistic infections in children with HIV infection include *Pneumocystis carinii* pneumonia (PCP) and recurrent serious bacterial infections with organisms including *S. pneumoniae* and *H. influenzae* type b. Cryptococcosis and toxoplasma infections are much rarer in children than in adults with HIV infection. Cancers most commonly found in children with HIV infection include lymphomas, leiomyomas and Kaposi's sarcoma, but all cancers are much less common in children than in adults with HIV infection.

Because the normal range for the number of $CD4^+$ T cells changes with age, so does the number that defines immunodeficiency, and CD4% is often used (Table 134.6). Classification of children with HIV infection incorporates both clinical and immunologic information (Table 134.7). Before antiretroviral treatment was available, median survival for children with HIV infection in the USA was approximately 8 years (Table 134.8).[29] Survival is lower with lower $CD4^+$ T-cell counts and higher viral loads (Table 134.9).[30] Children diagnosed with symptomatic disease (CDC category B) or those with poor growth in the first 6 months of life, have more rapidly progressive disease and shorter survival.[31]

Table 134.2 Factors affecting vertical transmission of HIV.

FACTORS AFFECTING VERTICAL TRANSMISSION OF HIV	
Viral factors	• Increased transmission with high virus load • Syncytium-inducing phenotype (SI) does not increase transmission risk • Non-syncytium-inducing (NSI or macrophage tropic) increases transmission risk • HIV-1 is transmitted more readily than HIV-2
Maternal factors	• Advanced disease (low CD4, high CD8 or symptoms of AIDS) increases transmission risk • Primary infection is associated with increased transmission • Primiparous women may transmit HIV more frequently • Maternal Epstein–Barr virus shedding increases transmission risk • Maternal antiretroviral therapy reduces perinatal transmission risk • Vitamin A deficiency is associated with increased transmission risk • Maternal cigarette smoking may increase transmission risk • Other infections (condylomata or other sexually transmitted diseases) may increase transmission • Combined maternal infection with HIV-1 and HIV-2 may protect against transmission
Obstetric events	• First-born of twins has increased infection risk compared to second-born • Rupture of membranes >4 hours increases transmission risk, especially in preterm infants • Maternal bleeding during pregnancy increases transmission risk • Fetal scalp electrode increases risk of transmission • Elective cesarean section reduces perinatal transmission
Fetoplacental factors that increase transmission risk	• Chorioamnionitis • Placenta previa • Prematurity increases risk of peripartum transmission, but not in-utero transmission
Infant factors	• HLA type and maternal–infant HLA concordance • CCR5 chemokine receptor haplotype • Fetal immune response (responsiveness of cord blood leukocytes to HIV *env* determinants may be protective)
Postnatal factors important in transmission	• Breast-feeding increases transmission by 14–16% and breast-feeding longer than 15 months multiplies that risk • Maternal nipple lesions or mastitis increase transmission risk • Maternal seroconversion during breast-feeding increases transmission risk • Infant thrush at <6 months of age increases transmission in breast-feeding infants

With the availability of antiretroviral treatment, disease progression has been slowed considerably, with a change in the median age at death from 6 months to 3.6 years in a European study.[28] However, in areas of the world where treatment is not readily available, rapid disease progression and early death remain common. In Malawi, in a cohort of 190 children with perinatally acquired HIV infection, 89% were dead by 3 years, and only 1% were free of symptoms.[32] In South Africa, newborns co-infected with HIV and tuberculosis, syphilis or cytomegalovirus (CMV) had mean age at death of only 3.5 months, and 83% were dead by 9 months.[33]

At birth, infants who have HIV infection are on average 0.28kg lighter and 1.64cm shorter than those without HIV infection[34] born to women with HIV infection. Because both weight and length are affected, children with HIV infection appear symmetrically small, with average body mass index by 18 months of age.[34] Poor growth by 6 months of age is an indicator of rapid disease progression.[31] Growth failure is not usually secondary to neuroendocrine dysfunction, but may be at least partially related to reduced energy intake.

HIV-1 RNA has been found in cerebrospinal fluid of children with HIV infection, and clinical manifestations of this CNS involvement are common, with 9% of patients showing signs of progressive neurologic involvement by 12 months of age,[26] and 21% diagnosed with encephalopathy by 24 months of age.[35] A wide range of manifestations of neurologic involvement is possible, from developmental delay identified only by prospective testing, to profound cognitive deficits and motor disorders, including signs of pyramidal tract dysfunction, movement disorders and ataxia.[36] Some patients have isolated cognitive dysfunction, whereas others have primarily motor abnormalities and many have a mixed pattern of involvement. The clinical course of illness may be static, it may transiently plateau, or it may be progressive. Progression of cognitive and motor delays occurred by 30 months of age in 50% of 114 prospectively evaluated infants with perinatally acquired HIV infection, even in the absence of overt encephalopathy. In children who have HIV infection, small head circumference is common even without encephalopathy,[34] and microcephaly may occur in over half of the children with HIV-associated encephalopathy. Abnormalities on computerized tomography (CT) of the brain were found in 86% of 83 symptomatic children with HIV infection; these abnormalities included ventricular enlargement, cortical and cerebellar atrophy, and cerebral calcifications.[37] Basal ganglia calcifications associated with disruption of the blood–brain barrier and perivascular calcium deposits can be found in children with HIV encephalopathy.

Pulmonary lymphoid hyperplasia (PLH) and lymphoid interstitial pneumonitis (LIP) are focal (PLH) to diffuse (LIP) lymphocytic infiltratitve diseases of the lung. They begin as asymptomatic interstitial nodular pulmonary infiltrates with hilar and mediastinal lymphadenopathy on chest radiograph, and they may progress to an illness characterized by chronic cough and slowly or intermittently progressive hypoxemia associated with clubbing of the digits.

Table 134.3. Prevention of HIV transmission from pregnant women to their infants.[18]

PREVENTION OF HIV TRANSMISSION FROM PREGNANT WOMEN TO THEIR INFANTS[18]
1. Suggest the use of ZDV, antiretroviral therapy a. ZDV, following the regimen from ACTG Protocol 076
Pregnant women
During pregnancy: ZDV 200mg/dose q8h or 300mg/dose q12h po, beginning after 14 weeks of gestation and continuing until labor begins
During labor: ZDV iv during labor: 2mg/kg load over 0.5–1 hour followed by 1mg/kg per hour iv infusion. Add ZDV for infusion to 5% dextrose in water for concentration of ≤4mg/ml
Before scheduled cesarean section: iv ZDV regimen should be infused at least 3 hours before the cesarean section
Newborn infants
ZDV 2mg/kg/dose po q6h (ZDV 2.6mg/kg/dose po q8h being investigated. Prematures: 1.5mg/kg/dose po q12h 1st 2 weeks, then 2mg/kg/dose po q8h >2 weeks.) Start within 8–12 hours of age. Give 6 weeks of total therapy, if HIV DNA PCR negative. Adjust dose for weight gain as needed. Check hematocrit at 4 weeks. If HIV DNA PCR positive, repeat to confirm and refer to specialist for treatment.
b. Other combinations of prepartum and postpartum therapy can reduce perinatal transmission, including shorter courses of ZDV, with or without lamivudine, and a single prepartum and postpartum dose of nevirapine[18]
2. Avoid procedures that may increase the risk of exposure of the child to maternal blood and secretions (e.g. scalp electrode, scalp pH, etc.)
3. Avoid artificial rupture of membranes unless medically indicated. Rupture of membranes >4 hours increases the risk of MTCT of HIV
4. Cesarean section has been shown to decrease risk of vertical HIV transmission. Cesarean section may be considered if maternal HIV RNA PCR >1000
5. Wash the baby promptly
6. Advise against breast-feeding of the infant, and educate the mother about safe alternatives

PLH–LIP is frequently associated with generalized lymphadenopathy and salivary gland enlargement and, even though it is an AIDS-defining illness, it is associated with prolonged survival compared with survival in other patients with AIDS. Compared to children with PCP, those with PLH–LIP are older (usually over 1 year of age), have less tachypnea and fever, lower lactate dehydrogenase, higher total immunoglobulins and higher titers to Epstein–Barr virus (EBV) antigens.[38] PLH–LIP is pathogenically linked to infection with EBV as well as HIV, and it improves with immune system improvement with antiretroviral therapy. Corticosteroid therapy (e.g. oral prednisone) may be of benefit in selected patients.

Cardiac abnormalities are common. Children with HIV infection have faster heart rate, higher left ventricular mass and lower left ventricular function than uninfected children.[39] HIV genome has been identified in cardiac myocytes and in pericardial fluid in three infants with pericardial effusions and sudden death.[40] Children with rapid disease progression have higher resting heart rate and respiratory rate than other infants with perinatally acquired HIV, and chronic heart disease was found in 53% of 34 children with HIV who died before 5 years of age.[41] Of 81 children with HIV infection evaluated in one study, arrhythmias occurred in 35%, unexpected cardiac arrest in 9%, transient congestive heart failure in 10% and chronic congestive heart failure in 10%.[42] Patients who have encephalopathy may be at highest risk for chronic congestive heart failure and cardiac arrest.[42]

Nephropathy affects 3–40% of children with HIV infection, is more common in blacks, and occurs late in the course of disease. The most common pathologic findings are focal glomerulosclerosis and mesangial hyperplasia associated with lymphohistiocytic tubulointerstitial infiltrates.[43] Although renal disease may be associated with renal failure, it is not usually the cause of death in children with HIV infection.

The occurrence of opportunistic infections in children with HIV infection varies with age and $CD4^+$ T-cell count (Table 134.10).[44] *Pneumocystis carinii* pneumonia in adults occurs late in the course of HIV infection, when T-cell immunodeficiency has progressed enough for this chronic pulmonary colonizer to reactivate and cause acute hypoxemia. In children, PCP occurs at an early age, with peak age of onset at 3–6 months of age.[45] This probably represents primary infection with *P. carinii*, and 20–30% of cases are in children with $CD4^+$ T-cell counts of more than 1500/mm^3.[46,47] Compared with the chronic presentation of PLH–LIP in older children, PCP is characterized by acute onset of fever, tachypnea with rib retraction, significant hypoxemia with diminished breath sounds, wheezes and rhonchi.[38] Chest radiograph may be normal but it usually shows bilateral interstitial and alveolar infiltrates. Diagnosis can be made by using special stains to identify cysts or trophozoites in fluid from induced sputum, bronchoalveolar lavage or lung biopsy. Even though treatment with trimethoprim–sulfamethoxazole (co-trimoxazole) is better tolerated in children than adults, the case fatality rate from PCP in infancy is 33%, which is higher than that in adults.

Serious bacterial infections with organisms including *S. pneumoniae* and *H. influenzae* type b are common in children with HIV infection (see Tables 134.5 and 134.10), and AIDS is defined by two or more episodes of sepsis, pneumonia, meningitis, bone or joint infection, or deep abscess in 2 years.[25] Otitis media, sinusitis and bronchitis are also common manifestations of the B-cell defect that accompanies HIV infection in children, and are caused by the usual childhood respiratory pathogens *S. pneumoniae*, *H. influenzae* and group A streptococci until late stages of immunosuppression, when *Staphylococcus aureus* and *Pseudomonas aeruginosa* may be more common. While intravenous immune globulin (IVIG) has been shown to decrease the number of bacterial infections in selected

CDC CLASSIFICATION FOR CHILDREN (<13 YEARS OF AGE) WITH HIV INFECTION	
Clinical categories	**Diagnostic criteria**
N: Not symptomatic No signs or symptoms of HIV infection or only one of the conditions listed in category A	If <18 months of age two positive results on separate determinations from one or more of the following: (a) HIV culture, (b) HIV PCR or (c) HIV p24 antigen If ≥18 months HIV antibody positive by repeatedly reactive ELISA and confirmatory test (e.g. Western Blot or IFA)
A: Mildly symptomatic Two or more of the conditions listed, but none of the conditions listed in categories B or C	Lymphadenopathy (≥0.5cm at more than two sites; bilateral at one site) Hepatomegaly Splenomegaly Dermatitis Parotitis Recurrent or persistent upper respiratory infection, sinusitis or otitis media
B: Moderately symptomatic Symptoms of HIV infection other than those listed for categories A or C. Examples include but are not limited to those listed	Anemia (<8), neutropenia (<1000) or thrombocytopenia (<100,000) persisting ≥30 days Bacterial meningitis, pneumonia or sepsis (single episode) Candidiasis, oropharyngeal thrush, persisting >2 months in children >6 months old Cardiomyopathy CMV infection, onset before 1 month of age Diarrhea, recurrent or chronic Hepatitis Herpes simplex virus (HSV) stomatitis, recurrent (more than two episodes within 1 year) HSV bronchitis, pneumonitis or esophagitis with onset before 1 month of age Herpes zoster (shingles) – two episodes or more than one dermatome Leiomyosarcoma Lymphoid interstitial pneumonia (LIP) or pulmonary lymphoid hyperplasia (AIDS defining, report to State) Nephropathy Nocardiosis Persistent fever (lasting >1 month) Toxoplasmosis, onset before 1 month of age Varicella, disseminated (complicated chickenpox)
C: Severely symptomatic Any condition listed in the 1987 surveillance case definition for AIDS with the exception of LIP	Serious bacterial infection; two in 2 years: sepsis, pneumonia, meningitis, bone or joint infection, abscess of organ or body cavity (excludes otitis media, skin or mucosal abscesses and indwelling catheter infections) Candidiasis, (esophageal, tracheal, bronchial, pulmonary) Coccidioidomycosis, disseminated or extrapulmonary Cryptococcosis, extrapulmonary Cryptosporidiosis or isosporiasis >1 month duration CMV disease (onset >1 month), other than liver, spleen or lymph nodes Encephalopathy: >1 finding for >2 months and no illness that explains: (a) failure to attain or loss of milestones or intellectual ability shown by neuropsychologic tests; (b) impaired brain growth or acquired microcephaly shown by OFC measurements or brain atrophy on CT scan or MRI (serial imaging needed if <2 years old); (c) acquired symmetric motor deficit with at least two of: paresis, pathologic reflexes, ataxia or gait disturbances Herpes simplex (ulcer >1 month duration or pneumonia or esophagitis >1 month old) Histoplasmosis, disseminated or extrapulmonary Kaposi's sarcoma Lymphoma, primary, in brain Lymphoma, B cell, non-Hodgkin's lymphoma *Mycobacterium tuberculosis*, disseminated or extrapulmonary Mycobacterium infection, noncutaneous, extrapulmonary or disseminated (except leprosy) *Pneumocystis carinii* pneumonia Progressive multifocal leukoencephalopathy Salmonella (nontyphoid) sepsis, recurrent Toxoplasmosis of the brain, onset >1 month old Wasting syndrome in absence of other illness that explains: (a) weight loss >10% of baseline or (b) downward crossing of ≥2 percentile lines on the weight chart in a child ≥1 year or (c) <5th percentile on weight for height on two consecutive measures ≥30 days apart plus (a) chronic diarrhea (≥2 loose stools/day for ≥30 days) or (b) documented fever for ≥30 days, intermittent or constant

Table 134.4 CDC classification for children (<13 years of age) with HIV infection: diagnostic criteria for clinical categories N, A, B and C. Adapted from Centers for Disease Control and Prevention.[25]

CLINICAL FINDINGS IN CHILDREN WITH HIV INFECTION				
Clinical finding	By 6 months (%) (n=66)	By 9 months (%) (n=70)	By 12 months (%) (n=75)	Older children (%)
Anemia	20	33	37	
Serious bacterial infection				55
– One	18	31	37	
– Two	5	9	15	
Persistent oral candidiasis	18	24	27	48
Generalized lymphadenopathy	17	31	39	90
Failure to thrive	17	30	30	62
Hepatomegaly	17	27	35	86
Splenomegaly	15	24	29	69
Thrombocytopenia	14	17	19	
Pneumocystis carinii pneumonia	9	16	15	
Persistent diarrhea	8	10	13	17
Hepatitis	6	9	13	
Other opportunistic infections	5	9	11	31
Progressive neurologic disease	5	7	9	34
Persistent fever	2	7	9	
Lymphoid interstitial pneumonitis	0	1	5	28
Parotitis	0	1	1	10
Cancers (lymphomas)	0	0	0	7
Asymptomatic	36	27	21	

Table 134.5 Clinical findings in children with HIV infection. Adapted from Forsyth *et al.*[26] and Pahwa *et al.*[27]

CDC CLASSIFICATION FOR CHILDREN (<13 YEARS OF AGE) WITH HIV INFECTION						
Immunologic categories	Age of child					
	<12 months		1–5 years		6–12 years	
	Cells/μl	(%)	Cells/μl	(%)	Cells/μl	(%)
1. No suppression	≥1500	(≥25)	≥1000	(≥25)	≥500	(≥25)
2. Moderate suppression	750–1499	(15–24)	500–999	(15–24)	200–499	(15–24)
3. Severe suppression	<750	(<15)	<500	(<15)	<200	(<15)

Table 134.6 CDC classification for children (<13 years of age) with HIV infection.[25] Immunologic categories based on age-specific CD4+ T-cell counts and percent of total lymphocytes.

SUMMARY OF PEDIATRIC HIV CLASSIFICATION				
Immunologic categories (see Table 134.6)	Clinical categories			
	N: No signs/symptoms	A: Mild signs/symptoms	B[H]: Moderate signs/symptoms	C[H]: Severe signs/symptoms
1. No suppression	N1	A1	B1	C1
2. Moderate suppression	N2	A2	B2	C2
3. Severe suppression	N3	A3	B3	C3

Table 134.7 Summary of pediatric HIV classification. Children whose HIV infection status is not confirmed are classified by placing the letter E (for perinatally exposed) before the classification code (e.g. EN1). H, both category C and lymphoid interstitial pneumonitis in category B are reportable to state health departments as AIDS. Adapted from Centers for Disease Control and Prevention.[25]

pediatric patients with HIV infection,[48,49] in patients being treated with trimethoprim–sulfamethoxazole (co-trimoxazole) prophylaxis there is no added benefit of IVIG.[50] Children who may benefit from IVIG for prophylaxis of recurrent infections are those with hypogammaglobulinemia or bronchiectasis from recurrent pulmonary infections.

Although HIV is not itself oncogenic, children with HIV infection do have an increased risk of malignancy.[51] Kaposi's sarcoma, although rarer in children than in adults, is found in children with HIV infection.[52] Non-Hodgkin's lymphoma, predominantly of B-cell origin, is the most common malignancy reported in children with HIV infection, and lymphomas of T-cell origin also occur. Many lymphomas are

TIME IN EACH STAGE AND SURVIVAL TIME FROM BEGINNING OF EACH STAGE				
Stage	Mean time in stage (months)	Median survival (months)	Mean survival (months)	% Surviving 5 years
N	10	113	96	75
A	4	103	85	67
B	65	99	81	65
C	34	34	23	17

Table 134.8 Time in each stage and survival time from beginning of each stage in the absence of retroviral therapy. Adapted from Barnhart *et al.*[29]

CD4+ CELL COUNT, VIRUS LOAD AND RISK OF DEATH IN CHILDREN WITH HIV INFECTION				
CD4+%	>15%	>15%	<15%	<15%
HIV RNA PCR	<100,000	>100,000	<100,000	>100,000
Number of patients	103	89	24	36
Mortality rate at 5.1 years (%)	14.6	36.0	62.5	80.6

Table 134.9 CD4+ cell count, virus load and risk of death in children with HIV infection. Based on experience of 254 children enrolled in the NICHD IVIg Clinical Trial.[41,42] Mean age at entry was 3.41 years, and mean follow-up time was 5.1 years. Organon NASBA assay was used to measure plasma HIV RNA. Relative risk of death was 2.75 for each 1 log increase in HIV RNA and 1.33 for each 5 point decrease in CD4+%.[62] Adapted from Mofenson *et al.*[30]

OPPORTUNISTIC INFECTIONS IN 3331 CHILDREN WITH HIV INFECTION					
OI diagnosis	Number of events	Event rate/100 person years	Median age at OI diagnosis (years)	Median CD4% at OI diagnosis	% of patients with CD4 count <50 at time of OI diagnosis
Serious bacterial infection	879	15.1	3.5	17	23
Herpes zoster	199	2.9	7.6	13	27
Disseminated *Mycobacterium avium* complex	126	1.8	6.4	2	76
Pneumocystis carinii pneumonia	92	1.3	3.9	6	55
Candidiasis	87	1.2	4.8	4	60
Cryptosporidiosis	41	0.6	5.9	4	51
CMV retinitis	33	0.5	7.1	4	61
Tuberculosis	27	0.4	7.6	10	33
Other CMV disease	16	0.2	3.6	7	50
Fungal infection	8	0.1	12.3	3	65
Toxoplasmosis	4	0.06	11.5	4	100
Progressive multifocal leukoencephalopathy	4	0.06	10.8	2	100

Table 134.10 Opportunistic infections (OIs) in 3331 children with HIV infection. Adapted from Dankner *et al.*[44]

associated with EBV infection. Smooth muscle tumors, including leiomyomas and leiomyosarcomas, are specifically associated with HIV infection in children,[53] and occur late in the course of illness when the CD4+ T-cell count is low. Epstein–Barr virus genome has been found in the muscle cells of leiomyosarcomas from children with HIV infection, but not in such tumors from persons without HIV infection.[54]

DIAGNOSIS

Because many children with HIV infection remain asymptomatic for long periods of time, the clinical examination is not a sensitive test for the presence of infection. Infection with HIV in adults and children older than 18 months is presumptively diagnosed by using an enzyme-linked immunosorbent assay (ELISA) to screen blood for presence of antibody to HIV. A single positive ELISA is repeated, and if still positive, results are confirmed by Western blot for HIV-specific antibody.[55]

Children born to women with HIV infection passively acquire maternal IgG antibody to HIV, which can make the HIV IgG antibody ELISA reactive for 12–18 months after birth, even in infants not infected with HIV. Therefore, detection of virus or virus products is the preferred means of diagnosis because it can identify infected infants at a younger age.

Culture of HIV is the gold standard for diagnosis of HIV infection in infants under 18 months of age,[56] but DNA PCR is more widely available and has been shown to be equally sensitive. A single positive culture is not diagnostic of HIV infection in infants because 2–7% of children later found to be uninfected may have a positive culture within the first 6 months of life.[57–59] Therefore, at least two positive cultures should be obtained to confirm the diagnosis of HIV infection in children.

The PCR for HIV DNA is the most rapid and accurate method for identification of HIV infection in children under 18 months of age.[9,60,61] Sensitivity is 38% on the day of birth, 93% by day 14 of life and 96% by day 28.[10] False-positive results are possible, owing to laboratory error,[60] but two positive tests together are 98.5% accurate in identifying infection status, and using three tests performed after 1 month of age achieves 100% accuracy. The first positive HIV DNA PCR after perinatal infection may appear as late at 183 days of life.[10]

Two positive HIV DNA PCR tests are needed to diagnose HIV infection in infants. Two negative PCR tests performed at more than 1 month of age, with one at more than 4 months of age, reasonably exclude HIV infection.[62] Because of the importance of a negative test, PCR testing should include controls to assess DNA sample adequacy. Samples with inadequate DNA should be rejected, and not reported as negative. In the child with two negative HIV DNA PCR tests at more than 1 month of age and 2–4 months of age, ELISA for IgG to HIV should be performed at 18 months to confirm absence of infection (seroreversion). Primers for PCR differ in their ability to identify nucleic acid from non-clade B HIV, and in some settings special testing may be required to identify or exclude such infection (see Chapter 136).[63]

Measurement of HIV p24 antigen in blood is not sensitive enough to be used for early diagnosis of HIV infection in children, even if immune complex dissociated methods are used for sample preparation.

MANAGEMENT

Issues of immediate importance in the care of children born to women with HIV infection are:

- continued intervention to prevent HIV infection if possible (see Table 134.3);
- identification of infected infants; and
- institution of prophylactic therapy for PCP.

Independent of specific HIV-associated problems, certain health-related procedures are necessary for all children with HIV infection. Height and weight are measured at regular intervals and plotted on appropriate growth charts. The head circumference should be measured at least every 3 months until 2 years of age, in conjunction with a careful neurologic assessment. Developmental screening is recommended every 6 months until 24 months of age and yearly thereafter.

Respiratory status should be monitored closely for the possible acute onset of PCP in younger patients or the more insidious onset of PLH–LIP in older children. Symptoms or signs of heart failure should prompt evaluation, including chest radiograph, pediatric cardiology evaluation, electrocardiography and possibly echocardiography. A normal heart size on chest radiograph does not rule out cardiac dysfunction. Chest radiographs are indicated yearly for comparison with later films because of the frequency of pulmonary disease and the often subtle beginnings of PLH–LIP.

Ophthalmologic examinations are recommended annually for children treated with dideoxyinosine (ddI). For children who have CMV infection, more frequent eye examinations may be indicated.

Immunizations

Immunizations follow the schedule for infants and children recommended by the American Academy of Pediatrics (Table 134.11),[64] with the following caveats.

Polio

Enhanced-potency inactivated poliovirus vaccine (eIPV) should be given to infected children and to uninfected children when parents or siblings have HIV infection. Oral polio vaccine (OPV) should not be used.

Measles, mumps and rubella

In spite of a small risk of immunizing immunosuppressed patients with live vaccine, measles, mumps and rubella vaccine (MMR) should be given because of the high case fatality rate of measles for HIV-infected children. It may be better to give measles vaccine at 12 months to improve the probability of seroconversion. Second dose may be given as soon as 28 days later Measles vaccination of an adult with an extremely low $CD4^+$ T-cell count has resulted in vaccine-associated pneumonitis, and measles vaccine is not recommended for children with CD4% less than 15%. Immunoglobulin prophylaxis is indicated for HIV-infected children exposed to measles, even if they have been previously vaccinated for measles.

Influenza

Influenza vaccine is indicated for children with symptomatic HIV infection, as well as asymptomatic or uninfected children if they are living with family members who have HIV infection and who are ill.

Pneumococcus

Children up to 5 years of age, infected with HIV, are vaccinated with 7-valent conjugate vaccine. After age 5 years, use 23-valent polysaccharide vaccine. For children 10 years of age or under, a single revaccination is recommended 3–5 years after the initial dose. For children over 10 years of age, a single re-vaccination is recommended if 5 or more years has elapsed since the previous dose

Haemophilus influenzae type b

Administration of *H. influenzae* type b (Hib) conjugate vaccine follows standard recommendations for infants and consideration should be given for its administration to newly diagnosed children who are over 60 months of age.

IMMUNIZATION OF CHILDREN WITH HIV INFECTION		
Vaccinate following routine for children without HIV Infection	Special vaccinations to give children with HIV infection	Do not give these vaccines to children with HIV infection
Polio: eIPV	Influenza	Polio: OPV
DTP/DTaP	Pneumococcus	
MMR	BCG	
Hepatitis B	Varicella	
Hib-conjugate		

Table 134.11 Immunization of children with HIV infection. See text for details. DtaP, diphtheria, tetanus and acellular pertussis vaccine. Adapted from Centers for Disease Control and Prevention.[64]

Bacille Calmette–Guérin

Although bacille Calmette–Guérin (BCG) is not recommended for use in the USA,[65] the WHO recommends its use in asymptomatic infants in regions where risk of tuberculosis is high.[66]

Varicella

Vaccination with varicella vaccine is indicated for children with HIV infection in CDC class N1 or A1, with CD4% of at least 25%. Give two doses with a 3-month interval between them.[67] Not addressed by the CDC recommendations is the patient with prior symptoms and prior low CD4+ T-cell count (e.g. C3 in the past), now on triple antiretroviral therapy, asymptomatic, with CD4% over 25%. There are no data to assure the safety or efficacy of varicella vaccine under such circumstances. However, if such patients are clinically stable, with CD4% over 25% for more than 6 months, two-dose vaccination might be considered, with the understanding that safety and efficacy are not assured.

Laboratory monitoring

CD4+ T-cell count and percentage and a full blood cell count with differential are indicated every 3 months to evaluate the integrity of the immune system. Immunoglobulin concentrations are measured once for patients under 6 months of age to identify those patients with hypogammaglobulinemia.

Virus load is measured as the plasma HIV RNA concentration at 3-month intervals to help in the decision to begin or alter antiretroviral therapy. Virus load testing is also performed 4–8 weeks after beginning or changing therapy, to assess the effectiveness of therapy.[68]

Patients with specific clinical problems may require extra laboratory monitoring.

Antiretroviral therapy

Antiretroviral therapy is indicated for children with symptomatic HIV infection, independent of CD4+ T-cell count or virus load, but USA and European guidelines differ on the extent of symptoms that demand treatment (Table 134.12).[68,69] Since CD4+ T-cell count and virus load are predictive of disease progression and death in children with HIV infection (see Table 134.9) starting antiretrovirals in asymptomatic children with HIV infection may be based on either the CD4+ T-cell count, or on the virus load (see Table 134.12). Before starting therapy based on the CD4+ T-cell count or virus load, persistent abnormality should be confirmed by repeating at least once, with at least 1 week between tests.

Plasma HIV RNA concentrations early in life are higher than in adults with primary HIV infection, and they decline slowly over an undetermined time period toward the values observed in adults. A 'stable baseline' plasma HIV RNA concentration may not be reached in perinatally infected children until they are 3–6 years of age. Adult guidelines for therapy based on plasma HIV RNA concentration might be applicable to children over 30 months of age, suggesting institution of antiretroviral therapy for children in this age group with plasma HIV RNA of more than 55,000 to 100,000 copies/ml, independent of CD4+ T-cell count.[68,70]

Some authorities suggest that antiretroviral therapy is indicated in all children with HIV infection who are less than 1 year of age,[68] hoping that early therapy will suppress HIV replication more efficiently by reducing viral quantity and diversity. The potential benefits of this approach are speculative and need to be weighed against the risks of toxicity of therapy.[69,71]

Single-agent antiretroviral therapy should not be used in the treatment of children or adolescents with HIV infection (Table 134.13).[71] A combination of three drugs is regarded as optimal therapy, most commonly two nucleoside analog reverse transcriptase inhibitors (NRTIs) plus a protease inhibitor.[68–70] Most experience in children is with ZDV–3TC or ZDV–ddI plus NFV, or RTV, or LPV–RTV. D4T–3TC, and either d4T or ZDV plus ABC are also reasonable combinations of NRTIs to which a protease inhibitor may be added. An alternative triple combination regimen of two NRTIs plus one non-NRTI (e.g. NVP or EFV) is acceptable. Triple NRTI regimens are possible (e.g. ZDV–3TC–ABC). Regimens of two NRTIs alone may produce initial clinical benefit but do not produce sustained viral suppression. Compared to adults, infants and children have poor absorption and more rapid metabolism of antiretroviral medications, especially non-NRTI and protease inhibitor, and higher doses may be needed for children compared to adults.

ZDV and d4T should not be used together because of antiviral antagonism and diminished clinical effectiveness. ddC should not be combined with ddI, d4T or 3TC because of the potential for overlapping toxicity. IDV should not be used with SQV.

Intolerance of antiretroviral therapy can lead to dosage modification or discontinuation of therapy. Clinical symptoms – including

CLINICAL AND IMMUNOLOGIC CHARACTERISTICS THAT PROMPT INITIATION OF ANTIRETROVIRAL THERAPY IN CHILDREN WITH HIV INFECTION

Age group	Characteristic	Treatment recommendations	
		USA	Europe
Infant to 12 months	Any	Recommend for any infant <12 months of age	Consider for any infant <12 months of age
	Symptoms		Always start for CDC category C
	CD4 cell count		Always start for CD4 <20% or rapidly falling CD4
	Virus load		Always start if >1,000,000
Child >12 months	Symptoms	Recommend for CDC category A, B or C	Always start for CDC category C. Consider for CDC category B. Defer for CDC category N or A
	CD4 cell count	Recommend for CD4 <25% or rapidly falling CD4	Always start for CD4 <15%. Consider for CD4 <20%. Defer for CD4 >20%
	Virus load	Recommend for high or increasing virus load	Consider if >100,000

Table 134.12 Clinical and immunologic characteristics that prompt initiation of antiretroviral therapy in children with HIV infection. Adapted from Centers for Disease Control and Prevention[68] and Sharland *et al.*[69]

DOSAGE AND ADMINISTRATION OF ANTIRETROVIRALS FOR CHILDREN		
Drug name	**Recommended dosage**	**How supplied**
Nucleoside or nucleotide analog reverse transcriptase inhibitors (NRTIs)		
ZDV, zidovudine, azidothymidine, AZT, Retrovir	Premature infants 0–2 weeks: 1.5mg/kg/dose q12h po (1.0mg/kg/dose q12h iv) >2 weeks: 2.0mg/kg/dose q8h po (1.5mg/kg/dose q8h iv) Term infants 0–6 weeks: 2mg/kg/dose q6h po (1.5mg/kg/dose q6h iv), 4mg/kg/dose q12h po (1.5mg/kg/dose q6h iv) 4 weeks–13 years: 120–160mg/m^2/dose q8h po, 180mg/m^2/dose q12h po ≥13 years: 200mg/dose q8h po or 300mg/dose q12h po	Syrup: 10mg/ml Capsules: 100mg Tablets: 300mg Combivir: ZDV 300mg plus 3TC 150mg in a single tablet Trizivir: ZDV 300mg + 3TC 150mg + ABC 300mg Injection: 10mg/ml in 20ml vials
ddI, dideoxyinosine, didanosine, Videx	<3 months: 50mg/m^2/dose q12h po 3 months to <13 years: 90–135mg/m^2/dose q12h po or 240mg/m^2/dose q24h po ≥13 years, <60kg: tablets 125mg q12h po; powder 167mg q12h po; Videx EC 250mg q24h po ≥13 years, >60kg: tablets 200mg q12h po, powder 250mg q12h po, Videx EC 400mg q24h po	Chewable tablets*: 25mg, 50mg, 100mg, 150mg, 200mg Buffered powder packets: mix with water: 100mg, 167mg, 250mg Enteric-coated delayed release tabs (Videx EC): 125mg, 200mg, 250mg, 400mg Pediatric powder for oral solution mixed to final concentration of 10mg/ml
ddC, dideoxycytidine, zalcitabine, HIVID	<13 years: 0.01mg/kg/dose q8h po ≥13 years: 0.75mg q8h po	Syrup: 0.1mg/ml (investigational) Tablets: 0.375mg, 0.75mg
d4T, stavudine, Zerit	<30kg: 1mg/kg/dose q12h po 30–60kg: 30mg q12h po >60kg: 40mg q12h po	Solution: 1mg/ml Capsules: 15, 20, 30, 40mg Mix with apple sauce
3TC, lamivudine, Epivir	<1 month: 2mg/kg/dose q12h po <37.5kg: 4mg/kg/dose q12h po ≥37.5kg: 150mg/dose q12h po	Oral solution: 10mg/ml Tablets: 150mg Combivir: ZDV 300mg plus 3TC 150mg in a single tablet Trizivir: ZDV 300mg + 3TC 150mg + ABC 300mg
Abacavir, 1592U89, Ziagen, ABC	<37.5kg or 16 years: 8mg/kg/dose q12h po ≥37.5kg or 16 years: 300mg/dose q12h po	Oral solution: 20mg/ml Tablets: 300mg Trizivir: ZDV 300mg + 3TC 150mg + ABC 300mg
TDF, tenofovir disoproxil fumarate, Viread	<13 years: 210mg/m^2/dose q24h po (investigational) >13 years: 300mg q24h po	Tablets: 300mg
Non-nucleoside analog reverse transcriptase inhibitors (NNRTIs)		
NVP, nevirapine, Viramune	<3 months: 5mg/kg/dose q24h × 2 weeks, then 120mg/m^2/dose q12h × 2 weeks, then 200mg/m^2/dose q12h po <1m^2: 120–200mg/m^2/dose q12h po ≥1m^2: 200mg q12h po (maximum dose) Always start at half dose for 2 weeks, then to full dose if tolerated	Suspension: 10mg/ml Tablets: 200mg
DLV, delavirdine, Rescriptor	<13 years: dosage not established ≥13 years: 400mg/dose q8h po	Tablets: 100mg
EFV, DMP 266, efavirenz, Sustiva	<2 years: investigational >2 years: 650mg/m^2/dose q24h po ≥28kg (0.95m^2) and adults: 600mg/dose q24h po	Capsules: 50, 100, 200, 600mg

Table 134.13 Dosage and administration of antiretrovirals for children.[68,69,71,72] Combination therapy is recommended for treatment, and the preferred regimen is two NRTIs and one PI. Most experience in children is with ZDV/3TC or ZDV/DDI plus NFV or RTV. D4T/DDI, D4T/3TC and ZDV/ABC are also reasonable NRTI combinations to which a PI may be added. An alternative triple combination regimen of two NRTIs plus one NNRTI is acceptable but may be less likely to result in durable suppression of viral load. Regimens of two NRTIs alone may show initial clinical benefit but do not usually show sustained viral suppression. There is wide interperson variation in plasma concentration of antiretrovirals and therapeutic drug monitoring may be helpful to guide dose selection. Do not use monotherapy. Do not use the following combinations: ZDV/D4T; DDC/DDI; DDC/D4T; DDC/3TC; or IDV/SQV. Body surface area (BSA) = {[height (cm) × weight (kg)]/3600}^{2}. Adapted from Centers for Disease Control and Prevention[68] Sharland *et al.*,[69] Havens *et al.*[71] and Centers for Disease Control and Prevention.[72]

DOSAGE AND ADMINISTRATION OF ANTIRETROVIRALS FOR CHILDREN—CONT'D		
Drug name	**Recommended dosage**	**How supplied**
Protease Inhibitors (PIs)		
SQV, saquinavir, Invirase (hard gel), Fortovase (soft gel)	<16 years: 50mg/kg/dose q8h po (investigational) ≥16 years: 600mg/dose q8h po with fatty meal (Invirase: poorly absorbed: do not use), 1200mg/dose q8h po with fatty meal (Fortovase)	Hard gel capsules: 200mg Soft gel capsules: 200mg
RTV, ritonavir, Norvir	3 months–13 years: 400–450mg/m^2/dose q12h po ≥13 years: 600mg/dose q12h po	Oral solution: 80mg/ml Gel caps: 100mg Store in original bottle
IDV, indinavir, Crixivan	3–13 years: 500mg/m^2/dose q8h po ≥13 years: 800mg q8h po	Capsules: 200 and 400mg. Must be stored in original bottle
NFV, nelfinavir, Viracept	1 month–13 years: 30–50mg/kg/dose q8h po, 55–60mg/kg/dose q12h po (max. 2000mg/dose; investigational) ≥13 years: 750–1250mg/dose q8h po, 1250mg/dose q12h po (adolescents may need higher dose than adults)	Powder for oral suspension: 50mg/'level scoop', or 200mg/USA teaspoon (5ml) Tablet: 250mg
141W94, APV amprenavir, Agenerase	<3 years: not recommended 3–12 years: 20mg/kg/dose q12h or 15mg/kg/dose q8h po (liquid: 85% bioavailable, so use 22.5mg/kg/dose q12h or 17mg/kg/dose q8h to maximum of 2800mg/day) Adults: 1200mg/dose q12h po	Oral solution: 15mg/ml Tablets: 50mg, 150mg
LPV/r, Abbott-378/r, lopinavir/ritonavir, Kaletra	Children: 300/75 (LPV–RTV)mg/m^2/dose q12h po Adults: 400/100 (LPV–RTV)mg/dose q12h po, 533/133 (LPV–RTV)mg/dose q12h po if given with NVP	Oral solution: 400mg/100mg LPV–RTV per 5ml (80mg/20mg LPV–RTV per ml). Can store at room temp for 2 months Capsules 133.3mg/33.3mg LPV–RTV per capsules

Table 134.13 Cont'd. Dosage and administration of antiretrovirals for children.[68,69,71,72] Combination therapy is recommended for treatment, and the preferred regimen is two NRTIs and one PI. Most experience in children is with ZDV/3TC or ZDV/DDI plus NFV or RTV. D4T/DDI, D4T/3TC and ZDV/ABC are also reasonable NRTI combinations to which a PI may be added. An alternative triple combination regimen of two NRTIs plus one NNRTI is acceptable but may be less likely to result in durable suppression of viral load. Regimens of two NRTIs alone may show initial clinical benefit but do not usually show sustained viral suppression. There is wide interperson variation in plasma concentration of antiretrovirals and therapeutic drug monitoring may be helpful to guide dose selection. Do not use monotherapy. Do not use the following combinations: ZDV/D4T; DDC/DDI; DDC/D4T; DDC/3TC; or IDV/SQV. Body surface area (BSA) = $\{[\text{height (cm)} \times \text{weight (kg)}]/3600\}^2$. Adapted from Centers for Disease Control and Prevention[68] Sharland *et al.*,[69] Havens *et al.*[71] and Centers for Disease Control and Prevention.[72]

growth delay, new or worsening encephalopathy, or new or recurring opportunistic infections – are markers of progressive HIV disease, and may trigger a change in therapy. Rising plasma HIV RNA, or falling CD4+ T-cell counts, are markers of disease progression that may be used to guide a change in antiretroviral therapy.

Prevention of opportunistic infections

Guidelines for the prevention of opportunistic infections in adults and adolescents who have HIV infection established by the US Public Health Service and the Infectious Diseases Society of America, and endorsed by the American Academy of Pediatrics, have been published. Recommendations in this section follow those guidelines except as noted.

Prophylaxis for PCP is indicated for all children with prior PCP, for all children with a percentage of CD4+ T cells that is less than 15% and for all children with a CD4+ T-cell count less than those indicated in Table 134.14. Prophylaxis for PCP is indicated for all children born to women with HIV infection, and it should be started at 4–6 weeks of age, regardless of the child's CD4+ T-cell count or HIV infection status.[62,72] For children in whom HIV infection is reasonably excluded (usually by 4 months of age), PCP prophylaxis can be discontinued.

Children who have HIV infection should continue PCP prophylaxis until at least 12 months of age. Prophylaxis is discontinued at 12 months of age for children with HIV infection whose CD4+ T-cell counts during the first year of life have been over 750/mm^3 (15%) when regularly measured. Prophylaxis for PCP is continued after 12 months of age for children with HIV infection with any CD4+ T-cell count that was less 750/mm^3 (15%) during the first 12 months of life. For children between 12 and 24 months old who are not on prophylaxis, begin it if CD4+ T-cell counts are less than 750/mm^3 (15%). At 24 months, children with HIV infection who have been receiving PCP prophylaxis can discontinue treatment if CD4+ T-cell counts have all been over 500/mm^3 (15%) when regularly measured every 3 months. Prophylaxis for PCP is continued after 24 months of age for children with HIV infection with any CD4+ T-cell count that was less than 500/mm^3 (15%) during the first 24 months of life.

For HIV-infected children who are older than 24 months, PCP prophylaxis is begun when the CD4+ T-cell count drops below the critical levels outlined in Table 134.14. Usual PCP prophylaxis is trimethoprim–sulfamethoxazole 150mg/m^2 per day (5–7mg/kg per day) divided into two daily doses and given on Monday, Tuesday and Wednesday every week. Alternative regimens are shown in Table 134.15.

Children and adolescents who have HIV infection and a positive tuberculin skin test (more than 5mm induration) without evidence of active disease, prior antituberculous therapy or prior antituberculous prophylaxis should receive prophylactic isoniazid, 10–15mg/kg (to a maximum of 300mg per dose) once daily for 12 months. Such therapy should also be considered for skin test-negative children who are close contacts of persons with infectious tuberculosis, after active

NORMAL CD4+ T CELL COUNTS AND CD4+ T CELL COUNTS AT WHICH TO INITIATE PROPHYLAXIS FOR PCP AND MAC INFECTIONS			
Age	Normal CD4+ T cell count/mm^3, median[64]	CD4+ T cell count/mm^3 at which to start PCP prophylaxis[55]	CD4+ T cell count/mm^3 at which to start MAC prophylaxis[63]
1–11 months*	>3000	All*	<750
12–23 months	2600	750	<500
24–71 months	1700	500	<75
≥6 years	1000	200	<50

* Even patients for whom the diagnosis of HIV infection has not yet been confirmed should begin PCP prophylaxis at 4–6 weeks of age. For patients in whom HIV infection is reasonably excluded by at least two DNA PCR tests, PCP prophylaxis can be discontinued (usually at 4 months of age)[55]

Table 134.14 Normal CD4+ cell counts and CD4+ cell counts at which to initiate prophylaxis for *Pneumocystis carinii* pneumonia and *Mycobacterium avium* complex infections. Patients with prior PCP should receive prophylaxis. All patients should receive prophylaxis when the CD4% is less than 15%. Adapted from Centers for Disease Control and Prevention.[62,64,72]

PROPHYLAXIS OF PCP IN CHILDREN		
Drug	Dose	Comment
Trimethoprim–sulfamethoxazole	150mg/m^2/day ÷ q12h 3 days/week on consecutive days	Preferred regimen
	150mg/m^2/day po q24h on consecutive days	More marrow toxicity
	150mg/m^2/day ÷ q12h 7 days/week	More marrow toxicity
	150mg/m^2/day ÷ q12h po for 3 days/week alternate days	
Dapsone*	2mg/kg/day, as a single dose (max. 100mg)	Absorption equal at high/low gastric pH
Atovaquone	1–3 months old: 30mg/kg/dose po q24h 4–24 months old: 45mg/kg/dose po q24h >24 months old: 30mg/kg/dose po q24h	
Pentamidine	300mg monthly by aerosol inhalation via Respirgard II nebulizer	>5 years old
	4mg/kg every 2–4 weeks iv	Of unproven benefit

* Testing for G6PD deficiency is indicated before starting therapy because dapsone may induce hemolysis in G6PD deficient patients

Table 134.15 Prophylaxis of *Pneumocystis carinii* pneumonia in children. Adapted from Havens *et al.*[71]

tuberculous infection has been excluded. Rifampin (rifampicin), 10–20mg/kg (up to a maximum of 600mg per dose) given once daily is reasonable alternative prophylaxis if the strain to which the child was exposed is known to be resistant to isoniazid.[64]

Clarithromycin, 7.5mg/kg (up to a maximum of 500mg per dose) q12h is recommended for prevention of *Mycobacterium avium* complex (MAC) infections in children, based on age and $CD4^+$ T-cell count (see Table 134.14). Alternative regimens include azithromycin, 20mg/kg (up to a maximum of 1200mg per dose) once weekly; azithromycin 5mg/kg (up to a maximum of 250mg per dose) once daily; or rifabutin 5mg/kg (up to a maximum of 300mg per dose) once daily. Blood cultures for mycobacteria should be performed before beginning prophylaxis. Positive blood cultures prompt treatment with at least three drugs (e.g. clarithromycin, ethambutol and rifabutin). At the stage of infection when MAC prophylaxis is considered, patients may be on other medications that may interact with rifabutin. The advantages and disadvantages of beginning therapy should be carefully discussed with families.

Patients who have HIV infection and hypogammaglobulinemia may benefit from infusions of IVIG, 400mg once monthly to prevent serious bacterial infections. Intravenous immunoglobulin for prophylaxis of bacterial infections shows no additional benefit in children without hypogammaglobulinemia who are already receiving concurrent trimethoprim–sulfamethoxazole.

Varicella-zoster immune globulin is given to children who have HIV infection without prior varicella infection if they are exposed to chickenpox or zoster. Varicella-zoster immune globulin is not effective if given more than 96 hours after exposure. Prophylaxis with aciclovir is used for patients with frequently recurring zoster. The exact dose for this indication in children is unclear, but 5mg/kg q12h is a reasonable starting dose, increasing to as high as 10–20mg/kg q6–8h if breakthrough occurs.

Prophylaxis for CMV disease in children is not recommended at this time. Prophylaxis of herpes simplex virus disease and fungal infections in children follow guidelines for adults, with appropriate dose modifications.[64] Other prophylaxis may be indicated for patients with a variety of late complications of HIV infection.[64]

REFERENCES

1. World Health Organization. AIDS Epidemic Update, December, 2001. http://www.unaids.org/epidemic_update/report_dec.
2. Quinn TC. AIDS in the Americas: a public health priority for the region. AIDS 1990;4:709–24.
3. World Health Organization. Children and young people in a world of AIDS. http://www.unaids.org/publications/documents/children/children/JC656-Child&Aids-E.pdf.
4. The Working Group on Mother-to-Child Transmission of HIV. Rates of mother-to-child transmission of HIV-1 in Africa, America, and Europe: results from 13 perinatal studies. JAIDS 1995;8:506–10.
5. MacDonald KS, Embree J, Njenga S, *et al.* Mother–child class I HLA concordance increases perinatal human immunodeficiency virus type 1 transmission. J Infect Dis 1998;177:551–6.
6. Kostrikis LG. Impact of natural chemokine receptor polymorphisms on perinatal transmission of human immunodeficiency virus type 1. Teratology 2000;61:387–390.
7. Auger I, Thomas P, DeGruittola V, *et al.* Incubation periods for pediatric AIDS patients. Nature 1988;336:575–7.
8. Bryson YJ, Luzuriaga K, Sullivan JL, Wara DW. Proposed definitions for *in utero* versus intrapartum transmission of HIV-1. N Engl J Med 1992;326:1246–7.
9. Bertolli J, St. Louis ME, Simonds RJ. Estimating the timing of mother-to-child transmission of human immunodeficiency virus in a breast-feeding population in Kinshasa, Zaire. J Infect Dis 1996;174:722–6.
10. Dunn DT, Brandt CD, Krivine A, *et al.* The sensitivity of HIV-1 DNA polymerase chain reaction in the neonatal period and the relative contributions of intra-uterine and intra-partum transmission. AIDS 1995;9:F7–11.
11. Nduati R, John G, Mbori-Ngacha D, *et al.* Effect of breastfeeding and formula feeding on transmission of HIV-1: a randomised clinical trial. JAMA 2000;283:1167–74.
12. Luzuriaga K, Sullivan JL. Viral and immunopathogenesis of vertical HIV-1 infection. In: Pizzo PA, Wilfert CM, eds. Pediatric AIDS: the challenge of HIV infection in infants, children, and adolescents. 3rd edition. Baltimore: Williams and Wilkins; 1998:89–104.
13. Wilfert CM, Wilson C, Luzuriaga K, Epstein L. Pathogenesis of pediatric human immunodeficiency virus type 1 infection. J Infect Dis 1994;170:286–92.
14. Barroga CF, Raskino C, Fangon MC, *et al.* The CCR5Δ32 allele slows disease progression of human immunodeficiency virus-1-infected children receiving antiretroviral treatment. J Infect Dis 2000;182:413–9.
15. Tressoldi E, Romiti ML, Boniotto M, *et al.* Prognostic value of the stromal cell-derived factor 1 3′A mutation in pediatric human immunodeficiency virus type 1 infection. J Infect Dis 2002;185:696–700.
16. Connor EM, Sperling RS, Gelber R, *et al.* Reduction of maternal–infant transmission of human immunodeficiency virus type 1 with zidovudine treatment. N Engl J Med 1994;331:1173–80.
17. Lallemant M, Jourdain G, Le Coeur S, *et al.* for the Perinatal HIV Prevention Trial (Thailand) Investigators. A trial of shortened zidovudine regimens to prevent mother-to-child transmission of HIV-1. N Engl J Med 2000;343:982–91.
18. Centers for Disease Control and Prevention. Public Health Service task force recommendations for the use of antiretroviral drugs in pregnant women infected with HIV-1 for maternal health and reducing perinatal HIV-1 transmission in the United States. MMWR Morb Mortal Wkly Rep 1998;47 (RR-2):1–30. Updated periodically at http://www.aidsinfo.nih.gov.
19. Cooper ER, Charurat M, Mofenson L, *et al.* Combination antiretroviral strategies for the treatment of pregnant HIV-1 infected women and prevention of perinatal HIV-1 transmission. J Acquir Immune Defic Synd Hum Retrovirol 2002;29:484–94.
20. Read JS, for the International Perinatal HIV Group. The mode of delivery and the risk of vertical transmission of human immunodeficiency virus type 1. N Engl J Med 1999;340:977–87.
21. Ioannides JP, Abrams EJ, Ammann A, *et al.* Perinatal transmission of human immunodeficiency virus type 1 by pregnant women with RNA virus loads <1000 copies/mL. J Infect Dis 2001;183:539.
22. American Academy of Pediatrics, Committee on Pediatric AIDS. Human milk, breastfeeding, and transmission of human immunodeficiency virus in the United States. Pediatrics 1995;96:977–9.
23. World Health Organization. New data on the prevention of mother-to-child transmission of HIV and their policy implications: Conclusions and recommendations. WHO technical consultation on behalf of the UNFPA/UNICEF/WHO/UNAIDS/ inter-agency task team on mother-to-child transmission of HIV, Geneva, 11–13 October, 2000. http://whqlibdoc.who.int/hq/2001/WHO_RHR_01.28.pdf.
24. Centers for Disease Control and Prevention. 1993 Revised classification system for HIV infection and expanded surveillance case definition for AIDS among adolescents and adults. MMWR Morb Mortal Wkly Rep 1992;41(RR-17):1–19.
25. Centers for Disease Control and Prevention. 1994 Revised classification system for human immunodeficiency virus infection in children under 13 years of age. MMWR Morb Mortal Wkly Rep 1994;43(RR-12):1–10.
26. Forsyth BWC, Andiman WA, O'Connor T. Development of a prognosis-based clinical staging system for infants with human immunodeficiency virus. J Pediatr 1996;129:648–55.
27. Pahwa S, Kaplan M, Fikrig S. Spectrum of human T-cell lymphotrophic virus type III infection in children. JAMA 1986;255:2299–305.
28. European Collaborative Study. Fluctuations in symptoms in human immunodeficiency virus-infected children: the first 10 years of life. Pediatrics 2001;108:116–22.
29. Barnhart HX, Caldwell MB, Thomas P. Natural history of human immunodeficiency virus disease in perinatally infected children: an analysis from the pediatric spectrum of disease project. Pediatrics 1996;97:710–6.
30. Mofenson LM, Korelitz J, Meyer WA *et al.* The relationship between human immunodeficiency virus type 1 RNA level, CD4 lymphocyte percent, and mortality risk in HIV-1 infected children. J Infect Dis 1997;175:1029–38.
31. Rich KC, Fowler MG, Mofenson LM, *et al.* Maternal and infant factors predicting disease progression in human immunodeficiency virus type 1-infected infants. Pediatrics 2000;105:1–6.
32. Taha TE, Graham SM, Kumwenda NI, *et al.* Morbidity among human immunodeficiency Virus-1 infected and uninfected African Children. Pediatrics 2000;106(6). http:www.pediatrics.org/cgi/content/full/106/6/e77.
33. Thillagavathie P, Adhikari M, Dhayendhree M, *et al.* Severe, rapidly progressive human immunodeficiency virus type 1 disease in newborns with coinfections. Pediatr Infect Dis J 2001;20:404–10.

34. Moye J, Rich KC, Kalish LA. Natural history of somatic growth in infants born to women infected by human immunodeficiency virus. J Pediatr 1996;128:58–69.
35. Cooper ER, Hanson C, Diaz C, *et al.* Encephalopathy and progression of human immunodeficiency virus disease in a cohort of children with perinatally acquired human immunodeficiency virus infection. J Pediatr 1998;132:808–12.
36. Gay CL, Armstrong FD, Cohen D, *et al.* The effects of HIV on cognitive and motor development in children born to HIV-seropositive women with no reported drug use: birth to 24 months. Pediatrics 1995;96:1078–82.
37. DeCarli C, Civitello LA, Brouwers P, Pizzo P. The prevalence of computed tomographic abnormalities of the cerebrum in 100 consecutive children symptomatic with the human immune deficiency virus. Ann Neurol 1993;34:198–205.
38. Rubinstein A, Morecki R, Silverman B, *et al.* Pulmonary disease in children with acquired immune deficiency syndrome and AIDS-related complex. J Pediatr 1986;108:498–503.
39. Lipshultz SE, Easley KA, Orav EJ, *et al.* Cardiovascular status of infants and children of women infected with HIV-1 (P^2C^2 HIV): a cohort study. Lancet 2002;360:368–73.
40. Kovacs A, Hinton DR, Wright D, *et al.* Human immunodeficiency virus type 1 infection of the heart in three infants with acquired immunodeficiency syndrome and sudden death. Pediatr Infect Dis J 1996;15:819–24.
41. Shearer WT, Lipshultz SE, Easley KA, *et al.* Alterations in cardiac and pulmonary function in pediatric human immunodeficiency virus type 1 disease progressors. Pediatrics 2000;105(1). http://www.pediatrics.org/cgi/content/full/105/1/e9.
42. Luginbuhl LM, Orav EJ, McIntosh K, Lipshultz SE. Cardiac morbidity and related mortality in children with HIV infection. JAMA 1993;269:2869–75.
43. Strauss J, Abitbol C, Zilleruelo G, *et al.* Renal disease in children with the acquired immunodeficiency syndrome. N Engl J Med 1989;321:625–30.
44. Dankner WM, Lindsey JC, Levin MJ, and the Pediatric AIDS Clinical Trials Group Protocol Teams 051, 128, 128, 144, 152, 179, 190, 220, 240, 254, 300 and 327. Pediatr Infect Dis J 2001;20:40–8.
45. Simonds RJ, Oxtoby MJ, Caldwell MB, Gwinn ML, Rogers MF. *Pneumocystis carinii* pneumonia among US children with perinatally acquired HIV infection. JAMA 1993;270:470–3.
46. European Collaborative Study Group: Dunn D, Newell ML, Ades T, Peckham C, DeMaria A. CD4 T cell count as predictor of *Pneumocystis carinii* pneumonia in children born to mothers infected with HIV. Br Med J 1994;308:437–40.
47. Simonds RJ, Lindegren ML, Thomas P, *et al.* Prophylaxis against *Pneumocystis carinii* pneumonia among children with perinatally acquired human immunodeficiency virus infection in the United States. N Engl J Med 1995;332:786–90.
48. National Institute of Child Health and Human Development Intravenous Immunoglobulin Study Group. Intravenous immune globulin for the prevention of bacterial infections in children with symptomatic human immunodeficiency virus infection. N Engl J Med 1991;325:73–80.
49. Mofenson LM, Moye J, Bethel J, Hirschhorn R, Jordan C. Prophylactic intravenous immunoglobulin in HIV-infected children with $CD4^+$ counts of 0.20×10^9/L or more. JAMA 1992;268:483–8.
50. Spector SA, Gelber RD, McGrath, *et al.* A controlled trial of intravenous immune globulin for the prevention of serious bacterial infections in children receiving zidovudine for advanced human immunodeficiency virus infection. N Engl J Med 1994;331:1181–7.
51. Mueller BU, Pizzo PA. Cancer in children with primary or secondary immunodeficiencies. J Pediatr 1995;126:1–10.
52. Chintu C, Athale UH, Patil PS. Childhood cancers in Zambia before and after the HIV epidemic. Arch Dis Child 1995;73:100–5.
53. Murphy SB, Chadwick EG. HIV and smooth muscle tumors. Pediatrics 1993;91:1020–1
54. McClain KL, Leach CT, Jenson HB, *et al.* Association of Epstein–Barr virus with leiomyosarcomas in young people with AIDS. N Engl J Med 1995;332:12–18.
55. Husson RN, Comeau AM, Hoff R. Diagnosis of human immunodeficiency virus infection in infants and children. Pediatrics 1990;86:1–10.
56. Burgard M, Mayaux MJ, Blanche S, *et al.* The use of viral culture and p24 antigen testing to diagnose human immunodeficiency virus infection in neonates. N Engl J Med 1992;327:1192–7.
57. McIntosh K, Comeau AM, Wara D, *et al.* The utility of IgA antibody to human immunodeficiency virus type 1 in early diagnosis of vertically transmitted infection. Arch Pediatr Adolesc Med 1996;150:598–602.
58. Newell ML, Dunn D, Maria AD, *et al.* Detection of virus in vertically exposed HIV-antibody-negative children. Lancet 1996;347:213–5.
59. Roques PA, Gras G, Parnet-Mathieu F, *et al.* Clearance of HIV infection in 12 perinatally infected children: clinical, virological and immunological data. AIDS 1995;9:F19–26.
60. Bremer JW, Lew JF, Cooper E. Diagnosis of infection with human immunodeficiency virus type 1 by a DNA polymerase chain reaction assay among infants enrolled in the Women and Infants' Transmission Study. J Pediatr 1996;129:198–207.
61. Owens DK, Holodniy M, McDonald TW, Scott J, Sonnad S. A meta-analytic evaluation of the polymerase chain reaction for the diagnosis of HIV infection in infants. JAMA 1996;275:1342–8.
62. Centers for Disease Control and Prevention. 1995 Revised guidelines for prophylaxis against *Pneumocystis carinii* pneumonia for children infected with or perinatally exposed to human immunodeficiency virus. MMWR Morb Mortal Wkly Rep 1995;44(RR-4):1–11.
63. Centers for Disease Control and Prevention. Guidelines for national human immunodeficiency virus case surveillance, including monitoring for human immunodeficiency virus infection and acquired immunodeficiency syndrome. MMWR Morb Mortal Wkly Rep 1999;48(RR-13):1–36.
64. Centers for Disease Control and Prevention. Guidelines for preventing opportunistic infections among HIV-infected persons – 2002 recommendations of the US Public Health Service and the Infectious Diseases Society of America. MMWR Morb Mortal Wkly Rep 2002:51(RR-8):1–60. http://www.aidsinfo.nih.gov
65. Centers for Disease Control and Prevention. The role of BCG vaccination in the prevention and control of tuberculosis in the United States: a joint statement by the Advisory Council for the Elimination of Tuberculosis and the Advisory Committee on Immunization Practices. MMWR Morb Mortal Wkly Rep 1996;45(RR-4):1–15.
66. World Health Organization Special Programme on AIDS and Expanded Program on Immunization. Consultation on human immunodeficiency virus (HIV) and routine childhood immunization. Wkly Epidemiol Rec 1987;62:297–9.
67. Centers for Disease Control and Prevention. Prevention of varicella: updated recommendations of the Advisory Committee on Immunization Practices (ACIP). MMWR Morb Mortal Wkly Rep 1999;48(RR-6):3.
68. Centers for Disease Control and Prevention. Guidelines for the use of antiretroviral agents in pediatric HIV infection. MMWR Morb Mortal Wkly Rep 1998;47(RR-4):1–43. http://www.aidsinfo.nih.gov.
69. Sharland M, Castelli Gattinara di Zub G, Thomas Ramos J, Blanche S, Gibb DM. PENTA guidelines for the use of antiretroviral therapy in paediatric HIV infection. 2002 www.ctu.mrc.ac.uk/penta/guidelin.pdf.
70. Centers for Disease Control and Prevention. Report of the NIH panel to define principles of therapy of HIV infection and guidelines for the use of antiretroviral agents in HIV-infected adults and adolescents. MMWR Morb Mortal Wkly Rep 1998;47(RR-5):1–83. http://www.aidsinfo.nih.gov.
71. Havens PL, Water DA, Cuene BE, McIntosh K, Yogev R. Caring for infants, children, adolescents and families with HIV infection. Wisconsin Department of Health and Social Services, Division of Health Publication POH 4498 (Rev. 01/01); 2001. http://www.mcw.edu/peds/infectdis.
72. Centers for Disease Control and Prevention. Guidelines for prophylaxis against *Pneumocystis carinii* pneumonia for children infected with human immunodeficiency virus. MMWR Morb Mortal Wkly Rep 1991;40(RR-2):1–11.

chapter

135 Special Problems in Women who have HIV Disease

Beverly E Sha & Constance A Benson

EPIDEMIOLOGY

The number and proportion of women who have HIV-1 infection in the USA have been gradually increasing. Of 41,960 persons reported to the Centers for Disease Control and Prevention (CDC) who had AIDS in 2000, 10,459 (25%) were women.[1] This contrasts with 1985 statistics, when 7% (534/8153) of people reported to the CDC who had AIDS were women. Based on 1999 vital statistics data, HIV-1 infection is the fifth leading cause of death for women aged 25–44 years and the third leading cause of death for African-American and Hispanic women in this age group. The racial distribution of women who had AIDS in 2000 was 62.6% African-American (45.9/100,000), 18.1% white (2.2/100,000) and 17.7% Hispanic (13.8/100,000).

Heterosexual transmission has surpassed injection drug use as the primary route for women acquiring HIV-1 infection in the USA. Geographically, the north-eastern and southern USA have reported the greatest number of cases. Current estimates are that 40,000 new infections occur annually in the USA, of which 30% are in women. Of newly infected women, estimates are that 75% acquired HIV-1 through heterosexual sex and 25% through intravenous drug use.

Worldwide 2001 UNAIDS estimates are that, of the 37.2 million adults living with HIV-1/AIDS, 17.6 million (47%) are women.[2] More than 70% live in sub-Saharan Africa. One in every 100 adults worldwide aged 15–49 years is HIV-1-infected. In sub-Saharan Africa, 8.4% of all adults in this age group are HIV-1 infected. More than 80% of all adults worldwide acquired HIV-1 infection via heterosexual intercourse.

TRANSMISSION

Factors that are important in male-to-female transmission of HIV-1 infection include:

- advanced disease in the infected source partner;
- plasma HIV-1 RNA level (and virus shedding in genital secretions);
- anal receptive intercourse;
- presence of genital ulcers;
- absence of condom use; and
- absence of zidovudine use.[3–6]

Factors associated with heterosexual female-to-male transmission of HIV-1 infection include:

- advanced disease in the infected source partner;
- plasma HIV-1 RNA level (and virus shedding in genital secretions);
- presence of genital ulcers;
- sexual intercourse during menses; and
- absence of condom use.

In developing countries, observational studies have also suggested an association of non-ulcerative sexually transmitted diseases with increased rates of HIV-1 transmission. For women, *Candida* vaginitis, bacterial vaginosis and use of depot medroxyprogesterone acetate have been associated with an increased incidence of HIV-1 infection. The efficiency of male-to-female transmission of HIV-1 has been estimated to be twice that of female-to-male transmission, although some studies have found equal rates of transmission between the sexes.[4,5]

CLINICAL FEATURES

Disease manifestations and progression

Overall, there are few differences in the incidence of nongynecologic opportunistic diseases between men and women who have HIV-1 infection, with the exception of a higher incidence of esophageal candidiasis as an AIDS-defining condition and a lower incidence of Kaposi's sarcoma reported among women.[7] It has been postulated that women may have a higher incidence of candidiasis due to vaginal colonization with yeast or hormonal influences, although data supporting these hypotheses are lacking.

Several studies have now demonstrated that women have lower plasma HIV-1 RNA levels than do men after controlling for age, the interval from seroconversion and the $CD4^+$ lymphocyte count.[8] Another study found that this sex difference in plasma HIV-1 RNA levels disappeared 5–6 years after seroconversion. Although women may progress to AIDS with lower viral loads, the time to progression to AIDS appears to be similar for men and women. Similarly, for HIV-1-infected men and women who have adequate access to health care and treatment, survival appears to be equivalent.[9,10]

Gynecologic manifestations

Infection

Gynecologic disorders are common in women who have HIV-1 infection.[11] Up to 50% of these women develop recurrent *Candida* vaginitis, which often precedes the development of oral or esophageal candidiasis. Several longitudinal cohorts have reported that 14–18% of women who have HIV-1 infection have or develop recurrent genital herpes simplex virus (HSV) infection, which can be more severe or refractory to treatment than among HIV-1-seronegative women.[10]

The relationship between HIV-1 and pelvic inflammatory disease (PID) in women is less clear. Several retrospective studies suggest that women presenting with PID have a high rate of co-infection with HIV-1 and that women who have HIV-1 infection with PID require surgical intervention more frequently because of abscess formation.[12] Prospective studies will be necessary to define this relationship and determine whether there are differences in response to therapy, microbiologic etiology and risk of recurrence or long-term sequelae.

Genital dysplasia

Cervicovaginal dysplasia is common in women who have HIV-1 infection.[11,13] Abnormal Papanicolaou smears were found in 38.3% of 1713 HIV-1-infected women and 16.2% of 482 women uninfected with HIV-1 but at risk, in the Women's Interagency HIV-1 Study cohort.[13] In multivariate analyses, risk factors for abnormal cytology included HIV-1 infection, low $CD4^+$ lymphocyte counts, high plasma HIV-1 RNA levels and detection of human papillomavirus (HPV). In follow-up of this cohort, HPV detection, $CD4^+$ lymphocyte count and plasma HIV-1 RNA levels predicted regression.[14] Rates of incidence, progression and regression of abnormal cytology did not differ between the HIV-1-uninfected controls and HIV-1-infected women with $CD4^+$ lymphocyte counts greater than 200 cells/ml and plasma HIV-1 RNA levels below 4,000 copies/ml. In another study, 20% (80/398) of HIV-1-seropositive women compared with 4% (15/357) of HIV-1-seronegative women had cervical intra-epithelial neoplasia (CIN) confirmed by colposcopy.[15] The presence of CIN was found to be independently associated with:

- HPV infection (odds ratio 9.8);
- HIV-1 infection (odds ratio 3.5);
- $CD4^+$ lymphocyte count less than 200/ml (odds ratio 2.7); and
- age greater than 34 years (odds ratio 2.0).

The rate of CIN in women who have HIV-1 infection with fewer than 200 $CD4^+$ lymphocytes/μl was 28% (27/95) compared with 19% (45/236) for those with higher $CD4^+$ lymphocyte counts.

Conflicting data exist regarding whether CIN and invasive cervical cancer have a more aggressive course or a less favorable response to therapy among women who have HIV-1 infection. In one study prior to the availability of highly active antiretroviral therapy (HAART), 62% of 127 women who had HIV-1 infection with CIN developed recurrent CIN within 36 months of treatment compared with 18% of HIV-1-seronegative controls.[16] During the 36-month follow-up period, progression to higher grade dysplasia, including one invasive cancer, occurred in 25% of women who had HIV-1 infection compared with 2% of controls. Recently, HIV-1-infected women in New York were reported to be at higher risk than HIV-1-seronegative women for other HPV-associated malignancies, including vulvar and anal cancers. Highly active antiretroviral therapy that reverses immunosuppression is likely to impact favorably on the rate of HPV detection and prevalence of genital tract and anal dysplasia.

The 2001 Consensus Guidelines for the management of women who have cervical cytologic abnormalities are detailed in Table 135.1.[17] These guidelines are not specific to women with HIV-1 infection but reflect updated terminology for reporting cervical cytology results, recent availability of HPV DNA testing and further follow-up data on the natural history of atypical squamous cells of undetermined significance/low-grade squamous intraepithelial lesions that were not available for the February 2002 US Public Health Service (USPHS) guidelines for cervical dysplasia screening in women who have HIV-1 infection.[18]

GUIDELINES FOR CERVICAL DYSPLASIA SCREENING OF WOMEN INFECTED WITH HIV-1	
Initial gynecologic examination with Papanicolaou smear	If normal, repeat in 6 months If atypical squamous cells of uncertain significance (ASCUS) proceed to colposcopy If atypical glandular cells proceed to colposcopy If low grade squamous intraepithelial lesion proceed to colposcopy If high grade squamous intraepithelial lesion, proceed to colposcopy
If initial two Papanicolaou smears are normal	Repeat annually as long as smears remain normal

Table 135.1 Guidelines for cervical dysplasia screening of women infected with HIV-1. These are based on the 2001 Consensus Guidelines and the United States Public Health Service Guidelines.[17,18]

Because *Candida* vaginitis, genital HSV disease, PID and cervical dysplasia are common in women who have HIV-1 infection, these conditions, along with other common sexually transmitted diseases such as gonorrhea, chlamydial infection and syphilis, should prompt a determination of HIV-1 risk factors and appropriate HIV-1 screening.

Menstrual cycle

The impact of HIV-1 infection on the menstrual cycle remains unknown. There are reports of increased rates of dysmenorrhea, oligomenorrhea, amenorrhea or menorrhagia, but these have been discounted by other studies.[19] Ongoing prospective observational studies of the epidemiology, manifestations and progression of HIV-1 disease in women should address these issues.

PREVENTION

Contraception

Condoms are important for preventing the transmission of HIV-1 and other sexually transmitted diseases. However, alone they may not be adequate to prevent pregnancy. Reported breakage rates for male condoms are less than 2% for vaginal and anal intercourse. An evaluation of the effectiveness of the female condom at preventing pregnancy in 147 women over a 6-month period demonstrated an annual failure rate of 26%. Among 86 women who reported using the condom consistently and correctly, the annual failure rate was still 11%.[20]

Hormonal contraceptives should be considered in addition to condoms for women who have HIV-1 infection, are sexually active and wish to avoid pregnancy. In view of the wide array of potential drugs available for antiretroviral therapy and prevention and treatment of opportunistic infections, the medications of women receiving hormonal agents should be critically reviewed to avoid drug–drug interactions such as:

- those that might lead to a reduction in the efficacy of hormonal agents; and
- those that may reduce the efficacy or increase the toxicity of other drugs in the presence of hormonal agents.

In particular, protease inhibitors and non-nucleoside reverse transcriptase inhibitors (NNRTIs) can affect the levels of hormonal agents. Table 135.2 details these interactions and recommendations for their concomitant use.[21]

Pregnancy

In the USA, in 1993, the rate of HIV-1 infection among women of childbearing age was 1.7 per 1,000 and there were between 1000 and 2000 perinatally infected infants born to 6000–7000 HIV-1-infected women. UNAIDS estimates for 2001 are that, worldwide, 4.3 million children under 15 years of age have died of AIDS; another 2.7 million are currently living with HIV-1/AIDS, of whom 800,000 were infected in 2001.[2]

Perinatal transmission can occur in utero and during labor and delivery, as well as postpartum, primarily through breast-feeding.[22,23] Excluding postpartum transmission through breast-feeding, data suggest that 80% of maternal–infant transmission occurs late in gestation or during labor and delivery.[24] Several studies have found that breast-feeding may increase the rate of transmission by 7–22% and thus breast-feeding is not recommended when safe alternatives are available.[23] The majority of infections transmitted through breast milk occur during the first few weeks or months of life, suggesting that postpartum maternal and/or infant antiretroviral therapy could further reduce transmission in breast-feeding populations.[25] Risk factors associated with transmission via breast-feeding include level of virus in the breast milk, mastitis, breast abscesses and maternal seroconversion during lactation.

Table 135.2 Drug interactions between antiretrovirals and oral contraceptives. Recommended adjustments are listed. Data from CDC.[21]

DRUG INTERACTIONS BETWEEN ANTIRETROVIRALS AND ORAL CONTRACEPTIVES				
		Recommendation		
Agent	Effect on oral contraceptive	No dose adjustment	No data	Use alternative agent or second method
Indinavir	Norethindrone levels ↑ 26% ethinylestradiol levels ↑24%	X		
Ritonavir	Ethinylestradiol levels ↓40%			X
Saquinavir			X	
Nelfinavir	Norethindrone levels ↓18% ethinylestradiol levels ↓47%			X
Amprenavir	Potential for interaction		X	X
Lopinavir	Ethinylestradiol levels ↓42%			X
Nevirapine	Ethinylestradiol levels ↓20%			X
Delavirdine			X	
Efavirenz	Ethinylestradiol levels ↑37% no data on norethindrone levels			X

Table 135.3 Maternal–infant transmission of HIV-1. Maternal, and labor and delivery factors that increase the risk of transmission.[22,26]

MATERNAL–INFANT TRANSMISSION OF HIV-1	
Maternal factors	Labor and delivery factors
Advanced maternal HIV disease Maternal p24 antigenemia Low maternal $CD4^+$ lymphocyte counts High maternal plasma HIV-1 RNA levels Acute maternal HIV infection during pregnancy Genital inflammation or maternal sexually transmitted disease at the time of delivery Episiotomy with severe lacerations Detectable genital tract HIV-1 RNA near delivery Breast-feeding	Chorioamnionitis Prolonged rupture of membranes (>4h) Premature delivery before 34 weeks gestation Use of fetal scalp electrodes Non-elective cesarean section delivery Lack of antiretroviral therapy

A number of maternal and delivery factors appear to influence the risk of transmission and are listed in Table 135.3.[22,26] In addition, the rate of maternal–infant transmission has been reported to be increased when maternal virus exhibits rapid or high titer replication in human peripheral blood mononuclear cells, T cell line tropism or resistance to neutralization by maternal serum. Among twin births, the firstborn twin is at greater risk of acquiring HIV-1 infection because of more prolonged exposure to maternal blood and secretions. Interventions currently recommended to reduce transmission include:

- avoidance of invasive monitoring whenever possible;
- avoidance of breast-feeding;
- the use of zidovudine with or without other antiretroviral therapy during pregnancy for the mother and in the peripartum and postpartum period for the infant;
- treatment of sexually transmitted disease or vaginitis; and
- elective cesarean section if plasma HIV-1 RNA level remains above 1,000 copies/ml near term.

Recently the USPHS published revised guidelines on the use of antiretroviral therapy in pregnant women.[27] Since the results of AIDS Clinical Trials Group (ACTG) 076, which demonstrated a 66% reduction in maternal–infant HIV-1 transmission with zidovudine use in the mother (100mg orally 5 times per day initiated at 14–34 weeks gestation), during labor and delivery (2mg/kg intravenous loading dose then 1mg/kg continuous infusion until delivery) and in the baby (2mg/kg orally q6h for the first 6 weeks of life) compared with placebo (7.6% vs 22.6% transmission, respectively), advancements have occurred in our understanding of the pathogenesis of HIV-1 disease and its treatment and management.[28] The precise mechanisms by which zidovudine diminishes maternal–infant transmission of HIV-1 remain unclear but they are probably multifactorial and include decreased maternal plasma HIV-1 RNA levels, resulting in decreased exposure of the fetus to the virus in utero, or of the infant at delivery, or both, thereby preventing infection becoming established in the fetus or infant. Additional analyses have now shown that transmission of HIV-1 occurs at all levels of $CD4^+$ lymphocyte counts and even in some women who have undetectable plasma HIV-1 RNA levels, although overall the risk of transmission is greater in women who have lower $CD4^+$ lymphocyte counts and higher plasma HIV-1 RNA levels, particularly at the time of delivery.[29] Detectable virus in the female genital tract at 38 weeks gestation has also been independently associated with maternal–infant transmission of HIV-1.[30]

It is important to stress that even intervening late in pregnancy can diminish the risk of transmission. Epidemiologic data from New York State showed decreased transmission to the infant when intravenous zidovudine was begun during labor followed by 6 weeks of oral zidovudine for the infant compared with no therapy (10% vs 27% transmission, respectively).[31] A study in Thailand randomized 397 HIV-1-infected pregnant women to receive placebo or zidovudine (300 mg q12h orally from 36 weeks gestation until onset of labor and 300 mg q3h orally from onset of labor until delivery).[32] There was an 18.9% transmission risk for women receiving placebo compared with a 9.4% transmission risk for women receiving zidovudine. Thus, transmission in this non-breast-feeding cohort was decreased by 50% with the use of a shorter course of zidovudine, oral dosing during labor and no infant treatment compared with a 66% reduction with the more complicated ACTG 076 regimen.

In an African breast-feeding cohort, the PETRA study compared a combination regimen of zidovudine and epivir of four varying durations in the mother and infant: (1) starting at 36 weeks gestation, orally intrapartum and for 1 week postpartum to the woman and infant; (2) starting during labor and for 1 week postpartum to the woman and infant; (3) during labor only to the woman; and (4) placebo.[33] Arms 1 and 2 reduced transmission to the infant by approximately 50% and 38%, respectively, as compared with the placebo arm. Arm 3 provided no reduction in transmission compared with placebo (16% vs 17%, respectively), suggesting that any potential benefit was negated by breast-feeding.

More recently, in Uganda, a two-dose nevirapine regimen was compared with a short-course zidovudine schedule.[34] At the onset of labor, women received either oral nevirapine, 200mg as a single dose, or oral zidovudine, 600mg loading dose followed by 300mg q4h until delivery. Infants received matched drug to their mothers, either oral single dose nevirapine 2mg/kg within 72 hours of birth or oral zidovudine 4mg/kg q12h for 7 days. In this breast-feeding population, the risk of HIV-1 transmission at birth was 10.4% in the zidovudine group and 8.2% in the nevirapine group. By 6–8 weeks postpartum, 21.3% of infants had acquired HIV-1 infection in the zidovudine group versus 11.9% in the nevirapine group ($p = 0.0027$). These data demonstrated that the two-dose nevirapine regimen reduced the risk of maternal–infant transmission by 47% compared with a truncated zidovudine regimen. Follow-up data from this study, however, documented the occurrence of K103N mutations in virus recovered from up to 15% of women who were randomized to nevirapine, a mutation conferring cross-class resistance to NNRTIs.[35] These data may have implications for future treatment of women who received this regimen.

All pregnant women should be offered HIV-1 testing. In general, current recommendations are to approach the treatment of the HIV-1-infected pregnant woman as if she were not pregnant and strive for maximal suppression of viral replication. Nevertheless, knowledge that limited data exist regarding toxicity of the 16 Food and Drug Administration (FDA)-approved antiretroviral agents to the developing fetus and the infant must also be taken into account. Tables 135.4 and 135.5 summarize the current information known about reverse

REVERSE TRANSCRIPTASE INHIBITORS					
Agent	Transmission to fetus prevented*	FDA approved		FDA pregnancy category†	Placental transfer (%)
		Neonates	Children		
Zidovudine	Yes	Yes	Yes	C	85
Didanosine	No	Yes	Yes	B	50
Lamivudine	Yes	No	≥3 months	C	100
Stavudine	No	No	≥1 months	C	76 (rhesus monkeys)
Zalcitabine	No	No	No	C	30–50 (rhesus monkeys)
Abacavir	No	No	≥3 months	C	Yes (rats)
Nevirapine	Yes	No	≥2 months	C	100
Delavirdine	No	No	No	C	?
Efavirenz	No	No	≥3 years	C	100 (rhesus monkeys)
Tenofovir	No	No	No	B	Yes (rat, monkey)

* Randomized trial showing benefit.
† A, adequate and well controlled studies of pregnant women fail to demonstrate a risk to the fetus during the first trimester and no evidence of risk during later trimesters; B, animal studies fail to demonstrate a risk to the fetus but no adequate studies exist in pregnant women; C, animal studies demonstrate risk or have not been conducted, and safety in human pregnancy has not yet been determined – however, the benefit of the drug may still outweigh the risk; D, positive evidence of human fetal risk exists based on adverse reaction data but benefits may still outweigh the risks.

Table 135.4 Reverse transcriptase inhibitors. Data from CDC.[27]

PROTEASE INHIBITORS					
Agent	Transmission to fetus prevented*	FDA approved		FDA pregnancy category†	Placental transfer
		Neonates	Children		
Nelfinavir	No	No	≥2 years	B	Minimal
Indinavir	No	No	No	C	Minimal
Ritonavir	No	No	≥2 years	B	Minimal
Saquinavir	No	No	No	B	Minimal
Amprenavir	No	No	≥4 years	C	?
Lopinavir/ritonavir	No	No	≥ 6 months	C	?

* Randomized trial showing benefit.
† A, adequate and well controlled studies of pregnant women fail to demonstrate a risk to the fetus during the first trimester and no evidence of risk during later trimesters; B, animal studies fail to demonstrate a risk to the fetus but no adequate studies exist in pregnant women; C, animal studies demonstrate risk or have not been conducted, and safety in human pregnancy has not yet been determined – however, the benefit of the drug may still outweigh the risk; D, positive evidence of human fetal risk exists based on adverse reaction data but benefits may still outweigh the risks.

Table 135.5 Protease inhibitors. Data from CDC.[27]

transcriptase inhibitors and protease inhibitors with regard to FDA approval status, placental transfer and carcinogenicity data. To date, neither pre-term delivery nor birth defects have been clearly associated with any antiretroviral agent; however, data are limited, particularly for infants exposed to combination therapy. Only efavirenz should be avoided in the first trimester, because of evidence of teratogenicity in rhesus macaques at human doses. A French group reported eight cases of mitochondrial dysfunction among 1754 uninfected infants who received zidovudine or the combination of zidovudine and epivir in utero and/or after birth. Two of these children developed progressive neurologic dysfunction and died. This syndrome has not been detected in over 20,000 children born to HIV-1-infected women in the USA.

On the basis of this information, the USPHS has drafted the following guidelines for the treatment of HIV-1-infected pregnant women.[27]

If the woman has had no prior antiretroviral therapy, treatment should be based on standard indications. However, at a minimum the three-part zidovudine regimen as outlined in ACTG 076 should be administered. In a meta-analysis, antenatal antiretroviral prophylaxis primarily with zidovudine alone was shown to reduce transmission for women who have plasma HIV-1 RNA levels to below 1000 copies/ml at or near delivery compared with no antenatal therapy (1% vs 9.8%, respectively).[36] Many experts feel comfortable substituting zidovudine 300mg q12h orally for the maternal component. Combination therapy is recommended for women who have a plasma HIV-1 RNA level over 1000 copies/ml. Consideration can be given to delaying the initiation of therapy until after 10–12 weeks gestation, which is thought to be the critical time for fetal organogenesis.

If the HIV-1-infected pregnant woman is already on antiretroviral therapy when pregnancy is diagnosed, then therapy should in general be continued, even in the first trimester. If the decision is made to stop therapy during the first trimester owing to concerns about teratogenicity, all drugs should be stopped and then restarted simultaneously in order to minimize the development of resistance.

Zidovudine should be incorporated into the regimen whenever feasible; however, if resistance or intolerance precludes its use, zidovudine should still be administered intravenously intrapartum and to the baby as outlined above. Additionally, zidovudine and stavudine should not be co-administered. Some experts would also recommend zidovudine in combination with other antiretroviral agents for infants born to mothers who have known or suspected zidovudine resistance.

For women receiving standard antenatal antiretroviral therapy, the addition of the two-dose nevirapine regimen did not further reduce transmission rates and, as previously discussed, resulted in the development of mutations conferring resistance to NNRTIs.[37,38] Thus, for women who do not achieve adequate viral suppression near delivery, cesarean section is recommended and the addition of the two-dose nevirapine regimen is not.

If an HIV-1-infected woman presents in labor and no prior antiretroviral therapy has been given, four antiretroviral treatment options are recommended:

- single-dose nevirapine 200 mg orally to the mother as soon as possible and nevirapine 2mg/kg orally to the infant at 48 hours of life;
- oral zidovudine and epivir to the mother until delivery followed by 1 week of zidovudine and epivir to the infant;
- intrapartum intravenous zidovudine until delivery, and zidovudine to the newborn for 6 weeks; or
- the two-dose nevirapine regimen combined with intrapartum intravenous zidovudine and 6 weeks of zidovudine for the newborn.

Infants born to HIV-1-infected mothers who have received no antiretroviral therapy during pregnancy or intrapartum should still receive zidovudine for the first 6 weeks of life. Consideration may also be given to treating the infant with additional antiretroviral medications. The mother's therapy should be re-evaluated after delivery in both these situations.

Resistance testing is available to guide antiretroviral therapy choices. The International AIDS Society–USA Panel and Euro-Guidelines Group for HIV-1 Resistance recommend that all pregnant women who have detectable viremia have resistance testing performed prior to initiating or changing antiretroviral therapy. The USPHS recommends resistance testing for HIV-1-infected pregnant women based on standard indications, which include the following settings: acute infection, failing a current regimen, or high likelihood of having resistant virus based on community resistance patterns or known drug resistance in the woman's source partner. While underlying resistance can affect the ability to achieve maximal viral suppression, it is not clear that the presence of mutations increases the likelihood of transmission to the infant. Resistant virus has been transmitted to infants; however, women who have zidovudine resistance mutations have not consistently transmitted infection to their infants at higher rates and, in some cases where transmission has occurred, wild-type virus was transmitted. When less than potent antiretroviral regimens (zidovudine monotherapy or dual nucleoside analogues) are administered to pregnant HIV-1-infected woman because antiretroviral therapy is not indicated for the women herself or the woman chooses to minimize exposure to antiretroviral therapy during pregnancy, development of resistance can occur and can potentially limit future treatment options.

A meta-analysis of 15 prospective cohort studies, conducted in an era when pregnant HIV-1-infected women received no antiretroviral therapy or zidovudine monotherapy, showed that elective cesarean section decreased the risk of maternal–infant transmission of HIV-1 compared with other modes of delivery.[39] For women on zidovudine, transmission was 2% with elective cesarean section and 7.3% with other modes of delivery. Because transmission rates are expected to be below 2% for women on potent antiretroviral therapy with controlled viremia, the American College of Obstetricians and Gynecologists' Committee on Obstetric Practice recommends cesarean section before the onset of labor for women who have plasma HIV-1 RNA levels above 1,000 copies/ml near term. The cesarean section should be performed at 38 weeks gestation without amniocentesis to assess for fetal lung maturity. For a scheduled cesarean section, intravenous zidovudine should be started 3 hours before surgery. Cesarean section has greater morbidity than vaginal delivery but current data suggest that HIV-1 infected women have similar complications to those in uninfected women.

Duration of ruptured membranes is also associated with an increased risk of transmission. For the first 24 hours of membrane rupture, a meta-analysis of the same 15 studies used to assess the benefit of cesarean section showed a 2% increase in transmission for every additional hour of membrane rupture.[40] Cleansing the birth canal with a 0.25% chlorhexidine solution q4h until delivery did not reduce transmission in one study, except when membranes were ruptured more than 4 hours before delivery.[41] Whether or not non-elective cesarean section to shorten the duration of ruptured membranes or labor will further reduce transmission rates is currently unknown.

Safety monitoring guided by the pregnant woman's specific antiretroviral therapy should be performed. Routine hematologic and hepatic enzyme monitoring is recommended for women on zidovudine. Women receiving nucleoside reverse transcriptase inhibitors (NRTIs) should also be assessed for development of lactic acidosis and hepatic steatosis with frequent liver enzyme and electrolyte monitoring in the third trimester. Recently, cases of fatal lactic acidosis have been reported in pregnant women receiving prolonged courses of didanosine and stavudine. When other alternatives are available, this combination should be avoided during pregnancy. Women on protease inhibitors should be monitored for development of hyperglycemia. In general, the $CD4^+$ lymphocyte count and plasma HIV-1 RNA level should be monitored every 3–4 months. A plasma HIV-1 RNA level should be obtained at 34–36 weeks gestation to guide decisions on mode of delivery. A level II ultrasound is recommended to assess the fetus for women on combination antiretroviral therapy.

In the future, ongoing or planned studies will certainly provide more information regarding the use of the newer NRTIs, NNRTIs, nucleotide analogues, protease inhibitors and combination regimens for the treatment of pregnant women and the prevention of transmission to the fetus/infant. Studies are also ongoing to assess the feasibility of rapid HIV-1 testing for women who present in labor with unknown HIV-1 status. In the meantime, HIV-1-infected pregnant women should be referred for participation in clinical trials whenever possible and be reported to the appropriate agencies that collect safety and teratogenicity data. In the USA, the Antiretroviral Pregnancy Registry can be reached at www.APRegistry.com.

In general, pregnant women who have HIV-1 infection should receive prophylaxis for opportunistic infections appropriate for their stage of disease.[18] For *Pneumocystis carinii* pneumonia prophylaxis, some experts recommend avoiding trimethoprim–sulfamethoxazole and dapsone in the first trimester, and trimethoprim–sulfamethoxazole close to term to reduce the risk of kernicterus in the infant. Aerosolized pentamidine can be substituted during these time periods. While rifabutin and the macrolides have not been studied in pregnant women, those at high risk of disseminated *Mycobacterium avium* complex disease may benefit from the use of these medications after the first trimester. Azithromycin is favored owing to its safety profile because clarithromycin is teratogenic in animals. Pregnant women who have a positive purified protein derivative skin test for tuberculosis should also receive isoniazid prophylaxis after the first trimester. Pregnant women should also avoid eating raw or undercooked meat and avoid contact with cat feces to diminish the risk of toxoplasmosis. Good handwashing techniques should be employed for prevention of cytomegalovirus (CMV) disease, particularly in women who are health care workers or who have children in day care settings.[18] For CMV-seronegative women who require blood transfusions, only CMV-seronegative blood products should be used.[18]

Several studies have now demonstrated no adverse effect of pregnancy on the progression of HIV-1 disease for women who have $CD4^+$ lymphocyte counts above 200 cells/μl.[42] Unfortunately, women who have more advanced HIV-1 disease may not tolerate pregnancy as well and may have a higher rate of spontaneous abortion, prematurity, low birth weight infants and other complications of pregnancy.[43]

REFERENCES

1. Centers for Disease Control and Prevention. HIV/AIDS surveillance report, 2000. Atlanta: US Department of Health and Human Services, Public Health Service; 2000;12:1–48.
2. UNAIDS. Report on global HIV/AIDS epidemic: December 2001. http://www.unaids.org.
3. Musicco M, Lazzarin A, Nicolosi A, *et al.* Antiretroviral treatment of men infected with human immunodeficiency virus type 1 reduces the incidence of heterosexual transmission. Arch Intern Med 1994;154:1971–6.
4. De Vincenzi I, European study group on heterosexual transmission of HIV. A longitudinal study of human immunodeficiency virus transmission by heterosexual partners. N Engl J Med 1994;331:341–6.
5. Royce RA, Sena A, Cates W Jr., Cohen MS. Sexual transmission of HIV. N Engl J Med 1997;336:1072–8.
6. Quinn TC, Wawer MJ, Sewankambo N, *et al.* Viral load and heterosexual transmission of human immunodeficiency virus type 1. N Engl J Med 2000;342:921–9.
7. Fleming PL, Ciesielski CA, Byers RH, Castro KG, Berkelman RL. Gender differences in reported AIDS-indicative diagnoses. J Infect Dis 1993;168:61–7.
8. Sterling TR, Vlahov D, Astemborski J, Hoover DR, Margolick JB, Quinn TC. Initial plasma HIV-1 RNA levels and progression to AIDS in women and men. N Engl J Med 2001;344:720–5.
9. Cozzi LA, Pezzotti P, Dorrucci M, Phillips AN, Rezza G. HIV disease progression in 854 women and men infected through injecting drug use and heterosexual sex and followed for up to nine years from seroconversion. Italian Seroconversion Study. Br Med J 1994;309:1537–42.
10. Sha BE, Benson CA, Pottage JC Jr, *et al.* HIV infection in women: an observational study of clinical characteristics, disease progression, and survival for a cohort of women in Chicago. J Acquir Immune Defic Syndr Hum Retrovirol 1995;8:486–95.
11. Korn AP, Landers DV. Gynecologic disease in women infected with human immunodeficiency virus type 1. J Acquir Immun Defic Syndr Hum Retrovirol 1995;9:361–70.
12. Hoegsberg B, Abulafia O, Sedlis A, *et al.* Sexually transmitted disease and human immunodeficiency virus infection among women with pelvic inflammatory disease. Am J Obstet Gynecol 1990;163:1135–9.
13. Massad LS, Riester KA, Anastos KM, *et al.* Prevalence and predictors of squamous cell abnormalities in Papanicolaou smears from women infected with HIV-1. J Acquir Immune Defic Syndr 1999;21:33–41.
14. Massad LS, Ahdieh, Benning, *et al.* Evolution of cervical abnormalities among women with HIV-1: Evidence from surveillance cytology in the Women's Interagency HIV Study. J Acquir Immune Defic Syndr 2001;27:432–42.
15. Wright TC, Ellerbrock TV, Chiasson MA, *et al.* Cervical intraepithelial neoplasia in women infected with human immunodeficiency virus: prevalence, risk factors, and validity of Papanicolaou smears. Obstet Gynecol 1994;84:591–7.
16. Fruchter RG, Maiman M, Sedlis A, *et al.* Multiple recurrences of cervical intraepithelial neoplasia in women with the human immunodeficiency virus. Obstet Gynecol 1996;87:338–44.
17. Wright TC Jr, Cox JT, Massad LS, Twiggs LB, Wilkinson EJ for the 2001 ASCCP-Sponsored Consensus Conference. 2001 Consensus Guidelines for the management of women with cervical cytological abnormalities. JAMA 2002;287:2120–9.
18. United States Public Health Service/Infectious Disease Society of America Prevention of Opportunistic Infections Working Group. 2001 USPHS/Infectious Disease Society of America guidelines for the prevention of opportunistic infections in persons infected with human immunodeficiency virus. http://www.hivatis.org; 2001:1–65.
19. Shah PN, Smith JR, Wells C, *et al.* Menstrual symptoms in women infected by the human immunodeficiency virus. Obstet Gynecol 1994;83:397–400.
20. Centers for Disease Control and Prevention. Update: barrier protection against HIV infection and other sexually transmitted diseases. MMWR Morb Mortal Wkly Rep 1993;42:589–91.
21. Centers for Disease Control and Prevention. Guidelines for using antiretroviral agents among HIV-infected adults and adolescents. Recommendations of the panel on clinical practices for treatment of HIV. MMWR Morb Mortal Wkly Rep 2002;51(RR-7):1–56.
22. Peckham C, Gibb D. Mother-to-child transmission of the human immunodeficiency virus. N Engl J Med 1995;333:298–302.
23. The Italian register for HIV infection in children. Human immunodeficiency virus type 1 infection and breast milk. Acta Paediatr Suppl 1994;400:51–8.
24. Kourtis AP, Bulterys M, Nesheim SR, Lee FK. Understanding the timing of HIV transmission from mother to infant. JAMA 2001;285:709–12.
25. Ndauti R, John G, Mbori-Ngacha D, *et al.* Effect of breast-feeding and formula feeding on transmission of HIV-1: a randomized clinical trial. JAMA 2000;283:1167–74.
26. Landesman SH, Kalish LA, Burns DN, *et al.* Obstetrical factors and the transmission of human immunodeficiency virus type 1 from mother to child. N Engl J Med 1996;334:1617–23.
27. Perinatal HIV Guidelines Working Group. Public Health Service Task Force recommendations for use of antiretroviral drugs in pregnant HIV-1-infected women for maternal health and interventions to reduce perinatal HIV-1 transmission in the United States. http://www.hivatis.org; 2002:1–49.
28. Connor EM, Sperling RS, Gelber R, *et al.* Reduction of maternal–infant transmission of human immunodeficiency virus type 1 with zidovudine treatment. N Engl J Med 1994;331:1173–80.
29. Sperling RS, Shapiro DE, Coombs RW, *et al.* Maternal viral load, zidovudine treatment, and the risk of transmission of human immunodeficiency virus type 1 from mother to infant. N Engl J Med 1996;335:1621–9.
30. Chuachoowong R, Shaffer N, Siriwasin, *et al.* Short-course antenatal zidovudine reduces both cervicovaginal human immunodeficiency virus type 1 RNA levels and risk of perinatal transmission. J Infec Dis 2000;181:99–106.

31. Wade NA, Birkhead GS, Warren BL, *et al.* Abbreviated regimens of zidovudine prophylaxis and perinatal transmission of the human immunodeficiency virus. N Engl J Med 1998;339:1409–14.
32. Shaffer N, Chuachoowong R, Mock PA, *et al.* Short-course zidovudine for perinatal HIV-1 transmission in Bangkok, Thailand: A randomised controlled trial. Lancet 1999;353:773—80.
33. Saba J on behalf of the PETRA Trial Study Team. Interim analysis of early efficacy of three short ZDV/3TC combination regimens to prevent mother-to-child transmission of HIV-1: the PETRA trial. 6th Conference on Retroviruses and Opportunistic Infections, Chicago, IL, January 1999: Abstract S-7.
34. Guay LA, Musoke P, Fleming T, *et al.* Intrapartum and neonatal single-dose nevirapine compared with zidovudine for prevention of mother-to-child transmission of HIV-1 in Kampala, Uganda: HIVNET 012 randomised trial. Lancet 1999;354:795–802.
35. Eshleman SH, Mracna M, Guay LA, *et al.* Selection and fading of resistance mutations in women and infants receiving nevirapine to prevent HIV-1 vertical transmission (HIVNET 012). AIDS 2001;15:1951–7.
36. Ioannidis JPA, Abrams EJ, Ammann A, *et al.* Perinatal transmission of human immunodeficiency virus type 1 by pregnant women with RNA virus loads <1000 copies/ml. J Infect Dis 2001;143:539–45.
37. Dorenbaum A, Cunningham CK, Gelber RD, *et al.* Two-dose intrapartum/newborn nevirapine and standard antiretroviral therapy to reduce perinatal HIV transmission: a randomized trial. JAMA 2002;288:189–98.
38. Cunningham CK, Britto P, Gelber RD *et al.* Genotypic resistance analysis in women participating in PACTG 316 with HIV-1 RNA >400 copies/ml. 8th Conference on Retroviruses and Opportunistic Infections. Chicago, IL, February 2001: Abstract 712.
39. Read JS for the International Perinatal HIV Group. The mode of delivery and the risk of vertical transmission of human immunodeficiency virus type 1: a meta-analysis of 15 prospective cohort studies. N Engl J Med 1999;34:977–87.
40. The International Perinatal HIV Group. Duration of ruptured membranes and vertical transmission of HIV-1: a meta-analysis from 15 prospective cohort studies. AIDS 2001;15:357–68.
41. Biggar RJ, Miotti PG, Taha TE, *et al.* Perinatal intervention trial in Africa: effect of a birth canal cleansing intervention to prevent HIV transmission. Lancet 1996;347:1647–50.
42. Hocke C, Morlat P, Chene G, *et al.* Prospective cohort study of the effect of pregnancy on the progression of human immunodeficiency virus infection. Obstet Gynecol 1995;86:886–91.
43. Temmerman M, Chomba EN, Ndinya-Achola J, *et al.* Maternal human immunodeficiency virus-1 infection and pregnancy outcome. Obstet Gynecol 1994;83:495–501.

chapter 136

Practice Point

Diagnosis of HIV in newborns

Peter L Havens

In the absence of intervention, children born to women who have HIV infection have about a 25% chance of being infected with HIV. Children born to women who have HIV infection need:

- therapy to prevent HIV infection;
- testing to identify infected infants; and
- institution of therapy to prevent *Pneumocystis carinii* pneumonia (PCP).

Pathogenesis

Perinatal transmission of HIV occurs in utero (about 25–30% of perinatal infections) and in the peripartum period (about 70%). Breast-feeding results in late postnatal HIV transmission in another 14–16% of infants.

Clinical features

Because many children who have HIV infection remain asymptomatic for long periods of time, the clinical examination is not a sensitive test for the presence of infection.

Diagnosis

In adults and children older than 18 months of age, HIV infection is diagnosed using an enzyme-linked immunosorbent assay (ELISA) to screen blood for the presence of antibody to HIV. A single positive ELISA should be repeated, and repeatedly positive tests should be confirmed by Western blot for HIV-specific IgG antibody.

Children born to women who have HIV infection passively acquire maternal IgG antibody to HIV, which can make the HIV IgG antibody ELISA and Western blot reactive for up to 18 months after birth, even in infants not infected with HIV. Therefore, positive tests for IgG antibody to HIV do not confirm the diagnosis of HIV infection in children less than 18 months of age but rather identify infants who are at risk of being infected. However, two or more negative HIV IgG antibody tests (ELISA) performed with an interval of at least 1 month in children over 6 months of age can be used to 'reasonably exclude' HIV infection among children without clinical evidence of HIV disease or previous positive laboratory evidence of HIV infection, such as HIV DNA polymerase chain reaction (PCR) or culture.

Immunoglobulin A does not cross the placenta as readily as IgG, and immunoassays for HIV-specific IgA have been developed to allow serologic diagnosis of children born to women who have HIV infection. Although these assays are 89–100% specific by 1–2 months of age, false-positive tests in the first week of life and low sensitivity as late as 6 months of age limit their usefulness in clinical practice.

Culture of HIV has been considered the gold standard for diagnosis of HIV infection in infants less than 18 months of age. Because up to 7% of children who are later found to be uninfected may have a positive culture within the first 6 months of life, at least two positive cultures are necessary to confirm the diagnosis of HIV infection in infants. Cultures are difficult and costly to perform, they can only be performed in special laboratories and they take a long time to produce a result; therefore, their clinical practicality is limited.

Polymerase chain reaction for HIV DNA is the most rapid and accurate method for identification of HIV infection in children less than 18 months of age. Sensitivity is 38% on the day of birth, 93% by day 14 of life and 96% by day 28. False-positive results are possible from laboratory error but two tests performed on separate samples are 98.5% accurate in identifying infection status and using three tests performed after 1 month of age achieves almost 100% accuracy.

Infants infected with HIV in utero have a positive HIV DNA PCR at birth and are at high risk of rapidly progressive symptomatic HIV infection. Infants infected in the peripartum period have negative HIV DNA PCR in the first few days of life, but in those infants HIV DNA PCR tests may be positive by as early as 2 weeks of age and 96% are positive by 1 month of age. Infants infected by breast-feeding may have negative HIV DNA PCR until after 6 months of age (Table 136.1).

Polymerase chain reaction for HIV RNA may be more sensitive than DNA in very young infants, and two positive HIV RNA PCR tests performed on separately collected blood samples are diagnostic of HIV infection in infants and children. HIV RNA PCR is not routinely recommended for screening at-risk infants because negative HIV RNA PCR testing does not exclude HIV infection. However, for infants infected with non-clade B HIV isolates, HIV RNA PCR using methods developed to include non-clade B RNA sequences may be preferable to standard HIV DNA PCR, which is less sensitive for identifying non-clade B virus.

Measurement of HIV p24 antigen in blood is not sensitive enough to be used for early diagnosis of HIV infection in children, even if immune complex dissociated methods are used for sample preparation. However, repeatedly positive HIV p24 antigen tests are diagnostic of HIV infection.

Management

The details of management of infants born to women who have HIV infection are shown in Table 136.2.

HIV INFECTION AND USUAL PATTERN OF TEST RESULTS IN NEWBORNS OF WOMEN WHO HAVE HIV INFECTION							
HIV infection category		Test	Infant's age at time testing performed and usual result of testing				
			Day of birth	1 month	4 months	>6 months	18 months
Not infected	Seroreverter (nontransmitted maternal infection)	ELISA/Western blot	+	+	+	+/−	−
		HIV DNA PCR	−	−	−	−	−
Infected	In utero	ELISA/Western blot	+	+	+	+	+
		HIV DNA PCR	+	+	+	+	+
	Perinatal	ELISA/Western blot	+	+	+	+	+
		HIV DNA PCR	−	±	+	+	+
	Via breast milk	ELISA/Western blot	+	+	+	+	+
		HIV DNA PCR	−	−	±	+	+

Table 136.1 HIV infection and usual pattern of test results in newborns of women who have HIV infection.

LABORATORY MONITORING AND TREATMENT OF INFANTS BORN TO WOMEN WHO HAVE HIV INFECTION		
Age	Category of intervention	Test or treatment indicated
Newborn	Evaluation	ELISA for antibody to HIV (and Western blot if ELISA is positive); a well documented history of HIV infection in mother can replace ELISA testing in the newborn
		HIV DNA PCR
		Complete blood count with differential, alanine transaminase, bilirubin and glucose if mother taking protease inhibitors during pregnancy
	Treatment	Zidovudine for prophylaxis against vertical transmission (see Chapter 134)
		Advise against breast-feeding if safe alternatives are available
4 weeks	Evaluation	HIV DNA PCR
	Treatment	Continue zidovudine; hematocrit (optional; to check for anemia from azidothymidine)
6 weeks	Treatment	Stop zidovudine (assuming the HIV DNA PCR at birth and 4 weeks are negative)
		Begin treatment with trimethoprim–sulfamethoxazole for prophylaxis against Pneumocystis carinii pneumonia
4 months	Evaluation	HIV DNA PCR (if earlier testing negative)
	Treatment	Stop treatment with trimethoprim–sulfamethoxazole if the 4-month HIV DNA PCR returns and is negative, but continue if HIV DNA PCR test is positive
18 months	Evaluation	ELISA for antibody to HIV (Western blot confimation if ELISA positive); if negative, in the presence of previously negative HIV DNA PCR test and absence of symptoms of HIV infection, then the patient is a 'seroreverter', and HIV infection is definitively excluded at the present time; if positive, repeat
HIV culture may be used in place of HIV DNA PCR testing. Any positive culture or HIV DNA PCR is repeated as soon as possible to confirm the diagnosis. Patients diagnosed with HIV infection are treated as outlined in Chapter 134.		

Table 136.2 Laboratory monitoring and treatment of infants born to women who have HIV infection.

Prevention of perinatal transmission (see Chapter 135)

One regimen to prevent perinatal transmission of HIV includes 6 weeks of zidovudine therapy in the newborn infant. Breast-feeding increases the risk of perinatal transmission of HIV, so, in areas of the world where safe alternatives to breast-feeding are readily available, women who have HIV infection should be advised not to breast-feed their infants.

Prophylaxis of *Pneumocystis carinii* pneumonia

All children born to women who have HIV infection should be started on PCP prophylaxis at 4–6 weeks of age, regardless of $CD4^+$ T cell count or HIV infection status. The most common drug regimen for prophylaxis is trimethoprim–sulfamethoxazole, trimethoprim 150mg/m^2/day and sulfamethoxazole 750mg/m^2/day q12h and given 3 days weekly (see Chapter 134, Fig. 134.14). For children in whom HIV infection is reasonably excluded, PCP prophylaxis can be discontinued. Prophylaxis against PCP should be continued until at least 12 months of age in children found to be infected with HIV, independent of their $CD4^+$ T cell count.

Follow-up visits

A baseline visit with the primary care provider is recommended. Follow-up visits at 2- to 3-month intervals to primary practitioners are adequate for most children, with timing determined in part by the immunization schedule in infancy. Diagnostic testing for HIV follows the schedule outlined in Table 136.2. An office visit is not necessary each time laboratory testing is performed.

The uncertainty of an indeterminate infection status is difficult for families. An initial visit or discussion with personnel experienced in the care of children who have or who are at risk for HIV infection can give families an opportunity to learn about the illness and the follow-up needed. Children who are found to be infected with HIV should follow the care recommendations outlined in Chapter 134.

Further reading

American Academy of Pediatrics. Evaluation and medical treatment of the HIV-exposed Infant. Pediatrics 1997;99:909–17.

Centers for Disease Control and Prevention. 1995 Revised guidelines for prophylaxis against *Pneumocystis carinii* pneumonia for children infected with or perinatally exposed to human immunodeficiency virus. MMWR Morb Mortal Wkly Rep 1995;44(RR-4):1–11.

Dunn DT, Brandt CD, Krivine A, *et al.* The sensitivity of HIV-1 DNA polymerase chain reaction in the neonatal period and the relative contributions of intra-uterine and intra-partum transmission. AIDS 1995;9:7–11.

Jenny-Avital ER, Beatrice ST. Erroneously low or undetectable plasma human immunodeficiency virus type 1 (HIV-1) ribonucleic acid load, determined by polymerase chain reaction, in West African and American patients with non-B subtype HIV-1 infection. Clin Infect Dis 2001; 32:1227–30.

Leroy V, Newell ML, Dabis F, *et al.* International multicentre pooled analysis of late postnatal mother-to-child transmission of HIV-1 infection. Lancet 1998;352:597–600.

Newell ML, Dunn D, Maria AD, *et al.* Detection of virus in vertically exposed HIV-antibody-negative children. Lancet 1996;347:213–5.

Owens DK, Holodniy M, McDonald TW, Scott J, Sonnad S. A meta-analytic evaluation of the polymerase chain reaction for the diagnosis of HIV infection in infants. JAMA 1996;275:1342–8.

Roques PA, Gras G, Parnet-Mathieu F, *et al.* Clearance of HIV infection in 12 perinatally infected children: clinical, virological and immunological data. AIDS 1995;9:19–26.

Zaman MM, Recco RA, Haag R. Infection with non-B subtype HIV type 1 complicates management of established infection in adult patients and diagnosis of infection in newborn infants. Clin Infect Dis 2002;34:417.

chapter 137

Diagnostic Tests for HIV Infection and Resistance Assays

Daniel R Kuritzkes

INTRODUCTION

Since the first human immunodeficiency virus (HIV-1) was isolated in 1983 and the first antibody detection tests were marketed in 1985, laboratory tests for the diagnosis and monitoring of HIV infection have evolved constantly. Technologic advances have led to the development of clinical assays that permit the precise quantification of plasma virus levels, detect the presence of key drug resistance mutations or generate recombinant viruses for phenotypic drug resistance testing. Indeed, few areas in medicine have witnessed such rapid and widespread adaptation of molecular biologic tools to everyday patient management.

DIAGNOSTIC TOOLS FOR HIV INFECTION

Serologic assays

Assays have been developed for detection of HIV antibodies in serum, whole blood, saliva, urine and dried blood collected on filter paper.

Enzyme-linked immunosorbent assay

Most laboratories screen for anti-HIV-1 and anti-HIV-2 antibodies by means of an enzyme-linked immunosorbent assay (EIA) based on antigens that consist of viral lysates or recombinant or synthetic proteins corresponding to the immunodominant epitopes from two HIV-1 subtype B variants (LAI and MN strains) and HIV-2 subtype A (ROD strain). These tests are therefore able to detect anti-HIV-1 and anti-HIV-2 antibodies. Current antigen sandwich EIAs have a sensitivity and specificity that approach 100%.[1] In contrast to earlier tests, which detected only IgG antibodies, third-generation HIV EIAs detect all classes of anti-HIV antibodies, considerably shortening the time to diagnosis following acute infection. However, these assays may fail to detect antibodies to the highly divergent HIV-1 subtypes from groups N and O.

Rapid tests

Diagnostic tests based on red cell or particle agglutination as well as dot blot assays have been developed that permit rapid diagnosis of HIV-1 infection. In laboratory comparisons, sensitivity and specificity are similar to those of the EIA, but performance may be somewhat lower in the field.[2] The simplicity and wide operating temperature of these tests make them ideally suited for use in resource-poor settings. Rapid tests are also useful for diagnosis of HIV infection in women during labor and delivery, and to establish the infection status of source patients following an occupational needlestick injury.

Home testing

'Home testing' for HIV infection in fact refers to home collection of a fingerstick blood sample, which is applied to a filter paper, dried and mailed directly to a central laboratory for analysis. Anonymity is preserved by the use of code numbers to identify specimens and their senders. Results and counseling are provided over the telephone. In the USA, fewer than 1% of samples submitted for testing during the first year of availability were positive, suggesting that these tests serve primarily to reassure the worried well.

Western blot

Despite a specificity of >99%, a reactive HIV EIA has a relatively low positive predictive value when applied to populations at low risk for HIV infection. Thus, a confirmatory test is essential to exclude false-positive results. The Western blot (WB) method is currently the most widely used. In a WB, viral proteins are separated by polyacrylamide gel electrophoresis and transferred by blotting onto a nitrocellulose strip. The strips are then reacted with the test serum to determine which, if any, viral proteins are recognized by patient antibodies. Figure 137.1 shows a typical WB positive for HIV-1, with the different reactive proteins. Alternatively, immunoblotting uses recombinant HIV-1 or HIV-2 proteins or synthetic peptides applied as individual strips or spots to a plastic support. Immunoblots are simpler to standardize than Western blots and are more sensitive in cases of recent seroconversion, but are more expensive. Because they use a limited number of synthetic proteins, immunoblots are less likely to detect antibodies to uncommon HIV-1 subtypes.

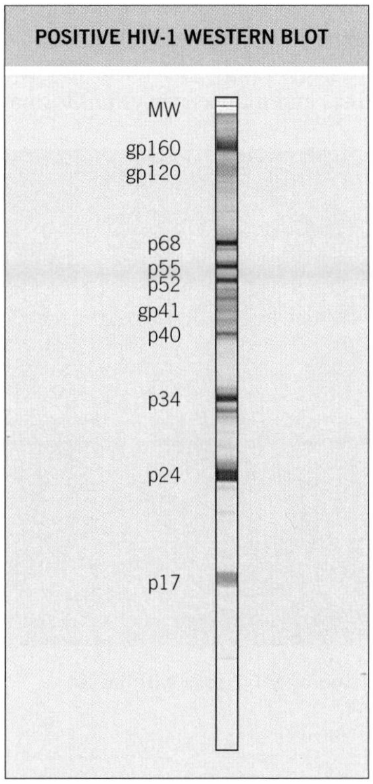

Fig. 137.1 Positive HIV-1 Western blot. The binding of the patient's antibodies to viral antigens coated on the strip is revealed by an enzyme-labeled antihuman globulin. gp160, gp120 and gp41 are *env* gene products. p55, p24 and p17 are *gag* gene products. p68, p52 and p34 are *pol* gene products. MW, molecular weight of the viral proteins.

Strain serotyping

Differentiating between HIV-1 and HIV-2

Serologic differentiation is based on the detection of specific antibodies against the HIV-2 transmembrane protein (gp36) by Western blot or immunoblot assay. Monospecific EIAs for HIV-2 also are available for differentiation. Epitope differences between the immunodominant regions of HIV-1 and HIV-2 generally are sufficient for adequate serologic differentiation.

Serotypic differentiation of HIV-1 group M subtypes

The use of peptides corresponding to the V3 loop of the different group M subtypes can identify the infecting subtype with acceptable predictive value relative to genotyping. Alternatively, competitive peptide EIAs can be used. However, phylogenetic analysis of *pol* sequences obtained at the time of genotypic resistance testing (see below) offers a more convenient approach to subtype identification.

HIV isolation

HIV can be isolated from blood, plasma, cerebrospinal fluid (CSF), genital secretions or tissue by co-culture with lymphocytes from a seronegative donor that have been stimulated with phytohemagglutinin and interleukin-2 before use. Viral replication is revealed by p24 antigen production in the culture supernatant. A positive culture provides direct evidence of HIV-1 infection, but virus culture is rarely necessary to establish a diagnosis. Morever, HIV culture has been supplanted for diagnostic purposes by polymerase chain reaction (PCR)-based assays; its use is limited primarily to specific research applications.

Virus isolation is successful in more than 95% of individuals infected with HIV-1, but sensitivity is lower in patients with higher $CD4^+$ cell counts. For a given $CD4^+$ cell count, the rate of HIV-2 isolation is significantly lower.[3] CD8 T cells that are present in peripheral blood mononuclear cells (PBMCs) exert an antiviral effect and may prevent outgrowth of virus in vitro. Therefore, it is often necessary to remove these cells in vitro in order to recover virus from patients on effective antiretroviral therapy.

Tropism

It has long been known that HIV-1 strains isolated from patients with AIDS can be more virulent in vitro than those isolated from asymptomatic persons. These strains, found in the later stages of immunodepression, are termed 'T lymphotropic' because they are able to multiply in T-lymphocyte lines and induce syncytium formation in the MT2 cell line (Fig. 137.2). Syncytium-inducing strains are observed in up to 50% of patients in the later stages of infection. Emergence of SI variants is associated with an accelerated decline in $CD4^+$ lymphocyte counts.[4] Nearly all strains isolated during seroconversion usually are non-SI and macrophage tropic and are incapable of multiplying in T-cell lines.

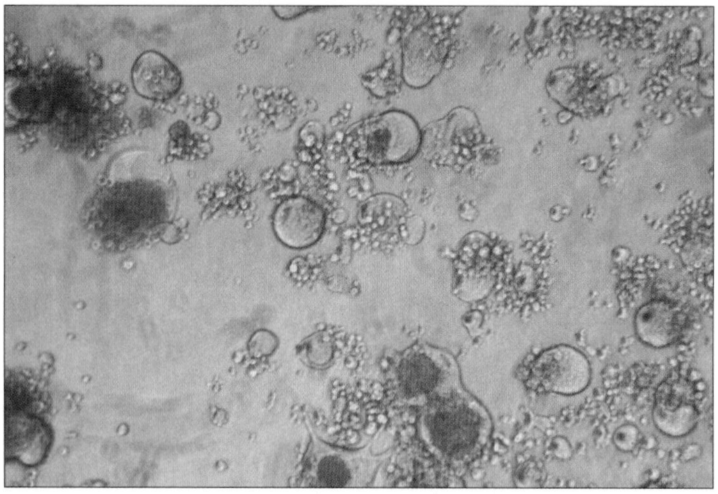

Fig. 137.2 Syncytia formed by infection of MT-2 cells with an X4 (syncytium-inducing) isolate of HIV-1.

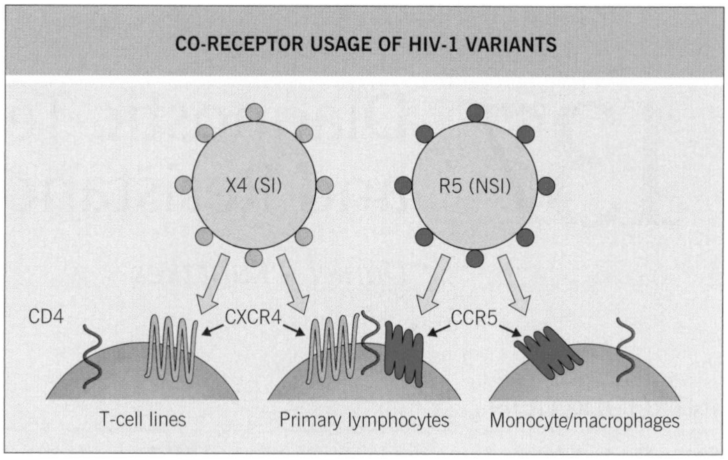

Fig. 137.3 Relationship between co-receptor usage and cellular tropism of HIV-1.

A biologic basis for the switch in tropism associated with the SI phenotype was provided by discovery of the chemokine co-receptors for HIV. CCR5 is expressed by monocytes and primary T cells, but expression of this co-receptor is lost by T-cell lines. Conversely, CXCR4 is expressed by activated T cells and T-cell lines, but not by monocytes. Lymphotropic (SI) strains preferentially use the CXCR4 co-receptor, whereas macrophage-tropic (non-SI) strains use the CCR5 co-receptor (Fig. 137.3). Amino acid differences in certain hypervariable regions of gp120 determine co-receptor specificity. Consequently, SI strains now are referred to as X4 strains (because they use the CXCR4 co-receptor) and non-SI strains as R5 strains (because they use the CCR5 co-receptor). Occasionally duotropic (R5/X4) viruses are isolated. These viruses are able to use both CCR5 and CXCR4 co-receptors and can infect monocytes and $CD4^+$ lymphocytes with similar efficiency. It is thought that R5/X4 viruses represent intermediate forms in the evolution of SI viruses from non-SI strains.

At present, characterizing the co-receptor usage of patient isolates has little clinical utility and tests to distinguish R5 and X4 viruses are not routinely available. However, such knowledge might become important if HIV-1 entry inhibitors that specifically inhibit CCR5 or CXCR4 binding are developed for treatment of HIV-1 infection.

Viral antigen detection

Circulating HIV-1 capsid (p24) antigen can be detected by qualitative or quantitative antigen-capture EIA. High titers of p24 antigen are present during acute infection prior to seroconversion. Subsequently, p24 antigen is complexed with p24-specific antibodies and becomes undetectable in most asymptomatic patients. With advancing disease, p24 antibody titers fall and the antigen once again becomes detectable (a poor prognostic sign). Qualitative assays for p24 antigen are useful in diagnosing HIV-1 infection prior to seroconversion, but quantitative assays have been replaced by more sensitive viral RNA assays. A modified assay that dissociates p24 antigen–antibody complexes by heat treatment may provide an affordable alternative to RNA assays for quantifying plasma viremia in resource-poor countries.[5]

Viral nucleic acid detection

HIV-1 DNA polymerase chain reaction

Presence of integrated proviral HIV-1 DNA can be detected by qualitative PCR. Conserved sequences in *gag* or *pol* are amplified and the PCR product is detected by hybridization using an enzyme- or radiolabeled oligonucleotide probe. Under appropriate conditions, experienced laboratories can achieve a sensitivity and specificity of 100% in detecting subtype B virus.[6] However, sensitivity is lower in individuals with higher $CD4^+$ cell counts due to the lower titer of circulating infected PBMCs, and in patients with nonsubtype B infection. HIV-1 DNA PCR assays are used almost exclusively for early diagnosis of infection in neonates. These tests have limited utility in adults, but occasionally may be useful in resolving cases in which results of serologic tests are ambiguous.

Quantitative HIV-1 RNA assay

The development of sensitive and precise assays for quantifying HIV-1 RNA in plasma led to novel insights into HIV-1 pathogenesis and helped establish complete suppression of detectable virus replication as the appropriate goal of antiretroviral therapy. Use of these assays is now standard in the management of HIV-1-infected patients in the developed world.

Several different assay formats have been developed for HIV-1 RNA quantification. In PCR-based assays (Amplicor HIV-1 Monitor, Roche Molecular Systems), HIV-1 RNA is converted into DNA by reverse transcription followed by PCR amplification of the DNA. The PCR product is detected by hybridization to an enzyme-conjugated probe specific for HIV-1, and quantified by reacting bound probe with a substrate that undergoes a color change, as in an ELISA. The branched DNA assay (Quantiplex HIV-1 RNA, Bayer Nucleic Acid Diagnostics) uses nonenzymatic means to amplify the signal from HIV RNA. In this assay, viral RNA is 'captured' by hybridization to complementary oligonucleotides that are bound to the wells of a microtiter plate. The captured viral RNA target is then hybridized to branched oligonucleotides (hence the name 'branched' DNA assay), which in turn are hybridized to enzyme-conjugated oligonucleotides that can be quantified as above. The NASBA assay (HIV-1 RNA QT, Organon-Teknika) is similar in concept to the RT-PCR assay except that reactions occur at one temperature. A fourth assay, based on DNA hybridization and colorimetric detection (Digene Diagnostics), has been developed, but is not yet widely available.

Performance characteristics of the three commercially available assays are similar (Table 137.1), and studies have demonstrated the excellent correlation between plasma RNA titers in a given plasma sample tested by the three techniques. All three assays have a lower limit of quantification of approximately 50–80 copies/ml. Assay sensitivity can be extended by concentrating plasma virus from larger sample volumes. Although detection limits of 3–5 copies/ml are achievable by such means, these assays are much less precise at plasma HIV-1 RNA titers below 200 copies/ml.[7] Once infection becomes established, steady-state plasma virus levels are relatively stable, varying by 0.3–0.4 $\log_{10}$ copies/ml over weeks to months. Given these factors, changes of greater than 0.5–0.7 $\log_{10}$ (3- to 5-fold) are likely to reflect significant changes in HIV-1 replication.[8]

Although most strains of HIV-1 that circulate in North America belong to subtype B, more than 10 different subtypes are found around the world. The HIV-1 Monitor 1.0 (RT-PCR) assay is significantly less sensitive for detecting HIV-1 from subtypes A, E and F as compared with the Quantiplex version 3.0 (bDNA) assay.[9] Plasma HIV-1 RNA levels that appear to be lower than expected in a patient with advanced disease can be a clue to infection with a nonsubtype B strain. Incorporation of alternative primer sets in the new version of the HIV-1 Monitor assay (version 1.5) has improved the ability of this assay to detect diverse HIV-1 subtypes.

PERFORMANCE CHARACTERISTICS OF PLASMA HIV-1 RNA ASSAYS

	RT-PCR (Roche)	bDNA (Bayer)	NASBA (Organon Teknika)
Linear range (copies/ml)	$400–8 \times 10^5$	$75–5 \times 10^5$	$80–4 \times 10^7$
Interassay variation ($\log_{10}$ SD)	0.12–0.22	0.05–0.17	0.038–0.261
Specimen volume	200μl	2ml	100μl–1ml
Preferred anticoagulant	EDTA/ACD	EDTA	EDTA/ACD/HEP

ACD, acid citrate dextran; EDTA, ethylenediaminetetra-acetic acid; HEP, heparin

Table 137.1 Performance characteristics of plasma HIV-1 RNA assays. The range of the 'ultrasensitive' RT-PCR assay is 50–50,000 copies/ml.

Drug resistance assays

A variety of assays are available for assessing drug resistance, including:

- genotypic assays, in which nucleotide sequencing of viral genetic material is used to detect the presence or absence of critical drug resistance mutations; and
- phenotypic assays, in which the concentration of drug necessary to inhibit virus replication in vitro is estimated in a drug susceptibility assay.

Each method has potential advantages and disadvantages. An important limitation of both approaches is that they provide a measure of the characteristics of the predominant viral species but do not indicate the presence of minor species that may emerge as resistant variants during subsequent treatment (Table 137.2).

Genotypic tests of HIV-1 drug resistance

Several approaches to genotyping are available, ranging from full-length sequencing of the target gene to point mutation assays, which focus only on a particular mutation of interest. The most commonly used genotypic assays rely on automated DNA sequencing. Using this technique, the nucleotide sequence of some or all of the gene of

COMPARISON OF GENOTYPIC AND PHENOTYPIC DRUG RESISTANCE TESTS FOR HIV

Type of assay	Advantages	Disadvantages
Genotypic assays	Rapid turn-around time Appearance of resistance mutations may precede change in phenotype Widely available	Genotype may not correlate with phenotype Require expert interpretation Fail to detect minor species Unable to assess mutational interactions
Phenotypic assays	Direct measure of viral drug susceptibility Assess net effect of mutational interactions and cross-resistance patterns	Cost Longer turn-around time Fail to detect minor species Appropriate cut-offs not defined for all drugs

Table 137.2 Comparison of genotypic and phenotypic drug resistance tests for HIV.

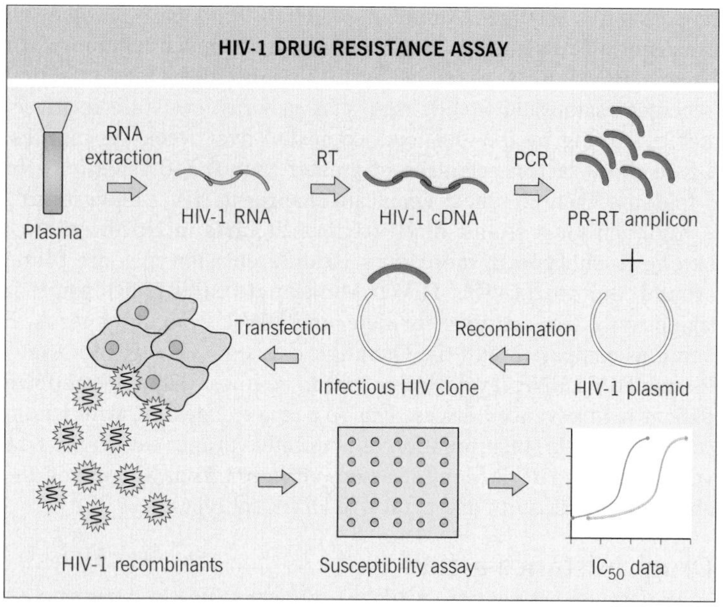

Fig. 137.4 HIV-1 drug resistance assay. RT, reverse transcription reaction; cDNA, complementary DNA; PR-RT, protease and reverse transcriptase gene; IC_{50}, 50% inhibitory concentration.

interest (e.g. protease (PR) or reverse transcriptase (RT)) is obtained, then translated into the predicted amino acid sequence in order to determine whether specific mutations are present or absent. Automated sequencing offers the most complete data on viral genotype, but generates more information than is needed for most clinical purposes. For example, HIV-1 RT has 550 amino acids, but mutations at only a small number of these positions are implicated in drug resistance. Therefore, interpretation of the genotype is needed in order to help distinguish which changes are merely polymorphisms and which might be significantly associated with drug resistance.

In most commercially available genotypic tests, viral RNA is extracted from a sample of plasma and reverse transcribed into complementary DNA in the laboratory (Fig. 137.4). The PR- and RT-coding regions of the cDNA are then amplified by PCR, and the nucleotide sequence of the PCR product is determined on an automated DNA sequencer. Some laboratories use specific diagnostic kits that provide standardized reagents needed for the RT-PCR and DNA sequencing steps. Generally, these kits are part of an HIV genotyping system that includes equipment for running the sequencing assays and software for interpreting assay results. The TRUGENE HIV-1 genotyping kit and OpenGene DNA sequencing system and the ViroSeq HIV-1 Genotyping System are approved for clinical use by the US Food and Drug Administration (FDA) in conjunction with the appropriate FDA-cleared interpretation algorithm; approval of the PE/Applied Biosystems HIV-GT kit is pending. Other laboratories employ so-called 'home brew' assays using reagents, primers and interpretive algorithms developed individually by each laboratory.

Other types of genotypic resistance assays, such as the line probe assay (LiPA), differential probe hybridization assays or real-time PCR assays using selective PCR primers, are designed to provide more limited information by testing for the presence or absence of specific mutations at particular codons. These assays are faster than standard genotypic tests and may be more sensitive at detecting minor species. However, because these tests do not generate a comprehensive sequence, information needed to interpret complex genotypes might be missing. Furthermore, the tests must be reconfigured to include important new mutations as they are defined.

The frequency of false-positive and false-negative results is <1% for genotypic assays when assessed using samples that carry predominantly mutant or predominantly wild-type virus populations. However, sensitivity for detecting presence of a mutation is variable when both wild-type and mutant viruses are present as a mixture. In general, mutant species must constitute 10–20% of the population to be detected by standard sequencing methods. Some mutations may go undetected unless they are present as the majority species.

Phenotypic tests of HIV-1 drug resistance

Drug susceptibility tests with HIV-1 usually are performed using a recombinant virus assay, in which the viral genes of interest (e.g. PR and RT) are introduced into a plasmid that carries all of the other viral genes needed for replication in cell culture (see Fig. 137.4).[10,11] Modification of the assay allows introduction of the integrase (IN) or envelope (ENV) genes in order to determine susceptibility to integrase inhibitors and entry inhibitors, respectively. Using these assays, small differences in susceptibility can be detected (~2- to 4-fold compared with control). Phenotypic assays are more complex and labor intensive than genotypic assays. Automation makes it possible to test many samples simultaneously, and allows for high throughput. However, the cost and complexity of the automation limit availability of these assays to a few reference laboratories.

Viral fitness and replication capacity assays

Accumulation of drug resistance mutations can decrease the replication capacity of the virus. In the absence of drug, resistant variants are significantly less fit than wild-type and are replaced by wild-type virus if antiretroviral therapy is interrupted.[12] Viral fitness can be assessed by growth competition assays, in which the relative replication of two or more viral species is tested in the same culture.[13] Alternatively, viral replication capacity can be measured by a modification of the phenotypic resistance assay. At present, the clinical utility of these assays remains undefined.

Therapeutic drug monitoring

Therapeutic drug monitoring (TDM) is used to maintain plasma levels of a drug within a defined therapeutic range in order to maximize efficacy and minimize toxicity. Plasma concentrations of antiretroviral drugs following administration of a standardized dose show considerable interpatient variation. In theory, TDM of antiretroviral agents could lead to dosage adjustments that would correct for this variation. Although measuring the plasma concentration of most antiretroviral drugs is relatively straightforward, establishing a therapeutic range is more difficult. Consequently, the data needed to guide dosage adjustment for currently available antiretroviral drugs given a particular plasma concentration are lacking. Moreover, in the case of nucleoside RT inhibitors, concentration–response relationships have not been demonstrated consistently. Nevertheless, TDM is likely to prove useful for non-nucleoside RT inhibitors and protease inhibitors, and efforts to generate the information needed to establish clinical utility of TDM are underway.

CLINICAL USE OF HIV DIAGNOSTIC TESTS

Diagnosing acute HIV-1 infection

After exposure to the virus, HIV RNA can be detected from day 12 and p24 antigen from days 14–16 (Fig. 137.5). Detection of HIV-1 p24 antigen has a sensitivity of approximately 90% and a specificity of 100% in the diagnosis of acute infection.[14] HIV-1 RNA assays have a sensitivity of 100% in diagnosing acute infection, but at the cost of lowered specificity (97%). Because of the potential social and legal ramifications of a false-positive HIV-1 test, and the need to perform additional testing to clarify a patient's HIV infection status, some experts prefer p24 antigen assays in this setting. However, false-positive HIV-1 RNA tests usually have titers less than 10,000 copies/ml, whereas HIV-1

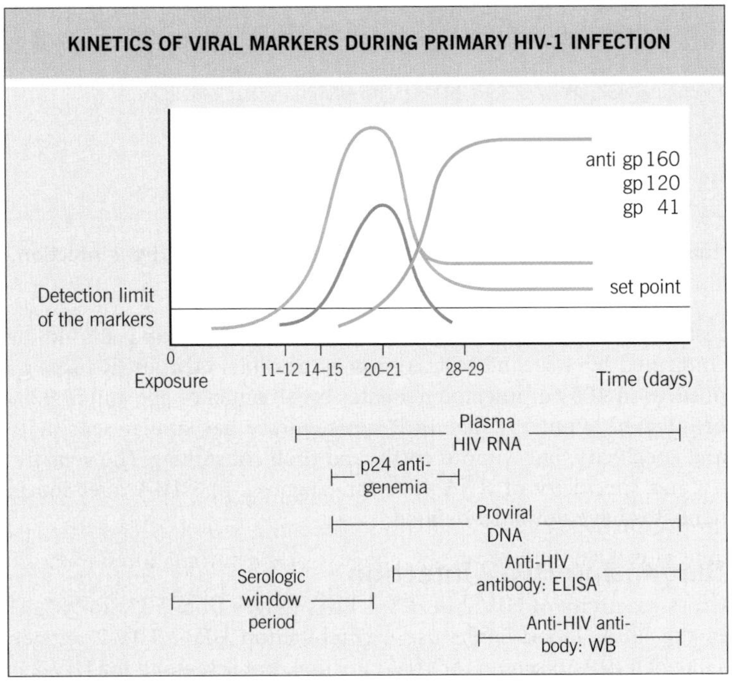

Fig. 137.5 Kinetics of viral markers during primary HIV-1 infection. The first positive viral marker is plasma RNA 11–12 days after infection. p24 Antigenemia is detectable on day 14 or 15. The first anti-HIV antibodies are detectable by third-generation ELISAs on days 20–21. (Pink, plasma HIV RNA; purple, p24 antigenemia; blue, anti-HIV antibody).

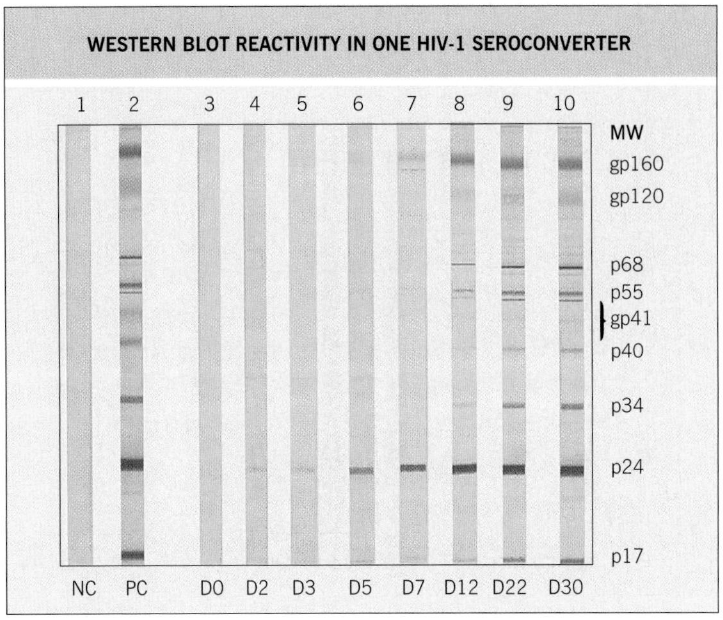

Fig. 137.6 Western blot reactivity in one HIV-1 seroconverter. Lanes 1 and 2, negative (NC) and positive controls (PC). Lanes 3–10, serial samples collected on days (D) 0, 2, 3, 5, 7, 12, 22 and 30. Day 0 corresponds to the first collected sample. Anti-p24 was the first antibody detected, rapidly followed by anti-gp160, p55, p40 and gp120. Later, gp41 and p18 are weakly reactive.

DIAGNOSIS OF ACUTE AND EARLY HIV INFECTION	
EIA negative	• p24 Antigen positive, or • Plasma HIV-1 RNA >10,000 copies/ml
EIA positive	• Evolving WB pattern, and/or • EIA-negative by 'detuned' assay

Table 137.3 Diagnosis of acute and early HIV infection.

RNA levels generally exceed 100,000 copies/ml in primary infection. Thus, plasma HIV-1 RNA testing might be used in selected cases where a history of recent exposure and symptoms consistent with acute HIV-1 infection provide a high index of suspicion (Table 137.3).

The first antibodies are detectable on day 21. However, the kinetics of these markers can vary according to the patient and infecting strain; antibodies against non-B subtypes may be less well recognized early after infection.[15] It is generally agreed that beyond week 6 after infection antibodies are detectable in almost all patients. Reactivity by WB lags behind seroconversion by EIA. Therefore, a positive EIA and negative or evolving WB can provide evidence of recent infection, particularly if antibodies directed against gag proteins are present (Fig. 137.6). A fully reactive WB usually develops within 6 months.[16] Recent seroconverters can also be identified by use of a less sensitive ('detuned') third-generation EIA. Patients infected within 5–6 months prior to testing are reactive on the sensitive EIA but nonreactive on the detuned EIA. A two-step algorithm using a sensitive/less sensitive EIA testing strategy can correctly identify nearly all recent seroconverters.[15]

Diagnosing chronic HIV-1 infection

Testing for HIV antibodies is a two-stage process: samples that test positive by an initial screening assay are retested to exclude clerical or laboratory error and a confirmatory assay is performed on repeatedly reactive sera to verify that the antibodies are directed against HIV antigens. Screening in industrialized countries generally is based on the EIA and in most resource-poor countries on rapid kits. In some countries (France, Switzerland) two different kits must be combined for screening purposes to reduce the risks linked to human error and the possible failure of one test. The possibility of false positivity means that positive screening tests must always be confirmed with highly specific tests.

The WB is the most commonly used confirmatory test, although indirect immunofluorescence assays are used occasionally. Confirmation of a reactive EIA by positive WB establishes the diagnosis of HIV infection. A negative WB suggests a false-positive EIA or acute infection (see above). Criteria for interpretation of HIV-1 WBs have been developed by several groups, but no uniform standard has been adopted (Table 137.4).[17]

CRITERIA FOR WB INTERPRETATION

Organization	Criteria
American Red Cross	At least one band from each structural gene product (*gag*, *pol* and *env*)
US Centers for Disease Control and Prevention and Association of State and Territorial Public Health Directors Directors	Reactivity to any two of p24, gp41or gp120/160
Consortium for Retrovirus Serology Standardization	p24 or p31 and one of gp41 or gp120/160
Du Pont	p24 and p31 and gp41 or gp120/160
World Health Organization	Reactivity to two envelope glycoproteins

Table 137.4 Criteria for Western blot interpretation.

WESTERN BLOT PATTERNS OF NINE SAMPLES

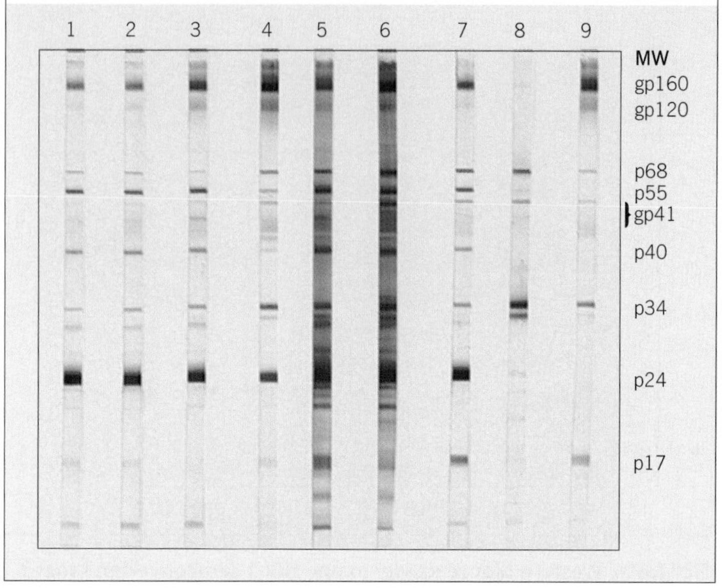

Fig. 137.7 Different Western blot patterns of nine samples. Samples 1, 2 and 3 are from recent seroconverters infected by HIV-1 subtype B. Western blot is weakly reactive on gp41 and *pol* products. Patient 4 has a slight decrease in *gag* products by WB. Patients 5 and 6 are fully WB reactive. Patient 7 is a recent seroconverter infected by HIV-1 subtype A. gp120 and gp41 are weakly reactive. Patient 8 is infected with HIV-1 group O. The WB pattern is highly suggestive of infection by a variant, with no *env* reactivity and strong *pol* reactivity. Patient 9 is in the terminal phase of AIDS, with disappearance of *gag* reactivity.

Careful interpretation of the WB can be highly informative (Fig. 137.7).

- A complete pattern (all bands) with reactivity at least as strong as that of the positive control is suggestive of infection dating back more than 6 months.
- Absent or weak reactivity with proteins p68, p52 and p34 (*pol* gene products) is suggestive of recent primary infection (less than 6 months). Follow-up of the kinetics of appearance of these antibodies will confirm recent seroconversion.
- A fall in reactivity to the core proteins p55, p40 and p24 is found in patients infected many years previously.
- Weak reactivity with *env* gene products and strong reactivity with *pol* gene products can point to nonsubtype B infection.

Occasionally, individuals at low risk of infection are identified through screening as having repeatedly positive EIAs and persistent indeterminate WBs. This situation arises most often in patients with rheumatoid arthritis, systemic lupus erythematosuis or polyclonal gammopathy. Such individuals usually are not HIV infected; a negative HIV-1 DNA PCR test can provide additional reassurance.

Diagnosing HIV-1 infection in children

Transplacental passage of IgG leads to a reactive EIA and positive WB that decrease with time. Passively transmitted antibodies disappear by the age of 15 months; their persistence beyond this time is diagnostic of HIV-1 infection in the infant. Serologic screening of the mother should be offered routinely at the outset of all pregnancies. If the mother is HIV negative despite the existence of risk factors, the result should be checked before delivery, as primary infection is possible during pregnancy.

Early diagnosis of mother-to-child transmission (MTCT) is based on the detection of nucleic acids or the virus in several samples. Current guidelines recommend testing infants born to HIV-infected mothers at age 48 hours, 1–2 months and 3–6 months.[18] A positive test suggests the possibility of HIV-1 infection, and should be confirmed by a second test as soon as possible. DNA PCR tests are positive in 40% of infected neonates by 48 hours of age and in 93% of infected infants by day 14;[19] virus culture has similar sensitivity and specificity, but is more costly and time consuming. The sensitivity and specificity of RNA tests for diagnosis of HIV-1 infection in neonates have not been defined.

EPIDEMIOLOGIC RISK FACTORS ASSOCIATED WITH HIV-2 INFECTION
• Sexual contact or needle sharing with HIV-2-infected individual • Person originating from HIV-2-endemic region • Receipt of blood transfusion in an HIV-2-endemic region • Child born of an HIV-2-infected mother

Table 137.5 Epidemiologic risk factors associated with HIV-2 infection.

Diagnosing HIV-2 infection

Cross-reactivity of HIV-2 in HIV-1 EIAs ranges from 50% to 93%.[20] In the USA, blood banks use a combination HIV-1/HIV-2 antigen sandwich EIA to screen for HIV infection, but screening for HIV-2 is not routinely performed in other settings. Therefore, an HIV-2-specific EIA should be obtained when the epidemiologic setting suggests the possibility of HIV-2 infection (Table 137.5).

Virus load monitoring

Plasma HIV-1 RNA levels are correlated with disease stage. Patients who have symptomatic HIV infection or AIDS have significantly higher virus loads than do those with asymptomatic infection. The plasma HIV-1 RNA titer is also a powerful predictor of the risk of disease progression and death at all stages of disease. The change in plasma HIV-1 RNA level in response to treatment also provides important clinical information. Analyses from several large clinical trials show a significant correlation between the magnitude of plasma HIV-1 RNA reduction from baseline and the extent of clinical benefit.[21] Conversely, a rise in plasma HIV-1 RNA level suggests failure of a treatment regimen to suppress virus replication.

Analysis of the virologic response to therapy reveals the importance of the nadir achieved in plasma HIV-1 RNA levels as a marker for the duration of virus suppression.[22] Several studies also show that the early response to treatment is predictive of long-term outcome. Substantial increases in the CD4 cell count may be sustained even if plasma viremia remains detectable, so long as virus load remains significantly below the pretreatment baseline.

Samples should be collected in EDTA tubes and plasma separated and stored at $-70°C$ until testing. Although HIV-1 RNA is stable in plasma at room temperature for up to 48 hours, samples should be processed within 6 hours if possible. Because clinical events that lead to immune activation can cause transient increases in virus load, plasma HIV-1 RNA testing should not be performed within 4 weeks of intercurrent infection or vaccination.

Treatment guidelines recommend obtaining two measurements of plasma HIV-1 RNA to determine the baseline or 'set-point' virus load.[23] Virus load testing should be performed immediately prior to initiating treatment and repeated within 2–8 weeks of starting treatment in order to assess the initial response to a regimen. In treatment-naive patients the plasma HIV-1 RNA level should drop by at least 1.0 $\log_{10}$ within 4–8 weeks of starting an initial antiretroviral regimen; by week 16 plasma virus should be undetectable (below 50 copies/ml) in most patients. More than 24 weeks may be required for plasma virus titers to fall below the limit of detection in patients with high pretreatment levels of viremia (above

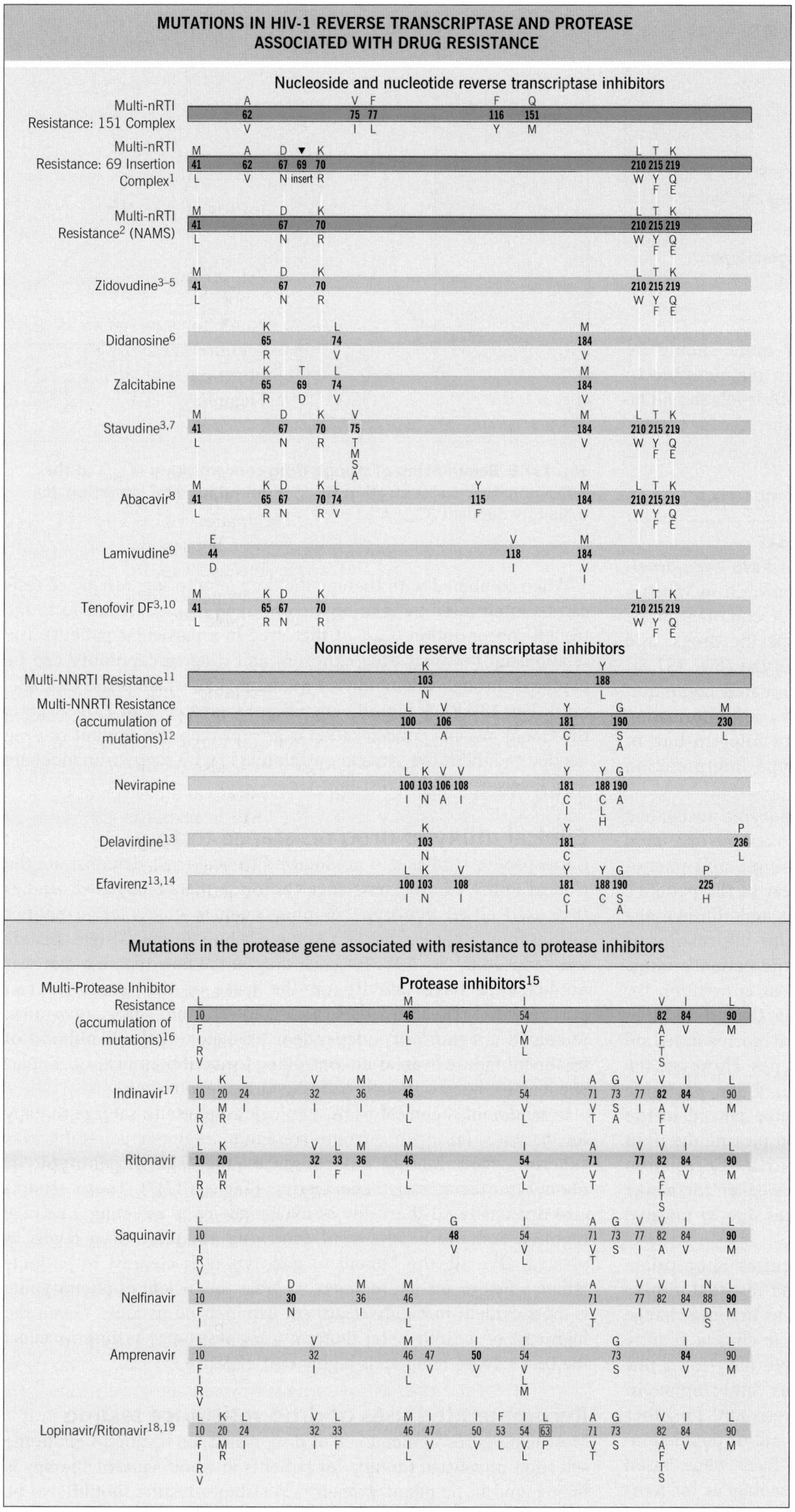

Fig. 137.8 Mutations in HIV-1 reverse transcriptase and protease associated with drug resistance. Wild-type amino acids are shown above the bar, and mutant amino acids are shown below the bar. Numbers indicate amino acid position. Vertical bars indicate cross-resistance. Bold-face indicates major protease inhibitor resistance mutations. Complete explanation of figure and footnotes available at www.iasusa.org. From D'Aquila *et al.*[28], reprinted with permission.

USEFUL WEBSITES FOR INTERPRETING HIV-1 GENOTYPIC RESISTANCE TESTS	
International AIDS Society-USA	www.iasusa.org
Stanford HIV RT and Protease Sequence Database	http://hivdb.stanford.edu
Los Alamos National Laboratory	http://hiv-web.lanl.gov
RetroGram	www.retrogram.com

Table 137.6 Useful websites for interpreting HIV-1 genotypic resistance tests.

100,000 copies/ml). Declines of 0.5 $\log_{10}$ or more should be expected within 8 weeks following a change in regimen due to treatment failure. Subsequently, plasma HIV-1 RNA levels should be repeated every 3–4 months in order to monitor the success of antiretroviral therapy.

CLINICAL USE OF DRUG RESISTANCE TESTING

Interpreting HIV-1 drug resistance tests

Various systems for interpreting HIV-1 genotypes have been developed. Most interpretations use a 'rules-based' approach in which a group of experts determine which mutations or combination of mutations are associated with resistance to specific drugs, and establish an algorithm for interpreting the genotype (Fig. 137.8). These algorithms are used as the basis of automated computer-generated reports, but require periodic updating as new information becomes available. Alternatively, clinicians may refer to one of a number of online websites that offer genotype interpretation (Table 137.6).

An alternative approach to interpreting genotypic resistance tests is the 'virtual' phenotype. This approach makes use of a large database (>30,000 samples) with paired genotypic and phenotypic data. Viruses with genotypes that are similar to the patient's virus are identified by searching the database and the average IC_{50} of these matching viruses is calculated. This information is then used to estimate the likely phenotype of the patient's virus. The actual and virtual phenotype show excellent correlation for most drugs. The strength of this approach is that it reduces complex genotypic data to simple phenotypic categories based on a rational, data-driven analysis of similar genotypes. However, the virtual phenotype only provides an estimate of the *probable* phenotype of the patient's virus. The confidence placed in the result depends on the number of matches and on picking the right codons to incorporate into the database search. Correlation between actual and virtual phenotype will be weaker for newer drugs or in cases where there are fewer matches due to unusual genotypes.

Interpreting phenotypic resistance tests requires appropriate definition of the 'cut-off' between susceptible and resistant viruses for each drug. Ideally, cut-offs would be defined as the fold-change in susceptibility that corresponds to a reduction in clinical activity of the drug in question. Such data are available only for a few drugs, however, including abacavir, tenofovir and lopinavir. Consequently, definitions of 'susceptible' and 'resistant' for other antiretroviral drugs are based on assay variation and/or population-based susceptibility data for wild-type viruses. Even when based on virologic response data, cut-offs can be misleading, as for most drugs there is a continuous relationship between susceptibility and antiviral activity. Thus, it might be more realistic to consider drugs as having greater or lesser activity against viruses that are more or less susceptible.

RELATIONSHIP OF TROUGH DRUG CONCENTRATION (C_{min}) TO THE 50% INHIBITORY CONCENTRATION (IC_{50}) REQUIRED FOR VIRAL INHIBITION

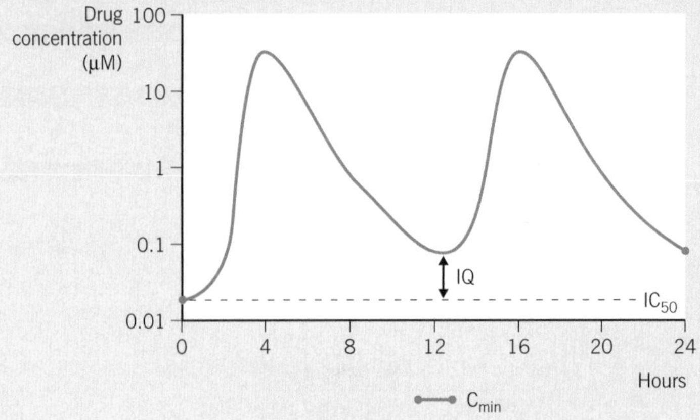

Fig. 137.9 Relationship of trough drug concentration (C_{min}) to the 50% inhibitory concentration (IC_{50}) required for viral inhibition. IQ, inhibitory quotient (C_{min}:IC_{50}).

When combined with therapeutic drug monitoring, resistance tests can be interpreted by relating the observed IC_{50} of an isolate to the trough concentration (C_{min} of that drug in a particular patient). The relationship between drug exposure and drug susceptibility can be explored through the inhibitory quotient (IQ), which is the C_{min}:IC_{50} ratio (Fig. 137.9). A high IQ (significantly greater than 1.0) suggests the trough plasma concentration is greater than the amount of drug needed to inhibit the virus in question; a low IQ suggests inadequate drug levels or a highly resistant virus.

Clinical utility of drug resistance testing

Retrospective studies and randomized clinical trials demonstrate the clinical utility of drug resistance testing. A meta-analysis of studies that used either genotype or phenotype to characterize patient viruses found that the risk of virologic failure during salvage therapy was reduced by 30–50% for each drug in the new regimen that was predicted to have activity on the basis of the resistance test performed.[24] These studies also showed that drug resistance remained a significant independent predictor of the likelihood of treatment failure even after controlling for treatment history. Similar results have been obtained with the virtual phenotype.

In randomized clinical trials, virologic response to salvage therapy for patients failing a current treatment regimen generally was superior when therapy was chosen on the basis of genotypic or phenotypic drug resistance testing (Table 137.7). These studies also demonstrated the value of expert advice in selecting a salvage regimen and the necessity of achieving adequate drug levels in plasma. Overall, the benefit of genotyping is clearest in patients failing a first or second regimen, whereas the benefit of phenotyping is most evident in highly treatment-experienced patients. Given the high cost of antiretroviral therapy, using resistance testing to select the best salvage regimen is highly cost-effective.[25]

Recommended uses of drug resistance testing

Most experts recommend use of drug resistance testing to guide the selection of salvage therapy for patients in whom current therapy is failing, and in pregnant women.[26] Resistance testing should also be considered for patients with acute or recent HIV infection. Given the evidence that transmission of drug-resistant HIV-1 is on the rise,[27] testing of all patients prior to initiation of antiretroviral therapy is reasonable where affordable.

Table 137.7 Randomized trials of HIV-1 drug resistance testing.

RANDOMIZED TRIALS OF HIV-1 DRUG RESISTANCE TESTING			
	Study	**Result**	**Reference**
Genotyping	VIRADAPT	Genotyping superior to SOC	Durant *et al.*[29]
	GART	Genotyping + expert advice superior to SOC	Baxter *et al.*[30]
	ARGENTA	Genotyping superior to SOC in more adherent, less treatment-experienced patients	Cingolani *et al.*[31]
	NARVAL	Genotyping superior to SOC in patients with lower VL, less treatment experience	Maynard *et al.*[32]
	HAVANA	Genotyping and expert each superior to SOC, best in combination	Tural *et al.*[36]
	CERT	No benefit of genotyping	Wegner *et al.*[33]
Phenotyping	VIRA 3001	Phenotyping superior to SOC	Cohen *et al.*[34]
	NARVAL	No benefit of phenotyping	Maynard *et al.*[32]
	CCTG 575	Phenotyping superior to SOC in highly treatment-experienced patients	Haubrich *et al.*[35]
	CERT	Phenotyping superior to SOC in highly treatment-experienced and NNRTI-experienced patients	Wegner *et al.*[33]

SOC, standard of care; VL, virus load; NNRTI, nonnucleoside reverse transcriptase inhibitors

For treatment-experienced patients, resistance testing will be most informative if samples are obtained while the patient continues on the failing regimen. Once a regimen is stopped, there is the possibility that residual wild-type virus will rapidly overgrow the less fit drug-resistant mutants, giving a potentially misleading test result. To ensure accurate results, testing should be reserved for patients with virus load above 1000 copies/ml. If resistance to a drug is identified, then that drug is likely to have little or no activity and should be avoided, if possible. Similarly, if resistance to a drug has ever been identified, it is safe to assume that resistant virus persists, even if not detected in a current sample. Absence of resistance in the context of treatment failure may be evidence of nonadherence or a pharmacologic barrier to drug activity.

Ultimately, the best choice of therapy for an individual patient should be determined by taking into account all the information available, including history, disease stage, virus load, CD4 count and patient preferences. Although resistance testing is a useful tool, it is not a substitute for sound clinical judgment.

REFERENCES

1. Ward JW, Grindon AJ, Feorino PM, Schable C, Parvin M, Allen JR. Laboratory and seroepidemiologic evaluation of an enzyme immunoassay for antibodies to HTLV-III. JAMA 1986;256:357–61.
2. Kassler WJ, Haley C, Jones WK, Gerber AR, Kennedy EJ, George JR. Performance of a rapid, on-site human immunodeficiency virus antibody assay in a public health setting. J Clin Microbiol 1995;33:2899–902.
3. Simon F, Matheron S, Tamalet C, *et al.* Cellular and plasma viral load in patients infected with HIV-2. AIDS 1993;7:1411–7.
4. Koot M, Keet IPM, Vos AHV, *et al.* Prognostic value of HIV-1 syncytium-inducing phenotype for rate of $CD4^+$ cell depletion and progression to AIDS. Ann Intern Med 1993;118:681–8.
5. Schupbach J, Flepp M, Pontelli D, Tomasik Z, Luthy R, Boni J. Heat-mediated immune complex dissociation and enzyme-linked immunosorbent assay signal amplification render p24 antigen detection in plasma as sensitive as HIV-1 RNA detection by polymerase chain reaction. AIDS 1996;10:1085–90.
6. Jackson JB, Drew J, Lin HJ, *et al.* Establishment of a quality assurance program for human immunodeficiency virus type 1 DNA polymerase chain reaction assays by the AIDS Clinical Trials Group. J Clin Microbiol 1993;31:3123–8.
7. Erice A, Brambilla D, Bremer J, *et al.* Performance characteristics of the QUANTIPLEX HIV-1 RNA 3.0 assay for detection and quantitation of human immunodeficiency virus type 1 RNA in plasma. J Clin Microbiol 2000;38:2837–45.
8. Yen-Lieberman B, Brambilla D, Jackson B, *et al.* Evaluation of a quality assurance program for quantitation of human immunodeficiency virus type 1 RNA in plasma by the AIDS Clinical Trials Group Virology Laboratories. J Clin Microbiol 1996;34:2695–701.
9. Nolte FS, Boysza J, Thurmond C, Clark WS, Lennox JL. Clinical comparison of an enhanced-sensitivity branched-DNA assay and reverse transcription-PCR for quantitation of human immunodeficiency virus type 1 RNA in plasma. J Clin Microbiol 1998;36:716–20.
10. Hertogs K, Bloor S, de Vroey V, *et al.* A novel human immunodeficiency virus type 1 reverse transcriptase mutational pattern confers phenotypic lamivudine resistance in the absence of mutation 184V. Antimicrob Agents Chemother 2000;44:568–73.
11. Petropoulos CJ, Parkin N, Limoli K, *et al.* A novel phenotypic drug susceptibility assay for human immunodeficiency virus type 1. Antimicrob Agents Chemother 2000;44:920–8.
12. Deeks S, Wrin T, Liegler T, *et al.* Virologic and immunologic consequences of discontinuing combination antiretroviral-drug therapy in HIV-infected patients with detectable viremia. N Engl J Med 2001;344:472–80.
13. Lu J, Kuritzkes DR. A novel recombinant virus assay for comparing the relative fitness of HIV-1 reverse transcriptase variants. J Acquir Immune Defic Syndr 2001;27:7–13.
14. Daar ES, Little SJ, Pitt J, *et al.* Diagnosis of primary HIV-1 infection. Ann Intern Med 2001;134:25–9.
15. Janssen RS, Satten GA, Stramer S, *et al.* New testing strategy to detect early HIV-1 infection for use in incidence estimates and for clinical and prevention purposes. JAMA 1998;280:42–8.
16. Jackson JB. Human immunodeficiency virus (HIV)-indeterminate western blots and latent HIV infection. Transfusion 1992;32:497–9.
17. CDC. Interpretation and use of the western blot assay for serodiagnosis of human immunodeficiency virus type 1 infections. MMWR Morb Mortal Wkly Rep 1989;38:S1–S7.
18. Anonymous. Guidelines for the use of antiretroviral agents in pediatric HIV infection. www.hivatis.org, 2000.
19. Dunn DT, Brandt CD, Krivine A, *et al.* The sensitivity of HIV-1 DNA polymerase chain reaction in the neonatal period and the relative contributions of intra-uterine and intra-partum transmission. AIDS 1995;9:F7–11.
20. Hirsch MS, Brun-Vezinet F, Clotet B, *et al.* Antiretroviral drug resistance testing in adults infected with human immunodeficiency virus type 1: 2003 recommendations of an international AIDS society-USA panel. Clin Infect Dis 2003;37:113–28.
21. Marschner IC, Collier AC, Coombs RW, *et al.* Use of changes in plasma levels of human immunodeficiency virus type 1 RNA to assess the clinical benefit of antiretroviral therapy. J Infect Dis 1998;177:40–7.
22. Raboud JM, Rae S, Hogg RS, *et al.* Suppression of plasma virus load below the detection limit of human immunodeficiency virus kit is associated with longer virologic response than suppression

below the limit of quantitation. J Infect Dis 1999;180:1347–50.
23. Panel on Clinical Practices for Treatment of HIV Infection convened by the Department of Health and Human Services (DHHS). Guidelines for the use of antiretroviral agents in HIV-infected adults and adolescents. www.hivatis.org, 2001.
24. de Gruttola V, Dix L, d'Aquila R, *et al.* The relation between baseline HIV drug resistance and response to antiretroviral therapy: re-analysis of retrospective and prospective studies using a standardized data analysis plan. Antiviral Ther 2000;5:41–8.
25. Weinstein MC, Goldie SJ, Losina E, *et al.* Use of genotypic resistance testing to guide HIV therapy: clinical impact and conservativeness. Ann Intern Med 2001;134:440–50.
26. Hirsch MS, Brun-Vézinet F, d'Aquila RT, *et al.* Antiretroviral drug resistance testing in adult HIV-1 infection: recommendations of an International AIDS Society-USA Panel. JAMA 2000;283:2417–26.
27. Little S, Routy J, Daar E, *et al.* Antiretroviral drug susceptibility and response to initial therapy among recently HIV-infected subjects in North America. N Engl J Med 2002;347:385–94.
28. D'Aquila RT, Schapiro JM, Brun-Vézinet F, *et al.* Drug resistance mutations in HIV-1. Topics HIV Med 2002;10:11–15.
29. Durant J, Clevenbergh P, Halfon P, *et al.* Drug-resistance genotyping in HIV-1 therapy: the VIRADAPT randomized controlled trial. Lancet 1999;353:2195–9.
30. Baxter JD, Mayers DL, Wentworth DN, *et al.* A randomized study of antiretroviral management based on plasma genotypic antiretroviral resistance testing in patients failing therapy. AIDS 2000;14:F83–93.
31. Cingolani A, Antinori A, Rizzo MG, *et al.* Usefulness of monitoring HIV drug resistance and adherence in individuals failing highly active antiretroviral therapy: a randomized study (ARGENTA). AIDS 2002;16:369–79.
32. Maynard JL, Vray M, Mourand-Joubert L, *et al.* Phenotypic or genotypic resistance testing for choosing antiretroviral therapy after treatment failure: a randomized trial. AIDS 2002;16:727–36.
33. Wegner S, Wallace M, Tasker S, *et al.* Long-term clinical efficacy of resistance testing: results of the CERT trial (abstract 158). Antiviral ther 2002;7:S129.
34. Cohen CC, Hunt S, Sension M, *et al.* A randomized trial assessing the impact of phenotypic resistance testing on antiretroviral therapy. AIDS 2002;16:1–10.
35. Haubrich R, Keiser P, Kemper C, *et al.* CCTG 575: a randomized, prospective study of phenotype testing versus standard of care for patients failing antiretroviral therapy (abstract 80). Antiviral Ther 2001;6(Suppl.1):63.
36. Tural C, Ruiz L, Holzer C, *et al.* Clinical utility of HIV genotyping and expert advice. The Havara

chapter 138

Principles of Management in the Developed World

Julio SG Montaner, Peter Phillips & Valentina Montessori

INTRODUCTION

The management of HIV infection continues to evolve as treatments, treatment strategies, laboratory investigations and our understanding of pathogenesis have changed. Not only is viral load testing now available but viral resistance assessments and pharmacokinetic measurements of antiretroviral agents are crossing over from the research laboratory to clinical practice. Improved longevity with better antiretroviral therapy has also been associated with increased incidence, awareness and understanding of various adverse effects of antiretroviral therapy. These include osteoporosis, lactic acidemia, disorders of fat accumulation and fat wasting (lipodystrophy), dyslipidemias, glucose intolerance, hypertension, hepatic toxicity and liver failure.

Traditionally, the $CD4^+$ lymphocyte count has been regarded as the key surrogate marker for prognostic staging and therapeutic monitoring of HIV-infected individuals. Then new molecular techniques became available to detect circulating virion-associated HIV RNA in plasma. The availability of HIV viral load testing led to a major revision of our understanding of the natural history of HIV disease.[1–7] The notion of a prolonged phase of virologic latency antedating the symptomatic phase of the disease has been replaced by one of continuous viral replication from the time of infection until the terminal phases of the illness. It became clear that an ongoing high viral turnover is directly responsible for the ultimate destruction of the immune system.[3] The rate of $CD4^+$ lymphocyte loss will ultimately be dependent on the balance between viral replication, hence $CD4^+$ lymphocyte destruction, and $CD4^+$ lymphocyte production (see Chapter 130).

Antiretroviral therapy has been shown to decrease AIDS-related death rates, opportunistic infections and hospitalizations.[8–12] The potency of the immunologic recovery seen with antiretroviral therapy has, in fact, been associated in some patients with recognition of previously subclinical infection and has been coined an 'immune reconstitution syndrome'.[13,14] Immune reconstitution has also led to an ability to discontinue prophylaxis and even suppressive therapy for opportunistic infection in some settings.[15,16]

In the past few years an awareness of the need to intervene for HIV with antiretroviral therapies at the correct moment has emerged. Long-term therapy has become associated with various adverse effects as well as incomplete adherence to medications – often leading to the development of drug-resistant strains of virus. Although the 'hit early, hit hard' philosophy has played a role in the management of HIV, current thinking has seen the pendulum swing back to a 'watchful waiting' scenario.[17,18]

LABORATORY MARKERS OF DISEASE PROGRESSION

Three assays are currently available to quantify plasma HIV-1 viral load. These are commonly referred to as reverse transcriptase polymerase chain reaction (RT-PCR), branched chain DNA and nucleic acid sequence-based amplification. All three assays are generally comparable from a technical standpoint. They are also similar in their reproducibility and physiologic variability. The lower threshold of detection is in the range of 200–500 copies/ml, with the newer RT-PCR assays having a lower limit of detection of 50 copies/ml. The variability of the assays is approximately $0.3\log_{10}$ within the dynamic range of the test. As a result, a $0.5\log_{10}$ change in HIV RNA level is generally regarded as a significant viral load change in the context of antiretroviral therapy. It should be noted that intercurrent events (such as infections) or vaccinations can transiently but substantially increase plasma viral load.[19–22]

Levels of viral replication appear to be set soon after primary infection.[23] Plasma RNA viral load has been correlated with disease progression and death in a seropositive cohort of untreated gay men using archival samples.[24] Patients were divided into four equal groups (quartiles) based on their viral load levels (Table 138.1). In contrast to the close relationship between baseline viral load and outcome, baseline $CD4^+$ lymphocyte count failed to show a similar gradient among quartiles for the risk of disease progression or death. Furthermore, among the three quartiles with the highest $CD4^+$ lymphocyte count, no differences in these outcomes were observed.

These data also provided conclusive evidence of the independence of viral load from $CD4^+$ lymphocyte counts with regard to prognosis. Among patients who had a $CD4^+$ lymphocyte count of more than $500/mm^3$, there was a significant difference in time to death according to whether the baseline viral load was above or below the median (10,190 copies/ml). The 10-year survival was 70% and 20%, for the low- and high-viral-load groups, respectively; both groups had a median $CD4^+$ lymphocyte count of approximately $780/mm^3$. Similarly, among those who had a baseline $CD4^+$ lymphocyte count below 500/ml, a significantly shorter survival was associated with a baseline HIV RNA greater than the median (17,320 copies/ml), despite similar baseline $CD4^+$ counts within the groups.

Despite the integral role of plasma viral load in HIV management, the $CD4^+$ count continues to be an important and useful test, helping to determine where a patient is on the continuum of HIV disease. In adults, a $CD4^+$ lymphocyte count range of approximately 400–1400 $cells/mm^3$ is considered normal. Counts below 200 $cells/mm^3$ are associated with increased risk of opportunistic infection.

RELATIONSHIP BETWEEN VIRAL LOAD AND OUTCOME

Viral load (HIV RNA copies/ml)	Progression to AIDS at 5 years (%)	Median time to AIDS (years)	Progression to death at 5 years (%)	Median estimated survival (years)
≤4530	8	>10	5	>10
4531–13,020	26	7.7	10	9.5
13,021–36,270	49	5.3	25	7.4
>36,270	62	3.5	49	5.1

Table 138.1 Relationship between viral load and outcome. These viral load thresholds specifically apply to the study group under the particular circumstances of the study. Caution should be exercised when extrapolating to specific clinical situations. The values obtained will vary depending on assay methodology. Also, samples run on a real-time basis are likely to be higher than those specified here. Adapted from Mellors *et al.*[24]

The CD4+ lymphocyte count is usually reported as a fraction (or percentage) and an absolute count. Although the absolute CD4+ lymphocyte count is usually sufficient to guide the clinical management of a given patient, it must be noted that under specific circumstances this may be misleading. For example, patients who have undergone splenectomy typically have a relatively high absolute CD4+ count. In such patients the CD4+ lymphocyte fraction is a more appropriate reflection of their immunologic status. It is therefore advisable to monitor the CD4+ lymphocyte fraction in tandem with the CD4+ count at all times to ensure that these are in general agreement.

Substantial diurnal variation is shown by CD4+ counts; they are lowest in the morning and highest in the evening. In normal individuals the evening CD4+ lymphocyte count can be nearly double what it is in the morning. Although the normal physiologic variation may be reduced in HIV-infected patients, it is still recommended that specimens for CD4+ counting in HIV-infected patients be collected in the morning. Patients should be advised to avoid alcohol, smoking and exercise before collection of the specimen. Other factors that may affect the count include acute infections such as common viral illnesses, certain pharmaceutical agents such as corticosteroids, vaccinations and stress. The results may also be influenced by differing laboratory methodologies. Short-term fluctuations in CD4+ lymphocyte counts of up to 30% have been shown to occur in HIV-infected individuals who are clinically stable.[5] In addition, correlation between CD4+ lymphocyte count and clinical status can be quite different from one patient to the next. Overall, it is important to monitor the trends in CD4+ counts over time rather than placing too much emphasis on a single reading.[25,26]

From a practical standpoint it is useful to consider the CD4+ lymphocyte count as indicative of the level of immunosuppression or, better yet, 'the immunologic damage that has already occurred'. On the other hand, the plasma viral load better illustrates disease activity and therefore 'the damage that is about to occur'. The prognostic contribution of viral load determinations at any level of CD4+ lymphocyte count is illustrated in Figure 138.1. Clinical trials have demonstrated conclusively that a change in plasma HIV-1 RNA viral load is associated with a change in the rate of disease progression.[27–29] In this context, a treatment-induced 10-fold ($1\log_{10}$) reduction in plasma HIV-1 RNA was associated with a decrease of approximately 50% in the relative risk of death.

On the basis of these data, CD4+ lymphocyte counts and plasma viral load should be measured every 3–4 months in stable HIV-infected adults as part of their routine evaluation. More frequent determinations are warranted under special circumstances, such as when introducing antiretroviral therapy. It should be noted that the use of other surrogate markers such as β_2-microglobulin, C1q or immune complexes, erythrocyte sedimentation rate and neopterin are no longer recommended in clinical practice.

Advances in the research laboratory are becoming important in the clinical care of patients. Testing for resistance to antiretrovirals can now identify drugs that perhaps should be excluded from a new regimen (see Chapter 137).[30] However, the factors influencing successful therapy are multiple and include the patient's adherence to the regimen and serum or intracellular drug levels, in addition to many others – not only susceptibility testing. Therapeutic drug monitoring of patients receiving nelfinavir-based therapy was recently shown to improve virologic outcomes in a pilot study.[31] Further trials are currently underway aimed to characterize better the optimal use of therapeutic drug monitoring. Until these results are available, therapeutic drug monitoring should be regarded as an experimental tool to be used selectively in special cases, such as patients requiring dose adjustments due to unusual toxicities or those receiving poorly characterized drug combinations.

PROGNOSTIC CONTRIBUTION OF VIRAL LOAD DETERMINATIONS AT DIFFERENT CD4+ LEVELS

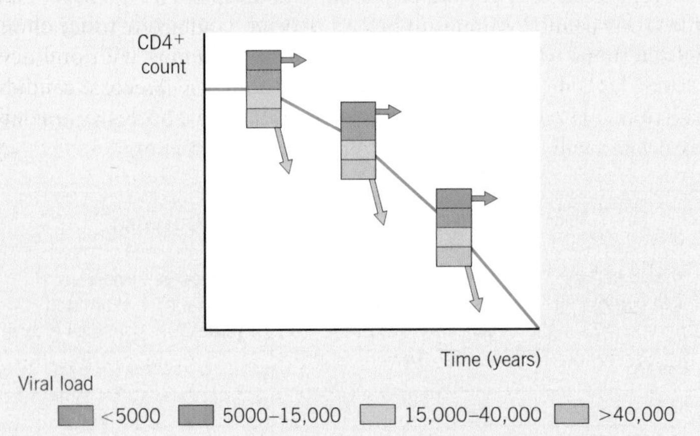

Fig. 138.1 Prognostic contribution of viral load determinations at different CD4+ levels. For a given CD4+ lymphocyte count, individuals with high viral load will have a more rapid decline in CD4+ count and therefore a worse clinical prognosis (demonstrated by the downward shift of the survival curve). The viral load is an independent predictor of rapidity of disease progression. A more aggressive virus phenotype – syncytium-inducing versus non-syncytium-inducing – may also adversely affect prognosis, as may viral strains that are resistant to antiretroviral medications.

BASELINE EVALUATION

Baseline evaluation of an infected individual should include a complete history and physical examination. Counseling should be given regularly. Laboratory tests are also very important, particularly before the start of a treatment program. These should include those listed in Table 138.2.

In terms of blood counts, it is worth noting that anemia, neutropenia and thrombocytopenia are common in patients who have HIV infection. Absolute lymphopenia should raise suspicion of advanced disease. The criterion for the tuberculin skin test is that an induration of 5mm or more in diameter after a 5 tuberculin units purified protein derivative (PPD) test should be regarded as a positive response in an HIV-infected individual; isoniazid prophylaxis

LABORATORY TESTS FOR BASELINE EVALUATION OF HIV-INFECTED PATIENTS

- Plasma HIV RNA viral load
- CD4+ lymphocyte count, absolute and percentage
- Complete blood count and differential and platelet count
- Liver (aspartate aminotransferase, lactate dehydrogenase, alkaline phosphatase, bilirubin) and renal (blood urea nitrogen, creatinine) profiles
- Creatine phosphokinase, amylase, uric acid and triglycerides
- Hepatitis B, hepatitis C, syphilis, cytomegalovirus (CMV) and toxoplasmosis serologies
- Tuberculin skin test
- Cultures and smears for sexually transmitted diseases, as indicated by the history and physical examination
- Sputum cultures and smears for mycobacteriae, as indicated by history and physical examination
- Chest radiograph
- Urinalysis
- Pregnancy test
- Papanicolaou's smear test (if appropriate)
- Eye fundoscopy if the CD4+ count is <100/ml

Table 138.2 Laboratory tests for baseline evaluation of HIV-infected patients.

should therefore be considered. A negative response in persons who have advanced HIV disease does not rule out infection with *Mycobacterium tuberculosis*, as such individuals may be anergic.[32,33]

FOLLOW-UP ASSESSMENT

The routine follow-up of a stable asymptomatic HIV-positive patient should include a history and physical examination as well as plasma viral load and $CD4^+$ lymphocyte count every 3–4 months. Counseling should take place at each visit. Patients should also have an opportunity to discuss the most recent trends in management and antiretroviral therapy.

Symptomatic patients and those who have AIDS require active drug therapy and as such they should be seen at least monthly. More frequent and additional laboratory investigations may be warranted for patients presenting with co-morbidities such as viral hepatitis (B or C) or psychiatric illness.

GENERAL APPROACH TO THE SYMPTOMATIC PATIENT

Not every illness in an HIV-infected patient is attributable, or unique, to HIV infection or AIDS. HIV-infected patients, like everyone else, are susceptible to all the usual illnesses. In fact, as a result of the immune dysfunction that characterizes HIV infection even before the development of overt AIDS, patients typically present with often repeated bouts of common illnesses, such as seborrheic dermatitis, eczema, angular cheilitis, shingles, onychomycosis, sinusitis or community-acquired pneumonia. When signs and symptoms appear, management should be the same as in uninfected individuals.

When $CD4^+$ lymphocyte counts are within the normal range, immune function in adults is almost normal and opportunistic infections are unlikely. The work-up does not usually require any special initiatives. However, it should be noted that some conditions, such as tuberculosis, Kaposi's sarcoma or lymphomas, can occur at any level of $CD4^+$ lymphocyte count. One should have a higher index of suspicion for opportunistic infections as the $CD4^+$ lymphocyte count falls below normal, and particularly once it is below 200 cells/mm^3 or below a $CD4^+$ lymphocyte fraction of 15%.[34]

PROPHYLACTIC TREATMENTS AND VACCINATIONS

Prevention plays a major role in the management of HIV-infected individuals. The following interventions should be considered when a newly diagnosed patient is evaluated.

Tuberculin skin test

A tuberculin skin test should be performed. If there is induration of 5mm or more in diameter, then prophylaxis with isoniazid 5mg/kg daily (maximum 300mg/day) for 12 months should be initiated, along with pyridoxine to reduce the risk of isoniazid toxicity.[32] Prophylaxis may also be indicated in patients at high risk of tuberculosis who have cutaneous anergy or household contact with someone with active tuberculosis, patients who have chest radiograph findings suggestive of previous tuberculosis who do not have a history of adequate treatment, or patients who have not previously received isoniazid prophylaxis or tuberculosis treatment.[32–34] A positive tuberculin skin test should be interpreted with caution among immigrants, who may have received tuberculosis vaccine during childhood.

Vaccination against common pathogens

While antigen recognition is still intact, it is essential to boost humoral immunity against certain common pathogens. Recommended vaccines include polyvalent vaccine against *Streptococcus pneumoniae* (Pneumovax) given once, and influenza vaccine given annually in the autumn.[35,36] The evidence in favor of the latter, however, remains controversial. Tetanus toxoid updates should be offered as necessary, and hepatitis B vaccination should be encouraged for any susceptible patient. Male homosexual HIV-positive men should also receive hepatitis A vaccine. The inactivated polio vaccination should be given to any patient who is traveling. Table 138.3 summarizes additional travel-related vaccine advice. Vaccines against *Haemophilus influenzae* type b and *Neisseria meningitidis* are at present not widely recommended.

VACCINATION AGAINST COMMON TRAVEL-RELATED PATHOGENS

Vaccine	Comments
	In general, live vaccines should be avoided
Measles	Not recommended for travelers who are severely immunocompromised*
Typhoid	The inactivated parenteral typhoid vaccine should be given instead of the live, attenuated oral vaccine
Yellow fever	Live vaccine of uncertain safety in HIV†
Hepatitis A	A killed vaccine that should be used as for non-HIV-infected travelers‡
Diphtheria–tetanus	A killed vaccine that should be used as for non-HIV-infected travelers
Japanese encephalitis	A killed vaccine that should be used as for non-HIV-infected travelers
Rabies	A killed vaccine that should be used as for non-HIV-infected travelers

* Measles vaccine is recommended for nonimmune travelers. However, measles vaccine is not recommended for travelers who are severely immunocompromised; immune globulin should be considered for measles-susceptible, severely immunosuppressed travelers who are anticipating travel to measles endemic countries.
† Travelers with asymptomatic HIV infection who cannot avoid potential exposure to yellow fever should be offered the choice of vaccination. All travelers should avoid mosquito bites.
‡ In the setting of immunosuppression, these vaccines may not offer complete protection.

Table 138.3 Vaccination against common travel-related pathogens.

Prophylaxis and treatment for opportunistic infections (see Chapter 123)

As shown in Table 138.4, as HIV disease progresses prophylaxis and treatment of opportunistic infections become increasingly important. Recurrent genital herpes outbreaks may be dealt with using either intermittent treatment or regular suppressive therapy with oral acyclovir, depending on the frequency of the attacks.[37] Mucosal candidiasis may be treated with topical agents or systemic azoles as needed. Systemic azole therapy is usually needed as the immunodeficiency progresses. In some patients intermittent or even continued suppressive therapy with systemic azoles may be warranted to control frequent relapses.

More than 80% of untreated HIV infected individuals will have at least one episode of *Pneumocystis carinii* pneumonia (PCP) during their lifetime. Prophylaxis against PCP is indicated if the $CD4^+$ lymphocyte count is below 200/mm^3, if the $CD4^+$ lymphocyte fraction is below 15%, if there is a history of recurrent *Candida* infections, or if there are chronic constitutional symptoms such as persistent unexplained fevers and weight loss. All patients should be offered PCP prophylaxis after an episode of PCP (secondary prophylaxis). Prophylaxis against PCP should also be offered to any patient who has had an AIDS-defining illness. The preferred regimen consists of one double-strength tablet of trimethoprim–sulfamethoxazole daily.[37] Alternatively, dapsone 100mg q24h, atovaquone 1500 mg q24h or aerosol pentamidine 300mg once a month can be used. Before starting prophylaxis, patients should be assessed to rule out active pulmonary

PROPHYLAXIS AND TREATMENT FOR OPPORTUNISTIC INFECTIONS	
CD4+ lymphocyte count (no/ml)	**Management strategy**
>500	• General counseling (safer sex, nutrition, etc.) • History and physical examination every 3–6 months • Plasma viral load and CD4+ count every 3–6 months • Pneumovax, annual influenza vaccinations • Tuberculin skin test and INH prophylaxis if indicated • Update diphtheria–pertussis–tetanus (tetanus toxoid for adults) and inactivated polio vaccinations • Hepatitis B vaccine if at risk • Syphilis serology
<500	• Antiretroviral therapy followed by plasma viral load 1 month later • Plasma viral load and CD4+ count every 3–4 months • Herpes suppression if frequent recurrences (more than 4–6 outbreaks/year) • Relevant history, physical and laboratory investigations at least monthly if symptomatic, diagnosed with AIDS or on antiretroviral therapy
<200	• Start prophylaxis for PCP
<100	• Plasma viral load and CD4+ count every 3–4 months • Start prophylaxis for toxoplasmosis if seropositive and not on trimethoprim–sulfamethoxazole
<75	• Consider MAC prophylaxis
<50	• Screening by an ophthalmologist for cytomegalovirus (CMV) retinitis, to be repeated at 3- to 6-monthly intervals; consider CMV prophylaxis

Table 138.4 Prophylaxis and treatment for opportunistic infections.

disease. In the context of continued use of highly active antiretroviral therapy (HAART), patients having adequate responses, such as HIV RNA levels below 50 copies/ml and a CD4+ lymphocyte count recovery to 200 cells/mm³ or more for at least 3 months should be encouraged to discontinue either primary or secondary PCP prophylaxis.[38,39]

Prophylaxis for toxoplasmosis is indicated for those patients who have positive serum IgG for toxoplasmosis and CD4+ lymphocyte count less than 100/mm³. It is worth noting that trimethoprim–sulfamethoxazole, as indicated for PCP prophylaxis, is also effective against toxoplasmosis.[37] As with PCP, prophylaxis may be discontinued for patients who experience HAART-induced immune reconstitution associated with an increase in the CD4+ lymphocyte count to more than 200/mm³ for at least 3 months. Toxoplasma prophylaxis should be restarted if CD4+ lymphocyte counts fall to less than 100/mm³.

There are currently insufficient data for a recommendation regarding the advisability of discontinuing secondary prophylaxis although this is increasingly being done without ill effects once the CD4+ lymphocyte count is above 200/mm³ for at least 3 months with the use of effective HAART.

As disease progresses, prophylaxis for *Mycobacterium avium* complex (MAC) with intermittent azithromycin or daily clarithromycin may also be considered once the CD4+ lymphocyte count is below 50/mm³. MAC prophylaxis can be safely discontinued in patients who have responded to HAART with increased CD4+ counts to more than 100 cells/mm³ for at least 3 months.[15] Prophylaxis should be restarted if the CD4+ level falls to below 50 cells/mm³. Once the CD4+ lymphocyte count is below 100/mm³, screening by an ophthalmologist for cytomegalovirus retinitis should be encouraged, and this should be repeated at 3- to 6-monthly intervals thereafter, while the CD4+ count remains below 100/mm³.

ANTIRETROVIRAL THERAPY

The objective of antiretroviral therapy use is to prevent disease progression and prolong survival while maintaining quality of life. Long-term nonprogression will be achieved by reducing plasma viral load below 50 copies/ml on a long-term basis. The use of combinations of antiretrovirals with no overlapping toxicity and demonstrated antiviral additive to synergistic effect is recommended to maximize the duration of the antiviral response.[18]

Since 1996, triple drug combination antiretroviral therapy has been shown to decrease morbidity and mortality dramatically in symptomatic and asymptomatic HIV-1 infected individuals.[8–10,24,40–42] Recommendations for the initiation of therapy have been crafted based on thresholds of CD4+ lymphocyte counts and plasma HIV-1 RNA that reflect the risk for disease progression in natural history and observational studies as well as randomized clinical trials.[30,43–47] The optimal time for initiation of therapy, however, has not been defined. Recent work has characterized rates of disease progression to AIDS or death for CD4+ and plasma viral load thresholds in treated patients.[17,48–50] In an analysis of a population-based cohort of 1200 HIV-1 infected patients, Hogg *et al.*[17] demonstrated low rates of disease progression to AIDS and death (<3% at 12 months) among patients starting antiretroviral therapy with CD4+ lymphocyte counts of 200 cells/mm³ or more, independent of HIV-RNA levels. In their study, disease progression to AIDS and death clustered among patients starting therapy with CD4+ lymphocyte counts below 200 cells/mm³. From these results, it appears that 200 cells/mm³ represents a critical CD4+ threshold below which the short-term clinical effectiveness of antiretroviral therapy is at least partially compromised. Currently, it is recommended that all symptomatic individuals, as well as those who have CD4+ lymphocyte counts below 250/mm³, be treated with HAART. The risk–benefit ratio associated with earlier intervention (i.e. 250–350 or 350–500/mm³) remains to be clarified. Patients who have 250–350/mm³ CD4+ lymphocyte counts should be monitored closely with repeated CD4+ counts, given that rapid declines in CD4+ lymphocytes can occur, particularly among those who have HIV RNA levels of more than 30,000 copies/ml. In such instances, monthly monitoring may be appropriate.

The effectiveness of antiretroviral therapy relies not only on the appropriate time of initiation of treatment but also on the degree to which patients are able to adhere to therapy. Incomplete adherence to antiretroviral treatment has been associated with premature virologic failure.[51] Intermittent adherence increases the risk of having suboptimal drug levels, which in turn may increase the likelihood of drug resistance.[52,53] Moreover, resistance to one drug is frequently associated with cross-resistance to other members of the same class,[54,55] thus limiting future treatment options (see Chapter 140). Furthermore, not only has incomplete adherence been associated with premature virologic failure but it has also been linked with increased risk for mortality.[56] Thus, the challenges of effectively treating HIV with antiretrovirals includes attention to both the optimal time for initiation of therapy and the means to maximize adherence.

Prior to initiating antiretroviral therapy, a long-term treatment strategy should be developed considering the possibility of intolerance and treatment failure due to resistance. Consideration must be given to enhancing compliance – with simpler regimens more likely to be effective. The current goal of therapy is to suppress plasma viral load below the level of quantitation of the assay (less than 50 copies/ml) on a long-term basis. If a patient experiences drug toxicity, brief cessation of all medications is recommended. Decreasing dosage or stopping only one medication is not to be encouraged as this will promote the development of resistance. If plasma viral load rebounds despite ongoing therapy, consider noncompliance and resistance as the most likely causes. A confirmed detectable plasma HIV RNA level

ANTIRETROVIRAL MEDICATIONS			
Drug	**Dosage**	**Comments**	**Cost**
Nucleoside reverse transcriptase inhibitors (NRTIs)			
Zidovudine (AZT)	400–600mg q24h in 2 divided doses	Most common adverse effects: nausea, headache, rash, anemia, leukopenia, elevated liver enzymes, elevated lactic acid and elevated CPK Should not be combined with D4T	$$
Lamivudine (3TC)	150mg bid	Most common adverse effect is neutropenia (rare)	$$
Didanosine (ddl)	35–49kg: 100mg q12h over 50kg: 200mg q12h Full daily dose can be given once a day	Main common adverse effects: gastrointestinal intolerance, pancreatitis, gout, reversible peripheral neuropathy Should not be combined with ddC Should be taken NPO	$
DDI-EC	Over 50kg: 400mg q24h		
Zalcitabine (ddC)	0.75mg q8h	Most common adverse effects: reversible peripheral neuropathy, mouth ulcers, pancreatitis Should not be combined with d4T or ddl Relatively weak risk–benefit ratio limits usefulness	$
Stavudine (d4T)	40–60kg: 30mg q12h Over 60kg: 40mg q12h	Reversible peripheral neuropathy Lactic acid elevations (rarely fatal) Should not be combined with AZT	$$
Tenofovir	300mg q24h	Most common adverse effect: gastrointestinal upset, low phosphate	$$$
Abacavir (ABC)	300mg q12h	Most common adverse effect is a hypersensitivity reaction, which may be characterized by fever, rash, myalgias, arthralgias, malaise. Reaction may be *fatal* if medication is continued or patient is rechallenged	$$$
Non-nucleoside reverse transcriptase inhibitors (NNRTIs)			
Nevirapine (NVP)	200mg q24h for 2 weeks then increase to 200mg q12h Full daily dose can be given once a day	Most common adverse effects: rash, elevated liver enzymes	$$
Delavirdine (DLV)	400mg q8h	Most common adverse effect is rash	$$
Efavirenz (EFV)	600mg q24h (or 300mg q12h)	Most common adverse effects: central nervous system toxicity ('hangover', drowsiness), rash	$$$
Protease inhibitors (PIs)*			
Saquinavir (INV – Invirase®)	Very poor bioavailability unless combined with RTV When given with RTV use INV/RTV 400mg/400mg q12h *or* 1000mg/100mg q12h *or* 1600mg/100mg q24h	Most common adverse effect is elevated liver enzymes Better tolerability (i.e. gastrointestinal) and similar PK to FTV when used with RTV boosting	$$$$
Saquinavir (FTV – Fortovase®)	1200mg q8h *or* 1000mg/100mg q12h *or* 1600mg/100mg q24h	Most common adverse effect is gastrointestinal toxicity and elevated liver enzymes Better bioavailability than INV in the absence of RTV	$$$$
Ritonavir (RTV)	600mg q12h	Most common adverse effects: gastrointestinal upset, diarrhea, circumoral paresthesias, elevated liver enzymes, hypertriglyceridemia Most common use at present is as a PI booster at low doses (i.e. 100mg–400mg q24h)	$$$$
Indinavir (IDV)	800mg q8h Can be given with RTV boosting: IDV 800mg/RTV 100mg q12h	Most common adverse effects: elevated liver enzymes, nephrolithiasis, hypertension, ingrown toenails, benign hyperbilirubinemia	$$$$
Lopinavir/ritonavir (LPV/RTV)	3 capsules q12h Dose should be increased to 4 capsules q12h if used with EFZ or NVP and in the presence of moderately to highly PI-resistant HIV	Actually two drugs combined in one capsule Most common adverse effects: gastrointestinal upset	$$$$
Amprenavir (APV)	1200mg q12h Can be used with RTV at a dose of 600mg APV/100mg RTV q12h	Most common adverse effects: rash, gastrointestinal upset	$$$$$
Nelfinavir (NFV)	750mg q8h	Most common adverse effect is gastrointestinal upset, mostly diarrhea	$$$$

*PIs have multiple drug interactions and may be associated with various metabolic adverse effects such as diabetes mellitus, hyperlipidemias or lipodystrophy (limb and face wasting and accumulation of abnormal fat deposits)

Table 138.5 Antiretroviral medications.

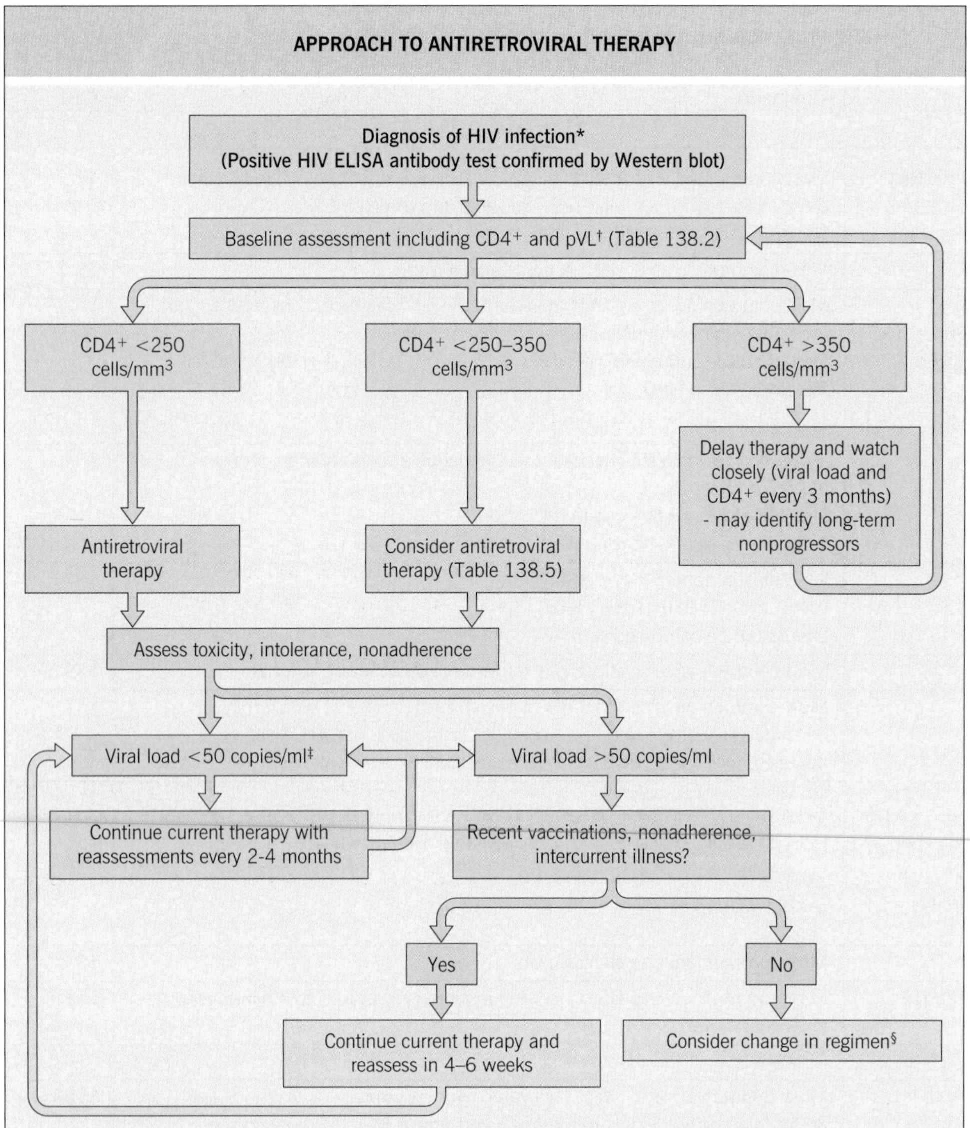
APPROACH TO ANTIRETROVIRAL THERAPY
Diagnosis of HIV infection*
(Positive HIV ELISA antibody test confirmed by Western blot)
Baseline assessment including CD4+ and pVL† (Table 138.2)
CD4+ <250 cells/mm3
CD4+ <250–350 cells/mm3
CD4+ >350 cells/mm3
Delay therapy and watch closely (viral load and CD4+ every 3 months) - may identify long-term nonprogressors
Antiretroviral therapy
Consider antiretroviral therapy (Table 138.5)
Assess toxicity, intolerance, nonadherence
Viral load <50 copies/ml‡
Viral load >50 copies/ml
Continue current therapy with reassessments every 2-4 months
Recent vaccinations, nonadherence, intercurrent illness?
Yes
No
Continue current therapy and reassess in 4–6 weeks
Consider change in regimen§

* If a patient presents with a history of possible exposure to HIV, with or without a history of a recent mononucleosis-like illness, consider HIV seroconversion. In this setting, the HIV antibody may be negative or 'indeterminate' and a p24 antigen may be positive. These patients should be referred to specialists with experience in interpreting these results.
† Frequency of re-evaluation in untreated patients will vary depending on HIV RNA levels (e.g. <30,000 copies/ml at 3 months; > 100,000 copies/ml at 1 month.
‡ The goal of therapy is to suppress viral replication to prevent the emergence of resistant strains and therefore, prolong the durability of the antiviral response. A goal of pVL <50 copies/ml is recommended as this is the lower limit of quantitation common to all currently available clinical assays. As the newer, more sensitive assays become available, the goal may be revised.
§ Given the currently available therapeutic alternatives, it is reasonable to delay a change in therapy until there is definitive evidence of rebound of viral replication. Full suppression of viral replication represents a very attractive therapeutic strategy, however, if this goal cannot be reached, the interim aim should become partial suppression of viral replication (i.e. pVL below baseline and below 10,000–20,000 copies/ml, as long as the CD4 count remains stable and there is no clinical evidence of disease progression).

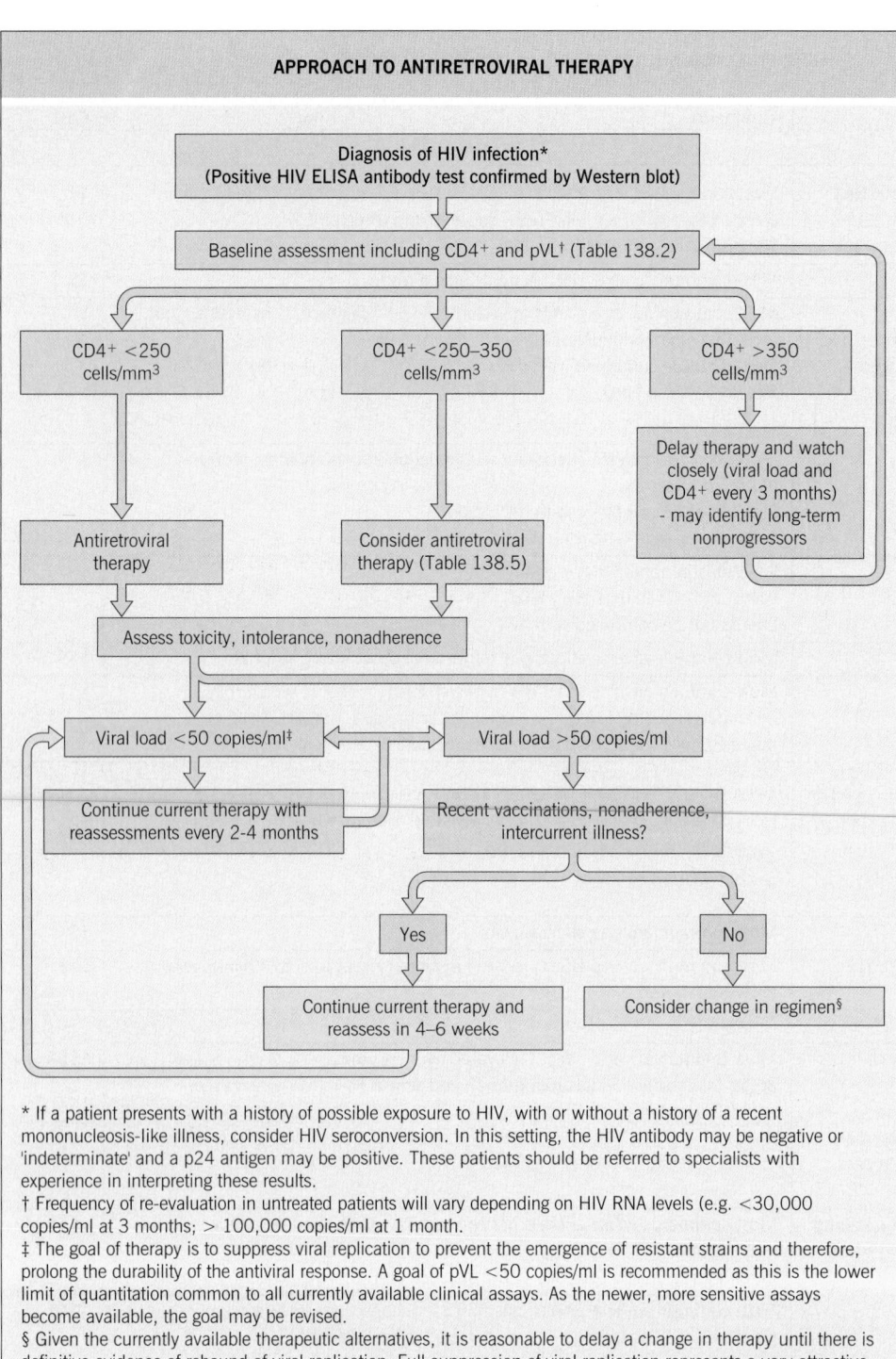

Fig. 138.2 Approach to antiretroviral therapy. PI, protease inhibitors.

in an adherent patient indicates virologic failure. At such time the treatment should be re-evaluated and possibly changed to an alternative fully suppressive regimen to avoid development of resistance. Table 138.5 summarizes the currently available antiretroviral agents. For further discussion, refer to Chapters 139 and 204. An approach to antiretroviral therapy is suggested in Figure 138.2.

PRINCIPLES IN CHANGING THERAPY

Currently, drug failure is defined in virologic terms as the occurrence of a confirmed viral load rebound in the absence of other obvious explanation (e.g. treatment interruption, intercurrent illness or immunizations). A change in therapy in this setting will only be carried out after careful evaluation of prior drug exposure, prior response to therapies, prior tolerability and toxicity issues, as well as the results of resistance testing done on a real time basis and on stored samples. It is critically important to understand and correct the determinants of prior treatment failure in any given individual. This must be done before a change in therapy is implemented. Failure to address these issues effectively will invariably compromise the chances of success with the new regimen. Whenever possible, pharmacokinetic issues (past and present) should also be evaluated. Multiple variables are operational when changing regimens in the context of virologic failure in a given clinical case. As such, guidelines cannot replace expert advice in this setting. It is critical, therefore, that the decision of when to change and what to change to be arrived at under the guidance of an experienced practitioner.

When a decision to change therapy for sustained virologic failure is made, the new regimen should be one with the highest probable effectiveness, as predicted by the patient's complete drug history and the resistance test result, as well as the highest likelihood of tolerability and adherence. New regimens should contain at least two, and if possible three, drugs deemed to be active. The viruses that replicate during treatment failure may not be resistant to all of the drugs in the failing regimen. However, latently infected lymphocytes may harbor archived viruses that are resistant to drugs used in the past but are not detected by routine resistance testing in the plasma. Frequently, shared-resistance mutations conferred by an individual drug lead to cross-resistance among drugs in the same class, complicating the choice of alternative regimens.

With the currently approved non-nucleoside reverse transcriptase inhibitors (NNRTIs), the risk of complete NNRTI-class cross-resistance is high when an NNRTI-containing regimen fails. With protease inhibitors, intraclass cross-resistance is not so predictable. Depending on the pattern of resistance, an alternative protease inhibitor (or a combination of protease inhibitors) can often be selected. With nucleoside reverse transcriptase inhibitors (NRTIs), the extent of class cross-resistance is greater than anticipated previously, and the level of resistance to alternative drugs (e.g. to stavudine) is more difficult to infer from genotype or phenotype testing results. In rare circumstances, multidrug resistance to NRTIs may develop through a unique pathway of resistance. Alternative regimens must therefore be assessed on a case-by-case basis, based on predicted resistance patterns.

In the absence of virologic or immunologic failure, a regimen may pose problems due to adherence, intolerance or toxicity. Detailed discussion of the management of all possible antiretroviral-related toxicities is beyond the scope of this review. In general, as long as the antiviral potency of the regimen is preserved, exchanging an individual component of the regimen to deal with a toxicity problem is acceptable. The closer the agents are in terms of their potency and resistance profile, the easier and safer the change will be – for instance, replacing stavudine with zidovudine in a patient who has anemia, or zidovudine with stavudine in a patient who has neuropathy. Similarly, replacing nevirapine in a patient who has central nervous system toxicity with epavirenz would be generally safe and effective. Drug substitutions become more complicated as patients present with a history of prior drug exposure and/or failure to multiple regimens. In such cases, changes in therapy should only be performed under the guidance of an experienced physician.

SUMMARY

The overall management of the patient who has HIV infection is dictated by the level of disease activity, as indicated by the plasma viral load and by the degree of immunodeficiency. The latter is best characterized – in the absence of symptoms – by the $CD4^+$ lymphocyte count. As with any chronic disease, the primary care physician is best situated to co-ordinate care in an ongoing fashion in close collaboration with experienced specialists. Because of the multiple complexities associated with the use of currently available antiretroviral therapy regimens, it is best to reserve their use to those with an expertise in this rapidly evolving field. As signs and symptoms of specific diseases appear, referral for special investigation and treatment should be encouraged.

REFERENCES

1. Pantaleo G, Graziosi C, Demarest JM, *et al.* HIV infection is active and progressive in lymphoid tissue during the clinically latent stage of disease. Nature 1993;362:355–8.
2. Embretson J, Zupancic M, Ribas JL, *et al.* Massive covert infection of helper T lymphocytes and macrophages by HIV during the incubation period of AIDS. Nature 1993;362:359–62.
3. Piatak MJ, Saag MS, Yang LC, *et al.* High levels of HIV-1 in plasma during all stages of infection determined by competitive PCR. Science 1993;259:1749–54.
4. Ho DD, Neumann AU, Perelson AS, *et al.* Rapid turnover of plasma virions and CD4 lymphocytes in HIV-1 infection. Nature 1995;373:123–6.
5. Wei X, Ghosh SK, Taylor ME, *et al.* Viral dynamics in human immunodeficiency virus type 1 infection. Nature 1995;373:117–22.
6. Perelson AS, Neumann AU, Markowitz M, Leonard JM, Ho DD. HIV-1 dynamics in vivo: virion clearance rate, infected cell life-span, and viral generation time. Science 1996;271:1582–6.
7. Coffin JM. HIV population dynamics in vivo: implications for genetic variation, pathogenesis, and therapy. Science 1996;267:483–9.
8. Hammer SM, Squires KE, Hughes MD, *et al.* A controlled trial of two nucleoside analogues plus indinavir in persons with human immunodeficiency virus infection and CD4 cell counts of 200 per cubic millimeter or less. N Engl J Med 1997;337:725–33.
9. Cameron DW, Heath-Chiozzi M, Danner S, *et al.* Prolongation of life and prevention of AIDS complications in a randomized controlled clinical trial of ritonavir in patients with advanced HIV disease. Lancet 1998;351:543–9.
10. Montaner JSG, Reiss P, Cooper D, *et al.* A randomized, double-blind trial comparing combinations of nevirapine, didanosine, and zidovudine for HIV-infected patients. The INCAS Trial. Italy, The Netherlands, Canada and Australia Study. JAMA 1998;279:930–7.
11. Palella FJ Jr, Delaney KM, Moorman AC, *et al.* Declining morbidity and mortality among patients with advanced human immunodeficiency virus infection. HIV Outpatient Study Investigators. N Engl J Med 1998;338:853–60.
12. Hogg RS, Yip B, Kully C, *et al.* Improved survival among HIV-infected patients after the initiation of triple-drug antiretroviral regimens. Can Med Assoc J 1999;160:659–65.
13. DeSimone JA, Pomerantz RJ, Babinchak TJ. Inflammatory reactions in HIV-1-infected persons after initiation of highly active antiretroviral therapy. Ann Intern Med 2000;133:447–54.
14. Domingo P, Torres OH, Ris J, Vazquez G. Herpes zoster as an immune reconstitution disease after initiation of combination antiretroviral therapy in patients with human immunodeficiency virus type-1 infection. Am J Med 2001;110:605–9.
15. El-Sadr WM, Burman WJ, Grant LB, *et al.* Discontinuation of prophylaxis for *Mycobacterium avium* complex disease in HIV-infected patients who have a response to antiretroviral therapy. N Engl J Med 2000;342:1085–92.
16. Ledergerber B, Mocroft A, Reiss P, *et al.* Discontinuation of secondary prophylaxis against *Pneumocystis carinii* pneumonia in patients with HIV infection who have a response to antiretroviral therapy. N Engl J Med 2001;344:168–74.
17. Hogg RS, Yip B, Chan KJ, *et al.* Rates of disease progression by baseline CD4 cell count and viral load after initiating triple-drug therapy. JAMA 2001;286:2568–77.
18. Carpenter CCJ, Fischl MA, Hammer SM, *et al.* Antiretroviral therapy for HIV infection in 1996. Recommendations of an international panel. JAMA 1996;276:146–54.
19. Staprans SI, Hamilton BL, Follansbee SE, *et al.* Activation of virus replication after vaccination of HIV 1-infected individuals. J Exp Med 1995;182:1727–37.
20. O'Brien WA, Grovit-Ferbas K, Namazi A, *et al.* Human immunodeficiency virus-type 1 replication can be increased in peripheral blood of seropositive patients after influenza vaccination. Blood 1995;86:1082–9.
21. Raboud JM, Montaner JSG, Conway B, *et al.* Variation in plasma RNA levels, CD4 cell counts and p24 antigen levels in clinically stable men with human immunodeficiency virus infection. J Infect Dis 1996;174:191–4.
22. Saag MS, Holodniy M, Kuritzkes DR, *et al.* HIV viral load markers in clinical practice: recommendations of an International AIDS Society–USA Expert Panel. Nat Med 1996;2:625–9.
23. Mellors JW, Kinsley LA, Rinaldo CRJ, *et al.* Quantitation of HIV-1 RNA in plasma predicts outcome after seroconversion. Ann Intern Med 1995;122:573–9.
24. Mellors JW, Rinaldo CR Jr, Gupta P, *et al.* Prognosis in HIV-1 infection predicted by the quantity of virus in plasma. Science 1996;272:1167–70.
25. Hughes MD, Stein DS, Gundacker HM, *et al.* Within-subject variation in CD4 lymphocyte

count in asymptomatic human immunodeficiency virus infection: implications for patients monitoring. J Infect Dis 1994;169:28–36.
26. Raboud JM, Haley L, Montaner JSG, *et al.* Quantification of the variation due to laboratory and physiologic sources of the CD4 lymphocyte counts of clinically stable HIV infected individuals. J Acquir Immune Defic Syndr 1995;10(Suppl.2):S67–73.
27. Delta Coordinating Committee. Delta: a randomized double-blind controlled trial comparing combinations of zidovudine plus didanosine or zalcitabine with zidovudine alone in HIV-infected individuals. Lancet 1996;348:283–91.
28. Hammer SM, Katzenstein DA, Hughes MD, *et al.* A trial comparing nucleoside monotherapy with combination therapy in HIV-infected adults with CD4 cell counts from 200 to 500 per cubic millimeter. N Engl J Med 1996;335:1081–90.
29. O'Brien WA, Hartigan PM, Martin D, Esinhart J. Changes in plasma HIV-1 RNA and $CD4^+$ lymphocyte count relative to treatment and progression to AIDS. N Engl J Med 1996;334:426–31.
30. Hirsch MS, Brun-Vezinet F, D'Aquila RT, *et al.* Antiretroviral drug resistance testing in adult HIV-1 infection. Recommendations of an International AIDS Society–USA Panel. JAMA 2000;283:2417–26.
31. Burger DM. Therapeutic drug monitoring (TDM)of nelfinavir (NFV) 1250 mg bid in treatment-naive patients improves therapeutic outcome after one year: results from ATHENA (abstract). Presented at the 2nd International Workshop on Clinical Pharmacology of HIV Therapy, Nordwijk, the Netherlands, 2–4 April 2001.
32. Centers for Disease Control. Tuberculosis and human immunodeficiency virus infection: recommendations of the Advisory Committee for the Elimination of Tuberculosis. MMWR Morb Mortal Wkly Rep 1989;38:236–50.
33. Centers for Disease Control. Guidelines for preventing the transmission of tuberculosis in health-care settings with special focus on HIV-related issues. MMWR Morb Mortal Wkly Rep 1990;39(RR-17):1–29.
34. Centers for Disease Control. Purified protein derivative (PPD)–tuberculin anergy and HIV infection: guidelines for anergy testing and management of anergic persons at risk of tuberculosis. MMWR Morb Mortal Wkly Rep 1991;40(RR-5):27–32.
35. Centers for Disease Control. Update on adult immunization recommendations of the Immunization Practices Advisory Committee (ACIP). MMWR Morb Mortal Wkly Rep 1991;40(RR-12):1–94.
36. Centers for Disease Control. Recommendations of the Advisory Committee on Immunization Practices (ACIP): use of vaccines and immune globulins for persons with altered immunocompetence. MMWR Morb Mortal Wkly Rep 1993;42(RR-4):1–18.
37. Kaplan JE, Masur H, Holmes KK, *et al.* USPHS/IDSA guidelines for the preventions of opportunistic infections in persons infected with human immunodeficiency virus: disease-specific recommendations. Clin Infect Dis 1995;21(Suppl.1):S32–43.
38. Furrer HF, Egger M, Opravil M, *et al.* Discontinuation of primary prophylaxis against *Pneumocystis carinii* pnuumonia in HIV-1-infected adults treated with combination antiretroviral therapy. Swiss HIV Cohort Study. N Engl J Med 1999;340:1301–5.
39. De Quiros JCL, Miro JM, Pena JM, *et al.* and the Grupo de Estudio del SIDA 04/98. A randomized trial of the discontinuation of primary and secondary prophylaxis against *Pneumocystis carinii* pneumonia after highly active antiretroviral therapy in patients with HIV infection. N Engl J Med 2001;344:159–67.
40. Carpenter, CCJ, Cooper DA, Fischl MA, *et al.* Antiretroviral therapy in adults. Updated recommendations of the International AIDS Society–USA Panel. JAMA 2000;283:381–90.
41. Gazzard B, Moyle G on behalf of the BHIVA Guidelines Writing Committee. 1998 revision to the British HIV Association guidelines for antiretroviral treatment of HIV seropositive individuals. Lancet 1998;352:314- 6.
42. Panel on Clinical Practices for the Treatment of HIV Infection. Guidelines for the use of antiretroviral agents in HIV-infected adults and adolescents. Washington, DC: US Department of Health and Human Services/Henry J Kaiser Family Foundation; 2000.
43. Grabar S, Le Moing V, Goujard C, *et al.* Clinical outcome of patients with HIV-1 infection according to immunologic and virologic response after 6 months of highly active antiretroviral therapy. Ann Intern Med 2000;133:401–10.
44. Voldberding PA, Lagokos SW, Grimes JM, *et al.* A comparison of immediate with deferred zidovudine therapy for asymptomatic HIV-infected adults with CD4 cell counts of 500 or more per cubic millimeter. AIDS Clinical Trial Group. N Engl J Med 1995;333:401–7.
45. Mellors JW, Munoz A, Giorgi JV, *et al.* Plasma viral load and $CD4^+$ lymphocytes as prognostic markers of HIV-1 infection. Ann Intern Med 1997;126:946–54.
46. Phillips AN, Staszewski, Weber R, *et al.* Viral load changes in response to antiretroviral therapy according to the baseline CD4 lymphocyte count and viral load. Presented at the Fifth International Congress on Drug Therapy in HIV Infection, Glasgow, 22–26 October 2000. AIDS 2000;14 (Suppl.4):S3, abstract PL3.4.
47. Cozzi Lepri A, Phillips AN, d'Arminio Monforte A, *et al.* When to start HAART in chronically HIV-infected patients? A collection of pieces of evidence from the ICONA study. Presented at the Fifth International Congress on Drug Therapy in HIV Infection, Glasgow, 22–26 October 2000. AIDS 2000;14 (Suppl.4):S3, abstract PL3.5.
48. Chen R, Westfall A, Coud G, *et al.* Long-term survival after initiation of antiretroviral therapy. Presented at the Eighth Conference on Retroviruses and Opportunistic Infections, Chicago, IL, 4–8 February 2001, abstract 341.
49. Sterling TR, Chaisson RE, Bartlett JG, Moore RD. $CD4^+$ lymphocyte level is better than HIV-1 plasma viral load in determining when to initiate HAART. Presented at the Eighth Conference on Retroviruses and Opportunistic Infections, Chicago, IL, 4–8 February 2001, abstract 519.
50. Karon J, Cohn D, Thompson M, Buskin S, *et al.* Late initiation of antiretroviral therapy (at $CD4^+$ lymphocytes <200 cells/mL) is associated with increased risk of death. Presented at the Eighth Conference on Retroviruses and Opportunistic Infections, Chicago, IL, 4–8 February 2001, abstract 520.
51. Descamps D, Flandre P, Calvez V, *et al.* Mechanisms of virologic failure in previously untreated HIV-infected patients from a trial of induction-maintenance therapy. JAMA 2000;283:205–11.
52. Vanhove GF, Schapiro JM, Winters MA, Merigan TC, Blaschke TF. Patients compliance and drug failure in protease inhibitor monotherapy. JAMA 1999;276:1955–6.
53. Markowitz M, Saag M, Powderly WG, *et al.* A preliminary study of ritonavir an inhibitor of HIV-1 protease, to treat HIV-1 infection. N Engl J Med 1995;333:1534–9.
54. Tisdale M, Myers RE, Maschera B, Parry NR, Oliver NM, Blair ED. Cross-resistance analysis of human immunodeficiency virus type 1 variants individually selected for resistance to five different protease inhibitors. Antimicrob Agents Chemother, 1995;39:1704–10.
55. Condra JH, Schleif WA, Blahy OM, *et al.* In vivo emergency of HIV-1 variants resistant to multiple protease inhibitors. Nature 1995;374:569–71.
56. Hogg RS, Heath K, Bangsberg D, *et al.* Intermittent use of triple combination therapy is predictive of mortality at baseline and after 1 year of follow-up. AIDS 2002;16:1051–8.

chapter

139 Antiviral Therapy

Stefano Vella & Marco Floridia

INTRODUCTION

HIV infection is a chronic disease in which, in the absence of appropriate treatment, high-level viral replication occurs continuously for years, even during the clinically latent phase and in the absence of symptoms and opportunistic infections. Symptoms and opportunistic infections typical of full-blown AIDS usually start occurring 10–12 years after HIV infection. Both viral and cellular turnover show fast kinetics, particularly during primary infection and, later, during the AIDS stage.[1] Viral replication drives the progression of HIV disease and viral load levels are highly predictive of the subsequent risk of disease progression and death.[2] Residual viral replication due to incomplete suppression in the presence of drugs is also responsible for the development of viral resistance to antiretroviral drugs, which further contributes to treatment failure and disease progression.[3] Antiviral treatment should therefore be aimed at obtaining maximal and sustained suppression of HIV replication. Indeed, suppression of HIV replication is associated with a significant delay in the progression to AIDS and increased survival, particularly in previously untreated patients.[4]

Plasma HIV-1 RNA levels and $CD4^+$ lymphocyte counts represent the main tools in the monitoring of antiretroviral treatment.[5] Previously untreated patients are expected to reach undetectable HIV plasma levels in no more than 4–6 months, with a concomitant rise in $CD4^+$ lymphocyte counts. Different drug combinations can produce this effect. It must, however, be stressed that 'undetectable' plasma HIV RNA level does not mean eradication of the virus at other sites (lymphoid tissues, central nervous system, semen). Studies on the effects of therapy in these compartments are ongoing,[6] but eradication of the virus is not considered a realistic goal for the moment.

Even with potent regimens, virologic failure of treatment (i.e. persistently elevated HIV plasma levels in the presence of treatment) is frequent. It may depend on different factors, which include low therapeutic adherence, presence of drug-resistant HIV strains, low drug levels in plasma or tissues and other still undetermined factors. Targeted strategies are being developed in order to improve treatment efficacy, including the development of new drugs with improved formulation and administration schedule, increased potency and reduced toxicity.

The availability of an increasing number of drugs and the rapidly evolving scientific information have made HIV treatment an extremely complex field. Treatment should be supervised by experts, and several national and international guidelines have been developed in order to help in the clinical management of HIV-infected adults and adolescents, pregnant women, infants and children, and uninfected individuals who have occupational exposure to HIV. Proper information for patients and their full involvement in each therapeutic decision are essential elements of a successful response to treatment.

This chapter also addresses the issue of resistance, mostly from the point of view of its clinical implications. Treatment in specific clinical settings such as primary/acute HIV infection and pediatric infection, and the prevention of HIV transmission in the occupational setting are discussed in more detail in Chapters 122, 134 and 117, respectively. Thus, this chapter focuses mainly on the treatment of established HIV infection. The following text summarizes the antiviral activity, toxicity profiles and clinical efficacy of drugs and combinations of drugs that are already available. Some information on drugs under initial clinical evaluation is also presented.

ANTIRETROVIRAL DRUGS

Until 1987, no drug was available for the treatment of HIV infection. In 1987, zidovudine was widely introduced into clinical practice and zidovudine monotherapy remained the basis of treatment for some years[7] until it became evident that its benefit was limited.[8] Subsequent experience of switching from zidovudine to another nucleoside reverse transcriptase inhibitor or adding a different nucleoside to a prolonged zidovudine regimen was limited in extent.[9] Development of resistance was common with all these drugs and was associated with clinical failure.

Nucleoside monotherapy was finally deemed to be a suboptimal treatment when clinical trials and viral load measurements clearly indicated that two-nucleoside regimens were able to induce a more obvious and prolonged effect on viral load and $CD4^+$ counts, and to delay progression and increase survival.[4,10] In 1995 available protease inhibitors (PIs), in combination with reverse transcriptase inhibitors, produced a further reduction of HIV replication, often to undetectable levels, and a clinical benefit in intermediate and advanced disease.[11] Non-nucleoside reverse transcriptase inhibitors (NNRTIs), introduced after 1996, have also proved to be highly effective and have become widely used in clinical practice.

It is therefore now clear that the optimal treatment of HIV infection is a potent combination of drugs (termed highly active antiretroviral therapy, HAART), as already established for other important complex diseases such as cancer and tuberculosis. Most of the currently recommended potent regimens are based on a dual nucleoside 'backbone' plus a NNRTI or a PI (with the option of adding low-dose ritonavir to another PI for pharmacoenhancement). Three-nucleoside regimens including abacavir are also increasingly used because these regimens are easy to administer and are dual-class-sparing (i.e. allow deferred use of PIs and NNRTIs).

Many substances are active against HIV in vitro, and almost every step of the HIV replicative cycle is currently being analyzed to identify specific targets of antiviral treatment (Fig. 139.1).

At present, available antiretroviral drugs include six nucleoside reverse transcriptase inhibitors (zidovudine, didanosine, zalcitabine, stavudine, lamivudine and abacavir), one nucleotide reverse transcriptase inhibitor (tenofovir disoproxil fumarate), three NNRTIs (nevirapine, delavirdine and efavirenz) and six HIV PIs (saquinavir, ritonavir, indinavir, nelfinavir, amprenavir and lopinavir; Table 139.1). Their mechanism of action and clinical characteristics are briefly summarized, together with those of some other drugs that are in an advanced phase of evaluation and could enter clinical practice in the next few months or years.

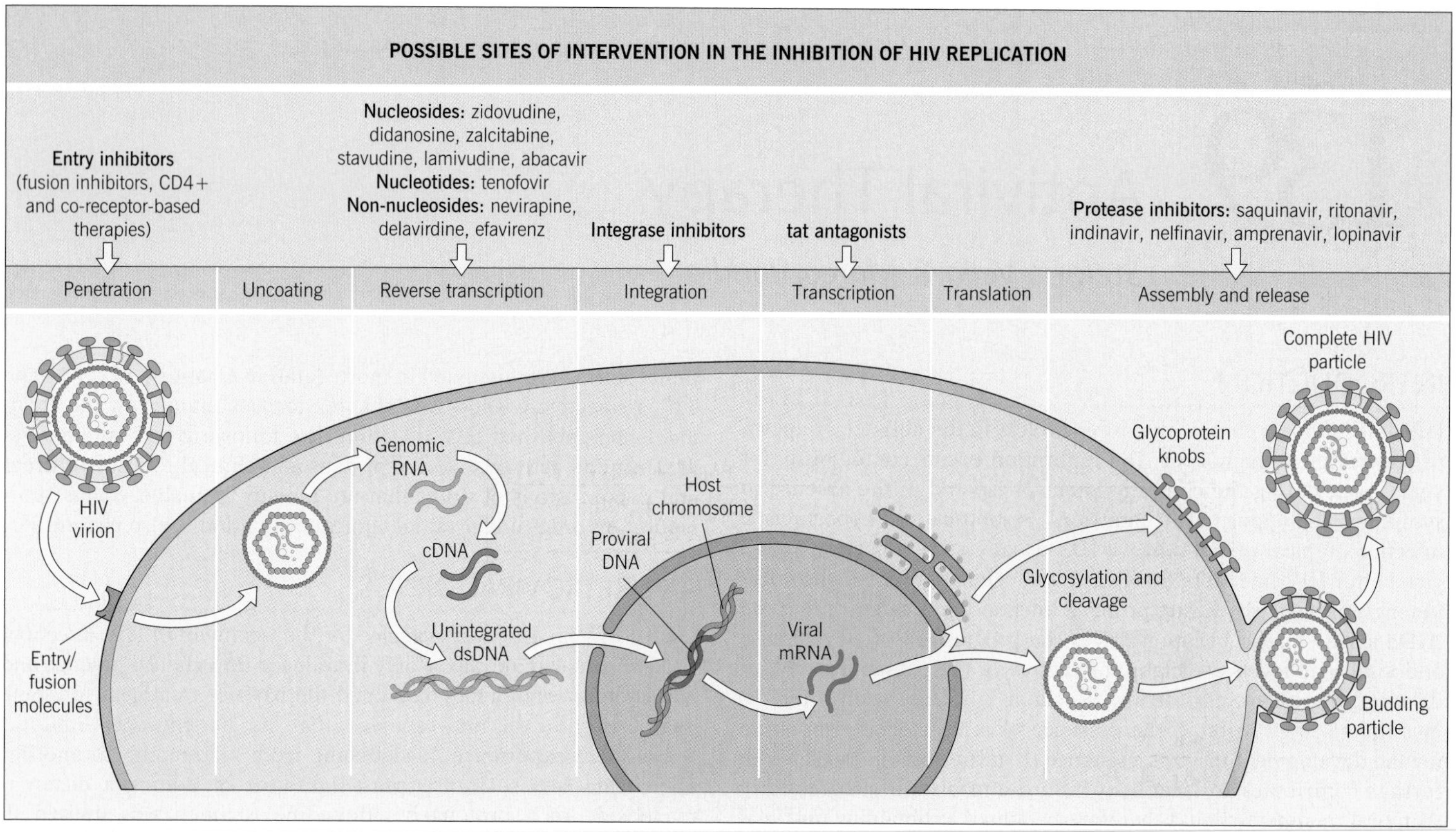

Fig. 139.1 Possible sites of intervention in the inhibition of HIV replication.

REVERSE TRANSCRIPTASE INHIBITORS

Reverse transcriptase inhibitors act through at least two mechanisms. First, as 'chain terminators', they block the elongation of the DNA chain through blockage of further nucleosides. This mechanism is characteristic of the nucleoside and nucleotide analogues and depends on the intracellular phosphorylation of the drugs to the corresponding triphosphate. Second, they act by competition/binding of the reverse transcriptase in functionally essential sites; NNRTIs act only through this mechanism and not as 'chain terminators'. Nucleoside analogues have in general good oral bioavailability, are only minimally bound to plasma proteins and are excreted through the kidneys. Because of these metabolic characteristics, they have relatively few interactions with other drugs as compared with PIs. Cerebrospinal fluid (CSF) to plasma ratios may be variable, ranging between 10% and 80%. They are generally active on HIV-1 and HIV-2. Non-nucleoside reverse transcriptase inhibitors are characterized by an HIV-1-restricted antiviral activity and are generally metabolized by the liver; interactions with other drugs with hepatic metabolism may occur. Their binding to plasma protein can also be higher than that with nucleoside analogues, and binding site displacement effects are possible. Data on their penetration into the central nervous system (CNS) are scarce.

Concerns were recently raised for the occurrence of mitochondrial toxicity due to inhibition of DNA γ-polymerase by nucleoside analogues. Although the clinical correlates of mitochondrial disfunction are poorly defined, a variety of clinical situations have been ascribed to this condition: chronic hyperlactatemia, with possible evolution into potentially fatal lactic acidosis with hepatomegaly and hepatic steatosis (three fatal cases reported in pregnant women receiving didanosine plus stavudine); pancreatitis, neuropathy, myopathy and cardiomyopathy; sporadic cases of severe and potentially fatal neurologic involvement in HIV-negative children exposed in utero to nucleoside analogues; and possibly, some of the features of the lipodystrophy syndrome (see below).[12] At present, lactic acidosis is considered to be the most serious condition associated with treatment with nucleoside analogues.

Zidovudine

Zidovudine (or azidothymidine; AZT) was the first drug approved for the treatment of HIV. It can be used in combination with most of the other antiretroviral drugs, with the exception of stavudine, and is available as dual co-formulation with lamivudine and as triple co-formulation with lamivudine and abacavir. The currently recommended dose is 600mg (200mg q8h or 300mg q12h). If tolerability is compromised by side effects, the dose of zidovudine is often reduced to 100mg q8h. It should be noted that, although currently available data suggest that 100mg q8h can have a favorable effect on surrogate markers, the clinical effectiveness of this dose has not been established. Pediatric dosages are about 180mg/m^2 q6h. Oral availability is approximately 60%. The drug concentrates in the semen, crosses the placenta and has good penetration into the CSF. Drugs inhibiting its glucuroconjugation, such as probenecid, valproic acid, naproxen, indomethacin and oxazepam, should be used with caution; methadone may increase zidovudine concentrations in serum.

The main adverse reactions include anemia, leukopenia, nausea, headache, insomnia and reversible myositis, with raised creatine phosphokinase (CPK) levels. Macrocytosis is a common hallmark of treatment with zidovudine.

Didanosine

Didanosine (ddI) is a nucleoside analogue to be administered in doses adjusted according to body weight: 200mg q12h or 400mg q24h in patients whose body weight is above 60kg, and 125mg q12h or 250mg q24h in patients whose body weight is below 60kg. Recommended dosage in children is on average 200mg/m^2 q24h (as oral solution). Didanosine is rapidly degraded at low pH and must

ANTIRETROVIRAL DRUGS AVAILABLE FOR HAART COMBINATION REGIMENS			
Class	Drug		Dosage
Nucleoside reverse transcriptase inhibitors	Zidovudine (AZT)	Retrovir®*†	200mg q8h or 300mg q12h
	Didanosine (ddl)	Videx®	>60kg: 200mg (tablets) or 250mg (powder) q12h, 400mg q24h (tablets or EC capsules) <60kg: 125mg (tablets) or 167mg (powder) q12h; 250mg q24h (tablets or EC capsules)
	Zalcitabine (ddC)	Hivid®	0.75mg q8h
	Lamivudine (3TC)	Epivir®*†	>50kg: 150mg q12h <50kg: 2mg/kg q12h
	Stavudine (d4T)	Zerit®	>60kg: 40mg q12h <60kg: 30mg q12h
	Abacavir (ABC)	Ziagen®†	300mg q12h
Nucleotide reverse transcriptase inhibitors	Tenofovir	Viread®	300mg q24h
Non-nucleoside reverse transcriptase inhibitors	Delavirdine (DLV)	Rescriptor®	400mg q8h
	Nevirapine (NVP)	Viramune®	200mg q24h for 2–4 weeks, then 200mg q12h
	Efavirenz (EFV)	Sustiva®	600mg q24h
Protease inhibitors	Saquinavir (SAQ)	Invirase® (HGC)‡	HGC: 400mg q12h, to be used only with ritonavir
		Fortovase® (SGC)§	SGC: 1200mg q8h
	Ritonavir (RTV)	Norvir®	300mg q12h, escalate to 600mg q12h in 2 weeks
	Indinavir (IDV)	Crixivan®	800mg q8h
	Nelfinavir (NFV)	Viracept®	750mg q8h or 1250mg q12h
	Amprenavir (APV)	Agenerase®	>50kg: 1200mg q12h <50kg: 20mg/kg q12h (max. 2400mg daily total)
	Lopinavir (LPV)	Kaletra®¶	400mg lopinavir + 100mg ritonavir q12h

* Also available (300mg AZT+ 150mg 3TC) as Combivir®. † Also available (300mg AZT+ 150mg 3TC+ 300mg ABV) as Trizivir®. ‡ Hard-gel capsule. § Soft-gel capsule. ¶ Only available as Kaletra® (133.3mg lopinavir + 33.3mg ritonavir).

Table 139.1 Antiretroviral drugs available for highly active antiretroviral therapy combination regimens.

be taken on an empty stomach. The oral bioavailability of didanosine is about 35–40%, and lower penetration than with zidovudine into the CNS has been reported. The metabolism is likely to involve the same pathways as those responsible for the elimination of endogenous purines.

The main adverse effects associated with didanosine therapy include gastrointestinal intolerance, diarrhea, hyperamylasemia, pancreatitis, peripheral neuropathy, hyperuricemia, hypertriglyceridemia and, rarely, rhabdomyolysis and lactic acidosis. Side effects appear to be more frequent in patients who have advanced disease. Concomitant use of pancreotoxic or neurotoxic drugs may increase the risk of pancreatitis and peripheral neuropathy respectively.

Zalcitabine

Zalcitabine (ddC) is a nucleoside analogue generally used in combination with zidovudine. Dosage is 0.75mg q8h for a total of 2.25mg/day. In patients weighing less than 50kg, half dosing is recommended. It has good bioavailability (80%); when administered with food, adsorption is reduced by 14% and time to achieve peak plasma concentrations approximately doubles from 0.8 hours to 1.6 hours.

The main adverse effects associated with zalcitabine therapy include peripheral neuropathy and painful mouth and penile ulcers. Nausea, dysphagia, anorexia, diarrhea, headache and myalgias have also been observed. Less frequently, rash, hyperamylasemia and pancreatitis have occurred in the context of zalcitabine therapy. Because of the common risk of peripheral neuropathy and pancreatitis, concomitant administration of didanosine or stavudine and zalcitabine is not recommended.

Lamivudine

Lamivudine (3TC), a nucleoside analogue inhibitor of the reverse transcriptase, is to be used in combination with zidovudine or stavudine. The recommended dose is 150mg q12h in adults (2 mg/kg q12h in patients below 50kg) and 8mg/kg/day in children. Because of the increased concentration of lamivudine in patients who have renal impairment, doses must be reduced in the presence of a creatinine clearance below 50ml/min. A dosage of 2mg/kg q12h is recommended in patients whose body weight is below 50kg. Lamivudine can be taken with food and its bioavailability is about 86% in adolescents and adults and 66% in children. Trimethoprim–sulfamethoxazole can increase the concentrations of the drug. Lamivudine can cross the blood–brain barrier, but to a limited extent, with CSF to plasma ratios of 6% in adults and 15% in children.

The main adverse effect associated with lamivudine therapy is reversible neutropenia. This can be exacerbated with zidovudine use and advanced HIV disease. Sporadic cases of pancreatitis and rash have also been reported. In pediatric patients receiving lamivudine, an increased frequency of pancreatitis has been reported, suggesting that particular caution is needed in children who have a previous history or at risk of pancreatitis. The drug has also shown in-vitro activity against hepatitis B virus (see Chapter 125).

Stavudine

The recommended dose of stavudine (d4T) is 40mg q12h (30mg q12h if weight is less than 60kg). The drug should be taken at least 1 hour before meals and has good bioavailability (80%); its terminal half-life is about 1.3 hours (3.5 hours intracellularly). It crosses the blood–brain barrier, although variable CSF to blood ratios have been reported. Elimination seems to occur by excretion in the urine (as unchanged drug) and by elimination through endogenous pathways. Pharmacokinetics in patients who have hepatic impairment are similar to those in patients who have normal hepatic function. Within the cell, zidovudine-5'–monophosphate may inhibit the production of stavudine-5'–monophosphate, suggesting that zidovudine and stavudine may be antagonistic and should therefore not be co-administered in combination.[13] This antagonism has been documented in vivo.

The main adverse effect associated with stavudine therapy is peripheral neuropathy, which is more frequent at higher doses (i.e. 40mg q12h), in advanced disease and in patients who have a previous history of neuropathy. The neuropathy is usually reversible at the cessation of treatment. A mild degree of bone marrow inhibition has also been reported, with moderate macrocytosis. Asymptomatic increases in liver function tests are also possible in about 10% of treated patients, and a small number of cases of pancreatitis have been observed. The risk of asymptomatic hyperlactatemia and lactic acidosis may be greater with stavudine than with other nucleoside analogues, particularly when used in combination with didanosine. Stavudine is also linked to the loss of peripheral fat (lipoatrophy).

Abacavir

Abacavir is the only guanosine analogue among the nucleoside reverse transcriptase inhibitors. After a unique phosphorylation pathway it is converted to carbovir triphosphate and subsequently metabolized by hepatic glycuroconjugation and renal excretion. The recommended dosage is 300mg q12h (with or without food). Central nervous system penetration (0.18 CSF:plasma ratio) and activity on viral load is probably superior to first-generation nucleoside analogues. It is increasingly being used in three-nucleoside combination regimens as a co-formulation with zidovudine and lamivudine. There is some degree of cross-resistance with other nucleoside analogues (didanosine, zalcitabine and lamivudine).

The toxicity profile is characterized, together with relatively nonspecific adverse events (diarrhea, nausea, abdominal pain, asthenia, headache, transaminase and creatinine increases) by a potentially serious hypersensitivity reaction (fever with nausea or vomiting, asthenia or flu-like symptoms, often accompanied by rash), which requires permanent discontinuation of the drug because of the risk of life-threatening reactions associated with drug rechallenge.[14]

Tenofovir

Tenofovir disoproxil fumarate is a prodrug that in vivo is converted to tenofovir, an acyclic nucleoside phosphonate, which represents a nucleotide analogue of adenosine 5'-monophosphate with inhibitory activity against HIV reverse transcriptase. The recommended dosage is 300mg q24h, to be taken with food in order to increase bioavailability. It is mainly excreted through the kidneys and the potential for interactions based on cytochrome P450 enzymes is considered to be low. Resistance profile of tenofovir seems to be unique among nucleoside reverse transcriptase inhibitors, with a limited degree of cross-resistance with other nucleoside analogues that needs to be further defined.

Information on toxicity profile is restricted to short-term side effects, mainly represented by gastrointestinal symptoms, asthenia and headache. Because of its renal metabolism, it is not currently recommended in patients who have low values of creatinine clearance. At present, clinical experience is more limited than with other nucleoside analogues, but preliminary results suggest that three-drug regimens (two nucleoside reverse transcriptase inhibitors plus one NNRTI) that include tenofovir may induce viral load reductions and $CD4^+$ lymphocyte increases comparable to those obtained with other commonly used three-drug regimens.

Nevirapine

Nevirapine (NVP) is the first compound to be approved among HIV NNRTIs. Recommended dosing is 200mg orally once daily for the initial 2 weeks, to be increased to 200mg q12h thereafter. Bioavailability is approximately 65%. Skin rash is the most common adverse event and may occur in up to 30% of nevirapine-treated patients by 24 weeks. In less than 5% of patients rash may be severe and, although rare, Stevens–Johnson syndrome has been described. Headache, diarrhea, nausea, fatigue, drowsiness, fever, chills, and joint and muscle aches are also reported. Hepatotoxicity usually occurs in the first 12 weeks of treatment, is more common in women and may be severe or fatal.

Delavirdine

Delavirdine (DLV) is another approved NNRTI. Recommended dosing is 400mg orally q8h. Adverse effects are headache, skin rash – generally maculopapular – fatigue, gastric intolerance, change in body temperature, increase in liver enzymes, faintness, dizziness or lightheadedness, changes in stools and leg cramps. Delavirdine inhibits cytochrome P450 enzymes, and various drug–drug interactions have been described when it is associated with PIs.

Efavirenz

Efavirenz is a NNRTI that can be administered once daily (600mg at bedtime, with or without food) because of a long plasma half-life. The main adverse effect associated with efavirenz is dizziness. Other CNS symptoms such as abnormal dreams, insomnia, hallucination and euphoria may also occur. Nausea, rash and hypersensitivity reactions have also been reported. Major congenital abnormalities have been observed in monkeys whose mothers were treated with efavirenz during pregnancy. Women on efavirenz treatment must therefore avoid pregnancy.

Like nevirapine, being an inducer of the P450 (CYP) 3A4 cytochrome isozyme, efavirenz can reduce the concentrations of drugs (such as indinavir, saquinavir or lopinavir) that are metabolized by this enzyme. It should not be administered with terfenadine, astemizole, cisapride, midazolam and triazolam because competition for the CYP3A4 isozyme may occur, leading to severe side effects. The resistance profile indicates cross-resistance with other NNRTIs.

PROTEASE INHIBITORS

Protease inhibitors act on the binding to the catalytic site of the HIV aspartic protease. This enzyme is critical in the post-translational processing of the polyprotein products of *gag* and *gag–pol* genes into the functional core proteins and viral enzymes, respectively. Its inhibition leads to the release of immature, noninfectious viral particles. Most of the PIs are compounds that mimic the part of the structure of Gag–Pol protein that is recognized by HIV protease.

Protease inhibitors, as nucleoside analogues, are active on HIV-1 and HIV-2, and have shown antiviral activity in primary human lymphoid and monocytic cell lines and against a variety of viral strains. However, unlike inhibitors of reverse transcriptase, which provide no protection in established in-vitro infection, PIs are active in chronically infected cells. Finally, PIs are active as the administered compound and do not need intracellular phosphorylation. Although these factors may imply a prolonged activity in a wider range of cells, many PIs are significantly bound to plasma proteins, with subsequent reduction in cellular uptake and, thus, intracellular levels. The possibility of achieving elevated blood levels is also affected by the bioavailability of these drugs, which is usually lower than that of reverse transcriptase inhibitors, mostly because of limited absorption and first-pass hepatic metabolism.

Protease inhibitors are generally dependent on the cytochrome P4503A hepatic isozyme for metabolism and can compete with other substrates of this enzyme. When the metabolism of other drugs that are dependent on the same enzyme is inhibited, the blood levels of these drugs can increase dramatically and toxic interactions may occur. This phenomenon has been evaluated for many of the compounds that are frequently used in patients who have HIV disease, and it has been shown that the combination of nucleoside analogues and PIs does not generally lead to untoward effects, although important pharmacokinetic interactions are possible for rifabutin, ketoconazole, rifampin (rifampicin), astemizole, terfenadine, cisapride and other drugs that are dependent on the P4503A hepatic isozyme for metabolism; therefore, attention should be paid before prescribing these drugs together with PIs. However, the concomitant administration of PIs and other drugs with hepatic metabolism may lead to decreased levels of these drugs (see Chapter 141).

Metabolic complications have recently emerged in patients treated with PIs. These include glucose metabolism abnormalities (hyperglycemia or diabetes), hyperlipidemia (mainly hypertriglyceridemia, with or without associated hypercholesterolemia), lipodystrophy or abnormal fat distribution (accumulation in the posterior neck, upper back and central abdomen). The pathogenesis of these abnormalities is still unclear and further studies are needed to define the role played by HIV infection, individual predisposing factors and treatment with specific drugs in the development of these complications.

Available data on the penetration of PIs into the CNS indicate that this is generally low, suggesting that, for optimal clinical use, these drugs should be combined with antiretrovirals that enter the CNS. The rapid development of resistance using reduced doses of PIs indicates that full dosage and adequate compliance should be maintained whenever possible. Protease inhibitors are generally used in combination with reverse transcriptase inhibitors or with another PI, taking advantage of a boosting effect on drug concentrations that occurs when PI are coadministered. The boosting effect, related to inhibitory activity on P450, is most pronounced with ritonavir, which is therefore commonly combined at low dosages (100mg q12h) with other PIs.

Saquinavir

Saquinavir (SQV) was the first PI to be approved in combination with other antiretrovirals for the treatment of HIV infection. A new formulation soft gel with enhanced bioavailability, to be administered at a dosage of 1200mg q8h or at lower dosages with ritonavir q12h, has actually replaced the previous formulation in clinical practice. Saquinavir has a low bioavailability (approximately 4% because of limited absorption and extensive first-pass metabolism). The drug should be taken with food, because drug bioavailability is significantly reduced in the fasting state. The drug is consistently tissue-bound, inactivation is rapid and elimination is predominantly nonrenal.

Diarrhea, abdominal discomfort or pain, headache, nausea, mouth ulcers, dizziness, numbness or tingling in limbs, rash, muscle aches and tiredness have been reported with increased frequency among patients taking saquinavir.

Ritonavir

Ritonavir (RTV) is a PI with potent antiviral activity in vivo. Recommended dosing is 600mg orally q12h. It should be taken with meals if possible. Bioavailability is about 60–70%, with minor differences in the blood levels between the nonfasted and fasted state. Ritonavir is approximately 98–99% plasma-protein-bound. After oral administration, 86% of the given radiolabeled dose was recovered in the feces and less than 4% in the urine. Ritonavir has a marked interference with hepatic metabolic enzymes, mainly represented by inhibition of the cytochrome P450 isoenzyme CYP3A, which can lead to remarkably increased blood levels of other drugs sharing the same metabolic process; these therefore must be avoided in patients receiving ritonavir. It is increasingly, and almost exclusively, used at low dosage as a pharmacokinetic enhancer of other PIs; ritonavir administration (100 or 200mg q12h) significantly increases the plasma levels of other PIs, allowing achievement of therapeutic plasma levels with lower doses and with more convenient schedules (q12h instead of q8h). Significant hepatic impairment is likely to induce a marked decrease in the metabolism and elimination of ritonavir.

The most common clinical side effects are circumoral paresthesias and diarrhea and/or vomiting. Headache, fever, numbness and tingling, muscle weakness and lightheadedness have also been described. Gastrointestinal side effects may be reduced by starting ritonavir alone and then adding the other drugs and gradually increasing ritonavir dosages over 7–10 days. The most frequently reported laboratory abnormalities have been liver enzyme elevations and elevations in blood lipids. Ritonavir should be used with caution among patients at high risk of bleeding, such as hemophiliacs.

Indinavir

Indinavir (IDV) is a PI of similar potency to ritonavir. Recommended dosing is 800mg q8h orally. Indinavir is rapidly absorbed in the fasted state, with a bioavailability of approximately 60%; a decrease in blood levels by approximately 80% is seen when the drug is administered with a high-fat meal, whereas lighter meals have no relevant effect on pharmacokinetics. Binding of indinavir to human plasma proteins is about 60% and metabolism is P450 dependent. After oral administration of a single 400mg dose, over 80% of radioactivity is detected in the feces, with a mean recovery in the urine of 19%; renal clearance studies suggest a secretory component in excretion, which may play a role, together with the observed supersaturation of the urine with indinavir dosages above 600mg, in the formation of indinavir urinary crystals.

Nephrolithiasis and microscopic hematuria can occur in 10–28% of treated patients, and a high fluid intake (at least 2 l/day) is therefore recommended to prevent this complication. Another laboratory side effect that has been frequently associated with indinavir sulfate is hyperbilirubinemia and, at times, jaundice. Other side effects include nausea, vomiting, diarrhea, rash, fatigue and headache.

Nelfinavir

Although introduced later than other PIs, nelfinavir (NFV) is widely used in clinical practice because of its relatively good tolerability/activity ratio. In clinical trials and observational studies, the use of nelfinavir together with nucleoside analogues has resulted in significant and sustained reductions in viral load and in marked increases in $CD4^+$ lymphocyte counts. It can be administered both q12h (1250mg per dose) or q8h (750mg per dose).

The tolerability profile is relatively good compared with other PIs, with diarrhea representing the most commonly observed adverse event and a main cause for drug discontinuation. Other PI-related adverse events may also occur, such as lipid and glucose abnormalities and possible increase in risk of bleeding in patients who have hemophilia. Resistance studies suggest that, if under treatment virus mutates along a specific mutation pathway (D30N), the efficacy of other PIs may be relatively preserved (see Chapter 137).

Lopinavir

Lopinavir is a very potent inhibitor of HIV-1 protease. Its bioavailability is greatly enhanced by coadministration of ritonavir and is therefore co-formulated at a 4:1 ratio with ritonavir (capsules: 133.3mg lopinavir/33.3mg lopinavir; oral solution 80mg lopinavir/20mg ritonavir per ml). Recommended dosage is 400/100mg q12h with food. Data on clinical progression are not yet available. Lopinavir has been used in patients in whom previous treatment has failed and in previously untreated patients. Available data indicate that the drug has high potency on viral load and $CD4^+$ lymphocyte counts, and efficacy both in salvage regimens and in previously untreated patients. Lopinavir is principally metabolized by the liver, and shares many of the drug interactions and contraindications common to other PIs.

The safety profile of the drug is not fully assessed because of the small number of patients as yet studied. The main adverse events observed in clinical trials were diarrhea and other gastrointestinal complaints. Hyperlipidemia is also relatively common. Rash was observed in some children. The high potency characteristics make this drug a potentially important element in the design of particularly potent first-line drug regimens or salvage strategies.

Amprenavir

Amprenavir (APV) is a PI approved for use in both adults and children. It is available both as capsules and as oral solution and can be administered q12h, without restrictions in terms of food timing. Coadministration of ritonavir, as for other PIs, improves amprenavir pharmacokinetic parameters and allows dosage reductions. There are limited data from controlled trials comparing amprenavir and other PIs in terms of efficacy.

The safety profile is also only partially assessed because of the relatively recent introduction of the drug. Preliminary data suggest that amprenavir is relatively well tolerated, with gastrointestinal disturbances and rash representing the main events leading to treatment discontinuation in early trials. Oral/perioral paresthesias have also been observed. The drug is metabolized by the P450 isozyme system and shares some of interactions and contraindications common to other PIs. Amprenavir should be avoided in patients who have sulfonamide allergy. Judging from the evidence of in vitro studies and on preliminary observations in vivo, the drug might also have, as compared with other PIs, a lower impact on metabolic status and on lipodystrophy. The resistance mutation profile is also potentially interesting, suggesting lower potential for cross-resistance with other drugs of this class. These specific tolerability and resistance characteristics, if confirmed by further evaluations, may prove useful in the design of sequential therapeutic strategies against HIV.

NEW INVESTIGATIONAL AGENTS (see also Chapter 204)

A number of novel nucleoside (nucleotide) reverse transcriptase inhibitors (NRTIs), NNRTIs and PIs are currently in development. Desirable characteristics of this new generation of drugs include easier administration schedule, perfected pharmacokinetics, potency, tolerability and the ability to inhibit HIV viruses that are resistant to the existing agents.

TMC125, a new NNRTI, showed high antiviral effect in preliminary studies based on small samples of patients. In treatment-experienced patients failing efavirenz- or nevirapine-containing therapy, TMC125 administered at a dose of 900mg q12h for 7 days decreased the median viral load by approximately $1\log_{10}$ copies/ml compared with baseline.[15] Diarrhea and headache were the most frequent adverse effects reported by patients taking the drug.

Tipranavir, a new PI, administered together with a small dose of ritonavir in patients who were failing multiple PIs, showed an interesting resistance profile. After more than 1 year of tipranavir/ritonavir treatment, only 2% of the clinical isolates (5/41) exhibited a reduced susceptibility to tipranavir. Moreover, the number of mutations in the protease gene at baseline did not influence the virologic response to tipranavir/ritonavir, and tipranavir/ritonavir treatment did not affect the susceptibility of HIV to other PIs.[16] These data indicate that resistance to tipranavir is uncommon in HIV-positive patients who have failed multiple PI-containing regimens, either at baseline or after 1 year of treatment.

Atanazavir is a new once-daily PI in development that seems to be characterized by a favorable metabolic profile; the drug in antiretroviral-naive individuals had no negative impact on levels of total cholesterol, low-density lipoprotein or triglyceride.

Although current antiretroviral treatment is still based on reverse transcriptase and PIs, inhibitors of the entry/fusion process of HIV into the target cell (T20 and T1249) gave important results in preliminary clinical trials and are likely to join the therapeutic repertoire soon, mainly as components of salvage regimens. In addition, integrase inhibitors are also entering clinical evaluation.

The chemokine receptors CCR5 and CXCR4, which represent co-receptors used by HIV strains in addition to CD4 to enter target cells, are also potentially important therapeutic targets. Antiretroviral agents that inhibit HIV-1 entry by blocking these co-receptors are being developed and some of them recently entered phase I studies.

NEWLY RECOGNIZED ADVERSE EVENTS OBSERVED IN PATIENTS UNDERGOING POTENT ANTIRETROVIRAL THERAPY

In addition to drug-specific adverse events, the long-term use of potent antiretroviral therapy has highlighted a number of adverse events that were previously not recognized. Some of these events appear to be associated with a specific class of drugs, such as mitochondrial toxicity and lactic acidosis with NRTIs or hyperglycemia with PIs; in other cases the association with a single class of drugs is less evident and the pathogenesis of the adverse events is poorly understood (e.g. metabolic disturbances, fat maldistribution, bone abnormalities). All these events may seriously jeopardize adherence and continuation of antiretroviral treatment and therefore represent a major problem in clinical management.

Possible manifestations of NRTI-related mitochondrial toxicity include cardiomyopathy, myopathy, peripheral neuropathy, pancreatitis, proximal renal tubular dysfunction, hepatic steatosis and lactic acidosis. However, it needs to be considered that many effects associated with mitochondrial toxicity are difficult to distinguish from effects associated with HIV infection itself.

Fat distribution changes (also commonly described as lipodystrophy) represent a major event in terms of clinical relevance. This syndrome may present with atrophic changes (peripheral fat loss involving face and limbs), hypertrophic changes (visceral or dorsocervical fat accumulation, breast enlargement) or both. A dysmetabolic profile involving hyperglycemia, hyperlipidemia and hyperinsulinemia is frequently but not always associated with the lipodystrophy syndrome. A common case definition is still lacking, pathogenesis is uncertain and treatment strategies have proved unsatisfactory so far in terms of efficacy. The impact of metabolic changes on incidence of cardiovascular disease is also poorly defined. Although a number of biochemical and vascular abnormalities have been reported, observational studies have yielded conflicting results, with some studies showing association between potent antiretroviral therapy and increased risk of cardiovascular disease and others not indicating an increased number of cardiovascular events following introduction of potent antiretroviral therapy regimens. Bone abnormalities have also been reported, with no clear association with any specific class of antiretroviral drugs; the abnormalities observed include avascular osteonecrosis, osteopenia and osteoporosis, sometimes in association with metabolic changes.

Although lack of a standard case definition complicates characterization, diagnosis and tracking, the morphologic changes have a real and substantial impact on quality of life. Cardiovascular sequelae of dyslipidemia appear to be minimal in the short term but long-term outcome is unknown. So far, management approaches of fat redistribution syndromes and of metabolic toxicities are largely empirical. Only a few of them are based on short-term controlled studies: antiretroviral therapy switches, exercise and diet, anabolic steroids, recombinant human growth hormone (rhGH), testosterone, metformin, thiazolidinediones and plastic surgery for fat redistribution syndromes; lifestyle modification (diet, exercise), use of lipid-lowering agents and switching to non-PI regimens for dyslipidemic syndromes.

HIV RESISTANCE TO ANTIRETROVIRAL DRUGS

Definition and biologic basis of resistance

Emergence of HIV resistance to all classes of antiretroviral drugs used until now has been described. Although other factors may play a role in determining the loss of efficacy of antiretroviral treatment, drug resistance plays a major role in this phenomenon, and great attention is paid to possible strategies to prevent or delay it.

How treatment can affect resistance

Because resistant variants may exist before treatment and evolve under selective pressure, therapy can address viral resistance in three ways:

- by maximizing the suppression of viral replication;
- by using drugs where multiple mutations are required for resistance; and
- by forcing the emergence of variants that result in attenuated replication or decreased virulence (see Chapter 137).

Resistance to nucleoside analogues

HIV variants with decreased susceptibility were first reported in clinical isolates in 1989 for zidovudine, followed by reports of drug-resistance to the other nucleoside analogues and PIs. Advanced disease stage, baseline low $CD4^+$ lymphocyte count and high RNA plasma levels are strongly predictive of the development of resistance. With zidovudine (as with some PIs), resistance appears to be the consequence of a stepwise accumulation of mutations. For other drugs, such as didanosine and zalcitabine, the mechanisms and the molecular correlates of resistance are less clear, although a number of mutations responsible for reduced susceptibility have been identified.

Resistance to zidovudine is the most widely explored in its molecular and clinical aspects. It is related to the ordered emergence of HIV variants with mutations at reverse transcriptase codons 215, 70, 41, 67 and 219, with wild-type strains showing a generally narrow range of IC_{50}–IC_{90}. From a clinical point of view, zidovudine resistance has been shown to predict a more rapid progression of HIV disease, although the clinical significance of resistance to the dideoxynucleosides has not yet been completely defined. High-level resistance to didanosine or zalcitabine has not been reported to date and there is no clear explanation for these findings. Cross-resistance has been reported and multidrug resistance has been observed after combination therapy with nucleoside analogues.

Development of resistance may not necessarily represent an entirely negative event; under treatment with lamivudine, resistance occurs rapidly in vivo, associated with a substitution at codon 184. This codon change may antagonize the effect of zidovudine resistance mediated by the 215 (and 41) mutations, leading to a restored phenotypic sensitivity to zidovudine.[17] This mechanism, however, does not seem to be effective in all cases, with dual zidovudine/lamivudine resistance also observed.

Resistance to non-nucleoside reverse transcriptase inhibitors

Non-nucleoside reverse transcriptase inhibitor use in monotherapy is associated with a rapid development of resistance, which initially suggested a limited usefulness in clinical practice. However, when these drugs were used in triple combination regimens with nucleoside analogues, resistance did not occur in patients who had a sustained viral load suppression to undetectable levels, supporting the concept that resistance occurs as a direct consequence of viral replication. Many NNRTIs have a common pattern of resistance, and this limits sequential use of these drugs because of cross-resistance.

Resistance to protease inhibitors

As for the other classes of antiretrovirals, reduced sensitivity has been reported for all tested PIs, with some strains exhibiting cross-resistance to different PIs after in-vitro or in-vivo drug exposure.[18] The patterns of mutations, however, appear to be more complex than for reverse transcriptase inhibitors, with a higher number of sites involved and higher variability in the temporal patterns and combinations of mutations leading to 'phenotypic' resistance; this suggests that the protease can adapt differently and perhaps more easily than the reverse transcriptase under the genetic pressure induced by drugs. At present, although about 20 codons have been identified as possible mutation sites, several different genetic profiles can be identified and can therefore be employed in designing sequential treatment.

Resistance to entry/fusion inhibitors

Unfortunately, HIV resistance should be expected with any class of drugs used. The increasing clinical use of fusion inhibitors in HIV-infected patients has recently highlighted the occurrence of resistance in some patients receiving the fusion inhibitor enfuvirtide (T-20) in monotherapy.[19]

Clinical implications of drug resistance

Resistance may be a consequence of incomplete viral suppression (in the presence of antiretroviral drugs) and this what usually occurs during the virologic failure of first-line therapy. On the other hand, resistance may be a *cause* of incomplete viral suppression if mutations pre-exist, which is the case with patients failing second- and third-line regimens.

In all cases, the presence of drug resistance, together with other factors (low antiviral potency of the regimen, poor adherence, pharmacokinetic interactions) may compromise the effectiveness of treatment. Information on resistance status is therefore considered useful both in instituting antiretroviral treatment in previously untreated patients and in managing therapeutic decisions in patients already on antiviral therapy. There is, however, uncertainty about the weight of resistance data in clinical decisions, because available resistance tests are as yet not fully validated and are based on different techniques. In the interpretation of results, absence of resistance (through genotypic or phenotypic testing) does not rule out the possibility of resistant virus in small quantities or in tissue reservoirs. Conversely, evidence of resistance, although indicating a potential reduction in the activity of the drug, should always prompt (before instituting treatment changes) a careful technical interpretation of the resistance test used, longitudinal evaluation of viral load and $CD4^+$ trends over time, an estimate of adherence to treatment and a review of concomitant treatments potentially interfering with drug efficacy. Further studies are needed to define which resistance test(s) will be more adequate in clinical management. Until their validation, changes in HIV RNA levels, together with treatment history, represent the dominant parameters that should guide treatment changes, and the additional information provided by resistance testing should at present be included in a global evaluation of the patient's response to treatment.

HIV TREATMENT STRATEGIES

Principles

The treatment of HIV infection is one of the most rapidly evolving fields in medicine. Advances in basic research, the development of new technologies for the monitoring of therapy, the continuous introduction of new drugs into clinical practice and the relentless dissemination of the results of recent trials contribute to create new expectations and to suggest new strategies for optimal management of the disease. The dynamics of HIV-1 replication in vivo strongly suggest that HIV should definitely be 'hit hard' with potent combinations of antiretroviral drugs to minimize the negative consequences of HIV replication and genetic evolution. Recent data, however, have indicated that replication-competent HIV may survive, even in the presence of highly active treatment, within latently infected cells in the blood or in tissue reservoirs and 'sanctuary sites' inaccessible to treatment in lymphoid tissues, bone marrow and other macrophage-rich tissues and organs.

More studies are needed to define the size and distribution of the latent/infected cellular population, the impact of treatment on HIV load in latent reservoirs, and the extent to which immune reconstitution is possible in already immunocompromised patients.

A variety of therapeutic guidelines have been developed to keep clinical practice up to date, as far as possible, with the data emerging from basic and clinical research. The recommendations currently represent an authoritative reference in the field.[20] National guidelines have been published, in the USA[21] and in many other countries.

When to start treatment

Early initiation of therapy with a combination of antiretroviral drugs has been shown to produce more durable clinical benefit than the initiation of therapy in advanced disease. Therapy should be started before the development of symptoms and fall of $CD4^+$ lymphocyte count to low levels, using regimens able to induce and maintain maximal viral suppression and to prevent the emergence of resistant strains. Moreover, because even complete inhibition of viral replication may not be able, in the long term, to prevent the selection of resistance mutants if they exist at a high enough frequency before therapy, treating very early in the course of the infection (i.e. at or immediately before seroconversion), when the virus population is at its most homogenous, may be more beneficial. For these reasons, in the mid-late 1990s, the treatment philosophy for many HIV/AIDS physicians and patients was 'treat early, treat hard'.

However, more recently, the growing appreciation of the difficulties of taking antiretroviral therapy on a long-term basis, the adverse effects of many antiretroviral drugs and regimens, and their negative impact on quality of life has led to a re-evaluation of this early intervention strategy. With 'eradication' not on the horizon, the goal of therapy must now be redirected toward the long-term management of a chronic infection. The decision of when to initiate treatment is now based first on the patient's disease stage, because its clear that a symptomatic patient should always be treated. For an asymptomatic patient, the decision should be driven mainly by the $CD4^+$ lymphocyte count (which is an immediate predictor of progression) and the plasma HIV-1 RNA level (which is an indicator of the level of actual HIV replication and predicts the subsequent rate of loss of $CD4^+$ lymphocytes). Other elements should, however, be factored into the decision to start treatment: the patient's commitment to therapy and a knowledge of the limitations of current regimens.

Therefore, the decision to initiate therapy in asymptomatic patients should be based on prognosis as determined by the $CD4^+$ T cell count and RNA level. Despite the fact that serious complications of HIV infection do not frequently occur when $CD4^+$ lymphocytes are still above $200/mm^3$, a reasonable approach is to start treatment if $CD4^+$ lymphocytes decrease below $300–350/mm^3$ and to treat independently of $CD4^+$ if viral load is particularly high (plasma HIV RNA >50,000–100,000 copies/ml). In any case, treatment should be started only when the patient has been educated regarding therapy and is committed to adherence.

A situation that may indicate treatment is primary/acute HIV infection; when viral load is generally remarkably high, the infection disseminates in several reservoirs and the interaction between HIV and the immune system establishes a 'set point' of viremia, which is predictive of the subsequent course of the disease. It now seems clear that this condition can be clinically identified in some patients, allowing a timely intervention that could potentially have positive consequences on the course of the disease. Whether it is possible to discontinue therapy after a prolonged period of adequate suppression is the subject of ongoing trials (see Chapter 122).

What to start with

With combination therapy representing the key to an effective treatment, achieving a low or undetectable viral load is dependent on the availability of a sufficient number of drugs with as wide a specificity of action as possible, and by a rational design of combination regimens (Table 139.2). An optimal combination regimen should fulfill several requirements, the first of which is a high antiviral potency. Although viral suppression in vitro is indicative of the drug's efficacy, a better estimate is obtained by measuring the effect of the regimen on HIV viral load in vivo. Indeed, some of the new drugs and regimens have recently proved effective in reducing the number of plasma HIV-1 RNA copies by $3\log_{10}$ from baseline, compared with the mean $0.5–1\log_{10}$ reduction that is characteristic of most of the first-generation, monotherapy regimens, with a more durable response in terms of $CD4^+$ and HIV RNA (Fig. 139.2). Similarly, and perhaps more importantly, regimens characterized by a substantial proportion of patients achieving durably 'undetectable' viral load should be given priority in clinical practice.

CRITERIA FOR THE SELECTION OF COMBINATION REGIMENS
• High and sustained antiviral activity in vivo (able to induce at least $2\log_{10}$ reduction in viral load; able to achieve 'undetectable' HIV-1 RNA level in >70% of patients)
• Simultaneous targeting of multiple viral enzymes
• Wide spectrum cell specificity (e.g. lymphocytes/macrophages, active/resting)
• Wide spectrum tissue activity (lymph nodes, other sanctuary sites, CNS)
• Absence of cross-toxicity patterns
• Induction of 'favorable' mutations (reduced replicative capacity, reversal of resistance, enhanced 'fidelity')
• Absence of cross-resistance (allowing a higher number of subsequent options)
• Favorable pharmacokinetic interactions (e.g. increase in plasma concentrations of one of the drugs used)
• Accessibility, tolerability, compliance and therapeutic index

Table 139.2 Criteria for the selection of combination regimens.

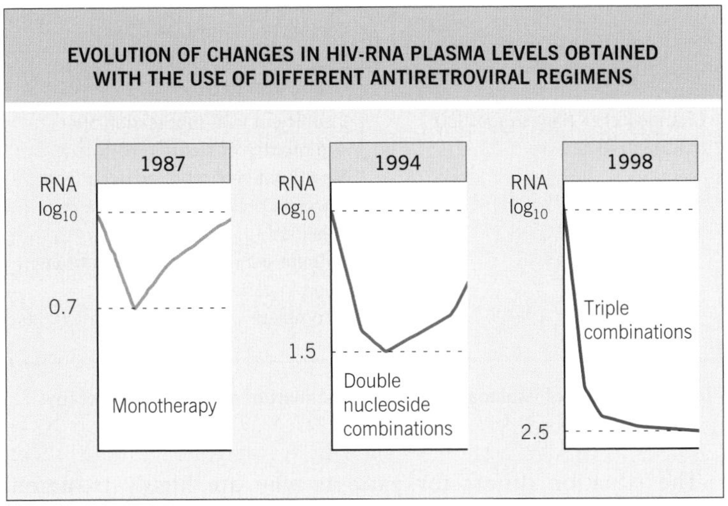

Fig. 139.2 Evolution of changes in HIV RNA plasma levels obtained with the use of different antiretroviral regimens.

As for any combination therapy, the drugs selected should also show different toxicity and resistance profiles and be characterized by distinct tissue or cellular specificity to ensure a more generalized viral suppression in the body. Of particular relevance are:

- penetration into the CNS, because of its possible role in preventing HIV-associated neurologic disease;
- possible differences in antiviral activity among resting or activated cells, according to specific phosphorylation profiles of nucleoside analogues in different cells;[22] and
- wide cell and enzyme target profiles – two or more drugs 'convergent' against the same HIV enzyme can reduce the possibility of viral 'escape' of variants with functional mutations, whereas combining reverse transcriptase and PIs may allow activity on acutely and chronically infected cells, adding effectiveness to the regimen.

Another important tool in designing treatment is represented by information on the resistance profile of the drugs, the impact of drug-induced mutations on the replicative characteristics of the virus and sensitivity to other drugs that have been previously used or could be used sequentially. Pharmacokinetics also represent an important aspect in the design of the regimen because an adequate knowledge and rational use of drug interactions allows a simpler administration schedule and an increased potency regimen. Finally, it must always be considered that HIV infection is a long-term disease mostly affecting young people; in this condition, as for other chronic diseases necessitating continuous treatment, tolerability, compliance and accessibility are important factors that must carefully be considered in the design of treatment to ensure compliance and efficacy.

In conclusion, factors determining therapeutic efficacy are certainly linked to the quality of the antiretroviral agents (potent combinations, tolerability, convenient dosing, affordability) but also to the health care provider (who should be accessible in working with patients, give clear instructions and counseling, and use an individualized approach) and to patient commitment and motivation to treatment (conducive lifestyle, family support).

Different combinations of drugs belonging to the three classes have shown similar activity and efficacy in the short to mid term. Considerations in the selection of the most appropriate regimen for the individual patient may include potency; side effect profile; patient's predicted adherence, with potential effect on quality of life and pill burden; the potential for maintenance of future options in terms of drug class sparing and cross-resistance profile; the presence of co-morbid conditions and medications; and, finally, in certain clinical circumstances and geographic areas, the potential for primary acquisition of resistant viral strains.

The most widely used regimens include:

- PI (± low-dose ritonavir) + two NRTIs (NNRTI-sparing regimen);
- NNRTI + two NRTIs (PI-sparing regimen); and
- three NRTIs, including abacavir (PI/NNRTI-sparing regimen).

Other combinations under clinical investigation include a regimen with drugs belonging to all three classes (1–2 PIs + NNRTI + 1–2 NRTIs) and a combination that excludes NRTIs (PI/low-dose ritonavir + NNRTI).

All available regimens have both advantages and disadvantages. For PI-containing regimens the advantages include the solidity of available clinical data, the longest experience, high potency and a relatively high genetic barrier to resistance. Combinations of two PIs are increasingly being used instead of a single PI because they have pharmacokinetic advantages and possibly increase the PI regimen's potency while greatly improving adherence to therapy. Addition of a low dose of ritonavir (100 or 200mg q12h) to saquinavir, indinavir or amprenavir improves the pharmacokinetic profile, reduces pill burden, lowers the dose frequency, lowers the costs and obviates the need for administration of PIs on an empty stomach. A co-formulation of lopinavir + ritonavir has recently been introduced. Disadvantages of PI-containing regimens are mainly represented by the high risk of metabolic complications, which, in the long term, may occur in a considerable proportion of patients (>40%).

Advantages of NNRTI-containing regimens, which appears to be equipotent to PI-containing regimens, include very low pill burden and convenience. The main disadvantage, together with some relevant although organ-focused toxicities, is the low genetic barrier to resistance, which limits the use of other members of this class.

Combinations composed only of NRTIs have the advantage of deferring the use of two classes of antiretroviral (the PIs and the NNRTIs). For patients who have high viral loads, more data are needed regarding the efficacy of triple NRTI regimens. The long-term consequences of NRTI additive toxicities are unknown. In addition, most available efficacy data refer to combinations including abacavir, with which serious hypersensitivity reactions may occur in about 5% of patients at institution of therapy.

Specific consideration is necessary for the selection of the most appropriate NRTI backbone combination. As initial treatment often fails, it is likely that a sequence of NRTIs will be given during the lifetime of an HIV-infected patient. The best NRTI backbone to be used first to give the optimum chance of the second regimen being successful is currently unknown and is under evaluation in strategic trials. In general we rarely use zalcitabine because of its significant potential for neurotoxicity and the need for q8h administration. Clinical data suggest that stavudine and zidovudine should not be given in combination. There is recent evidence of increased toxicity when stavudine and didanosine were used together and therefore we are less enthusiastic about this combination at the present time. We tend not to recommend abacavir and nevirapine together as initial therapy because there is evidence that the nevirapine rash may complicate the management of suspected abacavir hypersensitivity.

Most of the experience for initial therapy has been accumulated regarding zidovudine plus lamivudine, or stavudine plus lamivudine. Tenofovir plus lamivudine has also been shown in prospective trails to be effective and well tolerated. Zidovudine plus didanosine has been extensively studied in the past but issues of palatability relating to the didanosine formulation precluded widespread use of this combination. More recently, with the availability of an enteric-coated formulation of didanosine, this has been circumvented and the new formulations allow once-daily dosing, which is particularly attractive for certain patients. Despite the limited data available for abacavir in the initial regimen, this agent has worked well, particularly with lamivudine or as part of a zidovudine and lamivudine triple combination. However a recent study comparing zidovudine and lamivudine plus efavirenz to zidovudine and lamivudine plus abacavir suggested the three-nucleoside combination was inferior as initial therapy. Finally, the likelihood of potential toxicities will ultimately help us to decide what is the best backbone NRTI combination for a given patient.

Changing treatment

The success of antiretroviral treatment can be evaluated in different ways. From a laboratory point of view, sustained maximal viral load reduction is certainly proof of the activity of the selected regimen on HIV replication, together with a sustained rise in $CD4^+$ lymphocyte counts. However, we should not lose sight of the need for improved clinical outcome (in terms of opportunistic infections, symptomatic HIV disease and survival) and of the need to preserve the patient's quality of life.

Criteria for changing therapy (Table 139.3) include:

- a suboptimal reduction in plasma viremia after initiation of therapy;
- re-appearance of viremia after suppression to undetectable;
- significant increases in plasma viremia from the nadir of suppression; and
- declining numbers of $CD4^+$ T cells.

To exert a significant effect on the viral 'background' of the patient, changes should therefore be implemented before complete virologic failure, selecting at least two potent drugs not previously used by the patient with appropriate toxicity and resistance profiles. However, because of the lack of many options for changing treatment, one must not prematurely abandon a given regimen. In patients who have very high baseline RNA levels, maximal suppression may not be seen until after 12–24 weeks of potent therapy. Moreover, a careful assessment of adherence must also be made before deciding to switch the patient to a new therapeutic regimen.

Any discussions on salvage strategies requires a definition of treatment failure. For the adherent patient on an initial treatment regimen, confirmed detectable plasma HIV-1 RNA (>50 copies/ml) should be considered evidence of treatment failure. Continued treatment with the same regimen in this situation will eventually lead to development of high-level drug resistance and diminishes the likelihood that salvage regimens will be successful. Thus, for the patient who has clear treatment options, early switching could maximize the chances for therapeutic success of the next treatment regimen and preserve future options.

USE OF VIRAL LOAD IN THE MANAGEMENT OF ANTIRETROVIRAL THERAPY	
Parameter	**Recommendation**
Plasma HIV RNA levels that should lead to close monitoring and consideration of starting treatment, regardless of laboratory or clinical status	50,000–100,000 copies/ml or more
Target HIV RNA level after initiation of treatment	Undetectable
Suggested frequency of HIV RNA measurement	At baseline: two measurements, 3–4 weeks apart One measurement 4–6 weeks after starting therapy, to confirm antiviral activity of the regimen For patients starting at very high baseline RNA levels, maximal suppression may not be seen until 12–24 weeks, when HIV RNA should be remeasured Plasma HIV-RNA should thereafter be checked every 3–4 months, in conjunction with CD4 count (shorter intervals in proximity of critical decisions)
Change in HIV RNA suggesting treatment failure	Insufficient viral suppression after 4–6 months of starting treatment Significant viral rebound in patients who had previously undetectable viral load Definite trend toward pre-treatment levels in patients who have incomplete viral suppression

Table 139.3 Use of viral load in the management of antiretroviral therapy.

The situation differs for patients who are highly treatment experienced and for whom fewer options remain. In such cases, a more conservative approach may be warranted. Usually, virologic escape is followed by immunologic deterioration and eventually clinical evolution. However, the time lag between HIV RNA rebound and clinical failure varies from patient to patient, and it has become clear that $CD4^+$ lymphocyte count may remain high even in the presence of a clear rebound in HIV RNA.

Before making any decisions about changes in antiretroviral treatment, it is important to determine why the current regimen is failing, in order to avoid choosing an inappropriate remedy. In particular, factors such as drug resistance, inadequate drug exposure due to poor adherence, absorption and pharmacokinetics, and persistence of HIV in viral reservoirs all represent major causes of failure that should be investigated in depth before switching to a different regimen.

General criteria for the choice of second-line regimens

Unfortunately, because of the large degree of cross-resistance occurring within all antiretroviral drug classes, the options that actually exist are limited, especially for patients experiencing their second or third failure. In this heavily pre-treated population, both observational and prospective studies have shown quite disappointing results for any investigated salvage regimens.

Different studies have demonstrated that 90–95% adherence to a NRTI/PI regimen is required to achieve/maintain full suppression. In addition to patient information and training, future opportunities to improve adherence may include once-daily NRTI dosing (didanosine, lamivudine, abacavir), once-daily PI dosing (saquinavir/ritonavir, lopinavir/ritonavir, indinavir/ritonavir), directly observed therapy, simplification after suppression, use of NRTI-class-sparing regimens and phosphokinase manipulation.

The path to be followed in the face of a confirmed treatment failure could be summarized as follows:

- review antiretroviral history;
- assess adherence and tolerability;
- distinguish first, second, multiple failures;
- consider newer agents through expanded access or clinical trials;
- consider phosphokinase enhancement; and
- perform resistance testing to identify susceptible drugs/drug classes.

Use of resistance testing

The most important issue in clinical practice is the relatively high level of cross-resistance among drugs in the same classes. Sequential utility in the case of resistance is almost nonexistent with NNRTIs and only moderate with PIs or NRTIs. The rationale for resistance testing in patient management includes demonstration of the correlation between drug resistance and virologic response to new regimen when prior therapy has failed; the fact that drug resistance is an independent risk factor for poor virologic response after controlling for HIV-1 RNA level, $CD4^+$ lymphocyte count and treatment history; and the fact that virologic failure is not inevitably accompanied by resistance to all drugs in the regimen.

Although representing a major advantage for the management of HIV patients, the routine use of resistance tests in the clinical setting has still to be validated. In general, whereas resistance is generally a good predictor of the probable failure of a drug, susceptibility is no guarantee of success. It is becoming a common belief, therefore, that these assays have their major application in predicting which drugs not to use, rather than which are likely to be successful. Their best current application is therefore in the design of salvage regimens. Indeed, several retrospective and a few prospective studies have shown that, at least in the short term, a higher response rate is likely to occur when a salvage regimen is selected on the basis of genotype/phenotype testing results (see Chapter 137).[23–27]

Finally, transmission of drug-resistant virus at primary HIV infection is a growing phenomenon. Data from the USA show that the prevalence of high level resistance to NNRTI and PIs has increased in the last year compared with 1996–8.[28] Continuing surveillance is required and many suggest that drug resistance testing should be performed in patients who have primary HIV infection before initiating antiretroviral therapy.

FUTURE PERSPECTIVES

The development of new drugs within existing antiretroviral classes may provide patients with potent agents that have improved tolerability profiles and are more convenient to take than current drugs. However, as has happened in the recent history of antiretroviral therapy, a major impact has been made by the careful evaluation of new treatment strategies.

Treatment simplification strategies are necessary to improve patient adherence and hence outcome. A number of antiretroviral switch regimens have been proposed and/or studied in order to prevent or alleviate antiretroviral-associated toxicities, as well as to improve adherence. There are two main types of switching:

- PI switch regimen (i.e. from a PI-based regimen to a triple NRTI or one NNRTI/two NRTIs regimen); or
- NRTI-sparing switch (i.e. from one PI or NNRTI/two NRTIs regimen to one containing a PI and a NNRTI in order to minimize the risk of mitochondrial toxicity).

Many patients now being treated had marginal indications for therapy based on current guidelines and may be able to remain off therapy for a substantial period of time following a period of full viral suppression and $CD4^+$ gain. Structured or strategic treatment interruption has raised many practical and theoretical questions. This must be seen as a research tool and cannot be recommended apart from in controlled trials.

Despite impressive progress, much work remains to be done. In Western countries, increasing progress in antiretroviral therapy will result from new data obtained in clinical trials, a better knowledge of the pathophysiology of the disease, an increased awareness of the long-term toxicity of drugs and of viral cross-resistance, and the availability of new drugs.

Finally, we cannot forget that, on a global scale, the recent impressive therapeutic gains have only benefited 10% of those infected in the world. In the southern hemisphere the epidemic is reversing decades of development and widening the gap between rich and poor nations.

The dramatic inequalities between rich and poor nations in caring for persons living with HIV/AIDS highlight the moral imperative to develop strategies to increase access to life-saving treatments for the majority of infected people. The impact that AIDS is having on societies and communities makes it not only the most dramatic health emergency of our times but also the major developmental threat to populations and countries in the southern hemisphere. This is why – in addition to humanitarian and ethical reasons – there is an urgent need to start reversing this catastrophe and to bring HIV care and medicines to the developing world.

Although this may be seen as one of the most difficult scientific, social, political and economic challenges of our century, universal access to HIV treatment should be seen as the ultimate goal.

REFERENCES

1. Wei X, Ghosh SK, Taylor ME, *et al.* Viral dynamics in human immunodeficiency virus type 1 infection. Nature 1995;373:117–22.
2. Mellors JW, Kinsley LA, Rinaldo CR Jr, *et al.* Prognosis in HIV-1 infection predicted by the quantity of virus in plasma. Science 1996;272:1167–70.
3. D'Aquila RT, Johnson VA, Welles SL, *et al.* Zidovudine resistance and HIV-1 disease progression during antiretroviral therapy. Ann Intern Med 1995;122:401–8.
4. Hammer S, Katzenstein D, Hughes M, *et al.* A trial comparing nucleoside monotherapy with combination therapy in HIV infected adults with CD4 cell counts from 200 to 500 per cubic millimeter. N Engl J Med 1996;335:1081–90.
5. O'Brien WA, Hartigan PM, Martin D, *et al.* Changes in plasma HIV-1 RNA and $CD4^+$ lymphocyte counts and the risk of progression to AIDS. N Engl J Med 1996;334:426–31.
6. Perelson AS, Essunger P, Cao Y, *et al.* Decay characteristics of HIV-1 infected compartments during combination therapy. Nature 1997;387:188–91.
7. Volberding PA, Lagakos SW, Koch MA, *et al.* Zidovudine in asymptomatic human immunodeficiency infection. A controlled trial in person with fewer than 500 CD4-positive cells per cubic millimeter. N Engl J Med 1990;322:941–9.
8. Concorde Coordinating Committee. Concorde: MRC/ARNS randomised double-blind controlled trial of immediate and deferred zidovudine in symptom-free HIV infection. Lancet 1994;343:871–81.
9. Kahn JO, Lagakos SW, Richman DD, *et al.* A controlled trial comparing continued zidovudine with didanosine in human immunodeficiency virus infection. N Engl J Med 1992;327:581–7.

10. Delta Coordinating Committee. Delta: a randomised double-blind controlled trial comparing combinations of zidovudine plus didanosine or zalcitabine with zidovudine alone in HIV-infected individuals. Lancet 1996;348:283–91.
11. Deeks SG, Smith M, Holodniy M, Kahn JO. HIV-1 protease inhibitors. JAMA 1996;277:145–53.
12. Brinkman K, Smeitink J, Romijn J, Reiss P. Mitochondrial toxicity induced by nucleoside analogue reverse transcriptase inhibitors is a key factor in the pathogenesis of antiretroviral therapy related lipodystrophy. Lancet 1999;354:1112–5.
13. Ho H-T, Hitchcock MJ. Cellular pharmacology of 2′-3′-dideoxy-2′-3′-didehydrothymidine, a nucleoside analog active against human immunodeficiency virus. Antimicrob Agents Chemother 1989;33:844–9.
14. Foster RH, Faulds D. Abacavir. Drugs 1998;55:729–36.
15. Gazzard B, Pozniak A, Arasteh K, *et al.* TMC125, a next-generation NNRTI, demonstrates high potency after 7 days therapy in treatment-experienced HIV-1-infected individuals with phenotypic NNRTI resistance. In: 9th Conference on Retroviruses and Opportunistic Infections, Seattle, WA, 24–28 February 2002:Abstract 4.
16. Schwartz R, Kazanjian P, Slater L, *et al.* Resistance to tipranavir is uncommon in a randomized trial of tipranavir/ritonavir (TPV/RTV) in multiple PI-failure patients (BI 1182.2). In: 9th Conference on Retroviruses and Opportunistic Infections, Seattle, WA, 24–28 February 2002:Abstract 562.
17. Larder BA, Kemp SD, Harrigan R. Potential mechanism for sustained antiretroviral efficacy of AZT–3TC combination therapy. Science 1995;269:696–9.
18. Tisdale M, Myers RE, Maschera B, *et al.* Cross-resistance analysis of human immunodeficiency virus type 1 variants individually selected for resistance to five different protease inhibitors. Antimicrob Agents Chemother 1995;39:1704–10.
19. Wei X, Decker JM, Liu H, *et al.* Emergence of resistant Human Immunodeficiency virus type 1 in patients receiving fusion inhibitor (T-20) monotherapy. Antimicrob Agents Chemother 2002;46:1896–905.
20. Yeni P, Hammer SM, Carpenter CC, *et al.* Antiretroviral treatment for adult HIV infection in 2002: updated recommendations of the International AIDS Society-USA Panel. JAMA 2002;288:222–35.
21. US Public Health Service. Guidelines for the use of antiretroviral agents in HIV-infected adults and adolescents. Updated 4 February 4 2002. Available at: http://www.hivatis.org/trtgdlns.html#Adult.
22. Gao, WY, Shirasaka T, Johns DG, *et al.* Differential phosphorylation of azidothymidine, dideoxycytidine, and dideoxyinosine in resting and activated peripheral blood mononuclear cells. J Clin Invest 1993;91:2326–33.
23. Baxter JD, Mayers DL, Wentworth DN, *et al.* A randomized study of antiretroviral management based on plasma genotypic antiretroviral resistance testing in patients failing therapy. CPCRA 046 Study Team for the Terry Beirn Community Programs for Clinical Research on AIDS. AIDS 2000;14:F83–93.
24. Tural C, Ruiz L, Holtzer C, *et al.* Clinical utility of HIV-1 genotyping and expert advice: the Havana trial. AIDS 2002;16:209–18.
25. Cingolani A, Antinori A, Rizzo MG, *et al.* Usefulness of monitoring HIV drug resistance and adherence in individuals failing highly active antiretroviral therapy: a randomized study (ARGENTA). AIDS 2002;16:369–79.
26. Cohen CJ, Hunt S, Sension M, *et al.* A randomized trial assessing the impact of phenotypic resistance testing on antiretroviral therapy. AIDS 2002;16:579–88.
27. Meynard JL, Vray M, Morand-Joubert L, *et al.* Phenotypic or genotypic resistance testing for choosing antiretroviral therapy after treatment failure: a randomized trial. AIDS 2002;16:727–36.
28. Grant RM, Hecht FM, Warmerdam M, *et al.* Time trends in primary HIV-1 drug resistance among recently infected persons. JAMA 2002;288:181–8.

chapter
140 Immunobased Therapies

Richard B Pollard & Michelle Onorato

INTRODUCTION

Paralleling the development of more effective and better tolerated antiretroviral therapy for HIV infection has been the growing interest in developing alternative therapeutic approaches. Recent appreciation of the limitations and adverse effects of long-term antiretroviral therapy led to continued exploration of immune-based therapy for HIV infection. Both enhancement of HIV-specific immune responses and stimulation of general immune responses are potential strategies for immune-based therapies of HIV infection that are being developed. Table 140.1 outlines these approaches, which may be of particular value in the treatment of later stage patients, whose high levels of viremia and previous exposure to therapy place them at greatest risk of developing resistance to therapeutic agents and who also have the greatest need for a restoration of normal immune function. However, such interventions must be used with care to avoid compromising the effects of highly active antiretroviral therapy (HAART), which has significant antiviral and immunologic activity.

ENHANCEMENT OF HIV-SPECIFIC IMMUNITY

There are four approaches to the enhancement of HIV-specific response:

- structured treatment interruption or treatment cycling eventually resulting in viral rebound and rechallenge;
- administration of HIV-specific therapeutic and prophylactic vaccines (which are discussed in detail in Chapter 118);
- administration of passive immunotherapy, via either transfer of pooled immunoglobulin from people who have HIV infection or monoclonal antibodies to specific viral epitopes; and
- passive transfer of specific cell populations in an effort to enhance immune responsiveness to HIV.

A better understanding of host response to HIV infection, both by cellular immune responses and by the antibody response (particularly neutralizing antibody response), has led to refinement of the above strategies. However, enhancement of the HIV-specific immune response does not necessarily lead to improved clearance of the virus.

STRATEGIES OF IMMUNOBASED THERAPY	
Enhancement of HIV-specific immunity	Therapeutic vaccine Transfer of HIV-specific cell populations Transfer of pooted immune sera Transfer of monoclonal antibody
General immune enhancement	Inhibition of proinflammatory cytokines Administration of immune modulators (i.e. interleukin (IL)-2, IL-12, interferon (IFN)-α)

Table 140.1 Strategies of immunobased therapy.

Therapeutic vaccination

Although early attempts to enhance HIV-specific immunity by immunization with HIV-specific antigens in the era prior to effective antiretroviral therapy did result in enhanced lymphoproliferative response, these apparent immunologic benefits did not lead to improved clinical outcome with respect to disease progression or control of viral replication. Clinical trials of various gp120 vaccines in patients with early and later stage HIV infection did not show an effect on viral replication or rate of CD4 cell decline[1] despite immunologic response to immunization (particularly in the higher CD4 group). Another therapeutic vaccine tested extensively in clinical trails is the gp120 depleted Remune® product, which has been shown to induce LPA responses in several cohorts; although in a large multicenter US trial clinical benefit was not observed.[2,3] However, the lack of benefit seen in the setting of continued viral replication, prior to treatment with effective antiretroviral therapy, may be due to the already maximal benefit of antigen-driven responses in these subjects and so the role of therapeutic vaccination in stimulating HIV-specific immunity and providing antigenic stimulation may be quite different in the setting of undetectable levels of circulating virus. Several approaches are being explored to induce immune response to envelope, internal coat and accessory protein epitopes; these include recombinant proteins, peptide, naked DNA, viral vectors and prime-boost combinations. In addition to exploring the types of vaccines that will prove effective in therapeutic vaccination, there is great interest in therapeutic vaccination in conjunction with other immune modulators, such as administration of interleukin-2 and the ALVAC vaccine, or vaccination in combination with treatment cycling.

Structured treatment interruption

Structured treatment interruption (STI) was first proposed as a strategy to boost HIV-specific responses capable of controlling viral replication after the report of a patient treated during primary HIV infection with effective antiretroviral therapy who was able to control viral replication for a prolonged period after cycling on and off therapy twice; this patient demonstrated T-cell-mediated immunity without detectable neutralizing antibodies to HIV.[4] Further study of STI in patients treated early in the course of HIV infection showed that, in many patients, control of viremia could be achieved by T- cell-mediated immune response.[5,6] However, because the success of the autologous immunization during STI depends on a robust immune response, the promise of this strategy in the chronically HIV-infected patient is less clear, given the wider variation in immune response that can be induced in this patient population. The Swiss-Spanish Study is the largest clinical trial of STI in chronically infected patients. Subjects were treated for 2 weeks off followed by 8 weeks on HAART; this was repeated for four cycles, then therapy was interrupted until viral load rebounded to >5000 copies/ml. All but nine of 54 subjects reached this threshold within 12 weeks, including all subjects with baseline viral loads of >100,000 copies/ml, suggesting this approach has limited value in chronic infection. Also, patients with highest viral loads and lowest CD4 counts at baseline were the most likely to be unable to achieve undetectable levels of viremia after resumption of therapy. The degree of virologic control and duration of suppression in these chronically infected patients seem to depend on the magnitude of cell-mediated responses. Although exposure to circulating virus results in mobilization of HIV-specific T-cell response, suppression is transient as these T-cell populations are eventually exhausted in the face of continued viral replication.[7–9]

HIV-specific cytotoxic T-lymphocyte responses

The interaction between HIV-1 and the cellular immune response is central to the immunopathogenesis of HIV infection, and delineation of this interaction may lead to interventions that can change the natural history of HIV infection.

Much attention has been focused on understanding the cellular immune response following primary infection as it is responsible in part for a several log drop in viral replication following the initial burst of viremia. Primary infection, with its high levels of viremia, is also the time when the virus begins to develop genetic diversity in response to selective pressures exerted by the host immune response. This dynamic interaction at the initial phase of HIV infection sets the stage for the natural history of HIV infection.

Several studies have suggested that the cell-mediated immune response, rather than specific neutralizing antibody, is the main mechanism responsible for this initial control of viral replication.

The first piece of evidence is the finding that HIV-specific cytotoxic T lymphocytes (CTLs) can be found just as high levels of viremia begin to abate and before the rise in neutralizing antibody titers, suggesting that the CTL response is responsible for declines in initial viremia.[10,11] In addition, the HIV-1-specific CTL response is demonstrable as early as 21 days following clinical presentation with primary infection and is directed at diverse epitopes within many of the HIV-1 gene products.[11]

Nonhuman primate models of primary infection with simian immunodeficiency virus (SIV) show a remarkably parallel sequence of events; within 4 weeks of detecting SIV p27 antigen in blood and SIV RNA in the extrafollicular and sinusoidal areas of lymphoid tissue, p27 antigen is cleared. Increased numbers of $CD8^+$ lymphocytes are detected in the periphery and in lymph nodes at the same time as this plasma viremia is declining. Humoral and cellular SIV-specific immune responses can be detected within 2 weeks of initial infection. Therefore, both human and simian data suggest that the remarkable containment of initial viremia is largely due to both humoral and cellular immune responses.[12]

Further study has shown that, although the CTL response during primary infection develops to multiple antigenic determinants, this repertoire is more limited than would be predicted. It is this limitation that perhaps allows the virus, with its genetic diversity, a chance to escape immune surveillance by mutating critical epitopes.[11,13] Indeed, in a patient with early HIV infection, serial observations revealed an early CTL response aimed at a highly immunodominant epitope in gp160. However, with a mutation resulting in a single amino acid change, an escape mutant emerged that could not be recognized by epitope-specific CTLs. Therefore, the CTL response can exert selective pressure, which drives the emergence of resistant virus, just as is seen with antiretroviral therapy.[14] Implications of this finding include:

- vaccine strategies that result in CTL response to multiple co-dominant epitopes; and
- the importance of concurrent antiretroviral and immune-based approaches to therapy of HIV infection.

Data from natural history studies as well as study of long-term non-progressors with HIV-1 infection suggest that the immunopathogenesis of HIV infection is influenced by the quality of the CTL response. For example, CTL activity is preserved in the long-term nonprogressors, which is in stark contrast to vertically infected children, who generally have little CTL response and rapid progression of clinical disease.[14,15] Furthermore, longitudinal studies of CTL response over time show a steady decline in HIV-1-specific CTL precursor cells, paralleling the decline in the ability of $CD8^+$ lymphocytes to suppress HIV replication with progressive infection.[16]

Transfer of HIV-specific cell populations

Given the importance of cell-mediated immunity both in primary infection and in the asymptomatic nonprogressors, the ex vivo propagation and expansion of lymphocyte populations and reinfusion of expanded cell populations to people who have HIV infection is a potential treatment strategy that is currently being explored. One study examined the ex-vivo expansion of unfractionated lymphocytes from an HIV-negative identical twin and infusion of the expanded cell population to the HIV-infected twin. This appeared to be safe, and to result in increases in $CD4^+$ lymphocyte counts in the twin who had the infection.[17]

Dendritic cells, which are key in developing T-cell-dependent immunity by activating quiescent T cells, including naive T cells, and by inducing CD4 and CD8 killer T cells, are also being explored as an HIV-specific cell population that could help boost CTL response to HIV. Sensitized enriched populations of dendritic cells have been used to enhance CTL response in patients with lymphoma and melanoma, as well as other malignancies, with demonstrated immunologic and some clinical benefit.[18–21] Clinical trials will employ this strategy comparing CTL responses in patients immunized with ALVAC alone versus those who receive subcutaneous reinfusion of populations of ALVAC-exposed dendritic cells.

Another approach is the adoptive transfer of $CD8^+$ lymphocytes following expansion. Preliminary reports suggest that these re-infused cells have little CTL activity, and that the majority are rapidly cleared from the circulation. The administration of $CD8^+$ lymphocytes expanded ex vivo with interleukin (IL)-2 has been investigated as a potential therapy for Kaposi's sarcoma.[22]

Another strategy under investigation is the administration of HIV-specific autologous CTL cell lines that have been selected in vitro and expanded for reinfusion; the safety and effects on immunologic parameters of this approach are currently under study. The finding that $CD4^+$ lymphocytes can be expanded in vitro in the presence of three antiretroviral drugs holds promise for autologous expanded $CD4^+$ lymphocytes as therapy as well.[23]

The limitations of these approaches are:

- the enormous investment in cell culture facilities;
- careful quality control; and
- the variable half-life of the reinfused cells, necessitating repeated administrations.

Transfer of pooled immune sera

The strategy of transferring pooled antibodies from donors who have HIV infection or of monoclonal antibodies directed against HIV is of interest not only as a potential prophylactic measure to prevent infection in exposed seronegative individuals, but also as an attempt to enhance antiviral activity in the serum of individuals who already have HIV infection. This could occur not only by neutralization of the virus, but perhaps also by enhancement of antibody-dependent cellular cytotoxicity and increased complement-mediated lysis. The long half-life of antibodies makes this approach particularly attractive, as intermittent therapy at bimonthly intervals may be practical. The drawbacks of this approach again relate to the genetic diversity of HIV and the potential for the development of mutants not recognized by the more specific antibody preparations. In addition, the vast amount of circulating viral antigen could potentially lead to the formation of immune complexes, resulting in adverse effects due to their deposition in various tissues, although to date there have been no reported adverse events after these infusions that can be related to immune complex deposition.

Trials of polyclonal antisera

Two controlled trials evaluating the effect of HIV immune plasma on disease progression in HIV-positive individuals have been published. One reported no benefit;[24] in the second, in which patients received either immune plasma or plasma from negative donors every 2 weeks for 1 year, there was a significant decrease in the number of opportunistic infections in subjects receiving immune sera.[25] Others have reported preliminary results of similar strategies, using pooled hyperimmune plasma or a sterile filtered pooled high-titer anti-HIV plasma preparation (treated with β-propiolactone to inactivate any HIV that may be present).[26,27]

The role of hyperimmune anti-HIV intravenous immunoglobulin (IVIG) in preventing perinatal transmission has also been assessed. In a phase 1–2 double-blind controlled study by the pediatric AIDS Clinical Trials Group (ACTG), 28 maternal–infant pairs were randomized to receive either HIV hyperimmune IVIG or placebo (IVIG) beginning at between 20 and 30 weeks of gestation; all of the mothers enrolled were receiving zidovudine. Mothers received infusions every 28 days until delivery; infants received a single infusion within 12 hours of birth. All mothers and infants received zidovudine as per the ACTG 076 protocol. Sustained suppression of immune complex dissociated p24 antigenemia was seen in the treated women, although no change was seen in quantitative HIV RNA. Infants in the treatment group had higher levels of p24 antibody at birth, confirming transplacental transfer of antibody from the HIV hyperimmune IVIG infusions.[28]

Further studies are necessary before the significance of these results and the potential for specific immunoglobulin as therapy are fully understood.

Various trials have also examined the efficacy of IVIG without specific anti-HIV activity and consistently show no effect on HIV-related virologic or immunologic parameters, although IVIG may have a role in reducing the frequency of bacterial infections.[29]

Transfer of monoclonal antibody

Another approach that has been considered is the administration of specific monoclonal antibodies to various epitopes of HIV. This has been limited by concerns that the virus would acquire resistance to specific antibodies, although this may be overcome by administering antibody combinations that are directed at more than one neutralizing epitope. Another obstacle to clinical trials of specific monoclonal antibodies is the expense of the large-scale production that would be required.

The first step in developing monoclonal antibodies to be tested in clinical trials is to identify epitopes that will induce antibodies that will result in anti-HIV activity. Most attention to date has focused on antibodies to various surface epitopes of HIV, either to the V3 loop, C4 and gp41 or, in the case of F105 (a monoclonal antibody), directed against the CD4 binding site. Combinations of these antibodies in vitro show at least additive activity and, against some strains of HIV, synergistic activity.

The F105 antibody has been evaluated in a dose-escalating phase 1–2 ACTG trial; half-lives of the antibody were prolonged, but there was no change in HIV titers.[30]

GENERAL IMMUNE ENHANCEMENT

The availability of cytokine inhibitors that could potentially counteract the overproduction of cytokines seen in HIV infection and of general immune stimulators has led to interest in manipulating the immune system as a therapeutic tool.

Theoretically, the general immune stimulation or suppression that may result from these manipulations may hasten the rate of HIV progression, particularly as there is concern that stimulation of certain cell populations may enhance HIV replication. Therefore, active antiretroviral therapy has to be administered concurrently with any of these modulators of the immune system.

Inhibition of proinflammatory cytokines

The cytokine that has been most extensively studied is tumor necrosis factor (TNF)-α because:

- it is produced in large quantities in HIV infection; and
- it upregulates HIV expression in vitro.

Pentoxifylline, thalidomide and corticosteroids have all been studied as potential therapies because they inhibit TNF-α production.

Pentoxifylline

Studies of the use of pentoxifylline in people who have HIV infection have shown a decrease in TNF-α mRNA; however, in a controlled trial of pentoxifylline at the highest tolerable dosages, no significant antiviral effect was detected.[29] It seems that the benefit is seen mainly in patients who have high pretreatment levels of TNF-α. This observation led to the initiation of a placebo-controlled trial of pentoxifylline in people who have HIV infection with active pulmonary tuberculosis in Uganda, because they have very high levels of circulating TNF-α. The patients enrolled in this study had relatively early HIV infection, with a mean $CD4^+$ lymphocyte count of 380/μl, and did not receive other antiretroviral therapy. Patients in the pentoxifylline arm had lower levels of HIV RNA than the control arm and reduced levels of β_2-microglobulin; however, no difference was observed in the two groups with regard to new AIDS-defining illness or survival.[31–34]

Thalidomide

Thalidomide is also known to inhibit production of TNF-α and has been shown to inhibit HIV-1 replication in vitro. A placebo-controlled trial has shown benefit in the treatment of HIV-associated oral and esophageal aphthous ulcers. Of note, patients in the thalidomide arm appeared to have increases in HIV-1 RNA, underscoring the importance of concurrent antiretroviral therapy.[35,36]

Corticosteroids

The observation that corticosteroids appear to benefit patients with HIV-associated nephropathy has led to interest in them for interrupting cytokine activity, but there are insufficient controlled data to evaluate their use.

Ciclosporin

Ciclosporin has been proposed as an immunomodulatory agent with potential activity in HIV infection. A phase 2 trial of ciclosporin versus placebo in patients with early HIV infection ($CD4^+$ lymphocyte count >500/μl) has been completed; although the drug was well tolerated in this population, it had no effect on level of immune activation or CD4 count at the dose studied. However, Pantaleo and others reported a positive effect of a limited course of ciclosporin A when given in conjunction with HAART to patients during primary HIV infection as compared with HAART alone. The group that received ciclosporin showed acute benefit in terms of restoration of normal $CD4^+$ cell number and proportion, which was seen more than a year after the ciclosporin was stopped. It appears that dampening of T-cell activation during primary infection may have lasting immunologic benefit.[37]

Cyclophosphamide

Administration of cytotoxic therapy has been postulated as a way to reduce the cellular reservoir of HIV in chronically infected patients on HAART. A study, ACTG 380, was designed to address this question: 10 treatment-naive individuals were randomized to receive either antiretroviral therapy alone or escalating doses of cyclophosphamide after they had achieved a viral load of <50 copies/ml. The drug was well tolerated, but no difference was seen between the two groups in terms of peripheral blood or lymphoid HIV DNA levels.[38]

Enhancement of immune response via cytokines and lymphokines: administration of immune modulators

Recent studies of administration of immune modulators have focused mainly on IL-2 and interferon (IFN)-α.

Interferon-α

Low-dose oral IFN-α has been studied with and without concurrent antiretroviral administration; there appears to be little benefit with regard to antiviral activity. Subcutaneous IFN-α in combination with other antiviral agents has also been evaluated. The most positive data regarding IFN-α to date are for its use in the treatment of HIV-associated thrombocytopenia. Patients in two uncontrolled studies showed benefit with regard to platelet levels at low doses of this agent.[39–42] In general, systemic administration of IFN-α has resulted in unacceptable toxicity and marginal benefit in patients who have HIV infection, limiting its clinical usefulness, although the use of pegylated interferon as an antiviral agent for HIV infection is being tested in clinical trials.

Interleukin-2

Interleukin-2 has emerged as a potentially exciting agent for immune-based therapy of HIV infection. Results of a small trial of intermittent intravenous IL-2 (5-day continuous infusions every 8 weeks) are encouraging. Of patients who had baseline $CD4^+$ lymphocyte counts over 200/μl, 60% showed sustained increases in $CD4^+$ lymphocyte counts following treatment. This increase in $CD4^+$ lymphocyte count was seen over a 14-month follow-up of these patients, although no change was seen in plasma HIV RNA levels or levels of p24 antigenemia. In patients who had a baseline $CD4^+$ lymphocyte count of less than 100/μl, no benefit was seen in terms of $CD4^+$ lymphocyte count. However, the transient rise in viral load reported in preliminary studies of IL-2 use in patients who have later stage HIV infection was not seen in this study, presumably because of concurrent antiretroviral therapy.[43,44]

A major drawback of this approach is the frequency of continuous intravenous therapy, and so trials of subcutaneous or intermittent intravenous IL-2 are in progress. ACTG 328 is a trial of intravenous IL-2 with HAART versus subcutaneous IL-2 with HAART versus HAART alone. Primary analysis at weeks 60 and 84 showed marked and sustained increases in $CD4^+$ cells counts. Furthermore, significant increases in naive and memory $CD4^+$ cells were seen along with increases in $CD25^+$, $CD28^+$ and $CD95^+$ subpopulations in both treatment arms. Assessment of AIDS-defining events suggested a lower incidence of progression to AIDS in the two treatment arms compared with HAART alone. Two other long-term studies (SILCAT and ESPRIT) are underway examining the benefit of IL-2 in patients receiving HAART, but will require several years of follow-up to gather adequate clinical end-point data.

Interleukin-12

Interleukin-12 is currently in phase 1 clinical trials. It is known to increase natural killer lymphocyte and CTL activity in vitro and to be deficient in people who have HIV-1 infection. It is hoped that treatment will stimulate the development of T-helper type 1 lymphocytes, reverting the shift to T-helper type 2 predominance that is seen in HIV infection and may be a detrimental consequence of the host response to HIV-1 infection.[45] In a preliminary study, IL-12 was well tolerated in doses of up to 100ng/kg in patients with <50 CD4 cells/mm³, and up to 300ng/kg in a group with higher CD4 counts. Although IL-12 administration resulted in significant dose-related decreases in serum neopterin, no change in LPA response to HIV or *M. avium-intracellulare* was seen; nor was any change in serum IFN-γ levels or HIV RNA levels seen.[46]

Granulocyte-macrophage colony-stimulating factor

Granulocyte-macrophage colony-stimulating factor (GM-CSF) is another immune modulator that has been examined for its effect on HIV disease progression. ACTG 5041 was a two-step clinical trial with an initial randomized, placebo-controlled phase, followed by a open label phase, which looked at the effect of GM-CSF on CD4 counts and HIV viral loads in patients with stable, quantifiable viral loads. Initial analysis showed a trend toward higher viral load and higher CD4 counts in the treatment group at 16 weeks.[47]

CONCLUSION

In summary, both pharmacologic and immunologic approaches to new interventions for HIV infection have yielded a number of encouraging agents and potential combinations of agents. The challenge is to sort out which strategies are likely to result in long-term clinical benefit with minimum toxicity in the setting of planning therapy for a chronic disease such as HIV infection. In a rapidly changing environment of new antiretrovirals, the position of immunologic therapy will have to be carefully understood. Major developments in the suppression of HIV with significant improvements in immune function have been reported. However, whether immune function can be restored with antiretroviral therapy alone is unclear at present. It is likely that immune-based therapies will be an important adjuvant to antiretroviral therapy in some patient populations.

REFERENCES

1. Schooley RT, Spino C, Kuritzkes D, *et al.* For the ACTG 209 and 214 Study Teams. Two double blinded, randomized, comparitive trials of 4 human immunodeficiency virus type 1 envelope vaccines in HIV-1-infected individuals across a spectrum of disease severity: AIDS Clinical Trials Group 209 and 214. J Infect Dis 2000;182:1357–64.
2. Moss RB, Wallace MR, Giermakowska WK, *et al.* Phenotypic analysis of human immunodeficiency virus type 1 cell mediated immune responses after treatment with an HIV-1 immunogen. J Infect Dis 1999;180:641–8.
3. Maino VC, Suni MA, Wormsley SB, *et al.* Enhancement of HIV-1 antigen specific $CD4^+$ T cell memeory in patients with chronic HIV type 1 infection receiving an HIV type–1 immunogen. AIDS Res Hum Retroviruses 2000;16:539–47.
4. Lisziewicz J, Rosenberg E, Lieverman J, *et al.* Control of HIV despite the discontinuation of antiretroviral therapy. N Engl J Med 1999;340:1683–4.
5. Rosenberg ES, Altfield M, Poon SH, *et al.* Immune control of HIV-1 after early treatment of acute infection. Nature 2000;407:523–6.
6. Ortiz GM, Nixon DF, Trkola A, *et al.* HIV-1 specific immune responses in subjects who temporarily contain virus replication after duscintinuation of highly active antiretroviral therapy. J Clin Invest 1999;104:R13–8.
7. Papasavvas E, Ortiz GM, Gross R, *et al.* Enhancement of human immunodeficiency virus type-1 specific CD4 and CD8 T cell responses in chronically infected persons after temporary treatment interruption. J Infect Dis 2000;182:766–75.
8. Carcelain C, Tubaina R, Samri A, *et al.* Transient mobilization of human immunodeficiency virus

specific CD4 T-helper cells fails to control virus rebounds during intermittent antiretroviral therapy in chronic HIV-1 infection. J Virol 2001;75:234–41.
9. Ruiz L, Carcelain C, Martinez-Picardo J, *et al.* HIV dynamics and T-cell immunity after three structured treatment interruptions in chronic HIV infection. AIDS 2001;15:F19–27.
10. Koup RA, Safrit JT, Cao Y, *et al.* Temporal association of cellular immune responses with initial control of viremia in primary HIV-1 syndrome. J Virol 1994;68:4650–5.
11. Pantaleo G, Demarest JF, Soudeyns H, *et al.* Major expansion of $CD8^+$ T cells with a predominant Vb usage during the primary immune response to HIV. Nature 1994;370:463–7.
12. Safrit JT, Andrews CA, Zhu T, *et al.* Characterization of HIV-1 specific cytotoxic T lymphocyte clones isolated during acute seroconversion: recognition of autologous virus sequences within a conserved imunodominant epitope. J Exp Med 1994;179:463–72.
13. Borrow P, Lewicki H, Hahn BH, *et al.* Virus specific $CD8^+$ cytotoxic T-lymphocyte activity associated with control of viremia in primary HIV-1 infection. J Virol 1994;68:6103–10.
14. Reimann KA, Tenner-Racz K, Racz P, *et al.* Immunopathogenic events in acute infection of rhesus monkeys with SIV of macaques. J Virol 1994;68:2362–70.
15. Coullin I, Culmann-Penciolelli B, Gomard E, *et al.* Impaired CTL recognition due to genetic variations in the main immunogenic recognition of the HIV-1 Nef protein. J Exp Med 1994;180:1129–34.
16. Borrow P, Lewicki H, Wei X, *et al.* Antiviral pressure exerted by HIV-1 specific cytotoxic T lymphocytes during primary infection demonstrated by rapid selection of CTL escape virus. Nature Med 1997;3:205–11.
17. Walker R, Larson M, Cartert C, *et al.* Adoptive immunotherapy using activated expanded synergistic lymphocytes in HIV-infected identical twins [Abstract WS-B286]. IX International Conference on AIDS/IV STD World Congress. Berlin; 1993:71.
18. Hsu FJ, Benike C, Fagoni F, *et al.* Vaccination of patients with B-cell lymphoma using autologous antigen-pulsed dendritic cells. Nat Med 1996;2:52–8.
19. Holtl L, Rieser C, Papesh C, *et al.* $CD83^+$ blood dendrititic cells as a vaccine for immunotherapy of metastatic renal cell cancer. Lancet 1998;352:1358.
20. Murphy GP, Tjoa BA, Simmons SJ, *et al.* Phase II prostate cancer trial; report of a study involving 37 patients with disease recurrence following primary treatment. Prostate 1999;39:54–9.
21. Thurner B, Haendle I, Roder C, *et al.* Vaccination with MAGE-3A1 peptide-pulsed mature, monocyte-derived dendritic cells expands specific cytotoxic. T cells and induces regression of some metastasis in advanced stage IV melanoma. J Exp Med 1999;190:1669–78.
22. Klimas N, Fletcher M, Walling J, *et al.* Response of Kaposi's sarcoma to autologous CD8 cells expanded and activated *ex vivo* and re-infused with rIL-2 [Abstract WSB152]. IX International Conference on AIDS/IV STD World Congress. Berlin; 1993:58.
23. Wilson CC, Wong JT, Rosenthal TM, *et al.* Ex-vivo expansion of $CD4^+$ T lymphocytes from HIV-1 seropositive perso in the absence of ongoing viral replication [Abstract 111]. In: Abstracts of the First National Conference on Human Retroviruses. Washington DC: American Society for Microbiology; 1993:75.
24. Jacobson JM, Colman N, Ostrow NA, *et al.* Passive immunotherapy in treatment of advanced HIV infection. J Infect Dis 1993;298:305.
25. Lefrere JJ, Vittecoq D. The French Passive Immunotherapy Collaborative Study Group. Passive immunotherapy in AIDS: results of a double blind randomized phase II study [Abstract L12]. In: Abstracts of the First National Conference on Human Retroviruses. Washington DC: American Society for Microbiology; 1993:29.
26. Karpas A, Bainbridge S. Passive immunization in HIV disease [Abstract PO-A28–0659]. IX International Conference on AIDS/IV STD World Congress. Berlin; 1993:244.
27. Levy J, Youvan T. The California Physician Study Group for PHT. Efficacy and safety of passive hyperimmune therapy in HIV disease [Abstract PO-B28–2149]. IX International Conference on AIDS/IV STD World Congress. Berlin; 1993:493.
28. Lambert SJ, Mofenson LM, Fletcher CV, *et al.* for the Pediatric Aids Clinical Trials Group Protocol 185 Pharmacokinetic Study Group. Safety and pharmacokinetics of hyperimmune anti-HIV immunoglobulin administered to HIV-infected pregnant women and their newborns. J Infect Dis 1997;175:283–91.
29. Pollard RB, Forrest BD. Immunologic therapy for HIV-infected individuals, 1993–1994. AIDS 1994:8(Suppl.1):S295.
30. Wolfe EJ, Samore MH, Cavacini LA, *et al.* Pharmacokinetics of F105, a monoclonal antibody, in subjects with HIV infection. Clin Pharmacol Ther 1996;59:662–7.
31. Dezube BJ, Lederman ML, Spritzler JG, *et al.* High-dose pentoxyphylline in patients with AIDS inhibition of tumor necrosis factor production. J Infect Dis 1995;171:1628–32.
32. DeZube BJ, Lederman MM, Pardee AB, *et al.* Pentoxyphyline decreases tumor necrosis factor and may decrease HIV replication in AIDS patients [Abstract PO-B26–2142]. IX International Conference on AIDS/IV STD World Congress. Berlin; 1993:492.
33. Mole L, Margolis D, Holodniy M. A pilot study of pentoxyphylline in HIV-infected patients with $CD4^+$ lymphocytes less than 400 cells/mm^3 [Abstract PO-B26–2116]. IX International Conference on AIDS/IV STD World Congress. Berlin; 1993:488.
34. Wallis RS, Nsubuga P, Whalen C, *et al.* Pentoxyphylline therapy in human immunodeficiency virus positive persons with tuberculosis: a randomized, controlled trial. J Infect Dis 1996;174:727–33.
35. Jacobson JM, Greenspan JS, Spritler J, *et al.* Thalidomide for the treatment of oral aphthous ulcers in patients with human immunodefiency virus infection. NIADS AIDS Clinical Trails Group. N Engl J Med 1997;336:1487–93.
36. Wohl, D, Aweeka F, Schmidt JL, *et al.* Safety, tolerability, and pharmacokinetic effects of thalidomide in patients infected with Human Immunodeficiency virus: ACTG 267. J Infect Dis 2002;185:1359–63.
37. Rizzardi GP, Harai A, Capiluppi B, *et al.* Treatment of primary Hiv-1 infection with cyclosporin A coupled with highly active antiretroviral therapy. J Clini Invest 2002;109:688.
38. Bartlett JA, Silberman M, Miralles GD, *et al.* Antiretroviral therapy plus cyclophosphamide to diminish HIV-DNA in lymphoid tissues. Abstract #16. 8th Conference on Human Retroviruses and Opportunistic Infections, Chicago, 2001.
39. Jablonowski H, Mauss S, Knechten H, *et al.* Combination therapy with zidovudine and low dose alpha interferon in HIV seropositive patients with rapidly declining $CD4^+$ lymphocyte counts [Abstract PO-B28–2148]. IX International Conference on AIDS/IV STD World Congress. Berlin; 1993:493.
40. Nadler J, Toney J, Holt D, *et al.* Comparison of Retrovir, HIVID, and Wellferon vs Retrovir and HIVID in HIV-infected patients without AIDS [Abstract 688]. XXXIII Interscience Conference on Antimicrobial Agents and Chemotherapy. New Orleans: American Society for Microbiology; 1993:245.
41. Vianelli N, Catani L, Gugliotta L, *et al.* Recombinant alpha interferon 2b in the treatment of HIV-related thrombocytopenia. AIDS 1993;7:823–7.
42. Fabris F, Sgarabotto D, Zanoan E, *et al.* The effect of a single course of alpha-2b-interferon in patients with HIV-related and chronic idiopathic immune thrombocytopenia. Autoimmunity 1993;14:175–9.
43. Kovacs JA, Baseler M, Lane HC, *et al.* Increases in CD4 T lymphocytes with intermittent courses of IL-2 in patients with HIV infection. N Engl J Med 1995;332:567–75.
44. Kovacs JA, Vogel S, Albert JM, *et al.* Controlled trial of interleukin-2 infusion in patients infected with the human immunodeficiency virus. N Engl J Med 1996;335:1350–6.
45. Foli A, Saville MW, Baseler MW, *et al.* Effects of the Th1 and Th2 stimulatory cytokines interleukin-12 and interleukin-4 on HIV replication. Blood 1995;85:2114–23.
46. Jacobson MA, Spritzler J, Landay A, *et al.* For the ACTG 325 Protocol Team. A phase I, placebo-controlled trail of multi-dose recombinant human interleukin-12 in patients with HIV infection. AIDS 2002;16:1147–54.
47. Jacobson J, Lederman M, Spritzler J, *et al.* The effects of GM-CSF on Plasma HIV-1 RNA and CD4 Lymphocyte counts In HIV-1 Infected subjects receiving concomitant potent antiretroviral therapy. Abstract, 9th Conference on Retroviruses and Opportunistic Infections, Seattle 2002.

chapter

141 Practice Points

a. The role of resistance typing

Peter Reiss, Charles Boucher & Stefano Vella

Introduction

The circulating plasma HIV-1 RNA level reflects the extremely high rate of virus replication that occurs in the lymphoid tissue, with billions of new virions being produced each day throughout all stages of HIV infection, including the period of clinical latency. Within the first year of primary HIV-1 infection, the level at which plasma HIV-1 RNA plateaus is strongly predictive of the rate of progression to HIV-associated disease and death. Furthermore, the degree to which HIV-1 replication can be inhibited by antiretroviral therapy in a sustained fashion, as determined by increasingly sensitive techniques to measure reductions in plasma HIV-1 RNA levels, is an important determinant of the clinical benefit of treatment. Both the nadir plasma HIV-1 RNA level that is reached and the time to reach the nadir determine the sustainability of the virologic response to treatment. Thus, the principal goal of modern-day antiretroviral therapy is to reduce virus replication as much as possible for as long as possible. Unfortunately, one of the factors that jeopardizes the achievement of this goal is the danger that viral drug resistance may develop.

Pathogenesis

The principal targets of currently available antiretroviral agents are the HIV-1 reverse transcriptase and protease enzymes. The viral genes that encode these two enzymes are prone to the development of mutations because the HIV-1 reverse transcriptase is highly error-prone when reverse transcribing viral RNA into proviral DNA, the characteristic step in the viral life cycle during each round of replication of a retrovirus, including HIV-1. Given the extremely high replication rate of HIV-1, mutations in the HIV-1 reverse transcriptase and protease-encoding genes, including those that confer drug resistance, can be expected to be generated on a daily basis and to be present in a patient in a minority of virus subpopulations, even in the absence of antiretroviral drug pressure. Thus, in the absence of sufficient drug pressure, such as the use of any current antiretroviral monotherapy or of insufficiently potent combination therapy, pre-existing drug-resistant viruses eventually show preferential growth that results in treatment failure (Fig. 141a.1). This forms the basis for the current standard of giving treatment with highly active antiretroviral therapy (HAART) using potent combinations of multiple antiretrovirals.

Clinical features

Clinically, a harbinger of the possible emergence of retroviral drug resistance is the repeated demonstration of levels of plasma HIV-1 RNA above the quantification limit of the assay being used, after HIV-1 RNA levels, following the institution of therapy, have become undetectable using the same assay. It is important to realize that this is not necessarily immediately accompanied by a decline in blood $CD4^+$ lymphocyte numbers or by the development of clinical symptoms. It is therefore crucial that patients being treated with HAART are monitored by regular determination of plasma HIV-1 RNA levels, so that the emergence of potential retroviral drug resistance can be noted in a timely manner.

Investigations

Although rebound of plasma HIV-1 RNA during HAART to detectable levels may indicate retroviral drug resistance, other causes for drug failure need to be considered to determine the subsequent approach to treatment in such patients. Certain of the combinations of antiretrovirals currently used for HAART dictate the use of large numbers of pills according to strict administration schedules, with different requirements for each drug in the combination with respect to timing, possibility of co-administration and concomitant consumption of food. Consequently, it is understandable why lack of continuous patient adherence to these often complicated treatment regimens is increasingly becoming apparent as an important determinant of HAART failure. Thus, taking the patient's history with respect to treatment adherence is crucial when evaluating 'drug' failure. Therapeutic drug monitoring by determining plasma levels, particularly of HIV protease and non-nucleoside reverse transcriptase inhibitors (NNRTIs), may yield additional information in judging patient compliance with therapy. Furthermore, such monitoring may identify patients who, despite proper compliance, have insufficient drug exposure because of variation between individuals in pharmacokinetics and/or pharmacodynamics of protease inhibitors or NNRTIs, or because of drug interactions that result from the use of certain concomitant medications.

Poor patient adherence leads to insufficient drug pressure and results in increased virus replication and emergence of virus resistant to those antiretroviral agents that are being continued (see Fig. 141a.1). This is

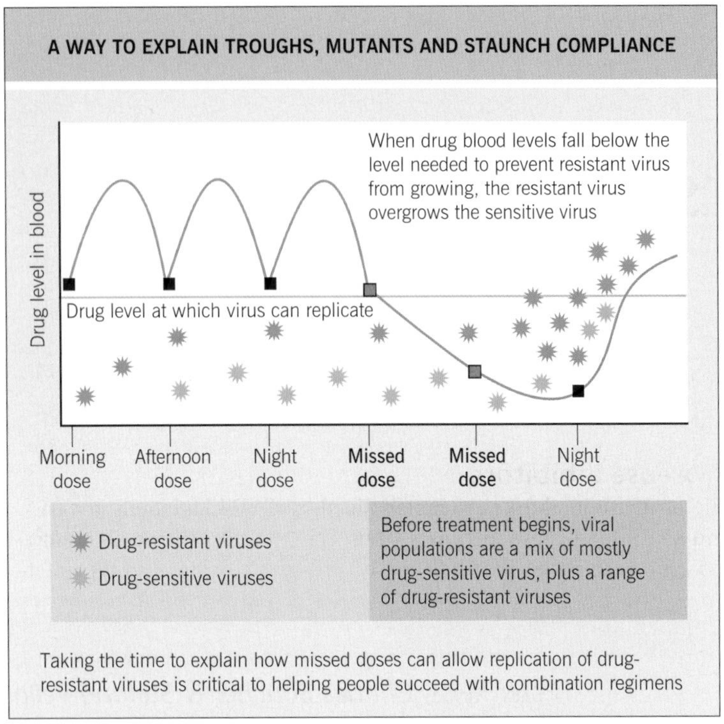
A WAY TO EXPLAIN TROUGHS, MUTANTS AND STAUNCH COMPLIANCE
When drug blood levels fall below the level needed to prevent resistant virus from growing, the resistant virus overgrows the sensitive virus
Drug level in blood
Drug level at which virus can replicate
Morning dose
Afternoon dose
Night dose
Missed dose
Missed dose
Night dose
Drug-resistant viruses
Drug-sensitive viruses
Before treatment begins, viral populations are a mix of mostly drug-sensitive virus, plus a range of drug-resistant viruses
Taking the time to explain how missed doses can allow replication of drug-resistant viruses is critical to helping people succeed with combination regimens

Fig. 141a.1 A way to explain troughs, mutants and staunch compliance. Relationship between lack of patient adherence to treatment, insufficient drug levels and emergence of resistance. Adapted with permission from Mascolini M. The drugs we've got ... the drugs we're getting ... beyond blood: a three part look at the Fourth Conference on Retroviruses and Opportunistic Infections. J Int Assoc Physicians AIDS Care 1997;3:30.

seen most rapidly and is most pronounced for those agents that are particularly vulnerable to resistance development, such as lamivudine and the currently available NNRTIs.

The measurement of retroviral drug resistance of circulating virus can be carried out with both genotypic and phenotypic assays (see also Chapters 137 and 204). Genotypic assays, which identify the presence of specific mutations in defined gene sequences (e.g. the HIV reverse transcriptase or protease genes), are relatively rapid to perform but only provide an indirect measure of resistance and do not necessarily correlate with phenotypic assays, a problem particularly pronounced for HIV protease inhibitors. Moreover, certain of these assays cannot detect the presence of minority populations of viruses (i.e. those that comprise <20% of total plasma viral RNA), which harbor potentially resistance-conferring mutations. Phenotypic assays, which measure the in-vitro growth capacity of a virus isolate in the presence of increasing concentrations of a drug, are a more direct measure of resistance but are labor-intensive, slower to perform and (like genotypic assays) may be insensitive to minority populations of virus. Finally, it is important to realize that the cut-off for determining phenotypic susceptibility or resistance of a virus to a particular drug should be judged in relation to the concentration of that drug that is achieved in vivo. Resistance to a drug that is present when dosed in its usual manner could be overcome by increasing the dose of the drug as long as increasing drug concentrations are not hampered by loss of tolerability. This demands the availability of drugs with a wider therapeutic margin than is currently the case.

Further standardization and validation of the currently available resistance assays in relation to the drug levels achieved in the patient will become increasingly important to enhance the usefulness of resistance testing in guiding therapeutic choices in individual patients.

Management

Several prospective randomized clinical trials have now demonstrated an improved short-term (6–12 months) virologic outcome for patients who had failed to maintain adequate virus suppression on their current treatment, when treatment was adjusted based on genotyping and/or phenotyping as compared with clinical judgment only. In addition, these trials have demonstrated that the benefit of resistance testing is enhanced by providing the clinician not just with a result of resistance testing but also with expert advice on how to interpret and use this result. Clearly, given the significant degree of cross-resistance between drugs within each of the three currently available classes of antiretrovirals, the usefulness of resistance testing is hampered by the lack of available alternative agents. This is also reflected in the relatively small degree of improved virologic outcome in the above-mentioned trials. Whether to change therapy and which alternative drugs to use in patients who are failing treatment will always remain a multifactorial decision-making process. This will involve not only the use of resistance testing assisted by expert interpretation and advice but at the same time obtaining a detailed history of prior antiretroviral exposure, knowledge of patterns of cross-resistance, and information concerning patients' adherence and drug level monitoring. The increasing availability of rapid and reliable HIV drug-resistance assays is likely to help not only to guide the choice of therapy in patients who have become resistant to prior treatment, but also to select initial treatment in certain circumstances. Examples of these are the choice of initial treatment in regions that have a high prevalence of primary HIV infection with drug-resistant strains, in infants who have become perinatally infected despite the use of antiretroviral therapy by their mothers, and in the setting of drug prophylaxis following accidental or sexual exposure to HIV from a known source. In patients failing therapy with a history of exposure to multiple prior drugs and drug regimens, the usefulness of resistance testing will to a large extent remain dependent on the development and introduction of novel drugs that do not exhibit cross-resistance to the current armamentarium. (See also Chapters 137, 138 and 204.)

Further reading

Boucher CAB. HIV drug resistance tests are here to stay. Curr Opin Infect Dis 1999;12:27–32.

Richman DD. Drug resistance and its implications in the management of HIV infection. Antivir Ther 1997;2:41–58.

Vella S. Advances in the virology of HIV infection and implications for clinical management. AIDS Clin Care 1998;10:17–9.

b. Drug interactions in HIV and AIDS

Charles W Flexner & Stephen C Piscitelli

Introduction

The recognition and management of pharmacokinetic and pharmacodynamic drug interactions is a major factor in choosing drugs and designing dosage regimens for the HIV-infected patient. Complex, multidrug regimens have become the standard of care and clinicians must be aware of the potential need for dosage alterations with combination therapy. Many of the antiretrovirals in current use can alter concentrations of concomitantly administered drugs or have their own concentrations altered by other agents. These interactions can be detrimental or beneficial to the patient.

Nucleoside reverse transcriptase inhibitors

The nucleoside reverse transcriptase inhibitors (NRTIs) are primarily eliminated by renal mechanisms and thus they are not generally involved in clinically significant pharmacokinetic interactions. These agents can be used with protease inhibitors and non-nucleoside reverse transcriptase inhibitors (NNRTIs) without the need for dosage alterations. Two NRTIs – zidovudine and abacavir – are eliminated in part by hepatic glucuronidation. Inducers of glucuronyl transferase activity could modestly lower plasma concentrations of these agents, although the clinical significance of this is uncertain since the active metabolites are intracellular nucleoside triphosphates.

Nucleoside reverse transcriptase inhibitors may interact pharmacodynamically with agents that have similar side-effect profiles. Increased bone marrow toxicity may be observed when zidovudine is used with other drugs capable of bone marrow suppression, such as ganciclovir and sulfamethoxazole. Didanosine and stavudine are associated with pancreatitis and should be used with caution in those receiving other agents with known pancreatic toxicity, such as pentamidine. Patients receiving combinations of didanosine, stavudine and zalcitabine should be counseled on the signs and symptoms of peripheral neuropathy and pancreatitis. Several NRTIs have been associated with lactic acidosis and should be used cautiously with other agents causing hyperlactatemia, such as metformin. The combination of didanosine and stavudine has been particularly associated with lactic acidosis and should be avoided.

The NRTI tenofovir increases the plasma levels of concomitantly administered didanosine and may increase the toxicity of didanosine if standard doses are used. A dose reduction to didanosine 250mg daily is recommended.

Non-nucleoside reverse transcriptase inhibitors

Nevirapine and efavirenz are moderate inducers of cytochrome P450 (CYP) 3A4. Both agents have been shown to decrease the area under the concentration–time curve (AUC) of amprenavir, indinavir and saquinavir (Table 141b.1). These agents should not be used with saquinavir, unless in combination with ritonavir, because of a large decrease in the saquinavir AUC.

Efavirenz affects other drug-metabolizing enzymes and may act as a P450 inhibitor in certain situations. It increases concentrations of ritonavir and nelfinavir by approximately 20% presumably through inhibition of CYP450 pathways. In general, no dosage adjustments are required with these combinations.

Delavirdine is a moderate inhibitor of the CYP 3A4 enzyme and can increase concentrations of saquinavir 5-fold and indinavir 3-fold (see Table 141b.1). Serious toxicity could occur if delavirdine is used with certain 3A4 substrates, such as the nonsedating antihistamines astemizole and terfenadine (no longer marketed in the USA), cisapride (also no longer marketed), certain benzodiazepines or ergot derivatives (Table 141b.2). Absorption of delavirdine can be affected by changes in gastric pH and its administration should be separated from didanosine, antacids and H_2-blockers.

Protease inhibitors

The protease inhibitors are metabolized by CYP450, mainly by 3A4, and can inhibit these enzymes. Thus, they possess the same contraindications as noted above with delavirdine. Ritonavir has the greatest degree of inhibition and is associated with the largest number of observed and potential drug interactions. Amprenavir, indinavir and nelfinavir have a moderate potential to cause interactions and saquinavir has the fewest drug interactions described.

The potent inhibition of CYP 3A4 by ritonavir can be used to optimize the AUC of saquinavir, which previously required ingestion of up to 18 large capsules per day. Concomitant administration with ritonavir results in a 20-fold increase in steady-state saquinavir concentrations, allowing for a dosage reduction of saquinavir to as little as 400mg q12h, while maintaining high blood concentrations. Once-daily combinations of 1600mg saquinavir with 100mg of ritonavir are under investigation. This combination was successful at suppressing HIV replication in clinical trials in protease inhibitor-naive subjects. The combinations of ritonavir with amprenavir, indinavir or lopinavir show similar activity.

In addition to enzyme inhibition, ritonavir and nelfinavir possess moderate enzyme-inducing properties and decrease concentrations of a number of co-administered agents (see Table 141b.2). Ritonavir

CONSEQUENCES OF SELECTED CYP450-MEDIATED DRUG INTERACTIONS

	Agents affected	Consequence
CYP450 inhibitors Amprenavir Cimetidine Clarithromycin Delavirdine Erythromycin Grapefruit juice Itraconazole Indinavir Ketoconazole Nelfinavir Ritonavir	Amprenavir, benzodiazepines, calcium channel antagonists, indinavir, lopinavir, rifabutin, saquinavir, terfenadine	Increased concentration of co-administered drug and possible increased therapeutic effect or toxicity
CYP450 inducers Carbamazepine Efavirenz Nelfinavir Nevirapine Phenobarbital Phenytoin Rifabutin Rifampin (rifampicin) Rifapentine St John's wort	Amprenavir, calcium channel antagonists, indinavir, lopinavir, methadone, oral contraceptives, saquinavir	Decreased concentration of co-administered drug and possible decreased therapeutic effect

Table 141b.1 Consequences of selected cytochrome P450-mediated drug interactions.

SPECIFIC CONTRAINDICATED DRUGS WITH POTENTIAL FOR SERIOUS DRUG INTERACTIONS		
Agent or drug class	**Interacting drugs**	**Consequence**
Terfenadine, astemizole and cisapride*	CYP450 inhibitors (macrolides, delavirdine, protease inhibitors, azole antifungals)	Decreased metabolism with increased concentrations and potential for cardiac toxicity
Long-acting benzodiazepines (alprazolam, midazolam)	CYP450 inhibitors	Decreased metabolism with potential for oversedation
Ergot derivatives	CYP450 inhibitors	Decreased metabolism with potential for cardiovascular toxicity
Protease inhibitors	CYP450 inducers (efavirenz, rifampin, St John's wort)	Increased metabolism with decreased concentrations and potential for resistance and treatment failure
* Removed from the US market.		

Table 141b.2 Specific contraindicated drugs with potential for serious drug interactions.

and nelfinavir also increase glucuronyl transferase activity. Ethinyl estradiol and progesterone concentrations can be decreased by concomitant administration of these two protease inhibitors, necessitating alternative forms of birth control. Amprenavir appears to be an inducer of drug-metabolizing enzymes in some circumstances.

Combining protease inhibitors with ritonavir can offer additional advantages to patients. For example, indinavir requires three times daily administration on an empty stomach or with a light meal. When administered in combination with ritonavir, it can be dosed twice daily with food and still produce high plasma concentrations.

Certain enzyme-inducing agents can produce profound decreases in the concentrations of protease inhibitors. For example, rifampin (rifampicin) has been shown to decrease the saquinavir AUC by 80% and the indinavir AUC by 65%. The resulting low blood levels have the potential to promote drug resistance and treatment failure, so indinavir and saquinavir should be avoided in patients receiving rifampin. Other potent enzyme inducers, such as phenytoin, phenobarbital and carbamazepine, could produce similar reductions.

Management of drug interactions

A careful review of patient medication profiles is essential to managing drug interactions in the HIV-infected patient. This should include complementary and alternative medicines, since agents such as St John's wort induce CYP 3A4 and can reduce concentrations of indinavir and presumably other protease inhibitors. Clinicians need to have a general understanding of certain 'red flag' drugs that are potent inhibitors and inducers of CYP450 (i.e. ritonavir, efavirenz, etc.). In this era of complex regimens, a table of recommended dosages for each combination of protease inhibitors or NNRTIs should be immediately available.

Patient counseling is critically important when complex antiretroviral regimens are prescribed. Patients must be instructed on how to take their medications with regard to timing and content of meals. In some cases, a written daily calendar of medications and times of administration may be useful to the patient and may improve adherence. Proper separation of dosing of certain drugs (i.e. didanosine and indinavir) must be explained and can also be documented on a daily dosage planner.

The HIV clinician can use a variety of interventions to manage drug interactions. Selection of a drug with fewer interactions should be considered if warranted by the clinical situation. For example, azithromycin is not metabolized by CYP450 and has far fewer drug interactions compared with other macrolides. Also, drugs that can be administered once or twice daily may be useful to lessen food-related interactions or dosage separation problems. Finally, clinicians should be aware of and try to avoid drugs with overlapping toxicities. However such combinations are sometimes unavoidable and patients who receive these agents must be closely monitored for the development of toxicity.

Further reading

Flexner C. HIV protease inhibitors (review). N Engl J Med 1998;338:1281–92.

Flexner C. Dual protease inhibitor therapy in HIV-infected patients: pharmacologic rationale and clinical benefits (review). Ann Rev Pharmacol Toxicol 2000;40:651–76.

Flexner C, Piscitelli SC. Drug-drug interactions in human immunodeficiency virus infection. In: DeClercq E, ed. Antiretroviral therapy. Washington DC: ASM Publications; 2001:339–50.

Flexner C, Piscitelli SC. AIDS drug administration and interactions. In: Dolin R, Masur H, Saag S, eds. AIDS therapy. New York: Churchill Livingstone; 1999:785–97.

Flexner C, Acosta E, Piscitelli SC. Managing drug-drug interactions in HIV disease: an interactive website for AIDS care providers. Healthcare Communications/Medscape, Inc. Available at http://www.medscape.com.

Piscitelli SC, Gallicano KD. Interactions among drugs for HIV and opportunistic infections (review). N Engl J Med 2001;34:984–96.

Piscitelli SC, Burstein AH, Chaitt D, Alfaro RM, Falloon J. Indinavir concentrations and St John's wort. Lancet 2000;355:547–8.

Piscitelli SC, Flexner C, Minor JR, Polis MA, Masur H. Drug interactions in HIV-infected patients (review). Clin Infect Dis 1996;23:685–93.

c. How to manage the hepatitis C virus co-infected HIV patient

Stanislas Pol, Anaïs Vallet-Pichard, Hélène Fontaine, Pascal Lebray & Rodolphe Sobesky

Interactions between HIV and the hepatitis C virus (HCV) were widely studied before the introduction of highly active antiretroviral therapy (HAART). The latter has markedly modified the prognosis of HIV infection, resulting in a significant decrease in morbidity and mortality that may now reveal liver-related complications. Since the improvement in treating HCV infection paralleled the progress in treating HIV, the question is now how to manage HIV–HCV co-infected patients.

Why evaluate HIV–hepatitis C virus co-infection?

Consequences of HIV–hepatitis C virus co-infection

Anti-HCV antibodies are frequently detected in HIV-infected patients, especially in hemophiliacs and intravenous drug users (around 70–90%), and are usually associated with active infection as assessed by detectable HCV viremia. This prevalence may be underestimated in case of delayed seroconversion and seroreversions.

It has recently been suggested that genotype 1b HCV may worsen the natural history of HIV in hemophiliacs and drug users. Moreover, HCV infection (and active intravenous drug use) has been suggested as an important factor in the morbidity and mortality of HIV-1-infected patients. Liver disease associated with HCV is an important cause of morbidity (8.6% of admissions) and mortality (4.8%) in HIV–HCV co-infected patients.

On the other hand, HIV significantly modifies the natural history of HCV infection:

- by increasing levels of HCV viremia;
- by significantly increasing the risk of mother-to-child or sexual transmission (from a mean of 6% to 20% and from 0% to 3%, respectively);
- by increasing (2- to 5-fold) and accelerating the risk of cirrhosis: this translates into a significantly increased yearly progression of the fibrosis score in co-infected subjects depending on the CD4 cell count level (<200 cells/mm^3) and possibly chronic alcohol consumption; and
- by increasing the risk of fibrosing cholestatic hepatitis, related to direct cytotoxicity of HCV in case of high viremia leading to accumulation of viral proteins in the endoplasmic reticulum and hepatocyte death.

The pathophysiology of HCV-related chronic hepatitis is not fully understood. Immune-mediated mechanisms are mainly involved but a direct cytotoxicity of the high HCV viremia cannot be excluded. Infection with HIV may have a direct cytopathic effect on liver cells or may modify the pattern of cytokine production, leading to production of fibrogenic factors or to decrease in antifibrogenic factors.

Impact of highly active antiretroviral therapy

Late consequences of HCV-related chronic liver disease were probably overshadowed by the extrahepatic causes of deaths, related to severe immune deficiency. Given the increasing frequency of HCV–HIV co-infection, the significant increase of cirrhosis in immunocompromised patients and the significant improvement in survival with therapeutic progress in the field of anti-HIV therapy, the next few years may see the occurrence of symptomatic liver disease leading ultimately to hepatic carcinoma in HIV–HCV co-infected patients, underlining the need for early diagnostic procedures and therapeutic strategies.

Improvement in immunity could be deleterious in case of diseases involving immune-mediated mechanisms, such as chronic viral hepatitis. Antiretroviral therapy restores both CD4 and CD8 cells (directed against specific HCV antigens), which may participate in the pathologic deterioration. Several cases of liver deterioration paralleling immune restoration in HCV–HIV co-infected patients have been reported. Thus, a careful liver follow-up in HCV–HIV co-infected patients on triple combination antiretroviral therapy is required.

Antiretroviral therapy, by improving immune status, could decrease HCV viral load and thus the severity of HCV liver disease if direct viral cytotoxicity is, at least partially, responsible for the histopathologic lesions of chronic hepatitis. However, there is no significant variation in HCV RNA load after 3, 6 or 9 months of triple therapy in HCV–HIV co-infected subjects, as compared with baseline values, suggesting that HAART will not decrease HCV-related liver disease associated with HCV replication.

All antiviral drugs have potential toxicity. Nucleoside reverse transcriptase inhibitors cause rare but severe hepatitis, which is due to a mitochondrial cytopathy with severe microsteatosis and lethal lactic acidosis. Non-nucleoside reverse transcriptase inhibitors are responsible for clinical hepatitis in 2–5% of cases, which are sometimes severe (0.1% of cases) and are associated with signs of hypersensitivity in two-thirds of cases. Drug-related hepatitis in association with protease inhibitors is observed in 2–8.5% of treated patients, with a predilection for patients co-infected with HCV or HBV. In most cases of drug-related hepatitis, liver biochemical abnormalities resolve after discontinuation of the drug and do not relapse after changing of protease inhibitor. The rate of HAART withdrawal in relation to hepatotoxicity is around 2% without significant difference regarding the type of antiretroviral treatment.

Drug-related hepatitis may participate in the deterioration of liver histology, as well as hepatitis of immune function restoration, direct cytotoxicity of HCV and other usual causes of liver damage, including alcohol toxicity (Fig. 141c.1).

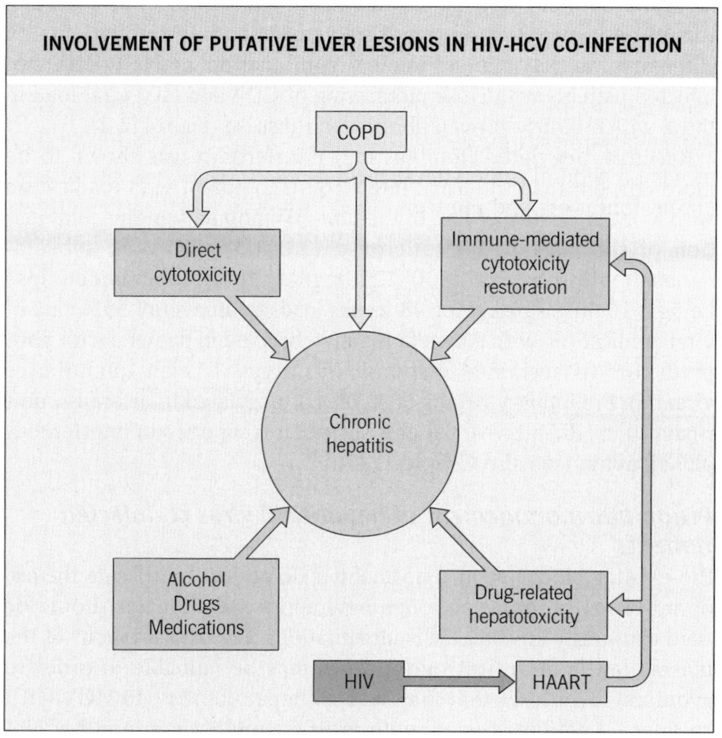

Fig. 141c.1 Involvement of putative liver lesions in HIV–HCV co-infection.

Therapeutic implications

Treatment of hepatitis C virus infection in co-infected patients

The increased risk of cirrhosis in HCV–HIV co-infected patients, the histologic deterioration under anti-HIV therapy related to immune restoration, direct viral cytotoxicity or drug toxicity, and the increase in survival of HIV-infected patients underline the need for reliable anti-HCV antiviral therapies. An important issue is to distinguish who among HIV–HCV co-infected patients should receive anti-HCV treatment with the aim of eradicating HCV.

In co-infected patients, interferon alone led to a low rate of viral eradication (around 15%) with significant side-effects but a low impact on the HIV status.

The standard treatment of HCV infection is now the combination of ribavirin and interferon. Ribavirin, a nucleoside analogue, has no clear effect as monotherapy on HCV or HIV and is now currently given in combination with interferon-α in treating hepatitis C in HIV-infected patients. The ribavirin–interferon-α combination results in a 40% rate of HCV eradication in the non-HIV population with a range from 15% to 80% according to the virologic (genotype and quantitative viremia) and pathologic (fibrosis) predictive factors and to the duration of therapy (6 or 12 months). Sustained viral eradication is usually associated with a long-lasting resolution and histologic improvement or normalization.

The results of the ribavirin–interferon combination in HIV co-infected patients have been reported. In-vitro inhibition of the phosphorylation by ribavirin of zidovudine, stavudine and zalcitabine has been reported but it does not seem to clearly modify the efficacy of HAART in vivo. By contrast, in vitro, ribavirin may positively interfere with phosphorylation of didanosine and the combination didanosine, ribavirin and interferon is highly synergistic and increases the side-effects of didanosine, especially lactic acidosis and pancreatitis.

The combination of interferon-α and ribavirin may lead, in naive HCV–HIV co-infected patients, to an overall 25% rate of sustained eradication, with a good tolerance, especially at the immunologic level. This low rate of sustained response is expected since cirrhosis, high pretreatment viremia and high genomic heterogeneity, predictors of poor response, are more frequent in co-infected patients. In summary, we recommend such a combination in HCV–HIV co-infected patients with close monitoring of CD4 and HIV viral load in those with a biopsy-proven fibrotic liver disease (Fig. 141c.2).

Recently, pegylated (long-lasting) interferon-α was shown to be more efficient than the usual interferon-α to obtain viral eradication with a better quality of life. In the non-HIV population, the combination of the pegylated interferon-α (1.0–1.5µg/kg/week subcutaneously) with ribavirin (800–1200mg/day, the recommended dose being >10.6mg/kg/day) for 48 weeks leads to an overall 55% rate of viral eradication, with a benefit mainly observed in patients with poor predictors of sustained response (genotype 1, high quantitative viremia). Preliminary results of studies of pegylated interferon-α plus ribavirin in HIV positive patients suggest it is superior to interferon-α plus ribavirin (see also Chapter 125).

Pragmatic management of hepatitis C virus co-infected patients

Pre-existing biochemical abnormalities do not contraindicate the use of antiretroviral drugs although nevirapine and ritonavir should be used cautiously. In some difficult situations, the measurement of the plasma levels of antiretroviral drugs may be valuable in order to avoid any overdoses that may lead to hepatotoxicity. In HCV–HIV co-infected patients treated with protease inhibitor, a monthly biochemical follow-up is warranted in the first 3 months after introduction of any new antiretroviral drug and then every 3 months in order to identify potential drug-related toxicity. An increase in ALT levels (>5-fold the upper normal value, but the rate of increase is more important than the absolute values) should lead to a switch of the protease inhibitor or to the introduction of a non-nucleoside reverse transcriptase inhibitor. Biochemical liver abnormalities occurring with non-nucleoside reverse transcriptase inhibitor should lead to treatment withdrawal, especially if cutaneous signs of hypersensitivity are associated. However, the interpretation of such biochemical liver abnormalities is difficult, raising the question of drug-related hepatitis but also of other toxic causes such as alcohol, cocaine, or metamphetamine.

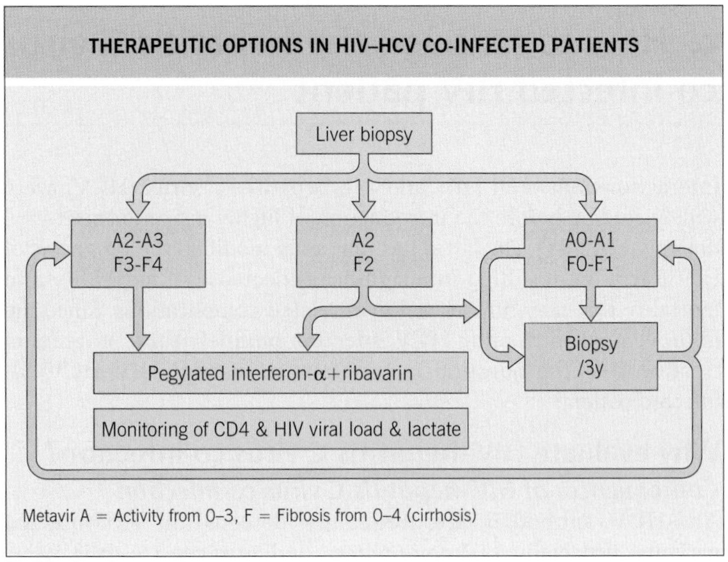

Fig. 141c.2 Therapeutic options in HIV–HCV co-infected patients.

An unsolved question is the respective place of anti-HCV and anti-HIV therapies. In clinical practice, most HIV patients are referred to the hepatologist while receiving HAART and the question is not relevant. In the future, physicians will have to consider the priority of each treatment according to liver histology and immune status. Given the chance of complete eradication of HCV-associated chronic hepatitis, anti-HCV therapy should be considered a priority and be treated first if the CD4 lymphocyte count is not less than 300 cells/mm^3. A marked inflammatory activity or fibrosis (A2–A3 or F3–F4) indicates a need for anti-HCV treatment in order to avoid deleterious evolution; in contrast, a low inflammatory activity or fibrosis (A0–A1 or F0–F1) does not necessarily indicate anti-HCV treatment but a liver follow-up by biopsy and biochemical evaluation of fibrosis every 3 years. In intermediate situations (A2–F2), the choice to treat or not to treat should be based mainly on the predictive factors, including genotype and quantitative viremia (see Fig. 141c.2).

In conclusion, physicians should be aware of the potential risk of:

- symptomatic liver disease in HCV–HIV co-infected patients in the era of antiretroviral therapy;
- liver deterioration paralleling immune function restoration;
- lack of impact of active antiretroviral therapy on HCV load; and
- potential drug-related hepatitis that may modify the natural history of HCV-related liver disease.

Liver biopsies should be regularly performed to identify patients with severe liver disease who require early anti-HCV therapy (see Fig. 141c.2) under close monitoring of the immune status.

Further reading

Benhamou Y, Bochet M, Di Martino V, *et al.* Liver fibrosis progression in HIV-HCV coinfected patients. The Multivirc Group. Hepatology 1999;30:1054–8.

Boyer N, Marcellin P, Degott C, *et al.* Recombinant intrferon-alpha for chronic hepatitis C in patients positive for antibody to human immunodeficiency virus. J Infect Dis 1992;165:723–6.

Greub G, Ledergerber B, Battegay M, *et al.* Clinical progression, survival, and immune recovery during antiretroviral therapy in patients with HIV-1 and hepatitis C virus co-infection. Lancet 2000;356:1800–5.

John M, Flexman J, French MAH. Hepatitis C virus associated hepatitis following treatment of HIV-infected patients with HIV protease inhibitors: an immune restoration disease? AIDS 1998;12:2289–93.

Lafeuillade A, Hittinger G, Chapadaud S. Increased mitochondrial toxicity with ribavirin in HIV/HCV coinfection. Lancet 2001;357:280–1.

Landau A, Batisse D, Van Huyen JP, *et al.* Efficacy and safety of combination therapy with interferon-alpha 2b and ribavirin for chronic hepatitis C in HIV infected patients. AIDS 2000;14:839–44.

Manns MP, MacHutchinson JG, Gordon S, *et al.* Peg-Interferon alfa-2b plus ribavirin compared to Interferon alfa-2b plus ribavirin for the treatment of chronic hepatitis C:24 week treatment analysis of a multicenter, multinational phase III randomized controlled trial. Hepatology 2000;32:297A.

Mc Hutchinson JG, Gordon SC, Schiff ER, *et al.* Interferon alfa-2b alone or in combination with ribavirin as initial treatment for chronic hepatitis C. N Engl J Med 1998;339:1485–92.

Soriano V, Rodriguez-Rosado R, Garcia-Samaniego J. Management of chronic hepatitis C in HIV-infected patients. AIDS 1999;13:539–46.

Soriano V, Rodriguez-Rosado R, Perez-Olmeda M, *et al.* Interferon plus ribavirin for chronic hepatitis C in HIV-infected patients. AIDS 2000;14:2409–10.

Vento S, Garofano T, Renzini C, *et al.* Enhancement of hepatitis C virus replication and liver damage in HIV-coinfected patients on antiretroviral combination therapy. AIDS 1998;12:116–7.

d. How to manage hyperlipidemia in the HIV patient

Judith Currier

Typical case

A 45-year-old woman with HIV infection presents to establish primary care. She was diagnosed with HIV during pregnancy 7 years ago. Initially her $CD4^+$ T cell count was 450 cells/mm^3. She was treated with ZDV monotherapy for 8 months during her pregnancy and stopped all therapy 1 month postpartum. She restarted treatment 2 years ago when her $CD4^+$ T cell count was 225 cells/mm^3 and her HIV RNA is 65,000 copies/ml. She has maintained an undetectable HIV RNA on her current regimen of stavudine, lamivudine and nelfinavir. She has no family history of diabetes or heart disease. She has not had a menstrual period for 3 years. She smokes one pack of cigarettes per day. Her physical examination is normal and her blood pressure is 142/80mmHg. Fasting lipid values include triglycerides of 420mg/dl (4.75mmol/l), total cholesterol 260mg/dl (6.73mmol/l) and HDL cholesterol 28mg/dl (0.73mmol/l). Lipid values prior to starting treatment are not available. Does this patient have a clinically significant dyslipidemia and, if so, what are the options for management?

Dyslipidemia in HIV infection

The dyslipidemia associated with HIV infection may be a consequence of HIV infection per se, a direct effect of the antiretroviral agents used to treat HIV infection or it may be secondary to central adiposity and insulin resistance that can occur during treatment. Currently marketed protease inhibitors (PIs) differ slightly in their ability to cause dyslipidemia, whereas in general non-PI-containing regimens have been found to have less of an effect on lipids. Median increases in total cholesterol of 40–60mg/dl (1.04–1.55mmol/l) and triglyceride increases of 80–100mg/dl (0.90–1.13mmol/l) have been reported in studies examining currently marketed PIs. The magnitude of the effect on lipids may vary for different PI combinations. Patients with untreated advanced HIV infection have been noted to have a pattern of low HDL cholesterol and increased triglycerides.

Estimating cardiovascular risk

The long-term significance of dyslipidemia in HIV-infected individuals is not completely known. The patterns of lipid abnormalities most commonly observed in patients with HIV infection might be expected to result in increased cardiovascular morbidity. In many cases both antiretroviral therapies and HIV infection per se are thought to contribute. Large studies are currently underway to determine the incidence of cardiovascular events and atherosclerosis in HIV-infected individuals and the relative contribution of the identified risk factors. Preliminary recommendations for the management of dyslipidemia in HIV-infected individuals have been developed from existing guidelines applicable to the general population.

The National Cholesterol Education Program (NCEP) guidelines are a reasonable starting point for considering the need for intervention. These guidelines utilize threshold values of LDL cholesterol and consider the following as important risk factors for cardiovascular disease: current cigarette smoking, diabetes, hypertension, family history of coronary heart disease and HDL cholesterol. The first step in evaluating cardiovascular risk is to determine whether two or more risk factors are present. If so, then an estimate of the 10-year cardiovascular risk using the Framingham scoring system is suggested. In our example the patient has several classic risk factors for cardiovascular diseases; she is a smoker with untreated hypertension who is postmenopausal and she also has low HDL cholesterol and elevated total cholesterol. Using Tables 141d.1–7 adapted from the NCEP ATP III guidelines, we can total her points for each of the risk factors to discover that she has a total of 23 points, which correlates with an estimated 10-year cardiovascular risk of over 20%. This is considered a high risk, similar to that of someone with established coronary heart disease.

The reliance on LDL cholesterol complicates the use of NCEP guidelines in the management of patients with HIV infection. When the value for triglycerides exceeds 400mg/dl (4.52mmol/l), calculation of LDL cholesterol from the total cholesterol and HDL is not accurate. Direct measurement of LDL is not available in many settings and hence it may be reasonable to base decisions for intervention on the values of non-HDL cholesterol. The value for non-HDL cholesterol is the total cholesterol minus HDL cholesterol. In our example, the value for non-HDL cholesterol would be 260 − 28 = 232mg/dl (6.0mmol/l). The NCEP ATP III guidelines include goals for non-HDL cholesterol in addition to LDL cholesterol and these are included in Table 141d.8.

Management

Now that we have established that the patient in this example requires intervention for her dyslipidemia, we can consider the options for management. The first steps would include discussing her diet and lifestyle. The importance of smoking cessation and treatment of her hypertension should be addressed. These modifiable risk fac-

CALCULATING CARDIOVASCULAR RISK IN WOMEN: AGE	
Age	Points
20–34	−7
35–39	−3
40–44	0
45–49	3
50–54	6
55–59	8
60–64	10
65–69	12
70–74	14
75–79	16

Table 141d.1 Calculating cardiovascular risk in women: age. (Adapted from Expert Panel 2001)

CALCULATING CARDIOVASCULAR RISK IN WOMEN: TOTAL CHOLESTEROL					
Total cholesterol	Points				
	Age 20–39	Age 40–49	Age 50–59	Age 60–69	Age 70–79
<160	0	0	0	0	0
160–199	4	3	2	1	1
200–239	8	6	4	2	1
240–279	11	8	5	3	2
≥280	13	10	7	4	2

Table 141d.2 Calculating cardiovascular risk in women: total cholesterol. (Adapted from Expert Panel 2001)

CALCULATING CARDIOVASCULAR RISK IN WOMEN: SMOKING					
Smoking status	Points				
	Age 20–39	Age 40–49	Age 50–59	Age 60–69	Age 70–79
Nonsmoker	0	0	0	0	0
Smoker	9	7	4	2	1

Table 141d.3 Calculating cardiovascular risk in women: smoking. (Adapted from Expert Panel 2001)

CALCULATING CARDIOVASCULAR RISK IN WOMEN: SYSTOLIC BLOOD PRESSURE		
Systolic blood pressure (mmHg)	Untreated	Treated
<120	0	0
120–129	1	3
130–139	2	4
140–159	3	5
≥160	4	6

Table 141d.4 Calculating cardiovascular risk in women: systolic blood pressure. (Adapted from Expert Panel 2001)

CALCULATING CARDIOVASCULAR RISK IN WOMEN: HDL CHOLESTEROL	
HDL (mg/dl)	Points
≥60	−1
50–59	0
40–49	1
<40	2

Table 141d.5 Calculating cardiovascular risk in women: HDL cholesterol. (Adapted from Expert Panel 2001)

CALCULATING CARDIOVASCULAR RISK IN WOMEN: TOTAL THE POINTS	
Risk factors	Case example
Age	3
Total cholesterol	8
Smoking	7
Systolic blood pressure	3
HDL cholesterol	2
Total	23

Table 141d.6 Calculating cardiovascular risk in women: total the points. (Adapted from Expert Panel 2001)

CALCULATING CARDIOVASCULAR RISK IN WOMEN: POINT TOTAL AND 10-YEAR RISK ASSESSMENT	
<9	<1
10–12	1
12–14	2
15	3
16	4
17	5
18	6
19	8
20	11
21	14
23	22
24	27
≥25	≥30

Table 141d.7 Calculating cardiovascular risk in women: point total and 10-year risk assessment. (Adapted from Expert Panel 2001)

CALCULATING CARDIOVASCULAR RISK IN WOMEN: NCEP III RISK CATEGORIES AND NON-HDL CHOLESTEROL GOALS		
Risk level	LDL cholesterol	Non-HDL cholesterol
CHD or risk equivalent	<100	<130
>2 Risk factors and <20% risk	<130	<160
0–1 Risk factor	<160	<190

Table 141d.8 Calculating cardiovascular risk in women: NCEP III Risk Categories and Non-HDL Cholesterol Goals. (Adapted from Expert Panel 2001)

tors should be addressed prior to considering altering her currently successful antiretroviral regimen. Her diet should be reviewed and she should be given information on a low-fat (with reduced saturated fat), low-cholesterol diet. Given her calculated level of cardiovascular risk, additional measures to lower her non-HDL cholesterol are likely to be needed.

The additional measures for management of this patient's dyslipidemia include alteration in her antiretroviral regimen and the use of lipid-lowering agents. There are currently limited data to guide clinicians in this regard. Several studies have suggested a benefit of substituting a non-nucleoside analogue such as nevirapine or efavirenz as a reasonable option for patients who are well suppressed on a PI-containing regimen with dyslipidemia. The nucleoside analogue abacavir can also be substituted for the PI component of the regimen; however, in patients with a history of prior nucleoside analogue monotherapy the substitution of abacavir may be associated with an increased risk of virologic failure due to pre-existing nucleoside resistance mutations. The patient in this example received monotherapy with zidovudine for 8 months during an earlier pregnancy and this may increase her risk of failing an abacavir substitution. In our case, substitution of nelfinavir with nevirapine or efavirenz would be my preference for initial management of her dyslipidemia. If the patient is reluctant to change her therapy, the use of lipid-lowering agents should then be considered if changes in diet are not successful.

There are currently limited data on the efficacy of lipid-lowering therapy in patients with HIV infection. The HMG-CoA reductase inhibitors (statins) are generally the first-line intervention for lipid disorders in the general population. Important drug interactions between the statin agents lovastatin and simvastatin and the PIs have been reported and these agents are not currently recommended. The statin agent least likely to interact with PIs is pravastatin. Drug interactions are unlikely to occur with the use of fibric acid derivatives gemfibrozil and fenofibrate. Preliminary results of clinical trials evaluating the use of either gemfibrozil and statin agents have been reported. In the case above, with elevations in both triglycerides and non-HDL cholesterol, the use of gemfibrozil at a dose of 600mg po twice daily 30 minutes prior to meals in addition to dietary advice would be a reasonable first approach if substituting the nelfinavir with a non-nucleoside were not an option. If there was no response after 3 months consideration should be given to adding a statin agent–pravastatin at a dose of 20mg po qd. Close monitoring for hepatotoxicity and myopathy is warranted when statin and fibrate agents are used concurrently. Again, substituting the PI component of the regimen would be preferable to adding a second lipid-lowering agent.

As the treatment of HIV infection has evolved into the management of a chronic disease more emphasis is being placed on preventing long-term complications from both the disease and the therapies used to treat it. Currently, it is not known whether patients with HIV infection who sustain increases in lipids are at the same risk as would be expected if these lipid changes occurred spontaneously. It is important for clinicians to be aware of these issues and to screen patients for lipid disorders. Attention to modifiable cardiac risk factors such as smoking, diet and level of physical activity is critical and should not be overlooked. In settings where the underlying cardiovascular risk appears to be high, further interventions with lipid-lowering agents or modification of the antiretroviral regimen may be warranted.

Further reading

Dubé MP, Sprecher D, Henry WK, *et al.* Preliminary guidelines for the evaluation and management of dyslipidemia in adults infected with human immunodeficiency virus and receiving antiretroviral therapy: recommendations of the Adult AIDS Clinical Trial Group Cardiovascular Disease Focus Group. Clin Infect Dis 2000;31:1216–24.

Drechsler H, Powderly WG. Switching anti-retroviral therapy: a review. Clin Infect Dis 2002;35:1219–30.

Expert Panel on Detection, Evaluation, and Treatment of High Blood Cholesterol in Adults. Executive summary of the third report of the National Cholesterol Education Program (NCEP) Expert Panel on Detection, Evaluation, and Treatment of High Blood Cholesterol in Adults (Adult Treatment Panel III). JAMA 2001;285:2486–97.

Fichtenbaum CJ, Gerber JG, Rosenkranz SL, *et al.* Pharmacokinetic interactions between protease inhibitors and statins in HIV seronegative volunteers: ACTG study A5047. AIDS 2002;16:569–77.

Frost PH, Havel RJ. Rationale for use of non-high-density lipoprotein cholesterol rather than low-density lipoprotein cholesterol as a tool for lipoprotein cholesterol screening and assessment of risk and therapy. Am J Cardiol 1998;81:26B–31B.

Henry K, Melroe H, Huebesch J, Hermundson J, Simpson J. Atorvastatin and gemfibrozil for protease-inhibitor-related lipid abnormalities. Lancet 1998;352:1031–2.

Martinez E, Conget I, Lozano L, *et al.* Reversion of metabolic abnormalities after switching from HIV-1 protease inhibitors to nevirapine. AIDS 1999;13:805–10.

Martinez E, Garcia-Viejo MA, Blanco JL, *et al.* Impact of switching from human immunodeficiency virus type 1 protease inhibitors to efavirenz in successfully treated adults with lipodystrophy. Clin Infect Dis 2000;31:1266–73.

Miller J, Carr A, Brown D, Cooper DA. A randomised, double-blind study of gemfibrozil (GF) for the treatment of protease inhibitor-associated hypertriglyceridaemia [abstract 540]. 8th Conference on Retroviruses and Opportunistic Infections. February 4–8, 2001; Chicago. Available at: http://www.retroconference.org/2001/abstracts/abstracts/abstracts/540.htm.

Moyle GJ, Lloyd M, Reynolds B, Baldwin C, Mandalia S, Gazzard BG. Dietary advice with or without pravastatin for the management of hypercholesterolaemia associated with protease inhibitor therapy. AIDS 2001;15:1503–8.

Murphy RL, Brun S, Hicks C, *et al.* ABT-378/ritonavir plus stavudine and lamivudine for the treatment of antiretroviral-naive adults with HIV-1 infection: 48-week results. AIDS 2001;15:F1–F9.

Periard D, Telenti A, Sudre P, *et al.* Atherogenic dyslipidemia in HIV-infected individuals treated with protease inhibitors. Circulation 1999;100:700–5.

Purnell JQ, Zambon A, Knopp RH, *et al.* Effect of ritonavir on lipids and post-heparin lipase activities in normal subjects. AIDS 2000;14:51–7.

Thomas JC, Lopes-Virella MF, del Bene VE, *et al.* Use of fenofibrate in the management of protease inhibitor-associated lipid abnormalities. Pharmacotherapy 2000;20:727–34.

van der Valk M, Gisolf EH, Reiss P, *et al.* Increased risk of lipodystrophy when nucleoside analogue reverse transcriptase inhibitors are included with protease inhibitors in the treatment of HIV-1 infection. AIDS 2001;15:847–55.

e. Managing the patient with multidrug-resistant HIV

Pablo Tebas

Frequency of the problem

Unfortunately, because of difficulty with adherence to antiretroviral treatment or the sequential use of partially suppressive regimens when therapy was initiated, a very significant proportion of patients with HIV infection develop multidrug-resistant HIV. In a recent survey of the ongoing HIV Costs and Service Utilization Study (HCSUS), approximately 63% of the patients under care had a detectable viral load at the time of the last determination, 78% of those had resistance to at least one drug and more than 50% were resistant to two. These data suggest that more than 100,000 patients in the USA alone (or half of the total number of patients in care) are infected with viruses that are resistant to antiretroviral drugs. HIV disease is like other infectious diseases, such as tuberculosis or malaria, in which the development of resistance is a frequent clinical problem. The problem of drug resistance in HIV is more common among subjects receiving therapy and those who are in care than among patients who have never received treatment.

Primary resistance to HIV therapies is rising alarmingly among new and chronically infected individuals in the developed world. Unfortunately, this problem will also affect the developing world when antiretroviral therapy becomes more widely available. Primary resistance is more frequently seen with nucleoside reverse transcriptase inhibitors, since these are the drugs that have been used for the longest period of time. It is increasing among non-nucleoside reverse transcriptase inhibitors and protease inhibitors. The goal is to prevent this problem by the intelligent use of antiretroviral medications and resistance testing. Despite these efforts, the use of antiretroviral therapy will always be associated with the development of resistance. Clinicians will frequently face patients for whom no therapeutic options are readily available.

Therapeutic options for the patient who has multidrug-resistant HIV

When the number of treatment options is limited, the clinician must select between discontinuing a costly, and potentially ineffective toxic treatment that is increasing the risk of accumulating multiple resistance mutations, or maintaining a partially suppressive regimen in the hope that this approach will delay the appearance of immunologic and clinical failure.

Several considerations are important in this all too frequent situation. First, virologic failure is not equivalent to immunologic and clinical failure. A recent study indicates that the median period of time between virologic and immunologic failure is 36.4 months (3 years). The delay between virologic and immunologic failure seems to be associated with the decreased replicative fitness of viruses that harbor protease-inhibitor-associated resistance mutations. Viruses with multiple mutations are less cytopathic in vitro than wild-type isolates. Second, discontinuing therapy in the patient with multidrug-resistant virus is associated with the overgrowth of wild-type virus after approximately 12 weeks. This switch to wild type as the predominant quasispecies in the patient is associated with a significant decay in the $CD4^+$ T cell count, rapid progression of HIV disease and, in some cases, serious opportunistic infections. Third, there is growing evidence that the rates of clinical progression are low in patients who continue antiretroviral therapy in the presence of virologic failure. These subjects maintain their $CD4^+$ cell numbers, especially if the viral load is maintained below the natural set point of the patient (the HIV RNA load before the initiation of antiretroviral therapy).

Based on the above, most experienced clinicians would maintain a partially suppressive regimen in a patient with limited therapeutic options, especially if the disease is in an advanced stage. The goal of therapy in this situation shifts from complete suppression of viral replication to partial suppression to prevent immunologic and clinical decline.

Many clinicians also maintain lamivudine in these patients because the presence of the M184V mutation (usually associated with the use of lamivudine) may enhance susceptibility to zidovudine, stavudine or tenofovir. These drugs are frequently used individually as part of combination regimens in the patient with multidrug resistance. The presence of this mutation also stabilizes the reverse transcriptase of the virus and makes it less prone to make errors, which are associated with the development of resistance. This effect may be overcome by an accumulation of nucleoside associated mutations (also known as NAMs): M41L, E44D, D67N, K70R, V118I, L210W, T215Y/F and K219Q/E (see Chapters 137 and 204).

Other authors have suggested the used of multidrug combination regimens (six or more drugs), also called 'mega-HAART regimens', in this situation. Occasionally, significant antiviral activity has been observed; however, these regimens are complicated to use, especially in patients with adherence problems (as is usually the case in patients with multidrug resistance). They are also associated with significant side effects, drug–drug interactions and increased cost. The use of therapeutic drug monitoring (measuring antiretroviral drugs levels, and adjusting dosages accordingly) might be necessary in these cases.

Although some authors have suggested that transient discontinuation of antiretroviral treatment might 'resensitize' the virus and make it susceptible to previously used antiretroviral agents, this phenomenon is probably short-lived because of 'archived' resistance of the integrated HIV in the T cell memory reservoirs. This approach might work better in the patient who has some therapeutic options left, and should always be undertaken with extreme caution because of the high risk of significant clinical deterioration in the patient who has advanced disease.

In the patient with multidrug-resistant HIV, it is also critically important to maintain all prophylactic regimens that the subject should be taking at the recommended $CD4^+$ T cell count thresholds. Thus, it is important to maintain *Pneumocystis carinii*, *Toxoplasma* and *Mycobacterium avium* complex prophylaxis if indicated. It is probably also a good idea to increase the frequency of the clinical visits to once every month or two, so opportunistic infections can be readily identified and treated.

New drug availability

Before the licensing agencies (e.g. the Food and Drug Administration in the USA) grant full approval, new drugs often become available as part of compassionate use and expanded access programs. The clinician frequently is pressed and tempted to add this 'single' new drug to the regimen that the patient is taking, hoping to obtain at least a partial virologic and clinical benefit in a patient with very limited options. The decision to do this should be based on the clinical situation of the patient and the types of drugs available. For some classes of drugs, such as non-nucleoside reverse transcriptase inhibitors and fusion inhibitors, resistance develops very quickly if those drugs are not used as part of fully suppressive regimens. With other classes of drugs, such as protease inhibitors or nucleoside/nucleotide analogues, resistance takes longer to develop and durable virologic and potentially clinical benefits might be obtained.

For compounds where the threshold for developing resistance is low, it might be reasonable to wait until more drugs become available and a combination regimen with a good chance of response can be developed. For drugs with a higher threshold for resistance, immediate use might be advisable, especially in the patient who is clinically deteriorating. For example, enfuvirtide (also known as T-20) is a peptide fusion inhibitor that binds to the HR-1 domain of gp41. Its use has been associated with significant decreases in viral load when used as monotherapy, and improvements in the viral load response of otherwise optimized rescue regimens. HIV becomes resistant to this drug very quickly if it is not used as part of a fully suppressive antiretroviral regimen. Resistance mutations in the gp41 envelope gene have been identified primarily at positions 36 to 45 of the first heptad repeat (HR1) region. On the other hand, tenofovir, a recently approved nucleotide, was evaluated as an 'intensification' (the addition of a single drug to a failing antiretroviral regimen) in Gilead study 907. The virologic benefits (approximately half a log decrease in HIV viral load) were still present after 48 weeks of treatment.

If the patient is clinically failing antiretroviral therapy or the addition of a single drug is being considered, it is important to maximize the benefits of the background regimen that the patient is taking. Phenotypic resistance testing might have an edge over genotypic or 'virtual phenotype' testing (a genotype test with an automatic interpretation linked to a large database of geno-phenotypes) in this very complicated situation (see Chapter 137). It might better identify which drugs maintain a residual activity in vitro in a patient who has limited therapeutic options. It also might provide a measurement of 'replicative capacity' of the patient's virus.

The use of the replication capacity assay

Replicative fitness is the ability of a species or strain of virus to compete against others in a defined environment; for example, a wild-type virus is more 'fit' than a virus with multidrug resistance in a environment where there is no drug, but the reverse is true in the presence of antiretroviral therapy. To evaluate replicative fitness, it is necessary to conduct very cumbersome assays in which the two different strains to be tested compete against each other. Recently a 'replication capacity assay' has been provided as part of the phenotypic assay (see Chapter 137). In this assay patient-derived HIV reverse transcriptase or protease undergoes a single round of replication. The vector contains a luciferase gene that permits quantitation of replication, which is then compared to the level of replication of a wild-type HIV reference strain. The result is provided as the ratio of the patient strain replication to the wild-type (reference) strain replication. Normally, multidrug-resistant viruses have replication capacity values less than 1. Theoretically, the lower the number the less fit the virus is.

The number of studies using this assay is limited. Changes in the results obtained with this assay predicted the change in viral load when therapy was discontinued in patients with evidence of multidrug resistance. Based on those results and the results of small-cohort studies, some clinicians are using this assay to guide therapy in the patient with multidrug resistance by selecting combination regimens that lower the replication capacity of the predominant quasispecies of the patient. However, clinical validation of the utility of this assay is still lacking. Until then this approach might lead to unnecessary changes of otherwise well-tolerated regimens. Ensuring that the viral load is kept as low as possible, preferably below the natural set point of the patient, might be another approach to handle the patient who has limited therapeutic options.

Further reading

Deeks SG, Hoh R, Grant RM, *et al.* CD4+ T cell kinetics and activation in human immunodeficiency virus-infected patients who remain viremic despite long-term treatment with protease inhibitor-based therapy. J Infect Dis 2002;185:315–23.

Deeks SG, Wrin T, Liegler T, *et al.* Virologic and immunologic consequences of discontinuing combination antiretroviral-drug therapy in HIV-infected patients with detectable viremia. N Engl J Med 2001;344:472–80.

SECTION

6

GEOGRAPHIC AND TRAVEL MEDICINE

Seth F Berkley
Keith PWJ McAdam

chapter 142

Geography of Infectious Diseases

Mary E Wilson

INTRODUCTION

Infectious diseases vary by geographic region and population, and they change over time.[1] Increasingly, humans are moving from one region to another, thereby becoming exposed to a variety of potential pathogens and also serving as part of the global dispersal process.[2] Microbes picked up at one time and in one place may manifest in disease far away in time and place. Because many microbes have the capacity of persisting in the human host for months, years or even decades, the relevant time frame for study of exposures becomes a lifetime. Furthermore, microbes also move and change and reach humans via multiple channels.

Caring for patients in today's world requires an understanding of the basic factors that underlie the geography of human diseases and events that cause shifts in the distribution and burden of specific diseases. Current technology contributes to massive population movements and rapid shifts in diseases and their distributions, but it also provides communication channels that can aid clinicians who care for patients with complicated medical problems. This chapter reviews the factors that shape the global distribution of infectious diseases and the forces that are expected to shift distributions in the future. Several examples are used to illustrate the broad range of factors that affect the distribution and expression of infectious diseases.[3]

Many authors have traced the origins and spread of specific infectious diseases through human history. A century and a half ago, John Snow noted that epidemics of cholera followed major routes of commerce and appeared first at seaports when entering a new region.[4] Yersinia pestis, the cause of plague, accompanied trade caravans and moved across oceans with rats on ships. Exploration of the New World by Europeans introduced a range of human pathogens that killed one-third or more of the local populations in some areas of the Americas. The plants and animals introduced as a result of this exploration have also had profound and long-lasting consequences for the ecology and economics of the new environment.[5] The speed, reach and volume of today's travel are unprecedented in human history and offer multiple potential routes to move biologic species around the globe. Pathogens of animals and plants are being transported as well and this can affect global food security.[6] This chapter focuses only on pathogens that directly affect human health and on their sources (Table 142.1). When thinking about geography of human infections, it is useful to consider both the origin of the organism and the conveyor or immediate source for the human (Fig. 142.1).

This chapter addresses three key issues:

- factors influencing geographic distribution: why are some infectious diseases found only in focal geographic regions or in isolated populations?
- factors influencing the burden of disease: why does the impact from widely distributed infections vary markedly from one region or one population to another? and
- factors influencing emergence of disease: what allows or facilitates the introduction, persistence and spread of an infection in a new region and what makes a region or population resistant to the introduction of an infection?

FACTORS INFLUENCING GEOGRAPHIC DISTRIBUTION

In past centuries, lack of interaction with the outside world could allow an infection to remain geographically isolated. Today, most infections that are found only in focal areas have biologic or geoclimatic constraints that prevent them from being introduced into other geographic regions. For example, the fungus *Coccidioides immitis*, which causes coccidioidomycosis, thrives in surface soil in arid and semiarid areas with alkaline soil, hot summers and short, moist winters; it is endemic in parts of south-western USA, Mexico and Central and South America. People become infected when they inhale arthroconidia from soil. An unusual wind storm in 1977 lifted soil from the endemic region and deposited it in northern California, outside the usual endemic region.[7] In general, infection is associated with residence in or travel through the endemic region. However, because the fungus can persist in the human host for years, even decades, after initial infection (which may be mild and unrecognized), disease may be diagnosed far from the endemic regions.

Vectors

Many microbes require a particular arthropod vector or animal host and hence inhabit circumscribed regions and may be unable to survive in other habitats. Malaria is a vector-borne infection that cannot persist in a region without a competent vector. The presence of a competent vector is a necessary but not sufficient condition for human infection. The mosquito must have a source of malarial parasites (gametocytemic human who may be asymptomatic), an appropriate incubation period to allow development of the parasite to a form that is infective via a bite, and access to other humans. Prevailing temperature and humidity must allow the mosquito to survive long enough for the malarial parasite to undergo maturation to reach an infective state for humans. Competent vectors exist in many areas without malaria transmission, because the other conditions are not met. These areas are at risk of the introduction of malaria, as illustrated by several recent examples in the USA and elsewhere.[8,9]

Malaria was endemic in many parts of the USA into the 20th century (Fig. 142.2), with estimates of more than 600,000 cases in 1914.[9] Even before extensive mosquito control programs were instituted, transmission declined. Demographic factors (population shifts from rural to urban areas), improved housing with screened doors and windows and the availability of treatment were among the factors that may have contributed to this decrease.

The flavivirus dengue is transmitted primarily by the widely distributed mosquito, *Aedes aegypti*, which is well adapted to human habitats. This viral infection has now become a major and growing problem in many tropical and subtropical regions throughout the world (see below).

The distribution of onchocerciasis in Africa is notable for its association with rivers.[10] The reason becomes clear by understanding that the vector of this filarial parasite, the black fly (genus *Simulium*), lays her eggs on vegetation and rocks of rapidly flowing rivers and

ORIGINS AND CONVEYORS OF HUMAN PATHOGENS		
Origin or carrier	**Conveyor or immediate source**	**Examples of disease**
Humans	Humans	HIV, syphilis, hepatitis B
Humans	Humans (air-borne pathogen)	Measles, tuberculosis
Soil	Soil, air-borne	Coccidioidomycosis
Soil	Food	Botulism
Animals	Water	Leptospirosis
Humans	Mosquitoes	Malaria, dengue
Humans	Soil	Hookworm, strongyloidiasis
Animals	Ticks	Lyme disease
Animals, humans	Sand flies	Leishmaniasis
Animals	Animals	Rabies
Rodents	Rodent excreta	Hantaviruses
Humans	Water, marine life	Cholera
Humans or animals (with snails as essential intermediate host)	Water	Schistosomiasis
Humans	Food	Typhoid fever
Animals	Water	Cryptosporidiosis, giardiasis

Table 142.1 Origins and conveyors of human pathogens. Some pathogens have multiple potential sources.

usually inhabits a region within 5–10km on either side of a river. Another name for onchocerciasis, river blindness, describes the epidemiology as well as one consequence of infection.

Some pathogens have a complex cycle of development that requires one or more intermediate hosts. Distribution may remain relatively fixed, even when infected humans travel widely, if other regions do not supply the right combination and geographic proximity of hosts (Fig. 142.3). Although persons with schistosomiasis visit many regions of the world, the parasite cannot be introduced into a new region unless an appropriate snail host is present, excreted eggs (in urine or feces) are released into water where they reach the snail hosts and humans subsequently have contact with the untreated water.[11]

Many hantaviruses exist worldwide with distributions that are still being defined. Each hantavirus seems to have its specific rodent reservoir with which it has evolved. As with many zoonoses, humans are incidental to the survival of the virus in rodents, yet humans can develop severe and sometimes fatal disease if they happen to enter an environment where they are exposed to the virus. Undoubtedly, other rodent-associated viruses and other pathogens (as well as pathogens associated with other animals or insects) with the capacity to infect humans will be identified as humans enter unexplored environments in the future.

Lassa and Ebola viruses are other viruses that have focal distributions, although the reservoir host for Ebola virus has not yet been defined. Because these infections can be spread from person to person, secondary household and nosocomial spread in several instances has amplified what began as an isolated event. Lack of adequate resources in hospitals in many developing regions contributes to the spread of infections within hospitals and to persons receiving outpatient care, such as those receiving injections.

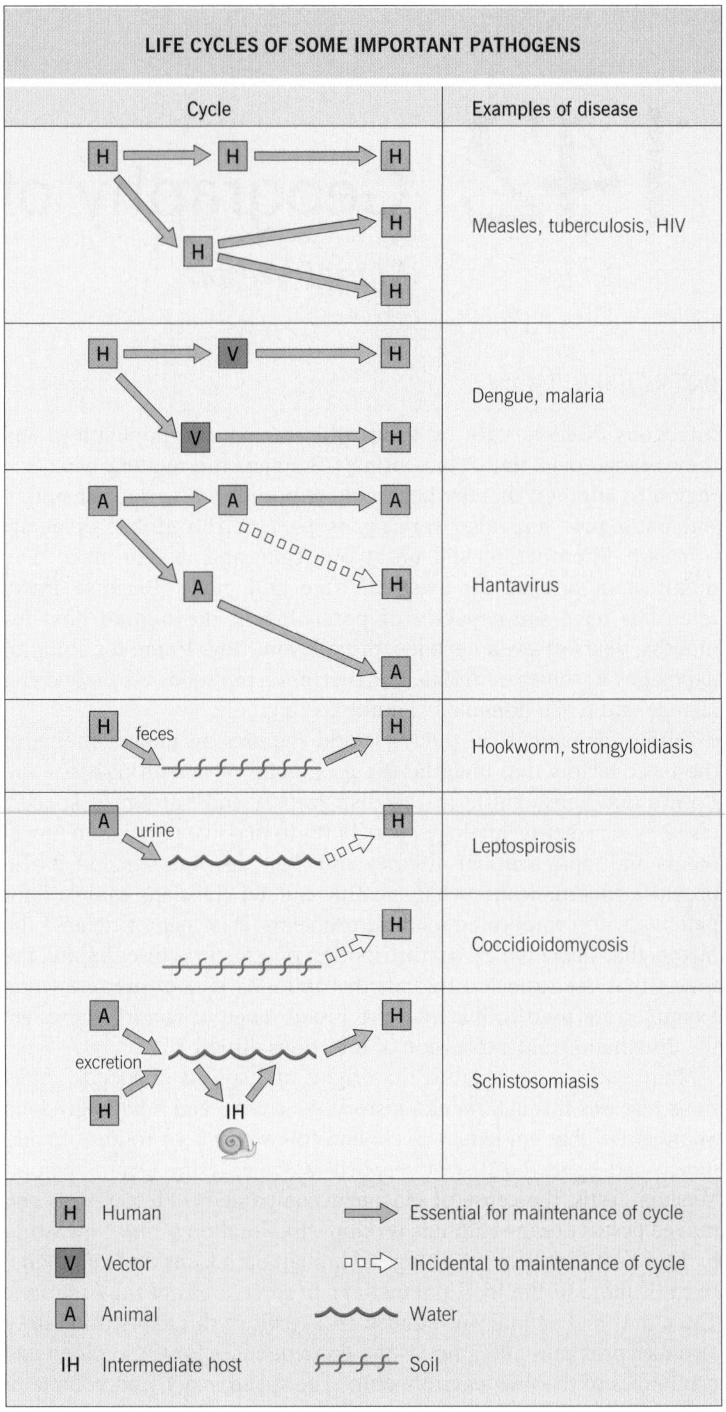

Fig. 142.1 Life cycles of some important pathogens.

Cultural practices can lead to unusual infections in isolated areas. Residents of the highlands of Papua New Guinea developed kuru after ingestion (or percutaneous inoculation) of human tissue during the preparation of the tissues of dead relatives.

Thus, the presence of a pathogen in a region may reflect the biologic properties of the organism, its need for a certain physicochemical environment or its dependence on specific arthropods, plants or animals to provide the milieu where it can sustain its lifecycle (Table 142.2). The presence of a pathogen in a region does not necessarily equate with human disease, because mechanisms must exist for the pathogen to reach a susceptible human host for human disease to occur. Sometimes it is only with exploration of new regions or changes in land use that humans place themselves in an environment where they come into contact with microbes that were

AREAS IN THE USA THOUGHT TO BE ENDEMIC FOR MALARIA DURING THE YEARS 1882–1912

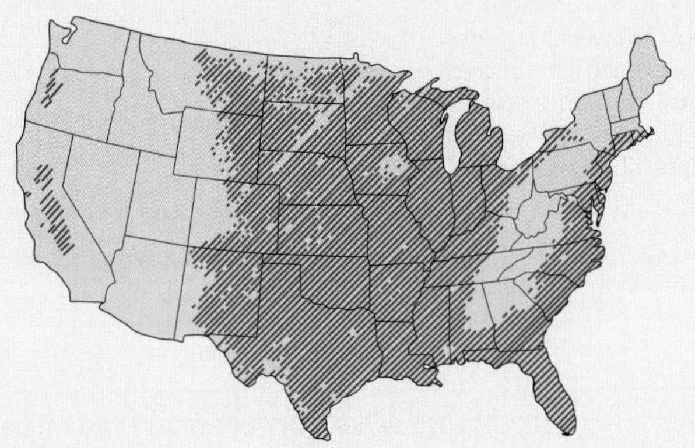

Fig. 142.2 Areas of the USA thought to be endemic for malaria during the years 1882–1912.

WORLDWIDE DISTRIBUTION OF SCHISTOSOMIASIS

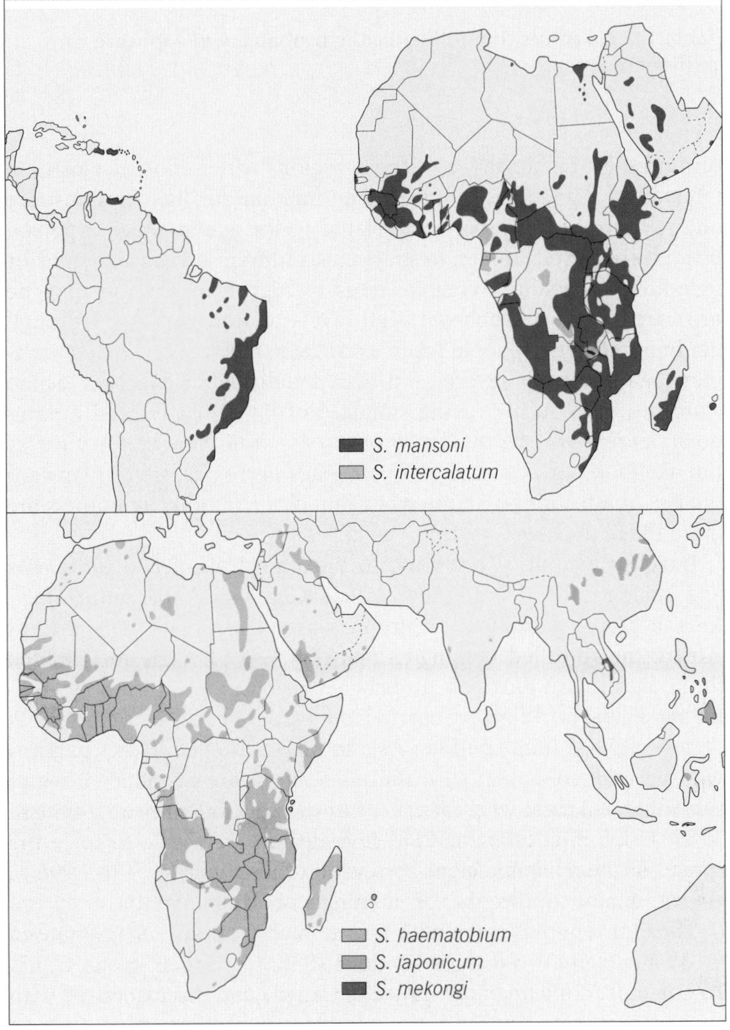

Fig. 142.3 Worldwide distribution of schistosomiasis.

previously unrecognized as human pathogens. Preferences for specific foods, certain preparation techniques or cultural traditions may place one population at a unique risk for infection.

BIOLOGIC ATTRIBUTES OF ORGANISMS THAT INFLUENCE THEIR EPIDEMIOLOGY

- Host range
- Duration of survival in host
- Route of exit from host
- Route of entry into human
- Virulence
- Capacity to survive outside host
- Resistance to antimicrobials and chemicals

Table 142.2 Biologic attributes of organisms that influence their epidemiology.

MODES OF TRANSMISSION FOR MAJOR GLOBAL INFECTIOUS DISEASES

Mode of transmission	% of total
Person-to-person	65
Food-borne, water-borne or soil-borne	22
Insect-borne	13
Animal-borne	0.3

Table 142.3 Modes of transmission for major global infectious diseases. The figures are based on an estimated 17.3 million deaths due to infectious diseases in 1995, as reported by the World Health Organization.[12]

FACTORS INFLUENCING THE BURDEN OF DISEASE

Among the infectious diseases that impose the greatest burden of death globally, most are widely distributed: respiratory tract infections (e.g. influenza, *Streptococcus pneumoniae* and others), diarrheal infections, tuberculosis, measles, AIDS and hepatitis B.[12] Most of these infections are spread from person to person. The World Health Organization estimated that about 65% of infectious diseases deaths globally in 1995 were due to infections transmitted from person to person (Table 142.3).[12]

Burden from these diseases is unevenly distributed across populations and among different countries. Poor sanitation, lack of clean water, crowded living conditions and lack of vaccination contribute to the disproportionate burden from many of these infections in developing regions of the world. In industrialized countries, pockets of high risk persist. Disadvantaged populations have higher rates of tuberculosis, HIV and many other infectious and noninfectious diseases. Rates of reported cases of tuberculosis vary widely by region (Table 142.4).[13] Variation also exists within countries. Figure 142.4 shows the effect of crowded living conditions on rates of tuberculosis in England and Wales in 1992.[14] Among welfare applicants and recipients addicted to drugs or alcohol in New York City, the rate of tuberculosis was 744 per 100,000 person years or more than 70 times the overall rate for the USA.[15] The impact of an infection derives not only from the risk of exposure but also from the access to effective therapy. For example, treatment of a patient with active tuberculosis can cure the individual and eliminate a source of infection for others in the community.

Neonatal tetanus, which was estimated to kill 459,000 persons (mostly neonates) in 1995,[12] is caused by a widely distributed bacterium, but the disease predominates in areas where pregnant women and their infants are not protected by immunization with tetanus toxoid. Diphtheria, controlled in many parts of the world,

RATES OF REPORTED CASES OF TUBERCULOSIS WORLDWIDE BY REGION (2000)		
Region	**Rate per 100,000 population**	**Range of rates***
Africa	115	17–635
Americas	28	0–151
Eastern Mediterranean	28	4–628
Europe	42	0–160
South East Asia	91	32–153
Western Pacific	48	0–253

* Highest and lowest rates reported by countries in region.

Table 142.4 Rates of reported cases of tuberculosis worldwide by region (2000). Source: WHO Report. Global tuberculosis control. Geneva: WHO; 2002.

RATES OF TUBERCULOSIS IN ENGLAND AND WALES (1992)

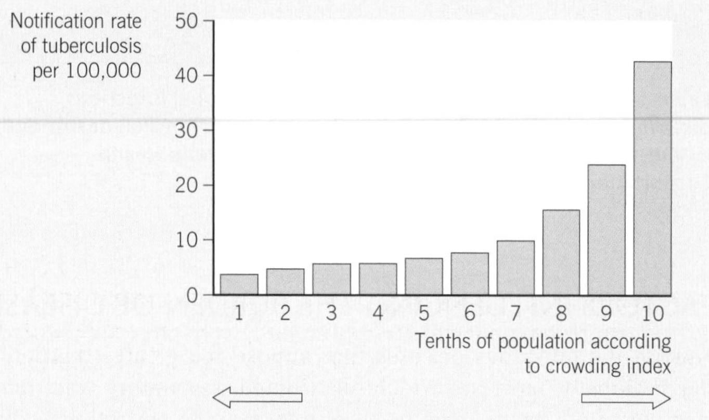

Fig. 142.4 Rates of tuberculosis in England and Wales by crowding index (1992). Adapted from Bhatti *et al.*[14]

FACTORS THAT INFLUENCE THE TYPES AND ABUNDANCE OF MICROBES IN A COMMUNITY

- Geoclimatic conditions
- Socio-economic conditions
- Public health infrastructure
- Urban versus rural environment
- Density and mobility of population
- Season of the year

Table 142.5 Factors that influence the types and abundance of microbes in a community.

FACTORS THAT INFLUENCE THE PROBABILITY OF EXPOSURE TO PATHOGENS

- Living accommodation
- Level of sanitation
- Occupational and recreational activities
- Food preparation and preferences
- Sexual activities and other behavior
- Contact with pets and other animals
- Time spent in the area

Table 142.6 Factors that influence the probability of exposure to pathogens.

resurged in new independent states of the former Soviet Union in the 1990s, a reminder of the tenuous control over many infectious diseases. Populations in other countries also felt the impact as cases related to exposures in the Russian Federation were reported in Poland, Finland, Germany and the USA. Serologic studies in America and Europe suggest that up to 60% of adults may be susceptible to diphtheria.

Travelers to tropical and developing regions of the world can pick up geographically focal, often vector- or animal-associated infections (such as malaria and dengue), but travelers most often acquire infections with a worldwide distribution that are especially common in areas lacking good sanitation. Food- and water-borne infections are common and lead to traveler's diarrhea, which is caused by multiple agents (including *Escherichia coli, Salmonella* spp., *Shigella* spp., *Campylobacter* spp. and others), typhoid fever and hepatitis A. Respiratory tract infections may be acquired from other travelers from all over the globe during the crowding that occurs in travel (e.g. in buses, airplanes, terminals and on cruise ships) as well as from persons in the local environment. Tables 142.5 and 142.6 note factors that influence the types and abundance of microbes in a community and the probability of exposure to pathogens.

Hepatitis A virus remains a common cause of infection in developing regions of the world although it is not considered a major cause of morbidity or mortality in those regions where most persons are infected at a young age and become immune for life. The presence and severity of symptoms are related to the age at which a person becomes infected. Infection in young children is typically mild or inapparent. Persons living in areas of high transmission may be unaware of the presence of high levels of transmission, although nonimmune, older people (such as travelers) who enter the environment may develop severe, and occasionally fatal, infection. Some countries with an improving standard of living have noted a paradoxic increase in the incidence of disease from hepatitis A virus as the likelihood of exposure at a young age decreases, shifting upward the age of infection to a time when jaundice and other symptoms are more likely to occur.

Travelers may also contribute to the spread of infectious diseases and influence the global burden of these diseases. *Neisseria meningitidis*, a global pathogen, occurs in seasonal epidemics in parts of Africa: the so-called meningitis belt (Fig. 142.5).[16] Irritation of the throat by the dry, dusty air probably contributes to invasion by colonizing bacteria. Pilgrims carried an epidemic strain of group A *N. meningitidis* from southern Asia to Mecca in 1987. Other pilgrims who became colonized with the epidemic strain introduced it into sub-Saharan Africa, where it caused a wave of epidemics in 1988 and 1989. Using molecular markers, investigators were able to trace the spread of the epidemic clone to several other countries.[17] In 1996 in Africa, major outbreaks of meningococcal meningitis occurred (>185,000 reported cases with a case fatality rate of ~10%) caused by *N. meningitidis* serogroup A, clone III-1.[18] A virulent group C, ET-15 strain of *N. meningitidis* spread in Canada and was associated with an increased case fatality rate and a higher proportion of cases in persons over the age of 5 years.[19] In these examples, the virulence of the microbe and travel and trade acted synergistically to change the epidemiology and burden of disease. In the spring of 2000 serogroup W135 *N. meningitidis* caused an outbreak of infection in pilgrims to the Hajj and subsequently spread to their contacts and others around the world. Studies using serotyping, multilocus sequence typing, multi-

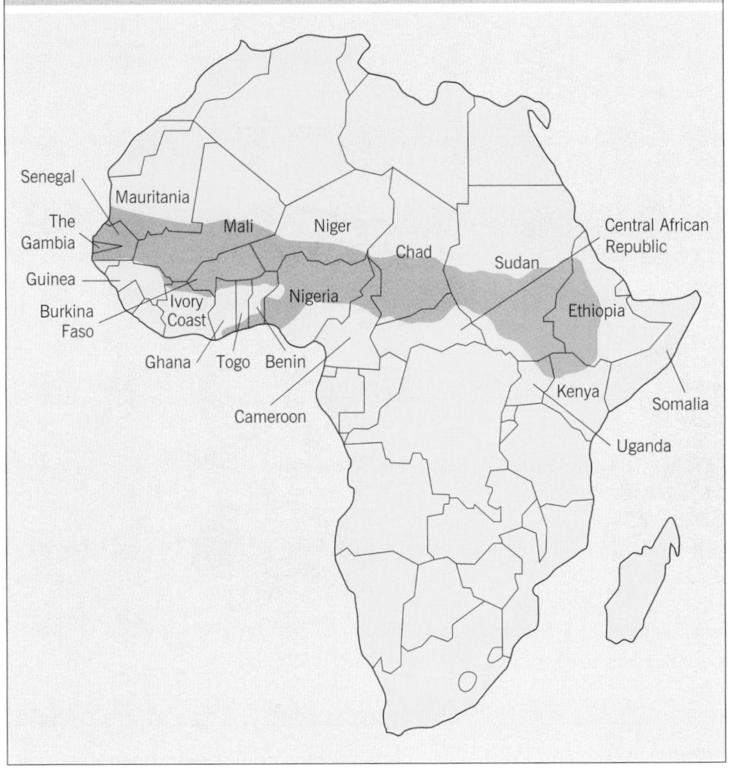

Fig. 142.5 Meningitis belt in Africa.

locus DNA fingerprints and other techniques found identical W135 isolates in multiple countries. Pilgrims are required to receive a meningococcal vaccine but before this outbreak, pilgrims from many countries received a vaccine that protected against serotype A but not W135. The vaccine reduces risk of disease but does not prevent oropharyngeal carriage of *N. meningitidis*.[20]

FACTORS INFLUENCING EMERGENCE OF DISEASE

Regular, rapid movement of persons from tropical regions to major urban areas throughout the world raises concerns that unusual infections could be introduced into an environment where they could spread to large populations. How likely is this? Microbes are repeatedly carried around the globe, yet endemic regions for many infections remain relatively fixed. Most examples of the appearance of a microbe or disease in a region are not followed by sustained spread.

In order to assess the potential for a pathogen to be introduced into a new population, information is required about the biologic properties of the organism, the region and population being considered and the mechanisms of transmission (see Table 142.1). The key factor that determines whether a pathogen can survive and spread in a new environment is its basic reproductive rate, which is the average number of successful offspring a pathogen can produce. To become established in a new host population, a parasitic species must have a basic reproductive rate that exceeds one offspring per pathogen.[21] The concept is simple but invasion and persistence are affected by a range of biologic, social and environmental factors.

Certain factors restrict the introduction and spread or persistence of infection in a region (Table 142.7); many of these are discussed above. Before measles vaccine was introduced, the epidemiology of measles exhibited marked periodicity in large populations, with peaks typically occurring every 2–3 years.[22] In general, a community size of about 250,000 is necessary to provide a sufficient number of susceptible people to sustain the virus. In small island communities

FACTORS THAT RESTRICT INTRODUCTION AND SPREAD OF INFECTIONS
• Geoclimatic factors that cannot support vector or intermediate host • Genetics of human population, making it genetically resistant or relatively resistant • Immunity of human population, making it not susceptible because of past infection with same or related microbe or via vaccination • Demographic factors (e.g. size and density of population will not support sustained transmission of diseases such as measles) • Social and behavioral factors (absence of activities such as iv drug use and unprotected sex with multiple partners) • Food preparation habits and local traditions (e.g. certain dishes not eaten, food always well cooked) • High-quality housing, sanitation, public health infrastructure • High standard of living, good nutrition, lack of crowding

Table 142.7 Factors that restrict the introduction and spread of infections.

(or other isolated populations), outbreaks typically occur only after periodic introductions from outside. Size and density of a population thus influence the epidemiology of some infections. It has been suggested that measles as it has been known in the 20th century could not have established itself much before 3000 BC because before that time human populations had not achieved sufficient size to sustain the virus. Measles could not have persisted in nomadic, hunting communities.

Examples of emerging pathogens

It is instructive to look at examples of infections that have recently undergone major shifts in distribution and to review the key factors that have influenced their geographic spread. They are a reminder of the complexity of the interactions among host, microbe and the environment. A recurring theme is the movement of humans who introduce pathogens into a new region (see also Chapter 4).

Human immunodeficiency virus and other pathogens carried by humans

Organisms that survive primarily or entirely in the human host and are spread from person to person (e.g. by sexual or other close contact or by droplet nuclei) can be carried to any part of the world. The spread of HIV in the past two decades to all parts of the world is a reminder of the rapid and broad reach of travel networks. Although the infection has also spread via blood and shared needles, it has been the human host engaging in sex and reproduction who has been the origin for the majority of the infections worldwide. Person-to-person spread accounted for the rapid world-wide distribution of SARS (severe acute respiratory syndrome), a coronavirus infection, in the spring of 2003.

Drugs or vaccines injected by reused inadequately sterilized needles and syringes have been and continue to be an important means of spread of blood-borne infections, such as hepatitis C, hepatitis B and HIV, in some parts of the world.[23]

A large outbreak of antibiotic-resistant shigellosis involving more than 50% of the estimated 12,700 persons at a mass gathering in North Carolina, USA, was followed by nationwide dissemination of the organism and outbreaks in at least three other states.[24] Using molecular techniques coupled with epidemiologic data, investigators were able to show the emergence of multiple drug-resistant tuberculosis clones in New York and their dissemination in New York and to at least four other cities in the USA.[25] It is not only the pathogens carried by humans that are relevant. Humans also carry resistance and virulence factors that can be transferred to and exchanged with other microbes.[26]

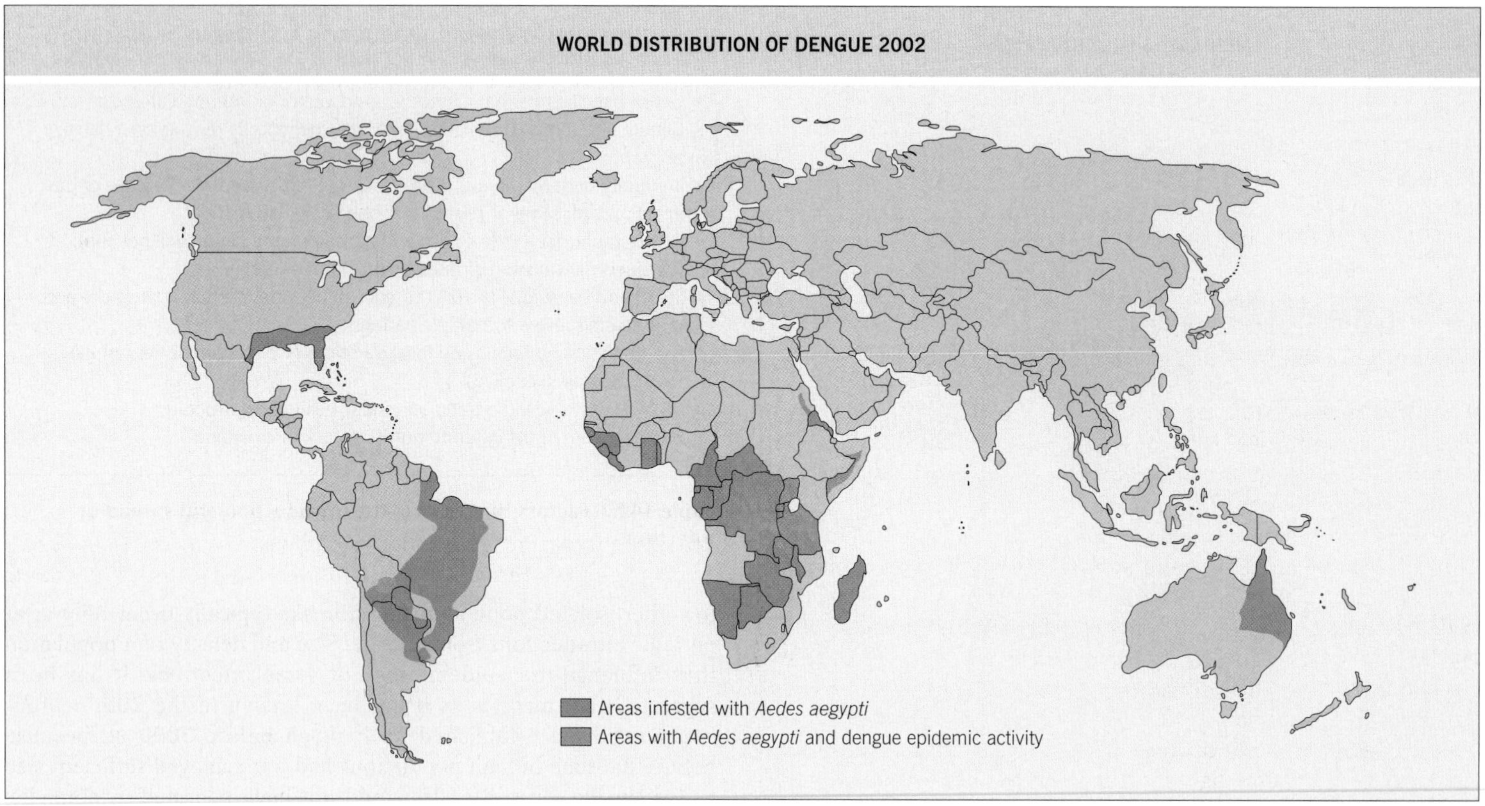

Fig. 142.6 Areas reporting dengue fever and areas with a competent vector (2002). Many areas with a competent vector do not report dengue epidemic activity. Data from the Centers for Disease Control and Prevention.[16]

Dengue fever

Dengue fever is a mosquito-borne viral infection that has now spread to most tropical and subtropical regions of the world and threatens to continue to increase in incidence and severity. Viremic humans regularly enter regions infested with *Aedes aegypti*, the principal vector of dengue, transporting the virus for new outbreaks. Infection can spread rapidly and outbreaks are sometimes massive, involving >30% of the population. Because four serotypes of dengue virus exist and infection with one serotype does not confer lasting immunity against other serotypes, a person can be infected more than once. The risk of developing severe dengue (e.g. dengue shock syndrome or dengue hemorrhagic fever, DSS or DHF) after repeat infection is 82–103 times greater than after primary infection.[27] In an outbreak in Cuba, 98.5% of cases of DSS or DHF were in persons with a prior dengue infection. The rate of DSS or DHF was 4.2% in persons with prior dengue infection who became infected with a new serotype.[28] Geographic regions where multiple serotypes are circulating have continued to expand, setting the stage for more severe consequences of infection. Factors that have aided the spread of dengue include increasing (and rapid) travel to and from tropical regions; expansion of the regions infested with *Aedes aegypti*; increasing urbanization, especially in tropical areas, which has provided large, dense populations; the use of nonbiodegradeable and other containers that make ideal breeding sites for the mosquito; and lack of support for vector control programs.

Most of the world population growth is occurring in tropical and developing regions. The expectation is that more urban areas in tropical regions will reach the critical population size, perhaps somewhere between 150,000 and 1 million people, to permit sustained transmission of dengue and to increase the risk of the severe forms of infection, dengue hemorrhagic fever and dengue shock syndrome.[29] But travelers are also at risk and the 90 laboratory-diagnosed infections in travelers returning to the USA in 1998 represented a 70% increase from 1997.[30]

It is instructive to ask not only where dengue occurs but also where it does not. Although large dengue epidemics occurred in the USA earlier in this century, only a handful of cases have been acquired in the USA in recent years, despite the presence of epidemic disease in adjacent areas of Mexico and the presence of a competent vector (*Aedes aegypti*) in south-eastern USA (Fig. 142.6).[16] It is possible that the presence of screened dwellings and air conditioning may make an area relatively resistant to the introduction of infection, even if a competent vector infests a region.

Cholera

Cholera is an ancient disease that is continuing to spread and to change. In 1991 it entered Latin America for the first time in more than a century and spread rapidly from Peru to infect persons throughout the region. By 1996, more than 1.4 million cases had been reported to cause more than 10,000 deaths.[31] In 1992, a novel strain of cholera, classified as *Vibrio cholerae* 0139 Bengal, emerged in India and Bangladesh, causing major epidemics in India, Bangladesh and other Asian countries. Travelers carried infections back to Europe, the USA and Japan. This new strain was unusual in that it was the first non-01 strain that could cause epidemics. Persons in cholera-endemic regions who had immunity to the well-known cholera strains were susceptible to this new strain. The already licensed vaccines did not protect against *V. cholerae* 0139.

Cholera illustrates the complex interactions between microbe, environment and host.[32] Epidemics are seasonal in endemic regions. *V. cholerae* lives in close association with marine life, binding to chitin in crustacean shells and colonizing surfaces of algae, phytoplankton, zooplankton and water plants. *V. cholerae* can persist within the aquatic environment for months or years, often in a viable but dormant state, nonculturable by usual techniques. Environmental factors, including temperature, salinity, pH and sea-water nutrients, affect the persistence, abundance and viability of the organisms, and hence have a striking influence on human epidemics.

Under conditions of population crowding, poor sanitation and lack of clean water, cholera can have a devastating impact, as was shown by the massive outbreak of El Tor cholera in Rwandan refugees in Goma, Zaire, which caused 12,000 deaths in July 1994.[33]

The organism can be carried by humans, who sometimes have few or no symptoms, and introduced into new regions. Trade probably also plays a critical role. Ballast water, picked up by boats in multiple locations and discharged at another time and place, carries a wide range of species, including many that have no direct impact on human health.[34–36] In studies of the ballast and bilge of cargo ships in the USA Gulf of Mexico, researchers were able to identify *V. cholerae* identical to the strains causing epidemic disease in Latin America.[37]

Food-borne disease

The globalization of the food market means pathogens from one region can appear in another; some are common pathogens with a worldwide distribution but others are not. An outbreak of cholera in Maryland, USA, was traced to imported, contaminated commercial frozen coconut milk.[38] Alfalfa sprouts grown from contaminated seed sent to a Dutch shipper caused outbreaks of infections with *Salmonella* spp. on two continents, in at least Arizona and Michigan in the USA and in Finland.[39] Commercial movement of fruits and vegetables redistributes resistance factors along with the microbes. Tracing the source after an infection has been diagnosed can be convoluted and often is not carried out unless disease is severe, lethal or epidemic or involves a highly visible person or population.

Travel and trade are key features in the epidemiology of the infection *Cyclospora*, a cause of gastroenteritis. Recognized for many years in multiple regions of the world, cases were often associated with living in or travel to areas where sanitary facilities were poor. Most of the experience in the USA with the disease was in overseas travelers. In the summer of 1996, a large outbreak occurred in persons who had not traveled. Over a period of a few months, 1465 cases of cyclosporiasis were reported from 20 states. The outbreak was linked to eating raspberries imported from Guatemala.[40] During some seasons of the year up to 70% of selected fruits and vegetables sold in the USA come from developing countries.

Schistosomiasis

Seemingly unrelated events can profoundly alter the epidemiology of infectious diseases in humans. Changes in the way land is used is an important one. In Egypt, prevalence of *Schistosoma mansoni* infection increased from 21.7% in 1985 to 42.1% in 1992 among settlers in a region where recent irrigation projects had reclaimed land from the desert. The irrigation water came from the Nile River or its irrigation dams, which made it likely that snail vectors would be introduced into the new regions. Many settlers to the area were already infected and so contributed to the contamination of the waters because sanitary treatment of human excreta was generally unavailable. New settlers came from other regions and had little or no pre-existing immunity to schistosomiasis, making them especially vulnerable to the consequences of infection.[41]

In Senegal, extensive agricultural development and the building of two large dams led to the introduction of *Schistosoma mansoni* into the Senegal river basin.[42] The first case was discovered in 1988. Infection spread rapidly and the prevalence of schistosomiasis reached 45–70% by 1990.

Visceral leishmaniasis

In the past, visceral leishmaniasis in Brazil was primarily a rural disease. Recently, however, several cities have reported large outbreaks of visceral leishmaniasis.[43] Reasons for the change in epidemiology include geoclimatic and economic factors (drought, lack of farm land, famine) leading to migration of large numbers of persons, who settle in periurban areas where they live in densely crowded shanties, lacking basic sanitation. The presence of domestic animals, such as dogs, chickens and horses, in and adjacent to human dwellings provides ample sources of blood meals for the sand fly, the vector of leishmaniasis. Outbreaks have occurred in many cities in Brazil, including Teresina, São Luis and Natal. Children and young people have been most affected. Malnutrition also can contribute to the severity of the disease.

Disease–disease interactions can also alter the epidemiology of infections. Visceral leishmaniasis has become an important infection in HIV-infected people in Spain and other areas where the two diseases co-exist.[44] The presence of HIV leads to increased risk of progression of infection; late appearance of disease can occur years to decades after exposure in an endemic region, leading to the appearance of cases of leishmaniasis in regions distant from endemic areas. A common consequence is missed or delayed diagnosis.

Movement of vectors and other species

Movement today involves all forms of life and the movement of non-human species can affect infections in humans. *Aedes albopictus* introduced into the USA via used tyres shipped from Asia[45] has since become established in at least 21 contiguous states of the USA and in Hawaii. *Aedes albopictus* can transmit dengue and is a competent laboratory vector of La Crosse, yellow fever and other viruses. It is also hardier than many other mosquito species and therefore may spread widely and be extremely difficult to eradicate. Multiple strains of eastern equine encephalitis virus have been isolated from *Aedes albopictus* in Florida.

An example from the past illustrates the potential consequences of the introduction of a mosquito vector into a new region. In March 1930, an entomologist in Natal, Brazil, came upon *Anopheles gambiae* larvae in a small, wet, grassy field between a railway and a river.[46] He was surprised, because the usual habitat for this mosquito was Africa. Investigation revealed that the probable route of entry into South America was via boats that made mail runs between Dakar in Senegal and Natal in Brazil, covering the 3300km in less than 100 hours. In Dakar the boats were anchored a distance from the shore within easy flight range of *A. gambiae*. In Brazil, over the ensuing years, the mosquito spread along the coastal region and inland. Natal, as an ocean port, terminus of two railway lines and the hub of truck, car and river transportation, was well suited for dissemination of *A. gambiae* into the region. Although malaria already existed in the region, the local mosquitoes were not efficient vectors. *Anopheles gambiae*, in contrast, lived in close proximity to humans, entered houses, sought human blood and was an efficient biter. In 1938 and 1939, devastating outbreaks of malaria killed more than 20,000 persons. In this instance, the simple introduction of a new vector into a region led to severe problems. Fortunately, an intensive (and expensive) eradication campaign was effective.

Current transportation systems regularly carry all forms of life, including potential vectors, along with people and cargo.[47] In an experiment carried out several years ago, mosquitoes, house flies and beetles in special cages were placed in wheel bays of 747 aircraft and carried on flights lasting up to 7 hours. Temperatures were as low as −62°F (−52°C) outside and ranged from 46 to 77°F (8–25°C) in the wheel bays. Survival rates were greater than 99% for the beetles, 84% for the mosquitoes and 93% for the flies.[48] Occasional cases of so-called airport malaria – cases of malaria near airports in temperate regions – attest to the occasional transport and survival of a commuter mosquito long enough to take at least one blood meal in the new environment.[49]

In the USA, transportation of racoons in the late 1970s from Florida to the area between Virginia and West Virginia (in order to stock hunting clubs) unintentionally introduced a rabies virus variant into the animals of the region. From there, the rabies enzootic spread for hundreds of miles, reaching racoons in suburban and densely

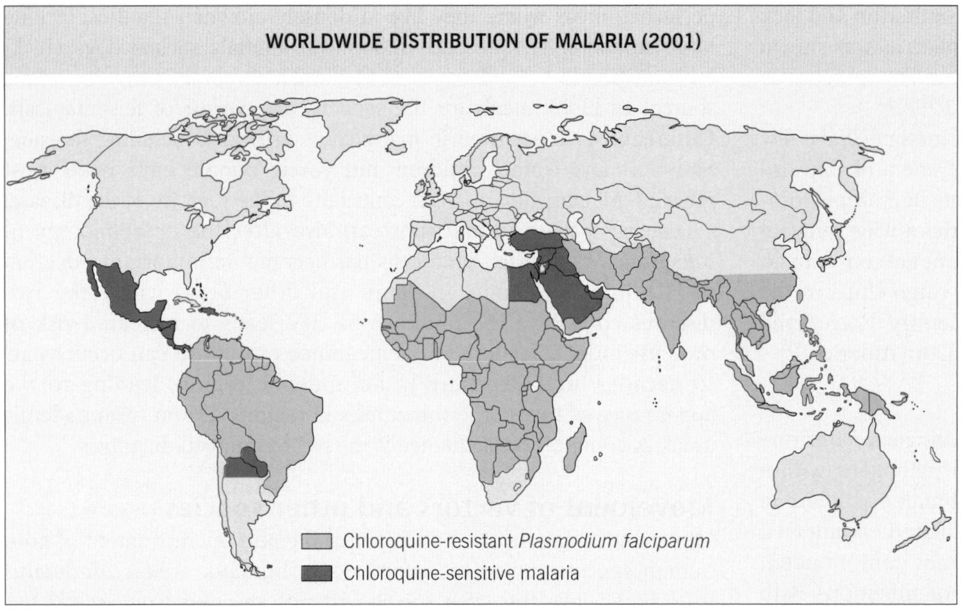

Fig. 142.7 Worldwide distribution of malaria (2001). Data from the Centers for Disease Control and Prevention.[16]

populated regions of the north-east USA. Spill-over of the rabies virus variant into cats, dogs and other animal populations and direct racoon–human interactions have had extremely costly and unpleasant consequences.[50]

GEOGRAPHIC INFLUENCES ON DIFFERENTIAL DIAGNOSIS

Geographic exposures influence how one thinks about probable diagnoses in a given patient. In Mexico, for example, more than 50% of patients with late-onset seizures have CT evidence of the parasitic infection, neurocysticercosis.[51] In Peru, 29% of persons born outside Lima who had onset of seizures after age 20 years had serologic evidence of cysticercosis.[52] In northern Thailand, melioidosis is a common cause of sepsis, accounting for 40% of all deaths from community-acquired sepsis.[53]

In considering the consequences of exposures in other geographic regions, relevant data in assessing the probability of various infections include the duration of visit, activities and living conditions during the stay and the time lapsed since the visit. Among British travelers to West Africa, the relative risk of malaria was 80.3 times higher for persons staying for 6–12 months than among those staying 1 week.[54] In Malawi, the risk of schistosome infection increased directly with duration of stay. Seroprevalence was 11% for those present for 1 year or less, but this increased to 48% among those present for 4 years or longer.[55] In a study of persons with cysticercosis, the average time between acquisition of infection and onset of symptoms was about 7 years.[56]

For malaria, it is necessary to know not only whether infection can be acquired in a specific location but also the types of parasites present and the patterns of resistance to antimalarial agents. As chloroquine resistance has spread, maps now typically highlight the few remaining areas of chloroquine sensitivity. Because the resistance to antimalarial agents is a dynamic process, with levels of resistance generally increasing over time (involving *Plasmodium vivax* in some areas as well as *P. falciparum*), it is essential to base decisions about chemoprophylaxis and treatment on up-to-date information. Figure 142.7 shows the distribution of malaria and resistance patterns globally as of 2001.

Expression of disease may vary depending on age of first exposure, immunologic status of the host, genetic factors and the number and timing of subsequent exposures. Temporary residents of endemic regions have different patterns of response to a number of helminths from those of long-term residents. In cases of loiasis, temporary residents have immunologic hyperresponsiveness, high-grade eosinophilia and severe symptoms that are not seen in long-term residents of the same area.[57] Genetic factors can affect susceptibility to infection or expression of disease. Some persons, for example, are genetically resistant to infection with parvovirus because they lack appropriate receptors on their erythrocytes.[58] Persons lacking Duffy factor cannot be infected with the malarial parasite, *P. vivax*.

CONCLUSION

Knowledge about the geographic distribution of diseases is essential for informed evaluation and care of patients, who increasingly have had exposures in multiple geographic regions. Infectious diseases are dynamic and will continue to change in distribution. Changes in virulence and shifts in resistance patterns will also require ongoing surveillance and communication to health care providers. Multiple factors favor even more rapid change, perhaps in unexpected ways, in the future: rapidity and volume of travel, increasing urbanization (especially in developing regions), the globalization of trade, multiple technologic changes that favor mass processing and broad dispersal and the backdrop of ongoing microbial adaptation and change, which may be hastened by alterations in the physicochemical environment.

REFERENCES

1. Wilson ME. A world guide to infections: diseases, distribution, diagnosis. New York: Oxford University Press; 1991.
2. Wilson ME. Travel and emergence of infectious diseases. Emerg Infect Dis 1995;1:39–46.
3. Wilson ME. Infectious diseases: an ecological perspective. BMJ 1995;311:1681–4.
4. Winkelstein W Jr. A new perspective on John Snow's communicable disease theory. Am J Epidemiol 1995;142(suppl):S3–S9 [Citing: Snow J. On the mode of communication of cholera. London: John Churchill; 1849].
5. Crosby AW Jr. The Columbian exchange. Westport, Connecticut: Greenwood Press; 1972.
6. Wilson ME, Levins R, Spielman A, eds. Disease in evolution: global changes and emergence of infectious diseases. New York: New York Academy of Sciences; 1994.
7. Flynn NM, Hoeprich PD, Kawachi MM, *et al.* An unusual outbreak of windborne coccidioidomycosis. N Engl J Med 1979;301:358–61.
8. Maldonado YA, Nahlen BL, Roberto RR, *et al.* Transmission of *Plasmodium vivax* malaria in San Diego County, California, 1986. Am J Trop Med Hyg 1990;42:3–9.
9. Zucker J. Changing patterns of autochthonous malaria transmission in the United States; a review of recent outbreaks. Emerg Infect Dis 1996;2:37–43.
10. World Health Organization. Report of a WHO expert committee on onchocerciasis control. Geneva: World Health Organization Technical Report Series, No. 852; 1995.
11. World Health Organization. Prevention and control of schistosomiasis and soil-transmitted helminthiasis. Report of a WHO expert committee, 2002. Geneva: World Health Organization Technical Report Series, No.912.
12. World Health Organization. The world health report 1996. Fighting disease, fostering development. Geneva: World Health Organization; 1996.
13. World Health Organization. Tuberculosis. Weekly Epidemiol Rec 1997;72:117–22.
14. Bhatti N, Law MR, Morris JK, Halliday R, Moore-Gillon J. Increasing incidence of tuberculosis in England and Wales: a study of the likely causes. BMJ 1995;310:967–9.
15. Fineberg HV, Wilson ME. Social vulnerability and death by infection. N Engl J Med 1996;334:859–60.
16. Centers for Disease Control and Prevention. Health information for international travel 2001–2002. Atlanta, Georgia: Department of Health and Human Services; 2001.
17. Moore PS, Reeves MW, Schwartz B, Gellin BG, Broome CV. Intercontinental spread of an epidemic group A *Neisseria meningitidis* strain. Lancet 1989;2:260–3.
18. World Health Organization. Meningitis in Chad. Weekly Epidemiol Rec 1998;73:126–6.
19. Whalen CM, Hockin JC, Ryan A, Ashton F. The changing epidemiology of invasive meningococcal disease in Canada, 1985 through 1992. Emergence of a virulent clone of *Neisseria meningitidis*. JAMA 1995;273:390–4.
20. Taba MK, Achtman M, Alouso JM, *et al.* Serogroup W135 meningococcal disease in Hajj pilgrims. Lancet 2000;356:2159.
21. Anderson RM, May RM. Infectious diseases of humans. Dynamics and control. Oxford: Oxford University Press; 1991.
22. Cliff A, Haggett P, Smallman-Raynor M. Measles. An historical geography of a major human viral disease from global expansion to local retreat, 1940–1990. Oxford: Blackwell Publishers; 1993.
23. Drucker E, Alcabes PG, Marx PA. The injection century: massive unsterile injections and the emergence of human pathogens. Lancet 2001;358:1989–92.
24. Wharton M, Spiegel RA, Horna JM, *et al.* A large outbreak of antibiotic-resistant shigellosis at a mass gathering. J Infect Dis 1990;162:1324–8.
25. Bifani PJ, Plikaytis BB, Kapur V, *et al.* Origin and interstate spread of a New York City multidrug-resistant *Mycobacterium tuberculosis* clone family. JAMA 1996;275:452–7.
26. Okeke IN, Edelruan R. Dissemination of antibiotic-resistant bacteria across goegraphic borders. Clin Infect Dis 2001;33:364–9.
27. Thein S, Aung MM, Shwe TH, *et al.* Risk factors in dengue shock syndrome. Am J Trop Med Hyg 1997;56:566–72.
28. Guzman MG, Kouri G, Valdes L, *et al.* Epidemiologic studies on dengue in Santiago de Cuba, 1997. Am J Epidemiol 2000;152:793–9.
29. Kuno G. Review of the factors modulating dengue transmission. Epidemiol Rev 1995;17:321–35.
30. Centers for Disease Control and Prevention. Imported dengue – United States, 1997 and 1998. MMWR 2000;49:248–53.
31. Sanchez JL, Taylor DN. Cholera. Lancet 1997;349:1825–30.
32. Colwell RR. Global climate and infectious disease: the cholera paradigm. Science 1996;274:2025–31.
33. Goma Epidemiology Group. Public health impact of Rwandan refugee crisis: what happened in Goma, Zaire, in July, 1994. Lancet 1995;345:339–44.
34. Carlton JT, Geller JB. Ecological roulette: the global transport of non-indigenous marine organisms. Science 1993;261:78–82.
35. Committee on Ship's Ballast Operations, Marine Board, Commission on Engineering and Technical Systems, National Research Council. Stemming the tide. Controlling introductions of nonindigenous species by ships' ballast water. Washington DC: National Academy Press; 1996.
36. Ruiz GM, Rawlings TK, Dobbs FC, *et al.* Invasion biology: global spread of microorganisms by ships. Nature 2000;408(6806):49–50.
37. McCarthy SA, McPhearson RM, Guarino AM. Toxigenic *Vibrio cholerae* O1 and cargo ships entering the Gulf of Mexico. Lancet 1992;339:624–5.
38. Taylor JT, Tuttle J, Pramukul T, *et al.* An outbreak of cholera in Maryland associated with imported commercial frozen fresh coconut milk. J Infect Dis 1993;167:1330–5.
39. Mahon BE, Ponka A, Hall WN, *et al.* An international outbreak of *Salmonella* infections caused by alfalfa sprouts grown from contaminated seeds. J Infect Dis 1997;175:876–82.
40. Herwaldt BL, Ackers M-L, Cyclospora Working Group. An outbreak in 1996 of cyclosporiasis associated with imported raspberries. N Engl J Med 1997;336:1548–56.
41. El-Sayed HF, Rizkalla NH, Mehanna S, Abaza SM, Winch PJ. Prevalence and epidemiology of *Schistosoma mansoni* and *S. haematobium* infection in two areas of Egypt recently reclaimed from the desert. Am J Trop Med Hyg 1995;52:194–8.
42. Stelman FF, van der Werf M, Talla I, Niang M, Gryseels B. Four years' follow-up of hepatosplenic morbidity in a recently emerged focus of *Schistosoma mansoni* in northern Senegal. Trans R Soc Trop Med Hyg 1997;91:29–30.
43. Jeronimo SMB, Oliveira RM, Mackay S, *et al.* An urban outbreak of visceral leishmaniasis in Natal, Brazil. Trans R Soc Trop Med Hyg 1994;88:386–8.
44. Canto-Lara SB, Perez-Molina JA, Guerrero A, *et al.* Clinicoepidemiologic characteristics, prognostic factors, and survival analysis of patients coinfected with human immunodeficiency virus and *Leishmania* in an area of Madrid, Spain. Am J Trop Med Hyg 1998;58:436–43.
45. Reiter P, Sprenger D. The used tire trade: a mechanism for the worldwide dispersal of container-breeding mosquitoes. J Am Mosq Control Assoc 1987;3:494–501.
46. Soper FL, Wilson DB. *Anopheles gambiae* in Brazil, 1930–1940. New York City: The Rockefeller Foundation; 1943.
47. Lounibos LP. Invasions by insect vectors of human disease. Ann Rev Entomol 2002;47:233–66.
48. Russell RC. Survival of insects in the wheel bays of a Boeing 747B aircraft on flights between tropical and temperate airports. Bull WHO 1987;65:659–62.
49. Isaacson M. Airport malaria: a review. Bull WHO 1989;67:737–43.
50. Fishbein DB, Robinson LE. Rabies. N Engl J Med 1993;329:1632–8.
51. Medina M, Roasa E, Rubio F, Sotelo J. Neurocysticercosis as the main cause of late-onset epilepsy in Mexico. Arch Intern Med 1990;150:325–7.
52. Garcia HH, Gilman R, Martinez M, *et al.* Cysticercosis as a major cause of epilepsy in Peru. Lancet 1993;341:197–200.
53. Chaowagul W, White HJ, Dance DAB, *et al.* Melioidosis: a major cause of community-acquired septicemia in northeastern Thailand. J Infect Dis 1989;159:890–9.
54. Phillips-Howard PA, Radalowicz A, Mitchell J, Bradley DJ. Risk of malaria in British residents returning from malarious areas. BMJ 1990;300:499–503.
55. Cetron M, Chitsulo L, Sullivan JJ, *et al.* Schistosomiasis in Lake Malawi. Lancet 1996;348:1274–8.
56. Dixon HBF, Harvreaves WH. Cysticercosis (*T. solium*): a further ten years' clinical study, covering 284 cases. Q J Med 1944;13:107–21.
57. Klion AD, Massoughbodji A, Sadeler BC, Ottesen EA, Nutman TB. Loiasis in endemic and nonendemic populations: immunologically mediated differences in clinical presentation. J Infect Dis 1991;163:1318–25.
58. Brown KE, Hibbs JR, Gallinella G, *et al.* Resistance to parvovirus B19 infection due to lack of virus receptor (erythrocyte P antigen). N Engl J Med 1994;330:1192–6.

chapter

143 Pretravel Advice and Immunization

David R Hill

The pretravel care of the international traveler is entirely preventive medicine.[1] The first step in providing this care is to assess the health risk of a particular trip. This is done by determining a traveler's itinerary (not only the country of destination, but also the areas within the country that will be visited) and the types of accommodation. For example, a prolonged research expedition to the shores of Kenya's Lake Victoria will expose the traveler to more health risks than a short business trip to Nairobi. The epidemiology of infectious disease health risks can be found in several publications[2–4] and Internet sites (See Sources of Information and Keystone *et al*[5]) (Fig. 143.1). The duration of travel is also important. With longer trips there will be a cumulative risk of disease as well as the possibility that the traveler will become increasingly lax in preventive measures such as malaria chemoprophylaxis.[6] Finally, the purpose of the trip needs to be determined.

The next step is to assess the traveler's current health. Although more than 25% of individuals travel with chronic medical conditions, these generally do not interfere with the traveler's plans. Nevertheless, consideration of specific vaccines or prophylactic medications will need to be matched against the traveler's health. Once assessed, the traveler should be given vaccines, medications and preventive advice. Education about illness avoidance may be the most cost-effective measure, but it is difficult to ensure compliance. Finally, each traveler should be informed how to access medical care during travel and on return. With constantly changing epidemiology of disease and patterns of microbial resistance, complexity of travel itineraries and newly released vaccines and preventive medications, most travelers should be cared for in specialized travel clinics that have trained personnel, carry all vaccines and provide accurate preventive advice.[7]

IMMUNIZATIONS

It is helpful to divide immunizations into three categories (Table 143.1):

- recommended as part of routine health maintenance irrespective of international travel;
- may be required for entry into a country; and
- recommended because of risk during travel.

It is imperative that adequate records are kept for immunizations. This includes the type and dose of vaccine, date of administration, manufacturer and lot number, site of administration and administrator's signature. Adverse reactions to vaccines should be reported to the appropriate monitoring agency. Prior to administration of any vaccine patients should undergo informed consent procedures. The use of vaccine information sheets will help to explain to travelers the benefits and risk of each vaccine. These are often available from vaccine manufacturers or can be downloaded from the Centers for Disease Control and Prevention (CDC): www.cdc.gov/nip/publications/vis.

Most vaccines may be administered simultaneously at different sites. Patient tolerance, therefore, usually dictates how many may be given at any one time. A few rules do apply. Live viral vaccines should be either given together or separated by at least 1 month and immunoglobulin should not be given less than 5 months before or less than 2 weeks after measles, mumps or rubella vaccines and 3 weeks after varicella vaccine.[8] Other specific conditions are discussed later. The major travel vaccines, their administration schedule and side effects are listed in Table 143.2. Full manufacturer's prescribing information should be consulted before administration of each vaccine, as schedules, doses and products often differ between countries.

Immunizations for routine health maintenance

The pretravel visit is an ideal time to update routinely recommended immunizations. In most areas of the world this includes tetanus-diphtheria, pertussis, measles, mumps and rubella, polio, pneumococcal, influenza and, increasingly, hepatitis B vaccines. Many older adults have never been adequately immunized against tetanus and diphtheria or have waning serologic evidence of protection because of failure to receive regular boosters. In the USA this has translated into tetanus cases, most of which occur in adults over the age of 50 years. Diphtheria has occurred in regions where vaccine coverage has declined secondary to population migration or failure of the infrastructure for vaccination. These regions include some countries in Latin America, the Caribbean, Africa, Asia and Eastern Europe. All travelers should have completed a primary series against tetanus-diphtheria and then received boosters on a 10-yearly basis. Because a tetanus-prone wound requires a booster if more than 5 years have elapsed since immunization, some travelers may benefit from vaccination at this interval, particularly if it would be difficult to obtain vaccination overseas.

Although many countries only require a single dose of live measles vaccination in childhood, in 1989 the USA adopted a two-dose policy in response to an increase in measles cases. This means

THREE CATEGORIES OF IMMUNIZATION		
Routine health care	**Required**	**Recommended because of exposure**
Tetanus-diphtheria	Yellow fever	Hepatitis A
Varicella	(Cholera)	Typhoid
Measles (mumps, rubella)		Meningococcal
Haemophilus influenzae type b		Rabies
Polio		Japanese B encephalitis
Pertussis		Tick-borne encephalitis
Influenza		
Pneumococcal		
Hepatitis B		

Table 143.1 Three categories of immunization. Note that cholera vaccination is no longer required as a condition of entry to any country.

IMMUNIZATIONS FOR FOREIGN TRAVEL						
Vaccine	**Type**	**Route**	**Schedule**	**Indications**	**Precautions and contraindications**	**Side-effects**
Toxoids						
Tetanus-diphtheria	Adsorbed toxoids	im	Primary: 3 doses, first 2, 4–8 weeks apart; 3rd dose 6–12 months later Booster: every 10 years	All adults	First trimester of pregnancy Hypersensitivity or neurologic reaction to previous doses Severe local reaction	Local reactions Occasional fever, systemic symptoms Arthus-like reactions if history of multiple boosters Rare: systemic allergy
Inactivated bacterial vaccines						
Cholera	Phenol-killed *Vibrio cholera* (4×10^9/ml)	im, sc or id	Primary: 2 doses 1 week to 1 month apart, ≥6 days before travel Booster: every 6 months	Oral vaccines preferred No longer required by individual countries No longer available in USA	Safety in pregnancy not known Previous severe local or systemic reaction No protection against *V. cholerae* 0139	Local reaction of pain, erythema and induration lasting 1–2 days Occasional fever, malaise
Cholera	Killed, whole cell *Vibrio cholerae* with recombinant B subunit of cholera toxin	Oral	Primary: 2 doses at 0 and ≥7 days Booster: 6 months to 2 years	No longer required for international travel May give some protection against enterotoxigenic *E. coli* (traveler's diarrhea) Not available in USA	Hypersensitivity to previous dose	Mild gastrointestinal side-effects
Streptococcus pneumoniae	Polysaccharide containing 23 serotypes 7-valent conjugate vaccine available (see text)	sc or im	Primary: single dose Booster: recommended for high-risk patients after 5 years	≥5 years old and at increased risk of pneumococcal disease and its complications Healthy adults 65 years or older	Safety in pregnancy not known Previous pneumococcal vaccination (relative)	Mild erythema and pain at injection site in c.50% Systemic reaction in <1% Arthus-like reaction with booster doses
Neisseria meningitidis	Polysaccharide containing serotypes (A, C, Y, W135) (serotype C conjugate vaccine available in some countries)	sc	Primary: 1 dose Booster (after 5 years): not officially recommended. May be given after 3–5 years	Travel to areas with epidemic meningococcal disease Asplenia or certain complement deficiency states	Safety in pregnancy is not known	Infrequent, mild local reactions
Typhoid	Heat-phenol-inactivated *Salmonella typhi* (10^9/ml)	sc	Primary: 2 doses given ≥4 weeks apart Booster: every 3 years	Risk of exposure to typhoid fever No longer available in USA	Previous severe local or systemic reaction Acetone-killed vaccines should not be given id Pregnancy	Frequent local reaction of pain; swelling and induration lasting 1–2 days Occasional systemic reaction, can be severe
Typhoid	Vi polysaccharide	im	Primary: 1 dose Booster: every 2 years	Risk of exposure to typhoid fever	Safety in pregnancy not known Hypersensitivity to vaccine components	Local pain and induration in 10–20% Systemic reaction in <5%

Table 143.2 Immunizations for foreign travel. Manufacturer's full prescribing information should be consulted because vaccines, doses and schedules may differ among countries. Only major precautions, contraindications and side-effects are listed. Indications are discussed in more detail in the text. Immunocompromised host refers to persons immunocompromised because of immunodeficiency disease, leukemia, lymphoma, generalized malignancy or AIDS, or immunosuppressed from therapy with corticosteroids, alkylating agents, antimetabolites or radiation.

IMMUNIZATIONS FOR FOREIGN TRAVEL (continued)

Vaccine	Type	Route	Schedule	Indications	Precautions and contraindications	Side-effects
Attenuated live bacterial vaccine						
Typhoid	Attenuated Ty21a strain of *Salmonella typhi*	po	Primary: 1 capsule every other day for 4 doses Booster: every 5 years	Risk of exposure to typhoid fever	Safety in pregnancy not known Immunocompromised host Children <6 years Acute febrile or gastrointestinal illness Antibiotics or mefloquine (separate the doses by ≥24h) Capsules must be refrigerated	Infrequent gastrointestinal upset, rash
Cholera	Live, attenuated CVD 103-HgR strain of *V. cholerae*	Oral	Primary: single dose Booster: 6 months	No longer required for international travel Not available in USA	Safety in pregnancy is not known Immunocompromised host Antibiotics (separate dose by ≥24h) Complete vaccination at least 1 week before malaria chemoprophylaxis	Mild nausea, cramping and diarrhea in about 2%
Attenuated live virus vaccines						
Measles	Attenuated live virus: monovalent form or combined with rubella (MR) ± mumps (MMR)	sc	Primary: 2 doses, first at 12–15 months, 2nd at 4–12 years of age. For adults, 2 doses separated by ≥1 month Booster: none	People born after 1956 who have not had documented measles or received 2 doses of live vaccine	Pregnancy Immunocompromised host; can be considered for asymptomatic HIV-infected persons (see text) History of anaphylaxis to eggs or neomycin Recent (<5 months) administration Ig	Temperature ≥39.4°C, 5–21days after vaccination in 5–15% Transient rash in 5% Local reaction if previously immunized with killed vaccine (1963–67): 4–55%
Mumps	Attenuated live viral	sc	Primary: 1 dose (usually given as part of MMR vaccine) Booster: none	People born after 1956 who have not had documented mumps	Pregnancy Immunocompromised host History of anaphylaxis to eggs or neomycin Recent (<5 months) administration of Ig	Mild allergic reactions uncommon Rare: parotitis
Poliomyelitis	Attenuated live virus, trivalent	po	Primary: 3 doses, the first 2 given at a 6–8 week interval, the third 8–12 months later Booster: 1 oral dose	<18 years old Boost previously immunized people; complete series in partially immunized adults No longer used for vaccination in USA	Immunocompromised host or immunocompromised contacts of recipients	Rare: paralysis Occasional outbreaks

Table 143.2 (Continued)

IMMUNIZATIONS FOR FOREIGN TRAVEL (continued)						
Vaccine	**Type**	**Route**	**Schedule**	**Indications**	**Precautions and contraindications**	**Side-effects**
Attenuated live virus vaccines *cont.*						
Rubella	Attenuated live virus	sc	Primary: 1 dose (usually given as part of MR or MMR) Booster: none	All people, particularly women of childbearing age, without documented illness or receipt of live vaccine at ≥12 months of age	Pregnancy Immunocompromised host History of anaphylaxis to neomycin Recent (<5 months) administration of Ig	Post pubertal women: up to 40% have joint pains, transient arthritis, beginning 3–25 days after vaccination, persisting 1–11 days Frank arthritis in <2%
Varicella	Attenuated live virus	sc	Primary: children of 1–12 years, 1 dose; >12 years, 2 doses at a 4–8 week interval	≥12 months old and no history of varicella	Pregnancy Immunocompromised host Potential for rare transmission of vaccine virus to susceptible hosts Recent (<5 months) administration of Ig	Local pain and induration in 20% Fever in 15% Localized or systemic mild varicella rash in 6%
Yellow fever	Attenuated live virus	sc	Primary: 1 dose, 10 days to 10 years before travel Booster: every 10 years	As required by individual countries	Avoid in pregnant women, unless high-risk travel Infants <9 months Immunocompromised host Hypersensitivity to eggs	Mild headache, myalgia, fever, 5–10 days after vaccination in 2–5% Rare: immediate hypersensitivity, multiorgan system failure (see text)
Inactivated virus vaccines						
Hepatitis A	Inactivated	im	Primary: 2 doses, 2nd dose after 6–24 months provides long-term (≥10 years) protection Booster: not currently recommended	Travel to developing countries Used in routine immunization of children in some regions of USA (see text) Some travelers may benefit from pre-vaccine hepatitis A testing	Safety in pregnancy is not known	Local reaction of pain and tenderness in <20% Occasional fever in <5%
Hepatitis B	Yeast-derived recombinant hepatitis B surface antigen	im	Primary: 3 doses at 0, 1 and 6 months. Can accelerate vaccine schedule (see text) Booster: not routinely recommended	Health care workers in contact with blood Residence or sexually active in areas of high endemicity for HBsAg Contact with blood, body fluids, or blood-contaminated medical or dental instruments	Pregnancy is not a contraindication in high-risk persons Hypersensitivity to vaccine components	Mild local reactions in 10–20% Occasional fever, headache, fatigue and nausea

Table 143.2 (Continued)

IMMUNIZATIONS FOR FOREIGN TRAVEL (continued)

Vaccine	Type	Route	Schedule	Indications	Precautions and contraindications	Side-effects
Inactivated virus vaccines *cont.*						
Hepatitis A and B antigens combined	Inactivated virus (A) plus recombinant hepatitis B surface antigen	im	Primary: 3 doses at 0, 1 and 6 months Booster: not currently recommended	Travelers at risk for both hepatitis A and B; lower age limit of vaccination varies between countries Give at least 2 doses of vaccine before departure to protect against hepatitis A	Safety in pregnancy is not known Hypersensitivity to vaccine components	Local reactions in ~35% Systemic symptoms of headache and fatigue, similar to single antigen preparations
Poliomyelitis	Killed poliomyelitis virus, trivalent enhanced potency	sc	Primary: 3 doses, first 2 at a 4–8 week interval; 3rd 6–12 months after 2nd Booster: 1 lifetime dose	Travel to polio-endemic countries	Safety in pregnancy not known Anaphylactic reactions to streptomycin or neomycin	Mild local reaction
Influenza	Inactivated whole and split influenza A and B virus	sc	Annual vaccination with current vaccine	≥6 months old and at increased risk of complications from influenza Healthy adults >50 years old Medical care personnel Travelers at risk	First trimester of pregnancy is a relative contraindication Anaphylaxis to eggs	Mild local reactions in <33% Occasional systemic reaction of malaise and myalgia: begins 6–12h after vaccination; lasts 1–2 days Rare: allergic reaction
Japanese B encephalitis	Inactivated virus	sc	Primary: 3 doses at weekly intervals Booster: 1 dose at 3-year intervals	Travel to areas of risk with rural exposure or prolonged residence	Pregnancy Allergy to mice or rodents History of anaphylaxis or urticaria	Local mild reactions lasting 1–3 days in 20% Systemic symptoms of fever, myalgia, headache or GI upset, in 10% Severe reactions with urticaria, rash, angioedema, or respiratory distress (0.01–1%)
Rabies	Inactivated virus	im or id	Pre-exposure: 3 doses at days 0, 7, and 21 or 28 Booster: depends upon risk category and is based upon serologic testing at specified intervals	Itinerary and activities that place traveler at risk of rabies	Allergy to previous doses May be given in pregnancy if indicated id route should be completed ≥30 days before travel id route should not be used with concurrent chloroquine or mefloquine id dosing no longer available in USA	Local reactions in ~30% Mild systemic reactions: headache, nausea, aches, dizziness in ~20% Rare: neurologic illness Immune-complex reactions with booster doses of human diploid cell vaccine occurring 2–21 days after vaccination, in 6%

Table 143.2 (Continued)

IMMUNIZATIONS FOR FOREIGN TRAVEL (continued)						
Vaccine	**Type**	**Route**	**Schedule**	**Indications**	**Precautions and contraindications**	**Side-effects**
Inactivated virus vaccines *cont.*						
Tick-borne encephalitis	Inactivated virus	im	Primary: 3 doses at 0, 1 and 9–12 months Booster: 3 years	Hiking, camping in areas of risk; exercise tick avoidance	Safety in pregnancy is not known Hypersensitivity to previous doses	Occasional local reactions of swelling, redness or swollen regional lymph nodes Infrequent fever, headache Rare neuritis
Passive prophylaxis						
Immunoglobulin	Fractionated Ig (primarily IgG)	im	Travel $<$3 months: 0.02ml/kg Travel $>$3 months: 0.06ml/kg every 4–6 months	For prevention of hepatitis A Some travelers may benefit from pretravel hepatitis A antibody testing	Not to be given less than 2 weeks after (3 weeks for varicella) or 5 months before, measles mumps and rubella, or varicella vaccines	Transient local discomfort Rare systemic reaction

Table 143.2 (Continued)

ACCELERATED IMMUNIZATION OF CHILDREN UNDER 2 YEARS OF AGE			
Vaccine	No. of doses after which protection may be achieved	Earliest age at which dose may be given	Interval (weeks)
Diphtheria–tetanus–pertussis	3	6 weeks	≥4
Measles	1	6 months	
Polio (oral)	3	6 weeks	≥6
Polio (inactivated)	3	6 weeks	≥4
Haemophilus influenzae type b	2	6 weeks	≥4
Hepatitis B	2	newborn	≥4

Table 143.3 Accelerated immunization of children under 2 years of age. The data shown are for children who will travel to developing areas and require protection faster than by the routine schedule. Protection conferred by these schedules may not be complete. Children vaccinated with measles at under 12 months of age should be revaccinated at 12–15 months. In polio-endemic countries, the first oral polio dose may be given in the newborn period but three additional doses should be given, the first at 6 weeks of age and then at 4-week intervals.

that adults born in 1957 and after, a time before which it is assumed that measles infection was universal, should have received two doses of live vaccine. Measles vaccine coverage may be limited in developing countries, particularly those in the African and Eastern Mediterranean regions, so it is important to ensure adequate protection in travelers.[9] It may be helpful in some travelers to perform serologic testing for immunity to measles and rubella.

Pneumococcal and influenza vaccines are routine for healthy, older adults (≥65 years), who make up nearly 15% of all travelers. In addition to the older adult, those with chronic illness who would be adversely affected by pneumococcal pneumonia or influenza, such as persons who have HIV or AIDS, diabetes or chronic pulmonary, renal, hepatic or cardiac disease, should be vaccinated. Pneumococcal vaccine should also be administered to those with hemoglobinopathies and functional or surgical asplenia, and influenza vaccine to health care workers, children up to the age of 18 years on chronic aspirin therapy, pregnant women in their second and third trimesters, and to healthy adults and others if they desire it. Influenza strains included in the vaccine are selected on the basis of worldwide influenza activity during the season preceding vaccine manufacture. The risk of influenza is year round in tropical areas and between April and September in countries in the southern hemisphere. Outbreaks can occur out of season when persons from diverse regions of the world congregate in close quarters, such as on cruise ships.

Routine vaccination of children is important. Children should receive vaccines that are age recommended; however, the schedule may be advanced if a child is traveling before they would have received a scheduled vaccine and the risk during their trip is sufficient (Table 143.3).[3] In the USA vaccines recommended in childhood are measles, mumps and rubella, polio, *Haemophilus influenzae* type b, diphtheria-pertussis-tetanus (DPT), hepatitis B, varicella and pneumococcal. An acellular pertussis vaccine has been incorporated into the DPT vaccine to decrease the risk of febrile reactions from the pertussis component. A 7-valent conjugate vaccine against *Streptococcus pneumoniae* has been introduced for children aged 2–23 months (and in high-risk older children), and in some countries a conjugate *Neisseria meningitidis* type C is administered.[10] Other countries routinely administer BCG vaccine for the prevention of tuberculosis.

Required immunizations

The only vaccine that may be required for international travel is yellow fever vaccine. Yellow fever is prevalent throughout the Amazon basin of South America and sub-Saharan Africa between 15° north and 10° south of the equator. It is one of the diseases that is re-emerging and expanding into new regions and in recent years has caused the deaths of unvaccinated short-term tourists to infected areas.[11] Travelers to rural regions in the endemic zone for yellow fever (areas with the appropriate ecology for transmission, but without cases) and to areas actually infected with yellow fever should receive vaccine. Infected areas are listed in the CDC publication *Summary of health information for international travel* which can be accessed on-line at the CDC travel website: www.cdc.gov/ travel/bluesheet.htm. Other countries that have no reported cases of yellow fever and are not in the endemic zone may require vaccination of travelers arriving from yellow fever countries. The specific regulations governing this may be found in the respective CDC and World Health Organization (WHO) publications, *Health information for international travel*[3] and *International travel and health. Vaccination requirements and health advice*.[4] Yellow fever vaccination has to be recorded in the International Certificate of Vaccination (see Sources of Information). In addition to vaccine, travelers should protect themselves against the daytime-biting *Aedes* mosquito (Table 143.4).

MOSQUITO AVOIDANCE	
Repellents	DEET-containing products (≤35%) Apply to exposed areas of skin
Protective clothing	Long sleeves and trousers may be impregnated with permethrin-containing sprays or solutions
Screens and netting	May be impregnated with permethrin-containing sprays or solutions
Pyrethroid insecticide sprays and coils	May be sprayed or burned in enclosed areas

Table 143.4 Mosquito avoidance. For avoidance of *Anopheles* malaria mosquitoes, precautions should be exercised from dusk to dawn. *Aedes* spp. mosquitoes, which transmit dengue and yellow fever, are active in the daytime hours.

There have been recent reports of multiorgan system failure in apparently normal hosts following yellow fever vaccine.[12] There was increased risk with advancing age of the vaccine recipient, particularly in those over the age of 75 years. Considering that these cases are rare, there have been no changes made to vaccine recommendations. Health care providers should ensure that vaccine is only administered to persons traveling to infected or endemic areas.[12a]

Cholera vaccine is no longer required for international travel, although some local authorities may act outside international health regulations and request documentation. The removal of cholera vaccination for travelers is likely because of the very low risk of disease in travelers, the variable efficacy of vaccines against cholera and the lack of a clear role of vaccination in the control of cholera in nonepidemic settings.[13] In addition, the only vaccine which was available for US travelers (a whole-cell, inactivated vaccine which was poorly tolerated and had a limited duration of efficacy) is no longer being produced. Cholera is endemic throughout Latin America, Asia and Africa. *Vibrio cholerae* 01 circulates in all areas and *V. cholerae* 0139 in Asia. More than 85% of cholera cases are reported from Africa.[14]

Two oral vaccines are now available in many countries outside the US.[13,15] One is live attenuated (Mutachol®, Berna) and the other is inactivated (Dukoral®, SBL Vaccine AB). These vaccines are well tolerated and provide improved protection (60–80% protective efficacy depending upon age of the recipient) compared with the parenteral, inactivated vaccine. They may be considered for individuals, often health care or relief workers, living in a highly endemic area under poor sanitary conditions.

Smallpox vaccine has not been required for international travel since 1982 following the global eradication of smallpox in 1977. There has been renewed interest in smallpox vaccine with concerns about a potential use of smallpox in a bioterrorist attack. New guidelines for the existing vaccinia virus vaccine are being developed.[16]

Immunizations recommended because of risk

The following vaccines are recommended because there is a risk of exposure during travel to particular regions of the world or during travel under certain conditions such as poor sanitation. There are three vaccine-preventable diseases transmitted because of poor food and beverage hygiene: hepatitis A, typhoid fever and polio (for information on cholera see above).

Hepatitis A is the most common vaccine-preventable infection with a risk of 1–10 cases per 1000 travelers (Fig. 143.1), and can be acquired even during 'first-class' trips.[17,18] For this reason most travelers should receive protection. The first step is counseling about safe food and liquids and then providing either passive protection with immunoglobulin or active protection with one of the inactivated vaccines. Immunoglobulin provides immediate protection with antibodies that are circulating for 2–6 months. Because of its shorter duration of protection and a decreased acceptance by both provider and traveler because it is a blood product, most protection against hepatitis A is now done with inactivated vaccines.

There are several inactivated vaccines marketed throughout the world.[19] Two of the most completely studied are Havrix® (GlaxoSmithKline) and Vaqta® (Merck). These vaccines provide long-term protection with efficacy rates exceeding 90%. On the basis of mathematical models, two doses of vaccine should provide protection for at least 10–20 years. The use of inactivated vaccines in other risk groups such as raw seafood eaters, sewer workers, men who have sex with men, illegal drug users, persons with chronic liver disease and health care workers is being debated. In the USA vaccine is administered as part of routine childhood immunization in regions with high endemic rates of hepatitis A, e.g. the south-west USA.[20]

The first dose of an inactivated hepatitis A vaccine should be administered at least 2 weeks before departure, but for immediate protection immunoglobulin plus vaccine may be given simultaneously in separate sites. However, indirect information suggests that protection begins immediately following immunization with inactivated vaccines.[21,22] Travelers with a high likelihood of previous hepatitis A infection may benefit from hepatitis A antibody testing to avoid unnecessary vaccination if they are positive. These include those born before 1945, those born and raised in developing countries and those with a history of jaundice.[17,20]

Protection against both hepatitis A and B may be achieved with the use of a combined antigen vaccine, Twinrix® (GlaxoSmithKline), in a three-dose schedule. Two doses of vaccine should be given before departure to ensure protection against hepatitis A since a lower concentration of antigen is used in this preparation compared with the single antigen hepatitis A vaccines.

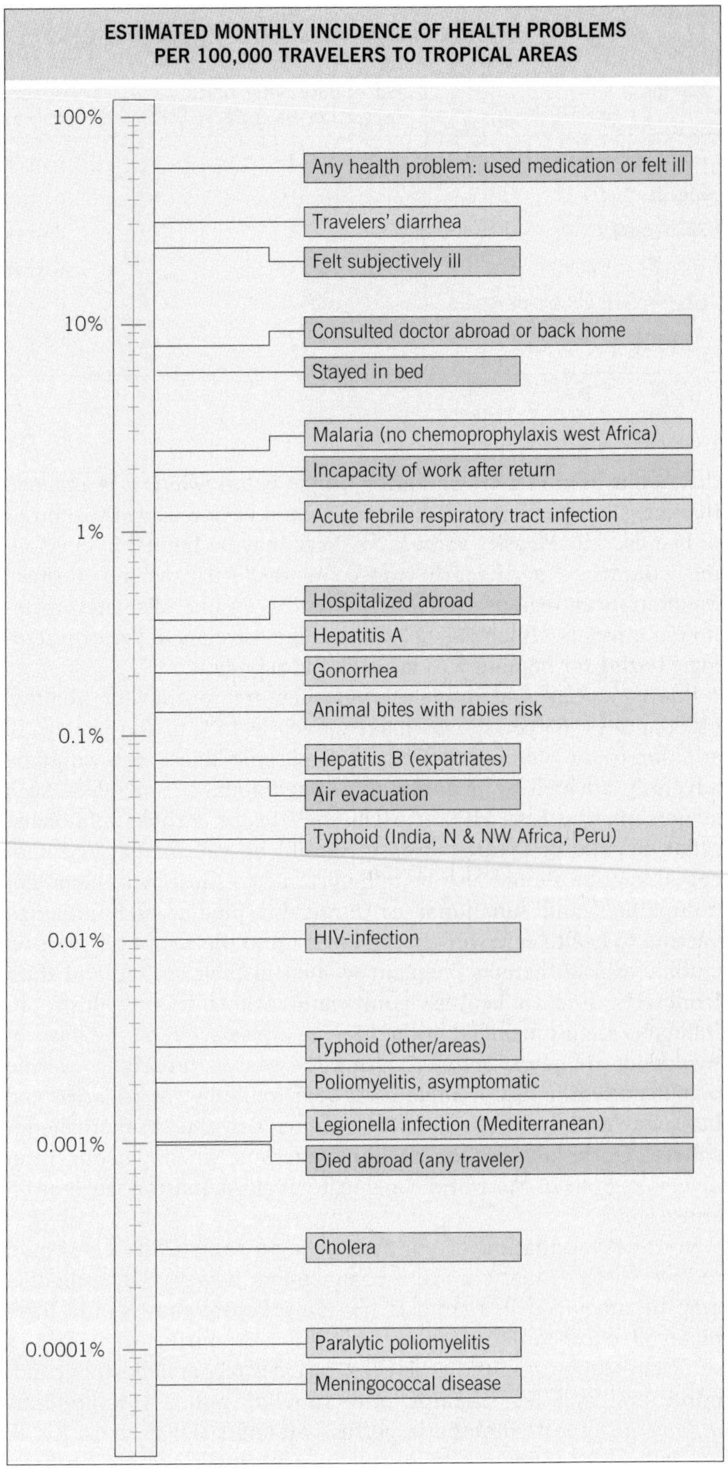

Fig. 143.1 Estimated monthly incidence of health problems for travelers to tropical areas. Adapted from reference[18].

Hepatitis E is enterically transmitted in the developing world, particularly during periods of high rainfall. In travelers, most cases have originated from India. Pregnant women have a high mortality. Immunoglobulin and the current hepatitis vaccines do not prevent hepatitis E so food and liquid hygiene is the best prevention (see Chapter 214).

Most cases of imported typhoid in the USA have been acquired in Mexico, although travel to the Indian subcontinent represents the highest risk with 1–4 cases per 10,000 travelers.[23] Multidrug-resistant *Salmonella typhi* is also common. There are three vaccines for protection (see Table 143.2) but production of the whole-cell inactivated vaccine was discontinued in the USA in 2000. These vaccines have similar efficacy rates (60–70%) but they differ widely in method of administration and side-effects.[24,25] The whole-cell inactivated vaccine may have uncomfortable local and systemic side-effects. Although it is inexpensive, its main place is in providing protection for children aged 6–24 months, an age range when the other vaccines are not effective. The oral, live-attenuated vaccine (Ty21a) is well tolerated, effective in children older than 4 years and provides protection for 5 years. If a traveler is on mefloquine for malaria prophylaxis or taking antibiotics, they should wait at least 24 hours before taking the Ty21a vaccine so that its replication will not be inhibited. A polysaccharide vaccine that uses the Vi antigen of *S. typhi* is given in a single intramuscular dose and is effective for 2–3 years. For persons who cannot take the oral vaccine because of time or compliance issues or for children between the ages of 2 and 4 years, this vaccine may be the one of choice. Conjugate vaccines in development should provide higher levels of protection.[26]

All travelers should have completed a primary series against poliomyelitis. Because the risk of polio during travel is low, a polio booster is not given routinely. Also, efforts at global eradication of polio have dramatically decreased the risk associated with travel to many areas of the world;[27] the western hemisphere was declared polio free in September 1994, the Western Pacific region in October 2000 and the European region in June 2002. The Indian subcontinent and Africa account for most polio cases each year.

At-risk travelers who have completed a primary series of vaccine should receive a one-time adult booster with the enhanced-potency inactivated polio vaccine (eIPV). Production of the oral vaccine was discontinued in the USA in January 2000 to eliminate the rare risk of flaccid paralysis from this vaccine. Those who have never completed a primary series should complete one.

Immunizations recommended because of exposure during certain activities or risk behavior include those against hepatitis B, *Neisseria meningitidis*, rabies, Japanese B encephalitis, tick-borne encephalitis and plague.

In an effort to control hepatitis B infection in the USA, vaccination is now included during routine childhood immunization. Unimmunized health care workers who will reside in endemic regions should receive the hepatitis B vaccine. Protection against both hepatitis A and B is now available in a combination vaccine (see section on hepatitis A). The vaccination schedule for hepatitis B (Engerix® only, GlaxoSmithKline) may be accelerated to 0, 1 and 2 months with a booster at 6–12 months. It can be further accelerated by giving doses at 0, 7 and 21 days; 65% will seroconvert at 28 days.[28]

Meningococcal vaccine is recommended for travelers to areas with high risk of meningococcal disease such as the meningitis belt of sub-Saharan Africa (particularly during the months from December through June).[29] Saudi Arabia requires it for religious pilgrims during the Hajj. Neither the bivalent (A, C) or quadrivalent vaccine (A, C, Y, W135) contains serogroup B, but this serogroup is less frequently a cause of meningitis in endemic regions. A conjugate group C vaccine is being used in some European countries and Canada for protection of children.[10] In the USA it is recommended that first-year university students consider vaccination.

All travelers should be counseled about rabies. In much of the developing world rabies is transmitted through the bite of a dog (see Chapter 153), although other mammals (e.g. bats, cats, foxes) may transmit the virus. Rabies-free countries may be determined by consulting the CDC[3] or going on-line to the Rabnet site of the WHO (oms2.b3e.jussieu.fr/rabnet/). All bites should be thoroughly cleansed with soap and water; postexposure rabies prophylaxis should then be obtained. Regimens may differ throughout the world, but if prophylaxis is administered properly with rabies antiserum (either a human or equine product) plus vaccine, the traveler should be protected.[30] If there is any question as to the potency of vaccine a traveler may have received, they should have serology checked upon return and postexposure treatment initiated while awaiting serologic evidence of protection (see Chapter 219).

Pre-exposure protection against rabies is considered for those traveling to endemic areas for 1 month or more, for persons with high-risk travel over a shorter period or for persons who will have difficulty obtaining safe and effective postexposure rabies biologics. Pre-exposure prophylaxis eliminates the need for rabies immune globulin which can be difficult to obtain in many areas of the world. Most pre-exposure vaccination is now administered intramuscularly to ensure adequate development of immunity.

Japanese B encephalitis is a viral encephalitis in Asia transmitted by the *Culex* spp. mosquito. The complete listing of risk areas and seasons of transmission may be found in *Health information for international travel*.[3] It is recommended that persons receive vaccine if they will have prolonged residence in endemic areas or will engage in high-risk activities such as camping, bicycling or field work. Rural Asia, particularly where rice and pigs are farmed, is the highest risk area; the pigs act as a reservoir for the virus and the rice fields as a breeding ground for the mosquito vector. The vaccine would probably receive wider use but for the serious, rare (approximately 0.1–5 per 1000) hypersensitivity reactions. About 20% of vaccinees have mild local and systemic reactions but serious allergic reactions, including anaphylaxis, urticaria, angio-edema and respiratory distress, have occurred at intervals ranging from minutes to as long as 1 week after vaccination.[31] Reactions can occur after any of the three doses. The traveler should remain in the waiting room for 30 minutes after receipt of vaccine and not travel within 10 days of completing the series in case a reaction occurs during flight or on arrival in the country of destination. Patients who have a history of allergies or urticaria may be at a slightly higher risk of severe reaction, so they should be vaccinated only after careful consideration.

Plague (see Chapter 176) is a rare disease for international travelers. Seven countries have reported cases each year from 1995 through 1999: Madagascar, Tanzania, Peru, USA, China, Mongolia and Vietnam. The vaccine is of uncertain efficacy and is generally not recommended. The rare adult traveler with exceptionally high exposure can take tetracycline or doxycycline chemoprophylaxis and children can take sulfonamides.

Tick-borne encephalitis is a viral meningoencephalitis spread by *Ixodes* ticks throughout forested areas of Eastern and Central Europe, and Siberia in the spring and summer months. Unpasteurized dairy products in endemic areas may also transmit the virus. There are two inactivated vaccines (Encepur®, Chiron, and FSME-Immun®, Baxter AG), but they are not available in the USA and require three doses over a year to achieve full protection, which is not practical or possible for most travelers. Travelers to these areas should exercise precautions against ticks by the use of protective clothing, repellents and insecticides. These measures will help to prevent Lyme disease, which is also transmitted throughout Europe and the USA by the bite of *Ixodes* ticks. Production of a Lyme disease vaccine in the USA was recently discontinued.

Tuberculosis is endemic in many parts of the world. The incidence of infection can be as high as eight cases per 1000 person-months; this rate was seen in PPD-negative health care personnel working in tuberculosis-endemic regions.[32] Most children reared outside the USA have received the BCG vaccine in childhood. BCG vaccine is not advocated for travel except for children who will have unavoidable, close exposure to persons with untreated tuberculosis.[33] Long-term travelers should receive pretravel and post-travel tuberculin (purified protein derivative) skin testing to check for conversion and, therefore, infection. The post-travel skin test should be administered 1 month or more after return.

Table 143.5 Immunization of the pregnant traveler. Adapted from references [3] and [4].

IMMUNIZATION OF THE PREGNANT TRAVELER			
Vaccine		Is the vaccine safe?	Notes
Bacterial	Tetanus–diphtheria	Yes	Should ideally wait until after first trimester of pregnancy
	Pneumococcal	Yes	
	Meningococcal	Yes	Probably safe but has not been studied conclusively
	Typhoid		
	Killed	No	
	Live-attenuated	Not known	Vaccination should generally be avoided
	Vi polysaccharide	Not known	May be given with high-risk exposure; vaccine of choice in pregnancy
	Cholera		
	killed	No	
	oral	Not known	
	BCG	No	
Viral	Poliomyelitis		
	Inactivated	Yes	
	Live-attenuated	Yes	
	Yellow fever	Yes	Should generally be avoided, but may be given with high-risk exposure
	Measles, mumps, rubella	No	
	Influenza	Yes	Should ideally wait until after first trimester of pregnancy
	Rabies	Yes	
	Japanese B encephalitis	Not known	Should generally be avoided, but may be given with high-risk exposure
	Hepatitis B	Yes	
	Hepatitis A		
	Immunoglobulin	Yes	
	Inactivated	Not known	Should generally be avoided, but may be given with high-risk exposure
	Tick-borne encephalitis	Not known	Should generally be avoided, but may be given with high-risk exposure
	Varicella	No	

Immunization in special groups

Two major groups of travelers require special consideration before immunization – pregnant women and immunocompromised hosts, particularly those who have HIV or AIDS. For pregnant women, any vaccine should have a clear indication to avoid potential adverse fetal effects (Table 143.5).[3,4,34] Although many inactivated vaccines may be given safely, those that have the potential for major systemic side effects, such as whole-cell typhoid vaccine, should be avoided. Measles, mumps and rubella, and the varicella vaccine should not be given, although data have not clearly demonstrated adverse outcomes when women have received rubella vaccine. Although yellow fever vaccine strain virus may be transmitted to the unborn child, this has not been associated with fetal abnormalities.[35] Other vaccines are likely to be safe, but there is insufficient experience to make a clear recommendation.

HIV-infected patients are another group to consider separately (Table 143.6).[36,37] All travelers should be asked about HIV risk factors before vaccination. Then the safety, immunogenicity and efficacy of the vaccine need to be balanced against the risk of the disease. It is generally agreed that immunogenicity decreases with advanced disease; a $CD4^+$ lymphocyte count of <200–400 cells/ml or <25% by age-specific percentages correlates with decreased immunogenicity. Although it has not been clearly studied, this may also be a cut-off point for an increased risk of adverse consequences of live viral vaccines. If assurance of immunity is needed, then post-vaccination serology should be obtained.

In addition to vaccination, HIV-infected travelers should consider the health risks associated with travel to developing regions. Many enteric infections, such as *Salmonella, Cyclospora* and *Cryptosporidium*, and systemic infections such as leishmaniasis and tubercu-

Table 143.6 Immunization in HIV infection. Data from references [3] and [4].

IMMUNIZATION IN HIV INFECTION			
Vaccine		Is the vaccine safe?	Notes
Bacterial	Tetanus-diphtheria	Yes	
	Pneumococcal	Yes	
	Meningococcal	Yes	
	Typhoid		
	Killed	Yes	
	Live-attenuated	Not known	Safety is not known and vaccination should be avoided
	Vi polysaccharide	Yes	
	Cholera		
	Parenteral	Yes	
	Oral, attenuated	No	
	Oral, killed	Not known	
	BCG	No	
	Tick-borne encephalitis	Not known	Safety is not known and vaccination should be avoided
Viral	Poliomyelitis		
	Inactivated	Yes	
	Live-attenuated	No	
	Yellow fever		Probably safe in persons without immunosuppression (e.g. CD4 count ≥200 cells/mm³), but has not been conclusively studied
	Measles		Can be given to persons without severe immunosuppression (e.g. CD4 count ≥200 cells/mm³)
	Influenza	Yes	
	Rabies	Yes	
	Japanese B encephalitis	Not known	Safety is not known and vaccination should be avoided
	Hepatitis B	Yes	
	Hepatitis A		
	Immunoglobulin	Yes	
	Inactivated	Yes	
	Varicella		Can be considered for children without severe immunosuppression (e.g. CD4% of >25%)

losis are more prevalent and can be prolonged and difficult to treat in HIV-infected individuals. The ability to access sophisticated medical care may also be an issue.

TRAVELER'S DIARRHEA

Traveler's diarrhea is the most common illness in developing areas of the world and affects 30–50% of travelers.[38] Illness usually begins in the first week after arrival and is typically mild, characterized by three or more loose to watery stools with nausea, abdominal cramping and malaise. Fever is usually less than 101°F (38°C) and vomiting is unusual. In most cases, illness is self-limiting over 3–5 days. Dysentery with tenesmus and bloody stools occurs in less than 10% of patients. Although most individuals can continue with their activities, 20–30% will need to alter plans. Enterotoxigenic *Escherichia coli* accounts for about 50% of the known causes, and *Shigella*, *Salmonella* and *Campylobacter* spp. for a large proportion of the other bacteria (see Chapter 144). Viruses cause 10–20% of cases and protozoa cause 5–10%. New etiologic agents are being described continually; some of the most recent ones have been *Cryptosporidium* and *Cyclospora* spp. and new types of *E. coli*, such as enteroaggregative types. The incidence of diarrhea does not seem to decline with increasing time of residence in developing areas.

Prevention

A full description of the prevention and treatment of traveler's diarrhea can be found in Chapter 43. The best prevention is care in the selection of food and liquids. Although most travelers understand the importance of being careful, many still make errors soon after arrival overseas. Foods and liquids that are likely to be contaminated are ground-grown greens and vegetables, incompletely cooked or poorly stored meats and seafood, untreated water and ice cubes, unpasteurized milk products and food from street vendors. Thus, travelers should restrict themselves to commercially prepared or heated beverages, recently and thoroughly cooked meats and greens, and fruits that can be peeled by the traveler. Water may be purified by bringing it to the boil or by halogenating (iodine or chlorine preparations) and then filtering it with a filter of pore size ″1μm.[39] The cysts of *Cryptosporidium* spp. and *Cyclospora* (and eggs of helminths) are likely to be halogen resistant, so water potentially contaminated with these parasites should be filtered or boiled.

Several nonantimicrobial agents have been used to prevent diarrhea. Bismuth subsalicylate is modestly effective either in tablet (2 tablets (252mg/tablet), q6h) or liquid form (2 oz qid), decreasing the incidence of diarrhea by about 65%. It should not be taken by individuals who are allergic to salicylates, who are taking large doses of them for other reasons or are on anticoagulant therapy. It can decrease the absorption of doxycycline. Ingestion of prophylactic *Lactobacillus* spp. does not confer significant protection and antimotility agents such as loperamide and diphenoxylate should not be taken preventively.

Antibiotics are effective for prophylaxis but they may be associated with side effects, contribute to bacterial resistance and are not practical for travelers going for more than 2–3 weeks. There are also many areas of the world that have sulfonamide-resistant and tetracycline-resistant bacteria, making these agents less effective. Therefore, most persons should not be given prophylaxis and it should be reserved for travelers in whom an episode of diarrhea would have extreme consequences.

Treatment

If the traveler becomes ill, prompt treatment should be initiated with hydration (see Chapter 161 for a full discussion of rehydration). Commercial rehydration packets combining electrolytes, sugar and bicarbonate are easy to use and, for small children, are probably safer than home-made preparations. They are widely available throughout the developing world or can be purchased before travel. Infants who are breast-feeding should continue nursing. As diarrhea improves, the diet can be increased by adding bland foods (breads and cereals, potatoes, soups, bananas, fish and chicken) in frequent small meals.

Mild disease may be treated with bismuth subsalicylate. This reduces the number of loose stools by about 50%, but does not begin to work until about 4 hours after taking it. Antimotility agents such as loperamide rapidly decrease cramping and loose stools. They should be avoided if there is blood in the stool or a fever >101.5°F (38.5°C). Because most episodes of diarrhea are self-limiting, symptomatic therapy alone may be sufficient.

A short course of antibiotics will often improve diarrhea within 1 day. Antibiotics combined with loperamide may control symptoms within hours, but there has been variable success with this approach depending upon the etiologic agent.[40,41] The wide prevalence of sulfonamide and tetracycline resistance in *E. coli, Salmonella, Shigella* and *Campylobacter* spp. has made the fluoroquinolones such as ciprofloxacin, norfloxacin, ofloxacin and levofloxacin the most commonly recommended antibiotics in treatment. In Asia where *Campylobacter* may be resistant to the fluoroquinolones, azithromycin may be used. This agent can also be safely given to children. Antibiotics are prescribed for up to 3 days, but single-dose therapy may be sufficient.[42] Medical care should be sought by persons with dysentery if self-treatment does not result in improvement within 24 hours, or in cases of severe dehydration. Diarrhea that persists after return should be evaluated (see Chapter 144 for a full discussion of persistent diarrhea) for causes ranging from functional bowel disease to infection with *Giardia* or *Cyclospora* spp. to tropical sprue.

MALARIA PREVENTION

Malaria is one of the most important diseases to prevent as it can be fatal. The type of malaria and risk of acquisition vary by destination and reason for travel, but worldwide there are approximately 10,000 cases in returned travelers. Over 80% of cases of the most severe form of malaria, *Plasmodium falciparum*, are acquired by travelers on trips to Africa, where resistance to chloroquine is widespread and transmission may occur in urban and rural areas. Deaths in travelers can almost always be prevented by adherence to mosquito avoidance, compliance with appropriate chemoprophylaxis and prompt recognition of malaria symptoms and consequent initiation of treatment.[43]

Malaria is transmitted by the *Anopheles* mosquito, which is most active during the nighttime hours from dusk to dawn. During these times travelers should wear loose-fitting cotton clothing which covers their arms and legs, apply repellents to exposed areas of skin and sleep in enclosed areas behind screens or under netting (see Table 143.4). The most effective repellents are those that contain *N,N*-diethyl-3-methylbenzamide (DEET).[44] There is no need to exceed a concentration of 20–35%. DEET-containing repellents are safe to use in children and pregnant women, but should be used sparingly to avoid systemic absorption and rare neurologic toxicity. Travelers should not apply repellents to mucous membranes and irritated skin and should wash them off when coming indoors. Residual insecticide preparations (e.g. permethrin-containing compounds) can be applied to clothing and netting to kill insects rather than only repel them. Mosquito coils and sprays containing pyrethroids may be used in enclosed sleeping areas.

Chemoprophylaxis needs to be taken on a regular basis during travel and for a period of time after return that depends on which medications were taken (Table 143.7). Many cases of malaria occur not because of drug resistance but because of poor compliance. Fifty to sixty per cent of short-term travelers will be completely compliant and less than this number of long-term travelers. The choice of a chemoprophylactic regimen should be based on risk of exposure, types of parasites prevalent in the travel destination and health status of the traveler. Up-to-date sources should be consulted before prescribing any antimalarial.[3,4]

Chloroquine as a single agent is effective only in areas where *P. falciparum* is not present or remains sensitive: Mexico, Central America west and north of the Panama Canal, the Dominican Republic and Haiti, Egypt, most areas of the Middle East and parts of China. Travelers to other risk areas in Africa, Asia and Latin America will need to take mefloquine, a new combination medication called Malarone® (atovaquone/proguanil, GlaxoSmithKline), doxycycline or add proguanil to chloroquine.

In the USA, mefloquine and Malarone® are the drugs of choice for travel to areas with chloroquine-resistant *P. falciparum*.[3] Mefloquine is highly efficacious in preventing malaria but concern has been expressed by both health care providers and travelers as to the drug's potential for side effects. When it is taken in prophylactic doses, minor GI and neuropsychiatric events occur in 5–30% of users.[45] The neuropsychiatric side effects may include sleep disturbance, vivid dreams, mood changes, anxiety, headache and dizziness. Serious adverse events such as psychosis are rare with an occurrence of about one case per 13,000 users.[46]

Contraindications to mefloquine are a known hypersensitivity to the drug, a history of seizures or psychiatric disorder, an underlying cardiac conduction abnormality, but not the use of β-blockers for blood pressure control. It is likely to be safe in pregnancy, but should be avoided if possible during the first trimester. Some travel health consultants prescribe mefloquine 2–3 weeks before departure to assess patient tolerance and allow a switch to other agents if there is a problem.[4] Seventy per cent of adverse reactions occur during the first three doses. Loading doses of the drug are usually not advocated.

Malarone® is a fixed combination antimalarial containing atovaquone and proguanil.[47,48] It is available in the US, Canada and

PROPHYLAXIS OF MALARIA		
Drug	**Adult dose**	**Pediatric dose**
Chloroquine	300mg base (500mg salt) orally, once/week, beginning 1 week before travels, weekly whilst traveling and for 4 weeks after travel	5mg/kg base (8.3mg/kg salt), once per week (not to exceed adult dose)
Mefloquine	250mg salt orally, once/week	<15kg: 5mg of salt/kg/week 15–19kg: 1/4 tablet/week 20–30kg: 1/2 tablet/week 31–45kg: 3/4 tablet/week >45kg: 1 tablet/week
Atovaquone/proguanil (A/P) (Malarone®)	250mg A/100mg P 1 tablet daily, beginning 1–2 days before travel and for 7 days after travel	62.5mg A/25mg P 11–20kg: 1 tablet daily 21–30kg: 2 tablets daily 31–40kg: 3 tablets daily >40kg: adult dosing
Doxycycline	100mg orally, once/day, beginning 1–2 days before travel and for 4 weeks after travel	>8 years of age: 2mg/kg orally, once/day, not to exceed adult dose
Proguanil	200mg orally, once/day Used in combination with chloroquine	<2 years: 50mg/day 2–6 years: 100mg/day 7–10 years: 150mg/day >10 years: 200mg/day
Primaquine	15mg base (26.3mg salt) orally, once/day for 14 days Used to eradicate extraerythrocytic stage	0.3mg/kg base (0.5mg/kg salt) Orally, once/day for 14 days

Table 143.7 Prophylaxis of malaria. Full manufacturer's prescribing instructions should be consulted on dosing guidelines as they may vary between countries. Information from reference[3].

many European countries and comes in both adult and pediatric formulations. It is effective in treatment and prophylaxis of all malaria species, although experience with non-falciparum species is limited. It is started the day before exposure to malaria, continued daily and discontinued 7 days after leaving the malarious area. It has causal prophylactic effect (kills developing hepatic-stage parasites but not the hypnoziotes of *P. virax* or *P. ovale*) which allows the shortened period of time post travel. It is ideally targeted for short-term travelers to areas of risk.

Rural, forested, border areas of Thailand with Myanmar (formerly Burma) and Cambodia have multidrug-resistant *P. falciparum* malaria; the few travelers to these areas should take daily doxycycline for prophylaxis. Malarone may also be effective in these areas. Doxycycline is also an alternative medication for those intolerant of mefloquine, although it cannot be given to children under the age of 8 and to pregnant women. Doxycycline should be swallowed with a large volume of liquid to prevent esophageal irritation. It may predispose to vaginal yeast infection and act as a photosensitizer.

The combination of chloroquine plus proguanil has been recommended for areas in which there is chloroquine-resistant *P. falciparum* malaria but only a small risk of acquisition, such as India.[4] It is in these limited risk areas that US and European recommendations differ; the CDC no longer recommends this combination.[3] Health practitioners should consult the appropriate source for their country.

All travelers need to be told that no antimalarial is 100% protective and that they can develop malaria in spite of being compliant with prophylaxis. If they develop a fever or flu-like illness overseas that could be malaria, they should seek medical care. Their evaluation needs to include a blood smear performed by a competent laboratory, because the sensitivity of symptoms or physical findings alone is low. The use of self-administered diagnostic kits (dipstick tests) is controversial as travelers can have difficulty in using and interpreting these tests.[49] If medical care cannot be obtained within 24 hours the traveler can consider self-treatment. The combination drug sulfadoxine/pyrimethamine (Fansidar, three tablets at one time) may be taken in many areas of the world except where there is resistant disease such as in South East Asia.[4] There, quinine alone or with doxycycline or tetracycline can be used. Malarone is another option for standby treatment. Fansidar should not be taken by those with a sulfonamide allergy. Halofantrine has excellent activity against all species of malaria but it should not be used as standby therapy because of potentially fatal cardiac side effects in predisposed individuals.[50]

Travelers who have had prolonged exposure to malaria in areas of *P. vivax* and *P. ovale* activity can consider primaquine to eradicate hepatic-stage parasites. Before taking primaquine a glucose-6-phosphate dehydrogenase (G-6-PD) test should be obtained. Primaquine cannot be given to pregnant women because the G-6-PD status of the fetus cannot be determined. Chloroquine-resistant *P. vivax* has been described primarily from South East Asia (Papua New Guinea and Irian Jaya) with sporadic cases from Myanmar, India and Guyana and Brazil, but is unusual. Primaquine resistance may also occur.

Pregnant women should not travel to malarious areas unless absolutely necessary, because of the added risk of complications of malaria during pregnancy. Chloroquine is safe. Mefloquine can be taken after the first trimester (and may be safe in the first trimester), although the US Food and Drug Administration has not approved mefloquine use in pregnancy. Doxycycline and primaquine are contraindicated and there is insufficient data on Malarone®.

ENVIRONMENTAL RISK

Travel to the tropics is associated with increased heat and humidity; the traveler will need to take into account the effects these changes may have on their health. These can range from a feeling of malaise and tiredness to increased loss of salt and water with resultant dehydration. Travelers should maintain hydration, limit exercise and sleep in a cool environment, particularly if they are elderly or have chronic medical problems. Excessive sun exposure should be avoided by wearing loose-fitting cotton clothing to cover exposed skin, wearing hats and using sunscreens with a sun protection factor of at least 15. Water insolubility may extend the life of the sunscreen. If the patient is taking doxycycline for malaria prophylaxis, it is particularly important to limit sun exposure. In addition to protecting the skin against sunburn, it should be kept dry and clean to avoid cellulitis and dermatophyte infection.

Travelers to altitudes above 2500–3000 meters may experience acute mountain sickness (AMS) or the more severe high-altitude pulmonary edema, retinal hemorrhage and cerebral edema.[51] AMS is characterized by headache, nausea, vomiting, insomnia and lassitude and may affect up to 50% of persons. The risk of illness can be lessened by acclimatization: spending a few days at intermediate altitudes of 1500–2200 meters and gradually ascending, sleeping at elevations no more than 300–500 meters higher each night. Acetazolamide, a carbonic anhydrase inhibitor, may be taken to assist acclimatization. It is given at a dose of 125–250mg orally twice daily, starting 2 days before being at altitude and for several days at altitude. It has also been used to treat mild symptoms of AMS. Dexamethasone may be used to treat AMS but in severe illness the safest course is always to descend.[51] Acetazolamide is contraindicated in persons with sulfonamide allergy.

Jet lag is a common problem, particularly when more than five time zones are crossed. It is easier to travel west and lengthen the day than to travel east and shorten the day. In order to help with jet lag, several methods have been proposed. Exposure to bright light after arrival may help. Taking a short to intermediate-acting benzodiazepine or a pyrazolopyrimidine can help travelers to fall asleep and maintain sleep, which decreases the contribution of exhaustion to the effects of time zone adjustment. Melatonin, which is secreted during the night hours, has also been studied.[52] A dose of 5–8mg taken at night for the first few nights may be helpful but the purity and effectiveness of over-the-counter preparations have not been documented and the effectiveness of this approach is controversial.

The risk of deep venous thrombosis (DVT) and pulmonary embolism has received recent attention. DVTs can occur in as many as 5% of persons flying for 10–15 hours and who have cardiovascular risk factors. Some of these will go on to have pulmonary embolism.[53] At-risk travelers should maintain their hydration, exercise at regular intervals and consider wearing below-the-knee support stockings to decrease the risk.

BEHAVIORAL RISK

Although health care providers and travelers tend to focus on infectious and medical illness, the most important contributor to severe morbidity and mortality, particularly in young adults, is accidents and injuries.[18,54] To prevent assault and theft, travelers should not wear jewellery and ostentatious clothing and they should travel in groups, avoiding high-risk urban areas, particularly at night. The US State Department posts travel advisory and safety information at: http://travel.state.gov/. Motor vehicle safety can be enhanced by riding in vehicles with seat belts, avoiding excessive speed and not driving at night. One should avoid riding in the back of open bed trucks and overcrowded buses. When swimming, travelers should be aware of undercurrents and never dive into unknown waters.

Sexually transmitted diseases, including HIV, gonorrhea, syphilis and chancroid, are prevalent. In some countries in sub-Saharan Africa nearly 50% of sexually active adults may be HIV positive. In parts of Latin America, South East Asia and China, HIV has increased exponentially.[55] Although condoms and spermicides may help to prevent transmission, the safest course is abstinence. In spite of these statistics, many travelers continue to engage in high-risk sexual behavior, often without the protection of condoms.[56] In all situations, alcohol contributes to increased risk behavior.

OTHER DISEASES AND CONSIDERATIONS

Dengue fever, a viral disease (see Chapter 184) transmitted by *Aedes* mosquitoes, has seen a resurgence throughout Asia, sub-Saharan Africa, the Caribbean basin and Latin America and has become a theoretical risk in the south-eastern USA.[57] Recent outbreaks have also occurred in Hawaii. Dengue is characterized by the sudden onset of fever, headache, myalgias and arthralgias, abdominal discomfort, rash and mild liver abnormalities. Severe disease can progress to a hemorrhagic shock syndrome. There is no vaccine currently available for prevention, so travelers need to exercise precaution against this daytime feeding mosquito. Complying with the measures outlined in Table 143.4 will help to prevent not only dengue and malaria, but also the other less common insect-transmitted diseases such as leishmaniasis, trypanosomiasis, filariasis and rickettsial infection. East African trypanosomiasis has recently been seen in several travelers to Tanzanian game parks.[58]

Schistosoma spp. (see Chapter 167) can infect travelers who swim in fresh water in endemic areas of the Caribbean, South America, Africa and Asia. Travelers to these areas should avoid all fresh-water swimming unless it is in a chlorinated pool. Letting water stand for 48 hours or warming it to 50°C for 5 minutes will render it safe from the *Schistosoma* parasites. Fresh-water swimming, particularly after periods of flooding, can be a risk for acquisition of leptospirosis.

Although the viral hemorrhagic fevers – Ebola, Lassa and Marburg (see Chapter 183) – garner a great deal of media attention, they are generally not a risk for travelers. Current outbreaks of disease can be followed by subscribing to the listserv ProMED or by checking the disease outbreak sites of the WHO and CDC web pages (see Sources of Information). Any returning traveler who is suspected of having a viral hemorrhagic fever should be managed according to WHO guidelines.[59]

Access to medical care overseas can be accomplished in several ways. Travelers can purchase a travel health insurance package that should include the following: help in locating medical care, paying for the care upfront and, if necessary, providing for emergency evacuation. There are several air ambulance and insurance companies (www.travel.state.gov/medical.html). Embassies or consulates may provide names of physicians and mission hospitals can be a source of care. Tattooing, injections and dental instruments should be avoided to decrease the risk of acquiring blood-borne pathogens such as hepatitis B and C and, less likely, HIV. The International Association of Medical Assistance to Travelers (www.iamat.org) will provide a list of English-speaking physicians throughout the world. A small first-aid kit that contains analgesics, bandages, a thermometer and any over-the-counter medications frequently used is helpful as it is often difficult to find even the simplest medicines overseas.

Finally, it is important to alert travelers to recognize major problems, such as fever, persistent diarrhea or rash, that may occur after return. Although routine posttravel follow-up for short-term travelers is usually not necessary, anyone who experienced major illness overseas or new-onset illness after return should be evaluated.[60] After a history, physical examination and targeted laboratory testing, a predominant syndrome can be described and a differential diagnosis generated. Each potential diagnosis can be matched against its incubation period, geographic area of risk, frequency of occurrence and the traveler's preventive measures. The appropriate evaluation and interventions should then be pursued. A more detailed discussion of individual syndromes and diseases is provided in other chapters.

SOURCES OF INFORMATION

There are a number of helpful sources of information in travel medicine. Major ones are listed.

United States resources

Centers for Disease Control and Prevention (USA)

- *Health information for international travel*, published annually. Atlanta, GA: DHHS. This can be purchased in hard copy (+1 877-252-1200), ordered on-line at http://bookstore.phf.org, or downloaded from the CDC travel medicine home page.
- Travel medicine home page: www.cdc.gov/travel/index.htm
- Morbidity and Mortality Weekly Report: www.cdc.gov/mmwr

US State Department

- Travel advisories: http://travel.state.gov
- Medical Information for Americans Traveling Abroad (has information on travel medical insurance and air ambulance companies): www.travel.state.gov/medical.html

World Health Organization

- *International travel and health. Vaccination requirements and health advice*. Geneva: World Health Organization, published annually. This can be purchased in hard copy (+41 22 791 24 76), ordered on-line at bookorders.who.int:8080/newaccess/anglais/home1.jsp or viewed at www.who.int/ith
- Home page: www.who.int/home-page
- Emerging infections: www.who.int/csr/don/en
- Weekly Epidemiologic Record: www.who.int/wer
- Rabnet (rabies epidemiology and biologics availability): http://oms2.b3e.jussieu.fr/rabnet

Canadian resources

- Health Canada – Travel Medicine: www.travelhealth.gc.ca
- Committee to Advise on Tropical Medicine and Travel: www.hc-sc.gc.ca/pphb-dgspsp/tmp-pmv/catmat-ccmtmv/index.html

United Kingdom resources

- Communicable Disease Report: www.phls.co.uk/publications/cdr/index.html
- Department of Health: www.doh.gov.uk/traveladvice/index.htm
- Fit for Travel – Scotland: www.fitfortravel.scot.nhs.uk/

European Surveillance website: www.eurosurveillance.org

International Association of Medical Assistance to Travelers

- IAMAT, 417 Center Street, Lewiston, NY 14092 (+1 716 754-4883), email: info@iamat.org
- Home page: www.iamat.org

International Society of Travel Medicine

- PO Box 871089, Stone Mountain, GA 30087–0025, USA (+1 770 736-7060); email: istm@istm.org
- *Journal of Travel Medicine*. BC Decker Inc, Hamilton, Ontario, Canada (+1 905 522-7017).
- Home page: www.istm.org
- Travel clinic directories: www.istm.org/disclinics.html

American Society of Tropical Medicine and Hygiene

- 60 Revere Street, Suite 500, Northbrook, IL 60062, USA (+1 847 480-9592); email: astmh@astmh.org.
- Homepage: www.astmh.org
- Travel clinic directories: www.astmh.org/scripts/clinindex.html

Royal Society of Tropical Medicine and Hygiene

- Manson House, 26 Portland Place, London W1B 1EY, UK (+44 (0)20 7580-2127).
- Home page: www.rstmh.org

ProMed Electronic Network

- This is a communication system to monitor emerging infectious diseases (sometimes unverified). To subscribe send an email message to majordomo@promedmail.org and in your message type 'subscribe promed' and your name.

International certificate of vaccination

- In US, order through US Government Printing Office, Superintendent of Documents, Mail Stop: SSOP, Washington DC 20402-9328 (+1 866 512-1800). Order on-line at: http://bookstore.gpo.gov/index.html
- Also available through the WHO: call +41 22 791 24 76 or order on-line at bookorders.who.int:8080/newaccess/anglais/home1.jsp

Commercial travel medicine databases

- Travax EnCompass (Shoreland Inc, US): www.shoreland.com
- Travax (Travel Medicine – Scotland): www.travax.scot.nhs.uk
- MASTA (England): www.masta.org
- Exodus Software Ltd (Ireland): www.exodus.ie
- Edisan (Médecine des Voyages – France): www.edisan.fr
- Tropimed® (Switzerland, Germany, USA): www.tropimed.com

Textbooks of travel medicine

- DuPont HL, Steffen R, eds. Textbook of travel medicine and health, 2nd ed. Hamilton, Ontario: BC Decker; 2001.
- Keystone JS, Kozarsky PE, Nothdurft HD, *et al*, eds. Travel medicine. London: Harcourt; 2003.
- Zuckerman JN, ed. Principles and practice of travel medicine. New York: John Wiley; 2001.

REFERENCES

1. Ryan ET, Kain KC. Health advice and immunizations for travelers. N Engl J Med 2000;342:1716–25.
2. Wilson ME. A world guide to infections. Diseases, distribution, diagnosis. Oxford: Oxford University Press; 1991.
3. Centers for Disease Control and Prevention. Health information for international travel, 2001–2002. Atlanta, GA: US Department of Health and Human Services; 2001.
4. World Health Organization. International travel and health. Vaccination requirements and health advice. Geneva: World Health Organization; 2002.
5. Keystone JS, Kozarsky PE, Freedman DO. Internet and computer-based resources for travel medicine practitioners. Clin Infect Dis 2001;32:757–65.
6. Hill DR. Issues for long-term and expatriate travelers. In: Cook GC, ed. Travel-associated disease. London: Royal College of Physicians; 1995:101–20.
7. Hill DR. Starting, organizing and marketing a travel clinic. In: Keystone JS, Kozarsky PE, Nothdurft HD, Freedman DO, Connor BA, eds. Travel medicine, London: Harcourt; 2003.
8. Centers for Disease Control and Prevention. General recommendations of the Advisory Committee on Immunization Practices and the American Academy of Family Physicians. MMWR 2002;51(No. RR-2):1–35.
9. Centers for Disease Control and Prevention. Global measles control and regional elimination, 1998–1999. MMWR 1999;48:1124–30.
10. MacLennan J. Meningococcal group C conjugate vaccines. Arch Dis Child 2001;84:383–6.

11. Centers for Disease Control and Prevention. Fatal yellow fever in a traveler returning from Amazonas, Brazil, 2002. MMWR 2002;51:324–5.
12. Centers for Disease Control and Prevention. Fever, jaundice, and multiple organ system failure associated with 17D-derived yellow fever vaccination, 1996–2001. MMWR 2001;50:643–5.
12a. Centers for Disease Control annd Prevention. Yellow fever vaccine; recommendations of the Advisory Committee on Immunization Practices (ACIP). MMWR 2002;51(No.RR-17):1–10.
13. World Health Organization. Cholera vaccines. WHO position paper. Wkly Epidemiol Rec 2001;76:117–24.
14. World Health Organization. Cholera, 2000. Wkly Epidemiol Rec 2001;76:233–40.
15. Ryan ET, Calderwood SR. Cholera vaccines. Clin Infect Dis 2000;31:561–5.
16. Medical Letter. Drugs and vaccines against biological weapons. Med Lett Drug Ther 2001;43:87–9.
17. Steffen R, Kane MA, Shapiro CN, *et al.* Epidemiology and prevention of hepatitis A in travelers. JAMA 1994;272:885–9.
18. Reid D, Keystone JS, Cossar JH. Health risks abroad: general considerations. In: DuPont HL, Steffen R, eds. Textbook of travel medicine and health, 2nd ed. Hamilton, Ontario: BC Decker; 2001:3–10.
19. Committee to Advise on Tropical Medicine and Travel (CATMAT). Statement on hepatitis A vaccines for travelers. An Advisory Committee Statement (ACS). Can Commun Dis Rep 2001;27:3–12.
20. Centers for Disease Control and Prevention. Prevention of hepatitis A through active or passive immunization: recommendations of the Advisory Committee on Immunization Practices (ACIP). MMWR 1999;48(No. RR-12):1–37.
21. Werzberger A, Mensch B, Kuter B, *et al.* A controlled trial of a formalin-inactivated hepatitis A vaccine in healthy children. N Engl J Med 1992;327:453–7.
22. Sagliocca L, Amoroso P, Stroffolini T, *et al.* Efficacy of hepatitis A vaccine in prevention of secondary hepatitis A infection: a randomised trial. Lancet 1999;353:1136–9.
23. Mermin JH, Townes JM, Gerber M, *et al.* Typhoid fever in the United States, 1985–1994. Changing risks of international travel and increasing antimicrobial resistance. Arch Intern Med 1998;158:633–8.
24. Engels EA, Falagas ME, Lau J, *et al.* Typhoid fever vaccines: a meta-analysis of studies on efficacy and toxicity. BMJ 1998;316:110–15.
25. World Health Organization. Typhoid vaccines. WHO position paper. Wkly Epidemiol Rec 2000;75:257–64.
26. Lin FY, Ho VA, Khiem HB, *et al.* The efficacy of a *Salmonella typhi* Vi conjugate vaccine in two-to-five-year-old children. N Engl J Med 2001;344:1263–9.
27. Centers for Disease Control and Prevention. Progress toward global poliomyelitis eradication, 2000. MMWR 2001;50:320–2,331.
28. Bock HL, Löscher T, Scheiermann N, *et al.* Accelerated schedule for hepatitis B immunization. J Travel Med 1995;2:213–17.
29. Greenwood B. Meningococcal meningitis in Africa. Trans Roy Soc Trop Med Hyg 1999;93:341–53.
30. Centers for Disease Control and Prevention. Human rabies prevention – United States, 1999: recommendations of the Advisory Committee on Immunization Practices (ACIP). MMWR 1999;48 (No. RR-1):1–21.
31. World Health Organization. Japanese encephalitis vaccines. WHO position paper. Wkly Epidemiol Rec 1998;73:337–44.
32. Cobelens FGJ, van Deutekom H, Draayer-Jansen IWE, *et al.* Risk of infection with *Mycobacterium tuberculosis* in travellers to areas of high tuberculosis endemicity. Lancet 2000;356:461–5.
33. Centers for Disease Control and Prevention. The role of BCG vaccine in the prevention and control of tuberculosis in the United States: a joint statement by the Advisory Council for the Elimination of Tuberculosis and the Advisory Committee on Immunization Practices. MMWR 1996;45(No. RR-4):1–18.
34. Samuel BU, Barry M. The pregnant traveler. Infect Dis Clin North Am 1998;12:325–54.
35. Nasidi A, Monath TP, Vandenberg J, *et al.* Yellow fever vaccination and pregnancy: a four-year prospective study. Trans Roy Soc Trop Med Hyg 1993;87:337–9.
36. Rousseau MC, Moreau J, Delmont J. Vaccination and HIV: a review of the literature. Vaccine 1999;18:825–31.
37. Karp CL. Preparation of the HIV-infected traveler to the tropics. Cur Infect Dis Rep 2001;3:50–8.
38. DuPont HL, Ericsson CD. Prevention and treatment of traveler's diarrhea. N Engl J Med 1993;328:1821–7.
39. Backer H. Water disinfection for international and wilderness travelers. Clin Infect Dis 2002;34:355–64.
40. Ericsson CD, DuPont HL, Mathewson J, *et al.* Treatment of traveler's diarrhea with sulfamethoxazole and trimethoprim and loperamide. JAMA 1990;263:257–61.
41. Petruccelli BP, Murphy GS, Sanchez JL, *et al.* Treatment of traveler's diarrhea with ciprofloxacin and loperamide. J Infect Dis 1992;165:557–60.
42. Adachi JA, Ostrosky-Zeichner L, DuPont HL, *et al.* Empirical antimicrobial therapy for traveler's diarrhea. Clin Infect Dis 2000;31:1079–83.
43. Kain KC, MacPherson DW, Kelton T, *et al.* Malaria deaths in visitors to Canada and in Canadian travellers: a case series. Can Med Assoc J 2001;164:654–9.
44. Fradin MS, Day JF. Comparative efficacy of insect repellents against mosquito bites. N Engl J Med 2002;347:13–18.
45. Schlagenhauf P. Mefloquine for malaria chemoprophylaxis 1992–1998: a review. J Travel Med 1999;6:122–33.
46. Weinke T, Trautmann M, Held T, *et al.* Neuropsychiatric side effects after the use of mefloquine. Am J Trop Med Hyg 1991;45:86–91.
47. Kain KC, Shanks GD, Keystone JS. Malaria chemoprophylaxis in the age of drug resistance. I. Currently recommended drug regimens. Clin Infect Dis 2001;33:226–34.
48. Overbosch D, Schilthuis H, Bienzle U, *et al.* Atovaquone-proguanil versus mefloquine for malaria prophylaxis in nonimmune travelers: results from a randomized, double-blind study. Clin Infect Dis 2001;33:1015–21.
49. Jelinek T, Grobusch MP, Nothdurft HD. Use of dipstick tests for the rapid diagnosis of malaria in nonimmune travelers. J Travel Med 2000;7:175–9.
50. Centers for Disease Control and Prevention. Sudden death in a traveler following halofantrine administration – Togo, 2000. MMWR 2001;50:169–70, 179.
51. Hackett PH, Roach RC. High-altitude illness. N Engl J Med 2001;345:107–14.
52. Spitzer RL, Terman M, Williams JB, *et al.* Jet lag: clinical features, validation of a new syndrome-specific scale, and lack of response to melatonin in a randomized, double-blind trial. Am J Psychiatry 1999;156:1392–6.
53. Lapostolle F, Surget V, Borron SW, *et al.* Severe pulmonary embolism associated with air travel. N Engl J Med 2001;345:779–83.
54. MacPherson DW, Guerillot F, Streiner DL, *et al.* Death and dying abroad: the Canadian experience. J Travel Med 2000;7:227–33.
55. Joint United Nations Programme on HIV/AIDS (UNAIDS) and World Health Organization (WHO). AIDS epidemic update. Geneva: WHO; 2002.
56. Matteelli A, Carosi G. Sexually transmitted diseases in travelers. Clin Infect Dis 2001;32:1063–7.
57. Guzman MG, Kouri G. Dengue: an update. Lancet Infect Dis 2002;2:33–42.
58. Jelinek T, Bisoffi Z, Bonazzi L, *et al.* Cluster of African trypanosomiasis in travelers to Tanzanian national parks. Emerg Infect Dis 2002;8:634–5.
59. World Health Organization. Viral hemorrhagic fever. Management of suspected cases. Wkly Epidemiol Rec 1995;70:249–52.
60. MacLean JD, Libman M. Screening returning travelers. Infect Dis Clin North Am 1998;12:431–43.

chapter 144

Diarrhea and Food-borne Illness

Andrew T Pavia

INTRODUCTION

It has been said that 'travel broadens the mind and loosens the bowels'. Although diarrhea is not the most serious travel-related condition, it is by far the most common illness among travelers and expatriates from developed countries who visit less developed nations.[1] In the first 2 weeks abroad, 20–50% of travelers will develop diarrhea. A large proportion will still have symptoms when they return home. In one study, 12% first developed symptoms after returning home. Travelers' diarrhea is usually defined as the passage of three or more unformed stools with associated symptoms, including nausea, vomiting, abdominal pain or cramps, tenesmus or passage of mucus or blood. The median duration of symptoms is 2–3 days, but 10–15% have symptoms lasting more than 1 week. In two large studies, 0.9% of Swiss travelers[1] and 1.7% of Peace Corps volunteers[2] developed persistent diarrhea lasting more than 1 month.

The risk of developing diarrhea is related to destination, the age and mode of travel and the care taken in selecting food and drink (Fig. 144.1). The highest incidence of diarrhea is associated with travel to or residence in Africa, Asia, the Middle East and Latin America. Intermediate risk areas include central and southern Europe and some Caribbean islands. The incidence is highest among children younger than 2 years old[3] and among young adults (age 15–24).[4,5] Eating in private homes is generally safer than eating in restaurants and, not surprisingly, eating food from street vendors is associated with markedly increased risk. The prevalence of diarrhea episodes peaks in the first few weeks and declines with prolonged residence in an endemic region.

The range of causative pathogens and the clinical spectrum of diarrheal illness among travelers parallel diarrheal illness among children living in the country. Intensive studies of the etiology of travelers' diarrhea over the past 30 years have shown a wide range of causative agents. The most important pathogens among travelers are, in decreasing order of frequency, enterotoxigenic *Escherichia coli* (ETEC), *Shigella* spp., *Campylobacter jejuni*, *Salmonella* spp., *Plesiomonas shigelloides*, noncholera *Vibrio* spp. and *Aeromonas* spp. (Table 144.1).[6–9] More than one pathogen is isolated in 10–20%. Rotavirus has been detected in 0–24% of travelers with diarrhea, but generally is found with similar frequency among asymptomatic travelers. *Cyclospora* has been recently described as a cause of travelers' diarrhea,[10] as have microsporidia sp.[11] Enteroadherent *E. coli* which demonstrate local, diffuse or aggregative adherence to HEp-2 cells have been implicated in travelers' diarrhea.[12,13] Recent data demonstrate that these organisms are a frequent cause of illness, perhaps second only to ETEC.[14]

PRESENTING SIGNS AND SYMPTOMS THAT POINT TO A DIAGNOSIS

Acute diarrhea

It is difficult to make an etiologic diagnosis for most episodes of diarrhea in the returning traveler. Most illness is of moderate severity and resolves spontaneously; empiric antimicrobial therapy is highly effective. ETEC is the most common pathogen, yet it cannot be detected in most clinical laboratories. Because of the wide range of potential pathogens, an unfocused laboratory evaluation will be far reaching and expensive. Therefore, a stepwise focused approach is recommended. There is substantial overlap in the clinical manifestations of different pathogens and it is impossible to determine reliably the etiology of travelers' diarrhea based on the presentation.[15,16] Nonetheless, clinical and epidemiologic clues can point to a diagnosis and are a valuable guide to therapy and diagnostic approach (Table 144.2).

Vomiting

Illnesses that manifest as vomiting alone are generally short-lived and less likely to be seen after the traveler returns. Toxin-mediated food-borne illness caused by *Staphylococcus aureus* or *Bacillus cereus* may occur among travelers because of exposure to foods that were not adequately refrigerated. Vomiting may be the only symptom among adults with viral gastroenteritis. Vomiting and intense abdominal pain that persists may suggest anisakiasis. This syndrome is caused by invasion of the gastric or intestinal mucosa by larvae of *Anisakis* spp. or *Pseudoterranova* spp. after eating raw fish, including herring, salmon, cod, halibut, pollack, greenling and mackerel.

Watery diarrhea

Acute watery diarrhea is the most common presentation of travelers' diarrhea; ETEC is the most frequent cause of this syndrome. Vomiting is present in 10–20% of patients. Vomiting may suggest gastroenteritis caused by Norwalk-like viruses (norovirus), astrovirus or calicivirus rather than ETEC infection.[17] The sudden onset of vomiting after a short incubation period suggests toxin-mediated food-borne illness caused by *Staph. aureus* or *B. cereus*. Explosive watery diarrhea that is short-lived may be caused by preformed toxin from *Clostridium perfringens* or *B. cereus*. Outbreaks of food-borne illness caused by preformed toxin, Norwalk virus, ETEC and *Shigella* spp. have been common on cruise ships. Airline meals have been implicated in outbreaks of *Shigella* and cholera.

A history of seafood ingestion suggests infection with *Vibrio parahaemolyticus*, *Vibrio cholerae* non-O1, other *Vibrio* spp. or *Aeromonas* spp. Profuse dehydrating diarrhea may occasionally be caused by toxigenic *V. cholerae* O1 or O139. The diarrhea caused by *Cryptosporidia* and *Cyclospora* spp. is most often watery, profuse and prolonged; fever is uncommon.[10,18]

Although most acute diarrhea among travelers will not be associated with a larger outbreak, physicians should be alert to this possibility. Prompt reporting of cases (along with the travel history) to local or national public health authorities may lead to identification of widely dispersed outbreaks.

Inflammatory or bloody diarrhea

Symptoms of inflammatory diarrhea include the passage of bloody or mucoid stools, high fever, abdominal pain and tenesmus; white

Fig. 144.1 Food-borne transmission probably accounts for the majority of diarrheal illness in travelers and expatriates. The high rates of shigellosis and campylobacteriosis compared with cholera among travelers in cholera-endemic areas suggest that they may be better able to avoid exposure to contaminated water than to contaminated food.

blood cells are often present in the stool. Approximately 10–20% of episodes of diarrhea will be bloody. Pathogens associated with inflammatory or bloody diarrhea include *Shigella* spp., *C. jejuni*, nontyphoidal *Salmonella* spp., *V. parahaemolyticus, Entamoeba histolytica, P. shigelloides, Clostridium difficile* and enteroinvasive *E. coli* (EIEC). Of these, *Shigella* spp. and *Campylobacter* spp. are the most common in most settings. *Vibrio parahaemolyticus* is common among Japanese travelers and should be suspected if there is a history of seafood consumption. *Clostridium difficile* should be considered in a patient who has previously been treated with antimicrobials. The presence of fecal leukocytes suggests infection with an invasive organism, most often *Shigella* spp., *Campylobacter* spp. or *Salmonella* spp. Leukocytes are not invariably present in these infections; assays for fecal lactoferrin have greater sensitivity and specificity than microscopy but are not widely used.[19] In one study, fecal leukocytes were detected by microscopy in 67% of patients who have *Shigella* infection,[20] 24% of those with *Campylobacter* and 27% of those with *Salmonella*. Fecal leukocytes are strikingly absent in amebic dysentery caused by *E. histolytica*.

Patients who have typhoid fever may present with diarrhea and abdominal pain, and diarrhea is a more common manifestation of typhoid among children. In some instances, diarrhea may persist for 1–2 weeks; fecal leukocytes are usually present. The stepwise increase in fever along with associated symptoms, such as headache, confusion, weakness, cough or myalgia, should raise the suspicion of typhoid. A febrile patient who has a relatively slow pulse should be suspected of having typhoid.

Among sexually active homosexual men, proctitis caused by *Neisseria gonorrhoeae* or *Chlamydia trachomatis* can potentially be mistaken for inflammatory diarrhea if a sexual history is not obtained. Another diagnostic pitfall is the failure to consider malaria in a person with high fevers, headaches and myalgias, because patients who have acute malaria may complain of diarrhea or vomiting.

Diarrhea with neurologic symptoms

Several types of food-borne illness that have distinctive neurologic manifestations may occur in travelers.[21] Nausea, vomiting, diarrhea and abdominal cramps followed by paresthesias, myalgias, arthralgias, reversal of hot and cold sensation and a sensation of loose teeth are symptoms of ciguatera poisoning. Ciguatera follows ingestion of large predatory reef fish, usually barracuda, grouper, amberjack and snapper, which contain high concentrations of toxins produced by dinoflagellates. Symptoms may persist for anything from several days to months. Shellfish that contain toxins from the toxin-producing planktonic dinoflagellates (*Gonyaulax catenella* and *Gymnodinium breve*) cause paralytic and neurotoxic shellfish poisoning. Paralytic shellfish poisoning manifests after an incubation period of between 5 minutes and 4 hours, with symptoms of paresthesias of the mouth, lips, face and fingers, followed by dysarthria, dysphonia, muscle weakness and respiratory compromise. The symptoms of neurotoxic shellfish poisoning are similar but less severe.

Because of the relatively long incubation period of food-borne botulism (median 24 hours, range 12 hours to 7 days) and the potential subtlety of symptoms, travelers with this disease might not

ETIOLOGY OF DIARRHEA IN TRAVELERS BY REGION

Organism	Nepal (%)	South East Asia (%)	India (%)	Latin America (%)	Africa (%)
Enterotoxigenic *E. coli*	20–28	6–30	24	26–72	25–75
Enteroadherent *E. coli*	13–18	3–8	19	15	–
Enteroinvasive *E. coli*	0–3	0–3	–	2	0
Shigella	10–23	2–7	10	0–22	0–15
Campylobacter	4–28	15–58	3	2–15	1–5
Salmonella	3–4	3–17	10	0–16	0–5
Yersinia	0–2	1–3	–	–	0
Vibrio spp.	0–1	5–13	5	–	3
Plesiomonas	4	2–13	7	–	2–7
Aeromonas			3	–	2
Rotavirus	3–11	8	5	0–24	0–6
Giardia	9–16	0–2	2	0–36	0
Entamoeba histolytica	3	–	5	–	0
Cryptosporidium	4–5	1–2	2	–	0–2
Cyclospora	11	–	–	–	–
No pathogen	40–53	25–42	45	22–50	29–64

Table 144.1 Etiology of diarrhea in travelers by region. Results are compiled from studies of varying populations ranging from short-term tourists to military personnel and Peace Corps volunteers. Not all pathogens were sought in all studies. Adapted from references[6–9,29].

CHARACTERISTICS OF SELECTED FOOD-BORNE ILLNESSES						
Organism	**Incubation period in hours median (range)**	**Vomiting**	**Diarrhea**	**Fever**	**Other symptoms**	**Common vehicles**
Histamine fish poisoning (scombroid)	5 min to 1 hour	+	+++	−	Headache, flushing, urticaria	Tuna, mackerel, bonito, mahi-mahi, bluefish
Staphylococcus aureus	3 (1–6)	+++	++	−		Ham, poultry, cream-filled pastries, potato and egg salad
Bacillus cereus (emetic syndrome)	2 (1–6)	+++	+	−		Fried rice
Ciguatera	2(1–6)	+	++	−	Paresthesias, myalgias, headache, arthralgia	Barracuda, snapper, grouper, amberjack
Bacillus cereus (diarrheal syndrome)	9 (6–16)	+	+++	−	Abdominal cramps	Beef, pork, chicken
Clostridium perfringens	12 (6–24)	+	+++	−	Abdominal cramps	Beef, poultry, gravy
Vibrio cholerae non-O1	11 (5–96)	+	+++	+++	Abdominal cramps, bloody diarrhea (25%)	Fish, shellfish
Vibrio parahaemolyticus	15 (4–96)	++	+++	++	Abdominal cramps, headache, bloody diarrhea (rare)	Fish, shellfish
Norwalk virus	24 (12–48)	+++	+++	++	Headache, myalgias	Water, ice, shellfish, salads
Shigella spp.	24 (7–168)	+	+++	+++	Abdominal cramps, bloody diarrhea	Lettuce, street food
Enterotoxigenic *Escherichia coli*	36 (16–72)	+	+++	+	Abdominal cramps, headache, myalgias	Ice, water, produce
Vibrio cholerae O1	48 (6–120)	++	+++	+	Dehydration	Shellfish
Salmonella spp.	36 (12–72)	+	+++	++	Abdominal cramps, headache, myalgias	Beef, poultry, pork, eggs, dairy products, vegetables, fruit
Campylobacter jejuni	48 (24–168)	+	+++	+++	Abdominal cramps, bloody diarrhea, myalgias	Poultry, milk
Clostridium botulinum	18 (6–240)	++	++	−	Dysarthria, diplopia, dry mouth, paralysis	Canned food, fermented seafood, garlic under oil, dried salted fish

−, rare symptom (<10%); +, infrequent symptom (11–33%); ++, frequent symptom (33–66%); +++, classic symptom.

Table 144.2 Characteristics of selected food-borne and diarrheal illnesses of importance to travelers, arranged by incubation period.

present until after their return home. Symptoms include dysphagia, dysphonia, blurred vision, dry mouth and diplopia; up to 50% will initially have nausea, vomiting and diarrhea. Home canning and unregulated commercial canning pose a risk of food-borne botulism. Type E botulism is associated with foods of marine origin, and travelers with a taste for exotic food might be at risk. Vehicles of type E botulism include fermented seal and whale blubber, and dried salted whitefish.

Persistent diarrhea

Persistent diarrhea is usually defined as diarrhea that lasts for 14 days or more. Although only about 3% of travelers will have diarrhea lasting at least 2 weeks and perhaps 1% will have symptoms for more than 1 month, these patients account for many physician visits and a substantial amount of time lost from work.[1] The etiology of persistent diarrhea in travelers (Table 144.3) has not been systematically investigated and is not well understood.[22]

Protozoal agents are relatively uncommon causes of acute travelers' diarrhea, but are much more likely to be responsible for protracted illness.[11] *Giardia lamblia* has long been recognized as a cause of prolonged diarrhea, often associated with bloating, malabsorption and offensive flatus. The incubation period is 1–2 weeks. *Cryptosporidium parvum* infections cause prolonged illness even in immunocompetent hosts. In one study of Finnish travelers and in several outbreaks in the USA, the median duration of diarrhea ranged from 9 to 12 days. *Cyclospora cayetanensis* is a recently described cause of diarrhea (originally referred to as blue-green algae, cyanobacteria-like organism and coccidia-like), which has been identified in North, South and Central America, Africa, Europe and Asia. In studies in Nepal, and in produce-associated outbreaks in North America, the illness was intermittent, lasted a median of 7 weeks and was associated with anorexia, weight loss and pronounced fatigue.[10,18] *Isospora belli* can also cause persistent diarrhea; it was identified in 1.4% of military personnel with persistent diarrhea in Vietnam. *Entamoeba histolytica* and *Dientamoeba fragilis* are less common protozoal causes in travelers. Helminths may occasionally cause persistent diarrhea, including *Strongyloides stercoralis, Schistosoma mansoni, Trichuris trichiura* and *Capillaria philippinensis*. Schistosomiasis should be considered if there is fever, hepatosplenomegaly, eosinophilia and a history of immersion in fresh water in an endemic region. Eosinophilia strongly suggests helminthic infection but is unusual in protozoal disease. The exception to this rule is isosporiasis, in which eosinophilia is common. However, eosinophilia may be an unrelated finding, caused by coexistent helminthic infection with agents such as hookworm, which is not responsible for the diarrhea.

Bacterial agents are also important causes of persistent diarrhea. ETEC, *Shigella* spp., *Campylobacter* spp., *P. shigelloides* and *Aeromonas hydrophila* may cause prolonged diarrhea. These infections may be associated with passage of blood and mucus. Enteroadherent *E. coli* strains are important causes of persistent diarrhea in children in tropical countries[23,24] and they may be important in travelers as well.[14,25] Three classes are currently recognized by adherence pattern to HEp-2 cells. Locally adherent *E. coli* include most classic EPEC

CAUSES OF PERSISTENT DIARRHEA IN TRAVELERS AND EXPATRIATES		
Infectious		
Persistent bacterial infection *Salmonella* spp. *Campylobacter* spp. *Yersinia* spp. Enteroadherent *E. coli* (3 subgroups) *Clostridium difficile* *Aeromonas* spp. *Plesiomonas* spp.	**Persistent protozoal infection** *Giardia lamblia* *Cryptosporidium parvum* *Cyclospora cayetanensis* *Entamoeba histolytica* *Isospora belli* *Dientamoeba fragilis* *Balantidium coli*	**Helminth infections** *Strongyloides stercoralis* *Schistosoma* spp. *Capillaria philippinensis*
Noninfectious		
Dietary Lactose intolerance Osmotic diarrhea	**Gastrointestinal pathology** 'Postdysenteric irritable bowel syndrome' Crohn's disease Ulcerative colitis Bacterial overgrowth Celiac disease Collagenous colitis	
Unclassified (likely infectious)		
Tropical sprue Chronic idiopathic ('Brainerd') diarrhea		

Table 144.3 Causes of persistent diarrhea in travelers and expatriates. Within each category, the causes are listed in roughly the order of frequency. Enteroadherent *Escherichia coli* includes three subgroups of organisms, grouped on the basis of patterns of adherence to HEp-2 cells: enteroaggregative, locally adherent (EPEC) and diffusely adherent.

strains. Diffusely adherent *E. coli* are currently of uncertain significance. Enteroaggregative *E. coli* (EAggEC) display a unique 'stacked brick' adherence and may elaborate a unique enterotoxin. Studies in adult volunteers show that some strains cause prolonged illness in normal hosts but suggest that there is substantial heterogeneity.[22]

In many patients who have persistent diarrhea the infectious etiology will not be identifiable despite intensive investigation. In some patients, lactose intolerance may be present. Small bowel overgrowth with aerobic and anaerobic flora may follow acute enteric infection and lead to chronic non-specific symptoms. Gastrointestinal problems such as inflammatory bowel disease and carcinoma of the colon may occur coincidentally with travel or perhaps be exacerbated or unmasked by acute travelers' diarrhea. A syndrome of intermittent diarrhea and abdominal pain after acute enteric infection in patients who have no demonstrable infections, structural abnormality or evidence of malabsorption has been termed postdysenteric irritable bowel syndrome, for lack of a better term. These patients usually improve over time and appear to respond to fiber supplement and dietary modification.

Tropical sprue is a rare but serious syndrome of persistent diarrhea, usually seen in persons who have resided overseas for prolonged periods. It is suggested by symptoms of chronic malabsorption, including bulky, greasy stools, weight loss, anemia and neuropathy. Some travelers with persistent diarrhea appear to have a disease resembling 'Brainerd diarrhea', named after a town in Minnesota, USA, where a large outbreak of chronic diarrhea occurred as a result of consumption of unpasteurized milk.[26] This illness is characterized by 10–20 daily bouts of painless, urgent watery diarrhea, and lasts 1–2 years. Water-borne outbreaks of this illness have occurred in Illinois, USA, and among travelers to the Galapagos Islands.

DIFFERENTIAL DIAGNOSIS BY GEOGRAPHICAL AREA

Studies of travelers' diarrhea from different geographic areas are summarized in Table 144.1. Varying microbiologic techniques limit direct comparison of studies. However, ETEC is the most common organism in virtually all regions. *Campylobacter* infections have been identified more commonly in studies of travelers, expatriates and military personnel from Nepal and South East Asia. *Vibrio* and *Aeromonas* infections have been primarily reported among travelers to South East Asia. *Giardia* and *Cryptosporidium* infections have been prominent among travelers to St Petersburg, Russia. *Capillaria philippinensis* has only been reported in the Philippines region. Certain regions appear to be at high risk for tropical sprue: Puerto Rico, Haiti, the Dominican Republic, India, Nepal, Myanmar (formerly Burma) and the Philippines.

Season may also provide a clue to the likely etiology: ETEC infections are most common during the wetter and warmer season in several regions. Studies among travelers to Mexico and Morocco found that *Campylobacter* infections are more common in the winter months.

INVESTIGATIONS TO CONFIRM THE DIAGNOSIS

The evaluation of the returned traveler with diarrhea should begin with a careful travel history and details of the onset, duration and character of the symptoms. The presence of signs of inflammatory diarrhea (fever, bloody or mucoid stools) raises the likelihood of infection with an invasive pathogen and usually should lead to obtaining cultures for *Shigella* spp., *Salmonella* spp. and *Campylobacter* spp. Fecal lactoferrin is a more sensitive assay to identify polymorphonuclear cells, but staining a fresh stool specimen with methylene blue is quick and inexpensive and can be used in resource-poor settings to identify patients most likely to benefit from antimicrobial therapy. An additional benefit is that *Giardia* trophozoites may be identified occasionally. Seafood consumption will raise the likelihood of *Vibrio* or *Plesiomonas* infection. The incubation period, if known, is helpful. Incubation periods of less than 18 hours suggest toxin-mediated food-borne illness and further diagnostic testing is not helpful. Incubation periods of more than 5 days suggest diarrhea caused by protozoa or helminths.

Acute diarrhea

In patients who have milder illness of less than a few days' duration, rehydration and an antidiarrheal medication (loperamide or bis-

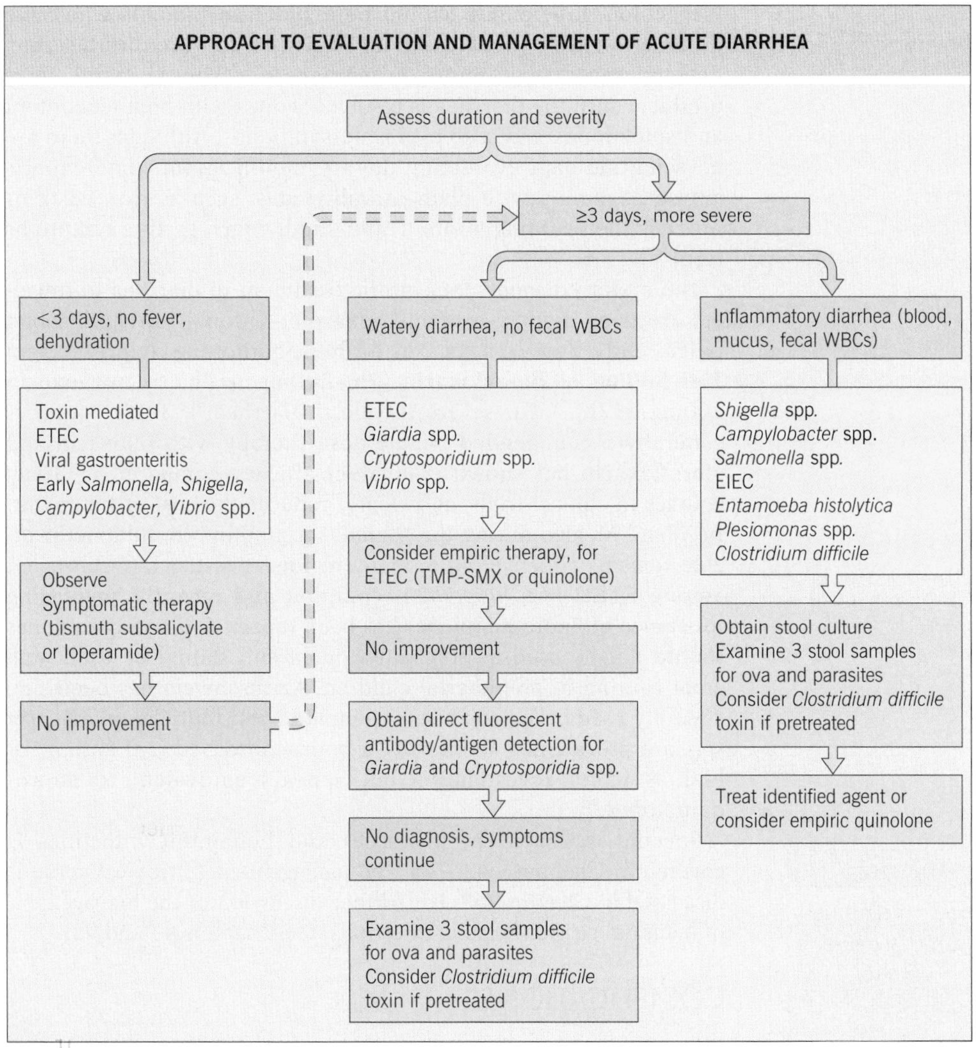

Fig. 144.2 A suggested approach to the evaluation and management of acute diarrhea in the returned traveler. The most likely pathogens for each scenario are given.

muth subsalicylate) alone may suffice (Fig. 144.2). For patients who have moderate to severe acute watery diarrhea, many physicians favor an initial empiric course of antimicrobial therapy (see below). ETEC is the most likely organism in this setting. If watery diarrhea persists despite empiric antimicrobial therapy, *Giardia, Cryptosporidium* and *Cyclospora* infection should be considered. Antigen detection assays for *Giardia* spp. and *Cryptosporidium* spp. are more sensitive than routine examination of stools for ova and parasites and can be performed initially.[11] If symptoms continue, three liquid stool samples should be examined for ova and parasites. In settings in which resources are limited, an empiric trial of metronidazole (250mg q8h) can be used as a therapeutic trial to treat *Giardia* infection.

For patients who have inflammatory diarrhea or dysentery and those who have failed antimicrobial therapy, stool cultures for *Shigella* spp., *Salmonella* spp. and *Campylobacter* spp. and up to three ova and parasite examinations to look for *E. histolytica* are indicated. In patients who have taken antibiotics, assays for *C. difficile* toxin should be performed.

Persistent diarrhea

Persistent diarrhea warrants a more complete evaluation. The evaluation can be time consuming, costly and frustrating. The approach should be stepwise (Fig. 144.3). At least one specimen should be examined for bacterial agents. Selective media such as thiosulfate citrate bile salts sucrose agar may enhance recovery from *Vibrio* spp., but many strains can be identified from conventional media such as McConkey agar if the laboratory is alerted to look for oxidase-positive organisms. A careful parasitologic examination of three liquid stools should include concentration techniques and staining to improve the identification of *Isospora* spp. and *Cyclospora* spp., because both respond well to treatment with trimethoprim–sulfamethoxazole (co-trimoxazole). If a potential pathogen is identified, it does not prove causation, but a trial of specific therapy is warranted. Identification of enteroinvasive, enterotoxigenic and enteroadherent *E. coli* strains requires carefully standardized adherence assays and DNA probes, which are only available in research laboratories. Because diagnosing these infections is impractical, a trial of 5–7 days of a fluoroquinolone may be reasonable. When diarrhea persists, especially if there is weight loss, bloody stools or symptoms of malabsorption, a complete evaluation for malabsorption and endoscopy with biopsies should be considered. HIV infection should always be considered in unexplained chronic diarrhea.

The management of persistent diarrhea is difficult if diagnostic resources are limited. A trial of antimicrobial therapy, preferably with a fluoroquinolone, can be given. If this fails, and symptoms suggest *Cyclospora* or *Isospora* infection, a 2-week trial of trimethoprim–sulfamethoxazole (co-trimoxazole) can be considered. Empiric therapy with metronidazole for persistent diarrhea may treat giardiasis, *Balantidium coli* and *C. difficile*.

IMMEDIATE MANAGEMENT

All patients who have diarrheal illness need careful attention to hydration. In adults, oral rehydration with mineral water, weak tea or dilute fruit juice along with a source of sodium chloride (salty crackers, dilute broth) is usually sufficient. Oral rehydration

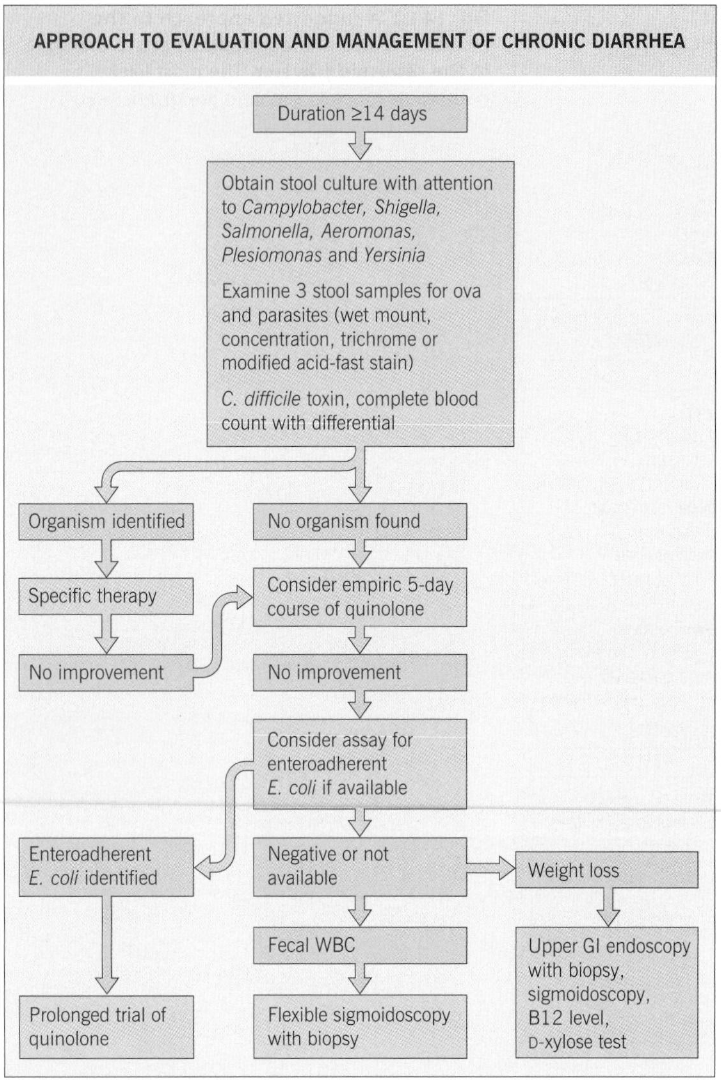
APPROACH TO EVALUATION AND MANAGEMENT OF CHRONIC DIARRHEA
Duration ≥14 days
Obtain stool culture with attention to *Campylobacter, Shigella, Salmonella, Aeromonas, Plesiomonas* and *Yersinia*
Examine 3 stool samples for ova and parasites (wet mount, concentration, trichrome or modified acid-fast stain)
C. difficile toxin, complete blood count with differential
Organism identified
No organism found
Specific therapy
Consider empiric 5-day course of quinolone
No improvement
No improvement
Consider assay for enteroadherent *E. coli* if available
Enteroadherent *E. coli* identified
Negative or not available
Weight loss
Fecal WBC
Upper GI endoscopy with biopsy, sigmoidoscopy, B12 level, D-xylose test
Prolonged trial of quinolone
Flexible sigmoidoscopy with biopsy

Fig. 144.3 A suggested approach to the evaluation and management of chronic diarrhea in the returned traveler. The presence of significant weight loss or evidence of malabsorption should influence the pace and aggressiveness of the evaluation. This approach is designed for use in a Western setting.

solutions such as the WHO/UNICEF oral rehydration solution or commercial products such as Pedialyte or Ricelyte take advantage of glucose-coupled transport and provide more physiologic replacement of fluid, sodium, bicarbonate and potassium (see Chapters 161 and 222). They should be used for young children and persons with significant dehydration. Popular remedies such as tea, soft drinks and sports drinks are very low in sodium and should not be used alone. Bismuth subsalicylate has been clearly shown to provide symptomatic relief.[27] Antimotility agents such as loperamide (4mg initially followed by 2mg after each loose stool) provide prompt decrease in the number of stools. Short-term use of loperamide has been proven safe in studies of travelers' diarrhea and can be used in addition to antimicrobials. Because of the risk of toxic megacolon, loperamide should be avoided in patients who have dysentery and in young children. Patients who have diarrhea may develop secondary lactose intolerance and should avoid dairy products until the diarrhea is resolved. Foods with high fat content and spicy foods may also aggravate symptoms. Although there are no scientific data evaluating dietary modification, some experts advise beginning with plain carbohydrates, such as rice, pasta or breads, then adding protein and finally fats as the symptoms resolve.

The preferred agents for empiric treatment of diarrhea in travelers are trimethoprim–sulfamethoxazole, 1 double-strength tablet twice daily for 3 days, or a fluoroquinolone (ciprofloxacin 250–500mg q12h, ofloxacin 200–300mg q12h, or norfloxacin 200mg q12h).[28] For severe travelers' diarrhea, a 3-day course is generally recommended. Single-dose therapy with ofloxacin and ciprofloxacin has shown equivalent efficacy compared to 3-day courses in clinical trials, and clearly reduces the cost of treatment. In inland Mexico during the summer, trimethoprim–sulfamethoxazole remains effective but in many regions, resistance to this agent among ETEC and *Shigella* is common and recently, increasing resistance to fluoroquinolones has been reported. Fluoroquinolones should not be used in pregnant women and should be used with great caution in prepubertal children. Azithromycin has been successfully used in regions where quinolone-resistant *Campylobacter* spp. are prevalent.[29] Rifaxamin, a poorly absorbed oral antimicrobial, is under investigation but appears equivalent to fluoroquinolones.[30]

Specific treatment of protozoal and helminthic infections is covered in Chapters 242–246. The management of tropical sprue is discussed in Chapter 163. For further discussion of the management of bacterial gastrointestinal infections, see Chapters 43 and 93.

COMPLICATIONS

Most cases of diarrhea in travelers are self-limiting. Serious electrolyte abnormalities are uncommon in adults, with the exception of those with toxigenic *V. cholerae*. Inappropriate rehydration solutions may lead to hyponatremia or hypokalemia, especially in children and those on diuretics. Hypoglycemia and seizures are less common complications.

Rectal complaints are common in patients who have chronic diarrhea. Hemorrhoids can result in rectal bleeding, which may be confused with bloody diarrhea. Weight loss, skin changes, anemia and neuropathy caused by folate and vitamin B12 deficiency are complications of malabsorption caused by chronic diarrhea resulting from giardiasis, strongyloidiasis, tropical malabsorption and sprue. Extraintestinal complications of amebiasis are unusual but can include liver and brain abscesses.

Although diarrheal illnesses remain among the leading killers of children, the greatest impact of diarrhea on adults is economic. In addition to the effect on tourist income in developing countries and the direct medical costs, diarrhea among travelers results in a substantial amount of lost productivity.[1,31] Despite recent advances, improved strategies for prevention, treatment and diagnosis are still needed.

REFERENCES

1. Steffen R, Rickenbach M, Wilhelm U, *et al.* Health problems after travel to developing countries. J Infect Dis 1987;156:84–91.
2. Addiss DG, Tauxe RV, Bernard KW. Chronic diarrhoeal illness in US Peace Corps volunteers. Int J Epidemiol 1990;19:217–18.
3. Pitzinger B, Steffen R, Tschopp A. Incidence and clinical features of traveler's diarrhea in infants and children. Pediatr Infect Dis J 1991;10:719–23.
4. von Sonnenburg F, Tornieporth N, Waiyaki P, *et al.* Risk and aetiology of diarrhoea at various tourist destinations. Lancet 2000;356:133–4.
5. Steffen R, Collard F, Tornieporth N, *et al.* Epidemiology, etiology, and impact of traveler's diarrhea in Jamaica. JAMA 1999;281:811–17.
6. Black RE. Epidemiology of travelers' diarrhea and relative importance of various pathogens. Rev Infect Dis 1990;12:S73–S79.
7. Taylor DN, Houston R, Shlim DR, *et al.* Etiology of diarrhea among travelers and foreign residents in Nepal. JAMA 1988;260:1245–8.
8. Jiang ZD, Lowe B, Verenkar MP, *et al.* Prevalence of enteric pathogens among international travelers with diarrhea acquired in Kenya (Mombasa), India (Goa), or Jamaica (Montego Bay). J Infect Dis 2002;185:497–502.
9. Hoge CW, Shlim DR, Echeverria P, *et al.* Epidemiology of diarrhea among expatriate residents living in a highly endemic environment. JAMA 1996;275:533–8.
10. Hoge CW, Shlim DR, Rajah R, *et al.* Epidemiology of diarrhoeal illness associated with coccidian-like organism among travellers and foreign residents in Nepal. Lancet 1993;341:1175–9.
11. Okhuysen PC. Traveler's diarrhea due to intestinal protozoa. Clin Infect Dis 2001;33:110–14.
12. Mathewson JJ, Johnson PC, DuPont HL, *et al.* A newly recognized cause of travelers' diarrhea: enteroadherent Escherichia coli. J Infect Dis 1985;151:471–5.
13. Glandt M, Adachi JA, Mathewson JJ, *et al.* Enteroaggregative Escherichia coli as a cause of traveler's diarrhea: clinical response to ciprofloxacin. Clin Infect Dis 1999;29:335–8.
14. Adachi JA, Jiang ZD, Mathewson JJ, *et al.* Enteroaggregative Escherichia coli as a major etiologic agent in traveler's diarrhea in 3 regions of the world. Clin Infect Dis 2001;32:1706–9.
15. Mattila L. Clinical features and duration of traveler's diarrhea in relation to its etiology. Clin Infect Dis 1994;19:728–34.
16. Ericsson CD, Patterson TF, Dupont HL. Clinical presentation as a guide to therapy for travelers' diarrhea. Am J Med Sci 1987;294:91–6.
17. Hyams KC, Bourgeois AL, Merrell BR, *et al.* Diarrheal disease during operation Desert Shield. N Engl J Med 1991;325:1423–8.
18. Herwaldt BL. Cyclospora cayetanensis: a review, focusing on the outbreaks of cyclosporiasis in the 1990s. Clin Infect Dis 2000;31:1040–57.
19. Huicho L, Garaycochea V, Uchima N, *et al.* Fecal lactoferrin, fecal leukocytes and occult blood in the diagnostic approach to childhood invasive diarrhea. Pediatr Infect Dis J 1997;16:644–7.
20. Taylor DN, Bodhidatta L, Echeverria P. Epidemiologic aspects of shigellosis and other causes of dysentery in Thailand. Rev Infect Dis 1991;13(suppl 4):S226–30.
21. Pavia AT. Approach to acute foodborne and waterborne disease. Semin Pediatr Infect Dis 1994;5:222–30.
22. Taylor DN, Connor BA, Shlim DR. Chronic diarrhea in the returned traveler. Med Clin North Am 1999;83:1033–52.
23. Bhan MK, Raj P, Levine MM, *et al.* Enteroaggregative *Escherichia coli* associated with persistent diarrhea in a cohort of rural children in India. J Infect Dis 1989;159:1061–4.
24. Cravioto A, Tello A, Navarro A, *et al.* Association of *Escherichia coli* HEp-2 adherence patterns with type and duration of diarrhoea. Lancet 1991;337:262–4.
25. Bourgeois AL, Gardiner CH, Thornton SA, *et al.* Etiology of acute diarrhea among United States military personnel deployed to South America and west Africa. Am J Trop Med Hyg 1993;48:243–8.
26. Osterholm MT, MacDonald KL, White KE, *et al.* An outbreak of a newly recognized chronic diarrhea syndrome associated with raw milk consumption. JAMA 1986;256:484–90.
27. Johnson PC, Ericsson CD, DuPont HL, *et al.* Comparison of loperamide with bismuth subsalicylate for the treatment of acute travelers' diarrhea. JAMA 1986;255:757–60.
28. DuPont HL, Ericsson CD. Prevention and treatment of traveler's diarrhea. N Engl J Med 1993;328:1821–7.
29. Kuschner RA, Trofa AF, Thomas RJ, *et al.* Use of azithromycin for the treatment of Campylobacter enteritis in travelers to Thailand, an area where ciprofloxacin resistance is prevalent. Clin Infect Dis 1995;21:536–41.
30. DuPont HL, Jiang ZD, Ericsson CD, *et al.* Rifaximin versus ciprofloxacin for the treatment of traveler's diarrhea: a randomized, double-blind clinical trial. Clin Infect Dis 2001;33:1807–15.
31. Thoren A. Enteric infections in the traveler: a socioeconomic perspective. Chemotherapy 1995;1:16–19.

chapter

145 Fever

Anthony D Harries

INTRODUCTION

There has been a marked increase in international travel in the past 20 years and it is estimated that over 50 million people from industrialized countries visit the developing world each year.[1] Infectious diseases cause considerable morbidity among travelers and fever in returning travelers, including children, has become a relatively common clinical problem.[2–7] Fever is an elevation of body temperature above the peak normal range and is normally considered to be present if the oral temperature is above 100.2°F (37.8°C).

As a result of the high prevalence of infections and parasitic diseases in the tropics, febrile illnesses are more common after a visit to tropical countries than after a visit to more developed countries. In one report, about 3% of 8000 German-speaking Swiss tourists reported a high fever or chills after a short-term visit to a tropical country compared with 1% of tourists who visited Greek or Canary Islands.[8] Among returned travelers who are managed in specialist tropical disease centers, fever tends to be a common clinical problem. For example, of 1084 patients admitted to the Hospital for Tropical Diseases, London, UK, during a 12-month period, nearly 50% presented with 'fever'.[9]

Travelers are liable not only to the usual causes of fever seen in temperate climates, but also to more exotic infections such as malaria, dengue fever and typhus. Because some tropical infections, such as malaria, may be rapidly fatal if undiagnosed or poorly treated and others, such as typhoid fever, can be a public health risk, this chapter focuses on the diagnosis and management of fever in travelers returned from tropical countries.

CLINICAL FEATURES

The common final diagnoses in febrile patients returned from the tropics and admitted to centers specializing in tropical medicine are malaria, typhoid fever, viral hepatitis and dengue fever (Table 145.1). In an appreciable proportion of patients the cause of fever is one that occurs worldwide such as an upper respiratory tract infection, community-acquired pneumonia and urinary tract infection. In addition, many fevers are undiagnosed and settle spontaneously and presumably are due to a non-specific viral infection.

History

A detailed history allows an appropriate differential diagnosis to be made and is useful in guiding initial investigations. Specific presenting symptoms and a full medical history (including a drug history) must be documented. Although complaints such as headache, lassitude and sweating have no useful diagnostic or localizing value, other symptoms such as cough and pleuritic chest pain (suggesting pneumonia) or dysuria and loin pain (suggesting acute pyelonephritis) may provide a clue to the anatomic site of disease. Several important travel-related topics also must be addressed.

Travel history

Arrival and departure dates, countries visited, duration of stay in each country, places visited within each country and activities should be precisely determined. Most tropical infections are transmitted more easily in rural than in urban areas. The backpacker or volunteer who travels in such areas and has closer contact with the local population therefore has a greater risk of acquiring a tropical infection than the person who stays in first-class hotels in the capital city. However, the affluent traveler who stays in air-conditioned hotels is sometimes at risk of contracting enteric bacterial infections and respiratory infections such as Legionnaires' disease.

A knowledge of incubation periods will help to eliminate the possibility of several potential infections and to narrow the differential diagnosis (Table 145.2). For example, malaria would not be considered in a febrile patient whose potential exposure was less than 7 days earlier. Likewise, dengue fever would be unlikely in a patient who had returned from an endemic area more than 10 days previously. Some tropical infections such as malaria due to *Plasmodium vivax* or *Plasmodium ovale*, African trypanosomiasis and visceral leishmaniasis may present weeks, months or even years after departure from the tropics (see Chapters 157, 166 and 172).

Vaccination and prophylaxis

A history of vaccination against yellow fever, hepatitis A and hepatitis B virtually rules out these infections. If there is doubt about vaccination status, it is important to check vaccination certificates as patients may be confused about what inoculations they have received.[10] Oral and injectable typhoid vaccines are from 70% to 90% effective and prophylactic intramuscular human immunoglobulin against hepatitis A is effective for up to 6 months, with the protective efficacy declining with increasing time after administration. Childhood vaccinations against polio, measles and diphtheria may not be protective if boosters have not been given (see Chapter 143).

With the progressive spread of drug-resistant *Plasmodium falciparum* malaria and the recent emergence of chloroquine-resistant *P. vivax*, no chemoprophylactic antimalarial regimen is 100% protective even if compliance is excellent.[1,11] Poor compliance with chemoprophylaxis, both during and after travel, increases the risk of breakthrough malaria. Antimosquito measures (screened rooms for sleeping, pyrethroid-impregnated bed nets and insect repellents) provide useful additional protection, and if they are used during travel in endemic areas they will decrease the risk of contracting malaria.

Specific exposures

Sometimes there are unique exposures that point to a specific diagnosis (Table 145.3).[2,6] African tick typhus is strongly suspected if there is a history of a tick bite followed by fever, rash, regional lymphadenopathy and skin eschar. Unprotected sexual intercourse with commercial sex workers in high HIV seroprevalence areas in sub-Saharan Africa or parts of Asia may point to a diagnosis of acute HIV syndrome in a patient with a 'glandular fever'-like illness. Leptospirosis should be considered as a cause of fever in adventure travelers who have freshwater contact (such as rafting) in South East Asia.[12] It is also useful to find out whether the patient traveled in a party and if so whether other members have also been ill. There have been several outbreaks of acute schistosomiasis

COMMON FINAL DIAGNOSES IN THE RETURNED TRAVELER WITH 'FEVER'			
	Hospital for Tropical Diseases, London[9]	McGill Centre for Tropical Disease, Montreal[4]	Hospital for Tropical Disease, London[5]
Number of patients	523	587	195
Percentage with:			
Malaria	44	32	42
Hepatitis	11	6	3
Dengue fever	–	2	6
Typhoid fever	5	2	2
Respiratory infection	5	11	4
Urinary tract infection	2	4	3
Diarrheal illness	3	5	7
No diagnosis	7	25	25

Table 145.1 Common final diagnoses in the returned traveler with 'fever'.

USUAL INCUBATION PERIODS FOR SELECTED INFECTIONS	
Short (about 1 week or less)	• Arboviral infections (including dengue fever) • Enteric bacterial infections • Legionnaires' disease • Relapsing fever (*Borrelia* spp.) • Crimean–Congo hemorrhagic fever • Plague
Intermediate (1–3 weeks)	• Malaria • Typhoid fever • Typhus • African trypanosomiasis (*Trypanosoma brucei rhodesiense*) • Viral hemorrhagic fevers (e.g. Lassa, Marburg, Ebola) • Brucellosis • Leptospirosis
Long (>3 weeks)	• Malaria • Viral hepatitis • Acute schistosomiasis • HIV infection • Miscellaneous infections (e.g. amebic liver abscess, brucellosis, melioidosis, visceral leishmaniasis, African trypanosomiasis (*Trypanosma brucei gambiense*), filarial lymphangitis)

Table 145.2 Usual incubation periods for selected infections.

SPECIFIC EXPOSURES THAT ASSIST IN THE DIAGNOSIS OF INFECTIONS	
Exposure	**Infection or disease**
Raw or uncooked foods	Enteric bacterial infections, viral hepatitis
Untreated water	Enteric bacterial infections, viral hepatitis
Unpasteurized milk	Brucellosis, salmonellosis, abdominal tuberculosis
Fresh water swimming	Schistosomiasis, leptospirosis
Promiscuous sexual contact	HIV infection, viral hepatitis B, syphilis, gonococcal bacteremia
Mosquito bite	Malaria, dengue fever, filarial lymphangitis
Tick bite	Typhus, borreliosis, Crimean–Congo hemorrhagic fever, babesiosis
Louse bite	Typhus, borreliosis
Tsetse fly bite	African trypanosomiasis
Reduviid bug bite	Chagas' disease
Sand fly bite	Visceral leishmaniasis, arboviruses
Animal contact	Q fever, brucellosis, anthrax, viral hemorrhagic fevers, histoplasmosis, rabies, plague
Infected person contact	Viral hemorrhagic fevers (Lassa, Ebola, Marburg, Crimean–Congo), viral hepatitis, typhoid fever, meningococcal disease

Table 145.3 Specific exposures that assist in the diagnosis of infections.

('Katayama fever') among parties of nonimmune travelers after exposure to infected fresh water in sub-Saharan Africa.[13] A 'swimmers itch' may occur at the time of schistosomal cercarial penetration, followed several weeks later by a febrile illness associated with eosinophilia. In the spring of 2003, an acute febrile respiratory illness with sometimes severe pneumonia was described initially in southern China and Vietnam. The syndrome, severe acute respiratory syndrome (SARS) spread to all continents due to air travel and is associated with considerable morbidity and mortality. It is presumably of viral origin with the leading candidate being a member of the corona virus family.

Physical examination

Temperature patterns

The temperature and pulse rate must be measured initially and regularly thereafter. Some patients who are being investigated for fever are in fact afebrile or the fever may settle spontaneously before a diagnosis is reached. Such patients should be reassured and discharged because it is usually unrewarding to pursue investigations retrospectively.[9] For patients with a documented fever, the height of the temperature curve may assist in establishing a diagnosis. High temperatures above 106.8°F (41.5°C) are uncommon and may be caused by infections such as malaria, bacteremia, meningoencephalitis and typhoid fever or by noninfectious disease such as heat stroke, intracerebral hemorrhage and drugs.

Although fever patterns are not pathognomonic for particular infections, they can occasionally provide diagnostic clues:

- a pattern of short paroxysms of high fever accompanied by rigors and separated by periods when the temperature is normal (intermittent fever) is often a feature of malaria, pyogenic abscesses, miliary tuberculosis and bacteremia;
- paroxysms occurring every third or every fourth day occur typically with *P. vivax* and *P. ovale* (benign tertian malaria) and *P. malariae* (benign quartan malaria), respectively;

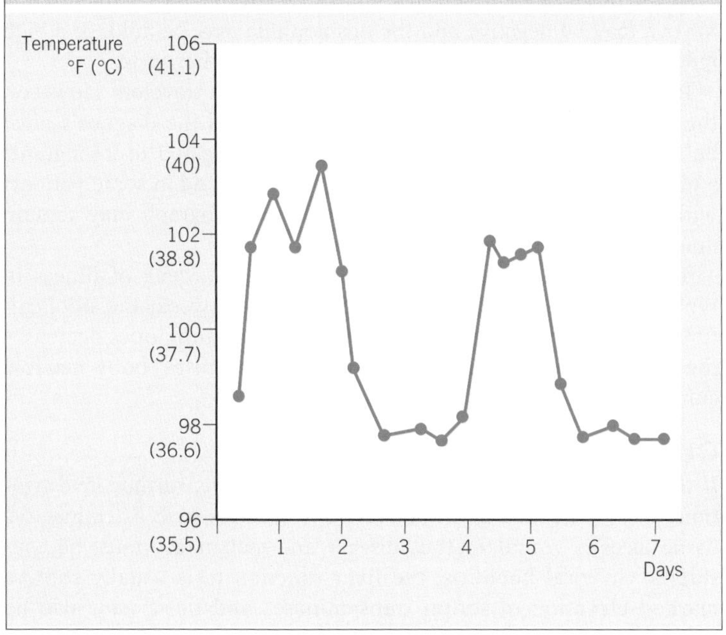

Fig. 145.1 Temperature pattern in a patient with dengue fever.

- a temperature that remains elevated throughout the day with minor fluctuations (continuous fever) may be caused by typhoid fever or typhus;
- dengue fever typically presents with 'saddle back' fever (i.e. two febrile periods separated by an afebrile interval of 1–3 days' duration, as shown in Fig. 145.1);
- several episodes of fever alternating with periods of normal temperature may occur in relapsing fever due to *Borrelia* spp.

For every 1.8°F (1°C) that the temperature rises above normal, the pulse rate rises by about 10–15 beats/minute. A slower pulse rate than is predicted from the temperature chart (relative bradycardia) is sometimes seen in typhoid fever, meningitis, brucellosis and Legionnaires' disease; it may also indicate factitious fever.

Physical signs

Physical findings in many tropical infections are non-specific and often overlap, although it can be rewarding to carefully examine the skin (Table 145.4), the liver, spleen and lymph nodes, and any other organ system associated with symptoms. Generalized lymphadenopathy is a feature of many infections, although a localized enlarged tender lymphadenopathy (bubo) suggests plague and tenderness over lymphatic vessels suggests filarial lymphangitis. Hepatosplenomegaly occurs in several tropical infections such as malaria, viral hepatitis and typhoid fever. Tender hepatomegaly suggests amebic liver abscess and splenomegaly of more than 10cm below the left costal margin suggests visceral leishmaniasis.

The absence of physical signs can be helpful. Malaria is an unlikely diagnosis in the febrile patient who has lymphadenopathy or a maculopapular rash.

Differential diagnosis by geographic area

Several infections have a worldwide distribution among tropical countries. These include malaria, dengue fever, hepatitis, typhoid fever, tuberculosis, HIV infection and amebic liver abscess. However, the risks of infection can be higher in certain geographic regions (see Chapter 142):

- among travelers from Europe and North America, malaria due to *P. falciparum* occurs most often after travel to sub-Sahara Africa, whereas malaria due to *P. vivax* is more common after travel to India and South East Asia;[14,15]
- travelers to Central and South America are particularly at risk of dengue fever due to the growing incidence of the infection in this region;[16]
- although schistosomiasis occurs widely, Katayama fever in travelers is usually a result of exposure in sub-Saharan Africa;[17] and
- high HIV infection rates are found in commercial sex workers in sub-Saharan Africa and increasingly in India, Thailand and Cambodia;
- SARS in travellers to South East Asia.

SKIN LESIONS THAT PROVIDE DIAGNOSTIC CLUES

Skin lesion	Infection
Eschar	Tick typhus, scrub typhus, anthrax
Chancre	African trypanosomiasis
Rose spots on trunk	Typhoid fever
Urticaria	Acute schistosomiasis
Orbital edema (bilateral)	Trichinosis
Orbital edema (unilateral)	Chagas' disease
Maculopapular rash	Dengue fever, other arbovirus infections, viral hemorrhagic fever, typhus, leptospirosis, meningococcal bacteremia, syphilis, African trypanosomiasis
Petechiae and hemorrhage	Viral hemorrhagic fever, meningococcal bacteremia, louse-borne relapsing fever, louse-borne typhus

Table 145.4 Skin lesions that provide diagnostic clues.

TROPICAL INFECTIONS WITH LIMITED GEOGRAPHIC DISTRIBUTION

Region	Infection
Sub-Saharan Africa	• African trypanosomiasis • Ebola, Lassa and Marburg viral hemorrhagic fever • Specific arbovirus infections (e.g. Rift Valley fever) • African tick typhus
Asia and South East Asia	• Scrub typhus • Japanese encephalitis
South and Central America	• Chagas' disease • Specific arbovirus infections (e.g. Argentine hemorrhagic fever)

Table 145.5 Tropical infections with limited geographic distribution.

Some infections have limited geographic distribution (Table 145.5). In sub-Saharan Africa, trypanosomiasis has a sporadic distribution in rural savanna areas and game forests, so the safari enthusiast has the highest risk of acquiring this disease. African tick typhus due to *Rickettsia africae*[18] and Asian scrub typhus due to *R. tsutsugamushi*[19] are contracted by walking in grass or scrubby vegetation in the countryside.

DIAGNOSIS

Initial investigations include:

- thick and thin blood films for malaria parasites plus a simple diagnostic strip test (*Para*Sight F test) for *P. falciparum*,
- full blood count with differential white cell count,
- urinalysis, and
- chest radiograph (if indicated).

Thick and thin blood films plus simple diagnostic strip test for *Plasmodium falciparum*

Malaria is a great 'imitator' of other diseases and blood films should always be examined for malaria parasites if the patient has visited an endemic area. Thick films have greater sensitivity for identifying malaria parasites, whereas thin films are better for differentiating the species and, in *P. falciparum* infection, for estimating the degree of parasitemia. The films should be examined by someone who has relevant experience to avoid missing a low-grade parasitemia. Sometimes no parasites are found in blood films as a result of ongoing malaria chemoprophylaxis, partial antimalarial treatment or sequestration of parasitized red cells in deep capillaries in the case of *P. falciparum* infection. A simple diagnostic strip test for *P. falciparum* malaria (*Para*Sight F test, Becton Dickinson Advanced Diagnostics), which detects a water-soluble antigen produced by the blood stages of *P. falciparum*, has high sensitivity and specificity for the initial assessment of *P. falciparum* in returning travelers.[20] The test does not remove the need for blood film examination but has a useful role in screening, especially where laboratory staff are not experienced in diagnosing malaria. If malaria is still suspected despite negative initial screening, blood films and a *Para*Sight F test should be repeated and smears of blood-stained tissue from an intradermal puncture may help in difficult cases (see Chapter 166). Hemolytic jaundice and thrombocytopenia are valuable pointers to malaria, although thrombocytopenia may also be due to an arbovirus infection or bacteremia.

Blood films are essential in the diagnosis of relapsing fever (*Borrelia* spp.) and acute infection with trypanosomiasis (*Trypanosoma brucei rhodesiense*). Spirochetes of *Borrelia* spp. are plentiful and easily recognized, whereas several blood films may need to be examined to find trypanosomes.

Differential white blood cell count

This simple investigation can be rapidly performed and the results help to focus the differential diagnosis and further investigations (Table 145.6).[21]

In patients who have a neutrophil leukocytosis, the additional findings of anemia, raised serum alkaline phosphatase and elevated right hemidiaphragm on chest radiography strongly suggest amebic liver abscess. Liver ultrasound may initially be negative, but the amebic immunofluorescent antibody test is very sensitive and usually positive in proven cases.

At the onset of acute schistosomiasis (Katayama fever), microscopy for ova may be negative and the eosinophilia may be mild, so a high index of suspicion may be required to make the diagnosis.

Tuberculosis is rarely contracted by short-term travelers. However, the risk increases with the duration of stay and the diagnosis must be strongly considered and aggressively investigated in immigrants and foreign students. Diagnosis can be difficult and in some patients with disseminated tuberculosis, the chest radiograph may remain normal until after treatment has started.

Blood cultures are often positive in the first week of illness in typhoid fever and in the second and subsequent weeks the stool cultures become positive. Previous treatment with antibiotics decreases the positive yield of blood cultures; in these cases, bone marrow culture may prove more sensitive.

Other investigations

If the initial screening tests prove nondiagnostic, further investigations will be needed and noninfectious diseases such as connective tissue disease, granulomatous disease and malignancy must be considered. In viral hepatitis, the liver function tests usually show a marked elevation of serum transaminases and these may also be mildly to moderately raised in malaria, typhoid fever and typhus. It is advisable to store an 'acute' serum specimen for antibody detection that can be used with a paired convalescent specimen at a later date.

MANAGEMENT

Recognition and treatment of malaria

The first step in management is to ensure that malaria due to *P. falciparum* is diagnosed and correctly treated (Table 145.7). Falciparum malaria in the returning traveler can be regarded as severe or complicated if:

- the patient is unable to take oral medication,
- there is any sign of specific organ failure,
- parasitemia is greater than 2%, or
- there is hypoglycemia.[22,23]

If falciparum malaria is suspected in an ill patient but no malaria parasites are found, it is reasonable to treat the patient empirically

DIFFERENTIAL WBC COUNT AND DIAGNOSTIC POSSIBILITIES		
WBC differential	**Diagnostic possibilities**	**Further investigations**
Neutrophil leukocytosis	• Bacteremia • Deep sepsis • Amebic liver abscess • Relapsing fever • Leptospirosis	Blood culture Ultrasound, CT scan Ultrasound, serology Blood films Serology, culture of body fluids
Eosinophilia	• Schistosomiasis • Fascioliasis • Trichinosis • Lymphatic filariasis	Serology, microscopy of stool, urine, rectal snips Serology Creatinine phosphokinase, serology Nocturnal blood film, serology
Leukopenia	• Brucellosis • Disseminated tuberculosis • Visceral leishmaniasis	Serology, blood and bone marrow culture Biopsies (multiple sites), CT scans Serology, bone marrow or spleen aspirate for amastigotes
Normal WBC count and differential	• Arbovirus infection • Typhus • Typhoid fever	Serology Serology Blood and stool culture

Table 145.6 Differential white blood cell (WBC) count and diagnostic possibilities.

IMMEDIATE MANAGEMENT FOR THE RETURNED TRAVELER WITH FEVER
Step 1: Blood films for malaria parasites (if from endemic area)
Step 2: Malaria parasites identified • Uncomplicated falciparum malaria – treat with quinine sulfate and pyrimethamine-sulfadoxine **or** mefloquine **or** halofantrine **or** artemether • Non-falciparum malaria – treat with chloroquine • Complicated falciparum malaria – treat with parenteral quinine or quinidine together with pyrimethamine-sulfadoxine **or** artesunate **or** artemether
Step 3: Malaria suspected, patient ill, no parasites identified • Treat as for complicated falciparum malaria – *Para*Sight F test useful for diagnosis of falciparum malaria and serology useful for retrospective diagnosis • Blood cultures followed by antibiotics as for suspected bacteremia
Step 4: Possibility of viral hemorrhagic fever (VHF) • Obtain expert advice • If possibility of VHF is high, no further blood specimens or body secretions sent to the routine laboratory until VHF excluded • If VHF confirmed, transfer patient to special isolation facility and perform all investigations in a high-security laboratory
Step 5: Clinical diagnosis made but unconfirmed by tests • Perform appropriate investigations first and commence empiric treatment
Step 6: No clinical diagnosis and patient not seriously ill • Avoid empiric treatment and perform appropriate investigations
Step 7: Exotic tropical infection identified • Consider transfer to hospital facility specializing in tropical medicine

Table 145.7 Immediate management for the returned traveler who was fever.

with parenteral quinine. Several sets of blood cultures should also be taken and antibiotics started as treatment for a possible bacteremia. Blood films for malaria parasites should be examined daily during treatment and other causes of fever rigorously pursued (see Chapter 166).

Exclusion of viral hemorrhagic fever

The rare possibility of viral hemorrhagic fever should be considered in all febrile patients who have been in endemic areas during the 3 weeks before the onset of illness. Lassa, Ebola, Marburg and Crimean–Congo hemorrhagic fever viruses can all be transmitted from person to person through close contact with infected blood or other body secretions, so placing health and laboratory personnel at high risk. These infections are serious and cause a high mortality, although ribavirin (tribavirin) is useful in treating Lassa fever and Crimean–Congo hemorrhagic fever.[24] Clinical diagnosis is difficult as the differential diagnosis is wide (see also Chapters 183 and 186a).

Particular risk factors for travelers to endemic areas include:

- camping in the bush,
- staying in rural farming areas,
- contact with sick animals, and
- tick bites.

If viral hemorrhagic fever is suspected, it is vital to seek expert advice promptly.[25] Many such patients in fact have falciparum malaria, which in its own right requires rapid diagnosis and treatment.

Empiric treatment

If a clinical diagnosis has been made with or without initial screening tests, empiric treatment can be commenced while awaiting results of specific investigations. For example, in suspected typhoid fever, treatment can be commenced with a quinolone antibiotic after three sets of blood cultures and a stool culture have been obtained. African tick typhus can be diagnosed on clinical grounds and treated with doxycycline.

If no diagnosis has been made after the initial screening procedures and the patient is not seriously ill, empiric treatment is best avoided and investigations are continued as appropriate. For a deteriorating patient who has suspected disseminated tuberculosis, it is sometimes justified to start (and observe the response to) empiric therapy with specific antituberculosis drugs such as isoniazid, pyrazinamide and ethambutol while awaiting results of mycobacterial cultures.

Exotic tropical infections

Exotic tropical infections, such as African trypanosomiasis or visceral leishmaniasis, are uncommon and cases are best referred to specialist tropical centers because treatment is potentially toxic, of long duration and requires expert parasitologic monitoring.

Infection control procedures

Many tropical infections, such as malaria, dengue fever and typhus, can be managed without special isolation facilities. Typhoid fever, some enteric bacterial infections, viral hepatitis, HIV infection and plague can be transmitted from person to person, and appropriate measures must be instituted to prevent transmission. The rare viral hemorrhagic fevers are extremely dangerous and suspected cases should be managed in a high-security isolation facility (see Chapter 186a).

COMPLICATIONS

Many of the common infections in returned travelers do not cause long-term sequelae and are not transmitted to immediate family members. However, some arbovirus infections (including dengue fever) are associated with postviral fatigue syndromes, hepatitis B and hepatitis C can cause chronic active hepatitis and liver cirrhosis, and almost all patients infected with HIV will eventually develop features of AIDS.

If *P. vivax* or *P. ovale* malaria is not treated with an appropriate course of primaquine, relapsing malaria can occur for several years after leaving a malaria-endemic area, and trypanosomiasis with central nervous system involvement may relapse after inadequate treatment with melarsoprol B.

Some pathogens may be transmitted to family members either by the enteric route (e.g. *Salmonella typhi* in the chronic typhoid carrier, hepatitis A and E), by sexual intercourse (HIV, hepatitis B and C) and by nasopharyngeal spread (*Neisseria meningitidis*). In such cases, family members must be counseled and offered appropriate vaccination (hepatitis B) or chemoprophylaxis (*N. meningitidis*).

Viral infections are usually associated with prolonged immunity to the particular virus serotype, but most bacterial or parasitic infections in the short-term traveler confer no useful immunity for the future. Malaria acquired during last year's visit to Africa will not protect against malaria for next year's African safari!

REFERENCES

1. Ryan ET, Kain KC. Health advice and immunizations for travellers. N Engl J Med 2000;342:1716–25.
2. Strickland GT. Fever in the returned traveller. Med Clin North Am 1992;76:1375–92.
3. Saxe SE, Gardner P. The returning traveller with fever. Infect Dis Clin North Am 1992;6:427–39.
4. MacLean JD, Lalonde RG, Ward B. Fever from the tropics. Travel Med Advisor 1994;5:27.1–14.
5. Doherty JF, Grant AD, Bryceson ADM. Fever as the presenting complaint of travellers returning from the tropics. Q J Med 1995;88:277–81.
6. Humar A, Keystone J. Evaluating fever in travellers returning from tropical countries. Br Med J 1996;312:953–6.
7. Klein JL Millman GC. Prospective, hospital based study of fever in children in the United Kingdom who had recently spent time in the tropics. Br Med J 1998;316:1425–6.
8. Steffen R, Rickenbach M, Wilhelm U, *et al.* Health problems after travel to developing countries. J Infect Dis 1987;156:84–91.
9. Bryceson A. Imported fevers. In: Pounder RE, Chiodini PL, eds. Advanced medicine 23. London: Baillière Tindall; 1987:336–43.
10. Teichmann D, Grobusch MP, Wesselmann H, *et al.* A haemorrhagic fever from Cote d'Ivoire. Lancet 1999;354:1608.
11. Bradley DJ, Warhurst DC. Malaria prophylaxis: guidelines for travellers from Britain. Br Med J 1995;310:709–14.
12. van Crevel R, Speelman P, Gravekamp C, *et al.* Leptospirosis in travellers. Clin Infect Dis 1994;19:132–4.
13. Visser LG, Polderman AM, Stuiver PC. Outbreak of schistosomiasis among travellers returning from Mali, West Africa. Clin Infect Dis 1995;20:280–5.
14. Svenson JE, MacLean JD, Gyorkos TW, *et al.* Imported malaria. Clinical presentation and examination of symptomatic travelers. Arch Intern Med 1995;155:861–8.
15. Muentener P, Schlagenhauf P, Steffen R. Imported malaria (1985–95): trends and perspectives. Bull World Health Organ 1999;77:560–6.
16. Guzman MG, Kouri G. Dengue: an update. Lancet Infectious Diseases 2002;2:33–42.
17. Doherty JF, Moody AH, Wright SG. Katayama fever: an acute manifestation of schistosomiasis. Br Med J 1996;313:1071–2.
18. Raoult D, Fournier PE, Fenollar F, *et al. Rickettsia africae*, a tick-borne pathogen in travelers to sub-Saharan Africa. N Engl J Med 2001;344:1504–10.
19. McDonald JC, Maclean JD, McDade JE. Imported rickettsial disease: clinical and epidemiologic features. Am J Med 1988;85:799–805.
20. Cropley IM, Lockwood DNJ, Mack D, *et al.* Rapid diagnosis of falciparum malaria by using the *Para*Sight F test in travellers returning to the United Kingdom: prospective study. Br Med J 2000;321:1484–5.
21. Bell DR. Lecture notes on tropical medicine, 4th ed. Oxford: Blackwell Science; 1996.
22. Molyneux M, Fox R. Diagnosis and treatment of malaria in Britain. Br Med J 1993;306:1175–80.
23. World Health Organization, Communicable Diseases Cluster. Severe falciparum malaria. [Severe and complicated malaria, third edition]. Trans Roy Soc Trop Med Hyg 2000;94(Suppl.1):S1/1–90.
24. Fischer-Hoch SP, Khan JA, Rehman S, *et al.* Crimean–Congo haemorrhagic fever treated with oral ribavirin. Lancet 1995;346:472–5.
25. World Health Organization. Viral hemorrhagic fevers – management of suspected cases. Wkly Epidemiol Rec 1995;352:49–52.

chapter

146 Coma and Confusion

Geoffrey Pasvol

INTRODUCTION

Although infrequent, the management of returning travelers with signs of confusion and/or any level of impaired consciousness, ranging from disorientation to coma, presents a particular challenge to the clinician.[1,2] The management of any comatose patient is difficult because of the wide number of possible diagnoses (Table 146.1)[3] and because the urgency for diagnosis and specific treatment constitutes a medical emergency.[4] In addition to all the common non-infection-related etiologies, such as those associated with trauma (e.g. subdural hematoma), hyperpyrexia, alcohol poisoning, drug overdose, cerebrovascular lesions and diabetes mellitus, the differential diagnosis will also include more exotic and less well-known causes of coma that could result from the patient's travels. Travel can also be associated with many factors that could exaggerate and complicate an acute confusional state, such as alcohol intoxication or withdrawal, psychologic stress, sleep deprivation, jet lag and sensory overload. Confusion in elderly travelers is especially common, even in the presence of non-neurologic conditions such as pneumonia and urinary or biliary tract infections. The combination of air travel, dehydration, alcohol ingestion and relative hypoxia can be enough to induce confusion in elderly travelers.

Patients from tropical destinations may also present with multiple pathologies, for example an HIV-positive patient with *Salmonella* sepsis or a patient who has cerebral malaria and meningitis.

The most common consideration for any traveler returning from an area where malaria is endemic and presenting with a decreased level of consciousness is the possibility of malaria, although equally important diagnostic possibilities are meningitis and encephalitis. In any patient presenting with an alteration in conscious state, it is imperative to exclude malaria either as a cause or complicating factor by means of a thick and thin blood film.

CLINICAL FEATURES

For patients with confusion or coma it is important to obtain a history from accompanying travelers or attending ambulance or aircraft cabin crew (Table 146.2). It is important to establish whether the onset of confusion or coma was rapid or gradual, part of an ongoing known disease process, unpredictable in someone with a known underlying condition (e.g. epilepsy) or entirely unexpected. The patient may present with rambling speech, abnormally aggressive behavior, disorientation, impairment of memory, hallucinations or any decrease in level of consciousness, including coma. Fever or the history of fever suggest the presence of an infection.

Examination needs to be careful and thorough. The level of consciousness may be best monitored serially using the Glasgow Coma Scale.[5] Since the reticular activating system in the brain stem plays such an important role in consciousness level, elucidation of signs of brain stem involvement is essential. This requires careful attention to pupillary size and response to light. Any change might suggest uncal herniation as might occur in conditions that cause unevenly distributed changes in intracranial pressure. The oculocephalic ('doll's eye') and oculovestibular (elicited by instilling ice cold water into the external auditory meatus) responses may be tested to indicate whether the brain stem is intact. The corneal response is usually retained until coma is deep. Brain stem involvement may also manifest as an abnormality in respiratory pattern with tachypnea, long-cycle periodic breathing or Cheyne–Stokes respiration. This should not be confused with the deep sighing breathing of metabolic acidosis (Kussmaul's breathing) or that due to a respiratory cause.

Examination of the fundi is important, with special attention to the appearances of papilledema, hemorrhage and the changes of hypertensive or diabetic retinopathy.

Patients who have **malaria** have a history of travel to an endemic area, often with inadequate or no prophylaxis. They may present with complications, other than cerebral malaria, that may impair consciousness (e.g. repeated convulsions or even status epilepticus, metabolic acidosis, hypoglycemia, sepsis, respiratory involvement with hypoxia, renal failure and severe anemia; see Chapter 166).[6] A history of mosquito bites neither suggests nor refutes the diagnosis. The shortest possible incubation period for falciparum malaria is about 7 days and patients who have progressed to confusion or coma have usually been ill for a number of days, often with a flu-like illness.

In children it is important to distinguish cerebral malaria from transient postictal coma, which may last anything up to an hour after a fit. It is also important in cases of malaria to determine that the decreased level of consciousness is not due to sedative drugs (e.g. benzodiazepines) or hypoglycemia. In cerebral malaria the gag reflex is usually preserved. Grinding of the teeth (bruxism) has been observed in some patients. Examination of the fundus may reveal retinal hemorrhages, extramacular whitening and vessel changes in which the vessels turn white in isolated segments, especially at branch points.

Typhoid is suggested by travel to a highly endemic area, particularly the Indian subcontinent, and a compatible food history. Symptoms are predominantly abdominal, with a fever and a dry cough. The symptomatology is generally not abrupt and has an onset over a few days with increasing fever. The so-called characteristic features of typhoid, such as rose spots (Fig. 146.1), relative bradycardia, pea soup stools or constipation, may be absent. The early neurologic manifestations of typhoid are often subtle, with mild disorientation and a 'glazed', vacant look.

A wide range of **viral infections**, especially arboviral, may present with neurologic manifestations, including dengue fever, which is the most frequent in travelers. Patients with dengue may have a characteristic blanching erythematous rash, which is often confused with sunburn. In more severe infections there may be petechiae and even evidence of frank hemorrhage into the skin. West Nile virus more commonly causes fever, arthralgia and a rash rather than alterations in consciousness. Japanese B encephalitis is more dramatic and can produce a severe meningoencephalitis with altered sensorium. It can also cause a newly recognized polio-like acute flaccid paralysis syndrome.

CAUSES OF CONFUSION AND COMA IN A TRAVELER	
Infections	**Other**
Cerebral malaria	Drug-induced
Bacterial meningitis	Alcohol abuse
Viral meningitis	Cerebrovascular accidents,
Encephalitis including arboviral such as:	including subarachnoid
Dengue	hemorrhage
Japanese B	Head trauma
West Nile	Dehydration
Viral hemorrhagic fevers	Hepatic encephalopathy (e.g.
Lassa	hepatitis)
Marburg	Renal failure
Ebola	Hypoglycemia
Typhoid	Diabetic ketoacidosis
AIDS-related infections	Epilepsy and postepileptic states
Toxoplasmosis	Space-occupying lesions
Cryptococcal meningitis	(especially abscess or tumors)
Tuberculous meningitis	
AIDS dementia	
Protozoan infections	
Trypanosomiasis	
Toxoplasmosis	
Naegleria	
Acanthamoeba	
Relapsing fevers (Louse and tick-borne)	
Other spirochetal infections	
Leptospirosis	
Lyme disease	
Neurosyphilis	
Helminthic infections	
Schistosomiasis	
Cysticercosis	
Hydatid disease	
Strongyloidiasis	
Paragonimiasis	
Angiostrongylus	
Rabies	
Any severe infection, especially septicemia, endocarditis, pneumonia (especially Legionnaires' disease), pyelonephritis or cholecystitis	

Table 146.1 Causes of confusion and coma in a traveler.

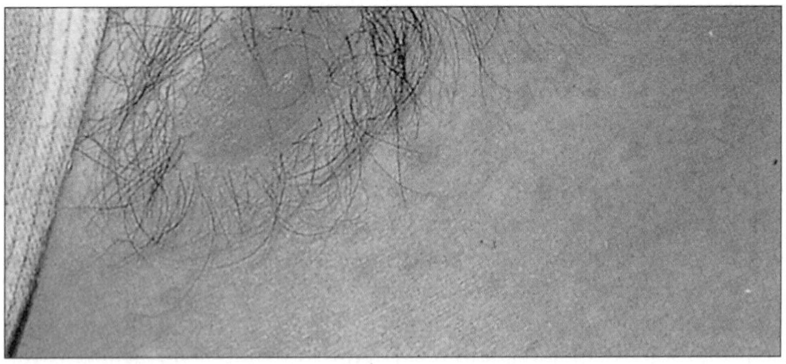

Fig. 146.1 Rose spots. In *Salmonella typhi* and *S. paratyphi* infections (enteric fever) classic rose spots of 1–3mm diameter can be found, especially on the abdominal wall, lower thorax and back of the trunk. These are small erythematous macular lesions, which tend to come and go during infection. Courtesy of Anthony Bryceson.

Incubation of the **viral hemorrhagic fevers** (which include Lassa, Ebola, Marburg and Crimean–Congo hemorrhagic fevers) ranges from 3 to 21 days. Symptoms include sustained fever, malaise and headache as well as muscle and joint pains. Nausea, diarrhea and vomiting may occur. In the case of Lassa fever there is often a history of travel to west Africa, contact with infectious patients and a characteristic illness beginning with pharyngitis and circumoral pallor. Ebola and Marburg diseases may produce a measles-like rash after 4–7 days. Overt bleeding is a late or terminal event in these infections.[7]

In **trypanosomiasis** there may be a history of travel to game parks in east Africa and a painful tsetse fly bite followed by a local chancre, a rash (Fig. 146.2) and lymphadenopathy.

Leptospirosis occurs worldwide, particularly in those participating in recreational water sports or working with animals. It is usually the patients with jaundice, conjunctival hemorrhage (Fig. 146.3) and renal failure that present with confusion.

Lyme disease due to *Borrelia burgdorferi* more commonly leads to fatigue and personality disorders than alterations in conscious level.

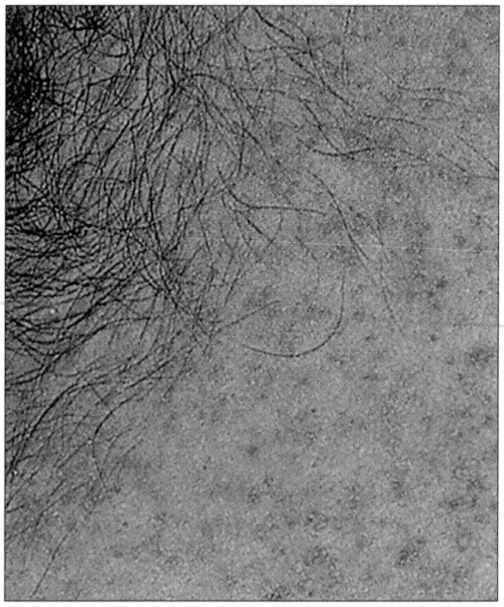

Fig. 146.2 Trypanosomal rash. In fair-skinned individuals, each peak of fever may be accompanied by a remarkable skin eruption in the form of annular patches of erythema. In other cases, the rash may be more generalized, as seen here on the sixth day of an infection with *Trypanosoma brucei rhodesiense.* Courtesy of Anthony Bryceson.

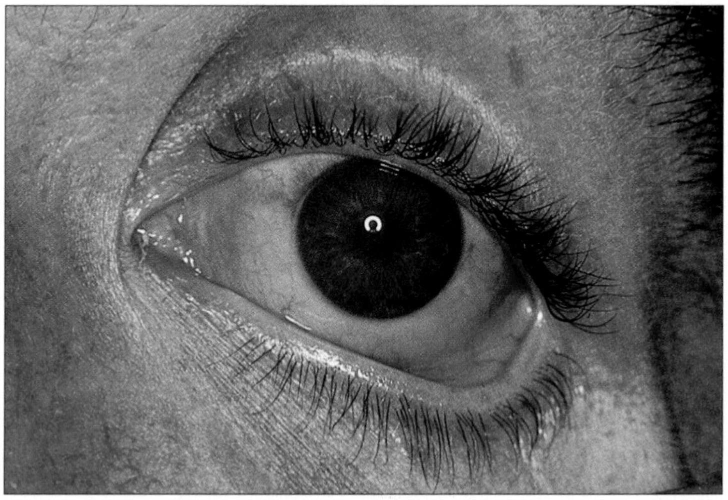

Fig. 146.3 Subconjunctival hemorrhages and jaundice in leptospirosis. Asymptomatic or atypical infection probably occurs in 90% of cases and, in some tropical areas, leptospirosis may account for up to 15% of all patients with undiagnosed pyrexia. While this form can be mild, the infection may develop into a generalized septic form with confusion within 1–2 weeks. This is characterized by fever, myalgia and often subconjunctival hemorrhages. The patient illustrated was in the second week following the onset of symptoms. The most dangerous form (Weil's disease) may be very severe and can involve several organs, with jaundice, renal failure, haemorrhagia, vascular collapse and obtundation.

FEATURES SUGGESTING THE CAUSE OF CONFUSION AND COMA IN A TRAVELER

Symptom or sign	Possible diagnosis
General	
Fever	Malaria Meningitis/encephalitis
Jaundice	Malaria Hepatic encephalopathy, especially hepatitis
Lymphadenopathy, oral thrush, shingles scar	HIV infection associated with cerebral toxoplasmosis, cryptococcal meningitis or tuberculous meningitis
Venepuncture marks	Injection drug abuse
Dehydration	Diabetic coma
Acidotic breathing	Severe malaria Diabetic ketoacidosis Renal failure
Sweating	Malaria Hypoglycemia
Rash	Meningococcal infection Dengue fever Louse-borne typhus Erythema migrans of Lyme disease
Game park visit and tsetse fly bite	Trypanosomiasis
Hyperpigmentation	Addisonian crisis (tuberculosis)
Drug history	Mefloquine or chloroquine Isoniazid Cannabis Other drug abuse (e.g. opiates, cocaine, barbiturates, amphetamines)
Recent head injury	Concussion Contusion Laceration Subdural hematoma
Fetor	Alcohol intoxication or withdrawal Diabetic ketoacidosis
Water contact	Leptospirosis Cerebral schistosomiasis Cysticercosis Cerebral hydatid

Symptom or sign	Possible diagnosis
Cardiovascular	
Bradycardia (relative)	Typhoid Yellow fever
Irregular pulse, significant murmur	Cerebral embolus, endocarditis
Raised blood pressure	Hypertensive encephalopathy
Low blood pressure, postural drop	Hypoadrenalism
Respiratory	
Cyanosis, hypoxia	Respiratory failure
Respiratory distress	Severe pneumonia Severe malaria
Consolidation	Meningitis (including tuberculous) Cerebral abscess
Abdominal	
Pain, constipation, diarrhea	Typhoid
Jaundice	Hepatitis Leptospirosis Severe malaria
Neurologic	
Cuts, abrasions, fractures	Trauma
Neck stiffness, positive Kernig's or Brudzinski's sign	Meningitis Meningoencephalitis Subarachnoid hemorrhage
Seizures	Malaria Idiopathic epilepsy Focal neurologic lesions
Constricted pupils	Opiate drug abuse Organophosphate poisoning
Retinal hemorrhage	Cerebral malaria
Subhyaloid hemorrhage	Subarachnoid hemorrhage
Decerebrate/decorticate rigidity	Cerebral malaria
Focal neurologic deficits as suggested by hemiplegia, unequal pupil size, external ophthalmoplegia, asymmetric reflexes	Cerebral abscess Cerebral tumor (e.g. pituitary adenoma)

Table 146.2 Features suggesting the cause of confusion and coma in a traveler.

Relapsing fevers. In louse-borne relapsing fevers due to *Borrelia recurrentis* and tick-borne fevers due to *Borrelia duttonii* there may be a history of a visit to an endemic area and evidence of a bite that develops into an eschar associated with a more generalized rash. Tick-borne relapsing fever is usually milder than the louse-borne form.

Neurosyphilis patients can present with a history of a gradual onset of confusion.

Helminthic infections, which sometimes involve the central nervous system, need to be considered especially when the clinical findings suggest a focal lesion. These infections more commonly present with a fit than with confusion. They include neurocysticercosis (*Taenia solium*), hydatid disease due to *Echinococcus granulosis* or *Echinococcus multilocularis* and schistosomiasis. Less likely are *Strongyloides stercoralis*, *Trichinella spiralis* from under-

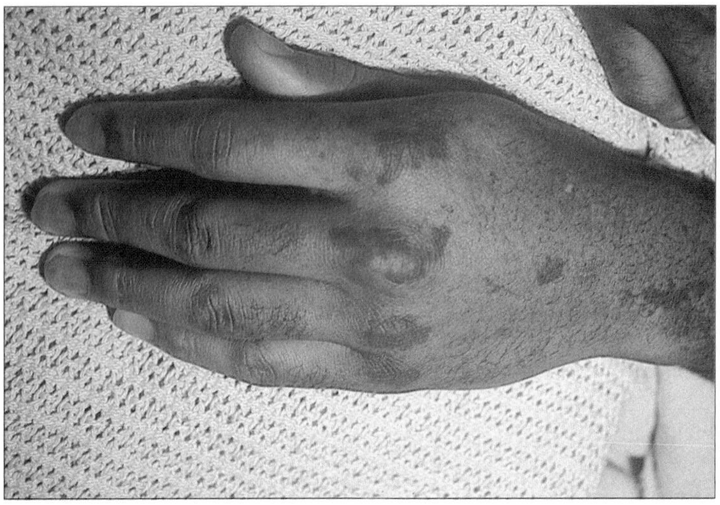

Fig. 146.4 Meningococcal septicemia. Meningococcal infections are common in the tropics, most notably in the relatively dry 'meningococcal belt' of sub-Saharan Africa, stretching from Senegal and the Gambia in the west to Ethiopia in the east. The nonblanching skin rash and the petechiae and purpura are often difficult to see in individuals with pigmented skin, as is demonstrated in this patient.

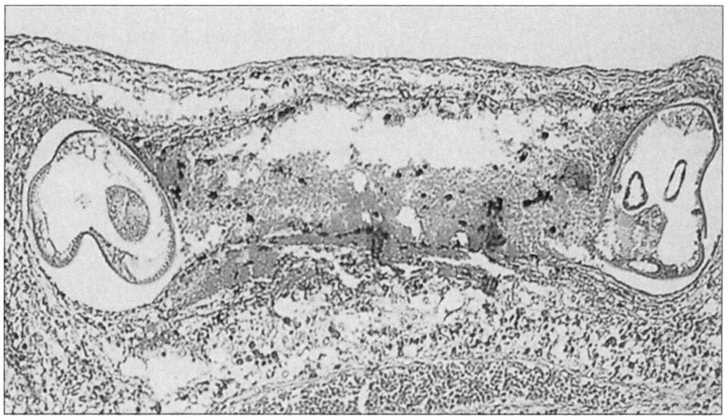

Fig. 146.5 Section of *Angiostrongylus cantonensis* larvae in meninges of human brain. Humans may be infested by ingesting third-stage larvae in raw or inadequately cooked intermediate hosts such as snails, prawns, frogs or fish, or in contaminated salads. The larvae migrate to the brain, where they cause eosinophilic meningitis or meningoencephalitis. The diagnosis is aided by the serologic examination of paired specimens, using a specific antigen from adult worms. Courtesy of Colonel JC Crook, RAMC.

cooked meat (usually pork) and *Paragonimiasis* spp. from freshwater crustaceans.

Cerebral abscesses of whatever cause are another important differential in focal neurologic presentations. It is important to ensure that these do not relate to infective endocarditis.

Meningitis and encephalitis. If acquired when traveling, these infections do not necessarily differ from meningitis and encephalitis occurring elsewhere. The meningococcal rash is sometimes difficult to see in individuals with pigmented skin (Fig. 146.4). The specific cause of an encephalitis may be suggested by the region of travel (see below) and this applies especially to some of the less common causes of viral meningitides and encephalitides. Eosinophilic meningitis due to *Angiostrongylus cantonensis* (rat lungworm) is found in South East Asia, the Pacific Basin and more recently in the Caribbean. While most cases occur sporadically and are self-limited, outbreaks have been reported and neurologic sequelae and sometimes death do occur. Headache with raised intracranial pressure associated with paresthesias or hyperesthesias, and cerebrospinal fluid (CSF) pleocytosis, with or without eosinophilia, in a traveler should alert clinicians to the possibility of eosinophilic meningitis (Fig. 146.5). Amebic infection due to *Naegleria fowleri* (usually from freshwater) and *Acanthamoeba* spp. from brackish warm water can lead to a meningoencephalitis.

While **rabies** and **tetanus** usually occur in the setting of an individual who is conscious, brain stem rabies is an exception and can present with profound obtundation.

Drug (heroin, cocaine, barbiturate or amphetamine) **and alcohol abuse** are important considerations in the differential diagnosis in returning travelers who are confused. A history of personality change and self-neglect, together with sleep disturbance and poor appetite, are suggestive factors. Needle tracks, superficial thrombophlebitis or bruising are telltale signs. **Insecticide poisoning** is another possibility, which is particularly common in India and Sri Lanka. Occasionally **antimalarials**, most notably mefloquine and chloroquine, can lead to neuropsychiatric symptoms and manifest as confusion in a traveler.

It is important to determine whether the unconsciousness developed suddenly or gradually. The former might suggest a subarachnoid hemorrhage, whereas the onset of coma due to trypanosomiasis or an intracranial tumor is gradual except when there is hemorrhage into a tumor. The onset of coma in malaria may be heralded by a grand mal seizure.

Symptoms and signs that may suggest the cause of confusion and coma in a traveler are given in Table 146.2.

If there are any indications in the history of risk factors for HIV infection or any findings on clinical examination suggesting HIV infection, such as oral candidiasis, generalized lymphadenopathy or shingles, an HIV test should be done. This is important as the causes of coma, and therefore the clinical approach, are quite different in the HIV and non-HIV setting.[8] In an HIV-positive individual, diagnoses such as toxoplasmosis, tuberculosis, cryptococcal and coccidioidal meningitis, as well as HIV dementia, become important. A simple algorithm for distinguishing between some of the important diagnoses in the traveler with confusion or coma is shown in Figure 146.6.

Differential diagnosis by geographic area

In attempting to distinguish the different causes of confusion and coma in the traveler, a clear history of the exact details of travel can be helpful and sometimes diagnostic.

The majority of cases of falciparum malaria are acquired in sub-Saharan Africa and the Indian subcontinent. A few cases are acquired in Papua New Guinea and Vanuatu and occasionally in South East Asia and South America. Knowledge of the rainy season in a particular area and the altitude of the places visited can also assist in the assessment of the risk of malaria.

Typhoid occurs worldwide, but especially in the Indian subcontinent.

The major endemic areas for louse-borne relapsing fever are the highlands of Ethiopia and Burundi. Tick-borne disease has a much wider distribution in both the Old and New Worlds.

Dengue fever is most frequent in travelers who have visited the Caribbean, Central and South America and most of Asia, but is also acquired in west Africa.

Lassa fever is endemic in rural west Africa. Most cases have been acquired by health care workers in the rural areas of Nigeria, Liberia and Sierra Leone.

Ebola virus disease has occurred in central (Zaire, Congo, Uganda, Sudan and Gabon) and west Africa (Ivory Coast).

Japanese B encephalitis is most commonly found in rural areas of Asia, tick-borne encephalitis virus in central Europe and Murray Valley encephalitis virus in Australia. West Nile virus is found across much of Africa, southern Europe and the Middle East. Recent outbreaks of West Nile encephalitis have occurred in several parts of the USA and in Israel.

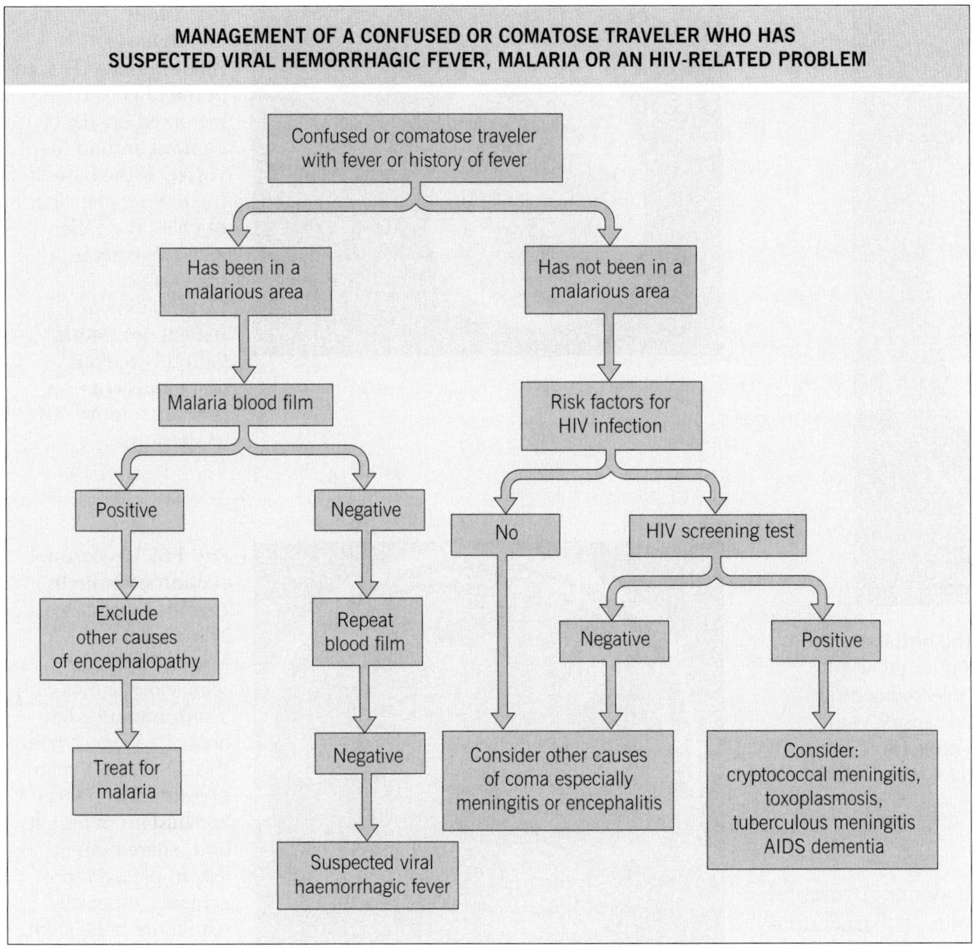

Fig. 146.6 Management of a confused or comatose traveler who has suspected viral hemorrhagic fever, malaria or an HIV-related problem.

Marburg virus disease has occurred in laboratory workers handling the African green monkey from Uganda. Crimean–Congo hemorrhagic fever has occurred in sporadic outbreaks in the areas indicated by its name (e.g. Greece, Turkey and Albania) and in east and west Africa, central Asia and the former USSR. Transmission is by tick bite.

Lyme disease occurs in the north east, mid-west and western USA and many parts of Europe, including Scandanavia.[9]

DIAGNOSIS

All patients who are in a coma require blood tests for glucose (and lactate), electrolytes, urea and creatinine, liver function tests, a full blood count, prothrombin time, a screen for drug abuse if suspected and, in certain cases, arterial blood gas measurement.

Malaria must be excluded for all patients with a fever (or a history of fever) who have visited a malaria-endemic area (see Chapter 166). The cornerstone in the diagnosis of malaria is provided by thick and thin blood films, which may need to be repeated if negative or if there is any doubt. Malaria can be responsible for coma even after the parasites have cleared, especially in the context of renal failure (Fig. 146.7).

In typhoid the most important investigations are blood, bone marrow and stool cultures.

For suspected trypanosomiasis, lymph node aspiration and examination of the blood and CSF for the parasite may be required.

Leptospirosis and Lyme disease are usually clinical diagnoses and are confirmed serologically.

Suspicion of the very many other causes of confusion and coma in a returning traveler will dictate specific further investigations.

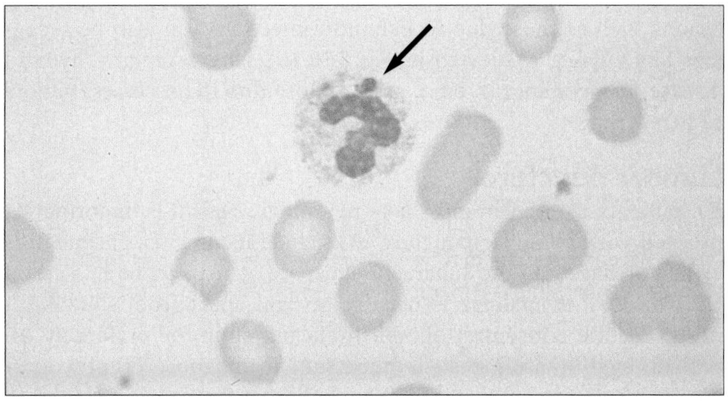

Fig. 146.7 Peripheral blood film of a patient with past malaria. The patient had returned 5 days previously from Malawi, having been treated there for malaria. At this stage no parasites were visible on the film. She was confused and delirious on admission and was found to have a profound acidosis (pH 6.98) and acute renal failure, thought to be due to the malaria. She was hypotensive, which suggested a secondary bacterial infection, and was found to have a *Salmonella* sepsis. Secondary bacterial infections are not uncommon in severe malaria associated with immunosuppression. The only evidence on blood film for malaria was the presence of malarial pigment (hemozoin) in many of the neutrophils, one of which is demonstrated here (arrow).

Computerized tomography

A contrast-enhanced computerized tomography (CT) scan of the brain should be carried out if there is any suspicion of raised intracranial pressure, as suggested by focal neurologic signs, which include abnormal patterns of respiration, loss of oculocephalic (doll's

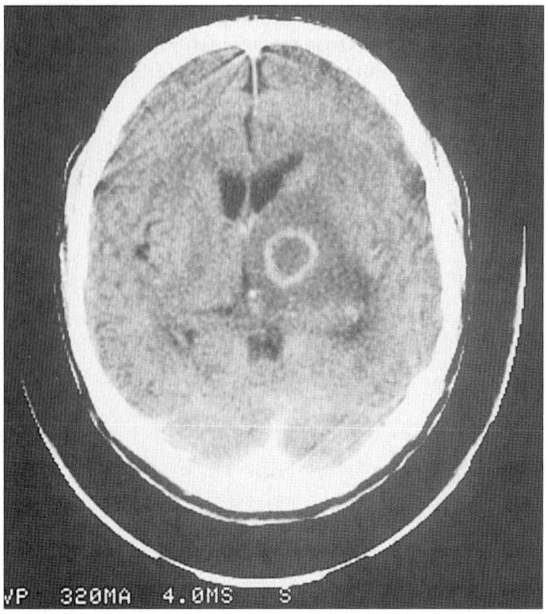

Fig. 146.8 Toxoplasmosis. This patient presented to the hospital confused, with a right-sided stroke. An astute doctor requested an HIV test, which was positive. The CT scan carried out with injected contrast shows a typical ring-enhancing lesion in the left internal capsule with considerable surrounding edema. Further lesions were noted on different sections. The *Toxoplasma* IgG was positive and the patient made a full response to anti-*Toxoplasma* therapy.

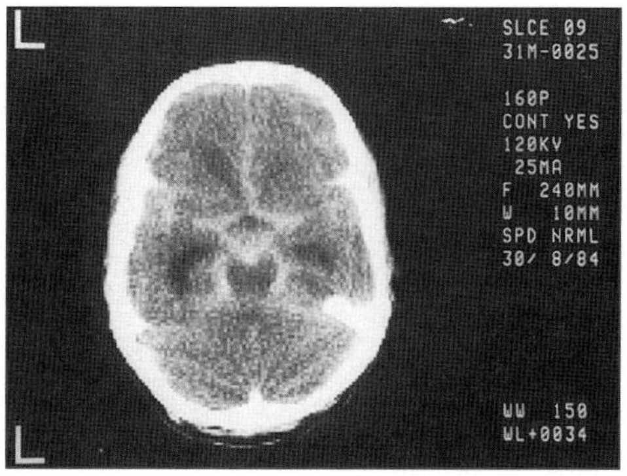

Fig. 146.9 Tuberculous meningitis. A CT scan of the brain showing increased uptake of contrast around the vessels at the base of the brain in the circle of Willis in a patient with tuberculous meningitis. Obtundation in a patient presenting with tuberculous meningitis is an indication for the use of steroids.

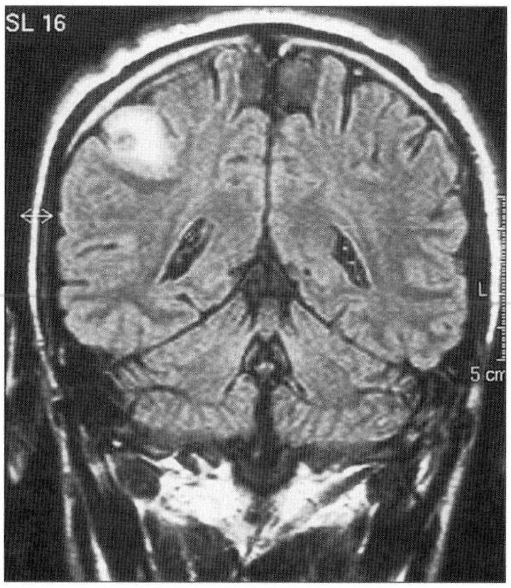

Fig. 146.10 Coronal section of brain in cerebral cysticercosis. This magnetic resonance imaging scan shows a cyst with a surrounding white area of edema. While this 22-year-old man presented with focal convulsions of his left arm, edematous lesions placed more centrally, especially within the brain stem, can lead to both confusion and coma.

eye) or oculovestibular (caloric) reflexes, or papilledema. A cerebral abscess, cerebrovascular event, subdural hematoma, subarachnoid hemorrhage or significant cerebral edema may be diagnosed in this way. If the patient has HIV infec-tion, features suggestive of toxoplasmosis (Fig. 146.8), a tuberculous lesion (Fig. 146.9), cryptococcal meningitis or cerebral atrophy may be detected. Space-occupying lesions such as those due to helminth infections can also be recognized by CT (e.g. cysticercosis (Fig. 146.10), schistosomiasis, hydatid disease, paragonimiasis, etc.), as can those due to abscesses, tumors or hemorrhage.

Lumbar puncture

For patients with fever and stable neurologic signs it is important to proceed with a lumbar puncture to exclude meningitis, encephalitis or hemorrhage into the subarachnoid space, which can be missed on CT. The CSF in malaria is usually normal apart from showing a raised lactate concentration. An India ink stain, or preferably an antigen agglutination test, is necessary to diagnose cryptococcal meningitis. In trypanosomiasis examination of the CSF is essential to determine whether there is central nervous system involvement with the presence of trypanosomes, leukocytes above 4/μl and/or protein above 0.4g/l. The CSF must also be examined to determine the extent of neurologic involvement in syphilis.

Magnetic resonance imaging

This is of particular value for a suspected demyelinating illness such as a viral encephalitis, for which the sensitivity of CT is limited, and in situations of brain stem or cerebellar involvement.

MANAGEMENT

Coma is a life-threatening condition until vital functions are stabilized and the underlying cause is identified and corrected. The first priority for a comatose patient is to preserve vital functions. Resuscitation may be necessary, paying special attention to airway protection, support of respiration and circulation, and the urgent treatment of hypoglycemia after blood has been taken for various biochemical, hematologic, microbiologic and toxicologic tests. Other metabolic causes of coma other than hypoglycemia, such as acidosis, electrolyte abnormalities and drug intoxication, may need urgent attention. Once the patient is stable the next priority is to establish a diagnosis, which is critical if specific therapy is to be instituted.

All patients who have confusion or are comatose should be managed using the highest level of care appropriate for the particular health care setting. Unconscious patients may need to be moved to the intensive therapy unit. The risk of infection to others needs to be reviewed initially for all travelers, especially if there is any suspicion that the patient has a viral hemorrhagic fever or if he or she is to be moved to a ward area rather than to an isolation unit (see Chapter 186a). Until a diagnosis is made, drugs should be used sparingly. Haloperidol (5–30mg) or chlorpromazine (25–50mg) given intramuscularly may be used for restless or confused patients at risk of injuring themselves or attending staff and to allow diagnostic procedures such as imaging (CT or magnetic resonance imaging) or lumbar puncture. Haloperidol has fewer sedative and hypotensive effects and can be administered by different routes. Travelers with confusion will be in unfamiliar surroundings and are disoriented with regard to time, place and person. It is important that, during recovery, simple but firm communication as to the location and date, a visible clock and the presence of a relative are considered in the overall management of such patients.

REFERENCES

1. Plum F, Posner J. Diagnosis of stupor and coma, 3rd ed. Philadelphia: Davis; 1980.
2. Shakir RA, Newman PK, Poser CM, eds. Tropical neurology. London: WB Saunders; 1996.
3. Peters W, Pasvol G, eds. Tropical medicine and parasitology. London: Mosby; 2002
4. Bates D. The management of medical coma. J Neurol Neurosurg Psychiatry 1993;56:589–98.
5. Teasdale G, Jennett B. Assessment of coma and impaired consciousness. A practical scale. Lancet 1974;2:81–4.
6. Pasvol G, Clough B, Carlsson J, Snounou G. The pathogenesis of severe falciparum malaria. In: Pasvol G, ed. Malaria. Baillière's Clinical Infectious Diseases. London: Baillière Tindall; 1995:249–70.
7. Advisory Committee on Dangerous Pathogens. Management and control of viral haemorrhagic fevers. London: The Stationery Office; 1996.
8. Price R. Neurological complications of HIV infection. Lancet 1996;348:445–52.
9. Pfister H-W, Wilske B, Weber K. Lyme borreliosis: basic science and clinical aspects. Lancet 1994;343:1013–9.

chapter 147

Skin Rashes and Ulcers

Roderick J Hay

INTRODUCTION

In most developing and tropical countries skin disease is the second or third most common reason for presentation in primary health care. The majority of the diseases that are seen are infective and easily treatable. It is therefore not surprising that people who have visited tropical areas should return with skin disease and are often alarmed that this may have been acquired during their stay overseas. It is important to consider the possible predisposing factors that may have affected the acquisition of skin disease.

PREDISPOSING FACTORS THAT POINT TO A DIAGNOSIS

Diseases endemic to specific geographic areas

As with other diseases, some skin conditions are confined to specific endemic areas. Most of these are infectious diseases and geographic localization depends on climate or the presence of an appropriate vector or host. Examples include onchocerciasis and cutaneous leishmaniasis, in which climatic factors and the appropriate vectors are both specific to certain regions. Endemic dermatoses are not necessarily restricted to the tropics – other infections show similar geographic restrictions. For example, erythema chronicum migrans, an annular erythema caused by primary infection with *Borrelia burgdorferi*, may be acquired during a visit to an area in the USA, Scandinavia or Central Europe, where Lyme disease is endemic.[1]

Activities that predispose to skin disease

Certain activities expose travelers to unusual environments that may affect the development of skin disease. These vary from overland trekking through desert or rainforest to sunbathing on the beach. The beach, in particular, is a potential source of skin diseases, including those due to sun exposure (e.g. discoid lupus erythematosus, polymorphic light eruption) as well as the acquisition of larva migrans from sitting in contaminated sand. Trekking exposes the traveler to other noninfectious hazards, such as contact with plants that may cause allergic or irritant contact dermatitis. Under this heading, reactions to drugs, such as antimalarials, that have been taken during the trip should also be considered.

Climate

Climatic conditions also affect the development of skin disease. Factors identified as important include increased ambient temperature or high levels of atmospheric humidity, both of which have an effect on bacterial growth on the epidermis. Infections due to *Staphylococcus aureus* are much more common in hot and humid climates than in colder climates. Some other infections, such as pityriasis versicolor, are also more frequent in hot and humid environments.

Table 147.1 shows a list of additional questions that are important in taking a history from a patient returning from a trip overseas.

MAKING A DIAGNOSIS

It is important to differentiate between:

- skin diseases in travelers that were already present before the patient left home and skin diseases to which the patient is susceptible and that may have been exacerbated during travel;
- skin diseases that have been caused by exposure to a different climate or environment; and
- newly acquired skin diseases that are normally confined to the area visited.

Skin disease seen in travelers can therefore be considered under the following three main headings.

Conditions made worse by travel

Almost any pre-existing skin condition can be affected by travel, although certain conditions are more likely to present for treatment on return. These include acne vulgaris, which is often considerably worsened in a tropical environment with rapid spread of new pustular lesions. Pre-existing photosensitivity (which includes polymorphic light eruption, discoid lupus erythematosus and solar urticaria) is also exacerbated by sun exposure. Atopic eczema behaves differently in different environmental conditions. For instance, it may be improved by exposure to mild sunlight and sea-bathing, but it is usually made worse by very hot and humid conditions. It is also exacerbated by travel to very cold areas, because this increases skin dryness.

Some forms of dermatophytosis are also more common in the tropics and patients who have pre-existing tinea pedis, for instance, often have an exacerbation when visiting a hot climate; the infection may spread beyond the initial site to affect other areas such as the groin or trunk.

Conditions acquired by exposure to different environmental conditions

Although it is always possible for patients to acquire new skin diseases under different environmental conditions (e.g. light-exacerbated psoriasis), the common presentations are very specific to travel.

Pityriasis versicolor is a common superficial fungal infection that is caused by *Malassezia* yeasts, which are normal commensals on the skin surface.[2] They become pathogenic under certain conditions, one of which is climatic change and sun exposure. The condition presents with widespread scaly hypopigmented or hyperpigmented macules, which tend to become confluent on the trunk and neck (Fig. 147.1). It is not itchy and discoloration is the usual reason for seeking medical help, often a few weeks after return from overseas. Although the definitive diagnosis is best made by microscopic examination of skin scrapings, a simple measure is to demonstrate the presence of fine scales by scratching the lesions. The treatment is ketoconazole shampoo, topical azole antifungal creams (e.g. clotrimazole, miconazole) or oral ketoconazole (200mg daily for 3–5 days) or itraconazole (200mg daily for 5 days). There is no reliable way of preventing this infection, although some habitual sufferers treat themselves

ADDITIONAL USEFUL QUESTIONS IN TAKING A HISTORY FROM TRAVELERS WITH SKIN LESIONS
What countries have you visited during your vacation or trip? Try to find out where they have been within these countries and any potential exposures (e.g. camping by a fast-flowing river in an area endemic for onchocerciasis). Also, it is important to find out whether they were traveling rough or using luxury hotels – there is sometimes a difference in disease exposure.
Before you went overseas did you have any skin problems? Find out about potential reactions to sunlight and atopic disease, acne, etc.
What sort of things did you do on your trip – bathing in the sea or lake, trekking, sunbathing on a beach?
Were you taking any medications during your stay overseas?

Table 147.1 Additional useful questions in taking a history from travelers with skin lesions.

Fig. 147.1 Pityriasis versicolor. The rash shows confluent scaly macules.

during their vacations with a single application of selenium sulfide or ketoconazole shampoo.

A related condition, often misdiagnosed as acne, is *Malassezia* folliculitis, which characteristically presents with small itchy pustules on the shoulders and upper chest after sun exposure.[3] The distribution and the itching, as well as the absence of comedones, distinguish this condition from acne. It too responds best to oral itraconazole or ketoconazole.

Infections acquired specifically overseas

Although the common infections seen in tropical communities are scabies, bacterial pyoderma, pediculosis and fungal infections (Table 147.2), they are not as common in travelers as in local people. They are usually acquired as a result of close contact (rather than casual contact) with infected people and they are particularly associated with overcrowding in houses. Likewise, tropical ulcer (see below), which is very common in certain areas of the tropics, is seldom seen in visitors unless they stay for long periods and share the living conditions of the local inhabitants.

Specific examples of conditions acquired overseas are discussed below.

INSECT BITE REACTIONS

Most people become tolerant of the biting insect fauna of their local area; for example, reactions to mosquito bites decline with increasing age owing to sensitization to mosquito salivary antigens.[4] (There

SKIN SYMPTOMS AND SIGNS IN TRAVELERS AND POTENTIAL INFECTIVE CAUSES	
Generalized itching Scabies Schistosomiasis	**Urticaria** Strongyloidiasis Schistosomiasis
Localized itching Onchocerciasis **Abscesses** *Staphylococcus aureus* infection Melioidosis	**Ulcers** Insect bites Leishmaniasis Streptococcal ecthyma *Corynebacterium diphtheria* Tungiasis Tick-bite fever African trypanosomiasis
Nodules Reations to insect bites Larva migrans Dirofilariasis Onchocerciasis Tungiasis Leishmaniasis	**Scaly rashes** Dermatophytosis (e.g. tinea imbricata) **Annular erythema** Borreliosis

Table 147.2 Skin symptoms and signs in travelers and potential infective causes.

are exceptions to this in people in whom severe hypersensitivity persists.) However, exposure to a new set of antigens from mosquitoes has been associated with an increased level of sensitivity and it is therefore not surprising that insect bites are a very common cause of complaint in travelers. The range of clinical manifestations of bite reactions includes small papules, blisters, dermal nodules and small ulcers. In particular, it is not uncommon for these to become secondarily infected by *Streptococcus* spp. or *Staphylococcus aureus*, which make lesions become more indurated and weepy.

Clues to the diagnosis of prolonged bite reactions are the presence of multiple itchy lesions, in some cases clustering on exposed sites, and a history of evolution over a few days. It is important, though, to exclude secondary infection and treat with appropriate antibiotics. In some cases, cutaneous leishmaniasis may present with indurated itchy papules and nodules that may mimic bites where, of course, they originated. If in doubt, a skin biopsy is often helpful, because a dense polymorphic cellular infiltrate in the debris with large numbers of eosinophils is highly suggestive of a bite reaction.

Other common bite or sting reactions that may be found in travelers, apart from scorpion sting and snake bite, which require more immediate attention, include jellyfish stings and sea urchin granulomas.

Jellyfish stings[5] usually present with a linear rash on an exposed area. The rash typically consists of multiple papules or small bullae. However, patients usually know what has caused this reaction because the symptoms are virtually instantaneous. Application of cool packs or vinegar may provide immediate relief. In severe cases, such as those due to the Portuguese man-of-war jellyfish, stings may be accompanied by systemic symptoms such as fever, diarrhea and cardiovascular shock.

The spines of sea urchins cause localized clusters of small dermal granulomas. The presence of spines can, if necessary, be confirmed by radiograph. However, in addition, sarcoid-like granulomas that do not contain spines may form in the area of the puncture wound; these persist for months. Recent studies suggest that a small proportion of such wounds may be infected with *Mycobacterium marinum*.[6] Once again, patients know the cause of a sea urchin injury but may delay consultation until their return from overseas. The main treatment is removal of spines if these are still present.

This may be difficult if much time has elapsed after the injury, and broad-spectrum antibiotic cover is also advisable.

Tunga penetrans (the jigger flea) may cause a localized tender nodule on the feet and toes. It may ulcerate and is usually itchy. It is usually covered with a small crust or pustule but where this is carefully removed the presence of a dark posterior segment can be seen. Treatment is by covering the lesion with Vaseline and once the larva appears it can be removed by forceps; alternatively excision after exploration is usually curative. Myasis or infestation with fly larva can also occur and although this affects other sites, the presentation, a tender nodule or ulcer, is similar.

BACTERIAL INFECTIONS

These are not common in travelers except when they are secondary to some pre-existing skin lesions such as insect bites or varicella.[7] Cutaneous diphtheria is still possible in patients who have been traveling rough in some areas such as the Saharan region, and it should be considered in those presenting with ulcers that are covered with a grayish slough. Tropical ulcer, a synergistic bacterial infection, is rare in travelers.[8] One condition that is seen regularly in those working or vacationing in some parts of the Mediterranean region or Africa is the initial ulcer of tick bite or boutonneuse fever. This is caused by *Rickettsia conori*, which is endemic in eastern Africa and some Mediterranean countries.[9] The presence of a necrotic localized ulcer, and often a fine macular rash, in a patient who has an undiagnosed fever is highly suggestive; patients can sometimes describe the tick that caused the reaction. The treatment is with doxycycline (200mg daily for 7 days).

FUNGAL INFECTIONS

Most of the unusual endemic fungus infections are exceptionally rare in travelers, although existing infections may be exacerbated.[10] However, two fungal infections that may occur are *Scytalidium* infections and tinea imbricata.

Scytalidium dimidiatum, a plant pathogen, and *S. hyalinum* are both found in a wide range of tropical environments and both cause superficial infections that mimic those caused by the dermatophyte *Trichophyton rubrum*. Although they are not common in travelers, they occasionally cause nail infections which in Caucasians may present with patchy melanonychia (black discoloration of the nail-plate; Fig. 147.2).[11] Treatment is difficult, because neither of these infections responds to conventional antifungal agents.

Trichophyton concentricum is a dermatophyte that causes the infection tinea imbricata in remote areas of the Western Pacific and in Central and South America. It may occur in travelers, particularly if they have been traveling rough. It presents with very typical lesions with concentric rings of scales.[12] It responds best to oral terbinafine (250mg daily) or itraconazole (200mg daily).

PARASITIC INFECTIONS

The common diseases of the developing world, such as scabies and pediculosis, are also seen in travelers. A variety of parasitic diseases are seen in those spending short periods in the tropics.

Cutaneous leishmaniasis

This is discussed in detail elsewhere (see Chapter 172). Leishmaniasis can affect travelers who have visited a wide range of countries in the Middle East, Africa and Central and South America. It is also seen in certain areas of Europe around the Mediterranean such as northern Greece, Turkey, Spain and the Balearic Islands, although it is not common in these areas.[13,14]

Patients present with either single or multiple lesions. These range in morphology from indurated nodules to ulcers. Occasionally they form a chain of nodules along a lymphatic vessel, as in sporotrichosis (see Chapter 13). The typical history is that they appear like an insect bite that persists after return home. It is important to take a biopsy of such lesions.

Onchocerciasis

Onchocerciasis (see Chapters 170 and 174) may appear in those traveling to endemic areas of Africa, Central and South America and the Yemen.[15] The usual skin presentation of onchocerciasis in the traveler is acute papular onchodermatitis[16] with localized areas of small itchy papules that are often confined unilaterally to a limb or the waist or shoulder region. There is also a form of dermal edema that resembles *peau d'orange* (Fig. 147.3). The diagnosis is made by demonstrating microfilariae in skin snips. The skin changes in travelers are often very subtle and the presence of localized itching and a history of travel, often involving camping by a river, are helpful clues.

Cutaneous larva migrans

Cutaneous larva migrans (creeping eruption; see Chapter 174) is not uncommon in travelers, particularly those who have visited tropical beaches, and is caused by skin infection with animal hookworm larvae such as *Ancyclostoma brasiliense, A. caninum* and *Uncinaria stenocephala*. Often, patients have returned from a vacation during which they have sat on the beach. Lesions present with an itchy

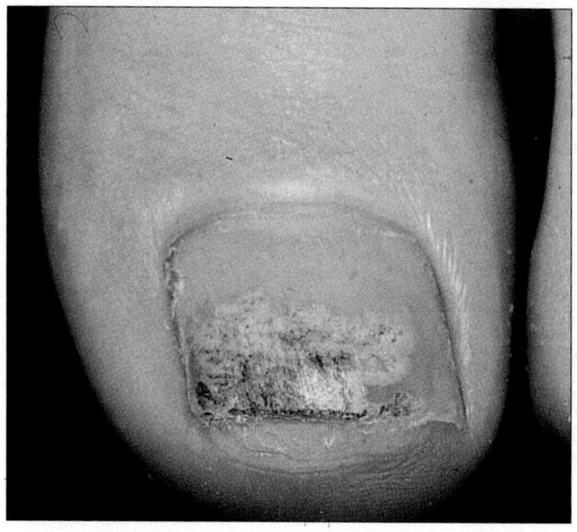

Fig.147.2 Onychomycosis caused by *Scytalidium dimidiatum* in a traveler.

Fig.147.3 Acute papular onchodermatitis. There is a combination of dermal edema and a papular rash.

cluster of lesions on an exposed site such as the legs or buttocks. The morphology of the lesions varies. In some cases there is a typical sinuous track, but in other cases the lesions are nodular but grouped in a specific area. In cases where the lesion is clearly worm-like, diagnosis is easy; otherwise it may be necessary to biopsy lesions. Treatment with albendazole (400mg daily for 3 days) is usually curative.[17]

Other parasites

Other tropical parasites very occasionally cause imported infections in travelers.

Cercarial dermatitis

Cercarial dermatitis[18] presents as an itchy rash that often occurs after swimming. Patients describe intense itching after exposure to water, sometimes accompanied by papules or small weals. Although it is usually a harmless symptom caused by contact with avian cercaria in areas that are endemic for schistosomiasis, it can be an early symptom of exposure to pathogenic schistosomes.

Katayama fever

In patients returning from areas that are endemic for schistosomiasis, the development of urticaria, joint pains and fever should be regarded with suspicion, because it is an early sign of sensitization in the early stages of schistosomiasis.[19] These symptoms usually occur several weeks after exposure.

Dirofilariasis

This occurs in several regions – Africa, the Far East, South America and the southern USA. The cutaneous infection is due to *Dirofilaria* species such as *D. tenuis* or *D. ursi*. Patients present with a localized itchy papule or nodule, which is often near the eye, elsewhere on the face or on the chest.[20] The diagnosis is made by biopsy.

Other important parasitic infections such as dracunculiasis, loiasis and lymphatic filariasis are uncommon in travelers, but have all been reported occasionally.

DRUG REACTIONS

Many patients take medications during trips overseas, including antimalarial agents, antidiarrheal agents and antihistamines. All may produce skin lesions; some drugs (e.g. tetracyclines) may cause photodermatitis. It is important to take an adequate drug history in those returning from overseas. The most common cause of drug rashes in this group are the antimalarial agents:

- chloroquine can cause a range of different rashes, but the main reactions are lichenoid (lichen planus-like) reactions and pruritus;
- mepacrine causes a diffuse yellowish pigmentation of the skin;
- mefloquine can cause pruritus and urticaria;
- pyrimethamine combined with sulfodoxine can cause urticaria, erythema multiforme and toxic epidermal necrolysis – it is thought that the skin reactions are largely due to the sulfonamide component; and
- quinine can cause erythema and flushing and pruritus.

It is important to obtain a drug history to ensure that all medications, including antimalarial agents, that were taken during the trip are considered in making the diagnosis of any skin rash.

ULCERS

Ulceration of the skin is a common and important physical sign. Diagnosis of ulcers depends on the underlying clinical situation, the evolution of the condition, the area affected and the appearance. Many of the conditions discussed above may develop into small ulcers. These include leishmaniasis, insect bites and boutonneuse fever. However, there are others that are important not to miss.

Tropical ulcer

Tropical ulcer is a common condition in remote parts of the tropics mainly seen in children and teenagers and affecting the lower limbs.[8] The lesion usually starts with mild discomfort and overlying hyperpigmentation on the skin that progresses over a few days until the skin breaks down and sloughs revealing an underlying ulcer. The ulcer, therefore, is often described as occurring rapidly.

Tropical ulcer is mainly seen in Africa, India, the West Pacific and part of Indonesia and the Philippines. The disease is due to a combined infection by a number of different bacteria together with a fusiform bacterium, *Fusobacterium ulcerans*, and an as yet unidentified spirochete. The disease is associated with poor living conditions and exposure to stagnant water and mud. *Fusobacterium ulcerans* has been isolated from mud in endemic areas.

The lesion is often clean on first presentation, round, with smooth edges (Fig. 147.4a). It generally starts on the lower leg or ankle and in about 10% of cases it progresses to become an irregular, enlarged and chronic ulcer (Fig. 147.4b). The condition heals well in most patients with simple cleansing and treatment with penicillin. However, early grafting may be necessary where healing is delayed.

The differential diagnosis of tropical ulcer includes yaws, diphtheritic ulcer and leishmaniasis.

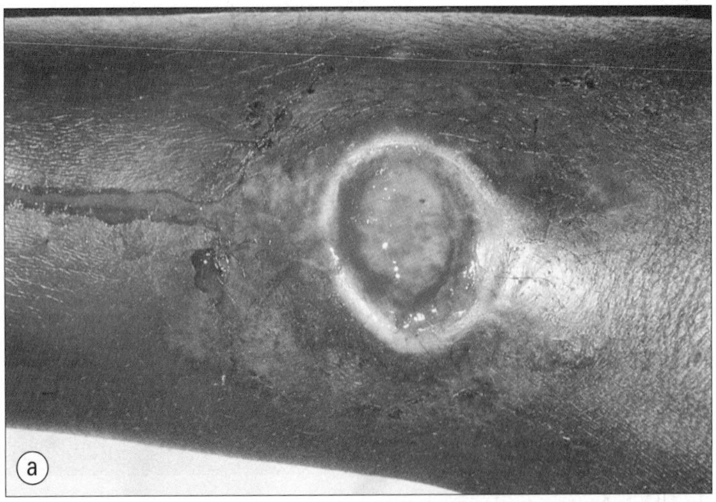

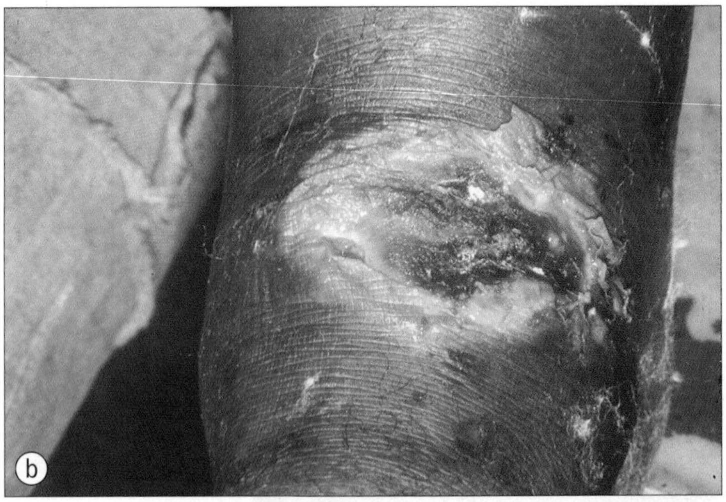

Fig.147.4 Tropical ulcer. (a) Acute. (b) Chronic.

- The primary lesion of yaws is usually more exophytic and appears to stand out from the skin. It may then ulcerate before the development of secondary lesions. Although it was once controlled, yaws has resurfaced in some of the previous endemic areas of West Africa and the West Pacific, areas where tropical ulcer may also occur.
- Diphtheritic ulcer is uncommon but the lesion is more irregular and the base is covered with a gray to yellow slough. It is more often seen in desert or semidesert areas.
- Leishmaniasis can be distinguished by its slower speed of onset with a skin nodule often with surrounding plaque breaking down to produce ulceration. Inflammation around the ulcer is more intense.

Overall tropical ulcer is unlikely to occur in the traveler unless the area visited is remote and the patient has lived under local conditions.

Buruli ulcer

This condition is not often seen in travelers although it is sometimes considered.[21] Once again, it occurs in the remote parts of Africa, particularly Central and West Africa, and the West Pacific. Cases have been reported from Australia. It is caused by *Mycobacterium ulcerans* and usually affects children and young adults. Like tropical ulcer, there is an association with exposure to water. The ulceration starts as a small raised nodule that breaks down to develop into an extensive undermined and irregular ulcer that may extend for 10 cm or more. Treatment is largely surgical. The undermining is characteristic.

Other ulcers seen in travellers

Mycobacterium marinum causes ulceration of the skin preceded by the development of a nodule. In many cases it causes a characteristic form of spread involving local lymphatics (sporotrichoid or lymphangitic). The primary ulcer is followed by secondary nodules that may break down and discharge. While typically this is an infection seen in those handling tropical fish at home, it can be acquired naturally by swimming in shallow coastal waters. *Mycobacterium marinum* is a natural pathogen of fish.

Streptococcal ecthyma is also seen frequently in the tropics. This is a more severe form of impetigo where the whole epidermis and part of the dermis is involved in necrosis to give 1–2cm punched-out ulcers. It is often a secondary infection (e.g. on an insect bite or following chickenpox). It responds slowly to penicillin. It may be seen in returned travelers at the site of scratches or bites.

There is no reason why travelers cannot develop the same types of ulceration abroad as at home and the differential diagnosis should include:

- stasis, arterial or diabetic ulcers;
- ulcers due to vasculitis such as polyarteritis nodosa; and
- hemoglobinopathy-associated ulcers (e.g. sickle cell disease).

Taking a thorough history of the time course of onset of ulceration and any relevant background information is very important. Where necessary, it may also be useful to biopsy the edge of ulcers as this may provide further diagnostic information. Histology from the central area is only rarely useful.

CONCLUSION

Skin disease is common and patients not infrequently present with lesions that appear to have been acquired during the course of foreign travel. In making the diagnosis, it is important to remember that the majority of such cases are due to skin conditions that are just as likely to occur at home as overseas. However, in some patients, the condition is a genuine imported infection that has followed exposure during the course of travel.

REFERENCES

1. Berger BW. Dermatologic manifestations of Lyme disease. Rev Infect Dis 1989;11(Suppl.6):S1475–81.
2. Faergemann J. Lipophilic yeasts in skin disease. Semin Dermatol 1985;4:173–84.
3. Back O, Faergemann J, Hornquist R. Pityrosporum folliculitis: a common disease of the young and middle aged. J Am Acad Dermatol 1985;12:56–61.
4. Penneys NS, Nayar JK, Bernstein H, *et al.* Mosquito salivary gland antigens identified by circulating human antibodies. Arch Dermatol 1989;125:219–22.
5. Auerbach PS. Marine envenomations. N Engl J Med 1990;325:486–9.
6. De la Torre C, Vega A, Carracedo A, Toribio J. Identification of *Mycobacterium marinum* in sea-urchin granulomas. Br J Dermatol 2001;145:114–6.
7. Wortman P. Bacterial infections of the skin. Curr Probl Dermatol 1993;5:196–204.
8. Robinson DC, Adriaans B, Hay RJ, *et al.* The epidemiology and clinical features of tropical ulcer. Int J Dermatol 1988;27:49–53.
9. Marschang A, Nothdurft HD, Kumlien S, *et al.* Imported rickettsioses in German travelers. Infection 1995;23:94–7.
10. Allen AM, King RD. Occlusion, carbon dioxide and fungal skin infections. Lancet 1978;i:360–2.
11. Jones SK, White JE, Jacobs PH, *et al. Hendersonula toruloidea* infection of the nails in Caucasians. Clin Exp Dermatol 1985;10:444–7.
12. Logan R, Kobza-Black A. Tinea imbricata in a British nurse. Clin Exp Dermatol 1988;13:232–3.
13. Desjeux P. The increase in risk factors for leishmaniasis worldwide. Trans Roy Soc Trop Med Hyg 2001;95:239–43.
14. Hepburn NC, Tidman MJ, Hunter JA. Cutaneous leishmaniasis in British troops from Belize. Br J Dermatol 1993;128:63–8.
15. Elgart ML. Onchocerciasis and dracunculosis. Dermatol Clin 1989;7:323–30.
16. Murdoch M, Hay RJ, Mackenzie CD, *et al.* A new clinical classification for the skin lesions of onchocerciasis. Br J Dermatol 1993;129:260–9.
17. Orihuela AR, Torres JR. Single dose of albendazole in the treatment of cutaneous larva migrans. Arch Dermatol 1990;126:398–9.
18. Baird JK, Wear DJ. Cercarial dermatitis. The swimmers' itch. Clin Dermatol 1987;5:88–91.
19. Cheever AW. Schistosomiasis. Infection versus disease and hypersensitivity. Am J Pathol 1993;142:699–702.
20. Harzeberg AJ, Boyd PR, Gutierrez Y. Subcutaneous dirofilariasis in Collier Country, Florida, USA. Am J Surg Pathol 1995;19:934–9.
21. Semret M, Koromihis G, MacLean JD, Libman M, Ward BJ. *Mycobacterium ulcerans* infection (Buruli ulcer): first reported case in a traveller. Am J Trop Med Hyg 1999;61:689–93.

chapter

148 Sexually Transmitted Diseases

Mark W Tyndall

INTRODUCTION

The incidence of sexually transmitted diseases (STDs) in the returned traveler is not known as reporting systems are sporadic, diagnosis is difficult and self-treatment is common. The risk of STD is directly related to the frequency of sexual contact, choice of sexual partner and type of exposure. Despite considerable risk, surveys conducted among travelers show that up to 25% have new sexual partners, contact with commercial sex workers is common, condom use is inconsistent and perceived risk of infection is underestimated.[1–6]

Increased international travel through tourism, business and migration has dramatically changed the patterns of STD transmission.[7–10] Many of the most popular travel destinations in Africa, Asia and the Caribbean are regions with high STD prevalence, high rates of prostitution and little capacity to implement effective STD control. The AIDS epidemic tragically illustrates how the spread of sexually transmitted pathogens transcends international borders and frustrates control efforts.[11–14]

PREVENTION

Prevention of STDs among travelers is of the highest priority and should be discussed prior to departure. Contracting an STD pathogen while traveling may have serious short-term and long-term implications. Counseling should include the promotion of responsible sexual behavior, including abstinence, condom use and avoiding commercial sex. Prevention efforts to date have been inadequate as shown in surveys of both departing and returning travelers.[3–5]

CLINICAL FEATURES

Sexually transmitted disease pathogens can broadly be divided into those that cause nonulcerative lesions and those that cause ulcerative lesions. For clinical management, the nonulcerative pathogens can be further divided into anatomic sites. The most common presentation for men is urethritis, followed by epididymitis, prostatitis and proctitis. Infection involving the lower genital tract is the most common presentation in women and includes cystitis, vulvitis, vaginitis, urethritis and cervicitis. HIV infection, multiple concurrent STDs or other infectious complications, however, may alter this simplified clinical approach.

Urethritis in men

The etiology of urethritis in men has traditionally been divided into gonococcal and nongonococcal infections. This classification was developed due to the characteristic presentation of *Neisseria gonorrhoeae*, which is generally symptomatic and involves profuse, purulent, urethral discharge, occurring 2–5 days following sexual contact. The less severe clinical presentation of mucoid discharge and/or dysuria has been associated with nongonococcal infections, which include *Chlamydia trachomatis, Ureaplasma urealyticum, Mycoplasma genitalium* and *Trichomonas vaginalis*. These infections have longer incubation periods of 1–6 weeks. Nongonococcal urethritis is more often asymptomatic (10–30%) and may therefore go undiagnosed. Where available, etiologic diagnostic testing should be performed due to the poor sensitivity and specificity of a clinical diagnosis.

Mucopurulent cervicitis

Most serious infections of the lower genital tract in women involve *N. gonorrhoeae* and *C. trachomatis*, either of which may result in ascending infections with severe consequences. These organisms are clinically indistinguishable and cause urethritis and/or cervicitis. Vaginal discharge and dysuria are the most common clinical presentations, but are extremely variable and the conditions are easily confused with vaginitis. Asymptomatic infections are common (>50%) and may only be detected when complications occur. Herpes simplex virus is also associated with inflammation of the urethra and cervix, but does not result in ascending infections.

Other causes of vaginal discharge

The major causes of vaginitis are *Trichomonas vaginalis*, *Candida albicans* and bacterial vaginosis. These are difficult to distinguish clinically and may occur together. Vulvitis and cystitis also present with lower genitourinary tract symptoms and must be distinguished from vaginal infections.

- Trichomoniasis typically presents with profuse, yellow-green, frothy vaginal discharge with erythema of the vaginal wall.
- Candidiasis presents with pruritus and white curd-like discharge. It is extremely common in women during child-bearing years and the role of sexual transmission remains controversial.
- Bacterial vaginosis presents with malodorous white vaginal discharge and is characterized by a change in normal vaginal flora. This process is likely multifactorial and, despite being a common diagnosis at STD clinics, it is not considered to be sexually transmitted.
- Vulvitis may be due to *C. albicans*, herpes simplex virus (HSV) or human papillomavirus (HPV). Pruritus, burning discomfort, edema and erythema are the common manifestations. In cases of HSV and HPV infection, characteristic lesions may be seen on close examination.
- Cystitis, which may be related to sexual activity, can usually be excluded from sexually transmitted infections by history and urine culture.

Other nonulcerative sexually transmitted diseases

Other nonulcerative STDs that may be seen in the returned traveler include:

- genital warts, caused by HPV types 6 and 11, which affect genital and anal regions and can range from asymptomatic lesions to large confluent masses;
- molluscum contagiosum, which is a benign, self-limited, papular condition affecting the skin and mucous membranes, with lesions characterized by central umbilication;

- pubic lice, caused by *Phthirus pubis*, which present with itching and inflammation in the pubic area. The lice can usually be seen by the naked eye and infestation is usually self-limited; and
- scabies, caused by *Sarcoptes scabiei*, is commonly sexually transmitted and may lead to severe inflammation and excoriation in the genital region, mimicking other infections.

Genital ulceration

Genital ulcer disease (GUD) is most commonly caused by HSV, syphilis or chancroid (Fig. 148.1), although in some regions donovanosis and lymphogranuloma venereum should be considered. Occasionally scabies, trichomoniasis and nonsyphilis spirochetes may present as genital ulcers. The differential diagnosis also includes noninfectious causes such as a fixed drug eruption, Behçet's syndrome, Reiter's syndrome, trauma and malignancy. Table 148.1 describes the classic clinical presentation of the major infectious etiologies but, as with other STDs, there is considerable variation in presentation and mixed infections are common.[15,16]

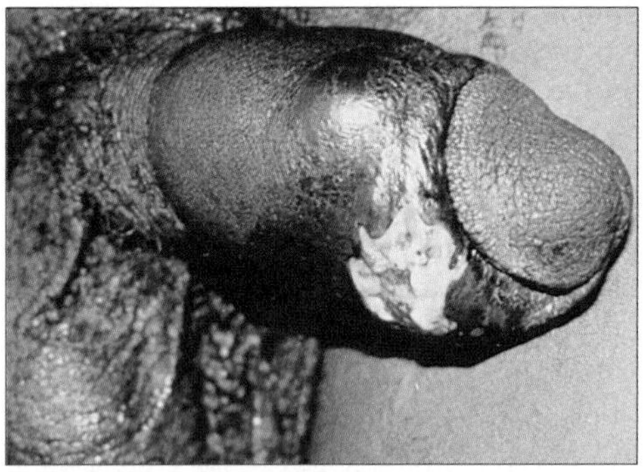

Fig. 148.1 Chancroid. Characteristic purulent lesion with ragged borders, friable base and surrounding inflammation.

CLINICAL FEATURES OF GUD

Infection (pathogen)	Incubation period	Clinical features and natural history
Syphilis (*Treponema pallidum*)	Primary (14±28 days)	Single, rounded, well-defined borders, nontender, indurated base; may occur in extragenital sites; resolves spontaneously in 3±6 weeks
	Secondary (1±12 weeks following primary lesion)	Systemic features; papular rash classically affecting palms and soles; condylomata lata in moist areas
	Tertiary (uncommon) (years)	Neurosyphilis; cardiovascular syphilis; late benign syphilis
Chancroid (*Haemophilus ducreyi*)	4±10 days	Single or multiple, deep, painful, ragged borders; inguinal swelling (bubo) occurs in 30% and may suppurate; progressive and destructive
Herpes (HSV-2)	2±7 days	Multiple vesicular ulcers, which break down; superficial and painful; resolve spontaneously in 1±3 weeks, but may recur
Granuloma inguinale or donovanosis (*Calymmatobacterium granulomatis*)	1±10 weeks	Single or multiple elevated, painless, beefy red; progressive verrucous lesions; systemic illness
Lymphogranuloma venereum (*Chlamydia trachomatis* serovars L1, L2, L3)	Primary disease (3±12 days)	Penile and urethral which resolves spontaneously in days; urethritis
	Secondary disease (10±30 days)	Lymph node disease; persistent and destructive; inguinal swelling (groove sign); proctitis, lymphangitis; sinus formation; systemic illness

Table 148.1 Clinical features of genital ulcer disease.

SEXUALLY TRANSMITTED DISEASES WITH THE GREATEST GLOBAL SIGNIFICANCE

The persistent viral STDs, which include HIV-1, HIV-2, human T-lymphocyte leukemia/lymphoma virus-1 (HTLV-1), cytomegalovirus, HSV, HPV and hepatitis B and hepatitis C viruses, represent the most serious long-term health risks for the sexually active traveler. Ironically, most of these infections do not present with genital symptoms. Table 148.2 shows the estimated sexual transmission efficiency and clinical manifestations of these viral agents. There is convincing evidence that the transmission of these viral pathogens is facilitated by other genital infections, both ulcerative and nonulcerative.[17–19]

Historically, the complications of STDs have primarily affected women, manifesting with severe local disease, pelvic inflammatory disease, infertility and complications in pregnancy. Although this remains true, the persistent viral infections pose serious long-term risks for both men and women:

- HIV infection continues as a global pandemic with heterosexual transmission being the predominant route of infection;
- HPV is widespread and has resulted in high rates of cervical cancer, especially among women in developing countries;

PERSISTENT VIRAL STDs: TRANSMISSION EFFICIENCY, CLINICAL MANIFESTATIONS AND EPIDEMIOLOGY

Virus	Estimated efficiency of sexual transmission	Clinical manifestations	Endemic areas
HIV-1	Low–moderate	Immunosuppression/AIDS	Sub-Saharan Africa, India, South East Asia
HIV-2	Low–moderate	Immunosuppression/AIDS	West Africa
HTLV-1	Unknown	Adult T-lymphocyte leukemia/lymphoma, HTLV-1-associated myelopathy or tropical spastic paraparesis	Japan, Caribbean
Cytomegalovirus	Moderate–high	Systemic disease in the immunosuppressed	South East Asia, Africa
HSV-1 and HSV-2	Moderate–high	Recurrent genital ulcers	Worldwide
HPV	Moderate–high	Cervical cancer in women, anal cancer in men, recurrent genital warts	Worldwide
Hepatitis B virus	Moderate–high	Chronic hepatitis, cirrhosis, hepatic failure, carcinoma	South East Asia, Africa
Hepatitis C virus	Low	Chronic hepatitis, cirrhosis, hepatic failure, carcinoma	Worldwide

Table 148.2 Persistent viral sexually transmitted diseases: transmission efficiency, clinical manifestations and epidemiology.

- hepatitis B produces chronic liver disease and liver cancer and the role of sexual transmission is important;
- sexual transmission of hepatitis C virus appears to be less efficient than that of hepatitis B virus, but does occur;
- herpesviruses type 1 and type 2, and cytomegalovirus are now widespread global infections with major implications in the immunocompromised; and
- the implications of retroviruses (e.g. HTLV-1), other than HIV, lead to a range of illnesses and sexual contact may play a role in transmission.

DIAGNOSIS

Laboratory diagnosis

The diagnostic work-up for STDs in the returned traveler does not differ significantly from the approach used for locally acquired infections, although knowledge of the geographic distribution of infection may assist with the differential diagnosis. Although an efficient and rational approach to diagnosis should be taken, it may be necessary to order several diagnostic tests simultaneously because of the poor sensitivity and specificity of clinical examination, the propensity of STD pathogens to occur together and the variability in test performance. In addition, the potential complications of infection and the risk of further transmission demand that the infection is identified and treated expeditiously.

Test availability, patient circumstances and controversies in test performance preclude rigid diagnostic algorithms. In general, first-line tests should include microscopy, which can be conducted in a clinic setting and may provide a rapid diagnosis. Media-based cultures and serology require 48–72 hours, but are inexpensive and should be used as first-line tests when available. Tissue culture and amplification procedures are the most expensive tests and should be used with restraint. It is anticipated that with the development, commercial availability and affordability of sensitive and specific amplification procedures, many of the current culture-based methods will be replaced. Table 148.3 outlines the specimen collection and diagnostic testing available for the most common nonulcerative and ulcerative pathogens.

The risk of HIV infection and other viral STDs introduces a special problem in the approach to patient care. Presentation with a bacterial STD is essentially a marker for potential exposure to viral STDs. Among viral STDs the focus initially is on HIV infection, which arguably has the most serious consequences, and early treatment may alter disease progression. Most HIV screening currently tests for both HIV-1 and HIV-2, although the transmission of HIV-2 remains unusual outside West Africa. Screening for other persistent viral infections should be evaluated on an individual basis. For other viruses, the risk is not immediate and there are no specific interventions to block or delay chronic infection. The implications for current and future sex partners, however, are important and screening may be warranted.

DIAGNOSTIC TESTING FOR PATHOGENS CAUSING NONULCERATIVE AND ULCERATIVE INFECTIONS

Infection (pathogen)	Specimen collection	Diagnostic tests
Gonorrhea (*Neisseria gonorrhoeae*)	Men: meatal swab/urine; women: cervical swab/urine	Gram stain (Gram-negative diplococci) or media culture or nucleic acid amplification (LCR/PCR)
Chlamydiosis (*Chlamydia trachomatis*)	Men: endourethral swab/urine; women: cervical swab/urine	Tissue culture or ELISA or nucleic acid amplification (LCR/PCR)
Trichomoniasis (*Trichomonas vaginalis*)	Men: endourethral swab/urine; women: vaginal fluid	Microscopy (motile trichomonads) or media culture
Candidiasis (*Candida albicans*)	Women: vaginal fluid	Microscopy (wet mount or potassium hydroxide preparation showing yeast and mycella); media culture
Bacterial vaginosis (*Gardnerella vaginalis*, mycoplasmas, anaerobic bacteria)	Women: vaginal fluid	Microscopy (clue cells), vaginal pH <4.5, potassium hydroxide test, white discharge
Syphilis (*Treponema pallidum*)	Serum	Nontreponemal serology: RPR, VDRL; treponernal serology: MHA-TP, FTA-ABS
	Ulcer scrapings	Dark-field microscopy
Chancroid (*Haemophilus ducreyi*)	Ulcer swab or bubo aspirate	Media culture, nucleic acid amplification (PCR)
Herpes (HSV-2)	Ulcer swab	Tissue culture, nucleic acid amplification (PCR)
		Type-specific HSV-2 antibody serology
Donovanosis (*Calymmatobacterium granulomatis*)	Ulcer tissue or scrapings	Giemsa or Wright staining (identify Donovan bodies)
Lymphogranuloma venereum (*Chlamydia trachomatis* serovars L1,2,3)	Serum	Serology (complement fixation or immunofluorescent antibody tests)
	Ulcer scrapings	Tissue culture

Table 148.3 Diagnostic testing for pathogens causing nonulcerative and ulcerative infections in men and women. FTA-ABS, fluorescent treponemal antibody-absorbed test; LCR, ligase chain reaction; MHA-TP, microhemagglutination-*Treponema pallidum*; RpR, rapid plasma reagin; VDRL, Venereal Disease Reference Laboratories test.

Diagnosis by geographic region

A comprehensive picture of the global epidemiology of STDs is not available. Much of what is known about the geographic prevalence of infection is based on ad hoc surveys in selected populations.[6] The highest prevalence of STDs is found in resource-poor countries, which have the least capacity for monitoring and recording information. Sporadic cases and outbreaks of STDs are common and can occur in any region.

Prevalence figures for HIV-1 infection, which are more complete, generally indicate that it is common in regions in which other STDs are prevalent such as sub-Saharan Africa and South and South East Asia. Sexually transmitted diseases are prevalent in any geographic area that is characterized by poverty, prostitution and social disruption.

Genital ulcer diseases are one group of STDs for which knowledge of the geographic distribution may be useful. They appear to occupy specific geographic niches, knowledge of which may aid in the differential diagnosis. Table 148.4 indicates regions where etiologic-specific GUDs are endemic.

The persistent viral STDs have spread globally, although endemic regions are well described (see Table 148.2). Although HIV-1 infection has been the most lethal of these viral pathogens, cervical cancer caused by HPV and hepatic diseases caused by hepatitis B virus have serious consequences and are much more prevalent globally.

Knowledge of antibiotic resistance patterns in various geographic locations may be useful for empiric therapy, but as with STD prevalence figures, the data are sparse and the patterns change rapidly. In high-prevalence regions, the capacity to monitor antibiotic resistance and disseminate this information is inadequate. It is the returned traveler who fails to respond to recommended antimicrobials who

GEOGRAPHIC DISTRIBUTION OF GUD	
GUD	**Endemic areas**
Syphilis	Sub-Saharan Africa, India, eastern Europe
Chancroid	Sub-Saharan Africa, South East Asia, central America
Herpes	Worldwide
Granuloma inguinale (donovanosis)	South-east India, New Guinea, Caribbean, Brazil, Vietnam, Japan, central Australia, Zambia, South Africa
Lymphogranuloma venereum	East Africa, West Africa, South East Asia, South America, Caribbean

Table 148.4 Geographic distribution of genital ulcer disease.

may indicate emerging resistance. In fact, penicillinase-producing *N. gonorrhoeae*, which is now found globally, was first isolated from an American traveler returning from South East Asia.[19] The overuse and misuse of antimicrobials has promoted the emergence of *N. gonorrhoeae* resistance to penicillin, tetracycline and fluoroquinolones in many parts of the world.[20] Although the recommended empiric treatments should be available and effective for most returning travelers, ongoing surveillance for emerging resistance is a priority for reference laboratories.

MANAGEMENT

An STD in a returned traveler has major implications beyond diagnosis and treatment. The psychologic stress can range from minimal to debilitating. Issues of confidentiality, reporting and contact tracing may result in serious social disruption. Infection with a persistent viral infection may have long-term health consequences. An experienced health care team that can request appropriate diagnostic testing, monitor response to treatment, provide counseling, organize contact tracing and arrange longer term follow-up is essential.

The immediate management will be guided by a detailed history, including frequency of sexual exposure, type of exposure (e.g. oral, anal, vaginal), selection of partner (e.g. commercial sex worker, traveling companion), use of condoms and previous treatment (e.g. local, self-administered). It is not uncommon for travelers to have sought treatment abroad and often these individuals do not know what they received.

A thorough genital examination is important, despite the limitations of establishing an accurate etiologic diagnosis. This is especially true for women, for whom complications of infection are common and multiple anatomic sites might be involved. If an STD is suspected but rapid diagnostic testing is unavailable or inconclusive, empiric treatment is required, due to the risk of:

- developing complications,
- transmission to other partners, and
- potential loss to follow-up.

Table 148.5 summarizes the recommended treatments for the major nonulcerative and ulcerative pathogens. It is recommended that the treatment for gonorrhea always include treatment for chlamydia and that the treatment for chancroid always include treatment for syphilis. Beyond this, the choice of empiric treatment must be based on:

- severity of illness,
- knowledge of local infections,
- availability of diagnostic tests, and
- opportunity for follow-up.

Contact tracing in the returned traveler is generally concerned with informing and screening any sexual partners since returning. This is usually carried out by public health authorities who respond to

RECOMMENDED TREATMENT FOR NONULCERATIVE AND ULCERATIVE STDS		
Infection		**Empiric treatment**
Nonulcerative	Gonorrhea	Cefixime 400mg po single dose or ciprofloxacin 500mg po single dose or ceftriaxone 125mg im single dose
	Chlamydiosis	Azithromycin 1g po single dose, doxycycline 100mg po q12h for 7 days
	Trichomoniasis	Metronidazole 2g po single dose
	Ureaplasma infection	Doxycycline 100mg po q12h for 7 days
	Bacterial vaginosis	Metronidazole 2g po single dose
Ulcerative	Syphilis	Benzathine penicillin G 2.4 million units im single dose
	Chancroid	Azithromycin 1g po single dose or Ceftriaxone 250mg im single dose or Ciprofloxacin 500mg po q12h for 3 days or Erythromycin 500mg po q8h for 7 days
	Herpes	Aciclovir 400mg po q8h for 7–10 days or Aciclovir 200mg po five times a day for 7–10 days or Famciclovir 250mg q8h po for 7–10 days or Valaciclovir 1g po q12h for 7–10 days
	Lymphogranuloma venereum	Doxycycline 100mg po q12h for 21 days or erythromycin 500mg po q6h for 21 days
	Donovanosis	Doxycycline 100mg po q12h for at least 21 days or Trimethoprim–sulfamethoxazole one DS q12h for at least 21 days

Table 148.5 Recommended treatment for nonulcerative and ulcerative STDs.

reports of STDs in the community. With the variability in symptoms and delays in seeking treatment, it is not uncommon to transmit infection and many imported STDs are diagnosed only after symptoms appear in secondary contacts.

HIV-1 screening

Perhaps the most difficult issue for the returned traveler is whether to screen for persistent viral infections. This may be a concern of returned travelers and should be discussed by the health care worker if it is not. The decision for HIV-1 screening must be made after an informed discussion and a careful evaluation of the risk. Testing for HIV-1 should be strongly recommended for those who:

- have engaged in unprotected sex with a commercial sex worker;
- present with any GUD (especially chancroid);
- have failed standard treatment;
- have developed a flu-like illness associated with the STD (which may indicate a seroconversion illness); or
- are pregnant.

Testing should also be offered to anyone contracting an STD while traveling in high-prevalence areas, including those who are worried but well.

REFERENCES

1. Hawkes S, Hart G, Bletsoe E, Shergold C, Johnson A. Risk behaviour and STD acquisition in genitourinary clinic attenders who have travelled. Genitourin Med 1995;71:351–4.
2. Mendelsohn R, Astle L, Mann M, Shahmanesh M. Sexual behaviour in travellers abroad attending an inner-city genitourinary medicine clinic. Genitourin Med 1996;72:43–6.
3. Mulhall B, Hu M, Thompson M, *et al.* Plamed sexual behaviour of young Australian visitors to Thailand. Med J Aust 1993;158:530–5.
4. Tveit KS, Nilsen A, Nyfors A. Casual sexual experience abroad in patients attending an STD clinic and at high risk for HIV infection. Genitourin Med 1994;70:12–4.
5. Ford K, Wirawan N, Fajans P, Thorpe L. AIDS knowledge, risk behaviors, and factors related to condom use among male commercial sex workers and male tourist clients in Bali, Indonesia. AIDS 1995;9:751–9.
6. Abdullah AS, Fielding R, Hedley AJ, Travel, sexual behaviour, and the risk of contracting sexually transmitted diseases. Hong Kong Med J 1998;4:137–44.
7. DeSchryver A, Meheus A. Epidemiology of sexually transmitted diseases: the global picture. Bull World Health Organ 1990;68:639–54.
8. Mulhall BP. Sexually transmissible diseases and travel Br Med Bull 1993;49:394–411.
9. Mabey D, Mayaud P. Sexually transmitted diseases in mobile populations. Genitourin Med 1997;173:18–22.
10. Gras MJ, van Benthem BH, Coutinho RA, van den Hoek A. Determinants of high-risk sexual behavior among immigrant groups in Amsterdam: implications for interventions. J Acquir Immune Defic Syndr 2001;28: 166–72.
11. Vittecoq D, May T, Roue RT. Acquired immunodeficiency syndrome after travelling in Africa: an epidemiological study in seventeen caucasian patients. Lancet 1987;ii:612–4.
12. Hawkes S, Hart G, Johnson A, *et al.* Risk behaviour and HIV prevalence in international travellers. AIDS 1994;8:247–52.
13. Allard R, Lambert G. Knowledge and beliefs of international travellers about the transmission and prevention of HIV infection. Can Med Assoc J 1992;146:353–9.
14. von Reyn CF, Mann JM, Chin J. International travel and HIV infection. Bull World Health Organ 1990;68:251–9.
15. DiCarlo R, Martin D. The clinical diagnosis of genital ulcer disease in men. Clin Infect Dis 1997;25:292–8.
16. O'Farrell N, Hoosen A, Coetzee K, van den Eixle J. Genital ulcer disease: accuracy of clinical diagnosis and strategies to improve control in Durban, South Africa. Genitourin Med 1994;70:7–11.
17. Laga M, Manoka A, Kivuvu M, *et al.* Non-ulcerative sexually transmitted diseases as risk factors for HIV-1 transmission. AIDS 1993;7:95–102.
18. Plummer FA, Simonsen JN, Cameron DW, *et al.* Co-factors in female-male transmission of human immunodeficiency virus type 1. J Infect Dis 1991;163:233–9.
19. Ashford W, Golash R, Hemming V. Penicillinase-producing *Neisseria gonorrhoeae*. Lancet 1976;ii:657–8.
20. Ye S, Su X, Wang Q, Yin Y, Dai X, Sun H. Surveillance of antibiotic resistance of Neisseria gonorrhoeae isolates in China, 1993–1998. Sex Transm Dis 2002;29:242–5.

chapter 149

Jaundice

Hilton C Whittle

INTRODUCTION

The common afflictions experienced by the returned traveler are diarrhea and malaise.[1] However, jaundice in the returned traveler excites fears of highly infectious and serious exotic infections. In fact, since the advent of vaccines for hepatitis A virus and hepatitis B virus, jaundice in returned travelers is unusual and is equally likely to be due to mundane causes that are common in the developed world.

Jaundice is caused by the accumulation of bilirubin, resulting in yellow discoloration of the sclera and the skin. It is exacerbated when an infection causing hemolysis or hepatic damage occurs in a person who has pre-existing liver damage or in a person who has a congenital tendency to hemolysis.[2] The discussion in this chapter is limited to frank jaundice that is due to infection in a traveler recently returned from a developing country or a nonendemic zone or in a repatriated person who has worked or resided in such a place.

HISTORY

A precise and thorough history is the key to diagnosis. In the excitement and drama of the onset of jaundice, especially if it is associated with mental confusion, the vital question of the recent whereabouts of the patient may be overlooked.

Figures 149.1 and 149.2 show the distribution of some exotic viral infections that can cause jaundice. The duration of stay, mode of travel and lifestyle at home and abroad, including eating, drinking and sexual and drug habits, affect the risk of infection during travel. For example, a young student adventurer intent on meeting and living like the locals is obviously in danger of being infected through contaminated food, water or insects. Pot-holing, caving and fresh water sports represent a risk for leptospirosis. Did this young traveler attend a local health center to receive injections or a blood transfusion? On the other hand, a businessman frequenting luxury hotels and nightclubs is in less danger of endemic infections but is at higher risk of alcoholic hepatitis and sexually transmitted hepatitis B. Drug abuse is common among some travelers, who share cheap drugs and dirty needles with their local counterparts, thus placing themselves at high risk of viral hepatitis and other infections. An expatriate doctor, nurse or researcher working with contaminated blood in a rural hospital is in obvious danger of needle-stick injuries, which can transmit viral and other infections that may cause hepatitis and jaundice. Other obvious questions, which are often forgotten, relate to illness in fellow travelers, outbreaks of infection with or without jaundice in local communities, and exposure to toxins such as methyl alcohol in local potions or the ingestion of raw shellfish or other inadequately cooked food. Behind all these questions is the crucial one; is this person likely to have been nonimmune before exposure to infection during travel in an endemic or epidemic area?

Past medical history

The past medical history contains essential information. Was the traveler immunized against hepatitis A virus, hepatitis B virus, yellow fever and typhoid? What antimalarials did the traveler take? Does the traveler use recreational drugs such as ecstasy or cocaine or take other medications, such as isoniazid, dapsone or methyldopa, that may cause hepatitis? Was local food eaten and local water drunk? Was any attempt made to prevent mosquito bites? A previous history of chronic liver disease due to alcohol or viral hepatitis or a tendency to hemolysis (as in some hemoglobinopathies or enzyme deficiencies, such as glucose-6-phosphate dehydrogenase deficiency) may explain exacerbation of jaundice associated with infections of the liver.

SIGNS, SYMPTOMS AND DIFFERENTIAL DIAGNOSIS

A simple classification of jaundice and a list of common infectious causes is found in Table 149.1, and their likely geographic origins are shown in Figures 149.1 and 149.2. Other noninfectious causes of jaundice must also be kept in mind (e.g. alcoholic and other causes of cirrhosis, autoimmune hepatitis, gallstones or metastases blocking the bile ducts, drugs such as isoniazid or chlorpromazine, and poisons such as aflatoxin).

A full and thorough clinical examination is obviously mandatory and this must include a good examination of cerebral function. If cerebral function is disturbed, jaundice may be due to hypoglycemia, which is found in severe malaria, especially in children, or it may be due to liver damage itself; headache and meningeal irritation are common in leptospirosis. Signs of chronic liver disease should be looked for because chronic liver disease is sometimes the backdrop to a fulminant infection.

Hemorrhage in skin or mucosa suggests viral hemorrhagic fever, relapsing fever, leptospirosis, severe bacteremia (e.g. meningococcemia) or fulminant hepatitis itself. Assess the size of the liver. If it is small and hard, cirrhosis may be the cause; if it is large and severely tender, ascending cholangitis, flukes or gallstones may be the cause; if there is localized tenderness between the ribs, or inflamed localized swelling, an amebic abscess or another type of abscess may be the cause. The chest should be examined carefully and radiography performed if possible. Severe pneumonia can cause jaundice; a raised diaphragm on the right suggests liver abscess.

Other diagnostic clues

The incubation period is of obvious importance, whether a patient presents with an infection while traveling or after returning. Thus, hepatitis B virus, which has an incubation period of up to 6 months, may cause jaundice long after the holiday is forgotten,[3] whereas the acute hemorrhagic fevers present within 3–6 days of infection, often precipitating emergency removal from the area of travel.[4] The incubation period of leptospirosis is of intermediate duration, being 7–12 days,[5] similar to that of malaria, although the incubation of malaria may be prolonged as a result of inadequate use of prophylactic or curative drugs.[6]

Blood transfusion

In tropical or developing countries blood transfusion is fraught with danger because screening procedures are often not as rigorous

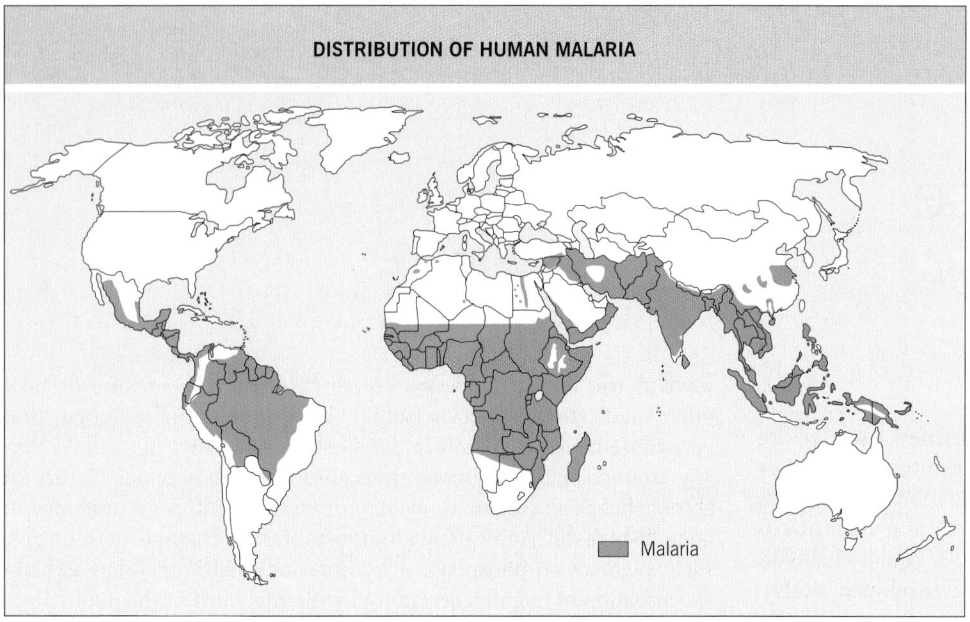

Fig. 149.1 Distribution of human malaria.

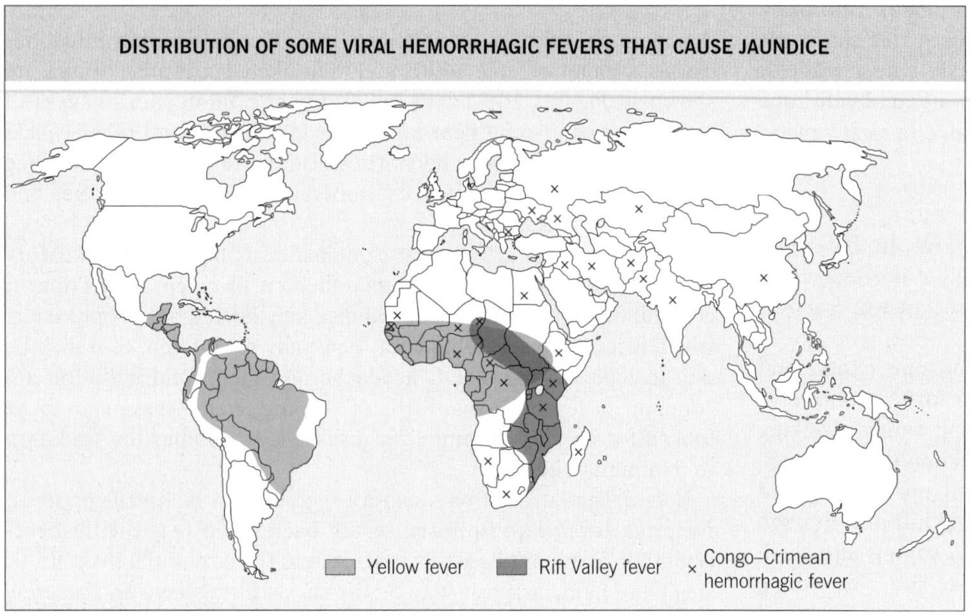

Fig. 149.2 Distribution of some viral hemorrhagic fevers that cause jaundice.

DIFFERENTIAL DIAGNOSIS OF JAUNDICE DUE TO INFECTION IN THE RETURNED TRAVELER				
Type of jaundice		**Cause**	**Diagnostic test**	**Comments**
Prehepatic	Hemolysis	Malaria; *Bartonella* spp.	Thick and thin blood film	Hemolysis is severe in 'blackwater' fever; *Bartonella* spp. are found in Columbia, Peru, Ecuador
Hepatic	Viruses	Hepatitis viruses A–E, hemorrhagic fevers (yellow fever, Rift Valley fever, Crimean–Congo hemorrhagic fever)	Serum IgM antibody, antigen detection tests, polymerase chain reaction	Was patient transfused? Any local outbreak of jaundice? Jaundice is uncommon in most hemorraghic fevers
	Bacteria, spirochetes	Any severe bacteremia, leptospirosis	Blood culture, micro-agglutination test	Any contact with infected soil or water?
	Protozoa	Amebic or pyogenic liver abscess	Amebic antibodies	East coast of Africa, Mexico and South East Asia are notorious 'hot' spots
Posthepatic	Bile duct obstruction	*Ascaris*, liver flukes, clonorchiasis opisthorchiasis, fascioliasis	Examination of stool for eggs	Unusual in schistosomiasis. Has traveler been eating raw fish?

Table 149.1 Differential diagnosis of jaundice due to infection in the returned traveler.

as in the Western world. Malaria, hepatitis B, C and D viruses, Epstein–Barr virus and cytomegalovirus are possible blood-borne agents that may cause jaundice, especially in subjects who have underlying immunodeficiencies or who are pregnant. Travelers in developing countries should avoid blood transfusions if possible.

Malaria

Malaria is probably the most common cause of fever in the returned traveler. Jaundice caused by massive hemolysis and a degree of hepatocellular necrosis may be manifest during severe *Plasmodium falciparum* malaria in adults, and milder forms are apparent in *Plasmodium vivax* and *Plasmodium ovale* malaria. Underlying liver disease or red cell enzyme deficiencies exacerbate this tendency, and primaquine used to treat *P. vivax* and *P. ovale* may precipitate hemolytic jaundice in some patients who have glucose-6-phosphate dehydrogenase deficiency (see Chapter 166).

Hepatitis viruses

Hepatitis viruses are the next most common cause of fever in the returned traveler, although a minority of those infected develop jaundice.[7] The incubation periods of hepatitis A and E virus are around 15–50 days after contact with infected food or water. Pregnant women are particularly prone to severe hepatitis E virus infection.[8] Hepatitis B, which has a much longer incubation period of 3–6 months, may be transmitted in contaminated blood or needles, as may hepatitis C, which has an incubation period of 2 months. Fever accompanied by general malaise is seldom ascribed to these viruses (see Chapter 48).[9]

Yellow fever and other hemorrhagic fevers

Yellow fever causes jaundice in 1 in 10 infections; Rift valley fever and Crimean–Congo hemorrhagic fever are less common causes. The other hemorrhagic fevers – Lassa, Junin, Ebola, Marburg, Hanta or Dengue – are not noted to cause jaundice, except occasionally in very severe cases (see Chapter 183). All cause hemorrhage and some degree of hepatic and renal damage, the latter being manifest by uremia and proteinuria.

Yellow fever is characterized by the acute onset of fever, chills, muscle aches, nausea and vomiting, followed by jaundice. The pulse may be slower than expected from the degree of fever. Leukopenia is common. After a brief remission of a day or more, a toxic state may develop, with liver and renal failure. Serologic diagnosis is achieved by demonstrating antigen or viral DNA in serum or liver or by IgM antibody.

There are two types of transmission cycle, a sylvatic or jungle cycle involving *Aedes* spp. of mosquitoes and nonhuman primates and an urban cycle involving humans and *Aedes aegypti*. Endemic areas now include parts of Africa and Latin America (see Chapter 222).

Leptospirosis

Weil's disease, a severe form of leptospirosis, is characterized by jaundice, fever, rashes, which may be hemorrhagic, and renal failure.[5] Severe headache, conjunctivitis and myalgia are characteristic, along with a history of working in an environment infested by rats. The organism, which lurks in contaminated food, soil and water, enters through abrasions in the skin or through intact mucous membranes (see Chapter 181).

Relapsing fever

The louse-borne type of relapsing fever is particularly likely to cause jaundice and petechiae in its severe form.[10] The more common, tick-borne form of relapsing fever seldom causes jaundice (see Chapter 182).

Bacterial infections

Severe bacterial infections caused by *Salmonella typhi*, *Streptococcus pneumoniae*, *Staphylococcus aureus* or *Neisseria meningitidis* can cause mild jaundice, especially in patients who have cirrhosis or hemoglobinopathies. *Bartonella bacilliformis*, which is endemic in the western Andes, infects red blood cells and causes hemolytic anemia and jaundice.

Differential diagnosis by geographic area

Knowledge of the geography of infections causing jaundice is essential when weighing the relative risk of each. However, the risk is also related to the level of endemicity and, in the case of malaria, to the level of drug resistance; these are variable within countries and often poorly documented. Thus, the following notes are offered only as a rough guide and should be interpreted with caution.

Malaria

The worldwide distribution of malaria is shown in Figure 149.1.[6]

Africa

Sub-Saharan tropical Africa is the major focus of *P. falciparum* malaria. *Plasmodium malariae* is widespread, but *P. vivax* is uncommon. Low-level transmission of *P. vivax* occurs in northern Africa. Chloroquine resistance is now widespread in Africa.

Asia

Plasmodium vivax is common in India, Pakistan, Sri Lanka and New Guinea, whereas multidrug-resistant *P. falciparum* occurs in many parts of South East Asia, New Guinea and the islands of the Pacific.

Americas

Plasmodium vivax is the common cause of malaria in central America, whereas *P. falciparum* predominates in Haiti and both infections are found in the low-lying areas of South America.

Hepatitis viruses

Hepatitis A and B viruses are very widespread.[7] The level of endemicity is low in northern Europe and North America, intermediate in southern Europe and high in Africa, India, Asia and parts of South America. Thus, if the risk of hepatitis A virus infection to the unvaccinated British person traveling in France and Scandinavia is considered to be 1, the relative risk in Spain is 5, in eastern Europe 20, in the Middle East 85, in sub-Saharan Africa 235, in South America and the Caribbean 243 and in the Indian subcontinent a massive 1835.[11]

Hepatitis E virus infection, which occurs in large outbreaks transmitted mainly to young adults by the fecal–oral route, has been described in Afghanistan, India, Pakistan, South East Asia, Ethiopia, Yemen, Mexico and in a colossal outbreak in the Xinjiang region of China.[8] Sporadic disease is also a major problem in India and, no doubt, in other parts of the developing world where it is yet to be diagnosed. Even more hepatitis viruses await discovery.

Viral hemorrhagic fevers

The distribution of the viral hemorrhagic fevers that are most likely to cause jaundice are shown in Figure 149.2.[12]

During outbreaks, yellow fever is transmitted by mosquitoes from monkeys to humans and from human to human. Hunters, expatriate or otherwise, may be exposed to mosquitoes infected from monkeys.

Rift Valley fever virus, a bunyavirus, is mainly a disease of sheep and goats but it can be transmitted to humans by mosquitoes or by direct contamination from infected animals.

Crimean–Congo hemorrhagic fever is transmitted mainly by ticks but air-borne infections occur in both hospital and laboratory environments.

Spirochetes

Leptospirosis occurs worldwide.[5] Infected rodents that associate with infected domestic animals, such as cattle, horses, pigs and dogs, are the chief source of infection. Farmers and other people working with or in contact with these animals are infected by their urine. Louse-borne relapsing fever is endemic in the highlands of Ethiopia but outbreaks occur in Sudan, Somalia, western Africa and Vietnam.

Protozoa

Entamoeba histolytica is very widespread.[13] It can cause colitis and hepatic abscess, which is occasionally associated with jaundice. The invasive form is prevalent in the forest zones of western Africa and on the east coast of Africa, in the whole of South East Asia and in Mexico and the west coast of South America.

Metazoa

Ascaris lumbricoides, which is very widespread, is the most common metazoic cause of obstructive jaundice. Relapsing cholangitis caused by *Opisthorchis* sp. occurs in north and north-eastern Thailand, Laos and Cambodia, where humans may eat infected raw fish, which are the second intermediate hosts. The parasite usually cycles between its definitive hosts (cats, dogs and fish-eating mammals). Clonorchiasis, caused by *Clonorchis sinensis*, is associated with eating raw fish in Japan, Korea, China, Taiwan and Vietnam, and occasionally causes an obstructive cholangitis. Fascioliasis is common in sheep in many parts of the world. The common causative organism, *Fasciola hepatica*, is cycled through snails. Infected water cress grown in snail-infested waters is the common source of infection in humans. Extensive outbreaks of fascioliasis have occurred in France and Cuba but infections are also found in the USA, including Hawaii, the Middle East and Asia.[14]

DIAGNOSIS

First-line tests

Simple dipstick tests for both blood and urine are available to measure levels of glucose, bilirubin and urobilinogen. Conjugated bilirubin in the urine indicates hepatocellular or obstructive jaundice; the froth after the urine is shaken is yellow and the urine is dark brown. Urobilinogen, which can be detected by dipstick or Ehrlich's reagent, indicates hemolysis. Biochemical tests for serum conjugated and unconjugated bilirubin, serum aspartate, alanine aminotransferase and alkaline phosphatase are useful in differentiating the two types of jaundice. Viral hemorrhagic fevers are distinguished from viral hepatitis by aspartate aminotransferase concentrations being disproportionally high compared with the alanine aminotransferase concentrations. Blood glucose and urinary protein should be measured if the patient's level of consciousness is altered. Thick and thin blood films may reveal malaria parasites or spirochetes; leukocytosis with a predominance of polymorphs suggests bacteremia, leptospirosis, amebic abscess or cholangitis. Stool microscopy may show ova of *Ascaris*, *Opisthorchis*, *Clonorchis* or *Fasciola* organisms.

Specialized tests

These are outlined in Table 149.1 but are usually available only at centers specializing in tropical diseases or at large public health laboratories. Serum IgM antibody tests have the advantage of early diagnosis using a single specimen. Antigen detection tests are also becoming available for malaria and may prove very useful because microscopy, although simple in concept, requires experience and skill if mistakes are to be avoided. Polymerase chain reaction tests are now available for most human viral infections. They are rapid, reliable and safe for samples that are inactivated during the extraction procedure.

MANAGEMENT

General measures

Acute hepatitis is often poorly managed, especially in its severe form, which is characterized by deep jaundice, liver flap of the hands and confusion or coma. Signs of previous chronic liver disease, such as spider angioma, a small liver, ascites and a history of alcohol abuse, bode ill, as does the presence of renal failure. Full details of the complexities of the management of severe liver failure and severe infections can be found in standard texts.

Specific treatment

The primary issue at stake is what the likely cause of the jaundice is and whether this is treatable (Table 149.2). Good clinical skills and simple diagnostic tests, available even in resource-poor countries, allow a rational decision, which often hinges on the following questions.

BASIS OF TREATMENT OF COMMON INFECTIONS THAT CAUSE JAUNDICE

Infection	Therapeutic agent	Comment
Severe malaria	Quinine or artemether	Quinine resistance increasing in South East Asia
Viruses	Ribavirin	Ebola and possibly Crimean–Congo hemorrhagic fever virus[15]
Leptospirosis	Penicillin or tetracycline	Jarisch–Herxheimer reaction in severe infection
Relapsing fever	Tetracycline, or erythromycin for pregnant women and children	Jarisch–Herxheimer reaction common in severe louse-borne type; relapse common in tick-borne type
Amebic liver abscess	Metronidazole or tinidazole	Aspirate if large
Ascaris	Mebendazole	Surgery often required for obstructive jaundice
Clonorchis, Opisthorchis	Praziquantel	Only one dose necessary
Fascioliasis	Triclabendazole or bithionol	Multiple courses may be required

Table 149.2 Basis of treatment of common infections that cause jaundice.

- Is the jaundice due to underlying liver disease?
- Is it due to a virus that is not treatable?
- Is it due to an infection that is treatable?

Other considerations

Important and agonizing decisions hinge on whether the patient should be treated locally or referred to a specialist hospital or, in extreme cases, to a high-containment facility. The decision is doubly difficult if the patient presents in a developing or resource-poor country because transport by air is expensive and may endanger the patient and, if the cause of the jaundice is highly infectious, the vehicle and other people in it may be contaminated.

In this respect the viral hemorrhagic fevers are greatly feared, although in these cases the most likely routes of human–human transmission are by direct contact, blood and contaminated syringes rather than by aerosol droplets.[4] However, the patient may be confused, bleeding and severely infected by high titers of virus and thus should be isolated when the diagnosis of viral hemorrhagic fever is suspected, and attendants should be protected by gowns, mask and gloves.[16]

Patients who have yellow fever are usually viremic only during the first 4 days of illness. By the time hepatitis occurs they pose little risk except from residual virus in viscera. The exact duration of viral excretion and level of infectivity of convalescent patients who have other hemorrhagic fevers is variable, but there is no evidence of long-term chronic carriage.

The proper disposal of excreta after inactivation by disinfectants is mandatory even in small hospitals or clinics. Laboratory specimens should be kept in sealed, plastic containers and handled and stored with care. They may be highly infectious (see Chapter 186a).[4]

In summary, when in a developing country do not transfer the patient unless there is a strong reason to think that this will be of real benefit to the patient. This caveat applies to any patient who has acute viral hepatitis; it is simpler, cheaper and easier to send specimens. In a developed country, most patients will be sent to a specialist hospital, particularly if the exact cause of viral hepatitis is not known. Other infections are more likely to be treated locally.

PREVENTION AND PROPHYLAXIS

Sensible behavior should be the order of the day; travelers should eat well-cooked food and drink boiled water, sleep under a mosquito net, preferably one treated with insecticide, and bring their own sterile needle and syringe if they need an injection.[17] Immunization status should be checked well before traveling because optimal regimens are available for vaccines against yellow fever, hepatitis A or B virus, rabies and meningococcal disease. These regimens should be used before entering an endemic or epidemic area, especially if the traveler intends to stay there. Booster polio and tetanus vaccines are also available.

REFERENCES

1. Steffen R, Lobel HO. Travel medicine. In: Cook G, ed. Manson's tropical diseases. London: WB Saunders; 1966:407–20.
2. Elias E. Jaundice. In: Weatherall DJ, Ledingham JGG, Warrell DA, eds. Oxford textbook of medicine, vol. 2. Oxford: Oxford University Press; 1966:2054–60.
3. Wright TL, Lau JYN. Clinical aspects of Hepatitis B infection. Lancet 1993;342:1340–4.
4. Peters CJ, Jahrling PB, Khan AS. Patients infected with high-hazard viruses: scientific basis for control. Arch Virol 1996;(Suppl.2):141–68.
5. Sitprija V. Leptospirosis. In: Weatherall DJ, Ledingham JGG, Warrell DA, eds. Oxford textbook of medicine, vol. 1. Oxford: Oxford University Press 1996:698–703.
6. Whittle H, van Hemsbroek MB. Malaria. In: Lankinen KS, Bergstrom S, Makela PH, Peltomaa M, eds. Health and disease in developing countries. London: Macmillan 1994;147–62.
7. Hall AJ. Hepatitis in travellers: epidemiology and prevention. Br Med Bull 1993;49:382–93.
8. Skidmore SJ. Hepatitis E. Br Med J 1995;310:414–5.
9. Doherty JF, Grant AD, Bryceson ADM. Fever as the presenting complaint of travellers returning from the tropics. Q J Med 1995;88:277–81.
10. Warrell DA. Other Borrelia infections. In: Weatherall DJ, Ledingham JGG, Warrell DA, eds. Oxford textbook of medicine, vol. 1. Oxford: Oxford University Press 1996; 692–7.
11. Behrens R, Collins M, Botto B, Heptonstall J. Risk for British travellers of acquiring hepatitis A. Br Med J 1995;311:193.
12. Simpson DIH. Arbovirus infections. In: Cook GC, ed. Manson's tropical diseases. London: WB Saunders; 1996:615–65.
13. Knight R. Amoebiasis. In: Weatherall DJ, Ledingham JGG, Warrell DA, eds. Oxford textbook of medicine, vol. 1. Oxford: Oxford University Press 1996:825–34.
14. Harinasuta T, Bunnag D. Liver, lung and intestinal trematodiasis. In: Warren KS, Mahmoud AAF, eds. Tropical and geographical medicine. New York: McGraw-Hill; 1990:473–89.
15. Fischer-Hoch SP, Khan JA, Rahman S, Mirza S, Khurshid M, McCormick JB. Crimean–Congo haemorrhagic fever treated with oral ribavirin. Lancet 1995;346:472–5.
16. Fischer-Hoch SP, Tomori O, Nasidi A, *et al.* Review of cases of nosocomial Lassa fever in Nigeria: the high price of poor medical practice. Br Med J 1995;311:857–9.
17. Blair DC. A week in the life of a travel clinic. Clin Microbial Rev 1997;10:650–73.

chapter 150

Eosinophilia in the Returned Traveler

Peter F Weller

INTRODUCTION

Eosinophilia represents increased numbers of eosinophils in the blood and/or tissues and is defined as when eosinophils exceed 450/μl blood. Eosinophilia can be a feature of a diverse array of infectious, allergic, neoplastic and other diseases (Table 150.1).[1]

Of the infectious etiologies, helminthic parasites are the predominant agents associated with eosinophilia. Therefore, for travelers returning from brief or prolonged stays in regions where parasitic infections are endemic, infections with various helminths are likely causes of eosinophilia.[2] Analyses of the frequency or risks for developing eosinophilia in travelers are not available. One retrospective study of asymptomatic expatriates who had returned from the tropics indicated that the sensitivity of eosinophil counts as a screening test for acquired infections due to filariasis, schistosomiasis or strongyloidiasis was 38%, with a positive predictive value of 9%. It concluded that in this population eosinophil counts contributed little to detecting these three parasitic infections if asymptomatic patients had full stool examinations and specific serologic testing.[3] Nevertheless, eosinophilia provides a valuable clue to the presence of many helminthic infections.

Travelers who have eosinophilia differ from other eosinophilic patients:

- first, as a consequence of their travel, they may have had recent exposures to infectious agents or medications that cause eosinophilia;
- second, the duration of travel, whether brief or prolonged, constitutes a definable time period for the onset of potential infection – the limited exposure period of travelers is important because they may return with infections in early stages of evolution; and
- third, travelers do not usually have any previous exposure to helminthic parasites, and so their response to helminths may differ from that of residents in endemic areas who have had lifelong exposure to helminthic infections – several helminthic infections result in more pronounced immune reactions and eosinophilia in travelers or temporary residents than in long-term inhabitants.

Evaluation of eosinophilia in a traveler is therefore largely targeted at helminthic infections, although other etiologies for eosinophilia must also be considered.

ETIOLOGIES OF EOSINOPHILIA IN TRAVELERS

Bacterial and viral infections

Acute bacterial or viral infections characteristically produce eosinopenia. The development of a bacterial, viral or protozoan (i.e. malaria) infection in patients who have eosinophilia due to helminthic or allergic diseases suppresses the blood eosinophilia.

Eosinophilia may accompany HIV infection for several reasons:

- leukopenia may lead to an increased eosinophil percentage in the absence of a true eosinophilia;
- reactions to medications may elicit eosinophilia;
- eosinophilia may arise from adrenal insufficiency resulting from cytomegalovirus and other infections in patients who have AIDS;
- a modest and rarely marked eosinophilia is observed in some patients who have HIV infection; and
- eosinophilia accompanies eosinophilic folliculitis in HIV infection.

Eosinophilia is also seen with human T-cell lymphotropic virus-1 (HTLV-1) infections.

Fungal infections

Two fungal diseases are associated with eosinophilia:

- aspergillosis, in the form of allergic bronchopulmonary aspergillosis; and
- coccidioidomycosis.

Eosinophilia is a feature of primary coccidioidal infection and at times disseminated coccidioidomycosis. In travelers to the south western USA, where *Coccidioides immitis* is endemic, eosinophilia may reflect infection with this organism.

Protozoan infections

Infections with single-celled protozoan parasites do not elicit blood eosinophilia. This is true of all intestinal-, blood- and tissue-infecting protozoa with two exceptions: *Dientamoeba fragilis* and *Isospora belli*.

Helminthic infections

Infections with many helminthic parasites elicit eosinophilia (Table 150.2).[4] Although eosinophilia can be a hematologic indicator of helminthic infections, neither the absence of blood eosinophilia nor the presence of only low-grade or episodic eosinophilia excludes such infections. The eosinophilic response to helminths is determined both by the host's immune response and by the parasite, including its distribution, extent of tissue migration and development within the infected host.

For several types of helminth infections, the migration of infecting larvae or subsequent developmental stages through the tissues is greatest early in infections and at these times the eosinophilia will be most marked (Table 150.3). For a detailed description of the parasitology see Chapters 174 & 246.

Eosinophilia may be absent in established infections when the parasites are antigenically sequestered within tissues (e.g. intact echinococcal cysts) or present only in the intestinal lumen (e.g. adult *Ascaris*, tapeworms).

For some established infections, there may be episodic blood eosinophilia. Intermittent leakage of fluids from echinococcal cysts can elicit episodic increases in blood eosinophilia and allergic (urticaria, bronchospasm) reactions. For tissue-dwelling helminths, the eosinophilia may increase during the migration of adult parasites, as in loiasis and gnathostomiasis.

Intestinal nematodes

Ascaris lumbricoides infections

These are acquired by ingesting fecally derived eggs, which may contaminate agricultural products or foods. Larvae derived from the

DISEASES ASSOCIATED WITH EOSINOPHILIA	
'Allergic' diseases	Atopic and related diseases Medication-related eosinophilias
Infectious diseases	Parasitic infections, mostly helminth infections (see Table 150.2) Specific fungal infections: allergic bronchopulmonary aspergillosis; coccidioidomycosis Other infections – infrequent, including HIV-1 and HTLV-1 infections
Hematologic and neoplastic disorders	Hypereosinophilic syndrome Leukemia Lymphomas, including nodular sclerosing Hodgkin's disease Tumors Mastocytosis
Diseases with specific organ involvement	Skin and subcutaneous diseases, including urticaria, bullous pemphigoid, eosinophilic cellulitis (Well's syndrome), episodic angioedema with eosinophilia Pulmonary diseases, including acute or chronic eosinophilic pneumonia, allergic bronchopulmonary aspergillosis Gastrointestinal diseases, including eosinophilic gastroenteritis Neurologic diseases (e.g. eosinophilic meningitis) Rheumatologic diseases, especially Churg–Strauss vasculitis; also eosinophilic fasciitis Cardiac diseases (e.g. endomyocardial fibrosis) Renal diseases, including drug-induced interstitial nephritis, eosinophilic cystitis; dialysis
Immunologic reactions	Specific immune deficiency diseases: hyper-IgE syndrome, Omenn's syndrome Transplant rejection: lung, kidney, liver
Endocrine	Hypoadrenalism: Addison's disease, adrenal hemorrhage
Other	Atheroembolic disease Irritation of serosal surfaces, including peritoneal dialysis Inherited, sarcoidosis, inflammatory bowel disease

Table 150.1 Diseases associated with eosinophilia.

HELMINTHIC PARASITIC DISEASES ASSOCIATED WITH EOSINOPHILIA	
Ancylostoma caninum *Angiostrongylus cantonensis* *Angiostrongylus costaricensis* Anisakiasis Ascariasis *Capillaria philippinensis* Clonorchiasis Coenurosis Cysticercosis Dicroceliasis Dirofilariasis Dracunculiasis Echinococcosis Echinostomiasis Fascioliasis Fasciolopsiasis Filariases: lymphatic (*Wuchereria* spp., *Brugia* spp.), loiasis, mansonelliasis, onchocerciasis, tropical pulmonary eosinophilia	Gnathostomiasis Heterophyiasis Hookworm (*Ancylostoma* spp., *Necator* spp.) Hymenolepsiasis Metagoniamiasis *Nanophyetus salminocola* Opisthorchiasis Paragonimiasis Schistosomiasis: schistosome dermatitis, *Schistosoma mansoni, Schistosoma haematobium, Schistosoma japonicum, Schistosoma intercalatum* Sparganosis Strongyloidiasis Trichinosis Trichostrongyloidiasis Trichuriasis Visceral larva migrans: *Toxocara canis, Bayllascaris* spp

Table 150.2 Helminthic parasitic diseases associated with eosinophilia.

HELMINTHIC PARASITIC DISEASES CAUSING MARKED EOSINOPHILIA	
Disease	**Notes**
Angiostrongylus costaricensis	
Ascariasis	Early transpulmonary larval migration, often absent when mature
Hookworm infection	Early transpulmonary larval migration, often mild when mature
Strongyloidiasis	
Trichinosis	
Visceral larva migrans	Primarily pediatric
Gnathostomiasis	
Filariasis: tropical pulmonary eosinophilia	
Filariasis: loiasis	Especially in expatriates
Filariasis: onchocerciasis	
Flukes: schistosomiasis	During early infection in people who are not immune (Katayama fever)
Flukes: fascioliasis	During early infection
Flukes: clonorchiasis	During early infection
Flukes: paragonimiasis	During early infection
Flukes: fasciolopsiasis	During early infection

Table 150.3 Helminthic parasitic diseases causing marked eosinophilia (>3000/mm^3).[5]

eggs pass hematogenously to the liver and lungs. About 1–2 weeks after infection, larvae in the lungs penetrate from the capillaries into the alveoli and mature into third-stage larvae. These ascend the tracheobronchial tree and are swallowed to enter the intestine. In the intestine, the larvae mature into adult male and female worms, which begin producing eggs 2–3 months after the initial infection.

The first manifestations of *Ascaris* infections during the transpulmonary passage of larvae produce a syndrome of eosinophilic pulmonary infiltrates (Loeffler's syndrome).[5,6] Symptoms develop when the larvae are within the lungs, about 9–12 days after ingesting the *Ascaris* eggs. A nonproductive cough, burning substernal discomfort, low-grade fever and wheezing are common. Eosinophilia increases after several days of symptoms and resolves slowly over many weeks. Chest radiographs reveal round or oval infiltrates up to several centimeters in size, which clear over many weeks.

A diagnosis of early-phase pneumonic ascariasis is made with certainty by detecting *Ascaris* larvae in respiratory secretions or gastric aspirates. At least 40 days must elapse before the intrapulmonary larvae responsible for *Ascaris* pneumonia will have matured to produce eggs detectable on stool examinations. Negative stool examinations during or soon after acute infection do not exclude *Ascaris* as an etiology. Finding that the stools are free of eggs during pneumonic involvement but contain *Ascaris* eggs 2–3 months later supports the role of *Ascaris* as the etiologic agent of acute eosinophilia and pneumonitis.

Hookworm

Infections with hookworms (*Necator americanus* or *Ancylostoma duodenale*) are acquired when larvae in fecally contaminated soil penetrate the skin. Even brief exposures of travelers to contaminated soil may be sufficient because as few as three larvae can produce infection. Larval penetration of the skin often produces a pruritic maculopapular eruption, and in those who have been previously infected there are serpiginous tracks of larval migration, as in cutaneous larva migrans.

In experimental infections pulmonary symptoms have not developed (although larvae penetrate through to the lungs), but gastrointestinal symptoms, including nausea, diarrhea, vomiting and abdominal pain, are common. Blood eosinophilia increases after 2–3 weeks and peaks after 5–9 weeks of infection.

In untreated hookworm infections the eosinophilia slowly diminishes, but the eosinophil count can remain elevated for several years due to the attachment of adult worms to the intestinal mucosa. Eggs are detectable in feces about 6–8 weeks after infection with *N. americanus*. The larvae of *A. duodenale* may persist within the tissues before returning to the intestine so egg laying can be delayed. Cutaneous larva migrans from other animal hookworm species is commonly associated with eosinophilia when humans become infected as accidental hosts.

Tissue and intravascular nematodes

Filariasis

Infection occurs following the introduction of infective larvae by biting insect vectors (see Chapter 170). Early infections with lymphatic-dwelling (*Brugia* and *Wuchereria* spp.) filariae can cause lymphadenitis, lymphangitis and eosinophilia, usually without detectable microfilaremia. Infections with *Loa loa* in long-term residents of endemic areas in equatorial West and Central Africa are manifested by microfilaremia, episodic angioedema (Calabar swellings), transocular migration of adult worms and modest eosinophilia. In contrast, among those who acquire loiasis after temporary residence, microfilaremia is less common, episodic angioedema is more severe and elevations in serum IgE, antifilarial antibody titer and eosinophilia are more pronounced. Eosinophilia and inflammatory reactions are more prominent in acute filariasis among previously nonimmune patients who exhibit immunologic hyperresponsiveness to infection than among long-term residents of endemic regions who develop partial immunity to infections.

Trichinosis

Trichinosis is acquired by consuming the meat of carnivores that contains viable encysted larvae of *Trichinella* spp. The muscle phase of trichinosis begins about 1 week after infection when the larvae from the intestine disseminate hematogenously and begin to encyst in striatal muscle. Patients may experience subconjunctival, retinal and subungual splinter hemorrhages, and periorbital and facial edema. As the larvae encyst in muscle, myalgias, fatigue, elevated muscle enzymes and eosinophilia develop. Eosinophilia is present in over 90% of those who have symptomatic trichinosis and abates slowly over months. As *Trichinella* spp. are globally distributed, travelers are at risk of acquiring trichinosis if they ingest undercooked meats from domestic and wild pigs, wart hogs, boars, bears, walruses or horses containing *Trichinella* larvae.

Visceral larva migrans

The ingestion of eggs of the dog ascarid, *Toxocara canis*, produces a syndrome of visceral larva migrans. This is most common in young children who ingest soil contaminated with fecally derived eggs and is less frequently seen in adults, when it is potentially acquired by ingesting foods contaminated with *Toxocara canis* eggs. Most infections are subclinical and marked only by blood eosinophilia. Eosinophilia is also prominent with heavier infections.

Trematodes

Acute schistosomiasis

Schistosomiasis (see Chapter 167) is acquired by exposure of the skin to fresh water containing cercariae of *Schistosoma* spp. A distinct syndrome of acute schistosomiasis (Katayama fever) develops principally in previously unexposed individuals who have heavy infections. Patients develop fever, chills, anorexia, weight loss, abdominal pain, diarrhea, urticaria, myalgias, a dry cough and bronchospasm 2–8 weeks after infection. Blood eosinophilia is very prominent. In the later stage of this syndrome, antischistosomal antibodies develop and egg laying begins and schistosome eggs become detectable in the stools, urine and rectal mucosa. The syndrome is self-limiting and resolves over 1–2 months, but can be shortened by treatment with corticosteroids and antischistosomal therapy.

Paragonimiasis

Paragonimiasis (see Chapter 168) results from infection with the lung fluke (*Paragonimus* spp.). *Paragonimus westermani* is endemic in Asia, whereas other *Paragonimus* spp. cause infections in other regions of the world. Infection is acquired by ingesting freshwater crabs or crayfish that harbor metacercariae. After ingestion, the metacercariae excyst in the duodenum, penetrate the gastrointestinal wall and migrate within the peritoneal cavity. Most young flukes penetrate the diaphragm to migrate within the pulmonary parenchyma, where they become surrounded by an inflammatory infiltrate and later a fibrous capsule. After 7–8 weeks of infection mature flukes begin egg production within the capsule, which enlarges and ruptures, often into a bronchiole.

Eosinophilia is most pronounced in the early phase of paragonimiasis. In this phase, larval migration into the pleural cavity may result in a pleurisy and exudative eosinophil-rich pleural effusions. Chest radiographs reveal transient migratory pulmonary infiltrates and eosinophilia is prominent.

Diagnosis of early-phase paragonimiasis before egg production has been initiated is difficult and often based presumptively on compatible clinical findings in a patient who has eosinophilia and a history of exposure in an area where paragonimiasis is endemic.

Fascioliasis

Infection with *Fasciola hepatica*, the liver fluke of sheep and cattle, is acquired by ingesting cysts attached to aquatic plants (e.g. wild watercress). In early-stage fascioliasis marked eosinophilia is common as the parasites burrow into the liver and enter the bile ducts. The symptoms may be minimal or include fever, abdominal pain, malaise, pruritus, urticaria and coughing. Hepatomegaly and cholestatic liver function test abnormalities develop. Because there are no eggs in the stool or biliary or duodenal fluid samples until about 3 months after infection, the diagnosis of acute fascioliasis will be suggested by the triad of fever, marked eosinophilia and hepatomegaly.

Intestinal flukes

Eosinophilia is prominent in the early stages of infections with several intestinal flukes. *Fasciolopsis buski* is acquired by ingesting metacercariae on water plants such as water chestnuts, *Metagonimus yokogawai* or *Heterophyes heterophyes* by ingesting metacercariae in raw or undercooked fish, and *Nanophyetus salminocola* by ingesting salmon.

Chronic helminthic infections

One hallmark of helminthic infections in addition to their characteristic elicitation of eosinophilia is their ability to survive within infected human hosts for prolonged periods of time. Some can cause eosinophilia lasting for years (e.g. hookworm, strongyloidiasis, filiariasis, hepatic trematodes). In contrast to their early phases, the diagnostic stages of the helminthic parasites will have formed in mature infections.

Other travel-related causes of eosinophilia

Ectoparasites (e.g. scabies) may be associated with eosinophilia. Eosinophilia can also accompany adverse drug reactions and can occur with numerous travel-related medications.

EVALUATION OF EOSINOPHILIA IN TRAVELERS

History

Although many helminths are widely distributed, some have more discrete geographic distributions.[7] The parasite causing clonorchiasis is found in Asia. *Angiostrongylus cantonensis*, a cause of eosinophilic meningitis, is principally but not exclusively found in the Pacific Basin. Of filarial parasites, *Loa loa* is limited to Central and West Africa and *Onchocerca volvulus* is found in equatorial Africa and elevated regions in Central America.

Dietary history is pertinent for several helminthic infections, including anisakiasis (raw fish), fish tapeworm (fish), *N. salminocola* (salmon), *Taenia solium* (pork), *Taenia saginata* (beef), fascioliasis (watercress), fasciolopsiasis (horse chestnut), gnathostomiasis (freshwater fish, eels, frogs, snakes and poultry and pigs fed on fish), *A. cantonensis* (land snails or slugs, freshwater shrimps, crabs, some marine fish) and trichinosis (pork, boar, bear meat, horse meat, walrus, wart hog). Exposure in sheep-rearing areas is pertinent for *Echinococcus granulosus*.

A history of swimming in or having contact with fresh water is relevant in areas where there is snail-borne schistosomiasis. Contact with fresh or salt water followed by a rash on water-exposed skin and eosinophilia suggests schistosome dermatitis, which can be caused by avian schistosome species. Skin contact with soil potentially contaminated with human or dog feces, as may occur by walking barefoot or occupational exposure, is relevant for the acquisition of cutaneous larva migrans, hookworm or *Strongyloides* infections.

Clinical features

Because diagnostic-stage parasites are not detectable in early helminthic infections, the clinical findings are especially important:

- trichinosis is suggested by eosinophilia in a patient who has myositis, periorbital edema and subungual splinter hemorrhages;
- in strongyloidiasis, a migratory serpiginous linear urticarial eruption ('larva currens') due to larvae migrating in the skin is a pathognomonic manifestation experienced by some patients;
- urticaria can be a feature of several helminthic infections, including acute ascariasis, strongyloidiasis, acute schistosomiasis, acute fascioliasis and echinococcosis;
- angioedematous subcutaneous (Calabar) swellings and subconjunctival migrations of adult worms are cardinal manifestations of *Loa loa* infections; and
- gnathostomiasis causes subcutaneous swellings with eosinophilia.

Investigations

Although stool examinations help in the identification of enteric helminths, many helminths capable of eliciting eosinophilia, either tissue- or blood-dwelling helminths or those causing early-phase enteric infections, cannot be identified by fecal examination. Among the established helminthic infections capable of inducing eosinophilia that are not diagnosable from stool examinations are trichinosis, filariasis, anisakiasis, gnathostomiasis, visceral larva migrans and echinococcosis. Even some intestinal helminths, notably hookworm and *Strongyloides*, may not be readily detectable on routine stool examinations.

Other diagnostic tests include examination of respiratory secretions (sputum, bronchoalveolar lavage fluid) for larvae of *Strongyloides*, hookworm and ascaris, or for eggs of *Paragonimus* spp.

For a diagnosis of filariasis, blood should be examined for microfilariae by blood filtration. Blood-borne microfilariae include those of:

- lymphatic-dwelling *Wuchereria bancrofti* and *Brugia* spp. – generally the yield is greatest from night-time blood samples;
- *Loa loa* – yield is greatest from morning samples; and
- *Mansonella perstans* and *Mansonella ozzardi*.

Skin snips should be obtained to detect the microfilariae of *Onchocerca volvulus*, *M. ozzardi* and *M. streptocerca*. Urine is examined for the eggs of *Schistosoma haematobium*. Tissue biopsies may help in diagnosing trichinosis (muscle biopsy), schistosomiasis (rectal biopsy, liver biopsy) and loaisis or gnathostomiasis (involved soft tissues).

Serologic testing can be valuable for several helminthic parasites. For *Strongyloides stercoralis*, enzyme-linked immunosorbent assay serology has proved useful, even when stool examinations are unrevealing. Because of the difficulty in detecting this parasite and its potential for persisting and causing later serious infections, serologic evaluation for strongyloidiasis is indicated for a patient who has eosinophilia. Serologic tests are the most expedient way for diagnosing visceral larva migrans. In trichinosis diagnostic serologic titers may not rise until the third week of infection. Serologic tests are also helpful in diagnosing schistosomal and filarial infections, cysticercosis and echinococcosis. In echinococcosis, the serology may be negative, even when there are obvious lesions; the tests are positive in only 50% of patients who have isolated pulmonary lesions and in 85–90% of those who have hepatic hydatid cysts (Chapter 169).

Management

Treatment should be directed at identified parasites. Although some advocate presumptive therapy with mebendazole or thiabendazole for undiagnosed eosinophilias in travelers, it is preferable to pursue an etiologic diagnosis for eosinophilia and to exclude the presence of undetected intestinal or extraintestinal helminths. This is especially important because *Strongyloides stercoralis*, with its potential for long-term persistence, may cause prolonged eosinophilia.

Following the initiation of anthelmintic therapy, blood eosinophilia may increase for several weeks before subsiding. The magnitude of the post-treatment eosinophilia correlates with the number of parasites present before treatment and is an immune reaction to killed parasites. Resolution of eosinophilia can be monitored as one measure of the efficacy of anthelmintic therapy, with hematologic studies being repeated in the months after therapy.

Complications

Sustained blood eosinophilia (the idiopathic hypereosinophilic syndrome) can lead to cardiac complications, including the development of intraventricular thrombi and endomyocardial fibrosis with secondary mitral or tricuspid regurgitation.[8] Most patients who have eosinophilia develop no endomyocardial damage, but such damage has been noted occasionally in Americans and Europeans who have eosinophilia due to loiasis and acute trichinosis. Patients who have sustained eosinophilia should be monitored by echocardiography.

REFERENCES

1. Weller PF. Eosinophilia and eosinophil-related disorders. In: Adkinson NF Jr, Yunginger JW, Busse WW, Bochner BS, Holgate ST, Simons FE, eds. Allergy: principles and practice, 6th ed. St. Louis: Mosby; 2001.
2. Harries AD, Myers B, Bhattacharrya D. Eosinophilia in Caucasians returning from the tropics. Trans Roy Soc Trop Med Hyg 1986;80:327–8.
3. Libman MD, MacLean JD, Gyorkos TW. Screening for schistosomiasis, filariasis, and strongyloidiasis among expatriates returning from the tropics. Clin Infect Dis 1993;17:353–9.
4. Wilson ME, Weller PF. Eosinophilia. In: Guerrant RL, Walker DH, Weller PF, eds. Tropical infectious diseases: principles, pathogens and practice. Philadelphia: WB Saunders; 1999;1400–19.
5. Weller PF. Eosinophilia in travelers. Med Clin North Am 1992;76:1413–32.
6. Weller PF. Parasitic pneumonias. In: Pennington JE, ed. Respiratory infections: diagnosis and management, 3rd ed. New York: Raven Press; 1994:695–714.
7. Wilson ME. Worldwide distribution of infections. A world guide to infections. Disease, distributions, diagnosis. New York: Oxford University Press; 1991:179–203.
8. Weller PF, Bubley GJ. The idiopathic hypereosinophilic syndrome. Blood 1994;83:2759–79.

chapter

151 Cough and Respiratory Tract Infections

Thomas C Jones

EPIDEMIOLOGY

Acute respiratory illness (ARI) is common throughout the world. As a result, respiratory illness is common among travelers.[1] There are over 4 million childhood deaths due to ARI each year in the developing world.[2] Especially common causes of these deaths are:

- respiratory syncytial virus (15–20%),
- pneumococcal pneumonia (20%),
- hemophilus pneumonia (10–20%),
- postmeasles pneumonia (15%),
- pertussis (10%), and
- parainfluenza virus (7–10%).

These statistics show that the traveler is highly exposed to respiratory pathogens. It has been reported that 2.2% of travelers return with symptoms of rhinitis and 1–2% have acute respiratory tract infection with fever.[1] These infections are primarily due to respiratory viruses but mycoplasma, legionella and other less common organisms also contribute.

Atypical causes of respiratory illness can occur in the traveler because of exposure to unusual microbes. Although these illnesses are rare, they are very important for the physician caring for a traveler with respiratory illness because they are potentially serious, transmissible and treatable. Although pneumonia due to *Streptococcus pneumoniae*, *Mycoplasma pneumoniae*, *Mycobacterium tuberculosis* or influenza makes up less than 0.001% of diseases in travelers, it can account for up to 10% of cases of febrile disease involving the respiratory tract presenting to a physician. These patients must be diagnosed and managed in the same way as nontraveling patients with community-acquired pneumonia.[3,4] Hidden in this group of travelers with pneumonia are a few patients whose diseases are specifically a result of exposure to agents or environmental conditions associated with their travel. These diseases may be misdiagnosed because of their rarity.

This chapter is directed at the microbial causes of respiratory illness, and of cough in particular. Nonmicrobial causes can also affect the traveler and require carefully managed medical intervention.

PATHOGENESIS AND PATHOLOGY

The physician caring for the traveler with cough must be aware of the potential causes, both common and rare, of respiratory disease throughout the world. Toxins, allergens, viruses, mycoplasma, chlamydia, rickettsia, bacteria, fungi, protozoa and helminths may each be responsible for respiratory signs and symptoms.

Toxins or allergens

A cause of cough in travelers is exposure to respiratory toxins or allergens that are not present in his or her home environment. Some of these, along with their associated pulmonary illnesses, are listed in Table 151.1. High levels of air pollution in large cities can cause respiratory tract irritation and exacerbate cough. A new environment may also expose an allergic traveler to grasses, pollens and dust in much higher concentrations than normal. This is particularly a problem for the young traveler, who may not have developed full immunotolerance for potential allergy-producing substances. For example, among Cambodian refugees on the Thailand border, the most common respiratory illness, 'Khao-I-Dang lung', was due primarily to dust inhalation.

Of special relevance to the traveler is exposure to unusual concentrations of respiratory allergens such as inhaled fungi. The best example of this is bronchopulmonary aspergillosis, caused by inhalation of *Aspergillus* spp. (see Chapter 237). In 'farmer's lung', the likely allergenic organisms are various molds that accumulate in silos.

Viral, mycoplasmal, chlamydial and rickettsial causes

The microbial agents in these groups that cause respiratory symptoms are listed in Table 151.2, along with their most common related illnesses. As in the home environment, respiratory viruses cause a significant number of the pulmonary signs and symptoms that affect travelers.[1,3] The traveler enters an environment that is foreign to his or her immune system and is likely to develop illness due to the different rhinoviruses, adenoviruses and other respiratory viruses that are prevalent in the communities visited.

The chances of contracting a viral illness during air travel are enhanced by crowding, spread of respiratory droplets and by rapid turnover of dry cool air, which reduces airway defenses. Alcohol and fatigue further increase the likelihood of an overt respiratory illness shortly after returning home.

TOXINS AND ALLERGENS AS CAUSES OF RESPIRATORY SIGNS AND SYMPTOMS IN THE TRAVELER

Causative agent		Main pulmonary disease
Toxins	Smoke fumes	Rhinitis, bronchitis, pneumonia
	Carbon monoxide, sulfur dioxide, ozone	Bronchitis
	Halides, phosgene, pesticides	Bronchitis, pneumonia
Environment	Hypobaric conditions during air travel	Stress bronchoconstriction, hypoxia
	Mountain sickness	Pulmonary edema
Allergens	Dust and mites	Rhinitis, conjunctivitis, bronchitis, asthma
	Pollens and grasses	Rhinitis, conjunctivitis, bronchitis, asthma
	Aspergillus spp. (allergic bronchopulmonary aspergillosis)	Asthma, eosinophilic pneumonia
	Molds (farmer's lung)	Eosinophilic pneumonia

Table 151.1 Toxins and allergens as causes of respiratory signs and symptoms in the traveler.

VIRAL, MYCOPLASMAL, CHLAMYDIAL AND RICKETTSIAL CAUSES OF COUGH IN TRAVELERS			
	Condition/microbial agent	**Sources of infection**	**Main illness**
Viruses	Influenza	Worldwide, varied seasons, epidemics, pandemics	Fever, bronchitis, pneumonia
	Rhinovirus, adenovirus and other respiratory viruses	Worldwide, varied seasons	Rhinitis, pharyngitis, bronchitis
	Hantavirus	Worldwide	Respiratory distress syndrome
	Chickenpox, measles	Contact with infected patient	Fever, pneumonia, rash
	Coronavirus	Contact with infected patient	Fever, severe pneumonia, SARS
Mycoplasmas	Atypical pneumonia: *Mycoplasma pneumoniae*	Worldwide, crowding	Acute pneumonia
Chlamydiae	*Chlamydia pneumoniae*	Worldwide	Acute pneumonia
	Chlamydia trachomatis	Worldwide, children	Paroxysmal cough, pneumonia
	Psittacosis: *Chlamydia psittaci*	Contact with psittacine birds	Acute pneumonia
Rickettsiae	Q fever: *Coxiella burnetii*	Contact with sheep, cattle, goats, ticks	Acute pneumonia

Table 151.2 Viral, mycoplasmal, chlamydial and rickettsial causes of cough in travelers.

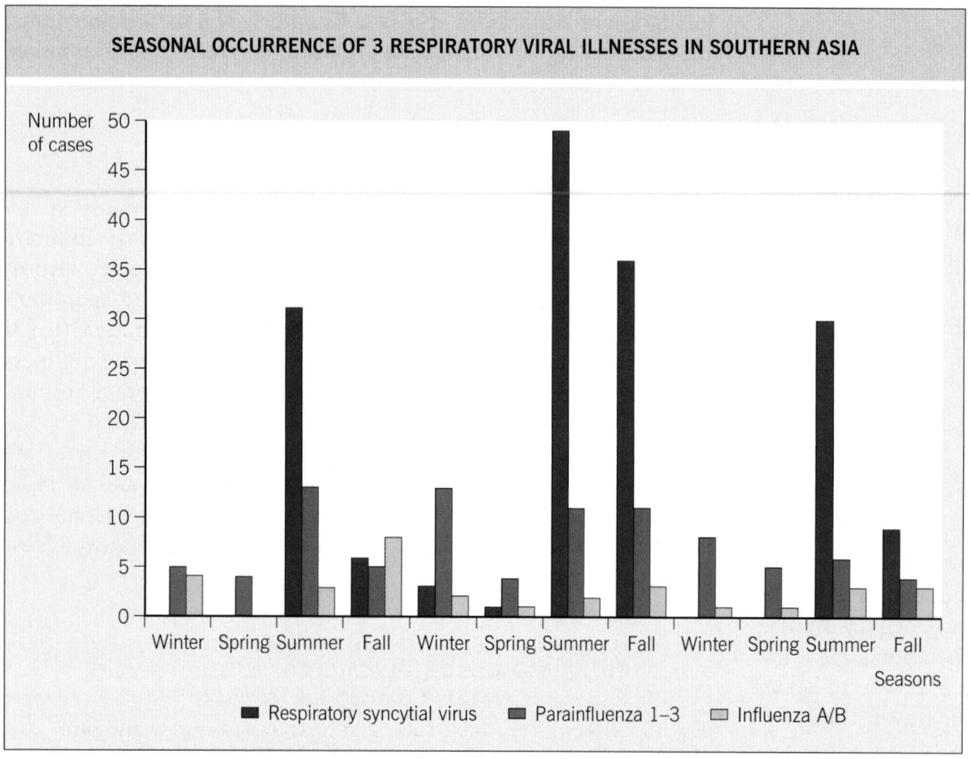

Fig. 151.1 Respiratory illness in southern Asia (February 1985 to December 1987). Data modified from reference[5].

Seasonal patterns related to the spread of viruses differ in various parts of the world. For example, many respiratory viruses that are spread from December to April in the northern hemisphere are spread from May to September in the southern hemisphere, and most often during the rainy season in tropical countries. Figure 151.1 shows the frequency of three groups of viruses in southern India during different seasons over a 3-year period. The highest prevalence occurred in the summer and fall, rather than the winter as recorded in temperate regions in the north.[5]

The most important and best-documented virus in travelers is influenza. For example, during the pandemic of 1957, influenza reached the USA from Asia, beginning at a conference in the midwest and spreading throughout the country as the participants returned home.[6] Another example comes from the war in Vietnam, when military personnel in the Philippines often had holidays in Hong Kong. In 1968, thousands of cases of influenza occurred among these people and their contacts in the Philippines owing to the new antigenically shifted virus (H3N2) that had emerged that year in Asia. A recently recognized epidemic due to a Coronavirus has emerged from Asia. This new virus causes the illness now termed Severe Acute Respiratory Syndrome (SARS).[7–9]

A newly recognized cause of respiratory illness is hantavirus, which is transmitted as aerosolized virus from rodents. It has caused localized epidemics in many parts of the world including the USA, Europe, South America and Asia.

In the past, careful attention has been given to the possibility that a traveler with the first respiratory signs of smallpox might infect a large number of people on the airplane or at the airport before the tell-tale signs of cutaneous eruption had appeared. Smallpox remains a threat as an agent of bioterrorism and patients with chickenpox or measles could have only cough and fever at the beginning of the illness. It is important for the physician caring for a traveler with cough to document any potential exposure to these diseases.

BACTERIAL AND FUNGAL CAUSES OF COUGH IN TRAVELERS			
	Condition/infecting agent	Geographic distribution and sources of infection	Main illness
Bacteria	Pneumococcal pneumonia	Worldwide	Acute pneumonia
	Tuberculosis	Worldwide, infected patients	Chronic pneumonia
	Legionellosis	Aerosolized water, cooling systems	Acute pneumonia
	Bordetella pertussis	Worldwide	Acute glottitis and chronic cough
	Actinomycosis	Worldwide, soil	Draining sinuses, chronic pneumonia
	Plague: *Yersinia pestis*	Infected patients or rodents, fleas	Lymphadenitis, pneumonia
	Meningococcal pneumonia	Worldwide epidemics, central Africa	Pharyngeal carriage, pneumonia, meningitis
	Tularemia	Contact with infected small mammals	Lymphadenitis, pneumonia
	Bacillus anthracis	Animal hides, bioterrorism	Skin lesions, pneumonia
	Melioidosis	South East Asia	Pneumonia, systemic illness
Fungi	Histoplasmosis	Worldwide, decayed vegetation, bat caves	Erythema nodosum, acute or chronic pneumonia, hilar adenopathy
	Coccidioidomycosis	Aerosolized soil, south-west USA	Acute or chronic pneumonia
	Paracoccidioidomycosis	South America	Acute or chronic pneumonia
	Blastomycosis	Southern USA	Pharyngeal lesion, pneumonia
	Cryptococcosis	Contact with feces from pigeons	Pneumonia, meningitis
	Penicilliosis	Northem Thailand	Skin lesions, pneumonia
	Pneumocystis pneumonia	Worldwide, pneumocystis	Acute pneumonia in those who are immunodeficient (i.e. HIV)
	Aspergillosis	Worldwide	Aspergilloma: pneumonia in those who are immunodeficient

Table 151.3 Bacterial and fungal causes of cough in travelers.

Mycoplasmal pneumonia can cause cough in travelers. *M. pneumoniae* is transmitted in crowded conditions, as has been demonstrated among military recruits. There are three important chlamydial causes of pneumonias:

- *Chlamydia pneumoniae*, an increasing cause of community-acquired pneumonia,
- *Chlamydia trachomatis*, particularly in children, and
- *Chlamydia psittaci*, the cause of psittacosis.

Psittacosis is transmitted by contact with either psittacine birds such as parrots or with people who have psittacosis. Although rare in wild birds, psittacosis occurs when birds are housed together.

Q fever is a cause of pneumonia in those exposed to rickettsia aerosolized from or in the secretions of infected farm animals. Small epidemics have occurred in many parts of the world, and have been well studied in Australia, California, Israel and Switzerland. A detailed history of possible exposure to these microbes is the key to correct diagnosis.

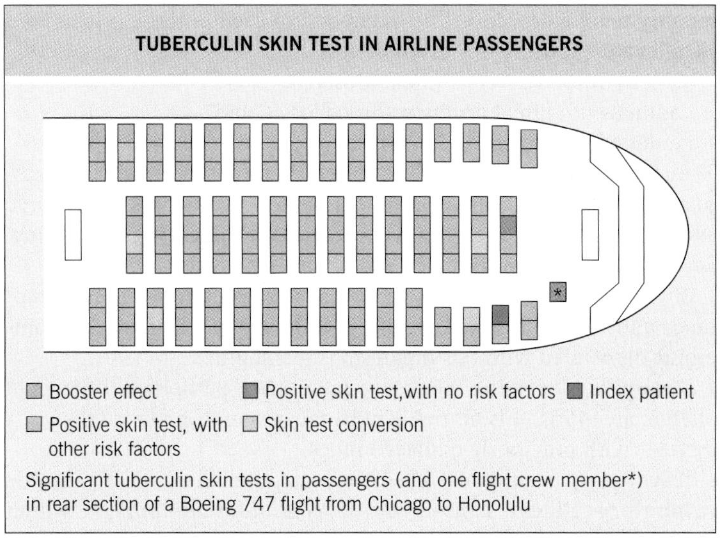

Fig. 151.2 Significant tuberculin skin tests in passengers and one flight crew member in the rear section of a Boeing 747 flight from Chicago to Honolulu.

Bacterial and fungal causes

Table 151.3 lists bacterial and fungal causes of cough in travelers. The most common cause of bacterial pneumonia among travelers is the same as among nontravelers – *Strep. pneumoniae*. This must always be considered in a recently returned traveler who has acute symptoms of fever, cough, purulent sputum and chest pain.

Legionellosis has recently been identified as an important disease among travelers because of the presence of the organism in the air conditioning systems and spas of hotels and ships.[10,11]

M. tuberculosis is a major cause of lung disease worldwide. Recently, spread of the infection among airline passengers has been reported.[12] Figure 151.2 shows a diagram of the rear section of the airplane and the evidence that six passengers and one flight crew member were exposed to tuberculosis during the 11-hour flight. Tuberculosis is particularly noteworthy at present because it is increasing in frequency after being brought under partial control early in the 20th century and as it now demonstrates increased multiantibiotic resistance.

Pneumonia caused by the plague bacillus *Yersinia pestis* must be considered in the differential diagnosis of pneumonia for a patient who has been in countries where plague may occur near ports or among wild rodent populations.[13] The pulmonary disease occurs in an environment where the more common from of the disease (bubonic plague) is being reported. Epidemic spread of this organism to the patient's contacts and health care workers may occur and is a true medical emergency.

Tularemia is another potential cause of pneumonia in those exposed to small wild animals or those who have been bitten by infected flies or ticks. Tularemia is geographically restricted and outbreaks have occurred in North America, Europe, the former Soviet Union and Japan (*Francisella tularensis*). Anthrax can be acquired by exposure to animals during slaughter, or to their hides or fur, and if the organism, *Bacillus anthracis*, is used as an agent of bioterrorism.

Pertussis, caused by the organism *Bordetella pertussis*, has been controlled by vaccine in most countries but because of incomplete immunization of children in many regions of the world, and waning immunity in adults, travelers are at risk. Recent outbreaks have occurred in the former Soviet Union and among adults in Europe.[14] It

PROTOZOAL AND HELMINTHIC CAUSES OF COUGH IN A TRAVELER			
	Condition/infecting agent	Sources of infection	Main illness
Protozoa	Malaria	Mosquitoes in Africa, Asia, South America	Fever, hemolysis, hepatitis, 'flu syndrome'
	Amebiasis	Tropics and subtropics	Fever, liver abscess, secondary pneumonia
Helminths	Filariasis	Worldwide, mainly tropics, particularly India	Eosinophilic pneumonia
	Strongyloidiasis	Contact with fecally contaminated soil	Transient pneumonia, diarrhea, severe pneumonia in those who are immunodeficient
	Ascariasis	Ingestion of fecally contaminated food or water	Transient pneumonia, intestinal obstruction
	Paragonimiasis	Ingestion of raw crabs	Chronic pneumonia
	Echinococcosis: *Echinococcus granulosus*	Contact with dog feces in cattle or sheep regions	Hepatic or lung cyst
	Echinococcus multilocularis	Contact with feces of wild carnivores in the northern hemisphere	Chronic invasive lung lesion
	Acute schistosomiasis	Contact with cercariae while swimming	Fever, dry cough

Table 151.4 Protozoal and helminthic causes of cough in a traveler.

can be the cause of both acute upper respiratory illness and prolonged paroxysmal cough. The illness is underdiagnosed because physicians have become unfamiliar with the characteristic 'gasping' cough and because special PCR or serologic tests are required for diagnosis.

Other infrequent causes of either an acute or chronic cough in the traveler include melioidosis, brucellosis, actinomycosis and pulmonary meningococcosis. The likelihood of each of these is increased by relevant exposure, for example to:

- soil in South East Asia (melioidosis);
- animals or animal products (brucellosis); and
- epidemic meningococcal disease.

The most important fungal disease acquired by the traveler is histoplasmosis. This is particularly common in travelers who have explored bat caves or areas where dead and decaying trees allow aerosolization of the organism *Histoplasma capsulatum*.[15]

Cryptococcus neoformans can be aerosolized from pigeon droppings and lead to respiratory illness, although the illness most commonly associated with this organism is meningitis.

Aspergillus fumigatus can cause pulmonary pathology other than allergic alveolitis. It is more likely to cause symptomatic disease in a traveler with previously damaged lungs.

Travelers to south-west USA may acquire an acute or chronic respiratory illness caused by *Coccidioides immitis*,[16] which is inhaled with contaminated soil. Diagnosis requires the use of appropriate serologic tests and application of skin test antigens. In South America a similar disease is caused by *Paracoccidioides brasiliensis*. Blastomycosis is endemic in the southern USA. Penicilliosis, caused by *Penicillium marneffei*, has recently been recognized in Thailand. It causes skin lesions and pulmonary symptoms.

Protozoal and helminthic causes

Table 151.4 lists important protozoa and helminths that can cause cough in a traveler. The most important protozoal cause of respiratory illness is malaria, not because the lung usually exhibits the pathology of malaria but because early in the infection malaria is often misdiagnosed as 'flu syndrome'.[17]

Entamoeba histolytica infection (amebiasis) must be considered in travelers with cough. Although the lung may be involved in severe amebiasis, cough is more commonly caused by an amebic liver abscess elevating the right diaphragm; this results in segmental atelectasis of the lung and the patient presents with a secondary bacterial pneumonia. Even without this complication, the patient may present with cough due to diaphragmatic irritation and chest pain due to the enlarged inflamed liver.

Among the most interesting patients are travelers with eosinophilia and cough (see Chapter 150). After evaluating the patient for hypersensitivity reactions that can cause cough, allergic aspergillosis and asthma, helminthic causes need to be considered. Three diseases are due to the migration phase of helminths:

- *Ascaris lumbricoides* is acquired by ingesting the eggs in fecally contaminated food or water;
- *Schistosoma* spp. are acquired by exposure to lakes or rivers containing infected cercariae; and
- *Strongyloides stercoralis* is acquired by walking near fecal deposits.

These helminths cause transient, usually undetected, febrile pulmonary illnesses unless, as in the case of strongyloidiasis, the traveler is immunosuppressed, in which case a serious and potentially fatal pneumonia may develop.

Tropical pulmonary eosinophilia (Weingarten's syndrome) is usually due to *Wuchereria bancrofti* or *Brugia malayi* and is found mainly in southern Indians and in Indonesians. Symptoms are characterized by cough, wheezing, fever with eosinophilia and fluffy infiltrates on chest X-ray. *Dirofilaria* can cause similar symptoms but usually present as a 'coin lesion' on chest X-ray.[18]

Paragonimiasis, caused by *Paragonimus* spp., most commonly *P. westermani*, is characterized by chronic cough and pulmonary symptoms very similar to those of tuberculosis. It is acquired by ingesting uncooked fresh-water crabs that contain the intermediate stage of the organism. The diagnosis is made by identifying the characteristic operculated eggs in sputum or stool.

Echinococcus multilocularis causes disease in wild animals in the northern parts of the world. Exposure to the feces of the primary hosts (wild wolves, dogs and other carnivores) primarily through eating contaminated berries or plants can lead to infection, which is manifest as progressive invasion and damage to the liver and lung. *Echinococcus granulosus* can be transmitted by the feces of dogs in domestic farms. This helminth occasionally causes lung cysts, although usually the abdominal viscera are involved.

PREVENTION

Physicians should advise appropriate vaccinations for travelers visiting potentially epidemic regions (e.g. influenza, pertussis, measles and even pneumococcal vaccine[19] and BCG[20] in some situations). Of course, influenza strains and pneumococcal serotypes may differ in the visited areas from those contained in the vaccines. Physicians should warn travelers of any epidemics in the regions to be visited. Care regarding exposure to new agents (such as SARS) includes wearing face masks and protection against spread by finger/hand contact on contaminated surfaces.

CLINICAL FEATURES

The time and character of the onset of cough must be carefully recorded because these will be closely related to its cause and so to the differential diagnosis and treatment. For example, respiratory symptoms caused by toxins or allergens occur within hours of exposure, viral illnesses occur 3–5 days after exposure and slowly progressive diseases such as tuberculosis may bring the patient to the physician weeks or months after exposure.

The nature of the patient's illness – fever, malaise and chest pain, the rapidity of onset and the degree of associated general toxicity – can distinguish acute illnesses (e.g. influenza, malaria, pneumococcal pneumonia, legionellosis, plague, psittacosis) from more chronic diseases (e.g. tuberculosis, melioidosis, paragonimiasis, tropical pulmonary eosinophilia).

The type of cough may be helpful; for example, the paroxysmal cough of chlamydial infection or pertussis can be distinguished from the rhinitis and cough of viral infections caused by rhinoviruses.

Signs and symptoms in organs other than the lung may provide important clues to the etiology, for example:

- fever and splenomegaly in malaria;
- lymphatic buboes and marked toxicity in plague;
- hepatic tenderness in amebiasis; and
- meningitis in cryptococcosis and meningococcal disease.

In many conditions, symptoms are most common in patients with pre-existing pulmonary disease. For example, on exposure to allergens or viruses asthmatic patients may wheeze and be short of breath or may present with cough and increased respiratory secretions, whereas patients with pre-existing chronic pulmonary disease may simply show a deterioration in pulmonary function demonstrated by dyspnea.

DIAGNOSIS

There are a number of questions that should be asked of the traveler with cough (Table 151.5). Once answered, the physician can begin to focus on whether special tests need to be done for unusual diseases. A flow chart for the diagnosis and treatment of cough in the traveler is shown in Figure 151.3

Immediate tests should include:

- a complete blood count and differential;
- chest radiography;
- sputum and blood culture;
- sputum Gram stain and acid-fast stain; and
- as appropriate on the basis of history of exposure, serologic or polymerase chain reaction (PCR) tests for mycoplasma, influenza, legionella, psittacosis, pertussis and the specific tests for the more unusual diseases listed above.

Patients with fever, malaise and cough who have returned from an endemic malaria area should have a malaria smear. If the patient has eosinophilia, stool and sputum examination for helminth eggs or larvae should be considered. If the patient has a leukocytosis, investigations should include serologic testing for amebiasis in addition to appropriate cultures for bacteria and fungi.

QUESTIONS TO ASK A PATIENT WHO HAS TRAVELED
Where/when/how long?
• Which countries did you visit?
• What time of year was your trip?
• How long was the trip and when did you return?
Medical history
• Do you have a history of allergy; if so to what?
• Do you have a history of lung disease such as bronchitis, emphysema, tuberculosis, bronchiectasis?
Special activities
• Did you visit caves or assist in activities such as clearing trees or debris?
• Did you experience dry, dusty or moist environmental conditions?
• Did you eat uncooked vegetables, berries or fish, or drink untreated water?
Special contacts
• Did you inhale dust, smoke or toxic fumes?
• Did you have contact with domestic or wild animals?
• Did you have contact with ill people? What illness?
• Were you bitten by mosquitoes, ticks or other arthropods?

Table 151.5 Questions to ask a patient who has traveled.

Differential diagnosis

To determine whether a patient has a common, easily managed infection or one that is difficult to diagnose and manage is a major task for the physician. A key decision to be made is whether hospitalization and full work-up are indicated (Fig. 151.3). Malaria smears or sputum examinations for paragonimus eggs on each traveler would be inappropriate. However, viewing every illness as 'flu syndrome' is inviting disaster. The correct diagnosis is arrived at by a balanced review of the detailed history, the type and severity of the signs and symptoms, and the initial laboratory tests.

Sometimes the differential diagnostic process must include the response to initial treatment. This will be helpful, for example, in distinguishing pneumococcal pneumonia, in which a response generally occurs within a few days, from other bacterial pneumonias. A diagnosis of tropical eosinophilia may not be confirmed until the patient has responded to diethylcarbamazine.

Most importantly, the physician must imagine being in the environment the traveler has been in. He or she will then take the right steps towards the correct diagnosis and treatment.

MANAGEMENT

The appropriate treatment will become clear as the correct diagnosis is made. Empiric therapy with antibiotics is seldom necessary; however, hospitalization followed by appropriate cultures and therapy for the most likely serious diagnoses is appropriate for an acutely ill patient with pneumonia. Depending on the history, in some patients with respiratory infections not requiring hospitalization, macrolide antibiotic therapy is appropriate.

Patients with respiratory symptoms after exposure to chickenpox or measles should be advised that a rash may follow and that they should avoid putting others at risk of acquiring the infection. It should be determined whether the patient has an immunodeficiency that warrants the use of immunoglobulins. The possibility of contagious disease in a traveler should be immediately reported to local public health authorities and the Centers for Disease Control in the USA.

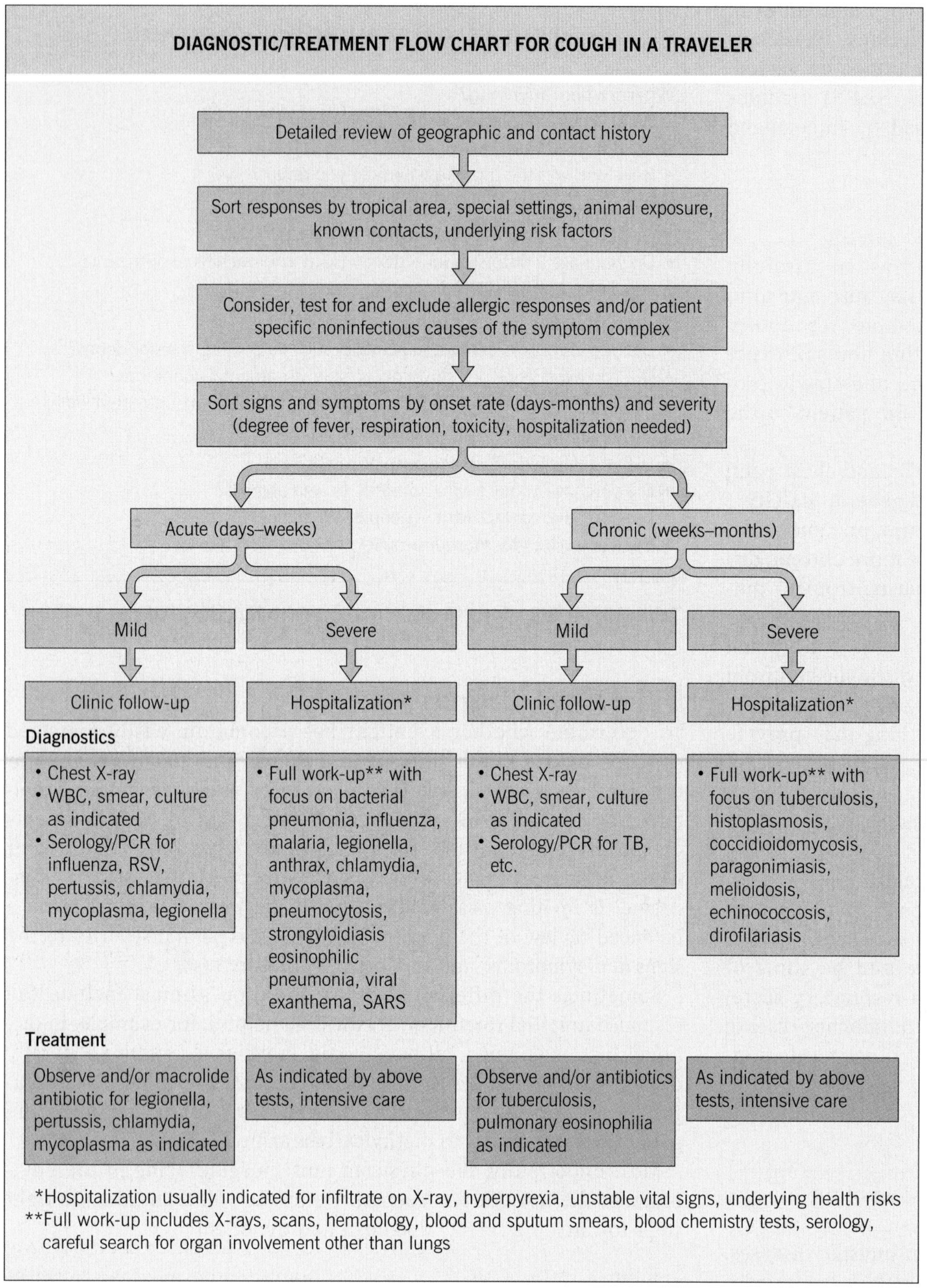
DIAGNOSTIC/TREATMENT FLOW CHART FOR COUGH IN A TRAVELER
Detailed review of geographic and contact history
Sort responses by tropical area, special settings, animal exposure, known contacts, underlying risk factors
Consider, test for and exclude allergic responses and/or patient specific noninfectious causes of the symptom complex
Sort signs and symptoms by onset rate (days-months) and severity (degree of fever, respiration, toxicity, hospitalization needed)
Acute (days–weeks)
Chronic (weeks–months)
Mild
Severe
Mild
Severe
Clinic follow-up
Hospitalization*
Clinic follow-up
Hospitalization*
Diagnostics
• Chest X-ray • WBC, smear, culture as indicated • Serology/PCR for influenza, RSV, pertussis, chlamydia, mycoplasma, legionella
• Full work-up** with focus on bacterial pneumonia, influenza, malaria, legionella, anthrax, chlamydia, mycoplasma, pneumocytosis, strongyloidiasis eosinophilic pneumonia, viral exanthema, SARS
• Chest X-ray • WBC, smear, culture as indicated • Serology/PCR for TB, etc.
• Full work-up** with focus on tuberculosis, histoplasmosis, coccidioidomycosis, paragonimiasis, melioidosis, echinococcosis, dirofilariasis
Treatment
Observe and/or macrolide antibiotic for legionella, pertussis, chlamydia, mycoplasma as indicated
As indicated by above tests, intensive care
Observe and/or antibiotics for tuberculosis, pulmonary eosinophilia as indicated
As indicated by above tests, intensive care
*Hospitalization usually indicated for infiltrate on X-ray, hyperpyrexia, unstable vital signs, underlying health risks
**Full work-up includes X-rays, scans, hematology, blood and sputum smears, blood chemistry tests, serology, careful search for organ involvement other than lungs

Fig. 151.3 Diagnostic/treatment flow chart for cough in travelers.

REFERENCES

1. Steffen R, Rickenbach M, Wilhelm U, Helminger A, Schar M. Health problems after travel to developing countries. J Infect Dis 1988;156:84–91.
2. Berman S. Epidemiology of acute respiratory infections in children in developing countries. Rev Infect Dis 1991;13(Suppl.6):S454–62.
3. Fass RJ. Aetiology and treatment of community-acquired pneumonia in adults: an historical perpective. J Antimicrob Chemother 1993;32(Suppl.A):17–27.
4. Leeper KV Jr. Severe community-acquired pneumonia. Semin Respir Infect 1996;11:96–108.
5. John TJ, Cherian T, Steinhoff MC, Simoes EA, John M. Etiology of acute respiratory infections in children in tropical Southern India. Rev Infect Dis 1993;13(Suppl.6):S463–9.
6. Kilbourne ED. Epidemiology of influenza. In: Kilbourne ED, ed. Influenza viruses and influenza. New York: Academic Press;1975:483.
7. Peiris J, Lai S, Poon L, *et al.* Coronavirus as a possible cause of severe acute respiratory syndrome. Lancet 2003;361:1319–25.
8. Ksiazek TG, Erdman D, Goldsmith CS, *et al.* A novel coronavirus associated with severe acute respiratory syndrome. N Engl J Med 2003;348:1947–58.
9. Drosten C, Günther S, Preiser W, *et al.* Identification of a novel coronavirus in patients with severe acute respiratory syndrome. www.nejm.org April 10, 2003.
10. Castellani-Pastoris M, Benedetti P, Greco D, *et al.* Six cases of travel-associated legionnaires' disease in Ischia involving four countries. Infection 1992;20:73–7.
11. Jernigan DB, Hofmann J, Cetron MS, *et al.* Outbreak of legionnaires' disease among cruise ship passengers exposed to a contaminated whirlpool spa. Lancet 1996;347:494–9.
12. Kenyon TA, Valway SE, Ihle WW, Onorato IM, Castro KG. Transmission of multi-drug resistant Mycobacterium tuberculosis during a long airplane flight. N Engl J Med 1996;334:933–8.
13. Doll JM, Zeitz PS, Ettestad P, *et al.* Cat-transmitted fatal pneumonic plague in a person who traveled from Colorado to Arizona. Am J Trop Med Hyg 1994;51:109–14.
14. Schmitt-Grohé S, Cherry JD, Heininger H, *et al.* Pertussis in German adults. Clin Infect Dis 1995;21:860–6.
15. Suzuki A, Kimura M, Kimura S, Shimada K, Miyaji M, Kaufman L. An outbreak of acute pulmonary histoplasmosis among travelers to a bat-inhabited cave in Brazil. Kansenshogaku Zasshi 1995;69:444–9.
16. Lefler E, Weiler RD, Merzbach D, Ben-Izhak O, Best LA. Traveler's coccidioidomycosis: case report of pulmonary infection diagnosed in Israel. J Clin Microbiol 1992;30:1304–6.
17. Albert S, Schroter A, Bratzke H, Brade V. Post-mortem diagnosis of tropical malaria. Dtsch Med Wochenschr 1995;120:18–22.
18. Udwadia FE. Tropical eosinophilia: a review. Respir Med 1993;87:17–21.
19. Editorial. Pneumococcal vaccination for travel to Spain? Lancet 1992;340:84–5.
20. Stevens JP, Daniel TM. Bacille Calmette-Guérin immunization of health care workers exposed to multi-drug resistant tuberculosis: a decision analysis. Tubercul Lung Dis 1996;77:315–21.

chapter 152

Lymphadenopathy, Splenomegaly and Anemia

Tom Doherty

INTRODUCTION

Lymphadenopathy is a common feature of many infectious diseases. It may be generalized or localized to one group of lymph nodes. Usually, the cause is obvious; it is commonly the result of local sepsis. Both non-specific viral infections and bacterial skin infections are common among travelers. Occasionally, however, lymphadenopathy may be due to something more exotic, particularly in travelers returning from tropical parts of the world.

Splenomegaly implies an underlying systemic illness. Anemia, unless it is very mild and has an obvious cause, requires further evaluation. Both splenomegaly and anemia are uncommon among returned travelers but both should be sufficient reason for further investigations.

'Travelers' are a heterogeneous group of people – young people in search of a bit of excitement, members of the international business community, people returning from developed countries to their original country of origin, aid workers, volunteers, missionaries and, increasingly, holidaymakers. With such an ill-defined group, it is difficult to make precise recommendations that apply to everyone. Travelers may well suffer from 'exotic' conditions such as brucellosis or Katayama fever; however, it is worth emphasizing that some pre-existing or relatively mundane disease may often explain their symptoms. For example, 9% of travelers returning from the tropics who required admission to hospital with a febrile illness were found to have a urinary tract infection, community-acquired pneumonia or a streptococcal sore throat, and another 25% were assumed to have a non-specific viral infection that settled spontaneously.

LYMPHADENOPATHY

A diagnosis of lymphadenopathy is usually a clinical one; it is therefore subjective and not uncommonly wrong. Other conditions to bear in mind include:

- abscesses, particularly in the early stages before they have become fluctuant;
- cystic lesions (in the context of tropical diseases, cysticerci and *Trichinella* deserve special mention);
- lipoma and other similar lesions such as dermoid tumors;
- aneurysms, particularly if they are full of clotted blood and therefore less likely to be pulsatile;
- migratory helminthic infections, particularly gnathostomiasis, the Calabar swellings associated with loaiasis, and onchocercal nodules;
- pyomyositis, which can develop spontaneously; and
- myiasis or 'tumbu fly'.

A list of those conditions that are associated with lymphadenopathy and of conditions that do not usually give rise to lymphadenopathy is shown in Table 152.1.

Presenting signs and symptoms that point to a diagnosis

As with any clinical problem, the diagnosis should be based on a full and detailed history and thorough general examination. In the case of returned travelers, it is essential to determine not only where they went and when they returned but precisely what they did when they were away. One useful maxim is to try to answer four questions: why did this person, from this place, develop these symptoms at this time?

A point that may be useful and is often overlooked is a person's occupation. For example, people traveling on business and staying in international hotels are unlikely to contract trypanosomiasis but agriculturists working in rural areas are more likely to do so. Tsetse flies, the vector for African trypanosomiasis, exist only in rural parts of Africa, and their bites are extremely painful and unlikely to be forgotten. A full sexual history is important. People traveling alone may be at higher risk of acquiring sexually transmitted diseases. A dietary history is often overlooked and may provide a clue to a possible diagnosis of brucellosis (from unpasteurized milk or cheese, and more often from camel's milk than cow's milk) or gnathostomiasis (from raw fish or crustaceans). The combination of alcohol intolerance, pruritus and eosinophilia combined with lymphadenopathy is suggestive of Hodgkin's lymphoma. HIV seroconversion illness can exactly mimic infection with Epstein–Barr virus (EBV). Kikuchi's disease, which causes painful, usually unilateral, cervical lymphadenopathy and a fever, is most often seen in young Japanese women.

The size of palpable lymph nodes is worth noting. In general, palpable lymph nodes less than 0.5cm in diameter are unlikely to have clinical significance, particularly in thin people. The site of the palpable lymph nodes is also important – local sepsis is more likely to result in localized lymphadenopathy than in lymphadenopathy that is generalized. Epitrochlear lymphadenopathy is of particular significance as it suggests an underlying systemic disease, specifically secondary syphilis, HIV, or a reticulosis. Remember the anatomy – lesions of the perineum drain to the inguinal group of nodes while lesions of the testes, for example, drain to the para-aortic nodes and, ultimately, to the neck. Pre-auricular nodes usually react to a lesion of the eye or to pathogens that invade through the conjunctiva. Do not forget to examine the teeth, particularly in the context of cervical lymphadenopathy.

The consistency of enlarged lymph nodes is often claimed to be of diagnostic importance. Lymphadenopathy that is due to an infectious process is often tender and asymmetric. Lymph nodes that are enlarged as a result of lymphoma are usually described as matted and 'rubbery', whereas fixed, hard, or 'craggy' nodes are more suggestive of a metastatic lesion. In practice, in most cases, such information is subjective and unreliable, and other associated findings are of greater significance. The combination of lymphadenopathy with either hepatomegaly or splenomegaly suggests a generalized process rather than local sepsis, as does the presence of anemia.

Differential diagnosis by geographic area

Many infectious diseases that give rise to lymphadenopathy are ubiquitous, particularly viral infections such as EBV, sexually transmitted diseases such as syphilis or HIV, and tuberculosis. Others

CAUSES OF LYMPHADENOPATHY		
	Causes	**Notes**
Common	Local sepsis Tonsillitis EBV Non-specific viral infection	Cause is usually obvious Particularly streptococcal Palatal petechiae, splenomegaly, atypical lymphocytes
Less common but important	HIV seroconversion illness HIV (established disease) Kaposi's sarcoma Tuberculosis Trypanosomiasis Toxoplasmosis Secondary syphilis Dengue fever Chancroid Lymphoproliferative disorder Neoplasia Sarcoidosis Leishmaniasis Typhus	Transient lymphadenopathy Permanent lymphadenopathy Localized lymphadenopathy in early infection with chancre; generalized lymphadenopathy in late infection Lymphadenopathy occurs in 50% of cases; usually mild Usually inguinal lymphadenopathy Usually metastatic lymphadenopathy Particularly hilar lymphadenopathy Cutaneous and visceral Usually painful eschar
Uncommon	*Wuchereria bancrofti* *Brugia malayi* Parvovirus Q fever Lymphogranuloma venereum Castleman's disease Rheumatoid arthritis Systemic lupus erythematosus Leptospirosis Still's disease Pityriasis rosea Cat-scratch fever	
Rare	Lepromatous leprosy Erythema nodosum leprosum Bartonellosis Tularemia Anthrax Diphtheria Plague Kikuchi's disease Ehrlichiosis Behçet's syndrome Wegener's granulomatosis Midline granuloma Whipple's disease Weber–Christian disease Podoconiosis	 Often tender Extremely tender 'buboes'

Table 152.1 Causes of lymphadenopathy (continued over page).

have relatively well-defined areas of transmission. For example, leishmaniasis is uncommon in western and southern Africa but appears to be spreading from countries bordering the Mediterranean south into Sudan and northern Kenya, and it also occurs in Central and South America and throughout much of the Indian subcontinent. Bartonellosis is confined to the Americas. Dengue is particularly common in South East Asia, West Africa and the Caribbean and often causes epidemics.

Investigations to confirm the diagnosis

In most cases, the cause of regional lymphadenopathy is obvious and requires little further investigation, if any. A throat swab may confirm a clinical suspicion of a streptococcal sore throat (and rule out the possibility of diphtheria) and a skin swab may be useful in determining appropriate antibiotic therapy for skin sepsis.

In those cases where the lymphadenopathy is more generalized, and particularly when there are systemic features, further investigations may be warranted. A normal full blood count with differential white blood cell count is reassuring. A blood film, looking specifically for atypical lymphocytes, is suggestive of infection with EBV, although atypical lymphocytes also are a feature of other viral infections and toxoplasmosis. Both the Paul–Bunnell test and monospot test for EBV may be negative in patients with the infection, and EBV serology is a more sensitive investigation.

Serologic markers for toxoplasmosis may provide useful information, particularly if facilities are available for measuring IgM as well

CAUSES OF LYMPHADENOPATHY—CONT'D		
	Causes	**Notes**
Infections usually not associated with lymphadenopathy	Brucellosis	
	Loaiasis	
	Onchocerciasis	Secondary infection of scratched skin may result in lymphadenopathy
	Malaria	
	Hepatitis	
	Typhoid	Lymphadenopathy has been reported in chronic salmonellosis
	Tuberculoid leprosy	
	Schistosomiasis	May occur in acute disease
	Flaviviruses	
	South American trypanosomiasis (chronic form)	
	Intestinal helminths	
	Strongyloides spp.	
	Hydatid disease	
	Cholera	
	Tetanus	
	Melioidosis	
	Cysticercosis	
	Amebiasis	
	Fascioliasis	

Table 152.1 Causes of lymphadenopathy—Cont'd.

as IgG. A negative Venereal Disease Research Laboratory (VDRL) test virtually excludes secondary syphilis. HIV antibody tests may be negative during a seroconversion illness, and measurement of p24 antigenemia or HIV RNA may be more informative. Serologic markers exist for cytomegalovirus and parvovirus infections, although their clinical relevance is questionable. *Leishmania* serology is nearly always negative in patients with cutaneous disease but almost always positive in those with visceral disease, as long as they are not also infected with HIV. Most patients with both HIV and visceral leishmaniasis do not mount a serologic response.

For patients with a history of systemic upset or chronic disease, markers of inflammation such as the erythrocyte sedimentation rate, C-reactive protein and serum albumin concentration may be helpful. However, the erythrocyte sedimentation rate may be greatly elevated in residents of tropical countries, particularly in Africa, as a result of non-specific hyperglobulinemia. A Mantoux test is usually positive in patients with tuberculous lymphadenopathy, unless they have miliary disease or hypoalbuminemia.

Imaging may also be useful. A chest radiograph may provide evidence of hilar lymphadenopathy and suggest sarcoidosis or tuberculosis. Abdominal ultrasonography with or without computerized tomography (CT) scanning may not only confirm the presence of intra-abdominal lymphadenopathy but also enable accurate biopsy material to be obtained. Sometimes, isotope scanning with either indium or gallium may define an unexpected local source of infection.

In certain cases, where the diagnosis is in doubt (and particularly in the context of systemic illness), more invasive investigations are warranted. Fine-needle aspiration of enlarged lymph nodes may provide a diagnosis in case of tuberculosis, trypanosomiasis and neoplastic disease. In most sites, open biopsy of enlarged lymph nodes can be performed under local anesthesia and, although it is helpful to cut across the excised node to discover tuberculous caseation, histologic examination of the tissue obtained may be necessary to provide the answer. In general terms it is advisable not to choose inguinal nodes for biopsy – those in the neck are more likely to generate useful information.

Bone marrow aspiration and liver biopsy specimens may occasionally be required to confirm or refute a diagnosis of tuberculosis or a lymphoproliferative disorder. Liver biopsy is of particular significance in patients with lymphomas as it provides information regarding the staging of the disease. To reduce the risk of iatrogenic complications, it may be appropriate to obtain biopsy material under direct imaging, either ultrasound or CT, where such facilities are available. Beware of taking biopsies from inguinal nodes in patients with suspected lymphatic filariasis – both lymphatic leakage and secondary infections occur not uncommonly.

Complications

Lymphadenopathy is unlikely to lead to any serious complications. Tuberculous nodes, especially *Mycobacterium bovis* infections in the neck, not uncommonly break down and suppurate – and the addition of oral steroids to antituberculous therapy may reduce the degree of scarring should this occur. Similarly, metastatic lymph nodes may ulcerate, but usually in the late stages of the disease. Very large intrathoracic lymph nodes can compress the major airways and other structures. The treatment depends on the nature of the underlying condition.

SPLENOMEGALY

Presenting signs and symptoms that point to a diagnosis

Splenomegaly may be part of an acute febrile illness or of a more chronic underlying process. Commonly, the differential diagnosis for these two situations differs, although there is some overlap. A list of the causes of splenomegaly is provided in Table 152.2.

Malaria

In a traveler recently returned from the tropics with a febrile illness, the most important diagnosis is *Plasmodium falciparum* malaria; this must be excluded. In acute malaria, the spleen is often enlarged, although not greatly so; however, the absence of clinical splenomegaly is of little value in excluding the diagnosis. In a series of 482 cases of malaria admitted to a single hospital in Canada over a 12-year period, only 24% had detectable splenomegaly at the time of admission.

CAUSES OF SPLENOMEGALY	
Mild splenomegaly	*Malaria* *EBV* *Hepatitis* *Typhoid and other salmonelloses* *Tuberculosis* *Dengue fever* *Katayama fever* *Toxoplasmosis* *Cytomegalovirus* *HIV* *Leptospirosis* *Brucellosis* *Sepsis* *Trypanosomiasis* *Histoplasmosis* Rheumatoid arthritis Systemic lupus erythematosus Hemaglobinopathies Sarcoidosis Lepromatous leprosy and erythema nodosum leprosum Amyloidosis
Moderate splenomegaly	Lymphoproliferative disorder Subacute bacterial endocarditis Splenic abscess Portal hypertension due to *chronic schistosomiasis*
Marked splenomegaly	*Visceral leishmaniasis* *Hyperreactive malarious splenomegaly* Myelofibrosis Chronic myeloid leukemia Glycogen storage diseases

Table 152.2 Causes of splenomegaly. Each section reflects the importance and/or frequency of the various conditions. The italic type shows the conditions that are more likely to occur in travelers.

Tropical splenomegaly syndrome, recently reclassified as hyperreactive malarial splenomegaly, is a poorly understood condition. It is uncommon in travelers but does occur. Several diagnostic criteria have been proposed, including hyperglobulinemia, pancytopenia, strongly positive malaria serology (particularly IgM), a negative blood film for malaria parasites and perisinusoidal lymphocytosis on liver biopsy specimens. The condition represents an inappropriate immunologic response to malaria. Usually the splenomegaly responds to long-term treatment with antimalarial drugs, either weekly chloroquine, daily proguanil or both. Those cases that prove refractory usually turn out to be misdiagnosed cases of lymphoma.

Dengue fever

Dengue fever commonly mimics malaria and is increasing both in frequency and in geographic distribution. The 'classical' rash of dengue fever is petechial, but in practice it is more often morbilliform in the early stages, at least in travelers. A generalized erythematous reaction that blanches with pressure is suggestive of the diagnosis, but both these signs are difficult to see, particularly on dark skin (Fig. 152.1). The combination of severe low back pain, pain in the long bones and retro-orbital pain, particularly when this is accentuated by extreme lateral gaze, is very suggestive of a diagnosis of dengue. Although splenomegaly is unusual among children with the disease in endemic areas, most travelers with dengue have some degree of splenomegaly.

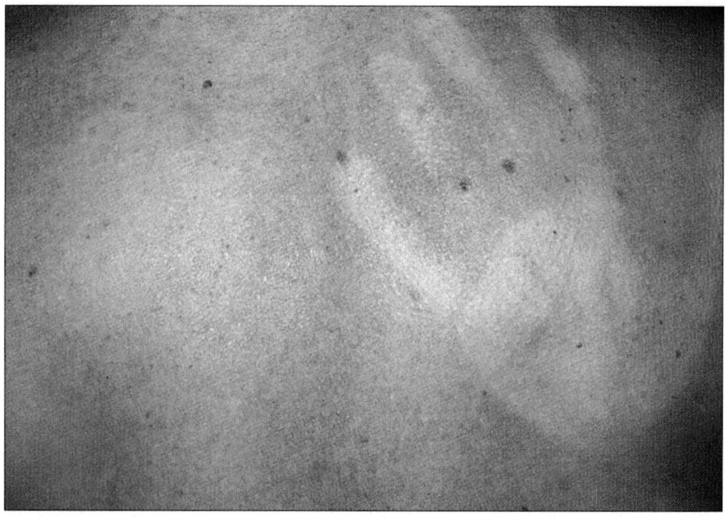

Fig. 152.1 Early rash of dengue fever.

Typhoid

Splenomegaly is a common feature of patients with typhoid fever, particularly in the second week of the illness, and it also occurs in patients with nontyphoid salmonelloses and in patients with *Shigella* infections. Several features suggest a diagnosis of typhoid. Usually, patients with the disease are clinically extremely unwell; cough, abdominal pain with either constipation or diarrhea, and neurologic symptoms may all occur. Although the fever of malaria may spike and return to normal values, patients with typhoid usually have fevers that fluctuate to some extent but rarely return to baseline. The value of features such as a relative bradycardia has been overemphasized. Rose spots (pale pink papules on the upper trunk extending into the axillae) are difficult to see, even on Caucasian skin, and occur at least as commonly with nontyphoid salmonelloses as with typhoid. Splenomegaly is common, but again its absence does not rule out the diagnosis.

Epstein–Barr virus infection

Epstein–Barr virus (EBV) infection is common in tropical countries, particularly in Africa. It causes an acute febrile illness, often associated with a sense of misery, lethargy and profound malaise. Splenomegaly occurs in most cases; usually there is associated lymphadenopathy with or without palatal petechiae, both of which are uncommon in malaria or typhoid. An idiosyncratic morbilliform rash after ampicillin is an avoidable but characteristic sign. Although EBV infection is more common among children and young adults, it can cause severe disease even in late middle age, and has been associated with acute splenic rupture.

Visceral leishmaniasis

Kala-azar, or visceral leishmaniasis, is widely distributed in India and is currently epidemic in southern Sudan and northern Kenya. In addition, its frequency is increasing and its epidemiology is changing in response to the immunosuppression associated with HIV. Visceral leishmaniasis is found in as many as 17% of HIV-positive symptomatic people in southern Mediterranean countries.

Classically, it presents as a chronic febrile illness associated with considerable systemic upset and associated wasting. The spleen is usually firm and grossly enlarged. Pancytopenia is common. *Leishmania* serology is invariably positive in immunocompetent people but in only about 40% of patients co-infected with HIV. The parasite is often identifiable in biopsies of the reticuloendothelial system, including bone marrow, spleen, lymph nodes and liver tissue.

Schistosomiasis

Katayama fever is a poorly understood immunologic condition that is apparently triggered by the onset of ovulation by maturing schistosomulae, which usually occurs 4–6 weeks after exposure to infected water. It occurs most commonly in people who have not previously been exposed to schistosomiasis and is less common with *Schistosoma haematobium* than with either *Schistosoma mansoni* or *Schistosoma japonicum*. Only a small minority of people who become infected with schistosomiasis develop the syndrome – probably fewer than 1%.

A diagnosis of Katayama fever can only be made on clinical grounds, as there is no definitive investigation. As it occurs in response to ovulation, examination of stool or urine for schistosome ova is usually negative and serologic responses only become positive once the acute symptoms have resolved. Splenomegaly occurs in approximately 25% of affected people, usually in combination with a brisk rise in the total eosinophil count and non-specific changes in liver function tests. Urticarial reactions and hepatomegaly may also occur.

Splenomegaly is also a feature of established schistosomiasis, commonly the result of portal hypertension resulting from the periportal hepatic fibrosis associated with *S. mansoni*. However, although long-term sequelae of this kind may be common in endemic areas, they are very rare among travelers. As the liver damage that results from schistosomiasis is the result of fibrosis induced by a granulomatous response to egg antigens (with a characteristic pattern on liver biopsy), hepatic function is usually preserved when assessed with conventional liver function tests. Schistosomal serology is usually, but not always, positive. Often the adult worms have died of old age by the time the diagnosis is made, and therefore ova are not commonly found in stool or urine or in rectal snips. Similarly, eosinophilia, associated with early infection, is uncommon in established disease.

HIV

The seroconversion illness of HIV infection mimics that of EBV infection, and transient splenomegaly, lymphadenopathy, atypical lymphocytosis and a morbilliform rash may all occur. As the acute illness resolves, the spleen returns to normal. However, as the HIV syndrome continues, both lymphadenopathy and splenomegaly may recur as part of the AIDS-related complex.

Other causes of splenomegaly

Patients with acute hepatitis may have splenomegaly but the diagnosis is relatively easy to confirm. Leptospirosis is uncommon among travelers but has been reported, particularly in military personnel; exposure may occur during white-water rafting and pot-holing. Tuberculosis, brucellosis, trypanosomiasis and histoplasmosis are all uncommon among travelers but each does occur. Infectious endocarditis is well recognized as a cause of splenomegaly but is no more common among travelers than among the indigenous population. Equally, noninfectious causes of splenomegaly, such as autoimmune disease and lymphoproliferative disorders, may need to be excluded. Adult Still's disease is an uncommon condition and one that is difficult to diagnose; it is therefore easily missed, but the clinical picture includes fever and splenomegaly.

ANEMIA

Anemia is uncommon among travelers. When it does occur, the differential diagnosis is very similar to that among the indigenous population. Broadly speaking, anemia results from one or a combination of: a deficiency of iron, folate or vitamin B12; chronic blood loss; decreased red cell survival; chronic disease; or bone marrow aplasia.

Any patient with significant anemia for which there is no immediately obvious cause should ideally be admitted to hospital for investigation. The basic work up for any such patient should follow conventional lines, including a full history and clinical examination. Questions regarding blood loss, menorrhagia, systemic upset, nutrition, use of nonsteroidal anti-inflammatory drugs and pre-existing disorders such as abnormal red cell phenotypes are obviously important. Examination should focus particularly on the mucous membranes (for evidence of bleeding), the spleen and lymph nodes (for evidence of an underlying inflammatory process), a rectal and vaginal exam-ination where appropriate (for evidence of blood loss or malabsorption), and some assessment of nutritional status.

A few particular diagnoses deserve special mention. Chronic malaria, especially due to infection with *Plasmodium vivax*, can present with marked anemia and splenomegaly, but anemia is relatively uncommon in travelers with acute *P. falciparum* infection. Visceral leishmaniasis invariably results in some degree of anemia, and the anemia may be profound. Tropical sprue appears to be decreasing in frequency; although it has been reported most commonly from the Indian subcontinent, sporadic cases do occur among travelers to sub-Saharan Africa, and often these patients have a macrocytic anemia. Intestinal helminthic infections are often cited as a cause of anemia; in practice, this is very unlikely in returning travelers. Of the common intestinal helminths, only hookworm actually consume blood from the host. Each worm only consumes 0.6–1.0ml of blood per day and, in common with other helminthiases (except *Strongyloides* sp.), hookworms are unable to multiply within the gastrointestinal tract. Although people who live in tropical areas, particularly children, may have very high worm burdens as a result of repeated infection, and often survive on a poor diet with the added burden of repeated malaria attacks – all factors that make anemia very likely – such factors are uncommon in adult travelers.

INVESTIGATIONS TO CONFIRM THE DIAGNOSIS OF SPLENOMEGALY AND/OR ANEMIA

A suggested schedule for the investigation of travelers with either splenomegaly or anemia is shown in (Table 152.3). A few points are worth emphasizing. Malaria can only be excluded after repeated blood film examinations, particularly in those patients with low parasitemia and in those taking chemoprophylactic agents. Mefloquine, in particular, has a long half-life and may delay the time taken for symptoms to develop. Alternative strategies – for example, the use of dipstick techniques such as the ICT test – may replace microscopy in the future, particularly in settings where staff have relatively little experience in identifying low-density infections.

Aspiration of the spleen to confirm a diagnosis of visceral leishmaniasis is a relatively safe procedure; however, it should only be performed by experienced practitioners and ideally under ultrasound control. Any aspirate should be cultured as well as subjected to microscopy; the polymerase chain reaction is now the method of choice for identifying the infecting strain of *Leishmania*. As with liver biopsy, the procedure should only be undertaken once clotting indices and a platelet count have been measured and a supply of compatible and safe blood identified.

Fiberoptic endoscopy to biopsy the mucosa of the small intestine is the investigation of choice in cases of suspected sprue. Endoscopy has the added advantage of enabling aspiration of jejunal fluid, which can be examined for the presence of *Giardia* or *Strongyloides* spp. in particular. It is worth remembering that celiac disease is not confined to children; it can present even in late middle age. Measurement of anti-endomysial antibodies may be useful.

Other serologic tests may be useful but several measurements may be necessary to confirm a diagnosis and a change in titer may be

SUGGESTED REASONS FOR SPLENOMEGALY AND ANEMIA IN A PATIENT RECENTLY RETURNED FROM ABROAD	
Initial investigations	Thick and thin blood films for malaria (repeated several times) Blood cultures (repeated several times) Full blood count (red cell indices, white cell count, evidence of hypersplenism) Blood film examination (atypical lymphocytes; red cell morphology; evidence of hemolysis)
If anemia predominates	Serum iron Transferrin, total iron binding capacity Red cell folate Vitamin B12 Fecal occult blood (repeated several times) Hemoglobin electrophoresis Also consider: bone marrow aspirate endoscopy
Serologic investigations	EBV Toxoplasmosis Cytomegalovirus Malaria immunofluorescent antibody test Schistosomal ELISA Brucella Leishmania Widal agglutination test HIV Histoplasmosis Acute and convalescent sera for dengue fever and other flaviviruses
Imaging	Abdominal ultrasound and CT Chest radiography Indium-labeled white blood cell scan Labeled red blood cell survival scan
Tissue diagnosis	Liver biopsy Splenic aspiration

Table 152.3 Suggested reasons for splenomegaly and anemia in a patient recently returned from abroad. ELISA, enzyme-linked immunosorbent assay.

more valuable than a single reading. Imaging techniques are very useful – sarcoidosis, for example, gives a characteristic appearance on chest radiograph. Tissue biopsy of bone marrow, liver or spleen may well be indicated, particularly in more complicated cases, and biopsies that are taken under either ultrasound or CT guidance are rather more likely to provide useful material.

Further reading

Arnow PM, Flaherty JP. Fever of unknown origin. Lancet 1997;350:575–80.

Alvar J, Gutierrez-Solar B, Molina R, *et al.* Prevalence of *Leishmania* infection among AIDS patients. Lancet 1992;339:1427.

Bloor M, Thomas M, Hood K, *et al.* Differences in sexual risk behaviour between young men and women travelling abroad from the UK. Lancet 1998:352:1664–8.

Cobelens FGJ, van Deutekom H, Draayer-Jansen IWE, *et al.* Risk of infection with *Mycobacterium tuberculosis* in travellers to areas of high tuberculosis endemicity. Lancet 2000;356:461–5.

Day JH, Behrens RH. Delay in onset of malaria with mefloquine prophylaxis. Lancet 1995;345:398.

Doherty JF, Grant AD, Bryceson ADM. Fever as the presenting complaint of travellers returning from the tropics. Q J Med 1995;88:277–81.

Doherty JF, Moody AH, Wright SG. Katayama fever: an acute manifestation of schistosomiasis. Br Med J 1996;313:1071–2.

Humar A, Keystone J. Evaluating fever in travellers returning from tropical countries. BMJ 1996;312:953–6.

O'Brien D, Tobin S, Brown GV, Torresi J. Fever in returned travelers: review of hospital admissions for a 3-year period. CID 2001;33:603–9.

Ryan ET, Wilson ME, Kain KC. Illness after international travel. N Engl J Med 2002;347:505–16.

Singh N, Valecha N, Sharma VP. Malaria diagnosis by field workers using an immunochromatographic test. Trans R Soc Trop Med Hyg 1997;91:396–7.

Svenson JE, MacLean JD, Gyorkos TW, Keystone J. Imported malaria: clinical presentation and examination of symptomatic travellers. Arch Intern Med 1995;155:861–8.

chapter

153 Animal Bites and Rabies

Charles E Rupprecht

INTRODUCTION

An estimated 4.4 million persons sustain animal bites annually in the USA.[1] These bites range in severity from insignificant to fatal maulings. Sequelae include disfigurement, dismemberment, envenomation, localized infection of soft tissues and deep structures, as well as rabies and other systemic infections.[2]

Rabies is a viral zoonosis transmitted via the saliva of infected mammals. The virus spreads to the central nervous system, causing an encephalomyelitis which progresses to coma and death. On average, 1–2 cases of human rabies and 5000–10,000 cases of animal rabies are reported in the USA each year, 90% diagnosed in wild animals.[3] Worldwide, an estimated 50,000 cases of human rabies occur per year according to the World Health Organization. Between 1960 and 1979, eight (22%) of the 37 cases of human rabies diagnosed in the USA were acquired abroad, whereas 13 (33%) of the 39 cases of human rabies that occurred since 1980 were acquired outside the USA.[3,4]

PRESENTING SIGNS AND SYMPTOMS THAT POINT TO THE DIAGNOSIS

Patients either present for first aid immediately after a bite or considerably later with signs and symptoms of a bite-related infection.

It is important to determine the extent of the injury and the structures involved in the bite. Feline teeth can penetrate deeply into tendons, bones and joints, in contrast to dog bites, which are more likely to devitalize large areas of soft tissue by crushing injury.[5] Besides the common organisms that are isolated from bite wounds, which include *Staphylococcus, Streptococcus* and *Corynebacterium* spp., the type of animal involved can also help to implicate other specific pathogens that are known to cause well-defined syndromes (Table 153.1). When a patient presents with cellulitis 12–24 hours after cat bite, the likely agent is *Pasteurella multocida* rather than the patient's skin flora, which usually requires an incubation period of 24 hours or longer. Although specific case histories have documented etiologic agents associated with animal bites other than those listed in Table 153.1 (e.g. *Francisella* spp., *Yersinia* spp., nonoxidative Gram-negative rods, etc.), these other instances appear rather uncommon.

Rabies virus is transmitted in the saliva of mammals, almost always by a bite. Rabies in humans has an incubation period of 1–3 months, but occasionally periods may be as short as a week or last as long as several years. Early symptoms include a nonspecific flu-like prodromal illness with headache, fatigue and fever associated with paresthesiae at the site of the bite or proximal to it. These symptoms are followed by the onset of an acute neurological phase with anxiety, irritability and other behavioral changes. Some patients develop classic 'furious' rabies, characterized by periods of hyperactivity, disorientation, hallucinations and other bizarre behaviors alternating with periods of calm. Additional signs and symptoms can include autonomic instability manifested as hyperthermia, tachycardia and hypersalivation, as well as hydrophobia and aerophobia. This phase of disease rapidly progresses to seizures, coma and death, usually within 10 days of the first onset. Occasionally, patients present with 'dumb' rabies and develop flu-like symptoms, paralysis and finally disorientation, coma and death.

DIFFERENTIAL DIAGNOSIS BY GEOGRAPHIC AREA

Most people who sustain an animal bite are able to provide an adequate history of the type of animal, the location and the circumstances that may have provoked the event. Thus, the differential diagnosis is not directly related to the type of trauma that caused the injury, but rather to the organisms that are likely to result in infection due to the bite. Comprehensive lists of bacterial flora that have been cultured from the mouths and bite wounds of various animals have been published elsewhere, together with case reports of rare exotic pathogens that have been transmitted by a bite at least once. In general, the organisms that most often cause bite-related infections are the Gram-positive skin flora of the victim and the bacteria that reside in the animal's mouth, which are predominantly Gram-negative rods and anaerobes.[5] There is no known variation to this generalization by major geographic regions.

In rabies, however, there is significant geographic variability in both the incidence and the species that are likely to transmit the virus. In the early 1940s in the USA, dogs were the predominant reservoir for rabies.[3] With the utilization of rabies vaccines for domesticated dogs and stray animal control laws, the total number of cases of canine rabies decreased substantially and wildlife rabies cases increased. Today, on the eastern coast of the USA, the predominant reservoir for rabies is the racoon. In California and the upper and lower mid-west, skunks account for the majority of animal rabies cases. Rabid bats have been diagnosed in all of the continental states of the USA.[3] A case of rabies occured recently in a bat-handler in Scotland. Outside the USA, regions of South East Asia, Africa and Latin America have large populations of stray dogs that are unvaccinated, and in these regions an unprovoked dog bite should always lead to active consideration of rabies. Figure 153.1 illustrates the predominant types of rabid animals in different regions. The World Health Organization maintains a list of countries that are supposedly rabies free or that have achieved secondary elimination (internet access: http://www.rabnet.who.int). Knowledge of this situation can help in deciding whether patients should receive postexposure prophylaxis (PEP).

INVESTIGATIONS TO CONFIRM THE DIAGNOSIS

Specific diagnostic tests may have limited value in the initial evaluation of animal bites. Radiographs can be used if there is concern about fractures or embedded foreign bodies. Cultures of fresh bite wounds are likely to produce positive results, but not all patients will develop infection. If infection results, the recovered organisms may not be the cause. Patients presenting later with established infections should be evaluated according to standard procedures for skin and soft tissue infections. Such evaluations should include a white blood

PATHOGENS ASSOCIATED WITH BITES FROM SPECIFIC ANIMALS		
Animal	**Pathogen**	**Comments**
Dog	*Capnocytophaga canimorsus*	Causes a sepsis syndrome in asplenic patients
Cat	*Bartonella henselae* *Pasteurella multocida*	The agent of cat-scratch disease Causes an aggressive soft-tissue infection, usually within 24 hours of inoculation
Macaque	Herpesvirus simiae (B virus)	Macaques can be asymptomatic carriers, whereas the disease is fatal in other monkeys; postexposure prophylaxis not routinely recommended; documented infections can be treated with aciclovir[6]
Rat	*Streptobacilus moniliformis* *Spirillum minus*	Cause of rat-bite fever; occurs 7–10 days after a bite with fever, chills, headache, rash on palms and soles, and arthritis Cause of rat-bite fever; longer incubation period with fever and regional adenopathy; arthritis and rash less prominent
Fresh-water species	*Aeromonas hydrophila*	Snake and leech bites have also resulted in *Aeromonas* infections
Salt-water species	*Vibrio* spp.	Can present with an ulcerating lesion at the site of inoculation and bacteremia
Mammal	Rabies	All mammals are capable of transmitting rabies by biting, but carnivores and bats predominate

Table 153.1 Pathogens associated with bites from specific animals.

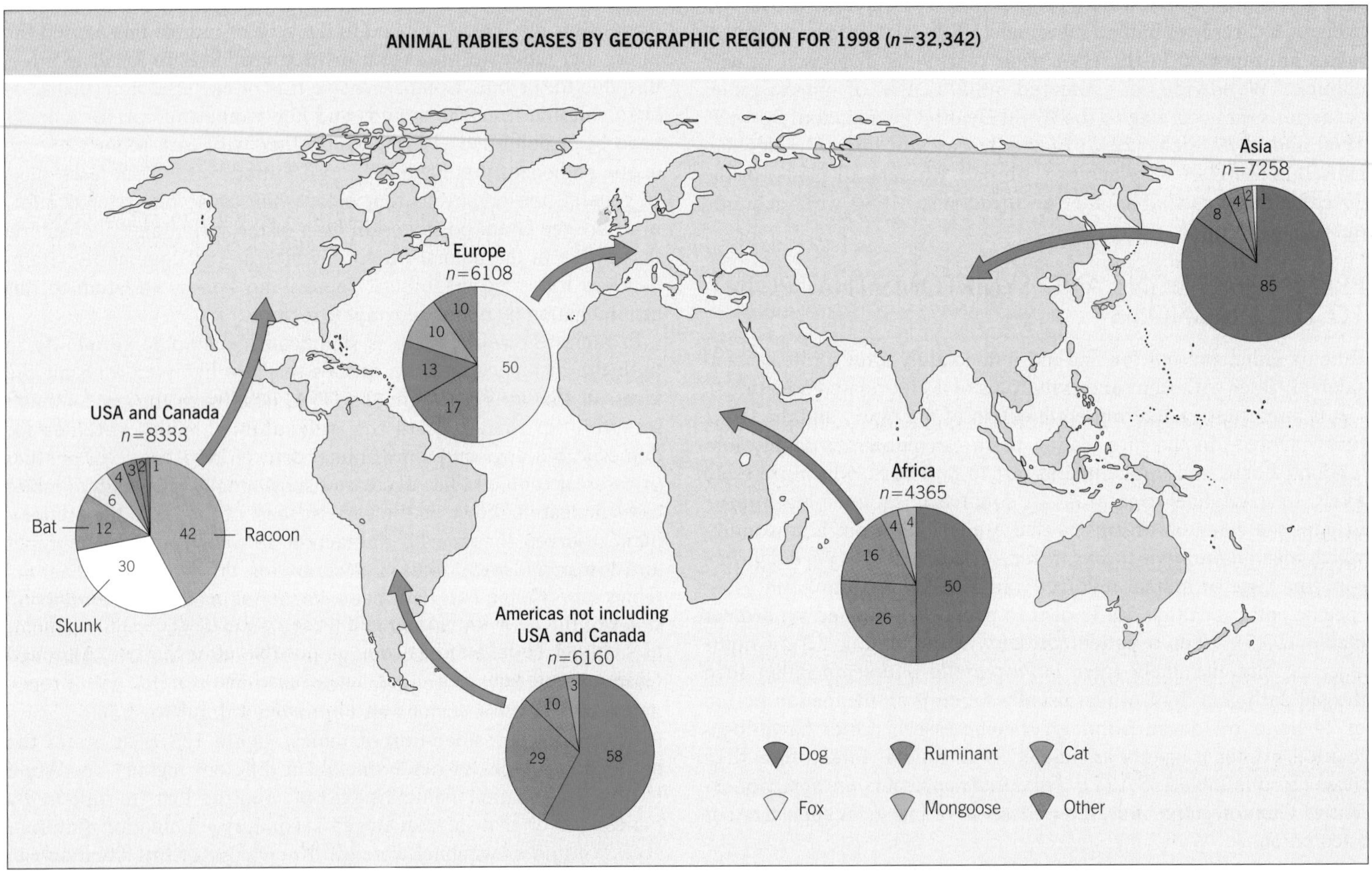

Fig. 153.1 Animal rabies cases by geographic region for 1998. A total of 32,342 cases are displayed here. According to WHO sources in the 34th World Survey (Via Rabnet document, 2000, WHO/CDS/CSR/APH/99.6), based upon data from 110 countries reporting out of 193 members, wildlife rabies predominates in some regions, such as the USA and Canada, whereas dogs remain a significant reservoir in many other countries. Values shown are percentages. (Note: Rabies has been diagnosed among bats in Australia but these do not appear in the above report.)

cell count and appropriate cultures that can be used later to adjust ad hoc antimicrobial therapy.

Before the onset of symptoms, there are no diagnostic tests for assessing exposure to rabies virus. Rather, to rule out the likelihood that a patient has been exposed to the virus, the biting animal should be captured and either put into quarantine for observation over a sufficient time frame or euthanized so that appropriate samples of brain tissue can be examined for the presence of rabies virus antigen, using the direct fluorescent antibody test http://www.cdc.gov/ncidod/dvrd/rabies/professional/publications/DFA_diagnosis/DFA_protocol-b.htm). The length of time a domestic animal needs to be under observation to determine if it was rabid at the time of the bite

RECOMMENDATION FOR RABIES POSTEXPOSURE PROPHYLAXIS			
Geographic area	Mammals*	Prophylaxis recommendations†‡	
		Bite	Non-bite
Group 1: Rabies enzootic or suspected in species involved in the exposure	Bat, racoon, skunk, fox, coyote; mongoose in Puerto Rico; stray dogs and cats along border with Mexico	Treat	Treat
Group 2: Rabies not enzootic in species involved in the exposure but reported in other animals in region (e.g. most of continental USA)	Most wild carnivores (wolf, cougar, bobcat, bear, etc.)	Treat	Treat or consult
	Domestic dogs, cats and ferrets	Observe or consult	Observe or consult
	Wild rodents and lagomorphs, except groundhogs	Consult or do not treat	Do not treat
	Livestock	Consult or do not treat	Do not treat
Group 3: Rabies not enzootic in species involved in the exposure and only sporadic reports in region (e.g. Pacific North-West)	Dogs, cats, other domestic animals and many wild terrestrial animals	Consult or do not treat	Consult or do not treat
Group 4: Rabies not reported in region (e.g. Hawaii, Guam, Samoa, Virgin Islands, etc.)	Any terrestrial mammal	Do not treat	Do not treat

* All mammals are susceptible to rabies, but reservoirs include bats and certain carnivores. Small rodent bites are common, but almost never require prophylaxis.
† 'Consult' means consultation with a knowledgeable state or local health department, especially if the animal is not available for testing or observation. If the risk of rabies in the species involved in the exposure is considered low and the animal's brain is available for testing, prophylaxis may sometimes be delayed for up to 48 hours, pending the results of laboratory diagnosis. A healthy domestic dog, cat or ferret that bites a person should be confined and observed for 10 days. Any illness in the animal should be evaluated by a qualified veterinarian and reported immediately to the local health unit. If signs suggestive of rabies develop, human prophylaxis is begun immediately. If the suspected animal is determined to be a stray dog, cat or ferret, rather than confined, it may be euthanized, the head removed and the package shipped, under refrigeration, for examination by a qualified diagnostic laboratory.
‡ Rabies may develop in ~<1 to >70% of untreated humans bitten by a rabid animal (depending in part upon species, route, dose, severity, etc.) and in ~<0.1 to 1–2% of those untreated after direct exposure to a rabid animal but not bitten (e.g. licked on an open wound or mucous membrane, or scratched).

Table 153.2 Recommendation for rabies postexposure prophylaxis. The regimens are applicable for all age groups, including children. The deltoid area is an acceptable site of vaccination in adults and older children; the outer aspect of the thigh may be used in younger children. Vaccine should never be administered in the gluteal area. People who are previously vaccinated are those with a history of pre-exposure vaccination with HDCV, PCEC or RVA, prior postexposure prophylaxis with HDCV, PCEC or RVA, or previous vaccination with any other type of rabies vaccine and documented history of antibody response to the prior vaccination. HDCV, human diploid cell vaccine; RVA, rabies vaccine absorbed; PCEC, purifed chick embryo cell. Information from Centers for Disease Control and Prevention, 1999.[9]

depends on the species of animal. In practice, only domestic dogs, cats and ferrets undergo a 10-day observation period. Other animals are usually euthanized because the length of the viral shedding period has not been determined.[7] Rabies should be included in the differential diagnosis of any suspected acute progressive viral encephalitis, regardless of a history of animal bite.[8] Once a patient develops symptomatic rabies, available diagnostic tests include assays for viral antibodies in the serum or cerebrospinal fluid (CSF); viral isolation from CSF or saliva; viral antigen detection in biopsies of skin, corneal impressions or brain tissue; and reverse transcription polymerase chain reaction of saliva, CSF or related tissues (such as salivary glands or brain tissue).[3,4,8,9]

A thorough history of the type of animal, the location and the circumstances surrounding the incident should be noted. Many animal bites are provoked.[5] Unprovoked attacks by animals exhibiting unusual behavior are more likely to be rabies exposures.[9] If the bite was caused by an animal that is likely to have rabies in that particular geographic location, that animal should be confined or euthanized.[9] If the animal tests positive or if it is unavailable for testing, the patient should receive rabies PEP (Table 153.2). Regardless of the length of the interval between true rabies exposure and presentation of the healthy patient, PEP should be initiated as soon as possible after the bite. Although rabies is uniformly fatal once symptoms have started, with proper intervention the disease is essentially completely preventable.

IMMEDIATE MANAGEMENT

One of the most important steps in the initial management of animal bites to decrease the incidence of infection, including rabies, is aggressive cleansing of the wounds with copious irrigation and debridement of devitalized tissue. Issues that remain controversial are whether to apply primary sutures to the wound and whether to prescribe prophylactic antibiotics.

Most bites that receive medical attention within a few hours can be cleaned and sutured immediately, especially if rabies is not a concern, so as to avoid the opportunity of viral contamination to deeper tissues. Otherwise, wounds are packed, observed and either sutured later or allowed to heal by secondary intention. Prophylactic antibiotics may be indicated for some high-risk events, such as facial bites and involvement of deep structures such as tendons and joints.[5] In addition, patients should be up to date with tetanus vaccination.

COMPLICATIONS

Figure 153.2 illustrates the case of a person from the USA who was bitten by a dog while traveling abroad.[10] There were multiple opportunities to receive PEP, yet it did not occur. Patients traveling to rabies-endemic regions who are likely to be more than 24–48 hours away from appropriate medical care are candidates for pre-exposure vaccination.[9] They should be counseled that, despite pre-exposure vaccination, boosters would be required if they were to be bitten.

Recommendations for reducing the frequency of animal bites include both education and public policy initiatives. Potential owners of animals should be discouraged from trying to tame or handle wildlife, such as racoons or bats, and should consider more docile breeds of dog. Behavioral training should be directed at both dogs and children to ensure that animals are properly socialized and that children are taught proper conduct around animals. Responsible pet ownership should be promoted and all stray and wildlife should be avoided.[7,9]

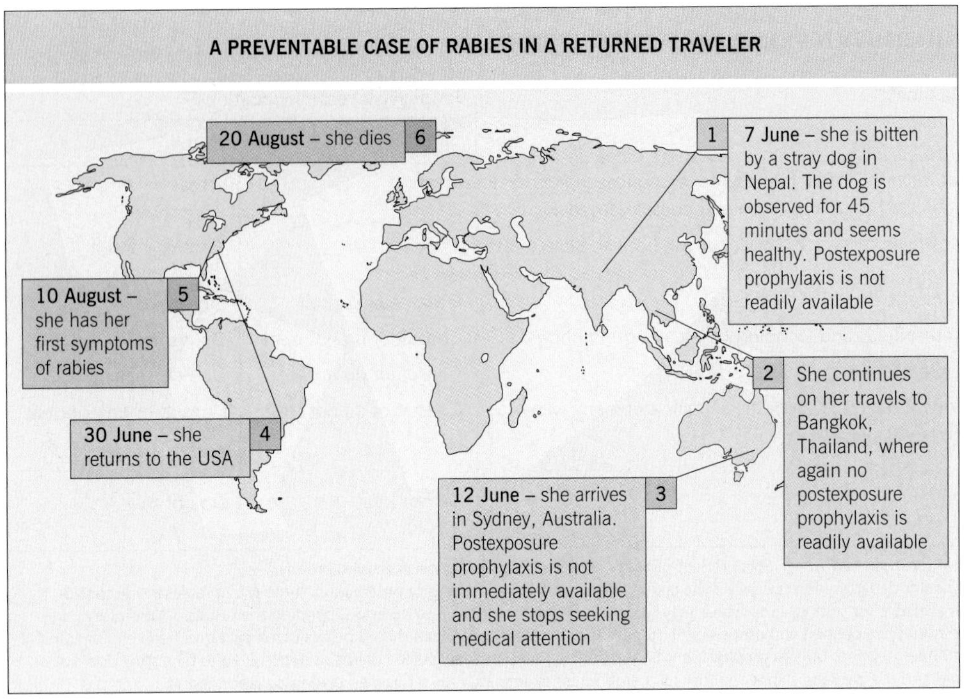

A PREVENTABLE CASE OF RABIES IN A RETURNED TRAVELER
20 August – she dies 6
1 7 June – she is bitten by a stray dog in Nepal. The dog is observed for 45 minutes and seems healthy. Postexposure prophylaxis is not readily available
10 August – she has her first symptoms of rabies 5
2 She continues on her travels to Bangkok, Thailand, where again no postexposure prophylaxis is readily available
30 June – she returns to the USA 4
12 June – she arrives in Sydney, Australia. Postexposure prophylaxis is not immediately available and she stops seeking medical attention 3

Fig. 153.2 A preventable case of rabies in a returned traveler. The patient had been traveling for 6 months. She did not receive pre-exposure rabies vaccine and despite multiple opportunities, did not receive postexposure prophylaxis.[10]

REFERENCES

1. Weiss HB, Friedman DI, Coben JH. Incidence of dog bite injuries treated in emergency departments. JAMA 1998;279:51–3.
2. Mitmooupitak C, Tepsumethanon V, Raksaket S, Nayuthaya AB, Wilde H. Dog-bite injuries at the Animal Bite Clinic of the Thai Red Cross Society in Bangkok. J Med Assoc Thai 2000;83:1458–62.
3. Krebs JW, Noll HR, Rupprecht CE, Childs JE. Rabies surveillance in the United States during 2001. J Am Vet Med Assoc 2002;221:1690–701.
4. Noah DL, Drenzek CL, Smith JS, *et al.* The epidemiology of human rabies in the United States, 1980 to 1996. Ann Intern Med 1998;128(11):922–30.
5. Greigo RD, Rosen T, Orengo IF, Wolf JE. Dog, cat, and human bites: a review. J Am Acad Dermatol 1995;33:1019–29.
6. Holmes GP, Chapman LE, Stewart JA, *et al.* Guidelines for the prevention and treatment of b-virus infections in exposed persons. Clin Infect Dis 1995;20:421–39.
7. National Association of State Public Health Veterinarians. Compendium of animal rabies prevention and control, 2003. MMWR 2003;S2(No. RR-5):1–6.
8. Centers for Disease Control and Prevention. Human rabies – Iowa, 2002. MMWR 2003;52:47–8.
9. Centers for Disease Control and Prevention. Human rabies prevention – United States, 1999: Recommendations of the Advisory Committee on Immunization Practices (ACIP). MMWR 1999;48 (no. RR-1):1–21.
10. Centers for Disease Control and Prevention. Human rabies – New Hampshire, 1996. MMWR 1997;46:267–70.

chapter

154 Leprosy

Warwick J Britton

EPIDEMIOLOGY

Leprosy is a chronic infection of the skin and nerves with *Mycobacterium leprae* which, although rarely fatal, is a significant cause of disability. Over the past decade there have been dramatic changes in the prevalence of leprosy since the introduction of multidrug therapy (MDT).[1,2] As a result of the shorter duration of therapy and more intensive control programs, the number of registered leprosy patients receiving chemotherapy has fallen from 10–12 million to 600,000 in 2000.[3] The annual case detection rate, however, has remained unchanged at approximately 700,000 new patients/year. This contributes to the pool of 2–3 million patients with permanent nerve impairment as a consequence of leprosy.

Leprosy is widely distributed in tropical and warm temperate countries and 1.3 billion people live in regions where there is active transmission of *M. leprae*. There has been a reduction in the number of endemic countries (prevalence rate >1/10,000) from 122 in 1985 to 15 in 2000,[3] mainly in Africa, Asia and Latin America. Currently 83% of registered cases occur in only six countries:

- India (accounting for 64% of all registered cases); and
- Brazil, Myanmar, Madagascar, Nepal and Mozambique, in order.[3]

Because of the long incubation period of leprosy, an individual from an endemic country may develop leprosy years after migration elsewhere. Delay in diagnosis is usually longer in nonendemic than endemic regions and therefore leprosy should be considered as a diagnostic possibility in any person who is from an endemic country and who has chronic lesions of the skin or peripheral nerves.

Subclinical infection with *M. leprae* is far more common than overt disease.[4] Analysis of *M. leprae*-specific immune responses[5] has demonstrated that *M. leprae* infection is common after exposure, but the majority of individuals control the infection.

The major mechanism of transmission of *M. leprae* is through nasal secretions, particularly from lepromatous patients.[4] Organisms probably enter through the mucosa of respiratory tracts and, if not controlled, they disseminate to the skin and peripheral nerves. Other possible modes of transmission include breast milk from mothers with untreated lepromatous disease and rare cases of cutaneous inoculation. Although infection with *M. leprae* has been documented in wild armadilloes and some primates, zoonotic transmission does not contribute to human disease.

Proximity to leprosy patients is important in transmission, and the relative risk for disease for household contacts is 8- to 10-fold greater for lepromatous cases and 2- to 4-fold greater for tuberculoid cases.[4] Nevertheless, the majority of leprosy cases are sporadic.

Genetic factors influence both the development of leprosy and the pattern of disease. Whole genome screening has identified susceptibility loci on chromosome 10p13, close to the gene for the mannose receptor C type 1,[6] and the HLA region with linkage to both the HLA class II and tumor necrosis factor genes,[7] in Indian and Brazilian patients respectively. The HLA locus also affects the pattern of disease; HLA-DR2 and DR3 are associated with tuberculoid disease and HLA-DQ1 with lepromatous leprosy.[5] Racial and geographic factors also influence the type of leprosy, with lepromatous leprosy being less common in Africans than Indians and most common in Chinese and Caucasians.

The incidence of leprosy peaks in two age groups (10–15 and 30–60 years of age) and there is a male predominance in most regions of about 2:1.[4] The incubation period varies widely from months to over 30 years, but is usually prolonged, averaging 4 years for tuberculoid and 10 years for lepromatous leprosy. In contrast to tuberculosis, there is no definite evidence for an association between HIV infection and clinical leprosy,[8] although one study suggested an increase in HIV prevalence in leprosy patients in Tanzania.[9]

PATHOGENESIS AND PATHOLOGY

Although *M. leprae* was the second bacterium to be associated with a human disease, it still cannot be cultivated in vitro. The organism is capable of limited multiplication in mouse footpad, with a doubling time of 11–13 days, and this has permitted drug sensitivity studies.[10] *Mycobacterium leprae* is an acid-fast, Gram-positive bacillus and is an obligate intracellular parasite with tropism for macrophages and Schwann cells. The bacilli show preference for growth in cooler regions of the body. The unique characteristic of *M. leprae* is its predilection to infect Schwann cells. The receptor complex on the Schwann cell is the G-domain of the laminin $\alpha2$ chain in the basal lamina of Schwann cells and the laminin receptor, α-dystroglycan.[11] A number of ligands on the surface of *M. leprae* bind to this complex, including the specific trisaccharide of phenolic glycolipid (PGL)-I and a 21kDa surface protein.

Genetic and structural analyses have confirmed that *M. leprae* is a member of the family Mycobacteriacae. A major advance has been the sequencing of genome of an Indian isolate of *M. leprae*.[12] The genome contains 1605 genes encoding proteins and 50 genes for stable RNA molecules. Remarkably, half of the functional genes in the *M. tuberculosis* genome are absent, being replaced by many inactivated or pseudogenes. This gene decay has removed entire metabolic pathways and regulatory genes, particularly those involved in catabolism. This may render the leprosy bacillus dependent on host metabolic products and may explain its long generation time and inability to grow in culture.[12] The availability of the *M. leprae* and other mycobacterial genomes has major implications for the development of new antimycobacterial drugs[13] and *M. leprae*-specific diagnostic reagents. The complex cell wall contains important targets of the immune response, including a species-specific PGL-I and immunomodulatory lipoarabinomannan. The cell wall biosynthetic pathways are relatively intact in *M. leprae*, despite the loss of other genes, indicating that these represent the essential genes for the formation of a minimal mycobacterial cell wall.[14] *Mycobacterium leprae* is relatively inert and the host immune response is responsible for most of the tissue damage.

The manifestations of leprosy form a wide clinical spectrum determined by immunopathologic responses to the organism (Fig. 154.1).[15] Patients who have the polar forms of tuberculoid

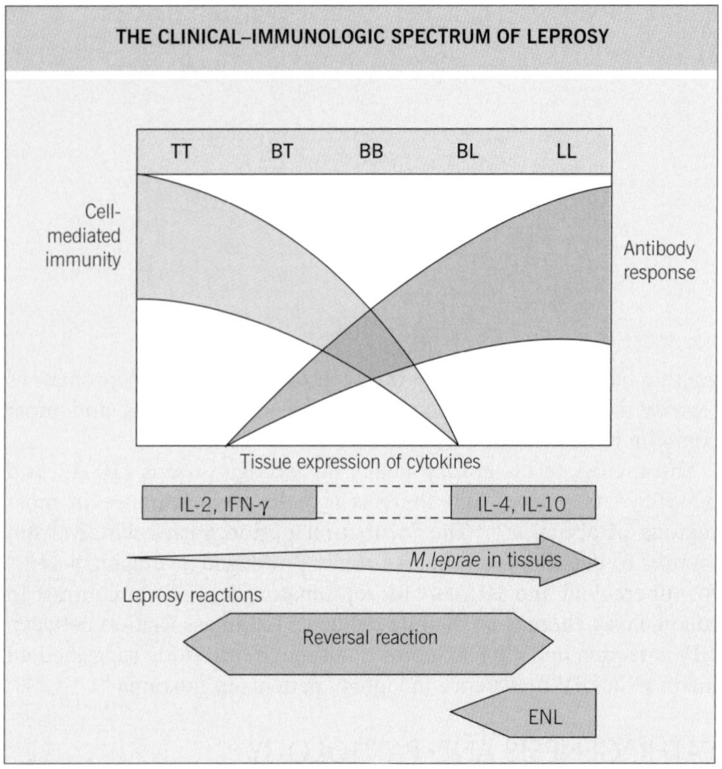

Fig. 154.1 The clinical–immunologic spectrum of leprosy. This reflects the underlying host immunity as measured by the T-cell and antibody responses to *M. leprae*. Spontaneous fluctuations in the immune response are responsible for reversal reactions and erythema nodosum leprosum (ENL). TT, tuberculoid leprosy; BT, borderline tuberculoid; BB, mid-borderline leprosy; BL, borderline lepromatous leprosy; LL, lepromatous leprosy; IFN, interferon; IL, interleukin.

(TT) and lepromatous leprosy (LL) are immunologically stable, but those who have the intermediate types of borderline-tuberculoid (BT), mid-borderline and borderline-lepromatous (BL) leprosy are immunologically unstable and subject to either a gradual decline toward the lepromatous pole or upgrading reversal reactions (RRs; see Fig. 154.1). In TT a vigorous cellular response to *M. leprae* limits the disease to a few well-defined skin patches or nerve trunks.[15] The lesions are infiltrated by interferon-γ secreting $CD4^+$ T cells, which form well-demarcated granulomas containing epithelioid and multinucleate giant cells around dermal nerves.[5] Few, if any, bacilli are demonstrable. Cellular immunity may be confirmed by in-vitro lymphocyte responses to *M. leprae* antigens or skin test reactivity. Intradermal injection of heat-killed *M. leprae* causes a transient swelling at 48 hours in a sensitized subject (Fernandez reaction), followed by the development of a granulomatous nodule at 3–4 weeks (Mitsuda reaction).[5,15] The latter confirms an individual's capacity to mount a T-cell response to *M. leprae*. Antibody responses to *M. leprae* are absent or low titer.

The hallmark of LL is the absence of *M. leprae*-specific cellular immunity and this results in uncontrolled proliferation of the bacilli with extensive infiltration of the skin and nerves and numerous lesions.[5] Histologically, the dermis contains foamy macrophages filled with multiple bacilli and a scattering of $CD4^+$ and $CD8^+$ lymphocytes, but no organized granulomas.[15] There are high titers of antibodies to *M. leprae*-specific PGL and protein antigens. In borderline cases a progressive reduction in cellular responses is associated with a greater bacillary load, more frequent skin and nerve lesions and increasing antibody levels.

The dynamic nature of the immune response to *M. leprae* is responsible for spontaneous fluctuations in the clinical pattern, termed leprosy reactions:[16]

- a type 1 reaction is usually an 'upgrading' RR caused by increased cellular reactivity to mycobacterial products, results in edema and acute inflammation of skin lesions and nerves, is most common in borderline patients and is a major cause of nerve damage; and
- a type 2 reaction or erythema nodosum leprosum (ENL) is a systemic inflammatory response to the deposition of extravascular immune complexes, leading to neutrophil infiltration and activation of complement in multiple organs,[9] and is accompanied by high circulating levels of tumor necrosis factor α and systemic toxicity.

PREVENTION

The chief means of preventing leprosy is the interruption of transmission by treating those with infectious leprosy early. Multidrug therapy was introduced because of the increasing spread of primary and secondary dapsone resistance worldwide.[1] Its advantages are its proven efficacy[2] and improved compliance, which is related to the limited duration of therapy and its monthly observed component (see Management, below). Furthermore, early treatment before the onset of nerve damage reduces the long-term disability associated with leprosy.[3,17] The effectiveness of MDT has prompted a World Health Organization (WHO) co-ordinated campaign to implement MDT in all endemic countries, with the aim of reducing the prevalence rate of leprosy to less than 1/10,000.[3] This has been successful, with 15 countries left to attain this goal. Importantly, however, the case detection rate has not yet fallen, probably because of the prolonged incubation period of clinical leprosy, indicating that control programs must be sustained.

The response to immunization with *M. bovis* BCG has been variable, but in a major trial in Malawi BCG induced 50% protective efficacy against clinical leprosy, both tuberculoid and lepromatous forms.[18] Reimmunization enhanced the protective effect by a further 50%. The benefit of BCG has been confirmed in subsequent case-control studies. Extensive BCG immunization of children in endemic countries has probably made a significant contribution to the decline of leprosy. The addition of heat-killed *M. leprae* to BCG did not increase the observed protective efficacy of BCG in two trials.[18] Other experimental vaccines are being tested against leprosy infection at present.

Leprosy is commonly associated with poverty and overcrowding, and improved socioeconomic conditions have contributed to the decline of leprosy in Europe and some Asian countries.

CLINICAL FEATURES

Types of leprosy

Indeterminate leprosy

This is the earliest form and occurs as a single slightly hypopigmented, ill-defined macule in children, who are often contacts of leprosy patients.[19] The majority of these lesions are self-limiting and resolve without therapy. A minority (<25%) develop into defined lesions within the clinical spectrum.

Tuberculoid leprosy

These lesions occur as 1–3 large asymmetric macules or plaques with sharply defined borders and hypopigmented anesthetic centers (Fig. 154.2).[19,20] Although leprosy lesions are usually hypopigmented, in light skins the macules may appear erythematous or dyschromic. Involvement of sweat glands and hair follicles results in dryness and loss of hair. Enlarged cutaneous nerves may be palpable at the edge of the lesion, but nerve trunk involvement is minimal.

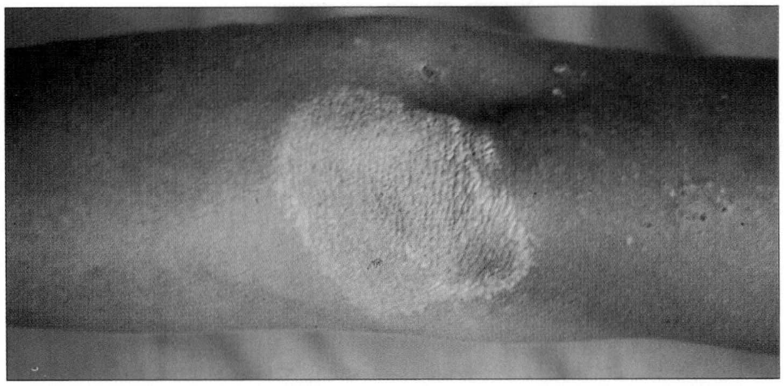

Fig. 154.2 Tuberculoid leprosy. Single hypopigmented anesthetic plaque with raised border and dry surface.

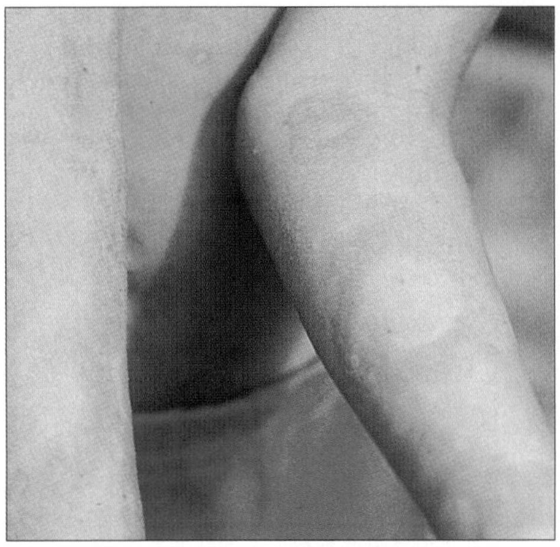

Fig. 154.4 Mid-borderline leprosy. Characteristic target lesion with raised erythematous annular border and 'punched-out' central area with impaired sensation.

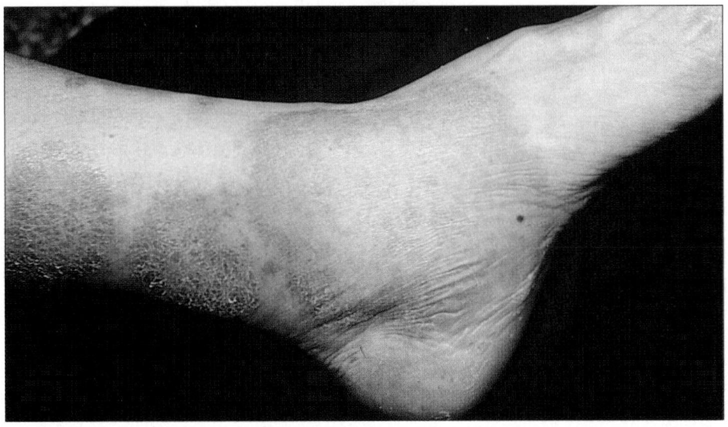

Fig. 154.3 Borderline tuberculoid leprosy. Three large well-defined erythematous patches with reduced sensation, spreading borders and satellite lesions.

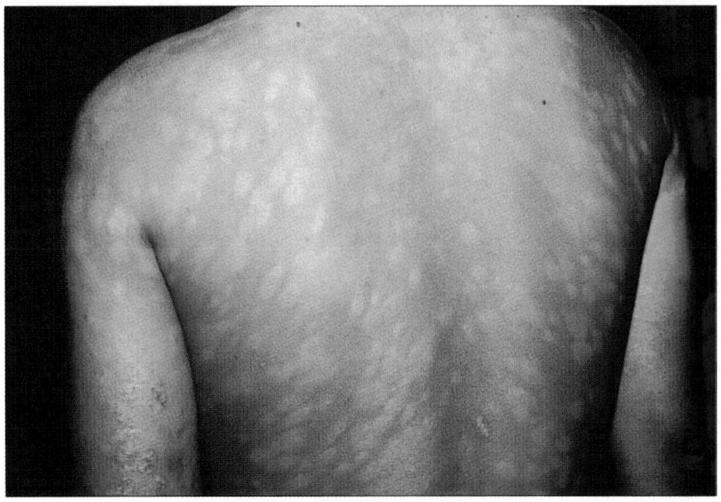

Fig. 154.5 Lepromatous leprosy. Multiple, small, slightly erythematous macules with intact sensation and symmetric distribution. The skin smears of both the lesions and intervening skin are positive for acid-fast bacilli.

Borderline tuberculoid leprosy

This is the commonest form of leprosy. The skin lesions resemble those in TT leprosy, but are more frequent and variable in appearance and their borders are less well demarcated (Fig. 154.3). The outline may be irregular with adjacent 'satellite' lesions suggesting local spread. Occasionally, large patches of BT leprosy may involve a whole limb. Asymmetric enlargement of several peripheral nerves is usual and patients may present with muscle weakness or trauma secondary to sensory impairment. Progressive nerve damage is common.

Mid-borderline leprosy

This is the most immunologically unstable form with the propensity to shift rapidly toward BT leprosy during a reversal reaction or to downgrade toward BL leprosy. The skin lesions are numerous and vary in size, shape and distribution. They may be hypopigmented or erythematous. The characteristic 'target' lesion has a broad, erythematous border with a vague outer edge and 'punched-out' pale center with sensory impairment (Fig. 154.4).

Borderline lepromatous leprosy

In borderline lepromatous leprosy there are numerous small erythematous macules, which initially may be limited in distribution, but become progressively more symmetric.[19] Papules, nodules and succulent plaques may develop and, in contrast to tuberculoid leprosy, the lesions have normal sensation. The intervening skin is normal. Widespread nerve involvement is typical, especially if the patient has downgraded from BT leprosy.

Lepromatous leprosy

This is a systemic disease with a generalized bacteremia leading to widespread involvement of the skin and other organs.[19] The first manifestation may be a diffuse infiltration of the dermis, causing a smooth shiny appearance of the skin. More typically, there are numerous symmetrically distributed macules, papules or nodules (Figs 154.5 and 154.6). Progressive thickening of the skin results in coarsening of the facial features and nodular thickening of the ear lobes. With time the eyebrows and eyelashes become thinned.

Bacillary infiltration is responsible for gradual tissue damage in the involved organs. The nasal mucosa is infiltrated at an early stage, resulting in discharge and obstruction. Erosion of the cartilage and nasomaxillary bones results in perforation of the nasal septum, collapse of the nose and saddle-nose deformity. Laryngeal involvement produces hoarseness and stridor. Direct bacillary involvement of the eye causes keratitis and iritis.

Infiltration of the dermal nerves results in a peripheral sensory loss similar to that of a 'glove and stocking' neuropathy,[19] which leaves the skin susceptible to ulceration and secondary infection. Reactional episodes cause edema of the feet, shins and hands. Dactylitis develops in the hands and feet and, together with trauma and osteomyelitis, results in phalangeal erosion.

Both testicular infiltration and orchitis contribute to testicular atrophy and secondary gynecomastia. Glomerulonephritis may occur and is usually associated with ENL. Secondary amyloidosis is a consequence of recurrent ENL reactions.

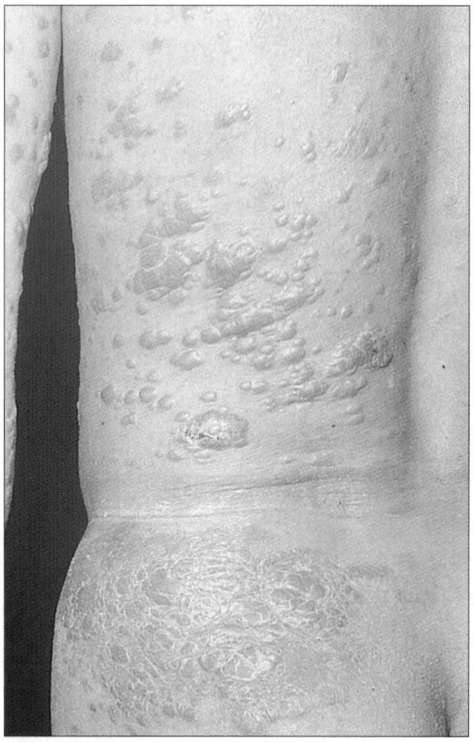

Fig. 154.6 Nodular lepromatous leprosy. Diffuse infiltration of the skin by multiple nodules of varying size, each teeming with bacilli.

Peripheral nerve involvement

The nerves of predilection occur at superficial sites where the nerve trunks are cooler, more readily traumatized and often anatomically constricted.[19] These include the:

- ulnar nerve at the medial epicondyle of the humerus,
- median nerve at the wrist,
- lateral popliteal nerve at the neck of the fibula,
- posterior tibial nerve behind and inferior to the medial maleolus, and
- radial nerve in the humeral groove posterior to the deltoid insertion.

Easily palpated superficial cutaneous nerves include the:

- superficial radial nerve at the wrist,
- greater auricular nerves,
- supraorbital nerve, and
- sural nerves.

These nerves should be examined for enlargement and associated weakness and sensory loss. The resulting muscle imbalance leads to the characteristic deformities of clawhand, footdrop, clawtoes and wristdrop. Autonomic nerve dysfunction contributes to impaired sweating and dry skin, which is subject to cracking, infection and poor healing. The combination of insensitive feet and clawtoes leads to recurrent plantar ulceration, a major cause of disability.

In pure neural (PN) leprosy the nerve trunks are affected without any skin lesions. On biopsy the neural lesions tend to be 'lepromatous' in appearance and PN leprosy involving more than one nerve should be treated as multibacillary (MB).

Before and during therapy the function of the commonly involved nerves should be assessed at regular intervals by voluntary muscle and sensory testing (preferably with nylon monofilaments) to determine whether there is ongoing nerve function impairment. This may presage the onset of a reversal reaction before nerve pain or typical skin lesions develop. Nerve function impairment may develop or worsen despite effective chemotherapy, and early recognition and therapy prevent permanent nerve damage.[16,17] Patients with pre-existing nerve damage at diagnosis and MB patients are at greatest risk for new nerve function impairment and should be carefully monitored.[17]

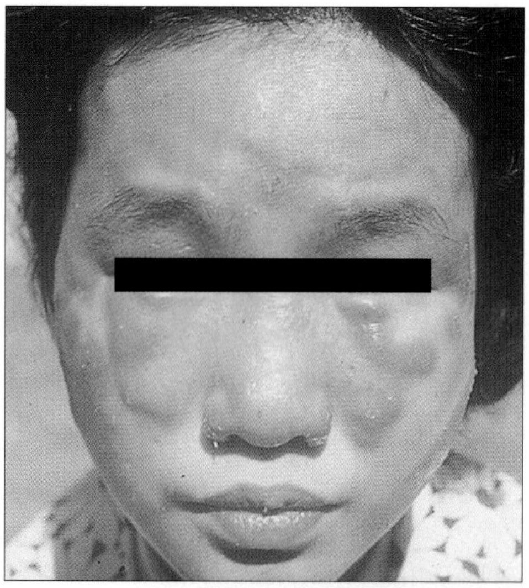

Fig. 154.7 Reversal reaction. Erythema and edema in the facial lesions of a patient who has borderline-tuberculoid leprosy undergoing an upgrading reversal reaction.

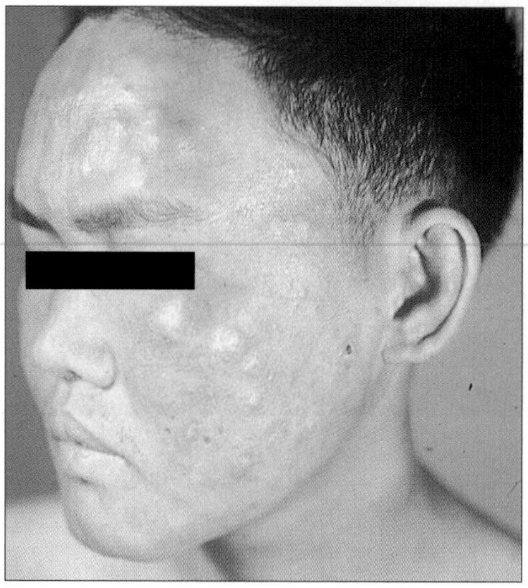

Fig. 154.8 Erythema nodosum leprosum. Tender papules associated with fever, arthralgia and acute neuritis in a patient who has lepromatous leprosy.

Leprosy reactions

Reversal reactions

These develop in about one-third of patients who have BT-BL leprosy, usually within the first 6 months of treatment.[16] They present with:

- increased inflammation in established BT-BL skin lesions or new swollen lesions in BL and subpolar LL patients (Fig. 154.7),
- acute neuritis with pain or tenderness in the involved nerve and loss of function, and
- recent (<6 months) or progressive nerve function impairment in the absence of painful nerves.

Silent neuritis responds to therapy for the RR.[21] Patients who have a particular risk of developing a RR are those who have facial patches, more extensive disease involving more than two body areas or *M. leprae*-specific IgM anti-PGL antibodies.

Erythema nodosum leprosum

This once affected 30–50% of BL and LL patients, but the frequency and severity of ENL have reduced since the regular use of clofazimine in MDT.[2] It may develop at any stage of therapy, but usually within the first year, and is often recurrent. An episode begins with fever and malaise and the rapid emergence of painful erythematous nodules, typically over the extensor surfaces of the limbs.[20] In severe cases widespread nodules may form pustules and ulcerate (Fig. 154.8). Painful neuritis is the most common complication. Erythema nodosum leprosum has features of widespread immune complex deposition and these may include small vessel vasculitis, iridocyclitis, polyarthritis, orchitis, lymphadenitis and glomerulonephritis.

Recurrent or uncontrolled ENL reactions can result in the development of secondary amyloidosis (amyloid A protein) within 3 months.

Eye involvement

Involvement of branches of the facial and trigeminal nerves results in lagophthalmos and corneal anesthesia, respectively, and if combined there is a considerable risk of ulceration and infection of the exposed insensitive cornea.[22]

In 25–30% of patients who have LL, infiltration of the anterior segment of the eye causes a superficial punctate keratitis and iridocyclitis, which may be painless and only recognized by slit-lamp examination. Iridocyclitis is exacerbated during episodes of ENL, but can occur independently of overt reactions. The iritis may be complicated by glaucoma or cataract, both of which contribute to leprosy-associated blindness (see Chapter 20).

DIAGNOSIS

A diagnosis of leprosy is usually straightforward if it is suspected as a cause of any skin or peripheral nerve lesion in a person from an endemic country. The cardinal signs of leprosy[19,20] are:

- skin patch with sensory loss,
- nerve enlargement, and
- acid-fast bacilli (AFB) in the skin.

The presence of one or more of these features establishes the diagnosis, which should be confirmed with a full-thickness skin biopsy. Approximately 70% of all leprosy patients can be diagnosed by the single sign of a skin patch with sensory loss, but 30% of patients, including many MB patients, may not present with this sign, indicating the importance of nerve enlargement as an additional sign and the importance of clinical suspicion for the diagnosis.

Acid-fast bacilli are best demonstrated in slit-skin smears, which should be taken from the edges of at least two lesions and both ear lobes.[23] If these are not available a skin biopsy should be stained for AFB with a modified Wade–Fite stain. The extent of the bacillary load can be quantitated as a bacterial index[10] on a logarithmic scale of 1+ to 6+. The percentage of solid staining AFB in smears, the morphologic index,[10] is an indirect measure of the viability of leprosy bacilli. In PN leprosy a biopsy from a sensory nerve such as the superficial radial nerve may be diagnostic. Polymerase chain reaction (PCR) can be used to identify *M. leprae* DNA and, together with PCR-based detection of rifampin (rifampicin)-resistant strains, it is a valuble tool for epidemiologic studies.[24]

Lepromin testing and serology may be used for accurate classification of patients in research studies. Antibodies to PGL and other *M. leprae*-specific protein antigens are present in MB patients and their titer falls with effective therapy.[5] In patients who have BL and LL, evidence of chronic inflammation includes anemia, hypergammaglobulinemia, elevated serum amyloid A protein and positive antinuclear and anticardiolipin autoantibodies.

Other skin diseases can be differentiated from tuberculoid leprosy by the absence of anesthesia in the lesions and the presence of nerve involvement elsewhere.[20,23] Lepromatous skin lesions are not anesthetic and biopsy may be necessary to distinguish these from those due to other systemic infections such as leishmaniasis and secondary syphilis and other nodular or infiltrative skin conditions. Other causes of nerve enlargement such as primary amyloidosis and familial polyneuropathy are excluded by biopsy and family history.

MANAGEMENT

Successful management of leprosy requires prolonged drug treatment and careful monitoring for complications and it is essential to enlist the patient as an ally in this process. The patient should be educated about:

- the importance of compliance,
- the first symptoms of a reaction, and
- the elements of self-care needed to prevent secondary tissue damage if there is sensory nerve impairment.

The most important step in disability prevention is the early initiation of bactericidal drug therapy.

Antileprosy drugs

Dapsone

This is an important antileprosy drug because of its bactericidal effect at full dosage, low cost and low toxicity.[2] When used alone stepwise dapsone resistance emerges as a major problem,[1] but this is prevented by combination therapy. Mild hemolytic anemia is common, but is only severe in the presence of glucose-6-phosphate dehydrogenase deficiency, which should be excluded where possible. Occasionally dapsone allergy, and rarely agranulocytosis, may develop after 2–6 weeks.

Rifampin

Rifampin is a key component of MDT because it is the most effective bactericidal drug against *M. leprae* when given either daily or monthly.[2,10] Toxicity is low with monthly dosage, although thrombocytopenia, hepatitis and a flu-like syndrome occasionally occur. It must be used with at least one other effective drug to prevent rifampin resistance. Tuberculosis should always be excluded before monthly rifampin is started (see Chapters 37 and 202). Rifapentine is a long-acting rifamycin-derivative that is more bactericidal than rifampin in mice and is currently being tested in humans.

Clofazimine

This is a fat-soluble dye that is deposited within the skin, fat stores and macrophages. It has similar bactericidal activity to that of dapsone,[2,15] and also a significant anti-inflammatory effect. It is relatively nontoxic and its only disadvantage is the associated development of a reddish skin pigmentation, which resolves after the drug has been discontinued. When used in high doses for prolonged periods, clofazimine is deposited in the small intestinal wall and can cause diarrhea and pain.

Other drugs

Three additional drugs have proved effective against *M. leprae* in human and mouse studies:[2,23]

- the fluoroquinolones ofloxacin and moxifloxacin have moderate bactericidal activity and infrequent side-effects involving the gastrointestinal tract and central nervous system;
- minocycline, the only fat-soluble tetracycline, has moderate anti-*M. leprae* activity. It has proved effective in patients with LL and has low toxicity in adults when used as long-term therapy for acne and so is a useful alternative drug for leprosy; and
- clarithromycin has modest bactericidal activity.

Multidrug therapy

The principle underlying MDT is the use of three drugs when the bacterial load is high in MB leprosy to treat and prevent the emergence of dapsone-resistant strains. Two drugs are sufficient for paucibacillary disease. Since its introduction in 1982,[1] MDT has proved highly effective and over 10 million patients have been treated with few treatment failures and remarkably low relapse rates of about 0.1/100 patient-years.[2,3,25]

Multibacillary multidrug therapy

This is recommended for adult patients with BB, BL, LL, smear-positive BT and PN leprosy. In leprosy control programs in endemic countries, a simplified form of classification is employed, based on the number of patches, so that MB leprosy >5 patches and paucibacillary (PB) ″5 patches. Multibacillary MDT comprises:

- rifampin, 600mg once a month, supervised administration;
- dapsone, 100mg/day, self-administered; and
- clofazimine, 300mg once a month, supervised administration; 50mg/day, self-administered.

Originally, MB-MDT was continued for at least 2 years and then until the skin smears became negative.[1] In subsequent field trials a fixed duration of MB-MDT for 2 years was as effective[2] and this was utilized in control programs with very low rates of relapse.[25] Patients who have MB leprosy and a skin smear bacterial index of 4+ or over may require a longer duration of therapy.[2] More recently in 1998, the WHO recommended that MB-MDT of 12 months duration may be sufficient for use in control programs.[25] Although the results of continuing clinical trials comparing 12 and 24 month duration MB-MDT are not available as yet, 12 month MB-MDT is currently used in leprosy control programs in endemic countries.

Some authorities in developed countries prefer to use more frequent doses of rifampin and continue to treat until the smears are negative, which can take 5–8 years. One approach is to double the dose of rifampin to 600mg daily for two consecutive days each month,[23] while others use daily rifampin 450–600mg for 2–3 years with dapsone and clofazimine. There is no evidence, however, that daily rifampin is more effective than when given once monthly.

If clofazimine is unacceptable because of pigmentation or if dapsone hypersensitivity occurs, minocycline (100mg daily) or ofloxacin (400mg daily) may be substituted.[25] Patients who have rifampin intolerance require two new drugs, minocycline and ofloxacin, along with clofazimine (50mg/day) for 6 months and then either drug with clofazimine for another 18 months.

Paucibacillary multidrug therapy

This is recommended for indeterminate, TT and smear-negative BT leprosy[2] and in the control programs for patients with ″5 patches. PB-MDT comprises:

- rifampin, 600mg once a month, supervised administration; and
- dapsone, 100mg/day, self-administered.

This is continued for 6 months. If the skin smear is positive at any site, the patient is given MB-MDT. If a RR develops after completion of chemotherapy, then MDT should be recommenced while on prednisone.[23]

In some countries patients with solitary leprosy skin lesions are common. A large field study in India established that the combination of rifampin (600mg), ofloxacin (400mg) and minocycline (100mg) was almost as effective as PB-MDT in the treatment of patients with single smear-negative skin lesions and no nerve involvement, although the follow-up period was only for 18 months.[26] This regimen is helpful for treating carefully selected patients in endemic countries with a high proportion of single lesion cases, but should be reserved for this setting.

Treatment for reactions

Patients who have RRs, including silent nerve function impairment, require high-dose corticosteroids for a prolonged duration to permit nerve function recovery.[16] Prednisone is started at 40mg/day and increased to 60mg/day if there is no response, and then to 120mg/day if necessary. Once there is evidence of improvement on serial voluntary muscle and sensory testing, the dose is reduced over 6 weeks to 20mg/day and this is continued for some months before gradual removal. Therapy is usually required for 4–6 months, but often for longer durations in MB leprosy.[23] It is important to maintain treatment with antimycobacterial drugs to reduce the bacillary load. Adequate analgesia is essential along with physical support during the period of active neuritis. This therapy can be successfully administered without admission if other infections and medical problems are excluded. The expected recovery rate for nerve function is 60–70%,[16] but may be up to 88% in patients with no nerve damage at diagnosis who develop acute neuropathy during MDT.[27] Recovery is less in those with pre-existing nerve function impairment or with chronic or recurrent reactions.

Mild ENL responds to aspirin or nonsteroidal anti-inflammatory drugs, increased clofazimine dosage and rest. Moderate or severe episodes and those with neuritis require prednisone, usually starting at 40–60mg/day.[16] The response is rapid, but as ENL is liable to become corticosteroid dependent the prednisone should be withdrawn over 2–3 months. Clofazimine at a higher daily dose of 300mg suppresses ENL after 4–6 weeks and can be used to prevent further episodes.

If the ENL is poorly controlled or recurs, it usually responds to thalidomide, 400mg/day for 2–3 weeks, and then 100–200mg/day as maintenance.[16] Thalidomide inhibits the release of tumor necrosis factor from macrophages and results in prompt relief. Its use, however, is severely limited by its teratogenicity and should be restricted to male and postmenopausal patients under strict supervision. Thalidomide may cause a peripheral neuropathy, but this has not been reported in leprosy patients.

Eye involvement is common and iritis requires local treatment with corticosteroid and atropine drops.[22]

Other therapies

Prevention of disability is an important component of care.[28] Regular monitoring of nerve function will reveal early reversible RRs. Patients with irreversible nerve function impairment must learn to care for insensitive hands and feet and be provided with appropriate footwear. Plantar ulceration requires prolonged rest for healing. Physiotherapy and reconstructive surgery for clawhands and clawfeet, footdrop and lagophthalmos may prevent further tissue damage and restore appearance, and facial deformity can be corrected by plastic surgery.[28] Community-based rehabilitation is proving effective in assisting patients with persistent nerve impairment to return to full participation in their own communities.[29]

Websites

http://genolist.pasteur.fr/Leproma. Web-based tool for extracting information about annotations from the *M. leprae* genome database.

http://www.who.int/lcp/. Provides access to WHO documents on the epidemiology and treatment of leprosy, including the 7th Report of WHO Expert Committee on Leprosy, and information on MDT and leprosy elimination campaigns.

REFERENCES

1. World Health Organization Study Group on Chemotherapy of Leprosy. Wld HH Org Tech Rep Ser No. 675. Geneva: World Health Organization; 1982.
2. World Health Organization Study Group on Chemotherapy of Leprosy. Wld HH Org Tech Rep Ser No. 847. Geneva: World Health Organization; 1994.
3. World Health Organization. Leprosy global situation. Wkly Epidemiol Rec 2002;77:1–8.
4. Nordeen SK. Epidemiology of leprosy. In: Hastings RC, ed. Leprosy, 2nd ed. Edinburgh: Churchill Livingstone; 1994:29–48.
5. Britton WJ. Immunology of leprosy. Trans Roy Soc Trop Med Hyg 1993;82:508–14.
6. Siddiqui MR, Meisner S, Tosh K, *et al.* A major susceptibility locus for leprosy in India maps to chromosome 10p13. Nat Genet 2001;27:439–41.
7. Shaw MA, Donaklson IJ, Collins A, *et al.* Association and linkage of leprosy phenotypes with HLA class II and tumour necrosis factor genes. Genes Immunol 2001;2:196–204.
8. Lucas S. Human immunodeficiency virus and leprosy. Lepr Rev 1993;64:97–103.
9. van den Broek J, Chum HJ, Swai R, O'Brien RJ. Association between leprosy and HIV infection in Tanzania. Int J Lepr Other Mycobact Dis 1997;65:203–10.
10. Rees RJW, Young DB. The microbiology of leprosy. In: Hastings RC, ed. Leprosy, 2nd ed. Edinburgh: Churchill Livingstone; 1994:49–86.
11. Rambukkana A. Molecular basis for the peripheral nerve predilection of *Mycobacterium leprae.* Curr Op Microbiol 2001;4:21–7.
12. Cole ST, Eiglmeier K, Parkhill J, *et al.* Massive gene decay in the leprosy bacillus. Nature 2001;409:1007–11.
13. Grosset JH, Cole ST. Genomics and the chemotherapy of leprosy. Lepr Rev 2001;72:429–40.
14. Brennan PJ, Vissa VD. Genomic evidence for the retention of the essential mycobacterial cell wall in the otherwise defective *Mycobacterium leprae.* Lepr Rev 2001;72:415–28.
15. Ridley DS, Jopling WH. Classification of leprosy according to immunity. J Lepr 1966;34:255–73.
16. Britton WJ, Lockwood DNJ. Leprosy reactions: current and future approaches to management Baitlière's Clin Infect Dis 1997;4:1–23.
17. Saunderson P, Gebre S, Desta K, Byass P, Lockwood DNJ. The pattern of leprosy-related neuropathy in the AMFES patients in Ethiopia definitions, incidence, risk factors and outcome. Lepr Rev 2000;71:285–308.
18. Karonga Prevention Trial Group. Randomised controlled trial of single BCG, repeated BCG, or combined BCG and killed *Mycobacterium leprae* vaccine for prevention of leprosy and tuberculosis in Malawi. Lancet 1996;348:17–24.
19. Pfaltzgraff RE, Ramu G. Clinical leprosy. In: Hastings RC, ed. Leprosy, 2nd ed. Edinburgh: Churchill Livingstone; 1994:237–87.
20. Bryceson A, Pfaltzgraff RE. Leprosy, 3rd ed. Edinburgh: Churchill Livingstone; 1990.
21. van Brakel WH, Khawas IB. Silent neuropathy in leprosy: an epidemiological description. Int J Lepr Other Mycobact Dis 1994;65:350–60.
22. Joffrion VC. Ocular leprosy. In: Hastings RC, ed. Leprosy, 2nd ed. Edinburgh: Churchill Livingstone; 1994:353–66.
23. Waters MFR. Leprosy. In: Weatherall DJ, Ledingham JGG, Warrell DA, eds. Oxford textbook of medicine, 3rd ed. Oxford: Oxford University Press; 1996:667–79.
24. Honore N, Roche PW, Grosset JH, *et al.* A method for the rapid detection of rifampin-resistant isolates *Mycobacterium leprae.* Lepr Rev 2001;72:441–8.
25. World Health Organization Expert Committee on Leprosy. 7th report. Wld HH Org Tech Rep Ser No. 874. Geneva: World Health Organization; 1998.
26. Gupte MD. Field trials of a single dose of the combination rifampicin-ofloxacin-minocycline (ROM) for the treatment of paucibacillary leprosy. Lepr Rev 2000;71:S77–80.
27. Croft RP, Nicholls PG, Richardus JH, Smith WCS. The treatment of acute nerve function impairment in leprosy: results from a prospective cohort study in Bangladesh. Lepr Rev 2000;71:154–68.
28. Srivasasin H. Rehabilitation in leprosy. In: Hastings RC, ed. Leprosy, 2nd ed. Edinburgh: Churchill Livingstone; 1994:411–48.
29. Nicholls PG. Guidelines for social and economic rehabilitation. Lepr Rev 2000;71:422–65.

chapter

155 Ectoparasites

Wallace Peters

EPIDEMIOLOGY

Definition and nomenclature

In the strictest sense, an ectoparasite is defined as a parasite that derives its nourishment from the skin, as distinct from an endoparasite, which lives inside the body of the host. For this chapter, the definition has been adjusted to include both parasites that derive their nourishment from the skin and parasites that live within the skin and subcutaneous tissues. Not included here are skin-invading protozoa of the genus *Leishmania* that are relatively common in returning travelers from endemic areas (see Chapter 172). Purely hematophagous parasites, such as mosquitoes and ticks (see, for example, Chapter 11, Fig. 11.3 and Chapters 166 and 179) are of major public health importance, especially as vectors of viral and protozoal diseases, and many groups of these invertebrates are more or less cosmopolitan. However, the parasites themselves are most unlikely to be found in direct association with travelers returning to temperate climates from endemic tropical and subtropical areas. The reader is referred, therefore, to Chapters 14, 166 and 179 & 247 and other publications for information on these parasites.[1–3] This chapter particularly considers the various species of arthropods that may invade and may become apparent in the returned traveler (Table 155.1).

Geographic distribution

The arthropods referred to below, some of which have relatively well-defined geographic distributions in warm regions (see Table 155.1), are often found in returning travelers. Current infestations with mites and ticks that have been acquired abroad are rarely seen, although their sequelae may still be apparent. However, myiasis such as that caused by *Cordylobia anthropophaga*, also called the Tumbu or mango fly, is common in parts of sub-Saharan Africa and that caused by *Dermatobia hominis*, the human botfly, is not infrequently acquired by travelers to rural areas of Central and South America. The Tumbu fly lays batches of 200–300 eggs on dry soil in shaded areas. Domestic dogs are most frequently infested by the first instar larvae, but humans are also commonly infected. *Dermatobia hominis* infests many species of domestic and wild animals and is a serious pest of cattle in some endemic areas of the New World.

The sand, chigoe or jigger flea, *Tunga penetrans*, has a wide distribution within Central and South America, west and east Africa as well as some parts of the Indian subcontinent. The larvae are found mainly in dry, sandy soil where they mature into very small adults that actively seek a mammalian or avian host. Pigs are commonly infested in or around houses, where humans are also readily attacked.

Infestation with other arthropods, such as the New World screwworm *Cochliomyia hominivorax*, formerly a very serious, destructive pest of cattle and occasionally of humans, as well as the Congo floor maggot *Auchmeromyia senegalensis*, are now rare and unlikely to be acquired by travelers.[1,4] Myiasis caused by other species of flies (see Table 155.1) is uncommon and not likely to be found in the returning traveler. Any suspicious object recovered from such indi-viduals should, however, be referred for specialist identification.

Mites such as *Sarcoptes scabiei* and harvest mites of various species are cosmopolitan.[5,6] Scabies or pediculosis caused by body, head or pubic lice (Figs 155.1 and 155.2) may of course be acquired during travel anywhere through contact with infected people and may be diagnosed only after return home. The bites of anopheline mosquitoes may result in malaria that becomes manifest only after some time, as may certain viral infections transmitted by mites, ticks, mosquitoes or other hematophagous ectoparasites[1,3,7,8] (see also Chapters 166, 179 & 247, Figs 247.1–247.12).

PATHOGENESIS AND PATHOLOGY

Immunologic responses of the skin

The skin is a complex organ with complicated immune regulatory and effector functions, which involve both cellular and humoral responses to invasion by ectoparasites.[9] In order to survive within the skin and subcutaneous tissues, the parasites have evolved a number of ways in which they, in turn, modulate the host's immune response. Invading larvae of myiasis-causing flies produce proteases that facilitate their penetration of the dermal tissues as well as providing nutrition. The host response to the foreign proteins is intense and comprises a massive cellular response to both the foreign protein and the bulky, growing organism, with eosinophils and macrophages being predominant.[5] Although much research has been conducted in recent years into the parasite–host relationship of invasive arthropods, it has been directed mainly at those of veterinary importance and little detail is known about the parasites that affect humans. In areas endemic for Tumbu flies, for example, a marked level of cellular immunity, first localized but later more general, develops after prolonged and repeated exposure.[5]

Pathology

The pustular skin lesions associated with invasive larvae of myiasis-causing flies present a similar histologic picture of a fistulous track leading to a dermal cavity. This is densely infiltrated by macrophages, eosinophils and plasma cells. As the larva grows, it extends its posterior end toward the surface, through which its respiratory tubes project in the form of a pair of spiracles in a chitinous plate. The general appearance is of an acutely inflamed furuncle. As such larvae mature they push outward and are eventually extruded to the exterior, where they fall to the ground and pupate.

The pathology of *T. penetrans* is different since it is the adult female that actively burrows its way into the skin of the feet or under the toenails until her head reaches the papillary dermis. The posterior end of the insect, which bears the respiratory spiracles and sexual organs, remains at the surface. As the flea feeds and grows, its eggs develop until its abdomen becomes a pea-sized sac from which several hundred eggs are released to the exterior, a few at a time. The flea becomes encased in an inflammatory, foreign body granuloma, which may be surrounded by microhemorrhages.

CLASSIFICATION, COMMON NAMES AND GEOGRAPHIC DISTRIBUTION OF THE MAJOR ECTOPARASITES THAT AFFECT HUMANS					
Class	**Order/suborder**	**Genera and species**	**Common name**	**Geographic distribution**	**Notes**
Arachnida	Acari (mites)	*Trombicula* spp.	Scrub mites	Cosmopolitan	Include vectors of viruses, rickettsias
		Sarcoptes scabei		Cosmopolitan	Cause of scabies
	Acari (ticks)	Ixodidae and Argasidae	Hard and soft ticks	Cosmopolitan	Include many vectors of viruses, rickettsias, *Borrelia, Babesia, Ehrlichia* spp.
Insecta	Diptera	Many genera and species	Including biting and myiasis flies		
	Nematocera	Numerous genera and spp.	Mosquitoes, *Simulium*, etc.	Cosmopolitan	Major vectors of malaria, viruses, helminths
	Brachycera	*Chrysomyia bezziana*	Old World screw-worm	Widespread in tropical Africa, South East Asia and the south west Pacific	Common cause of cutaneous myiasis in South East Asia
		Cochliomyia hominivorax	New World screw-worm	Central and South America	Causes massively destructive myiasis
		Lucilia spp.	Greenbottles	Cosmopolitan	Facultative wound myiasis
		Calliphora spp.	Bluebottles	Cosmopolitan	Facultative wound myiasis
		Auchmeromyia senegalensis	Congo floor maggot	Sub-Saharan Africa	Sucks blood but no myiasis
		Cordylobia anthropophaga	Tumbu, mango fly	Sub-Saharan Africa	Causes furuncular myiasis
		Wohlfahrtia spp.	Flesh flies	Mainly in the South Palearctic region	Can cause tissue destruction
		Dermatobia hominis	Human botfly	Central and South America	Causes furuncular myiasis
		Oestrus ovis	Sheep nasal botfly	Cosmopolitan	Larvae may invade nose, eye
		Hypoderma spp.	Warble, botflies	Cosmopolitan	Causes 'creeping eruption'
	Siphonaptera	Numerous genera and spp.	Fleas	Cosmopolitan	Vectors of plague, rickettsias, helminths
		Tunga penetrans	Chigger, jigger flea, chigoe	Central and South America, tropical Africa, India	Female invades dermis (especially of the foot) to develop and lay eggs
	Phthiraptera	Numerous genera and spp.	Biting and sucking lice	Cosmopolitan	
		Pediculus humanus	Body and head louse	Cosmopolitan	Vector of rickettsias, *Borrelia* spp.
		Phthirus pubis	Pubic louse	Cosmopolitan	

Table 155.1 Classification, common names and geographic distribution of the major ectoparasites that affect humans. Parasites that derive their nourishment from the skin and parasites that live within the skin and subcutaneous tissues are included.

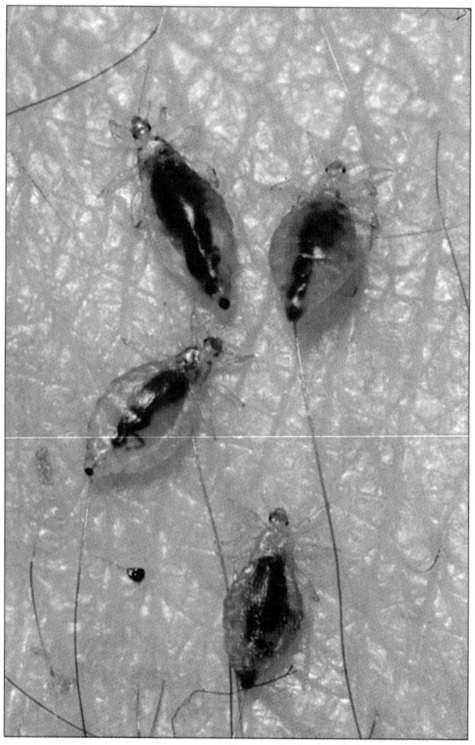

Fig. 155.1 Adult *Pediculus humanus corporis* (the body louse) feeding. These insects are not only a source of considerable skin irritation but also the vectors of epidemic typhus and trench fever. Courtesy of Dr med H Lieske. With permission from Peters and Pasvol.[7]

Fig. 155.2 The 'crab louse', *Phthirus pubis*. The crab louse, which is commonly acquired during sexual intercourse, infests not only the pubic region but also other sites, including the eyelashes. Courtesy of Dr med H Lieske. With permission from Peters and Pasvol.[7]

PREVENTION

The newly hatched larvae of *C. anthropophaga* live on the ground where they are attracted to warm skin, which they can rapidly penetrate with the aid of oral hooks and backward pointing body spines (Fig. 155.3). They are also attracted to clothing, for example underwear bearing human body odors. Prevention of infection involves not lying directly on potentially contaminated ground as well as not laying washing on the ground to dry, a common practice in many tropical areas.

Dermatobia hominis (Fig. 155.4) has a more complex life cycle. The female lays its eggs individually on various species of biting flies. When these take a blood meal the eggs hatch and the emerging larvae rapidly invade the mammalian host's skin, in which they begin to develop. No rational method of prevention is therefore available. The avoidance of sites that are known to be frequented by *T. penetrans*, for example chicken houses and farm buildings, and especially the wearing of solid footwear help to prevent infection with this flea. It is also important not to disperse eggs when removing the adult females (see below).

CLINICAL FEATURES

The clinical features of furuncular myiasis are similar for all species. The infection site is inconspicuous at first but a small, reddened papule develops within about 24 hours. The papule itches intermittently but especially at night. As the larva grows within the dermal cavity over the next 2–3 weeks a dome-like swelling develops on the skin surface with a surrounding area of inflammatory edema. Itching may become intense and a throbbing pain may be present. At the center of the dome a hole develops, through which the posterior tip of the larva bearing its spiracles emerges, together with a purulent, bloody exudate. As the larva grows it moults twice; this process is often accompanied by severe pain. The clinical course runs for 14–16 days in infestation with *C. anthropophaga* but up to 1 month with *D. hominis*. Lymphangitis and regional lymphadenopathy are common from about weeks 2–4 of infestation. During this time the larva repeatedly protrudes its posterior end through the hole in the skin but rapidly withdraws if contacted (Fig. 155.5). Eventually the mature larva forces its way out of the skin, causing little pain, and drops to the ground to pupate. The skin lesion usually heals rapidly and only a pigmented scar marks the site of the lesion (Fig. 155.6).

Infection with *T. penetrans* initially causes itching and sometimes pain; multiple lesions are common. The sites most commonly attacked are the skin of the feet and under the toenails. As the insect grows it produces a firm nodule, the surface of which becomes hyperkeratotic with a central, black spot. This is the site of the projecting spiracles. Secondary infection with pyogenic bacteria is common and may be associated with lymphangitis and regional lymphadenopathy. Infection with tetanus bacilli is a particular hazard.

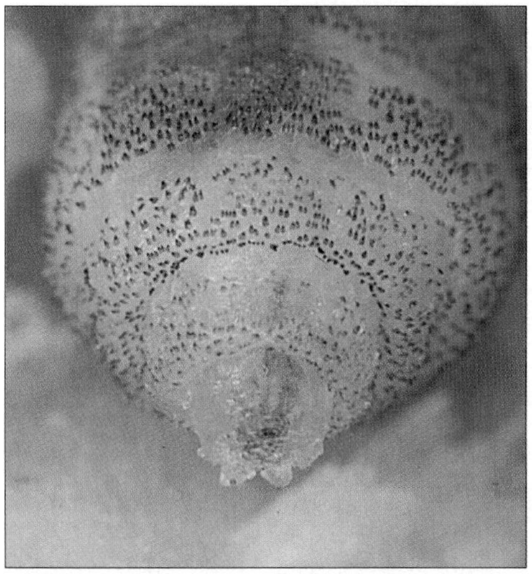

Fig. 155.3 Third instar larva of *Cordylobia anthropophaga*, the Tumbu fly. The powerful mouth hooks, with which the larva feeds, are seen as long, dark bars. With permission from Peters.[1]

Fig. 155.4 Adult female *Dermatobia hominis*. The fly lays eggs on blood-sucking insects such as mosquitoes or on ticks. After about 1 week larvae hatch from the eggs to infest the skin of a human or other warm-blooded host, which is fed on by the phoretic host. Courtesy of Dr AJ Shelley. With permission from Peters.[1]

Fig. 155.5 Second instar larva of *Dermatobia hominis* after surgical removal. The characteristic rows of dark spines are seen clearly. Courtesy of Dr RP Lane. With permission from Peters and Pasvol.[7]

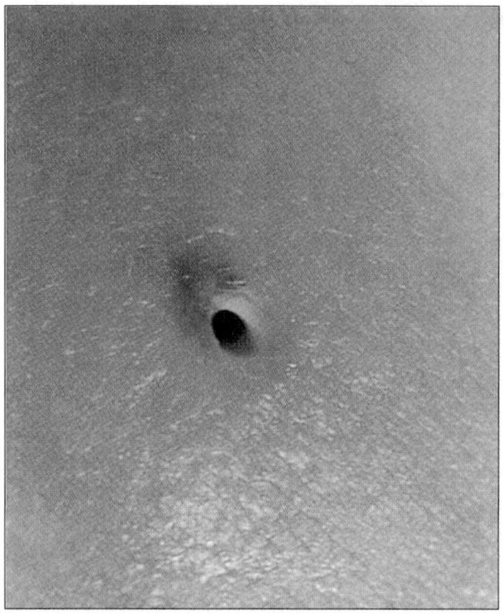

Fig. 155.6 Cavity left in the skin of the back of a woman who returned to Europe from an African holiday with multiple furuncular lesions caused by larvae of *Cordylobia anthropophaga*. Note the marked surrounding inflammation. Courtesy of Professor T Rufli. With permission from Peters.[1]

DIAGNOSIS

Any pustule of several days' or weeks' duration in a returning traveler should lead to a presumptive diagnosis of myiasis, and the travel history will immediately give a clue to the possible species involved. The presence of a central dark point in the pustule containing a spiracular plate or even a protruding larval extremity confirms the diagnosis but a specialist examination of any larva removed from the lesion may be required to confirm the species involved. Similarly, the presence of tender nodules on the feet or under the toenails should give rise to a possible diagnosis of tungiasis. In this case, too, the posterior end of the flea may be observed in the center of the skin overlying the nodule.

The differential diagnosis of myiasis includes infection with pyogenic bacteria or an embedded foreign body with secondary infection. Lesions of tungiasis may resemble plantar or subungual warts or acute infective paronychia. Multiple, serpiginous, subcutaneous lesions, especially on the feet (Fig. 155.7), buttocks or hands should give rise to a suspicion of skin invasion by ground-dwelling, infective larvae of dog hookworms ('creeping eruption', see Chapters 174 and 246).

MANAGEMENT

Attempts to express the embedded larvae of flies such as *C. anthropophaga* or *D. hominis* by squeezing the pustules are likely to do more harm than good. If the surface pore through which the spiracles of *C. anthropophaga* protrude is covered with paraffin for some hours, the larva can sometimes be pulled out with forceps (Fig. 155.8) but this is rarely successful with *D. hominis*.

In endemic areas of Central and South America, it is claimed that the larva can be tempted to emerge if the lesion is covered with a piece of pork fat for 24 hours or so, but this is not a method that one would suggest for use in returning travelers! In most cases it is best to remove the larva surgically after infiltrating round the lesion with an appropriate local anesthetic (see Fig. 155.5). This also facilitates removal of the larva because it is anesthetized. If necessary, the cavity can be curetted and, if it is large, it can be stitched, after which it can be left to granulate. The wound usually heals in about 1 week, leaving a pigmented scar.

Gravid *T. penetrans* (Fig. 155.9) should also be removed surgically. Inhabitants of endemic areas often extract the flea with a sharp sliver of bamboo or a razor blade, frequently inadvertently breaking open the insect's abdomen in the process and releasing the eggs to continue the insect's life cycle. The residual cavity in the skin, which must be kept clean to minimize secondary bacterial contamination, usually heals rapidly but secondary infection may require appropriate antibiotic therapy.

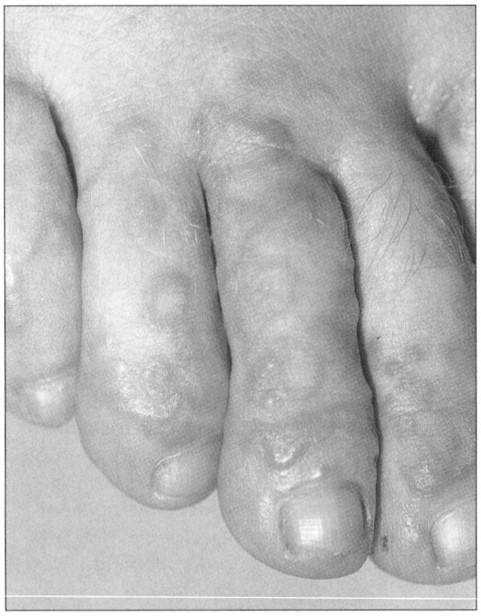

Fig. 155.7 Cutaneous larva migrans ('creeping eruption') due to invasion of infective larvae of the dog hookworm *Ancylostoma caninum*. This condition may be mistaken for infestation with the larvae of ectoparasitic arthropods. The lesions respond rapidly to treatment with albendazole or ivermectin. With permission from Peters and Pasvol.[7]

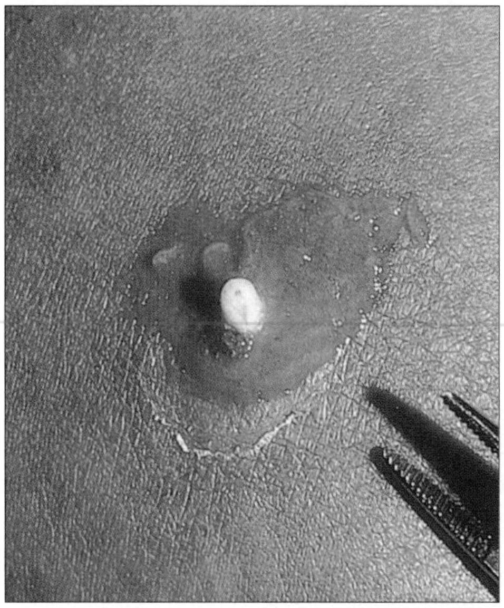

Fig. 155.8 Extracting a larva of *Cordylobia anthropophaga* after covering it with paraffin. The pair of black spiracles can just be seen in the center of the posterior tip of the larva. Courtesy of Professor A Bryceson. With permission from Peters and Pasvol.[7]

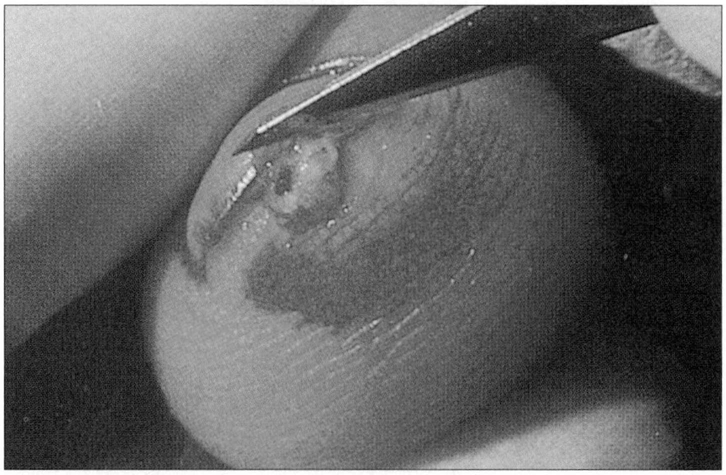

Fig. 155.9 Surgical extraction of a gravid female *Tunga penetrans*. Care must be taken not to disrupt the abdomen and release the eggs. Courtesy of Professor C Curtis. With permission from Peters.[1]

REFERENCES

1. Peters W. A colour atlas of arthropods in clinical medicine. London: Wolfe Publishing Ltd; 1992.
2. Goddard J. Physician's guide to arthropods of medical importance. Boca Raton: CRC Press; 1993.
3. See also the following pages on the Worldwide Web that contain numerous secondary links to ectoparasites: http://www.soton.ac.uk/~ceb/EctoEndodirectory/medecto.htm and http://www.ent.iastate.edu/List/medical_entomolgoy.html.
4. Hall MJR, Smith KGV. Diptera causing myiasis in man. In: Lane RP, Crosskey RG, eds. Medical insects and arachnids. London: Chapman and Hall; 1993:429–69.
5. Alexander JO. Arthropods and human skin. Berlin: Springer-Verlag; 1984.
6. Schaller KF, ed. Colour atlas of tropical dermatology and venerology. Berlin: Springer-Verlag; 1994.
7. Peters W, Pasvol G. Tropical medicine and parasitology, 5th ed. London: Mosby-Wolfe; 2002.
8. Cook GC, Zumla A, eds. Manson's tropical diseases, 21st ed. London: WB Saunders; 2002.
9. Wikel SK, ed. The immunology of host-ectoparasitic arthropod relationships. Oxford: CAB International; 1996.

chapter

156 Endemic Treponematoses

André Z Meheus & Om P Arya

The endemic treponematoses include yaws (also known as buba, framboesia, parangi and pian), endemic syphilis (also known as bejel, dichuchwa and sklerjevo) and pinta (also known as azul, carate and mal de pinto), all of which are chronic bacterial infections. The causative organisms (*Treponema pallidum* subsp. *pertenue*, *T. pallidum* subsp. *endemicum* and *Treponema carateum*, respectively) are morphologically and serologically indistinguishable from *T. pallidum* subsp. *pallidum*, which is the causative organism of venereal syphilis.

Small genetic differences, (a single base pair change) have been identified between the organisms of the venereal and nonvenereal (endemic) treponematoses.[1–3] However, none of these genetic variations identified so far can differentiate one subspecies from another and it remains unresolved whether they are all the same or different organisms. Nevertheless, there are significant clinical and epidemiologic differences.[4]

EPIDEMIOLOGY

Historic perspective

The endemic treponematoses, because of the disfigurement and disability they cause, were a major public health problem in the pre-antibiotic era. In 1948, the World Health Organization (WHO) and the United Nations International Children's Emergency Fund (UNICEF) sponsored a global control program. This involved 46 countries and brought these diseases under control with the help of long-acting penicillin. Unfortunately, the diseases were not eradicated and the lack of continuing vigilance allowed persistence of endemic foci in some countries, resulting in resurgence of these disease in the 1980s.

Geographic distribution

The endemic treponematoses are now largely confined to communities in remote rural areas living in poor, overcrowded and unhygienic conditions. Yaws occurs mainly in the warm, humid areas of Africa, South East Asia and the Pacific, the Caribbean and Central and South America. Endemic syphilis occurs mainly in the arid areas of sub-Saharan Africa and among the nomadic people of the Arabian peninsula. Pinta occurs mainly in Central and South America (among Indian tribes in the Amazon region and adjacent areas). Cases of imported yaws and endemic syphilis are sometimes encountered in the countries of the northern hemisphere, where clinicians may need to include them in the differential diagnosis.

INCIDENCE AND PREVALENCE

Accurate incidence and prevalence data are unavailable. The most recent estimate by WHO in 1995 yields a global prevalence of 2.5 million cases, including 460,000 infectious cases.

Age and sex

Yaws and endemic syphilis usually occur in children aged 2–14 years. For pinta the range is 10–30 years. The sexes are probably equally affected.

Mode of transmission

Yaws and pinta are transmitted by direct skin-to-skin contact with infectious lesions, transmission being facilitated by a breach in the skin of the recipient. The role of nonbiting flies in the transmission is uncertain. In the case of endemic syphilis, because the initial lesions are often in or around the mouth, the infection spreads by direct contact (e.g. older children kissing their younger siblings) and by indirect contact through infected communal eating or drinking utensils.

PATHOLOGY

Yaws and endemic syphilis affect skin and bones, whereas pinta is confined to the skin.

The basic pathology in endemic treponematoses is the same as in venereal syphilis. However, the vascular changes in the endemic treponematoses are less marked. A recent study of skin biopsies from yaws patients showed numerous plasma cells but few T and B cells; the treponemes were found mostly in the epidermis, whereas in venereal syphilis they were demonstrated mainly in the dermis and dermal–epidermal junction.[5] Because these differences are relative, they cannot be used to differentiate yaws from venereal syphilis.

In pinta, there is loss of melanin in basal cells, the presence of many melanophages in the dermis and the absence of inflammatory cells and treponemes in the achromic lesions.[6]

Contrary to occasional reports, endemic treponematoses are not believed to be associated with congenital transmission or with involvement of the cardiovascular and nervous systems.

PREVENTION

Essential in prevention of the endemic treponematoses is not only to identify and treat clinical cases but also to recognize that the presence of clinical cases in a community necessitates an immediate search for further clinical and latent cases, which also must be treated.

The preventive measures include:

- strengthening and improving accessibility of the primary health care facilities;
- training of clinicians to detect and treat patients and to examine and treat household and other obvious contacts;
- health education of the population;
- improvement in the standard of living and in personal and environmental hygiene; and
- provision of soap and water and clothing to children.

CLINICAL FEATURES

The incubation period is 9–90 days (mean 21 days).

Yaws

Early stage

The initial or primary lesion ('mother yaw') appears at the site of infection on an exposed part of the body. It may be a localized maculopapular eruption or a papule, which may develop into a large papilloma 2–5cm in diameter. It is painless but itchy and may ulcerate as a result of scratching. It may heal in 3–6 months with or without scarring. Secondary lesions, which are the result of lymphatic and hematogenous spread of organisms, appear a few weeks to 2 years after the primary lesion. They may consist of multiple excrescences, often resembling the initial papilloma. The papillomas may ulcerate and the exudate may dry to form a yellow crust which, when removed, gives the lesion an appearance of a raspberry (hence the name 'framboesia'). The lesions may be irregular, crescentic or discoid in shape and on moist areas may mimic condylomata lata of venereal syphilis. They are rather florid and become more numerous in the rainy season (Fig. 156.1). They may last up to 6 months and heal with or without scarring. Infectious relapses may occur for 5 years and, rarely, for 10 years.

Other manifestations include:

- regional lymphadenopathy;
- palmar and plantar lesions, which may be painful, resulting in a crab-like gait; and
- osteoperiostitis of the proximal phalanges of the fingers (dactylitis) or of long bones, causing nocturnal bone pains.

The patient may at any time enter latency, with only serologic evidence of the infection.

Late stage

About 10% of patients develop late lesions after 5 years or more of untreated infection. The late stage is characterized by gummatous lesions of skin, bones and overlying tissues. The manifestations, some of which also occur in early stage but are now more destructive, include:

- hyperkeratosis of palms and soles with deep fissuring;
- juxta-articular subcutaneous nodules;
- more extensive osteoperiostitis of long bones (e.g. sabre tibia);
- hyperostosis of the nasal processes of the maxillae ('goundou'); and
- ulceration of the palate and nasopharynx (rhinopharyngitis mutilans; Fig. 156.2) with secondary infection resulting in foul-smelling discharge ('gangosa').

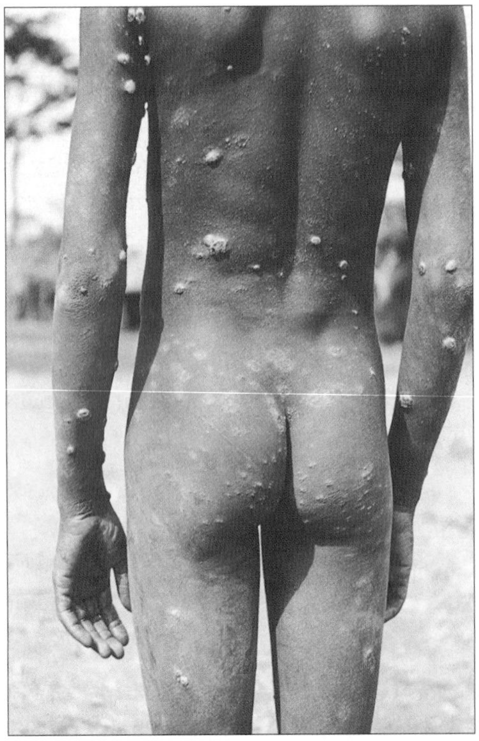

Fig. 156.1 Mixed early yaws lesions: papillomata, ulceropapillomatous lesions and squamous macules. Courtesy of WHO, Geneva.

Endemic syphilis

The primary lesion is seldom seen. The early manifestations include mucous patches (i.e. shallow painless ulcers on the lips and in the oropharynx) and other mucocutaneous and bone lesions resembling those of venereal syphilis and yaws. Papilloma favor warm and moist areas and occur as split papules or angular stomatitis at the labial commissures (Fig. 156.3). Later, the patient may enter the latent phase, which may be prolonged; after this some patients develop late lesions, which are similar to those seen in yaws.

Pinta

Pinta is confined to the skin and is the mildest of all treponematoses. The primary lesion, appearing at the site of entry of *T. carateum* on an exposed part of the body, is an itchy, red, scaly

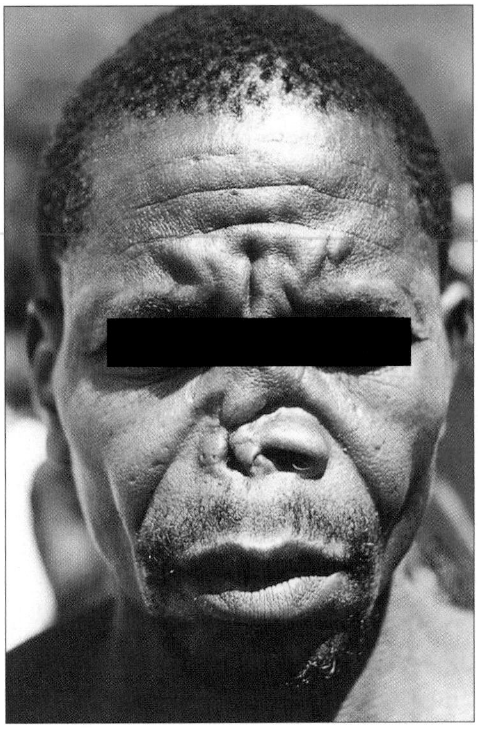

Fig. 156.2 Gangosa in late stage of yaws (rhinopharyngitis mutilans; occurs also in endemic syphilis). Courtesy of WHO, Geneva.

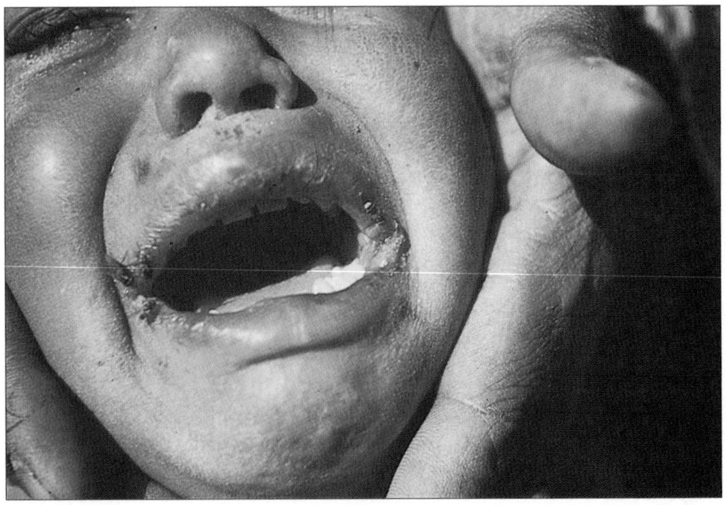

Fig. 156.3 Angular stomatitis (also called split papules) of endemic syphilis; these lesions are also found in early yaws. Courtesy of Dr GM Antal.

papule, sometimes associated with satellite lesions and regional lymphadenopathy. The secondary stage develops several months later, in other areas, with the appearance of pintids, which are similar to the initial lesions. These are also itchy. In due course, they undergo a variety of color changes from red to copper-colored, gray and bluish-black. The lesions remain infectious for many years.

The late lesions are characterized by varying degrees of hypochromia, discoloration, atrophy and achromia. Sometimes these features are seen in the same area.

Attenuated endemic treponematoses

In areas of reduced transmission, the clinical expression of endemic treponematoses can be much milder (a few or even a single papilloma) or many of the infected subjects can be asymptomatic.[4] In the Gambia, 9.3% of pregnant women were seropositive for a treponemal infection; children of seropositive mothers showed no signs of congenital syphilis and there was no increase in perinatal, neonatal or child deaths. No clinical signs of endemic treponematoses were found, indicating the asymptomatic nature of the infection.[7,8]

HIV infection and endemic treponematoses

As yet, no information is available on any interaction between HIV infection and endemic treponematoses.

DIFFERENTIAL DIAGNOSIS

In endemic areas, an accurate clinical diagnosis can be made in the presence of classic lesions. This will, however, necessitate appropriate training of clinicians, especially in view of the rather milder forms being encountered. The difficulties arise when there are no clinical lesions (i.e. latent cases), when venereal syphilis is also locally prevalent and when the patient is an immigrant from an endemic area presenting at a clinic in a nonendemic country. Differentiation from venereal syphilis is important because of social stigma implications. A careful and detailed history (including that of mother, father and siblings when appropriate) and thorough physical examination are always essential.

Apart from venereal syphilis, the conditions to be considered for differential diagnosis include:

- skin sepsis, scabies, fungal infection, lichen planus, plantar warts, psoriasis and tungiasis in a patient who has early skin lesions;
- tropical ulcer, cutaneous leishmaniasis, mycotic lesions and leprosy in a patient who has gummatous ulceration; and
- tuberculosis and sickle cell disease in a patient who has dactylitis.

Pinta may need to be differentiated from pityriasis versicolor, tinea corporis, vitiligo, leprosy and chloasma.

DIAGNOSIS

There is no test that can differentiate the treponematoses (including venereal syphilis) from one another. The diagnosis of treponemal infection is confirmed by the demonstration of treponemes (but beware of nonpathogenic commensals) in a wet preparation of the material from early lesions by dark-field microscopy or in the biopsy material stained by the silver impregnation technique.

Serologic tests (rapid plasma reagin (RPR) or Venereal Disease Research Laboratory (VDRL) nontreponemal tests; *T. pallidum* hemagglutination assay (TPHA) or fluorescent treponemal antibody absorption (FTA-ABS) treponemal (i.e. specific) tests) should be carried out in all cases, but their interpretation requires expertise. The treponemal tests are particularly useful to confirm a reactive nontreponemal test (exclusion of false positives). A reactive treponemal test may indicate a current infection or a past infection ('serologic scar'). Radiologic evidence of osteoperiostitis may assist in the diagnosis.

If the differentiation from venereal syphilis is difficult, the patient should be managed as for venereal syphilis.

MANAGEMENT

Penicillin remains the drug of choice. Long-acting benzathine penicillin G, given intramuscularly in a single session, is preferred. The dose is 600,0000 units (0.45g) for children under the age of 6 years; 1.2 million units (0.9g) for those aged 6–15 years; and 2.4 million units (1.8g) for those over 15 years. The dose may be divided, half to be given into each buttock. While it is recognized that treponematoses have remained exquisitely sensitive to penicillin, there is a recent report of penicillin treatment failures of yaws in Papua New Guinea.[9] Three penicillin treatment failures have also been observed in Ecuador.[10] The distinction between relapse, re-infection or true resistance is difficult to make but these clinical failures are worrisome and should be further researched.

Although there is little information on the use of drugs other than penicillin to treat these conditions, oral erythromycin or tetracycline 500mg q6h for 15 days or oral doxycycline 100mg q12h for 15 days are likely to be effective for those allergic to penicillin. Children between 12 and 15 years of age should receive half that dose. Tetracyclines (including doxycycline) are not recommended for pregnant and breast-feeding women and for children under the age of 12 years.

Contacts

Arrangements should be made to examine and, if appropriate and after proper explanation, to treat the household contacts and other close contacts.

Prognosis and follow-up

The lesions become noninfectious within 24 hours after the injection of penicillin. Whereas treatment in early stages should result in cure in almost 100% of patients, it will not reverse any destructive change in late stages. Rapid plasma reagin (or VDRL) titers should decline within 6–12 months, becoming negative in about 2 years. However, in a small proportion of cases, especially if treated in late stages, the RPR (or VDRL) may remain positive, albeit in low titer (i.e. below 1:8). The specific tests (i.e. TPHA, FTA-ABS) will remain positive throughout life.

REFERENCES

1. Noordhoek GT, Hermans PAN, Paul AN, *et al.* *Treponema pallidum* subspecies *pallidum* (Nichols) and *T. pallidum* subspecies *pertenue* (CDC 2575) differ in at least one nucleotide, comparison of two homologous antigens. Microb Pathog 1989;6:29–42.
2. Centurion-Lara A, Castro C, Castillo R, *et al.* The flanking regions sequences of the 15-kDa lipoprotein gene differentiate pathogenic treponemes. J Infect Dis 1998;177:1036–40.
3. Cameron CE, Castro C, Lukehart SA, *et al.* Sequence conservation of glycerophosphodiester phosphodiesterase among *Treponema pallidum* strains. Infect Immun 1999;67:3168–70.
4. Antal GM, Lukehart SA, Meheus AZ. The endemic treponematoses. Microbes Infect 2002;4:83–94.
5. Engelkens HJH, ten Kate FJW, Judanarso J, *et al.* The localization of treponemes and characterization of the inflammatory infiltrate in skin biopsies from patients with primary or secondary syphilis, or early infectious yaws. Genitourin Med 1993;69:102–7.
6. Marquez F. Pinta. In: Canizares O, ed Clinical tropical dermatology. Oxford: Blackwell Scientific Pulbications; 1975:86–92.
7. Greenwood AM, D'Allessandro U, Sisay F, *et al.* Treponemal infection and the outcome of pregnancy in a rural area of the Gambia, West Africa. J Infect Dis 1992;166:842–6.
8. Meheus A. Treponemal infection and pregnancy outcome in West Africa (letter). J Infect Dis 1994;169:701–2.
9. Backhouse JL, Hudson BJ, Hamilton PA, *et al.* Failure of penicillin treatment of yaws on Karkar Island, Papua New Guinea. Am J Trop Med Hyg 1998;59:388–92.
10. Anselmi M, Araujo E, Narváez PJ, *et al.* Yaws in Ecuador: impact of control measures on the disease in the Province of Esmeraldas. Genitourin Med 1995;71:343–6.

chapter

157 African Trypanosomiasis

David G Lalloo

EPIDEMIOLOGY

African trypanosomiasis (sleeping sickness) causes considerable mortality and morbidity across much of the African continent. Approximately 45,000 cases were reported to the World Health Organization (WHO) in 1999, but the true burden of disease is thought to be much higher, with estimates of between 300,000 and 500,000 individuals being infected.[1,2] Intensive control activities in the 1950s and 1960s were extremely successful in reducing the incidence of disease but a lack of resources and civil conflict in many of the most heavily affected countries has led to re-emergence of the disease as a major health problem.

African trypanosomiasis occurs in two distinct clinical forms: an acute form, caused by *Trypanosoma brucei rhodesiense*, transmitted in endemic situations by savanna *Glossina morsitans* group flies and in epidemic situations by a 'riverine' species, namely *Glossina fuscipes*; and a more chronic form caused by *Trypanosoma brucei gambiense*, transmitted by the riverine species *Glossina palpalis*, *Glossina tachinoides* and *G. fuscipes* (Fig. 157.1).[3,4] *Trypanosoma b. rhodesiense* is distributed in east and central Africa between Ethiopia and Botswana. It is a zoonosis with several game animal reservoirs; in the epidemic cycle, cattle are an important reservoir. *Trypanosoma b. gambiense* is found from Uganda west to Senegal and south through Zaire to Angola; humans are the prime reservoir of infection (Fig. 157.2, Table 157.1).[2]

PATHOGENESIS

Members of the genus *Trypanosoma* are parasitic in the blood and tissues of vertebrates and are transmitted by blood-sucking insects. A developmental cycle occurs in the gut and sometimes in the salivary glands of the insect vectors with the production of infective metacyclic trypanosomes; mammals acquire the infection by the bite of the tsetse fly vector. Trypanosomes are microscopic, varying in length from 15μm to 35μm, and are highly active when observed under the microscope.[4]

Metacyclic trypanosomes inoculated during tsetse feeding multiply locally in extracellular spaces and induce the typical 'chancre' (Fig. 157.3), with a marked local tissue response characterized by vasculitis, perivascular mononuclear cell infiltration, edema and local tissue damage. Trypanosomes enter the lymphatics and multiply within lymph nodes, leading to parasitemia 5–12 days after infection. Antigenic variation of the surface glycoproteins causes successive waves of parasitemia as the parasite evades the host immune response.[5]

Parasites enter the central nervous system (CNS) via the choroid plexus or by transcytosis across endothelial cells to cause a lymphocytic meningoencephalitis, which particularly affects the brain stem, although cortical areas and the cerebellum are also involved.[6] Perivascular infiltration with lymphocytes, plasma cells, macrophages and characteristic morular cells occurs; microglia and astrocytes proliferate and there is neuronal destruction and demyelination. Similar lesions also occur in the heart, serous membranes and endocrine organs.

Polyclonal activation of B lymphocytes leads to elevation of IgM concentrations. Heterophile antibodies, rheumatoid factor, immune complexes and autoantibody production may occur. Some neuropsychiatric manifestations may be biochemically induced; elevated prostaglandin D_2 concentrations have been found in advanced *T. b. gambiense* infection, which may be responsible for the circadian sleep disorders.[7]

PREVENTION

There are two major components of sleeping sickness control: detection and treatment of cases, and vector control. In *T. b. rhodesiense* areas, patients who present with symptoms of early parasitemia (passive surveillance) can be treated at local rural centers: in epidemics, rapid deployment of active surveillance using blood film screening and the establishment of effective local treatment centers is important (Fig. 157.4). In *T. b. gambiense* areas, limited clinical symptoms in the early stages require active surveillance. Individuals can be screened using gland aspiration or rapid antigen tests (e.g. the card agglutination test for trypanosomes, CATT). Although prophylactic measures such as 6-monthly intramuscular injections of pentamidine have been suggested for populations most at risk, concerns about development of drug resistance and the masking of second-stage infections means that this is no longer advocated.[2]

Vector control using insecticide-impregnated traps and targets has been demonstrated to be effective in epidemics of *T. b. gambiense* in the Congo[8] and in epidemics of *T. b. rhodesiense* transmitted by *G. fuscipes* in Uganda.[9] Sterile insect release methods may also be useful in reducing vector populations.[10] Residual insecticide application to *Glossina* resting sites, insecticide spraying and the clearing of riverine habitat have been used in the past but resource and environmental considerations means that these can no longer be considered. In epidemic situations, treatment of the cattle reservoir by cattle trypanocides may also be a strategy for prevention of human sleeping sickness.[11]

CLINICAL FEATURES

A local skin lesion, the chancre, may develop at the site of inoculation (see Fig. 157.2). This is a raised, tender, edematous papule that rapidly increases in size with surrounding local edema, erythema and local lymphadenopathy. Chancres resolve after 2–3 weeks; they are common in *T. b. rhodesiense* infections, but rare in *T. b. gambiense* infections. Trypanosomes subsequently invade lymphatics and blood, leading to the hemolymphatic stage (stage I) and may invade the central nervous system and cerebrospinal fluid (CSF), leading to meningoencephalitis (stage II). *Trypanosoma b. gambiense* causes a mild but protracted illness over months or years, which is followed by the late development of meningoencephalitis. In contrast, *T. b. rhodesiense* causes a severe, acute, febrile disease, with rapid progression to meningoencephalitis and death within months.[2,12,13]

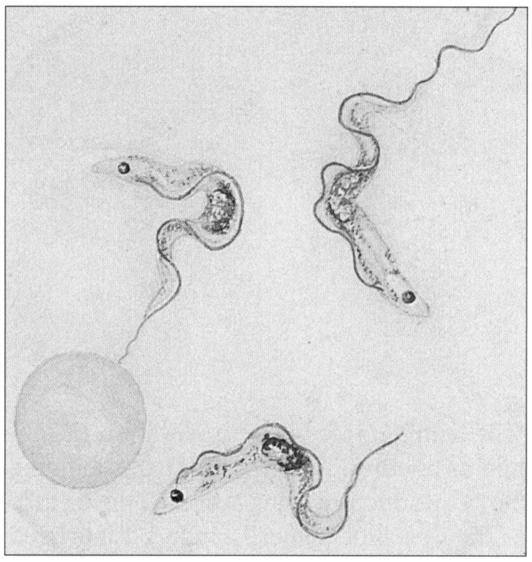

Fig. 157.1 The causative organisms of sleeping sickness in humans. Reproduction of Dutton's original drawing of *Trypanosoma brucei gambiense* from the blood of a man. The organisms possess nucleus kinetoplast and flagella, and their relative size can be assessed from the red blood cell diameter of 7μm.

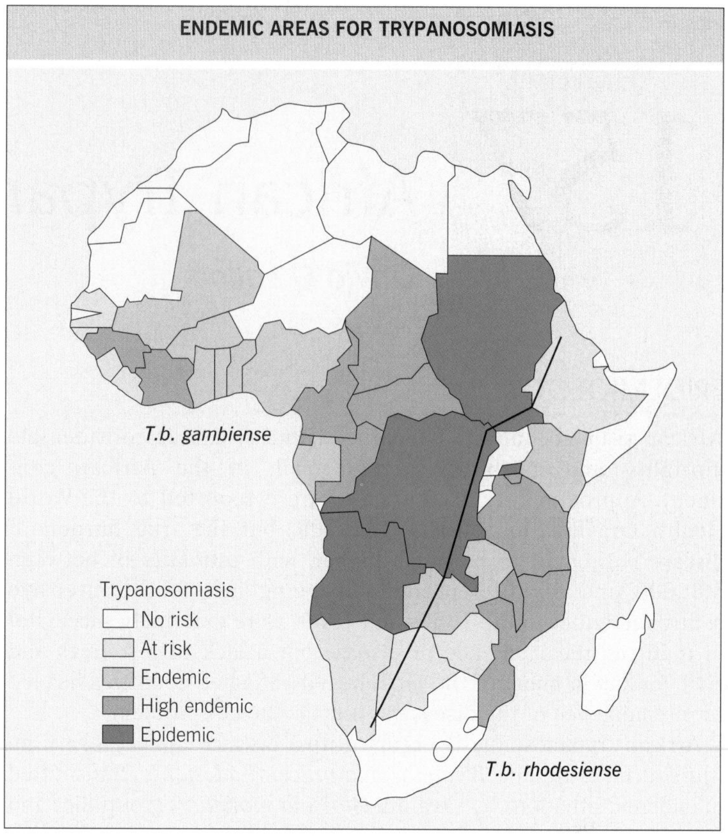

Fig. 157.2 Endemic areas for trypanosomiasis.

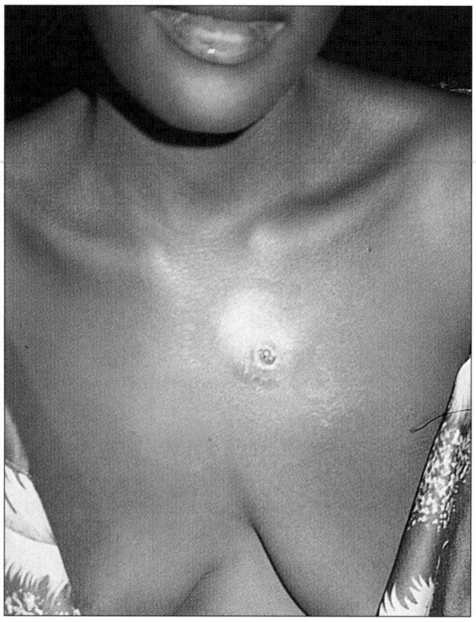

Fig. 157.3 Typical chancre of a patient infected with *Trypanosoma brucei rhodesiense*. The chancre develops at the site of the infecting fly bite.

Hemolymphatic trypanosomiasis (stage I)

The characteristic clinical features of hemolymphatic trypanosomiasis comprise:

- episodes of fever, often accompanied by chills and rigors, malaise and prostration;
- headache;
- joint pains; and
- loss of weight.

In *T. b. gambiense* infections the disease slowly increases in severity as it progresses. Lymphadenopathy occurs in *T. b. gambiense* infections, and enlargement of the posterior cervical glands is character-

Table 157.1 Epidemiology and distribution of the human trypanosomiases.

EPIDEMIOLOGY AND DISTRIBUTION OF THE HUMAN TRYPANOSOMIASES		
	Trypanosoma brucei gambiense	*Trypanosoma brucei rhodesiense*
Distribution	Uganda to Senegal and Angola	Ethiopia south to Botswana and east of Rift Valley
Vector	*Glossina palpalis, tachinoides, fuscipes*; feed on any available host	*Glossina morsitans, pallidipes, swynnertoni*; host is game or cattle
Acquisition	Sites of high human–vector contact: river crossings, sacred groves, streams; end of dry season in Guinea savannas; peridomestic transmission in derived humid savanna; plantations of coffee and cocoa	Human penetration into savanna woodland; associated occupations (e.g. hunting, fishing, gathering of firewood and honey)
Epidemic characteristics	Lack of control (surveillance, diagnosis, treatment and vector control) as a result of expansion of human reservoir	Changes of habitat; intense human–fly–cattle contact for *G. fuscipes* transmission; encroachment on human habitation for *G. morsitans* transmission
Animal reservoirs	Pigs; to a lesser extent other domestic animals, rarely game animals	Game animals in endemic situation (bushbuck and hartebeest); cattle in epidemic situation

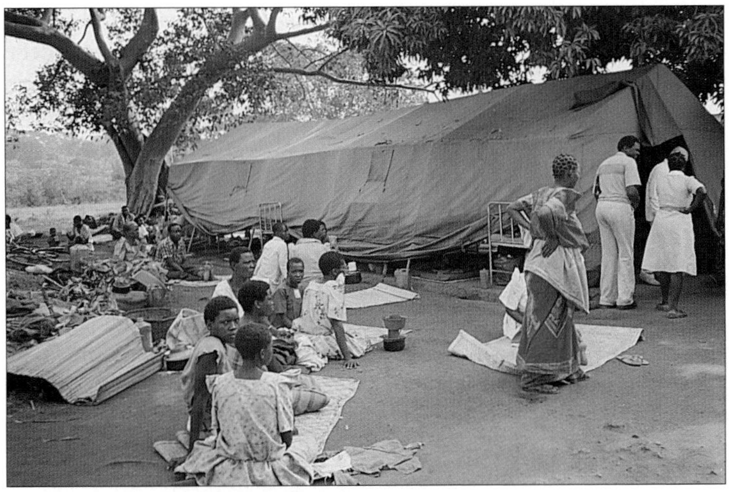

Fig. 157.4 Emergency treatment center Uganda. This center was established to provide facilities for the care and treatment of patients with sleeping sickness during the epidemic in Busoga.

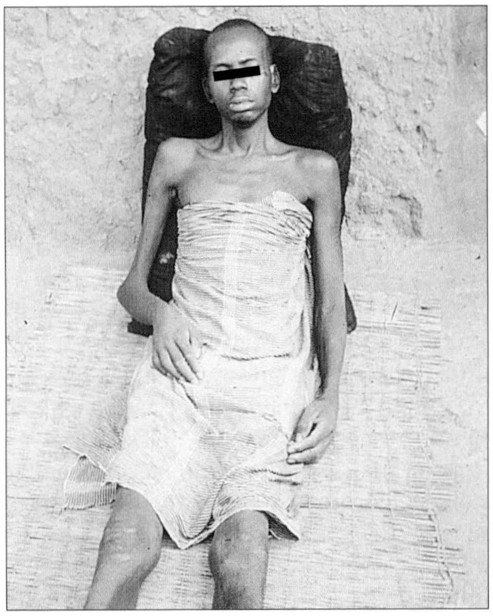

Fig. 157.5 Comatose terminal stage patient with sleeping sickness. Note the degree of cachexia.

istic (Winterbottom's sign). Lymph nodes are moderately enlarged, firm and discrete. Splenomegaly occurs in around one-third of cases, and may be associated with hepatomegaly. A fleeting erythematous rash ('circinate erythema') on the trunk or upper extremities is evident in light skinned people. There are focal areas of edema, facial puffiness, dependent edema and serous effusions including ascites, pleural effusions and pericardial effusions. Myocarditis occurs especially in *T. b. rhodesiense* infections.[12,13]

Meningoencephalitic trypanosomiasis (stage II)

In *T. b. rhodesiense* infections, cerebral involvement occurs within weeks of the onset of infection, whereas in *T. b. gambiense* infections meningoencephalitis may be delayed several years after initial infection. Headache becomes more severe and protracted. Personality changes may occur early, especially in *T. b. gambiense* infections, with apathy, lack of attention, loss of appetite, antisocial behavior and paranoid or delusional states. Abnormalities of sleep are characteristic and result from disturbance of normal circadian rhythms. Diurnal and inappropriate somnolence is often associated with nocturnal insomnia.

Neurologic features include tremors, muscle fasciculation, increased muscle tone and rigidity, choreic and athetotic movements. The gait is affected early with progressive ataxia. Speech is slow, slurred, or incoherent. Convulsions and hemiplegia can occur. Pyramidal tract and cranial nerve lesions are less common. Kerandel's sign refers to deep hyperesthesia, often with a delayed response to painful stimuli. Intractable pruritus is a feature of *T. b. gambiense*, especially in the later stages. Ocular manifestations can include iritis, chorioretinitis and papilledema.

The course of the disease is a relentless deterioration to a stuporose state, with cachexia, wasting and progressive malnutrition (Fig. 157.5). Patients become increasingly difficult to rouse and pass into deepening coma and death. This is relatively rapid in *T. b. rhodesiense* but may be protracted over months or years in *T. b. gambiense*. Intercurrent infections, especially bronchopneumonia, are common in the late stages of the disease. In *T. b. gambiense*, amenorrhea and impotence are common.[12–14]

Sleeping sickness in special groups

Although sleeping sickness is less common in children than adults, the clinical course of infection in children may be more severe and, with *T. b. rhodesiense* infection, progression to meningoencephalitis may be even more rapid than in adults.[15] Congenital infection has been described in *T. b. gambiense*.

Trypanosomiasis caused by *T. b. rhodesiense* or *T. b. gambiense* may occur in tourists and visitors to endemic areas. Severe early infections with high peripheral parasitemia are most common in travelers, characterized by a severe systemic illness with fever, anemia, biochemical abnormalities and circulating immune complexes. Thrombocytopenia is common and there may be evidence of a coagulopathy and disseminated intravascular coagulation. Most travelers do not develop CNS involvement, although delayed diagnosis may be a problem outside endemic areas, especially if no chancre is present.[16]

DIAGNOSIS

Routine laboratory tests demonstrate normal white cell counts, raised erythrocyte sedimentation rate, anemia, thrombocytopenia, low serum albumin and elevated serum IgM.

Parasitologic diagnosis

Diagnosis of sleeping sickness is dependent on finding trypanosomes in the chancre, blood, lymph gland juice or CSF – either in unfixed or unstained preparations, when moving parasites are observed, or in stained preparations. Blood films are usually positive in *T. b. rhodesiense* infection but parasitologic diagnosis may be difficult in chronic *T. b. gambiense* disease; high levels of parasites are often only found during a fever. Repeated examination and concentration techniques such as microhematocrit centrifugation may improve diagnostic sensitivity. *Trypanosoma b. gambiense* may also be diagnosed by finding parasites in aspirates from enlarged cervical lymph glands.

Diagnosis of second stage (CNS) disease requires examination of CSF. Before lumbar puncture, a single dose of suramin eliminates trypanosomes from the blood, avoiding the risk of contamination of CSF with trypanosoma.[2,12] Parasites may be found in the centrifuged deposit, which should be examined within 15 minutes of the lumbar puncture. A raised CSF cell count (>5/mm^3) or raised CSF protein are also suggestive of CNS infection.

Immunologic diagnosis

A number of serologic tests have been developed; CATT is particularly useful for rapid preliminary screening of large populations for *T. b. gambiense* infection. A more recent approach to indirect detection of parasites is the use of an antigen detection test (CIATT) to detect *T. b. rhodesiense* in serum and CSF. This may be useful for following the response to therapy.[17]

Differential diagnosis

In endemic areas, *T. b. rhodesiense* is most common in certain occupational groups such as hunters, game wardens and fishermen, although all members of the community may be affected. Transmission of *T. b. gambiense* occurs at places of contact between humans and water, and both sexes and all age groups are affected. Outside endemic areas, trypanosomiasis caused by *T. b. rhodesiense* should be considered in travelers from eastern and southern Africa (especially those who have visited game parks) who present with an acute severe febrile illness. *Trypanosoma b. gambiense* infections may present months or years after exposure, with a febrile illness or neuropsychiatric features.

Chancres may be confused with insect bites, skin infections, an eschar or cutaneous anthrax. Early hemolymphatic disease mimics a wide range of febrile illnesses, especially malaria, relapsing fever, typhoid, brucellosis and arboviral infections. Occasionally, myocarditis may dominate the clinical picture. The differential diagnosis of meningoencephalitis includes a wide range of inflammatory cerebral infections; in particular, cryptococcal or tuberculous meningitis complicating HIV infection needs to be excluded. The neuropsychiatric presentations of trypanosomiasis may be confused with a variety of psychiatric syndromes, especially when personality change or psychotic behavior predominate. Late-stage disease may also mimic focal neurologic disorders, parkinsonism and space-occupying cerebral lesions.

MANAGEMENT

Treatment of sleeping sickness depends upon the stage of disease; a lumbar puncture is therefore crucial to determine whether there is evidence of CNS involvement. At least one dose of suramin or pentamidine should be given to clear blood parasites before a lumbar puncture is performed to prevent inoculation of parasites into CSF at the time of lumbar puncture. There have been few recent advances in the chemotherapy of trypanosomiasis and the number of available drugs is limited (Table 157.2).[18] Most treatment regimens are relatively toxic and it is therefore important to diagnose and treat nutritional deficiencies or intercurrent infections; routine anthelmintic and antimalarial treatment is often given. Hemolymphatic trypanosomiasis is treated with suramin or pentamidine; the latter is only effective in *T. b. gambiense* infection. Meningoencephalitis requires treatment with drugs that cross the blood–brain barrier in trypanocidal concentrations. The mainstays of therapy are arsenical drugs, particularly melarsoprol, used since the beginning of the 20th century. Eflornithine and nifurtimox are also used for the treatment of late-stage *T. b. gambiense* infections. In most individuals, drugs rapidly clear parasitemia or CNS parasites, but relapses occur and 2-year cure rates are the best estimate of drug efficacy. Treatment responses vary according to the drug, severity of illness and geographic location.

Hemolymphatic trypanosomiasis

Suramin is given intravenously as a 10% solution. Fever, nausea, vomiting and urticaria are common but the most severe side-effect is an idiosyncratic anaphylactic reaction, which is infrequent (1 in 2000–4000) but may be more common in the presence of onchocerciasis. Proteinuria and renal failure may also occur. Intramuscular or intravenous pentamidine isethionate or pentamidine methanesulfonate are alternatives to suramin in *T. b. gambiense* infection and are usually well tolerated. Side-effects include a histamine-like reaction with hypotension and circulatory collapse, hypoglycemia and, after prolonged administration, hyperglycemias and diabetes; adrenaline (epinephrine) and glucose should be available when this drug is administered.

Meningoencephalitic trypanosomiasis

Melarsoprol is a trivalent arsenical compound that crosses the blood–brain barrier. A number of treatment schedules have been used, most lasting for 4–5 weeks. However, shorter 10-day treatment regimens have recently been shown to be effective in *T. b. gambiense* infection.[19] Thrombophlebitis and cellulitis following extravascular leakage are common (Fig. 157.6). The most important side-effect is reactive arsenic encephalopathy, which occurs in 2–10% of patients, usually after the third or fourth dose. Presentation is usually as an acute deterioration in conscious level often heralded by convulsions. There is an associated case fatality rate of 10–50%. Prophylactic prednisone (prednisolone) reduces the incidence of reactive arsenic encephalopathy in *T. b. gambiense* (but not *T. b. rhodesiense*) infection.[20]

Other toxicity is also common – a peripheral neuropathy occurs in up to 10% of patients and skin reactions, hepatic and renal toxicity are also seen; hemolysis may occur in glucose-6-phosphate dehydrogenase deficiency. Treatment with melarsoprol normally leads to a striking improvement in the mental and physical condition of patients with sleeping sickness. However, recent data suggest that rates of relapse following melarsoprol therapy are increasing.[18]

DRUGS CURRENTLY USED FOR THE TREATMENT OF SLEEPING SICKNESS

Drug	Species	Indication	Route	Typical dosage regimen	Side-effects
Suramin	*Trypanosoma brucei rhodesiense* *(Trypanosoma brucei gambiense)*	Stage 1	Slow iv infusion	Day 1: 5mg/kg test dose Day 3: 10mg/kg Days 5,11,23,30: 20mg/kg	Anaphylaxis Cutaneous reactions
Pentamidine	*T. b. gambiense*	Stage 1	im/iv	7–10 doses of 4mg/kg daily (or alternate days)	Local reactions (im) Hypotension Hypoglycemia
Melarsoprol	*T. b. rhodesiense* *T. b. gambiense*	Stage 2	iv infusion	Three series of four daily doses of1.2–3.6mg/kg, each separated by 7–10 days	Arsenical encephalopathy Peripheral neuropathy Dermatitis
Eflornithine	*T. b. gambiense*	Stage 2	iv infusion (po)	400mg/kg daily in four divided doses for 7–14 days	Diarrhea Pancytopenia Convulsions
Nifurtimox (under evaluation)	*T. b. gambiense* *?T. b. rhodesiense*	Stage 2	po	15–20mg/kg daily in three divided doses for 14 days	Anemia Neurologic side-effects

Table 157.2 Drugs currently used for the treatment of sleeping sickness.

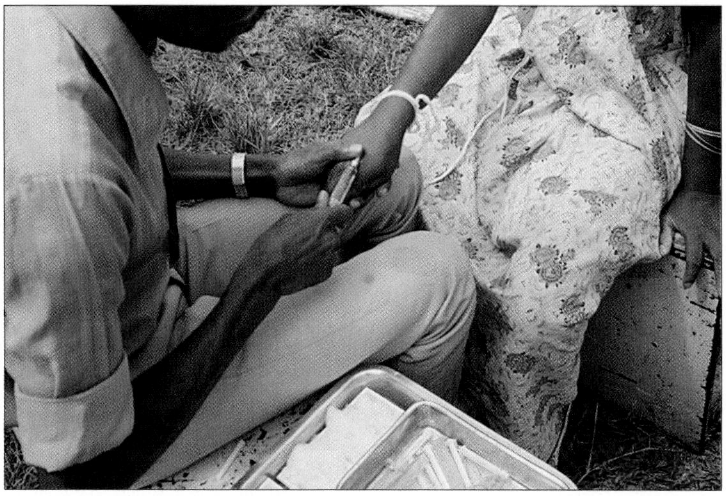

Fig. 157.6 Treatment of a patient with an intravenous injection of melarsoprol. It is vital to adhere to the schedules of treatment and to have a scrupulous technique of injection in order to avoid destruction of local tissue as a result of leakages of the melarsoprol suspended in propylene glycol.

Eflornithine (difluoromethyl-ornithine, DFMO) is an ornithine decarboxylase inhibitor that is effective in the treatment of stage 1 and stage 2 *T. b. gambiense* infection but is poorly effective against *T. b. rhodesiense*. Most current regimens use intravenous administration, although oral preparations are being evaluated. The drug is less toxic than melarsoprol. Standard courses last 14 days; 7-day courses have been advocated but appear to be less effective in new cases of sleeping sickness.[21] Eflornithine may be particularly useful for the treatment of late-stage *T. b. gambiense* infection when the organism has become resistant to melarsoprol.

Nifurtimox is a drug that has occasionally been used in the treatment of arsenic-refractory *T. b. gambiense*, with reported response rates that vary from 50% to 80%. Its role is still being evaluated.[18]

Post-treatment follow-up

Following treatment, patients should be reviewed every 3 months for 6 months and then 6-monthly for 2 years to identify episodes of relapse, which may occur after both early and late-stage disease. In late-stage infection, the CSF abnormalities improve slowly after treatment and values usually return to normal within 1–2 years; CSF examination should be repeated before discharge and routinely at follow-up to detect parasites or a rising cell count. Relapse in *T. b. gambiense* following treatment with suramin or pentamidine is often treated with melarsoprol; eflornithine can also be used. Relapse in *T. b. rhodesiense* is usually treated with a second course of melarsoprol; nifurtimox may be effective if further relapse occurs but more data are needed.[2] Combination therapy has also been used in the treatment of relapse but there are inadequate data to determine its role at present.

Acknowledgement

This chapter is a revision of the original chapter by Dr DH Smith and Professor DH Molyneux in the first edition.

REFERENCES

1. World Health Organization. The program for surveillance and control of African trypanosomiasis. http://who.int/emc/disease/tryp/sleeping_sickness.pdf.
2. World Health Organization. Control and surveillance of African trypanosomiasis. Technical Report Series No 881. Geneva: World Health Organization; 1998.
3. Molyneux DH. Current public health status of the trypanosomiases and leishmaniases. In: Hide G, Mottram JC, Coombs GH, Holmes PH, eds. Trypanosomiasis and leishmaniasis: biology and control. Wallingford, UK: Commonwealth Agricultural Bureau International; 1997:39–50.
4. Molyneux DH, Ashford RW. The biology of *Trypanosoma* and *Leishmania*, parasites of man and domestic animals. London: Taylor & Francis; 1983.
5. Barry JD. The biology of antigenic variation in African trypanosomes. In: Hide G, Mottram JC, Coombs GH, Holmes PH, eds. Trypanosomiasis and leishmaniasis: biology and control. Wallingford, UK: Commonwealth Agricultural Bureau International; 1997:89–107.
6. Enanga B, Burchmore RJ, Stewart ML, *et al.* Sleeping sickness and the brain. Cell Mol Life Sci 2002;59:845–58.
7. Pentreath VW, Rees K, Owolabi OA, *et al.* The somnogenic T lymphocyte suppressor prostaglandin D2 is selectively elevated in cerebrospinal fluid of advanced sleeping sickness patients. Trans R Soc Trop Med Hyg 1990;84:795–9.
8. Gouteux JP, Sinda D. Community participation in the control of tsetse flies. Large scale trials using the pyramidal trap in the Congo. Trop Med Parasitol 1990;41:49–55.
9. Lancien J. Lutte contre la maladie du sommeil dans le sud est Ouganda par le piégeage des glossines. Ann Soc Bel Med Trop 1991;71(Suppl.1):35–47.
10. Schofield CJ, Maudlin I. Trypanosomiasis control. Int J Parasitol 2001;31:614–9.
11. Fevre EM, Coleman PG, Odiit M, *et al.* The origins of a new *Trypanosoma brucei rhodesiense* sleeping sickness outbreak in eastern Uganda. Lancet 2001;358:625–8.
12. Ormerod WE. Pathogenesis and pathology of trypanosomiasis in man. In: Mulligan HW, ed. The African trypanosomiases. London: George Allen & Unwin/Ministry of Overseas Development; 1970:587–601.
13. Apted FIC. Clinical manifestations and diagnosis of sleeping sickness. In: Mulligan HW, ed. The African trypanosomiases. London: George Allen & Unwin/Ministry of Overseas Development; 1970:661–83.
14. Burri C, Nkunku S, Merolle A, *et al.* Efficacy of new, concise schedule for melarsoprol in treatment of sleeping sickness caused by *Trypanosoma brucei gambiense*: a randomised trial. Lancet 2000;355:1419–25.
15. Triolo N, Trova P, Fusco C, *et al.* Report on l7 years of studies of human African trypanosomiasis caused by *T. gambiense* in children 0–6 years of age. Med Trop 1985;45:251–7.
16. Sinha A, Grace C, Alston WK, *et al.* African trypanosomiasis in two travelers from the United States. Clin Infect Dis 1999;29:840–4.
17. Asonganyi T, Doua F, Kibona SN, Nyasulu YM, Masake R, Kuzoe F. A multi-centre evaluation of the card indirect agglutination test for trypanosomiasis (TrypTect CIATT). Ann Trop Med Parasitol 1998;92:837–44.
18. Legros D, Ollivier G, Gastellu-Etchegorry M, *et al.* Treatment of human African trypanosomiasis – present situation and needs for research and development. Lancet Infect Dis 2002;2:437–40.
19. Burri C, Nkunku S, Merolle A, *et al.* Efficacy of new, concise schedule for melarsoprol in treatment of sleeping sickness caused by *Trypanosoma brucei gambiense*: a randomised trial. Lancet 2000;355:1419–25.
20. Pepin J, Milord F, Guern C, *et al.* Trial of prednisolone for prevention of melarsoprol-induced encephalopathy in gambiense sleeping sickness. Lancet 1989;1:1246–50.
21. Pepin J, Khonde N, Doua F, *et al.* Short course eflornithine in Gambian trypanosomiasis: a multicentre randomised trial. Bull WHO 2000;78:1284–95.

chapter 158

Other Parasitic Infections of the Central Nervous System

Euan M Scrimgeour

This chapter reviews parasitic infections of the central nervous system (CNS), with brief reference to trypanosomiasis and cerebral malaria (see Chapters 146, 157, 166 and 173).

EPIDEMIOLOGY

Numerous species of protozoa and helminths parasitize man, especially in tropical and developing countries where environmental conditions promote mass transmission. Many sources of infection exist (Table 158.1). Table 158.2 lists parasites that can invade the CNS as adults, larvae or ova, depending upon the species, and gives their principal geographic distribution. It excludes parasitic Diptera, whose maggots occasionally invade the brain from the eye, nose or ear, and ticks that cause tick bite paralysis.

Many parasitic diseases are zoonoses. Examples, identifying the mammalian hosts, include:

- toxoplasmosis (cats and rodents),
- South American trypanosomiasis (domestic and wild animals),
- Rhodesian trypanosomiasis (antelopes, cattle),
- angiostrongyliasis (rodents),
- gnathostomiasis (fish-eating mammals),
- trichinosis (pigs and rats),
- toxocariasis (dogs and cats),
- schistosomiasis japonica (domestic animals and rodents), and
- echinococcosis (dogs and herbivores).

Gambian trypanosomiasis, schistosomiasis mansoni and schistosomiasis haematobium are essentially anthroponotic. In taeniasis solium (*T. solium*) humans are the definitive host but the larval cysticerci are found in pigs.

Relatively few parasites commonly involve the CNS. In some (e.g. *Plasmodium falciparum, Trypanosoma* spp., *Toxoplasma gondii, Angiostrongylus cantonensis* and *Taenia solium* (cysticercosis)), it is part of the life cycle. In others, it is accidental (e.g. eosinophilic meningoencephalitis caused by the racoon ascarid *Bayliscaris procyonis*).

Large populations are exposed to the risk of CNS parasitism. Worldwide, toxoplasmosis is probably the most prevalent neurotropic parasitosis. Schistosomiasis affects 200 million people, with prevalence rates of 10–80% in endemic areas. About 50 million individuals have African trypanosomiasis (prevalence 50–70/10,000 in endemic areas) and some 20 million – including thousands of migrants from South and Central America living in North America – have trypanosomiasis cruzi (Chagas' disease). In South East Asia and Oceania, angiostrongyliasis is common although diagnosis is infrequent.[1] Because CNS involvement is often underdiagnosed and silent, it is difficult to estimate prevalence and incidence rates. However, autopsy studies of patients with cysticercosis in Peru, Mexico, India and Zimbabwe have shown CNS infection rates of 0.5–3%, usually without clinical sequelae; in Mexico, 80% were asymptomatic.[2] Schistosomiasis japonica affects 70 million people and 2–5% of cases develop CNS complications.[3] Clinical evidence of CNS involvement is uncommon in infections with S. mansoni and S. haematobium, but autopsy studies in Zimbabwe, Nigeria, Egypt and Brazil have revealed ova in the brain in 3–28% and in the spinal cord in 0.3–2% of cases.[4] Worldwide, cerebral malaria is the most commonly diagnosed manifestation of CNS parasitism; in African children with severe falciparum malaria, 30–70% have this complication.[5]

PATHOGENESIS AND PATHOLOGY

Parasites invade the CNS as adults, larvae or ova, through the systemic circulation or retrogradely via the vertebral venous system (Fig. 158.1). Clinical sequelae depend upon the nature and number of parasites and the immune response. Immune evasion is exhibited by many parasites (e.g. *Toxoplasma gondii, Trypanosoma* spp.), with minimal tissue reaction.

In falciparum malaria, maturation of the trophozoite to the schizont requires sequestration of the parasitized erythrocyte by cytoadherence in capillaries, including those of the CNS. This is usually without clinical sequelae in immune subjects, but in cerebral malaria massive sequestration obstructs capillaries, the most plausible explanation for coma.[5] In acute African trypanosomiasis trypomastigotes rapidly invade the brain. They may become dormant but later, in stage II of the disease, especially in Gambian trypanosomiasis, they cause nonsuppurative encephalomyelitis (see Chapter 157).

Migrating larvae of the nematodes *Angiostrongylus cantonensis, Gnathostoma spinigerum, Toxocara canis* and *Toxocara cati, Trichinella spiralis*, occasionally *Loa loa, Mansonella perstans, Ascaris lumbricoides* and *Dirofilaria immitis* (the dog heartworm) produce transient focal cerebral lesions or eosinophilic meningoencephalitis.[6,7] *Bayliscaris procyonis* and the saprophytic soil nematode *Micronema deletrix* have also been incriminated. *Angiostrongylus cantonensis*, and others that cannot complete their life cycle in humans, die after a few weeks.

Certain trematode ova and larvae can involve the CNS. In early schistosomiasis, anomalous migration of worms to the CNS is followed by a cell-mediated response to ova deposition to form a periovular granuloma.[8] When the subsequent humoral response to adult worms and egg antigens is excessive, Katayama fever occurs, especially in *Schistosoma japonicum* infection, with fever, eosinophilia and self-limiting encephalopathy or myelopathy. In chronic schistosomiasis, retrograde passage of ova and occasionally worms, through Batson's vertebral venous plexus, may result in myelopathy or cerebral lesions. This also occurs in *S. haematobium* infection with obstructive uropathy. When hepatosplenic schistosomiasis develops, ova pass through portopulmonary anastomoses to the lungs and reach the systemic circulation through arteriovenous shunts or by pulmonary veins (see Fig. 158.1). Schistosomal cor pulmonale also promotes cerebral embolization of ova. Ova in the CNS may incite little histologic reaction, but the development of a granuloma, focal vasculitis, localized infarction or rarely subarachnoid or cerebral hemorrhage can result.[4] In paragonimiasis, flukes migrate from lung to brain through the soft tissues of the neck.

SOURCES OF PARASITE INFECTION AND RESULTING DISEASE		
Source of infection		**Disease**
Food	Salads	Amebiasis, angiostrongyliasis, ascariasis, cysticercosis
	Raw aquatic plants	Fascioliasis
	Uncooked vegetables	Angiostrongyliasis, echinococcosis, cysticercosis
	Uncooked pork	Trichinosis, taeniasis solium, sparganosis
	Uncooked beef	Toxoplasmosis
	Uncooked freshwater fish	Gnathostomiasis, diphyllobothriasis, heterophyiasis, metagonimiasis
	Uncooked freshwater crayfish or crabs	Paragonimiasis, angiostrongyliasis
	Uncooked snakes, frogs*	Sparganosis
	Uncooked land molluscs (e.g. *Achatina fulica* snails)	Angiostrongyliasis
Fresh water	Skin contact	Schistosomiasis
	Nasal contact	*Naegleria fowleri* meningoencephalitis
	Consumption	Sparganosis, dracontiasis, amebiasis
Other environmental sources	Geophagy	Toxoplasmosis, toxocariasis, ascariasis, hydatidosis
	Soil	Strongyloidiasis
	Airborne	*Acanthamoeba castellani* meningoencephalitis, ascariasis
Arthropods	Mosquito (*Anopheles* spp.)	Falciparum malaria
	Mosquito (*Culex* spp.)	Bancroftian filariasis, dirofilariasis
	Midge (*Culicoides* spp.)	Mansonellosis
	Tsetse fly (*Glossina* spp.)	Rhodesian and Gambian trypanosomiasis
	Blackfly (*Simulium* spp.)	Onchocerciasis
	Chrysops flies	Loiasis
	Reduviid bugs (e.g., *Triatoma* spp.)	American trypanosomiasis (Chagas' disease)
Other sources	Blood transfusion/contaminated syringes and needles	Falciparum malaria, American trypanosomiasis (Chagas' disease) toxoplasmosis
	Cardiac, renal transplant	Toxoplasmosis
	Transplacental	American trypanosomiasis (Chagas' disease), toxoplasmosis
	Autoinfection†	Cysticercosis, strongyloidiasis

* In South East Asia, frogs applied as a poultice may transmit sparganosis
† Patient with taeniasis solium inadvertently consumes eggs he or she has passed in feces

Table 158.1 Sources of parasite infection and resulting disease.

In cysticercosis, the larval oncospheres reach cerebral and meningeal capillaries and mature to cysticerci in the gray matter and meninges. The spinal cord is largely spared. Cysticerci survive silently for 2–10 years. Intense inflammation follows their death and antibodies appear in the cerebrospinal fluid (CSF). Healing, with fibrosis and calcification, follows. If the oncosphere enters the subarachnoid space or ventricles, then chronic meningitis with hydrocephalus may result.[2] Rarely, parasites produce large cystic lesions (e.g. in paragonimiasis, hydatidosis and coenurosis). In dracontiasis an extradural abscess containing an adult worm may compress the spinal cord, and in diphyllobothriasis an adult tapeworm competes with the host for vitamin B12 and can produce myelopathy (see Chapter 168).

Immunodeficiency and central nervous system parasitism

Immunodeficient patients are susceptible to the same parasites as the immunocompetent. Falciparum malaria is not more common in patients with HIV/AIDS but the parasite count may be increased. In toxoplasmosis, following acute infection, cysts containing the resting phase bradyzoites remain dormant in muscle, heart, brain or choroid for decades. (The risk of a nonimmune subject developing toxoplasmosis following organ transplant from a seropositive donor is 50% for cardiac and 20% for renal transplant.) In immunodeficiency states (e.g. AIDS, leukemia and lymphomas, inherited immunodeficiency syndromes, systemic lupus erythematosus, immunosuppressive drug therapy, radiotherapy, etc.), reactivation of bradyzoites produces multiplying tachyzoites, with cerebral abscess formation (see Chapter 127). Reactivation results from impaired interferon-γ dependent cell-mediated and humoral immunity.[10] In AIDS, this occurs when the CD4 lymphocyte count falls below 350 cells/mm^3. Trypanosomiasis cruzi spares the brain in the immunocompetent (except children), but in immunodeficiency (in AIDS, CD4 cell count <200/mm^3), often after symptom-free decades, reactivation produces cardiomyopathy and acute, multifocal, necrotizing meningoencephalitis or a cerebral granuloma.[10] Other opportunistic parasites that invade the CNS include free-living amoebae (eg. *Acanthomoeba culbertsoni* and *Balamuthia mandrillaris)*, which produce chronic granulomatous meningoencephalitis,[11] and the intestinal microsporidium *Encephalitozoon cuniculi*, which disseminates to produce encephalopathy.[12] Some *Strongyloides stercoralis* larvae normally hatch in the jejunum, penetrate the intestinal mucosa, migrate through the lungs and return to the jejunum as adults. In immunodeficiency, especially in human T-cell lymphoma virus 1 (HTLV-1) infection, *Strongyloides* hyperinfection may develop with massive tissue invasion, encephalitis and complicating *Escherichia coli* meningitis.

PREVENTION

Control and prevention of parasite infections are based on health education for exposed populations and visitors to endemic regions (see Table 158.1) and implementation of public health measures. Vector control includes destruction of breeding habitats, spraying with insecticides and controlling freshwater snails. As a rule, it is impossible to control zoonoses effectively.

Important personal precautions include (see also Chapter 143):

PARASITES THAT CAUSE GENERALIZED OR FOCAL OR SPACE-OCCUPYING LESIONS AND THEIR PRINCIPAL GEOGRAPHIC DISTRIBUTION			
Parasite		**CNS disease**	**Geographic distribution**
Protozoa	*Acanthamoeba castellani**	Meningoencephalitis	Worldwide
	Balamuthia mandrillaris	Meningoencephalitis	Worldwide
	Encephalitozoon cuniculi	Encephalitis	Worldwide
	*Entamoeba histolytica**	Meningoencephalitis	Tropics, subtropics
	*Naegleria fowleri**	Meningoencephalitis	Worldwide
	Plasmodium falciparum	Cerebral malaria	Tropics, subtropics
	Toxoplasma gondii	Encephalitis, SOL brain	Worldwide
	Trypanosoma brucei gambiense	Encephalitis	West Africa eastward to Rift Valley
	Trypanosoma brucei rhodesiense	Encephalitis	Central and East Africa
	Trypanosoma cruzi	Meningoencephalitis	Central and South America
Helminths			
Nematodes	*Angiostrongylus cantonensis*	Meningoencephalitis	South East Asia, Oceania
	*Ascaris lumbricoides**	SOL brain	Worldwide
	*Bayliscaris procyonis**	Meningoencephalitis	North America
	*Mansonella perstans**	Meningoencephalitis	Tropical Africa
	*Dirofilaria immitis**	Meningitis	Worldwide
	*Dracunculus medinensis**	SOL spinal cord	Tropical Africa, Asia and Brazil
	*Loa loa**	Meningoencephalitis	Central and West Africa
	Gnathostoma spinigerum	Meningoencephalitis	Far East
	*Micronema deletrix**	Meningoencephalitis	North America
	*Onchocerca volvulus**	SOL brain	West Africa, South America, Yemen
	*Strongyloides stercoralis**	Meningoencephalitis	Tropics, subtropics
	Trichinella spiralis	Meningoencephalitis	Worldwide
	Toxocara canis, Toxocara cati	SOL brain	Worldwide
	*Wuchereria bancrofti**	SOL brain	Tropics, subtropics
Trematodes	*Fasciola hepatica**	SOL brain	Worldwide, sheep-farming countries
	*Heterophyes heterophyes**	SOL brain and cord	Far East, Middle East
	*Metagonimus yokogawi**	SOL brain and cord	Far East, Europe
	Paragonimus westermani	SOL brain and cord	Far East, tropical Africa, South America
	Schistosoma japonicum	SOL brain and cord	Far East, Philippines, Indonesia (Sulawesi)
	Schistosoma mansoni	SOL brain and cord	Africa, Middle East, South America
	Schistosoma haematobium	SOL brain and cord	Africa, Middle East
	Schistosoma intercalatum	Myelopathy	Sâo Tomé e Príncipe
Cestodes	*Diphyllobothrium latum**	Myelopathy	Russia, Canada and subartic Europe
	Echinococcus granulosus (hydatidosis)	SOL brain and cord	Worldwide
	*Echinococcus multilocularis**	SOL brain and cord	Northern Europe, Canada, Japan
	Spirometra spp. (sparganosis)*	SOL brain and cord	South East Asia, North America
	Taenia multiceps (coenurosis)*	SOL brain and cord	Worldwide
	Taenia solium (cysticercosis)	SOL brain and cord	Worldwide, South America

* CNS disease is infrequent or rare.
SOL, space-occupying lesion.

Table 158.2 Parasites that cause generalized or focal or space-occupying lesions and their principal geographic distribution. Parasites of the order Diptera, whose maggots may invade the CNS, and ticks that cause tick bite paralysis are excluded. Note that related species of some parasites listed produce similar symptomology (e.g. *Angiostrongylus mackerrasae* in Queensland, Australia, *Angiostrongylus malayensis* in Malayasia and Indonesia, and numerous *Paragonimus* spp. in different parts of the world).

- avoidance of drinking water or eating salads or uncooked food (vegetables, meat, freshwater fish, crustaceans or terrestrial molluscs) in regions where contamination by various protozoa and helminths is probable;
- efforts to discourage children from geophagy (risk of toxoplasmosis and toxocariasis from cat and dog excreta, respectively);
- regular anthelmintic treatment of pet dogs and cats;
- prevention of skin exposure to fresh water in regions endemic for schistosomiasis;
- prevention of arthropod bites (protective clothing, use of insect repellent creams and mosquito nets);
- effective prophylaxis for falciparum malaria;
- screening patients who have been exposed to strongyloidiasis prior to immunosuppressive therapy; and
- trimethoprim–sulfamethoxazole prophylaxis for toxoplasmosis in AIDS when the CD4 count falls below 350/mm^3.

CLINICAL FEATURES

Most parasitic CNS infections lack specific diagnostic features. Diagnosis depends on suspecting a parasitic etiology and obtaining a history of residence in an endemic area (at any time from recent to remote, depending upon the parasite suspected), when exposure to infection may have occurred. The latter often requires a searching inquiry because patients are usually ignorant of the ways in which infection is contracted. Clinicians unfamiliar with this complex field must refer to a differential diagnosis checklist, remembering that multiple parasite infections are common in the tropics.

Major neurologic syndromes

Cerebral malaria

Fever, coma, absence of meningitis or focal neurologic signs (in the early stages) and presence of falciparum trophozoites in the blood

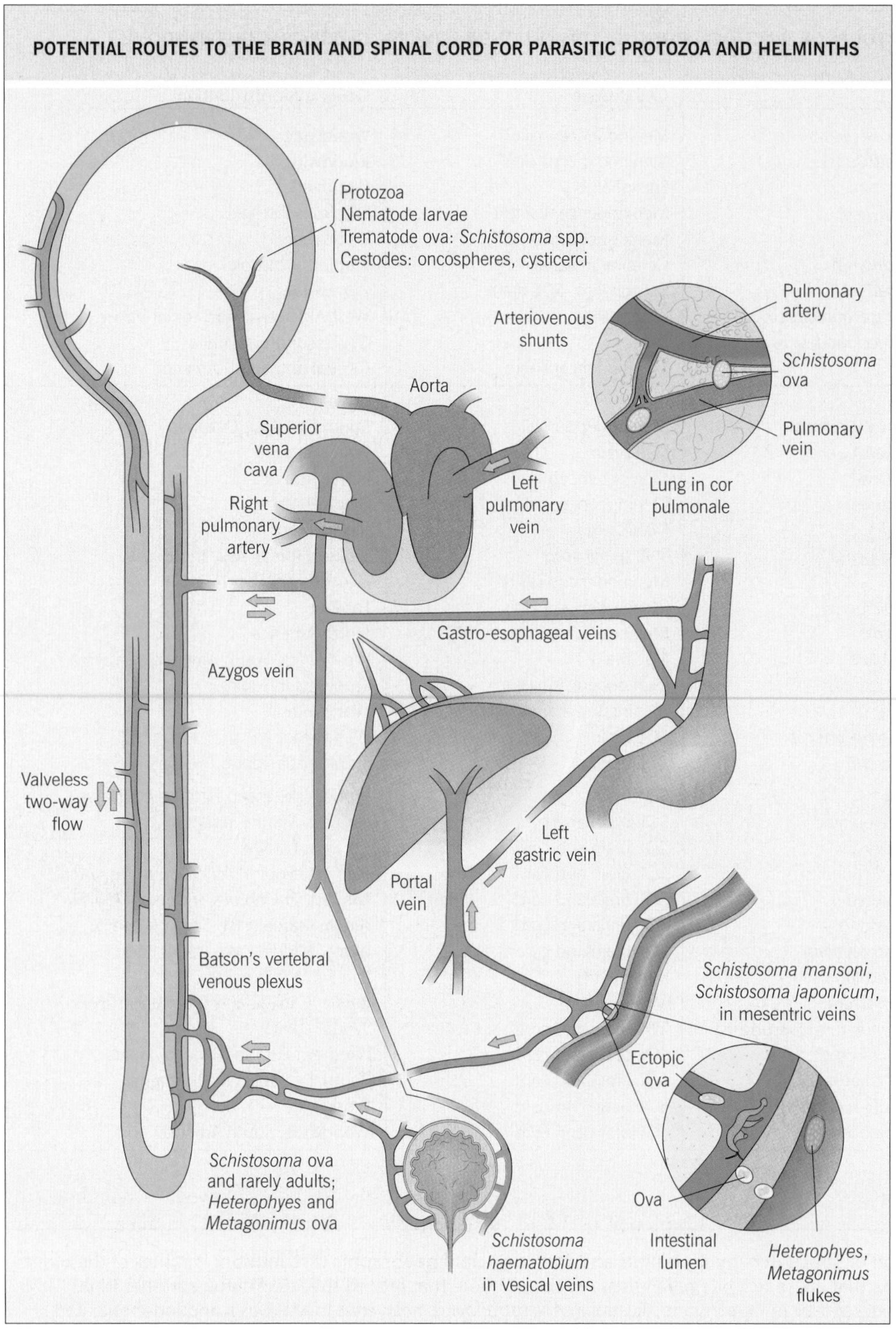

Fig. 158.1 Potential routes to the brain and spinal cord for parasitic protozoa and helminths. Collateral circulation (e.g. in hepatosplenic schistosomiasis with portal hypertension) allows ova to embolize via portopulmonary anastomoses to the lung and thence to the systemic circulation. Batson's vertebral venous plexus allows retrograde access to the spinal cord and brain by parasites and/or ova.

suggest cerebral malaria. Alternative causes in a person who coincidentally has falciparum parasitemia include encephalitides, various systemic and toxic infections, and heat stroke.[5]

Trypanosomiasis

In stage II of African trypanosomiasis (sleeping sickness), chronic encephalomyelitis develops. This presents with change of personality, apathy, extrapyramidal signs including tremor, chorea, expressionless facies and reversal of sleep rhythm (see Chapter 157). Acute American trypanosomiasis causes meningoencephalitis in children.

Meningitis or meningoencephalitis

A specific helminthic cause is suggested by periorbital edema and generalized myositis (trichinosis) or subcutaneous migratory swellings followed by CNS complications (gnathostomiasis).[6] In angiostrongyliasis (history of eating raw *Achatina* snails), signs may fluctuate markedly; the patient may have headache, confusion, severe generalized dysesthesia, neck stiffness and various focal neurologic signs but later the same day the patient may be almost symptom free. Fever is often absent.[1,7] Other migrating larval nematodes can produce similar variable features.

Focal or space-occupying lesions

Parasitic space-occupying lesions in the CNS are usually without diagnostic features (see Table 158.2). However, cysts in the third ventricle (e.g. cysticercus, hydatid or coenurus cysts) cause intermittent internal hydrocephalus with periodic headache and loss of consciousness.

Toxoplasmosis

Immunodeficient patients developing reactivation toxoplasmosis, with abscess formation usually in the basal ganglia, present with low-grade fever, headache, seizures, raised intracranial pressure and hemiparesis. Diffuse encephalitis is less frequent.

Cysticercosis

Acute infection presents with headache, diffuse hyperesthesia and myalgia. The first manifestation may be seizures, developing months or years after exposure to infection. Careful examination of the whole skin surface may reveal firm, painless, pea-sized, subcutaneous nodules in 50% or more of patients.[2] Differentiation from other causes of seizures is required.

Schistosomiasis

In *S. japonica* infection, and less frequently in *S. mansoni* and *S. haematobium* infections, ova in the CNS may cause seizures or present as a space-occupying lesion. There may be no other evidence of schistosomiasis.

Myelopathy

Myelopathy is uncommon in parasitic infection, except in schistosomiasis.[14] Asymptomatic deposition of ova in the spinal cord is frequent in *S. haematobium* infection but *S. mansoni* is the usual cause of myelopathy; it is uncommon in *S. japonicum* infection. *S. intercalatum* was incriminated in two cases from Sâo Tomé e Príncipe. The usual presentation is acute, flaccid, areflexic paraparesis caused by a granuloma in the conus medullaris but spasticity is present in higher lesions. Acute massive necrosis of the lower cord, presumably immunologically mediated, has been described in Brazil. The differential diagnosis includes tuberculosis, neoplasia and HTLV-1 infection. In diphyllobothriasis, megaloblastic anemia is present in association with posterior column degeneration.

Ophthalmic involvement by parasites

Reports of direct or immunologic involvement of the eye by parasites are extensive and include the following.

- Iritis: *Toxoplasma gondii*, *Trypanosoma gambienese* and *rhodesiense*, *Leishmania donovani*, *Onchocerca volvulus*, *Wuchereria bancrofti*, *Dirofilaria immitis*, *Toxocara* spp., *Gnathostoma spinigerum* and cysticerci.
- Choroidoretinitis: *T. gondii* (bilateral, congenital; unilateral, acquired), *O. volvulus*, *Angiostrongylus cantonensis*, *Toxocara* spp., *Loa loa*, *Schistosoma mansoni*, cysticerci and *Armillifer armillatus* (pentastomid larvae).
- Optic neuritis: *T. gondii*, *Trypanosoma gambiense* and *rhodesiense*, *O. volvulus*, *A. cantonensis* and *Paragonimus westermani*.
- Orbital myositis: *Trypanosoma cruzi*.
- Orbital or retro-orbital mass or lesion: *Trichinella spiralis*, *G. spinigerum*, *S. mansoni*, *Fasciola hepatica*, *P. westermani*, *Echinococcus granularis* cyst, cysticerci and *Taenia brauni* coenurus (in tropical Africa).

The maggots of various Diptera can invade the eye (e.g. *Oestrus ovis*), ear or nose (e.g. *Cochliomyia hominivorax*), rarely extending to the brain.

Tick bite paralysis

In Australia, Africa, America and south east Europe, various hard (ixodid) and soft (argasid) ticks possess salivary neurotoxins. Between 1 and 6 days after it starts feeding, symmetric, ascending, flaccid paralysis appears, reaching the facial and bulbar muscles. Pain, fever and sensory abnormalities are absent. Death may result from respiratory failure. Recovery follows removal of the tick.

DIAGNOSIS

Cerebral malaria

The demonstration of ring forms of *Plasmodium falciparum* in the blood and exclusion of other causes of coma (including normal CSF) are the basic diagnostic criteria.

African trypanosomiasis: sleeping sickness

Trypanosomes may be present in blood films. The enzyme-linked immunosorbent assay (ELISA) IgM is positive in 90%. Suramin is given prior to lumbar puncture (LP) to destroy blood tryptomastigotes that might otherwise enter the CSF. The CSF contains lymphocytic pleocytosis, raised protein and normal glucose levels and occasionally motile tryptomastigotes. Polymerase chain reaction (PCR) may detect *Trypanosoma* DNA in CSF. Computerized tomography (CT) and magnetic resonance imaging (MRI) scans show brain edema (see also Chapter 157).

Meningitis or meningoencephalitis

Examination of the CSF is essential. This is often deferred if papilledema or CT scan evidence of raised intracranial pressure is present, but if an early diagnosis is critical (e.g. to detect tuberculous meningitis) cisternal or LP to aspirate a small sample of CSF is justified. In protozoal infections, lymphocytosis, normal glucose and mildly raised protein levels are typical. Similar findings are present in helminthic meningoencephalitis, but eosinophilia is usually present. Nonparasitic causes of eosinophilic meningitis include Hodgkin's disease, polyarteritis nodosa and occasionally bacterial or viral meningitis. Micro-organisms observed include amebae in primary amebic meningoencephalitis, tryptomastigotes in African trypanosomiasis and in *T. cruzi* infections in children (and immunodeficient adults), and occasionally larval worms in angiostrongyliasis and in disseminated strongyloidiasis.

Other investigations may point to the diagnosis. Stool may contain larvae in strongyloidiasis and sputum ova or larval worms in many helminthic infections (see Chapters 165 and 246). In filarial diseases, microfilariae may appear in the peripheral blood at night (Bancroftian filariasis), at noon (loiasis) or at any time (mansonellosis) or in a skin snip (onchocerciasis). In trichinosis, biopsy of a tender muscle may reveal larvae.

Focal or space-occupying lesions

Basic parasitologic investigations may explain focal or space-occupying lesions. The stool may contain ova in *S. mansoni* and *S. japonicum* infections, paragonimiasis, fascioliasis, heterophyiasis, metagonimiasis and diphyllobothriasis. The terminal drops of urine may contain ova of *S. haematobium*. Multiple rectal snips may reveal schistosome ova of all species. In paragonimiasis, and occasionally schistosomiasis, the sputum contains ova.

The CSF in toxoplasmosis and cysticercosis reveals a lymphocytic pleocytosis and raised protein and occasionally reduced glucose levels. In schistosomiasis, a modest lymphocytosis is typical and protein and glucose levels are usually normal, whereas in paragonimiasis, eosinophilia is accompanied by raised protein levels. Eosinophilia is present in only 25% of cases of cerebral hydatidosis.

Immunodiagnostic tests for protozoa and helminths (see Chapters 245 and 246).

When organisms cannot be detected, antibody or antigen detection tests in serum and/or CSF confirm exposure or support diagnosis.[14] Investigations include immunoblot, monoclonal antibody tests and PCR for DNA detection. Immunodiagnosis is especially useful in the following: toxoplasmosis (ELISA, PCR for antigens); trypanosomiasis; neurocysticercosis (ELISA is 90% specific in blood, and almost 100% in CSF; immunoblot may be negative if few cysticerci are present); echinococcosis (IHAT positive in 60% of sera); and schistosomal myelopathy (ELISA in the CSF is positive in >75% of cases). To confirm active infection with *T. cruzi*,[15] xenodiagnosis is performed utilizing laboratory-raised vector reduviid bugs to feed on the patient (see Chapter 173).

Ultrasonography of the liver or CT or MRI scans of the abdomen detect amebic and hydatid hepatic cysts (the latter calcify), *F. hepatica* flukes in bile ducts or periportal fibrosis (pathognomonic of hepatosplenic schistosomiasis). Chest radiography and CT scans may reveal pulmonary paragonimiasis, hydatid cyst (noncalcifying) or schistosomal cor pulmonale. In schistosomal myelopathy, myelography typically reveals an intramedullary lesion of the conus with a complete block between T12 and L1. Computerized tomography or MRI may identify a granuloma; occasionally diffuse cord edema is observed, as in the Katayama syndrome.

Computerized tomography and MRI scans assist diagnosis of cerebral parasitic space-occupying lesions. Toxoplasmosis presents as one or more low-density lesions, usually ring enhancing (Fig. 158.2). In early cysticercosis, small nonenhancing hypodense lesions are present. Later, a hyperdense center (the scolex) develops (Fig. 158.3), with ring enhancement when it dies (Fig. 158.4). Finally, calcification supervenes.[2] Plain radiographs may show multiple calcified cysticerci in muscle. In hydatid cyst, the CT scan is the most definitive investigation; dead cysts calcify. The CT/MRI scan in paragonimiasis reveals cystic calcified lesions containing flukes, in schistosomiasis a contrast-enhancing granuloma, and in sparganosis a granuloma containing a worm. Other investigations (e.g. gallium-67 scans and positron emission tomography) are useful but non-specific for identifying inflammatory foci.

Finally, whenever the diagnosis is in doubt, brain or spinal cord biopsy under CT guidance is required.

Immunodeficient patients

Meningitis in immunodeficiency (e.g. AIDS) is more likely to be caused by cryptococcosis or tuberculosis than parasites. In meningoencephalitis in South or Central American patients, Chagas' disease should be considered. Rarer causes include chronic granulomatous meningoencephalitis (caused by *Acanthomoeba culbertsoni* or *Balamuthia mandrillaris*) diagnosed by brain biopsy. Encephalopathy in disseminated microsporidiosis is diagnosed by identifying *Encephalitozoon cuniculi* cysts in the urine. Cerebral space-occupying lesions are most likely to be caused by toxoplasmosis (10% of cases in North America, up to 50% in Africa) or tuberculoma. In North America, 2% are due to primary CNS lymphomas; the specific investigation is thallium-201 single photon emission CT. In South America, a 'chagoma' caused by *T. cruzi* should be considered (Fig. 158.5). Many other opportunistic infections can produce space-occupying lesions (e.g. nocardiosis, cryptococcoma, aspergilloma and syphilitic gumma). Myelopathy is most likely to be caused by tuberculosis but many other causes, including toxoplasmosis and HTLV-1 infection, must be considered.

MANAGEMENT

Specific treatment of parasite infections listed in Table 158.1 is discussed in the relevant chapters. Here, the management of the major CNS parasitic disease syndromes is summarized.

Cerebral malaria

Any comatose patient who has suspected or diagnosed falciparum malaria should be treated at once with intravenous quinine (after assessing blood glucose), pending further evaluation (see Chapter 166). Corticosteroid drugs are not helpful.

African trypanosomiasis: sleeping sickness

Suramin is given to clear trypanosomes from the blood. After 1 week, melarsoporol is administered. Eflornithine is effective in Gambian trypanosomiasis only (see Chapters 157 and 209).

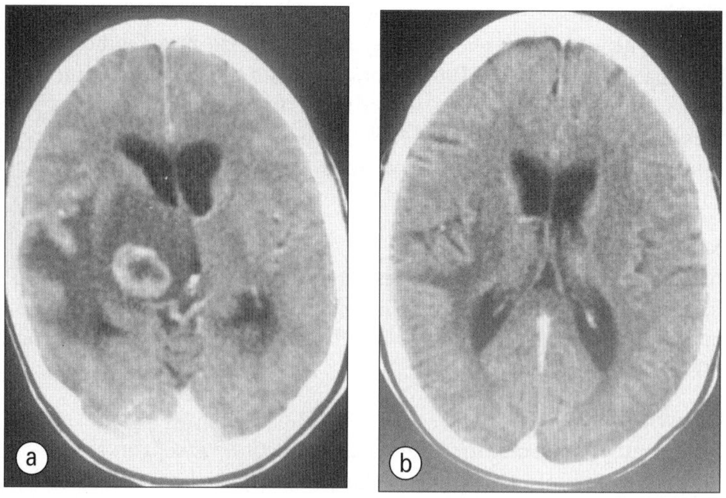

Fig. 158.2 Toxoplasma abscess. (a) This CT brain scan shows a toxoplasma abscess in the left internal capsule, compressing the lateral ventricles. Contrast demonstrates a typical ring-enhancing effect. (b) Same patient after 17 days of treatment with pyrimethamine and sulfonamide showing resolving abscess.

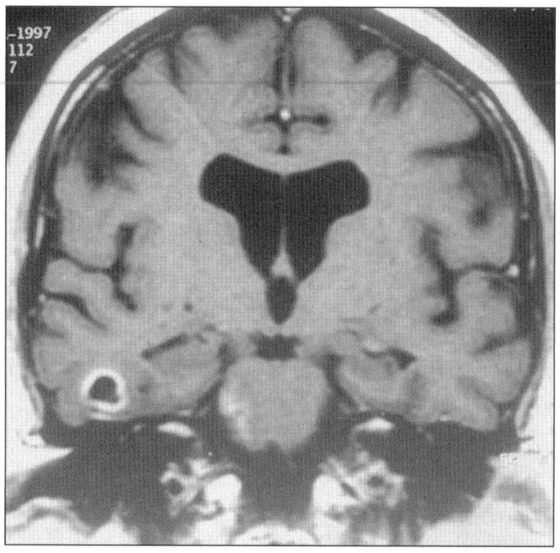

Fig. 158.3 Coronal MRI of brain showing living cysticercus, with the scolex appearing as a hyperintense center ('pea in the pod' appearance). There is no visible inflammatory reaction.

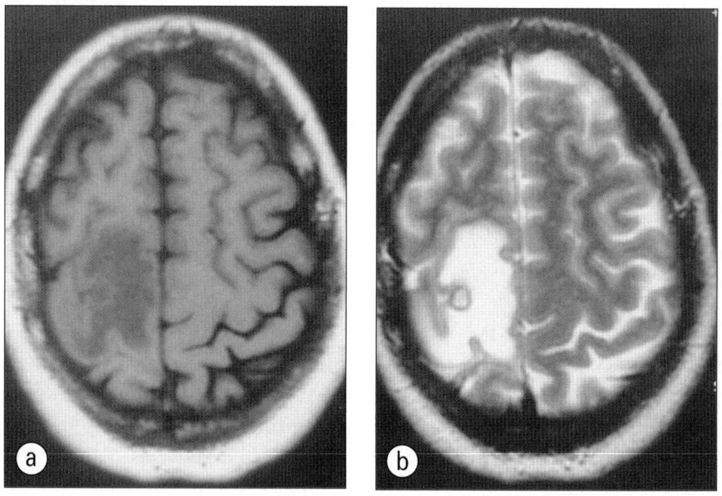

Fig. 158.4 Cerebral cysticercus. (a) This MRI of brain shows a dying cysticercus surrounded by intense inflammation. (b) Post-contrast MRI T2-weighted image demonstrating the isointense wall of the cyst and surrounding hyperintense edema.

Meningitis and meningoencephalitis

When a parasitic cause is diagnosed, corticosteroid treatment (prednisolone 1–2mg/kg/day) should be considered if there is raised intracranial pressure or if the patient is seriously ill. If

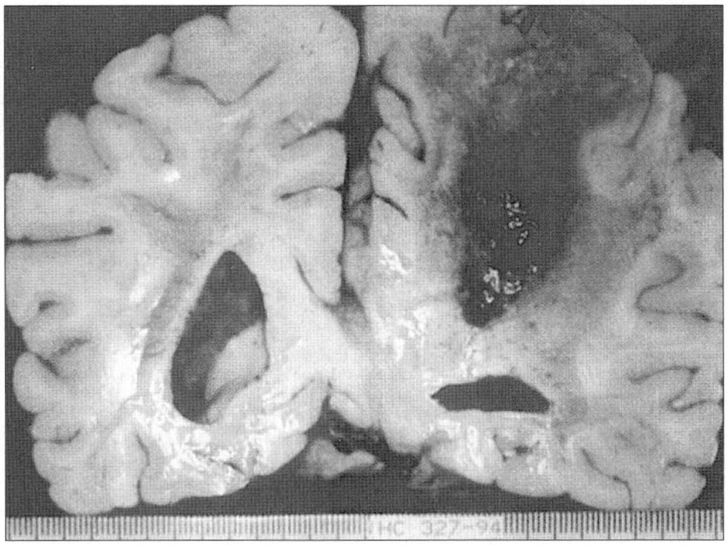

Fig. 158.5 Extensive necro-hemorrhagic lesions of the right cerebral hemisphere in an AIDS patient with reactivated acute Chagas' disease. Courtesy of Professor L Chimelli.

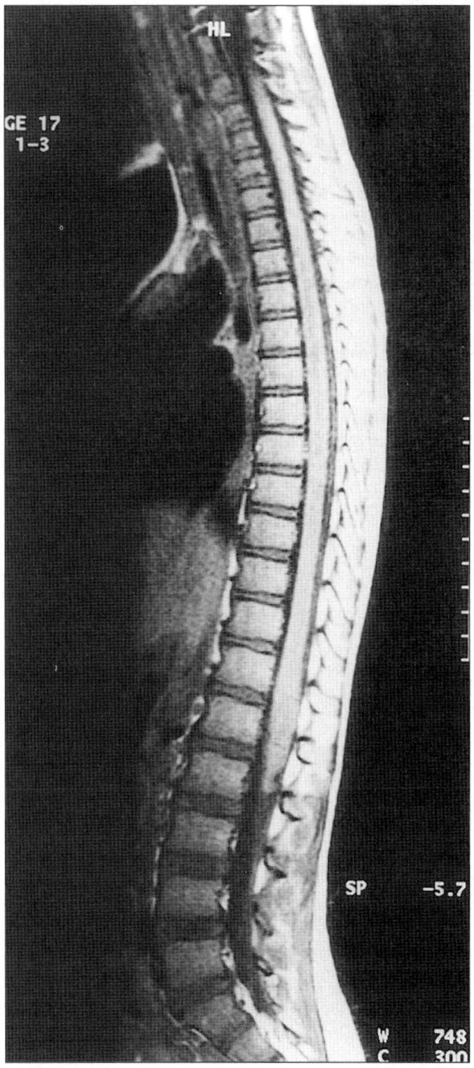

Fig. 158.6 MRI of the spinal cord of a 9-year-old Omani boy with acute schistosomiasis mansoni, who presented with transverse myelitis (vertical scale in cms). Extensive cord edema from the first thoracic vertebral level to the conus medullaris is present (arrows). He recovered and was ambulant after 2 weeks treatment with prednisone and praziquantel.

specific treatment is lacking (e.g. in angiostrongyliasis, trichinosis, gnathostomiasis and toxocariasis), it may be the only option other than repeated LP to reduce pressure. Diethylcarbamazine and thiabendazole have been tried in toxocariasis and albendazole in gnathostomiasis (together with corticosteroids) with some evidence of benefit.

Focal or space-occupying lesions

In cystericercosis, when living cysticerci are present, praziquantel (without corticosteroids, which reduce its efficacy) 10–20mg/kg q8h for 21 days, sometimes increased to 25mg/kg q8h for up to 30 days,[2] is advocated. Albendazole (with preceding corticosteroid therapy) 15mg/kg/day for 1 week has replaced praziquantel in some centers. Seizures are controlled by anticonvulsants. Despite the apparent benefit of these drugs, if untreated, the majority of cysts disappear without sequelae within 1 year. Surgery should be avoided unless the cysticercus is blocking the third ventricle.

In schistosomiasis, praziquantel 40mg/kg is routinely given as a single dose; 60mg daily for 3 days may achieve more complete eradication of worms. Suspected schistosomal myelopathy should be treated conservatively with praziquantel. When this develops acutely in the Katayama syndrome, with edema of the spinal cord (Fig. 158.6), adjunctive, high-dose corticosteriod treatment is essential. Schistosomal myelopathy may improve even after several months of paraplegia. Surgery is required if there is deterioration despite treatment. If schistosomal myelopathy is encountered unexpectedly at operation, only a biopsy should be obtained.[4] It is difficult to know when schistosomiasis has been cured; antibody titers decline slowly and antigen detection may be negative although some worms persist (see Chapter 167).

Cerebral paragonimiasis is treated conservatively with praziquantel or bithionol. Hydatid cysts are completely excised, first administering praziquantel or albendazole. Surgical resection is required for a sparganum and for a coenurus (with adjunctive praziquantel).

Treatment of central nervous system parasitism in immunodeficiency

Standard treatment applies for most parasitic infections. The immune status should be improved if possible (e.g. highly active antiretroviral treatment in AIDS). If brain biopsy is not possible, empiric treatment for suspected toxoplasmosis in an IgG-seropositive patient (IgM remains negative) is pyrimethamine and sulfadiazine or high-dose trimethoprim–sulfamethoxazole. A convincing response within a week to 10 days supports the diagnosis. Lifelong trimethoprim–sulfamethoxazole prophylaxis follows recovery. When *Toxoplasma* IgG is negative, an intracerebral space-occupying lesion is treated either as a tuberculoma or a primary CNS lymphoma. In South America, early treatment of Chagas' meningoencephalitis (which may coexist with toxoplasmosis) with benznidazole is imperative. No effective treatment for chronic granulomatous meningitis exists (see Chapters 173 and 244). Cerebral microsporidiosis (*Encephalitozoon cuniculi*) is almost invariably fatal, but has responded temporarily to albendazole (Chapters 209 and 243). Hyperinfection with strongyloidiasis responds to ivermectin and broad-spectrum antibiotics for the usual coexistent *E. coli* meningitis.

REFERENCES

1. Scrimgeour EM. *Angiostrongylus cantonensis* in East New Britain, Papua New Guinea. Trans Roy Soc Trop Med Hyg 1984;78:774–5.
2. Wadia NH. Neurocysticercosis. In: Shakir RA, Newman PK, Poser CM, eds. Tropical neurology, London: WB Saunders; 1996:247–73.
3. Liu LX. Spinal and cerebral schistosomiasis. Semin Neurol 1993;13:189–200.
4. Scrimgeour EM, Gajdusek DC. Involvement of the central nervous system in *Schistosoma mansoni* and *S. haematobium* infection. Brain 1985;108:1023–38.
5. Warrell DA. Cerebral malaria. In: Shakir RA, Newman PK, Poser CM, eds. Tropical neurology. London: WB Saunders; 1996:213–45.
6. Punyagupta S, Bunnag T, Jathjudatta P. Eosinophilic meningitis in Thailand: clinical and epidemiological characteristics of 162 patients with myeloencephalitis probably caused by *Gnathostoma spinigerum*. J Neurol Sci 1990;96:241–56.
7. Punyagupta S, Juttijudata P, Bunnag T. Eosinophilic meningoencephalitis in Thailand. Clinical studies of 484 typical cases probably caused by *Angiostrongylus cantonensis*. Am J Trop Med Hyg 1975;24:921–31.
8. Pitella JEH. Neuroschistosomiasis. Brain Pathol 1997;7:649–62.
9. Suzuki Y. Host resistance in the brain against *Toxoplasma gondii*. J Infect Dis 2002;185(Suppl.1):558–65.
10. Gluckstein D, Ciferri F, Ruskin J. Chagas' disease: another cause of cerebral mass in the acquired immunodeficiency syndrome. Am J Med 1992;92:429–32.
11. Martinez AJ, Visvesvara GS. Free-living, amphizoic and opportunistic amebas. Brain Pathol 1997;7:583–98.
12. Weber R, Deplazes P, Flepp M, *et al.* Cerebral microsporidiosis due to *Encephalitozoon cuniculi* in a patient with human immunodeficency virus infection. N Engl J Med 1997;336:474–8.
13. Scrimgeour EM. Non-traumatic paraplegia in Northern Tanzania. Br Med J 1981;283:975–8.
14. Garcia LS, Bruckner DA. Antibody and antigen detection in parasite infections. In: Garcia LS, Bruckner DA, eds. Diagnostic medical parasitology. Washington: AJM Press, 1997:473–86.
15. Spina-Franca A, Livramento JA, Machado LR, Yasuda N. *Trypanosoma cruzi* antibodies in the cerebrospinal fluid: a search using complement fixation and immunofluorescence reactions. Arq Neuropsiquiatr 1988;46:374–8. (Article in Portuguese).

chapter

159 Epidemic Bacterial Meningitis

Montse Soriano-Gabarró, Nancy E Rosenstein, Robert Pinner & David Stephens

INTRODUCTION

Bacterial meningitis remains a major cause of morbidity and mortality throughout the world. *Neisseria meningitidis* is unique among major causes of bacterial meningitis for its ability to cause large epidemics, especially in sub-Saharan Africa. This chapter focuses on *N. meningitidis* (the meningococcus) and epidemic bacterial meningitis.

EPIDEMIOLOGY

Although acute bacterial meningitis can be caused by a variety of organisms, until recently three-quarters of all cases were caused by *Haemophilus influenzae* type b (Hib), *Streptococcus pneumoniae* and *N. meningitidis*.[1] The introduction of effective Hib conjugate vaccines in industrialized countries has led to a dramatic decline in the incidence of Hib meningitis and other invasive Hib disease.[2] The Hib conjugate vaccines are progressively being introduced into routine childhood vaccination programs in developing countries with the support of the Global Alliance for Vaccines and Immunizations (GAVI), the World Health Organization (WHO) and other partners (http://www.vaccinealliance.com). Routine use of a new 7-valent pneumococcal conjugate vaccine in infants has recently been adopted in the USA.[3] Additional vaccine and disease burden data are needed to inform decision-making for the introduction of pneumococcal conjugate vaccines in developing countries. Serogroup C meningococcal conjugate vaccines have been developed and have been introduced in the UK, other European countries and Canada.[4] Other meningococcal conjugate vaccines are under development.[5]

Haemophilus influenzae type b, pneumococci and meningococci can each cause sporadic disease and case clusters, but *N. meningitidis* is the major agent of epidemic bacterial meningitis. Endemic meningococcal disease is estimated to cause 120,000 cases per year worldwide; during epidemics, attack rates can reach 1000 times baseline rates. When epidemic meningococcal disease occurs, it commands public health attention and calls for a large-scale public health response.[6] The case-fatality rate of meningococcal disease is 5–25% and, among survivors, there is also considerable morbidity, including persistent neurologic sequelae.

Humans are the only natural host of meningococci. The organisms are spread through close contact with nasopharyngeal secretions. Only a fraction of those who are exposed to meningococci develop clinical infections; 10% of individuals carry the organism asymptomatically in the nasopharynx and can transmit it to others.

The African meningitis belt (Fig. 159.1), originally characterized by Lapeysonnie in 1963,[7] is a broad region that extends from Ethiopia in the east to Senegal in the west and includes portions of 10–15 countries.[7,8] The following three consistent epidemiologic features characterize epidemics in the African meningitis belt:

- an increase in the rate of meningococcal disease compared with historic trends;
- a shift in age-specific incidence rates, with a higher proportion of disease in older children and young adults; and
- clonality of the organism causing epidemics.

In this region, high rates of sporadic infections (1–20 cases per 100,000 population) occur in annual cycles with large-scale epidemics (usually caused by serogroup A but occasionally by serogroup C and more recently by serogroup W-135) superimposed periodically. In the countries of the African meningitis belt, epidemics with incidence rates as high as 1000 cases per 100,000 population have occurred every 8–12 years over at least the past 50 years. In addition, major epidemics have occurred in adjacent countries not usually considered part of the African meningitis belt (e.g. Kenya, Tanzania).

In periods of endemic disease the highest attack rates occur among young children but during some epidemic situations a higher proportion of cases occur in older children and young adults.[9] Small local epidemics, often unrecognized at a national level, may precede major epidemics. Typically, once an epidemic begins to expand, it does so rapidly, reaching a peak within a few weeks and, in the absence of extensive vaccination, lasting for several months. A countrywide epidemic may consist of a series of smaller epidemics, centered at the village or province level.

Neisseria meningitidis can be classified into serogroups based on the structural and antigenic differences in the capsular polysaccharide expressed. The epidemic potential varies among the serogroups. Among the nine serogroups that cause invasive disease, serogroups A, B, C and, more recently, W-135 have been associated with epidemic disease. Less common serogroups, including Y and X, have also recently been associated with disease clusters in some parts of the world.[10]

Serogroup A

Although epidemics of serogroup A meningococcal disease were common in industrialized countries early in the 20th century, they have been rare or absent in these countries since the end of the Second World War. In the past 20 years, limited epidemics concentrated among groups of low socio-economic status have occurred in Finland and New Zealand, with attack rates below 15 cases per 100,000 people in the population. In contrast, in the developing world, attack rates can exceed 1% of the population. In the past 20 years, intense group A epidemics have occurred in Brazil, Mongolia, Nepal and various regions in sub-Saharan Africa.

Between 1996 and 1998, the largest epidemic ever reported (over 350,000 cases – probably a substantial underestimate) occurred in the African meningitis belt, with more than 10 countries recording large increases in the number of cases of serogroup A meningococcal disease. Although rapid detection and early response to epidemics can reduce illness and deaths through prompt vaccination campaigns, the region was not adequately prepared to implement comprehensive control efforts. The medical and economic impact of this epidemic was substantial. Essential services and personnel were diverted and limited health budgets strained to cope with the epidemic.

The potential for global dissemination of an epidemic-associated serogroup A strain is evident from an epidemic caused by one clonal group, identified by multilocus enzyme electrophoresis (MLEE) as

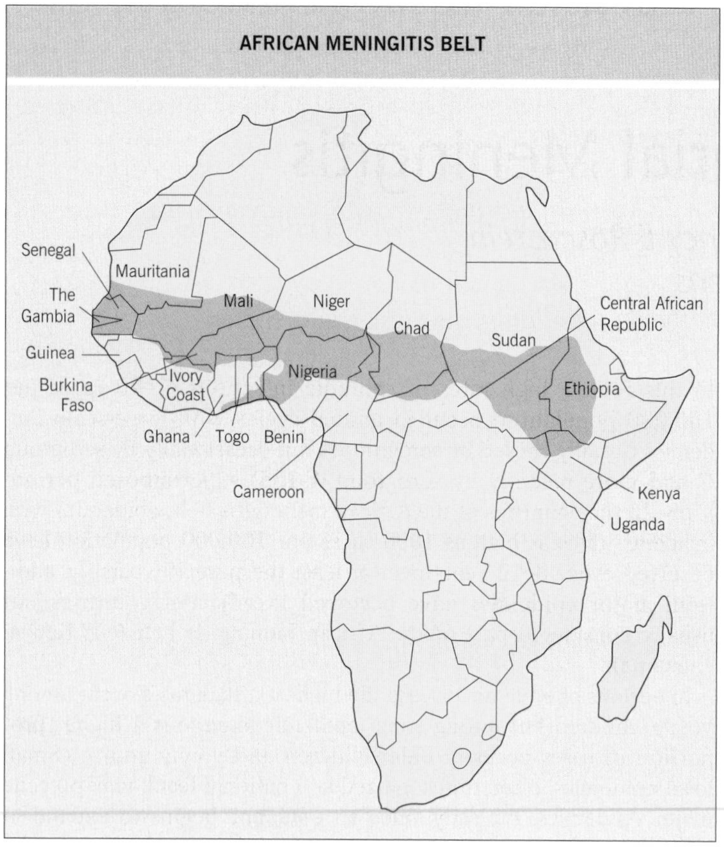

Fig. 159.1 The African meningitis belt.

ET-III-1 complex. Epidemics of group A meningococcal disease caused by this clonal group occurred in Nepal in 1983 and 1984, and in Pakistan and New Delhi, India, in 1985, and may have caused earlier epidemics in China. In 1987, an epidemic of group A meningococcal disease caused by ET-III-1 strains occurred in association with the annual Moslem pilgrimage (Hajj) to Mecca.[11] The epidemic started among persons from south Asian countries, including Nepal. As the pilgrims returned to their home countries, meningococci belonging to this complex were carried throughout the world, causing secondary epidemics among pilgrims and their contacts and eventually in their immediate communities. Isolated secondary cases did occur in industrialized countries but, for reasons not entirely clear, did not spread to the general community.[12] In 1987, strains belonging to the ET-III-1 complex then caused widespread epidemics in the meningitis belt of sub-Saharan Africa, including countries traditionally considered outside the meningitis belt, such as Kenya (1989), Tanzania (1990) and Burundi (1992). During 1996, ET-III-1 strains were again responsible for the large epidemics that occurred in the African meningitis belt. Other large-scale movement or displacement of populations, such as refugees, may pose similar risks.

Serogroup B

Serogroup B meningococcal disease, a major cause of sporadic disease in industrialized countries, has been associated with epidemics with attack rates of between 10 and 50 per 100,000 population, which are generally lower than in the major serogroup A epidemics. In the late 1970s, a serogroup B strain belonging to a clonal group known as ET-5 emerged in north western Europe and caused epidemics in Norway (1974–5), the UK (1974–6), Iceland (1976) and Denmark (1981).[13] Intercontinental spread of clones from this group has been documented and was probably responsible for subsequent epidemics in Cuba (1980), Chile (1985) and Brazil (1987). Starting in 1989, an epidemic of serogroup B meningococcal disease occurred in Oregon and Washington, USA, due to the ET-5 clone, with attack rates peaking in 1996 that were seven times higher than the US national average;[14] since 2001 these rates have decreased. An ongoing serogroup B epidemic has been affecting New Zealand since 1991 with annual rates of 16.9 cases per 100,000 population; highest incidence rates are found among Maori and Pacific Island children.[15]

Serogroup C

Serogroup C meningococcus, like serogroup A, can cause endemic disease, small clusters and major epidemics, such as those that occurred in Brazil (1972) and Vietnam (1977). Although attack rates in serogroup C epidemics are usually lower than in serogroup A epidemics, they can reach high levels. During a serogroup C epidemic in Burkina Faso in 1979, attack rates exceeded 500 cases per 100,000 population. Serogroup C strains identified as a single enzyme complex, ET-37, have been found to be responsible for a number of recent epidemics and a large proportion of cases of endemic disease in the USA, Canada, Europe and Latin America.

Serogroup Y

Serogroup Y meningococcal disease has been recognized as a cause of endemic disease in some populations in the USA since the 1970s. Beginning in 1988, the proportion of meningococcal disease due to serogroup Y increased in the USA from 2% (in 1988–91) to 26% (in 1996–8). From 1999–2001, about one-third of meningococcal disease in the USA was due to serogroup Y.[16] Smaller increases have been reported in Canada, Sweden and Israel. Serogroup Y is often associated with pneumonia and disease among older age groups, as compared with serogroups B and C.

Serogroup W-135

Serogroup W-135 meningococcus has recently emerged as a cause of epidemic disease. This serogroup is responsible for only 2–5% of endemic disease worldwide. However, an epidemic of serogroup W-135 meningococcal disease occurred concurrently with a serogroup A epidemic during the 2000 Hajj in Saudi Arabia, with a serogroup W-135 attack rate of 9 cases per 100,000 population. The serogroup W-135 isolates causing the epidemic belonged to the ET-37 complex as defined by MLEE and were designated as the (W)ET-37 clone.[17] In 2000 and 2001, following this epidemic, cases of serogroup W-135 meningococcal disease were identified in Europe, North America, the Middle East, Asia and Africa, associated with returning Hajj participants or their contacts. Carriage of serogroup W-135 meningococci was observed among returning Hajj pilgrims.[18,19]

In 2002, the first major W-135 meningococcal disease epidemic occurred in Burkina Faso. More than 13,000 suspected meningitis cases and 1,400 deaths were reported, with an overall attack rate of 104 cases per 100,000 population (Ministry of Health/WHO/Centers for Disease Control and Prevention (CDC), unpublished data).[20] Serogroup W-135 isolates found in Burkina Faso in 2002 belong to the ET-37 complex and were closely related to the Hajj 2000 isolates (Ministry of Health/WHO/CDC, unpublished data). These strains were also closely related to serogroup W-135 ET-37 complex strains found in sporadic cases or carriage in other parts of the world since the 1970s, suggesting expansion of an existing clonal group rather than introduction of a new one.[17]

The potential for dissemination of serogroup W-135 meningococcal disease epidemics in African meningitis belt countries is of great concern, given the clonal association between these two recent epidemics and the fact that historically serogroup A meningococcal disease epidemics caused by the ET-III-1 complex were first seen during the Hajj in 1987 and subsequently caused epidemics in multiple regions of sub-Saharan Africa.

RISK FACTORS

Individual host factors that predispose to invasive meningococcal infections include functional or anatomic asplenia, properdin deficiency, congenital and acquired immunoglobulin deficiencies and terminal or C3 complement deficiency.[21] In addition, genetic polymorphisms such as tumor necrosis factor (TNF) promoter region polymorphisms, mannose-binding protein abnormalities, plasminogen activator and inhibitor expression and cytokine induction have been linked with severity of meningococcal disease. People infected with HIV may be at increased risk of meningococcal disease, although the risk is probably lower than that for pneumococcal infections.

In the African meningitis belt, both sporadic and epidemic disease are characterized by seasonality, with increased rates during the dry season (December to May) and rapid decline with the onset of the annual rains. Low humidity and blowing dust may damage the mucosal membranes or inhibit mucosal defenses, leading to an increase in the proportion of those who acquire the meningococcus and develop invasive disease. Poor and crowded living conditions and smoke exposure are associated with meningococcal disease. These environmental and economic factors may result from people clustering in poorly ventilated dwellings and may facilitate the spread and risk of disease. Concurrent or preceding upper respiratory infections have also been implicated in several meningococcal disease epidemics and may contribute to their seasonality.[22] These viral or mycoplasmal 'cofactors' may increase transmission and susceptibility by damaging mucosal membranes, by causing transient immune suppression and by enhancing coughing and sneezing.

Other risk factors for meningococcal disease have been difficult to characterize because they may vary between industrialized and developing countries, between endemic and epidemic disease and among illnesses caused by the different serogroups. Differences between strains may lead to variability in exposure to the organism, in acquisition of carriage and in progression to invasive disease. Furthermore, factors that place an individual person at risk of sporadic disease may differ from risk factors for an epidemic.

Meningococcal disease epidemics are usually caused by strains that are clonal, as noted by the intercontinental spread of the serogroup A III-1 clone and serogroup W135 ET-37. In contrast, the overall population structure of meningococci is panmetric. These invasive strains appear to possess particular virulence factors that confer the capacity to be transmitted more effectively, cause increased invasive disease or have antigenic characteristics not recognized by the population, leading to enhanced susceptibility. Waxing and waning of the immunologic susceptibility of a population may contribute to the apparent periodicity of meningococcal epidemics. The striking phenomenon of meningococcal epidemics results from a complex interaction that involves strain characteristics, population characteristics and cofactors such as smoking and upper respiratory tract infections.

PATHOGENESIS AND PATHOLOGY

The human nasopharynx is the natural reservoir of *N. meningitidis* and the site from which meningococci are transmitted by aerosol or secretions to others, spread to adjacent mucosal surfaces (e.g. in the lower respiratory tract) and invade and gain access to the bloodstream to produce systemic disease.[21] Meningococci overcome clearance (e.g. mucus and ciliary activity) and other local host defenses in order to attach to and multiply on this mucosal surface (i.e. colonization). The meningococcus is carried asymptomatically in the nasopharynx by 5–10% of adults in nonepidemic periods. In closed populations (e.g. among military recruits) nasopharyngeal carriage rates can be greater than 50%. Nasopharyngeal colonization is an important immunizing process that may protect against future systemic illness.

The nasopharynx also appears to be a major site of mucosal invasion of meningococci and other meningitis pathogens. Crossing of the nasopharyngeal epithelium by meningococci allows access to subepithelial tissues and blood vessels. Meningococci may also penetrate nasopharyngeal epithelium damaged by environmental factors such as smoking or by viral or mycoplasmal co-infections.[22] In meningococcal disease, systemic illness usually follows acquisition of the organism in the nasopharynx within 2–10 days. Successful penetration through this epithelial barrier of even a few organisms that are capable of surviving in the bloodstream may be sufficient to cause systemic disease.

Survival of meningococci after invasion into the bloodstream is determined by both organism-specific and host-specific factors. Encapsulation, outer membrane proteins, lipo-oligosaccharide, inhibition or defects in serum bactericidal activity (both bactericidal antibody and complement) and, to a lesser extent, opsonophagocytic activity are involved. Levels of bacteremia correlate with the release of inflammatory cytokines (interleukins 1 and 6 and TNF-α), which are important in the pathogenesis of meningococcemia.

The mechanism by which meningococci cross the blood–brain barrier and enter the cerebrospinal fluid is not well characterized. Endothelial cell invasion, which is important in meningococcemia, may also be involved in the invasion of the central nervous system. Meningitis results from bacterial survival and multiplication in the cerebrospinal fluid, the release of inflammatory cytokines and other host factors (e.g. nitric oxide), leukocyte infiltration across the blood–brain barrier and breakdown of the blood–brain barrier with edema, coagulation and ischemia.[23]

PREVENTION

Epidemic bacterial meningitis are primarily caused by serogroups A, C and W-135. The persistence of large serogroup A epidemics of meningococcal disease in developing countries and their virtual disappearance in industrialized countries suggests that continued improvements in the standard of living in developing countries may decrease the occurrence of epidemic meningococcal disease. For now, however, prevention of serogroup A meningococcal disease epidemics focuses on vaccination. The recent serogroup W-135 epidemics in Saudi Arabia and Burkina Faso and the possible spread of this clone to other parts of the world indicates the need for broadly based meningococcal vaccines, including the development of non-serogroup-specific vaccines.

Vaccination

Meningococcal A, C, Y and W-135 polysaccharide vaccines are composed of purified capsular polymers. In adults and in children over 2 years of age, antibodies develop rapidly after vaccination and protection is achieved within 7–10 days. These vaccines have high efficacy in adults; however, antibody levels decline over 2–3 years. Following the occurrence of epidemics in military populations, military recruits in some countries have been routinely vaccinated at the start of their military service. Because these vaccines are generally poorly immunogenic in young children and have limited duration of efficacy, meningococcal A, C, Y and W-135 polysaccharide vaccines have not widely been used in routine childhood immunization programs.

Meningococcal capsular polysaccharide vaccines are distributed in freeze-dried form, injectable by intramuscular route and available either as a bivalent A/C vaccine or as a quadrivalent A/C/Y/W-135 vaccine, containing 50μg of each antigen per dose. They are generally well tolerated, with the most common side-effects being pain and redness at the injection site.

The polysaccharide vaccines can be useful in control of epidemics of meningococcal disease. During the 1996 epidemic in northern

Ghana, vaccination campaigns reduced the number of cases by an estimated 23%.[24] Data collected during the epidemic of meningococcal disease in northern Ghana in 1996–7 was used to assess the potential effect of different vaccination strategies. A strategy of using disease incidence thresholds to trigger vaccination campaigns after the epidemic was started would have prevented 61% of cases. A similar proportion of cases (61%) could have been prevented if routine childhood and adult immunization had been used, assuming that a high vaccine coverage rate had been achieved and maintained before the epidemic.[24]

The decision about when to initiate a vaccination campaign and who to vaccinate is complicated. Vaccination campaigns are expensive and logistically difficult, involving a large commitment of resources. Vaccinating large numbers of people on the basis of only a few cases of meningococcal disease may result in wasted efforts if the epidemic fails to materialize. The WHO has published guidelines for detecting and responding to meningococcal disease epidemics; these guidelines include recommendations about approaches to surveillance, case management, and formation of epidemic response teams[25] as well as recently revised recommendations on the use of threshold incidence rates to predict epidemics and trigger early decisions to implement campaigns.[26]

Following the meningococcal disease epidemics in 1996–8 in Africa, the WHO and other international agencies created the International Coordination Group (ICG) with the objective of better assuring international co-ordination to epidemic response.[27] The ICG manages a security stock of the bivalent A/C polysaccharide vaccine, specific treatment and injection material for use in epidemic emergencies. Since 1997 a stock of approximately 7 million doses of bivalent A/C vaccine has been maintained. Every year countries experiencing epidemics have used the ICG mechanism to rapidly obtain quantities of high-quality vaccine and injection materials at preferential prices.

Meningococcal A/C/Y/W-135 polysaccharide vaccines are not assured by the ICG and are produced in limited quantities worldwide. The serogroup W-135 meningococcal disease epidemic in Burkina Faso in 2002 has represented a major challenge to the ICG and international community, given the major shortage of meningococcal A/C/Y/W-135 vaccines for use in Africa. Early in 2003, a serogroup A/C/W-135 meningococcal polysaccharide vaccine (trivalent vaccine) has been produced in limited quantities for use in African countries with the prospect of increased production in the following years.

Conjugate serogroup A and A/C/Y/W-135 vaccines are currently being developed, using methods similar to those used for Hib conjugate vaccines, in which capsular polysaccharides are covalently linked to carrier proteins to convert the T-cell-independent polysaccharide to a T-cell-dependent antigen.[28] The first clinical trials with a meningococcal serogroup A and C conjugate vaccine were conducted in the Philippines and the USA. In the late 1990s, the safety and immunogenicity of a meningococcal A/C conjugate vaccine was evaluated in infants from Niger. This and other studies have shown that meningococcal conjugate vaccines are safe, improve immune response in infants, prime immunologic memory and lead to a booster response to subsequent doses.[29,30]

At the end of 1999, conjugate C meningococcal vaccines were introduced in the UK among children and young adults under 18 years of age. Rates of meningococcal disease in the UK were approximately 2 per 100,000 population, and 30–40% of cases were caused by serogroup C.[31] Age-specific vaccine efficacy is estimated to be 89% in children under 12 months, 89% in children aged 12–24 months and 94% in adolescents aged 15–17 years.[32,33] Although serogroup carriage rates are low, preliminary data on the effect of a serogroup C meningococcal conjugate vaccine on carriage suggest that the conjugate vaccine may reduce carriage of serogroup C meningococci, which implies that it may decrease transmission, leading to herd inmmunity.[33] No significant increases have occurred so far in carriage of meningococci expressing other disease-associated serogroups.[33] Serogroup C conjugate vaccines have also recently been introduced in several European countries and Canada.

The newly created Meningitis Vaccine Project (funded by the Bill and Melinda Gates Foundation) seeks to promote and facilitate development of meningococcal serogroup A and serogroup A/C/Y/W-135 conjugate vaccines at a reasonable price for use in Africa.[34] Production of vaccines will be followed by introduction into some of the poorest nonindustrialized countries in the African meningitis belt. As has been demonstrated for the Hib vaccine, meningococcal conjugate vaccines could have a major impact on prevention of meningococcal disease. If these conjugate vaccines prove to be capable of providing a durable antibody response, particularly in infants and young children, then integrating them into routine childhood immunization, especially in hyperendemic areas of sub-Saharan Africa, would appear to be warranted.

Because the capsule of serogroup B meningococci is identical to human cell antigens (N-CAM) and is poorly immunogenic in humans, vaccine development has largely focused on outer membrane protein vaccines. The immunogenicity and protective efficacy of vaccines against several serogroup B outer membrane proteins have been recently evaluated; results have been encouraging, although questions remain about their effectiveness against heterologous strains and in young children.[35,36]

Chemoprophylaxis

Most people become infected after contact with asymptomatic carriers rather than with persons who have meningococcal disease, but close contacts of patients (e.g. those living in the same home) have a 500–800 times increased risk of developing disease.[37] Antimicrobial chemoprophylaxis of close contacts of patients who have meningococcal disease remains the primary preventive measure after the occurrence of sporadic cases. Systemic antibiotics that eliminate nasopharyngeal carriage include rifampin (rifampicin), ciprofloxacin and ceftriaxone. Nasopharyngeal cultures are not useful in determining who should receive chemoprophylaxis. Mass chemoprophylaxis is not currently recommended to control meningococcal disease epidemics, given that meningococcal vaccines constitute a better epidemic control strategy.

Travelers

Since the 1987 outbreak associated with the Hajj, pilgrims to Mecca have been required to show proof of vaccination against meningococcal disease on entry to Saudi Arabia. Because of the serogroup W-135 meningococcal disease outbreak in 2000, pilgrims are now required to show proof of vaccination with quadrivalent (A/C/Y/W-135) polysaccharide vaccine when entering Saudi Arabia. For other travelers, guidelines for immunization against meningococcal disease vary. Vaccination with the quadrivalent A/C/Y/W-135 polysaccharide vaccine may benefit persons traveling to or residing in countries that are undergoing an epidemic or have hyperendemic disease, particularly if contact with the local population will be prolonged.[38]

CLINICAL FEATURES

The clinical presentation of epidemic meningococcal meningitis is similar to that of other forms of acute purulent meningitis (see Chapter 22), with sudden onset of headache, fever, nausea, vomiting, photophobia, neck stiffness and alteration in mental state. Some patients who have meningococcal meningitis, but not all, have an asso-

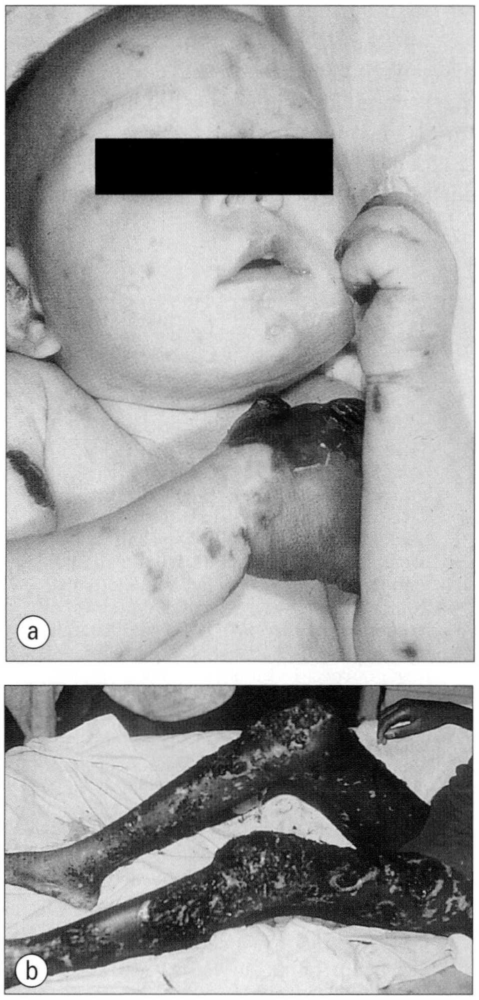

Fig. 159.2 Meningococcal septicemia with purpura fulminans. (a) In an infant and (b) in an adult.

ciated purpuric or petechial rash. This may be less common in adults and is difficult to recognize in dark-skinned people. Meningococcal sepsis is characterized by abrupt onset of fever and the characteristic petechial or purpuric rash, which is often severe (purpura fulminans; Fig. 159.2) and may be associated with the rapid onset of hypotension, acute adrenal hemorrhage (Waterhouse–Friderichsen syndrome) and multiple organ failure. In infants under 1 year of age, the presentation may be atypical with slow onset, absence of neck stiffness and the presence of bulging fontanelle.

DIAGNOSIS

Diagnosis is strongly suspected based on clinical findings of headache, fever, stiff neck and a petechial or purpuric rash. Meningococcal meningitis is confirmed by a lumbar puncture, which classically shows purulent or turbid cerebrospinal fluid, elevated white blood cell count, elevated protein level and decreased glucose, and a Gram stain showing Gram-negative diplococci (often intracellular). Meningococci can be grown on Mueller–Hinton or chocolate agar. Rapid antigen detection, by latex agglutination or countercurrent immunoelectrophoresis, can identify specific serogroup capsular antigens in cerebrospinal fluid. Blood cultures are commonly positive. If a rash is present, a skin biopsy can be examined for Gram-negative diplococci. Serogroup specific polymerase chain reaction (PCR) techniques have been used, primarily in industrialized countries, for the diagnosis of meningococcal disease; rapid PCR techniques for use in Africa are under development.

In the midst of an epidemic in a developing country, the flood of patients may overwhelm the health facilities and laboratory capacity. As soon as a meningococcal epidemic has been confirmed, rapid initiation of treatment and initiation of prevention measures take priority. Laboratory confirmation of cases throughout the epidemic is encouraged, mainly for epidemics of serogroup W-135 meningococcal disease.

MANAGEMENT

Many antimicrobial agents, including penicillin, remain active against meningococci (Table 159.1), but choice of antibiotic is increasingly threatened by drug resistance, lack of central nervous system penetration and cost. Since the emergence of sulfa-resistant meningococcal strains in the 1960s, sulfa drugs are no longer considered suitable as initial therapy. Third-generation cephalosporins, such as ceftriaxone, are excellent but currently expensive alternatives in developing countries. Recently, meningococcal isolates with increased resistance to penicillin have been recognized in the USA, Spain and Canada

ANTIBIOTIC TREATMENT, CHEMOPROPHYLAXIS AND VACCINATION FOR EPIDEMIC MENINGOCOCCAL MENINGITIS	
Treatment in an outbreak setting in developing countries[22]	Long-acting chloramphenicol (e.g. tifomycin) in oil suspension, single dose: Adults, 3.0g (6ml); children 1–15 years, 100mg/kg; children <1 year, 50mg/kg
Other treatment options	Penicillin G 18–24 megaunits/day iv in divided doses q4h (250,000 units/kg/day) Ceftriaxone 1–2g iv q12h (100mg/kg/day) If penicillin-allergic: chloramphenicol 100mg/kg/day im in divided doses q6h
Vaccination (generally limited to epidemics or to travelers to endemic areas)	A/C/Y/W-135 vaccine or A/C vaccine given as single 0.5ml sc injection Decreased efficacy in children <2 years of age; vaccine efficacy wanes after 3–5 years
Chemoprophylaxis (recommended for close contacts of cases)	Rifampin (rifampicin): Adults, 600mg po q12h for 2 days; children >1 month, 10mg/kg po q12h for 2 days; children <1 month, 5mg/kg po q12h for 2 days Ciprofloxacin: Adults, 500mg po (single dose) Ceftriaxone: Adults, 250mg im (single dose); children <15 years, 125mg im (single dose)

Table 159.1 Antibiotic treatment, chemoprophylaxis and vaccination for epidemic meningococcal meningitis.

and isolates with increased resistance to chloramphenicol have been recognized in Vietnam and France;[39–41] however, the clinical significance and potential impact on treatment is unclear.

The care of a large number of patients during an epidemic in a developing country makes repeated injections with crystalline penicillin or even ceftriaxone impractical. A single intramuscular dose of an oily suspension of chloramphenicol has been shown to be as effective as a 5-day course of crystalline penicillin in the treatment of meningococcal meningitis[42] and it is a useful first-line therapy during epidemic periods in developing countries. If the patient fails to improve within 48 hours, a second dose should be administered and other causes of bacterial meningitis should be considered. Management of sporadic cases consists of intravenous penicillin or ceftriaxone or, if the patient is allergic to penicillin, chloramphenicol.

REFERENCES

1. Greenwood BM. Selective primary health care: strategies for control of disease in the developing world. XII. Acute bacterial meningitis. Rev Infect Dis 1984;6:374–89.
2. Adams WG, Deaver KA, Cochi SL, *et al.* Decline of childhood *Haemophilus influenzae* type b disease in the Hib vaccine era. JAMA 1993;269:221–6.
3. Centers for Disease Control and Prevention. Preventing pneumococcal disease among infants and young children. MMWR Morb Mortal Wkly Rep 2000; 49(RR09):1.
4. Miller E, Salisbury D, Ramsay M. Planning, registration, and implementation of an immunisation campaign against meningococcal serogroup C disease in the UK: a success story. Vaccine 2001; 20:S58–67.
5. Lepow ML, Perkins, BA, Hughes, PA, *et al.* Meningococcal vaccines. In: Plotkin SA, Orenstein WA, eds. Vaccines, 3rd ed. Philadelphia: WB Saunders; 1999:711–27.
6. Murray CJL, Lopez AD. Global health statistics: a compendium of incidence, prevalence, and mortality estimates for over 200 conditions. Boston: Harvard School of Public Health on behalf of the World Health Organization and the World Bank; 1996:283–309.
7. Lapeyssonie L. La meningite cerebro-spinale en Afrique. Bull WHO 1963;28(Suppl.1):3–114.
8. Greenwood BM. The epidemiology of acute bacterial meningitis in tropical Africa. In: Williams JD, Burnie J, eds. Bacterial meningitis. London: Academic Press; 1987:61–91.
9. Peltola H, Kataja JM, Maekela PH. Shift in the age-distribution of meningococcal disease as a predictor of an epidemic? Lancet 1982;2:829–30.
10. Gagneux SP, Hodgson A, Smith TA, *et al.* Prospective study of a serogroup X *Neisseria meningitides* outbreak in Northern Ghana. J Infect Dis 2002; 185:618–26.
11. Novelli VM, Lewis RG, Dawood ST. Epidemic group A meningococcal disease in Hajj pilgrims. Lancet 1987;2:863.
12. Moore PS, Harrison LH, Telzak EE, *et al.* Group A meningococcal carriage in travelers returning from Saudi Arabia. JAMA 1988;260:2686–9.
13. Fischer M, Perkins BA. *Neisseria meningitidis* serogroup B: emergence of the ET-5 complex. Semin Pediatr Infect Dis 1997;8:50–6.
14. Diermayer M, Hedberg K, Hoesly F, *et al.* Epidemic serogroup B meningococcal disease in Oregon: the evolving epidemiology of the ET-5 strain. JAMA 1999; 281:1493–7.
15. Baker MG, Martin DR, Kieft CE, *et al.* 10-year serogroup B meningococcal disease epidemic in New Zealand: descriptive epidemiology, 1991–2000. J Pediatr Child Health 2001;37:S13–9.
16. Active Bacterial Core Surveillance Report. *Neisseria meningitidis*, 2000. Altanta, GA: Centers for Disease Control; 2000. http://www.cdc.gov/ncidod/dbmd/abcs/survreports.htm.
17. Mayer LW, Reeves MW, Al-Hamdan N, *et al.* The 2000 outbreak of W-135 meningococcal disease: not emergence of a new W-135 strain, but clonal expansion within the ET-37 complex. J Infect Dis 2002;185:1596–605.
18. Centers for Disease Control and Prevention. Assessment of risk for meningococcal disease associated with the Hajj 2001. MMWR Morb Mortal Wkly Rep 2001;50:221.
19. Wilder-Smith A, Barkham TMS, Earnest A, *et al.* Acquisition of W135 meningococcal carriage in Hajj pilgrims and transmission to household contacts: prospective study. Br Med J 2002;517:365–6.
20. World Health Organization. Meningococcal disease, serogroup W-135, Burkina Faso. Preliminary Report, 2002. Wkly Epidemiol Rep 2002;18:152–5.
21. Stephens DS, Hajjeh RA, Baughman WS, *et al.* Sporadic meningococcal disease in adults: results of a 5-year population-based study. Ann Intern Med 1995;123:937–40.
22. Moore PS, Hierholzer J, Dewitt W, *et al.* Respiratory viruses and mycoplasma as cofactors for epidemic group A meningococcal meningitis. JAMA 1990;264:1271–5.
23. Quagliarello V, Scheld WM. Bacterial meningitis: pathogenesis, pathophysiology, and progress. N Engl J Med 1992;327:864–72.
24. Woods CW, Armstrong G, Sackey SO, *et al.* Emergency vaccination against epidemic meningitis in Ghana: implications for the control of meningococcal disease in West Africa. Lancet 2000; 355:30–3.
25. World Health Organization Working Group. Control of epidemic meningococcal diseases. WHO Practical Guidelines. Lyon: Édition Fondation Marcel Merieux; 1995.
26. World Health Organization. Detecting meningococcal meningitis epidemics in highly-endemic African countries. WHO recommendation. Wkly Epidemiol Rec 2000;75:306–9.
27. World Health Organization. http://www.who.int/disease-outbreak-news/n2001/april/ICG.html.
28. Anderson EL, Bowers T, Mink CM. Safety and immunogenicity of meningococcal A and C polysaccharide conjugate vaccines in adults. Infect Immun 1994;62:3391–5.
29. Campagne G, Garba A, Fabre P, *et al.* Safety and immunogenicity of three doses of a *Neisseria meningitidis* A + C diphtheria conjugate vaccine in infants from Niger. Pediatr Infect Dis J 2000;19:144–50.
30. Soriano-Gabarro, M, Stuart JM Rosenstein NE. Vaccines for the prevention of meningococcal disease in children. Semin Pediatr Infect Dis 2002;13:182–9.
31. Public Health Laboratory Service. Vaccination programme for group C meningococcal infection is launched. CDR Wkly 1999;9:261–4.
32. Miller E, Borrow R, Kaczmarski E, *et al.* Update on meningococcal conjugate vaccination programme in England and Wales: herd immunity, vaccine efficacy, and validation of serological correlated. 13th International Pathogenic *Neisseria* Conference, September 2002, Oslo, Norwey; Session IX (Vaccines):60.
33. Maiden MCJ, Stuart JM, UK Meningococcal Carriage Group. Carriage of serogroup C meningococci 1 year after meningococcal C conjugate polysaccharide vaccination. Lancet 2002;359:1829.
34. Bill and Melinda Gates Foundation. The Bill & Melinda Gates Foundation announces grant for the elimination of epidemic meningitis in sub-Saharan Africa. Announcement, 30 May 2002. Washington: Bill & Melinda Gates Foundation; 2002. http://www.gatesfoundation.org/globalhealth/infectiousdiseases/vaccines/announcements/announce-382.htm.
35. De Moraes JC, Perkins BA, Camargo MC, *et al.* Protective efficacy of a serogroup B meningococcal vaccine in São Paulo, Brazil. Lancet 1992;340:1074–8.
36. Rosenstein NE, Perkins BA, Stephnes DS, *et al.* Meningococcal disease. N Engl J Med 2001;344:1378–88.
37. Meningococcal Disease Surveillance Group. Analysis of endemic meningococcal disease by serogroup and evaluation of chemoprophylaxis. J Infect Dis 1976;134:201–4.
38. Centers for Disease Control, National Center for Infectious Diseases. Traveler's health website. http://www.cdc.gov/travel/index.htm.
39. Jackson LA, Tenover FC, Baker C, *et al.* Prevalence of *Neisseria meningitidis* relatively resistant to penicillin in the United States, 1991. Meningococcal Disease Study Group. J Infect Dis 1994;169:438–41.
40. Sáez-Nieto JA, Lujan R, Berrón S, *et al.* Epidemiology and molecular basis of penicillin-resistant *Neisseria meningitidis* in Spain: a 5-year history (1985–1989). Clin Infect Dis 1992;14:394–402.
41. Galimand M, Gerbaud G, Guibordenche M, *et al.* High level chloramphenicol resistance in *Neisseria meningitidis*. N Engl J Med 1998;339:868–74.
42. Pecoul B, Varaine F, Keita M, *et al.* Long-acting chloramphenicol versus intravenous ampicillin for treatment of bacterial meningitis. Lancet 1991;338:862–6.

chapter 160

Eye Infections in the Tropics

Robin Bailey

This chapter discusses the contribution of infection to the major blinding diseases of the tropics and the ocular features associated with common tropical infections. In tropical practice, visual prognosis in both major blinding infections and simple trauma is often worsened by late presentation, secondary infection and inappropriate use of traditional eye medicines.

MAJOR BLINDING INFECTIONS OF THE TROPICS

Cataract, vitamin A deficiency, trachoma and onchocerciasis are classically considered to be associated with blindness in developing countries, although community-based studies of the causes of blindness have only been conducted in a few countries.[1,2] In two of these diseases, trachoma and onchocerciasis, and in two other important tropical infectious diseases, leprosy and measles, infection and the host response to it play prominent and contrasting roles in the pathogenesis of blindness and other ocular complications. These are discussed below.

TRACHOMA

Trachoma is a chronic follicular keratoconjunctivitis caused by infection with *Chlamydia trachomatis*, almost exclusively of serotypes A, B, Ba and C. (The 'genital' *C. trachomatis* serotypes D–K may cause disease that is indistinguishable from trachoma, but this is rare.) Trachoma is characterized by scarring sequelae of the conjunctiva after repeated infections (see Chapters 18 and 236).

Epidemiology

Trachoma is one of the most common infectious diseases; it is estimated that 500 million people are exposed to infection, and in 1995 the World Health Organization estimated that 6 million people have been blinded by trachoma.[1] As a result of demographic trends, 12 million further cases of blindness are expected within 30 years.[3] It is a disease of poverty, associated with poor personal and environmental hygiene, and it was common in much of Europe and North America during the 19th century. The map (Fig. 160.1) shows the current distribution of active trachoma based on reports reaching the WHO. 'Endemic' disease is considered to be present if there is more than 10% prevalence in school-aged children. Trachoma is found in northern and sub-Saharan Africa, the Middle East and the Indian subcontinent. There are also foci in parts of Central and South America, Australia and the Pacific.

In trachoma-endemic communities, the main reservoir of infection is the eyes of affected children; active trachoma is unusual among adults, and there is evidence that most transmission of trachoma occurs within the family[4,5] as a result of close contact between young children and their mothers and other caregivers. Transmission is favored by poor environmental and personal hygiene, lack of water for washing, inadequate sleeping space, inadequate disposal of rubbish or sewage, and the proximity of domestic animals. It is considered to take place via fingers and fomites. Recent evidence implicates the bazaar fly *Musca sorbens*, which prefers to breed in fresh human feces on the ground, as a mechanical vector of trachoma in conditions of poor sanitation.[6,7] The relative importance of these means of transmission probably varies from one community to another.

Pathogenesis

There is evidence that the pathologic features of trachoma are not the result of direct tissue damage but are immunologically mediated. A single infection with *C. trachomatis* usually leads to a self-limiting follicular conjunctivitis, and repeated episodes appear to be necessary for the development of intense inflammation and of scarring sequelae. The most characteristic histologic finding in active trachoma is the presence of follicles, which resemble germinal centers, in the superior tarsal conjunctiva. Subsequently subconjunctival scarring occurs and contraction of the scars causes distortion of the tarsal plate, entropion and trichiasis (inturned eyelashes).

Evidence from animal models suggests that cellular immune mechanisms are of primary importance in limiting and clearing chlamydial infection. There is evidence that scarred subjects have a reduced capacity for clearance of chlamydial infection, which occurs by way of specific T helper-1 lymphocyte responses[8] and possibly by way of cytotoxic lymphocyte activity.[9] Tumor necrosis factor-α has pro-inflammatory and antichlamydial activity and appears to participate in the process by which repeated episodes of intense disease lead to scarring.[10] Transforming growth factor-β, a cytokine with established fibrogenic properties, is expressed to a greater extent in the conjunctivae of scarred subjects[11] and is also directly implicated in the scarring process. Antibodies to a chlamydial heat shock protein, HSP 60, are also associated with scarring in both the eye and the genital tract, but it is uncertain whether these reflect a causal role for this antigen or an epiphenomenon.

Prevention

The goal of prevention is to reduce transmission to a level at which exposure to reinfection does not occur often enough to cause blinding trachoma. Measures focused on improving personal and community hygiene, such as adequate water supplies and control of *Musca sorbens* through pit latrine provision, are likely to reduce the incidence of trachoma. A study of community education targeted at face washing showed that, with intense effort, reductions in trachoma prevalence are possible but that they were not well sustained.[12] Treatment of active cases with topical antibiotics may be effective temporarily, but such a strategy usually results in rapid reinfection either from an extraocular reservoir or from members of the household or community who are subclinically infected or incubating disease. In order to produce an effective reduction in the infectious reservoir in a community, whole families, households or communities may need systemic treatment. There is no vaccine at present.

Clinical features

In endemic communities, *C. trachomatis* infection is usually acquired early in childhood and the progressive scarring and distortion of the

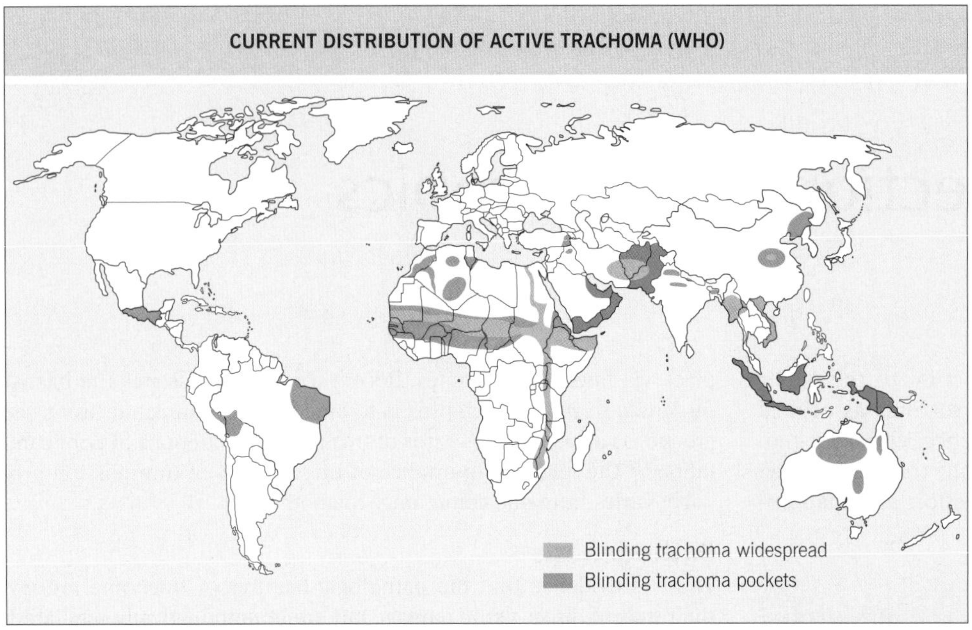

Fig. 160.1 Current distribution of active trachoma (WHO).

eyelid may lead to corneal scarring and blindness, usually in late middle age. In severely affected communities signs of trachoma can be found in over 90% of children aged between 1 and 2 years, and blindness rates may approach 25% of those over 60 years. In most endemic areas, there is no sex difference in prevalence or incidence until after adolescence, but both active trachoma and its scarring sequelae are more common in women, probably reflecting their closer contact with children.

Subjects who have trachoma typically have few symptoms until the final stages, when inturned eyelashes (trichiasis) develop. Secondary bacterial infection may play a role in the mucopurulent conjunctivitis, nasal discharge and chronic otitis media seen in some patients.

The most prominent sign of active trachoma is the presence of lymphoid follicles, which are usually found on the superior tarsal conjunctiva and can be easily visualized by everting the upper eyelid, although they may also occasionally be found at the corneoscleral junction (limbal follicles). The presence of five or more of these pale yellow or white spots with a diameter <0.5mm is needed in the central area of the superior tarsal conjunctiva to meet the accepted definition of trachomatous inflammation of follicular grade (TF; Fig. 160.2). Active trachoma is also associated with capillary congestion of the conjunctiva, visible either as small red dots (papillae) or as obscuration of the normally visible tarsal blood vessels. If the blood vessels are obscured in more than half of the central area over the tarsal plate, trachomatous inflammation of intense grade (TI) is said to be present (Fig. 160.3). Neovascularization of the cornea or 'pannus' is associated with active inflammatory disease and in trachoma typically involves the superior corneal margin.

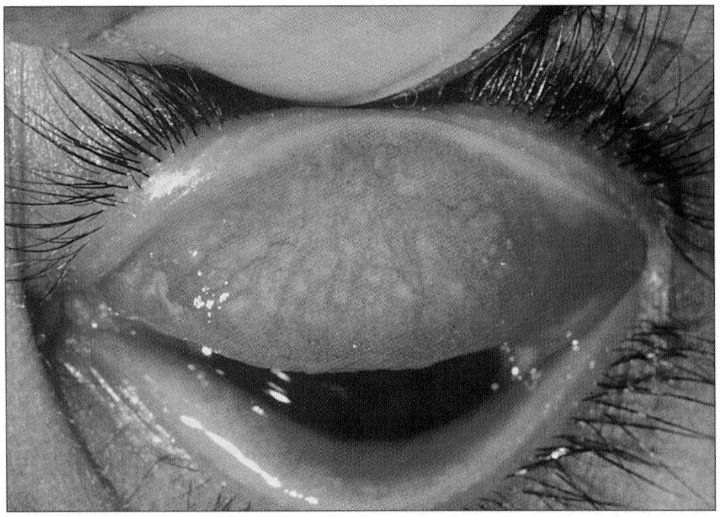

Fig. 160.2 Everted eyelid showing follicular trachoma (TF). Courtesy of the WHO Program for the Prevention of Blindness.

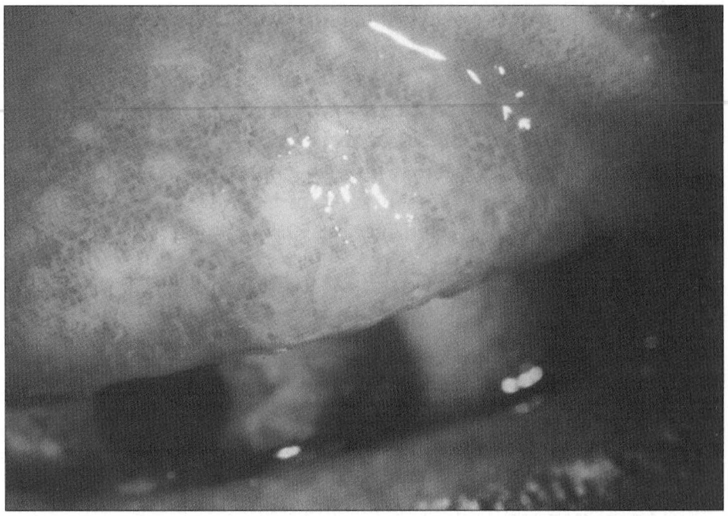

Fig. 160.3 Everted eyelid showing intense inflammatory trachoma. Follicles are also present.

Conjunctival scars (which, if clearly visible, would be graded trachomatous scarring (TS)) are initially small and stellate, but eventually become broad and confluent (Fig. 160.4). The scars contract, causing distortion of the tarsal plate and loss of its normal protective functions and resulting in inturning of the lashes (trichiasis, which is graded TT if any lash is deviated towards the eyeball), which rub on the cornea (Fig. 160.5). This can lead to corneal opacity and ultimately to blindness from abrasion of the cornea. Limbal follicles resolve to leave small depressions at the limbus known as 'Herbert's pits' (see Fig. 160.4).

Trachoma may be confused with other conditions producing a follicular conjunctivitis (Table 160.1). With the exception of viral conjunctivitis, which is acute and self-limiting, the other conditions in Table 160.1 are never endemic in a community; however, limbal follicles or Herbert's pits (Fig. 160.4) are the only clinical sign unique to trachoma[13] and these do not occur even in a majority of cases.

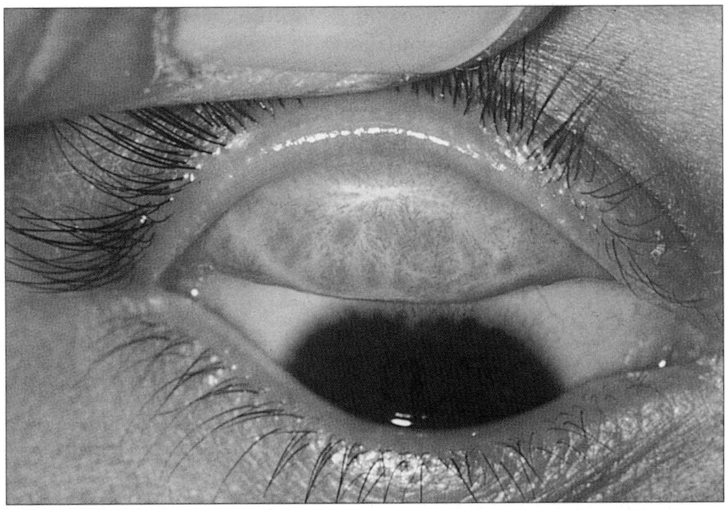

Fig. 160.4 Everted eyelid showing trachomatous scarring (TS). There are also Herbert's pits visible at the corneoscleral junction. Courtesy of the WHO Program for the Prevention of Blindness.

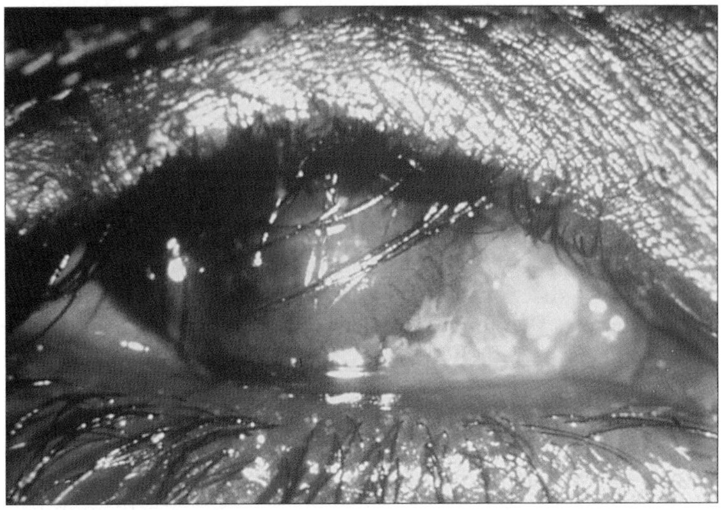

Fig. 160.5 Trachomatous trichiasis (TT) and secondary corneal opacity. Courtesy of the WHO Program for the Prevention of Blindness.

Table 160.1 Causes of follicular conjunctivitis.

CAUSES OF FOLLICULAR CONJUNCTIVITIS	
Cause	**Comments**
Folliculosis	Follicles are few and occur in the inferior fornix without inflammation or hyperemia; a common finding
Viral infections	Acute, self-limiting with signs of resolution in 2 weeks
Trachoma	
'Inclusion conjunctivitis' and other ocular chlamydial infections	Also caused by ocular chlamydial infection, often with genital serotypes; frequently unilateral
'Toxic' follicular conjunctivitis:	
Molluscum contagiosum	Caused by spillage of contents of molluscum lesions on eyelids
Drug induced	Follows use of eye medications for months or years
Eye cosmetics	Granules of cosmetic seen in follicles
Bacterial infections: *Moraxella* spp. and others	Angular blepharitis with *Moraxella lacunata*; seen in adolescent girls who share eye make-up
Axenfeld's chronic follicular conjunctivitis	Reported in institutionalized children and native Americans; probably a mild form of trachoma[11]
Chronic follicular conjunctivitis of Thygeson	Outbreak in a Californian high school that contained trachoma cases; features compatible with mild active trachoma[11]
Parinaud's oculoglandular syndrome	Associated with pathogens invading through the conjunctivae; associated with systemic malaise and gross pre-auricular lymphadenopathy; some cases associated with exposure to cats and may be due to feline strains of *Chlamydia psittaci*; many other causes (e.g. syphilis, lymphogranuloma venereum, tuberculosis, tularemia)
Vernal catarrh	Occurs in atopic subjects; characteristic appearance with giant 'cobblestone' papillae

Diagnosis

Trachoma is usually diagnosed on clinical grounds. The simplified grading scheme including TF, TI, TS and TT has been developed by the World Health Organization for public health purposes.[14] Several laboratory tests can be used to confirm a diagnosis of trachoma, but these are rarely available in endemic areas. Chlamydial infection is characterized by blue intracytoplasmic inclusions in Giemsa-stained epithelial cell scrapings. The organism can be cultured in cell monolayers, visualized in smears using direct fluorescent antibody methods, or detected by enzyme immunoassay. Deoxyribose nucleic acid amplification by polymerase chain reaction and ligase chain reaction based on target sequences in the common plasmid pCT1 of *C. trachomatis* are the most sensitive methods described for demonstrating ocular chlamydial infection.[15]

Management

Individual sporadic cases are normally treated with 1% tetracycline ointment topically q12h for 6 weeks. A single oral dose of azithromycin (20mg/kg) is also effective.[16] Treatment of patients in endemic areas is usually compromised by rapid reinfection, as discussed above, and mass treatment or systemic treatment may need to be considered. Trichiasis can be treated by epilation, but this normally provides only temporary relief and lid surgery is usually needed to prevent blindness. Tarsal rotation[17] is the operation of choice. The

International Trachoma Initiative currently supports azithromycin donation to trachoma control programs as a component of the SAFE (Surgery Antibiotic treatment Facial cleanliness and Environmental improvement) strategy endorsed by the WHO.

ONCHOCERCIASIS

Pathogenesis

In the eye, as in the rest of the body, pathology is due to an inflammatory reaction to dead microfilariae of *Onchocerca volvulus*. As these can be found in the cornea, the anterior chamber, the iris, the lens, the retina and the choroid, onchocercal lesions may involve all these sites. In the conjunctiva and iris, an immunohistochemical study has found that chronic ocular onchocerciasis is associated with predominant infiltration by $CD8^+$ lymphocytes and is associated with major histocompatibility complex class II antigen expression in resident cell populations, suggesting activation (see Chapters 18 and 246).[18]

Clinical features

Eye involvement in onchocerciasis is usually bilateral and affects men more commonly than women.

Punctate or 'snowflake' keratitis occurs as inflammatory cells accumulate around dead microfilariae, and it may respond to topical corticosteroids. Sclerosing keratitis, in which neovascularization and scarring develop nasally and temporally in the cornea and then extend inwards from the inferior limbal margin to involve the whole surface to produce a total corneal scar, has been a common cause of blindness, particularly in savannah regions. Microfilariae may be visible in the anterior chamber with a slit lamp, often as movement that is closely associated with the posterior corneal surface. Inflammatory reactions may produce iritis, and cataract may also contribute to reduced vision. In the posterior segment of the eye, choroidoretinal atrophy, with clumping and breaking up of the retinal pigment epithelium, and associated optic atrophy may follow onchocercal chorioretinitis (leading to the 'Hissette–Ridley' fundus). These changes in the posterior segment contribute further to visual loss and there is no specific treatment.

MEASLES

Pathogenesis

Measles virus infection and its consequences are a major risk to sight in tropical practice. In Africa they cause about 50% of childhood blindness, usually from corneal scarring.[19] Although measles virus infects the corneal epithelium and the conjunctiva, its devastating effects on the cornea are the result of secondary processes, which include infection, acute vitamin A deficiency, exposure and the effects of traditional eye medicines. Measles virus-associated immunosuppression appears to be responsible for reactivation of herpes simplex virus, which has been found in corneal ulcers after measles,[20] and gut involvement appears to precipitate acute vitamin A deficiency in those with marginal reserves.

Clinical features

The direct effects of measles on the eye are a punctate keratitis and sometimes conjunctival lesions that are analogous to Koplik's spots, which normally resolve without sequelae. Corneal ulceration and keratomalacia with liquefaction of the cornea and the whole eye may supervene in acute vitamin A deficiency. Secondary ulceration due to herpes simplex virus may be typically dendritic or modified by other factors as discussed below. If subjects are too sick or dehydrated to close their eyes, corneal dryness and exposure ulceration may result, and in tropical practice, traditional medicines are frequently applied and may contribute to secondary infection and a worse prognosis. Subjects who have ocular complications of measles should be treated with vitamin A, topical antibiotics and measures to avoid corneal exposure.

LEPROSY

Pathogenesis

In leprosy three main mechanisms operate in the eye to cause pathology. Overwhelming bacterial infection in lepromatous leprosy may lead to atrophy of the involved tissues. The eye may be involved in type I reactions (reversal reactions), in which motor and sensory nerve loss is prominent, and in type II reactions, in which inflammation within the eye is prominent. As elsewhere in the body, it is the reactions that cause most damage, manifesting as visual loss and blindness in the case of the eye.

Clinical features

Lepromatous leprosy may be characterized by limbal lepromata, painless yellow or pink nodules at the corneoscleral junction. Chalky deposits may be associated with corneal invasion by *Mycobacterium leprae*. The iris may become thin and atrophic, and pathognomonic 'iris pearls', which are calcified foci of dead leprosy bacilli, appear as white nodules on the surface of the iris.[20] Type I reactions involving the fifth cranial nerve can result in corneal anesthesia and lagophthalmos (inability to close the eyes) may occur if the seventh cranial nerve is involved. Together these produce a cornea that is both anesthetic and exposed, and therefore requires protection. Eye health education, blinking exercises, protective spectacles and surgical procedures such as tarsorrhaphy may all be needed.[20] Type II reactions may cause acute or chronic iritis, which requires treatment with topical corticosteroids and mydriatics, or scleritis, which may require systemic treatment with corticosteroids and clofazimine (see Chapter 154).

CLINICAL ASPECTS OF EYE INVOLVEMENT IN COMMON TROPICAL INFECTIONS

BACTERIAL INFECTIONS

Tuberculosis

Primary tuberculosis may affect the conjunctiva with nodular lesions and associated chronic conjunctivitis that is not responsive to standard topical treatment. In miliary disease, tubercles may be found in the conjunctiva, the iris or the choroid. Phlyctenular conjunctivitis and granulomatous uveitis may be associated with tuberculosis but are not specific for it. Optic neuritis may complicate tuberculous basal meningitis.

Sexually transmitted diseases

Ocular gonococcal infection, usually as a result of autoinoculation from the genital tract, causes an acute purulent conjunctivitis that may progress rapidly to corneal ulceration and perforation in the absence of appropriate treatment.

Gonococcal ophthalmia neonatorum, acquired by an infant passing through an infected birth canal, is similarly threatening to sight and usually presents in the first week of life as a bilateral purulent conjunctivitis.[21]

Ocular autoinoculation from genital *C. trachomatis* infection causes a clinical picture identical to trachoma, except that it is commonly unilateral. Among infants born to infected mothers, 30% develop chlamydial ophthalmia neonatorum, which is usually a self-limiting bilateral mucopurulent conjunctivitis presenting within 2 weeks of delivery. In a small proportion of cases, pneumonia and permanent lung sequelae follow. Thus chlamydial and gonococcal ophthalmia neonatorum both require systemic and topical therapy.

Iritis, retinal vasculitis, optic neuritis and disseminated chorioretinitis may be features of secondary acquired syphilis (see Chapter 75).

Other bacterial infections

Petechiae may be seen at the conjunctiva in meningococcal meningitis; conjunctivitis, anterior uveitis and even panophthalmitis may complicate meningococcemia. Diphtheria may present with a membranous conjunctivitis, lid edema and local effects of exotoxin. Cholera with rapid dehydration has been associated with the acute development of cataracts. Rose spots in typhoid fever may involve the conjunctiva. The clinical picture of Parinaud's syndrome (follicular or granulomatous conjunctivitis, pre-auricular lymphadenopathy, often with systemic malaise) is associated with pathogen invasion via the conjunctiva and may be seen with tuberculosis, syphilis, tularemia and lymphogranuloma venereum. Brucellosis has been associated with chronic granulomatous uveitis. Dilatation of the conjunctival vessels and subconjunctival hemorrhages may be presenting features of leptospirosis or typhus.

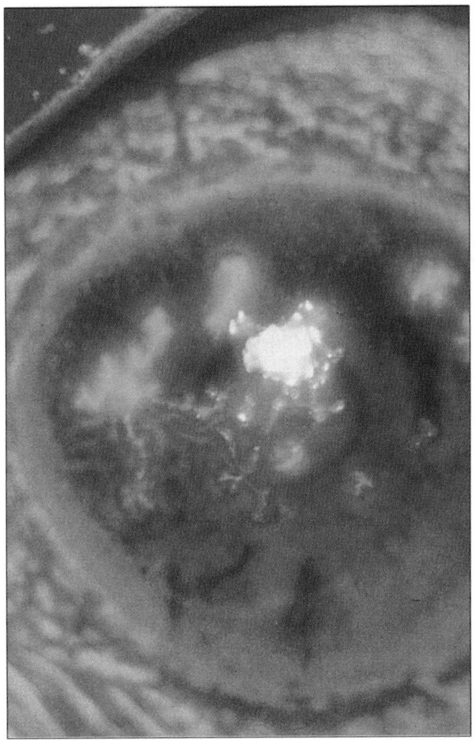

Fig. 160.6 Typical dendritic ulcer caused by herpes simplex virus, visualized with fluorescein staining.

PARASITIC INFECTIONS

Retinal hemorrhages may be seen in malaria and may be the earliest sign of cerebral involvement. Unilateral edema of the eyelid (Romaña's sign) may be seen in American trypanosomiasis if the inoculation site is in the region of the eye. Chorioretinitis is the most common ocular manifestation of toxoplasmosis. An ocular larva migrans syndrome (larvae migrating within the eye) may be seen with *Toxocara* spp. and *Gnathostoma* spp., and *Loa loa* typically migrates under the conjunctiva. Egg granulomas may occur in the conjunctiva or choroid in schistosomiasis. Cysticerci of *Taenia solium* may occur within the eye, often subretinally.

VIRAL INFECTIONS

Herpes simplex virus, which has a worldwide distribution, can have devastating effects on the eye. In many tropical environments this is the most common cause of corneal ulceration, often occurring as a complication of measles or causes of high fever such as malaria. A narrow, branching, dendritic ulcer that is best seen with fluorescein staining is typical (Fig. 160.6), but in tropical practice the time to presentation and inappropriate use of traditional eye medicines often modify this, leading to larger ameboid ulcers. If available, idoxuridine or aciclovir drops should be given very frequently until epithelial healing takes place.

Infection with HIV may itself cause a retinopathy with cotton wool spots, indicating ischemic damage to the retina. Cytomegalovirus retinopathy does not seem to be common in tropical practice, but syphilis, tuberculosis and herpes simplex virus infections and their associated ocular manifestations are more common among HIV patients. Kaposi's sarcoma may involve the eyelid or conjunctiva.

FUNGAL INFECTION AND SUPPURATIVE KERATITIS

Corneal ulceration, usually arising from mismanaged traumatic corneal abrasion, is prone to secondary colonization and infection with both bacteria and filamentous fungi. This results in a suppurative keratitis: an infected corneal ulcer with or without pus in the anterior chamber (hypopyon). The management of this condition depends on demonstrating a causative pathogen on culture or corneal scraping or on a local knowledge of the patterns of infection commonly encountered. A recent study in Ghana and India found that infected ulcers were commonly colonized with bacteria, *Streptococcus* spp. (India) or *Pseudomonas* spp. (Ghana), or fungi, *Fusarium* or *Aspergillus* spp.[22]

REFERENCES

1. Thylefors B, Negrel AD, Pararajasegaram R, Awadzi K. Global data on blindness. Bull World Health Organ 1995;73:115–21.
2. Faal H, Minassian D, Sowa S, Foster A. National survey of blindness and low vision in The Gambia: results. Br J Ophthalmol 1989;73:82–7.
3. Schachter J, Dawson CR. The epidemiology of trachoma predicts more blindness in the future. Scand J Infect Dis 1990;69(suppl):55–62.
4. Barenfanger J. Studies on the role of the family unit in the transmission of trachoma. Am J Trop Med Hyg 1975;24:509–15.
5. Bailey RL, Hayes LJ, Pickett M, Whittle HC, Ward ME. The molecular epidemiology of trachoma in a Gambian village. Br J Ophthalmol 1994;78:813–7.
6. Emerson PM, Lindsay SW, Walraven GEL, Faal H, Bogh C, Lowe K, Bailey R. Effect of fly control on trachoma and diarrhoea. Lancet 1999;353:1401–3.
7. Emerson PM, Bailey R, Mahdi OSM, Lindsay SW. Transmission ecology of the fly *Musca sorbens*, a putative vector of trachoma in The Gambia. Trans Roy Soc Trop Med Hyg 2000;94:28–32.
8. Holland MJ, Bailey RL, Hayes LJ, Whittle HC, Mabey DCW. Conjunctival scarring in trachoma is associated with depressed cell-mediated immune responses to chlamydial antigens. J Infect Dis 1993;168:1528–31.
9. Holland MJ, Conway D, Blanchard TJ, *et al.* Synthetic peptides based on *C. trachomatis* antigens identify CTL responses in subjects in a trachoma endemic population. Clin Exp Immunol 1997;107:44–9.
10. Conway D, Holland M, Bailey R, *et al.* Scarring trachoma is associated with polymorphism in the TNF-alpha gene promoter and with elevated TNF-alpha in tear fluid. Infect Immun 1977;65:1003–6.
11. Bobo L, Novak N, Mkocha H, *et al.* Evidence for a predominant proinflammatory conjunctival

cytokine response in individuals with trachoma. Infect Immun 1996;64:3273–9.
12. West S, Munoz B, Lynch M, *et al.* Impact of face washing on trachoma in Kongwa, Tanzania. Lancet 1995;345:155–8.
13. Dawson CR. Trachoma. In: Schachter J, Dawson CR, eds. Human chlamydial infections. Lyttleton, Massachusetts: PSG Publishing Company; 1978:61.
14. Thylefors B, Dawson CR, Jones BR, West SK, Taylor HR. A simple system for the assessment of trachoma and its complications. Bull World Health Organ 1987;65:477–83.
15. Bobo L, Munoz B, Viscidi R, Quinn T, Mkocha H, West S. Diagnosis of *Chlamydia trachomatis* eye infection in Tanzania by polymerase chain reaction/enzyme immunoassay. Lancet 1991;338:847–50.
16. Bailey RL, Arullendran P, Whittle HC, Mabey DCW. Randomised controlled trial of single-dose azithromycin in treatment of trachoma. Lancet 1993;342:453–6.
17. Reacher MH, Munoz B, Alghassany A, Daar AS, Elbualy M, Taylor HR. A controlled trial of surgery for trachomatous trichiasis of the upper lid. Arch Ophthalmol 1992;110:667–74.
18. Chan CC, Ottesen EA, Awadzi K, Badu R, Nussenblatt RB. Immunopathology of ocular onchocerciasis. 1. Inflammatory cells infiltrating the anterior segment. Clin Exp Immunol 1989;77:367–73.
19. Whittle HC, Sandford-Smith S, Kogbe O, Dossetor J, Duggan M. Severe ulcerative herpes of mouth and eye following measles. Trans Roy Soc Trop Med Hyg 1979;73:66–9.
20. Ffytche T. Ocular leprosy. J Commun Eye Health 1989;2:1.
21. Klauss V. Newborn conjunctivitis (ophthalmia neonatorum). J Commun Eye Health 1988;1:2–4.
22. Leck AK, Thomas PA, Hagan M, *et al.* Aetiology of suppurative corneal ulcers in Ghana and south India, and epidemiology of fungal keratitis. Br J Ophthalmol 2002;86:1211–15.

chapter 161

Secretory Diarrheas: Cholera and Enterotoxigenic *Escherichia coli*

Richard A Cash & Davidson H Hamer

INTRODUCTION

Cholera, the most severe of the secretory diarrheas, can cause dehydration and death within hours of onset in a severely purging individual. Although less likely to lead to dehydration than cholera, a more common cause of secretory diarrhea is enterotoxigenic *Escherichia coli* (ETEC); see Chapter 144). Although morbidity and mortality from cholera tend to be greatest in epidemic settings, ETEC infections occur more commonly as sporadic cases, especially in travelers to or children living in developing regions of the world.

Treatment programs that emphasize oral rehydration therapy have greatly reduced mortality from cholera and other watery dehydrating diarrheas worldwide, although diarrhea still remains the second most important cause of death in children in developing countries. Diarrheal disease is also a major cause of morbidity in the USA, where physicians are consulted for more than eight million episodes annually[1] and there is a yearly reported average of approximately 300 diarrheal deaths for children under 5 years of age, with most deaths related to dehydration.[2]

EPIDEMIOLOGY

Vibrio cholerae

Although the Bangladesh region has been the traditional home of cholera, the current pandemic – the seventh recorded in modern times – began in Indonesia in 1961 before traveling to the Indian subcontinent, the Middle East, the Soviet Union, Sub-Saharan Africa and finally to South America in 1991. The organism associated with the current pandemic is an El Tor biotype. The South American epidemic that began in Peru in January 1991 caused over a million cases in the first 3 years. The disease occurred in all age strata since the population had no protective antibody. Unboiled drinking water, unwashed fruits or vegetables and food or water from street vendors were implicated in this explosive outbreak.[3]

A newly described toxigenic non-01 strain, now designated *Vibrio cholerae* 0139 Bengal, was first identified in 1992 in southern India and Bangladesh.[4]

Cholera occurs sporadically along the Gulf Coast of the USA, mainly in Texas and Louisiana.[5] Among the millions of American travelers to endemic areas in foreign countries, only 42 imported cases of cholera were reported in the USA in the period 1965–1991.[6]

Humans are the only host for *V. cholerae* and carriers (about 5% following exposure) are seen only with the El Tor biotype. Contaminated water is the primary vehicle for spread, but certain foods have been implicated in some epidemics, especially if washed with contaminated water or, in the case of seafood (especially crustaceans and bivalves), harvested from water containing *V. cholerae*.[3] Person-to-person transmission is uncommon and health personnel rarely acquire cholera. Reduced gastric acidity, whether idiopathic or caused by drugs (e.g. H_2-blockers, proton pump inhibitors), or previous gastrectomy increases susceptibility to infection. The inoculum of *V. cholerae* leading to natural infection is not known, but samples of water sources epidemiologically linked to outbreaks rarely contain more than 10^3 organisms/ml. *Vibrio cholerae* 01 can enter into a viable nonculturable state but still retain its pathogenicity. The bacterium can also survive on aquatic vegetation (i.e. water hyacinth) and in the hindgut mucosa of zooplankton. Both of these factors might account for the low vibrio counts in contaminated water and explain where *V. cholerae* resides in the noncholera season.[7]

Enterotoxigenic *Escherichia coli*

These infections are also acquired from other humans as animal strains of ETEC are host specific. Like cholera, the major vehicles of infection are contaminated food and beverages.

Infection occurs primarily in children, with the highest incidence in the tropics, where the reported annual incidence of ETEC-related diarrhea in children varies from 15% to 50%.[8] Reports of ETEC infection in the USA have generally demonstrated a low incidence in most cities. However, ETEC is the most common cause of diarrhea in those traveling from North America or northern Europe to areas of the developing world where diarrheal disease is prevalent.

PATHOGENESIS AND PATHOLOGY

Acute bacterial diarrhea can be classified into:

- toxigenic types, in which an enterotoxin is the major if not exclusive pathogenic mechanism; and
- invasive types, in which the organism penetrates the mucosal surface as the primary event, but enterotoxin may be produced as well.

Diarrheal toxins can be grouped broadly into two categories:

- cytotonic, producing fluid secretion by activation of intracellular enzymes such as adenylate cyclase without causing any damage to the epithelial surface; and
- cytotoxic, causing injury to the mucosal cell as well as inducing fluid secretion but not primarily by activation of cyclic nucleotides.

Both *V. cholerae* and ETEC produce cytotonic enterotoxins.

There have been several exciting developments in the area of pathogenesis during recent years, including the finding that the structural genes for the cholera toxin are encoded by a filamentous bacteriophage.[9]

Vibrio cholerae

Vibrio cholerae is an aerobic, motile, Gram-negative rod that is shaped like a comma. Toxigenic *V. cholerae* that agglutinate in 01 antiserum are the main cause of epidemic cholera. The two major biotypes of *V. cholerae* 01, classic and El Tor, can both produce identical severe watery diarrhea. Although the percentage of mild and moderate cases is higher with El Tor infections, there are more cases of El Tor and thus more severe illness is caused by this biotype. The major serotypes associated with clinical disease are Inaba and Ogawa. The clinical features of illness caused by different sero- and biotypes of *V. cholerae* 01 are virtually indistinguishable.

All wild strains of *V. cholerae*, including 0139, elaborate the same enterotoxin: a protein molecule composed of two subunits, A and B.

The B subunit is responsible for binding to the receptor on the mucosa, whereas the A subunit is responsible for binding and activation of adenylate cyclase located on the inner cellular membrane. *Vibrio cholerae* requires both the cholera enterotoxin and toxin-coregulated pili (required for intestinal colonization) for full virulence.

The secretory diarrhea seen in cholera is caused by the action of the toxin on the epithelial cells of the small intestine. There appears to be a differential action on the mucosal cells characterized by:

- a direct secretory effect on the crypt cells; and
- an antiabsorptive effect on the villous cells.

Fluid loss originates in the duodenum and upper jejunum; the ileum is less affected. The colon is usually in a state of absorption because it is relatively insensitive to the toxin. The large volume of fluid produced in the upper intestine overwhelms the capacity of the lower bowel to absorb it.

The electrolyte composition of the stool is isotonic with plasma and the effluent has a low protein concentration. No inflammatory cells are visible on microscopic examination. Stool of heavily purging patients has very little odor except for a slightly 'fishy' smell.

Enterotoxigenic *Escherichia coli*

Inspired by the discoveries in cholera, investigators focused on *E. coli* as a possible cause of acute toxigenic diarrheal disease and found that some strains of *E. coli* elaborated an enterotoxin similar to the toxin of *V. cholerae*. There are two types of enterotoxins produced by ETEC with some species producing both or one:[10]

- the heat-labile toxin (LT) is a protein that is destroyed by heat and acid, acts like cholera toxin by activating adenylate cyclase, thereby causing secretion of fluid and electrolytes into the intestinal lumen, and shares antigenic components with cholera toxin; and
- the heat-stable toxin (ST) has no biochemical similarity to cholera toxin, is able to withstand heating to 212°F (100°C) and activates guanylate cyclase.

As is the case with *V. cholerae*, ETEC must elaborate both adherence factors and enterotoxin in order to be pathogenic.

PREVENTION

The four possible approaches to preventing cholera and ETEC infection are:

- avoidance of potentially contaminated water and food;
- prophylactic antibiotics;
- other prophylactic medications; and
- immunization.

Food and water precautions

These are necessary to prevent diarrhea and other diseases transmitted by the fecal–oral route. In endemic areas, if the quality of water is in doubt, bottled or boiled water should be used. Carbonated beverages are safer than noncarbonated ones as the organisms are very sensitive to the lower pH (4.0–5.0). Tea and coffee prepared with boiling water are generally safe. Food should be well cooked and eaten hot if possible. Snacks prepared by street vendors carry a higher risk, especially if the food is not well cooked. In coastal areas of Louisiana and Texas, seafood, especially crustaceans, should be well cooked.[6]

Prophylactic antibiotics and other prophylactic medications

Prophylactic antibiotics should not be used for cholera, especially on a mass scale, as resistance may develop. Antimicrobials have been extensively studied for the prevention of diarrhea in travelers.[10] Studies employing trimethoprim–sulfamethoxazole have shown protection rates of 71–95%. Similar rates have been observed with norfloxacin and ciprofloxacin. The prophylactic use of antibiotics should generally be discouraged, however, as it increases the risk of adverse reactions to the agent used and may enhance antimicrobial resistance.

Bismuth subsalicylate has been used for prevention, based on its antimicrobial and antisecretory properties, but provides only modest protection and must be taken daily at high doses, creating side-effects (black tongue and stool, tinnitus) that many find unacceptable.

Immunization

People infected with ETEC develop antibodies against the enterotoxin and colonization factors. Those living in high-risk areas appear to develop immunity as the attack rate for symptomatic infections for resident adults is much less than for visitors. At present there are no commercial vaccines for ETEC. An experimental ETEC oral killed vaccine has proven to be safe and immunogenic and field tests are now under way.[11]

Exposure to vibrios, whether by actual infection or asymptomatic carriage, causes an elevation of vibriocidal antibody. Protection is related to, but not guaranteed by, the presence of vibriocidal antibody titer. In endemic areas, vibriocidal activity increases with age, as acute cholera in endemic areas is a disease of young children. Antitoxin titers rise slowly after acute infection and remain elevated for months. Natural immunity is short term (3–6 months), biotype and serotype specific, and primarily vibriocidal, with some antitoxin component. The susceptibility of adults in cholera-endemic areas to *V. cholerae* 0139 Bengal strain indicated that these populations were immunologically naive and that previous exposure to *V. cholerae* 01 and its toxin provided incomplete cross-protection.

The current commercially available cholera vaccine is a parenteral killed whole-cell preparation that provides approximately 50% protection from disease for 3–6 months. Cholera vaccine has no protective value in epidemics as it requires two doses and takes weeks to be effective. As the risk of contacting cholera is small and the vaccine has limited effectiveness, the World Health Organization (WHO) recommends that a vaccine not be required for routine international travel and most countries no longer require a cholera vaccination for entry.

Limited immunity to the toxin can be achieved by injecting the B subunit of cholera toxin. By combining the B subunit with a killed *V. cholerae* vaccine, an oral vaccine with a protective efficacy of about 85% has been evaluated in field trials.[12,13] Several genetically engineered vaccines for both *V. cholerae* O1 and O139 have been developed and have provided some promising results.[14]

CLINICAL FEATURES

For cholera and ETEC, like many other infectious diseases, there is a spectrum of clinical manifestations, from an asymptomatic carrier state to the person with one loose stool to a desperately ill patient with severe dehydration.

Cholera

After an incubation period of 16–72 hours, the initial stage of cholera is characterized by a feeling of fullness. This is soon followed by diarrhea, which accelerates over the next few hours to frequent purging. There may be nausea and vomiting. As the purging increases in frequency and volume, the stool becomes liquid and the color changes from brown to green to yellow and finally to 'rice water' (so named because it looks like water left over after boiling a pot of rice).

All of the clinical signs and symptoms of cholera can be ascribed to fluid and electrolyte losses. The stool is isotonic with plasma,

ELECTROLYTE COMPOSITION OF INFECTIOUS DIARRHEA AND FLUID THERAPIES				
	Electrolyte concentrations (mmol/l)			
	Sodium	Potassium	Chloride	Bicarbonate
Stool				
Cholera, adult	124	16	90	48
Cholera, child	101	27	92	32
Non-specific diarrhea, child	56	25	55	14
Intravenous therapy				
Lactated Ringer's solution	130	4	109	28*
Dhaka solution	133	13	98	48
Oral rehydration therapy				
WHO formula	90	20	80	30
Pedialyte	45	20	35	30†
Ceralyte	70	20	60	30†

* Equivalent from lactate conversion
† Equivalent base in the form of citrate

Table 161.1 Electrolyte composition of infectious diarrhea and fluid therapies.

although there is an inordinate loss of potassium and bicarbonate (Table 161.1). With increasing fluid loss the external signs of dehydration are:

- the pulse progresses from rapid to thready;
- skin turgor decreases (often difficult to assess in infants and the elderly);
- the patient may develop 'washerwoman's hands';
- urine specific gravity increases; and
- urine volume decreases.

Breathing becomes deep and rapid as factors leading to respiratory alkalosis attempt to compensate for the metabolic acidosis brought on by the profound loss of bicarbonate in the stool. Metabolic acidosis may mask hypokalemia, which occurs in severely malnourished children or patients on diuretics. Severely dehydrated patients may present in hypovolemic shock which, if not immediately treated, can lead to cardiovascular collapse and, uncommonly, to renal failure. Mild fever may be a feature, but there are no signs of sepsis. Diarrhea can persist for up to 5 days in the untreated patient.

Enterotoxigenic *Escherichia coli* infection

There is nothing distinctive about the clinical presentation of ETEC infection. Following an incubation period of 24–48 hours, the patient develops a sense of intestinal distress (cramping is uncommon), followed shortly thereafter by watery diarrhea. As in cholera, the illness ranges from mild to quite severe, although it rarely leads to the profound dehydration seen in cholera. Although most people have 3–5 loose stools/day, about 20% of cases have 6–15 watery bowel movements/day. The average duration of illness is 3–5 days. Strains that produce only ST cause a milder attack of diarrhea than LT-producing strains, but cause more vomiting and constitutional symptoms.[15]

DIAGNOSIS

Cholera

Cholera should be suspected in patients with watery diarrhea that has little odor (especially during the periods of heavy purging), and which on microscopic examination fails to reveal formed cellular elements such as erythrocytes and leukocytes. If fresh unstained cholera stool is examined under a dark-field microscope, spiral shaped organisms will be seen to have a 'shooting star' pattern of motility; they are immobilized by antisera. If cholera is suspected, fresh stool should be cultured on thiosulfate citrate bile salts (TCBS) sucrose medium. A colorimetric test that uses monoclonal antibodies can be used to identify *V. cholerae* rapidly in clinical specimens with a high degree of sensitivity and specificity.[16]

Enterotoxigenic *Escherichia coli* infection

Diagnosis of ETEC in a routine bacteriologic laboratory is difficult and generally impractical; ETEC cannot be differentiated from non-pathogenic strains of *E. coli* on routine culture on MacConkey agar and special tests such as enzyme immunoassays, DNA probes or polymerase chain reaction are required to determine virulence factors at either the genotypic or phenotypic level.

MANAGEMENT

The major goal of treatment is replacement of fluid and electrolytes lost in the diarrheal stool. The traditional route of fluid administration has been intravenous, but oral rehydration solutions (ORSs) have proved equally effective and safe for all but the most severely dehydrated, heavily purging patients.[17] The mortality from even severe cholera should be less than 1% with proper fluid therapy (in contrast to as much as 50% if untreated). The composition of intravenous solutions and ORS is directly related to the electrolyte composition of secretory diarrhea (see Table 161.1).

Oral rehydration therapy is based on the physiologic principle that glucose enhances sodium absorption in the small intestine, even in the presence of secretory losses caused by bacterial toxins. From practical, economic and logistic perspectives, ORS is the preferred treatment in developing countries. It is also the treatment of choice for mild-to-moderate diarrhea in both children and adults in the USA and it can be used for maintenance therapy in patients with severe diarrhea after initial parenteral fluid replacement.[18]

The volume and rate of fluid replacement are based on the patient's degree of dehydration (Table 161.2).[18] The patient is thirsty when mildly dehydrated and begins to show the physical signs of dehydration without vascular collapse when fluid loss is moderate. Clinical signs of dehydration become evident after 4–5% of body weight has been lost. The level of dehydration may be difficult to determine in the elderly and often goes unrecognized. A changing

ASSESSMENT OF DEHYDRATION			
Physical finding or symptom	No signs of dehydration (loss of <2.5% body weight)	Some dehydration (loss of 2.5–10% body weight)	Severe dehydration (loss of >10% body weight)
Mental status	Alert, appears well	**Irritable, restless**	**Lethargic or unconscious, floppy infant**
Eyes	Normal	Sunken	Very sunken and dry
Tears	Present	Absent	Absent
Oral mucosa, tongue	Moist	Dry	Dry
Thirst	Absent, drinks normally	**Thirsty, drinks eagerly**	**Drinks poorly or is unable to drink**
Fontanelle	Normal	Sunken	Very sunken
Skin pinch	Goes back rapidly	**Goes back slowly**	**Goes back very slowly**

Table 161.2 Assessment of dehydration. Physical findings highlighted in bold type are important signs in the assessment of dehydration. Adapted from Tacket *et al.*[14]

mental status may be an early sign. After rehydration has been completed, the amount given should be at least equal to that lost in the stool. The most common reason for treatment failure with either intravenous fluids or ORS is that insufficient amounts are given. Vomiting is not a contraindication to the use of ORS; rather, ORS should be given in smaller, more frequent sips until emesis stops, which is usually within the first 4 hours of therapy. Figures 161.1–161.3 illustrate the dramatic effect that ORS fluid replacement has on the rehydration of an adult cholera patient.

The ORS formula recommended by the WHO has been used effectively in hundreds of millions of cases. Recent studies have suggested that an ORS formula that has a lower content of sodium chloride and glucose may be better absorbed in children, therefore resulting in a need for less ORS.[18] Others have suggested, however, that the change in formula provided only marginal improvement in stool output that is more than offset by a negative net salt balance and its consequences, especially in the adult cholera patient.[19] An inexpensive alternative to glucose-based ORS is a solution in which starch derived from rice or other cereals is substituted for glucose. The taste of cereal-based solutions is more appealing to some, but additional preparation time is required and heating (and fuel use) may be necessary.

Eating during an acute episode of watery diarrhea is an important aspect of effective treatment. The traditional approach of dietary abstinence, which restricts the intake of necessary calories, has no place in the treatment. Diarrhea may be prolonged if a child is starved during the illness, and so it is particularly important to restart feeding as soon as the child is able to accept food. Breast-feeding should not be discontinued. Full-strength dairy products may increase diarrhea in some individuals as a result of lactose intolerance, and so should be avoided during the episode of acute diarrhea in those not dependent upon milk as the principal source of caloric intake. Alcohol and beverages that contain caffeine or methylxanthine such as coffee or tea may increase intestinal motility, so they should be avoided.

Antimicrobial agents can be useful in the treatment of cholera as the duration of an episode, volume of stool output and period of *V. cholerae* excretion can be reduced with effective therapy (Table 161.3).[20] A 3-day course of tetracycline is effective; there is no proven value in lengthening the duration of therapy to 4 or more days. A single-dose ciprofloxacin (1g in adults) is also effective in the treatment of *V. cholerae* O1 or O139.[21]

Antimotility drugs such as loperamide have little place in the treatment of watery diarrhea in children in developing countries. The same can be said for various absorbing agents such as kaolin or pectin. Literally hundreds of antidiarrheal remedies can be found in pharmacies and assorted medical establishments throughout the world. Many products contain a combination of drugs, most of them therapeutically ineffective and others potentially dangerous.

Although few studies have evaluated the treatment of ETEC infections (as a distinct group) with antibiotics, short courses of therapy with trimethoprim–sulfamethoxazole or fluoroquinolones such as ciprofloxacin will reduce the mean duration of diarrhea in travelers who frequently have ETEC as the underlying enteropathogen.[10] Results with single-dose therapy of acute traveler's diarrhea with fluoroquinolones are also encouraging.

Travelers to areas with high rates of diarrhea would be advised to take two or more 1-liter ORS packets and, if possible, a collapsible 1-liter container for accurate measurement of water.

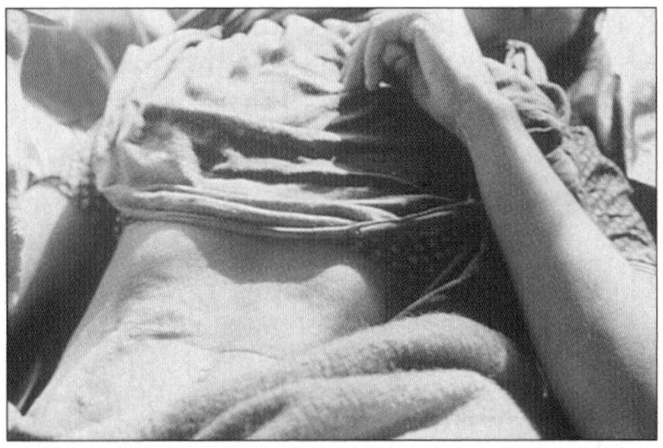

Fig. 161.1 Severe dehydration from cholera. Decreased skin turgor in a severely dehydrated cholera patient. Courtesy of the International Centre for Diarrhoeal Diseases Research, Bangladesh.

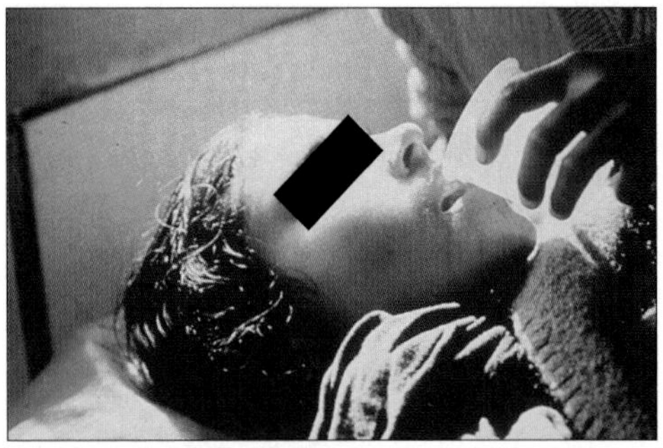

Fig. 161.2 Oral rehydration. The patient is immediately given ORS to correct her dehydration. Courtesy of the International Centre for Diarrhoeal Diseases Research, Bangladesh.

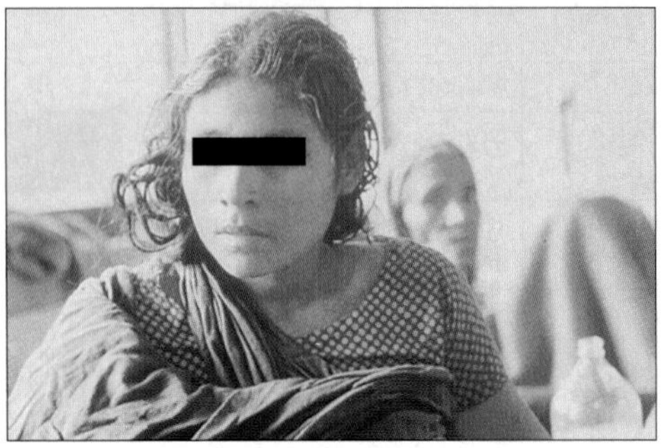

Fig. 161.3 Complete recovery from cholera after rehydration. The patient 24 hours later is completely rehydrated on ORS alone. Courtesy of the International Centre for Diarrhoeal Diseases Research, Bangladesh.

ANTIMICROBIAL THERAPY OF CHOLERA

	First-line therapy	Alternatives*
Adults	Tetracycline 500mg po q6h for 3 days Single dose of doxycycline 300mg po	Single dose of ciprofloxacin 1000mg po Erythromycin 250mg po q6h for 3 days Trimethoprim–sulfamethoxazole 160mg/800mg po q12h for 3 days Furazolidone 100mg po q6h for 3 days
Children	Tetracycline 12.5mg/kg po q6h for 3 days Single dose of doxycycline 6mg/kg po†	Erythromycin 10mg/kg po q8h for 3 days Trimethoprim–sulfamethoxazole (5mg/kg trimethoprim plus 25mg/kg sulfamethoxazole) po q12h for 3 days Furazolidone 1.25mg/kg po q6h for 3 days

* For use when resistant organisms are suspected or documented present or if the patient has a history of an allergic reaction to the first-line therapy
† Not recommended for use in children under 8 years of age as it may lead to permanent discoloration of teeth

Table 161.3 Antimicrobial therapy of cholera.

REFERENCES

1. Garthright WE, Archer DL, Kvenberg JE. Estimates of incidence and costs of intestinal infectious diseases in the United States. Publ Health Rep 1988;103:107–15.
2. Glass RI, Lew JF, Gangarosa RE, *et al.* Estimates of morbidity and mortality rates for diarrheal diseases in American children. J Pediatr 1991;118:S27–33.
3. Mujica OJ, Quick RE, Palacios AM, *et al.* Epidemic cholera in the Amazon: the role of produce in disease risk and prevention. J Infect Dis 1994;169:1381–4.
4. Cholera Working Group. Large epidemic of cholera-like disease in Bangladesh caused by *Vibrio cholerae* O139 synonym Bengal. Lancet 1993;342:387–90.
5. Morris JG, Black RE. Cholera and other vibrioses in the United States. N Engl J Med 1991;312:343–50.
6. Weber JT, Levine WC, Hopkins DP, Tauxe RV. Cholera in the United States, 1965–1991. Risks at home and abroad. Arch Intern Med 1994;154:551–6.
7. Colwell RR. Global climate change and infectious disease: the cholera paradigm. Science 1996;274:2025–31.
8. Hamer DH, Gorbach SL. Infectious diarrhea and bacterial food poisoning. In: Feldman M, Scharschmidt BF, Sleisenger MH, eds. Gastrointestinal disease, 6th ed. Philadelphia: WB Saunders; 1998.
9. Waldor MK, Mekalanos J. Lysogenic conversion by a filamentous phage encoding cholera toxin. Science 1996;272:1910–4.
10. Sack RB. Enterotoxigenic *Escherichia coli*: identification and characterization. J Infect Dis 1980;142:279–86.
11. Savarino SV, Brown FM, Hall E, *et al.* Safety of an oral killed enterotoxigenic *Echerichia coli*—Cholera toxin B subunit in Egyptian Adults. J Infect Dis 1998;177:796–9.
12. Clemens JD, Harris JR, Sack DA, *et al.* Field trial of oral cholera vaccines in Bangladesh: results of one year follow-up. J Infect Dis 1988;158:60–8.
13. Sanchez JL, Vasquez B, Begue RE, *et al.* Protective efficacy of oral whole cell recombinant-B-subunit cholera vaccine in Peruvian military recruits. Lancet 1994;344:1273–6.
14. Tacket CO, Losonsky G, Nataro JP, *et al.* Initial clinical studies of CVD 112 *Vibrio cholerae* O139 live oral vaccine: safety and efficacy against experimental challenge. J Infect Dis 1995;172:883–6.
15. Merson MH, Sack RB, Islam S, *et al.* Disease due to enterotoxigenic *Escherichia coli* in Bangladeshi adults: clinical aspects and a controlled trial of tetracycline. J Infect Dis 1980;141:702–8.
16. Hasan JAK, Huq A, Tamplin ML, Siebeling RJ, Colwell RR. A novel kit for rapid detection of *Vibrio cholerae* O. J Clin Microbiol 1994;32:249–52.
17. Duggan C, Santosham M, Glass RI. The management of acute diarrhea in children: oral rehydration, maintenance, and nutritional therapy. MMWR Morb Mortal Wkly Rep 1992;RR-16:1–20.
18. CHOICE Study Group. Multicenter randomised double-bind clinical trial to evaluate the efficacy and safety of a reduced osmolarity oral rehydration salt solution in children with acute watery diarrhea. Pediatrics 2001;1071:613–18.
19. Hirschhorn, N, Nalin DR, Cash RA, *et al.* Formulation of oral rehydration solution. Lancet 2002; 360:340–341.
20. World Health Organization Programme for Control of Diarrhoeal Diseases. Management of the patient with cholera. Geneva: World Health Organization; 1992:WHO/CDD/SER/91.15 Rev. 1.
21. Khan WA, Bennish M, Seas C, *et al.* Randomized controlled comparison of single-dose ciprofloxacin and doxycycline for cholera caused by *Vibrio cholerae* O1 or O139. Lancet 1996;348:296–300.

chapter
162 Tropical Malabsorption and Sprue

Gerald T Keusch

INTRODUCTION

Tropical malabsorption and sprue are clinical syndromes of still uncertain pathogenesis, although many possibilities have been proposed over the years. These syndromes are expressed as a continuous spectrum of manifestations from asymptomatic malabsorption with mild histologic changes of the small bowel (tropical enteropathy) to persistent diarrhea with laboratory evidence of malabsorption (tropical malabsorption), extending to an overt clinical malabsorptive disease, tropical sprue, in which severe villous atrophy is associated with steatorrhea, chronic diarrhea and a wasting syndrome. Some of these episodes can be proven to be infectious in nature, and household or community outbreaks have been described. The term 'post-infectious tropical malabsorption' is used by a number of authorities for such illnesses.[1] In other patients, the onset of malabsorption is insidious, and no specific intestinal infection is ever documented. However, there is no evidence that tropical enteropathy is a precursor lesion for overt tropical malabsorption or sprue. As a result, tropical malabsorption and sprue have become paradigms of illnesses acquired in the tropics by native and long-term expatriate residents alike, in which infection, malabsorption and malnutrition interact to a varying extent in individual patients to cause an illness with similar overlapping manifestations.

EPIDEMIOLOGY

Definition and nomenclature

Because there is no specific diagnostic test or universally agreed definitions for this syndrome, tropical malabsorption and sprue are defined by a constellation of clinical and laboratory findings, often including the response to therapy.

Tropical enteropathy is a biochemical and histologic process occurring in residents or visitors to the tropics, in which D-xylose malabsorption[2] is associated with alteration of the small bowel villus architecture from the normal finger-like villus to a shorter, broader, tongue-like structure, with lymphocyte infiltration of the mucosa. There may be no symptoms or mild diarrhea and minimal weight loss. Tropical malabsorption is defined as clinical malabsorption associated with an identified infection, whereas in tropical sprue no etiology is found. Both are more severe than tropical enteropathy; that is, they are associated with more profound malabsorption of two or more unrelated nutrients (including carbohydrate, fat or vitamin B12), more severe villus atrophy and more intense clinical symptoms, which if not treated last for months. The associated clinical conditions include megaloblastic anemia and, on occasion, neurologic complications of vitamin B12 deficiency.

Typically, tropical enteropathy and malabsorption or sprue develop during a period of residence of months to years in the tropics, especially in the Caribbean and the Indian subcontinent, although cases are also reported from Africa[3] and other areas of Asia[4] (Fig. 162.1). Neither condition is commonly contracted by short-term visitors to the tropics.

In southern India, epidemic waves of tropical malabsorption were documented over years, typically associated with fever, leading to the speculation that a specific infectious agent was responsible.[5] In some cases, a 'corona virus-like' structure was observed in biopsy specimens of small bowel, although a specific enteric virus was not isolated.[6] Preparations for a prospective field study to isolate and identify the agent were made, but epidemic sprue subsequently disappeared and the investigators have been unable to do the study since.

PATHOGENESIS AND PATHOLOGY

Asymptomatic tropical enteropathy

With the development of safe and simple instruments for biopsy of the small bowel approximately 40 years ago, a new entity, tropical enteropathy, was defined. Studies in Bangladesh[7] and Thailand[8] in the mid-1960s reported that apparently healthy residents of these countries had shortened villi, deepened crypts and lymphocyte infiltration of the lamina propria of the jejunum compared with apparently healthy residents of industrialized nations. When simple intestinal function studies were carried out, these subjects were generally lactase deficient and malabsorbed xylose but not fat or vitamin B12. Studies of Peace Corps volunteers living in the community in Thailand demonstrated that they acquired the same histopathologic lesion and intestinal functional abnormalities during the first year in the country, and some progressed to overt tropical sprue, whereas US military personnel in the same country living in more sanitary conditions and generally eating on a military base retained a more normal mucosa and normal function.[8] Studies of Bangladeshi subjects and former American residents of Pakistan living in the USA demonstrated that the lesions of tropical enteropathy regress after a few years.[9,10] These studies suggest that living in a fecally contaminated environment with poor sanitation in which water and food commonly contain large numbers of enteric micro-organisms is the basis for the structural and functional intestinal lesions of tropical enteropathy.

Pathologic and pathophysiologic changes

The essential features of tropical enteropathy develop in early childhood, when the finger-like villi of the small bowel of neonates become shorter and broader, with increased crypt thickness, reduced ratio of villus length to crypt length, more frequent mitotic figures and increased cellularity of the lamina propria with lymphocytes and plasma cells.[11] The enterocyte turnover rate is increased, suggesting enterocyte injury with compensatory increase in cell generation in the crypts. Studies in acute epidemic tropical sprue in India have shown focal degeneration of crypt cells at a time when villus cells are intact, which argues for a primary insult to the crypt cells. With the reduced mature villus absorptive surface, carbohydrate absorption, commonly measured by the xylose tolerance test, is diminished as well. This is associated with the failure to absorb as much as 5% of the energy content of the diet in some studies. Abnormal gut permeability as measured by the lactulose–mannitol test has been shown in such subjects.

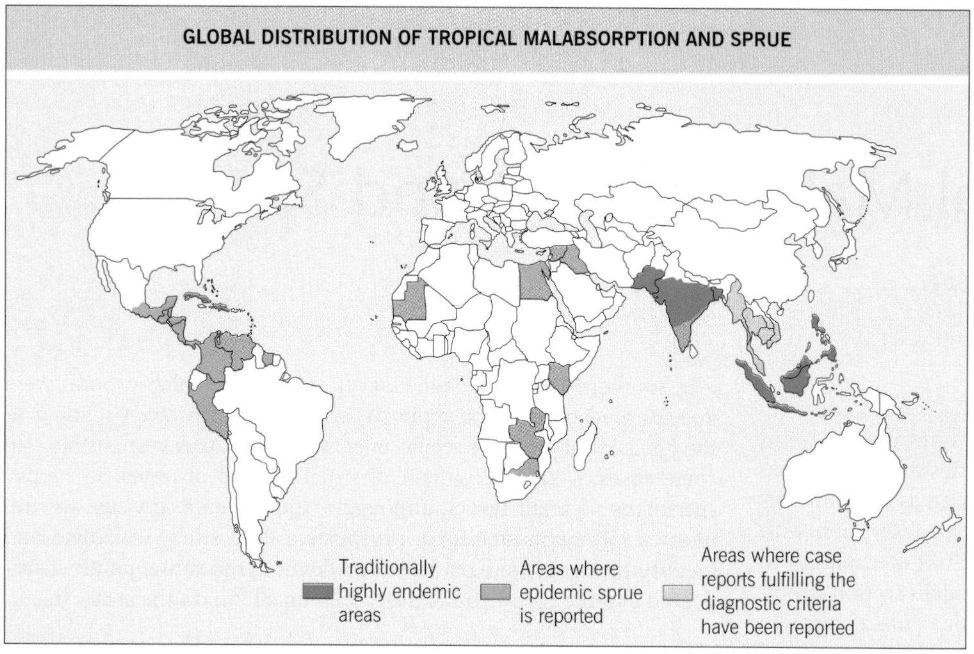

Fig. 162.1 Global distribution of tropical malabsorption and sprue. Tropical malabsorption and sprue in central equatorial Africa remains largely unexplored or unreported.

With the development of tropical sprue, greater damage of villus cells is noted, including disturbed brush border, dilated rough endoplasmic reticulum, loss of mitochondrial cristae and an increase in lysosomes. This is associated with extrusion of damaged villus cells, and an increase in cells with pyknotic nuclei, surrounded by lymphocytes and plasma cells. Fat droplets are present in the cytoplasm, in the thickened basement membrane and in the lamina propria. These changes reverse with prolonged residence in industrialized countries.[10]

It is difficult to document the sequence of physiologic changes that occur in tropical malabsorption and sprue. However, delayed small intestinal transit time may be an early and common event. Cook[1] postulates that the process is initiated by epithelial cell injury, probably postinfectious, leading to the release of enteroglucagon, which in turn results in intestinal stasis, secondary bacterial overgrowth and malabsorption. Cultures of small bowel fluid obtained by aspiration in sprue patients reveals high numbers of bacteria, including a variety of Gram-negative rods (*Escherichia coli*, *Klebsiella pneumoniae*, *Enterobacter cloacae*, *Citrobacter freundii*, *Serratia marcescens* and others). Enterocyte injury is reflected in the increased permeability of the intestine as measured by increased urinary lactulose excretion following an oral dose of lactulose. Colonic function is often abnormal, with increased losses of water and electrolytes; this correlates with the level of free unsaturated fatty acids in stool.

If the diagnosis is restricted to adults without HIV infection who have persistent diarrhea, clinical malabsorption and wasting, the number of patients meeting the case definition of tropical malabsorption and sprue has diminished remarkably over the past 20 years throughout the world. The reasons for this remain speculative, although some authorities believe the increased use of antibiotics for acute diarrhea, prompt attention to dehydration and nutritional status during and after acute diarrhea, and improved environmental hygiene in many developing countries may account for the observations. With more aggressive nutritional and antimicrobial therapy, mortality rates have dropped dramatically in the non-HIV-infected population.

PREVENTION AND RISK FACTORS

Other than residence in the tropics and acute or recurrent diarrhea, no specific risk factors have been identified. Although genetic factors have been suspected for a long time, and some HLA associations are reported,[12] no specific genes mediating susceptibility have been found. Presumably eating foods that are prepared in a sanitary environment and, therefore, are likely to be less contaminated may be useful in preventing the illness.

CLINICAL FEATURES

There are generally no clinical manifestations of tropical enteropathy in indigenous populations of the tropics; expatriates may experience a moderate increase in stool number, with softer stools and modest weight loss. Acquired lactase deficiency can result in clinical lactose intolerance, presenting as the acute onset of cramps and diarrhea after ingestion of lactose-containing dairy products. With the progression to tropical malabsorption and sprue, stool bulk usually increases and the classic manifestations of steatorrhea develop, including foul-smelling, greasy stools that float. This may be accompanied by bloating, belching, borborygmi and flatus. Continuing malabsorption is manifested by anorexia and progressive weight loss, which can be profound. Progressive vitamin deficiency (e.g. of vitamin B12 and folate) leads to megaloblastic anemia, with fatigue and limited exercise tolerance and, rarely, severe neurologic complications of vitamin B12 deficiency (subacute combined degeneration of the spinal cord).

DIAGNOSIS

The requirement for a diagnosis of tropical malabsorption and sprue is the intestinal lesion, for which small bowel biopsy is necessary. Biopsy has become much simpler than it used to be with the advent of endoscopy, which can also be used to diagnose giardiasis and strongyloidiasis and to obtain small bowel fluid for culture. There is, however, no reason to biopsy patients for suspected tropical enteropathy if they have no clinical manifestations. Malabsorption of multiple nutrients should be documented; the classic tests are carbohydrate tolerance tests (xylose or lactose), 3-day fecal fat excretion and the Schilling test for vitamin B12 absorption. Breath tests for carbohydrate absorption, small bowel overgrowth, bile salt deconjugation and intestinal transit time, as well as intestinal permeability as evaluated by the lactulose–mannitol test, are useful adjuncts to help to characterize the pathophysiologic lesion more fully. A simple full blood count and examination of the cells can document megaloblastic anemia, which suggests the value of measuring vitamin B12 and folate levels. Small bowel overgrowth is a common finding in tropical sprue, but culture of the small bowel contents is not necessary. It is, however, mandatory to look for specific treatable causes of the

DIFFERENTIAL DIAGNOSIS OF TROPICAL MALABSORPTION AND SPRUE	
Category	**Cause**
Malabsorption syndromes	Tropical malabsorption or sprue Celiac sprue Short bowel syndromes (trauma, surgery) Blind loop syndromes Venous or lymphatic obstruction (constrictive pericarditis, idiopathic tropical cardiomyopathy, filariasis)
Digestive conditions	Chronic calcific pancreatitis Bite salt deficiency (chronic liver disease, ileal tuberculosis)
Infectious diseases	Parasitic infections (*Giardia lamblia, Cryptosporidium parvum, isospora belli, Strongyloides stercoralis, Capillaria philippinensis*, leishmaniasis and others) Viral infections (HIV, possibly Burkitt's lymphoma) Bacterial infections (enteroaggregative *Escherichia coli*, possibly others)

Table 162.1 Differential diagnosis of tropical malabsorption and sprue.

malabsorption syndrome by culture and examination of stool for enteric bacteria and parasites, often supplemented by a string test for *Giardia* spp. and *Strongyloides* spp. In endemic areas such as the Indian subcontinent, a dye contrast study or endoscopy may be indicated to rule out intestinal tuberculosis.

Differential diagnosis

Giardia lamblia, one cause of acute travelers' diarrhea, may progress to a malabsorption syndrome with steatorrhea that mimics tropical sprue. It seems likely that one of the earliest described cases of tropical sprue in Barbados was, in reality, giardiasis.[13] Persistent diarrhea (symptoms continuing for a minimum of 2 weeks) is a hallmark of tropical sprue; however, most patients who have this complaint do not have this syndrome. Many are infected with a limited list of infectious agents, including *G. lamblia*, *Cyclospora cayetanensis* and *Cryptosporidium parvum*, and on occasion a bacterium such as enteroaggregative *Escherichia coli*, *Campylobacter jejuni* or *Aeromonas hydrophila*. Such patients respond to specific treatment for the infection (see Chapter 144).

Other illnesses overlap the clinical manifestations of tropical malabsorption and sprue (Table 162.1).[14] Since the mid 1980s, persistent diarrhea and malabsorption have been common manifestations of AIDS, especially in the tropics. These episodes are often due to opportunistic infections with *Cryptosporidium parvum*, *Isospora belli* or a *Microsporidium* spp. Other causes of persistent diarrhea and malabsorption in the tropics include parasitic hyperinfection syndromes with *Strongyloides stercoralis* or *Capillaria philippinensis*, or persistent enteritis with *Salmonella typhimurium*, *Shigella* spp. or *Campylobacter jejuni*. HIV itself appears to be capable of infecting enterocytes, resulting in a chronic diarrhea–malabsorption syndrome known as AIDS enteropathy.[15] By convention, such specific infections and AIDS enteropathy in patients with HIV infection are not classified as tropical malabsorption or sprue, even though the pathophysiology may be similar if not identical.

Several other specific causes of malabsorption may present in the tropics and are distinct from tropical malabsorption and sprue. These include gluten-induced enteropathy, intestinal tuberculosis, Burkitt's lymphoma, kala-azar and even pellagra in maize-eating cultures. Gluten sensitivity can appear for the first time during residence in the tropics, and this can be readily confused with tropical sprue, as can the less common Whipple's disease.

Persistent diarrhea in infants in the tropics, whether or not the infant is HIV seropositive, is usually accompanied by carbohydrate malabsorption and failure to thrive; this is not classified as tropical malabsorption or sprue. This is considered to be a postinfectious malabsorption syndrome, whether or not the etiology is identified.

MANAGEMENT

Treatment for specific causes of infectious malabsorption syndromes in the tropics does not differ from treatment in industrialized countries. Thus, the drugs of choice are now:

- metronidazole (2g/day for 3 days) or tinidazole (a single dose of 2g) for *G. lamblia*;
- albendazole (400mg q12h for 7 days) or thiabendazole (25mg/kg q12h for 3 days) for *S. stercoralis*; and
- albendazole (400mg q12h for 7 days) for *C. philippinensis*.

Patients who have AIDS and have *C. parvum* infections and malabsorption are optimally managed when combination antiretroviral therapy is given, but this is not possible in many tropical countries because of the cost of the drugs. *Isospora belli* responds to trimethoprim–sulfamethoxazole (co-trimoxazole) 160mg/800mg q6h for 10–14 days, even without antiretroviral therapy, but relapse is common when therapy stops; therefore chronic suppressive therapy is recommended (160mg/800mg three times weekly). When no specific etiology is discovered, therapy is directed toward the elimination of small bowel overgrowth with an antibiotic. Tetracycline is commonly used for this, and doses as low as 250mg q8h for 4 weeks are usually successful. Metronidazole is an alternative (500mg/day) because the anaerobic flora may be the primary culprits. The antibiotic regimen is usually supplemented with oral folic acid (5mg q12h) for 3 months; however, folic acid alone may be sufficient to reverse all manifestations of the illness.

REFERENCES

1. Cook GC. Aetiology and pathogenesis of post-infective tropical malabsorption (tropical sprue). Lancet 1984;1:721–3.
2. Keusch GT, Plaut AG, Troncale FJ. The interpretation and significance of the xylose tolerance test in the tropics. J Lab Clin Med 1970;75:558–65.
3. Thomas G, Clain DJ. Endemic tropical sprue in Rhodesia. Gut 1976;17:877–87.
4. Van Duijnhoven EM, Rijken J, Theunissen PH. Postinfectious tropical malabsorption and the differences from non-tropical sprue (celiac disease). Ned Tijdschr Geneeskd 1993;137:2552–4.
5. Mathan VI, Baker SJ. Epidemic tropical sprue and other epidemics of diarrhea in south Indian villages. Am J Clin Nutr 1968;21:1077–87.
6. Baker SJ, Mathan M, Mathan VI, Jesudoss S, Swaminathan SP. Chronic enterocyte infection with coronavirus: one possible cause of the syndrome of tropical sprue? Dig Dis Sci 1982;27:1029–43.
7. Lindenbaum J. Small intestine dysfunction in Pakistanis and Americans resident in Pakistan. Am J Clin Nutr 1968;21:1023–9.
8. Keusch GT, Plaut AG, Troncale FJ. Subclinical malabsorption in Thailand. II. Intestinal absorption in American military and Peace Corps personnel. Am J Clin Nutr 1972;25:1067–73.
9. Lindenbaum J, Gerson CD, Kent TH. Recovery of small-intestinal structure and function after residence in the tropics. I. Studies in Peace Corps volunteers. Ann Intern Med 1971;74:218–22.
10. Gerson CD, Kent TH, Saha JR, Siddiqi N, Lindenbaum J. Recovery of small-intestinal structure and function after residence in the tropics. II. Studies in Indians and Pakistanis living in New York City. Ann Intern Med 1971;75:41–8.
11. Wood GM, Gearty JC, Cooper BT. Small bowel morphology in British, Indian, and Afro-Caribbean subjects: evidence of tropical enteropathy. Gut 1991;32:256–9.
12. Menendez-Corraga R, Nettleship E, Santiago-Delpin EA. HLA and tropical sprue. Lancet 1986;2:1183–5.
13. Bartholomew C. William Hillary and sprue in the Caribbean: 230 years later. Gut 1989;30:17–21.
14. Overbosch D, Ledeboer M. 'The tropics in our bathroom': chronic diarrhoea after return from the tropics. Scand J Gastroenterol 1995;212:43–7.
15. Greenson JK, Belitsos PC, Yardley JH, Bartlett JG. AIDS enteropathy: occult enteric infections and duodenal mucosal alterations in chronic diarrhea. Ann Intern Med 1991;114:366–72.

chapter

163 Typhoid Fever

John Richens

EPIDEMIOLOGY

Typhoid fever is a special form of salmonellosis that is confined to humans and characterized by prominent systemic symptoms. It is often lumped with the closely related paratyphoid illnesses under the term 'enteric fever'. Typhoid has been virtually eliminated from more affluent countries, but high levels of transmission occur notably in the Indian subcontinent, in Indonesia, in much of sub-Saharan Africa and in parts of South and Central America. Point-source outbreaks of typhoid occasionally occur in industrialized countries when contaminated foods are imported or when measures to protect the community from excreting carriers break down. Apart from this, the majority of cases of typhoid seen in industrialized countries occur in travelers returning from endemic areas.

Typhoid has been estimated to cause 33 million infections per year.[1] Community-based studies of typhoid transmission in areas of high endemicity have shown annual incidences reaching 1200 per 100,000 of the population. Transmission rates can be high both in dry weather, when access to water is poor and personal hygiene declines, and with the onset of rains, when contaminated matter is washed into water catchment areas.

PATHOGENESIS AND PATHOLOGY

At the macroscopic level, the main effects of typhoid infection are to be seen in the lymphoid tissue of the ileum known as Peyer's patches, which display an initial hypertrophy and subsequent ischemia and necrosis (Fig. 163.1). At the microscopic level, systemic *Salmonella* infections such as typhoid are characterized by the location of organisms predominantly within macrophages, where their virulence is closely linked to an ability to survive within 'spacious' phagosomes[2] and to trigger an acute inflammatory response capable of producing harmful local ischemia and necrosis. At the moleculer level, recently identified triggers of the acute inflamatory response include a caspase-1 dependent necrosis,[3] the release of interleukin (IL)-1β and IL-18, and the release of bacterial lipopolysaccharide.

Following ingestion, typhoid bacilli multiply within the bowel lumen. They then pass through epithelial cells to reach the lamina propria and are conveyed from there to the mesenteric lymph nodes. From these nodes, organisms reach the bloodstream via the thoracic duct and, in the course of a transient primary bacteremia, the infection seeds to other reticuloendothelial sites. During the incubation period of 1–2 weeks, organisms multiply silently within sites to which they have been seeded by the primary bacteremia. The onset of symptoms correlates with the spill-over into the blood of large numbers of organisms from primarily infected sites. Infection now disseminates widely throughout the liver, spleen and bone marrow. The gallbladder is an important reservoir of infection that constantly delivers more bacilli to the intestine and Peyer's patches via the bile. It has recently been suggested this re-exposure of Peyer's patches to antigen produces a reaction analagous to the Schwartzman reaction and Koch phenomenon resulting in necrosis (Fig. 163.2).[4]

As the infection progresses, non-specific changes associated with systemic sepsis appear in many organs, such as the heart, brain and kidneys, culminating in circulatory collapse in the most severely affected patients. The local effects of ischemia and necrosis of typhoid nodules in Peyer's patches may lead to perforating intestinal ulcers. The mortality of untreated typhoid used to be about 10%. The majority of patients mount an effective immune response involving a mix of cell-mediated, humoral and mucosal elements.

PREVENTION

There are three broad strategies that can be used to interrupt the transmission of typhoid. The first is to identify and eradicate *Salmonella typhi* from infected people (patients or carriers), primarily through the use of antibiotic therapy. This will include both the management of typhoid patients and measures to detect and treat asymptomatic carriers.

The second strategy is to take measures to prevent ongoing transmission by people who are known to be infected but in whom treatment measures have failed or have not yet produced results. This includes such measures as safe disposal of infected urine and feces from patients, prevention of nosocomial transmission and legislation to exclude chronic carriers in whom eradication measures have failed from food-handling professions.

The third strategy involves protective measures that can be taken by people who may be exposed to risk of infection. These measures include avoidance of unsafe water and food in areas of typhoid transmission and typhoid vaccination.

The identification and treatment of carriers are dealt with in the section on Management, below. In areas of typhoid endemicity, tap water is unsafe when water supplies are contaminated by raw effluent, and foodstuffs (such as fresh vegetables) are unsafe when washed with such water. *Salmonella typhi* thrives in a wide range of foods. Notable outbreaks have occurred in association with dairy products, including ice cream, processed meats and shellfish, which efficiently concentrate *Salmonella* spp. from sea water that has been contaminated by untreated effluent.[5]

A range of vaccines have been developed for typhoid.[1] None of them is wholly effective and protection may be overcome by heavy inocula of bacteria. Because efficacy data on typhoid vaccines come principally from studies that have been conducted in endemic areas, where higher levels of naturally acquired immunity are present, the degree of protection for previously unexposed people tends to be overestimated.

Vaccines that are currently available do not offer concomitant protection against paratyphoid strains. A recent meta-analysis of published studies of vaccines against typhoid reported 3-year cumulative efficiencies of 73% for two doses of the parenteral whole-cell vaccine, 55% for a single dose of the parenteral Vi vaccine and 51% for three doses of the oral Ty21a vaccine.[6] Local and systemic reactions are common with whole-cell vaccines and abdominal symptoms may occur with the oral vaccine.

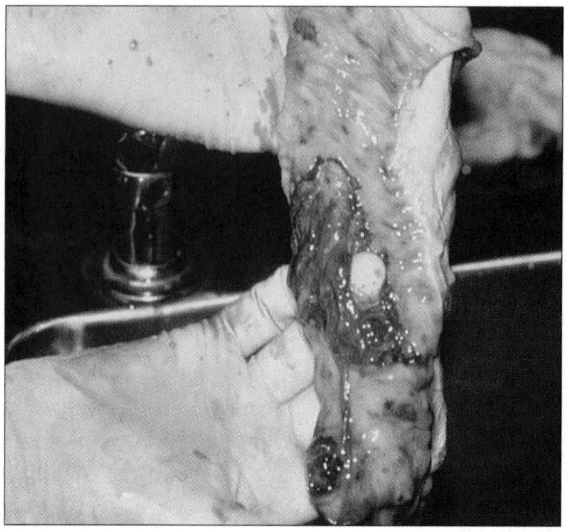

Fig. 163.1 Perforating typhoid ulcer of the terminal ileum. This large, necrotic ulcer covered in dark brown slough is on the antimesenteric side of the distal ileum. A gloved fingertip is seen within the large perforating ulcer that caused the patient's death. Reproduced with permission.[22]

CLINICAL FEATURES

Typhoid affects the sexes equally. In endemic areas it shows a predilection for children and young adults.

The majority of patients with typhoid seen in affluent countries present with the triad of persistent fever, headache and abdominal symptoms (mainly abdominal pain and diarrhea or constipation). Their symptoms rarely progress beyond this stage. In developing countries, patients tend to present later and are more likely to be seen with the vast array of less common symptoms and complications that are associated with typhoid.

The fever of typhoid has special characteristics that help to differentiate it from other fevers. The onset is typically gradual and in the early part of the infection a persistent high fever with relatively little diurnal variation is common. Rigors are not typical of early typhoid but they may be observed in the second and third weeks of untreated infection. Prominent temperature–pulse dissociation is a well-known feature of typhoid but it is not invariably present, nor is it unique to typhoid.

Headache is a prominent feature of typhoid and its absence should cast considerable doubt on the diagnosis.

The primary focus of typhoid within the small bowel gives rise to a variety of abdominal symptoms. Gastroenteritic symptoms (diarrhea, abdominal pain, nausea, vomiting) are prominent in some patients (more so in children), but constipation is equally well known. Severe diarrhea has been described in AIDS patients who have typhoid. The absence of abdominal symptoms does not exclude typhoid and in some patients the systemic symptoms very much dominate the clinical picture. A dry cough is a common feature of typhoid and scattered wheezes may be audible on auscultation.

As the infection progresses, typhoid patients may display a variety of neuropsychiatric manifestations.[7] A depressed, apathetic appearance may occur first and progress later to an agitated, twitching delirium before the onset of coma. Typhoid presenting with psychotic symptoms is well known in Africa and India. Such neuropsychiatric manifestations carry important prognostic significance, the mortality in a study from Indonesia being 50% in patients with marked confusion.[8]

Findings on examination

When examining patients with suspected typhoid, a search should be made for the classic rose spots that develop in 60% of Caucasian patients at about the 10th day. Lesions are less common and also less easy to discern on dark skins. Rose spots tend to be quite few in number, are most likely to be found on the skin of the abdomen (Fig. 163.3) and can extend to the chest, back and upper arms.

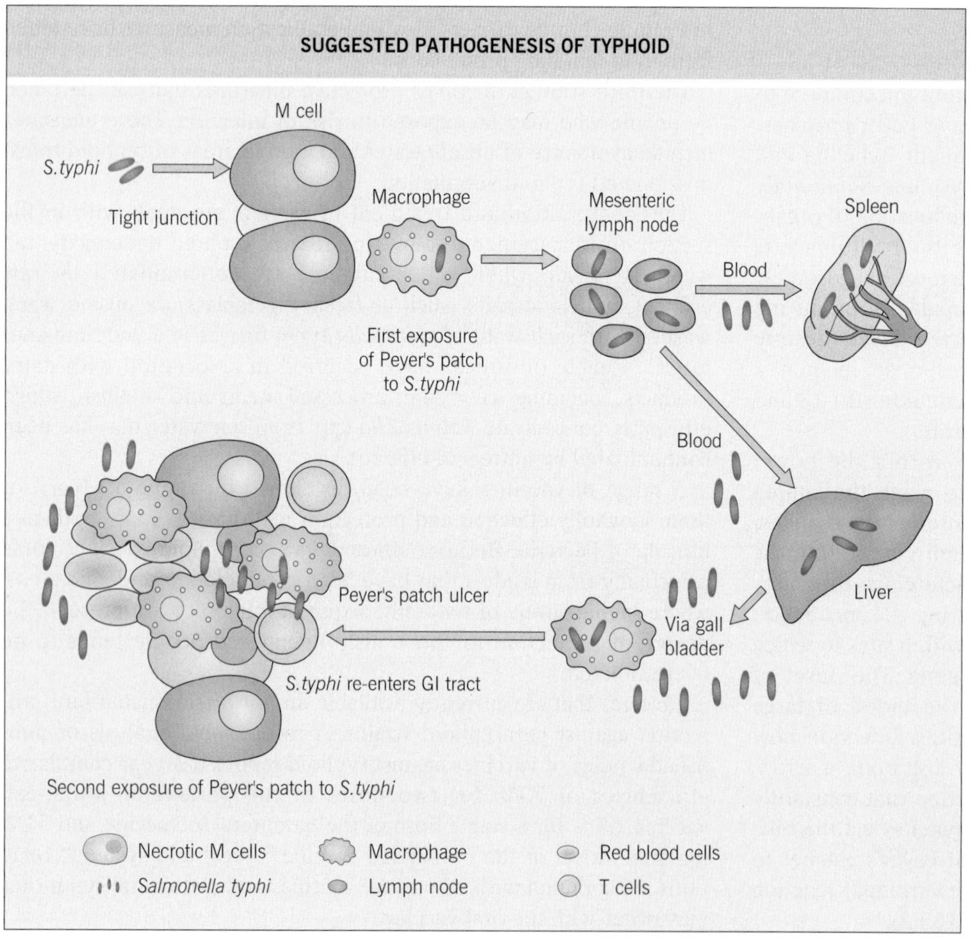

Fig. 163.2 Suggested pathogenesis of typhoid. A Schwartzman-type reaction occurs when Peyer's patches are re-exposed to Salmonella typhi following initial uptake, hematogenous dissemination and return to small intestine via gallbladder.[4]

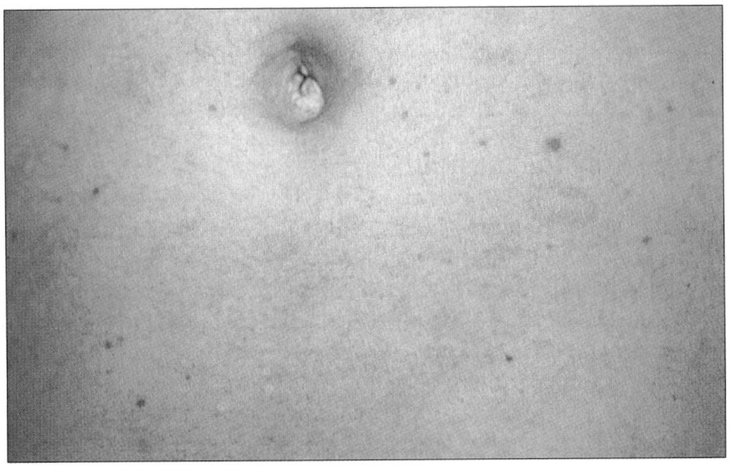

Fig. 163.3 Typhoid rose spots. The abdomen is the best place to look for these lesions, which appear at the end of the first week and are usually quite sparse. They usually take the form of pink macules that blanch when the skin is stretched, but they may take on a more purpuric, nonblanching character, as in this patient. Reproduced with permission.[22]

Typically, they appear as small pink macules that blanch with pressure. Purpuric lesions may also be found. More florid versions of the same rash are associated with paratyphoid.

Abdominal examination may reveal enlargement of the liver and spleen in some cases and a diffuse abdominal tenderness is often present. In more serious cases gaseous abdominal distention occurs and this may herald the onset of the acute abdomen that accompanies ileal perforation.

Clinical assessment of patients should also include an assessment of the mental state and hemodynamic status, because hypotension and mental abnormalities carry important prognostic significance.

Complications

The important complications of typhoid are:

- bleeding and perforation of ileal ulcers,
- circulatory collapse in severely ill patients,
- relapse following treatment, and
- long-term carriage of infection.

A comprehensive list of the complications of typhoid, most of which are rare and seen mainly in patients in whom there has been a delay in diagnosis and treatment, is presented in Table 163.1.

COMPLICATIONS OF TYPHOID.
Abdominal complications
Intestinal perforation
Intestinal hemorrhage
Hepatitis
Cholecystitis
Spontaneous splenic rupture
Rupture and hemorrhage of mesenteric nodes
Pancreatitis
Genitourinary complications
Urinary retention
Glomerulonephritis
Pyelonephritis
Cystitis
Orchitis
Cardiovascular complications
Myocarditis
Pericarditis
Endocarditis
Electrocardiographic abnormalities
Phlebitis and arteritis
Deep venous thrombosis
Gangrene
Shock
Sudden death
Respiratory complications
Bronchitis
Pneumonia
Laryngeal ulceration
Glottal edema
Neuropsychiatric complications
Delirium
Psychosis
Depression
Deafness
Meningitis
Encephalomyelitis
Transverse myelitis
Upper motor neuron signs
Extrapyramidal disorders
Impairment of co-ordination
Optic neuritis
Peripheral and cranial neuropathy
Guillain–Barré syndrome
Pseudotumor cerebri
Hematologic complications
Anemia
Disseminated intravascular coagulation
Hemoloysis
Hemolytic–uremic syndrome
Focal infections
Abscesses of brain, liver, spleen, breast, thyroid, muscle, lymph nodes
Parotitis
Pharyngitis
Osteitis
Arthritis
Other complications
Myopathy
Hypercalcemia
Decubitus ulceration
Abortion
Development of chronic carrier state
Relapse

Table 163.1 Complications of typhoid. Most of these complications occur rarely and are seen mainly in patients in whom there has been a delay in diagnosis and treatment.

DIAGNOSIS

The clinical features of typhoid are often non-specific and many other causes of fever may have to be entertained. The most dangerous condition that requires exclusion is usually falciparum malaria. Vasculitic conditions, notably temporal arteritis, can masquerade as typhoid. Complicated cases of typhoid may present with pneumonia, nephritis, meningitis or psychosis.

The definitive diagnosis of typhoid requires isolation of *S. typhi*. Less definitive but sometimes more rapid evidence of infection can be obtained by demonstrating the presence of *S. typhi* antigens in body fluids or of antibodies to those antigens.

Culture

Salmonella typhi can be grown from feces, urine, blood, bone marrow, bile or rose spots. The highest yield is obtained from bone marrow, which can continue to yield positive cultures in patients who have been exposed to effective antibiotic therapy before culture attempts. Fine-needle aspiration methods can be used to minimize patient discomfort.

Serology and antigen detection

The tube agglutination tests originally developed by Widal and others to demonstrate a serologic response to *S. typhi* continue to enjoy widespread use, but the interpretation of such tests has many pitfalls. Preferably, they should be used in conjunction with more reliable methods. A 4-fold rise of antibodies to *S. typhi* O, H or Vi antigens provides support for a diagnosis of typhoid in culture-negative patients. High levels of antibody are found in some healthy people in endemic areas and after vaccination. Some patients fail to mount a response to specific antigens. A modification of the Widal test carried out as a slide agglutination using commercially available antigens offers a useful way of obtaining rapid support for a diagnosis of typhoid. Detection of *S. typhi* antigens in urine can also be used for rapid diagnosis of typhoid.[9]

Hematologic and biochemical findings

Patients with typhoid commonly have leukopenia. Hemoglobin and platelet counts may show a modest reduction.

Biochemical findings commonly include a modest degree of hyponatremia and hypokalemia and modest elevation of transaminase levels. Occasionally, a typhoid hepatitis develops with more pronounced derangements of liver function tests.

Imaging

Chest radiography may be prompted in typhoid patients by the presence of cough and abnormal auscultatory findings. Usually, the appearance of the chest radiograph is normal, but occasionally typhoid presents with, or is complicated by, a secondary pneumonia. Abdominal sonography may demonstrate enlargement of the liver and spleen, prominent mesenteric lymph nodes and, in the event of perforation, abdominal fluid collections.

MANAGEMENT

A decision about initiating therapy must be made according to the patient's condition and the likelihood of typhoid. Initiation of fluorinated quinolone therapy will bring rapid relief of symptoms to typhoid patients but delay in initiating therapy carries few hazards for mild cases. At least one trial has reported no difference in outcome for children with uncomplicated typhoid treated with and without antibiotics[10] and management without antibiotics is well validated for other forms of uncomplicated salmonella diarrhea.[11]

Antibiotics for typhoid

Chloramphenicol was shown to be effective in the treatment of typhoid in 1950 and for many years it was considered the treatment of choice. Later studies showed equally good results from treatment with amoxicillin and trimethoprim–sulfamethoxazole.

The management of typhoid has been complicated over the past 30 years by the emergence all over the world of strains that are multiply resistant to these antibiotics. In the search for newer antibiotics with good activity against multiple-resistant strains of *S. typhi*, most of the attention has been on fluorinated quinolones, extended-spectrum cephalosporins and, more recently, azithromycin. Randomized comparisons of quinolones and cephalosporins suggest that the quinolones tend to give higher cure rates and more rapid defervescence,[12] whilst azithromycin is proving useful in areas with emerging quinolone resistance.

The incidence of long-term carriage and relapse after treatment with quinolones also appears to compare favorably with other antibiotics. An important concern about quinolone use has been its suitability for pregnant women and children, but there is now an increasing amount of evidence that quinolones are superior to alternative agents and that children can be treated safely with these drugs.[13] Many different fluorinated quinolones have been tried in the treatment of typhoid and most appear to be effective. Fleroxacin[14,15] has the advantage of once-daily oral treatment and recent trials have indicated that as little as 3 days treatment are sufficient for children with uncomplicated typhoid in Vietnam. To summarize, most authorities would prefer quinolones over cephalosporins for the treatment of multiple-resistant typhoid in all age groups.[12] The optimal duration of treatment for typhoid is not clearly established. Short courses of quinolone therapy often work well for those resident in endemic areas but may be less adequate for travelers. Treatment recommendations for typhoid are listed in Table 163.2. Quinolone resistance is being reported increasingly from Asian countries. A UK reference

TREATMENT OPTIONS FOR PATIENTS WITH TYPHOID						
Drug	**Daily dose**	**Route**	**Doses/day**	**Duration**	**Comments**	**Key trials**
Fluorinated quinolones						
Ciprofloxacin	0.5–1g	po/iv	2	7–14 days	Rapid fever clearance and low relapse rates. Short courses (as little as 3 days) work well for those living in endemic areas. Longer duration may be required for nonimmune travelers	Arnold *et al.*[16]
Fleroxacin	400mg	po/iv	1			
Ofloxacin	800mg	po/iv	2			
Pefloxacin	800mg	po/iv	2			
Extended-spectrum cephalosporins						
Cefixime	20mg/kg	po	1	7–14 days	Slower response rates and higher treatment failure than with quinolones. Short course therapy more likely to fail. Less concern about toxicity in pregnancy and children	Cao *et al.*[17]
Ceftriaxone	50–60mg/kg	im/iv	2			
Azalides						
Azithromycin	500mg	po	1	7 days	Compares favorably with quinolone therapy. Useful in areas with quinolone resistance. Not validated in severe typhoid	Chinh *et al.*[18]

Table 163.2 Treatment options for patients with typhoid. These treatments are suitable for most patients infected with multiple-resistant strains of *Salmonella typhi.*

laboratory has reported quinolone resistance in 23% of 179 infections investigated in 1999.[19] Such cases may respond to prolonged maximum dose quinolone therapy, a cephalosporin or azithromycin.

Management of severe typhoid

Trials of quinolones in typhoid have mostly been conducted in patients with mild disease. So far there are few data on the impact of quinolones and the optimal duration of therapy in patients with severe typhoid. Work conducted in Indonesia in the 1980s defined a group of patients, on the basis of circulatory and mental findings, who were at greatly increased risk of a fatal outcome.[8] The criteria for 'severe' typhoid were mental confusion (or more profound alterations of conscious level) or shock, defined as systolic blood pressure of below 12kPa (90mmHg) in adults and 10.67kPa (80mmHg) in children under 12 years, associated with evidence of decreased organ perfusion – peripheral shutdown, oliguria after rehydration (<0.3ml/kg urine output per hour) or an abnormal state of consciousness. In a randomized controlled trial involving patients who met these criteria, the administration of high-dose dexamethasone (3mg/kg infused intravenously over 30 minutes, followed by eight further doses of 1mg/kg q6h) resulted in a case fatality rate of 10.0% compared with one of 55.6% in controls not treated with corticosteroids.[8]

Ileal perforation and hemorrhage

In a small number of patients, one or more of the ileal Peyer's patch ulcers progresses to full perforation, resulting in an acute abdomen. The onset of symptoms can be gradual with perforation occurring against a steadily increasing background level of abdominal pain. Gas under the diaphragm may be demonstrable radiographically and ultrasound can be used to locate feculent fluid collections. The outcome of patients with perforation is greatly improved by prompt diagnosis, full preoperative resuscitation, early surgery and the addition of metronidazole to the antibiotic regimen. Conservative management of perforation, although once in vogue, is no longer advocated[20] because available data suggest poorer outcomes, but no controlled trials have ever been undertaken. Hemorrhage from ileal ulcers may accompany perforation or it may occur in isolation. A minority of bleeds require transfusion; life-threatening hemorrhage is rare.

Relapse

Typhoid shows a natural tendency to relapse in about 10% of patients. Relapse occurs about 2 weeks after recovery from the initial episode and usually takes the pattern of the initial episode in milder and shorter form. *Salmonella typhi* isolates from relapsing patients show the same antibiotic susceptibilities as isolates from the initial episode and thus treatment with the same drugs is feasible. Lower relapse rates have been reported since the introduction of fluorinated quinolones in typhoid management.

Typhoid carriers

Typhoid carriers play a central role in typhoid transmission and the detection and management of carriers are central to the control of epidemics. Excretion of organisms may occur during acute illness, during the convalescent phase and, in a small proportion of those infected, it continues for life. After treatment of typhoid, a series of stool and urine specimens should be cultured for *S. typhi*. In the first 3 months following infection, most carriers identified excrete on a temporary basis only and the only intervention called for is strict personal hygiene and safe disposal of excreta. Anyone still excreting *S. typhi* at 3 months is likely to become a long-term carrier. Detection of persistently high Vi antibody offers an additional way of screening for long-term carriers. Successful eradication of long-term carriage can be achieved using ciprofloxacin 750mg q12h or norfloxacin 400mg q12h orally for 4 weeks.[21]

Chronic typhoid carriage is more likely in the presence of chronic diseases of the liver (opisthorchiasis), gallbladder (cholelithiasis) or urinary tract (nephrolithiasis or schistosomiasis), and treatment of these associated conditions facilitates antibiotic eradication of *S. typhi*.

REFERENCES

1. Ivanoff B, Levine MM, Lambert PH. Vaccination against typhoid fever: present status. Bull World Health Organ 1994;72:957–71.
2. Alpuche-Aranda CM, Berthiaume EP, Mock B, *et al.* Spacious phagosome formation within mouse macrophages correlates with *Salmonella* serotype pathogenicity and host susceptibility. Infect Immun 1995;63:4456–62.
3. Brennan MA, Cookson BT. *Salmonella* induces macrophage death by caspase-1 dependent necrosis. Mol Microbiol 2000;38:31–40.
4. Everest P, Wain J, Roberts M, *et al.* The molecular mechanisms of severe typhoid fever. Trends Microbiol 2001;9:316–9.
5. Christie AB. Typhoid and paratyphoid fevers. In: Christie AB, ed. Infectious diseases: epidemiology and clinical practice, 4th ed, vol. 1. Edinburgh: Churchill Livingstone; 1987:100–64.
6. Engles EA, Falagas M, Lau J, Bennish ML. Typhoid fever vaccines: a meta-analysis of studies on efficiency and toxicity. Br Med J 1998;316:110–6.
7. Osuntokun BO, Bademosi O, Ogunremi K, Wright SG. Neuropsychiatric manifestations of typhoid fever in 959 patients. Arch Neurol 1972;27:7–13.
8. Hoffman SL, Punjabi NH, Kumala S, *et al.* Reduction of mortality in chloramphenicol-treated severe typhoid fever by high-dose dexamethasone. N Engl J Med 1984;310:82–8.
9. West B, Richens JE, Howard PF. Evaluation in Papua New Guinea of a urine coagglutination test and a Widal slide agglutination test for rapid diagnosis of typhoid fever. Trans Roy Soc Trop Med Hyg 1989;83:715–7.
10. Chiu CH, Lin TY, Ou JT. A clinical trial comparing oral azithromycin, cefixime and no antibiotics in the treatment of acute uncomplicated Salmonella enteritis in children. J Pediatr Child Health 1999;35:372–4.
11. Sirinavin S, Garner P. Antibiotics for treating salmonella gut infections (Cochrane Review). Cochrane Library, Issue 2, 2002. Oxford: Update Software.
12. White NJ, Parry CM. The treatment of typhoid fever. Curr Opin Infect Dis 1996;9:298–302.
13. Bethell DB, Hien TT, Phi LT, *et al.* The effects on growth of single short courses of fluoroquinolones. Arch Dis Child 1996;74:44–6.
14. Tran TH, Nguyen MD, Hunyh DH, *et al.* A randomised comparative study of fleroxacin and ceftriaxone in enteric fever. Trans Roy Soc Trop Med Hyg 1994;88:464–5.
15. Duong NM, Vinh Chau NV, Van Anh DC, *et al.* Short course fleroxacin in the treatment of typhoid fever. JAMA Southeast Asia 1995;11:6–11.
16. Arnold K, Hong CS, Nelwan R, *et al.* Randomized comparative study of fleroxacin and chloramphenicol in typhoid fever. Am J Med 1993;94:195S–200S.
17. Cao XT, Kneen R, Nguyen TA, *et al.* A comparative study of ofloxacin and cefixime for treatment of typhoid fever in children. Pediatr Infect Dis 1999;18:245–8.
18. Chinh NT, Parry CM, Ly NT, *et al.* A randomized controlled comparison of azithromycin and ofloxacin for treatment of multidrug-resistant or nalidixic acid-resistant enteric fever. Antimicrob Agents Chemother 2000;44:1855–9.
19. Threlfall EJ, Ward LR. Decreased susceptibility to ciprofloxacin in *Salmonella enterica* serotype typhi, United Kingdom. Emerg Infect Dis 2001;7:448–50.
20. Butler T, Knight J, Nath SK, *et al.* Typhoid fever complicated by intestinal perforation: a persisting fatal disease requiring surgical managmenet. Rev Infect Dis 1985;7:244–56.
21. Gotuzzo E, Guerra JG, Benavente L, *et al.* Use of norfloxacin to treat chronic typhoid carriers. J Infect Dis 1988;157:1221–5.
22. Weatherall D, Ledinghan J, Warrell D, eds. Oxford textbook of medicine. Oxford: Oxford University Press; 1995:561–2.

chapter

164 Amebiasis and Other Protozoan Infections

Adolfo Martínez-Palomo & Martha Espinosa-Cantellano

INTRODUCTION

In terms of its morbidity and mortality, invasive amebiasis is the most important protozoan infection of the gastrointestinal tract. Most of this chapter is therefore devoted to this disease. Giardiasis and cryptosporidiosis are also frequently encountered in geographic and travel medicine and are briefly discussed.

Amebiasis is the infection of the human gastrointestinal tract by the protozoan parasite *Entamoeba histolytica*. The motile form of the parasite, the trophozoite, lives in the lumen of the large intestine, where it multiplies and differentiates into the cyst, the resistant form responsible for transmitting the infection. Trophozoites can invade the colonic mucosa and produce dysentery and through blood-borne spread give rise to extraintestinal lesions, mainly liver abscesses. The course of dysentery is usually self-limiting, but amebic liver abscess is potentially fatal unless diagnosed promptly and treated appropriately.

During the past 20 years there has been growing evidence in the fields of biochemistry, immunology, molecular biology, clinical medicine and epidemiology that many asymptomatic intestinal infections formerly attributed to 'nonpathogenic' strains of *E. histolytica* are caused by a different species of ameba, namely *E. dispar*. This species is morphologically identical to *E. histolytica*, but has a non-invasive nature, as suggested by Brumpt in 1925 (see Chapter 242).[1]

AMEBIASIS

EPIDEMIOLOGY

Invasive amebiasis is a major health and social problem in certain areas of Africa, Asia and Latin America. In most industrialized countries, however, severe amebiasis is much less common, but knowledge of the disease is still important in these areas because failure to identify an amebic infection can result in a lethal outcome (e.g. intestinal amebiasis may be treated as chronic ulcerative colitis). In addition, high infection rates can exist among certain immigrant groups and epidemic outbreaks can occur in institutions such as schools or psychiatric hospitals. A major increase in intestinal amebic infections has been detected in male homosexual populations in several large cities of the USA, Canada and England with point prevalence rates varying from 20% to 31%. In these populations most reported cases are asymptomatic, probably because many of the infections are caused by *E. dispar*. In Japan, however, invasive amebiasis due to *E. histolytica* is not uncommon among sexually active male homosexuals.

In areas of high prevalence invasive amebiasis is characteristically endemic. In 1984 it was estimated that 40 million people worldwide developed disabling colitis or liver abscesses. At least 40,000 deaths that year were attributable to amebiasis, mostly as a consequence of liver abscesses.[2] Therefore, on a global scale, amebiasis is the third most common parasitic cause of death, behind only malaria and schistosomiasis. More recent data on the morbidity and mortality of amebiasis are lacking.

Symptomatic intestinal amebiasis occurs in all age groups, whereas liver abscesses are mostly seen in adult males. The people who pose the greatest risk of transmitting the infection are those who pass cysts of *E. histolytica*, especially if they are involved in food preparation and handling. In endemic areas a variety of conditions, including poor education, poverty, overcrowding, inadequate and contaminated water supplies and poor sanitation, favor fecal–oral transmission from one person to another.

PATHOGENESIS AND PATHOLOGY

The lytic and invasive characteristics of *E. histolytica* are related to multifactorial mechanisms that include:

- striking trophozoite motility and phagocytic capacity; and
- release of membrane pore-forming peptides and proteases that produce contact-dependent lysis of target cells and degradation of extracellular matrix components.[3]

Invasion of the colonic and cecal mucosa by *E. histolytica* begins in the interglandular epithelium. Cell infiltration around invading amebae leads to rapid lysis of inflammatory cells and tissue necrosis. Acute inflammatory cells are therefore seldom found in biopsy samples or in scrapings of rectal mucosal lesions. The ulcerations may deepen and progress under the mucosa to form typical 'flask ulcers', which extend into the submucosa, producing abundant microhemorrhages (Fig. 164.1). This explains the finding of hematophagous amebae in stool specimens and rectal scrapings, which are the best indication of the amebic nature of a case of dysentery or bloody diarrhea. Macroscopically, the ulcers are initially superficial, with hyperemic borders, a necrotic base and normal mucosa between the sites of invasion. Progression of the lesions may result in a loss of the mucosa and submucosa covering the muscle layers and eventually lead to rupture of the serosa. Recent advances in the study of amebic pathogenicity have started to unravel the molecular basis of the pathologic findings in invasive amebiasis.[4]

Complications of intestinal amebiasis include perforation, direct extension to the skin and dissemination, mainly to the liver. Amebae probably spread from the intestine to the liver through the portal circulation. The extent of liver involvement bears no relationship to the degree of intestinal amebiasis, and the two conditions do not necessarily coincide. The early stages of hepatic amebic invasion have not been studied in humans. In experimental animals, inoculation of *E. histolytica* trophozoites into the portal vein produces multiple foci of neutrophil accumulation around the parasites, followed by focal necrosis and granulomatous infiltration (Fig. 164.2). As the lesions increase in size, the granulomas are gradually replaced by necrosis until the lesions coalesce and necrotic tissue progressively occupies an increasing proportion of the liver. Hepatocytes close to the early lesions show degenerative changes, which lead to necrosis, but direct contact between liver cells and amebae is very rarely observed.[5] Human liver abscesses consist of areas in which the parenchyma has been completely replaced by a semisolid or liquid material (Fig. 164.3) composed of necrotic material and a few cells. Neutrophils are generally absent and amebae tend to be located at the periphery of the abscess. Liver abscesses may heal, rupture or disseminate.

If appropriately treated, invasive amebic lesions almost invariably heal without the formation of scar tissue whether localized in the large intestine, liver or skin. The absence of fibrotic tissue following regeneration is particularly striking in the liver.

PREVENTION

The main reservoir of *E. histolytica* is humans. The infection has a prepatent period ranging from 2 days to 4 months. The transmissibility period of untreated intestinal infections is variable as cysts have been demonstrated in feces for as long as 2 years. The cysts may remain viable and infective for a few days in feces. Because they are killed by desiccation, cyst-laden dust is not infective. Cysts are also killed by temperatures higher than 154.4°F (68°C), and so boiled water is safe to use. The amount of chlorine usually used to purify water is insufficient to kill cysts; higher concentrations of chlorine are effective, but the water must be dechlorinated before use.[6]

Invasive amebiasis could be controlled through improvements in living standards and the establishment of adequate sanitary conditions in countries where the disease is prevalent. Strategies should be aimed at:

- the community, through the improvement of environmental sanitation including water supply, food safety and health education to prevent fecal–oral transmission; and
- the individual, through early detection and treatment of cases of infection and/or disease.[7]

Cases of invasive amebiasis require prompt chemotherapy and asymptomatic carriers should be treated if infected with *E. histolytica*. Mass chemotherapy of high-risk populations has been attempted with only partially successful results. Individual or collective chemoprophylaxis is not indicated.[8]

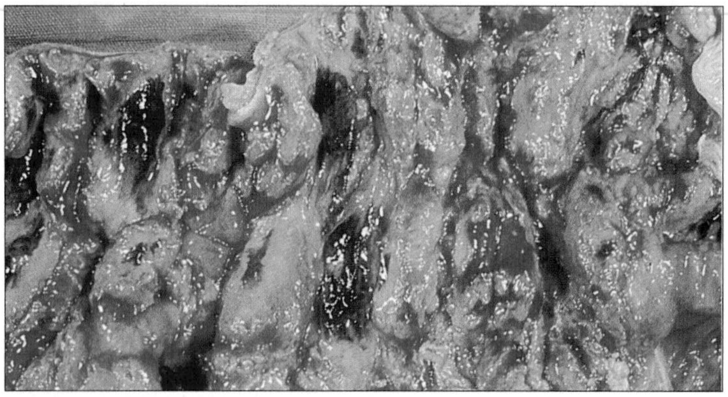

Fig. 164.1 Pathology specimen from a fatal case of human amebic colitis. Deep ulcerations into the submucosa have produced abundant hemorrhages. Courtesy of Dr Jesús Aguirre García, Hospital General de México, Secretaria de Salud.

CLINICAL FEATURES

Intestinal amebiasis

The clinical spectrum of intestinal *E. histolytica* infection ranges from the asymptomatic carrier state and acute colitis to fulminant colitis with perforation, depending upon the host's nutritional status and susceptibility, including age and, probably, differences in the virulence of amebic strains.

Invasive intestinal amebiasis usually manifests as an acute rectocolitis. Most patients present with a nontoxic dysenteric syndrome and constitutional symptoms are not as prominent as in *Shigella* dysentery. The onset of acute rectocolitis is gradual and 85% of patients have intense abdominal pain. Initially there are loose watery stools, but these rapidly become blood-stained and contain mucus. Tenesmus occurs in 50% of patients and is always associated with rectosigmoidal involvement. Watery diarrhea or loose stools without blood may be present for a few days, particularly if the distal colon is involved.[9]

Amebic liver abscess

This is the most common extraintestinal form of invasive amebiasis. Amebic abscesses occur in all age groups, but are 10 times more frequent in adults than in children and are more common in males than in females. Although liver abscess develops after intestinal infection, patients rarely have associated amebic rectocolitis, but the large intestine is colonized with *E. histolytica* in more than 70% of cases. Lesions are usually single and localized to the right lobe of the liver in the posterior, external and superior portions.

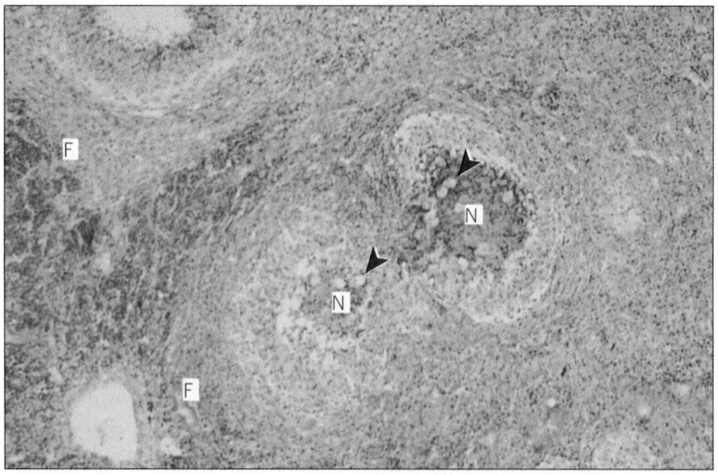

Fig. 164.2 Experimental amebic liver abscess. Two characteristic granulomas can be observed with several trophozoites (arrowheads) around its necrotic center (N) and epithelioid cells limiting the lesion, surrounded by an area of fibrosis (F).

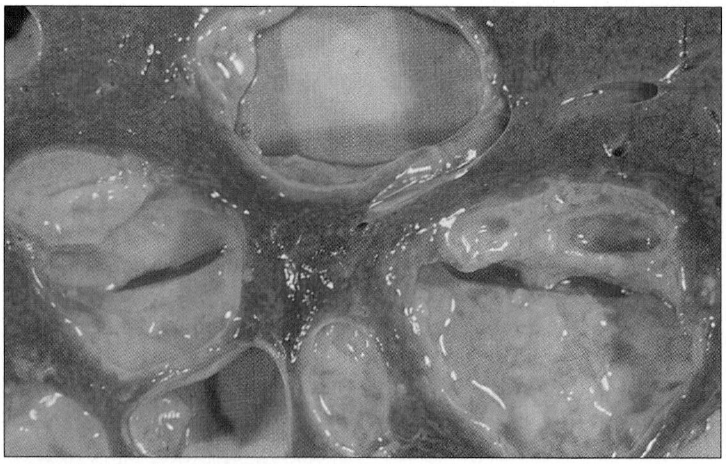

Fig. 164.3 Human amebic liver abscess. Multiple abscesses, one cavitated, can be observed occupying virtually all lobes of the liver parenchyma, which is replaced by a semisolid material. Courtesy of Dr Jesús Aguirre García, Hospital General de México, Secretaría de Salud.

In most patients, mainly those under 30 years of age and children, the clinical presentation and course of the disease are typical (Table 164.1). The onset is abrupt, with pain in the upper abdomen and high fever. The pain is intense and constant, radiating to the scapular region and right shoulder; it increases with coughing, deep breathing or when the patient rests on the right side. When the abscess is located in the left lobe, the pain tends to be felt in the epigastrium and may radiate to the left shoulder. Fever is present in most cases; it varies between 100.4°F (38°C) and 104°F (40°C), frequently in spikes, but is sometimes constant over several days, with rigors and profuse sweating. There is anorexia and rapid weight loss and approximately one-third of patients have nonproductive cough. Nausea and vomiting may occur and in some cases there may be diarrhea or dysentery. Physical examination reveals a pale wasted patient who has an enlarged tender liver. Digital pressure in the right lower intercostal spaces produces intense pain and there is often marked tenderness on percussion over the right lower ribs in the posterior region. Movement of the right side of the chest and diaphragm is greatly restricted, as is the intensity of respiratory sounds. Older patients may present with a chronic and milder nonspecific febrile illness, hepatomegaly, anemia and abnormal liver function tests.[9]

Complications

Amebic liver abscesses commonly produce thoracic complications, particularly pleurisy with a nonpurulent pleural effusion, rupture into the bronchial tree and, less commonly, rupture into the pleural cavity or amebic pericarditis. Rupture into the abdomen occurs in approximately 8% of patients who have amebic liver abscess; only rarely do abscesses rupture into the gallbladder, stomach, duodenum, colon or inferior vena cava. Occasionally, an abscess may erode through the abdominal wall and reach the skin. Secondary infection of amebic liver abscesses is an uncommon complication, which can be suspected when the patient presents with a severe toxic state and there is lack of response to antiamebic chemotherapy.[10]

CLINICAL FEATURES OF AMEBIC LIVER ABSCESS	
Clinical feature	**Proportion of cases (%)**
Symptoms for <2 weeks	37–66
Symptoms for 2–4 weeks	20–40
Symptoms for 4–12 weeks	16–42
Symptoms for >12 weeks	5–11
Fever	71–98
Abdominal pain	62–98
Diarrhea	14–66
Cough	10–32
Weight loss	33–53
Tender liver	80–95
Hepatomegaly	43–93
Epigastric tenderness	22
Rales, rhonchi	8–47
Jaundice	10–25
White cell count >10,000/mm³ (10 × 10⁹/l)	63–94
Hemoglobin <2g/dl (20g/l)	25–90
Elevated transaminases	26–50
Elevated alkaline phosphatase	38–84
Elevated bilirubin	10–25
Increased erythrocyte sedimentation rate	81

Table 164.1 Clinical features of amebic liver abscess. Data from Martínez-Palomo and Ruiz-Palacios.[3]

DIAGNOSIS

Intestinal amebiasis

Rectosigmoidoscopy and colonoscopy of benign cases show small ulcerations with linear or oval contours, 3–5mm in diameter and covered by a yellowish exudate containing many trophozoites. In the great majority of cases rectosigmoidoscopy and immediate microscopic examination of rectal smears for the presence of motile hematophagous trophozoites of *E. histolytica* are the most important diagnostic procedures. The microscopic examination of amebae has several drawbacks, including the requirement for a skilled technician and the need to perform the examination on fresh clinical specimens. Cyst detection usually requires concentration methods including flotation or sedimentation procedures. In cases of colonic invasive amebiasis serologic detection of antiamebic antibodies is positive in approximately 75% of cases. Reliable and sensitive assays such as immunoassay or hybridization using gene probes to distinguish *E. histolytica* from *E. dispar* infections are already in the market, but still unavailable to clinical laboratories in developing countries due to high costs. However, initial pilot studies have produced excellent results using specific diagnostic reagents.[11]

Amebic liver abscess

This condition should be suspected, particularly in endemic areas or if there is a history of travel to those countries, in patients who present with a spiking fever, weight loss and abdominal pain in the upper right quadrant or epigastrium and tenderness in the liver area. Other signs include leukocytosis, an elevated alkaline phosphatase and an elevated right diaphragm in chest radiographs. Liver imaging with sonography or computerized tomography will demonstrate a space-occupying lesion in 75–95% of cases depending upon the procedure used and course of the illness. This should be followed by testing for antiamebic antibodies, which are elevated in more than 90% of cases. The tests currently used are indirect hemagglutination, counterimmunoelectrophoresis and enzyme immunoassays. The antibody response is directly related to the duration of the illness. It may be negative during the first week after onset and titers reach a peak by the second or third month, decreasing to lower but still detectable levels by 9 months.[3]

Differential diagnosis

The differential diagnosis of amebic liver abscess should include pyogenic abscess and neoplasm (see also Chapter 49). Pyogenic abscess is more common in older patients who have a previous history of hepatobiliary diseases, abdominal sepsis, appendicitis, diverticulitis or abdominal surgery. These patients are more likely to present with jaundice, pruritus and septic shock. Hepatomegaly and an elevated diaphragm in the chest radiographs are uncommon and amebic serology is negative. Aspiration is indicated for microscopy and culture if there is a space-occupying lesion and negative serology.

Liver neoplasm is a differential diagnosis when the patient is febrile and wasted and has vague abdominal discomfort. Neoplasms produce distinct images, particularly on CT scanning, and testing for tumor markers such as alpha fetoprotein or carcinoembryonic antigen is useful.

Stool microscopy for the identification of trophozoites or cysts of *E. histolytica* is of value for the diagnosis of amebic liver abscess because, as mentioned above, many patients have associated asymptomatic intestinal amebiasis.

MANAGEMENT

Metronidazole and related nitroimidazole compounds have contributed greatly to decreasing the morbidity and mortality rate of amebiasis. They are reasonably well tolerated and despite their reported carcinogenic effect in rodents and their mutagenic potential in bacteria, no such effects have been reported in humans. Emetine hydrochloride, dehydroemetine and chloroquine, which have activity against the organism, are seldom used now.

Amebic liver abscess should be treated with chemotherapy; surgery is rarely indicated. The recommended oral dosage for metronidazole is 1g q12h for 5–10 days for an adult and 30–50mg/kg/day in three divided doses for 10 days for children. The intravenous route is highly effective for patients who have a complicated hepatic abscess; the recommended dosage in those cases is 500mg q6h for 5–10 days. In many cases of amebic hepatic abscess, a favorable response is obtained following the third day of treatment, but administration of the drug for 10 days increases the rate of cure to nearly 95%. Other nitroimidazole derivatives may be effective within 1–3 days but in view of the serious nature of amebic liver abscess as a disease, there is little reason to shorten the duration of therapy. Despite some isolated reports of failure in the treatment of amebic liver abscess with metronidazole, in-vitro studies and experiments with animal models of liver abscess have not demonstrated the existence of metronidazole-resistant strains of ameba. In 85% of cases liver imaging reveals resolution of amebic abscesses within 6 months of treatment; the remaining 15% of cases still show imaging defects 3 years after treatment.[3]

Oral administration of metronidazole is occasionally accompanied by symptoms of gastrointestinal upset such as abdominal pain, nausea and vomiting. Additionally, patients often report a metallic taste and a brownish discoloration of the urine. Undesirable reactions are observed on ingesting alcoholic beverages, probably due to inhibition of alcohol dehydrogenase. Metronidazole and its derivatives should not be administered during the first trimester of pregnancy and should only be prescribed under strict supervision during the second and third trimesters because of their ability to cross the placental barrier and rapidly enter the fetal circulation. The effect of these drugs on fetal development is unknown. Similarly, because of their elimination in breast milk, they are not recommended for nursing mothers; breast-feeding should be suspended if metronidazole is prescribed. To prevent recurrences and transmission, patients who have amebic liver abscess treated with metronidazole should also be treated with a luminal amebicide because up to two-thirds of them have asymptomatic intestinal colonization with *E. histolytica*. The most frequently used amebicides with luminal action are diloxanide furoate, di-iodohydroxyquin and paromomycin.

Current indications for percutaneous drainage of an amebic liver abscess are:

- imminent rupture of a large abscess;
- as a complementary therapy to shorten the course of the disease when the response to chemotherapy has been slow; and
- when pyogenic or mixed infection is suspected.

Drainage should be carried out under ultrasound or CT guidance. Catheters should not be left in for drainage and should be rapidly removed to avoid contaminating the track and skin.

Indications for surgical drainage include:

- imminent rupture of an inaccessible liver abscess, especially of the left lobe;
- a risk of peritoneal leakage of necrotic fluid after aspiration; and
- rupture of a liver abscess.

Monitoring the patient's condition

A prompt diagnosis and adequate chemotherapy will control most cases of liver abscess produced by *E. histolytica*. In general, a full clinical recovery and disappearance of the liver lesions (as confirmed by CT scanning) can be expected for uncomplicated cases. The prognosis is favorable in the absence of severe malnutrition or alcoholism, age over 50 years, multiple lesions, signs of peritonitis, evidence of toxemia or a history of operative treatment for amebiasis. A poor prognosis is associated with ascites or coma, especially if in a patient over 50 years or if the patient has severe jaundice, signs of peritonitis or toxemia.

GIARDIASIS

Giardiasis is a common infection of the human small intestine by the protozoan parasite *Giardia lamblia*. Most patients are asymptomatic, but an unspecified percentage of those infected develop acute or chronic symptoms. Acute manifestations include a sudden onset of explosive, watery, foul diarrhea with flatulence, cramps and abdominal distention and absence of blood, mucus or cellular exudate in the stools. Subacute or chronic infections may be accompanied by flatulence, mushy foul stools, cramps and abdominal distention. Spontaneous resolution of the infection seems to be common. Diagnosis is carried out by finding trophozoites or cysts on microscopic examination of the stools. Treatment is usually effective with metronidazole, tinidazole or furazolidone. Metronidazole is the drug of choice.

Extraintestinal complications of giardiasis are rare and include chronic cholecystitis with pain in the right upper quadrant of the abdomen, perhaps as a consequence of the presence of trophozoites in the gallbladder. In addition, granulomatous hepatitis and cholangitis have been reported in association with chronic diarrhea, weight loss, fever, hypoalbuminemia and anemia. In all of these reports, eradication of the parasite with specific chemotherapy has produced a rapid improvement of symptoms and a resolution of the histologic changes when liver biopsy has been performed. For a fuller description of the clinical and laboratory aspects of giardiasis see Chapters 46 and 242.

CRYPTOSPORIDIOSIS

Cryptosporidium are intestinal protozoan parasites of domestic and wild animals and have recently been found to be an uncommon cause of debilitating diarrhea in humans. In immunocompetent patients the infection is usually self-limiting and the symptoms include diarrhea, abdominal pain, nausea, vomiting and anorexia. In contrast, in immunocompromised patients, particularly those who have AIDS, the symptoms may last for several months and produce profound weight loss. The diagnosis is based on the microscopic finding of *Cryptosporidium* in stool samples using acid-fast stains to differentiate the parasite from yeasts (see also Chapters 46, 127 and 243).

An effective treatment for cryptosporidiosis in humans is not yet available. Paromomycin may have modest activity, but has not proved to be efficacious in controlled trials.

Cryptosporidium infection of the gallbladder and biliary tract has been found in 10–26% of patients who have AIDS and results in acalculous cholecystitis, extrahepatic bile duct stenosis and sclerosing cholangitis. Sonographic or CT imaging show an enlarged gallbladder with a thickened wall, dilated or irregular intra- and extrahepatic biliary ducts and a normal or stenotic distal common bile duct. Diagnosis is made histologically after cholecystectomy or ampullary biopsy or by examination of the bile for oocysts. Among patients who have HIV infection who are exposed to *Cryptosporidium*, those who have a $CD4^+$ T cell count less than 50 cells/mm^3 have an increased risk of developing biliary symptoms and of death within 1 year after the infection. Paromomycin treatment decreases stool frequency and oocyst excretion, but biliary disease progresses despite long-term therapy. Operative treatment includes cholecystectomy and sphincterotomy, with variable therapeutic success.[12]

REFERENCES

1. Brumpt E. Étude sommaire de l' '*Entamoeba dispar*' n. sp. Amibe à kystes quadrinucléés, parasite de l'homme. Bull Acad Méd (Paris) 1925;94:943–52.
2. Walsh JA. Prevalence of *Entamoeba histolytica* infection. In: Ravdin JI, ed. Amebiasis: human infection by *Entamoeba histolytica*. New York: Wiley; 1988:93–105.
3. Martínez-Palomo A, Ruíz-Palacios G. Amebiasis. In: Mahmoud AAF, Warren KE, eds. Tropical and geographical medicine. New York: McGraw-Hill; 1989:327–44.
4. Espinosa-Cantellano M, Martínez-Palomo A. Pathogenesis of intestinal amebiasis: from molecules to disease. Clin Microbiol Rev 2000;13:318–31.
5. Tsutsumi V, Mena-López R, Anaya-Velázquez F, Martínez-Palomo A. Cellular bases of experimental amebic liver abscess formation. Am J Pathol 1984;117:81–91.
6. Martínez-Palomo A, Espinosa-Cantellano M. Intestinal amoebae. In: Cox FEG, Kreier JP, Wakelin D, eds. Topley & Wilson's Microbiology and microbial infections. New York: Arnold; 1998;5:157–77.
7. Martínez-Palomo A, Martínez-Báez M. Selective primary health care: strategies for control of disease in the developing world. X. Amebiasis. Rev Infect Dis 1983;5:1093–102.
8. World Health Organization. Prevention and control of intestinal parasitic infections. World Health Organ Tech Rep Ser 1987;749.
9. Sepúlveda B, Treviño-García Manzo N. Clinical manifestations and diagnosis of amebiasis. In: Martínez-Palomo A, ed. Amebiasis. Human parasitic diseases. Amsterdam: Elsevier; 1986:169–88.
10. Adams EB, MacLeod IN. Invasive amebiasis. II. Amebic liver abscess and its complications. Medicine 1977;56:325–34.
11. Petri WA, Haque R, Lyerly D, *et al*. Estimating the impact of amebiasis on health. Parasitol Today 2000;16(8):320–1.
12. Fayer R, Speer CA, Dubey JP. The general biology of Cryptosporidium. In: Fayer R, ed. Cryptosporidium and cryptosporidiosis. Boca Raton: CRC Press; 1997:1–41.

chapter

165 Ova, Cysts and Parasites in the Stool

Peter L Chiodini

INTRODUCTION

The objective in the diagnosis of parasitic disease is to find the parasite and, for most infections, microscopy remains the 'gold standard'. If the specimen is examined by a competent microscopist, then a rapid, highly specific diagnosis can be obtained. However, the very need for experienced laboratory staff is also the weakness of microscopy as a diagnostic method, because well-trained pathologists and laboratory technologists are in short supply, especially in those areas of the world where parasitic disease is most prevalent. New methods for detection of parasite antigens by enzyme-linked immunosorbent assay (ELISA), 'dipstick' technology or detection of parasite DNA are coming into routine use. Optimum diagnosis requires:

- an understanding of the life cycles of the parasites and of their geographic distribution;
- examination of freshly collected samples, preserved where appropriate; and
- the use of the correct parasite isolation method and stain for those parasites potentially present in a given specimen.

When helminth eggs or larvae are found in the stool, the adult worms are usually situated in the bowel. Exceptions to this rule are:

- *Fasciola* spp., *Clonorchis* spp. (Fig. 165.1) and *Opisthorchis* spp., the adults of which live in the bile ducts;
- *Schistosoma* spp., paired adult worms of which live in the mesenteric or perivesical veins; and
- *Paragonimus* spp., the adults of which reside in the lungs.

The protozoa whose cysts or trophozoites are detected in stool samples are all primarily parasites of the gastrointestinal tract, although extraintestinal spread occurs in *Entamoeba histolytica* infection and in *Cryptosporidium parvum* or microsporidial infections in immunocompromised hosts (see Chapter 46).

Geographic distribution

The geographic distribution of the common parasites that can be diagnosed by stool examination is shown in Table 165.1.[1]

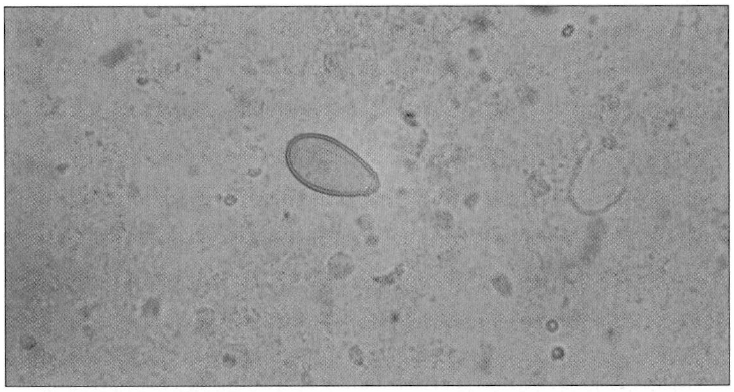

Fig. 165.1 Ovum of *Clonorchis*. Large, operculated ova in fecal specimen.

INVESTIGATIONS TO CONFIRM THE DIAGNOSIS

Relevant information

The test request form should state the patient's clinical symptoms and signs, where the patient is normally resident and whether there has been any recent overseas travel, stating the particular location visited if so. If the patient is immunocompromised, this should also be stated because it should prompt the diagnostic laboratory to perform tests for parasites such as microsporidia, which might otherwise be omitted.

Sample collection

Unless the fecal sample is properly collected and taken care of, it will be of no value for diagnosis. A clean, dry container is essential; urine and water destroy protozoal trophozoites and dirt renders identification more difficult. Approximately 100g of feces is required. Ideally, the sample should be brought to the laboratory as soon as it is passed, to avoid deterioration of protozoal trophozoites. Diarrheal specimens and specimens containing blood or mucus should be examined promptly after receipt in the laboratory because such samples may contain motile amebic or flagellate trophozoites, which may become rounded and non-motile and be missed if examination is delayed. Where amebic dysentery is suspected, the laboratory should be advised that a 'hot' stool is being submitted, to permit its examination within 20 minutes of being passed. (It should be noted that the term 'hot stool' refers to the urgency of the request. The stool should not be heated but merely prevented from cooling significantly by prompt delivery to the laboratory.) With the exception of 'hot' stools, samples that cannot be examined on receipt should be stored at 39°F (4°C).

Rectal scrapes for amebae should be placed directly on to a microscope slide by the clinician performing the proctoscopy. A drop of 0.9% sodium chloride solution kept at 98.6°F (37°C) is added and a coverslip is applied. The scrapes are then taken directly to the laboratory, which should be informed in advance so that the specimen can be examined on receipt.

Rectal snips for schistosome eggs should be placed directly onto a microscope slide by the clinician taking them, a drop of 0.9% sodium chloride added and then a coverslip applied. The snips need to be examined promptly in the laboratory in order to prevent them from drying up.

Many laboratories routinely advise preservation of fecal samples as soon as possible, either immediately after collection or on receipt by the laboratory. Examples of preservation fluids include formalin, merthiolate–iodine–formalin and sodium acetate–acetic acid–formalin. The choice of preserving fluid is influenced by the subsequent technique to be used. For example, formalin is not a suitable fixative if permanently stained fecal smears are to be prepared.

Visual observation of the fecal sample

The macroscopic appearance of the fecal sample can sometimes give a clue to the underlying pathology; for example, the pale fatty

GEOGRAPHIC DISTRIBUTION OF THE COMMON PARASITES THAT CAN BE DIAGNOSED BY STOOL EXAMINATION		
Widespread, especially in areas of poor sanitation		**Organism**
Protozoa		*Giardia intestinalis (lamblia)* *Entamoeba histolytica* and *Entamoeba dispar* *Cryptosporidium parvum* *Isospora belli* *Cyclospora cayetanensis* *Dientamoeba fragilis* *Blastocystis hominis* Microsporidia (various species)
Helminths	Nematodes	*Strongyloides stercoralis* Hookworm *Ascaris lumbricoides* *Trichuris trichiura* *Enterobius vermicularis*
	Cestodes	*Hymenolepis nana* *Hymenolepis diminuta* *Taenia saginata*
Focal distribution		**Geographic areas**
Helminths Nematodes	*Capillaria philippinensis*	Philippines, Thailand, Egypt, Indonesia
Cestodes	*Taenia solium*	Central and South America, southern Asia, China, parts of Africa
	Diphyllobothrium latum	Russia, parts of North and South America, potential for transmission in eastern Scandinavia and eastern Europe
Trematodes	*Schistosoma haematobium* (ova occasionally seen in stool rather than urine)	Africa, eastern Mediterranean, Indian Ocean Islands, western Asia
	Schistosoma mansoni	Arabian peninsula, Africa, parts of South America, some Caribbean islands
	Schistosoma japonicum	China, Indonesia, Philippines, Thailand
	Paragonimus spp.	Asia, Africa, Central and South America (including China, Taiwan, Thailand, Cambodia, Nigeria, Peru, Ecuador)
	Clonorchis spp. and *Opisthorchis* spp.	Far East, eastern Europe, former Soviet Union
	Fasciola gigantica	Southern and South East Asia, Africa
	Fasciola hepatica	Parts of Europe, the Middle East, Africa, Central and South America.
	Fasciolopsis buski	Asia
	Heterophyids (including *Heterophyes* spp. and *Metagonimus*)	Asia, Siberia, Turkey, the Balkans

Table 165.1 Geographic distribution of the common parasites that can be diagnosed by stool examination. Data from the World Health Organization.[1]

stool of malabsorption may suggest giardiasis. The presence or absence of blood, mucus and exudate are noted. Adult nematodes (e.g. *Ascaris*, *Enterobius*) or tapeworm proglottids may also be seen in the specimen.

Preparation for microscopic examination

A formalin–ether or formalin–ethyl acetate concentration method should be performed on all fecal samples examined for parasites. This increases the numbers of ova, cysts and larvae per given volume by approximately 20-fold but does not improve the yield of trophozoites, which are usually destroyed by this method. Direct microscopy should be done on all unformed and liquid samples. This permits detection of amebic or flagellate trophozoites and provides information on the presence of any exudate in the stool (e.g. fecal leukocytes). All fecal specimens should be examined for the presence of *Cryptosporidium*. If laboratories are unable to do this, a minimum requirement is that all specimens from children up to and including 15-year-olds be tested.[2] Ideally, a permanently stained direct fecal smear should be prepared from all stool samples. Where resources are limited, its application may be restricted to bloody, liquid or semiformed stools. Permanently stained smears can reveal the presence of intestinal parasites that are either destroyed or missed by the formalin–ether or ethyl acetate concentration method. A plan for testing stool specimens is given in Figure 165.2.

Reporting criteria

Ideally, the presence of all parasites should be reported, especially in the case of protozoan cysts, whether or not they are considered to be pathogens. If the practice of the laboratory is to report all parasites, the report should then state whether they are regarded as pathogens. The stage of the parasite should also be stated:

- for protozoa, whether cysts or trophozoites were seen; and
- for helminths, whether adult worms or their eggs were detected and the developmental stage of any larva found.

Morphology

The microscopic appearances of common protozoan cysts and trophozoites are summarized in Tables 165.2 and 165.3.

Particular care must be taken to distinguish oocysts of *Cyclospora* spp. from those of *Cryptosporidium* spp. because both are acid-fast in fecal smears stained with modified Ziehl–Neelsen stain (see Table 165.3).[3,4]

It is important to note that cysts of *E. histolytica* and *Entamoeba dispar* cannot be distinguished from each other morphologically but, if amebic trophozoites are evident in a fresh stool preparation, the presence of ingested erythrocytes within them is diagnostic of *E. histolytica*. However, macrophages can also ingest erythrocytes, which can lead to confusion with amebae. Permanently stained preparations may be required to resolve the diagnosis.

Microsporidial spores can be visualized in a thin fecal smear by non-specific fluorescence[5] using calcofluor or uvitex 2B stains, but the presence of microsporidial spores must be confirmed using a modified trichrome stain[6] as small fungi and some artefacts may also fluoresce.[7] With the modified trichrome stain, the spores are seen as oval, pinkish structures with a polar vacuole, often with a diagonal line across the spore. Size varies according to species, with an approximate range of 1.5–3μm for the microsporidia found in human feces.

A key to identifying eggs of the common intestinal helminths is given in Figure 165.3.[1]

Nematode larvae in fresh fecal specimens are usually the result of *Strongyloides* spp. infection. However, if an unfixed stool sample more than 12–24 hours old is received, hookworm eggs (Fig. 165.4) may hatch to release larvae, which then need to be distinguished from those of *Strongyloides*. When seen in fecal concentrates, rhabditiform larvae of hookworm are 100–150μm × 15–17μm in size, with a long (15μm) buccal cavity. The esophagus occupies one-third of the body length and has two swellings. The hookworm larva has a small (7μm) genital primordium and the anal pore is 80μm from the

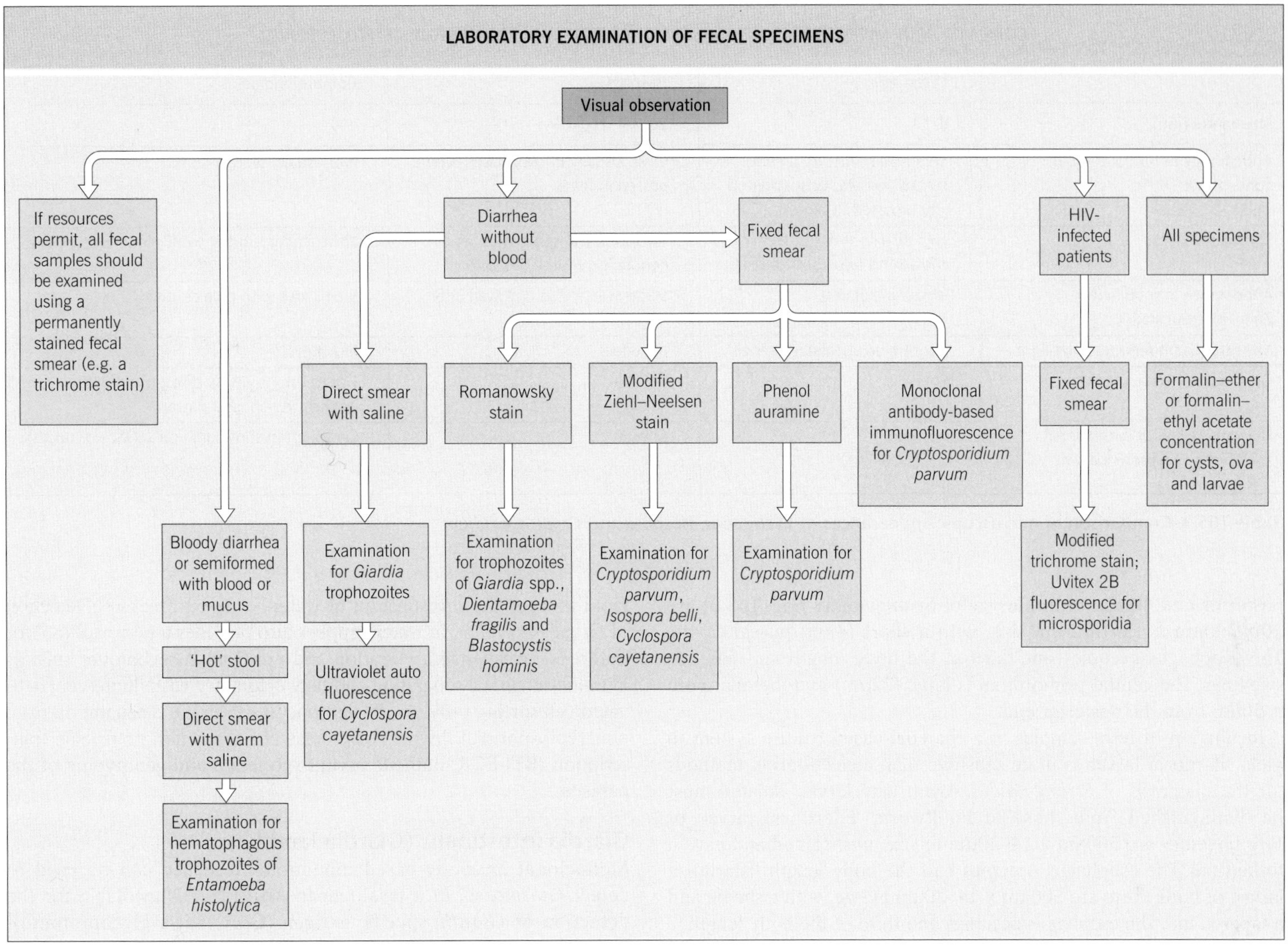

Fig. 165.2 Laboratory examination of fecal specimens.

MORPHOLOGY OF COMMON PROTOZOAL CYSTS AND TROPHOZOITES IN FECAL SAMPLES

Species	Cyst				Trophozoite
	Size (μm)	Number of nuclei	Chromidial bar	Glycogen inclusion	
Entamoeba hartmanni	7–9	1–4	Blunt, round end-young cyst	Diffuse	Clear pseudopodia
Entamoeba histolytica/dispar	9–14.5	1–4	Blunt, round end-young cyst	Diffuse	Ingested RBC (*E. histolytica* only), clear pseudopodia
Entamoeba coli	14–30	1–8	Seldom seen, sharp, splintered	Diffuse	Blunt pseudopodia, sluggish movement
Iodamoeba butschlii	9–15	1	–	One compact mass	Rarely seen
Endolimax nana	6–9	4 (pin-point)	–	–	–
Dientamoeba fragilis	No cyst stage				Small, angular, two nuclei
			Refractile inclusion		
Giardia intestinalis (lamblia)	8–12	4 (not obvious)	Clear axostyle	–	Pear shaped, two nuclei, undulating flagella, little motility
Chilomastix mesnili	5–6	1	Axostyle	–	Size similar to *Giardia*, pointed tail, rapid motility
Trichomonas hominis	5–6	1	–	–	Undulating membrane
Enteromonas hominis	No cyst stage				Small, three flagellae

Table 165.2 Morphology of common protozoal cysts and trophozoites in fecal samples.

COMPARISON OF MICROSCOPIC APPEARANCES OF *CYCLOSPORA, ISOSPORA* AND *CRYPTOSPORIDIUM*			
	Cyclospora	*Isospora*	*Cryptosporidium*
Size range (μm)	8–10	20–33 × 10–19	4–6
Appearance in formalin-ether concentrate	Spherical refractile, greenish central morula. Unsporulated when passed in feces	Oval. Usually unsporulated when passed in feces	Not usually seen
Sporulated occyst	Two oval sporocysts, each containing two sporozoites	Two spherical sporocysts, each containing four sporozoites	Spherical or slightly ovoid; four sporozoites
Appearance in modified Ziehl–Neelsen stain	Irregular staining	Stains well, often cyst wall only	Stains well with pale center
Appearance under ultraviolet light	Bright blue autofluorescence	No effect	No effect
Fluorescence with auramine	Poor	Variable	Good; bright yellow discs, often with erythrocyte-shaped pattern
Fluorescence with monoclonal antibody to *Cryptosporidium*	Absent	Absent	Good; often shows line on surface of oocyst

Table 165.3 Comparison of microscopic appearances of *Cyclospora, Isospora* and *Cryptosporidium*.

posterior end. Rhabditiform larvae of *Strongyloides* (Fig. 165.5) are 200–300μm × 15–18μm in size, with a short (4μm) buccal cavity. The esophagus occupies one-third of the body length and has two swellings. The genital primordium is large (22μm) and the anal pore is 50μm from the posterior end.

Incubation of fecal samples in a charcoal-based culture system to yield filariform larvae is more sensitive than concentration methods for the diagnosis of *Strongyloides*. Again, any larvae isolated must be distinguished from those of hookworm. Filariform larvae of *Strongyloides* are 500μm × 14–20μm in size, unsheathed and have a forked tail. The esophagus occupies half the body length. Filariform larvae of hookworm are 500μm × 14–20μm in size, with a sheath and a tapered tail. The esophagus occupies one-third of the body length.

Serodiagnosis by ELISA provides a useful screening method for the diagnosis of *Strongyloides* but it exhibits some cross-reactivity with other nematode infections, which can render interpretation difficult.

Alternative methods to classical microscopy for the diagnosis of cysts, ova and larvae in the stool

In recent years there has been increasing interest in the development of new methods to detect parasites in fecal samples.

Cryptosporidium parvum

Cryptosporidial infection in humans is most commonly due to *C. parvum*, but *Cryptosporidium felis*, *Cryptosporidium muris* and *Cryptosporidium meleagridis* have been identified in immunocompromised individuals. *Cryptosporidium parvum* has two genotypes, type 1 (human-derived) and type 2 (animal- and human-derived), and it has been suggested that they may represent two distinct species.[8]

Oocysts of *C. parvum* can be detected with improved specificity by fluorescence microscopy using *Cryptosporidium*-specific monoclonal antibody. It is often possible to demonstrate a 'suture' line on the oocyst surface using this method. Cryptosporidial infection can also be diagnosed by an antigen-capture ELISA[9] for the detection of oocyst antigen in stool supernatant. The test has a reported sensitivity of 94% and specificity of 99% compared with microscopy. Using fluorescence-labeled probes for real-time detection of *Cryptosporidium* and melting curve analysis of the polymerase chain reaction (PCR) products to differentiate species and genotypes, the genetic polymorphism in the small subunit ribosomal RNA of *Cryptosporidium* can be exploited to detect and speciate cryptosporidia infecting humans. This provides a rapid tool for the investigation of water-borne outbreaks.[10] Detection of *Cryptosporidium* in water supplies also provides a powerful tool for outbreak investigation. Filtration and purification techniques such as immuno-magnetic separation and flow cytometry with fluorescent activated cell sorting provide efficient oocyst capture and separation from noncryptosporidial debris. Polymerase chain reaction or reverse transcription (RT)-PCR methods permit speciation and genotyping of the parasite.[11]

Giardia intestinalis (Giardia lamblia)

Monoclonal antibody-based immunofluorescence can be used to detect *Giardia* sp. in a fecal smear. An ELISA is available for the detection of *Giardia*-specific antigen (GSA)-65, a glycoprotein of molecular weight 65kDa, in aqueous extracts of feces.[12] The assay has a reported sensitivity of 98–100% compared with conventional fecal microscopy and has the substantial advantage of analyzing many samples simultaneously without the subjectivity of microscopy.

Entamoeba histolytica and Entamoeba dispar

Understanding of human amebiasis has been transformed by the demonstration that the organism formerly known as *E. histolytica* is, in fact, two separate species, *Entamoeba histolytica* and *E. dispar*, the cysts of which are morphologically identical.[13] *Entamoeba histolytica* is pathogenic to humans; *E. dispar* is not. If cysts of *E. histolytica* or *E. dispar* are found in a fecal sample, further evaluation is required in order to determine whether *E. histolytica* is present. Amebic serology, if positive, supports the diagnosis of *E. histolytica* but, especially in areas where amebiasis is common, seropositivity may be related to past infection rather than to current infection. Furthermore, sensitivity of serology is low in asymptomatic amebic cyst passage.

Entamoeba histolytica infection can be diagnosed by an ELISA that detects antigen by using antibodies to the galactose adhesin of *E. histolytica*.[14] Reported sensitivity and specificity for identification of *E. histolytica* antigen are 92.6% and 96.7% respectively, compared with positive specimens in which *E. histolytica* could be identified by zymodeme analysis. Correlation between zymodeme analysis and the antigen detection ELISA is 94.7%.

Detection of *E. histolytica* and *E. dispar* in fecal samples can be undertaken by PCR-solution hybridization enzyme-linked immunoassay (PCR-SHELA).[15,16] The PCR assay is based on primers specific for a 145bp DNA sequence in *E. histolytica* and a 133bp DNA sequence in *E. dispar*. These are based on highly repeated sequences in

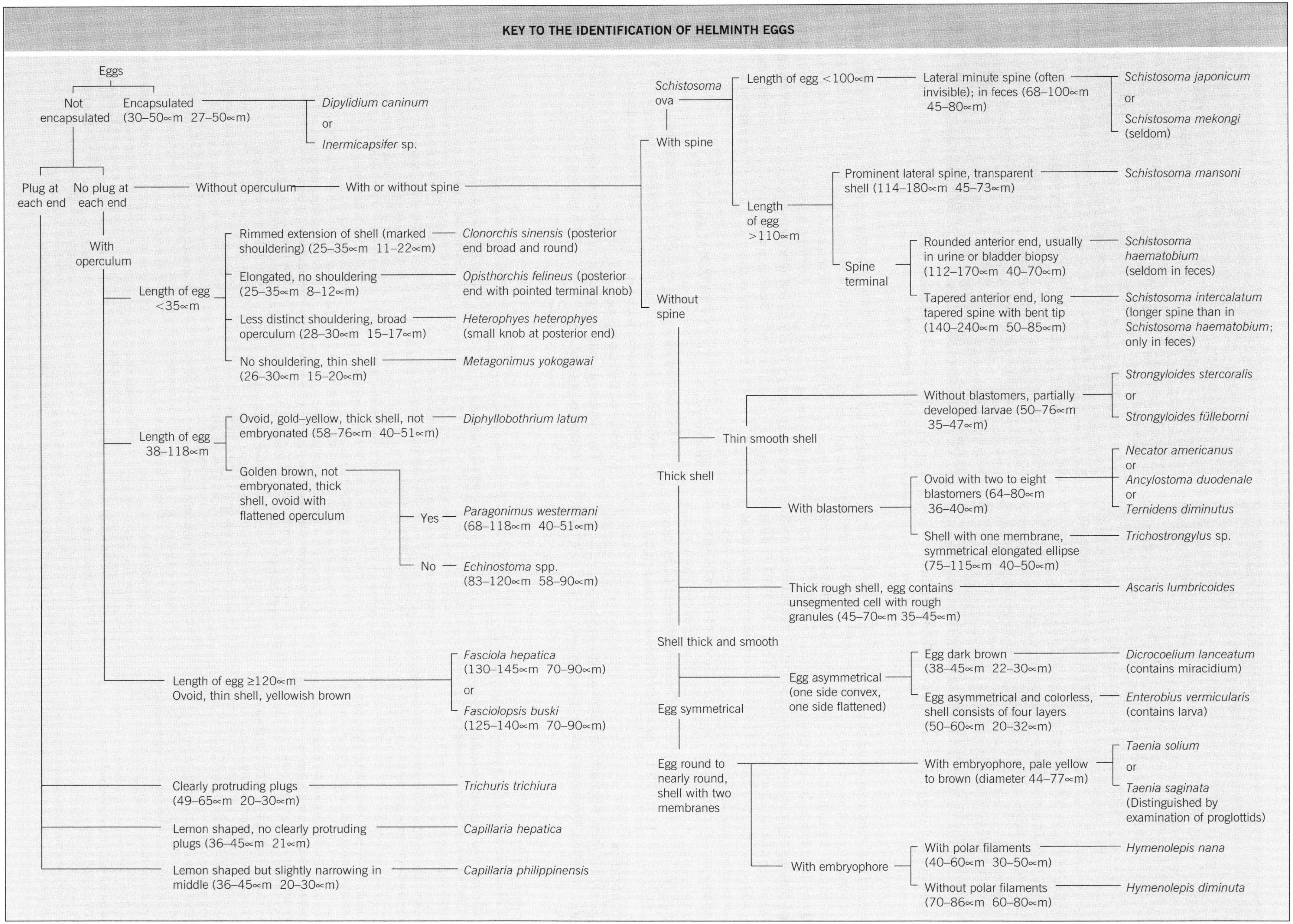

Fig. 165.3 Key to the identification of helminth eggs. Adapted from the World Health Organization.[1]

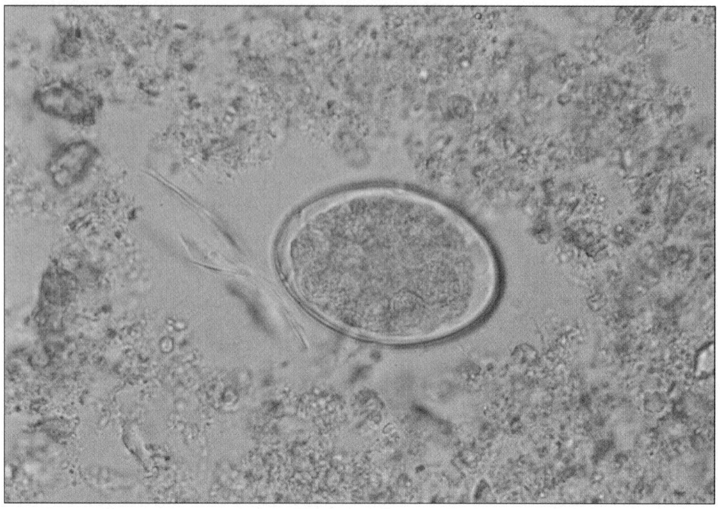

Fig. 165.4 Ovum of *Diphyllobothrium latum* in a fecal specimen.

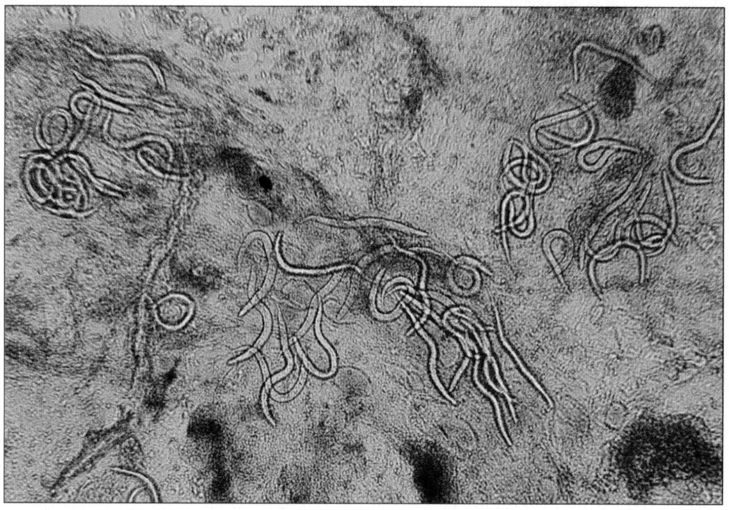

Fig. 165.5 Numerous rhabditiform larvae of *Strongyloides* in a duodenal juice specimen.

ribosomal DNA episomes, several hundred of which are present in each amebic trophozoite. Hybridization of PCR product to probes labeled with 5′ digoxigenin (for *E. histolytica*) and 5′ fluorescein (for *E. dispar*) is followed by colorimetric detection using peroxidase-labeled antidigoxigenin and peroxidase-labeled antifluorescein. The method is reported to identify 10^{-1} *E. histolytica* and 1–10 *E. dispar* trophozoites per gram of feces when they are present separately, and 10 *E. histolytica* and 100 *E. dispar* trophozoites per gram of feces in the presence of 10^6 trophozoites per gram of feces of the other species. When this assay was applied to 18 clinical specimens from which *E. histolytica* or *E. dispar* had been cultured and identified by isoenzyme analysis, the PCR-SHELA gave the correct result in each case.

Microsporidia

Microscopy for these organisms requires a high level of expertise and is time-consuming. Diagnosis can be aided by use of species-specific immunofluorescence of microsporidial spores,[17] when sensitivity comparable to that achieved by PCR has been reported,[18] and by PCR.[19] One study comparing light microscopy and PCR for the detection of microsporidia in fecal specimens[20] recorded 89% sensitivity and 98% specificity for PCR, compared with 80% sensitivity and 95% specificity for light microscopy. Neither species-specific immunofluorescence nor PCR for these emerging pathogens is widely available at present.

TREATMENT AND COMPLICATIONS

Provided samples have been examined by a competent microscopist, identification of named parasitic ova, cysts or parasites in a fecal sample is diagnostic, and so specific treatment can be given. Empiric treatment is, therefore, rarely required.

The treatment and complications of these infections are discussed in Chapters 46 and 209.

REFERENCES

1. World Health Organization. Intestinal parasites. In: Basic laboratory methods in medical parasitology. Geneva: World Health Organization; 1991:67–79.
2. Crook P, Mayon-White R, Reacher M. Enhancing surveillance of cryptosporidiosis: test all faecal specimens from children. Commun Dis Public Health 2002;5:112–3.
3. Chiodini PL. A 'new' parasite: human infection with *Cyclospora cayetanensis*. Trans R Soc Trop Med Hyg 1994;88:369–71.
4. Eberhard ML, Pieniazek NJ, Arrowood MJ. Laboratory diagnosis of *Cyclospora* infections. Arch Pathol Lab Med 1997;121:792–7.
5. Van Gool T, Snidjers F, Reiss P, *et al.* Diagnosis of intestinal and disseminated microsporidial infections in patients with HIV by a new rapid fluorescence technique. J Clin Pathol 1993;46:694–9.
6. Weber R, Bryan DT, Owen RL, Wilcox CM, Gorelkin L, Visvesvara GS. Improved light microscopical detection of microsporidial spores in stool and duodenal aspirates. N Engl J Med 1992;326:161–6.
7. Garcia LS. Laboratory identification of the microsporidia. J Clin Microbiol 2002;40:1892–901.
8. Sestak K, Ward LA, Sheoran A, *et al.* Variability among *Cryptosporidium parvum* and genotype 1 and 2 immunodominant surface glycoproteins. Parasite Immunol 2002;24:213–9.
9. Sloan LM, Rosenblatt JE. Evaluation of enzyme-linked immunosorbent assay for detection of *Cryptosporidium* spp. in stool specimens. J Clin Microbiol 1993;31:1468–71.
10. Limor JF, Lal AA, Xiao L. Detection and differentiation of *Cryptosporidium* parasites that are pathogenic for humans by real-time PCR. J Clin Microbiol 2002;40:2335–8.
11. Quintero-Betancourt W, Peele PR, Rose JB. *Cryptosporidium parvum* and *Cyclospora cayetanensis*: a review of laboratory methods for detection of these waterborne parasites. J Microbiol Methods 2002;49:209–24.
12. Rosoff JD, Sanders CA, Sonnad SS, *et al.* Stool diagnosis of giardiasis using a commercially available enzyme immunoassay to detect *Giardia*-specific antigen 65 (GSA 65). J Clin Microbiol 1989;23:1997–2002.
13. Jackson TF. *Entamoeba histolytica* and *Entamoeba dispar* are distinct species; clinical, epidemiological and serological evidence. Int J Parasitol 1998;28:181–6.
14. Haque RK, Kress S, Wood T, *et al.* Diagnosis of pathogenic *Entamoeba histolytica* infection using a stool ELISA based on monoclonal antibodies to the galactose-specific adhesin. J Infect Dis 1993;167:247–9.
15. Aguirre A, Warhurst DC, Guhl F, Frame I. Polymerase chain reaction-solution hybridization enzyme-linked immunoassay (PCR-SHELA) for the differential diagnosis of pathogenic and non-pathogenic *Entamoeba histolytica*. Trans R Soc Trop Med Hyg 1995;89:187–8.
16. Britten D, Wilson SM, McNerney R, Moody AH, Chiodini PL, Ackers JP. An improved colorometric PCR-based method for detection and differentiation of *Entamoeba histolytica* and *Entamoeba dispar* in faeces. J Clin Microbiol 1997;35:1108–11.
17. Lujan HD, Conrad JT, Clark CG, *et al.* Detection of microsporidia spore-specific antigens by monoclonal antibodies. Hybridoma 1998;17:237–43.
18. Cisse OA, Ouattara A, Thellier M, *et al.* Evaluation of an immunofluorescent-antibody test using monoclonal antibodies against *Enterocytozoon bieneusi* and *Encephalitozoon intestinalis* for diagnosis of intestinal microsporidiosis in Bamako (Mali). J Clin Microbiol 2002;40:1715–8.
19. Franzen C, Muller A, Hartmann P, *et al.* Polymerase chain reaction for diagnosis and species differentiation of microsporidia. Folia Parasitol (Prague) 1998;45:140–8.
20. Rinder H, Janitschke K, Aspock H, *et al.* Blinded, externally controlled multicenter evaluation of light microscopy and PCR for detection of microsporidia in stool specimens. Diagnostic Multicenter Study Group on Microsporidia. J Clin Microbiol 1998;36:1814–8.

chapter 166

Malaria

Geoffrey Pasvol

INTRODUCTION

Malaria is an infection caused by the coccidian protozoan parasite of the genus *Plasmodium* carried by female *Anopheles* spp. mosquitoes. The clinical disease in humans may vary widely according to the species of parasite – *Plasmodium falciparum, Plasmodium vivax, Plasmodium ovale* or *Plasmodium malariae* – and the genetics, immune status and age of the host. These variables have a major influence on all aspects of the disease, including epidemiology, pathogenesis, clinical features and management.

EPIDEMIOLOGY

Geographic distribution

Wherever temperatures are favorable and humans and mosquitoes co-exist, there is the potential for malarial transmission. Malaria certainly existed until the mid-20th century in Europe, especially in Italy, as well as in northern parts of Asia adjoining the former USSR. Almost 2 billion people are at risk of malaria in endemic areas and each year it is estimated that up to 250 million clinical cases occur and over 1 million die, largely among infants and young children in Africa.[1,2]

Malaria occurs throughout the tropics and subtropics, especially where the temperature exceeds the 60.8°F (16°C) isotherm (see Chapter 245 and Fig. 166.1). The four species of malaria parasites that affect humans differ in their geographic distributions:

- *P. falciparum* is most common in sub-Saharan Africa and Melanesia (Papua New Guinea and the Solomon Islands);
- *P. vivax* is found mainly in Central and South America, North Africa, the Middle East and within the Indian subcontinent;
- *P. ovale* is found predominantly in West Africa but also in Asia; and
- *P. malariae* occurs worldwide, although most cases occur in Africa.

With modern air travel, individuals with malaria can be rapidly transported within hours to any part of the world and malaria is the single most common imported infection occurring in travelers.

There have been occasional reports of 'airport malaria' where infected mosquitoes have been imported on board aircraft into a nonendemic area of the world where they infect local inhabitants who have not traveled.

A few outbreaks have also been documented in nonendemic areas where environmental conditions have become optimal for the transmission of disease by local susceptible mosquitoes becoming infected after biting individuals who have obtained their infection elsewhere (e.g. as occurred in New York in the summer of 1993). In addition, there is now the threat of a global climate change. If the predictions of a 3.6°F (2°C) rise by the year 2100 become a reality, this might lead to the spread of malaria back into areas previously affected by malaria.

Malaria can also be transmitted by blood and blood products.

The epidemiology of malaria depends upon a complex interplay between the:

- host (humans),
- vector (mosquito), and
- malarial parasite.

Population density and prevalence of infection among children are important factors because children tend to have both high parasitemias and rates of carriage of the sexual forms of the parasite (gametocytes), which are necessary for transmission of the infection. Paradoxically, in the 2 weeks after effective treatment of *P. falciparum* malaria, the numbers of gametocytes in the blood rises, so that while the patient improves clinically, mosquitoes biting the patient during this time are more likely to transmit infection.

The longevity of the mosquito is also crucial because it needs to be of sufficient duration to allow for full development of the parasite. Ambient temperatures have a major impact, because higher temperatures significantly shorten this period of maturation in the mosquito (the extrinsic incubation period) and increase transmission. Seasonal rainfall dramatically increases the breeding of mosquitoes.

Where malaria prospers, human societies prosper the least and there is a striking correlation between malaria and poverty. The effects of malaria are felt on diverse areas including fertility, population growth, savings and investment, worker productivity, absenteeism, premature mortality and medical costs.

PATHOGENESIS AND PATHOLOGY

Malaria is one of the few infective agents of humans that invades red cells.[3,4] All four species of malarial parasites that infect humans have a similar life cycle that alternates between human and mosquito (see Chapter 245). The clinical symptoms and signs are produced by the asexual forms of the parasite, which invade and destroy red cells, localize in critical organs and tissues in the body, and induce the release of many proinflammatory cytokines (see Fig. 166.2), of which tumor necrosis factor (TNF)-α is thought to be the most important. The sporozoites injected by the bite of the infected mosquito, the exoerythrocytic parasites, which subsequently develop in the liver, and the sexual forms of the parasite (macro- and microgametocytes), which arise from the asexual forms do not cause clinical disease.

Invasion of red cells

Merozoites in the peripheral blood invade red cells (and occasionally platelets) and the rate and degree to which the parasite multiplies appear to relate to disease severity in nonimmune individuals. Invasion is a highly specific, ordered and sequential process in which the invasive form, the merozoite, attaches to a susceptible red cell, reorients itself so that its apical end is apposed to the red cell membrane, and then slowly moves into a localized invagination.[5] The entire process of invasion is completed within 30 seconds. In falciparum malaria the erythrocyte binding antigen (EBA 175) and/or merozoite surface proteins (MSP-1 and MSP-2) appear to interact with the red cell sialoglycoproteins (glycophorins), whereas in *P. vivax* infection, the red cell Duffy antigen on the uninfected red cell is involved (see Table 166.1). There is surprising redundancy in the

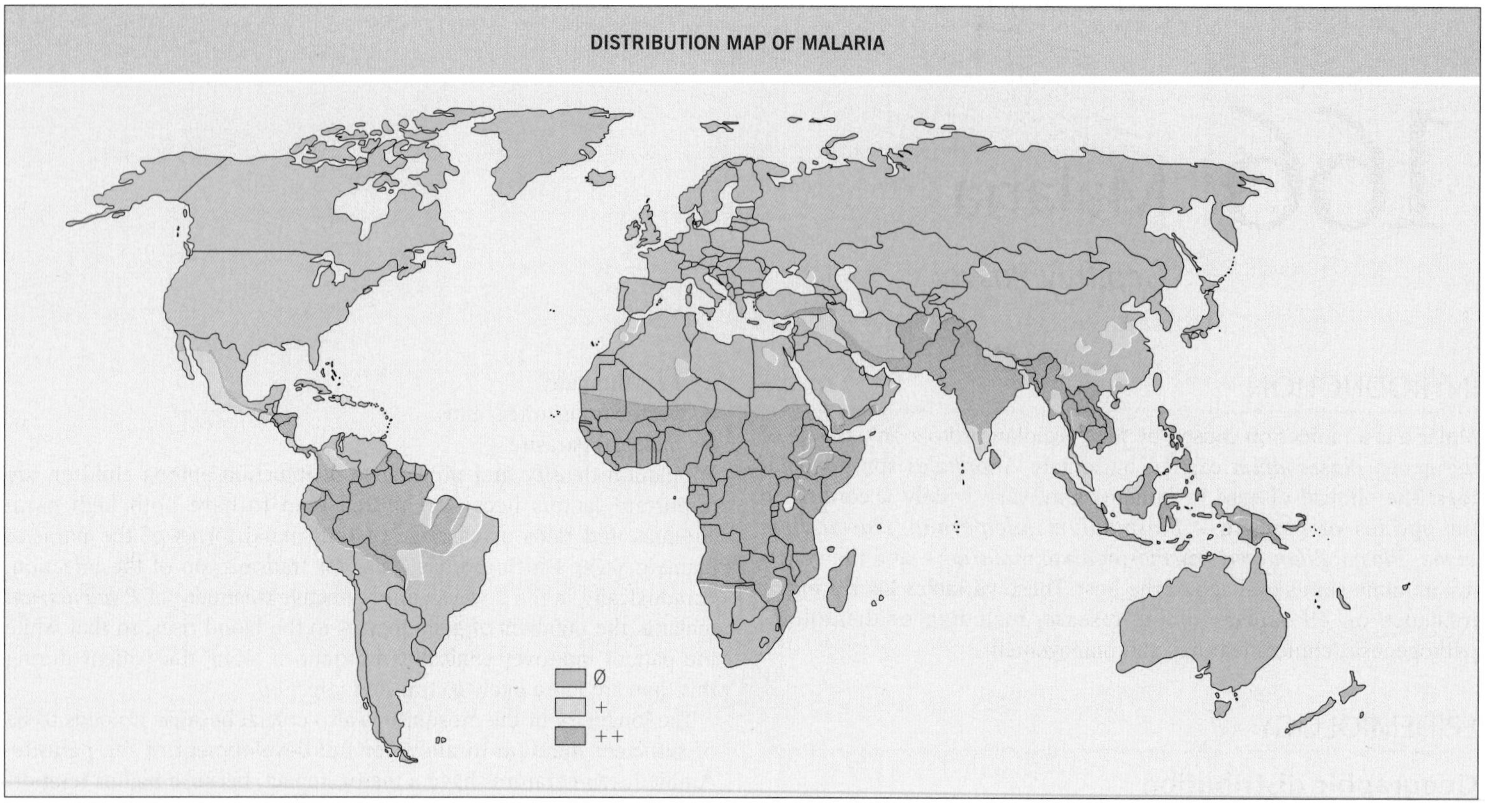

Fig. 166.1 Distribution map of malaria. Despite intensive control measures over the past 50 years, malaria is still widely distributed in the tropics and subtropics. The breakdown of large-scale vector control operations and the emergence of multidrug-resistant parasites have even led to an increase in the incidence of malaria in some regions. O, areas where malaria has disappeared, been eradicated or never existed; +, areas with limited risk; ++, areas where malaria transmission occurs. (Adapted from WHO 1999, Map No. WHO 99419 EF.) Courtesy of Dr C Lavaissiere.

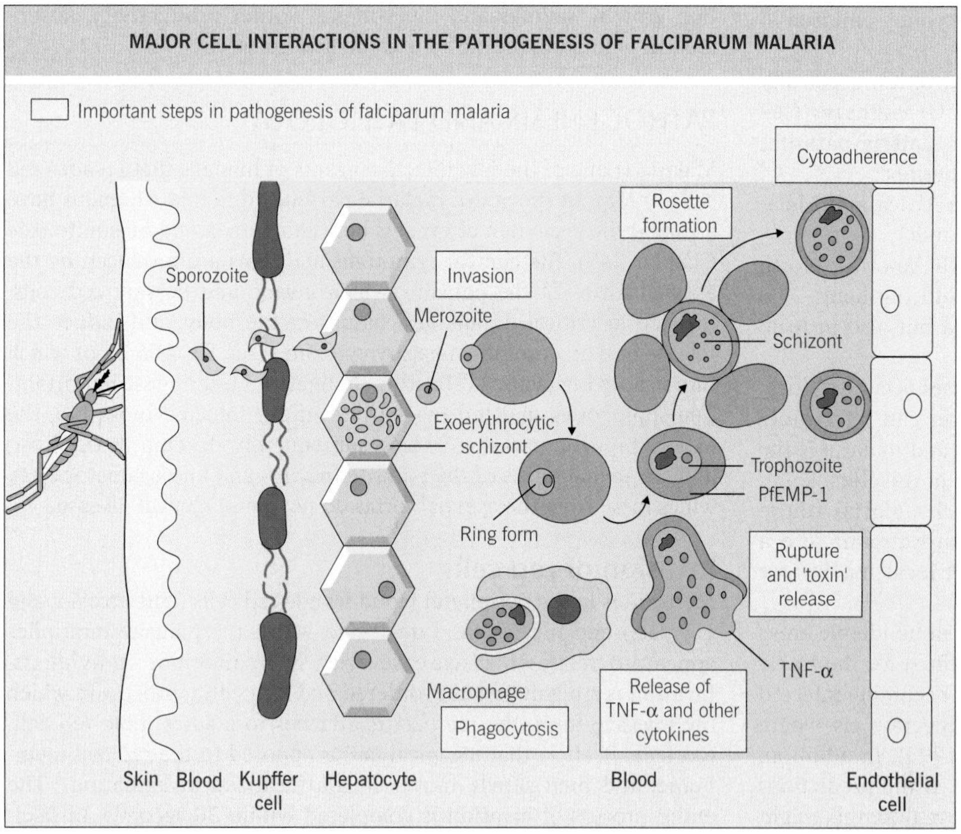

Fig. 166.2 Major cell interactions in the pathogenesis of falciparum malaria. The injected sporozoites invade hepatocytes. Merozoites released from rupturing liver schizonts invade red cells. The parasite matures via the ring to the trophozoite to the erythrocytic schizont stage. Such schizonts can bind to uninfected red cells (rosette formation) or to the endothelial cells lining the postcapillary venules (cytoadherence). When the mature schizont ruptures, 'toxin'-like molecules are released which induce the release of proinflammatory cytokines such as TNF-α.

invasion pathways of *P. falciparum* and a number of sialoglycoprotein and nonsialoglycoprotein pathways have been identified.

Attachment and orientation is followed by interiorization accompanied by deformation of the red cell membrane. Although each merozoite of *P. falciparum* can theoretically produce from 16 to 32 new merozoites every 48 hours, a more realistic figure *in vivo* is between three and 10. It is only recently (largely because of technical difficulties) that parasite multiplicative ability within red cells (i.e. the ability to invade) has been shown to relate to disease severity.

MAJOR INTERACTIONS OF RED CELL INVASION, ROSETTING, CYTOADHERENCE AND TNF INDUCTION AND SOME OF THE MOLECULES INVOLVED IN THE PATHOGENESIS OF FALCIPARUM MALARIA				
	Invasion	**Rosetting**	**Cytoadherence**	**TNF induction**
Parasite-induced molecules	Erythrocyte-binding antigen (EBA-175) Merozoite surface protein-1 (MSP-1) MSP-2/4/5 Apical membrane antigen (AMA) Rhoptry-associated protein (RAP-1) RAP-2 RAP-3	*Plasmodium falciparum* erythrocyte membrane-1 (PfEMP-1) Rosettins	PfEMP-1 PfEMP-3 Histidine-rich protein-1 (HRP-1) Ring surface protein-1 + 2 (RSP1/2) Modified band-3 (Pfalhesin) Cytoadherence-linked asexual gene protein (CLAG)	Glycosylphosphatidylinositol (GPI)-anchored molecules Phospholipid Hemazoin
Molecules of host cell origin	Glycophorin A (Gp-A) Gp-B Gp-C Sialic acid α2–3 linkage Sialic acid independent pathways-as yet unspecified	CD36 Rosettins Blood group A Complement receptor-1 (CR1)	CD36 Thrombospondin Intercellular adhesion molecule (ICAM-1) (ICAM-2) Vascular cellular adhesion molecule (VCAM-1) Platelet endothelial cellular adhesion molecule (PECAM-1) E-selectin P-selectin Chondroitin sulfate A (CSA) Hyaluronic acid (HA) Heparan sulfate-like glycosaminoglycans (GAG) $\alpha_v\beta_3$ integrin	CD 36 on monocyte/macrophages Red cell membrane
Molecules in the host serum/plasma	Immunoglobulin	Nonimmune IgM Immune immunoglobulin Other undefined factors	Immune immunoglobulin	Unknown

Table 166.1 Major interactions of red cell invasion, rosetting, cytoadherence and TNF induction and some of the molecules involved in the pathogenesis of falciparum malaria.

Cytoadherence

Cytoadherence, the process whereby mature infected cells specifically bind to endothelial cells in postcapillary venules, appears to play a central role in the pathogenesis of falciparum malaria, possibly by localizing mature forms of the parasite in critical organs such as the brain.[6] In addition, cytoadherence of mature parasites:

- prevents their passage through the spleen, a major site of parasite destruction;
- localizes maturing parasites at sites of reduced oxygen tension, which favors parasite growth; and
- may facilitate the invasion of uninfected red cells.

However, despite these effects many studies have failed to find an association between cytoadherence and severe disease.[7] Cytoadherent parasites presumably lead to microvascular obstruction, although the role and extent of this obstruction remain unclear. Cytoadherence may also serve to localize the effect of parasite toxins, which lead to endothelial cell activation and damage as a result of cytokine release.

The molecular interactions that occur in cytoadherence have been studied in some detail. During parasite maturation a number of regular, symmetrically arranged 'knobs' appear on the surface of the infected cell. These knobs are thought to be the sites at which the parasitized red cell attaches to the endothelial cell. A number of high-molecular weight parasite proteins protrude from these knobs, of which the best known is the *P. falciparum* erythrocyte membrane protein (PfEMP)-1 coded for by the *var* (variant) genes. A single parasite may be capable of expressing up to 50 variants of PfEMP-1. Other possible adhesive parasite antigens on the infected red cell surface include a molecule called sequestrin and a modified form of band 3 (the main anion transporter of the red cell) called pfalhesin.

In turn PfEMP-1 may bind to a number of potential receptors on the surface of endothelial cell. These include:

- the adhesion molecule CD36;
- the bridging molecule thrombospondin (a major component of the platelet a granule);
- two members of the immunoglobulin superfamily – intercellular adhesion molecule 1 (ICAM-1) and vascular cell adhesion molecule;
- E-selectin; and

- the recently described glycosaminoglycan, chondroitin sulfate A (see Table 166.1).

Whether PfEMP-1 is the molecule that binds to all of the above molecules has yet to be established. It appears that ICAM-1 and CD36 are the major ligands;[8] ICAM-1 acts as a rolling receptor, whereas CD36 and thrombospondin seem to be involved in more stable interactions. Cytokines, especially TNF-α, can upregulate the expression of ICAM-1. How cytoadherence leads to severe pathology remains an unresolved issue.

Rosetting

In rosetting, red cells containing the more mature stages of parasite bind uninfected red cells to their surface. The mechanisms by which rosetting leads to disease remain obscure, but may involve microcirculatory obstruction. Rosetting falciparum parasites have been associated with severe disease,[9] but both *P. vivax* and *P. ovale* are capable of rosetting without causing severe disease. The specific molecules involved in rosetting on the infected and uninfected red cell have not been fully characterized, although PfEMP-1 and small (between 20 and 40kDa) molecular weight 'rosettins' on the parasitized cell and CD36 and the ABO blood group molecules on the uninfected cell have been implicated (see Table 166.1). Most recently the complement receptor CR1, which is present at low levels (approximately 250 copies per cell) on uninfected cells, has been implicated as binding to PfEMP-1 and playing a role in rosetting.[10]

Parasite toxins and cytokines

The paroxysmal increase of many cytokines, notably TNF-α and interferon-γ, during a febrile episode and coinciding with rupture of schizont-infected red cells suggests the release of a toxin. Attempts to identify a definitive malarial 'toxin' remain unproductive. Parasite molecules anchored in the red cell membrane by a glycosyl phosphotidylinositol (GPI) structure are favored candidates, but other molecules have been proposed, including an as yet undefined phospholipoprotein molecule and protease-sensitive components associated with malarial pigment (hemozoin). Antibodies to GPI anchors are associated with a lack of disease in adults. However, even products from lysed uninfected red cells are capable of inducing cytokine release from macrophages.

Different falciparum parasite lines vary in their capacity to stimulate TNF-α from macrophages. It is not known whether this observation is due to a quantitative or qualitative attribute of the toxin or why infection by *P. vivax*, sometimes leading to TNF levels comparable with falciparum malaria, results in relatively benign disease. This may be because *P. vivax* does not exhibit cytoadherence which would localize effects of the parasite in critical organs such as the brain.

It is proposed that such a malarial toxin or toxins lead to the release of the cytokines TNF-α interferon-γ and interleukin (IL)-1 among others. There is a good correlation between high levels of TNF-α and the outcome of falciparum malaria. Production and release of TNF-α could account for the fever, leukocytosis, enhanced sequestration, hypoglycemia, acidosis and dyserythropoiesis, and possibly even the impaired consciousness observed in malaria. In addition, TNF-α may upregulate the expression of adhesion molecules such as ICAM-1 and other receptors that bind the parasitized red cell. Other cytokines may be synergistic.

Pathophysiologic events leading to cerebral malaria

There is a debate as to whether the major mechanism in the pathogenesis of malaria is:

- ischemia due to obstruction of the microcirculation by sequestering parasites; or
- release of mediators induced by the parasite toxin(s).

A model of the pathogenesis of cerebral malaria due to *P. falciparum* needs to take into account the delicate interplay between both factors, which may prove to be equally relevant. For example, sequestration, the result of rosetting and cytoadherence of infected cells, would not only lead to microvascular obstruction, but could also localize the effect of parasite toxins when released by rupturing schizonts.

In cerebral malaria there appears to be no reduction in total cerebral blood flow, although blood flow is low relative to the cerebral arterial oxygen content.[11] Cerebral malaria can occur in the absence of a localized inflammatory cell response, direct tissue invasion, a breakdown in the blood–brain barrier, cerebral edema, disseminated intravascular coagulation and hypoglycemia. The cerebrospinal fluid in cerebral malaria shows no increase in cell number or protein concentration and may only show a raised lactate concentration, and in some cases, especially in children, a raised opening pressure.[12] A raised cell count or protein concentration should cause one to think of an alternative or additional diagnosis.

Raised intracranial pressure has been invoked in the pathogenesis of cerebral malaria in children in Africa, but its role in adult disease has yet to be determined, although the volume of the brain is increased, probably as a result of sequestration and compensatory vasodilation of the cerebral vasculature.[13]

Tissue infarction is not a major feature of cerebral malaria. In addition, the majority of patients who recover from coma due to malaria appear to have few, if any, neurologic sequelae, in contrast to those resulting from other neurologic infections of equal severity.

Small microhemorrhages may occur around capillaries and venules, but there are few platelets or microthrombi.

The syndrome of cerebral malaria appears to be related to the tight packing of schizonts in the small capillaries of the brain.[14] This process is brought about by sequestration, which in turn results from cytoadherence, rosetting or the decreased deformability of infected cells or a combination of these factors.

PREVENTION

There are a number of points in the malaria parasite's life cycle where the infection can be interrupted. This mainly involves reduced mosquito contact and the use of antimalarial chemoprophylaxis. Vaccination against malaria is currently not a reality.

Antimosquito measures

In endemic areas those at risk should:

- sleep in properly screened rooms;
- use mosquito nets without holes and impregnated with permethrin and tucked in carefully under the mattress before nightfall;
- wear long-sleeved clothing and long trousers when outdoors after sunset; and
- use other adjuncts – insect spray (usually containing permethrin) and mosquito coils or repellents such as diethyltoluamide, DEET or citronella.

For those living in highly endemic areas, the use of permethrin-impregnated bednets has been found to reduce both malarial morbidity and mortality. However, problems remain regarding cost, state of repair of the net, regular impregnation and how the bednets might change the rate of acquisition of immunity and consequently the pattern of disease, especially relating to severity. By protecting the very young against the severe manifestations of malaria, it is argued that severe complications may be deferred until they are older, but this remains a theoretic possibility only.

Malarial chemoprophylaxis

The spread of drug-resistant *P. falciparum* malaria and awareness that some of the more effective combination drugs, such as pyrimethamine with sulfadoxine (Fansidar) and pyrimethamine with dap-

BRIEF GUIDELINES FOR THE CHEMOPROPHYLAXIS OF MALARIA		
Chemoprophylaxis	**Area to be visited**	**Dose/comments**
None	North Africa (Morocco, Algeria, Tunisia, Libya, tourist areas of Egypt) Tourist areas of South East Asia (Thailand, Philippines, Hong Kong, Singapore, Bali, China)	Antimosquito measures should still be applied. Risk of other vector-borne diseases still possible
Chloroquine **or** proguanil (Paludrine)	Middle East (including summer months in rural Egypt and Turkey) Central America Rural Mauritius	300mg base (2 tablets) once per week 200mg (2 tablets) once per day
Chloroquine and proguanil	Indian subcontinent Afghanistan and Iran South America	Doses as above. Also indicated: • in pregnancy (safe) • in children (liquid formulations) • when other antimalarials cannot be tolerated
Mefloquine (Lariam), doxycycline or Malarone (each tablet contains atovaquone 250mg and proguanil 100mg)	Sub-Saharan Africa, e.g. Cameroon, Kenya, Malawi, Tanzania, Uganda, Zaire, Zambia All rural areas of SE Asia, Papua New Guinea, Solomon Islands and Vanuatu	*Mefloquine*: 250mg (1 tablet) per week. Use especially in areas of high risk. Use up to 1 year Contraindicated in epilepsy and psychiatric disorders *Doxycycline*: 100mg per day. Beware light sensitization *Malarone*: Start 1 day before entry, during and 1 week after exit from a malarious area
Doxycycline	As above and mefloquine-resistant parts of South East Asia	100mg daily Can be used as an alternative to mefloquine, Malarone or chloroquine and proguanil where these are not tolerated

Table 166.2 Brief guidelines for the chemoprophylaxis of malaria. Specialist advice should be sought for details.

sone (Maloprim) and amodiaquine (Camoquin), may rarely have severe and sometimes fatal side-effects[15] have complicated malarial chemoprophylaxis. The risk of contracting malaria in any given country or situation needs to be weighed constantly against the risk of a serious adverse reaction to any drug used. In the absence of adequate data, this becomes difficult. Compliance is of extreme importance because, although those who comply poorly have a similar attack rate, their risk of death is much greater than that of individuals on no prophylaxis.

A brief guide to antimalarial chemoprophylaxis is shown in Table 166.2. If there is any doubt, specialist advice should be sought (see also Chapter 143). Chemoprophylaxis should start 1 week before entering an endemic area (to ensure adequate blood levels and to evaluate any potential side-effects), and continue while within such an area and for 4 weeks after return except in the use of Malarone which can be commenced on the day before entry into a malarious area and continue for a week after leaving. Chloroquine, two tablets (300mg base) once a week, together with proguanil, two tablets (200mg) daily, is one of the safest and most inexpensive regimens, but is of diminishing efficacy. These drugs have only minor side-effects, the commonest being difficulty in visual accommodation in the case of chloroquine and mouth ulcers with proguanil. There is increasing use of mefloquine one tablet (250mg) weekly, doxycycline one tablet (100mg) daily and Malarone one tablet daily, by travelers to sub-Saharan Africa, Papua New Guinea and the Solomon Islands because of chloroquine resistance.[15] The main side effects of mefloquine are neuropsychiatric and are of varying severity. Doxycycline can lead to light sensitization and Malarone can cause gastroenterological upset.

More detailed and specialist advice should be sought in specialized circumstances, including for:

- long-term visitors,
- children under 12 years of age,
- individuals who have drug allergies, immunosuppression because of disease or therapy, or epilepsy, and
- women who are pregnant.

In individuals born and living in an endemic area chemoprophylaxis should be made available for those with sickle cell disease and pregnant women.

Vaccination

An effective and safe malarial vaccine is still not available. A live attenuated whole sporozoite vaccine has been shown to work, but only on a very small scale and is impractical for widespread use. Results with the SPf66 vaccine, a synthetic peptide, have proved disappointing. Most recently a vaccine using part of the circumsporozoite protein linked to hepatitis B surface antigen and administered in a formulation with a novel adjuvant has shown preliminary promise but protection appears short-lived. A DNA-based vaccine has also been tested.[16]

CLINICAL FEATURES

The most frequent presentation of malaria is that of a pronounced febrile illness with rigors. However, the clinical features of malaria can be extremely diverse because the parasitized red cell circulates to every organ and tissue within the body and therefore has the

MANIFESTATIONS OF SEVERE MALARIA REQUIRING SPECIAL MANAGEMENT	
Manifestation	**Comment**
Cerebral malaria	Coma with peripheral parasitemia and other causes of encephalopathy excluded
Severe anemia	Normocytic anemia with hemoglobin <50g/l (5gm/dl) (<15% hematocrit) in presence of parasitemia >10,000/μl
Respiratory distress	Pulmonary edema or adult respiratory distress syndrome
Renal failure	Urine output of less than 400ml/24h (or less than 12ml/kg in children) and a serum creatinine >3.0mg/dl (265μmol/l)
Hypoglycemia	Whole blood glucose <40mg/dl (2.2mmol/l)
Circulatory collapse (shock)	Systolic blood pressure less than 70mmHg or core skin temperature difference >18°F (10°C)
Coagulation failure	Spontaneous bleeding or laboratory evidence of disseminated intravascular coagulation
Impaired consciousness of any degree, prostration, jaundice, intractable vomiting, parasitemia ≥2%	In nonimmune individuals should be managed as severe malaria (i.e. with parenteral antimalarials)

Table 166.3 Manifestations of severe malaria requiring special management.

potential for producing a wide variety of pathology. In endemic areas the manifestations of severe disease in children are mainly those of cerebral malaria, often with convulsions, respiratory distress and severe anemia (Table 166.3), whereas adults are more likely to develop multiorgan failure (e.g. renal failure) and are less likely to have convulsions or severe anemia. Complications of prolonged malarial infection such as hyperactive malarial splenomegaly (HMS) and nephrotic syndrome due to *P. malariae* infection are rare in travelers.

Mild malaria

The incubation period for malaria is variable, but under optimal conditions may be as short as 7 days and in exceptional cases up to 20 years, as in the case of *P. malariae* infections. The majority (>90%) of *P. falciparum* infections in travelers occur within 6 weeks of leaving an endemic area.

The clinical presentation of mild malaria with rigors is well known. There is usually a history of travel to or residence within an endemic area. A history of even the best compliance with the most effective antimalarial chemoprophylaxis cannot exclude the diagnosis. There may be a prodromal period of tiredness and aching. The features of a classic paroxysm are:

- an abrupt onset of an initial 'cold stage' associated with dramatic rigors in which the patient visibly shakes;
- an ensuing 'hot stage' during which the patient may have a temperature of well over 104°F (40°C), may be restless and excitable, and may vomit or convulse; and
- finally, the sweating stage, during which the patient defervesces and may fall asleep.

Such a paroxysm may last 6–10 hours and a prolonged asymptomatic period may follow and last 38–42 hours in the case of *P. vivax* and *P. ovale* infections and 62–66 hours in *P. malariae* infections. In *P. falciparum* infections the periodicity of fever tends to be less predictable and the fever may be continuous. There may be an accompanying headache, cough, myalgia (flu-like symptoms), diarrhea and mild jaundice.

Malaria is rarely, if ever, the cause of lymphadenopathy, pharyngitis or a rash, and alternative explanations need to be considered for these specific symptoms.

Severe malaria

Definitions of the clinical manifestations of severe falciparum malaria are included in Table 166.3.[17] However, many of these definitions are for study purposes in order to compare data from different parts of the world, especially for the standardization of clinical trials, and must be taken in context. For example, any degree of impairment of consciousness, prostration, jaundice or evidence of renal impairment, especially in a nonimmune individual, should be taken seriously. Furthermore, parenteral therapy is regarded by many as necessary for a parasitemia of 2% or above in a nonimmune patient and in the presence of vomiting.

Cerebral malaria

Cerebral malaria in which the patient passes from drowsiness into coma may develop insidiously over a few days or abruptly within 1–2 hours and is often heralded by a convulsion. The majority of patients have no focal neurologic signs, but there may be a wide variety of neurologic manifestations such as a cranial nerve palsy, monoplegia or hemiplegia, extensor posturing, decerebrate or decorticate rigidity, conjugate or even dysconjugate eye movements, grinding of the teeth (bruxism) or hiccoughs. Some patients have retinal hemorrhages (Fig. 166.3), sometimes with extramacular whitening of

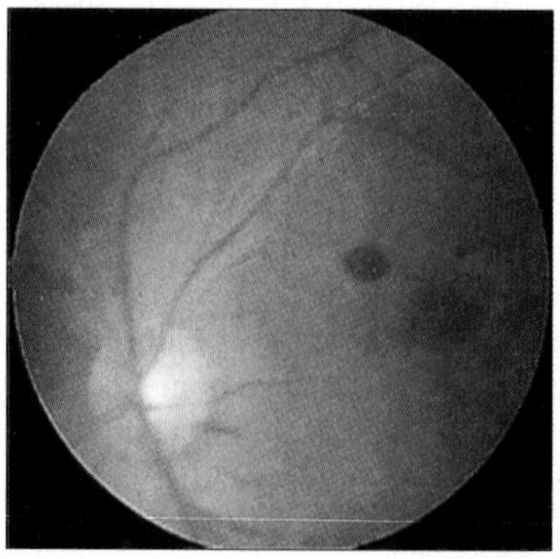

Fig. 166.3 Retinal hemorrhage in severe *falciparum* malaria. Examination of the fundus is important in the physical examination of a patient with severe *falciparum* malaria as it can give some indication as to prognosis. In this case the hemorrhage is near the macula. Such hemorrhages have been found in as many as 18–30% of patients with cerebral malaria. In children, additional changes of extramacular whitening and changes in which the vessels turn white in isolated segments, often at branch points, occur.

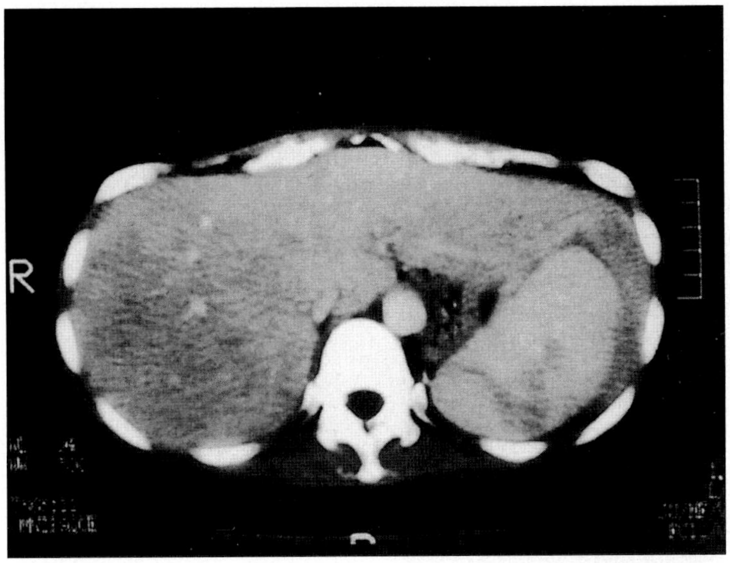

Fig. 166.4 Massive hepatosplenomegaly in a patient with severe malarial anemia due to *P. falciparum*. This CT scan of the abdomen was taken in a traveler from West Africa who, after a prolonged history of fevers, presented with a hemoglobin concentration of less than 50g/l. The scan shows a massively enlarged liver, the left lobe of which is encircling an equally enlarged spleen.

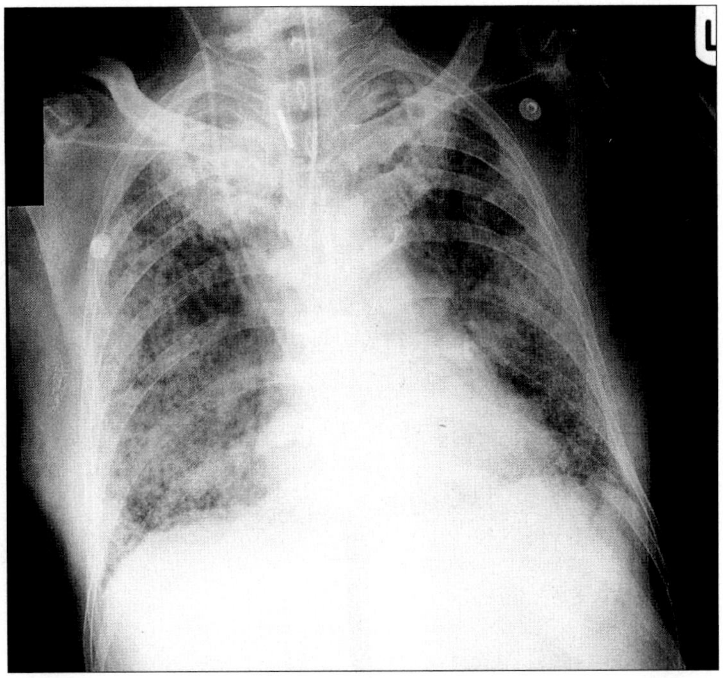

Fig. 166.5 Chest radiograph of a patient with acute respiratory distress sydrome (ARDS) due to *falciparum* malaria. This X-ray shows new, bilateral, diffuse, homogeneous pulmonary infiltrates without cardiac failure, fluid overload, chest infection or chronic lung disease in an adult with severe *falciparum* malaria. The prognosis is poor. This condition is rare in children.

the fundus and retinal vessel changes where they turn white in isolated segments, particularly at branch points. Coma in malaria may not only be due to primary neurologic involvement, but may also be part of a prolonged postictal state, status epilepticus or a severe metabolic disorder such as acidosis or hypoglycemia. Thus drowsiness and coma may be the result of a number of different pathological processes.

Anemia

The anemia of falciparum malaria is both complex and multifactorial.[18,19] The fall in hemoglobin is often far in excess of what can be accounted for by the loss of infected red blood cells alone. The major mechanisms in the pathogenesis of anemia are those of:

- red cell destruction because of rupture of infected cells, removal of uninfected cells due to antibody sensitization or other physicochemical changes, and increased reticuloendothelial activity, particularly in organs such as the spleen; and
- decreased red cell production due to marrow hypoplasia as seen in acute infections and dyserythropoiesis, a morphologic appearance that in functional terms results in ineffective erythropoiesis.

Two clinical presentations of anemia predominate which represent the ends of a clinical spectrum.

- Severe acute malaria in which anemia supervenes but only after a few days of severe illness such as cerebral malaria. There may be respiratory distress with acidosis, cardiac failure (often difficult to diagnose in children), poor tissue perfusion and death. There is shortened red cell survival (hemolysis) and evidence of bone marrow suppression despite the progressive fall in hematocrit.
- Severe anemia in patients in whom the illness has developed insidiously over a period of days or sometimes weeks (Fig. 166.4). These patients are often very young children living in endemic areas and are anemic when first seen. They have splenomegaly of varying degree and the peripheral blood film may show only scant asexual parasitemia. The bone marrow often shows a picture of dyserythropoiesis, although in this setting erythropoietin levels may be raised but not necessarily appropriate for the degree of anemia. In many cases gametocytes and malarial pigment are seen in phagocytic cells. Because the development of this type of anemia is slow, there is adaptation to the low hematocrit and the clinical condition may often conceal the severity of the underlying anemia.

Respiratory distress

Respiratory distress is manifest by rapid labored breathing and sometimes abnormal rhythms of respiration.[20] In children there may be intercostal recession, use of the accessory muscles of respiration and flaring of the alar nasae, making it difficult to differentiate from an acute respiratory infection.

Respiratory distress in patients with malaria may be the result of a number of pathologies:

- respiratory compensation for a profound metabolic acidosis in the majority of cases;
- a direct effect of the parasite or raised intracranial pressure on the respiratory center in the brainstem;
- secondary lung infection as a consequence of immunosuppression;
- air hunger as a result of severe anemia; and
- pulmonary edema as a consequence of hypoalbuminemia, iatrogenic fluid overload or direct alveolar capillary damage by parasites and neutrophils leading to the acute respiratory distress syndrome (Fig. 166.5);
- overuse of anticonvulsants, particularly phenobarbitone which depresses the respiratory center drive.

Identification of these different causes of respiratory distress is important as they each require different modalities of management.

Acidosis

Acidosis (base excess $\leq$12) or acidemia (pH $<$7.3) in malaria indicates a poor prognosis and can be due to a number of causes:[21]

- poor tissue perfusion, in some cases due to hypovolemia, leading to reduced oxygen delivery;
- lactate production by the parasite;
- lactate generation as a result of cytokine activity, especially TNF, in the acute phase response;

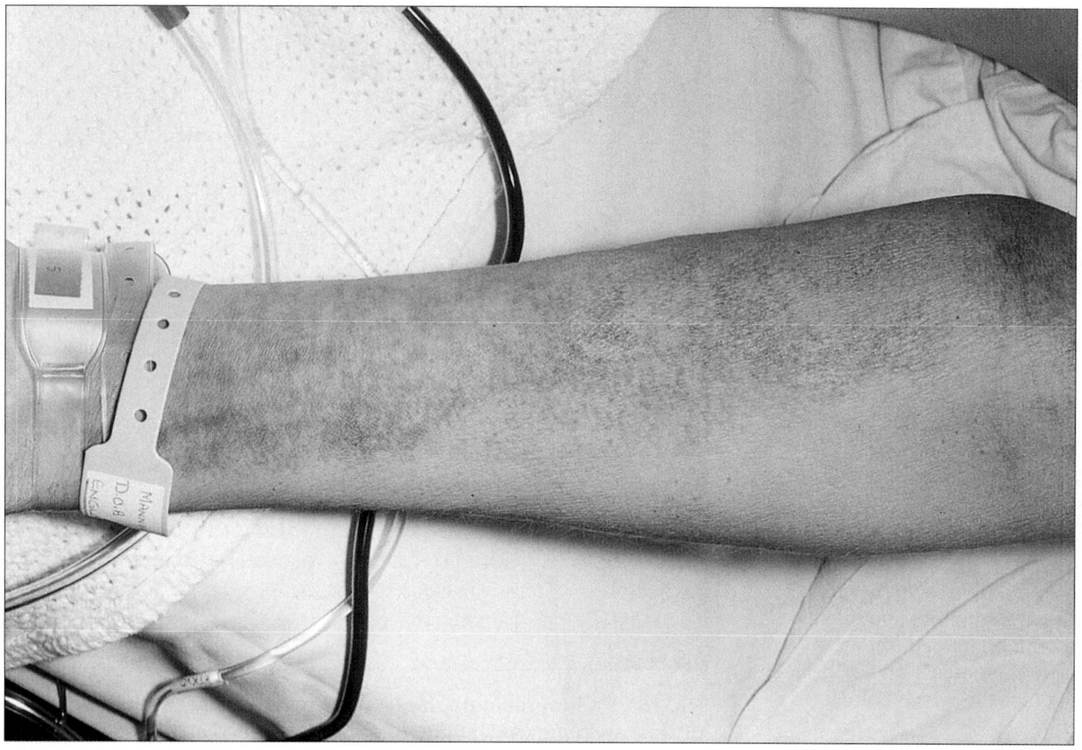

Fig. 166.6 Disseminated intravascular coagulation in *falciparum* malaria. Bleeding into the skin seen in a patient with a thrombocytopenia, a prolonged prothrombin time, increased fibrinogen degradation products and hypofibrinogenemia. The patient had no signs of cerebral malaria.

- reduced hepatic blood flow and therefore lactate clearance;
- impaired renal function and therefore acid excretion; and
- exogenous acids due to aspirin (salicylate) administration.[22]

Hypoglycemia

The characteristic clinical manifestations of hypoglycemia may not be evident in malaria, often because the patient is already unconscious. Suspicion of this important complication is often circumstantial: on admission in children and during quinine therapy in adults. The cause of hypoglycemia is multifactorial:[23]

- depletion of glucose stores because of starvation or malnutrition;
- malabsorption of glucose due to decreased splanchnic blood flow;
- increased tissue metabolism of glucose;
- parasite utilization of glucose;
- cytokine-induced impairment of gluconeogenesis; and
- hyperinsulinemia due to quinine therapy.

Anaerobic metabolism of glucose leads to acidemia and the production of lactate. Acidemia (blood pH <7.3) and hyperlactatemia are important prognostic factors in severe malaria. Acidemia is associated with respiratory rhythm abnormalities (especially a slow respiratory rhythm) and death.

Shock

Unlike the sepsis syndrome, shock is relatively rare in severe malaria. In most cases the blood pressure of patients with malaria is at the lower end of the normal range, probably due to vasodilatation. Marked hypotension in a few cases may be the result of dehydration, but is more commonly due to concomitant sepsis. Care should be taken to look for signs of sepsis, especially septicaemia and respiratory and urinary tract infection.

Bleeding

Bleeding due to the commonly occurring thrombocytopenia in malaria is rare. Bleeding is more likely to occur in the setting of disseminated intravascular coagulation (Fig. 166.6). However, more often there is only subtle activation of the coagulation cascade with a reduction in antithrombin III concentration, an increase in thrombin–antithrombin III complexes and a reduction in factor XII and prekallikrein activities, which do not appear to be clinically significant.[24]

Fig. 166.7 Blackwater fever. Urine specimen on admission (left) and days 2, 3 and 4 in a cross-Africa traveler with *falciparum* malaria on quinine treatment, showing the characteristic dark urine of blackwater fever, which showed gradual clearing. The same patient presented with a fever 1 week later and when treated presumptively for malaria with quinine, developed dark urine once again. Renal function was only mildly impaired.

Renal involvement and blackwater fever

A degree of renal impairment, often due to hypovolemia but not always clinically evident, almost always occurs in severe malaria. Acute renal failure, which is less common, may occur in malaria both during the acute parasitemic phase, but also after parasite clearance.[25] In addition, the acute renal failure of malaria may be nonoliguric. Although the urinary manifestation of blackwater fever may be dramatic (Fig. 166.7), occurring in the setting of glucose-6-phosphate dehydrogenase (G6PD) deficiency or a semi-immune patient given quinine, it does not invariably lead to renal failure and appears to be considerably more benign than the classically described syndrome.[26]

Differential diagnosis

Malaria may have little to distinguish it from other febrile illnesses. In the absence of a travel history, malaria can be transmitted in 'airport malaria' where infected mosquitoes are brought from endemic areas on planes or due to autochthonous spread during a hot summer in a nonendemic area where infected individuals pass the infection on to the local mosquito population. Malaria must also be considered in patients with a fever after blood transfusion, organ transplantation or needlestick injury. A critical step in the diagnosis of malaria, especially outside endemic areas, is consideration of the possibility of this diagnosis. A travel history should now be a routine part of any clinical consultation, especially in patients with a fever. Malaria needs to be excluded in any febrile patient in or returning from an endemic country whether or not they have been taking antimalarials. No antimalarial at present can guarantee absolute protection.

Malaria is a great mimic and must enter the differential diagnosis of a number of clinical presentations.

- In the acute presentation fever due to malaria needs to be differentiated from typhoid, viral illnesses such as dengue fever and influenza, brucellosis and respiratory and urinary tract infections. Less common causes of tropical fevers include leishmaniasis, trypanosomiasis, rickettsial infections and relapsing fevers.
- The coma of cerebral malaria need to be differentiated from meningitis (including tuberculous meningitis), encephalitis, enteric fevers, trypanosomiasis, brain abscess and other causes of coma (see Chapter 153).
- The anemia of malaria can be confused with other common causes of hemolytic anemia in the tropics such as that due to the hemoglobinopathies (e.g. sickle-cell disease, thalassemia), G6PD deficiency, and the South East Asian form of ovalocytosis. The anemia of malaria must be differentiated from that of iron, folate or vitamin B12 deficiency.
- The renal failure of malaria must be distinguished from renal impairment due to massive intravascular hemolysis seen in G6PD deficiency, sickle-cell disease, leptospirosis, snake envenomation, use of traditional herbal medicines and chronic renal disease resulting from glomerulonephritis and hypertension.
- The jaundice and hepatomegaly of malaria must be distinguished from that of viral hepatitis (A, B and E, cytomegalovirus and Epstein–Barr virus infections), leptospirosis, yellow fever, biliary disease and drug-induced disease, including alcohol.

Clinical diagnosis on its own is notoriously inaccurate and may be incorrect in up to 50% of cases.

DIAGNOSIS

The definitive diagnosis of malaria is made by prompt microscopic examination of thick and thin blood films. There is no need to wait for a fever peak before carrying out a blood film as parasites are often present throughout the red cell cycle. Malarial chemoprophylaxis should be withheld during investigation for malaria as antimalarials can suppress peripheral parasitemia.

The most common abnormality on full blood count is thrombocytopenia, especially in the nonimmune. This is thought to be largely splenic pooling of platelets but also platelet activation.[34] The total white count is usually in the normal range but often there is a lymphopenia on presentation due to lymphocyte redistribution and more recently, apoptosis of lymphocytes has been identified in falciparum malaria.[35]

Thick blood films

One or two drops of blood from a fingerprick are stirred in a circle on a glass slide, allowed to air dry and then stained with Giemsa or Field's

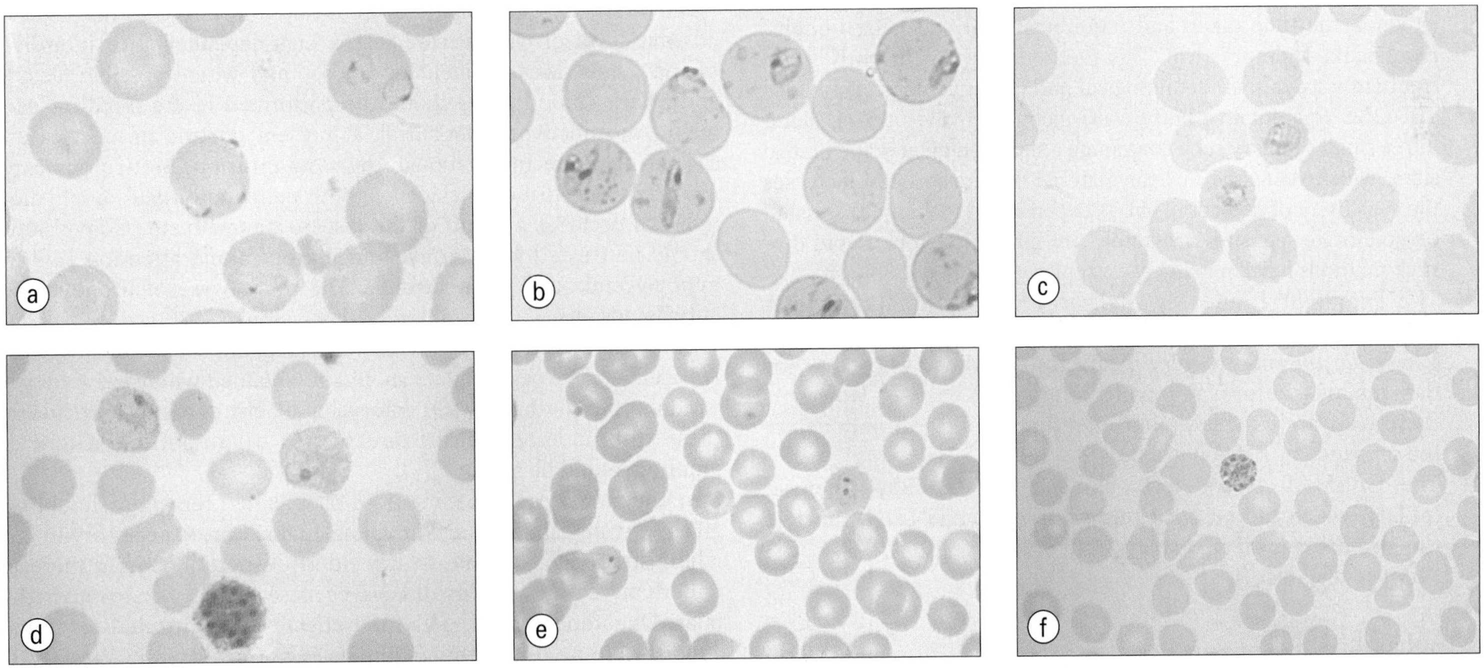

Fig. 166.8 Thin blood films from patients with malaria. (a) Delicate small ring forms of *Plasmodium falciparum* showing multiply infected red cells and a characteristic 'appliqué' form in the uppermost parasite in the central red cell where the parasite appears as if it is applied to the surface, rather than within the red cell. (b) Ring forms of *P. falciparum* in a heavy infection and where the pH of the stain is 7.2 rather than 6.7 showing the irregular, basophilic Maurer's clefts in the cytoplasm of infected cells characteristic of *P. falciparum*. (c) Very early trophozoites of *P. falciparum* in the peripheral blood film of a patient with severe disease. The relative size and presence of pigment indicate the greater maturity of the parasite and may indicate a poorer prognosis. (d) Peripheral blood film from a patient with *vivax* malaria showing mixed ring and schizont forms. The ring forms are far more fleshy and ameboid and the cytoplasm of the infected cell shows the characteristic regular and eosinophilic Schüffner's dots, which help in diagnosis. (e) Peripheral blood film from a patient with *ovale* malaria showing a small ring form on the left, which could quite easily be mistaken for *P. falciparum*. The larger central parasite has enlarged the cell into an oval shape and has also formed a fimbriated fringe at the upper pole of the cell. (f) Peripheral blood film from a patient with *malariae* malaria showing the characteristic rosette schizont with daughter merozoites (usually eight) around a central piece of pigment (*hemazoin*). The ring forms of this species characteristically form a band stretching across the width of the red cell.

stain. With this method, the red cells lyse whereas the white cells and parasites remain intact. Parasites are identified by recognizing both the eosinophilic nucleus and the basophilic cytoplasm of the malarial parasite. Parasite density can be related to the number of white cells present. This method has far greater sensitivity than the thin blood film.

Thin blood films

A thin film is produced by spreading a small drop of blood across a slide using the edge of a second slide, thereby producing a monolayer of red cells. Fixation is usually with methanol and the staining technique is as for the thick blood film (optimally at pH 7.2). The red cells remain intact. The thin blood film allows accurate speciation of the parasite and quantitation, in which the number of parasites is related to the number of red cells present. It is important that parasites are accurately recognized, as platelets or debris can often be mistaken for parasites. The size, shape and stippling of the red cell cytoplasm help in the speciation of the parasite. Examples of the four species are shown in Figure 166.8.

Other valuable information can be obtained from the blood film, especially in severe disease. Careful staging of the parasites in the peripheral blood can indicate disease severity as the presence of more mature parasites may reflect a greater proportion of sequestered parasites and indicate more severe disease (Fig. 166.8).[27] The presence of malarial pigment in more than 5% of neutrophils provides some indication of the total parasite load and is associated with a poor prognosis.[28]

Other methods

Malaria can be diagnosed using other methods, but each has its own drawbacks with regard to time, cost or being nonquantitative or nonspecific.

- The polymerase chain reaction is useful for making an accurate species diagnosis and detecting low level parasitemias, but its expense, the time taken and requirement for specialized equipment make it impractical. This methodology is currently more frequently used in epidemiological and pharmacological studies.
- The QBC (quantitative buffy coat) method involves taking blood into a small capillary tube containing a float and an acridine orange stain, which stains the nuclear material of parasites and increases the sensitivity of detection, but its expense and inability to speciate or quantitate parasites accurately are limiting factors. Rapid dipstick methods have in many cases replaced this methodology.
- The ParaSight F and the Malaria PF antigen capture tests use a monoclonal antibody to the histidine-rich protein 2 of *P. falciparum* and are very useful tests in those who have not had malaria before, requiring minimal expertise. However, these tests are expensive, not quantitative and can only detect the presence of *P. falciparum*.
- The OptiMAL test detects parasite lactate dehydrogenase (pLDH) which can be distinguished from human LDH. This test can also distinguish *falciparum* from *vivax* infections.
- Autopsy diagnosis.

MANAGEMENT

Once a definitive diagnosis of malaria has been made treatment with specific antimalarial drugs can be initiated.[29]

Non-*falciparum* malaria

Malaria due to *P. vivax, P. ovale* or *P. malariae* requires a standard course of treatment with chloroquine, which usually leads to defervescence (Table 166.4). Chloroquine-resistant asexual forms of *P. vivax* have recently been documented and may require quinine treatment. In the case of *P. vivax* and *P. ovale* malaria treatment with an 8-aminoquinoline (primaquine) is given to eradicate the exoerythrocytic forms, especially the hypnozoites responsible for relapses. Levels of G6PD should be measured in all patients before they are given primaquine, an oxidant drug which can lead to major hemolysis in G6PD-deficient individuals. Treatment with primaquine should be delayed until after delivery and/or breastfeeding in pregnant women. Primaquine-resistant *vivax* hypnozoites have been identified which require more prolonged (often 3 weeks) and higher dose (22.5mg/day) therapy.

Falciparum malaria

Mild falciparum *malaria*

In endemic areas the treatment of malaria in children involves the use of drugs that are locally affordable and appropriate. For this reason mild *falciparum* malaria in many parts of Africa is still treated with chloroquine as for non-*falciparum* malaria and recrudescences are treated with pyrimethamine/sulfadoxine (Fansidar). For travelers and in areas where there is resistance to chloroquine and pyrimethamine/sulfadoxine, the mainstay of treatment is oral quinine sulfate used as shown in Table 166.4, followed by the use of pyrimethamine/sulfadoxine or doxycycline to eradicate remaining asexual forms of the parasite. Mefloquine may be used and more recently drug combinations such as atovaquone with proguanil (Malarone) and artemether/lumefantrine (Coartemether) have been successfully used. Whichever drug is used, parasitemia may paradoxically rise in the first 24–36 hours and is not generally indicative of treatment failure.

Severe falciparum *malaria*

The management of severe *falciparum* malaria constitutes a medical emergency.[29] The diagnosis needs to be confirmed microscopically and intravenous access obtained as soon as possible. Depending upon the clinical manifestations, the investigations detailed in Table 166.5 should be carried out.

Patients with severe malaria should be transferred to the highest possible level of clinical care (e.g. a high-dependency or intensive therapy unit). Measurement of glucose and where possible lactate and arterial blood gases should be performed in the initial assessment. An effective antimalarial, at present quinine in most cases, should be given intravenously by slow infusion. Meticulous care must be given to fluid balance as both dehydration and overhydration can occur as a result of the disease or treatment. Convulsions should be treated with intravenous diazepam and attention paid to hypoglycemia and hyponatremia. The routine use of prophylactic anticonvulsants is unwarranted.

Blood should be taken for cross-matching and coagulation studies. A baseline electrocardiogram should be obtained with careful observation of the rhythm and QT interval in elderly patients, particularly those with underlying heart disease, and where possible a cardiac monitor should be set up.

In endemic areas a loading dose of quinine (20mg/kg) should be given to young children and fit young adults. Care is necessary in the administration of quinine to the elderly, especially where there is underlying cardiovascular disease because of the risks of arrhythmias. Quinidine can be safely and effectively substituted for intravenous quinine (intravenous quinine is not available in the USA). Cardiac dysrhythmias and hypotension may occur and therefore quinidine should be administered in an ICU setting.

Recent evidence in childhood malaria has shown that blood transfusion may be of benefit in patients who have respiratory distress and metabolic acidosis.[30] In units with appropriate facilities complicated hyperparasitemia may be treated with exchange transfusion. The use of exchange transfusion is controversial,[31] but should be considered where safe blood is available for all patients in whom the parasitemia exceeds an arbitrary 30% and for those in whom parasitemia is lower, but who:

SUMMARY OF THE DRUG TREATMENT OF MALARIA			
Type of malaria	**Drug**	**Dose**	**Comments**
Non-*falciparum* malaria	Chloroquine phosphate or sulfate (each tablet contains 150mg base)	Loading dose 600mg, 300mg 6 hours later, then 300mg daily for 2 days (i.e. 10 tablets)	Chloroquine and primaquine resistance now documented for *vivax* malaria
	Followed in *vivax* and *ovale* malaria by primaquine	15mg daily for 14 days	Not given in G6PD deficiency or 45mg weekly for 6 weeks with monitoring for hemolysis. Not given in pregnancy
***Falciparum* malaria**			
Mild (A range of treatments can be used depending on availability of drugs and choice of local practice)	Quinine sulfate	10mg (salt)/kg (usually 600mg) q8h po for 3–7 days (at a practical level when parasite clearance has been achieved for 24 hours)	Almost all patients develop cinchonism (ringing in the ears, deafness, nausea, vomiting, etc.) and especially if they have liver or renal impairment. Reduce dose to q12h if the parasite count is falling
	Followed by: doxycycline or pyrimethamine/sulfadoxine (Fansidar)	200mg loading dose, then 100mg daily for 6 days Single dose of three tablets (each tablet contains 500mg sulfadoxine and 25mg pyrimethamine)	Not for children or in pregnancy Mainly for malaria from West Africa; doxycycline is preferred with increasing resistance to Fansidar in Africa
	Atovaquone and proguanil (Malarone)	Four tablets daily for 3 days (each tablet contains atovaquone 250mg and proguanil 100mg)	Fewer side-effects than quinine – mainly gastrointestinal. Caution as newly approved drug
	Artemether and lumefantrine (Riamet)	Four tablets q12h for six doses (each tablet contains artemether 20mg and lumefantrine 120mg)	Relatively few side-effects. Caution as newly approved drug
	Mefloquine	750mg as a single dose, repeated after 6 hours	Contraindicated in early pregnancy and in patients who have a neuropsychiatric history
Severe	Quinine dihydrochloride	10mg (salt) per kg, q8h until parasites cleared, then doxycycline or Fansidar as above when the patient can take medication orally	Can induce hypoglycemia and cardiac arrhythmias; a loading dose 20mg/kg can be given to young otherwise healthy patients when hyperparasitemia cannot be treated by exchange transfusion
Severe – newer regimens	Artemether (a qinghaosu (artemesinin) derivative)	3.2mg/kg iv followed by 1.6mg/kg daily (usual adult dose 160mg followed by doses of 80mg)	An alternative to quinine given im. Doxycycline usually required as recrudescences are common
	Artesunate	2.4mg/kg iv followed by 1.2mg/kg at 12 and 24h; then 1.2mg/kg daily (usual adult dose 120mg followed by doses of 60mg)	Can be given intravenously as it is water soluble Also requires doxycycline as recrudescences are common
	Quinidine gluconate	7.5mg/kg q8h over 4h until patient can swallow	For emergencies and in the USA where intravenous quinine is not available. Requires ECG monitoring

Table 166.4 Summary of the drug treatment of malaria. G6PD, glucose-6-phosphate dehydrogenase.

- have manifestations of severe complicated malaria;
- have underlying medical complaints, such as diabetes mellitus and ischemic heart disease;
- are elderly; or
- are pregnant.

During the course of treatment useful parameters for monitoring progress should include twice-daily parasite counts, regular pH and blood gas measurements and, where appropriate, measurement of glucose and lactate concentrations and renal function.

Each patient needs to be assessed individually. During an infusion of quinine it is essential to monitor blood glucose carefully.

Elective ventilation needs to be considered where facilities are available, especially if there is severe acidosis, clear evidence of raised intracranial pressure or respiratory failure of any cause. Further details of investigations and management are given in Table 166.5.

Cerebral malaria

Antimalarials form the mainstay of treatment for cerebral malaria. A number of adjuvant therapies such as corticosteroids and heparin have been tried, but have not been shown to be effective. Some children and a few adults show evidence of raised intracranial pressure,

INVESTIGATIONS IN THE MANAGEMENT OF MALARIA		
Investigation	**Relevance**	**Management**
Full blood count		
Hemoglobin	Often not anemic on presentation; an indicator of duration of infection	Generally threshold for transfusion is high (e.g. <7.5g/dl (75g/l) in adults, <5g/dl (50g/l) with respiratory distress in children in an endemic area); self-recovery is generally rapid once the parasites have been removed
White blood cells	Normal in uncomplicated cases; often lymphopenic; in severe malaria a neutrophil leukocytosis is common	Generally none; secondary bacterial infection is common in severe cases and will require antibiotics
Platelets	Often low	Bleeding in the absence of DIC is uncommon
Blood film and parasite count	Essential for diagnosis and continuing management if high; more mature forms or pigment in ≥5% neutrophils indicates a poor prognosis (see text)	Depending upon setting and severity (see text) exchange transfusion might be required
Electrolytes		
Sodium	Often low; some cases are due to the syndrome of inappropriate antidiuretic hormone secretion, others due to an inability to secrete free water	Self-correcting with treatment
Potassium	Normal unless high due to acute renal failure	Dialysis may be necessary
Creatinine	Normal or high	Dialysis may be necessary
Calcium	Often low in severe cases	May need replacement especially if the QT interval is prolonged on the electrocardiogram
Magnesium	Can be low	May need replacement especially if the QT interval is prolonged on the electrocardiogram
Glucose and lactate		
Glucose	Often low in severe cases in children and also during quinine administration in adults; often there is an absence of classical symptoms and signs of hypoglycemia	Regular monitoring of glucose in severe cases; immediate administration of 50ml 50% glucose (0.5–1.0gm/kg in children)
Lactate	Raised in severe cases; good prognostic and progress marker from hour to hour; important to measure in spinal fluid if lumbar puncture performed	Important to ensure good tissue perfusion, especially by correction of any hypovolemia
Coagulation		
Including prothrombin time, thrombin time, D-dimers (or fibrinogen degradation products) and platelets	Activated in almost all cases of malaria to some degree	Fresh frozen plasma and platelets might be required if there is clinical evidence of bleeding
Liver function tests		
Albumin	Often low in acute infection	Does not require correction unless clinically relevant; danger of fluid overload and pulmonary edema
Transaminases	Can be moderately raised; if very high consider other concomitant infections (e.g. hepatitis)	Quinine dosage may need modification (e.g. reduction to q12h regimen)
Alkaline phosphatase	Not raised in malaria	If raised think of other causes
C-reactive protein	Raised in acute attack	Useful for daily monitoring in severe cases
Blood gases		
pH	Acidosis important in the prognosis of severe cases	Requires adequate fluid replacement, possible blood transfusion in anemic cases and avoidance (if possible) of epinephrine if inotropes are required[33]
Partial pressure of oxygen	Hypoxia uncommon unless there is pulmonary edema or infection	Oxygen
Partial pressure of carbon dioxide	Can be low in acidosis	
Bicarbonate	Low in acidosis	Replacement unlikely to help in acidemia
Other investigations		
Quinine levels	Free rather than total quinine levels are relevant to efficacy and toxicity. (α_1-acid glycoprotein (α_1-AGP) is the main quinine binding plasma protein)	Not generally helpful in management; maintain at 10–15mg/l according to parasite sensitivity and for quinidine 4–6mg/l
Electrocardiograph monitoring (corrected QT (QTc) interval)	Interval can be prolonged in nonimmune patients, especially if there is an underlying cardiac disorder	Quinine dosage may be need to be reduced
Blood and urine culture	Patients often acquire a secondary infection (most commonly respiratory, renal tract or sepsis) due to immunosuppression	May require systemic antibiotics
Lumbar puncture (only when patient is stable)	Relevant in very young and elderly and when other causes of encephalopathy, especially meningitis, must be excluded	Appropriate antimicrobial chemotherapy

Table 166.5 Investigations in the management of malaria. The feasibility of these investigations and their management will depend upon the severity of disease and availability of facilities. DIC, disseminated intravascular coagulation.

in which case a therapeutic trial of an osmotic agent such as mannitol may be attempted.

Acute renal failure

Dialysis or hemofiltration may be required. The indications are similar to those for any other form of renal failure. Nonoliguric renal failure may be managed conservatively.

Acidosis

Adequate fluid replacement avoiding fluid overload is essential. Sodium bicarbonate has not been shown to be of any benefit and may worsen acidosis. Transfusion of anemic patients has been shown to improve severe acidosis and reduce lactate concentration in young children.[30] Early hemodifiltration and ventilation may be used according to availability. The inotrope epinephrine (adrenaline) should be avoided unless absolutely necessary as it may worsen the acidosis, unlike dopamine, dobutamine and norepinephrine (noradrenaline).[32] Aspirin can also exacerbate metabolic acidosis.

Bacterial superinfection

Bacterial superinfection is common in malaria and must be suspected, particularly if the fever remains high despite antimalarial treatment or if there is evidence of septicemia or focal sepsis (e.g. pneumonia or urinary tract infection).

Adjunctive therapies

Many adjunctive therapies have been tried in malaria but few, if any, have been shown to be of benefit. The use of anti-TNF antibodies has been disappointing, leading only to a decrease in fever but no difference in clinical outcome. Corticosteroids are clearly not indicated in the treatment of acute cerebral malaria. The role of iron chelators and heparin remains unresolved, as does the use of an anti-TNF agent, pentoxifylline.

The role of mannitol in patients who have evidence of raised intracranial pressure, dichloroacetate in patients who have hyperlactatemia and the free radical scavenger, desferrioxamine, remain unclear.

REFERENCES

1. Bremen J. The ears of the hippopotamus: manifestations, determinants, and estimates of the malaria burden. Am J Trop Med Hyg 2001;64(suppl):1–11.
2. Marsh K. Malaria – a neglected disease? Parasitology 1992;104(suppl):53–69.
3. Pasvol G, Clough B, Carlsson J, Snounou G. The pathogenesis of severe falciparum malaria. In: Pasvol G, ed. Malaria. London: Baillière Tindall; 1995:249–70.
4. Miller L, Baruch D, Marsk K, Doumbo O. The pathogenic basis of malaria. Nature 2002;415:673–9.
5. Mitchell GH, Bannister LH. Malaria parasite invasion: interactions with the red cell membrane. Crit Rev Oncol Hematol 1988;8:225–310.
6. Berendt A, Ferguson D, Newbold C. Sequestration in *Plasmodium falciparum* malaria: sticky cells and sticky problems. Parasit Today 1990;6:247–54.
7. Marsh K, Marsh VM, Brown J, Whittle HC, Greenwood BM. *Plasmodium falciparum*: the behavior of clinical isolates in an *in-vitro* model of infected red blood cell sequestration. Exp Parasitol 1988;65:202–8.
8. Turner GD, Morrison H, Jones M, *et al.* An immunohistochemical study of the pathology of fatal malaria. Evidence for widespread endothelial activation and a potential role for intercellular adhesion molecule-1 in cerebral sequestration. Am J Pathol 1994;145:1057–69.
9. Carlson J, Helmby H, Hill AVS, Brewster D, Greenwood BM, Wahlgren M. Human cerebral malaria: association with erythrocyte rosetting and lack of anti-rosetting antibodies. Lancet 1990;336:1457–60.
10. Rowe J, Moulds J, Newbold C, Miller L. *P. falciparum* rosetting mediated by a parasite-variant erythrocyte membrane protein and complement-receptor 1. Nature 1997;388:292–5.
11. Warrell DA, White NJ, Veall N, *et al.* Cerebral anaerobic glycolysis and reduced cerebral oxygen transport in human cerebral malaria. Lancet 1988;2:534–8.
12. Newton CR, Kirkham FJ, Winstanley PA, *et al.* Intracranial pressure in African children with cerebral malaria. Lancet 1991;337:573–6.
13. Looareesuwan S, Wilairatana P, Krishna S, *et al.* Magnetic resonance imaging of the brain in patients with cerebral malaria. Clin Infect Dis 1995;21:300–9.
14. MacPherson G, Warrell M, White N, Looareesuwan S, Warrell D. Human cerebral malaria. A quantitative ultrastructural analysis of parasitised erythrocyte sequestration. Am J Pathol 1985;119:385–401.
15. Bradley D, Bannister B. Guidelines for the prevention of malaria in travellers from the United Kingdom. Commun Dis Public Health 2001;4:84–101.
16. Richie T. Saul A. Progress and challenges for malarial vaccines. Nature 2002;415:694–701.
17. World Health Organization. Severe falciparum malaria. Trans Roy Soc Trop Med Hyg 2000;94(suppl 1).
18. Abdalla S, Weatherall D, Wickramasinghe S, Hughes M. The anaemia of *P. falciparum* malaria. Br J Haematol 1980;46:171–83.
19. Phillips RE, Pasvol G. Anaemia of *Plasmodium falciparum* malaria. Baillière's Clin Haematol 1992;5:315–30.
20. Marsh K, Forster D, Wariuru C, *et al.* Indicators of life-threatening malaria in African children. N Engl J Med 1995;332:1399–404.
21. English M, Sauerwein C, Wariuru C, *et al.* Acidosis in severe childhood malaria. Q J Med 1997;90:263–70.
22. English M, Marsh V, Amukoye E, Lowe B, Murphy S, Marsh K. Chronic salicylate poisoning and severe malaria. Lancet 1996;347:1736–7.
23. Krishna S, Waller DW, ter KF, *et al.* Lactic acidosis and hypoglycaemia in children with severe malaria: pathophysiological and prognostic significance. Trans Roy Soc Trop Med Hyg 1994;88:67–73.
24. Clemens R, Pramoolsinsap C, Lorenz R, Pukrittayakamee S, Bock H, White N. Activation of the coagulation cascade in severe falciparum malaria through the intrinsic pathway. Br J Haematol 1994;87:100–5.
25. Sowunmi A. Renal function in acute falciparum malaria. Arch Dis Child 1996;74:293–8.
26. Chau T, Day N, Van Chuong L, *et al.* Blackwater fever in Southern Vietnam: a prospective descriptive study of 50 cases. Clin Infect Dis 1996;23:1274–81.
27. Silamut K, White NJ. Relation of the stage of parasite development in the peripheral blood to prognosis in severe falciparum malaria. Trans Roy Soc Trop Med Hyg 1993;87:436–43.
28. Nguyen PH, Day N, Pram TD, Ferguson DJ, White NJ. Intraleucocytic malaria pigment and prognosis in severe malaria. Trans Roy Soc Trop Med Hyg 1995;89:200–4.
29. White N. The treatment of malaria. N Engl J Med 1996;335:800–5.
30. English M, Waruiru C, Marsh K. Transfusion for respiratory distress in life-threatening childhood malaria. Am J Trop Med Hyg 1996;55:525–30.
31. Looareesuwan S, Phillips R, Karbwang J. *Plasmodium falciparum* hyperparasitaemia: use of exchange transfusion in seven patients and a review of the literature. Q J Med 1990;75:471–81.
32. Riddle M, Jackson J, Sanders J, Blazes D. Exchange transfusion as an adjunct therapy in severe *Plasmodium falciparum* malaria: a meta-analysis. Clin Infect Dis 2002;34:1192–8.
33. Day N, Phu N, Bethell D, *et al.* The effects of dopamine and adrenaline infusions on acid–base balance and systemic haemodynamics in severe infection. Lancet 1996;348:219–23.
34. Skudowitz RB, Katz J, Lurie A, Levin J, Metz J. Mechanisms of thrombocytopenia in malignant tertian malaria. BMJ 1973;2:515–7.
35. Kemp K, Akanmori BD, Adabayeri V, *et al.* Cytokine production and apoptosis among T cells from patients under treatment for *Plasmodium falciparum* malaria. Clin Exp Immunol 2002;127:151–7.

chapter 167

Schistosomiasis

Adel AF Mahmoud

INTRODUCTION

Schistosomiasis is the most significant helminthic infection in humans because of its global prevalence, the protean nature of its associated disease manifestations and the remarkable difficulties encountered in attempts to control its spread.[1] Humans may be infected with one of five species: *Schistosoma haematobium, Schistosoma mansoni, Schistosoma japonicum, Schistosoma mekongi* and *Schistosoma intercalatum*.

EPIDEMIOLOGY

The geographic distribution of schistosomiasis in endemic areas is dependent on the availability of a considerable reservoir of infection in humans or, in the case of *S. japonicum*, in domestic animals and specific snail intermediate hosts. Transmission necessitates a set of cultural, social and health habits that facilitate the spread of infection. In addition, this infection is extending its geographic distribution to new areas because of irrigation projects[2] or massive population movement. The main areas of endemicity of the five schistosome species responsible for the bulk of human infection are given in Table 167.1.[3] Attention should always be given to the nonuniform distribution of infection in any specific locality; endemicity, therefore, must be precisely mapped out. Detailed information on geographic distribution is unfortunately missing in most circumstances.

The schistosomes, similar to most other helminthic infections of humans, have a unique biologic characteristic in that they do not replicate within their definitive host. With the availability of procedures to quantify infection, it is therefore possible to appreciate several unique epidemiologic features of schistosomiasis. In endemic countries children encounter infection in their early years of life (4–6 years). Prevalence of infection increases with age and peaks in the age group 15–20 years. This age-dependent prevalence of infection is a constant finding in all endemic areas, irrespective of the peak percentage of infected individuals.[4] Intensity of infection, which is a measure of the number of eggs excreted in urine or feces and consequently is an estimate of worm load, follows a similar pattern to prevalence in the age group 5–20 years. Infection intensity increases with age to peak at age 15–20 years; thereafter the curves of prevalence and intensity diverge. Although prevalence remains stable, intensity of infection decreases remarkably, so that by age 30 years or older the number of eggs quantified in urine or stools is significantly lower than peaks achieved in persons a decade younger. The age-specific dependence of intensity of infection may be explained by acquisition of immunity or change in water exposure patterns of individuals living in endemic areas.[5,6]

Another of the remarkable epidemiologic features of schistosomiasis in the populations of endemic areas is its overdispersed distribution.[7] This means that among infected individuals most harbor low worm burden and only a minority (5–15%) are heavily infected. What determines the susceptibility to heavy infection is not known, but age (the young acquire heavier infection) and/or genetic susceptibility[8] are among the better recognized factors.

Expression of disease manifestations caused by schistosome infection is a multifactorial process. It depends on the species of the parasite and where ova are trapped in host tissues. Within the different species and perhaps geographic strains, a heterogeneity of disease manifestations is appreciated. For example, a considerable percentage of children infected with *S. haematobium* will complain of dysuria and hematuria, and objective evaluation of blood in urine demonstrates positive results in up to 80% of examined populations. In contrast, in children and young adults infected with any of the intestinal schistosomes, no more than 10–20% will complain of gastrointestinal symptoms or show signs of hepatosplenomegaly. Although the high prevalence of symptoms in *S. haematobium*-infected individuals may be related to the anatomic localization of worms and ova, the paucity of specific clinical features in intestinal schistosomiasis raises the possibility of additional pathogenetic factors such as age, genetic makeup and degree of immune responsiveness.[9]

PATHOGENESIS AND PATHOLOGY

Disease manifestations caused by schistosome infection are multiple, not only because of the several species that infect humans but also because of the multiple stages of the pathogen within the human host and the myriad responses it elicits. A summary of the main pathogenetic mechanisms in acute and chronic schistosomiasis is given in Table 167.2. Acute schistosomiasis is seen more commonly in infections with either *S. mansoni* or *S. japonicum*. It may manifest either as cercarial dermatitis, which is caused by the development of humoral and cellular immune responses to invading cercariae or as Katayama fever, which is probably a serum sickness-like illness caused by antigen–antibody complex deposition and proinflammatory cytokines in response to the maturing worms and the shower of egg antigens that follow.[10]

In contrast to the general immunologic nature of pathogenesis in acute schistosomiasis, the causes of disease in the chronic stages are mainly localized in specific sites within infected individuals. Central to the pathology of chronic infection is egg deposition and the subsequent host granulomatous response. Mature worms begin oviposition 6–9 weeks after cercarial invasion. Egg deposition occurs intravascularly in the small venous tributaries of the measenteric or vesical plexuses. Through the secretion of enzymes, and perhaps aided by urinary tract or intestinal movement, the parasite eggs find their way to the lumen of these viscera where they are carried to the outside via urine or stools. A proportion of parasite eggs, however, fail to traverse from the venous lumen to visceral cavities and are either retained locally in host tissues or carried via venous blood to distant organs such as liver, lung, etc. At these sites, the effector arms of the host immune system mount a granulomatous response to enclose the parasite ova (Fig. 167.1). The response is initiated by cell-mediated mechanisms and is regulated by multiple humoral and cytokine cascades. The result is a space-occupying lesion that may obstruct portal blood flow through the liver, leading to portal hypertension, or may obstruct urine flow through the ureters, leading to

GEOGRAPHIC DISTRIBUTION OF HUMAN SCHISTOSOMES					
Species	Africa	Middle East	Asia	Americas	Caribbean
S. haematobium	+	+	+	+	+
S. mansoni	+	+	+	–	–
S. japonicum	–	–	+	–	–
S. mekongi	–	–	+	–	–
S. intercalatum	+	–	–	–	–

Table 167.1 Geographic distribution of human schistosomes.

PATHOGENETIC MECHANISMS IN HUMAN SCHISTOSOMIASIS			
Syndrome	Parasite stage	Immunologic mechanisms	
		Induction	Regulation
Swimmer's itch	Cercarial	Humoral and cellular	Undefined
Acute stage	Adults and eggs	Antigen–antibody complexes	Undefined
Chronic stage			
Granuloma	Eggs	Cell mediated	Antigens, cells, cytokines
Fibrosis	Egg antigens	Cell mediated	Cytokines

Table 167.2 Pathogenetic mechanisms in human schistosomiasis.

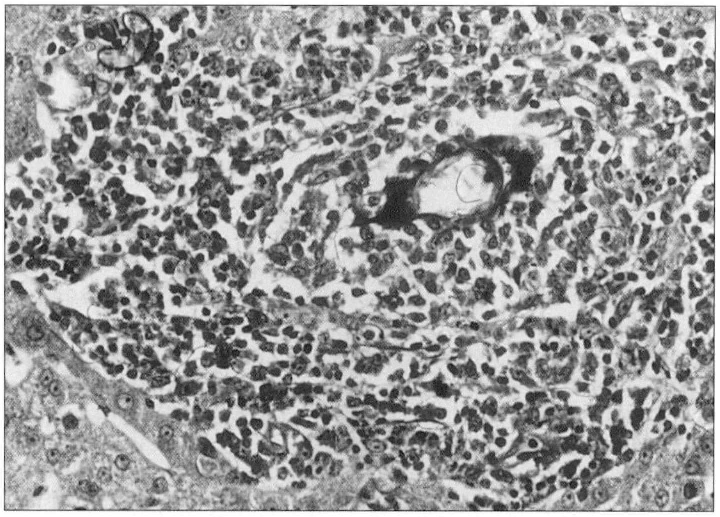

Fig. 167.1 The basic pathologic lesions of intestinal schistosomiasis. A liver biopsy is depicted with egg deposition, granuloma formation and fibrosis in the periportal areas. Courtesy of Professor MA Madwar.

hydroureters and hydronephrosis. The nidus for these granulomatous lesions is the parasite eggs with their multiple antigens that are recognized by the host. The miracidia within the eggs, however, survive for only 6–8 weeks and then die, thus eliminating the continuous antigenic stimulation. The result is a decrease in granuloma size, but more significant is tissue healing through fibrosis. Such mechanisms lead to the permanence of schistosomal tissue injury and hemodynamic effects.

PREVENTION

For individuals traveling to areas endemic for schistosomiasis, prevention simply means no contact with infected bodies of fresh water. Because the distribution of infection in most endemic areas is not clearly demarcated, avoidance of all fresh-water sources is most prudent. Of particular importance is the unreliability of equating fast-running water with less chance of infection. Anticercarial preparations may be applied under special circumstances, but their widespread use has not been tested. In contrast, prevention in people living in endemic areas is complex and multifaceted. It reflects the degree of education, economic growth and cultural and recreational practices. Four strategies have been used and are still in use: molluscciding; provision of sanitary water and sewage disposal; chemotherapy delivered to infected individuals as mass chemotherapy or targeting treatment to specific segments of infected populations; and economic and social development in general. Each of these strategies has its limitations and none has achieved widespread and sustained control of infection or disease in endemic areas. Significant effort is given to discovery of antischistosome vaccines. Although such a goal is important, understanding of the complexity of the organisms and the host immune responses has not resulted to date in a practical vaccination strategy.[11]

CLINICAL FEATURES

The clinical manifestations of disease caused by schistosomiasis are related not only to the species of the parasite but also to intensity of infection, genetic make-up of the host and other interactions with infectious and nutritional conditions. It is, therefore, essential to use the clinical descriptions that follow with a full understanding that the phenotypic expression of disease caused by schistosomiasis is multifactorial in nature.

The first major set of clinical manifestations of schistosomal infection occurs during its acute phase and results in varying degrees of morbidity in association with the five species responsible for the bulk of human infection. Swimmer's itch or cercarial dermatitis is a maculopapular itchy rash that usually occurs 1–2 days after exposure. The rash is related to cercarial invasion and, therefore, it usually occurs in areas of the skin that are exposed to infected waters. Cercarial dermatitis has been reported more often in newly exposed persons in endemic areas. The lesions are usually self-limited and require little medical attention. A more severe form of cercarial dermatitis occurs after human exposure to avian schistosomes. These helminths are endemic in many parts of the world, including North America. Exposure usually occurs in spring when transmission of the parasites in their natural habitat begins. The maculopapular eruptions are more severe and recur with each exposure.

A few weeks after schistosome infection occurs (4–8 weeks) some individuals exhibit systemic manifestations of acute schistosomiasis.[12] This is the more common manifestation seen in travelers who return after exposure to infection in endemic areas. The symptoms include fever, malaise, general aches and, upon examination, lymphadenopathy and hepatomegaly may be detected. Most of these individuals will show moderate peripheral blood eosinophilia, positive serology for schistosomiasis and schistosome eggs may be demonstrated in their excreta. Acute schistosomiasis is more prevalent in individuals newly exposed to the helminth, particularly those experiencing heavy exposure. The condition has resulted in a few reported fatalities, but the majority survive.

Chronic schistosomiasis and its sequalae and interactions with other clinical conditions occur within several months to several years after infection. Symptoms, signs and pathologic lesions are species specific. Clinical features are described according to the parasite species below.

Urinary schistosomiasis

Symptoms and signs related to *S. haematobium* infection are seen in a considerable proportion of infected individuals, significantly more often than in those infected with any of the other species of schistosome. Furthermore, these features are seen earlier in the course of infection. In endemic areas children infected with *S. haemotobium* will complain of hematuria, which may be terminal, dysuria and frequency. Urine examination may show evidence of hematuria, proteinuria and cellular markers of inflammation.[13] The prevalence of these symptoms varies from 40% to 80% of infected individuals. Ultrasonographic examination of the urinary tract, which is the current suggested investigative modality, demonstrates thickening of urinary bladder wall, granulomas, hydronephrosis and sometimes evidence of bladder and ureteric calcification. At this stage of disease, the functional abnormality in the urinary tract is bladder neck obstruction. Later the course of disease may be complicated by frequent urinary tract bacterial infection, bladder or ureteric stone formation, renal functional abnormalities and ultimately kidney failure. In several endemic areas there is a strong epidemiologic association with squamous cell carcinoma of the bladder, which occurs characteristically in the age group 30–50 years.[14]

Intestinal/hepatic schistosomiasis

Clinical features that are specifically linked to any of the four intestinal species of schistosomes (*S. mansoni, S. japonicum, S. mekongi* and *S. intercalatum*) are seen in a relatively small proportion of infected individuals. Most of the clinical descriptions available report on either *S. mansoni* or *S. japonicum* infection. Established infection with either of these two species results in intestinal and/or hepatic disease.[15] The intestinal presentations are characterized by vague abdominal pains and bloody diarrhea; the latter feature is usually mild, not dysenteric in nature and variable in course. Liver disease manifests originally as hepatomegaly that is subsequently associated with evidence of portal hypertension, including splenomegaly and development of portosystemic collaterals, particularly at the esophagogastric junction and anterior abdominal wall (Fig. 167.2). Liver function tests at this stage are preserved because of the slow rate of development of the portal hypertension, because of the fibrotic and not cirrhotic pathologic changes in the liver, and because of arterialization of the hepatic blood supply that preserves parenchymal cell perfusion and oxygenation. The late stages of liver disease are associated with fibrosis and shrinking of organ size (Fig.

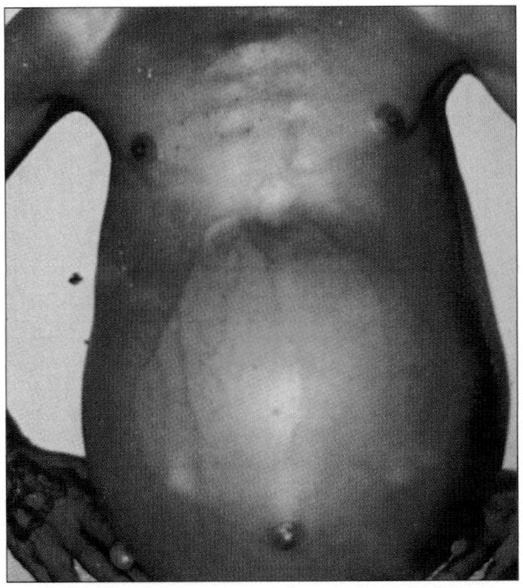

Fig. 167.2 Late manifestations of disease caused by *Schistosoma mansoni* infection. Note marked ascites and collateral circulation on anterior abdominal wall. Courtesy of Professor MA Madwar.

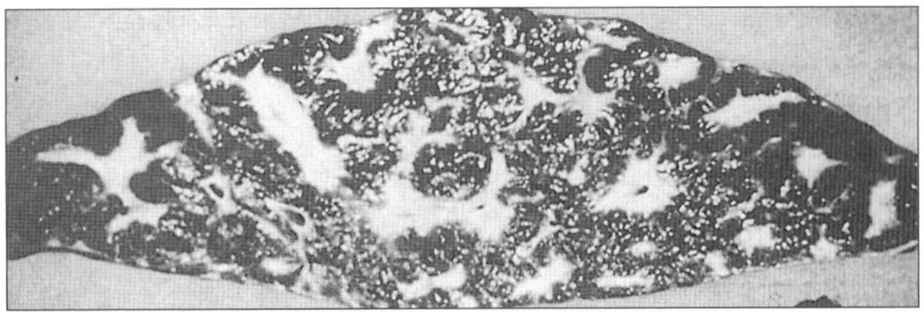

Fig. 167.3 Advanced liver fibrosis in portal tracts (clay pipe-stem). Courtesy of Professor MA Madwar.

167.3), extensive splenomegaly, ascites, repeated episodes of hematemesis and finally hepatic failure. The phenotypic expression of hepatic disease in schistosomiasis may not only relate to intensity of infection but also to intercurrent infections, such as viral hepatidites,[16,17] and the genetic constitution of the host.

Schistosomal disease may affect other organs in the body;[1] examples include cor pulmonale, cerebral or transverse myelitis, and cutaneous and genital manifestations. In general, these are less frequent than the previously described features and are usually seen in populations of endemic areas.

DIAGNOSIS

Infection with any of the schistosome species should be suspected in a variety of clinical presentations, as indicated above. A high index of suspicion, obtaining accurate geographic history and enquiry about possible exposure to infected water bodies are, therefore, elementary but essential steps in approaching the individual who possibly has schistosomal infection. Epidemiologic evaluation of infection in travelers necessitates similar examination of others who were exposed. Diagnosis is based on demonstrating the presence of parasite eggs or on serologic evidence (see Chapter 246).[18] Schistosome eggs may be detected in urine samples (for *S. haematobium*). Urine should preferably be collected between 1100h and 1300h, when egg passage is maximal. Sedimentation or filtration allows more sensitive diagnosis and quantification. The usefulness of detecting hematuria with reagent strip and correlating its presence with *S. haematobium* infection has been demonstrated in several studies in endemic areas. This practice, however, is not recommended for the returning occasional traveler in the developed world because of the multiple etiologies of hematuria. For intestinal schistosomes stool examination is performed by any of several concentration techniques, the Kato being the easiest and providing quantitative data. Assessing the parasite burden is important in appreciating the degree of tissue damage and in following up success of therapy. Diagnostic methods that are based on egg identification in urine or stool samples may also be combined with ova hatching to determine their viability. Serologic testing gives evidence for current or past infection by demonstrating antigen-specific antibodies; in the USA these tests are available in some state laboratories or at the Centers for Disease Control and Prevention. Serology for schistosomiasis detects antibodies against several stages of the parasite. It usually converts within 1–2 weeks after exposure and remains positive for a long period, even after chemotherapeutic cure. The test as performed has no useful quantitative value and does not differentiate present from past infection. Antigen detection techniques are also available that allow examination of serum or urine and may be helpful in determining the viability of the worms and their numbers.[19] The decision to work up a person with positive history depends on specific exposure and on the symptoms and signs related to schistosomiasis.

Other diagnostic tests include tissue examination for parasite eggs. Samples may be obtained from rectal mucosa, bladder and liver biopsies, or from other tissues. Care should be taken when examining tissue for schistosome eggs to identify the parasite species, the viability of the miracidia contained within the egg shells and any evidence of calcification. Clinical diagnosis of schistosomiasis based on symptoms or signs without laboratory or serologic evidence should not be used, except in rare circumstances. These include peripheral blood eosinophilia in those suspected of having acute schistosomiasis, the characteristic liver or urinary tract pathology seen upon ultrasonographic examination or the rare central nervous system and other ectopic disease manifestations.

MANAGEMENT

Praziquantel is the current drug of choice for treating active infection with any of the five schistosome species.[20] The drug is administered orally 40mg/kg body weight in one dose for *S. haematobium*, *S. mansoni* or *S. intercalatum* infection, and 60mg/kg body weight in three divided doses over 1 day for *S. japonicum* or *S. mekongi* infection. Praziquantel administration is usually not associated with significant side-effects; however, in those with heavy burdens, abdominal pain, nausea and vomiting may occur. The drug is effective in producing parasitologic cure in approximately 80% of treated individuals and achieves over 90% reduction of egg counts in the remaining individuals. Follow-up urine or stool examination within 3 months is advised to assess efficacy of therapy. Praziquantel therapy in early infection also will result in reversal of pathologies such as hepatomegaly, bladder wall thickening or hydroureters. In established pathologic conditions, such as portal hypertension or extensive hydronephrosis, no reversal of pathology may be accomplished.

Treatment of the chronic sequelae of schistosomiasis may necessitate measures other than specific chemotherapy. For example, management of individuals with end-stage liver or kidney disease should be handled along general medical practices. Corrective surgical procedures for portal hypertension or urinary tract anatomic alterations also may be necessary in some cases.

REFERENCES

1. Mahmoud AAF, ed. Schistosomiasis. London: Imperial College Press; 2001:1–510.
2. El-Sayed HF, Rizkalla NH, Mehanna S, Abaza SM, Winch PJ. Prevalence and epidemiology of *Schistosoma mansoni* and *S. haematobium* infection in two areas of Egypt recently reclaimed from the desert. Am J Trop Med Hyg 1995;52:194–8.
3. Citsuho L, Engels D, Montresor A, Savioli L. The global status of schistosomiasis and its control. Acta Trop 2000;77:41–51.
4. Guyatt HL, Smith T, Gryseels B, *et al.* Aggregation in schistosomiasis: comparison of the relationships between prevalence and intensity in different endemic areas. Parasitology 1994;109:45–55.
5. Warren KS. Regulation of prevalence and intensity of schistosomiasis in man: immunology or ecology. J Infect Dis 1973;127:595–609.
6. Woodhouse MEJ, Ndamba J, Bradley DJ. The interpretation of intensity and aggregation data for infections of *Schistosoma haematobium*. Trans Roy Soc Trop Med Hyg 1994;88:520–6.
7. Anderson R, May RM. Infectious diseases of humans: dynamics and control. Oxford: Oxford University Press; 1991.
8. Zinn-Justin A, Marquet S, Hillaire D, Dessein A, Abel L. Genome search for additional human loci controlling infection levels by *Schistosoma mansoni*. Am J Trop Med Hyg 2001;65:754–8.
9. Ross AGP, Bartley PB, Sleigh AC, *et al.* Schistosomiasis. N Engl J Med 2002;346:1212–20.
10. de Jesus AR, Silva A, Santana LB, *et al.* Clinical and immunologic evaluation of 31 patients with acute schistosomiasis mansoni. J Infect Dis 2002;185:98–105.
11. James SL, Colley DG. Progress in vaccine development. In: Mahmoud AAF, ed. Schistosomiasis. London: Imperial College Press; 2001:469–95.
12. Visser LG, Polderman AM, Stuiver PC. Outbreak of schistosomiasis among travelers returning from Mali, West Africa. Clin Infect Dis 1995;20:280–5.
13. King CH. Disease in schistosomiasis haematobia. In: Mahmoud AAF, ed. Schistosomiasis. London: Imperial College Press; 2001:265–95.
14. World Health Organization. International Agency for Research on Cancer Monographs on the evaluation of carcinogenic risks to humans. Schistosomes, liver flukes and *Helicobacter pylori*. Geneva: WHO; 45–119.
15. Mahmoud AAF. Schistosomiasis and other trematode infections. In: Kasper DL, Brunwald E, Fauci AS, Hauser SL, Longo DL, Jameson JL, eds. Harrison's principles of internal medicine, 16th ed. New York: McGraw-Hill; 2003.
16. Gad A, Tanaka E, Orii K, *et al.* Relationship between hepatitis C virus infection and schistosomal liver disease: not simply an additive effect. J Gastroenterol 2001;36:753–8.
17. Yu DB, Ross AG, Williams GM, *et al.* Determinants of hepato- and spleno-megaly in Human, China: cross-sectional survey data from areas endemic for schistosomiasis. Ann Trop Med Parasitol 2001;95:707–13.
18. Peters PAS, Kazura JW. Update on diagnostic methods for schistosomiasis. In: Mahmoud AAF, ed. Baillière's Clinical Tropical Medicine and Communicable Diseases. Schistosomiasis. 1987;2:419–33.
19. Al-Sherbiny MM, Osman A, Hancock K, *et al.* Application of immunodiagnostic assays: detection of antibodies and circulating antigens in human schistosomiasis and correlation with clinical findings. Am J Trop Med Hyg 1999;60:960–6.
20. King CH, Mahmoud AAF. Drugs five years later: praziquantel. Ann Intern Med 1989;110:290–6.

chapter
168 Cestode and Trematode Infections

Guy Baily

INTRODUCTION

Cestode and trematode worms are highly specialized, ubiquitous flatworm parasites infecting both vertebrate and invertebrate animals. Typically, they have a complex life cycle that involves more than one host species harboring stages of the parasite that differ markedly in morphology. Most of these parasites are restricted in their range of host species, particularly in the definitive host of the adult reproductive worms. From among the enormous number of known parasitic flatworms, humans are the preferred host of only a handful, with rather more being capable of incidental or paratenic human infection.

Despite this variety, the life cycles of the parasites that infect humans have certain features in common. The strategy of the trematode parasites is to use aquatic snails as an amplification host. Snails are infected by a first larval stage hatched from eggs that have entered the aquatic environment in the waste products (most often feces) of a definitive host. For the blood flukes that cause schistosomiasis, the larvae (known as cercaria) released by the snails invade directly through skin or mucous membranes in contact with infected water. Other human trematode parasites cause infection through ingestion and rely on their cercaria 'hitching a lift' by encysting on an item of human diet present in the aquatic environment. Adult cestodes are tapeworms that live in the gut of their definitive hosts. Intermediate hosts are infected by ingesting ova, which develop into a sessile larval form, often with a cystic structure, in their tissues. The life cycle is completed when these infected tissues are eaten by a suitable definitive host. The larval forms of cestode parasites often have serious consequences for the function of the intermediate host and are among the most grave human helminthic infections. (Schistosomiasis is discussed in Chapter 167 and hydatid disease in Chapter 169.)

CYSTICERCOSIS

Epidemiology and prevention

Cysticercosis is infection with the larval or metacestode stage of the pork tapeworm *Taenia solium*. It is acquired as a feco-oral infection from human tapeworm carriers and is therefore a disease of poor sanitation. Historically it occurred worldwide but it has now been largely eliminated from affluent countries through sanitation and meat inspection. The prevalence is strongly influenced by local customs in both diet and animal husbandry. It remains common in Central and South America, south Asia and China, and locally in Africa. A postmortem prevalence of nearly 2% has been reported from Mexico City. Individuals can protect themselves through the ordinary hygienic precautions employed against other feco-oral infections. Mass treatment campaigns with praziquantel can reduce cysticercosis by eliminating tapeworm infections; this may be a useful additional benefit of praziquantel use in schistosomiasis control in Africa.

Pathogenesis and pathology

Ingested *T. solium* ova are activated by exposure to the gastric and duodenal environments into invasive larval forms, termed oncospheres. These migrate into the tissues, where they develop into a sessile cyst about 1cm across and surrounded by a host-derived capsule. Almost any tissue may be infected but skeletal muscle and the central nervous system, where cysts may be a little larger, are the preferred sites. Significant clinical sequelae are related to neurologic involvement (Fig. 168.1). Unless they are degenerating, cysts elicit very little immune response.

Clinical features

Most people who have cysticerci in their brain have no attributable symptoms. Much the commonest consequence is epilepsy, which is often focal. Where cysticercosis is prevalent, it may account for more than one-third of cases of adult-onset epilepsy.[1] Other neurologic manifestations are very varied. Focal neurologic syndromes may occur, including paralysis, extrapyramidal movement disorders and spinal cord syndromes. When there are many cysts, raised intracranial pressure may be the dominant problem. If untreated, this may lead to permanent loss of cerebral function with dementia and cortical blindness.

In children, who tend to mount a more substantial local immune response, a subacute encephalitis syndrome, with fitting and global changes in cerebral function, may occur.[2]

A minor abnormality of cerebrospinal fluid, mild pleocytosis or slightly elevated protein, can be found in around half of cases of neurocysticercosis; this is a reflection of how commonly cysts have some contact with the meninges. Much less commonly, cysticerci in the larger subarachnoid spaces, especially the cisterna magna, give rise to a clinical presentation of chronic meningitis with headache and global deterioration in cerebral function associated with markedly abnormal cerebrospinal fluid.[3] This may progress to hydrocephalus through obstruction of the ventricular foramina.

Cysticerci in the eye are not uncommon. Usually they are sited in the vitreous or under the retina, where they give rise to visual scotomata. Any significant inflammatory response is likely to result in loss of vision. Serious clinical consequences from cysts at other extraneurologic sites are very rare.

Diagnosis

A clinical diagnosis of neurocysticercosis is seldom possible because the neurologic presentation is never specific and could reflect a number of disease processes. For this reason it may be considerably underdiagnosed in the resource-poor regions where it is most prevalent. Occasionally, evidence of extracranial cysticercosis provides a clue to the origin of neurologic disease (e.g. palpable subcutaneous cysticerci or spindle-shaped calcification of muscle cysts seen on radiography). Eosinophilia is seldom present in established infection. Serology for cysticercosis is available in a number of centers and, although it is not completely sensitive and despite some cross-reactivity among other cestode infections, it provides a very valuable

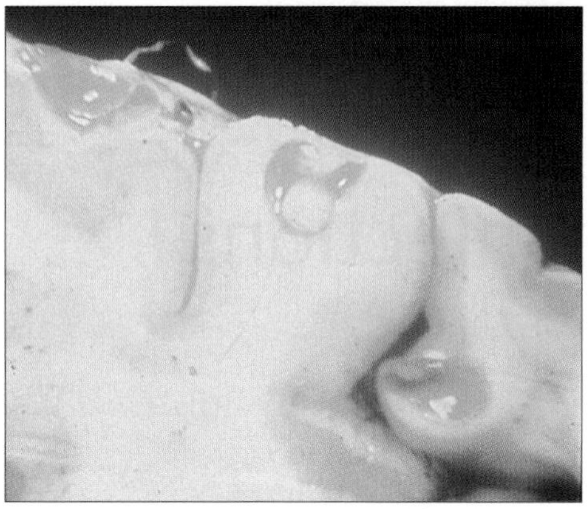

Fig. 168.1 Cysticerci in the brain.

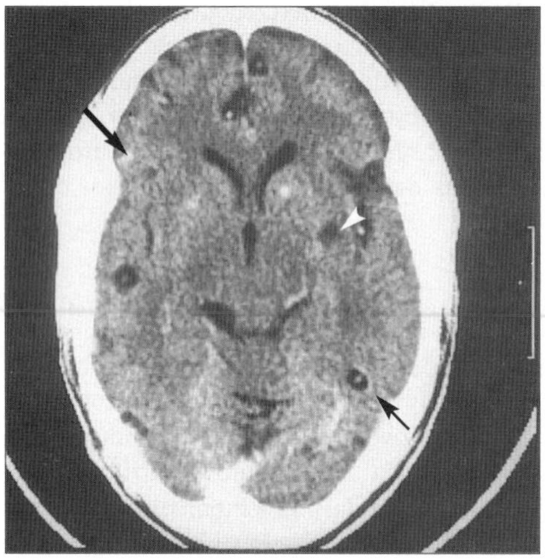

Fig. 168.2 Computerized tomography appearances in neurocysticercosis. Viable cysts appear as radiolucent defects (arrowhead). The central protoscolex appears as a radiodense spot in about 50% (small arrow). Cysts that show ring enhancement are probably degenerating. Calcified cysts (large arrow) are dead and will not benefit from specific therapy.

screening tool for neurology patients in endemic countries.[4] Cysticerci can usually be visualized with intracranial imaging (Fig. 168.2). Magnetic resonance imaging is superior to computerized tomography (CT) for intraventricular cysticerci, cysticerci in the posterior fossa and spinal disease.

Management

Anthelmintic drug therapy is now widely used for neurocysticercosis, although its exact role remains controversial. Much of this controversy results from the complexity of the natural history of the disease. Cysts that enhance on CT are inflamed and likely to be degenerating. Prospective studies have shown that they will almost always disappear within a year without specific treatment.[5] This is the usual sequence of events in children unless they are heavily infected. Nonenhancing cysts, often seen in adults, are likely to persist. Praziquantel in large doses (40mg/kg daily orally for 15 days) has been shown to reduce the size and number of nonenhancing parenchymal brain lesions and to lessen fitting.[6] Albendazole (15mg/kg daily orally for 1 month) appears to be at least as effective.[7]

The value of anthelmintics for other clinical presentations is not well documented. On balance, children who have enhancing lesions can reasonably be managed with corticosteroids, symptomatic treatment such as fit control and close follow-up. Nonenhancing parenchymal cysts should be treated with anthelmintics.

The principal complication of both praziquantel and albendazole treatment is acute raised intracranial pressure, which may occasionally be life-threatening. It can be largely prevented with corticosteroids, although this may reduce the efficacy of praziquantel. Practice varies, but a favored opinion is that anthelmintic treatment for cysticercosis should always be accompanied by corticosteroids (e.g. dexamethasone 2mg q12h for 3 days).

Shorter courses of both albendazole and praziquantel may improve CT appearances but are not yet sufficiently established to be generally recommended.[8] Finally, surgery retains a place, particularly in the management of ventricular cysts and hydrocephalus.

OTHER LARVAL CESTODE INFECTIONS

Coenurosis

Humans are occasionally infected by the metacestode larvae of *Taenia multiceps*, which is normally maintained between dogs and sheep. The metacestode is a coenurus; it is a large cyst, more than 2cm in diameter, with multiple invaginated protoscolices, most often localizing in the brain. It is a rare illness but one with a wide geographic distribution.[9] Biopsy is necessary for diagnosis once a large cyst has been identified by imaging. Surgical excision has been advocated; the value of anthelmintics is unknown.

Sparganosis

Sparganosis is infection with the migratory plerocercoid larvae of cestodes of the genus *Spirometra*. These have an aquatic life cycle, similar to *Diphyllobothrium* spp. The larvae ascend the aquatic food chain from invertebrates such as *Cyclops* to reptiles and amphibians. Humans may become infected from drinking water that contains infected *Cyclops* spp., from eating inadequately cooked frog or snake meat, or from using the skin of these animals to dress wounds and sore eyes, as is the custom in some parts of eastern Asia. It is an uncommon but widespread disease in warm climates.

Clinically, there is a localized subcutaneous inflammatory swelling, which migrates rather slowly and contains a single worm-like sparganum (Fig. 168.3). The eye may be damaged by adjacent lesions; entry of the worm into the brain is rare but may be devastating. Excision of the worm is the only reliably effective treatment.

TAPEWORM INFECTIONS

Taeniasis

Humans are the only definitive host for two *Taenia* spp: *T. saginata*, the beef tapeworm; and *T. solium*, the pork tapeworm (Fig. 168.4). Infection is acquired by eating undercooked infected beef or pork, respectively. The clinical consequences of taeniasis are generally trivial and are limited to minor abdominal symptoms, such as occur in irritable bowel syndrome. *Taenia saginata* generates highly motile proglottids (pale, rectangular tapeworm segments) that may cause distress by emerging spontaneously from the anus. *Taenia* spp. do not appear to have any significant nutritional effect on their host. The principal concern in taeniasis is that *T. solium* may give rise to cysticercosis in the same host through feco-oral autoinfection.[10]

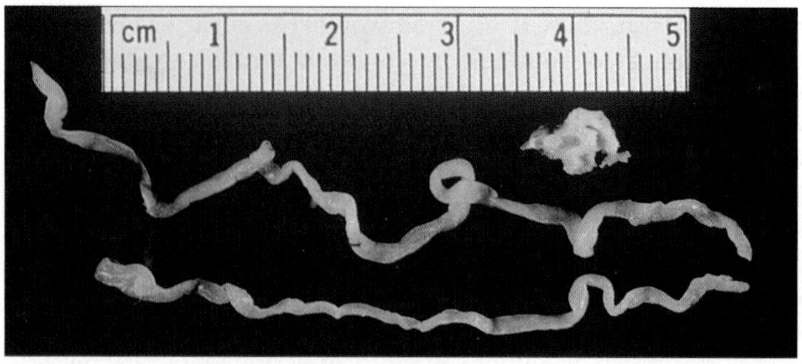

Fig. 168.3 A sparganum worm dissected from an inguinal mass.

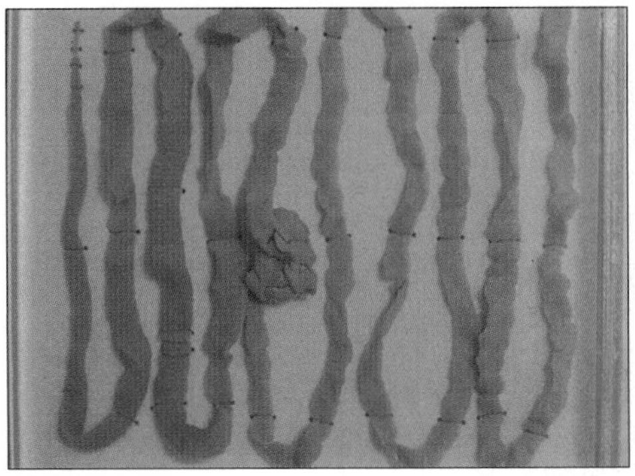

Fig. 168.4 *Taenia saginata.* A mature worm may be over 33 feet (10m) long.

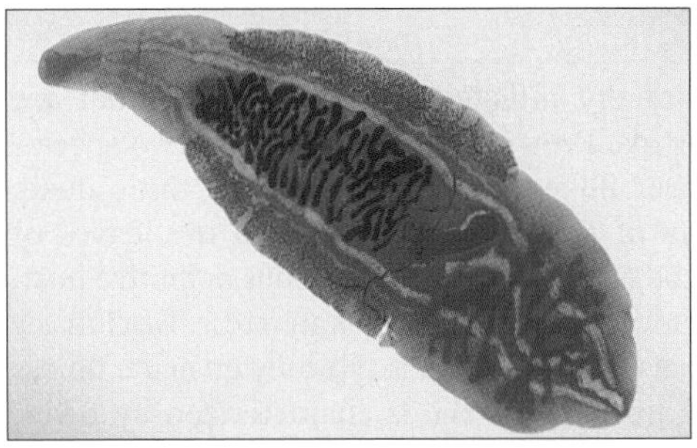

Fig. 168.5 An adult liver fluke (*Clonorchis sinensis*). The worm is typically about 0.75 inches (2cm) in length.

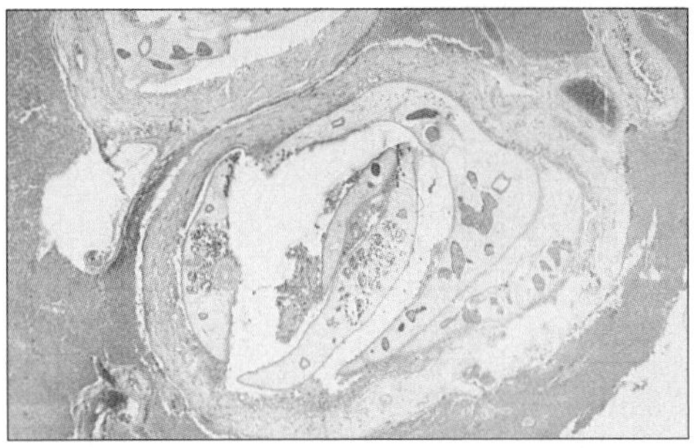

Fig. 168.6 Low-power section of a human bile duct containing adult *Clonorchis sinensis* flukes.

Diphyllobothriasis

Diphyllobothrium spp. are a large group of tapeworms that include a complex aquatic phase in their life cycle, ascending the food chain in fish. The species adapted to humans is *Diphyllobothrium latum*. Most human infection now occurs in Russia. Humans acquire infection by eating inadequately cooked or preserved fish. A large tapeworm, up to 33 feet (10m) long, develops in the small bowel; multiple infections are common. Clinical consequences, as with other tapeworm infections, are minor. Tapeworm anemia, described principally from Finland, was an association between diphyllobothriasis and deficiency of vitamin B12. It has not been recorded for several decades and is of historic interest only.[11] A variety of other *Diphyllobothrium* spp. may infect humans, principally in the sub-Arctic and the northern Pacific areas. Prevalences of up to 30% have been recorded in Canadian Inuit communities for *Diphyllobothrium dendriticum*. Clinical consequences of these infections are not well documented, but they are also thought to be minor.

Hymenolepis

The dwarf tapeworm, *Hymenolepis nana*, has the unique distinction among cestodes of being able to complete its life cycle within a single human host. Ova ingested from the environment encyst within a villus of the small bowel epithelium and, after a few days, evaginate a protoscolex. This develops into a new tapeworm only 1.6 inches (4cm) long in the gut lumen. The worm is thus transmitted directly between humans as a feco-oral infection. It is strongly associated with poor sanitation and is common in warm countries, especially among children, in whom prevalences may exceed 10%. In addition to abdominal symptoms, some systemic features such as headache and irritability occur, and eosinophilia is common. There is evidence that heavy infections may contribute to growth retardation.[12]

Zoonotic tapeworms

Various tapeworms that are not primarily adapted to humans may nevertheless occasionally cause human infection. *Hymenolepis diminuta* is a parasite of rats and mice, using their fleas as an intermediate host. Similarly, *Dipylidium caninum* passes between dogs and their fleas. Both are occasional sources of human infection worldwide, principally in children, through the accidental ingestion of fleas. There are no known serious clinical consequences.

Diagnosis and management of tapeworm infections

The diagnosis of tapeworm infection is by direct microscopy of feces for the detection of ova which, within the genera *Taenia* and *Diphyllobothrium*, cannot be readily speciated. Entire proglottids or larger worm portions may sometimes be seen. Treatment with a single dose of praziquantel at 10mg/kg is effective for all the human tapeworms except *H. nana*, for which at least 20mg/kg should be given.

LIVER FLUKE INFECTIONS

Epidemiology and prevention

There are three closely related trematodes, *Clonorchis sinensis*, *Opisthorchis viverrini* and *Opisthorchis felineus*, which for clinical purposes can be considered as one entity; the human liver flukes (Fig. 168.5). Aquatic snails are infected when human feces containing ova contaminate their environment. Cercaria released from the snails encyst under the scales of freshwater fish and will infect a new human host if eaten raw. Thus, either the sanitary disposal of feces or the thorough cooking of fish will interrupt transmission. The liver flukes are almost entirely restricted to eastern Asia and some foci in Siberia. Local prevalences may reach 35%.[13]

Pathogenesis and pathology

Ingested larvae migrate from the duodenum through the ampulla into the biliary tract, developing into adult flukes within small bile ducts in the liver, where they may live for many years. Pathologic consequences arise from the constant abrasion and inflammation of the bile duct in contact with the rough tegument of the flukes (Fig. 168.6). With time the bile duct walls become fibrotic and thickened and the liver becomes enlarged. The gallbladder is frequently abnormal, with distension, irregular thickening, or stones.

Clinical features

Light infections are likely to be asymptomatic. Heavier infection may be associated with right hypochondrial pain and other abdominal symptoms.[14] Significant complications include biliary obstruction and acute cholangitis. There is a strong association between liver fluke infections, especially with *O. viverrini*, and cholangiocarcinoma, which may be among the leading causes of mortality in highly endemic areas.[15]

Diagnosis and management

Liver fluke infection can be sensitively detected by stool microscopy with appropriate concentration technique – the fecal egg burden is a guide to the worm burden, which is in turn proportional to the severity of the pathology. A single dose of praziquantel 40mg/kg is usually effective, although more prolonged treatment may be preferable in heavier infections.

FASCIOLIASIS

Humans are also occasionally infected with liver flukes that are primarily adapted to animals. Principal among these are two species of *Fasciola*: the sheep liver fluke, *F. hepatica*; and the cattle fluke, *F. gigantica*. The cercaria of *Fasciola* spp. encyst on the leaves of aquatic plants, hoping to be eaten by their herbivorous definitive host. Humans are most often infected through wild watercress. Fascioliasis is uncommon but widely distributed. There is typically an acute illness as larvae migrate to the liver; this stage is characterized by fever, eosinophilia and painful hepatomegaly. Even in established infection, ova are difficult to find in the stool, so the diagnosis depends on serology. This is the only human flatworm infection that is unresponsive to praziquantel. Corticosteroids will alleviate much of the immune-mediated acute illness. Bithionol is the established specific treatment, but few physicians have much experience with this drug.[16]

LUNG FLUKE INFECTIONS

Epidemiology

Several trematodes in the genus *Paragonimus* cause human infection. Cases have been reported from most tropical areas but the principal foci are in eastern Asia and central and western Africa. *Paragonimus* cercaria encyst in the gills and other organs of fresh water crustaceans such as crabs and crayfish. Where these are customarily eaten raw or lightly cooked, human paragonimiasis is likely to occur.

Pathogenesis and pathology

Ingested larvae migrate through the intestinal wall and cross the diaphragm to enter the lungs, where they mature, inhabiting a host-derived fibrous capsule typically in the upper zones of the lungs. Pathologic consequences may result from the inflammatory response to larval migration or from the local effects of established adult worms. Occasionally worms develop in ectopic sites, most significantly in the brain, where the inflammatory response is likely to be very destructive.

Clinical features

The pattern of disease differs between *Paragonimus* spp. Mature flukes give rise to a chronic, low-grade, cavitating pulmonary disease. There is chronic sputum production and often hemoptysis. In the African disease, extrapulmonary manifestations are not a feature, but Asian parasites may give rise to migratory subcutaneous inflammatory swellings and more seriously to an eosinophilic meningitis with a variety of focal or global neurologic features.[17]

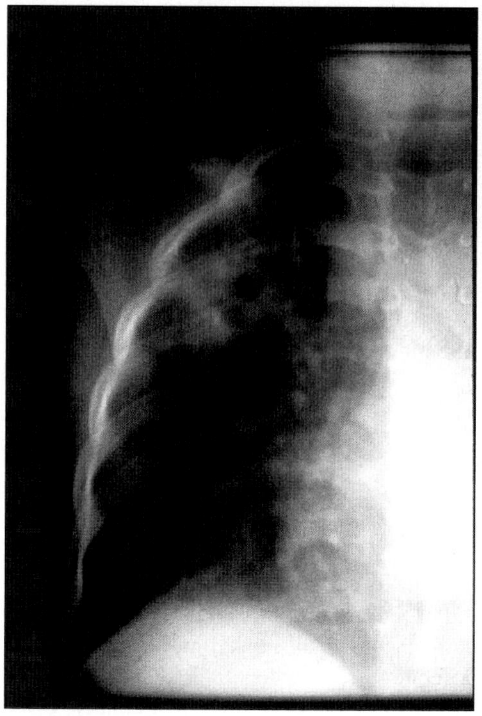

Fig. 168.7 Shadowing in the right upper zone with cavitation in a 6-year-old-boy with an African lung fluke infection (*Paragonimus uterobilateralis*).

Diagnosis and management

Diagnosis is by the detection of characteristic ova in the sputum or stool (which they reach via the larynx and esophagus). Serologic tests are also available. The chest radiograph is often abnormal but not diagnostic. Typical appearances are of a cavitating disease in the upper zones; this is easily confused with tuberculosis (Fig. 168.7). Eosinophilia is common. Praziquantel at a dose 25mg/kg q8h for 3 days is very effective.[18]

INTESTINAL FLUKE INFECTIONS

There are a variety of trematodes in eastern Asia that can inhabit the human intestine, most notably *Fasciolopsis buski*, which is principally a parasite of pigs. Symptoms are generally absent or mild but heavy *Fasciolopsis* infections can result in significant malabsorption. Intestinal flukes are almost always eliminated by a single dose of praziquantel at 15mg/kg.

REFERENCES

1. Medina MT, Rosas E, Rubio-Donnadieu F, Sotelo J. Neurocysticercosis as the main cause of late-onset epilepsy in Mexico. Arch Intern Med 1990;150:325–7.
2. Rangel R, Torres B, del Bruto O, Sotelo J. Cysticercotic encephalitis: a severe form in young females. Am J Trop Med Hyg 1987;36:387–92.
3. Chandramuki A, Nayak P. Subacute and chronic meningitis in children – an immunological study of cerebrospinal fluid. Indian J Pediatr 1990;57:685–91.
4. Mason PR, Houston S, Gwanzura L. Neurocysticercosis: experience with diagnosis by ELISA serology and computerised tomography in Zimbabawe. Cent Afr J Med 1992;38:149–54.
5. Mitchell WG, Crawford TO. Intraparenchymal cerebral cysticercosis in children: diagnosis and treatment. Pediatrics 1988;82:76–82.
6. Sotelo J, Escobedo F, Rodriguez-Carbajal J, Torres B, Rubio-Donnadieu F. Therapy of parenchymal brain cysticercosis with praziquantel. N Engl J Med 1984;310:1001–7.
7. Cruz M, Cruz I, Horton J. Albendazole versus praziquantel in the treatment of cerebral cysticercosis. Trans R Soc Trop Med Hyg 1991;85:244–7.
8. Sotelo J, del Brutto OH, Penagos P, *et al.* Comparison of therapeutic regimen of anticysticercal drugs for parenchymal brain cysticercosis. J Neurol 1990;237:69–72.
9. Templeton AC. Anatomical and geographical location of human coenurus infection. Trop Geogr Med 1971;23:105.
10. Diaz-Camacho S, Candil-Ruiz A, Uribe-Beltran A, Willms K. Serology as an indicator of *Taenia solium* tapeworm infections in a rural community in Mexico. Trans R Soc Trop Med Hyg 1990;84:563–6.
11. Von Bonsdorff B. Diphyllobothriasis in man. London: Academic Press; 1977.
12. Khalil HM, el Shimi S, Sarwat MA, Fawzy AF, el Sorougy AO. Recent study of *Hymenolepis nana* infection in Egyptian children. J Egypt Soc Parasitol 1991;21:293–300.
13. Giboda M, Ditrich O, Scholz T, Viengsay T, Bouaphanh S. Current status of food-borne parasitic zoonoses in Laos. Southeast Asian J Trop Med Public Health 1991;22:56–61.
14. Pungpak S, Viravan C, Radomyos B, *et al.* *Opisthorchis viverrini* infection in Thailand: studies on the morbidity of the infection and resolution following praziquantel treatment. Am J Trop Med Hyg 1997;56:311–4.
15. Elkins DB, Mairiang E, Sithithaworn P, *et al.* Cross-sectional patterns of hepatobiliary abnormalities and possible precursor conditions of cholangiocarcinoma associated with *Opisthorchis viverrini* infection in humans. Am J Trop Med Hyg 1996;55:295–301.
16. Farag HF, Salem A, el-Hifni SA, Kandil M. Bithionol (Bitin) treatment in established fascioliasis in Egyptians. J Trop Med Hyg 1988;91:240–4.
17. Jaroonvesama N. Differential diagnosis of eosinophilic meningitis. Parasitol Today 1988;88:262–6.
18. Udonsi JK. Clinical field trials of praziquantel in pulmonary paragonimiasis due to *Paragonimus uterobilateralis* in endemic populations of the Igwun Basin, Nigeria. Trop Med Parasitol 1989;40:65–8.

chapter

169 Hydatid Disease

Bruno Gottstein

Echinococcus spp. are cestode parasites commonly known as small tapeworms of carnivorous animals. Their medical importance lies in the infection of humans by the larval stage of the parasites, predominantly including two species:

- *Echinococcus granulosus*, which is the causative agent of cystic hydatid disease (or cystic echinococcosis, CE); and
- *Echinococcus multilocularis*, which causes alveolar echinococcosis (AE).[1,2]

Two other species, namely *Echinococcus vogeli* and *Echinococcus oligarthrus*, are extremely rarely found in humans and are therefore not covered in this chapter.

EPIDEMIOLOGY

Echinococcus granulosus

Echinococcus granulosus lives as a small intestinal tapeworm of dogs and occasionally other carnivores. The shedding of gravid proglottids or eggs in the feces occurs within 4–6 weeks after infection of the definitive host (Fig. 169.1). Ingestion of eggs by intermediate host animals or humans results in the release of an oncosphere into the gastrointestinal tract, which then migrates to primary target organs such as liver and lungs, and less frequently to other organs (Fig. 169.2). Usually, the fully mature metacestode (i.e. hydatid cyst) develops within several months or years.

Infections with *E. granulosus* occur worldwide, predominantly in countries of South and Central America, the European and African part of the Mediterranean area, the Middle East and some sub-Saharan countries, Russia and China. The annual incidence rates of diagnosed human cases/100,000 inhabitants vary widely, for example 13 in Greece, 143 in some provinces of Argentina, 197 in the Hinjang province of China and 220 in the Turkana district of Kenya. Most cases observed in Europe and the USA are associated with immigrants from highly endemic areas. Various strains of *E. granulosus* have been described, and differ especially in their infectivity for intermediate hosts such as humans. The most important strains for human infection include sheep and cattle as intermediate hosts.

Echinococcus multilocularis

The natural life cycle of *E. multilocularis* involves predominantly red and arctic foxes as definitive hosts (Fig. 169.3), but domestic dogs or house cats can also become infected and represent an important infection source for humans in highly endemic areas.[3] In the definitive host, egg production starts as early as 28 days after infection. After egg ingestion by a rodent or a human, larval maturation will occur within the liver tissue in more than 98% of the cases (see Fig. 169.2); subsequent metastases may occur in adjacent or distant tissues. Proliferation occurs by exogenous budding of metacestode tissue with a progressive tumor-like growth.

The geographic distribution of *E. multilocularis* is restricted to the northern hemisphere. In North America, the cestode is present in the subarctic regions of Alaska and Canada. The parasite has been discovered in its wildlife cycle in several other states, therefore indicating an apparent expansion of distribution within the North–Central American continent.

In Europe, relatively frequent reports of AE in humans occur in central and eastern France, Switzerland, Austria and Germany. The Asian areas where *E. multilocularis* occurs include the whole zone of tundra, from the White Sea eastward to the Bering Strait, covering large parts of the Soviet Union, China and northern Japan.

Worldwide there are scant data on the overall prevalence of human AE. Some well-documented studies demonstrate a generally low prevalence among affected human populations. The annual mean incidence of new cases in different areas including Switzerland, France, Germany and Japan has therefore been reported to vary between 0.1 and 1.2/100,000 inhabitants.[1,2]

PATHOGENESIS AND PATHOLOGY

Echinococcus granulosus

Cystic echinococcosis (cystic hydatid disease) is clinically related to the presence of one or more well-delineated spherical primary cysts, most frequently formed in the liver, and then in the lungs and other organs such as kidney, spleen, brain, heart and bone (see Fig. 169.2). Tissue damage and organ dysfunction result mainly from this gradual process of space-occupying displacement of vital host tissue, vessels or parts of organs. Consequently, clinical manifestations are primarily determined by the site, size and number of the cysts, and are therefore highly variable. Accidental rupture of the cysts can be followed by a massive release of cyst fluid and hematogenous or other dissemination of protoscolices. Occasionally, this results in anaphylactic reactions and multiple secondary cystic echinococcosis (as protoscolices can develop into secondary cysts within the intermediate host).

The histology of a typical hydatid cyst exhibits the germinal layer as the primary site of parasite development (see Fig. 169.1). It is surrounded by a parasite-derived thick laminated layer, which is rich in aminocarbohydrates, as shown by periodic acid–Schiff positivity. The germinal layer forms protoscolices and brood capsules within the cyst lumen. Granulae, calcareous corpuscules and occasionally free daughter cysts are often observed. The parasite evokes an immune response, which is involved in the formation of a host-derived adventitious capsule. This often calcifies uniquely in the periphery of the cyst, one of the typical features found in imaging procedures. In the liver there may be cholestasis. Commonly, there is pressure atrophy of the surrounding parenchyma. Immunologically, the coexistence of elevated quantities of interferon (IFN)-γ, interleukin (IL)-4, IL-5, IL-6 and IL-10 observed in most of hydatid patients supports Th1 and Th2 cell activation in CE. In particular, Th1 cell activation seemed to be more related to protective immunity, whereas Th2 cell activation was related to susceptibility to disease.[4]

Echinococcus multilocularis

In infected humans the *E. multilocularis* metacestode (larva) develops primarily in the liver (see Fig. 169.2). Occasionally, secondary lesions form metastases in the lungs, brain and other organs. The

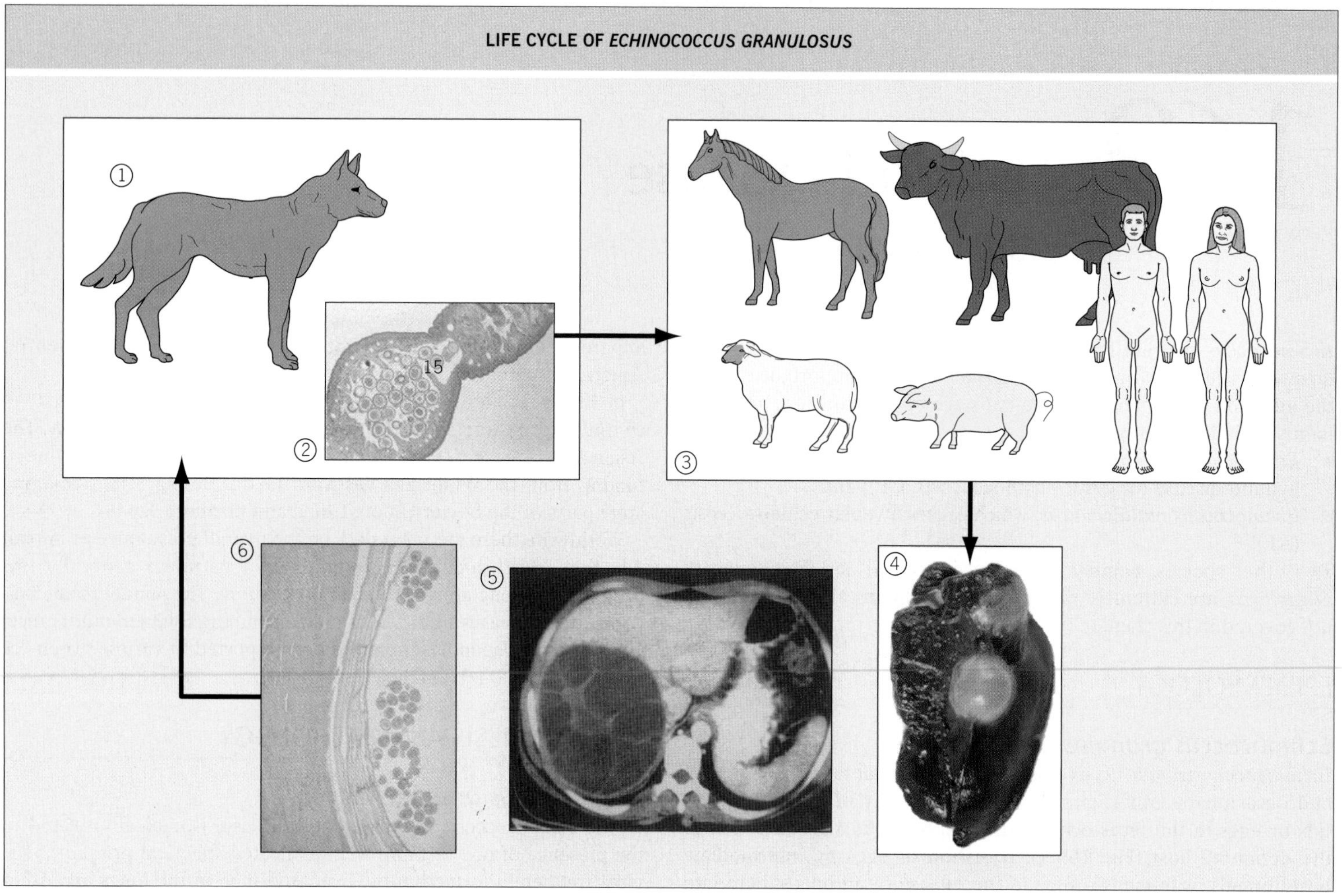

Fig. 169.1 Life cycle of *Echinococcus granulosus*. Adult tapeworms parasitize the small intestine of definitive hosts, mainly dogs (1). Parasite proglottids and eggs are shed with the feces (2), such eggs being infectious for intermediate hosts including humans (3). Hydatid cyst formation occurs predominantly in the liver (4), but also in lungs and other organs. Imaging techniques such as CT (5) demonstrate well-delineated, fluid-filled, usually unilocular bladder-like lesions. Internal daughter cysts may be visible in larger cysts as septated segments within the primary cyst. Histologically, the cyst by itself consists of a very thin inner germinal and nucleated layer with a predominantly syncytial structure (6). The germinal layer is externally protected by an acellular laminated layer of variable thickness. The endogenous formation of brood capsules and protoscolices is a prerequisite for completion of the life cycle (6), which occurs when definitive hosts ingest protoscolex-containing hydatid cysts.

typical lesion appears macroscopically as a dispersed mass of fibrous tissue with a conglomerate of scattered cavities with diameters ranging from a few millimeters to centimeters in size. In advanced chronic cases, a central necrotic cavity containing a viscous fluid may form, and rarely there is a bacterial superinfection. The lesion often contains focal zones of calcification, typically within the metacestode tissue.

Histologically, the hepatic lesion is characterized by a conglomerate of small vesicles and cysts demarcated by a thin laminated layer with or without an inner germinative layer (see Fig. 169.3). Parasite proliferation is usually accompanied by a granulomatous host reaction, including vigorous synthesis of fibrous and germinative tissue in the periphery of the metacestode, but also necrotic changes centrally. In contrast to lesions in susceptible rodent hosts, lesions from infected human patients rarely show protoscolex formation within vesicles and cysts.

Genetic and immunologic host factors are responsible for the resistance shown by some patients in whom there is an early 'dying out' or 'abortion' of the metacestode.[5] Therefore, not everyone infected with *E. multilocularis* is susceptible to unlimited metacestode proliferation and develops symptoms 5–15 years after infection.[2,3] The host mechanisms modulating the course of infection are most likely of an immunologic nature, including primarily T cell interactions. Thus, the periparasitic granuloma, mainly composed of macrophages, myofibroblasts and T cells, contains a large number of $CD4^+$ T cells in patients with abortive or died-out lesions, whereas in patients with active metacestodes the number of $CD8^+$ T cells is increased. An immunosuppressive process is assumed to downregulate the lymphoid macrophage system. Conversely, the status of cured AE is generally reflected by a high in-vitro lymphoproliferative response. The cytokine mRNA levels following *E. multilocularis* antigen stimulation of lymphocytes show an enhanced production of Th2-cell cytokine transcripts IL-3, IL-4 and IL-10 in patients, including a significant IL-5 mRNA expression in patients and not in healthy control donors.[6] The phenomenon of immunologic or constitutional resistance may be dependent upon a potential immunogenetic predisposition associated with HLA-DR.[7,8] Conversely, lack of Th cell activity such as in advanced AIDS is associated with a rapid and unlimited growth and dissemination of the parasite in AE.[9]

PREVENTION

Prevention of both CE and AE focuses primarily on veterinary interventions to control the extent and intensity of infection in definitive host populations, which may indirectly be approached by controlling the prevalence in animal intermediate hosts also. The first includes

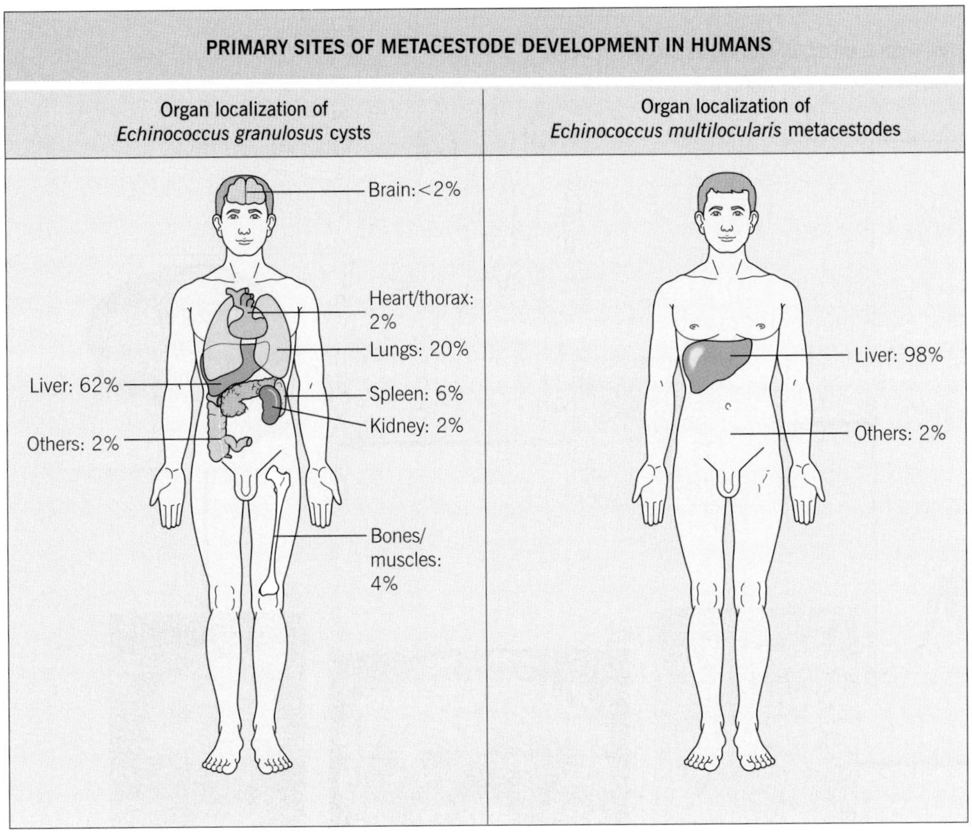

Fig. 169.2 Primary sites of metacestode development in humans. Organ distribution of the primary sites of metacestode development for *Echinococcus granulosus* (cystic echinococcosis) and *Echinococcus multilocularis* (alveolar echinococcosis) in human disease.

regular pharmacologic treatment and taking sanitary precautions for handling pets or meat to prevent infection and egg excretion, respectively.[10] For the second, a vaccine for ruminant intermediate hosts is in evaluation.[11] Prevention of human infection is strategically very difficult.

CLINICAL FEATURES

The initial phase of primary infection is always asymptomatic. The infection may then remain asymptomatic for years or even decades depending upon the size and site of the developing cyst or metacestode mass. After a highly variable incubation period, the infection may become symptomatic due to a range of different events.

Cystic echinococcosis

Depending on the size and the site of the developing hydatid cyst, the infection can remain asymptomatic for months, years or even longer. After a highly variable incubation period, the infestation may become symptomatic due to a range of different events.

- The growing cyst exerts pressure on or induces dysformation of adjacent tissues, thus inducing dysfunction of the affected organ or vascular compromise. In the case of hepatic CE, signs and symptoms may include hepatomegaly with or without a palpable mass in the right upper quadrant, right epigastric pain, nausea, vomiting and occasionally cholestatic jaundice. In inoperable cases, hepatic compromise may lead to biliary cirrhosis and the Budd–Chiari syndrome.

  Infestation of the lungs may present with chronic cough, hemoptysis, bilioptysis, pneumothorax, pleuritis, lung abscess and parasitic lung embolism.

  Rare but often catastrophic infestations can affect the heart or the brain. In the heart this can present as tumor, pericardial effusion up to tamponade, complete heart block and sudden death. In the spine and brain presentation is as a tumor with neurologic symptoms. Hydatid disease should be considered as a cause of stroke in young patients.
- A cyst may rupture and spill its content into the adjacent site. Rupture into the biliary tree will mimic biliary colic or result in cholestatic jaundice and cholangitis or pancreatitis. This is the presenting symptom in 5–25% of patients. Ruptures in the liver but also in the lungs and other organs may result in acute anaphylactic shock reactions which usually represent the initial and life-threatening manifestation.
- The cyst can become superinfected; in hepatic hydatid disease this occurs in about 9% of patients and is an indication for rapid surgical intervention.[12]

The majority of patients with CE have single organ involvement with solitary cysts. Simultaneous involvement of two or more organs is observed in 10–15% of patients, depending on the geographic origin of the patient and the strain of the parasite. In hepatic CE, the right lobe is more frequently affected than the left lobe. Cyst size varies usually between 1 and 15cm in diameter. Cyst growth ranges between a size increase of a few millimeters (1/3 of the patients) to approximately 10mm (most of the patients); 1/10 of the patients exhibit a rapid increase with an annual average of 30mm. In Europe, the average age of patients at diagnosis is 36 years. Approximately 10% of the CE cases occur in children, and the rate of lung involvement is significantly increased among this group of young patients. Pulmonary cysts occasionally become superinfected and this is best detected by computerized tomography (CT) scanning. The ratio of males to females may vary dependent on the geographic area but is statistically not significant overall.

Hepatic alveolar echinococcosis

In patients with hepatic AE, the size of the liver lesion will range between a few millimeters up to 50cm or more when patients present for diagnosis and initial treatment.[2] Typical calcifications occur in 70% of cases and central or peripheral necrotic cavities are also found in approximately 70% of cases. Clinical signs at diagnosis

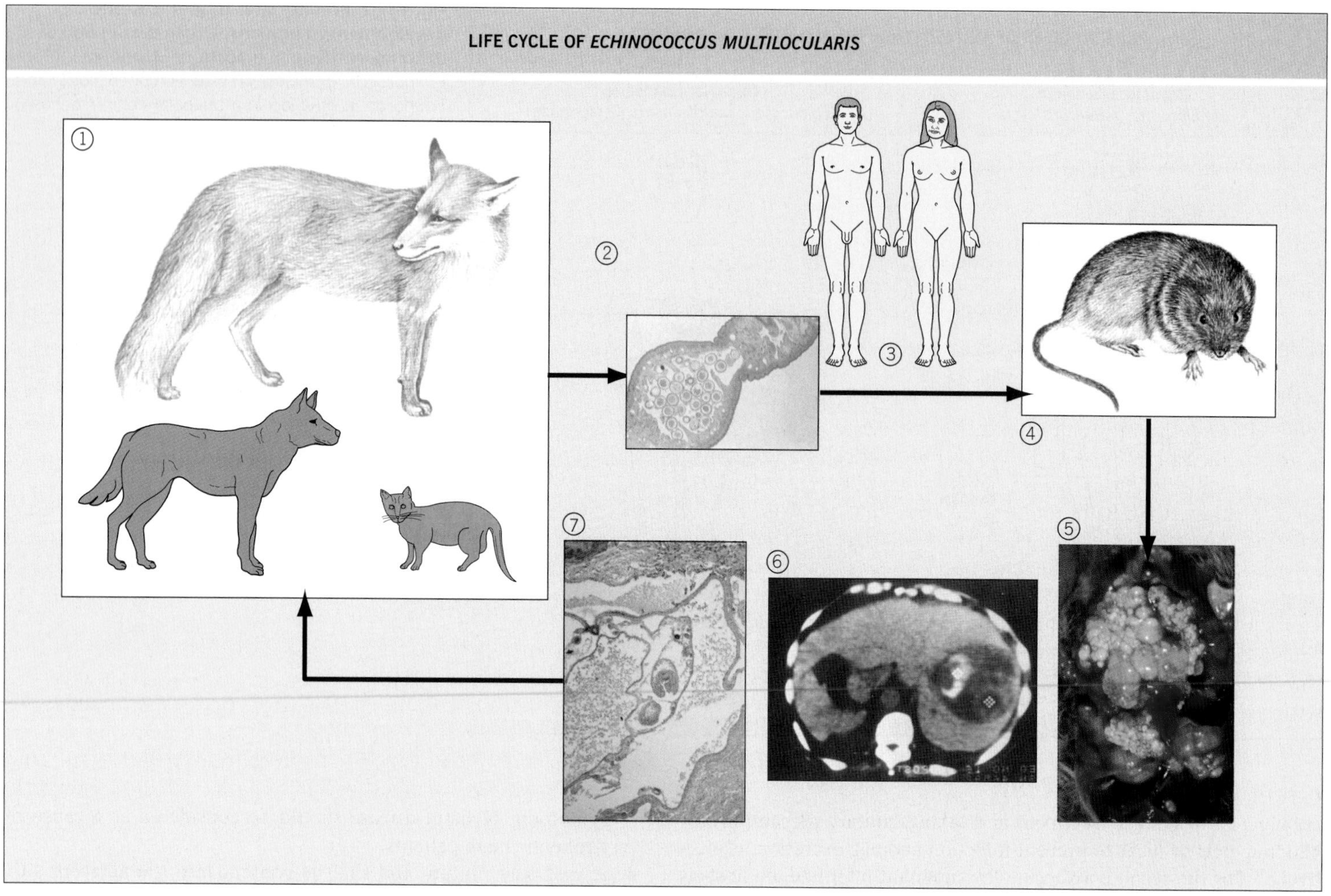

Fig. 169.3 Life cycle of *Echinococcus multilocularis*. This involves predominantly foxes as definitive hosts (1) and occasionally other carnivores such as domestic dogs or house cats. Egg production by the tapeworm starts as early as 28 days after infection (2). Eggs must be ingested by a suitable intermediate host (3), including humans and various rodent species (4). As a result, the parasite metacestode primarily becomes established in the liver. Macroscopically, the typical lesion is characterized by a dispersed mass of fibrous tissue with a multitude of interconnected vesicles ranging from a few millimeters to centimeters in size (5). The lesion often contains focal necrotic zones with scattered calcifications, as demonstrated by CT (6). Histologically, the hepatic lesion consists of a conglomerate of small vesicles and cysts demarcated by a thin laminated layer with or without an inner germinal layer and, predominantly in the rodent intermediate host, protoscolex formation (7). Oral ingestion of protoscolex-containing metacestodes by definitive hosts completes the life cycle.

include hepatomegaly–cholestasis–jaundice, secondary biliary cirrhosis, liver abscess, portal hypertension and Budd–Chiari syndrome. The disease starts frequently with non-specific symptoms such as epigastric pain or cholestatic jaundice. In complicated cases, evidence of secondary biliary cirrhosis and/or cholangitis will be found. Evidence of cholestasis is frequently present, while transaminases are only rarely and moderately elevated, in particular when there is central necrosis. One of the most feared complications is infection of a necrotic cavity and/or obstructed bile ducts, which are associated with very high mortality due to development of septic shock. Distant metastases can occur late in the disease; these have been described in brain, spine, lung and bone. Metastatic disease occurs in approximately 10–20% of patients.

The growth rate of the metacestode tissue is usually slow in immunocompetent patients. Analysis by CT scans indicated an average volume increase of 15ml/year for progressive forms of AE. In Europe, the average age of AE patients at diagnosis is 55 years.[2] Young children rarely develop AE, unless the cellular immune system is compromised.[9] The ratio of males to females varies geographically, but any variation is not statistically significant.

DIAGNOSIS

Echinococcus granulosus

In most cases, imaging procedures together with serology will yield the diagnosis. Sonography is the primary diagnostic procedure of choice for hepatic cases, although false positives occur in up to 10% of cases due to the presence of nonechinococcal serous cysts, abscesses or tumors.[2] The main diagnostic features of hydatid disease include:

- separation of the membrane from the wall,
- daughter cysts, and
- ruptured cysts.

Computerized tomography is the best investigation for detecting extrahepatic disease and volumetric follow-up assessment; magnetic resonance imaging (MRI) assists in the diagnosis by identifying changes in the intra- and extrahepatic venous systems. Ultrasonography is also helpful in following up treated patients as successfully treated cysts become hyperechogenic. Calcification of variable degree occurs in about 10% of the cysts.

Aspiration cytology appears to be particularly helpful in the detection of pulmonary, renal and other nonhepatic lesions for which imaging techniques and serology do not provide appropriate diagnostic support. The viability of aspirated protoscolices can be determined by microscopic demonstration of flame cell activity and trypan blue dye exclusion. Anti-Ag5 monoclonal antibody has been used for the detection of the respective antigen in diagnostic fine-needle aspiration biopsies (FNABs) from patients with suspected CE.[13] Immunodiagnostic tests to detect serum antibodies or circulating antigens are used to support the clinical diagnosis of CE.[14] The indirect hemagglutination tests and the enzyme-linked immunosorbent assay using *E. granulosus* hydatid fluid antigen are diagnostically relatively sensitive for hepatic cases (85–98%). For pulmonary cysts the diagnostic sensitivity is markedly lower (50–60%) and for multiple organ involvement it is very high (90–100%). These tests are usually used for primary serologic screening. Specificity is low for other cestode infections. To increase specificity, primary seropositive sera are retested using a confirmation test such as immunoblotting for a relatively specific 8kDa/12kDa hydatid fluid polypeptide antigen.[14]

Serologic studies to follow-up patients with CE postoperatively have emphasized the detection of circulating immune complexes or antigens. The detection of circulating parasite antigens proved useful for monitoring the course of disease and for assessing the extent of surgical removal of parasite lesions.[14]

Besides skin tests and basophil degranulation tests, diagnostic cellular immunodiagnosis has focused on in-vitro lymphoproliferative responses to *E. granulosus* antigens. The diagnostic sensitivity of cell-mediated immunodiagnosis is 75%, including the finding of seronegative patients with a positive proliferation test.[14]

Echinococcus multilocularis

Among the imaging procedures, ultrasonography, CT and MRI are of greatest diagnostic value, none of those being uniquely superior.[15] Irregularly dispersed clusters of calcifications on plain abdominal radiographs may give the first clue as to the etiology of the disease; the percentage of calcifications within the lesions increases from 30% to nearly 100% as the disease progresses. Hyperechogenic and hypoechogenic zones characterize the lesions. The cystic appearance may reflect central necrotic cavities. Similar findings can be found on CT and the lesions are typically not enhanced with contrast medium. The lesions are heterogeneous hypodense masses with irregular contours and lacking well-delineated walls. Hilar involvement can lead to liver atrophy, which is easily visualized by CT. Ultrasonography is the preferred imaging procedure for mass screening programs. Magnetic resonance imaging adds to diagnosis, in particular in cases with appropriate organ localization such as brain and bone, and to visualize pathologically altered microstructures in certain affected organs. Thus, MRI can give a precise analysis of the different components of the parasitic lesions such as necrosis and fibrosis.[15] However, in contrast to CT microcalcifications are not visualized by MRI. Assessing the parasite viability in vitro following therapeutic interventions may be of tremendous advantage when compared with the invasive analysis of resected or biopsied samples. Such alternatives may be offered by magnetic resonance spectrometry or positron emission tomography. The latter technique has recently been used for assessing the efficacy of chemotherapy in AE.[16]

Immunodiagnosis represents a valuable secondary diagnostic tool complementary to imaging procedures and is useful for confirming the nature of the etiologic agent.[14] Serologic tests are more reliable in the diagnosis of AE than CE. The use of purified *E. multilocularis* antigens such as the Em2 antigen or recombinant antigens II/3–10 (identical to EM10 and Em18) exhibits diagnostic sensitivities ranging between 91% and 100%, with overall specificities of 98–100%.[14] These antigens allow discrimination between the alveolar and the cystic forms of disease with a reliability of 95%. Seroepidemiologic studies reveal asymptomatic preclinical cases of human AE as well as cases in which the metacestode has died at an apparently early stage of infection (see above).[3] Serologic tests are, however, of limited value for assessing the efficacy of treatment and chemotherapy. The best respective information is provided by the detection of anti-II/3–10 (and Em18) antibodies, a status reflecting the presence of viable metacestode lesions. Cellular immune tests show that the in-vitro lymphoproliferative response to *E. multilocularis* antigen stimulation is high in cured patients who have had radical surgery and in patients with dead lesions, and is significantly lower in patients who have had partial or no surgical resection.

Histopathologic and immunohistochemic procedures to analyze surgically resected samples or biopsies obtained by FNAB include the use of species-specific MAbs such as MAbG11[17] or molecular techniques such as polymerase chain reaction.[18]

MANAGEMENT

The management of CE and AE follows the strategy recommended in the manual on echinococcosis published in 2001 by the Office International des Epizooties and the World Health Organisation.[10]

Echinococcus granulosus

Surgery remains the mainstay in the treatment of hepatic hydatid disease. Cystectomy and pericystectomy offer a good chance for cure and should be undertaken wherever possible. Occasionally, formal hepatic resection will be required. Radical surgery – either pericystectomy or resection – is possible in 50–85% of cases. In the absence of complications this can be achieved with little mortality and an acceptable morbidity. Recently, laparoscopic pericystectomy has been demonstrated to be as safe and effective as open laparotomy in selected cases with hepatic and/or splenic involvement.[19]

If surgical removal of the cyst is contraindicated, treatment of CE has several alternatives such as PAIR (Puncture, Aspiration, Injection of an heminthicide and Reaspiration), chemotherapy or 'wait and observe' approach.

Basically, indications for hepatic surgery include large liver cysts with putatively multiple daughter cysts; single liver cysts, situated superficially, which may rupture spontaneously or as a result of trauma; bacterially superinfected cysts; cysts communicating with biliary tree and/or exerting pressure on adjacent vital organs; brain, heart and kidney cysts; and spinal and bone cysts. Relative contraindications are inoperable cases as defined for surgical procedures in general; patients with cysts difficult to access; and abortive cysts either partly or totally calcified.

A direct communication between the hydatid cyst and the biliary tree may contraindicate the use of protoscolicidal solutions, which can cause chemical cholangitis leading to sclerosing cholangitis. Formalin should not be used for this reason. Effective protoscolicides with a relatively low risk of toxicity are 70–95% ethanol or 15–20% hypertonic saline solution.

Preoperative chemotherapy with albendazole or mebendazole is indicated for reducing the risk of secondary echinococcosis after operation and should begin at least 4 days before surgery and be continued for at least 1 or preferably more months. Diagnostic puncture of hydatid cysts harbors the risk of cyst rupture and dissemination of protoscolices and is therefore not recommended.

PAIR has become well justified in selected cases but it still needs to be practiced by experienced specialists.[20] Indications for PAIR are patients refusing surgery; infected cysts not communicating with the biliary vessel system; inoperable patients (see contraindications for surgery, above); pregnant patients; children >3 years; anechoic lesion ≥5cm in diameter; cysts with a regular double laminated layer; cysts with more than five septal divisions; multiple cysts (≥5cm in diameter) in different liver segments; relapse after surgery; and failure to respond to chemotherapy. Relative contraindications for PAIR are inaccessible or risky location of the cyst in the liver; multiple septal divisions; cysts with echogenic lesions; inactive cysts or calcified lesions; communicating cysts; cysts located in the lung and bones; and some others. It should not be performed when exophytic cysts or dilated bile ducts are observed on preoperative imaging.

Treatment with benzimidazoles (preferably albendazole) is highly recommended for 4 days prior to intervention. After successful instillation of protoscolicides and re-aspiration, benzimidazoles should be given for 3 months.

Treatment of nonresected cysts with benzimidazoles (albendazole or mebendazole) results in cyst disappearance in 30% of cases; in 30–50% of patients there is cyst degeneration or a significant reduction in cyst size and in 20–40% of patients the cysts show no morphologic change.[10] Indications for chemotherapy include inoperable patients as listed above.

The formerly conventional dosage of albendazole (10–15mg/kg/day in several 1-monthly courses with 14-day intervals) included three courses at minimum, and more than six courses were usually not necessary. This strategy is more commonly replaced by continuous treatment, which demonstrated equal or improved efficacy without increased adverse effects when compared with cyclic treatment.[21] For mebendazole, the usual dosage is 40–50mg/kg/day for at least 3–6 months. Praziquantel has been proposed as an additional antiprotoscolicidal drug to be given once a week in a dose of 40mg/kg along with benzimidazoles. It is also recommended before and after surgery/PAIR when there is a risk of cyst rupture and release of protoscolices.

Echinococcus multilocularis

The following strategies are commonly accepted for treatment of AE:

- the first choice of treatment is radical surgical resection of the entire parasitic lesion from the liver and other affected organs in all operable cases, with excision of the parasitic lesion following the rules of radical tumor surgery;
- concomitant chemotherapy for all cases after radical surgery or after nonsurgical interventional procedures;[21] and
- long-term chemotherapy for inoperable or only partially resectable cases and all patients after liver transplantation.[10]

Presurgical chemotherapy is not indicated for AE. The daily dosage for albendazole and mebendazole treatment is the same as for CE. For albendazole, continuous treatment is well tolerated for a duration up to 6 years, and is replaced by the former discontinuous scheme (see above) only in cases with side-effects related to medication. For mebendazole, plasma drug levels should be over 74ng/ml (250nmol/l). Generally, the duration of treatment is at least 2 years after radical surgery or continuously for many years for inoperable cases or if resection is incomplete.

As an ultimate goal liver transplantation has been proposed for a selected group of patients who have inoperable AE and chronic liver failure. However, the indications are limited and focus on cases with extensive lesions restricted to the liver and secondary liver disease leading to chronic liver failure;[22] relapse is frequent and caused by extrahepatic metacestodes, which rapidly proliferate under immunosuppressed conditions.

REFERENCES

1. Gottstein B, Reichen J. Echinococcosis/Hydatidosis. In: Cook GC and Zumla A, eds. Manson's Tropical Diseases, 21st ed. Philadelphia: Saunders/Elsevier; 2002;1561–82.
2. Amman RW, Eckert J. Cestodes: *Echinococcus*. Gastroenterol Clin North Am 1996;25:655–89.
3. Gottstein B, Saucy F, Deplazes P, *et al.* Is a high prevalence of *Echinococcus multilocularis* in wild and domestic animals associated with increased disease incidence in humans? Emerg Infect Dis 2001;7:408–12.
4. Rigano R, Profumo E, Siracusano A. New perspectives in the immunology of *Echinococcus granulosus* infection. Parassitologia 1997;39:275–7.
5. Rausch RL, Wilson JF, Schantz PM, McMahon BJ. Spontaneous death of *Echinococcus multilocularis*: cases diagnosed serologically by Em2-ELISA and clinical significance. Am J Trop Med Hyg 1987;36:576–85.
6. Sturm D, Menzel J, Gottstein B, Kern P. Interleukin-5 is the predominant cytokine produced by peripheral blood mononuclear cells in alveolar echinococcosis. Infect Immun 1995;63:1688–97.
7. Gottstein B, Bettens F. Association between HLA-DR13 and susceptibility to alveolar echinococcosis. J Infect Dis 1994;169:1416–7.
8. Eiermann TH, Bettens F, Tiberghien P, *et al.* HLA and alveolar echinococcosis. Tissue Antigens 1998;52:124–9.
9. Sailer M, Soelder B, Allerberger F, Zaknun D, Feichtinger H, Gottstein B. Alveolar echinococcosis in a six-year-old girl with AIDS. J Pediatr 1997;130:320–3.
10. Pawlowski ZS, Eckert J, Vuitton DA, *et al.* Echinococcosis in humans: clinical aspects, diagnosis and treatment. In: Eckert J *et al.*, eds. WHO/OIE Manual on echinococcosis in humans and animals. Paris: WHO/OIE; 2001:20–71.
11. Lightowlers MW, Flisser A, Gauci CG, Heath DD, Jensen O, Rolfe R. Vaccination against cysticercosis and hydatid disease. Parasitol Today 2000;16:191–6.
12. Salinas JC, Torcal J, Lozano R, Sousa R, Morandeira A, Cabezali R. Intracystic infection of liver hydatidosis. Hepatogastroenterology 2000;47:1052–5.
13. Stefaniak J. Fine needle aspiration biopsy in the differential diagnosis of the liver cystic echinococcosis. Acta Tropica 1997;67:107–11.
14. Siles-Lucas S, Gottstein B. Review: molecular tools for the diagnosis of cystic and alveolar echinococcosis. Trop Med Int Health 2001;6:463–75.
15. Reuter S, Nüssle K, Kolokythas O, *et al.* Alveolar liver echinococcosis: a comparative study of three imaging techniques. Infection 2001;29:119–25.
16. Reuter S, Schirrmeister H, Kratzer W, Dreweck C, Reske SN, Kern P. Pericystic metabolic activity in alveolar echinococcosis: assessment and follow-up by positron emission tomography. Clin Infect Dis 1999;29:1157–63.
17. Diebold-Berger S, Khan H, Gottstein B, Puget E, Frossard JL, Remadi S. Cytologic diagnosis of isolated pancreatic alveolar hydatid disease with immunologic and PCR analyses – a case report. Acta Cytol 1997;41:1381–6.
18. Kern P, Frosch P, Helbig M, *et al.* M. Diagnosis of *Echinococcus multilocularis* infection by reverse-transcription polymerase chain reaction. Gastroenterology 1995;109:596–600.
19. Seven R, Berber E, Mercan S, Eminoglu L, Budak D. Laparoscopic treatment of hepatic hydatid cysts. Surgery 2000;128:36–40.
20. Odev K, Paksoy Y, Arslan A, *et al.* Sonographically guided percutaneous treatment of hepatic hydatid cysts: long-term results. J Clin Ultrasound 2000;28:469–78.
21. Reuter S, Jensen B, Buttenschoen K, Kratzer W, Kern P. Benzimidazoles in the treatment of alveolar echinococcosis: a comparative study and review of the literature. J Antimicrob Chemother 2000;46:451–6.
22. Bresson-Hadni S, Miguet JP, Lenys D, *et al.* Recurrence of alveolar echinococcosis in the liver graft after liver transplantation. Hepatology 1992;16:279–80.

chapter
170 Filariasis

Eric A Ottesen

INTRODUCTION

Lymphatic filariasis, onchocerciasis and loiasis are the three most important filarial infections of humans (Table 170.1) and for two of these three diseases (lymphatic filariasis and onchocerciasis) there are now major public health initiatives to control or eliminate them completely.[1–4] All of these infections are caused by parasites transmitted by biting arthropods (mosquitoes or flies). Each goes through a complex life cycle that includes a slow maturation (often 3–12 months) from the infective larval stage, carried by the insects, to the adult worm that resides either in the lymph nodes and adjacent lymphatics or in the subcutaneous tissue. The offspring of the adults, the microfilariae, are 200–350μm in length and either circulate in the blood (lymphatic filariasis and loiasis) or migrate through the skin (onchocerciasis), awaiting ingestion by the insect vectors in which they develop infectivity for humans to continue this complex life cycle (see Chapter 246).

EPIDEMIOLOGY

Lymphatic filariasis

There are 120 million people in at least 80 countries of the world who are infected with lymphatic filarial parasites, and it is estimated that 1000 million people (20% of the world's population) are at risk of acquiring infection.[1,3] Of these infections, 90% are caused by *Wuchereria bancrofti*, whose only host is humans, and most of the remainder are caused by *Brugia malayi*. The major vectors for *W. bancrofti* are culicine mosquitoes in most urban and semiurban areas, anopheline mosquitoes in the more rural areas of Africa and elsewhere, and *Aedes* spp. in many of the endemic Pacific islands. For the *Brugia* parasites, *Mansonia* spp. serve as the major vector, but in some areas anopheline mosquitoes are responsible for transmitting the infection. *Brugia* parasites are confined to areas of eastern and southern Asia, especially India, Malaysia, Indonesia, the Philippines and China.

Onchocerciasis

There are 17 million people in 35 endemic countries who are infected with *Onchocerca volvulus*; 95% of these people live in sub-Saharan Africa.[2,4] Humans are the exclusive host for *O. volvulus*; there is no nonhuman reservoir of infection. Blackflies of several *Simulium* spp. are the vectors of infection, and because the larvae of these flies require fast-flowing water for their development, transmission is limited to those areas within the flight range of the flies that breed in such rivers. Thus, the distribution of onchocerciasis ('river blindness') is very much determined by the river systems and tributaries in Africa, Yemen and the Americas, where the infection is endemic.

Loiasis

Loa loa infects approximately 12 million people in the rainforest belt of western and central Africa and equatorial Sudan, where the *Chrysops* vector flies can easily find breeding spots. Although *L. loa* can be found in a number of nonhuman African primates, there is little or no cross-infection between the cycles of *L. loa* in humans and in nonhuman primates.

PATHOGENESIS AND PATHOLOGY

The pathology associated with filariases results from a complex interplay of the pathogenic potential of the parasite, the immune response of the host and external ('complicating') bacterial and fungal infections.[5,6]

Lymphatic filariasis

Although genital abnormalities (especially hydrocele) and lymphedema or elephantiasis are the most recognizable clinical entities associated with lymphatic filarial infections (Fig. 170.1), earlier changes can be detected when lymphoscintigraphy[4] or ultrasound techniques are used,[5] including lymphatic dilatation with abnormal lymphatic function. These can occur with and without an inflammatory response. Secondary host inflammatory responses, including responses to bacterial and fungal superinfections of tissues with compromised lymphatic function, cause most of the progression and physical destruction associated with elephantiasis.

The pathology in lymphatic filariasis that is immune mediated most commonly derives from the lymphatic obstructive consequences of the responses to dead or dying worms in the lymphatics, but in the syndrome of tropical pulmonary eosinophilia, the pathogenesis is distinctly different[7] and results from immunologic hyperresponsiveness to the microfilaria-stage parasites.

Onchocerciasis

Most of the significant pathology in onchocerciasis affects the skin (Fig. 170.2) or the eyes. There are both noninflammatory and inflammatory routes to tissue damage.[6] In 'steady-state', chronic *O. volvulus* infections, between 10,000 and 500,000 microfilariae are produced each day. These microfilariae migrate through the skin, inducing little inflammatory response; however, the elaboration of collagenases, elastases and other enzymatic molecules leads to hyperpigmentation, atrophy and thinning of the skin (see Fig. 170.2). Superimposed inflammatory reactions to dying microfilariae result in episodic papular dermatitis. In the eyes, these inflammatory responses result either in a characteristic punctate keratitis and, ultimately, anterior segment blindness or in uveitis and retinal lesions that can lead to posterior segment blindness. The possibility that a bacterium (*Wolbachia* spp.) that is an endosymbiont living within *O. volvulus* has a role in the pathogenesis of onchocerciasis has recently been advanced.[8]

Loiasis

'Calabar' swellings, the angio-edematous lesions characteristic of loiasis, have been less well studied. Presumably, these are immune-mediated inflammatory responses to migrating subcutaneous adult worms (Fig. 170.3) and are more common in the immunologically

PRINCIPAL FILARIAL DISEASES							
Disease	**Number of people infected worldwide**	**Parasite**	**Vector**	**Principal clinical manifestations**	**Distribution**	**Location of microfilariae within the body**	**Periodicity**
Lymphatic filariasis	120 million	*Wuchereria bancrofti*	Mosquitoes	Lymphedema, elephantiasis, genital pathology (hydrocele)	Tropics worldwide	Blood	Nocturnal (95%), 'subperiodic' (5%)
		Brugia malayi	Mosquitoes	Lymphedema, elephantiasis	Asia, India, Philippines	Blood	Nocturnal (75%), 'subperiodic' (25%)
Onchocerciasis	17 million	*Onchocerca volvulus*	Blackflies	Dermatitis, blindness	Africa (95%), Americas, Yemen	Skin	Minimal
Loiasis	12 million	*Loa loa*	Deer flies	Angio-edema, 'eyeworm'	Africa	Blood	Diumal

Table 170.1 Principal filarial diseases.

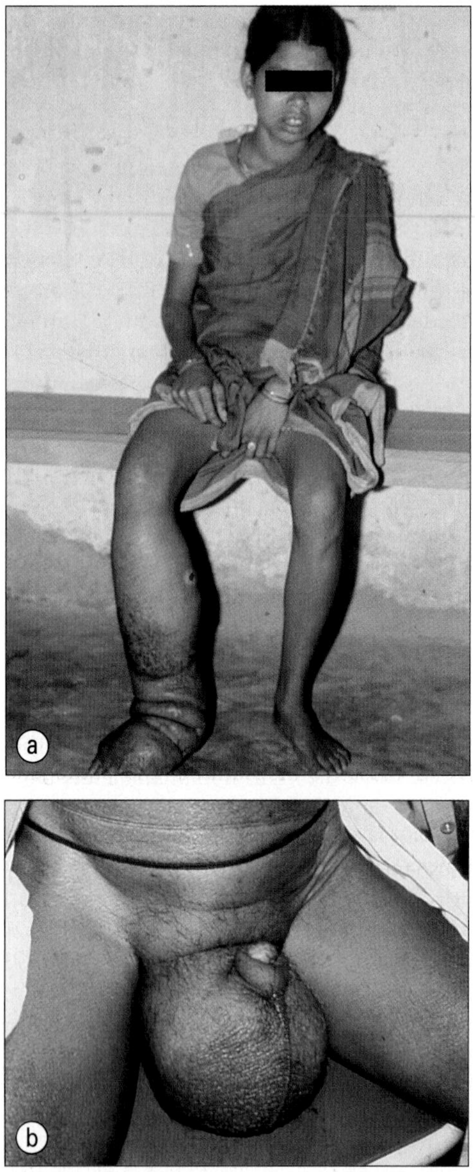

Fig. 170.1 Elephantiasis. (a) Already advanced elephantiasis in a 14-year-old Indian girl who has bancroftian filariasis. Although such clinical expression of filarial disease is more commonly seen in adults, infection in endemic areas is usually established in early childhood. (b) Scrotal elephantiasis in an adult man who has bancroftian filariasis.

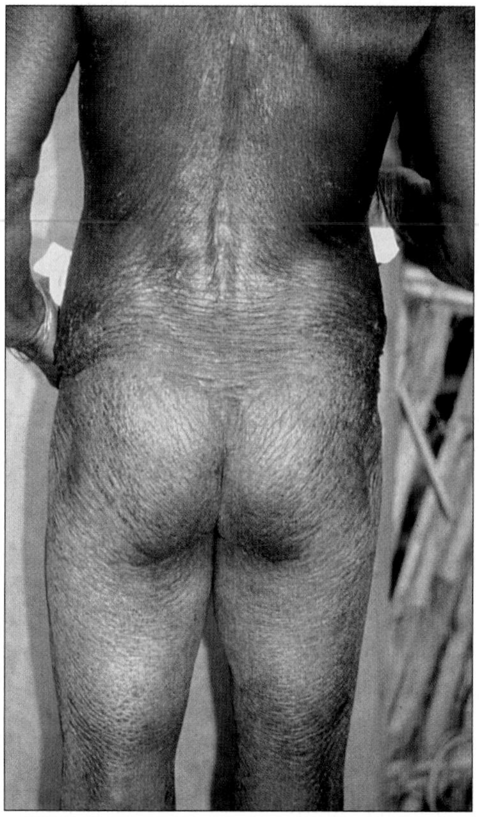

Fig. 170.2 Onchocerciasis. Evidence of excoriation caused by the patient's trying to relieve the maddening pruritus caused by onchocerciasis. Note also the marked dermal atrophy associated with chronic infection.

naive. Not common in untreated patients, but increasingly problematic in populations receiving ivermectin for co-endemic onchocerciasis, is a central nervous system (CNS) depression syndrome leading to coma or even death.[9] Its pathogenesis is suspected to involve inflammatory responses to dying microfilariae in cerebral vessels, but many details remain uncertain.

PREVENTION

Filarial infections can be acquired only from vector-borne infective larvae. Therefore, prevention of infection can be achieved either by decreasing contact between humans and vectors, generally through vector control efforts, or by decreasing the amount of infection the vector can acquire, through treating the human host.

Lymphatic filariasis

Population-based prevention

Efforts to decrease filariasis in populations through mosquito-vector control have usually proved ineffective owing to high cost and the long lifespan of the parasite (4–8 years). More recently, especially with the advent of extremely effective single-dose, once-yearly, two-drug regimens (albendazole 400mg plus either ivermectin 200μg/kg or diethylcarbamazine (DEC) 6mg/kg), the alternative approach of decreasing microfilariae in the population has been preferred.[10]

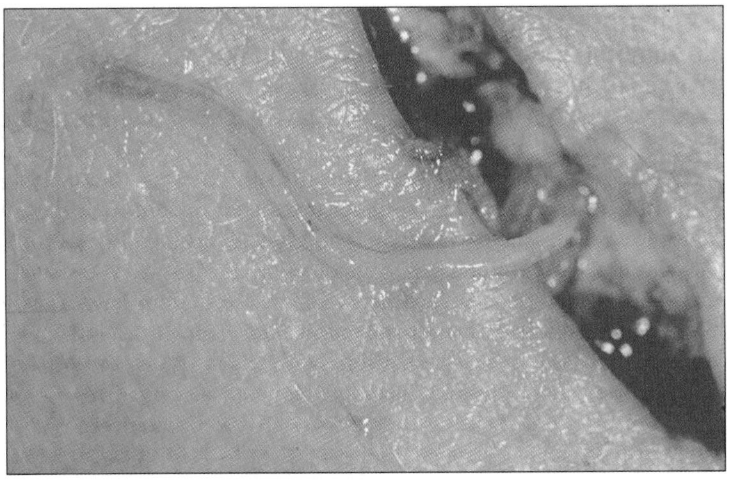

Fig. 170.3 ***Loa loa* adult worm.** The worm has been teased from the subcutaneous tissue after incision was made through a small pruritic papule (0.5cm in diameter) in an expatriate patient who had loiasis. Such papules can occur spontaneously or after treatment with DEC.

Indeed, it is this strategy that forms the basis of the new Global Program to Eliminate Lymphatic Filariasis undertaken by the World Health Organization (WHO) and a global alliance of public and private sector partners.[3]

Individual-based prevention

Contact with infected mosquitoes can be decreased through the use of personal insect repellents, bednets or insecticide-impregnated materials. Alternatively, suggestive evidence from animal models and some limited experience in human populations indicate that a prophylactic regimen of DEC (6mg/kg/day for 2 days each month) could provide effective protection against infection.

Onchocerciasis

Population-based prevention

A program to prevent onchocerciasis in 11 West African countries has been undertaken by the WHO, the United Nations Development Programme and the World Bank. It was initially based on eliminating the blackfly vectors of the infection for a period that needed to exceed the lifespan of all adult *O. volvulus* worms (12–15 years) in that area. This 'Onchocerciasis Control Program' has now run for more than 25 years and been extraordinarily successful in 'reclaiming' both land and lives of people otherwise severely compromised by onchocercal disease.[4] However, because this approach is both expensive and difficult, a new strategy for treatment and consequent prevention of infection through the use of once-yearly ivermectin in affected populations has been undertaken in all of the remaining African countries where onchocerciasis is endemic.[4]

Individual-based prevention

Decreased contact with infected blackflies through protective clothing and repellents is helpful in preventing infection. Although no prophylactic treatment regimen has yet been defined, recent studies employing monthly doses of ivermectin in cattle exposed to the related parasite *Onchocerca ochengi* show a dramatic prophylactic effect of ivermectin, but studies have not yet been undertaken to see whether similar prophylactic efficacy can be shown for ivermectin in humans as well.

Loiasis

Population-based prevention

No specific prevention efforts in populations have been undertaken.

Individual-based prevention

There are good data that repeated use of DEC (300mg weekly or 6mg/kg/day for 2 days each month in adults) is effective prophylaxis against acquisition of *L. loa* infection.[11]

CLINICAL FEATURES

Lymphatic filariasis

Chronic manifestations

Hydrocele, even though it is found only with *W. bancrofti* infections (and not *Brugia* infection), is the most common clinical manifestation of lymphatic filariasis. Uncommon in childhood, it is seen more frequently after puberty and there is a progressive increase in prevalence with age.[12] In many endemic communities, 40–60% of all adult males have hydrocele. It often develops in the absence of overt inflammatory reactions and, indeed, many patients who have hydrocele also have microfilariae circulating in the blood. The localization of adult worms in the lymphatics of the spermatic cord leads to a thickening of the cord so that the cord is palpable on physical examination of most patients. Hydroceles can become massive but still occur without the development of lymphedema or elephantiasis in the penis and scrotum[13] (see Fig. 170.1).

Although lymphedema can also develop in the absence of overt inflammatory reactions and in the early stages be associated with microfilaremia, the development of elephantiasis (either of the limbs or the genitals) is most frequently associated with a history of recurrent inflammatory episodes. Patients who have chronic lymphedema or elephantiasis are rarely microfilaremic. Very important in the progression of these lesions is the fact that the redundant skin folds, cracks and fissures of the skin provide havens for bacteria and fungi to thrive and intermittently penetrate the epidermis, leading to either local or systemic infections.

Chyluria, another of the chronic filarial syndromes, is caused by the intermittent flow of intestinal lymph (chyle) through ruptured lymphatics into the renal pelvis and subsequently into the urine. The mechanisms underlying this have not been well defined and the clinical course is known to be intermittent. Nutritional compromise can, however, be severe in patients who have chronic chyluria; special diets (low-fat and high-protein, supplemented with fluids) can often be helpful.[13]

Acute manifestations

There are four distinct acute manifestations of lymphatic filariasis, each with a different set of causative mechanisms and pathogenic implications.

The first and most important is acute inflammation of the limbs or scrotum that is related to bacterial or fungal superinfection of tissues with already compromised lymphatic function.[7]

Another type of 'filarial fever' was confused with this picture in the past. In this second type, the inflammation is initiated in the lymph node (commonly the inguinal node) with 'retrograde' extension down the lymphatic tract and an accompanying 'cold' edema. Here the inflammation appears to be immune mediated and less frequent (10–20% of cases) than the episodes of inflammation initiated by dermal infection.[13]

A third acute filarial syndrome is tropical pulmonary eosinophilia, a distinctly different syndrome caused by an immunologic hyperresponsiveness to filarial infection.[7] It is characterized by:

- extremely high levels of peripheral blood eosinophilia;
- asthma-like symptoms;
- restrictive (and often obstructive) lung disease;
- very high levels of specific antifilarial antibodies; and
- an excellent therapeutic response to appropriate antifilarial treatment with DEC.

It occurs with a frequency of less than 1% of all filariasis cases, but it is a severe condition that can lead to chronic interstitial fibrosis and pulmonary failure.

The fourth (and least commonly recognized) form of acute inflammatory reaction is that seen early after infection, particularly in expatriates who are exposed to and acquire filarial infection for the first time. Lymphangitis occurs around developing larval and early adult stages in these patients, associated with acute eosinophilic inflammation.[7]

Asymptomatic presentations

Of all the patients who have lymphatic filariasis, at least half appear clinically asymptomatic, although they have microfilariae circulating in their blood and essentially all have hidden damage to their lymphatic or renal systems.[14]

A second asymptomatic 'presentation' exists in people who do not have demonstrable microfilaremia but who do have parasite antigen in the blood (which will disappear after appropriate treatment). The clinical features and long-term sequelae of infection in this group remain to be defined.

A variety of other syndromes co-existing with filariasis are found in filarial-endemic regions and because they show some evidence of therapeutic response to DEC they have been regarded as possible manifestations of lymphatic filariasis. These include arthritis (typically monoarticular), endomyocardial fibrosis, tenosynovitis, thrombophlebitis, lateral popliteal nerve palsy and others. Although future studies may strengthen an etiologic relationship with filariasis, such presentations cannot now be confidently attributed to filarial infection.

Onchocerciasis

Chronic presentations

Most damage from onchocerciasis occurs in the skin and eye. Subcutaneous nodules (generally 1–6cm in diameter) can be palpated superficially. However, most of the skin activity is a waxing and waning of maculopapular rashes, which are essentially always accompanied by itching (see Fig. 170.1),[2] presumably because of allergic responses to dying microfilariae. During the long course of infection, the skin becomes extensively damaged, losing much of its elasticity and even pigmentation. Indeed, when the skin over the inguinal nodes (which often are enlarged owing to their continual stimulation by dying microfilariae) becomes so atrophic that it cannot support the underlying lymph nodes, the clinical presentation of 'hanging groin' occurs.

In the eye, acute changes are those associated with dying microfilariae and the local inflammatory reactions that they induce.[2] In the cornea, 'fluffy opacities' (inflammatory cells associated with the dying microfilariae) can lead to punctate keratitis, but in prolonged and heavy infection, inflammation in the cornea results in sclerosing keratitis, whereas inflammatory responses located elsewhere in the eye lead to iridocyclitis, choroidoretinitis or optic atrophy. Complications of these inflammatory eye processes also include glaucoma and cataract.

Loiasis

The two most characteristic clinical features of loiasis are the passage of an adult filarial worm across the eye ('eye worm'), often in an otherwise asymptomatic person, and Calabar swellings. Calabar swellings are localized areas of erythema and angio-edema that may be 5–10cm or more in size. Often they occur in the extremities and last for several days before regressing spontaneously. If the inflammatory reaction extends to nearby joints or peripheral nerves, corresponding symptoms may develop. Routine radiographs of people in endemic areas may reveal calcified dead worms lying between the metacarpals.

Expatriate syndrome

Recently, this 'new' filarial syndrome has been recognized as one of clinical and immunologic hyperresponsiveness that is found in expatriate visitors to regions endemic for loiasis *and other filariases*. These people manifest prominent signs and symptoms of inflammatory reactions (including allergic reactions) to the mature or maturing parasites. In loiasis, these manifestations have included primarily Calabar swellings, hives, rashes and occasionally asthma. In bancroftian filariasis (when military personnel or other migrants to endemic areas have acquired these infections), the manifestations have usually been lymphangitis, lymphadenitis and genital pain (from inflammation of the associated lymphatics), with hives, rashes and other 'allergic-like' manifestations, including blood eosinophilia.[7]

DIAGNOSIS

Except for *W. bancrofti* infections, diagnosis of filarial infections depends on the direct demonstration of the parasite (almost always microfilariae) in blood or skin specimens using relatively cumbersome techniques and having to take into account the periodicity (nocturnal or diurnal) of microfilariae in blood (see Table 170.1). Most alternative methods based on detection of antibodies by immunodiagnostic tests have not proved to be satisfactory because of their failure to distinguish between active and past infections and their problems with specificity. There is good evidence, however, that recombinant antigens will greatly improve the value of such antibody-based immunodiagnostics in the future.

Lymphatic filariasis

Antigen detection

Circulating filarial antigen detection with almost complete specificity and high sensitivity should now be regarded as the 'gold standard' for diagnosing *W. bancrofti* infections.[15] Two commercial forms of this assay are available. One is based on the methodology of an enzyme-linked immunosorbent assay and yields semiquantitative results; the other is based on a simple card (immunochromatographic) test and yields only qualitative (positive or negative) answers. No such test is currently available for brugian filariasis.

Microfilaria detection

Before the development of the circulating filarial antigen assay, detection of microfilariae in blood was the standard approach to diagnosing lymphatic filarial infection, and it is the one still required today for both brugian filariasis and those situations where the antigen detection test is not available for bancroftian filariasis. Such assessments must take into account the possible nocturnal periodicity of the parasites when the the optimal time for drawing blood is chosen; this is between 10.00pm and 2.00am for most brugian filariasis and bancroftian infections.[1,13] The simplest technique for examining blood or other fluids (e.g. hydrocele fluid or articular effusions) is to spread 20μl evenly over a clean slide that is dried and then stained with Giemsa or a similar stain. A wet smear may also be made by diluting 20–40μl of anticoagulated blood with water or 2% saponin, which will lyse the red blood cells but allow the microfilariae to remain motile and thus more readily identifiable. The larger the blood volumes examined, the greater will be the likelihood of detecting low levels of parasitemia. Other concentration techniques are also available.[13]

Clinical diagnosis

Many lymphatic filariasis patients are amicrofilaremic and therefore the diagnosis of these infections must be made 'clinically'.[16] For amicrofilaremic syndromes other than tropical eosinophilia syndrome (see Chapter 150), serologic findings based on detecting IgG_4 antibodies have proved helpful, because this subclass of IgG has greater diagnostic specificity and is stimulated by the presence of active infection. Such antibody analyses also are particularly helpful in diagnosing the 'expatriate syndrome', in which background (i.e. pre-exposure) levels of IgG and especially of IgG_4 antibodies to filarial antigens are very low, so that elevated levels have significant diagnostic implications in association with the clinical presentation.[16]

Eosinophilia is a frequent concomitant of all filarial syndromes but is diagnostically helpful only when the eosinophil levels are extremely high (as in tropical eosinophilia or the expatriate syndrome).

Onchocerciasis

Parasitologic techniques are most commonly used to diagnose onchocerciasis.[2] Microfilariae can be visualized directly in the anterior chamber fluid of the eye by slit-lamp examination of patients who have been 'prepared' by remaining for 2 minutes in a head-down position to allow microfilariae to drift forward into the anterior chamber. Skin microfilariae can be visualized after a skin snip has removed the most superficial layers of skin with either a corneoscleral punch or a small needle and disposable razor blade to obtain approximately 1mg of a bloodless piece of skin. This sample is then placed in saline or water for examination for the emergence of microfilariae after 30 minutes to 24 hours. Alternative tests include a polymerase chain reaction on skin-snip specimens or a patch test, in which DEC is incorporated into a cream that is placed on the skin, covered by gauze and the area later observed for development of papular dermatitis resulting from the death of the microfilarial parasites. Also, subcutaneous or deep nodules (generally 1–6cm in size) can be detected by palpation or ultrasound, and the adult worms they contain can be identified histologically in specimens that have been removed surgically.

Loiasis

Diagnosis of loiasis remains dependent on direct parasitologic identification (most frequently microfilariae in the blood) or indirect serologic approaches in association with a compatible clinical presentation and exposure history.[16] *Loa loa* microfilarial periodicity in the blood means that blood sampling must be done near midday (usually between 12.00pm and 2.00pm). Treatment with DEC of some amicrofilaremic patients who have suspected loiasis can induce an inflammatory nodule which, on biopsy, frequently discloses an adult worm surrounded by acute inflammatory cells. Eosinophilia and antifilarial antibodies are important diagnostic tools in expatriates with extensive exposure to infection.[16] Radiographic assessment is of little diagnostic value in these patients, but because hypereosinophilia resulting from loiasis has been associated with endomyocardial disease, echocardiography is of value in establishing whether cardiac damage has occurred.

MANAGEMENT

Lymphatic filariasis

Treatment of the infection

Remarkable advances in treating lymphatic filarial infection have recently been achieved, but most of these have focused not on individual patients but on the community. Community reduction of microfilaremia through once-yearly treatment of parasites has been described already. Few clinical trials, however, have focused on optimizing treatment of the individual patient, so there is still insufficient data to permit recommendation for a change from the older treatment regimens (DEC 6mg/kg/day for 12 days in bancroftian filariasis and for 6 days in brugian filariasis).[1] These regimens can be repeated at intervals of 1–6 months if necessary but, interestingly, essentially the entire effectiveness of a 'course' of DEC results from the first dose.[17] Ivermectin, although very effective in decreasing levels of microfilaremia, appears not to kill adult worms and thus it cannot be expected to cure infection completely. Albendazole, on the other hand, appears to kill the adult worms after prolonged courses (2–3 weeks) and to inhibit production of microfilariae after single doses (400mg)[18] but optimization of its usage is just now beginning.

Therefore, for treating infection in individual patients, single or repeated courses of DEC are still recommended. However, because the use of DEC in patients who have either onchocerciasis or loiasis can be unsafe (see below), it is important that individual patients who have bancroftian filariasis who live in areas endemic for these other infections should be examined for co-infection with these parasites before being treated with DEC.

Both diethylcarbamazine and, ivermectin, given separately at the doses necessary to treat microfilaremic patients, have minimal or no-side-effects per se. However, their rapid killing of the microfilariae releases enough antigen to overwhelm the modulating effects of the host's immune system and to induce a variety of side reactions.[19] These occur in proportion to the microfilarial levels before treatment and include headaches, fever, myalgia, lymphadenopathy and occasionally rash, itching and other symptoms. Although the most severely affected patients can also experience postural hypotension, generally these reactions are well managed through the use of antipyretics, antihistamines or, in the most severe instances, corticosteroids. In the tropical eosinophilia syndrome, as there are no microfilariae in the blood, there is no exacerbation of symptoms, but rather a steady improvement over the 2–4 weeks during which DEC is administered.

Treating the disease

Although it is important to try to cure the infection itself, management of the consequences of that infection (particularly the lymphedema, elephantiasis and genital pathology) is what is often of greatest concern to the patient. For early disease manifestations, it has been shown repeatedly that community treatment of infection with either intermittent (monthly, 6-monthly or yearly) drug administration or the steady use of DEC-fortified table or cooking salt leads to clinical improvement, with decreases in hydrocele size and prevalence and in regression of early lymphedema.

In more chronic states, patients with hydroceles or related urogenital pathology must be subjected to surgical procedures in order to obtain relief.[20]

The most dramatic change in managing patients with lymphatic filariasis has come from the recent recognition that bacterial and fungal superinfections of tissues with compromised lymphatic function play a prominent and progressively exacerbating role in disease development, so that careful attention to these infections can dramatically improve the outcome.[13] Rigorous hygiene in the affected limbs removes much of the excess stress on the lymphatic system and allows it (although still functionally compromised) to handle much more of the extracellular fluid. Management regimens should include the following:

- twice-daily washing of the affected parts with soap and water;
- raising the affected limb at night;
- regular exercise of the affected limb to promote lymph flow;
- keeping the nails clean;
- wearing shoes; and
- the use of antiseptic or antibiotic creams to treat small wounds or abrasions.

The addition of elastic bandages and other adjunctive measures can further improve results.

These same intensive local hygiene efforts and antibiotic ointments can also decrease the frequency of recurrent infection episodes in patients who have elephantiasis of the penis or scrotum but, unfortunately, specific guidelines for management have not yet been developed for successfully reversing such anatomic distortions caused by the infection.

Noninvasive management of chyluria relies on nutritional support, especially replacement of fat-rich diets with high-protein, high-fluid diets supplemented where possible with medium-chain triglycerides.[13] Surgery, the sclerosing effects of lymphangiography or, often, time alone can also lead to the cessation of the lymphatic leakage into the renal pelvis, collecting system and urine.

Onchocerciasis

Complete cure of *O. volvulus* infections is difficult to achieve because the only drug available that kills the adult worms is intravenous suramin, which is highly toxic, difficult to administer and probably not even indicated.[2]

Rather, for most patients, because the pathology is generally associated with the microfilarial stage of the parasite, treating to kill the microfilariae both rids the patients of existing symptoms and protects them from development of further eye lesions. The safest, most effective microfilaricide is ivermectin at the recommended dosage of 150–200μg/kg; in various settings it has been repeated at 12-, 6- or even 3-monthly intervals. For individual patients, the frequency of treatment can best be determined by the rate at which symptoms (primarily itching and rash) recur. For individual patients, optimal management requires a thorough eye examination before initial treatment to ensure that no microfilariae are present, since it is the inflammatory complications of treatment with microfilaricides that must be avoided, especially in the eye. If there are microfilariae in the eye, the most conservative approach to treatment would include administration of prednisone 1 day before the dose of ivermectin is given and for 2 days after it. Short courses of corticosteroids have little negative effect on the microfilaricidal activity of ivermectin, and they are clearly effective in diminishing the side reactions caused by killing the microfilariae.

The side reactions that follow treatment of onchocerciasis with ivermectin (or, earlier, with DEC) have been termed the Mazzotti reaction. They consist primarily of headache, fever, pruritus, adenopathy, rash and, occasionally, postural hypotension.[21] Although pronounced after DEC, they are much milder after ivermectin and are self-limiting (beginning within hours of treatment and persist-ing as long as 4–5 days); they can be managed satisfactorily with antipyretics, analgesics, antihistamines and, if necessary, systemic corticosteroids.

Because adult worms, which are not killed by either ivermectin or DEC, continue to shed microfilariae for up to 12–15 years, symptoms may recur and require additional treatment over an extended period of time.

Loiasis

The approach to treatment of loiasis depends on the clinical presentation. In patients who do not have microfilaremia, DEC 6–8mg/kg/day for 3 weeks is the optimal treatment and results in cure of approximately half of the patients. Repeated courses of the drug are indicated when patients become symptomatic again and each repeated treatment results in additional patient cures.[22]

For microfilaremic patients, the approach to treatment is more difficult because the side reactions induced by the dying microfilariae can include CNS effects and even death. Such severe reactions rarely, if ever, occur in patients who have blood microfilaria counts of less than 2000/ml of blood (drawn at the time of day for peak parasitemia). However, even in a very controlled, hospital setting, when highly microfilaremic loiasis patients were treated with DEC (initially at very low dosages – 0.25mg/kg – and then increased progressively), there were still some patients in whom there was development of a post-treatment encephalopathy and death. This was not prevented, even when corticosteroids were co-administered.[23] When ivermectin is used instead of DEC, the clearance of microfilaremia from the blood is very much slower and not so complete. While it is very much safer than DEC, both in terms of the systemic side reactions that it elicits (which are similar to those of the Mazzotti reaction) and in terms of avoiding the catastrophic neurologic complications in patients with extremely high levels of microfilaremia (15,000–100,000/ml), ivermectin has still led to instances of CNS deterioration, coma and death. With optimal clinical care, the transient CNS compromise of such ivermectin-treated patients can be managed successfully and catastrophic results minimized. However, the treatment of loa-endemic populations with ivermectin (usually as part of national programs linked to the African Program for Onchocerciasis Control[4] or the Global Program to Eliminate Lymphatic Filariasis[3]) often is rendered in remote areas without access to optimal medical management. Therefore, this potential complication of treatment provides a major challenge that must be overcome before these massive public health initiatives can be successful in the loa-endemic regions of Africa.

If patients experience an adult *L. loa* crossing the eye below the conjunctiva, such worms can be removed through simple surgical incision of the conjunctiva, but because usually there are multiple parasites within the patient, a single procedure may not be curative.[24]

REFERENCES

1. WHO Expert Committee on Filariasis. Fifth Report. Lymphatic filariasis: the disease and its control. WHO Tech Rep Ser 1992;821:1–71.
2. WHO Expert Committee on Onchocerciasis. Fourth Report. WHO Tech Rep Ser 1995;852:1–103.
3. Ottesen EA. The global programme to eliminate lymphatic filariasis. Trop Med Int Health 2000;5:591–4.
4. Richards FO, Boatin B, Sauerbrey M, Seketeli A. Control of onchocerciasis today: status and challenges. Trends Parasitol 2001;17:558–63.
5. Dreyer G, Noroes J, Figueredo-Silva J, *et al.* Pathogenesis of lymphatic disease in Bancroftian filariasis: a clinical perspective. Parasitol Today 2000;16:544–8.
6. Ottesen EA. Immune responsiveness and the pathogenesis of human onchocerciasis. J Infect Dis 1995;171:659–71.
7. Kumaraswami V. The clinical manifestations of lymphatic filariasis. In: Nutman TB, ed. Lymphatic filariasis. London: Imperial College Press; 2000:103–26.
8. Saint AA, Blackwell NM, Hall LR, *et al.* The role of endosymbiotic Wolbachia bacteria in the pathogenesis of river blindness. Science 2002;295:1892–5.
9. Boussinesq M, Gardon J, Gardon-Wendel N, *et al.* Three probable cases of *Loa loa* encephalopathy following ivermectin treatment of onchocerciasis. Am J Trop Med Hyg 1998;58:461–9.
10. Ottesen EA, Duke BOL, Karam M, Behbehani K. Strategies and tools for the elimination of lymphatic filariasis. Bull World Health Organ 1997;75:491–503.
11. Nutman TB, Miller KD, Mulligan M, *et al.* Diethylcarbamazine prophylaxis for human loiasis: results of a double-blind study. N Engl J Med 1988;319:752–6.
12. Witt C, Ottesen EA. Lymphatic filariasis: an infection of childhood. Trop Med Int Health 2001;6:582–606.
13. Addiss DG, Dreyer G. Treatment of lymphatic filariasis. In: Nutman TB, ed. Lymphatic filariasis. London: Imperial College Press; 2000:151–200.
14. Dreyer G, Ottesen EA, Galdino E, *et al.* Renal abnormalities in microfilaremic patients with Bancroftian filariasis. Am J Trop Med Hyg 1992;46:745–51.
15. Weil GJ, Lammie PJ, Weiss N. The ICT filariasis test: a rapid format antigen test for diagnosis of bancroftian filariasis. Parasitol Today 1997;13:401–4.
16. Ottesen EA. Filarial infections. Infect Disease Clin North Am 1993;7:619–33.
17. Noroes J, Dreyer G, Santos A, *et al.* Assessment of the efficacy of diethylcarbamazine on adult *Wuchereria bancrofti in vivo.* Trans Roy Soc Trop Med Hyg 1997;91:78–81.
18. Ottesen EA, Ismail MM, Horton J. The role of albendazole in programmes to eliminate lymphatic filariasis. Parasitol Today 1999;15:382–6.

19. Dreyer G, Coutinho A, Miranda D, *et al.* Treatment of bancroftian filariasis in Recife, Brazil: a two-year comparative study of the efficacy of single treatments with ivermectin or diethylcarbamazine. Trans Roy Soc Trop Med Hyg 1995;89:98–102.
20. DeVries CR. The role of the urologist in the treatment and elimination of lymphatic filariasis worldwide. BJU Int 2002;89(Suppl.1):37–43.
21. Francis H, Awadzi K, Ottesen EA. The Mazzotti reaction following treatment of onchocerciasis with diethylcarbamazine: clinical severity as a function of infection intensity. Am J Trop Med Hyg 1985;34:529–36.
22. Klion AD, Ottesen EA, Nutman TB. Effectiveness of diethylcarbamazine in treating loiasis acquired by expatriate visitors to endemic regions: long-term follow-up. J Infect Dis 1994;169:604–10.
23. Carme B, Boulesteix J, Boutes H, Puruehnce MF. Five cases of encephalitis during treatment of loiasis with diethylcarbamazine. Am J Trop Med Hyg 1991;44:684–90.
24. Eveland LK, Yermakov V, Kenney M. *Loa loa* infection without microfilaraemia. Trans Roy Soc Trop Med Hyg 1975;69:354–5.

chapter 171

Infections in Sickle Cell Disease

Graham R Serjeant

DEFINITION

Sickle cell disease is a 'generic' term that embraces a group of genotypes characterized by pathology associated with the presence of sickle hemoglobin (HbS). This abnormal hemoglobin (Hb) results from a single amino acid substitution of valine for glutamic acid at position 6 in the β-chain. Inheritance of this abnormal gene from one parent and a normal gene for HbA from the other results in the harmless carrier state, the sickle cell trait. Sickle cell trait (AS genotype) is excluded from the definition of sickle cell disease because it causes no clinical problems in the great majority of subjects unless they are exposed to hypoxic environments such as high altitude or respiratory depression. The principal genotypes of sickle cell disease include:

- homozygous sickle cell (SS) disease, in which the abnormal HbS gene is inherited from both parents;
- sickle cell HbC (SC) disease, in which the gene for HbS is inherited from one parent and the gene for HbC from the other. HbC is the second most common abnormal Hb among people of West African origin; and
- inheritance of the sickle cell gene with one of the genes for β-thalassemia.

The β-thalassemia genes reduce the synthesis of β-chains; the degree of β-chains produced determines the amount of HbA. This inhibits sickling, and influences the hematology and clinical course. Several molecular mutations causing β-thalassemia have been described in association with HbS. In sickle cell β^0-thalassemia there is no HbA and a generally severe course, whereas a variety of sickle cell β^+-thalassemia syndromes result in variable amounts of HbA and variable clinical courses. The most common form of sickle cell β^+-thalassemia among peoples of African origin results in 20–30% of HbA and a very mild clinical course.

DISTRIBUTION AND PREVALENCE

In equatorial Africa, the prevalence of the sickle cell trait commonly reaches 20–30%. Contrary to the common belief that the sickle cell gene is confined to peoples of African ancestry, the gene is widespread in populations around the Mediterranean (Sicily, northern Greece, southern Turkey, the Levant and northern Africa), eastern Saudi Arabia and central India. HbC is a marker of west African ancestry, reaching prevalences of 20% in parts of Ghana and Burkina Faso, falling to 3–5% in Nigeria, and not occurring in central or east Africa, Saudi Arabia, Greece or central India.

In Nigeria, where approximately 25% have the sickle cell trait, it is estimated that SS disease occurs once in every 50 births, or in 100,000 births annually. The prevalence of SS disease at later ages is determined by the mortality of this genotype, which in Africa is often very high with infrequent survival to adult life. In Jamaica, the relative frequencies of the four major genotypes at birth (Table 171.1) are also influenced at later ages by their relative mortality, which is greater in SS disease and $S\beta^0$-thalassemia. The prevalence of these four major genotypes among African–Americans and among the UK population of Afro-Caribbean origin are similar to those in Jamaica (because of similar gene frequencies), although the increasing population of direct African origin has markedly increased trait and disease frequencies in the UK. In all populations, the prevalence of sickle cell disease at birth is determined by the gene frequency but at later ages is influenced by the relative survival of affected patients; in hospital-based populations frequency is influenced by the relative severity, which determines presentation.

PATHOGENESIS AND PATHOLOGY

On deoxygenation, HbS molecules form rigid linear structures (polymers), which increase the intracellular viscosity and deform red cells into an abnormal 'sickled' shape. This can be reversed on oxygenation but after several sickle–unsickle cycles, these cells may become permanently deformed. These less deformable red cells have difficulty negotiating the capillary beds where normal red cells with an average diameter of 7μm must bend and fold to traverse a capillary measuring 3μm. As a result, these abnormal red cells become prematurely destroyed (hemolysis) and may also block blood flow (vaso-occlusion).

Accelerated hemolysis results in anemia, jaundice, an increased prevalence of pigment gallstones and marked bone marrow expansion with high metabolic demands. The consequences of vaso-occlusion are determined by the site of the occlusion, but may include strokes, retinal ischemia, acute chest syndrome, a variety of splenic pathologies and chronic leg ulcers. Some manifestations, such as bone marrow necrosis, are influenced by both the hemolytic and vaso-occlusive components giving rise to dactylitis, the painful crisis, and avascular necrosis of long bones and femoral head. In these conditions, the pathology is confined to areas of active bone marrow activity, where the metabolic demands are believed to exceed the supply, which has been diminished either by vaso-occlusion or, more likely, by shunting of blood away from the active marrow.

The pathologies of particular relevance to infections in sickle cell disease are the accelerated bone marrow activity, the prevalence of leg ulcers, acute chest syndrome and – most important of all – the early loss of splenic function. These processes are most marked in SS disease and sickle cell β^0-thalassemia, and less marked in the generally mild conditions of SC disease and sickle cell β^+-thalassemia.

The spleen in sickle cell disease

The spleen acts like a filter in the circulation, removing damaged red cells and bacteria from the bloodstream. It achieves this function by requiring red cells to squeeze between endothelial cells (Fig. 171.1) as the blood traverses from the cordal tissue to the splenic sinuses before returning to the circulation. In addition to the filtering mechanism, the spleen also represents a large mass of reticuloendothelial tissue that is in intimate contact with the circulation and is important in the production of specific antibodies. These are particularly important if the liver is to participate actively in the removal of blood-borne antigens. Splenectomy removes these protective mechanisms and, in patients

RELATIVE FREQUENCY OF PRINCIPAL GENOTYPES OF SICKLE CELL DISEASE IN JAMAICA	
Genotype	**Frequency at birth**
Homozygous sickle cell (SS) disease	1 in 300
Sickle cell-hemoglobin C (SC) disease	1 in 500
Sickle cell β^+-thalassemia	1 in 3000
Sickle cell β^0-thalassemia	1 in 7000

Table 171.1 Relative frequency of principal genotypes of sickle cell disease in Jamaica. In these data, sickle cell β^+-thalassemia refers to the common Jamaican form with 20–25% HbA.

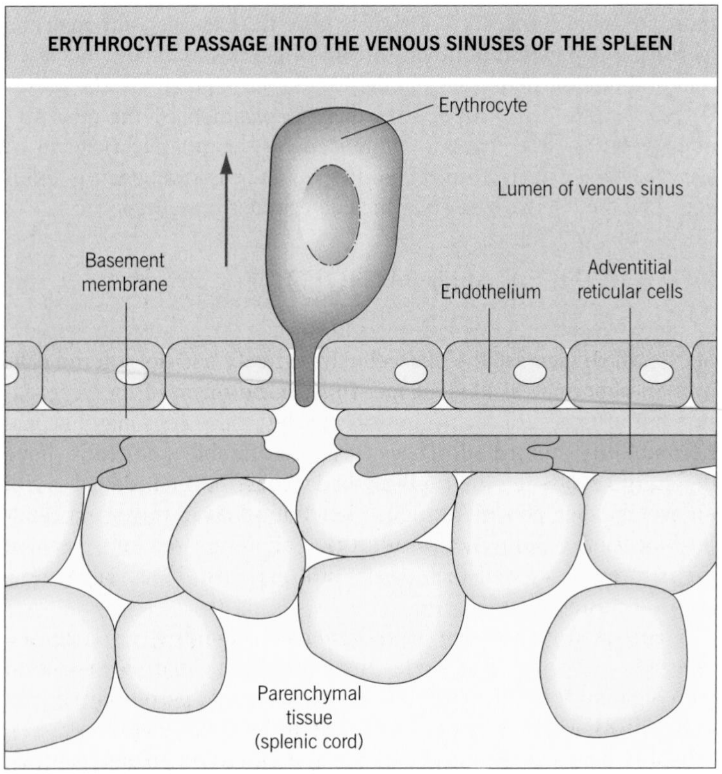

Fig. 171.1 Erythrocyte passage into the venous sinuses of the spleen. A red cell passing between endothelial cells (arrow shows direction of movement) from the cordal tissue to the vascular sinus. Sickle cells do not have this deformability, so they accumulate in the spleen. Modified from Weiss.[1]

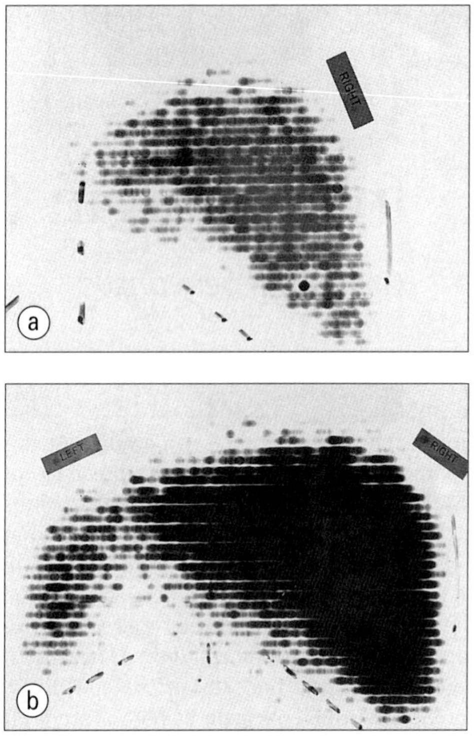

Fig. 171.2 ^{99m}Technetium sulfur colloid scans (posterior view) in a 2-year old child with SS disease and splenomegaly. (a) The scan shows hepatic uptake but no splenic uptake. (b) A repeat scan 6 days after a blood transfusion shows restoration of splenic uptake of colloid. From Pearson *et al.*[5]

without sickle cell disease, splenectomy has been calculated to increase the risk of sepsis 50- to 60-fold (see Chapter 109).

In sickle cell disease, the abnormal red cells damage splenic function early in life. Even when the spleen is clinically enlarged, splenic uptake of ^{99m}technetium sulfur colloid is abnormal;[2] and elevated pitted red cell counts, which suggest abnormal splenic function, may occur as early as 6 months of age, and are seen in 20% of SS children by 1 year of age and in 40% by 2 years of age.[3] This loss of splenic function appears to be directly related to the susceptibility to infection[4] and may be reversed by chronic transfusion in young children (Fig. 171.2).[5] It is also delayed in SS patients with high levels of fetal Hb (HbF), which inhibit sickling and allow persistence of splenic function in SS patients in eastern Saudi Arabia.[6]

CLINICAL FEATURES

Bacterial infection

Streptococcus pneumoniae

The susceptibility to pneumococcal sepsis in SS disease is well substantiated and was first reported in 1928. The relative risk has been calculated to be at least 20 times that in the general population, and age-specific incidence rates are highest before the age of 2 years and fall sharply after 5 years.[7] Infection is closely linked to the appearance of clinical splenomegaly before 6 months of age.[8]

Prophylactic penicillin markedly reduces this risk, whether given orally[9] or by depot monthly intramuscular injection,[10] and has now become routine for children with severe genotypes (SS disease, Sβ^0-thalassemia). Although there is some evidence of an increased risk in SC disease, the risk is not generally considered of sufficient magnitude to justify routine prophylaxis in the milder genotypes (SC disease, Sβ^+-thalassemia). The maximum risk from pneumococcal sepsis in Jamaica is in the first 3 years of life (Fig. 171.3), and depot injections of penicillin during that period prevent infection. It is unclear when to stop but the current Jamaican protocol provides intramuscular penicillin monthly from 4 months to 4 years with a single dose of 23-valent pneumococcal vaccine at the time of the last penicillin injection. Intramuscular injections are preferred in Jamaica to avoid the problems of compliance, which may compromise the twice-daily oral penicillin generally favored in the USA. Twice-daily erythromycin may be used in children who are allergic to penicillin. The nonconjugated capsular polysaccharide pneumococcal vaccine does not confer adequate protection in young children, but its immunogenicity improves with the age of the patient, and preliminary data suggest that protective levels against many of the serotypes are achieved by the vaccine given at 4 years of age.

Two recent factors may cause these policies to be reassessed: the increasing prevalence of penicillin-resistant pneumococci, which may account for 20–50% of isolations in children with SS disease in the USA; and the development of a conjugate pneumococcal vaccine, which may be effective given at 2, 4 and 6 months, and is currently under assessment. Preliminary data suggest this vaccine may generate what are believed to be protective levels of antibody but potential disadvantages are the high cost and the less comprehensive coverage (7- or 9-valent) compared with the standard 23-valent nonconjugate vaccine.

This susceptibility to the pneumococcus has not been shown in all sickle cell populations, and several studies on the bacteriology of

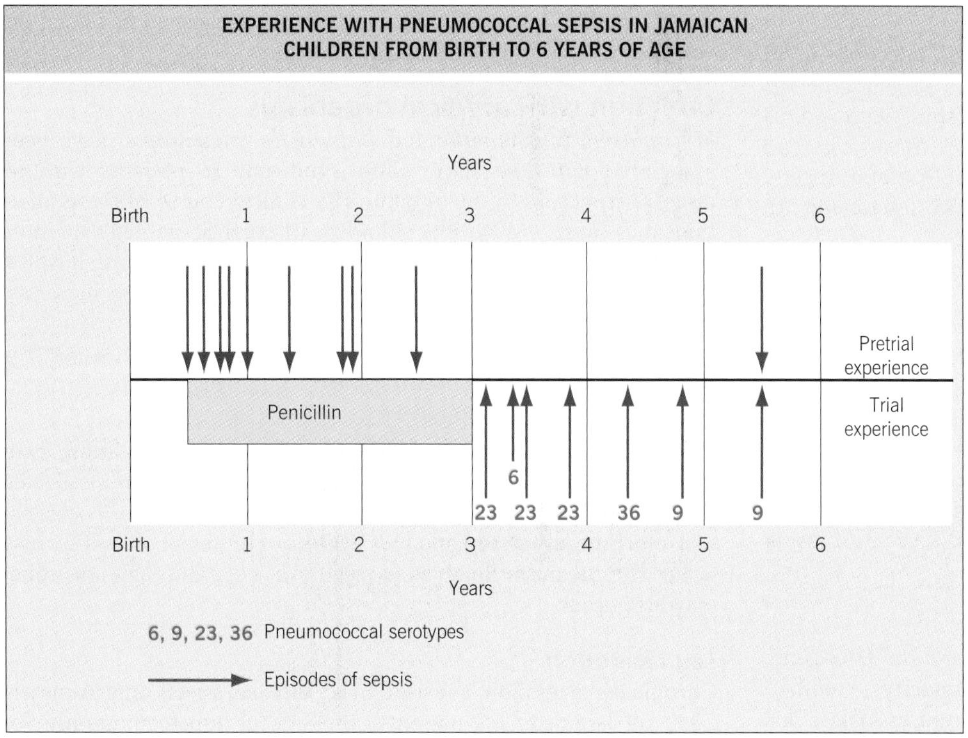

Fig. 171.3 Experience with pneumococcal sepsis in Jamaican children from birth to 6 years of age. Pre-trial experience shows that sepsis episodes commenced at 6 months and 9 or 10 episodes occurred before 3 years. During penicillin prophylaxis from 6 months to 3 years, no episodes occurred but seven episcodes occurred after cessation of penicillin. The numbers by the arrows refer to pneumococcal serotypes.

septic children with SS disease in Nigeria[11] and Uganda revealed the most common agents to be *Klebsiella* spp., staphylococci, *Salmonella* spp. and *Escherichia coli,* with a paucity of *S. pneumoniae*. Possible interpretations of this infrequency of pneumococci include the early use of over-the-counter penicillin, the rapid demise of septicemic patients so that they do not reach hospital, the environmental dominance of Gram-negative organisms, or the intriguing postulate that malaria-induced splenomegaly may allow persistence of splenic function.[11] The role of the pneumococcus in SS disease in equatorial Africa must be clarified if governments are to be advised to spend limited resources on pneumococcal prophylaxis programs in sickle cell disease.

Haemophilus influenzae *type b*

It seems likely that children with SS disease are also more prone to *Haemophilus influenzae* type b (Hib) infection, which has been increasing in importance with the advent of effective pneumococcal prophylaxis.[12] Extensive data from the US Cooperative Study of Sickle Cell Disease showed an incidence rate of 0.45 per 100 patient-years under 6 years of age, not significantly different from the incidence in the normal black population;[6] however, a susceptibility of 20–160 times that in the normal population has been proposed from other studies.[13] Although the risks of Hib infection in SS disease are unclear, prophylaxis appears justified and may be effected by conjugated Hib vaccines given between 2 and 6 months of age.[14]

Salmonella

There is a long-standing and well-recognized susceptibility to *Salmonella* osteomyelitis in SS disease, and a less well-recognized association with *Salmonella* sepsis. In a Jamaican study, half of the *Salmonella* isolations from blood occurred without obvious bone involvement and were associated with a 22% mortality because the potential significance of *Salmonella* spp. in a septic patient often went unrecognized.[15] On the other hand, none of the patients with *Salmonella* isolations associated with bone involvement died because the increased awareness of the association led to the early use of specific therapy against *Salmonella* spp.

Salmonella osteomyelitis is believed to be a secondary infection of avascular bone marrow, and its distribution reflects that of the underlying bone marrow necrosis. The complication may become superimposed upon dactylitis in young children and should be suspected if the swelling is marked or there is high fever, in which case a surgical opinion should be sought regarding drainage; infection may be followed by a premature epiphysial fusion and a permanent shortening of affected small bones. At later ages, osteomyelitis may follow bone marrow necrosis in the shafts of the long bones, ribs or sternum, pelvis and vertebrae. Infection of the avascular femoral head may be particularly difficult to diagnose, but this can lead to very rapid dissolution and extensive bone damage. Diagnosis depends on positive blood culture, and the diagnostic yield may be increased by invasive procedures such as bone marrow aspirate or trephine biopsies. The differential diagnosis of sterile avascular necrosis and osteomyelitis is a difficult clinical challenge and even bone scanning techniques have generally been unhelpful, the diagnosis resting on clinical judgment. Treatment is by specific antibiotics against *Salmonella* spp., such as chloramphenicol, ampicillin, trimethoprim–sulphamethoxazole (co-trimoxazole), or third-generation cephalosporins. Surgical drainage and the removal of sequestra may be necessary for complete healing and, even after apparent recovery, patients are prone to recurrence, sometimes years later, suggesting that the organisms remain dormant or loculated.

The source of *Salmonella* organisms in SS disease remains unknown, but common speculations include microinfarction of the gut wall in patients carrying *Salmonella*, or gallbladder colonization associated with gallstones and an abnormal gallbladder wall. However, a recent study showed no association with gallstones or with indices of vaso-occlusion, and *Salmonella* isolation from stools is only occasionally reported in patients with *Salmonella* osteomyelitis. The high prevalence of *Salmonella enteritidis*, which accounted for one-third of all isolations in the Jamaican series, suggests a dietary source; an intriguing possibility is carriage of *Salmonella* spp. by white cells, which would have the ironic effect of introducing the organism to the site of initially sterile avascular necrosis. More work is needed on the method of acquisition of *Salmonella* spp. in SS disease.

Escherichia coli

The extent of the increased risk of *Escherichia coli* infections in SS disease is unknown, but a significant excess of the SS genotype has been noted among black children admitted to hospital with serious infection and diagnosed as having *E. coli* sepsis.[16] *Escherichia coli* sepsis has also been associated with osteomyelitis and stroke. Urinary tract infections appear more common in SS disease and are a likely origin of *E. coli* sepsis.

Splenectomy and infection

Splenectomy, which may avoid morbidity and potential deaths in acute or chronic red cell sequestration, may be deferred because of concerns over loss of the splenic contribution to immune competence. However, the spleen in such patients is already immune compromised and no increase in severe infections or deaths occurred in 130 splenectomized SS patients when compared with 130 age- and sex-matched SS controls over the same period.[17] If indicated, splenectomy in SS disease should not be deferred for fear of losing persistent splenic immune function.

Malaria

There is a special relationship between malaria and the HbS gene, which was initially noted because malaria endemicity tended to coincide with high frequencies of the sickle cell trait in Africa. This has been the basis of many studies, which have reached general agreement that during a critical period in early childhood (between the loss of passively acquired maternal immunity and the development of active immunity), the presence of the sickle cell trait confers some protection against malaria. The mechanism remains controversial and may be multifactorial, but increased sickling of parasitized red cells has been demonstrated and may serve to identify the host cell to the spleen and brings about its more effective removal. The maintenance of high frequencies of the sickle cell gene in areas of falciparum malaria led to the hypothesis of balanced polymorphism, proposing that a survival advantage in the sickle cell trait was balanced by the disadvantage and presumed loss of two genes in the early deaths occurring in SS disease. For patients with SS disease, malaria is believed to be a major cause of morbidity and mortality; further hemolysis being superimposed upon that already present. Some African workers suggest that such patients do not die of malaria but succumb to symptoms that are related to sickle cell disease but are precipitated by malaria.

Viral infection

Patients with SS disease are not intrinsically more prone to viral infections. Antibody responses to viral vaccines appear normal and infection rates by human parvovirus are similar in SS disease and AA controls. The greater exposure to blood transfusion may render patients more prone to transfusion-acquired viral infections such as hepatitis C virus and HIV.

Human parvovirus infection appears to be the cause of aplastic crisis in SS disease, but this reflects a difference in response rather than an increased susceptibility. Human parvovirus infection colonizes and destroys red cell precursors in the bone marrow, but the virus becomes neutralized by specific antibody, and bone marrow function returns after 7–10 days. In SS disease, the red cell survival may be as short as 7–10 days and, unless oxygen delivery is maintained by transfusion, the aplastic crisis may result in death. Human parvovirus displays the general characteristics of a viral infection – most affected patients are under 15 years of age, epidemics occur at 3- to 4-year intervals, and there is high infectivity between siblings. The risk of aplasia among susceptible siblings of an affected patient is 50% within 3 weeks. A human parvovirus vaccine has been developed but it is still awaiting clinical trial.

Infection with atypical organisms

Mycoplasma pneumoniae and *Chlamydia pneumoniae* have been associated with the acute chest syndrome in patients with SS disease, especially in the autumn. The clinical course of these infections may be severe but it is unknown whether SS patients are more prone to develop these infection. The increased rate of hospital admission among SS patients also exposes them to an increased chance of hospital-acquired infections.

Other mechanisms of infection

Gallstones

The rapid hemolysis and consequent high excretion of bilirubin leads to increased gallstone formation, which occurs in 50% of unselected SS patients by the age of 25 years. Jamaican experience[18] suggests that most are asymptomatic, but acute or chronic cholecystitis may occur. The organism involved is usually *E. coli*, although anaerobes may also occur.

Leg ulceration

Chronic leg ulceration, a feature of SS disease, affects approximately 70% of Jamaican SS patients; they occur most commonly for the first time between 15 and 20 years of age and run a healing–relapsing course. The ulcer surface is commonly colonized by *Staphylococcus aureus*, *Pseudomonas aeruginosa* and β-hemolytic streptococci, but these ulcers are rarely associated with evidence of systemic infection. A possible association between ulcer-borne β-hemolytic streptococci and glomerular disease with proteinuria has been suggested, similar to the association between skin carriage of this organism and acute glomerulonephritis described from Trinidad, but subsequent analysis has indicated that, although both leg ulceration and proteinuria increased with age, there was no relationship between the two after correction for age. Leg ulcers occasionally act as a portal of entry for tetanus.

The lack of evidence for systemic infection in leg ulceration suggests a limited role for antibiotic therapy, although infection with *P. aeruginosa* may occasionally be associated with ulcer deterioration and poor healing.

Acute chest syndrome

The acute chest syndrome is a pneumonia-like pathology with elements of infection, infarction, pulmonary sequestration and fat embolism. It is a major cause of morbidity and the most common single cause of mortality at all ages after 2 years. The contribution of primary infection is controversial, and, although early studies reported pathogens in approximately half the cases in children aged under 3 years, recent studies have found evidence of bacterial infection in only 4–14% of episodes. Furthermore, the poor response to antibiotics and the striking improvement in many cases following transfusion has favored a vascular pathology rather than an infective one. Infections with the atypical agents *M. pneumoniae* and *C. pneumoniae* have been mentioned above.

CONCLUSION

Patients with sickle cell disease are susceptible to some but not all infections. However, any infective illness coinciding with sickle cell disease may precipitate sickle-related complications, such as painful crisis, by inducing fever and possibly dehydration from vomiting and diarrhea.

REFERENCES

1. Weiss L. The red pulp of the spleen: Structural basis of blood flow. Clin Haematol 1983;12:375–93.
2. Pearson HA, McIntosh S, Ritchey AK, *et al.* Developmental aspects of splenic function in sickle cell diseases. Blood 1979;53:358–65.
3. Pearson HA, Gallagher D, Chilcote R, *et al.* Developmental pattern of splenic dysfunction in sickle cell disorders. Pediatrics 1985;76:392–7.
4. Falter ML, Robinson MG, Kim OS, *et al.* Splenic function and infection in sickle cell anemia. Acta Haematol 1973;59:154–61.
5. Pearson HA, Cornelius EA, Schwartz AD, *et al.* Transfusion reversible asplenia in young children with sickle-cell anemia. N Engl J Med 1970;283:334–7.
6. Al-Awamy B, Wilson WA, Pearson HA. Splenic function in sickle cell disease in the Eastern Province of Saudi Arabia. J Pediatr 1984;104:714–7.
7. Zarkowsky HS, Gallagher D, Gill FM, *et al.* Bacteremia in sickle hemoglobinopathies. J Pediatr 1986;109:579–85.
8. Rogers DW, Vaidya S, Serjeant GR. Early splenomegaly in homozygous sickle-cell disease: an indicator of susceptibility to infection. Lancet 1978;2:963–5.
9. Gaston MH, Verter JI, Woods G, *et al.* Prophylaxis with oral penicillin in children with sickle cell anemia. N Engl J Med 1986;314:1593–9.
10. John AB, Ramlal A, Jackson H, *et al.* Prevention of pneumococcal infection in children with homozygous sickle cell disease. Br Med J 1984;288:1567–70.
11. Akuse RM. Variation in the pattern of bacterial infection in patients with sickle cell disease requiring admission. J Trop Paediatr 1996;42:318–23.
12. Lee A, Thomas P, Cupidore L, *et al.* Improved survival in homozygous sickle cell disease: lessons from a cohort study. Br Med J 1995;311:160–2.
13. Powers D, Overturf G, Turner E. Is there an increased risk of Haemophilus influenzae septicemia in children with sickle cell anemia? Pediatrics 1983;71:927–31.
14. Gigliotti F, Feldman S, Wang WC, *et al.* Immunization of young infants with sickle cell disease with a *Haemophilus influenzae* type b saccharide-diphtheria CRM_{197} protein conjugate vaccine. J Pediatr 1989;114:1006–10.
15. Wright J, Thomas P, Serjeant GR. Septicemia caused by salmonella infection; an overlooked complication of sickle cell disease. J Pediatr 1997;130:394–9.
16. Robinson MG, Halpern C. Infections, *Escherichia coli*, and sickle cell anemia. JAMA 1974;230:1145–8.
17. Wright JG, Hambleton IR, Thomas PW, *et al.* Postsplenectomy course in homozygous sickle cell disease. J Pediatr1999;134:304–9.
18. Walker TM, Hambleton IR, Serjeant GR. Gallstones in sickle cell disease: observations from the Jamaican Cohort Study. J Pediatr 2000;136:80–5.

chapter

172 Leishmaniasis

Robert N Davidson

EPIDEMIOLOGY

Protozoa of the genus *Leishmania* can cause cutaneous (CL), mucocutaneous (MCL) and visceral (VL, kala-azar) leishmaniasis. The distribution of the leishmaniases is shown in Figures 172.1 and 172.2. About 10 million cases of CL and 400,000 cases of VL occur annually.[1] A country by country review has been published by the World Health Organization (WHO).[2] Phlebotomine sandflies transmit leishmaniasis, either to humans from a wide range of infected animals as a zoonosis, or from human to human. Transmission varies geographically depending upon climate, habitat, season and opportunities for sandfly contact. However, the numbers of all forms of leishmaniasis are increasing in many areas. For example, in Brazil, the increase in VL and CL is due to deforestation, which brings humans into close contact with animal reservoirs and forest vectors of *Leishmania braziliensis* and other species. In north Africa and the Middle East, irrigation projects have resulted in increased numbers of gerbils and construction of new townships in these areas has led to marked increases in endemic CL caused by *Leishmania major*. Breakdown of the infrastructure in Afghanistan has caused outbreaks of urban CL due to *Leishmania tropica*.

Visceral leishmaniasis

This is caused by *Leishmania donovani*, *Leishmania infantum* and *Leishmania chagasi* (see Fig. 172.1); the latter two species are indistinguishable. A reduction of dichlorodiphenyltrichloroethane (DDT) spraying against malaria vectors in India and Bangladesh has been blamed for the present epidemic of VL (due to *L. donovani*), which affects hundreds of thousands annually. From 1984 to 1999 there was a major epidemic of VL (*L. donovani*) in southern and then eastern Sudan brought on by population movement, famine, civil war and ecologic change.[3,4] In Europe prior to widespread use of effective antiretrovirals, 20–70% of cases of VL (due to *L. infantum*) were co-infected with HIV, and 1.5–9% of AIDS patients had VL.[5] Co-infections of HIV and *Leishmania* are increasingly reported from Africa, India and South America.

Serologic and leishmanin skin test surveys suggest that subclinical self-healing infection occurs more frequently than clinical VL, particularly where *L. infantum* or *L. chagasi* is involved.[6] In epidemics involving *L. donovani*, however, most infections are symptomatic, and the mortality rate is high.[7]

Cutaneous leishmaniasis

In the Old World, *L. tropica* causes anthroponotic CL in villages, towns and cities; *L. major* causes zoonotic CL in those living or working near gerbil burrows. Smaller numbers of CL cases are caused by *L. infantum* in Europe and *Leishmania aethiopica* in Ethiopia and parts of Kenya. In the New World CL is mainly caused by members of the *Leishmania mexicana* complex (*L. mexicana mexicana*, *L. m. amazonensis*, *L. m. venezuelensis*) and the *Leishmania braziliensis* complex (*L. braziliensis braziliensis*, *L. b. panamensis*, *L. b. guyanensis*, *L. b. peruviana*; see Fig. 172.2).[8,9]

PATHOGENESIS AND PATHOLOGY

Infected macrophages rely mainly on nitric oxide production as an innate mechanism for killing *Leishmania* spp.; this is specifically inhibited by the parasite, which is able to multiply in the parasitophorous vacuole. Eventually infected macrophages rupture and amastigotes are taken up by new phagocytic cells. Macrophages and dendritic cells present *Leishmania* antigens to T cells and this results in either:

- an effective cellular immune response – a T-helper (Th)1 pattern; or
- an ineffective humoral response – a Th2 pattern).

In the Th1 response, T cells activate macrophages by releasing the cytokines interferon (IFN)-γ and interleukin (IL)-2. In the Th2 response, T cells release cytokines IL-4, IL-5, IL-10 and transforming growth factor (TGF)-β, which inhibit macrophages from killing *Leishmania* spp. (see Chapter 2). Although each *Leishmania* sp. produces a typical pattern of disease, host cellular immunity will determine whether:

- a clinical or subclinical infection results;
- the disease is visceral, cutaneous or mucocutaneous;
- lesions are few or diffuse; and
- response to treatment is complete or partial.[10]

PREVENTION

Helpful measures for individual protection are wearing long sleeves and trousers, using insect repellents and impregnating mosquito nets and clothing with permethrin.[11]

In the community, known animal reservoirs can be controlled, for example by bulldozing gerbil burrows, destroying infected dogs, or providing the dog population with deltamethrin-impregnated collars. Active case finding and treatment of patients who have VL and post-kala-azar dermal leishmaniasis (PKDL) caused by *L. donovani* and CL caused by *L. tropica* should reduce human-to-human transmission. Early case finding has been helped by the use of serologic tests that are suitable for field use, mainly the direct agglutination (DAT) test and rapid test strips using a recombinant antigen, rK39.[12,13] Sandflies remain susceptible to residual insecticides and spraying of homes or fogging of streets will reduce the density of peridomestic sandflies.

Two doses of a vaccine, combining killed *Leishmania* promastigotes and live bacillus Calmette–Guérin (BCG), were more than 70% protective against CL in Ecuador;[14] in Iran one dose of a similar vaccine was ineffective[15] and in Sudan a similar vaccine did not prove effective against VL.[16]

CLINICAL FEATURES

Visceral leishmaniasis

In VL, amastigotes disseminate throughout the reticuloendothelial system. After an incubation period of 2–8 months (range 10 days to

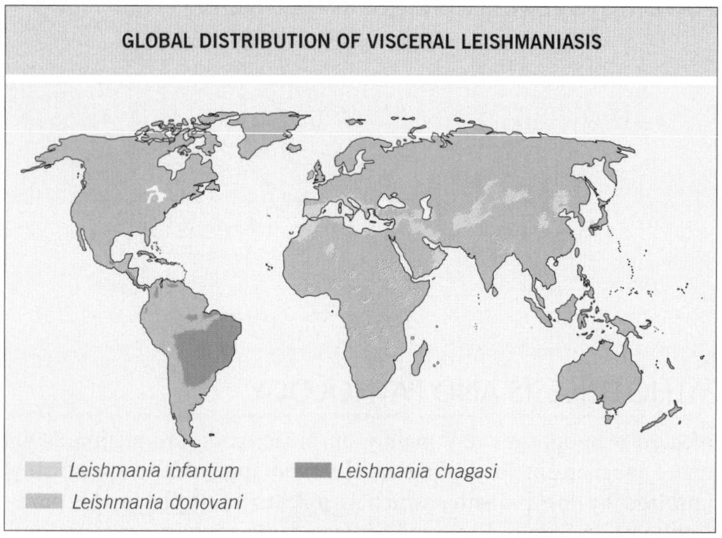

Fig. 172.1 Global distribution of visceral leishmaniasis. More than 90% of VL cases occur in India/Nepal/Bangladesh, Sudan/Ethiopia and Brazil.

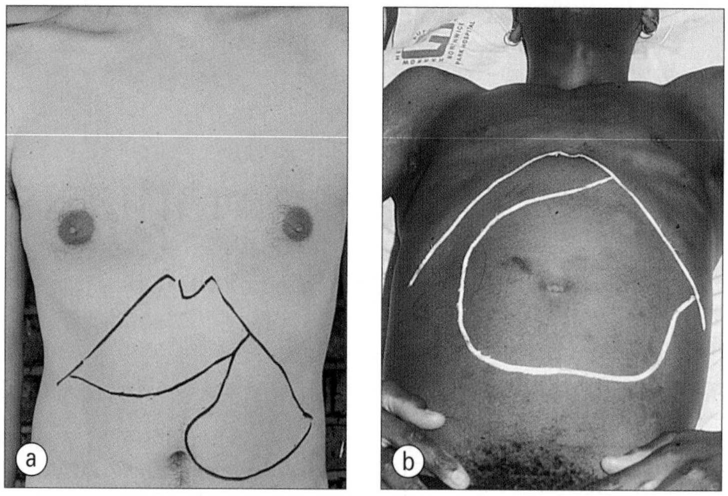

Fig. 172.3 Visceral leishmaniasis. (a) Hepatosplenomegaly and pallor in a 29-year old Italian man. (b) Splenomegaly and pallor in a 23-year old Angolan. Both complained of weight loss, fatigue and fever of several weeks' duration.

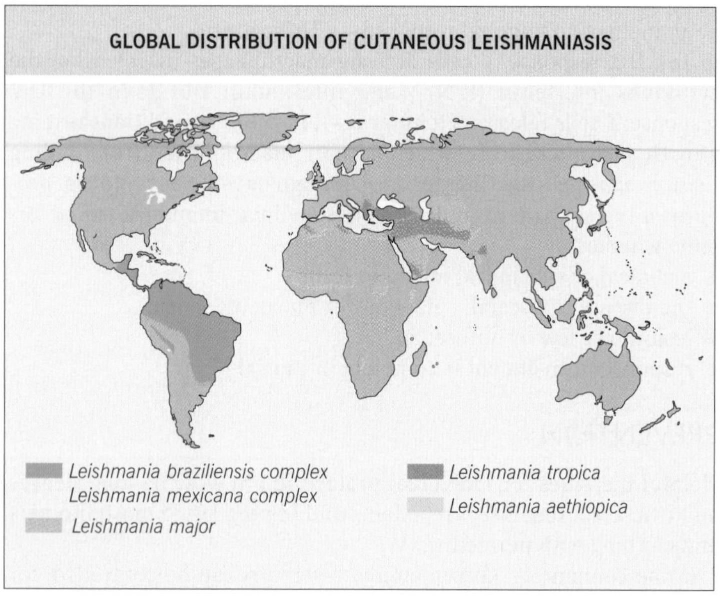

Fig. 172.2 Global distribution of cutaneous leishmaniasis. More than 90% of CL cases occur in the regions of Brazil/Peru, Algeria, Saudi Arabia and Syria/Iraq/Iran/Afghanistan.

over 2 years), the patient develops pyrexia, wasting and hepatosplenomegaly, which may become massive (Fig. 172.3). Males and females are equally affected in Sudan but outdoor activities make males more frequently affected in Kenya, Uganda, India and some other areas. Most cases in Europe are seen in children.

The onset can be ill-defined, and months elapse before the patient presents with fever, discomfort from an enlarged spleen, abdominal swelling, weight loss, cough or diarrhea. In some patients, such as those who are infected during an epidemic, the disease has an abrupt onset with high fever and rapid progression resulting in prostration, weakness, dyspnea and acute anemia.

The physical signs (Table 172.1) depend upon the duration of the disease, the nutritional state of the patient and the presence of complications. Patients who present late are thin, with wasted muscles. Hair changes and pedal edema may accompany hypoalbuminemia, but ascites is rare. Hyperpigmentation of the face, hands, feet and abdomen is characteristic of VL in India (kala-azar means 'black sickness'). The spleen is massively enlarged, often reaching the left or even right iliac fossa. It is smooth and nontender unless there has been a recent infarct. The liver is moderately enlarged in one-third of cases. Lymphadenopathy is common only in African patients, in whom unimpressive, peanut-sized lymph nodes are often palpable in the groins. Jaundice, mucosal and retinal hemorrhage, and episcleri-

FEATURES OF VISCERAL LEISHMANIASIS *(LEISHMANIA DONOVANI)*

Clinical feature	Proportion affected (%)
Age <9 years	22 (*L. infantum* and *L. chagasi* more commonly affect children and infants)
Age <15 years	44
Fever	83–100
Wasting	70–100
Loss of appetite	62–74
Uncomfortable spleen	81–88
Cough	72–83
Epistaxis	44–55
Diarrhea	25–55
Vomiting	2–37
Splenomegaly	93 (adults), 98 (children)
Hepatomegaly	55–65
Lymphadenopathy	55–86 (uncommon outside Africa)
Jaundice	2–7
Edema	2–7
Laboratory findings	**Proportion (%)**
Globulin >30g/l	98
Albumin <30g/l	88
Anemia	61–92
Leukopenia	84
Thrombocytopenia	73
Elevated bilirubin	17
Elevated liver transaminases	22
Elevated alkaline phosphatase	40
Positive *Leishmania* serology	95
Parasitologically proven	96

Table 172.1 Features of visceral leishmaniasis *(Leishmania donovani)*. The duration of symptoms is 2–4 months but is shorter in children.

tis are occasional features. After several weeks to months of illness, approximately 90% of patients who have VL will die, often as a result of uncontrolled bleeding, secondary bacterial pneumonia, tuberculosis or dysentery, or other infections such as cancrum oris.

Leishmaniasis in patients who are immunosuppressed or have HIV infection

Visceral leishmaniasis caused by *L. infantum* occurs as an opportunistic infection among patients co-infected with HIV (typically $CD4^+$ lymphocytes <200 cells/mm^3),[6] patients on corticosteroid treatment and patients who have undergone organ transplantation or thymectomy. Travel to an endemic area may have been years previously. The clinical features are often atypical; the symptoms may be vague, the laboratory abnormalities may be less severe and hepatosplenomegaly may be absent or unimpressive. Amastigotes may be found unexpectedly in bone marrow aspirates or skin biopsies of febrile HIV-positive patients. Amastigotes may be found in unusual cells (e.g. circulating neutrophils). Gastrointestinal symptoms may predominate and amastigotes of *Leishmania* spp. found in rectal or duodenal biopsies. *Leishmania* serology is negative in one-third of immunosuppressed patients. Such patients may respond well to antileishmanial treatment only to relapse 2–12 months later. Alternatively, the response to treatment may be incomplete or the patient may be completely nonresponsive or experience exaggerated drug toxicity. In Ethiopia, *L. donovani* infection in HIV-infected patients is clinically indistinguishable from VL in HIV-negative patients. However, those who have HIV co-infection have around 30% mortality during treatment, rising to about 50% by 6 months, and have higher rates of relapse and PKDL.[17]

Cutaneous leishmaniasis has been reported in patients who have HIV infection in Africa and South America. The lesions often resemble those of diffuse cutaneous leishmaniasis (DCL, see below).

Viscerotropic Leishmania tropica

Nine US soldiers who served in the Persian Gulf area in 1990–1 were found to have systemic infection caused by viscerotropic *L. tropica*.[18] They experienced a non-specific febrile illness with fatigue, arthralgia and diarrhea. Some soldiers recovered spontaneously, whereas others progressed and developed a chronic condition with adenopathy or splenomegaly. Most responded to treatment with sodium stibogluconate.

Post-kala-azar dermal leishmaniasis

After successful treatment for VL due to *L. donovani* (but not *L. chagasi* or *L. infantum*), patients may develop a rash called PKDL.

In Africa, PKDL occurs toward the end of apparently successful treatment or within a few weeks or months later. In Sudan, PKDL occurs in approximately 55% of patients who have VL, including those who have had subclinical VL.[19] In India, PKDL is less common, and occurs months to years after VL. Occasionally, PKDL is acute and severe, resulting in desquamation of skin and mucosae. More commonly, it is characterized by the development of hypopigmented patches, nodules and plaques. Parasites are infrequent or absent from the biopsies. People who have PKDL may act as a reservoir of *L. donovani* between outbreaks.

Cutaneous leishmaniasis

In CL (Fig. 172.4) amastigotes multiply in dermal macrophages near the site of inoculation, typically on the arms, legs, face or ears. The lesions may be:

- nodular or ulcerative; and
- single or with multiple satellite nodules or lymphangitic spread.

The most typical lesion of CL is a chronic ulcer with a diameter of 2–5cm and indurated margins. The ulcer may be covered by a fibrinous crust or there may be an exudate. It is painful if large or secondarily infected.

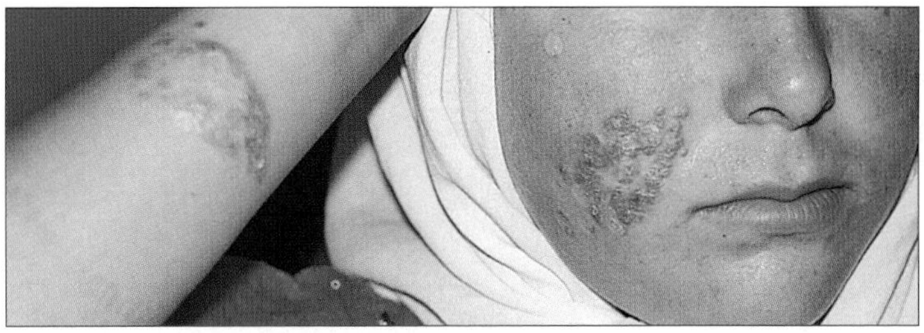

Fig. 172.4 Cutaneous leishmaniasis. *Leishmania tropica* recidivans leishmaniasis lesions on the face and forearm of a Syrian girl. These had been present for 4 years with slow healing in the center and multiple recurrences despite courses of intralesional meglumine antimonate.

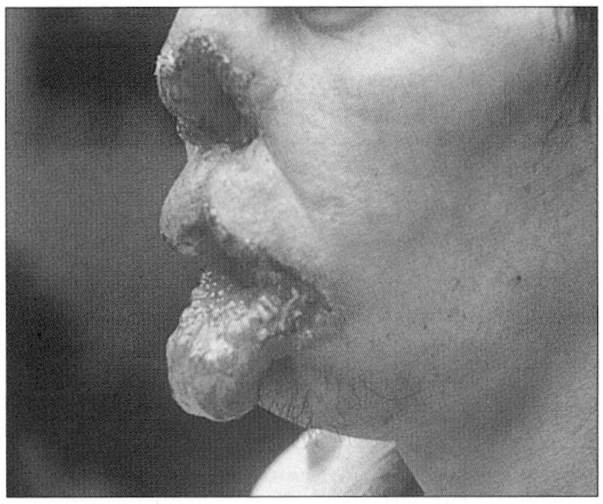

Fig. 172.5 Mucocutaneous leishmaniasis. A young man from Peru who had a 2-year history of slow enlargement of the lips and ulceration of the nostrils. Courtesy of Professor Luis Valda Rodriguez.

The histologic picture is of an intense lymphoid and monocytic infiltrate with granulomas. A 'tissue-paper' scar remains after healing. The spontaneous healing rate differs for each species and is typically:

- less than 5 months for *L. major*;
- less than 8 months for *L mexicana*; and
- approximately 1 year for *L. tropica* and *L. braziliensis*.[8]

There are two chronic forms of CL. Difuse cutaneous leishmaniasis is rare but disfiguring. Widespread plaques containing huge numbers of amastigotes persist for decades. People who have DCL are anergic to leishmanin, but do not have visceral dissemination or systemic symptoms. It is caused mainly by *L. aethiopica* in Africa and *L. amazonensis* in South and Central America. Leishmaniasis recidivans is a chronic, nonhealing or relapsing cutaneous infection, seen mainly with *L. tropica* infection in the Middle East. These patients are hypersensitive to leishmanin and organisms are rarely identified (see Fig. 172.4).

Mucocutaneous leishmaniasis

Mucocutaneous leishmaniasis (MCL; Fig. 172.5) occurs in approximately 3–10% of cases of CL due to *L. b. braziliensis*; it is commonest in Peru and Bolivia. The mucosal lesions usually manifest months to years after the cutaneous sores have healed, but cases of simultaneous CL and MCL occur, as do cases that have no history of CL. Usually the tip of the nose, nasal cartilage or upper lip are involved first with a painless induration or ulceration. The condition may remain static or there may be extension over months to years into the nasopharynx, palate, uvula, larynx and upper airways. The nose may be destroyed.

Biopsies show a chronic inflammatory and granulomatous infiltrate with very few amastigotes. Cultures of biopsies are usually positive for *L. braziliensis* but this may require repeated attempts. Less

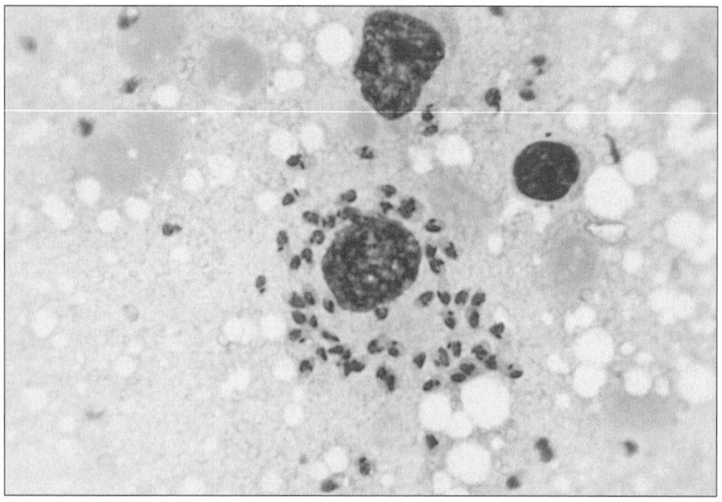

Fig. 172.6 Amastigotes (Leishman–Donovan bodies) in bone marrow aspirate from a patient who had *Leishmania infantum* visceral leishmaniasis and AIDS. The nucleus and kinetoplast stain deeply with Giemsa and give the organism its characteristic appearance. *Histoplasma* spp. are the main source of mistaken identification in bone marrow smears, but lack these structures. Amastigotes measure 2–3μm in length and are found within macrophages in tissue sections, but usually lie free in smears because infected macrophages burst as they are smeared.

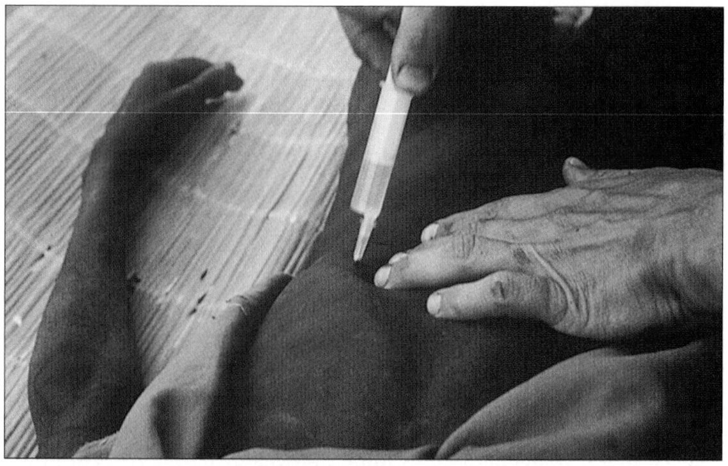

Fig. 172.7 Splenic aspiration. The picture shows a splenic aspirate being performed under field conditions on a child suffering from *Leishmania donovani* kala-azar in south Sudan. The procedure is simple, painless and safe if the prothrombin time is normal and the platelet count is above 40×10^9/l. Palpate the spleen and mark its outline. Using a 1.25 inch (30mm) long 21-gauge needle attached to a 5ml syringe, penetrate the skin over the spleen. Withdraw the plunger 1ml and plunge the needle into the spleen upwards at an angle of 45° and withdraw immediately, maintaining suction. The tiny amount of material obtained is sufficient for culture and smear. Courtesy of Drs Robert Wilkinson and Jill Seaman.

severe oral or nasal mucosal involvement rarely occurs with other species, such as *L. infantum*, and this often indicates an underlying immune defect.

DIAGNOSIS

Parasitologic diagnosis

Leishmaniasis is suggested by clinical features and supported by serologic or skin tests but should be confirmed by finding or culturing the parasite. *Leishmania* spp. may be isolated from material taken from reticuloendothelial tissue or from biopsies of skin or mucosal lesions. Some of the sample is smeared onto glass slides stained with Giemsa stain, and examined for amastigotes (Fig. 172.6). The rest of the sample is inoculated into suitable media and cultured at 78.8–82.4°F (26–28°C) and a positive culture will produce microscopically visible motile promastigotes within 2 weeks.

In VL, positive yields from smears of aspirates are of the following order: spleen, more than 95%; bone marrow or liver, 70–85%; lymph node (Africa), 58–65%; and buffy coat of blood up to 70%.[12] Cultures yield about another 10% in good hands. The technique of splenic aspirate is shown in Figure 172.7.

In CL, DCL, PKDL and MCL, slit skin smears are taken from the raised edge of the CL ulcer or center of the nodule (Fig. 172.8; see Chapter 154). Amastigotes are most abundant in fresh CL lesions and are very numerous in DCL. Conversely, they are infrequent in old CL lesions, in MCL and in PKDL.

Immunologic diagnosis

In VL, 95% of cases have positive serology for *Leishmania* with high titers using DAT, the immunofluorescent antibody test (IFAT) or enzyme-linked immunosorbent assay.[12] The leishmanin skin test is invariably negative, indicat-ing antigen-specific anergy and an absence of Th1 cell-mediated immunity.

In CL, *Leishmania* serology may be weakly positive and the leishmanin skin test is usually positive. In MCL and PKDL, both serology and the leishmanin skin test are usually positive. In DCL, there is anergy and both serology and the leishmanin skin test are negative.

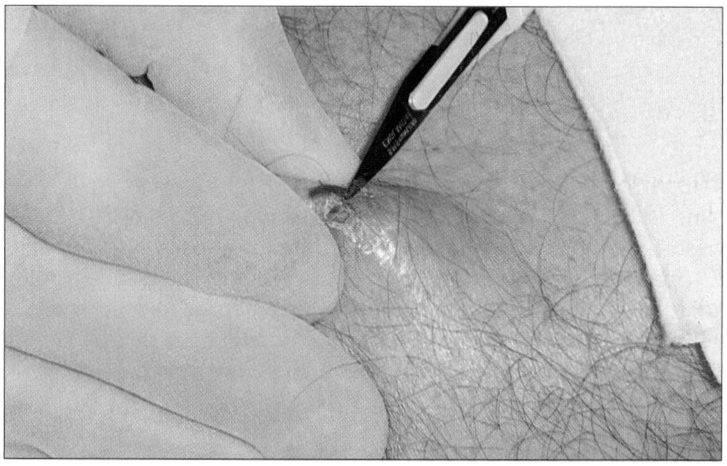

Fig. 172.8 Slit skin smear. The picture shows a slit skin smear being taken from the edge of a chronic *Leishmania infantum* ulcer obtained in Malta. Smears are taken from the raised edge of the ulcer or center of the nodule, where amastigotes are most abundant. The skin is cleaned and then firmly pinched throughout the procedure to squeeze away blood. A 5mm-long and 3mm-deep incision is made and then the scalpel is turned through 90° and the blade is used to scrape the edge of the slit. A line of tissue scrapings is gently streaked on to a slide and the process is repeated until two or three lines of scrapings are present on at least two slides. Further scrapings and fluid oozing from the pinched slit are put into culture medium.

MANAGEMENT

First-line agents

Pentavalent antimonials

Pentavalent antimonials (Sb^v) have been used for millions of cases since the 1940s.[8,9,20] Sodium stibogluconate contains Sb^v 100mg/ml; meglumine antimonate contains 85mg/ml. In the systemic treatment of VL, CL and MCL, a single daily dose of Sb^v of 20mg/kg is used for 28 days. Intravenous injections are less painful than intramuscular injections. Courses of up to 3 months are used for PKDL. Primary resistance to Sb^v is seen in approximately 1% of cases in Africa and up to 60% in parts of India. Relapse rates should be less than 5%, but secondary Sb^v resistance is likely to develop in patients who relapse unless they are retreated very thoroughly.

Toxicity

This relates to the daily and cumulative dose of Sb^v, as well as to unknown factors; for example, toxicity is almost never seen in patients treated for PKDL, whereas patients who have VL regularly have symptoms suggestive of toxicity and occasional sudden deaths occur in VL patients that might be due to arrhythmias. Children tolerate Sb^v better than adults and may be given higher doses per unit of body surface area. Before starting treatment, ideally a full blood count, biochemistry profile and electrocardiograph should be obtained. Patients should be hospitalized during systemic Sb^v therapy and, where possible, blood tests and electrocardiographs should be repeated twice weekly. Hospital-based Sb^v treatment is usually impossible in endemic countries, where Sb^v is administered by a nurse to outpatients without the facilities for monitoring toxicity. Nonetheless, serious adverse events are rare and deaths due to Sb^v very rare, even in severely debilitated VL patients.[9,20]

The toxicity is reversible and includes an elevation of serum amylase and liver enzymes, arthralgia and myalgia, thrombocytopenia, leukopenia, anorexia and thrombophlebitis. Patients may complain of lethargy, headache, nausea, vomiting, a metallic taste or pruritus. The most common electrocardiograph changes are ST-segment and T-wave changes; prolongation of the corrected QT interval to more than 0.5s is an indication to temporarily discontinue therapy.[21] Toxicity can usually be managed by stopping Sb^v treatment for 1–2 days. If toxicity recurs the daily dose should be reduced. Acute renal failure, thrombocytopenia, arthritis, tremors and exfoliative dermatitis occur occasionally.

Pancreatic toxicity is a common complication; asymptomatic hyperamylasemia is very common, and symptomatic[22] and even fatal[23] Sb^v-associated pancreatitis have been reported.

Intralesional administration

When used intralesionally, approximately 1ml of undiluted Sb^v is infiltrated into the base and edges of a CL lesion. The injections are repeated every 2–3 days for up to 2–3 weeks. There are no systemic side-effects, but the injections are painful.

Amphotericin B

Amphotericin B deoxycholate is a very powerful antileishmanial and is a first-line drug in India. Amphotericin B is remarkably nontoxic in the regimens used for Indian VL. The optimal regimen is 20 doses of 1mg/kg on alternate days.[24]

Amphotericin B is the drug of choice for advanced MCL, for which Sb^v treatment is often ineffective, and total doses of 30mg/kg are used.

Amphotericin B has not been systematically assessed for CL or PKDL.

Lipid-associated amphotericin B

These compounds are all taken up by macrophages and therefore target amphotericin B to the site of infection, achieving very high levels in liver and spleen. All have lower toxicity than amphotericin B but are more expensive.

Liposomal amphotericin B (AmBisome®) is rapidly effective and nontoxic for VL in Europe[25] and is of value for VL in Sudan[26] and India.[27] The usual regimen is a total dose of 20–30mg/kg, given as at least five daily doses of 3–4mg/kg over a period of 10–21 days. Very short courses of liposomal amphotericin B 1mg/kg daily for 5 days, or 5mg/kg as a single dose, have a high cure rate in India[27] but are unlikely to be effective in Sudan.[26] A few complicated cases of CL have been successfully treated with long courses of liposomal amphotericin B.

Amphotericin B cholesterol dispersion (Amphocil®) has been used for Brazilian VL at a dosage of 2mg/kg/day for 7 or 10 days.[28] Amphotericin B lipid complex (Abelcet®) has been used successfully for Indian VL in a regimen of 3mg/kg on consecutive or alternate days for five doses.[29]

Second-line drugs

Miltefosine

Miltefosine is the first oral drug with demonstrated efficacy against kala-azar, the dose in adults who have VL being 50mg twice daily for 28 days.[30] It is teratogenic, so cannot be given to pregnant women or women who could become pregnant within 6 months after treatment. Experience thus far is limited to India, where it has been licensed.

Paromomycin (aminosidine)

Paromomycin may be synergistic with Sb^v, a suitable regimen in VL being paromomycin 15–17mg/kg/day plus Sb^v 20mg/kg/day, given together for 17 days.[31] Paromomycin as a single agent is safe and effective at doses of up to 16–20mg/kg/day for 30 days, the optimal regimen being 15mg/kg/day for 21 days.[32]

Pentamidine

Pentamidine is too weak to be routinely used for VL, although short courses – seven doses of 2mg/kg on alternate days or four doses of 3mg/kg on alternate days – are effective for New World CL.[33]

Immunotherapy

Interferon-γ added to Sb^v improves the cure rates for relapsed or Sb^v-unresponsive VL and MCL[34] but toxicity and expense exclude it from routine use.

Granulocyte–macrophage colony-stimulating factor combined with Sb^v in the treatment of VL induces a more rapid increase in leukocyte count and fewer secondary infections[35] but cannot be recommended for routine use.

Second-line oral agents

Ketoconazole is effective for CL caused by *L. major* and *L. mexicana*, but less effective against *L. tropica*, *L. aethiopica* and *L. braziliensis*. Fluconazole[36] or itraconazole have similar efficacy and are better tolerated. Imidazoles cannot reliably cure VL or PKDL and there are no studies of their use in the treatment of MCL.

Allopurinol has been assessed in the treatment of all forms of leishmaniasis but has not shown consistent benefit.

Topical treatment

Topical aminosidine 15% in methylbenzethonium chloride applied twice daily for 10–30 days is effective in the treatment of *L. major* CL.[37] Preparations without methylbenzethonium chloride are of little value.

Monitoring response to treatment

Visceral leishmaniasis

Intercurrent infections such as malaria, tuberculosis and dysentery must be treated, and good hydration and nutritional supplements should be provided.

If responding, the patient will be afebrile within 1 week and clinical and laboratory abnormalities will improve within 2 weeks.

After successful treatment, amastigotes will be absent from aspirates and culture will be negative, and these should be confirmed before treatment is stopped. The patient should be reviewed during 6–12 months after treatment. Slight splenomegaly may persist for several months. Most relapses occur within 6 months. Body weight, spleen size, full blood count, serum albumin concentration and erythrocyte sedimentation rate are all sensitive markers of recurrent VL. A relapse rate of less than 5% is expected for immunocompetent patients but more than 80% for patients who also have HIV infection. Maintenance with intravenous pentamidine every 2–4 weeks or amphotericin B once or twice weekly may be useful to prevent or delay relapse for patients who have HIV infection but its efficacy is unproven.

A second course of Sb^v may be used successfully to treat a relapse of VL but a different drug such as amphotericin B is probably more effective.

For patients who have HIV co-infection, relapses may be less severe than the first attack and accompanied by vague, minor or atypical clinical features. For such patients, the benefit to be gained from any treatment must be weighed against the adverse effects of prolonged or repeated courses of toxic drugs.

Cutaneous leishmaniasis

Treatment is necessary if the lesions are large, multiple, disfiguring or overlie a joint. Intralesional Sb^v is cheap and usually effective but CL due to *L. braziliensis* should be treated systemically to reduce the risk of subsequent MCL. Most relapses of CL will occur within 12 months.

Mucocutaneous leishmaniasis

Untreated MCL will slowly progress to produce extensive mutilating lesions. Early lesions respond better to treatment[38] but the response is slow and relapses are common. Corticosteroids should be added if the larynx or airways are involved, to prevent edema complicating the start of treatment. Relapse may occur up to several years after treatment, so prolonged clinical follow-up is necessary.

REFERENCES

1. Marsden PD. Selective primary health care: strategies for the control of disease in the developing world. XIV. Leishmaniasis. Rev Infect Dis 1984;6:763–4.
2. World Health Organization. Information on the epidemiology and control of the leishmaniases by country or territory. WHO/LEISH/91.30. Geneva: World Health Organization; 1991.
3. Seaman J, Mercer AJ, Sondorp E. The epidemic of visceral leishmaniasis in western Upper Nile, southern Sudan: course and impact from 1984–1994. Int J Epidemiol 1996;25:862–71.
4. Zijlstra EE, Ali MS, El Hassan AM, *et al.* Clinical aspects of kala-azar in children from the Sudan: a comparison with the disease in adults. J Trop Pediatr 1992;38:17–20.
5. Davidson RN. AIDS and leishmaniasis. Genitourinary Med 1997;73:237–9.
6. Badaro R, Jones TC, Carvalho EM, *et al.* New perspectives on a subclinical form of visceral leishmaniasis. J Infect Dis 1986;154:1003–11.
7. Seaman J, Mercer AJ, Sondorp HE, Herwaldt BL. Epidemic visceral leishmaniasis in southern Sudan: treatment of severely debilitated patients under wartime conditions and with limited resources. Ann Intern Med 1996;124:664–72.
8. Bryceson ADM. Leishmaniasis. In: Cook GC, ed. Manson's tropical diseases, 20th ed. London: WB Saunders; 1996:1213–45.
9. Berman JD. Human leishmaniasis: clinical diagnostic and chemotherapeutic developments in the last 10 years. A review. Clin Infect Dis 1997;24:684–703.
10. Gaafar A, Kharazmi A, Ismail A, *et al.* Dichotomy of the T cell response to *Leishmania* antigens in patients suffering from cutaneous leishmaniasis: absence or scarcity of Th1 activity is associated with severe infections. Clin Exp Immunol 1995;100:239–45.
11. Soto J, Medina F, Dember N, Berman J. Efficacy of permethrin-impregnated uniforms in the prevention of malaria and leishmaniasis in Colombian soldiers. Clin Infect Dis 1995;21:599–602.
12. Zijlstra EE, Ali MS, El-Hassan AM, *et al.* Kala-azar: a comparative study of parasitological methods and the direct agglutination test in diagnosis. Trans R Soc Trop Med Hyg 1992;86:505–7.
13. Sundar S, Reed SG, Singh VP, Kumar PC, Murray HW. Rapid accurate field diagnosis of Indian visceral leishmaniasis. Lancet 1997;351:563–5.
14. Armijos RX, Weigel MM, Aviles H, Maldonado R, Racines J. Field trial of a vaccine against new world cutaneous leishmaniasis in an at-risk child population – safety, immunogenicity, and efficacy during the first 12 months of follow-up. J Infect Dis 1998;177:1352–7.
15. Sharifi I, Fekri AR, Aflatoninan MR, *et al.* Randomised vaccine trial of single dose of killed *Leishmaninia major* plus BCG against anthroponotic cutaneous leishmaniasis in Bam, Iran. Lancet 1998;351:1540–3.
16. Khalil EA, El Hassan AM, Zijlstra EE, *et al.* Autoclaved *Leishmania major* vaccine for prevention of visceral leishmaniasis: a randomised, double-blind, BCG-controlled trial in Sudan. Lancet 2000;356:1565–9.
17. Ritmeijer K, Veeken H, Melaku Y, *et al.* Ethiopian kala-azar: generic sodium stibogluconate and Pentostam are equivalent; HIV coinfected patients have a poor outcome. Trans R Soc Trop Med Hyg 2003; in press.
18. Magill AJ, Grogl M, Gasser RA, Sun W, Oster CN. Visceral infection caused by *Leishmania tropica* in veterans of Operation Desert Storm. N Engl J Med 1993;328:1383–7.
19. Zijlstra EE, El Hassan AM, Ismael A, Ghalib HW. Endemic kala-azar in eastern Sudan: a longitudinal study on the incidence of clinical and subclinical infection and post-kala-azar dermal leishmaniasis. Am J Trop Med Hyg 1994;51:826–36.
20. Herwaldt BT, Berman JD. Recommendations for treating leishmaniasis with sodium stibogluconate (Pentostam) and review of pertinent clinical studies. Am J Trop Med Hyg 1992;46:296–306.
21. Hepburn NC, Nolan J, Fenn L, *et al.* Cardiac effects of sodium stibogluconate: myocardial, electrophysiological and biochemical studies. Q J Med 1994;87:465–72.
22. Gasser RA Jr, Magill AJ, Oster CN, Franke ED, Grogl M, Berman JD. Pancreatitis induced by pentavalent antimonial agents during treatment of leishmaniasis. Clin Infect Dis 1994;18:83–90.
23. McBride MO, Linney M, Davidson RN, Weber JN. Pancreatic necrosis following treatment of leishmaniasis with sodium stibogluconate. Clin Infect Dis 1995;21:710.
24. Thakur CP, Sinha GP, Pandey AK. Comparison of regimens of amphotericin B deoxycholate in kala-azar. Indian J Med Res 1996;103:259–63.
25. Davidson RN, di Martino L, Gradoni L, *et al.* Short course treatment of visceral leishmaniasis with liposomal amphotericin B (AmBisome). Clin Infect Dis 1996;22:938–43.
26. Seaman J, Boer C, Wilkinson R, *et al.* Liposomal amphotericin B (AmBisome) in the treatment of complicated kala-azar under field conditions. Clin Infect Dis 1995;21:188–93.
27. Sundar S, Agrawal G, Rai M, Makharia MK, Murray HW. Treatment of Indian visceral leishmaniasis with single or daily infusions of low dose liposomal amphotericin B: randomised trial. Br Med J 2001;323:419–22.
28. Dietze R, Milan EP, Berman JD, *et al.* Treatment of Brazilian kala-azar with a short course of Amphocil (amphotericin B cholesterol dispersion). Clin Infect Dis 1993;17:981–6.
29. Sundar S, Agrawal NK, Sinha PR, Horwith GS, Murray HW. Short-course, low-dose amphotericin B lipid complex therapy for visceral leishmaniasis unresponsive to antimony. Ann Intern Med 1997;127:133–7.
30. Sundar S, Makharia A, More DK *et al.* Short-course of oral miltefosine for treatment of visceral leishmaniasis. Clin Infect Dis 2000;31:1110–3.
31. Seaman J, Pryce D, Sondorp HE, Moody A, Bryceson ADM, Davidson RN. Epidemic visceral leishmaniasis in Sudan: a randomized trial of aminosidine plus sodium stibogluconate versus sodium stibogluconate alone. J Infect Dis 1993;168:715–20.
32. Thakur CP, Kanyok TP, Pandey AK, Sinha GP, Messick C, Olliaro P. Treatment of visceral leishmaniasis with injectable paromomycin (aminosidine). An open-label randomized phase-II clinical study. Trans R Soc Trop Med Hyg 2000;94:432–3.
33. Soto J, Buffet P, Grogl M, Berman J. Successful treatment of Colombian cutaneous leishmaniasis with four injections of pentamidine. Am J Trop Med Hyg 1994;50:107–11.
34. Squires KE, Rosenkaimer F, Sherwood JA, Forni AL, Were JB, Murray HW. Immunochemotherapy for visceral leishmaniasis: a controlled pilot trial of antimony versus antimony plus interferon-gamma. Am J Trop Med Hyg 1993;48:666–9.
35. Badaro R, Nascimento C, Carvalho JS, *et al.* Recombinant human granulocyte macrophage colony stimulating factor reverses neutropenia and reduces secondary infections in visceral leishmaniasis. J Infect Dis 1994;170:413–8.
36. Alrajhi AA, Ibrahim EA, De Vol EB, Khairat M, Faris RM, Maguire JH. Fluconazole for the treatment of cutaneous leishmaniasis caused by *Leishmania major.* N Engl J Med 2002;346:891–5.
37. El-On J, Livshin R, Evan-Paz Z, Hamburger D, Weinrauch L. Topical treatment of cutaneous leishmaniasis. J Invest Dermatol 1986;87:284–8.
38. Franke ED, Llanos Cuentas A, Echevarria J, *et al.* Efficacy of 28 day and 40 day regimens of sodium stibogluconate (Pentostam) in the treatment of mucosal leishmaniasis. Am J Trop Med Hyg 1994;51:77–82.

chapter

173 Chagas' Disease (American Trypanosomiasis)

Michael A Miles

EPIDEMIOLOGY

Chagas' disease was first described by the Brazilian scientist Carlos Chagas in 1907.[1] The causative agent, *Trypanosoma cruzi*, is a kinetoplastid protozoan parasite. It is transmitted to mammals by blood-sucking triatomine bugs (order Hemiptera, family Reduviidae, subfamily Triatominae) not by their bite but by contamination of the host with *T. cruzi*-infected bug feces. Secondary routes of transmission include:

- blood transfusion;
- organ transplant;
- transplacental transmission; and
- orally by consumption of food contaminated with triatomine bug feces or of uncooked meat from infected mammals.

Infective forms (metacyclic trypomastigotes) of *T. cruzi* gain entry to the mammalian host from triatomine feces by penetrating mucous membranes or abraded skin. Trypomastigotes can then enter nonphagocytic or phagocytic cells, in which they transform to amastigotes and divide by binary fission to produce a pseudocyst. Before rupture of the pseudocyst amastigotes transform to trypomastigotes, which upon release re-enter cells or circulate in the blood (Fig. 173.1) from where they are picked up when the host is again attacked by bugs.

Multiplication within the insect vector occurs by binary fission as the epimastigote stage in the intestinal tract. Triatomines acquire *T. cruzi* infection only by feeding on an infected host and not by transovarial transmission. They are highly susceptible to infection and once infected usually remain infective for life.

The trypomastigote, amastigote and epimastigote life cycle stages are distinguished by the position of a discrete organelle, the kinetoplast, in relation to the nucleus and by the presence or absence of a free flagellum (see Diagnosis, below). Organisms at all stages of the life cycle can be grown in culture.[2]

The majority of triatomine bug species[3] are found in the New World and *T. cruzi* is restricted to the Americas. A few bug species cause widespread and abundant household infestation, principally:

- *Triatoma infestans* (Argentina, Bolivia, Brazil, Chile, Paraguay, Peru and Uruguay);
- *Rhodnius prolixus* and *Triatoma dimidiata* (northern South America and Central America);
- *Panstrongylus megistus* (central and eastern Brazil); and
- *Triatoma brasiliensis* (north eastern Brazil).

The natural habitats of triatomines are trees, burrows and rocks, where they feed on mammals, birds and reptiles. All mammals, but not birds or reptiles, are considered to be susceptible to *T. cruzi* infection and the organism has been reported in more than 150 mammal species of 24 families. Domestic dogs, guinea pigs, cats, rats and mice living in houses may therefore be important domestic reservoir hosts. In addition, chickens, although not infected, are a significant factor because they can sustain large bug infestations. The most common sylvatic reservoir host of *T. cruzi* is the opossum, *Didelphis*. Sylvatic cycles of *T. cruzi* transmission are found from southern Argentina and Chile (latitude 46° south) to northern California (latitude 42° north), although human infection is rare in the USA and sporadic in the Amazon basin because local vectors have not adapted to colonize houses.[4]

Serologic surveys indicate that more than 10 million people carry *T. cruzi* in the Americas, with prevalence rates of more than 70% in some communities. In some endemic localities seropositivity rates among blood donors may reach 20%. Transmission cycles have been described as:

- enzootic, with rare human infections but sympatric sylvatic transmission (as in USA; Amazon basin);
- discontinuous, with separate domestic and sylvatic transmission cycles involving different triatomine vector species (as in Southern Cone countries, see below); and
- continuous, with overlapping domestic and sylvatic transmission cycles involving the same triatomine vector species (as in parts of Venezuela).[5]

The initial, acute phase of *T. cruzi* infection may be asymptomatic (see Clinical features, below) and is not commonly reported. Although 10% of acute phase infections in children may be fatal, the epidemiologic importance of Chagas' disease also arises from chronic infection. Once *T. cruzi* infection has been acquired, in the absence of treatment it is usually retained for life.

Trypanosoma cruzi frequently invades heart muscle and smooth muscle of the alimentary tract. Up to 30% of chronic infections have been reported to lead to chagasic cardiomyopathy, electrocardiograph (ECG) abnormalities and sudden death or progressive heart disease. Associated chronic phase syndromes are mega-esophagus and megacolon (see below).

Biochemical studies and genotyping have demonstrated that *T. cruzi* is genetically diverse. Two principal subspecific groups have been identified and named *T. cruzi* I and *T. cruzi* II, the latter with five subgroups (a–e). *Trypanosoma cruzi* I predominates in the Amazon basin and in endemic countries north of the Amazon; *T. cruzi* II is the predominant cause of Chagas' disease throughout the Southern Cone countries of South America.[6] The disparate distribution of *T. cruzi* strain groups has been circumstantially linked to regional differences in the severity of chronic Chagas' disease.[6] *Trypanosoma cruzi* I hybrids have been generated in the laboratory from clonal parental genotypes.[7] Phylogenetic evidence indicates that genetic exchange may have contributed significantly to the evolution of *T. cruzi*.[7,8] Genetic exchange may facilitate the spread of virulent and drug-resistant strains, or the extension of host range.[7]

PATHOGENESIS AND PATHOLOGY

The pathogenesis of Chagas' disease is still somewhat enigmatic. Many infected individuals who survive the acute phase show no progression to chronic disease. Pathogenesis has been described as involving an inflammatory response, focal neurologic damage and, in some cases, resurgence of a chronic inflammatory response that may be triggered by autoimmunity. An immunocompromised state may lead to reactivation of infection, producing symptoms typical of the acute phase.

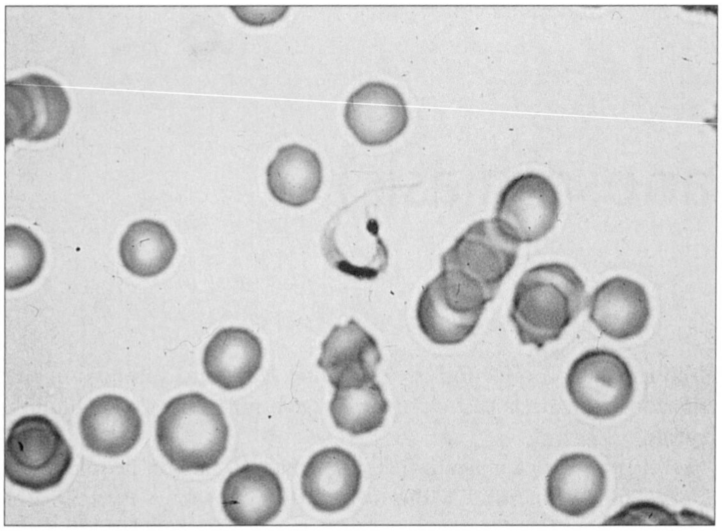

Fig. 173.1 *Trypanosoma cruzi* C-shaped trypomastigote in Giemsa-stained thin blood film.

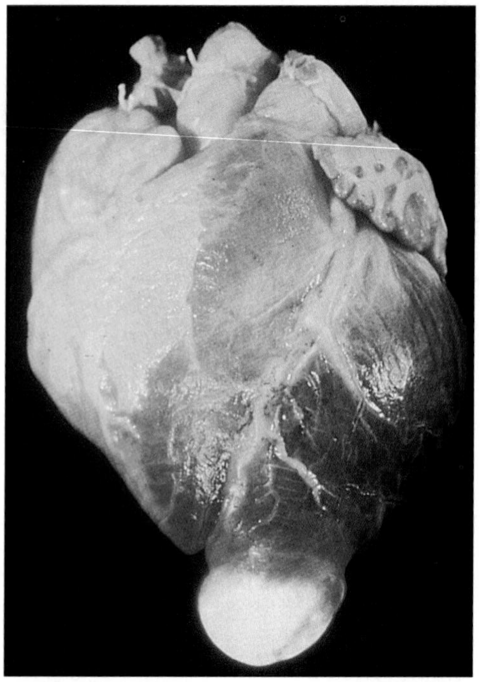

Fig. 173.2 Apical aneurysm of the left ventricle in chronic Chagas' disease. Courtesy of Dr JS Oliveira.

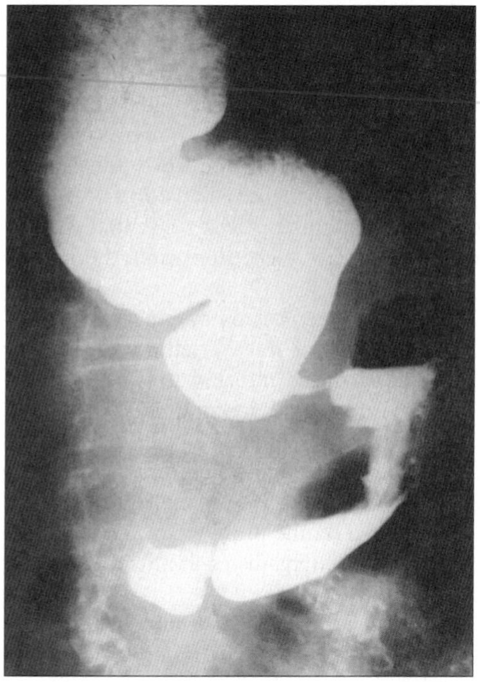

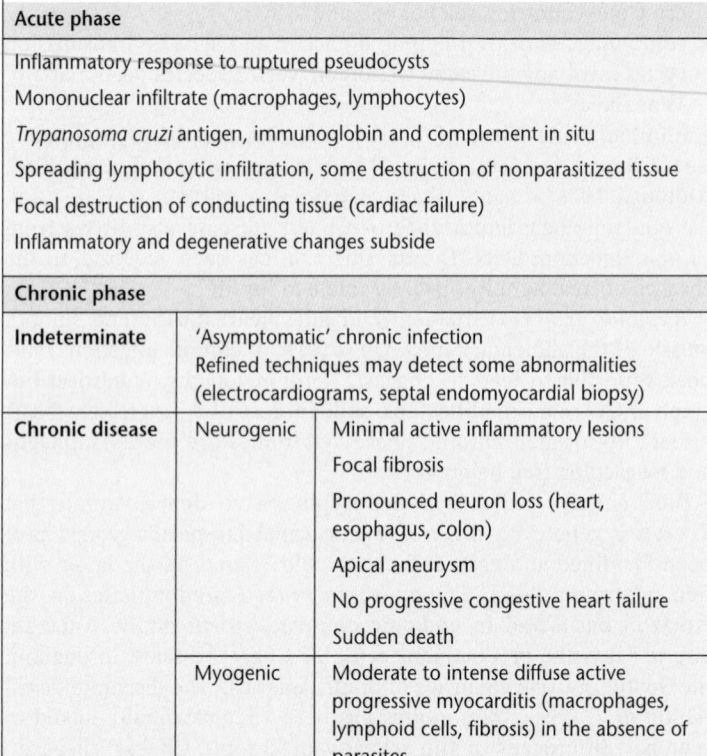

Fig. 173.3 Mega-esophagus on radiograph. Courtesy of Dr JS Oliveira.

PHASES OF CHAGAS' DISEASE		
Acute phase		
Inflammatory response to ruptured pseudocysts Mononuclear infiltrate (macrophages, lymphocytes) *Trypanosoma cruzi* antigen, immunoglobin and complement in situ Spreading lymphocytic infiltration, some destruction of nonparasitized tissue Focal destruction of conducting tissue (cardiac failure) Inflammatory and degenerative changes subside		
Chronic phase		
Indeterminate	'Asymptomatic' chronic infection Refined techniques may detect some abnormalities (electrocardiograms, septal endomyocardial biopsy)	
Chronic disease	Neurogenic	Minimal active inflammatory lesions Focal fibrosis Pronounced neuron loss (heart, esophagus, colon) Apical aneurysm No progressive congestive heart failure Sudden death
	Myogenic	Moderate to intense diffuse active progressive myocarditis (macrophages, lymphoid cells, fibrosis) in the absence of parasites Progressive congestive heart failure

Table 173.1 Phases of Chagas' disease.

Local multiplication at the portal of entry of *T. cruzi* may lead to a skin lesion or conjunctivitis (see Clinical features, below) with a local inflammatory response. Pseudocyst rupture in the heart or other organs generates an inflammatory response with infiltration of lymphocytes, monocytes and/or polymorphonuclear cells (Table 173.1). In those surviving acute phase infection, intracellular multiplication and parasitemia in the blood subside, although trypomastigotes may still be detectable by sensitive methods (see Diagnosis, below).

Focal lesions in the conducting system of the heart are associated, both clinically and experimentally, with corresponding ECG abnormalities. The pathogenesis of this 'neurogenic' form of chronic Chagas' disease is thought to depend upon irreversible neuron loss in the acute phase, exacerbated by further loss with age, such that a threshold is reached beyond which organ function is perturbed. Electrocardiogram abnormalities or aperistalsis of the alimentary tract then ensue, with organ enlargement, or mega syndromes. Gross pathology of the heart consists of megacardia and focal thinning of the myocardium, especially at the apex of the left ventricle, which may lead to apical aneurysm formation, which is considered to be pathognomonic of chronic chagasic cardiomyopathy (Fig. 173.2). Apical aneurysm can be produced experimentally without *T. cruzi* infection by inoculating catecholamines, suggesting that it may be associated with sympathetic dominance. Chagasic mega-esophagus (Fig. 173.3) is more common than chagasic megacolon (Fig. 173.4) and either or both may be associated with chagasic cardiomyopathy.[9]

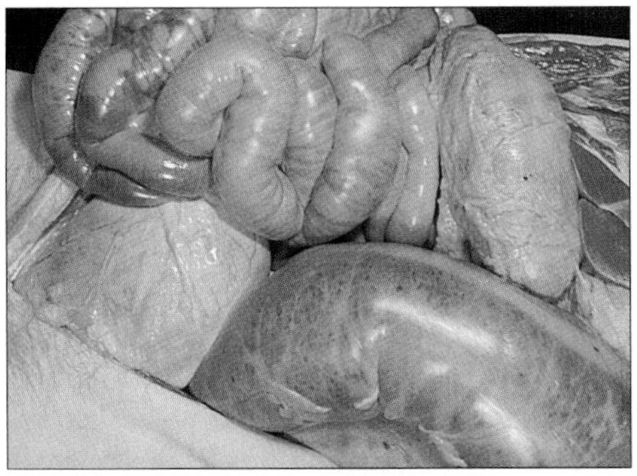

Fig. 173.4 Megacolon. Courtesy of Dr JS Oliveira.

Some patients who have chronic 'myogenic' Chagas' disease present with a renewed inflammatory response and a progressive diffuse myocarditis associated with a slow decline in cardiac function. It has been proposed that this pathology can be explained by an autoimmune pathogenesis. It is known that antigens released from ruptured pseudocysts may spread from the immediate site of infection, and be adsorbed to uninfected cells. This may lead to an extension of focal damage and the release of normally sequestered host antigens, which could precipitate autoimmunity. Candidate cross-reactive epitopes between *T. cruzi* and mammalian tissues have also been described, including the C-terminus of the *T. cruzi* ribosomal P protein, and myosin epitopes. It is not clear whether autoantibodies are markers of pathology or have a causal role.[10]

A tentative overall explanation of the pathogenesis of Chagas' disease is that:

- direct and indirect focal neuronal damage in the acute phase may with time culminate in ECG abnormalities and sudden death or mega syndromes; and
- in a proportion of patients there is autoimmune reactivation of the inflammatory response and progressive myocarditis.

The Pan American Health Organization has produced a review of Chagas' disease and the nervous system.[11]

PREVENTION

There is no vaccine for Chagas' disease. Crude or fractionated antigens can protect experimental animals against a normally fatal challenge infection. Prospects for vaccine development are remote because of the alleged involvement of autoimmunity in the pathogenesis of Chagas' disease and the impracticality of vaccine trials. Immunotherapy has been proposed but not devised, and is likely to be of limited use and not cost-effective.

Chagas' disease is maintained by poverty and poor housing, which prevent families and communities from controlling domestic triatomine populations. Prevention of new cases of vector-borne *T. cruzi* infection relies on insecticide spraying, health education and improved housing. Screening or treatment of donor blood, and of organ donors and recipients are also essential measures.

Pyrethroids, which have low toxicity and high residual activity, are the insecticides of choice for killing triatomines. Control campaigns are organized and run in three phases – preparatory, attack and vigilance:

- during the preparatory phase the distribution of dwellings is mapped, the number of infested houses assessed and the second and third phases are costed and planned;
- in the attack phase all houses and peridomestic buildings are sprayed, irrespective of the known presence of bug infestation; and
- in the vigilance phase a community surveillance system reports residual or new triatomine bug infestations, eliciting a rapid re-spraying response for those houses affected.[12]

Blood for transfusion and organ donors or recipients can be screened by one of several serologic methods. In highly endemic areas, if serology cannot be performed, blood may be treated with crystal violet (at 250mg/l) and stored at 39.2°F (4°C) for a minimum of 24 hours, which will kill *T. cruzi* trypomastigotes.

Serology is also crucial for monitoring the success of control programs. Children born after control campaigns are initiated should be serologically negative, except for some of those under 9 months of age who will retain transplacentally transferred IgG from seropositive mothers (see Diagnosis, below). Seropositivity in the relevant age group will pinpoint residual triatomine bug infestation and vector-borne transmission or sporadic cases of congenital transmission of infection from mother to child (see Diagnosis and Clinical features, below). To monitor control campaigns serology can be used economically to screen:

- entire populations of countries or endemic regions; and
- selected populations in areas of high seroprevalence or on the edges of endemic areas where new epidemic outbreaks might occur.

These well-established control principles have lead to a Southern Cone initiative to eliminate *Triatoma infestans* from the southern countries of South America (Argentina, Bolivia, Brazil, Chile, Paraguay, Peru and Uruguay).[13] The cost of prevention in this way is a small proportion of the economic burden of the diagnosis, management and treatment of acute and chronic Chagas' disease. The Southern Cone program has stimulated ministries of health to invest in triatomine control and has led to a dramatic reduction in domestic infestation over wide areas. The success of the program is assisted by the fact that *T. infestans* is thought to be restricted to domestic habitats throughout its range, except in Bolivia where it is also found in feral guinea pig colonies. Surveillance programs are being planned to protect the Amazon basin from immigration by domestic triatomine species and to report adaptation of local sylvatic bugs to colonization of houses.[4,14]

The prospects for vector control in northern South America and Central America are less straightforward, as in some regions domestic bugs may be continuously replenished from nearby sylvatic foci. Morphologic similarities between *Rhodnius* spp.[15] may, however, have led to an overestimation of the degree of movement between sylvatic and domestic bug populations. Andean and Central American initiatives to control Chagas' disease have been launched in an effort to mimic the success of the Southern Cone program.[16]

CLINICAL FEATURES

Acute phase *T. cruzi* infections are most common in children. If bug feces contaminate the eye, metacyclic trypomastigotes may penetrate the conjunctiva, leading to unilateral conjunctivitis and periophthalmic edema known as Romaña's sign (Fig. 173.5). If the portal of entry is the skin, a cutaneous lesion (chagoma) may result. Occasionally multiple chagomas may be seen in acute phase infections in infants. With both sites there may be regional lymphadenopathy and local infiltration of lymphocytes and monocytes. Further clinical signs during the acute phase may include fever, hepatosplenomegaly, generalized lymphadenopathy, facial or generalized edema, rash, vomiting, diarrhea and anorexia. There may be early ECG abnormalities, including sinus tachycardia, increased PR interval, T-wave changes and low QRS voltage. The incubation period between exposure to infection and the appearance of symptoms may be as short as 2 weeks but can be as long as several months if infection results from blood transfusion. Shorter incubation times in vector-borne infections may be due to the adaptation of metacyclic organisms to rapid invasion of cells, whereas trypomastigotes in contaminated transfusion blood may less efficiently invade the heart or other organs.

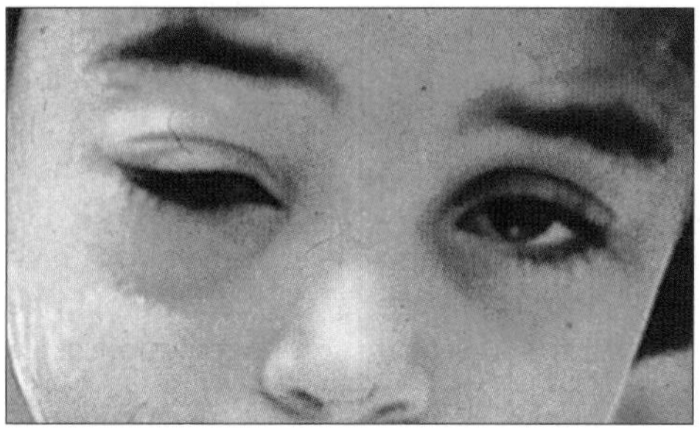

Fig. 173.5 Romaña's sign.

General lymphadenopathy and splenomegaly are common in patients who have acquired infection by blood transfusion.[17]

Signs of congenital infection may include fever, edema, metastatic chagomas and neurologic signs such as convulsions, tremors and weak reflexes, and apnea. Hepatosplenomegaly is also common in congenital infections. The ECG picture in congenital cases is usually normal but there may be low-voltage complexes, decreased T-wave height and increased atrioventricular (AV) conduction time.[17]

Meningoencephalitis is infrequent in adults but more common in infants and carries a poor prognosis. Meningoencephalitis is also common in those immunocompromised by AIDS, as the organism frequently traverses the blood–brain barrier in these patients.[18]

Individuals who recover from the acute phase may lead entirely normal lives without any further signs. Indeed, one of the first cases described by Carlos Chagas, a young girl called Berenice, lived into her eighth decade with no associated illness, even though *T. cruzi* was isolated from her on several occasions and late into life. After a symptom-free indeterminate phase of unpredictable duration, ECG abnormalities typical of chronic Chagas' disease arise in up to 30% of patients who recover from the acute phase. Cardiac signs include dysrhythmias, palpitations, chest pain, edema, dizziness, syncope and dyspnea. The most typical reported ECG changes are right bundle branch block and left anterior hemiblock, but there may also be AV conduction abnormalities, including complete AV block. Many different types of dysrhythmia may occur, including sinus bradycardia, sinoatrial block, ventricular tachycardia, primary T-wave changes and abnormal Q waves. The severity of heart disease is graded according to the extent of the disturbance. Radiography of the thorax is a useful aid for detecting cardiac enlargement (megacardia).[17]

Signs of mega-esophagus include loss of peristalsis, regurgitation and dysphagia. Megacolon may be associated with failure of defecation and severe constipation. In both cases there may be progressive dilatation of the organs, which is clinically graded to describe severity.[9,19]

Differential diagnosis includes distinction from all other types of heart disease and ECG abnormalities, but changes such as right bundle branch block and left anterior hemiblock associated with a history of exposure to *T. cruzi* infection (see Diagnosis, below) are indicative.[20] Megacolon due to Hirschsprung's disease is usually recognizable, in part because of its rarity in adults.[9]

DIAGNOSIS

During the acute phase of infection circulating trypomastigotes may be detectable by direct microscopy of unstained wet-blood preparations. Several methods can be attempted to improve the sensitivity of parasitologic diagnosis. These include microscopy of:

- Giemsa-stained thick blood films;
- the buffy coat layer after centrifugation of hematocrit capillaries (with care to avoid exposure to infection);
- centrifugation sediment from recently separated serum (Strout's method); and
- centrifugation sediment after lysis of red blood cells with 0.87% ammonium chloride.

All these methods may fail, even in the acute phase of infection, if the parasitemia is low. A more sensitive method of parasitologic diagnosis is the process known as xenodiagnosis, in which triatomine bugs from laboratory colonies maintained on birds are fed on the suspect patient. The fed bugs are then dissected about 20–25 days later and the hind gut contents are examined for the presence of *T. cruzi* epimastigotes. The hind gut and rectum are drawn out into a drop of sterile physiologic saline, mixed with a blunt instrument such as a microspatula, and examined for the typical motile epimastigotes and trypomastigotes. Care must be taken to avoid infection during this procedure and bugs are usually dissected behind a small Perspex screen or, if available, in a microbiologic safety cabinet. It is also necessary to ensure that colony bugs are not infected with the monoxenous flagellate *Blastocrithidia triatomae*, which may be found in *T. infestans*.

Culture of venous blood on to a blood agar base medium may be used as an alternative to xenodiagnosis[21] but demands better laboratory facilities, is difficult to perform under field conditions and seldom achieves the sensitivity of xenodiagnosis.

In the chronic phase of Chagas' disease xenodiagnosis is still the parasitologic method of choice throughout most of Latin America.

Detection of DNA by the polymerase chain reaction (PCR) may be an adjunct to parasitologic diagnosis for research purposes but is not a routine clinical procedure.[22] In areas where *Rhodnius prolixus* is a vector of *T. cruzi*, xenodiagnosis may yield the nonpathogenic human trypanosome *Trypanosoma rangeli*. Frequently, *T. rangeli* infections in *Rhodnius* spp. can be identified by the presence of long, slender (up to 80μm) epimastigotes, by the smaller kinetoplast and the capacity to invade the bug salivary glands (*T. rangeli* is transmitted by inoculation not by contamination).

Serum antibody is usually detectable within a few days of *T. cruzi* infection and usually persists for life unless the infection is elim-inated by chemotherapy. Rarely, serologic reversion may occur without treatment. There is an initial IgM response and a sustained IgG response, which is detectable by a variety of assays. Commonly used tests are the indirect fluorescent antibody test (IFAT), the enzyme-linked immunosorbent assay (ELISA) and the indirect hemagglutination test. Washed organisms (IFAT) or lysates of epimastigotes grown in vitro (ELISA) are used as antigens. Around 50% of seropositive cases may yield a positive parasitologic result by careful xenodiagnosis.

No universal specific, highly sensitive, recombinant antigen is yet available.[23,24] Diagnostic assays must be standardized adequately to determine cut-off titers, with positive and negative control sera, and it is advisable to establish reference laboratories for checking assay reproducibility. Cross-reactions may occur, especially with visceral and cutaneous leishmaniasis, which may be sympatric (co-exist in the same geographic area) with Chagas' disease. Infants born of seropositive mothers may be seropositive until up to 9 months of age due to transplacental transfer of IgG. Seropositivity in such infants using an IgM-specific conjugate suggests congenital infection.

Short-term visitors to endemic areas are extremely unlikely to acquire Chagas' disease and, if infection is suspected through exposure to triatomine bug bites or blood transfusion, serologic status may be used to exclude more likely causes of heart disease (Fig. 173.6).

Strain groups of *T. cruzi* may be identified using enzyme electrophoresis or DNA amplification of kinetoplast minicircle DNA, or ribosomal and mini-exon gene targets, but the identification of infecting strain is not yet a proven prognostic indicator. Antibody recognition of the *T. cruzi* II specific epitope of a mucin-like protein is reported to be associated with confirmed Chagas' disease in patients from Argentina, Brazil and Chile.[25] This is not surprising, because *T. cruzi* II predominates in human populations in this region, whereas *T. cruzi* I predominates in endemic countries north of the Amazon

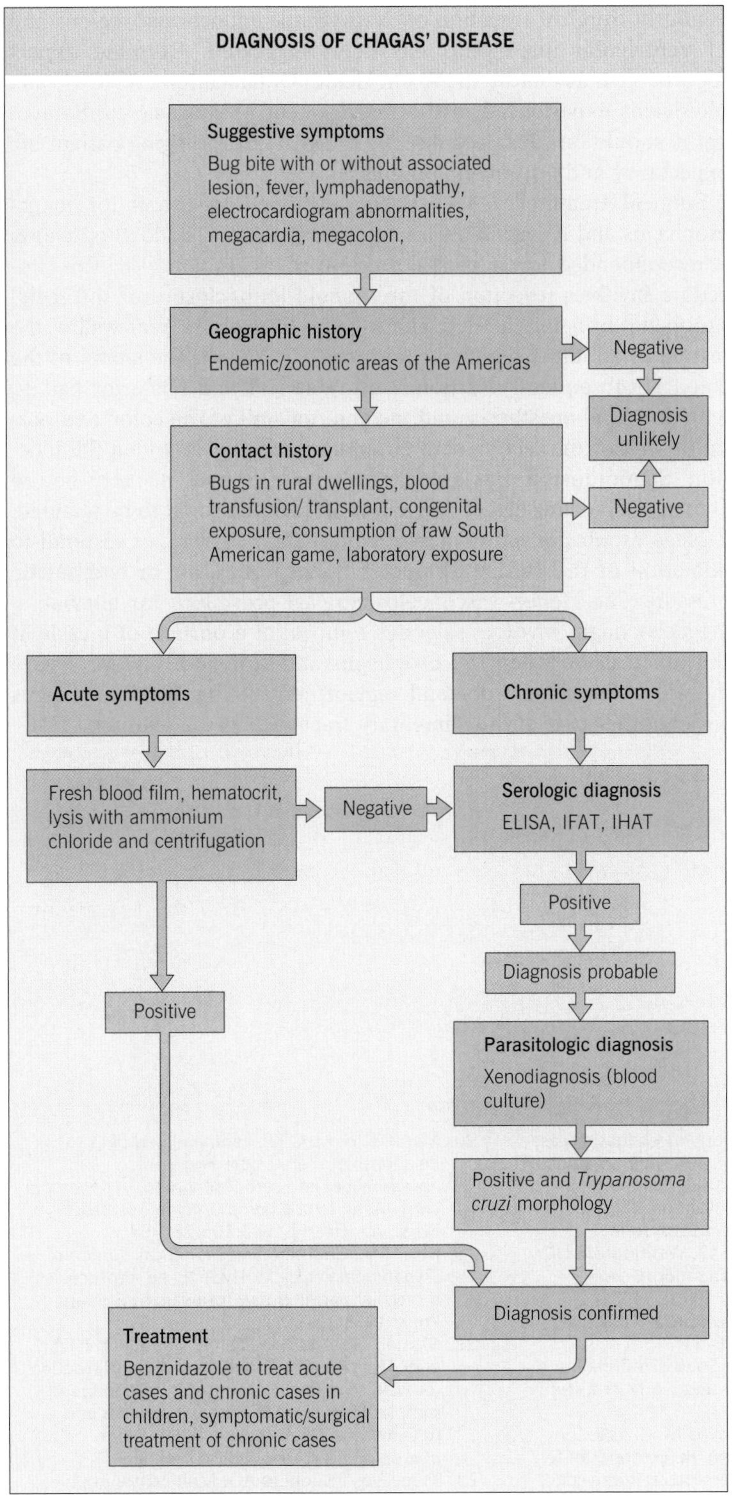

Fig. 173.6 Diagnosis of Chagas' disease. ELISA, enzyme-linked immunosorbent assay; IFAT, indirect fluorescent antibody test; IHAT, indirect hemagglutination test.

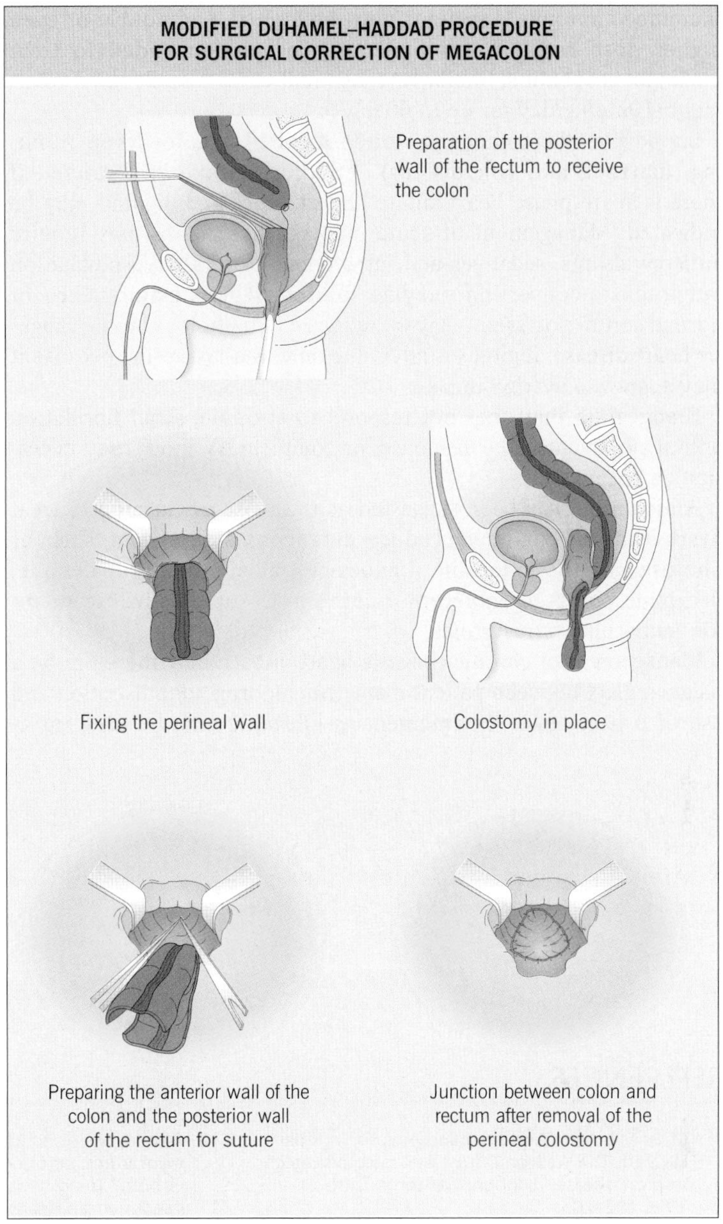

Fig. 173.7 Modified Duhamel–Haddad procedure for surgical correction of megacolon.[9,19,27]

basin. Chagasic myocardiopathy occurs in *T. cruzi* I endemic regions of northern South America and Central America, even though chagasic megacolon and mega-esophagus appear to be rare or absent.

MANAGEMENT

The oral synthetic nitrofuran nifurtimox has been used for treatment of Chagas' disease but is no longer readily available. The sole drug to treat *T. cruzi* infection is now benznidazole, which is an orally delivered nitroimidazole. The drug is given at 5–7mg/kg/day orally for adults, in two divided doses, for 60 days using 100mg tablets. Children tolerate higher doses of 10mg/kg/day given in two divided doses. Side-effects include rashes, fever, nausea, peripheral polyneuritis and leukopenia, and rarely agranulocytosis. Adverse effects may lead to interruption of treatment.

Chemotherapy is recommended during the acute phase of infection as it suppresses the parasitemia and may be life-saving, and for chronic cases in children, who are less susceptible to side-effects.[26] Elimination of infection is not guaranteed. Chemotherapy for chronic Chagas' disease in adults is more controversial as the pathogenesis might be largely attributable to acute phase damage. Adult chronic cases are thus not always treated because:

- the contribution of continued low-level infection to pathogenesis is uncertain[10];
- side-effects may cause interruption of treatment;
- treatment often fails to eliminate the organism; and
- cure is difficult to prove (negative parasitology is not sufficiently sensitive to prove absence of infection and reversion of serology may take decades).

Immunocompromised patients must be treated, and double or even higher dose rates, if tolerated, may be recommended to treat meningoencephalitis. Similarly, congenital cases also demand treatment (10mg/kg/day for up to 60 days).

Supportive chemotherapy is often required (e.g. for fever, vomiting, diarrhea and convulsions).[17] Sodium intake is restricted if there is acute-phase heart failure and diuretics and digitalis may be indicated. Management of acute meningoencephalitis may require anticonvulsants, sedatives and intravenous mannitol. Vasodilatation (angiotensin-converting enzyme inhibitors) and maintenance of normal serum potassium may be required initially for chronic chagasic heart disease; digitalis is advisable only as a last resort because it may aggravate dysrhythmias.

Bradycardia that does not respond to atropine, atrial fibrillation with a slow ventricular response, or complete AV block may necessitate a pacemaker.

Amiodarone has been suggested as the most useful drug to treat dysrhythmias, but may produce cutaneous side-effects, such as photosensitivity. Lidocaine (lignocaine), mexiletine, propafenone, flecainide and β-adrenoreceptor antagonists are effective treatment for ventricular extrasystoles.

Management of chronic chagasic heart disease may therefore be a balancing act between patient management, drug administration and use of a pacemaker. In emergencies lidocaine may be used intravenously. Surgical resection of dysrhythmic endocardial regions and of ventricular aneurysms has been suggested. Detailed expert reports, such as that by the World Health Organization (WHO),[17] and physicians experienced in the management of chagasic cardiomyopathy should be consulted directly to assist in prolonging patient life expectancy and optimizing prognosis.

Surgical treatments have been developed in Brazil for mega-esophagus and megacolon. The modified Duhamel–Haddad operation is recommended for surgical correction of megacolon.[9,19,27] This procedure involves resection of the sigmoid loop, closure of the rectal stump and bringing the descending colon through the rear wall of the rectum as an initial perineal colostomy (Fig. 173.7). The stump of the colon is subsequently sectioned into anterior and posterior halves, with peridural anesthesia, and the anterior wall of the colon and posterior wall of the rectum sutured in an inverted V to widen the junction. Sigmoidostomy as a separate operation and recovery before Duhamel–Haddad surgery may allow more of the colon to be retained.

Mega-esophagus may improve with dietary control, or respond to dilatation of the cardiac sphincter using probes, air or hydrostatic pressure. The Heller–Vasconcelos surgical procedure for alleviating megaesophagus involves selective removal of a portion of muscle at the junction between the esophagus and stomach.[27] More severe mega-esophagus may demand replacement of the distal esophagus with another part of the alimentary tract such as the jejunum.

REFERENCES

1. Miles MA. New World trypanosomiasis. In: Cox FEG, ed. The Wellcome Trust illustrated history of tropical diseases. London: Wellcome Trust; 1996;192–205.
2. Miles MA. New World trypanosomiasis. In: Topley & Wilson's microbiology and microbial infections. London: Edward Arnold 1997:283–302.
3. Lent H, Wygodzinsky P. Revision of the Triatominae (Hemiptera, Reduviidae), and their significance as vectors of Chagas disease. Bull Am Mus Nat Hist 1979;163:123–520.
4. Coura JR, Junqueira AC, Fernandes O, Valente SA, Miles MA. Emerging Chagas disease in Amazonian Brazil. Trends Parasitol 2002; 18:171–6.
5. Miles MA. The epidemiology of South American trypanosomiasis: biochemical and immunological approaches and their relevance to control. Trans R Soc Trop Med Hyg 1983;77:5–23.
6. Gaunt M, Miles M. The ecotopes and evolution of triatomine bugs (Triatominae) and their associated trypanosomes. Mem Inst Oswaldo Cruz 2000; 95:557–65.
7. Gaunt MW, Yeo M, Frame IA, *et al.* Mechanism of genetic exchange in American trypanosomes. Nature 2003;421:936–9.
8. Machado CA, Ayala FJ. Nucleotide sequences provide evidence of genetic exchange among distantly related lineages of *Trypanosoma cruzi*. Proc Natl Acad Sci USA 2001, 98:7396–401.
9. Miles MA. Chagas disease and chagasic megacolon. In: Kamm MA, Lennard-Jones JE, eds. Constipation. Petersfield, UK: Wrightson Biomedical; 1994; 205–10.
10. Girones N, Fresno M. Etiology of Chagas disease myocarditis: autoimmunity, parasite persistence, or both? Trends Parasitol 2003;19:19–22.
11. Pan American Health Organization. Chagas disease and the nervous system. Scientific publication no. 547. Washington, DC: Pan American Health Organisation; 1994:1–354.
12. Dias JCP. Control of Chagas disease in Brazil. Parasitol Today 1987;3:336–41.
13. Schofield CJ, Dias JCP. The Southern Cone initiative against Chagas disease. Adv Parasitol 1998;42:1–27.
14. Miles MA, de Souza AA, Povoa M. Chagas disease in the Amazon basin. III. Ecotopes of ten triatomine bug species (Hemiptera: Reduviidae) from the vicinity of Belém, Pará, Brazil. J Med Entomol 1981;18:266–78.
15. Monteiro FA, Escalante AA, Beard CB. Molecular tools and triatomine systematics: a public health perspective. Trends Parasitol 2001;17:344–7.
16. Dias JC, Silveira AC, Schofield CJ. The impact of Chagas disease control in Latin America: a review. Mem Inst Oswaldo Cruz, 2002;97:603–12.
17. World Health Organization. Control of Chagas disease. Technical report series 905. Geneva: World Health Organization; 2002:1–109.
18. Rocha A, de Meneses AC, Da Silva AM, *et al.* Pathology of patients with Chagas disease and acquired immunodeficiency syndrome. Am J Trop Med Hyg 1994;50:261–8.
19. Moreira H, de Rezende JM, Sebba F, *et al.* Chagasic megacolon. Colo-Proctology 1985;7:260–7.
20. Maguire JH, Mott KE, Lehman JS, *et al.* Relationship of electrocardiographic abnormalities and seropositivity to *Trypanosoma cruzi* within a rural community in northeast Brazil. Am Heart J 1983;105:287–94.
21. Miles MA. Culturing and biological cloning of *Trypanosoma cruzi*. In: Hyde JE, ed. Protocols in molecular parasitology. Totowa, NJ: Humana Press; 1993:15–28.
22. Marcon GE, Andrade PD, de Albuquerque DM, *et al.* Use of a nested polymerase chain reaction (N-PCR) to detect *Trypanosoma cruzi* in blood samples from chronic chagasic patients and patients with doubtful serologies. Diagn Microbiol Infect Dis 2002; 43:39–43.
23. Moncayo A, Luquetti AO. Multicentre double blind study for evaluation of *Trypanosoma cruzi* defined antigens as diagnostic reagents. Mem Inst Oswaldo Cruz 1990;85:489–95.
24. Da Silveira JF, Umezawa ES, Luquetti AO. Chagas disease: recombinant *Trypanosoma cruzi* antigens for serological diagnosis. Trends Parasitol 2001; 17:286–91.
25. Di Noia JM, Buscaglia CA, De Marchi CR, Almeida IC, Frasch AC. A *Trypanosoma cruzi* small surface molecule provides the first immunological evidence that Chagas disease is due to a single parasite lineage. J Exp Med 2002; 195:401–13.
26. Urbina JA. Specific treatment of Chagas disease: current status and new developments. Curr Opin Infect Dis 2001; 14:733–41.
27. Raia AA. Manifestações digestivas da moléstia de Chagas. São Paulo, Brazil: Sarvier; 1983:1–277.

chapter

174 Migrating Worms

Stephen H Gillespie

INTRODUCTION

Somatic migration of larvae is a normal part of the life cycle of many nematode pathogens, for example *Ascaris lumbricoides*. However, some nematodes are able to invade the human host but are unable to complete their development into adults. In this circumstance the somatic migration stage is prolonged and gives rise to the condition of visceral larva migrans. The most common cause of this syndrome is the canine ascarid *Toxocara canis*, although more rarely *Gnathostoma* larvae and *Angiostrongylus* spp. and the dog hookworms are implicated.

TOXOCARA CANIS

LIFE CYCLE

Toxocara canis is a pathogen of canids, including the domestic dog and feral fox. Ingested eggs hatch in the intestine and the larvae invade the wall and migrate through the liver and lungs. Passing through four larval moults, mature larvae are coughed up and adults develop in the small intestine. This classic ascarid migration occurs mainly in dogs less than 6 months old. In older dogs larval maturation is halted at the second larval stage (L_2), and the larvae migrate and persist in the tissues. Larvae reactivate in pregnant bitches during week 6 of gestation, cross the placenta and are excreted in milk to infect puppies. This mechanism of transmission is very efficient, so that almost all dogs are infected. In dogs, adult worms continue to lay eggs until they are expelled, usually when the dog is about 6 months old. The fertilized eggs must mature in the soil for 2–4 weeks before they are infectious (Figs 174.1 and 174.2). In humans, *T. canis* eggs hatch and larvae invade in the same way but are unable to develop beyond the L_2 stage and continue to migrate through the body for a prolonged period.[1] Humans, along with many other animals, are paratenic hosts. Infection can follow ingestion of fertilized embryonated eggs or uncooked tissue of another paratenic host.

EPIDEMIOLOGY

Serologic studies among adults show that between 2% and 8% of the population has evidence of previous infection. Seroprevalence in children is higher, up to 35% in warm, moist tropical areas with poor sanitary conditions. Symptomatic disease typically occurs in children, with a male predominance. The peak incidence of visceral larva migrans occurs between 3 and 7 years of age and the peak incidence of ocular disease occurs between 7 and 10 years of age. Infection is commonly associated with dog ownership and pica. Several occupational groups that have an excess contact with dogs (e.g. kennel workers) have increased risk of infection, but symptomatic disease is rare in adults. Fecal–oral transmission of infection by ingestion of fertilized mature eggs is the main route of acquisition of *T. canis*. Public parks are thought to be an important source of infection. There have been a few reports of outbreaks of *T. canis* infection associated with the ingestion of raw meat containing L_2 larvae. Examples include undercooked chicken and a Lebanese dish that includes raw sheep liver.[2]

PATHOGENESIS

The L_2 larvae of *T. canis* excrete a complex mixture of glycoproteins, the excretory antigens (*Toxocara* excretory secretory antigens, TES or TEX) from the larval surface. These antigens activate complement, stimulate cytokine production and have potent elastase, acetylcholinesterase and superoxide dismutase activities.[3] As larvae migrate through the tissue there is an intense inflammatory response to TES. The symptoms and signs of toxocariasis are a consequence of this immune response. When the larval load is high there is an intense systemic response, leading to the syndrome of visceral larva migrans (see below). If a larva is trapped in the retina, the inflammatory response is localized, leading to ocular complications such as endophthalmitis or uveitis. Healing of the lesion may be followed by fibrosis with the potential for retinal traction and detachment.[4]

CLINICAL FEATURES

Visceral larva migrans

This syndrome was clearly described in Paul Beaver's initial report as consisting of prolonged fever, cough, wheeze, hepatosplenomegaly and eosinophilia.[5] Since then, more subtle clinical symptoms and signs have been associated with infection, including failure to thrive, urticaria and abdominal pain, and clinicians may include toxocariasis in the differential diagnosis of children with asthmatic symptoms, chronic non-specific abdominal pain, failure to thrive and anemia in addition to the classic visceral larva migrans syndrome (Tables 174.1 and 174.2).[6–9] Rarely, heavy infections are associated with myocarditis and a fatal outcome. Associations between toxocariasis and asthma and between toxocariasis and seizures have been made, but a clear etiologic role for *T. canis* has not been identified.

Ocular infection

The pattern and severity of ocular disease depend on the age of the child, the location of the lesion and the immune response. In younger children early lesions may go unrecognized and untreated, so that they present only in routine medical examinations, by which time treatment may not be effective. Ocular toxocariasis may present with endophthalmitis or uveitis. Vision may be reduced by the presence of inflammatory cells in the ocular medium or damage may be caused by a retinal granuloma. Macular lesions can cause a complete loss of vision. Ocular toxocariasis is usually unilateral, but bilateral disease has been reported in up to 3% of series.[4]

Diagnosis

As *T. canis* does not complete its life cycle in humans, adult worms do not develop and eggs cannot be found in the stool. The diagnosis

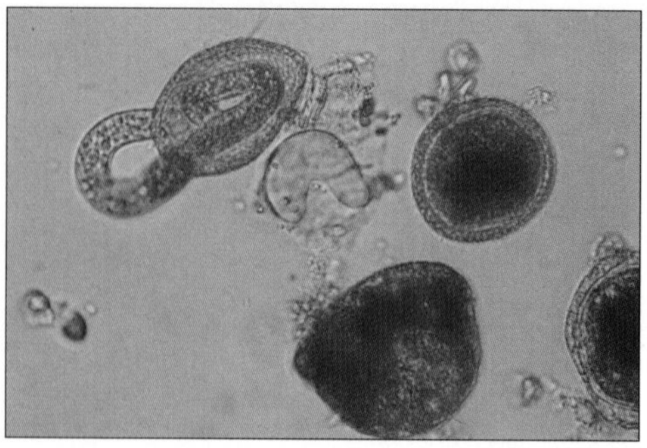

Fig. 174.1 Fully embryonated egg of *Toxocara canis* hatching. To the right are two unfertilized eggs.

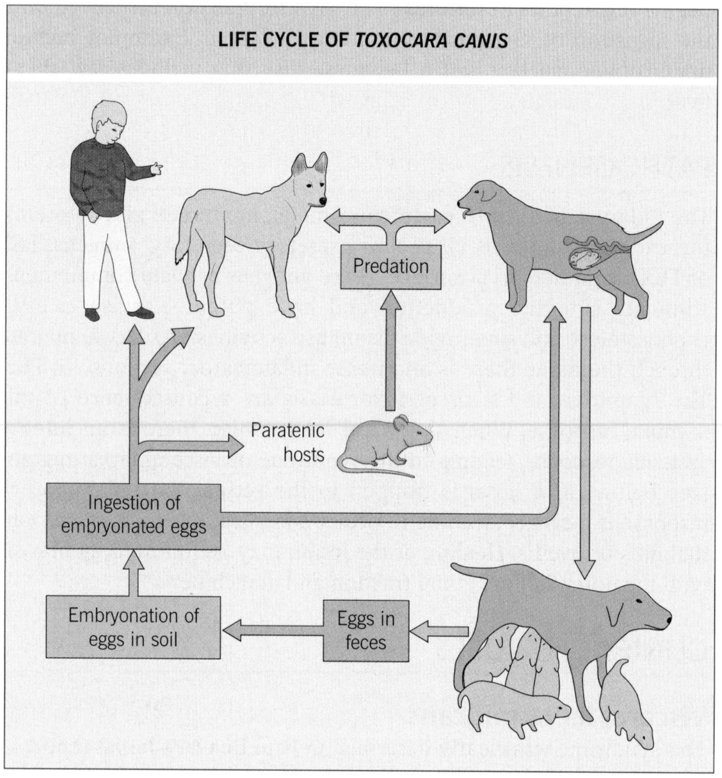

Fig. 174.2 Life cycle of *Toxocara canis*. This demonstrates the importance of transplacental transmission in maintaining canine infection, and the role of young dogs in transmitting infection to humans.

of toxocariasis depends on serologic methods and hematologic parameters. An antibody capture enzyme immunoassay, based on TES antigens, is used worldwide. This test has proved sensitive and specific, with few cross-reactions with other helminth parasites.[10] Alternative diagnostic approaches have included IgE-specific antibody testing and detection of TES antigens, but none of these techniques has proved sufficiently robust for routine clinical diagnosis.[11] There is evidence that IgE detection, although less sensitive, does make the diagnosis of cases of eosinophilia where the serum IgG test is negative. Also serum IgE becomes negative after treatment and has been proposed as a method of following patients who have been given anthelmintic agents.[12]

TREATMENT

The natural history of visceral larva migrans tends toward resolution over a period of weeks or months. Treatment should be considered when the severity or prolonged nature of the symptoms makes it necessary. A single comparative trial showed no enhanced clinical benefit for albendazole over thiabendazole.[13] Albendazole 400mg for 7 days is probably the treatment of choice, although diethyl carbamazine and thiabendazole are alternatives.

CLINICAL SYMPTOMS OF TOXOCARIASIS: COMPARISON OF STUDIES

Feature	No of patients (%)			
	Harrison-Synder[6]	Huntley *et al.*[7]	Taylor *et al.*[8]	Gillespie[9]
Pica	100	90	NR	10
Fever	55	80	33	39
Cough	20	80	68	46
Wheeze	20	63	51	28
Abdominal pain	0	0	63	32
Failure to thrive	NR	39	NR	4
Anemia	40	NR	NR	4
No symptoms	0	0	NR	12
Male sex	75	66	NR	60
Eosinophilia	100	100	NR	77

Table 174.1 Clinical symptoms of toxocariasis: comparison of studies. NR, none recorded.

SIGNS OF CLINICAL TOXOCARIASIS: COMPARISON OF STUDIES

Feature	No of patients (%)			
	Harrison-Synder[6]	Huntley *et al.*[7]	Taylor *et al.*[8]	Gillespie[9]
Hepatomegaly	85	65	26	15
Splenomegaly	40	NR	8	11
Lympadenopathy	NR	8	62	21
Bronchospasm	NR	43	NR	17
Skin lesions	NR	22	5	5

Table 174.2 Signs of clinical toxocariasis: comparison of studies. NR, none recorded

In ocular disease therapy is directed toward reducing the severity of the inflammatory response. There is no controlled trial evidence to suggest whether specific anthelmintic therapy is beneficial. There are several reports that support the value of therapy with both albendazole and corticosteroids.[14,15] Vitrectomy and surgical correction of retinal detachment is beneficial in approximately half of patients with retinal traction.[16] Laser treatment of retinal granuloma has been described but its benefit has not been systematically assessed in comparison with other therapy.

PREVENTION AND CONTROL

Control measures are directed toward reducing contact between children and infective eggs. Because eggs require a period of embryonation in soil, contamination of soil in public parks is an important target for control measures. Dog owners should be encouraged to worm their dogs regularly and to clean up after their pets have defecated. This may be supported by local legislation punishing promiscuous canine defecation in public areas with fines. It is especially important that children's play areas should be made dog proof and children should be encouraged to wash their hands thoroughly after playing in a park.

ANGIOSTRONGYLUS CANTONENSIS

Angiostrongylus cantonensis is a nematode parasite closely related to hookworm. The life cycle involves two hosts, a vertebrate and a snail in which the infective larvae develop. Humans become infected when they eat slugs or snails or fruits and vegetables on which larvae have been shed in slime. Humans are abnormal hosts for *A. cantonensis* and severe symptoms may result: eosinophilic meningitis, eosinophilic meningoencephalitis and eosinophilic radiculomyeloencephalitis.

A closely related species, *Angiostrongylus costaricensis*, causes abdominal symptoms that may mimic acute appendicitis or ileitis and is found in Central America.[17] Treatment with benzimidazoles may be beneficial.

Infection with *A. cantonensis* principally occurs in South East Asia, Oceania, India, Madagascar, Côte d'Ivoire and Egypt, but a new focus of infection has been described in the Caribbean.[18] Treatment may exacerbate symptoms by releasing parasite antigens, and management with corticosteroids may be beneficial, although experience is limited.

GNATHOSTOMIASIS

Gnathostomia spinigerum is the commonest species associated with human gnathostomiasis. The organism has a complex life cycle involving an adult in the intestinal wall of the cat and eggs in the feces, which are ingested by a water-dwelling cyclops and are subsequently ingested by fish, snakes and amphibians. Human infection arises by eating raw or undercooked fish or by handling ducks or chickens that have eaten intermediate hosts. The larvae are unable to complete their life cycle in humans and migrate through the tissues for prolonged periods. The disease principally presents as migratory cutaneous swellings but, more seriously, invasion of the central nervous system or ocular disease may develop, causing eosinophilic meningitis, which may involve the spinal cord. Meningitis in gnathostomiasis is frequently fatal. In the eye, the parasite can produce severe inflammation and hemorrhagic lesions. Treatment is unsatisfactory although some have recommended the use of benzimidazoles for treatment.

ANCYLOSTOMA CANINUM AND *ANCYLOSTOMA BRAZILIENSE* INFECTIONS

Dog hookworms cannot complete their life cycle in noncanine hosts and may cause cutaneous larva migrans.[19] Cutaneous larva migrans does not occur after the first exposure to *Ancylostoma caninum* and *A. braziliense* larva, suggesting that the disease is due to hypersensitivity to larval secretions. The lower extremities are more often affected, with eruptions on the feet making up almost two-thirds of all cases. Infection is commonly reported in patients returning from tropical travel. Lesions may be found in the upper legs, urogenital region and on the arms and trunk. Lesions on the head are extremely rare but have been described.[19] The lesions are intensely itchy, red and edematous and show a worm-like migratory pathway under the skin. However, recent studies indicate that *A. caninum* can achieve a wider migration and is implicated in the condition of eosinophilic enteritis.[20] Eosinophilic enteritis is characterized by abdominal pain that is often colicky moving to the periumbilical region or right of the iliac fossa. It usually lasts up to 1 month. It is associated with anorexia, nausea and diarrhea, and some patients can be sufficiently ill to present with an acute abdominal condition that may mimic acute appendicitis or intestinal obstruction.[21]

The diagnosis of cutaneous larva migrans is made on the basis of the characteristic clinical features. The laboratory has no role to play in diagnosis. Eosinophilia is only a feature of a minority of cases. The total serum IgE is usually normal and other serologic tests for helminth infections are unhelpful. In eosinophilic enteritis the patient has significant eosinophilia and a high total IgE level but these laboratory features may be absent in some patients. The diagnosis is made histologically using tissue biopsies obtained during colonoscopy.[20] Aphthous ulcers can be seen in the cecum and terminal ileum on colonoscopy. Laparotomy, when performed for a suspected diagnosis of appendicitis, often reveals an inflamed ileum with intense serositis and enlarged mesenteric lymph nodes. Antibodies to the excretory-secretory antigens of adult *A. caninum* patients can be found in more than 85% of patients with eosinophilic enteritis by antibody capture enzyme-linked immunosorbent assay.

Cutaneous larva migrans is readily treated by application of 10% thiabendazole paste and an occlusive dressing for 24 hours. In severe cases systemic treatment with albendazole or ivermectin may also be used. Eosinophilic enteritis is readily treated with 200mg mebendazole. Failure to respond within 24 hours would suggest an alternative diagnosis.

REFERENCES

1. Lloyd S. *Toxocara canis*: the dog. In: Lewis JW, Maizels RM, eds. *Toxocara* and toxocariasis. London: British Society of Parasitology; 1993.
2. Glickman LT. Epidemiology of toxocariasis. In: Lewis JW, Maizels RM, eds. *Toxocara* and toxocariasis. London: British Society of Parasitology; 1993.
3. Maizels RM, Gems DH, Page AP. Synthesis and secretion of TES antigens from *Toxocara canis* infected larvae. In: Lewis JW, Maizels RM, eds. *Toxocara* and toxocariasis. London: British Society of Parasitology; 1993.
4. Gillespie SH, Dinning WJ, Voller A, Crowcroft NS. The spectrum of ocular toxocariasis. Eye 1993;7:415–8.
5. Beaver PC. The nature of visceral larva migrans. J Parasitol 1969;55:3–12.
6. Harrison-Snyder C. Visceral larva migrans. Pediatrics 1961;28:85–91.
7. Huntley CC, Costas MC, Lyerly A. Visceral larva migrans syndrome: clinical characteristics and immunological studies. Paediatrics 1965;36:523–6.
8. Taylor MR, Keane CT, O'Connor P, Mulvihill E, Holland C. The expanded spectrum of *Toxocaral* disease. Lancet 1988;1:692–5.
9. Gillespie SH. The clinical spectrum of toxocariasis. In: Lewis JW, Maizels RM, eds. *Toxocara* and toxocariasis. London: British Society of Parasitology; 1993.
10. de Savigny DH, Voller A, Woodruff AW. Toxocariasis: serological diagnosis by enzyme immunoassay. J Clin Pathol 1979;32:284–8.
11. Gillespie SH, Bidwell D, Voller A, Robertson BM, Maizels RM. Diagnosis of human toxocariasis by antigen capture enzyme linked immuno-absorbent assay. J Clin Pathol 1993;46:551–4.
12. Magnaval JF, Fabre R, Maurieres P, Charlet JP, de Larrard B. Evaluation of an immunoenzymatic assay detecting specific anti-*Toxocara* immunoglobulin E for diagnosis and post treatment follow-up of human toxocariasis. J Clin Microbiol 1992;30:2269–74.
13. Strucher D, Schubarthi P, Gualzata M, Gottstein B, Oettli A. Thiabendazole vs albendazole in treatment of toxocariasis: a clinical trial. Ann Trop Med Parasitol 1989;83:473–8.
14. Dinning WJ, Gillespie SH, Cooling RJ, Maizels RM. Toxocariasis: a practical approach to the management of ocular disease. Eye 1988;2:580–2.
15. Barisani-Asenbauer T, Maca SM, Hauff W, *et al.* Treatment of ocular toxocariasis with albendazole. J Ocul Pharmacol Ther 2001;17:287–94.
16. Amin HL, McDonald HR, Han DP, *et al.* Vitrectomy update for macular traction in ocular toxocariasis. Retina 2000;20:80–5.
17. Piris M, Gutierrez Y, Minini C, *et al.* Fatal human pulmonary infection caused by an *Angiostrongylus*-like nematode. Clin Infect Dis 1995;20:59–65.
18. Slom TJ, Cortese MM, Gerber SI, *et al.* An outbreak of eosinophilic meningitis caused by *Angiostrongylus cantonensis* in travelers returning from the caribbean. N Engl J Med 2002;346:668–75.
19. Jelinek T, Maiwald H, Northdurft HD, Loscher T. Cutaneous larva migrans in travelers: synopsis of histories, symptoms and treatment of 98 patients. Clin Infect Dis 1994;19:1062–6.
20. Croese J, Loukas A, Opdebezck J, Fairley S, Prociv P. Human enteric infection with canine hookworms. Ann Intern Med 1994;20:369–74.
21. Croese J, Fairley S, Loukas A, Hack J, Stronach P. A distinctive aphthous ileitis linked to *Ancylostoma caninum*. J Gastroenterol Hepatol 1996;11:524–31.

chapter 175

Melioidosis

David AB Dance

INTRODUCTION

The term 'melioidosis' refers to infections caused by the Gram-negative bacillus *Burkholderia* (formerly *Pseudomonas*) *pseudomallei*, which is recognized increasingly as a public health problem in some tropical regions.[1] The considerable recent progress in our understanding of the pathogenesis of this infection and the sequencing of the bacterial genome contrast starkly with our poor knowledge of the epidemiology and distribution of the disease worldwide.[2]

EPIDEMIOLOGY

The distribution of melioidosis is shown in Figure 175.1. Most cases are diagnosed in South East Asia and northern Australia. The disease is probably under-recognized elsewhere (e.g. half the recent cases diagnosed in the UK originated from the Indian subcontinent). Imported infection is seen mainly in immigrants or soldiers serving in endemic areas, but occasionally occurs in tourists.

Burkholderia pseudomallei is a saprophyte found in soil and surface water, particularly rice paddies, in endemic areas. A closely related, arabinose-assimilating, avirulent organism, *Burkholderia thailandensis*, is similarly distributed, and may give rise to confusion, particularly in serologic tests. Humans and a wide range of other animals acquire infection from contact with soil (e.g. through rice farming), probably by inoculation or inhalation.[3] Recent clusters of infection in Australia have also been associated with contamination of potable water supplies.[2] Most cases present during the rainy season, when people are maximally exposed to the organisms in the environment.[3,4] Animal-to-human and person-to-person spread, iatrogenic infection and laboratory-acquired infection have all been reported occasionally. All ages may be affected, with a peak from 40–60 years. Males are more often affected than females.[3,4]

PATHOGENESIS AND PATHOLOGY

The outcome of infection with *B. pseudomallei* depends on a balance between the virulence of the organism, the size of inoculum and the resistance of the host. Between 50% and 70% of patients who have melioidosis have predisposing underlying diseases, especially diabetes mellitus but also chronic renal disease, malignancy, immunosuppressive treatment (e.g. corticosteroids), liver disease, alcohol or drug abuse, pregnancy and cystic fibrosis.[3,4] Interferon (IFN)-γ appears to play a key role in controlling the infection in experimental animals. Recent studies have shown that capsular polysaccharide is a major virulence determinant in *B. pseudomallei*, possibly by reducing intracellular killing.[5] Other potential virulence factors include lipopolysaccharide, a lethal exotoxin, various enzymes (lecithinase, lipase, proteases and acid phosphatase), type III secretion systems and a siderophore. Several of these appear to be encoded on 'pathogenicity islands', possibly acquired by horizontal transfer.[2] Intracellular survival of *B. pseudomallei* probably contributes to the recalcitrant nature of melioidosis.

Burkholderia pseudomallei causes localized abscesses or granulomas at the site of primary infection, depending on the duration of the lesion. Invasion of the bloodstream leads to sepsis, which may in turn result in metastatic foci of infection in other tissues. The host response may also contribute to pathogenesis, because serum levels of several cytokines, including IFN-γ, tumor necrosis factor, interleukin (IL)-6 and IL-8, are also correlated with mortality.

PREVENTION

Because *B. pseudomallei* is ubiquitous in the environment in endemic areas, avoidance of the organism is virtually impossible. No *B. pseudomallei* vaccine has been developed for human use, although several experimental vaccines are under development and some have been used on animals. The organism should be handled in containment level 3 facilities in the laboratory. Patients should ideally be cared for in standard isolation, although person-to-person spread is very rare.

CLINICAL FEATURES

None of the clinical classifications of melioidosis is entirely satisfactory. Infections may be acute or chronic and localized or disseminated, but one form of the disease may progress to another and individual patients are often difficult to categorize. Several reviews of the clinical features of melioidosis have been published.[4,6] The manifestations of the disease in Australia are similar to those in Thailand, although prostatic abscesses and neurologic involvement are more frequently described and parotid abscesses less often.[4]

Mild and subclinical infections

Antibodies to *B. pseudomallei* are very common yet disease is rare, so the majority of infections are presumably mild or asymptomatic. A flu-like illness associated with seroconversion has been reported.

Latent infections

Unusually for a bacterial infection, long periods of latency (up to 29 years) may occur before the disease becomes apparent, which usually happens during intercurrent stress (hence the name 'the Vietnamese time bomb').

Septic melioidosis

Positive blood cultures are found in 46–60% of cases of culture-positive melioidosis.[4,6] Most of these cases present with a picture of fulminant sepsis syndrome with a short history of high fever and rigors, although some patients have a less acute, typhoidal picture with a remittent fever. Only half have evidence of a primary focus of infection, usually in the lung or skin and subcutaneous tissues. Confusion and stupor, jaundice and diarrhea may also be prominent features. Initial investigations usually reveal:

- anemia;
- a neutrophil leukocytosis;
- coagulopathy; and
- evidence of renal and hepatic impairment.

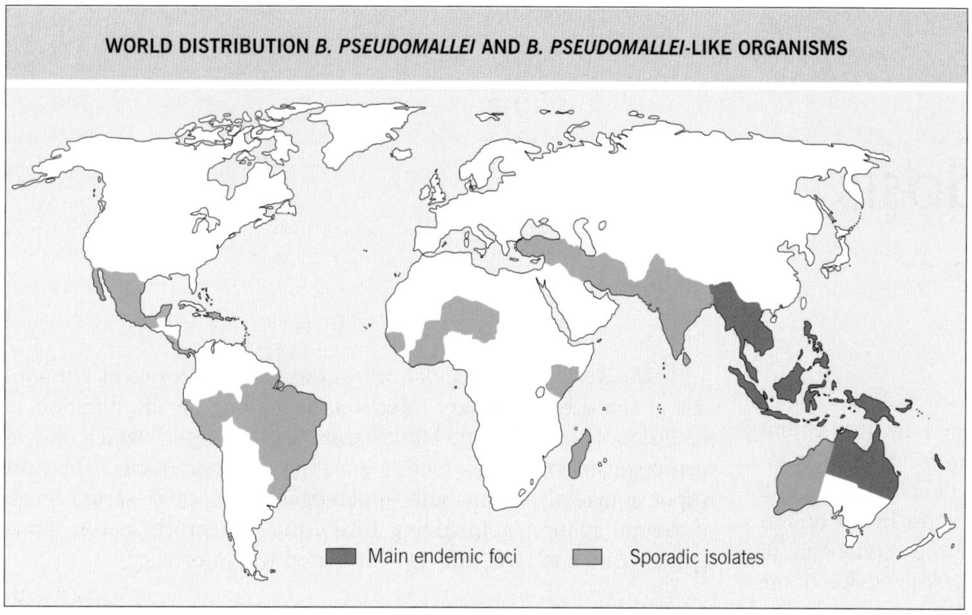

Fig. 175.1 World distribution of *Burkholderia pseudomallei* and *Burkholderia pseudomallei*-like organisms. The boundaries are political and are not intended to define the true limits of distribution. With permission from Dance.[1]

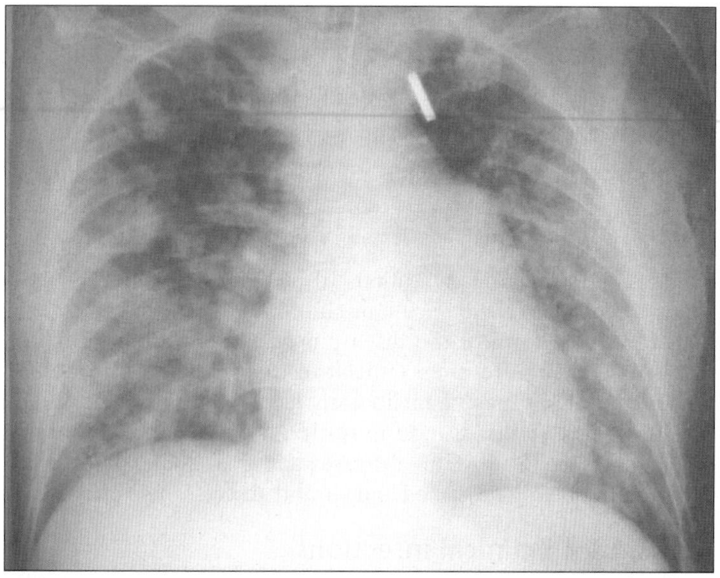

Fig. 175.2 Chest radiograph of patient who has septic melioidosis. Note the multiple areas of consolidation scattered throughout both lung fields (blood-borne pneumonia). With permission from Prof N J White.

Patients often deteriorate rapidly, developing widespread metastatic foci, metabolic acidosis with Kussmaul's breathing, and shock, and many die within 48 hours of hospital admission. Poor prognostic features include absence of fever, leukopenia, azotemia and abnormal liver function tests.[6]

If the patient survives the acute phase, the manifestations of metastatic septic foci become prominent. An abnormal chest radiograph is found in 60–80% of patients, the most common pattern being widespread, nodular shadowing (Fig. 175.2). Multiple liver and splenic abscesses are common.[7] Cutaneous pustules or subcutaneous abscesses occur in 10–20% of cases.[6] Other common sites for secondary lesions include the urinary tract (kidneys and prostate gland), bones and joints. Involvement of the central nervous system may comprise cerebral abscesses or a syndrome of peripheral motor weakness, brain stem encephalitis, aseptic meningitis and respiratory failure.[4]

Localized melioidosis

Localized melioidosis is most common in the lung, where it usually causes a subacute cavitating pneumonia accompanied by profound weight loss. This may be confused with tuberculosis, although relative sparing of the apices and the infrequency of hilar adenopathy may help to distinguish the two. Any lung zone may be affected, although there is a predilection for the upper lobes. Complications include pneumothorax, empyema, purulent pericarditis and ultimately progression to sepsis. Acute suppurative parotitis (Fig. 175.3) is a characteristic manifestation of melioidosis in children in Thailand, although it is rarely reported elsewhere. Localized *B. pseudomallei* infection may affect any other tissue or organ (e.g. cutaneous and subcutaneous abscesses, lymphadenitis, osteomyelitis and septic arthritis, liver or splenic abscesses, cystitis, pyelonephritis, prostatic abscesses, epididymo-orchitis, keratitis, brain abscesses and mycotic aneurysms).

DIAGNOSIS

Melioidosis should be considered in any patient who has sepsis or abscesses who has ever visited an endemic area, particularly if the patient has an underlying disease such as diabetes mellitus. Microscopy of a Gram-stained smear of pus or sputum is neither specific nor sensitive but immunofluorescent microscopy, which is only available in a few centers, offers the best opportunity of making a rapid diagnosis. Definitive diagnosis depends on isolation and identification of *B. pseudomallei* from cultures of blood or clinically affected sites (e.g. pus, sputum). It is important to alert the laboratory to the suspicion of melioidosis. Preliminary culture results should be available within 48 hours, although identification may be delayed in nonendemic areas because microbiologists are not familiar with the organism. Several rapid diagnostic techniques for the detection of *B. pseudomallei* antigens or nucleic acids have been developed, but these are not yet sufficiently sensitive or specific to be widely used.[9]

The serologic test most widely used in endemic areas is an indirect hemagglutination (IHA) test, although other assays that detect IgG antibodies give similar results. There is a need for internationally standardized serologic tests. High background seropositivity means that false-positive reactions are common in people from endemic areas,[6] but a single high IHA titer (>1:40) in someone

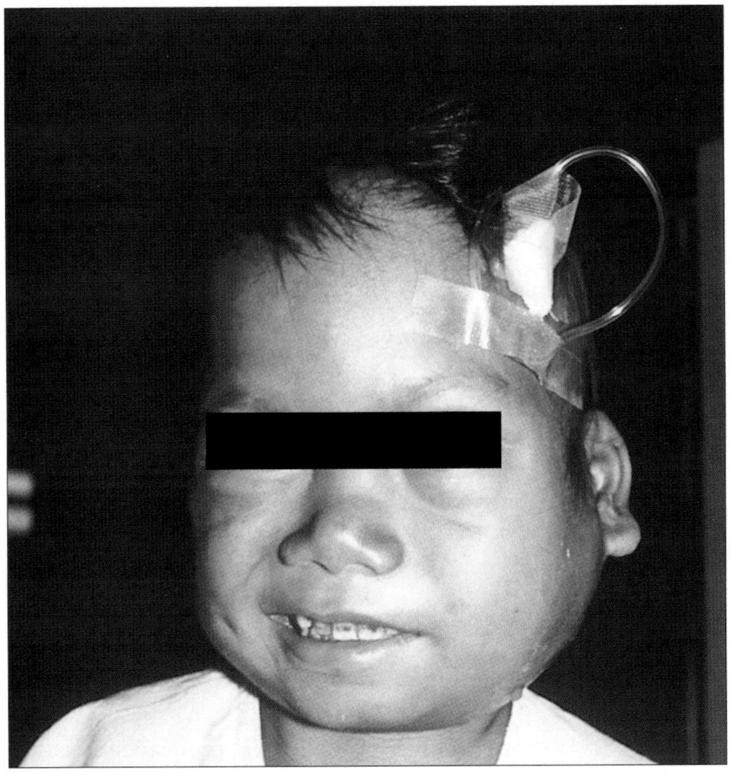

Fig. 175.3 Acute suppurative parotitis. This form of melioidosis accounts for around one third of pediatric cases in north east Thailand, but has rarely been reported elsewhere. With permission from Dance *et al.*[8]

from a nonendemic area, or a rising titer, may be diagnostically useful. Tests for specific IgM (e.g. indirect immunofluorescence, enzyme-linked immunosorbent assay) correlate better with disease activity and, along with measurement of C-reactive protein, they may be useful during follow-up of patients on treatment. Imaging, including the use of labeled white cell scans, is also useful in determining the initial extent of dissemination and monitoring the response to treatment.

MANAGEMENT

Supportive treatment

Patients who have septic melioidosis usually require aggressive supportive treatment, including correction of volume depletion and septic shock, respiratory and renal failure, and hyperglycemia or ketoacidosis. Abscesses should be drained whenever possible.

Specific treatment

Burkholderia pseudomallei is intrinsically resistant to many antibiotics, including aminoglycosides and early β-lactams, and a failure to respond to these agents is characteristic of melioidosis.[6] Several recent studies have shown that the mortality of acute severe melioidosis can be substantially reduced by newer β-lactam agents such as ceftazidime, imipenem, amoxicillin–clavulanic acid and cefoperazone-sulbactam, with or without trimethoprim–sulfamethoxazole.[10] Very encouraging results have also been reported from Australia using meropenem plus trimethoprim–sulfamethoxazole.[4] The role of granulocyte colony-stimulating factor, which has also been used as adjunctive treatment in Australia, remains to be determined. Ceftazidime or a carbapenem are currently the treatments of choice and should be given in full doses (ceftazidime 120mg/kg/day, imipenem and meropenem 60mg/kg/day, or a dose appropriately adjusted for renal function) for 2–4 weeks according to the clinical response.

Following parenteral treatment, prolonged oral antibiotics are needed to prevent relapse, which occurs in up to 23% of patients and is more common in patients who have more severe disease. The proportion of patients who relapse can be reduced to less than 10% if antibiotics are given for 20 weeks.[10] The combination of chloramphenicol (40mg/kg/day), doxycycline (4mg/kg/day) and trimethoprim–sulfamethoxazole (10mg/kg trimethoprim plus 50mg/kg sulfamethoxazole per day) has been associated with a lower relapse rate than amoxicillin–clavulanic acid (60mg/kg amoxicillin plus 15mg/kg clavulanic acid per day). Lately the chloramphenicol has been omitted from this regimen without apparent detriment[11] and trimethoprim–sulfamethoxazole alone has been used in Australia,[4] although doxycycline alone and fluoroquinolones are inadequate. Amoxicillin–clavulanic acid is preferable in children and pregnant or lactating women. In patients who have mild localized disease, any of the oral regimens described above may be used.

OUTCOME AND FOLLOW-UP

Even with optimal treatment, the mortality from acute severe melioidosis is high (30–47% in Thailand, 19% in Australia).[4,9] In patients who survive, there is often chronic morbidity resulting both from the disease itself and from the underlying conditions. Patients require long-term follow-up to detect relapse. Susceptibility tests should be carried out on isolates obtained during or after treatment, because resistance may emerge in 5–10% of cases.

REFERENCES

1. Dance DAB. Melioidosis: the tip of the iceberg? Clin Microbiol Rev 1991;4:52–60.
2. Dance DAB. Melioidosis. Curr Opin Infect Dis 2002;15:127–32.
3. Suputtamongkol Y, Hall AJ, Dance DAB, *et al.* The epidemiology of melioidosis in Ubon Ratchatani, northeast Thailand. Int J Epidemiol 1994;23:1082–90.
4. Currie BJ, Fisher DA, Howard DM, *et al.* Endemic melioidosis in tropical northern Australia: a 10-year prospective study and review of the literature. Clin Infect Dis 2000;31:981–6.
5. Reckseidler SL, Deshazer D, Sokol PA, *et al.* Detection of bacterial virulence genes by subtractive hybridisation: identification of capsular polysaccharide of *Burkholderia pseudomallei* as a major virulence determinant. Infect Immun 2001;69:34–44.
6. Chaowagul W, White NJ, Dance DAB, *et al.* Melioidosis: a major cause of community-acquired septicemia in northeastern Thailand. J Infect Dis 1989;159:890–9.
7. Chong VFH, Fan YF. The radiology of melioidosis. Australas Radiol 1996;40:244–9.
8. Dance DAB, Davis TM, Wattanagoon Y, *et al.* Acute suppurative parotitis caused by *Pseudomonas pseudomallei* in children. J Infect Dis 1989;159:654-60.
9. Zysk G, Splettstösser WD, Neubauer H. A review on melioidosis with special respect on molecular and immunological diagnostic techniques. Clin Lab 2000;46:119–30.
10. Chaowagul W. Recent advances in the treatment of severe melioidosis. Acta Trop 2000;74:133–7.
11. Chetchotisakd P, Chaowagul W, Mootsikapun P, *et al.* Maintenance therapy of melioidosis with ciprofloxacin plus azithromycin compared with co-trimoxazole plus doxycycline. Am J Trop Med Hyg 2001;64:24–7.

chapter 176

Plague

David T Dennis & Kenneth L Gage

Plague is an acute, life-threatening zoonosis caused by the bacterium *Yersinia pestis*. The disease is best known for three devastating pandemics, including the Black Death of the Middle Ages. Plague is primarily a disease of rodents, and humans typically acquire the disease as a result of being bitten by rodent fleas, less commonly by handling infected animals, and rarely by inhaling infectious respiratory particles. Urban, rat-borne plague outbreaks have historically been responsible for most human plague cases; in recent decades, however, plague has occurred typically in remote, rural populations. The three principal clinical forms of plague are bubonic plague, septic plague and pneumonic plague. The most common of these is bubonic plague, an acute illness characterized by fever and one or more enlarged tender lymph nodes (buboes) that usually appear in the groin or the axillary or cervical regions proximal to the site of an infective inoculation. Bacteremia and sepsis occur when lymphatic defenses have been breached, and plague pneumonia can arise secondarily as a result of blood-borne seeding of the lungs. Occasionally, pneumonic plague spreads from person to person, most often in crowded, substandard living conditions.

Plague is often fatal when not diagnosed and treated with appropriate antibiotics early in the course of infection. The aminoglycosides, tetracyclines and chloramphenicol are the antibiotics most commonly used to treat plague. Pneumonic plague patients should be isolated under respiratory droplet precautions until no longer infectious, and it is recommended that persons who have been in close contact with pneumonic plague patients be placed on antimicrobial prophylaxis and monitored for fever. Prevention and control of plague relies on environmental sanitation, human and animal disease surveillance, flea and rodent control, and early detection, treatment and isolation of cases, as indicated. Plague is considered to be an important potential weapon of bioterrorism.

EPIDEMIOLOGY

Agent

Yersinia pestis is a Gram-negative, microaerophilic coccobacillus belonging to the family Enterobacteriaceae (see Chapter 228). The entire genome of *Y. pestis* has been decoded, showing that the organism recently evolved from *Yersinia pseudotuberculosis*, a gut pathogen.[1] It is nonmotile and nonsporulating, does not ferment lactose and exhibits bipolar staining with Wayson's, Giemsa's or Wright's stains. Growth occurs in a variety of media at a wide range of temperatures (39–104°F (4–40°C); optimal 82–86°F (28–30°C)) and pH values (5.0–9.6; optimal 7.2–7.6). It is a facultative intracellular pathogen that normally grows in extracellular environments; importantly, it invades, multiplies within and is transported by phagocytes during the initial phases of infection.[2]

Genetic factors that enable *Y. pestis* to survive in its mammalian hosts and flea vectors and be transmitted between them are outlined in Table 176.1.[2–6] Some factors are expressed selectively at temperatures and environments encountered in fleas or mammals. For example, hemin storage locus (*hms*) products are expressed in the low temperature environment of the flea, apparently enabling the bacteria to form the gut blockages necessary for their survival and efficient transmission.[2,6]

Three biotypes of *Y. pestis*, which are classified according to their ability to ferment glycerol and reduce nitrate, have been correlated with the three principal plague pandemics. The biotype that spread around the world during the third pandemic beginning in the late 19th century is termed the orientalis biotype; it occurs alone in South East Asia, portions of Africa, Madagascar and in the Western Hemisphere. The antiqua biotype occurs in parts of Africa, southeastern Russia and in Central Asia. The mediaevalis biotype, thought to have been responsible for the Black Death, occurs in natural foci around the Caspian Sea. Results of typing by restriction fragment length polymorphism analysis of rRNA genes (ribotyping) supports these distinctions and has shown chromosomal rearrangements in the orientalis biotype after its spread around the world about 100 years ago.[7]

Life cycle

Understanding the epidemiology of plague requires a working knowledge of the ecology of *Y. pestis* and its transmission cycles. In general, *Y. pestis* is maintained in both enzootic and epizootic cycles involving various sylvatic and commensal rodent species and their fleas (Fig. 176.1).[8] Historically, the commensal black or roof rat, *Rattus rattus*, the sewer rat, *Rattus norvegicus*, and their fleas (especially the oriental rat flea, *Xenopsylla cheopis*) have been the principal sources of epidemics of plague and its pandemic spread.

During interepizootic periods the plague bacterium is maintained in 'silent' enzootic cycles involving populations of wild rodents that exhibit variable responses to *Y. pestis* infection. The most susceptible members of an enzootic host population are likely to develop high bacteremias and serve as suitable sources for infecting feeding fleas. Other members of the same population of rodents develop little or no bacteremia and infect few fleas. These more resistant animals will, however, survive to reproduce and are likely to have offspring that vary in their susceptibility to plague, a factor that promotes the survival of enzootic host populations and yet allows the transmission cycle to be maintained. Most enzootic host species also have relatively high reproductive rates, which further promotes the ongoing introduction of susceptible, nonimmune animals into the population.[9] Under certain conditions, plague is likely to spread from enzootic hosts to more susceptible rodent species (epizootic hosts), causing explosive epizootics and massive die-offs. Commensal rats and certain burrowing rodents, such as prairie dogs, marmots and various ground squirrels, are among the most important epizootic hosts.

Humans and other incidental hosts of *Y. pestis* are not directly involved in maintaining its natural cycle. *Yersinia pestis* can, however,

PROPOSED VIRULENCE AND TRANSMISSION FACTORS FOR *YERSINIA PESTIS*		
Genomic element	**Virulence or transmission factor**	**Proposed role in virulence or transmission**
9.5kb plasmid (pesticin plasmid; a 19kb dimer of this plasmid also exists)	Pesticin sensitivity (*pst*)	Loss of sensitivity to pesticin (a bacteriocin) is associated with reduced siderophore binding capability (affects iron uptake)
	Plasminogen activator (*pla*)	Fibrinolytic activity (important for dissemination)
70–75kb plasmid (low calcium response plasmid)	*Yersinia* outer proteins (Yops – genes found in the Yop virulon, a type III secretion system; includes *lcrV* or V antigen)	Proposed functions vary among Yops and include: translocation of other Yops (effectors) across cell membranes; disturbance of phagocyte cytoskeleton dynamics (interferes with phagocytosis); blocking production of proinflammatory cytokines and interfering with ability of B and T cells to be activated by means of antigen receptors (immunosuppression); or binding thrombin (interferes with thrombin–platelet aggregation)
100–110kb plasmid	Murine toxin (*ymt*)	Required for survival in fleas; also has β-adrenergic antagonist activity in rats and mice but not guinea pigs, rabbits, dogs or nonhuman primates
	F1 'capsular' antigen (*caf1*)	Resistance to phagocytosis by monocytes
Chromosomal	Pigmentation (*pgm* locus, includes genes of *hms* locus, high pathogenicity island and *ybt* operon)	Pigment-positive strains bind hemin and appear pigmented on culture media containing Congo Red; *pgm* locus contains genes of the high pathogenicity island (HPI), which is found in other Yersiniae and certain related enteric bacteria; the HPI contains the *ybt* (yersiniabactin) operon, which encodes genes of a siderophore-based iron uptake system; the *pgm* locus also contains the *hms* locus, which must be functional for 'blocking' to occur in the flea vector (blocking is required for efficient transmission of plague by fleas)
	Endotoxin (lipopolysaccharide)	Lipopolysaccharide release responsible for major pathogenic effects of plague sepsis, systemic inflammatory response syndrome and associated adult respiratory distress syndrome, cytokine activation, complement cascade, DIC, bleeding, unresponsive shock and organ failure
	Serum resistance (lipopolysaccharide in part)	Resistance to complement-mediated lysis; proposed to be related in part to lipopolysaccharide structure
	pH 6 antigen (*psa*)	Entry into naive macrophages; assists in delivery of Yops into phagocytic cells

Table 176.1 Proposed virulence and transmission factors for *Yersinia pestis*.

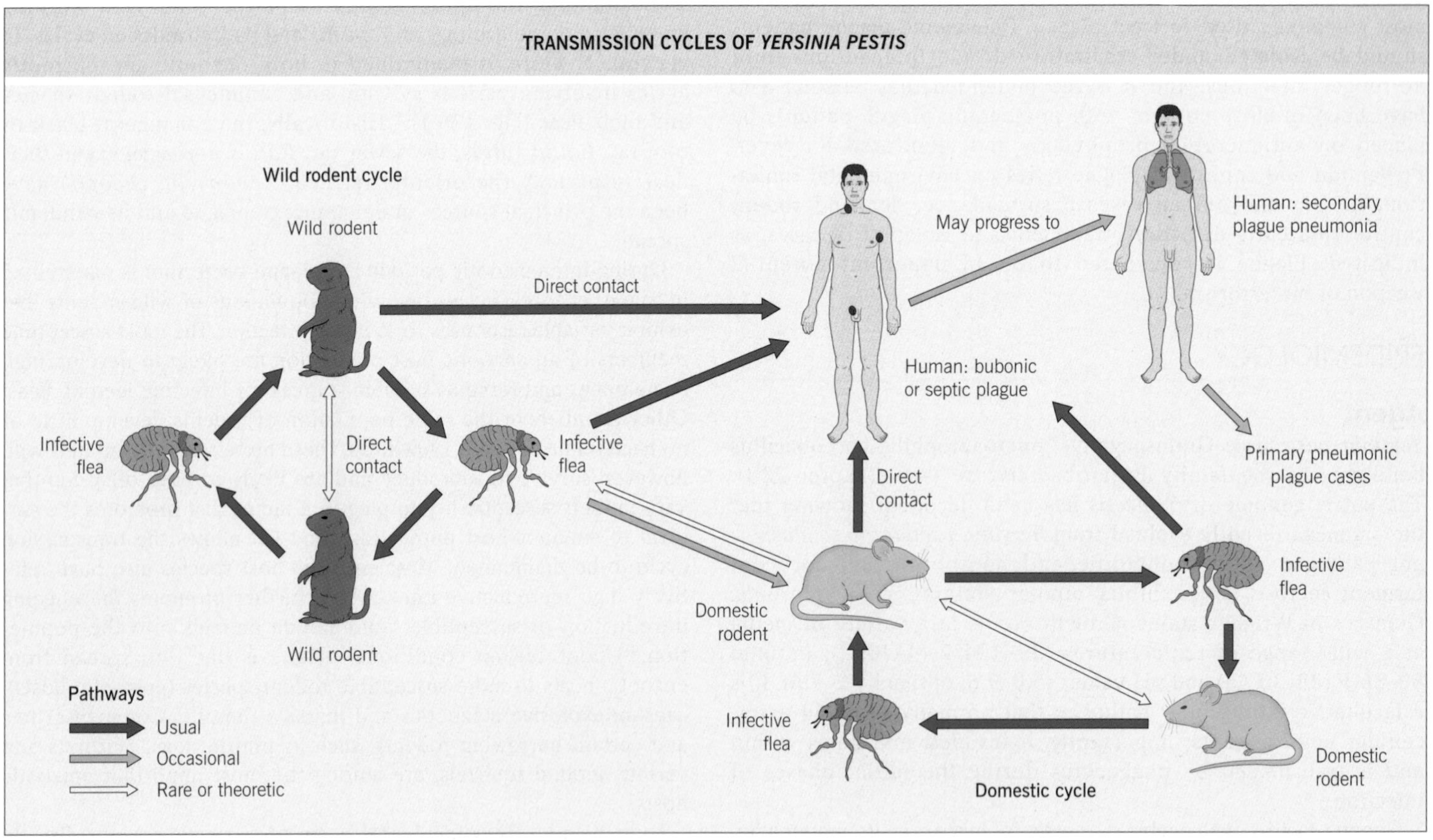

Fig. 176.1 Transmission cycles of *Yersinia pestis*.

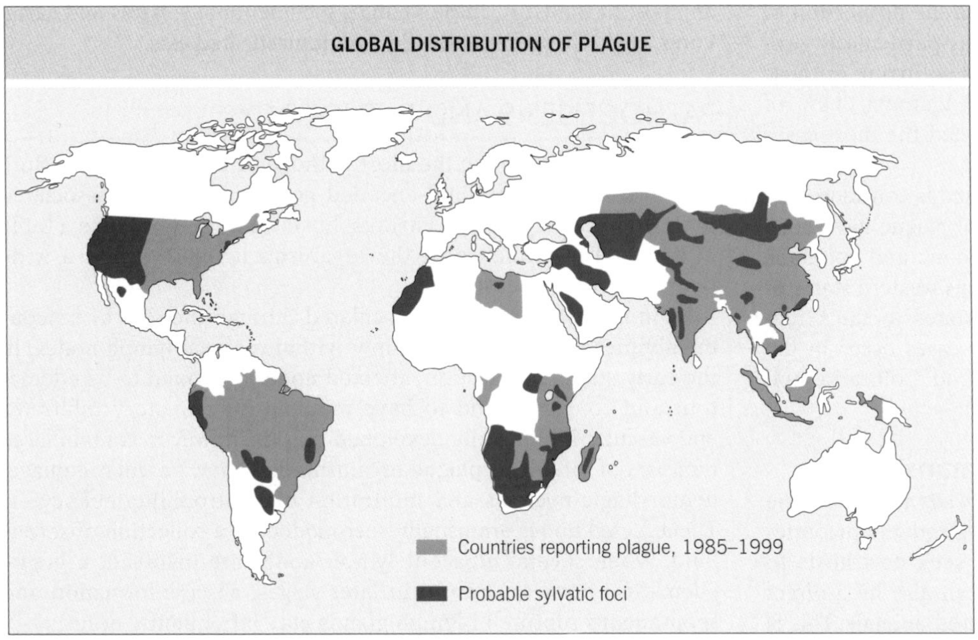

Fig. 176.2 Global distribution of plague. Compiled from sources of the WHO, the Centers for Disease Control and Prevention, and the individual countries.

be directly transmitted from one person to another by respiratory secretions, causing primary plague pneumonia in the recipient (see Fig. 176.1).

Geographic distribution

Plague foci are widely distributed throughout the world, and human cases are typically reported from 10 or so countries each year.[10] Countries reporting human or animal plague at some time in the past 15 years are shown in Figure 176.2.

Populations affected

Plague is mostly a public health problem of impoverished populations living under substandard conditions. It typically affects inhabitants of rural villages in the developing world that are heavily infested with susceptible rodent hosts and their fleas. Urban rat-borne plague is now unusual around the world, occurring most recently in Madagascar in the 1990s. In the USA, most persons acquire plague from exposures to infection around rural residential properties, which often have poorly maintained woodpiles, abandoned vehicles, dilapidated buildings and other debris that provide favorable harbor for rodents. Cases also occasionally arise among campers, hikers, hunters and others exposed to plague in natural settings.

In the absence of control measures, plague has the potential to spread from rural areas to population centers, including major cities and ports, either through unintended transport of infected rats and fleas or through direct exchange of infection between contiguous rodent populations.[8] Occasionally, persons incubate plague while traveling (peripatetic plague), develop plague pneumonia and transmit plague to others along the way or at their destination. The risk of plague to persons visiting endemic areas for business or tourism is, in general, extremely low.

Disease incidence

The International Health Regulations of the World Health Organization (WHO) require prompt reporting of human plague cases to the WHO.[11] Twenty-four countries reported to the WHO a total of 33,948 cases (mean of 2263 cases per year) and 2653 (8% fatality rate) deaths during the years 1985–99 (Table 176.2).[10] Countries in eastern and southern Africa, and the adjacent island of Madagascar, reported 77% of these cases, with the remaining cases occurring in Asia (17%) and the Americas (6%). Madagascar alone reported 28% of the cases reported to WHO from 1985 to 1999 and Tanzania accounted for almost another 20% of cases. The recent re-emergence of plague, both urban and rural, in southeastern Africa

REPORTED CASES OF PLAGUE IN HUMANS BY COUNTRY (1985–99)

Region	Country	Number of cases	Number of deaths
Africa	Botswana	173	12
	Congo	3008	607
	Kenya	44	8
	Madagascar	9650	795
	Malawi	665	15
	Mozambique	1787	28
	Namibia	2865	110
	Tanzania	6646	478
	Uganda	556	61
	Zambia	320	27
	Zimbabwe	418	35
	Total	**26,132**	**2176**
Americas	Bolivia	135	22
	Brazil	293	6
	Ecuador	17	16
	Peru	1436	74
	USA	144	14
	Total	**2025**	**132**
Asia	China	361	53
	India	876	54
	Indonesia	6	0
	Kazakhstan	18	6
	Laos	10	0
	Mongolia	82	30
	Myanmar	815	6
	Vietnam	3623	196
	Total	**5791**	**345**
World totals		**33,948**	**2653**

Table 176.2 Reported cases of plague in humans by country, 1985–99.

and Madagascar has been striking.[12,13] The rise in the proportion of cases reported from Africa and Madagascar was particularly pronounced in the 1990s, and the number of cases occurring in these countries has remained high. During 1985–99, Vietnam (11% of world total) and Peru (4% of world total) reported the most cases from Asia and the Americas, respectively.

Plague was introduced into the USA in 1900 and is considered an emerging disease there.[13] More than 400 cases of plague have been reported in the USA since 1950. Although enzootic and epizootic plague occurs in rural areas of 17 of the contiguous western states of the USA, extending from the Pacific coastal states to the Great Plains states and eastern Texas, 80% of human cases occur in the southwestern states of New Mexico, Arizona and Colorado, and approximately 10% in California.[13,14]

Sources of infection and risks for humans

Flea bites are the most common source of *Y. pestis* infection. The risk of plague for humans increases greatly during rodent epizootics when large numbers of *Y. pestis*-infected fleas seek new hosts to replace those killed by plague. Human plague can also be a direct result of handling tissues or body fluids of infected animals. This is an important source of plague among persons who hunt and skin marmots (*Marmota* spp.) in Central Asia and northern China, and occasionally this is the source of plague in the USA in persons who handle the carcasses of infected prairie dogs, rabbits and carnivores.[8] Pet owners and veterinary staff may become infected with *Y. pestis* while caring for domestic cats that develop oropharyngeal or pneumonic plague from having ingested infected rodents.[15] Outbreaks of plague have occurred in Saudi Arabia, Libya and Jordan as a result of persons handling and consuming infected camel and goat meat.[16]

Primary pneumonic plague occurs when persons inhale infectious respiratory secretions. This usually arises in the setting of an outbreak of bubonic plague in which some persons who develop secondary pulmonary infection spread infection to others through infectious respiratory droplets, starting a chain of respiratory transmission. Persons living in the same quarters as a pneumonic plague patient and persons attending the sick, such as family members and health care personnel, are especially at risk. *Yersinia pestis* is classified as a category A agent of potential danger as a weapon of bioterrorism because it could be aerosolized and cause outbreaks of severe or fatal illness, create panic, and requires special actions for medical and public health preparedness (see Chapter 6).[17,18] The release of an aerosol of *Y. pestis* in a biologic terrorism event would be expected to result in an outbreak of respiratory plague with potential for person to person spread. Under natural conditions, primary pneumonic plague usually comprises only a small fraction of the total number of cases in any plague-endemic region (less than 2% in the USA); nevertheless, this form of plague is extremely dangerous because of a high case fatality rate and the risk of epidemic spread.[19]

Seasonality

Flea-borne cases of human plague in the temperate Northern Hemisphere are most likely to occur between late spring and the end of summer when epizootic transmission peaks.[8] In tropical and semitropical plague foci, transmission may vary between a wet, relatively cool season and another season of hotter, drier weather, with the numbers of cases being lowest during the latter period.[20] Although flea-borne cases of human plague are occasionally reported during 'off-season' months in various plague foci, particularly those in tropical or semitropical regions, they are rare in other areas such as the USA. Most 'off-season' (winter) cases in the temperate Northern Hemisphere occur among hunters or trappers handling infected animals. In the USA, these animals include rabbits, hares and carnivores, such as coyotes and wild and domesticated cats.

PATHOGENESIS AND PATHOLOGY

Yersinia pestis is among the most pathogenic bacteria known. Both chromosomal and plasmid-encoded gene products are associated with adaptability to its various hosts and to virulence (Table 176.1).[2–6] The virulence of the organisms is expressed in a wide range of severe disease.[21–25]

Yersinia pestis organisms inoculated through the skin or mucous membranes travel to and multiply within regional lymph nodes. In the early stages of infection, affected nodes are found to be edematous and congested and to have minimal inflammatory infiltrates and vascular injury. Fully developed buboes, however, contain large numbers of infectious plague organisms and show vascular damage, hemorrhagic necrosis and infiltration of neutrophilic leukocytes. The affected nodes are usually surrounded by a collection of serous fluid. When several adjacent lymph nodes are involved, a boggy edematous mass can result. In later stages, abscess formation and spontaneous rupture of lymph glands may infrequently occur.

Plague sepsis in the absence of signs of localized infection, such as a bubo, is termed primary septic plague. It can result from direct entry of *Y. pestis* through broken skin or mucous membranes or from the bite of an infective flea. Secondary septic plague can occur in the course of bubonic or pneumonic plague when lymphatic or pulmonary defenses are breached and the plague bacillus enters and multiplies within the bloodstream. Bacteremia is common in all forms of plague; septicemia is less common and immediately life-threatening.

Yersinia pestis can invade and cause disease in almost any organ, and untreated infection usually results in widespread and massive tissue destruction. Diffuse interstitial myocarditis with cardiac dilatation, multifocal necrosis of the liver, diffuse hemorrhagic splenic necrosis and fibrin thrombi in renal glomeruli, are commonly found in fatal cases.[19,21,22,24] If disseminated intravascular coagulation (DIC) occurs, it results in thrombosis within the microvasculature, necrosis and bleeding, with widespread cutaneous, mucosal and serosal petechiae and ecchymoses. Gangrene of acral parts, such as fingers and toes, may occur in the late stages of this process (Fig. 176.4).

Primary plague pneumonia, which results from inhalation of infective respiratory particles, usually begins as a lobular process and then extends by confluence, becoming lobar and then multilobar. Typically, plague organisms are numerous in the alveoli and in pulmonary secretions. Secondary plague pneumonia arising from hematogenous seeding of the lungs typically begins more diffusely as an interstitial process, with plague bacilli most numerous in the interstitial spaces. In untreated cases of both primary and secondary plague pneumonia, the usual pathologic findings are diffuse pulmonary congestion, edema, hemorrhagic necrosis and scant neutrophilic infiltration.[19,24]

PREVENTION AND CONTROL

Plague prevention and control is best accomplished by a combination of:

- environmental sanitation;
- awareness campaigns to promote avoidance of potential infective exposures; and
- early detection of human and animal plague to focus remedial environmental actions and to institute early treatment of cases, infection control procedures and prophylaxis of exposed persons, as indicated.

In endemic areas, public health services must provide a continuing system of human and animal plague surveillance, epidemiologic investigations and control actions.

The principal environmental remediation measures during outbreaks of human plague or dangerous epizootics are insecticidal flea control, rodent control and sanitation. Flea control should be carried out before or in conjunction with the killing of rodents to reduce the chances that infected fleas will feed on humans.[8,26]

A killed, whole-cell plague vaccine has limited availability and usefulness. It was available in the USA until the late 1990s, but is no longer being manufactured there. Use of this vaccine was limited primarily to certain groups that were thought to be at high risk, including research laboratory workers, biologists working with susceptible animal populations and some military personnel. The efficacy of this vaccine was never evaluated in clinical trials, and evidence for vaccine protection was based on animal experiments, immunogenicity studies in humans and observations on its use in USA servicemen during the Vietnam conflict. It was thought to be protective against flea-borne exposures but to be only partially protective, if at all, against respiratory exposures. Primary immunization consisted of a series of three injections followed by boosters at intervals of 6 months or more.[27] Research is underway to develop improved plague vaccines that are likely to be protective against airborne routes of exposure, but it is unknown when these vaccines will be approved and commercially available. At present, the most promising candidates are recombinant subunit vaccines that express both the F1 and V antigens of *Y. pestis*.[28] Interest in developing an effective plague vaccine has increased greatly in recent years because of concerns about bioterrorism and biowarfare.

In the event of an outbreak of plague, measures should be taken to rapidly control spread, as described in international regulations and manuals of plague control.[11,26] These measures include:

- determining the source;
- defining the geographic limits of activity;
- establishing active surveillance;
- laboratory confirmation of cases, and isolation of pneumonic cases;
- rapid treatment of cases and others at risk of infection, including close contacts of symptomatic pneumonic plague cases; and
- control of fleas and rodents in plague-infected areas, in port facilities and on ships and other conveyances.

CLINICAL FEATURES

Bubonic plague

Bubonic plague has a usual incubation period of 2–6 days, occasionally longer. Typically, the patient experiences the acute onset of chills, fever that rises within hours to 100.4°F (38°C) or higher, myalgias, arthralgias, headache and a profound lethargy. Soon, usually within 24 hours, tenderness and pain occur in one or more regional lymph nodes proximal to the site of inoculation of the plague bacillus. The femoral and inguinal groups of nodes are most commonly involved, axillary and cervical nodes less so, varying with the site of inoculation. The enlarging bubo or buboes become progressively swollen, painful and tender, sometimes exquisitely so. Typically, the patient guards against palpation and limits movement, pressure and stretching around the bubo. The surrounding tissue often becomes edematous, sometimes markedly, and the overlying skin may be reddened, warm and tense (Fig. 176.3). Inspection of the skin surrounding the bubo or distal to it may reveal the site of a flea bite marked by a small papule, pustule, scab or ulcer (phlyctenule). Larger furuncular lesions, sometimes with eschars that are similar to those caused by tularemia, occur rarely. The bubo of plague differs from lymphadenitis of most other causes by its rapid onset, extreme tenderness, surrounding edema, accompanying signs of toxemia and absence of cellulitis or obvious ascending lymphangitis.

If treated in the uncomplicated state with an appropriate antimicrobial agent, bubonic plague usually responds quickly, with defervescence and resolution of other systemic manifestations over a 2- to 5-day period. Buboes often remain enlarged and tender for a week or more after treatment has begun and infrequently become fluctuant. Without effective antimicrobial treatment, typical bubonic plague patients manifest an increasingly toxic state of fever, tachycardia, lethargy leading to prostration, agitation and confusion and, occasionally, convulsions and delirium. Mild forms of bubonic plague, called pestis minor, have been described in South America and elsewhere; in these cases, the patients are ambulatory and only mildly febrile and have subacute buboes.

Differential diagnostic possibilities for bubonic plague include streptococcal or staphylococcal adenitis, tularemia, cat-scratch disease, mycobacterial infection, acute filarial lyphadenitis, chancroid and strangulated inguinal hernia.

Septic plague

Septic plague is manifest as a rapidly progressive, overwhelming endotoxemia.[21–25] Primary sepsis occurs in the absence of regional lymphadenitis, and the diagnosis of plague is often not suspected until results of blood culture are reported by the laboratory. Furthermore, patients who have septic plague often present with gastrointestinal symptoms such as nausea, vomiting, diarrhea and abdominal pain, making misdiagnosis even more likely. If it is not treated early with appropriate antibiotics and aggressive supportive care, septic plague is usually fulminant and fatal. Petechiae, ecchymoses, bleeding from puncture wounds and orifices, and ischemia of acral parts are manifestations of DIC (Fig. 176.4). Refractory hypotension, renal shutdown, obtundation and other signs of shock are pre-terminal events. Acute respiratory distress syndrome, which

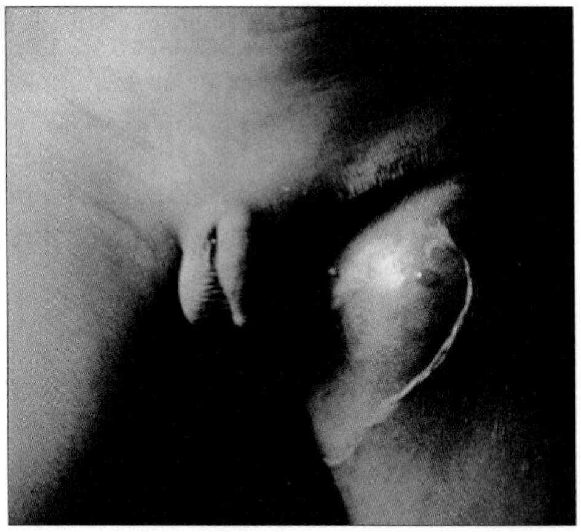

Fig. 176.3 Left inguinal and femoral buboes, demonstrating surrounding edema and overlying desquamation.

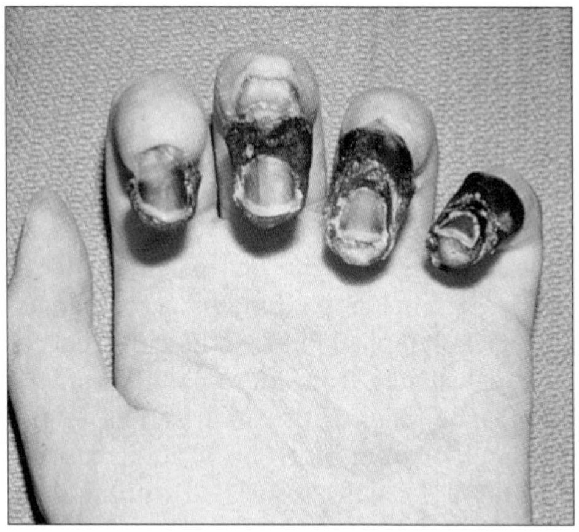

Fig. 176.4 Septic plague patient who demonstrated disseminated intravascular coagulation, bleeding into the skin and acral gangrene as a late manifestation.

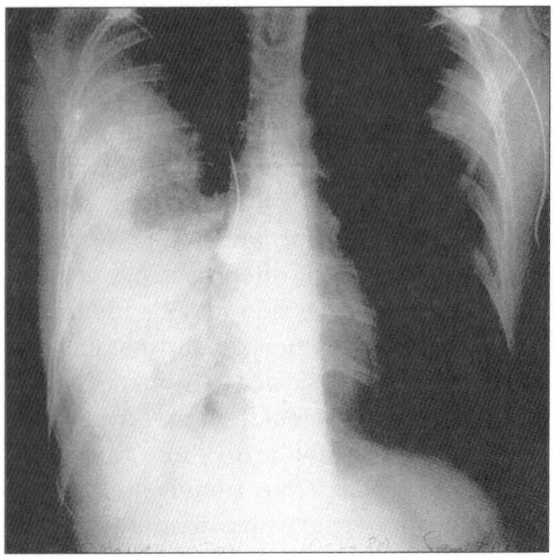

Fig. 176.5 Chest radiograph of a patient who has primary plague pneumonia, showing extensive infiltrates in the right middle and lower lung fields.

can occur at any stage of septic plague, may be confused with other conditions such as hantavirus pulmonary syndrome.

Differential diagnostic possibilities include septicemia caused by other bacterial infections, including other Gram-negative bacteria, meningococcemia, bacterial endocarditis and tularemia.

Pneumonic plague

Pneumonic plague is the most rapidly developing and fatal form of plague.[19,21,22,24] The incubation period for primary pneumonic plague is usually 3–5 days (range 1–6 days). The onset is most often sudden, with chills, fever, headache, body pains, weakness, dizziness and chest discomfort. Cough, sputum production, increasing chest pain, tachypnea and dyspnea typically predominate on day 2 of the illness, and these features may be accompanied by hemoptysis, increasing respiratory distress, cardiopulmonary insufficiency and circulatory collapse. In primary plague pneumonia, the sputum is most often watery or mucoid, frothy and blood-tinged, but it may become frankly bloody. Chest signs in primary plague pneumonia may indicate localized pulmonary involvement in the early stage; a rapidly developing segmental consolidation may be seen before bronchopneumonia occurs in other segments and lobes of the same and opposite lung (Fig. 176.5). Liquefaction necrosis and cavitation may develop at sites of consolidation and leave significant residual scarring.

Plague pneumonia arising from metastatic spread (secondary pneumonic plague) typically manifests first as a diffuse interstitial pneumonitis in which sputum production is scant, and is more likely to be inspissated and tenacious in character than the sputum found in primary pneumonic plague.

Differential diagnostic possibilities include other bacterial conditions such as tularemia, community-acquired bacterial pneumonias such as mycoplasma pneumonia, Legionnaires' disease and staphylococcal or streptococcal pneumonia. Viral pneumonias to be differentiated include influenzal pneumonitis, hantaviral pulmonary syndrome and pneumonia caused by respiratory syncitial virus or cytomegalovirus infection. Q fever may need to be considered.

Other manifestations

Meningitis is an unusual manifestation of plague. In the USA there were 12 (3%) cases of meningitis among the total 390 cases of plague reported in the period from 1947 to 1996.[14] All these cases were complications of treated bubonic plague and all the patients survived. Plague occasionally presents as pharyngitis accompanied by fever, sore throat and cervical lymphadenitis. In its early stages, this may be clinically indistinguishable from more common infectious causes of pharyngitis. Plague pharyngitis can arise in primary form from respiratory exposures or from ingestion of undercooked tissues of infected animals, and it is usually associated with marked cervical glandular enlargement. Inoculation of *Y. pestis* through the conjunctiva can result in oculoglandular plague.

DIAGNOSIS

Except in outbreak situations, a high index of clinical suspicion and a careful clinical and epidemiologic history and physical examination are required to make a timely diagnosis of plague. A delayed or missed diagnosis is associated with a high case fatality rate,[14] and infected travelers who seek medical care after they have left endemic areas are especially at risk. Laboratory tests for plague are highly reliable when conducted by persons experienced with *Y. pestis*, but such expertise is usually limited to selected reference laboratories.

When plague is suspected, clinical specimens should be obtained promptly for microbiologic studies, chest radiographs taken and specific antimicrobial therapy initiated pending confirmation of diagnosis. Blood and other clinical materials such as bubo aspirates, sputum, tracheal washes, swabs of skin lesions or pharyngeal mucosa and cerebrospinal fluid, as indicated, should be inoculated onto suitable media (e.g. brain–heart infusion broth, sheep blood agar, chocolate agar or MacConkey agar).[29] Bubo aspirates typically yield only small amounts of serosanguinous fluid and 1–2ml of saline may need to be injected first to obtain adequate material for diagnosis. Smears of each specimen should be stained with Gram's, Wayson's or Giemsa's stain. Direct fluorescent antibody testing is a useful presumptive diagnostic procedure available at some reference laboratories. An acute-phase serum specimen should be collected for *Y. pestis* antibody testing, followed by a convalescent-phase specimen collected 3–4 weeks later. For diagnosis in fatal cases, tissues, including buboes and samples of liver, spleen, lungs and bone marrow, should be collected at autopsy for culture, fluorescent antibody testing and histologic studies, including possible immunohistochemical staining. Cary Blair medium or a similar holding medium can be used to transport *Y. pestis*-infected tissues. Presumptive identification of *Y. pestis* can be made by polymerase chain reaction or antigen capture enzyme-linked immunosorbent assay. A recently developed rapid immunogold dipstick assay designed to detect *Y. pestis* antigens in patient samples also appears highly promising.[30]

Laboratory confirmation of plague depends on isolation of *Y. pestis* from body fluids or tissues. When the patient's condition allows, several blood cultures taken over a 45-minute period before treatment will usually result in successful isolation of the bacterium. *Yersinia pestis* strains are readily distinguished from other Gram-negative bacteria by polychromatic and immunofluorescence staining properties, characteristics of growth on microbiologic media, biochemical profiles and confirmatory lysis by the *Y. pestis*-specific bacteriophage. Laboratory mice and hamsters are susceptible to *Y. pestis* and are used in specialized laboratories to make isolations from contaminated materials and for virulence testing.

In the absence of a cultural isolation, a diagnosis of plague can be made by the demonstration of a 4-fold or greater change in serum antibodies to *Y. pestis* antigen using passive hemagglutination testing. A serum antibody titer of 128 or greater in a single serum sample from a patient who has a compatible illness and who has not received plague vaccine is also diagnostic. A few plague patients will develop detectable antibodies as soon as 5 days after the onset of illness, most seroconvert 1–2 weeks after onset, a few seroconvert 3 or more weeks after onset and a few (<5%) fail to seroconvert. Early specific antibiotic treatment may delay seroconversion by several weeks. After seroconversion, positive serologic titers diminish gradually over months to years. Enzyme-linked immunosorbent assays for detecting IgM and IgG antibodies to *Y. pestis* have been found to be useful in identifying antibodies in early infection and in differentiating them from antibodies developed in response to previous vaccination.

TREATMENT GUIDELINES FOR PLAGUE

Drug		Dosage	Route of administration
Streptomycin	Adults	1g q12h	im
	Children	15mg/kg q12h*	im
Gentamicin	Adults	1–1.5mg/kg q8h†	im or iv
	Children	2.0–2.5mg/kg q8h	im or iv
	Infants/neonates	2.5mg/kg q8h	im or iv
Tetracycline	Adults	0.5g q6h	po
	Children >8 years old	6.25–12.5mg/kg q6h	po
Doxycycline	Adults	100mg q12h	po or iv
	Children >8 years old and >45kg	100mg q12h	po or iv
	Children >8 years old and <45kg	2.2mg/kg q12h	po or iv
Chloramphenicol	Adults	12.5mg/kg q6h‡	po or iv
	Children >1 year old	12.5mg/kg q6h‡	po or iv

* Not to exceed 2g/day
† Daily dose should be reduced to 3mg/kg as soon as clinically indicated
‡ Up to 100mg/kg per day initially. Dosage should be adjusted to maintain plasma concentrations at 5–20μg/ml. Hematologic values should be monitored closely

Table 176.3 Treatment guidelines for plague.

Plague patients typically have white blood cell counts of 10,000–25,000/mm^3 with a predominance of early stage polymorphonuclear leukocytes. Leukemoid reactions with white cell counts as high as 50,000/mm^3 or more can occur.

MANAGEMENT

Untreated, plague is fatal in over 50% of patients who have bubonic disease and in nearly all patients who have septic or pneumonic plague. The overall mortality rate in plague cases in the USA in the past 25 years has been approximately 15%.[14] Fatalities are almost always due to delays in seeking treatment, misdiagnosis and delayed or incorrect treatment. Rapid diagnosis and appropriate antimicrobial therapy (Table 176.3) are essential.[31]

Streptomycin has long been considered the drug of choice for treating plague, but gentamicin is increasingly being used in its place because of its wider availability and ease of administration, and it is currently recommended for use in managing patients in a bioterrorism attack.[18] Tetracyclines or chloramphenicol are effective alternatives to the aminoglycosides. Chloramphenicol is indicated for conditions in which high tissue penetration is important, such as plague meningitis, pleuritis, endophthalmitis or myocarditis. It may be used separately or in combination with an aminoglycoside. Although doxycycline has, because of its ease of administration and rapid action, become the tetracycline of choice for treating plague, clinical trials of its efficacy have not been performed. Trimethoprim–sulfamethoxazole (co-trimoxazole) has been used successfully to treat bubonic plague, but it is not considered a first-line choice. *Yersinia pestis* is highly sensitive to several fluoroquinolones, and ciprofloxacin has been recommended as an alternative antimicrobial for treating plague cases in the event of a bioterrorism attack.[18] Penicillins, cephalosporins and macrolides have a suboptimal effect and should not be used to treat plague. In general, antimicrobial treatment should be continued for 7–10 days or for at least 3 days after the patient has become afebrile and has made a clinical recovery. Patients begun on intravenous antibiotics may be switched to oral regimens as indicated by clinical response. Improvement is usually evident 2–3 days from the start of treatment, even though fever may continue for several more days.

Complications of delayed treatment of plague include DIC, adult respiratory distress syndrome and other consequences of bacterial sepsis. Patients who have these disorders require intensive monitoring and close physiologic support. Buboes may require surgical drainage if they threaten to rupture spontaneously. Abscessed nodes can be a cause of recurrent fever in patients who have otherwise made satisfactory recovery; the cause may be occult if intrathoracic or intra-abdominal nodes are involved. Viable *Y. pestis* organisms have been isolated from affected nodes 1–2 weeks after clinical recovery from acute disease. Strains of *Y. pestis* that are resistant to antimicrobials have only rarely been isolated from humans. Such resistant strains have usually involved partial resistance to a single agent only and have not been associated with treatment failure. Recently, however, a multidrug-resistant strain of *Y. pestis* was isolated from a bubonic plague patient in Madagascar.[32] This isolate was resistant at high levels to all first-line antibiotics recommended for treating plague (including tetracycline, streptomycin and chloramphenicol). Resistance was plasmid-mediated and transferable to other strains of *Y. pestis* and to *Escherichia coli*. Fortunately, surveillance for multidrug-resistant *Y. pestis* in Madagascar and elsewhere has not disclosed any other such resistant strains. Isolated instances of strains resistant to streptomycin or tetracycline are occasionally reported.

Antimicrobials are recommended in some situations as prophylaxis against plague.[27,31] Postexposure treatment for 7 days with a tetracycline, chloramphenicol or trimethoprim–sulfamethoxazole is recommended for persons who have been in close contact with a pneumonic plague patient in the previous 7 days. Prophylaxis with doxycycline or ciprofloxacin has been recommended in the event of a bioterrorism attack.[18] Short courses of antimicrobial prophylaxis are sometimes recommended for household members of bubonic plague patients because of possible rodent flea exposures. Prophylaxis is only rarely warranted for people who visit or reside in an area where plague is occurring. Isolation and respiratory droplet precautions are recommended for managing patients with pneumonic plague, including the use of masks for persons caring for these patients while they are infectious. The use of masks may be an important measure for interrupting person to person transmission in the event of a pneumonic plague outbreak. Respiratory plague patients are generally considered to be noncontagious following 48 hours of antibiotic treatment.

REFERENCES

1. Parkhill J, Wren BW, Thompson NR, *et al.* Genome sequence of *Yersinia pestis*, the causative agent of plague. Nature 2001;413:523–7.
2. Hinnebusch BJ. Bubonic plague: a molecular genetic case history of the emergence of an infectious disease. J Mol Med 1997;75:645–52.
3. Perry RD, Fetherston JD. *Yersinia pestis* – etiologic agent of plague. Clin Microbiol Rev 1997;10:35–66.
4. Smego RA, Frean J, Koornhof HJ. Yersiniosis I: Microbiological and clinicoepidemiological aspects of plague and non-plague *Yersinia* infections. Eur J Clin Microbiol Infect Dis 1999;18:1–15.
5. Koornhof HJ, Smego RA Jr, Nicol M. Yersiniosis II. The pathogenesis of *Yersinia* infections. Eur J Clin Microbiol Infect Dis 1999:18:87–112.
6. Hinnebusch BJ, Rudolph AE, Cherepenov P, *et al.* Role of murine toxin in survival of *Yersinia pestis* in the midgut of the vector flea. Science 2002:296:733–5.
7. Guiyoule A, Grimont F, Iteman I, *et al.*. Plague pandemics investigated by ribotyping of *Yersinia pestis* strains. J Clin Microbiol 1994;32:634–41.
8. Gage KL. Plague. In: Collier L, Balows A, Sussman M, Hausler WJ, eds. Topley and Wilson's microbiology and microbial infections, vol. 3, 9th edition. London: Arnold Publications; 1998:885–903.
9. Poland JD, Barnes AM. Plague. In: Beran GW, ed. CRC handbook series in zoonoses, section A: bacterial, rickettsial, and mycotic diseases. Boca Raton, Florida: CRC Press; 1979:93–112.
10. World Health Organization. Human plague in 1998 and 1999. Wkly Epidemiol Rec 2000;75:338–9.
11. World Health Organization. International health regulations (1969). Geneva: World Health Organization; 1983.
12. Chanteau S, Ratsifasoamanana L, Rasoamanana B, *et al.* Plague, a reemerging disease in Madagascar. Emerg Infect Dis 1998;4:101–4.
13. Dennis DT. Plague as an emerging disease. In: Scheld WM, Craig WA, Hughes JM, eds. Emerging infections 2. Washington DC: ASM Press; 1998:169–83.
14. Centers for Disease Control and Prevention. Fatal human plague. MMWR Morb Mortal Wkly Rep 1997;278:380–2.
15. Gage KL, Dennis, DT, Orloski KA, *et al.* Cases of cat-associated plague in the western US, 1977–1998. Clin Infect Dis 2000;30:893–900.
16. Christie AB, Chen TH, Elberg SS. Plague in camels and goats: their role in human epidemics. J Infect Dis 1980;141:724–6.
17. Khan AS, Morse S, Lillibridge S. Public health preparedness for biological terrorism in the USA. Lancet 2000;356:1179–82.
18. Englesby TV, Dennis DT, Henderson DA, Bartlett JG, *et al.*, for the Working Group on Civilian Biodefense. Plague as a biological weapon: medical and public health management. JAMA 2000;283:2281–90.
19. Wu L-T. A treatise on pneumonic plague. Geneva: League of Nations Health Organization; 1926.
20. Cavanaugh DC, Marshall JD Jr. The influence of climate on the seasonal prevalence of plague in the Republic of Vietnam. J Wildlife Dis 1972;8:85–94.
21. Butler T. Plague and other yersinia infections. New York: Plenum Press; 1983.
22. Crook LD, Tempest B. Plague – a clinical review of 27 cases. Arch Intern Med 1992;152:1253–6.
23. Hull HF, Montes JM, Mann JM. Septicemic plague in New Mexico. J Infect Dis 1987;155:113–8.
24. Dennis D, Meier F. Plague. In: Horsburgh CR, Nelson Am, eds. Pathology of emerging infections. Washington DC: ASM Press; 1997:21–47.
25. Campbell GL, Dennis DT. Plague and other *Yersinia* infections. In: Fauci AS, Braunwald E, Isselbacher KJ, *et al.*, eds. Harrison's principles of internal medicine, 14th edition. New York: McGraw-Hill; 1998:975–83.
26. Gratz NG. Control of plague transmission. In: Plague manual, epidemiology, distribution, surveillance and control. Geneva: World Health Organization; 1999:97–131.
27. Centers for Disease Control and Prevention. Prevention of plague. Recommendations of the Advisory Committee on Immunization Practices (ACIP). MMWR Morb Mortal Wkly Rep 1996;45(RR–14):1–15.
28. Williams ED. Plague vaccine research and development. J Appl Microbiol 2001;91:606–8.
29. Aleksic S, Bockemuhl J. *Yersinia* and other Enterobacteriaceae. In: Murray PR, Baron EJ, Pfaller MA, *et al.*, eds. Manual of clinical microbiology, 7th edition. Washington DC: ASM Press; 1999:483–96.
30. Chanteau S, Rahalison L, Foulon J, *et al.* Development and testing of a rapid diagnostic test for bubonic and pnuemonic plague. Lancet 2003;361:211–6.
31. Dennis DT. Plague. In: Rakel RE, Bope ET, eds. Conn's current therapy. Philadelphia: WB Saunders; 2001:115–7.
32. Galimand, MA, Guiyole G, Gerbaud B, *et al.* Multidrug resistance in *Yersinia pestis* mediated by a transferable plasmid. N Engl J Med 1997;337:677–80.

chapter
177 Tularemia

David T Dennis

Tularemia is an uncommon, potentially severe bacterial zoonosis caused by *Francisella tularensis*. The natural cycle of the causative organism involves maintenance of infection in a wide diversity of animal hosts and in certain hard ticks. Transmission of *F. tularensis* to humans, which are incidental hosts, occurs by several modes, including bites by infective ticks and other arthropods, direct inoculation of *F. tularensis* through skin or mucous membranes from handling infectious materials, ingestion of contaminated water or food, or by inhalation of contaminated aerosols or dusts. The agent of tularemia is widely distributed in temperate and subarctic regions of North America and Eurasia. Human infection results in various clinical presentations of varying severity depending on the route of inoculation, the dose and virulence of the infecting strain, and the host defenses. The most common clinical form, ulceroglandular tularemia, presents as an illness with fever, an ulcer at the site of inoculation and regional lymphadenitis. Several other forms occur involving various organ systems. Tularemia is considered to be an important potential weapon of bioterrorism (see Chapter 6).

EPIDEMIOLOGY

Agent

Francisella tularensis (formerly *Pasteurella tularensis*) is a small, facultatively intracellular, Gram-negative coccobacillus. The organism has a lipidated envelope and is able to survive under favorable conditions for several weeks in water, moist soil and decaying animal carcasses. *Francisella tularensis* strains may be divided into two main groups by virulence testing, biochemical reactions and epidemiologic features. Formerly, it was thought that strains of the more virulent type, termed Jellison type A (*F. tularensis* subsp. *tularensis*), were restricted to North America. Recent molecular studies have shown that some *F. tularensis* strains found in Central Asia and in Japan share significant genetic homology with *F. tularensis* subsp. *tularensis*.[1] The less virulent Jellison type B strains (*F. tularensis* subsp. *holarctica*) are found throughout Eurasia, and they are also found widely in North America. A closely related subspecies, *Francisella tularensis* subsp. *novicida*, has been associated with febrile illness in a small number of patients in North America. *Francisella tularensis* is considered to be a potential agent of bioterrorism because it can be weaponized as an aerosol, could result in large numbers of casualties, and because it requires special actions for medical and public health preparedness.[2]

Life cycle

Francisella tularensis is widespread in nature and has been recovered from more than 100 species of wild mammals, at least nine species of domestic animals (including cats, dogs and cattle), numerous species of birds, some amphibians and fish, and more than 50 species of arthropods.[3,4] The principal natural cycles of the agent involve maintenance of infection in wild mammalian hosts, such as lagomorphs (wild hares and rabbits), terrestrial rodents (especially voles and meadow mice) and aquatic rodents (water rats, muskrats, beaver). Certain species of hard ticks are able to maintain infection from one developmental stage to another. Transmission among animals is accomplished by the bites of blood feeding arthropods or by direct exposures to contaminated materials in the environment (Fig. 177.1).[3,4] Predation and cannibalism may also contribute to the natural cycle.

Humans become infected:

- when they intrude into the arthropod-borne cycle and are bitten by ticks, which are true biologic vectors, or by blood-feeding flies or mosquitoes that have contaminated mouthparts;
- by handling or ingesting infectious animal tissues or fluids;
- by ingestion of contaminated water or food; or
- by inhalation of infective aerosols or dusts.

Occasional cases occur following infective bites or scratches by cats,[5] or other carnivores or predators with contaminated mouths or claws. Although the agent is highly infectious, requiring only 10–50 organisms to regularly cause experimental infections of humans, person–person transmission has not been documented.

Geographic distribution

Tularemia is endemic throughout much of the Nearctic and Palaearctic regions between latitudes 30°N and 71°N. This includes all of North America from the Arctic Circle to northern Mexico, much of Eurasia and some states of northern Africa along the Mediterranean coast.[3,4] In North America, the highest incidence of tularemia in humans occurs in south-central, south-eastern, Great Plains and Rocky Mountain regions of the USA (Fig. 177.2),[6] but cases have been reported throughout the continental USA, across Canada, and in Mexico as far south as Guadalajara. In Eurasia, the disease occurs most frequently in Scandinavia and in states of the former Soviet Union. Tularemia also occurs sporadically throughout most of Europe, in some areas of the Near East and Middle East, in Central Asia and in Mongolia. It has not been documented in Central or South America, Australia or Africa outside the Mediterranean littoral.

Populations affected

Tularemia is a rural disease. It affects persons of all ages and both sexes. Groups at highest risk include:

- hunters and trappers, wildlife specialists, animal skinners and dressers, butchers and others who handle potentially infective animal carcasses;
- rural residents, especially farmers, who are exposed to water, soils and dusts contaminated by infected wild animals, such as meadow voles, lagomorphs and aquatic mammals; and
- persons exposed in enzootic areas to bites by certain hard ticks, tabanid flies or mosquitoes.[7–10]

Disease incidence

Global incidence figures are not available. In Eurasia, recent outbreaks involving hundreds of cases each have been reported from Scandinavia,[10] Kosovo[11] and Spain,[12] and outbreaks involving

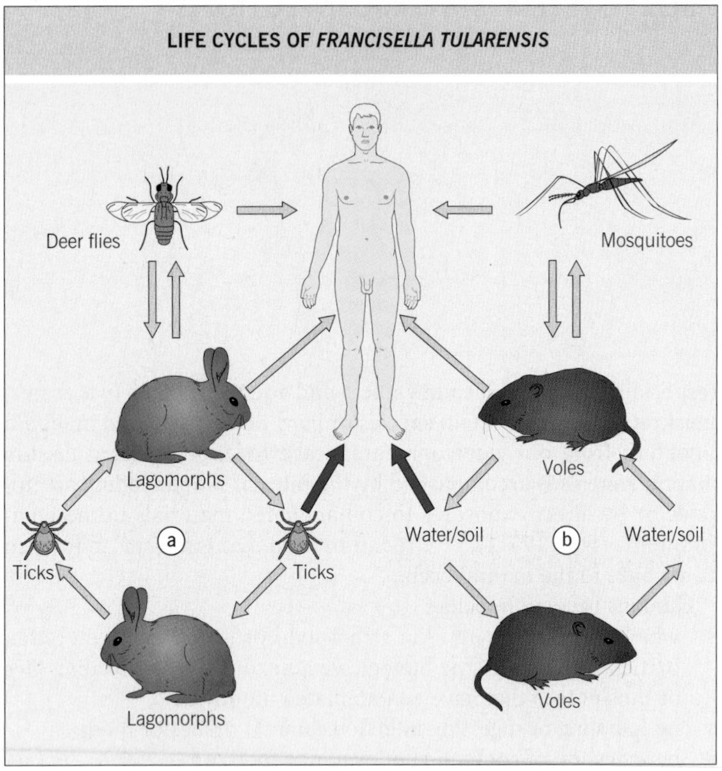

Fig. 177.1 Life cycles of *Francisella tularensis*. The two major life cycles in nature are shown. In cycle (a), which is dominant in North America, *F. tularensis* is maintained predominantly among lagomorphs and hard ticks. In cycle (b), which is dominant in Eurasia, *F. tularensis* is principally maintained among cricetine rodents, especially field voles and mice, water voles and other aquatic rodents. Humans are incidental hosts that are infected by tick vectors and by the bites of flies or mosquitoes that have contaminated mouthparts, by direct contact with infected animal carcasses or other contaminated materials, by ingestion of contaminated matter or by inhalation of infectious aerosols or dusts.

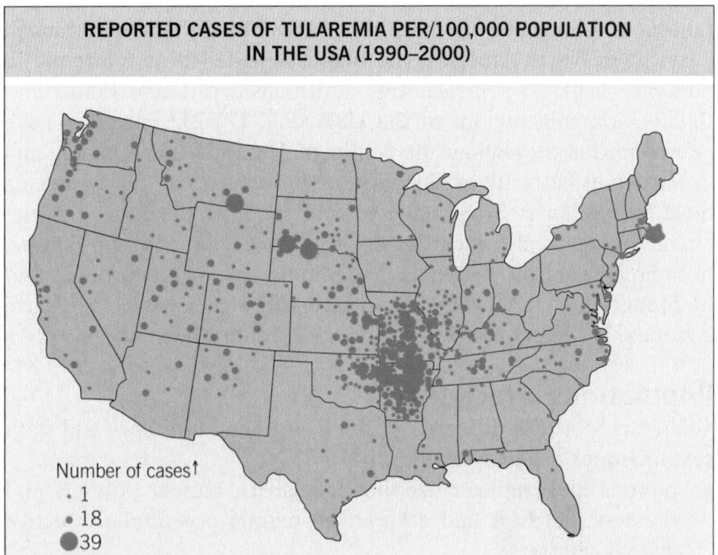

Fig. 177.2 Reported cases of tularemia per 100,000 population in the USA, 1990–2000.

thousands of persons have been reported in the past from the former Soviet Union. Tularemia incidence is relatively stable in the USA, where the disease has been in steady decline since 1945.[6] In the period 1990–2000, a total of 1368 cases were reported from 44 states, averaging 124 cases (range 86–193) per year. Four states accounted for 56% of all reported cases: Arkansas (315 cases), Missouri (265 cases), South Dakota (96 cases) and Oklahoma (90 cases). The age distribution was bimodal, with highest incidence rates in the age groups 5–9 years and 75 years of age and older. Males predominated in all age groups. Disease onsets peaked in the period May–August (70% of all cases), although cases were reported from all months of the year.[6]

Sources of human infection

Eurasia

Cricetine rodents (especially, meadow voles, lemmings, water voles and muskrats), water and soil contaminated by these animals, hares (*Lepus* spp.) and bites by contaminated mosquitoes (especially *Aedes cinereus* and *Aedes excruscians*) are the principal sources of human tularemia in Eurasia.[3,4] Mosquito-borne infection occurs in forested and marshy Scandinavian and Baltic regions. Sporadic cases also result in Eurasia from bites by infected ticks and by blood-feeding flies. Outbreaks of tularemia among farmers have been described in Europe following respiratory exposure to dusts from contaminated stored and fresh mown hay,[13,14] and among workers in agricultural processing plants exposed to contaminated water sprays. Ingestion of water and food contaminated by infected rodents or hares has also resulted in outbreaks in the region, such as recently reported from Kosovo and Turkey.[11,15] In Japan, the disease has historically been associated with the trapping, handling and eating of wild hares.

North America

The principal animal sources of infection in North America are the cottontail rabbit (*Sylvilagus* spp.), wild hares and rodents (muskrats, beaver, voles, ground squirrels).[3,4,7] The agent is vectored by certain species of hard ticks, especially the dog tick, *Dermacentor variabilis*, the lone star tick, *Amblyomma americanum*, and the Rocky Mountain wood tick, *Dermacentor andersoni*.[3,4] Biting tabanid flies, especially deer flies (*Chrysops* spp.), mechanically transmit the infection.[9] The epidemiology of tularemia in North America has changed significantly since the 1930s and 1940s, when the disease most commonly called 'rabbit fever' had a much higher incidence and when cases were more likely to be linked to the hunting, dressing and butchering of wild rabbits and hares than to arthropod bites.[16,17]

Seasonality

Mosquito-borne transmission in Eurasia peaks in the summer months. In North America, a peak of tularemia cases in the spring and summer months is associated mostly with bites by ticks and blood-feeding flies, and a second peak in the late autumn and winter is associated with handling infected animals, especially among hunters and trappers.[17]

PATHOGENESIS AND PATHOLOGY

The principal pathologic changes in localized disease occur at the cutaneous site of inoculation and in the regional lymph nodes draining the site; when the disease is disseminated, the lungs, spleen, lymph nodes, liver and skin are most often involved.[18–20] The primary skin lesion begins as a papule several days following inoculation. The papule rapidly progresses to a vesicle that erodes and develops into an ulcer, which is typically 2–3cm in diameter with an irregular slightly raised and erythematous border. The base is necrotic, and frequently covered with a thick dark scab that can mimic the eschar of cutaneous anthrax (Fig 177.3). Affected lymph nodes show hemorrhagic necrosis and may suppurate. Secondary skin lesions have also been described in tularemia, including papular and papulovesicular lesions, erythema nodosum and erythema multiforme.

Francisella tularensis is a facultative intracellular organism, and the response to infection has a prominent component of cell-mediated immunopathology.[21] Histologically, the early disease is characterized by focal suppurative necrosis. The central area of necrosis is at first composed primarily of polymorphonuclear leukocytes and macrophages, which may be replaced by epithelioid cells in more advanced lesions. A wall of fibroblasts may surround the acute inflammatory reaction. Later, smaller lesions may be indistinguishable from miliary tubercles. A frequent finding on pathologic examination of affected lungs is small (3–12mm), yellowish, necrotic subpleural nodules. Patchy interstitial infiltrates are common in pneumonic tularemia; bronchopneumonia is found in about 30% of cases, and lobar pneumonia with consolidation of an entire lobe in about 15% of pneumonic cases. Lung abscesses occasionally occur. Hilar lymph nodes may be inflamed and enlarged.

Prevention

Persons exposed in endemic areas to ticks, biting flies or mosquitoes should, when feasible, wear protective clothing, tuck their trouser legs into their socks and apply repellents containing diethyltoluamide (DEET) to skin and clothing as directed by the manufacturer. Permethrin-based products can be applied to clothing to kill ticks and biting flies on contact. Frequent examinations should be made to identify and remove ticks on clothing and skin. Persons should always avoid direct contact with sick or dead animals, and hunters, trappers, dressers and butchers should wear impervious gloves when skinning and handling wild animal carcasses. Recently, an outbreak of pneumonic tularemia occurred in Massachusetts, USA, among landscapers using power tools that typically raise environmental dusts,[22] and the use of fine particle masks while engaged in these activities has been suggested as a possible means of reducing infective inhalation exposures.

Live attenuated vaccines have been used to protect laboratory personnel who routinely work with *F. tularensis*. Vaccines have also been used in an attempt to reduce the incidence of disease among rural residents of highly endemic areas of the former Soviet Union. A live attenuated tularemia vaccine was until recently available in the USA under investigational new drug (IND) protocol; its manufacture is currently under Food and Drug Administration review. Persons exposed to a laboratory accident possibly resulting in aerosolization or inoculation of *F. tularensis* should be considered for prophylactic antibiotic administration or placed on fever watch and closely monitored for early signs of illness.

CLINICAL FEATURES

The primary forms of tularemia include:[18–20]

- ulceroglandular tularemia (45–85% of cases),
- glandular tularemia (10–25% of cases),
- oculoglandular tularemia (<5% of cases),
- typhoidal (septic) tularemia (<5% of cases),
- oropharyngeal tularemia (<5% of cases), and
- pneumonic (inhalation) tularemia (<5% of cases).

The incubation period is usually 2–5 days (range 1–14 days). Onset is sudden; typically, the patient has fever of 100–104°F (38–40°C) and a constellation of non-specific manifestations including chills, headache, generalized body aches (often prominent in the lumbosacral region), nausea, weakness, cough and chest pain.[18–20] Without treatment, nonspecific symptoms usually persist for several weeks. Sweats, chills, progressive weakness and weight loss characterize the continuing illness. Any of the principal forms of tularemia may be complicated by bacteremic spread that may lead to secondary sepsis, tularemic pneumonia, meningitis or other metastatic infection.

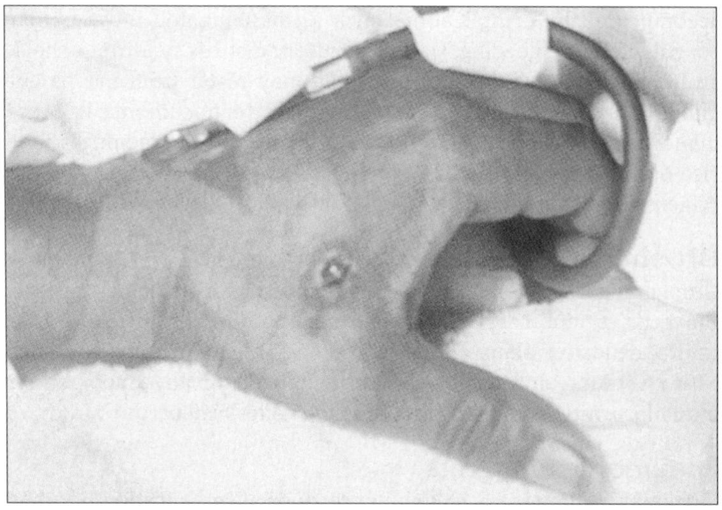

Fig. 177.3 Tularemic ulcer with eschar formation after percutaneous inoculation of *Francisella tularensis*.

Before antibiotics became available, the overall mortality rate from infections with the more severe type A strains was in the range of 5–10%; however, a considerably higher fatality rate was reported for typhoidal and pneumonic forms of disease. Untreated, infections with type B strain have been associated with a fatality rate of only 1–3%. In the USA, the fatality rate for all forms in recent years has been less than 2%.[23]

Ulceroglandular tularemia

A local papule appears at the site of inoculation at the time of, or shortly after, the onset of fever and other generalized symptoms. This becomes vesiculated and pustular, and then ulcerates within a few days of its first appearance. Typically, the ulcer is tender, has an indolent character and may be covered by a scab (Fig. 177.3). By the time of ulceration, painful lymphadenitis occurs in one or more adjacent nodes in the afferent pathway. In persons infected by handling contaminated materials, the epitrochlear nodes (8%) and the axillary nodes (65%) are the most commonly affected. In persons infected by arthropod bites, the femoral–inguinal nodes (64%), the axillary nodes (24%) and the cervical nodes (6%) are commonly involved.[20] In some cases, an abscessed node may suppurate, create a sinus tract and discharge purulent material to the outside.

Oculoglandular tularemia

Oculoglandular tularemia (Parinaud's syndrome) follows contamination of the conjunctival sac. Ulceration may occur on the conjunctiva, which becomes severely inflamed, with marked edema and vasculitis. Characteristically, there is painful swelling of nodes draining the periorbital tissues, such as the preauricular, submandibular and cervical chain nodes.

Glandular tularemia

Glandular tularemia differs from the ulceroglandular type only in not having the local cutaneous ulceration. It is more likely to follow arthropod-borne inoculation than direct percutaneous inoculation of the hands and fingers of persons handling infected animal tissues.

Typhoidal tularemia

Typhoidal tularemia presents as an acute illness without localizing signs.[20] The diagnosis is most often made by the identification of *F. tularensis* in cultures of the blood. Abdominal pain, diarrhea and vomiting may be prominent in the early illness. Sepsis may occur and the systemic inflammatory response syndrome may ensue, rarely accompanied by complications such as disseminated intravascular coagulation and bleeding, acute respiratory distress syndrome, shock and organ failure. Typhoidal tularemia may result from inapparent inhalation exposures, that then progresses to pneumonia in more than 50% of cases; infection of the kidneys and the meninges may also occur. In some cases, the upper gastrointestinal tract may be the principal target organ in typhoidal tularemia.

Oropharyngeal tularemia

Oropharyngeal tularemia is acquired by ingesting inadequately cooked game, or contaminated water or food. The patient may develop a painful exudative pharyngitis or tonsillitis, or a stomatitis, sometimes with ulceration, and tender cervical lymphadenopathy. Suppuration, fistula formation and drainage of cervical nodes may occur.[11]

Pneumonic tularemia

Pneumonic tularemia is a common secondary complication of other forms of tularemia. Infrequently, primary pneumonia arises from inhalation of an infective aerosol or dust. In addition to fever, chills, fatigue and other generalized symptoms of infection, pulmonic manifestations include cough (usually with minimal sputum production), chest discomfort, sometimes with pleuritic pain, dyspnea, tachypnea and occasionally mild hemoptysis. *Francisella tularensis* was weaponized for aerosol delivery by biowarfare programs during and after the Second World War, and it is assumed that this would be the most likely mode of delivery in a potential terrorism attack. The expected result would be an outbreak of pneumonic tularemia and non-specific febrile illness (typhoidal tularemia) beginning 3–5 days after exposure; this might at first be difficult to distinguish from the many usual causes of community-acquired infection. It is possible that an aerosol exposure could also result in cases of oropharyngeal and oculoglandular tularemia. Since naturally acquired tularemia is almost entirely a rural disease, bioterrorism should quickly be suspected should a cluster of cases occur in an urban population. The recognition, and medical and public health management of tularemia as a weapon of bioterrorism has recently been outlined.[2]

DIAGNOSIS

The presumptive diagnosis of tularemia is made by clinical examination combined with information on potentially infective exposures. Differential diagnostic possibilities are many, as follows:

- in persons who have glandular or ulceroglandular disease they include plague, sporotrichosis, cat-scratch fever, lymphogranuloma venereum, streptococcal or staphylococcal lymphadenitis, toxoplasmosis, mycobacterial infection, chancre and chancroid;
- in persons who have oropharyngeal tularemia, other bacterial and viral causes of stomatitis, pharyngitis and cervical adenitis must be considered, such as streptococcal infection, infectious mononucleosis, mycobacterial infection, adenoviral infection and diphtheria;
- in persons who have pneumonia, they include mycoplasmal pneumonia, chlamydial pneumonia, Legionnaires' disease, staphylococcal or streptococcal pneumonitis, *Haemophilus influenzae* pneumonia, plague, histoplasmosis and tuberculosis; and
- in persons who have typhoidal tularemia, they include bacterial endocarditis, disseminated mycobacterial or fungal infection, typhoid fever, brucellosis, listeriosis, leptospirosis, Q fever, plague and other causes of sepsis.

The clinical diagnosis of tularemia is confirmed by cultural isolation of *F. tularensis* or diagnostic rises in serologic titers.[24] The organism can be grown in routine culture systems; however, clinical suspicion of tularemia is critical in directing selection of the correct (cysteine-enriched) culture media that favors growth of *Francisella* spp. In addition to culture, materials other than blood should be streaked on glass slides for presumptive diagnosis by direct fluorescent antibody testing. The agglutination reaction for combined IgM and IgG immunoglobulins is the routine serological procedure in use in most laboratories. Reference laboratories use microagglutination methods that are more sensitive than tube agglutination procedures. Antibody titers usually do not rise before 10 days or more of illness onset. A 4-fold rise in titer between acute and convalescent serum specimens, or a single titer of 1:160 or greater is considered diagnostic for *F. tularensis* infection. Potentially useful diagnostic procedures include enzyme-linked immunoassay, immunoblotting for IgM antibodies, polymerase chain reaction assays immunochromatographic handheld assays, and DNA probes, but these are still in the experimental stages of development.[25] Many routine diagnostic laboratories have policies that exclude work on *F. tularensis* because it readily aerosolizes from culture and is notorious as a cause of laboratory-acquired infections.[26] Biosafety level 2 precautions are essential for routine procedures, and biosafety level 3 precautions are required for safe manipulation of cultures and for animal studies.[27]

MANAGEMENT

Patients are best managed under hospital care until a full diagnostic evaluation and satisfactory treatment response has occurred. Streptomycin, which is bactericidal, is the drug of choice based on experience and efficacy. It is given to adults intramuscularly in a dosage of 0.5–1.0g q12h for 10 days. Gentamicin, an acceptable alternative, is given parenterally in an adult dosage of 3–5mg/kg per day, once daily or in equal divided doses at 8-hour intervals[28] for 10 days. A tetracycline (most commonly, doxycycline) or chloramphenicol may be used in place of an aminoglycoside, especially in less severely ill patients, but use of these bacteriostatic agents occasionally results in primary treatment failures, and dosage schedules of at least 14 days are recommended to prevent relapses. Oral or parenterally administered ciprofloxacin has been used to treat adults and children with good success in standard doses for 10 days.[29] Patients begun on parenterally administered antimicrobials can switch to oral administration when clinically indicated. *Francisella tularensis* organisms routinely produce β-lactamase and are resistant to β-lactam antibiotics and azithromycin, but they are generally highly susceptible to aminoglycosides, tetracyclines, chloramphenicol and quinolones.[30,31] Penicillins and cephalosporins are not effective and should not be used. Typically, fever and general symptoms of acute infection begin to regress within 24–48 hours of initiation of appropriate antibiotic administration. Factors associated with a poor outcome include delays in seeking medical care, or delays in diagnosis and treatment, and underlying medical disorders, such as diabetes or alcoholism.[32] Standard (universal) precautions only are required for purposes of hospital infection control.[2] Postexposure prophylactic antibiotic treatment of close contacts is not recommended because human to human transmission is not known to occur.

REFERENCES

1. Ellis J, Oyston PCF, Green M, et al. Tularemia. Clin Microbiol Rev 2002; 15:631–46.
2. Dennis DT, Inglesby TV, Henderson DA, *et al.* Tularemia as a biological weapon: medical and public health management. JAMA 2001;285:2763–73.
3. Hopla CE, Hopla AK. Tularemia. In: Beran GW, Steele, JH, eds. Handbook of zoonoses, 2nd edition, section A: bacterial, rickettsial, chlamydial, and mycotic. Boca Raton, Florida: CRC Press; 1994:11–26.
4. Bell JF. Tularemia. In: Steele JG, ed. CRC handbook series in zoonoses, vol. 2. Boca Raton, Florida: CRC Press; 1980:161–93.
5. Capellan J, Fong IW. Tularemia from a cat bite: case report and review of feline-associated tularemia. Clin Infect Dis 1993;16:472–5.
6. Centers for Disease Control and Prevention. Tularemia–United States, 1990–2000. MMWR Morb Mortal Wkly Rep 2002;51:181–4.
7. Jellison WL. Tularemia in North America. Missoula, Montana: University of Montana; 1974:1–276.
8. Markowitz LE, Hynes NA, de la Cruz P, *et al.* Tick-borne tularemia: an outbreak of lymphadenopathy in children. JAMA 1985;254:2922–5.
9. Klock LE, Olsen PF, Fukushima T. Tularemia epidemic associated with the deerfly. JAMA 1973;226:149–52.
10. Eliasson H, Lindbäck J, Nuorti JP, *et al.* The 2000 tularemia outbreak: a case–control study of risk factors in disease-endemic and emergent areas, Sweden. Emerg Infect Dis 2002;8:956–60.
11. Reintjes R, Dedushaj I, Gjini A, *et al.* Tularemia investigation in Kosovo: case control and environmental studies. Emerg Infect Dis 2002;8:69–73.
12. Perez-Castrillon JL, Bachiller-Luque P, Martin-Luquero M, *et al.* Tularemia epidemic in northwestern Spain: clinical description and therapeutic response. Clin Infect Dis 2001;33:573–6.
13. Syrjälä H, Kujala P, Myllylä V, *et al.* Airborne transmission of tularemia in farmers. Scand J Infect Dis 1985;17:371–5.
14. Dahlstrand S, Ringertz O, Zetterberg B. Airborne tularemia in Sweden. Scand J Infect Dis 1971;3:7–16.
15. Helvaci S, Gedikoglu S, Akalin H, *et al.* Tularemia in Bursa, Turkey: 205 cases in ten years. Eur J Epidemiol 2000;16:271–6.
16. Boyce JM. Recent trends in the epidemiology of tularemia in the United States. J Infect Dis 1975;131:197–9.
17. Taylor JP, Istre GR, McChesney TC, *et al.* Epidemiological characteristics of human tularemia in the southwest-central states, 1981–1987. Am J Epidemiol 1991;133:1032–8.
18. Francis E. A summary of present knowledge of tularemia. Medicine 1928;7:411–32.
19. Dienst FT. Tularemia: a perusal of three hundred thirty-nine cases. J Louisiana State Med Soc 1963;115:114–27.
20. Evans ME, Gregory DW, Schaffner W, *et al.* Tularemia: a 30-year experience with 88 cases. Medicine 1985;64:251–69.
21. Tärnvik A. Nature of protective immunity to *Francisella tularensis*. Rev Infect Dis 1989;11:440–51.
22. Feldman K, Enscore R, Lathrop S, *et al.* Outbreak of primary pneumonic tularemia on Martha's Vineyard. N Engl J Med 2001;345:1601–6.
23. Dennis DT. Tularemia. In: Wallace RB, ed. Maxcy-Rosenau-Last public health and preventive medicine. 14th edition. Stamford, CT: Appleton and Lange; 1998:354–7.
24. Wong JD, Shapiro DS. *Francisella*. In: Murray PR, Baron EJ, Pfaller MA, *et al.*, eds. Manual of clinical microbiology. 7th edition. Washington, DC: American Society Microbiology Press; 1999:647–51.
25. Grunow R, Splettstoesser W, McDonald S, *et al.* Detection of *Francisella tularensis* in biological specimens using a capture enzyme-linked immunosorbent assay, and immunochromatographic handheld assay, and a PCR. Clin Diagn Lab Immunol 2000;7:86–90.
26. Pike RM. Laboratory-associated infections: summary and analysis of 3921 cases. Health Lab Sci 1976;13:105–14.
27. US Department of Health and Human Services. Laboratory biosafety level criteria. In: Richmond JY, McKinney RW, eds. Biosafety in microbiology and biomedical laboratories. 4th edition. Washington, DC: Dept of Health and Human Services; 1999:17–52.
28. Enderlin G, Morales L, Jacobs RF, *et al.* Streptomycin and alternative agents for the treatment of tularemia: review of the literature. Clin Infect Dis 1994;19:42–7.
29. Johansson A, Berglund L, Sjöstedt A, *et al.* Ciprofloxacin for treatment of tularemia. Clin Infect Dis 2001;33:267–8.
30. Ikaheimo I, Syrjälä H, Karhukorpi J, *et al.* In vitro antibiotic susceptibility of *Francisella tularensis* isolated from humans and animals. J Antimicrob Chemother 2000;46:287–90.
31. Johansson A, Urich SK, Chu, MC, *et al.* In vitro susceptibility to quinolones of *Francisella tularensis* subspecies *tularensis*. Scand J Infect Dis 2002;34:327–30.
32. Penn RL, Kinasewitz GT. Factors associated with a poor outcome in tularemia. Arch Intern Med 1987;147:265–8.

chapter

178 Diphtheria

Androulla Efstratiou

EPIDEMIOLOGY

Mass immunization with diphtheria toxoid during the 1940s and 1950s resulted in the virtual elimination of diphtheria in many countries by the 1970s as a result of the introduction of the Expanded Program on Immunization by the World Health Organization (WHO). However, an all-time low of 623 reported cases in the WHO European Region was reached in 1980, which is in contrast to the total global figure of 97,811. Since 1989, major resurgence was observed in Europe, centered mostly in the newly independent states (NIS) of the former Soviet Union. The epidemic within the NIS commenced in 1990 and affected all 15 countries of the NIS by the end of 1994. In 1990, the number of reported cases was 1481 and peaked at 50,449 in 1995. In 1995, cases in the NIS accounted for 88% of reported cases globally (56,966). As a result of vigorous action taken in the NIS and collaboration between the epidemic countries and various international agencies, the incidence began to decline in 1996 (Fig. 178.1). The decreasing trend has continued; the number of cases reported in 1999 and 2000 was approximately 1500.[1] There is therefore evidence of progress toward control of the epidemic in the NIS since 1996. Diphtheria control is still urgently required in Georgia, Kyrghyzstan, Latvia, the Russian Federation and Tajikistan. During 2001–2, Latvia had the highest rate of diphtheria in Europe and the reasons for the resurgence in Latvia are unclear.[2] The overall situation within the European Region is still considered to be of high priority by the WHO.

A major contribution toward the control of these epidemics has been the formation of a specific microbiologic and epidemiologic global network for diphtheria. Initially, the European Laboratory Working Group on Diphtheria (ELWGD) was formed in 1993 at the request of WHO, with participation from primarily European countries.[3] During the past 7 years the network has expanded significantly and now comprises participants from 40 countries worldwide. The Diphtheria Surveillance Network (DIPNET) continues its collaborative and co-ordinated approach to support countries to improve diphtheria surveillance for early detection of cases and contacts by accurate microbiologic surveillance and the establishment of a network of national and international laboratories (http://www.phls.org.uk/inter/diphtheria/menu.htm).

Small epidemics are also occurring in other parts of the world, including South East Asia, India, Pakistan, Bangladesh and South America.[4] All these outbreaks and epidemics strongly emphasize the need for maintaining full immunization coverage and clearly demonstrate that, when immunization programs are disrupted by social, political or other changes, the disease may return. Vaccine-induced immunity does not last for life and various serologic studies in developed countries have shown that many adults are potentially susceptible, particularly when immunization courses are incomplete.

Increasing international travel and migration from areas where the disease is prevalent clearly indicate the need for maintaining clinical awareness of the disease, particularly among travelers from these areas and their contacts. All these epidemics have been classically associated with the causative agent of diphtheria, namely toxin-producing *Corynebacterium diphtheriae*. However, more recently within Europe, there have also been increasing reports of diphtheria caused by toxigenic *Corynebacterium ulcerans*. The latter is a known veterinary pathogen and causes mastitis in cattle and other domestic and wild animals. Toxigenic strains of *C. ulcerans* have been associated with classical diphtheria as well as milder symptoms. At least one death in the UK has recently been attributed to such an infection.[5]

PATHOGENESIS AND PATHOLOGY

The pathogenesis of the disease is complex. Virulence is thought to be associated with the production of an exotoxin by the causative organisms, potentially toxigenic corynebacteria, *C. diphtheriae* or *C. ulcerans*. The *C. diphtheriae* genome has now been sequenced and the complete genome is finished and is currently undergoing annotation and analysis. The annotation has revealed a number of interesting features that should provide an insight into the life and pathogenicity of the organism (sequence data: http://www.sanger.ac.uk/Projects/C_diphtheriae/).

Humans are the only known reservoir for *C. diphtheriae*. The mode of transmission is usually by direct contact with a patient or a carrier by aerosol transmission. More rarely, contact with articles contaminated with discharges from lesions or infected material can also occur.

Corynebacterium ulcerans, however, has always been regarded as a zoonosis and has always traditionally been associated with the ingestion of unpasteurized dairy products. In the UK, there has been recent documentation of toxigenic *C. ulcerans* in domestic cats with chronic rhinitis.[6] There had previously been no reports in the literature of infection among small domestic animals with *C. ulcerans,* so the implications are unclear. The risk to humans is greatest in household contacts of the cats and other very close human contacts who may examine them, such as veterinary surgeons. Overall, the bacteria do not actively invade deep tissues or the blood but tend to multiply locally and produce diphtheria toxin. Despite the proven role of the toxin, toxigenicity does not appear to be synonymous with pathogenicity because strains that do not produce toxin can survive for long periods in the upper respiratory tract and are also able to cause disease, ranging from relatively mild pharyngitis to severe tonsillitis and, in rare instances, systemic disease such as endocarditis.

PREVENTION

Diphtheria is notifiable in all countries of Europe and North America. It is imperative that all cases be rapidly identified and properly investigated according the WHO guidelines.[7] Cases are usually classified as suspected, probable or confirmed and are definitively described in the WHO manual. Local European guidelines are also available, in particular within the UK, where clinical recommendations have also been established for the management of toxigenic *C. ulcerans* cases. The advice is similar to that given for

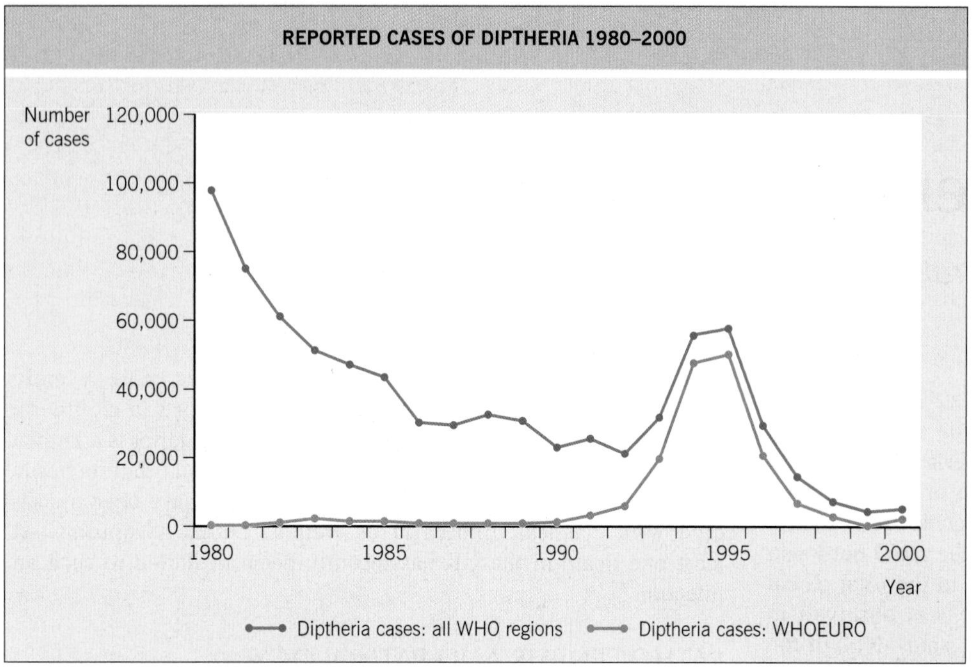

Fig. 178.1 Reported cases of diphtheria 1980–2000. Cases reported to the WHO worldwide and within the WHO European Region.

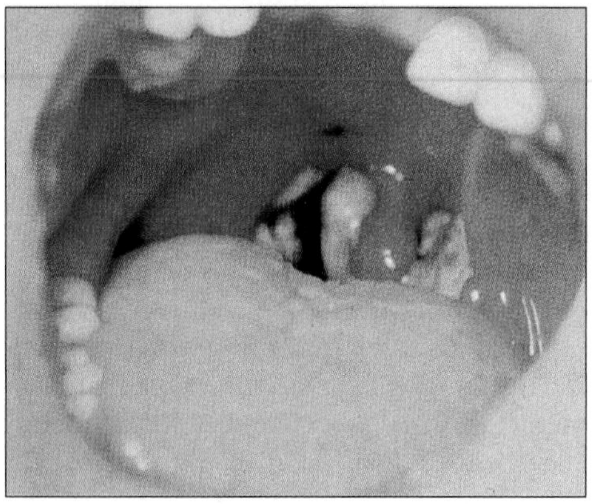

Fig. 178.2 Characteristic diphtheria pseudomembrane in a child. Courtesy of Dr Norman Begg.

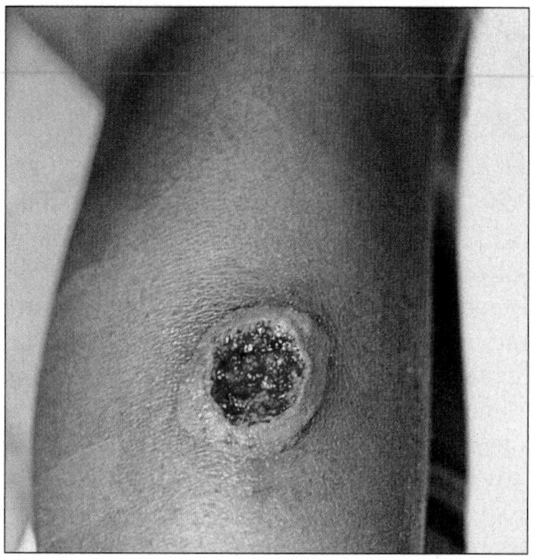

Fig. 178.3 Characteristic diphtheria lesion of the lower limb, showing the classic rolled, 'crater-like' edge and eschar.

toxigenic *C. diphtheriae* with management of close contacts as well as index cases.[5] The main aim of prevention and control of diphtheria is to eradicate toxigenic corynebacteria from the community and to maintain adequate levels of protective immunity by active immunization. Published data have indicated that, for example, approximately 38% of adult UK blood donors are susceptible to diphtheria. A significant trend of decreasing immunity with increasing age is apparent from many recent serologic studies.[8,9] The recommendations and guidelines for immunization strategies are given by many health authorities and consist of primary immunization (e.g. within the UK three doses for children aged 2–4 months with an interval of 1 month between each dose) and reinforcing immunization (preschool booster dose and another booster just before leaving school for all teenagers). However, in any country where an epidemic situation exists or is imminent, aggressive mass immunization of high-risk groups must be implemented. Low levels of immunity in adults and a gradual increase in the percentage of children not immunized with at least three doses of adsorbed diphtheria–tetanus–pertussis vaccine pose a danger for recurrence of diphtheria, as seen in eastern Europe.[10,11]

CLINICAL FEATURES

Diphtheria is usually classified according to its site of manifestation; there are two major 'forms' of disease the classic respiratory condition and nonrespiratory (cutaneous) diphtheria. The clinical manifestations vary from place to place and from time to time depending on a range of host and environmental factors that are not fully understood. The most important factor is individual immunity to the toxin, which is mediated either by neutralizing antibody induced by toxoid or by natural immunity.

The incubation period for the disease is 2–5 days, occasionally longer. The first symptoms are malaise, low-grade fever, sore throat and loss of appetite. A pseudomembrane forms in the throat and may extend into the lungs (Fig. 178.2). The disease is usually subdivided into three stages: early, late and severe. Each stage is associated with the isolation of the causative organism and the presence of the pseudomembrane. The pseudomembrane adheres to underlying tissue and the tissue bleeds when attempts are made to remove it. This feature is useful for diagnosing diphtheria because pseudomembranes caused by other infectious agents are not adherent.

In the early stage of disease, manifestations are localized in the upper respiratory tract or in skin lesions, leading to the severe stage resulting in toxic circulatory collapse, severe edema of the neck, submucosal or skin petechial hemorrhages and acute renal insufficiency. The late stage is associated with neurologic and cardiologic features owing to the dissemination of the toxin to the major organs. This results in extensive cardiac and neurologic damage: myocarditis, blurred vision and paralysis of the soft palate, diaphragm and limbs. Between 10% and 25% of patients who have clinical respiratory diphtheria develop some form of myocardial damage and up to 75% develop a neuropathy. Symptoms may range from pharyngitis with low-grade fever in faucial diphtheria to partial or even complete respiratory obstruction due to the formation of the pseudomembrane in laryngeal or tracheobronchial diphtheria.

Cutaneous diphtheria is a chronic condition associated with the tropics; it is prevalent within South East Asia. The characteristic lesions are difficult to treat and they often take months even years to heal. They are quite marked in their appearance with a characteristic rolled, 'crater-like' edge (Fig. 178.3). The lesions are covered with an eschar, a hard bluish-gray membranous scar that is slightly raised. The lesion, therefore, acts as a potential reservoir for transmission and spread of the pharyngeal form of the disease. Cutaneous diphtheria lesions proved to be the 'vehicles' of transmission of the organism in the outbreak that occurred in the USA in the late 1970s among the Skid Row alcoholics.[12]

DIAGNOSIS

The presumptive clinical diagnosis of respiratory diphtheria is based on the presence of the pseudomembrane. However, in many instances, particularly in countries where the disease is uncommon, diagnosis is often difficult and diphtheria may be misdiagnosed or confused with other diseases such as severe streptococcal sore throat, glandular fever or even Vincent's angina. This thus highlights the importance of the microbiologic diagnosis of the disease, and isolation and confirmation of the causative organism, toxigenic *C. diphtheriae* or *C. ulcerans* (see Chapter 226). However, bacteriologic diagnosis should be complementary to the clinical diagnosis and should not delay immediate and specific treatment of the patient. A throat swab and, if possible, samples of the membrane should be collected and cultured. The most important test is, of course, the test to detect diphtheria toxin. Guidelines for the microbiologic diagnosis of diphtheria are described in the WHO manual for the laboratory diagnosis of the disease.[13] Guidelines that incorporate the laboratory and clinical diagnosis of *C. ulcerans* are described further in the UK guidelines.[14] Current approaches to laboratory diagnosis in Europe and beyond have recently been updated.[15]

Close (household and kissing) contacts may be asymptomatic carriers or at risk of developing the disease and they should also be sampled by taking throat swabs. Local public health authorities must be alerted if a suspected case has been identified; the appropriate measures for swabbing, contact tracing and management (including immunization and antibiotic prophylaxis) should be initiated. Guidelines for the control, treatment and management of the disease, cases and contacts have been outlined by the WHO.[7] A travel, medical and immunization history of the suspected case and close contacts should be ascertained.

MANAGEMENT

Because patients who have suspected respiratory diphtheria may deteriorate rapidly, treatment should not be delayed and should not depend solely upon the result from the microbiology laboratory. In suspected cases, treatment should commence with diphtheria antitoxin, antibiotics and strict isolation. The three main areas of therapy are essentially:

- administration of diphtheria antitoxin;
- administration of antibiotics; and
- strict isolation procedures.

Diphtheria antitoxin

Administration of diphtheria antitoxin (hyperimmune horse serum) aims at neutralizing circulating toxin that has not yet bound to tissue. The dose of antitoxin depends on the severity of the disease and the site and extent of the pseudomembrane. Before administration of antitoxin the patient must be tested for sensitivity to horse serum and, if necessary, desensitized. Usually, in cases of tonsillar or pharyngeal diphtheria, the dose is 15,000–40,000 units of antitoxin by intramuscular or intravenous injection; in severe forms, doses as high as 80,000–100,000 units are given.[7]

Antibiotics

Antibiotics are essential for eradicating the organism and eliminating its spread but they are not a substitute for antitoxin treatment. Penicillin (0.5–1.0g q6h orally) or erythromycin (500mg q6h) is recommended. Antibiotic therapy should be continued for 14 days. Antibiotics are also important for eradicating colonization in contacts and for postexposure prophylaxis.[7] At present, there is no significant, relevant antimicrobial resistance among *C. diphtheriae*; however, erythromycin resistance has been reported from South East Asia.[16,17]

Isolation procedures

Patients should be cared for in strict isolation and attended by staff whose immunization history is documented. Before patients are discharged they should be confirmed as 'culture-negative' for *C. diphtheriae* or *C. ulcerans* by collection of three swabs at 24-hour intervals and also given a booster dose of diphtheria toxoid, because natural infection does not necessarily confer immunity. It is important also to monitor the cardiac status closely with early intervention if appropriate (e.g. pacing for cardiac conduction disturbances and therapy for arrhythmias).

Cutaneous diphtheria

For cutaneous diphtheria, vigorous cleaning of the wound with soap and water is recommended in addition to antibiotic therapy. It is also advisable to take respiratory tract swabs from both the index case and close household contacts. Some authorities also advocate the use of antitoxin therapy because toxic sequelae have been documented among patients who have cutaneous disease.[7]

SUMMARY

In summary, it is important to consider the following practical points:

- the diagnosis of diphtheria should be considered in travelers returning from endemic and epidemic areas or from areas where recent cases have occurred;
- a history of the immunization status of the patient does not necessarily exclude the diagnosis of diphtheria;
- microbiologic confirmation is essential for the definitive diagnosis but treatment must not be delayed pending confirmation; and
- expert opinion should be sought early and contacts must be actively followed up.

Acknowledgements

We gratefully acknowledge the European Commission (EC), Fourth Framework programmes, Biomed 2, BMH4.CT.98.3793; INCO-Copernicus ICT.98.0302 and EC DG SANCO S12.324473 (2001CVG4-012) for funding aspects of the surveillance activities within the European Region.

REFERENCES

1. Emiroglu N. Diphtheria in the European Region of WHO. Seventh International Meeting of the European Laboratory Working Group on Diphtheria, Vienna, Austria, June 2002. Abstract 1.1:33–34. London: Public Health Laboratory Service; 2002:
2. Griscevica A. Epidemic of diphtheria in Latvia. Seventh International Meeting of the European Laboratory Working Group on Diphtheria, Vienna, Austria, June 2002. Abstract 3.3:55–6.
3. Efstratiou A, Roure C, Members of the European Laboratory Working Group on Diphtheria. The European Laboratory Working Group on Diphtheria: a global microbiologic network. J Infect Dis 2000;181(Suppl.1):S146–51.
4. Efstratiou A, George RC. Microbiology and epidemiology of diphtheria. Rev Med Microbiol 1996;7:31–42.
5. Bonnet JM, Begg NT. Control of diphtheria: guidance for consultants in communicable disease control. Commun Dis Public Health 1999;2:242–9.
6. PHLS. Toxigenic *Corynebacterium ulcerans* in cats. Commun Dis Rep Wkly 2002; 14 March.
7. Begg N. Manual for the management and control of diphtheria in the European Region. The expanded program on immunization in the European region of WHO. Copenhagen: World Health Organization; 1994:ICP/EPI 038(B).
8. Maple PAC, Efstratiou A, George RC, Andrews NJ, Sesardic D. Diphtheria immunity in UK blood donors. Lancet 1995;345:963–5.
9. Edmunds WJ, Pebody RG, Aggerbeck H, *et al.* The seroepidemiology of diphtheria in Western Europe. ESEN Project. European Sero-Epidemiology Network. Epidemiol Infect 2000;125:113–25.
10. Markina SS, Maksimova NM, Vitek CR, Bogatyreva EY, Monisov AA. Diphtheria in the Russian Federation in the 1990s. J Infect Dis 2000;181(Suppl.1):S27–34.
11. Galazka A. Implications of the diphtheria epidemic in the former Soviet Union for immunization programs. J Infect Dis 2000;181(Suppl.1):S244–8.
12. Harnisch JP, Tronca E, Nolan CM, Turck M, Holmes KK. Diphtheria among alcoholic urban adults. A decade of experience in Seattle. Ann Intern Med 1989;111:71–82.
13. Efstratiou A, Maple PAC. Manual for the laboratory diagnosis of diphtheria. The expanded program on immunization in the European region of WHO. Copenhagen: World Health Organization; 1994:ICP/EPI 038(C).
14. Efstratiou A, George RC. Laboratory guidelines for the diagnosis of infections caused by *Corynebacterium diphtheriae* and *C. ulcerans*. Commun Dis Public Health 1999;2:250–7.
15. Efstratiou A, Engler KH, Mazurova IK, Glushkevich T, Vuopio-Varkila J, Popovic T. Current approaches to the laboratory diagnosis of diphtheria. J Infect Dis 2000;181(Suppl.1):S138–45.
16. Engler KH, Warner M, George RC. In vitro activity of ketolides HMR3004 and HMR3647 and seven other antimicrobial agents against *Corynebacterium diphtheriae.* J Antimicrob Chemother 2001;47:27–31.
17. Kneen R, Pham NG, Solomon T, *et al.* Penicillin vs. erythromycin in the treatment of diphtheria. Clin Infect Dis 1998;27:845–50.

chapter 179

Scrub Typhus and Other Tropical Rickettsioses

Philippe Parola & Didier Raoult

INTRODUCTION

Rickettsioses (also called typhus) are infectious diseases caused by obligate intracellular bacteria formerly grouped in the order Rickettsiales. These organisms were first described as short, Gram-negative rods that retained basic fuchsin when stained by the method of Gimenez.[1] Recent developments in molecular taxonomic methods have resulted in the reclassification within the Rickettsiales.[1] However, four groups of diseases are still usually called rickettsioses. These include:

- scrub typhus due to *Orientia tsutsugamushi*;
- diseases due to bacteria of the genus *Rickettsia* (including the spotted fever group and the typhus group);
- ehrlichioses due to bacteria within the family Anaplasmataceae (ehrlichioses have not, however, been properly demonstrated to occur in the tropics); and
- Q-fever, which is due to *Coxiella burnetii*.

DIFFERENTIAL DIAGNOSIS BASED ON REGION

The agents of rickettsioses are associated with arthropods including ticks, mites, fleas and lice, which may act as vectors, reservoirs and/or amplifiers of the organisms. Most of these vectors favor specific optimal environmental conditions, biotopes and hosts. These factors determine the geographic distribution of the vector and consequently the risk area for the rickettsioses. This is particularly true when vectors are also reservoirs of pathogens, as seen in the case of ticks for most spotted fever group rickettsioses.[1,2] Thus, although some rickettsioses are distributed worldwide (i.e. Q-fever, murine typhus), a specific area is usually associated with specific diseases. Therefore, most rickettsioses are geographic diseases. Table 179.1 presents the rickettsioses occurring in tropical areas of Africa, Asia, America and Australia.[1,2]

EXPOSURE

Most rickettsioses are transmitted to humans by arthropods. Thus, exposure to the disease is closely linked to exposure to the arthropod vectors. Furthermore, although *C. burnetii*, the agent of Q-fever, has been found to infect more than 40 species of ticks throughout the world, the role of ticks in human infections is not confirmed. In fact, Q-fever is usually acquired by the ingestion or inhalation of virulent organisms from infected mammals, mostly goats, sheep and cats, and their products.[2]

Chiggers

'Chiggers' is the commonly used name of several species of larval-stage, trombiculid mites, which are the vectors (and reservoirs) of scrub typhus due to *Orientia tsutsugamushi*. Risk areas range from typical tropical secondary growth (scrub) vegetation in the Asia-Pacific region to temperate zones and even the Himalayas. Although scrub typhus is essentially an occupational disease among rural residents engaged in agricultural or gathering activities, travelers or soldiers in the field may be infected when entering the biotope of the vectors.[3]

Ticks

Ticks are obligate hematophagous acarins that parasitize every class of vertebrate throughout the world and may bite people. Ticks are not only vectors but also reservoirs of most of the currently known spotted fever group rickettsiae. Ecologic characteristics of the tick are keys for the epidemiology of tick-borne diseases. For example, the brown dog tick *Rhipicephalus sanguineus*, which is the vector of *Rickettsia conorii*, lives in dog environments (kennels and human houses) and has a low affinity for people. Cases of Mediterranean spotted fever are sporadic in endemic areas and most cases are encountered in urban areas. In contrast, *Amblyomma hebraeum*, which are vectors of *Rickettsia africae* in southern Africa, emerge from their habitats and actively attack animals, particularly nearby ruminants. They also feed readily on people that enter their biotopes. Furthermore, numerous ticks can attack a host at the same time. These ticks are highly infected by rickettsiae. Thus, cases of African tick-bite fever often occur as grouped cases among subjects entering the bush (e.g. during a safari) and people can suffer several tick bites simultaneously.[2,4]

House mouse mite

The house mouse mite (*Liponyssoides sanguineus*) has been described as a vector of *R. akari*, the agent of rickettsialpox. These hematophagous arthropods maintain *R. akari* among house mice (*Mus musculus*) and may transmit the disease when biting people. Exposure to the mite is linked to contact with house mice. However, *Rickettsia akari* has been also identified in Korean voles (*Microtus fortis pelliceus*).

Fleas

Fleas are hematophagous insects. The rat flea *Xenopsylla cheopis* is the main vector of murine typhus due to *Rickettsia typhi*, whereas rodents, mainly *Rattus norvegicus* and *Rattus rattus*, act as reservoirs. It is generally accepted that most people become infected when flea feces containing *R. typhi* contaminate disrupted skin or are inhaled into the respiratory tract.[1] Infections may result from flea bites as well. Exposure to rat fleas is linked to exposure to rats. The diseases are urban as well as rural. Fleas are also suspected to be the vectors of the emerging infection due to *Rickettsia felis*. Cat fleas (*Ctenocephalides felis*), dog fleas (*C. canis*) and human fleas (*Pulex irritans*) are all possible vectors, but the disease cycle has not yet been described.

Lice

Human body lice (*Pediculus humanus corporis*) are insects that live in human clothing. They thrive during periods of cold weather, particularly in conditions or areas of reduced hygiene maintenance, poverty and wars. The body louse is the vector of *Bartonella quintana* (the agent of trench fever), *Borrelia recurrentis* (agent of relapsing fever) and *Rickettsia prowazekii* (the agent of epidemic typhus). Until recently, epidemic typhus was considered to be endemic only in Ethiopia. However, an outbreak of typhus in approximately

TROPICAL RICKETTSIOSES THROUGHOUT THE WORLD					
Location by continent	**Vectors**	**Disease**	**Agent**	**Specific areas**	**Risk of exposure**
Africa	**Ticks**				
	Rhipicephalus sanguineus	Mediterranean spotted fever	*Rickettsia conorii*	Mediterranean area (Algeria, Tunisia, Morocco, Libya, Egypt) Kenya, Somalia, Central African Republic, Zimbabwe and South Africa	Urban (2/3) and rural (1/3)
	Amblyomma sp.	African tick-bite fever	*R. africae*	Sub-Saharan Africa	Rural area. Safari
	Hyalomma marginatum	Unnamed	*R. aeschlimmanii*	Morocco, Zimbabwe, South Africa	
	H truncatumyalomma[*]	Unnamed	'*R. mongolotimonae*'	Niger[*]	
	Fleas				
	Xenopsylla cheopis (rat flea)	Murine typhus	*R. typhi*	Ubiquitous. High prevalence in coastal areas	Contact with rats and rat fleas
	Pulex irritans (human flea)[*]	Flea-borne spotted fever	*R. felis*	Ethiopia[*]	Lack of hygiene
	Lice				
	Pediculus humanus corporis	Epidemic typhus	*R. prowazekii*	Ethiopia, Burundi, Rwanda, Uganda, Algeria	Civil war, refugee camps, lack of hygiene in cold or mountainous areas
Americas	**Ticks**				
	Amblyomma cajennense	Rocky Mountain spotted fever	*R. rickettsii*	Central America (Mexico, Panama, Costa Rica), South America (Brazil, Colombia)	Rural areas
	Amblyomma spp.	African tick-bite fever	*R. africae*	West Indies	Rural areas
	Fleas				
	Xenopsylla cheopis (rat flea)	Murine typhus	*R. typhi*	Ubiquitous	Contact with rats and rat fleas
	Ctenocephalides felis (cat flea)[*]	Flea-borne spotted fever	*R. felis*	Texas, California, Mexico, Brazil, Peru	
	Lice				
	Pediculus humanus corporis	Epidemic typhus	*R. prowazekii*	Peru and Andean area	Lack of hygiene in mountainous area
Asia	**Ticks**				
	Rhipicephalus sanguineus	Indian tick typhus	*R. conorii* Indian	India. Suspected in Thailand	
	Ixodes granulatus[*]	Flinders Island spotted fever	*R. honei*	Thailand[*]	
	Ixodes ovatus *Dermacentor taiwanensis* *Haemaphysalis longicornis* *Haemaphysalis flava*	Oriental or Japanese spotted fever	*R. japonica*	Japan[†]	Agricultural activities, bamboo cutting
	Ixodes ovatus,[*] *I. persulcatus,*[*] *I. monospinus*[*]	Unnamed	*R. helvetica*	Japan.[†] Suspected in Thailand	
	Haemaphysalis asiaticum[*]	Unnamed	'*R. mongolotimonae*'	China (Inner Mongolia)[*,†]	
	Dermacentor nuttalli, D. marginatus	North-Asian tick typhus	*R. sibirica*	Northern China, former USSR (Asian republics, Siberia), Armenia, Pakistan	
	Haemaphysalis concinna *Dermacentor silvarum*	Unnamed	'*R. heilongjiangii*'	North-eastern China	
	Fleas				
	Xenopsylla cheopis (rat flea)	Murine typhus	*R. typhi*	Ubiquitous	
	Ctenocephalides felis (cat flea)[*]	Flea-borne spotted fever	*R. felis*	Thailand	
	Trombiculid acarins				
	Leptothrombidium spp.	Scrub typhus	*Orientia tsutsugamushi*	Asia-Pacific region from Korea to Papua New Guinea and Queensland, Australia, and from Japan to India and Afghanistan	Rural activities Agricultural activities Soldiers in the field
	Lice				
	Pediculus humanus corporis	Epidemic typhus	*R. prowazekii*	China. India (Kashmir)	Civil war, refugee camps, lack of hygiene in cold or mountainous areas
	House mouse mite				
	Liponyssoides sanguineus	Rickettsialpox	*R. akari*	Korea[‡]	

Table 179.1 Tropical rickettsioses throughout the world. Note that Q-fever due to *C. burnetii* is distributed worldwide (except in New Zealand).

TROPICAL RICKETTSIOSES THROUGHOUT THE WORLD—CONT'D					
Location by continent	**Vectors**	**Disease**	**Agent**	**Specific areas**	**Risk of exposure**
Australia	**Ticks**				
	Unknown	Flinders Island spotted fever	*R. honei*	Flinders Island, north-eastern Australia	
	Ixodes holocyclus	Queensland tick typhus	*R. australis*	North-eastern Australia	
	Fleas				
	Xenopsylla cheopis (rat flea)	Murine typhus	*R. typhi*	Ubiquitous	Contact with rats and rat fleas
	Trombiculid acarins				
	Leptothrombidium spp.	Scrub typhus	*Orientia tsutsugamushi*	Northern Territory and Western Australia, Queensland, Australia	Rural activities Agricultural activities Soldiers in the field

* Suspected by detection of the pathogen in the relevant arthropod
† Although not included in tropical areas, Japan and China are mentioned regarding the aspects of travel medicine
‡ Isolated from voles (*Microtus fortis pelliceus*)

Table 179.1 Tropical rickettsioses throughout the world—cont'd.

100,000 people was reported during the civil war in Burundi in 1997, in addition to cases that were reported in Peru, Russia, the USA, Algeria and France in the 1990s.[5] Epidemic typhus, then, must still be considered a potential major health risk in tropical countries; this is thought to be particularly true of refugee camps in the cooler mountainous areas. Infected body lice always die within 1–2 weeks (red louse disease). People, therefore, are considered to be the major reservoirs of this disease. *Rickettsia prowazekii* is transmitted to people by infected louse feces (in which *R. prowazekii* survives for weeks), through aerosols (thought to be the main route of infection for health workers attending patients) or by skin autoinoculation, following scratching.

CLINICAL FEATURES

Scrub typhus

Symptoms occur usually 7–10 days after the chigger's bite. A papule at the bite site that later ulcerates, forming a black crust of eschar (Figs 179.1 and 179.2), is typically associated with fever, regional lymphadenopathy, a macular or maculopapular rash, headache and myalgia. However, eschar and rash may be absent or unnoticed.[3]

Spotted fevers

These diseases include tick-borne rickettsioses, rickettsialpox due to *R. akari*, and the emerging flea-borne infection due to *R. felis*. Generally, the clinical symptoms of spotted fever group rickettsioses begin 6–10 days after the arthropod bite and typically include fever, headache, muscle pain, rash, local lymphadenopathy and a characteristic inoculation eschar ('tache noire') at the bite site.[1] However, the main clinical signs vary depending on the rickettsial species involved and therefore may allow us to distinguish between the diseases. For example, African tick-bite fever is characterized by the occurrence of multiple inoculation eschars and grouped cases, due to the fact that numerous highly infected *Amblyomma* may attack and bite many people in several places at the same time.[4] In contrast, in cases of Mediterranean spotted fever due to *R. conorii*, a single eschar is usual because of the low likelihood of the tick biting people and a low rate of infection of the ticks. Details of each pathogen and clinical pictures are presented elsewhere (see Chapter 14).

Murine typhus

Murine typhus is a mild disease with non-specific signs. The incubation period is 7–14 days and at presentation the classic triad of fever, headache and skin rash is observed in less than 15% of cases. Later in the disease progression, fever and headache occur more frequently than rash. Rash is present in less than 50% of patients and is often transient or difficult to observe. Nausea, vomiting, abdominal pain, diarrhea, jaundice, confusion and seizures have also been reported.[1]

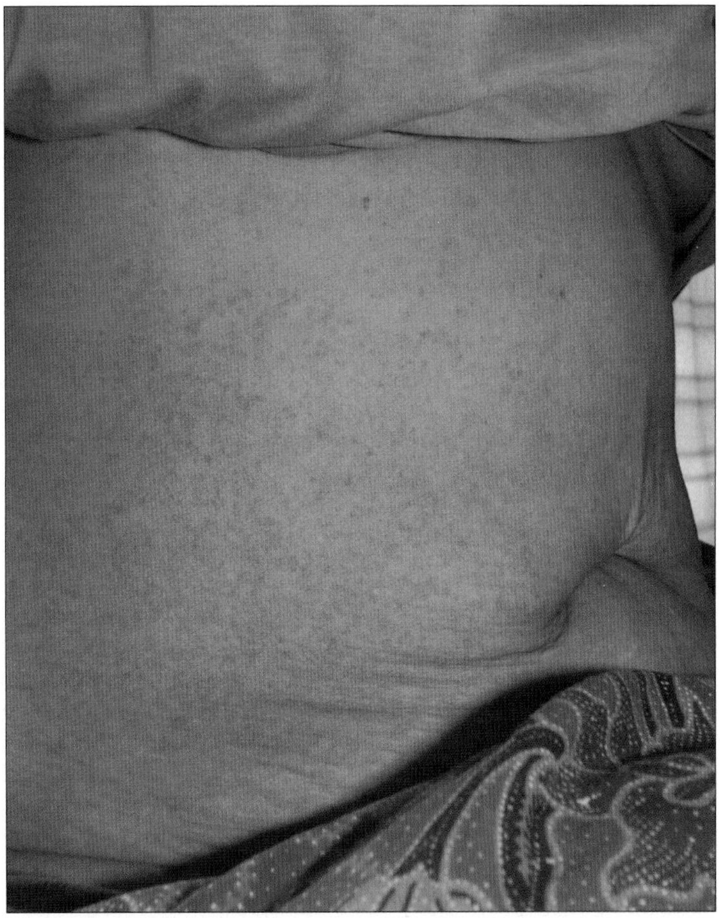

Fig. 179.1 Macular rash in a patient with scrub typhus.

Epidemic typhus

The incubation period is about 10–14 days. Patients develop malaise and vague symptoms before the abrupt onset of signs including fever (100%), headache (100%) and myalgia (70–100%). Other common

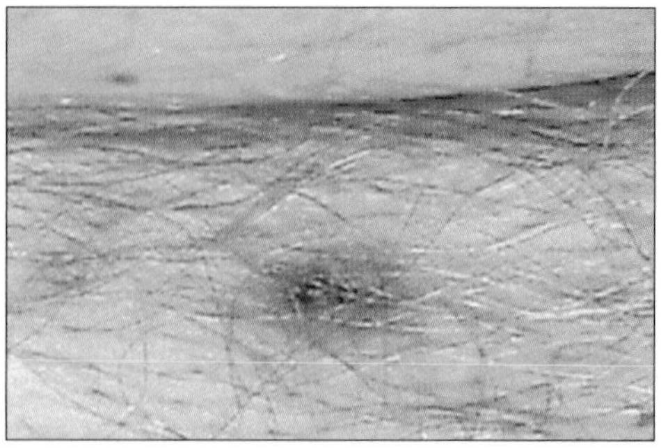

Fig. 179.2 Eschar at the bite site, a hallmark of rickettsial diseases.

signs include nausea or vomiting, coughing and neurologic involvement ranging from confusion to stupor and coma. Diarrhea, pulmonary involvement, myocarditis, splenomegaly and conjunctivitis may also occur. Most patients (20–80%) develop a skin rash that classically begins on the trunk of the body and spreads to the limbs. It may be macular, maculopapular or petechial and may be difficult to detect on darker skin tones. Epidemic typhus may be confused with typhoid. Recrudescence of epidemic typhus, also called Brill–Zinsser disease, can appear many years after the acute disease and has milder symptoms.[5]

Acute Q-fever

This disease is usually mild, with up to half of the infected people being asymptomatic. A self-limited febrile syndrome or 'pseudo-flu' occurs most frequently in symptomatic patients, but in more serious cases there might be hepatitis, pneumonitis and prolonged fever[2] (see Chapter 235).

INVESTIGATIONS

Routine laboratory investigation

Common non-specific laboratory abnormalities in rickettsioses include leukocyte count abnormalities, anemia and thrombocytopenia. Hyponatremia, hypoalbuminemia and hepatic and renal abnormalities may also occur.[3]

Serology

Serological tests are the most valuable tools in the diagnosis of rickettsioses.[1] The Weil–Felix test, the oldest serologic assay for rickettsioses, is based on the detection of antibodies to various *Proteus* antigens that cross-react with rickettsiae (*P. vulgaris* OX2 with spotted fever rickettsiae, *P. vulgaris* OX19 with typhus-group rickettsiae and *P. mirabilis* OXK with *O. tsutsugamushi*). Although it lacks both specificity and sensitivity, it is still used in many tropical countries. However, immunofluorescence is currently considered the reference method for the diagnosis of spotted fever group and typhus group. Cross-absorption of sera and Western blotting can be used to differentiate infections within rickettsial antigens when cross-reactions occur. For scrub typhus, the major surface protein antigen is the 56kDa protein including group-specific and strain-specific epitopes. However, several major serotypes (Karp, Kato, Gilliam, Kawasaki and Boryon) have been shown to present sufficient cross-reactivity with antigen from other strains to be used for serologic diagnosis. Immunofluorescence and immunoperoxidase assays are the most reliable serologic tools, but dot blot immunoassay and enzyme-linked immunosorbent assay tests have been developed and are commercially available. For Q-fever, the antigenic variation of *C. burnetii* is extremely useful to differentiate between the acute and chronic forms of the disease. Indeed, when isolated from animals or humans, *C. burnetii* expresses phase I antigen and is highly infectious. After subculture in the laboratory, there is an antigenic variation of *C. burnetii* to phase II form, which is less infectious. In acute Q-fever, antibodies to phase II antigens predominate and their titer is higher than the phase I antibody titer. On the other hand, in chronic forms of the disease, elevated anti-phase I antibodies are uniformly detected.

Culture

The growth of rickettsiae in reference laboratories requires living host cells (animal mouse models, embryonated eggs) or cell cultures (VERO, L929, HEL or MRC5 cells), as well as a P3 safety level laboratory. The centrifugation shell-vial technique using HEL fibroblasts is the reference method. Rickettsiae can be seen in tissue by Giemsa or Gimenez staining or by immunodetection methods.[1]

Molecular tools

Polymerase chain reaction and sequencing methods are useful, sensitive and rapid tools to detect and identify rickettsiae in blood and skin biopsies (the inoculation eschar being the most useful specimen).[1,2,4] Primers amplifying sequences of several genes can be used for typhus group and spotted fever group rickettsiae, including *OmpA, OmpB, gltA* and gene D. Polymerase chain reaction amplification and sequencing of the 56kDa protein gene of *O. tsutsugamushi* have also been developed. Q-fever can also be diagnosed by molecular tools. Arthropods may also be used as epidemiologic tools. For example, *R. prowazekii* was detected in lice collected from refugees in Burundi after having been sent to our laboratory in Marseille to confirm the presence of epidemic typhus.

COMPLICATIONS

Spotted fever group rickettsioses range from mild to severe and fatal diseases. For example, to date no mortalities or severe complications have been reported in patients with African tick-bite fever, whereas the mortality rate may be as high as 2.5% for Mediterranean spotted fever.[1,2,4]

Murine typhus is usually a mild disease, although severe forms requiring hospitalization have been reported. Signs in untreated patients last for 7–14 days after which there is usually a rapid return to health.

Epidemic typhus is a potentially fatal disease. Without treatment, mortality rates are 10–30% depending on the presence of other underlying conditions and the patient's nutritional state.[1]

Scrub typhus is a public health problem in Asia; about 1 million cases occur each year and 1 billion people may be exposed. The severity of the disease varies from asymptomatic to fatal (up to 30%), depending on the susceptibility of the host and/or the virulence of the strain.[3]

Chronic Q-fever represents the development of the acute disease in predisposed hosts. It may present as endocarditis in patients with underlying heart valve lesions or, more rarely, as vascular aneurysms, graft infections, chronic bone infections or pseudotumors of the lung.

MANAGEMENT

Empiric treatment of rickettsioses is started before laboratory confirmation of the diagnosis.

Unless contraindicated, doxycycline is the preferred treatment of scrub typhus and the usual adult oral dose is 100mg twice daily for 7 days. Tetracycline 500mg q6h for 7 days may also be used. Chloramphenicol is the common alternative to the tetracyclines. The usual adult dosage is 500mg q6h for 7 days or 50–75mg/kg/day in children. Based on preliminary studies, rifampin (1-week 600–900mg/day oral treatment) and azithromycin (500mg on the first day followed by 250mg daily for 2–4 more days) may be proposed as alternatives to doxycycline and chloramphenicol.

The treatment of choice for spotted fever rickettsioses is 200mg doxycycline/day for 1–7 days depending on the severity of the disease. In children and pregnant women, macrolides including josamycin (50mg/kg/day in children or 3g/day in adults) and roxythromycin, but not erythromycin, can be used for 8 days.

The treatment of choice for murine and epidemic typhus is a single 200mg dose of oral doxycycline usually leading to defervescence within 48–72 hours.

PREVENTION

There are no vaccines currently available for travelers against scrub typhus and other tropical rickettsioses. Thus prevention is mainly based on avoiding the arthropod bite.

Currently, the best method to avoid tick, flea and chigger bites comprises two components: topical DEET (N,N-diethyl-m-toluamide) repellent applied to exposed skin and treatment of clothing with permethrin, which kills arthropods on contact. These products are commercially available in a wide variety of formulas. Bites may also be limited by wearing long trousers that are tucked into boots. People staying in infested area should be advised to check their bodies routinely for the presence of arthropods. Any tick found attached should be removed immediately using blunt, rounded forceps.

In the case of epidemic typhus, louse eradication (e.g. in refugee camps) is the most important preventive measure and is essential in the control of outbreaks. Since body lice live only in clothing, the simplest method of delousing is to remove and then destroy or wash and boil all clothing. Dusting of all clothing with 10% DDT, 1% malathion or 1% permethrin is also a rapid and effective method of killing body lice and reduces the risk of re-infestation.

REFERENCES

1. Raoult D, Roux V. Rickettsioses as paradigms of new or emerging infectious diseases. Clin Microbiol Rev 1997;10:694–719.
2. Parola P, Raoult D. Ticks and tick-borne bacterial human diseases, an emerging infectious threat. Clin Infect Dis 2001;32:897–928. (Erratum: Clin Infect Dis 2001;33:749.)
3. Watt G, Kantipong P, Jongsakul K, Watcharapichat P, Phulsuksombati D, Strickman D. Doxycycline and rifampicin for mild scrub-typhus infections in northern Thailand: a randomised trial. Lancet 2000;356:1057–61.
4. Raoult D, Fournier PE, Fenollar F, *et al.* *Rickettsia africae*, a tick-borne pathogen in travelers to sub-Saharan Africa. N Engl J Med 2001;344:1504–10.
5. Raoult D, Roux V. The body louse as a vector of reemerging human diseases. Clin Infect Dis 1999;29:888–911.

chapter 180

Brucellosis

Finn T Black

EPIDEMIOLOGY

Brucellosis, also known as undulant fever or Malta fever, is a zoonosis caused by bacteria of the genus *Brucella*. The disease exists worldwide, with the highest prevalence in the Mediterranean countries, Asia, Africa and Central and South America. Around 500,000 new cases are reported annually worldwide, of which fewer than 100 are in the USA,[1] but brucellosis is probably underreported.

Brucellosis is transmitted to humans by direct contact with infected animals, by ingestion of unpasteurized milk or milk products, through cuts and abrasions or by inhalation of aerosols. In many European countries and in the USA it is mainly an occupational disease occuring in abattoir workers, butchers and farmers. Veterinary surgeons may become infected by accidental inoculation of live attenuated *Brucella* vaccine. Person–person transmission is extremely rare.

Four *Brucella* spp. can cause infection in humans:

- *Brucella melitensis*, which is found in goats, sheep and camels, is the most widespread and is the most virulent;
- *Brucella abortus*, which is found in cattle and camels, is less virulent;
- *Brucella suis*, which is found in pigs, is also less virulent; and
- *Brucella canis*, which is found in dogs, is the least common.

Other animals, including wildlife, may provide a reservoir for brucellae.[2]

PATHOGENESIS

Brucellae are facultative intracellular bacteria that are able to survive and multiply within mononuclear phagocytes. The mechanism is poorly understood but seems to include the suppression of degranulation of myeloperoxidase-containing granules, suppression of phagosome–lysosome fusion and production of protective enzymes.

The host reaction to brucellae is the formation of granulomas. *Brucella melitensis* and *B. suis* cause the most severe disease with caseating granulomas. Granulomas eventually heal with fibrosis and calcification.

Humoral antibodies seem to play some role in protection against reinfection. The control of the infection, however, depends on cell-mediated immunity.[2]

PREVENTION

The prevention of human brucellosis is dependent on the elimination of brucellosis in domestic animals. The use of veterinary vaccines for *B. abortus* and *B. melitensis* together with pasteurization of milk has resulted in a dramatic decrease in the incidence of human brucellosis. There is no effective vaccine available for *B. suis*. People at high risk of infection, such as veterinary surgeons and abattoir workers, should wear protective clothing. Laboratory-acquired brucellosis can be prevented by adherence to biosafety level 3 precautions. No effective vaccine is available for human use. Travelers to high endemic areas should be advised not to drink unpasteurized milk.

CLINICAL FEATURES

Brucellosis is a systemic infection that can involve any organ or organ system. The incubation period is normally between 2 and 4 weeks, but it may be months. The onset of clinical disease can be acute or insidious. Subclinical infection has been observed. Brucellosis is characterized by numerous somatic complaints in contrast to the few abnormal physical findings. Hepatosplenomegaly is present in 20–60%, depending on the species of *Brucella*, and mild lymphadenopathy is present in 10–20%. The non-specific symptoms (e.g. fever, sweats, anorexia, fatigue, myalgia, malaise, headache and depression) are common and may mimic diseases such as tuberculosis, toxoplasmosis, mononucleosis, hepatitis, systemic lupus erythematosus, typhoid and many others.

When symptoms related to a single organ or organ system are dominant it is often referred to as localized disease. The most common complications are listed in Table 180.1. The term 'chronic brucellosis' should be reserved for patients who have complaints of ill health for more than 12 months.[2] This includes patients who have relapsing illness or persisting focal infection and patients complaining of weakness, fatigue and depression, but with no objective signs of infection and no elevation of IgG antibody titer. This last group is believed to suffer from a psychoneurosis or a syndrome akin to chronic fatigue syndrome (see Chapter 94).

Complications

Osteoarticular complications

Osteoarticular complications affect 20–40% of patients. Sacroiliitis is the most common reported complication, especially when *B. melitensis* predominates.[3] The characteristic radiographic findings are blurring of articular margins and widening of the sacroiliac space. The clinical presentation is systemic symptoms and pain.

Spondylitis is most often seen in the lumbosacral region in elderly men, probably reflecting pre-existing anomalies in the spine, and it may be complicated by paraspinal abscesses (Fig. 180.1). The main symptoms are fever and vertebral pain. The typical radiographic findings are epiphysitis of vertebrae and narrowing of the intervertebral disc (Fig. 180.2). Bone scans and computerized tomography scans may detect infection earlier than radiography.[4]

Differential diagnosis includes tuberculosis, fungal and pyogenic osteomyelitis, multiple myeloma and metastatic carcinoma.

Arthritis especially involves the hips, knees and ankles.

Gastrointestinal complications

Up to 70% of patients have intestinal complaints such as anorexia, nausea, vomiting, abdominal pain, diarrhea or constipation. The liver is probably always involved, but liver function tests are usually only mildly abnormal. Cirrhosis does not seem to follow *Brucella* infection.

Pulmonary complications

Respiratory symptoms are reported in 15–25% of patients. They range from flu-like symptoms to bronchitis, interstitial pneumonitis, lung abscesses, hilar lympadenopathy and lung effusions.

COMMON COMPLICATIONS OF BRUCELLOSIS	
Organ system	**Patients (%)**
Cardiovascular	1–2
Endocarditis	0–2
Cutaneous	5–10
Gastrointestinal	50–70
Genitourinary	1–5
Orchitis	1–4
Neurologic	2–4
Osteoarticular	20–40
Sacroiliitis	10–15
Spondylitis	8–10
Pulmonary	15–25

Table 180.1 Common complications of brucellosis

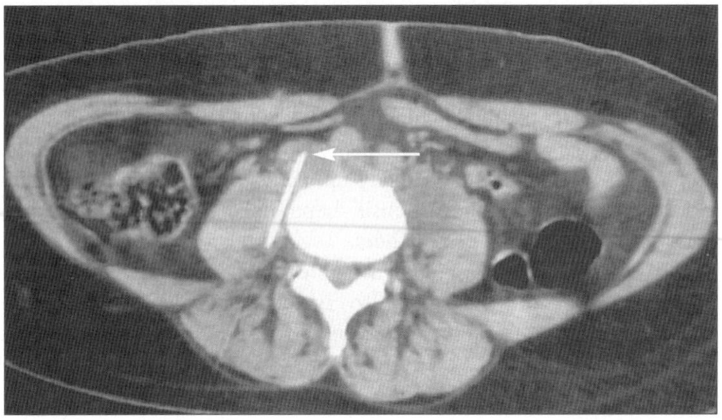

Fig. 180.1 CT scan of fine needle aspiration of paraspinal abscess (arrow) in a patient with brucellosis.

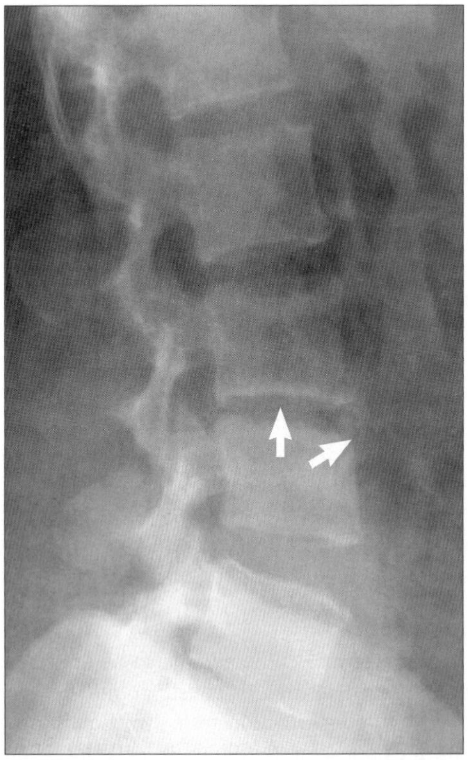

Fig. 180.2 Radiograph of the lumbar spine in a patient who has discitis and spondylitis of L_{3-4} caused by brucellosis. Note the reduced disc space and the destruction of the upper articular margins of L_4 (arrows).

Genitourinary complications

Complications from the genitourinary tract are rare. Acute orchitis or epididymo-orchitis with signs of systemic infection do occur and interstitial nephritis, glomerulonephritis and pyelonephritis resembling tuberculosis have been described. Brucellosis during pregnancy is rare but it can result in abortion like any other systemic infection.

Neurologic complications

Depression is a common complaint, but invasion of the central nervous system occurs in only 2–4% of cases. It usually presents as acute or chronic meningitis. Encephalitis, polyradiculopathy, psychosis and meningovascular complications have also been described.[5] Analysis of cerebrospinal fluid reveals elevated protein, lymphocytic pleocytosis, low to normal glucose and most often intraspinally produced specific antibodies. Brucellae are isolated from cerebrospinal fluid in less than 30% of patients.

Cardiovascular complications

Endocarditis, although rare, is the main cause of death related to brucellosis.[6] The aortic valve is involved more often than the mitral valve. Other complications include mycotic aneurysms, myocarditis and pericarditis.

Cutaneous involvement

Cutaneous manifestations of brucellosis consist mainly of transient non-specific lesions including erythema nodosum, petechiae, vasculitis, papules and rashes.

DIAGNOSIS

Because the symptoms of brucellosis are non-specific, it is crucial that the attending physician anticipate the probability of the disease. A certain diagnosis of brucellosis is made when brucellae are isolated from blood, bone marrow or other body fluids or tissues. Most laboratories employ rapid isolation methods for blood cultures. However, these cultures need to be maintained for up to 30–40 days to successfully isolate *Brucella* spp. Bone marrow cultures are more sensitive than blood cultures in acute brucellosis and tend to remain positive later in the course of the infection, even during antimicrobial treatment.

The serum agglutination test is the simplest, best standardized and most widely used test.[8] It measures both IgG and IgM antibodies; IgM antibodies are removed by pretreating the serum with 2-mercaptoethanol. Antibodies to *Vibrio cholerae, Francisella tularensis* and *Yersinia enterocolitica* can give false-positive reactions. False-negative reactions due to blocking antibodies are seen and dilutions of 1:640 should be made. A titer >1:160 is normally considered positive, as is a 4-fold or greater rise in titer.

Most patients who have acute infection develop IgM and IgG antibodies. The IgG antibodies persist as long as the infection is active and they increase with relapse and decrease with cure. The enzyme-linked immunosorbent assay appears to be more sensitive than and as specific as the serum agglutination test. It is rapid, easy to perform and can be automated.[9] The polymerase chain reaction has also been shown to be a very sensitive and specific rapid diagnostic test.[7]

MANAGEMENT

Doxycycline is the most effective single drug for treatment of brucellosis because of its excellent activity against brucellae, its penetration into cells and its passage over the blood–brain barrier.[10] Because of the high relapse rate (5–40%) with single drug therapy, a combination of two or three drugs is usually recommended. Uncomplicated brucellosis is treated with oral doxycycline 200mg q24h plus oral rifampin (rifampicin) 600–900mg q24h for 3–6 weeks. An alterna-tive is oral doxycycline for 3–6 weeks plus an intramuscular amino-glycoside (e.g. streptomycin 1g q12h or gentamicin 240mg q24h) for 2–3 weeks. Children less than 8 years of age and pregnant women should not be treated with doxycycline.

Instead, oral trimethoprim–sulfamethoxazole can be used (20mg/kg sulfamethoxazole and 4mg/kg trimethoprim q12h in children for 3–6 weeks, 800mg sulfamethoxazole and 160mg trimethoprim q12h in adults for 3–6 weeks) plus intramuscular gentamicin (5mg/kg q24h in children for 1 week and 240mg q24h in adults for 1 week). Gentamicin can be replaced by oral rifampin (10–20mg/kg q24h in children for 3–6 weeks, 600mg q24h in adults for 3–6 weeks).

Complications

Complications of brucellosis such as meningitis and endocarditis require longer courses of therapy, directed by the response.[2] In severe cases, a combination of three agents is often recommended (e.g. doxycycline and aminoglycoside plus rifampin or trimethoprim–sulfamethoxazole and aminoglycoside plus rifampin). Endocarditis often requires additional surgical intervention.[6]

Many other antimicrobial agents have shown in-vitro activity against *Brucella* spp., including fluoroquinolones, third-generation cephalosporins and azithromycin. However, when these drugs are administered alone the relapse rates are unacceptable and they should be kept as second-line drugs until further studies have been carried out.

With chemotherapy the overall mortality rate is less than 2%.

REFERENCES

1. Centers for Disease Control and Prevention. Summary of notifiable diseases, United States, 1995. MMWR Morb Mortal Wkly Rep 1995;44:53.
2. Young EJ. An overview of human brucellosis. Clin Infect Dis 1995;21:238–90.
3. Ariza J, Pujol M, Valverde J, *et al.* Brucellar sacroiliitis: findings in 63 episodes and current relevance. Clin Infect Dis 1993;16:761–5.
4. Ariza J, Gudiol F, Valverde J, *et al.* Brucellar spondylitis: a detailed analysis based on current findings. Rev Infect Dis 1985;7:656–64.
5. McLean DR, Russel N, Khan MY. Neurobrucellosis: clinical and therapeutic features. Clin Infect Dis 1992;15:582–90.
6. Jacobs F, Abramowicz D, Vereerstraeten P, Le Clerc JL, Zech F, Thys JP. Brucella endocarditis: the role of combined medical and surgical treatment. Rev Infect Dis 1990;12:740–4.
7. Zerva L, Bourantas K, Mitka S, Kansouzidou A, Legakis NJ. Serum is the preferred clinical specimen for diagnosis of human brucellosis. J Clin Microbiol 2001;39:1661–4.
8. Young EJ. Serologic diagnosis of human brucellosis: analysis of 214 cases by agglutination tests and review of the literature. Rev Infect Dis 1991;13:359–72.
9. Osoba AO, Balkhy H, Memish Z, *et al.* Diagnostic value of Brucella ELISA IgG and IgM in bacteremic and non-bacteremic patients with brucellosis. J Chemother 2001;1(Suppl.):54–9.
10. Hall WH. Modern chemotherapy for brucellosis in humans. Rev Infect Dis 1990;12:1066–99.

chapter

181 Leptospirosis

Charles N Edwards

EPIDEMIOLOGY

Leptospirosis is caused by pathogenic serovars of *Leptospira*, of which 17 species are now recognized, defined by DNA–DNA hybridization. The disease is maintained in nature by chronic renal infection of mammals and is probably the most widespread zoonosis.[1] Human infection follows exposure to infected animals, either directly or indirectly through contaminated soil and water. Leptospires survive for days or weeks in warm, damp, slightly alkaline conditions, especially in still or slowly moving fresh water in the temperate summer and in damp soil and water in the tropics, especially in the rainy season.

Over 230 serovars of leptospires are recognized – the most ubiquitous serovars and their reservoir are *icterohaemorrhagiae*, usually derived from rats (*Rattus norvegicus*), and a number of serovars associated with domestic livestock animals, such as *hardjo* (cattle) and *pomona* (pigs). Other serovars are more restricted in their distribution, such as *lai*, which causes most cases of human infection in China and the Korean peninsula.

In temperate climates, leptospirosis is acquired mainly through recreational or occupational exposure, but in tropical regions exposure through avocational activities is more widespread.[2] Leptospirosis is an important cause of febrile illness in tourists returning from the tropics, particularly those involved in adventure tourism.[3] The reported incidence of leptospirosis in developed countries is declining and the disease is no longer reportable in the USA. The burden of disease is greatly underestimated in the tropical developing world.

PATHOGENESIS AND PATHOLOGY

Leptospires gain access to the circulation through penetration of abraded skin or intact mucous membranes, disseminate and ultimately penetrate various tissues. This action results in a systemic illness with a wide spectrum of clinical features. A systemic vasculitis with endothelial injury is the basic microscopic finding in the disease. Damaged endothelial cells usually show varying degrees of swelling, denudation and necrosis. Leptospires have been documented in large- and medium-sized blood vessels and capillaries in various organs. The major affected organs are:

- the kidneys, with a diffuse tubulointerstitial inflammation and tubular necrosis;
- the lungs, usually congested, with focal or massive intra-alveolar hemorrhage; and
- the liver, which shows cholestasis associated with mild degenerative changes in hepatocytes.

Whether a direct toxic effect of the leptospires or immune complex deposition causes the vascular injury is unclear. Production of humoral antibodies (IgM in the second and third weeks, IgG later) produces inflammatory responses such as meningoencephalitis and anterior uveitis. During recovery leptospires continue to be excreted in the urine for some days.

PREVENTION

Prevention measures are based upon an awareness of the epidemiology of disease occurring in a region.

Rodent control should be attempted where appropriate and feasible. Occupational protective clothing is effective in groups at risk. In some high-risk groups (e.g. soldiers on jungle maneuvers), oral chemoprophylaxis with doxycycline 200mg weekly is effective,[4] but there have been few attempts to use this approach on a large scale, such as after massive flooding.

Vaccines for human use are licensed in France, China, Japan and Cuba.[5] The large number of serovars makes general protection of human populations by immunization almost impossible. Vaccines for use in dogs and livestock animals historically have been unable to prevent renal infection and thus the reservoir state, and generally have not generated lasting immunity to acute infection. A new generation of vaccines for use in cattle appears to stimulate a cell-mediated immune response and overcomes the limitations of earlier vaccines.[6]

CLINICAL FEATURES

Humans become ill 7–12 days after exposure to leptospires. The majority of patients (90%) experience a mild febrile illness while a minority (10%) have a severe illness called Weil's syndrome. A biphasic course of illness can be seen in all patients. The first or septicemic phase is characterized by a sudden onset of fever, retro-orbital headache, chills, myalgias classically involving the paraspinal, calf and abdominal muscles, conjunctival suffusion (Fig. 181.1), vomiting, prostration and a skin rash, which may be maculopapular or purpuric. Defervescence of fever occurs after 5–7 days in this phase.

The second or immune phase is characterized by the appearance of IgM antibodies. Symptoms recur and signs of meningitis may develop in up to 50% of cases. In severe cases, fever may persist and be associated with renal insufficiency or failure, pulmonary hemorrhage, varying levels of jaundice and myocarditis. Death, occurring in 10–15% of these severe cases, is thought to be due to pulmonary hemorrhage or cardiac failure and arrhythmias secondary to myocarditis. Chest radiographs may reveal numerous abnormalities including segmental opacities or a diffuse pneumonitis.

Clinical laboratory investigations reveal red and white cells in the urine with albuminuria. An elevated white cell count, thrombocytopenia and a high creatinine phosphokinase are commonly observed. When the bilirubin is elevated, the transaminases are only mildly elevated.

The differential diagnosis of leptospirosis includes dengue fever, malaria, influenza and several other acute febrile illnesses depending on the geographic location.

DIAGNOSIS

Because of the broad spectrum of symptoms and the wide differential diagnosis, a high index of clinical suspicion is required if appropriate diagnostic tests are to be made.[7] During the first week of

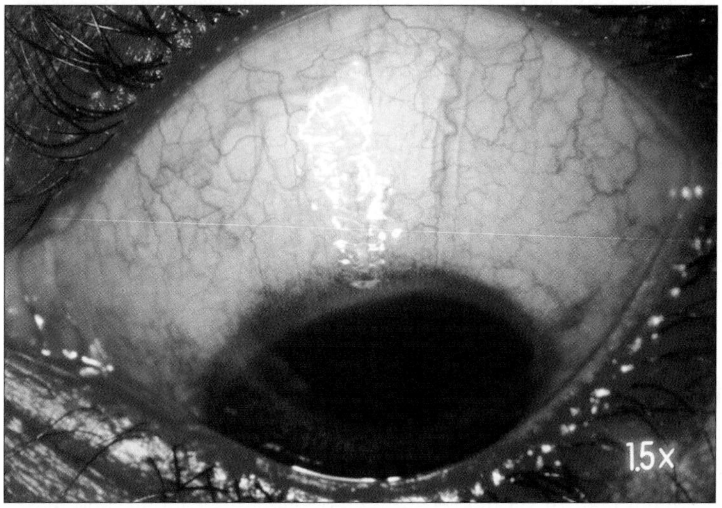

Fig. 181.1 Conjunctival suffusion and jaundice.

illness leptospiremia occurs, while in the second week leptospires are excreted in urine and are found in the cerebrospinal fluid of patients with meningitis. Isolation of the organism requires special media and may take several weeks of incubation, and thus does not contribute to individual patient diagnosis. Detection of leptospiral DNA by polymerase chain reaction is more sensitive than culture, but has yet to be optimized.

A strong IgM antibody response, which appears about 5–7 days after onset of symptoms, may be detected using several commercial assays. The microscopic agglutination test is a complex assay that detects antibodies against live antigen suspensions and is performed only in reference laboratories. Diagnosis using this assay requires paired acute and convalescent sera. This test yields information about the presumptive infecting serogroup and thus has epidemiologic value. In endemic areas, single elevated titers must be interpreted with caution because antibodies persist for years after acute infection.

Direct microscopic examination of clinical samples is of little value, but immunohistochemical staining of autopsy specimens is a valuable diagnostic tool.[8]

MANAGEMENT

Patients with mild or anicteric disease usually get better without treatment. Doxycyline 100mg daily has been shown to shorten the duration of the illness.[9] Hospitalization is recommended for severe cases. Excellent supportive care with particular attention to fluid and electrolyte balance and pulmonary and cardiac function is critical. Renal failure should be treated by peritoneal or hemodialysis. Until the efficacy of antibiotics in this severe illness is resolved, patients should be treated with intravenous penicillin G (benzylpenicillin)[10] or cefotaxime.

REFERENCES

1. World Health Organization. Leptospirosis worldwide, 1999. Wkly Epidemiol Rec 1999;74:237–42.
2. Levett PN. Leptospirosis: re-emerging or re-discovered disease? J Med Microbiol 1999;48:417–18.
3. Haake DA, Dundoo M, Cader R, *et al.* Leptospirosis, water sports, and chemoprophylaxis. Clin Infect Dis 2002;34:e40–3.
4. Takafuji ET, Kirkpatrick JW, Miller RN, *et al.* An efficacy trial of doxycycline chemoprophylaxis against leptospirosis. N Engl J Med 1984;310:497–500.
5. Martínez Sánchez R, Pérez Sierra A, Baró Suárez M, *et al.* Evaluación de la efectividad de una nueva vacuna contra la leptospirosis human en grupos en riesgo [Evaluation of the effectiveness of a new vaccine against human leptospirosis in groups at risk]. Rev Panam Salud Publica 2000;8:385–92.
6. Naiman BM, Alt D, Bolin CA, Zuerner R, Baldwin CL. Protective killed *Leptospira borgpetersenii* vaccine induces potent Th1 immunity comprising responses by CD4 and gammadelta T lymphocytes. Infect Immun 2001;69:7550–8.
7. Levett PN. Leptospirosis. Clin Microbiol Rev 2001;14:296–326.
8. Zaki SR, Spiegel RA. Leptospirosis. In: Nelson AM, Horsburgh CR, eds. Pathology of Emerging Infections 2. Washington DC: American Society for Microbiology; 1998:73–92.
9. McClain JBL, Ballou WR, Harrison SM, Steinweg DL. Doxycycline therapy for leptospirosis. Ann Intern Med 1984;100:696–8.
10. Edwards CN, Nicholson GD, Hassell TA, Everard COR, Callender J. Penicillin therapy in icteric leptospirosis. Am J Trop Med Hyg 1988;39:388–90.

chapter
182 Relapsing Fever

David A Warrell & Eldryd HO Parry

INTRODUCTION

Repeated abrupt episodes of fever, separated by afebrile periods, give relapsing fever its name. There are two forms:

- tick-borne relapsing fever, caused by various *Borrelia* spp.; and
- louse-borne relapsing fever, caused by *Borrelia recurrentis*.

The two diseases differ in their epidemiology, clinical features and management (see Chapter 230).

EPIDEMIOLOGY

The epidemiology of the relapsing fevers has been considered in a number of studies.[1]

Tick-borne relapsing fever

Borrelia–*tick complex*

Different species of soft ticks of the genus *Ornithodoros* (Argasidae) and of *Borrelia* spirochetes are involved in different parts of the world:

- in central and western USA and Mexico, *Ornithodoros hermsi, Ornithodoros parkeri* and *Ornithodoros turicata* with *Borrelia hermsi, Borrelia parkeri* and *Borrelia turicatae*;
- in Central and South America (chiefly in Colombia and Venezuela, with a focus around northern Argentina, Bolivia and Paraguay), *Ornithodoros rudis* (*O. venezuelensis*) with *Borrelia venezuelensis*;
- in east, central and southern Africa, *Borrelia duttonii* with the *Ornithodoros moubata* complex;
- in Senegal and some other parts of north and east Africa and the Middle East, *Borrelia crocidurae* with *Ornithodoros sonrae* (*O. erraticus* small form);
- in the Middle East, Iran and a belt stretching eastward through Uzbekistan and other countries of the former Soviet Union to western China, *Borrelia persica* with *Ornithodoros tholozani* (*O. pappilipes*); and
- in north Africa and the Iberian peninsula, *Borrelia hispanica* with *Ornithodoros erraticus*.

The soft tick vectors are found in dry savanna areas and scrub, particularly rodent burrows, caves, piles of timber and dead trees, or in the roof spaces and beneath the floors of log cabins – anywhere that small rodents can establish their nests. Unlike louse-borne relapsing fever, tick-borne relapsing fever is a zoonosis, except for *B. duttonii* infection, which is transmitted only between humans. The vertebrate reservoir, which varies with the ecology of the area, may be various species of rodent (rats, gerbils, mice, squirrels, chipmunks) or even dogs and some birds. Ticks become infected when they feed on an infected animal (or human) and in turn they infect the next host either by a bite, when infected saliva is injected, or perhaps when infected coxal fluid contaminates mucosal membranes.

Humans are accidentally infected when they are in contact with infected ticks. In eastern Africa, humans have displaced rodents and have become the reservoir for the *O. moubata–B. duttonii* complex. This also occurs in Senegal.[2] A tick remains infected for life and can survive prolonged starvation. The female can transmit the spirochete transovarially to its offspring, so that the infection is enzootic among ticks and awaits the reservoir animal or human to infect. Borrelias are not found in tick feces.

Tick-borne relapsing fever is endemic in most continents except Australasia and the Pacific region. In western Senegal, a recent survey revealed a prevalence of 1% among children.[2] At one health center in Rwanda, 1650 proven cases are treated each year (6% of all patients) and the disease is prevalent in the Dodoma region of Tanzania.

Louse-borne relapsing fever

This classic epidemic disease of armies, refugees and immigrants remains endemic in the highlands of Ethiopia and adjacent countries, hilly areas of Yemen and some parts of the Peruvian and Bolivian Andes.[3] The human body louse, *Pediculus humanus*,[4] and head louse, *Pediculus capitis*, are obligate blood-sucking ectoparasites that ingest borrelias when they feed on humans and then transmit the organism when they are crushed against broken skin or rubbed on a mucous membrane such as the conjunctiva, so that spirochetes in their celomic fluid enter the person's blood. Unlike ticks, lice cannot infect their progeny. Humans are the only reservoirs of this infection.

Louse-borne relapsing fever thrives where people are crowded and poor, where a cold, wet climate (as in the highlands of Ethiopia) encourages them to wear clothes that harbor lice, where water for washing may be scarce and where agents to kill lice are unavailable. The clothes of an infected person teem with lice, particularly around the waist and the buttocks, and lice move from person to person. In the highlands of Ethiopia, the disease flares up in the rainy season because people are crowded and cold. The prevalence of lice is higher during the rainy season but the prevalence of lice in the communities where louse-borne relapsing fever is endemic is high and constant, and it is linearly related to the intensity of infection in an individual person. Rarely, relapsing fevers are diagnosed in travelers who have returned from endemic areas, in intravenous drug users and in recipients of blood transfusions.

PATHOGENESIS

Relapses are due to fresh antigenic variants of borrelias. Extra chromosomal DNA in linear plasmids recombines to activate the genes that control variable major protein synthesis.[5] Experimentally, spirochetes persist in the brain or eye in immunodeficient animals even though they are apparently cleared from the peripheral blood.[6]

PREVENTION

Tick-borne relapsing fever can be prevented if ticks are suppressed, if rodents are controlled and if travelers avoid sleeping in places where ticks or their rodent reservoir could be abundant, such as poorly maintained log cabins. Rodent-proofing of such cabins is feasible in some places, such as the North Rim of the Grand Canyon.[7] There are sporadic cases in travelers in the Middle East, Africa and Europe, and small outbreaks in the USA (e.g. Browne Mountain, the Grand

Canyon) during the vacation season or among those who have worked or stayed in caves, but the risk of transmission of borrelias from an infected tick to humans is not high. Ticks can be eliminated with pyrethroids, benzene hexachloride, malathion or dichlorodiphenyltrichloroethane (DDT).

Prevention of louse-borne relapsing fever depends on breaking transmission from louse to the susceptible population, and this can only be achieved by eradicating the body louse. Infected clothing should be washed and treated with chlorine bleach and an insecticide. The lice are abundant in hair, which must be shaved off or washed and treated too. This is better than giving tetracycline to people at risk of relapsing fever.[8]

CLINICAL FEATURES

Tick-borne relapsing fever

The bite of the tick is painless and produces no eschar. Therefore, it may not be noticed. An incubation period of 3–18 days follows, long enough that potential exposure may be forgotten.

The first symptoms are explosive: fever, headache, muscle and joint pains, extreme fatigue with prostration and drenching episodes of sweating.[9] Epistaxis, abdominal pain, diarrhea and cough may follow. In 5–10% of patients neurologic symptoms and signs, which are the most important clinical problem, manifest as a wide range of focal deficits and are typically transient. They include paresthesias, cranial nerve palsies (especially VII) and visual symptoms, and hemiparesis or paraparesis. Meningeal symptoms, which are usually accompanied by a lymphocytic pleocytosis, are rare. Various erythematous rashes and petechiae may also be seen. The density of spirochetemia governs the clinical severity. Symptoms abate after a few days – the duration depends on the severity of the initial episode – only to recur about 7–15 days later. As many as eight relapses may occur, but they become steadily less severe. Few cases remain undiagnosed for so long. Pregnancy is interrupted in up to a third of cases.

Louse-borne relapsing fever

There is a very wide range of clinical features, from a mild and insignificant fever to a disease that affects many systems in a critically ill person.[1] Typically, after an incubation period of 4–17 (average 7) days, the first symptoms are fever, chills, headache, muscle and body aches, fatigue, dizziness, anorexia and nightmares. Then, in at least 50% of patients, there is evidence of bleeding, commonly manifest as epistaxis, subconjunctival hemorrhage (Fig. 182.1) and petechial hemorrhages, especially on the trunk. An enlarged and tender liver, often with an enlarged spleen, is palpable in as many as 50% of cases in some outbreaks, and about half of these are jaundiced. The respiratory system is affected in about 15% of cases. Cough may indicate pneumonia but it may also precede clinical pulmonary edema. Rarely, there are manifestations of adult respiratory distress syndrome.

Transient myocardial damage may lead to pulmonary edema, which is an additional hazard during treatment. Neurologic and meningeal signs, transient focal deficits and, ominously, a confusional state and coma are less common than in tick-borne relapsing fever. Fetal loss is very common in pregnant women.

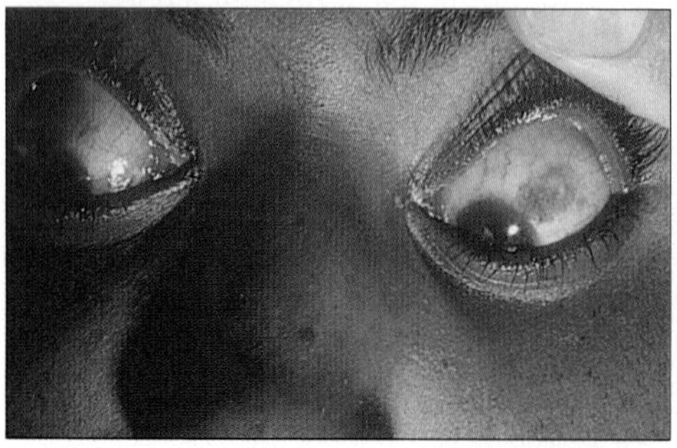

Fig. 182.1 Ethiopian patient who has louse-borne relapsing fever 4 days after the start of febrile symptoms, showing subconjunctival hemorrhages and jaundice.

Spontaneous crisis and Jarisch–Herxheimer reaction

The clinical course of relapsing fever, especially louse-borne relapsing fever, is usually terminated either by a mild 'spontaneous crisis' on about day 5 of the untreated illness or by a Jarisch–Herxheimer reaction. This much more severe reaction is induced by, and follows 1–3 hours after, antimicrobial treatment.[1,10] The patient becomes restless 1–3 hours after treatment. Frank rigors may develop and the temperature, respiratory rate, pulse rate and blood pressure increase rapidly. There may be associated vomiting, diarrhea, coughing, musculoskeletal pains and delirium, and some patients die of hyperpyrexia at the height of the fever. During the ensuing flush phase of this endotoxin-like reaction, there is profuse sweating, intense vasodilatation with a fall in mean arterial pressure and a slow decline in temperature over the next 6–12 hours. Fatalities during this phase are due to hypovolemic shock or acute pulmonary edema resulting from myocarditis. The incidence of Jarisch–Herxheimer reactions varies from 30% to almost 100% in different published reports.

A borrelial pyrogen, an outer membrane variable major lipoprotein[11,12] released by the action of antimicrobial agents, stimulates an explosive release of cytokines from macrophages through NF-κB,[13] principally tumor necrosis factor (TNF)-α, interleukin (IL)-6, IL-8 and IL-1β, just before the start of the clinical manifestations of the Jarisch–Herxheimer reaction (Fig. 182.2).[14] The reaction is unaffected by corticosteroids, is delayed by meptazinol (an opiate agonist–antagonist) and can be prevented by a polyclonal antibody against TNF if this is given just before antimicrobial treatment.[15]

LABORATORY FINDINGS

Spirochete density in peripheral blood may exceed 500,000/mm³. There is a peripheral neutrophil leukocytosis but, during the

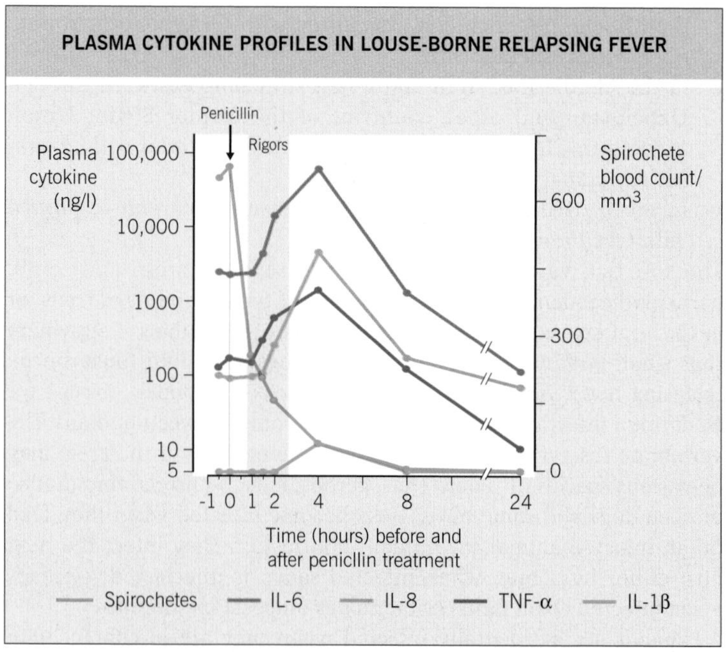

Fig. 182.2 Plasma cytokine profiles in louse-borne relapsing fever. These profiles are from an Ethiopian patient treated with penicillin (at time 0 on the horizontal axis). There is a sharp increase in (TNF)-α, IL-6 and IL-8 concentrations at the start of the phase of violent rigors.

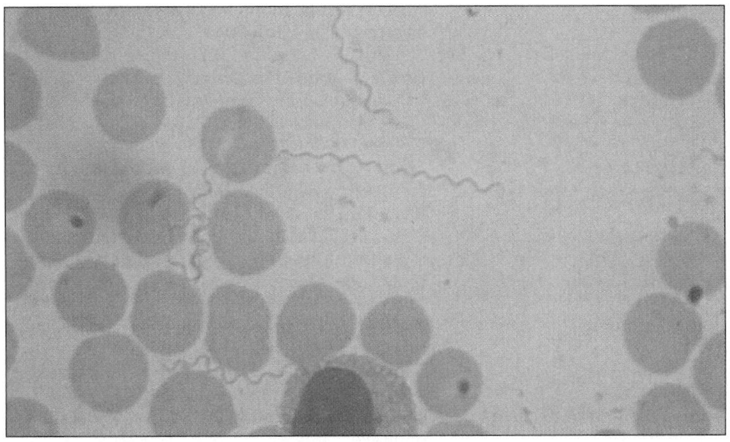

Fig. 182.3 Thin blood smear from an Ethiopian patient who has louse-borne relapsing fever (Giemsa stain), showing numerous spirochetes.

Jarisch–Herxheimer reaction or spontaneous crisis, there is a transient profound fall in leukocyte count. Thrombocytopenia is common and there is a coagulopathy attributable partly to hepatic dysfunction and partly to disseminated intravascular coagulation with increased fibrinolytic activity. Biochemical evidence of hepatocellular damage is found in most patients.[1] A few patients show transient, mild renal impairment. A mild neutrophil–lymphocyte pleocytosis has been described.

DIAGNOSIS

If the patient has an acute fever and has traveled in the tropics, it is essential to do a blood film to look for malarial parasites. This may also reveal the spirochetes of tick-borne relapsing fever, which will be recognized in a thin or thick blood film (Fig. 182.3). In suspected tick-borne relapsing fever, the spirochetes must be searched for repeatedly; in louse-borne relapsing fever the higher and more persistent spirochetemia is more easily detected. In suspected cases of tick-borne relapsing fever, blood must be taken at the height of a relapse because it is unlikely to reveal borrelias between relapses.

The serologic response in tick-borne relapsing fever may be helpful but *Borrelia burgdorferi*, the organism responsible for Lyme disease, leads to production of antibodies, mainly to 41kDa and 60kDa antigens, which cross-react with the antiborrelial immunoglobulins of tick-borne relapsing fever. This is due to conserved antigenic epitopes expressed by borrelias.[16,17] Both *B. duttonii* and *B. recurrentis* have been cultivated in vitro.[18]

In the clinical diagnosis of a traveler at risk, two less common causes of episodic recurrent fever are possible: trench fever (caused by *Bartonella quintana*) if the traveler might have been in contact with the body louse, or rat-bite fever (caused by *Spirillum minus*).

The differential diagnosis of a febrile patient with jaundice, petechial rash, spontaneous systemic bleeding and hepatosplenomegaly includes, apart from relapsing fevers, falciparum malaria, yellow fever and other viral hemorrhagic fevers (such as Rift Valley fever in the Horn of Africa), viral hepatitis, rickettsial infections, especially louse-borne typhus, which has the same epidemiologic predispositions as louse-borne relapsing fever, and leptospirosis. Secondary infections, known to complicate louse-borne relapsing fever, include bacillary dysentery, salmonellosis, typhoid, typhus, malaria and tuberculosis.

PROGNOSIS

Reported case fatalities during epidemics have exceeded 40% but this can be reduced to less than 5% with antimicrobial treatment, provided that appropriate ancillary treatment is given during the life-threatening Jarisch–Herxheimer reaction. Deaths during relapses are most unusual and occur only in tick-borne relapsing fever.

MANAGEMENT

The principles of treatment are:

- to eliminate spirochetemia and prevent relapses, using antibiotics;
- to monitor the patient very carefully through the Jarisch–Herxheimer reaction; and
- to restore and maintain circulating volume during the 24 hours after starting antibiotic treatment.

Antibiotic agents

The choice of agents is based on clinical experience.[19]

Tick-borne relapsing fever

Doxycycline 100mg per day for 10 days is recommended for adults. For pregnant women and young children, erythromycin can be used.

Louse-borne relapsing fever

A single 500mg oral dose of tetracycline or erythromycin stearate is effective. In severely ill patients who are likely to vomit, effective parenteral treatment consists of either a single intravenous dose of tetracycline hydrochloride (250mg)[20] or, for pregnant women and children, a single intravenous dose of erythromycin lactobionate (300mg for adults, 10mg/kg for children). In mixed epidemics of louse-borne relapsing fever and louse-borne typhus, a single oral dose of doxycycline 100mg has proved effective. Penicillins and chloramphenicol are also effective.[20]

Supportive treatment

Postural hypotension and cardiac arrhythmias are prevented by nursing the patient flat in bed for 24 hours after antibiotic treatment. Hyperpyrexia and hypovolemia must be prevented. Acute heart failure with pulmonary edema responds to intravenous furosemide (frusemide) and digoxin. Bleeding and clotting problems are treated with vitamin K, platelets and clotting factor concentrates. Complicating infections, notably typhoid, salmonellosis, bacillary dysentery, tuberculosis, malaria and typhus in some endemic situations, must be treated appropriately.

REFERENCES

1. Bryceson ADM, Parry EHO, Perine PL, *et al.* Louse-borne relapsing fever: a clinical and laboratory study of 62 cases in Ethiopia and a reconsideration of the literature. Q J Med 1970;39:129–70.
2. Trape JF, Duplanter JM, Bouganali H, *et al.* Tick borne borreliosis in West Africa. Lancet 1991;337:473–5.
3. Raoult D, Birtles RJ, Montoya M, *et al.* Survey of three bacterial louse-associated diseases among rural Andean communities in Peru: prevalence of epidemic typhus, trench fever and relapsing fever. Clin Infect Dis 1999;29:434–6.
4. Raoult D, Roux V. The body louse as a vector of re-emerging human diseases. Clin Infect Dis 1999;29:888–911.
5. Barbour AG. Antigenic variation of a relapsing fever *Borrelia* species. Ann Rev Microbiol 1990;44:155–71.
6. Cadavid D, Bundoc V, Barbour AG. Experimental infection of the mouse brain by a relapsing fever *Borrelia* species: a molecular analysis. J Infect Dis 1993;168:143–51.
7. Paul WS, Maupin G, Scott-Wright AO, Craven RB, Dennis DT. Outbreak of tick-borne relapsing fever at the north rim of the Grand Canyon: evidence for effectiveness of preventive measures. Am J Trop Med Hyg 2002;66:71–5.

8. Sundnes KO, Haimanot AT. Epidemic of louse-borne relapsing fever in Ethiopia. Lancet 1993;342:1213–5.
9. Dworkin MS, Schwan TG, Anderson DE. Tick-borne relapsing fever in North America. Med Clin North Am 2002;86:417–33.
10. Warrell DA, Pope HM, Parry EHO, Perine PL, Bryceson ADM. Cardiorespiratory disturbance associated with infective fever in man: studies of Ethiopian louse-borne relapsing fever. Clin Sci 1970;39:123–45.
11. Vidal V, Scragg IG, Cutler SJ, *et al.* Variable major lipoprotein is a principal TNF-inducing factor of louse-borne relapsing fever: comparison of tetracycline and slow-release penicillin. J Infect Dis 1998;147:898–909.
12. Scragg IG, Kwiatkowski D, Vidal V, *et al.* Structural characterization of the inflammatory moiety of a variable major lipoprotein of *Borrelia recurrentis*. J Biol Chem 2000;275:937–41.
13. Udalova IA, Vidal V, Scragg IG, Kwiatkowski D. Direct evidence for involvement of NF-κB in transcriptional activation of tumor necrosis factor by a spirochetal lipoprotein. Infect Immun 2000;68:5447–9.
14. Negussie Y, Remick DG, De Forge LE, *et al.* Detection of plasma tumor necrosis factor, interleukin 6 and 8 during the Jarisch–Herxheimer reaction of relapsing fever. J Exp Med 1992;175:1207–12.
15. Fekade D, Knox K, Hussein K, *et al.* Prevention of Jarisch–Herxheimer reactions by treatment with antibodies against tumor necrosis factor a. N Engl J Med 1996;335:311–5.
16. Schwan TG, Gage KL, Karstens RH, *et al.* Identification of the tick-borne relapsing fever spirochete *Borrelia hermsii* by using a species-specific monoclonal antibody. J Clin Microbiol 1992;30:790–5.
17. Schwan TG, Schrumpf ME, Hinnebusch BJ, *et al.* GlpQ: an antigen for serological discrimination between relapsing fever and Lyme borreliosis. J Clin Microbiol 1996;34:2483–92.
18. Cutler SJ, Akintunde CO, Moss J, *et al.* Successful *in-vitro* cultivation of *Borrelia duttonii* and its comparison with *Borrelia recurrentis*. Int J Syst Bacteriol 1994;49:1793–9.
19. Perine PL, Teklu B. Antibiotic treatment of louse-borne relapsing fever in Ethiopia: a report of 377 cases. Am J Trop Med Hyg 1983;32:1096–100.
20. Warrell DA, Perine PL, Krause DW, Bing DH, MacDougal SJ. Pathophysiology and immunology of the Jarisch–Herxheimer-like reaction in louse-borne relapsing fever: comparison of tetracycline and slow-release penicillin. J Infect Dis 1983;147:898–909.

chapter 183

Viral Hemorrhagic Fevers

Joseph B McCormick

INTRODUCTION

Viral hemorrhagic fevers (VHFs) are endemic in every continent with the possible exception of Australia. The diseases are characterized by an acute onset and high fever, and in some cases, a high mortality rate. The bleeding by which they are known is a complication of severe disease, but the underlying pathology is a leaky capillary syndrome with prominent pulmonary edema. Death, when it occurs, is usually due to hypovolemic shock with or without adult respiratory distress syndrome (ARDS).

VIROLOGY AND NATURAL HISTORY

These diseases, almost all zoonoses, are caused by a range of enveloped RNA viruses. Humans are not part of the natural history of these viruses, and therefore infection of humans is an accident, usually the consequence of intrusion into the ecologic niche of the virus. The viruses belong to four major families – Bunyaviridae, Arenaviridae, Filoviridae and Flaviviridae (Table 183.1).

The bunyaviruses Crimean–Congo hemorrhagic fever virus (CCHFV), hantaviruses and Rift Valley fever virus (RVFV) cause VHF in humans. Crimean–Congo hemorrhagic fever virus is spread by ticks and occurs widely across Africa, south-eastern Europe, the Middle East and Asia. Hantaviruses are found throughout the world as natural silent infections in many rodents. A hantavirus in the USA, a pathogen of deer mice, causes the hantavirus pulmonary syndrome (HPS). Rift Valley Fever virus is mosquito borne and causes an acute illness in livestock and wild animals as well as humans.

Arenaviruses also infect rodents, the most important being Lassa virus, which is confined to West Africa, and the South American hemorrhagic fever viruses, of which four are known and cause VHF. The filoviruses, Ebola and Marburg viruses, are a unique family of filamentous viruses known as Filoviridae, from Africa. African filovirus infections have a high mortality rate, but recently described Asian filoviruses have not, so far, been seen to be pathogenic for humans.

The Flaviviridae include yellow fever virus (see Chapter 222) and dengue virus (see Chapter 184), which are both spread by mosquitoes.

Other viruses can cause hemorrhagic fever, such as those causing Kyasanur Forest disease and Omsk hemorrhagic fever, but these are confined to very local areas and are not discussed in detail here. Neither are viruses such as West Nile virus, which, although common and causing increasing numbers of cases in a widening geographic area, rarely cause hemorrhagic disease (and is covered in Chapter 222).

EPIDEMIOLOGY

These infections are primarily rural diseases in developing communities occurring in areas where there is substantial contact with rodents, ticks or mosquitoes and usually with poor facilities for medical care. They are often undiagnosed, particularly single sporadic cases. Much of our knowledge of these diseases is the result of outbreak investigation, and rarely based on experience with endemic sporadic infections. Most of these infections are predominant in the poor. Some of these infections are also transmissible from person to person, such as Lassa virus, Ebola virus and CCHFV. These are particularly notorious for causing nosocomial outbreaks. Only dengue and occasionally yellow fever are seen in the cities where large populations of humans form effective reservoirs along with the abundant mosquitoes that act as both reservoirs and transmitters of the viruses. However, as a result of the increasing mobility of populations everywhere, infected patients can and do appear almost anywhere in the world. Missionaries and medical staff working in remote areas are at risk, but often more likely to reach tertiary care facilities than locals. Large epidemics of VHF can kill thousands of people, such as with yellow fever. Some viruses, particularly filoviruses, have only ever emerged in small epidemics, but their very high mortality rates have given them a notoriety perhaps disproportionate to the number of people actually infected. Monkeys and chimps appear to be as sensitive (or even more so) to the filoviruses as are humans. As a result, there have been many cases of monkey infection now documented, including their onward transmission to humans. There is no evidence, however, that chimps or monkeys are the natural reservoir.

DIAGNOSIS AND CLINICAL FEATURES

The most critical element in the clinical diagnosis in nonendemic areas is to take a thorough history covering the incubation period (3 to a maximum of 4 weeks before the onset of fever). The element that alerts the physician to VHF (and usually indicates which one it is likely to be) is the contact the patient has had with known ecologic niches (see Table 183.1). The history must include:

- a thorough travel history, particularly in Africa, and contact with known severely ill febrile individuals;
- any possible contact with ticks, fresh animal blood, rodent urine or blood, wild animals or mosquitoes and other insects;
- any recent camping in exotic and potentially endemic areas;
- any entry into bat caves; and
- attendance at ceremonial funerals.

Usually these risks occur in rural and remote areas. A medical care provider or other worker who might have had contact with blood from a primary case should also alert the physician to possible VHF.

The essential clinical features (Table 183.2) are a short history of fever, which is usually high and of sudden or rapid onset. Severe body pains and headache are prominent and may be excruciating. Other features may include severe pharyngitis, nausea and vomiting, petechiae, oozing from the gums and bradycardia. Proteinuria is common. Peripheral white blood cell counts are often low very early in disease, but may go up dramatically later, and therefore the presence of neutrophilia may falsely indicate a bacterial disease and be misleading. Thrombocytopenia is common and platelet function is often impaired, even in the presence of low normal platelet counts. Partial thromboplastin times may be prolonged, but prothrombin times are relatively unaffected. Disseminated intravascular coagulation

EPIDEMIOLOGIC CHARACTERISTICS OF THE MOST IMPORTANT VHFs								
	Arenaviruses*		Filoviruses		Bunyaviruses			Flaviviruses
	Lassa virus	**Junin, Machupo, Guanarito, Sabia**	**Ebola**	**Marburg**	**Hantavirus**	**Crimean–Congo**	**Rift Valley fever**	**Yellow fever**
Geography	West Africa	South America, North America	Central and West Africa	East and Central Africa	Worldwide	Europe, Asia, Africa	Africa	South America and Africa
Primary source of infection	Rodent (*Mastomys natalensis*)	Rodent (*Calomys, Zygodontomys* sp.)	Unknown; possibly bats		Rodents; species depends on location	Tick-borne, (>27 species)	Mosquito	Mosquito-borne (*Aedes* and *Hemogogus* spp.)
Transmission	Nosocomial Rodent to human/ person to person	Rodent to human	Nosocomial; possibly reservoir to human; person to person; also infected chimps and possibly monkeys can transmit to humans		Rodent to human	Nosocomial tick to human; possibly animal to human; possibly person to person	Mosquito to human; possibly animal to human via blood	Mosquito to human (human reservoir in outbreaks)
Risk factors	Close contact *Mastomys* rural West Africa; close contact infected persons	Contact rodents in circumscribed agricultural areas South America, possibly North America	Close contact infected blood or secretions from infected persons; environmental risk unknown (possibly caves for Marburg)		Contact with rodent or rodent urine in dust; laboratory	Tick bites; contact with infected livestock; contact with blood or secretions from infected persons	Mosquito bites rural Africa	Mosquito bites rural West Africa and South American rainforests
Treatment	Responds to ribavirin when treated early	Junin responds to immune plasma given early; all may respond to ribavirin	No present treatment; does not respond to ribavirin		Ribavirin may be beneficial early; trial and current use in China; open-label trial in USA for acute pulmonary disease was inconclusive	Sensitive to ribavirin; several published reports of successful case treatment	Sensitive to ribavirin; limited data in monkeys; no human data	No therapy; does not respond to ribavirin
Vaccine	Vaccinia vectored glycoprotein vaccine protects primates Development of human vaccine possible	Attenuated vaccine to Junin virus has greatly reduced cases in Argentina; no vaccine available for others	Protection in small animal studies. Protection of primates not clear	Nothing available	M gene DNA vaccine expressing glycoproteins 1 and 2 protects small animals from challenge and elicits neutralizing antibody in Rhesus monkeys; also formalin-inactivated vaccine but no trial data	Killed vaccine available in Eastern Europe and China, but no published trials	Attenuated vaccine for animals, none for humans	Live attenuated vaccine since 1940s; one of the most effective vaccines ever

* Arenaviruses have been isolated from wood rats in the south-western USA – their capacity to cause human infection is uncertain

Table 183.1 Epidemiologic characteristics of the most important viral hemorrhagic fevers.

KEY CLINICAL FEATURES OF VHFs										
	Arenavirus		Filovirus			Bunyavirus				Flavivirus
	Lassa virus	South American	Ebola**	Marburg	Reston*	Old World hantavirus	New World hantavirus	Crimean–Congo	Rift Valley fever	Yellow fever
Untreated case fatality (%)	16–20	16	50–90	6–50	0	1–15	45–50	10–>50	1–2	20–50
Cardiovascular system										
Thrombocytopenia	+	+++	+++	+++	–	++	+	+++	++	++
Oozing	++	++	+++	+++	–	++	–	+++	++	+++
Petechiae	–	+++	+	+	–	+++		+		
Ecchymoses			++	++	–		–	++		
Circulatory shock	+++	+++	+++	+++	–	+++	+++	+++	+++	+++
Tissue edema	++		+	+	–	+	–			
Major hemorrhage	+	+	++	++	–	+	–	++	+	++
Central nervous system										
Encephalopathy	+++	+	+	+	–	–	–	+		
Ataxia	+	++				+				
Deafness	++									
Blindness			+							
Mood alteration	+	+	+	+				++		
Intracranial bleeding						+				
Other major systems										
Renal	–	–	+/–	+/–	–	+++	+			+
Pulmonary (ARDS)	+++	+	++	+	–	+	+++			+
Hepatic	+	+	+	+	–	+	+	+	+	+++

+ Denotes present to differing degrees indicated by number of marks
– Denotes absence
No mark indicates no reliable data
* Reston is not a human pathogen
** Viruses from West and Central Africa appear to vary with those in West and North Central Africa; may be less virulent and with lower case fatality than Central Africa

Table 183.2 Key clinical features of viral hemorrhagic fevers.

is not a feature of VHF except as a complication of the general deterioration of patients in the terminal phase.

As the disease progresses hypovolemic shock, pulmonary edema and frank bleeding ensue. Aspartate aminotransferase (AST) is usually raised and virtually all VHFs distinguish themselves from viral hepatitis because the AST is disproportionately high compared with alanine aminotransferase (ALT). Ratios of AST to ALT may be as high as 11 to 1, and the level of AST also reflects prognosis. Patients are rarely jaundiced (except in yellow fever) and the bilirubin is usually normal.

The viruses are pantropic, primarily targeting the reticuloendothelial system. There are usually high titers of virus in the blood and tissues. The central nervous system is relatively spared, but encephalopathy and neurologic sequelae such as ataxia and deafness can occur, particularly in the early convalescent phase. Viruses are rarely recovered from the cerebrospinal fluid.

Care must be taken in collecting, handling and transporting specimens, and consultation with the laboratory is essential. Gloves must be worn at all times and the specimens clearly labeled as hazardous. Blood samples should preferably be drawn into a vacuum tube system. Specimens for transport should be transferred to a leakproof plastic container and double-wrapped in leakproof containers in which they can be transported to a suitable reference laboratory (see Chapter 222).

Laboratory diagnosis may be provided by several methods, depending on the virus in question by:

- presence of virus-specific IgM in the serum;
- presence of viral RNA, usually in serum or white cells, demonstrated by a reverse transcriptase polymerase chain reaction (PCR);
- presence of viral antigen through enzyme-linked immunosorbent assay (ELISA) for specific viral antigens in serum or blood;
- isolating the virus from serum; or
- demonstrating a 4-fold rise in antibody titer;

Sera may be inactivated for serology by gamma irradiation or, if this is unavailable, heating at 140°F (60°C) for 30 minutes. Immunofluorescence assays and ELISAs detect both virus antibody and antigen. More recently, molecular techniques such as PCR performed directly on serum or tissues to detect viral RNA have been found to be rapid, reliable and safe, and while they are more widely available, they are not always available in the areas endemic for VHFs. No truly successful diagnostic system has yet been developed that can be easily and uniformly applied in the remote areas where these diseases occur. New advances in PCR offer the most likely method.

MANAGEMENT

Viral hemorrhagic fevers are self-limiting diseases, and if the patient can be brought through the acute crisis recovery is rapid and complete, although fatigue and general weakness may persist well after the acute disease. The main challenge of acute disease is careful management of fluid balance. Patients often present with a high hematocrit due to dehydration. Despite this, pulmonary edema is a real risk and patients should be infused with caution. Blood and platelet replacement may be necessary. Full intensive care support may be required including mechanical ventilation, monitoring of central venous pressure and dialysis. Seizures and arrhythmias will need to be controlled. Any necessary operation (e.g. obstetric intervention) should be carried out. Pregnant patients are a major challenge. They often present with absent fetal movements and the survival of the mother in Lassa fever has been shown to depend upon the presence of aggressive obstetric intervention to remove the dead fetus.

Lassa virus and CCHFV are highly treatable using the antiviral agent ribavirin, provided therapy is instituted as early as possible in the course of the disease (see Table 183.1). Therapy with immune plasma has also been advocated, but efficacy has never been demonstrated except for Argentine hemorrhagic fever. Disseminated intravascular coagulation is not an underlying feature and heparin is contraindicated. Early accurate diagnosis and good intensive care support are the most important underlying principles for the physician.

Patients who have VHF do not travel well because their cardiovascular system is often unstable and trauma is likely to induce bleeding. It is therefore advised that moving a suspected patient is avoided wherever possible. Moving the patient also exposes a greater number of people to secondary infection. Patients may be managed quite successfully in standard hospital isolation rooms with rigorous barrier nursing because these diseases do not transmit from person to person by aerosol.

PREVENTION

The fearsome reputation of some of these viruses comes from their ability to spread to medical staff and patients in facilities where poor training and inadequate materials for barrier nursing lead to blood-to-blood contact with the virus, for example as a result of a needlestick injury, blood spill on unprotected damaged skin or mouth- to-mouth resuscitation. In some countries, the re-use of needles and syringes has produced devastating nosocomial outbreaks. There are also reports of outbreaks among surgical teams who have unwisely performed laparotomies on infected patients. In these circumstances, the mortality rate has been high.

The key to the prevention of nosocomial transmission in both endemic and nonendemic areas has consistently been good hospital and laboratory practice, with strict isolation of febrile patients and rigorous use of gloves and disinfection.

A small number of named personnel should undertake direct care and be kept fully informed about the nature of the virus and the precautions to be taken. Intensive care, operative interventions and air evacuation in the absence of any local hospital facility should not be denied because they do not pose substantial threats to a well-trained staff accustomed to simple barrier nursing techniques. Aerosol spread in hospitals has not been documented; indeed, there is much published evidence showing that this is not a major hazard. Past recommendations for strict isolation of patients in a plastic isolator have been abandoned in favor of simple strict barrier nursing. This practice presents no excess risk to hospital personnel and allows substantially better care of the patient.

The major factor in nosocomial transmission is the combination of unawareness of the possibility of the disease by a worker who is also inattentive to the requirements of effective barrier nursing. Contacts should be carefully assessed and monitored. Postexposure prophylaxis may be offered where appropriate. Once the diagnosis has been considered and appropriate precautions instituted, the risk of nosocomial transmission is very small (<1%).

A high risk of infection is associated with direct percutaneous or mucosal contact with blood or body fluids and prophylaxis with ribavirin should be offered after exposure to CCHFV and arenaviruses. Other contacts (includes most unprotected contact with blood or body fluids) may safely be observed daily for the development of a persistent high fever for 3 weeks from the last date of contact. The practice of following up airline passengers who do not have any direct physical contact and other low-risk contacts with Lassa fever virus has been discontinued (see Practice Point 186a).

The 1988 USA Centers for Disease Control and Prevention Guidelines for the Management of Patients with VHFs therefore recommend routine patient isolation in a single room, preferably but not necessarily with a negative air pressure gradient from the hallway through an anteroom to the patient room. Staff education, use of gloves, gowns and masks, and rigorous disinfection with fresh liquids are mandatory. The recommendations issued for patient management and handling of clinical specimens from patients who have AIDS are adequate for the containment of VHFs. The major event to be avoided is direct contact with the blood or other fluid or excretions from an acutely infected patient.

Lassa and Ebola viruses in particular are robust and even withstand some drying. Blood from severely ill patients may contain as much as 10^9 infectious units/ml. However, all the viruses can be inactivated by heat, detergents, chlorine, formalin and ultraviolet radiation (including sunshine). Disinfection can be accomplished by washing with 0.5% phenol in detergent, 0.5% hypochlorite solution, formaldehyde, glutaraldehyde or paracetic acid. Care should be taken to ensure solutions are freshly and correctly made up and time allowed for disinfectant to work on spills.

Finally, a major hazard of VHFs, particularly viruses such as Ebola virus, is the fear and press attention they receive. A single case can be quite traumatic for an institution unless the situation is carefully handled. A measured and informed approach from a collaborative team of doctors, nurses, administrators and others is needed. Careful education of all medical staff, emphasizing the real risks and the ways to avoid them and allaying unnecessary fears, and avoiding panic will result in appropriate management of the patient, and avoid secondary infections. Press attention can be quite disruptive and is best managed by the sharing of accurate and regular information.

Details of appropriate management and containment facilities, contact handling, surveillance, laboratory procedures and resource laboratories have been published.

FURTHER READING

Baize S, Eric M, Leroy E, *et al.* Defective humoral responses and extensive intravascular apoptosis are associated with fatal outcome in Ebola virus-infected patients. Nature Med 1999;5:423–6.

Bwaka MA, Bonnet MJ, Calain P, *et al.* Ebola hemorrhagic fever in Kikwit, Democratic Republic of the Congo: clinical observations in 103 patients. J Infect Dis 1999;179(Suppl.1):S1–7.

Centers for Disease Control and Prevention. Guidelines for the management of viral hemorrhagic fevers. MMWR Morb Mortal Wkly Rep 1988;37:3.

Chen HX, Qiu FX, Dong SJ, *et al.* Epidemiological studies on hemorrhagic fever with renal syndrome in China. J Infect Dis 1986;154:394–8.

Enria D, Briggiler AM, Fernandez JH, Levis SC, Maiztegui JI. Importance of dose of neutralizing antibodies in treatment of Argentine haemorrhagic fever with immune plasma. Lancet 1984;ii:255–6.

Fisher-Hoch SP, Hutwagner L, Brown B, McCormick JB. Effective vaccine for lassa fever. J Virol 2000;74:6777–83

Fisher-Hoch SP, Khan JA, Rehman S, *et al.* Crimean–Congo hemorrhagic fever treated with oral ribavirin. Lancet 1995;346:472–5.

Fisher-Hoch SP, McCormick JB. Arenaviruses. In: Warrell D, ed. The Oxford textbook of medicine, 3rd ed. Oxford: Oxford University Press; 1996:429–38.

Fisher-Hoch SP, McCormick JB. Filoviruses. In: Zuckerman AJ, Banatvala JE, Pattison JR, eds. Principles and practices of clinical virology, 3rd ed. Chichester: John Wiley and Sons; 1995.

Fisher-Hoch SP, Platt GS, Lloyd G, Simpson DI, Neild GH, Barrett AJ. Haematological and biochemical monitoring of Ebola infection in rhesus monkeys: implications for patient management. Lancet 1983;2:1055–8.

Holmes GP, McCormick, JB, Trock SC, *et al.* Lassa fever in the United States: investigation of a case and new guidelines for management. N Engl J Med 1990;323:1120.

Huggins JW, Hsiang CM, Cosgriff TM, *et al.* Prospective, double-blind, concurrent, placebo-controlled, clinical trial of intravenous ribavirin therapy of hemorrhagic fever with renal syndrome (HFRS). J Infect Dis 1991;164:1119–27.

Ksiazek TG, Rollin PE, Williams AJ, *et al.* Clinical virology of Ebola hemorrhagic fever (EHF): virus, virus antigen, and IgG and IgM antibody findings among EHF patients in Kikwit, Democratic Republic of the Congo, 1995. J Infect Dis 1999;179(Suppl.1):S177–87.

Leroy EM, Baize S, Lu CY, *et al.* Diagnosis of Ebola haemorrhagic fever by RT-PCR in an epidemic setting. J Med Virol 2000;60:463–7.

Maiztegui JI. Clinical and epidemiological patterns of Argentine hemorrhagic fever. Bull World Health Organ 1975;52:567–75.

McCormick JB, King IJ, Webb PA, *et al.* A case–control study of clinical diagnosis and course of Lassa fever. J Infect Dis 1987;155:445–14.

McCormick JB, King IJ, Webb PA. *et al.* Lassa fever: effective therapy with ribavirin. N Engl J Med 1986;314:20–6.

Monath TP. The flaviviruses. In: Field BN, ed. Virology. New York: Raven Press; 1990.

Mupapa K, Massamba M, Kibadi K, *et al.* Treatment of Ebola hemorrhagic fever with blood transfusions from convalescent patients. International Scientific and Technical Committee. J Infect Dis 1999;179(Suppl.1):S18–23.

Swanepoel R, Gill DE, Shepherd AJ, *et al.* The clinical pathology of Crimean–Congo hemorrhagic fever. Rev Infect Dis 1989;11(Suppl.4):S794–800.

World Health Organization. Ebola haemorrhagic fever in Zaire, 1976: report of an International Commission. Bull World Health Organ 1978;56:271–93.

chapter 184

Dengue Fever/ Dengue Hemorrhagic Fever

Scott B Halstead

The dengue viruses (types 1, 2, 3 and 4) are enveloped ssRNA viruses of the Flaviviridae family. Transmission from human to human is by the mosquito *Aedes aegypti*, which bites in the daytime, is adapted to human habitats and has a strong preference for human blood meals. It breeds in relatively clean water stored for drinking or washing purposes in a variety of containers, and in rainwater that collects in manmade containers (e.g. tires, plastic containers, bottles, pails, tanks, cisterns, shallow wells).

The population explosion since World War II and subsequent migration from rural to urban areas have resulted in large cities, deteriorating urban environments and the spread of *A. aegypti* to almost all tropical countries.[1,2] All four dengue virus types are now endemic around the globe. Of the 2.5 billion inhabitants of these areas, it is estimated that about 50–100 million individuals become infected by dengue viruses each year. Since the end of World War II, a syndrome first recognized in South East Asia – dengue hemorrhagic fever/dengue shock syndrome (DHF/DSS) – has spread globally (see Fig. 184.1), resulting in hundreds of thousands of hospitalizations and thousands of deaths each year.[2] Travelers to most tropical areas are at risk of dengue infection. In 2001, Hawaii experienced a 6-month epidemic of dengue type 1 transmitted by *Aedes albopictus*.

PATHOGENESIS

Dengue hemorrhagic fever/DSS is an immunopathologic syndrome that occurs in:

- infants infected for the first time who have acquired maternal dengue antibody in utero;[3] and
- children and, less commonly, adults during a second dengue virus infection.[4,5]

Enhancing antibodies appear to be responsible for DHF/DSS. From protective levels at birth, maternal dengue antibodies degrade from neutralizing to enhancing concentrations over a period of 2–10 months.[3] Non-neutralizing antibodies, even in very small numbers, form infectious immune complexes with dengue viruses.[6] These attach efficiently to the Fc receptors of mononuclear phagocytes (macrophages, monocytes, Kupffer cells). The virus then attaches to receptors and fuses through adjacent plasma membrane, extruding viral RNA into the cytosol. The net effect is enhanced infection – more cells infected more rapidly than without enhancing antibody, a phenomenon now documented in humans.[7] Sequential infection in children over 1 year of age accounts for 85% of cases of DHF/DSS. In this setting, enhanced infections occur when antibody from a first infection fails to cross-neutralize a second dengue virus type.[8]

Only viruses of South East Asian origin appear to produce DHF/DSS.[9,10] In the American genotype dengue 2 virus, the occurrence of dengue 1-like epitopes results in significant cross-reaction and some level of protection in persons immune to dengue 1 virus.[11]

The mediator of DSS has not yet been identified. Recent data suggest that IL-2, interferon-γ and tumor necrosis factor released as a result of interactions between activated T cells and infected macrophages may damage postcapillary endothelial junctions. Dengue hemorrhagic fever/DSS is more severe in:

- whites and Asians (versus black people);[12,13]
- females (versus males); and
- well-nourished (versus malnourished) children.[2]

PREVENTION

Aedes aegypti is a furtive black-and-white striped mosquito that often bites shadowed areas of the skin on the back of the neck, arms and legs. Most dengue infections are acquired at home. Prevention consists of scrupulous destruction and control of breeding sites. All unwanted containers should be discarded, buried or filled with sand.[2] Salt prevents eggs from hatching in water-filled ant traps and water coolers. Standing water that needs to be conserved can be treated with a 1% sand granule formulation of Abate, 1ppm [0,0′-(thiodi-*p*-phenylene) 0,0,0,0′-tetramethylphosphorothioate].

Larvivorous small fish can provide reliable control of mosquito larvae. Adult mosquitoes can be destroyed by pyrethrin knock-down sprays or organophosphate sprays delivered in microdroplets. However, source reduction is always the best method of preventing dengue infections.

For travelers to tropical countries, the only practical method of prevention is to avoid mosquito bites. Topical repellents are effective, but prevention comprises avoiding daytime visits to high-risk areas.

A tetravalent live-attenuated dengue vaccine is in the final stages of development.

CLINICAL FEATURES

Most primary dengue infections in children and many in adults are silent. Dengue infection presents clinically as three overlapping syndromes: undifferentiated fever, dengue fever syndrome and DHF/DSS.[2] The early signs and symptoms of overt dengue infections are common to many acute viral, bacterial and parasitic infections. The pathophysiologic presentation of classic DSS (history of recent high fever, thrombocytopenia, elevated hematocrit and hypotension or narrow pulse pressure) is unique in infectious diseases. Presumptive diagnosis of dengue fever or DHF requires a careful travel history to establish possible exposure to dengue infection. The differential diagnoses for the dengue fever and viral hemorrhagic fever syndromes are shown in Table 184.1.

Undifferentiated fever

This occurs in young children and is a mild febrile illness lasting 1–3 days, often with upper respiratory signs.

Dengue fever syndrome

This occurs in adolescents and adults. After an infective mosquito bite, there is an incubation period of 3–8 days, followed by a sudden onset of fever with severe headache, pain behind the eyes, backache, chills, lack of appetite, gastrointestinal disturbances and generalized

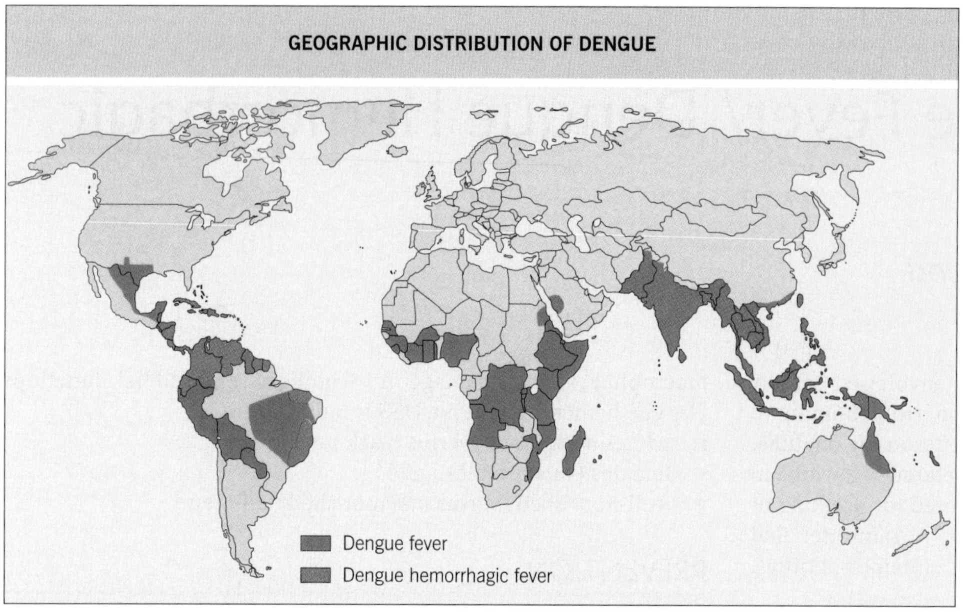

Fig. 184.1 Geographic distribution of dengue.

DIFFERENTIAL DIAGNOSIS OF DENGUE FEVER AND DENGUE HEMORRHAGIC FEVER

Dengue fever syndrome

- *Mosquito-transmitted febrile exanthems*
  - chikungunya (Africa, Asia)
  - o'nyong nyong (Africa)
  - West Nile (US, Europe, Africa, Asia)
- *Insect transmitted – no rash*
  - sandfly fever (Europe, Middle East)
  - Rift Valley fever (Africa, Egypt)
  - Ross River fever (Australia, Pacific Islands)
  - Oropouche (Amazon basin)
- *Febrile diseases in dengue-endemic areas*
  - most acute viral and bacterial infections
  - malaria
  - yellow fever
  - leptospirosis
  - scrub typhus
  - viral hepatitis

Hemorrhagic fevers

- *Ubiquitous*
  - meningococcemia
- *Viral hemorrhagic fevers*
  - mosquito-borne: Rift Valley fever, yellow fever
  - tick-borne: Crimean-Congo HF, Omsk HF, Kyasanur Forest disease
  - infectious secretions/tissues: Argentine HF, Bolivian HF, Venezuelan HF, Lassa fever, Marburg disease, Ebola HF, hemorrhagic fever with renal syndrome

Table 184.1 Differential diagnosis of dengue fever and dengue hemorrhagic fever.

pains in the muscles and bones ('breakbone fever'). A maculopapular rash usually appears on the trunk between the third and fifth day of the illness, spreading to the face and extremities. Fever is accompanied by leukopenia, relative lymphocytosis and moderate thrombocytopenia. Dengue fever may be complicated by bleeding, particularly in menstruating women or adults who have peptic ulcer disease.[14] The illness usually lasts for about 4–10 days. Convalescence may be accompanied by prostration and depression.

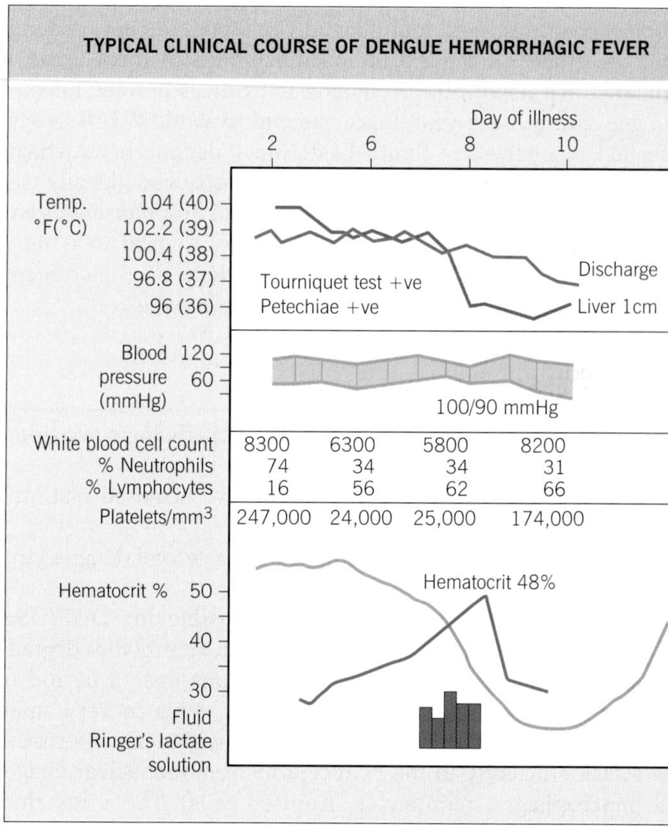

Fig. 184.2 Typical clinical course of dengue hemorrhagic fever.

DENGUE HEMORRHAGIC FEVER/DENGUE SHOCK SYNDROME

This is an acute vascular permeability syndrome accompanied by abnormal hemostasis. Although both adults and children develop the syndrome, children are inherently more susceptible due to greater capillary fragility,[5,15,16] with a characteristic illness progression (Fig. 184.2). A relatively mild first phase with abrupt onset of fever, malaise, vomiting, headache, anorexia and cough may be followed after 2–5 days by a rapid deterioration and physical collapse due to hypovolemia secondary to increased vascular permeability.[17]

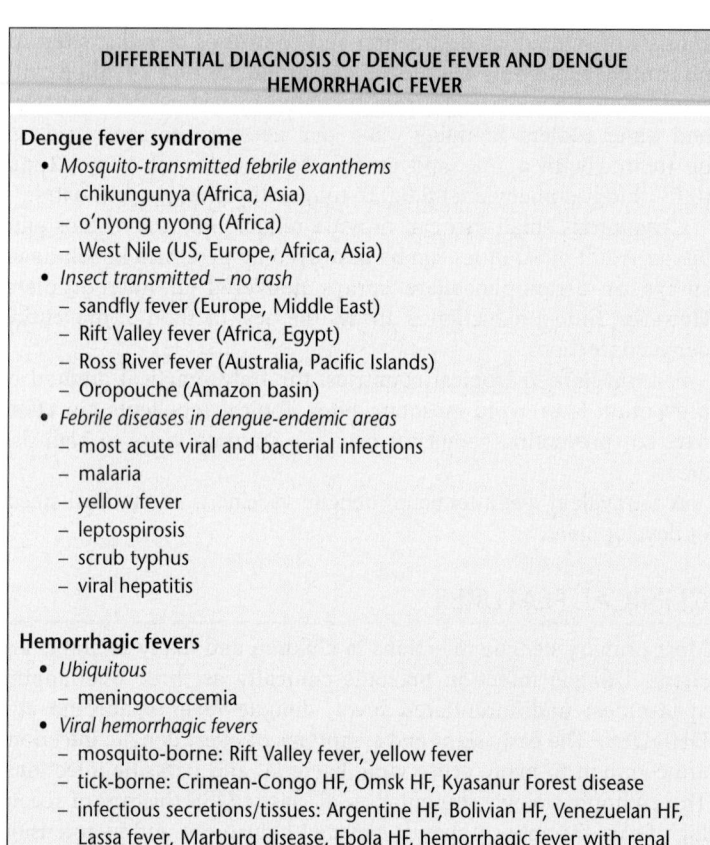

In this second phase, as the temperature becomes normal the patient may have cold clammy extremities, a warm trunk, flushed face, circumoral cyanosis, diaphoresis, restlessness, irritability and midepigastric pain. Respirations and pulse are rapid. Blood pressure may exhibit narrow pulse pressure (20mmHg) or low systolic and diastolic pressures. Scattered petechiae may be seen on the forehead and extremities along with spontaneous ecchymoses, easy bruising and bleeding at venepuncture sites.

As the disease progresses, the liver is usually palpable two or three fingerbreadths below the costal margin, firm and nontender. Chest radiography shows unilateral (right) or bilateral pleural effusions. Sonograms show ascites and perivesicular edema. Approximately 10% of patients have gross ecchymoses or gastrointestinal bleeding. Laboratory abnormalities include thrombocytopenia, elevated hematocrit and abnormal levels of liver enzymes. Convalescence is fairly rapid for children who recover after a 24–36-hour period of crisis.

In addition to classic DSS, adults may have a stormy, often fatal course characterized by elevated liver enzymes, hemostatic abnormalities and gastrointestinal bleeding.

DENGUE HEMORRHAGIC FEVER/DENGUE SHOCK SYNDROME

	Case definition	Grading	Management
DHF	• Fever of 2 or more days duration	I Positive tourniquet test	• Oral rehydration fluids in outpatient department
DHF	• Hematocrit increase ≥20% recovery level	II Bleeding manifestations	• If hematocrit increases, hospitalize • Monitor pulse rate, hematocrit, urine output Infuse 5% dextrose in Ringer's lactate 7ml/kg/h
DHF	• Thrombocytopenia ≤100,000/mm3		
DHF / DSS	• Narrow pulse pressure (≤20mmHg) or hypotension for age	III Circulatory failure IV Profound shock	• If hematocrit increases, add colloid • With improvement reduce infusion rate to avoid overhydration

Fig. 184.3 Dengue hemorrhagic fever/dengue shock syndrome. Case definition, clinical staging and treatment strategies for DHF/DSS.

MANAGEMENT

Dengue fever

Dengue fever should be treated supportively. Aspirin is avoided because it may exacerbate the bleeding tendency. Patients who go into shock with normal or falling hematocrit levels should be investigated for gastrointestinal bleeding.[14]

Dengue hemorrhagic fever/dengue shock syndrome

Dengue hemorrhagic fever/dengue shock syndrome is life-threatening and requires immediate evaluation of vital signs, hemoconcentration, dehydration, urine output and electrolyte imbalance (Fig. 184.3). Close monitoring for at least 48 hours is essential because shock may occur or recur precipitously early in the disease. Patients who are cyanotic or have labored breathing should be given oxygen.

Rapid intravenous replacement of fluid and electrolytes using normal saline can often sustain patients until they have a spontaneous recovery.[2,17] Colloid preparations, such as dextran 70, should be given if the pulse pressure is 10mmHg or less or the hematocrit remains elevated after fluid replacement.[18] Care should be taken to avoid overhydration, which is heralded by a fall in hematocrit and a wide pulse pressure. Diuretics may be necessary. Fresh frozen plasma, whole blood, platelets or heparin (if there is laboratory evidence of severe consumptive coagulopathy), together with rigorous replacement of fluid and protein with colloids, may be required if bleeding complicating DHF/DSS is sufficiently severe. Bleeding is thought to be due to one or more platelet abnormalities.[19]

Chloral hydrate or diazepam may be necessary to manage agitated children.

Corticosteroids, vasopressors, α-adrenergic blocking agents and aldosterone have no role in treatment. Salicylates are contraindicated.

The etiology can be established by recovering the virus from the acute-phase serum, usually on or before the fifth day after the onset of fever. An IgM antibody-capture enzyme-linked immunosorbent assay on serum obtained between 7 days and 2 months after the onset of the fever enables identification of a recent dengue infection. Increases in antibody titer can be detected by hemagglutination inhibition or neutralization tests on paired sera (optimally separated by 2 weeks).[20]

REFERENCES

1. Gubler DJ. Epidemic dengue/dengue hemorrhagic fever as a public health, social and economic problem in the 21st century. Trends Microbiol 2002;10:100–3.
2. Halstead SB. Dengue and dengue hemorrhagic fever. In: Feigin RD, Cherry JD, eds. Textbook of pediatric infectious diseases, vol II, 5th ed. Philadelphia: WB Saunders; 2002.
3. Kliks SC, Nimmannitya S, Nisalak A, Burke DS. Evidence that maternal dengue antibodies are important in the development of dengue hemorrhagic fever in infants. Am J Trop Med Hyg 1988;38:411–19.
4. Sangkawibha N, Rojanasuphot S, Ahandrik S, *et al.* Risk factors in dengue shock syndrome. A prospective epidemiological study in Rayong, Thailand. I The 1980 outbreak. Am J Epidemiol 1984;120:653–69.
5. Guzman MG, Kouri G, Valdes L, *et al.* Epidemiological studies on dengue, Santiago de Cuba, 1997. Am J Epidemiol 2000;152:793–9.
6. Halstead SB. Pathogenesis of dengue: challenges of molecular biology. Science 1988;239:476–81.
7. Vaughn DW, Green S, Kalayanarooj S, *et al.* Dengue viremia titer, antibody response pattern and virus serotype correlate with disease severity. J Infect Dis 2000;181:2–9.
8. Kliks SC, Nisalak A, Brandt WE, Wahl L, Burke DS. Antibody-dependent enhancement of dengue virus growth in human monocytes as a risk factor for dengue hemorrhagic fever. Am J Trop Med Hyg 1989;40:444–51.
9. Leitmeyer KC, Vaughn DW, Watts DM, *et al.* Dengue virus structural differences that correlate with pathogenesis. J Virol 1999;73:4738–47.
10. Watts DM, Porter K, Putvatana R, *et al.* Failure of secondary infections with American genotype dengue 2 viruses to cause dengue haemorrhagic fever. Lancet 1999;354:1431–4.
11. Kochel T, Watts DM, Halstead SB, *et al.* Neutralization of American genotype dengue 2 viral infection by dengue 1 antibody may have prevented dengue haemorrhagic fever in Iquitos, Peru. Lancet 2002;360:310–12.
12. Guzman MD, Kouri GP, Bravo J, Soler M, Vazquez S, Mories C. Dengue hemorrhagic fever in Cuba, 1981: a retrospective sero-epidemiologic study. Am J Trop Med Hyg 1990;42:179–84.
13. Halstead SB, Streit TG, Lafontant JG, *et al.* Absence of dengue hemorrhagic fever despite hyperendemic dengue virus transmission. Am J Trop Med Hyg 2001;65:180–3.

14. Tsai CJ, Kuo CH, Chen PC, Chang Chen CS. Upper gastrointestinal bleeding in dengue fever. Am J Gastroenterol 1991;86:33–55.
15. Guzman MG, Kouri G, Bravo J, Valdes L, Vasquez S, Halstead SB. Effect of age on outcome of secondary dengue 2 infections. Int J Infect Dis 2002;6:118–24.
16. Bethell DB, Gamble J, Pham PL, *et al.* Noninvasive measurement of microvascular leakage in patients with dengue hemorrhagic fever. Clin Infect Dis 2001;32:243–53.
17. Cohen S, Halstead SB. Shock associated with dengue infection. I. The clinical and physiologic manifestations of dengue hemorrhagic fever in Thailand. J Pediatrics 1966;68:448–56.
18. Ngo NT, Kneen R, Wills B, *et al.* Acute management of dengue shock syndrome: a randomized double-blind comparison of 4 intravenous fluid regimens in the first hour. Clin Infect Dis 2001;32:204–13.
19. Krishnamurthi C, Kalayanarooj S, Cutting MA, *et al.* Mechanisms of hemorrhage in dengue without circulatory collapse. Am J Trop Med Hyg 2001;65:840–7.
20. Technical Guide. Dengue haemorrhagic fever: diagnosis, treatment, prevention and control, 2nd ed. Geneva: World Health Organization, 1997.

chapter 185

Anthrax

Mehmet Doganay

INTRODUCTION

Anthrax is an ancient disease that was rarely seen outside certain well-defined geographic areas, except as an occasional occupational hazard, but which has recently assumed greater importance as a result of its potential use as an agent of bioterrorism.

EPIDEMIOLOGY

Anthrax is usually a disease of herbivores and only incidentally infects humans. This infection still persists in arid and semiarid regions of the Middle East, in Africa, Asia, South America and Haiti. Humans almost invariably acquire anthrax directly or indirectly from infected animals. The main route of transmission is contact with or inhalation of *Bacillus anthracis* spores.[1,2] Human cases may occur in an agricultural or an industrial environment.[1,3]

Agricultural cases have occurred in individuals who came into contact with sick or dead animals in rural areas. In certain impoverished communities, livestock owners are forced to slaughter animals at the first sign of infection in order to salvage the meat, hair and hides because of economic problems. Farmers, butchers, knackers, shepherds and veterinarians are therefore the most frequently infected. Anthrax is also reported in women spinning wool with hand spindles and in carpet weavers.[1,3,4] Another route of infection is by ingestion of raw or undercooked meat from an infected carcass.[5] Travelers should be aware that, in certain societies, some traditional meals are made of raw meat and are consumed without any cooking or preservation methods. In our series of 113 cases of anthrax, 89 patients gave a history of handling of, or contact with infected dead animals or their products. In four cases, there was a history of consumption of meat from the carcass of a diseased cow or sheep. The source of infection in the remaining 20 cases could not be determined but they were clearly agricultural in origin.[6]

There is also an infection risk after contact with a commercial product prepared from inadequately treated wool or leather. For example, a human case of cutaneous anthrax was acquired from contact with imported souvenir drums with drumheads made of goatskin and another case was most probably acquired from a purchased wool coat. A fatal case of inhalation anthrax was also recorded in a home weaver as a result of contact with imported yarn from Pakistan that contained animal fibers.[1,3]

Insect vectors, such as horseflies, have been reported to transmit *B. anthracis* from an infected animal to a second animal. They could also theoretically infect humans by mechanical transfer but this has not been well documented.[1,3]

Industrial anthrax occurs as a result of the inhalation of spore-laden dust or other aerosols or contact with spores. In the industrial environment, spores in dust clouds created from the handling of dry hides, skins, sheep wool, goat hair, bone meal and the like are inhaled or spread through contact with the skin of workers. Most cases in industrialized countries are associated with exposure to animal products, particularly goat hair, imported from countries in which anthrax is endemic.[1,3,7]

Records of person-to-person spread are very rare; an unqualified nursing orderly in Zimbabwe acquired an anthrax lesion on his finger as a result of removing dressings from a patient who had cutaneous anthrax, and communal loofahs were found to be responsible for, spreading infection from person to person in the Gambia. Laboratory-acquired infections occur occasionally.[1,3] In 2001 there was an outbreak of anthrax in the USA that apparently resulted from the deliberate distribution of spores in the postal system, resulting in a number of cases of both cutaneous and inhalational anthrax.[2]

CLINICAL FEATURES

The disease occurs primarily in three forms: cutaneous, respiratory and gastrointestinal. Sepsis and meningitis can rarely develop after the lymphohematogenous spread of *B. anthracis* from a primary lesion (cutaneous, gastrointestinal or pulmonary).

Cutaneous anthrax

Cutaneous anthrax accounts for 95% of human cases. The spore is introduced to the skin via a cut, abrasion or insect bite. The incubation period ranges from 1 to 19 days, usually 2–7 days. The lesion begins as a pruritic papule. The papule enlarges and a ring of vesicles develops around the papule at day 2–4 of the disease. Vesicular fluid may be a hemorrhagic exudate (Fig. 185.1). This area is surrounded by a small ring of erythema and marked edema develops. Unless there is secondary infection, there is no pus and the lesion is not painful, although painful lymphadenitis may occur in the regional lymph nodes. Eventually, the vesicle or vesicular ring ruptures, discharging a clear fluid, and a central depressed black necrotic lesion known as an eschar is formed (Fig. 185.2). Edema extends some distance from the lesion. The eschar begins to resolve about 10 days after the appearance of the initial papule. Resolution is slow (2–6 weeks), regardless of treatment (Fig. 185.3).[1,7–9]

The lesion is usually 1–3cm diameter and remains round and regular. Rarely, a lesion may be larger and irregularly shaped. Systemic symptoms, including low-grade fever, malaise and headache, may be present. The cutaneous reaction may be severe in some patients and is characterized by significant local and spreading edema associated with blebs, bullae, induration, chills and fever (see Fig. 185.2b). Clinical symptoms may be more severe if the lesion is located in the face, neck or chest. In these more severe forms, clinical findings are high fever, toxemia, regional painful adenomegaly and extensive edema; shock and death may ensue (Fig. 185.4).[6–11]

More than 90% of the lesions occur in exposed areas such as the face, neck, arms or hand. The site of infection often reflects the occupation of the patient. Workers who carry hides or carcasses on their shoulders are prone to infection on the back of the neck. Handlers of contaminated animal products tend to be infected on the arms, wrists and hands. The patients generally have a single cutaneous lesion but sometimes they have two or more. For example, if the

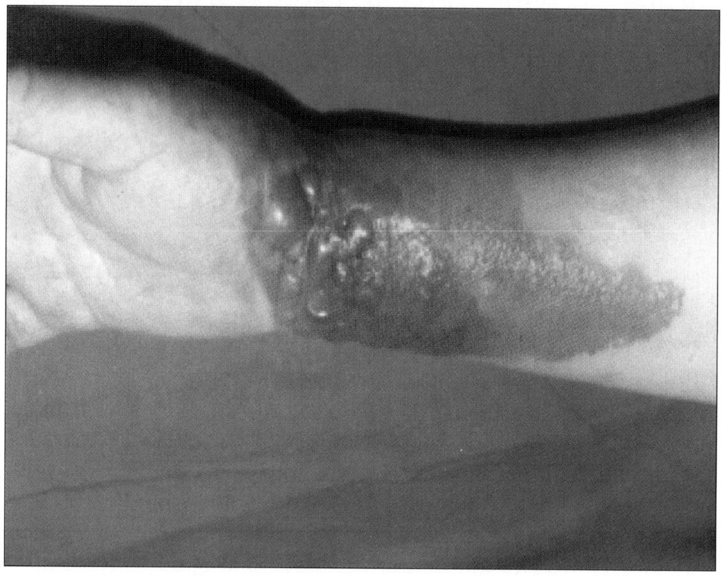

Fig. 185.1 A cutaneous anthrax lesion with extensive erythema and hemorrhagic bullae on the wrist.

infection has been acquired by skinning an infected dead animal with hands and arms, multiple lesions can be seen on hands, wrists and arms. Atypical localization can also be seen.[1,3,4,6,7] The distribution of lesions in 114 cases of anthrax treated in our clinic is shown in Table 185.1. A skin lesion was seen on the hand and fingers in the majority of cases. Lesions localized to other anatomic sites were less frequently observed.

Gastrointestinal anthrax

Ingestion of *B. anthracis* in contaminated food or drink can cause gastrointestinal anthrax. The incubation period is commonly 3–7 days. There are two clinical forms of gastrointestinal anthrax: intestinal and oropharyngeal.[1,5,7,8]

The symptoms of intestinal anthrax are initially non-specific and include nausea, vomiting, anorexia and fever. With progression of the illness, abdominal pain, hematemesis, bloody diarrhea and massive ascites occur, and signs suggestive of acute abdomen appear. Then toxemia and shock develop, followed by death. The lesions occur most commonly on the wall of the terminal ileum or cecum. The stomach, duodenum, upper ileum and large bowel are occasionally affected.[1,7]

Oropharyngeal anthrax is less common than the gastrointestinal form. The lesion is generally localized in the oral cavity, especially on the buccal mucosa or tongue, or the tonsils, and the posterior wall of the pharynx. In some cases, the lesion may be present in two or more places in the gastrointestinal system, oropharynx and intestine. The oral lesion is generally 2–3cm in diameter and covered with a gray pseudomembrane surrounded by extensive edema. When infection is localized on the tonsils, the affected tonsil is also intensely edematous and covered with pseudomembrane. The main clinical features are sore throat, dysphagia, fever and painful regional lymphadenopathy in the neck. The illness progresses rapidly and edema develops around the lymph node and may extend to the upper anterior chest wall. Bacteremia may develop. The infection leads to toxemia and acute respiratory distress syndrome. Shock and coma ensue. In some cases, toxemia leads to sudden death. Despite intensive medical therapy, the mortality is about 50%.[5]

Inhalation anthrax

This natural form of anthrax was previously almost always caused by industrial exposure to spores; however, the most serious outbreaks of anthrax in 1979 in Sverdlovsk and in October 2001 in America are new and notable exceptions.[2,12]

Inhalation anthrax shows a biphasic clinic pattern with a mild initial phase followed by an acute and severe second phase. After an incubation period of 1–6 days (up to 43 days in the event at Sverdlovsk), the illness begins with mild fever, fatigue, malaise, myalgia, nonproductive cough and some chest or abdominal pain.

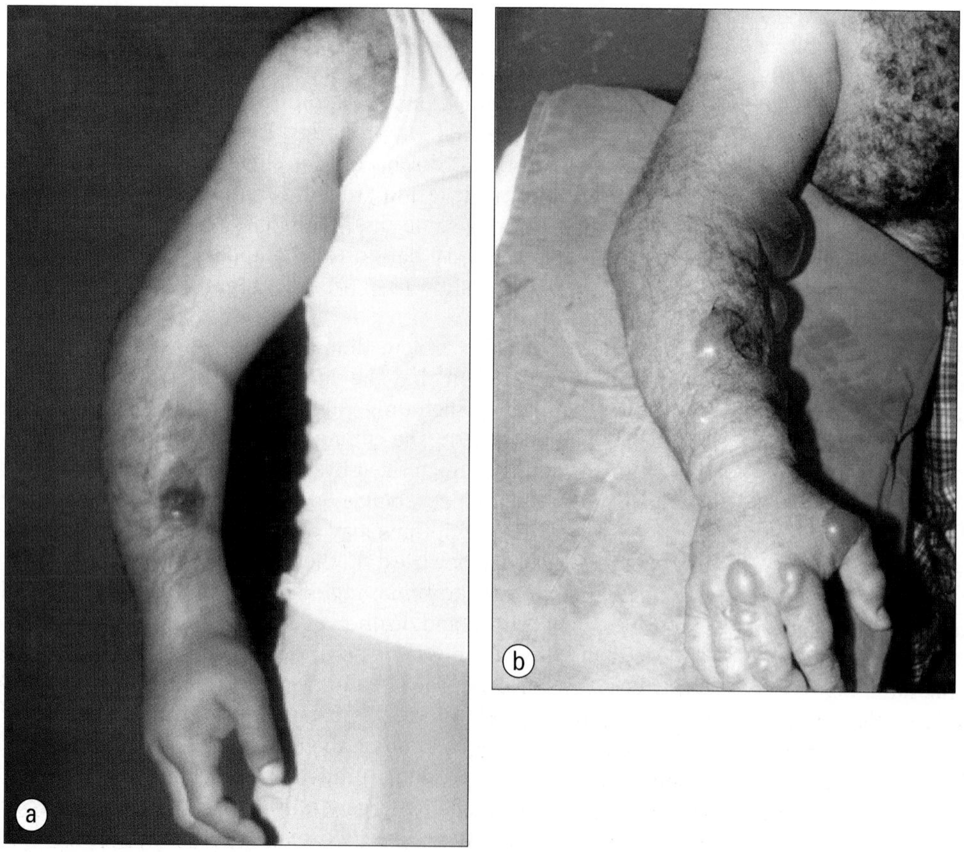

Fig. 185.2 Cutaneous anthrax. (a) A well developed lesion on the right forearm (third day of disease). (b) The extension of the skin lesion in the same patient on the sixth day. Extensive edema, induration and bullous changes have occurred over the last 3 days despite antibiotic therapy. Antibiotic therapy does not prevent inflammatory reactions.

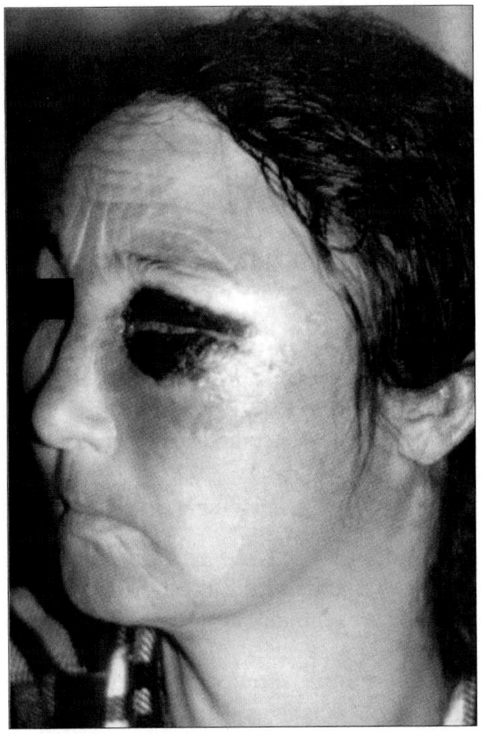

Fig. 185.3 A dried black anthrax eschar on the eyelids on the 15th day of therapy (third week of the disease). The lesion healed leaving a deep scar. Courtesy of Professor O Ural, Konya, Turkey.

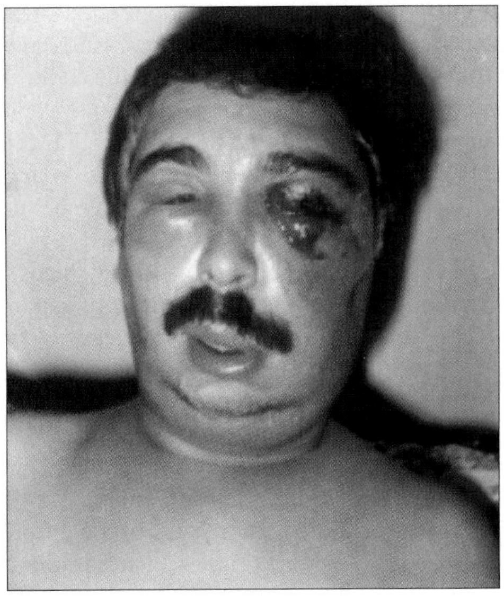

Fig. 185.4 An anthrax lesion of the eyelids surrounded by erythema and massive edema extending from the left eye to the right and down to and beyond the neck. Such extensive edema is characteristic of anthrax. This lesion healed with therapy and left a deep scar.

DISTRIBUTION OF LESIONS IN 114 CASES OF ANTHRAX		
Site of lesion	No. of cases	No. of deaths
Cutaneous	**107**	**0**
Hands and fingers	79	
Wrist and arms	10	
Eyelid and face	11	
Neck	2	
Foot and leg	5	
Oropharyngeal	**6**	**3**
Tonsil	5	
Tongue	1	
Meningitis	**1**	**1**

Table 185.1 Distribution of lesions in 114 cases of anthrax.

The disease progresses to the second phase within 2–3 days. The second phase is characterized by high fever, toxemia, dyspnea and cyanosis. Hypothermia and shock develop, resulting in death. In up to half of patients, meningitis develops as a complication.[7,13]

Anthrax meningitis

The meningeal form of anthrax is very rare. The world's literature contains approximately 100 cases of anthrax meningitis, with a mortality rate of over 90%.[8,14]

Meningitis may be a complication of the three forms of primary anthrax. The most common portal of entry is skin (52%) and then the lungs (22.9%). Anthrax meningitis also occurs in cases of gastrointestinal anthrax. The organisms can spread to the central nervous system by hematogenous or lymphatic routes. The primary focus of infection can not be determined in about 10% of cases and it is called primary anthrax meningitis. Blood cultures are positive for *B. anthracis* in 70% of patients who have meningitis.[14]

The clinical presentation includes sudden onset of fever, fatigue, myalgia, headache, nausea, vomiting, agitation, seizures, delirium and meningeal symptoms. The initial signs are followed by rapid neurologic deterioration and death. The cerebrospinal fluid is often bloody and contains many Gram-positive bacilli.[7,8,14]

Anthrax sepsis

Sepsis may occur by spreading of *B. anthracis* via lymphohematogenous route from a primary lesion. Sepsis is rarely seen in patients who have cutaneous anthrax; it is more commonly seen in patients who have inhalation and gastrointestinal anthrax. Clinical features include fever, respiratory distress and changing mental status. Severe toxemia and shock may lead to death in a short time.[5,8]

COMPLICATIONS

Some 10–20% of untreated cases of cutaneous anthrax might be expected to result in death. With treatment, the mortality rate is less than 1%. Toxemic shock due to massive edema, airway obstruction by compression on the trachea from edematous swelling around the neck, deep scar tissue, deep tissue necrosis and secondary infection are all recorded as complications in cases of cutaneous anthrax.[1,7,8] In our 107 cases of cutaneous anthrax, toxemic shock occurred in two cases, airway obstruction in two, eyelid deformity in two, temporal artery inflammation in one, and secondary infection and deep tissue necrosis in two.[6,10,11]

Serious complications such as sepsis and meningitis can be seen in inhalation anthrax and gastrointestinal anthrax. These complications are less frequently seen in cutaneous anthrax. The mortality rate in industrial-related inhalation anthrax is over 80%, despite treatment. Gastrointestinal anthrax is also a potentially fatal disease. Mortality is greater than 50%. If an early diagnosis is made and an appropriate treatment is given, the disease can be cured.[1,5,7,8,13]

DIFFERENTIAL DIAGNOSIS

A history of exposure to contaminated animal materials, occupational exposure and living in an endemic area are all important clues for the suspicion of anthrax.[3,8]

Cutaneous anthrax should be suspected when the patient describes a painless, pruritic papule, surrounding vesicles and edema, usually on an exposed part of the body. The ulcerative eschar of cutaneous anthrax must be differentiated from other papular and ulcerative lesions that present with regional lymphadenopathy. If regional lymphadenopathy together with a purulent lesion is present, a cutaneous anthrax lesion may be superinfected with pyogenic bacteria such as staphylococci. The differential diagnosis should include ecthyma gangrenosum, rat-bite fever, ulceroglandular tularemia, plague, glanders, orf, rickettsialpox, erysipelas, staphylococcal skin and lymph node infection, syphilitic chancre and cutaneous tuberculosis.[7–9,13] Occasionally, the cutaneous reaction may be severe. A severe cutaneous anthrax lesion involving the face, neck and anterior chest wall must be differentiated from orbital cellulitis, dacryocystitis and deep tissue infection of the neck. Necrotizing soft tissue infections – particularly group A streptococcal infections and gas gangrene – and severe cellulitis due to staphylococci should also be considered in the differential diagnosis of severe forms of cutaneous anthrax. Gas and abscess formation are not observed in patients who have cutaneous anthrax.[7–9]

Intestinal anthrax mimics food poisoning (in the early stages), acute abdomen of other causes and hemorrhagic gastroenteritis, particularly necrotizing enteritis due to *Clostridium perfringens*.[7,8] In the differential diagnosis of oropharyngeal anthrax, streptococcal pharyngitis, Vincent's angina, Ludwig's angina, parapharyngeal abscess and deep tissue infection of the neck should be considered.[5]

The clinical picture of anthrax meningitis is acute hemorrhagic meningitis. Differential diagnosis should include acute meningitis of other bacterial etiology and subarachnoid hemorrhage. In the differential diagnosis of anthrax sepsis, sepsis due to other bacteria should be considered.[7,8]

The initial symptoms of inhalation anthrax are non-specific and clinical presentation is similar to those of atypical pneumonia from other causes and cardiovascular collapse with noninfectious causes.[7,13] More details on inhalation anthrax are given in Chapter 231.

INVESTIGATIONS

The investigation of a potential exposure to the infectious agent is very important for suspicion of anthrax. However, the source of infection cannot be determined in some cases.

The well-developed lesion of cutaneous anthrax is readily recognized by its central eschar, ring of vesicles and accompanying edema. Swabs are appropriate for collecting vesicular exudates for microscopy and bacterial culture. In a well formed eschar, in which vesicular exudate is absent, the edge of the eschar can be lifted up with forceps and fluid obtained by a capillary tube. A smear is made from the material and is stained with polychrome methylene blue and examined microscopically for the presence of the pink-staining encapsulated bacilli (McFadyean reaction). The samples are also inoculated on blood agar.[1,8]

For the isolation of *B. anthracis* in patients who have suspected gastrointestinal anthrax, swabs from oropharyngeal lesion, vomit, fecal specimens, blood and ascites samples are obtained. Specimens likely to be contaminated with commensal flora should be cultured on polymyxin-lysozyme-EDTA-thallous acetate (PLET) agar as a selective medium for *B. anthracis*.[1,8]

Radiographic examination of the chest usually reveals widening of the mediastinum in inhalation anthrax. Parenchymal infiltration and pleural effusion can also be seen. Direct examination of a smear of pleural fluid or blood, stained with polychrome methylene blue or Gram stain, may show encapsulated bacilli. *Bacillus anthracis* can be isolated from the cultures of these specimens. Culture of nasal swabs has been used for the determination of inhalation exposure to *B. anthracis*.[2,7,13]

Blood or cerebrospinal fluid smear stained with polychrome methylene blue should be examined for the encapsulated bacilli and blood or/and cerebrospinal fluid cultures are taken for the isolation of *B. anthracis* in cases of sepsis or meningitis.[7,8,14]

Serologic tests are also useful for diagnosis of anthrax. For routine confirmation of anthrax infection or in monitoring the response to the anthrax vaccine, a determination of antibodies against protective antigen alone appears to be satisfactory. Diagnosis may be confirmed serologically by demonstrating an increase in antibody titers; two or more serum samples taken 2–4 weeks apart will give greater diagnostic reliability. If only one serum sample is collected, it will be of greater diagnostic value if collected more than a week after the onset of symptoms.[15]

New diagnostic techniques include immunohistochemical testing of clinical specimens by using *B. anthracis* capsule and cell wall antibody and, most recently, by *B. anthracis*-specific polymerase chain reaction. These new rapid methods may become useful in early diagnosis and in culture-negative patients.[2,7]

MANAGEMENT

Viable *B. anthracis* organisms disappear from the lesions of cutaneous anthrax within a few hours of the initiation of treatment with parenteral penicillin G. Given the severity of disease, however, patients who have suspected anthrax should receive immediate empiric therapy pending definitive diagnosis. Penicillin G has been the drug of choice, an alternate being doxycycline (although recently ciprofloxacin has been added as a first line agent – see below). Treatment is usually continued for 7–10 days. Naturally occurring strains have also been sensitive to erythromycin, cefazolin, tetracycline, chloramphenicol, gentamicin and ciprofloxacin (see also Chapter 226).

The recommendations for antibiotic use in the setting of a bioterrorism attack are based upon a small series of cases in humans, studies in experimental animals and the knowledge that strains may have been engineered for antibiotic resistance.[16] Because of the rapid course of bioterrorism-related symptomatic inhalation anthrax, early antibiotic administration is essential. Limited early information from the 2001 anthrax attacks suggest that those treated with two or more intravenous antibiotics active for *B. anthracis* had a greater chance of survival.[2] Although small numbers make these observations statistically inconclusive, given the severity of the illness, this seems prudent. The treatment of choice has been ciprofloxacin, with doxycycline as an alternative. An aminoglycoside is often added. Once clinically stable, patients are switched to oral regimens but, because of the risk of delayed germination of spores, it has been suggested that antibiotic therapy should be continued for at least 60 days.

PREVENTION

The mainstay of prevention of anthrax is the avoidance of contaminated animals or animal products. An inactivated acellular vaccine exists and is used mostly in occupational and military settings. This vaccine is not recommended for normal travelers unless there is likely to be occupational exposure. A live attenuated vaccine has been produced and used in the former Soviet Union. Accelerated development is underway to produce safer and more effective vaccines.

REFERENCES

1. Quinn CP, Turnbull PCB. Anthrax. In: Collier L, Balouas A, Sussman M, eds. Topley-Wilson's microbiology and microbial infections. Vol. 3, Bacterial infections. London: Edward Arnold 1998:799–818.
2. Jernigan JA, Stephens DS, Ashford DA, *et al.* Bioterrorism-related inhalational anthrax: the first 10 cases reported in the United States. Emerg Infect Dis 2001;7:933–44.
3. Brachman PS. Anthrax. In: Evans SA, Brachman PS, eds. Bacterial infections of humans, epidemiology and control. New York: Plenum; 1991:75–86.
4. Amidi S, Dutz W, Kohout E, Ronaghy A. Human anthrax in Iran: report of 300 cases and review of literature. Z Tropenmed Parasit 1974;25:96–104.
5. Doganay M, Almac A, Hanagasi R. Primary throat anthrax: a report of six cases. Scand J Infect Dis 1986;18:415–9.
6. Doganay M. Human anthrax in Turkey. Salisbury Med Bull 1996;87(Special Suppl.):8.
7. Dixon T, Meselson M, Guillemin J, Hanna PC. Anthrax. N Engl J Med 1999;341:815–86.
8. Turnbull PCB, Böhm R, Cosivi O, *et al.* Guidelines for the surveillance and control of anthrax in humans and animals. Geneva: World Health Organization; 1998.
9. Doganay M, Aygen B. Cutaneous anthrax (photo quiz). Clin Infect Dis 1997;25:607, 725.
10. Doganay M, Bakir M, Dokmetas I. A case of cutaneous anthrax with toxaemic shock. Br J Dermatol 1987;117:659–62.
11. Doganay M, Aygen B, Inan M, Kandemir O, Turnbull P. Temporal artery inflammation as a complication of anthrax. J Infect Dis 1994;28:311–4.
12. Meselson M, Guillemin J, Hugh-Jones M, *et al.* The Sverdlovsk anthrax outbreak of 1979. Science 1994;266:1202–8.
13. Swartz MN. Recognition and management of anthrax: an update. N Engl J Med 2001;345:1621–6.
14. Koshi G, Lalitha MK, Daniel J, Chacko A, Pulimood BM. Anthrax meningitis, a rare clinical entity. J Assoc Physicians India 1981;29:59–62.
15. Turnbull PCB, Doganay M, Lindeque PM, Aygen B, McLaughlin J. Serology and anthrax in humans, livestock and Etosha National Park wildlife. Epidemiol Infect 1992;108:299–313.
16. Inglesby TV, O'Toole T, Henderson DA, *et al.* Anthrax as a biologic weapon, 2002. Updated recommendations for management. JAMA 2002;287:2236–52.

chapter
186 Practice Points

a. Management of a patient who has suspected viral hemorrhagic fever

Steven M Opal

Introduction

Continued expansion of human populations into tropical rain forests, economic pressures and changing ecologic conditions around equatorial regions of the world have increased the risk of exposure to a variety of tropical viral diseases. Global markets and expanded international trade in combination with improved access to remote areas by expanded international airline transportation makes it feasible that these viral illnesses could spread worldwide. Physicians in endemic areas must be aware of the potential threat of viral hemorrhagic illnesses. Moreover, physicians in nonendemic regions must recognize the potential risk of hemorrhagic viral illness in international travelers from tropical regions. Animal handlers in primate research laboratories throughout the world are also at risk. Regrettably, these viral agents are potentially exploitable as a bioterrorist weapon as well. It is essential that health care facilities develop a plan to manage viral hemorrhagic fever (VHF) even if the chances of seeing such patients seem remote.

It is important that physicians are aware of the potential risk of tropical VHFs for several reasons:

- to ensure appropriate diagnosis and management of index cases;
- to provide advice, counseling and possible prophylaxis to close contacts;
- to minimize the risk of nosocomial transmission among health care workers (HCWs) caring for such patients; and
- to contact public health authorities immediately in the event of a possible outbreak of VHF.

Strict adherence to basic infection control techniques and some advance planning will minimize the risk to HCWs and allow rapid, compassionate and safe care of affected patients.

Microbiology and pathogenesis

Hemorrhagic viruses in which person-to-person transmission has been documented include representatives of the arenavirus, bunyavirus and the filovirus groups. The most important examples are Lassa fever, Ebola virus and Marburg virus, and Crimean–Congo hemorrhagic fever, caused by a tick-transmitted bunyavirus (see Chapter 222). Lassa, Ebola, Marburg and Crimean–Congo hemorrhagic fever viruses are particularly important to recognize because nosocomial transmission to HCWs is a real possibility. Although the animal reservoir and mode of transmission to humans is reasonably well understood for Lassa and Crimean–Congo hemorrhagic fevers, the method of transmission of Ebola virus and Marburg virus remain an unsolved mystery.

These viral syndromes share many overlapping clinical features in humans. After an incubation period of between 3 and 21 days, patients develop the abrupt onset of fever, headache, myalgia, sore throat, respiratory symptoms, abdominal pain, nausea, vomiting, diarrhea and conjunctivitis with associated pharyngitis and cervical lymphadenitis. A macular skin eruption may occur in infections with Ebola and Marburg virus; this is less common in Lassa and Crimean–Congo hemorrhagic fever. Various degrees of mucosal and cutaneous hemorrhage occur associated with thrombocytopenia and disseminated intravascular coagulation. The geographic location or travel history of the patient is most useful in distinguishing between the different types of VHFs before virologic confirmation.

The viruses share rapid growth potential and the ability to invade a variety of cell types, resulting in high-grade viremia. The patient's blood and body fluids become potentially contagious to others who come in direct contact with them. Transmission may also occur through handling of bodies during burial rituals, as demonstrated in recent Ebola outbreaks in central Africa. Although many other febrile illnesses, such as malaria, typhoid fever, meningococcemia, arboviral infections and leptospirosis, may present in a similar fashion, infection control measures must be instituted to guard against potential transmission of VHFs until the diagnosis is established.

Diagnosis and management

Recent improvements in the serologic diagnosis of VHFs now make it possible to make a specific diagnosis in the majority of acutely ill patients. An antigen-capture enzyme-linked immunosorbent assay (ELISA) has been developed for Ebola virus and may allow rapid diagnosis in acutely ill patients. Specific IgM and IgG capture ELISA antibody studies are available for serologic diagnosis in convalescent samples. Unfortunately, diseases such as Ebola virus infection, in

INFECTION CONTROL METHODS FOR SUSPECTED VHFs	
Isolation method	**Comments**
Isolation room	In the past, the negative pressure room was the ideal and still may be used where available. However, the patient can be managed through strict contact isolation, universal blood and body substance precautions and enhanced prevention measures in the handling of blood and body fluids
Personnel and visitors	Traffic flow into the patient's room should be restricted. A daily record of those who enter and leave the patient's room should be kept. Only essential personnel should be exposed to the patient and the patient's body fluids
Personal protection	Fluid-impervious gowns, gloves, face shields or surgical masks with eye protection (goggles); if cough, vomiting or extensive hemorrhage, respirators with filters (high-efficiency particulate air respirators) and leg and shoe coverings should be worn
Clinical samples	Clinical samples should be placed in plastic sealed bags and transported in a leak proof container without contaminating the external surfaces. Samples should be handled in a biologic safety cabinet (biosafety level III). Serum should be pretreated with a polyethylene glycol phenolic for 1 hour before handling. Automated analyzers should be disinfected with 1:100 dilution of bleach after use. Fixation of blood smears and tissue samples will inactivate the virus and can be handled in a routine manner
Decontamination of the environment and of linen	Contaminated environmental surfaces should be disinfected using a registered hospital disinfectant or 1:100 dilution of bleach. Soiled linens can either be decontaminated by use of an autoclave or incineration. Hot cycle laundering with bleach may be acceptable.
Human excrement and blood and body fluids	As an added precaution, human excreta, blood and body fluids should be decontaminated by 1:100 dilution of bleach for at least 5 minutes before disposal
Surgical procedures and autopsy	If a surgical procedure or autopsy is essential, extreme precautions must be used to avoid blood contamination. Double gloves, full face shields with high-efficiency particulate air filtration, water-impervious gowns and shoe covers should be worn. Every effort should be taken to avoid generation of an aerosol. Deceased persons should not be embalmed. The body should be placed in leakproof, sealed material and cremated or buried in a sealed casket

Table 186a.1 Infection control methods for suspected viral hemorrhagic fevers.

which mortality rates exceed 75%, do not often allow the opportunity to study convalescent samples. Virus isolation from the blood and body secretions of acutely ill patients is the definitive diagnostic method. This is, of course, a severe biohazard and it should only be attempted in biosafety level IV facilities. Reverse transcription and polymerase chain reaction for specific viral RNA is also a useful diagnostic method in patients who have viral hemorrhagic illnesses. Many of these methodologies are unavailable in regions of the world where these diseases are endemic. For this reason, the recent development of an immunochemical staining method for skin biopsy samples is particularly valuable. This method allows for fixation of tissues at the site of diagnosis and eliminates the biohazard of transportation of infected human tissues.

Routine diagnostic methods to evaluate other common febrile illnesses should not be delayed because of suspected VHF. In particular, care must be taken to exclude falciparum malaria, which may be fatal if unrecognized and left untreated. In practice, most cases of suspected VHF turn out to be malaria. Universal precautions when handling blood and body secretions should suffice to protect HCWs from hemorrhagic viruses (see Chapter 183).

Infection control methods

The viruses are transmitted through direct contact with the patient or the patient's secretions. There is a remote risk of airborne transmission based upon studies with nonhuman primates, and one potential transmission by respiratory aerosol in a patient who had Lassa fever with extensive pulmonary involvement has been reported. Therefore, the primary infection control strategy is strict contact isolation, universal blood and body substance precautions, and enhanced preventive measures in the handling of blood and body fluids. Body substances are contagious during the acute febrile illness, but there is no evidence of transmission during the incubation phase of the illness. The guidelines listed in Table 186a.1 should be instituted in patients who have suspected VHF.

Postexposure prophylaxis

The arenavirus that causes Lassa fever is susceptible to ribavirin, and this antiviral agent may be of some value to HCWs exposed to blood or body fluids (e.g. by percutaneous needlestick accident). Passive immunotherapy with plasma from surviving patients with high-titer antibody has been shown to be of limited benefit in the prevention of VHF.

Reporting

It is essential that patients who have suspected VHF are reported to public health authorities as soon as possible. This allows a coordinated response to a potential epidemic situation and ensures that diagnostic and therapeutic efforts will be handled appropriately. Expert international assistance may be necessary should a VHF occur in an international traveler.

Further reading

Centers for Disease Control and Prevention. Outbreak of Ebola viral hemorrhagic fever – Zaire, 1995. MMWR Morb Mortal Wkly Rep 1995;44:381–2.

Centers for Disease Control and Prevention. Update: management of patients with suspected viral hemorrhagic fever – United States. MMWR Morb Mortal Wkly Rep 1995;44:475–9.

Holmes GP, McCormick JB, Trock SC. Lassa fever in the United States – investigation of a case and new guidelines for management. N Engl J Med 1990;323:1120–3.

Peters CJ. Emerging infections – Ebola and other filo viruses. West J Med 1996;164:36–8.

Peters CJ. Many viruses are potential agents of bioterrorism. ASM News 2002;68:168–73.

Peters CJ, Sanchez A, Feldmann H, Rollin PE, Nichol S, Ksiaek TG. Filo viruses as emerging pathogens. Semin Virol 1994;5:147–54

b. Follow-up of the traveler who has swum in Lake Malawi

Nick J Beeching

Introduction

Lake Malawi is a huge freshwater resource 630km long and 50km wide in Central Africa, providing essential food and income for a large proportion of Malawians and people of the other nations that border its shores (Fig. 186b.1). Over the past two decades it has become a major attraction for both 'local' tourists and for backpackers and overlanders from outside Africa, with the associated development of hotels and facilities for watersports such as scuba diving and windsurfing. These are especially found in the south around Cape Maclear and Monkey Bay, where the shores are relatively shallow and the snail vectors for *Schistosoma haematobium* have become established. Further north and centrally, the ecology of the lake differs, with deep water close to the land. Bilharzia was recognized by early European visitors to Malawi and was noted in 50% of lakeshore inhabitants in the early 1900s. It has become more widely established since then, particularly with the development of irrigation schemes. The predominant species is *Schistosoma haematobium*, but small pockets of *Schistosoma mansoni* also exist.

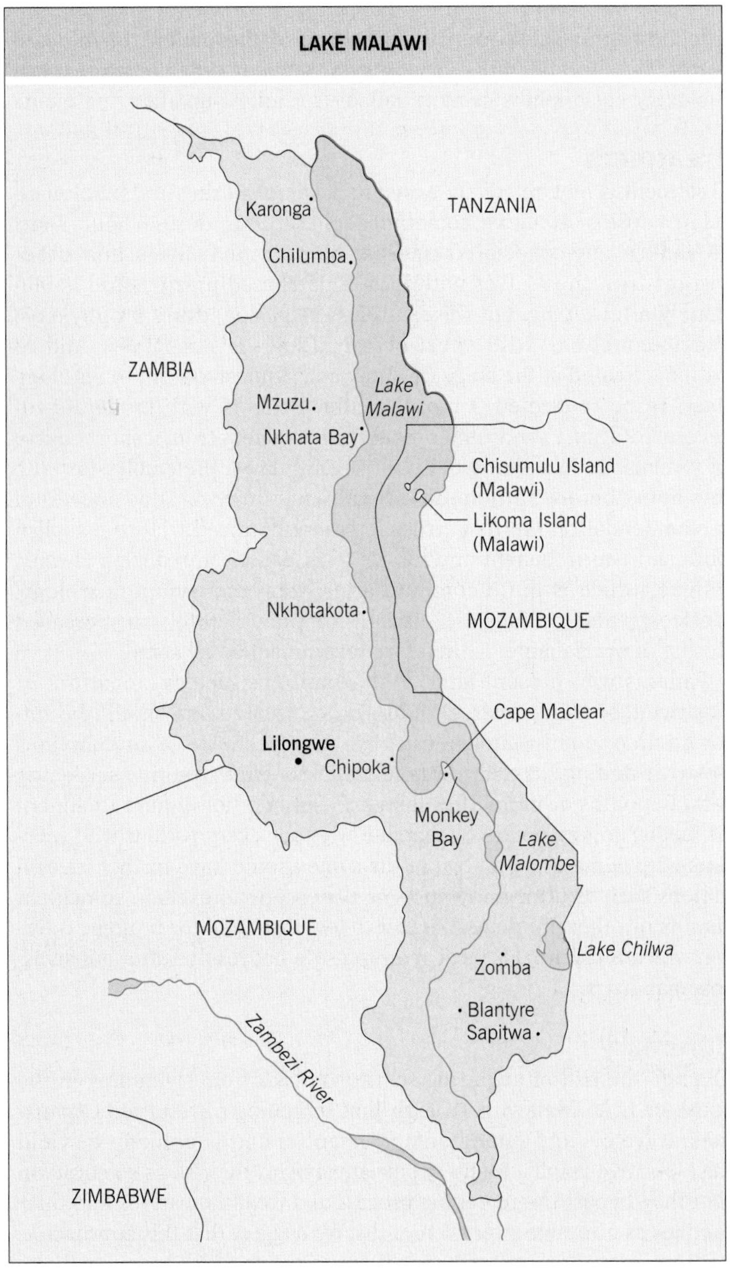

Fig. 186b.1 Lake Malawi.

Schistosomiasis has become a common diagnosis in expatriates and short-term tourists in Malawi. Similar risks are already well-recognized for visitors to the Dogon area of Mali or to the waters of the Kariba Dam and the Zambesi, but Lake Malawi has overtaken these sites as the main source of the many cases of schistosomiasis imported annually from Africa to the UK and elsewhere. A large case–control study showed that 33% of foreigners in Malawi had serologic evidence of exposure to infection, the highest risk being associated with repeated exposure to the lake, especially around Cape Maclear. Our own experience of screening groups of returned travelers is that 75% of those who spend a week scuba diving at Cape Maclear will have clinical or asymptomatic laboratory evidence of infection. People are at risk from showers and swimming pools that are fed directly with unchlorinated lake water as well as from paddling and swimming. Brief exposure is sufficient; we recently screened students from the same school who had spent 48 hours only at two locations around the lake. Of those camping near Cape Maclear 90% (19/21) had been infected, compared with none of 17 students camping on Likoma Island, another popular tourist spot.

General approach to the traveler who has swum in Lake Malawi

The general approach to the traveler who has swum in Lake Malawi is the same as that for any other traveler, including the need to exclude malaria in febrile patients. A detailed travel and exposure history must be taken, including the precise timing, frequency, type and locations of any freshwater contact. Previous travel and possible schistosomal risk activity should be checked along with pre-existing illnesses including atopy and urologic or gastrointestinal problems. Enquiries should routinely review adherence to antimalarial chemoprophylaxis and mosquito avoidance measures, and the use of measures that might reduce schistosomal load such as vigorous rubbing of the skin immediately after immersion, or pre-exposure use of anti-schistosomal soaps or permethrin on the skin.

Only a minority of people will remember experiencing 'swimmer's itch', lasting from a few to 48 hours after swimming, caused by penetration of the skin by cercariae. This does not reliably predict later symptoms, which first appear in a substantial minority of patients 3–8 weeks after exposure, as the 'Katayama syndrome,' which is related to an immunologic reaction to final migration of schistosomules around the body and the onset of oviposition by the maturing flukes (see Chapter 167). Typical symptoms include fever, headache, malaise, wheezing, dry cough and dyspnea. Transient urticarial rashes are common (Fig. 186b.2), and lymphadenopathy and hepatosplenomegaly may be found on examination. Usually this is a diagnosis of exclusion and the supportive laboratory finding of eosinophilia exceeding $2 \times 10^9/l$ is not always present. We have seen cases misdiagnosed as glandular fever due to coincident lymphocytosis, false-positive slide tests for infectious mononucleosis and mild disturbance of liver function tests. Transient shadows may be seen on chest radiographs.

Whether or not patients have experienced earlier symptoms, continued oviposition from 3 to 6 months after exposure may then cause symptoms related to the organs involved. *Schistosoma haematobium* principally affects bladder, prostate and seminal vesicles and typical complaints are of terminal hematuria, perineal discomfort and, in males, alteration in the consistency (thin or lumpy) or color (yellow

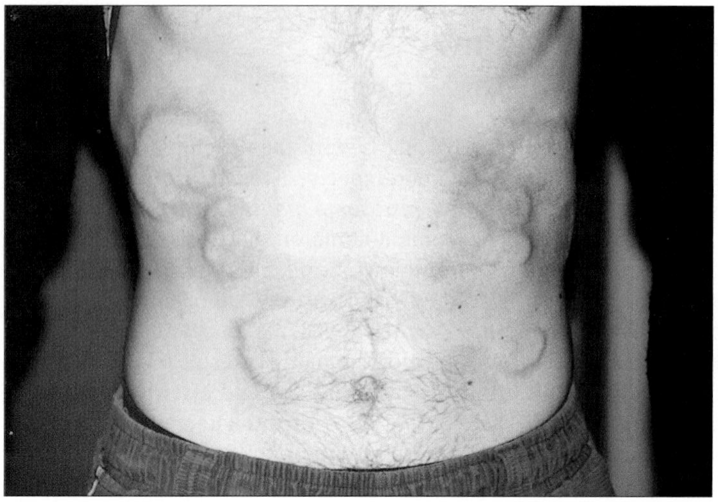

Fig. 186b.2 Giant urticaria associated with Katayama syndrome after swimming in Lake Malawi. Courtesy of Dr ME Jones, Edinburgh.

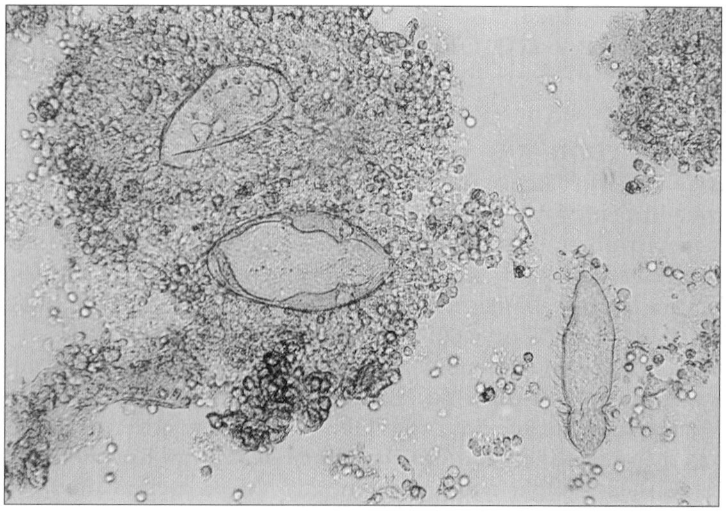

Fig. 186b.3 Empty ovum case and hatched miracidium of *Schistosoma haematobium* in semen. Note oligospermia, which usually resolves after treatment.

or frank blood) of semen. Women occasionally notice a wart-like genital granuloma. *Schistosoma mansoni* primarily affects the large bowel, leading to blood in feces and alteration in bowel habit, but the anatomic location of both species has considerable overlap. Symptoms are more common with *S. haematobium* infections and may be associated with non-specific fatigue.

The long-term outcome of untreated, relatively light infections of visitors is unknown, but is likely to be benign and not to lead to the complications caused by chronic and repeated infections of inhabitants of endemic areas, such as bladder cancer and portal or pulmonary hypertension (see Chapter 167). However, a small minority of travelers develop central nervous system complications such as epilepsy or spinal cord damage due to ectopic deposition of ova, and the general expert consensus is that all exposed travelers should be screened and treated.

Screening

The minimum investigations, whether or not symptoms are present, should include an absolute eosinophil count, testing of urine for blood, and microscopy for ova in feces and on a filter of a 4-hour mid-day urine specimen. 'Routine' urine microscopy is insufficiently sensitive. Semen microscopy may become positive earlier than urine or feces, and males can be asked to provide a sample for microscopy, particularly if being screened in the first few months after water exposure (Fig. 186b.3). If the index of clinical suspicion remains high and other tests are negative, a squash preparation of a fresh rectal biopsy can be examined for ova. Viability of ova, hence current infection, can be inferred from the observation of active flame cells within the miracidium developing in the ovum. Eosinophilia is only found in about 50% of patients in the chronic phase of infection.

The rather crude serologic tests available from European reference centers include an enzyme-linked immunosorbent assay (ELISA) using circumoval protein as antigen to detect circulating antischistosomal antibodies. These become positive from about the time of oviposition, but seroconversion may take up to 6 months and late follow-up screening is essential for those who are asymptomatic and who have negative tests before this time. The serologic tests available from the US Centers for Disease Control and Prevention become positive soon after exposure to infection, and discriminate between *S. haematobium* and other species. Once positive, serology remains positive for years and titers may even increase during the first year after treatment. Follow-up serologic tests after treatment are not, therefore, useful as a test of cure or even for distinguishing reinfection after subsequent re-exposure of the patient to infected water. The disappearance of any symptoms or other positive tests, including eosinophilia, is more reliable for follow-up after treatment.

Treatment

Treatment is now relatively easy and harmless, using oral praziquantel in a dose of 40mg/kg, sometimes split into two doses 6 hours apart to reduce any associated nausea. Many scuba divers and other visitors treat themselves with locally purchased praziquantel immediately after diving, but this is useless as postexposure prophylaxis. Praziquantel has little effect on migrating schistosomules, and so patients treated at the stage of Katayama syndrome symptomatology need to be re-treated 3 months later. Patients with moderate-to-severe Katayama syndrome probably also benefit from a short course of prednisone (e.g. 40mg daily for several days), preferably started a few hours before anthelmintic treatment. However, this anecdotal recommendation merits a prospective randomized trial to establish both short-term benefit and longer term benefit in reducing chronic fatigue, which is quite common after Katayama symptomatology. Coticosteroids reduce the efficacy of praziquantel, so increased dosing of praziquantel is therefore recommended by some.

Patients who present later, with symptoms such as hematuria or positive laboratory tests, should also be treated and should be followed up 6 months later to establish disappearance of any previous positive findings. Asymptomatic travelers with negative screening tests 6 months or more after lake exposure do not require treatment or further follow-up. It is debatable whether every patient who presents with hematuria and ova in the urine should have further investigations such as ultrasonography or cystoscopy to exclude coincident tumors or other problems. We have a low threshold for urologic referral, which is essential if local symptoms do not resolve after antischistosomal drugs.

Summary

Overall, the risk of acquiring schistosomiasis from swimming in the south of Lake Malawi is so high that screening of returned expatriates, travelers and immigrants is essential and is unlikely to yield false-positive results. Many expatriates regard the risk as so common that they bypass the screening process and treat themselves and their families as a routine every 6 months. We suggest that this approach is inappropriate for the occasional traveler who has swum in Lake Malawi (or similar freshwater bodies), who should be fully assessed before possible treatment with an anthelmintic that is only available on a named-patient basis outside the tropics.

Further reading

Cetron MS, Chitulo L, Sullivan JJ, *et al.* Schistosomiasis in Lake Malawi. Lancet 1996;348:1274–6.

Cooke GS, Lalvani A, Gleeson FV, Conlon CP. Acute pulmonary schistosomiasis in travelers returning from Lake Malawi. Clin Infect Dis 1999;29:836–9.

Day JH, Grant AD, Doherty JF, Chiodini PL, Wright SG. Schistosomiasis in travellers returning from sub-Saharan Africa. Br Med J 1996;313:268–9.

Harries AD, Cook GC. Acute schistosomiasis (Katayama fever): clinical deterioration after chemotherapy. J Infect 1987;14:159–61.

Joubert JJ, Evans C, Schutte CHJ. Schistosomiasis in Africa and international travel. J Travel Med 2001;8:92–9.

King M, King E. The story of medicine and disease in Malawi. Blantyre, Malawi: Montfort Press; 1992.

Leutscher P, Ravaoalimalala VE, Raharisolo C, *et al.* Clinical findings in female genital schistosomiasis in Madagascar. Trop Med Int Health 1997;3:327–32.

McKenna G, Schousboe M, Paltridge G. Subjective change in ejaculate as symptom of infection with *Schistosoma haematobium* in travellers. Br Med J 1997;314:1000–1.

Welby SB, Wyatt G, Squire B, Bailey W. An outbreak of schistosomiasis among medical students returning from Malawi, Central Africa. Travel Med Int 1999;17:169–72.

Whitty CJM, Mabey DC, Armstrong M, Wright SG, Chiodini PL. Presentation and outcome of 1107 cases of schistosomiasis from Africa diagnosed in a non-endemic country. Trans R Soc Trop Med Hyg 2000;94:531–4.

c. Indications for exchange transfusion in severe malaria

Robin Bailey

Introduction

Patients with high proportions of their red cells parasitized by *P. falciparum* are at increased risk of developing all the complications of severe malaria. It has been suggested that this risk is proportional to the parasitemia and thus that exchange transfusion might benefit some patients with very high parasite counts. The rationale for exchange transfusion is that physical removal of infected red blood cells from the circulation and their replacement by healthy and unparasitized red cells will:

- lower the parasite burden more quickly than chemotherapy alone;
- reduce the antigenic load and its concomitant burdens of parasite-derived toxins and metabolites and the host responses to them;
- correct anemia and improve the oxygen-carrying capacity and microcirculatory properties of the blood.

With these theoretical benefits come dangers of the procedure, including hypocalcemia, hemodynamic disturbance, transfusion reactions and infection.

The use of exchange transfusion has been reported in over 200 patients since 1974. A recent meta-analysis of eight studies involving 279 subjects with severe malaria found no evidence for a survival benefit and concluded that the evidence base supporting its use was inadequate, with publication bias and a tendency for more severely ill patients to receive exchange transfusion being particular difficulties in the interpretation of published studies. No adequately powered randomized controlled trial has been conducted and it is doubtful whether such a trial could be conducted given the logistic difficulties and the number of centers that would need to be involved. However, the balance of expert opinion favors its use as an adjunct to optimal chemotherapy in extreme situations.

When should exchange transfusion be considered?

Exchange transfusion only becomes an option if large amounts of adequately screened, pathogen-free and properly cross-matched blood are available, there are adequate monitoring facilities in a high-care environment, and the exchange itself can be carried out safely. The benefits may be greatest where nonimmune patients have high parasitemias and have not responded to optimal chemotherapy.

The WHO suggests the following indications for exchange transfusion in patients receiving optimal chemotherapy.

- Parasitemia of greater than 30%.
- Parasitemia of greater than 10% in the presence of severe or complicated disease, especially cerebral malaria, acute renal failure, adult respiratory distress syndrome or jaundice, or severe anemia.
- Parasitemia of greater than 10% not responding to optimal chemotherapy after 12–24 hours.
- Parasitemia of greater than 10% and poor prognostic features (for example, elderly patients or late-stage schizonts in the peripheral blood).

There are some problems in basing decisions on the parasitemia. Although high parasite densities imply severity, the reverse is not always true, particularly in nonimmune persons where there may be wide differences between the proportions of the burden of parasitized cells circulating in the peripheral blood as opposed to sequestered in the microvasculature. Serial blood films at 6–12 hour intervals may reveal rapid changes in parasitemia, especially in synchronous infections, even with optimal treatment. In particular, the relation between the peripheral blood and total body parasite burden depends on the stage of the parasite development. If early *P. falciparum* trophozoites are predominant the peripheral parasitemia is likely to be more representative of the parasitized cell burden in the body and, presumably, more easily removed by exchanging. The later pre-schizont and schizont stages sequester in the microvasculature, a phenomenon believed to be responsible for the cerebral and renal manifestations of severe malaria. Thus although the presence of late-stage schizonts on the peripheral blood film may indicate that another cycle of replication is imminent, a greater proportion of the parasitized red cells are sequestered and thus not accessible to removal during exchange transfusion.

Methods of exchange transfusion

Traditionally double-lumen catheters or venesection/transfusion through separate lines have been used to perform manual exchanges, usually of six units of blood, one unit at a time. This is time consuming and inevitably causes some hemodynamic disturbance. The use of cell separator hardware and software to remove only the red cell fraction and replace it with donor red cells in a single automated isovolemic procedure of 'erythrocytapheresis' is preferable as the method of choice where the expertise and facilities are available, for example in hematology departments in developed country settings.

Conclusion

Exchange transfusion as an adjunct to optimal chemotherapy in severe malaria is recommended by many centers, especially for high parasitemias in nonimmune patients. This cannot be considered an evidence-based recommendation, but it is supported by expert opinion for the indications listed above. A definitive randomized controlled trial is needed, but would be difficult to carry out.

Further reading

Field JW. Blood examination and prognosis in acute falciparum malaria. Trans Roy Soc Trop Med Hyg 1949;43:33–48.

Macallan DC, Pocock M, Robinson GT, Parker-Williams J, Bevan DH. Red cell exchange, erythrocytapheresis, in the treatment of malaria with high parasitaemia in returning travellers Trans Roy Soc Trop Med Hyg 2000;94(4):353–6.

Riddle MS, Jackson JL, Sanders JW, Blazes DL. Exchange transfusion as an adjunct therapy in severe Plasmodium falciparum malaria: a meta-analysis. Clin Infect Dis 2002;34:1192–8.

White NJ, Chapman D, Watt G. The effects of multiplication and synchronicity on the vascular distribution of parasites in falciparum malaria. Trans Roy Soc Trop Med Hyg 1992;86:590–7.

WHO. Severe falciparum malaria. Trans Roy Soc Trop Med Hyg 2000;94(suppl 1):1–90.

d. What are the treatment options for a pregnant patient with malaria?

Edgar Dorman & Caroline Shulman

Definition of the problem

Falciparum malaria is responsible for massive maternal and perinatal morbidity and mortality globally. The clinical features in pregnancy depend to a large extent on the immune status of the woman, which in turn is determined by her previous exposure and continued exposure to malaria.

In pregnant women with little or no pre-existing immunity, such as travelers or women from nonendemic areas, infection is associated with extremely high risks of both maternal and perinatal mortality. Women of all parities are affected and are at 2–3 times greater risk of developing severe disease than nonpregnant women. They are also at approximately three times greater risk of dying if they do develop severe disease. Severe disease in pregnant women has been associated with 20–30% maternal mortality and at least a 60% risk of miscarriage, premature delivery or neonatal death. Particular dangers are hyperpyrexia, hypoglycemia, severe hemolytic anemia, cerebral malaria and pulmonary edema. The hyperpyrexia can precipitate miscarriage or premature labor. Hypoglycemia may be severe and refractory and may be associated with fetal heart rate abnormalities. It may be present prior to commencement of treatment but is particularly common in patients treated with quinine, due to quinine-induced hyperinsulinism. Although hypoglycemia usually presents as an alteration in the woman's conscious level or as abnormal behavior, often with sweating and an increased respiratory rate or dyspnea, it may be asymptomatic. Pulmonary edema associated with malaria in pregnancy is usually due to abnormal capillary permeability and can occur without positive fluid balance, as acute respiratory distress syndrome.

In areas of moderate or high transmission (holo- or hyperendemic), including large parts of sub-Saharan Africa, adults usually have a high level of immunity to malaria, maintained by continued exposure to infection. During pregnancy, this immunity is altered and pregnant women are at greater risk of infection than nonpregnant women. Primigravidae are affected most, with the risk decreasing in each successive pregnancy. In women with substantial pre-existing immunity, severe disease is uncommon and infection is frequently asymptomatic. However, even when asymptomatic, placental parasitization is common, whereby infected red cells sequester in the placenta in the intervillous space and malaria in pregnancy is associated with the development of severe maternal anemia and low birth-weight delivery. The low birth weight is mediated through a combination of intrauterine growth restriction (IUGR) and prematurity. Because it is asymptomatic, malaria may go unsuspected and undetected, particularly as the peripheral film may be negative despite placental infection (Fig. 186d.1).

The other species of malaria are not associated with severe disease and usually present with fever, although infection with *Plasmodium vivax* during pregnancy is associated with mild anemia and low birth-weight delivery.

Clinical cases

Case 1 – nonimmune

A 37-year-old West African woman presented to a London maternity department at 29 weeks' gestation in her first pregnancy, with a 5-day history of fever. She had recently returned to London, her home for the past 2 years. On admission her temperature was 103.1°F (39.5°C), pulse 130 beats/min (bpm) and, blood pressure 108/56mmHg. She was conscious and responsive. Her urine contained protein ++ on ward testing and was sent for culture (subsequently negative). Her uterus was soft and fetal size was appropriate for 29 weeks. There was a fetal tachycardia (180 bpm) with a suspicious pattern: a flat trace with reduced short-term variability (<5 bpm). Her initial investigation results were as follows: hemoglobin (Hb) 8.2g/dl, white blood cell (WBC) count $18 \times 10^9/1$ and platelets $66 \times 10^9/1$. Apart from her thrombocytopenia, her coagulation screen was normal. Two hours after admission her malaria film was reported to be positive with a 10% *Plasmodium falciparum* parasitemia. Her blood sugar was subsequently found to be 2.6mmol/l.

The patient was transferred to the intensive care unit and commenced on an infusion of 10% dextrose after a bolus of 50%. She received a loading dose of intravenous quinine 20mg/kg over 4 hours. In view of the hyperparasitemia, she was transferred to a tertiary referral unit for consideration of exchange transfusion. She required two top-up transfusions over the subsequent 3 days but her para-

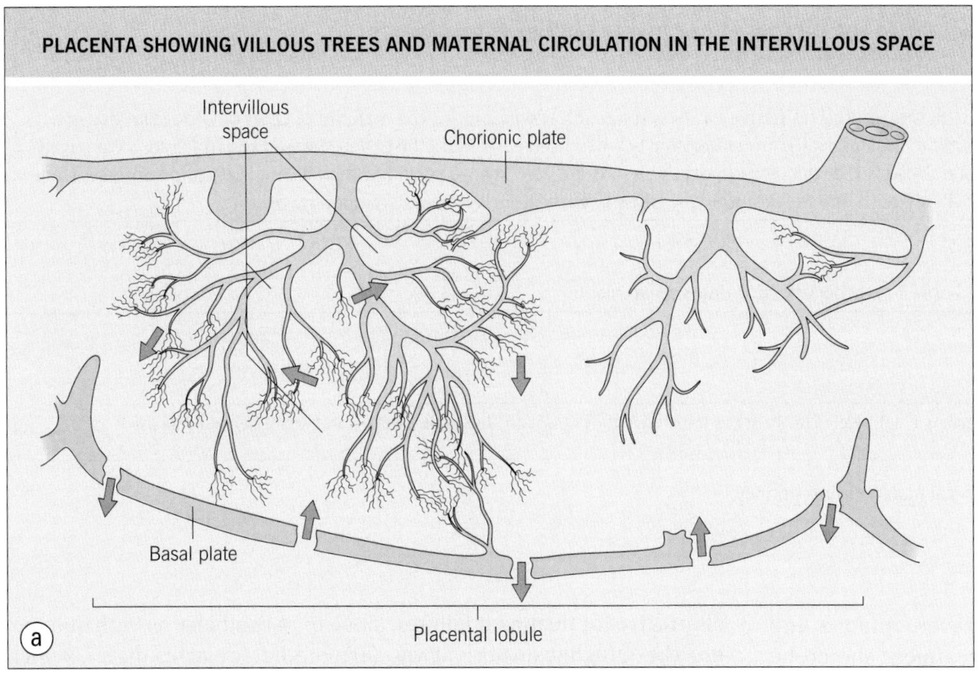

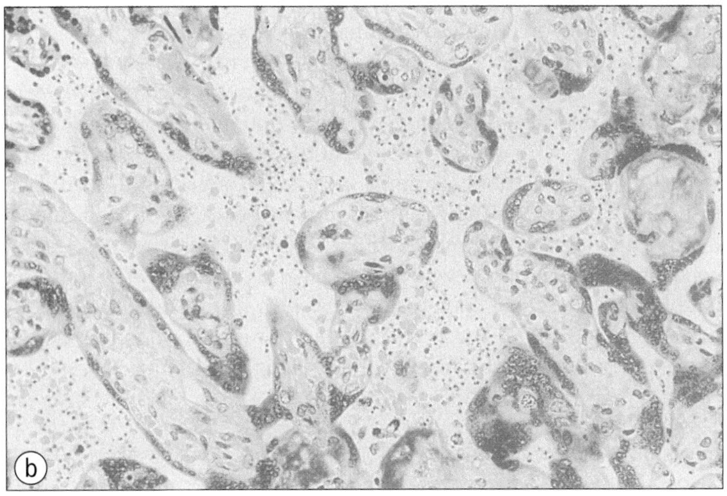

Fig. 186d.1 Heavy placental sequestration of malaria parasites is a common feature of malaria in pregnancy. (a) Placenta showing villous trees and maternal circulation in the intervillous spaces (broad arrows). (b) Photomicrograph showing trophozoites in maternal red blood cells in the intervillous spaces.

sitemia decreased and was negative after day 5. The patient remained well thereafter.

Ultrasound assessment on day 2 revealed an appropriately grown fetus with normal amniotic fluid volume. There was bilateral notching of the uterine artery Doppler waveforms with raised resistance indices, suggesting a degree of placental dysfunction. The umbilical artery and fetal arterial Doppler studies were normal. Over the subsequent 5 days the uterine artery Doppler waveforms normalized and remained normal throughout the rest of the pregnancy. However, subsequent serial scans for growth demonstrated IUGR, despite normal Dopplers.

HIV testing was undertaken during antenatal follow-up and the patient was found to be HIV positive. For this reason and because of the IUGR, she was delivered by cesarian section at 37 weeks' gestation.

Case 2 – semi-immune

A 26-year-old woman from East Africa presented at 24 weeks' gestation for antenatal booking. She was an asylum seeker who had arrived in the UK 2 weeks previously. She reported no specific symptoms other than tiredness and lethargy. Routine booking investigations were carried out. All results were unremarkable apart from the hemoglobin (6.2g/dl with iron-deficient indices). The patient was recalled to clinic and was subsequently admitted for transfusion of four units of packed cells. She was followed up in the clinic and 4 weeks later was severely anemic again (Hb 6.5g/dl). On this occasion stool was sent for microscopy and a malaria film was requested. Further transfusion of packed cells was arranged. The stool microscopy and malaria film were reported to be negative. However, the patient complained of flu-like symptoms over the ensuing days and a further malaria film was positive (*P. falciparum* $<1\%$ parasites seen). After treatment with oral quinine for 5 days followed by sulfadoxine-pyrimethamine (SP), the patient recovered. She had no further episodes of anemia during the antenatal period.

Diagnosis

The investigation of a patient with suspected falciparum malaria in pregnancy should be treated with great urgency.

Thick and thin blood films, stained with Giemsa, should be examined by an experienced microscopist. If the film is negative, it should be repeated if the patient remains symptomatic. Rapid dipstick tests (such as the ICT card test or OPTIMAL) are available as an aid to diagnosis in addition to microscopy. However, they are not as sensitive as microscopy in the hands of an experienced microscopist.

Blood and urine should be cultured to exclude other infections and in the comatose patient, lumbar puncture should be considered to exclude meningitis, providing there is no evidence of raised intracranial pressure.

DRUGS THAT CAN BE USED FOR TREATMENT OF CLINICAL MALARIA IN PREGNANCY	
In any trimester	• Quinine • Chloroquine: though widespread drug resistance has now made this redundant for the majority of cases of falciparum malaria. • Sulfadoxine-pyrimethamine: theoretical risk of teratogenicity when used early in the first trimester and of kernicterus when used late in the third trimester. However, evidence suggests these risks are very low, so provided there is not likely to be drug-resistant disease, it can be used at any gestation for symptomatic disease, as the risks will be outweighed by benefits.
In the second and third trimesters only	• Artemisin derivatives • Amodiaquine • Mefloquine: to be used only if no other effective drugs are available
Drugs that are contraindicated in pregnancy	• Halofantrine • Primaquine • Doxycycline
NB: No drug is safe enough for treating malaria in pregnancy if there is a high level of resistance to the drug in the population. The most effective drug available should be used	

Table 186d.1 Drugs that can be used for treatment of clinical malaria in pregnancy.

In a woman from an endemic country with severe anemia and suspected asymptomatic disease, presumptive treatment should be given even if a blood slide is negative, as illustrated by the second case history.

Management

Nonimmune pregnant women with malaria are more ill, more hypoglycemic and deteriorate more rapidly than nonpregnant patients and should be managed jointly by a physician and an obstetrician with an interest in materno-fetal medicine. As well as monitoring the parasitemia, regular hemoglobin, platelet counts and blood sugar measurements should continue during the course of the infection. The priority is to treat the mother. Delivery should not be contemplated until her condition is stabilized. Evidence of fetal compromise may resolve during the course of treatment, as in the first case history.

Unless there is multidrug resistance, quinine is the first-line drug for all symptomatic falciparum malaria infections in pregnancy. It is safe for use at any gestation, although it may have some weak oxytocic activity. In clinical practice, quinine use is not associated with premature labor and the greatest risk factor for premature labor is fever in the inadequately treated patient. If there is doubt about the malaria species, treatment with quinine should be commenced, pending confirmation from a reference laboratory.

In nonsevere disease, oral therapy with quinine should be given at a dose of 10mg salt/kg (maximum 600mg) q8h. If severe tinnitus or deafness occurs, dosage should be reduced to q12h. After 5 days or after clearance of parasitemia, whichever is the longer, a single treatment dose of SP may be given and quinine discontinued. Where possible, SP should be avoided both in the first trimester, due to the theoretical risk of teratogenicity, and near to term, due to the theoretical risk of kernicterus in the newborn. Both of these risks appear extremely low, however, and it can be used if alternatives are not available.

In severe disease, intravenous therapy should be instituted, converting to oral treatment as above as soon as the patient can swallow. A loading dose of quinine dihydrochloride 20mg/kg (maximum 1400mg) should be infused over 4 hours. Eight hours after the start of treatment, maintenance therapy with 10mg/kg over 4 hours should be started and repeated every 8 hours.

Malaria imported from parts of Thailand, Papua New Guinea and elsewhere in South East Asia may be resistant to quinine, SP and other drugs. Mefloquine may remain effective for these infections but it should be used with caution in pregnancy. The other effective alternative for treatment failures, alone or in combination with quinine, are the Qinghausu derivatives (artemether or artesunate), which appear safe in pregnancy and which the World Health Organization recommends for treatment of quinine-resistant severe malaria.

Careful attention should be paid to fluid balance in any patient with falciparum malaria, specifically avoiding the use of fluid challenges in response to oliguria, as this may precipitate pulmonary edema.

Transfusion with packed cells should be given slowly in any severely anemic patient. Patients with high parasitemia should be transfused earlier, as their hemoglobin will continue to fall due to hemolysis, despite treatment. In patients with parasitemia >10%, exchange transfusion allows physical clearance of parasites from the circulation. Exchange transfusion may also be considered at lower parasitemia levels in the presence of pre-rupture schizonts in the peripheral film, as this indicates an escalating parasitemia.

Conclusion

In nonimmune women, malaria in pregnancy is a dangerous condition associated with a high risk of maternal and perinatal mortality. Particular dangers are hyperpyrexia, hypoglycemia, severe hemolytic anemia, cerebral malaria and pulmonary edema. Even in immune women, falciparum malaria in pregnancy is associated with severe maternal anemia and low birth-weight delivery.

Malaria should be considered likely in any febrile patient with a travel history in the past year and treatment commenced for falciparum malaria if there is any doubt about the diagnosis. Severe or complicated malaria should be managed in an ITU setting and should involve early liaison between obstetricians and experts in tropical medicine.

Pregnant women should be advised against travel to malaria-endemic areas and if travel is unavoidable, advice on personal protection and chemoprophylaxis must be given.

Further reading

Bulmer JN, Rasheed FN, Francis N, Morrison L, Greenwood BM. Placental malaria. I. Pathological classification. Histopathology 1993;22:211–18.

Looareesuwan S, White NJ, Silamut K, Phillips RE, Warrell DA. Quinine and severe falciparum malaria in late pregnancy. Lancet 1985;2:4–8.

Luxemburger C, Ricci F, Nosten F, Raimond D, Bathet S, White NJ. The epidemiology of severe malaria in an area of low transmission in Thailand. Trans Roy Soc Trop Med Hyg 1997;91:256–62.

McGready R, Cho T, Cho JJ, *et al.* Artemisin derivatives in the treatment of falciparum malaria in pregnancy. Trans Roy Soc Trop Med Hyg 1998;92:430–3.

Meek SR. Epidemiology of malaria in displaced Khmers on the Thai-Kampuchean border. Southeast Asian J Trop Med Public Health 1988;19:243–52.

Nosten F, McGready R, Simpson J, *et al.* The effects of *P. vivax* in pregnancy. Lancet 1999;354:546–9.

Shulman CE, Dorman EK. Clinical features of malaria in pregnancy. In: Gilles HM, ed. Essential malariology, 4th ed. London: Arnold; 2002:219–35.

Shulman CE. Malaria in pregnancy: its relevance to safe-motherhood programmes. Ann Trop Med Parasit 1999;93(Suppl.1):S59–66.

Shulman CE, Marshall T, Dorman EK, *et al.* Malaria in pregnancy: adverse effects on haemoglobin levels and birthweight in primigravidae and multigravidae. Trop Med Int Health 2001;6:770–8.

Steketee RW, Wirima JJ, Hightower AW, Slutsker L, Heymann DL, Breman JG. The effect of malaria and malaria prevention in pregnancy on offspring birthweight, prematurity, and intrauterine growth retardation in rural Malawi. Am J Trop Med Hyg 1996;55(1 Suppl.):33–41.

World Health Organization. Severe falciparum malaria. Trans Roy Soc Trop Med Hyg 2000;94(Suppl.1):S1–90.

e. Treatment of dysentery in a pregnant woman

Lucia Larson

Introduction

Encountering dysentery or debilitating diarrhea in a pregnant woman sets the physician on a challenging path. Fetal health is inextricable from maternal health, making concerns about morbidity doubly important. Physiologic stresses of severe diarrhea may be well tolerated by a young woman but they may not be when she is pregnant. Furthermore, her unborn child relies for its survival on maternal volume status by way of placental blood flow. The dysenteric pregnant woman should be hospitalized immediately if at all possible. The clinician must work quickly to ensure hydration, to establish a diagnosis and to select a rational management plan.

Pathogenesis

Etiologic considerations are the same for pregnant and nonpregnant patients but there are a few specific organisms to which a pregnant woman may be particularly predisposed. Noninfectious causes of dysentery should also be considered, particularly inflammatory bowel disease.

For example, physiologic changes of pregnancy may place the patient at risk for contracting or manifesting certain conditions. Cellular immunity is suppressed, predisposing the woman to intracellular pathogens, such as *Listeria* spp. The decreased gastrointestinal motility of pregnancy may allow for higher concentrations of enteric pathogens to accumulate in the bowel lumen, leading to more severe enteric illness. This, in combination with increased mucosal vascularity, may increase systemic access of enteric pathogens.

The normal physiology of pregnancy can obscure diagnosis in the dysenteric patient. Leukocytosis is common. Uterine enlargement complicates the abdominal examination. Common symptoms of pregnancy can delay recognition of disease or lead to interventions that place the patient at risk of more significant dysenteric disease. For example, decreased bowel motility and laxity of the gastroesophageal sphincter, both caused by elevated estrogen levels, can cause severe gastroesophageal reflux and intestinal bloating and cramping. These symptoms may obscure the early recognition of enteric infections in pregnant women.

Microbiology

The classic bacterial organisms associated with dysenteric disease are *Salmonella* spp. and *Shigella* spp., with the former more commonly associated with bacteremia and a carrier state. Enterohemorrhagic strains of *Escherichia coli* are an increasingly recognized cause of bloody diarrhea and may cause severe dysentery in pregnant women (Chapter 43). In addition, a number of cases of postpartum hemolytic uremic syndrome have had evidence of Shiga toxin-producing *Escherichia coli* infection.

Listeria monocytogenes infection typically causes a febrile diarrheal illness in pregnancy. Pregnancy is the most common independent risk factor for infection with *Listeria* spp., which are invasive, intracellular bacterial pathogens. Most reported cases of listeriosis in otherwise immunocompetent hosts are in pregnant women, particularly in the third trimester. Transplacental infection of the fetus and amnion, with severe outcomes, is well described even with mild maternal illness, making aggressive detection and treatment essential. The patient who has listeriosis may have additional signs and symptoms, including myalgia, pharyngitis or meningitis. She may, unfortunately, present only with a mild febrile diarrheal illness and intrauterine fetal death, which should focus the clinician immediately on *Listeria* spp. (Chapter 63).

Campylobacter spp. are increasingly common agents of diarrheal illness that can afflict patients by multiple pathogenic mechanisms (Chapter 43). Symptoms are often suggestive of appendicitis, bowel perforation or inflammatory bowel disease. *Campylobacter* spp. have been described as a cause of abortion, chorioamnionitis and perinatal sepsis. *Salmonella* spp. have also been documented to cause transplacental infection causing fetal loss, neonatal sepsis and even episiotomy site infection. These pathogens should be vigorously pursued in pregnant women who have diarrheal illness.

Parasitic infections deserve consideration in the pregnant patient who has diarrhea. *Entamoeba histolytica* may cause severe amebic colitis without typical symptoms of amebic dysentery in pregnant women. *Giardia lamblia*, although not a classic cause of dysentery, is problematic in pregnancy. Achlorhydria and any form of immunodeficiency each enhance risk of infection. Although pregnancy has never been identified as an independent risk factor for giardiasis, the disease may easily be missed in the pregnant patient who has intermittent bouts of gastrointestinal distress. Misdiagnosis can range from psychosomatic illness to hyperemesis gravidarum (Chapter 242). Giardia has not been known to cause intrauterine or fetal infection.

Clinical features

What is most striking about pregnant women with any major illness is how quickly they can become severely ill, making early diagnosis and treatment essential. Pregnant women have at least a 20% greater plasma volume than nonpregnant women, with corresponding requirements for fluid intake. They and their fetuses tolerate fluid losses poorly, whether from diarrhea, fever or the decreased fluid intake that often accompanies enteric illness. Decreased peripheral vascular tone with vasodilatation contributes to a tendency for postural hypotension or presyncopal symptoms that may develop rapidly.

In the course of any significant infectious illness, particularly one with tissue invasion or associated Gram-negative bacteremia, the previously healthy pregnant woman is at substantial risk of developing pulmonary edema owing to the lowered colloid oncotic pressure of the gravid state. This is true even before rigorous hydration. A high index of suspicion for pulmonary edema is warranted in assessing and managing the pregnant patient with any infection. Her fetus will not tolerate hypoxemia as well as she does.

Many features of dysentery in pregnancy are no different from those in the nonpregnant patient; these include fever, abdominal cramping and bloody diarrhea. In *Shigella, Salmonella* and *Campylobacter* enteritis, the abdomen may be so tender that peritonitis is suspected. Peritoneal signs may be difficult to distinguish from chorioamnionitis in pregnancy. Vigilance and serial clinical examinations are essential to ensure prompt and proper diagnosis.

As with any infectious illness in a pregnant patient, infectious diarrhea or dysentery may present as preterm labor. In addition, the fetus may show signs of distress because of decreased uterine blood flow resulting from maternal volume depletion, hypoxemia or other physiologic alterations.

Investigations

When evaluating the pregnant woman who has a dysentery-like illness, it is important to account for normal physiologic changes of pregnancy (Table 186e.1).

Blood cultures may provide the definitive diagnosis in diarrhea caused by *Salmonella* spp. or *Listeria* spp. If the patient is febrile, it is appropriate to culture all potentially infected body fluids, such as urine, stool and even amniotic fluid. Where there is a question of peritonitis or chorioamnionitis as well, amniocentesis is appropriate and is best performed by a qualified obstetrician.

A Gram stain of a stool specimen to look for evidence of mononuclear or polymorphonuclear white blood cells can quickly focus further investigations. Most importantly, bacterial isolates of enteric pathogens should undergo antibiotic susceptibility testing to avoid repeated trials of ineffective multiple antibiotics that lead to unnecessary and potentially injurious drug exposures in pregnant patients.

Ulcerative colitis or colonic Crohn's disease is often diagnosed by a flexible sigmoidoscope examination and biopsy, strategies with no excess risk in pregnancy. Occasionally, radiographic imaging of the abdomen is warranted. Fetal risks of radiation exposure must be weighed carefully against the risk of delayed or inaccurate diagnosis. However, fetal well-being depends on maternal well-being. A pregnant woman should not be denied a potentially life-saving diagnostic intervention, nor should it be delayed on account of her pregnancy.

Management

After an appropriate diagnostic evaluation (Table 186e.2) empiric antimicrobial agents need to be considered. Further, if there is any suspicion of an infection that may be life threatening to the mother or fetus, such as listeriosis, then empiric therapy should be instituted. Precautions should be taken to prevent neonatal infection should a delivery occur at the time of an active maternal infection.

Numerous sources of information are available on the safety of antibiotics in pregnant women. Most readily available is the manufacturer's package insert, which usually includes a 'pregnancy category'. These categories are not always consistently applied. It is therefore wise to seek more detailed information from other sources, such as the online resources that are widely available in medical libraries and hospital pharmacies.

The number of commonly recommended antibiotics for diarrheal diseases is small. None of them are known teratogens. Ampicillin and other β-lactam antibiotics (with the potential exception of ticarcillin) have a strong record of safety in pregnancy and are best administered in doses at the upper end of the therapeutic range for women in the second and third trimesters owing to altered pharmacokinetics.

Metronidazole is teratogenic in experimental animals and its use in pregnancy is controversial in some settings. Its use is probably warranted when the patient has a severe illness, such as symptomatic amebiasis. Fluoroquinolones are more controversial. As human data are scant, this class of agents is best avoided in pregnant women owing to the risk of arthropathy in the developing fetus, which has been well characterized in animal models. For all potential causes of dysenteric illness where fluoroquinolones are considered first-line therapy, alternative agents exist that have better characterized safety risk profiles in pregnancy. Tetracyclines (which carry the risk of hepatotoxicity and staining of permanent teeth), chloramphenicol (which suppresses bone marrow), and prolonged courses of aminoglycosides (which are ototoxic) are best avoided in pregnancy if possible. Macrolides are generally safe, but even

NORMAL LABORATORY FINDINGS IN PREGNANCY

Test	Increased	Unchanged	Decreased	Comment
Hemoglobin and hematocrit			✓	Red cell indices unchanged
Leukocyte count	✓			
Platelet count		✓		
Blood urea nitrogen			✓	
Serum creatinine			✓	Usually less than 0.6mg/dl (<53μmol/l)
Sodium		✓		
Potassium			✓	
Chloride		✓		
Bicarbonate			✓	
Alanine aminotransferase		✓		
Aspartate aminotransferase		✓		
Bilirubin		✓		
Alkaline phosphatase	✓			
Albumin			✓	
Creatinine clearance	✓			1.5–2 times baseline

Table 186e.1 Normal laboratory findings in pregnancy.

MANAGEMENT OF THE PREGNANT WOMAN WHO HAS DYSENTERY

1. Hospitalization
2. Fluid and electrolyte replacement
3. Oxygen monitoring
4. Fetal evaluation by an obstetrician
5. Begin diagnostic evaluation
6. Empiric therapy if indicated

Table 186e.2 Management of the pregnant woman who has dysentery.

erythromycin has been occasionally associated with hypertrophic pyloric stenosis in infancy. Sulfa drugs should be avoided in the third trimester because of the potential increased risk of kernicterus. Trimethoprim-sulfamethoxazole (co-trimoxazole) has been associated in some studies with cleft palate when administered to rats at high doses, and it has the potential for interference with folate metabolism, raising concern about potential neural tube defects in the developing fetus. However, these have not been shown to be significant risks for humans.

The clinician unaccustomed to the uncertainties of prescribing in pregnancy may find little reassurance in such data. Absolute risk from a given agent in a given situation may be minimal, but the anxiety created by the unknown can be substantial. It must be remembered that delay of needed therapy may offer far more risk to the fetus than the therapy itself. Thus, as in the early stages of patient evaluation, the clinician must resist being paralyzed by indecision and the unknown regarding therapies. Rather, it is appropriate and wise to seek additional information. Most important, open and honest discussion of uncertainties with the patient and her obstetrician will serve all parties well.

Further reading

Armon PJ. Amoebiasis in pregnancy and puerperium. Br J Obstet Gynaecol 1978;85:264–9.

Burrow GN, Ferris TF. Medical complications during pregnancy, 4th ed. Philadelphia: WB Saunders; 1995.

Creasy RK, Resnik R. Maternal–fetal medicine: principles and practice, 3rd ed. Philadelphia: WB Saunders; 1994.

Friedman JM, Polifka JE. The effects of drugs on the fetus and nursing infant: a handbook for health care professionals. Baltimore: Johns Hopkins University Press; 1996.

Lee R, Rosene-Montella K, Barbour LA, Garner PR, Keely E. Medical care of the pregnant patient. Philadelphia: American College of Physicians; 2000.

Simor AE, Karmali MA, Jadavji T, Rosco M. Abortion and perinatal sepsis associated with *Campylobacter* infection. Rev Infect Dis 1986;8:397–402.

Tobak MA, Hart MD, Osborn LM. *Campylobacter* enteritis: prenatal and perinatal implications. Am J Obstet Gynecol 1983;147:845–6.

Van der Klooster JM, Roelofs HJM. Management of *Salmonella* infections during pregnancy and puerperium. Netherlands J Med 1997;51:83–6.

SECTION

7

ANTI-INFECTIVE THERAPY

Scott M Hammer
S Ragnar Norrby

chapter

187 Principles of Anti-infective Therapy

Vito R Iacoviello & Stephen H Zinner

The science of antimicrobial chemotherapy began in the last century, during which time we have witnessed a dramatic reduction in morbidity and mortality due to infections caused by common bacterial agents, only to be presently threatened by the worldwide emergence of antibiotic-resistant bacteria. Antimicrobial resistance limits the usefulness of antimicrobial agents, and careful attention to appropriate antimicrobial use might mitigate the extinction of these life-saving drugs. The past century also saw the introduction of effective chemotherapy directed against fungi and viruses as well as protozoa and parasitic organisms. This chapter focuses on the principles that guide appropriate use as well as an understanding of the mechanisms of action, pharmacokinetics and pharmacodynamics, indications and clinical selection of antimicrobial agents.

ANTIBIOTICS

General principles of antibiotic selection

The selection of appropriate antibiotic therapy depends on a number of important factors. First, antibiotics are useful only for the treatment of bacterial infections, and so general confirmation of the presence of such an infection is critical. The clinical presentation of an obvious pyogenic infection with such features as fever, purulent cough or exudate, shaking chills, tachycardia, diaphoresis and a localized inflammatory site in the chest, abdomen, urinary tract, joint or meninges, or on the skin should prompt appropriate diagnostic tests. These usually include blood cultures and smears and cultures from the clinically obvious infected site. Samples of pus, purulent exudate, cerebrospinal fluid, synovial fluid, urine or other likely infected material should be examined microscopically with a Gram-stained smear. If a predominating pathogen is strongly suggested on this examination, then the choice of antimicrobial agent is facilitated. Appropriate use of bacteriologic cultures and new molecular techniques such as DNA probes and polymerase chain reaction will help in selecting the most appropriate antibiotic and limit antibiotic resistance resulting from the selective pressure of unbridled antibiotic use.

Often, the presence of a bacterial infection is suspected simply on clinical grounds and there is no direct source of pus or other material for culture. In office practice of medicine, many patient encounters are via the telephone and antibiotic selection is often made in the absence of a physical or laboratory examination. Although the majority of these encounters are for viral infections, in those cases where bacterial infection is more probable, a reasonable choice of antimicrobial can be made based on the usual pathogens responsible for the symptoms in question. For example, purulent tonsillitis with fever and tender adenopathy is likely to be caused by *Streptococcus pyogenes*, as is uncomplicated cellulitis on an extremity. A carbuncle or furuncle is often caused by *Staphylococcus aureus* and uncomplicated cystitis with fever or pyelonephritis is usually due to infection with *Escherichia coli* or other enteric Gram-negative bacteria. Other clinical presentations may suggest the presence of *Neisseria gonorrhoeae*, *Chlamydia trachomatis*, *Mycoplasma pneumoniae* or *Streptococcus pneumoniae*, among others. In these situations it might be possible to select appropriate antibiotics directed against these specific pathogens (Table 187.1).[1] When empiric therapy is prescribed in these situations, the provider must be aware of local susceptibility patterns. Antibiotics that might have sufficed a decade or more ago now may be less effective as a result of increasing antibiotic resistance.

As a general rule, whenever possible appropriate clinical specimens should be obtained to attempt a culture-proven diagnosis so that the most effective antibiotic can be selected for targeted therapy and for the correct duration. Cultures are also important to isolate the infecting organism and determine the presence of antibiotic resistance. Unnecessary use of antibiotics for prophylaxis and for probable nonbacterial infections, as well as excessively prolonged courses for uncomplicated bacterial infections, should be avoided.

Bacteriostasis and bactericidal effects

Antibiotics exert an antibacterial effect that results either in inhibition of bacterial growth (bacteriostasis) or in bacterial killing (bactericidal effect). While not always specific for a given antibiotic and a particular bacterial pathogen, bacteriostatic antibiotics include tetracyclines, sulfonamides, clindamycin and chloramphenicol as examples. However, chloramphenicol is bactericidal against pneumococci, meningococci and *Haemophilus influenzae*. Aminoglycosides, β-lactams and fluoroquinolones are bactericidal against most susceptible bacterial pathogens. Macrolide and azalide antibiotics may be inhibitory or bactericidal depending on drug concentrations, bacterial inocula and growth rates.[2] Some organisms, notably *Enterococcus* spp., require two agents to effect bacterial killing – a cell-wall-active agent such as a penicillin or glycopeptide plus an aminoglycoside are required for bactericidal activity, although either drug alone might induce an inhibitory or bacteriostatic effect.[3]

Some infections, such as uncomplicated bacterial cystitis, may be adequately treated with antibiotics that inhibit bacterial growth, such as sulfonamides. If bacterial multiplication is arrested, then normal host defenses including micturition and dilution with uninfected urine from the upper urinary tract will help to eradicate the infection. More invasive bacterial infections such as meningitis, bacterial endocarditis, peritonitis and bacteremia are best treated with bactericidal agents. Similarly, host factors might determine the choice of bactericidal versus bacteriostatic agents. In general, in neutropenic patients or patients who have other immune defects, bacterial infections are best treated with bactericidal drugs.[4]

Bactericidal antibiotics differ in the time course of bacterial killing. Some agents, such as cephalosporins, penicillins and penems, show time-dependent killing and produce maximal effect approximately 6–8 hours after exposure. Higher concentrations of antibiotic do not produce a greater bactericidal effect. The percentage of time during a given dosing interval that antibiotic concentration is above the minimal inhibitory concentration for a given organism (time above MIC) is the pharmacodynamic parameter that predicts the effect of time-dependent antibiotics (see below). Other antibiotics such as aminoglycosides and fluoroquinolones produce concentration-dependent killing. With these antibiotics

COMMON CLINICAL SITES FOR BACTERIAL INFECTIONS IN ADULTS, FREQUENTLY ENCOUNTERED ORGANISMS AND APPROPRIATE ANTIBIOTICS		
Infection site	**Common bacterial etiology**	**Appropriate antibiotics***
Oropharynx, tonsil	*Streptococcus pyogenes*	Penicillin V ×10 days, azithromycin, second-generation cephalosporin, clindamycin, erythromycin, clarithromycin
Acute sinusitis	*Streptococcus pneumoniae, Haemophilus influenzae, Moraxella catarrhalis*, group A streptococcus	Amoxicillin, ampicillin–clavulanate, cefpodoxime, cefuroxime axetil, cefdinir, fluoroquinolone
Acute exacerbation of chronic bronchitis	*S. pneumoniae, H. influenzae, M. catarrhalis*	Mild: amoxicillin, doxycycline, trimethoprim–sulfamethoxazole, oral cephalosporin Severe: ampicillin–clavulanate, azithromycin, oral cephalosporin, levofloxacin, gatifloxacin, moxifloxacin
Pneumonia, community-acquired, smoker	*S. pneumoniae, H. influenzae, M. catarrhalis*	Outpatient: azithromycin, fluoroquinolone, second-generation cephalosporin
Pneumonia, community-acquired, non-smoker	*M. pneumoniae, Chlamydia pneumoniae, S. pneumoniae*	As above
Pneumonia, community-acquired	As above	Inpatient: third-generation cephalosporin, plus erythromycin or azithromycin, fluoroquinolone
Urinary tract infection, uncomplicated cystitis	Enterobacteriaceae	Trimethoprim–sulfamethoxazole, trimethoprim, fluoroquinolone
Pyelonephritis	Enterobacteriaceae, *Enterococcus* sp.	Fluoroquinolone, ampicillin plus gentamicin, third-generation cephalosporin, ticarcillin–clavulanate, ampicillin–sulbactam, piperacillin–tazobactam
Urethritis, gonococcal	*Neisseria gonorrhoeae*	Ceftriaxone, cefixime, ciprofloxacin, ofloxacin
Urethritis, non-gonococcal	*Chlamydia* sp., *Mycoplasma hominis, Ureaplasma* sp.	Doxycycline, azithromycin
Pelvic inflammatory disease	*N. gonorrhoeae, Chlamydia* sp., *Bacteroides* sp., Enterobacteriaceae, *Streptococcus* sp.	Ofloxacin or levofloxacin plus metronidazole, ceftriaxone plus doxycycline, cefotetan or cefoxitin plus doxycycline, ampicillin–sulbactam plus doxycycline
Prostatitis, <35 years old	*N. gonorrhoeae, Chlamydia* sp.	Ofloxacin, ceftriaxone plus doxycycline
Prostatitis, >35 years old	Enterobacteriaceae	Fluoroquinolone, trimethoprim–sulfamethoxazole
Gastroenteritis	*Shigella* sp. *Salmonella* sp., *Campylobacter* sp., *Escherichia coli* 0157H7	Fluoroquinolone
Cholecystitis	Enterobacteriaceae, enterococci, anaerobes	Ampicillin–sulbactam, piperacillin–tazobactam, imipenem, meropenem
Diverticulitis	Enterobacteriaceae, anaerobes, enterococci	Ampicillin–sulbactam, piperacillin–tazobactam, imipenem, meropenem, metronidazole plus fluoroquinolone
Spontaneous bacterial peritonitis	Enterobacteriaceae, *S. pneumoniae*	Cefotaxime, ceftriaxone, ticarcillin–clavulanate, piperacillin–tazobactam, ampicillin–sulbactam
Cellulitis	Group A streptococcus, *Staphylococcus aureus*	Nafcillin, oxacillin, first-generation cephalosporin, erythromycin, ampicillin–clavulanate
Septic arthritis, monoarticular, sexually active	*N. gonorrhoeae*	Ceftriaxone, cefotaxime, ceftizoxime
Septic arthritis, monoarticular, not sexually active	*S. aureus, Streptococcus* sp., Gram-negative rod	Nafcillin or oxacillin plus third-generation cephalosporin or ciprofloxacin
Septic arthritis, prosthetic	*Staphylococcus epidermidis, S. aureus*, Enterobacteriaceae, *Pseudomonas* sp.	Vancomycin plus ciprofloxacin or aztreonam, or ceftazidime or cefepime
Osteomyelitis	*S. aureus*	Nafcillin, oxacillin, first-generation cephalosporin, vancomycin
Meningitis	*S. pneumoniae, N. meningitidis*	Ceftriaxone ± vancomycin
Endocarditis, native valve	*Viridans* streptococcus, other streptococcal species, enterococci, staphylococci	Penicillin or ampicillin, plus nafcillin–oxacillin, plus gentamicin; vancomycin plus gentamicin
Endocarditis, prosthetic valve	*S. epidermidis, S. aureus*	Vancomycin plus gentamicin ± rifampin

* This is a general overview, the choice of antibiotics must consider the resistance pattern in any given geographic area (e.g. penicillin and macrolide resistance in *S. pneumoniae*; ampicillin and trimethoprim–sulfamethoxazole resistance among *E. coli*), as well as adjustments based on the identified etiologic agent and susceptibility testing.

Table 187.1 Common clinical sites for bacterial infections in adults, frequently encountered organisms and appropriate antibiotics. This table is not intended to be all-inclusive. Specific infections are considered in detail in other chapters.

higher concentrations produce more rapid and more complete bacterial killing. The ratio of maximal drug concentration to MIC (C_{max}/MIC) and the ratio of the area under the concentration–time curve (AUC) to MIC (AUC/MIC) are pharmacodynamic predictors of the effect of concentration-dependent antibiotics. The clinical significance of these differences is not clear, primarily because clinical trials are usually designed to test different doses rather than different dosing intervals.[5]

Postantibiotic effects

Bacterial growth may be inhibited following exposure to an antibiotic even after the drug concentration has fallen far below the MIC. This is known as the postantibiotic effect (PAE) and is determined in vitro by observing bacterial growth after the drug has been removed. Animal models have been described to measure PAE in vivo.[6] Postantibiotic effects vary with different drugs and micro-organisms. For example, prolonged PAEs have been reported after aminoglycoside or fluoroquinolone exposure to Gram-negative rods, whereas most β-lactam antibiotics exhibit shorter PAEs. It has been reported that PAEs in animal models may be longer than those measured in vitro.[6] Postantibiotic leukocyte enhancement (PALE) considers enhanced white blood cell killing of organisms that have just been exposed to antibiotic. It can add to the inherent PAE of a given drug–organism pair. Both PAE and PALE contribute to the dosing interval; drugs exhibiting prolonged PAEs may be dosed less frequently.

Antibiotic resistance

Bacteria have evolved complex mechanisms to resist the action of antibiotics. The mechanisms are discussed in detail in Chapter 189. Although some organisms (e.g. *Enterococcus gallinarum*) are inherently resistant to some antibiotics, much of the impetus for bacterial resistance is believed to relate to excessive antibiotic use. It is remarkable that such mechanisms exist because widespread antibiotic use has been available for only 60 years. Bacteria may exhibit antibiotic resistance based on the elaboration of an enzyme that renders the antibiotic ineffective. There are a large number of β-lactamases produced by many different bacteria that hydrolyze the β-lactam ring of penicillins, cephalosporins and penems.[7] Examples of common β-lactamases include a penicillinase of *S. aureus*, which is responsible for penicillin-resistant staphylococci, and TEM-1 β-lactamase in *E. coli*, which mediates ampicillin resistance. Some of these enzymes are responsible for inactivation of broad-spectrum cephalosporins (extended spectrum β-lactamases (ESBLs) such as OXA-11, OXA-14 in *Pseudomonas aeruginosa*, SHV-2 in *Klebsiella pneumoniae* and TEM 3–29, also in *K. pneumoniae* and other Enterobacteriaceae). β-Lactamase genes may be found on plasmids and transposons or may be chromosomally mediated. Aminoglycoside antibiotics may be inactivated by bacterial enzymes, which result in phosphorylation, acetylation or nucleotidylation. Transposons or plasmids may transfer these modifying enzymes.

Bacteria can increase the elimination of antibiotics by upregulating efflux mechanisms, as is seen with macrolide antibiotics and Gram-positive cocci carrying the *mef* gene.[8] Other bacteria resist antibiotics by altering their cell wall structure to reduce permeability through outer or internal membranes. Alterations in the shape or number of porin channels make it difficult for antibiotics to transfer from the external milieu to the ribosomal targets within the organism. These mechanisms have been found in imipenem resistant *P. aeruginosa* and other Gram-negative rods.[9]

Still other bacteria can modify the target site of antibiotic action rendering the usual binding impossible. Mutations in *gyrA* or *gyrB* genes responsible for DNA gyrase production alter the binding sites for fluoroquinolone antibiotics. Vancomycin resistance in enterococci is mediated by *vanA* or *vanB* genes that encode cell-wall proteins that have altered affinity for the antibiotic.[10] Ribosomal binding sites might be modified by methylation in macrolide-resistant bacteria and mutations in the DNA-dependent RNA polymerase mediate resistance to rifampin (rifampicin). Rifampin resistance may develop rapidly during therapy as a result of one-step bacterial mutations. For this reason, rifampin is rarely used alone except in the four-dose regimen used for meningococcal prophylaxis.

There is growing evidence to suggest that increasing antibiotic use results in increased rates of antibiotic resistance.[11,12] Global travel, worldwide food distribution, antibiotics in animal feed and other products, as well as poor adherence to infection control techniques enhance the spread of antibiotic resistance.[13] Within hospitals or hospital units, it has been possible to show decreased resistance associated with decreased use of a given antibiotic. However, it has been more difficult to show clearly a reduction in resistance in the community associated with such usage changes.[14] Since antibiotics are found in foods, animal feeds, battleship paints, household products and other sources, this difficulty is not surprising. Common sense dictates that limited and appropriate use of these resources will limit the emergence of resistance. Patients who exhibit no evidence of bacterial infections should be encouraged to accept other therapeutic agents for symptom relief and to decrease their demand for unnecessary antibiotics. Several novel population interventions are in progress to test new approaches to the control of antibiotic resistance in the community.[15] Maximizing infection control efforts within the hospital and global education of physicians and patients will help to reduce the emergence of resistance. Optimizing dosing using pharmacokinetic/pharmacodynamic principles also might be successful.[5]

Although the classic teaching has been to select appropriate older antibiotics to which organisms are susceptible and use the lowest successful dose, in order to minimize the selection of resistant organisms perhaps the use of the most active or most potent antibiotics might be preferred. In the early part of the last century Ehrlich wrote, '*frapper fort et frapper vite*' ('hit hard and hit fast').[16] This might translate today into the use of rapidly bactericidal drugs that achieve concentrations at the infection site high enough to eradicate all the infecting organisms and thus minimize the opportunity for the development of resistance. Whether this approach will result in less antibiotic resistance remains to be tested clinically.

Determinants of the antimicrobial effect

In-vitro and in-vivo techniques

The activity of an antibiotic against an isolated pathogenic bacterium may be expressed using a number of techniques. The most frequently used of these methods are disc diffusion tests (such as the Kirby-Bauer method in North America, or Stokes or the BSAC method in Europe), and the determination of the MIC of the antibiotic. Disc susceptibility testing involves the agar inoculation of an approximated number of bacteria as a 'lawn', with the overlaying of antibiotic-impregnated discs. After overnight incubation, zones of inhibition appear around the discs impregnated with antibiotics to which the organism is susceptible (Fig 187.1a). MIC testing used to be done by agar or broth dilution, but now most laboratories use an ingenious antibiotic-impregnated strip, the E-test (Fig 187.1b) or other automated techniques. In the USA, the National Committee for Clinical Laboratory Standards (NCCLS) sets 'breakpoints' for the MIC based on the integration of MICs with achievable antibiotic levels in serum and tissues, clinical pharmacology and data from in-vitro and animal models.[17] Typically these results are presented to the clinician as a report of 'sensitive', 'intermediate' or 'resistant'. Determinations of MIC are rough guides to the susceptibility of an isolated pathogen and these values form the usual basis for antibiotic selection. In clinical situations, bacterial concentrations might be larger than those used in the in-vitro determination. Pharmacokinetic considerations are not included in the MIC determination, and pharmacokinetic and pharmacodynamic parameters are important in predicting outcome (see below).

Determinations of MIC might not provide the most complete assessment or optimal prediction of the likely outcome of antibiotic therapy. Minimal inhibitory concentration values correlate with the ability of an antibiotic to inhibit a given bacterium under specified laboratory conditions. In some clinical situations, such as bacterial endocarditis, it is useful to know the ability of an antibiotic to kill the infecting organism. The minimal bactericidal concentration (MBC) can be determined using microtiter plate well or tube dilutions of antibiotic inoculated with a known concentration of the isolated infecting organism. After overnight incubation and subsequent quantitative subculture of the non-turbid wells or tubes, the concentration of drug that produces a

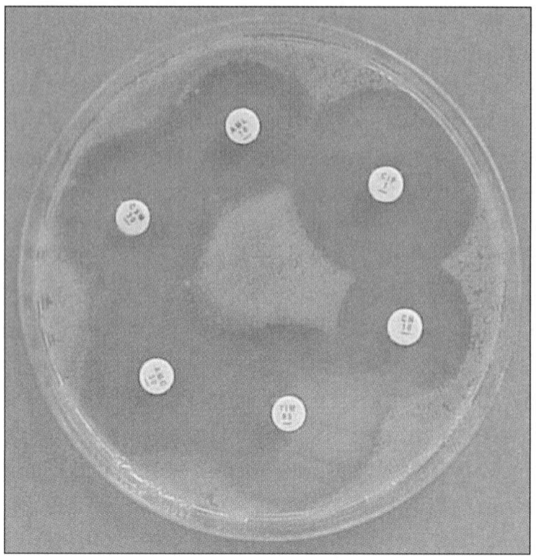

Fig. 187.1 (a) A disc diffusion sensitivity plate showing a fully sensitive coliform tested against a typical range of first-line antibiotics. Courtesy of Dr M Cubbon, Brighton, UK.

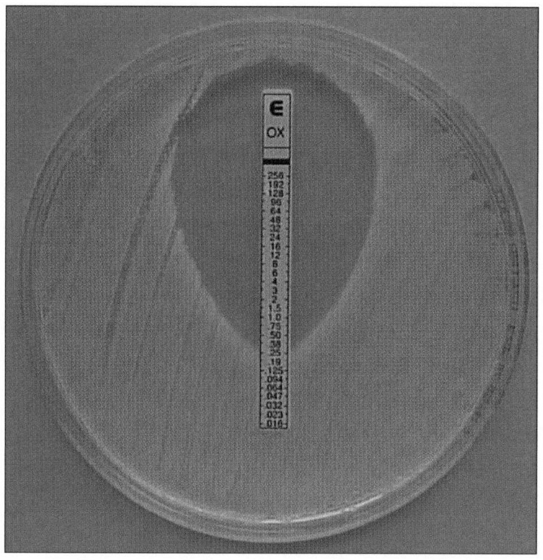

Fig. 187.1 (b) An E-test showing a methicillin-sensitive *S. aureus*. The MIC of oxacillin for this strain is 0.25 mg/L, and is obtained by noting the point at which the zone of inhibition intersects with the test strip. Courtesy of Dr M Cubbon, Brighton, UK.

99% or 99.9% reduction in the starting inoculum determines the MBC. For research purposes bacterial killing curves are studied using known bacterial inocula and antibiotic concentrations that approximate achievable serum levels. The time course of bacterial killing is determined by sampling and bacterial quantitation. In some clinical situations it is useful to determine the ability of various dilutions of serum sampled after an antibiotic dose to kill a standardized inoculum of the patient's infecting organism. The serum bactericidal assay is performed infrequently today but it has been used to estimate the adequacy of an antibiotic regimen in patients who have bacterial endocarditis or in bacteremic neutropenic patients.[18,19]

The effects of antibiotic combinations also can be studied in vitro. Various techniques have been introduced to apply increasing concentrations of two antibiotics to known concentrations of bacteria. These include antibiotic-impregnated disc approximations, tube dilution tests, microtiter well methods, replicator plating techniques and bacterial killing concentrations. Experimental animal models have also been used to study the effects of antibiotic combinations.

Antibiotic combinations may be judged as additive when their activities can be summed, synergistic when the effect is greater than the sum of each drug's activity (i.e. the MIC of each drug in the presence of the other is reduced significantly) or antagonistic when the effect of the drugs in combination is less than the sum of each alone. Although several techniques have been described,[20] the study of antibiotic combinations is not routinely performed in clinical microbiology laboratories and this information is rarely available to the clinician.

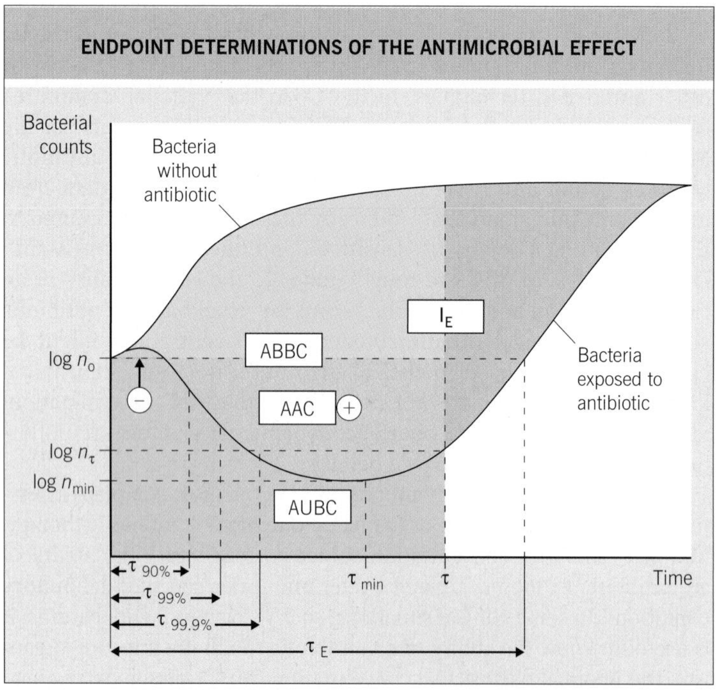

Fig. 187.2 End-point determinations of the antimicrobial effect. See text for details. Redrawn with permission of the American Society for Microbiology from Firsov *et al.*[22]

In-vitro pharmacodynamic models have been introduced in the past two decades to incorporate pharmacokinetic and pharmacodynamic parameters into in-vitro predictions of the antimicrobial effect.[21] These models mimic human antibiotic dosing and can be used to study the relationship of pharmacodynamics to the antimicrobial effect (see below). These models have been used to describe additional end-point determinations of the antimicrobial effect. In the presence of changing concentrations of antibiotic following a simulated dose, several bacterial end points can be used[22] (Fig. 187.2). These include the time to reduction of the starting inoculum by 90%, 99% or 99.9% (t_{90}, t_{99}, $t_{99.9}$); the difference between the starting inoculum and the number of bacteria at the nadir of the killing and regrowth curve (n_0–n_{min}); the time to the nadir of the kill curve (t_{min}), n_{min} itself; the viable count at the end of the usual dosing interval, τ, (n_τ); and several integral end points that reflect areas above or below the bacterial time curve. The integral end points may be related to the dosing interval, τ, such as the area under the bacterial curve (AUBC), the area above the curve (AAC) or the area between the curves in the presence and absence of antibiotic (ABBC); or the area may extend beyond the dosing interval and reflect the area between the control growth curve and the curve in the presence of a simulated antibiotic dose (intensity of the effect, I_E).[23] Of these, I_E has been shown most comprehensively to reflect the antimicrobial effect in in-vitro dynamic models.

Animal models

A variety of animal models have been developed and used to study optimal dosing and scheduling of antibiotics as well as antimicrobial pharmacodynamics. Animal and human pharmacokinetics differ significantly, especially in small animals. Although these models are rarely used clinically, they are quite important in the preclinical evaluation of antimicrobials. Specific models might be particularly useful in developing appropriate therapeutic regimens for bacterial endocarditis or meningitis, for example. In the endocarditis model, New Zealand rabbits are used and an intravascular catheter is inserted to cross the heart valve.[24] The catheter remains in place and organisms are introduced intravenously to establish typical bacterial vegetations similar to those that occur in clinical endocarditis. Meningitis models have been described in many animal systems and usually involve a stereotactic injection of bacteria directly into the cerebrospinal fluid.[25] Other models have been developed for peritonitis and intra-abdominal abscess, pyelonephritis, pneumonia and osteomyelitis. The neutropenic mouse thigh infection model of Craig and colleagues has been particularly helpful in correlating pharmacodynamic parameters with outcome.[26]

Antibiotic pharmacology

As with all drugs, pharmacologic considerations aid in the appropriate selection of antibiotics. Antibiotics may be administered orally or intravenously (and less often via the intramuscular route). Oral antibiotics must be absorbed via the gastrointestinal tract. Bioavailability, F, refers to 'the fraction of the administered dose that is absorbed intact'.[27] The bioavailability of intravenously administered antibiotics is 100%. The bioavailability of orally administered antibiotics is dependent on absorption across the gastrointestinal tract and ranges from 20% for sulfasalazine to up to 100% for sulfadiazine, ciprofloxacin, nitrofurantoin and cefaclor, for example. To be effective at the site of infection, antibiotics must be well distributed in the tissues. In general, lipophilic agents (e.g. chloramphenicol) and uncharged or nonpolar drugs (e.g. fluoroquinolones) are able to cross biologic membranes and achieve effective concentrations in tissues. The apparent volume of distribution of an antibiotic, V_d, is calculated by dose/plasma concentration and may reflect the ability of the drug to enter inflammatory cells and tissues. Distribution is affected by the protein binding of the drug in plasma and, in general, very highly bound drugs (e.g. >95%) may not cross biologic membranes as well as less highly bound drugs. However, as most of this binding to albumin and other plasma proteins is in reversible equilibrium, the clinical significance of protein binding remains confusing. In general, very highly protein bound antibiotics can be expected to penetrate into cerebrospinal fluid and abscesses less than drugs with lower degrees of protein binding.[28]

PHARMACOKINETIC AND PHARMACODYNAMIC PARAMETERS THAT AFFECT ANTIBIOTIC THERAPY

Parameters		Details
Pharmacokinetic	F	Bioavailability, fraction of the administered dose absorbed intact; intravenous drugs have 100% bioavailability; oral drugs vary with absorption and are usually less bioavailable than intravenous forms
	C_{max}	Maximal serum concentration after single or multiple doses
	t_{max}	Time after drug administration to reach C_{max}
	$t_{1/2\ elim}$	Elimination half-life; time to reduce peak serum concentration by 50%
	AUC	Area under the concentration–time curve (relates to total drug exposure following a dose)
Pharmacodynamic	C_{max}/MIC, Peak/MIC	Ratio of the maximum serum concentration to the MIC (predicts activity of concentration dependent bactericidal antibiotics)
	AUC/MIC	Ratio of the area under the concentration–time curve to the MIC (also predicts activity of concentration dependent bactericidal antibiotics)
	t>MIC, t_{eff}	Time above the MIC; the duration of time during a dosing interval that serum concentration remains above the MIC (predicts activity of time-dependent bactericidal antibiotics)

Table 187.2 Pharmacokinetic and pharmacodynamic parameters that affect antibiotic therapy.

Metabolism is another important consideration in the selection of antibiotics. A rapidly metabolized drug that is excreted by the kidney in an inactive form would not be an appropriate choice for the treatment of urinary tract infections, for example. Some drugs are metabolized in the liver by the cytochrome P450 system and as such may interact with other drugs metabolized via this system. Metabolism is a critical determinant of drug interactions and these must be understood and appreciated when patients receive multiple pharmaceutical interventions.

A clear understanding of the elimination half-life and excretion of antibiotics also influences selection. Drugs with a short half-life are rapidly eliminated and need more frequent administration to produce high levels of the antibiotic at the site of infection. Drugs with a longer half-life are often more convenient because single daily dosing is usually effective. Drugs that are primarily excreted via the kidney often need dose adjustment in the face of renal insufficiency; drugs primarily excreted via the hepatic and biliary system might accumulate inappropriately in patients who have hepatic insufficiency. Although antibiotics are not usually thought to be highly toxic drugs, some concentration-related adverse effects are likely to be more prevalent in the face of dysfunctional organs of excretion.

The pharmacokinetic variables that are most useful in antibiotic chemotherapy include bioavailability (F), maximal serum concentration (C_{max}), time to reach C_{max} (t_{max}), elimination half-life ($t_{1/2}$) and area under the drug concentration curve following a dose (AUC; Table 187.2).

Recently, pharmacodynamics has been popularized in the antibiotic field. Antibiotic pharmacodynamics can be described as the interrelations between pharmacokinetics (drug concentrations) and the antibacterial effects that result from these concentrations in, for instance, serum, tissues and body fluids. The most useful pharmacodynamic variables (see Table 187.2) include the ratio of the area under the 24-hour concentration–time curve to the MIC (AUC_{24}/MIC), the ratio of C_{max} to MIC (Peak/MIC) and the time during a given dosing interval that the serum concentration remains above the MIC (time above MIC, t>MIC, t_{eff}).

Pharmacokinetic/pharmacodynamic (PK/PD) variables are of increasing interest as possible predictors of the antimicrobial effect. Such parameters may be exploited to develop optimal dosing regimens, although there are relatively few clinical studies to test the ability of these parameters to predict outcome. One such clinical study suggested that C_{max}/MIC was useful in predicting outcome of levofloxacin treatment for several different infections.[29]

Other in-vitro and clinical studies suggest that PK/PD parameters might be exploited to minimize the emergence of resistant organisms during exposure or therapy. It remains to be determined whether PK/PD-based antibiotic prescribing and dosing can reduce adverse effects and costs while providing an optimal antibacterial effect.

Antibiotics in general are very safe drugs. However, adverse effects of antibiotics do occur and include gastrointestinal events (nausea, vomiting, diarrhea, antibiotic-associated colitis, pseudomembranous colitis), cutaneous reactions (rash, urticaria, Stevens–Johnson Syndrome), neurologic symptoms (agitation, insomnia, seizures), hepatic dysfunction, renal insufficiency, anemia, agranulocytosis and thrombocytopenia, among others. Some adverse events associated with antibiotics are idiosyncratic or hypersensitivity reactions and some are related to their concentration in serum and tissues. For example, prolongation of the QT_c interval with macrolide and other antibiotics might increase at higher drug concentrations as a result of either increased dose or decreased elimination.[30] Some hepatic toxicities are also related to dose and duration, and toxicity in general is dose-limiting for many antibiotics. Careful attention to appropriate use and dosing should reduce antibiotic-associated toxicity.

Choice of antibiotics for empiric therapy

Combinations: monotherapy versus multiple antibiotics

A single antibiotic is usually sufficient for the treatment of most bacterial infections. In some situations more than one antibiotic is prescribed. Most commonly two or more antibiotics are administered because the diagnosis is not obvious or not clearly established. Antibiotics are often combined in presumed mixed bacterial infections such as intra-abdominal abscesses or peritonitis, where antibiotics with activity against facultative Gram-negative rods, such as ampicillin plus gentamicin or a quinolone or third-generation cephalosporin, are combined with an antianaerobic agent such as metronidazole or clindamycin. For some specified infections such as pelvic inflammatory disease, multiple organisms, including *C. trachomatis*, *N. gonorrhoeae* and facultative and strict anaerobic Gram-negative rods, are assumed to be present and in fact might not be cultured. Antibiotic combinations are often prescribed for this infection.

Early studies of carbenicillin plus aminoglycosides in severe *Pseudomonas aeruginosa* infections suggested that these two antibiotics were more effective than either alone; this has led to the routine use of two antibiotics for infections caused by this organism. This concept has recenly been challenged, but the importance of high concentrations of bactericidal antibiotics remains cogent.[31] Optimal results for pseudomonal infections might require two active agents. Even more clearly, bacteremic infections caused by *Enterococcus faecalis* are best treated with a combination of a cell-wall-active penicillin or glycopeptide plus an aminoglycoside (assuming that high-level resistance to one or both agents is not present).[32] Some studies of bacterial endocarditis caused by viridans streptococci and bacteremia caused by *Staphylococcus aureus* suggest better outcomes with combination therapy.

Antibiotics also might be combined to minimize or prevent the selection of resistant organisms. This is most clearly demonstrated with *Mycobacterium tuberculosis*, where use of two or more antimycobacterial agents (depending on the likely inoculum size) reduces the likelihood of selecting for resistant bacteria. Whether this also applies to pyogenic bacteria is not definitively proven.

Antibiotic combinations (e.g. an aminoglycoside and an antipseudomonal β-lactam) were initially recommended for the treatment of presumed bacterial infections in febrile, neutropenic patients. Prolonged and profound granulocytopenia places these immunocompromised patients at particular risk for Gram-negative rod bacteremia. Although combination therapy is still considered acceptable for these patients, several potent antibiotics (such as imipenem, meropenem, cefepime and ceftazidime) are currently acceptable for single-agent empiric therapy.[4]

Duration of therapy

For most acute bacterial infections in the respiratory or urinary tracts, the duration of therapy can be short (e.g. from 3 to 7 or 10 days). In the early antibiotic era, patients who had pneumococcal pneumonia were successfully treated with courses of antibiotics that lasted for 3–5 days after the patient became afebrile. Modern therapy duration may be inappropriately based on standardized clinical trials needed for drug registration purposes. There is a trend now for shorter courses of treatment for some respiratory infections such as acute bacterial exacerbations of chronic bronchitis. Rigid adherence to 10- to 14-day treatment regimens for many acute infections is probably not necessary and may contribute to excess antibiotic use, increased adverse effects and complications of therapy, as well as the emergence of resistant organisms.

Subacute and more chronic infections such as endocarditis and osteomyelitis are treated for prescribed lengths of time. Six weeks of intravenous therapy is often required for bacterial osteomyelitis and 4 weeks is usually prescribed for patients who have bacterial endocarditis (although 2-week treatment courses are clearly effective for certain organisms, e.g. viridans streptococci; see Chapters 52 & 59).

Route of administration

The intravenous administration of antibiotics is preferred for patients who are critically ill or bacteremic, or in whom gastrointestinal absorption cannot be guaranteed. For most acute bacterial infections (e.g. pneumonia, pyelonephritis) it is possible to switch to oral therapy with the same or comparable agents when the patient has stabilized and vital signs are returning toward normal.[33] Fluoroquinolone antibiotics are particularly useful in these situations, assuming that the infecting organism is susceptible. Home administration of intravenous antibiotics is now entirely possible and preferable for long-term treatment with these drugs for infections such as endocarditis and osteomyelitis, where high concentrations at the site of infection are desired.

Topical use of antibiotics is limited to specific infections.[34] Although minor cutaneous infections might respond to topical therapy, some evidence suggests that sensitization via this route is frequent for some agents. Excessive use of topical antibiotics may lead to increased bacterial resistance. Topical administration may be employed to treat bacterial conjunctivitis with ciprofloxacin, trachoma with tetracycline, and acne with clindamycin, tetracycline or erythromycin, for example. Topical aminoglycosides have been useful in the prophylaxis and treatment of burns and burn wound infection (see Chapter 85). Topical mupirocin (its only formulation) is used to treat impetigo and nasal carriage of *S. aureus*. Polymyxin and neomycin are used in topical therapy of minor wound infections. Adverse effects seen with intravenous or oral administration of the same drug can certainly occur following topical therapy.

Cost, restricted use policy and formulary constraints

Antibiotics comprise a significant portion of the pharmacy budget for most hospitals and managed care plans. The appropriate use of first-line agents for proven or strongly suggested bacterial infections should help to control these costs. The cost to pharmaceutical companies to develop a new antibiotic may be as high as US$800,000,000. Increasing regulatory requirements and safety concerns clearly contribute to these costs. Incentives for continued development of antibiotics in the face of rising rates of bacterial resistance are clear societal needs, and these factors also contribute to the high cost of these drugs.

Some hospitals adopt policies to restrict use of certain antibiotics to infectious disease clinicians or other designated experts. Although these schemes have been shown to reduce costs and improve appropriate antibiotic use, their success is tied to continual monitoring and control of antibiotic prescribing.[35] Most successful programs include physician education to sustain their impact. Many managed care organizations limit their formularies to less expensive and older drugs. The impact of these policies on clinical outcome and resistance development is under study.[15]

Antibiotic use in special populations

Special considerations modify the use of antibiotics at the extremes of age, in the presence of renal or hepatic insufficiency, in pregnancy and in the presence of foreign bodies. In neonates and infants less than 1 year of age, dosing is often based on the body mass index. In elderly patients the fever and leukocytosis associated with bacterial infections may be blunted or absent, making diagnosis more problematic. Antibiotic dosing must consider the aging-related slight decline in gastrointestinal absorption and decreases in renal function associated with nephron loss. Drug interactions are particularly worrisome in the elderly because of the large number of drugs that such patients may be taking. QT_c prolongation might be enhanced when some antibiotics are combined with other classes of drugs known to increase the QT_c interval. Metronidazole may interact with warfarin,

resulting in increased effect of the anticoagulant. Loop diuretics may increase aminoglycoside-related ototoxicity. Adherence to drug regimens should be stressed as elderly patients may find the addition of any new agent confusing, even for a short course of therapy. Side effects are also more common in elderly patients.[36]

The dosing of some antibiotics, notably those primarily excreted by the kidney, must be reduced in the presence of renal insufficiency. The more severe the renal failure the more the dose or its interval must be altered. Patients on hemodialysis or peritoneal dialysis need special dosing modifications to supplement antibiotics (usually those of low molecular weight) that are removed during the procedures. For some drugs, such as aminoglycosides, the dosing interval can be extended and/or the dose itself reduced according to the estimated creatinine clearance. Some adverse effects of frequently used antibiotics are increased in patients who have renal insufficiency. For example, seizures may be seen with usual dosing of imipenem or quinolones, and hearing loss may occur with erythromycin. Several tables have been published to guide the appropriate dosing of antibiotics in patients who have renal insufficiency.[1,37]

In the face of hepatic failure additional considerations affect the choice or dose of antibiotic. Drugs excreted by the liver such as metronidazole, tetracycline and clindamycin often need dose adjustment in hepatic failure. In the presence of large-volume ascites, some antibiotics might need to be administered in a larger dose to ensure appropriate concentrations at the site of infection.

Antibiotic selection in pregnancy is determined by the specific infections under treatment. Penicillins and cephalosporins are generally considered safe in pregnant women, and aminoglycosides also can be used if needed. Trimethoprim–sulfamethoxazole and other sulfonamides may be used in pregnancy but not in the last few months because of their effect on bilirubin conjugation and the risk of kernicterus in neonates. Fluoroquinolones, tetracyclines and chloramphenicol should not be used in pregnancy.

The treatment of infections in the presence of foreign bodies such as intravascular or bladder catheters and orthopedic prostheses is covered elsewhere (see Chapters 53). As foreign bodies may be coated with a microbiologic biofilm, agents that reduce bacterial mucus, slime or biofilm production, even if they are not bacteriostatic or bactericidal for the infecting organisms, might be useful in conjunction with other antibacterial agents. Macrolides and fluoroquinolones have been shown to reduce bacterial mucoid production.[38] In most cases, infected foreign bodies need to be removed to resolve the infection completely.

Prophylaxis

Surgical prophylaxis is discussed in Chapter 190. Medical prophylaxis against bacterial infections is limited to specific indications, such as the prevention of *S. pyogenes* infection in patients who have known rheumatic fever or to reduce the possibility of bacterial endocarditis in patients who have known valvular cardiac disease and are undergoing dental, gastrointestinal or genitourinary procedures. Prophylaxis against traveler's diarrhea is not usually recommended (but empiric therapy is preferred, see Chapter 143). Inappropriate or excessive use of prophylactic antibiotics is likely to contribute to the increased incidence of antibiotic resistance.

New targets for antibiotics

With increasing antibiotic resistance and few new antibiotics in the pharmaceutical pipeline, it is urgent to begin to identify new bacterial targets and novel approaches to antimicrobial chemotherapy. Several lines of work have begun to find new inhibitors of bacterial efflux pumps, biofilm production, essential bacterial protein secretion, membrane proteins, signaling systems, DNA replication and bacterial cell division. Identification of bacterial genomes also has revealed important potential targets and functional genomics should allow opportunities for new drug development.[39] Recent work on quorum sensing by bacteria also might provide new chemotherapy targets.[40]

ANTIFUNGAL THERAPY

Health care providers are faced with increasing numbers of patients who are susceptible to severe, invasive fungal infections. Multiple factors play a role, including chemotherapy-induced neutropenia, immunosuppression secondary to chronic infections such as HIV, and immunosuppression related to organ transplantation, as well as exposure to lengthy courses of broad-spectrum antibiotics. These agents are used to treat documented infections and increasingly for prophylaxis of invasive fungal infection in these at-risk patients. Prior to the late 1970s only amphotericin B and flucytosine were available for the treatment of serious fungal infections. In the past two decades many new agents have been developed and approved, and new classes of antifungals are now entering clinical trials. Treatment of specific fungal infections is covered in detail in Chapters 111, 126 and 237–241; here the classes of antifungal agents, mechanisms of action and the emerging topics of antifungal pharmacodynamics and resistance are outlined briefly.

Amphotericin B, a polyene, and its newer formulations remain the mainstay of antifungal therapy for severe infection. The mechanisms of action primarily include binding to ergosterol, the principal sterol in the fungal cell membrane, leading to permeability changes and cell death. Secondary actions include the generation of oxidative metabolites and free radicals, as well as stimulation of host macrophages. The newer formulations (lipid complex, colloidal dispersion, cholesteryl complex and liposomal amphotericin B) offer some reduced toxicity and the ability to deliver higher drug concentrations. Amphotericin B is active against a wide variety of fungi; it is fungicidal against many of these but fungistatic against others. Some fungi (*Pseudallescheria boydii*, *Fusarium* spp., *Trichosporon* spp. and some *Candida* spp.) demonstrate reduced amphotericin B susceptibility, while others have developed frank resistance.[41]

Nystatin, a tetraene-diene, was the first antifungal polyene. It has broad antifungal activity similar to that of amphotericin B. Nontopical formulations are presently being investigated and may prove to be efficacious, given this agent's fungicidal properties.

Flucytosine, a low-molecular-weight, synthetic pyrimidine analogue, is taken up by the fungal cell wall and, after enzymatic modification, causes RNA miscoding and inhibition of DNA synthesis. Flucytosine has activity against *Candida* spp., *Cryptococcus neoformans*, *Saccharomyces cerevisiae* and some dematiaceous molds. At clinically achievable doses it is fungistatic. When flucytosine is used as monotherapy, resistance emerges rapidly and thus it is usually used in combination with amphotericin B or fluconazole. Resistance can emerge from mutations that affect production of uridine monophosphate pyrophosphorylase, cytosine permease or cytosine deaminase, or increased pyrimidine production. Toxicity includes bone marrow suppression, which is most evident when used in combination with amphotericin B. This occurs as a consequence of the high rate of renal impairment with amphotericin B and subsequent high flucytosine levels. Recent pharmacokinetic studies have suggested that flucytosine may be safer and more effective at lower and less frequent dosing.[42]

As a class the azoles act by inhibiting fungal cytochrome-P450-dependent conversion of lanosterol to ergosterol, ultimately leading to altered cell membrane properties and inhibition of cell growth. The imidazoles clotrimazole, ketoconazole and miconazole have two nitrogens in the five-member ring whereas the triazoles have three. For many years ketoconazole was the only available oral agent for the treatment of systemic fungal infections. Because of difficulty with absorption, substantial toxicity and disappointing treatment

ANTIVIRAL DRUGS: NON-HIV				
Agent	**Mechanism of action**	**Antiviral activity**	**Mechanism of resistance**	**Toxicity/side effects**
Aciclovir	Inhibits DNA polymerase, chain terminator. Requires viral thymidine kinase and cellular enzymes	HSV-1, HSV-2, VZV, CMV (much less activity), EBV (in vitro)	Mutations in thymidine kinase (more common) and mutations in DNA polymerase	Intravenous: phlebitis, crystalline nephropathy. Confusion, delirium, lethargy, tremors, nausea, vomiting, lightheadedness, diaphoresis, rash
Adefovir	Nucleotide analogue	HBV	As of 2000, no mutations	Renal impairment at >30mg q24h
Amantadine	Inhibits transmembrane protein M2, reduced uncoating of viral genome	Influenza A	Point mutation in gene encoding transmembrane domain M2 protein	Nervousness, anxiety, lightheadedness, confusion, insomnia
Cidofovir	Acyclic nucleoside phosphonate (does not require a virus-specific thymidine kinase)	HSV-1, HSV-2, VZV, EBV, CMV	Mutations in DNA polymerase	Severe nephrotoxicity, neutropenia, ocular hypotony, metabolic acidosis. Carcinogenic, teratogenic
Famciclovir	Prodrug to penciclovir	See penciclovir	See penciclovir	Headache, nausea, diarrhea, vomiting, pruritus, LFT abnormalities
Fomivirsen (intravitreal)	Antisense oligonucleotide	CMV	In-vivo resistance not seen	Iritis, vitreitis, increased ocular pressures, visual changes
Foscarnet	Noncompetitive inhibitor of viral DNA polymerase (does not require thymidine kinase)	HSV-1, HSV-2, VZV, CMV, EBV, influenza A, influenza B, HBV, HIV	In CMV, single mutation in conserved region of DNA polymerase	Renal impairment, electrolyte disturbances, seizures, anemia, neutropenia, fever, nausea, vomiting, diarrhea, headache
Ganciclovir	Inhibitor of DNA polymerase, also competitive inhibitor of deoxyguanosine triphosphate (monophosphorylation by infection-induced kinases in HSV and VZV, and viral-encoded phosphotransferase in CMV-infected cells)	HSV-1, HSV-2, VZV, CMV, EBV, HHV-6	One or more point mutations in UL97, mutations in CMV DNA polymerase	Bone marrow suppression, fever, rash, increased LFTs, nausea, vomiting, eosinophilia, seizures, confusion, encephalopathy
Interferon-α	Induces changes in infected/exposed cells to promote resistance to infecting virus. Produces proteins that inhibit RNA synthesis, cleaves cellular and viral DNA, inhibits messenger RNA, alters cell membranes, inhibits release of replicated virions	Papillomavirus, HCV, HBV, HDV, HIV	Fever, headache, chills, arthralgias, myalgias, fatigue, dizziness, neutropenia, thrombocytopenia, somnolence, depression, cognitive changes, suicidal ideation, increased LFTs, altered thyroid function, nausea, vomiting, diarrhea	
Lamivudine	Competitively inhibits viral reverse transcriptase, terminates proviral DNA chain extension	HBV, HIV	Mutations at YMDD locus (conserved domain reverse transcriptase)	Low-dose equivalent to placebo. High dose: headache, fatigue, insomnia, myalgias, arthralgias, diarrhea, rash, lactic acidosis, hepatomegaly
Lobucavir	Guanosine analogue	HBV	Mild anorexia, dizziness, abdominal pain. Clinical testing halted with concerns for carcinogenesis	

Table 187.3 Antiviral drugs: non-HIV.

results in immunocompromised patients, it has largely been replaced by the triazoles.

The triazoles are less susceptible to degradation and have greater target specificity, increased potency and an expanded activity spectrum. The first generation triazoles fluconazole and itraconazole are active against dermatophytes, *Candida albicans* and some non-*albicans* candidal species; in addition, itraconazole has activity against *Aspergillus* spp. and some dematiaceous molds. Fluconazole is generally fungistatic and itraconazole is both fungicidal and fungistatic depending on the fungal strain. Second-generation triazoles include posaconazole, ravuconazole and the FDA-approved voriconazole. These drugs have enhanced target activity especially against *Aspergillus* spp., specificity and a wide spectrum of activity. Available data show that voriconazole is well tolerated, with rash, fever and visual disturbances reported most frequently. Like the triazoles, these agents also appear to be both fungicidal and fungistatic depending on the specific organism. As a group they have potential for substantial drug–drug interactions with agents metabolized by the cytochrome system.[43]

The echinocandins inhibit the synthesis of 1,3-β-D-glucan, a polysaccharide in the cell wall of many pathogenic fungi. Glucan fibrils are involved in the maintenance of osmotic integrity of the cell wall as well as playing a role in cell division and growth. Caspofungin, micafungin and anidulafungin all possess potent, broad antifungal activity against *Candida* and *Aspergillus* spp. They are not metabolized through the cytochrome P450 system. In-vitro models have demonstrated both fungicidal and fungistatic properties. Caspofungin has recently been approved by the US Food and Drug Administration (FDA) for the treatment of candidemia and invasive aspergillosis in patients refractory to or intolerant of other therapies.

ANTIVIRAL DRUGS: NON-HIV				
Agent	**Mechanism of action**	**Anti-viral activity**	**Mechanism of resistance**	**Toxicity/side effects**
Oseltamivir	Neuraminidase inhibitor	Influenza A, influenza B	Mutations in viral neuraminidase and viral hemagglutinin	Nausea, vomiting
Penciclovir (topical)	Incorporated into DNA molecule	HSV-1, HSV-2, VZV, EBV (less so), CMV (less so), HBV (in vitro)	Mutations in thymidine kinase and mutations in DNA polymerase	Topical same as placebo
Pleconaril	Capsid binding compound prevents viral attachment to cells and/or release of viral RNA from the capsid	Picornaviruses (enterovirus, rhinovirus)	Observed in vitro but clinical significance not clear	Crystalluria
Ribavirin	Guanosine analogue, three possible mechanisms: competitive inhibition of host enzymes, inhibition of viral RNA polymerase complex, inhibition of messenger RNA formation	RSV, HCV (clinically); but also influenza A, influenza B, mumps, measles, parainfluenza, herpesviruses, togavirus, bunyavirus, adenovirus, Coxsackie virus, hemorrhagic fever virus, HAV, HBC, Lassa fever virus, Hantaan virus, ?Hantavirus	Anemia, hyperbilirubinemia, elevated uric acid, nausea, headache, lethargy. Teratogenic, mutagenic, embryotoxic, gonadotoxic	
Rimantadine	Inhibits transmembrane protein M2, reduced uncoating of viral genome	Influenza A	Point mutation in gene encoding transmembrane domain M2 protein	Nervousness, anxiety, lightheadedness, confusion, insomnia (much less so than amantadine)
Trifluridine (topical)	Pyrimidine nucleoside	HSV-1, HSV-2, CMV, vaccinia, some adenoviruses		
Valganciclovir	Metabolized to ganciclovir	See ganciclovir	See ganciclovir	Bone marrow suppression, fever, nausea, headache, vomiting, insomnia, abdominal pain, peripheral neuropathy, paresthesias, potential carcinogen
Zanamivir (aerosolized/ intranasal)	Neuraminidase inhibitor	Influenza A, influenza B	Mutations in viral neuraminidase and viral hemagglutinin	Nasal, throat discomfort, bronchospasm in asthmatics

CMV, cytomegalovirus; EBV, Epstein–Barr virus; HAV, hepatitis A virus; HBV, hepatitis B virus; HCV, hepatitis C virus; HDV, hepatitis D virus; HHV, human herpesvirus; HSV, herpes simplex virus; LFT, liver function test; RSV, respiratory syncytial virus; VZV, varicella-zoster virus.

Table 187.3—cont'd.

Sordarins exert their antifungal effect by selective inhibition of fungal protein synthesis by interacting with translocation elongation factor 2 and the large ribosomal subunit stalk rpP0. In vitro, they have shown fungicidal activity against *C. albicans*, some non-*albicans* species, *C. neoformans*, as well as some other yeast-like fungi and endemic molds.

There is little doubt that severe invasive fungal infections will continue to be clinically challenging, especially in immunocompromised patients. In addition to minimizing the use of broad-spectrum antibiotics, limiting immunosuppression to the lowest safe doses and protecting HIV-infected patients by judicious use of antiretrovirals, there will still be a need for newer and safer antifungal agents. In addition we need more studies investigating the pharmacodynamics and pharmacokinetics of already available agents in order to offer patients safer and equally, if not more, efficacious treatment options. Readily available and clinically relevant resistance testing would be a major advance in the therapy of these infections.

ANTIVIRAL THERAPY

Specific therapy for viral infections has become possible only recently. The discovery of many potent and effective antiviral drugs as well as marked improvements in diagnostic techniques that allow more rapid identification of viral infections have made effective therapy possible. Although most viral infections are usually self-limiting, others are overwhelming and devastating, with significant morbidity and mortality. Antiviral therapy is now available for herpesviruses, hepatitis C virus (HCV) and hepatitis B virus (HBV), papillomavirus, influenza and HIV, among others. Antiviral drugs share the common principle of being virustatic; they are only active against replicating viruses and do not affect latent virus. Therapeutic approaches to viral infections share very little other common ground. Some infections require monotherapy for very brief periods of time (aciclovir for herpes simplex virus), others require dual therapy for prolonged periods of time (α-interferon/ribavirin for HCV), while others require multiple drug therapy for indefinite periods of time (HIV).[44] Table 187.3 briefly summarizes the antiviral activity, resistance mechanisms and more common toxicities of the non-HIV antivirals.[44,45] Chapters 205 to 207 address specific antiviral agents.

The approaches to treatment of HIV infection are in constant flux. Like other infections, cure is the goal; however, like other viral infections, cure is not possible at this time, although suppression of viral replication and preservation of the immune system are short-term goals of therapy. In less than two decades antiretroviral therapy has emerged as a great success but it remains an enormous challenge.

ANTIVIRAL DRUGS: HIV		
Agent	**Mechanism of action**	**Toxicity/side effects**
Abacavir	Nucleoside reverse transcriptase inhibitor	Hypersensitivity syndrome, rash, fever, nausea, vomiting, diarrhea, abdominal pain, elevated LFTs
Amprenavir	Protease inhibitor	Nausea, vomiting, diarrhea, rash, oral paresthesias, dysgeusia, mood disorder
Atazanavir	Protease inhibitor	Increased unconjugated bilirubin, gastrointestinal symptoms
DAPD	Nucleoside reverse transcriptase inhibitor	Nausea, vomiting, diarrhea, abdominal pain, hepatitis
Delavirdine	Non-nucleoside reverse transcriptase inhibitor	Rash, headache, Stevens–Johnson syndrome
Didanosine	Nucleoside reverse transcriptase inhibitor	Nausea, vomiting, diarrhea, abdominal pain, peripheral neuropathy, pancreatitis
Efavirenz	Non-nucleoside reverse transcriptase inhibitor	Dizziness, difficulty concentrating, nausea, vomiting, diarrhea, rash, flu-like symptoms
Emtricitabine	Nucleoside reverse transcriptase inhibitor	Nausea, diarrhea, headache
Enfurvirtide	Fusion inhibitor	Injection site inflammation
Hydroxyurea	Potentiates didanosine, may facilitate immune reconstitution	Myelosuppression, stomatitis, leg ulcers
Indinavir	Protease inhibitor	Nephrolithiasis, nausea, dysgeusia, benign hyperbilirubinemia
Interleukin-2	Peripheral expansion of existing $CD4^+$ lymphocytes	Nausea, vomiting, diarrhea, fever, asthenia, pruritus
Lamivudine	Nucleoside reverse transcriptase inhibitor	No significant toxicity, peripheral neuropathy, pancreatitis
Lopinavir	Protease inhibitor	Nausea, asthenia, diarrhea
Nelfinavir	Protease inhibitor	Diarrhea
Nevirapine	Non-nucleoside reverse transcriptase inhibitor	Dizziness, rash, difficulty concentrating, nausea, vomiting, diarrhea, flu-like symptoms
Ritonavir	Protease inhibitor	Dysgeusia, nausea, vomiting, diarrhea, circumoral paresthesias, increased triglycerides, LFTs, CPK and uric acid
Saquinavir	Protease inhibitor	Nausea, vomiting, diarrhea, headache
Stavudine	Nucleoside reverse transcriptase inhibitor	Peripheral neuropathy
Tenofovir	Nucleoside reverse transcriptase inhibitor	Nausea, vomiting, diarrhea, headache, elevated LFTs and CPK
Tipranovir	Protease inhibitor	Nausea, vomiting, diarrhea
Zalcitabine	Nucleoside reverse transcriptase inhibitor	Oral ulcers, peripheral neuropathy, pancreatitis
Zidovudine	Nucleoside reverse transcriptase inhibitor	Anemia, neutropenia, nausea, vomiting, myositis, neuropathy
CPK, creatine phosphokinase; LFT, liver function test		

Table 187.4 Antiviral drugs: HIV.

There is no doubt that antiretroviral therapy has saved lives; however, this has occurred at considerable expense, including morbidity due to immediate side effects and long-term metabolic toxicities, as well as recognition of serious drug–drug interactions and the emergence of highly resistant virus. Much attention has been focused on combination studies, including older work that revealed potential antagonistic antiretroviral combinations. More recent pharmacokinetic and pharmacodynamic studies have revealed drug–drug combinations with reduced toxicity and improved efficacy. Newer agents and new formulations have allowed for simpler therapeutic regimens, which hopefully will add the benefit of improved adherence and consequently decreased resistance. These agents are no longer used only for the treatment of chronically infected patients but also to treat acutely infected patients, to prevent maternal–child transmission and as prophylaxis against infection following sexual exposure or exposure in a health care setting. Table 187.4 briefly outlines the agents used in the treatment of HIV infection. Chapters 139 and 204 address antiretroviral agents and the therapy of HIV infection in detail.

The list of available agents to combat both HIV and non-HIV viral infections is expanding rapidly. In addition to new agents, the agents already available are being manipulated by using them in combination at lower, less toxic doses against viruses for which they were not initially investigated and stretching their pharmacology to optimize efficacy and minimize toxicity. As with antibiotics, increased use of antiviral agents will lead to resistance, a major impediment that warrants constant attention.

ANTIPARASITIC THERAPY

Parasitic infections are major causes of significant morbidity and mortality worldwide. In developing countries, lack of resources for many basic services has allowed vector-borne illnesses to persist and propagate. In developed countries health care providers are more frequently encountering parasitic infections as a consequence of increased international travel and a growing number of patients immunocompromised by HIV, antineoplastic therapies and chronic medication-induced immunosuppression.

Although new agents have been introduced in recent years, advances in antiparasitic therapy have lagged behind antibacterials, antivirals and antifungals. The reasons for this are multifactorial and include lack of in-depth knowledge of the life cycle and potential targets for many of these organisms, lack of financial incentives for pharmaceutical companies to invest in drug development for infections not frequently encountered in the developed world, and hesitancy to invest the monies needed to pursue FDA approval for drugs already developed.

Antiparasitic drugs can loosely be characterized as antiprotozoal or anthelmintic, although some agents do have activity against both. They are used in the treatment of acute infections and also in chronic infections. Prophylactic use is increasing in international travelers. For many agents the mechanisms of action are incompletely understood, and this is especially true for many antimalarials. Anthelmintic agents can be characterized as inhibitors of metabolic pathways, inhibitors of neuromuscular function or drugs that disrupt reproduction and larval development.[46,47]

Resistance to antiparasitic therapy is most clearly recognized in the antimalarials. Recent studies have suggested potential resistance mechanisms (p-glycoprotein involved in efflux of the antimalarial) but these explanations are just beginning.[48] Antiparasitic agents are discussed in detail in Chapter 209, and parasites and the treatment of parasitic infections are covered throughout the text under organ-specific infections, Infections in the Immunocompromised Host, HIV and AIDS, Geographic and Travel Medicine, and Clinical Microbiology.

SUMMARY

Antimicrobial therapy is one of the great advances of the last century. Currently, there are many classes of antimicrobials with activity against most agents of infection, including bacteria and mycobacteria, rickettsiae, fungi, viruses and parasites. Appropriate use of these drugs should include applications of their pharmacology to specifically diagnosed or suspected infections. Doses should be adequate to ensure eradication of the pathogens when possible and the duration of treatment should follow standard regimens based on carefully performed clinical trials. Physicians should be encouraged to use these agents sparingly and only for their proven indications. Excessively long courses, inappropriate prophylactic use, unnecessary combinations and failure to consider the impact of each prescription on the bacterial ecology will ultimately limit the lifespan and usefulness of these life-saving drugs. Careful and thoughtful diagnosis should precede the use of antimicrobial agents and knowledge of their adverse event profiles and potential for drug interactions are prerequisites for their appropriate use. Appropriate antimicrobial use will not only reduce selection of resistant organisms but is likely to improve patient care by reducing adverse effects, toxicities, drug–drug interactions and cost.

REFERENCES

1. Gilbert DN, Moellering RC Jr, Sande MA, eds. The Sanford guide to antimicrobial therapy 2002, 32nd ed. Hyde Park, VT: Antimicrobial Therapy Inc.; 2002:2–46.
2. Haight TH, Finland M. Observations on mode of action of erythromycin. Proc Soc Exp Biol Med 1952;81:88–93.
3. Moellering RC Jr, Wennersten C, Weinberg AN. Studies on antibiotic synergism against enterococci. I. Bacteriologic studies. J Lab Clin Med 1971;77:821–8.
4. Hughes WT, Armstrong D, Bodey GP, *et al.* 2002 guidelines for the use of antimicrobial agents in neutropenic patients with cancer. Clin Infect Dis 2002;34:730–51.
5. Craig WA. Pharmacokinetic/pharmacodynamic parameters: rationale for antibacterial dosing of mice and men. Clin Infect Dis 1998;26:1–12.
6. Craig WA. Post-antibiotic effects in experimental infection models: relationship to in-vitro phenomena and to treatment of infection in man. J Antimicrob Chemother 1993;31(Suppl.D):149–58.
7. Medeiros AA. Evolution and dissemination of beta-lactamases accelerated by generations of beta-lactam antibiotics. Clin Infect Dis 1997;24(Suppl.1):S19–45.
8. Levy SB. Active efflux, a common mechanism for biocide and antibiotic resistance. J Appl Microbiol 2002;92(Suppl.):55–64S.
9. Livermore DM. Interplay of impermeability and chromosomal beta-lactamase activity in imipenem resistant *Pseudomonas aeruginosa.* Antimicrob Agents Chemother 1992;36:2046–8.
10. Eliopoulos GM. Vancomycin-resistant enterococci. Mechanism and clinical relevance. Infect Dis Clin North Am 1997;11:851–65.
11. Doern GV. Antimicrobial use and the emergence of antimicrobial resistance with *Streptococcus pneumoniae* in the United States. Clin Infect Dis 2001;33(Suppl.3):S187–92.
12. Steinke D, Davey P. Association between antibiotic resistance and community prescribing: a critical review of bias and confounding in published studies. Clin Infect Dis 2001;33(Suppl.3):S193–205.
13. Boyce JM. Consequences of inaction: importance of infection control practices. Clin Infect Dis 2001;33(Suppl.3):S133–7.
14. Levin BR. Minimizing potential resistance: a population dynamics view. Clin Infect Dis 2001;33(Suppl.3)S161–9.
15. Belongia EA, Naimi TS, Gale CM, *et al.* Antibiotic use and upper respiratory infections: a survey of knowledge, attitudes and experience in Wisconsin and Minnesota. Prevent Med 2002;34:346–52.
16. Ehrlich P. Chemotherapeutics: scientific principles, methods, and results. Lancet 1913;4694:445–51.
17. Ferraro MJ. Should we reevaluate antibiotic breakpoints? Clin Infect Dis 2001;33(Suppl.3):S227–9.
18. Weinstein MP, Stratton CW, Ackley A, *et al.* Multicenter collaborative evaluation of a standardized serum bactericidal test as a prognostic indicator in infective endocarditis. Am J Med 1985;78:262–9.
19. Sculier JP, Klastersky J. Significance of serum bactericidal activity in gram-negative bacillary bacteremia in patients with and without granulocytopenia. Am J Med 1984;76:429–35.
20. Eliopoulos GM, Moellering RC Jr. Antimicrobial combinations In: Lorian V, ed. Antibiotics in laboratory medicine, 4th ed. Baltimore: Williams & Wilkins;1996:330–96.
21. Lewis D, Reeves D, Wiedemann B, *et al.*, eds. Methodology and evaluation of *in-vitro* models of antimicrobial chemotherapy. J Antimicrob Chemother 1985;15(Suppl.A):1–326.
22. Firsov AA, Vostrov SN, Shevchenko AA, *et al.* Parameters of bacterial killing and regrowth kinetics and antimicrobial effect examined in terms of area under the concentration-time curve relationships: action of ciprofloxacin against *Escherichia coli* in an *in vitro* dynamic model. Antimicrob Agents Chemother 1997;41:1281–7.
23. Firsov AA, Lubenko IY, Portnoy YA, *et al.* Relationships of the area under the curve/MIC ratio to different integral endpoints of the antimicrobial effect: gemifloxacin pharmacodynamics in an *in vitro* dynamic model. Antimicrob Agents Chemother 2001;45:927–31.
24. Durack TD, Beeson PB, Petersdorf RG. Experimental bacterial endocarditis. 3. Production and progress of the disease in rabbits. Br J Exp Pathol 1973;54:142–51.
25. Tauber MG, Doroshow CA, Hackbarth CJ, *et al.* Antibacterial activity of beta-lactam antibiotics in experimental meningitis due to *Streptococcus pneumoniae.* J Infect Dis 1984;149:568–574.
26. Vogelman B, Gudmundsson S, Leggett J, *et al.* Correlation of antimicrobial pharmacokinetic parameters with therapeutic efficacy in an animal model. J Infect Dis 1988;158:831–47.
27. Kitteringham NR, Park BK. Pharmacokinetics. In: O'Grady F, Lambert HP, Finch RG, Greenwood D, eds. Antibiotic and chemotherapy. New York: Churchill Livingstone; 1997:44–69.
28. Bergeron MG. Tissue penetration of antibiotics. Clin Biochem 1986;19:90–100.
29. Preston SL, Drusano GL, Berman AL, *et al.* Pharmacodynamics of levofloxacin: a new paradigm for early clinical trials. JAMA 1998;279:125–9.
30. Bertino JS JR, Owens RC Jr, Carnes TD, *et al.* Gatifloxacin-associated corrected QT interval prolongation, torsades de pointes, and ventricular fibrillation in patients with known risk factors. Clin Infect Dis 2002;34:861–3.
31. Kashuba AD, Nafziger AN, Drusano GL, *et al.* Optimizing aminoglycoside therapy for nosocomial pneumonia caused by gram-negative bacteria. Antimicrob Agents Chemother 1999;43:623–9.
32. Zimmerman RA, Moellering RC Jr, Weinberg AN. Enterococcal resistance to antibiotic synergism. Antimicrob Agents Chemother 1970;10:517–21.
33. Sevinc F, Prins JM, Koopmans RP, *et al.* Early switch from intravenous to oral antibiotics: guidelines and implementation in a large teaching hospital. J Antimicrob Chemother 1999;43:601–6.
34. Kaye ET. Topical antibacterial agents. Infect Dis Clin North Am 2000;14:321–39.
35. Briceland LL, Nightingale CH, Quintiliani R, *et al.* Antibiotic streamlining from combination therapy to monotherapy utilizing an interdisciplinary approach. Arch Intern Med 1988;148:2019–22.
36. Stalam M, Kaye D. Antibiotic agents in the elderly. Infect Dis Clin North Am 2000;14:357–69.
37. Livornese LL Jr, Slavin D, Benz R, *et al.* Use of antibacterial agents in renal failure. Infect Dis Clin North Am 2000;14:371–90.
38. Bui KQ, Banevicius MA, Nightingale CH, *et al.* *In vitro* and *in vivo* influence of adjunct clarithromycin on the treatment of mucoid *Pseudomonas aeruginosa.* J Antimicrob Chemother 2000;45:57–62.
39. Cassell GH, Mekalanos J. Development of antimicrobial agents in the era of new and reemerging infectious diseases and increasing antibiotic resistance. JAMA 2001;285:601–5.
40. Bassler BL. Small talk: cell-to-cell communication in bacteria. Cell 2002;109:421–4.
41. Patel R. Antifungal Agents. Part I. Amphotericin B preparations and flucytosine. Mayo Clin Proc 1998;73:1205–25.
42. Groll AH, Piscitelli SC, Walsh TJ. Antifungal pharmacodynamics: concentration–effect relationships *in vitro* and *in vivo.* Pharmacotherapy 2001;21:133–48S.
43. Patel R. Antifungal agents. Part II. The azoles. Mayo Clin Proc 1999;74:78–100.
44. Drugs for non-HIV viral infections. Med Lett 1999;41 (issue 1069).
45. Keating MR. Antiviral agents for non-human immunodeficiency virus infections. Mayo Clin Proc 1999;74:1266–83.
46. Liu LX, Weller PF. Antiparasitic drugs. N Engl J Med 1996;334:1178–84.
47. Rosenblatt JE. Antiparasitic agents. Mayo Clin Proc 1999;74:1161–75.
48. Despommier DD, Gwadz RW, Hotez PJ, Knirsch, CH. Parasitic diseases, 4th ed. New York: Apple Trees Productions; 2000:287–93.

chapter
188 Mechanisms of Action

Francoise Van Bambeke, Didier M Lambert, Marie-Paule Mingeot-Leclercq & Paul M Tulkens

ANTIBIOTICS THAT ACT ON THE CELL WALL

The basis of the bacterial cell wall is peptidoglycan, a polymer that contains alternating residues of glucosamine and muramic acid in β-1→4 linkage. The carboxyl groups of muramyl residues are substituted by short peptides (usually pentapeptides such as L-Ala-D-Glu-D-Asp-D-Ala-D-Ala, L-Ser-D-Glu-D-Asp-D-Ala-D-Ala or Gly-D-Glu-D-Asp-D-Ala-D-Ala). Cell-wall-active antibiotics act by inhibiting the activity of enzymes involved in the synthesis of the precursors or in the reticulation of peptidoglycan.

β-lactams

The β-lactam nucleus is the basic building block of an exceptionally large class of antibiotics, all of which share a common mode of action but have quite distinct properties in terms of spectrum, pharmacokinetics and activity against resistant strains (see Chapter 193).

Chemical structure

All antibiotics in this class contain a cyclic amide called β-lactam, but different classes have been described according to the nature of the cycle or of the heteroatom included in the cycle. The main classes are (Fig. 188.1):

- penams – β-lactams with a five-membered ring containing a sulfur atom (penicillins);
- clavams – β-lactamase inhibitors that contain a five-membered ring with an oxygen as heteroatom (e.g. clavulanic acid; some sulfur analogs have also been reported);
- carbapenems – five-membered rings with a double bond (e.g. thienamycin, imipenem);
- penems – five-membered unsaturated ring with a sulfur atom (faropenem);
- cephems – six-membered unsaturated rings with a sulfur atom (cephalosporins);
- oxacephems – the oxygen analogs of cephems (latamoxef); and
- monobactams – cyclic amides in a four-membered ring (azetidine) with a methylcarboxylate function in the case of nocardicins and a sulfonate in the case of the other monobactams (e.g. aztreonam).

Other representatives members of the β-lactams are thiacephems, dethiacephems, dethiacephams, heterocephems and cephams, as well as diverse bicyclic systems.

Some non-β-lactam analogs have been also reported but seem to be of little interest.

Mode of action

β-lactams act primarily as inhibitors of the synthesis of the cell wall, by blocking the action of transpeptidases (Fig. 188.2).[1]

Specialized acyl serine transferases or transpeptidases are involved in the assembly of the bacterial cell wall. The structural properties of β-lactams mimic the D-Ala-D-Ala sequence in that the distance between the carboxylate and the cyclic amide is similar. Thus, these antibiotics act as a false substrate for D-alanyl-D-alanyl transpeptidases. The carboxylate or the sulfonate of the β-lactams react with a serine residue of the transpeptidases [also called penicillin-binding proteins (PBPs)] to give an acyl enzyme, with the formation of a covalent bond (Fig. 188.3).[2] The acylated enzyme is inactive. Such a mechanism is called suicide inhibition or mechanism-based enzyme inactivation. Transpeptidases are located in the perisplamic space, which is directly accessible in Gram-positive bacteria. In Gram-negative bacteria, β-lactams have to cross the outer membrane of the bacteria either through the membrane (by passive diffusion) or via porin channels.

The perturbations induced by the β-lactams in cell wall formation explain the inhibition of the growth of the bacteria, but the bactericidal effect results from indirect mechanisms (mostly the activation of autolytic enzymes). β-lactams are active only against rapidly dividing bacteria.

DIVERSITY OF BETA-LACTAM ANTIBIOTICS

Structure	Group	Examples
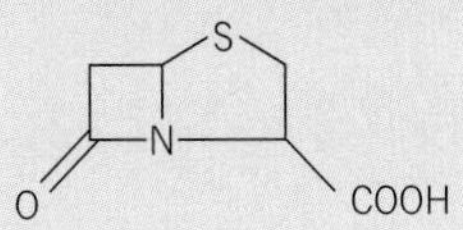	Penam	Penicillins
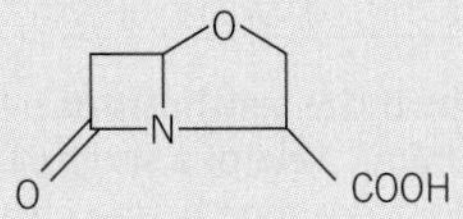	Clavam	β-lactamase inhibitors (clavulanic acid)
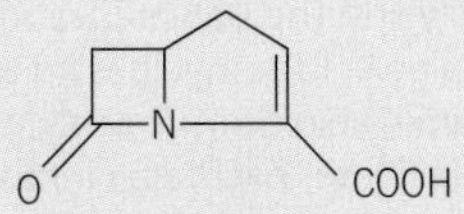	Carbapenem	(Thienamycin, imipenem)
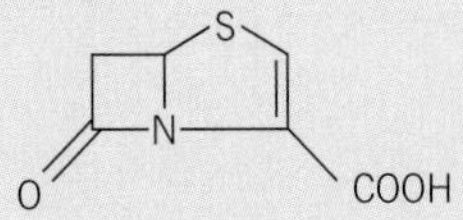	Penem	(Faropenem)
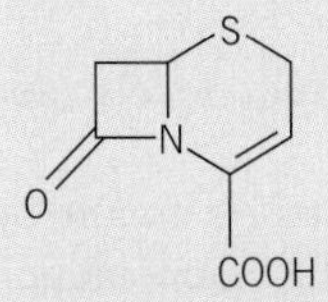	Cephem	Cephalosporins
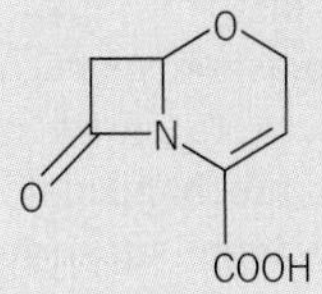	Oxacephem	(Latamoxef)
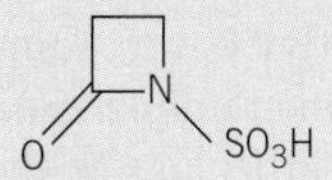	Monobactam	(Aztreonam)

Fig. 188.1 Diversity of β-lactam antibiotics: main ring structures, names and representative antibiotics.

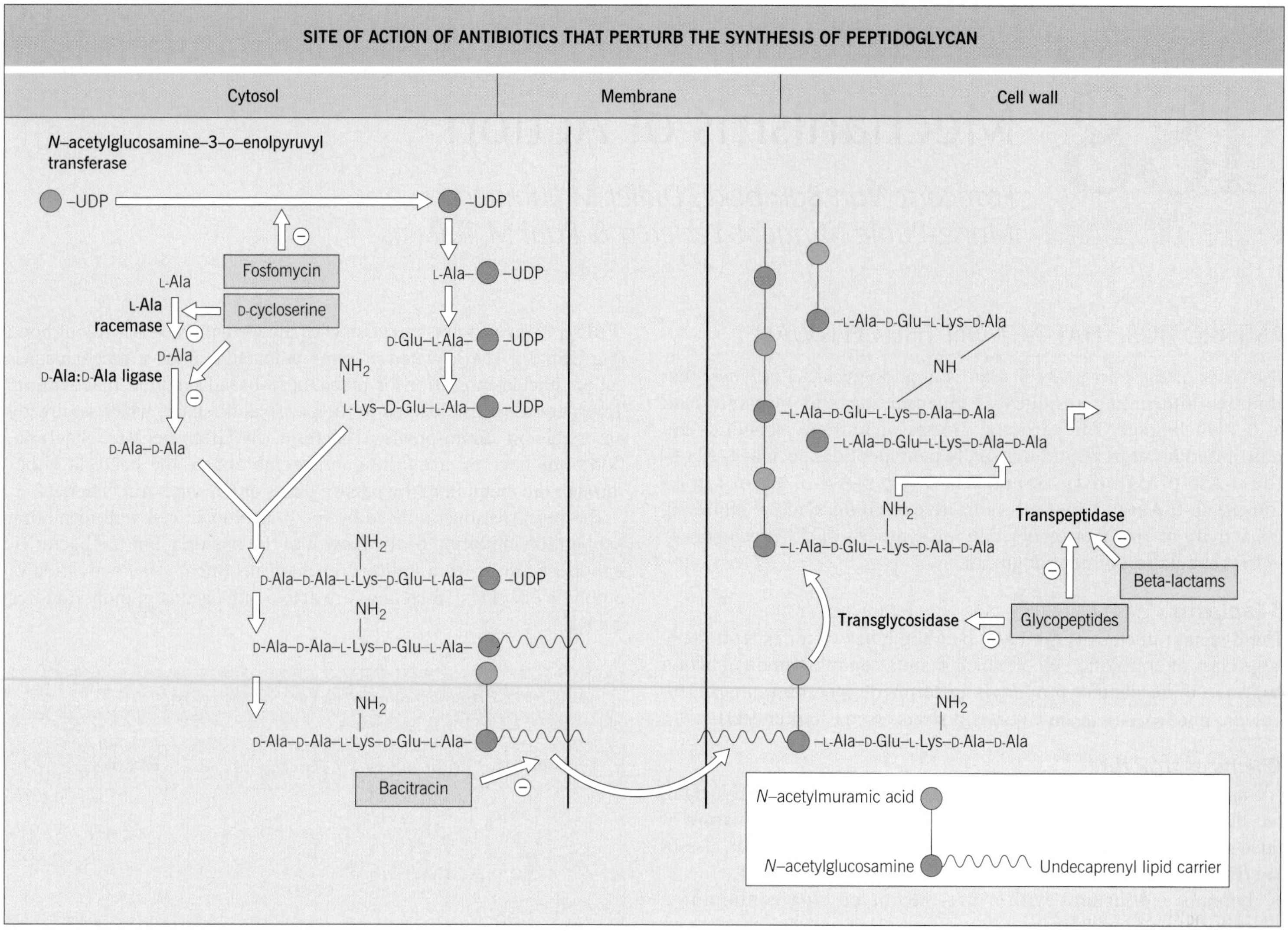

Fig. 188.2 Site of action of antibiotics that perturb the synthesis of peptidoglycan. The peptidoglycan unit is formed in the cytosol of bacteria by the binding to uridine diphosphate (UDP)-*N*-acetylmuramic acid of a short peptide (the nature of which differs between bacteria). This precursor is then attached to a lipidic carrier and added to *N*-acetylglucosamine before crossing the bacterial membrane. At the cell surface peptidoglycan units are reticulated by the action of transglycosylases (catalyzing the polymerization between sugars) and of transpeptidases (catalyzing the polymerization between peptidic chains). The antibiotics act as follows: fosfomycin is an analog of phosphoenolpyruvate, the substrate of the *N*-acetylglucosamine-3-*o*-enolpyruvyl transferase synthesizing *N*-acetylmuramic acid from *N*-acetylglucosamine and phosphoenolpyruvate; cycloserine is an analog of D-Ala and blocks the action of D-Ala racemase and D-Ala:D-Ala ligase; bacitracin inhibits the transmembrane transport of the precursor; vancomycin binds to D-Ala–D-Ala termini and thus inhibits the action of transglycosylases and transpeptidases; and β-lactams are analogs of D-Ala–D-Ala and suicide substrates for transpeptidases.

Resistance

Resistance to β-lactams may occur at four different levels (see Chapter 189):

- first, access to the PBPs in Gram-negative bacteria might be abolished by an alteration of porin channels – this phenomenon predominantly affects highly water-soluble β-lactams;
- second, the antibiotic concentration in the periplasmic space of Gram-negative organisms such as *Pseudomonas aeruginosa* or *Escherichia coli* can be reduced by active efflux mechanisms[3] – the corresponding pumps are characterized by a large substrate specificity, conferring cross-resistance to antibiotics from unrelated classes and by an ill-explained selectivity for some β-lactams (e.g. meropenem is a better substrate than imipenem);
- modification of PBPs can also be observed, in particular, for the PBP2, which is indeed an essential protein involved in the 'shaping' of the bacteria – resistant strains (methicillin-resistant staphylococci), produce a PBP2 protein with a very low affinity for β-lactams and other PBPs can also show the same decreased affinity;
- the fourth and most abundant mechanism is the production of hydrolyzing enzymes called β-lactamases[2,4–7] – these enzymes are serine proteases enzymes that cleave the β-lactam ring by opening the amide bond and the corresponding genes may either be carried on chromosomes (and their expression may be constitutive or inducible) or on plasmids – this system of resistance is very efficient because these enzymes are secreted out of the cell wall in Gram-positive bacteria and in the perisplamic space in Gram-negative bacteria, and the affinity for β-lactams is greater than that for PBPs.

Most β-lactamases open the β-lactam ring in exactly the same way as transpeptidases, but the major difference is that the hydrolysis rate is far quicker in the case of β-lactamase than in the case of PBP (see Fig. 188.3). In other words, the speed of hydrolysis of the acyl enzyme is higher and explains the high efficiency of β-lactamases. The turnover of PBPs and β-lactamases is indeed very different (1 β-lactam per hour and 1000 β-lactams per second respectively). Analytic data and genetic studies of β-lactamases show a high level of structural homology, which suggests that both derive from a common ancestor. A number of β-lactams have been

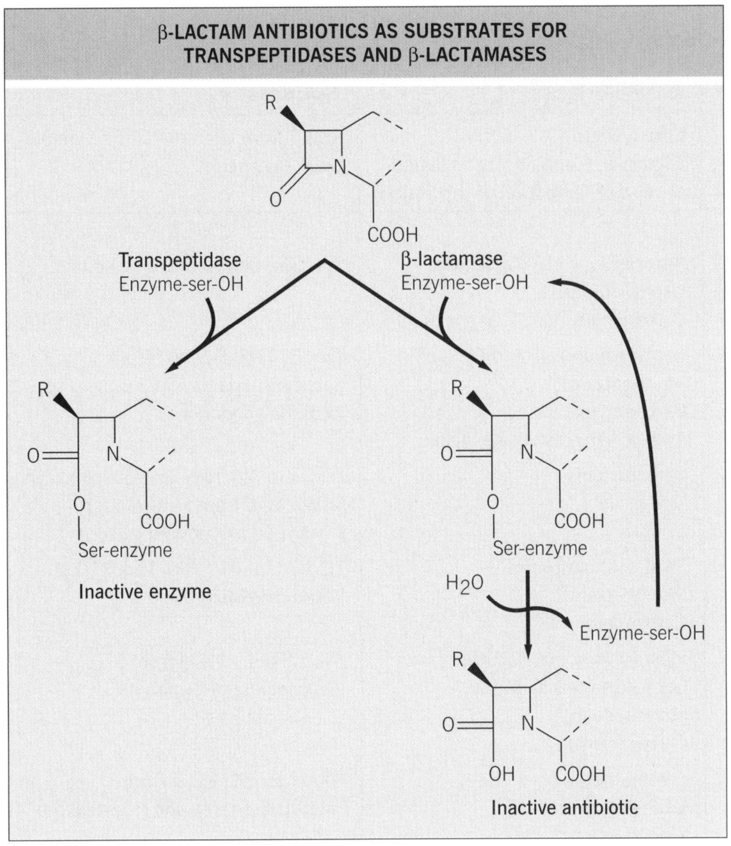

Fig. 188.3 β-Lactam antibiotics as substrates for transpeptidases and β-lactamases. The left part of the illustration shows how a β-lactam covalently binds to the transpeptidases. Hydrolysis of this acylated enzyme is very slow (one β-lactam per hour), making the enzyme inactive. The right part of the illustration shows that the same reaction occurs in the case of a β-lactamase. Hydrolysis of the acylated enzyme is, however, very rapid (1000 β-lactams per second), making the antibiotic inactive and regenerating the enzyme for a new cycle of hydrolysis.

made resistant to β-lactamases by appropriate steric hindrance or change in conformation (Fig. 188.4), giving rise to the large number of successive generations of penicillins and cephalosporins. β-lactamases, however, have an extraordinary plasticity and inevitably develop activity against all new derivatives at a fast pace (Table 188.1).

Thanks to their specific structure, clavams are poor antibiotics but bind tightly to β-lactamases. Given in combination with β-lactams, they provide protection unless the bacteria produces β-lactamases. Some β-lactamases can also hydrolyze the clavams.

Pharmacodynamics

β-lactams are relatively slow-acting antibiotics and show only limited post-antibiotic effects. They must therefore be present at a concentration above the minimum inhibitory concentration (MIC) as long as possible (from 40% in moderately severe infections to probably much more and perhaps up to 100% in severe, life-threatening infections). Conversely, concentrations higher than 4–5 times the MIC provides little gain in activity so frequent dosing is more appropriate than infrequent administration of large doses (administration by continuous infusion is being developed, but may encounter difficulties due to the intrinsically fragile character of the β-lactam ring, making the molecules potentially unstable in aqueous media).[8]

Glycopeptides

Chemical structure

Glycopeptide antibiotics (vancomycin, teicoplanin) contain two sugars and an aglycone moiety made of a relatively highly conserved heptapeptide core, in which two amino acids bear a chloride substituent. The aglycone fraction is responsible for the pharmacologic activity of the molecule, whereas the sugars are thought to modulate its hydrophilicity and its propensity to form dimers (see below). As a result of their large size, glycopeptides are not only unable to cross the outer membrane of Gram-negative bacteria (which explains their inactivity against these organisms), but are also unable to penetrate inside bateria, which limits them to an extracellular target.

Mode of action

Glycopeptide antibiotics inhibit the late stages of cell wall peptidoglycan synthesis (see Fig. 188.2). Glycopeptides bind to D-Ala-D-Ala terminals of the pentapeptide-ending precursors localized at the outer surface of the cytoplasmic membrane. At the molecular level, glycopeptides form a high affinity complex with D-Ala-D-Ala by establishing hydrogen bounds via their aglycone moiety.[9] The strength of this binding is, however, greatly enhanced either by :

- dimerization of the glycopeptide molecules (mediated by their sugars and the chloride atoms substituents on the aglycone – as observed in vancomycin); or
- anchoring of glycopeptide molecules in the membrane by a fatty acyl chain substituent (as observed in teicoplanin).[10]

The subsequent steric hindrance around the pentapeptide terminals blocks the reticulation of peptidoglycan by inhibiting the activity of transglycosylases (responsible for the new dissacharide–pentapeptide subunit on the nascent peptidoglycan) and of transpeptidases (catalyzing the formation of interpeptide bridges).[9]

Resistance

Resistance to glycopeptides results from substituting a D-lactic acid in place of terminal D-Ala of the pentapeptide. Although this does not prevent the action of the transpeptidase, it prevents the binding of the glycopeptides because of the loss of one crucial hydrogen bound.[9]

Pharmacodynamics

Glycopeptide antibiotics show a very slow bactericidal activity, which is not very dose-dependent, for reasons that are unclear. It has been proposed that their inhibition of cell wall synthesis blocks the growth of bacteria and therefore the synthesis of DNA, RNA and proteins, whereas the autolytic enzymes could continue to function. As their activity is time-dependent, glycopeptides need repeated

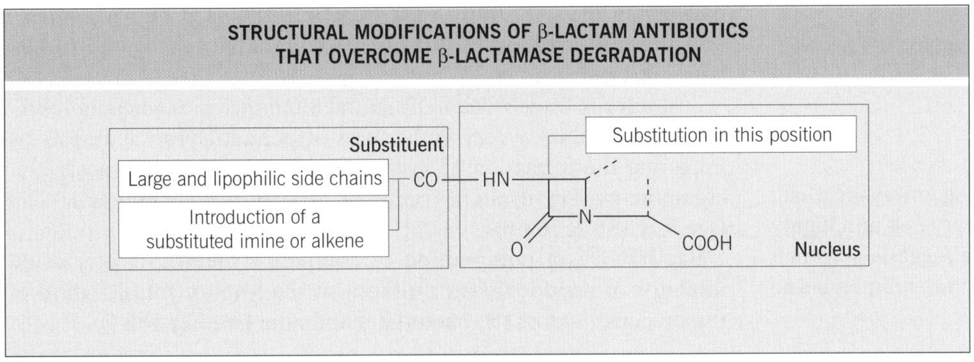

Fig. 188.4 Structural modifications of β-lactam antibiotics that overcome β-lactamase degradation. A first strategy, applied in penicillins, cephalosporins, oxacephems and monobactams consists of the introduction of a large side chain on the nucleus, possibly containing a substituted imine or alkene. A second strategy, applied in oxacephems and cefoxitin consists of the introduction of a methoxy group on the β-lactam ring.

FUNCTIONAL CLASSIFICATION OF β-LACTAMASES				
Group	**Molecular class**	**Preferred substrates**	**Active β-lactams**	**Typical examples**
Group 1: serine cephalosporinases not inhibited by clavulanic acid	C	Cephalosporins I and II (>> cephalosporins III, monobactams, penicillins)	Carbapenems Temocillin (cephalosporins III and IV, variable upon level of expression)	AmpC from Gram-negative; variable upon the species
Group 2: serine β-lactamases				
2a: penicillinases inhibited by clavulanic acid	A	Penicillins (penicillin, ampicillin >> carbenicillin >> oxacillins)	Amoxicillin + clavulanic acid Cephalosporins Carbapenems	Penicillinases from Gram-positive
2b: broad-spectum β-lactamases inhibited by clavulanic acid	A	Penicillins (penicillin, ampicillin >> carbenicillin >> oxacillins) Cephalosporins I and II	Cephalosporins III and IV, Monobactams* Carbapenems Amoxicillin + clavulanic acid	TEM-1, TEM-2, SHV-1 from Enterobacteriacea, *Haemophilus* spp. *Neisseria gonorrhoeae*
2be: extended-spectrum β-actamases inhibited by clavulanic acid (ESBL)	A	Penicillins Cephalosporins I II III (IV) Monobactams	Carbapenems Temocillin	TEM-3 to -26 from Enterobacteriacea SHV-2 to -6 from *Klebsiella* spp. K1-OXY from *Klebsiella oxytoca*
2br: broad-spectrum β-lactamases with reduced binding to clavulanic acid	A	Penicillins	Most cephalosporins Monobactams* Carbapenems	TEM-30 to -41 (=IRT-1 to IRT-12) from *Escherichia coli*
2c: carbenicillin-hydrolyzing β-lactamases generally inhibited by clavulanic acid	A	Penicillins Carbenicillin (Cephalosporins I and II)	Piperacillin + tazobactam Cephalosporins III and IV Monobactams* Carbapenems	PSE-1, PSE-3, PSE-4 from *Pseudomonas aeruginosa*
2d: cloxacillin-hydrolyzing β-lactamaxes generally inhibited by clavulanic acid	D	Penicillins Cloxacillin Cephalosporins I and II	Carbapenems Cephalosporins III Monobactams* Piperacillin + tazobactam	OXA-1 to -11, PSE-2 from Enterobacteriacea and *P. aeruginosa*
2e: cephalosporinases inhibited by clavulanic acid	A	Cephalosporins I and II	Cephalosporins III and IV Monobactams* Penems	FPM-1 from *Proteus vulgaris* Cep-A from *Bacteroides fragilis*†
2f: carbapenem-nonmetallo-hydrolyzing β-lactamases	A	Penicillins Cephalosporins Carbapenems	(Cephalosporins III and IV) (Monobactams*)	NMC-A, IMI-1 from *Enterobacter cloacae* Sme-1 from *Serratia marcescens*
Group 3: Metallo β-lactamases inhibited by EDTA	B	Most β-lactams, including carbapenems	Monobactams*‡	L-1, XM-A from *Stenotrophomonas maltophilia* CcrA from *Bacteroides fragillis* A2h, CphA from *Aeromonas hydrophila* IMP-1 in *Pseudomonas* spp. and *Serratia* spp.
Group 4: Penicillinases not inhibited by clavulanic acid		Penicillins, including carbenicillin and oxacillin	Monobactams*†‡ and generally carbapenems	SAR-2 from *Burkholderia cepacia*

* Monobactams are not active on Gram-positive bacteria
† Penems are the only molecules active in this case
‡ Remain active for most of the rare published studies

Table 188.1 Functional classification of β-lactamases. The number of enzymes as well as their spectrum of activity is continually evolving. Data from Bush *et al.*[6]

administration, yet, they show a moderate (2-hour) postantibiotic effect, which combined with their long half-life (6 hours for vancomycin, and more than 24 hours for teicoplanin), makes continuous infusion of less interest than for β-lactams.

Glycopeptides show, at least *in vitro*, a synergistic effect with aminoglycosides, probably by facilitating the penetration of these polar molecules into bacteria.

Future developments

New derivatives with a hydrophobic substituent (e.g. oritavancin) act against vancomycin-resistant strains and show a very fast and highly concentration-dependent bactericidal effect, which suggests a distinct mode of action that could involve drug dimerization and membrane destabilization.[11]

Other agents that act on cell wall synthesis

D-cycloserine is a broad-spectrum antibiotic active through its similarity with D-Ala (see Fig. 188.2; Fig. 188.5), inhibiting the conversion of L-Ala into D-Ala (reaction catalyzed by a racemase) and the dimerization of D-Ala (reaction catalyzed by the D-Ala: D-Ala ligase).[12]

Fosfomycin, which bears structural similarities to phospho-*enol*-pyruvate, inhibits a very early stage of peptidoglycan synthesis by impairing the formation of uridine diphosphate (UDP)-*N*-acetylglucosamine-*enol*-pyruvate, a precursor of UDP-*N*-acetylmuramic acid (see Figs 188.2, 188.5).[13]

Bacitracin is a polypeptide of complex structure. It acts as an inhibitor of peptidoglycan synthesis at the level of translocation of the precursor across the bacterial membrane (see Fig. 188.2).[14]

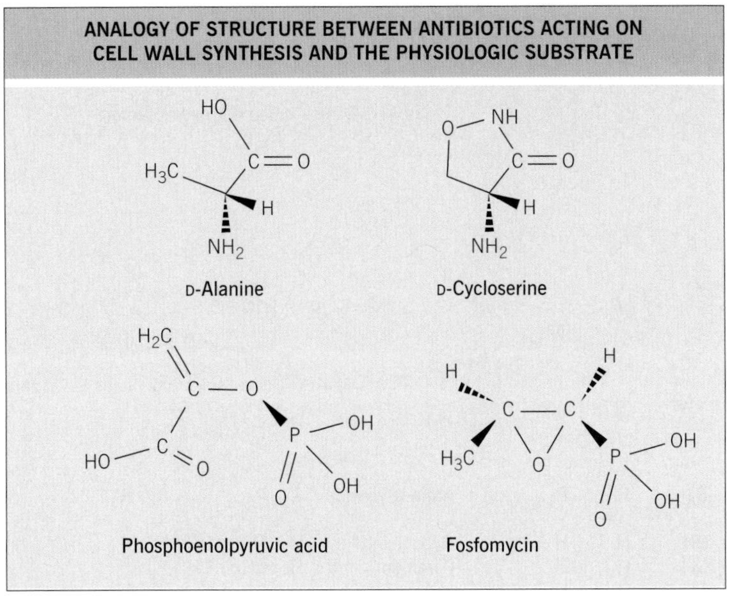

Fig. 188.5 Analogy of structure between antibiotics acting on cell wall synthesis and the physiologic substrate. The two antibiotics act as analogs of the corresponding substrate.

ANTIBIOTICS THAT ACT ON PROTEIN SYNTHESIS

Bacterial ribosomes comprise:

- a 30S subunit, which binds mRNA and initiates the protein synthesis; and
- a 50S subunit, which binds aminoacyl tRNA, catalyzes the peptide bond formation and controls the elongation process.

The main sites identified in the ribosome are the donor peptidyl site (P-site), where the growing peptide chain is fixed, and the acceptor aminoacyl site (A-site), where peptide bond formation occurs.

Aminoglycosides

Chemical structure

Streptomycin was discovered in 1944, but this compound had a relatively limited spectrum of activity. Several other compounds, with a broader spectrum of activity, especially towards aerobic and facultative Gram-negative bacilli, were extracted from bacteria or semisynthesized over the subsequent 20 years (aminoglycosides from kanamycin or gentamicin families). In the 1970s, netilmicin and amikacin demonstrated the possibility of developing compounds active against strains resistant to earlier aminoglycosides.

Aminoglycosides are made of several aminated sugars joined by glycosidic linkages to a dibasic cyclitol.[15] The latter is streptidine in streptomycin and derivatives, fortamine in the fortimicin series, and two-deoxystreptamine in most aminoglycosides used clinically. The two-deoxystreptamine moiety links to cyclic sugars either at positions 4 and 5 (neomycin and paromomycin) or 4 and 6 (kanamycin, tobramycin, amikacin and dibekacin in the kanamycin family; gentamicin C_1, C_{1a}, C_2, and isepamicin in the gentamicin family, sisomicin and netilmicin; Fig. 188.6). All compounds are positively charged at physiologic pH.

Bacterial targeting

Aminoglycosides selectively disturb the protein synthesis of bacteria because they bind to the 30S subunit of bacterial ribosomes, which does not exist in eukaryotic cells. However, molecules that display a hydroxyl function in C6′ in place of an amino function affect also protein synthesis in cultured mammalian cells, as do high doses of gentamicin, probably through nonspecific binding to ribosomes or nucleic acids.

Mode of action

As a result of their highly polar character, aminoglycosides are unable to diffuse through membranes, and therefore require specific mechanisms of transport. Their passage across the outer membrane of Gram-negative bacteria occurs by a process that is not energy dependent and involves the drug-induced disruption of Mg^{2+} bridges between adjacent lipopolysaccharide molecules. By contrast, their transport across the cytoplasmic (inner) membrane is dependent upon electron transport, and is therefore termed energy-dependent phase I (EDP-I). The greater the transmembrane electrical potential, the greater the antibacterial effect of the aminoglycoside. In an anaerobic environment, at low external pH and in high osmolar culture media, this transmembrane electrical potential is decreased, which explains the low activity against anaerobes as well as in purulent collections.

Once in the bacterial cytosol, aminoglycosides bind to the aminoacyl site of the 30S subunit of ribosomes[17] (and, to a lesser extent, to specific sites of the 50S subunit), again through an energy-dependent process (EDP-II), disturbing the elongation of the nascent peptide. Their mechanism of action is complex, involving inhibition of the transfer of the peptidyl tRNA from the A-site to the P-site and impairment of the proofreading process that controls translational accuracy. The latter action leads to misreading or premature termination in protein synthesis. The final effects vary somewhat from one compound to another, which possibly explains differences in the killing rates. The aberrant proteins may be inserted into the cell membrane, which results in altered permeability and further stimulation of aminoglycoside transport.

Resistance

Resistance occurs mostly by the production of enzymes that inactivate the functions responsible for activity of the natural aminoglycosides (Fig. 188.7, see Chapter 189). Semisynthetic derivatives (e.g. netilmicin, amikacin, isepamicin) were therefore made specifically to afford protection against these enzymes. However, whereas previously resistant bacteria harbored only one of a very few types of enzymes, the simultaneous production of several enzyme types is increasingly more common, causing multiple resistance. It is believed that most of these enzymes have physiologic effects on natural substrates and acted on aminoglycosides only opportunistically in the initial introduction of these antibotics. However, point mutations and selection may have quickly increased their specificity and efficacy.[18,19]

A second mechanism of resistance is membrane impermeability, which confers resistance to all aminoglycosides. Its molecular mechanism is unclear.

Pharmacodynamics

Aminoglycosides demonstrate a rapid, concentration-dependent bactericidal effect and an important postantibiotic effect (probably because of a largely irreversible binding to the ribosomes). A once-a-day regimen is therefore the optimal mode of administration for these antibiotics, allowing elevated serum peak concentrations (over eight times the MIC, thereby maximizing efficacy while minimizing toxicity) to be reached .

Aminoglycosides show a synergistic activity with antibiotics that act on cell wall synthesis, because they facilitate the penetration of aminoglycosides into the bacteria. In contrast, their activity is antagonized by bacteriostatic agents such as chloramphenicol and tetracyclines, probably by inhibition of their energy-dependent uptake and by interference with the movement of the ribosome along mRNA.

Future developments

Efforts are being undertaken in two directions:

- to increase the binding affinity while retaining binding selectivity; and

STRUCTURAL FORMULAE OF THE 2-DEOXYSTREPTAMINE-CONTAINING AMINOGLYCOSIDES

4, 6-Disubstituted deoxystreptamine

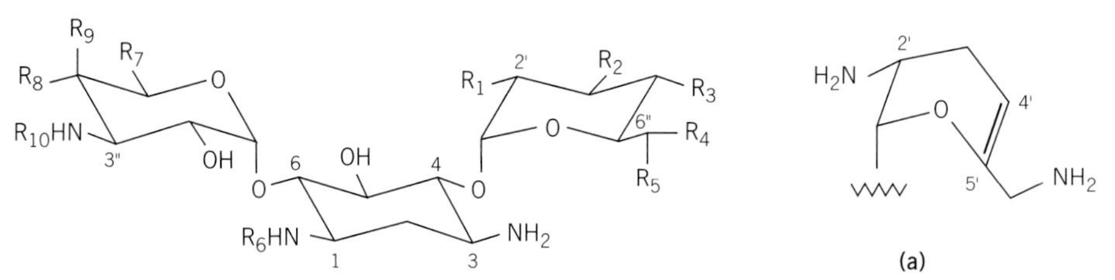

(a)

	Aminoglycoside	R_1	R_2	R_3	R_4	R_5	R_6	R_7	R_8	R_9	R_{10}
Kanamycins	**Kanamycin A**	OH	OH	OH	H	NH_2	H	CH_2OH	OH	H	H
	Kanamycin B	NH_2	OH	OH	H	NH_2	H	CH_2OH	OH	H	H
	Kanamycin C	NH_2	OH	OH	H	OH	H	CH_2OH	OH	H	H
	Amikacin	OH	OH	OH	H	NH_2	COR	CH_2OH	OH	H	H
	Tobramycin	NH_2	H	OH	H	NH_2	H	CH_2OH	OH	H	H
	Dibekacin	NH_2	H	H	H	NH_2	H	CH_2OH	OH	H	H
	Arbekacin*	NH_2	H	H	H	NH_2	COR	CH_2OH	OH	H	H
Gentamicins	**Gentamicin C_1†**	NH_2	H	H	CH_3	$NHCH_3$	H	H	CH_3	OH	CH_3
	Gentamicin C_{1a}†	NH_2	H	H	H	NH_2	H	H	CH_3	OH	CH_3
	Gentamicin C_2†	NH_2	H	H	CH_3	NH_2	H	H	CH_3	OH	CH_3
	Gentamicin C_{2b}†	NH_2	H	H	H	$NHCH_3$	H	H	CH_3	OH	CH_3
	Gentamicin B†	OH	OH	OH	H	NH_2	H	H	CH_3	OH	CH_3
	Isepamicin†	OH	OH	OH	H	NH_2	COR	H	CH_3	OH	CH_3
	Sisomicin	–	–	–	–	–	H	H	CH_3	OH	CH_3
	Netilmicin	–	–	–	–	–	R	H	CH_3	OH	CH_3

R=$CHOHCH_2NH_2$; R=$CHOH(CH_2)_2NH_2$; R=CH_2CH_3 (a)=primed sugar for sisomicin and netilmicin

*In Japan

†Commercially availiable **gentamicin** is a mixture of C1, C1a and C2 in a ratio of 30, 30 and 40%, respectively

4, 5-Disubstituted deoxystreptamine

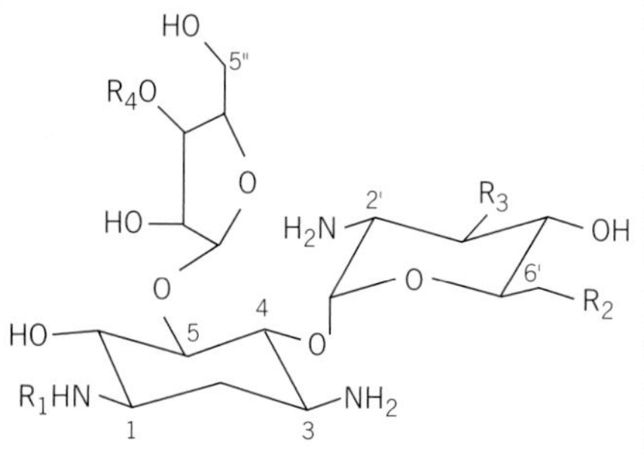

Aminoglycoside	R_1	R_2	R_3	R_4	R_5
Neomycin B	H	NH_2	OH	X	H
Paromomycin I	H	OH	OH	X	H
Lividomycin A	H	OH	H	X	Mannose
Ribostamycin	H	NH_2	OH	H	
Butirosin B	Y	NH_2	OH	H	

X= Y=

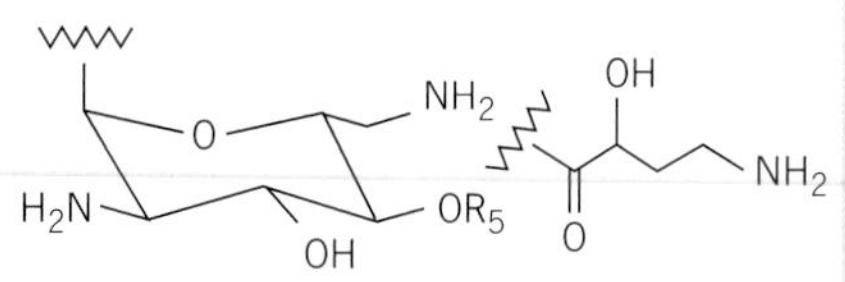

Fig. 188.6 Structural formulae of the 2-deoxystreptamine-containing aminoglycosides. The numbering of the atoms shown here follows the recommendations from Nagabushe *et al.*[16] with the primed numbers (′) being ascribed to the sugar attached to C4 of the 2-deoxystreptamine (as this C is of the R configuration) and the doubly primed numbers (″) being ascribed to the sugar attached to either the C6 (S configuration) for the 4,6-disubstituted 2-deoxystreptamine or the C5 (R configuration) for the 4,5-disubstituted 2-deoxystreptamine. Molecules indicated in bold denote the aminoglycosides in widespread clinical use.

- to develop new aminoglycoside derivatives resistant to these enzymes.

Although some derivatives have been made by pharmacochemical approaches, little success has been obtained. A more innovative approach could be to use our understanding of the aminoglycoside-inactivating enzymes to produce enzyme inhibitors or to design totally new aminoglycoside derivatives that would be intrinsically resistant to these enzymes.

Tetracyclines

Chemical structure

The first tetracyclines discovered were isolates from *Streptomyces* spp. (tetracycline, oxytetracycline), whereas more recent long-acting compounds (doxycycline, minocycline) are semisynthetic. All such molecules, contain four hydrophobic fused rings, which are diversely substituted, but principally by oxygenated hydrophilic groups (see Chapter 200).

Bacterial targeting

Tetracyclines penetrate the outer membrane of Gram-negative organisms through porins. Accumulation inside the bacteria depends on the pH gradient between the cytosol and the external medium, but it is unclear whether transmembrane transport occurs by diffusion or via a proton-driven carrier. The main argument in favor of the latter is that it could explain the selective action of tetracyclines by preferential transport in bacterial cells (Fig. 188.8).

Mode of action

Tetracyclines interfere with the initiation step of protein synthesis (see Fig. 188.8). More precisely, they inhibit the binding of aminoacyl tRNA to the A-site of the ribosome. The 7S protein and the 16S RNA show the best affinity for tetracyclines, and are therefore the main targets involved pharmacologically.[20] This binding inhibits the fixation of a new aminoacyl tRNA on the ribosome. At higher concentrations, tetracyclines also bind to the 23S RNA, which is part of the peptidyl transferase region of the ribosome. However, the enzymatic activity of this site does not seem not to be disturbed by tetracyclines. Additional actions on ribosomal functions have been proposed:[21]

- tetracyclines bind, or at least protrude, in the P-site, thanks to the change in ribosome conformation in the post-translocational state; and
- tetracyclines modify the ribosome conformation at the head of the 30S subunit and at the interfacial side of the 50S subunit.

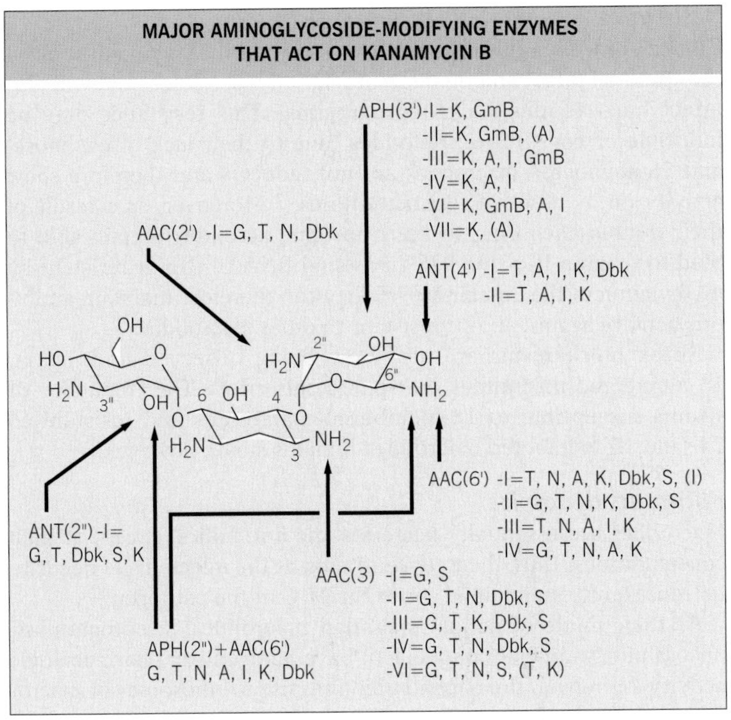

Fig. 188.7 Major aminoglycoside-modifying enzymes that act on kanamycin C. This aminoglycoside is susceptible to the largest number of enzymes. The *N*-acetyltransferases (AACs) affect amino functions and the o-nucleotidyltransferases affect hydroxyl functions. Each group of enzymes inactivates specific sites, but each of these sites can be acted upon by distinct isoenzymes (Roman numerals) with different substrate specificities (phenotypic classification). At least one enzyme is bifunctional and affects both positions 2″ (*o*-phosphorylation) and 6′ (*N*-acetylation). The main aminoglycosides used clinically on which these enzymes act are amikacin (A), dibekacin (DbK), commercial gentamicin (G), gentamicin B (Gmb), kanamycin A (K), isepamicin (I), netilmicin (N), sisomicin (S) and tobramycin (T). The drug abbreviations that appear in parentheses are those for which resistance was detectable *in vitro* although clinical resistance was not conferred. Data from Shaw *et al.*[19]

More recently, it has been shown that tetracyclines have chondroprotective effects in inflammatory arthritis models, an action related to their ability to inhibit the expression of nitric oxide synthases induced by inflammatory conditions.[22] Clinical evaluation is, however, needed to document further the potential usefulness of tetracyclines as modulators of the inflammatory response. A possible application would be the treatment of arthritis of bacterial origin (e.g. Lyme disease).

Resistance

Resistance to tetracyclines is now widespread, and is related to a decrease in the bacterial drug content caused by an active drug efflux (see Fig. 188.8).[23] Efflux mechanisms appear more important and are somehow largely, but not entirely unrelated to the drug structure (see fluoroquinolones and macrolides below; see also Chapter 189).

Pharmacodynamics

Tetracyclines are essentially bacteriostatic, but demonstrate persistent effects. They need to be administered at intervals short enough, in terms of the drug half-life, to maintain their serum level above the infecting organism's MIC for as long as possible. The total dose administered also appears to be important.

Future developments

Glycylcyclines are tetracyclines derivatives that bear a glycyl substituent and are able to bind to the tetracycline binding site on the ribosome.[24] Their main advantage is that they conserve their activity against strains with acquired resistance to conventional tetracyclines by the production of efflux pumps or by a mechanism of ribosomal

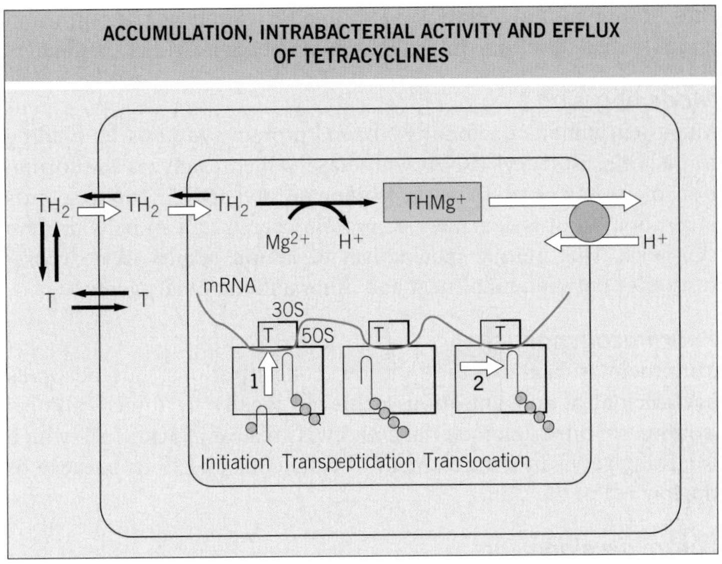

Fig. 188.8 Accumulation, intrabacterial activity and efflux of tetracyclines. Tetracyclines diffuse freely through the extracellular membrane of Gram-negative bacteria. Penetration inside bacteria is an energy-dependent process depending on the pH and Mg^{2+} gradient between the extracellular medium of Gram-positive bacteria or the periplasmic medium of Gram-negative bacteria and the intracellular medium. Only the protonated form is highly diffusible, so accumulation is favored by lowering of the extracellular pH. Once inside the cytosol the tetracycline molecule forms a nondiffusible complex with Mg^{2+}. This type of complex with a bivalent cation is also the substrate of the efflux pumps present in the membrane of resistant bacteria and acting as H^+ antiports (pink circle). The antibacterial action of the teracyclines (T) is due to the binding to the 30S subunit of the ribosomes. In the pretranslocational state, tetracyclines inhibit the binding of aminoacyl tRNA (arrow 1) to the A-site (yellow part of the ribosome). In the post-translocational state, tetracyclines protrude in the P-site (white part of the ribosome) and inhibit the binding of the peptidyl tRNA (arrow 2). Data from Geigenmüller and Nierhaus[21] and Yamaguchi *et al.*[23]

protection (acquisition of a gene that encodes a Tet protein, (i.e. an elongation factor able to displace the tetracycline bond on the ribosome). However, mutants resistant to glycylcyclines have already been selected *in vitro*, with the possibility that such mutants may emerge in clinical strains.

Fusidic acid

Chemical structure

Fusidic acid is a steroid-like structure and a member of the fusidane class. It is used in its sodium salt form.

Mode of action

Fusidic acid prevents the dissociation of the complex formed by guanosine diphosphate, the elongation factor 2 and the ribosome. It thereby inhibits the translocation step of the peptidyl tRNA from the P-site to the A-site of the ribosome and, therefore, the elongation of the nascent polypeptide chain.

Pharmacodynamics

Fusidic acid is bacteriostatic, but may be bactericidal at high concentrations.

Mupirocin

Chemical structure

Mupirocin contains a short fatty acid side chain (9-hydroxynonanoic acid) linked to monic acid by an ester linkage. Mupirocin is also called pseudomonic acid because its major metabolite is derived from submerged fermentation by *Pseudomonas fluorescens*. Pseudomonic acid A is responsible for most of the antibacterial activity;

three other minor metabolites of similar chemical structure and antimicrobial spectrum are called pseudomonic acids B, C, and D.

Mode of action

Mupirocin inhibits bacterial RNA and protein synthesis by binding to bacterial isoleucyl tRNA synthetase, which catalyzes the formation of isoleucyl tRNA from isoleucine and tRNA. This prevents incorporation of isoleucine into protein chains, and so halts protein synthesis. This unique mechanism of action results in no cross-resistance between mupirocin and other antimicrobial agents.[25]

Pharmacodynamics

Mupirocin is bacteriostatic at low concentrations, but becomes bactericidal at concentrations achieved locally by topical administration. *In vitro* antibacterial activity is greatest at acidic pH, which is advantageous in the treatment of cutaneous infections because of the low pH of the skin.

Future developments

The recognition of the peculiar mode of action of mupirocin has triggered a large genomic-based research towards similar targets at the level of the other amino acids.[26]

Macrolides

Chemical structure

The main active macrolides are 14-, 15- or 16-membered lactone rings, substituted by two sugars, of which one bears an aminated function. Erythromycin, the first clinically developed macrolide, is a natural product. Most of the molecules developed in the mid 1980s are semisynthetic derivatives, and have been designed to be stable in acidic milieu. They are therefore essentially characterized by an improved oral bioavailability. 16-membered macrolides are intrinsically acid stable. In 15-membered macrolides (azithromycin), an additional aminated function is inserted in the lactone ring, conferring to this subclass of molecule the name of 'azalides'. They are acid stable and characterized by an exceptionally large volume of distribution and prolonged half-life. Ketolides are 14-membered macrolides in which the cladinose is replaced by a keto function and which possess in their macrocycle a carbamate linked to an alkyl-aryl extension (Fig. 188.9).[27] They are also intrinsically acid stable. Moreover, they remain active against most of the strains resistant to other macrolides.

Bacterial targeting

Macrolides specifically bind to the 50S subunit of the ribosomes (more precisely, to the 23S rRNA), which does not exist in eukaryotic cells.

Mode of action

Macrolides reversibly bind to the peptidyl transferase center, located at the 50S surface, which results in multiple alterations of the 50S subunit functions.[28,29] While macrolides bind to the domain V of the 23S rRNA, ketolides have a dual anchoring to the ribosome. They not only bind to domain V, like other macrolides, but also bind to domain II of 23S rRNA (see Fig. 188.9).[30,31] This additional binding involves the carbamate extension, which is absent in conventional macrolides.[27] Because of their double interaction, ketolides are characterized by a higher affinity for their target and therefore by an improved efficacy. Macrolides are classically thought to block the peptide bond formation or the peptidyl tRNA translocation from the A- to the P-site. However, additional consequences of macrolides binding to ribosomes have been reported. A proposal is that they could also favor the premature dissociation of peptidyl tRNA from the ribosome during the elongation process, leading to the synthesis of incomplete peptides.[28] A further suggestion is that erythromycin prevents the assembly of the 50S subunit, but this does not appear to be applicable to other macrolides.

Resistance

Clinically meaningful resistance occurs primarily by modification of the bacterial target and therefore affects all macrolides (and will also affect lincosamides and streptogramins). This resistance may be inducible or constitutive. Ketolides (due to their lack of cladinose) and 16-membered macrolides are not inducers and therefore show activity on a subset of resistant strains.[27] Moreover, as a result of their double anchoring to the ribosome, ketolides remain able to bind to domain II of the 23S ribosomal RNA of strains resistant by methylation of the domain V.[30–32] They can therefore maintain antibiotic activity against strains resistant to other macrolides.

Efflux mechanisms are also now being observed and, again, 16-membered macrolides are spared this effect. The frequency of strains susceptible to 16-membered macrolides and resistant to 14- and 15-membered macrolides remains small, however.

Pharmacodynamics

Macrolides are essentially bacteriostatic antibiotics, except at high concentrations. Thus, their concentration at the infected site needs to be consistently maintained above the MIC of the pathogen.[33]

As their mode of action is similar, macrolides, streptogramins, lincosamides and chloramphenicol have antagonistic pharmacologic activity. Moreover, the common binding site to ribosomes of macrolides, streptogramins, and lincosamides shows that a mutation of the target causes cross-resistance to these three classes of antibiotics.

Future developments

Efforts are still being made to discover macrolide derivatives active against bacteria resistant to the macrolides used at the present time in the clinics. Research in the field of ketolides is still active. Erythromycylamines modified at their cladinose moiety show activity against inducible resistant strains and also against strains resistant through the production of efflux pumps.

Lincosamides

Chemical structure

Lincomycin and its 7-chloro-7-deoxy derivative, clindamycin, comprise a propylhygrinic acid linked to an aminosugar.

Mode of action

Lincosamides bind to the 50S ribosomal subunit and have a mode of action similar to that of macrolides.[29] They inhibit early chain elongation by interfering with the transpeptidase reaction.

Resistance

The main mechanism of resistance to lincosamides is similar to that found in resistance to macrolides and streptogramins, and consists of alteration of the 50S subunit. Rare cases of enzymatic inactivation of the antibiotic have also been described for clindamycin (adenylation reaction).

Pharmacodynamics

Lincosamides are bacteriostatic, and are antagonists of macrolides and streptogramins, which bind at the same site on the ribosomes.

Streptogramins

Chemical structure

Streptogramins are antibiotics that comprise a pair of synergistic constituents, namely a depsipeptide (group I) and a lactone macrocycle (group II). The combination of quinupristin and dalfopristin is used in the clinic.[34]

Mode of action

Streptogramins bind to the 50S subunit of bacterial ribosomes and interfere with the protein synthesis by a double mechanism, involving an inhibition of the incorporation of the aminoacyl tRNA in the ribo-

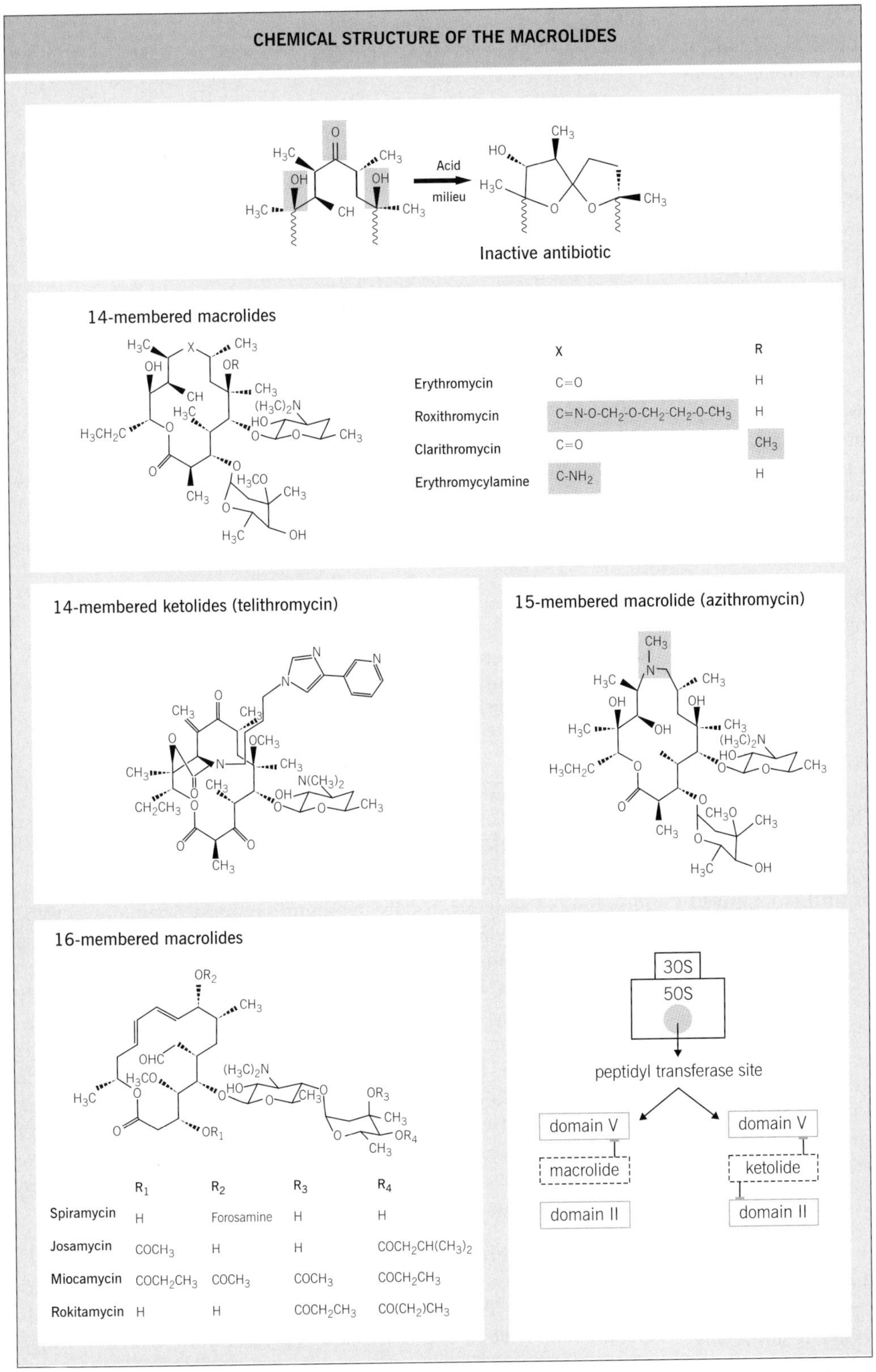

Fig. 188.9 Chemical structure of the macrolides. The upper panel shows the degradation of erythromycin in the gastric milieu (substituents responsible for the instability of the miolecule are shown in gray). 16-membered macrolides and ketolides are intrinsically stable. The structural modifications conferring stability in acidic milieu to 14- and 15-membered macrolides are highlighted in gray in the middle panel. The lower panel compares the binding of macrolides and ketolides to the petidyl transferase site of the 50S subunit of ribosomes. Macrolides are characterized by a single anchoring point and ketolides by a double anchoring point, which increases the affinity of ketolides for wild type and methylated ribosomes.

somes and of the translation of the mRNA. The synergy between the two components could be due to a modification of the conformation of the ribosome caused by the binding of the group I component, which exposes a site of fixation for the group II component.[28]

Resistance

Resistance by mutation of the ribosomal target will also result in resistance to macrolides and lincosamides. Resistance to streptogramins alone is rare and occurs by enzymatic inactivation (involving an hydrolase and an acetylase).

Pharmacodynamics

Streptogramin constituents are highly synergistic and show a dose-dependent bactericidal activity if given together.[33] In addition, they increase the antibiotic activity of aminoglycosides and rifamycins.

Streptogramins also exhibit prolonged bacteriostasis, which consists of a delay of regrowth when the antibiotic concentration falls under its MIC. This could be interpreted as a consequence of the persistent binding of the drug to its target.

Future developments

Streptogramins are not largely used today. However, their potential role for bacteria resistant to other antibiotics (MRSA, vancomycin-resistant enterococci) may reactivate research in this area.

Chloramphenicol and thiamphenicol

Chemical structure

Chloramphenicol and thiamphenicol are based on dichloroacetamide bearing a diversely substituted phenyl group (see Chapter 200).

Bacterial targeting
Chloramphenicol acts principally by binding to the 50S subunit of the bacterial ribosomes. However, it can also interact with mitochondrial ribosomes of eukaryotic cells, which results in its toxicity.

Mode of action
Chloramphenicol enters the bacteria by an energy-dependent process. Its antibiotic activity results from competitive inhibition of aminoacyl tRNA binding to the peptidyl transferase domain of the 50S subunit. This induces conformational changes of this part of the ribosomes, which slows or even inhibits (at high enough concentrations) the incorporation of the aminoacyl tRNA and, therefore, the transpeptidase reaction.[35]

Resistance
Resistance to chloramphenicol derives mainly from the production of a specific acetyl transferase that inactivates the antibiotic.[36] The gene encoding the transferase is often located on plasmids that also confer resistance to other antibiotic classes. Another mechanism of resistance is reduced entry of the drug into the bacteria.

Pharmacodynamics
Chloramphenicol is bacteriostatic. It competes in binding to the ribosomes with macrolides and lincosamides, making its combination with these drugs useless.

Oxazolidinones

Chemical structure
Oxazolidinones are totally synthetic molecules. The first derivatives endowed with antimicrobial activity were described at the end of the 1970s. Structures were then refined on the basis of structure–activity relationships[37] to give rise so far to linezolid, the first clinically available molecule (Fig. 188.10). The 5-(S)-configuration of the oxazolidinone ring is essential for activity, which is further improved by its substitution by an N-fluorinated aryl group and a C5 acylaminomethyl group.

Mode of action
Oxazolidinones inhibit protein synthesis at an earlier step that other antibiotics acting on the ribosome. Their binding site is located in the vicinity of the peptidyl transferase center of the 50S subunit.[38] This interaction prevents the formation of the initiation ternary complex which associates $tRNA^{met}$, mRNA, and the 50S subunit of the ribosome,[39] and therefore the binding to the ribosome as well as the synthesis of peptide bonds, and the translocation of $tRNA^{met}$ into the P-site.[40]

Resistance
Because of the unique mode of action of oxazolidinones, there is no cross-resistance with other antibiotics acting on protein synthesis. The introduction of linezolid in clinics is too recent to draw any conclusion concerning the incidence and mechanisms of resistance. Case reports of resistant clinical isolates emerging during therapy have, however, been published.[41] Mutation of the 23S rRNA *in vitro* confers resistance to linezolid.[38]

Pharmacodynamics
Oxazolidinones are bacteriostatic, time-dependent antibiotics, with a short post-antibiotic effect.[41] They can compete for binding to the 50S subunit of the ribosome with other antibiotics (e.g. lincosamides, chloramphenicol).

Future developments
Other molecules are currently under investigation. Efforts are essentially directed towards broadening the spectrum of activity and increasing intrinsic activity.

STRUCTURAL ACTIVITY RELATIONSHIP FOR LINEZOLID, THE FIRST OXAZOLIDINONE, AND MODE OF ACTION

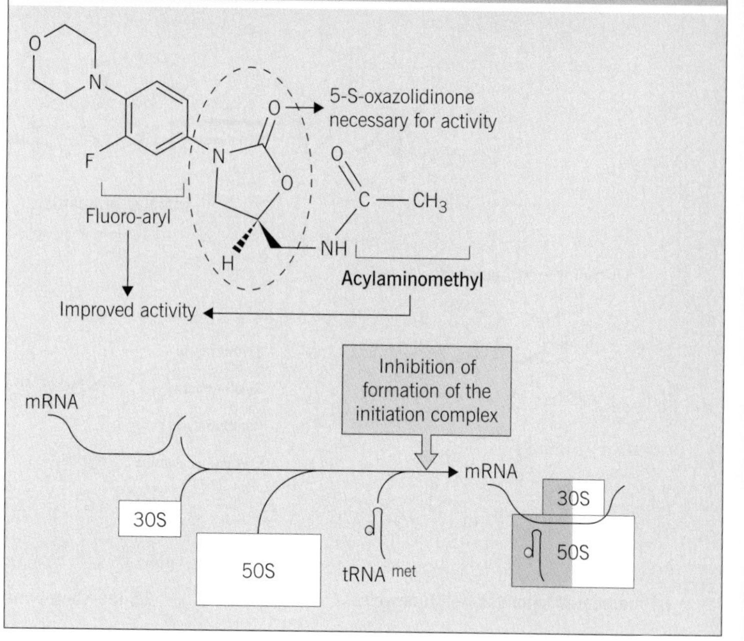

Fig. 188.10 Structural activity relationship for linezolid, the first oxazolidinone, and mode of action. The drug prevents the formation of the ternary complex between mRNA, ribosome subunits and $tRNA^{met}$ necessary for protein synthesis.

DRUGS THAT AFFECT NUCLEIC ACIDS

Fluoroquinolones

Chemical structure
Fluoroquinolones are totally synthetic products originally derived from nalidixic acid (see Chapter 198). All current compounds have a dual ring structure, with nitrogen at C1, a free carboxylate at C3 and a carbonyl at C4. A fluorine substituent at C6 usually greatly enhances activity, whereas the substituents at C7, C8 and N1 modulate the spectrum, pharmacokinetics and side-effects of the drugs (Fig. 188.11).[42] In this respect, new molecules (among which moxifloxacin and gatifloxacin are now used in the clinic) have been designed to better cover Gram-positive organisms, keep activity against Gram-negative organisms and also be, to some extent, active against anaerobes.[43] They all present a small hydrophobic substituent on N1 and a diaminated small-sized ring substituent in 7.

Bacterial targeting
Fluoroquinolones cross the outer membrane of Gram-negative bacteria via porins. Their affinity for the bacterial target is 1000 times greater than that of the corresponding eukaryotic enzyme, which ensures their specificity.

Mode of action
Fluoroquinolones inhibit the activity of topoisomerases, which are enzymes responsible for the supercoiling of the DNA (DNA gyrase) and relaxation of supercoiled DNA (topoisomerase IV). Both enzymes have a similar mode of action, which implies:
- binding of DNA to the enzyme;
- cleavage of the DNA;
- passage of the DNA segment through the DNA gate;
- resealing of the DNA break and the release from the enzyme.

Gyrase and topoisomerase IV are tetramers made of two types of subunits, namely two GyrA or ParC that catalyze DNA cutting and resealing, and two GyrB or ParE responsible for the transduction and binding of adenosine triphosphate. The main target of fluoro-

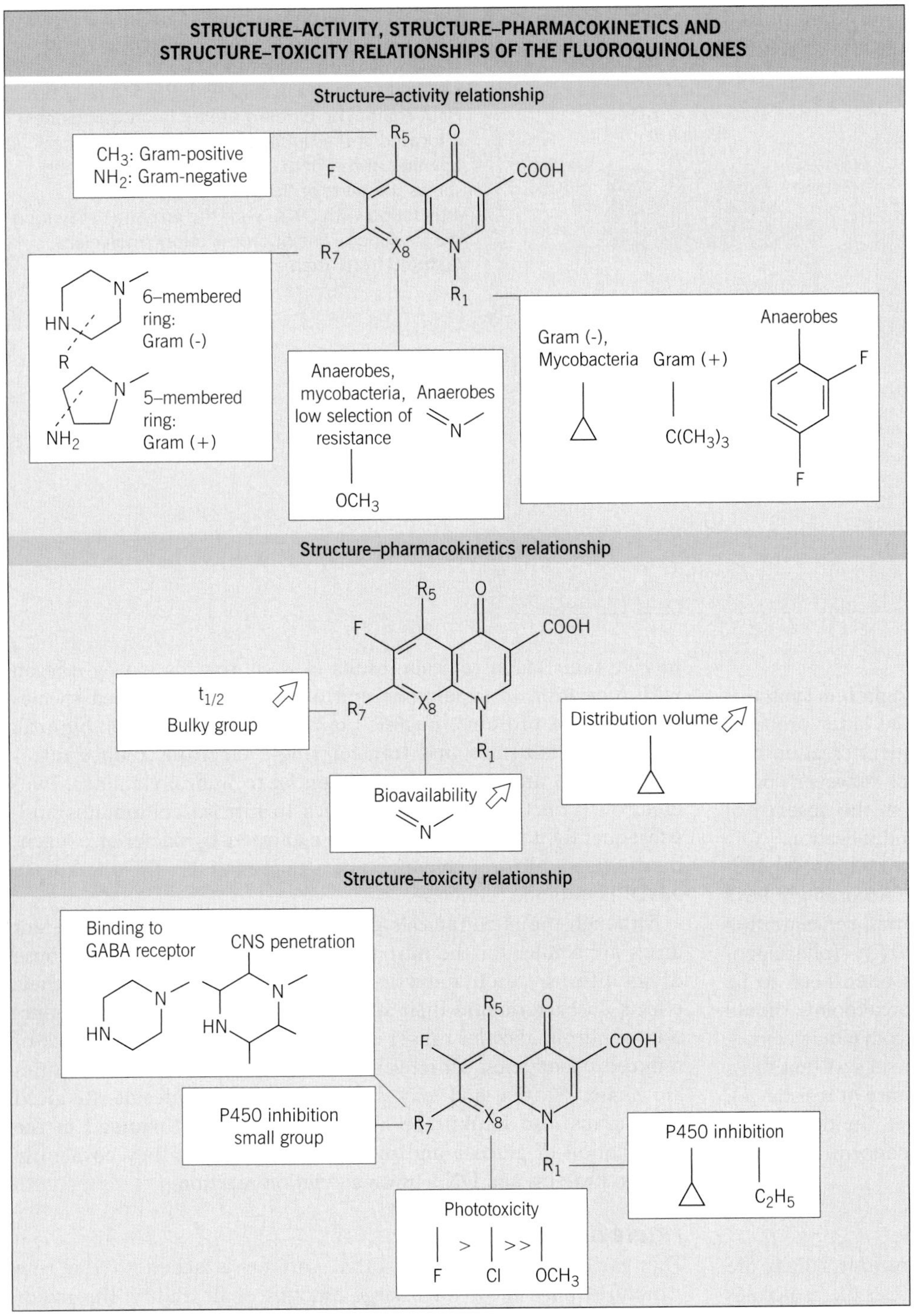

Fig. 188.11 Structure–activity, structure–pharmacokinetics and structure–toxicity relationships of the fluoroquinolones. These considerations form the basis of the rational development of the new molecules of this class, which have a very extended spectrum (including Gram-positive bacteria and anaerobes), a long half-life and minimal phototoxicity and metabolic interactions.

quinolones is DNA gyrase in Gram-negative bacteria and topoisomerase IV in Gram-positive bacteria.[44]

Fluoroquinolones form a ternary complex with DNA and the enzyme (Fig. 188.12).[45] This binding site for fluoroquinolones is formed during the gate-opening step of the double-stranded DNA. Cooperatively, four fluoroquinolone molecules are fixed to single-stranded DNA. Their stacking is favored by the presence of coplanar aromatic rings in their structure and by the tail-to-tail interactions between the substituents at N1. Interaction with DNA occurs by hydrogen bonds or via Mg^{2+} bridges established with carbonyl and carboxylate groups. Interaction with the enzyme is mediated by the fluorine at C6 and substituents at C7. The binding of the fluoroquinolones stabilizes the cleavable complex (formed by the cut DNA and the enzyme) and leads to the dissociation of the enzyme subunits. The latter action is observed only for potent molecules or at higher concentrations.

Quinolones have other effects on bacterial cells, such as induction of the DNA repair response, which involves three proteins (RecA, LexA and RecBCD). Induced RecA cleaves the repressor part of the SOS regulon (LexA), stimulating repair of damage caused by fluoroquinolones to DNA. Induced RecBCD binds to the chromosome at the double-strand break created by the ternary complex of topoisomerase–DNA–quinolone, and results in mutagenesis as well as increased cell survial in the presence of quinolones. This system therefore protects against the antibacterial activity of fluoroquinolones.[42]

Resistance

Resistance occurs mostly by mutation of the topoisomerases (reducing drug-binding ability), by porin impermeability or by efflux. These mechanisms affect all fluoroquinolones and result in progressive slight increases in the MIC. New fluoroquinolones may remain active against resistant strains based upon higher intrinsic activity, which is a structure-related property. In particular, the presence of a methoxy substituent in position 8 reduces the potential for selecting resistant mutants (see Fig. 188.11).[46]

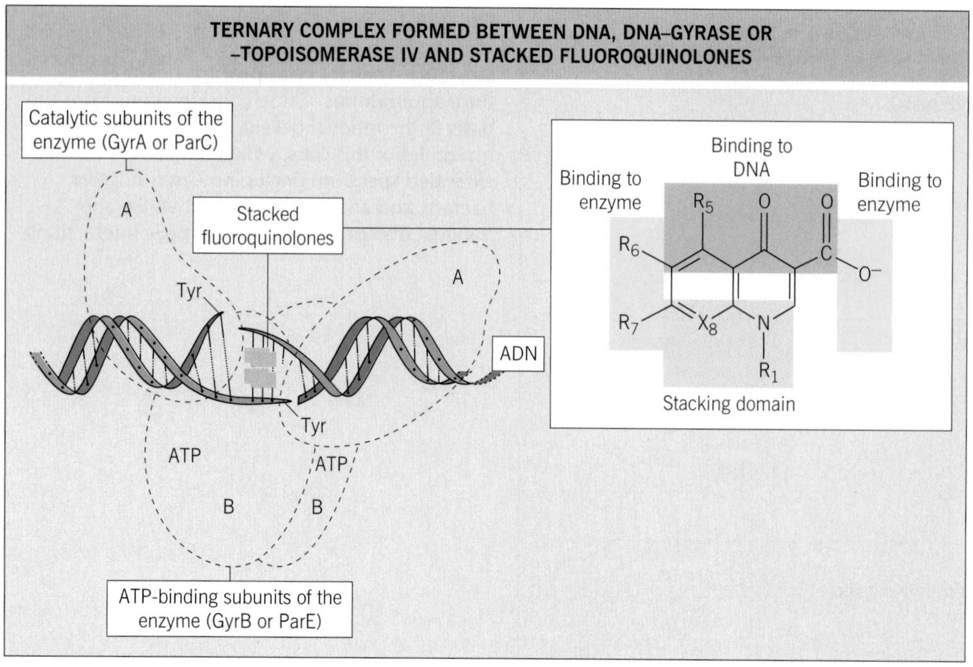

Fig. 188.12 Ternary complex formed between DNA, DNA–gyrase or –topoisomerase IV and stacked fluoroquinolones. Subunits A form covalent bonds via Tyr122 with the 5′ end of the DNA chain. The binding site for fluoroquinolones is located in the bubble formed during the local opening of the DNA molecule. The right panel shows the parts of the antibiotic molecules interacting with DNA, with the enzyme or favoring the stacking of the fluoroquinolone molecules. Adapted from Shen *et al.*[45]

Pharmacodynamics

The mechanism described above requires RNA and protein synthesis as well as cell division for bactericidal action. The latter probably results from cutting of the DNA and the subsequent creation of a barrier for its transcription. Alternative mechanisms, however, confer bactericidal activity to certain molecules either in the absence of protein and RNA synthesis or without bacterial multiplication.

The activity of fluoroquinolones is largely concentration dependent, but these drugs show also persistent effects. Accordingly both the peak/MIC and the 24-hour area under the serum concentration curve (AUC)/MIC ratios are important for activity (pharmacodynamic studies have shown that effective doses often need to be considerably higher than was originally tought; breakpoints should be revised to lower values, and based on pharmacodynamic considerations, should be <1µg/ml;[47] recent studies also suggest that the a peak/MIC ratio >10 protects or retards the emergence of resistance). Fluoroquinolones also show a postantibiotic effect, the duration of which varies according to the pathogen, drug concentration and period of exposure.

Future developments

New molecules with extended spectrum and high intrinsic activity are still in development, among which des-fluoroquinolones (i.e. molecules lacking the F substituent in position 6).[48] When applied to molecules of high intrinsic activity, this structural change was shown to not affect activity while maintaining the mode of action of fluoroquinolones. These molecules have also a low potential for selecting resistance.

Nitroimidazoles and nitrofurans

Chemical structure

The nitroheterocyclic drugs include nitrofuran and nitroimidazole compounds (Fig. 188.13).

Mode and spectrum of action

The activity of nitroheterocyclic drugs requires activation of the nitrogroup attached to the imidazole or furan ring, which must undergo single- or two-electron enzymatic reduction in the bacteria.[49–51] Single-electron reduction of nitroaromatics is most frequently catalyzed by flavoenzyme dehydrogenase electrotransferases and bacterial oxygen-sensitive nitroreductases. Under aerobic conditions, the single electron reduction of nitroaromatics to give their anion radicals results in their reoxidation by oxygen with formation of superoxide and other activated oxygen species that damage proteins, nucleic acids, and lipids. Under hypoxic conditions, enzymes that transfer single electrons reduce nitroaromatics to amines or, less frequently, to hydroxylamines. Two-electron reduction of nitroaromatics to nitroso compounds and, subsequently, to hydroxylamines is catalyzed by bacterial oxygen-insensitive nitroreductases and mammalian DT-diaphorase NADPH:quinone reductase.

Although the nitro radicals generated by reduction of the parent drugs are similar for the nitroimidazoles and the nitrofurans, these drugs differ by their reduction potential, and, therefore in their effects on bacteria and their spectrums of activity. Thus, the reduction of nitroimidazoles causes depletion in the intracellular stock of reduced coenzymes. Moreover, reduced forms of these antibiotics are highly reactive and may damage the DNA molecule. Reduced nitrofurans also inhibit the activity of enzymes involved in the degradation of glucose and pyruvate. In addition, they covalently bind to proteins and DNA by an alkylation reaction.

Future developments

The variety of substitutions that can be attached to the ring structures may allow for a large amount of flexibility. The major interest in these drugs is the use of 2-nitroimidazole probes as radiosensitizers of hypoxic cells on a cell-to-cell basis and for non-invasive detection.

Ansamycins

Chemical structure

Ansamycins, which are macrocyclic antibiotics, are lipophilic and therefore easily diffuse through membranes. They comprise two aromatic rings (containing a quinone), connected by a long chain (or 'ansa' – hence the name given to this class of antibiotics), which confers a rigid character to the whole molecule.

Mode of action

Ansamycins inhibit the initiation of DNA transcription to mRNA and therefore the subsequent protein synthesis.[52] The RNA polymerase contains five subunits $(\alpha_2\beta\beta'\sigma)$:

- α subunits establish contact with transcription factors;
- β' subunit is a basic polypeptide that binds DNA;

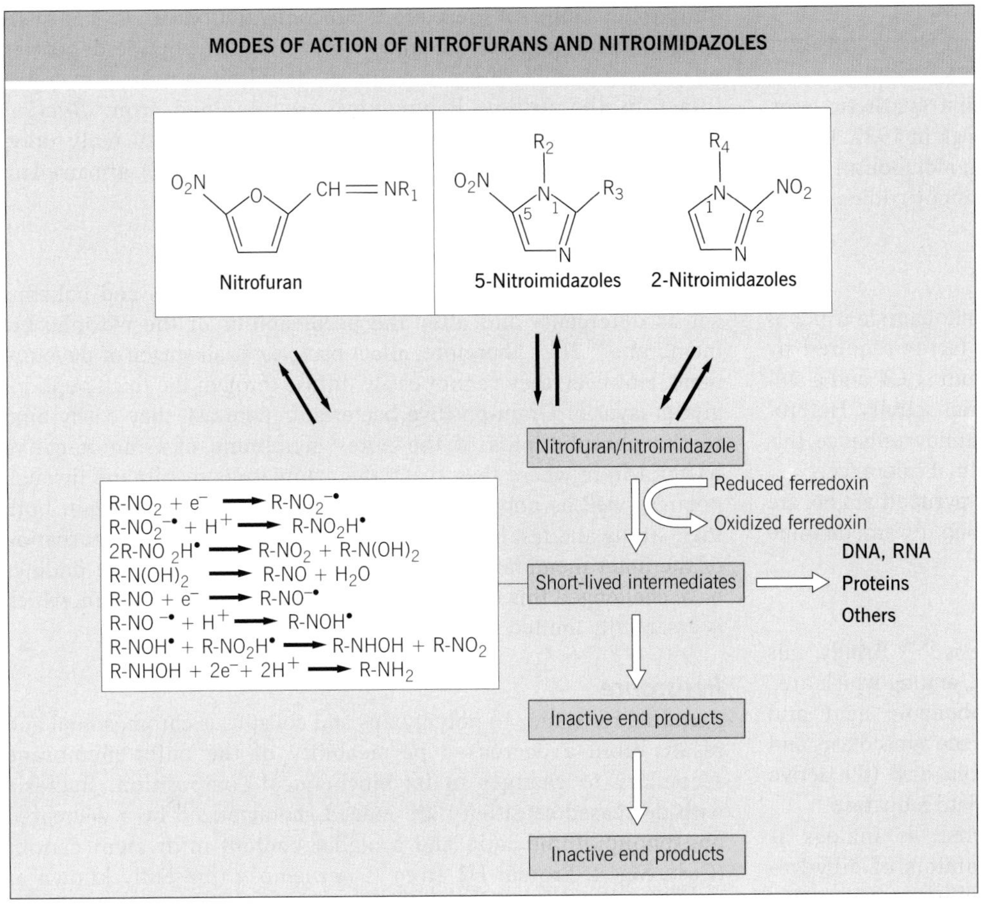

Fig. 188.13 Modes of action of nitrofurans and nitroimidazoles. The modes of action include passage through the cell membrane, reduction to highly reactive products, interaction with intracellular targets and release of inactive end products.

- β subunit is an acidic polypeptide and is part of the active site;
- σ-subunit initiates the transcription and then leaves the polymerase nucleus.

The core polymerase ($\alpha_2\beta\beta'$) therefore retains the ability to synthesize RNA but is defective in its ability to bind and initiate DNA transcription.

Inhibition by rifamycins follows binding of the antibiotic to the β subunit of the RNA polymerase or, to a lesser extent, of the DNA–RNA complex. This binding is mediated by hydrophobic interactions between the aliphatic ansa chain and the β subunit. The precise site of binding has been identified only partly, by studying mutants in RNA polymerase that have acquired resistance to rifampin (rifampicin). All the mutations that affect drug binding belong to three clusters of amino acids in the central domain of the β subunit.

Inhibition of transcription caused by rifamycins is essentially noncompetitive. A model has been proposed in which rifamycins block the translocation event during transcription initiation, without hindering the synthesis of the first phosphodiester bridge between the two first nucleotide triphosphates of the mRNA molecule.[53] Specificity of action depends on the fact that ansamycins alter mammelian cell metabolism only at concentrations 10,000 times those necessary to cause bacterial cell death (Fig. 188.14).

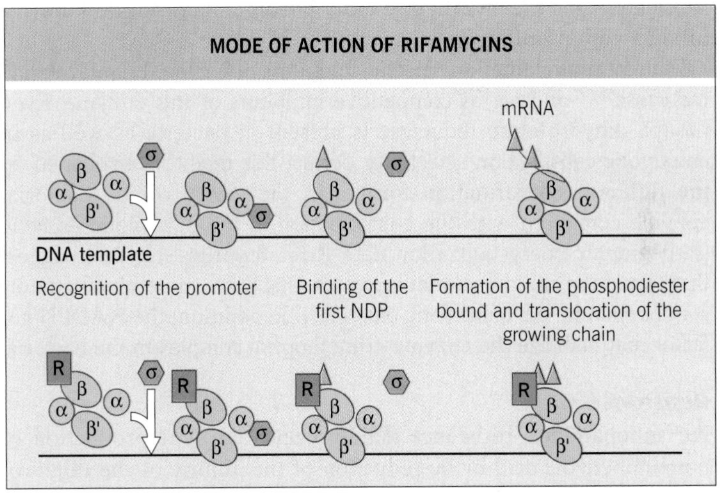

Fig. 188.14 Mode of action of rifamycins. Synthesis of mRNA by RNA polymerase is shown in the upper panel and inhibition by rifamycins (R in the green squares) is shown in the lower panel. The RNA polymerase core is made up of four subunits, of which the β′ subunit binds to the DNA template and the β subunit binds the ribonucleotide diphosphate (NDP; triangle). The σ factor only participates to the intiation step by allowing for the recognition by the enzyme core of promoter sequences on the DNA template. Rifamycins bind to the β subunit. They do not interfere with the binding of the nucleotide diphosphate, but rather inhibit the transcription initiation either by impairing the formation of the first phosphodiester bond or the translocation reaction of the newly synthesized dinucleotide.

Pharmacodynamics

Rifamycins are bactericidal – an effect that results either from the high stability of the complex formed between rifampin and the enzyme or from the formation of superoxide ions on the quinone ring of the antibiotic molecule. As their action is to hinder bacteria multiplication, they are, at least *in vitro*, antagonists to antibiotics that require active bacterial growth to exert their activity (β-lactams) or other antibiotics that act on protein synthesis (macrolides and aminoglycosides). This antagonism is, however, not observed *in vivo*, because of the different distribution of these antibiotics (intracellular for rifamycins; extracellular for β-lactams and aminoglycosides). Their postantibiotic effect is longlasting because of the irreversible nature of their binding. The efficient cell penetration of ansamycins gives them excellent activity against sensitive intracellular organisms.

Future developments

Benzoxazinorifamycins constitute a new group of semisynthetic molecules that show greatly enhanced activity against *Mycobacteria* spp., the main clinical target of this class of antibiotics.[54]

ANTIMETABOLITES

Sulfonamides and diaminopyrimidines

Prontosil (sulfamidochrysoidine) was one of first synthetic compounds with antibacterial activity found by Domagk in 1932. In fact, this product was a prodrug and elucidation of its metabolism led to the development of the sulfonamides. With diaminopyridines, they inhibit the folate pathway in bacteria.

Chemical structure

Sulfonamides are derived from *p*-aminobenzenesulfonamide which is a structural analog of *p*-aminobenzoic acid, a factor required by bacteria for folic acid synthesis. A free amino group at C4 and a sulfonamide group at C1 are required for antibacterial activity. Heterocyclic or aromatic rings substituting the sulfonamide enhance this activity by modifying absorption and gastrointestinal tolerance.

Diaminopyrimidines, such as trimethoprim and pyrimethamine, are pyrimidines substituted at C5 by an aromatic group. Pyrimethamine has an additional substituent at C6.

Mode of action

Sulfonamides inhibit tetrahydrofolic acid synthesis.[55,56] Briefly, this synthesis requires successive enzymatic reactions, among which are:

- formation of pteroic acid from *p*-aminobenzoic acid and dihydropteridin catalyzed by the dihydropteroate synthetase, and
- reduction of dihydrofolic acid in tetrahydrofolic acid (the active form of folic acid) catalyzed by the dihydrofolate reductase.

Sulfonamides act via a double mechanism. First, as analogs as *p*-aminobenzoic acid, they are competitive inhibitors of dihydropteorate synthetase. Second, they can also function as alternative substrates for the synthetase and become incorporated into a product with pteridine.

Diaminopyrimidines are specific inhibitors of bacterial dihydrofolate reductase[55,56] and act as competitive inhibitors of this enzyme. Even though dihydrofolate reductase is present in bacteria as well as in eukaryotic cells, action selectivity occurs; this might be explained by the different conformation formed in the cavity of the bacterial enzyme compared with the conformation in the eukaryotic enzyme [radiographic cocrystallization data (trimethoprim–enzyme) suggest that trimethoprim in bacterial enzymes establishes more binding interactions than in the eukaryotic enzymes]. In addition, the NADPH cofactor may stabilize the enzyme–trimethoprim complex in the bacteria.

Resistance

For sulfonamides, resistance mainly occurs by hyperproduction of *p*-aminobenzoic acid or by reduction of the affinity of the dihydrofolate reductase for the antibiotic, which causes resistance to the whole class. For diaminopyrimidines, resistance mostly occurs by enzyme mutations that prevent binding [a single point mutation (e.g. Phe98→Tyr) is sufficient to prevent any binding of trimethoprim to the enzyme, because of the loss of a critical hydrogen bound].[57]

Pharmacodynamics

Sulfonamides are only bacteriostatic. Their combination with diaminopyrimidines confers to them a bactericidal activity because of synergism.

ANTIBIOTICS ACTING ON THE MEMBRANE

Cyclic polypeptides (polymyxins/colistins)

Chemical structure

These are a collection of cyclic, branched polypeptides (molecular masses about 1000Da) containing both cationic and hydrophobic aminoacids. Some of these are the D configuration or are non-DNA coded, which confers resistance to mammalian peptide-degrading enzymes (60–90% of a parenterally-administered dosis is excreted intact in the urine). Polymyxins are obtained from *Bacillus polymyxa* and colistins from *Aerobacillus colistinus*. Only polymyxin B and colistin A (identical to polymyxin E) are used in clinical practice.

Mode of action

Because of their amphipathic character, polymyxins and colistins act as detergents and alter the permeability of the cytoplasmic membrane.[58] They, therefore, affect bacteria at all stages of development. However, they cannot easily diffuse through the thick peptidoglycan layer of Gram-positive bacteria. In contrast, they easily bind to the phospholipids of the outer membrane of Gram-negative bacteria from where they reach the cytoplasmic membrane through polar as well as nonpolar channels. These properties explain both their strong and fast bactericidal activity through major perturbation of the inner membrane permeability properties (but recent findings have challenged this mechanism) and their narrow spectrum, which is essentially limited to Gram-negative organisms.

Resistance

Acquired resistance to polymyxins and colistins is chromosomal and results from a decreased permeability of the outer membrane secondary to changes in its biochemical composition. Bacteria with decreased sensitivity are indeed characterized by a decreased phospholipid/lipid ratio and a higher content in divalent cations (Ca^{2+}, Mg^{2+}). Protein H1 from *P. aeruginosa* (presently known as OprH) prevents binding of polymyxins and colistins to lipopolysaccharide and its overproduction has been correlated with less sensitivity [this change is, however, not sufficient *per se* and must be combined with other modifications of the membrane; two genes downstream to OprH (PhoP and PhoQ) coregulate OprH and polymyxin B resistance]. Although still exceptional, resistance to polymyxins and colistins has now been described in strains exhibiting multiple resistance to β-lactams and aminoglycosides.[59]

Pharmacodynamics

Colistin A and polymyxin B show concentration-dependent activity but no or little post-antibiotic effect (rapid regrowth after the concentration falls below the MIC), justifying the administration of repeated daily doses.[60]

Nonantibiotic pharmacologic and toxicologic properties related to chemical structure

As membrane-disrupting and lipid-binding agents, polymyxins and colistins display a number of non-antibiotic effects, some of which are potentially useful [inactivation of endotoxins (immobilized polymyxin B is currently used to remove endoxins from protein solutions), and synergy with serum bactericidal activities], but many others are highly detrimental to the host [activation of the alternate pathway of complement, mast cell degranulation with histamine release, decreased production of cytokines (but increased TNF-α release), increase in membrane conductance in epithelia, apoptosis].

Future developments

Because of the widespread emergence of resistance to other antimicrobials, polymyxins are being re-evaluated for chronic, difficult-to-treat infections (e.g. pulmonary infections in cystic fibrosis) and new, potentially less toxic derivatives are therefore being synthesized and evaluated.[61] The use of polymyxin B as an anti-endotoxin agent is also being investigated.[62]

REFERENCES

1. Ghuysen JM, Charlier P, Coyette J, *et al.* Penicillin, and beyond: evolution, protein fold, multimodular polypeptides, and multiprotein complexes. Microb Drug Resist 1996;2(2):163–75.
2. Goffin C, Ghuysen JM. Multimodular penicillin binding proteins, an enigmatic family of orthologs and paralogs. Microbiol Mol Biol Rev 1998;62(4):1079–1093.
3. Nikaido H. Antibiotic resistance caused by Gram-negative multidrug efflux pumps. Clin Infect Dis. 1998;27(Suppl.1):S32–41.
4. Ghuysen JM. Molecular structures of penicillin binding proteins and beta lactamases. Trends Microbiol 1994;2(10):372–80.
5. Livermore DM. Beta lactamases in laboratory and clinical resistance. Clin Microbiol Rev 1995;8(4):557–84.
6. Bush K, Jacoby GA, Medeiros AA. A functional classification scheme for beta lactamases and its correlation with molecular structure. Antimicrob Agents Chemother 1995;39(6):1211–33.
7. Bradford PA. Extended spectrum beta lactamases in the 21st century: characterization, epidemiology, and detection of this important resistance threat. Clin Microbiol Rev 2001;14(4):933–51.
8. Servais H, Tulkens PM. Stability and compatibility of ceftazidime administered by continuous infusion to intensive care patients. Antimicrob Agents Chemother 2001;45(9):2643–7.
9. Reynolds PE. Structure, biochemistry and mechanism of action of glycopeptide antibiotics. Eur J Clin Microbiol Infect Dis 1989;8(11):943–50.
10. Beauregard DA, Williams DH, Gwynn MN, Knowles DJ. Dimerization and membrane anchors in extracellular targeting of vancomycin group antibiotics. Antimicrob Agents Chemother 1995;39(3):781–5.
11. Nicas TI, Mullen DL, Flokowitsch JE, *et al.* Semisynthetic glycopeptide antibiotics derived from LY264826 active against vancomycin resistant enterococci. Antimicrob Agents Chemother 1996;40(9):2194–9.
12. Neuhaus FC, Lynch JL. The enzymatic synthesis of D-alanyl-D-alanine. III. On the inhibition of D-alanyl-D-alanine synthase by the antibiotic D-cycloserine. Biochemistry (US) 1964;3:471–480.
13. Schonbrunn E, Sack S, Eschenburg S, *et al.* Crystal structure of UDP *N*-acetylglucosamine enolpyruvyltransferase, the target of the antibiotic fosfomycin. Structure 1996;4(9):1065–75.
14. Stone KJ, Strominger JL. Mechanism of action of bacitracin: complexation with metal ion and C 55 isoprenyl pyrophosphate. Proc Natl Acad Sci USA 1971;68(12):3223–7.
15. Mingeot Leclercq MP, Glupczynski Y, Tulkens PM. Aminoglycosides: Activity and resistance. Antimicrob Agents Chemother 1999;43: 727–37.
16. Nagabushan TL, Miller GH, Weinstein MJ. Structure–activity relationships in aminoglycoside–aminocyclitol antibiotics. In: Whelton A, Neu HC, eds, The aminoglycosides. New York; Marcel Dekker, Inc.; 1982:3–27.
17. Yoshizawa S, Fourmy D, Puglisi JD. Structural origins of gentamicin antibiotic action. EMBO J 1998;17(22):6437–48.
18. Miller GH, Sabatelli FJ, Hare RS, *et al.* The most frequent aminoglycoside resistance mechanisms changes with time and geographic area: a reflection of aminoglycoside usage patterns? Aminoglycoside Resistance Study Groups. Clin Infect Dis 1997;24(Suppl.1):S46–62.
19. Shaw KJ, Rather PN, Hare RS, Miller GH. Molecular genetics of aminoglycoside resistance genes and familial relationships of the aminoglycoside modifying enzymes. Microbiol Rev 1993;57(1):138–63.
20. Oehler R, Polacek N, Steiner G, Barta A. Interaction of tetracycline with RNA: photoincorporation into ribosomal RNA of *Escherichia coli.* Nucleic Acids Res 1997;25(6):1219–24.
21. Geigenmüller U, Nierhaus KH. Tetracycline can inhibit tRNA binding to the ribosomal P site as well as to the A site. Eur J Biochem 1986;161(3):723–6.
22. Amin AR, Attur MG, Thakker GD, *et al.* A novel mechanism of action of tetracyclines: effects on nitric oxide synthases. Proc Natl Acad Sci USA 1996;93(24):14014–9.
23. Yamaguchi A, Udagawa T, Sawai T. Transport of divalent cations with tetracycline as mediated by the transposon Tn10 encoded tetracycline resistance protein. J Biol Chem 1990;265(9):4809–13.
24. Rasmussen BA, Gluzman Y, Tally FP. Inhibition of protein synthesis occurring on tetracycline resistant, TetM-protected ribosomes by a novel class of tetracyclines, the glycylcyclines. Antimicrob Agents Chemother 1994;38(7):1658–60.
25. Yanagisawa T, Lee JT, Wu HC, Kawakami M . Relationship of protein structure of isoleucyl tRNA synthetase with pseudomonic acid resistance of *Escherichia coli.* A proposed mode of action of pseudomonic acid as an inhibitor of isoleucyl tRNA synthetase. J Biol Chem 1994;269(39):24304–9.
26. Baltz RH, Norris FH, Matsushima P, *et al.* NA sequence sampling of the *Streptococcus pneumoniae* genome to identify novel targets for antibiotic development. Microb Drug Resist. 1998;4(1):1–9.
27. Bonnefoy A, Girard AM, Agouridas C, Chantot JF. Ketolides lack inducibility properties of MLS(B) resistance phenotype. J Antimicrob Chemother 1997;40(1):85–90
28. Vannuffel P, Cocito C. Mechanism of action of streptogramins and macrolides. Drugs 1996;51(Suppl.1):20–30.
29. Menninger JR. Mechanism of inhibition of protein synthesis by macrolide and lincosamide antibiotics. J Basic Clin Physiol Pharmacol 1995;6(3–4):229–50
30. Douthwaite S, Champney WS. Structures of ketolides and macrolides determine their mode of interaction with the ribosomal target site. J Antimicrob Chemother 2001;48(Suppl.T1):1–8.
31. Hansen LH, Mauvais P, Douthwaite S. The macrolide ketolide antibiotic binding site is formed by structures in domains II and V of 23S ribosomal RNA. Mol Microbiol 1999;31(2):623–31.
32. Liu M, Douthwaite S. Activity of the ketolide telithromycin is refractory to erm monomethylation of bacterial rRNA. Antimicrob Agents Chemother 2002;46(6):1629–33.
33. Carbon C. Pharmacodynamics of macrolides, azalides, and streptogramins: effect on extracellular pathogens. Clin Infect Dis 1998;27(1):28–32
34. Chant C, Rybak MJ. Quinupristin/dalfopristin (RP 59500): a new streptogramin antibiotic. Ann Pharmacother 1995;29(10):1022–7
35. Drainas D, Kalpaxis DL, Coutsogeorgopoulos C. Inhibition of ribosomal peptidyltransferase by chloramphenicol. Kinetic studies. Eur J Biochem 1987;164(1):53–8
36. Shaw WV. Chloramphenicol acetyltransferase: enzymology and molecular biology. CRC Crit Rev Biochem 1983;14(1):1–46
37. Park CH, Brittelli DR, Wang CL, *et al.* Antibacterials. synthesis and structure activity studies of 3 aryl 2 oxooxazolidines. 4. Multiply substituted aryl derivatives. J Med Chem 1992;35(6):1156–65
38. Kloss P, Xiong L, Shinabarger DL, Mankin AS. Resistance mutations in 23S rRNA identify the site of action of the protein synthesis inhibitor linezolid in the ribosomal peptidyl transferase center. J Mol Biol 1999;294(1):93–101.
39. Swaney SM, Aoki H, Ganoza MC, Shinabarger DL. The oxazolidinone linezolid inhibits initiation of protein synthesis in bacteria. Antimicrob Agents Chemother 1998;42(12):3251–5
40. Aoki H, Ke L, Poppe SM, Poel TJ, *et al.* Oxazolidinone antibiotics target the P site on *Escherichia coli* ribosomes. Antimicrob Agents Chemother 2002;46(4):1080–5;42(12):3251–5.
41. Diekema DJ, Jones RN. Oxazolidinone antibiotics. Lancet 2001;358(9297):1975–82.
42. Gootz TD, Brighty KE. Chemistry and mechanism of action of the quinolone antibiotics. In: Andriole VT, ed. The quinolones, 2nd edition. San Diego, Ca: Academic Press, 1998:29–80.
43. Blondeau JM. A review of the comparative *in vitro* activities of 12 antimicrobial agents, with a focus on five new respiratory quinolones. J Antimicrob Chemother 1999;43(Suppl.B):1–11.
44. Ferrero L, Cameron B, Manse B, *et al.* Cloning and primary structure *of Staphylococcus aureus* DNA topoisomerase IV: a primary target of fluoroquinolones. Mol Microbiol 1994;13(4):641–53.
45. Shen LL, Mitscher LA, Sharma PN, *et al.* Mechanism of inhibition of DNA gyrase by quinolone antibacterials: a cooperative drug–DNA binding model. Biochemistry 1989;28(9):3886–94
46. Dong Y, Zhao X, Domagala J, Drlica K. Effect of fluoroquinolone concentration on selection of resistant mutants of *Mycobacterium bovis* BCG and *Staphylococcus aureus.* Antimicrob Agents Chemother 1999;43(7):1756–8.
47. Pickerill KE, Paladino JA, Schentag JJ. Comparison of the fluoroquinolones based on pharmacokinetic and pharmacodynamic parameters [Review]. Pharmacotherapy 2000;20(4):417–28.
48. Schmitz FJ, Boos M, Mayer S, Kohrer K, Scheuring S, Fluit AC. *In vitro* activities of novel des-fluoro(6)quinolone BMS 284756 against mutants of *Streptococcus pneumoniae, Streptococcus pyogenes,* and *Staphylococcus aureus* selected with different quinolones. Antimicrob Agents Chemother 2002;46(3):934–5.
49. Castelli M, Malagoli M, Ruberto AI, *et al. In vitro* studies of two 5 nitroimidazole derivatives. J Antimicrob Chemother 1997;40(1):19–25.
50. Freeman CD, Klutman NE, Lamp KC . Metronidazole. A therapeutic review and update. Drugs 1997;54(5):679–708.
51. Aboagye EO, Lewis AD, Tracy M, Workman P.Bioreductive metabolism of the novel fluorinated 2 nitroimidazole hypoxia probe N-(2-hydroxy-3,3,3-trifluoropropyl)-2-(2-nitroimidazolyl) acetamide (SR-4554). Biochem Pharmacol 1997;54(11):1217–24.
52. Wehrli W, Knusel F, Schmid K, Staehelin M . Interaction of rifamycin with bacterial RNA polymerase. Proc Natl Acad Sci USA 1968;61(2):667–73.
53. Kumar KP, Reddy PS, Chatterji D. Proximity relationship between the active site of *Escherichia coli* RNA polymerase and rifampicin binding domain: a resonance energy transfer study. Biochemistry. 1992;31(33):7519–26.
54. Saito H, Tomioka H, Sato K, *et al. In vitro* antimycobacterial activities of newly synthesized benzoxazinorifamycins. Antimicrob Agents Chemother 1991;35(3):542–7.

55. Burchall JJ. Mechanism of action of trimethoprim and sulfamethoxazole II. J Infect Dis 1973;128:S437–441.
56. Zinner SH, Mayer KH. Sulfonamides and trimethoprim. In: Mandell GL, Bennett JE, Dolin R, eds. Principles and practice of infectious diseases, 4th edition. New York: Churchill Livingstone, 1995:354–63.
57. Gold HS, Moellering RC. Antimicrobial drug resistance. N Engl J Med 1996;335:1445–53.
58. Fidai S, Farmer SW, Hancock RE. Interaction of cationic peptides with bacterial membranes. Methods Mol Biol 1997;78:187–204.
59. Rahaman SO, Mukherjee J, Chakrabarti A, Pal S. Decreased membrane permeability in a polymyxin B resistant *Escherichia coli* mutant exhibiting multiple resistance to beta lactams as well as aminoglycosides. FEMS Microbiol Lett 1998;161(2):249–54.
60. Renard L, Gicquel M, Laurentie M, Sanders P. Effet bactéricide de la colistine vis a vis d'*Escherichia coli*. Modélisation et simulation de la relation pharmacocinétique pharmacodynamique pour la prédiction de l'efficacité en antibiothérapie vétérinaire. Vet Res 1996;27(1):23–32.
61. Weinstein J, Afonso A, Moss E Jr, Miller GH. Selective chemical modifications of polymyxin B. Bioorg Med Chem Lett 1998;8(23):3391–6.
62. Giacometti A, Cirioni O, Ghiselli R, et al. Therapeutic efficacy of intraperitoneal polymyxin B and polymyxin-like peptides alone or combined with levofloxacin in rat models of septic shock. J Antimicrob Chemother 2002;49:193–6.

chapter

189 Mechanisms of Antibacterial Resistance

Franz-Josef Schmitz & Ad C Fluit

INTRODUCTION

Although treatment of infections is often initiated empirically, the determination of bacterial susceptibility to an antimicrobial agent is an essential test in clinical microbiology because of widespread resistance to all classes of antimicrobial agents. Standardized methods for the determination of susceptibility and resistance have been formulated.[1] Bacterial isolates that are considered resistant to an antibiotic by these methods usually cannot be treated by this antibiotic, although the successful clinical outcome for isolates deemed susceptible is not guaranteed.

There is a strong correlation between the presence of some determinants of bacterial resistance and the outcome of antimicrobial therapy. The presence of a β-lactamase in *Neisseria gonorrhoeae* strongly correlates with penicillin treatment failure. The presence of the *mecA* gene in *Staphylococcus aureus* is highly predictive for treatment failure with oxacillin, and in fact oxacillin-resistant *S. aureus* (usually called methicillin-resistant *S. aureus* (MRSA) because of their resistance to the oxacillin analog methicillin) are by definition also considered resistant to all other β-lactam antibiotics.

However, the presence of a resistance gene is not equivalent to treatment failure. The gene should also be expressed in sufficient levels to lead to phenotypic resistance, and expression may differ depending on culture conditions or site of infection. For example β-lactamase production is common among Enterobacteriaceae but resistance to penicillins depends on the mode and amount of expression.

Antibiotic resistance can be divided into six basic groups depending on the mechanism involved:

- the presence of an enzyme that inactivates the antibiotic;
- the presence of an alternative enzyme for that inhibited by the antibiotic;
- mutation in the target, which reduces binding of the antibiotic to the target;
- modification of the target, which reduces binding of the antibiotic to the target;
- reduced uptake of the antibiotic; and
- active efflux of the antibiotic.

The genetic determinants for resistance against antimicrobial agents can be located on the bacterial chromosome or on plasmids. The analysis of resistance genes and their distribution through the use of modern DNA techniques has provided new insights into the mechanisms of resistance and the spread of resistance genes through hospitals and the community.

RESISTANCE TO β-LACTAM ANTIBIOTICS

Penicillin is the oldest β-lactam antibiotic; since its introduction we have witnessed the development of a whole array of β-lactam-based antibiotics, such as the first-generation cephalosporins through to the fourth-generation cephalosporins, carbapenems and monobactams. Almost immediately after the introduction of penicillin, resistance was observed in staphylococci. The β-lactam antibiotics interfere with cell wall synthesis by binding to the enzymes involved in the process. These enzymes are called penicillin-binding proteins (PBPs). Resistance to β-lactams is mainly caused by either the presence of β-lactamases, which destroy the lactam ring, or the presence of altered PBPs, which are not inhibited by these antibiotics. In Gram-positive bacteria the β-lactamase is excreted into the environment, and in Gram-negative bacteria the β-lactamase is excreted in the periplasm. Whether the β-lactam antibiotic is effective against the bacterium depends on a number of factors (Fig. 189.1), including:[2]

- the concentration of the antibiotic in the environment;
- the rate of entry through the outer membrane (in the case of Gram-negative bacteria);
- the amount of β-lactamase;
- the hydrolysis rate for the antibiotic by the β-lactamase; and
- the affinity of the PBPs for the antibiotic.

The number of β-lactamases has steadily risen since the introduction of penicillin. The β-lactamases have been classified according to their functional aspects.[3] This system is based on hydrolysis rates for a number of substrates and the level of inhibition by clavulanic acid, but simple point mutations may alter the classification. They have also been classified according to the nucleotide sequences that encode β-lactamase.[4] Classes A, B and D have a serine at their active site, whereas class B has a zinc atom at the active site. Class A enzymes are encoded mostly on plasmids, whereas class C enzymes are generally chromosomally encoded. Class A enzymes are generally constitutively expressed. Class C enzyme genes are present in almost all Gram-negative bacilli, except *Salmonella* spp., but their presence (e.g. in *Escherichia coli*) does not necessarily lead to resistance. Class C enzymes are usually inducible and a total of four genes are required for expression of β-lactamase activity. *Escherichia coli* possesses the *ampC*, *ampD* and *ampG* genes, but lacks the *ampR* gene. Why *E. coli* possesses three of these genes and lacks the fourth is unclear. Class D is a limited group of enzymes able to hydrolyze oxacillin; they are related to class C enzymes. Class B is of increasing importance because many act as carbapenemases. The β-lactamases range between 30 and 40kDa in size.

The commonest β-lactamases in Enterobactericeae are TEM-1, TEM-2 and SHV-1 (TEM are the first three letters of the patient from which the isolate came that harbored the first TEM β-lactamase; SHV stands for sulfhydryl variable). These are simple penicillinases and their activity can be inhibited by compounds such as clavulanic acid and tazobactam, thereby rendering penicillin derivatives active again. However, TEM and SHV enzymes can easily obtain a broader spectrum through mutations, which may lead to resistance against third-generation cephalosporins. Inactivation of aztreonam, ceftazidime, cefotaxime or ceftriaxone is considered an indication for the presence of such an extended-spectrum β-lactamase (ESBL). However, these antibiotics can also be inactivated by the overproduction of ampC. True ESBLs are determined by their inhibition with clavulanic acid.

Resistance to third-generation cephalosporins was first described in 1983 and was mediated by a plasmid encoding for a TEM-related

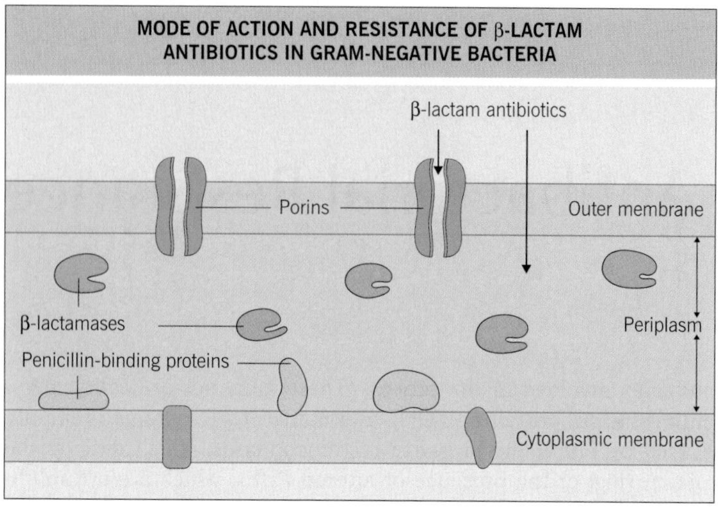

Fig. 189.1 Mode of action and resistance of β-lactam antibiotics in Gram-negative bacteria.

β-lactamase. The majority of ESBLs are found in *Klebsiella pneumoniae* isolates. Extended spectrum β-lactamases are encoded by plasmids, and these are highly transmissible. More than 60 TEM-type ESBLs have been described (Table 189.1).[5] In addition, more than 30 SHV-type ESBLs are known. Besides these common ESBL-types, some ESBLs have been described that do not belong to these two classes. Some plasmid-encoded cephalosporinases, which are also called cephamycinases, have properties similar to ampC but are produced constitutively. Spread of these genes through the hospital or the community may further endanger the use of cephalosporins.

Another group is formed by the carbapenemases. These enzymes are encoded chromosomally and inactivate the highly active carbapenems, imipenem and meropenem, but resistance is still rare.

Altered PBPs are also a major reason for resistance against β-lactam antibiotics. An altered PBP is involved in methicillin resistance in staphylococci. Both MRSA and methicillin-resistant *Staphylococcus epidermidis* (MRSE) are important causes of nosocomial infections. These infections are difficult to treat because both MRSA and MRSE are generally multiresistant and are susceptible to only a limited number of antibiotics.

This PBP2a is encoded by the *mecA* gene. Regulation of methicillin is complex. Expression can be heterogeneous and only a few cells express the phenotype, although all cells are genotypically identical and possess the *mecA* gene. Through mutation the resistance phenotype may become homogeneous. Expression is also influenced by the plasmid-encoded β-lactamase regulatory (blaR) systems blaR1 and blaI inducer-repressor system, which interacts with the mec-associated mecR1 and mecI system.[6] The *mec* determinant appears to originate in coagulase-negative staphylococci, which have a much higher prevalence of the gene, and horizontal transfer appears to take place on a regular basis. The *mecA* gene appears to be located on a transposon, but the genetic environment of the *mecA* gene may vary considerably among different strains of staphylococci, although there is a core region and some specific genetic determinants are frequently associated with the presence of *mecA* (Fig. 189.2).[7] Besides the presence of *mecA*, some methicillin-resistant strains are overproducers of β-lactamases.[8,9]

Resistance to penicillin in *Streptococcus pneumoniae* is also due to the presence of altered PBPs, and this mechanism can be responsible for chromosomally mediated penicillin resistance in *N. gonorrhoeae*.

RESISTANCE TO AMINOGLYCOSIDES

The first clinically effective aminoglycoside was streptomycin, which was isolated from *Streptomyces griseus* and first described in 1944. Numerous aminoglycosides have been isolated from species belonging to the genera *Streptomyces*, *Micromonospora*, *Bacillus* and *Pseudomonas*. Also, synthetic derivatives were produced, such as amikacin. Clinically, the most important aminoglycoside antibiotics are gentamicin, tobramycin, amikacin and streptomycin. They have a broad antimicrobial spectrum and are effective against both Gram-positive and Gram-negative organisms. However, they are not effective against anaerobes. Aminoglycosides bind to the ribosomes and thus interfere with protein synthesis (see Chapter 188).

Aminoglycosides enter the bacterial cell in several phases. In the first phase the aminoglycosides bind to anionic sites on the cell and, after binding, diffuse through outer membrane proteins. In *Pseudomonas aeruginosa* the entry is enhanced; the lipopolysaccharides of *P. aeruginosa* are rich in phosphate groups to which the aminoglycosides bind. This binding displaces magnesium ions, thus allowing entry of the aminoglycoside. The second and third phases are energy dependent and transport the aminoglycoside molecules across the cytoplasmic membrane. The lack of activity of aminoglycosides against anaerobes is explained by the fact that the transport of aminoglycosides across the cytoplasmic membrane depends on aerobic respiration.

Inactivation of aminoglycosides is the major mechanism of resistance against these antibiotics, but ribosomal modification and reduced permeability may also lead to resistance. The enzymes that are responsible for inactivation belong to three classes, depending on the type of modification that causes inactivation: phosphotransferases (APH), acetyltransferases (AAC) and nucleotidyltransferases (ANT). Each class is subdivided on the basis of the site of modification on the substrate and substrate specificity (Table 189.2). Often these enzymes are able to modify several closely related antibiotics, which is not surprising in view of their chemical similarity. The enzymes have to inactivate their targets before they reach the ribosomes and they appear to be either located inside the cell or associated with the inside or the outside of the cytoplasmic membrane.[10]

Resistance to aminoglycoside antibiotics is widespread and of clinical importance. It is observed in both Gram-negative and Gram-positive bacteria. Studies concerning the evolution of resistance using nucleotide sequencing clearly show that, at least within enzyme classes, the genes are related. For example, immunologic and hybridization tests have shown that the APH(3′) enzymes from streptococci and staphylococci are closely related, as are those enzymes on the Gram-negative transposons (Tn), Tn*5* and Tn*903*. However, there is far less homology between enzymes from Gram-negative bacteria compared to enzymes from Gram-positive bacteria. Nevertheless, the genes from Gram-negative bacteria appear to be more closely related to a gene of *Streptomyces fradiae*. In fact it was concluded that it is likely that gene transfer had taken place between these species. Aminoglycoside resistance genes are believed to have originated from genes involved in the production of aminoglycosides in aminoglycoside-producing species.[11]

Besides the transfer of genes between bacteria and aminoglycoside-producing species, transfer between Gram-positive and Gram-negative species has been documented.[12] It should be noted, however, that transfer of a functional resistance gene from one species or even within one species does not necessarily lead to the expression of resistance.

Aminoglycoside resistance in staphylococci is well documented.[13] Up to six genes have been identified. Often more than one resistance gene is present. One of the most remarkable aminoglycoside enzymes is the bifunctional AAC(6′)APH(2″) enzyme, which is found on Tn*4001* of *S. aureus* and in *Enterococcus faecalis* isolates. Nucleotide sequencing data suggest that the enzyme arose through the fusion of two genes, each encoding one of the partners. The epidemiology of Tn*4001* is well studied and illustrates that substitutions, insertions

CHARACTERIZATION OF TEM β-LACTAMASES

β-lactamase	Amino acid at position																
	21	39	42	69	104	153	164	165	182	237	238	240	244	265	268	275	276
TEM-1	L	Q	A	M	E	H	R	W	M	A	G	E	R	T	S	R	N
TEM-2		K															
TEM-3		K			K						S						
TEM-4	F				K						S			M			
TEM-5							S			T		K					
TEM-6					K		H										
TEM-7		K					S										
TEM-8		K			K		S				S						
TEM-9	F				K		S							M			
TEM-10							S					K					
TEM-11		K					H										
TEM-12							S										
TEM-13		K												M			
TEM-15					K						S						
TEM-16		K			K		H										
TEM-19											S						
TEM-20									T		S						
TEM-21		K			K	R					S						
TEM-22		K			K					G	S						
TEM-24		K			K		S			T		K					
TEM-25	F										S			M			
TEM-26					K		S										
TEM-27							H					K		M			
TEM-28							H					K					
TEM-29							H										
TEM-30													S				
TEM-31													C				
TEM-32				I					T								
TEM-33				L													
TEM-34				V													
TEM-35				L													D
TEM-36				V													D
TEM-37				I													D
TEM-38				V												L	
TEM-39				L				R									D
TEM-40				I													
TEM-41													T				
TEM-42		K	V								S	K		M			
TEM-43					K		H		T								
TEM-44		K											S				
TEM-45				L												Q	
TEM-46		K			K		S					K					
TEM-47											S	K		M			
TEM-48		F									S	K		M			
TEM-49		F									S	K		M	G		
TEM-50				L	K						S						D
TEM-51													H				
TEM-52					K				T		S						

Table 189.1 Characterization of the first 52 TEM β-lactamases. A, alanine; D, aspartic acid; E, glutamic acid; F, phenylalanine; G, glycine; H, histidine; I, isoleucine; K, lysine; L, leucine; M, methionine; N, asparagine; P, proline; Q, glutamine; R, arginine; S, serine; T, threonine; V, valine; W, tryptophan.

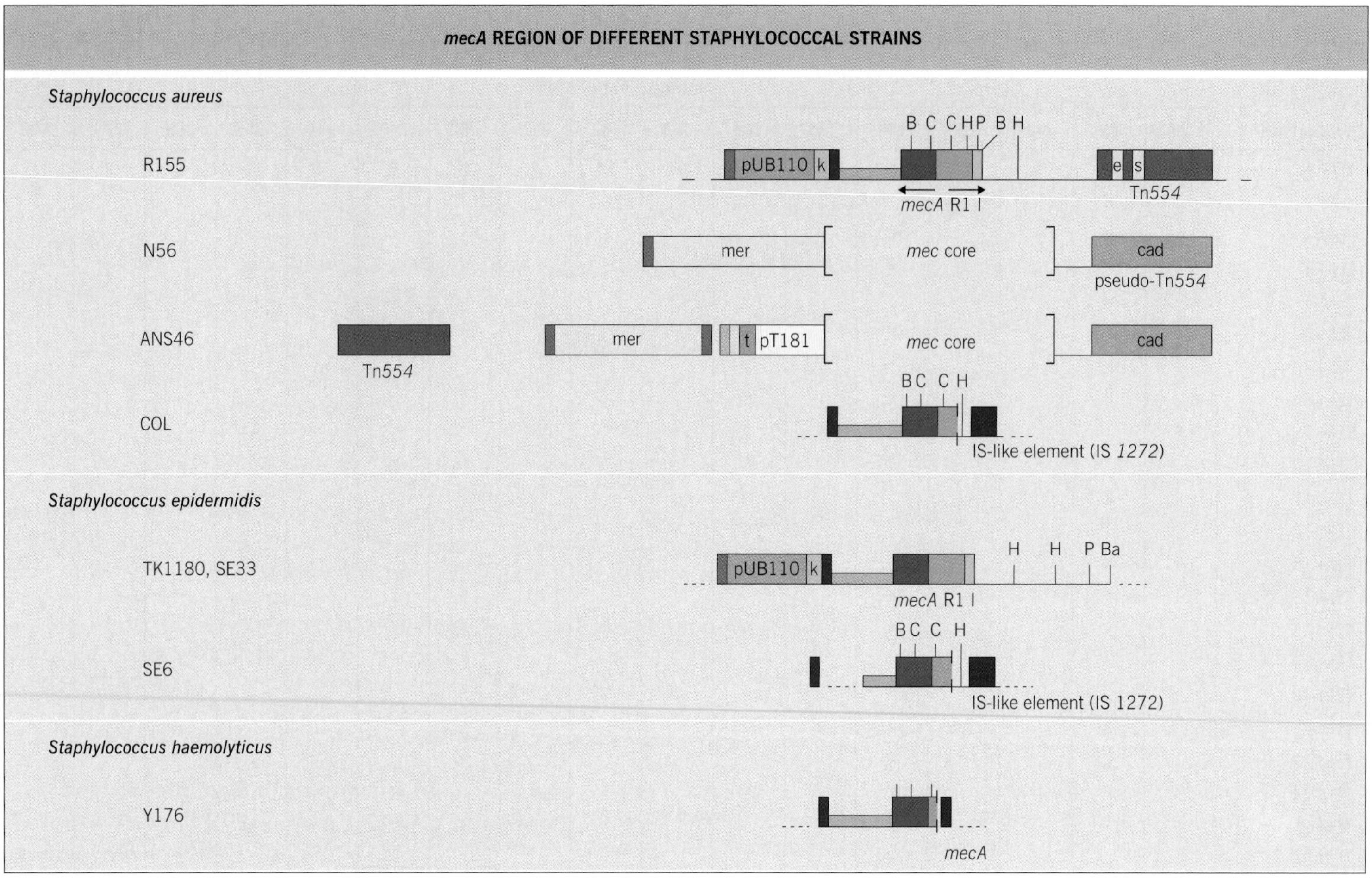

Fig. 189.2 *mecA* region of different staphylococcal strains. IS, insertin sequence; mecA, methicillin-resistant gene; R1, regulatory element; Tn, transposon; vertical lines, position on restriction enzyme cleavage sites.

and deletions play an important role in the adaptation of these elements to new hosts.

Hybridization studies in Australia showed that Tn*4001* could be present on the bacterial chromosome as well as on a number of structurally related plasmids, and this was linked to the rapid spread of gentamicin- and tobramycin-resistant *S. aureus* in Australia. The same transposon was also observed in the USA but with shorter inverted repeats and insertion sequences flanking the resistance gene.

The presence of multiple genes is also well known for other species, especially Gram-negative organisms, but the myriad aminoglycoside resistance genes makes it difficult to study the extent of this problem.

Initially, only resistance against the naturally occuring aminoglycosides was observed and only APH(3′)-II and APH(3′)-III were capable of modifying amikacin in vitro, but the introduction of this antibiotic quickly changed this. In the San Juan Veterans Administration Medical Center, the prevalence of amikacin resistance increased from 0.2 to 3.6% among aerobic Gram-negative bacilli in 4 years through the use of amikacin as a first-line antibiotic. Analysis of plasmids obtained from amikacin-resistant *Serratia marcescens* and *K. pneumoniae* showed that these were almost identical. This suggested that the plasmid disseminated through the hospital and that this dissemination occurred in a relatively short time span.[14]

Resistance to streptomycin is often caused by mutation of the S12 protein in the small ribosomal subunit (30S subunit).

RESISTANCE TO MACROLIDES, LINCOSAMIDES AND STREPTOGRAMINS

Macrolide, lincosamide and streptogramin (MLS) antibiotics are chemically distinct inhibitors of bacterial protein synthesis. Macrolides are composed of a minimum of two amino sugars or neutral sugars attached to a lactone ring of variable size. Macrolides can be subdivided according the chemical structure of their lactone ring (into 14-membered, 15-membered or 16-membered lactone ring macrolides). These classes differ in their pharmacokinetic properties and in their responses to bacterial resistance mechanisms. Lincosamides are alkyl derivatives of proline and are devoid of a lactone ring. Streptogramin antibiotics are mixtures of naturally occurring cyclic peptide compounds. They are composed of two factors, A and B (e.g. pristinamycin II and I, virginiamycin M and S), with synergistic inhibitory and bactericidal activities[15,16] (see Chapter 194).

Intrinsic resistance to macrolide, lincosamide and streptogramin B (MLS_B) antibiotics in Gram-negative bacilli is due to low permeability of the outer membrane to these hydrophobic compounds.

Three different mechanisms of acquired MLS resistance have been described in Gram-positive bacteria. First, target modification alters a site in 23S rRNA that is common to the binding of MLS_B antibiotics. Modification of the ribosomal target confers cross-resistance to MLS_B antibiotics (MLS_B-resistant phenotype) and remains the most frequent mechanism of resistance, although enzymatic modification of the antibiotics and active efflux appear to be increasingly prevalent.[15,17,18]

Target modifications

Macrolide, lincosamide and streptogramin antibiotics bind to 50S ribosomal subunits and inhibit elongation of peptide chains. Resistance to MLS_B antibiotics is mostly due to acquisition of erythromycin resistance methylase (*erm*) genes that encode enzymes that N^6-dimethylate an adenine residue of 23S rRNA. The precise site of methylation has been located in a highly conserved region of the

CHARACTERISITICS OF AMINOGLYCOSIDE-MODIFYING ENZYMES			
Enzyme subclass	**Number of different genes described that encode enzymes capable of the same aminoglycoside modification**	**Modification**	**Distribution**
AAC(1)	1		
AAC(3)-I	2	Gentamicin	Gram-negative bacteria
AAC(3)-II	3	Gentamicin, tobramycin	Gram-negative bacteria
AAC(3)-III	3	Gentamicin, tobramycin	Gram-negative bacteria
AAC(3)-IV	1	Gentamicin, tobramycin	Gram-negative bacteria
AAC(3)-VI	1	Gentamicin	Gram-negative bacteria
AAC(3)-VII	1		Fungi
AAC(3)-VIII	1		Fungi
AAC(3)-IX	1		Fungi
AAC(3)-X	1		Fungi
AAC(6′)-I	9	Amikacin	Gram-negative and Gram-positive bacteria
AAC(6′)-II	2	Gentamicin, tobramycin	Gram-negative bacteria
AAC(6′)-III	1		Gram-negative bacteria
AAC(6′)-APH(2″)	1	Amikacin, gentamicin, tobramycin	Gram-positive bacteria
AAC(2′)I	1	Gentamicin, tobramycin	Gram-negative bacteria
ANT(2″)-I	3	Gentamicin, tobramycin	Gram-negative bacteria
ANT(3″)-I	1	Streptomycin	Gram-negative bacteria
ANT(4′)-I	1	Amikacin, tobramycin	Gram-positive bacteria
ANT(4″)-I	1	Amikacin, tobramycin	Gram-negative bacteria
ANT(6)-I	1	Streptomycin	Gram-positive bacteria
ANT(9)-I	1		Gram-positive bacteria
APH(3′)-I	3		Gram-negative bacteria
APH(3′)-II	1		Gram-negative bacteria
APH(3′)-III	1	Amikacin	Gram-positive bacteria
APH(3′)-IV	1		Gram-positive bacteria
APH(3′)-V	3		Fungi
APH(3′)-VI	2	Amikacin	Gram-negative bacteria
APH(3′)-VII	1		Gram-negative bacteria
APH(3″)-I	2	Streptomycin	Fungi
APH(6)-I	4	Streptomycin	Fungi
APH(4)-I	2		Gram-negative bacteria, fungi

Table 189.2 Characteristics of aminoglycoside-modifying enzymes. Only the clinically relevant antibiotics are listed. AAC, acetyltransferase; ANT, nucleotidyltansferase; APH, phosphotransferase.

rRNA. Nucleotide alterations in 23S rRNA, both mutational and post-transcriptional, cluster in the peptidyltransferase region in 23S rRNS domain V, providing a physical basis and a common location for MLS_B antibiotic sites of action. Methylation of rRNA probably leads to a conformational change in the ribosome that results in decreased affinity and leads to co-resistance to all MLS_B antibiotics. This suggests that the binding sites for these drugs overlap or at least functionally interact. Streptogramin A-type antibiotics are unaffected, and synergy between the two components of streptogramin against MLS-resistant strains is maintained.

A sequence comparison of *erm* genes from various bacterial species and results of hybridization experiments under stringent conditions led to the recognition of at least nine classes of resistance determinants (Table 189.3). Because a number of these genes cross-hybridize, clinical isolates can be assigned to one of four hybridization classes: *ermA*, *ermC*, *ermAC* and *ermF*. This gene distribution is relatively species specific. The amino acid sequences of the methylases encoded by these determinants are related, indicating that the *erm* genes are derived from a common ancestor, possibly belonging to an antibiotic producer. However, various degrees of similarity among the enzymes can be observed.

Expression of MLS_B resistance can be constitutive or inducible. The character of resistance is not related to the class of *erm* determinant but, rather, depends on the sequence of the regulatory region upstream from the structural gene for the methylase. Regulation by these regions occurs by a translational attenuation mechanism in which mRNA secondary structure influences the level of translation. In laboratory mutants and clinical isolates, single nucleotide changes, deletions or duplications in the regulatory region convert inducibly resistant strains to constitutively resistant ones that are cross-resistant to MLS_B antibiotics.

Expression of MLS resistance in staphylococci may be constitutive or inducible. When expression is constitutive, the strains are resistant to all MLS_B antibiotics. Streptogramin A-type antibiotics escape

DISTRIBUTION OF *erm* GENES IN CLINICALLY IMPORTANT BACTERIAL SPECIES		
Hybridization class	**Gene**	**Host**
ermA	*ermA*	*Staphylococcus aureus* Coagulase-negative staphylococci
ermAM	*ermP*	*Clostridium perfringens*
	ermZ	*Clostridium difficile* *Enterococcus faecalis*
	ermBC	*Escherichia coli* *Lactobacillus reuteri*
	ermAM	*Streptococcus sanguis* *Streptococcus pneumoniae* *Streptococcus agalactiae* *Streptococcus pyogenes*
ermC	*ermB*	*Staphylococcus aureus* *Bacillus subtilis* *Lactobacillus* spp.
	ermC	*Staphylococcus aureus* Coagulase-negative staphylococci
	ermM	*Staphylococcus epidermidis*
ermF	*ermF*	*Bacteroides fragilis* *Bacteroides ovatus*

Table 189.3 Distribution of *erm* genes in clinically important bacterial species. Data from Leclercq and Courvalin.[15]

resistance, and synergy with streptogramin B-type antibiotics is retained. When expression is inducible, the strains are resistant to 14- and 15-membered macrolides only. The 16-membered macrolides, the commercially available lincosamides and the streptogramin antibiotics remain active. This dissociated resistance is due to differences in the inducing abilities of MLS antibiotics; only 14- and 15-membered macrolides are effective inducers of methylase synthesis in staphylococci.

Resistance to MLS antibiotics in streptococci can also be expressed constitutively or inducibly. However, unlike the situation with staphylococci, various macrolides or lincosamides may act as inducers to various degrees. Thus, in streptococci, whether inducible or constitutive, ribosomal methylation leads to cross-resistance among macrolides, lincosamides and streptogramin B antibiotics.

In addition, alterations in ribosomal protein L4 account for resistance in pneumococcal strains selected in vitro by macrolide passage. The presence of alterations in the L4 ribosomal protein is consistent with the interpretation that this protein is in contact with or near the peptidyltransferase region in domain V of 23S rRNA. Thus, this alteration may act indirectly to alter 23S rRNA confirmation.[19] In some cases, these modifications also reduce the in-vitro activities of ketolides, derivatives of macrolides, which were designed in order to act against macrolide-resistant micro-organisms.

Antibiotic inactivation

Unlike target modification, which causes resistance to structurally distinct antibiotics, enzymatic inactivation confers resistance only to structurally related drugs.[15,17–19]

Enzymes (ErmA and ErmB) that hydrolyze the lactone ring of the macrocyclic nucleus and phosphotransferases (type I (*mphA*) and type II) that inactivate macrolides by introducing a phosphate on the 2′-hydroxyl group of the amino sugar have been reported in members of the family Enterobacteriaceae and in *S. aureus*. The gene *linA* mediates resistance to lincosamides. The product of *linA* has been partially purified and demonstrated to act as a lincosamide O-nucleotidyl transferase. Lactonases that are capable of cleaving the macrocyclic lactone ring structure of type B streptogramins have been identified in staphylococci (*vgb* gene). Two staphylococcal-related determinants, *vat* and vat_B, encoding an acetyltransferase that inactivates type A streptogramins, have been characterized. The *vat* and *vgb* genes are adjacent to each other on plasmid pIP630. This vat–vgb region is flanked by inverted copies of the insertion sequence IS*257*, suggesting a role for this element in dissemination of these determinants.

Active efflux

The presence of multicomponent macrolide efflux pumps in staphylococci (msrA, msrB) and *N. gonorrhoeae* (mtr), as well as an efflux system in streptococci (mefA, mefE), has also been documented.[20–23] *msr* genes confer resistance only to 14- and 15-membered ring macrolides. Recent epidemiologic surveys have shown that some erythromycin-resistant strains of pneumococci and group A streptococci have been shown to have the M phenotype, namely resistance to macrolides but susceptibility to lincosamide and streptogramin B antibiotics. These strains contain the *mefA* or *mefE* gene coding for an efflux pump for 14- and 15-membered macrolides. The presence of a plasmid-mediated gene, *vga*, encoding for a putative ATP-binding protein, has been associated with an active efflux of streptogramin A group compounds. An overview on macrolide resistance genes was recently published.[19]

RESISTANCE TO FLUOROQUINOLONES

Fluoroquinolone antibiotics exert their antibacterial effects by inhibition of certain bacterial topoisomerase enzymes, namely DNA gyrase (bacterial topoisomerase II) and topoisomerase IV.[13,23–26] These essential bacterial enzymes alter the topology of double-stranded (ds) DNA within the cell. In most bacteria, the chromosome exists as a single circle of dsDNA, which is maintained in a highly negatively supercoiled state. This energetically activated form is required for critical cellular processes such as replication and transcription.

Deoxyribonucleic acid gyrase and topoisomerase IV are heterotetrameric proteins composed of two subunits, designated A and B. The genes encoding the A and B subunits are referred to as *gyrA* and *gyrB* (DNA gyrase) or *parC* and *parE* (DNA topoisomerase IV (*grlA* and *grlB* in *S. aureus*)).

Deoxyribonucleic acid gyrase is the only enzyme that can effect supercoiling of DNA. Inhibition of this activity by fluoroquinolones is associated with rapid killing of the bacterial cell. Topoisomerase IV also modifies the topology of dsDNA, but whereas DNA gyrase seems to be important for maintenance of supercoiling, topoisomerase IV is predominantly responsible for separation of daughter DNA strands during cell division.

In Gram-negative organisms, DNA gyrase is the primary target for quinolones, whereas topoisomerase IV appears to be the primary target in *Staphylococcus aureus* and *Streptococcus pneumoniae.* In Gram-positive species, mutations in genes encoding topoisomerase IV appear to precede mutations in DNA gyrase. Nevertheless, in *S. pneumoniae* it has been shown that different quinolones can have different primary targets in the same bacterial species (i.e. quinolone structure determines the mode of antibacterial action). Thus, the primary target seems to be dependent on the bacterial species as well as on the quinolone structure.

Target modification

Alterations of the target enzymes appear to be the most dominant factors in expression of resistance to quinolones.[13,23–27] Many Gram-negative fluoroquinolone-resistant organisms contain a *gyrA* mutation, resulting in inhibition of supercoiling of DNA and elevated minimum inhibitory concentrations (MICs; Table 189.4). The first molecular characterization of a quinolone resistance mutation in *gyrA* was reported

ALTERATIONS IN DNA GYRASE SUBUNIT A CONFERRING QUINOLONE RESISTANCE	
Organism	**Amino acid substitution**
Acinetobacter baumanni	Gly 81 → Val Ser 83 → Leu
Aeromonas salmonicida	Ser 83 → Ile Ser 83 → Ile Ala 67 → Gly
Coxiella burnetti	Glu 87 → Gly
Campylobacter jejuni	Ala 70 → Thr
Campylobacter lari	Thr 86 → Ile Asp 90 → Ala, Asn Ser 83 → Arg Glu 87 → Lys, Gly Thr 86 → Ile Pro 104 → Ser
Enterobacter cloacae	Ser 83 → Leu
Escherichia coli	Ala 67 → Ser Gly 81 → Cys, Asp Ser 83 → Leu, Trp, Ala Ala 84 → Pro Asp 87 → Asn, Val, Thr, Gly, His
Enterococcus faecalis	Ser 83 → Ile Gln 106 → His, Arg
Helicobacter pylori	Asn 87 → Lys Ala 88 → Val Asp 91 → Gly, Asn, Tyr Asp 91 → Asn Ala 97 → Val
Mycobacterium avium	Ala 90 → Val
Mycobacterium smegmatis	Ala 90 → Val Asp 94 → Gly
Mycobacterium tuberculosis	Gly 88 → Cys Ala 90 → Val Ser 91 → Pro Asp 94 → Asn, His, Gly, Tyr, Ala
Neisseria gonorrhoeae	Ser 83 → Phe Ser 83 → Phe Asp 87 → Asn
Pseudomonas aeruginosa	Thr 83 → Ile Asp 87 → Tyr, Asn, Gly, His
Shigella dysenteriae *Salmonella typhi* *Salmonella typhimurium*	Ser 83 → Leu Ser 83 → Phe Ser 83 → Phe, Tyr Asp 87 → Gly, Tyr, Asn Ala 119 → Glu Ala 67 → Pro Gly 81 → Ser Ser 83 → Ala Asp 87 → Asn
Staphylococcus aureus	Ser 84 → Leu, Ala, Phe Ser 85 → Pro Glu 88 → Lys, Gly
Staphylococcus epidermidis	Ser 84 → Phe

Table 189.4 Alterations in DNA gyrase subunit A conferring quinolone resistance. The Ser 83 to Phe substitution for *Neisseria gonorrhoeae* is based on *Escherichia coli* sequence. Adapted from Everett and Piddock.[24]

in 1988 from *E. coli*. The mutations found were situated in a relatively hydrophilic region of the polypeptide and close to a tyrosine residue at amino acid 122 at the active site, which has been shown to be the site covalently bound to the DNA. The small region from codon 67 to 106 was designated the quinolone resistance determining region (QRDR). In almost all instances, amino acid substitutions within the QRDR involve the replacement of a hydroxl group with a bulky hydrophobic residue. This suggests that mutations in *gyrA* induce changes in the binding site conformation or charge (or both) that may be important for interactions between quinolones and DNA gyrase.

Although quinolones are thought to interact primarily with the A subunit of DNA gyrase, there are mutations in the B subunit that also confer quinolone resistance in some species, such as *E. coli*. However, the frequency of *gyrB* mutations has been shown to be relatively low compared with the frequency of *gyrA* mutations in clinical isolates of *E. coli* and other Gram-negative organisms. Until now, no *gyrB* mutations have been reported as resulting in cross-resistance between quinolones and the B subunit inhibitors coumermycin and novobiocin. This is consistent with evidence that suggests that the GyrB protein comprises two distinct domains: an *N*-terminal domain containing the sites for hydroloysis of adenosine triphosphate and binding of coumermycin, and a *C*-terminal domain containing the QRDR of GyrB.

Topoisomerase IV is a secondary target for fluoroquinolone action in *E. coli* in the absence of a sensitive DNA gyrase. Mutations in *parC* result in further decreased susceptibility. These mutations in *parC* have been shown to occur at Ser80 and Glu84, which are analogous to codons Ser83 and Asp87 of *E. coli gyrA*, and to be common in fluoroquinolone-resistant clinical isolates of *E. coli*. A mutation has also been reported in the *parE* gene that results in decreased fluoroquinolone susceptibility. However, as in the case with *gyrB*, such mutations appear to be rare in clinical isolates.

In *Staphylococcus aureus*, topoisomerase IV is the primary target of fluoroquinolones. Strains with mutations in *gyrA* and *gyrB* without *grlA* mutations resulting in high-level fluoroquinolone resistance can be isolated by single-step selection with fluoroquinolones in *E. coli* but not in *S. aureus*. Previously, 116 clonally unrelated *S. aureus* isolates originating from nine different countries were screened for mutations in the *gyr* and *grl* gene loci.[27] In correlating the characterized mutations to the resulting MIC of ciprofloxacin, it is clear that all studied isolates without the *grlA* mutation at position Ser80 were susceptible to ciprofloxacin. All ciprofloxacin-resistant isolates had the *grlA* mutation Ser80 in combination with either a Ser84 mutation or a Glu88 mutation within the *gyrA* gene. In two isolates a Ser80 to Phe mutation was combined with no mutations in the *gyrA* gene, resulting in a MIC value for ciprofloxacin of 2μg/ml, which, although elevated from a wild-type level, is still below the breakpoint for resistance. These data support the finding that in *S. aureus*, *grlA* mutations precede *gyrA* mutations in developing resistance to ciprofloxacin. Combinations of single point mutations within the *gyrA* gene from various species have been shown to be associated with higher MIC values for ciprofloxacin than single point mutations. Similarly, two combinations of single point mutations within *grlA*, of a Glu84 to Val mutation or a Ala48 to Thr mutation in combination with a Ser80 to Phe mutation, were associated with relatively higher ciprofloxacin MIC values (64–256μg/ml) than only a single Ser80 to Phe mutation (8–64μg/ml). Sequence data show that some *grlA* and *gyrA* mutations are conserved in both MRSA and methicillin-sensitive *S. aureus* from unrelated clones of *S. aureus* isolated from different countries.

Topoisomerase IV mutations have now been characterized in several other organisms. In *Streptococcus pneumoniae* topoisomerase IV also appears to be the primary target for fluoroquinolone action. Ciprofloxacin-resistant mutants of *S. pneumoniae* were generated by stepwise selection at increasing drug concentrations. First-step mutants exhibiting low-level resistance had no detectable changes in their topoisomerases QRDR, suggesting altered permeation or another novel resistance mechanism. Second step mutants exhibited an alteration in ParC at Ser79 to Tyr or Ser79 to Phe or at Ala84 to Thr. Third and fourth step mutants displaying high-level ciprofloxacin resistance were found to have, in addition to ParC alteration, a change in GyrA at residues equivalent to *E. coli* GyrA resistance hot spots Ser83 and Asp87 or in GyrB at Asp435 to Asn, equivalent to *E. coli* Asp426. ParC mutations preceded those in GyrA, suggesting that topoisomerase IV is the primary topoisomerase target and gyrase the secondary target for ciprofloxacin in *S. pneumoniae*. Additionally, it has been shown that in *S. pneumoniae* different quinolones can have different primary targets. The targeting of DNA gyrase by sparfloxacin in *S. pneumoniae* but of topoisomerase IV by ciprofloxacin indicates that target preference can be altered by change in quinolone structure.

Decreased uptake

Deoxyribose nucleic acid gyrase and topoisomerase IV are both located in the cytoplasm of the bacterial cell. In order to reach their targets, fluoroquinolone antibiotics must traverse the cell envelope. In Gram-positive bacteria this consists of the cell wall and a single membrane, whereas in Gram-negative bacteria the fluoroquinolone must first cross the outer membrane. Changes in the cell envelope of Gram-negative bacteria, particularly in the outer membrane, have been associated with decreased uptake and increased resistance to fluoroquinolones.[23–26] Some of these changes may be due to the effect of quinolones or *gyrA* mutations, or both, on differential expression of outer membrane proteins, because it has been shown that *gyrA*-mediated changes in supercoiling of DNA can affect the expression of porin genes. In contrast, decreased uptake has not been demonstrated to be a mechanism of resistance in Gram-positive bacteria.

Active efflux

Increased efflux as a mechanism of fluoroquinolone resistance has been reported in fluoroquinolone-resistant *Staphylococcus aureus*. The *norA* gene encodes the multidrug efflux pump NorA.[28] The NorA protein has a hydropathic amino acid profile consistent with a location in the cytoplasmic membrane and it exhibits a low level of fluoroquinolone efflux, with a preference for hydrophilic fluoroquinolones. Efflux is an active process and can be inhibited by protonophores. NorA-mediated fluoroquinolone resistance is due to overexpression of the wild-type gene *norA*. In *P. aeruginosa*, resistance to fluoroquinolones as well as to a number of other antimicrobial agents has often been associated with decreased accumulation and increased expression of outer membrane proteins, often with concomitant increase in cytoplasmic membrane proteins. Resistance is due to overexpression of one or more efflux systems (i.e. OprK) capable of removing fluoroquinolones and other antibiotic compounds. *Escherichia coli* has also been shown to possess efflux systems, notably EmrAB and AcrAB.[24]

MAR operon

Escherichia coli and a number of other organisms possess mechanisms that provide intrinsic protection against a wide range of chemically unrelated toxic substances, including quinolone antibiotics. Multiple antibiotic resistance (MAR) in *E. coli* has been shown to be the result of mutations in the *mar* locus of the *E. coli* chromosome. A homolog of the *mar* locus exists in other members of the Enterobacteriaceae as well as in other bacteria. In *E. coli*, the *mar* locus consists of two divergently expressed operons, marC and marRAB, both of which are required for full expression of the MAR phenotype. Expression of the MAR phenotype, whether by induction or mutation, protects the cells from fluoroquinolone killing at up to four times the MIC. This may be more clinically important than the relatively modest increases in MIC associated with MAR because cells that escape death would have the potential to mutate to higher levels of fluoroquinolone resistance.[23,24,29]

LOCATION OF THE TETRACYCLINE-RESISTANCE DETERMINANTS	
Plasmid	**Chromosome**
TetA–E	TetB (rare)
TetX	–
TetG, TetH	–
TetK	TetK
TetL	TetL (rare)
TetM (rare)	TetM
TetO	TetO
TetP	–
–	TetQ
TetS	–
–	OtrA–C

Table 189.5 Location of the tetracycline-resistance determinants. TetK can be associated with an integrated plasmid. Tet, tetracycline-resistance determinant; Otr, oxytetracycline-resistance determinant. Data from Roberts.[30]

RESISTANCE TO TETRACYCLINES

Tetracyclines probably penetrate bacterial cells by passive diffusion. Tetracycline acts by reducing the affinity of the A and P sites of the 30S ribosomal subunit for aminoacyl transfer RNA, resulting in the inhibition of protein synthesis.[13,23,30–33]

A growing number of bacterial species are acquiring resistance to the bacteriostatic activity of tetracycline. Until now, at least 16 tetracycline-resistance (Tet) determinants and three oxytetracycline-resistance (Otr) determinants, first found in oxytetracyline-producing *Streptomyces* spp., have been described and characterized, with new Tet determinants being identified continually. Of these determinants, at least 13 are frequently associated with plasmids, whereas others are on the chromosome (Table 189.5). Resistance to tetracyclines is primarily due to acquisition of Tet determinants rather than to mutation of existing chromosomal genes.

The two widespread mechanisms of bacterial resistance do not destroy tetracycline: one is mediated by energy-dependent efflux pumps; and the other involves an elongation-factor G-like protein that confers ribosome protection. Both mechanisms are widespread among Gram-negative and Gram-positive bacteria (Tables 189.6 and 189.7). Oxidative destruction of tetracycline has been found in a few species. Nevertheless, the enzymatic inactivation of the antibiotic is not thought to be important in nature. The classification of Tet determinants according to their mechanism of resistance is shown in Table 189.8.

Reduced intracellular concentration of tetracycline

Because the ribosome is the target, antibiotic activity of tetracycline depends on the presence of the drug in the cytoplasm. A reduced tetracycline concentration in the cytoplasm can be achieved by two means:[13,23,30–33]

- the permeability of the cell envelope may be lowered; or
- tetracycline may be pumped out of the cytoplasm in an energy-dependent fashion.

Bacteria differ in their cell wall composition, causing differences in permeability and hence insensitivity to antibiotics. The peptidogly-

DISTRIBUTION OF TETRACYCLINE-RESISTANCE DETERMINANTS AMONG GRAM-NEGATIVE BACTERIA			
Efflux		Ribosomal protection and/or efflux	
Genus	**Tet determinant**	**Genus**	**Tet determinant**
Actinobacillus	TetB	*Bacteroides* (anaerobic spp.)	TetM, Q, X
Aeromonas	TetA, B, D, E	*Campylobacter*	TetO
Citrobacter	TetA, B, C, D	*Eikenella*	TetM
Edwardsiella	TetA, D	*Fusobacterium* (anaerobic spp.)	TetM
Enterobacter	TetB, C, D	*Haemophilus*	TetB, M
Escherichia	TetA, B, C, D, E	*Kingella*	TetM
Klebsiella	TetA, D	*Neisseria*	TetM
Moraxella	TetB	*Prevotella* (anaerobic spp.)	TetQ
Pasteurella	TetB, D, H	*Veillonella* (anaerobic spp.)	TetM
Plesiomonas	TetA, B, D		
Proteus	TetA, B, C		
Pseudomonas	TetA, C		
Salmonella	TetA, B, C, D, E		
Serratia	TetA, B, C		
Shigella	TetA, B, C, D		
Vibrio	TetA, B, C, D, E, G		
Yersinia	TetB		

Table 189.6 Distribution of tetracycline-resistance determinants among Gram-negative bacteria. Ribosomal-protection encoding genes have not yet been found in enteric genera, and when these genes are cloned into *Escherichia coli* the level of resistance to tetracycline conferred is relatively low. Tet, tetracycline-resistance determinant. Data from Roberts.[30]

can layer surrounding most Gram-positive bacteria does not reduce cytoplasmic accumulation of low molecular weight antibiotics such as tetracycline. In contrast, the outer membrane of Gram-negative bacteria is an effective permeability barrier for hydrophobic compounds. The effects of permeability barriers are usually supported by additional resistance mechanisms to achieve high-level resistance. Energy-dependent efflux of tetracycline causes high-level resistance in bacteria by itself. Two different types of efflux pumps are involved in tetracycline resistance: multidrug-resistance pumps and tetracycline-specific transporters. A multidrug-resistance pump belonging to the Acr family is responsible for the reduced tetracycline accumulation in *P. aeruginosa*. Furthermore, *E. coli* has a chromosomal multidrug resistance efflux system that is associated with the *mar* locus. Multidrug efflux pumps transport their substrate straight out of the cell into the surrounding medium. In contrast to the broad substrate range of multidrug transporters, many of the efflux pumps identified in Gram-positive and Gram-negative bacteria specifically transport tetracycline (see Table 189.8). The efflux proteins exchange a proton for a tetracycline–cation complex and are antiporter systems. Efflux determinants from Gram-negative bacteria (TetA–E, TetG–H) share a common genetic organization, which is different from the one in Gram-positive bacteria. Both Gram-negative and Gram-positive contain a structural and a repressor gene that are expressed in opposite directions from overlapping operator regions. The Gram-positive *tetK* and *tetL* genes encoding tetracycline-efflux proteins are regulated by mRNA attenuation in a similar way to that described for Gram-positive *erm* genes encoding rRNA methylase and *cat* genes encoding chloramphenical acetyltransferases.

Tetracycline-specific exporters pump their substrate into the periplasm and not across the outer membrane, as found for the multidrug efflux pumps.

Protection of the ribosome

Protection of the ribosome from the action of tetracycline as a mechanism of tetracycline resistance was discovered in streptococci. Tetracycline resistance can result from production of a protein that interacts with the ribosome such that protein synthesis is unaffected by the presence of the antibiotic. To date, six classes of Tet determinants that confer tetracycline resistance on the level of protein synthesis have been identified (see Table 189.8). Most of the work on the mechanism of ribosomal protection has been done on TetM. The ribosomal protection proteins encoded by the other classes have an amino acid sequence similarity of at least 40% to TetM. Therefore, the mechanism of action may be similar for all ribosomal protection proteins. TetM ribosomal protection protein resembles elongation factors (EFs) in three properties:

- it has amino acid sequence similarity to EF-G (which translocates the peptidyl transfer RNA during protein synthesis) and EF-Tu;
- it has a ribosome-dependent guanosine triphosphatase activity; and
- it seems to confer resistance by reversible binding to the ribosome.

However, to date, the biochemical basis of tetracycline resistance mediated by TetM remains unclear. One possibility is that TetM stabilizes the ribosome–transfer RNA interaction in the presence of tetracycline.[13,23,30–33]

RESISTANCE TO CHLORAMPHENICOL

Chloramphenicol is a bacteriostatic antibiotic that binds to the 50S ribosomal subunit and inhibits the peptidyltransferase step in protein synthesis. Resistance to chloramphenicol is mostly due to inactivation of the antibiotic by a chloramphenicol acetyltransferase (CAT) enzyme that acetylates the antibiotic. Chloramphenicol resistance most commonly results from the acquisition of plasmids that encode CAT, but in certain Gram-negative bacteria decreased outer membrane permeability can confer resistance to chloramphenicol and structurally unrelated compounds.[13,23]

Enzyme inactivation

Chloramphenicol contains two hydroxyl groups that are acetylated in a reaction catalyzed by CAT. Monoacetylated and diacetylated derivatives are unable to bind to the 50S ribosomal subunit to inhibit prokaryotic peptidyltransferase. Expression of the *cat* genes in *Staphylococcus aureus*, *Streptococcus pneumoniae* and *Enterococcus faecalis* is typically inducible, and expression appears to be regulated by translational attenuation in a similar manner to the *erm* genes

DISTRIBUTION OF TETRACYCLINE-RESISTANCE DETERMINANTS AMONG GRAM-POSITIVE BACTERIA	
Genus	**Tet determinant**
Actinomyces	TetL
Aerococcus	TetM, O
Bacillus	TetK, L
Clostridium (anaerobic spp.)	TetK, L, M, P
Corynebacterium	TetM
Enterococcus	TetK, L, M, O
Eubacterium	TetK, M
Gardnerella	TetM
Gernella	TetM
Lactobacillus	TetO
Listeria	TetK, L, M, S
Mobiluncus (anaerobic spp.)	TetO
Mycobacterium (acid-fast bacteria)	TetK, L, OtrA, B
Mycoplasma (cell-wall-free bacteria with a Gram-positive metabolism)	TetM
Peptostreptococcus (anaerobic spp.)	TetK, L, M, O
Staphylococcus	TetK, L, M, O
Streptococcus	TetK, L, M, O
Streptomyces (multicellular bacteria)	TetK, L, OtrA, B, C
Ureaplasma (cell-wall-free bacteria with a Gram-positive metabolism)	TetM

Table 189.7 Distribution of tetracycline-resistance determinants among Gram-positive bacteria. Tet, tetracycline-resistance determinant; Otr, oxytetracycline-resistance determinant. Data from Roberts.[30]

CLASSIFICATION OF TETRACYCLINE-RESISTANCE DETERMINANTS ACCORDING TO THEIR MECHANISM OF RESISTANCE			
Efflux	**Ribosomal**	**Enzymatic**	**Unknown**
TetA–E	TetM	TetX	OtrC
TetG–H	TetO		
TetK	TetS		
TetL	TetQ		
TetA (P)	TetB (P)		
OtrB	OtrA		

Table 189.8 Classification of tetracycline-resistance determinants according to their mechanism of resistance. Tet, tetracycline-resistance determinant; Otr, oxytetracycline-resistance determinant. Data from Roberts.[30]

conferring resistance to macrolides. The *cat* gene is preceded by a nine-amino acid leader peptide, and the leader mRNA can form a stable stem-loop structure, which masks the ribosome binding site of the *cat* gene. Chloramphenicol appears to cause the ribosome to stall on the leader sequence, opening the stem-loop structure, thereby exposing the *cat* ribosome binding site and allowing *cat* expression. In Gram-negative bacteria, resistance to chloramphenicol is usually mediated by plasmid-mediated or transposon-mediated genes that are generally expressed constitutively.

Decreased permeability

In Gram-negative bacteria, resistance may also be due to chromosomal mutations that result in decreased outer membrane permeability. In *P. aeruginosa*, nonenzymatic chloramphenicol resistance is associated with the presence of the *clmA* gene. The ClmA protein appears to result in reduced expression of the outer membrane porins OmpA and OmpC and decreased chloramphenicol uptake. In *E. coli*, resistance to chloramphenicol and structurally unrelated antibiotics is part of the MAR phenotype.[34]

RESISTANCE TO GLYCOPEPTIDES

The glycopeptide antibiotics vancomycin and teicoplanin inhibit cell wall synthesis in Gram-positive bacteria by interacting with the terminal D-alanyl–D-alanine (D-Ala–D-Ala) group of the pentapeptide side-chains of peptidoglycan precursors. This interaction prevents the transglycosylation and transpeptidation reactions required for polymerization of peptidoglycan. Almost all bacteria synthesize peptidoglycan terminating in D-Ala–D-Ala, but the exclusion limits of the porin proteins of Gram-negative outer membranes prevent transport of the glycopeptides, and so only Gram-positive species are susceptible to clinically achievable concentrations of this class of antibiotics.

Glycopeptide resistance in enterococci

The vancomycin enterococci can be divided into six different phenotypic groups: A, B, C, D, E and H (Table 189.9).[13,23,35–40]

The origin of the *van* genes in enterococci is not known. The *vanA* gene has 52% amino acid sequence identity to the D-Ala–D-Ala ligase of *Salmonella* spp. and can complement a temperature-sensitive ligase mutant of *E. coli*. The D-Ala–D-Ala ligase is responsible for the production of the D-Ala–D-Ala dipeptide, which in Gram-positive bacteria is the target for glycopeptide antibiotics. The *vanB* and *vanC* genes are also both highly comparable in sequence to D-Ala ligases.

VanA resistance phenotype

The *vanA* gene is carried within a transposon together with several other genes, many but not all of which are required for the expression of resistance to vancomycin. The VanA product is a D-Ala–D-lactate (D-Lac) ligase. The *vanH* gene apparently encodes an enzyme that catalyzes the conversion of pyruvate to D-lactic acid. The VanA ligase uses this as a substrate to form the depsipeptide D-Ala–D-Lac, which is than incorporated into an alternative, vancomycin-resistant peptidoglycan precursor (Fig. 189.3). The VanX protein appears to cleave the D-Ala–D-Ala dipeptide, decreasing the amount of substrate that is available for the formation of the normal pentapeptide. The VanX protein does not hydrolyze the D-Ala–D-lactate pentapeptide or pentadepsipeptide.

Most vancomycin-resistant strains of enterococci also produce a carboxypeptidase. The structural gene for this carboxypeptidase in VanA-harboring strains is *vanY*. The carboxypeptidase may reduce the levels of the normal precursor so that the alternative precursor predominates. The *vanY* gene, however, is not required for resistance to cyclic glycopeptides. The inducible nature of glycopeptide resistance in most VanA enterococci suggests that expression is regulated at the genetic level. The genes *vanR* and *vanS* are involved in the regulation of VanA resistance, and the analysis of the amino acid sequences of the gene products has indicated similarity with two-component signal transducing regulatory systems that sense and respond to environmental stimuli. VanR seems to act as a transcriptional activator and seems to be stimulated by VanS. The phosphorylated VanR peptide acts on a promoter that lies between *vanS* and *vanH* and from which the *vanH*, *vanA* and *vanX* genes are cotranscribed. The environmental stimulus that triggers the initial phosphorylation of VanS has not been identified, but it is probably related to the presence of vancomycin and its interaction with the D-Ala–D-Ala target site, which inhibits transglycosylation. In addition to the high-level glycopeptide resistance mediated by the *vanH*, *vanA*, *vanX* and *vanY* genes, a second mechanism of resist-

Table 189.9 Resistance to enterococcal glycopeptides. Adapted from Shlaes and Rice.[35]

GLYCOPEPTIDE RESISTANCE IN ENTEROCOCCI						
Resistance	**Acquired**					**Intrinsic**
Phenotype	VanA	VanB	VanD	VanG	VanE	VanC
MIC (mg/l)						
Vancomycin	64–1000	4–1000	64–128	8–16	16	2–32
Teicoplanin	16–512	0.5–1	4–64	0.5	0.5	0.5–1
Expression	Inducible		Constitutive	?	Inducible	Constitutive Inducible
Location	Plasmid Chromosome		Chromosome	?	Chromosome	Chromosome
Modified target	D-Ala–D-Lac			D-Ala–D-Ser		

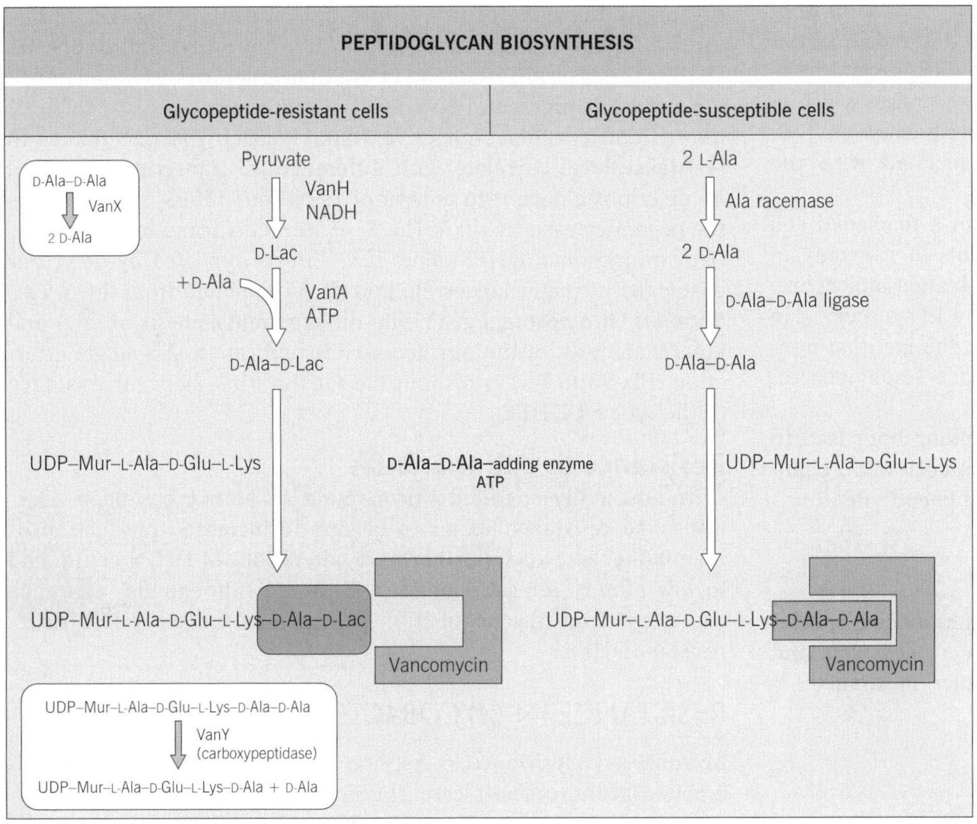

Fig. 189.3 Peptidoglycan biosynthesis. ATP, adenosine triphosphate, Lac, lactate; UDP, uridine diphosphate. Adapted from Shlaes and Rice.[35]

ance exists. The *vanZ* gene mediates resistance to teicoplanin while vancomycin MICs are unaffected. The mechanism by which the VanZ peptide confers this low-level teicoplanin resistance has yet to be established.

VanB and VanC resistance phenotypes

The drug resistance of VanB-harboring strains appears to be similar to that of VanA-harboring strains, except that the VanB-harboring strains originally described remained susceptible to teicoplanin. However, it has become clear that glycopeptide-resistant enterococci containing the *vanB* gene are phenotypically diverse, exhibiting a wide range of vancomycin MICs, including high-level resistance. In addition, the emergence of mutants that express *vanB* constitutively has been described. Resistance mediated by *vanB* may also be transferable, with the gene located either on the chromosome or on plasmids. The *vanC* resistance determinants are present on the chromosome in *Enterococcus casseliflavus* and *Enterococcus gallinarum* and are intrinsic characteristics of these species. VanC-harboring enterococci have low-level resistance to vancomycin and remain susceptible to teicoplanin. The pentapeptide that results from the action of the VanC ligase terminates in D-Ala–D-Ser. This substitution probably reduces vancomycin binding, albeit not to the same degree as the depsipeptide found in VanA and VanB enterococci. Insertional inactivation of *vanC* caused reversion to vancomycin susceptibility, suggesting the existence of a second chromosomal ligase that synthesizes vancomycin-susceptible precursors.

VanC-harboring strains with high-level resistance to glycopeptides as a result of the acquisition of the *vanA* gene cluster have also been isolated. The biochemical basis for the VanC phenotype displayed by most isolates of *E. casseliflavus* and *Enteroccocus flavescens* remains to be clarified in detail. Two genes, designed *vanC-2* and *vanC-3*, have been identified in these species. There is extensive similarity between the *vanC-2* or *vanC-3* gene and the *vanC* gene, now designated *vanC-1*, from *E. gallinarum*, although they do not cross-hybridize.

Glycopeptide resistance in staphylococci

Resistance to glycopeptides among staphylococci is phenotypically diverse[40] *S. aureus* strains resistant to vancomycin have been obtained in vitro either by selection of resistant mutants or by the conjugational transfer of *vanA* from enterococci.[41] Recently, the first vancomycin-resistant *S. aureus* isolate has been detected in the

USA. This strain contained the *vanA* gene, probably originating from a vancomycin-resistant *E. faecium* isolate. One of the enterococcal plasmids containing the *vanA* gene was found to be able to transfer to a strain of *S. aureus* and to be able to express resistance to vancomycin in an inducible fashion, and the resultant staphylococcal strain appears to have stably inherited the resistance.[41] Probably the same mechanism has appeared now in vivo. Teicoplanin-resistant derivatives of teicoplanin-susceptible *S. aureus* strains have also been obtained in vitro.

Recently, *S. aureus* isolates with reduced vancomycin susceptibility were described worldwide (GISA isolates – isolates with reduced susceptibility to glycopeptides).[40] As far as has been studied, all of these isolates contained thickened cell walls. Furthermore, all of them with the exception of the Illinois isolate showed a reduced cross-linking when compared with isogenic revertants. Interestingly, only some of them (Michigan, New Jersey, Duesseldorf) showed a reduction in D-glutamic acid amidation.[40] The data described so far on GISA strains seem to indicate that, depending on the strain studied, several independent mutations have been accumulated in these strains, which in various combinations lead to the observed resistance phenotype.

Probably the following mechanisms are associated with the appearance of GISA strain:[40]

- accelerated cell wall synthesis, which leads to a thickened cell wall capable of affinity trapping large amounts of vancomycin and shielding the membrane-associated lipid II target molecules;
- most probably caused by the accelerated cell wall synthesis – in addition, cross-linking will be reduced due to the fact that non-amidated precursors are poor substrates for the staphylococcal transpeptidation reaction; and
- since lower nonamidation and lower cross-linking both lead to even higher consumption of vancomycin per unit cell wall weight, they also contribute positively to the resistance phenotype.

Glycopeptide resistance in other Gram-positive species

Glycopeptide resistance is intrinsic in some Gram-positive species such as *Lactobacillus* spp., *Leuconostoc* spp., *Pedicoccus* spp. and *Erysipelothrix rhusiopathiae*. The exact resistance mechanism is these species has not yet been clarified.

RESISTANCE TO TRIMETHOPRIM AND SULFONAMIDES

Trimethoprim and sulfonamides are synthetic agents that affect the biosynthesis of tetrahydrofolic acid, an essential derivative used in amino acid and nucleotide synthesis.[13,23,42–44] Sulfonamides are analogs of *p*-aminobenzoic acid. They competitively inhibit the enzyme dihydropteroate synthase (DHPS), which catalyzes the condensation of dihydropteridine with *p*-aminobenzoic acid synthesis. Trimethoprim is an analog of dihydrofolic acid. It compeptitively inhibits the enzyme dihydrofolate reductase (DHFR). Dihydrofolate reductase catalyzes the reduction of dihydrofolic acid to tetrahydrofolic acid, the final step in tetrahydrofolic acid synthesis. Trimethoprim–sulfamethoxazole (co-trimoxazole) is a combination of trimethoprim with a sulfonamide.

Intrinsic resistance to trimethoprim and sulfonamides

Outer membrane impermeability results in trimethoprim and sulfonamide resistance in *P. aeruginosa*. Intrinsic resistance to trimethoprim in a number of species is due to host DHFR enzymes with low affinity for the drug. Folate auxotrophs such as *Enterococcus* spp. and *Lactobacillus* spp. that are able to use exogenous pre-formed folates exhibit reduced susceptibilities to sulfonamides and trimethoprim.

Resistance to trimethoprim

Both high- and low-level resistance has been reported in several species. In some cases, chromosomally encoded trimethoprim resistance may be due to

- overproduction of the host DHFR;
- mutations in the DHFR structural gene *folA*; or
- mutations that inactivate thymidylate synthetase, an enzyme that converts deoxyuridylate to thymidylate.

These *thy* mutants require exogenous thymine or thymidine for DNA synthesis and are thus resistant to folate pathway antagonists.

High-level resistance to trimethoprim in enterobacteria is almost always caused by the acquisition of DNA that specifies a trimethoprim-resistant DHFR with an altered active site. At least 11 modified DHFRs have been characterized in Gram-negative organisms. In staphylococci, trimethoprim resistance is encoded by the *dfrA* gene, which encodes a trimethoprim-resistant type S1 DHFR. The transposon encoded *dfrA* gene appears to be responsible for both high- and low-level trimethoprim resistance in *S. aureus* and coagulase-negative staphylococci. The differences in resistance level correlate with differences in transcription caused by deletions adjacent to a copy of IS*257* in Tn*4003*, which affects the promoter used by *dfrA*. The *S. epidermidis* trimethoprim-sensitive chromosomal DHFR gene *dfrC* differs from *dfrA* by only four base pairs, strongly suggesting that *dfrA* originated from the *S. epidermidis* chromosomal gene. Site-directed mutagenesis of *dfrA* and kinetic analyses of the purified DHFRs indicate that a single alteration (Phe98 to Tyr) is responsible for the trimethoprim resistance of the type S1 DHFR.

Resistance to sulfonamides

Chromosomally encoded sulfonamide resistance has been described and resistance seems to be due to increased production of *p*-aminobenzoic acid. Furthermore, alterations of DHPS could lead to low affinity for sulfonamides. Acquired sulfonamide resistance can result from the acquisition of plasmids that encode a drug-resistant DHPS.

RESISTANCE IN *MYCOBACTERIUM TUBERCULOSIS*

Mycobacterial resistance to first-line antimicrobial agents is a considerable concern to health care. The slow growth rate of *M. tuberculosis* and the serious consequences of inappropriate therapy make the study of the mechanisms of antibiotic resistance of particular importance. The main antibiotics for the treatment of mycobacterial infections are isoniazid and rifampin (rifampicin). Resistance was reported soon after the introduction of isoniazid in 1952. Isoniazid acts by inhibiting an oxygen-sensitive pathway in the mycolic acid biosynthesis of the cell wall. The mechanism of resistance appears to multifactorial, and genetic modifications in a number of genes may have an effect. These genes include the *katG* gene-encoded catalase, the isoniazid target encoding *inhA* gene, the *oxyR* and neighboring *aphC* genes and their intergenic region.[45]

The molecular basis of rifampin resistance is understood better. Rifampin interferes with RNA synthesis. At least eight amino acid substitutions in the rpoB subunit of RNA polymerase have been described as conferring resistance.[46]

MULTIPLE RESISTANCE

Bacteria are often resistant to more than one antimicrobial agent. Multiple resistance is conferred by three mechanisms:

- reduced permeability,
- active efflux, and
- multiple resistance genes.

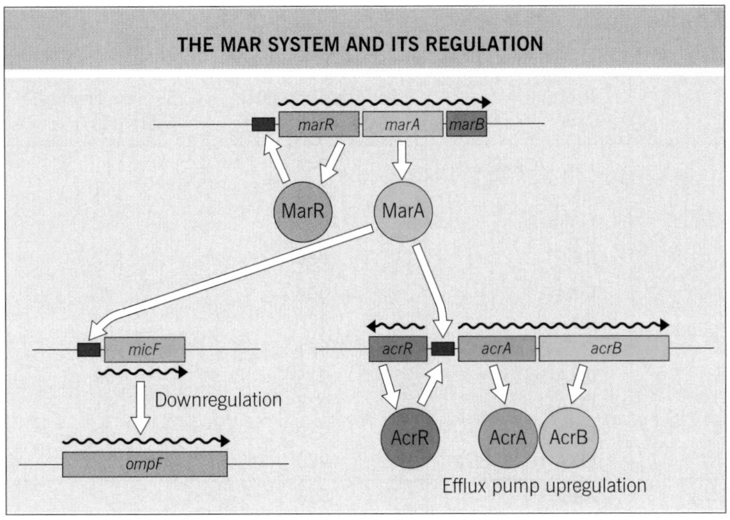

Fig. 189.4 The MAR system and its regulation.

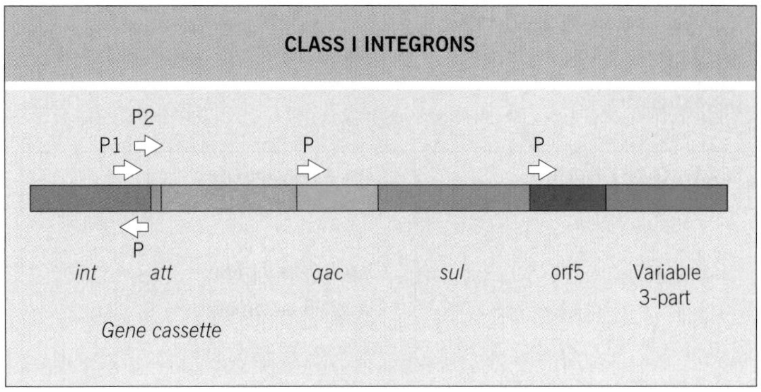

Fig. 189.5 Class I integrons. Open arrows point in the direction of transcription from each promotor site. orf, open reading frame.

Reduced permeability is generally caused by alteration in the cell wall of the bacterium, especially the reduced expression of porins. The best studied is the outer membrane protein (omp) ompF, from *E. coli.*

Multidrug resistance pumps may play an important role in antibiotic resistance. Several families of these efflux pumps have been described in both Gram-positive and Gram-negative bacteria. Some of these pumps not only recognize diverse classes of antibiotics, but also a number of disinfectants such as chlorhexidine.[47] In the so-called MAR system in *E. coli*, reduced uptake and active efflux are combined in a single regulatory system. The MAR system was discovered by Levy and coworkers, who observed that resistant mutants were obtained at a frequency of 10^{-7} when *E. coli* was plated on agar media containing either tetracycline or chloramphenicol. Usually, mutants obtained with one antibiotic were also resistant to the other, but cross-resistance to β-lactams, puromycin, rifampin and nalidixic acid was also observed. Genetic mapping studies revealed that a three-gene operon, containing the *marRAB*, was involved (Fig. 189.4).

Sequencing studies revealed that resistant mutants had either mutations in the putative operator–promoter region of the operon or in the *marR* gene. The MarR product acts as a negative regulator for the mar operon. The MarA product is required for resistance. The MarA product is supposed to act on at least two different promoter regions. The first is involved in the expression of OmpF protein. Expression of OmpF is regulated by the *micF* gene. Transcription of this gene leads to the production of an antisense RNA for the ompF mRNA. Stimulation of micF RNA production by the MarA product causes reduced translation of the OmpF mRNA owing to its blockage by the micF antisense RNA and thereby reduced permeability through OmpF. The MarA product also interacts with the acr operon. This operon encodes two subunits of an efflux pump. Inactivation of this efflux system results in hypersensitivity to a wide variety of antimicrobial agents. The expression of the acr operon appears to regulated by AcrR, the product of the third gene of this operon. MarA apparently interacts with the binding of AcrR to its operator, resulting in increased expression of the two subunits of the efflux pump. However, the expression of the pump is also increased by a variety of environmental stimuli, such as ethanol and high concentrations of salt, but these stimuli apparently do not operate through either MarA or AcrR. Despite the detailed molecular knowledge about this mechanism of multiple resistance, its clinical impact is not clear.[48]

Multiple resistance caused by the presence of a number of different resistance genes can originate from the sequential acquisition of mutations or resistance genes, but often these genes are transferred as complete units. These units are located either on transposons or multiresistance plasmids that have acquired these genes over time. An example of plasmid-borne multiple resistance comes from a study into eight strains of *Enterococcus*[49] that were resistant to chloramphenicol, erythromycin, minocycline and tetracycline. Genetic analysis showed that all these genes were transferred on a conjugative plasmid, except in the case of three strains. In these strains the chloramphenicol and erythromycin resistance was located either on a nonconjugative plasmid or on the chromosome.

Transposons, easily mobilizable genetic elements that range in size from a few kilobases to more than 150 kilobases, are an important source for the spread of antibiotic resistance. Numerous different transposons have been described and many of them carry one or more antibiotic resistance determinants. Resistance to any class of antimicrobial agent may be encoded on a transposon. Transposons may integrate either in plasmids or the bacterial chromosome and may be present in multiple copies, thereby enhancing their effectiveness in the expression of resistance. A number of transposons have been well studied. These include Tn*5*, Tn*7*, Tn*10* and Tn*21* from Gram-negative bacteria and Tn*554*, Tn*916* and Tn*4001* from Gram-positive bacteria.[50] Transposition may be very efficient and the spread of Tn*4001* described above is an example. Tn*916*, found in *E. faecalis*, was one of the first conjugative transposons discovered. It encodes resistance against tetracycline and chloramphenicol. Tn*916* is a member of a large family of related conjugative transposons, but other families have also been described. Conjugative transposons are not limited to Gram-positive bacteria; they are also present in Gram-negative bacteria. Tn*916* has also been found in *N. gonorrhoeae* for example. Conjugative transposons have a somewhat different mechanism of transfer from the more common transposons such as Tn*5* and Tn*10*, but they are well equipped for dissemination between species, although transfer is regulated. For some conjugative transposons, this transfer may be upregulated (by up to 10,000 times) by antibiotics, which enhances the dissemination of antibiotic resistance determinants. In addition, these conjugative transposons may mobilize co-resident plasmids, which also may carry antibiotic resistance determinants, resulting in the transfer of multiple antibiotic resistance.[51]

Integrons are a special group of genetic elements. The most common are class I integrons, but two other classes are known as well. The class I integrons are characterized by two conserved sequences (CSs). The 5′-CS contains the *int* gene, which encodes a protein homologous to other members of the integrase family. The 3′-CS consists of the *qacEΔ1*[52] and *sulI*[53] genes and an open reading frame, orf5.[54] The *qacEΔ1* and *sulI* genes define resistance against quaternary ammonium compounds and sulfonamide, respectively (Fig. 189.5). Integration of gene cassettes by the integrase takes places between the conserved segments. Cassettes can also be excised by the integrase and cassettes can exist as free circular DNA molecules. This process can also lead to the rearrangement of the

GENE CASSETTES					
Gene cassettes			**Protein**	**Length of cassette (base pairs)**	**59-base element (base pairs)**
Resistance to β-lactams	Class A β-lactamases	*blaP1*	PSE-1/CARB-2	1044	111
		blaP2		1044	111
		blaP3	CARB-4	>1023	>92
	Class B β-lactamase	bla_{IMP}	IMP-1	880	127
	Class D β-lactamases	*oxa1*	OXA-1	1004	90
		oxa2	OXA-2	876	70
		oxa3	OXA-3	>861	>56
		oxa5	OXA-5	915	106
		oxa7	OXA-7	874	65
		oxa9	OXA-9	957	69
		oxa10	OXA-10 (PSE-2)	920	111
Resistance to aminoglycosides	Aminoglycoside adenylyltransferases	*aadA1a*	AAD(3″)	856	60
		aadA1b	AAD(3″)	856	60
		aadA2	AAD(3″)	856	60
		aadB	AAD(2″)	591	60
	Aminoglycoside acetyltransferases	*aacA1*	AAC(6′)-Ia	>778	
		aacA4	AAC(6′)-Ib	637	70
		aacA (orfB)	AAC(6′)-Id	526	72
		aacA7	AAC(6′)-II	591	112
		aacA	AAC(6′)-IIa	628	60
		aacA	AAC(6′)-IIb	653	97
		aacC1	AAC(3)-Ia	577	109
		aacC	AAC(3)-Ib	>498	>34
Resistance to chloramphenicol	Chloramphenicol acetyltransferases	*catB2*	CATB2	739	72
		catB3	CATB3	715	60
		catB5	CATB5	>677	>25
	Chloramphenicol exporter	*cmlA*	CmlA	1549	70
Resistance to trimethoprim	Class A dihydrofolate reductases	*dfrA1*	DHFRIa	577	95
		dfrA5	DHFRV	568	87
		dfrA7	DHFRVII	617	134
		dfrA12	DHFRXII	584	90
		dfrA14	DHFRIb	>523	>43
	Class 8 dihydrofolate reductases	*dfrB1*	DHFRIIa	485	57
		dfrB2	DHFRIIb	384	57
		dfrB3	DHFRIIc	408	57
Resistance to streptothricin	Streptothricin acetyltransferase	*sat*	SAT-2	584	60
Resistance to antiseptics and disinfectants	Quaternary ammonium compound exporter	*qacE*	QacE	587	141
Unidentified orfs		orfA		501	69
		orfC		507	60
		orfD		320	60
		orfE		262	60
		orfF		320	60

Table 189.10 The first gene cassettes.

order of cassettes in an integron. Each gene cassette has an imperfect inverted repeat element. This so-called 59-base pair element, which may vary in length between 57 and 141 base pairs, is unique for each gene cassette.[55] At least 42 gene cassettes have been described, including genes defining resistance against β-lactam antibiotics, aminoglycosides, trimethoprim, chloramphenicol and antiseptics and disinfectants (Table 189.10).[56] Generally the cassettes do not have promoters, but transcription occurs from one of two promoter sequences present in the 5′-CS. Integrons are widespread in Enterobacteriaceae but are also found in pseudomonads. Isolates may carry more than one integron.[57] Remarkably, the 59-base pair elements show a close relationship with *Vibrio cholerae* repetitive sequences; these are 123–126 base pairs in length and there may be up to 100 copies. The role of these sequences is unknown, but if they are part of gene cassettes, then integration of gene cassettes may play a significant role in bacterial evolution.[55]

CONCLUSION

Worldwide antibiotic resistance is widespread and increasing. The best-known examples are MRSA, vancomycin-resistant enterococci, penicillin-resistant *Streptococcus pneumoniae* and ESBL-carrying Enterobacteriaceae. Studies into the molecular mechanisms of antimicrobial resistance help us to understand the problem and to monitor outbreaks, but other measures are required to quell the spread of resistance genes. Local, national and international antimicrobial surveillance studies are required to gain insight into trends in antimicrobial resistance on which empiric treatment of patients can be based. However, only the prudent use of antibiotics and infection prevention measures will limit or even prevent the spread of antibiotic resistance.

It is not only the use of antimicrobial agents for the treatment of humans that plays a role in the spread of resistance; their use for the treatment of animals also plays a role. The practice in animal husbandry of using antibiotics in subtherapeutic concentrations as growth enhancers is a particular cause for concern. This practice started in the 1950s. In the 1960s it became controversial and experts questioned the wisdom of adding antibiotics to feed owing to the emergence of multidrug-resistant Enterobacteriaceae. (In fact, the first multidrug-resistant Enterobactericeae had been observed in the 1950s.) In 1966 a multi-resistant *Salmonella* strain ingested via food caused an outbreak that resulted in six deaths. Many studies were issued, but on a political level little action has been taken and the controvesy continues today. An example is avoparcin, which gives rise to cross-resistance to vancomycin. Evidence was recently provided that transfer of vancomycin-resistant enterococci from animals to humans may be possible.[58] Although transfer of resistant strains from animals to humans has been demonstrated, it is often contended that strains of bacteria living in animals are not able to survive in humans because they are not well adapted. However, animal strains of at least some multiresistant strains are able to survive for weeks in humans. They may not cause disease directly, but they provide a reservoir of resistance determinants, which can spread easily between strains and species.[59]

Interestingly, in Europe the use of avoparcin has been high and the use of vancomycin in hospitals low, but the levels of vancomycin-resistant enterococci causing infections in patients are low. In the USA avoparcin was not used in feed and the amount of vancomycin used in hospitals was high and vancomycin-resistant enterococci are often isolated from patients. This suggests that the use of antibiotics in hospitals may pose a greater threat for the spread of resistance than use of subtherapeutic concentrations of antibiotics in feed.

Therefore, inappropriate use of antibiotics in both veterinary and medical practice contributes to the spread of antibiotic resistance, a situation that leads to potentially untreatable common infections.

REFERENCES

1. National Committee for Clinical Laboratory Standards. Performance standards for antimicrobial susceptibility testing. Supplement tables. Wayne, Pennsylvania: National Committee for Clinical Laboratory Standards; 1998:M100–S8.
2. Livermore DM. Beta-lactamases: quantity and resistance. Clin Microbiol Infect 1997;3(Suppl.4):10–19.
3. Bush K, Jacoby GA, Medeiros AA. A functional classification scheme for beta-lactamases and its correlation with molecular structure. Antimicrob Agents Chemother 1995;39:1211–33.
4. Ambler RP. The structure of beta-lactamases. Phil Trans R Soc Lond [Biol] 1980;289:321–31.
5. Jacoby G. Nomenclature of TEM beta-lactamases. J Antimicrob Chemother 1997;39:1–3.
6. Brakstad OG, Maeland JA. Mechanisms of methicillin resistance in staphylococci. Acta Path Microbiol Immunol Scand 1997;105:264–76.
7. Archer GL, Niemeyer DM. Origin and evolution of DNA associated with resistance to methicillin in staphylococci. Trends Microbiol 1994;2:343–7.
8. Dominguez MA, Linares J, Martin R. Molecular mechanisms of methicillin resistance in *Staphyloccus aureus*. Microbiologica 1997;13:301–8.
9. Chambers HF. Methicillin resistance in staphylococci: molecular and biochemical basis and clinical implications. Clin Microbiol Rev 1997;10:781–91.
10. Perlin MH, Lerner SA. Localization of an amikacin 3′-phosphotransferase in *Escherichia coli*. Antimicrob Agents Chemother 1981;17:537–43.
11. Thomson CJ, Gray GS. The nucleotide sequence of streptomycete aminoglycoside phosphotransferase gene and its relationship to phosphotransferases encoded by resistance plasmids. Proc Natl Acad Sci USA 1983;80:5190–4.
12. Trieu-Cuot P, Courvalin P. Evolution and transfer of aminoglycoside resistance genes under natural conditions. J Antimicrob Chemother 1986;18(Suppl.C):93–102.
13. Paulsen IT, Firth N, Skurray RA. Resistance to antimicrobial agents other than beta-lactams. In: Crossley B, Archer GL, eds. The staphylococci in human disease. New York: Churchill Livingstone; 1997:175–212.
14. Gaynes R, Groisman E, Nelson E, Casaban M, Lerner SA. Isolation, characterization, and cloning of a plasmid-borne gene encoding a phosphotransferase that confers high-level amikacin resistance in enteric bacilli. Antimicrob Agents Chemother 1988;32:1379–84.
15. Leclercq R, Courvalin P. Bacterial resistance to macrolide, lincosamide, and streptogramin antibiotics by target modification. Antimicrob Agents Chemother 1991;35:1267–72.
16. Cocito C, Di Giambattista M, Nyssen E, Vannuffel P. Inhibition of protein synthesis by streptogramins and related antibiotics. J Antimicrob Chemother 1997;39(Suppl.A):7–13.
17. Weisblum B. Erythromycin resistance by ribosome modification. Antimicrob Agents Chemother 1995;39:577–85.
18. Weisblum B. Insights into erythromycin action from studies of its activity as inducer of resistance. Antimicrob Agents Chemother 1995;39:797–805.
19. Fluit AC, Visser MR, Schmitz FJ. Molecular detection of antimicrobial resistance Clin Microbiol Rev 2001;14:836–71.
20. Sutcliffe J, Tait-Kamradt A, Wondrack L. *Streptococcus pneumoniae* and *Streptococcus pyogenes* resistant to macrolides but sensitive to clindamycin: a common resistance pattern mediated by an efflux system. Antimicrob Agents Chemother 1996;40:1817–24.
21. Tait-Kamradt A, Clancy J, Cronan M, *et al.* *mefE* is necessary for the erythromycin-resistant M phenotype in *Streptococcus pneumoniae*. Antimicrob Agents Chemother 1997;41:2251–5.
22. Jones RN, Cormican MG, Wanger A. Clindamycin resistance among erythromycin-resistant *Streptococcus pneumoniae*. Diagn Microbiol Infect Dis 1996;25:201–4.
23. Quintiliani R, Courvalin P. Mechanisms of resistance to antimicrobial agents. In: Murray PR, Baron EJ, Pfaller MA, Tenover FR, Yolken RH, eds. Manual of clinical microbiology. Washington: ASM Press; 1995:1308–26.
24. Everett MJ, Piddock LJV. Mechanisms of resistance to fluoroquinolones. In: Kuhlmann J, Dahlhoff A, Zeiler HJ, eds. Quinolone antibacterials. Berlin: Springer-Verlag; 1998:259–97.
25. Schmitz FJ, Higgins P, Meyer S, Fluit AC, Dalhoff A. Activity of quinolones against gram-positive cocci: mechanisms of drug action and bacterial resistance. Eur J Clin Microbiol Infect Dis 2002;21:647–59.
26. Nakamura S, Yoshida H, Bogaki M, Nakmuar M, Kojima T. Quinolone resistance mutations in DNA gyrase. In: Andoh T, Ikeda H, Oguro M, eds. Molecular biology of DNA topoisomerases and its application to chemotherapy. London: CRC Press; 1993:135–43.
27. Schmitz FJ, Jones ME, Hofmann B, *et al.* Characterization of *grlA, grlB, gyrA* and *gyrB* mutations in 116 unrelated isolates of *Staphylococcus aureus* in relation to minimal inhibitory concentrations of ciprofloxacin. Antimicrob Agents Chemother 1998;42:1249–52.
28. Kaatz GW, Seo SM, Ruble CA. Efflux-mediated fluoroquinolone resistance in *Staphylococcus aureus*. Antimicrob Agents Chemother 1993;37:1086–94.
29. Cohen SP, McMurry LM, Hooper DC, Wolfson JS, Levy SB. Cross-resistance to fluoroquinolones in multiple-antibiotic-resistant (Mar) *Escherichia coli* selected by tetracycline or chloramphenicol: decreased drug accumulation associated with membrane changes in addition to OmpF reduction. Antimicrob Agents Chemother 1989;33:1318–25.
30. Roberts MC. Epidemiology of tetracycline-resistance determinants. Trends Microbiol 1994;2:353–7.
31. Schnappinger D, Hillen W. Tetracyclines: antibiotic action, uptake, and resistance mechanisms. Arch Microbiol 1996;165:359–69.
32. Burdett V. tRNA modification activity is necessary for Tet(M)-mediated tetracycline resistance. J Bacteriol 1993;175:7209–15.
33. Speer BS, Shoemaker NB, Salyers AA. Bacterial resistance to tetracycline: mechanisms, transfer, and clinical significance. Clin Microbiol 1992;5:387–99.
34. McMurray LM, George AM, Levy SB. Active efflux of chloramphenicol in susceptible *Escherichia coli* strains and in multiple-antibiotic-resistant (Mar) mutants. Antimicrob Agents Chemother 1994;38:542–46.
35. Shlaes DM, Rice LB. Bacterial resistance to the cyclic glycopeptides. Trends Microbiol 1994;2:385–8.
36. Arthur M, Courvalin P. Genetics and mechanisms of glycopeptide resistance in enterococci. Antimicrob Agents Chemother 1993;37:1563–71
37. Bugg TDH, Wright GD, Dutka-Malen S, Arthur M, Courvalin P, Walsh CT. Molecular basis for vancomycin resistance in *Enterococcus faecium* BM 41147: biosynthesis of a depsipeptide peptidoglycan precursor by vancomycin resistance proteins VanH and VanA. Biochemistry 1991;30:10408–15.
38. Hayden MK, Trenholme GM, Schultz JE, Sahm DF. In vivo development of teicoplanin resistance in a VanB *Enterococcus faecium*. J Infect Dis 1993;167:1224–7.
39. Leclercq R, Dutka-Malen S, Brisson-Noël A, *et al.* Resistance of enterococci to aminoglycosides and glycopeptides. Clin Infect Dis 1992;15:495–501.
40. Geisel R, Schmitz FJ, Fluit AC, Labischinski H. Emergence, mechanism, and clinical implications of reduced glycopeptide susceptibility in

Staphylococcus aureus. Eur J Clin Microbiol Infect Dis 2001;20:685–97.
41. Noble WC, Virani Z, Cree RGA. Cotransfer of vancomycin and other resistance genes from *Enterococcus faecalis* NCTC 12201 to *Staphylococcus aureus.* FEMS Microbiol Lett 1992;93:195–8.
42. Amyes SGB, Towner KJ. Trimethoprim resistance; epidemiology and molecular aspects. J Med Microbiol 1990;31:1–19.
43. Hamilton-Miller JMT. Reversal of activity of trimethoprim against gram-positive cocci by thymidine, thymine, and folates. Antimicrob Agents Chemother 1988;22:35–9.
44. Radström P, Swedberg G, Sköld O. Genetic analysis of sulfonamide resistance and its dissemination in gram-negative bacteria illustrate new aspects of R plasmid evolution. Antimicrob Agents Chemother 1991;35:1840–8.
45. Drobniewski FA, Wilson SM. The rapid diagnosis of isoniazid and rifampicin resistance in *Mycobacterium tuberculosis* – a molecular story. J Med Microbiol 1998;47:189–96.
46. Telenti A, Honore N, Bernasconi C, *et al.* Genotypic assessment of isoniazid and rifampin resistance in *Mycobacterium tuberculosis*: a blind study at reference laboratory level. J Clin Microbiol 1997;35:719–23.
47. Lewis K, Hooper DC, Ouellette M. Multidrug resistance pumps provide broad defense. ASM News 1997;63:605–10.
48. Miller PF, Sulavik MC. Overlaps and parallels in the regulation of intrinsic multiple-antibiotic resistance in *Escherichia coli.* Mol Microbiol 1996;21:441–8.
49. Pepper K, Horaud T, LeBougunec C, De Cespedes G. Location of antibiotic resistance markers in clinical isolates of *Enterococcus faecalis* with similar antibiotypes. Antimicrob Agents Chemother 1987;31:1394–402.
50. Mobile DNA. Berg DE, Howe MM, eds. Washington DC: American Society for Microbiology; 1989.
51. Salyers AA, Shoemaker NB, Stevens AM, Li LY. Conjugative transposons: an unusual and diverse set of integrated gene transfer elements. Microbiol Rev 1985:679–90.
52. Paulsen IT, Littlejohn TG, Rådström P, Sköld O, Swedberg G, Skurray RA. The 3′ conserved segment of integrons contains a gene associated with multidrug resistance to antiseptics and disinfectants. Antimicrob Agents Chemother 1993;35:761–8.
53. Sundström L, Rådström P, Swedberg G, Sköld O. Site-specific recombination promotes linkage between trimethoprim and sulfonamide resistance genes. Sequence characterization of *dhfrV* and *sulI* and a recombination active locus on Tn*21*. Mol Gen Genet 1988;213:191–201.
54. Stokes HW, Hall RM. A novel family of potentially mobile DNA elements encoding site specific gene-integration functions: integrons. Mol Biol 1989;3:1669–83.
55. Recchia GD, Hall RM. Origins of the mobile gene cassettes found in integrons. Trends Microbiol 1997;5:389–94.
56. Recchia GD, Hall RM. Gene cassettes: a new class of mobile element. Microbiology 1995;141:3015–27.
57. Jones M, Peters E, Weersink A, Fluit A, Verhoef J. Widespread occurrence of integrons causing multiple resistance in bacteria. Lancet 1997;349:1742–3.
58. Das I, Fraise A, Wise R. Are glycopeptide-resistant enterococci in animals a threat to human beings? Lancet 1997;349:997–8.
59. Feinman SE. Antibiotics in animal feed-drug resistance revisited. ASM News 1998;64:24–30.

chapter 190

Antibiotic Prophylaxis in Surgery

Joseph S Solomkin

INTRODUCTION

The prevention of surgical site infection (SSI) remains a focus of attention because wound infections continue to be a major source of expense, morbidity and even death. The US Centers for Disease Control and Prevention (CDC) refers to postoperative wound infections as 'surgical site infection' and divides these into superficial (involving skin and subcutaneous tissue) and deep (involving the fascia and muscle) incisional infections, and organ/space infections.

A patient who develops a wound infection while hospitalized has an approximately 60% greater risk of being admitted to the intensive care unit, and an attributable extra hospital stay of 6.5 days, at an extra direct cost of $3000. Risk of re-admission within 30 days is five times more likely for infected patients, at a cost of more than $5000.[1,2]

The epidemiologic data testifying to the significance of SSI are overwhelming. Surgical site infections are the third most frequently reported nosocomial infection, accounting for 14–16% of nosocomial infections in hospitalized patients. Approximately 40% of nosocomial infections occurring among surgical patients are SSIs, two-thirds of which affect the incision and one-third involve organ/space infection. Three-quarters of deaths of surgical patients with SSI are attributed to that infection, nearly all of which are organ/space infections.[3]

Because of the importance of these infections following operation, considerable effort has been expended to identify other potentially controllable variables that influenced infection rates. A major review of this subject and an extensive list of recommendations for preoperative patient preparation and operating room environment has recently been published by the Hospital Infection Control Practices Advisory Committee (HICPAC) of the CDC.[4]

An early finding of surveillance research was that there were variations in infection rates by surgeon. In an extension of the Hawthorne effect, in which the act of studying a human process improves results, it was then shown that the existence of a wound surveillance system and the reporting of the results normalized surgeon-specific infection rates.[5] This information supported the development of hospital-based surgical wound surveillance programs as a quality monitoring and improvement activity.[6] The trend to more rapid hospital discharge has, however, significantly decreased the accuracy of these programs, which are dependent upon in-hospital examination of wounds and reporting, and no generally applicable technique has replaced it. Surgeon and patient questionnaires have been employed, as well as computerized screens for physician visits and antibiotic prescribing. None have been found as reliable as wound inspection.[7–10] So, we are now flying blind and an appreciation for the fundamental mechanisms involved in preventing wound infection gains in importance.

This chapter describes current notions of risk factors for SSIs and discusses problems relating to knowing what our infection rates really are. The chapter will then provide recommendations for practices and describe the data supporting these practices. Guidelines published by several expert groups have created a near uniform approach to antibiotic usage for prophylaxis. Nonetheless, it is important to note that administration of systemic anti-infectives is only part of a broad program of infection control involving adequate operating room ventilation, sterilization, barrier usage and delicate surgical technique.[11]

RISK FACTORS FOR SURGICAL SITE INFECTION

Information on appropriateness of antimicrobial prophylaxis is of considerable significance because of the cost of infection that might have been prevented had prophylaxis been given and, conversely, the cost of providing antimicrobial therapy to a very large number of patients if the yield is only the prevention of a relatively small number of infections or even the prevention of no infection. The costs of providing therapy extend far beyond the acquisition and administration charges. They include costs of treating adverse reactions and the more ominous potential cost of dealing in future times with drug-resistant bacteria. Therefore, enormous effort has been expended to identify factors that increase the risk of infection and would, at least potentially, suggest providing antimicrobial prophylaxis.

Whether surgical prophylaxis has any substantial impact on bacterial resistance patterns is unknown but unlikely. In comparison to the raw tonnage of antibiotics prescribed in the community for upper respiratory infections, the amount provided to surgical patients for prophylaxis is quite small. Furthermore, within the hospital, antimicrobial resistance is principally engendered in the intensive care units. The intensive care unit is home to patients at great risk of infection by virtue of acute and chronic disease and by the insertion of a range of monitoring and infusion catheters. These elements lower the inoculum needed to initiate infection and provide portals of entry.

HISTORICAL ASPECTS

Administration of antibiotics to decrease the incidence of postoperative wound infection is a surprisingly recent strategy. The investigational background for the use of anti-infectives for this purpose was developed only in the 1950s and 1960s, considerably later than the initial availability of anti-infectives.[12] In fact, early studies of anti-infective prophylaxis, performed in the 1950s, reported either no decrease in infection rates or even higher rates than control. These results are explained by the fact that anti-infectives were begun only in the postoperative period. During the late 1950s and 1960s, important developments were made to rationalize antimicrobial prophylaxis. The most fundamental was definition of the decisive period, the time following wound contamination that antibiotics would still reduce the incidence of infection.

WOUND CLASSIFICATION SYSTEMS FOR IDENTIFYING RISK OF INFECTION

It is assumed that at least three categories of variables serve as predictors of SSI risk:

- those that estimate the intrinsic degree of microbial contamination of the surgical site;
- those that measure the duration of the operation and other less easily quantifiable elements of the procedure; and
- those that serve as markers for host susceptibility.

In 1964, the National Research Council sponsored an examination of the efficacy of ultraviolet irradiation, and that provided the data to validate a wound classification scheme describing risk of infection in relation to the extent of wound contamination.[13] That document is a landmark in this area, and the classification scheme has remained useful to the present day. This classification is presented in Table 190.1. A clear connection between the contaminating flora at various surgical sites and subsequent infecting pathogens was established. This microbiologic correlation included the recognition of the role of anaerobes in postoperative wound infection and abscess formation.

Two subsequent CDC efforts, the SENIC project (Study of the Efficacy of Nosocomial Infection Control) and NNIS (National Nosocomial Infection Surveillance), sought to examine these other variables as predictors of infection.[3,14] These showed that even within the category of clean wounds, the SSI risk varied from 1.1 to 15.8% (SENIC) and from 1.0 to 5.4% (NNIS), depending on the presence of other risk factors.

The size of these studies is truly phenomenal. Information was collected on 58,498 patients undergoing operations in 1970 to develop a simple multivariate risk index. Analyzing 10 risk factors with stepwise multiple logistic regression techniques, they developed a model that combined information on four of the risk factors to predict a patient's probability of getting a wound infection. Information was then collected on another sample of 59,352 surgical patients seen in 1975–6 to validate the proposed index.

SURGICAL WOUND CLASSIFICATION

Class	Description	Definition
I	Clean	An uninfected operative wound in which no inflammation is encountered and the respiratory, alimentary, genital or uninfected urinary tract is not entered. In addition, clean wounds are primarily closed and, if necessary, drained with closed drainage. Operative incisional wounds that follow nonpenetrating (blunt) trauma should be included in this category if they meet the criteria
II	Clean–contaminated	An operative wound in which the respiratory, alimentary, genital or urinary tracts are entered under controlled conditions and without unusual contamination. Specifically, operations involving the biliary tract, appendix, vagina and oropharynx are included in this category, provided no evidence of infection or major break in technique is encountered
III	Contaminated	Open, fresh, accidental wounds. In addition, operations with major breaks in sterile technique (e.g. open cardiac massage) or gross spillage from the gastrointestinal tract, and incisions in which acute nonpurulent inflammation is encountered are included in this category
IV	Dirty–infected	Old traumatic wounds with retained devitalized tissue and those that involve existing clinical infection or perforated viscera This definition suggests that the organisms causing postoperative infection were present in the operative field before the operation

Table 190.1 Surgical wound classification.[13]

The variables that were significantly and independently associated with subsequent SSI included:

- an abdominal operation;
- an operation lasting over 2 hours,
- a surgical site with a wound classification of either contaminated or dirty/infected and
- an operation performed on a patient having at least three discharge diagnoses.

Each of these variables contributes one point when present, and the risk index varies from 0 to 4. This means that each variable has the same significance as any other. Using this index predicted SSIs about twice as well as relying on wound classification. With the simplified index, a subgroup, consisting of half the surgical patients, can be identified in whom 90% of the surgical wound infections will develop. By the inclusion of factors measuring the risk due to the patient's susceptibility as well as that due to the level of wound contamination, the simplified index predicts surgical wound infection risk about twice as well as the traditional classification of wound contamination.

The problem with this system is that it is not operation specific and depends on variables collected after the operation (at discharge). To further refine the risk scoring system, a second study was then performed through the NNIS System from 44 hospitals from January 1987 through December 1990.[14] A risk index was developed to predict a surgical patient's risk of acquiring a surgical wound infection. The risk index score, ranging from 0 to 3, is the number of risk factors present from among the following:

- a patient with an American Society of Anesthesiologists preoperative assessment score of 3, 4 or 5;
- an operation classified as contaminated or dirty-infected; and
- an operation lasting over T hours, where T depends upon the operative procedure being performed.

The surgical wound infection rates for patients with scores of 0, 1, 2 and 3 were 1.5, 2.9, 6.8 and 13.0, respectively. The risk index is a significantly better predictor of surgical wound infection risk than the traditional wound classification system and performs well across a broad range of operative procedures.

It is important to note that this system provides little insight into risk of infection in clean or clean–contaminated wounds, other than identifying a correlation with length of operation.

SURVEILLANCE TECHNIQUES FOR IDENTIFYING SURGICAL SITE INFECTIONS: WHAT YOU GET IS WHAT YOU LOOK FOR

Given the clinical and economic importance of SSIs, all hospitals are required to have a program to monitor the incidence of postoperative infections. The methods for monitoring such infections were developed at a point in time when most surgical procedures were occurring in the hospital and patients were generally hospitalized for the procedure and remained in hospital for several days post-operatively. One of the weak points, in fact, of the SENIC and NNIS data presented above is that they by and large relied on in-hospital patient monitoring. Identification and reporting schemes for infections occurring outside the hospital were not well developed or tested. This means that the available data primarily address major surgical procedures, primarily done for intra-abdominal or intrathoracic pathology, for which patients were confined in hospital.

It is known that approximately half of SSIs occur post-discharge, with most occurring within 21 days after operation.[10] Although SSIs occurring after hospital discharge cause substantial morbidity, their epidemiology is not well understood, and methods for routine post-discharge surveillance have not been validated. A post-discharge surveillance program including self-reporting of infections by patients and return of questionnaires by patients and surgeons is labor and resource intensive. A variety of techniques have been tested, including physician questionnaires, direct patient contacts and computer screens of pharmacy, outpatient, microbiologic and re-admission databases. None has been found superior to others, and it is likely that as more and more elements of patients' medical care are computerized, automated surveillance systems will become increasingly effective.

ACCEPTED INDICATIONS FOR ANTI-INFECTIVE PROPHYLAXIS

There is a wide consensus on specific procedures that warrant antimicrobial prophylaxis. Consensus statements by the Surgical Infection Society, the Infectious Diseases Society of America, the American Society of Hospital Pharmacists, the Canadian Infectious Diseases Society and the French Society of Anesthesia and Intensive Care all agree on a number of indications (Table 190.2).[15–19] There is also considerable agreement as to which procedures do not warrant prophylaxis.

Controlled trials of antimicrobial prophylaxis in minimally invasive procedures have recently been reported. In low risk laparoscopic cholecystectomy and arthroscopic surgery, routine prophylaxis is not indicated.[20] In contaminated laparoscopic procedures, such as high-risk cholecystectomy and bowel surgery, it is best to apply the standards for similar open procedures.

In many areas of antibiotic administration sufficient numbers of studies have been carried out to allow synthesis of the data.[21–25] While there is some skepticism regarding this process, termed meta-analysis, there is no doubt that it is useful in selected situations where the primary literature is of good quality, heterogeneity in the response to treatment is small and well-understood, and there is a specific, critical parameter of outcome. Prophylaxis lends itself well to this, in that much of the literature is of good quality, the response to therapy is uniform, and the outcome parameter (SSI) is a specific and well-defined event.

It is worthwhile to note that one benefit of meta-analysis is the identification of benefit early in the evolution of a practice concept, thereby sparing many patients either the extra risk that their procedure might carry were prophylaxis not given or the extra risk of an adverse event from receiving a medication that would not benefit them. This is perhaps best illustrated with regards to antibiotic prophylaxis for elective colon surgery.

PATHOGENS CAUSING SSIs AND ANTIMICROBIAL DRUGS OF CHOICE FOR PROPHYLAXIS

Procedure	Likely pathogen(s)	Drug/dosing	For history of anaphylactoid reactions
Clean procedures for which prophylaxis is accepted	*Staphylococcus aureus* and *Staphylococcus epidermidis*	Cefazolin 1g preoperatively	Clindamycin 600mg or vancomycin 1g
Head and neck procedures entering the oropharynx; esophageal procedures	Streptococci; oropharyngeal anaerobes (e.g. peptostreptococci)	Cefazolin 1g preoperatively	Clindamycin 600mg or vancomycin 1g
High-risk gastroduodenal and biliary	Enterobacteriaceae and streptococci	Cefazolin 1g preoperatively	Quinolone selected for low cost††
Placement of all grafts, prostheses or implants	*S. aureus*; coagulase-negative staphylococci	Cefazolin 1g preoperatively	Clindamycin 600mg or vancomycin 1g
Cardiac	*S. aureus*; coagulase-negative staphylococci	Cefazolin 1g preoperatively	Clindamycin 600mg or vancomycin 1g
Neurosurgery	*S. aureus*; coagulase-negative staphylococci	Cefazolin 1g preoperatively	Clindamycin 600mg or vancomycin 1g
Breast	*S. aureus*; coagulase-negative staphylococci	Cefazolin 1g preoperatively	Clindamycin 600mg or vancomycin 1g
Orthopedic – total joint replacement, closed fractures/use of nails, bone plates, other internal fixation devices, functional repair without implant/device, trauma	*S. aureus*; coagulase-negative staphylococci; Gram-negative bacilli	Cefazolin 1g q8h × 3	Gentamicin 2mg/kg + clindamycin 600mg q12h × 2
Noncardiac thoracic – thoracic (lobectomy, pneumonectomy, wedge resection, other noncardiac mediastinal procedures), closed tube thoracostomy	*S. aureus*; coagulase-negative staphylococci; *Streptococcus pneumoniae*; Gram-negative bacilli	Cefazolin 1g × 1	Clindamycin 600mg
Vascular	*S. aureus*; coagulase-negative staphylococci	Cefazolin 1g × 1	Clindamycin 600mg
Appendectomy*	Gram-negative bacilli; anaerobes	Cefazolin 1g + metronidazole 500mg q8h × 3 or cefotetan 1g × 1 or cefoxitin 1g × 4	Quinolone selected for low cost†† + metronidazole 500mg q12h × 2
Colorectal	Gram-negative bacilli; anaerobes	Cefazolin 1g + metronidazole 500mg preoperatively or cefotetan 1g preoperatively or cefoxitin 1g†	Quinolone selected for low cost†† + metronidazole 500mg preoperatively
Obstetric and gynecologic	Gram-negative bacilli; enterococci; group B streptococci; anaerobes	Cefazolin 1g preoperatively	Quinolone selected for low cost†† + metronidazole 500mg preoperatively
Urologic (may not be beneficial if urine is sterile)	Gram-negative bacilli	Cefazolin 1g preoperatively	Quinolone selected for low cost preoperatively††

* For nonperforated appendicitis. If perforated, treatment is therapeutic
† Re-dose if procedure lasts >4 hours
†† Ciprofloxacin, levofloxacin, gatifloxacin or moxifloxacin

Table 190.2 Pathogens causing surgical site infections and antimicrobial drugs of choice for prophylaxis.

CHOICE OF ANTI-INFECTIVES FOR PROPHYLAXIS

It is certainly not necessary to cover the entire spectrum of contaminants of a surgical wound. The anticipated pathogens from various operative sites are detailed in Table 190.2.

Little investigational work has been done on appropriate dosing. In general, doses of the selected agent that would be used for the treatment of established infection are recommended. The more important issue for prophylaxis concerns the need to maintain effective antibiotic levels throughout the procedure. This is typically accomplished by providing repetitive dosing for lengthy procedures. This is in part a function of the half-life of the agent selected, and is an additional argument in favor of agents such as cefazolin that have half-lives approaching 2 hours. A current recommendation is to re-dose the patient at intervals of twice the half-life of the agent provided. It is important to note that increasing the dose of an agent provides less benefit than shortening the dosing interval because drug clearance is logarithmic.

A large number of studies now document effective prophylaxis with no further dosing after the patient leaves the operating room.[26]

Gastroduodenal procedures

Prophylaxis is recommended for most gastrointestinal procedures. The density of organisms and proportion of anaerobic organisms progressively increase along the gastrointestinal tract, so the recommendation depends on the segment of gastrointestinal tract entered during the procedure. The intrinsic risk of infection associated with procedures entering the stomach, duodenum and proximal small bowel is quite low and does not support a routine recommendation for prophylaxis. However, any disease or therapeutic intervention that decreases gastric acidity causes a marked increase in the number of bacteria and the risk of wound infection. Therefore, previous use of antacids, histamine blockers or a proton pump inhibitor qualifies the patient for prophylaxis. Prophylaxis is also indicated for procedures treating upper gastrointestinal bleeding. Stasis also leads to an increase in bacterial counts, and so prophylaxis is warranted in procedures to correct obstruction. In addition, the intrinsic risk of infection in patients with morbid obesity and advanced malignancy is sufficiently high to warrant prophylaxis in these cases. Although the local flora is altered in these patients, cefazolin provides adequate prophylaxis and is the recommended agent.

Generally, elective surgery on the stomach or duodenum for ulcer disease is often not included in those procedures requiring prophylaxis. The highly acidic environment results in a very low endogeneous bacterial density, and rates of postoperative infection without prophylaxis are low. High-risk gastroduodenal procedures include operations for cancer, gastric ulcer, bleeding, obstruction and perforation, as well as operation in the presence of acid-reducing medical or surgical therapy. Prophylaxis is also recommended for gastric procedures for morbid obesity.

Colorectal procedures

Colorectal procedures have a very high intrinsic risk of infection and warrant a strong recommendation for prophylaxis. Several studies have demonstrated efficacy with rates of infection decreasing from over 50% to less than 9%. Antibiotics are directed at Gram-negative aerobes and anaerobic bacteria.

Mechanical cleansing

Commonly used colon preparation routines have changed substantially in that most patients self-administer these regimens at home and are admitted to hospital the morning of surgery. All prophylactic regimens begin with a mechanical bowel preparation, intended to greatly reduce the amount of feces present. Most commonly, polyethylene glycol (PEG) regimens are used. It is worth noting that the true value of these preparative activities is primarily to facilitate the operative procedure. Several trials have recently documented that mechanical cleansing does not alter wound infection rates if systemic antibiotic prophylaxis is used.

A current standard is a 4-liter PEG preparation. Bowel preparation with bisacodyl and 2 liters of PEG is reportedly more acceptable to patients than a 4-liter regimen and is equally effective in cleansing the colon.

It is important to be aware of the fluid losses that occur following PEG preparations. Compared with patients who receive inpatient preparation, patients receiving outpatient preparation require significantly more intraoperative fluid and colloid administration, greater amounts of fluid in the first 24 hours postoperatively and significantly more postoperative fluid challenges. Patients with multiple medical problems may not tolerate extensive fluid shifts; therefore, other preoperative arrangements, such as inpatient or outpatient intravenous fluid therapy, need to be considered to minimize complications that may outweigh potential cost savings.

Another alternative is 90ml of sodium phosphate (NaP) and bisacodyl. This is available in kit form. In one study comparing the two, patient tolerance to NaP was superior to PEG with less trouble drinking the preparation, less abdominal pain, less bloating and less fatigue. The preparations clear the colon equally well. Patients undergoing afternoon surgery may take their preparation early in the morning so that they have nothing by mouth for 6 hours before operation.

These regimens decrease fecal bulk but do not decrease the concentration of bacteria in the stool. In fact, the risk of infection with mechanical preparation alone is still 25–30%. The gastrointestinal side-effects of the osmotic mechanical preparations now used complicate the oral administration of antibiotics.

Antibiotics

In the USA, it is common to use a regimen of erythromycin base and neomycin given at 1 p.m., 2 p.m. and 11 p.m. (1g of each drug per dose) the day before a colorectal procedure scheduled for 8 a.m. Times of administration are shifted according to the anticipated time of starting the procedure, with the first dose given 19 hours before operation. Metronidazole can be substituted for erythromycin. If this regimen is used, there is no advantage to also providing parenteral prophylaxis.

Outside the USA, however, oral nonabsorbable antibiotic preparation have largely been abandoned in favor of parenteral treatment. A major systematic review has recently been reported for colorectal prophylaxis.[27,28] This review examined trials published between 1984 and 1995, and some 147 trials were suitable for analysis. These included over 23,0000 patients and 70 different regimens were tested. The results confirmed that the use of antimicrobial prophylaxis is effective for the prevention of surgical wound infection after colorectal surgery. There was no significant difference in the rate of surgical wound infections between many different regimens. However, certain regimens were found to be inadequate. Inadequate regimens included metronidazole alone (which lacks activity again facultative and aerobic Gram-negative organisms), doxycycline alone, piperacillin alone (which lacks activity against anaerobes), and oral neomycin plus erythromycin on the day before operation. The addition of an effective parenteral agent reduced infection rates seen with neomycin–erythromycin to the same level as that seen with the parenteral agent alone. Several trials showed extra benefit of oral antibiotics if inadequate parenteral antibiotics such as metronidazole alone or piperacillin alone were employed. These authors found that a single dose administered immediately before the operation (or short-term use) is as effective as long-term postoperative antimicrobial prophylaxis.

This study also found no evidence to suggest that the new-generation cephalosporins are more effective than first-generation cephalosporins. Antibiotics selected for prophylaxis in colorectal surgery should be active against both aerobic and anaerobic bacteria. No additional benefit was observed in six trials that compared parenteral anti-infectives alone with parenteral plus topical.

Oral or topical application of antibiotics in addition to the parenteral administration of appropriate anti-infectives is of no benefit. Antibiotics selected for prophylaxis in colorectal surgery should be active against both aerobic and anaerobic bacteria. Administration should be timed to make sure that the tissue concentration of antibiotics around the wound area is sufficiently high when bacterial contamination occurs. Guidelines should be developed locally to achieve a more cost-effective use of antimicrobial prophylaxis in colorectal surgery.

Prophylaxis is also recommended for appendectomy. Although the intrinsic risk of infection is low for uncomplicated appendicitis, the preoperative status of the patient's appendix is typically not known. Cefotetan or cefoxitin are acceptable agents, although a high rate of *Bacteroides fragilis* resistance to cefotetan has recently been identified.[29]

Metronidazole combined with a quinolone is also an acceptable regimen. For uncomplicated appendicitis, coverage need not be extended to the postoperative period. Complicated appendicitis (e.g. with accompanying perforation or gangrene) is an indication for antibiotic therapy, thereby rendering any consideration of prophylaxis irrelevant.

Biliary tract procedures

The recommendations for antibiotic prophylaxis for procedures of the biliary tract depend on the presence of specific risk factors. In general, prophylaxis for elective open cholecystectomy (either open or laparoscopic) may be regarded as optional. Risk factors associated with an increased incidence of bacteria in bile and thus of increased risk for postoperative infection include age over 60 years, disease of the common duct, diagnosis of cholecystitis, presence of jaundice and previous history of biliary tract surgery. Only one factor is necessary to establish the patient as high risk. In most cases of symptomatic cholelithiasis meeting high-risk criteria, cefazolin is an acceptable agent. Agents with theoretically superior antimicrobial activity have not been shown to produce a lower postoperative infection rate.

Neurosurgical procedures

Studies evaluating the efficacy of antibiotic prophylaxis in neurosurgical procedures have shown variable results. Nonetheless, prophylaxis is currently recommended for craniotomy, laminectomy and shunt procedures. Coverage targets *Staphylococcus aureus* or *Staphylococcus epidermidis.*

Head and neck procedures

For procedures entailing entry into the oropharynx or esophagus, coverage of aerobic cocci is indicated. Prophylaxis has been shown to reduce the incidence of severe wound infection by approximately 50%. Either penicillin or cephalosporin-based prophylaxis is effective. Cefazolin is commonly used. Prophylaxis is not indicated for dentoalveolar procedures, although prophylaxis is warranted in immunocompromised patients undergoing these procedures.

General thoracic procedures

Prophylaxis is routinely used for nearly all thoracic procedures. Antimicrobial prophylaxis is particularly important when there is high likelihood of encountering high numbers of micro-organisms during the procedure. Pulmonary resection in cases of partial or complete obstruction of an airway is a procedure in which prophylaxis is clearly warranted. Likewise, prophylaxis is strongly recommended for procedures entailing entry into the esophagus. Although the range of micro-organisms encountered in thoracic procedures is extensive, most are sensitive to cefazolin, which is the recommended agent.

Cardiac procedures

Prophylaxis against *S. aureus* and S. *epidermidis* is indicated for patients undergoing cardiac procedures. Although the risk of infection is low, the morbidity of mediastinitis or a sternal wound infection is great. Numerous studies have evaluated antibiotic regimens based on penicillin, first-generation cephalosporins, second-generation cephalosporins or vancomycin. Cardiopulmonary bypass reduces the elimination of drugs, and so additional intraoperative doses typically are not necessary.

Antistaphylococcal penicillins and first-generation cephalosporins have traditionally been the prophylactic antibiotics of choice for patients undergoing cardiothoracic operations. Recently published studies have claimed improved outcomes with respect to postoperative wound infection when second-generation cephalosporins were used for prophylaxis.

A meta-analysis of placebo-controlled trials of cardiothoracic prophylaxis demonstrated a consistent benefit from the administration of antibiotic prophylaxis, with an approximate 5-fold reduction in wound infection rate.[22] The second-generation cephalosporins, cefamandole and cefuroxime, performed better than cefazolin, with an approximate 1.5-fold reduction in wound infection rate. Administration of prophylaxis beyond 48 hours was not associated with improved infectious outcomes.[22]

Obstetric and gynecologic procedures

Prophylaxis is indicated for cesarean section and abdominal and vaginal hysterectomy. Numerous clinical trials have demonstrated a reduction in risk of wound infection or endometritis by as much as 70% in patients undergoing cesarean section. For cesarean section, the antibiotic is administered immediately after the cord is clamped to avoid exposing the newborn to antibiotics. Despite the theoretic need to cover Gram-negative and anaerobic organisms, studies have not demonstrated a superior result with broad-spectrum antibiotics compared with cefazolin. Therefore, cefazolin is the recommended agent.

When 25 randomized controlled trials of antibiotic prophylaxis that used rigorous protocols were analyzed,[25] overall 21.1% (373 of 1768) of the patients who did not receive antibiotic prophylaxis had serious infections after abdominal hysterectomy. Among patients who received any antibiotics, 9.0% (166/1836) had serious postoperative infections. Cefazolin was evaluated in 615 patients. The differences in the prevalence of infection between women who received prophylaxis and women who did not receive prophylaxis were statistically significant (any antibiotics, $p=0.00001$; cefazolin, $p=0.00021$) The authors concluded that preoperative antibiotics are highly effective in the prevention of serious infections associated with total abdominal hysterectomy, and that they should be used routinely. They also noted that the use of controls who receive no treatment is no longer justified in trials of antibiotic prophylaxis for total abdominal hysterectomy.

Urologic procedures

The range of potential urologic procedures and intrinsic risk of infection vary widely. In general, it is recommended that preoperative sterilization of the urine be achieved if clinically feasible. For procedures entailing the creation of urinary conduits, recommendations are similar to those for procedures pertaining to the specific segment of the intestinal tract being used for the conduit. Procedures not requiring entry into the intestinal tract and performed in the context of sterile urine are regarded as clean procedures. It should be recognized, however, that prophylaxis for specific urologic procedures has not been fully evaluated.

Orthopedic procedures

Antibiotic prophylaxis is clearly recommended for certain orthopedic procedures. These include the insertion of a prosthetic joint, ankle fusion, revision of a prosthetic joint, reduction of hip fractures, reduction of high-energy closed fractures and reduction of open fractures. Such procedures are associated with a risk of infection of 5–15%, but this is reduced to less than 3% by the use of prophylactic anti-biotics.[3] *Staphylococcus aureus* and *S. epidermidis* predominate in wound or joint infections. Cefazolin provides adequate coverage. The additional use of aminoglycosides and extension of coverage beyond the operative period is common but lacks supportive evidence.

Noncardiac vascular procedures

Available data support the recommendation for coverage of procedures using synthetic material, those requiring groin incisions and those affecting the aorta. Cefazolin is the recommended agent because most infections are caused by *S. aureus* or S. *epidermidis.* Prophylaxis is not recommended for patients undergoing carotid endarterectomy.

Anti-infective prophylaxis for clean procedures

The biggest controversy regarding antibiotic prophylaxis centers around prophylaxis for clean surgery. Prophylaxis has prevented postoperative wound infection after clean surgery in a majority of clinical trials with sufficient power to identify a 50% reduction in risk. The low control rates of infection means that very large studies must be carried out to see a significant effect; studies of more than 1000 procedures are needed to detect such reductions reliably.

The major study on this subject was a randomized, double-blind trial of 1218 patients undergoing herniorrhaphy or surgery involving the breast, including excision of a breast mass, mastectomy, reduction mammoplasty and axillary-node dissection.[30] The prophylactic regimen was a single dose of cefonicid (1g intravenously) administered approximately half an hour before surgery. The patients were followed up for 4–6 weeks after surgery.

The patients who received prophylaxis had 48% fewer probable or definite infections than those who did not. For patients undergoing a procedure involving the breast, infection occurred in 6.6% of the cefonicid recipients (20 of 303) and 12.2% of the placebo recipients (37 of 303); for those undergoing herniorrhaphy, infection occurred in 2.3% of the cefonicid recipients (7 of 301) and 4.2% of the placebo recipients (13 of 311). There were comparable reductions in the numbers of definite wound infections, wounds that drained pus and those infected with *S. aureus*. There were comparable reductions in the need for postoperative antibiotic therapy, nonroutine visits to a physician for problems involving wound healing, incision and drainage procedures, and re-admission because of problems with wound healing.

An observational study was then carried out on the effects of antibiotic prophylaxis on definite wound infections:[31] 3202 patients undergoing herniorrhaphy or selected breast surgery procedures were identified preoperatively and monitored for 4 or more weeks; 34% of patients received prophylaxis at the discretion of the surgeon; 86 definite wound infections (2.7%) were identified. Prophylaxis recipients were at higher risk for infection, with a higher proportion of mastectomies, longer procedures and other factors. Patients who received prophylaxis experienced 41% fewer definite wound infections and 65% fewer definite wound infections requiring parenteral antibiotic therapy after adjustment for duration of surgery and type of procedure. Additional adjustment for age, body mass index, the presence of drains, diabetes and exposure to corticosteroids did not change the magnitude of this effect. The effect of prophylaxis was similar for all procedures studied.

The argument then is not whether such therapy lowers infection rates but rather whether it is worth the cost. Additionally, the control infection rate is so low that physicians will not be aware of a decreased infection rate unless very careful surveillance is performed, and then only for patients from several practices. Comparing one effective regimen with another, as has been done with colorectal surgical prophylaxis, is simply not going to happen. Effective regimens are effective against *S. aureus* and other pathogens that may be carried in the nares or on the skin. In addition, relatively long half-life in the serum and low cost are important considerations. Cefazolin is a good prophylaxis agent for many clean surgical procedures.

To justify the use of prophylaxis for clean procedures at a single institution, an accurate assessment of infection rates must be available. This requires a considered effort at post-discharge follow-up. When these data are available, the risk/benefit ratio can be more knowledgeably assessed. Without accurate information on infection rates by procedure, known risk factors described above may serve as guides. Extremes of age, poor nutritional status, diabetes and obesity are recognized as significant additional risk factors.

The use of systemic prophylaxis for hernia repairs entailing the insertion of mesh is considered desirable because the morbidity of infected mesh in the groin is substantial. However, no prospective trials demonstrate the effectiveness or necessity of this practice. Modified radical mastectomy and axillary node dissection also warrant prophylaxis because wounds near or in the axilla have an intrinsic risk of infection. If prophylaxis is desired or indicated for any of these procedures, cefazolin is the agent of choice.

Laparoscopic and thoracoscopic procedures

Specific data supporting a recommendation of antibiotic prophylaxis for laparoscopic or thoracoscopic procedures are lacking. Therefore, pending the availability of new data, recommendations for the same procedure performed using the 'open technique' should be followed.

REFERENCES

1. Jarvis WR. Selected aspects of the socioeconomic impact of nosocomial infections: morbidity, mortality, cost, and prevention [see comments]. Infect Control Hosp Epidemiol 1996;17:552–7.
2. Kirkland KB, Briggs JP, Trivette SL, Wilkinson WE, Sexton DJ. The impact of surgical-site infections in the 1990s: attributable mortality, excess length of hospitalization, and extra costs [see comments]. Infect Control Hosp Epidemiol 1999;20:725–30.
3. Horan TC, Culver DH, Gaynes RP, Jarvis WR, Edwards JR, Reid CR. Nosocomial infections in surgical patients in the United States, January 1986–June 1992. National Nosocomial Infections Surveillance (NNIS) System. Infect Control Hosp Epidemiol 1993;14:73–80.
4. Mangram AJ, Horan TC, Pearson ML, Silver LC, Jarvis WR. Guideline for prevention of surgical site infection, 1999. Centers for Disease Control and Prevention (CDC) Hospital Infection Control Practices Advisory Committee. Am J Infect Control 1999;27:97–132.
5. Cruse PJ, Foord R. The epidemiology of wound infection. A 10-year prospective study of 62,939 wounds. Surg Clin North Am 1980;60:27–40.
6. Olson M, O'Connor M, Schwartz ML. Surgical wound infections. A 5-year prospective study of 20,193 wounds at the Minneapolis VA Medical Center. Ann Surg 1984;199:253–9.
7. Byrne DJ, Lynch W, Napier A, Davey P, Malek M, Cuschieri A. Wound infection rates: the

importance of definition and post-discharge wound surveillance. J Hosp Infect 1994;26:37–43.
8. Reimer K, Gleed C, Nicolle LE. The impact of postdischarge infection on surgical wound infection rates. Infect Control. 1987;8:237–40.
9. Ferraz EM, Ferraz AA, Coelho HS, *et al.* Postdischarge surveillance for nosocomial wound infection: does judicious monitoring find cases? Am J Infect Control 1995;23:290–4.
10. Fields CL. Outcomes of a postdischarge surveillance system for surgical site infections at a Midwestern regional referral center hospital. Am J Infect Control 1999;27:158–64.
11. Mangram AJ, Horan TC, Pearson ML, Silver LC, Jarvis WR. Guideline for prevention of surgical site infection, 1999. Hospital Infection Control Practices Advisory Committee [see comments]. Infect Control Hosp Epidemiol 1999;20:250–78.
12. Altemeier WA. Control of wound infection. J R Coll Surg Edinb 1966;11:271–82.
13. Ad Hoc Committee of the Committee on Trauma, Division of Medical Sciences National Academy of Science – National Research Council. Postoperative wound infections: the influence of ultraviolet irradiation of the operating room and of various other factors. Ann Surg 2000;160(Suppl.2):1–192.
14. Culver DH, Horan TC, Gaynes RP, *et al.* Surgical wound infection rates by wound class, operative procedure, and patient risk index. National Nosocomial Infections Surveillance System. Am J Med 1991;91:152S–7S.
15. Anonymous. ASHP therapeutic guidelines on antimicrobial prophylaxis in surgery. American Society of Health-System Pharmacists. Am J Health Syst Pharm 1999;56:1839–88.
16. Page CP, Bohnen JM, Fletcher JR, McManus AT, Solomkin JS, Wittmann DH. Antimicrobial prophylaxis for surgical wounds. Guidelines for clinical care [published erratum appears in Arch Surg 1993;128(4):410]. Arch Surg 1993;128:79–88.
17. Waddell TK, Rotstein OD. Antimicrobial prophylaxis in surgery. Committee on Antimicrobial Agents, Canadian Infectious Disease Society [see comments]. CMAJ 1994;151:925–31.
18. Dellinger EP, Gross PA, Barrett TL, *et al.* Quality standard for antimicrobial prophylaxis in surgical procedures. Infectious Diseases Society of America. Clin Infect Dis 1994;18:422–7.
19. Anonymous. The French Society of Anesthesia and Resuscitation. Recommendations for the practice of antibiotic prophylaxis in surgery. Current status 1999. Chirurgie 1999;124:441–7.
20. McGuckin M, Shea JA, Schwartz JS. Infection and antimicrobial use in laparoscopic cholecystectomy. Infect Control Hosp Epidemiol 1999;20:624–6.
21. Fallon WFJ, Wears RL. Prophylactic antibiotics for the prevention of infectious complications including empyema following tube thoracostomy for trauma: results of meta-analysis. J Trauma 1992;33:110–6.
22. Kreter B, Woods M. Antibiotic prophylaxis for cardiothoracic operations. Meta-analysis of thirty years of clinical trials. J Thorac Cardiovasc Surg 1992;104:590–9.
23. Langley JM, LeBlanc JC, Drake J, Milner R. Efficacy of antimicrobial prophylaxis in placement of cerebrospinal fluid shunts: meta-analysis. Clin Infect Dis 1993;17:98–103.
24. Meijer WS, Schmitz PI, Jeekel J. Meta-analysis of randomized, controlled clinical trials of antibiotic prophylaxis in biliary tract surgery [see comments]. Br J Surg 1990;77:283–90.
25. Mittendorf R, Aronson MP, Berry RE, *et al.* Avoiding serious infections associated with abdominal hysterectomy: a meta-analysis of antibiotic prophylaxis [see comments]. Am J Obstet Gynecol 1993;169:1119–24.
26. McDonald M, Grabsch E, Marshall C, Forbes A. Single- versus multiple-dose antimicrobial prophylaxis for major surgery: a systematic review [see comments]. Aust NZ J Surg 1998;68:388–96.
27. Glenny AM, Song F. Antimicrobial prophylaxis in colorectal surgery. Qual Health Care 1999;8:132–6.
28. Song F, Glenny AM. Antimicrobial prophylaxis in colorectal surgery: a systematic review of randomized controlled trials [published erratum appears in Br J Surg 1999;86(2):280]. Br J Surg 1998;85:1232–41.
29. Snydman DR, Jacobus NV, McDermott LA, *et al.* National survey on the susceptibility of *Bacteroides fragilis* group: report and analysis of trends for 1997–2000. Clin Infect Dis 2002;35(Suppl.1):S126–34.
30. Platt R, Zaleznik DF, Hopkins CC, *et al.* Perioperative antibiotic prophylaxis for herniorrhaphy and breast surgery. N Engl J Med 1990;322:153–60.
31. Platt R, Zucker JR, Zaleznik DF, *et al.* Prophylaxis against wound infection following herniorrhaphy or breast surgery. J Infect Dis 1992;166:556–60.

chapter 191

Home Therapy with Antibiotics

Benjamin P Howden & M Lindsay Grayson

INTRODUCTION

Most antibiotics given at home are administered orally. However, over the past 20 years, home intravenous antimicrobial therapy has developed as an important component of health care delivery. Over a quarter of a million patients are treated in the USA annually in this manner.[1] The use of home intravenous antimicrobial therapy was first reported in 1974 for children who had cystic-fibrosis-associated pneumonia and subsequently for patients who had osteomyelitis.[2,3] In addition to the USA, home intravenous antimicrobial therapy is now a common treatment modality in many regions, including Europe and Australia.

This chapter focuses on the home antibiotic treatment of patients who, because of the serious nature of their infections, would otherwise require in-hospital therapy. The use of intravenous antimicrobial therapy outside the hospital has been termed outpatient parenteral antimicrobial therapy (OPAT) in the USA, and hospital-in-the-home (HITH) in some other parts of the world.[1,4] These programs are useful both for patients who have infections requiring prolonged intravenous antibiotic therapy (e.g. osteomyelitis or endocarditis) and for patients who have common infections such as cellulitis, in whom in-hospital admission may be avoided entirely. The potential advantages and disadvantages of OPAT are summarized in Table 191.1, but a crucial component for successful OPAT is that patients are clinically stable and have appropriate home circumstances. Although there have been very few randomized trials of OPAT, those that have been done, as well as the many published case series, have reported good treatment outcomes.[5,6]

MODELS FOR HOME INTRAVENOUS ANTIMICROBIAL THERAPY

The delivery of high-quality, safe home therapy is best achieved by an OPAT team consisting of physicians, nurses and pharmacists who use clearly delineated treatment protocols.[6,7] Physicians should be experienced in the treatment of infectious diseases and have a good understanding of antimicrobial pharmacokinetics to allow appropriate decisions regarding the selection and duration of therapy, as well as drug monitoring. Since nursing staff administer therapy, they have regular contact with the patient and carer(s) and are often the initial contact when problems arise. Outpatient parenteral antimicrobial therapy pharmacists assist in the choice and mode of therapy, drug supply and compounding.

Many OPAT units have an infusion center (generally located within a hospital or clinic) where patients can be medically reviewed and receive directly observed therapy. outpatient parenteral antimicrobial therapy can be administered either by a nurse visiting the patient at home, the patient receiving treatment in an infusion center, or patients (or their relatives) self-administering therapy. Self-administration requires a well-motivated patient and carer who are capable of being educated regarding safe drug administration. It can be particularly useful for patients requiring prolonged or multidose therapy, or for those who require repeated courses of intravenous therapy (e.g. patients who have cystic fibrosis). The keys to a successful OPAT program include:

- a well structured OPAT team;
- appropriate patient selection based on medical need and suitability for treatment at home;
- informed patient and carer consent;
- careful monitoring of patients for response to therapy and adverse events; and
- 24 hour access to OPAT staff, particularly for emergencies.

The decision to accept a patient for home intravenous antimicrobial therapy should be based on medical need and appropriateness and should not be driven by bureaucratic or economic factors.

TECHNOLOGY USED IN OUTPATIENT PARENTERAL ANTIMICROBIAL THERAPY

Recent advances in medical technology have allowed development of new venous access devices and drug delivery systems that have improved the safety of home intravenous antibiotic administration.

Venous access devices

The optimal choice of vascular access is generally based on a number of factors, including the proposed treatment duration, the medication to be infused and the type of delivery system to be used.

Peripherally inserted central catheters

Peripherally inserted central catheters (PICCs) are a convenient form of intravenous access for OPAT therapy. They are made of flexible silicone, are introduced into the cubital vein and advanced into the superior vena cava, and are easily held in position with an adhesive dressing. Advantages of PICCs include the fact that they can be inserted and removed in the outpatient setting, are very durable, can be kept patent with an infrequent saline flush and have a relatively low infection rate.[8] Because of their central positioning, they are suitable for administration of concentrated antibiotic solutions such as used in continuous-infusion dosing.

Peripheral intravenous cannulae

Peripheral intravenous cannulae are generally used for short-duration therapy, but to minimize the risk of phlebitis they should be changed every 2–3 days. Thus, nursing staff need to be skilled in cannula insertion.

Long-term central venous catheters

These catheters (e.g. Hickman's, Port-A-Cath) are occasionally used in patients who have few other options for intravenous access, or who require them for administration of parenteral nutrition or cancer chemotherapy. In-hospital admission and anesthesia are generally required for insertion; however, they have a low infection rate and provide effective access for patients who require prolonged or repeated intravenous therapy.

POTENTIAL ADVANTAGES AND DISADVANTAGES OF OPAT	
Potential advantages	**Potential disadvantages**
Patient at home with family Continue work, school Decreased nosocomial infections Fewer cannula-associated infections Improved utilization of hospital beds Patient sense of empowerment Reduced health care costs (possible)	Disruption to home environment Increased patient/family stress Non-adherence with therapy Misuse of intravenous access Decreased supervision Feeling of abandonment Inappropriate antibiotic selection Non-adherence to bed rest, leg elevation Potential for unnecessarily prolonged duration of OPAT because of less medical incentive to stop treatment

Table 191.1 Potential advantages and disadvantages of outpatient parenteral antimicrobial therapy. Adapted from Howden and Grayson.[6]

Drug delivery systems

Like the choice of intravenous access, the optimal OPAT drug delivery system is influenced by the agent to be delivered and the proposed treatment duration.[6,9]

Direct push

Intravenous injection over 5–10 minutes is useful for antibiotics such as cephalosporins and penicillins. Spring-loaded devices are available that can deliver an intravenous push using small (e.g. 10–20ml) syringes.

Gravity

Drug administration by gravity is usually used for agents that require dilution in larger volume solutions (e.g. 100–1000ml) before infusion, or where infusions require administration over an extended period of time (e.g. vancomycin, amphotericin B).

Controlled-rate infusion devices

A number of compact, battery-operated, computerized infusion pumps are available that can be programmed to deliver antibiotic by either continuous infusion or intermittent bolus. They can be readily carried in a small bag around the waist or neck, and allow the patient to continue with normal activities while receiving therapy. These pumps are generally expensive to purchase but are reusable and most models will alarm if the intravenous line becomes blocked or develops in-line air bubbles. Nonprogrammable continuous-infusion devices are also available that are either spring-loaded or elastomeric – in these the tension in either the spring or the elastomeric 'bladder' propel the infusion. Although these pumps are cheaper, they are generally not reusable and will not alarm if the infusion is interrupted. Both devices are ideal for the continuous infusion of antimicrobials that are stable in solution over a 24-hour period and that have optimal activity when stable high serum concentrations are maintained (e.g. antistaphylococcal penicillins).[10–12]

INTRAVENOUS ANTIBIOTIC REGIMENS

Although there may be a tendency for the practicalities of home antibiotic administration to influence the choice of antibiotic used (e.g. once-daily agents), the principles used for appropriate antibiotic prescribing should be similar to those applied to patients managed in hospital. Appropriate antimicrobial agent(s) include those with the narrowest antibacterial spectrum appropriate for the responsible pathogen, most practical dosing regimen and lowest purchase and delivery costs. Patient-specific factors are also important, such as avoiding aminoglycosides in patients who have significant renal impairment. Antibiotics that can be administered by continuous infusion or that have a long serum half-life (and therefore require infrequent dosing) are most appropriate for OPAT. Agents, such as ceftriaxone or glycopeptides, that are simple to use because they require only once-daily dosing but often have an antibacterial spectrum that is broader than necessary for many indications should be used only cautiously. Antibiotics that would be considered optimal for in-hospital use should, where possible, be used for OPAT, although in some cases these may require innovative delivery methods.

Beta-lactams

The clinical efficacy of β-lactams against many pathogens is related to the proportion of the dosing interval during which the serum drug concentrations are maintained above the minimum inhibitory concentration (MIC) of the infecting pathogen(s).[10] Thus, β-lactams with a short half-life (e.g. penicillin, ampicillin, antistaphylococcal penicillins) should either be dosed frequently (e.g. q4–6h, which is generally impractical for OPAT) or administered by continuous infusion. There is increasing experience with the successful use of continuous-infusion antistaphylococcal penicillins (e.g. flucloxacillin, oxacillin) and some cephalosporins (e.g. ceftazidime) for the treatment of a range of conditions, including osteomyelitis, endocarditis and pneumonia.[11–13] Limiting factors with continuous-infusion administration include the availability and cost of accurate drug delivery devices and the instability in solution of some agents (e.g. ampicillin) after compounding (Table 191.2).

Cephalosporins such as ceftriaxone, which have a sufficiently long serum half-life to allow once-daily dosing, can be extremely useful for OPAT. Similarly, recent studies in which oral probenecid was used to prolong the half-life of the first-generation cephalosporin cefazolin have established that this combination given once-daily is effective in the treatment of conditions such as cellulitis.[14,15]

Aminoglycosides

A number of clinical studies suggest that administration of aminoglycosides (e.g. 4–5mg/kg/d gentamicin) as a once-daily dose rather than as two or three divided doses is associated with similar efficacy and probably reduced toxicity as compared with multidosing regimens when treating Gram-negative infections.[23] Once-daily gentamicin is now the preferred regimen when treating infections such as pyelonephritis, cholangitis and moderate–severe Gram-negative pneumonia. However, data regarding the efficacy of once-daily aminoglycoside therapy is limited or lacking in some settings, including pregnancy, neonates, burns patients, cystic fibrosis and some cases of endocarditis; in these situations, the use of once-daily aminoglycosides may not be appropriate.

Glycopeptides

Glycopeptides (e.g. vancomycin, teicoplanin) are effective against many Gram-positive pathogens. Vancomycin generally needs to be administered twice daily over at least 1–2 hours, while teicoplanin, after initial loading, may be given rapidly once daily. Although glycopeptides have been used in OPAT because of their infrequent dosing requirements, they are usually only an appropriate choice when used to treat resistant bacteria such as methicillin-resistant *Staphylococcus aureus* (MRSA), or patients who are anaphylactic to β-lactams. The efficacy of teicoplanin in some situations has been questioned and the emergence of resistant pathogens such as vancomycin-resistant enterococci reinforce the view that glycopeptides should only be used when clearly indicated.[6]

OPAT TREATMENT REGIMENS, MONITORING AND POTENTIAL COMPLICATIONS					
Condition	**Intravenous regimen**	**Oral alternative available**	**Monitoring***	**Complications and side effects**	**Comments and references**
Cellulitis	**Recommended**: cefazolin 2g iv q12h *or* 2g q24h + probenecid 1g po q24h **Alternative**: ceftriaxone (1g iv q24h)	Yes†	Clinical response	Nausea and drug interactions a potential problem with probenecid	Cefazolin has narrower antimicrobial spectrum than ceftriaxone[14–17]
Osteomyelitis and septic arthritis (MSSA)	**Recommended**: antistaphylococcal penicillin‡ 8–12g/d by continuous infusion for 4–6 weeks **Alternative**: vancomycin 1g iv q12h for 4–6 weeks	Usually none	Clinical response Inflammatory markers Drug levels	Nausea, vomiting, liver dysfunction from antistapylococcal penicillin	Vancomycin generally reserved for patients who have β-lactam allergy[11,12]
Endocarditis (*viridans* streptococci, uncomplicated)§	**Recommended**: ceftriaxone 2g iv q24h for 4 weeks **Alternative**: ceftriaxone 2g iv q24h + gentamicin 3mg/kg q24h for 2 weeks *or* penicillin 8.4g/d by continuous infusion for 4 weeks	None	Clinical response Echocardiogram Gentamicin levels Audiometry Renal function	Cardiac decompensation Emboli Renal or vestibular damage from aminoglycosides	Most authorities recommend 2–3 doses of gentamicin per day for endocarditis Published reports regarding continuous infusion penicillin are limited, although this regimen is recommended by some authors[18–20]
Endocarditis (MSSA)	**Recommended**: antistaphylococcal penicillin‡ 8–12g/d by continuous infusion for 6 weeks	None	Clinical response Echocardiogram Drug levels	Nausea, vomiting, liver dysfunction from antistaphylococcal penicillin	Uncomplicated disease and in-hospital stabilization crucial prior to OPAT[11,12]
Pyelonephritis	**Recommended**: gentamicin 4–6mg/kg/d iv *or* ceftriaxone 1g iv q24h	Yes†	Clinical response Renal function Aminoglycoside levels Urine microscopy and culture	Renal or vestibular damage from aminoglycosides	Complete 14 days therapy with oral agents Exclude prostatitis
Pneumonia (moderate severity – pneumonia severity index III)	**Recommended**: ceftriaxone 1g iv q24h	Yes†	Clinical response Chest radiography	Respiratory failure	Careful patient selection[7,21]
Cystic fibrosis (infective exacerbation)	**Recommended**: cefepime 2g iv q12h + tobramycin 4–6mg/kg q24h iv	None	Clinical response Chest radiography		Treatment guided by results of sputum culture
Meningitis	**Recommended**: ceftriaxone (2g iv q24h–q12h)	None	Clinical response	Seizures	Tice *et al.*[22]
Cytomegalovirus (CMV) disease (induction therapy)	**Recommended**: ganciclovir 5mg/kg iv q12h for 2–3 weeks	Yes†	Clinical response CMV antigenemia or viral load	Neutropenia	May follow with long-term suppressive therapy
Invasive fungal infection (e.g. cryptococcal meningitis)	**Recommended**: amphotericin B 0.6–1.5mg/kg daily or 3 times per week	Yes†	Clinical response Cerebrospinal fluid glucose, antigen titer Renal function, electrolytes	Renal impairment Hypokalemia Nausea, chills	

* Generally, all patients receiving OPAT should have routine hematology and biochemistry monitored weekly.
† See Table 191.3.
‡ Includes nafcillin, oxacillin, flucloxacillin.
§ Native valve, no complications, penicillin MIC of organism <0.1mg/ml.
MSSA, methicillin-susceptible *Staphylococcus aureus*

Table 191.2 Outpatient parenteral antimicrobial therapy treatment regimens, monitoring and potential complications. Adapted from Howden and Grayson.[6]

Antiviral agents

Ganciclovir is effective for both acute treatment and long-term suppression of serious cytomegalovirus disease and is administered once or twice daily. Such regimens are suitable for OPAT administration, although the availability of oral ganciclovir and the recent availability of the highly bioavailable valganciclovir have reduced the need for long-term intravenous suppressive therapy and may avoid the need for intravenous induction therapy in some patients.[24] Other intravenous antiviral agents (e.g. foscarnet) may occasionally be used in OPAT.

INDICATIONS FOR HOME INTRAVENOUS ANTIMICROBIAL THERAPY

A wide variety of infections can be safely and conveniently treated with OPAT, should such treatment be appropriate (see Table 191.2).[4,6,25] Although this latter point may seem rather obvious, there is a growing body of data to support the use of some highly bioavailable oral antibiotic regimens for conditions such as osteomyelitis and pyelonephritis – conditions that previously were thought to require intensive parenteral therapy (Table 191.3). Infections that are relatively common and generally require only brief OPAT include cellulitis, pyelonephritis, pneumonia, bacterial meningitis and infective exacerbations associated with chronic lung disease. Such patients do not generally need long-term venous access and ideally can be treated with agents that require only infrequent dosing (e.g. once or twice daily). Serious diseases that are often suitable for OPAT include endocarditis, osteomyelitis, septic arthritis, deep abscesses (e.g. brain, psoas, liver – generally after initial drainage), and invasive fungal and cytomegalovirus disease in transplant recipients and HIV-infected patients. Since these conditions usually need prolonged intravenous antibiotic therapy, long-term venous access (e.g. PICC) is often required and innovative treatment regimens (e.g. continuous-infusion agents) may be appropriate, depending on the responsible pathogen(s). Although these conditions are not common, they are often large consumers of in-hospital bed days; hence, OPAT may substantially improve in-hospital bed utilization by treating a relatively small number of patients.

Patient selection

Appropriate patient selection is a crucial component in ensuring a safe and successful OPAT program. Both patient-specific and disease-specific factors are important in the decision to accept a patient for OPAT (Fig. 191.1). In particular, special care should be taken when assessing for OPAT, elderly or isolated patients, who often do not cope well with medical illness, and patients who have serious

ORAL ANTIBIOTICS WITH EXCELLENT BIOAVAILABILITY THAT MAY BE AN ALTERNATIVE TO INTRAVENOUS THERAPY

Antibiotic	Adult dose	Peak serum concentration (μg/ml)	Key indications	Notable side effects
Fluoroquinolones:				
Ciprofloxacin	500–750mg q12h	1.8–2.8	UTI, OM, GI, STI	GI symptoms, rash, dizziness, headache
Ofloxacin	400mg q12h	4.0–6.0	UTI, RTI, OM, GI, STI	Seizures in elderly patients
Levofloxacin	500mg q24h	5.7	UTI, RTI	
Gatifloxacin	400mg q24h	4.2–4.6	RTI, STI	QT prolongation, drug interactions, rash, occasional hypoglycemia, dizziness, GI symptoms
Moxifloxacin	400mg q24h	4.5	RTI, STI	
Macrolides:				
Azithromycin	500mg q24h	0.4	RTI, STI, Myc	GI symptoms, rash, drug interactions
Clarithromycin	250–500mg q12h	0.8–3.0	RTI, Myc, HPY	GI symptoms, rash, drug interactions
Metronidazole	200–500mg q8h	6.2–25	ANA, C diff	GI symptoms, peripheral neuropathy
Clindamycin	150–600mg q6h	2.5–8.0	SKN, ANA	GI symptoms, pseudomembranous colitis, rash
Cephalosporins:				
Cefixime	400mg q24h	3–5	RTI, UTI, STI	Rash, GI symptoms
Cefpodoxime	100–200mg q12h	2.9	RTI, STI	Rash, GI symptoms
TMP–SMX	160/800mg tabs (1q12h to 2 q6h)	1–2/40–60 (1 tab)	UTI, RTI, PCP, *Nocardia*	Rash, GI symptoms, neutropenia, thrombocytopenia, renal dysfunction
Doxycycline	100mg q24h–q12h	1.5–2.1	RTI, STI, malaria	GI symptoms, photosensitivity, fetal effects
Oxazolidinones:				
Linezolid	600mg q12h	15–20	SKN, RTI (resistant organisms)	GI symptoms, rash, thrombocytopenia
Antivirals:				
Valganciclovir	900mg q24h–q12h	4.0–8.8 (ganciclovir)	CMV disease	Neutropenia, diarrhea
Valacyclovir	500mg q24h to 1g q6h	5.0 (1g q6h)	HSV, VZV	Headache, nausea, diarrhea
Famciclovir	125–500mg q8h	2.8–4.0 (500mg)	HSV, VZV	Headache, nausea
Triazoles:				
Fluconazole	100–400mg q24h	20–30 (400mg)	Cryptoc, *Candida*	Rash, GI symptoms, elevated liver enzymes, drug interactions
Itraconazole	100–400mg q24h	0.4–2.0*	Dermatophytes, *Candida*, molds, dimorphic fungi	Rash, GI symptoms, elevated liver enzymes, drug interactions

* Use of the itraconazole formulated in cyclodextrin leads to improved oral absorption and higher serum levels.

ANA, anaerobic infection; C diff, *Clostridium-difficile*-associated diarrhea; CMV, cytomegalovirus; Cryptoc, *Cryptococcus neoformans.*; GI, infective diarrhea; HPY, *Helicobacter pylori*; HSV, herpes simplex virus; Myc, mycobacterial infection; OM, osteomyelitis; PCP, *Pneumocystis carinii* pneumonia; RTI, respiratory infection; SKN, skin and soft tissue infection; STI, some sexually transmitted infections; TMP–SMX, trimethoprim-sulfamethoxazole; UTI, urinary tract infection; VZV, varicella-zoster virus.

Table 191.3 Oral antibiotics with excellent bioavailability that may be an alternative to intravenous therapy. Data on peak serum concentration from Kucers *et al.*[26] and Gilbert *et al.*[27]

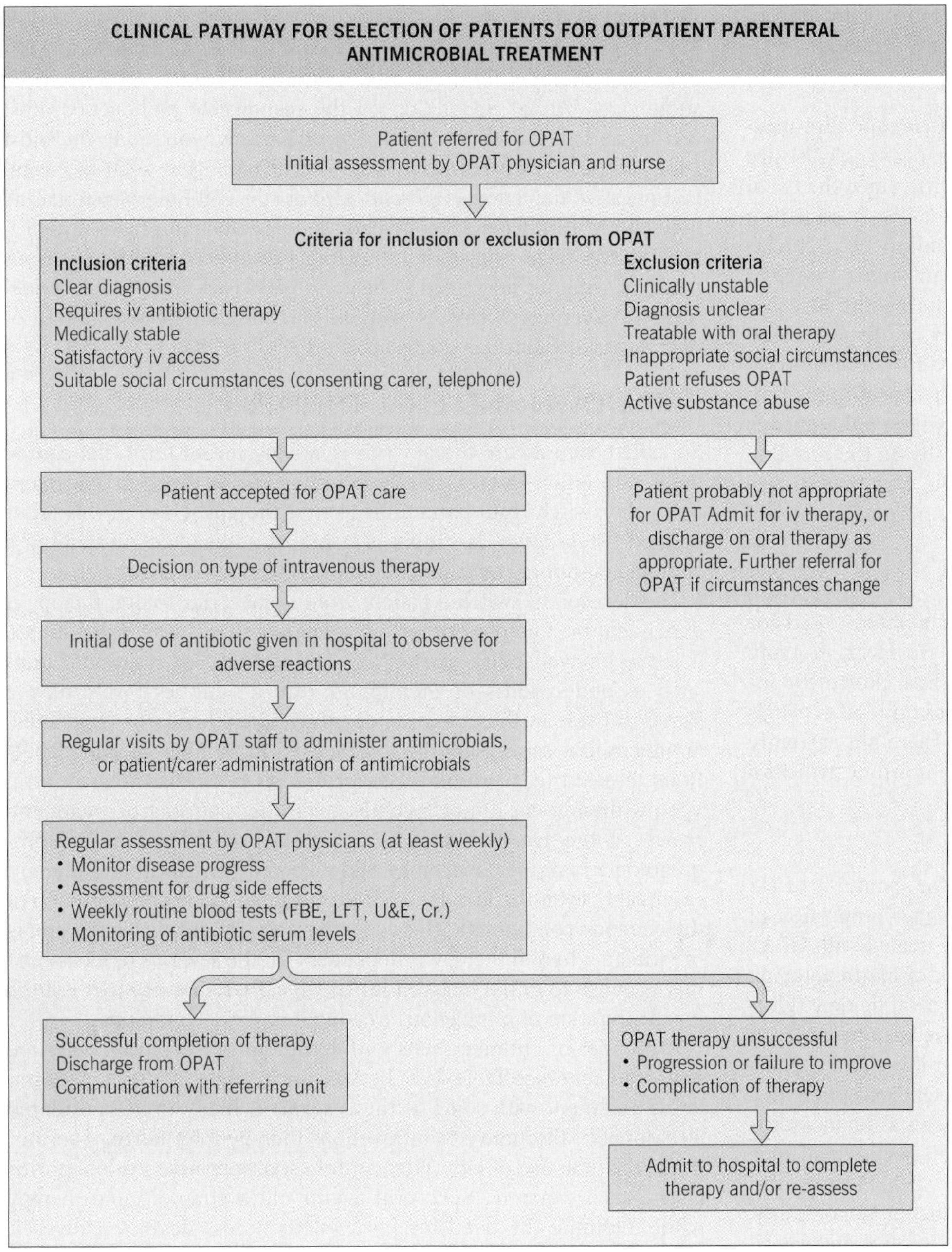

Fig. 191.1 Clinical pathway for selection of patients for outpatient parenteral antimicrobial treatment of infections.

diseases such as endocarditis, where potentially catastrophic disease-related complications can occur.

Patient-specific factors

Factors that may be potential contraindications to OPAT include:

- patients who live alone or in isolated areas, or who do not have a telephone or other means of rapid communication;
- active substance abuse;
- aggressive patients, relatives or pets – these generally argue against patient suitability for OPAT care, since OPAT nurse safety is crucial; and
- the presence of a language barrier between patient and staff that cannot be overcome with the assistance of interpreters or family members – this suggests that safety at home cannot be assured and that in-hospital therapy may therefore be more appropriate.

Disease-specific factors

A clearly defined diagnosis is important before embarking on OPAT. Patients who have common, less serious, conditions such as cellulitis can often be transferred directly from the emergency department to the OPAT program, avoiding in-hospital admission. Patients who have more serious conditions such as endocarditis, osteomyelitis and meningitis generally require a period of inpatient assessment, treatment and stabilization before transfer to an OPAT program to complete their treatment course.

Disease-specific indications

General recommendations for disease-specific therapy are outlined in Table 191.2. However, further discussion regarding some common conditions is warranted.

Cellulitis

Cellulitis is usually the most common indication for OPAT. Since *Streptococcus pyogenes* and *Staphylococcus aureus* are the most frequent responsible pathogens, treatment with a first-generation cephalosporin or antistaphylococcal penicillin is often appropriate. Numerous US studies have demonstrated the efficacy of once-daily ceftriaxone 1–2g for cellulitis, although the appropriateness of this relatively broad-spectrum agent for this indication has been questioned. The first-generation cephalosporin cefazolin, when given 2g twice daily, or 2g once daily together with oral probenecid 1g once daily, is effective. Both regimens have comparable clinical efficacy to that of once-daily ceftriaxone and represent practical, appropriate OPAT treatment options.[14–16] Subsequent switching to oral agents such as dicloxacillin (500mg q6h), cephalexin (500mg q6h) or clindamycin (300mg q6h) after initial improvement usually results in cure.

Pyelonephritis

Gentamicin (4–5mg/kg intravenously q24h), ceftriaxone (1g intravenously q24h) or ciprofloxacin (500–750mg orally q12h) are appropriate empiric single agents for pyelonephritis, since the usual pathogens are often Gram-negative bacilli. Ampicillin or penicillin may also be given empirically to treat possible enterococcal infections, although this is an uncommon pathogen in young patients. Antibiotic selection should be reviewed once the results of urine and blood cultures are available. Recent studies have demonstrated that oral fluoroquinolones are highly effective for treatment of many cases of pyelonephritis, and they may be considered as an alternative to parenteral therapy for patients in whom adherence is assured.[28] Although ciprofloxacin would not usually be the first-line choice for in-hospital care of pyelonephritis, the fact that its use may avoid the need for intravenous access offers a significant practical advantage.

Community-acquired pneumonia

Ceftriaxone 1–2g once daily is the agent most commonly used for the home intravenous treatment of pneumonia. However, in many regions ceftriaxone would not be the drug of first choice for in-hospital care of community-acquired pneumonia and the drug's broad spectrum of activity may be unnecessary. There are currently few data regarding the OPAT use of continuous-infusion penicillin for community-acquired pneumonia.

Endocarditis

The treatment of endocarditis currently accounts for about 5% of US OPAT treatment courses but almost certainly a higher proportion of treatment days.[29] Endocarditis can be successfully treated with OPAT but poses a particular problem because of the risk of life-threatening complications.[7,11,12] Outpatient parenteral antimicrobial therapy selection criteria for patients who have endocarditis have been proposed.[30] They suggest that most patients who have endocarditis should generally be managed in hospital for the initial 2 weeks. One exception may be patients with uncomplicated viridans streptococcal endocarditis who have rapidly become afebrile and cleared their bacteremia; such patients may be suitable for transfer home after 1 week. Patients who have complicated endocarditis (heart failure, conduction abnormality, perivalvular abscess), aortic valve disease, prosthetic valve endocarditis, acute endocarditis or infection caused by virulent organisms such as *S. aureus* should generally be managed primarily as inpatients.

Various OPAT options for common pathogens are shown in Table 191.2. Ceftriaxone (2g/d) has been most commonly used for the home treatment of uncomplicated viridans streptococcal endocarditis; it appears to be effective when given either alone for 4 weeks or together with an aminoglycoside for 2 weeks.[18–20] Monitoring of renal and auditory function is particularly important if aminoglycosides are being used for prolonged periods. Although there are some case reports of treatment with intermittent-dose (and occasionally continuous-infusion) penicillin via a computerized pump for viridans streptococcal endocarditis, this is not currently a common OPAT regimen.

There are a number of reports of successful OPAT for staphylococcal endocarditis. Treatment options include the use of antistaphylococcal penicillins given by computerized pump as a continuous infusion or by intermittent bolus.[11–13] Vancomycin may be used in β-lactam-allergic patients but appears to be less effective than β-lactams for susceptible staphylococcal strains.[31] There are very limited OPAT data for endocarditis caused by other organisms such as enterococci, HACEK organisms, and fungi. Outpatient parenteral antimicrobial therapy for endocarditis generally requires central venous access (e.g. PICC) and close weekly clinical and drug monitoring.

Osteomyelitis

Most forms of osteomyelitis require 4–6 weeks of parenteral antimicrobial therapy, although the treatment duration and need for surgery may differ depending on the responsible pathogen(s), host factors and the bone involved. *Staphylococcus aureus* is the most common cause of osteomyelitis, but other pathogens such as coagulase-negative staphylococci, *Pseudomonas* spp. and Enterobacteriaceae may be involved when osteomyelitis is nosocomial in origin or associated with foreign bodies or intravenous drug abuse.[32] Thus, various treatment options may need to be considered (see Table 191.2). Long-term intravenous access is generally required unless oral fluoroquinolones are considered appropriate.[32,33]

STEP-DOWN AND ORAL THERAPY

So-called 'step-down' therapy is a relatively recent term that can be applied to either the transfer from in-hospital to OPAT management or to the switch from parenteral to oral therapy. Used in this latter context, 'step-down' is simply a fashionable means of describing a routine component of managing many infectious diseases.

The decision to switch a patient from intravenous to oral therapy is dependent on a number of factors, including the nature of the disease and the bioavailability of effective oral agents. For some infections such as endocarditis or meningitis, oral antibiotics rarely play a significant role in therapy as, once intravenous therapy is completed, antimicrobials can usually be stopped. For a number of other infectious diseases (e.g. osteomyelitis or cytomegalovirus disease) intravenous therapy has, until recently, been the mainstay of treatment. However, the availability of more potent oral therapy (e.g. fluoroquinolones, valganciclovir) may allow an early switch to oral therapy, or possibly even the avoidance of intravenous therapy altogether. For the common conditions such as cellulitis and pyelonephritis the timing of switching to oral therapy is dependent on the severity of illness and the response to initial intravenous therapy. There are no strict criteria for the duration of intravenous treatment in these conditions.

A number of antimicrobials with excellent oral bioavailability are now available (see Table 191.3). As clinical trials evidence accumulates, treatment with some of these agents is likely to be considered a reasonable alternative to intravenous therapy for a range of serious infections; the use of ciprofloxacin for Gram-negative pyelonephritis is one such example. Such oral agents allow simple home therapy while avoiding the need for intravenous access devices. However, ensuring such agents have an appropriate spectrum of activity (not too broad) and that patients adhere to these oral regimens will be crucial to avoid the emergence of resistance and treatment failures.

MONITORING PATIENTS RECEIVING OUTPATIENT PARENTERAL ANTIMICROBIAL THERAPY

Patients require careful monitoring while receiving both OPAT and oral therapy. Although the home environment has many advantages for the patient, the careful regular monitoring that generally occurs in hospital is not present at home. In general, patients should be reviewed by the OPAT physician at least once a week, usually in the outpatient department or office. Specific factors to assess on review include:

- patient's reaction to OPAT;
- response to therapy;
- drug side effects; and
- other complications (e.g. venous cannula infection).

Routine hematology and biochemistry, as well as serum drug levels, are also often monitored weekly.

Since in some situations more frequent reviews, or even emergency assessments, may be necessary, all good OPAT programs should have a system to manage these.

SUMMARY

Given recent trends worldwide, an increasing proportion of medical care that previously would have been administered in hospital is likely to be delivered at home. To be successful, patient selection should be based primarily on medical suitability rather than economic considerations. Ensuring appropriate antibiotic selection, safe delivery systems and continuity of care will be key challenges.

REFERENCES

1. Tice AD. Outpatient parenteral antimicrobial therapy. Infect Dis Clin North Am 1998;12:xi–xii.
2. Rucker RW, Harrison GM. Outpatient intravenous medications in the management of cystic fibrosis. Pediatrics 1974;54:358–60.
3. Antoniskis A, Anderson BC, Van Volkinburg EJ, *et al.* Feasibility of outpatient self-administration of parenteral antibiotics. West J Med 1978;128:203–6.
4. Grayson ML. Hospital in the home – is it worth the hassle? Med J Aust 1998;170:262–3.
5. Caplan GA, Ward JA, Brennan NJ, *et al.* Hospital in the home: a randomised controlled trial. Med J Aust 1999;170:156–60.
6. Howden BP, Grayson ML. Hospital-in-the-home treatment of infectious diseases. Med J Aust 2002;176:440–5.
7. Williams DN, Rehm SJ, Tice AD, *et al.* Practice guidelines for community-based parenteral anti-infective therapy. Clin Infect Dis 1997;25:787–801.
8. Ng PK, Ault MJ, Ellrodt AG, *et al.* Peripherally inserted central catheters in general medicine. Mayo Clin Proc 1997;72:225–33.
9. Schleis TG, Tice AD. Selecting infusion devices for use in ambulatory care. Am J Health Syst Pharm 1996;53:868–77.
10. Turnidge JD. The pharmacodynamics of beta-lactams. Clin Infect Dis 1998;27:10–22.
11. Howden BP, Richards MJ. The efficacy of continuous infusion flucloxacillin in home based therapy for serious staphylococcal infections and cellulitis. J Antimicrob Chemother 2001;48:311–44.
12. Leder K, Turnidge JD, Korman TM, *et al.* The clinical efficacy of continuous-infusion flucloxacillin in serious staphylococcal sepsis. J Antimicrob Chemother 1999;43:113–8.
13. Gilbert DN, Dworkin RJ, Raber SR, *et al.* Drug therapy: outpatient parenteral antimicrobial-drug therapy. N Engl J Med 1997;337:829–38.
14. Grayson ML, McDonald M, Gibson K, *et al.* Once-daily intravenous cefazolin plus oral probenecid is equivalent to once-daily intravenous ceftriaxone plus oral placebo for the treatment of moderate-to-severe cellulitis in adults. Clin Infect Dis 2002;34:1440–8.
15. Brown G, Chamberlain R, Goulding J, *et al.* Ceftriaxone versus cefazolin with probenecid for severe skin and soft tissue infections. J Emerg Med 1996;14:547–51.
16. Leder K, Turnidge JD, Grayson ML. Home-based treatment of cellulitis with twice-daily cephazolin. Med J Aust 1998;169:519–22.
17. Deery HG. Outpatient parenteral anti-infective therapy for skin and soft tissue infections. Infect Dis Clin North Am 1998; 12: 935–49.
18. Francioli P, Etienne J, Hoigne R, *et al.* Treatment of streptococcal endocarditis with a single daily dose of ceftriaxone sodium for 4 weeks. Efficacy and outpatient treatment feasibility. JAMA 1992;267:264–7.
19. Francioli P, Ruch W, Stamboulian D. Treatment of streptococcal endocarditis with a single daily dose of ceftriaxone and netilmicin for 14 days: a prospective multicenter study. Clin Infect Dis 1995;21:1406–10.
20. Sexton DJ, Tenenbaum MJ, Wilson WR, *et al.* Ceftriaxone once daily for four weeks compared with ceftriaxone plus gentamicin once daily for two weeks for treatment of endocarditis due to penicillin-susceptible streptococci. Endocarditis Treatment Consortium Group. Clin Infect Dis 1998;27:1470–4.
21. Fine MJ, Auble TE, Yealy DM, *et al.* A prediction rule to identify low-risk patients with community-acquired pneumonia. N Engl J Med 1997;336:243–50.
22. Tice AD, Strait K, Ramey R, *et al.* Outpatient parenteral antimicrobial therapy for central nervous system infections. Clin Infect Dis 1999;29:394–9.
23. Munckhof WJ, Grayson ML, Turnidge JD. A meta-analysis on the safety and efficacy of aminoglycosides given either once daily or as divided doses. J Antimicrob Chemother 1996;37:645–63.
24. Martin DF, Sierra-Madero J, Walmsley S, *et al.* The Valganciclovir Study Group. A controlled trial of valganciclovir as induction therapy for cytomegalovirus retinitis. N Engl J Med 2002;346:1119–26.
25. Tice AD, ed. Outpatient parenteral antibiotic therapy. Management of serious infections. Part II: Amenable infections and models for delivery. Hosp Pract 1993;28(Suppl.2):5.
26. Kucers A, Crowe S, Grayson ML, Hoy J. The use of antibiotics. 5th ed. Oxford: Butterworth Heinemann; 1997.
27. Gilbert DN, Mollering RC Jr, Sande MA, eds. The Sanford guide to antimicrobial therapy. 32nd ed. Hyde Park, VT: Antimicrobial Therapy, Inc.; 2002.
28. Mombelli G, Pezzoli R, Pinoja-Lutz G, *et al.* Oral vs intravenous ciprofloxacin in the initial empirical management of severe pyelonephritis or complicated urinary tract infections: a prospective randomized clinical trial. Arch Intern Med 1999;159:53–8.
29. Rehm SJ. Outpatient intravenous antibiotic therapy for endocarditis. Infect Dis Clin North Am 1998;12:879–901.
30. Andrews MM, von Reyn CF. Patient selection criteria and management guidelines for outpatient parenteral antibiotic therapy for native valve infective endocarditis. Clin Infect Dis 2001;33:203–9.
31. Wood CA, Wisniewski RM. β-lactam versus glycopeptides in treatment of subcutaneous abscesses infected with *Staphylococcal aureus.* Antimicrob Agents Chemother 1994;38:1023–6.
32. Lew DP, Waldvogel FA. Osteomyelitis. N Engl J Med 1997;336:999–1007.
33. Gentry LO. Antibiotic therapy for osteomyelitis. Infect Dis Clin North Am 1990;4:485–99.

chapter 192

Short-course Antibiotic Therapy

Debby Ben David, Gili Regev-Yochay & Ethan Rubinstein

INTRODUCTION

The length of antibiotic course of therapy has been rarely studied in conventional infections while in tuberculosis, malaria and, interestingly, in venereal diseases it has been investigated thoroughly. The reasons for this discrepancy may be that in out-of-hospital studies, where compliance has always been a problem, investigators attempted to formalize the shortest possible course, to increase patient adherence and reduce the medical workload and costs. In the hospital until 15 years ago, the questions of compliance and cost were not as vital as they are today. In addition, the issue of bacterial resistance was 20 years ago of far less importance and wide implication as it is today. The introduction of new bactericidal agents with a rapid onset of action as well as better definition of patient population and deeper understanding of pharmacodynamics have also contributed to the shortening of antibiotic therapy courses. The best possible examples are the single-dose therapy for gonorrhea with ceftriaxone, cefixime, ciprofloxacin, ofloxacin, azithromycin or doxycycline. The reduction of the very long courses of tuberculosis treatment from around 18–24 months to much shorter periods (4–6 months in immunocompetent hosts[1] due in part to the introduction of rifampin, a highly bactericidal agent) and the introduction of directly observed therapy (DOT), which assured better compliance and therefore lower rates of resistance development, have lead to shorter therapy courses. The ability to treat meningococcal meningitis in children with 4 days of ceftriaxone therapy or even a single administration of long-acting penicillin,[2] or in adults for 2 days with ceftriaxone or for 4 days with penicillin G also demonstrates the changes occurring in our understanding of the necessary length of therapeutic periods. In hospitals also, the reduction of presurgical prophylaxis to a single dose,[5] with no untoward effect on wound infection, but with a significant reduction in resistant Gram-negative wound isolates, demonstrates the utility of short and ultra-short therapy (and prophylaxis) courses.

A course of therapy is conventionally defined as the time period during which an antimicrobial is administered. Due to the presence of counterfeit agents with decreased activity, irregular absorption and other uncontrolled parameters, a better definition may be the period during which therapeutic concentrations are maintained at the site of infection.

The advantage of a short therapy (or prophylaxis) period is that patient compliance improves with the reduction of the number of dosages to be administered and the time period necessary for a full treatment course.[3] A short-term therapy course is conventionally less expensive than prolonged courses because of the decreased amounts of drugs used and decreased cost of physicians, medical personnel and laboratory tests associated with more prolonged courses. In short-course therapy, if the full course is interrupted, there is less waste of unused antibiotics. Obviously when fewer antibiotics are prescribed the risk of adverse events and drug–drug interaction would be less. There is less risk of bacterial resistance development of the treated pathogen as well as of commensals if therapy is short. This has been shown to be true in the community,[4] where therapy of URTI in children for >7 days increased the risk of selection of penicillin-resistant *Strep. pneumoniae* (PRSp; OR = 3.5, 95% CI 1.3–9.8) compared to shorter treatment courses, as well as in the hospital, where prophylaxis of >48 hours increased the risk of acquired antibiotic resistance of Enterobacteriaceae and enterococci (OR 1,6, CI 1.1–2.6) compared to prophylaxis of <48 hours.[5] There is potentially less harm done to the environment in the immediate vicinity of the patient and less risk to his family members of becoming carriers of resistant bacteria, if fewer antibiotics are excreted and secreted from the patient into his immediate surroundings.

Evidently there is a lower limit under which short-course therapy becomes ineffective. Thus, for example, it was shown that for uncomplicated cystitis in women short therapy of 3 days was as effective as 5 days and as 7 days therapy with β-lactam antibiotics, trimethoprim-sulfamethoxazole and fluoroquinolones. Nevertheless, reduction of the therapy course to <3 days was associated with an increasing rate of relapses and is thus not recommended.[6] In endocarditis also, reducing the duration of therapy to less than 28 days in aortic valve endocarditis was associated with unsatisfactory results compared with conventional duration of therapy. Another example is the observation that treating staphylococcal bacteremia for <10 days was associated with a high relapse rate.[7] Similarly, in catheter-related *Staph. aureus* bacteremia, antistaphylococcal therapy for >14 days was associated (albeit not significantly) with favorable outcome, fewer complications and less attributable death.[8] Other investigators also confirmed the need for 10–15 days, therapy for catheter-associated bacteremia.

A successful abbreviated treatment course depends on several mandatory factors on the part of the patient, pathogen, infection and therapeutic agent, as detailed in Table 192.1.

The patient needs to be fully immunocompetent to be able to be cured with short courses of therapy and needs the full number of active leukocytes and macrophages. He needs to be able to produce adequate antibodies and to mount a satisfactory cell-mediated immune response. He must have adequate concentration of albumin to carry the antibiotic in the circulation and to have adequate distribution of intra- and extracellular water to allow the agent to penetrate or diffuse to the sites of infection.

The pathogen involved must be highly susceptible to the administered agent and not have the tendency to develop resistance to the agent used (low spontaneous mutation rate). The pathogen should preferably be extracellular and should be able to divide frequently enough to allow for prolonged antibiotic-vulnerable periods. The pathogen, at the site of infection, should preferably be in a planktonic form and not adherent to solid phases like bone and cartilage.

The infection should be at a site that is easily accessible to antibiotics; thus infections in sanctuaries like the brain, the prostate and eye are not good candidates for abbreviated therapy courses. The infection should not be life threatening and should not be localized in or around foreign bodies to which the pathogen is adherent and at which it forms a biofilm. It should be caused by a single pathogen and should not be an abscess, empyema, granuloma, etc., that would

FEATURES NECESSARY FOR SUCCESSFUL ABBREVIATED THERAPY COURSES			
Patient factors	**Pathogen factors**	**Infection factors**	**Antibiotic factors**
Immunocompetence	Susceptible to antibiotics	At an easily accessible site	Bactericidal
Adequate WBC	Low spontaneous mutation rate	Not as a biofilm	Rapid onset of action
Normal albumin level	Extracellular	Lack of foreign body	Lack of propensity to induce mutations
Adequate hydration	Rapid multiplication rate	Not life-threatening	Easy penetration to tissues
Adequate compliance		Caused by a single pathogen	Active against nondividing bacteria
		Not a closed space infection	Not affected by adverse conditions
		Lack of adverse environmental factors	
		Early infectious state	

Table 192.1 Features necessary for successful abbreviated therapy courses.

not allow antibiotics to penetrate or that have conditions of low pH, WBC debris and other factors that inhibit antibiotic action. Experience has shown that infections on mucosal surfaces (like upper and lower respiratory tract infections, intestinal infections and genitourinary infections) are best suited for abbreviated courses of therapy while infections in bones, joints, the brain or intracellular infections are not suited for such treatment modality.

In order for the agent to be successful in abbreviated mode therapy, it has to be bactericidal and act rapidly, be associated with the lowest rate of resistance induction, be able to penetrate easily to tissues and body fluids (that is, having a low molecular weight and being lipophilic) and be present at the site of infection in sufficiently high concentrations for those agents with concentration-dependent killing (e.g. aminoglycosides, fluoroquinolones and imidazoles) and in concentrations above the MIC for long enough periods for agents that possess time-dependent bacterial killing (β-lactams, macrolides, glycopeptides, etc.).[9]

GROUP A STREPTOCOCCAL PHARYNGITIS

Therapy of group A streptococcal (GAS) pharyngitis is intended to prevent both suppurative and nonsuppurative complications (rheumatic fever and perhaps poststreptococcal glomerulonephritis).

The treatment currently recommended by the American Heart Association, Infectious Disease Society of America and other organizations is 10 days of penicillin.[10] Prevention of acute rheumatic fever is believed to require eradication of the infecting streptococci from the pharynx, an effect that depends on prolonged rather than high-dose penicillin therapy.

The efficacy of 10-day treatment with penicillin was first documented in the early 1950s. By 1953 the American Heart Association recommended treatment of GAS pharyngitis with oral penicillin for 10 days.[11] In 1981 Schwartz *et al* re-evaluated the duration of treatment in a study which compared patients with proven GAS infection treated for 7 or 10 days with penicillin V in 8 hourly regimens.[12] They concluded that the 10-day regimen was more effective than a 7-day regimen in eradicating GAS, but also concluded that persistence of GAS after adequate therapy may be common. It is now accepted that approximately 15% of patients continue to harbor the original infecting GAS serotype in their pharynx after completing a course of oral penicillin.[10]

Gerber *et al*[13] compared 5 versus 10 days of penicillin V treatment in a randomized controlled trial. Patients in the two treatment groups were comparable with respect to clinical findings, compliance and serologic response to GAS. The same serotype of GAS was present in the follow-up in 18% of the 73 patients treated for 5 days versus 6% of 99 patients treated for 10 days. Thus, the need for 10 days of penicillin V treatment was confirmed.

Macrolides are an alternative choice, especially for penicillin-allergic patients. Several studies have examined short courses of various macrolides as an optional treatment for GAS pharyngitis. McCarty *et al*[14] compared clarithromycin to penicillin V and demonstrated comparable rates of clinical success and a higher eradication rate with clarithromycin (94% vs 78%). Boccazzi *et al*[15] compared a 3-day azithromycin regimen to 5-day cefibuten. They showed a somewhat higher eradication rate after cefibuten than after azithromycin treatment. Yet, the widespread use of macrolides has been associated with the development of resistance by GAS and this should limit the use of macrolides for GAS pharyngitis only to penicillin-allergic patients.

Oral cephalosporins are also highly effective in treating streptococcal pharyngitis. A meta-analysis of 19 studies suggested that streptococcal eradication rates and clinical cure rates attained with these agents are even slightly higher than those achieved with penicillin.[16]

Since the mid-1990s several randomized controlled studies have been carried out to compare shorter therapeutic courses (4–5 days of treatment) of cephalosporins with either the standard 10-day penicillin V regimen or with 10-day treatment with cephalosporins. These studies demonstrated that the shorter treatments were equivalent or superior in bacteriological eradication and clinical response. However, none of these studies evaluated the incidence of post-streptococcal sequelae. The general concern that shorter treatment courses might lead to an increased incidence of post-streptococcal sequelae was increased by clusters of rheumatic fever which occurred in the USA in the late 1980s.

Two recent large-scale European studies were performed by Adam *et al*,[17] to compare short-course treatments with the standard 10-day penicillin treatment. They evaluated 4782 culture-proven cases of GAS pharyngitis and also measured the incidence of post-streptococcal sequelae for a follow-up of 1 year. They examined 5-day regimens with six antibiotics that have been shown effective in previous trials: amoxicillin/clavulanate, ceftibuten, cefuroxime axetil, loracarbef, clarithromycin and erythromycin estolate. The 5-day regimens were as effective as the 10-day penicillin treatment. Both bacteriologic eradication and clinical success rates were equivalent. However, among the patients treated with the short course there were four cases of poststreptococcal late sequelae (three cases of rheumatic fever and one glomerulonephritis), while only one patient in the 10-day penicillin group developed glomerulonephritis. The authors claim that the poststreptococcal sequelae in these cases could not be definitely related to the streptococcal episode treated in the study according to their histories. A separate evaluation for cefuroxime axetil (5-day) versus penicillin (10-day) showed equivalence with no streptococcal sequelae.

In summary, abbreviated courses (less than 10 days) of penicillin V were unsuccessful. Short courses of macrolide drugs have led to equivalent clinical and bacterial eradication results, but the concern of resistance development in GAS should limit these drugs to treating penicillin-allergic patients. Short courses of cephalosporins were equivalent or slightly better in clinical and bacterial eradication, but it is difficult to prove that poststreptococcal sequelae will not increase with these treatments and the concern about antibiotic resistance should probably limit these drugs to treating special cases. In addition, most of these agents are more expensive than penicillin, even when administered for short courses. Therefore, the best choice is probably still penicillin.

OTITIS MEDIA

Acute otitis media (AOM) remains one of the most common bacterial infections in childhood and the leading indication for antimicrobial use in this population. The objective of treating AOM is achieving a rapid clinical relief and preventing complications such as mastoiditis, meningitis, jugular vein thrombosis, etc. Failure to eradicate the causative pathogens in the middle ear was shown to lead to a higher risk of relapse and long-term sequelae. Thus, most expert panels have recommended treating children with AOM. However, other studies demonstrated that even among bacterial infections, the majority will resolve spontaneously, with only a minor advantage of antibiotic treatment over nontreatment, and thus have recommended withholding antimicrobial treatment entirely in some or all cases of AOM unless symptoms persist or worsen.[18]

Most clinical guidelines and expert panels still recommend 10 days of β-lactams (first drug of choice being amoxicillin) for most patients, some limiting this treatment to children younger than 2 years, and allowing a shorter course of treatment (5 days) for older children.[19]

Recently, interest in shortening the course of antibiotic therapy from the traditional 10 days to 5 days has emerged for the reasons previously mentioned. Cefpodoxime, cefdinir and azithromycin are the only oral antibiotics currently approved by the US FDA for 5-day short-course therapy of AOM.

A meta-analysis[20] of randomized, controlled trials of shortened antibiotic therapy in AOM suggested that a 5-day course of a short-acting antibiotic was an effective treatment. However, patient subgroup sizes were too small to provide a reliable estimate of the risk of treatment failure in children younger than 2 years. Yet it is precisely children in this age group who gain the greatest benefit from treatment and who have the highest risk of treatment failure.

When evaluating the results of AOM studies it is particularly important to critically review the criteria used for diagnosis and for assessing outcome. In some of the previous trials, a combination of middle ear effusion and one or more nonspecific signs or symptoms has been considered sufficient. Outcomes in some of the studies have been based on symptomatic response alone, without regard to specific tympanic membrane findings, thus permitting inclusion of patients who do not actually have AOM but have otitis media with effusion (OME), a condition that is self-limiting and with minor symptoms.

In summary, abbreviated 5-day courses have been shown to be equivalent to standard therapies in children older than 2 and may be equivalent in those younger than 2 years who do not attend a daycare center. Children younger than 2 years of age who attend a daycare center should continue to receive the standard 10-day treatment in order to achieve good clinical success and prevent relapses.

ACUTE BACTERIAL SINUSITIS

Acute bacterial sinusitis is a common upper respiratory tract infection, with an estimated 20 million cases reported in the US annually. There are no specific clinical features to distinguish between bacterial and viral etiologies. It is, however, accepted that patients who have symptoms of rhinosinusitis (purulent nasal secretions and maxillary facial pain) for less than 7 days are unlikely to have bacterial infection. The presence of symptoms for more than 7 days is a sensitive but nonspecific predictor of bacterial sinusitis. Two recent meta-analyses[21,22] have concluded that antibiotics are statistically more efficacious than placebo in reducing symptoms, although their benefit is relatively small. It is generally recommended that treatment should be initiated with narrow-spectrum agents, e.g. amoxicillin, doxycycline or trimethoprim-sulfamethoxazole (TMP-SMX); however, these recommendations do not consider the increasing incidence of penicillin-resistant *Strep. pneumoniae* as a causative pathogen. The Sinus and Allergy Health Partnership guidelines for treatment of bacterial rhinosinusitis recommend stratifying patients according to severity of disease, rate of progression, recent antibiotic exposure and local resistance data.[23] Recommendations for initial therapy for adults with mild disease who have not received antibiotics include the following choices: amoxicillin/clavulanate, amoxicillin (1.5–3g/day), cefpodoxime proxetil or cefuroxime axetil. However, the duration of therapy is not indicated in these guidelines.

As the optimal duration of antimicrobial treatment for acute sinusitis has not been adequately studied until recently, the duration of treatment was not well defined and was therefore generally based on physician preference. The standard duration of antibiotic treatment for acute bacterial sinusitis ranges between 7 and 14 days. All the controlled studies published between 1990 and 2002 that compared the efficacy of short-course treatment (fewer than 7 days) with that of a long course (more than 7 days) showed equivalent clinical and bacteriologic efficacy results for 3–5 days, compared with 8–14 days of therapy with all agents studied. A single randomized, double-blind, placebo-controlled study[24] has compared amoxicillin/clavulanate administrated for 5 days with a 10-day course. Risk factors for failure in the abbreviated course were a history of more than four bouts of sinusitis during the 2 years prior to therapy or a history of surgical drainage. Thus, longer treatment courses might be indicated for certain risk groups. Further studies are needed to resolve this question.

Azithromycin has a prolonged half-life ranging between 2 and 5 days and a slow release from tissues. These properties suggest that a short course of azithromycin could be comparable to prolonged antimicrobial therapy. Several studies demonstrated high efficacy of azithromycin in acute sinusitis when administrated for 3–5 days. The response rates are comparable with those of prolonged therapy.

In summary, several studies have demonstrated similar efficacy of a short antimicrobial course compared with 8–14 days of antimicrobial treatment. Nevertheless, most studies included patients with maxillary sinusitis and the results cannot be extrapolated to patients with frontal, ethmoidal and sphenoidal or pan-sinusitis. It is important to emphasize that most studies did not verify the bacterial etiology of sinusitis by the use of sinus punctures. As most cases of acute rhinosinusitis are caused by viruses and less than 2% are complicated by bacterial infection and since there are no specific clinical features to distinguish between bacterial and viral etiologies, the true efficacy of prolonged antibiotic therapy compared to short-course therapy is difficult to assess.

COMMUNITY-ACQUIRED PNEUMONIA

There are no controlled trials that compare short antimicrobial courses in community-acquired pneumonia (CAP) with long courses (more than 7 days). The Infectious Disease Society of America[25] recommends treating pneumonia caused by *Strep. pneumoniae* until the patient is afebrile for 72 hours. Pneumonia caused by bacteria that can cause necrosis of pulmonary parenchyma (e.g. *Staph. aureus* or *P. aeruginosa*) should be treated for longer than 2 weeks, and pneumonia caused by atypical pathogens (e.g. *M. pneumoniae* or *C. pneumoniae*) should be treated for at least 2 weeks. However, these recommendations are not based on randomized clinical trials and are supported by expert opinion only.

ACUTE EXACERBATION OF CHRONIC OBSTRUCTIVE PULMONARY DISEASE

Approximately 5% of Americans in their middle and late years have chronic bronchitis, which predisposes them to frequent episodes of illness. Acute infectious exacerbation of chronic obstructive pulmonary disease (AE-COPD) contributes considerably to the morbidity and mortality of this population. The benefit of antibiotics in AE-COPD in reducing mortality and morbidity has been demonstrated in several randomized placebo-controlled studies. A meta-analysis has demonstrated a small but statistically significant improvement due to antibiotic therapy in acute exacerbations of COPD.[26]

The administration of therapy for 10–14 days has been the standard treatment. A large number of studies have been published during the last few years which support the use of short-course antimicrobial therapy in AE-COPD. Most studies used different antibiotic regimens that compared the efficacy of a short course (fewer than 7 days) with that of a long course (more than 7 days). All trials enrolled patients with a clinical diagnosis of AE-COPD. Across studies involving 6629 patients published between 1988 and 2001, clinical and bacteriologic efficacy of various classes of antibiotics were equivalent for 3–5 days compared with 8–14 days of therapy.

The new fluoroquinolones have a wide antimicrobial activity (including penicillin-resistant *Strep. pneumoniae, H. influenzae* and atypical pathogens), favorable pharmacokinetics and pharmacodynamics, including high bio-availability, extensive distribution into respiratory fluids, long elimination half-life and potent and rapid killing. Based on their pharmacokinetic and pharmacodynamic profile, a shorter course of fluoroquinolones could have equivalent efficacy to the traditional 10–14 days therapy for AE-COPD. Several randomized trials have demonstrated high efficacy of the new fluoroquinolones in the treatment of AE-COPD. Abbreviated courses of various fluoroquinolones of 5 days' duration had similar efficacy compared to standard duration therapy.

In summary, most studies have demonstrated similar efficacy of a short course of antimicrobial therapy in AE-COPD compared with standard duration therapy. Therefore, abbreviated therapy should be considered for AE-COPD.

URINARY TRACT INFECTIONS

When considering treatment for UTI the prognosis of the untreated infection and the long-term results to be expected from therapy should be measured and compared to the side-effects, cost and inconvenience of different therapeutic regimens. As the prognosis of UTI in nonpregnant adult women is excellent and reinfection is common, therapy probably makes little contribution to the patient's well-being other than alleviating the symptoms. Hundreds of patients have been followed for years with persistent or recurrent infections without documenting progression of renal disease caused by the infection.

Bacteriuria in the elderly is associated with degenerative and debilitating diseases, but does not seem to aggravate the underlying condition. Routine treatment of asymptomatic bacteriuria in the elderly is thus not recommended by most experts.

Asymptomatic as well as symptomatic bacteriuria in preschool children with vesicourethral reflux can result in stunted growth of the kidney, scar formation and, rarely, renal failure. Bacteriuria in pregnancy may also have serious implications – for example, preterm deliveries, low birth weight, etc. Thus, treatment of children and pregnant women is most likely to be beneficial. Symptomatic patients, regardless of age, should be adequately treated, even when infection is likely to recur.

In the past, 7–10 days of therapy were routinely recommended for patients with lower urinary tract symptoms. However, in recent years it has become apparent that most women with lower UTI have only a superficial mucosal infection that can be cured with much shorter courses of therapy, even with a single dose of an antimicrobial agent.

Short-course therapy for UTI with sulfonamides has been intensively studied and more than 70 reports have been published. A meta-analysis of these trials revealed that a single-dose therapy was less effective than longer duration regimens (87% eradication vs 94%), but 3-day regimens were equivalent to longer duration treatments and were associated with lower rates of adverse events.[6] Several trials have demonstrated the efficacy of a single-dose of ciprofloxacin; however, this drug, like most agents studied, appeared to be more effective when given as a 3-day regimen.[27]

Since then, several randomized controlled studies have confirmed that low-dose, short courses (3 days) of fluoroquinolones and short-course TMP-SMX are superior to 7-day treatments of many commonly used drugs (fluoroquinolones, TMP-SMX and nitrofurantoin), mainly due to the lower rate of adverse events.[28–30]

β-Lactam short-course studies revealed that all β-lactam regimens (amoxicillin, pivamecillinam, cefadroxil, etc.) were less effective when given in a shorter than 7 day regimen, demonstrating higher recurrence and lower eradication rates with the short courses.

To summarize: β-lactam and nitrofurantoin short-course regimens have failed and are less effective than the standard 7-day regimens. Three-day regimens of TMP-SMX are equivalent to longer duration treatments and may be the drug of choice in areas in which resistance to this drug is low. Three-day regimens of fluoroquinolones are equivalent to longer duration regimens and may be more effective than 3-day regimens of TMP-SMX in areas where resistance to the latter is high.

INTESTINAL INFECTIONS

These infections would be the most amenable to abbreviated courses of therapy as in most instances the pathogen is located on the epithelial surface or has penetrated the intestinal epithelial cell but does not proceed to invade other tissues. The pathogen is classically a rapidly dividing bacteria, there is no foreign body and the peristalsis of the intestine would inhibit biofilm formation. The major obstacles to abbreviated therapy are the penetration of the antibiotic into the intestinal lumen and into the epithelial cells, the adverse effect of fecal material on the antibacterial activity of the agent (binding to fecal material), and the inactivation of the antimicrobial agent by neighboring bacteria that may produce extracellular enzymes, e.g. β-lactamases, aminoglycoside-inactivating enzymes, etc.

In shigellosis, a randomized double-blind controlled trial compared 5 days of therapy with ciprofloxacin or azithromycin in 70 hospitalized adults men in Bangladesh.[31] Clinical success (determined as disappearance of loose stools on day 5 and temperature <37.8° on day 3) and bacteriological eradication rates were equal in both groups. A study in 135 Vietnamese children with bacillary dysentery, in a region with a high rate of multidrug-resistant shigellosis (of 63 isolates, 62% were MDR), compared the conventional therapy of nalidixic acid (55mg/kg for 5 days) with two doses of ofloxacin (total 15mg/kg). Resolution times for fever and diarrhea were similar, excretion time for stool pathogens was longer in the nalidixic acid group, there were 25% treatment failures in the nalidixic acid group compared to 10% in the ofloxacin group ($p>0.1$). The authors concluded that the two regimens were equally effective and thus a preference for the shorter therapy was obvious.[32]

TYPHOID FEVER

Typhoid fever has traditionally been treated with 10–14 days of therapy with chloramphenicol, ceftriaxone, etc. Attempts have been made to shorten this treatment period from 10–14 days to 5–7 days but the long-term relapse rate remained undefined.[33] The current practice is to administer systemic antibiotic until the patient defervesces and to continue with an oral cephalosporin for a total of 10–14 days. The fluoroquinolones, because of their *in vitro* activity against Salmonellae, intracellular penetration and transepithelial intestinal elimination reaching high intraepithelial concentrations, were considered attractive for shorter treatments of typhoid fever and other systemic salmonellosis.[34] Seven days of treatment with ciprofloxacin 500mg twice daily were compared with azithromycin 1g initial oral dose followed by 500mg once daily for 6 additional days in 123 Egyptian patients. Cure was similar in the two groups with similar time to defervescence in both groups with no relapse in either group.[35] When ofloxacin 5-day course (200mg twice daily) was compared with ceftriaxone 3g once daily for 3 days, ofloxacin cured 100% of patients (22/22) while ceftriaxone cured 18/25 patients (72%) ($p\leq0.01$) with defervescence in the ofloxacin group occurring far earlier than in the ceftriaxone group.[36] In a study that compared ofloxacin 3 days to 5 days in MDR typhoid fever in 438 patients in Vietnam, both regimens were equally effective.[37] For fluoroquinolone-resistant and nalidixic acid-resistant *S. typhi* (NARST) treated with ofloxacin, the time for blood clearance was double (156h) that for susceptible strains and a third of the NARST patients required retreatment (compared to 0.4% of the susceptible strains). NARST-infected patients were, however, effectively treated with short-course (5 days) azithromycin therapy with rapid defervescence, sterilization of stool cultures and no relapses.[38]

ENDOCARDITIS

In 1971, Paul Beeson wrote that in cases where signs and symptoms were favorable, 2- or 3-week therapy was sufficient whereas in abacteremic patients, in those with long-standing disease, those with large vegetations and those with relatively resistant organisms, it is wiser to continue therapy for 6–10 weeks. Today infections with penicillin-susceptible streptococci and *Streptococcus bovis* (with a penicillin MIC of ≤0.1μg/ml) require a 2-week regimen of ceftriaxone or penicillin G combined with gentamicin as long as the patient does not have extracardiac foci of infections, myocardial abscesses or prosthetic valve endocarditis. When the pathogen is relatively resistant to penicillin (MIC ≥0.1 but ≤0.5μg/ml) penicillin (or ceftriaxone) for 4 weeks are required accompanied in the first 2 weeks by gentamicin. In right-sided staphylococcal endocarditis in intravenous drug abusers, 2-week therapy with methicillin (or nafcillin) combined with gentamicin is effective.[39,40] The reason for shortening the therapy duration may be greater awareness of the possibility of endocarditis that is now supported by echocardiography, allowing for earlier diagnosis, and a deeper understanding of the pharmacokinetics and pharmacodynamics of the antibiotics used for treating this infection.

NOSOCOMIAL INFECTIONS

The widespread use of antibiotics in hospitals has substantial implications for the cost of care, side effects and spread of resistant micro-organisms. Generally, nosocomial infections are treated for 10–14 days. However, there are no randomized clinical studies evaluating the optimal duration of antimicrobial treatment in most nosocomial infections. As the majority of the hospitalized patients who develop infections are critical patients, immunocompromised or patients who have undergone surgery, or elderly and those with foreign bodies, an abbreviated antimicrobial course could lead to therapeutic failure or relapse. On the other hand, prolonged antimicrobial therapy exposes these patients to drug toxicity and the emergence of resistant micro-organisms at an individual level and also influences the hospital or unit ecology.

Nosocomial pneumonia

Respiratory tract infections account for approximately 50% of all antibiotics prescribed in intensive care units. The American Thoracic Society recommends that the duration should be adapted to the severity of the disease, the time to clinical response and the micro-organism involved.[41] Prolonged antimicrobial treatment is recommended for the following situations: multilobar involvement, cavitation and isolation of *P. aeruginosa* or *Acinetobacter* spp. and pneumonia associated with bacteremia. A short antimicrobial treatment (7–10 days) is recommended for *Staph. aureus* and *H. influenzae* pneumonia.

A prospective nonrandomized clinical study in ventilator-associated pneumonia (VAP) evaluated the efficacy of a clinical guideline restricting the total duration of antimicrobial therapy to 7 days.[42] The mean duration of treatment in the first period was 14.8 days compared to 8.6 days. No significant differences in hospital mortality and hospital lengths of stay were found between the two study groups. However, patients in the before-evaluation group were more likely to develop a second episode of VAP compared with those in the after-evaluation group (24.0% vs 7.7%, $p = 0.030$).

Currently there are no randomized clinical studies comparing the efficacy of shorter antimicrobial treatment courses in severe VAP. However, in many cases, antibiotic treatment is prescribed for pulmonary infiltrates without pneumonia. Because VAP in the ICU has a high attributable mortality, empiric antimicrobial treatment is prescribed when new pulmonary infiltrates appear, despite a low likelihood of infection. In a randomized clinical study,[43] patients with low likelihood of nosocomial pneumonia (CPIS <6) were randomized to receive ciprofloxacin (experimental group) for 3 days or standard therapy (choice and duration of antibiotics at the physician's discretion). Antibiotics were continued beyond 3 days in 90% of patients in the standard therapy compared with 28% in the ciprofloxacin group. The duration of antibiotics in patients with CPIS <6 and no other documented infection was 3 days compared to 9.8 days in the standard therapy group. Mortality and length of hospital stay did not differ between the two groups. Nevertheless, antimicrobial resistance or superinfection was documented in 15% of patients in the ciprofloxacin group compared with 35% in the control group. Antimicrobial cost was significantly lower in the ciprofloxacin group. Such an approach, in patients with mild-moderate nosocomial pneumonia, including VAP, may lead to significantly lower antimicrobial therapy costs, antimicrobial resistance rates and superinfections. A recent French study[44] compared 8 vs. 15 days of antibiotic therapy in 401 VAP patients. No excess motility or pulmonary infections were detected on day 28 in the short treatment group, favoring short duration therapy for patients with ICU-VAP.

Catheter-related bloodstream infections

Currently, there are no randomized controlled clinical trials evaluating the optimal duration of therapy for bloodstream infection.

Patients with catheter-related bacteremia are separated into those with complicated infections (e.g. endocarditis, septic thrombosis) and those with uncomplicated infections. Patients with an uncomplicated infection should receive 10–14 days of antimicrobial therapy. Patients with complicated bacteremia should receive a prolonged course of antimicrobial therapy (4–6 weeks). There are no randomized trials evaluating the efficacy of abbreviated courses.

Nosocomial *Staph. aureus* bacteremia is a serious and common disease often associated with serious complications including septic thrombosis, infective endocarditis, osteomyelitis and metastatic abscesses. Despite several studies, the optimal duration of antimicrobial treatment for catheter-related *Staph. aureus* bacteremia (CRSAB) remains unknown. In the past, CRSAB has been treated for 4–6 weeks, but recent studies have reported a low complication rate when the duration of treatment was 10–14 days. In several retrospective studies among patients with CRSAB and no early complications, a 10–15-day course of parenteral antibiotics was equivalent to longer courses of therapy.[45] However, treatment with antimicrobial agents for less than 10 days appeared to be inadequate due to a high rate of relapse. Delayed removal of the catheter is associated with a high rate of relapse. A meta-analysis of studies reporting outcome for patients with *Staph. aureus* bacteremia treated with short-course therapy (≤2 weeks) has identified 11 studies.[46] Late complication rates ranged from 0% to 29% and the relapse rate was 6.1%. However, most of the studies were uncontrolled.

No controlled trials have assessed the optimal duration of antibiotic treatment of catheter-related bloodstream infection due to Gram-negative bacilli. Randomized trials are necessary to determine the optimal duration of treatment for bloodstream infection caused by various micro-organisms.

CONCLUSION

In summary, there is good evidence for shortening antibiotic therapy provided the correct treatment is applied to the appropriate patient in a well-defined patient population for a clearly defined infection caused by a known pathogen with known antibiotic susceptibilities. Most effort in this field was dedicated to infections that can be treated on an outpatient basis; for severe infections, length of therapy still needs additional data.

REFERENCES

1. Cohn DL, Catlin BJ, Peterson KL, *et al.* A-62 dose, 6 months therapy for pulmonary and extrapulmonary tuberculosis: a twice weekly directly observed and cost-effective regimen. Ann Intern Med 1990;112:407–15.
2. MacFarlane JT, Anjorin FL, Cleland PJ, *et al.* Single injection treatment of meningococcal meningitis. 1. Longterm penicillin. Trans Roy Soc Trop Med Hyg 1979;73:693–7.
3. Kardas P. Patient compliance in antibiotic treatment for respiratory tract infections. J Antimicrob Chemother 2002;49:897–903.
4. Guillemot D, Carbon C, Balkau B, *et al.* Low dose and long treatment duration of beta-lactam: risk factors for carriage of penicillin-resistant Streptococcus pneumoniae. JAMA 1998;279:365–70.
5. Habarth S, Samore NH, Lichtenberg D, Carmeli Y. Prolonged antibiotic prophylaxis after cardiovascular surgery and its effect on surgical site infection and antimicrobial resistance. Circulation 2000;101:2916–22.
6. Warren JW, Abrutyn E, Hebel JR, *et al.* Guidelines for antimicrobial treatment of uncomplicated acute bacterial cystitis in women. Clin Infect Dis 1999;29:745–58.
7. Iannini P, Crossley K. Therapy of Staphylococcus aureus bacteremia associated with a removable focus of infection. Ann Intern Med 1976;84:558–60.
8. Zeylemaker MM, Jaspers CA, van Kraaij MG, Visser MR, Hoepelman IM. Long term infectious complications and their relation to treatment duration in catheter-related Staphylococcus aureus bacteremia. Eur J Clin Microbiol Infect Dis 2001;20:380–4.
9. Craig WA. Does the dose matter? Clin Infect Dis 2001;15(suppl 3):S233–7.
10. Bisno AL, Gerber MA, Gwaltney JM Jr, *et al.* Diagnosis and management of Group A streptococcal pharyngitis: a practice guideline. Clin Infect Dis 1997;25:574–83.
11. Breese BB, Bellows MT, Fischel EE, *et al.* Prevention of rheumatic fever: statement of the American Heart Association Council on rheumatic fever and congenital heart disease. JAMA 1953;151:141–3.
12. Schwartz RH, Wientzen RL, Pedreira F, Feroli EJ, Mella GW, Guandolo VL. Penicillin V for group A streptococcal pharyngotonsillitis – a randomized trial of seven vs ten days therapy. JAMA 1981;246:1790–5.
13. Gerber MA, Randolph MF, Chanatry J, Wright LL, DeMeo K, Kaplan EL. Five vs ten days of penicillin V therapy for streptococcal pharyngitis. Am J Dis Child 1987;141(2):224–7.
14. McCarty J, Hedrick JA, Gooch WM. Clarithromycin suspension vs. penicillin V suspension in children with streptococcal pharyngitis. Adv Ther 2000;17(1):14–26.
15. Boccazzi A, Tonelli P, Angelis M, Bellussi L, Passali D, Careddu P. Short course therapy with ceftibuten vs azithromycin in pediatric streptococcal pharyngitis. Pediatr Infect Dis J 2000;19(10):963–7.
16. Pichichero ME, Margolis PA. A comparison of cephalosporins and penicillins in the treatment of Group A streptococcal pharyngitis: a meta-analysis supporting the concept of microbial copathogenicity. Pediatr Infect Dis J 1991;10:275–81.
17. Adam D, Scholz H, Helmerking M. Short-course antibiotic treatment of 4782 culture proven cases of group A streptococcal tonsillopharyngitis and incidence of poststreptococcal sequelae. J Infect Dis 2000;182:509–16.
18. Van Buchem FL, Dunk JH, van Hof MA. Therapy of acute otitis media: myringotomy, antibiotics or either? A double-blind study in children. Lancet 1981;2:883–7.
19. Dowell SF, Butler JC, Giebink GS, *et al.* Acute otitis media: management and surveillance in an era of pneumococcal resistance – a report from the drug-resistant Streptococcus pneumoniae Therapeutic Working Group. Pediatr Infect Dis J 1999;18:1–9.
20. Kozyrkij A, Hildes Ripstein E, *et al.* Treatment of acute otitis media with shortened course of antibiotics: a meta-analysis. JAMA 1998;279:1738–42.
21. Williams JW Jr, Aguilar C, Makela M, *et al.* Antibiotic therapy for acute sinusitis: a systematic literature review. Acute Respiratory Infections Module of the Cochrane Database of Systematic Reviews. Oxford: Update Software; 1997.
22. Zucher DR, Balk E, Engels E, *et al.* Agency for Health Care Policy and Research Publication No. 99-E016: Evidence Report/Technology Assessment Number 9. Diagnosis and treatment of acute bacterial rhinosinusitis. Available at: www.ahrq.gov/clinic/sinussum.htm
23. Sinus and Allergy Health Partnership. Antimicrobial treatment guidelines for acute bacterial rhinosinusitis. Otolaryngol Head Neck Surg 2000;123(suppl 1):4–32.
24. Gehanno P, Beauvillain C, Bobin S, *et al.* Short therapy with amoxicillin/clavulanate and corticosteroids in acute sinusitis: results of a multicentere study in adults. Scand J Infect Dis 2000;32:679–84.
25. Bartlett JG, Dowell SF, Mandell LA, *et al.* Practice guidelines for the management of community acquired pneumonia in adults. Clin Infect Dis 2000;31:347–82.
26. Saint S, Bent S, Vittinghoff E, Grady D. Antibiotics in chronic obstructive pulmonary disease exacerbations. A meta-analysis. JAMA 1995;273:957–60.
27. Iravani A, Tice AD, McCarty J, *et al.* Short-course ciprofloxacin treatment of acute uncomplicated urinary tract infection in women: the minimum effective dose. Arch Intern Med 1995;155:485–94.
28. McCarty JM, Richard G, Huck W, *et al.* A randomized trial of short-course ciprofloxacin, ofloxacin, or trimethoprim/sulfamethoxazole for the treatment of acute urinary tract infection in women. Ciprofloxacin Urinary Tract Infection Group. Am J Med 1999;106(3):292–9.
29. Iravani A, Klimberg I, Briefer C, Munera C, Kowalsky SF, Echols RM and the UTI Group. A trial comparing low-dose, short-course ciprofloxacin and standard 7-day therapy with co-trimoxazole or nitrofurantoin in the treatment of uncomplicated urinary tract infection. J Antimicrob Chemother 1999;43:67–75.
30. Hooton TM, Winter C, Tiu F, Stamm WE. Randomized comparative trial and cost analysis of 3-day antimicrobial regimens for treatment of acute cystitis in women. JAMA 1995;273:41–5.
31. Khan WA, Seas C, Dhar U, Salam MA, Bennish ML. Treatment of shigellosis: V comparison of azithromycin and ciprofloxacin. A double blind randomized controlled trial. Ann Intern Med 1997;126:697–703.
32. Vinh H, Wain J, Chinh MT, *et al.* Treatment of bacillary dysentery in Vietnamese children: two doses of ofloxacin versus 5 days nalidixic acid. Trans Roy Soc Trop Med Hyg 2000;94:323–6.
33. Moosa A, Rubidge CJ. Once daily ceftriaxone vs. chloramphenicol for treatment of typhoid fever in children. Pediatr Infect Dis J 1989;8:696–699.
34. Alam MN, Haq SA, Das KK, *et al.* Efficacy of ciprofloxacin in enteric fever: comparison of treatment durations in sensitive and multidrug resistant Salmonella. Am J Trop Med Hyg 1995;53:306–11.
35. Girgis NI, Butler T, Frenck RW, *et al.* Azithromycin versus ciprofloxacin for treatment of uncomplicated typhoid fever in a randomized trial in Egypt that included patients with multidrug resistance. Antimicrob Agents Chemother 1999;43(6):1441–4.
36. Smith MD, Duong NM, Hoa NT, *et al.* Comparison of ofloxacin and ceftriaxone for short-course treatment of enteric fever. Antimicrob Agents Chemother 1994;38:1716–20.

37. Tran TH, Bethell DB, Nguyen TT, *et al.* Short-course of ofloxacin for treatment of multidrug-resistant typhoid. Clin Infect Dis 1995;20:917–23.
38. Chinh NT, Parry CM, Thi Ly N, *et al.* A randomized controlled comparison of azithromycin and ofloxacin for treatment of multidrug-resistant or nalidixic acid-resistant enteric fever. Antimicrob Agents Chemother 2000;44:1855–9.
39. Mylonakis E, Calderwood SB. Infective endocarditis in adults. N Engl J Med 2001;345:1318–30.
40. Working Party of the British Society for Antimicrobial Chemotherapy. Antibiotic treatment of streptococcal, enterococcal, and staphylococcal endocarditis. Heart 1998;79:207–10.
41. American Thoracic Society. Hospital-acquired pneumonia in adults: diagnosis, assessment of severity, initial antimicrobial therapy, and preventive strategies. A consensus statement. Am J Respir Crit Care Med 1996;53:1711–25.
42. Ibrahim EH, Ward S, Sherman G, Schaiff R, Fraser VJ, Kollef MH. Experience with a clinical guideline for the treatment of ventilator-associated pneumonia. Crit Care Med 2001;29:1109–15.
43. Singh N, Rogers P, Atwood CW, Wagener MM, Yu VL. Short-course empiric antibiotic therapy for patients with pulmonary infiltrates in the intensive care unit. Am J Respir Crit Care Med 2000;165:505–11.
44. Chastre J, Wolff M, Fagon JY, Chevert A and Pneum A. Trial group comparison of two durations of antibiotic therapy to treat ventilator-associated pneumonia. 99th American Thoracic Society Meeting 2003. Seattle, Washington, USA. Abstract 353226.
45. Malanoski GJ, Samore MH, Pefanis A, Karchmer AW. Staphylococcus aureus catheter-associated bacteremia. Minimal effective therapy and unusual infectious complications associated with arterial sheath catheters. Arch Intern Med 1995;155:1161–6.
46. Fowler VG Jr, Sanders RS, Corey GR, *et al.* Outcome of Staphylococcus aureus bacteremia according to compliance with recommendations of infectious diseases specialists: experience with 244 patients. Clin Infect Dis 1998;27:478–86.

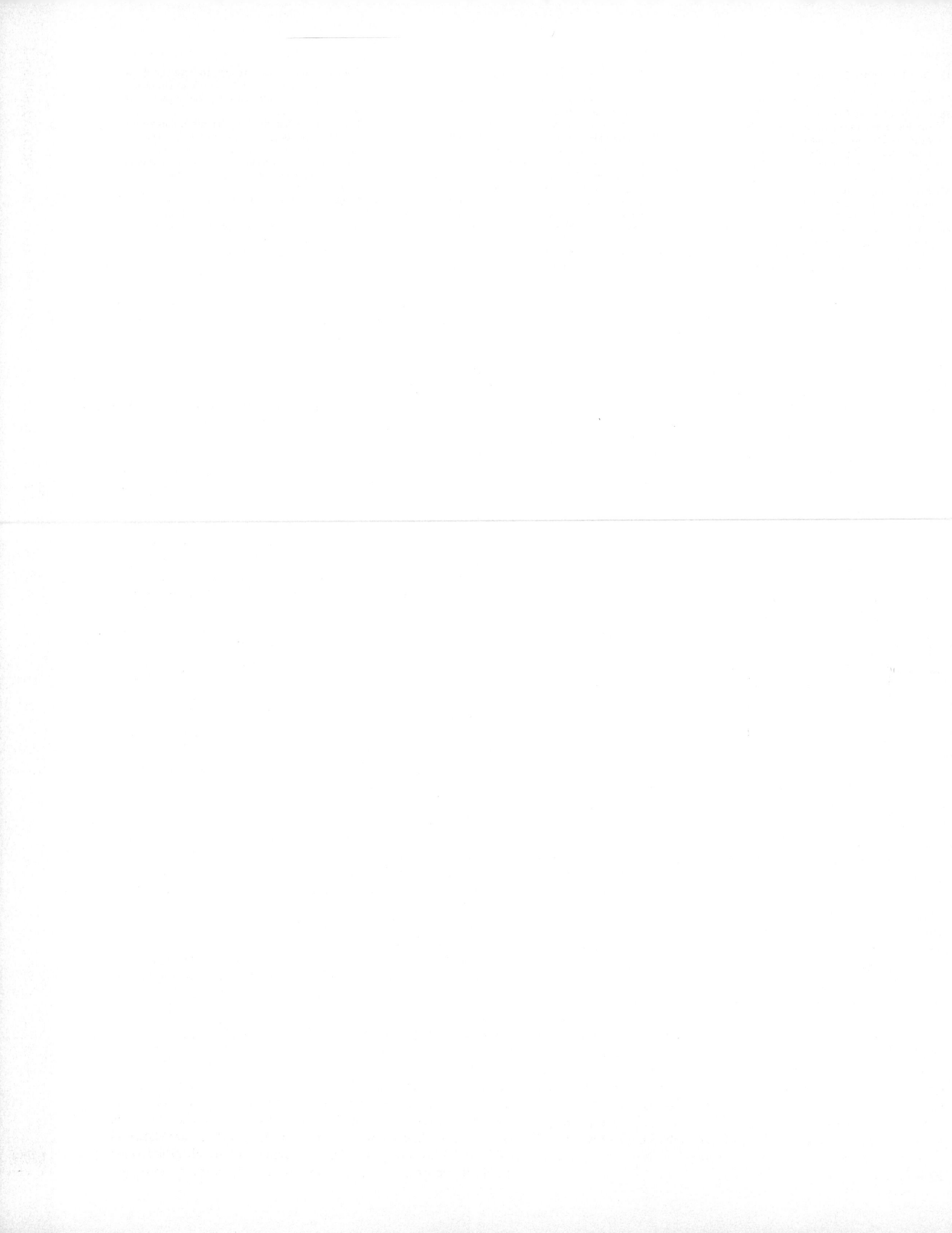

chapter 193

β-Lactam Antibiotics

Jason S Kendler & Barry J Hartman

INTRODUCTION

In 1928, Alexander Fleming observed that a mold of the genus *Penicillium* inhibited the growth of bacteria in culture.[1] Over a decade later in 1941, Florey, Chain and Abraham used penicillin for the first time in patients with staphylococcal and streptococcal infections.[2,3] More than a half century later, the β-lactam antibiotics remain the mainstay of treatment for a variety of bacterial infections (Table 193.1) and now include:

- penicillins (natural penicillins, penicillinase-resistant penicillins, aminopenicillins, carboxypenicillins and ureidopenicillins);
- cephalosporins (first-, second-, third- and fourth-generation);
- monobactams;
- carbapenems; and
- β-lactamase inhibitor combinations.

PENICILLINS

The natural penicillins are used primarily for the treatment of selected Gram-positive and anaerobic infections as well as selected Gram-negative infections. The penicillinase-resistant penicillins are primarily used for the treatment of infections due to staphylococci, but are also active against other Gram-positive organisms. The aminopenicillins have a similar spectrum of activity as the natural penicillins, but have additional coverage of Gram-negative organisms including many Enterobacteriaceae. When used in conjunction with β-lactamase inhibitors, they have extended coverage against Gram-positive, Gram-negative and anaerobic organisms that produce β-lactamases, which normally hydrolyze these agents. The carboxypenicillins and ureidopenicillins cover Gram-negative bacilli that are resistant to the aminopenicillins, in particular *Pseudomonas aeruginosa*. The carboxypenicillins and ureidopenicillins can also be used in conjunction with β-lactamase inhibitors for extended activity against β-lactamase-producing organisms.

Cephalosporins

The first-generation cephalosporins have excellent activity against Gram-positive cocci, but can also treat some community-acquired Gram-negative infections. The second-generation cephalosporins have improved Gram-negative coverage compared with that of the first-generation cephalosporins, and selected agents (i.e. cefoxitin and cefotetan) have excellent activity against anaerobes. Third-generation cephalosporins have further improved Gram-negative coverage; ceftazidime is used for *P. aeruginosa* infections, but has limited Gram-positive coverage. Ceftriaxone, a third-generation cephalosporin, not only has excellent Gram-negative activity but also provides excellent coverage of *Streptococcus pneumoniae* and other viridans streptococci. The fourth-generation cephalosporins (cefepime is the only drug available in the USA at this time) have excellent Gram-positive and Gram-negative coverage. No cephalosporin has any activity against *Enterococcus* spp.

Monobactams

The monobactams (aztreonam is the only available agent in this class) are effective only against aerobic Gram-negative organisms and have no activity against Gram-positive organisms or anaerobes.

Carbapenems

The carbapenems (imipenem, meropenem and ertapenem) have the broadest bacterial coverage of the β-lactam antibiotics, treating most infections with Gram-positive, Gram-negative and anaerobic bacteria.

Mechanism of action

β-Lactam antibiotics are bactericidal. Their mechanism of action involves interference with bacterial cell wall synthesis. More specifically, they attach to penicillin-binding proteins on the inner surface of the bacterial cell membrane, thereby interrupting the transpeptidation process that cross-links the amino acids of the individual petidoglycan components of the forming bacterial cell wall. Ultimately, loss of viability and, in some bacteria, lysis occurs as the result of the activation of autolytic enzymes through a poorly understood mechanism.[4] Of all β-lactam agents, only the carbapenems possess an extended inhibitory effect on bacterial growth after levels of these agents are below inhibitory levels (postantibiotic effect). In fact, only the carbapenem class of β-lactam antibiotics exhibits concentration-dependent killing – maximal bactericidal activity occurs at 4–5 times the minimum inhibitory concentration (MIC) of the organism, whereas all other β-lactam classes (penicillins, cephalosporins, monobactams) exhibit time-dependent killing pharmacodynamics (activity is greatest only during a period when the concentration is above the MIC) and there is no postantibiotic effect. In addition, regrowth of bacteria occurs rapidly after withdrawal of cephalosporins.

Bacterial resistance

Three major mechanisms lead to bacterial resistance to β-lactam antibiotics:

- failure of the antibiotic to penetrate the bacterial cell membrane;
- alterations in the penicillin-binding proteins that reduce the binding affinities of the β-lactams (intrinsic resistance);[5] and
- bacterial production of β-lactamases, which hydrolyze the β-lactam ring and render it inactive.

The most important and most common cause of resistance is the production of β-lactamases.[6] Strategies to combat resistance, including the use of β-lactamase inhibitors, are discussed later in this chapter.

PHARMACOKINETICS AND DISTRIBUTION

Absorption

The β-lactams have variable absorption from the gastrointestinal tract. Some agents, such as the antipseudomonal penicillins and methicillin, are acid-labile and cannot be taken orally. The absorption characteristics and pharmacokinetics of the β-lactams are shown in Table 193.2. Of note, amoxicillin is almost totally absorbed when administered orally whereas ampicillin is only partially absorbed.

THE DIFFERENT CLASSES OF β-LACTAM ANTIBIOTICS AND SAMPLE INDICATIONS FOR SELECTED AGENTS			
Class of β-lactam	**Example**	**Route**	**Sample indication**
Penicillins			
Natural penicillin	Penicillin V (phenoxymethyl penicillin)	po	Streptococcal pharyngitis
	Penicillin G (benzylpenicillin)	iv	Neurosyphilis
Penicillinase-resistant penicillin	Flucloxacillin	po	Cellulitis
	Nafcillin	iv	*Staphylococcus aureus* endocarditis
Aminopenicillin	Amoxicillin	po	Endocarditis prophylaxis
	Ampicillin	iv	*Listeria monocytogenes meningitis*
Amidinopenicillin	Piv-mecillinam	po	Urinary tract infection
Carboxypenicillin	Ticarcillin	iv	*Pseudomonas aeruginosa* pneumonia
Ureidopenicillin	Piperacillin	iv	Cholangitis
Cephalosporins			
First-generation	Cephalexin	po	Cellulitis
	Cefazolin	iv	Prophylaxis before surgery
Second-generation	Cefuroxime	po	Sinusitis
	Cefaxitin	iv	Intra-abdominal infection
Third-generation	Cefixime	po	*Escherichia coli* urinary tract infection (cystitis)
	Ceftriaxone	iv	Pneumococcal meningitis
	Ceftazidime	iv	*P. aeruginosa* pneumonia
Fourth-generation	Cefepime	iv	Septicemia secondary to Enterobacteriaceae resistant to other agents
Monobactam	Aztreonam	iv	Gram-negative septicemia
Carbapenems	Imipenem	iv	Monotherapy for intra-abdominal infections
	Meropenem	iv	Monotherapy for ultra-abdominal infections
	Ertapenem	iv	Complicated skin and soft tissue infections
β-Lactamase inhibitors	Clavulanic acid (+ amoxicillin)	po	Animal bite
	Clavulanic acid (+ ticarcillin)	iv	Neutropenic sepsis
	Sulbactam (+ ampicillin)	iv	Head and neck infection
	Tazobactam (+ piperacillin)	iv	Nosocomial sepsis

Table 193.1 The different classes of β-lactam antibiotics and sample indications for selected agents.

The presence of food in the stomach can delay absorption and can lower the peak serum concentration attainable for some β-lactams, such as ampicillin, cefaclor, cefixime and ceftibuten. In contrast, food can increase the absorption of cefuroxime and cefpodoxime.

Distribution

Following absorption, β-lactams are variably bound to serum proteins, mostly albumin. Protein-bound drug does not exert antimicrobial activity, but binding is reversible. In general, the degree to which a β-lactam antibiotic is protein bound does not influence the decision to use the antibiotic and the effect of protein binding on drug efficacy is not clear.[14] Excretion of the β-lactams is primarily renal (glomerular filtration and tubular secretion) and, in general, the serum half-life of these drugs is short.

Procaine penicillin G and benzathine penicillin G are intramuscular preparations that are absorbed slowly, allowing for longer dosing intervals, but the half-life of the drug is the same. Nafcillin, the ureidopenicillins (20–30%), cefoperazone (70%), ceftriaxone (40%) and cefotetan (20%) have significant excretion in bile.[10]

Imipenem is inactivated by an enzyme present on the renal brush border, dehydropeptidase I. Cilastatin is a dehydropeptidase inhibitor administered along with imipenem to prevent subtherapeutic levels of the antibiotic in urine. Cilastatin does not possess any antimicrobial activity nor does it alter the pharmacokinetics of other drugs.[15]

The β-lactam antibiotics achieve therapeutic concentrations in most tissues such as lung, kidney, bone, muscle and liver, and in secretions such as synovial fluid, pleural fluid, pericardial fluid, peritoneal fluid and bile. The microenvironment that may be found in an abscess, including a low pH, the presence of neutrophils and associated proteins, and low oxygen tension, does not inhibit the function of β-lactam antibiotics. However, β-lactams do not penetrate host cells and are therefore ineffective against intracellular organisms. Low concentrations of β-lactams are found in prostatic secretions, brain tissue, intraocular fluid and cerebrospinal fluid (CSF; Fig. 193.1). In the presence of inflammation, however, concentrations in the CSF are much higher, accounting for the efficacy of some β-lactams in the treatment of meningitis.[16] The penicillins and cephalosporins can penetrate the aqueous humor of the eye, but do not reach therapeutic levels in the posterior chamber.

ROUTE OF ADMINISTRATION AND DOSAGE

β-Lactams are available for oral, intravenous and intramuscular use. Generic and trade names, routes of administration and standard dosages for adult and pediatric patients with normal renal function are listed in Table 193.3. In dosing the β-lactam antibiotics, it is important to remember that:

- food can have an effect on oral absorption (e.g. food decreases absorption of ampicillin); and
- absorption of both cefuroxime and cefpodoxime are decreased by H_2-blockers or nonabsorbable antacids.[17]

In general, high doses of a β-lactam antibiotic should be used in patients who are neutropenic and for severe infections such as bacteremia, meningitis and otitis media in children. Dosages must be reduced in patients with renal failure (with the exception of nafcillin, cefoperazone and ceftriaxone) and in neonates, in whom renal function is not yet fully developed. Dosages of nafcillin, the ureidopenicillins and cefoperazone must be reduced in patients with severe liver disease (see Dosage in special circumstances, below).

INDICATIONS

The β-lactam antibiotics can be effectively used for the treatment of a variety of infections. These agents are widely distributed following administration and are routinely used in the treatment of sinusitis, otitis, pharyngitis, epiglottitis, dental infections, bronchitis, pneumonia, meningitis, infections of the genitourinary tract (including cervicitis and urethritis caused by *Neisseria gonorrhoeae*), peritonitis, biliary and gastrointestinal infections, skin and soft tissue infections, osteomyelitis, septic arthritis and infection of prosthetic devices, including venous access catheters. The choice of antibiotic and recommended duration of therapy for these infections is discussed in the chapters on the specific diseases. The remainder of this section focuses on the use of the β-lactam antibiotics in special circumstances. Table 193.4 summarizes the relative susceptibilities of various micro-organisms to the β-lactam antibiotics.

PHARMACOKINETICS FOR SELECTED β-LACTAM ANTIBIOTICS					
Generic name	**Oral absorption (%)**	**Effect of food on absorption**	**Protein binding (%)**	**Serum half-life (h)**	**Biliary excretion (%)**
Penicillins					
Amoxicillin/clavutanic acid	75/–	–/Increases	20/9–25	1.0/1.0	
Ampicillin/sulbactam	40/–	Decreases/–	20/38	0.8–1.5/1.0	3/–
Azlocillin	0		30	0.8–1.5	20–30
Bacampicillin		None	20	1.1	
Carbenicillin	30				0
Cloxacillin	50	Decreases			
Dicloxacillin	50	Decreases	95	0.7	
Methicillin			35–60	0.5–1.0	
Mezlocillin	0		16–42	1.0	20–30
Nafcillin	Erratic	Decreases	85	0.5	60–70
Oxacillin	30	Decreases	93	0.5	
Penicillin G	20	Decreases	60	0.5	
Penicillin V	60	None	80	0.6	
Piperacillin/tazobactam	0		16–30/30	0.6–1.2/1.0	20–30/–
Ticarcillin/clavulanic acid	0/–		45/9–25	1.2/1.0	4/–
Cephalosporins					
First-generation					
Cefadroxil		None	20	1.4	
Cefazolin			80	1.4–2.0	
Cephalexin	95	None	20	0.7–1.1	
Cephalothin			65	0.5–1.0	
Cephapirin			45–60	0.4	
Cephadrine	90	None	10	0.7–1.3	
Second-generation					
Cefaclor	52–95	Decreases	25	0.6–0.9	
Cefamandole			75	0.5–1.0	
Cefdinir	16–25	–	60–70	1.7	–
Cefmetazole			75	1.2	
Cefonicid			>90	4.5	
Cefotetan			88	3–4.6	20
Cefoxitin			41–75	0.7–1.1	
Cefprozil	95	None	36	1.3	
Ceftibuten		Decreases		2–2.4	
Cefuroxime	30–52	Increases	50	1.2–1.9	
Loracarbef	90	Decreases	25	1.0	
Third-generation					
Cefditoren	14	Increased with fatty meal	88	1.6	–
Cefixime	40–50	Delays peak	65	3–4	
Cefoperazone			82–93	2.0	70
Cefotaxime			37	1.0	8
Cefpodoxime	30–50	Increases	22–33	2.1–2.8	
Ceftazidime			<10	1.9	<1
Ceftizoxime			30	1.7	<1
Ceftriaxone			85–95	5.8–8.7	40
Fourth-generation					
Cefepime			20	2	
Monobactam					
Aztreonam			55	1.5–2.0	10
Carbapenems					
Ertapenem	–	–	85–95	4	–
Imipenem/cilastatin			20/40	1–3/1.0	
Meropenem			2	1.0	

Table 193.2 Pharmacokinetics for selected β-lactam antibiotics.[7–13] Absence of information is due to either lack of information or no effect.

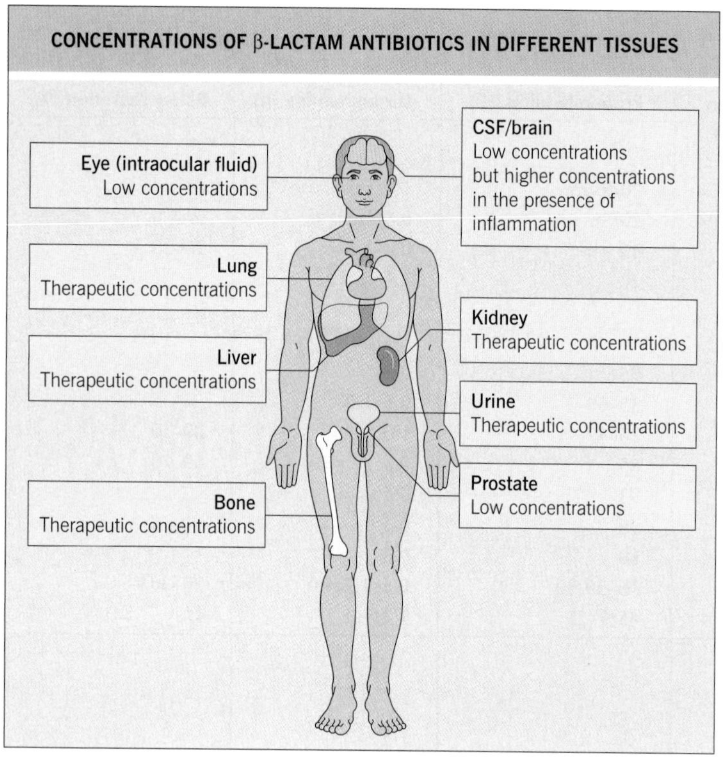

Fig. 193.1 Concentrations of β-lactam antibiotics in different tissues.

Prophylaxis

Antimicrobial prophylaxis in surgery (see also Chapter 190)

β-Lactam antibiotics are commonly used to decrease the incidence of infection for selected surgical procedures.[18] A single dose of cefazolin has been shown to decrease the incidence of wound infection for selected 'clean' procedures and is used commonly for cardiac, noncardiac thoracic, vascular, orthopedic, ophthalmic and neurosurgical procedures. For 'clean–contaminated' procedures in which colonized mucosa is violated, such as head and neck surgery, abdominal surgery and gynecologic surgery, antibiotic prophylaxis may also be used. Cefazolin or ampicillin–sulbactam can be used before head and neck surgery. Patients who are obese, who have reduced intestinal motility or who have decreased gastric acidity may be at high risk for infection following abdominal surgery and may also be candidates for prophylaxis with cefazolin.

Similarly, patients undergoing biliary tract surgery who are at high risk of infection due to advanced age, acute cholecystitis, a nonfunctioning gallbladder, obstructive jaundice, or choledocholithiasis may benefit from preoperative cefazolin. In the setting of acute appendicitis, cefoxitin or cefotetan have been shown to decrease the incidence of infection postoperatively. Women undergoing vaginal or abdominal hysterectomy, emergency cesarean section or first trimester abortion may be candidates for antibiotic prophylaxis with cefazolin or other agents.

Antibiotics should be used not only as prophylaxis but also as treatment for 'dirty' surgical procedures in which the surgical site is obviously contaminated by bacteria (e.g. a perforated viscus). Antimicrobial prophylaxis in surgery is summarized periodically in the publication *The Medical Letter*.[18]

Prophylaxis is not routinely recommended for patients undergoing cardiac catheterization, gastrointestinal endoscopy, herniorrhaphy, varicose vein surgery, most plastic surgery, arterial puncture, thoracentesis, paracentesis, repair of simple lacerations, outpatient treatment of burns, dental extractions or root canal therapy. Antimicrobial prophylaxis before breast surgery is controversial. A recent study suggests that antibiotic prophylaxis for endoscopic retrograde cholangiopancreatography does not prevent cholangitis.[19]

Endocarditis prophylaxis

Patients who have underlying cardiac or congenital valvular abnormalities are candidates for antibiotic prophylaxis when they undergo procedures that can cause transient bacteremia. Cardiac conditions that place a patient at increased risk of endocarditis include prosthetic valves, a previous history of endocarditis, most congenital cardiac abnormalities (except an isolated secundum atrial septal defect), rheumatic and other acquired valvular dysfunction, hypertrophic cardiomyopathy and mitral valve prolapse when accompanied by regurgitation.

Procedures that can cause transient bacteremia and may place a patient at risk of endocarditis include:

- dental procedures (including professional cleaning),
- tonsillectomy and/or adenoidectomy,
- surgical procedures involving intestinal or respiratory mucosa,
- rigid bronchoscopy,
- sclerotherapy for esophageal varices,
- esophageal dilatation,
- gallbladder surgery,
- cystoscopy,
- urethral dilatation,
- urethral catheterization and/or urinary tract surgery if there is infection,
- prostatic surgery, and
- incision and drainage of infected tissue.

The antibiotic of choice for prophylaxis for dental, oral or upper respiratory tract manipulations is a single dose of amoxicillin 2g taken orally 1 hour before the procedure. For high-risk patients undergoing genitourinary or gastrointestinal procedures, ampicillin 2g intravenously with gentamicin 1.5mg/kg intravenously should be given within 30 minutes of starting the procedure and then ampicillin or amoxicillin 1g orally should be given 6 hours later. Alternatives exist for patients who are allergic to penicillins.[20]

Rheumatic fever prophylaxis

Because patients who have had acute rheumatic fever are at risk of recurrent attacks if they have group A streptococcal infections, the American Heart Association recommends prophylaxis with penicillin for these patients. The dose is either a single injection of benzathine penicillin G 1.2 million U intramuscularly every 4 weeks or penicillin V 250mg orally q12h. It seems that prophylaxis can be safely discontinued in patients with a history of carditis after 10 years or at age 25. In patients without a history of carditis, prophylaxis can be stopped after 5 years or at age 18. The decision to stop prophylaxis, however, must be individualized because a patient who is at continued risk of streptococcal infection (e.g. teacher or pediatrician) may benefit from continued antibiotic prophylaxis (see also Chapter 60).[21]

Pneumococcal infections

Penicillin is the antibiotic of choice for infections (such as pneumonia, bacteremia or meningitis) caused by susceptible strains of *S. pneumoniae*. However, an increasing proportion of isolates of this pathogen are resistant to penicillin. Intermediate resistance is defined as a strain with an MIC of 0.1–1μg/ml and high-level resistance is defined by an MIC greater than or equal to 2μg/ml. The E test (an antibiotic strip with graded concentrations) is a convenient and reliable method for the detection of penicillin or cephalosporin resistance in pneumococci.[22] In the early 1990s, 4–5% of clinical isolates in the USA were found to be either intermediately or highly resistant to penicillin.[23,24] In a study that examined isolates collected from outpatients at different sites in the USA between 1994 and 1995, 14.1%

β-LACTAMS – SPECTRUM OF ACTIVITY, TRADE NAMES, ROUTES OF ADMINISTRATION AND DOSAGE IN PATIENTS WITH NORMAL RENAL FUNCTION					
Class	**Antimicrobial spectrum**	**Generic name**	**Trade name**	**Route**	**Adult dose (pediatric dose) for normal renal function**
Penicillins					
Natural penicillins	Gram-positives, anaerobes, selected Gram-negatives	Penicillin V	Betapen, Ledercillin, Pen-Vee, Robicillin, S-K penicillin, V-cillin, Veetids	po	250–500mg q6h (25–50mg/kg/day divided q6h)
		Penicillin G, benzathine	Bicillin, Permapen	im	600,000–1.2 million U every 1–4 weeks (300,000–600,000U every 1–4 weeks for weight <27kg; 900,000–1.2 million U every 1–4 weeks for weight >27kg)
		Penicillin G, procaine	Crysticillin, Duracillin, Wycillin	im	600,000–1.2 million U q12–24h
		Penicillin G, sodium or potassium		iv	1–4 million U q4h
Penicillinase-resistant penicillins	Penicillin-resistant *Staphylococcus aureus* and *Staphylococcus epidermidis*. Also active against streptococci	Cloxacillin	Tegopen	po	250–500mg q6h
		Dicloxacillin	Dynapen, Pathocil, Veracillin	po	125–500mg q6h (12–25mg/kg/day divided q6h)
		Flucloxacillin*	Floxapen	po im/iv	500mg q6h 1–2g q6h
		Methicillin	Celbenin, Staphcillin	im/iv	1–2g q4–6h
		Nafcillin	Unipen	im/iv po	1–2g q4–6h (50mg/kg/day divided q4–6h) 250–500mg q4–6h
		Oxacillin	Bactocill, Prostaphlin	im/iv po	1–2g q4–6h (50–100mg/kg/day divided q4–6h) 250–500mg q4–6h
Aminopenicillins	Same as penicillin G plus added Gram-negative cocci and Enterobacteriaceae	Amoxicillin	Amoxil, Larotid, Polymax	po	250–500mg q8h (20–40mg/kg/day divided q8h)
		Ampicillin	Alpen, Amcil, Omipen, Penbritin, Polycillin, Principen, Probampcin, Totacillin	po im/iv	250–500mg q6h 1–2g q4–6h (50–200mg/kg/day divided q4–6h)
		Bacampicillin		po	400–800mg q12h (25mg/kg/day divided q12h)
	β-Lactamase inhibitors expand Gram-positive, Gram-negative and anaerobic coverage	Amoxicillin–clavulanic acid	Augmentin	po	250–500mg q8–12h or 875mg q12h (20–40mg/kg/day divided q8–12h)
		Ampicillin–sulbactam	Unasyn	im/iv	1.5–3.0g q6h
Carboxypenicillins	Gram-negative aerobic rods resistant to ampicillin, including *Pseudomonas aeruginosa*	Ticarcillin	Ticar	im/iv	3–4g q4–6h (200–300mg/kg/day divided q4–6h)
		Ticarcillin–clavulanic acid	Timentin	iv	3.1g q4–6h (200–300mg/kg/day ticarcillin divided q4–6h)
Ureidopenicillins	Similar to carboxypenicillins	Azlocillin	Azlin	im/iv	3–4g q4–6h (90–120mg/kg/day divided q6–8h)
		Mezlocillin	Mezlin	im/iv	3–4g q4–6h (300mg/kg/day divided q4h)
		Piperacillin	Pipral, Pipracil	im/iv	3–4g q4–6h
		Piperacillin–tazobactam	Zosyn	iv	3.375g q4–6h
Cephalosporins					
First-generation	Gram-positive cocci and some community-acquired Gram-negative bacilli	Cefadroxil	Duricef, Ultracef	po	1–2g/day q24h or q12h (30mg/kg/day divided q12h)
		Cefazolin	Ancef, Kefzol	im/iv	0.5–1.5g q6–8h (25–100mg/kg/day divided q6–8h)
		Cephalexin	Biocef, Keflex, Keftab	po	250–500mg q6h (25–100mg/kg/day divided q6h)
		Cephalothin	Keffin, Seffin	im/iv	0.5–2g q4–6h (100mg/kg/day divided q4–6h)
		Cephapirin	Cefadyl	im/iv	0.5–2g q4–6h
		Cephradine	Anspor, Velosef	po im/iv	1–2g/day divided q6–12h 1g q6h

Table 193.3 β-Lactams – spectrum of activity, trade names, routes of administration and dosage in patients with normal renal function.[9] *Not available in the USA. Note that the trade name may differ in other parts of the world.

β-LACTAMS – SPECTRUM OF ACTIVITY, TRADE NAMES, ROUTES OF ADMINISTRATION AND DOSAGE IN PATIENTS WITH NORMAL RENAL FUNCTION					
Class	**Antimicrobial spectrum**	**Generic name**	**Trade name**	**Route**	**Adult dose (pediatric dose) for normal renal function**
Cephalosporins —cont'd					
Second-generation	Improved Gram-negative coverage as compared with first-generation; some agents have activity against anaerobes	Cefaclor	Ceclor	po	250–500mg q8h (20–40mg/kg/day divided q8h)
		Cefamandole	Mandol	im/iv	0.5–1.0g q4–8h (50–100mg/kg/day divided q4–8h)
		Cefdinir	Omnicef	po	300mg po q12h or 600mg po q24h (7mg/kg po q12h or 14mg/kg po q24h)
		Cefmetazole	Zefazone	im/iv	2g q6–12h
		Cefonicid	Monocid	im/iv	1–2g q24h
		Cefotetan	Cefotan	im/iv	1–2g q12h
		Cefoxitin	Mefoxin	im/iv	1–2g q6–8h (80–160mg/kg/day divided q6h)
		Cefprozil	Cefzil	po	250–500mg q24h or divided q12h (7.5–15mg/kg/day divided q12h)
		Ceftibuten	Cedax	po	400mg q24h (9mg/kg/day)
		Cefuroxime	Ceftin	po	250–500mg q12h (20–30mg/kg/day divided q12h)
			Kefurox, Zinacef	im/iv	0.75–1.5g q8h (50–240mg/kg/day divided q8h)
		Loracarbef	Lorabid	po	200–400mg q12h (15–30mg/kg/day divided q12h)
Third-generation	Improved Gram-negative coverage; excellent *Streptococcus pneumoniae* coverage (ceftriaxone, cefotaxime), modest staphylococcal coverage, excellent *P. aeruginosa* coverage (ceftazidime, cefoperazone)	Cefditoren	Spectracef	po	200–400mg po q12h
		Cefixime	Suprax	po	400mg/day q24h or divided q12h (8mg/kg/day q24h or divided q12h)
		Cefoperazone	Cefobid	im/iv	2–4g q12h
		Cefotaxime	Claforan	im/iv	1–2g q4–12h (50–180mg/kg/day divided q4–6h)
		Cefpodoxime	Vantin	po	200mg q12h (10mg/kg/day q24h or divided q12h)
		Ceftazidime	Fortaz, Tazicef, Tazidime	im/iv	1–2g q8–12h (90–150mg/kg/day divided q8h)
		Ceftizoxime	Cefizox	im/iv	0.5–4g q8–12h (150–200mg/kg/day divided q6–8h)
		Ceftriaxone	Rocephin	im/iv	1–2g q24h (50–100mg/kg/day divided q12–24h)
Fourth-generation	Excellent Gram-positive and Gram-negative coverage (including *P. aeruginosa*)	Cefepime	Maxipime	im/iv	0.5–2g q12h
Monobactam	Gram-negatives including *P. aeruginosa*, but no Gram-positives and no anaerobes	Aztreonam	Azactam	im/iv	0.5–2g q6–12h
Carbapenems	Excellent activity against Gram-positives, Gram-negatives (including *P. aeruginosa*) and anaerobes	Ertapenem	Invanz	im/iv	1g q24h
		Imipenem–cilastatin	Primaxin	im/iv	0.25–1g q6–8h
		Meropenem	Merrem	iv	1–2g q8h (60–120mg/kg/day divided q8h)

Table 193.3 β-lactams – spectrum of activity, trade names, routes of administration and dosage in patients with normal renal function–cont'd.[9]
*Not available in the USA. Note that the trade name may fiffer in other parts of the world.

had intermediate resistance and 9.5% were highly resistant.[25] Because of the emergence of resistance, some suggest that suspected cases of pneumococcal pneumonia and meningitis should be treated with vancomycin and/or a third-generation cephalosporin such as ceftriaxone until susceptibilities are known (see Chapter 34). There have been reports of failure of third-generation cephalosporins in the treatment of penicillin-resistant pneumococcal meningitis, again suggesting that vancomycin should be included until susceptibilities are known.[26]

Staphylococcal infections

Soon after the introduction of penicillin for the treatment of staphylococcal infections, penicillinase-producing strains became so common that it was no longer effective. Penicillinase-resistant penicillins (nafcillin, oxacillin, methicillin, dicloxacillin, cloxacillin and flucloxacillin) are now the agents of choice for susceptible strains of *Staphylococcus aureus*. Other β-lactam antibiotics that are effective in the treatment of staphylococcal infections are:

- the aminopenicillins in combination with a β-lactamase inhibitor (ampicillin–sulbactam or amoxicillin–clavulanate);
- the antipseudomonal penicillins in combination with a β-lactamase inhibitor (ticarcillin–clavulanate, piperacillin–tazobactam); and
- the carbapenems (ertapenem, imipenem and meropenem).

The first-generation cephalosporins, which are as effective as the penicillinase-resistant penicillins in the treatment of staphylococcal

SUSCEPTIBILITIES OF MICRO-ORGANISMS TO β-LACTAM ANTIBIOTICS						
Generic name	**Streptococci**	**Penicillinase-producing *S. aureus****	**Enterococci**	**Enteric Gram-negative bacilli†**	***Pseudomonas aeruginosa***	**Anaerobes**
Penicillins						
Amoxicillin	+++	0	+++	+	0	+
Amoxicillin–clavulanate	+++	++	+++	+++	0	+++
Ampicillin	+++	0	+++	+	0	+
Ampicillin–sulbactam	+++	++	+++	+++	0	+++
Azlocillin	++	0	+	++	+++	++
Bacampicillin	+++	0	+++	+	0	+
Carbenicillin	++	0	+	++	++	+
Cloxacillin	++	+++	0	0	0	0
Dicloxacillin	++	+++	0	0	0	0
Flucloxacillin	++	+++	0	0	0	0
Methicillin	++	+++	0	0	0	0
Mezlocillin	++	0	++	++	+++	++
Nafcillin	++	+++	0	0	0	0
Oxacillin	++	+++	0	0	0	0
Penicillin	+++	0	+++	0	0	+
Piperacillin	+++	0	++	++	+++	+
Piperacillin–tazobactam	+++	++	++	+++	+++	+++
Ticarcillin	+++	+	+	++	+++	++
Ticarcillin–clavulanate	+++	++	+	+++	+++	+++
Cephalosporins						
Cefaclor	++	++	0	++	0	+
Cefadroxil	++	++	0	++	0	+
Cefamandole	++	++	0	++	0	+
Cefazolin	+++	+++	0	+	0	+
Cefditoren	+++	++	0	++	0	+
Cefdinir	+++	++	0	++	0	0
Cefepime	+++	++	0	+++	+++	+
Cefixime[1]	+++	0	0	+++	0	+
Cefmetazole	++	+	0	++	0	++
Cefonicid	++	++	0	++	0	+
Cefoperazone	+	+	0	++	++	+
Cefotaxime	++	++	0	+++	+	+
Cefotetan	++	+	0	++	0	+++
Cefoxitin	++	+	0	++	0	+++
Cefpodoxime	+++	++	0	++	0	++
Cefprozil	++	+	0	++	0	+
Ceftazidime	+	+	0	+++	+++	+
Ceftibuten	++	0	0	+	0	0
Ceftizoxime	++	+	0	++	+	++
Ceftriaxone	+++	+	0	+++	+	+
Cefuroxime	+++	++	0	++	0	+
Cephalexin	+++	+++	0	+	0	+
Cephalothin	+++	+++	0	+	0	+
Cephapirin	++	+	0	++	0	+
Cephradine	++	+	0	++	0	+
Loracarbef	+++	+++	0	++	0	+
Monobactams						
Aztreonam	0	0	0	+++	+++	0
Carbapenems						
Ertapenem	+++	+++	+	+++	0	+++
Imipenem	+++	+++	++	+++	+++	+++
Meropenem	+++	+++	++	+++	+++	+++

1. Discontinued in the USA. MMWR 2002;51:1052.

Table 193.4 Relative susceptibilities to β-lactam antibiotics. *Methicillin-sensitive *Staphylococcus aureus* and *S. epidermidis*. All methicillin-resistant *S. aureus* and *S. epidermidis* are resistant to all β-lactams. †Primarily *Escherichia coli, Klebsiella pneumoniae, Enterobacter cloacae, Enterobacter aerogenes* and *Proteus mirabilis.*

infections, require less frequent dosing and may be used in patients with a history of mild penicillin allergy.

It is extremely important to remember that isolates of *S. aureus* or *Staphylococcus epidermidis* that are resistant to methicillin should be considered to be resistant to all other β-lactam antibiotics, including the cephalosporins and carbapenems, even if in-vitro testing suggests otherwise.[27]

Gram-positive bacilli

Penicillin G is the treatment of choice for:

- infections (oral-cervicofacial, thoracic, abdominal) due to actinomycosis;
- elimination of the carrier state of diphtheria;
- infections (pulmonary, cutaneous, gastrointestinal) due to anthrax;
- gas gangrene caused by species of *Clostridium* spp.; and
- erysipeloid caused by *Erysipelothrix rhusiopathiae.*

Either penicillin G or ampicillin may be used for infections caused by *Listeria monocytogenes*. No cephalosporin has any activity against *L. monocytogenes.*

Infections caused by Gram-negative organisms including *Pseudomonas aeruginosa*

The β-lactam antibiotics that have activity against *P. aeruginosa* are ticarcillin, carbenicillin, azlocillin, mezlocillin, piperacillin, ceftazidime, cefoperazone, cefepime, aztreonam, imipenem and meropenem. During treatment of pseudomonal infections, resistance to all β-lactam agents used as sole therapy has been observed.[28] For this reason, a suitable β-lactam antibiotic is generally used in conjunction with an aminoglycoside.

Antipseudomonal penicillins are often used in conjunction with a β-lactamase inhibitor – for example ticarcillin–clavulanic acid or piperacillin–tazobactam – to extend their spectrum. The β-lactamase inhibitor does not usually confer activity against *Pseudomonas* spp. that are resistant to the β-lactam because the mechanism of resistance is not due to β-lactamase production.[29] Treatment failures of nosocomial pneumonia caused by *P. aeruginosa* have occurred when piperacillin–tazobactam was used in the dose recommended by the manufacturer (3.375g intravenously q6h), and so this agent should be used in higher doses and in conjunction with an aminoglycoside when treating infections caused by or thought to be caused by *P. aeruginosa*.

The development of drug-resistant isolates of *P. aeruginosa* and other Gram-negative bacilli has become a problem in nosocomial infections. These micro-organisms are commonly found in intensive care units where patients can be on broad-spectrum antibiotics for prolonged periods of time. Many organisms produce inducible and extended-spectrum β-lactamases. In fact, certain bacteria (*Citrobacter freundii* and *Serratia* spp., *Proteus, Providencia, Pseudomonas, Enterobacter* and *Acinetobacter*) have developed resistance to cephalosporins during therapy.[30,31] Many recommend the concurrent use of an aminoglycoside in conjunction with a cephalosporin for the treatment of infections caused by these bacteria to prevent therapeutic failures.

Because of its broad antibiotic spectrum of activity against Gram-negative organisms resistant to other antibiotics, imipenem is frequently used in the treatment of nosocomial infections. Alternatives to the use of imipenem for resistant Gram-negative infections are now available and are discussed in the following two paragraphs.

Cefepime is a fourth-generation cephalosporin that is effective in the treatment of severe infections of the lower respiratory and urinary tracts, the skin and soft tissue, the female reproductive tract and neutropenic patients with fever. It has been shown to be more effective than ceftazidime in the treatment of pneumonia in patients with cystic fibrosis where *P. aeruginosa* is a common pathogen.[32] In addition to having activity against strains of *P. aeruginosa* resistant to ceftazidime, cefepime has also shown activity against *Enterobacter* spp. that are resistant to other β-lactam antibiotics.[33] It has a low potential for inducing bacterial resistance, excellent activity against nonenterococcal streptococci and activity against staphylococci similar to that of cefotaxime. It has little or no activity against *Bacteroides fragilis* and other anaerobes.

Meropenem is a carbapenem antibiotic that has a very broad spectrum of activity, similar to that of imipenem. Imipenem has more activity than meropenem against staphylococci and enterococci, but meropenem provides better coverage of *Pseudomonas, Enterobacter, Klebsiella, Morganella, Providencia, Alcaligenes, Aeromonas, Moraxella, Kingella, Actinobacillus, Pasteurella* and *Haemophilus* spp.[34,35] In one in-vitro study many isolates of *P. aeruginosa* resistant to imipenem were found to be sensitive to meropenem.[36] Meropenem has been effective in abdominal infections, meningitis in children and adults, community-acquired and nosocomial pneumonia, and neutropenic fever.[37]

Anaerobic infections

Anaerobic bacteria may play a significant role in brain abscess, dental infection, sinusitis, lung abscess, intra-abdominal abscess and bone and soft tissue infection. β-Lactam antibiotics have been used extensively in the treatment of anaerobic infections, but there is a trend for an increased resistance of anaerobes to some β-lactam antibiotics. As with the aerobes, the most common mechanism of resistance is the production of β-lactamase.[38]

Most *Clostridium* strains (with the exception of some strains of *C. ramosum, C. clostridiforme* and *C. innocuum*) remain susceptible to penicillin. Penicillin resistance is increasingly seen in the genus *Fusobacterium*, most commonly in *F. varium* and *F. mortiferum,* and although generally still sensitive to penicillin, the MICs for *F. nucleatum* have increased. Penicillin resistance is a major problem encountered in the treatment of infections caused by *B. fragilis* and other *Bacteroides* spp.

Penicillin is more effective than nafcillin against anaerobes. Ticarcillin, mezlocillin and piperacillin also have excellent activity against anaerobes, although there has been an increase in *B. fragilis* strains resistant to ticarcillin. Of the β-lactamase stable cephalosporins, cefoxitin, cefotetan, cefmetazole and ceftizoxime all show activity against anaerobes. Cefoxitin remains the most active cephalosporin against *B. fragilis*. Resistance to these cephalosporins is seen with some species of *Clostridium, Fusobacterium* and non-spore-forming Gram-positive rods. The first-generation cephalosporins such as cefazolin and cephalothin have poor activity against the Gram-negative anaerobes whereas the third-generation cephalosporins cefotaxime, cefoperazone and ceftriaxone have only modest activity (resistance seen in 30–60% of strains) and are therefore not the agents of choice for the empiric treatment of anaerobic infections. Cefotaxime has a desacetyl metabolite that works synergistically with the parent compound in the treatment of some anaerobic species in vitro, but is still not a primary agent for anaerobic infections in vivo. Ceftazidime has poor activity against both Gram-positive and Gram-negative anaerobes.

β-Lactamases are responsible for most resistance to β-lactam antibiotics in anaerobes. The β-lactamases in the *B. fragilis* group are typically cephalosporinases, whereas those in non-fragilis *Bacteroides* spp., *Clostridium* spp. and *F. nucleatum* are penicillinases. Almost all *B. fragilis* isolates produce β-lactamases. β-Lactamase production has not been reported in strains of *Clostridium perfringens.*

The addition of a β-lactamase inhibitor increases the activity of some of the β-lactams against β-lactamase producing anaerobes, in particular *Bacteroides* spp., and so ticarcillin–clavulanate, piperacillin–tazobactam, amoxicillin–clavulanate and ampicillin–

sulbactam are effective. The most active β-lactam agents against anaerobic isolates in the USA are imipenem, meropenem and ertapenem. Interestingly, in Japan, anaerobe resistance to imipenem is becoming a clinical problem, but this has not yet occurred in the USA. Aztreonam has no activity against anaerobes and must be used with other agents when treating mixed aerobic and anaerobic infections.[39]

Central nervous system infections (meningitis)

Certain β-lactam antibiotics are able to penetrate inflamed meninges and are commonly used to treat meningitis (e.g. penicillin G, ampicillin, nafcillin, oxacillin, cefotaxime, ceftizoxime, ceftriaxone, ceftazidime and meropenem). The most common pathogens in a series of adult patients with meningitis in descending order were *S. pneumoniae*, *Neisseria meningitidis* and *L. monocytogenes*.[40] In the pediatric population, *Haemophilus influenzae* also plays a role, but disease caused by this organism is less frequent as a result of the *H. influenzae* B vaccine. Penicillin G at a dose of 20–24 million U/day intravenously q4h for 14 days is the treatment of choice for susceptible strains of *S. pneumoniae*. The existence of resistance may necessitate the use of ceftriaxone and/or vancomycin until sensitivities are known. In an animal model, a combination of ceftriaxone and vancomycin was found to be synergistic against penicillin-resistant pneumococci.[41]

Penicillin or ampicillin are usually sufficient to treat *N. meningitidis* meningitis; however, a few β-lactamase producing strains have been seen and ceftriaxone has been used effectively. β-Lactams are not sufficient to eliminate the carrier state of *N. meningitidis*, and so rifampin (rifampicin) must be given at the completion of therapy. The agent of choice for the treatment of meningitis due to *L. monocytogenes* is ampicillin or penicillin alone or in combination with gentamicin; of note, the cephalosporins have no activity against this organism.

In children, the preferred agents for the treatment of *H. influenzae* meningitis are the third-generation cephalosporins cefotaxime or ceftriaxone.[42] There are several case reports that document the failure of cefuroxime to treat meningitis caused by *H. influenzae*[43] and there are instances where patients on cefuroxime have developed *H. influenzae* meningitis while being treated with cefuroxime for a non-meningeal infection caused by this organism. These failures are thought to occur as a result of resistant organisms or as a result of the inoculum effect whereby an increase in the inoculum of bacteria can significantly increase the apparent MIC/minimum bactericidal concentration (MBC) of the antibiotic to above attainable levels. A randomized trial found that ceftriaxone resulted in less hearing impairment and sterilized the CSF earlier than cefuroxime when used as treatment for meningitis in children.[44]

Patients with staphylococcal meningitis (which is usually seen after trauma or neurosurgical procedures) are best treated with high doses of nafcillin or oxacillin if the organism is susceptible. *Pseudomonas aeruginosa* meningitis has been effectively managed with ceftazidime, and meropenem may prove to be an alternative.[37]

Corticosteroids have been shown to reduce the neurologic sequelae of meningitis. In an animal model, corticosteroid treatment diminished the penetration of ceftriaxone into the CSF and markedly diminished the penetration of vancomycin.[45] Levels of rifampin in the CSF were not affected and the use of ceftriaxone with rifampin was successful in the treatment of meningitis in this model, whether or not the animal received corticosteroids. However, a recent prospective, randomized, double-blind trial demonstrated that the use of dexomethasone early in the treatment of patients with bacterial meningitis resulted in improved morbidity and mortality, particularly for patients with pneumococcal meningitis.[45a]

Biliary system infections (cholangitis)

Infection of the biliary tract generally occurs if there is an abnormality such as gallstones, strictures or a stent. Infection rarely complicates malignant obstruction of the biliary tree. In the obstructed biliary tract, there is very little excretion of any antibiotic. For example, biliary excretion of cefoperazone is responsible for 70% of the excretion of this compound, yet no levels are detectable in the biliary tract when there is an obstruction. However, after an obstruction in the biliary tree is relieved, therapeutic levels of antibiotics can be achieved within 24 hours.[46] The β-lactams that achieve significantly higher biliary than serum levels are nafcillin, mezlocillin, piperacillin, cefamandole, cefmetazole, cefoperazone and ceftriaxone. Ampicillin and carbenicillin achieve concentrations in the bile equal to or greater than those in serum. Interestingly, biliary levels are higher after oral amoxicillin or ampicillin than they are after intravenous administration. Biliary concentrations of ticarcillin, cefazolin, cefotaxime, ceftazidime and cefuroxime are all less than serum concentrations.[47]

For this reason, the ureidopenicillins mezlocillin and piperacillin are commonly used in biliary tract infections. Cefoperazone has been successful in the treatment of biliary infections. Cefoxitin, cefuroxime and ceftriaxone are also commonly used in conjunction with an aminoglycoside in patients with cholangitis.

In patients undergoing biliary surgery, adequate serum levels of antibiotic have been shown to be more important than biliary levels when the goal is to reduce postoperative infection.

Intra-abdominal infections (see Chapter 47)

Intra-abdominal infections, such as acute appendicitis, penetrating abdominal trauma and bowel perforation, are generally polymicrobial in nature and caused by a combination of aerobic, anaerobic and facultative anaerobic organisms. Historically, a regimen consisting of clindamycin and an aminoglycoside was the first to demonstrate superior efficacy in treating patients with penetrating abdominal trauma.[48] Since then, a number of studies have confirmed the efficacy of the β-lactam antibiotics alone or in combination with other agents for various intra-abdominal infections.[49] Cefoxitin, imipenem, cefotetan, piperacillin and ticarcillin–clavulanic acid have all been shown to be effective in treating intra-abdominal infections when used as monotherapy. Meropenem has been shown to have efficacy similar to that of imipenem for the treatment of intra-abdominal sepsis.[50,51] Ertapenem has similar efficacy in treating intra-abdominal infections as piperacillin–tazobactam.[52–54] The combination of clindamycin with either ceftazidime or aztreonam has been successful in the treatment of intra-abdominal infections. Failures of ampicillin–sulbactam have occurred when pseudomonal infections occur.

Although enterococci are commonly isolated from intra-abdominal infections (14–33%), many physicians do not include anti-enterococcal therapy in the initial treatment of these infections. There is a high incidence of enterococcal superinfections when moxalactam and ceftazidime are used; this phenomenon is not seen with cefotaxime, ceftizoxime or imipenem. 'Breakthrough' enterococcal infections occur in patients who have been hospitalized for long periods of time with persistent or recurrent intra-abdominal sepsis or who are immunosuppressed.[55]

Spontaneous bacterial peritonitis

Few studies have evaluated the efficacies of different antibiotics in the treatment of spontaneous bacterial peritonitis (SBP). The organisms that typically cause SBP are the Gram-negative bacilli (especially *Escherichia coli* and *Klebsiella* spp.), Gram-positive cocci (including pneumococci, other streptococci, enterococci and staphylococci) and anaerobes. When used in conjunction with an aminoglycoside, ampicillin had a cure rate of 76% in one study. Cefotaxime was shown to be more effective (cure rate 85%) than ampicillin and tobramycin (cure rate 56%) in another study of severe infections in patients with cirrhosis of which approximately 75% were SBP. In another uncontrolled study, amoxicillin and clavulanic acid had a cure rate of 80% for SBP. Aztreonam monotherapy has been associated with Gram-positive superinfection. Therefore, if aztreonam is to be used for SBP, then an additional antibiotic providing Gram-positive coverage is needed.[56,57]

Pancreatitis and its complications (see Chapter 47)

The prophylactic use of antibiotics in uncomplicated acute pancreatitis is controversial. Early studies that used ampicillin, an antibiotic that does not achieve therapeutic levels in pancreatic tissue, showed no benefit. However, several recent studies have shown a potential benefit. Patients with acute necrotizing pancreatitis treated with imipenem for 14 days had a lower incidence of pancreatic sepsis than those not treated; however, a trend toward a decreased mortality rate was not statistically significant.[58] A study that used cefuroxime in patients with acute necrotizing pancreatitis found that rates of bacteremia and mortality were both lower than those of controls.[59]

It is clear that β-lactam antibiotics have a role in the management of infectious complications of pancreatitis such as abscess or infected pseudocyst. The agents commonly used in addition to cefuroxime and imipenem include ticarcillin–clavulanic acid, piperacillin–tazobactam, ampicillin–sulbactam and meropenem.

Endovascular infections (endocarditis) (see Chapter 59)

A recent review provides guidelines for the treatment of endocarditis in adults.[60] The drug of choice for the treatment of endocarditis caused by the viridans streptococci is penicillin G. Depending upon the drug susceptibility of the organism, gentamicin can be added for part or all of the course and the duration of treatment can be 2–6 weeks. Alternatively, a 4-week course of ceftriaxone can be used.[61]

Enterococcal endocarditis is best treated with ampicillin or penicillin in combination with an aminoglycoside for 4–6 weeks.

The treatment of choice for native-valve endocarditis caused by *Staphylococcus aureus* is nafcillin or oxacillin for 4–6 weeks. Gentamicin has been used for the first 3–5 days to decrease the number of days of bacteremia, but has not been shown to change the outcome.[62]

Intravenous drug users with right-sided staphylococcal endocarditis have been successfully treated with 2 weeks of nafcillin and tobramycin.[63] Prosthetic valve endocarditis with coagulase-negative staphylococci is optimally treated with nafcillin or oxacillin (if the organism is sensitive) in combination with rifampin and gentamicin (for the first 2 weeks) for at least 6 weeks.

Endocarditis caused by the slow-growing fastidious Gram-negative organisms *Haemophilus parainfluenzae, H. aphrophilus, Actinobacillus actinomycetemcomitans, Cardiobacterium hominis, Eikenella corrodens* and *Kingella kingae* (the HACEK group) can be treated with ampicillin and gentamicin for 4 weeks or ceftriaxone alone for 4 weeks.

Neutropenic fever

β-Lactam antibiotics (for those who are not allergic to them) are the agents of choice for the management of fever in patients with cancer and treatment-induced neutropenia. Because life-threatening infections can occur with Gram-negative rods, including *P. aeruginosa*, ticarcillin–clavulanic acid is used in conjunction with an aminoglycoside for the treatment of neutropenic fever in our institution. However, monotherapy with agents such as ceftazidime or imipenem has also been shown to be effective.[64] A combination of an extended-spectrum β-lactam antibiotic with a third-generation cephalosporin (a double β-lactam combination) has also been found to be effective.[65] In patients allergic to the penicillins, aztreonam provides excellent coverage of the Gram-negative bacilli and is an acceptable alternative, along with Gram-positive coverage, such as vancomycin (see Chapter 100).

Lyme disease

Early infection caused by *Borrelia burgdorferi* can be managed with either amoxicillin or doxycycline. Since co-infection with *Ehrlichia* spp. is known to occur in many areas, many clinicians now prefer to use doxycycline. For later manifestations of Lyme disease, however, the β-lactams are the agents of choice. Lyme carditis can be successfully treated with either a 2-week course of ceftriaxone or intravenous penicillin G. Lyme meningitis and Lyme arthritis can also be treated with ceftriaxone or penicillin G, but for 2–4 weeks. A 30-day treatment course of amoxicillin and probenecid has been used for the treatment of Lyme arthritis. In pregnant women, doxycycline cannot be used, amoxicillin is used in early Lyme disease and intravenous penicillin G is used for disseminated early Lyme disease or any manifestation of late disease (see Chapter 54).[66,67]

Syphilis

Parenteral penicillin G is the preferred agent for treating all stages of syphilis and is the only therapy that has proved effective for neurosyphilis, syphilis in pregnancy and congenital syphilis.[68] Primary and secondary syphilis can be treated with a single dose of benzathine penicillin G (2.4 million U in adults, 50,000U/kg intramuscularly in children up to the adult dose). Late latent syphilis is treated with benzathine penicillin G 2.4 million U intramuscularly every week for 3 weeks. Procaine penicillin can be used where benzathine penicillin in unavailable, and there are alternatives for patients who are allergic to penicillin (see Chapter 75).

It is important to remember that patients being treated for any of the spirochete diseases – syphilis, Lyme disease or borreliosis – may develop a Jarisch–Herxheimer reaction, which may produce fever, tachycardia, chills, headaches, sore throat, malaise, myalgias, arthralgias, rash and, rarely, hypotension. This reaction has been observed in approximately 50% of patients treated for primary syphilis and 75% of patients with secondary syphilis.[69] Generally, it occurs a few hours after the first dose of penicillin, lasts for only a few hours and does not occur with subsequent doses of the antibiotic. Pre-treatment of patients with louse-borne relapsing fever (caused by *Borrelia recurrentis*) with hydrocortisone or acetaminophen does not prevent the Jarisch–Herxheimer reaction.[70] It is important to distinguish the reaction from penicillin allergy so that appropriate treatment is not discontinued.

DOSAGE IN SPECIAL CIRCUMSTANCES

Renal impairment

The majority of the β-lactam antibiotics are excreted almost entirely via the renal route, and so dose adjustments are necessary in the presence of kidney disease. Failure to reduce the dose of penicillin in uremic patients has resulted in toxicity, most notably encephalopathy.[71] As biliary secretion plays a major role in the excretion of ceftriaxone, cefoperazone, nafcillin and oxacillin, the doses of these antibiotics do not need to be adjusted in renal failure. Because biliary secretion plays a lesser, although significant role in the excretion of the ureidopenicillins, the dosages of these drugs do not have to be reduced as much as for the other penicillins. Some β-lactams must be re-dosed after peritoneal dialysis, which removes variable amounts of the drug. With the exception of ceftriaxone, cefoperazone, cefonicid, mezlocillin, methicillin, nafcillin, cloxacillin, dicloxacillin and oxacillin, the β-lactams need must re-dosed following hemodialysis. Specific dose adjustments are needed for patients with renal impairment and for patients on hemodialysis or peritoneal dialysis (Table 193.5).

Hepatic impairment

The dosages of some β-lactams must be adjusted in patients with severe hepatic disease. As a result of reduced desacetylation in

DRUG DOSAGES IN PATIENTS WITH RENAL FAILURE									
Generic name	**Dose in normal renal function**	**Max. daily dose with normal renal function**	**Adjustment in dose (D) or interval (I)**	**GFR (ml/min) >50**	**GFR (ml/min) = 10–50**	**GFR (ml/min) <10**	**Supplement after HD**	**Supplement with PD**	**CVVHD**
Penicillins									
Amoxicillin	250–500mg q8h	1.5g/day	I	q8h	q8–12h	q24h	Yes	250mg q12h	
Amoxicillin–clavulanate	250–500mg q8h		I	q8h	q8–12h	q24h	Yes		
Ampicillin	0.25–2g q4–6h	12g/day	I	q6h	q6–12h	q12–24h	Yes	250mg q12h	
Ampicillin–sulbactam	1.5–3g q6h		I	q6–8h	q12–24h	q24h			1.5–3g q8–12h
Azlocillin	2–3g q4h	18g/day	I	q4–6h	q6–8h	q8h	Yes	Dose for GFR<10	
Dicloxacillin	250–500mg q6h	2g/day	D	100%	100%	100%	No	No	
Methicillin	1–2g q4h	12g/day	I	q4–6h	q6–8h	q8–12h	No	No	
Mezlocillin	1.5–4g q4–6h	24g/day	I	q4–6h	q6–8h	q8h	No	No	
Nafcillin	1–2g q4–6h	12g/day		100%	100%	100%	No	No	1–2g q4h
Oxacillin	1–2g q4–6h	12g/day		100%	100%	100%	No	No	
Penicillin G	0.5–4MU q4–6h	24MU/day	D	100%	75%	20–50%	Yes	Dose for GFR <10	4 million U q6–8h
Penicillin V	250–500mg q6h	2g/day	D	100%	100%	100%	Yes	Dose for GFR <10	
Piperacillin	3–4g q4h	24g/day	I	q4–6h	q6–8h	q8–12h	Yes	Dose for GFR <10	3–4g q8h
Piperacillin–tazobactam	3.375g q4–6h		D&I	3.375g q6h	2.25g q6h	2.25g q8h	Yes – 0.75g	Dose for GFR <10	2.25–3.375g q8h
Ticarcillin	3g q4h	24g/day	D&I	1–3g q4h	1–2g q8h	1–2g q12–24h	Yes – 3g	Dose for GFR <10	
Ticarcillin–clavulanate	3.1g q4–6h		D&I	3.1g q4–6h	2g q4–8h	2g q12h	Yes – 3.1g	3.1g q12h	
Cephalosporins									
First-generation									
Cefadroxil	0.5–1g q12h	2g/day	I	q12h	q12–24h	q36h	Yes – 0.5–1g	250mg q8–12h	
Cefazolin	0.5–2g q8h	12g/day	I	q8h	q12h	q24–48h	Yes – 0.5–1g	0.5g q12h	1g q8h
Cephalexin	250–500mg q6h	4g/day	I	q8h	q12h	q12h	Yes	Dose for GFR <10	
Cephalothin	0.5–2g q6h	8g/day	I	q6h	q6–8h	q12h	Yes	1g q12h	
Cephapirin	0.5–2g q6h	8g/day	I	q6h	q6–8h	q12h	Yes	1g q12h	
Cephradine	0.25–2g q6h	8g/day	D	100%	50%	25%	Yes	Dose for GFR <10	
Second-generation									
Cefaclor	250–500mg q8h	1.5g/day	D	100%	50–100%	50%	Yes – 250mg	250mg q8–12h	
Cefamandole	0.5–2g q4–8h	12g/day	I	q6h	q6–8h	q12h	Yes – 0.5–1g	0.5–1g q12h	

Table 193.5 Drug dosages in patients with renal failure.[7,11,72–75] CVVHD, continuous venovenous hemodialysis. GFR, glomerular filtration rate; HD, hemodialysis; PD, peritoneal dialysis.

DRUG DOSAGES IN PATIENTS WITH RENAL FAILURE									
Generic name	**Dose in normal renal function**	**Max. daily dose with normal renal function**	**Adjustment in dose (D) or interval (I)**	**GFR (ml/min) >50**	**GFR (ml/min) = 10–50**	**GFR (ml/min) <10**	**Supplement after HD**	**Supplement with PD**	**CVVHD**
Cephalosporins —cont'd									
Cefdinir	300mg po q12h	600mg/day	I	q12h	q24h (GFR <30)	q24h	Yes 300mg and then 300mg every other day		
Cefmetazole	2g q6–12h	8g/day	I	q12–16h	q24h	q48h	Yes	Dose for GFR <10	
Cefonicid	1–2g q24h	2g/day	D&I	0.5g q24h	0.1–0.5g q24–48h	0.1g/1–5 days	No	No	
Cefotetan	1–2g q12h	6g/day	I	q12h	q12–24h	q48h	Yes – 1g	1g/day	
Cefoxitin	1–2g q6–8h	12g/day	I	q8h	q8–12h	q24–48h	Yes – 1g	1g/day	
Cefprozil	250–500mg q12h	1g/day	D&I	250–500mg q12h	250mg q12–16h	250mg q24h	Yes – 250mg	Dose for GFR <10	
Ceftibuten	400mg/day		D	100%	25–50%	25%			
Cefuroxime – po	250–500mg q12h	1g/day		100%	100%	100%	Yes	Dose for GFR <10	
Cefuroxime – iv	0.75–1.5g q8h	6g/day	I	q8h	q8–12h	q24h	Yes	Dose for GFR <10	1.5g q8h
Loracarbef	200–400mg q12h	800mg/day	I	q12	q24h	every 3–5 days	Yes		
Third-generation									
Cefditoren	200–400mg po q12h	800mg/day	D&I	200–400mg q12h	200mg q12h	200mg q24h (GFR < 30)			
Cefixime	250mg q12h	500mg/day	D	100%	75%	50%	Yes – 300mg	200mg/day	
Cefoperazone	1–2g q12h	12g/day	D	100%	100%	100%	Yes – 1g	No	1g q12h
Cefotaxime	1–2g q4–12h	12g/day	I	q6h	q8–12h	q24h	Yes – 1g	1g/day	1g q8–12h
Cefpodoxime	200mg q12h	400mg/day	I	q12h	q16h	q24–48h	Yes – 200mg	Dose for GFR <10	
Ceftazidime	1–2g q8h	6g/day	I	q8–12h	q24–48h	q48h	Yes – 1g	0.5g/day	1g q12h
Ceftizoxime	0.5–2g q8–12h	12g/day	I	q8–12h	q12–24h	q24h	Yes – 1g	0.5–1g/day	
Ceftriaxone	1–2g q24h	4g/day		100%	100%	100%	Yes	750mg q12h	1–2g q24h
Fourth-generation									
Cefepime	0.25–2g q12h	4g/day	I	q12h	q16–24h	q24–48h	Yes – 1g	Dose for GFR <10	1g q12h
Monobactam									
Aztreonam	1–2g q8–12h	8g/day	D	100%	50–75%	25%	Yes – 0.5g	Dose for GFR <10	1g q8–12h
Carbapenems									
Ertapenem	1g iv q24h	1g/day	D	q24h	0.5g q24h (GFR <30)	0.5g q24h	150mg Supplement if dosed within 6 hours prior to HD	Dose for GFR <10	
Imipenem–cilastatin	0.25–1g q6h	4g/day	D&I	250–500mg q6–8h	250mg q6–12h	125–250mg q12h	Yes	Dose for GFR <10	250mg q6–12h
Meropenem	0.5–2g q8h	6g/day	D&I	1g q8h	0.5–1g q12h	250–500mg q24h	Yes	Dose for GFR <10	1g q12h

Table 193.5 Drug dosages in patients with renal failure–cont'd.[7,11,72–75] CVVHD, continuous venovenous hemodialysis. GFR, glomerular filtration rate; HD, hemodialysis; PD, peritoneal dialysis.

patients with liver disease, the half-life of cefotaxime may increase slightly, but the half-life of cefoperazone may increase significantly and dosage reductions are required. Although biliary excretion plays a role in the excretion of ceftriaxone, no dose adjustment is needed in patients with liver disease.

Extremes of age

Dose reductions of the β-lactam antibiotics should be made in the elderly in the presence of renal dysfunction (see Table 193.5). Otherwise, elderly patients tolerate standard doses of the β-lactam antibiotics.

Because neonates do not have fully developed renal function, special modifications in dosage are necessary. In addition, because children have a high risk of cholestatic complications with ceftriaxone, another agent should be used when possible (see Adverse reactions and interactions, below).

β-Lactams in pregnancy

The penicillins, the β-lactamase inhibitors and the cephalosporins, aztreonam and meropenem (as of May, 1997) are considered category B in pregnancy (Table 193.6). This means that animal studies have shown no risk to the fetus, but adequate human studies have not been performed, or that animal studies have shown risk and human studies have shown no risk. When they are indicated, these antibiotics are commonly used in clinical practice in pregnant women.

Imipenem–cilastatin and moxalactam are pregnancy category C, meaning that animal studies show toxicity to the fetus and human studies are inadequate. However, the benefit of using these drugs may exceed the risk of not treating a serious infection in a pregnant woman when no alternatives exist.[76] Meropenem, category B, may be a suitable alternative to imipenem, category C, for infections with resistant Gram-negative aerobic organisms.

β-Lactam antibiotics that are not protein bound are transported across the placenta and reach the drug levels that are present in maternal serum. β-Lactams that are highly protein-bound reach only low concentrations in amniotic fluid and the fetus.[77]

As a general principle, the β-lactam antibiotics have accelerated elimination and lowered plasma concentrations in pregnant women as compared with nonpregnant women. As a result, the dose or frequency of administration should be increased in pregnant women.[76]

PREGNANCY CATEGORIES OF THE β-LACTAM ANTIBIOTICS	
Class of β-lactam	Pregnancy category
Penicillins – all	B
β-Lactamase inhibitors – all	B
Cephalosporins – all	B
Moxalactam	C
Aztreonam	B
Imipenem–cilastatin	C
Meropenem	B
Ertapenem	B

Table 193.6 Pregnancy categories of the β-lactam antibiotics (as of May 1997). Category B means that animal studies have shown no risk to the fetus, but adequate human studies have not been performed, or animal studies have shown risk and human studies have shown no risk. Category C means that animal studies show toxicity to the fetus and human studies are inadequate.

ADVERSE REACTIONS AND INTERACTIONS

Adverse reactions that occur with the β-lactam antibiotics are summarized in Table 193.7.

ADVERSE REACTIONS WITH β-LACTAM ANTIBIOTICS	
Reaction	Examples
Local	Pain, induration, tenderness at sile of im injection; burning during iv administration, phlebitis
Hypersensitivity	Rash, pruritus, urticaria, fever, chills, Stevens–Johnson syndrome, anaphylaxis
Gastrointestinal	Diarrhea, nausea, vomiting, abdominal pain, *Clostridium difficile* diarrhea
Hematologic	Eosinophilia, leukopenia, anemia, positive Coombs' test, hemolytic anemia, neutropenia, lymphopenia; thrombocytosis, thrombocytopenia, elevated prothrombin time, bleeding, abnormal clotting time, abnormal platelet aggregation
Hepatic	Elevated transaminases (aspartate transaminase, alanine transaminase), hepatitis, elevated alkaline phosphatase, elevated bilirubin
Renal	Elevated blood urea nitrogen and creatinine, falsely elevated creatinine, casts in urine
Central nervous system	Headache, dizziness, somnolence, confusion, tremor, myoclonus, seizures, encephatopathy
Genitourinary	Vaginitis
Superinfection	Thrush, vaginal candidiasis, infection with resistant bacteria

Table 193.7 Adverse reactions with β-lactam antibiotics.

Allergic reactions

The most common adverse event associated with the use of β-lactam antibiotics is an allergic reaction. The reported frequency of allergic reaction to penicillin varies from 0.7 to 10%, and anaphylaxis, the most feared reaction, occurs in 0.004–0.015% of patients.[78] A maculopapular rash occurs late in the treatment course of 2–3% of patients receiving a course of penicillin. Ampicillin and amoxicillin induce rashes in a higher percentage than other β-lactams of patients treated (5.2–9.5%) and almost invariably cause a rash when given during acute infectious mononucleosis (Epstein–Barr virus) or cytomegalovirus, and rarely when given to patients with acute lymphocytic leukemia. Such patients may tolerate β-lactam antibiotics when re-challenged after the acute illness has resolved. Reactions to penicillins are characterized according to the time of onset following administration of the drug:

- immediate reactions occur in the first hour;
- accelerated reactions occur 1–72 hours after drug administration; and
- late reactions occur 72 hours or more after starting a course of the antibiotic.

Both immediate and accelerated reactions may result in urticaria and anaphylaxis.

Previous exposure to penicillin does not seem to increase the risk of penicillin allergy. However, it is clear that people who have had allergic reactions to penicillin have a higher risk of allergic reactions than people who have tolerated therapy in the past. In patients with a history of penicillin allergy, re-challenge with penicillin results in acute reactions in an estimated 65% of patients, anaphylaxis in 5–10% and fatal anaphylaxis in 0.2–0.5%.

Skin testing is a useful technique in the evaluation of patients with a history of penicillin allergy, but is not useful as a screening test for the general population because many skin test positive patients without a history of penicillin allergy can tolerate penicillin therapy. Skin testing is not useful for identifying non-IgE-mediated adverse drug reactions such as drug fever.

Although fatalities have occurred as a result of the skin test itself, the procedure is generally regarded as safe. A wide range in the incidence of positive skin tests in patients with a previous history of penicillin allergy has been noted (8.75–63%), and therefore a significant proportion of patients who give a history of penicillin allergy can tolerate the drug.[79] In one large study, penicillin skin testing allowed the safe use of penicillin in 90% of patients who gave a history of penicillin allergy.[80] The incidence of positive skin test results in patients who have tolerated penicillin in the past range from 4 to 7%.[81] When penicillin is administered to patients with a previous history of penicillin allergy, but with a negative skin test, the overall reaction rate (early and accelerated) is low and similar to the rate of allergy reported in the general population. In addition, the reactions are generally mild and self-limiting. In one study, only 1.2% of patients who had a history of penicillin allergy and a negative skin test had a possible IgE-mediated reaction.[82] Anaphylaxis has occurred in patients with negative skin tests, but is extremely rare. Skin test reactivity declines with time in patients with a history of penicillin allergy. People with dermatitis and allergic rhinitis do not have an increased risk of penicillin allergy, but the risk may be increased for atopic individuals.[83]

Patients with a history of penicillin allergy are four times as likely to have a reaction to first-generation cephalosporins than patients without a history of allergy (8.1 vs 1.9%). Second- and third-generation cephalosporins have an incidence of skin reaction (rash) ranging from 1 to 3%, similar to the incidence of rash with penicillin. Anaphylaxis, however, is uncommon with cephalosporins. There seems to be a lower incidence of allergy to second- and third-generation cephalosporins in patients with a history of penicillin allergy. Patients with allergy to penicillins should be considered allergic to the carbapenems, but there seems to be no cross-reactivity with aztreonam. No major adverse reactions to aztreonam have been reported, but rarely patients will develop a rash. There is more allergic cross-reactivity among penicillin derivatives than among cephalosporin derivatives. However, allergic cross-reactivity between cephalosporin derivatives is greater than cross-reactivity between cephalosporins and penicillins.[84] For example, a patient who is known to be allergic to ceftriaxone is more likely to be allergic to ceftazidime than a patient who is known to be allergic only to penicillin.[85]

At times, it may be necessary to administer penicillin to patients with a previous severe reaction to the drug. For instance, penicillin is the only acceptable treatment for a pregnant woman with syphilis. Effective methods of desensitization have been described,[86] but adverse reactions are common and the patient should be in an intensive care unit for close monitoring.

Hematologic effects

Hematologic toxicity is rare, but leukopenia (occurring in 0.2% of patients on mezlocillin in one study) has been observed when the penicillins or cephalosporins are used at high doses,[87] and also rarely with imipenem. Counts return when the drug is discontinued, and lower dosages can often be tolerated without neutropenia. Isolated eosinophilia can occur in patients on cephalosporins (1–7%). A Coombs' positive hemolytic anemia is rarely observed with the penicillins[88] and cephalosporins.[89]

Dose-dependent defects of platelet aggregation and a prolongation of the bleeding time can be seen with carbenicillin and ticarcillin and can occur with all of the penicillins at high doses. Clinically significant bleeding can occur but is uncommon.[90] Hypoprothrombinemia has occurred frequently with cephalosporins that possess a methylthiotetrazole (MTT) group (cefamandole, cefoperazone, cefotetan, moxalactam, cefmetazole, cefmonoxime), which may interfere with the activation of factors II, VII, IX and X, and may also prevent the activation of vitamin K.[84,90,91] Patients with renal failure, malnutrition, intra-abdominal infection or recent gastrointestinal surgery seem to be at the highest risk and may benefit from weekly prophylaxis with vitamin K when being given one of these antibiotics.[89] The frequent occurrence of bleeding complications with moxalactam has led to minimal use of this antibiotic.[92] No coagulation abnormalities have been associated with imipenem.

Isolated thrombocytopenia rarely complicates the use of the β-lactam antibiotics. An immune mechanism has been documented.[93] Thrombocytopenia can occur as soon as 5 days after the initiation of the antibiotic and generally resolves when the agent is withdrawn.[94,95]

Renal effects

Interstitial nephritis, characterized by fever, rash, eosinophilia, proteinuria, hematuria, eosinophiluria and occasionally renal insufficiency can be seen with the penicillins, most commonly methicillin.[96] β-Lactam antibiotics that exist as sodium salts, particularly carbenicillin and ticarcillin, can induce hypokalemia.[97] Cephalothin can cause renal damage that histopathologically resembles that of nafcillin.[98] The concurrent use of aminoglycosides may add to the nephrotoxicity of cephalosporins[99] such as cephalothin. About 1% of patients on ceftazidime have elevated blood urea nitrogen or creatinine, but these are generally not clinically significant.[100] The sodium load of some penicillins can be high, most notably with ticarcillin (4.7mEq/g), but also with ampicillin, methicillin, penicillin G, azlocillin, mezlocillin and pipercillin, thereby posing a problem for patients with congestive heart failure.

Neurologic effects

Many of the β-lactams can cause neurotoxicity and, in particular, seizures. Seizures have been reported following the use of penicillin,[70] ampicillin, amoxicillin, oxacillin, nafcillin, carbenicillin, ticarcillin, piperacillin, cefazolin, cefonicid, cephalexin, ceftazidime and imipenem. Benzylpenicillin, cefazolin and imipenem have the highest neurotoxic potential of the β-lactam antibiotics. In fact, seizures occur in 0.4–1.5% of patients taking imipenem.

Several risk factors that may predispose a patient to neurotoxicity have been identified, for example:

- high doses;
- renal insufficiency;
- disruption of the blood–brain barrier,
- pre-existing central nervous system (CNS) disease;
- advanced age;
- concurrent administration of nephrotoxic drugs;
- concurrent drugs that may reduce the seizure threshold; and
- concurrent administration of other β-lactam antibiotics.[101]

Neurotoxicity of penicillins is clearly related to elevated CSF antibiotic levels, such as may occur when high doses are being used in patients with impaired renal function. Penicillin levels in CSF should not exceed 5mg/l. Seizures have occurred in patients receiving meropenem only if they have underlying CNS abnormalities.

Gastrointestinal effects

Gastrointestinal upset and diarrhea are common side-effects of the β-lactams. Enterocolitis caused by *Clostridium difficile* may result from use of any of the β-lactams, but particularly ampicillin.

Hepatitis is a rare side-effect of carbenicillin,[102] mezlocillin and nafcillin, and resolves after discontinuation of therapy. Hepatitis as a result of intravenous oxacillin can occur as early as 2 days into treatment, is thought to result from a hypersensitivity reaction, does not appear to be dose-related, and is reversible on discontinuation of the drug.[103,104] Mild elevations in transaminases and alkaline phosphatase also occur with the cephalosporins and carbapenems, but the drug can usually be continued.[105] Serum transaminases become elevated in 2–4% of patients receiving aztreonam.

Gallbladder sludge formation[106,107] and cholelithiasis[108] have occurred in patients on ceftriaxone. Children, patients receiving prolonged or high doses, and patients on total parenteral nutrition appear to be at risk of this complication.

A disulfuram-like reaction has been associated with the cephalosporins with an MTT group.[109,110] Patients taking these agents and then ingesting alcohol have developed flushing, tachycardia, diaphoresis, headache, nausea, vomiting and dizziness.

Other reactions

Local side-effects of the β-lactam antibiotics are not uncommon. At the intramuscular injection site, patients may experience pain, tenderness and edema. Thrombophlebitis can occur in up to 5% of patients receiving parenteral therapy with some agents.

Other reactions to penicillin are less common. Serum sickness, consisting of fever, urticaria, joint pains and angioneurotic edema, can occur and, rarely, exfoliative dermatitis, the Stevens–Johnson syndrome and allergic vasculitis. Late-onset morbilliform rashes can develop as a result of penicillin therapy and may disappear, even if the penicillin is continued, but desquamation can occur.

Drug interactions

The most clinically important drug interaction with the β-lactam antibiotics occurs with probenecid, a uricosuric and renal tubular blocking agent. Probenecid causes a 2- to 4-fold increase in the peak serum concentration of the β-lactam antibiotics. It also prolongs serum levels for these antibiotics. It is used most often with penicillin (e.g. in the treatment of gonococcal infections), but can also be used with ampicillin, methicillin, oxacillin, cloxacillin and nafcillin. The recommended dose in adults is 2g/day in divided doses, and in children a 25mg/kg initial dose is followed by 40mg/kg/day in four divided doses (adult dose used for children who weigh over 50kg). The mechanism of action involves not only inhibition of renal tubular secretion of the β-lactams, but also a decrease in the apparent volume of distribution of the drug.[111] Probenecid has little effect on the serum levels of imipenem and aztreonam and has no effect on drug levels of ceftazidime. Adverse reactions, including anaphylaxis, can occur with probenecid and the clinician must also be aware that toxicity can result from supratherapeutic levels of the β-lactam antibiotics when used with probenecid.

As cephalosporins with the MTT side-chain can interfere with hemostasis, care must be taken when using these antibiotics in patients taking warfarin.

Synergistic activity against various bacteria occurs when the penicillins, cephalosporins, carbapenems and monobactams are used in conjunction with aminoglycosides.[112–114] However, using two β-lactam antibiotics together may result in either synergy or antagonism.

The bactericidal effect of ampicillin may be reduced when other antibiotics (chloramphenicol, erythromycin, sulfa drugs and tetracycline) are used simultaneously. The clinical significance of this is unclear.

When ampicillin is used in patients who are taking oral contraceptive agents, breakthrough bleeding may occur and the contraceptive may be less effective.

Piperacillin and ticarcillin must be used cautiously in any patient on vecuronium because the neuromuscular blockade can be further prolonged. Piperacillin can also lower serum levels of tobramycin if the drugs are used together.

REFERENCES

1. Fleming A. On antibacterial action of cultures of *Penicillium*, with special reference to their use in isolation of *B. influenzae*. Br J Exp Pathol 1929;10:226–36.
2. Chain E, Florey HW, Gardner AD, *et al.* Penicillin as chemotherapeutic agent. Lancet 1940;2:226–8.
3. Abraham EP, Chain E, Fletcher CM, *et al.* Further observations on penicillin. Lancet 1941;2:177.
4. Tomasz A. From penicillin-binding proteins to the lysis and death of bacteria: a 1979 view. Rev Infect Dis 1979;1:434–65.
5. Georgopapadakou NH. Penicillin-binding proteins and bacterial resistance to beta-lactams. Antimicrob Agents Chemother 1993;37:2045–53.
6. Livermore DM. Beta-lactamases in laboratory and clinical resistance. Clin Microbiol Rev 1995;8:557–84.
7. Physicians' desk reference, 51st ed. Montvale, NJ: Medical Economics Company, Inc; 1997.
8. Abramowicz M, ed. Cefditoren (Spectracef) – a new oral cephalosporin. Med Lett 2002;44:5–6.
9. Abramowicz M, ed. Cefdinir – a new oral cephalosporin. Med Lett 1998;40:85–6.
10. Solomkin JS. Use of new beta-lactam antibiotics for surgical infections. Surg Clin North Am 1988;68:1–24.
11. Livornese LL Jr, Benz RL, Ingerman MJ, Santoro J. Antibacterial agents in renal failure. Infect Dis Clin North Am 1995;9:591–614.
12. Ennis DM, Cobbs CG. The newer cephalosporins. Infect Dis Clin North Am 1995;9:687–713.
13. Bush LM, Calmon J, Johnson CC. Newer penicillins and beta-lactamase inhibitors. Infect Dis Clin North Am 1995;9:653–86.
14. MacGregor RR, Graziani AL. Oral administration of antibiotics: a rational alternative to the parenteral route. Clin Infect Dis 1997;24:457–67.
15. Hellinger WC, Brewer NS. Imipenem. Mayo Clin Proc 1991;66:1074–81.
16. Mandell GL, Petri WA Jr. Penicillins, cephalosporins, and other beta-lactam antibiotics. In: Hardman JG, Limbird LE, Molinoff PB, Ruddon RW, Gilman AG, eds. Goodman and Gilman's the pharmacological basis of therapeutics. New York: McGraw-Hill; 1996:1073–101.
17. Fassbender M, Lode H, Schaberg T, Borner K, Koeppe P. Pharmacokinetics of new oral cephalosporins, including a new carbacephem. Clin Infect Dis 1993;16:646–53.
18. Abramowicz M, ed. Antimicrobial prophylaxis in surgery. Med Lett 1995;37:79–82.
19. van den Hazel SJ, Speelman P, Dankert J, *et al.* Piperacillin to prevent cholangitis after endoscopic retrograde cholangiopancreatography. Ann Intern Med 1996;125:442–47.
20. Dajani AS, Taubert KA, Wilson W, *et al.* Prevention of bacterial endocarditis. Recommendations by the American Heart Association. JAMA 1997;277:1794–801.
21. Berrios X, del Campo E, Guzman B, Bisno AL. Discontinuing rheumatic fever prophylaxis in selected adolescents and young adults. Ann Intern Med 1993;118:401–6.
22. Jorgensen JH, Ferraro MJ, McElmeel ML, Spargo J, Swenson JM, Tenover FC. Detection of penicillin and extended-spectrum cephalosporin resistance among *Streptococcus pneumoniae* clinical isolates by use of the E test. J Clin Microbiol 1994;32:159–63.
23. Caputo GM, Appelbaum PC, Liu HH. Infections due to penicillin-resistant pneumococci. Arch Intern Med 1993;153:1301–10.
24. Friedland IR, McCracken GH Jr. Management of infections caused by antibiotic-resistant *Streptococcus pneumoniae*. N Engl J Med 1994;331:377–82.
25. Gold HS, Moellering RC Jr. Antimicrobial-drug resistance. N Engl J Med 1996;335:1445–53.
26. John CC. Treatment failure with use of a third-generation cephalosporin for penicillin-resistant pneumococcal meningitis: case report and review. Clin Infect Dis 1994;18:188–93.
27. Chambers HF. Methicillin-resistant staphylococci. Clin Microbiol Rev 1988;1:173–86.
28. Slack MPE. Antipseudomonal beta-lactams. J Antimicrob Chemother 1981;8:165–70.
29. Abramowicz M, ed. Piperacillin/tazobactam. Med Lett 1994;36:7–9.
30. Sanders CC, Sanders WE Jr. Microbial resistance to newer generation beta-lactam antibiotics: clinical and laboratory implications. J Infect Dis 1985;151:399–406.
31. Collatz E, Gutmann L, Williamson R, Acar JF. Development of resistance to beta-lactam antibiotics with special reference to third-generation cephalosporins. J Antimicrob Chemother 1984;14(Suppl.B):13–21.
32. Cunha BA, Gill MV. Cefepime. Med Clin North Am 1995;79:721–32.
33. Sanders WE Jr, Tenney JH, Kessler RE. Efficacy of cefepime in the treatment of infections due to

multiply resistant *Enterobacter* species. Clin Infect Dis 1996;23:454–61.
34. Edwards JR. Meropenem: a microbiological overview. J Antimicrob Chemother 1995;36(Suppl.A):1–17.
35. Jorgensen JH, Maher LA, Howell AW. Activity of meropenem against antibiotic-resistant or infrequently encountered gram-negative bacilli. Antimicrob Agents Chemother 1991;35:2410–4.
36. Vogt K, Hahn H. Meropenem versus imipenem against multiresistant *Pseudomonas* [Abstract 162]. Antiinfect Drugs Chemother 1996;14:69.
37. Abramowicz M, ed. Meropenem – a new parenteral broad-spectrum antibiotic. Med Lett 1996;38:88–90.
38. Nord CE, Hedberg M. Resistance to beta-lactam antibiotics in anaerobic bacteria. Rev Infect Dis 1990;12(Suppl.2):231–4.
39. Johnson CC. Susceptibility of anaerobic bacteria to beta-lactam antibiotics in the United States. Clin Infect Dis 1993;16(Suppl.4):371–6.
40. Durand ML, Calderwood SB, Weber DJ, *et al.* Acute bacterial meningitis in adults. N Engl J Med 1993;328:21–8.
41. Friedland IR, Paris M, Ehrett, Hickey S, Olsen K, McCracken GH Jr. Evaluation of antimicrobial regimens for treatment of experimental penicillin- and cephalosporin-resistant pneumococcal meningitis. Antimicrob Agents Chemother 1993;37:1630–6.
42. Tunkel AR, Wispelwey B, Scheld WM. Bacterial meningitis: recent advances in pathophysiology and treatment. Ann Intern Med 1990;112:610–23.
43. Arditi M, Herold BC, Yogev R. Cefuroxime treatment failure and *Haemophilus influenzae* meningitis: case report and review of literature. Pediatrics 1989;84:132–5.
44. Schaad UB, Suter S, Gianella-Borradori A, *et al.* A comparison of ceftriaxone and cefuroxime for the treatment of bacterial meningitis in children. N Engl J Med 1990;322:141–7.
45. Paris MA, Hickey SM, Uscher MI, Shelton S, Olsen KD, McCracken GH Jr. Effect of dexamethasone on therapy of experimental penicillin- and cephalosporin-resistant pneumococcal meningitis. Antimicrob Agents Chemother 1994;38:1320–4.
45a. de Gans J, van de Beek D. Dexamethasone in adults with bacterial meningitis. N Engl J Med 2002;347:1549-56.
46. Van den Hazel SJ, Speelman P, Tytgat GNJ, Dankert J, van Leeuwen DJ. Role of antibiotics in the treatment and prevention of acute and recurrent cholangitis. Clin Infect Dis 1994;19:279–86.
47. Dooley JS, Hamilton-Miller JMT, Brumfitt W, Sherlock S. Antibiotics in the treatment of biliary infection. Gut 1984;25:988–98.
48. Gorbach SL. Antibiotic treatment of anaerobic infections. Clin Infect Dis 1994;18(Suppl.4):305–10.
49. Gorbach SL. Treatment of intra-abdominal infections. J Antimicrob Chemother 1993;31(Suppl.A):67–78.
50. Geroulanos SJ. Meropenem versus imipenem/cilastatin in intra-abdominal infections requiring surgery. J Antimicrob Chemother 1995;35(Suppl.A):191–205.
51. Wilson SE. Carbapenems: monotherapy in intra-abdominal sepsis. Scand J Infect Dis 1995;96(Suppl.):28–33.
52. Abramowicz M, ed. Ertapenem (Invanz) – a new parenteral carbapenem. Med Lett 2002;44:25–6.
53. Graham DR, Lucasti C, Malafia O, *et al.* Ertapenem once daily versus piperacillin–tazobactam four times per day for treatment of complicated skin and skin-structure infections in adults: results of a prospective, randomized, double blind multicenter study. Clin Infect Dis 2002;34:1460–7.
54. Ortiz-Ruiz G, Caballero-Lopez J, Friedland IR, *et al.* A study evaluating the efficacy, safety and tolerability of ertapenem versus ceftriaxone for the treatment of community acquired pneumonia in adults. Clin Infect Dis 2002;34:1076–83.
55. Dougherty SH. Role of enterococcus in intraabdominal sepsis. Am J Surg 1984;148:308–12.
56. Garcia-Tsao G. Spontaneous bacterial peritonitis. Gastroenterol Clin North Am 1992;21:257–75.
57. Bhuva M, Ganger D, Jensen D. Spontaneous bacterial peritonitis: an update on evaluation, management, and prevention. Am J Med 1994;97:169–75.
58. Pederzoli P, Bassi C, Vesentini S, Campedelli A. A randomized multicenter clinical trial of antibiotic prophylaxis of septic complications in acute necrotizing pancreatitis with imipenem. Surg Gynecol Obstet 1993;176:480–3.
59. Sainio V, Kemppainen E, Puolakkainen P, *et al.* Early antibiotic treatment in acute necrotising pancreatitis. Lancet 1995;346:663–7.
60. Wilson WR, Karchmer AW, Dajani AS, *et al.* Antibiotic treatment of adults with infective endocarditis due to streptococci, enterococci, staphylococci, and HACEK microorganisms. JAMA 1995;274:1706–13.
61. Francioli P, Etienne J, Hoigne R, Thys J, Gerber A. Treatment of streptococcal endocarditis with a single daily dose of ceftriaxone sodium for 4 weeks. JAMA 1992;167:264–67.
62. Korzeniowski O, Sande M. Combination antimicrobial therapy for *Staphylococcus aureus* endocarditis in patients addicted to parenteral drugs and in nonaddicts. Ann Intern Med 1982;97:496–503.
63. DiNubile MJ. Short-course antibiotic therapy for right-sided endocarditis caused by *Staphylococcus aureus* in injection drug users. Ann Intern Med 1994;121:873–6.
64. Pizzo PA, Hathorn JW, Hiemenz J, *et al.* A randomized trial comparing ceftazidime alone with combination antibiotic therapy in cancer patients with fever and neutropenia. N Engl J Med 1986;315:552–8.
65. Pizzo PA. Management of fever in patients with cancer and treatment-induced neutropenia. N Engl J Med 1993;328:1323–32.
66. Rahn DW, Malawista SE. Lyme disease: recommendations for diagnosis and treatment. Ann Intern Med 1991;114:472–81.
67. Abramowicz M, ed. Treatment of Lyme disease. Med Lett 1997;39:47–8.
68. Centers for Disease Control and Prevention. 1993 Sexually transmitted diseases treatment guidelines. MMWR Morb Mortal Wkly Rep 1993;42(RR-14):27–46.
69. Gelfand JA, Elin RJ, Berry FW Jr, Frank MM. Endotoxemia associated with the Jarisch–Herxheimer reaction. N Engl J Med 1976;295:211–3.
70. Butler T, Jones PK, Wallace CK. *Borrelia recurrentis* infection: single-dose antibiotic regimens and management of the Jarisch–Herxheimer reaction. J Infect Dis 1978;137:573–7.
71. Bloomer HA, Barton LJ, Maddock, RK Jr. Penicillin-induced encephalopathy in uremic patients. JAMA 1967;200:131–3.
72. Hoody DW. Antimicrobial dosing in continuous renal replacement therapy. Infectious Disease News, May 2002:10.
73. Joos B, Schmidli M, Keusch G, *et al.* Pharmacokinetics of antimicrobial agents in anuric patients during continuous venovenous haemofiltration. Nephrol Dial Transplant 1966;11:1582–5.
74. Joy MS, Matzke GR, Armstrong DK, Marx MA, Zarowitz BJ. A primer in continuous renal replacement therapy for critically ill patients. Ann Pharmacother 1998;32:362–75.
75. Davies JG, Kingswood JC, Sharpstone P, Street MK. Drug removal in continous haemofiltration and haemodialysis. BJHM 1995;54:524–8.
76. Heikkila A, Erkkola R. Review of beta-lactam antibiotics in pregnancy. Clin Pharmacokinet 1994;27:49–62.
77. Depp R, Kind AC, Kirby WMM, Johnson WL. Transplacental passage of methicillin and dicloxacillin into the fetus and amniotic fluid. Am J Obstet Gynec 1970;107:1054–7.
78. Idsoe O, Guthe T, Willcox RR, De Weck AL. Nature and extent of penicillin side-reactions, with particular reference to fatalities from anaphylactic shock. Bull World Health Organ 1968;38:159–88.
79. Sullivan TJ, Wedner HJ, Shatz GS, Yecies LD, Parker CW. Skin testing to detect penicillin allergy. J Allergy Clin Immunol 1981;68:171–80.
80. Gadde J, Spence M, Wheeler B, Adkinson NF Jr. Clinical experience with penicillin skin testing in a large inner-city STD clinic. JAMA 1993;270:2456–63.
81. Lin RY. A perspective on penicillin allergy. Arch Intern Med 1992;15:930–7.
82. Sogn DD, Evans R III, Shepherd GM, *et al.* Results of the National Institute of Allergy and Infectious Diseases collaborative clinical trial to test the predictive value of skin testing with major and minor penicillin derivatives in hospitalized adults. Arch Intern Med 1992;152:1025–32.
83. Green GR, Rosenblum A. Report of the penicillin study group – American Academy of Allergy. J Allergy Clin Immunol 1971;48:331–43.
84. Saxon A, Beall NG, Rohr AS, Adelman DC. Immediate hypersensitivity reactions to beta-lactam antibiotics. Ann Intern Med 1987;107:204–15.
85. Kelkar PS, Li JTC. Current concepts: cephalosporin allergy. N Engl J Med 2001;345;804–9.
86. Sullivan TJ. Drug allergy. In: Middleton E, Reed C, Ellis E, *et al.*, eds. Allergy: principles and practice, 4th ed. St. Louis: CV Mosby; 1993:1523–34.
87. Parry MF, Neu HC. The safety and tolerance of mezlocillin. J Antimicrob Chemother 1982;9(Suppl.A):273–80.
88. Kerr RO, Cardamone J, Dalmasso AP, Kaplan ME. Two mechanisms of erythrocyte destruction in penicillin-induced hemolytic anemia. N Engl J Med 1972;287:1322–5.
89. Bang NU, Kammer RB. Hematologic complications associated with beta-lactam antibiotics. Rev Infect Dis 1983;5(Suppl.2):380–91.
90. Sattler FR, Weitekamp MR, Ballard JO. Potential for bleeding with the new beta-lactam antibiotics. Ann Intern Med 1986;105:924–31.
91. Nichols RL, Wilker MA, McDevitt JT, Lentnek AL, Hosutt JA. Coagulopathy associated with extended-spectrum cephalosporins in patients with serious infections. Antimicrob Agents Chemother 1987;31:281–5.
92. Pakter RL, Russell TR, Mielke CH, West D. Coagulopathy associated with the use of moxalactam. JAMA 1982;248:1100.
93. Garratty G. Immune cytopenia associated with antibiotics. Transfus Med Rev 1993;VII:255–67.
94. Christie DJ, Lennon SS, Drew RL, Swinehart CD. Cefotetan-induced immunologic thrombocytopenia. Br J Haematol 1988;70:423–6.
95. Hull RL, Brandon D. Thrombocytopenia possibly caused by structurally related third-generation cephalosporins. DICP Ann Pharmacother 1991;25:135–6.
96. Baldwin DS, Levine BB, McCluskey RT, Gallo GR. Renal failure and interstitial nephritis due to penicillin and methicillin. N Engl J Med 1968;279:1245–52.
97. Appel GB, Neu HC. The nephrotoxicity of antimicrobial agents. N Engl J Med 1977;296:663–70.

98. Barza M. The nephrotoxicity of cephalosporins: an overview. J Infect Dis 1978;137(Suppl.):60–73.
99. Wade JC, Petty BG, Conrad G, *et al.* Cephalothin plus an aminoglycoside is more nephrotoxic than methicillin plus an aminoglycoside. Lancet 1978;2:604–6.
100. Meyers BR. Comparative toxicities of third-generation cephalosporins. Am J Med 1985;79(Suppl.2A):96–103.
101. Schliamser SE, Cars O, Norrby SR. Neurotoxicity of beta-lactam antibiotics: predisposing factors and pathogenesis. J Antimicrob Chemother 1991;27:405–25.
102. Wilson FM, Belamaric J, Lauter CB, Lerner M. Anicteric carbenicillin hepatitis. JAMA 1975;232:818–21.
103. Onorato IM, Axelrod JL. Hepatitis from intravenous high-dose oxacillin therapy. Ann Intern Med 1978;89:497–500.
104. Bruckstein AH, Attia AA. Oxacillin hepatitis. Am J Med 1978;64:519–22.
105. Norrby SR. Side effects of cephalosporins. Drugs 1987;34(Suppl.2):105–20.
106. Heim-Duthoy KL, Caperton EM, Pollock R, Matzke GR, Enthoven D, Peterson PK. Apparent biliary pseudolithiasis during ceftriaxone therapy. Antimicrob Agents Chemother 1990;34:1146–9.
107. Park HZ, Lee SP, Schy AL. Ceftriaxone-associated gallbladder sludge. Gastroenterology 1991;100:1665–70.
108. Lopez AJ, O'Keefe P, Morrissey M, Pickleman J. Ceftriaxone-induced cholelithiasis. Ann Intern Med 1991;115:712–4.
109. Foster TS, Raehl CL, Wilson HD. Disulfiram-like reaction associated with a parenteral cephalosporin. Am J Hosp Pharm 1980;37:858–9.
110. Buening MK, Wold JS, Israel KS, Kammer RB. Disulfiram-like reaction to beta-lactams. JAMA 1981;245:2027–8.
111. Gibaldi M, Schwartz MA. Apparent effect of probenecid on the distribution of penicillins in man. Clin Pharmacol Ther 1968;9:345–9.
112. Rahal JR Jr. Antibiotic combinations: the clinical relevance of synergy and antagonism. Medicine 1978;57:179–95.
113. Davis BD. Bactericidal synergism between beta-lactams and aminoglycosides: mechanism and possible therapeutic implications. Rev Infect Dis 1982;4:237–45.
114. Eliopoulos GM, Moellering, RC Jr. Antibiotic synergism and antimicrobial combinations in clinical infections. Rev Infect Dis 1982;4:282–93.

chapter 194

Macrolides, Ketolides, Lincosamides and Streptogramins

Claude J Carbon & Ethan Rubinstein

INTRODUCTION

Macrolides, lincosamides and streptogramins are chemically unrelated compounds but they possess closely related properties, such as mechanisms of action, antibacterial spectrum, pharmacokinetics and pharmacodynamics, and clinical use. They are considered in parallel in this chapter.

Macrolides

Erythromycin is considered as the reference macrolide antibiotic. First reports on this compound appeared in 1952. Other natural macrolides were launched soon after this. In the past few decades, efforts have been made to generate new semisynthetic compounds with improved chemical, biologic and pharmacokinetic properties and fewer side effects. The recent modifications of the macrolides, leading to the new class of ketolides, seem to be promising because they allow persistent activity against some micro-organisms that are otherwise resistant to the macrolides.

Lincosamides

Two compounds represent the lincosamide group:

- lincomycin, which is currently of limited clinical use, and
- clindamycin, which is still currently used in the treatment of anaerobic and some parasitic infections.

Streptogramins

Streptogramins are a group of cyclic peptides produced by various *Streptomyces* spp. Pristinamycin and virginiamycin are water-insoluble mixtures of naturally occurring compounds. More recently, the synthesis of water-soluble derivatives has allowed the development of an injectable streptogramin, namely Synercid (RP 59500). A common pattern to streptogramins is that they are composed of at least two structurally unrelated molecules (group A and group B), which act synergistically against most susceptible bacteria.

STRUCTURE

Macrolides and ketolides

The chemical structure of the macrolides is characterized by a large lactone ring containing between 12 and 16 atoms of carbon to which are attached one or more sugars, mainly desosamine and cladinose, by way of glycosidic bonds. Simplified classifications of the macrolides divide the compounds according to the size of the lactone ring (i.e. 12-, 14-, 15- or 16-membered rings; Fig. 194.1).[1] Within each of these groups, compounds are classified according to their natural or semisynthetic origin. The lactone ring is modified by a hydroxyl or alkyl group, one ketone at C7 in the 12-membered macrolides, at C9 in the 14-membered macrolides, and one aldehyde in the 16-membered compounds. The only compound with a 15-membered ring, the azalide azithromycin, contains a tertiary amino group. Neutral or basic sugars can substitute one, two or three hydroxyl groups of the lactone ring, conferring a more or less basic character to the molecule. The most basic compounds are the most active.[2]

The 12-membered macrolides have never become important in clinical practice. Numerous derivatives have been synthesized from the 14-membered macrolides derivatives of erythromycin A.[3] Efforts at extending the biochemical modifications of the 16-membered compounds have been less productive. The objective of this research was to retain the antibacterial activity of erythromycin while improving acid stability and thereby enhancing bioavailability.

In order to overcome the problem of bacterial resistance to macrolides, attempts have been made to modify the basic structure of 14-membered compounds. This has led to new derivatives, called ketolides because a ketone group replaces the L-cladinose of erythromycin A in position 3, a sugar long considered as essential for the antibacterial activity of macrolides.[4] Several additional modifications have allowed the isolation of several molecules. One of them, telithromycin, is already marketed in a number of countries; the others are currently under preclinical or clinical investigation. The telithromycin molecule has a second site of modification at positions C11,12 of the lactone ring, where an alkylaryl extension has been added to a carbamate group.

Lincosamides

Lincomycin was isolated from *Streptomyces lincolnensis*. It is an alkyl derivative of proline that is composed of an amino acid linked to an amino sugar; it is devoid of a lactone ring. Clindamycin is closely related; a hydroxyl group was substituted by a chlorine atom in position 7.

Streptogramins

Streptogramins, as mentioned above, are composed of two unrelated molecules. Group A streptogramins are polyunsaturated macrolactones. Group B streptogramins are cyclic hexadepsipeptides. Table 194.1 presents a summary of streptogramins and lists the compounds available for clinical use.[5]

MODE OF ACTION

Macrolides, ketolides lincosamides and streptogramins, although chemically unrelated, have similar modes of action against bacteria. The hydrophobicity of these molecules explains why they penetrate poorly through the external membrane of Gram-negative bacilli, thus inducing a limited effect against these bacteria. Macrolides and lincosamides exhibit a slow bactericidal effect against susceptible pathogens. Both components A and B of streptogramins demonstrate a synergistic effect that is responsible for a more rapid bactericidal action against some bacteria in their spectrum of activity.

Macrolides and lincosamides inhibit protein synthesis by binding to the 50S subunit of prokaryotic ribosomes, especially to the peptidyl transferase domain of 23S ribosomal RNA, close to the *P* site. Sites of fixation are different for the different classes of drugs. However, they partially overlap. The key sites of interaction for

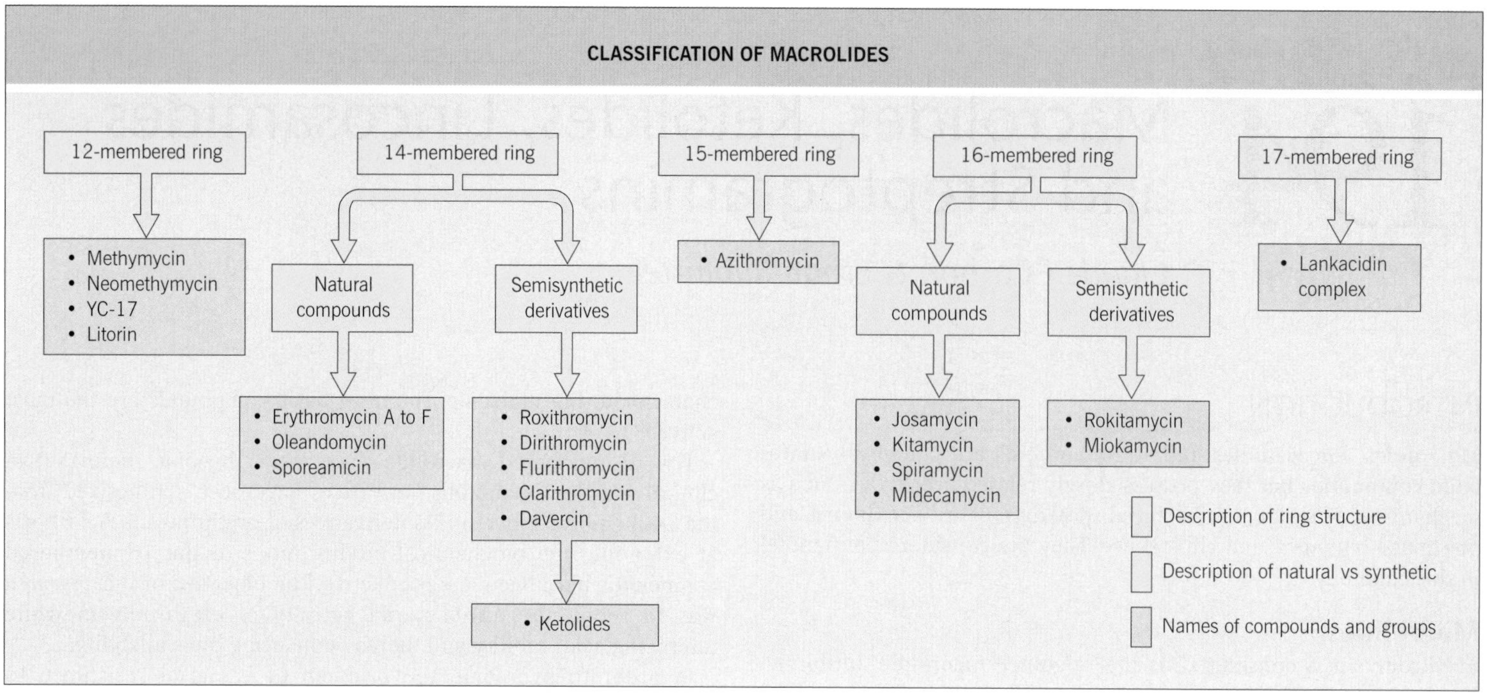

Fig. 194.1 Classification of macrolides. Adapted from Bryskier *et al.*[1]

STREPTOGRAMIN COMPOUNDS
Natural mixtures Pristinamycin (produced by *Streptomyces pristinaespiralis*) is a mixture of several molecules Virginiamycin (produced by *Streptomyces virginiae*)
Chemically defined natural molecules Group A streptogramins Pristinamycin II_A (synonym – streptogramin A) Pristinamycin II_B Group B streptogramins Pristinamycin I_A (synonym – streptogramin B) Pristinamycin I_C
Semisynthetic derivatives Synercid, for parenteral use, is a 30:70 mixture of quinupristin (derived from natural pristinamycin I_A) and dalfopristin (derived from natural pristinamycin II_B) RPR 106972, for oral use, is under clinical evaluation

Table 194.1 Streptogramin compounds. Data from Pechère.[5]

those drugs are at nucleotides A2058 and A2059 within domain V of the 23S RNA, A752 within domain II, and parts of ribosomal proteins L4 and L22, which together form a single drug-binding pocket. Telithromycin binds to wild-type ribosomes with 10-fold greater affinity than erythromycin A.[6] As a result of this binding, a blockade of the peptide bond formation has been reported, with an inhibition of peptide elongation during synthesis.[7] It has also been suggested that the binding could block the peptidyl-transfer (t)RNA translocation from the *A* to the *P* site of the ribosome.[8] Because some mutations can confer resistance simultaneously to macrolides and lincosamides, it is possible that both classes inhibit protein synthesis by stimulating peptidyl-tRNA dissociation from ribosomes.

The relevant target of macrolides and parent compounds against protozoan parasites such as *Toxoplasma gondii* remains unknown. Even very high concentrations have no effect on intracellular parasite survival in the parasitophorous vacuole, extracellular survival or invasion into the subsequent host cell. Replication with the second host cell is inhibited immediately upon entry, suggesting that a key event could be the establishment of the new parasitophorous vacuole.

Both group A and group B streptogramins bind to the ribosome and inhibit the translation of mRNA during the elongation step (Fig. 194.2).[5] Group A compounds interfere with the function of the peptidyl transferase. They block two steps of the peptide chain elongation process. Group B compounds interfere with the correct positioning of peptidyl-tRNA at the *P* site. They inhibit peptide bond formation, resulting in the release of incomplete peptide chains (see Chapter 188).

MECHANISMS OF RESISTANCE

Intrinsic resistance

As mentioned above, Gram-negative bacilli, in particular members of the family Enterobacteriaceae, *Pseudomonas* spp. and *Acinetobacter* spp., are resistant to macrolides, lincosamides and streptogramins owing to the relative impermeability of their cellular outer membrane to these hydrophobic compounds. However, concentrations of erythromycin far above those achievable in serum have proven efficacy against Gram-negative bacilli in the intestinal tract and have been used for intestinal selective decontamination. Furthermore, high intracellular levels achieved by the newest macrolides can inhibit some Gram-negative bacteria. Enterococci are resistant to lincosamides and *Enterococcus faecalis* is resistant to streptogramins. *Mycobacterium tuberculosis* is not susceptible.

Acquired resistance

Three mechanisms account for acquired resistance to the macrolides:[9–11]

- modification of the target of the antibiotics, by methylation or mutation;
- inactivation of the antibiotics; and
- active efflux.

POSSIBLE MOLECULAR ACTION OF STREPTOGRAMINS

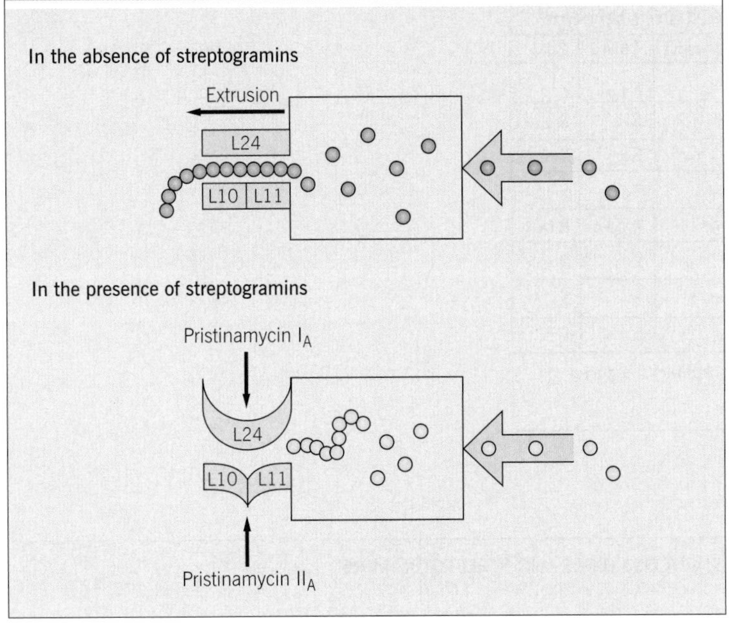

Fig. 194.2 Possible molecular action of streptogramins. In the absence of streptogramins, the exit channel for peptide chains is free. In the presence of streptogramins, type A may induce a conformational change of L10 and L11, leading to an increase in the association of type B streptogramins for L24 and to a constriction of the exit channel. L10, L11 and L24 are the main proteins of the exit channel of peptide chains. Adapted from Pechère.[5]

DISTRIBUTION OF *ERM* GENES IN CLINICALLY IMPORTANT BACTERIAL SPECIES

Hydridization class	Gene	Host
ermA	*ermA*	*Staphylococcus aureus* Coagulase-negative staphylococci
ermAM	*ermP*	*Clostridium perfringens*
	ermZ	*Clostridium difficile* *Enterococcus faecalis*
	ermBC	*Escherichia coli* *Lactobacillus reuteri*
	ermAM	*Streptococcus sanguis* *Streptococcus pneumoniae* *Streptococcus agalactiae* and *Streptococcus pyogenes*
ermC	*ermB*	*Staphylococcus aureus* *Bacillus subtilis* *Lactobacillus* spp.
	ermC	*Staphylococcus aureus* Coagulase-negative staphylococci
	ermM	*Staphylococcus epidermidis*
ermF	*ermF*	*Bacteroides fragilis* *Bacteroides ovatus*

Table 194.2 Distribution of *erm* genes in clinically important bacterial species. Data from Leclercq and Courvalin.[9,10]

In the first type of resistance, a single alteration in 23S rRNA confers cross-resistance to macrolides, lincosamides and group B streptogramins: the so-called MLS_B phenotype. The other two types confer resistance to structurally related compounds only.

Resistance by target methylation

Resistant strains produce an enzyme that demethylates an adenine residue in the 23S rRNA. This methylation leads to a conformational change in the ribosome, which in turn leads to co-resistance to MLS_B-type antibiotics. Streptogramin-A-type compounds are unaffected, and synergy between the two components of streptogramins against MLS_B-resistant strains is maintained. This enzyme production is under the control of erythromycin ribosome methylation (*erm*) genes. The distribution of *erm* genes among clinically important bacterial species is shown in Table 194.2. These genes may be located on chromosomes but are mainly present on plasmids or transposons. The existence of cross-transfer of genetic material from Gram-positive to Gram-negative bacteria under natural conditions has been demonstrated. In Gram-positive cocci, the expression of MLS resistance may be constitutive and the strains are therefore resistant to all macrolides, lincosamides and streptogramin-B-type compounds. Streptogramin-A-type antibiotics escape resistance, and the combination of group A and group B compounds still exhibits a synergistic bacteriostatic effect. However, depending on the level of resistance to the group B component, the in-vivo bactericidal activity of the combination can be limited, especially against *Staphylococcus aureus*. Resistance to macrolides, lincosamides and group B streptogramins can be divided into constitutive resistance, when the methylating enzyme is produced continuously, and inducible resistance, when the presence of an inducing antibiotic is required for enzyme production. When the expression of resistance is inducible, staphylococci are resistant to 14-membered and 15-membered macrolides. The 16-membered antibiotics, the lincosamides and the streptogramin antibiotics remain active, because only 14- and 15-membered macrolides are inducers of methylase synthesis. Ketolides are not inducers. In the case of streptococci, various macrolides and lincosamides can be inducers. Thus, among streptococci, there is a cross-resistance in any case, whether the expression of resistance is constitutive or inducible. As telithromycin is not an inducer of methylase production, it is effective against bacterial subpopulations harboring this type of resistance, but constitutively resistant bacteria are often resistant to telithromycin.[6]

Resistance among anaerobes (*Bacteroides* spp., *Clostridium* spp.) is mainly of the MLS_B constitutive phenotype, although inducibility has been reported. This resistance is either plasmid- or chromosome-mediated. Among *Campylobacter* spp., *Mycoplasma pneumoniae* and *Corynebacterium diphtheriae,* the resistance profile is of the MLS_B phenotype.

Resistance by target mutation

The clinical importance of this mechanism was only recently recognized, with identification of mutations at either A2058 or A2059 domain V of rRNA. A2058 and A2059 confer MLS_B resistance and ML resistance respectively. This mechanism has been identified in *Mycobacterium avium, Helicobacter pylori, Treponema pallidum* and *Streptococcus pneumoniae*. Mutations in ribosomal proteins L4 and L22 have been identified in *S. pneumoniae*.

Resistance by antibiotic modification

Various enzymes are responsible for this type of resistance by inactivation. This mechanism confers resistance to structurally related antibiotics only. Its clinical impact seems rather limited. Phosphotransferases encoded by *mph* (C) have been shown in *S. aureus*. Lincosamide nucleotidyltransferases encoded by *lnu*(A) and *lnu*(B) genes isolated in staphylococci and *Enterococcus faecium* inactivate

PHENOTYPIC AND GENOTYPIC RESISTANCE TO MACROLIDES RESULTING FROM DIFFERENT MECHANISMS						
Organism	Mechanism	Gene	Phenotype designation	Resistance phenotype		
				14–15M	16M	Cli
Staphylococci	Ribosomal methylation	*erm*	MLS_B inducible	R	s	s
			MLS_B constitutive	R	R	R
	Efflux	*msr*A	MS_B	R	S	S
	Lincosamide inactivation	*Lin*A	L	S	S	S
Streptococci and enterococci	Ribosomal inactivation	*erm*	MLS_B inducible	R or I	R or I	R or I
			MLS_B constitutive	R	R	R
	Efflux	*mef*A	M	R or I	S	S
Enterococcus faecium	Lincosamide inactivation	*lnu*B	L	S	S	s

14/15/16M, 14-, 15- or 16-membered macrolides; I, intermediate susceptibility; R, resistant; S, susceptible; s, reduced *in-vivo* susceptibility.

Table 194.3 Phenotypic and genotypic resistance to macrolides resulting from different mechanisms. Adapted from Leclercq.[11]

STAPHYLOCOCCAL RESISTANCE TO MACROLIDES, LINCOSAMIDES AND STREPTOGRAMINS									
Mechanism	Genotype	Erythromycin	Oleandomycin	16-membered macrolides	Lincomycin	Clindamycin	Streptogramin B-type antibiotics*	Streptogramin A-type antibiotics†	Streptogramin antibiotics
Target modification	*erm* (inducible)	R	S or R	S	S	S	S	S	S
	erm (constitutive)	R	R	R	R	R	R	R	S
Drug inactivation	*lin*A	S	S	S	R	S	S	S	S
	lsa	S	S	S	I	I	S	R	I
	saa-sbh	S	S	S	S or I	S or I	R	R	R
Active efflux	*erp*A (detected in coagulase-negative staphylococci only)	R	R	S	S	S	S	S	S
	*msr*A	R	R	S	S	S	R (after induction by erythromycin)	S	Not determined

*Pristinamycin factor I, virginiamycin factor S.
†Pristinamycin factor II, virginiamycin factor M.
I, intermediate resistance; R, resistance; S, susceptible.

Table 194.4 Staphylococcal resistance to macrolides, lincosamides and streptogramins. Adapted from Leclercq and Courvalin P.[9]

lincomycin and, to a lesser degree, clindamycin, which loses any bactericidal effect.

Resistance by active efflux

Two types of resistance by active efflux have been identified first in coagulase-negative staphylococci. The different types of resistance shown by bacteria are summarized in Tables 194.3 & 194.4. Resistance through active efflux is increasingly recognized in *Streptococcus pyogenes* and *S. pneumoniae*. The protein encoded by the macrolide efflux (*mef*)A or *mef*E gene causes resistance to 14- and 15-membered macrolides but not to other macrolides and lincosamides. This phenotype is called the M phenotype. Telithromycin does not appear to fit into this efflux pump and thus remains largely unaffected by *mef*.

Adequate in-vitro testing by combining disks of different MLS compounds may allow the interpretation of the phenotype of resistance and therefore help in choosing the best compound to use. The antibacterial effect of macrolides in vitro varies essentially according to the pH of the medium used; it decreases in acidic conditions and increases in alkaline conditions (see Chapter 188).

CLINICALLY RELEVANT SPECTRUM OF ACTIVITY

Macrolides

The clinical spectrum of macrolides (Table 194.5) is a function of several parameters:

- intrinsic activity;
- spread of resistance mechanisms;
- actual concentrations of active drug achieved in extracellular fluids; and
- intracellular concentrations able to reach intracellular pathogens.

CLINICALLY RELEVANT ANTIMICROBIAL SPECTRUM OF THE MACROLIDES				
Type of infection	**Extracellular bacteria**	**Intracellular bacteria**	**Mycobacteria**	**Parasites**
Upper or lower respiratory tract infections*	*Streptococcus pneumoniae* *Haemophilus influenzae* *Streptococcus pyogenes* *Moraxella catarrhalis* *Corynebacterium diphtheriae* *Bordetella* spp.	*Chlamydia pneumoniae* *Mycoplasma pneumoniae* *Legionella* spp.		
Sexually transmitted diseases	*Treponema pallidum* *Neisseria gonorrhoeae*	*Chlamydia trachomatis*		
Skin or soft tissue infections	*Streptococcus pyogenes* *Peptococcus* spp. *Peptostreptococcus* spp.			
Gastrointestinal infections	*Helicobacter pylori* *Campylobacter* spp.			*Cryptosporidium* spp.
Systemic infections	*Borrelia burgdorferi*	*Rickettsia* spp.	*Mycobacterium avium-intracellulare* *Mycobacterium leprae* *Mycobacterium fortuitum*	*Toxoplasma* sp.

Table 194.5 Clinically relevant antimicrobial spectrum of the macrolides. *; spectrum of clinical activity of telithromycin.

As discussed below in the sections on pharmacokinetics and pharmacodynamics, predicting in-vivo efficacy on the basis solely of extracellular levels of free drug is difficult with MLS compounds. Therefore, the clinically relevant spectrum can be better established on the basis of animal experiments and clinical trials than from in-vitro results and pharmacokinetic data alone.

The prevalence of resistance to macrolides such as erythromycin is highly variable among different countries.[12] Resistance of *S. aureus* to erythromycin ranges from 1% to 50%, with marked differences between community isolates (usually 70–90% susceptible) and hospital isolates, where less than 25% of methicillin-resistant *S. aureus* isolates remain susceptible. Generally more than 75% of methicillin-resistant *Staphylococcus epidermidis* are resistant to macrolides. An increase in the frequency of erythromycin resistance was noted in many hospitals when erythromycin was extensively used.[13] A similar phenomenon has been noted in Finland regarding the influence of macrolide prescription on the development of resistance of group A streptococci to erythromycin. In Finland, after a nationwide reduction in the use of macrolides for outpatient therapy, a significant decline in the frequency of erythromycin resistance among group A streptococci was observed.[12]

Resistance of *S. pneumoniae* to macrolides is also highly variable: 34% worldwide, with rates ranging from 77% in Asia to 7% in Australia. It is especially frequent in penicillin-resistant isolates. The efflux mechanism seems to be more frequent in the USA than in Europe, the *erm*-mediated mechanism being more frequent in Europe.[12] Telithromycin is active against 97.6% of erythromycin-resistant strains.

Enterococcal resistance has increased over the years and is probably a source of resistance in streptococcal species and staphylococci. Macrolide activity against *Haemophilus influenzae* is variable since the systemic levels of macrolides are similar to the minimum inhibitory concentration (MIC). Some strains of *H. influenzae* are resistant to clinically achievable blood levels of the macrolides. Some Gram-negative organisms, mainly *Campylobacter jejuni* and *H. pylori*, are major therapeutic targets of macrolides.

Some differences in terms of in-vitro activity and demonstration of in-vivo efficacy have been reported between erythromycin and the newest macrolide compounds (see Indications). However, it should be emphasized again that these compounds share the main resistance patterns with erythromycin.

Ketolides are active against Gram-positive cocci that are resistant to erythromycin by an efflux mechanism or by an inducible MLS_B mechanism.

Lincosamides

Lincosamides offer advantages of efficacy against anaerobes, including *Bacteroides* spp. (mainly *B. fragilis*), *Fusobacterium* spp., anaerobic cocci, *Clostridium perfringens* and other clostridia, certain non-spore-forming Gram-positive rods and *Capnocytophaga* spp. Resistance has been described with an increased incidence among anaerobes isolated from patients previously treated with clindamycin. The antiparasitic spectrum of clindamycin includes *Plasmodium* spp. and *T. gondii.*

Streptogramins

Streptogramins have a broad spectrum of antibacterial activity in vitro, roughly the same as that of the macrolides. However, interesting differences can be pointed out; the parenteral compound Synercid® is effective against staphylococci with the inducible type of resistance and against some of the constitutively resistant ones. Macrolide-resistant *S. pneumoniae* remain susceptible to streptogramins. These compounds are also active against constitutively macrolide-resistant strains of streptococci. Multiple-resistant *Enterococcus faecium* are susceptible in vitro to Synercid®.[14]

PHARMACOLOGY

Pharmacokinetics

Macrolides

The major drawback of earlier macrolides was their poor intestinal absorption (with large variations both within and between subjects), short half-life, high degree of binding to serum proteins (mainly the α-1 acid glycoprotein) and poor gastrointestinal tolerance. The main kinetic properties of macrolides are listed in Table 194.6.[15] It is important to note wide variations in peak serum concentrations, elimination half-lives and areas under the serum concentration curve (AUC). Furthermore, differences in terms of C_{max} (peak blood level) have been described for the different erythromycin preparations. Generally, the bioavailability of macrolides is low to moderate. Various factors may affect their absorption: the nature of the salt

PHARMACOKINETICS OF MACROLIDES AND AZALIDES						
Antibiotic	Oral dose (mg)	C_{max} (mg/l)	t_{max} (hours)	Half-life (hours)	Area under serum concentration curve (mg/l hour)	Protein binding (%)
Erythromycin base	500	2.00	3.7	2.0	7.7	74
Roxithromycin	300	10.8	1.6	11.9	116.9	95
Clarithromycin	400	2.1	1.7	4.7	17	70
Azithromycin	500	0.4	2.0	14	4.5	50
Dirithromycin	600	0.32	4.2	28	1.4	15–30
Spiramycin	6 MU	3.3	1	8	8.5	12 (albumin); 6 (α-1 acid glycoprotein)
Josamycin	500	1.2	1	2	7.9	10

Table 194.6 Pharmacokinetics of macrolides and azalides. C_{max}, peak blood level; t_{max}, time to maximum blood level.

that is administered (as mentioned above for erythromycin) and the presence of food. Therefore, specific conditions of oral administration should be checked for each compound (Table 194.7). The free fraction of macrolides diffuses into most tissues. Penetration into the cerebrospinal fluid is poor.

All macrolides exhibit intracellular accumulation mainly in polymorphonuclear leukocytes and macrophages; some of them have prolonged persistence of high intracellular levels. This phenomenon has also been observed in nonphagocytic cells and it has been proposed as the reason for the sustained bioactivity of macrolides against intracellular pathogens. Important variations in intracellular levels (with average intracellular to extracellular concentration ratios of more than 10) and half-lives have been described. The entry of macrolides into cells is rapid and almost complete within 15 minutes. The highest intracellular concentrations are currently achieved by azithromycin, which also has the longest intracellular half-life. The uptake rates of the compounds correspond to their lipid solubility, and this process is not saturable. The mechanisms underlying macrolide cellular uptake are still poorly understood, apart from the role of lipid solubility. One possible mechanism involves active transport systems, especially those used by nucleosides. A likely mechanism for the accumulation of macrolides involves their weak basic nature and the possibility of trapping by protonation within acidic cellular compartments, lysosomes and polymorphonuclear neutrophil granules.[16]

Efflux of macrolides from the cells into a drug-free medium is rapid but highly variable from one drug to another. It is therefore possible to distinguish three types of macrolides by comparing them with erythromycin:

- azithromycin, with low extracellular levels, high intracellular penetration, and long extracellular and intracellular elimination half-lives;
- roxithromycin, with relatively high serum levels and shorter half-life than azithromycin; and
- clarithromycin, which has properties of both compounds; some older compounds such as spiramycin and josamycin are also in this intermediate position.

Obviously, the high intracellular concentrations go a long way to explaining the high tissue concentrations that are observed following the administration of macrolides. The therapeutic relevance of these high intracellular levels is less clear. Indeed, high intracellular levels are a prerequisite for the cure of intracellular organisms. However, the location of the offending agent within the cell and the acidic intracellular pH are not always compatible with the expected effect. Furthermore, the concept of the transport of the drug to the infected focus by the means of phagocytic cells remain rather theoretic in the absence of direct proof that the release of the drug from the cell is able to maintain extracellular levels that are sufficient to inhibit extracellular bacteria.

The primary site of metabolism of macrolides is the liver, with the metabolites excreted into the bile. The cytochrome P450 enzymes play a key role. A lesser degree of metabolism occurs in kidneys and lungs. The known metabolic pathways exhibit some features that are common to many members of the class and others that are unique to specific compounds.[17] Within the 14-membered compounds, *N*-demethylation of desosamine and hydrolysis of cladinose are commonly observed. Some specific events can occur, such as the hydroxylation at C14 of clarithromycin, leading to a 14-hydroxy derivative, which acts synergistically with the mother compound on *H. influenzae*. Azithromycin, a 15-membered macrolide, is not highly metabolized; the unaltered parent compound accounts for 75% of drug-related substances excreted in humans. Within the family of 16-membered macrolides, cleavage of the 4″-O-acyl group on the terminal neutral sugar by liver esterases commonly occurs. In addition, oxidations at either the β-carbon of the 4″-ester or at the C14 of the lactone ring are frequently observed. Interactions of macrolides with hepatic enzymes, especially cytochrome P450-dependent mono-oxygenases, is very important. Several drug interactions involve this system, which controls the oxidative metabolism and elimination of medicinal compounds. Erythromycin and troleandomycin (a macrolide that is no longer available in most countries) exert a marked disturbance of liver cytochromes P450 of the 3A subfamily in humans. This is the consequence of three concomitant phenomena:

- the induction of a cytochrome P450 3A;
- its inactivation by the formation of an iron–metabolite complex caused by the strong binding of a nitrosoalkane metabolite derived from the macrolide to P450 iron(II); and
- the accumulation of this complexed P450 through its stability in the presence of degrading enzymes.

Three structural factors are important in the formation of inhibitory P450–iron–metabolite complexes during macrolide oxidation:

- the presence of an $N(CH_3)^2$ amine function;
- the accessibility of this amine function, which is required for the strong binding of the nitrosoalkane metabolite to heme; and
- the hydrophobicity of the molecule.

All macrolides that are prone to forming these complexes are good inducers of P450 3A. Metabolism can be affected by liver function abnormalities. Binding of α-1 acid-glycoprotein can be decreased by a reduction in the production of this protein, with a subsequent

MODE OF ADMINISTRATION OF MACROLIDES AND MODIFICATION OF DOSAGE IN SPECIFIC CONDITIONS					
Macrolides	Presentation	Route of administration	Dosage	Effect of food	Modification of dosage in specific conditions
Azithromycin	Capsules (250mg) Pediatric suspension or Granules	po po	500mg on day 1, then 250mg q24h 10mg/kg/day then 5mg/kg q24h	50% reduction in AUC	If creatinine clearance >30ml/minute, no modification If creatinine clearance <30ml/minute, situation uncertain Caution in severe hepatic failure
Clarithromycin	Tablets (250mg) Tablets (500mg modified release)	po	250–1000mg q12h	No effect	50% reduction in dose if creatinine clearance <30ml/minute No data in hepatic failure
Dirithromycin	Tablets (250mg)	po	500mg q24h	Increased bioavailability	50% reduction in dose if creatinine clearance <5ml/minute and in those aged over 80 years
Erythromycin lactobionate	Vials (500mg and 1000mg)	iv	2000mg/day by continuous infusion or 500mg q6h (infused over 1 hour) in adults; 30–40mg/kg/day in children	No effect	50% reduction in dose in case of renal failure Caution in the elderly
Erythromycin ethylsuccinate	Pediatric suspension or power (125mg and 250mg) Tablets (500mg and 1000mg)	po	30–50mg/kg/day in children 2000–3000mg/day in adults	No effect	Avoid in hepatic failure No modification in renal failure
Erythromycin propionate	Tablets (500mg)	po	500mg q12h	Decreased bioavailability	Avoid in hepatic failure Reduce dose in severe renal failure
Dihydrated erythromycin	Capsules (250mg)	po	500mg q12h	Decreased bioavailability	Avoid in hepatic failure Reduce dose in severe renal failure
Midecamycin diacetate	Tablets (400mg)	po	800mg q12h	No effect	Avoid in hepatic failure No modification in renal failure
Josamycin	Sachets (1000mg) Tablets (500mg) Pediatric suspension Granules	po	500–1000mg q12h	No effect	Avoid in hepatic failure No modification in renal failure
Roxithromycin	Tablets (100mg or 150mg) Pediatric suspension	po	150mg q12h 3mg/kg q12h	No effect	Avoid in case of hepatic failure No modification in renal failure
Spiramycin	Tablets (1.5×10^6 units or 3×10^6 units) Granules or suspension (1.5×10^6 units)	po iv	3×10^6 units q8–12h	No effect	No modification in renal failure

Table 194.7 Mode of administration of macrolides and modification of dosage in specific conditions.

increase in the free fraction of the macrolide. In normal conditions, the main route of elimination of macrolides is the liver. Renal elimination contributes little to total clearance. Changes in macrolide pharmacokinetics due to hepatic or renal impairment depend on the molecule considered, the route of administration and the extent of disturbance in renal or hepatic functions. Table 194.7 indicates the changes to be considered in the dosages in the case of renal or hepatic functional disturbances.

The route of administration of macrolides is usually oral, except for erythromycin and, in some countries, azithromycin and spiramycin, which have a parenteral form. The number of daily doses (usually two) depends on the elimination half-life of the drug and the severity of infection (see Table 194.7).

Ketolides

Telithromycin is administered orally at a 800mg od daily dose. (Max is 2.3mg/L, AUC 0.24h:12.5μg.h/mL; elimination half-life 9.8h.) The compound is 70% bound to serum proteins. Hepatic metabolism (through CYP 3 A4) represents 37% of the elimination process.

Lincosamides

Orally administered clindamycin has good bioavailability (about 90%), and food does not interfere with its absorption. Protein binding varies from 60% to 95%. Serum C_{max} is around 4.5mg/l after a 300mg dose. The elimination half-life is about 3 hours. Penetration into the cerebrospinal fluid is limited. Lincosamides are actively transported into phagocytic cells. Approximately 95% of administered clindamycin is excreted unchanged or is metabolized through the liver; 5% is excreted unchanged into the urine. Active metabolites represent 20% of the total amount excreted. Lincomycin can be administered orally or intravenously. The common doses for adults are 300mg q8h orally or 600mg q8h intravenously, and for children 10–30mg/kg/day (divided into three doses). No dose adjustment is necessary for patients who have renal insufficiency but a 50% reduction in the dose may be needed for patients who have severe hepatic impairment.

Streptogramins

The data on the pharmacokinetics of pristinamycin are very limited, owing to the complexity of the components of the commercial preparation, the number of metabolites and the great instability of the drug in biologic fluids. In some countries, pristinamycin is available for oral administration, 2–3g/day (50–100mg/kg/day in children), to be given as two to four doses. No dosage modification is needed in renal or hepatic failure.

The pharmacokinetic properties of the two components of Synercid® given intravenously in a 30:70 ratio (quinapristin:dalfopristin) at doses of 5, 10 and 15mg/kg have been studied in healthy human volunteers.[18] Mean maximal concentrations (mg/ml) were 1.3, 2.4 and 3.3 for quinupristin and 5.1, 7.1 and 8.5 for dalfopristin. Elimination half-lives ranged between 0.6 hours and 1 hour for quinupristin and between 0.3 hours and 0.4 hours for dalfopristin. Plasma clearance was high for both compounds: 1l/h/kg for quinupristin and 0.8l/h/kg for dalfopristin. The plasma levels of the active metabolite of dalfopristin were 20–45% those of the parent drug, showing a trend to increase with the dose. Synercid® must be administered by intravenous infusion using a central vein. The recommended doses are 7.5mg/kg q8–12h, depending on the organism responsible for infection and the severity of the infection.

Pharmacodynamics

Antibacterial mechanisms

Macrolides

The efficacy of macrolides against extracellular pathogens depends on the extracellular concentrations of free drug and the level of susceptibility of the organisms.[19] Macrolides exhibit a time-dependent bactericidal effect against most bacteria of their clinical spectrum, particularly against streptococci. They are slowly bactericidal and increasing the concentration has little influence on the rate of killing. The size of the inoculum affects the antistreptococcal effect and also antistaphylococcal activity. In the presence of serum, the MIC of some macrolides (e.g. roxithromycin, rokitamycin) against *S. pyogenes* increases 1- to 4-fold. In contrast, the MIC for *S. pneumoniae* does not change. The optimal effect is observed at pH 8, with a significant decrease in efficacy at pH less than 6. Against extracellular pathogens, the time during which the concentration of free extracellular drug is above the MIC is the major determinant of the efficacy of macrolides.

Ketolides

Telithromycin exhibits a concentration-dependent effect against *S. pneumoniae*, the AUC to MIC ratio being the best predictive factor of bacterial outcome both in animal and human studies.[20]

Streptogramins

The two components of Synercid® are bacteriostatic against MLS_B-susceptible and methicillin MLS_B inducibly resistant *Staphylococcus aureus*, whereas the MLS_B constitutively resistant strains are resistant to quinupristin. Synergy between antibiotics in vitro is a phenomenon found at concentrations close to the MIC, except for strains with constitutive resistance. High-level resistance to quinupristin does not significantly reduce the activity of the combination, and generally the MIC index is found to be less than 0.5. The bactericidal effect of Synercid® against *S. aureus* appears to be time-dependent but not concentration-dependent, because neither quinupristin nor dalfopristin alone is bactericidal. Synercid® is more rapidly bactericidal against *S. pneumoniae* (1h) than against *S. aureus* (6h); it is slowly active against *E. faecium*.

Postantibiotic effect

The presence of a postantibiotic effect (PAE) is a feature common to all macrolides (see Chapter 188). Several factors may affect the in-vitro PAE of these drugs.[21] The duration of this effect is longer with Gram-positive cocci than with *H. influenzae.* Increasing macrolide concentrations and exposure time prolongs the duration of PAE to a point of maximum response.

The PAE of Synercid® has been evaluated against a variety of bacteria, mainly staphylococci, pneumococci and streptococci. The PAE is constantly observed at concentrations above the MIC.[21]

Nonantibacterial pharmacologic effects

Erythromycin and 14-membered macrolides exhibit agonistic activity to motilin receptors and are therefore able to accelerate gastric emptying.

In relation to their high and prolonged intracellular concentrations in phagocytic and nonphagocytic cells, macrolides show an effect on some cellular functions (e.g. they enhance phagocytosis, bacterial killing and chemotaxis). These effects are observed mainly with very high extracellular levels. The macrolides with antibacterial effect have very few immunosuppressive effects, if any. Some molecules derived from this class of macrocyclic antibiotics, such as FK506, are used as immunosuppressive agents.

INDICATIONS

Macrolides in adult patients

Macrolides have a number of uses in both immunocompetent and immunocompromised patients (Table 194.8).[22]

In respiratory tract infections, the use of a macrolide as a first-line monotherapy is, in some areas, made difficult by a high rate of resistance of *S. pneumoniae* to erythromycin. In community-acquired pneumonia, the use of a macrolide in patients who are aged less than 60 years and who have no risk factors or signs of severe pneumonia has been proposed.[23] However, this point is considered controversial by some authors, who argue that the role of intracellular pathogens as etiologic agents of community-acquired pneumonia is limited in this subgroup of patients. As far as *Legionella pneumophila* or *Chlamydia pneumoniae* can be recognized or highly suspected as responsible for the infection, a macrolide is considered a useful therapy.[24] Finally, in cases of severe infection, the prescription of a combination of a β-lactam with a macrolide is recommended (see Chapter 34).[23]

Macrolides are used to treat some sexually transmitted diseases.[25] Azithromycin, given as a single dose of 1g, has been documented as effective in cervicitis and urethritis caused by *Chlamydia trachomatis*.[26] Conversely, such a short course of therapy is not effective in gonococcal infections, which require longer administration. For gonococcal infections and syphilis, macrolides are considered a second-choice treatment, even in cases of allergy to β-lactams, because more efficient alternatives exist. Activity of macrolides has been documented in donovanosis and lymphogranuloma venereum (see Chapters 74 & 78).

Given their limited activity against staphylococci, macrolides are not considered major agents in the therapy of skin and soft tissue infections, except when streptococci are highly suspected (impetigo) or documented, and in cases of allergy to β-lactams.

Azithromycin and clarithromycin have been evaluated as major components of the combinations that are active against *H. pylori*, including metronidazole and an inhibitor of the proton pump. The selection of strains with high-level resistance after the use of macrolide has been demonstrated as the major drawback of macrolide monotherapy. *Campylobacter jejuni* is highly susceptible in vivo to macrolides. However, the use of macrolides in acute gastroenteritis supposes a precise bacteriologic documentation (see Chapter 43). Azithromycin has been shown to be effective in typhoid fever.[27] The clinical experience remains limited and this drug is considered a second-choice alternative therapy.

The C16 macrolide spiramycin is marketed in a limited number of countries. Very few well-designed clinical studies have been performed. Some studies indicatethat its activity is equivalent to that of other macrolides in the major indications allowing the oral route. In some countries, spiramycin is considered as a drug of choice for the treatment of toxoplasmosis occuring during prenancy. Data on the efficacy of the compound in such an indication are of limited scientific value. Tolerance of spiramycin is good with very limited drug-drug interactions.

The impact of a large use of C16 macrolide in a community on the level of resistance of streptococci and pneumococci, actually depends on the respective prevalence of the different genotypes of resistance to macrolides amongst those organisms.

POTENTIAL USES OF MACROLIDES IN ADULT PATIENTS		
	Condition	**Comments**
Respiratory tract infections	Acute sinusitis	Not first-line agents
	Otitis media	Not first-line agents
	Pharyngitis	In cases of allergy to penicillins
	Acute exacerbation of chronic bronchitis	In areas with low rate of pneumococcal resistance to macrolides
	Community-acquired pneumonia	First-line drug in adults aged over 60 years and without risk factors, signs of severe pneumonia or evidence of pneumococcal infection; alternatives in cases of allergy to β-lactams; evidence of infection with *Legionella* spp. or *Chlamydia* spp.; combine with a β-lactam in severe cases
Sexually transmitted diseases	Chlamydial urethritis or cervicitis	Single dose (1g) or azithromycin
	Donovanosis or lymphogranuloma venereum	Demonstrated efficacy
	Syphilis	Alternatives to β-lactams (limited activity)
	Gonococcal infection	Alternatives to β-lactams (limited activity)
Skin and soft tissue infections	Streptococcal infections	Limited activity versus staphylococcal infections
Gastrointestinal infections	*Helicobacter pylori*	Azithromycin or clarithromycin in triple combinations
	Campylobacter jejuni	See text
	Typhoid fever	Azithromycin is an alternative to other therapies (limited experience)
Specific organisms	*Borrelia burgdorferi*	See text
	Rickettsia typhus group	See text
	Bartonella spp.	Azithromycin can be used in cat-scratch disease (limited experience)
Immunocompromised host	Mycobacteria (*Mycobacterium leprae, M. chelonae, M. fortuitum*)	See text
	Mycobacterial disseminated infections (*M. avium*)	In combination with other agents
	Toxoplasmal encephalitis	Minor alternative to other regimens (in combination)
	Cryptosporidial intestinal infection	Azithromycin has a limited activity at high doses
	Rhodococcus equi infection	Limited experience
	Bacillary angiomatosis	Activity has been demonstrated
Nonantibacterial use	Gastric paresis	Erythromycin has documented activity
Possible future uses	Atherosclerosis	Possible role in control of coronary restenosis and prevention

Table 194.8 Potential uses of macrolides in adult patients.

The use of azithromycin or clarithromycin in the treatment of Lyme disease remains speculative and some studies indicate that amoxicillin might be superior (see Chapter 54). Macrolides are active against *Rickettsia* spp. of the typhus group, and josamycin may be considered a safe alternative to treat Mediterranean spotted fever.[28] Both *Bartonella henselae* and *Bartonella quintana* are susceptible to macrolides. Azithromycin has been demonstrated to be of potential use in the treatment of cat-scratch disease (Chapter 91).[29] The clinical experience with macrolides is still limited in the treatment of other forms of infections caused by *Bartonella* spp. in immunocompetent patients.

Monthly regimens that include clarithromycin and minocycline have demonstrated a significant clinical efficacy in the treatment of lepromatous leprosy. Further investigations are needed to determine the proper dosage of both drugs.[30] Infections due to *Mycobacterium chelonae* and *M. fortuitum* may be susceptible to azithromycin or clarithromycin (see Chapter 3 and 233).[31]

Erythromycin is used for its effects on gastric and intestinal motility to treat gastric paresis or gastrointestinal disturbances in diabetic or postsurgical patients.

In immunocompromised patients, mainly those infected by HIV, the newest macrolides are considered helpful agents in the treatment of disseminated *M. avium* infections. Monotherapy with azithromycin or clarithromycin causes the rapid selection of resistant variants, and therefore a multiple combination is required. Neither azithromycin nor clarithromycin is very helpful in the treatment of encephalitis caused by *T. gondii* because they need to be given in high doses, often intravenously and in combination with other compounds. Azithromycin, even at high doses, has shown limited activity against diarrhea caused by *Cryptosporidium parvum*. Bacillary angiomatosis and some forms of *Rhodococcus equi* infections are susceptible to macrolides.

Macrolides have a number of potential prophylactic uses (Table 194.9). In surgical prophylaxis, erythromycin can be used in combination with neomycin and enemas for the preparation of the large bowel before surgery. Macrolides are included in the recommendations for the prevention of bacterial endocarditis in low-risk patients undergoing dental procedures who are intolerant of β-lactams.[32] There is a still limited experience in the use of azithromycin for the prevention of malaria.[33]

In immunocompromised hosts, macrolides are mainly used in the prevention of disseminated *M. avium* complex infection (see Chapter 129).[34] Azithromycin has been shown to be effective in primary prevention when given once weekly as has daily clarithromycin.[35] A combination of clarithromycin (or azithromycin) and another drug can be considered as an effective choice for the prevention of recurrences.

POTENTIAL PROPHYLACTIC USES OF MACROLIDES IN ADULT PATIENTS		
	Indication	Comments
Immunocompetent host	Surgical prophylaxis (large bowel preparation)	Oral therapy in combination with neomycin and enema
	Bacterial endocarditis	Alternatives to β-lactams in allergic patients
	Malaria	Limited experience with azithromycin
Immunocompromised host	Primary prevention of *Mycobacterium avium* complex infections	Weekly administration of azithromycin or daily clarithromycin has documented activity
	Prophylaxis of recurrences of *Mycobacterium avium* complex infections	Clarithromycin or azithromycin combined with another agent

Table 194.9 Potential prophylactic uses of macrolides in adult patients.

SPECIFIC USES FOR MACROLIDES IN PEDIATRIC PATIENTS		
	Indication	Comments
Upper respiratory tract infections	Acute otitis media	Not first-line choice Combine with sulfonamides
	Sinusitis	Not first-line choice
	Tonsillitis	Alternative to penicillin G and penicillin V in allergic patients
	Diphtheria	Eradication of acute and chronic carrier states
	Acute bronchitis	Antibiotic therapy has questionable efficacy
	Pneumonia	Not first-line choice as single agents Combination with β-lactam in severe cases if infections caused by *Legionella* spp. and *Chlamydia* spp. a concern
	Whooping cough	Shortens the duration of disease Eliminates carrier state
Skin and soft tissue infections	*Campylobacter jejuni* enteritis	Treatment of choice
	Ureaplasmal or chlamydial infections in neonates	Treatment of choice
Local uses	Acne	See text
	Conjunctivitis	Alternatives as prophylaxis of ophthalmia neonatorum
Prophylactic uses	Endocarditis	Alternatives to β-lactams in case of allergy
	Recurrences of rheumatic fever	Alternatives to β-lactams in case of allergy

Table 194.10 Specific uses for macrolides in pediatric patients. Data from Guay.[36]

Ketolides

Telithromycin has demonstrated equivalent activities to those of the comparators in the following indications: mild to moderate community-acquired pneumonia, acute exacerbations of chronic bronchitis, acute maxillary sinusitis and streptococcal pharyngitis, in adult patients at a single daily dose of 800mg. In most of those indications, a duration of treatment of 5 days has been shown to be acceptable.[20] Its use as a first-line choice for the treatment of community-acquired pneumonia is considered in many countries.

Use of macrolides in special circumstances

Some indications, more or less specific to children, are presented in Table 194.10.[36] Macrolides are no longer considered to be first-choice drugs in the treatment of otitis media, owing to major changes in the susceptibility of pneumococci to erythromycin.[37] The combination of a macrolide and a sulfonamide has been shown to increase the effect against *H. influenzae*. The use of macrolides in tonsillitis should be considered in patients who are intolerant to β-lactams in areas where group A streptococci have a low rate of resistance to erythromycin. The newest macrolides allow a reduction in the duration of treatment from 7–10 days to 4–5 days.[38] Topical preparations are used in the treatment of acne and for the prevention of ophthalmitis in neonates.

Table 194.11 gives some points to consider when choosing a particular compound once it has been established that the use of a macrolide is indicated. Efficacy for the indication should be the first point to be taken into consideration, together with the risk of side effects, drug interactions and poor patient compliance.

Table 194.7 mentions the modifications to be made in dosing in case of renal failure for the macrolides, and cautions around the use of those drugs in case of hepatic failure. In elderly patients, the degree of deterioration of the renal function should be taken into consideration to adapt the dose and dosing regimen of the intravenous forms of the macrolides. Also, as indicated in Table 194.12, special attention should be paid to drugs currently taken by the patients at the moment when a macrolide is prescribed. The same type of measures are to be envisaged with telithro-mycin. For this latter drug, no specific adaptation of the dose is needed in patients who have renal failure or in elderly patients. Similar reasoning is acceptable for lincosamides and synergistins. Macrolides and lincosamides are not contraindicated during pregnancy. There are no data regarding Synercid® in that

ADVANTAGES AND DISADVANTAGES OF SPECIFIC MACROLIDES		
Agent	Advantages	Disadvantages
Erythromycin	Long clinical experience Good documentation of efficacy Low cost	Poor bioavaliability Poor tolerance 2–4 doses per day Drug–drug interactions Acquired resistance
Roxithromycin	Increased absorption Decreased side effects Adequate extracellular levels Improved activity against mycobacteria than erythromycin	Drug–drug interactions Same resistance profile as erythromycin
Clarithromycin	Improved activity against some Gram-negative bacteria and some mycobacteria Increased absorption	Drug–drug interactions Same resistance profile as erythromycin
Azithromycin	High intracellular levels Improved activity against some Gram-negative bacteria and mycobacteria than erythromycin Limited drug–drug interactions Once-daily administration Short course of therapy Single dose in *Chlamydia trachomatis* infection	Poor extracellular levels Poor documentation in bacteremic pneumococcal diseases Same resistance profile as erythromycin
Dirithromycin	Improved biovailability than erythromycin Once-daily administration Few drug–drug interactions	Same resistance profile as erythromycin
Spiramycin	Improved bioavailability than erythromycin Good tolerance Limited drug interactions	Limited clinical documentation Same resistance profile as erythromycin
Josamycin	Good tolerance	Same resistance profile as erythromycin Drug–drug interactions

Table 194.11 Advantages and disadvantages of specific macrolides.

situation. However, the risks related to the infection caused by multiresistant organisms should be considered if Synercid® represents the only therapeutic option.

Future developments in macrolide use

The potential use of the newest compounds in the treatment of atherosclerosis, because of their activity against *C. pneumoniae*, one of the micro-organisms potentially involved in the pathogenesis of atherosclerosis, is the most attractive future development in the use of macrolides.[39] On the basis of controversial results, investigations are in progress to delineate their role in the therapy and possibly the prevention of the disease. Other areas of potential interest could be the effects of macrolides on the expression of bacterial virulence factors, the formation of bacterial biofilms and their use as immunomodulators.

Synergistins

Oral pristinamycin is marketed in a limited number of countries. It is used in minor or moderately severe infections such as community-acquired pneumonia and community-acquired staphylococcal infections. The development of the parenteral streptogramin Synercid® is focused on methicillin-resistant *S. aureus*, *E. faecium* resistant to glycopeptides, macrolide- or penicillin-resistant pneumococci, and the treatment of Gram-positive cocci infections in patients not able to tolerate a more conventional agent.[40]

Clindamycin

Clindamycin is used in polymicrobial infections outside the central nervous system, including intra-abdominal, gynecologic, bronchopulmonary, and skin and soft tissue infections.[41] Its use may be compromised by the development of resistance among staphylococci and some anaerobes such as *B. fragilis.* Clindamycin has been shown to improve the efficacy of doxycycline in the treatment of severe malaria caused by *Plasmodium falciparum* and that of quinine in the treatment of babesiosis.

Topically, clindamycin is used for the treatment of acne and bacterial vaginosis.

It is used in combination with pyrimethamine as an alternative for the treatment or prevention of *T. gondii* encephalitis in HIV-infected patients.[34]

MACROLIDE DRUG INTERACTIONS	
Erythromycin	Avoid concomitant use of theophylline, ergotamine, bromocriptine, warfarin, carbamazepine, triazolam, midazolam, alfentamil, cyclosporin, terfenadine, cisapride and astemizole Caution in the use of digoxin (increased bioavailability – check serum levels)
Josamycin	Avoid concomitant use of astemizole, cisapride, ergotamine, bromocriptine, terfenadine, triazolam Caution in the use of theophylline and cyclosporin
Roxithromycin	Avoid concomitant use of triazolam, midazolam, cisapride, astemizole and cyclosporin
Clarithromycin	Avoid concomitant use of terfenadine, carbamazepine, ergotamine and cisapride Take zidovudine 2 hours apart from macrolide Caution in the use of theophylline
Midecamycin	Avoid concomitant use of ergotamine, cisapride and bromocriptine Caution in the use of cyclosporin and warfarin
Dirithromycin	Caution in the use of cyclopsorin and cisapride (?)
Spiramycin	Caution in the use of levodopa and cisapride (?)
Azithromycin	Avoid concomitant use of ergotamine, cisapride and bromocriptine Caution with use of cyclosporin

Table 194.12 Macrolide drug interactions. Data from Guay.[36]

ADVERSE REACTIONS AND INTERACTIONS

Macrolides

Adverse reactions

In general, the macrolides have a high degree of safety.[36] The main adverse effects are referable to the gastrointestinal tract. Those effects are partly related to the dose-dependent prokinetic effects of the macrolides, with a higher incidence in young adults than in people over 70 years old. The 14-membered macrolides exhibit the most important effect on intestinal motility; the 16-membered have no such effects. These effects include nausea, vomiting, diarrhea and abdominal discomfort. Erythromycin is responsible for the highest percentages of gastrointestinal side effects, with values around 30% and a rate of discontinuation of therapy around 5%. These effects are significantly lower with the newest compounds, partly as a result of better bioavailability allowing lower oral doses (gastrointestinal side effects in between 3% and 10% of patients and discontinuation of therapy in 1–4%).

Reversible cholestatic hepatitis has been reported with erythromycin estolate, mainly in children, in about one case in 1000. A hypersensitivity mechanism has been suggested in view of the rapid development of cholestatic hepatitis in patients who have previous drug-induced hepatitis. Erythromycin estolate is contraindicated in pregnancy. The frequency of hepatitis with other erythromycin preparations, mainly ethylsuccinate, is much lower. In patients who have had a previous episode of hepatitis induced by erythromycin estolate, the other macrolides should be used with caution or even considered as contraindicated. No cases of hepatitis have been reported with the newest macrolides. Transient elevation of hepatic enzymes have been rarely reported; this has been observed in about 10% of patients receiving high doses of clarithromycin (2g/day or more).

Erythromycin can cause a dose-dependent, reversible hearing loss, usually in patients who have renal or hepatic impairment. Hearing loss has rarely been reported with high doses of clarithromycin.

Hypersensitivity reactions can be observed with any macrolide.

Prolongation of the QT interval on electrocardiography leading in some cases to recurrent *torsades de pointes* may rarely occur following erythromycin lactobionate administration. Cases of *torsades de pointes* have also been described in patients receiving clarithromycin and azithromycin. Telithromycin and presumably other ketolides have also the potential to cause a prolongation of the QT_c interval, especially in elderly patients who have predisposing conditions or those who are concurrently receiving drugs that are substrates for CYP2D6 and 3A4.[41] Macrolides should be used with caution in patients at risk of these disorders, such as elderly female patients, patients who have inborn prolonged QT_c interval, patients who have congestive heart failure, patients who have hypomagnesemia or hypokalemia, those on diuretic therapy and patients receiving concomitant drugs able to potentiate the toxic effects of the macrolide (e.g. antiarrhythmic agents from class II, amiodarone, certain antihistaminics, certain fluoroquinolones). Disturbances of the intestinal microbial flora, with selection of staphylococci, enterococci or *Candida* spp., have been reported. Like many other oral antimicrobial agents, macrolides can induce *Clostridium difficile* colitis.

Ketolides

The ketolides have a similar spectrum of adverse events as the macrolides. In clinical trials in which a daily dose of 800mg was used the adverse events rate and profile were similar to the comparator agent, with diarrhea (13.3%) and nausea (8.1%) being the most common; other less frequent adverse events were vomiting, abdominal pains and elevation of liver enzymes.[42] From more than 1.5 million patient treated with telithromycin, no unexpected adverse event was reported. QT_c prolongation was not reported. In 0.6% of the cases, blurred vision related to a transient, fully reversable, trouble with accomodation was reported.

Drug interactions

Apart from the interaction of macrolides with digoxin, which is related to the destruction by the macrolide of enteric flora that are partly responsible for digoxin metabolism, most of the interactions between macrolides and other drugs involve inhibition of drug metabolism via cytochrome P450 microsomal enzymes (see Pharmacology). Erythromycin and troleandomycin are the macrolides that are most involved in these interactions. Azithromycin, rokitamycin and spiramycin neither activate the cytochrome P450 nor form complexes with it, and therefore they are unable to modify the pharmacokinetics and metabolism of other drugs.[15] Clarithromycin, roxithromycin, josamycin and midecamycin induce cytochrome P450 isoenzymes but, unlike erythromycin, they do not form complexes with the glucocorticoid-inducible isoenzymes.

Some of these interactions suggest that the concomitant use of a macrolide and the other drug in question should be avoided. If the combination cannot be avoided, then serum concentrations of the concurrently administered drug should be monitored and patients observed for signs of toxicity. Table 194.12 summarizes the main macrolide drug–drug interactions and their clinical relevance.[36,42]

Streptogramins

Local pain and erythema in the vein used for infusion of this antibiotic has been frequent and dose-dependent. In 5% of patients this tolerance leads to discontinuation of the therapy and in more than 6% a change in the infusion site is required. Venous tolerability is improved by dissolving quinupristin–dalfopristin in larger quantities (over 250ml) of 5% dextrose and by using a central vein. Moderate and transient elevation of liver enzymes has also been reported in doses exceeding 10mg/kg. Itching, burning and erythema of the front of the neck and upper torso have also been reported in a few patients.[40] Arthralgia, myalgia, nausea and a rash are also common and elevation of liver enzymes are not uncommon. Synercid is a potent inhibitor of CYP3A4 and should be used with caution in patients taking drugs that are substrates of 3A4. Elevation of serum levels of nifedipine, midazolam and cyclosporin have been observed. Synercid has also the potential to prolong the QT_c interval when administered with drugs metabolized by 3A4 (e.g. cisapride).

Clindamycin

Adverse reactions include a morbilliform-rash, urticaria and, rarely, anaphylactoid reactions. Liver injury has also been reported rarely. Clindamycin-related diarrhea is reported in 2–30% of patients. It is usually a self-limiting problem, disappearing once clindamycin therapy is stopped. A small number of patients develop *C. difficile* colitis with various degrees of severity.[41]

REFERENCES

1. Bryskier A, Agouridas C, Gasc JC. Classification of macrolides antibiotics. In: Bryskier A, Butzler JP, Neu HC, Tulkens PM, eds. Macrolides. Oxford: Arnette Blackwell; 1993:5–66.
2. Mazzei T, Mini E, Novelli A, Periti P. Chemistry and mode of action of macrolides. J Antimicrob Chemother 1993;31(Suppl.C):1–9.
3. Neu HC. The development of macrolides: clarithromycin in perspective. J Antimicrob Chemother 1991;27(Suppl.A):1–9.
4. Agouridas C, Benedetti Y, Denis A, LeMartret O, Chantot JF. Ketolides: a new distinct class of macrolide antibacterials. Synthesis and structural characteristics of RU 004. In: Program Abstracts of the Interscientific Conference on Antimicrobial Agents and Chemotherapy, San Francisco, USA 1995;F-157.
5. Pechère JC. Streptogramins: a unique class of antibiotics. Drugs 1996;51(Suppl.1):13–9.
6. Douthwaite S, Champney WS. Structure of ketolides and macrolides determines their mode of interaction with the ribosomal target site. J Antimicrob Chemother 2001;48:1–8.
7. Aumercier M, Legoffic F. Mechanism of action of the macrolide and streptogramin antibiotics. In: Bryskier A, Butzler JP, Neu HC, Tulkens PM, eds. Macrolides. Oxford: Arnette Blackwell; 1993:115–23.
8. Menninger JR, Otto DD. Erythromycin, carbomycin and spiramycin inhibit protein synthesis in stimulating the dissociation of peptidyl-tRNA from ribosomes. Antimicrob Agents Chemother 1982;21:811–8.
9. Leclercq R, Courvalin P. Bacterial resistance to macrolide, lincosamide and streptogramin antibiotics by target modification. Antimicrob Agents Chemother 1991;35:1267–72.
10. Leclercq R, Courvalin P. Intrinsic and unusual resistance to macrolide, lincosamide and streptogramin antibiotics in bacteria. Antimicrob Agents Chemother 1991;35:1273–6.
11. Leclercq R. Mechanisms of resistance to macrolides and lincosamides: nature of the resistance elements and their clinical implications. Clin Infect Dis 2002;34:482–92.
12. Felmingham D. evolving resistance patterns in community-acquired respiratory pathogens: first results from the PROTEKT Global Surveillance Study. J Infect 2002;44:3–10.
13. Seppälä H, Klaukka T, Vuopio-Varkila J, *et al.* The effect of changes in the consumption of macrolide antibiotics on erythromycin resistance in group A streptococci in Finland. N Engl J Med 1997;337:441–6.
14. Finch RG. Antibacterial activity of quinupristin/dalfopristin (RP 59500): rationale for clinical use. Drugs 1996;51(Suppl.1):20–6.
15. Lode M, Boechk M, Schaberg T, Borner K, Koeppe P. Pharmacology of macrolides. In: Neu HC, Yong LS, Zinner SH, eds. The new macrolides, azalides and streptogramins. New York: Marcel Dekker; 1993;61–8.
16. Carlier MD, Zenerberg A, Tulkens PM. Cellular uptake and subcellular distribution of roxithromycin and erythromycin in phagocytic cells. J Antimicrob Chemother 1987;20(Suppl.1):47–56.
17. Periti T, Mazzei T, Mini E, Novelli A. Pharmacokinetic drug interactions of macrolides. Clin Pharmacokinet 1991;24:70.
18. Etienne SD, Montay G, Le Liboux A, Frydman A, Garaud JJ. A phase I, double-blind, placebo-controlled study of the tolerance and pharmacokinetic behaviour of RP 59500. J Antimicrob Chemother 1992;30(Suppl.A):123–31.
19. Carbon C. Pharmacodynamics of macrolides, azalides, and streptogramins: effect on extracellular pathogens. Clin Infect Dis 1998;27:28–32.
20. Shain S, Amsden GW. Telithromycin: the first of the ketolides. Ann Pharmacother 2002;36:452–64.
21. Craig WA, Gudmundsson S. Postantibiotic effect. In: Lorain V, ed. Antibiotics in laboratory medicine. Baltimore: Williams & Wilkins; 1991:403–31.
22. Charles L, Segreti J. Choosing the right macrolide antibiotic. Drugs 1997;53:349–57.
23. Bartlett JG, Dowell SF, Mandell LA, File TM, Musher DM, Fine MJ. Practice guidelines for the management of community-acquired pneumonia. Clin Infect Dis 2001;31:347–82.
24. Mundy LM, Oldach D, Auwaerter PG, *et al.* Implications for macrolide treatment in community-acquired pneumonia. Hopkins CAP Team. Chest 1998;113:1201–6.
25. Ridgway GL. Azithromycin in sexually transmitted diseases. Int J STD AIDS 1990;7(Suppl.1):1.
26. Magid D, Douglas JM Jr, Schwartz JS. Doxycycline compared with azithromycin for treating women with genital *Chlamydia trachomatis* infections: an incremental cost-effectiveness analysis. Ann Intern Med 1996;124:389–99.
27. Tribble D, Girgis N, Habile N, Butler T. Efficacy of azithromycin in typhoid fever. Clin Infect Dis 1995;21:1045–6.
28. Rolain JM, Maurin M, Vestris G, Raoult D. *In vitro* susceptibilities of 27 rickettsiae to 13 antimicrobials. Antimicrob Agents Chemother 1998;42:1537–41.
29. Chia JK, Nakata MM, Lami JL, Park SS, Ding JC. Azithromycin for the treatment of cat-scratch disease. Clin Infect Dis 1998;26:193–4.
30. Ji B, Jamet P, Perani EG, *et al.* Bactericidal activity of single dose of clarithromycin plus minocycline, with or without ofloxacin, against *Mycobacterium leprae* in patients. Antimicrob Agents Chemother 1996;40:2137–41.
31. Rapp RP, McCraney SA, Goodman NL, Shaddick DJ. New macrolide antibiotics: usefulness in infections caused by mycobacteria other than *Mycobacterium tuberculosis*. Ann Pharmacother 1994;28:1255–63.
32. Leport C, Horstkotte D, Burckhardt D. Antibiotic prophylaxis for infective endocarditis, from an international group of experts towards a European consensus. Eur Heart J 1995;16(Suppl.B):126–31.
33. Andersen SL, Oloo AJ, Gordon DM, *et al.* Successful double-blinded, randomized, placebo-controlled field trial of azithromycin and doxycycline as prophylaxis for malaria in western Kenya. Clin Infect Dis 1998;26:146–50.
34. USPHS/IDSA Prevention of Opportunistic Infections Working Group. 2001 Guidelines for the prevention of opportunistic infections in persons infected with human immunodeficiency virus. http://www.aidsinfo.nih.gov
35. Oldfield EC, Fessel WJ, Dunne MW, *et al.* Once weekly azithromycin therapy for prevention of *Mycobacterium avium* complex infection in patients with AIDS: a randomized, double-blind, placebo-controlled multicenter trial. Clin Infect Dis 1998;26:611–9.
36. Guay DRP. Macrolide antibiotics in paediatric infectious diseases. Drugs 1996;51:515–36.
37. Dagan R. Can the choice of antibiotics for therapy of acute otitis media be logical? Eur J Clin Microbiol Infect Dis 1998;17:1–5.
38. Tarlow MJ. Macrolides in the management of streptococcal pharyngitis/tonsillitis. Pediatr Infect Dis J 1997;16:444–8.
39. Gupta S, Leatham EW, Carrington D, *et al.* Elevated *Chlamydia pneumonia* antibodies, cardiovascular events, and azithromycin in male survivors of myocardial infarction. Circulation 1997;96:404–7.
40. Rubinstein E, Keller N. Future prospects and therapeutic potential of streptogramins. Drugs 1996;51(Suppl.1):27–31.
41. Falagas ME, Gorbach SL. Clindamycin and metronidazole. Med Clin North Am 1995,79:845–67.
42. Von Rosenstiel NA, Adam D. Macrolide antibacterials: drug interactions of clinical significance. Drug Saf 1995;13:105–22.

chapter
195 Oxazolidinones

Franklin D Lowy

The oxazolidinones are a relatively new family of bacteriostatic antimicrobials that are protein synthesis inhibitors. Because this new family works at the early stage of protein synthesis involving formation of the 70S initiation complex, there does not appear to be cross-resistance with other protein synthesis inhibitors. Originally developed as an agent for the treatment of bacterial and fungal infections of plants, the agents were subsequently found to have activity against Gram-positive bacteria. Upjohn originally developed two oxazolidinones, eperezolid and linezolid. Based on its more advantageous pharmacologic profile, linezolid was selected for further investigation. At present linezolid is the sole oxazolidinone available. The discussion below is therefore limited to this product. A number of comprehensive reviews of oxazolidinones and linezolid have recently been published.[1–3a]

PHARMACOKINETICS AND DISTRIBUTION

Linezolid has similar pharmacokinetics whether administered parenterally or orally. It is completely absorbed following oral administration achieving a bioavailability of 100%. Food causes a slight decrease in the rate of absorption but not in the overall amount absorbed. In normal volunteer studies peak plasma concentrations were achieved in 1–2 hours. Steady state concentrations were approximately 12 and 18mg/l following oral doses of 375 and 625mg twice daily respectively. Following intravenous administration of 625mg twice daily to volunteers for 7.5, days the steady state level was 3.8mg/l.[4,5] The half-lives of oral and intravenously administered linezolid are 5.4 and 4.8 hours, respectively. The drug is excreted by both renal and non-renal routes; 90% of circulating drug is not metabolized, but there are two inactive metabolites that are the result of oxidation of the morpholine ring. The P450 system does not appear to be involved in the metabolism of linezolid thus limiting the number of possible drug-drug interactions.

Linezolid is 31% bound to plasma proteins. It has a relatively large volume of distribution of 40–50l. Information on tissue penetration is still incomplete, however linezolid appears to penetrate well into tissue blister fluid, pulmonary alveolar macrophages, and sweat.[2,6] Preliminary studies suggest reasonable penetration of bone, fat and muscle. Mean ratios of linezolid in tissue fluid/plasma were 0.55, 1.2 and 0.71 for sweat, saliva and cerebrospinal fluid, respectively. There is little additional information at present on the tissue distribution of linezolid in humans.

ROUTE AND DOSAGE

As noted, linezolid can be administered orally or intravenously. Adjustment of dosage is not necessary when switching from one route to the other. The recommended dosage for serious infections such as nosocomial pneumonia or complicated skin and soft tissue infections is 600mg q12h. For uncomplicated infections including community acquired pneumonias or uncomplicated cutaneous infections 400mg q12h is adequate.

In patients with mild-to-moderate renal impairment (creatinine clearance 10–79ml/min) dosage adjustment is not necessary. However with more severe forms of renal disease dosage adjustment may be necessary.

The pharmacokinetics of linezolid appears unaffected by age. Dosage adjustment for the elderly is unnecessary. The clearance of linezolid is more rapid in children than in adults. As a result, the dose recommended for infants and children is 10mg/kg q8–12h. The only dosage schedule investigated to date in children has been q12h.

INDICATIONS

The oxazolidinones are primarily indicated for the treatment of bacterial infections caused by the Gram-positive staphylococci, streptococci and pneumococci, although their spectrum of antibacterial activity extends beyond these species. Linezolid has excellent *in-vitro* activity against staphylococcal species including methicillin-susceptible and resistant strains. There is little difference in the average minimal inhibitory concentrations (MICs) for methicillin-resistant and susceptible staphylococcal isolates. Linezolid is also active against the recently described *Staphylococcus aureus* isolates that are intermediate in susceptibility to glycopeptides – *Staph. aureus* with intermediate susceptibility to vancomycin (VISA) or *Staph. aureus* with intermediate susceptibility to glycopeptides (GISA) isolates.

In contrast with the protein synthesis inhibitor combination dalfopristin/quinupristin, linezolid is active against all enterococci, including *Enterococcus faecalis* and *Enterococcus faecium*, as well as those enterococcal strains that are vancomycin-resistant. It is also active against penicillin-susceptible and resistant *Streptococcus pneumoniae*, again with comparable MIC values (Table 195.1). In addition to these common Gram-positive pathogens, linezolid also has activity (MIC ≤4μg/ml) against some of the less frequently encountered Gram-positive organisms such as *Corynebacterium spp.*, *Bacillus spp.*, *Listeria monocytogenes*, *Erysipelothrix rhusiopathiae* and *Rhodococcus equi.*

Linezolid is moderately active against some anaerobes including *Clostridium spp.*, *Peptococcus spp.*, *Bacteroides fragilis* and *Fusobacterium nucleatum* and *F. meningosepticum*. It has limited activity against some Gram-negative bacteria such as *Moraxella*, *Bordetella* and *Haemophilus* spp. and has no activity against Enterobacteriaceae or *Pseudomonas* species. Of considerable interest for future development, is linezolid's *in-vitro* activity against *Mycobacterium tuberculosis* and *M. avium* complex.[7,8] This activity includes several multidrug resistant *M. tuberculosis* isolates. Chemical modification of linezolid is currently being explored to develop new drugs within the oxazolidinone class with enhanced antimycobacterial activity.

In animal studies linezolid has shown activity against methicillin-resistant *Staphylococcus aureus* (MRSA) and vancomycin-resistant *E. faecium* in the endocarditis model.[9,10] In a rabbit model of penicillin-resistant and susceptible pneumococcal meningitis, meningeal penetration of linezolid was good (38% of serum levels), however overall it was less effective than ceftriaxone.[11]

IN-VITRO ANTIMICROBIAL SUSCEPTIBILITY FOR LINEZOLID AGAINST COMMON GRAM-POSITIVE PATHOGENS			
Organism	**MIC (µg/ml) 50%***	**MIC(µg/ml) 90%**	**Overall (µg/ml)**
Staph. aureus **(n=2256)**			
Oxacillin susceptible	1–4	1–4	0.5–8
Oxacillin resistant	1–4	1–4	0.5–8
Coagulase-negative staphylococci (n=48)			
Oxacillin susceptible	0.5–2	1–4	0.25–4
Oxacillin resistant	0.5–2	1–2	0.5–4
β-haemolytic streptococci (n=47)	1–2	2–4	1–4
Strep. pneumoniae **(n=454)**			
Penicillin susceptible	0.5	1	<0.016–1
Penicillin resistant	0.5–1	1	0.06–4
Enterococcus **spp. (n=980)**			
Vancomycin susceptible	1–4	1–4	0.5–4
Vancomycin resistant	2–4	2–4	1–4

Source: adapted from ref 16 with original data in refs 26 and 31–36.
*Minimum concentration at which 50% of strains are inhibited.

Table 195.1 In-vitro antimicrobial susceptibility for linezolid against common Gram-positive pathogens. With permission from Diekema DJ, Jones RN, 2001.[1]

POTENTIAL CLINICAL INDICATIONS FOR THE USE OF LINEZOLID	
FDA-approved Indications **Nature of infection**	**Potential pathogens**
Skin & soft tissue (complicated)	MSSA, MRSA, *Streptococcus pyogenes, Streptococcus agalactiae*
Skin & soft tissue (uncomplicated)	MSSA, *Streptococcus pyogenes*
Infection with bacteremia	*Enterococcus faecium*
Nosocomial pneumonia	MRSA, MSSA, *Streptococcus pneumoniae* (penicillin susceptible)
Community-acquired pneumonia	*Streptococcus pneumoniae* (penicillin susceptible), MSSA
Potential future indications for linezolid	
Serious vancomycin-resistant *Enterococcus faecium* and *faecalis* infections or vancomycin-susceptible infections that are poorly responsive to therapy Serious MRSA, VISA (*Staphylococcus aureus* isolates that are intermediate in susceptibility to vancomycin), VRSA (vancomycin-resistant *Staphylococcus aureus*) infections, or infections that are poorly responsive to vancomycin therapy Complicated infections requiring long-term oral therapy with an antistaphylococcal or enterococcal agent where β-lactams cannot be used (e.g. chronic osteomyelitis) Treatment of infections (e.g. nosocomial pneumonia, endocarditis, meningitis) caused by highly resistant (but linezolid susceptible) Gram-positive bacteria where alternative agents are not available or are contraindicated Combination therapy for antimycobacterial infections where first- and second-line agents cannot be used	

MRSA, methicillin-resistant *Staphylococcus aureus;* MSSA, methicillin-susceptible *Staph. aureus*
VISA, *Staphylococcus aureus* with intermediate susceptibility to vancomycin

Table 195.2 Potential clinical indications for the use of linezolid.

At present linezolid is approved for the treatment of infections caused by vancomycin-resistant *E. faecium* with an associated bacteremia, nosocomial infections caused by both MRSA and methicillin-susceptible *Staph. aureus* (MSSA) as well as penicillin-susceptible *Staph. pneumoniae*, complicated skin and soft tissue infections caused by MRSA or MSSA, *Streptococcus pyogenes* and *Streptococcus agalactiae* and uncomplicated skin/soft tissue infections caused by MSSA and *Strep. pyogenes*.[12,13] It is also approved by the FDA for the treatment of community-acquired pneumonia due to *Staph. pneumoniae* (penicillin-susceptible) and MSSA (Table 195.2). Stevens *et al.*[14] recently reported that linezolid was comparable to vancomycin in the treatment of MRSA infections in a randomized open-label trial.

There is additional clinical and experimental experience with linezolid suggesting that it may ultimately have a broader therapeutic role although these other indications have not been FDA approved. These reports include the successful treatment of enterococcal endocarditis and meningitis (the latter a case of vancomycin-resistant *E. faecium*), MRSA prosthetic hip infections and the elimination of nasal carriage with *Staph. aureus*.[15–17] It is at present not clear how effective linezolid will be in the treatment of infections, such as endocarditis, that require bactericidal activity.

Linezolid is an important addition to the Gram-positive armamentarium. It is an alternative agent for the treatment of resistant Gram-positive infections (see Table 195.2). It has an antibacterial spectrum that is similar to vancomycin with advantageous pharmacokinetics. The availability of an oral preparation allows completion of therapy with the same therapeutic agent and therefore may help reduce the duration of hospital stays.[18]

Dosage in special circumstances

As noted above adjustment of dosage for moderate degrees of renal failure is not necessary. Because linezolid (as well as the linezolid metabolites) are cleared during hemodialysis, it is recommended that patients receive a supplemental dose following dialysis. For moderate degrees of hepatic disease dosage adjustment is not necessary.

ADVERSE REACTIONS AND INTERACTIONS

Linezolid has, in general, been well tolerated. The most common adverse events in the comparator-controlled trials were diarrhea (2.8–11%), nausea (3.4–9.6%) and headaches (0.5–11.3%).

Potentially, the most serious adverse event, thrombocytopenia, was seen in 2.4% of patients. It was seen most often during prolonged therapy (longer than 2 weeks) and resolved upon completion of therapy. Others have reported a higher incidence of thrombocytopenia.[19,20] As a result, hematologic monitoring of these parameters is recommended during prolonged therapy, especially for subjects who are already immunocompromised.

The oxazolidinones are monoamine oxidase (MAO) inhibitors. Linezolid appears to be a relatively weak MAO inhibitor. No evidence of adverse events related to this potential interaction has been reported to date. However, it is recommended that patients taking linezolid avoid tyramine-containing foods. There is also the potential for interaction with both serotonergic and adrenergic compounds.

REFERENCES

1. Diekema DJ, Jones RN. Oxazolidinone antibiotics. Lancet 2001;358:1975–82.
2. Perry CM, Jarvis B. Linezolid: a review of its use in the management of serious Gram-positive infections. Drugs 2001;61:525–51.
3. Clemett D, Markham A. Linezolid. Drugs 2000;59:815–27; discussion, 828.

3a. Moellering RC, Jr. Linezolid: the first oxazolidinorie antimicrobial. Ann intern Med 2003;138:135–142.

4. Stalker DJ, Wajszczuk CP, Batts DH. Linezolid safety, tolerance, and pharmacokinetics following oral dosing twice daily for 14.5 days. 37th Interscience Conference on Antimicrobial Agents and Chemotherapy, Toronto. Washington DC: American Society for Microbiology; 1997.
5. Stalker D, Wajszczuk CP, Batts DH. Linezolid safety, tolerance, and pharmacokinetics after intravenous dosing twice daily for 7.5 days. 37th Interscience Conference on Antimicrobial Agents and Chemotherapy, Toronto. Washington DC: American Society for Microbiology; 1997.
6. Conte JE Jr, Golden JA, Kipps JE. Intrapulmonary pharmacokinetics of linezolid. 40th Interscience Conference on Antimicrobial Agents and Chemotherapy, Toronto. Washington DC: American Society for Microbiology; 2000.
7. Cynamon MH, Klemens SP, Sharpe CA, Chase S. Activities of several novel oxazolidinones against *Mycobacterium tuberculosis* in a murine model. Antimicrob Agents Chemother 1999;43:1189–91.
8. Wallace RJ Jr, Brown-Elliott BA, Ward SC, Crist CJ, Mann LB, Wilson RW. Activities of linezolid against rapidly growing mycobacteria. Antimicrob Agents Chemother 2001;45:764–7.
9. Dailey CF, Dileto-Fang CL, Buchanan LV, *et al.* Efficacy of linezolid in treatment of experimental endocarditis caused by methicillin-resistant *Staphylococcus aureus.* Antimicrob Agents Chemother 2001;45:2304–8.
10. Patel R, Rouse MS, Piper KE, Steckelberg JM. Linezolid therapy of vancomycin-resistant *Enterococcus faecium* experimental endocarditis. Antimicrob Agents Chemother 2001;45:621–3.
11. Cottagnoud P, Gerber CM, Acosta F, Cottagnoud M, Neftel K, Tauber MG. Linezolid against penicillin-sensitive and -resistant pneumococci in the rabbit meningitis model. J Antimicrob Chemother 2000;46:981–5.
12. Rubinstein E, Cammarata S, Oliphant T, Wunderink R. Linezolid (PNU-100766) versus vancomycin in the treatment of hospitalized patients with nosocomial pneumonia: a randomized, double-blind, multicenter study. Clin Infect Dis 2001;32:402–12.
13. Stevens DL, Smith LG, Bruss JB, *et al.* Randomized comparison of linezolid (PNU-100766) versus oxacillin–dicloxacillin for treatment of complicated skin and soft tissue infections. Antimicrob Agents Chemother 2000; 44:3408–13.
14. Stevens DL, Herr D, Lampiris H, Hunt JL, Batts DH, Hafkin B. Linezolid versus vancomycin for the treatment of methicillin-resistant *Staphylococcus aureus* infections. Clin Infect Dis 2002;34:1481–90
15. Zeana C, Kubin CJ, Della-Latta P, Hammer SM. Vancomycin-resistant *Enterococcus faecium* meningitis successfully managed with linezolid: case report and review of the literature. Clin Infect Dis 2001;33:477–82.
16. Bassetti M, Di Biagio A, Cenderello G, *et al.* Linezolid treatment of prosthetic hip infections due to methicillin-resistant *Staphylococcus aureus* (MRSA). J Infect 2001;43:148–9.
17. Babcock HM, Ritchie DJ, Christiansen E, Starlin R, Little R, Stanley S. Successful treatment of vancomycin-resistant *Enterococcus* endocarditis with oral linezolid. Clin Infect Dis 2001;32:1373–5.
18. Li Z, Willke RJ, Pinto LA, *et al.* Comparison of length of hospital stay for patients with known or suspected methicillin-resistant *Staphylococcus* species infections treated with linezolid or vancomycin: a randomized, multicenter trial. Pharmacotherapy 2001;21:263–74.
19. Attassi K, Hershberger E, Alam R, Zervos MJ. Thrombocytopenia associated with linezolid therapy. Clin Infect Dis 2002;34:695–8.
20. Kuter DJ, Tillotson GS. Hematologic effects of antimicrobials: focus on the oxazolidinone linezolid. Pharmacotherapy 2001;21:1010–3.

chapter 196

Aminoglycosides

Richard Quintiliani Jr, Richard Quintiliani & Charles H Nightingale

INTRODUCTION

Despite predictions that aminogylcosides would in time become obsolete, or at best, of limited usage because of their ototoxic and nephrotoxic potential, they have increased in popularity and clinical importance. With continued usage since the 1940s, it has become apparent that their toxicity is modest as long as the dose is adjusted for renal function, and they are not administered for extended periods. In addition, with once-daily aminoglycoside dosing rather than the traditional intermittent dosing method, their toxicity has been reduced further.

A major reason for their increased use has been the increasing number of nosocomial infections by bacteria that are either initially resistant or develop resistance to β-lactam and the fluoroquinolone antibiotics. Many of these organisms have, however, not only retained their susceptibility to aminoglycosides, but seldom develop resistance during therapy. Unlike β-lactam antibiotics, which are often less active in the presence of high concentrations of bacteria, the aminoglycosides are not subject to this inoculum effect. In contrast to penicillins and cephalosporins, aminoglycosides continue to suppress regrowth of aerobic Gram-negative bacteria for hours after the blood levels fall below the minimum inhibitory concentrations (MICs) for these organisms.

Another important attribute of aminoglycosides is their ability to achieve an additive or synergistic effect against most aerobic Gram-negative bacilli and Gram-positive cocci when combined with β-lactam antibiotics and a similar effect against Gram-positive cocci when combined with vancomycin or teicoplanin.

BACKGROUND

The aminoglycosides were discovered following systematic screening of soil actinomycetes for the production of substances with antimicrobial activity. These compounds exhibited particular activity against aerobic Gram-negative bacilli and Gram-positive cocci. Streptomycin, the first clinically useful aminoglycoside, was isolated from *Streptomyces griseus* in 1944. Neomycin, kanamycin, tobramycin and paromomycin are also natural compounds that were subsequently isolated from various species of streptomyces. Gentamicin and sisomicin (not marketed in the USA) are natural products produced by *Micromonospora* spp. Amikacin and netilmicin are semisynthetic aminoglycosides derived from kanamycin and sisomicin, respectively. The suffix 'mycin' and 'micin' indicates that the compound was isolated directly or indirectly from *Streptomyces* spp. or *Micromonospora* spp., respectively.

CHEMISTRY

The chemical structures of the aminoglycosides are shown in Figure 196.1. All aminoglycosides include a central six-membered ring containing amino groups termed an aminocyclitol, which is linked to two or more amino- or non-amino-containing sugars by glycosidic bonds. Spectinomycin is a pure aminocyclitol and is often considered with the aminoglycosides, but is not strictly speaking an aminoglycoside because it contains neither aminosugars nor glycosidic bonds. For this reason, the complete group of compounds is more accurately referred to as aminoglycoside–aminocyclitol antibiotics.

Microbiologic activity

When evaluating the microbiologic activity of the aminoglycosides, it is useful to divide them into two groups:

- one that includes gentamicin, tobramycin, netilmicin and amikacin; and
- the other including streptomycin, neomycin, kanamycin, spectinomycin and paromomycin.

The former group of agents are closely similar in their microbiologic activity and clinical usage, whereas the latter group of drugs have more limited clinical indications.

Owing to the impressive broad-spectrum microbiologic activity of gentamicin, tobramycin, netilmicin and amikacin, they have gained wide popularity in the empiric treatment of patients in whom the suspected pathogens can be multiple (Table 196.1).

Although aminoglycosides alone do not inhibit enterococci and streptococci, they are often used in the therapy of serious infections caused by these organisms because of their frequent additive or synergistic effect when combined with other antibiotics.

In contrast to the cephalosporins and penicillins, the microbiologic effect of aminoglycosides is the same at low or high inocula of organisms.[1] This observation has particular relevance in the treatment of intra-abdominal infections where the density of bacteria may be high. In addition, aminoglycosides show a significant postantibiotic effect (PAE), which is the persistent suppression of bacterial growth after exposure to an antibiotic, against both Gram-negative and Gram-positive bacteria.[2] Except for the carbapenems such as imipenem and meropenem, β-lactams show no significant PAE against Gram-negative bacteria. The duration of the PAE with aminoglycosides that have activity against *P. aeruginosa* and Enterobacteriaceae is about 1–3 hours and 0.9–2 hours, respectively.[3] These PAEs are even longer if the once-daily aminoglycoside dosing technique discussed later in this chapter is used.

Absorption

Because of their highly charged nature, there is minimal absorption of aminoglycosides when given by mouth, topical application or rectal instillation.[4] Nevertheless, in patients with hepatic encephalopathy and renal impairment, large and frequent doses of neomycin have been associated with sufficient absorption into the systemic circulation to produce deafness.[5] Similarly, detectable blood levels of aminoglycosides can be found if they are used topically in burn patients with large areas of denuded skin. Because aminoglycosides penetrate extremely well into body spaces with large serosal surfaces (e.g. pleural space, peritoneal cavity, pericardial space, synovial fluid), it is unwise to instill them directly into these sites, and there have been reports of neuromuscular blockade (see Adverse reactions, below) associated with large doses injected into the peritoneal

CHEMICAL STRUCTURES OF THE AMINOGLYCOSIDES

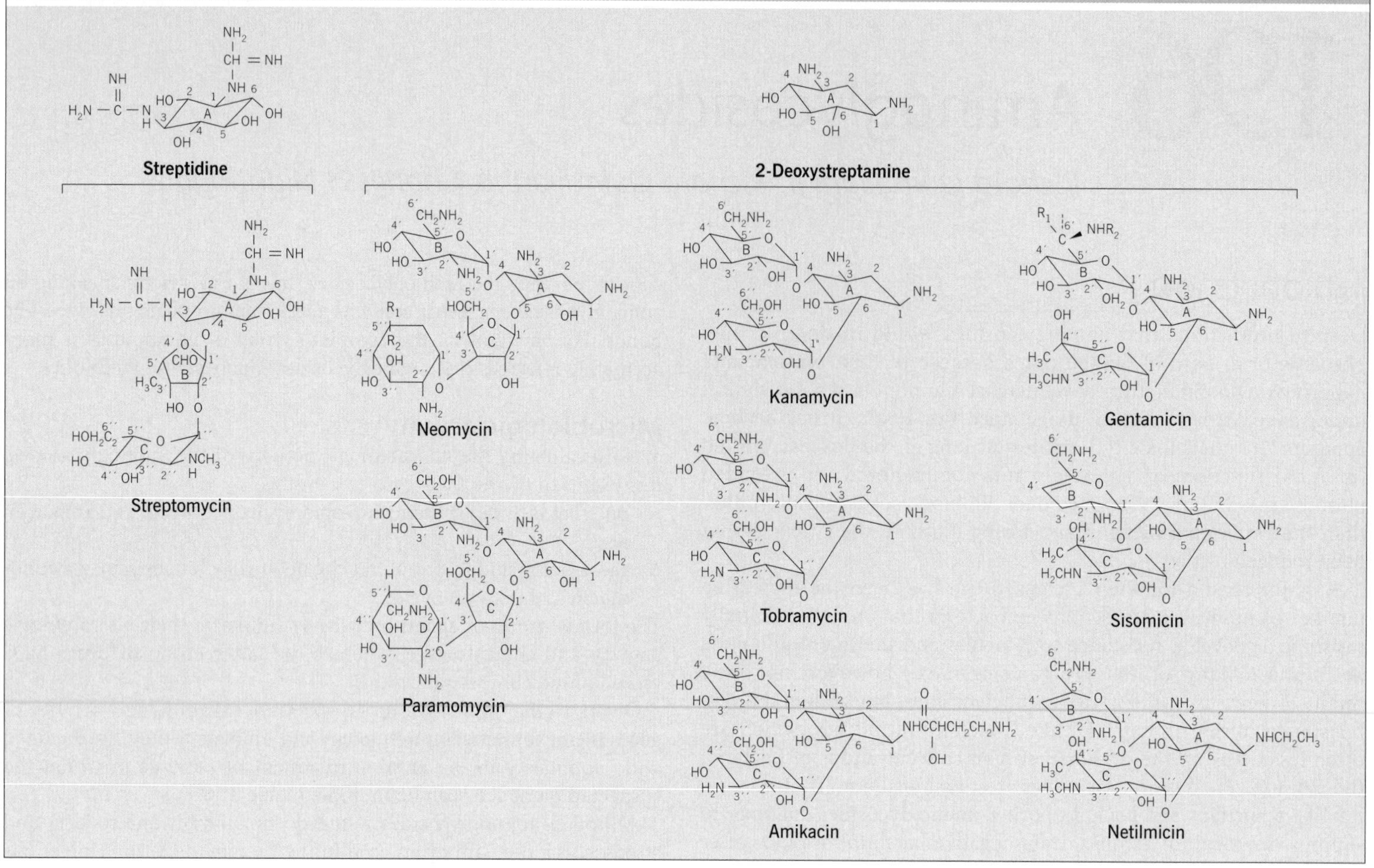

Fig. 196.1 Chemical structures of the aminoglycosides. All aminoglycosides include an aminocyclitol (a central six-membered ring containing amino groups), which is linked to two or more amino- or non-amino-containing sugars by glycosidic bonds. For streptomycin, the aminocyclitol ring is a streptidine, whereas for the remainder of the clinically available aminoglycosides it is 2-deoxystreptamine. Neomycin contains approximately equal amounts of neomycin B (R_1=H; R_2=CH_2NH_2) and neomycin C (R_1=CH_2NH_2; R_2=H). Kanamycin is principally kanamycin A, as shown. Gentamicin is gentamicin C complex with roughly equal amounts of C_1 (R_1=R_2=CH_3), C_{1a} (R_1=R_2=H) and C_2 (R_1=CH_3; R_2=H).

cavity.[6] Following endotracheal administration or aerosolization of aminoglycosides, systemic absorption is usually modest. However, significant concentrations can be achieved via aerosolized generators that use high pressure and small droplets (1–3mm).[7]

Distribution

Because aminoglycosides demonstrate linear pharmacokinetics, there is a direct proportionality between dose and area under the plasma concentration curve (AUC).[8] Although following an intravenous dose they exhibit a three-compartment model – initial distribution (alpha) phase, a rapid elimination (beta) phase and a slow elimination (gamma) phase – a one-compartment model can be used clinically for establishing dosage regimens.

After an intravenous or intramuscular dose of an aminoglycoside, peak serum concentrations occur in 30 and 45 minutes, respectively. In patients such as those with diabetes mellitus who have poor vascular perfusion into soft tissue structures, there may be a delay in the time to peak concentration. Because aminoglycosides are highly water soluble, their volume of distribution (Vd) is similar to that of the extravascular compartment. As predicted, the mean aminoglycoside concentration in interstitial fluid approximates the mean plasma concentration. Studies performed in normal adult volunteers have found a Vd of 0.2–0.3l/kg.[8] In patients with excess fluid in the extravascular space, as in patients with ascites or burns, the Vd is increased, whereas in markedly obese patients it is decreased.

The low serum protein binding (10%) of aminoglycosides increases the ease with which they are distributed into the extravascular space. In the unobstructed biliary tract, aminoglycoside levels are about 30% of the serum concentration; however, as with β-lactam antibiotics, bile levels are exceedingly low in the presence of biliary tract obstruction.

Aminoglycosides penetrate poorly into human cells because of the large size of the molecules, their low lipid solubility, and their high polycationic charge. High concentrations are observed only in specialized cells such as the tubular cells of the renal cortex and the hair cells of the ear, which have an active transport mechanism for aminoglycosides, and levels in these cells can even exceed those of plasma or interstitial fluid. Aminoglycoside levels can remain above therapeutic concentrations for extended periods of time (48–200 hours) as a result of renal tubular cell absorption and the prolonged release of aminoglycosides into urine.[9]

Aminoglycosides penetrate poorly into the cornea and the aqueous and vitreous humors of the eye.[10] In patients with serious eye infections such as bacterial endophthalmitis, direct intravitreal injections are usually needed. Subconjunctival injections achieve high aqueous humor levels. The penetration of aminoglycosides into cerebrospinal

MICROBIOLOGICAL ACTIVITY OF GENTAMICIN, TOBRAMYCIN, NETILMICIN AND AMIKACIN	
Susceptible	**Resistant**
Escherichia coli	Streptococci (e.g. *Streptococcus pneumoniae, Streptococcus pyogenes*)
Klebsiella spp.	*Enterococci*
Proteus mirabilis, Proteus vulgaris, Proteus penneri	Methicillin-resistant *Staph. aureus*
Providencia stuartii, Providencia alcalifaciens	Anaerobes
Enterobacter spp.	*Stenotrophomonas maltophilia*
Morganella morganii	*Burkholderia cepacia*
Salmonella spp.	*Flavobacterium* spp.
Shigella spp.	*Mycobacterium kansasii, Mycobacterium avium-intracellulare*
Serratia marcescens	*Burkholderia cepacia*
Citrobacter spp.	*Mycoplasma* spp.
Aeromonas spp.	*Rickettsiae*
Pseudomonas aeruginosa	Fungi
Acinetobacter baumannii, Acinetobacter lwoffi	Viruses
Methicillin-susceptible *Staph. aureus*, non-Staph. *aureus* spp. (e.g. *Staphylococcus epidermidis*)	
Yersinia pestis	
Francisella tularensis	
Brucella spp.	
Haemophilus influenzae	
Mycobacterium tuberculosis, selective atypical mycobacteria (e.g. *Mycobacterum fortuitum*)	
Neisseria meningitidis, N.gonorrhoeae	
Moraxella catarrhalis	
Legionella spp.	

Table 196.1 Microbiologic activity of gentamicin, tobramycin, netilmicin and amikacin.

fluid (CSF) is poor, both in the presence and absence of meningeal inflammation.[11] Penetration of gentamicin into CSF was studied in 26 patients aged 6–20 years with mumps meningoencephalitis after administration of a single intramuscular dose of 1.2–4.0mg/kg. Activity was found in only five of the 26 patients, with the highest level being 0.19μg/ml.[12]

Elimination

After a rapid distributive phase of 15–30 minutes, the elimination phase begins with 99% of the drug excreted unchanged in the urine and a half-life of 1.5–3.5 hours.[13] In patients with increased extravascular fluid, the Vd increases, resulting in a longer half-life. Because of this type of elimination, any impairment in renal function can result in considerable prolongation of the serum aminoglycoside half-life. There is active reabsorption of aminoglycoside into the proximal renal tubular cells, as indicated by the observation that renal clearance of these agents is somewhat less than that of simultaneous creatinine clearance. In neonates less than 1 week of age or in small premature babies, the half-life is typically prolonged to 8–11 hours.[14]

Following the elimination phase, there is a final extremely slow terminal elimination phase of 30–700 hours secondary to prolonged release from the proximal renal tubules back into the urine.[15] Because the amount of aminoglycoside eliminated is so low, it has no effect on dosing. Less than 1% of aminoglycoside is eliminated into feces, bile and saliva. Aminoglycosides are not metabolized.

Pharmacodynamic concepts

In the past 5 years, much has been learnt from animal models of infection, *in-vitro* pharmacodynamic studies, volunteer experiments and clinical trials that enable us to establish the best mode of antibiotic administration to maximize bacterial killing and minimize toxicity. From this information, we know that the higher the aminoglycoside concentration, the faster the rate of bacterial eradication.[16] As a result, this type of killing is designated concentration- or dose-dependent killing. For the aminoglycosides, the rate of bacterial eradication increases with increasing concentration up to approximately 10–12 times above their MICs.[17] Thereafter, increasing the concentration does not improve the rate of bacterial killing. If this favorable peak to MIC ratio is obtained, most bacteria die within a short period of time, and as a result the effect of the drug exposure time is minimal and can even be ignored.

In neutropenic and non-neutropenic animal models of infection, significantly more animals survive a potentially lethal challenge of bacteria if the animals are treated with a single large dose of an aminoglycoside than with the same dose divided on an 8-hour schedule.[18,19] Compared with intermittent dosing, once-daily dosing results in a larger probability that aminoglycoside concentrations will exceed the MIC by a factor of 10–12 times, and also result in a longer PAE with a lower chance for the emergence of aminoglycoside-resistant pathogens.[20]

ROUTE OF ADMINISTRATION AND DOSAGE

Once-daily dosing in adults

Recently, considerable attention has been given to using these pharmacodynamic concepts by giving the entire dose of the aminoglycoside on a once-daily basis in order to maximize bacterial killing and minimize toxicity. Different approaches have been used to monitor and adjust the dose in patients on once-daily aminoglycoside therapy with normal and diminished renal function to ensure adequate treatment and to minimize toxicity. In the USA, the most popular dosing method used by hospitals has been modelled after the one developed at Hartford Hospital, Hartford, Connecticut.[21] To optimize the serum peak to MIC ratio against *Pseudomonas aeruginosa*, the organism that most often warrants aminoglycoside therapy, a 7mg/kg dose is given. Through computer simulation of gentamicin and tobramycin concentrations versus time profile for once-daily dosing, 7mg/kg and 5mg/kg, respectively, would be the best dose to optimize the serum peak to MIC ratio (≥10) against *P. aeruginosa*, an organism that is typically inhibited by 2μg/ml of these agents. This dose, when diluted in 50ml of a compatible intravenous solution and given over 1 hour attains the target peak serum concentration of 20μg/ml (Fig. 196.2).

In this simulation, a one-compartment intravenous model was used with a fixed apparent Vd of the aminoglycoside of 0.3l/kg. In patients with normal renal function, the serum concentrations typically fall below 0.5μg/ml within 12 hours and then remain essentially undetectable for the remainder of the day (Fig. 196.3). This drug-free interval is crucial for reduced toxicity (see Adverse Reactions, below), for it allows a greater amount of aminoglycoside to egress from the renal tubular and inner ear cells than with the conventional intermittent dosing method.

In patients receiving the intermittent dosing approach of gentamicin or tobramycin (1.5mg/kg q8h), peak serum levels of only about 4–5μg/ml are obtained with a trough level still slightly above

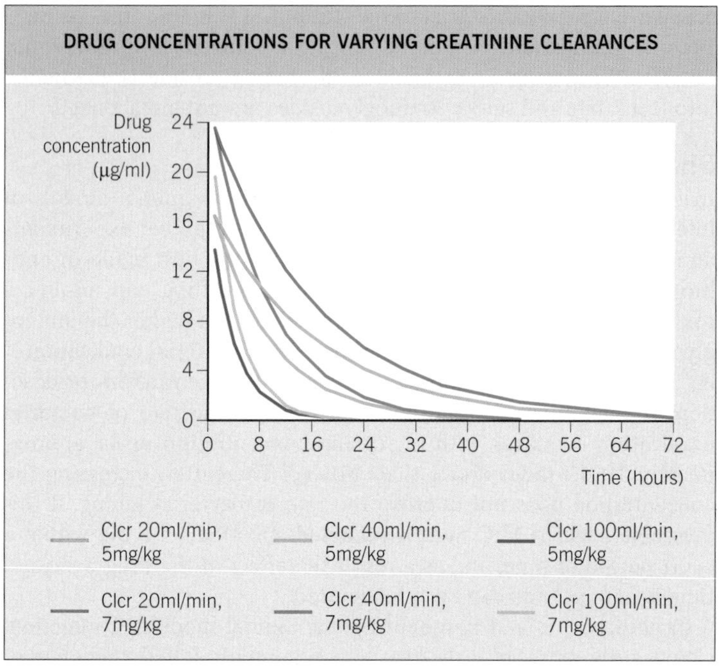

Fig. 196.2 Simulated concentration versus time profiles for once-daily 7mg/kg and 5mg/kg gentamicin regimens in patients with varying degrees of creatinine clearance (Clcr).

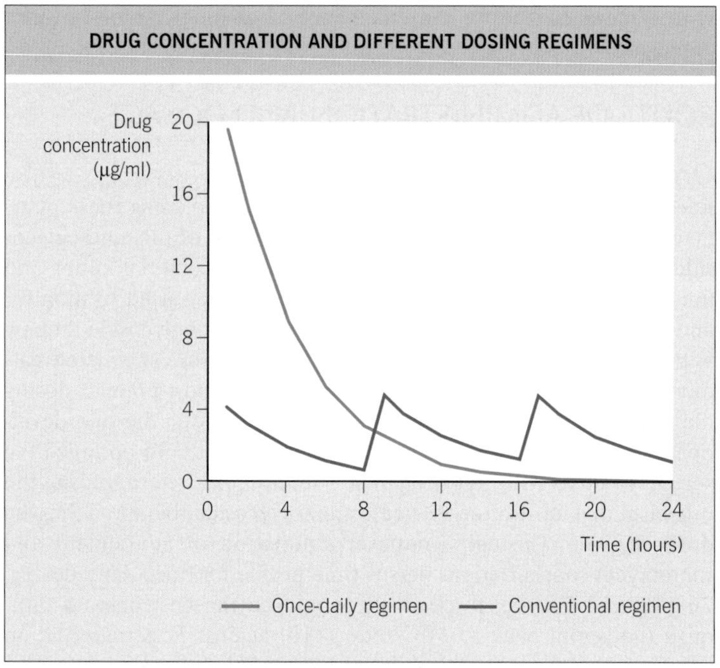

Fig. 196.3 Simulated concentration versus time profiles for once-daily (7mg/kg q24h) and conventional (1.5mg/kg q8h) gentamicin regimens in patients with normal renal function.

0.5μg/ml (see Fig. 196.3). Therefore, the absence of any prolonged drug-free period with intermittent dosing slows the egress of aminoglycosides from these cells, resulting in greater tissue accumulation. It is this lower accumulation of aminoglycosides with once-daily dosing than with intermittent dosing that results in less nephrotoxicity and ototoxicity (see below).

Although a dosing weight may be individualized for each patient, dosing is usually based on actual body weight unless the patient is obese [i.e. greater than 20% over ideal body weight (IBW)]. Calculation of IBW is accomplished by the following formulas:

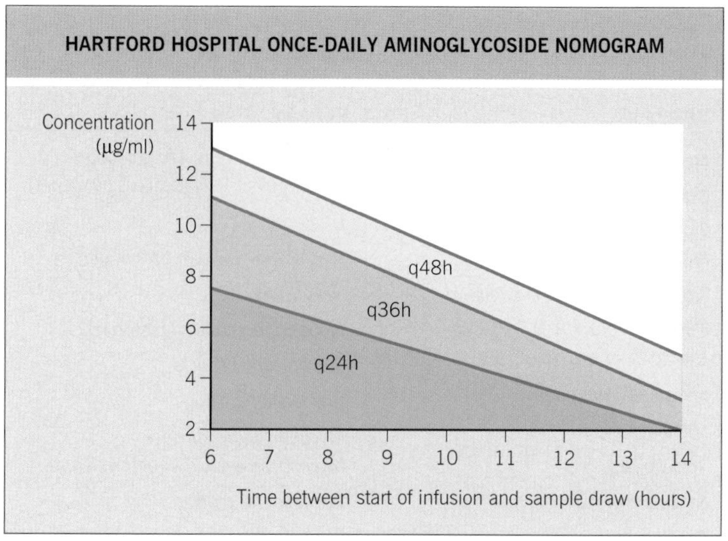

Fig. 196.4 Hartford Hospital once-daily aminoglycoside nomogram for gentamicin and tobramycin using the 7mg/kg dose.

- IBWmale = 50kg + 2.3kg for every inch (2.54cm) over 5 feet (1.524m);
- IBWfemale = 45.5kg + 2.3kg for every inch (2.54cm) over 5 feet (1.524m).

For the obese patient, a dosing weight can be calculated using the following: obese dosing weight = IBW + 0.4 (actual body weight – IBW).

Monitoring of patients on once-daily aminoglycoside therapy involves measuring a single random aminoglycoside serum concentration 6–14 hours following a 60-minute infusion of the 7mg/kg dose of gentamicin or tobramycin. Depending upon where the concentration falls on a nomogram (Fig. 196.4), the patient is then given the same 7mg/kg dose every 24, 36 or 48 hours. If the concentration falls on the line of the nomogram that separates the dosing intervals, then the longer interval is chosen. If the random level falls off the nomogram, then the dosing interval should be based on more frequent serum concentration determinations to decide on the most appropriate time for the next dose.

Although it is unnecessary to draw two serum samples in most patients, it may be necessary to obtain additional levels in some patients with rapidly changing creatinine clearance. If once-daily aminoglycoside therapy is continued beyond 4 days, a random concentration should be obtained on the fifth day, and then weekly thereafter. Serum creatinine should be measured every 2–3 days.

In certain patients the risk of toxicity is low and it is even unnecessary to obtain a random determination of the aminoglycoside level. This subset of patients includes adults under 60 years of age who have a normal serum creatinine concentration who are not receiving concurrent nephrotoxic agents (e.g. amphotericin B, ciclosporin, vancomycin) or contrast media, and are neither quadriplegic nor amputees. Even in this subset of patients, however, determinations of serum creatinine should be performed at 2- or 3-day intervals, and for those patients on once-daily therapy for longer than 5 days, a random serum aminoglycoside concentration should be obtained on the fifth day and weekly thereafter. Because of insufficient clinical or pharmacokinetic data or both, once-daily aminoglycoside dosing is not recommended for:

- those on chronic peritoneal dialysis or hemodialysis;
- pregnant women; and
- those with major burns (>20%), ascites or enterococcal endocarditis.

In hospitals where it is difficult to measure serum concentrations of gentamicin or tobramycin, the appropriate dosing interval can be selected based on the patient's creatinine clearance, which can be easily calculated by using the Cockcroft–Gault equation.[22] With this method, the creatinine clearance can be determined in males by multiplying (140–age) with (weight in kg) and then dividing this value by (serum creatinine concentration × 2), and in females, by using the same equation, but the calculated creatinine clearance is multiplied by 0.85. For those patients who have a creatinine clearance of ≥60, 40–60, and 20–40ml/min, the aminoglycoside should be given every 24, 36 and 48 hours, respectively.

In the USA, gentamicin and tobramycin are by far the most commonly used aminoglycosides. Nevertheless, a once-daily dose of amikacin could also be employed by administering a single dose of 15mg/kg with the dosing interval determined by the estimated creatinine clearance. In addition, because aminoglycosides exhibit linear pharmacokinetics, the amikacin dosing interval can also be determined by applying the same nomogram used for gentamicin and tobramycin by merely halving the random amikacin level obtained 6–14 hours after the infusion of a 15mg/kg dose.

Results from a number of studies using both neutropenic and non-neutropenic animal models of sepsis and clinical trials have shown that high peak concentrations and long dosing intervals of aminoglycosides improve efficacy and reduce toxicity.[23,24] In a recent meta-analysis comparing once-daily aminoglycoside with intermittent dosing in immunocompetent adults, once-daily dosing was equivalent with regard to bacteriologic cure, but showed a trend towards reduced mortality rates and reduced toxicity.[25]

In the largest outcome study in adults (2184 patients) treated with once-daily gentamicin or tobramycin, nephrotoxicity (as defined as an increase in serum creatinine concentration to 0.5mg/dl or more over baseline during aminoglycoside therapy) was detected in only 1.2% (27 patients) and ototoxicity in 0.1% (three patients).[21] The incidence of nephrotoxicity was significantly lower than the 3–5% observed from the same hospital when aminoglycosides were given in the conventional dosing technique. Furthermore, in the 27 patients referred to above, there were other possible explanations for nephrotoxicity (e.g. concomitant nephrotoxic agents, volume-related renal dysfunction). Of these patients 94% received gentamicin, 5% tobramycin and less than 1% amikacin. In the three patients who developed vestibular dysfunction, it was transient in two and permanent in the other, but this patient had received over 5 weeks of aminoglycoside therapy. The major exclusion criterion for once-daily aminoglycoside therapy was any patient who had enterococcal endocarditis.

The same investigators performed a detailed pharmacoeconomic analysis of their conversion program from intermittent to once-daily aminoglycoside and noted the movement to once-daily aminoglycoside dosing saved the hospital US$128,000 due to reductions in preparation, administration, monitoring and nephrotoxicity costs.[26] In a recent review of the economic impact of nephrotoxicity at six Philadelphia hospitals involving 1756 patients, it was determined that the mean total additional cost of an episode of aminoglycoside nephrotoxicity in a patient was US$2501. These costs were mainly related to a prolongation of hospital stay, additional consultations and increased laboratory tests and ancillary services.[27]

Once-daily dosing in children

Although the clinical outcome data on once-daily aminoglycoside dosing in children are much more limited, there is no reason why the same pharmacodynamic concepts should not apply. Although children have slightly higher Vd and elimination rates for drugs than adults, it is unlikely that these differences are of a significant magnitude to necessitate major changes in the once-daily aminoglycoside dosing method outlined above for adults. In fact, aminoglycoside dosing in children may require higher dosing. In children 6–12 months of age and those older than 1 year given a single intravenous dose of 20mg/kg dose of amikacin, the Vds were 0.5l/kg and 0.33l/kg, respectively.[28] Therefore, the Vd in children under 1 year of age is slightly higher than that of an adult, whereas that in children over 1 year of age is similar to that in adults. In addition, in this same study, the half-life in the younger children was longer than that in the older children and in adults, yet the peak and trough levels were similar. These observations suggest that children under 1 year of age require a higher single dose (20mg/kg) of amikacin than the dose (15mg/kg) in older children and in adults. Other studies using a 20mg/kg once-daily dose of amikacin in children undergoing bone marrow transplantation or with serious Gram-negative bacterial sepsis have shown no differences in efficacy or toxicity compared with standard intermittent dosing.[29,30]

Similarly, netilmicin given as a single 2mg/kg dose q8h, or gentamicin given as a single 6mg/kg/day dose or divided into two or three daily doses for treatment of infections in children showed no difference in clinical efficacy, ototoxicity or nephrotoxicity.[31] Identical results were also obtained in the treatment of 20 full-term neonates who received a single 4mg/kg dose of gentamicin given either once or in divided doses.[32]

Intermittent or traditional dosing

In the intermittent dosing technique, a loading dose is given and followed by a maintenance dose.[33] Because the loading dose is independent of renal function, it is the same in patients with abnormal or normal renal function. The loading dose should be calculated according to IBW as discussed above in the once-daily dosing method. The peak serum concentration is usually obtained 30–60 minutes after the infusion of the initial dose or after the first maintenance dose. The usual loading dose is:

- 2mg/kg for gentamicin, tobramycin and netilmicin; and
- 7.5mg/kg for amikacin and streptomycin.

In patients who have a creatinine clearance ≥90ml/min, the usual maintenance doses are:

- gentamicin 1.7mg/kg q8h;
- tobramycin 1.7mg/kg q8h;
- netilmicin 2.0mg/kg q8h;
- amikacin 7.5mg/kg q12h; and
- streptomycin 7.5mg/kg q12h.

The desired peak serum and trough concentrations are:

- 4–10μg/ml and 1–2μg/ml, respectively, for gentamicin, tobramycin and netilmicin; and
- 15–30μg/ml and 5–10μg/ml, respectively, for amikacin and streptomycin.

In patients with renal impairment, there are two ways to modify the dose, of which one is to lengthen the dosing interval and the other is to reduce the dose. Of these two methods, increasing the dosing interval is preferable because it provides the best peak to MIC ratios and thereby maximizes concentration-dependent bacterial killing. In this method the dose remains the same, but the dosing interval changes based on the patient's estimated creatinine clearance using the Cockcroft–Gault equation.[22]

For instance, in patients with an estimated creatinine clearance (ml/min) of 80–90, 50–80, 10–50 and <10, the dosing intervals become every 12h, 12–24h, 24–48h and 48–72h, respectively. The serum creatinine concentration should be measured every 3–5 days, and if it remains stable there is no reason to perform repeat measurements of peak and trough concentrations. If there is, however, a significant increase in serum creatinine concentration, then a new dosage is recalculated.

INDICATIONS

Use in patients with fever and neutropenia, sepsis syndrome and nosocomial infections

Gentamicin, tobramycin, netilmicin and amikacin have assumed a major clinical role for decades in the empiric treatment of the febrile neutropenic patient (see Chapter 100) and in patients with serious hospital-acquired infections (see Chapter 56) because of their broad spectrum of bactericidal activity against common and unusual Enterobacteriaceae, *P. aeruginosa*, and staphylococci. In addition, these agents usually exhibit synergy against these bacteria in combination with β-lactam antibiotics and against enterococci in combination with penicillins or vancomycin or teicoplanin. With the increasing usage of carbapenems such as imipenem and meropenem, and fluoroquinolones such as ciprofloxacin and ofloxacin, there has been a significant increase in the emergence of multiantibiotic resistant bacteria (e.g. *Burkholderia cepacia, Stenotrophomonas maltophilia,* enterococci), which often require treatment with an aminoglycoside alone or in combination with other antibiotics.

Although physicians often try to avoid aminoglycosides because of concerns for toxicity, these adverse events are actually infrequent, as discussed below, especially if one uses once-daily administration and avoids prolonged administration. Their low acquisition costs also make them attractive choices in the need for fiscal restraints in the health care system of all countries. In the USA, 100mg of gentamicin costs under US$1.

Once gentamicin and the carboxypenicillins (e.g. carbenacillin, ticarcillin), agents with antipseudomonal activity, became available, the usage of both kanamycin and polymyxin as part of a 'fever regimen' for neutropenic patients became negligible. As a result, the preferred empiric approach for febrile neutropenic patients or those considered to have a serious bacteremia became gentamicin and carbenicillin. With time, the empiric approach to patients such as these has remained quite similar in that the traditional approach remains an aminoglycoside in combination with an antipseudomonal penicillin (e.g. ticarcillin, piperacillin, mezlocillin, ticarcillin–clavulanate, piperacillin–tazobactam) or cephalosporin (e.g. ceftazadime, cefepime).

The choice of the antipseudomonal penicillin has changed to a greater use of the newer carboxypenicillin ticarcillin, or the ureidopenicillins mezlocillin or piperacillin. Because neither ticarcillin nor piperacillin has significant antistaphylococcal activity and the intrinsic activity of these drugs by themselves against anaerobes is moderate, these two agents are often given in their new formulations in which they are combined with a β-lactamase inhibitor such as clavulanate or tazobactam. In combination with these inhibitors, ticarcillin–clavulanate and piperacillin–tazobactam, are active against almost all anaerobes with MICs typically below 2μg/ml. The MICs of these penicillins by themselves against anaerobes such as *Bacteroides* spp. is about 32–64μg/ml.

Although the aminoglycosides are often used clinically in combination with β-lactams, the combination may lead to inactivation of both drugs. The reaction, which is time and concentration dependent, occurs by nucleophilic opening of the β-lactam ring and acylation of an amino group of the aminoglycoside resulting in a biologically inactive amide.[34,35] Gentamicin and tobramycin appear to be more susceptible to inactivation than amikacin or netilmicin. This phenomenon is probably clinically meaningful only in patients with significant renal failure in whom β-lactams accumulate to very high concentrations[36–39] On account of this interaction aminoglycosides should not be mixed with penicillins before infusion and serum samples used for aminoglycoside assay should be run immediately or frozen until used.

Gentamicin, tobramycin and amikacin usually exhibit the same activity against Enterobacteriaceae, although *Serratia marcescens* is somewhat more susceptible to gentamicin, whereas tobramycin is more active than the other aminoglycosides against *P. aeruginosa*. Some gentamicin-resistant *P. aeruginosa* remain susceptible to tobramycin. Because these enzymes are a poor substrate for amikacin, and occasionally netilmicin, these two aminoglycosides may be effective against organisms that are resistant to both gentamicin and tobramycin. However, with the use of once-daily aminoglycoside dosing, these modest differences in microbiologic activity appear to have little, if any, clinical relevance, except for isolated patients.

Vancomycin or teicoplanin (not available in the USA) is often added to the β-lactam–aminoglycoside combination in the initial treatment of the febrile neutropenic patient if one or more of the following findings are present:

- clinically suspected intravenous catheter-related infections;
- known colonization with β-lactam-resistant pneumococci or staphylococci (methicillin-resistant *Staphylococcus aureus* – MRSA);
- positive blood cultures for Gram-positive bacteria;
- evidence of cardiovascular impairment;
- patient on previous prophylaxis with a fluoroquinolone;
- abrupt increase in temperature to ≥104°F (40°C).

Therapy of enterococcal infections

Aminoglycosides are used in the therapy of systemic enterococcal infection because no single antibiotic by itself exhibits bactericidal activity against these bacteria. Usually the aminoglycoside, either gentamicin or streptomycin, is combined with either a penicillin or vancomycin to obtain a bactericidal effect, and this is crucial in the therapy of endocarditis. Although all enterococci are resistant to aminoglycosides based on achievable serum concentrations, synergistic activity with penicillins (usually ampicillin) or vancomycin results in effective therapy.

Therapy of enterococcal infection is, however, becoming more difficult owing to the increasing frequency of enterococcal isolates that have high-level resistance to aminoglycosides (MIC >2000μg/ml), penicillins and even vancomycin. Enterococci with high-level resistance to gentamicin contain the bifunctional aminoglycoside-modifying enzyme acetyltransferase (AAC) (6′)–phosphotransferase (APH) (2′), which abolishes synergy with all aminoglycosides except streptomycin. It is important to note that, although the bifunctional enzyme modifies amikacin and abolishes synergy with β-lactams and vancomycin, it does not lead to a resistant phenotype. For these reasons, amikacin should not be used against strains with high-level resistance to gentamicin even if the strain is reported to be susceptible. Streptomycin remains the only alternative for strains with high-level resistance to gentamicin. In the case of high-level resistance to streptomycin, this aminoglycoside should also not be used.

Treatment of other infections

Streptomycin

The major uses of streptomycin have been as part of combination therapy for enterococcal and mycobacteria infections and monotherapy for tularemia, brucellosis and plague (see Chapters 176, 177 and 180). The clinical role of streptomycin as well as the other aminoglycosides in the treatment of mycobacterial infections is discussed in detail in Chapters 37 and 38.

Paromomycin

Because paromomycin is too toxic following intravenous administration and is not absorbed following oral administration, its usage has been restricted to the treatment of intestinal infections, particularly cryptosporidiosis in patients who have AIDS.[40] The usual oral dose to treat cryptosporidiosis is 1g q12h for 1 month. For the treatment of intestinal amebiasis, the usual dose in adults and children is 25–35mg/kg/day q8h with meals for 5–10 days. Paromomycin has been used for treatment or prevention of traveler's diarrhea because it is also active against *Escherichia coli* and *Salmonella* spp.

Unlabeled uses of paramomycin include treatment of other parasitic infections such as:

- *Dientamoeba fragilis* (25–30mg/kg/day q8h for 7 days);
- *Diphyllobothrium latum, Taenia saginata, Taenia solium, Dipylidium caninum* (adults – 1g every 15 minutes for four doses; pediatric – 11mg/kg every 15 minutes for four doses); and
- *Hymenolepis nana* (45mg/kg/day for 5–7 days).

Like neomycin, paromomycin has been used to treat hepatic coma where the usual adult dose of neomycin is 4g/day in divided doses administered at regular intervals for 5–6 days. The activity of paromomycin closely parallels that of neomycin and kanamycin and there is complete cross-resistance between these agents.

Neomycin

Like paromomycin, neomycin is too toxic for systemic use. It has mainly been used by mouth as a prophylactic agent along with erythromycin in colonic surgery and in hepatic coma to reduce the number of aerobic enteric organisms. When it is used for preoperative prophylaxis for elective colorectal surgery, it usually given as a 1g oral dose along with a 1g oral dose of erythromycin, at 1p.m., 2p.m. and 11p.m. on the day before surgery. Metronidazole can be used in place of erythromycin and is usually given at 7p.m. and 11p.m. on the day before surgery.

In the treatment of hepatic coma, the usual dose in adults is 4–12g/day in divided doses, whereas in children the recommended dose is 50–100mg/kg/day in divided doses. Treatment is usually continued for 5–6 days. In patients with chronic hepatic insufficiency, neomycin may be required (in adults up to 4g/day) indefinitely.

The use of neomycin topically has been mainly for the treatment of external otitis media, usually with other antibiotics in the formulation.

Infections by Listeria *spp.,* Neisseria *spp. and* Haemophilus *spp.*

An infrequent use of gentamicin is to combine it with a penicillin, usually ampicillin, in the therapy of *Listeria monocytogenes* meningitis or endocarditis to achieve more rapid killing of the organism. In patients allergic to penicillin, trimethoprim–sulfamethoxazole (co-trimoxazole) can be used either alone or in combination with the gentamicin.

Although all aminoglycosides exhibit activity against *Neisseria* spp., only the aminocyclitol spectinomycin is used for gonococcal infection; this is, however, very uncommon because most gonococci are susceptible to third-generation cephalosporins and the fluoroquinolones such as ofloxacin and ciprofloxacin.

Haemophilus and *Legionella* spp. are often susceptible to aminoglycosides. Although their use as single agents for infections by these organisms has never been studied, it is useful to be aware that if a patient is on an aminoglycoside for some other infection, these organisms should be covered.

DOSING IN PATIENTS ON CHRONIC HEMODIALYSIS OR CHRONIC AMBULATORY PERITONEAL DIALYSIS

Because aminoglycosides are dialyzable, a supplemental dose should be given after each hemodialysis. The usual supplemental doses are:

- 1–2mg/kg for tobramycin and gentamicin;
- 2mg/kg for netilmicin; and
- 5–7mg/kg for amikacin.[41]

For patients on chronic ambulatory peritoneal dialysis (CAPD) who develop peritonitis without evidence of systemic infection, the aminoglycoside can be added directly to the dialysis fluid by one of two methods.[42] Most patients on CAPD have four 2l-exchanges/day with a dwell time of 6 hours:

- in the first method, 'therapeutic' concentrations (e.g. 4–8mg/l gentamicin, tobramycin or netilmicin; 6–12mg/l amikacin) are added to each bag of dialysis fluid; and
- in the second method, high concentrations (e.g. 20mg/l gentamicin, tobramycin or netilmicin; 60mg/l amikacin) are added to only one of the usual four exchanges of dialysis fluid.

ADVERSE REACTIONS

General

The major adverse effects associated with aminoglycosides include:

- neuromuscular blockade;
- nephrotoxicity; and
- ototoxicity (auditory and vestibular).

Aminoglycosides seldom produce hypersensitivity reactions, hematologic dyscrasias, hepatitis or drug fevers. Because they do not produce inflammatory reactions, they seldom produce phlebitis on intravenous injection, pain on intramuscular injection, or irritation of serosal surfaces on direct instillation into pleural space, joint space or the peritoneal cavity, or when incorporated into methylmethacrylate prosthetic joint cement. In addition, they are extremely well tolerated when injected into the CSF and have not been associated with epileptogenic reactions.

Neuromuscular blockade

The potential for neuromuscular blockade can be avoided if aminoglycosides are not given by bolus administration or instilled in large concentrations into the peritoneal cavity. Intravenous aminoglycosides should be administered over at least 20–30 minutes, especially if once-daily aminoglycoside therapy is used. The risk of neuromuscular blockade is increased in patients who are concomitantly receiving D-tubocurarine or succinylcholine, or possibly calcium channel blockers.[43,44] Infant botulism, myasthenia gravis, hypocalcemia and hypomagnesemia have also been associated with an increased risk for this adverse reaction.[45]

The classic manifestations of neuromuscular blockade include weakness of the respiratory musculature, flaccid paralysis and dilated pupils. Blockade results from the ability of aminoglycoside to prevent internalization of calcium into the presynaptic region of the axon, which is essential for the release of acetylcholine. When the neuromuscular blockade occurs, it can be rapidly reversed by the administration of calcium gluconate. With supportive care alone, in time, the blockade will resolve. Neomycin is the most likely aminoglycoside to cause this adverse reaction.

Nephrotoxicity

Except for spectinomycin, all aminoglycosides are capable of producing nephrotoxicity by interfering directly with renal tubular function and indirectly with glomerular filtration. Among the commonly prescribed aminoglycosides, such as gentamicin, tobramycin, netilmicin and amikacin, there appear to be no clinically relevant differences in toxicity. Using a definition of nephrotoxicity as a rise in serum creatinine concentration of 0.5mg/dl above the baseline, approximately 3–5% of patients on these agents develop this adverse reaction using standard dosing regimens.

Neomycin is the most nephrotoxic aminoglycoside and streptomycin the least. The most important molecular basis for nephrotoxicity appears to be the number of amino groups (NH_3). Neomycin, gentamicin, tobramycin, netilmicin, amikacin and streptomycin contain six, five, five, four, four and three amino groups, respectively.[46] The magnitude of the toxicity has been shown to be the greatest when the daily dose is divided into multiple small doses rather than as the same dose given once.[47] This observation has been the basis for the recent popularization of once-daily aminogycoside dosing (see Once-daily dosing, above). Loop diuretics such as ethacrynic acid aggravate aminoglycoside renal toxicity through volume depletion or hypokalemia or by increasing renal tubular uptake of aminoglycosides.

The concomitant use of aminoglycosides with vancomycin, *cis*-platinum, foscarnet, amphotericin B, methoxyflurane and intravenous radiocontrast agents has also been shown to accentuate nephrotoxicity.[48] Although elderly patients are traditionally considered to be at a higher risk for aminoglycoside nephrotoxicity, they may actually not be at an increased risk if one adjusts for an age-related decrease in glomerular filtration rate. High serum levels of aminoglycosides are not considered to be a risk factor for toxicity because there is a saturable movement of aminoglycosides into the renal tubular cell. Certain agents (e.g. potassium supplements, thyroid hormone, high-dose calcium, extended-spectrum penicillins) may reduce aminoglycoside toxicity, but there have been no controlled attempts to evaluate them.

Aminoglycosides bind to specific receptors on the proximal convoluted renal tubule causing an increased excretion of brush border enzymes, magnesium and calcium into the urine. Although there was considerable interest in using enzymuria as a marker of renal toxicity, it never became clinically useful because significant amounts can be detected in the urine even after a single dose. After binding to the renal cell, aminoglycosides are rapidly internalized into the cell by pinocytosis. Once inside the cell, they interfere with ribosomal-mediated protein synthesis and mitochondrial respiration, resulting in cell damage and necrosis.[49] Interference with liposomal enzyme production also occurs, resulting in a deposition of a material that resembles myelin by electron microscopy (myeloid bodies).[49] These myeloid bodies can be detected in the urine. Injury to the lysosome also results in an increased excretion of phospholipids into the urine (lysosome phospholipidosis).

The renal tubular cell is relatively resistant to the toxic effect of aminoglycosides as it takes several days of drug administration to produce functional or anatomic evidence of toxicity.[50] This is important since it reinforces the observation that the best way to prevent renal toxicity is to avoid prolonged administration of these agents. Even when renal tubular necrosis occurs, it is reversible, and surprisingly the renal tubule can even regenerate despite continued administration of the aminoglycoside.

Of equal clinical relevance is the observation that the aminoglycoside enzyme transfer system has a finite capacity for internalizing all aminoglycosides within the renal tubular cell.[51] This saturable transport system means that the amount of aminoglycoside that enters the cell is the same over 24 hours whether the dose is given in the traditional divided fashion or as a single dose. Because of the low or undetectable levels of aminoglycosides for 10–12 hours during the 24-hour period with once-daily dosing, most of the previously internalized drug gets transported out of the cell, resulting in less accumulation.

How damage of the renal tubular cell results in diminished glomerular filtration as indicated by an increase in serum creatinine concentration and the use of creatinine clearance remains controversial. The most frequent explanations mentioned include a release of vasoconstrictive hormones affecting the afferent arterioles, cellular debris obstructing nephrons, and a change in glomerular fenestrae.[48] After discontinuing aminoglycoside therapy, evidence of nephrotoxocity usually disappears within several days in the absence of other causes of nephrotoxicity.

The major clinical manifestations of distal nephron damage by aminoglycosides include:

- decreased urine concentrating ability; and
- polyuria.

Because of excessive magnesium losses in the urine, hypomagnesemia may occur, which in turn can lead to secondary hypocalcemia and hypokalemia.[52] Progression to anuric renal failure as a result of aminoglycoside nephrotoxicity is rare.

Ototoxicity

Auditory

Auditory toxicity occurs as a result of the accumulation of aminoglycosides in the perilymph of the inner ear with subsequent damage of the sensory cells of the organ of Corti. A reduction in the number of cochlear ganglion cells has also been reported as an additional cause of this adverse reaction.[53] Penetration of aminoglycosides into this space is facilitated by elevated trough levels, which impairs their back-diffusion into the plasma.

The exact mechanism by which aminoglycosides destroy hair cells is unknown, but possible explanations include saturation of the detoxification capabilities of the hair cells, binding of aminoglycosides to polyphosphinositides, mitochondrial dysfunction and inhibition of decarboxylase.[54]

Unlike patients with serious nephrotoxicity which is generally reversible, severe cochlear damage is usually permanent because cochlear hair cells do not regenerate. Interestingly, there may be a hereditary component to hearing loss caused by aminoglycosides due to a mutation of mitochondrial DNA.[55]

Symptoms of auditory toxicity include:

- hearing loss;
- tinnitus; and
- a sensation of fullness in the ear.

Although they may develop unilaterally or bilaterally, most patients experience symptoms in both ears. Both auditory and vestibular toxicity can occur in the same patient. The onset of symptoms may occur during or after cessation of treatment.

Cochlear toxicity is usually assessed by pure-tone audiometric testing of air and bone conduction by increasing the frequency from 0.5 to 8kHz. In general, an increase in threshold from the baseline of at least 15dB at any of two or more frequencies is considered to be a significant hearing loss.[56] The earliest signs of cochlear toxicity are usually detected at frequencies above 8kHz. Because perception of human speech occurs in the 0.3–3kHz range, significant cochlear damage can occur before the patient becomes aware of it. Many audiometers do not test for frequencies above 8kHz.

Clinical studies show that the incidence of cochlear toxicity due to aminoglycoside use varies from 5 to 15% with conventional intermittent dosing of aminoglycosides. The frequency varies and depends upon the method of establishing toxicity and whether the investigators include high-frequency loss. The frequency of ototoxicity may be less with once-daily aminoglycoside dosing, presumably because less drug accumulates in the perilymph.

In a guinea pig model evaluating the ototoxicity of amikacin, the investigators found that it was related to total perilymph accumulation rather than to peak concentrations.[57] Therefore, as in the renal tubular cell, there appears to be a saturable transport system into the sensory hair cells.

There is considerable controversy regarding the comparative potential for cochlear damage among the aminoglycosides, but it appears that there is little, if any, clinically relevant difference between gentamicin, tobramycin, amikacin and netilmicin. Compared with these agents, neomycin more often has a greater association with cochlear damage.

Risk factors for cochlear damage include:

- age (≥ 60 years);
- elevated plasma trough levels (i.e. drug accumulation);
- pre-existing ear disease;
- prolonged therapy;
- repeated treatment with aminoglycoside; and
- concomitant use of loop diuretics (e.g. ethacrynic acid) and other ototoxic drugs.[58]

Of these risk factors, duration of therapy remains the most important. When aminoglycosides are given for less than 10 days, toxicity is seldom a problem. In fact, if ototoxicity or nephrotoxicity occur during the first week of aminoglycoside usage, it is wise to search for another cause.

The potential for ototoxicity in humans with topical preparations remains controversial, but animal studies have shown sensorineural hearing loss with the administration of neomycin and gentamicin.[59] In a study of 44 children with chronic suppurative otitis media given topical preparations containing five different aminoglycosides (four neomycin; one gentamicin), there was no evidence of ototoxicity.[60]

Vestibular

As with cochlear toxicity, vestibular toxicity results from excessive accumulation of aminoglycoside in the perilymph of the inner ear, but the targets for damage differs and are the sensory hair cells of the vestibular epithelia located at the summit of the ampullar cristae.[61] Serious damage to these cells typically results in a permanent deficit because these sensory hair cells, like those of the organ of Corti, do not regenerate.

The risk factors for vestibular toxicity are identical to those mentioned above for auditory toxicity. As with cochlear damage, vestibular toxicity can occur during or after therapy and be unilateral or bilateral. Occasionally it occurs together with auditory toxicity.

Symptoms of vestibular toxicity include:

- nausea;
- vomiting;
- vertigo;
- nystagmus;
- difficulty with gait; and
- difficulty fixating on objects.

Difficulty with gait is especially prominent in the dark because of the loss of sight, which compensates for vestibular dysfunction.

The frequency of vestibular toxicity is difficult to establish because vestibular function testing is poorly standardized. The usual method is to record the response to caloric stimulation with water or air on an electronystagmogram. It is speculated that the frequency of vestibular toxicity is comparable to that of cochlear damage. Streptomycin more often has a much greater association with vestibular toxicity than neomycin, gentamicin, tobramycin and amikacin. This differential toxicity is the basis for the choice of streptomycin to obliterate vestibular function in patients with Ménière's disease.

REFERENCES

1. Moellering RC Jr. *In-vitro* antibacterial activity of the aminoglycoside antibiotics. Rev Infect Dis 1983;5(Suppl):212–32.
2. Zhbanel GG, Craig WA. Pharmacokinetic contributions to postantibiotic effects: focus on aminoglycosides. Clin Pharmacokinet 1994;27:377–92.
3. Isaksson B, Nilsson L, Maller R, *et al.* Postantibiotic effect of aminoglycosides on Gram-negative bacteria: evaluation by a new method. J Antimicrob Chemother 1988;22:23–33.
4. Weiss PJ, Andrew ML, Wright WW. Solubility of antibiotics in 24 solvents: use in analyses. Antibiot Chemother 1957;7:374–7.
5. Breen KJ, Bryant RE, Levinson JD, *et al.* Neomycin absorption in man. Ann Intern Med 1972;76:211–8.
6. Smavely SR, Hodges GR. The nephrotoxicity of antimicrobiol agents. Ann Intern Med 1984;101:92–104.
7. Ramsey BW, Dorkin HC, Eisenberg JD, *et al.* Efficacy of aerosolized tobramycin in patients with cystic fibrosis. N Engl J Med. 1993;328:1740–6.
8. Laskin OL, Longstreth JA, Smith CR, *et al.* Netilmicin and gentamicin multi-dosing kinetics in normal subjects. Clin Pharmacol Ther 1983;34:644–50.
9. Schentag JJ, Jusko WJ. Renal clearance and tissue accumulation of gentamicin. Clin Pharmacol Ther 1977;22:364–70.
10. Pflugfelder SC, Flynn HW. Infectious endophthalmitis. Infect Dis Clin North Am 1992;6:859–73.
11. Leedom JM, Wehrle PF, Mathies AW, *et al.* Gentamicin in the treatment of meningitis in neonates. J Infect Dis 1969;119:476–80.
12. Vacek V, Hyzlan M, Ckalova M. Penetration of antibiotics into the cerebrospinal fluid in inflammatory conditions. Int J Clin Pharmacol 1969;2:277–79.
13. Wilson TW, Mahon WA, Inaba T, *et al.* Elimination of tritiated gentamicin in normal human subjects and in patients with severly impaired renal function. Clin Pharmacol Ther 1973;14:815–22.
14. McCracken GH, Freij BJ. Clinical pharmacology of antimicrobial agents. In: Remington JS, Klein JO, eds. Infectious disease of the fetus and newborn infant, 3rd ed. Philadelphia: WB Saunders; 1990:1020–76.
15. Fabre J. Rudhardt M, Blanehard P, *et al.* Persistence of sisomicin and gentamicin in renal cortex and medulla compared with other organs and serum of rats. Kidney Int 1976;10:444–9.
16. Gilbert DN. Once-daily aminoglycoside therapy. Antimicrob Agents Chemother 1991;35:399–405.
17. Moore RD, Lietman PS, Smith CR. Clinical response to aminoglycoside therapy: importance of the ratio of peak concentration to minimal inhibitory concentration. J Infect Dis 1987;155:93–9.
18. Powell SH, Thompson WL, Luthe MA, *et al.* Once-daily vs continuous aminoglycoside dosing: efficacy and toxicity in animal and clinical studies of gentamicin, netilmicin, and tobramycin. J Infect Dis 1983;147:918–32.
19. Wood CA, Norton DR, Kohlhepp SJ, *et al.* The influence of tobramycin dosage regimens on nephrotoxicity, ototoxicity and antibacterial efficacy in a rat model of subcutaneous abscess. J Infect Dis 1988;158:13–22.
20. Craig WA, Audmundsson S. Postantibiotic effect. In: Lorain V, ed. Antimicrobics in the laboratory, 3rd ed. Baltimore: Williams and Williams; 1991:403–31.
21. Nicolau DP, Freeman CD, Belliveau PP, *et al.* Experience with a once-daily aminoglycoside program administered to 2184 adult patients. Antimicrob Agents Chemother 1995;39:650–5.
22. Cockroft DW, Gault MH. Prediction of creatinine clearance from serum creatinine. Nephron 1976;16:31–41.
23. Rozdzinski E, Kern WV, Reichle A, *et al.* Once-daily vs thrice-daily dosing of netilmicin in combination with β-lactam antibiotics as empirical therapy for febrile neutropenic patients. J Antimicrob Chemother 1993;31:585–98.
24. Prins JM, Buller HR, Kuijper EJ, Tange RA, Speelman P. Once vs thrice daily gentamicin in patients with serious infections. Lancet 1993;341:335–9.
25. Hatala R, Dinh T, Cook DJ. Once-daily aminoglycoside dosing in immunocompetent adults: a meta-analysis. Ann Intern Med 1996;124:717–25.
26. Lacy MK, Hitt CN, Nightingale CH, *et al.* The pharmacoeconomic benefit of once-daily aminoglycoside dosing. Drug Benefit Trends 1996;8:36–9.
27. Eisenberg JM, Koffer H, Gllick HA, *et al.* What is the cost of nephrotoxicity associated with aminoglycosides? Ann Intern Med 1987;107:900–9.
28. Marik PE, Havlik I, Monteagudo SE, Lipman J. The pharmacokinetics of amikacin in critically ill adult and pediatric patients: comparison of once-daily versus twice-daily dosing regimens. J Antimicrob Chemother 1991;27(Suppl C):81–9.
29. Marik PE, Lipman J, Kobilski A, Scribante J. A prospective randomized study comparing once-vs twice-daily amikacin dosing in critically ill adult and pediatric patients. J Antimicrob Chemother 1991;28:753–64.
30. Viscoli C, Dudley M, Ferrea G, *et al.* Serum concentrations and safety of single daily dosing of amikacin in children undergoing bone marrow transplantation. J Antimicrob Chemother 1991;27(Suppl.C):113–20.
31. Vigano A, Principi N, Brivio L, Tommasi P, Stasi P, Villa AD. Comparison of 5 milligrams of netilmicin per kilogram of body weight once daily versus 2 milligrams per kilogram thrice daily for treatment of Gram-negative pyelonephritis in children. Antimicrob Agents Chemother 1992;36:1499–503.
32. Langhendries JP, Battisti O, Bertrand JM, *et al.* Once-a-day administration of amikacin in neonates: assessment of nephrotoxicity and ototoxicity. Dev Pharmacol Ther 1993;20:220–30.
33. Dettli LC. Drug dosage in patients with renal disease. Clin Pharmacol Ther 1974;16:274–80.
34. Waitz JA, Drube CG, Moss EL Jr, *et al.* Biological aspects of the interaction between gentamicin and carbenicillin. J Antibiot 1972;25:219–25.

35. Benveniste R, Davies J. Structure–activity relationships among the aminoglycoside antibiotics: role of hydroxyl and amino groups. Antimicrob Agents Chemother 1973;4:402–9.
36. Thompson MIB, Russo ME, Saxon BJ, Atkinthor E, Matsen MJ. Gentamicin inactivation by piperacillin or carbenicillin in patients with end-stage renal disease. Antimicrob Agents Chemother 1982;21:268–73.
37. Ervin TR, Bullock WE, Nuttall CE. Inactivation of gentamicin by penicillins in patients with renal failure. Antimicrob Agents Chemother 1976;9:1004–11.
38. Blair DC, Duggan DO, Schroeder ET. Inactivation of amikacin and gentamicin by carbenicillin in patients with end-stage renal failure. Antimicrob Agents Chemother 1982;22:376–9.
39. Riff L, Jackson GG. Laboratory and clinical conditions for gentamicin inactivation by carbenicillin. Arch Intern Med 1972;130:887–91.
40. Bissuel F, Cotte L, Rabodnirina B, *et al.* Paromomycin: an effective treatment for cryptosporidial diarrhea in patients with AIDS. Clin Infect Dis 1994;18:447–9.
41. Golper TA, Wedel SK, Kaplan AA, *et al.* Drug removal during continuous arteriovenous hemofiltration: theory and clinical observations. Int J Artif Organs 1985;2:307–12.
42. Keanl WF, Everett ED, Golper TA, *et al.* Peritoneal dialyses-related peritonitis treatment recommendation. Perit Dial Int 1993;13:14–28.
43. Talbot PA. Potentiation of aminoglycoside-induced neuromuscular blockade by protons *in vitro* and *in vivo.* J Pharmacol Exp Ther 1987;241:686–94.
44. Gay CT, Marks WA, Riley HD Jr, *et al.* Infantile botulism. South Med J 1988;81:437–60.
45. Hokkanen E. The aggravating effect of some antibiotics on the neuromuscular blockade in myasthenia gravis. Acta Neurol Scand 1964;40:346–52.
46. Hummes HD. Aminoglycoside nephrotoxicity. Kidney Int 1988;33:900–11.
47. Bennett WM, Plamp CE, Gilbert DN, Parker RA, Porter GA. The influence of dosage regimen on experimental nephrotoxicity: dissociation of peak serum levels from renal failure. J Infect Dis 1979;140:576–80.
48. Appel GB. Aminoglycoside nephrotoxicity. Am J Med 1990;88(Suppl.C):16–20.
49. Beauchamp D, Gourde P, Bergeron MG. Subcellular distribution of gentamicin in proximal tubular cells, determined by immunogold labeling. Antimicrob Agents Chemother 1991;35:2173–9.
50. Gilbert DN, Bennett WM. Progress in the education of aminoglycoside nephrotoxicty. Contemp Issues Infect Dis 1984;1:121–52.
51. Dew RB, Susla GM. Once-daily aminglycoside treatment. Infect Dis Clin Pract 1996;5:12–29.
52. Shah GM, Kirchenbaum MA. Renal magnesium wasting associated with therapeutic agents. Miner Elect Metab 1996;17:58–64.
53. Hinojosa R, Lerner SA. Cochlear neural degeneration without hair cell loss in two patients with aminoglycoside ototoxicity. J Infect Dis 1987;156:449–55.
54. Hutchin T, Cortopassi G. Proposed molecular and cellular mechanism for aminoglycoside ototoxicity. Antimicrob Agents Chemother 1994;38:2517–20.
55. Prezant TR, Agapian JV, Bohlman MC, *et al.* Mitochondrial ribosomal RNA associated with both antibiotic-induced and non-syndromic deafness. Nature Genet 1993;4:289–94.
56. Brummett RE, Fox RE. Aminoglycoside-induced hearing loss in humans. Antimicrob Agents Chemother 1989;33:797–800.
57. Beubien AR, Ormsby E, Bayne A, *et al.* Evidence that amikacin ototoxicity is related to total perilymph area under the concentration–time curve regardless of concentration. Antimicrob Agents Chemother 1991;35:1070–4.
58. Moore RD, Smith CR, Lietman PS. Risk factors for the development of auditory toxicity in patients receiving aminoglycosides. J Infect Dis 1984;149:23–30.
59. Wright CG, Meyerhoff WL. Ototoxicity of otic drops applied to the middle ear in the chinchilla. Am J Otolaryngol 1984;5:166–76.
60. Merifield DO, Parker NJ, Nicholson NC. Therapeutic management of chronic suppurative otitis media with otic drops. Otolaryngol Head Neck Surg 1993;109:77–82.
61. Tran Ba Huy P, Manuel C, Meulemans A. Kinetics of aminoglycoside antibiotics in perilymph and endolymph in animals. In: Lerner SA, Matz GJ, Hawkins JE Jr, eds. Aminoglycoside ototoxicity. Boston: Little Brown; 1981:81–97.

chapter 197

Folate Inhibitors

S Ragnar Norrby

INTRODUCTION

Sulfonamides

Sulfonamides are competitive inhibitors of para-aminobenzoic acid (PABA), which is essential for folic acid synthesis in most bacteria, some protozoa and *Pneumocystis carinii* (Fig. 197.1).[1] A consequence of the mode of action is that sulfonamides lack activity against organisms for which PABA is not an essential metabolite (e.g. *Enterococcus* spp.). The eukaryotic cell does not use PABA and sulfonamides do not interfere with human folic acid synthesis.

Trimethoprim

Trimethoprim is a diaminopyrimidine that competitively inhibits dihydrofolate reductase.[1–3] Compared with many other diaminopyrimidines with antimicrobial activity (e.g. pyrimethamine), trimethoprim has a higher affinity for bacterial dihydrofolate reductase than for the human enzyme, thus reducing the risk of folic acid deficiency in the treated patient.[4] Pyrimethamine is also a competitive dihydrofolate reductase inhibitor. It has a high affinity for protozoal enzyme.

In addition to the above modes of action, it has been proposed that trimethoprim may inhibit the adhesion of bacteria to human mucosal cells.[5]

Combinations of sulfonamides and trimethoprim or pyrimethamine

Combinations of sulfonamides and trimethoprim or pyrimethamine interfere with two consecutive steps in the same metabolic chain in the micro-organism. This may lead to synergistic antimicrobial activity. The rationale for a fixed combination of trimethoprim and sulfamethoxazole is that, although both antibiotics alone are bacteriostatic, the combination may be bactericidal. The optimal trimethoprim–sulfamethoxazole (TMP–SMX) ratio for synergism is 1:20 and is obtained systemically with a 1:5 dosage combination.[6]

The clinical relevance of the synergism is difficult to prove in experimental infections and even more so in clinical trials. This has led to questioning of the clinical usefulness of the combination in comparison with trimethoprim alone for the treatment of bacterial infections.[7] An argument in favor of the combination is the possibility of the reduced risk of resistance; organisms initially susceptible to both sulfonamides and trimethoprim are less likely to develop resistance to combinations than to single drugs.

Folate inhibitor combinations are used for treating bacterial as well as fungal and protozoal infections. Because of the emergence of bacterial resistance and risks for adverse reactions, the sulfonamides have lost most of their usefulness as single agents. Emphasis will be put on combinations of sulfonamides and trimethoprim, especially the most widely used, namely TMP–SMX and pyrimethamine–sulfadoxine.

PHARMACOKINETICS

The sulfonamides are classically subdivided on the basis of their elimination time into short-acting (plasma half-life, $t_{1/2}$<8h), medium-acting ($t_{1/2}$=8–16h), long-acting ($t_{1/2}$=17–48h) and ultra-long-acting ($t_{1/2}$>48h). Sulfonamides used as single agents today are short- or medium-acting.

Plasma kinetics

The sulfonamides used today, as well as trimethoprim and pyrimethamine, are well absorbed after oral administration and have high bioavailability. Following an oral dose of 160mg of trimethoprim and 800mg of sulfamethoxazole, maximal plasma concentrations of 1.6–1.9mg/l and 26–41mg/l, respectively, are achieved.[8] After intravenous administration of 240mg trimethoprim and 1200mg sulfamethoxazole q12h, peak plasma concentrations in the steady state are about 6mg/l for trimethoprim and 180mg/l for sulfamethoxazole.[9] The protein binding of the sulfonamides varies from less than 50% for sulfadiazine to more than 90% for sulfadoxine. Importantly, sulfonamides bind firmly to albumin and may displace other compounds (e.g. bilirubin). In newborns this may lead to toxic levels of unbound bilirubin with a subsequent risk of 'kernicterus' (see Central nervous system reactions, below).

Distribution

Trimethoprim is lipid-soluble at physiologic pH and has a large volume of distribution (100–120l), whereas sulfamethoxazole is a weak acid with poor lipid solubility at pH values above 7, leading to a volume of distribution corresponding to that of the extracellular space (i.e. 12–18l). In tissues concentrations similar to or higher than those in plasma are achieved with trimethoprim, whereas considerably lower levels of sulfamethoxazole reach peripheral compartments. Concentration above the minimum inhibitory concentrations (MICs) of trimethoprim-susceptible strains are achieved in most tissues and tissue fluids. With sulfamethoxazole, the peripheral concentrations are sometimes so low that it should be questioned whether therapeutic levels are reached. All of the sulfonamides as well as trimethoprim achieve high urine concentrations.

Elimination

The main routes of elimination of sulfonamides, trimethoprim and pyrimethamine are via liver metabolism and renal excretion.[10] In patients who have normal renal function, half-life varies from less than 6 hours for sulfisoxazole and sulfamethizole to 11–17 hours for sulfamethoxazole and sulfadiazine and more than 200 hours for sulfadoxine. Trimethoprim has a half-life of about 15 hours and pyrimethamine is eliminated slowly, with a half-life of about 100 hours.

Kinetics in children

The kinetics of both sulfamethoxazole and trimethoprim differ between children and adults (Table 197.1). Elimination is faster in children, who must be given higher doses than adults.

ROUTE OF ADMINISTRATION AND DOSAGE

Most sulfonamides, trimethoprim and pyrimethamine are available for oral use. Trimethoprim, sulfamethoxazole and sulfadiazine are

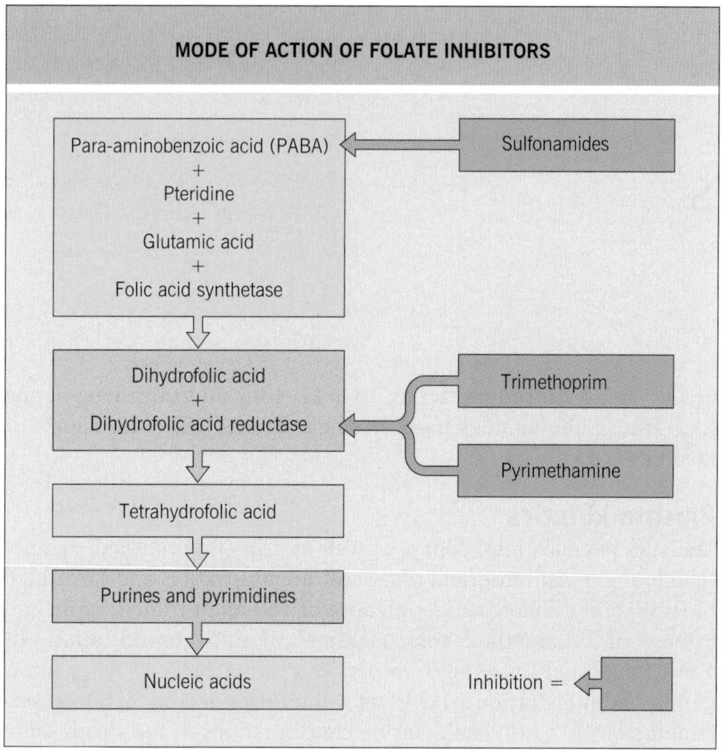

Fig. 197.1 Mode of action of folate inhibitors.

COMPARATIVE KINETICS OF TRIMETHOPRIM AND SULFAMETHOXAZOLE IN CHILDREN AND ADULTS

Parameter	Age (years)			
	<1	1–9	10–19	20–63
T dose (mg/kg)	32	20	14	13
S dose (mg/kg)	160	100	70	65
Peak T concentration (mg/l)	6.5	7.2	6.7	8.7
Peak S concentration (mg/l)	146	176	126	176
T volume of distribution (l/kg)	2.0	1.6	1.5	1.4
S volume of distribution (l/kg)	0.5	0.5	0.4	0.4
T plasma half-life (h)	11	5.6	10	16
S plasma half-life (h)	7.5	9.8	10	15

Table 197.1 Comparative kinetics of trimethoprim (T) and sulfamethoxazole (S) in children and adults.

also used intravenously; intravenous use of TMP–SMX is recommended when patients are unable to take the drug orally. Dosages for some of the sulfonamides and for combinations of sulfonamides and dihydrofolic acid inhibitors are given in Table 197.2.

INDICATIONS

Table 197.3 summarizes the current antibacterial spectrum of TMP–SMX; little information is available on the current activity of the individual components. The activity of TMP–SMX against enterococci is controversial. There are reports in the literature of enterococcal bacteremia during treatment with TMP–SMX despite full in-vitro sensitivity pre-therapy, and of high failure rates and rapid emergence of resistance in enterococcal urinary tract infections (UTIs).[11,12]

Reduced susceptibility or resistance to penicillin G by *Streptococcus pneumoniae* seems to be coupled to resistance to TMP–SMX

ADULT DOSAGES OF SOME FOLATE INHIBITORS

Drug	Indication and recommended dose for adults
Pyrimethamine	Malaria prophylaxis (with sulfadoxine) 25mg once weekly; malaria therapy (with sulfadoxine; Fansidar) 50–75mg as single dose; toxoplasmosis therapy (with sulfadiazine) 75–200mg loading dose followed by 25–100mg q24h for 3–6 weeks followed by 25–50mg q24h (maintenance therapy in AIDS)
Sulfadiazine	UTI (with trimethoprim, not licensed in USA) 410mg q12h; toxoplasmosis therapy (with pyrimethamine) 0.5–1.5g q6h
Sulfadoxine	Malaria prophylaxis 500mg once weekly (with pyrimethamine; Fansidar); malaria therapy 1–1.5g (with pyrimethamine; Fansidar) as single dose
Sulfamethizole	UTI 500mg q6h
Sulfamethoxazole (with trimethoprim)	UTI 1.6g single dose or 400–800mg q12h; systemic bacterial infections 800mg q12h; pneumocystis pneumonia treatment 18.75–25mg/kg q6h; pneumocystis pneumonia prophylaxis 800mg thrice weekly or daily
Sulfisoxazole	UTI 500mg q6h
Trimethoprim	UTI 100mg q12h or 200mg q24h; UTI (with sulfadiazine, not licensed in USA) 90mg q12h; UTI (with sulfamethoxazole) 320mg single dose or 80–160mg q12h; systemic bacterial infections (with sulfamethoxazole) 160mg q12h; pneumocystis pneumonia treatment (with sulfamethoxazole) 3.75–5mg/kg q6h; pneumocystis pneumonia prophylaxis (with sulfamethoxazole) 160mg thrice weekly or daily

Table 197.2 Adult dosages of some folate inhibitors. For pediatric doses, see the manufacturers' recommendations.

in a very high percentage of strains studied (Table 197.4).[13–16] Overall, resistance to TMP–SMX in pneumococci is a rapidly increasing problem.[17]

Streptococcus pyogenes is normally sensitive to TMP–SMX, but resistance has been reported in macrolide-resistant isolates.[18] Of other Gram-positive organisms, *Listeria monocytogenes* is susceptible to the combination.[19]

In *Escherichia coli* there is a very marked variation of susceptibility to TMP–SMX, not only between but also within countries. However, there is a clear trend towards increasing frequencies of resistance and in most countries 12% or more of *E. coli* isolates are resistant to trimethoprim and TMP–SMX.[20–22]

Shigella and *Salmonella* spp. also show varying sensitivity to TMP–SMX, with frequencies of resistance ranging from less than 5% to over 50%.

Several studies have indicated a relatively high frequency of selection of resistance to TMP–SMX in Enterobacteriaceae when the antibiotic is used therapeutically or, in particular, prophylactically.[23]

In *Haemophilus influenzae* also, reduced rates of susceptibility to TMP–SMX have been reported.[17]

The spectrum of the folate inhibitors also includes micro-organisms other than bacteria. The treatment of choice for *Toxoplasma gondii* remains a combination of pyrimethamine and sulfadiazine. The combination of sulfadoxine and pyrimethamine is used for treatment but less often for prevention of falciparum malaria in areas

SUSCEPTIBILITY OF COMMON BACTERIAL PATHOGENS TO TMP–SMX	
Generally susceptible species (>90% susceptible)	*Streptococcus pyogenes* *Staphylococcus saprophyticus* *Listeria monocytogenes* *Bordetella pertussis* *Yersinia enterocolitica* *Aeromonas* spp. *Burkholderia pseudomallei* *Burkholderia cepacia* *Stenotrophomonas maltophilia*
Varying susceptibility	*Streptococcus pneumoniae* *Staphylococcus aureus* Coagulase-negative staphylococci *Enterococcus* spp. *Escherichia coli* *Enterobacter* spp. *Klebsiella* spp. *Salmonella* spp. *Shigella* spp. *Campylobacter* spp. *Haemophilus influenzae* *Moraxella catarrhalis*
Resistance common	*Mycobacterium tuberculosis* *Pseudomonas aeruginosa* *Treponema pallidum* *Mycoplasma* spp.

Table 197.3 Susceptibility of common bacterial pathogens to trimethoprim–sulfamethoxazole.

CORRELATION BETWEEN REDUCED SUSCEPTIBILITY TO PENICILLIN AND RESISTANCE TO TMP–SMX IN STREPTOCOCCAL PNEUMONIA			
	Sensitivity* to TMP–SMX		
Reference	Penicillin S†	Penicillin R‡	All
Jorgensen[13]	439/467 (94%)	11/19 (58%)	450/486 (93%)
Shlbl[14]	ND	ND	204/358 (57%)‡
Liñares[15]	ND	1/68 (1.5%)	ND
Marton[16]	151/273 (55%)	1/77 (1.3%)	152/350 (43%)
Lehtonen[18]	39/56 (70%)	25/79 (32%)	64/135 (47%)

* MIC of trimethoprim of <2mg/l with a 1:19 TMP–SMX ratio.
† MIC <0.1mg/l.
‡ MIC >0.1mg/l.

Table 197.4 Correlation between reduced susceptibility to penicillin and resistance to trimethoprim–sulfamethoxazole in streptococcal pneumonia. ND, no data.

with chloroquine resistance. However, unlike *T. gondii*, for which no resistance against pyrimethamine–sulfadiazine has yet been reported, resistance against pyrimethamine–sulfadoxine is not uncommon in *Plasmodium falciparum* and might become a problem also in *Pneumocystis. carinii*.[24,25]

Use of sulfonamides alone

Sulfonamides for systemic use are recommended only for the treatment of uncomplicated UTIs. There are several arguments for reducing or abandoning such use:

- resistance to sulfonamides is relatively common in *E. coli* and other urinary pathogens;
- short-term treatment is poorly documented; and
- treatment times of 5 days or longer are associated with a risk of serious adverse reactions (see below).

CLINICAL USE OF TMP–SMX	
Type of infection	**Limitations**
Uncomplicated UTI	None for short-term therapy (single dose or 3 days)
Other types of UTI	Resistance and safety
Shigellosis	Resistance
Salmonellosis	Resistance
Enteric fever	Resistance
Travelers' diarrhea	Safety and resistance
Otitis media	Resistance
Community-acquired pneumonia	Resistance, safety
Melioidosis	Resistance, efficacy
Prophylaxis in immunocompromised patients	Safety, resistance, efficacy
Pneumocystis carinii pneumonia	None

Table 197.5 Clinical use of trimethoprim–sulfamethoxazole.

Use of trimethoprim–sulfamethoxazole

Trimethoprim–sulfamethoxazole has lost some of its usefulness through the emergence of resistance and increased awareness of the risk of adverse reactions, which may be serious or life-threatening.

Urogenital infections

Urogenital infections are the most common indications for TMP–SMX (Table 197.5). High frequencies of clinical and bacteriologic cure have been documented in women who have uncomplicated cystitis as well as in patients who have pyelonephritis, complicated UTIs or prostatitis.

Importantly, the use of TMP–SMX is well documented for single-dose or short-term treatment of uncomplicated cystitis in women.[26] It is equally effective if given for 3 days compared with treatment for 5–10 days, and a single dose is only slightly less effective than 3-day treatment. For other types of UTI, longer treatment times are required. In countries where resistant uropathogens are uncommon, single-dose or short-term TMP–SMX is an inexpensive and effective treatment of cystitis in women. For other types of infection, where longer treatment times are required, the relatively high frequency of potentially serious adverse reactions must be taken into account, and in adults a fluoroquinolone would probably be preferred in most patients.

Prostatitis is commonly treated with TMP–SMX and the few studies evaluating its use for this infection indicate a high degree of efficacy.[27]

For uncomplicated gonorrhea a single-dose of 640mg trimethoprim and 3200mg sulfamethoxazole was shown to be effective for 96% of 1069 patients and did not mask concurrent infections with *Treponema pallidum*.[28]

For *Haemophilus ducreyi* infections 160mg of trimethoprim plus 800mg sulfamethoxazole q12h for 3 days has given high cure rates, whereas shorter treatment times seem ineffective.[29,30]

Infections caused by *Chlamydia trachomatis* respond poorly to TMP–SMX.[30]

Enteric infections

These have been extensively treated with TMP–SMX because of its activity against *Salmonella* spp. (including *Salmonella typhi*), *Shigella* spp., *Vibrio cholerae* and enterotoxigenic *E. coli*. In a well-controlled trial in patients who had enteritis of verified etiology, the causative pathogens were eliminated on treatment day 2 in 41% of patients treated with TMP–SMX compared with 23% of those receiving placebo and 91% of patients on norfloxacin.[31]

A review of patients who had shigellosis showed that 97% of 149 patients treated with TMP–SMX responded clinically and 90% bacteriologically.[32] With the comparators (ampicillin, furazolidone or sulfadimidine) the clinical success rate was 78%. However, TMP–SMX may have lost some of its usefulness in shigellosis through the emergence of resistance.

Trimethoprim–sulfamethoxazole has been shown to be as effective as chloramphenicol for the treatment of enteric fever caused by susceptible strains of *S. typhi*.[33,34] However, a study comparing TMP–SMX with pefloxacin for this indication demonstrated a shorter time to defervescence with pefloxacin.[34]

In salmonellosis TMP–SMX is effective for treatment of invasive infections caused by sensitive strains, but, like other antibiotics, it seems less effective in eliminating the carrier state of *Salmonella* spp.[35]

Treatment of cholera should be aimed mainly at rehydration of the patients. However, antibiotics may reduce symptoms and shorten the duration of the carrier state of *V. cholerae*, thereby reducing the risk of transmission. Trimethoprim–sulfamethoxazole has proved effective in patients who have cholera and one study showed that it was better than tetracycline or sulfamethoxazole alone.[36]

In several studies TMP–SMX has been shown to be effective in preventing travelers' diarrhea.[37–39] However, it has also been found to select for resistance.[40] This aberration, plus the fact that serious adverse reactions are not uncommon, makes this type of prophylaxis of doubtful value.

Respiratory tract infections

Considering the etiology of such infections and the fact that the most important pathogen is *S. pneumoniae*, which at present is often resistant to TMP–SMX, the antibiotic has lost much of its usefulness in the treatment of community-acquired pneumonia. Also, its role in the treatment of acute exacerbations of chronic bronchitis should be questioned, although invasive pneumococcal infections are less common in this category of patients.

Trimethoprim–sulfamethoxazole has become a common alternative to β-lactam antibiotics for acute otitis media in children who have failed to respond to other antibiotics. This is probably due to its activity against *H. influenzae*. However, again the problem of resistant pneumococci limits its usefulness and TMP–SMX can not be recommended as empiric treatment.

In pneumonia caused by *Burkholderia pseudomallei*, melioidosis, TMP–SMX remains a choice for oral long-term treatment after standard treatment with ceftazidime, although some doubt exists about its effectiveness.[41]

Trimethoprim–sulfamethoxazole is the drug of choice for the treatment and prevention of *P. carinii* pneumonia.[42]

Other infections

Both trimethoprim and sulfamethoxazole penetrate the blood–cerebrospinal fluid barrier and the combination has been found to be effective in experimental bacterial meningitis.[43] Trimethoprim–sulfamethoxazole has therefore been used as a second-line drug for the treatment of bacterial meningitis. Favorable clinical results have been reported in the treatment of meningitis caused by *L. monocytogenes* as well as other types of meningitis.[44,45]

In patients who have brucellosis TMP–SMX can be considered a second-line drug.

Several studies have shown excellent clinical results with TMP–SMX, alone or in combination with aminoglycosides, in the treatment of actinomycosis or nocardiosis.[46]

A controversial field for the use of TMP–SMX is prophylaxis in neutropenic patients. Early studies showed significant protection against bacterial infections but others have shown the emergence of resistance, superinfections and high frequencies of side effects.[47] A reason for reassessing this indication is the possibility that some of these patients (e.g. those with megaloblastic leukemia) may be prone to develop serious hematologic side effects. Another argument against the use of TMP–SMX for prophylaxis in neutropenic patients is the possibility of reduced resistance to colonization with fecal flora.[4]

Pyrimethamine–sulfadiazine and pyrimethamine–sulfadoxine

Pyrimethamine–sulfadiazine remains the first-line drug combination for the treatment of toxoplasmosis.[48]

Pyrimethamine–sulfadoxine is an alternative for the treatment of *P. falciparum* malaria in areas with chloroquine resistance.[49] However, as pointed out above, resistance to pyrimethamine–sulfadoxine is not uncommon and safety aspects reduce its usefulness for prophylaxis.

DOSAGE IN SPECIAL CIRCUMSTANCES

Renal impairment results in prolonged elimination times. Table 197.6 gives dosages of sulfamethoxazole and trimethoprim in patients who had decreased renal function. This includes patients of advanced age. As pointed out, the above doses used in children should be higher than those in adults because of different kinetic profiles (see Table 197.1). All sulfonamides should be avoided in patients aged less than 6 weeks because of the risk of cerebral accumulation of free bilirubin (kernicterus). There are no recommendations for reduced dosage of folate inhibitors in patients who have hepatic disease. Most of the folate inhibitors pass to breast milk but at concentrations that make effects on the child unlikely. During pregnancy, trimethoprim and pyrimethamine should be avoided because of the possible risk of altered folate metabolism in the fetus. Sulfonamides should not be given during the last trimester of the pregnancy because of the risk of kernicterus.

ADVERSE REACTIONS AND INTERACTIONS

A summary of the potential adverse effects of folate inhibitors is given in Table 197.7.

EFFECT OF RENAL FUNCTION ON DOSAGE OF TRIMETHOPRIM AND SULFAMETHOXAZOLE

Creatinine clearance	Serum creatinine	Dosage
>25ml/min	<320μmol/l	Normal dose
15–25ml/min	320–405μmol/l	160mg trimethoprim + 800mg sulfamethoxazole q12h for 2 days and then every day until the serum concentration of sulfamethoxazole reaches >600μmol/l
<15ml/min	>405μmol/l	160mg trimethoprim + 800mg sulfamethoxazole q12h until the serum concentration of sulfamethoxazole reaches >600μmol/l

Table 197.6 Effect of renal function on dosage of trimethoprim and sulfamethoxazole.

ADVERSE ACTIONS OF FOLATE INHIBITORS IN HUMANS		
Body system	**Sulfonamides**	**Trimethoprim/pyrimethamine**
Central nervous system	'Kernicterus' in newborns	Aseptic meningitis, especially in patients who have collagen diseases
Liver	Toxic hepatitis	Probably none
Lung	None	None
Kidney	Crystalluria	Increased serum creatinine (inhibition of creatinine excretion)
Prostate/genitourinary	None	None

Table 197.7 Adverse actions of folate inhibitors in humans.

General safety profile

Several studies have shown a correlation between the treatment time and the risk of adverse reactions to TMP–SMX when used for uncomplicated UTIs.[26] As no differences have been found in the efficacy of short-term treatment and treatment for 5 days or longer, the use of TMP–SMX for more than 3 days for uncomplicated cystitis is discouraged.

Hematologic reactions

The mode of action of trimethoprim has caused concerns over possible bone marrow toxicity. Studies in patients treated for 1 month or more with TMP–SMX have shown moderate folate deficiency.[50–52] The possibility of immune reactions causing hematologic adverse effects has been proposed.[53]

Serious and even fatal hematologic adverse reactions to TMP–SMX have been reported. In a Swedish study of about 50 million daily doses an approximate frequency of fatal reactions to TMP–SMX was calculated to be 3.7/million treatments (data from SWEDIS, Medical Products Agency, Uppsala, Sweden). It was noteworthy that the mean age of the patients who died was 78 years (range 41–96 years) and that only three of 18 patients were below the age of 70. Taking into consideration the effect of aging on renal function, the doses of TMP–SMX were high. In addition, the treatment time was long (range 3–73 days, mean 17 days, median 12 days).

Pyrimethamine hematologic toxicity is less well described. Many use folinic acid to avoid folic acid deficiency. Support is lacking and hematologic reactions may very well be due to other mechanisms.

Skin, mucocutaneous and allergic reactions

These reactions may in some cases be serious, for example Stevens–Johnson or Lyell syndromes.[54,55] Such reactions seem to be related to the sulfonamide component rather than to trimethoprim.

It is worth noting that, in most reports on the safety of TMP–SMX or sulfonamides, skin reactions are only rarely reported in children. Possible explanations for this are the reduced risk for overdosing in children due to efficient elimination and less risk of sensitization to trimethoprim or sulfamethoxazole from previous exposures.

High numbers of serious cutaneous reactions have been reported following treatment with pyrimethamine–sulfadoxine.[56] Between 1974 and 1989, 126 cases of mucocutaneous syndromes were reported, giving an estimated risk of about 1.1/million treatments. This risk, which is most probably related to the sulfadoxine component, is considered to be high enough to discourage routine use of the combination for malaria prophylaxis.

Patients who have AIDS and *P. carinii* pneumonia and are treated with high doses of TMP–SMX have high frequencies of cutaneous reactions as well as other adverse reactions.[57–59] These reactions seem to be related to dose and treatment time, and many patients who have AIDS who have developed skin reactions later tolerate low-dose TMP–SMX prophylaxis against *P. carinii*.

Hepatic side effects

Cases of severe hepatic reactions to TMP–SMX have been reported and are most likely to be caused by the sulfonamide component.[60]

Gastrointestinal adverse reactions

Like many other orally administered antibiotics, TMP–SMX causes upper gastrointestinal adverse effects in some patients. Because of its low activity on the intestinal anaerobic flora it causes diarrhea only infrequently.

Renal safety

Sulfonamides with poor solubility can cause crystalluria. With sulfamethoxazole this does not seem to be a problem but, with sulfadiazine in high doses, crystalluria has been reported in AIDS patients who had toxoplasmal encephalitis.[61]

Increased serum creatinine in patients treated with TMP–SMX has been reported, but in most cases seems to be related to competitive inhibition of the renal excretion of creatinine by trimethoprim.[62]

Central nervous system reactions

Aseptic meningitis is related to trimethoprim therapy. Several cases have been reported in the literature with some over-representation of patients who have collagen vascular diseases (e.g. Sjögren's syndrome).[63,64] The pathogenesis remains obscure but seems to be of an allergic nature, with rapid onset and relapses after provocation.

Sulfonamides can cause central nervous system toxicity in newborns (kernicterus) because of displacement of bilirubin from albumin, resulting in toxic bilirubin concentrations in the brain.

INTERACTIONS BETWEEN TMP–SMX AND OTHER DRUGS	
Drug	**Interaction**
Sulfonylureas	Reduced clearance of tolbutamide; possible hypoglycemia
Dicoumarol	Reduced metabolism of dicoumarol
Warfarin	Reduced metabolism of warfarin
Digoxin	Reduced tubular secretion of digoxin
Procainamide	Reduced clearance of procainamide
Methotrexate	Possible increased risk of hematologic side effects
Ciclosporin A	Reversible decrease of renal function; risk of accumulation
Phenytoin	Reduced metabolism of phenytoin
Amantadine	Possible reduced excretion of amantadine
Zidovudine	Reduced excretion of TMP–SMX
Ritonavir	Reduced metabolism of sulfamethoxazole

Table 197.8 Interactions between trimethoprim–sulfamethoxazole and other drugs.

Drug–drug interactions

Considering the liver metabolism of trimethoprim, pyrimethamine and many of the sulfonamides, there is surprisingly little published on drug–drug interactions involving these drugs.[65,66] Table 197.8 lists possible interactions. The field needs further systematic evaluation, especially because TMP–SMX is likely to be used increasingly by patients who also receive other drugs (e.g. those who have AIDS and are treated for fungal and viral infections).

REFERENCES

1. Stokstad ELR, Jukes TH. Sulfonamide and folic acid antagonists: a historical overview. J Nutr 1987;11:1335–41.
2. Baccanari DP, Kuyper LF. Basis of selectivity of antibacterial diaminopyridines. J Chemother 1993;5:389–99.
3. Bowden K, Harris NV, Watson CA. Structure–activity relationships of dihydrofolate reductase inhibitors. J Chemother 1993;5:377–88.
4. Hughes WT. Trimethoprim and sulfonamides. In: Peterson PK, Verhoef J, eds. The antimicrobial agents annual, vol 1. Amsterdam: Elsevier; 1986:197–204.
5. Braga PC, Piatti G, Limoli A, Santoro T, Gazzola T. Inhibition of bacterial adhesion by sub-inhibitory concentrations of brodimoprim vs trimethoprim. J Chemother 1993;5:447–52.
6. Then R. Synergism between trimethoprim and sulphamethoxazole (letter). Science 1978;197:1301.
7. Brumfitt W, Hamilton-Miller JMT, Havard CW, Transley H. Trimethoprim alone compared to co-trimoxazole in lower respiratory tract infections; pharmacokinetics and clinical effectiveness. Scand J Infect Dis 1985;17:99–105.
8. Patel RB, Welling PG. Clinical pharmacokinetics of co-trimoxazole (trimethoprim/sulfamethoxazole). Clin Pharmacokinet 1980;5:405–23.
9. Spicehandler J, Pollock AA, Simberkoff MS, Rahal JJ Jr. Intravenous pharmacokinetics and *in vitro* bactericidal activity of co-trimoxazole. Rev Infect Dis 1982;4:562–5.
10. Siber GR, Gorham CC, Ericson JF, Smith AL. Pharmacokinetics of intravenous co-trimoxazole in children and adults with normal and impaired renal function. Rev Infect Dis 1982;4:566–78.
11. Goodhardt GL. *In vivo* versus *in vitro* susceptibility of enterococci to co-trimoxazole: a pitfall. JAMA 1984;252:2748–9.
12. Chattopadhya B. Trimethoprim–sulphamethoxazole in urinary infection due to *Streptococcus faecalis*. J Clin Pathol 1972;25:531–3.
13. Jorgensen JH, Doern GV, Maher LA, Howell AW, Redding JS. Antimicrobial resistance among respiratory isolates of *Haemophilus influenzae*, *Moraxella catarrhalis*, and *Streptococcus pneumoniae* in the United States. Antimicrob Agents Chemother 1990;34:2075–80.
14. Shibl AM, Hussein SS. Surveillance of *Streptococcus pneumoniae* serotypes in Riyadh and their susceptibility to penicillin and other commonly prescribed antibiotics. J Antimicrob Chemother 1992:29:149–57.
15. Liñares J, Oerez JL, Garau J, Murgui L, Martín R. Comparative susceptibilities of penicillin-resistant pneumococci to co-trimoxazole, vancomycin, rifampicin and fourteen β-lactam antibiotics. J Antimicrob Chemother 1984;13:353–9.
16. Marton A. Pneumococcal antimicrobial resistance: the problem in Hungary. Clin Infect Dis 1992;15:106–11.
17. Thornsberry C, Sahm DF, Kelly LJ, *et al.* Regional trends in antimicrobial resistance among clinical isolates of *Streptococcus pneumoniae*, *Haemophilus influenzae* and *Moraxella catarrhalis* in the United States. Results from the TRUST surveillance program 1999–2000. Clin Infect Dis 2002;34(Suppl.1):S4–16.
18. Lehtonen L, Houvinen P. Susceptibility of respiratory tract pathogens in Finland to cefixime and nine other antimicrobial agents. Scand J Infect Dis 1993;25:373–8.
19. Boisivon A, Guiomar C, Carbon C. *In vitro* bactericidal activity of amoxycillin, gentamicin, rifampicin, ciprofloxacin and co-trimoxazole alone or in combination against *Listeria monocytogenes*. Eur J Clin Microbiol Infect Dis 1990;9:206–9.
20. Manges AR, Johnson JRM Foxman B, O'Bryan TT, Fullerton KE, Riley LW. Widespread distribution of urinary tract infections caused by a multidrug-resistant *Escherichia coli* clonal group. N Engl J Med 2001;345:1007–13.
21. Karlowsky JA, Jones ME, Thornsberry C, Critchley I, Kelly LJ, Sahm DF. Prevalence of antimicrobial resistance among urinary tract pathogens Isolated from female outpatients across the US In 1999. Int J Antimicrob Agents 2001;18:121–7.
22. Brown PD, Freeman A, Foxman B. Prevalence and predictors of trimethoprim-sulfamethoxazole resistance among uropathogenic *Escherichia coli* isolates in Michigan. Clin Infect Dis 2002;34:1061–6.
23. Kauffman CA, Lipeman MA, Bergman AG, Mioduszewski J. Co-trimoxazole prophylaxis in neutropenic patients: reduction of infections and effects in bacterial and fungal flora. Am J Med 1983;74:599–607.
24. Wongsrichanalai C, Pickard AL, Wernsdorfer WH, Meshnick SR. Epidemiology of drug-resistant malaria. Lancet Infect Dis 2002;2:209–18.
25. Kovacs JA, Gill VJ, Meshnick S, Masur H. New insights into transmission, diagnosis, and drug treatment of *Pneumocystis carinii* pneumonia. JAMA 2001;286:2450–60.
26. Norrby SR. Short-term treatment of uncomplicated urinary tract infections in women. Rev Infect Dis 1990;12:458–67.
27. Meares EM Jr. Prostatitis: review of pharmacokinetics and therapy. Rev Infect Dis 1982;4:475–83.
28. Rahim G. Single-dose treatment of gonorrhoea. A report on 1,223 cases. Br J Vener Dis 1975;51:179–82.
29. Dylewski J, Nsanze H, D'Costa L, Slaney L, Ronald A. Trimethoprim sulphamethoxazole in the treatment of chancroid. Comparison of two single dose regimens with a five day regimen. J Antimicrob Chemother 1985;16:103–9.
30. Wilcox RR. How suitable are available pharmaceuticals for the treatment of sexually transmitted diseases? 1. Conditions presenting as genital discharges. Br J Vener Dis 1977;53:324–33.
31. Lolekha S, Patanchereon S, Thanangkul B, Vibulbandhitkit S. Norfloxacin versus co-trimoxazole in the treatment of acute bacterial diarrhoea: a placebo controlled study. Scand J Infect Dis 1988;56(Suppl.):35–45.
32. Nelson JD, Kusmiesz H, Shelton O. Oral or intravenous co-trimoxazole therapy for shigellosis. Rev Infect Dis 1982;4:546–50.
33. Keusch GT. Antimicrobial therapy for enteric infections and typhoid fever. Rev Infect Dis 1988;1(Suppl.1):199–205.
34. Hajji M, El-Mdajhri N, Benbachir M, Elî Filiali KM, Himmich A. Prospective randomized comparative trial of pefloxacin versus co-trimoxazole in the treatment of typhoid fever in adults. Eur J Clin Microbiol Infect Dis 1988;7:361–3.
35. Geddes AM, Fothergill R, Goodall JAD, Dorken PR. Evaluation of trimethoprim–sulphamethoxazole in treatment of salmonella infections. Br Med J 1971;3:451–4.
36. Cash RA, Northrop AS, Mizanur Rachman ASM. Trimethoprim and sulfamethoxazole in clinical cholera: comparison with tetracycline. J Infect Dis 1973;128(Suppl.):749–53.
37. DuPont HL, Evans DG, Rios N, Cabada FJ, Evans DJ Jr, DuPont MW. Prevention of travelers' diarrhea with co-trimoxazole. Rev Infect Dis 1982;4:533–9.
38. Ericsson CD, Johnson PC, DuPont HL, Morgan DR. Role of a novel antidiarrheal agent, BW942C, alone or in combination with co-trimoxazole in the treatment of travelers' diarrhea. Antimicrob Agents Chemother 1986;29:1040–6.
39. Ericsson CD, DuPont HL, Mathewson JJ, West MS, Johnson PC, Bitsura JM. Treatment of travelers' diarrhea with sulfamethoxazole and trimethoprim and loperamide. JAMA 1990;263:257–61.
40. Murray BE, Rensimer ER, DuPont HL. Emergence of high-level trimethoprim resistance in fecal *Escherichia coli* during oral administration of trimethoprim or trimethoprim–sulfamethoxazole. N Engl J Med 1982;306:130–5.
41. Sookprane M, Boonma P, Susaengrat W, Bhuripanyo K, Punyagupta S. Multicenter prospective randomized trial comparing ceftazidime plus co-trimoxazole with chloramphenicol plus doxycycline for treatment of severe doxycycline. Antimicrob Agents Chemother 1992;36:158–62.
42. Gallant JE, Moore RD, Cahisson RE. Prophylaxis for opportunistic infections in patients with HIV infection. Ann Intern Med 1994;120:932–44.
43. Mylotte JM, Bates TR, Sargeant KA, Matson RE, Beam TR Jr. Co-trimoxazole therapy of experimental *Escherichia coli* meningitis in rabbits. Antimicrob Agents Chemother 1981;20:81–7.
44. Levitz AJ, Quintiliani R. Co-trimoxazole for bacterial meningitis. Ann Intern Med 1984;100:881–90.
45. Spitzer PG, Hammer SM, Karchmer AW. Treatment of *Listeria* infections with co-trimoxazole: case report and review of the literature. Rev Infect Dis 1986;8:427–30.
46. Wallace RJ, Septimus EJ, Williams TW Jr, *et al.* Use of co-trimoxazole for the treatment of infections due to *Nocardia*. Rev Infect Dis 1982;4:315–25.
47. Welsh O, Sauceda E, Gonzalez J, Ocampo J. Amikacin alone and in combination with co-trimoxazole in the treatment of actinomycotic mycetoma. J Am Acad Dermatol 1987;17:443–8.
48. Vollard EJ, Clasener HAI, Janssen AJHM. Co-trimoxazole impairs colonization resistance in healthy volunteers. J Antimicrob Chemother 1992;30:685–91.
49. Georgiev VS. Management of toxoplasmosis. Drugs 1994;48:179–88.
50. Adagu IS, Wargurst DC, Ogala WN, Abdu-Aguye I, Bamgbola FO, Ovwigho UB. Antimalarial drug response of *Plasmodium falciparum* from Zaria, Nigeria. Trans R Soc Trop Med Hyg 1995;89:422–5.
51. Jenkins GC, Hughes DTD, Hall PC. A haematological study of patients receiving long-term treatment with trimethoprim and sulphonamide. J Clin Pathol 1970;23:392–6.
52. Hughes DTD, Jenkins GC, Gurney JD. The clinical, haematological and bacteriological

effects of long-term treatment with co-trimoxazole. J Antimicrob Chemother 1975;1:55–65.
53. Woods WG, Daigle AE, Hutchinson RJ. Myelosuppression associated with co-trimoxazole as prophylactic antibiotic in the maintenance phase of childhood acute lymphatic leukemia. J Pediatr 1984;105:639–44.
54. Bîttiger LE, Westerholm B. Adverse drug reactions during treatment of urinary tract infections. Eur J Clin Pharmacol 1977;11:439–42.
55. Lawson DH, Paice BJ. Adverse reactions to trimethoprim–sulfamethoxazole. Rev Infect Dis 1982;4:429–33.
56. Sturchler D, Mittleholzer ML, Kerr L. How frequent are notified severe adverse reactions to Fansidar? Drug Saf 1993;8:160–8.
57. Hughes WT, LaFon SW, Scott JD, Masur H. Adverse events associated with trimethoprim–sulfamethoxazole and ataquone during the treatment of AIDS-related *Pneumocystis carinii* pneumonia. J Infect Dis 1995;171:1295–301.
58. Hyperkalemia and high-dose trimethoprim–sulfamethoxazole. Ann Pharmacother 1995;29:427–9.
59. Roudier C, Caumes E, Rogeaux O, Bricaire F, Gentilini M. Adverse cutaneous reactions to trimethoprim–sulfamethoxazole in patients with the acquired immunodeficiency syndrome and *Pneumocystis carinii* pneumonia. Arch Dermatol 1994;130:1383–6.
60. Colucci CF, Cicero ML. Hepatic necrosis and trimethoprim–sulphamethoxazole. JAMA 1975;233:952–3.
61. Hein R, Brunkhorst R, Thon WF, Schedel I, Schmidt RE. Symptomatic sulfadiazine crystalluria in AIDS patients: a report of two cases. Clin Nephrol 1993;39:254–6.
62. Sandberg T, Trollfors B. Effect of trimethoprim on serum creatinine in patients with acute cystitis. J Antimicrob Chemother 1986;17:123–4.
63. Kremer I, Ritz R. Aseptic meningitis as an adverse effect of co-trimoxazole (letter). N Engl J Med 1983;308:1481.
64. Derbes SJ. Trimethoprim-induced aseptic meningitis. JAMA 1984;252:2865–6.
65. Carlson J, Wiholm BE. Trimethoprim associated aseptic meningitis. Scand J Infect Dis1987;19:787–91.
66. Salter AJ. Trimethoprim–sulfamethoxazole: an assessment of more than 12 years of use. Rev Infect Dis 1982;4:196–236.

chapter

198 Quinolones

Robin Howe & Alasdair MacGowan

INTRODUCTION

The quinolones are a heterogeneous group of synthetic antimicrobial agents. Originally deriving from 1,8-naphthyridine compounds (e.g. nalidixic acid), modern quinolones have evolved as shown in Figure 198.1 to give compounds initially with improved activity against Gram-negative bacteria (e.g. ciprofloxacin, ofloxacin) and more recently with greater activity against Gram positives (e.g. gatifloxacin, moxifloxacin). A number of broader spectrum agents have been developed (e.g. clinafloxacin, trovafloxacin) but have had to be withdrawn due to problems with toxicity.

Quinolones have excellent tissue and tissue fluid penetration so that they are suitable for infections in a wide range of organ systems. Adverse reactions are uncommon in marketed agents and relate mainly to the skin, the gastrointestinal system and central nervous system (CNS) and rarely warrant cessation of therapy. However, there are a number of potentially more serious adverse effects such as arthropathy, cardiotoxicity and phototoxicity. These occur as a class effect (although to different extents in different compounds) and have been a problem in drug development.

Modern fluoroquinolones are available in both intravenous and oral formulations. One of their major advantages has proved to be the ability to treat many serious infections with oral or intravenous–oral switch regimens, for example in the management of enteric fever, Gram-negative pyelonephritis, osteomyelitis, nosocomial pneumonia, severe exacerbations of both chronic bronchitis and cystic fibrosis. Many of the above previously demanded lengthy therapy with intravenous β-lactams, aminoglycosides or their combinations.

The activity of fluoroquinolones such as ciprofloxacin and ofloxacin in Gram-positive infections, notably those caused by pneumococci, has been disputed. Newer compounds, such as gatifloxacin and moxifloxacin, have markedly improved activity against Gram-positive pathogens and may find a place in the management of infections caused, for example, by penicillin-resistant pneumococci.

ANTIBACTERIAL SPECTRUM AND POTENCY

The antibacterial spectrum of quinolones is shown in Table 198.1. Quinolones are notable for the considerable knowledge that has been gained regarding structure–activity relationships.[1] The activity of the original naphthyridine and quinolone compounds (e.g. nalidixic acid) was limited to Gram-negative pathogens, primarily the Enterobacteriaceae, including Shigellae and Salmonellae. A major step forward in the development of the class was the addition of a fluorine at position 6, giving rise to the fluoroquinolones (Fig. 198.2). These agents are 10–100 times more active than their precursors against Gram-negative pathogens, including *Pseudomonas aeruginosa*, and have gained activity against the organisms causing atypical pneumonia. Potency, spectrum of activity and adverse effects/drug interactions are largely determined by substitutions at positions 1, 5, 6, 7 and 8:

- substitutions at position 1 (e.g. trovafloxacin) can alter potency (particularly against anaerobes) but may also affect interactions with theophyllines;
- substitutions at position 5 (e.g. grepafloxacin) can increase potency but may cause increased cardiotoxicity;
- substitutions at position 7 (e.g. moxifloxacin, gemifloxacin, garenoxacin) can increase activity against Gram-positive organisms and increase the plasma half-life;
- substitutions at position 8 (moxifloxacin, garenoxacin) can increase potency and reduce the rate selection of resistant mutants but can be associated with increased phototoxicity (sparfloxacin).

Early representatives such as ciprofloxacin only have borderline activity against Gram-positives pathogens. However, developments such as the addition at position 7 of a five-membered ring (gemifloxacin) or an azabicyclo group (moxifloxacin, garenoxacin) have brought increased Gram-positive activity. Unfortunately, this has been partly at the expense of some activity against *P. aeruginosa*. Agents with good activity against both Gram-positive and Gram-negative bacteria have been developed (e.g. clinafloxacin) but have been withdrawn due to toxicity problems.

Fluoroquinolones have good activity *in vitro* against many intracellular pathogens such as *Legionella* spp., *Mycoplasma* spp., *Ureaplasma urealyticum, Chlamydia* spp., *Brucella* spp., *Salmonella typhi* and *Coxiella burnettii*. This may be enhanced by the concentration of fluoroquinolones within cells (see below). As shown in Table 198.1, *Mycobacterium tuberculosis* is susceptible to most of the fluoroquinolones with greater activity displayed by most of the newer agents. Of the other Mycobacteria, *M. kansasii, M. marinum* and *M. fortuitum* tend to be fluoroquinolone susceptible, whereas *M. avium* complex, *M. chelonae* and *M. scrofulaceum* are more resistant.[2]

The quinolones are rapidly bactericidal against most susceptible species in a concentration-dependent manner and have a postantibiotic effect (PAE) of 2–4 hours. The pharmacodynamic determinants of efficacy are C_{max}/MIC (ratio of the maximum plasma concentration to MIC) and AUC_{0-24}/MIC (ratio of the area under the 24h drug concentration curve to MIC). Various groups have attempted to define the AUC_{0-24}/MIC ratio that would predict a successful outcome. It appears that the optimal ratio varies for different organisms so that a ratio of >125 has been proposed for infection caused by Gram-negative enteric pathogens and *P. aeruginosa*, but a much lower ratio of >34 is proposed for pneumococcal lower respiratory tract infections.[3,4]

MODE OF ACTION

Quinolones act by the rapid inhibition of bacterial DNA synthesis, leading to cell death. The primary targets are DNA gyrase and topoisomerase IV which are involved in the maintenance of the superhelical structure of DNA. Both enzymes are composed of two subunits that are homologous: DNA gyrase subunits encoded by *gyrA* and *gyrB*; topoisomerase IV encoded by *parC* (*grlA* in *Staphylococcus aureus*) and *parE* (*grlB* in *Staph. aureus*). Although inhibition of these enzymes is the most important determinant of antibacterial activity it appears that secondary activities may affect bactericidality.

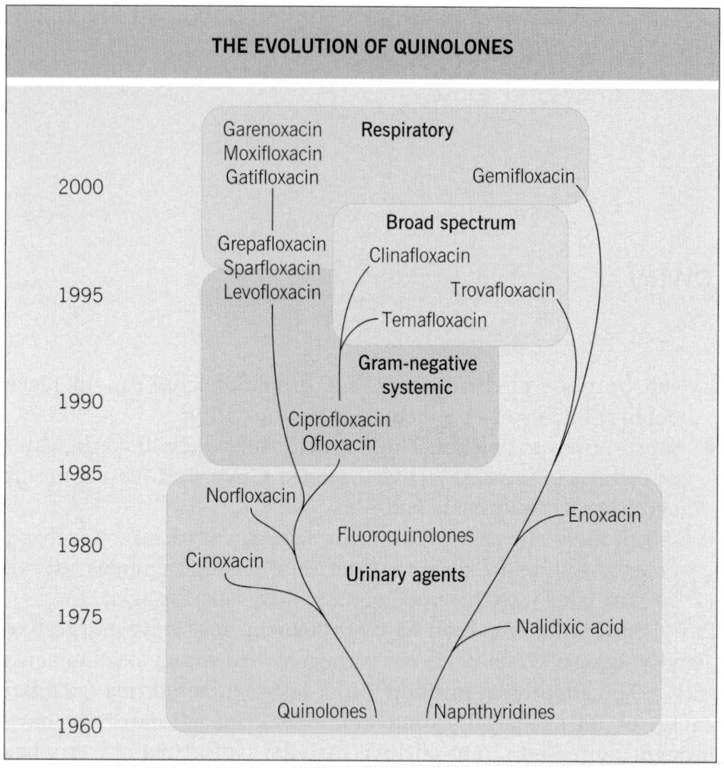

Fig. 198.1 The evolution of quinolones.

The addition of RNA and protein synthesis inhibitors or the use of high quinolone concentrations (which also inhibit RNA synthesis) can lead to a diminution in the cidality of some quinolones, suggesting that synthesis of some gene products contributes to the killing effect.

BACTERIAL RESISTANCE

The major mechanism for acquired resistance to quinolones is by mutational modification of the antimicrobial target site. Mutations around the active site of *gyrA* have been identified in many strains of *E. coli* and many other Gram-negative bacilli, giving rise to greater resistance to nalidixic acid than the fluoroquinolones. Alterations in *gyrB* are less common and cause lower levels of resistance.[5] The main site for resistance mutations in Gram positives such as *Staph. aureus* and *Streptococcus. pneumoniae* is the *parC* gene although mutations in *parE* have been described. In both Gram-negative and Gram-positive pathogens resistance develops in a stepwise fashion as mutations arise in one and then both targets. Following an initial mutation, the susceptibility to a quinolone will depend on the specificity of the agent for the alternative target. For example, in clinical practice it has been shown that an isolated *gyrA* mutation in *E. coli* will confer high-level resistance to nalidixic acid but only reduced susceptibility to ciprofloxacin. The acquisition of an additional *parC* mutation confers high-level resistance to ciprofloxacin.[6] For bacteria such as *P. aeruginosa* that inherently have less susceptibility to fluoroquinolones, a single mutation can give rise to clinically significant resistance.

Resistance to quinolones can also be achieved by active efflux of the drug from the bacterial cell. This has been best described in *P. aeruginosa* in which quinolone resistance has been associated with increased expression of the MexAB-OprM, MexCD-oprJ or MexEF-oprN efflux pumps.[7] In *E. coli* the pump is the acrAB-tolC system. Among Gram-positive pathogens, the *norA* pump has been described in *Staph. aureus* and the PmrA pump in *Strep. pneumoniae*.[8,9] On their own, efflux pumps will generally only cause low-level resistance and therefore may not be clinically important in inherently highly susceptible pathogens such as *E. coli*. However, the overexpression of efflux pumps becomes more significant in less susceptible organisms such as *P. aeruginosa*.

Resistance rates to quinolones have increased over the last decade. Ciprofloxacin resistance in the UK among *E. coli* increased from 0.8% to 3.7% between 1990 and 1999 when resistance was seen in 8.1% of *P. aeruginosa*.[10] Although methicillin-sensitive *Staph. aureus* is usually sensitive to fluoroquinolones, some clones of MRSA (e.g. EMRSA-16 seen in the UK) are resistant. Resistance among pneumococci remains uncommon although in some areas there is evidence that resistance is more common among penicillin-resistant pneumococci.[11]

Cross-resistance between fluoroquinolones is almost complete and minor differences in activity are not usually clinically exploitable. Cross-resistance to unrelated antimicrobials only occurs with overexpression of efflux pumps. In *P. aeruginosa*, for example, this leads to a low-level increase in resistance to chloramphenicol, tetracycline and macrolides.

PHARMACOKINETICS AND DISTRIBUTION

The quinolones are generally well absorbed and are widely distributed in body tissues and fluids, including the intracellular environment. They are excreted either by glomerular filtration or hepatic biotransformation or a combination of these routes, and by biliary or transintestinal elimination. Bio-availability is high and protein binding usually low to intermediate. Fluoroquinolone kinetics are summarized in Table 198.2.

Absorption

Fluoroquinolones are well and rapidly absorbed after oral administration and exhibit linear absorption kinetics so that doubling the dose produces twice the plasma level.[12] Peak plasma concentrations are usually present 1–2 hours after an oral dose. Absorption may be delayed by food and is impaired by co-administration of antacids and ferrous iron, and possibly by zinc in multivitamin preparations.

Distribution

The fluoroquinolones are extensively distributed to the tissues as can be seen in Table 198.3. Apparent volumes of distribution are usually 2–3l/kg although values for precursor compounds are lower (e.g. 0.5l/kg). Protein binding varies from 15–40% with norfloxacin, ofloxacin and ciprofloxacin[12] to 65% for gemifloxacin and higher still for garenoxacin and trovafloxacin (>80%).

Fluoroquinolones are concentrated approximately 10 times in polymorphoneutrophils (PMNs). Although it has been suggested that this may increase their *in vivo* efficacy against intracellular pathogens, there is evidence that the intracellular activity of different fluoroquinolones is variable, possibly related to where they are concentrated within the cell.[13] An additional result of the intracellular concentration of fluoroquinolones is that they may be transported by PMNs to a site of infection and then released.[14]

Elimination

Elimination half-lives vary from 1–2 hours for nalidixic acid to 3–5 hours for ciprofloxacin and 7–14 hours for newer agents.

Excretion of fluoroquinolones is primarily by renal glomerular filtration, hepatic metabolism and transintestinal elimination. The relative importance of glomerular filtration varies between agents and some compounds such as ofloxacin, levofloxacin and gatifloxacin exhibit minimal metabolism and are excreted largely unchanged in the urine. For these agents renal clearance almost equals total clearance and dose modification is required in renal

ACTIVITY OF QUINOLONES AGAINST COMMON PATHOGENIC BACTERIA										
Pathogen	Nalidixic acid	Norfloxacin	Ciprofloxacin	Ofloxacin	Levofloxacin	Grepafloxacin	Gemifloxacin	Gatifloxacin	Moxifloxacin	Garenoxacin
Streptococcus pneumoniae	>64	2–16	1–4	2–4	2	0.25	0.06	0.25	0.12	0.12
Staphylococcus aureus	>64	2	0.5–2	0.5–2	0.25	0.12	0.03	0.12	0.06	0.03
Enterococcus spp.	>64	8–16	1–8	2–8	2–8	1–16	0.25–>16	1–>16	0.5–4	0.5–8
β-Hemolytic streptococci	>64	4–8	2	4	1	0.25	0.03	0.5	0.25	0.12
Listeria spp.	NA	NA	1	2	1	NA	0.12	0.5	0.5	0.5
Haemophilus influenzae	1	0.25	0.03	0.03	0.03	0.016	0.015	0.03	0.06	0.03
Moraxella catarrhalis	4	0.25	0.06–0.25	0.12	0.06	0.015	0.03	0.12	0.12	0.03
Neisseria spp.	0.5	0.03	0.03	0.06	0.015	0.008	0.008	0.03	0.03	0.008
Escherichia coli	4–8	0.12–2	0.06–0.25	0.12–0.25	0.06–0.25	0.03	0.015	0.06–0.25	0.06	0.06–0.5
Klebsiella spp.	8–16	0.25–1	0.12–0.25	0.25–1	0.06–0.5	0.25–0.5	0.25	0.06–0.5	0.12–0.5	0.25–1
Enterobacter spp.	8–16	0.12–0.5	0.12–0.5	0.25–1	0.12–2	0.5–2	0.25–1	0.12–1	0.25	0.25–4
Salmonella spp.	2–4	0.25	0.12	0.25	0.25	0.015	0.06	0.06	0.25	0.12
Shigella spp.	8	0.25	0.12	0.25	0.03	0.008	0.008	0.03	0.06	0.03
Campylobacter spp.	8	0.25	0.12	0.25	0.12	NA	NA	0.12	0.06	0.12
Pseudomonas aeruginosa	>64	0.5–2	0.5–2	0.5–4	4	16	8	>4	8	16
Acinetobacter spp.	>64	>16	1–2	1–2	0.25–8	0.5–>16	0.5–>16	0.5–>16	0.25–16	0.12–8
Stenotrophomonas maltophilia	>64	NA	8	8	2–8	4	4	4	1	4
Bacteroides fragilis group	>64	16–32	4–16	8	2	8	1	1	0.5	0.5
Mycoplasma spp.	NA	4–16	1–2	1–2	0.5	0.12	0.12	0.12	0.12	0.06
Chlamydia spp.	NA	4–16	1–4	0.25–1	0.5	0.06	0.25	0.12	0.06	0.015
Legionella pneumophila	1	2	0.06	0.1	0.03	0.015	0.015	0.03	0.06	0.06
Mycobacterium tuberculosis	NA	2–8	1–4	0.5–2	1	NA	>4	0.25	0.12	2

Table 198.1 Activity of quinolones against common pathogenic bacteria: MIC_{90} (mg/l). NA, not available.

STRUCTURE OF QUINOLONES

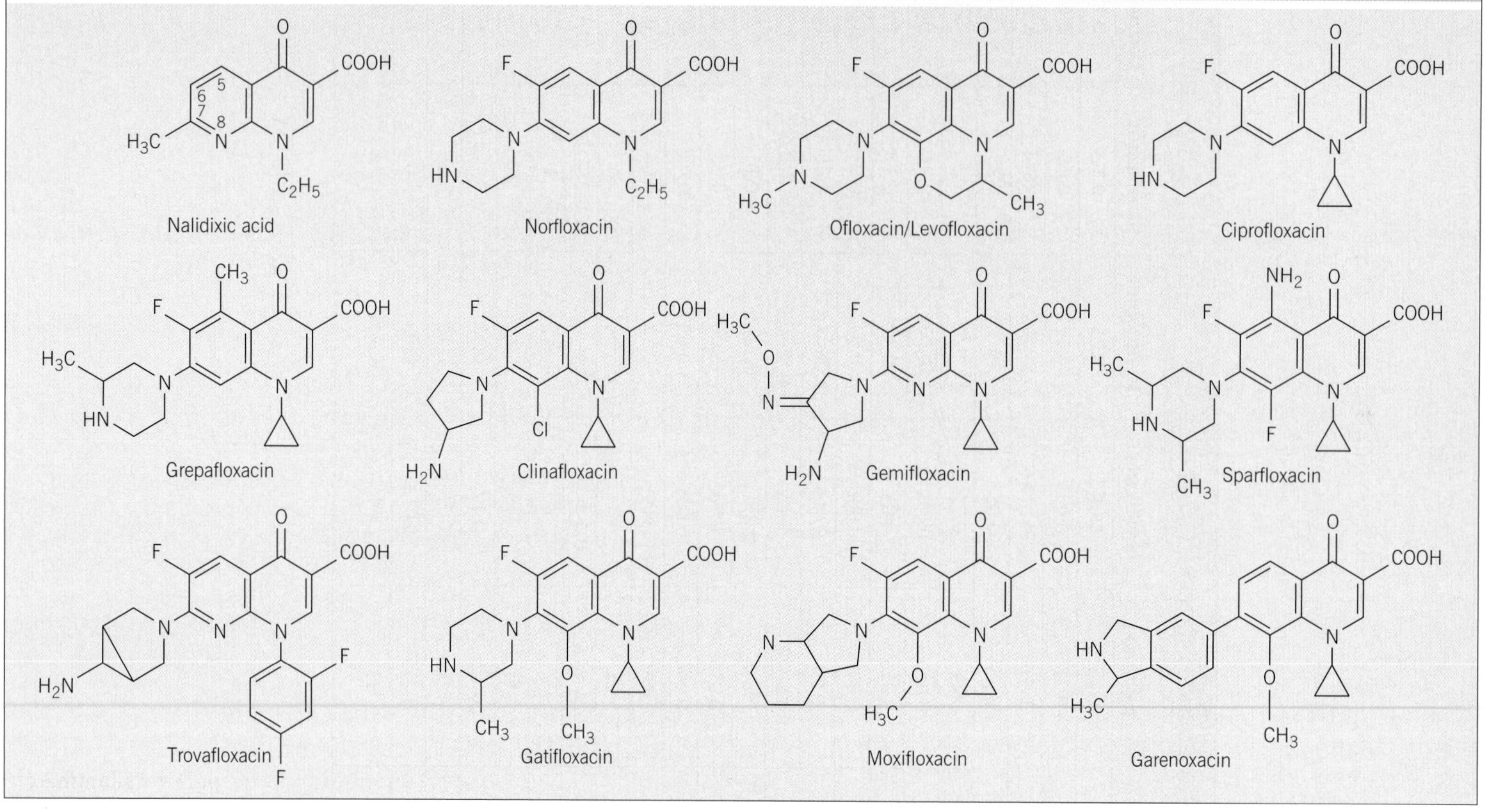

Fig. 198.2 Structure of quinolones.

BASIC PHARMACOKINETIC PARAMETERS OF QUINOLONES								
Agent	**Dose (g)**		**C_{max} (mg/l)**	**AUC_{0-24} (mg/lh)**	**$t^1/_2$ (h)**	**Protein binding %**	**% dose excreted unchanged in urine**	**Route**
Nalidixic acid	1	QDS	V	V	1.5	90	<1	po
Norfloxacin	0.4	BD	2	12.5	3	15	25–40	po
Ciprofloxacin	0.75	BD	3	30	4	40	30–50	po/iv
Ofloxacin	0.4	BD	6	80	7	30	70–85	po/iv
Levofloxacin	0.5	OD	6.4	54	7	40	85–90	po/iv
Grepafloxacin	0.4	OD	2.2	14	14	50	<10	po
Gatifloxacin	0.4	OD	4.6	37	9	20	70–80	po/iv
Gemifloxacin	0.32	OD	1.8	9	7	65	30	po
Moxifloxacin	0.4	OD	4.5	44	13	50	20	po/iv
Garenoxacin	0.4	OD	6.5	84	12.5	80	40	po/iv

Table 198.2 Basic pharmacokinetic parameters of quinolones. V, variable.

impairment.[12,15] Others, such as ciprofloxacin and moxifloxacin, have moderately extensive hepatic biotransformation (to oxo-, desethyl- and sulfo- derivatives – subsequently partly eliminated as inactive glucuronides in the bile). For these compounds renal clearance is half of the total clearance and dosage modification may not be required in renal impairment as long as other routes of elimination are intact.[16]

In hepatic impairment, the dosage of agents primarily cleared by the kidney (ciprofloxacin, ofloxacin and levofloxacin) rarely requires modification. However, for extensively metabolized drugs such as grepafloxacin, dose modification is necessary in patients with cirrhosis.

Fluoroquinolones that are not primarily eliminated by the kidney are present in significant quantities in the stool, partly by biliary excretion and, notably with ciprofloxacin, by transintestinal elimination. The majority is bound to ligands in the stool.

ROUTE OF ADMINISTRATION AND DOSAGE

Most agents are available in both oral and intravenous formulations. The high oral bio-availability of fluoroquinolones means that oral administration is adequate in most situations unless this route is unavailable. The manufacturer's dosage recommendations for quinolones are given in Table 198.4.

TISSUE DISTRIBUTION OF FLUOROQUINOLONES	
Tissue	**Tissue: plasma ratio**
Lung	
Bronchial mucosa	1.6
Epithelial lining fluid	2.1–8.7
Alveolar macrophages	11.8–21
CSF	
Uninflamed meninges	<0.1
Inflamed meninges	0.3–0.5
Brain tissue	0.9
Skin/soft tissue	
Skin	1.8
Muscle	3.3
Subcutaneous tissue	~1
Blister fluid	~1
Sweat	2.5
Prostate	
Prostatic tissue	2.1–5.7
Prostatic fluid	0.25
Seminal fluid	6–8
Eye	
Aqueous humor	0.5
Kidney	
Kidney tissue	~6
Urine	~100
Liver	
Hepatic tissue	4
Bile	6
Heart	
Myocardium	2–4
Heart valves	~1

Table 198.3 Tissue distribution of fluoroquinolones.

INDICATIONS

Early quinolones such as nalidixic acid were largely used for Gram-negative UTI and shigellosis. The development and evolution of fluoroquinolones have led to a number of agents with differences in spectrum of activity and therefore indications. Some, such as norfloxacin, are used almost exclusively for UTI. Agents such as ciprofloxacin and ofloxacin have been used for a broad range of infective syndromes. Newer compounds, such as levofloxacin, grepafloxacin, gatifloxacin and moxifloxacin, have improved activity against Gram-positive pathogens and may be more appropriate for respiratory tract infections.

Genitourinary tract infections

Uncomplicated lower urinary tract infection

Oral fluoroquinolone therapy is highly effective but to limit selection pressure for resistance should be used only when bacterial resistance precludes the use of other agents. Fluoroquinolones eradicate bowel reservoirs of uropathogenic *E. coli* and may reduce the incidence of early recurrence. Long-term suppression with low-dose norfloxacin or ciprofloxacin has been shown to be effective in preventing recurrent UTI in selected patients.[17,18]

Complicated ascending urinary tract infection

Fluoroquinolones given for 1–2 weeks are the recommended agents for the treatment of ascending or complicated UTI.[19] Oral ciprofloxacin has proved as efficacious as an intravenous regimen for initial empiric therapy.[20]

Prostatitis

Fluoroquinolones are concentrated in prostatic tissue and are recommended therapy for both acute and chronic bacterial prostatitis.[21] Ciprofloxacin for 28 days can give a clinical response of 98% in chronic bacterial prostatitis although relapse may occur in up to 40% of patients.[22]

Gonorrhoea

Single-dose oral therapy with ciprofloxacin or ofloxacin is equivalent to other parenteral single-dose regimens and is therefore a recommended choice in the management of uncomplicated urethral gonorrhea.[23] Pharyngeal and rectal disease also respond. However, quinolone resistance is emerging, particularly in South East Asia where high-level resistance can be found in up to 50% of isolates.[24]

Nongonococcal urethritis/cervicitis

The antichlamydial activity of fluoroquinolones varies and ofloxacin is the most potent of the established agents. A 7-day course of ofloxacin is as effective as doxycycline therapy.[25] Newer compounds such as moxifloxacin have excellent *in vitro* activity and may have a role in therapy.

Chancroid

A 3-day course of ciprofloxacin gives excellent cure rates, equivalent to standard β-lactam or trimethoprim–sulfamethoxazole (co-trimoxazole) therapy.[26]

Pelvic inflammatory disease

The ideal antimicrobial treatment for acute pelvic inflammatory disease has not been established by randomized clinical trials. However, ofloxacin is active against many of the potentially causal pathogens and is included in recommended treatment regimes.[23]

Respiratory tract infections

The fluoroquinolones ciprofloxacin and ofloxacin have been used extensively for upper and lower respiratory tract infections. However, there have been concerns regarding their activity against *Strep. pneumoniae*. Newer agents, such as gatifloxacin, gemifloxacin, moxifloxacin and garenoxacin, have improved activity against pneumococci, including macrolide- and penicillin-resistant strains, and are often termed 'respiratory quinolones'.

Sinusitis

Oral fluoroquinolones have comparable efficacy to macrolides or cephalosporins and give cure rates of >85% in acute sinusitis.[27–29]

Ear infections

Topical preparations of ofloxacin or ciprofloxacin are effective for the treatment of acute otitis media in children with tympanostomy tubes and for chronic suppurative otitis media.[30] Clinical cure rates of >85% for otitis externa can be obtained with the topical preparations. Malignant otitis externa, which is usually caused by *P. aeruginosa*, can be treated with oral ciprofloxacin. A prolonged course is required (3 months) and gives cure rates in excess of 90%.[31]

Acute exacerbations of chronic bronchitis

Fluoroquinolones are among the agents of choice for the management of moderate to severe exacerbations of chronic bronchitis. They have equivalent efficacy to macrolides or β-lactam/β-lactamase inhibitor combinations and achieve cure rates of >90%.[32,33]

Community-acquired pneumonia

Older quinolones are not indicated for pneumococcal pneumonia when alternative antibiotics are available. However, results with

DOSING RECOMMENDATIONS FOR QUINOLONES

	Nalidixic acid	Norfloxacin	Ofloxacin	Ciprofloxacin		Levofloxacin	Gatifloxacin	Moxifloxacin
	po	po	po/iv	po	iv	po/iv	po/iv	po/iv
Urinary tract infection	500–1000mg qds	400mg bd (3–21 days)	200mg bd (3–10 days)	100–500mg bd (3–14 days)	200–400mg bd (7–14 days)	250mg od (3–10days)	200–400mg od (3–10 days)	
Chronic bacterial prostatitis		400mg bd (28 days)	300mg bd (6 weeks)	500mg bd (28 days)	400mg bd (28 days)			
Acute sinusitis				500mg bd (10 days)	400mg bd (10 days)	500mg od (10–14 days)	400mg od (10 days)	400mg od (10 days)
Acute bacterial exacerbation of chronic bronchitis			400mg bd (10 days)	500–750mg bd (7–14 days)	400mg bd-tds (7–14 days)	500mg od (7 days)	400mg od (5 days)	400mg od (5 days)
Community-acquired pneumonia			400mg bd (10 days)			500mg od (7–14 days)	400mg od (7–14 days)	400mg od (7–14 days)
Skin and skin structure infection			400mg bd (10 days)	500–750mg bd (7–14 days)	400mg bd-tds (7–14 days)	500–750mg od (7–14 days)		400mg od (7 days)
Bone and joint infection				500–750mg bd (≥4–6 weeks)	400mg bd-tds (≥4–6 weeks)			
Intra-abdominal infection				500mg bd (7–14 days)	400mg bd (7–14 days)			
Infectious diarrhea				500mg bd (5–10 days)				
Uncomplicated urethral and cervical gonorrhea		800mg single dose	400mg single dose	250mg single dose			400mg single dose	
Nongonococcal cervicitis/urethritis			300mg bd (7 days)					
Pelvic inflammatory disease			400mg bd (10–14 days)					
Inhalational anthrax (postexposure)				500mg bd (60 days)	400mg bd (60 days)			

Table 198.4 Dosing recommendations for quinolones (from manufacturers' data sheets).

ciprofloxacin and ofloxacin suggest clinical response and bacterial eradication rates of 90% or greater and with levofloxacin, equivalence or superiority to ceftriaxone.[34] However, concerns have been raised regarding the efficacy of ciprofloxacin in severe pneumococcal pneumonia following reports of clinical failures.[35] Failures with levofloxacin have also been reported and in Europe it is suggested that it should be given at an increased dose of 500mg BD or in combination with benzyl penicillin in cases of severe pneumonia.[36,37] Newer agents such as gatifloxacin, gemifloxacin and moxifloxacin, which have improved activity against pneumococci and also atypical pathogens, show promising results in clinical trials with clinical cure rates in excess of 90%.[38] Although there are few specific data regarding infections with penicillin-resistant pneumococci, trovafloxacin gives clinical success rates of over 95%. Legionellosis can be successfully treated with quinolones such as ciprofloxacin, ofloxacin or levofloxacin. There are few clinical data to show whether or not they are superior to macrolides and often they are given in combination with a macrolide or rifampicin.[39]

Nosocomial pneumonia

A large-scale study of ciprofloxacin showed equivalence with imipenem in moderately to severely ill patients, most of whom required ventilation and treatment in an intensive care unit.[40] In the 20–25% with infection caused by *P. aeruginosa*, the results with both regimens were less satisfactory, underlining the need for combination therapy. Newer fluoroquinolones such as gemifloxacin, gatifloxacin and moxifloxacin have reduced *in vitro* potency against *P. aeruginosa* and will probably not have a role in the management of hospital-acquired pneumonia where *Pseudomonas* is a likely etiological agent.

Cystic fibrosis

Oral ciprofloxacin is effective for exacerbations caused by *P. aeruginosa*, producing results equivalent to those of standard β-lactam and aminoglycoside therapy. In the UK a 3-week course of ciprofloxacin combined with colistin is recommended for the treatment of early pseudomonal infection.[41]

Mycobacterial infections

Ofloxacin and ciprofloxacin have moderate activity against *Mycobacterium tuberculosis* and are bactericidal *in vivo*.[42] Their role in therapy is currently limited to use in combination regimens for the treatment of multiply drug-resistant *Mycobacterium tuberculosis* infection.[43] Newer agents such as moxifloxacin have enhanced antimycobacterial activity and animal studies suggest they may have a future role in antituberculous chemotherapy.[44]

As noted above, the susceptibility of nontuberculous mycobacteria to fluoroquinolones is variable. *Mycobacterium avium* complex is relatively resistant to quinolones. Nevertheless, the addition of ciprofloxacin to standard therapeutic combinations has been shown to be of benefit in HIV patients with disseminated disease.[45]

Skin and soft tissue infections

The fluoroquinolones give excellent results when compared with cephalosporins for the treatment of both uncomplicated and complicated skin and soft tissue infections.[46,47] However, more effective agents are routinely available for Gram-positive infections and usefulness in MRSA infections is limited by high rates of quinolone resistance.

Skeletal infections

Oral fluoroquinolones are highly effective for Gram-negative mixed acute (or chronic) contiguous osteomyelitis, giving cure rates of 80–90% after 3–6-month courses. They are also effective for post-surgical cases, salmonella osteitis and in some cases of chronic *P. aeruginosa* osteomyelitis (ciprofloxacin), although resistance may emerge causing a failure of treatment or relapse.[48] In patients with orthopedic prostheses infected with staphylococci, ciprofloxacin or ofloxacin in combination with rifampicin have been successfully used for conservative management (i.e. preserving the prosthesis).[49,50]

Gastrointestinal infections

Typhoid and paratyphoid fevers

Ciprofloxacin or ofloxacin are the agents of choice for typhoid and paratyphoid fevers.[51] Convalescent excretion states and long-term fecal carriage are rare after fluoroquinolone therapy, thereby reducing the human reservoir and possibly leading to a fall in incidence. Carriage states persisting after other antibiotic therapy may also respond to fluoroquinolones.

Decreased quinolone susceptibility has emerged in Asia over the last 10 years. Strains are typically resistant to nalidixic acid and have raised MICs of ciprofloxacin of 0.5–1mg/l. These strains are ciprofloxacin susceptible by NCCLS or BSAC criteria but there is evidence that infection by such strains responds less well to ciprofloxacin and longer courses or alternative agents are recommended.[52]

Salmonellosis

A 5–7-day course of oral fluoroquinolone is effective in reducing the duration and severity of severe salmonellosis.

Cholera

Three-day courses of oral fluoroquinolones are equal to standard trimethoprim-sulfamethoxazole or tetracycline regimens. A cure rate of >90% can be achieved with a single 1g dose of ciprofloxacin.[53]

Shigellosis

Fluoroquinolones are drugs of choice for invasive shigellosis. A single oral dose (ciprofloxacin 1g) is effective in adults.

Campylobacter

Fluoroquinolones have been used for gastrointestinal *Campylobacter* infections. However, resistance levels are increasing and may be as high as 50% in some areas of the world.[54]

Travelers' diarrhea

Ciprofloxacin or norfloxacin in full oral dosage for 5 days is effective for 80% of unprotected subjects who develop profuse diarrhea (>3–5 watery stools/day).

Other treatment indications

Ocular infections

Topical fluoroquinolones are effective for the treatment of bacterial conjunctivitis and keratitis. Penetration of systemic quinolones into the vitreous is relatively good but may not exceed the MICs of all likely pathogens. Intravitreal ciprofloxacin has been used in the treatment of endophthalmitis.[55]

Infections associated with chronic ambulatory peritoneal dialysis

Ciprofloxacin and ofloxacin have been used with success both orally and intraperitoneally. However, the emergence of resistant staphylococcal infection has limited their usefulness as monotherapy.

Q fever

Fluoroquinolones are active against *Coxiella burnetii in vitro* and a combination of a fluoroquinolone (ofloxacin) with doxycycline has been suggested for Q fever endocarditis.[56]

Anthrax

A 60-day course of ciprofloxacin is recommended for postexposure prophylaxis against anthrax.[57] In patients with inhalational anthrax a combination of ciprofloxacin plus another active agent (e.g. doxycycline) is recommended.[58]

Meningitis

Fluoroquinolones have been successfully used for Gram-negative meningitis.[59] Newer agents such as moxifloxacin show promising results in animal models of pneumococcal meningitis.[60] Trovafloxacin had comparable efficacy to ceftriaxone in a trial of pediatric meningitis.[61]

Chemoprophylaxis

Meningococcal infection

Single-dose (500mg) ciprofloxacin is effective in eradicating nasopharyngeal carriage in over 95% of subjects.[62]

Neutropenic patients

Norfloxacin, ofloxacin and ciprofloxacin have been widely used in the prophylaxis of opportunistic infection among neutropenic patients. Although prophylaxis has been shown to prevent febrile episodes of an infectious nature, current recommendations do not suggest their use due to concerns regarding the emergence and spread of antimicrobial resistance.[63]

Travelers' diarrhea

Once-daily prophylactic use of a fluoroquinolone (e.g. norfloxacin 400mg or ciprofloxacin 500mg) for the duration of potential exposure gives 75–90% protection from travelers' diarrhea caused by enterotoxigenic *E. coli* and other bacterial enteropathogens.

Surgical infections

Fluoroquinolones have been used effectively for the prevention of infection following transurethral prostatectomy and biliary surgery.

Pediatric use of fluoroquinolones

Pediatric use of fluoroquinolones has been limited by concerns regarding arthropathy observed in weight-bearing diarthrodial joints in juvenile dogs after prolonged high-dose administration. Nevertheless, accumulated experience has established some situations when the benefits of fluoroquinolones outweigh potential risks. These include typhoid fever, cholera and shigellosis, complicated UTI due to multiresistant pathogens, chronic suppurative otitis media caused by *P. aeruginosa*, multiresistant Gram-negative sepsis (including osteomyelitis), prophylaxis of meningococcemia (single-dose) and infection in neutropenia.

Treatment of pseudomonal infections in patients with cystic fibrosis is one of the commonest indications for the use of fluoroquinolones in children. Prolonged courses are often given but there has been little evidence of related arthropathy and fluoroquinolones continue to be widely used.

MANUFACTURERS' DOSAGE RECOMMENDATIONS FOR PATIENTS WITH RENAL IMPAIRMENT			
	Renal impairment		Hemodialysis/CAPD
	Mild	Moderate/severe	
Ciprofloxacin (iv)		200–400mg 18–24 hourly (CC = 5–29ml/min)	
Ciprofloxacin (po)	250–500mg bd (CC = 30–50ml/min)	250–500mg 18 hourly (CC = 5–29ml/min)	250–500mg od after dialysis
Ofloxacin	400mg od (CC = 20–50ml/min)	200mg od (CC <20ml/min)	
Levofloxacin	250mg od* (CC = 20–50ml/min)	250mg 48 hourly* (CC = 10–19ml/min)	250mg 48 hourly* (CC = 10–19ml/min)
Norfloxacin		400mg od (CC <30ml/min)	
Gatifloxacin		200mg od** (CC <40ml/min)	200mg od** (CC <40ml/min)
Moxifloxacin	No adjustment required		

CC, creatinine clearance
* Initial loading dose of 500mg
** Short courses up to 3 days do not require dosage alteration

Table 198.5 Manufacturers' dosage recommendations for patients with renal impairment.

DOSAGE IN SPECIAL CIRCUMSTANCES

Renal impairment

The extent to which the dosage requires modification is dependent on the degree of renal elimination. Table 198.5 shows the manufacturer's recommendations for selected quinolones. Essentially, agents such as ofloxacin and levofloxacin that are extensively renally excreted have the dose reduced to one-quarter of the normal daily dose in severe renal impairment and most other agents have the dose halved. However, as noted above, there is evidence that ciprofloxacin may not require dose modification as long as alternative routes of elimination are intact.[16] Moxifloxacin, which has only 20% renal excretion, does not require dose modification.

Hepatic impairment

Apart for extensively metabolized quinolones, such as pefloxacin, dose modification is not necessary in patients with hepatic impairment. However, experience with newer agents such as moxifloxacin in patients with severe liver failure (Child Pugh Class C) is limited.

Elderly patients

No specific changes in dosage are required for the elderly provided appropriate changes are made for reduced renal clearance.

Pediatrics

Optimal pediatric doses have not been established. Suggested doses of ciprofloxacin are 7.5–40mg/kg/day (oral) or 5–10mg/kg/day (intravenous) administered on a 8–12-hourly basis.

Pregnancy and lactation

Quinolones are not approved for use in pregnancy or during lactation.

ADVERSE REACTIONS AND INTERACTIONS

Adverse drug reactions

Fluoroquinolones are generally well tolerated although there are a number of potentially serious adverse effects that have been seen in some agents.[64] When adverse effects are reported, they are usually gastrointestinal (2–20%), dermatologic (0.5–3%) and CNS (0.5–2%) reactions which rarely necessitate withdrawal of therapy (1–3%). In most cases there are no specific age or racially related effects, but adverse drug reactions are more common in neutropenic patients and possibly in people who have AIDS.

Most fluoroquinolone adverse drug reactions are class effects, but incidence varies between compounds and can often be related to the specific structure of different agents. Certain group members have specific effects or more serious class effects that have led to restrictions on use or withdrawal. For example, the phototoxicity of sparfloxacin has restricted licensing by some registration authorities and temafloxacin, which caused hemolytic uremic syndrome and hypoglycemia, was withdrawn in 1992.

Gastrointestinal reactions

The usual reported symptoms are nausea, anorexia and dyspepsia. While diarrhea, abdominal pain and vomiting are less frequent, they are more likely to result in discontinuation of treatment. Antibiotic-associated diarrhea caused by *Clostridium difficile* is uncommon following fluoroquinolone therapy. Liver enzyme abnormalities occur in 2–3% of patients receiving fluoroquinolones and are usually mild and reversible. However, more severe liver abnormalities have been seen with some agents which, in the case of trovafloxacin, led to its withdrawal.

Dermatologic reactions

Although non-specific skin rashes, pruritus and urticaria have been reported, it is phototoxicity that has received most attention. This is a class effect and is thought to be related to the photodegradation of the fluoroquinolone and its ability to induce free radicals. The incidence and severity of phototoxicity differ between agents. Structurally, a fluorine moeity at position 8 causes more phototoxicity and sparfloxacin, which has this moiety, has caused a higher rate of phototoxicity. Phototoxic reactions are rare with ciprofloxacin, ofloxacin and levofloxacin. Gemifloxacin can cause a nonphototoxic rash which is seen particularly in female patients between the ages of 20 and 40 years.

Central nervous system reactions

These occur in less than 2% of patients with most fluoroquinolones and usually manifest as headache, dizziness, mild tremor or drowsiness. Convulsions occur rarely both as a primary effect and as a result of interactions with theophylline or nonsteroidal anti-inflammatory drugs (NSAIDs). Although the mechanism of quinolone toxicity has not been fully elucidated, it is believed to be due to inhibition of $GABA_A$ receptors.

Musculoskeletal effects

Fluoroquinolones as a class produce destructive arthropathy in weight-bearing, diarthrodial joints of juvenile animals, notably dogs, by production of cartilage erosions after prolonged high dosage. Some agents, notably precursors such as nalidixic acid, are considerably more likely to induce arthropathy. This effect has never been observed in human children and MRI follow-up and autopsy studies in children receiving both nalidixic acid and modern fluoroquinolones have revealed no evidence of joint damage.[65] Experience with ciprofloxacin in 1500 children noted reversible arthralgia in 3.2% of patients treated for pulmonary exacerbations of cystic fibrosis.[66]

Tendinitis occurs rarely as a class effect although it may be more common with concomitant corticosteroid therapy. The Achilles tendon is most commonly affected and patients are usually >50 years of age. MRI can be useful for early detection of damage and discontinuation is recommended at the first sign of tendon pain or inflammation.

Cardiovascular effects

Cardiotoxicity is manifest as prolongation of the QT interval with the potential to cause ventricular arrhythmias. The significance of this effect varies between agents and appears to be affected by substitutions at position 5 (see Fig. 198.2).[67] Adverse effects due to cardiotoxicity are rare although recently grepafloxacin was withdrawn voluntarily following reports of seven cardiac-related fatalities.

Other (rare) effects

Hypersensitivity occurs at a frequency of ~1%. Crystalluria and secondary interstitial nephritis are rare and relate to pH-associated solubility of fluoroquinolones in urine.

Interactions with other drugs

Interactions largely occur as a result of interference with fluoroquinolone absorption or by inhibition of biotransformation of unrelated drugs by the hepatic cytochrome P450 isoenzyme system. Central nervous system interactions due to GABA receptor inhibition occur with NSAIDs, notably fenbufen, and convulsions may follow, as reported with enoxacin.

Interactions affecting absorption of fluoroquinolones

The absorption of fluoroquinolones is reduced by up to 80% by co-administration of aluminium and magnesium-containing antacids, probably by the formation of insoluble complexes and, to a lesser extent, by calcium antacids, sucralfate and ferrous iron preparations. H_2-antagonists have no effect.

Interactions affecting drug metabolism

Fluoroquinolones reduce the hepatic clearance of xanthines via the P450 cytochrome system. The effect is most marked with enoxacin and grepafloxacin, but ciprofloxacin and pefloxacin also reduce clearance of theophylline by 30% and co-administration may result in theophylline toxicity, usually nausea but possibly convulsions. Dosage of theophylline should be interrupted or reduced and serum levels monitored if enoxacin, pefloxacin or ciprofloxacin is to be administered.

A similar effect, induced by the same fluoroquinolones, is responsible for inhibition of caffeine metabolism and resultant insomnia. Metabolism of warfarin, cimetidine and cyclosporin is affected much less by P450 cytochrome inhibition and interaction may not be clinically significant.

REFERENCES

1. Tillotson GS. Quinolones: structure-activity relationships and future predictions. J Med Microbiol 1996;44:320–4.
2. Vacher S, Pellegrin JL, Leblanc F, Fourche J, Maugein J. Comparative antimycobacterial activities of ofloxacin, ciprofloxacin and grepafloxacin. J Antimicrob Chemother 1999;44:647–52.
3. Forrest A, Nix DE, Ballow CH, Goss TF, Birmingham MC, Schentag JJ. Pharmacodynamics of intravenous ciprofloxacin in seriously ill patients. Antimicrob Agents Chemother 1993;37:1073–81.
4. Ambrose PG, Grasela DM, Grasela TH, Passarell J, Mayer HB, Pierce PF. Pharmacodynamics of fluoroquinolones against *Streptococcus pneumoniae* in patients with community-acquired respiratory tract infections. Antimicrob Agents Chemother 2001;45:2793–7.
5. Wiedemann B, Heisig P. Mechanisms of quinolone resistance. Infection 1994;22:S73–9.
6. McDonald LC, Chen FJ, Lo HJ, *et al.* Emergence of reduced susceptibility and resistance to fluoroquinolones in Escherichia coli in Taiwan and contributions of distinct selective pressures. Antimicrob Agents Chemother 2001;45:3084–91.
7. Zhang L, Li XZ, Poole K. Fluoroquinolone susceptibilities of efflux-mediated multidrug-resistant Pseudomonas aeruginosa, Stenotrophomonas maltophilia and Burkholderia cepacia. J Antimicrob Chemother 2001;48:549–52.
8. Piddock LJ, Johnson MM. Accumulation of 10 fluoroquinolones by wild-type or efflux mutant Streptococcus pneumoniae. Antimicrob Agents Chemother 2002;46:813–20.
9. Aeschlimann JR, Kaatz GW, Rybak MJ. The effects of NorA inhibition on the activities of levofloxacin, ciprofloxacin and norfloxacin against two genetically related strains of Staphylococcus aureus in an *in-vitro* infection model. J Antimicrob Chemother 1999;44:343–9.
10. Livermore DM, James D, Reacher M, *et al.* Trends of fluoroquinolone (ciprofloxacin) resistance in enterobacteriaceae from bacteremias, England and Wales, 1990–1999. Emerg Infect Dis 2002;8:473–8.
11. Goldsmith CE, Moore JE, Murphy PG, Ambler JE. Increased incidence of ciprofloxacin resistance in penicillin-resistant pneumococci in Northern Ireland. J Antimicrob Chemother 1998;41:420–1.
12. Lode H, Hoffken G, Boeckk M, Deppermann N, Borner K, Koeppe P. Quinolone pharmacokinetics and metabolism. J Antimicrob Chemother 1990;26(suppl B):41–9.
13. Carryn S, Van Bambeke F, Mingeot-Leclercq MP, Tulkens PM. Comparative intracellular (THP-1 macrophage) and extracellular activities of beta-lactams, azithromycin, gentamicin, and fluoroquinolones against Listeria monocytogenes at clinically relevant concentrations. Antimicrob Agents Chemother 2002;46:2095–103.
14. Mandell GL, Coleman E. Uptake, transport, and delivery of antimicrobial agents by human polymorphonuclear neutrophils. Antimicrob Agents Chemother 2001;45:1794–8.
15. Fillastre JP, Leroy A, Moulin B, Dhib M, Borsa-Lebas F, Humbert G. Pharmacokinetics of quinolones in renal insufficiency. J Antimicrob Chemother 1990;26(suppl B):51–60.
16. Jones EM, McMullin CM, Hedges AJ, *et al.* The pharmacokinetics of intravenous ciprofloxacin 400mg 12 hourly in patients with severe sepsis: the effect of renal function and intra-abdominal disease. J Antimicrob Chemother 1997;40:121–4.
17. Nicolle LE, Harding GK, Thompson M, Kennedy J, Urias B, Ronald AR. Prospective, randomized, placebo-controlled trial of norfloxacin for the prophylaxis of recurrent urinary tract infection in women. Antimicrob Agents Chemother 1989;33:1032–5.
18. Biering-Sorensen F, Hoiby N, Nordenbo A, Ravnborg M, Bruun B, Rahm V. Ciprofloxacin as prophylaxis for urinary tract infection: prospective, randomized, cross-over, placebo controlled study in patients with spinal cord lesion. J Urol 1994;151:105–8.
19. Warren JW, Abrutyn E, Hebel JR, Johnson JR, Schaeffer AJ, Stamm WE. Guidelines for antimicrobial treatment of uncomplicated acute bacterial cystitis and acute pyelonephritis in women. Infectious Diseases Society of America (IDSA). Clin Infect Dis 1999;29:745–58.
20. Mombelli G, Pezzoli R, Pinoja-Lutz G, Monotti R, Marone C, Franciolli M. Oral vs intravenous ciprofloxacin in the initial empirical management

of severe pyelonephritis or complicated urinary tract infections: a prospective randomized clinical trial. Arch Intern Med 1999;159:53–8.

21. Clinical Effectiveness Group (Association of Genitourinary Medicine and the Medical Society for the Study of Venereal Diseases). National guideline for the management of prostatitis. Sex Transm Infect 1999;75(suppl 1):S46–50.
22. Naber KG, Busch W, Focht J. Ciprofloxacin in the treatment of chronic bacterial prostatitis: a prospective, non-comparative multicentre clinical trial with long-term follow-up. The German Prostatitis Study Group. Int J Antimicrob Agents 2000;14:143–9.
23. CDC. 1998 Guidelines for treatment of sexually transmitted diseases. MMWR 1998;47:1–127.
24. Aplasca De Los Reyes MR, Pato-Mesola V, Klausner JD, *et al.* A randomized trial of ciprofloxacin versus cefixime for treatment of gonorrhea after rapid emergence of gonococcal ciprofloxacin resistance in The Philippines. Clin Infect Dis 2001;32:1313–8.
25. Mogabgab WJ, Holmes B, Murray M, Beville R, Lutz FB, Tack KJ. Randomized comparison of ofloxacin and doxycycline for chlamydia and ureaplasma urethritis and cervicitis. Chemotherapy 1990;36:70–6.
26. Naamara W, Plummer FA, Greenblatt RM, D'Costa LJ, Ndinya-Achola JO, Ronald AR. Treatment of chancroid with ciprofloxacin. A prospective, randomized clinical trial. Am J Med 1987;82:317–20.
27. Adelglass J, DeAbate CA, McElvaine P, Fowler CL, LoCocco J, Campbell T. Comparison of the effectiveness of levofloxacin and amoxicillin-clavulanate for the treatment of acute sinusitis in adults. Otolaryngol Head Neck Surg 1999;120:320–7.
28. Siegert R, Gehanno P, Nikolaidis P, *et al.* A comparison of the safety and efficacy of moxifloxacin (BAY 12-8039) and cefuroxime axetil in the treatment of acute bacterial sinusitis in adults. The Sinusitis Study Group. Respir Med 2000;94:337–44.
29. Clifford K, Huck W, Shan M, Tosiello R, Echols RM, Heyd A. Double-blind comparative trial of ciprofloxacin versus clarithromycin in the treatment of acute bacterial sinusitis. Sinusitis Infection Study Group. Ann Otol Rhinol Laryngol 1999;108:360–7.
30. Simpson KL, Markham A. Ofloxacin otic solution: a review of its use in the management of ear infections. Drugs 1999;58:509–31.
31. Gehanno P. Ciprofloxacin in the treatment of malignant external otitis. Chemotherapy 1994;40:35–40.
32. Anzueto A, Niederman MS, Haverstock DC, Tillotson GS. Efficacy of ciprofloxacin and clarithromycin in acute bacterial exacerbations of complicated chronic bronchitis: interim analysis. Bronchitis Study Group. Clin Ther 1997;19:989–1001.
33. Schaberg T, Ballin I, Huchon G, Bassaris H, Hampel B, Reimnitz P. A multinational, multicentre, non-blinded, randomized study of moxifloxacin oral tablets compared with co-amoxiclav oral tablets in the treatment of acute exacerbation of chronic bronchitis. J Int Med Res 2001;29:314–28.
34. File TM Jr, Segreti J, Dunbar L, *et al.* A multicenter, randomized study comparing the efficacy and safety of intravenous and/or oral levofloxacin versus ceftriaxone and/or cefuroxime axetil in treatment of adults with community-acquired pneumonia. Antimicrob Agents Chemother 1997;41:1965–72.
35. Gordon JJ, Kauffman CA. Superinfection with Streptococcus pneumoniae during therapy with ciprofloxacin. Am J Med 1990;89:383–4.
36. Zuck P, Bru JP. Treatment of community-acquired pneumonia with levofloxacin: 500mg once a day or 500mg twice a day? Presse Med 2000;29:1062–5.
37. British Thoracis Society. Guidelines for the management of community acquired pneumonia in adults. Thorax 2001;56(suppl 4):1–64.
38. Finch R, Schurmann D, Collins O, *et al.* Randomized controlled trial of sequential intravenous (i.v.) and oral moxifloxacin compared with sequential i.v. and oral co-amoxiclav with or without clarithromycin in patients with community-acquired pneumonia requiring initial parenteral treatment. Antimicrob Agents Chemother 2002;46:1746–54.
39. Dedicoat M, Venkatesan P. The treatment of Legionnaires' disease. J Antimicrob Chemother 1999;43:747–52.
40. Torres A, Bauer TT, Leon-Gil C, *et al.* Treatment of severe nosocomial pneumonia: a prospective randomised comparison of intravenous ciprofloxacin with imipenem/cilastatin. Thorax 2000;55:1033–9.
41. Cystic Fibrosis Trust. Antibiotic treatment for cystic fibrosis. Bromley, Kent: Cystic Fibrosis Trust; 2000.
42. Sirgel FA, Botha FJ, Parkin DP, *et al.* The early bactericidal activity of ciprofloxacin in patients with pulmonary tuberculosis. Am J Respir Crit Care Med 1997;156:901–5.
43. Berning SE. The role of fluoroquinolones in tuberculosis today. Drugs 2001;61:9–18.
44. Yoshimatsu T, Nuermberger E, Tyagi S, Chaisson R, Bishai W, Grosset J. Bactericidal activity of increasing daily and weekly doses of moxifloxacin in murine tuberculosis. Antimicrob Agents Chemother 2002;46:1875–9.
45. Keiser P, Nassar N, Skiest D, Rademacher S, Smith JW. A retrospective study of the addition of ciprofloxacin to clarithromycin and ethambutol in the treatment of disseminated Mycobacterium avium complex infection. Int J STD AIDS 1999;10:791–4.
46. Parish LC, Routh HB, Miskin B, *et al.* Moxifloxacin versus cephalexin in the treatment of uncomplicated skin infections. Int J Clin Pract 2000;54:497–503.
47. Gentry LO, Ramirez-Ronda CH, Rodriguez-Noriega E, Thadepalli H, del Rosal PL, Ramirez C. Oral ciprofloxacin vs parenteral cefotaxime in the treatment of difficult skin and skin structure infections. A multicenter trial. Arch Intern Med 1989;149:2579–83.
48. Lew DP, Waldvogel FA. Use of quinolones in osteomyelitis and infected orthopaedic prosthesis. Drugs 1999;58:85–91.
49. Zimmerli W, Widmer AF, Blatter M, Frei R, Ochsner PE. Role of rifampin for treatment of orthopedic implant-related staphylococcal infections: a randomized controlled trial. Foreign-Body Infection (FBI) Study Group. JAMA 1998;279:1537–41.
50. Drancourt M, Stein A, Argenson JN, Roiron R, Groulier P, Raoult D. Oral treatment of Staphylococcus spp. infected orthopaedic implants with fusidic acid or ofloxacin in combination with rifampicin. J Antimicrob Chemother 1997;39:235–40.
51. Akalin HE. Quinolones in the treatment of typhoid fever. Drugs 1999;58:52–4.
52. Wain J, Hoa NT, Chinh NT, *et al.* Quinolone-resistant Salmonella typhi in Viet Nam: molecular basis of resistance and clinical response to treatment. Clin Infect Dis 1997;25:1404–10.
53. Khan WA, Bennish ML, Seas C, *et al.* Randomised controlled comparison of single-dose ciprofloxacin and doxycycline for cholera caused by Vibrio cholerae 01 or 0139. Lancet 1996;348:296–300.
54. Piddock LJ. Quinolone resistance and Campylobacter spp. J Antimicrob Chemother 1995;36:891–8.
55. Smith A, Pennefather PM, Kaye SB, Hart CA. Fluoroquinolones: place in ocular therapy. Drugs 2001;61:747–61.
56. Levy PY, Drancourt M, Etienne J, *et al.* Comparison of different antibiotic regimens for therapy of 32 cases of Q fever endocarditis. Antimicrob Agents Chemother 1991;35:533–7.
57. Update. Investigation of anthrax associated with intentional exposure and interim public health guidelines, October 2001. MMWR 2001;50:889–93.
58. Update. Investigation of bioterrorism-related anthrax and interim guidelines for exposure management and antimicrobial therapy, October 2001. MMWR 2001;50:909–19.
59. Schonwald S, Beus I, Lisic M, Car V, Gmajnicki B. Ciprofloxacin in the treatment of gram-negative bacillary meningitis. Am J Med 1989;87:248S–249S.
60. Ostergaard C, Sorensen TK, Knudsen JD, Frimodt-Moller N. Evaluation of moxifloxacin, a new 8-methoxyquinolone, for treatment of meningitis caused by a penicillin-resistant pneumococcus in rabbits. Antimicrob Agents Chemother 1998;42:1706–12.
61. Saez-Llorens X, McCoig C, Feris JM, *et al.* Quinolone treatment for pediatric bacterial meningitis: a comparative study of trovafloxacin and ceftriaxone with or without vancomycin. Pediatr Infect Dis J 2002;21:14–22.
62. Dworzack DL, Sanders CC, Horowitz EA, *et al.* Evaluation of single-dose ciprofloxacin in the eradication of Neisseria meningitidis from nasopharyngeal carriers. Antimicrob Agents Chemother 1988;32:1740–1.
63. Hughes WT, Armstrong D, Bodey GP, *et al.* 2002 Guidelines for the use of antimicrobial agents in neutropenic patients with cancer. Clin Infect Dis 2002;34:730–51.
64. Lipsky BA, Baker CA. Fluoroquinolone toxicity profiles: a review focusing on newer agents. Clin Infect Dis 1999;28:352–64.
65. Ball P, Tillotson G. Tolerability of fluoroquinolone antibiotics. Past, present and future. Drug Saf 1995;13:343–58.
66. Kubin R. Safety and efficacy of ciprofloxacin in paediatric patients–review. Infection 1993;21:413–21.
67. Rubinstein E, Camm J. Cardiotoxicity of fluoroquinolones. J Antimicrob Chemother 2002;49:593–6.

chapter

199 Glycopeptides

Jihad Slim & Leon Smith

VANCOMYCIN

Vancomycin is a tricyclic glycopeptide antibiotic obtained from *Amycolaptosis orientalis*, which is found in the soil of Borneo and India. This antibiotic-producing bacterium was also known in the past as *Streptomyces orientalis* and *Nocardia orientalis*. Vancomycin has been used clinically since 1956 but recent improvements in its manufacture have increased its purity and reduced its toxicity. It is an extremely valuable and relatively safe antibiotic against the major Gram-positive organisms. In the past few years the emergence of resistance in enterococci, and especially in staphylococci, has become an important clinical issue.[1]

PHARMACOKINETICS AND DISTRIBUTION

Vancomycin is bactericidal and appears to exert its effect by binding to the precursor units of peptidoglycan synthesis (D-alanyle-D-alanine units) inhibiting the transpeptidase reaction. This step is necessary for cross-linking newly synthesized peptidoglycan precursors into a complete structure. The net result is an alteration of bacterial cell wall permeability. In addition, RNA synthesis is inhibited. Perhaps because of this dual mechanism of action, resistance to vancomycin is uncommon, although it has been reported in strains of enterococci, coagulase-negative staphylococci and a few strains of *Staphylococcus aureus*. Gram-negative organisms are not sensitive to vancomycin, perhaps because porin channels in the cell wall of the Gram-negative organism do not accommodate the large, bulky vancomycin molecule. Vancomycin exhibits concentration-independent (or time-dependent) bactericidal action against susceptible bacteria. It kills better in aerobic conditions than in anaerobic conditions.

Concomitant use with streptomycin or gentamicin is usually synergistic against susceptible pathogens, especially enterococci and *viridans* streptococci, while rifampin (rifampicin) exhibits synergism with vancomycin against most coagulase-negative staphylococci but not against *Staph. aureus*.

Generally, vancomycin is only administered intravenously, although oral administration is important in treatment of pseudomembranous colitis; the oral bioavailability of vancomycin is too low to treat systemic infections. Patients who have colitis, however, develop detectable serum levels after oral administration, especially if they have renal impairment.

A two- or a three-compartment model best explains the pharmacokinetics of vancomycin. A 500mg dose of vancomycin hydrochloride results in a mean peak serum concentration of approximately 30μg/ml immediately after infusion. Concentrations after 1 hour are approximately 6μg/ml, and after 6 hours they are approximately 3μg/ml. After a slow intravenous infusion of 1g vancomycin, peak serum levels are approximately 48μg/ml, with trough concentrations of 2μg/ml at 12 hours. Ideally, peak concentrations of approximately 30μg/ml and trough concentrations of 10μg/ml or less are desirable. After 24 hours, concentrations are less than 1μg/ml.[2–5]

Vancomycin is distributed into most body tissues and fluids, including pericardial, pleural, ascitic and synovial fluids (Table 199.1). Unless the meninges are inflamed, there is little diffusion into cerebrospinal fluid. Vancomycin is about 55% bound to serum protein. It is not known whether any metabolism takes place. Excretion is mainly by glomerular filtration, with about 80% of the drug excreted in 24 hours in the urine and only small amounts excreted in the feces. Owing to poor bioavailability, oral doses are excreted mainly in the feces. Vancomycin given by the oral route concentrates intraluminally in the distal gastrointestinal tract, resulting in high intraluminal vancomycin concentrations. There is approximately 1000μg/ml in the stool after a dose of 2g/day. Low serum concentrations may occur in patients who have a damaged intestinal mucosa.[3,4,7–10]

The kidneys eliminate vancomycin through glomerular filtration. Urine concentrations are approximately 300μg/ml after a 500mg intravenous dose, and tubular reabsorption is not important in the renal handling of vancomycin. Because vancomycin is eliminated via the renal route, it accumulates in the presence of renal insufficiency. The serum half-life of vancomycin in anuric patients is approximately 7 days, in contrast to 4–6 hours in adults who have normal

CONCENTRATION OF VANCOMYCIN IN BODY TISSUES AND FLUIDS

Body fluid or tissue	Dose	Route of administration	Sampling time (hours after administration of vancomycin dose)	Mean vancomycin concentration in sample (μg/ml)
Pericardial fluid	500mg	Intravenous	1.5–5.5	0.6–5.5
Lung	1g	Intravenous	6	1.3
Synovial fluid	500mg	Intravenous	1	5.7
Ascitic fluid	500mg	Intravenous	1.5–5.2	3.6
Bile	500mg	Intravenous	1	3.1
Urine	500mg	Intravenous	1	30–90
Stools	500mg	Oral	6	100–350

Table 199.1 Concentration of vancomycin in body tissues and fluids. Data from Cunha and Klein.[6]

ELIMINATION OF VANCOMYCIN

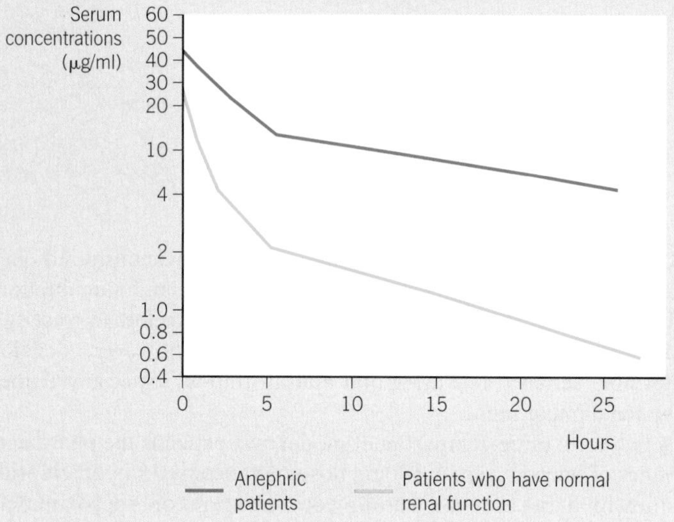

Fig. 199.1 Elimination of vancomycin by anephric patients and by patients who have normal renal function. Adapted with permission from Cunha *et al.*[11]

renal function (Fig. 199.1). If F60 or F80 polysulfone filters are used, significant amounts of vancomycin can be removed during hemodialysis.

ROUTE OF ADMINISTRATION AND DOSAGE

Adults and children who have normal renal function

The usual dose is 2g/day divided into two or four doses and administered intravenously at a rate no faster than 10mg/minute or over a total of at least 60 minutes.

Oral vancomycin is effective for pseudomembranous enterocolitis or staphylococcal enterocolitis, and the dose is 500–2000mg/day in three or four daily doses for 7–10 days.

For children the usual dosage is 10mg/kg q6h.

Vancomycin serum level is readily available in most laboratories and should be measured to monitor efficacy and prevent toxicity, especially in patients who have fluctuating renal function.

INDICATIONS

Most strains of *Staph. aureus* and *Staphylococcus epidermidis* are susceptible to vancomycin, as are streptococci (including enterococci), *Corynebacterium* spp. and *Clostridium* spp. (Table 199.2). Vancomycin is particularly useful against methicillin-resistant *Staphylococcus aureus* (MRSA) infections and for treating Gram-positive infections in patients who are allergic to penicillin. Some strains of Gram-positive bacteria – *Leuconostoc* spp., *Lactobacillus* spp., *Pediococcus* spp. and *Erysipelothrix* spp. – possess inherent resistance to vancomycin. Gram-negative bacteria, fungi, viruses and mycobacteria are resistant to vancomycin.

Synergistic bactericidal effects can be achieved when vancomycin is combined with aminoglycosides against enterococci and MRSA, but this increases possible renal toxicity. Vancomycin is useful against a wide variety of clinical infections caused by these organisms (Table 199.3), although it should not be used in patients who have meningitis unless absolutely necessary because of its poor penetration into the cerebrospinal fluid. Oral vancomycin is used for severe colitis caused by *Clostridium difficile*. Metronidazole should be used as the first-line agent for most cases of *C. difficile* related diarrhea. This limits the risk of overuse of vancomycin with its attendant risk of selection of vancomycin-resistant bacteria.

Susceptible organisms are usually sensitive to concentrations of 1–5μg/ml.

ORGANISMS TREATABLE BY VANCOMYCIN
Actinomyces spp.
Bacillus cereus and *Bacillus subtilis*
Clostridium difficile and other *Clostridium* spp.
Corynebacterium jeikeium and other *Corynebacterium* spp.
Enterococcus faecalis and *Enterococcus faecium*
Listeria monocytogenes
Staphylococcus spp. including *Staphylococcus aureus, Staphylococcus epidermidis* and methicillin-resistant staphylococci
Streptococcus spp. including *Streptococcus agalactiae* (group B streptococci), *Streptococcus bovis, Streptococcus pneumoniae, Streptococcus pyogenes* and *viridans* streptococci

Table 199.2 Organisms treatable by vancomycin. Resistant strains of enterococci and staphylococci may occur.

CONDITIONS TREATABLE BY VANCOMYCIN	
Diabetic foot ulcers	Skin and soft tissue infections
Endocarditis	Urinary tract infections
Osteomyelitis	Lower respiratory tract infections
Peritonitis	Intra-abdominal infections
Pneumonia	Bone and joint infections
Pseudomembranous colitis	Some forms of meningitis
Sepsis	

Table 199.3 Conditions treatable by vancomycin. These conditions are treatable by vancomycin if they involve the organisms listed in Table 199.2.

DOSAGES IN SPECIAL CIRCUMSTANCES

Vancomycin should be used with caution in patients who have renal failure because it can accumulate. High serum concentrations increase the possibility of developing ototoxicity and nephrotoxicity (see below). Dose adjustments are necessary and lower doses of the drug are recommended for patients who have renal dysfunction or in patients receiving other ototoxic or nephrotoxic drugs. Renal function tests should be performed routinely during therapy.

In patients who have impaired renal function, the patient can be given a loading dose of 15mg/kg with a daily maintenance dose in milligrams of 150 plus 15 times the creatinine clearance, which provides a steady state concentration of 20μg/ml.[12] Alternatively, a nomogram can be used.

Hemodialysis usually removes little or no vancomycin, and 1g (15mg/kg as a pediatric dose or for a small adult (<50kg)) every 7–10 days usually provides adequate serum concentrations in functionally anephric adults.

Patients on continuous ambulatory peritoneal dialysis can be given vancomycin intravenously with a loading dose of 23mg/kg and a maintenance dose of 17mg/kg every 7 days,[13] or 1.5mg/kg q6h.[14] Monitoring of serum concentrations is recommended.

Vancomycin dosage for neonates is 15mg/kg bolus followed by 10mg/kg q12h in the first week of life, q8h up to 1 month of age. For children it is administered at 10mg/kg q6h.

In premature infants and elderly patients, vancomycin dosage needs to be adjusted to their clearance of creatine.

Vancomycin serum concentrations must be monitored carefully in patients who have severe hepatic impairment since accumulation can occur.

Serum levels above 40μg/ml can be associated with nephrotoxicity, and ototoxicity.

ADVERSE REACTIONS

Too rapid an infusion of vancomycin can trigger histamine release, which may cause anaphylactoid reactions including fever, chills, sinus tachycardia, pruritus, paresthesiae, flushing, rash or redness in the face, neck, upper body, arms or back, and muscular spasms. It is seen infrequently now following the introduction of improved pharmacological formulations. In some cases, hypotension occurs. This histamine release reaction is often referred to as the 'red man' syndrome. Slowing the infusion rates, administering a histamine-1 blocker or lowering the size of the dose may reduce the incidence or severity of the reaction. These reactions usually resolve within 20 minutes but may persist for several hours. In animal studies, hypotension and bradycardia occurred in animals given large doses of vancomycin at high concentrations and rates. Such events are infrequent if vancomycin is given by slow infusion over 60 minutes. In studies of normal volunteers, infusion-related events did not occur when vancomycin was administered at a rate of 10μg/min or less.

Rarely, vancomycin causes nephrotoxicity. Renal failure is principally manifested by increased serum creatinine or blood urea nitrogen concentrations, especially in patients who have been given large doses of vancomycin. Rare cases of interstitial nephritis have also been reported. Most of these have occurred in patients who were given concomitant aminoglycosides or who had pre-existing kidney dysfunction. When vancomycin was discontinued, azotemia resolved in most patients. Generally the nephrotoxicity risk is minimized if trough serum concentrations are kept below 10μg/ml.

A few dozen cases of hearing loss associated with vancomycin have been reported; these occurred at serum concentrations of about 60–80μg/ml. Most of these patients had kidney dysfunction or a pre-existing hearing loss, were receiving concomitant treatment with an ototoxic drug, were dehydrated, or were bacteremic. Vancomycin-induced hearing loss can be manifested as either cochlear toxicity (causing tinnitus or hearing loss or both) or vestibular toxicity (causing ataxia, vertigo, nausea, vomiting and nystagmus). Reducing the serum levels may reverse the ototoxicity.

Orally administered vancomycin should be used with caution with cholestyramine or colestipol. These anion-exchange resins can bind vancomycin and reduce its effectiveness. If patients must take both drugs, doses should be administered several hours apart.

Concomitant use of parenteral vancomycin with other nephrotoxic drugs (e.g. aminoglycoside, cidofovir, foscavir, amphotericin B) can lead to additive nephrotoxicity.

RESISTANCE

There has been increasing concern about the emergence of vancomycin-resistant bacteria, especially enterococci. High-level resistance is mediated by a gene complex found on plasmids known as the VanA genotype. The phenotypic expression of vancomycin resistance (inducible and associated with teicoplanin resistance) is known as the VanA phenotype (see Chapter 189). The VanA phenotype is carried on a transposon designated as transposon (Tn) 1546, which carries clusters of seven genes that code for vancomycin resistance, five of which are required for the expression of the VanA phenotype. Intermediate-level resistance is mediated by the VanB gene cluster. These genes are transferable by conjugal plasmids and mediate the VanB resistance phenotype. Teicoplanin will not induce the expression of VanB resistance. Transfer of these genes between organisms can spread resistance.

This has led to recommendations by several governmental agencies to prevent vancomycin resistance. The guidelines from the Centers for Disease for Disease Control and Prevention in the USA state that vancomycin is not recommended for:

- routine surgical prophylaxis;
- treatment of single positive blood culture of coagulase-negative *Staphylococcus* spp.;
- empiric treatment of a febrile neutropenic patient in whom no evidence of Gram-positive infection exists;
- continued empiric therapy;
- selective decontamination of the gut;
- colonization with MRSA;
- primary treatment of pseudomembranous colitis;
- topical application or irrigation;
- treatment of methicillin-sensitive *Staphylococcus aureus* in dialysis patients;
- prophylaxis in continuous ambulatory peritoneal dialysis;
- systemic or local prophylaxis for indwelling central or local catheters; or
- Lyme disease.

TEICOPLANIN

Teicoplanin (formerly called teichomycin A) is a complex of five closely related glycopeptides that have the same heptapeptide base and an aglycone that contains aromatic amino acids, with D-mannose and *N*-acetyl-D-glucosamine as sugars, with a molecular weight of 1562–1891Da. Teicoplanin is structurally similar to vancomycin. It is produced from the actinomycete *Actinoplanes teichomyceticus*.

Teicoplanin is similar but not identical to vancomycin in its spectrum of activity. Minimum inhibitory concentrations (MICs) for most Gram-positive bacteria and anaerobes are comparable, but teicoplanin is less active against some strains of *Staphylococcus haemolyticus* (MIC 16–64mg/l compared to ≤4mg/l for vancomycin). Its ease of administration and its low toxicity potential make it a potential alternative to vancomycin for the treatment of Gram-positive aerobic and anaerobic bacteria, in both the immunocompetent and the immunocompromised host. In-vitro activity against most Gram-positive organisms is equal to or greater than that of vancomycin.

In both open and comparative clinical trials, teicoplanin has been well tolerated, and adverse reactions have rarely prompted discontinuation of treatment. Nephrotoxicity caused by teicoplanin is uncommon, even when it is used concomitantly with aminoglycosides or cyclosporin A. Favorable pharmacokinetics allow for intramuscular administration as well as intravenous bolus dosing and, after appropriate loading doses, maintenance therapy may be given on a once-daily basis. The combination of all of these factors makes teicoplanin an effective, safe alternative to vancomycin in the treatment of Gram-positive infections. Although it is widely used in Europe, it is still yet to be approved by the Food and Drug Administration in the USA.

PHARMACOKINETICS AND DISTRIBUTION

Teicoplanin binds to the terminal D-alanine–D-alanine sequence of peptides that form the bacterial cell wall and, by sterically hindering the transpeptidase and transglycosylation reaction, inhibits the formation of peptidoglycan. Teicoplanin is a large polar molecule and, as it cannot penetrate the lipid membrane of Gram-negative bacteria, they are resistant to it (see Chapter 188). Enterococci expressing VanA (high-level) vancomycin resistance are also resistant to teicoplanin. Teicoplanin is not significantly absorbed from the gastrointestinal tract but it can be administered intravenously or intramuscularly, in a once-daily dosing schedule. It has a long half-life of approximately 47 hours, allowing for once-daily dosing once therapeutic serum levels are attained. In a study in which healthy volunteers were given intravenous injections of teicoplanin, doses of 3mg/kg gave average peak plasma concentrations of 53.5μg/ml and doses of 6mg/kg gave average peak plasma concentrations of 111.8μg/ml.[15] Bioavailability after intramuscular injection of teicoplanin is 90%, with peak plasma concentration occurring 2 hours after injection.[15]

Teicoplanin is approximately 90% protein-bound. It is more lipophilic than vancomycin and has excellent penetration into tissues and tissue fluids with a large volume of distribution after intravenous administration. High concentrations are achieved in peritoneal and blister fluid, bile, liver, pancreas, mucosa and bone.[16] Penetration into cerebrospinal fluid across uninflamed meninges is poor.

Teicoplanin does not undergo extensive metabolism and is excreted almost entirely by the kidneys.[17] As with vancomycin, its half-life is prolonged by renal failure.[18] Neither hemodialysis nor peritoneal dialysis significantly affects the clearance of teicoplanin.

ADMINISTRATION AND DOSAGE

Dosing recommendations for adults who have normal renal function have been based both on pharmacokinetic properties and on results of open and comparative clinical trials. A single loading dose of 400mg on the first day followed by maintenance doses of 200mg/day (3mg/kg/day for pediatric dose) appears adequate for the treatment of urinary tract infections, skin and soft tissue infections and lower respiratory tract infections. For serious infections, including endocarditis, osteomyelitis and sepsis, it is necessary to maintain serum concentrations of teicoplanin at 10μg/ml or more.[19]

Treatment of endocarditis caused by *Staph. aureus* has been difficult with teicoplanin, especially when used as monotherapy.[19,20] In these cases, it is recommended that an aminoglycoside should be added and that teicoplanin trough levels should be maintained in the range of 20–60μg/ml.

INDICATIONS

The indications for the use of teicoplanin are similar to those for vancomycin (Table 199.4). They include Gram-positive infections caused by strains that are resistant to penicillin, cephalosporin or methicillin, or Gram-positive infections in patients who are allergic to penicillin. In addition, teicoplanin may be used for subacute bacterial endocarditis or surgical prophylaxis, in patients who are allergic to β-lactam drugs and as an alternative to vancomycin or metronidazole in the treatment of pseudomembranous colitis caused by *C. difficile* (approved in Europe).

Teicoplanin, alone or in combination with other antibiotics, has proved effective in the treatment of various Gram-positive infections, including sepsis, endocarditis, skin and soft tissue infections, osteomyelitis and lower respiratory infections. It has also been found to be effective in both prophylaxis and treatment of Hickman catheter infections in immunocompromised patients.[21,22] Specially prepared catheters loaded with teicoplanin have been developed and tested *in vitro* and have been shown to prevent bacterial colonization for at least 48 hours, thus showing promise for inhibiting early-onset catheter infections.[23] Teicoplanin has also been used along with other antibiotics for empiric treatment of febrile neutropenic patients and in the treatment of documented Gram-positive infections in neutropenic patients.[24,25]

INDICATIONS FOR THE USE OF TEICOPLANIN	
Infections with:	*Staphylococcus* spp., including methicillin-resistant strains *Streptococcus* spp., *Streptococcus agalactiae, Streptococcus bovis, Streptococcus pneumoniae, Streptococcus pyogenes* and *viridans* streptococci Enterococci *Clostridium* spp., including *Clostridium difficile* *Corynebacterium* spp., including *Corynebacterium jeikeium*
The following types of infection with the above organisms:	Sepsis Endocarditis Skin and soft tissue infections Osteomyelitis Lower respiratory tract infections Diarrhea associated with *Clostridium difficile* Nosocomial intravascular catheter infections (prophylaxis and treatment)

Table 199.4 Indications for the use of teicoplanin.

Oral teicoplanin is as effective as vancomycin in the treatment of diarrhea associated with *C. difficile*. A 10-day course of regimen of 100mg oral teicoplanin q12h was found to be as effective as 500mg oral vancomycin q6h.[26] Again, the risk of glycopeptide resistance development argues for the use of metronidazole for routine therapy for *C. difficile* associated diarrhea (see Chapter 44).

DOSAGE IN SPECIAL CIRCUMSTANCES

A dosage nomogram for teicoplanin has been designed,[27] based on the relationship between teicoplanin clearance and creatinine clearance and an average desired steady-state concentration of 20μg/ml. Although intravenous teicoplanin penetrates well into peritoneal fluid in normal patients, it does not penetrate well into the effluent of continuous ambulatory peritoneal dialysis patients and is not recommended for the treatment of peritonitis in these patients. Intraperitoneal teicoplanin has been effective in continuous ambulatory peritoneal dialysis patients who have Gram-positive peritonitis, however.

Another regimen for renal impaired patients includes a normal loading dose followed by doubling the dosage interval for patients who have a creatinine clearance of 30–80ml/minute and tripling the dosage interval for patients who have severe renal impairment (creatinine clearance <10ml/minute).

ADVERSE REACTIONS AND INTERACTIONS

Teicoplanin is generally well tolerated at therapeutic dosages, with side effects occurring in approximately 6–13% of the patients (Table 199.5).

Side effects (including nephrotoxicity) with teicoplanin are consistently less common than with vancomycin, even when teicoplanin is used concomitantly with aminoglycosides.[22,24] The incidence of red man syndrome or anaphylactoid reactions caused by teicoplanin administration is exceptionally low.

The commonest side effects were injection site intolerance, skin rash, bronchospasm and eosinophilia. Nephrotoxicity and ototoxicity are uncommon.

ADVERSE REACTIONS TO TEICOPLANIN	
Hypersensitivity	Skin rash Bronchospasm Anaphylaxis
Biochemical abnormalities	Increased liver function tests
Hematologic abnormalities	Eosinophilia
Local intolerance	Redness, pain (after intramuscular administration), phlebitis (after intravenous administration)
Non-specific reactions	Nausea Diarrhea Dizziness Tremor

Table 199.5 Adverse reactions to teicoplanin.

Like vancomycin, teicoplanin is bound and inactivated by bile binding resins such as cholestyramine.[28]

DAPTOMYCIN

Daptomycin is a ovel cyclic lipopeptide antibiotic derived from *Streptomyces roseosporus*. Its mechanism of action is not very well elucidated yet, but it is different from that of vancomycin and teicoplanin. It exerts bactericidal activity against Gram-positive organisms by binding to cell membranes in the presence of free ionized calcium.

Daptomycin has a relatively long plasma half-life, approximately 8.5 hours, which allow for once-daily administration; it is highly protein-bound.

The in-vitro spectrum of activity includes most aerobic and anaerobic Gram-positive bacteria, including vancomycin-resistant *Enterococcus*, vancomycin-intermediate *Staph. aureus*, methicillin-resistant *Staph. aureus* and *Staph. epidermidis*, penicillin-resistant pneumococcus, *C. difficile*, *Clostridium perfringens* and *Bacillus anthracis*.[29]

Resistance in naturally occurring *S. aureus* is unusual.

As of February 2002, phase III studies documented daptomycin's good tolerability and efficacy compared with vancomycin and anti-staphylococcal penicillin. The adverse event profile of 4mg/kg/day was similar to that of the standard dose of vancomycin.

Daptomycin may have an advantage over vancomycin, by virtue of its faster killing of *Staph. aureus* in vitro.[30]

ORITAVANCIN

Another glycopeptide in phase III studies, oritavancin differs from vancomycin by the addition of a lipophilic side chain (*N*3'-chlorobiphenyl) and of an aminated sugar (22-*O*-4-epivancosamine). This results in strongly amphiphilic molecule, which improves its ability to penetrate eucaryotic cells (e.g. macrophage) for better intracellular bactericidal activity.

Oritavancin is highly bound to human plasma protein (86–90%), and has a long terminal half-life, offering the potential of shorter treatment duration.[31] It is active against a broad range of Gram-positive organisms, including MRSA and vancomycin-resistant *Enterococcus*.

A double-blind controlled study in 517 patients who had complicated skin and skin-structure infection compared oritavancin 1.5mg/kg or 3 mg/kg for 3–7 days followed by oral placebo, versus vancomycin for 3–7 days followed by oral cephalexin, for a total therapy course of 10–14 days. At the conclusion of the study the three arms were comparable in efficacy and tolerability.[32]

REFERENCES

1. Smith TL, Pearson ML, Wilcox KR, *et al.* Emergence of vancomycin resistance in *Staphylococcus aureus*. N Engl J Med 1999;340:493–501.
2. American Medical Association. AMA drug evaluations. Chicago: American Medical Association; 1994:1535.
3. Bartlett JG. Antibiotic-associated pseudomembranous colitis. Rev Infect Dis 1979;1:530–9.
4. Fekety R. Vancomycin. Med Clin North Am 1982;66:175–81.
5. Kucers A, Bennet NM. The use of antibiotics, 4th ed. Philadelphia: JB Lippincott; 1988:1045.
6. Cunha BA, Klein NC. Vancomycin. In: Yoshikawa TT, Norman DC, eds. Antimicrobial therapy in the elderly patient. New York: Marcel Dekker; 1994:311.
7. Bartlett JG. Antibiotic-associated diarrhea. Infect Dis Pract 1992;16:1.
8. Fekety R, Silva J, Armstrong J, *et al.* Treatment of antibiotic-associated enterocolitis with vancomycin. Rev Infect Dis 1981;3(Suppl.):273–81.
9. Fekety R, Silva J, Kauffman C, *et al.* Treatment of antibiotic-associated *Clostridium difficile* colitis with oral vancomycin. Am J Med 1989;86:15–9.
10. Wilcox MH, Spencer RC. *Clostridium difficile* infection: responses, relapses and re-infections. J Hosp Infect 1992;22:85–92.
11. Cunha BA, Quintiliani R, Deglin JM, *et al.* Pharmacokinetics of vancomycin in anuria. Rev Infect Dis 1981;3(Suppl.):S269–72.
12. Nielsen HE, Hansen HE, Korsager B, Skov PE. Renal excretion of vancomycin in kidney disease. Acta Med Scand 1975;197:261–4.
13. Blevins RD, Halstenson CE, Salem NG, Matzke GR. Pharmacokinetics of vancomycin in patients undergoing continuous ambulatory peritoneal dialysis. Antimicrob Agents Chemother 1984;25:603–6.
14. Bunke CM, Aronoff GR, Brier ME, Sloan RS, Luft FC. Vancomycin kinetics during continuous ambulatory peritoneal dialysis. Clin Pharmacol Ther 1983;34:631–7.
15. Verbist L, Tjandramaga B, Hendrickx B, *et al.* In vitro activity and human pharmacokinetics of teicoplanin. Antimicrob Agents Chemother 1984;26:881–6.
16. Campoli-Richards DM, Brogden RN, Faulds D. Teicoplanin. A review of its antibacterial activity, pharmacokinetic properties and therapeutic potential. Drugs 1990;40:449–86.
17. Carver PL, Nightingale CH, Quintiliani R, *et al.* Pharmacokinetics of single and multiple dose teicoplanin in healthy volunteers. Antimicrob Agents Chemother 1989;33:82–6.
18. Falcoz C, Ferry N, Pozet N, *et al.* Pharmacokinetics of teicoplanin in renal failure. Antimicrob Agents Chemother 1987;31:1255–62.
19. Wilson APR, Gruneberg RN, Neu H. Dosage recommendations for teicoplanin. J Antimicrob Chemother 1993;32:792–6.
20. Presterl E, Graninger W, Georgopoulos A. The efficacy of teicoplanin in the treatment of endocarditis caused by Gram positive bacteria. J Antimicrob Chemother 1993;31:755–66.
21. Lim SH, Smith MP, Nachin SJ, *et al.* A prospective randomized study of prophylactic teicoplanin to prevent early Hickman catheter-related sepsis in patients receiving intensive chemotherapy for haematological malignancies. Eur J Haematol 1993;51(Suppl.54):10.
22. Smith SR, Cheesebrough JS, Makris M, *et al.* Teicoplanin administration in patients experiencing reactions to vancomycin. J Antimicrob Chemother 1989;23:810–2.
23. Jansen B, Jansen S, Peters G, Pulverer G. In-vitro efficacy of a central venous catheter ('HydroCath') loaded with teicoplanin to prevent bacterial colonization. J Hosp Infect 1992;22:93–107.
24. Chow AW, Jewesson PJ, Kureishi A, *et al.* Teicoplanin versus vancomycin in the empirical treatment of febrile neutropenic patients. Eur J Haematol 1993;51(Suppl.54):18.
25. Van der Auwera P, Aoun M, Meunier F. Randomized study of vancomycin versus teicoplanin for the treatment of Gram-positive bacterial infections in immunocompromised hosts. Antimicrob Agents Chemother 1991;35:451–7.
26. De Lalla F, Nicolin R, Rinaldi E, *et al.* Prospective study of oral teicoplanin versus oral vancomycin for therapy of pseudomembranous colitis and *Clostridium difficile*-associated diarrhea. Antimicrob Agents Chemother 1992;36:2192–6

27. Lam YWF, Kapusnik-Uner JE, Sachdeva M, *et al.* The pharmacokinetics of teicoplanin in varying degrees of renal function. Clin Pharmacol Ther 1990;47:655–61.
28. Pantosti A, Luzzi I, Cardines R, Gianfrilli P. Comparison of in vitro activities of teicoplanin and vancomycin against *Clostridium difficile* and their interactions with cholestyramine. Antimicrob Agents Chemother 1985;28:847–8.
29. Goldstein EJC, Citron DM. In vitro activity of daptomycin, quinupristin/dalfopristin, and linezolid against 275 Gram-positive aerobic and anaerobic organisms. Interscience Conference on Antimicrobial Agents and Chemotherapy 2000; abstract 2293 .
30. Snydman, DR. Daptomycin. Interscience Conference on Antimicrobial Agents and Chemotherapy 2000; abstract 1125.
31. Brown TJ. Protein binding of 14C-oritavancin. Interscience Conference on Antimicrobial Agents and Chemotherapy 2001; abstract 2193.
32. Wasilewski M. Equivalence of shorter course therapy with oritavancin vs vancomycin/cephalexin in complicated skin/skin structure infections. Interscience Conference on Antimicrobial Agents and Chemotherapy 2001; abstract UL-18.

chapter

200 Tetracyclines and Chloramphenicol

Kjell Alestig

TETRACYCLINES

INTRODUCTION

In 1948, Benjamin Duggar at the Lederle Laboratories isolated the first tetracycline, chlortetracycline, from a drop of Missouri mud containing a fungus producing a golden pigment. The fungus was therefore called *Streptomyces aureofaciens* and the antibiotic aureomycin.

In 1950 oxytetracycline was isolated from a strain of *Streptomyces rimosus* by workers at Charles Pfizer & Co. and in 1953 tetracycline was produced semisynthetically from chlortetracycline. Demeclocycline, derived from a mutant strain of *S. aureofaciens,* was introduced in 1957 and in the following years the semisynthetic derivatives rolitetracycline and methacycline were also introduced. A so-called second generation of long-acting tetracyclines, doxycycline and minocycline, were synthesized in 1966 and 1972 respectively.

Chemically, the tetracyclines have the structure of a hydronaphthacene nucleus containing four fused rings. The specific analogues are obtained by substitutions on the fifth, sixth or seventh position of the basic structure (Fig. 200.1).

MOLECULAR STRUCTURE OF SOME TETRACYCLINES

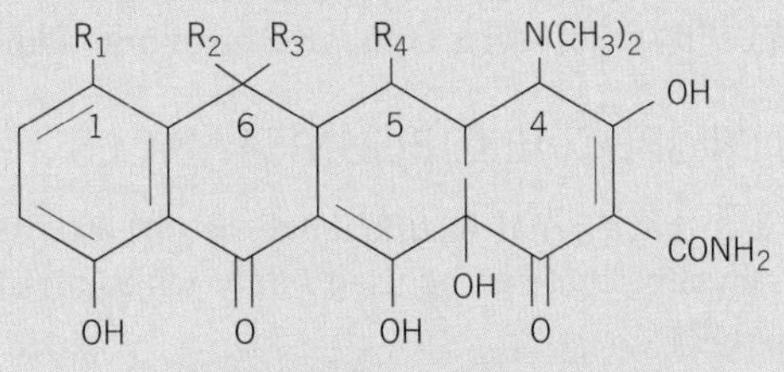

	R_1	R_2		R_3	R_4
Chlortetracycline	Cl	CH_3		OH	H
Oxytetracycline	H	CH_3		OH	OH
Tetracycline	H	CH_3		OH	H
Demeclocycline	Cl	OH		H	H
Methacycline	H		$-CH_2-$		OH
Doxycycline	H	CH_3		H	OH
Minocycline	$N(CH_3)_2$	H		H	H

Fig. 200.1 Molecular structure of some tetracyclines.

Tetracyclines are mainly bacteriostatic and they act by binding to the 30S subunits of the ribosomes in susceptible micro-organisms, thereby inhibiting protein synthesis.

There are few reasons to use any of the older tetracyclines; doxycycline and to some extent minocycline should be preferred because they are better absorbed and distributed than the older drugs. However, one exception may be that dermatologists often seem to prefer tetracycline or another first-generation drug for the treatment of acne.

ANTIMICROBIAL SPECTRUM

When they were introduced the tetracyclines were effective against a variety of Gram-positive bacteria and Gram-negative organisms within the Enterobacteriaceae group. Development of resistance has, however, led to restricted use of the drugs for infections caused by streptococci, staphylococci, *Escherichia coli* or *Proteus* spp. More important now is the tetracyclines' good activity against *Mycoplasma*, *Chlamydia* and *Rickettsia* spp., *Borrelia* spp. (especially *Borrelia burgdorferi*) and *Propionibacterium acnes* (Table 200.1).[1]

Doxycycline and minocycline often have a better activity in vitro than the other tetracyclines[2,3] but the differences are probably of little practical importance for clinical treatment.

RESISTANCE AGAINST TETRACYCLINES	
Generally susceptible species	*Mycoplasma pneumoniae* *Ureaplasma urealyticum* *Chlamydia* spp. *Rickettsia* spp. *Brucella* spp. *Francisella tularensis* *Propionibacterium acnes* *Borrelia burgdorferi* *Yersinia* spp.
Resistance common (great variations between countries)	Streptococci Staphylococci Enterobacteriaceae *Haemophilus influenzae* Meningococci Gonococci *Legionella pneumophila*
Resistance usually found	Enterococci *Proteus* spp. *Pseudomonas* spp. *Serratia* spp. *Bacteroides* spp.

Table 200.1 Resistance against tetracyclines.

RESISTANCE

Oral therapy with tetracyclines has a marked influence on the bowel flora and resistant strains may be quickly selected. This risk is somewhat reduced with doxycycline,[4] which is nearly completely absorbed.[5] Extensive use of tetracyclines leads to plasmid-mediated multiresistance, but chromosomal alterations may also occur.

Tetracyclines have been widely used in the veterinary field, not only to cure infections but also as a food additive to promote the growth of newborn animals. Penicillin and tetracyclines are not now permitted as growth stimulators within the European Union but are still used in the USA. In pigs, antibiotics promote an increase in weight of 8% and pigs are ready for slaughter 3 weeks earlier than animals that have not received antibiotics – an important economic advantage. This misuse of antibiotics is probably one important reason for the worldwide spread of tetracycline resistance within the Enterobacteriaceae group.[6–8] However, restrictions on the veterinary use of antibiotics have now been introduced in some countries. In Sweden the use of any antibiotic to promote the growth of animals was prohibited as early as in 1986, and similar legislation for the whole European Union is expected within the next few years.

Resistance to tetracyclines is now common among bacteria causing respiratory infections such as pneumococci, *Haemophilus influenzae* and *Moraxella catarrhalis*.[9]

PHARMACOKINETICS AND DISTRIBUTION

Clinical pharmacokinetics

After oral administration tetracyclines are absorbed from the stomach and the small intestine. Absorption is usually highest in the fasting state, but doxycycline and minocycline are also well absorbed with food. The degree of absorption and other pharmacokinetic parameters for some of the derivatives are shown in Table 200.2. The usually nearly complete absorption of doxycycline salts is reduced if the gastric pH is increased, as can occur in people who have atrophic gastritis or be caused by acid-reducing drugs. In some countries doxycycline is available in tablets bound to a polysaccharide, carragenate, which has been shown to increase absorption at higher pH.[10] There are also gelatin capsules available containing coated pellets of doxycycline hydrochloride that are resistant to gastric acid so that absorption will occur in the duodenum.[11]

Distribution

The tissue distribution of tetracyclines is clearly related to their different lipid solubility, which is higher for doxycycline than for all older tetracyclines. Doxycycline concentrations are therefore sufficient for treatment in the respiratory tract and lung tissue, the bile and the genital tract of both sexes.[12,13] Levels achieved in the central nervous system (CNS) are increased in chronic meningeal inflammation,[14] enabling treatment of neuroborreliosis.[15,16] Tetracyclines cross the placenta and bind to metal ions in fetal bone and teeth. They are also excreted in human milk.

Minocycline is even more lipid-soluble than doxycycline. This may not be an advantage because side effects such as vertigo and other CNS symptoms may be caused by increased drug concentrations in the cerebrosides of the brain.[17]

Elimination

Tetracyclines are metabolized in the liver in small amounts only, chlortetracycline being an exception with rapid metabolism. However, inducers of liver enzymes such as diphenylhydantoin may cause some metabolism of doxycycline. There is biliary excretion of tetracyclines to a varying degree and possibly enterohepatic circulation.

Tetracyclines are partly excreted by glomerular filtration. For minocycline this excretion is less than 10% but it is more than 50% for tetracycline.

Incomplete absorption will contribute to high concentrations in feces for the older tetracyclines. Only a small fraction of doxycycline is found in active form in feces, the larger part being bound as chelate.

Doxycycline may be given in normal doses to patients who have renal insufficiency and to those undergoing hemodialysis as the reduced renal excretion is compensated for by intestinal excretion of bound substance.[18] For minocycline, caution is recommended because of a larger risk of side effects.

ROUTE OF ADMINISTRATION AND DOSAGE

Peak serum levels after an oral dose of 500mg tetracycline or 200mg of doxycycline or minocycline are usually 3–5mg/l after 2 hours. Half-life in serum is longest for doxycycline (16–18 hours), followed by minocycline (11–13 hours) and tetracycline (8 hours). Doxycycline and minocycline can therefore be given once daily. A higher starting dose on day 1 is recommended in order to achieve a steady state level of the drug as early as possible. Dosages for adults are given in Table 200.3.

Doxycycline is also available for intravenous infusions but there is little difference in serum levels compared with oral administration.

DOSAGE IN SPECIAL CIRCUMSTANCES

In patients who have renal insufficiency or disease, doxycycline is the only tetracycline that can be used safely without risk of accumulation and toxicity.

PHARMACOKINETICS OF SOME TETRACYCLINES

	Tetracycline	Doxycycline	Minocycline
Oral absorption in fasting state (%)	80	90–93	100
Serum half-life (h)	6–12	18–22	13
Serum protein binding (%)	24–65	80–90	55–75
Lipid solubility in comparison with tetracycline	1	5	10
Excretion in urine (%) after oral administration	20	35–40	4–9

Table 200.2 Pharmacokinetics of some tetracyclines.

USUAL ADULT DOSAGES FOR SOME TETRACYCLINES

General name	Oral preparations: First dose	Oral preparations: Common dosage
Tetracycline	500mg	500mg q6h
Oxytetracycline	500mg	500mg q6h
Doxycycline	200mg	100mg q24h
Minocycline	200mg	100mg q12h

Table 200.3 Usual adult dosages for some tetracyclines. Doxycycline and minocycline may be given intravenously in the same doses. Higher doses of doxycycline are often used for sexually transmitted diseases and Lyme disease.

In patients who have hepatic disease tetracyclines should generally be avoided. If treatment is important, liver tests should be performed repeatedly during treatment. However, toxicity has mostly been observed when older tetracyclines have been used at high doses or given during pregnancy.

During pregnancy tetracyclines should be avoided because of the depressive effect on the skeleton of the child. In lactating patients a small amount of a tetracycline is excreted in the milk but is harmless to the baby.

In elderly patients kidney function is reduced according to age and the daily dose of a tetracycline should be reduced unless doxycycline is used.

INDICATIONS

Respiratory infections

Tetracyclines were first used for many types of respiratory tract infection. Because of increasing resistance in pneumococci and *H. influenzae*, they have been replaced in many areas by other antibiotics, mainly β-lactams.

Exacerbation of chronic bronchitis has been a classic indication for tetracyclines. Doxycycline has been found to be as effective as ampicillin. The advantage of one single dose per day may increase compliance in patients who have chronic respiratory diseases and many other medications (see Chapter 33).

Doxycycline is distributed to maxillary sinuses and can be used as a second-line drug in patients who have sinusitis and are allergic to β-lactams or in whom treatment with such drugs has failed.

Tetracyclines have good activity in pneumonias caused by *Mycoplasma pneumoniae*, *Chlamydia pneumoniae*, *Chlamydia psittaci* and *Coxiella burnetii*. Macrolides probably have an equal effect in infections caused by *M. pneumoniae* but clinical experience with the other infections is far greater with tetracyclines.

Sexually transmitted diseases

Tetracyclines are effective therapy for nongonococcal urethritis caused by *Chlamydia trachomatis* or *Ureaplasma urealyticum*. In an open evaluation of doxycycline in the treatment of urethritis and cervicitis caused by *C. trachomatis* the symptoms disappeared in 76%.[18] Treatment should usually be given for 10 days and concurrent treatment of sexual partners is recommended (see Chapter 74).

Tetracyclines are usually effective for the treatment of lymphogranuloma venereum and granuloma inguinale. Non-penicillinase-producing strains of gonococci are sensitive, which is an advantage in mixed infections with *C. trachomatis*.

Tetracyclines can be used as alternative therapy for syphilis in penicillin-allergic patients. Treatment time is 15 days for early disease and 30 days for later stages of the disease.

Lyme disease and ehrlichiosis

Doxycycline can be used in penicillin-allergic patients to treat erythema migrans and is as effective as penicillin in a dose of 200mg daily for 10 days. In erythema migrans with signs of dissemination such as multiple erythema and fever, doxycycline is often recommended as the primary drug. Treatment of neuroborreliosis with doxycycline 200mg daily for 2 weeks has given similar results to those achieved with penicillin G (see Chapter 54).[19]

Doxycycline is also the preferred drug for infections due to *Ehrlichia* spp (see Chapter 14).[20]

Other indications

Tetracyclines are very effective drugs for rickettsial infections (see Chapter 14). Doxycycline has been used for single-dose treatment of louse-borne typhus, but for other infections 7–10 days of treatment is usually needed. These infections can only be treated with tetracyclines or chloramphenicol. In children tetracyclines can often be given with minimal risk of staining the teeth if repeated treatments are avoided and the dose is kept as low as possible.

Doxycycline is also effective in a single dose for infections with *Borrelia recurrentis*. Tetracyclines are usually used in combination with other antibiotics such as streptomycin or rifampin (rifampicin) for brucellosis and tularemia.

For cholera in adults, tetracycline 500mg q6h for 5 days or a single dose of 300mg doxycycline have been recommended.[21]

Most tetracyclines have been used for oral treatment of chronic acne. The drugs have an antibacterial effect on *P. acnes* but also a general anti-inflammatory effect, which is probably of importance.[22] However, resistance of *P. acnes* to tetracyclines, including doxycyclines, has been reported from England and the USA. Cross-resistance does not include minocycline, which may be used clinically.[23]

Doxycycline may also be used for malaria prophylaxis in areas where *Plasmodium falciparum* is resistant to other antimalarial drugs.[24]

ADVERSE REACTIONS AND INTERACTIONS

Adverse drug reactions

All oral preparations of tetracyclines can cause nausea and epigastric discomfort. It is usually an advantage if the drugs can be taken with food without decreasing absorption, as with doxycycline and minocycline. Diarrhea is less common but may occur, especially when tetracyclines with low absorption are used.

Phototoxic reactions can occur with all tetracyclines.

Tetracyclines should not be used in children aged 8 years or less because of the risk of enamel hypoplasia and tooth discoloration. They should also not be used during pregnancy. Tetracyclines, except doxycycline, are contraindicated in patients who have renal impairment, because inhibition of protein synthesis increases azotemia from amino acid metabolism.

Vertigo and dizziness are CNS symptoms that occur with minocycline only and must be considered a major disadvantage of that antibiotic.

Hepatotoxicity and other severe organ reactions have occurred, mainly after parenteral therapy – often with high doses – and also when the drugs have had to be used during pregnancy.

Drug–drug interactions

Tetracyclines form chelate complexes with many drugs containing metal ions (Table 200.4). When combined with diuretics the risk of accumulation of urea increases, with the exception of doxycycline. Some drugs seem to stimulate liver enzymes, so increasing doxycycline metabolism and shortening its half-life.

DRUG INTERACTIONS WITH TETRACYCLINES

Interacting drug	Effect
Antacids with metal ions, calcium, zinc, iron, didanosine	Chelate formation and impaired absorption
Diuretics	Risk of increased serum urea concentration – not with doxycycline
Rifampin, phenobarbital, phenytoin, carbamazepine	Half-life of doxycycline shortened

Table 200.4 Drug interactions with tetracyclines.

CHLORAMPHENICOL

INTRODUCTION

Chloramphenicol was first isolated in 1947 from a sample of soil from Venezuela and the actinomycete was called *Streptomyces venezuelae*.

MODE OF ACTION AND SPECTRUM

Chloramphenicol inhibits protein synthesis by binding to the larger 50S subunit of the 70S ribosome. It is mainly a bacteriostatic agent but a bactericidal effect on some bacteria, such as *H. influenzae*, *Streptococcus pneumoniae* and *Neisseria meningitidis*, has been reported.

Chloramphenicol has a very broad spectrum, similar to that of tetracyclines, and it includes aerobic and anaerobic bacteria, spirochetes, rickettsias, chlamydias and mycoplasmas. It is very active against most anaerobic bacteria of clinical interest, including *Bacteroides fragilis*.

Chloramphenicol resistance can occur and is mediated by a bacterial enzyme, acetyltransferase, which inactivates the drug. This mechanism is R-factor-mediated, and epidemics of chloramphenicol-resistant typhoid fever and *Shigella* infections have occurred.

Unrestricted use of chloramphenicol seems to result in a resistance problem very similar to that observed with tetracyclines.

ROUTE OF ADMINISTRATION AND DOSAGE

Chloramphenicol is conjugated with glucuronic acid and is then excreted in active form by the kidneys. The metabolites are not toxic and dose reduction is not needed in renal insufficiency.

Chloramphenicol is a rather small lipophilic molecule and is well distributed in the body. The serum protein binding is about 44%. It reaches the CNS better than most other antibiotics and its concentration in the cerebrospinal fluid is often 30–50% of the serum concentration. Chloramphenicol also crosses the placenta and is found in breast milk.

Chloramphenicol is well absorbed (over 90%) after oral administration. Chloramphenicol 1g gives a serum concentration of 10mg/l and the half-life is 3–4 hours. It may also be given intravenously as a succinate ester but intramuscular injections should be avoided as absorption is unreliable.

INDICATIONS

Chloramphenicol is toxic and therefore it should be used carefully in systemic infections, when other alternatives are lacking. It can be used instead of tetracyclines for the treatment of rickettsial infections and for bacterial meningitis in the few patients who have an allergy to β-lactam drugs that includes third-generation cephalosporins and meropenem. It may also have a place as an oral alternative for CNS infections, especially brain abscesses.

Topical administration of chloramphenicol in drops or ointments is widely used for superficial bacterial infections of the eyes. Such treatment is still effective in comparison with the newer drugs such as quinolones or fusidic acid, which are also used locally for eye infections.[25,26]

ADVERSE REACTIONS AND INTERACTIONS

Adverse drug reactions

Neonates have a diminished ability to conjugate chloramphenicol and to excrete the active form in the urine. A dose of 25mg/kg/day should not be exceeded[27] otherwise the 'gray baby syndrome' may develop, with severe cyanosis and circulatory collapse.

Dose-related reversible bone marrow depression can occur in adults given high doses of more than 4g/day. The daily dose should not exceed 3g, and when the accumulated dose exceeds 25g reticulocytes should be checked regularly (e.g. twice weekly) until treatment is stopped.

A very severe reaction is aplastic anemia, which occurs with a frequency of 1/25,000–40,000 treatment courses.[28] No clear correlation to dose or duration of treatment has been observed and no route of administration is exempt from causing this catastrophic complication. There are also reports to indicate that the use of chloramphenicol may increase the risk of leukemia in children.[29]

Drug–drug interactions

As chloramphenicol is almost completely metabolized in the liver by cytochrome P450 enzymes, there is a possible risk of interactions with other drugs if they are metabolized by the same enzyme system. Chloramphenicol will decrease the rate of metabolism of tolbutamide, phenytoin, cyclophosphamide and warfarin. Rifampin may lower chloramphenicol concentrations by induced metabolism.

REFERENCES

1. Rylander M, Hallander HO. *In vitro* comparison of the activity of doxycycline, tetracycline, erythromycin and a new macrolide, CP 62993, against *Mycoplasma pneumoniae, Mycoplasma hominis* and *Ureaplasma urealyticum*. Scand J Infect Dis 1988;53(Suppl.):12–7.
2. Steigbigel NH, Reed CW, Finland M. Susceptibility of common pathogenic bacteria to seven tetracycline antibiotics *in vitro*. Am J Med Sci 1968;255:179–95.
3. Brogden RN, Speight TM, Avery GS. Minocycline: a review of its antibacterial and pharmacokinetic properties and therapeutic use. Drugs 1975;9:251–91.
4. Alestig K, Lidin-Janson G. The effect of doxycycline and tetracycline hydrochloride on the aerobic fecal flora. Scand J Infect Dis 1975;6:265–71.
5. Fabre J, Pitton JS, Kunz JP. Distribution and excretion of doxycycline in man. Chemotherapia 1966;11:73–85.
6. Levy SB, Fitzgerald GB, Macone AB. Changes in intestinal flora of farm personnel after introduction of a tetracycline-supplemented feed on a farm. N Engl J Med 1976;295:583–8.
7. Hirsch DC, Burton GC, Bleuden DC. The effect of tetracycline upon establishment of *Escherichia coli* of bovine origin in the alimentary tract of man. J Appl Bacteriol 1974;37:327–33.
8. Holmberg SD, Osterholm MT, Senger KA, Cohen ML. Drug-resistant *Salmonella* from animals fed antimicrobials. N Engl J Med 1984;311:617–22.
9. Doern GV. Trends in antimicrobial susceptibility of bacterial pathogens of the respiratory tract. Am J Med 1995;99(Suppl.6B):3–7S.
10. Grahnén A, Olsson B, Johansson G, Eckernäs S-Å. Doxycycline carragenate – an improved formulation providing more reliable absorption and plasma concentrations at high gastric pH than doxycycline monohydrate. Eur J Clin Pharmacol 1994;46:143–6.
11. Berger RS. A double-blind, multiple-dose placebo-controlled, cross-over study to compare the incidence of gastrointestinal complaints in healthy subjects given Doxy R and Vibramycin R. J Clin Pharmacol 1988;28:367–70.
12. Mandal AK, Thadepalli H, Bach VT. Doxycycline tissue levels in the respiratory tract. Postgrad Med 1979;1(Suppl.):81–6.
13. Mathisen W, Normann E, Taksdal S, Otnes B. Doxycycline levels in prostatic tissue and blood. Eur Urol 1975;1:157–8.
14. Dotevall L, Hagberg L. Penetration of doxycycline into cerebrospinal fluid in patients treated for suspected Lyme borreliosis. Antimicrob Agents Chemother 1989;33:1078–80.
15. Dotevall L, Alestig K, Hanner P, *et al.* The use of doxycycline in nervous system *Borrelia burgdorferi* infection. Scand J Infect Dis 1988;53:74–9.
16. Stiernstedt G. Therapeutic aspects of Lyme borreliosis. Clin Dermatol 1993;11:423–9.
17. Williams DN, Laughlin LW, Lee YH. Minocycline: possible vestibular side-effects. Lancet 1974;2:744–6.

18. Noguera X, Ferrer M, Ortda E, Lopez-Marin L. Evaluation of doxycycline in the treatment of urethritis and cervicitis caused by *Chlamydia trachomatis*. Clin Ther 1986;9(Suppl. A):33–7.
19. Schach von Wittenau M, Twomey TM. The disposition of doxycycline by man and dog. Chemotherapy 1971;16:217–28.
20. Dumler, JF, Walker DH. Tick-borne ehrlichioses. Lancet Infect Dis 2001;0: 21–8.
21. Farthing M, Feldman R, Finch R, *et al.* The management of infective gastroenteritis in adults. A consensus statement by an expert panel convened by the British Society for the Study of Infection. J Infect 1996;33:143–52.
22. Van Vlem B, Vanholder R, De Paepe P, Vogelaers D, Ringoir S. Immuno-modulating effects of antibiotics: literature review. Infection 1996;24:275–91.
23. Eady EA, Jones CE, Tipper JL, Cove JH, Cunliffe WJ, Layton AM. Antibiotic resistant propionibacteria in acne: need for policies to modify antibiotic usage. Br Med J 1993;306:555–6.
24. Pradines B, Spiegel A, Rogier C, *et al.* Antibiotics for prophylaxis of *Plasmodium falciparum* infections: in vitro activity of doxycycline against Senegalese isolates. Am J Trop Med Hyg 2000;62:82–5.
25. Power WJ, Collum LM, Easty DL, *et al.* Evaluation of efficacy and safety of ciprofloxacin ophthalmic solution versus chloramphenicol. Eur J Ophthalmol 1993;2:77–82.
26. Horven I. Acute conjunctivitis. A comparison of fusidic acid viscous eye drops and chloramphenicol. Acta Ophthalmol Copenh 1993;2:165–8.
27. Burns LE, Hodgman JE, Cass AB. Fatal circulatory collapse in premature infants receiving chloramphenicol. N Engl J Med 1959;261:1318–21.
28. Wallerstein RO, Condit PK, Kasper CK, *et al.* Statewide study of chloramphenicol therapy and fatal aplastic anemia. JAMA 1969;208:2045–50.
29. Shu XO, Linet MS, Gao RN, *et al.* Chloramphenicol use and childhood leukemia in Shanghai. Lancet 1987;2:934–7.

chapter 201

Nitroimidazoles: Metronidazole, Ornidazole and Tinidazole

S Ragnar Norrby

INTRODUCTION

The nitroimidazoles were developed as antimicrobial agents against protozoa, initially *Trichomonas vaginalis* and subsequently *Entamoeba histolytica* and *Giardia lamblia*. During the 1970s it was recognized that they are also highly active against strictly anaerobic bacteria, including difficult-to-treat organisms such as *Bacteroides fragilis* and *Clostridium difficile*. The mechanism(s) by which nitroimidazoles exert their antiprotozoan and antibacterial activities are not known in detail. It seems clear, however, that, after anaerobic reduction, the various derivatives interact with DNA and possibly other metabolic processes in bacteria and protozoa.[1,2] Although they are still used against protozoa, anaerobic infections and, recently, treatment of gastric ulcer caused by *Helicobacter pylori* have become the main indications for the nitroimidazoles. In addition they have also been used as radiosensitizing agents in patients who have solid tumors.

The nitroimidazoles that are available are metronidazole, tinidazole and ornidazole, but tinidazole and ornidazole are not available in the USA. In this chapter, the emphasis will be on metronidazole.

PHARMACOKINETICS

Following oral administration all nitroimidazoles are almost completely absorbed.[3] After rectal administration of metronidazole the absorption is estimated to be about 60%, with considerable variability between individuals. When given vaginally the bioavailability of metronidazole is 20% or less. Following a 400mg oral dose of metronidazole or tinidazole, peak plasma concentrations of about 10mg/l are achieved after 3–5 hours. Dose proportional kinetics have been seen for doses up to 2g. The concentrations after normal oral doses are well above the minimum inhibitory concentrations (MICs) for anaerobes but are borderline for *Gardnerella vaginalis*.

The nitroimidazoles are well distributed to peripheral compartments, including brain tissue and cerebrospinal fluid.[3] However, there are low concentrations (15% or less of concurrent serum levels) in subcutaneous fat.[4]

Nitroimidazoles are eliminated mainly via liver metabolism. The plasma half-life is about 8 hours for metronidazole and 12–13 hours for tinidazole. Metronidazole is partly metabolized to hydroxymetronidazole, which has a longer half-life (10–13 hours). Metronidazole elimination is prolonged in newborns and infants, and also in adults who have serious liver impairment (e.g. cirrhosis). Decreased renal function does not affect the half-life. The drugs are partly eliminated by hemodialysis. These antibiotics have no reported effects per se on the central nervous system, liver, lungs, kidneys, prostate or genitourinary system.

ROUTE OF ADMINISTRATION AND DOSAGE

The two most frequently used nitroimidazoles, metronidazole and tinidazole, are available for parenteral and oral use and also as suppositories and for vaginal administration. A metronidazole gel is used for periodontitis. Dosages of metronidazole are given in Table 201.1. Those of tinidazole and ornidazole are similar but, because their half-lives are longer, these drugs can be given q24h or q12h instead of q12h or q8h. Recommendations in the USA are normally for shorter dose intervals (i.e. q6h) for metronidazole than are indicated in Table 201.1. Considering the half-life, dose intervals shorter than q8h should not be needed and in most cases q12h regimens should be optimal.

In elderly patients the same doses should be used as in younger adults. Doses should be reduced in patients who have reduced liver function but full doses can be given irrespective of renal function. Metronidazole passes to breast milk but the concentrations achieved are unlikely to affect a child. There is no documentation on the use of metronidazole during pregnancy.

DOSAGES OF METRONIDAZOLE			
Type of infection	**Adult dose**	**Child dose**	**Duration of treatment (days)**
Trichomoniasis	2g	Not applicable	Single dose
Giardiasis	600mg q12h	15mg/kg q12h	6–7 days
Amebic dysentery	800mg q8h	20mg/kg q12h	5–10 days
Amebic abscess	800mg q8h	20mg/kg q12h	10 days
Vaginosis	400mg q12h	Not applicable	7 days
Helicobacter infection	400mg q8h	Not applicable	7–14 days
Clostridium difficile enteritis	800mg q8h	7.5mg/kg q12h	7–10 days
Anaerobic infections (treatment)	800mg q8h	7.5mg/kg q12h	7–14 days
Anaerobic infections (prophylaxis)	800mg	7.5mg/kg	Single dose

Table 201.1 Dosages of metronidazole. Child dose is for children aged 8 weeks or more.

INDICATIONS

Bacterial infections

The spectrum of activity of nitroimidazoles against strictly anaerobic bacteria is summarized in Table 201.2. No clinically important differences exist between the antianaerobic activities of the various derivatives in the group.[7] Nitroimidazoles are the most active antibiotics for the treatment and prevention of anaerobic infections and resistance is rare but has been reported.[8] However, their disadvantage is their lack of activity against aerobes. As anaerobic infections, with few exceptions, are mixed aerobic/anaerobic infections, nitroimidazoles are routinely combined with other antibiotics. The most common combinations are with cephalosporins or aminoglycosides. Anaerobic infections for which nitroimidazole use is well documented are brain

ACTIVITY OF METRONIDAZOLE AGAINST ANAEROBIC BACTERIA		
Organism	**Metronidazole MIC (mg/l) for 90% of isolates**	**Percent sensitive (NCCLS)**
Bacteroides fragilis	1–4	100
Prevotella spp.	4	100
Fusobacterium nucleatum	0.25–2	100
Fusobacterium spp.	0.25–4	100
Peptostreptococcus spp.	0.5–4	100
Propionibacterium acnes	>16	0
Clostridium difficile	0.5–4	100
Clostridium spp.	2–16	95

Table 201.2 Activity of metronidazole against anaerobic bacteria. NCCLS, National Committee for Clinical Laboratory Standards. Data from Wexler *et al.*[5] and Spangler *et al.*[6]

abscesses, intra-abdominal infections, gynecologic infections and antibiotic-associated diarrhea or colitis caused by *C. difficile*. For the latter infection, metronidazole should be preferred over oral vancomycin, which might increase the risk of selection of resistant Gram-positive aerobic bacteria (e.g. enterococci) in the lower intestinal tract.

Two bacterial species that are not obligate anaerobes have also been found to be sensitive to metronidazole treatment:

- *G. vaginalis*, implicated in the etiology of vaginosis, is susceptible to nitroimidazoles with MIC values higher (8–16mg/l) than for anaerobes;[9] and
- *H. pylori*, which causes gastric ulcers and has been correlated to gastric cancer, is often susceptible to nitroimidazoles. Metronidazole is one of several antibiotics that, in combination with other antibiotics, can be used for treatment of gastric ulcers caused by *H. pylori* despite the fact that resistance to metronidazole is not uncommon.[10]

Protozoal infections

The nitroimidazoles seem to be uniformly active against protozoa. However, resistance has been reported in *T. vaginalis* and in some cases the organisms have been resistant to metronidazole but more sensitive to tinidazole.[11] Nitroimidazoles are first-line treatment for giardiasis, amebiasis and trichomoniasis. For these infections there are few alternatives outside this group.[12] This is also the case for bacterial vaginosis.[13]

ADVERSE REACTIONS AND INTERACTIONS

Although nitroimidazoles have been found to be mutagenic and carcinogenic in animal studies, they are generally well tolerated in humans. One meta-analysis of more than 1300 pregnant women who had received metronidazole during their pregnancies showed no indication of teratogenicity.[14] The most common side effect is a metallic taste, especially when high doses are used. Reversible neuralgia has been reported in patients receiving high doses for prolonged periods. If combined with alcohol, metronidazole may cause an Antabuse-like reaction. Severe psychotic reactions have been reported in patients receiving metronidazole and disulfiram together, and so nitroimidazoles should not be given with disulfiram.

REFERENCES

1. Müller M. Action of clinically utilized 5-nitroimidazoles on microorganisms. Scand J Infect Dis 1981;(Suppl.26):31–41.
2. Tocher JH, Edwards DI. Evidence for the direct interaction of reduced metronidazole derivatives with DNA bases. Biochem Pharmacol 1994;48:1089–94.
3. Lau AH, Lam NP, Piscitelli SC, Wilkes L, Danziger LH. Clinical pharmacokinetics of metronidazole and other nitroimidazole anti-infectives. Clin Pharmacokinet 1992;23:328–64.
4. Badia JM, de la Torre R, Farre M, *et al.* Inadequate levels of metronidazole in subcutaneous fat after standard prophylaxis. Br J Surg 1995;82:479–82.
5. Wexler HM, Molitorius E, Finegold SM. The *in-vitro* activity of L-627 against anaerobic bacteria. J Antimicrob Chemother 1994;33:629–34.
6. Spangler SK, Jacobs MR, Appelbaum PC. Activity of WY-49605 compared with those of amoxicillin, amoxicillin–clavulanate, imipenem, ciprofloxacin, cefaclor, cefpodoxime, cefuroxime, clindamycin, and metronidazole against 384 anaerobic bacteria. Antimicrob Agents Chemother 1994;38:2599–604.
7. Belgian Collaborative Study Group. Belgian collaborative study of the in-vitro susceptibility of the *Bacteroides fragilis* group. Eur J Epidemiol 1988;4:360–5.
8. Snydman DR, Jacobus NV, McDermott LA, *et al.* Multicenter study of in vitro susceptibility of *Bacteroides fragilis* group, 1995 to 1996 with comparison of resistance trends from 1990 to 1996. Antimicrob Agents Chemother 1999;43:2417–22.
9. Kharsany ABM, Hoosen AA, van den Ende J. Antimicrobial susceptibilities of *Gardnerella vaginalis*. Antimicrob Agents Chemother 1993;37:2733–5.
10. Meyer JM, Silliman NP, Wang W, *et al.* Risk factors for *Helicobacter pylori* resistance in the United States: the surveillance of *H. pylori* antimicrobial resistance partnership (SHARP) study, 1993–1999. Ann Intern Med 2002;136:13–24.
11. Narcisi EM, Secor WE. In vitro effect of tinidazole and furazolidone on metronidazole-resistant *Trichomonas vaginalis*. Antimicrob Agents Chemother 1996;40:1121–5.
12. Neri A, Rabinerson D, Kaplan B. Bacterial vaginosis: drugs versus alternative treatment. Obstet Gynecol Surv 1994;49:809–13.
13. Walsh JH, Peterson WL. Treatment of *Helicobacter pylori* infection in the management of peptic ulcer disease. N Engl J Med 1995;333:984–91.
14. Burtin P, Taddio A, Aruburno O, Einarson TR, Koren G. Safety of metronidazole in pregnancy: a meta-analysis. Am J Obstet Gynecol 1995;172:525–9.

chapter

202 Antituberculosis Agents

John M Grange & Alimuddin Zumla

INTRODUCTION

Tuberculosis is at least as old as recorded human history, and a major preoccupation of the medical profession over the millennia has been the search for a cure for this 'Captain of all of these Men of Death', as the evangelist John Bunyan termed it. Numerous remedies have been described; many, such as bleeding, purging and John of Gaddeston's prescription of a mixture of pigeon's dung and weasel's blood were undoubtedly worse than useless. In 1782, Sir William Buchan remarked that, apart from a trip to the West Indies, milk was probably as effective as the entire pharmacopeia. In the Indian ayurvedic medical system, the malabar nut (*Adhatoda vasica*) was advocated and several British military doctors of the 19th century were impressed with its efficacy. In Europe, cod liver oil was widely used after its introduction by Percival in 1770; indeed, it was the most widely prescribed remedy at the Brompton Hospital for Consumptives, London, for several decades after its foundation in the mid-19th century. Owing to its high vitamin D content, it may well have had a positive effect because calcitriol, the active metabolite of this vitamin, is involved in the activation of human macrophages.

The discovery of the tubercle bacillus raised serious hopes that an effective remedy would soon be found and many workers attempted to develop immunotherapeutic agents. The best known of these attempts was Robert Koch's development of old tuberculin, but the British bacteriologist Sir Almroth Wright also conducted extensive studies, which are immortalized in George Bernard Shaw's play *The Doctor's Dilemma*.

It was, however, the discovery of streptomycin in 1944 by Albert Schatz and Selman Waksman in the USA that opened the door to effective therapy and led many health workers to believe that the disease would soon be conquered. Early jubilation turned to disappointment when it was found that patients treated with streptomycin often made an initial improvement but soon relapsed with disease because their tubercle bacilli became resistant to this agent. Fortunately, other active antituberculosis agents were soon discovered and, as a result of extensive trials initiated by Sir John Crofton in the UK, multidrug regimens that cured patients and prevented the emergence of drug resistance were developed.[1]

Therapy of tuberculosis with these early drug regimens, usually consisting of streptomycin, isoniazid and *para*-aminosalicylic acid, was beset with problems. Streptomycin had to be given by injection and *para*-aminosalicylic acid caused such severe gastrointestinal effects that patients often failed to comply with therapy. In addition, it was necessary to treat patients for 18–24 months in order to achieve a cure.

The second therapeutic revolution came in the early 1970s when regimens containing rifampin (rifampicin) were developed. The introduction of this drug had three major effects on the treatment of tuberculosis. First, the duration of therapy could be reduced to only 6 months so that the era of 'short course' therapy had arrived. Secondly, regimens could be entirely oral ones and thirdly, as a consequence, hospitalization could often be avoided.

Modern short course therapy, properly used, can achieve a cure in around 98% of patients and is among the most effective and cost-effective of all therapeutic interventions for a chronic disease.[2] Far from being conquered, however, tuberculosis remains one of the most prevalent causes of mortality and morbidity; it is responsible for one in seven deaths among young adults and it was declared a global emergency by the World Health Organization (WHO) in 1993. The problem is currently fueled by the HIV pandemic and the increasing prevalence of multidrug-resistant tuberculosis (MDRTB), and there is accordingly a very urgent need to develop new therapies and to use the available therapies in a much more responsible manner.

CLASSIFICATION

Antituberculous agents can be classified in several ways (Table 202.1). First, they can be divided into those that are synthetic molecules and those that are antibiotics or semisynthetic antibiotic derivatives. Second, they can be divided into agents with a broad spectrum of activity and use and those only active against mycobacteria or, specifically, members of the *Mycobacterium tuberculosis* complex. Third, they can be divided into the first-line drugs that form the basis of the modern short-course regimens advocated by the WHO and the second-line drugs, which are used in cases of drug resistance and where toxic reactions prevent the use of one or more first-line drugs. Finally, they can be divided into bacteriostatic and bactericidal agents, with the latter being further divided into those that are bactericidal in vitro and those that are able to sterilize lesions of tubercle bacilli in vivo (Table 202.2). This distinction is a clinically important one.

MODE OF ACTION AND PHARMACOKINETICS

Previously poorly understood, there have been considerable advances in recent years in our understanding of the genetic basis of action of the drugs used specifically for treating mycobacterial disease as a result of the successful sequencing of the genome of *M. tuberculosis*.[3]

The targets of streptomycin and other aminoglycosides, rifampin and the fluoroquinolones are the same in mycobacteria as in *Escherichia coli*, and resistance is due to single amino acid substitutions in the target proteins. Some other drugs, notably isoniazid, pyrazinamide, ethambutol, ethionamide and prothionamide, target specific components of the complex and lipid-rich mycobacterial cell wall. The mode of action and target genes are discussed under the individual drug headings below and are summarized in Table 202.3; the targets are shown in Figure 202.1. Most of the antituberculosis agents are readily absorbed from the gastrointestinal tract. Exceptions are streptomycin and other aminoglycosides, capreomycin and viomycin, which must therefore be given parenterally. Binding to serum proteins varies from agent to agent, as does entry into the cerebrospinal fluid (CSF). Agents that enter into the CSF poorly in health often pass the inflamed meninges so that therapeutically useful levels are achieved in cases of tuberculous meningitis. The pharmacokinetics of the conventional antimycobacterial drugs, their principal

SPECTRUM OF ACTIVITY, CLASS OF COMPOUND AND CROSS-RESISTANCES OF THE ANTITUBERCULOSIS AGENTS			
Agent	**Class of compound**	**Spectrum of activity**	**Cross resistance to other antituberculosis agents**
First-line agents			
Rifampin	Antibiotic	Broad	Other rifamycins
Isoniazid	Synthetic	Tubercle bacilli	None
Pyrazinamide	Synthetic	Tubercle bacilli	None
Ethambutol	Synthetic	Tubercle bacilli	None
Streptomycin	Antibiotic	Broad	Other aminoglycosides, viomycin, capreomycin
Second-line agents			
Thiacetazone	Synthetic	Tubercle bacilli	Ethionamide and prothionamide
para-aminosalicylic acid	Synthetic	Tubercle bacilli	None
Ethionamide and prothionamide	Synthetic	Tubercle bacilli	Thiacetazone
Capreomycin	Antibiotic	Tubercle bacilli	Aminoglycosides, viomycin
Viomycin	Antibiotic	Tubercle bacilli	Aminoglycosides, capreomycin
Cycloserine	Synthetic	Broad	None
Ofloxacin	Antibiotic	Broad	None

Table 202.1 Spectrum of activity, class of compound and cross-resistances of the antituberculosis agents. Agents that are active against tubercle bacilli (*Mycobacterium tuberculosis* complex) may also show activity against some other species of mycobacteria. Strains of *Mycobacterium bovis* are naturally resistant to pyrazinamide. There are only limited data on other activities of capreomycin and viomycin.

EFFICACY OF ANTITUBERCULOSIS AGENTS			
Agent	**Early bactericidal activity**	**Sterilizing activity**	**Prevention of emergence of drug resistance**
Rifampin	✓	✓✓	✓✓
Pyrazinamide	×	✓✓	×
Isoniazid	✓✓	✓	✓✓
Ethambutol	✓	×	✓
Streptomycin	×	×	✓
Thiacetazone	×	×	×

Table 202.2 Efficacy of antituberculosis agents. In sterilizing lesions, reducing viable bacterial population rapidly and preventing the emergence of drug resistance. ✓✓, good; ✓, fair; ×, poor. Data from Mitchison.

metabolites and routes of excretion are summarized in Tables 202.4 and 202.5 and are reviewed in depth elsewhere.[4]

DRUG TOXICITY

Although all antituberculosis drugs have some untoward side effects, drug toxicity is, in general, not a serious problem in modern short-course chemotherapy based on the first-line agents and is a small price to pay for the very real curative benefits. The major side effects are hepatotoxicity, peripheral neuropathy, mental disturbances, skin reactions (Figs 202.2–202.4) and fevers. Side effects are particularly likely to occur in HIV-positive patients and, of these, skin reactions due to thiacetazone are particularly serious and may be fatal.

The three principal drugs used in modern short-course regimens – isoniazid, rifampin and pyrazinamide – are all potentially hepato-

ANTITUBERCULOSIS AGENTS: TARGETS AND GENES FOR RESISTANCE		
Agent	**Target**	**Gene(s) encoding target(s) or those in which mutations conferring resistance occur**
Isoniazid	Mycolic acid synthesis	*inhA, katG, KasA, oxyR-ahpC*
Rifampin	DNA-dependent RNA polymerase	*rpoB*
Pyrazinamide	Fatty acid synthetase-1	*pncA*
Ethambutol	Arabinosyl transferase, involved in cell wall arabinogalactan synthesis	*embA, embB and embC*
Streptomycin	30S ribosomal subunit	*rspL* (encodes for ribosomal protein S12)
Other aminoglycosides	30S ribosomal subunit	genes encoding 16S-rRNA (and possibly *aac(2')* encoding aminoglycoside acetyltransferase)
Thiacetazone	Mycolic acid synthesis	Unknown
para-aminosalicylic acid	Mycobactin synthesis (?)	Unknown
Ethionamide and prothionamide	Mycolic acid synthesis	*inhA*
Macrolides	50S ribosomal subunit	Gene encoding peptidyl transferase region in 23S rRNA
Capreomycin and viomycin	50S or 30S ribosomal subunit	*vicA* (50S) or *vicB* (30S)
Clofazimine	Unknown; possibly RNA polymerase	–
Cycloserine	Peptidoglycan	*alrA*
Fluoroquinolones	DNA gyrase (topoisomerase)	*gyrA*

Table 202.3 Antituberculosis agents: targets and genes for resistance.

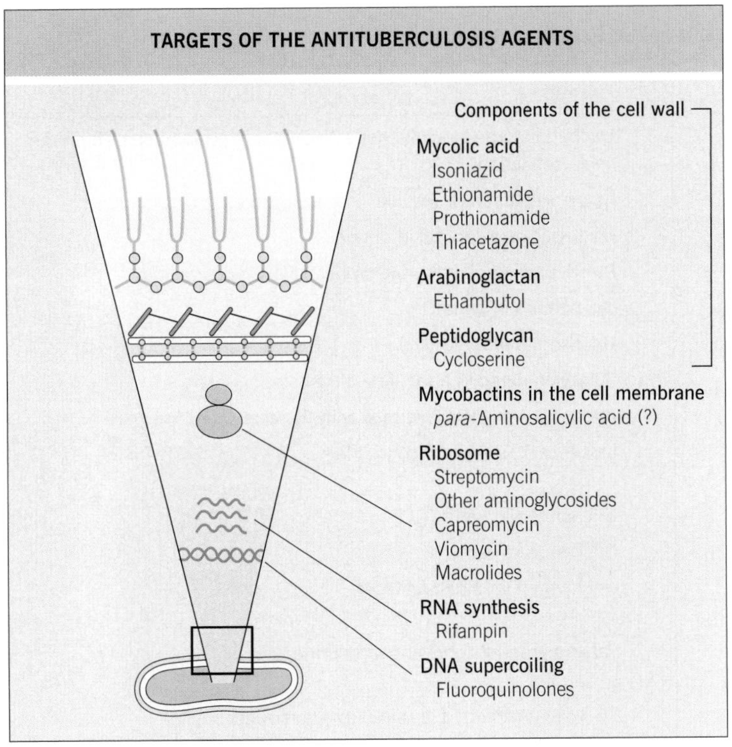

Fig. 202.1 Targets of the antituberculosis agents.

toxic, but this is seldom a problem in clinical practice. Some physicians, however, take a more cautious view and advocate regular liver function tests during therapy.[5] The adverse effects of the various drugs are discussed under the individual headings below and are summarized in Table 202.6.

FIRST-LINE DRUGS

Isoniazid (isonicotinic acid hydrazide)

The most widely used of all antituberculosis drugs, this is included in all modern regimens. It is also used as preventive monotherapy for infected (tuberculin-positive) persons, particularly in the USA.

It has a powerful bactericidal action against actively replicating tubercle bacilli and thus rapidly reduces infectiousness by reducing the number of viable bacilli in cavities. It has little or no activity against slowly replicating bacilli but is included in the continuation phase of modern short-course therapy to kill any rifampin-resistant mutants that commence replication. It inhibits the synthesis of mycolic acids – long-chain fatty acids that form an important part of the mycobacterial cell wall. Although mycolic acids are common to all mycobacteria, and similar molecules occur in the genera *Nocardia* and *Corynebacterium*, susceptibility to isoniazid is virtually restricted to the *M. tuberculosis* complex, although some strains of *Mycobacterium xenopi* and *Mycobacterium kansasii* are susceptible. Some, but not all, isoniazid-resistant strains of *M. tuberculosis* lack catalase–peroxidase activity because of point mutations in, or deletion of, the *katG* gene that encodes this enzyme. Conversely, many strains from south India have either weak catalase–peroxidase activity or none at all but are fully susceptible to isoniazid. Other mutations associated with isoniazid resistance occur in the *inhA* gene, which encodes for long-chain enoyl-acyl carrier protein reductase required for synthesis of mycolic acids, and the *oxyR–ahpC* genes that encode for antioxidant proteins.[6] Thus, several mutational changes induce isoniazid resistance and the predominant mutation(s) show geographic variations in their distribution.

Isoniazid is readily absorbed from the gastrointestinal tract and is converted to inactive metabolites, principally by acetylation, the rate of which is genetically determined. Thus, patients can be divided into rapid acetylators and slow acetylators, in whom the elimination half-lives of the drug are 0.5–1.5 hours and 2–4 hours respectively. About half of Caucasian and black patients but over 80% of Chinese and Japanese patients are rapid acetylators. If administered regularly, response to therapy is unaffected by acetylator status but drug interactions (see below) are more likely to occur in slow acetylators.

Owing to its widespread use since the 1950s, resistance to isoniazid is common and many strains that are resistant to other antituberculosis drugs, particularly to rifampin, are also resistant to isoniazid.

Adverse events are usually mild and are more likely to occur in slow acetylators. They include several neurologic effects, including

PHARMACOKINETICS OF THE ANTITUBERCULOSIS AGENTS			
Agent	**Binding to serum proteins**	**Absorption from gastrointestinal tract (time to reach peak serum level)**	**Entry into CSF (with healthy meninges)**
Isoniazid	Very low	Very rapid (30–60 minutes)	Good
Rifampin	High (up to 95%)	Rapid (2 hours)	Poor
Pyrazinamide	Very low	Rapid (1–2 hours)	Good
Ethambutol	Binds to erythrocytes	Rapid (2 hours); 80% of dose absorbed	Poor
Streptomycin	Moderate (30–35%)	Not absorbed	Poor
Thiacetazone	Not bound	Rapid (2 hours)	Limited data
para-aminosalicylic acid	High (60–65%)	Very rapid	Poor
Ethionamide and prothionamide	Limited data	Very rapid (30 minutes)	Good
Capreomycin	Limited data	Not absorbed	Poor
Viomycin	Limited data	Not absorbed	Poor
Clofazimine	Limited data	Slow (8–12 hours)	Limited data
Cycloserine	Not bound	Rapid (3 hours)	Good
Ofloxacin	Low	Rapid (1–1.5 hours)	Moderate

Table 202.4 Pharmacokinetics of the antituberculosis agents.

PRINCIPAL METABOLIC PRODUCTS AND EXCRETION OF THE ANTITUBERCULOSIS AGENTS		
Agent	**Principal metabolic products**	**Excretion**
Isoniazid	Acetyl derivatives: rate of acetylation is genetically controlled	Unchanged and as acetyl derivatives in urine (ratio depends on rate of acetylation)
Rifampin	Desacetyl derivative	As desacetylrifampin in bile
Pyrazinamide	Pyrazinoic acid	Mostly as pyrazinoic acid in urine
Ethambutol	Oxidation products and aldehydes	Mostly unchanged in urine; about 15% as metabolites
Streptomycin	None	Unchanged in urine
Other aminoglycosides	None	Unchanged in urine
Thiacetazone	Unknown	20% eliminated in urine, fate of remainder unknown
para-aminosalicylic acid	Acetylation products and glycine conjugates	About 80% in the urine, mostly in the acetylated form
Ethionamide and prothionamide	Sulfoxide (biologically active) and methyl derivatives	Less than 1% unchanged in urine
Capreomycin	None	Unchanged in urine
Viomycin	None	Unchanged in urine
Clofazimine	Very small amounts of unidentified metabolites	Unchanged in urine and feces
Cycloserine	Up to 35% converted to unidentified metabolites	Varying amounts unchanged in urine
Ofloxacin	5% metabolized to oxides and dimethyl derivatives	70–95% unchanged in urine, small amounts in bile

Table 202.5 Principal metabolic products and excretion of the antituberculosis agents.

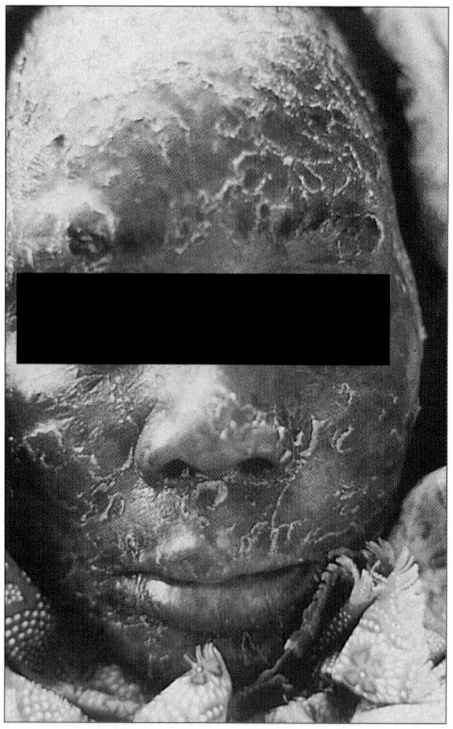

Fig. 202.2 Severe dermal reaction to isoniazid. Courtesy of Dr P Mwaba, Zambia.

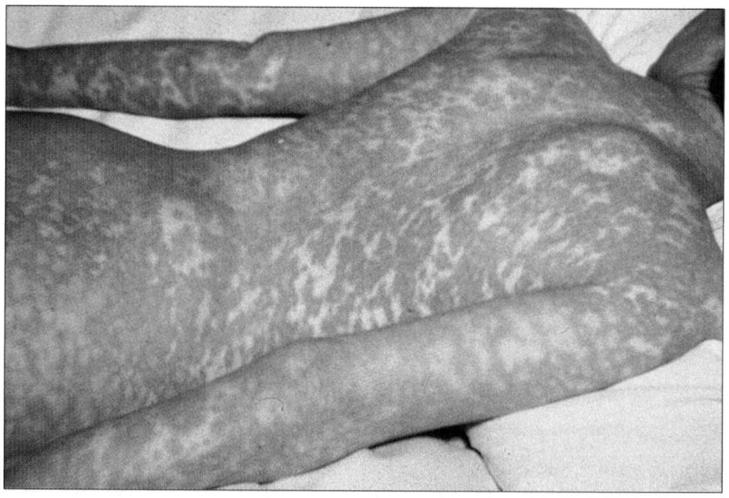

Fig. 202.3 Erythema multiforme reaction to rifampin. Courtesy of Dr P Mwaba, Zambia.

insomnia, restlessness, peripheral neuropathy, optic neuritis and various, but usually mild, psychiatric disturbances. More serious, but less common, neurologic effects include severe psychiatric disturbance and encephalopathy. The latter is particularly likely to occur in renal dialysis patients.[7]

Other adverse effects include hepatitis, particularly in patients aged over 35 years, arthralgia, fever and skin rashes. Very rare complications include hyperglycemia and agranulocytosis.

Adverse effects, particularly neurologic ones, are usually preventable by administration of pyridoxine (vitamin B_6) 10mg daily. In particular, pyridoxine should be given to patients who have liver disease, pregnant women, alcoholics, renal dialysis patients, HIV-positive patients, the malnourished and the elderly. Encephalopathy in renal dialysis patients may not respond to pyridoxine but usually resolves when isoniazid is withdrawn.[7]

Rifampin

This is one of the rifamycins, semisynthetic derivatives of rifamycin S, a fermentation product of *Amycolatopsis* (*Streptomyces*) *mediterranei*. Rifampin inhibits protein synthesis by a very specific inhibition of bacterial DNA-dependent RNA polymerase, thereby blocking the synthesis of mRNA. The corresponding mammalian enzyme is

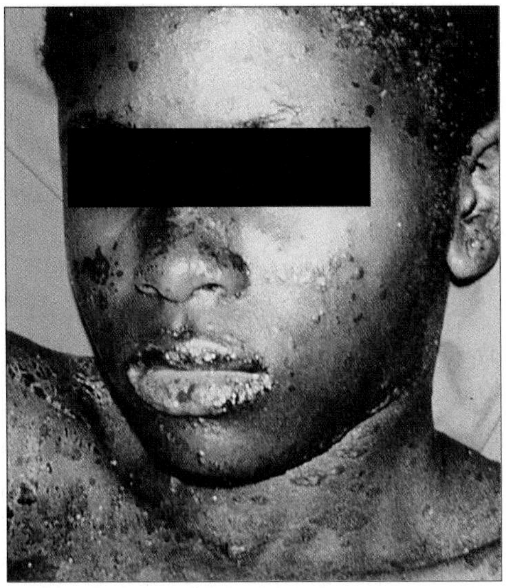

Fig. 202.4 Stevens–Johnson syndrome induced by thiacetazone. Courtesy of Dr P Mwaba, Zambia.

inhibited only by very high concentrations of rifampin. Resistance is due to single amino acid mutational changes in the *rpoB* gene, which encodes for the β subunit of the polymerase. Rifampin is the most effective of the antituberculosis drugs because it kills both rapidly dividing bacilli and those that exhibit only occasional short bursts of metabolism. Therefore, when cost considerations allow, it is given throughout the course of therapy. It is also used in the treatment of leprosy and for some other mycobacterial diseases.

Rifampin is rapidly absorbed from the gastrointestinal tract, although absorption is delayed if it is given with food, and it is widely distributed in the internal organs. Only small amounts enter the CSF in health but much more enters when the meninges are inflamed. Rifampin enters cells and is therefore active against intracellular mycobacteria. It is metabolized by hepatic microsomal enzymes to the desacetyl derivative, which is excreted in the bile. As this enzymatic activity is inducible, the rate of plasma clearance of rifampin increases as treatment proceeds. Although principally excreted in the bile, some rifampin and the desacetyl derivative enter the urine and impart an orange-red color to it. It also enters saliva and lachrymal secretions and may cause pink staining of soft contact lenses. The induction of microsomal enzymes may have clinically significant effects on the metabolism of several other drugs (see below).

Rifampin may cause an influenza-like syndrome, which, paradoxically, occurs less often if the drug is given daily rather than intermittently. It causes transient abnormalities in liver function and, occasionally, clinically evident hepatitis, although this is usually mild. Other adverse effects include gastrointestinal disturbances, skin rashes and antibody-mediated thrombocytopenia.

Acute renal failure is a rare complication, although in some regions it is more frequent; in one center in India it accounted for 11 of 607 (1.8%) of admissions for acute renal failure.[8] The renal prognosis is usually favorable. It typically occurs after reintroduction of rifampin and intermittent therapy is a risk factor.

Although the evidence that rifampin is teratogenic is very limited, it is best avoided if possible during the first 3 months of pregnancy. For the same reason, women receiving rifampin should avoid becoming pregnant. In this respect it is important to note that this drug interferes with the action of oral contraceptives.

Pyrazinamide (pyrazinoic acid amide)

This is regularly included in the initial intensive phase of short-course chemotherapy because it has the important property of killing intracellular tubercle bacilli and, possibly, extracellular bacilli in anoxic, acidic inflamed lesions. It is inactive in neutral or alkaline microenvironments. Its target is the fatty acid synthetase (FAS)-1 enzyme.[9] Pyrazinamide first requires conversion to pyrazinoic acid by mycobacterial pyrazinamidase enzymes encoded for by the *pncA* gene. Resistance is usually associated with mutations in this gene, which are detectable by a polymerase chain reaction (PCR)-based system,[10] and the enzymatic activity is not detectable in most pyrazinamide-resistant mutants of *M. tuberculosis* or in strains of *Mycobacterium bovis*, which are naturally resistant to this agent. A few pyrazinamide-resistant strains, however, lack mutations in the *pncA* gene, suggesting alternative mechanisms for resistance to this agent.[11]

It is readily absorbed from the gastrointestinal tract and freely enters the CSF, in which levels similar to those in plasma are found. It is metabolized in the liver; the metabolites, mostly pyrazinoic acid, are excreted in the urine.

Adverse effects are uncommon. It causes raised serum transaminase levels but overt hepatotoxicity, despite earlier reports, is uncommon. It should, however, be used with caution in alcoholics and in patients who have pre-existing hepatic disease, who should have regular liver function tests. Other adverse effects include anorexia, nausea, photosensitization of the skin,[12] arthralgia and gout caused by the inhibition of the excretion of uric acid by pyrazinoic acid.

Ethambutol

Ethambutol (*S,S′*-2,2′-(ethylenediimino)di-1-butanol) is now frequently used in short course therapy of tuberculosis as a fourth drug in the intensive phase of therapy. It is also included in therapeutic regimens for disease caused by other slowly growing mycobacteria, particularly *Mycobacterium avium* complex (MAC), *M. kansasii*, *M. xenopi* and *Mycobacterium malmoense*. In addition to its own activity, there is evidence that ethambutol may enhance the activity of some of the other drugs by affecting cell-wall permeability, particularly in the MAC but possibly also in multidrug-resistant strains of *M. tuberculosis*.[13]

Ethambutol inhibits the synthesis of the polysaccharide arabinogalactan, a macromolecule essential for the structural integrity of the mycobacterial cell wall, by inhibiting the enzyme arabinosyl transferase. Resistance is associated with mutations in the *embA, embB* and *embC* cluster of genes (principally *embB*), which encode for this enzyme.[14]

The drug is given orally and about 80% of the dose is absorbed from the gastrointestinal tract. Absorption is inhibited by antacids containing aluminum hydroxide. It does not cross the healthy meninges but up to 40% of the plasma level is found in the CSF in cases of tuberculous meningitis. It is mostly excreted unchanged in the urine but up to 15% is excreted as metabolites.

The principal side effect is optic neuritis, which may have an irreversible effect on vision. This complication is rare if the drug is given for no longer than 2 months at a daily dose of 25mg/kg body weight, or for longer at a dose not exceeding 15mg/kg. The 15mg/kg dose is used throughout therapy in some regimens. Nevertheless, care should be observed in the use of this drug, its recommended dose and duration of therapy should never be exceeded, and the patient should be informed of the risk of visual impairment and advised to discontinue the drug if such impairment occurs. Loss of color discrimination is the first sign of visual toxicity. Where facilities are available, visual acuity should be assessed before therapy and at intervals during it.

Most guidelines recommend that the drug should not given to children under the age of 5 years because their visual acuity cannot be readily assessed, even though ocular complications in such young children are extremely rare.

ADVERSE REACTIONS TO THE ANTITUBERCULOSIS AGENTS	
Agent	**Adverse reactions**
Isoniazid	
Uncommon reactions	Hepatitis, cutaneous hypersensitivity reactions including erythema multiforme, peripheral neuropathy
Rare reactions	Vertigo; convulsions; optic neuritis and atrophy; psychiatric disturbance; hemolytic anemia; aplastic anemia; dermal reactions including pellagra, purpura and lupoid syndrome; gynecomastia, hyperglycemia, arthralgia
Rifampin	
Uncommon reactions	Hepatitis, flushing, itching with or without a rash, gastrointestinal upsets, 'flu-like syndrome', headache
Rare reactions (usually associated with intermittent therapy)	Dyspnea, hypotension with or without shock, Addisonian crisis, hemolytic anemia, acute renal failure, thrombocytopenia with or without purpura, transient leucopenia or eosinophilia, menstrual disturbances, muscular weakness, pseudomembranous colitis
Pyrazinamide	
Common reactions	Anorexia
Uncommon reactions	Hepatitis, nausea and vomiting, urticaria, nausea, arthralgia
Rare reactions	Sideroblastic anemia, photosensitization, gout, dysuria, aggravation of peptic ulcer
Ethambutol	
Uncommon reactions	Optic neuritis, arthralgia
Rare reactions	Hepatitis, cutaneous hypersensitivity including pruritis and urticaria, photosensitive lichenoid eruptions, parasthesia of the extremities, interstitial nephritis
Streptomycin	
Uncommon reactions	Vertigo, ataxia, deafness, tinnitus, cutaneous hypersensitivity
Rare reactions	Renal damage, aplastic anemia, agranulocytosis, peripheral neuropathy, optic neuritis with scotoma, severe bleeding due to antagonism of factor V, neuromuscular blockade in patients receiving muscle relaxants and in those with myesthenia gravis
Other aminoglycosides	
Uncommon reactions	Cutaneous hypersensitivity, vertigo, deafness
Rare reactions	Renal damage, hypoglycemia, hypokalemia
Thiacetazone	
Common reactions	Gastrointestinal upsets, cutaneous hypersensitivity, vertigo, conjunctivitis
Uncommon reactions	Hepatitis, erythema multiforme, exfoliative dermatitis, hemolytic anemia
Rare reactions	Agranulocytosis
***para*-aminosalicylic acid**	
Common reactions	Gastrointestinal upsets
Uncommon reactions	Cutaneous hypersensitivity, hepatitis, hypokalemia
Rare reactions	Acute renal failure, hemolytic anemia, thrombocytopenia, hypothyroidism
Ethionamide and prothionamide	
Common reactions	Gastrointestinal upsets, salivation, metallic taste
Uncommon reactions	Cutaneous hypersensitivity, hepatitis
Rare reactions	Alopecia, convulsions, deafness, diplopia, gynecomastia, hypotension, impotence, psychiatric disturbance, menstrual irregularity, hypoglycemia, peripheral neuropathy
Capreomycin and viomycin	
Common reactions	Eosinophilia (with capreomycin), pain and induration at injection site
Uncommon reactions	Loss of hearing, vertigo, tinnitus, electrolyte disturbances including hypokalemia, leukopenia or leukocytosis
Rare reactions	Renal impairment, hepatitis, thrombocytopenia
Clofazimine	
Common reactions	Discoloration of skin and body fluids, nausea, vomiting, abdominal pain, diarrhea
Uncommon reactions	Dryness of skin, ichthyosis, photosensitivity
Rare reactions	Intestinal obstruction
Cycloserine	
Common reactions (especially with daily doses exceeding 500mg)	Convulsions, drowsiness, sleep disturbance, headache, tremor, vertigo, confusion, irritability, aggression and other personality changes, psychosis (sometimes with suicidal tendencies)
Uncommon reactions	Cutaneous hypersensitivity, hepatitis, megaloblastic anemia
Rare reactions	Congestive heart failure
Ofloxacin	
Uncommon reactions	Gastrointestinal upsets, headache, dizziness, insomnia, cutaneous hypersensitivity reactions
Rare reactions	Restlessness; convulsions; psychiatric disturbances including psychotic reactions and hallucinations; edema of face, tongue and epiglottis; disturbance of taste and smell; anaphylactoid reactions

Table 202.6 Adverse reactions to the antituberculosis agents.

Other side effects of ethambutol include skin rashes, arthralgia, peripheral neuritis, hyperuricemia and, rarely, jaundice and thrombocytopenia.

Streptomycin

This was the first of the antituberculosis drugs to be discovered and it still has an important role in the treatment of tuberculosis. It inhibits protein synthesis by binding to the 30S subunit of the bacterial ribosome. It is active in neutral or alkaline environments such as the cavity wall but not in the more acidic environment of the closed, inflammatory foci and is therefore not a good sterilizing drug. It is very poorly absorbed from the gastrointestinal tract and must be given parenterally.

Streptomycin is toxic for the eighth cranial nerve, including that of the fetus, and its use should therefore be avoided in pregnancy. Other adverse reactions include impairment of renal function and hypersensitivity reactions – usually mild skin rashes or fever but occasionally anaphylactic reactions or exfoliative dermatitis.

SECOND-LINE DRUGS

Aminoglycosides

In addition to streptomycin, the aminoglycosides kanamycin, amikacin and aminosidine (paromomycin) have activity against *M. tuberculosis*. Cross-resistance with streptomycin is usual. Kanamycin is included in some regimens for the treatment of MDRTB and amikacin in some regimens for the treatment of disease due to the MAC, particularly in HIV-positive patients. In common with streptomycin, these aminoglycosides are not absorbed from the gastrointestinal tract and must therefore be given parenterally.

Para-aminosalicylic acid

The mode of action of this bacteriostatic drug is not fully understood although there is some evidence that it inhibits the salicylate-dependent synthesis of the mycobactins – a class of iron-chelating lipids unique to the mycobacteria. It is readily absorbed from the intestine and rapidly acetylated in the liver. About 80% is excreted in the urine, mostly in the acetylated form.

It is rarely used as adverse effects are common. Gastrointestinal effects including nausea, abdominal pain and diarrhea occur in up to 30% of patients. Other adverse effects include thyroid dysfunction, crystalluria, blood dyscrasias and, rarely, Löffler syndrome and encephalitis.

Capreomycin and viomycin

These structurally closely related cyclic polypeptides are very rarely used and are seldom available. In common with the aminoglycosides, they inhibit protein synthesis by blocking ribosomal function. They are mutually completely cross-resistant and high-level resistance shows cross-resistance with the aminoglycosides. They are supplied as a water-soluble sulfate and, because they are not absorbed from the intestine, they are given by intramuscular injection. They do not readily enter cells or the CSF and are mostly excreted unchanged in the urine. Adverse effects include ototoxicity, nephrotoxicity and pain, bleeding and induration at the injection site.

Clofazimine

This is one of a group of iminophenazines originally developed for treatment of tuberculosis but now used principally for leprosy. It is occasionally used for treatment of MDRTB but there is only anecdotal evidence of efficacy. It was included in regimens for treatment of AIDS-related MAC infection but is now rarely used for this purpose on account of its toxicity in such patients.

Its mode of action is unclear. Some reports suggest that it potentiates intracellular killing by enhancing the generation of free oxygen radicals, whereas others suggest an interference with RNA polymerase activity. It is absorbed from the intestine; it has a very long half life – around 70 days – and is excreted in the urine and feces. Adverse effects include nausea, abdominal pain and diarrhea and, rarely, edema of the wall of the small intestine leading to subacute obstruction. It also causes skin discoloration, which may be a stigmatizing feature leading to nonadherence to therapy.

Ethionamide and prothionamide

Ethionamide (ethylthioisonicotinamide) and prothionamide (propylthioisonicotinamide) are closely related drugs that are structurally similar to isoniazid; in common with isoniazid they inhibit the synthesis of mycobacterial mycolic acids. Also in common with isoniazid, resistance is associated with mutations in the *inhA* gene encoding for long-chain enoyl-acyl carrier protein reductase but, surprisingly, cross-resistance to isoniazid does not develop. This may, in part, be explained by differences in the activation pathways of the two agents.[15] They are degraded into several metabolites in the liver and only a very small amount, less than 1%, is excreted unchanged in the urine.

The common occurrence of gastrointestinal irritation with these agents, even when they are given as enteric-coated tablets, limits their use in the treatment of tuberculosis. Prothionamide is slightly better tolerated and is used in some regimens for leprosy. Other adverse effects include skin reactions, hepatitis, impotence and gynecomastia in male patients, menstrual irregularities and various neurologic complications such as convulsions, mental disturbance and peripheral neuropathy.

Thiacetazone (acetylaminobenzaldehyde thiosemicarbazone)

In common with isoniazid, thiacetazone inhibits the synthesis of mycolic acid, but by a poorly understood mechanism. Resistance develops readily and is common in developing nations where, on account of its low cost, thiacetazone has been widely used. It is readily absorbed from the gastrointestinal tract. About 20% is eliminated in the urine but it is not known what happens to the remainder.

Adverse effects are common. Skin rashes frequently occur, particularly in patients of Chinese ethnic origin. A very high incidence of severe, sometimes fatal, skin reactions – exfoliative dermatitis and Stevens–Johnson syndrome – in HIV-positive patients has raised serious doubts as to the advisability of using this drug in regions where HIV-related tuberculosis is common. Less frequent adverse effects include gastrointestinal upsets, hepatitis, hemolytic anemia and, rarely, agranulocytosis.

Rifabutin and rifapentine

These are closely related to rifampin, being semisynthetic derivatives of rifamycin S. Although rifabutin (ansamycin) is considerably more active than rifampin in vitro, its in-vivo action against *M. tuberculosis* is similar to that of rifampin. Cross-resistance between the rifamycins is usual, so the place for rifabutin in the treatment of MDRTB is limited. Its principal use is for the prevention and treatment of HIV-related disease due to the MAC. Rifabutin, rifapentine and a new rifamycin derivative, benzoxazinorifamycin (KRM-1648), have long plasma half-lives and raise the possibility, currently under investigation, of once-weekly dosage for preventive therapy and during the continuation phase of therapy of active tuberculosis.[16]

Fluoroquinolones

Fluoroquinolones inhibit the enzyme DNA gyrase, which is responsible for the supercoiling of DNA. They have bactericidal activity against *M. tuberculosis* at clinically achievable levels in vitro, and there is increasing evidence that several of them, including ciprofloxacin, ofloxacin, sparfloxacin, levofloxacin and lomefloxacin, have a valuable place in the therapy of MDRTB.[17] Thus, for example, there is preliminary evidence that a combination of sparfloxacin, kanamycin and ethionamide is both safe and effective in the therapy of MDRTB.[18,19] Fluoroquinolones are readily absorbed from the gastrointestinal tract and enter tissues and fluids, including the CSF. Although metabolized to some extent by the liver, they are largely excreted unchanged in the urine. Doses therefore require modification in patients who have renal failure. Adverse effects include nausea and abdominal pain and various neurologic abnormalities including headache, vertigo, insomnia, restlessness, epileptiform attacks and psychiatric disturbances. They should be used with care in epileptic patients.

Cycloserine

This D-alanine analog inhibits synthesis of peptidoglycan. It is bacteriostatic and thus of limited efficacy, although it is used in some cases of MDRTB. Psychiatric symptoms, including psychotic episodes, occur commonly and further limit the usefulness of this drug, although the risk may to some extent be reduced by giving pyridoxine. Allergic skin rashes are rare. In-vitro synergy with β-chloro-D-alanine, another peptidoglycan inhibitor, has been demonstrated and suggests that therapy with a greatly reduced dose of cycloserine may be possible.[20]

Macrolides

These are broad-spectrum antibiotics that inhibit protein synthesis by binding to the ribosomal 50S subunit. Erythromycin is active against some mycobacteria in vitro and there are anecdotal reports of its efficacy in the treatment of post-BCG (bacillus Calmette–Guérin) abscesses and disease due to *M. kansasii* and *M. xenopi*. The newer macrolides, clarithromycin, azithromycin and roxithromycin, are more active than erythromycin against MAC, and clarithromycin is used to treat HIV-related disease due to MAC. They have limited in-vitro activity against *M. tuberculosis* but there is evidence that they act in synergy with rifampin and isoniazid against this species, particularly against intracellular bacilli.[21] Macrolides are well absorbed from the gastrointestinal tract and are excreted in urine. Adverse effects include gastrointestinal upsets with occasional cases of pseudomembranous colitis and various psychiatric disorders, including acute mania.

EXPERIMENTAL AGENTS

Research into novel therapy for tuberculosis is based on new use of old drugs, new delivery of old drugs, new drugs within old classes and new classes of drugs. A number of new rifamycins, macrolides, pyrazinamide analogues, nitroimidazoles and isonicotinoylhydrazones are being evaluated.[22–24] Synergy between antituberculosis agents and cell-wall assembly inhibitors is also a promising approach, which may overcome drug resistance and permit lower concentrations of toxic drugs to be used.[20,25]

Attempts to treat MDRTB by enhancing or modifying immune defense mechanisms have been made, either by the use of individual cytokines or bacterial adjuvants, and more clinical studies are indicated.[23,26]

Certain agents usually used for other infections may have useful activity against *M. tuberculosis*. For example, a combination of amoxicillin and clavulanic acid has in-vitro activity against *M. tuberculosis* and there is anecdotal evidence of a beneficial effect against MDRTB.[27] It has been suggested that metronidazole might kill dormant *M. tuberculosis* in anaerobic situations. Although one study indicates that addition of metronidazole to short-course regimens hastens the clinical improvement in cases of advanced pulmonary tuberculosis, information from studies on murine models of dormancy is conflicting.[28]

Dynamics of action of antituberculosis drugs in vivo and the design of therapeutic regimens

The aims of modern chemotherapeutic regimens are:

- to cure the patient;
- to reduce infectivity as rapidly as possible; and
- to prevent the emergence of drug resistance.

In order to cure patients, it is necessary to destroy all the tubercle bacilli in the tissues; if even a few survive, there is a high chance of relapse. In this respect, drugs that are bactericidal in vitro may not be able to effectively sterilize the tissues in vivo.[29] This difference occurs because tubercle bacilli in vivo are in a number of different physiologic states or 'compartments'. These physiologic 'compartments' are:

- freely dividing extracellular bacilli, found mainly in the cavity walls;
- slowly dividing bacilli, found within macrophages and in acidic, inflammatory lesions; and
- dormant and near-dormant bacilli, within cells and in firm caseous material.

The antituberculosis drugs vary in their ability to destroy bacilli in these compartments and in preventing the emergence of resistance to a second drug.

During chemotherapy with modern short-course regimens, the freely replicating bacilli in the walls of the cavities are rapidly killed; this is termed the early bactericidal effect. Subsequently, the slowly replicating and near-dormant bacilli are destroyed, but at a much slower rate.

Isoniazid plays a key role in achieving the early bactericidal effect because it is particularly effective in destroying the freely multiplying extracellular bacilli, particularly those in the walls of cavities. It has little or no effect on near-dormant bacilli and is therefore not a good sterilizing drug. Rifampin also contributes to the early bactericidal effect.

Ethambutol has bactericidal activity in the early stage of therapy but is not a sterilizing drug. Streptomycin is bactericidal in the slightly alkaline cavity walls but is likewise not a sterilizing agent because it is ineffective in the acidic environment within cells and caseous lesions. By contrast, pyrazinamide is effective within macrophages and acidic, anoxic inflammatory lesions, but not in the neutral or alkaline environment.

Thus, modern regimens commence with an intensive phase of therapy, usually lasting for 2 months, to optimize the early bactericidal effect, thereby eliminating most of the bacilli and rendering the patient noninfectious. The principal drugs used are:

- isoniazid (active against bacilli in the cavity walls);
- pyrazinamide (active against bacilli in acidic closed lesions); and
- rifampin (active against both).

In view of the widespread and increasing prevalence of drug resistance, many regimens now include a fourth agent, usually ethambutol but sometimes streptomycin. The daily drug doses are listed in Table 202.7 and the intermittent doses in Table 202.8.

The intensive phase is followed by a continuation phase, usually lasting 4 months, in which any remaining dormant or near-dormant bacilli are destroyed. For this purpose, rifampin is the most powerful sterilizing drug. Although isoniazid is not a sterilizing drug, it is, by its potent activity against replicating bacilli, very good at preventing the emergence of rifampin-resistant mutants. It is thus given together with rifampin throughout the regimen.

Accordingly, the most effective modern short-course regimens are based on a 2-month phase of rifampin, isoniazid, pyrazinamide and either ethambutol or streptomycin, followed by a 4-month phase of rifampin and isoniazid. The WHO has issued clear recommendations on drug regimens for the four categories of tuberculosis seen in clinical practice (Table 202.9).

In most regimens drugs are given daily but, provided that therapy is closely supervised so that all doses are taken, they may be given three times weekly during the continuation phase or, in some regimens, throughout. Such intermittent therapy renders the direct administration of the drugs less of a burden for both patients and supervisors.

There is general agreement, supported by clinical trials, that the modern chemotherapeutic regimens discussed above are suitable for the treatment of all types of tuberculosis, both pulmonary and non-

DAILY DOSES OF THE ANTITUBERCULOSIS AGENTS		
	Daily dose	
Agent	Adults	Children
Rifampin	450mg if body weight <50kg 600mg if body weight ≥50kg	10mg/kg to maximum of 600mg
Isoniazid	200–300mg	5mg/kg
Pyrazinamide	1.5g if body weight <50kg 2.0g if body weight ≥50kg	25mg/kg
Ethambutol	15mg/kg	As for adult
Streptomycin	750mg if body weight <50kg 1g if body weight ≥50kg 750mg if age ≥40 years 500mg if age ≥60 years	15mg/kg to maximum of 0.75g
Thiacetazone	150mg	50mg
para-aminosalicylic acid	10–12g	300mg/kg
Ethionamide and prothionamide	500mg if body weight <50kg 750mg if body weight ≥50kg	15–20mg/kg
Capreomycin	1g	Avoid
Viomycin	1g	Avoid
Cycloserine	500mg if body weight <50kg 750mg if body weight ≥50kg	Avoid
Ofloxacin	800mg	Avoid

Table 202.7 Daily doses of the antituberculosis agents.

DOSES OF THE FIRST-LINE ANTITUBERCULOSIS AGENTS IN THREE TIMES WEEKLY INTERMITTENT THERAPY		
Agent	Dose (mg/kg (adults and children))	Maximum dose
Isoniazid	15	750mg
Rifampin	15	600mg
Pyrazinamide	50	2.0g if body weight <50kg 2.5g if body weight ≥50kg
Ethambutol	30	1.8g
Streptomycin	15–20	750mg if body weight <50kg 1g if body weight ≥50kg

Table 202.8 Doses of the first-line antituberculosis agents in three times weekly intermittent therapy.

pulmonary, and even for life-threatening forms such as tuberculous meningitis. There is less agreement over the duration of therapy for non-pulmonary forms of tuberculosis; some physicians continue therapy for up to 12 months or even longer, particularly in the case of tuberculous meningitis, in which a relapse would be particularly devastating.

DRUG-RESISTANT TUBERCULOSIS

Resistance to any given anti-infective agent occurs by mutation at a low but constant rate, so that treatment with a single drug, however powerful, will inevitably lead to selection of resistant mutants.[5] The problem of treatment failure caused by the emergence of drug resistance became apparent soon after the introduction of antituberculosis chemotherapy and led to the universal advocacy of multiple-drug

PRINCIPAL ANTITUBERCULOSIS REGIMENS RECOMMENDED BY WHO		
Intensive phase	Continuation phase	Category of patient
HRZE (HRZS) for 2 months HRZE (HRZS) for 2 months HRZE (HRZS) for 2 months	HR daily for 4 months HR three times weekly for 4 months HE daily for 6 months	New patients with smear-positive pulmonary tuberculosis; extensive smear-negative pulmonary tuberculosis; severe nonpulmonary tuberculosis
HRZES for 2 months + HRZE for 1 month HRZES for 2 months + HRZE for 1 month	HRE daily for 5 months HRE three times weekly for 5 months	Cases of relapse, treatment failure or recommencing treatment after interruption
HRZ for 2 months HRZ for 2 months HRZ for 2 months	HR daily for 4 months HR three times weekly for 4 months HE daily for 6 months	New smear-negative pulmonary tuberculosis (other than those in the first category); less severe nonpulmonary tuberculosis
Treat as though drug-resistant		Case still positive after supervised retreatment

Table 202.9 Principal antituberculosis regimens recommended by the World Health Organization. E, ethambutol; H, isoniazid; R, rifampin; S, streptomycin; Z, pyrazinamide.

regimens. Under ideal conditions and in the absence of drug resistance, relapses after completion of a modern short-course chemotherapeutic regimen are uncommon and are mostly due to drug-susceptible bacilli.[24] Unfortunately, ideal treatment conditions are the exception rather than the rule and many deficiencies in the use of multiple-drug regimens has led to the increasing emergence of strains resistant to one or more drugs.[30]

Although resistance to isoniazid or streptomycin, or to both, is common, patients whose disease is caused by such resistant strains usually respond to short-course chemotherapy. Resistance to rifampin is much more serious, in view of the unique ability of this drug to eliminate near-dormant persisting bacilli. Many strains resistant to rifampin are also resistant to isoniazid and, because these drugs are the principal components of modern regimens, this combination renders such regimens ineffective. Thus, the term multidrug resistance has been adopted by the WHO to refer to strains that are resistant to these two drugs, with or without resistance to additional drugs.[31]

Two forms of drug resistance are encountered: acquired and primary (or initial). Acquired resistance is the result of suboptimal therapy that encourages the selective growth of mutants resistant to one or more drugs. Primary resistance is due to infection from a source case who has drug-resistant disease. In practice, it is often difficult to be sure that a patient who has apparent primary resistant tuberculosis has, in fact, not received any antituberculosis therapy, and some workers therefore prefer the term initial resistance. The division of resistance into acquired and primary forms is of epidemiologic value because an increasing incidence of the former indicates that drug regimens or the supervision of therapy are suboptimal, whereas the continuing occurrence of primary resistance indicates that the transmission of the disease in the community is not being adequately controlled.

The development of drug resistance is due to many avoidable failures in the management of the disease (Table 202.10).

The traditional explanation for treatment failure and emergence of drug resistance is noncompliance or nonadherence to therapy by the patient, thereby attempting to exonerate the health care services. While acknowledging that there will always be a small number of patients who will default on treatment in any situation, there is ample evidence that it is more often the health services than the patient that are at fault. In order to enhance effective tuberculosis control, the WHO has widely advocated the strategy of directly observed therapy, short course (DOTS). This is a six-point strategy incorporating:

- government commitment to tuberculosis control;
- provision of a regular supply of good-quality drugs free at the point of delivery;
- passive case finding by sputum microscopy;
- directly observed therapy;
- training and ongoing support of staff; and
- regular evaluation of the efficacy of the control program.

Combination drug preparations have been used to prevent patients from receiving monotherapy, but irregular and intermittent use of such preparations has led to drug and multidrug resistance.[30] In addition, the use of poorly formulated combination preparations has led to reduced bioavailability of the constituent agents and the risk of development of drug resistance.

There is no doubt that the blind addition of drugs to a failing regimen is very likely to generate multidrug resistance. Unfortunately, the determination of drug resistance is far from easy and most parts of the world lack the facilities for conducting drug susceptibility tests under good quality control. Errors are not uncommon even in the most sophisticated centers in the developed world and may be noticed only when laboratory reports are considered in the light of clinical data.

A combined initiative by the WHO and the International Union Against Tuberculosis and Lung Disease was launched in 1994 to perform a global survey of resistance to first-line antituberculosis drugs. The first report, published in 1997 and covering 35 countries, showed that resistance to these drugs was more widespread than was previously recognized and revealed certain areas with a very high incidence (Fig. 202.5).[32] These 'hotspots' included Estonia, Latvia, Russia, Argentina, China, the Dominican Republic and Côte d'Ivoire. The second report, published in 2000 and covering 72 countries, confirmed the widespread occurrence of MDRTB.[33] While, overall, the median prevalence of MDRTB in new cases was low, only 1% of all cases, a very high prevalence was found in the Henan province of China (35%), Ivanovo Oblast (Russian Federation; 32.4%), and Latvia (29.9%). Estonia showed 8.5% resistance to all four antituberculosis frontline drugs. On the other hand, no MDRTB was detected among new cases in Cuba, Finland, France and New Caledonia.

The situation in Russia is of particular concern.[34] Under the communist regime, tuberculosis in that country had been in decline for several decades, reaching an annual incidence of 34 cases per 100,000 population in 1991. Since the end of communism in 1991, however, the incidence of tuberculosis rose steadily to 85/100,000 by 1998. The cause of this upsurge appears to be a combination of poverty, malnutrition, poor housing, conflict and a fragmentation of health services. In addition, tuberculosis has flourished in overcrowded Russian prisons where there may be as many as 1 million prisoners, of whom 100,000 have active tuberculosis. The incidence of MDRTB is high; in one surveyed prison population it occurred in 24.6% of tuberculosis patients, rising to 92% among nonresponding cases. Despite implementation of a strict DOTS program in the prisons, and the use of WHO retreatment regimens for all new cases, there was a treatment failure rate of 35% in a tuberculosis referral prison in western Siberia.

The presence of HIV infection does not *per se* lead to an upsurge of MDRTB. Despite the increase in HIV-associated tuberculosis seen in most African countries, such an upsurge has not been documented. Exceptions include Mozambique and Côte d'Ivoire, where more than 3% of new cases are multidrug-resistant and in Yaonde, Cameroon, where the corresponding figure rises to 27.6%.

The problem of drug resistance is not encountered only in the developing nations. Several well documented epidemics of MDRTB have occurred in the USA, notably in New York City.[35] As mentioned above,

FACTORS LEADING TO SUBOPTIMAL THERAPY AND THE EMERGENCE OF DRUG AND MULTIDRUG RESISTANCE
Intermittent drug supplies
Use of time-expired drugs
Unavailability of combination preparations
Use of poorly formulated combination preparations
Prescription of inappropriate drug regimens
Unregulated over-the-counter sale of drugs, including cough mixtures containing isoniazid
Addition of single drugs to failing regimens in the absence of bacteriologic control
Poor supervision of therapy
Unacceptably high cost to patient in respect of the drugs, travel to the clinic and time off work

Table 202.10 Factors leading to suboptimal therapy and the emergence of drug and multidrug resistance.

GLOBAL DISTRIBUTION OF RESISTANCE TO ANTITUBERCULOSIS DRUGS

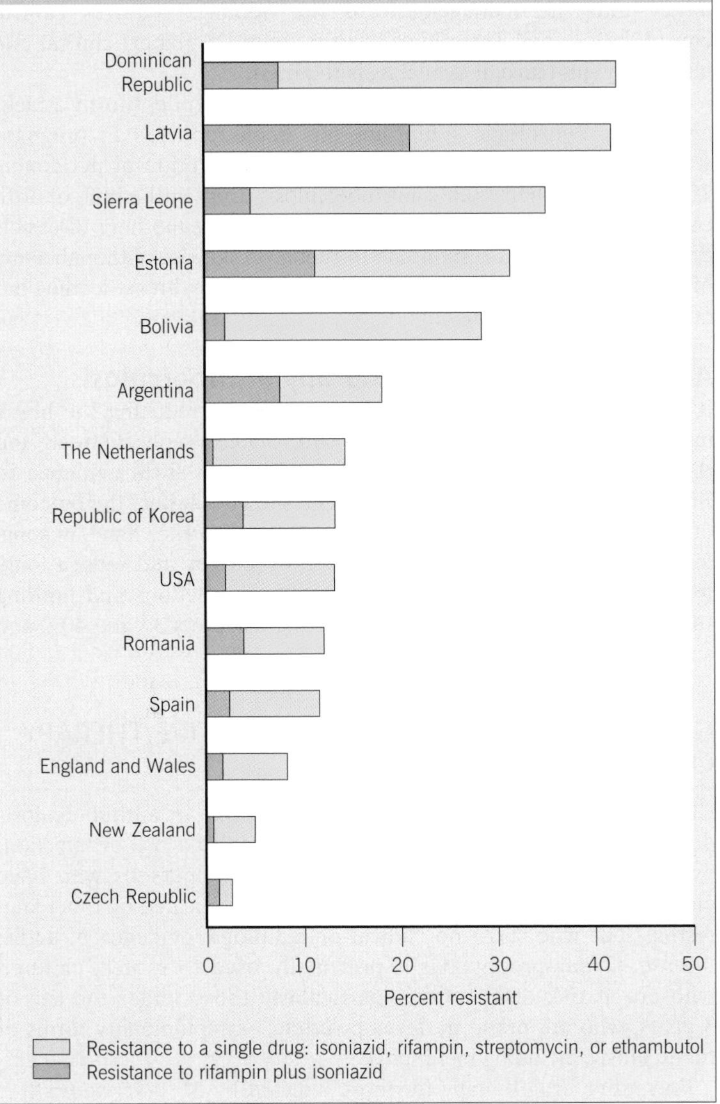

Fig. 202.5 Global distribution of resistance to antituberculosis drugs. The resistance is given as a percentage of all isolates. Data from the World Health Organization.[32]

HIV infection *per se* does not generate multidrug resistance and although such an association has been found in New York and some other regions it has not been found in others. The reason for the association, where it occurs, is that HIV infection facilitates outbreaks of tuberculosis in hospitals, prisons or common lodging facilities where such immunocompromised persons are crowded together. Thus, if the source case has MDRTB, a mini-epidemic of such disease will ensue. The first such outbreak in the UK occurred in 1995; four patients who presented with tuberculosis in mid-June had been exposed to the source case in April in a six-bed ward in an HIV unit in London.[36]

Ethnic minority communities, originating in countries where drug resistance is common, often have higher levels of drug resistance than the majority populations.[37]

The incidence of single-drug-resistant tuberculosis in a community can be reduced by establishment of good disease control programs.[38] This raises the question of whether the implementation of the WHO DOTS strategy would also reduce the incidence of MDRTB in a region. According to one mathematical model,[39] it would have such an effect, but the model assumes that multidrug-resistant strains of *M. tuberculosis* are less virulent than their drug-susceptible counterparts, an assumption for which there is no clear supporting evidence. Thus, further field studies are required to answer this important question.

PRINCIPLES FOR MANAGEMENT OF MULTIDRUG-RESISTANT TUBERCULOSIS
Single agents should never be blindly added to failing regimens
Before drug susceptibility tests become available, patients should be started on three agents that they have never received before
All therapy should be fully supervised (use of an injectable agent enhances adherence to therapy)
Therapy should last at least 24 months and should be continued for at least 18 months after bacteriologic conversion
Drug susceptibility tests should be repeated if cultures remain positive after 3 months of therapy

Table 202.11 Principles for management of multidrug-resistant tuberculosis.

Therapy of multidrug-resistant tuberculosis

Tuberculosis due to bacilli resistant to isoniazid alone usually responds to short-course drug regimens based on four drugs during the intensive phase but, by contrast, resistance to both isoniazid and rifampin (i.e. multidrug resistance) requires prolonged treatment with drugs that are much more costly, less effective and more toxic. The cost of such therapy is high; in the USA it can exceed $US250,000, compared with the cost of $US2000 for treating a patient who has drug-susceptible disease. The prognosis for patients who have MDRTB has improved considerably and, provided that the patient is diagnosed before severe lung damage has occurred and that the best supervised therapy and laboratory support is available, the outlook is good in the majority of cases. Under these optimal conditions, cure rates of 96% have been achieved.[40]

The successful management of MDRTB requires laboratory support and a team of dedicated supervisors of therapy, the so-called 'DOTS-plus' strategy.[41] Ideally regimens should be designed for each patient on the basis of in-vitro susceptibility. Various regimens have been used and there have been few comparisons between them. Currently used regimens are usually based on a fluoroquinolone with at least two other drugs to which the strain is susceptible such as kanamycin and ethionamide (or prothionamide).[18] Other agents include rifabutin, the new macrolides, amikacin, capreomycin, clofazimine, cycloserine and *para*-aminosalicylic acid. Great care and dedication is required for the successful management of MDRTB (Table 202.11).

In many parts of the world, neither these drugs nor the requisite laboratory support are available, and MDRTB is thus often fatal. Alternative forms of treatment such as immunotherapy are therefore urgently required.

TREATMENT OF PATIENTS IN SPECIAL CIRCUMSTANCES

Patients who have renal or hepatic disease

Modification of drug regimens and dosages may be required when there is substantial liver disease or renal impairment. The first-line drugs (rifampin, isoniazid, pyrazinamide, ethionamide) and also ethionamide and prothionamide are either completely metabolized or eliminated in the bile. They may therefore be used safely at the normal doses in patients who have renal impairment. Isoniazid occasionally causes encephalopathy in patients who have renal failure and in those on dialysis but the risk is reduced, although not eliminated, by administering pyridoxine.[7] Although ethambutol is mainly eliminated by the kidney it can be used in reduced doses in patients who have impaired renal function. Streptomycin and other aminoglycosides are eliminated entirely by the kidney and are potentially nephrotoxic and special care must be taken.

In severe renal failure the dose of isoniazid should be reduced to 200mg once daily (ensuring that pyridoxine is given to prevent peripheral neuropathy). Streptomycin and ethambutol are excreted by the kidney and adjustment to doses is necessary in renal failure. Streptomycin levels must be monitored and doses and spacing be adjusted to achieve a level of 4mg/ml to avoid toxicity. For patients on dialysis, streptomycin should be given 8 hours before commencing dialysis. Ethambutol dosages are dependent on creatinine clearances. For patients who have creatinine clearances between 50ml/min and 100ml/min, the dose is 25mg/kg three times weekly; at 30–50ml/min, the dose is 25mg/kg twice a week; and at 10–25ml/min the dose is 15mg/kg at 2-day intervals. Patients on hemodialysis may be given 25mg/kg ethambutol 6 hours before the procedure.

There is no clear evidence that the potentially hepatotoxic drugs rifampin and pyrazinamide are any more toxic in patients who have impaired hepatic function. Nevertheless, if they are used, hepatic function should be carefully and regularly monitored during therapy. Some physicians avoid them and treat such patients with isoniazid and ethambutol for 1 year, with the addition of streptomycin for the first 2–3 months. An alternative is to use a fluoroquinolone such as ofloxacin instead of rifampin.[42]

If rifampin is used, it should be used with caution; doses should be reduced in patients who have bilirubin concentrations exceeding 50mmol/l. Liver function should be regularly monitored, where possible, in alcoholics, the elderly, malnourished children and children under 2 years of age.

If jaundice develops during antituberculosis therapy, treatment should be stopped until the jaundice resolves. In many cases resumption of treatment does not cause a recurrence of the jaundice. If the patient is seriously ill with tuberculosis, he or she may be treated with streptomycin and ethambutol even in the presence of jaundice.

HIV-positive patients who have tuberculosis

The treatment of tuberculosis in HIV-positive patients (see also Chapter 129) follows the same well-established principles used in the treatment of non-HIV infected patients.[43] Despite a good bacteriologic response to treatment, patients who have HIV-related tuberculosis in Africa are almost four times as likely to die within 13 months of diagnosis than HIV-negative patients, with most deaths occurring during the first month of treatment.[44] This is largely due to other opportunistic infections but may also, in part, be due to an apparent synergistic immunosuppressive action of HIV infection and active tuberculosis. For this reason, prevention of tuberculosis is preferable to cure in HIV-positive persons (see below). Drug reactions tend to be more severe in HIV-positive patients than in HIV-negative patients. In particular, thiacetazone often causes severe dermal reactions, with some patients developing fulminant and potentially fatal exfoliative dermatitis. Drug interactions are also a particular problem in HIV-infected patients (see Chapter 129).

Pregnancy and the postpartum period

There is general agreement that the management of tuberculosis in pregnancy and in the postpartum period should be similar to that in other patients, although some advocate avoiding pyrazinamide. Short-course regimens seem to have a minimal risk of causing fetal abnormalities, and side effects in the pregnant woman are no higher than in those who are not pregnant.[45] Opinions concerning the safety of pyrazinamide differ because there are limited experimental data on its effect on the fetus but, notwithstanding this, it is often used, particularly in regions where drug resistance is common. Streptomycin is avoided owing to its ototoxic properties. The treatment of drug-resistant tuberculosis, especially MDRTB, during pregnancy and the management of the neonate requires careful consideration, and experience is very limited.[46] Expert clinical and laboratory guidance, if available, is required.

An increased incidence of isoniazid-related epileptiform attacks and other neurologic symptoms has been reported in pregnant women but these are preventable by the prescription of pyridoxine 10mg daily. Mothers taking antituberculosis drugs at the time of birth can care for their infants with little risk, unless the mother's disease is drug-resistant or not responding to therapy. Likewise, although some of the drugs enter the milk in small concentrations, breast-feeding has no adverse effects on the infant.[47]

Adjunct corticosteroid therapy in tuberculosis

It has been postulated that corticosteroids, by reducing the host's immune response, would allow dormant bacilli to replicate freely and thereby facilitate killing by the drugs. There is little evidence to support this, and their use has not been shown to affect the outcome of modern short-course chemotherapy.[48] On the other hand, in some forms of tuberculosis corticosteroids aid recovery and reduce long-term sequelae by suppressing inflammatory reactions and limiting subsequent scar formation. For details see Chapters 37 and 40.d and a review by Alzeer and FitzGerald.[49]

CHEMOPROPHYLAXIS AND PREVENTIVE THERAPY OF TUBERCULOSIS

Chemoprophylaxis is defined as the prescription of antituberculosis drugs for uninfected persons who are exposed to a risk of infection; preventive therapy refers to the treatment of persons who have already been infected with tubercle bacilli (as indicated by tuberculin testing) but who show no clinical or radiologic evidence of active disease. Chemoprophylaxis is principally used to protect children who are at risk of infections, particularly those under the age of 3 years, who are prone to develop serious extrapulmonary forms of tuberculosis, including meningitis.

Preventive drug therapy for those infected by *M. tuberculosis* (i.e. tuberculin reactors) is used in some countries, notably the USA, where tuberculosis is uncommon and where BCG is not used. Although highly efficacious, it is not without its problems. Isoniazid monotherapy, for up to 1 year, is the most widely used form of preventive therapy, although 6-month regimens are becoming more common. Although there is a theoretic risk of generating isoniazid resistance, this does not seem to happen in practice, probably because there are so few bacilli present. Hepatic toxicity has given cause for concern, particularly in older adults, and so such preventive therapy is not recommended for those aged over 35 years.[50]

Policies for the use of chemoprophylaxis vary from country to country. National guidelines should be consulted for indications for chemoprophylaxis and for the recommended drug regimens. In general, chemoprophylaxis in tuberculosis control in regions with a high incidence of tuberculosis has, in view of problems of compliance and organization, not played a major role in tuberculosis control programs.

Transplant recipients receiving corticosteroids and other immunosuppressive drugs are at risk of developing tuberculosis. It has been suggested that such patients should be given isoniazid 300mg, and pyridoxine 25–50mg daily if they have one or more of the following:[51]

- a history of inadequately treated tuberculosis;
- an abnormal chest radiograph;
- a positive tuberculin test of more than 10mm in diameter; and
- recent contact with a case of active tuberculosis.

Prophylaxis of tuberculosis in HIV-infected patients

In view of the very high risk of a co-infected person developing active tuberculosis, and the adverse effect of this disease on the immune status and survival of the patient, there is a very good theoretical case for provision of prophylactic treatment for those at risk. Several placebo-controlled studies of isoniazid monotherapy in patients co-infected with *M. tuberculosis* and HIV have shown that such chemoprophylaxis is effective.[52] In practice, serious problems have been encountered in diagnosing dual infection, ruling out active tuberculosis and ensuring compliance with therapy without breach of confidence or enhancement of stigma. Studies of varying design from Haiti, Zambia and Uganda have shown that chemoprophylaxis in HIV-infected adults significantly reduced the incidence of tuberculosis. The questions of how long the protection lasts, whether prophylactic treatment is safe and whether such therapy can lead to the emergence of drug-resistant strains of tuberculosis require attention.

Although prophylaxis leads to a reduction of the risk of tuberculosis by around 60% in tuberculin-skin-test-positive adults who have HIV infection, identifying HIV-infected individuals is difficult in resource-poor settings. A major problem is ensuring compliance with therapy.[53] The development of voluntary counseling and testing centres was seen as an effective tool to promote safer sex and to offer those who have HIV infection interventions such as preventive therapy for tuberculosis.

It is very important to ensure that HIV-positive persons receiving chemoprophylaxis do not have active tuberculosis or there is a strong risk of masking the disease and encouraging the emergence of drug resistance. It is also necessary to supervise the therapy, and this adds another burden to stretched tuberculosis control services.

Initially, 12-month courses of isoniazid monotherapy were evaluated but, subsequently, shorter combination regimens were also shown to be effective. These include a 3-month course of a rifamycin (rifampin or rifabutin) plus isoniazid, and a 2-month course of a rifamycin plus pyrazinamide, but the only clear advantage over isoniazid monotherapy is the shorter duration of treatment. A study in Zambia revealed that the 2-month combination regimens or 6 months of isoniazid, administered twice weekly, reduced the incidence of tuberculosis by about 40% compared with a placebo group, although the overall mortality due to all causes was not reduced.[54]

The relatively short-term benefit of preventive therapy is a further problem. By 18 months, the incidence of tuberculosis in those who receive prophylactic therapy is similar to that in those not receiving such therapy, indicating the need to consider repeated courses or, perhaps, lifelong prophylactic treatment.[55] As a general rule, prevention is more effective in those who have relatively limited immunosuppression (positive tuberculin tests, high lymphocyte counts and high hemoglobin levels). This, together with the difficulty in detecting co-infection, has led to the current recommendation to restrict preventive therapy to tuberculin positive, HIV-positive persons.

DRUG INTERACTIONS

Clinically significant interactions between the first-line antituberculosis drugs themselves are uncommon but such reactions could well occur when more complex regimens are used to treat MDRTB. Antituberculosis drugs may interact with drugs used to treat unrelated conditions (Table 202.12). Rifampin is the most important in this respect because it is a potent inducer of cytochrome isoenzymes involved in the metabolism of many drugs. The increased metabolism and clearance of these drugs may lead to therapeutic failure unless levels are adjusted and then readjusted when rifampin therapy ceases. Patients on oral contraceptives should be advised to use alternative forms of birth control.

CLINICALLY SIGNIFICANT DRUG INTERACTIONS WITH ANTITUBERCULOSIS AGENTS	
Effects opposed by rifampin	
Antiretroviral agents	Opioids
Azathioprine	Oral contraceptives
Corticosteroids	Phenytoin
Cyclosporin	Propranolol
Diazepam	Quinidine
Digoxin	Theophylline
Haloperidol	Tolbutamide
Imidazoles	Warfarin
Potentiates the effects of rifampin	
Trimethoprim–sulfamethoxazole	
Effects potentiated by isoniazid	
Phenytoin	
Carbamezapine	
Potentiates the effects of isoniazid	
Insulin	
Effects opposed by isoniazid	
Enflurane	
Opposes the effects of isoniazid	
Prednisone	
Antacids (inhibit absorbtion)	
Effects potentiated by streptomycin	
Neuromuscular blocking agents	
Effects potentiated by quinolones	
Aminophylline and theophylline	
Potentiates the effects of quinolones	
Cimetidine	
Opposes the effects of quinolones	
Antacids, iron preparations, sucralfate, didanosine (all inhibit absorbtion)	

Table 202.12 Clinically significant drug interactions with antituberculosis agents.

Rifampin reduces the plasma concentrations and half-lives of the imidazole and triazole antifungals and these agents reduce plasma levels of rifampin. Because some patients, notably those who are HIV-positive, may also require antifungal therapy, these interactions, which may lead to treatment failure, are of increasing importance.[56] Patients who are HIV-positive may also be receiving trimethoprim–sulfamethoxazole for prevention or treatment of *Pneumocystis carinii* infection. This agent significantly increases the serum levels and half-life of rifampin, leading to an increased incidence of adverse effects, including hepatotoxicity.[57]

Drug interactions with isoniazid are more pronounced in slow acetylators. The effects of isoniazid are potentiated by insulin and opposed by prednisone (prednisolone); its absorption from the intestine, and that of ethambutol and the quinolones, is inhibited by antacids containing aluminum hydroxide. The effects of carbamazepine and phenytoin are potentiated by isoniazid and those of enflurane are opposed.

A limited number of drug interactions with other antituberculosis agents have been described and reviewed.[58]

Drug interactions with antiretroviral agents

Protease inhibitors such as saquinavir, ritonavir, indinavir and nelfinavir all interact with rifampin.[58,59] Rifampin accelerates the metabolism of protease inhibitors (through induction of hepatic P450 cytochrome), resulting in subtherapeutic levels of the protease inhibitors and thereby increasing the risk of the development of viral resistance. In addition, protease inhibitors retard the metabolism of rifampin, resulting in increased serum levels and the likelihood of increased drug toxicity (see Chapter 129).

When prescribing antiretrovirals with antituberculosis drugs, it is important to refer to the latest guidelines on the subject since these are updated frequently. As new antiretroviral agents are being discovered and used, new interactions with antituberculosis drugs are being discovered. Updates on these periodically appear on the US Centers for Disease Control and Prevention website – http://www.cdc.gov/epo/mmwr/mmwr_rr.html.

Two pharmacokinetic issues complicate treatment: the possibility of malabsorption of drugs and the complex drug–drug interactions between antiretroviral and antituberculosis drugs described above. While HIV-infected patients who have tuberculosis commonly experience adverse drug interactions, current recommendations are that highly active antiretroviral therapy (HAART) is commenced early in patients who have advanced HIV disease ($CD4^+$ counts <100 cells/mm^3).[60] In clinically stable patients who have $CD4^+$ cells in excess of 100×10^6 cells/mm^3/l, HAART should be deferred until the continuation phase of tuberculosis treatment (i.e. after 2 months of antituberculosis therapy). The current recommendation in this case is to replace rifampin by rifabutin, a much less powerful inducer of cytochrome enzymes, and to commence or continue with the antiretroviral drugs.[61]

DRUG SUSCEPTIBILITY TESTING

The purpose of drug susceptibility testing is not to detect small numbers of drug-resistant mutants, which will inevitably be present in every patient who has tuberculosis and in every culture, but rather to determine whether the great majority of the bacilli are susceptible to levels of the drugs that are achieved clinically. In the developed nations with the requisite facilities, and particularly where MDRTB is common, susceptibility testing of all clinical isolates is definitely indicated.[62] In most developing countries, facilities for conducting drug susceptibility tests are very limited.

The epidemiologic importance of susceptibility testing has recently been emphasized by the need to monitor the global incidence and distribution of acquired and primary drug resistance. Unfortunately, susceptibility testing is expensive and time-consuming and requires good laboratory facilities, a high level of technical expertise and rigid quality-control procedures. There is no point in doing such testing unless high standards of accuracy can be maintained because much harm may be done by modifying regimens to include less effective and more toxic drugs on the basis of false reports of resistance.

Global surveys on drug resistance have been compromised by the variety of methods used for surveillance and for drug susceptibility testing and the lack of standardization of the methods. The WHO has therefore prepared guidelines for standardized surveillance techniques and has established a network of supranational reference laboratories to co-ordinate surveillance and to provide technical guidance and assistance.[32,63]

Methods of susceptibility testing

Methods for drug susceptibility testing can be divided into:

- those that are based on inhibition of bacterial growth on drug-containing standard media;
- those that detect growth inhibition by automated radiometric and related systems;
- those that use biologic indicators of bacterial viability, such as enzyme activity and bacteriophage replication; and
- those that use nucleic-acid-based technology to detect mutations in genes determining susceptibility to drugs.

Conventional techniques

Methods for drug susceptibility testing based on growth on conventional media are well established but have the great disadvantage that there is a long delay before results are available. Four methods are currently in use (Table 202.13).

In an (unpublished) investigation carried out by members of the European Society of Mycobacteriologists, there were only minor discrepancies between results obtained by different workers using the first three of the methods listed in Table 202.13. All these methods may be used either for direct susceptibility tests on smear-positive sputum or for indirect susceptibility tests on cultures. The relative merits and usefulness of these methods in differing circumstances are reviewed in several places.[64,65]

TECHNIQUES USED TO DETERMINE SUSCEPTIBILITY TO ANTITUBERCULOSIS AGENTS IN VITRO

Technique	Where technique is used	Description of technique
Proportion method	USA and some European countries	Drug-free and drug-containing media are inoculated with test strains and the colony counts are compared; strains are reported as resistant if the colony count on the drug-containing medium is over 1% of that on the drug-free medium
Absolute concentration method	Some parts of Europe	Based on growth on media containing doubling dilutions of a known concentration of drug, so that the minimal bactericidal concentrations of drugs may be determined
Resistance ratio method	UK and those countries influenced by British bacteriologists	Similar to the absolute concentration method except that results are expressed as the ratio of the drug concentration inhibiting the test and drug susceptible control strains, rather than as the actual inhibiting concentration
Disk diffusion method	Rarely used	Similar to absolute concentration method and resistance ratio method but technically simpler, as disks containing the drugs are placed on the solid media, thereby avoiding the need to prepare batches of media containing the various drugs

Table 202.13 Techniques used to determine susceptibility to antituberculosis agents in vitro.

Conventional tests for susceptibility to pyrazinamide pose particular problems because the drug acts only in acidic environments in which bacterial growth is poor. Thus, the tests require careful standardization and interpretation.

Rapid techniques

The radiometric technique has been widely used in the industrially developed countries.[66] It is more costly than the conventional methods but the rapidity of the results justifies the extra cost, especially where multidrug resistance is common. Susceptibility to all antituberculosis drugs, including pyrazinamide, can be determined by this method. Automated, nonradiometric systems for performing rapid drug susceptibility tests are increasingly used.[67] The latter systems are based on the unquenching of a fluorescent dye when oxygen is consumed by mycobacterial metabolism or on color changes in dyes when carbon dioxide is liberated from nutrients in the medium.

Several rapid methods for the detection of mutations in the *rpoB* gene conferring resistance to rifampin have been described; one of these, based on a number of DNA probes for wild-type and mutated regions of the gene (line hybridization assay), is available in a commercially available kit form. The sites of mutations responsible for resistance to some other antituberculosis drugs, including streptomycin, pyrazinamide, isoniazid and ethionamide, are also known, and so commercially available kits for rapid detection of resistance to these and other drugs may soon be available.[68]

Bacteriophages have been used to detect bacterial viability in the presence of antituberculosis agents.[69] Enzyme activity has been used for the same purpose and one rapid and inexpensive method is based on detection of nitrate reductase activity.[70]

CONCLUSIONS

Chemotherapy is the mainstay of tuberculosis control and modern short-course regimens are among the most effective and cost-effective of all therapeutic interventions for any human disease. Sadly, this potent intervention has been so badly used that tuberculosis remains the leading infectious cause of death worldwide and control of the disease is now seriously threatened by the emergence of multidrug resistance. Although recent advances in immunology and molecular biology may eventually yield novel preventive and therapeutic agents, the overwhelming need at the present time is ensure that the available disease control tools are universally deployed and used in the most effective ways possible.

REFERENCES

1. Ryan F. Tuberculosis: the greatest story never told. Bromsgrove, UK: Swift Publishers; 1992.
2. Murray CJL, DeJonghe E, Chum HJ, Nyangulu DS, Salomao A, Styblo K. Cost effectiveness of chemotherapy for pulmonary tuberculosis in three sub-Saharan African countries. Lancet 1991;338:1305–8.
3. Somoskovi A, Parsons LM, Salfinger M. The molecular basis of resistance to isoniazid, rifampin, and pyrazinamide in *Mycobacterium tuberculosis*. Respir Res 2001;2:164–8.
4. Winstanley PA. Clinical pharmacology of antituberculosis drugs. In: Davies PDO, ed. Clinical tuberculosis, 2nd ed. London: Chapman & Hall; 1998:225–42.
5. Mitchell I, Wendon J, Fitt S, Williams R. Antituberculous therapy and acute liver failure. Lancet 1995;345:555–6.
6. Drobniewski F, Wilson SM. The rapid diagnosis of isoniazid and rifampicin resistance in *Mycobacterium tuberculosis* – a molecular story. J Med Microbiol 1998;47:189–96.
7. Cheung WC, Lo CY, Lo WK, *et al.* Isoniazid induced encephalopathy in dialysis patients. Tubercle Lung Dis 1993;74:136–9.
8. Prakash J, Kumar NS, Saxena RK, Verma U. Acute renal failure complicating rifampicin therapy. J Assoc Physicians India 2001;49:877–80.
9. Zimhony O, Cox JS, McNeil M *et al.* Pyrazinamide inhibits the eucaryotic-like fatty acid synthetase 1 (FAS-1) of *Mycobacterium tuberculosis*. Nature Med 2000;6:1043–7.
10. Suzuki Y, Suzuki A, Tamaru A, Katsukawa C, Oda H. Rapid detection of pyrazinamide-resistant *Mycobacterium tuberculosis* by a PCR-based in vitro system. J Clin Microbiol 2002;40:501–7.
11. Bishop KS, Blumberg L, Trollip AP, *et al.* Characterisation of the *pncA* gene in *Mycobacterium tuberculosis* isolates from Gauteng, South Africa. Int J Tuberc Lung Dis 2001;5:952–7.
12. Maurya V, Panjabi C, Shah A. Pyrazinamide induced photoallergy. Int J Tuberc Lung Dis 2001;5:1075–6.
13. Gangadharam PRJ. New drugs and strategies for chemotherapy of tuberculosis. In: Gangadharam PRJ, Jenkins PA, eds. Mycobacteria, vol 2: Chemotherapy. London: Chapman & Hall; 1998:335–78.
14. Telenti A, Philipp WJ, Sreevatsan S, *et al.* The *emb* operon, a gene cluster in *Mycobacterium tuberculosis* involved in resistance to ethambutol. Nat Med 1997;3:567–70.
15. DeBarber AE, Mdluli K, Bosman M, Bekker LG, Barry CE. Ethionamide activation and sensitivity in multidrug-resistant *Mycobacterium tuberculosis*. Proc Natl Acad Sci USA 2000;97:9677–82.
16. Chapuis L, Ji B, Truffot-Pernot C, O'Brien RJ, Raviglione MC, Grosset JH. Preventive therapy of tuberculosis in immunocompetent and nude mice. Am J Respir Crit Care Med 1994;150:1355–62.
17. Bryskier A, Lowther J. Fluoroquinolones and tuberculosis. Expert Opin Investig Drugs 2002;11:233–58.
18. Singla R, Gupta S, Gupta R, Arora VK. Efficacy and safety of sparfloxacin in combination with kanamycin and ethionamide in multidrug-resistant pulmonary tuberculosis patients: preliminary results. Int J Tuberc Lung Dis 2001;5:559–63.
19. Berning SE. The role of fluoroquinolones in tuberculosis today. Drugs 2001;61:9–18.
20. David S. Synergic activity of D-cycloserine and beta-chloro-D-alanine against *Mycobacterium tuberculosis*. J Antimicrob Chemother 2001;47:203–6.
21. Luna-Herrera J, Reddy MV, Danneluzzi D, Gangadharam PRJ. Anti-tuberculosis activity of clarithromycin. Antimicrob Agents Chemother 1995;39:2692–5.
22. De Logu A, Onnis V, Saddi B, Congiu C, Schivo ML, Cocco MT. Activity of a new class of isonicotinoylhydrazones used alone and in combination with isoniazid, rifampicin, ethambutol, para-aminosalicylic acid and clofazimine against *Mycobacterium tuberculosis*. J Antimicrob Chemother 2002;49:275–82.
23. Schraufnagel DE. Tuberculosis treatment for the beginning of the next century. Int J Tuberc Lung Dis 1999;3:651–62.
24. Tomioka H. Prospects for development of new antimycobacterial drugs. J Infect Chemother 2000;6:8–20.
25. Bosne-David S, Barros V, Verde SC, Portugal C, David HL. Intrinsic resistance of *Mycobacterium tuberculosis* to clarithromycin is effectively reversed by subinhibitory concentrations of cell wall inhibitors. J Antimicrob Chemother 2000;46:391–5.
26. Johnson JL, Kamya RM, Okwera A, *et al.* Randomized controlled trial of *Mycobacterium vaccae* immunotherapy in non-Human Immunodeficiency Virus-infected Ugandan adults with newly diagnosed pulmonary tuberculosis. J Infect Dis 2000;181:1304–12.
27. Yew WW, Wong CF, Lee J, Wong PC, Chau CH. Do β-lactam–β-lactamase inhibitor combinations have a place in the treatment of multidrug-resistant pulmonary tuberculosis? Tubercle Lung Dis 1995;76:90–2.
28. Dhillon J, Allen BW, Hu YM, Coates AR, Mitchison DA. Metronidazole has no antibacterial effect in Cornell model of murine tuberculosis. Int J Tuberc Lung Dis 1998;2:736–42.
29. Mitchison DA. Hypothesis: the action of anti-tuberculosis drugs in short course chemotherapy. Tubercle 1985;66:219–25.
30. Mitchison DA. How drug resistance emerges as a result of poor compliance during short course chemotherapy for tuberculosis. Int J Tuberc lung Dis 1998;2:10–5.
31. Kochi A, Vareldzis B, Styblo K. Multidrug-resistant tuberculosis and its control. Res Microbiol 1993;144:104–10.
32. World Health Organization. Anti-tuberculosis drug resistance in the world. The WHO/IUATLD project on anti-tuberculosis drug resistance surveillance. Geneva: World Health Organization; 1997.
33. WHO/IUATLD Global Project on Anti-tuberculosis Drug Resistance Surveillance. Anti-tuberculosis drug resistance in the world. Report No. 2. Geneva: World Health Organization; 2000.
34. Perelman MI. Tuberculosis in Russia. Int J Tuberc Lung Dis 2000;4:1097–103.
35. Simone PM, Dooley SW. Drug resistant tuberculosis in the USA. In: Davies PDO, ed.

Clinical tuberculosis, 2nd ed. London: Chapman & Hall; 1998:265–87.
36. Communicable Disease Report. Outbreak of hospital acquired multidrug resistant tuberculosis. CDR Wkly 1995;5:161.
37. Festenstein F, Grange JM. Tuberculosis in ethnic minority populations in industrialised countries. In: Porter JDH, Grange JM, eds. Tuberculosis – an interdisciplinary perspective. London: Imperial College Press; 1999:313–38.
38. World Health Organization. Use DOTS more widely. WHO report on the tuberculosis epidemic. Geneva: World Health Organization; 1997.
39. Dye C, Williams BG. Criteria for the control of drug-resistant tuberculosis. Proc Natl Acad Sci USA 2000;97: 8180–85.
40. Bastian I, Colebunders R. Treatment and prevention of multidrug-resistant tuberculosis. Drugs 1999;58:633–61.
41. Farmer P. DOTS and DOTS-plus: not the only answer. Ann NY Acad Sci 2001;953:165–84.
42. Saigal S, Agarwal SR, Nandeesh HP, Sarin SK. Safety of an ofloxacin-based antitubercular regimen for the treatment of tuberculosis in patients with underlying chronic liver disease: a preliminary report. Gastroenterol Hepatol 2001;16:1028–32.
43. Scott JGM, Darbyshire JH. Management of mycobacterial infections in AIDS. In: Zumla A, Johnson M, Miller R, eds. AIDS and respiratory medicine. London: Chapman & Hall; 1997:177–98.
44. Anastasis D, Pillai G, Rambiritch V, Abdool Karim SS. A retrospective study of human immunodeficiency virus infection and drug-resistant tuberculosis in Durban, South Africa. Tubercle Lung Dis 1997;1:220–4.
45. Brost BC, Newman RB. The maternal and fetal effects of tuberculosis therapy. Obstet Gynecol Clin North Am 1997;24:659–3.
46. Signorini L, Matteelli A, Bombana E, *et al.* Tuberculosis due to drug-resistant *Mycobacterium bovis* in pregnancy. Int J Tuberc Lung Dis 1998;2:342–3.
47. Tran JH, Montakantikul P. The safety of antituberculosis medications during breastfeeding. J Hum Lact 1998;14:337–40.
48. Fox W. The current status of short-course chemotherapy. Bull Int Union Tuberc 1978;53:268–80.
49. Alzeer AH, FitzGerald JM. Corticosteroids and tuberculosis: risks and use as adjunct therapy. Tubercle Lung Dis 1993;74:6–11.
50. Israel HL. Chemoprophylaxis for tuberculosis. Respir Med 1993;87:81–3.
51. Qunibi WY, Al-Sibai MB, Taher S, *et al.* Mycobacterial infection after renal transplantation – a report of 14 cases and a review of the literature. Q J Med 1990;77:1039–60.
52. Wilkinson D. Drugs for preventing tuberculosis in HIV infected persons. In: Cochrane Database of Systemic Reviews, issue 4. Oxford: Update Software; 2000:CD000171.
53. Msamanga GI, Fawzi WW. The double burden of HIV infection and tuberculosis in sub-Saharan Africa. N Engl J Med 1997;337:849–51.
54. Pape JW, Jean SS, Ho JL, Hafner A, Johnson WD Jr. Effect of isoniazid prophylaxis on incidence of active tuberculosis and disease progression of HIV infection. Lancet 1993;342:268–72.
55. Whalen CC, Johnson JL, Okwera A, *et al.* A trial of three regimens to prevent tuberculosis in Ugandan adults infected with the human immunodeficiency virus. N Engl J Med 1997;337:801–8.
56. Lee BL, Safrin S. Interaction and toxicity of drugs used in patients with AIDS. Clin Infect Dis 1992;14:773–9.
57. Bhatia RS, Uppal R, Malhi R, *et al.* Drug interaction between rifampicin and co-trimoxazole in patients with tuberculosis. Hum Exp Toxicol 1991;10:419–21.
58. Grange JM, Winstanley PA, Davies PDO. Clinically significant drug interactions with anti-tuberculosis agents. Drug Saf 1994;11:242–51.
59. Dean GL, Edwards SG, Ives NJ, *et al.* Treatment of tuberculosis in HIV-infected persons in the era of highly active antiretroviral therapy. AIDS 2002;16:75–83.
60. Report. Clinical update: impact of HIV protease inhibitors on the treatment of HIV-infected tuberculosis patients with rifampin. Morb Mortal Wkly Rep 1996;45:921–5.
61. Centers for Disease Control. Prevention and treatment of tuberculosis among patients infected with human immunodeficiency virus: principles of therapy and revised recommendations. MMWR Morb Mortal Wkly Rep 1998;47(RR-20):1–58.
62. Centers for Disease Control. Initial therapy for tuberculosis in the era of multidrug resistance. Recommendations of the Advisory Council for the Elimination of Tuberculosis. MMWR Morb Mortal Wkly Rep 1993;42(RR-7):1–8.
63. Drobniewski F, Pablos-Méndez A, Raviglione MC. Epidemiology of tuberculosis in the world. Semin Respir Crit Care Med 1997;18:419–29.
64. Collins CH, Grange JM, Yates MD. Tuberculosis bacteriology. Organization and practice, 2nd ed. Oxford: Butterworth Heinemann; 1997.
65. Vareldzis BP, Grosset J, de Kantor I, *et al.* Drug resistant tuberculosis: laboratory issues. World Health Organization recommendations. Tubercle Lung Dis 1994;75:1–7.
66. Pfyffer GE, Bonato DA, Ebrahimzadeh A, *et al.* Multicenter laboratory validation of susceptibility testing of *Mycobacterium tuberculosis* against classical second-line and newer antimicrobial drugs by using the radiometric BACTEC 460 technique and the proportion method with solid media. J Clin Microbiol 1999;37:3179–86.
67. Tortoli E, Benedetti M, Fontanelli A, Simonetti MT. Evaluation of automated BACTEC MGIT 960 system for testing susceptibility of *Mycobacterium tuberculosis* to four major antituberculous drugs: comparison with the radiometric BACTEC 460TB method and the agar plate method of proportion. J Clin Microbiol 2002;40:607–10.
68. Shaw RJ, Taylor GM. Polymerase chain reaction: applications for diagnosis, drug sensitivity and strain identification of *M. tuberculosis*. In: Davies PDO, ed. Clinical tuberculosis, 2nd ed. London: Chapman & Hall; 1998:97–110.
69. Wilson SM, al-Suwaidi Z, McNerney R, Porter J, Drobniewski F. Evaluation of a new rapid bacteriophage-based method for the drug susceptibility testing of *Mycobacterium tuberculosis*. Nature Med 1997;3:465–8.
70. Angeby KA, Klintz L, Hoffner SE. Rapid and inexpensive drug susceptibility testing of *Mycobacterium tuberculosis* with a nitrate reductase assay. J Clin Microbiol 2002;40:553–5.

chapter 203

Miscellaneous Agents: Fusidic Acid, Nitrofurantoin and Spectinomycin

S Ragnar Norrby

This chapter deals with three antibiotics that are chemically different and have different antibacterial spectra and clinical uses.

FUSIDIC ACID

Fusidic acid has a steroidal chemical structure. It inhibits protein synthesis in Gram-positive bacteria.

PHARMACOKINETICS, ROUTE OF ADMINISTRATION AND DOSAGE

Fusidic acid is available for intravenous, oral or topical administration. The bioavailability after oral administration is 75–90% with tablets but only about 23% in children given a suspension.[1] After an oral dose of 500mg given as tablets, the initial plasma concentration is approximately 30mg/l and in steady state the concentration is about 100mg/l after a dosage of 500mg q8h. The protein binding is about 97%.

Fusidic acid is lipid-soluble and is efficiently distributed to peripheral compartments, including brain tissue, but excluding cerebrospinal fluid.[2] The elimination half-life is about 9 hours. Fusidic acid is eliminated mainly by conjugation to glucuronide in the liver and subsequent biliary excretion. Fusidic acid *per se* has no known effects on the central nervous system, lung, liver, kidney or prostate/genitourinary system.

The dosage of fusidic acid is:

- 500mg q8h orally or intravenously for adults; and
- 15–20mg/kg q12h for children.

Doses should be reduced in patients who have hepatic diseases, particularly biliary obstruction. Full doses can be given to patients who have renal insufficiency and to elderly. Because of the high protein binding, administration of fusidic acid should be avoided during the last trimester of pregnancy and to newborn children (risk for accumulation of bilirubin in the central nervous system – 'kernicterus').

INDICATIONS

The antibacterial spectrum of fusidic acid includes mainly *Staphylococcus aureus* but also coagulase-negative staphylococci and Gram-positive anaerobes, including *Clostridium difficile*.[3] In addition, fusidic acid has been found to be active against *Mycobacterium kansasii* and *Mycobacterium leprae*.[4,5] The antistaphylococcal spectrum includes methicillin-resistant strains, and sensitive strains typically have minimum inhibitory concentrations (MICs) of 0.25mg/l or less.[3]

Additive, synergistic or antagonistic antibacterial activity may result when fusidic acid is combined with other antibiotics.[3,6] The lack of predictive interaction between fusidic acid and other antibiotics is a problem because fusidic acid should be combined when used in systemic infections to avoid the possible emergence of resistance. In experimental staphylococcal endocarditis it was shown that, when fusidic acid was used as a single agent, resistance emerged in five of 12 animals, whereas no resistance was seen in animals treated with vancomycin plus fusidic acid.[7]

The spectrum of fusidic acid makes it one of the few antibiotics that can be used for the oral treatment of methicillin-resistant staphylococci. It should then preferably be combined with another antibiotic to avoid the emergence of resistance. Candidates for combinations with fusidic acid are clindamycin, rifampin (rifampicin), and possibly linezolid. Fusidic acid is widely used for the treatment of bone and joint infections due to *S. aureus*, usually combined with flucloxacillin, although there are no formal studies showing that the combination is better than flucloxacillin alone. Topical fusidic acid has been used to eliminate carriage of methicillin-resistant *S. aureus*.

ADVERSE REACTIONS AND INTERACTIONS

Intravenous fusidic acid causes local irritation and thrombophlebitis in about 15% of patients treated, and hemolysis may occur following rapid infusion (normal infusion time is 2 hours or more). In newborns fusidic acid may cause kernicterus. Fusidic acid may interact with coumarin derivatives and oral contraceptives, reducing the bioavailability of these drugs through interference with the fecal flora.

NITROFURANTOIN

Nitrofurantoin interacts with bacterial protein synthesis in aerobic bacteria.

PHARMACOKINETICS, ROUTE OF ADMINISTRATION AND DOSAGE

Nitrofurantoin is administered orally as a microcrystalline or macrocrystalline formulation, of which the latter has a slower absorption rate. Absorption is almost complete, with 2–4% of the dose being recovered from the feces.[8] Serum concentrations are not measurable, except in patients who have severe renal failure. This is because of destruction of nitrofurantoin in the tissues and, in particular, a very rapid renal elimination by glomerular filtration (20%) and tubular secretion, resulting in a serum half-life of only 20 minutes in patients who have normal renal function.[8] Excretion is complete within 6 hours after intake and urine concentrations achieved are 200–400mg/l after a dose of 100mg q8h. In patients who have renal failure – who should not be given nitrofurantoin – there are measurable but still very low serum and urine concentrations.[9] Nitrofurantoin has no effects on the central nervous system and does not affect the kidneys, the prostate or the genitourinary system. It may cause toxic hepatitis or allergic lung reactions (see below).

Therapeutic doses of nitrofurantoin are 50–100mg q8h or q6h for adults and 3mg/kg/day q12h or q8h for children. Prophylactically, the adult dose is 50–100mg at bedtime, and the pediatric dose is 1–2mg/kg. The duration of treatment when nitrofurantoin is used therapeutically should be 5–7 days. Dosages are not affected by liver function. Nitrofurantoin can be used during pregnancy and lactation.

INDICATIONS

Nitrofurantoin is active against aerobic Gram-negative and Gram-positive bacteria, including enterococci but excluding *Pseudomonas aeruginosa*.[10] Resistance is still rare in *Escherichia coli* but is frequently seen in *Klebsiella* spp.[11] Because nitrofurantoin loses most of its antibacterial activity in alkaline pH, it is not active against *Proteus*, *Morganella* and *Providencia* spp., even if susceptibility testing shows sensitivity. Nitrofurantoin should only be used for the treatment and prevention of urinary tract infections – complicated and uncomplicated bacterial cystitis.

In a study comparing 3-day treatment regimens of trimethoprim–sulfamethoxazole 160–800mg q12h, cefadroxil 500mg q12h, amoxicillin 500mg q8h and nitrofurantoin 100mg q6h for the treatment of uncomplicated cystitis in women, significantly better results were obtained with trimethoprim–sulfamethoxazole than with the other three regimens, which did not differ from each other.[12] Possible reasons for the lower activities of nitrofurantoin and the β-lactams are lack of activity on the fecal and vaginal flora and the short duration of treatment. Despite these findings, nitrofurantoin has a place in the therapy of cystitis, especially for pregnant women and children. However, the duration of treatment should be at least 5 days; similar efficacy results have been reported for trimethoprim–sulfamethoxazole and nitrofurantoin when they are used for 7 days.[13]

The use of a single dose of nitrofurantoin at night to prevent cystitis is documented, albeit with some study design deficiencies.[14]

ADVERSE REACTIONS

Table 203.1 lists the most important adverse reactions to nitrofurantoin. They occur at low frequencies (<0.5%).[15] The risk for these reactions can be markedly reduced by:

- avoiding long-term (>7 days) treatment, especially in the elderly;
- avoiding daily doses higher than 300mg in adults; and
- reducing the dosage for elderly patients and patients who have renal impairment.

Nitrofurantoin should not be used for patients who have renal failure because the urine levels are too low and there is an increased risk of adverse reactions. Upper gastrointestinal adverse reactions (nausea, vomiting, anorexia) may occur and seem to be more common with the old microcrystalline formulation than with the macrocrystalline one that is now used.[13]

SERIOUS ADVERSE REACTIONS TO NITROFURANTOIN

Adverse reaction	Risk factor
Eosinophilic lung infiltrates, fever	Prolonged treatment time, high doses
Pulmonary fibrosis	Elderly female patients, high doses
Polyneuropathy	High dose relative to renal function
Hepatitis	Long treatment time
Hemolytic anemia	Hereditary glucose-6-phosphate dehydrogenase deficiency

Table 203.1 Serious adverse reactions to nitrofurantoin.

SPECTINOMYCIN

Spectinomycin is an aminocyclitol antibiotic with a chemical structure similar to that of the aminoglycosides. Another similarity to the aminoglycosides is that spectinomycin acts by inhibiting bacterial protein synthesis at the 30S ribosomal level.[16]

PHARMACOKINETICS, ROUTE OF ADMINISTRATION AND DOSAGE

Spectinomycin is always given intramuscularly. It is rapidly and completely absorbed and a concentration of about 80mg/l is achieved after a dose of 2g.[17] Its protein binding is low (<5%) and it has an apparent volume of distribution of 0.3l/kg. The elimination is renal, with a half-life of about 1 hour. It has no reported effects *per se* on any organ system.

Spectinomycin is given as a single intramuscular dose of 2g for gonococcal urethritis and at a dose of 2g q12h for 3 days for disseminated gonorrhea. Dose reductions are not necessary in any patient category.

INDICATIONS AND ADVERSE REACTIONS

Spectinomycin was developed to act against the increasing number of strains of *Neisseria gonorrhoeae* resistant to β-lactam antibiotics and other drugs used to treat gonorrhea. Resistance to spectinomycin is uncommon in gonococci.[18] The only indication for spectinomycin is gonococcal urethritis. It is not usually a first-line choice but should be considered as an alternative to other, and often more effective, regimens, for instance in pregnancy when the patient is allergic to cephalosporins.[19]

REFERENCES

1. Borget P, Duhamel JF, Sorensen H, Roiro R. Pharmacokinetics of fusidic acid after a single dose of a new paediatric suspension. J Clin Pharmacol Ther 1993;18:171–7.
2. Mindermann T, Zimmerli W, Rajacic Z, Gratzl O. Penetration of fusidic acid into human brain tissue and cerebrospinal fluid. Acta Neurochir Wien 1993;121:12–4.
3. Drugeon HB, Caillon J, Juvin ME. In-vitro antibacterial activity of fusidic acid alone and in combination with other antibiotics against methicillin-sensitive and -resistant *Staphylococcus aureus*. J Antimicrob Chemother 1994;34:899–907.
4. Witzig RS, Franzblau SG. Susceptibility of *Mycobacterium kansasii* to ofloxacin, sparfloxacin, clarithromycin, azithromycin, and fusidic acid. Antimicrob Agents Chemother 1993;37:1997–9.
5. Franzblau SG, Chan GP, Garcia-Ignacio BG, *et al.* Clinical trials of fusidic acid for lepromatous leprosy. Antimicrob Agents Chemother 1994;38:1651–4.
6. Uri JV. Antibacterial antagonism between fusidic acid and ciprofloxacin. Acta Microbiol Hung 1993;40:141–9.
7. Fantin B, Leclercq R, Duval J, Carbon C. Fusidic acid alone or in combination with vancomycin for therapy of experimental endocarditis due to methicillin-resistant *Staphylococcus aureus*. Antimicrob Agents Chemother 1993;37:2466–9.
8. Reckendorf HK, Castringius RG, Spingler HK. Comparative pharmacodynamics, urinary excretion and half-life determinations of nitrofurantoin sodium. Antimicrob Agents Chemother 1962:531–42.
9. Kunin CM. More on antimicrobials in renal failure. Ann Intern Med 1968;69:397–401.
10. McOsker CC, Zhanel GG. Nitrofurantoin: mechanism of action and implications for resistance development in common uropathogens. J Antimicrob Chemother 1994;33(Suppl.A):23–30.
11. Karlowsky JA, Jones ME, Thornsberry C, Critchley I, Kelly LJ, Sahm DF. Prevalence of antimicrobialresistance among urinary tract pathogens isolated from female outpatients across the US in1999. Int J Antimicrob Agents 2001;18:121–7.
12. Hooton TM, Winter C, Tiu F, Stamm WE. Randomized comparative trial and cost analysis of 3-day antimicrobial regimens for treatment of acute cystitis in women. JAMA 1995;273:41–5.

13. Spencer RC, Moseley DJ, Greensmith MJ. Nitrofurantoin modified release versus trimethoprim or co-trimoxazole in the treatment of uncomplicated urinary tract infection in general practice. J Antimicrob Chemother 1994;33(Suppl.A):121–9.
14. Wiliams GJ, Lee A, Craig JC. Long-term antibiotics for prevention of recurrent urinary tract infections in children (Cochrane Review). In: Cochrane Database of Systemic Reviews, issue 4. Oxford: Update Software; 2001:CD001534.
15. D'Arcy PF. The comparative safety of therapies for urinary tract infection, with special reference to nitrofurantoin. In: Schröder FH, ed. Recent advances in the treatment of urinary tract infections. Royal Society of Medicine International Congress and Symposium Series No. 97. London: Royal Society of Medicine 1985:39–53.
16. Holloway WJ. Spectinomycin. Med Clin North Am 1982;66:169–73.
17. Wagner JG, Novak E, Leslie LG, Metzler CM. Absorption, distribution, and elimination of spectinomycin dihydrochloride in man. Int Z Klin Pharmakol Toxikol 1968;1:261–85.
18. Anonymous. Surveillance of antiniotic resistance in *Neisseria gonorrhoeae* in WHO Western Pacific region, 2000. Commun Dis Intell 2001;25:274–6.
19; Moran JS,Levine WC. Drugs of choice for the treatment of uncomplicated gonococcal infections. Clin Infect Dis 1995;20(Suppl 1):47–65.

chapter

204 Antiretroviral Agents

Scott M Hammer & Christine J Kubin

INTRODUCTION

The field of antiretroviral therapy is approaching its 20th anniversary. It began shortly after the discovery of HIV-1 in 1983, following which in-vitro cultivation of the virus permitted the screening of agents for antiviral activity. The availability of viral-specific targets (Fig. 204.1) has facilitated high throughput screening and rational drug design efforts, which resulted in the availability of 19 US Food and Drug Administration (FDA)-approved agents by mid-2003 (Table 204.1).

The availability of potent combination therapy has led to dramatic reductions in morbidity and mortality in the developed world.[1] Despite these advances, the challenges of adherence, toxicities and drug resistance have placed recognizable limits on the currently available agents. Thus, continued drug development is a necessity if further progress is to be made and, in this respect, cautious optimism is justified. The developmental horizon includes the potential for several new agents within existing drug classes and promising agents in the novel drug classes. The clinical use of antiretroviral agents involves a pathogenesis-based, combination treatment approach. The principles and approach to antiretroviral therapy and clinical monitoring tools are addressed in Chapters 138–140. The reader is also referred to published antiretroviral therapy guidelines from the Department of Health and Human Services[2] and the International AIDS Society – USA.[3] This chapter will review the characteristics of both approved and selected investigational agents. Although they will be discussed individually, it is critical to remember that these drugs must be used in appropriate combinations to provide sufficiently potent therapy to realize durable clinical benefits.

NUCLEOSIDE ANALOG REVERSE TRANSCRIPTASE INHIBITORS

Nucleoside analog reverse transcriptase inhibitors (NRTIs) were the first class of antiretroviral agents developed (Fig. 204.2). These drugs share a common mechanism of action. As purine or pyrimidine analogs, they require intracellular anabolic phosphorylation to triphosphate forms to be active inhibitors of the HIV reverse transcriptase. The NRTI triphosphates act as competitive inhibitors of the normal nucleoside triphosphates, are incorporated into the growing proviral DNA chain, and act as chain terminators.

Zidovudine

Description

Zidovudine – 3′-azido-,3′-deoxythymidine (AZT, ZDV; see Fig. 204.2) – is converted to ZDV triphosphate sequentially by cellular thymidine kinase, thymidylate kinase and nucleoside diphosphate kinase. Zidovudine triphosphate possesses a 100-fold greater selectivity for the HIV-1 reverse transcriptase than for the cellular DNA polymerase alpha, thus accounting for its viral specificity. The drug is active against HIV-1, HIV-2 and human T-cell lymphotropic virus type 1 (HTLV-1).

Pharmacokinetics and distribution

Zidovudine is rapidly and well absorbed following oral administration, but exhibits a mean systemic bioavailability of about 64% due to significant first-pass metabolism. Peak plasma concentrations of intravenous and orally administered ZDV range from 1.5 to 18μmol/l with single and multiple doses of 1–10mg/kg.[4] Zidovudine is highly lipophilic and widely distributed throughout the body.[5] Concentrations in the cerebrospinal fluid (CSF) in adults have ranged from 15 to 135% of plasma concentrations. Zidovudine is approximately 25% protein bound, primarily to albumin, and is primarily metabolized by hepatic 5′-glucuronidation forming a glucuronidated metabolite that is renally excreted.[5,6] The serum half-life of ZDV is approximately 1 hour.

Route and dosage

Zidovudine is available as capsule, tablet, oral liquid and intravenous preparations. The latter is used nearly exclusively intrapartum to prevent maternal–fetal HIV-1 transmission. Oral formulations are available as ZDV alone or in fixed dose combinations with lamivudine (Combivir) or with lamivudine and abacavir (Trizivir). The usual adult therapeutic dosage of ZDV is 300mg q12h.

Indications

Zidovudine was the first approved antiretroviral agent in the USA and has been a cornerstone of therapy throughout the nucleoside monotherapy, dual nucleoside therapy and multiple drug combination therapy eras. It is indicated for the treatment of HIV-1 infection in combination with other antiretroviral agents. Typically, it is paired with another NRTI to form a dual nucleoside component of a three- or four-drug regimen. The second NRTI is most commonly lamivudine or didanosine but should never be stavudine because of demonstrated antagonism.[7] In antiretroviral naive patients, these dual nucleoside components need to be prescribed with a protease inhibitor (PI), a non-nucleoside reverse transcriptase inhibitor (NNRTI) or the potent NRTI abacavir, to form a combination regimen capable of suppressing plasma HIV-1 RNA to less than 50 copies/ml. The use of ZDV in treatment-experienced patients should be guided by the previous treatment history and the results of drug resistance testing. The presence of NRTI class cross-resistance often limits the efficacy of ZDV in second- and third-line regimens.

Zidovudine plays a role in the prevention of HIV-1 acquisition in the following circumstances:

- as a cornerstone of regimens to prevent maternal–fetal transmission following the landmark findings of the AIDS Clinical Trials Group, Study 076, in which transmission was reduced by two-thirds;[8] (see Chapter 135)
- following accidental needle-stick exposure in health care workers; and
- following unprotected sexual exposure, as in cases of rape.

In the setting of the prevention of maternal–fetal transmission, published guidelines suggest including ZDV as part of the regimen irrespective of the treatment history of the mother. In the setting of accidental exposure, the risk of drug resistance in the index case should be factored into the choice of the appropriate prophylactic regimen.

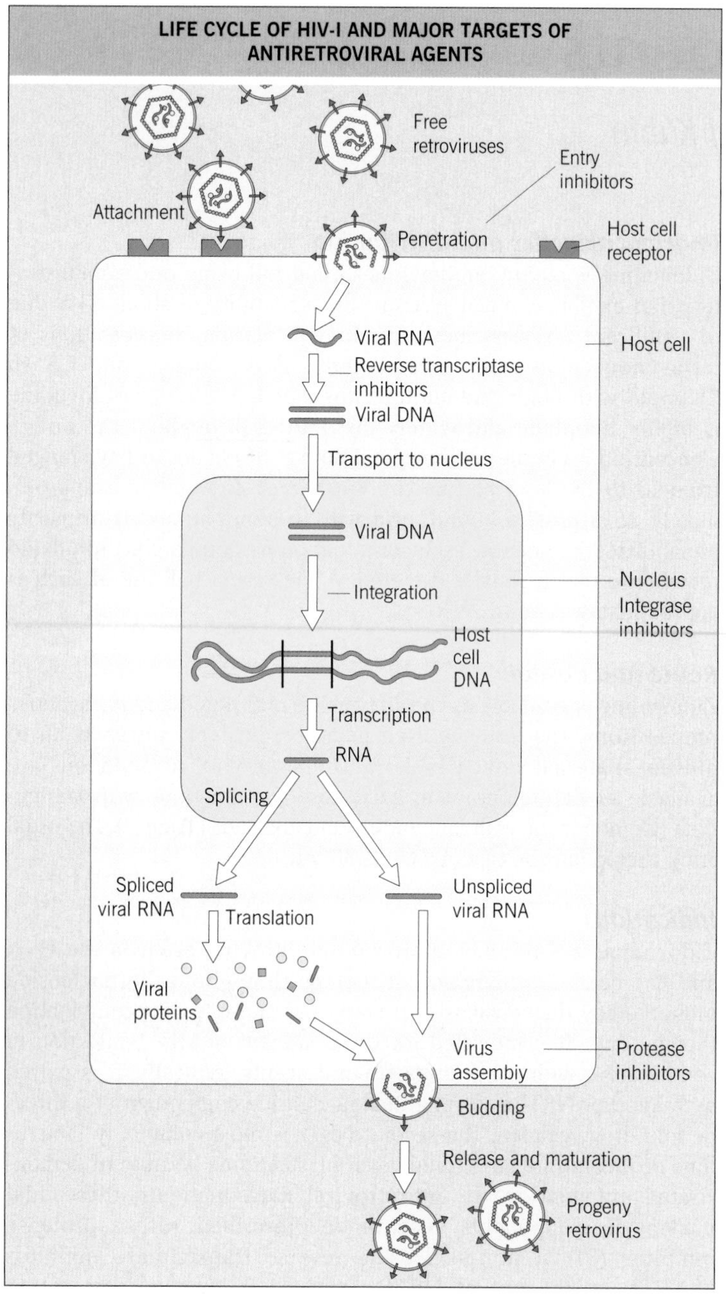

Fig. 204.1 Life cycle of HIV-1 and major targets of antiretroviral agents.

Resistance

Zidovudine, being the first antiretroviral agent in widespread use, became the first drug to which the development of drug resistance was described in 1989.[9] The mechanism of resistance is thought to be mediated by pyrophosphorolysis, which facilitates the removal of ZDV after its incorporation into the proviral DNA chain. Resistance to ZDV is mediated primarily by six mutations, which include M41L, D67N, K70R, L210W, T215F/Y and K219Q/E. High level ZDV resistance requires the accumulation of three to four mutations. These ZDV-associated mutations are now referred to as nucleoside analog-associated mutations (NAMs) because of the increasing recognition of their role in cross-resistance to other members of the NRTI and nucleotide RTI classes (Fig. 204.3). Resistance to ZDV can also be mediated by two multinucleoside resistance complexes: the Q151M complex (A62V, V75I, F116Y, Q151M) and a T69S 6bp insertion in the presence of NAMs (see Fig. 204.3).

Dosage in special circumstances

Dosage adjustment is necessary in patients with severe renal disease (Table 204.2). In patients with hepatic dysfunction, ZDV clearance is reduced and dosage modification is recommended. Limited data are available regarding specific dosage recommendations for patients with liver disease. Based on limited pharmacokinetic data in 14 patients with liver cirrhosis, a ZDV dose reduction by 50% or a doubling of the interval has been recommended.[6]

Zidovudine crosses the placenta with concentrations in the fetal circulation approximately 85% of maternal plasma concentrations. Teratogenic effects with ZDV have only been reported in rodents when exposed to lethal maternal doses (pregnancy category C).[10]

Adverse reactions and drug interactions

The major toxicities of ZDV include nausea, headache, anemia, neutropenia and myopathy (Table 204.3). Nucleoside reverse transcriptase inhibitor class toxicities are listed in Table 204.4. Clinically significant drug interactions are minimal because ZDV is predominantly renally excreted.

Didanosine

Description

Didanosine – 2′,3′-dideoxyinosine (ddI; see Fig. 204.2) – is sequentially converted intracellularly to 2′,3′-dideoxyinosine monophosphate by 5′-nucleotidase, and to 2′,3′-dideoxyadenosine monophosphate by adenylosuccinate synthetase and adenylosuccinate lyase. It is then converted to the ddA-triphosphate, which is the active form of the drug, possessing activity against HIV-1 and HIV-2.

Pharmacokinetics and distribution

Didanosine bioavailability varies from 21 to 54% following oral administration in adults. It is recommended that didanosine be

FDA APPROVED AGENTS			
Nucleoside/nucleotide reverse transcriptase inhibitors	**Non-nucleoside reverse transcriptase inhibitors**	**Protease inhibitors**	**Entry inhibitors**
Zidovudine (Retrovir) Didanosine (Videx, Videx EC) Zalcitabine (Hivid) Stavudine (Zerit) Lamivudine (Epivir) Abacavir (Ziagen) Tenofovir disoproxil fumarate (Viread) Emtricitabine (Emtriva)	Nevirapine (Virammune) Delavirdine (Rescriptor) Efavirenz (Sustiva)	Saquinavir (Invirase, Fortovase) Indinavir (Crixivan) Ritonavir (Norvir) Nelfinavir (Viracept) Amprenavir (Agenerase) Lopinavir/ritonavir (Kaletra) Atazanavir (Reyataz)	Enfuvirtide (Fuzeon)

Table 204.1 US Food and Drug Administration approved agents.

CHEMICAL STRUCTURES OF NUCLEOSIDE AND NUCLEOTIDE ANALOG REVERSE TRANSCRIPTASE INHIBITORS

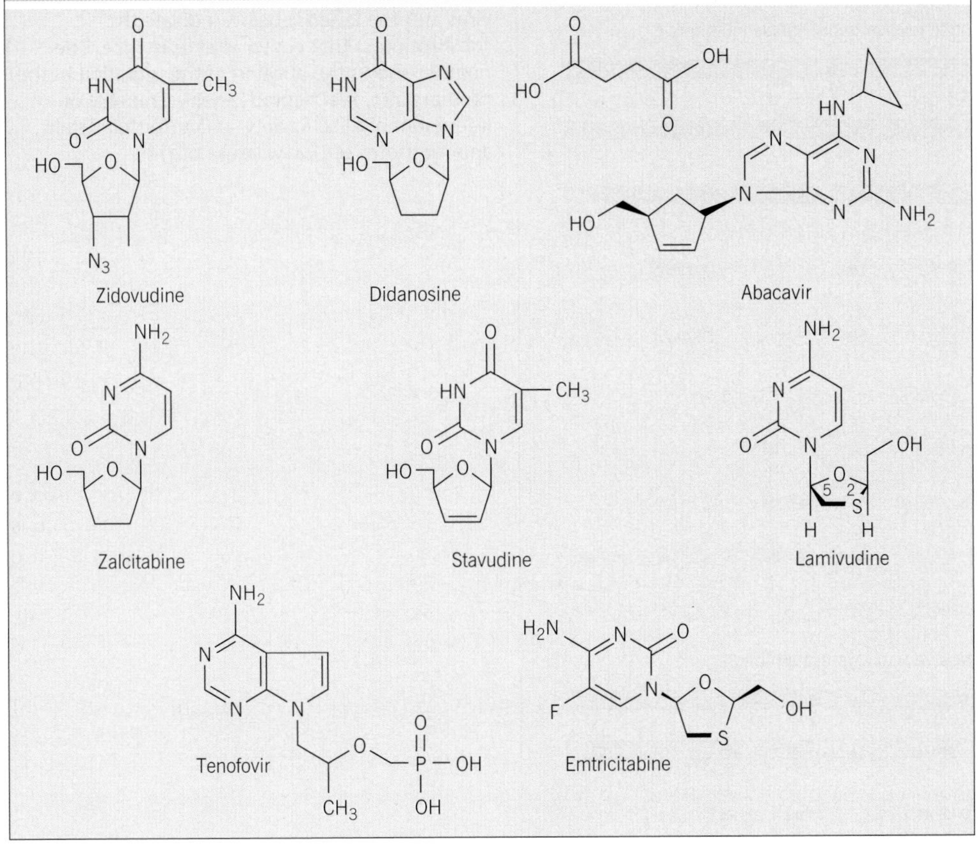

Fig. 204.2 Chemical structures of approved nucleoside analog reverse transcriptase inhibitors.

administered on an empty stomach to increase absorption. Administration of didanosine tablets and delayed release capsules with food decreases the didanosine area-under-the-curve (AUC) by approximately 55 and 19%, respectively. Didanosine exhibits linear pharmacokinetics with peak plasma concentrations ranging from 0.52 to 2.79mg/l after oral doses of 125–375mg q12h.[11] Results of pharmacokinetic studies suggest similar AUC values comparing the standard twice daily regimen to the same total daily dose administered once daily.[12] Didanosine is less than 5% protein bound. Concentrations in the CSF have been reported to be approximately 21% of those in plasma.[11] The plasma half-life of didanosine is short (<2 hours), but the in-vitro intracellular half-life of the triphosphate appears prolonged (>25 hours).[13] Didanosine is partially metabolized to ddATP or uric acid, or enters the purine metabolic pool.

Route and dosage

Didanosine is given orally and exists as enteric-coated capsules, chewable tablets (buffered), and powder for oral solution formulations. Dosage is weight based. The enteric-coated preparation improves tolerance and is administered once daily. The other formulations may be administered q24h or q12h. In adults, the usual dosage is 400mg q24h for those weighing over 60kg and 250mg q24h for those under 60kg.

Indications

Didanosine is indicated for the treatment of HIV infection in combination with other antiretroviral agents. It has proven efficacious throughout the monotherapy, dual therapy and potent combination therapy eras. Like ZDV, it is typically prescribed as part of the dual nucleoside component of three- to four-drug combination regimens. It is most commonly paired with ZDV or stavudine, although the toxicity of stavudine–didanosine has raised concerns about this combination (see below). Didanosine-containing dual NRTI components must be used with a PI and/or an NNRTI to provide a potent combination regimen. The drug can be used in both treatment naive and experienced patients. Its use in the latter situation should be driven by the treatment history and the drug resistance profile.

Hydroxyurea increases the intracellular activity of dideoxyadenosine triphosphate and has been studied in combination with didanosine or stavudine–didanosine. Although antiviral activity has been demonstrated, the blunting of CD4 cell responses and toxicity have dampened the enthusiasm for this adjunct to didanosine therapy.

Resistance

Low-fold changes in susceptibility to didanosine are sufficient to compromise the response to the drug and this must be recognized to properly interpret phenotypic resistance results. Genotypically, the signature mutation conferring didanosine resistance is L74V but K65R and M184V have also been associated with low-fold changes in susceptibility. The Q151M complex, the T69S insertions, and multiple NAMs also confer diminished susceptibility to didanosine (see Fig. 204.3).

Dosage in special circumstances

Didanosine clearance is significantly reduced in patients with renal disease and dosage modification is necessary (see Table 204.2). No dosage adjustment is recommended in patients with liver disease.

Didanosine crosses the placenta. Studies evaluating long-term carcinogenicity and teratogenicity have produced negative results (pregnancy category B).[10]

Adverse reactions and drug interactions

The major toxicities of didanosine include pancreatitis, peripheral neuropathy and diarrhea (see Table 204.3). The drug can also cause hepatotoxicity and has been associated with hepatotoxicity and

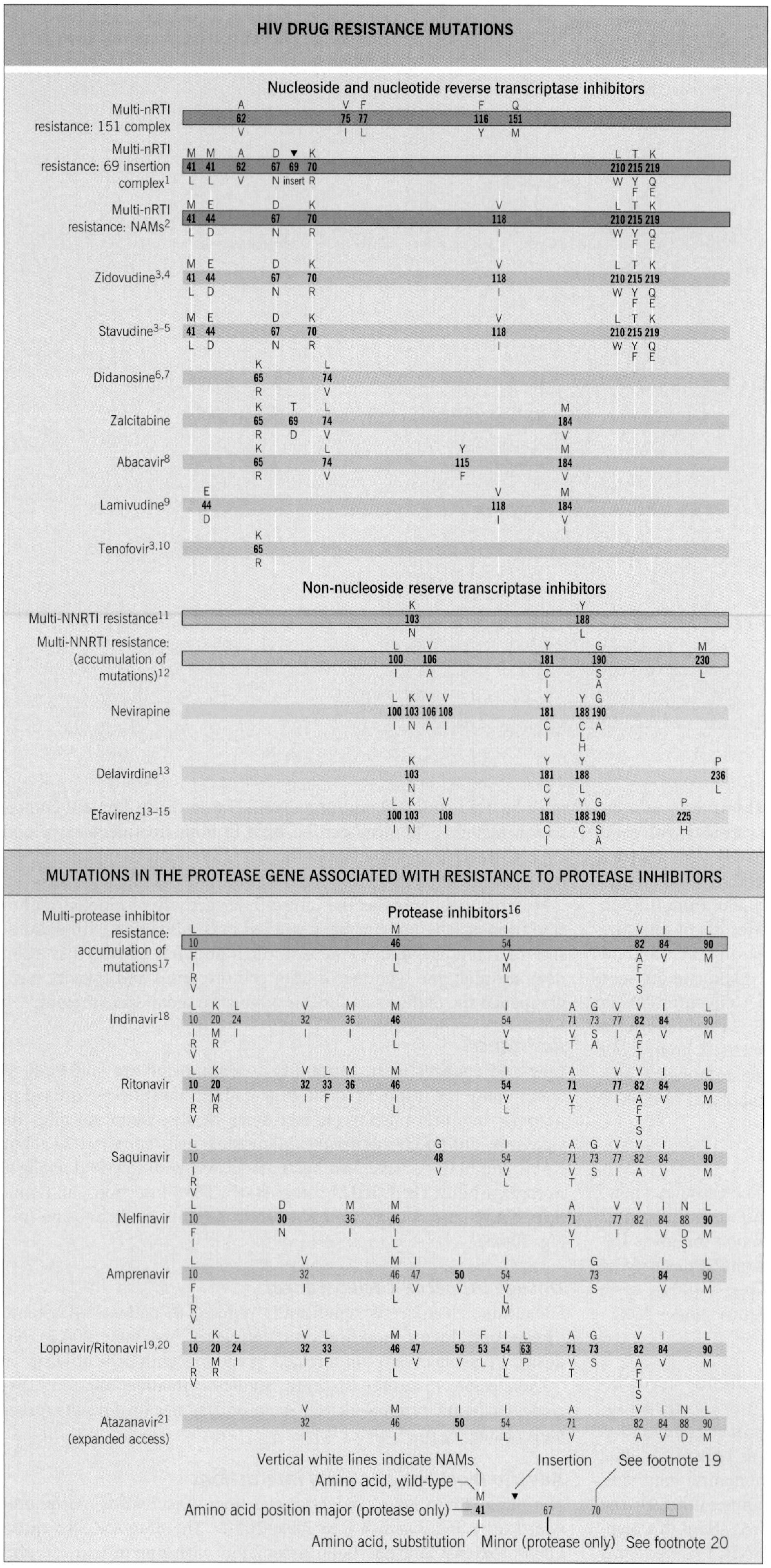

Fig. 204.3 HIV drug resistance mutations. For each amino acid residue the letter above the bar indicates the amino acid associated with wild-type virus and the letter(s) below indicate the substitution(s) that confer viral resistance. The number shows the position of the mutation in the protein. HR1, first heptad repeat. Courtesy of International AIDS Society – USA (for full details and footnotes see www.iasusa.org).

NUCLEOSIDE AND NUCLEOTIDE REVERSE TRANSCRIPTASE INHIBITOR DOSAGE MODIFICATIONS IN PATIENTS WITH RENAL DYSFUNCTION AND WITH DIALYSIS							
Drug	**Usual adult dose CrCl >50ml/min**	**CrCl 30–50ml/min**	**CrCl 10–30ml/min**	**CrCl <10ml/min**	**Hemodialysis***	**Peritoneal dialysis**	**Continuous renal replacement therapy**
Abacavir (po)	300mg q12h	300mg q12h	300mg q12h	300mg q12h	300mg q12h	300mg q12h	300mg q12h
Didanosine (po) ≥60kg	200mg q12h	100mg q12h	150mg q24h	100mg q24h	100mg q24h	100mg q24h	100mg q24h
<60kg	125mg q12h	75mg q12h	100mg q24h	75mg q24h	50–75mg q24h	75mg q24h	75mg q24h
Lamivudine (po)	150mg q12h	150mg q24h	100mg q24h	25–50mg q24h	25–50mg q24h	25–50mg q24h	50–150mg q24h
Stavudine (po) ≥60kg	40mg q12h	20mg q12h	20mg q24h	20mg q24h	20mg q24h	20mg q24h	N/A
<60kg	30mg q12h	15mg q12h	15mg q24h	15mg q24h	15mg q24h	15mg q24h	N/A
Tenofovir DF (po)	300mg q24h	Use not currently recommended in patients with CrCl <60ml/min	Use not currently recommended in patients with CrCl <60ml/min	Use not currently recommended in patients with CrCl <60ml/min	N/A	N/A	N/A
Zalcitabine (po)	0.75mg q8h	0.75mg q12h	0.75mg q12h	0.75mg q24h	0.75mg q24h	0.75mg q24h	N/A
Zidovudine (po)	300mg q12h	300mg q12h	100mg q8h	100mg q8h	100mg q8h	100mg q8h	100mg q8h

CrCl, creatinine clearance; N/A, specific dosing recommendations not available
* Drug should be administered after the hemodialysis session.

Table 204.2 Nucleoside and nucleotide reverse transcriptase inhibitor dosage modifications in patients with renal dysfunction and with dialysis.

NUCLEOSIDE AND NUCLEOTIDE REVERSE TRANSCRIPTASE INHIBITOR SPECIFIC TOXICITIES						
Zidovudine	**Didanosine**	**Zalcitabine**	**Stavudine**	**Lamivudine**	**Abacavir**	**Tenofovir DF**
Bone marrow suppression Anemia or neutropenia Gastrointestinal intolerance Headache Insomnia	Pancreatitis Peripheral neuropathy Nausea Diarrhea	Peripheral neuropathy Stomatitis Pancreatitis	Pancreatitis Peripheral neuropathy	Headache Nausea Diarrhea Insomnia Pancreatitis Neuropathy	Hypersensitivity reaction*	Asthenia Headache Diarrhea Nausea Vomiting

*Hypersensitivity reaction can be fatal: symptoms may include fever, rash, nausea, vomiting, malaise, fatigue, loss of appetite, and respiratory symptoms such as pharyngitis, dyspnea, or cough

Table 204.3 Nucleoside and nucleotide reverse transcriptase inhibitor specific toxicities.

NUCLEOSIDE REVERSE TRANSCRIPTASE INHIBITOR AND PROTEASE INHIBITOR CLASS TOXICITIES	
Nucleoside reverse transcriptase inhibitors	**Protease inhibitors**
Mitochondrial toxicity Lactic acidosis Hepatomegaly with steatosis Lipoatrophy	Gastrointestinal intolerance Fat redistribution Lipid abnormalities Insulin resistance and hyperglycemia Hepatitis Possible ↑ bleeding episodes in patients with hemophilia

Table 204.4 Nucleoside reverse transcriptase inhibitor and protease inhibitor class toxicities.

lactic acidosis when used in combination with stavudine in pregnant women. For NRTI class toxicities, see Table 204.4.

The didanosine buffered tablets have the potential for drug interactions with agents affected by concomitant antacid administration and with any agents that require gastric acidity for absorption. Clinically significant drug interactions have been reported between didanosine formulations and tenofovir disoproxil fumarate (tenofovir DF), delavirdine and indinavir. Administration of once daily didanosine enteric-coated capsules (Videx EC) 2 hours before tenofovir DF administered with a light meal resulted in an approximate 46% increase in didanosine exposure. Co-administration with a light meal resulted in an approximate 60% increase in didanosine exposure. Co-administration of the didanosine buffered tablets with tenofovir DF in the fasting state resulted in an approximate 44% increase in didanosine exposure. There appears to be no effect of either didanosine formulation on the levels of tenofovir DF. If didanosine and tenofovir are used concomitantly, the dosage of didanosine should be reduced to 250mg q24h. Simultaneous administration of didanosine buffered tablets with delavirdine and indinavir resulted in significant decreases in AUC by 20 and 84%, respectively. Consequently, delavirdine or indinavir should be administered 1 hour before didanosine buffered tablets.

Zalcitabine

Description

Zalcitabine – 2′,3′-dideoxycytidine (ddC; see Fig. 204.2) – is converted to its active, triphosphorylated form by cellular kinases. The drug is active against both HIV-1 and HIV-2.

Pharmacokinetics and distribution

Zalcitabine exhibits linear pharmacokinetics. Oral bioavailability exceeds 80%. Administration of zalcitabine with food decreases the rate and extent of absorption. With food, the peak concentration decreases 39%, bioavailability decreases 14% and the time to reach the peak concentration doubles.[14,15] Concentrations of zalcitabine in CSF have been reported as 14% of plasma levels.[16] Zalcitabine is not significantly metabolized and elimination is more dependent on renal mechanisms because approximately 75% of unchanged drug is recovered in the urine. The half-life of zalcitabine is less than 2 hours.

Route and dosage

Zalcitabine is available as a tablet formulation. It is administered orally with the usual adult dosage being 0.75mg q8h.

Indications

Major clinical end-point trials of zalcitabine reported in the mid-1990s in combination with ZDV demonstrated a clinical benefit to this combination over ZDV monotherapy in treatment naive patients.[17,18] Despite these findings, the drug has a very limited, if any, role in current antiretroviral therapy. Its limited potency, ineffectiveness in treatment-experienced patients and neurotoxicity contribute to the drug's current position as a low-priority agent.

Resistance

The genotypic patterns that confer reduced susceptibility to zalcitabine are similar to those reported for didanosine. They include K65R, L74V, M184V, multiple NAMs, the Q151M complex and the T69S insertions; T69D also confers zalcitabine resistance (see Fig. 204.3).

Dosage in special circumstances

Dosage adjustment is necessary in patients with renal disease (see Table 204.2). No dosage adjustment is necessary with hepatic impairment.

Zalcitabine crosses the placenta. Zalcitabine has been shown to be carcinogenic in rodents and teratogenic in mice and rats at high doses (pregnancy category C).[10]

Adverse reactions and drug interactions

The major toxicities of zalcitabine include peripheral neuropathy and pancreatitis (see Table 204.3). For NRTI class toxicities, see Table 204.4. Clinically significant drug interactions are minimal.

Stavudine

Description

Stavudine – 2′,3′-didehydro-3′-deoxythymidine (d4T; see Fig. 204.2) – is a thymidine analog that is converted to the active form, stavudine triphosphate, by a series of cellular kinases; the initial phosphorylation is the rate limiting step. The drug has activity against both HIV-1 and HIV-2.

Pharmacokinetics and distribution

Stavudine is rapidly absorbed and exhibits linear pharmacokinetics. Peak concentrations of about 0.9mg/l are achieved within 2 hours. The oral bioavailability is 82–86%. The mean serum half-life is short and ranges between 1 and 1.67 hours, with an intracellular half-life of about 3–4 hours. Protein binding is minimal. Stavudine penetrates into the CSF achieving levels approximately 40% of plasma levels.[19] Stavudine is excreted by renal and non-renal routes with approximately 50% of a dose excreted unchanged in the urine.[20]

Route and dosage

Stavudine is administered orally with the dosage weight adjusted. It is available in capsule and oral solution formulations. For adults weighing over 60kg, the dose is 40mg q12h; for those under 60kg, the dose is 30mg q12h. For the extended-release preparation of stavudine that is currently under investigation, the dose for persons over 60kg is 100mg q24h.

Indications

Like ZDV, stavudine is commonly used as part of dual NRTI components with lamivudine or didanosine. These are then typically combined with a PI, NNRTI or abacavir to form potent combination regimens. Stavudine can be used in treatment naive patients or as an alternative to ZDV in those patients who exhibit intolerance to ZDV in the first few weeks after initiation of therapy. The association of stavudine with lipoatrophy, perhaps more than with other NRTIs, has led to greater circumspection about using this agent in initial regimens. However, more data concerning the relative risks of the various NRTIs for peripheral lipoatrophy are needed. Its use in treatment-experienced persons should be dictated by the treatment history and the results of drug resistance testing.

Resistance

Low-fold changes in susceptibility can impair the response to stavudine in vivo and this is important to keep in mind in the interpretation of phenotypic resistance testing. Genotypically, the V75T has been thought to be a signature mutation for stavudine resistance but this mutation is only rarely seen in clinical isolates. Recent data suggest that stavudine and stavudine/didanosine can select for ZDV-associated mutations (NAMs) and the Q151M complex. Zidovudine and stavudine share cross-resistance at both the virion and enzyme levels. Zidovudine-resistant isolates should be considered resistant to stavudine (see Fig. 204.3).

Dosage in special circumstances

Stavudine requires dose adjustment in patients with renal disease (see Table 204.2). No dosage modification is recommended in patients with liver disease.

Stavudine crosses the placenta and teratogenicity studies in rodents were negative with a decrease in sternal calcium noted at high doses (pregnancy category C).[10]

Adverse reactions and drug interactions

The major toxicity of stavudine is peripheral neuropathy and the drug has been strongly implicated in peripheral lipoatrophy and mitochondrial dysfunction syndromes (see Table 204.3). For NRTI class toxicities, see Table 204.4. Clinically significant drug interactions are minimal.

Lamivudine

Description

Lamivudine – (-)2′,3′-dideoxy-3′-thiacytidine (3TC; see Fig. 204.2) – is the (-) enantiomer of a sulfur containing cytidine analog. This enantiomer was chosen on the basis of its potency and cytotoxicity profile. It is phosphorylated to its active form, lamivudine triphosphate, by cellular kinases. The drug is active against HIV-1 and HIV-2, and hepatitis B virus.

Pharmacokinetics and distribution

Lamivudine is well absorbed following oral administration with a mean bioavailability of over 80% in adults. Systemic drug exposure is not influenced by administration with food. Peak and trough concentrations of approximately 2μg/ml and 0.33μg/ml, respectively, have been achieved following oral administration of 150mg q12h.[21] The mean serum half-life is approximately 4–6 hours, with the intracellular half-life ranging from 10.5 to 15.5 hours.[22] Lamivudine is less than 36% protein bound. It penetrates the CSF, but the CSF to serum ratio is lower than that of other nucleoside analogs. Lamivudine is not significantly metabolized and is eliminated primarily unchanged via the kidney.

Route and dosage
Lamivudine is administered orally and is available in tablet and liquid formulations. The usual adult dosage is 150mg q12h but 300mg q24h dosing is being explored in clinical trials. The drug is also available as part of a fixed dose combination with ZDV (Combivir) and ZDV plus abacavir (Trizivir).

Indications
Lamivudine is one of the cornerstones of current antiretroviral therapeutics given its potency and excellent tolerability. It is commonly prescribed as part of the nucleoside component of initial regimens, typically paired with ZDV or stavudine. Recent data also suggest that it can be successfully paired with tenofovir DF. As noted previously, these dual NRTI components must be prescribed with a PI, an NNRTI or abacavir to create potent combination regimens. When lamivudine is not part of an initial regimen, it is useful in treatment-experienced patients if the key resistance mutation, M184V, is not present.

Lamivudine is widely used as part of maternal therapies and as part of maternal–fetal transmission interruption regimens. Concerns raised about potential fetal toxicity in a French study have not been borne out by larger reviews of experience in the USA.

Resistance
High-level phenotypic resistance (>500-fold change in susceptibility) quickly and nearly uniformly develops in patients treated with partially suppressive regimens containing lamivudine (e.g. dual nucleoside regimens). This is mediated through the lamivudine signature mutation, M184V. The latter has also been reported to increase the fidelity of the HIV reverse transcriptase and to decrease replicative fitness. The M184V mutation can delay the emergence of ZDV resistance and reverse ZDV resistance when the T215F/Y mutation is present. However, high-level ZDV/lamivudine co-resistance can develop when multiple ZDV associated mutations (NAMs) and the M184V are present.

Other genotypic correlates of resistance to lamivudine are the E44D and V118I mutations which, in the presence of NAMs, can reduce susceptibility to lamivudine in vitro; the clinical significance of these mutations, however, needs further confirmation. The Q151M complex and the T69S insertions also confer lamivudine resistance. Multiple NAMs alone, however, do not reduce susceptibility to lamivudine. This distinguishes lamivudine from the other approved NRTIs (see Fig. 204.3).

Dosage in special circumstances
Dosage adjustment is required in patients with renal disease (see Table 204.2). No dosage adjustment is necessary in patients with liver disease.

Lamivudine crosses the placenta. No carcinogenicity or teratogenicity has been observed in long-term animal studies (pregnancy category C).

Adverse reactions and drug interactions
Lamivudine is generally very well tolerated. Insomnia, headache, pancreatitis and peripheral neuropathy can occur (see Table 204.3). For NRTI class toxicities, see Table 204.4. Clinically significant drug interactions are minimal. Pancreatitis has been described in children.

Abacavir

Description
Abacavir sulfate – (1S, 4R)-4-[2-amino-6-(cyclopropylamino)-9H-purin-9-yl]-2-cyclo pentene-1-methanol (ABC; see Fig. 204.2) – is converted to carbovir intracellularly. Adenosine phosphotransferase catalyzes the first phosphorylation step. A cytosolic 5′-nucleotidase then converts abacavir monophosphate to carbovir monophosphate. Cellular kinases then complete the di- and triphosphorylation steps. Carbovir triphosphate is active against HIV-1 and HIV-2.

Pharmacokinetics and distribution
Abacavir is rapidly and well absorbed with a reported absolute oral bioavailability of approximately 83%. Administration with food does not significantly affect the oral bioavailability. Peak concentrations achieved following multiple dose administration of 300mg q12h were reported to be approximately 2.2mg/l.[23] The mean plasma half-life of abacavir is less than 2 hours. Abacavir is 50% protein bound. Its high lipophilicity facilitates its distribution and penetration into the CSF, where concentrations have been reported to be approximately 30% of plasma levels.[24] Abacavir undergoes extensive hepatic metabolism by alcohol dehydrogenase and glucuronyl transferase.

Route and dosage
Abacavir is administered orally and is available in tablet and oral solution formulations. The usual adult dosage is 300mg q12h but single daily dosing is being explored in clinical trials. As noted previously, abacavir is available in a fixed dose combination formulation with ZDV and lamivudine (Trizivir).

Indications
Abacavir's potency and efficacy has permitted a new option in antiretroviral naive patients – the triple NRTI regimen option. Data from two clinical trials comparing ZDV–lamivudine–abacavir with ZDV–lamivudine–indinavir have shown general comparability of these two combinations in intent-to-treat analyses.[25] More long-term efficacy data are needed in patients with high viral loads (e.g. >100,000 plasma HIV RNA copies/ml) and low CD4 cell counts (e.g. <50/mm^3) to provide clinicians with confidence about the triple NRTI option in this circumstance. Patients must be antiretroviral naive and harbor no NRTI-associated mutations to avoid a higher risk of virologic failure on this regimen.

Abacavir does not have to be solely reserved for the triple NRTI option and can be paired with any other NRTI as part of a PI- or NNRTI-based regimen. In previously naive individuals suppressed on a PI-containing regimen and harboring no NRTI-associated mutations, a switch of the PI to abacavir is virologically safe and can improve serum lipid abnormalities.[26] In treatment-experienced patients, abacavir's usefulness depends on the degree of cross-resistance that may have been conferred by previous NRTI therapy (see below).

Resistance
Changes in susceptibility of 8-fold or greater compromise the clinical efficacy of abacavir. Genotypically, a number of mutations confer resistance to abacavir. The M184V mutation alone confers a 2-fold change in abacavir susceptibility and the drug should still be useful in this situation. However, the M184V mutation in the presence of multiple NAMs and/or L74V and K65R will confer higher level abacavir resistance and compromise the drug's efficacy. The Q151M complex and the T69S insertion also confer abacavir resistance (see Fig. 204.3).

Dosage in special circumstances
Dosage adjustment is not necessary in patients with renal disease. No specific dosage modification is recommended in patients with liver disease.

Abacavir crosses the placenta. Developmental toxicity secondary to abacavir has been observed in rats (pregnancy category C).[24]

Adverse reactions and drug interactions
The major abacavir toxicity of concern is a hypersensitivity reaction, which has a 3–5% incidence and can be fatal (see Table 204.3). Abacavir hypersensitivity has been linked to the HLA B*5701 genotype.[27] For NRTI class toxicities, see Table 204.4. Clinically significant drug interactions are minimal.

Emtricitabine

Emtricitabine – 5-fluoro-1-[(2R,5S)-2-(hydroxymethyl)-1,3-oxathiolan-5-yl]cytosine (FTC, Coviracil) – is a cytidine analog with activity against HIV and hepatitis B. It is more potent than lamivudine in vitro and can be administered q24h. It has proven efficacy in phase III trials. Resistance is mediated by M184V, the same mutation, which confers resistance to lamivudine. The drug has generally been well tolerated.

Selected investigational nucleoside analog reverse transcriptase inhibitors

A number of NRTIs are currently under development with the objectives of improving pharmacokinetics, avoiding toxicities and/or targeting drug-resistant virus.

Amdoxovir

Amdoxovir – (-)-B-D-2,6-diaminopurane dioxolane (DAPD) – is a prodrug of dioxolane guanosine (DXG), an agent with both anti-HIV and hepatitis B activity. Dioxolane guanosine is active against NRTI-resistant strains except for those bearing the Q151M multinucleoside complex. Resistance to DAPD/DXG is mediated by K65R and L74V in vitro. The drug has shown dose-dependent antiviral activity in both naive and experienced patients in a short-term phase I trial.

Others

ACH-126, 443 (β-L-F-d4C) is a once daily NRTI with activity against NRTI-resistant strains and the potential for diminished mitochondrial toxicity given its L-nucleoside configuration. SPD-754 is the (-) enantiomer of dOTC (development of which was halted due to animal toxicity). SPD-754 is active against lamivudine and ZDV-resistant isolates in vitro and may have decreased potential for inducing mitochondrial toxicity. In vitro, K65R and V75I mutations can be selected. Clinical trial results with these two NRTIs are awaited.

NUCLEOTIDE ANALOG REVERSE TRANSCRIPTASE INHIBITOR

Tenofovir disoproxil fumarate

Description

Tenofovir DF – (R)-9-(2-phosphonomethoxypropyl)adenine (TDF; see Fig. 204.2) – is a prodrug of the nucleoside phosphonate 9-R-(2-phosphonomethoxypropyl)adenine (PMPA). Tenofovir DF represents a new class of antiretroviral agents, the nucleotide reverse transcriptase inhibitors (NtRTIs). These drugs differ from the NRTIs by having a phosphate group in the parent molecule. They thus require only diphosphorylation to be converted to their active compounds. Tenofovir DF is converted to tenofovir by serum esterases. Tenofovir is converted to its active diphosphate form serially by adenylate kinase and nucleotide diphosphate kinase. The drug is active against HIV-1, HIV-2 and hepatitis B virus.

Pharmacokinetics and distribution

Tenofovir is administered orally as a prodrug, tenofovir DF. The oral bioavailability of tenofovir is approximately 25 and 40% in the fasting and fed state, respectively, as compared with 1mg/kg intravenous dosing. Following oral administration of tenofovir DF 300mg q24h, mean steady state peak concentrations were reported as 303ng/ml with an estimated half-life of approximately 14 hours.[28] The intracellular half-life of tenofovir diphosphate ranges from 12 to 50 hours.[29] Tenofovir is primarily eliminated renally (70–80%) via a combination of glomerular filtration and active tubular secretion.

Route and dosage

Tenofovir DF is administered orally and is available in a tablet formulation. The usual adult dosage is 300mg q24h.

Indications

Tenofovir DF is approved for the treatment of HIV infection in combination with other antiretroviral agents. Its approval was based upon two randomized trials in treatment-experienced persons in which tenofovir DF was added to previous therapy. Plasma HIV-1 RNA declines of 0.6 $\log_{10}$ and modest CD4 cell rises were seen.[30] In antiretroviral-naive persons, the combination of tenofovir DF–lamivudine–efavirenz was comparable to a regimen of stavudine–lamivudine–efavirenz with respect to virologic suppression and CD4 cell increases.

Resistance

A phenotypic change in susceptibility of over 4-fold compromises the virologic response to tenofovir DF. The K65R is a signature mutation for tenofovir DF but its appearance in patients treated with tenofovir DF is infrequent. Four or more NAMs (especially M41L and L210W) and the T69S insertion also confer resistance to tenofovir DF. Interestingly, the M184V mutation enhances susceptibility to tenofovir DF, but the clinical significance of this finding is unclear. Specifically, the advisability of continuing lamivudine or abacavir to place selective pressure on the M184V mutation (to enhance susceptibility to tenofovir DF) in the setting of resistance to these drugs must be demonstrated in clinical trials before a formal recommendation can be made (see Fig. 204.3).

Dosage in special circumstances

Dosage adjustment and monitoring for drug toxicity are necessary in patients with renal disease. The pharmacokinetics of tenofovir have not been evaluated in patients with creatinine clearances less than 60ml/min and use in this patient population is not recommended until more information becomes available. The presence of hepatic insufficiency is likely to have a limited effect on tenofovir pharmacokinetics and no specific dosage modifications are recommended in this population.

Tenofovir is classified as pregnancy category B. In rats and rabbits, studies have found no evidence of impaired fertility or teratogenicity.

Adverse reactions and drug interactions

Neutropenia, headache, fatigue, pancreatitis, elevated creatinine and hypophosphatemia have been reported (see Table 204.3). As mentioned previously, concomitant use of tenofovir DF with didanosine increases exposure to didanosine and increases the potential for drug toxicity.

NON-NUCLEOSIDE REVERSE TRANSCRIPTASE INHIBITORS

The NNRTI class of antiretroviral agents is a chemically heterogeneous group of compounds that share a common mechanism of action. These agents differ from the NRTIs in that the parent compound is active and no intracellular metabolism is necessary. The drugs in this class allosterically bind in a noncompetitive fashion to a hydrophobic pocket near the active site of the reverse transcriptase and 'lock' the enzyme into an inactive state. The agents in this class also differ from NRTIs in that they are active against HIV-1 except for subtype O and are inactive against HIV-2 strains.

Nevirapine

Description

Nevirapine – 11-cyclopropyl-5,11-dihydro-4-methyl-6H-dipyrido [3,2-b:2',3'-][1,4]diazepin-6-one (NVP; see Fig. 204.4) – is the lead compound in this class and was the first NNRTI approved in the USA.

Pharmacokinetics and distribution

Nevirapine is well absorbed with an oral bioavailability of 90%. Absorption does not appear to be affected by co-administration with food or antacids. Maximum concentrations are achieved approximately 2 hours after an oral dose with a second peak occurring approximately 14 hours after a dose, presumably due to enterohepatic recycling.[31] Nevirapine exhibits linear pharmacokinetics. Following administration of a single 200mg and 400mg dose, a peak concentration of 7.5μmol/l and 12.8 μmol/l is achieved, respectively. Average steady state plasma concentrations are peak concentrations of 27.1μmol/l and trough concentrations of 15–17μmol/l following 200mg daily. Nevirapine is very lipophilic and widely distributed throughout the body.[32] It is approximately 60% protein bound. Concentrations in the CSF are approximately 45% of those achieved in plasma.[32] Nevirapine is primarily metabolized by the CYP3A4 and CYP2B6 isoenzymes to hydroxy-nevirapine metabolites and induces both these enzyme systems.[33] Auto-induction of its own metabolism has been demonstrated. The half-life of nevirapine is approximately 25–30 hours.

Route and dosage

Nevirapine is administered orally and is available as tablet and oral suspension formulations. The usual adult dosage is 200mg q24h for 14 days followed by 200mg q12h. This dose escalation regimen is recommended to reduce the incidence and severity of rash during treatment initiation.

Indications

Nevirapine is indicated for the treatment of HIV-1 infection in combination with other antiretroviral agents. Due to the vulnerability of nevirapine to single-step, high-level resistance, this drug needs to be used in potent combination regimens designed to suppress plasma HIV-1 RNA levels to less than 50 copies/ml. Partially suppressive regimens or poor drug adherence carry a high risk of engendering nevirapine resistance.

Combination regimens of NNRTI/dual NRTI are now among the recommended first-line therapies for treatment-naive patients. In individuals intolerant to the central nervous system (CNS) side-effects of efavirenz or in women of child-bearing age for whom access to effective contraception is problematic, nevirapine is an appropriate alternative to efavirenz. In previously naive persons who are virologically suppressed on a PI-containing regimen, a switch of the PI to nevirapine can maintain virologic suppression and improve serum lipid abnormalities.

Drug class cross-resistance among currently approved NNRTIs (nevirapine, delavirdine, efavirenz) severely limits the use of NNRTIs as alternative agents in NNRTI-experienced persons with virologic failure. However, in NNRTI-naive persons failing a PI- or triple NRTI-based regimen, this class of agents is critical to the ability to successfully construct a salvage regimen.[34] It is important, however, to be able to support the NNRTI component with at least two other active agents in the alternative regimen to try to avoid the rapid emergence of NNRTI resistance.

Nevirapine has assumed an important role in the prevention of maternal–fetal HIV transmission in the developing world.[35] A single dose of nevirapine to the mother and the infant can reduce HIV transmission by 50%. When added to combination therapy that the mother may be receiving, single-dose nevirapine has not been shown to further reduce HIV transmission in the developed world.[36]

In the prophylaxis of accidental needle-stick exposure in health care workers, the use of nevirapine should be limited given the reports of severe hepatotoxicity when used in this setting.

Resistance

Low-level changes in susceptibility to nevirapine (and other NNRTIs), of the order of 2.5- to 10-fold, are the result of natural polymorphisms in wild-type strains and do not affect the response to these agents. Higher level resistance compromises or eliminates the virologic response to nevirapine. Genotypically, the signature mutation for nevirapine is Y181C, but other nevirapine-associated mutations include L100I, K103N, V106A, V108I, Y188C/I/H and G190A (see Fig. 204.3).

Dosage in special circumstances

Dosage modification is not required for patients with renal dysfunction. Limited data are available in patients with hepatic impairment and no specific dosage modification is currently recommended.

Nevirapine is not associated with teratogenicity in rabbits or rats (pregnancy category C).[10] It rapidly crosses the placenta.

Adverse reactions and drug interactions

The major toxicities associated with nevirapine are rash and hepatotoxicity (which can be fatal; Table 204.5). Nevirapine is a moderate inducer of CYP3A4. Clinically significant drug interactions are summarized in Tables 204.6, 204.7 and 204.8.

Delavirdine

Description

Delavirdine – 1-(5-methanesulfonoamido-1H-indol-2-ylcarbonyl)-4-[3-(1-methylethylamino)pyridinyl]piperazine (DLV; see Fig. 204.4) – was the second approved NNRTI approved in the USA. Its use has been limited by the associated high pill burden.

Pharmacokinetics and distribution

Delavirdine is rapidly absorbed with peak concentrations occurring 1–2 hours after administration with an oral bioavailability of about 85%. Administration with food does not significantly affect steady state AUC within a dosage interval, trough plasma concentrations or time to peak concentrations, but reduces peak concentrations approximately 22%.[37] Absorption may be reduced in patients with gastric hypoacidity and with concomitant antacid administration. Delavirdine exhibits nonlinear pharmacokinetics. Mean C_{min} and C_{max} concentrations following delavirdine 400mg q8h are approximately 15μmol/l and 35μmol/l, respectively.[37] Delavirdine is approximately 98% protein bound. Penetration into the CSF is poor, with concentrations only 0.4% of plasma levels.[37] Delavirdine undergoes extensive metabolism into inactive metabolites primarily by CYP3A4 with less than 5% excreted unchanged in the urine. The mean half-life of delavirdine is approximately 6 hours.

Route and dosage

Delavirdine is administered orally and is available as a tablet formulation. The usual adult dosage is 400mg q8h.

NON-NUCLEOSIDE REVERSE TRANSCRIPTASE INHIBITOR SPECIFIC TOXICITIES

Nevirapine	Delavirdine	Efavirenz
Rash Hepatotoxicity	Rash Fatigue Nausea Diarrhea	CNS symptoms* Rash Hepatotoxicity

* CNS symptoms may include dizziness, insomnia, impaired concentration, somnolence, abnormal dreams, euphoria, confusion, agitation and hallucinations

Table 204.5 Non-nucleoside reverse transcriptase inhibitor specific toxicities.

DRUG INTERACTIONS BETWEEN NON-NUCLEOSIDE REVERSE TRANSCRIPTASE INHIBITORS AND PROTEASE INHIBITORS									
Drug affected	**Nevirapine (NVP)**	**Delavirdine (DLV)**	**Efavirenz (EFZ)**	**Saquinavir (SQV)**	**Indinavir (IDV)**	**Ritonavir (RTV)**	**Nelfinavir (NFV)**	**Amprenavir (APV)**	**Lopinavir/ritonavir (LPV/r)**
Nevirapine (NVP)						NVP AUC ↑			
Delavirdine (DLV)							DLV levels ↓ 50%		
Efavirenz (EFZ)	EFZ levels ↓ 22%			EFZ levels ↓ 12%; co-administration not recommended when SQV only PI		EFZ levels ↑ 21%			
Saquinavir (SQV)	SQV levels ↓ 25%	SQV levels ↑ 5-fold; consider Fortovase 800mg q8h + standard DLV dose	SQV levels ↓ 62%; combination not recommended when SQV only PI		SQV levels ↑ 4- to 7-fold	SQV levels ↑ 20-fold; consider Invirase or Fortovase 400mg q12h + RTV 400mg q12h	SQV levels ↑ 3- to 5-fold; consider Fortovase 800mg q8h or 1200mg q12h with standard NFV dose	SQV levels ↓ 19%	SQV levels ↑; consider SQV 800mg q12h with standard LPV/r dose
Indinavir (IDV)	IDV levels ↓ 28%; consider IDV 1000mg q8h + standard NVP dose	IDV levels ↑ >40%; consider IDV 600mg q8h + standard DLV dose	IDV levels ↑31%; consider IDV 1000mg q8h + standard EFZ dose			IDV levels ↑ 2- to 5-fold; dose IDV 400mg q12h + RTV 400mg q12h *or* IDV 800mg q12h + RTV 100 or 200mg q12h	IDV levels ↑ approximately 50%; consider IDV 1200mg q12h + NFV 1250mg q12h (limited data)	IDV levels ↓ 38%	IDV levels ↑; consider IDV 600mg q12h + standard LPV/r dose
Ritonavir (RTV)	RTV levels ↓ 11%	RTV levels ↑ 70%	RTV levels ↑ 18%; consider RTV 600mg q12h + standard EFZ dose						(Co-formulated with ritonavir)
Nelfinavir (NFV)	NFV levels ↑ 10%	NFV levels ↑ 2-fold	NFV levels ↑ 20%	NFV levels ↑ 20%	NFV levels ↑ 80%; consider 1200mg IDV q12h + NFV 1250mg q12h (limited data)	NFV levels ↑ 1.5 times; consider NFV 500–750mg q12h + RTV 400mg q12h			
Amprenavir (APV)			APV levels ↓ 36%; consider APV 1200mg q8h *or* APV 1200mg q12h + RTV 200mg q12h	APV levels ↓ 32%	APV levels ↑ 33%	APV levels ↑ 2.5-fold; consider APV 600mg q12h + RTV 100mg q12h *or* APV 1200mg q24h + RTV 200mg q24h	APV levels↑ 1.5-fold		APV levels ↑; consider APV 600–750mg q12h + standard LPV/r dose
Lopinavir/ritonavir (LPV/r)	LPV minimum concentration ↓ 55%; consider LPV/r 533/133mg q12h with standard NVP dose		LPV levels ↓ 40%; consider LPV/r 533/133mg q12h with standard EFZ dose						

AUC, area under the curve

Table 204.6 Drug interactions between non-nucleoside reverse transcriptase inhibitors and protease inhibitors.

DRUGS THAT ARE NOT RECOMMENDED FOR USE WITH NON-NUCLEOSIDE REVERSE TRANSCRIPTASE INHIBITORS			
Drug class	**Nevirapine**	**Delavirdine**	**Efavirenz**
Anticonvulsants		Phenytoin, phenobarbital, carbamazepine	
Antihistamines		Astemizole, terfenadine	Astemizole, terfenadine
Antimycobacterials	(Insufficient data)	Rifampin (rifampicin), rifabutin	Rifampin, rifabutin*
Ergot derivatives		Dihydroergotamine, ergonovine, ergotamine, methylergonavine	Dihydroergotamine, ergonovine, ergotamine, methylergonavine
Gastrointestinal drugs		Cisapride	Cisapride
Herbal products	St John's wort†	St John's wort†	St John's wort†
Lipid lowering agents		Simvastatin, lovastatin	
Neuroleptics		Pimozide	
Oral contraceptives	All oral contraceptives		Ethinyl estradiol and all oral contraceptives
Sedatives/hypnotics		Alprazolam, midazolam, triazolam	Midazolam, triazolam

* Increase daily dose of rifabutin 50%. Consider doubling rifabutin dose in regimens where rifabutin administered two or three times a week
† Co-administration of NNRTIs with St John's Wort is expected to substantially decrease NNRTI concentrations

Table 204.7 Drugs that are not recommended for use with non-nucleoside reverse transcriptase inhibitors.

Indications
Delavirdine is indicated for the treatment of HIV-1 infection in combination with other antiretroviral agents. Its use in clinical practice has been very restricted because of the high pill burden, the reluctance to use this agent if a severe reaction to nevirapine or efavirenz has occurred and the cross-resistance within this class of agents. One advantage the drug does have is its ability to raise the levels of co-administered PIs.

Resistance
Resistance to delavirdine is conferred primarily by the K103N, Y181C and Y188L mutations. The P236L mutation, which was described as a unique delavirdine-associated mutation in vitro, is only rarely seen in clinical isolates (see Fig. 204.3).

Dosage in special circumstances
Delavirdine does not require dosage adjustment in patients with renal dysfunction. No specific recommendations are available for patients with hepatic disease.

Delavirdine crosses the placenta. Carcinogenesis studies are incomplete, with teratogenicity (ventricular septal defects) shown in rats at doses equivalent to human therapeutic exposure (pregnancy category C).[10]

Adverse reactions and drug interactions
The major toxicities of delavirdine are rash, nausea, fatigue and diarrhea (see Table 204.5). Delavirdine is a potent inhibitor of CYP3A4 and has the potential for serious drug interactions and toxicity with selected agents. Clinically significant drug interactions are summarized in Tables 204.6, 204.7 and 204.8.

Efavirenz

Description
Efavirenz – (S)-6-chloro-4-(cyclopropylethynyl)-1,4-dihydro-4-(trifluoromethyl)-2H-3, 1-benzoxazin-2-one (EFZ; see Fig. 204.4) – is one of the most widely prescribed NNRTIs because of its potency, q24h administration and lower incidence of rash compared to nevirapine.

Pharmacokinetics and distribution
Efavirenz is well absorbed with peak concentrations achieved 5 hours after oral administration. Absorption appears unaffected by administration with meals containing a moderate fat content. When administered with high-fat meals, a mean increase in AUC of 50% has been shown, and concomitant administration with high-fat meals is not recommended. Efavirenz exhibits linear pharmacokinetics. Average steady state plasma C_{min} and C_{max} following oral administration of 600mg daily are approximately 6μmol/l and 13μmol/l, respectively.[32] Efavirenz is over 99% bound to plasma proteins, predominantly albumin, and crosses the blood–brain barrier, with CSF concentrations on average 0.69% of total plasma concentrations.[38] Efavirenz is metabolized in the liver, predominantly to inactive metabolites by CYP3A4 and CYP2B6. After multiple-dose oral administration, the half-life of efavirenz is approximately 40–55 hours. Efavirenz induces CYP3A4 in vivo, but has also been shown to inhibit CYP3A4, CYP2C9 and CYP2C19 in vitro.[39]

Route and dosage
Efavirenz is administered orally. The usual adult dosage is 600mg q24h, which is now available in a single tablet formulation.

Indications
Efavirenz is indicated for the treatment of HIV-1 infection in combination with other antiretroviral agents. Clinical trials have demonstrated the comparability of efavirenz-based regimens (i.e. combined with two NRTIs) with indinavir-based regimens in patients with both high and low viral loads. The drug now plays a major role in the initial treatment of antiretroviral-naive patients. Clinical trials have also demonstrated the value of efavirenz in patients with virologic failure, but the rapid emergence of NNRTI resistance can occur if the overall regimen potency is compromised by cross-resistance to the other components of the regimen.[34]

The drug should be avoided in patients with a history of significant psychiatric illness because of its CNS side-effect profile. It is also contraindicated in pregnancy because of demonstrated teratogenicity in primates.

Resistance
Resistance to efavirenz during in-vitro passage is mediated by mutations at the following positions: Y179D, Y181C, L100I, K103N and V108I. The drug maintains some degree of activity against viruses containing only the Y181C mutation, but virologic failure rates

SIGNIFICANT DRUG INTERACTIONS BETWEEN NON-NUCLEOSIDE REVERSE TRANSCRIPTASE INHIBITORS AND OTHER DRUGS				
		Nevirapine (NVP)	Delavirdine (DLV)	Efavirenz (EFZ)
Antiarrhythmics/ cardiac	Bepridil		↑ Bepridil; use with caution	
	Amiodarone, lidocaine, quinidine, flecainide, propafenone		↑ Antiarrhythmics (concentration monitoring recommended); use with caution	
	Dihydropyridine calcium channel blockers*		↑ Calcium channel blocker; use with caution	
Anticoagulant	Warfarin		↑ Warfarin; monitor international normalized ratio (INR)	Potential to ↑ or ↓ warfarin; monitor INR
Anticonvulsants	Phenobarbital, phenytoin, carbamazepine	Use with caution; monitor anticonvulsant levels	May ↓ DLV levels	Potential to ↓ anticonvulsant and/or ↓ EFZ; monitor anticonvulsant levels
Antifungals	Ketoconazole	↓ Ketoconazole AUC 63%; ↑ NVP levels approximately 15–30%; not recommended		Potential to ↓ antifungal
Antimycobacterials	Rifampin	↓ NVP C_{min} approximately 37%; not recommended	↓ DLV AUC approximately 97%; not recommended	↓ EFZ AUC approximately 26%; not recommended
	Rifabutin	↓ NVP C_{min} approximately 16%	↑ Rifabutin AUC 230%, ↓ DLV AUC 82%; not recommended	↓ Rifabutin AUC approximately 38%; consider rifabutin ↑ 50% or doubling of rifabutin when given two or three times a week
	Clarithromycin	↑ NVP approximately 26%; ↓ clarithromycin 30%	↑ Clarithromycin AUC 100%; reduce clarithromycin dose in patients with renal dysfunction	↓ Clarithromycin AUC approximately 39%; consider use of azithromycin
Corticosteroids	Dexamethasone		↓ DLV; use with caution	
Immunosuppressants	Ciclosporin Tacrolimus Rapamycin		↑ Immunosuppressant; monitor immunosuppressant levels	
Lipid lowering agents	Atorvastatin, Fluvastatin		↑ Statin levels; use with caution or consider pravastatin	
Narcotic analgesics	Methadone	↓ Methadone; monitor for withdrawal	↑ Methadone	↓ Methadone AUC approximately 52%; monitor for withdrawal
Oral contraceptives	Ethinyl estradiol	↓ Ethinyl estradiol approximately 20%; consider alternative method of contraception	↑ Ethinyl estradiol	↑ Ethinyl estradiol approximately 37%; not well characterized; consider alternative method of contraception
Miscellaneous	Sildenafil		↑ Sildenafil; do not exceed 25mg sildenafil in 48-hour period	
* Dihydropyridine calcium channel blockers: amlodopine, felodipine, isradipine, nifedipine, nicardipine, nimodipine, nisoldipine				

Table 204.8 Significant drug interactions between non-nucleoside reverse transcriptase inhibitors and other drugs.

are high when this mutation is present at baseline.[40] The most common mutation encountered clinically is K103N, which confers cross-resistance to efavirenz and delavirdine. Other clinically relevant mutations are L100I, V108I, Y188L, G190S/A and P225H. High-level resistance is seen with the double mutations K103N–V108I and L100I–K103N (see Fig. 204.3).

Dosage in special circumstances

No dosage adjustment is required in patients with renal disease. Following a single-dose study in patients with chronic liver disease, efavirenz C_{max} was reduced and the half-life increased with no significant change in AUC compared to healthy volunteers.[32] Administration of the standard dose with close monitoring for toxicity is recommended in patients with liver disease.

Efavirenz crosses the placenta. Teratogenicity has been noted in primates (pregnancy category C).[10]

Adverse reactions and drug interactions

The major toxicities associated with efavirenz are CNS related (e.g. impaired concentration, abnormal dreams, euphoria, anxiety and depression) and rash (see Table 204.5). As above, the drug is teratogenic in primates. Efavirenz acts as an inducer or inhibitor of CYP3A4 depending on the concomitantly administered drug. Clinically significant drug interactions are summarized in Tables 204.6, 204.7 and 204.8.

Selected investigational non-nucleoside reverse transcriptase inhibitors

Capravirine

Capravirine – 5-(3,5-dichlorophenyl)thio-4-isopropyl-1-(4-pyridyl) methyl-1H-imidazol-2-ylmethylcarbamate (CPV) – is active against a range of NNRTI-resistant isolates, including those bearing the K103N mutation. The drug has shown substantial antiviral activity in

CHEMICAL STRUCTURES OF NON-NUCLEOSIDE ANALOG REVERSE TRANSCRIPTASE INHIBITORS

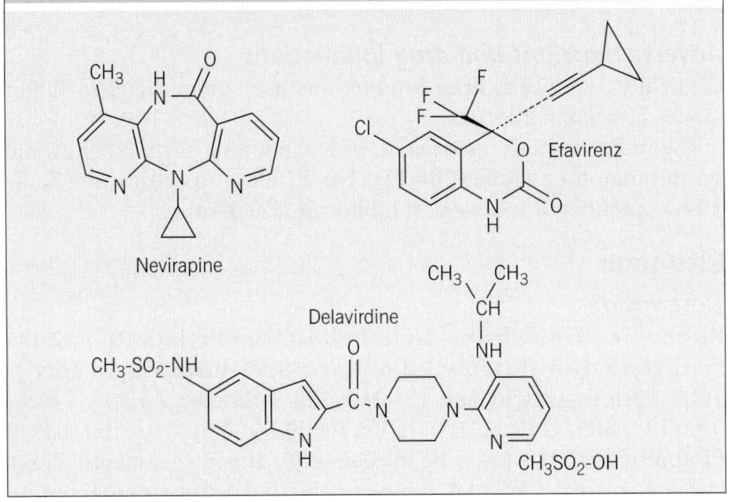

Fig. 204.4 Chemical structures of approved non-nucleoside reverse transcriptase inhibitors.

a phase I trial in naive patients. Development was temporarily halted because of animal toxicity but is now continuing.

TMC 125

TMC 125 is a diarylpyrimidine compound that has potency in the nanomolar range against a broad range of NNRTI-resistant isolates. The flexibility of the molecule and its high binding affinity likely account for these favorable characteristics. The drug has demonstrated substantial antiviral activity in short-term, phase I trials in naive and experienced subjects.

PROTEASE INHIBITORS

Mature HIV virions are produced as the virus buds off the cell surface and *gag* and *gag-pol* polyprotein precursors are cleaved by a virally encoded aspartyl protease. Successful inhibition of this enzyme marked a revolution in antiretroviral therapy starting in 1996. Enthusiasm for inclusion of this class of agents in initial regimens has waned with the growing awareness of the associated metabolic complications, but the value of this potent class of agents should not be forgotten. The six currently approved PIs are all peptidomimetic compounds, which bind to the active site of the enzyme and inhibit both HIV-1 and HIV-2.

Saquinavir

Description

Saquinavir – *N*-tert-butyldecahydro-2-[2(R)-hydroxy-4-phenyl-3-(S)-[[*N*-(2-quinolylcarbonyl)-L-asparaginyl]-amino]butyl](4aS,8aS)-isoquinoline-3(S)-carboxamide (SQV; Fig. 204.5) – was the first PI approved in the USA.

Pharmacokinetics and distribution

Saquinavir-hard gel capsule (hgc) is poorly bioavailable with the mean absolute bioavailability of a 600mg oral dose administered with food averaging 4%. This is presumed to be due to limited absorption and extensive first-pass metabolism.[41] The relative bioavailability of saquinavir-soft gel capsule (sgc) is estimated at over 3-fold higher than the hgc formulation. Absorption is improved upon administration with food or up to 2 hours after a meal. The mean C_{max} following oral administration of saquinavir-sgc 1200mg three times daily was 2477ng/ml. Saquinavir is approximately 97% bound to plasma proteins and is extensively hepatically metabolized to mono- and di-hydroxylated inactive compounds, primarily by CYP3A4 (>90%).[41] The half-life following intravenous administration is approximately 7 hours.

CHEMICAL STRUCTURES OF APPROVED PROTEASE INHIBITORS

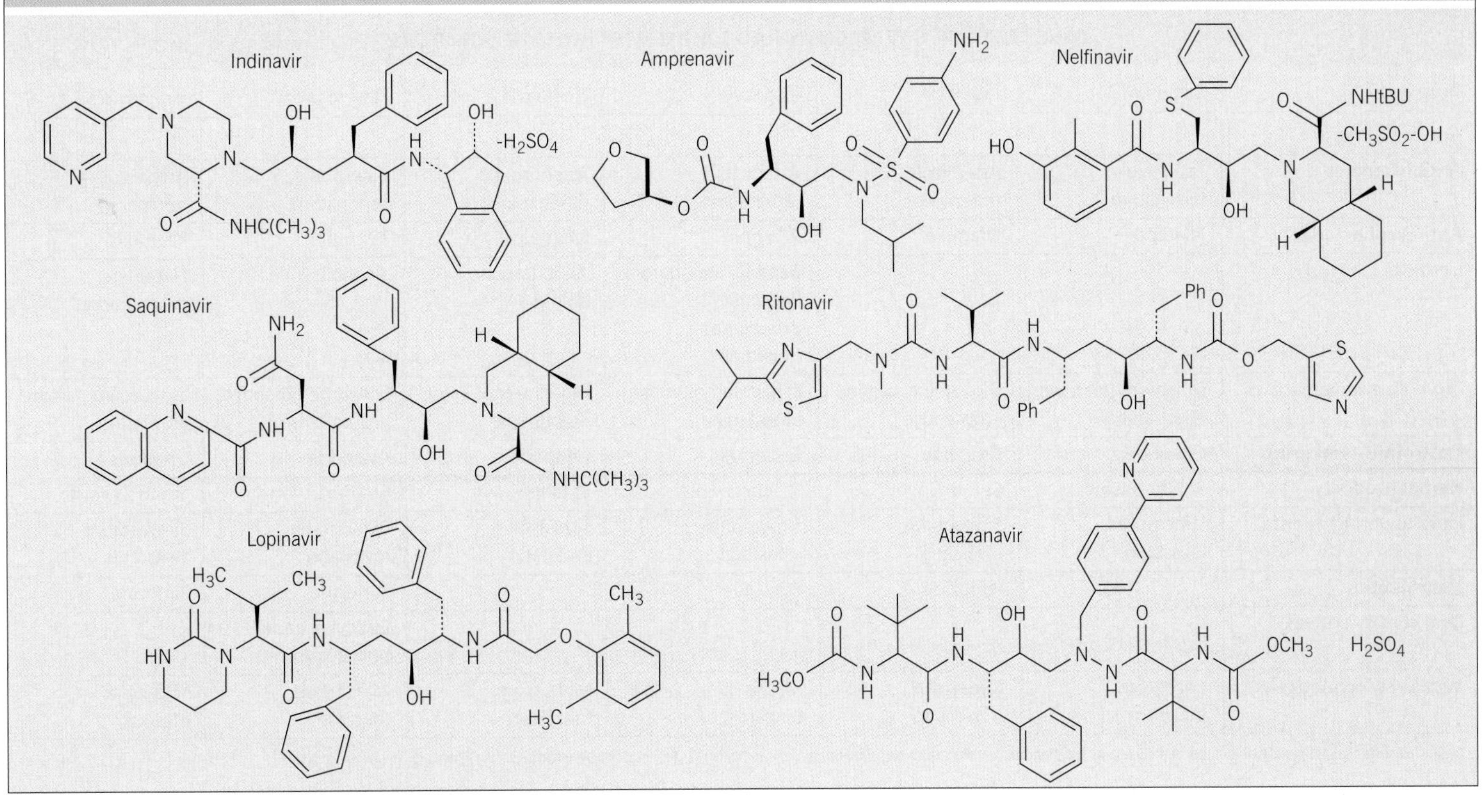

Fig. 204.5 Chemical structures of approved protease inhibitors.

Route and dosage

Saquinavir is administered orally and is available as hard-gel and soft-gel capsule formulations. In the absence of pharmacoenhancement, the approved dose of saquinavir-hgc in adults is 600mg three times daily but the drug should not be used in this fashion. Given its poor oral bioavailability, the hgc formulation should only be prescribed with low dose ritonavir enhancement. The dose of saquinavir-sgc is 1200mg three times daily. Low-dose ritonavir is also commonly used to decrease the pill burden associated with the sgc formulation. Under investigation are the following saquinavir–ritonavir dosage regimens: 1000mg/100mg q12h and 1600mg/200mg q24h.

Indications

Saquinavir is indicated for the treatment of HIV infection in combination with other antiretroviral agents. The drug is most commonly used with low-dose ritonavir enhancement and for initial therapy is typically combined with two NRTIs. For the management of treatment-experienced patients with virologic failure, saquinavir as part of single or dual PI ritonavir-enhanced regimens can prove useful depending upon the previous regimen, the results of drug resistance testing and the number of other active agents in the regimen.

Resistance

Resistance to saquinavir is mediated principally by the L90M and to a lesser extent the G48V mutation. Other codon alterations that can contribute to saquinavir resistance include L10I, I54L, A71V/T, G73S, V77I, V82A and I84V (see Fig. 204.3). L90M is one of the major PI mutations associated with drug class cross-resistance.

Dosage in special circumstances

Saquinavir does not require dosage adjustment in patients with renal disease. The pharmacokinetics of saquinavir have not been studied in patients with liver disease. No specific dosage recommendations are available in this patient population.

Saquinavir only minimally crosses the placenta. Animal studies have shown no mutagenicity or teratogenicity at 40–50% of AUC values achieved in humans (pregnancy catgory B).[10]

Adverse reactions and drug interactions

Clinically significant drug interactions are summarized in Tables 204.6, 204.9 and 204.10.

The major toxicity associated with saquinavir is gastrointestinal symptomatology (Table 204.11). For PI class toxicities, see Table 204.4. Saquinavir is a weak inhibitor of CYP3A4.

Ritonavir

Description

Ritonavir – 10-hydroxy-2-methyl-5-(1-methylethyl)-1-[2-(1-methylethyl)-4-thiazolyl]-3,6-dioxo-8,11-bis(phenylmethyl)-2,4,7,12-tetraazatridecan-13-oic-acid, 5-thiazolyl-methyl ester [5S-(5R*, 8R*, 10R*, 11R*)] (RTV; see Fig. 204.5) – was the second PI approved in the USA. Its intolerability at full therapeutic doses and its potent CYP3A4 inhibitory activity have combined to position this drug largely, if not exclusively, as a pharmacoenhancer of other PIs, including saquinavir, indinavir, amprenavir and lopinavir.

Pharmacokinetics and distribution

Ritonavir's oral bioavailability is estimated to range from 60 to 80%.[42] Relative to the fasting state, the AUC of ritonavir from the capsule formulation is approximately 15% higher when administered with food. For the oral solution, the AUC is decreased 7% when administered with food.[42] Following oral administration of ritonavir 600mg q12h, the C_{max} and C_{min} were reported as 11mg/l and 4mg/l, respectively. Ritonavir is greater than 98% protein bound, both to albumin and α_1-acid glycoprotein. Because of the high degree of protein binding, CSF concentrations are low and reported to be less than 0.05mg/l.[42] Ritonavir is extensively metabolized, primarily by CYP3A4 isoenzymes, with the CYP2D6 isoenzyme also contribut-

DRUGS THAT ARE NOT RECOMMENDED FOR USE WITH PROTEASE INHIBITORS						
Drug class	**Saquinavir**	**Indinavir**	**Ritonavir**	**Nelfinavir**	**Amprenavir**	**Lopinavir/r**
Anticonvulsants						
Antihistamines	Astemizole, terfenadine	Astemizole, terfenadine	Astemizole, terfenadine	Astemizole, terfenadine	Astemizole, terfenadine	Astemizole, terfenadine
Antimycobacterials	Rifampin*	Rifampin*	Rifampin*	Rifampin*	Rifampin*	Rifampin*
Cardiac			Bepridil, amiodarone, flecainide, propafenone, quinidine	Amiodarone, quinidine	Bepridil	Flecainide, propafenone
Ergot derivatives	Dihydroergotamine, ergotamine	Dihydroergotamine, ergotamine	Dihydroergotamine, ergotamine	Dihydroergotamine, ergotamine	Dihydroergotamine, ergotamine	Dihydroergotamine, ergotamine
Gastrointestinal drugs	Cisapride	Cisapride	Cisapride	Cisapride	Cisapride	Cisapride
Herbal products	St John's wort	St John's wort	St John's wort	St John's wort	St John's wort	St John's wort
Lipid lowering agents	Simvastatin, lovastatin	Simvastatin, lovastatin	Simvastatin, lovastatin	Simvastatin, lovastatin	Simvastatin, lovastatin	Simvastatin, lovastatin
Neuroleptics		Pimozide	Pimozide		Pimozide	Pimozide
Oral contraceptives					Ethinyl estradiol/ norethindrone	
Sedatives/hypnotics	Midazolam, triazolam	Midazolam, triazolam	Midazolam, triazolam	Midazolam, triazolam	Midazolam, triazolam	Midazolam, triazolam

* Rifampin decreases levels of protease inhibitors. Alternative antimycobacterial agents such as rifabutin (with dosage modification) should be considered.

Table 204.9 Drugs that are not recommended for use with protease inhibitors.

ing to the production of the isopropylthiazolyl oxidation metabolite.[42] The half-life of ritonavir ranges from 3 to 5 hours.

Route and dosage

Ritonavir is administered orally and is available in capsule and oral solution formulations. It is also available as a co-formulation with lopinavir (Kaletra). When administered as the sole PI, the adult dose of ritonavir is 600mg q12h. As noted, however, ritonavir's major role is as a pharmacoenhancer of other PIs, given the gastrointestinal intolerance conferred by full doses of this agent. Pharmacoenhancement doses depend upon the co-administered PI(s) and whether an inducer of CYP3A4, such as efavirenz or nevirapine, is also included in the regimen. Most typically, ritonavir doses of 100–200mg q12h are used in pharmacoenhanced regimens.

Indications

Ritonavir in full dose carries an indication for the treatment of HIV infection in combination with other antiretroviral agents. As a pharmacoenhancer, it is approved as a co-formulation with lopinavir. It is also commonly used in combination with saquinavir, indinavir and amprenavir.

Resistance

The major mutations conferring resistance to ritonavir are V82A/F/T/S and I84V. Other important mutations include L10F/I/R/V, K20M/R, V32I, L33F, M36I, M46I/L, I54V/L, A71V/T, V77I and L90M (see Fig. 204.3). Cross-resistance between indinavir and ritonavir is nearly complete. When used in low dose as a pharmacoenhancer of a second PI, the pattern of mutations that emerges with virologic failure may be influenced by the presence of ritonavir. The ability to boost the levels of other PIs has brought into focus the importance of pharmacodynamics in the treatment of HIV infection. The relationship of achievable drug concentrations to the 50% inhibitory concentration (IC_{50}) of the individual patient's virus has reinvigorated the concept of the inhibitory quotient in treating microbial pathogens. This has resulted in an attempt to define phenotypic susceptibility cut-offs that are clinically relevant and the consideration of whether therapeutic drug level monitoring has a role in the management of patients with drug-resistant virus.

Dosage in special circumstances

Renal disease is expected to have little effect on ritonavir pharmacokinetics and no dosage modification is necessary. In patients with mild-to-moderate hepatic insufficiency, the ritonavir pharmacokinetics varied little compared to patients with normal hepatic function when the dosage was reduced by 20%.[42] In addition, the elimination half-life increased from 4.6 hours in patients with normal hepatic function to 6.3 hours in patients with moderate hepatic disease. No specific dosage recommendations are available in patients with liver disease.

Less than 10% of ritonavir appears to cross the placenta. Ritonavir was not mutagenic in bacteria or mammalian cells and teratogenicity has only been seen in rats at maternally toxic doses (pregnancy category B).[10]

Adverse reactions and drug interactions

The major toxicities associated with ritonavir are headache, diarrhea, altered taste, circumoral and peripheral paresthesias and hyperlipidemia (see Table 204.11). For PI class toxicities, see Table 204.4. Ritonavir is the most potent inhibitor of the cytochrome P450 system of all the PIs. Ritonavir inhibits CYP3A4 and CYP2D6 and also increases glucuronosyltransferase activity. Ritonavir also induces CYP3A4 activity and has been shown to induce its own metabolism. Clinically significant drug interactions are summarized in Tables 204.6, 204.9 and 204.10.

Indinavir

Description

Indinavir – *N*-(2(R)-hydroxy-1(S)-indanyl)-2(R)-(phenylmethyl)-4(S)-hydroxy-5-[1-[4-(3-pyridylmethyl)-2(S)-(*N*-tert-butylcarbamoyl)piperazinyl]]pentanamide (IDV; see Fig. 204.5) – was the third PI approved in the USA and contributed substantially to ushering in the modern era of potent antiretroviral chemotherapy.

Pharmacokinetics and distribution

Indinavir is rapidly absorbed with peak concentrations occurring within 1 hour. The oral bioavailability is approximately 70%.[43] Administration of indinavir with meals containing high fat, carbohydrate, or protein significantly reduces the AUC by approximately 35–70% compared to the fasting state.[44] Food has little effect on the pharmacokinetics of indinavir when administered concomitantly with low-dose ritonavir. Steady-state peak and trough concentrations were 12.6μmol/l and 0.25μmol/l, respectively, after oral administration of 800mg q8h.[43] Indinavir is approximately 60% protein bound. Studies have shown that indinavir concentrations in the CSF are 2 and 6% of plasma concentrations 2 and 3.75 hours after administration, respectively.[45] A more recent study of indinavir pharmacokinetics in the CSF of eight adults infected with HIV found the free indinavir concentrations in the CSF to be approximately 15% of plasma levels.[46] Indinavir is extensively metabolized by CYP3A4 isoenzymes. The half-life of indinavir is approximately 1.8 hours.

Route and dosage

Indinavir is administered orally and is available as a capsule formulation. The dosage in adults is 800mg q8h in the absence of ritonavir enhancement or the concomitant use of efavirenz or nevirapine. Ritonavir reduces variation in the pharmacokinetic profile of indinavir, eliminates the food effect and converts indinavir to a twice daily agent. Indinavir/ritonavir combinations of 800mg/100mg, 800mg/200mg, 400mg/400mg and 400mg/100mg, respectively, have all been studied and are used clinically. The dose of indinavir should be increased to 1000mg q8h when used with the NNRTIs efavirenz or nevirapine because of the CYP3A4-inducing effect of these drugs (see Table 204.6). This effect can be blocked, however, by the concomitant use of ritonavir. Adequate hydration (approximately 1l of water per day) needs to be maintained to try to prevent nephrolithiasis.

Indications

Indinavir is indicated for the treatment of HIV infection in combination with other antiretroviral agents. There is a considerable published experience with indinavir establishing its clinical and long-term virologic efficacy.[47,48] It is one of the more commonly prescribed PIs for initial therapy, particularly in patients presenting with advanced disease. It is also useful in the management of antiretroviral failure if the patient's virus isolate remains susceptible and other active drugs remain available for inclusion in the regimen.

Resistance

The major PI mutations conferring resistance to indinavir are M46I/L, V82A/F/T and I84V. Other important mutations include L10I/R/V, K20M/R, L24I, V32I, M36I, I54V, A71V/T, G73S/A, V77I and L90M (see Fig. 204.3). Alterations at three or more codons are necessary before substantial changes in phenotypic susceptibility can be detected. Indinavir and ritonavir cross-resistance is nearly complete.

Dosage in special circumstances

Indinavir's pharmacokinetics are likely little affected by renal disease. In patients with mild-to-moderate hepatic insufficiency and cirrhosis, indinavir AUC was 60% higher following a single 400mg dose and the half-life was increased to 2.8 hours. It is recommended that the

SIGNIFICANT DRUG INTERACTIONS BETWEEN PROTEASE INHIBITORS AND OTHER DRUGS							
		Saquinavir (SQV)	**Indinavir (IDV)**	**Ritonavir (RTV)**	**Nelfinavir (NFV)**	**Amprenavir (APV)**	**Lopinavir/r (LPV; LPV/r)**
Antiarrhythmics/ cardiac	Amiodarone Lidocaine, quinidine, flecainide, propafenone, bepridil			May ↑ antiarrhythmic levels; use with caution			May ↑ antiarrhythmic levels; use with caution
	Dihydropyridine calcium channel blockers*		May ↑ calcium channel blocker levels; use with caution	May ↑ calcium channel blocker levels; use with caution			May ↑ calcium channel blocker levels; use with caution
Anticoagulant	Warfarin			May ↓ warfarin levels; use with caution			May affect warfarin levels; use with caution
Anticonvulsants	Phenobarbital, phenytoin, carbamazepine	May ↓ SQV levels; use with caution	May ↓ IDV levels; use with caution	May ↑ carbamazepine levels; may ↓ phenytoin levels; monitor anti-convulsant levels; use with caution	May ↓ NFV levels; monitor anti-convulsant levels; use with caution	May ↓ APV levels; monitor anti-convulsant levels; use with caution	May ↓ LPV levels; use with caution
Antifungals	Ketoconazole itraconazole	↑ SQV levels	Ketoconazole ↑ IDV AUC approximately 68%; itraconazole ↑ IDV levels; use with caution	↑ Ketoconazole AUC approximately 3.4-fold; ↑ RTV AUC approximately 18%	↑ NFV AUC approximately 35%	↑ APV AUC approximately 31%; ↑ ketoconazole AUC approximately 44%	↑ Ketoconazole AUC approximately 3-fold; ↑ itraconazole levels; use with caution
Antimycobacterials	Rifampin	↓ SQV AUC approximately 84%; not recommended unless using SQV + RTV	↓ IDV levels approximately 89%; not recommended	↓ RTV AUC approximately 35%; not recommended	↓ NFV AUC approximately 82%; not recommended	↓ APV AUC approximately 82%; not recommended	↓ LPV AUC approximately 75%
	Rifabutin	↓ SQV AUC approximately 43%; consider rifabutin 150mg 3 times per week when using SQV + RTV	↓ IDV AUC approximately 32%; ↑ rifabutin AUC approximately 204%; use with caution	↑ Rifabutin AUC 4-fold; consider rifabutin dose reduction to 150mg every other day or 3 times per week	↑ Rifabutin AUC approximately 207%; ↓ NFV AUC approximately 32%; consider rifabutin dose decrease by 50%	↓ APV AUC approximately 15%; ↑ rifabutin AUC approximately 193%; consider rifabutin dose decrease to 150mg daily or 300mg 3 times per week	↑ Rifabutin AUC approximately 3-fold; consider rifabutin dose reduction to 150mg every other day or 3 times per week
	Clarithromycin	↑ Clarithromycin AUC approximately 45%; ↑ SQV AUC approximately 177%	↑ Clarithromycin AUC approximately 53%; ↑ IDV AUC approximately 29%	↑ Clarithromycin AUC 77%; ↑ RTV AUC approximately 12%; ↓ clarithromycin dose in patients with renal dysfunction		↑ APV AUC approximately 18%	↑ Clarithromycin levels; ↓ clarithromycin dose in patients with renal dysfunction
Corticosteroid	Dexamethasone	May ↓ SQV levels; use with caution		May ↑ dexamethasone levels; use with caution			May ↓ LPV levels; use with caution

Table 204.10 Significant drug interactions between protease inhibitors and other drugs.

SIGNIFICANT DRUG INTERACTIONS BETWEEN PROTEASE INHIBITORS AND OTHER DRUGS—CONT'D							
		Saquinavir (SQV)	**Indinavir (IDV)**	**Ritonavir (RTV)**	**Nelfinavir (NFV)**	**Amprenavir (APV)**	**Lopinavir/r (LPV; LPV/r)**
Immunosuppressants	Ciclosporin tacrolimus, rapamycin			May ↑ immuno-suppressant levels; monitor levels; use with caution	May ↑ ciclosporin and tacrolimus levels; monitor levels		May ↑ immuno-suppressant levels; monitor levels; use with caution
Lipid lowering agents	Atorvastatin, fluvastatin	May ↑ statin levels; use with caution	May ↑ statin levels; use with caution	May ↑ statin levels; use with caution	↑ Atorvastatin levels approximately 74%; use with caution	May ↑ statin levels; use with caution	↑ Atorvastatin AUC approximately 5.8-fold; use with caution
Narcotic analgesics	Methadone			↓ Methadone AUC approximately 36%	May ↓methadone levels	↓ Methadone AUC approximately 35%	↓ Methadone AUC approximately 53%
	Meperidine			↓ Meperidine AUC approximately 62% and ↑ normeperidine AUC approximately 47%;			
Neuroleptics	Perphenazine, risperidone, thioridazine			Potential for ↑ neuroleptic levels; use with caution			
Oral contraceptives	Ethinyl estradiol		↑ Ethinyl estradiol AUC approximately 24%	↓ Ethinyl estradiol AUC approximately 40%; consider alternative method of contraception	↓ Ethinyl estradiol AUC approximately 47%; consider alternative method of contraception	↓ APV AUC approximately 22%; not recommended	↓ Ethinyl estradiol AUC approximately 42%; consider alternative method of contraception
Sedative/hypnotics	Clorazepate, diazepam, estazolam, flurazepam, zolpidem			Potential for ↑ sedative/ hypnotics levels; use with caution			
Miscellaneous	Sildenafil	↑ Sildenafil AUC approximately 210%; do not exceed 25mg sildenafil in 48-hour period	↑ Sildenafil AUC approximately 340%; do not exceed 25mg sildenafil in 48-hour period	↑ Sildenafil AUC approximately 11-fold; do not exceed 25mg sildenafil in 48-hour period	Potential for ↑ sildenafil levels; do not exceed 25mg sildenafil in 48-hour period	Potential for ↑ sildenafil levels; do not exceed 25mg sildenafil in 48-hour period	Potential for ↑ sildenafil levels; do not exceed 25mg sildenafil in 48-hour period
	Desipramine			↑ Desipramine AUC 145%; consider ↓ dosage of desipramine			
	Theophylline			↓ Theophylline AUC approximately 43%			

* Dihydropyridine calcium channel blockers: amlodopine, felodipine, isradipine, nifedipine, nicardipine, nimodipine, nisoldipine

Table 204.10 Significant drug interactions between protease inhibitors and other drugs—cont'd.

LIST OF PROTEASE INHIBITOR SPECIFIC TOXICITIES					
Saquinavir	Indinavir	Ritonavir	Nelfinavir	Amprenavir	Lopinavir/r
Nausea Diarrhea Abdominal pain Dyspepsia Headache	Nephrolithiasis Nausea Headache Asthenia Dizziness Rash	Nausea Vomiting Diarrhea Paresthesias (circumoral and extremities) Hepatitis Pancreatitis Asthenia Taste perversion ↑ Uric acid ↑ Creatine phosphokinase	Diarrhea	Nausea Vomiting Diarrhea Rash Oral paresthesias	Nausea Vomiting Diarrhea Asthenia

Table 204.11 List of protease inhibitor specific toxicities.

indinavir dose be reduced to 600mg q8h in patients with mild-to-moderate hepatic insufficiency due to cirrhosis.[43]

Indinavir crosses the placenta. In rats, carcinogenicity (an increased incidence of thyroid adenomas) and teratogenicity (increased incidence of supernumerary ribs and unilateral anophthalmia) have been shown (pregnancy category C).[10]

Adverse reactions and drug interactions

The major toxicities associated with indinavir include asymptomatic rises in indirect bilirubin and nephrolithiasis (see Table 204.11). For PI class toxicities, see Table 204.4. Indinavir is a moderate inhibitor of CYP3A4. Clinically significant drug interactions are summarized in Tables 204.6, 204.9 and 204.10.

Nelfinavir

Description

Nelfinavir – [3S-(3R*, 4aR*, 8aR*, 2′S*, 3′S*)]-2-[2′-hydroxy-3′-phenylthiomethyl-4′-aza-5′-oxo-5’-(2′′-methyl-3′′-hydroxy-phenyl)pentyl]decahydroisoquinoline-3-*N*-t-butyl-carboxamide (NFV; see Fig. 204.5) – was the fourth PI approved in the USA.

Pharmacokinetics and distribution

Following administration of nelfinavir 1250mg q12h, peak and trough plasma concentrations were reported as 4mg/l and 1.3–2.2mg/l, respectively. When administered in the fasting state, the AUC of nelfinavir is reduced 27–50%.[49] Nelfinavir should be administered with food. It is 98% bound to plasma proteins. Nelfinavir is hepatically metabolized by CYP450 isoenzymes, primarily CYP3A4 followed by CYP2C19, CYP2D6 and CYP2C9, to two active metabolites with the major oxidative metabolite (M8) exhibiting comparable in-vitro antiviral activity.[49,50] The half-life of nelfinavir is approximately 3.5–5 hours.

Route and dosage

Nelfinavir is administered orally and is available in tablet and oral powder formulations. The two approved dosage regimens in adults are 750mg q8h and 1250mg q12h.

Indications

Nelfinavir is indicated for the treatment of HIV infection in combination with other antiretroviral agents. It has been a mainstay of potent antiretroviral regimens for several years and has more commonly been used in the treatment of antiretroviral-naive patients (combined with two NRTIs) than as part of salvage regimens. It also has an established record of safety in pregnant women. Comparative clinical trials suggest that nelfinavir combined with two NRTIs is a less potent regimen than lopinavir–ritonavir or efavirenz-based regimens.[51]

Resistance

Resistance to nelfinavir may evolve along one of two pathways – either the D30N or the L90M. The factors that determine which pathway is chosen are not completely defined, but baseline polymorphisms and viral subtype may play a role. The D30N mutation by itself does not confer resistance to the other PIs and therefore successful alternative regimens in the face of virologic failure can often be constructed. When the L90M pathway is chosen, drug class cross-resistance may result. Additional relevant mutations include L10F/I, M36I, M46I/L, A71V/T, V77I, V82A/F/T/S, I84V and N88D/S (see Fig. 204.3).

Dosage in special circumstances

Dosage modification is not necessary in patients with renal disease. No dosage recommendations are available for patients with hepatic disease.

Nelfinavir concentrations in cord blood are low or undetectable compared to maternal concentrations (pregnancy category B). In animal studies, nelfinavir has not been found to be carcinogenic or teratogenic.[10]

Adverse reactions and drug interactions

The principal toxicity associated with nelfinavir is diarrhea (see Table 204.11). For PI class toxicities, see Table 204.4. Nelfinavir is a moderate inhibitor of CYP3A4. Clinically significant drug interactions are summarized in Tables 204.6, 204.9 and 204.10.

Amprenavir

Description

Amprenavir – (3S)-tetrahydro-3-furyl-*N*-[(1S, 2R)-3-(4-amino-*N*-isobutylbenzenesulfonamido)-1-benzyl-2-hydroxypropyl] carbamate (APV; see Fig. 204.5) – was the fifth PI approved in the USA. An amprenavir prodrug, GW 433908, designed to reduce pill size and burden, is under investigation.

Pharmacokinetics and distribution

Amprenavir is rapidly absorbed following oral administration. Peak concentrations of approximately 7.66μg/ml are achieved within 1 to

2 hours following administration of 1200mg q12h. The relative bioavailability of amprenavir oral solution is 14% less than amprenavir oral capsules. Effects of food on amprenavir pharmacokinetics (decreased AUC 23%) are not clinically significant except with high-fat meals, which should be avoided.[52] Amprenavir is approximately 90% protein bound, predominantly to α_1-acid glycoprotein. Amprenavir is hepatically metabolized by CYP3A4. The plasma half-life of amprenavir ranges from 7.1 to 10.6 hours.

Route and dosage

Amprenavir is administered orally and is available as capsule and oral solution formulations. The dosage in adults is 1200mg q12h when administered without ritonavir enhancement (which increases amprenavir levels) or concomitant efavirenz (which diminishes amprenavir levels). The size and number of amprenavir pills at standard dosing poses a problem for tolerance and drug adherence. Therefore, amprenavir is mostly used with low-dose ritonavir enhancement at a dose of 600mg/100mg q12h, respectively. The dose to use when combined with efavirenz is uncertain but some advise increasing the amprenavir/ritonavir doses to 750mg/200mg q12h, respectively, to ensure adequate amprenavir levels in the face of drug-resistant virus.

Indications

Amprenavir is indicated for the treatment of HIV infection in combination with other antiretroviral agents. Although efficacy for naive patients has been established, the pill burden has generally restricted the drug to the management of treatment-experienced persons. Clinical trials have demonstrated the efficacy of amprenavir in this circumstance[34] and it is now commonly used as part of dual ritonavir-enhanced regimens with lopinavir.

Resistance

Viral isolates resistant to the other approved PIs may remain susceptible to amprenavir. The major mutations conferring amprenavir resistance are I50V (a signature mutation) and I84V. Other important mutations include L10F/I/R/V, V32I, M46I/L, I47V, I54L/V/M, G73S and L90M (see Fig. 204.3).

Dosage in special circumstances

The effects of renal disease on amprenavir pharmacokinetics are limited and no dosage modification is necessary. The AUC of amprenavir in patients with moderate and severe cirrhosis is significantly greater than in patients with normal hepatic function. It is recommended that patients with a Child–Pugh score of 5–8 receive a reduced amprenavir dosage of 450mg q12h, and patients with Child–Pugh score of 9 to 12 receive a reduced amprenavir dosage of 300mg q12h. The oral solution of amprenavir contains propylene glycol (55%) and is contraindicated in patients with renal failure or hepatic failure, in pregnant women and in patients receiving disulfiram or metronidazole.

Amprenavir is classified as pregnancy category C. In rabbits and rats, an increased incidence of abortions (rabbits) and ossification defects (rabbits and rats) have been shown.[10]

Adverse reactions and drug interactions

The major toxicities associated with amprenavir include gastrointestinal symptomatology and rash (see Table 204.11). For PI class toxicities, see Table 204.4. Amprenavir is a moderate inhibitor of CYP3A4. Clinically significant drug interactions are summarized in Tables 204.6, 204.9 and 204.10.

Lopinavir (co-formulated with ritonavir)

Description

Lopinavir – [1S-[1R*, (R*), 3R*, 4R*]]-*N*-[4-[[2,6-dimethylphenoxy) acetyl]amino]-3-hydroxy-5-phenyl-1-(phenylmethyl)pentyl] tetrahydro-alpha-(1-methylethyl)-2-oxo-1(2H)-pyrimidine-acetamide (LPV; see Fig. 204.5) – was the sixth PI approved in the USA. It is co-formulated with ritonavir (lopinavir/r).

Pharmacokinetics and distribution

Lopinavir is poorly bioavailable because it is rapidly metabolized by NADPH and cytochrome P450 3A4/5-dependent enzyme systems. As such, lopinavir is co-formulated with ritonavir. Ritonavir inhibits the metabolism of lopinavir such that the AUC for lopinavir is increased over 100-fold when co-administered with ritonavir.[53] Administration of lopinavir/r with food increased the AUC by 48 and 80% for the capsule and liquid formulations, respectively. Lopinavir is approximately 98–99% protein bound, both to albumin and α_1-acid glycoprotein. At steady state, lopinavir peak and trough concentrations were reported as 9.6mg/l and 5.5mg/l following twice daily lopinavir/r 400/100mg.[53] Lopinavir undergoes extensive oxidative metabolism via CYP3A. The half-life of lopinavir/r has been reported to be approximately 6 hours.

Route and dosage

Lopinavir/r is administered orally and is available in capsule and oral solution formulations. Lopinavir/r capsules contain 133.3mg of lopinavir and 33.3mg of ritonavir. The usual adult dosage is 400mg/100mg q12h, respectively. When administered with efavirenz, the dose should be increased to 533mg/133mg q12h of lopinavir/r, respectively (see Table 204.6).

Indications

Lopinavir/r is indicated for the treatment of HIV infection in combination with other antiretroviral agents. In antiretroviral-naive patients, lopinavir/r in combination with two NRTIs has shown superior antiviral activity to nelfinavir plus two NRTIs.[51] Lopinavir/r has also shown substantial virologic efficacy in the treatment of NNRTI-naive subjects with both single and multiple PI experience. Lopinavir/r is also used in dual PI-enhanced regimens with amprenavir or saquinavir in the management of patients with drug-resistant virus. Formal studies of the efficacy of this latter approach are underway.

Resistance

The major mutations conferring lopinavir resistance are L10F/I/R/V, K20M/R, L24I, V32I, L33F, M46I/L, I47V, I50V, F53L, I54V/L, L63P, A71V/T, G73S, V82A/F/T/S, I84V and L90M (see Fig. 204.3). The pharmacoenhancement of lopinavir by ritonavir permits the drug to be active against viruses with up to 10- and possibly 40-fold changes in susceptibility to lopinavir.

Dosage in special circumstances

Dosage adjustment is not necessary in patients with renal disease. Close monitoring is advised in patients with liver disease. No specific dosage recommendations are available for this patient population.

Lopinavir has been shown to cross the placenta in rats. Developmental toxicities (skeletal variations and delayed ossification) have been shown in rats at maternally toxic doses (pregnancy category C).[10]

Adverse reactions and drug interactions

The principal toxicities associated with lopinavir/r include gastrointestinal symptomatology, hyperlipidemia and liver enzyme abnormalities (see Table 204.11). For PI class toxicities, see Table 204.4. Lopinavir is a moderate inhibitor of CYP3A4 and the combination of lopinavir with ritonavir (a potent CYP3A4 inhibitor) is likely to have drug interactions similar to those of full-dose ritonavir alone, but potentially to a lesser degree. Clinically significant drug interactions are summarized in Tables 204.6, 204.9 and 204.10

Atazanavir

Atazanavir sulfate – dimethyl (3S, 8S, 9S, 12S)-9-benzyl-3,12,di-tert-butyl-8-hydroxy-4,11-dioxo-6-(p-2pyridylbenzyl)-2,5,6,10,13-pentaazatetradecanedioate sulfate (ATV, Zrivada) – is an azapeptide PI whose advantage is q24h administration and the lack of induction of hyperlipidemia. Clinical trials reported to date in antiretroviral-naive patients have suggested that atazanavir sulfate in combination with two NRTIs has comparable efficacy to nelfinavir and efavirenz-based regimens, although in the latter study the efavirenz arm appeared to perform less well than in previously reported trials.[55] The use of atazanavir sulfate in treatment-experienced persons is currently under study. The drug, when administered without ritonavir pharmacoenhancement, has been reported to engender a signature mutation, I50L, in the setting of virologic failure. This mutation confers diminished susceptibility to atazanavir sulfate and appears to induce sensitization to other PIs. This characteristic may be exploitable in future treatment strategies. Other relevant mutations include V32I, M46I, I54L, A71V, V82A, I84V, N88S and L90M (see Fig. 204.3). The drug, in general, has been well tolerated, with an absence of hyperlipidemia a notable feature. The major toxicity noted thus far has been an asymptomatic rise in indirect bilirubinemia, not dissimilar to that seen with indinavir. PR and QT prolongation have also been seen at higher doses of the drug, but the clinical significance of this remains to be clarified.

Selected investigational protease inhibitors

Tipranavir

Tipranavir disodium – [R-(R*, R*)]-N-[3-[1-[5,6-dihydro-4-hydroxy-2-oxo-6-(2-phenylethyl)-6-propyl-2H-pyran-3-yl]propyl]phenyl]5-(trifluoromethyl)-2-pyridinesulfonamide disodium salt (TPV) – is a dihydropyrone, non-peptidic PI whose molecular advantage is the flexibility it can demonstrate in binding to the active site of the HIV protease. It is highly active against viral strains with diminished susceptibility to the approved PIs.[54] Tipranavir disodium is being developed for co-administration with low-dose ritonavir to diminish the pill burden and permit q12h dosing. The major toxicity seen thus far has been gastrointestinal-associated, which appears to be dose related. Clinical trial results reported to date have been promising with phase III studies pending. Its role will likely be in the management of patients with PI-resistant virus.

TMC 114

TMC 114 is a highly potent PI with in-vitro anti-HIV activity in the nanomolar range. The drug is a flexible molecule that binds tightly into the active site of the HIV protease. These qualities help to confer its potency against PI-resistant variants. Phase I trials of this agent are underway.

ENTRY INHIBITORS

Remarkable advances have been made in the past few years in our understanding of the HIV entry process. Specifically, the identification of HIV co-receptors (e.g. CCR5 and CXCR4) and the understanding of the events involved in fusion of the viral envelope with the cell membrane have created new therapeutic targets. Entry inhibitors can be divided into three subcategories: attachment inhibitors, chemokine receptor antagonists and fusion inhibitors.[56,57] Of these, the fusion inhibitors have demonstrated proven clinical efficacy and have come the furthest in development.

Enfuvirtide

Description

Enfuvirtide – $C_{204}H_{301}N_{51}O_{64}$, T-20 – is a 36-amino acid peptide derived from the HR2 region of HIV-1_{LAI}, which binds to the HR1 region of the HIV gp41 fusion peptide and prevents the coil–coil zipping reaction, which leads to six-helix bundle formation and eventual viral–host membrane fusion (Fig. 204.6). Enfuvirtide is active against both R5 and X4 viral strains with susceptibility influenced by the time that the gp41 HR1 target is exposed to the drug as the viral entry process proceeds. Co-receptor density and affinity may influence the susceptibility of HIV strains to enfuvirtide.

Pharmacokinetics and distribution

Enfuvirtide is rapidly digested by peptidases in the gastrointestinal tract and consequently is not orally bioavailable. Following subcutaneous dosing of enfuvirtide, the mean C_{max} and C_{min} at steady state were reported as 2626ng/ml and 972ng/ml, respectively, at 50mg q12h, and 4725ng/ml and 1774ng/ml, respectively, at 100mg q12h.[58] The time to maximal concentrations was approximately 4 hours. The serum half-life of enfuvirtide after intravenous administration has been reported as approximately 2 hours, but more sustained concentrations throughout the 12-hour dosing interval have been reported following subcutaneous administration.

Route and dosage

Enfuvirtide is administered by subcutaneous injection. The adult dosage is 90mg q12h.

Indications

Enfuvirtide is indicated for the treatment of HIV infection in combination with other antiretroviral agents. Given the parenteral nature of the drug and its activity against drug-resistant virus, its role lies in the management of patients with treatment failure in whom other options are constrained. It is important to try to have at least two (and preferably more) other active drugs to administer with enfuvirtide so that enfuvirtide-resistant virus does not quickly emerge. Two large phase III trials have demonstrated the efficacy of enfuvirtide when combined with background therapy optimized with the assistance of drug resistance testing. The enfuvirtide groups in both studies averaged a 0.9–1.0 $\log_{10}$ greater drop in plasma HIV-1 RNA than the control groups at 24 weeks.[59]

Resistance

Resistance to enfuvirtide has been documented to occur in vivo with most mutations mapping to positions 36–45 of the amino terminal (HR1 region) of gp41. The most commonly described mutations are G36D/S, I37V, V38A/M, Q39R, N42T and N43D (see Fig. 204.3). Interestingly, enfuvirtide-resistant viruses may be less fit than wild-type isolates. Thus an immunologic (and presumably clinical) benefit may persist beyond the point of virologic failure, similar to what has been described for PIs.

Dosage in special circumstances

The dose of the drug should not be influenced by renal or hepatic dysfunction given its peptide nature.

Adverse reactions and drug interactions

The major toxicity of enfuvirtide is injection site reaction, which occurs in a large proportion of patients to varying degrees. Bacterial infection at the injection sites can occur and has resulted in occasional bacteremia. A hypersensitivity syndrome has also been described.

Selected investigational entry inhibitors

Fusion inhibitors

T-1249 is a 39-amino acid peptide that binds to an overlapping but not identical region on the HR1 region of the HIV gp41 fusion peptide as enfuvirtide. It is somewhat more potent than enfuvirtide,

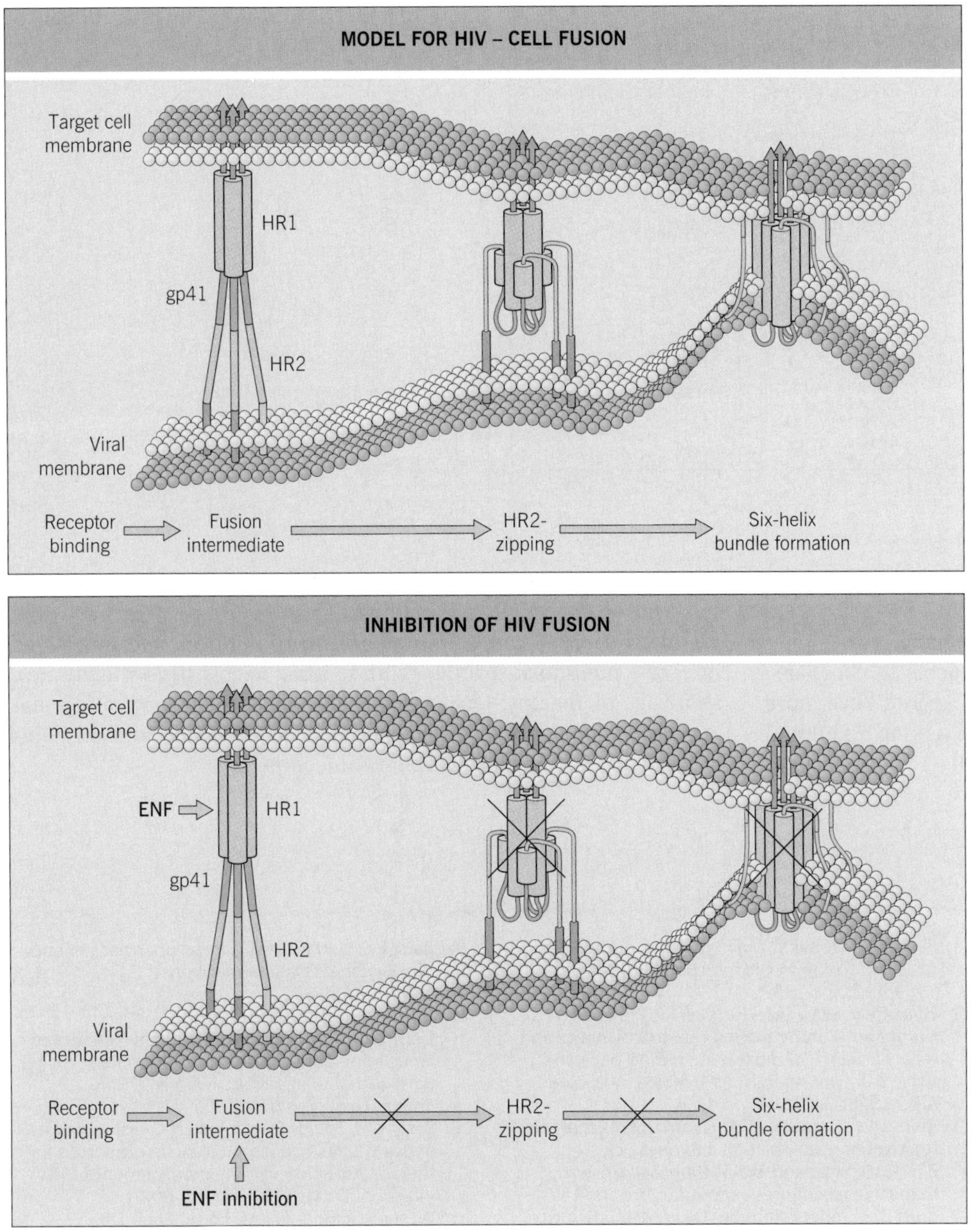

Fig. 204.6 Mechanism of HIV fusion with host cell membrane and its inhibition by enfuvirtide (ENF, T-20).

can be administered subcutaneously q24h and is active against enfuvirtide-resistant viruses in vitro. In a phase I study, dose-dependent decreases in plasma HIV-1 RNA have been reported.

Attachment inhibitors

Attachment inhibitors bind to HIV gp120 and prevent virion attachment to the cell surface receptors. Two compounds in development are PRO 542 and BMS 806. PRO 542 is a tetravalent CD4-IgG2 fusion protein that binds to gp120. Proof of principle has been established in a single-dose, phase I study.[60] BMS 806 is an orally bioavailable molecule that inhibits gp120/CD4 interactions by direct binding to gp120.[61] Resistance can be selected in vitro and is mediated by mutations in the binding site on gp120. Clinical trials of BMS 806 are planned.

Chemokine receptor antagonists

Chemokine receptor antagonists targeting both CCR5 and CXCR4 are under development. Approaches include a monoclonal antibody to CCR5 (PRO 140) and small molecule inhibitors of CCR5 (SCH-C, SCH-D, UK 427857, TAK compounds) and CXCR4 (AMD 3100, AMD 070).[62–65] Proof of principle in phase I human studies has been reported for SCH-C and AMD 3100. Development of the latter has been halted, however, due to limited potency.

INTEGRASE INHIBITORS

HIV integrase is essential for viral replication and has been a recognized target for several years. However, only recently have the characteristics of true integrase inhibitors been described and effective in-vitro screening approaches defined.[66,67] Two compounds, S-1360, a diketo acid, and L-870810, a naphthyridine compound, are currently in phase I trials. L-870810 has shown substantial antiviral activity in the SHIV rhesus macaque model.

FUTURE APPROACHES

Although entry and integrase inhibition are likely to represent the next major breakthroughs in antiretroviral chemotherapy, a number of other novel approaches are being intensively investigated and bear watching over the next few years. These include inhibition of nucleocapsid zinc fingers, alpha-defensins, interference with the HIV gag chaperone protein, TSG 101, and the exploding area of RNA interference (RNAi).[68–71]

LIST OF SELECTED INVESTIGATIONAL AGENTS				
Nucleoside reverse transcriptase inhibitors	Non-nucleoside reverse transcriptase inhibitors	Protease inhibitors	Entry inhibitors	Integrase inhibitors
Amdoxovir ACH-126, 443 SPD-754	Capravirine TMC 125	GW 433908 Tipranavir TMC 114	T-1249 PRO 542 BMS 806 PRO 140 SCH-C SCH-D UK 427857 AMD 070	S-1360 L-870810

Table 204.12 List of selected investigational agents.

CONCLUSION

The field of antiretroviral therapy has shown dramatic growth over the past 17 years with five drug classes now available to clinicians. On the near horizon, clinicians and patients are likely to have more choices within these existing drug classes as well as one additional class (i.e. integrase inhibitors) available (Table 204.12). Along with this will be the challenge of investigating and applying new drug regimens such as combinations of entry inhibitors and entry and integrase inhibitors, together with existing agents to formulate new strategies of therapy. On the more distant horizon, new molecular approaches hold promise for continued fundamental improvements in the treatment of those with HIV infection.

REFERENCES

1. Palella FJ Jr, Delaney KM, Moorman AC, *et al.* Declining morbidity and mortality among patients with advanced human immunodeficiency virus infection. HIV Outpatient Study Investigators. N Engl J Med 1998;338:853–60.
2. DHHS/Kaiser. Guidelines for the use of antiretroviral agents in HIV-infected adults and adolescents. Available at http://www.hivatis.org.
3. Yeni PG, Hammer SM, Carpenter CC, *et al.* Antiretroviral treatment for adult HIV infection in 2002: updated recommendations of the International AIDS Society–USA Panel. JAMA 2002;288:222–35.
4. Wilde MI, Langtry HD. Zidovudine. An update of its pharmacodynamic and pharmacokinetic properties, and therapeutic efficacy. Drugs 1993;46:515–78.
5. Klecker RW Jr, Collins JM, Yarchoan R, *et al.* Plasma and cerebrospinal fluid pharmacokinetics of 3′-azido-3′-deoxythymidine: a novel pyrimidine analog with potential application for the treatment of patients with AIDS and related diseases. Clin Pharmacol Ther 1987;41:407–12.
6. Acosta EP, Page LM, Fletcher CV. Clinical pharmacokinetics of zidovudine. An update. Clin Pharmacokinet 1996;30:251–62.
7. Havlir DV, Tierney C, Friedland GH, *et al.* In vivo antagonism with zidovudine plus stavudine combination therapy. J Infect Dis 2000;182:321–5.
8. Connor EM, Sperling RS, Gelber R, *et al.* Reduction of maternal–infant transmission of human immunodeficiency virus type 1 with zidovudine treatment. Pediatric AIDS Clinical Trials Group Protocol 076 Study Group. N Engl J Med 1994;331:1173–80.
9. Larder BA, Darby G, Richman DD. HIV with reduced sensitivity to zidovudine (AZT) isolated during prolonged therapy. Science 1989;243:1731–4.
10. Taylor GP, Low-Beer N. Antiretroviral therapy in pregnancy: a focus on safety. Drug Saf 2001;24:683–702.
11. Perry CM, Noble S. Didanosine: an updated review of its use in HIV infection. Drugs 1999;58:1099–135.
12. Hoetelmans RM, van Heeswijk RP, Profijt M, *et al.* Comparison of the plasma pharmacokinetics and renal clearance of didanosine during once and twice daily dosing in HIV-1 infected individuals. AIDS 1998;12:F211–6.
13. Ahluwalia G, Cooney DA, Hartman NR, *et al.* Anomalous accumulation and decay of 2′,3′-dideoxyadenosine-5′-triphosphate in human T-cell cultures exposed to the anti-HIV drug 2′,3′-dideoxyinosine. Drug Metab Dispos 1993;21:369–76.
14. Adkins JC, Peters DH, Faulds D. Zalcitabine. An update of its pharmacodynamic and pharmacokinetic properties and clinical efficacy in the management of HIV infection. Drugs 1997;53:1054–80.
15. Nazareno LA, Holazo AA, Limjuco R, *et al.* The effect of food on pharmacokinetics of zalcitabine in HIV-positive patients. Pharm Res 1995;12:1462–5.
16. Yarchoan R, Mitsuya H, Myers CE, Broder S. Clinical pharmacology of 3′-azido-2′,3′-dideoxythymidine (zidovudine) and related dideoxynucleosides. N Engl J Med 1989;321:726–38.
17. Delta: a randomised double-blind controlled trial comparing combinations of zidovudine plus didanosine or zalcitabine with zidovudine alone in HIV-infected individuals. Delta Coordinating Committee. Lancet 1996;348:283–91.
18. Hammer SM, Katzenstein DA, Hughes MD, *et al.* A trial comparing nucleoside monotherapy with combination therapy in HIV-infected adults with CD4 cell counts from 200 to 500 per cubic millimeter. AIDS Clinical Trials Group Study 175 Study Team. N Engl J Med 1996;335:1081–90.
19. Haas DW, Clough LA, Johnson BW, *et al.* Evidence of a source of HIV type 1 within the central nervous system by ultraintensive sampling of cerebrospinal fluid and plasma. AIDS Res Hum Retro 2000;16:1491–502.
20. Rana KZ, Dudley MN. Clinical pharmacokinetics of stavudine. Clin Pharmacokinet 1997;33:276–84.
21. Bruno R, Regazzi MB, Ciappina V, *et al.* Comparison of the plasma pharmacokinetics of lamivudine during twice and once daily administration in patients with HIV. Clin Pharmacokinet 2001;40:695–700.
22. Perry CM, Faulds D. Lamivudine. A review of its antiviral activity, pharmacokinetic properties and therapeutic efficacy in the management of HIV infection. Drugs 1997;53:657–80.
23. Weller S, Radomski KM, Lou Y, Stein DS. Population pharmacokinetics and pharmacodynamic modeling of abacavir (1592U89) from a dose-ranging, double-blind, randomized monotherapy trial with human immunodeficiency virus-infected subjects. Antimicrob Agents Chemother 2000;44:2052–60.
24. Hervey PS, Perry CM. Abacavir: a review of its clinical potential in patients with HIV infection. Drugs 2000;60:447–79.
25. Staszewski S, Keiser P, Montaner J, *et al.* Abacavir–lamivudine–zidovudine vs indinavir–lamivudine–zidovudine in antiretroviral-naive HIV-infected adults: a randomized equivalence trial. JAMA 2001;285:1155–63.
26. Opravil M, Hirschel B, Lazzarin A, *et al.* A randomized trial of simplified maintenance therapy with abacavir, lamivudine, and zidovudine in human immunodeficiency virus infection. J Infect Dis 2002;185:1251–60.
27. Mallal S, Nolan D, Witt C, *et al.* Association between presence of HLA-B*5701, HLA-DR7, and HLA-DQ3 and hypersensitivity to HIV-1 reverse-transcriptase inhibitor abacavir. Lancet 2002;359:727–32.
28. Barditch-Crovo P, Deeks SG, Collier A, *et al.* Phase I/II trial of the pharmacokinetics, safety, and antiretroviral activity of tenofovir disoproxil fumarate in human immunodeficiency virus-infected adults. Antimicrob Agents Chemother 2001;45:2733–9.

29. Robbins BL, Srinivas RV, Kim C, Bischofberger N, Fridland A. Anti-human immunodeficiency virus activity and cellular metabolism of a potential prodrug of the acyclic nucleoside phosphonate 9-R-(2-phosphonomethoxypropyl)adenine (PMPA), bis(isopropyloxymethylcarbonyl)PMPA. Antimicrob Agents Chemother 1998;42:612–7.
30. Schooley RT, Ruane P, Myers RA, *et al.* Tenofovir DF in antiretroviral-experienced patients: results from a 48-week, randomized, double-blind study. AIDS 2002;16:1257–63.
31. Cheeseman SH, Hattox SE, McLaughlin MM, *et al.* Pharmacokinetics of nevirapine: initial single-rising-dose study in humans. Antimicrob Agents Chemother 1993;37:178–82.
32. Smith PF, DiCenzo R, Morse GD. Clinical pharmacokinetics of non-nucleoside reverse transcriptase inhibitors. Clin Pharmacokinet 2001;40:893–905.
33. Erickson DA, Mather G, Trager WF, Levy RH, Keirns JJ. Characterization of the in vitro biotransformation of the HIV-1 reverse transcriptase inhibitor nevirapine by human hepatic cytochromes P-450. Drug Metab Dispos 1999;27:1488–95.
34. Hammer SM, Vaida F, Bennett KK, *et al.* Dual vs single protease inhibitor therapy following antiretroviral treatment failure: a randomized trial. JAMA 2002;288:169–80.
35. Guay LA, Musoke P, Fleming T, *et al.* Intrapartum and neonatal single-dose nevirapine compared with zidovudine for prevention of mother-to-child transmission of HIV-1 in Kampala, Uganda: HIVNET 012 randomised trial. Lancet 1999;354:795–802.
36. Dorenbaum A, Cunningham CK, Gelber RD, *et al.* Two-dose intrapartum/newborn nevirapine and standard antiretroviral therapy to reduce perinatal HIV transmission: a randomized trial. JAMA 2002;288:189–98.
37. Tran JQ, Gerber JG, Kerr BM. Delavirdine: clinical pharmacokinetics and drug interactions. Clin Pharmacokinet 2001;40:207–26.
38. Tashima KT, Caliendo AM, Ahmad M, *et al.* Cerebrospinal fluid human immunodeficiency virus type 1 (HIV-1) suppression and efavirenz drug concentrations in HIV-1-infected patients receiving combination therapy. J Infect Dis 1999;180:862–4.
39. Adkins JC, Noble S. Efavirenz. Drugs 1998;56:1055–64
40. Bacheler LT, Anton ED, Kudish P, *et al.* Human immunodeficiency virus type 1 mutations selected in patients failing efavirenz combination therapy. Antimicrob Agents Chemother 2000;44:2475–84.
41. Noble S, Faulds D. Saquinavir. A review of its pharmacology and clinical potential in the management of HIV infection. Drugs 1996;52:93–112.
42. Hsu A, Granneman GR, Bertz RJ. Ritonavir. Clinical pharmacokinetics and interactions with other anti-HIV agents. Clin Pharmacokinet 1998;35:275–91.
43. Plosker GL, Noble S. Indinavir: a review of its use in the management of HIV infection. Drugs 1999;58:1165–203.
44. Carver PL, Fleisher D, Zhou SY, Kaul D, Kazanjian P, Li C. Meal composition effects on the oral bioavailability of indinavir in HIV-infected patients. Pharm Res 1999;16:718–24.
45. Brinkman K, Kroon F, Hugen PW, Burger DM. Therapeutic concentrations of indinavir in cerebrospinal fluid of HIV-1-infected patients. AIDS 1998;12:537.
46. Haas DW, Stone J, Clough LA, *et al.* Steady-state pharmacokinetics of indinavir in cerebrospinal fluid and plasma among adults with human immunodeficiency virus type 1 infection. Clin Pharmacol Ther 2000;68:367–74.
47. Hammer SM, Squires KE, Hughes MD, *et al.* A controlled trial of two nucleoside analogues plus indinavir in persons with human immunodeficiency virus infection and CD4 cell counts of 200 per cubic millimeter or less. AIDS Clinical Trials Group 320 Study Team. N Engl J Med 1997;337:725–33.
48. Gulick RM, Mellors JW, Havlir D, *et al.* 3-year suppression of HIV viremia with indinavir, zidovudine, and lamivudine. Ann Intern Med 2000;133:35–9.
49. Jarvis B, Faulds D. Nelfinavir. A review of its therapeutic efficacy in HIV infection. Drugs 1998;56:147–67.
50. Lillibridge JH, Liang BH, Kerr BM, *et al.* Characterization of the selectivity and mechanism of human cytochrome P450 inhibition by the human immunodeficiency virus protease inhibitor nelfinavir mesylate. Drug Metab Dispos 1998;26:609–16.
51. Walmsley S, Bernstein B, King M, *et al.* Lopinavir–ritonavir versus nelfinavir for the initial treatment of HIV infection. N Engl J Med 2002;346:2039–46.
52. Adkins JC, Faulds D. Amprenavir. Drugs 1998;55:837–42.
53. Hurst M, Faulds D. Lopinavir. Drugs 2000;60:1371–9.
54. Larder BA, Hertogs K, Bloor S, *et al.* Tipranavir inhibits broadly protease inhibitor-resistant HIV-1 clinical samples. AIDS 2000;14:1943–8.
55. Piliero PJ. Atazanavir: a novel HIV-1 protease inhibitor. Expert Opin Investig Drugs 2002;11:1295–1301.
56. De Clercq E. Highlights in the development of new antiviral agents. Mini Rev Med Chem 2002;2:163–75.
57. De Clercq E. New developments in anti-HIV chemotherapy. Biochim Biophys Acta 2002;1587:258–75.
58. Kilby JM, Lalezari JP, Eron JJ, *et al.* The safety, plasma pharmacokinetics, and antiviral activity of subcutaneous enfuvirtide (T-20), a peptide inhibitor of gp41-mediated virus fusion, in HIV-infected adults. AIDS Res Human Retro 2002;18:685–93.
59. Chen RY, Kilby JM, Saag MS. Enfuvirtide. Expert Opin Investig Drugs 2002;11:1837–43.
60. Jacobson JM, Lowy I, Fletcher CV, *et al.* Single-dose safety, pharmacology, and antiviral activity of the human immunodeficiency virus (HIV) type 1 entry inhibitor PRO 542 in HIV-infected adults. J Infect Dis 2000;182:326–9.
61. Stephenson J. Researchers explore new anti-HIV agents. JAMA 2002;287:1635–7.
62. Strizki JM, Xu S, Wagner NE, *et al.* SCH-C (SCH 351125), an orally bioavailable, small molecule antagonist of the chemokine receptor CCR5, is a potent inhibitor of HIV-1 infection in vitro and in vivo. Proc Natl Acad Sci USA 2001;98:12718–23.
63. Takashima K, Miyake H, Furuta RA, *et al.* Inhibitory effects of small-molecule CCR5 antagonists on human immunodeficiency virus type 1 envelope-mediated membrane fusion and viral replication. Antimicrob Agents Chemother 2001;45:3538–43.
64. Trkola A, Ketas TJ, Nagashima KA, *et al.* Potent, broad-spectrum inhibition of human immunodeficiency virus type 1 by the CCR5 monoclonal antibody PRO 140. J Virol 2001;75:579–88.
65. Hendrix CW, Flexner C, MacFarland RT, *et al.* Pharmacokinetics and safety of AMD-3100, a novel antagonist of the CXCR-4 chemokine receptor, in human volunteers. Antimicrob Agents Chemother 2000;44:1667–73.
66. Hazuda DJ, Felock P, Witmer M, *et al.* Inhibitors of strand transfer that prevent integration and inhibit HIV-1 replication in cells. Science 2000;287:646–50.
67. Espeseth AS, Felock P, Wolfe A, *et al.* HIV-1 integrase inhibitors that compete with the target DNA substrate define a unique strand transfer conformation for integrase. Proc Natl Acad Sci USA 2000;97:11244–9.
68. Basrur V, Song Y, Mazur SJ, *et al.* Inactivation of HIV-1 nucleocapsid protein P7 by pyridinioalkanoyl thioesters. Characterization of reaction products and proposed mechanism of action. J Biol Chem 2000;275:14890–7.
69. Zhang L, Yu W, He T, *et al.* Contribution of human alpha-defensin 1, 2, and 3 to the anti-HIV-1 activity of CD8 antiviral factor. Science 2002;298:995–1000.
70. Demirov DG, Ono A, Orenstein JM, Freed EO. Overexpression of the *N*-terminal domain of TSG101 inhibits HIV-1 budding by blocking late domain function. Proc Natl Acad Sci USA 2002;99:955–60.
71. Jacque JM, Triques K, Stevenson M. Modulation of HIV-1 replication by RNA interference. Nature 2002;418:435–8.

chapter 205

Drugs for Herpesvirus Infections

John W Gnann Jr & Michelle R Salvaggio

INTRODUCTION

Over the last 25 years, the armamentarium of antiviral compounds has expanded from a handful of drugs with low potency and substantial toxicity to over two dozen drugs now in widespread clinical use. Initial attempts at antiviral drug development were thwarted by the complex interactions between viral and host cellular metabolism. Compounds that blocked viral replication also frequently caused unacceptable host cell toxicity. Many of the early drugs evaluated as antiviral therapeutics were serendipitously discovered through screening of compounds for anticancer activity. More recently, better understanding of molecular virology has permitted rational design of drugs specifically targeted for unique steps in the viral replication cycle. While most of the first-generation drugs were developed for treatment of infections caused by herpesviruses, new compounds are now entering clinical use for treatment of a variety of viruses, including respiratory viruses, enteroviruses and hepatitis viruses. Another emerging trend is the use of combinations of drugs for therapy of serious viral infections, pioneered in the field of HIV therapy.

DRUGS FOR TREATMENT OF HSV AND VZV INFECTIONS

Aciclovir and valaciclovir

Mechanism of action and in vitro activity

Aciclovir, 9-(2-hydroxyethoxymethyl) guanine, an acyclic analogue of guanosine, is a selective inhibitor of the replication of herpes simplex virus (HSV) types 1 and 2 and varicella-zoster virus (VZV).[1] Valaciclovir is an orally administered prodrug of aciclovir with improved pharmacokinetic properties. Aciclovir is converted to its monophosphate derivative by virus-encoded thymidine kinase (TK), a reaction that does not occur to any significant extent in uninfected cells (Fig. 205.1). Subsequent diphosphorylation and triphosphorylation steps are catalyzed by cellular kinases, producing high concentrations of aciclovir triphosphate within HSV- or VZV-infected cells. Aciclovir triphosphate inhibits viral DNA synthesis by competing with deoxyguanosine triphosphate as a substrate for viral DNA polymerase. Since aciclovir triphosphate lacks the 3′-hydroxyl group required for further DNA chain elongation, incorporation into viral DNA results in obligate chain termination. Viral DNA polymerase has much higher affinity for aciclovir triphosphate than does cellular DNA polymerase, resulting in little incorporation of aciclovir into cellular DNA. Aciclovir exhibits good *in vitro* activity against HSV-1, HSV-2 and VZV, with median inhibitory concentrations necessary to reduce plaque counts by 50% (IC_{50}) of 0.04, 0.10 and 0.50µg/ml, respectively. Human cytomegalovirus (CMV) is not inhibited by aciclovir at clinically achievable concentrations.

Pharmacokinetics and distribution

Following oral administration, aciclovir is slowly and incompletely absorbed, with bio-availability of about 15–30%. After oral administration of multiple doses of 200 or 800mg of aciclovir, mean plasma peak concentrations at steady state are about 0.6 and 1.6µg/ml, respectively. Steady-state peak plasma aciclovir concentrations after intravenous doses of 5 or 10mg/kg of body weight every 8 hours are about 10 and 20µg/ml, respectively. Plasma protein binding is less than 20%. Aciclovir penetrates well into most tissues, including the central nervous system (Table 205.1). Relative to plasma, aciclovir concentrations in cerebrospinal fluid, aqueous humor and breast milk are about 50%, 37% and 300%, respectively. Aciclovir is minimally metabolized and about 85% of an administered dose is excreted unchanged in the urine via glomerular filtration and renal tubular secretion. The terminal plasma half-life of aciclovir is 2–3 hours in adults and 3–4 hours in neonates with normal renal function, but is extended to about 20 hours in anuric subjects.

Valaciclovir is an orally administered prodrug of aciclovir designed to overcome the problem of poor oral bio-availability.[2] Valaciclovir, the L-valine ester of aciclovir, is well absorbed from the gastrointestinal tract via a stereospecific transporter and undergoes essentially complete first- pass conversion in the gut and liver to yield aciclovir and L-valine. With this prodrug formulation, bio-availability of aciclovir is about 54%, yielding peak plasma aciclovir levels that are 3–5-fold higher than those achieved with oral administration of the parent compound. Oral doses of 500mg or 1000mg of valaciclovir produce peak plasma aciclovir concentrations of 3.3 and 5–6µg/ml, respectively. After administration of valaciclovir at a dose of 2gm orally four times daily, plasma aciclovir area under the curve (AUC) values approximate those produced by aciclovir given intravenously at a dose of 10mg/kg every 8 hours. Following enzymatic conversion of valaciclovir to aciclovir, the antiviral spectrum of activity, pharmacokinetic properties and excretion are the same as those described above.

Route of administration and dosage

Aciclovir is available in topical, oral and intravenous formulations. Outside the United States, aciclovir is also available as a 3% preparation for ophthalmologic use. The dermatologic preparation consists of 5% aciclovir in a polyethylene glycol ointment base. Topical aciclovir is intended for treatment of minor mucocutaneous or genital HSV infections. Oral aciclovir preparations include a 200mg capsule, 400 and 800mg tablets, and a liquid suspension (200mg/5ml). Aciclovir sodium for intravenous infusion is supplied as a sterile water-soluble powder that must be reconstituted and diluted to a concentration of 50mg/ml.

The recommended dose of aciclovir will vary with the specific indication (see Table 205.2). Because of the greater intrinsic resistance of VZV to aciclovir, the doses required for treating VZV infections are higher than those used for HSV infections. In adults with normal renal function, oral aciclovir is given at a dose of 200mg (for HSV) to 800mg (for VZV) five times daily. The recommended dose of intravenous aciclovir is 5mg/kg every 8 hours for HSV infections or 10mg/kg every 8 hours for VZV infections, although higher doses

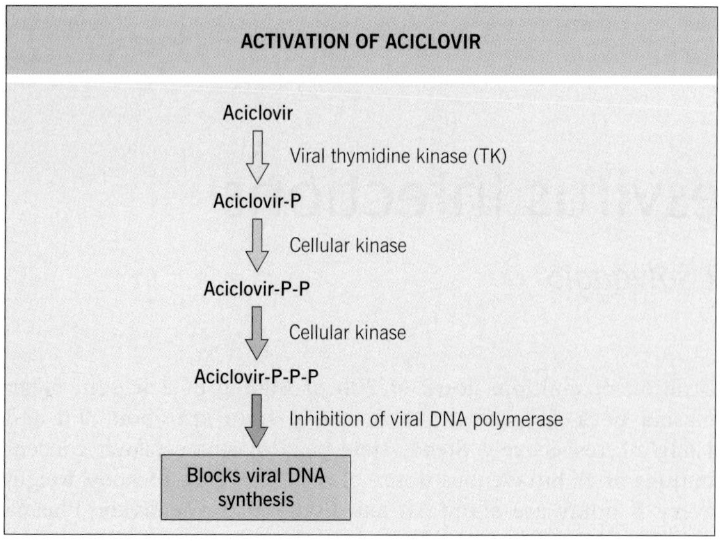

Fig. 205.1 Activation of aciclovir is dependent on monophosphorylation via viral thymidine kinase (TK). Aciclovir triphosphate inhibits the activity of viral DNA polymerase, thus blocking viral replication. Penciclovir and ganciclovir are activated by similar mechanisms.

(12–15mg/kg) are sometimes used for life-threatening infections, especially in immunocompromised patients.

Valaciclovir is available as 500mg and 1000mg tablets. The recommended doses are 500mg twice daily for episodic treatment of recurrent genital HSV infections and 1000mg three times daily for treatment of herpes zoster. A suspension preparation is not available.

Indications

HSV infections

Initial episodes of genital HSV infection can be treated with topical, oral or intravenous aciclovir. Intravenous aciclovir is the most effective treatment for initial genital herpes, but is not usually practical and should be reserved for patients with severe local disease or systemic complications. Oral aciclovir (200mg five times daily) is nearly as effective as intravenous therapy and significantly reduces the duration of symptoms, virus shedding and time to healing. Topical aciclovir is less effective than oral or intravenous therapy for initial genital herpes. Aciclovir treatment of acute HSV infection does not alter the risk of subsequent recurrences. Lesions associated with recurrent genital herpes are less severe than those seen in primary infection and the benefit from episodic therapy with oral aciclovir is relatively modest. A more effective approach in patients with frequent recurrences of genital herpes is to give aciclovir daily to prevent HSV reactivation. Daily administration of aciclovir will reduce the frequency of genital HSV recurrences in 90% of patients and a significant proportion will have no subsequent recurrences while taking suppressive medication. Titration of the dose of aciclovir (beginning with 400mg twice daily) may be required to establish the most effective dose. Periodic interruption of suppression to reassess the need for continued prophylaxis is recommended. There is no evidence of cumulative toxicity or emergence of drug-resistant

Table 205.1 Tissue distribution of aciclovir.*

TISSUE DISTRIBUTION OF ACICLOVIR*

	CSF/CNS	Lung	Liver	Kidney	Breast milk	Amniotic fluid	Heart
Aciclovir concentration (μg/ml)	10	26.7	26.7	206	66.7	<0.1–2.6	26.7

* Based on a steady-state plasma concentration (20.6μg/ml) after intravenous aciclovir dosing of 15mg/kg every 8 hours.[38]

Table 205.2 Indications for aciclovir therapy.

INDICATIONS FOR ACICLOVIR THERAPY

Infection	Route and dosage†
Genital HSV	
Initial episode	200mg po 5 times/d (or 400mg tid) × 10 days
Initial episode with complications	5mg/kg iv q8h × 5–7 days
Recurrent episodes	200mg po 5 times/d (or 400mg tid) × 5 days
Suppression	400mg po bid daily
Mucocutaneous HSV in immunocompromised patient	400mg po 5 times/d × 10–14 days*; or 5mg/kg iv q8h × 10 days
Disseminated or visceral HSV (including encephalitis)	10–15mg/kg iv q8h × 14–21 days
Neonatal HSV	10–15mg/kg iv q8h × 14–21 days*
Varicella (chickenpox)	
Normal host	20mg/kg (max. 800mg) po 4–5 times/d × 5 days
Immunocompromised patient	10–15mg/kg iv q8h × 7–10 days
Herpes zoster (shingles)	
Normal host	800mg po 5 times/d × 7–10 days
Immunocompromised patient (disseminated or visceral VZV)	10–15mg/kg iv q8h × 7–10 days

† Given doses are indicated for patients with normal renal function
* This indication is not approved by the US Food and Drug Administration

HSV in immunocompetent patients even after years of suppressive therapy.[3] Aciclovir suppression will also significantly reduce (but not eliminate) the frequency of asymptomatic viral shedding.[4]

In a study comparing valaciclovir (1000mg twice daily) with aciclovir (200mg five times daily) for treatment of first-episode genital herpes, both drugs were well tolerated and equivalent in efficacy.[5] For episodic treatment of recurrent genital herpes, valaciclovir (500mg twice daily for 3 days) reduced the duration of viral shedding and accelerated pain resolution and lesion healing.[6] For suppression of genital herpes, valaciclovir doses ranging from 250mg to 1000mg once daily and from 250mg to 500mg twice daily have been evaluated in clinical trials. A dose – response relationship is evident across the various valaciclovir regimens, with better suppression at higher doses, although all were significantly more effective than placebo. The recommended starting dose of valaciclovir for genital herpes suppression is 500–1000mg daily; patients who have breakthrough recurrences on this regimen may require 500mg twice daily for effective suppression. In general, aciclovir and valaciclovir are equally potent for suppression of genital herpes, although the once-daily dosing regimen for valaciclovir may be more convenient.

Oral aciclovir therapy can reduce the duration of symptoms for children with acute HSV gingivostomatitis. Topical aciclovir is relatively ineffective for recurrent herpes labialis. Treatment of herpes labialis with oral aciclovir (400mg five times daily for 5 days) offers some clinical benefit, if initiated during the prodromal or erythematous stage of lesion evolution. Oral aciclovir can be used for short-term prophylaxis of recurrent herpes labialis in situations where exposure to a known stimulus such as ultraviolet light is anticipated (e.g. a snow skiing or beach holiday). Patients with frequent recurrences of herpes labialis may benefit from long-term suppressive therapy with oral aciclovir (400mg twice daily), which can reduce the frequency of clinical recurrences by about 50%. A high-dose, short-course regimen of valaciclovir (e.g. 2g bid for 1 day) for treatment of herpes labialis has recently been approved in the United States.

Aciclovir prophylaxis of HSV infections is highly effective in severely immunocompromised patients, particularly those undergoing induction chemotherapy or organ transplantation. In bone marrow transplant recipients, aciclovir reduces the incidence of symptomatic HSV infection from approximately 70% to 10% and is especially valuable during the first 30 days following transplantation. A sequential regimen of intravenous followed by oral aciclovir (at doses ranging from 200mg three times daily to 800mg twice daily) for 3–6 months can virtually eliminate symptomatic HSV infections in organ transplant recipients. In immunocompromised patients with established mucocutaneous HSV infections, intravenous (5–10mg/kg every 8 hours) or oral aciclovir (400mg five times daily) can significantly reduce the duration of pain and accelerate lesion healing. Clinical experience suggests that intravenous aciclovir (10mg/kg every 8 hours) is the treatment of choice for disseminated or visceral HSV infection (e.g. pneumonitis, hepatitis, esophagitis, etc.) in immunocompromised patients, although data from controlled clinical trials are lacking.

HSV infection of the central nervous system is associated with substantial morbidity and mortality despite the use of antiviral therapy. Aciclovir was proven superior to vidarabine for HSV encephalitis and should be given intravenously at a dose of 10–15mg/kg for 14–21 days. Even with aggressive aciclovir therapy, the mortality rate at 6 months is 19% for patients with HSV encephalitis.

Neonatal herpes is a potentially devastating infection that can develop in infants born to mothers who are actively shedding HSV from the genital tract at the time of delivery. Intravenous aciclovir therapy can significantly reduce both morbidity and mortality among these infants. Studies are under way to establish the value of long-term aciclovir suppression for preventing progressive neurologic deterioration among surviving infants. Another promising approach currently under evaluation is the use of oral aciclovir or valaciclovir suppression during the third trimester in pregnant women with genital herpes. Data suggest that prophylaxis can significantly reduce the requirement for cesarian section due to active genital HSV lesions present at the onset of labor.[7]

VZV infections

Oral aciclovir therapy for immunocompetent children with chickenpox will reduce both the duration of fever and total lesion count if treatment is begun within 24 hours of disease onset. However, the benefits of aciclovir administration are relatively modest and many pediatricians consider antiviral treatment of chickenpox to be optional. In immunocompetent children, the dosage of oral aciclovir for chickenpox is 20mg/kg (up to a maximum of 800mg) four times daily. Varicella can be a more severe disease in adolescents and adults, with higher lesion counts and a greater risk of complications, especially pneumonitis. For this reason, aciclovir therapy (800mg orally five times daily for 7 days) is recommended for adolescents and adults who present within 24–48 hours of disease onset. Valaciclovir is also likely to be effective in this setting, but data from controlled clinical trials are lacking. Because of the high frequency of visceral involvement in immunocompromised children (or adults) with chickenpox, aggressive therapy with intravenous aciclovir (10mg/kg or 500mg/m^2 every 8 hours for 7–10 days) is warranted. Controlled trials of intravenous aciclovir in immunocompromised patients with varicella clearly demonstrated a significant reduction in the frequency of progression to VZV pneumonitis. Although no data from controlled trials are available, clinical experience suggests that intravenous aciclovir is the treatment of choice for patients with VZV infections complicated by visceral involvement (e.g. pneumonitis, encephalitis, etc.).

For treatment of herpes zoster in immunocompetent adults, oral aciclovir (800mg five times daily for 7 days) accelerates cutaneous healing and reduces the severity of acute neuritis. Benefits are maximized when treatment is initiated within 48 hours of appearance of lesions. Aciclovir does not alter the incidence of postherpetic neuralgia, but can accelerate the resolution of pain.[8] Aciclovir is especially beneficial for preventing ocular complications in patients with herpes zoster ophthalmicus. Severely immunocompromised patients (e.g. bone marrow transplant, cancer chemotherapy, etc.) with herpes zoster are at high risk for disseminated VZV infection and should be treated with intravenous aciclovir (10mg/kg every 8 hours). AIDS patients with herpes zoster can usually be treated effectively with oral therapy.

Valaciclovir (1000mg three times daily for 7 days) was compared with aciclovir (800mg five times daily for 7 days) in over 1000 immunocompetent patients (>50 years of age) with herpes zoster.[9] The progression of cutaneous healing was similar in the two treatment groups. Patients in the valaciclovir treatment group had a slightly shorter duration of zoster-associated pain (38 days versus 51 days). Extending valaciclovir therapy to 14 days did not result in any additional benefit. Both aciclovir and valaciclovir are effective for treatment of localized herpes zoster in immunocompetent patients if therapy is initiated within 72 hours of rash onset. Valaciclovir has the advantage of a simpler dosing regimen.

Other viral infections

While aciclovir is ineffective for established CMV infections, high-dose oral aciclovir or valaciclovir may have value for CMV prophylaxis in high-risk populations such as AIDS patients and organ transplant recipients.[10] Administration of aciclovir does not alter the course of infectious mononucleosis, but can induce regression

ACICLOVIR DOSAGE MODIFICATION FOR RENAL IMPAIRMENT			
Normal dosage regimen	CrCl (ml/min/1.73m²)	Adjusted dosage regimen	
		Dose	Dosing interval (h)
Aciclovir 200mg po q4h	>10	200mg	4 (5×/d)
	0–10	200mg	12
Aciclovir 400mg po q12h	>10	400mg	12
	0–10	200mg	12
Aciclovir 800mg po q4h	>25	800mg	4 (5×/d)
	10–25	800mg	8
	0–10	800mg	12
Aciclovir 5mg/kg iv q8h	>50	5mg/kg	8
	25–50	5mg/kg	12
	10–25	5mg/kg	24
	0–10	2.5mg/kg	24
Aciclovir 10mg/kg iv q8h	>50	10mg/kg	8
	25–50	10mg/kg	12
	10–25	10mg/kg	24
	0–10	5mg/kg	24
CrCl, creatinine clearance			

Table 205.3 Aciclovir dosage modification for renal impairment.

VALACICLOVIR DOSAGE MODIFICATION FOR RENAL IMPAIRMENT			
Normal dosage regimen	CrCl (ml/min)	Adjusted dosage regimen	
		Dose (mg)	Dosing interval (h)
Valaciclovir 1000mg q8h	>50	1000	8
	30–49	1000	12
	10–29	1000	24
	<10	500	24
Valaciclovir 1000mg q12h	>30	1000	12
	10–29	1000	24
	<10	500	24
Valaciclovir 500mg q12h	>30	500	12
	<30	500	24
Valaciclovir 1000mg q24h	>30	1000	24
	<30	500	24
Valaciclovir 500mg q24h	>30	500	24
	<30	500	48
CrCl, creatinine clearance			

Table 205.4 Valaciclovir dosage modification for renal impairment.

of EBV-induced oral hairy leukoplakia in HIV-infected patients. Aciclovir is not effective for treatment of chronic fatigue syndrome. It is considered the drug of choice for therapy of rare human infections caused by cercopithecine herpesvirus-1 (B virus). Aciclovir is not active against HIV; studies of the survival benefit of aciclovir therapy in AIDS patients have reached varying conclusions.

Dosage in special circumstances

Aciclovir is cleared primarily by renal mechanisms and dosage modification of aciclovir and valaciclovir is required for patients with significant renal dysfunction (see Tables 205.3, 205.4). The mean elimination half-life of aciclovir after a single 1g dose of valaciclovir is about 14 hours in patients with end-stage renal disease.[2] No specific dosage modification is required for patients with hepatic impairment. Aciclovir and valaciclovir are not approved for use in pregnancy, but have been widely used to treat serious HSV and VZV infections in pregnant women without evidence of maternal or fetal toxicity.[11]

Aciclovir AUC values after oral valaciclovir dosing are slightly higher in elderly individuals when compared with younger control groups, presumably due to declines in creatinine clearance associated with aging. Because no liquid valaciclovir preparation is available, experience with that drug in young children is limited.

Adverse reactions

Aciclovir is an extremely well-tolerated drug with very few significant adverse effects. With intravenous aciclovir therapy, inflammation and phlebitis may occasionally occur following localized drug extravasation. Renal dysfunction resulting from accumulation of aciclovir crystals in the kidney has been observed following administration of large doses of aciclovir by rapid intravenous infusion, but is uncommon and usually reversible. The risk of nephrotoxicity can be minimized by administering aciclovir by slow infusion (over 1 hour) and ensuring adequate hydration. A few reports have linked administration of aciclovir with CNS disturbances, including agitation, hallucination, disorientation, tremors and mild clonus. Neurotoxicity has most often been recognized in elderly patients with underlying CNS abnormalities and renal insufficiency. Patients receiving oral aciclovir therapy occasionally complain of nausea, diarrhea, rash or headache, but these possible adverse effects have not differed significantly between aciclovir and placebo recipients in large-scale clinical trials. Oral aciclovir therapy is rarely associated with neurotoxicity or nephrotoxicity. The safety of oral aciclovir for long-term administration has been established in patients receiving the drug for over 5 years for suppression of recurrent genital herpes.

At standard doses, valaciclovir is a very well-tolerated drug with few significant adverse effects.[12] Headache, nausea and abdominal pain have been reported, but the incidence of these symptoms has not differed between valaciclovir and placebo recipients in clinical studies. A syndrome of thrombotic microangiopathy (TMA) was described in some HIV-infected patients, receiving high-dose valaciclovir (8g/day) for prevention of CMV disease in a clinical trial; a causal relationship between high-dose valaciclovir and TMA has not been proven. The TMA-like syndrome, which is characterized by fever, microangiopathic hemolytic anemia, thrombocytopenia and renal dysfunction, has not been observed in immunocompetent patients receiving valaciclovir at approved doses (up to 3g/day). There is no contraindication to using valaciclovir at standard doses in HIV-infected patients.

Significant interactions between aciclovir and other drugs are extremely uncommon. Probenecid decreases the renal clearance of aciclovir and can prolong the plasma excretion half-life. Additive aciclovir-induced nephrotoxicity in patients receiving concomitant cyclosporin-A therapy has been suggested, but does not appear to be clinically important. Lethargy has been reported in a few patients receiving both aciclovir and zidovudine, but a causative role for aciclovir has not been established. Concomitant administration of cimetidine and probenecid reduces the rate of valaciclovir conversion to aciclovir, but the effect is not clinically significant.

Resistance

HSV resistance to aciclovir can develop through mutation of the viral genes encoding thymidine kinase or DNA polymerase. Most aciclovir-resistant clinical HSV isolates are TK deficient and are therefore unable to phosphorylate aciclovir.[13] Aciclovir-resistant HSV isolates are recovered only from immunocompromised patients. The most common clinical presentation of infection caused by aciclovir-resistant HSV is chronic, progressive mucocutaneous lesions. Approximately 5–6% of HSV isolates recovered from HIV-seropositive patients are aciclovir resistant (IC_{50}>2.0μg/ml). Aciclovir-resistant VZV isolates (less frequently encountered than resistant HSV isolates) are recovered almost exclusively from AIDS patients. Most clinical disease caused by aciclovir-resistant VZV has been limited to cutaneous involvement, often characterized by atypical lesions. TK-deficient HSV and VZV isolates will also be resistant to other drugs that require TK for activation, including ganciclovir and penciclovir. The drug of choice for treatment of aciclovir-resistant HSV or VZV disease is foscarnet, a viral DNA polymerase inhibitor that is not dependent on TK for activation.

Penciclovir and famciclovir

Mechanism of action and in vitro activity

Penciclovir, 9-(4-hydroxy-3-hydroxymethylbut-1-yl) guanine, is an acyclic guanine derivative that is similar to aciclovir in structure, mechanism of action and spectrum of antiviral activity. In HSV-or VZV-infected cells, penciclovir is first monophosphorylated by virally encoded TK and then further phosphorylated to the triphosphate moiety by cellular enzymes. Penciclovir triphosphate blocks viral DNA synthesis through competitive inhibition of viral DNA polymerase. Unlike aciclovir triphosphate, penciclovir triphosphate is not an obligate chain terminator and can be incorporated into the extending DNA chain. Compared with aciclovir triphosphate, intracellular concentrations of penciclovir triphosphate are much higher. For example, the half-life values for penciclovir triphosphate and aciclovir triphosphate in HSV-1 infected cells are 10 hours and 0.7 hour, respectively. However, this potential advantage is offset by a much lower affinity of penciclovir triphosphate for viral DNA polymerase. The *in vitro* activities of penciclovir against HSV-1, HSV-2 and VZV are similar to those of aciclovir, with median IC_{50} values of 0.4, 1.5 and 4.0μg/ml respectively, in MRC-5 cells.[14]

Just as valaciclovir is a prodrug of aciclovir, famciclovir is a prodrug of penciclovir. Because penciclovir is very poorly absorbed, famciclovir (the diacetyl ester of 6-deoxy-penciclovir) was developed as the oral formulation. The first acetyl side chain of famciclovir is cleaved by esterases found in the intestinal wall. On first pass through the liver, the second acetyl group is removed and oxidation catalyzed by aldehyde oxidase occurs at the 6 position, yielding penciclovir, the active antiviral compound.

Pharmacokinetics and distribution

Penciclovir is very poorly absorbed after oral administration. Intravenous infusion of penciclovir at 10mg/kg over 1 hour yields a peak plasma concentration of 12.1μg/ml. Plasma protein binding of penciclovir is <20%. The drug is cleared by renal tubular secretion and passive filtration. The plasma elimination half-life of penciclovir is about 2 hours and approximately 70% of the administered dose is recovered unchanged in the urine.

When administered as the famciclovir prodrug, the bio-availability of penciclovir is about 77%. Following a single oral dose of 250mg or 500mg of famciclovir, peak plasma penciclovir concentrations of 1.9 and 3.5μg/ml are achieved at 1 hour. The pharmacokinetics of penciclovir are linear and dose independent over a famciclovir dosing range of 125–750mg. Food slows famciclovir absorption and lowers the peak plasma penciclovir concentration, but does not alter the AUC value.

Route of administration and dosage

Famciclovir is available as 125mg, 250mg and 500mg tablets. Recommended dosages will vary with indication. The usual dose of famciclovir is 125mg twice daily for episodic therapy of recurrent genital herpes and 500mg three times daily for herpes zoster. The intravenous preparation of penciclovir has not been commercially released. A topical preparation of penciclovir is available as a 1% cream for treatment of HSV labialis.

Indications

Genital HSV infections.

Oral famciclovir reduced the duration of viral shedding and was comparable to oral aciclovir for accelerating healing and symptom resolution in patients with first-episode genital herpes. Famciclovir has not been approved for treatment of initial genital herpes in the United States, but 250mg orally three times daily for 5 days is likely to be effective.

Famciclovir was significantly superior to placebo for treatment of recurrent genital herpes.[15] When therapy was initiated by the patient at the time of symptom onset, famciclovir accelerated the events of healing and time to loss of pain.[15] The recommended dosage of famciclovir for episodic therapy of recurrent genital herpes is 125mg twice daily for 5 days.

Famciclovir is also effective for suppression of recurrent genital herpes.[16] In a multinational study of 455 patients, the time to first genital herpes recurrence was 336 days in the group receiving

Table 205.5 Oral antiviral therapy for genital herpes.

ORAL ANTIVIRAL THERAPY FOR GENITAL HERPES†			
Drugs	Initial episode	Recurrent episode	Suppression
Aciclovir	200mg 5 times/d (or 400mg tid*) × 10 days	200mg 5 times/d (or 400mg tid*) × 5 days	400mg bid daily
Famciclovir	125mg tid × 10 days*	125mg bid × 5 days	250mg bid daily
Valaciclovir	1000mg bid × 10 days	500mg bid × 3–5 days	500 or 1000mg once daily

† Recommended doses for immunocompetent adults with normal renal function
* This treatment regimen is not approved by the US Food and Drug Administration

famciclovir (250mg twice daily), compared with 47 days in the placebo group.[16] In the same study, 72% of subjects treated with famciclovir 250mg twice daily were recurrence free at 12 months, compared with 22% of placebo recipients.

Three drugs (aciclovir, valaciclovir and famciclovir) with proven efficacy for long-term suppression of recurrent genital herpes are now available. Few data from direct comparative trials have been published to guide the clinician in selecting the most effective treatment (see Table 205.5). All three of the compounds are safe and well tolerated. Considerations in selecting the appropriate drug may include cost and dosing convenience. For any patient, the goal is to establish a suppressive regimen that is effective, economical and convenient. For these drugs, a dose–response relationship exists, meaning that higher total daily doses generally produce more complete suppression. Clinicians may need to titrate the daily dose of the selected drug to identify optimal treatment for an individual patient.

Herpes labialis

Topical 1% penciclovir cream is applied every 2 hours while awake for treatment of herpes labialis. In placebo-controlled trials, topical penciclovir reduced the duration of viral shedding and accelerated lesion healing and pain resolution. Time to lesion healing was 0.7 days faster (4.8 days versus 5.5 days) for penciclovir-treated patients compared to the control group.

HSV infections in AIDS patients

Famciclovir (500mg twice daily) is comparable to aciclovir (400mg five times daily) for treatment of recurrent mucocutaneous (orolabial and anogenital) infections in HIV-infected patients. In a placebo-controlled trial, famciclovir (500mg twice daily) was also shown to be highly effective for suppression of recurrent mucocutaneous HSV infections in HIV-seropositive individuals.[17]

Herpes zoster

Famciclovir has been evaluated for treatment of dermatomal herpes zoster in immunocompetent patients. In a placebo-controlled clinical trial, famciclovir accelerated cutaneous healing and reduced the duration of viral shedding and postherpetic neuralgia.[18] In a subset of subjects over 50 years of age, the duration of postherpetic neuralgia was reduced from a median of 163 days to 63 days in the placebo and famciclovir treatment groups, respectively.[18] In the United States, the recommended dose of famciclovir for uncomplicated herpes zoster is 500mg three times daily. Doses of 250mg three times daily and 750mg once daily are approved in Europe and the United Kingdom.

Three drugs (aciclovir, valaciclovir and famciclovir) are currently available for treatment of uncomplicated herpes zoster in immunocompetent patients (see Table 205.6). The drugs are all well tolerated and appear to be comparable in clinical efficacy. In a large randomized clinical trial, valaciclovir and famciclovir were shown to be therapeutically

Table 205.6 Oral antiviral therapy for herpes zoster.

ORAL ANTIVIRAL THERAPY FOR HERPES ZOSTER†

Treatment options
- Aciclovir 800mg q4h (5 times daily) × 7–10 days
- Famciclovir 500mg q8h (3 times daily) × 7 days
- Valaciclovir 1000mg q8h (3 times daily) × 7 days

† Recommended doses for immunocompetent adults with normal renal function

equivalent for treatment of herpes zoster.[19] Because of their improved pharmacokinetic profiles and simpler dosing regimens, valaciclovir and famciclovir are preferred over aciclovir for this indication.

Herpes zoster in immunocompromised patients.

In a study of herpes zoster in bone marrow transplant or cancer patients, famciclovir (500mg three times daily) or aciclovir (800mg five times daily) for 10 days were shown to be therapeutically equivalent.[20] Famciclovir was also effective in an open-label study of herpes zoster therapy in HIV-seropositive patients.

Dosage in special circumstances.

Penciclovir is cleared predominantly by renal mechanisms, so adjustments of famciclovir dosing are required in patients with advanced renal insufficiency, as shown in Table 205.7. In patients with hepatic insufficiency, the rate of conversion of famciclovir to penciclovir is decreased, but the plasma AUC value for penciclovir is not significantly changed; no famciclovir dosage modification in hepatic impairment is necessary.[21] Plasma penciclovir concentrations are slightly higher in elderly patients treated with famciclovir due to age-related reduction in glomerular filtration rates, but dosage modifications on the basis of age are not required. Absorption after topical application is minimal and no dosage modifications are required for use of penciclovir 1% cream. No liquid preparation of famciclovir is currently available and few data regarding use in small children are available. Famciclovir has not been approved for use during pregnancy.

Adverse reactions

Safety data collected from over 3000 patients involved in clinical studies of famciclovir have shown the drug to be very safe and well tolerated.[22] The most frequently reported adverse experiences have included headache, nausea and diarrhea, but the frequency of these events was similar in both famciclovir and placebo recipients.

No clinically significant drug interactions have been noted with famciclovir. Co-administration of famciclovir with cimetidine or theophylline will increase the penciclovir AUC by about 20%. Co-administration of famciclovir and digoxin results in a 19% increase in the peak digoxin concentration, but no change in the AUC.

Topical penciclovir 1% cream is associated with no significant toxicities and has no known drug interactions.

Table 205.7 Famciclovir dosage modification for renal impairment.

FAMCICLOVIR DOSAGE MODIFICATION FOR RENAL IMPAIRMENT			
Normal dosage regimen	CrCl (ml/min)	Adjusted dosage regimen	
		Dose (mg)	Dosing interval (h)
Famciclovir 500mg q8h	>60	500	8
	40–59	500	12
	20–39	500	24
	<20	250	24
	HD	250	Post-HD
Famciclovir 125mg q12h	≥40	125	12
	20–39	125	24
	<20	125	24
	HD	125	Post-HD
Famciclovir 250mg q12h	>40	250	12
	20–39	125	12
	<20	125	24
	HD	125	Post-HD
Famciclovir 500mg q12h	≥40	500	12
	20–39	500	24
	<20	250	24
	HD	250	Post-HD

CrCl, creatinine clearance
FCV, famciclovir
HD, hemodialysis
Post-HD, after each hemodialysis

Resistance

The majority of clinically encountered aciclovir-resistant HSV and VZV isolates are TK deficient and thus will also be resistant to penciclovir, which requires viral TK for activation. However, some HSV strains that are aciclovir resistant by virtue of altered TK or DNA polymerase mutations may retain susceptibility to penciclovir. In general, however, penciclovir or famciclovir should not be considered as appropriate drugs for treatment of infections caused by aciclovir-resistant HSV or VZV.

Other drugs

Vidarabine

Vidarabine (adenine arabinoside) was the first intravenous antiviral drug accepted for widespread clinical use. Intravenous vidarabine was shown to be effective for herpes simplex encephalitis, neonatal HSV infections and for HSV and VZV infections in immunocompromised patients. Vidarabine, however, was not effective for aciclovir-resistant HSV infections in AIDS patients. Vidarabine 3% ophthalmic ointment is used for treatment of HSV keratoconjunctivitis. Vidarabine has now largely been replaced by more effective and less toxic antiviral drugs.

Trifluridine

Trifluridine is a fluorinated pyrimidine nucleoside with good *in vitro* activity against HSV. Trifluridine triphosphate is a competitive inhibitor of HSV DNA polymerase. Trifluridine is too toxic for systemic administration, but has been used successfully as a 1% ophthalmic solution for topical therapy of HSV keratitis. Topical trifluridine has also been used with moderate success for treatment of aciclovir-resistant mucocutaneous infections in AIDS patients.

Idoxuridine

Idoxuridine is an iodinated thymidine derivative with activity against HSV. Use of idoxurdine has been limited to topical application, since systemic administration is associated with significant myelosuppression. Idoxuridine (in topical 1% solution and 0.5% ointment formulations) has been used successfully for treatment of HSV keratitis, but has largely been replaced by topical trifluridine and aciclovir for this indication. Topical application of 15% idoxuridine in dimethyl sulfoxide was shown to shorten the course of herpes labialis in a placebo-controlled trial, and is available in Europe but not in the United States.

Brivudin

Brivudin (bromovinyldeoxyuridine; BVDU) is a highly potent antiviral agent with selective activity against HSV-1 and VZV. The drug has been evaluated for herpes zoster and varicella in both immunocompetent and immunocompromised populations and appears to be therapeutically equivalent to aciclovir. Because of concerns about potential toxicity, commercial development of brivudin has halted in most countries. The drug is available in Germany as a 125mg tablet and as a 0.1% ointment for ophthalmologic use.

n-Docosanol

n-Docosanol is a 22-carbon fatty alcohol with *in vitro* activity against several enveloped viruses, including HSV-1 and HSV-2. The drug acts by interfering with viral entry into target cells. In a multicenter, placebo-controlled study of 743 patients with recurrent herpes labialis (pooled data from two separate studies), 10% docosanol cream or placebo was applied five times a day within 12 hours of onset of prodrome or erythema. Median time to healing was reduced by 17 hours in the docosanol treatment group. n-Docosanol is available over the counter in a 2g tube of 10% cream and is indicated for recurrences of herpes labialis. It is to be applied to the area five times each day with the beginning of prodomal symptoms for a maximum of 10 days.[23]

DRUGS FOR TREATMENT OF CYTOMEGALOVIRUS INFECTIONS

Ganciclovir and valganciclovir

Mechanism of action and in vitro activity

Ganciclovir, 9-[(1,3-dihydroxy-2-propoxy) methyl] guanine, is a nucleoside analogue that is structurally similar to aciclovir, but has a hydroxymethyl group at the 3′ position of the acyclic side chain.[24] This relatively minor structural modification accounts for enhanced activity of ganciclovir against human CMV and also for the drug's greater toxicity. Ganciclovir triphosphate is a potent inhibitor of herpesvirus DNA replication, acting as both an inhibitor of and a substrate for viral DNA polymerase.[25] In HSV- or VZV-infected cells, monophosphorylation of ganciclovir is induced by viral TK, as also occurs with aciclovir. In CMV-infected cells, ganciclovir monophosphorylation is carried out by a protein kinase encoded by the UL97 gene. The di- and triphosphorylation steps are mediated by cellular kinases. On a molar basis, aciclovir triphosphate is actually a more potent inhibitor of CMV than is ganciclovir triphosphate. However, aciclovir is a poor substrate for phosphorylation by the UL97 gene product; consequently, the concentration of ganciclovir triphosphate in CMV-infected cells is 10-fold higher than that of aciclovir triphosphate. Furthermore, the half-life of ganciclovir triphosphate in CMV-infected cells is 16.5 hours, compared with 2.5 hours for aciclovir triphosphate. Ganciclovir triphosphate does not function as a chain terminator, and can be incorporated into elongating viral DNA (and, to a much lesser extent, human DNA) where it functions to slow DNA chain extension.

Ganciclovir and aciclovir have approximately comparable *in vitro* activity against HSV-1, HSV-2 and VZV. However, ganciclovir is much more active against CMV, with IC_{50} values of 0.1–1.8μg/ml against clinical isolates.

Pharmacokinetics and distribution

Intravenous infusion of ganciclovir at a dose of 5mg/kg yields peak and trough plasma levels of approximately 8 and 1μg/ml. Plasma protein binding is 1–2%. Reported plasma-to-CSF ratios for ganciclovir have ranged from 24% to 70%. Ganciclovir is not metabolized and is cleared by renal mechanisms, with an elimination half-life of about 3 hours. Ganciclovir is poorly absorbed after oral administration, with bio-availability of only 5–9%. Following oral dosing of ganciclovir at 1000mg three times daily, steady-state plasma peak and trough concentrations of 1.2 and 0.2μg/ml are achieved. To overcome the limited oral bio-availability of ganciclovir, a prodrug called valganciclovir has been developed.[26]

Valganciclovir, the L-valyl ester of ganciclovir, is rapidly and almost completely hydrolyzed to ganciclovir in the liver and intestinal wall. Bio-availability of ganciclovir is about 60% from the prodrug formulation and is significantly increased with food administration. Maximum plasma ganciclovir concentrations are 4–5-fold higher than those achieved after oral dosing with the parent drug. Oral valganciclovir doses of 450mg and 875mg once daily for 3 days produced peak plasma ganciclovir concentrations of 3.3 and 6.1μg/ml, respectively. The AUC of ganciclovir after administration of 900mg valganciclovir is about 26μg/ml/h, which is comparable to the AUC following administration of ganciclovir dosed at 5mg/kg intravenously.

Route of administration and dosage

Ganciclovir is available as an oral capsule, an intravenous formulation and as a delayed-release intraocular implant device. Recommended doses will vary with the indication. For treatment of acute CMV disease, the usual dose of intravenous ganciclovir is 5mg/kg every 12 hours. Oral ganciclovir, supplied as 250mg capsules, can be used for maintenance therapy of CMV disease at a dosage of 1000–2000mg three times daily, but has largely been replaced by oral valganciclovir.

Valganciclovir is available as a 450mg tablet. Recommended dose for induction therapy of acute CMV retinitis is 900mg by mouth with food twice daily for a total of 21 days, followed by maintenance therapy at a dose of 900mg by mouth once daily with food.

Indications

CMV retinitis

Ganciclovir was the first drug approved for treatment of CMV retinitis, a sight-threatening disease that occurs in AIDS patients and other immunocompromised hosts. The therapeutic approach for CMV retinitis is to halt disease progression with high-dose induction therapy, then prevent disease relapse by maintenance therapy continued for the duration of the immunosuppression.[27] The usual dose of ganciclovir for induction therapy is 5mg/kg given intravenous every 12 hours for 14–21 days. In uncontrolled studies, ganciclovir therapy halted progression of CMV retinitis in over 80% of patients. Without long-term maintenance therapy, virtually all AIDS patients will experience a relapse of retinitis within 30 days after induction therapy. Continuation of maintenance therapy can extend the interval to first relapse to a median of about 75 days. The usual maintenance regimen with intravenous ganciclovir is 5mg/kg once daily. High-dose oral ganciclovir (4500–6000mg daily) is almost as effective as intravenous ganciclovir for maintenance therapy and may be associated with fewer complications.

For oral therapy of CMV retinitis, ganciclovir has largely been supplanted by valganciclovir. In a study of 160 HIV-positive patients with newly diagnosed CMV retinitis, induction therapy with valganciclovir 900mg orally twice daily was shown to be as effective as ganciclovir given intravenously at 5mg/kg every 12 hours in halting progression of retinitis during the first 4 weeks of therapy.[28] Those receiving induction with valganciclovir experienced more diarrhea than those who received intravenous ganciclovir (19% vs 10%, $p = 0.11$), while those treated with intravenous ganciclovir developed more catheter-related events (9% versus 4%). The incidence of neutropenia was about 14% in both groups.[28] CMV retinitis is currently the only approved indication for valganciclovir.

Intravitreal injections of ganciclovir have been used effectively for treatment of CMV retinitis, although ganciclovir intraocular implants are a better option for patients who cannot tolerate systemic ganciclovir therapy. Median time to relapse of CMV retinitis is longer with ganciclovir intraocular implants then with oral or intravenous ganciclovir and their use should be strongly considered in patients whose retinal lesions are imminently sight threatening.[29] However, there is potential morbidity associated with surgical implantation of the devices, which must be replaced about every 6 months. Unlike systemic ganciclovir therapy, an intraocular implant will not prevent development of CMV retinitis in the contralateral eye or CMV disease in other organs.

Ganciclovir, valganciclovir, foscarnet and cidofovir (see below) are all effective for initial and maintenance therapy of CMV retinitis in AIDS patients (see Table 205.8). All of these drugs can be associated with significant toxicity; drug selection in an individual patient hinges, to some extent, on which adverse effects would be most tolerable. Ganciclovir is primarily myelosuppressive, while foscarnet and cidofovir are nephrotoxic. Ganciclovir would be preferred in a patient who has baseline renal dysfunction or who requires therapy with other nephrotoxic drugs. Conversely, foscarnet might be a better choice in a patient with significant baseline neutropenia. Despite the survival benefits for AIDS patients shown for foscarnet therapy in some studies, most clinicians use ganciclovir or valganciclovir for initial therapy on the basis of its more predictable adverse effects. Combination therapy (e.g. ganciclovir plus foscarnet) may be more effective for CMV disease in selected patients.

CMV gastrointestinal disease

In immunocompromised patients, CMV can cause esophagitis, gastritis, enteritis and especially colitis. Anecdotal data suggest that intravenous ganciclovir is effective for CMV colitis, although data from controlled studies are limited. In a placebo-controlled trial in AIDS

SYSTEMIC ANTIVIRAL THERAPY FOR CMV RETINITIS†		
Drugs	**Induction therapy***	**Maintenance therapy***
Ganciclovir	5mg/kg iv q12h × 14–21 days	5mg/kg iv daily or 1000–2000mg po tid daily
Valganciclovir	900mg po bid × 14–21 days	900mg po daily
Foscarnet	90mg/kg iv q12h (or 60mg/kg iv q8h) × 14–21 days	90–120mg/kg iv daily
Cidofovir	5mg/kg iv weekly × 2–3 weeks	5mg/kg iv every other week

† Recommended doses for adults with normal renal function
* Other therapeutic options include intraocular drug implants or intravitreal drug injections

Table 205.8 Systemic antiviral therapy for CMV retinitis.

patients with CMV colitis, intravenous ganciclovir (5mg/kg twice daily) reduced virus shedding, improved mucosal appearance by colonoscopic examination and reduced the incidence of extracolonic CMV disease; however, symptom scores between the ganciclovir and placebo groups were similar.[30] A placebo-controlled trial of ganciclovir for CMV gastrointestinal disease in bone marrow transplant recipients also failed to demonstrate symptomatic improvement. Despite these findings, ganciclovir continues to be used for treatment of CMV gastrointestinal disease on the strength of clinical experience. There is no consensus regarding the necessity or duration of maintenance therapy in this setting.

CMV pneumonitis

CMV pulmonary infections following allogeneic bone marrow transplantation are associated with very high mortality rates. In early clinical studies, ganciclovir therapy of CMV pneumonia did not result in improved survival. More recent studies have demonstrated that combination therapy with ganciclovir plus intravenous immune globulin is more effective than either intervention alone, resulting in survival rates over 50%. A commonly used regimen for active CMV pneumonia is intravenous ganciclovir 5mg/kg twice daily plus intravenous immune globulin (0.5g/kg every other day) for 14–21 days, followed by maintenance therapy with ganciclovir 5mg/kg daily for at least 2 more weeks.

Other CMV infections

Case reports and uncontrolled clinical trials have ascribed benefit to ganciclovir therapy for a variety of indications. In solid organ transplant recipients, ganciclovir has been reported to be effective for CMV hepatitis, CMV pneumonia and disseminated CMV syndrome. Improvement in CMV-induced polyradiculopathy and encephalitis has been described in AIDS patients treated with ganciclovir. Controlled studies are required to accurately assess the value of ganciclovir for these indications.

Prophylaxis of CMV disease

Intravenous ganciclovir administered to bone marrow transplant patients either pretransplantation or at the time of engraftment significantly reduced the incidence of CMV disease.[31,32] However, ganciclovir prophylaxis resulted in significant neutropenia, thus offsetting any survival benefit. An alternative scheme is to withhold ganciclovir until there is early laboratory evidence (e.g. by PCR or antigenemia assay) of CMV activation.[33] This approach permits initiation of therapy before CMV disease becomes symptomatic, while avoiding the risk of neutropenia associated with long-term ganciclovir administration. However, this 'pre-emptive' therapy approach is currently limited by lack of a sensitive, specific and readily available CMV diagnostic assay.

Benefits of intravenous ganciclovir therapy for prophylaxis of CMV infection in solid organ transplant recipients have varied with the transplant type, immunosuppressive regimen and CMV serologic status of the donor and recipient.[34] In general, high-risk patients (donor CMV positive, recipient CMV negative) require long-term (100 days) rather than short-term (28 days) prophylaxis to effectively prevent CMV disease. The 'pre-emptive therapy' approach discussed above has also been successfully employed for management of CMV disease in solid organ transplant recipients.[35] Oral ganciclovir and valganciclovir have shown promise for CMV prophylaxis in solid organ transplant recipients.

Dosage in special circumstances

Because ganciclovir is cleared by renal mechanisms, dosage reduction is necessary in patients with creatinine clearance of <70ml/min (see Table 205.9).[25] About 50% of an administered dose is removed during 4 hours of hemodialysis and dosing after dialysis is recommended. Valganciclovir dosage adjustment is required for patients with creatinine clearance <60ml/min; the drug is not recommended for patients on hemodialysis. No dosage adjustments for hepatic impairment are necessary. Ganciclovir is mutagenic, carcinogenic and causes reproductive toxicity in animal models.[25] Use of ganciclovir or valganciclovir in pregnant or nursing women is not recommended without careful consideration of the risk–benefit ratio. Data on ganciclovir use in children are currently limited, but the drug is being evaluated for therapy of congenital CMV infections.

Adverse reactions

The most important adverse effects of ganciclovir noted in AIDS patients being treated for CMV retinitis were neutropenia and thrombocytopenia. About 40% developed granulocytopenia (absolute neutrophil count <1000/mm^3) and 15% had thrombocytopenia (platelet count <50000/mm^3). Hematologic toxicity is also seen, although less commonly, in organ transplant recipients. Neutropenia and thrombocytopenia are usually reversible when ganciclovir therapy is discontinued. In many patients requiring ganciclovir therapy, neutropenia can be prevented or treated by co-administration of granulocyte colony-stimulating factor. Renal dysfunction has been reported in up to 20% of transplant recipients receiving ganciclovir prophylaxis, although this may be related to co-administration of other nephrotoxic drugs. In animal models, ganciclovir produces significant reproductive toxicity, especially azoospermia.[25] Valganciclovir appears to have similar hematological toxicity to intravenous ganciclovir. Pooled data from two different studies indicate that 50% patients developed granulocytopenia (absolute neutrophil count <1000/mm^3), 35% experienced anemia (hemoglobin <9.5g/dl) and 23% developed thrombocytopenia (platelets <100000/μl). Gastrointestinal complaints were also common: 41% reported diarrhea, 30% nausea, 21% vomiting and 15% abdominal pain.

In vitro, ganciclovir and zidovudine have mutually antagonistic antiviral activity, but this observation has not been shown to be clinically significant. Ganciclovir should be used with caution in

Table 205.9 Ganciclovir and valganciclovir dosage modification for renal impairment.

GANCICLOVIR AND VALGANCICLOVIR DOSAGE MODIFICATION FOR RENAL IMPAIRMENT			
Normal dosage regimen	CrCl (ml/min)	Adjusted dosage regimen	
		Dose	Dosing interval (h)
Ganciclovir 5mg/kg iv q12h	≥70	5mg/kg	12
	50–69	2.5mg/kg	12
	25–49	2.5mg/kg	24
	10–24	1.25mg/kg	24
	HD	1.25mg/kg	Post-HD (TIW)
Ganciclovir 5mg/kg iv q24h	≥70	5mg/kg	24
	50–69	2.5mg/kg	24
	25–49	1.25mg/kg	24
	10–24	0.625mg/kg	24
	HD	0.625mg/kg	Post-HD (TIW)
Ganciclovir 1000mg po q8h	≥70	1000mg	8
	50–69	500mg	8
	25–49	500mg	24
	HD	500mg	Post-HD (TIW)
Valganciclovir 900mg po bid	>60	900mg	12
	40–59	450mg	12
	25–39	450mg	24
	10–24	450mg	48
	HD	NR	–
Valganciclovir 900mg po qd	>60	900mg	24
	40–59	450mg	24
	25–39	450mg	48
	10–24	450mg	Twice weekly
	HD	NR	–

CrCl, creatinine clearance
HD, hemodialysis
Post-HD, after each dialysis
TIW, three times weekly
NR, not recommended

combination with other myelosuppressive drugs such as zidovudine because of the risk of additive hematologic toxicity. Probenecid can reduce renal clearance of ganciclovir, resulting in clinically significant increases in ganciclovir AUC. Seizures have been reported in patients receiving concomitant therapy with ganciclovir and imipenem.

Resistance

HSV and VZV isolates that are TK deficient and aciclovir resistant will also be cross-resistant with ganciclovir. Ganciclovir resistance *in vitro* is defined as an $IC_{50}>6\mu M$ (1.5μg/ml). CMV isolates resistant to ganciclovir have been produced in the laboratory and isolated from patients with CMV disease.[36] In a study of 72 AIDS patients treated with ganciclovir, five of 13 culture-positive patients treated for >3 months excreted resistant virus.[37] Ganciclovir-resistant CMV has been identified as a cause of retinitis, encephalitis and polyradiculopathy in AIDS patients. CMV resistance to ganciclovir is usually secondary to mutations in the UL97 gene, although alterations in the DNA polymerase gene have also been described. UL97 mutants remain susceptible to foscarnet, although polymerase mutants cross-resistant to both ganciclovir and foscarnet have been identified. Foscarnet or cidofovir are therapeutic options for treatment of disease caused by ganciclovir-resistant CMV.

Foscarnet

Mechanism of action and in vitro activity

Foscarnet (trisodium phosphonoformic acid) is an analogue of inorganic pyrophosphate that functions as a noncompetitive inhibitor of herpesvirus DNA polymerase.[38] Foscarnet blocks the pyrophosphate binding site, preventing cleavage of pyrophosphate from deoxynucleotide triphosphates. Viral DNA polymerase is inhibited at foscarnet concentrations 100-fold lower than those required to inhibit cellular DNA polymerase. Unlike the aciclovir-like drugs discussed above, foscarnet is not a nucleoside analogue, does not require intracellular activation by viral kinase and is not incorporated into the viral DNA chain. Therefore, thymidine kinase-deficient HSV and VZV isolates that are resistant to aciclovir will remain susceptible to foscarnet. Foscarnet has *in vitro* activity against HSV, VZV, CMV, EBV and HHV-6. The IC_{50} for most clinical isolates of CMV is in the range of 100–300μM, but varies considerably with the experimental conditions. Foscarnet can also inhibit viral reverse transcriptase and has *in vitro* activity against hepatitis B virus and HIV.[38]

Pharmacokinetics and distribution

Foscarnet has low oral bio-availability (approximately 17%) and is administered only by the intravenous route. Peak plasma concentrations after steady-state dosing at 60mg/kg every 8 hours or 90mg/kg every 12 hours are about 500μM and 700μM, respectively.[38] Plasma protein binding is about 15%. CSF foscarnet levels demonstrate wide interpatient variability, but average about 66% of plasma levels at steady state. Foscarnet is not metabolized and about 80% of an administered dose is excreted unchanged in the urine by glomerular filtration and tubular secretion within 36 hours. About 20% of the foscarnet dose is retained in bone, presumably due to the drug's structural similarity to inorganic phosphate. This results in a complex pattern of drug disposition, in which the initial elimination half-life is about 4.5 hours, followed by a prolonged terminal half-life of about 88 hours as drug is released from bone.[38] Plasma foscarnet levels are reduced about 50% following hemodialysis; dosing after dialysis is recommended.

Route of administration and dosage

Foscarnet is available only as an intravenous formulation. The usual dose for induction therapy of CMV retinitis is 90mg/kg every 12 hours, with a maintenance dose of 90–120mg/kg every 24 hours. When given via a central venous catheter, the drug can be diluted to 24mg/ml; for infusion through peripheral vein catheters, foscarnet must be diluted to 12mg/ml to avoid local phlebitis. The foscarnet dose must be administered over at least 1 hour using an intravenous infusion pump; bolus infusion can result in severe toxicity. A topical 3% foscarnet cream formulation has been evaluated for therapy of herpes labialis, but is not commercially available.

Indications

CMV retinitis

Intravenous foscarnet is approved for treatment of CMV retinitis in immunocompromised patients. In controlled clinical trials, foscarnet therapy was shown to significantly delay progression of CMV retinitis in AIDS patients.[39] As discussed above with ganciclovir, long-term maintenance with foscarnet is required to extend the time to subsequent relapse in patients with CMV retinitis. The recommended foscarnet dosage in patients with normal renal function is 90mg/kg every 12 hours for 14–21 days for induction, followed by 90–120mg/kg daily indefinitely. In a controlled trial comparing foscarnet with ganciclovir for CMV retinitis in AIDS patients, the two drugs were therapeutically equivalent for retinitis, but extended survival (12.6 versus 8.5 months) was shown in the foscarnet group.[40] Foscarnet clearly has antiviral activity against HIV, but it is uncertain whether this accounts for the survival benefit demonstrated in this and other studies. However, foscarnet therapy was significantly more toxic than ganciclovir and patients had to discontinue foscarnet three times more often because of adverse effects.[41] Limited clinical experience has shown intravitreal foscarnet to be effective for CMV retinitis. Foscarnet is an effective alternative therapy for some patients with retinitis caused by ganciclovir-resistant strains of CMV, although dually resistant isolates can rarely occur. Combination therapy with ganciclovir plus foscarnet has been used successfully to treat refractory CMV infections in AIDS patients.[42]

Other CMV infections

Evidence for foscarnet efficacy for CMV infections other than retinitis is derived primarily from uncontrolled studies and clinical experience. Foscarnet has been used to treat CMV pneumonia and CMV colitis in AIDS patients. Attempts to use foscarnet for therapy or prophylaxis of CMV infections in bone marrow transplant recipients have met with variable success.

Aciclovir-resistant HSV and VZV infections

Foscarnet is the drug of choice for treatment of infections caused by aciclovir-resistant HSV and VZV.[43] In a controlled trial, foscarnet was clearly superior to vidarabine for treatment of aciclovir-resistant mucocutaneous HSV infections in patients with AIDS.

Dosage in special circumstances

Foscarnet is excreted by renal mechanisms and dosage adjustment is required even for minor degrees of renal insufficiency (see Table 205.10). Serum creatinine should be monitored at least every other day during foscarnet therapy to assess the need for further dose adjustment. Dosage adjustment in hepatic impairment is not required. The safety of foscarnet during pregnancy has not been adequately evaluated and use is not recommended unless no other alternative therapy is available. Little information has been published regarding foscarnet safety and tolerance in neonates and children.

Adverse reactions

The most important adverse effect caused by foscarnet is nephrotoxicity.[41] Dose-limiting renal toxicity occurs in at least 15–20% of patients treated with foscarnet for CMV retinitis. The primary mechanism of renal toxicity appears to be acute tubular necrosis, although interstitial nephritis and crystalline nephropathy have also been described. Loading the patient with intravenous saline prior to foscarnet infusion can help reduce the risk of nephrotoxicity. In most cases, the renal dysfunction is reversible and serum creatinine will return to normal within 2–4 weeks after foscarnet therapy is discontinued. However, irreversible renal failure may occur in patients who are volume depleted or who receive concomitant therapy with other nephrotoxic medications. Foscarnet can induce a variety of electrolyte and metabolic abnormalities, most notably hypocalcemia.[44] Hypercalcemia, hypomagnesemia, hypokalemia and hypo- and hyperphosphatemia have also been reported. The acute decline in ionized serum calcium that can occur with foscarnet infusion may be due to formation of a complex between foscarnet and free calcium.[44] Further depletion of total serum calcium seen with

Table 205.10 Foscarnet dosage modification for renal impairment.

FOSCARNET DOSAGE MODIFICATION FOR RENAL IMPAIRMENT

Normal dosage regimen	CrCl (ml/min/kg)	Adjusted dosage regimen	
		Dose (mg/kg)	Dosing interval (h)
Foscarnet 90mg/kg q12h	>1.4	90	12
	>1.0–1.4	70	12
	>0.8–1.0	50	12
	>0.6–0.8	80	24
	>0.5–0.6	60	24
	>0.4–0.5	50	24
	<0.4	NR	–
Foscarnet 120mg/kg q24h	>1.4	120	24
	>1.0–1.4	90	24
	>0.8–1.0	65	24
	>0.6–0.8	105	48
	>0.5–0.6	80	48
	>0.4–0.5	65	48
	<0.4	NR	–

CrCl, creatinine clearance
NR, not recommended

long-term drug administration may be caused by renal calcium wasting, abnormal bone metabolism, concurrent hypomagnesemia or some combination of these factors. Foscarnet-induced electrolyte disturbances can predispose the patient to cardiac arrhythmias, tetany, altered mental status or seizures. It is mandatory that serum creatinine and electrolyte levels be closely monitored during foscarnet therapy. Foscarnet is much less myelosuppressive than ganciclovir, but anemia was reported in 10–50% of AIDS patients receiving foscarnet. Patients, especially uncircumcised males, may develop genital ulcerations due to local toxicity of high foscarnet concentrations in urine. Nausea and vomiting has been reported by 20–30% of patients receiving foscarnet. Other infrequent adverse effects include headache, diarrhea and abnormal liver function tests. When possible, foscarnet should be administered through a central venous line to avoid peripheral thrombophlebitis.

Specific drug interactions with foscarnet have not been described, although there is significant potential for additive toxicity. Concurrent therapy with foscarnet and intravenous pentamidine can result in severe and potentially fatal hypocalcemia. Concomitant administration of foscarnet with other potentially nephrotoxic drugs such as amphotericin B or aminoglycosides can compound the risk of serious nephrotoxicity. Foscarnet can be safely administered to patients receiving zidovudine, although there may be an increased risk of anemia.

Resistance

Although uncommon, foscarnet-resistant isolates of CMV, VZV and HSV have been encountered in AIDS patients receiving foscarnet therapy. Resistance is due to a mutation in the DNA polymerase gene which means that, in some circumstances, the foscarnet-resistant isolate may remain susceptible to aciclovir or ganciclovir. However, CMV isolates cross-resistant to both ganciclovir and foscarnet (containing both polymerase and UL97 mutations) have been recovered from AIDS patients. Cidofovir may be an effective alternative drug in this setting, but in vitro antiviral susceptibility testing is necessary to guide drug selection.

Cidofovir

Mechanism of action and in vitro activity

Cidofovir is a nucleotide analogue of cytosine monophosphate with potent broad-spectrum antiviral activity. Unlike aciclovir and other nucleoside analogues which require monophosphorylation by viral kinases for activation, cidofovir already carries a phosphonate group and does not require viral enzymes for conversion to cidofovir diphosphate, the active antiviral compound. Cidofovir diphosphate competitively inhibits the DNA polymerases of herpesviruses, thereby blocking DNA synthesis and viral replication. Cidofovir diphosphate inhibits viral DNA polymerases at concentrations much lower than those required to inhibit cellular DNA polymerases, accounting for its selectivity of action.[45] Cidofovir has potent in vitro activity against human CMV, with IC_{50} values in the range of 0.1–0.9μg/ml. Cidofovir retains activity against most CMV clinical isolates that are resistant to ganciclovir. Cidofovir also demonstrates in vitro activity against HSV and VZV (including TK-deficient, aciclovir-resistant isolates), adenovirus, poxvirus (including variola or smallpox virus) and human papillomavirus.

Pharmacokinetics and distribution

Serum cidofovir concentrations are dose proportional over a dosing range of 1.0–10.0mg/kg. Intravenous infusion of cidofovir at a dosage of 5mg/kg produces peak plasma concentrations of about 11μg/ml. The terminal half-life is 2.6 hours. Approximately 90% of the intravenous cidofovir dose is excreted by the kidneys within 24 hours, with clearance involving both glomerular filtration and tubular secretion. At cidofovir doses higher than 3mg/kg, concomitant administration of probenecid can block tubular secretion of cidofovir and reduce its renal clearance.[45] Cidofovir diphosphate and its metabolites have prolonged intracellular half-lives, which permit cidofovir to be effectively administered at extended dosing intervals.

Route of administration and dosage

Cidofovir for intravenous administration is supplied as 375mg of an aqueous solution (75mg/ml). The selected dose is diluted in 100ml of normal saline prior to administration. For induction therapy, the usual dose of cidofovir is 5mg/kg infused over 1 hour once weekly. The dose for maintenance therapy for CMV disease is 5mg/kg administered once every 2 weeks. To minimize nephrotoxicity, patients should receive 1 liter of normal saline intravenously over 1–2 hours immediately prior to cidofovir dose and an additional 1 liter of normal saline immediately following the cidofovir dose. Probenecid is given at a dose of 2g orally 3 hours before the cidofovir dose, then 1 doses at 2 hours and 8 hours after completion of the cidofovir infusion, for a total probenecid dose of 4g. Prodrugs of cidofovir (e.g. cyclic HPMPC) are under development.

Indications

CMV infections

Cidofovir has been approved in the United States for treatment of CMV retinitis. In a study of 48 AIDS patients with CMV retinitis, time to progression of disease was significantly longer in the cidofovir treatment group (120 days) compared with the deferred treatment group (22 days).[46,47] Cidofovir has also been shown to be effective for CMV retinitis in patients who have relapsed on, or were intolerant to, ganciclovir or foscarnet. Efficacy of intravenous cidofovir was similar to oral ganciclovir plus ganciclovir implant in 61 AIDS patients with CMV retinitis, but adverse effects differed between the two treatment groups.[48] These data indicate that intravenous cidofovir is effective for both initial and salvage therapy of CMV retinitis in AIDS patients.

Cidofovir has a potential role for pre-emptive treatment of CMV disease in bone marrow transplant recipients, but has been evaluated in only a limited number of patients and should currently be considered as second-line therapy.

HSV infections

Because cidofovir is not dependent on thymidine kinase for activation, the drug retains activity against aciclovir-resistant HSV. Published case reports suggest that cidofovir is effective for treatment of aciclovir- and foscarnet-resistant mucocutaneous HSV infections, but data from controlled clinical trials are currently lacking.[49] An investigational topical preparation of cidofovir has also been evaluated for this indication. Cidofovir gel (0.3% or 1%) applied topically to mucocutaneous HSV lesions in AIDS patients resulted in >50% reduction in lesion surface area in half of the cidofovir-treated patients. Six of 20 cidofovir-treated patients (versus 0 of 10 placebo-treated patients) had complete lesion healing.

Human papillomavirus

Cidofovir has potent *in vitro* activity against HPV. Topical preparations and intralesional injections are under evaluation for treatment of laryngeal papillomatosis and genital warts.

Poxvirus infections

Topical 3% cidofovir has been used on an investigational basis to treat severe cases of molluscum contagiosum. Cidofovir has activity against orthopoxvirus infections in animal models and has been suggested as a treatment for smallpox, monkeypox and disseminated vaccinia infections in humans.

Dosage in special circumstances

Because intravenous cidofovir can cause significant nephrotoxicity, initiation of therapy in patients with pre-existing renal dysfunction (serum creatinine >1.5mg/dl, calculated creatinine clearance ≤55ml/min or proteinuria >100mg/dl [≥2+]) is not recommended. Declining renal function during cidofovir therapy mandates dosage adjustment. If the serum creatinine increases by 0.3–0.4mg/dl above baseline, the cidofovir dose should be reduced from 5 to 3mg/kg. If the serum creatinine increases ≥0.5mg/dl above baseline or if proteinuria ≥3+ develops, cidofovir therapy should be discontinued. Dosage adjustment in patients with hepatic impairment is not required. Cidofovir is embryotoxic in animals and the drug should not be used during pregnancy unless there are no other therapeutic options. Cidofovir has not been systematically evaluated in children or elderly patients.

Adverse reactions

The most important safety concern with cidofovir therapy is nephrotoxicity. Pretreatment with intravenous hydration and probenecid (which blocks cidofovir tubular secretion) reduces the incidence of nephrotoxicity. In a clinical trial using cidofovir 5mg/kg plus probenecid, proteinuria occurred in five of 41 patients (12%) and elevated serum creatinine levels in two of 41 patients (5%). Neutropenia (ANC <750 WBC/ mm^3) was observed in 15% of cidofovir recipients.[46] Anemia, thrombocytopenia and hepatotoxicity have not been observed with cidofovir therapy. Ocular complications (including iritis, anterior uveitis and hypotony) have been described following intravenous or intravitreal cidofovir administration.

Probenecid, a benzoic acid derivative with a sulfa moiety, can cause allergic symptoms (e.g. fever, chills, rash) in patients allergic to sulfonamides. Patients with a history of severe sulfa hypersensitivity should not be treated with probenecid and, consequently, should not receive cidofovir. Other probenecid-related adverse effects include headache, nausea and vomiting, which can be minimized by administering the drug on a full stomach. In a CMV retinitis trial, probenecid-related adverse effects occurred in 23 of 41 patients (56%) and were dose limiting in three patients (7%).[46]

Cidofovir injections in rats were associated with mammary adenocarcinomas, but surveillance studies in treated patients have not demonstrated any excess frequency of tumors. Cidofovir administration causes embryotoxicity and impaired spermatogenesis in animals; male and female patients are advised to use adequate birth control during and for 3 months after completion of cidofovir therapy.

No specific drug interactions with cidofovir have been described, although concomitant therapy with other nephrotoxic drugs may result in additive toxicity. Probenecid, however, is known to alter the renal excretion of a wide variety of drugs. The dose of zidovudine should be reduced to 50% on days when probenecid administration is planned.

Resistance

Instances of clinical failure of cidofovir therapy due to drug resistance have been reported. CMV resistance to cidofovir results from a mutation in the viral polymerase gene and resistant isolates may exhibit cross-resistance to ganciclovir and/or foscarnet. *In vitro* susceptibility testing is necessary in this circumstance to guide appropriate drug selection.

Fomivirsen

Mechanism of action and in vitro activity

Fomivirsen is a 21-nucleotide phosphorothioate oligonucleotide designed as an antisense molecule with activity against CMV.[50] The oligonucleotide is complementary to mRNA from the immediate-early region 2 of CMV. Antisense inhibition of target gene expression, while necessary for optimal antiviral activity, only partially explains the activity of fomivirsen against CMV. Nonspecific interactions between the oligonucleotide and virus particles may prevent adsorption or lead to inhibition of enzymes required for viral DNA synthesis. Fomivirsen has activity against clinical CMV isolates, including isolates resistant to conventional antiviral drugs, with a median IC_{50} of 0.37μM in tissue culture.

In an open-label, dose-ranging study, increasing doses of fomivirsen were given to 22 AIDS patients (28 eyes) with refractory CMV retinitis. Decreased retinal CMV activity was noted in patients who received 300μg of fomivirsen by intravitreal injection every 1–2 weeks. In another study, 28 AIDS patients with newly diagnosed CMV retinitis (with less than 25% retinal involvement) were randomized to receive prompt treatment with fomivirsen or to defer treatment. In the treatment arm, 18 patients received 150μg of fomivirsen every week for 3 weeks then every other week. Median time to progression was 71 days in patients who received prompt treatment versus 14 days in the deferred group ($p = 0.0056$).

Pharmacokinetics and distribution

When cynomolgus monkeys were given 11, 57 or 115μg of fomivirsen intravitreally, maximum vitreal concentrations (ranging from 0.11 to 1.28μM) were achieved 2 days after injection of all doses. For the same dosages, retinal concentrations increased in a logarithmic pattern, with maximal concentration obtained 2 days after injection for all doses, ranging from 0.12 to 0.88μM. For the 115μg dose, the vitreal and retinal half-lives were 22 hours and 78 hours, respectively. Electrophoretic analyses of retina and vitreous specimens indicate the oligonucleotide is metabolized by exonucleolytic cleavage. Both intact drug and its metabolic products diffuse from the vitreous humor to the retina and it is hypothesized that the active metabolism occurs in both compartments.

Route of administration and dosage

Fomivirsen is supplied in single-use vials containing 0.25ml of 6.6mg/ml solution. Dosage for induction therapy of CMV retinitis is 330μg given intravitreally every other week for two doses. Maintenance therapy is 330μg given intravitreally every 4 weeks.

Indications

Fomivirsen is indicated for treatment of CMV retinitis in AIDS patients who have failed or are intolerant of other CMV therapies, including those with CMV that is resistant to ganciclovir and foscarnet. It is not recommended for use in patients who have received intravitreal or intravenous cidofovir. Fomivirsen is not indicated for systemic CMV therapy and will not protect the contralateral eye from involvement.

Dosage in special circumstances

As there is little systemic exposure to fomivirsen after intravitreal injection, no dose adjustments are required. This drug has not been studied in pregnant or lactating women or in pediatric or geriatric populations.

Adverse reactions

The most common adverse reactions reported were increased intraocular pressure and mild to moderate intraocular inflammation of the anterior and posterior chambers. The combined incidence of ocular reactions was 10–12% of patients treated every other week and 20% in patients treated weekly. Other adverse reactions reported in 5–20% patients included abnormal or blurred vision, conjunctival hemorrhage, retinal detachment and retinal edema. Topical steroids have been used with success to ameliorate some of these effects.

Resistance

A fomivirsen-resistant CMV isolate has been developed by exposing a laboratory strain to increasing concentrations of the drug. This resistant virus did not prove to have mutations which would have altered specificity for the fomivirsen target sequence. This provides more evidence that both antisense specific and nonspecific mechanisms are involved in the drug's activity against CMV. There have been no reports of formivirsen-resistant CMV isolates recovered from patients.

REFERENCES

1. Whitley RJ, Gnann JW. Acyclovir: a decade later. N Engl J Med 1992;327:782–9.
2. Perry CM, Faulds D. Valaciclovir: a review of its antiviral, pharmacokinetic properties and therapeutic efficacy in herpesvirus infections. Drugs 1996;52:754–72.
3. Fife KH, Crumpacker CS, Mertz GJ, *et al.* Recurrence and resistance patterns of herpes simplex virus following cessation of >6 years of chronic suppression with acyclovir. J Infect Dis 1994;169:1338–41.
4. Wald A, Zeh J, Barnum G, *et al.* Suppression of subclinical shedding of herpes simplex virus type 2 with acyclovir. Ann Intern Med 1996;124:8–15.
5. Fife KH, Barbarash RA, Rudolph T, *et al.* Valaciclovir versus acyclovir in the treatment of first-episode genital herpes infection. Results of an international, multicenter, double-blind, randomized clinical trial. Sex Transm Dis 1997;24:481–6.
6. Tyring SK, Douglas JMJ, Corey L, *et al.* A randomized, placebo-controlled comparison of oral valacyclovir and acyclovir in immunocompetent patients with recurrent genital herpes infections. Arch Dermatol 1998;134:185–91.
7. Brocklehurst P, Kinghorn G, Carney O, *et al.* A randomised placebo controlled trial of suppressive acyclovir in late pregnancy in women with recurrent genital herpes infection. Br J Obstet Gynaecol 1998;105:275–80.
8. Wood MJ, Kay R, Dworkin RH, *et al.* Oral acyclovir therapy accelerates pain resolution in patients with herpes zoster: a meta-analysis of placebo-controlled trials. Clin Infect Dis 1996;22:341–7.
9. Beutner KR, Friedman DJ, Forszpaniak C, *et al.* Valaciclovir compared with acyclovir for improved therapy for herpes zoster in immunocompetent adults. Antimicrob Agents Chemother 1995;39:1546–53.
10. Lowance D, Neumayer HH, Legendre CM, *et al.* Valacyclovir for the prevention of cytomegalovirus disease after renal transplantation. International Valacyclovir Cytomegalovirus Prophylaxis Transplantation Study Group. N Engl J Med 1999;340:1462–70.
11. Centers for Disease Control and Prevention. Pregnancy outcomes following systemic prenatal acyclovir exposure, June 1, 1984–June 30, 1993. MMWR 1993;42:806–9.
12. Acosta EP, Fletcher CV. Valacyclovir. Ann Pharmacother 1997;31:185–91.
13. Gaudreau A, Hill E, Balfour HHJ, *et al.* Phenotypic and genotypic characterization of acyclovir-resistant herpes simplex viruses from immunocompromised patients. J Infect Dis 1998;178:297–303.
14. Boyd MB, Safrin S, Kern EB. Penciclovir: a review of spectrum of activity, selectivity, and cross-resistance pattern. Antiviral Chemistry Chemother 1993;4 (suppl):3–11.
15. Sacks SL, Aoki FY, Diaz-Mitoma F, *et al.* Patient-initiated, twice-daily oral famciclovir for early recurrent genital herpes. A randomized, double-blind multicenter trial. JAMA 1996;276:44–9.
16. Diaz-Mitoma F, Sibbald RG, Shafran SD, *et al.* Oral famciclovir for the suppression of recurrent genital herpes (a randomized controlled trial). JAMA 1998;280:887–92.
17. Schacker T, Hu HL, Koelle DM, *et al.* Famciclovir for the suppression of symptomatic and asymptomatic herpes simplex virus reactivation in HIV-infected persons. Ann Intern Med 1998;128:21–8.
18. Tyring S, Barbarash RA, Nahlik JE, *et al.* Famciclovir for the treatment of acute herpes zoster: effects on acute disease and post-herpetic neuralgia: a randomized, double-blind, placebo-controlled trial. Ann Intern Med 1995;123:89–96.
19. Tyring SK, Beutner KR, Tucker BA, *et al.* Antiviral therapy for herpes zoster: randomized, controlled clinical trial of valacyclovir and famciclovir therapy in immunocompetent patients 50 years and older. Arch Fam Med 2000;9:863–9.
20. Tyring S, Belanger R, Bezwoda W, *et al.* A randomized, double-blind trial of famciclovir versus acyclovir for the treatment of localized dermatomal herpes zoster in immunocompromised patients. Cancer Invest 2001;19:13–22.
21. Perry CM, Wagstaff AJ. Famciclovir: a review of its pharmacological properties and therapeutic efficacy in herpesvirus infections. Drugs 1995;50:396–415.
22. Saltzman R, Jurewicz R, Boon R. Safety of famciclovir in patients with herpes zoster and genital herpes. Antimicrob Agents Chemother 1994;38:2454–7.
23. McKeough MB, Spruance SL. Comparison of new topical treatments for herpes labialis: efficacy of penciclovir cream, acyclovir cream, and n-docosanol cream against experimental cutaneous herpes simplex virus type 1 infection. Arch Dermatol 2001;137:1153–8.
24. Crumpacker CS. Ganciclovir. N Engl J Med 1996;335:721–9.
25. Faulds D, Heel RC. Ganciclovir. A review of its antiviral activity, pharmacokinetic properties and therapeutic efficacy in cytomegalovirus infections. Drugs 1990;39:597–638.
26. Curran M, Noble S. Valganciclovir. Drugs 2001;61:1145–50.
27. Jacobson MA. Current management of cytomegalovirus retinitis in AIDS: update on ganciclovir and foscarnet for CMV infections. Adv Exper Med Biol 1996;394:85–92.
28. Martin DF, Sierra-Madero J, Walmsley S, *et al.* A controlled trial of valganciclovir as induction therapy for cytomegalovirus retinitis. N Engl J Med 2002;346:1119–26.
29. Musch DC, Martin DF, Gordon JF, *et al.* Treatment of cytomegalovirus retinitis with a sustained-release ganciclovir implant. N Engl J Med 1997;337:83–90.
30. Dieterich DT, Kotler DP, Busch DF, *et al.* Ganciclovir treatment of cytomegalovirus colitis in AIDS: a randomized, double-blind, placebo-controlled multicenter study. J Infect Dis 1993;167:278–82.
31. Goodrich JM, Bowden RA, Fisher L, *et al.* Ganciclovir prophylaxis to prevent cytomegalovirus disease after allogenic marrow transplantation. Ann Intern Med 1993;118:173–8.
32. Winston DJ, Ho WG, Bartoni K. Ganciclovir prophylaxis of cytomegalovirus infection and disease in allogenic bone marrow transplant recipients: results of a placebo-controlled double-blind trial. Ann Intern Med 1993;118:179–84.
33. Boeckh M, Goodley TA, Myerson D, *et al.* Cytomegalovirus pp65 antigenemia-guided early treatment with ganciclovir versus ganciclovir at engraftment after allogenic marrow transplantation: a randomized double-blind study. Blood 1996;88:4063–71.
34. McGavin JK, Goa KL. Ganciclovir: an update of its use in the prevention of cytomegalovirus infection and disease in transplant recipients. Drugs 2001;61:1153–83.
35. Hibberd PL, Tolkoff-Rubin NE, Conti D, *et al.* Preemptive ganciclovir therapy to prevent cytomegalovirus disease in cytomegalovirus antibody-positive renal transplant recipients: a randomized controlled trial. Ann Intern Med 1995;123:18–26.
36. Limaye AP, Raghu G, Koelle DM, *et al.* High incidence of ganciclovir-resistant cytomegalovirus infection among lung transplant recipients receiving preemptive therapy. J Infect Dis 2002;185:20–7.
37. Drew WL, Miner RC, Busch DF, *et al.* Prevalence of resistance in patients receiving ganciclovir for serious cytomegalovirus infection. J Infect Dis 1991;163:716–19.
38. Wagstaff AJ, Bryson HM. Foscarnet: a reappraisal of its antiviral activity, pharmacokinetic properties and therapeutic use in immunocompromised patients with viral infections. Drugs 1994;48:199–226.
39. Palestine AG, Polis MA, DeSmet MD, *et al.* A randomized, controlled trial of foscarnet in the treatment of cytomegalovirus retinitis in patients with AIDS. Ann Intern Med 1991;115:665–73.
40. Studies of Ocular Complications of AIDS (SOCA) Research Group in collaboration with the AIDS clinical Trials Group. Mortality in patients with the acquired immunodeficiency syndrome treated with either foscarnet or ganciclovir for cytomegalovirus retinitis. N Eng J Med 1992;326:213–20.
41. Studies of Ocular Complications of AIDS (SOCA) Research Group. Morbidity and toxic effects associated with ganciclovir or foscarnet therapy in a randomized cytomegalovirus retinitis trial. Arch Intern Med 1995;155:65–74.
42. Studies of Ocular Complications (SOCA) of AIDS Research Group in collaboration with the AIDS Clinical Trials Group. Combination foscarnet and ganciclovir therapy vs. monotherapy for the treatment of relapsed cytomegalovirus retinitis in patients with AIDS. Arch Ophthalmol 1996;114:23–33.
43. Safrin S, Berger TG, Gilson I, *et al.* Foscarnet therapy in five patients with AIDS and acyclovir-resistant varicella-zoster virus infection. Ann Intern Med 1991;115:19–21.
44. Jacobson MA, Gambertoglio JG, Aweeka FT, *et al.* Foscarnet-induced hypocalcemia and effects of foscarnet on calcium metabolism. J Clin Endocrinol Metabol 1991;72:1130–5.
45. Lea AP, Bryson HM. Cidofovir. Drugs 1996;52:225–30.
46. Lalezari JP, Stagg RJ, Kuppermann BD, *et al.* Intravenous cidofovir for peripheral cytomegalovirus retinitis in patients with AIDS. Ann Intern Med 1997;126:257–63.
47. Studies of Ocular Complications of AIDS (SOCA) Research Group in collaboration with the AIDS

Clinical Trials Group. Parenteral cidofovir for cytomegalovirus retinitis in patients with AIDS: the HPMPC peripheral cytomegalovirus retinitis trial. Ann Intern Med 1997;126:264–74.
48. Studies of Ocular Complications of AIDS (SOCA) Research Group in collaboration with the AIDS Clinical Trials Group. The ganciclovir implant plus oral ganciclovir versus parenteral cidofovir for the treatment of cytomegalovirus retinitis in patients with acquired immunodeficiency syndrome: the Ganciclovir Cidofovir Cytomegalovirus Retinitis Trial. Am J Ophthalmol 2001;131:457–67.
49. LoPresti AE, Levine JF, Munk GB, *et al.* Successful treatment of acyclovir- and foscarnet-resistant herpes simplex virus type 1 lesion with intravenous cidofovir. Clin Infect Dis 1998;26:512–13.
50. Perry CM, Balfour JA. Fomivirsen. Drugs 1999;57:375–80.

chapter 206

Antiviral Agents against Respiratory Viruses

Michael Ison & Frederick G Hayden

M2 INHIBITORS

Overview

Amantadine and rimantadine are symmetric tricyclic amines that specifically inhibit the replication of influenza A viruses at low concentrations (<1.0μg/ml) by blocking the action of the M2 protein. M2, an acid-activated ion channel found only in influenza A viruses, is a membrane protein required for efficient nucleocapsid release after viral fusion with the endosomal membrane.

Amantadine and rimantadine share two concentration-dependent mechanisms of antiviral action.[1,2] Low concentrations of the drugs inhibit the ion channel function of the M2 protein, which inhibits viral uncoating or disassembly of the virion during endocytosis and, in H7 subtypes, alters HA maturation during viral assembly. Amantadine and rimantadine also increase the lysosomal pH, which in turn may inhibit virus-induced membrane fusion events for several enveloped viruses. However, such effects are generally not seen at drug concentrations observed in humans and clinically relevant antiviral activity is confined to influenza A viruses, although studies in chronic hepatitis C are in progress (see Table 206.1).

Resistance

Resistance to the two agents occurs as the result of amino acid substitutions in the transmembrane portion of the M2 protein. Although resistant wild-type virus is uncommonly found (<1%),[3] resistant viruses may rapidly emerge within 2–4 days after the start of therapy in up to 30% of patients.[4] Emergence of resistant virus does not appear to cause a rebound in illness in immunocompetent adults but may be associated with protracted illness and shedding in immunocompromised hosts.[5] Importantly, resistant virus can be spread to others and has caused failures of antiviral prophylaxis under close contact conditions, as in nursing homes and households.[4] The resistant virus appears to retain wild-type pathogenicity and causes an influenza illness indistinguishable from susceptible strains. Cross-resistance occurs to all M2 inhibitors without affecting susceptibility to the neuraminidase inhibitors and ribavirin.

Pharmacokinetics and distribution

Amantadine is rapidly absorbed, with a 53–100% bioavailability, and reaches peak plasma levels of 475μg/l within 4.5 hours after a 100mg dose in healthy adults.[6] The drug is predominantly excreted unchanged in the urine by glomerular filtration and tubular secretion. The plasma elimination half-life is about 11–15 hours in persons with normal renal function. Elimination is markedly prolonged in patients with renal impairment and decreases about 2-fold in the elderly so that dose adjustments are required (Table 206.3). Amantadine is widely distributed with salivary levels equivalent to those of blood and nasal mucus comparable to plasma at 8 hours after dosing.[7,8] Amantadine crosses the placenta and blood–brain barrier, with cerebrospinal fluid(CSF) levels equal to 56–96% of serum levels, and distributes in breast milk (see Table 206.2).

In experimental human influenza infection, a trough concentration at steady-state of 300μg/l, which corresponds to that observed after 200mg/day dosing, was associated with a lower infection rate than placebo.[8] Adverse events are dose related and daily doses of 200mg in young adults and 100mg in the elderly institutionalized are associated with excess central nervous system (CNS) adverse effects.[6]

Rimantadine has nearly complete oral bioavailability and achieves maximal plasma concentration 3–5 hours after ingestion. Peak concentrations average 416μg/l after a 200mg oral dose. Rimantadine levels in nasal secretions average 1.5 times those of plasma levels. The plasma half-life is long and ranges from 24 to 36 hours. Rimantadine undergoes extensive metabolism, including hydroxylation, conjugation and glucuronidation in the liver, before being excreted in the urine. Only 25% of the parent drug is excreted unchanged in the urine. Dose adjustments are recommended for advanced renal or hepatic failure and older age (see Table 206.3).

Route of administration and dosage

Amantadine and rimantadine come as 100mg tablets and a syrup formulation (50mg/5ml). In adults, the usual dose for treatment or prevention of influenza A infection is 100mg q12h for both drugs (see Table 206.3).

Indications

Amantadine and rimantadine are indicated for the prevention and treatment of influenza A virus illness. Most placebo-controlled studies of these drugs in the management of influenza have been conducted in previously healthy persons.[8]

Prophylaxis

Prophylaxis with amantadine or rimantadine is approximately 70–90% effective in preventing symptomatic influenza A infections.[9] Administration is advised for postexposure prophylaxis in nursing home populations at 100mg/day for 14 days or for at least 7 days after the last culture-confirmed illness in the ward or building; this regimen should be given with concomitant influenza vaccination for those not previously provided.[10] Rimantadine is better tolerated in this population.[11] Seasonal prophylaxis, during the 4–8 weeks of peak influenza virus circulation within the community, can be used for protection of high-risk patients who cannot tolerate immunization, who do not develop an adequate immune response to vaccine or when the strain circulating in the community does not match the vaccine strain. Postexposure prophylaxis in households appears protective when not used in conjunction with treatment of an ill index case.

Treatment

Amantadine or rimantadine therapy reduces duration of fever and symptoms in patients with documented influenza by about 1 day compared with placebo, when the medication is initiated within 48 hours of symptom onset.[12] Treatment is also associated with more rapid functional recovery[12] and resolution of small airways functional abnormalities. Studies comparing the therapeutic activity of

IN-VITRO ACTIVITY OF SELECTED AGENTS USED TO TREAT INFLUENZA			
Drug	Virus type/subtype	50% inhibitory concentration (IC_{50})	
		Cell culture (μM/l)	Neuraminidase enzyme (nM/l)
Amantadine[49]	A/H1N1	5.3–7.3	NA
	A/H3N2	1.1–4.4	NA
Rimantadine[49]	A/H1N1	0.6–0.62	NA
	A/H3N2	0.1–3.0	NA
Zanamivir[26]	A/H1N1	0.02–0.07	0.3–0.7
	A/H3N2	0.004–0.241	1.7–4.6
	B	0.03–0.15	1–17.0
Oseltamivir[50]	A/H1N1	0.02–0.094	0.69–2.2
	A/H3N2	0.0006–0.04	0.21–0.56
	B	0.091–0.16	0.8–24.0

Note: Concentrations for inhibition in cell culture are express in μM, whereas those for neuraminidase enzyme inhibition are expressed in nM. Results of representative publications.

Table 206.1 In-vitro activity of selected agents used to treat influenza.[26,49–51]

amantadine and rimantadine are few but generally show comparability.[12] Amantadine appears safe and efficacious in reducing length of fever and illness in children older than 2 years of age.[12] Pediatric studies have found variable clinical benefits relative to acetaminophen controls and document the frequent emergence of drug-resistant variants.[12]

Prospective controlled data to support the use of M2 inhibitors in treating severe influenza or in preventing complications are lacking; one retrospective study found no important differences in duration of illness or hospitalization between the amantadine-treated and untreated patients hospitalized with influenza.[13] In hematopoietic stem cell transplant (HSCT) and acute leukemia patients who received therapy with one of the M2 inhibitors, a reduced risk of progression to pneumonia (35% vs 76%) was found compared with no treatment.[14] However, emergence of resistance is common in such patients.[5] One retrospective study of nursing home residents suggested that early treatment might reduce lower respiratory complications.[15] Amantadine is ineffective for treating influenza B or C infections.

Dosage in special circumstances

Dosing of amantadine and rimantadine should be adjusted in the setting of renal failure (see Table 206.3). Neither M2 inhibitor is cleared by hemodialysis. Patients over 65 years of age should have the dose of both medications reduced to 100mg once daily to avoid side effects. Rimantadine needs dose adjustment to 100mg per day for serious hepatic insufficiency. Amantadine and rimantadine are embryotoxic and teratogenic in preclinical tests and amantadine may be associated with birth defects. As a result, neither drug should be used in pregnant women unless the benefits of therapy clearly outweigh the potential risks (pregnancy category C). The recommended pediatric dosage of both amantadine and rimantadine is 5mg/kg/day to a maximum of 150mg/day, divided twice daily in children younger than 10.[10]

Adverse effects and drug interactions

The most common side effects of the M2 inhibitors are minor CNS complaints (anxiety, difficulty concentrating, insomnia, dizziness, headache and jitteriness) and gastrointestinal upset. Patients who receive amantadine may develop antimuscarinic effects, orthostatic hypotension and congestive heart failure at low frequencies. Particularly in the elderly or those with renal failure, serious CNS side-effects due to amantadine, and less often rimantadine, include confusion, disorientation, mood alterations, memory disturbances, delusions, nightmares, ataxia, tremors, seizures, coma, acute psychosis, slurred speech, visual disturbances, delirium, occulogyric episodes and hallucinations.[8] Amantadine causes CNS side-effects in about 15–30% of persons, as well as dose-related abnormalities in psychomotor testing.[8] The incidence and severity of CNS adverse effects are less common with rimantadine.[11] Amantadine and possibly rimantadine may increase the risk of seizures in those with a history of seizures.

Concomitant ingestion of antihistamines or anticholinergic drugs increases the CNS effects of amantadine. Trimethoprim–sulfamethoxazole and triamterene–hydrochlorothiazide decrease the renal clearance of amantadine, which enhances the risk of CNS toxicity. Quinine and quinidine also reduce the clearance of amantadine. Co-administration with monoamine oxidase inhibitors may precipitate life-threatening hypertension. The drug does not appear to interact with the cytochrome P450 system. Cimetidine is associated with 15–20% increases and aspirin or acetaminophen with 10% decreases in plasma rimantadine concentrations, but such changes are unlikely to be of clincial significance.[16] Patients receiving either amantadine or rimantadine along with drugs affecting

PHARMACOKINETIC PROPERTIES OF ANTIVIRALS WITH ACTIVITY AGAINST INFLUENZA								
Drug	Dose	Route	C_{max} (μg/l)	T_{max} (h)	$AUC_{0-12\,hrs}$ (μg/ml·h)	$T_{1/2}$ (h)	B (%)	% Protein binding
Amantadine[7,8*]	200mg × 1	Oral (young)	510 (140)	2.1 (1)	10.2 (3.4)	14.4 (6)	62–93	67
		Oral (elderly)	800 (200)	2.2 (2.1)	17.6 (6.5)	19 (9.1)	53–100	
Rimantadine[7,8*]	200mg × 1	Oral (young)	240 (70)	4.6 (2.1)	9.8 (4.5)	36.5 (17.3)	75–93	40
		Oral (elderly)	250 (50)	4.0 (2.4)	11.5 (3.9)	36.5 (14.5)	NA	
Zanamivir[23**]	16mg × 1	Inhaled	39 (23–69)	0.75 (0.08–2)	0.03 (0.02–0.06)	3.6 (2.2–9.4)	4–17	10
	16mg 6 ×/d × 7 d	Inhaled	54 (34–96)	0.75 (0.25–1)	0.16 (0.09–0.32)	—	4–17	
Oseltamivir[31*]	100mg bid	Oral (18–55 yo)	439 (40.8)	3.5 (1)	3.85 (0.6)	6–10	79	42
		Oral (≥65 yo)	575 (83.3)	3.3 (1.4)	4.94 (1.0)	—	—	

C_{max} = maximum serum drug concentration; T_{max} = time to C_{max}; $T_{1/2}$ = serum elimination half-life; AUC = area under the serum drug concentration versus time for the dose interval; B = bioavailability (% of intravenous C_{max}). *Values are mean (SD); **values are median (range).

Table 206.2 Pharmacokinetic properties of antivirals with activity against influenza.[7,31,23]

Table 206.3 Agents used to prevent and treat influenza.[10]

AGENTS USED TO PREVENT AND TREAT INFLUENZA				
Drug	Usual adult dosage[+]		Dose adjustment state	Suggested dosage
	Prophylaxis	Treatment		
Amantadine	100mg bid	100mg bid	Age 1–9 years	5mg/kg to max of 150mg in two divided doses
			CrCl 30–50mL/min	100mg qd
			CrCl 15–30mL/min	100mg qod
			CrCl 10–15mL/min	100mg q week
			CrCl <10mL/min	100mg q week
			Age ≥65 years	100mg qd
Rimantadine	100mg bid	100mg bid	Age 1–9 years***	5mg/kg to max of 150mg in two divided doses
			CrCl <10mL/min	100mg qd
			Severe hepatic dysfunction	100mg qd
			Age ≥65 years	100mg qd
Zanamivir	2 puffs (10mg) qd**	2 puffs (10mg) bid	No dose adjustment needed	
Oseltamivir	75mg qd	75mg bid	CrCl <30mL/min¶	Treatment: 75mg qd Prophylaxis: 75mg qod
			≤15kg	30mg bid (2.5ml*)
			15–23kg	45mg bid (3.8ml*)
			23–40kg	60mg bid (5ml*)
			>40kg	75mg bid (6.2ml*)

Recommendations based on those provided by the Advisory Committee on Immunization Practices.[10] * Volume of suspension. § Hemodialysis contributes minimally to clearance. ¶ No treatment or prophylaxis dosing recommendations are available for patients undergoing renal dialysis. ** Investigational: not approved for prophylaxis by the US Food and Drug Administration. *** Investigational: not approved for treatment in children by the US Food and Drug Administration. + Duration of treatment is usually 5 days. Duration of prophylaxis depends on clinical setting.

CNS function, such as antihistamines, antidepressants or minor tranquilizers, should be monitored closely.

NEURAMINIDASE INHIBITORS

Overview

Influenza A and B viruses possess a surface glycoprotein with neuraminidase activity whereas influenza C viruses do not. This enzyme cleaves terminal sialic acid residues and destroys the receptors recognized by viral hemagglutinin. This activity is essential for release of virus from infected cells, for prevention of viral aggregates and for viral spread within the respiratory tract.[17] Zanamivir and oseltamivir are sialic acid analogues that potently and specifically inhibit influenza A and B neuraminidases by competitively and reversibly interacting with the active enzyme site.[18] These drugs are active against all nine neuraminidase subtypes in nature including the avian strains of influenza A H5N1 and H9N2 that infected humans (see Table 206.1).

Resistance

Zanamivir and oseltamivir carboxylate resistance in vitro results from mutations in the viral hemagglutinin and/or neuraminidase.[19,20] In the hemagglutinin variants, mutations in or near the receptor binding site make the virus less dependent on neuraminidase action, whereas neuraminidase mutations directly affect interaction with the inhibitors. The altered neuraminidases typically show reduced activity or stability and the mutated viruses usually have decreased infectivity in animals.[19] The particular neuraminidase mutation determines the degree of resistance and cross-resistance (i.e. R229K causes high-level resistance in oseltamivir but not zanamivir).[19] Several hemagglutin and neuraminidase mutants have been described in immunocompromised patients with prolonged virus shedding.[22] Oseltamivir-resistant variants have been recovered from <1% of treated adults and about 4% of treated children.[18] The possible clinical and epidemiologic significance of such variants requires study and a global Neuraminidase Inhibitor Susceptibility Network has been established to address these concerns.[20]

ZANAMIVIR

Pharmacokinetics and distribution

The oral bioavailability of zanamivir is low (<5%) and most clinical trials have used intranasal or dry powder inhalation delivery. The commercial dry powder formulation is mixed with lactose (5mg zanamivir per 20mg lactose). Following inhalation of the dry powder, approximately 7–21% is deposited in the lower respiratory tract and the remainder in the oropharynx.[23,24] Median zanamivir concentrations are above 1000ng/ml in induced sputum 6 hours after inhalation and remain detectable up to 24 hours (see Table 206.2). The peak plasma concentration averages 46μg/l after a single 16mg inhalation of zanamivir. The proprietary inhaler device for delivering zanamivir is breath activated and requires a co-operative patient.[25]

In both experimental and natural influenza, once-daily dosing appears protective.[26] Twice-daily administration is therapeutically active but increasing the dose frequency to four times per day does not appear to increase efficacy in treating natural influenza.[26] Intranasal dosing is protective against experimental infection but not natural infection and does not substantially increase the overall therapeutic response to inhaled zanamivir.

Route of administration and dosage

Zanamivir is delivered by inhalation with a proprietary breath-activated device (Diskhaler). The usual adult treatment dose is two inhalations (10mg) twice a day for 5 days.

Indications

Prophylaxis

Although not US Food and Drug Administration approved for prophylaxis, once-daily inhaled zanamivir for 4 weeks was 84% efficacious in preventing laboratory-confirmed illness with fever and 31% effective in preventing influenza infection, irrespective of symptoms.[26] When used for postexposure prophylaxis, inhaled zanamivir for 10 days reduced the risk of secondary influenza illness by 79% in households.[26] In nursing homes experiencing influenza outbreaks, inhaled zanamivir was more effective for prevention of influenza A illness than oral rimantadine, in part because of frequent resistance emergence to the M2 inhibitor.[26]

Treatment

In the USA zanamivir is indicated for the treatment of uncomplicated acute illness due to influenza A and B virus in adults and pediatric patients 7 years and older who have been symptomatic for no more than 2 days. Inhaled zanamivir in adults has consistently shown at least one less day of disabling influenza symptoms and most studies have found a reduction in the number of nights of disturbed sleep, in time to resumption of normal activities and in the use of symptom relief medications.[26,27] Similar therapeutic benefits have also been shown in children aged 5–12 years.[28] Greatest benefit was noted in patients who were febrile at the time of enrollment, those started on therapy within 30 hours after the onset of symptoms and in adults aged 50 years and older.[26] Zanamivir has also been associated with a 40% reduction in lower respiratory tract complications of influenza leading to antibiotics, particularly bronchitis and pneumonia.[29] It appears generally well tolerated and effective in treating influenza in patients with mild to moderate asthma or, less often, chronic obstructive pulmonary disease (COPD).[27,29] An uncontrolled study found zanamivir to be safe and possibly effective in allogeneic stem cell transplant recipients, although viral shedding persisted for an average of 2 weeks on therapy.[21] Further studies are needed in immunocompromised populations.

Dosage in special circumstances

Although the plasma elimination half-life increases with creatinine clearance ≤70ml/min, drug accumulation is negligible after inhalation and dose adjustment is not necessary for renal or hepatic dysfunction. Certain populations, particularly very young, frail or cognitively impaired patients, may have difficulty using the drug delivery system.[25]

Adverse effects and drug interactions

Topically applied zanamivir is generally well tolerated in controlled studies, including those involving patients with asthma and COPD.[27] No difference in adverse events between zanamivir and placebo (lactose) recipients has been found.[27] Less than 5% of zanamivir recipients have reported diarrhea, nausea, sinusitis, nasal signs and symptoms, bronchitis, cough, headache, dizziness and ear, nose and throat infections. Postmarketing reports indicate that bronchospasm may be an uncommon but potentially severe problem, particularly in patients with acute influenza and underlying reactive airways disease.[30] Anecdotal reports of hospitalization and fatality indicate that inhaled zanamivir should be used cautiously in such patients. Current guidelines advise against the use of zanamivir in patients with underlying airway disease, unless the patient is closely monitored and has a fast-acting inhaled bronchodilator available when inhaling zanamivir.[10]

Low bioavailability is associated with low exposure to circulating zanamivir and no clinically significant drug interactions have been recognized. In-vitro studies suggest that zanamivir does not inhibit or induce cytochrome P450 enzymes. The drug does not affect the immunogenicity of concomitant immunization with inactivated virus vaccines. It is uncertain whether inhaled zanamivir might reduce the immunogenicity of intranasal, live-attenuated vaccine if administered concurrently. Although not associated with teratogenic effects in preclinical studies, zanamivir should only be used in pregnancy when the potential benefit justifies the potential risk to the fetus (pregnancy category C).

OSELTAMIVIR

Pharmacokinetics and distribution

Oral oseltamivir ethyl ester is well absorbed and rapidly cleaved by esterases in the gastrointestinal tract, liver or blood. The bioavailability of the active metabolite, oseltamivir carboxylate, is estimated to be approximately 80% in previously healthy persons.[31] Mean peak oseltamivir carboxylate concentrations of 456μg/l are reached at 5 hours after oral administration of 150mg doses in healthy adults and the plasma elimination half-life is 6–10 hours (see Table 206.2). Although drug concentrations over time are 25–35% higher in the elderly at steady-state, no dose adjustment is deemed necessary. Administration with food appears to decrease the risk of gastrointestinal upset without decreasing bioavailability. Both the prodrug and parent are eliminated primarily unchanged through the kidney by glomerular filtration and anionic tubular secretion. The dose should be reduced by half for patients with a creatinine clearance less than 30ml/min.[32] Distribution is not well characterized in humans, but peak bronchoalveolar lavage levels are similar to plasma levels in animals.[31] Drug levels in middle ear fluid and sinus aspirates are similar to those in blood.[31]

There is no clear association between the plasma AUC for the oseltamivir carboxylate drug and viral titer after experimental infection; early therapy of experimental infection is associated with reduced median nasal lavage concentrations of interleukin-6, tumor necrosis factor-α and interferon-γ as compared with placebo.[31] In natural influenza, once-daily dosing appears as effective as twice-daily dosing for prevention of influenza illness.[31] Doses of 75mg and 150mg twice daily provide comparable antiviral and clinical effects in treatment of acute influenza A illness[31] and of experimental influenza B in adults.

Route of administration and dosage

Oseltamivir comes as 75mg tablets and as a suspension in bottles containing 25ml of suspension after constitution equivalent to 300mg oseltamivir base. The suspension comes in bottles containing 25ml of suspension after constitution equivalent to 300mg oseltamivir base. The typical adult dose for treatment is 75mg twice daily for 5 days and for prophylaxis is 75mg once daily. Pediatric dosing is based on weight and is outlined in Table 206.3.

Indications

In the USA oseltamivir is indicated for the treatment of uncomplicated acute illness due to influenza infection in patients 1 year and older who have been symptomatic for no more than 2 days and for the prophylaxis of influenza in adult patients and adolescents 13 years and older.

Prophylaxis

The efficacy of once-daily oseltamivir 75mg for 6 weeks in preventing influenza illness in healthy, nonimmunized adults was 84% and in preventing influenza infection irrespective of symptoms was 50%.[31] In immunized nursing home residents, the efficacy of prophylaxis was

92% against illness compared with placebo.[31] Similar efficacy was seen in a household-contact prophylaxis study,[31] and protection against influenza has been shown in children.[31]

Treatment

Oseltamivir 75mg twice daily for 5 days, when started within the first 2 days of symptoms, was associated with a shorter time to alleviation of illness (29–35 hours shorter) and with reductions in severity of illness, duration of fever, time to return to normal activity, quantity of viral shedding, duration of impaired activity, and complications leading to antibiotic use, particularly bronchitis, compared with placebo in previously healthy adults.[31] Preliminary analyses indicate that early treatment can reduce hospitalizations. In a pediatric study enrolling children between the ages of 1 and 12 years, oseltamivir 2mg/kg twice daily for 5 days significantly reduced illness duration and severity, time to resumption of full activities and the occurrence of complications leading to antibiotic use, particularly acute otitis media.[33] Little published information is available about therapeutic efficacy in elderly or high-risk persons, including those with underlying cardiopulmonary conditions or immunodeficiency.

Dosage in special circumstances

Oseltamivir dose should be reduced to 75mg once a day for treatment and 75mg every other day or 30mg of suspension daily for prophylaxis when a patient has a creatinine clearance of less than 30mg/dl. Doses of oseltamivir should be given after hemodialysis. The safety and pharmacokinetics in patients with hepatic impairment have not been evaluated. Oseltamivir should not be used in pregnant women unless the benefits of therapy clearly outweigh the potential risks (pregnancy category C). The recommended pediatric dosages are listed in Table 206.3.

Adverse effects and drug interactions

Oral oseltamivir is generally well tolerated and no serious end-organ toxicity has been found in controlled clinical trials. Oseltamivir is associated with nausea, discomfort and, less often, emesis in a minority of treated patients. Nausea and vomiting occur at approximately 10–15% excess in oseltamivir recipients. Gastrointestinal complaints are usually mild to moderate in intensity, usually resolve despite continued dosing and are ameliorated by administration with food.[34] Clinical studies comparing 75mg and 150mg twice daily doses found similar frequencies of adverse events with the two doses. Other infrequent possible adverse events include insomnia, vertigo and fever. Postmarking reports suggest that oseltamivir may be associated rarely with skin rash, hepatic dysfunction or thrombocytopenia.

No clinically significant drug interactions have been recognized. However, probenecid blocks tubular secretion and doubles the half-life of oseltamivir. Studies with amoxicillin, aspirin and acetaminophen have found no clinically important interactions. No interactions with the cytochrome P450 enzymes occur in vitro. Protein binding is below 10%. Oseltamivir should not affect the immunogenicity of concomitant vaccination with inactivated virus but might impair the immunogenicity of concurrent live-attenuated intranasal influenza vaccine.

RIBAVIRIN

Overview

Ribavirin is a guanosine analogue with a wide range of antiviral activity including influenza viruses, respiratory syncytial virus (RSV), parainfluenza viruses and adenoviruses. Ribavirin is rapidly phosphorylated by intracellular enzymes and the triphosphate inhibits influenza virus RNA polymerase activity and competitively inhibits the guanosine triphosphate-dependent 5′-capping of influenza viral messenger RNA. In addition, ribavirin depletes cellular guanine pools.[35,36] Although it has no antiviral activity when used alone, for the treatment of hepatitis C infection, the combination of ribavirin and interferon-α is more effective than interferon-α alone (see Chapter 207).

Pharmacokinetics and distribution

Oral ribavirin has a bioavailability of 33–45% in adults and children and achieves peak plasma concentrations of 0.6μg/ml 1–2 hours after ingestion of a 400mg dose in adults. Ribavirin has a short initial (0.3–0.7 hours) and long terminal-phase half-life (18–36 hours) and is eliminated by hepatic metabolism and renal clearance.[37–40] After aerosol administration, plasma levels increase with exposure and range from 0.2 to 1μg/ml. Respiratory secretions have levels of up to 1000μg/ml, which declines with a half-life of 1.4–2.5 hours.

Route of administration and dosage

Ribavirin comes in three formulations: oral, intravenous (investigational in the USA) and aerosol. Ribavirin for aerosolization is available as a 6g/100ml solution, which is diluted to a final concentration of 20mg/ml and delivered by small-particle aerosol for 12–18 hours with a proprietary device (SPAG-2 nebulizer). A higher concentration of aerosol solution (60mg/ml) has been given over 2 hours three times daily in some studies and appears well tolerated. Ribavirin also comes in 200mg tablets and sterile solution for injection.

Indications

Ribavirin aerosol is currently indicated for the treatment of severe RSV infection in children. Trials of aerosolized ribavirin for the treatment of severe RSV infection in infants have shown no consistent effect on duration of hospitalization time or mortality.[41] Earlier studies were confounded by the use of water aerosol as placebo, which may induce bronchospasm. Long-term follow-up of ribavirin recipients has likewise found no consistent benefits on pulmonary function.[41] Current guidelines recommend that aerosolized ribavirin be considered in the treatment of high-risk infants and young children, as defined by congenital heart disease, chronic lung disease, immunodeficiency states, prematurity and age <6 weeks, as well as for those hospitalized with severe illness.[41,42] Administration of a more concentrated aerosol solution (60mg/ml) over 2 hours thrice daily appears well tolerated and easier to administer.[43] Aerosolized ribavirin has shown minimal efficacy in treating influenza in hospitalized children.[44]

Ribavirin has also been studied for the treatment of RSV and parainfluenza virus infections in immunocompromised patients. Intravenous ribavirin appears to be ineffective in reducing RSV-associated mortality in human stem cell transplant with RSV pneumonia.[45] Aerosolized ribavirin may provide benefit in selected patient groups with less severe RSV disease. Survival is improved when treatment is started before respiratory failure or when infection is limited to the upper respiratory tract.[45] Although no prospective studies of aerosolized ribavirin alone versus combined ribavirin–antibody therapy (IVIG, RespiGam or palivizumab) have been reported, combination therapy may be more effective, particularly when started before severe respiratory distress.[45] In the management of parainfluenza virus (PIV) pneumonia in bone marrow transplant recipients, aerosolized ribavirin failed to improve 30-day mortality or reduce the duration of viral replication relative to no treatment.[45] Intravenous ribavarin may be beneficial in treating PIV or influenza virus infections in some immunocompromized patients.[46] High oral doses of ribavarin (30–60mg/kg/day in divided doses) have been used in early treatment of RSV and PIV infections in HSCT. High oral doses (8.4g over 2 days) provided modest benefit in acute influenza in otherwise healthy adults.[48]

Recently. oral and intravenous ribavirin have been used in treatment of SARS coronavirus illness with uncertain clinical and virologic effects. [48a, 48b]

Dosage in special circumstances

Systemic ribavirin is contraindicated in patients with creatinine clearance of less than 50mL/min and the dose should be reduced by one-third for patients under the age of 10 years. Dose adjustment is needed if there is a substantial decline in hematocrit and the drug should be discontinued if the hematocrit drops below 8.5g/dl. Ribavirin is contraindicated in pregnant women and in male partners of women who are pregnant because of teratogenicity of the drug. Pregnancy should be avoided during therapy and 6 months after completion of therapy in both female patients and in female partners of male patients taking ribavirin (pregnancy category X).

Adverse effects and drug interactions

Systemic ribavirin can cause a dose-related extravascular hemolytic anemia and, at higher doses, suppression of bone marrow release of erythroid elements. Severe anemia may require dose adjustment or cessation or use of erythropoietin. Aerosolized ribavirin can cause bronchospasm, mild conjunctival irritation, rash, psychologic distress if administered in a oxygen tent and, rarely, acute water intoxication. Bolus intravenous administration may cause rigors. Antagonism of both drugs occurs in vitro when ribavirin is combined with zidovudine; the in-vivo significance is unknown.

REFERENCES

1. Hay AJ. Amantadine and rimantadine: mechanisms. In: Richman DD, ed. Antiviral drug resistance. New York: Wiley; 1996:43.
2. Pinto LH, Holsinger LJ, Lamb RA. Influenza virus M2 protein has ion channel activity. Cell 1992;69:517–28.
3. Ziegler T, Hemphill ML, Ziegler ML, *et al.* Low incidence of rimantadine resistance in field isolates of influenza A viruses. J Infect Dis 1999;180:935–9.
4. Hayden FG. Amantadine and rimantadine: clinical aspects. In: Richman DD, ed. Antiviral drug resistance. New York: Wiley; 1996.
5. Englund JA, Champlin RE, Wyde PR, *et al.* Common emergence of amantadine- and rimantadine-resistant influenza A viruses in symptomatic immunocompromised adults. Clin Infect Dis 1998;26:1418–24.
6. Aoki FY, Sitar DS. Clinical pharmacokinetics of amantadine hydrochloride. Clin Pharmacokinet 1988;14:35–31.
7. Hayden FG, Minocha A, Spyker DA, Hoffman HE. Comparative single-dose pharmacokinetics of amantadine hydrochloride and rimantadine hydrochloride in young and elderly adults [published erratum appears in Antimicrob Agents Chemother 1986;30:579]. Antimicrob Agents Chemother 1985;28:216–21.
8. Hayden FG, Aoki FY. Amantadine, rimantadine, and related agents. In: Barriere SL, ed. Antimicrobial therapy and vaccines. Baltimore: Williams & Wilkins; 1999:1344–65.
9. Couch RB. Prevention and treatment of influenza. N Engl J Med 2000;343:1778–87.
10. Anonymous. Prevention and control of influenza: Recommendations of the Advisory Committee on Immunization Practices (ACIP). MMWR Morb Mortal Wkly Rep 2002;51:1.
11. Keyser LA, Karl M, Nafziger AN, Bertino JS Jr. Comparison of central nervous system adverse effects of amantadine and rimantadine used as sequential prophylaxis of influenza A in elderly nursing home patients. Arch Intern Med 2000;160:1485–8.
12. Jefferson TO, Demicheli V, Deeks JJ, Rivetti D. Amantadine and rimantadine for preventing and treating influenza A in adults. Cochrane Database of Systematic Reviews 2001;2.
13. Kaiser L, Hayden FG. Hospitalizing influenza in adults. In: Swartz MN, ed. Current clinical topics in infectious diseases. Malden: Blackwell Science; 1999:112–34.
14. La Rosa AM, Malik S, Englund JA, *et al.* Influenza A in hospitalized adults with leukemia and hematopoietic stem cell transplant (HSCT) recipients: risk factors for progression to pneumonia. 39th Infectious Diseases Society of America Meeting, San Francisco, 2001.
15. Bowles SK, Lee W, Simor AE, *et al.* Use of oseltamivir during influenza outbreaks in Ontario nursing homes, 1999–2000. J Am Geriatr Soc 2002;50:608–16.
16. Wills RJ. Update on rimantadine's clinical pharmacokinetics. J Respir Dis 1989;10:s20–s25.
17. Colman PM. Influenza virus neuraminidase: structure, antibodies, and inhibitors. Protein Sci 1994;3:1687–96.
18. Gubareva LV, Kaiser L, Hayden FG. Influenza virus neuraminidase inhibitors. Lancet 2000;355:827–35.
19. McKimm-Breschkin JL. Resistance of influenza viruses to neuraminidase inhibitors–a review. Antiviral Res 2000;47:1–17.
20. Zambon M, Hayden FG. Position statement: Global Neuraminidase Inhibitor Susceptibility Network. Antiviral Res 2001;49:147–56.
21. Johny A, Clark A, Price N, Carrington D, Oakhill A, Marks D. The use of zanamivir to treat influenza A and B infection after allogeneic stem cell transplantation. Bone Marrow Transplant 2002;29:113–15.
22. Gubareva LV, Matrosovich MN, Brenner MK, Bethell RC, Webster RG. Evidence for zanamivir resistance in an immunocompromised child infected with influenza B virus. J Infect Dis 1998;178:1257–62.
23. Cass LM, Brown J, Pickford M, *et al.* Pharmacoscintigraphic evaluation of lung deposition of inhaled zanamivir in healthy volunteers. Clin Pharmacokinet 1999;36:21–31.
24. Cass LM, Efthymiopoulos C, Bye A. Pharmacokinetics of zanamivir after intravenous, oral, inhaled or intranasal administration to healthy volunteers. Clin Pharmacokinet 1999;36:1–11.
25. Diggory P, Fernandez C, Humphrey A, Jones V, Murphy M. Comparison of elderly people's technique in using two dry powder inhalers to deliver zanamivir: randomised controlled trial. Br Med J 2001;322:577–9.
26. Dunn CJ, Goa KL. Zanamivir: a review of its use in influenza. Drugs 1999;58:761–84.
27. Murphy KR, Eivindson A, Pauksen K, *et al.* Efficacy and safety of inhaled zanamivir for the treatment of influenza in patients with asthma or chronic obstructive pulmonary disease: a double-blind, randomized, placebo-controlled multicentre study. Clin Drug Invest 2000;20:337–49.
28. Hedrick JA, Barzilai A, Behre U, *et al.* Zanamivir for treatment of symptomatic influenza A and B infection in children five to twelve years of age: a randomized controlled trial. Pediatr Infect Dis J 2000;19:410–7.
29. Lalezari J, Campion K, Keene O, Silagy C. Zanamivir for the treatment of influenza A and B infection in high-risk patients: a pooled analysis of randomized controlled trials. Arch Intern Med 2001;161:212–7.
30. Kent RS. Important revisions to safety labeling for Relenza (zanamivir for inhalation). Letter to physicians, July 2000: GlaxoWellcome, Inc. www.fda.gov/medwatch/safety/2000/relenz.htm.
31. McClellan K, Perry CM. Oseltamivir: a review of its use in influenza. Drugs 2001;61:263–83.
32. He G, Massarella J, Ward P. Clinical pharmacokinetics of the prodrug oseltamivir and its active metabolite Ro 64–0802. Clin Pharmacokinet 1999;37:471–84.
33. Whitley RJ, Hayden FG, Reisinger KS, *et al.* Oral oseltamivir treatment of influenza in children. Pediatr Infect Dis J 2001;20:127–33.
34. Insert. OP. Roche Laboratories Inc, Nutley, NJ, 07110.
35. Wray SK, Gilbert BE, Noall MW, Knight V. Mode of action of ribavirin: effect of nucleotide pool alterations on influenza virus ribonucleoprotein synthesis. Antiviral Res 1985;5:29–37.
36. Wray SK, Gilbert BE, Knight V. Effect of ribavirin triphosphate on primer generation and elongation during influenza virus transcription *in vitro.* Antiviral Res 1985;5:39–48.
37. Connor JD, Hintz M, van Dyke R. Ribavirin pharmacokinetics in children and adults during therapeutic trials. In: Smith J, ed. Clinical applications of ribavirin. Orlando, FL: Academic Press; 1984:107–23.
38. Laskin O, Longstreth J, Hart C, *et al.* Ribavirin disposition in high-risk patients for acquired immunodeficiency syndrome. Clin Pharmacol Therapeut 1987;41:546–55.
39. Connor E, Morrison S, Lane J, *et al.* Safety, tolerance, and pharmacokinetics of systemic ribavirin in children with human immunodeficiency virus infection. Antimicrob Agents Chemother 1993;37:532–9.
40. Paroni R, Del P, Borghi C, *et al.* Pharmacokinetics of ribavirin and urinary excretion of the major metabolite 1,2,4-triazole-3-carboxamide in normal volunteers. Int J Clin Pharmacol Ther Toxicol 1989;27:302–7.
41. Committee on Infectious Diseases American Academy of Pediatrics. Respiratory syncytial virus. Report of the Committee on Infectious Diseases, 25th edition. Elk Grove, IL: American Academy of Pediatrics; 2000:483–8.
42. American Academy of Pediatrics Committee on Infectious Diseases. Reassessment of indications for ribavirin therapy in respiratory syncytial virus infection. Pediatrics 1996;97:137–40.
43. Englund JA, Piedra PA, Jefferson LS, Wilson SZ, Taber LH, Gilbert BE. High-dose, short-duration ribavirin aerosol therapy in children with suspected respiratory syncytial virus infection. J Pediatr 1990;117:313–20.
44. Rodriguez WJ, Hall CB, Welliver R, *et al.* Efficacy and safety of aerosolized ribavirin in young children hospitalized with influenza: a double-blind, multicenter, placebo-controlled trial. J Pediatr 1994;125:129–35.
45. Ison MG, Hayden FG. Viral infections in immunocompromised patients: what's new with respiratory viruses? Curr Opin Infect Dis 2002;15:355–67.
46. Hohenthal U, Nikoskelainen J, Vainionpaa R, *et al.* Parainfluenza virus type 3 infections in a

hematology unit. Bone Marrow Transplantation 2001;27:295–300.
47. Chakrabarti S, Collingham KE, Holder K, *et al.* Pre-emptive oral ribavirin therapy of paramyxovirus infections after haematopoietic stem cell transplantation: a pilot study. Bone Marrow Transplantation 2001;28:759–63.
48. Stein DS, Creticos CM, Jackson GG, *et al.* Oral ribavirin treatment of influenza A and B. Antimicrob Agents Chemother 1987;31:1285–7.
48a. Peiris JS, Chu CM, Cheng VC, *et al.* Clinical progression and viral load in a community outbreak of coronavirus-associated SARS pneumonia: a prospective study. Lancet 2003;361:1767–72.
48b. So LK, Lau Ac, Yam LY *et al.* Development of a standard treatment protocol for severe acute respiratory syndrome. Lancet 2003;361:1615–7.
49. Burlington DB, Meiklejohn G, Mostow SR. Anti-influenza A activity of combinations of amantadine and ribavirin in ferret tracheal ciliated epithelium. J Antimicrob Chemother 1983;11:7–14.
50. Mendel DB, Tai CY, Escarpe PA, *et al.* Oral administration of a prodrug of the influenza virus neuraminidase inhibitor GS 4071 protects mice and ferrets against influenza infection. Antimicrob Agents Chemother 1998;42:640–6.
51. Bantia S, Parker CD, Ananth SL, *et al.* Comparison of the anti-influenza virus activity of RWJ-270201 with those of oseltamivir and zanamivir. Antimicrob Agents Chemother 2001;45:1162–7.

chapter 207

Drugs to Treat Viral Hepatitis

David F Gardiner & Marshall J Glesby

INTERFERONS

Interferons (IFNs) are a family of naturally occurring proteins produced by eukaryotic cells that function as cytokines in an early response to viral infection. Interferons do not have direct antiviral activity, but instead induce an antiviral state in exposed cells and activate other immune functions.

Interferons are broadly characterized as type I (IFN-α and -β), and type II (IFN-γ). Interferon-α and -β have primary antiviral activity while IFN-γ has more potent immunoregulatory functions.

Interferons act through cell surface receptors to induce a complex series of intracellular events, with inhibition of viral protein production appearing to be the primary target.[1] A variety of purified and recombinant IFN-α preparations is available for clinical use. The pharmaceuticals are termed 'IFN-alfa' to distinguish them from naturally occurring 'IFN-α'.

Recently, pegylated ('peg') varieties of IFN have become available. Pegylation involves the addition of a polyethylene glycol side-chain to the protein molecule, which extends the half-life significantly. Two formulations are currently available, pegIFN alfa-2a (Pegasys) and pegIFN alfa-2b (Peg Intron). PegIFN alfa-2a has a larger branched peg molecule of about 40kDa in size attached at several sites.[2] PegIFN alfa-2b has a smaller, linear peg molecule of about 12kDa attached at several sites. Their proposed mechanism of action is similar to that of standard IFNs.

Pharmacokinetics and distribution

Standard pharmacokinetic measurements may not be relevant for IFN therapy. Plasma levels of IFN-alfa are often undetectable after subcutaneous or intralesional administration, while the plasma elimination half-life ($t_{1/2}$) is 2–4 hours after intravenous administration. Interferon-alfa is well absorbed (approximately 80%) following intramuscular administration and peak plasma concentrations occur after approximately 5–8 hours.[3] Interferon-alfa is filtered through the glomeruli and then undergoes rapid proteolytic degradation during tubular resorption. Negligible amounts of IFN are excreted in the urine. A small percentage of the administered dose undergoes hepatic metabolism and biliary excretion. PegIFN alfa-2b reaches maximum concentrations by 20 hours and has a half-life of 40 hours. PegIFN alfa-2a reaches maximum concentrations by 72–96 hours and has a longer $t_{1/2}$ of 80 hours compared to pegIFN alfa-2b.

Route of administration and dosing

Interferons are administered systemically (subcutaneously or intramuscularly) for the treatment of chronic viral hepatitis and by intralesional injection for the treatment of condylomata acuminata. Dosages vary considerably according to the specific preparation and indication (Table 207.1).

Indications

Chronic hepatitis B virus infection

Interferon is approved for the treatment of chronic hepatitis B virus (HBV) infection. A response to IFN therapy is judged by a loss of HBV DNA and hepatitis B e antigen (HBeAg) from the plasma, along with biochemical and histologic improvements. A meta-analysis of 16 randomized trials examining IFN versus control found that loss of HBeAg occurred in 33% of patients while clearance of HBV DNA occurred in 37% of patients.[4] Control patients experienced these outcomes in only 12 and 17% of cases, respectively. Clinical predictors of response to IFN in patients infected with HBV include low level of HBV DNA, elevated serum transaminases and evidence of active hepatic inflammation.[5] As seen in Figure 207.1, IFN therapy is associated with significant adverse effects. Recent years have seen a variety of new and effective medications for the treatment of HBV infection with improved side-effect profiles compared to IFN. As a result of these therapies, discussed below, IFN is not considered first-line treatment for HBV infection by most clinicians (see also Chapter 48).

Hepatitis C virus infection

Treatment of acute hepatitis C virus (HCV) infection is still investigational; however, a recent study reported a 98% sustained virologic response rate with IFN monotherapy in this setting.[6] Treatment of chronic HCV infection is recommended in patients experiencing detectable HCV RNA levels higher than 50 IU/ml and with a liver biopsy showing portal or bridging fibrosis and moderate inflammation and necrosis.[7] A sustained virologic response (SVR) of HCV to therapy is defined as a HCV RNA assay <50 IU/ml at 24 weeks after therapy. Evaluation of data from combining results of two large prospective trials shows that IFN monotherapy results in SVR rates of less than 10% after 24 weeks of treatment and SVR rates less than 20% after 48 weeks of therapy.[8] Increasing doses of IFN provide increased responses, with concomitant increases in adverse reactions.

Hepatitis C virus has a half-life of about 3 hours and infection results in the production of about 12 billion virions daily. The dosing and pharmacokinetics of standard IFN described above result in wide variations in serum IFN levels and fluctuating antiviral activity. Pegylation of the IFN molecule maintains rapid absorption and rapid time to peak drug level, while providing a dramatically lengthened half-life. Studies show that the pegylated IFNs provide significantly improved response rates over standard IFNs. Monotherapy with pegylated IFNs yields SVR rates of 25–39% in treatment-naive patients with HCV infection.[9] These improved results over standard IFN apply to both pegIFN alfa-2a as well as pegIFN alfa-2b.[10,11]

Dosage in special circumstances

Guidelines for adjusting systemic IFN dosage in patients who have renal insufficiency are poorly defined. Only limited data are available regarding administration to patients who have decompensated liver disease, but IFN may be poorly tolerated in this population. In pregnant monkeys, IFN has abortifacient effects and should not be used in pregnant women unless the potential benefits clearly outweigh the potential risks to the fetus.

Adverse reactions

Interferon therapy is associated with an extensive list of toxicities (see Fig. 207.1). Most patients receiving IFN doses of over one

Table 207.1 Medication dosage regimens.

MEDICATION DOSAGE REGIMENS				
Disease	Therapy	Route	Dose	Duration
Chronic hepatitis B	IFN alfa-2b	sc or im	$30–35 \times 10^6$ IU per week administered as either 5×10^6 IU/day or 10×10^6 IU three times per week	16 weeks
	Lamivudine	po	100mg q24h	Optimal duration unknown
	Adefovir dipivoxil	po	10mg q24h	Optimal duration unknown
Chronic hepatitis C	IFN alfa-2a	sc or im	3×10^6 IU three times/week	48 weeks**
	IFN alfa-2b	sc or im	3×10^6 IU three times/week	48 weeks
	IFN alfacon	sc	9μg three times/week*	48 weeks
	PegIFN alfa-2a	sc	180μg/week	48 weeks
	PegIFN alfa-2b	sc	1.0μg/kg/week† or 1.5μg/kg/week‡	48 weeks
	Ribavirin	po	800–1200mg per day††	Co-administer with IFN

* Patients who fail therapy with IFN alfacon at standard dose may receive the drug at 15μg sc three times/week for 6 months
† Monotherapy
‡ Dual therapy with ribavirin
** An optimal duration of IFN therapy is not universally agreed upon. Most trials describe 24–48 weeks of IFN or IFN plus ribavirin therapy. Early viral response (EVR) defined as a >2 log drop in HCV viral load after 12 weeks may be predictive of patients who will have a successful response. (http//consensus.NIH.gov/cons/116/091202116cdc_statement.htm (NIH Consensus Statement Sept, 2002)). This duration is not reflected in most package inserts. Readers should examine specific large-scale trials of each regimen for more detailed information.
†† Optimal dose of ribavirin varies with the co-administration of IFN products as well as patient weight. Optimal dose ranges have not been uniformly determined. Readers should enquire to specific package inserts and recent dose finding trials.

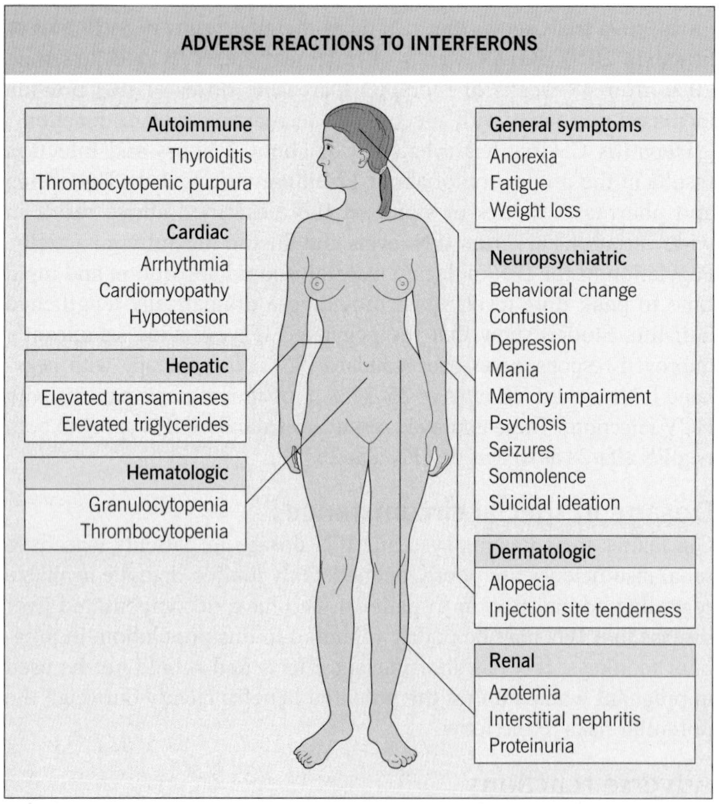

Fig. 207.1 Adverse reactions to interferons.

million units experience an 'influenza-like' syndrome characterized by fever, chills, headache, myalgias and arthralgias. These symptoms appear a few hours after the IFN injection, and they usually resolve within 12 hours. The symptoms can often be prevented by premedication with antipyretics. Tolerance develops in many patients with continued therapy. The most frequent dose-limiting adverse effects are leukopenia and thrombocytopenia. Before beginning IFN therapy, a baseline complete blood count, liver function profile, urinalysis, antinuclear antibody screen and thyroid function tests should be obtained.

The adverse events seen with pegylated IFN are similar to those seen with standard IFN. The most common hematologic toxicity associated with pegylated IFNs is neutropenia with as many as 18% of patients requiring dose adjustments as a result.[12] Dose reduction is often helpful in patients experiencing significant generalized or hematologic toxicity. The pegylated IFNs are also associated with psychiatric disturbances including depression, irritability, insomnia and suicidal ideation. Caution is warranted when using IFNs and pegIFNs in patients with a history of a psychiatric disorder.

RIBAVIRIN

Ribavirin is a guanosine analog that has a broad spectrum of antiviral activity. Its mechanism of action is not clearly defined, but it is believed to act against HCV by one or more of the following mechanisms:

- enhancing T-cell mediated immune responses to HCV by shifting the balance towards a T-helper-1 response;

- inhibiting cellular inosine monophosphate dehydrogenase, thereby decreasing the intracellular guanosine triphosphate pool needed for viral RNA replication;
- directly inhibiting HCV polymerase; and
- acting as an RNA virus mutagen, thereby reducing viral fitness.[13]

Ribavirin is well absorbed after oral administration, with bioavailability ranging from 33 to 69% of the dose, and about 40% of the drug being eliminated via the kidneys. The major side-effect of ribavirin is hemolytic anemia, which may necessitate discontinuation of therapy. Ribavirin is highly teratogenic and birth control is required if the drug is used by women of child-bearing age or their partners. The benefits of ribavirin monotherapy in HCV infection disappear rapidly when the treatment is discontinued and it is therefore not recommended. As detailed below, ribavirin is used in combination with IFN or pegIFN.

Retrospective analysis of phase III studies of pegIFN plus ribavirin reveal that response is inversely correlated with the patient's body weight. In the study by Manns *et al.*,[12] patients receiving at least 10.6mg/kg of ribavirin had significantly better response rates for the same doses of IFN. This suggests that higher weight-based dosing of ribavirin may lead to improved responses. A randomized clinical trial is now underway to resolve this issue.

COMBINATION THERAPY FOR HEPATITIS C VIRUS INFECTION

Ribavirin given in combination with IFN has been shown to be more effective than the use of IFN alone for the treatment of HCV.[14] An SVR may occur in up to 40% of patients treated with combination therapy compared with approximately 20% of patients treated with IFN alone. Studies combining pegIFN alfa-2b with ribavirin had a 54% SVR compared to a 47% SVR with standard IFN alfa-2b plus ribavirin.[12] The SVR in patients infected with HCV genotype 1, which is associated with a poorer response to therapy, was also improved (42 vs 33%). Trials of pegIFN alfa-2a plus ribavirin also demonstrate excellent responses.[15] Combination therapy for HCV may also be beneficial in patients co-infected with HIV. Preliminary results of a randomized trial in HCV/HIV co-infected patients suggest that pegIFN alfa-2a plus ribavirin is superior to standard IFN alfa-2a plus ribavirin, with 24-week virologic response rates of 44 versus 15%.[16] (See Chapter 125).

THERAPIES IN DEVELOPMENT FOR HEPATITIS C

Hepatitis C virus is a single-stranded (ss) RNA virus of about 9.4kb in length. It is translated into a single polypeptide prescursor, which is cleaved into several functional gene products, including structural proteins, RNA polymerase, helicase and serine protease.[17] Several drugs are in development to target key components of the viral life cycle, including inhibitors of serine protease as well as the helicase enzyme (Fig. 207.2). Ongoing clinical trials are investigating the potential antifibrotic effects of maintenance therapy with pegIFN alfa or colchicine for virologic nonresponders to IFN-based regimens. Interferon-γ is also under study as an antifibrotic agent.

NUCLEOSIDE AND NUCLEOTIDE ANALOGS

Nucleosides and nucleotides are the basic components of DNA and RNA in both prokaryotic and eukaryotic organisms. These molecules include a pentose sugar and a base moiety. A nucleotide differs from a nucleoside by the presence of one or more phosphate groups covalently bound to the molecule's sugar group. Intracellular phosphorylation is required before incorporation into the elongating nucleic acid chain. Pharmacologic analogs of these molecules have been developed for use in the treatment of several viral pathogens and

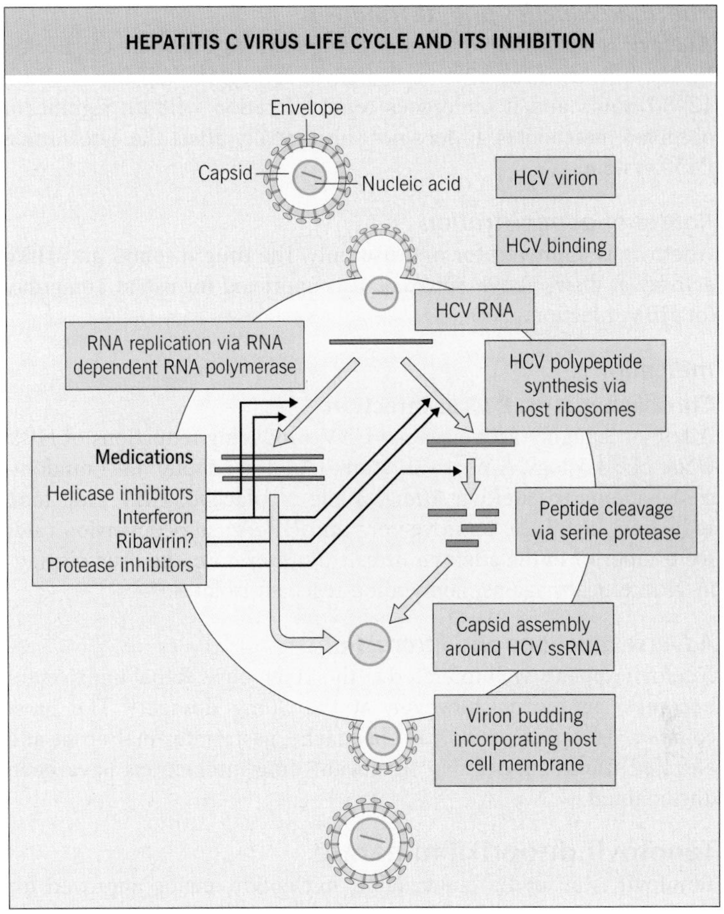

Fig. 207.2 Hepatitis C virus life cycle and its inhibition.

function either as nucleic acid chain terminators or as inhibitors of polymerase enzymes. Nucleoside analogs (phosphate absent) include lamivudine, famciclovir and lobucavir, while nucleotide analogs (phosphate present) are represented by adefovir and tenofovir. These drugs inhibit a critical step of the HBV life cycle where the reverse transcriptase activity of its DNA polymerase catalyzes the conversion of RNA to DNA.[18] Resistance to nucleoside analogs can be caused by mutations in the active site of the DNA polymerase enzyme, including the highly conserved amino acid motif YMDD.[19]

Lamivudine

Lamivudine was the first nucleoside analog approved for HBV infection. It is also used for the treatment of HIV infection. Detailed pharmacokinetic and distribution data are provided in Chapter 204. The dose used for HBV, 100mg q24h, is lower than that used for HIV. Lamivudine therapy is associated with a significant improvement in hepatic histology, normalization of hepatic enzymes and suppression of plasma HBV DNA.[20] In most patients, however, values return to baseline levels when lamivudine is discontinued. The emergence of drug-resistant HBV may limit the value of lamivudine for long-term therapy and may be associated with increases in serum liver transaminases.[21] Regimens combining lamivudine with other active compounds to enhance efficacy and limit the development of resistance are under investigation.[22]

Adefovir

Adefovir is approved for the treatment of HBV infection. Originally developed as an antiretroviral, it is associated with significant renal toxicity at the higher doses needed to inhibit HIV replication and is not approved for that indication.

Pharmacokinetics and distribution

Adefovir is administered as the prodrug adefovir dipivoxil. Unaffected by food, it achieves 60% oral bioavailability. Its half-life is about 12–30 hours and it undergoes renal excretion without significant observed metabolites. It does not substantially affect the cytochrome P450 system.

Routes of administration

Adefovir is approved for oral use only. The drug displays anti-HBV activity at doses above 5mg/day. It is approved for use at 10mg/day for HBV infection.

Indications

Chronic hepatitis B virus infection

Adefovir is highly active against HBV, producing reductions of HBV DNA of >3.5 logs. A phase III study (Adefovir Study 437) randomized patients to adefovir 10mg, 30mg or placebo; HBV viral load reduction, histologic improvement and HBeAg seroconversion rates were superior in the adefovir arms.[23] Furthermore, the drug displays in-vitro efficacy against lamivudine-resistant isolates.[24]

Adverse reactions and interactions

Adefovir appears well tolerated at the 10mg dose. Renal impairment becomes significant, however, at the 30mg dosage.[25] The most common adverse reactions are headache, gastrointestinal upset and elevated transaminases. No significant drug interactions have been documented.

Tenofovir disoprixil fumarate

Tenofovir is an orally bioavailable, nucleotide analog approved for HIV therapy. Detailed pharmacokinetic and distribution data are given in Chapter 204. Limited data suggest that the drug has activity against lamivudine-resistant HBV isolates.[26] Tenofovir may have potential for the treatment of HBV infection in patients co-infected with HIV.[26a]

Other nucleoside analogs in development

Emtricitabine

Emtricitabine has efficacy against HIV as well as HBV. Its activity against HBV may be greater than that seen with lamivudine. In a dose-ranging study of emtricitabine at 25, 100 and 200mg daily for 48 weeks, 38, 42 and 61% of patients had reductions in HBV DNA levels to below the level of quantification by Digene Hybrid Capture II assay (<4700 copies/ml), respectively, while 32, 38 and 50% in each arm experienced loss of HbeAg.[27]

Entecavir

Entecavir is an orally bioavailable nucleoside analog with a half-life of 110 hours. A dose-ranging study of entecavir at 0.01, 0.1 and 0.5mg versus lamivudine demonstrated reductions in HBV DNA of 2.4, 4.3 and 4.7 logs at each entecavir dose, respectively, compared with a 3.4 log reduction with lamivudine.[28] Preliminary results show efficacy against the lamivudine-resistant YMDD mutant.

Famciclovir (see also Chapter 205)

Famciclovir, an orally administered prodrug of penciclovir, is approved for the treatment of herpes simplex virus and varicella-zoster virus infections. It is effective in animal models of HBV infection and has significant antiviral effects in patients with chronic HBV infection.[29] Famciclovir may not suppress virus as effectively as lamivudine, as evidenced by a lower rate of HBeAg seroconversion.[30] Furthermore, the drug does not appear to suppress lamivudine-resistant HBV mutants.

Lobucavir

Lobucavir is a cyclobutyl analog of guanine with potent in-vitro activity against HBV. In a study of 81 patients with HBV infection, treatment with lobucavir resulted in a 3.5 log decrease in HBV DNA. Levels of HBV DNA were below the level of quantitation in 68% of patients. Unfortunately, the drug appears to be associated with carcinogenic potential in long-term animal studies, and it is not clear whether further drug development will continue.

COMBINATION THERAPY FOR HEPATITIS B VIRUS INFECTION

Studies of combination therapy involving nucleoside analogs plus IFN have yielded conflicting results thus far.[31] These combinations, as well as combinations of nucleoside analogs, await future definitive evaluations before they can be recommended.

REFERENCES

1. Novick D, Cohen B, Rubinstein M. The human interferon alpha/beta receptor: characterization and molecular cloning. Cell 1994;77:391–400.
2. Sharieff KA, Duncan D, Younossi Z. Advances in treatment of chronic hepatitis C: 'pegylated' interferons. Cleve Clin J Med 2002;69:155–9.
3. Wills R. Clinical pharmacokinetics of interferons. Clin Pharmacokinet 1990;19:390–9.
4. Wong DK, Cheung AM, O'Rourke K, Naylor CD, Detsky AS, Heathcote J. Effect of alpha-interferon treatment in patients with hepatitis B e antigen-positive chronic hepatitis B. A meta-analysis. Ann Intern Med 1993;119:312–23.
5. Brook MG, Karayiannis P, Thomas HC. Which patients with chronic hepatitis B virus infection will respond to alpha-interferon therapy? A statistical analysis of predictive factors. Hepatology 1989;10:761–3.
6. Jaeckel E, Cornberg M, Wedemeyer H, *et al.* Treatment of acute hepatitis C with interferon alfa-2b. N Engl J Med 2001;345:1452–7.
7. NIH. NIH Consensus statement, Sept, 2002. http//consensus.NIH.gov/cons/116/091202116 cdc_statement.htm.
8. Liang TJ, Rehermann B, Seeff LB, Hoofnagle JH. Pathogenesis, natural history, treatment, and prevention of hepatitis C. Ann Intern Med 2000;132:296–305.
9. Trepo C, Lindsay K, Niederau C, *et al.* Pegylated interferon alfa-2B (PEG-intron) mono-therapy is superior to interferon alfa-2B (intron A) for the treatment of chronic hepatitis C. J Hepatology 2000;32:29.
10. Heathcote EJ, Shiffman ML, Cooksley WG, *et al.* Peginterferon alfa-2a in patients with chronic hepatitis C and cirrhosis. N Engl J Med 2000;343:1673–80.
11. Lindsay KL, Trepo C, Heintges T, *et al.* A randomized, double-blind trial comparing pegylated interferon alfa-2b to interferon alfa-2b as initial treatment for chronic hepatitis C. Hepatology 2001;34:395–403.
12. Manns MP, McHutchison JG, Gordon SC, *et al.* Peginterferon alfa-2b plus ribavirin compared with interferon alfa-2b plus ribavirin for initial treatment of chronic hepatitis C: a randomised trial. Lancet 2001;358:958–65.
13. Lau JY, Tam RC, Liang TJ, Hong Z. Mechanism of action of ribavirin in the combination treatment of chronic HCV infection. Hepatology 2002;35:1002–9.
14. McHutchison JG, Gordon SC, Schiff ER, *et al.* Interferon alfa-2b alone or in combination with ribavirin as initial treatment for chronic hepatitis C. Hepatitis Interventional Therapy Group. N Engl J Med 1998;339:1485–92.
15. Fried MW, Shiffman ML, Reddy KR, *et al.* Peginterferon alfa-2a plus ribavirin for chronic hepatitis C virus infection. N Engl J Med 2002;347:975–82.
16. Chung RAJ, Alston B, Vallee M, *et al.* A randomized controlled trial of pegylated interferon alfa-2a with ribavirin vs interferon alfa-2a with ribavirin for the treatment of chronic HCV in HIV coinfection: ACTG A5071. Paper presented at 9th Conference on Retroviruses and Opportunistic Infections, Seattle, Washington. Alexandria,VA: Foundation for Retrovirology and Human Health; 2002:102.
17. Sharara AI, Hunt CM, Hamilton JD. Hepatitis C. Ann Intern Med 1996;125:658–68.
18. Malik AH, Lee WM. Chronic hepatitis B virus infection: treatment strategies for the next millenium. Ann Intern Med 2000;132:723–31.

19. Allen MI, Deslauriers M, Andrews CW, *et al.* Identification and characterization of mutations in hepatitis B virus resistant to lamivudine. Lamivudine Clinical Investigation Group. Hepatology 1998;27:1670–7.
20. Lai CL, Chien RN, Leung NW, *et al.* A one-year trial of lamivudine for chronic hepatitis B. Asia Hepatitis Lamivudine Study Group. N Engl J Med 1998;339:61–8.
21. Niesters HG, Honkoop P, Haagsma EB, de Man RA, Schalm SW, Osterhaus AD. Identification of more than one mutation in the hepatitis B virus polymerase gene arising during prolonged lamivudine treatment. J Infect Dis 1998;177:1382–5.
22. Jaeckel E, Manns MP. Experience with lamivudine against hepatitis B virus. Intervirology 1997;40:322–36.
23. Marcellin P, Chang TT, Lim SG, *et al.* Adefovir dipivoxil for the treatment of hepatitis B e antigen-positive chronic hepatitis B. N Engl J Med 2003; 348:808-16.
24. Xiong X, Flores C, Yang H, Toole JJ, Gibbs CS. Mutations in hepatitis B DNA polymerase associated with resistance to lamivudine do not confer resistance to adefovir *in vitro*. Hepatology 1998;28:1669–73.
25. Kahn J, Lagakos S, Wulfsohn M, *et al.* Efficacy and safety of adefovir dipivoxil with antiretroviral therapy: a randomized controlled trial. JAMA 1999;282:2305–12.
26. Ying C, De Clercq E, Nicholson W, Furman P, Neyts J. Inhibition of the replication of the DNA polymerase M550V mutation variant of human hepatitis B virus by adefovir, tenofovir, L-FMAU, DAPD, penciclovir and lobucavir. J Viral Hepat 2000;7:161–5.
26a. Ristig MB, Crippin J, Aberg JA, *et al.* Tenofovir disoproxil fumarate therapy for chronic hepatitis B in human immunodeficiency virus/hepatitis B virus-coinfected individuals for whom interferon-alpha and lamivudine therapy have failed. J Infect Dis 2002;186:1844-7.
27. Sykes A, Wakeford C, Rousseau F, Rigney A, Mondou E. Abstract 674–M. Antiviral efficacy and rate of development of resistance in patients treated 1 year for chronic HBV infection with FTC. Paper presented at 9th Conference on Retroviruses and Opportunistic Infections, Seattle, Washington. Alexandria,VA: Foundation for Retrovirology and Human Health; 2002:299.
28. Lai CL, Rosmawati M, Lao J, *et al.* Entecavir is superior to lamivudine in reducing hepatitis B virus DNA in patients with chronic hepatitis B infection. Gastroenterology 2002;123:1831-8.
29. Bartholomeusz A, Groenen LC, Locarnini S. Clinical experience with famciclovir against hepatitis B virus. Intervirology 1997;40:337–42.
30. Lai CL, Yuen MF, Cheng CC, Wong WM, Cheng TK, Lai YP. An open comparative study of lamivudine and famciclovir for the treatment of chronic hepatitis B infection. [Abstract]. Hepatology 1998;28:490A.
31. Barbaro G, Zechini F, Pellicelli AM, *et al.* Long-term efficacy of interferon alpha-2b and lamivudine in combination compared to lamivudine monotherapy in patients with chronic hepatitis B. An Italian multicenter, randomized trial. J Hepatol 2001;35:406–11.

chapter 208

Antifungal Agents

Shmuel Shoham, Andreas H Groll & Thomas J Walsh

Invasive fungal infections have evolved into important causes of morbidity and mortality in patients with severe underlying diseases. For more than three decades, treatment has been limited to amphotericin B (AmB) deoxycholate with or without flucytosine. Therapeutic options only emerged with the clinical development of fluconazole and itraconazole in the late 1980s. The past 10 years, however, have witnessed a major expansion in our antifungal armamentarium through the introduction of less toxic formulations of amphotericin B, the development of improved antifungal triazoles and the advent of the echinocandin lipopeptides, a new class of antifungal agents that target the fungal cell wall. This chapter reviews the clinical pharmacology of approved and investigational antifungal agents for treatment of invasive fungal infections.

POLYENE ANTIBIOTICS

Amphotericin B deoxycholate

Amphotericin B is a natural polyene macrolide antibiotic and consists of seven conjugated double bounds, an internal ester, a free carboxyl group and a glycoside side chain with a primary amino group (Fig. 208.1). It is amphoteric, virtually insoluble in water, and not orally or intramuscularly absorbed. For parenteral use, AmB has been solubilized with deoxycholate as micellar suspension, and this formulation has been available for now more than 40 years.

Mechanism of action

Amphotericin B primarily acts by binding to ergosterol, the principal sterol in the cell membrane of most fungi, leading to the formation of ion channels and concentration-dependent, cell death (Fig. 208.2). These pores, composed of AmB multimers, form most readily when ergosterol is present in the cell membrane.[1,2] With less avidity, the compound also binds to cholesterol, the main sterol of mammalian cell membranes, which is believed to account for most of its adverse effects. A second mechanism of action of AmB may involve oxidative damage of the cell through a cascade of oxidative reactions linked to its own oxidation and interactions with lipoproteins with formation of free radicals or an increase in membrane permeability.[3–6]

Antifungal activity

Amphotericin B has broad-spectrum antifungal activity that includes most fungi pathogenic in humans. Primary resistance has been associated with qualitative or quantitative variations in membrane sterols,[7] but it may also be related to increased catalase activity with decreased susceptibility to oxidative damage.[8–10] Resistance remains uncommon in *Cryptococcus neoformans* and *Candida* spp. although AmB appears somewhat less active against *Candida guilliermondii, Candida parapsilosis* and *Candida tropicalis*. *Candida lusitaniae* isolates are often resistant to AmB, and this resistance can develop during treatment.[11,12]. *Aspergillus* spp. and other opportunistic molds, but not the dimorphic molds, tend to have more variable susceptibility to AmB. *Aspergillus terreus, Fusarium* spp., *Pseudallescheria boydii, Scedosporium prolificans*, certain other dematiaceous fungi and *Trichosporon beigelii* may be resistant to AmB at concentrations safely achievable in patients.[11,13,14] Acquisition of secondary resistance has been anecdotally reported but its role as a clinical problem has not been fully defined.

Pharmacodynamics

Amphotericin B displays concentration-dependent fungicidal activity against susceptible *Candida albicans, C. neoformans* and *Aspergillus fumigatus* in time-kill assays and exhibits a postantifungal effect of up to 12 hours' duration against *C. albicans* and *C. neoformans* in vitro.[15–17] Studies in laboratory animals with experimental disseminated candidiasis suggest that peak serum level to MIC ratio correlates best with antifungal efficacy in vivo.[18] These findings support the notion that large doses will be most effective and that achievement of optimal peak concentrations is important.

Pharmacokinetics

After intravenous administration, AmB dissociates from its vehicle and becomes highly protein-bound before distributing predominantly into liver, spleen, bone marrow, kidney and lung. A unique property of AmB is that protein binding in plasma is enhanced with increasing drug concentration.[19] Clearance from plasma is slow with a terminal half-life of 5 days and longer.[20,21] Concentrations in body fluids other than plasma are generally low; however, despite mostly undetectable concentrations in the cerebrospinal fluid (CSF), AmB is effective in the treatment of fungal infections of the central nervous system. Amphotericin B is mostly excreted as unchanged drug in the urine and feces, and no metabolites have been identified.[20] Dose adjustment of AmB is not necessary in patients with unrelated renal or hepatic dysfunction. Because of its high protein binding, hemodialysis usually does not affect plasma concentrations of AmB. Infants and children appear to clear the drug from plasma more rapidly than adults, as indicated by a significant negative correlation between age and clearance.[22]

Adverse effects

Infusion-related reactions and nephrotoxicity of AmB are major problems and often limit therapy. Infusion-related reactions (fever, rigors, chills, myalgias, arthralgias, nausea, vomiting and headaches) are thought to be mediated by the release of cytokines from monocytes in response to the drug. They can be noted in up to 73% of patients during the first dose, but often improve during continued therapy.[23] Slowing the infusion rate or pre-medication with acetaminophen (10–15mg/kg), hydrocortisone (0.5–1.0mg/kg) or meperidine (0.2–0.5mg/kg) (pethidine, 25–50mg) may blunt these reactions. Continuous 24-hour infusion of AmB further reduces symptoms, but data on the antifungal efficacy of this dosing strategy is limited.[24] Cardiac arrhythmias and cardiac arrest caused by acute potassium release may occur with rapid infusion of under 60 minutes, especially if there is pre-existing hyperkalemia or renal impairment. True allergic reactions are rare.[25]

Amphotericin B-associated nephrotoxicity occurs as a result of alterations of membrane permeability in renal tubular and vascular

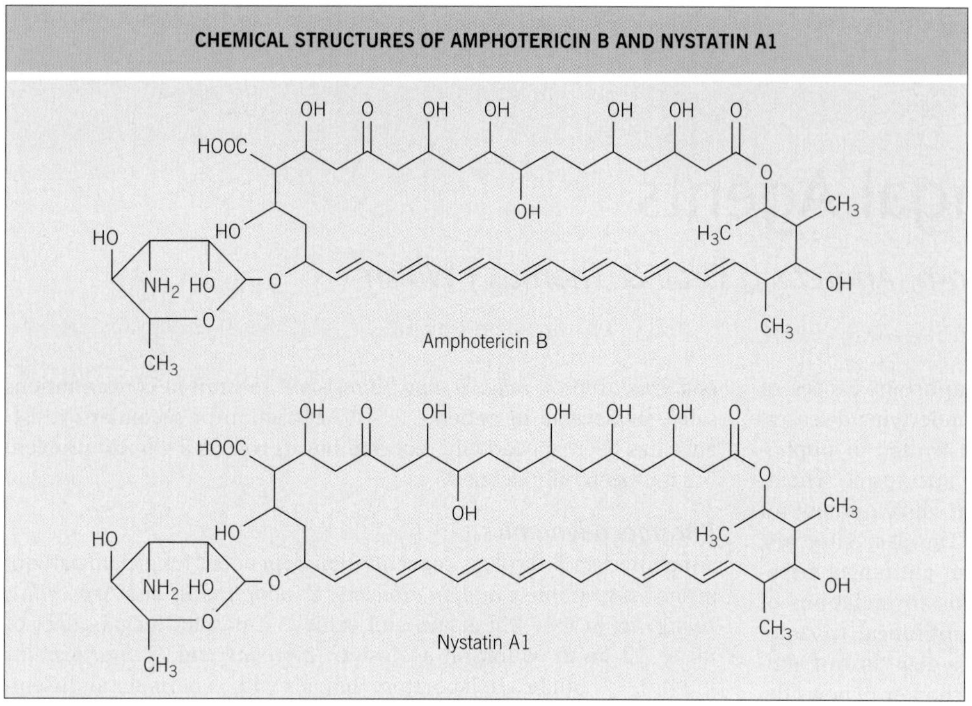

Fig. 208.1 Chemical structures of amphotericin B and nystatin A1.

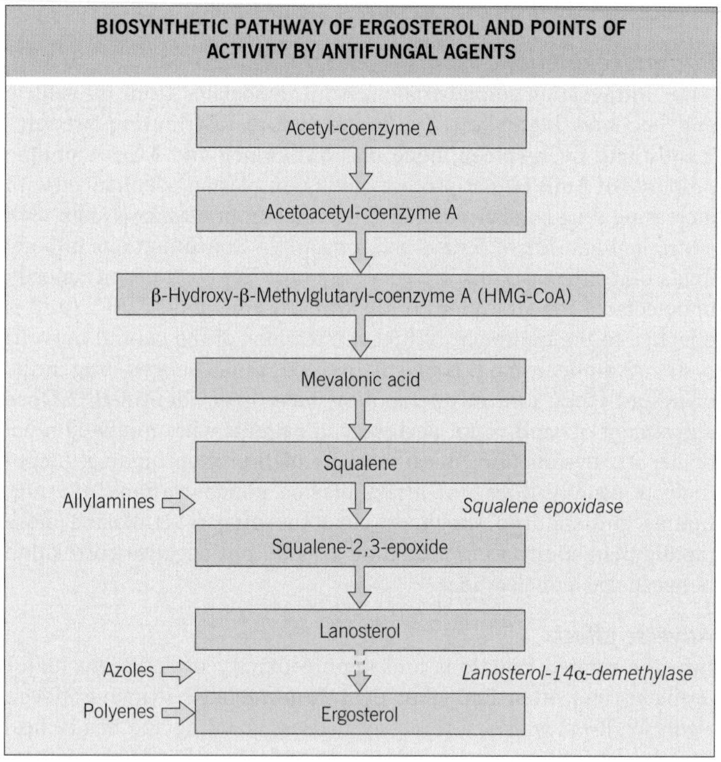

Fig. 208.2 Biosynthetic pathway of ergosterol and points of activity by antifungal agents.

smooth muscle cells. Tubular transport defects and decreased glomerular filtration rate caused by vasoconstriction are responsible for potassium and magnesium wasting, tubular acidosis, impaired urinary concentration ability and azotemia. Decreased renal blood flow and recurrent ischemia may lead to permanent structural nephrotoxic effects.[3] Hypokalemia can be quite refractory to replacement until hypomagnesemia is corrected. Tubular acidosis and impaired urinary concentration are rarely of clinical significance. Azotemia is common; in a large prospective clinical trial, the baseline serum creatinine rose by more than 100% in over one-third of 344 unstratified patients receiving AmB for empiric therapy of fever and neutropenia.[23] Risks of developing renal toxicity are related to dose and duration of therapy, concomitant use of nephrotoxic agents such as ciclosporin and amikacin, and pre-existing renal dysfunction.[26] Renal toxicity associated with the use of AmB has the potential to lead to renal failure and dialysis. Often, however, azotemia stabilizes on therapy and is usually reversible after discontinuation of the drug. Avoiding concomitant nephrotoxic agents, appropriate hydration and normal saline loading (0.9% sodium chloride 10–15ml/kg/day) may lessen the likelihood and severity of azotemia.

Other potentially relevant adverse effects of AmB include hypotension, hypertension, flushing, vestibular disturbances and a normocytic, normochromic anemia after chronic administration.[22] Amphotericin B deoxycholate is topically irritating; therefore, a central line should be used for infusion. Local instillation, including intrathecal administration, can cause focal areas of necrosis and should only be considered in conjunction with expert consultation.[27]

Drug interactions

In rats, AmB decreases the concentration of hepatic microsomal cytochrome P450 and inhibits propafenone metabolism.[28] Drug–drug interactions attributable to shared metabolic pathways have not been described in humans. Hypokalemia may be aggravated by corticosteroids, and hypomagnesemia may become especially profound in cancer patients with platinum-associated nephropathy. Amphotericin B therapy may enhance plasma levels and thereby toxicity of many renally cleared drugs, including aminoglycosides, vancomycin, fluorocytosine and ciclosporin. Cumulative renal toxicity has been seen when amphotericin B is given simultaneously with other nephrotoxic agents e.g., gentamicin, foscarnet or pentamidine. The simultaneous infusion of granulocytes has been associated with acute pulmonary reactions, and should therefore only be used with extreme caution. Treatment with fluconazole followed by AmB has been shown to reduce antifungal susceptibility in vitro and in vivo.[29] The sequential use of an azole followed by AmB should probably be avoided.

Indications and dosing

Despite its toxicity profile, AmB deoxycholate is still considered the drug of choice for the initial treatment of most life-threatening infections caused by susceptible organisms. Depending on both the type of infection and the host, the recommended daily dosage ranges from 0.5 to 1.5mg/kg/day administered over 2–4 hours as tolerated; the standard dosage for empiric therapy in persistently febrile neutropenic patients is 0.5–0.6mg/kg/day.[25] Continuous infusion of AmB deoxycholate may be associated with less toxicity;[24] however, this mode of administration is counterintuitive to the concentration-dependent pharmacodynamics of AmB and is therefore not recommended. Whether the enhanced plasma clearance in infants and young children has implications for dosing remains unknown. Currently, dosage recommendations for all pediatric age groups do not differ from those in adults. Treatment should be started at the full target dosage with careful bedside monitoring during the first infusion to allow for prompt intervention for infusion related reactions.

Therapeutic monitoring

Historically, it has been proposed that a plasma concentration at 1 hour after infusion of twice the MIC of the fungal isolate should be the target for treatment of yeast infections.[30] However, monitoring of AmB concentrations in plasma or CSF appears of little value, since relationships between plasma and tissue concentrations and clinical efficacy or toxicity have not been adequately characterized.[16]

Amphotericin B lipid formulations

During the past few years, three novel formulations of AmB have been approved in the USA and most of Europe:

- AmB colloidal dispersion (ABCD),
- AmB lipid complex (ABLC), and
- a small unilamellar vesicle liposomal formulation (L-AmB).

Because of their reduced nephrotoxicity in comparison to AmB deoxycholate, these compounds allow for the delivery of higher dosages of AmB. However, data from animal models also suggest that higher dosages are required for equivalent antifungal efficacy.

Physicochemical properties and pharmacokinetics

Because of differences in the physicochemical properties of their carriers, each of the lipid formulations confers its own distinct plasma pharmacokinetics properties to AmB. All three formulations, however, preferentially distribute to organs of the mononuclear phagocytic system (MPS), sequester lipid-associated drug within deep tissues and functionally spare the kidney. L-AmB, the only truly liposomal AmB, is composed of small spherical unilamellar lipid vesicles averaging 60–70nm in size. Following infusion the liposomal preparation has a prolonged circulation time in plasma, achieves strikingly high peak plasma concentrations and AUC values, and is only slowly taken up by the MPS. However, most of the AmB in plasma remains liposome-associated, and free unbound drug concentrations are low.[19,20]

Amphotericin B lipid complex, composed of ribbon-like lipid aggregates, is efficiently opsonized by plasma proteins and rapidly taken up by the MPS to achieve high concentrations of drug in the cellular components of blood, liver, lung and spleen. It exists as a depot in these tissues and free AmB is slowly released. Fungal and inflammatory cell lipases at the site of infection act to release the complexed AmB from the lipid carrier.[31]

Amphotericin B colloidal dispersion, a colloidal dispersion of microscopic disc-shaped particles, also preferentially collects in tissues of the MPS and free drug is slowly released over time. Drug levels in the plasma and kidney are low and terminal elimination half-life is long (Table 208.1).

Whether these distinct pharmacokinetic features translate into different pharmacodynamic properties is largely unknown. More recent experimental comparisons of all four formulations of AmB against defined invasive mycoses suggest potentially important differences in antifungal efficacy depending on agent, dose, type and site of infection.[13]

Safety and antifungal efficacy

Safety and antifungal efficacy of lipid formulations have been demonstrated in phase I and phase II studies in immunocompromised patients with a wide spectrum of underlying disorders.[32–34]

AMPHOTERICIN B FORMULATIONS AND LIPOSOMAL NYSTATIN: PHYSICOCHEMICAL PROPERTIES AND PHARMACOKINETIC PARAMETERS

	DAMB	ABCD	ABLC	LAMB	LNYS
Lipids (molar ratio)	Deoxycholate	Cholesterylsulfate	DMPC/DMPG (7:3)	HPC/CHOL/DSPG (2:1:0.8)	DMPC/DMPG (7:3)
Mol% drug	34	50	50	10	10
Lipid configuration	micelles	micelles	membrane-like	SUVs	MLVs
Particle diameter (μm)	0.05	0.12–0.14	1.6–11	0.08	0.32
Dosage (mg/kg)	1	5	5	5	4
C_{max} (μg/ml)	2.9	3.1	1.7	58	24
$AUC_{0-\infty}$ (μg/ml.h)	36	43	14	713	80
VD_{ss} (l/kg)	1.1	4.3	131	0.22	0.24
Cl (l/h/kg)	0.028	0.117	0.476	0.017	0.051
Half-life (h)	39	28	6–18	7–10	2–6

DAMB, amphotericin B deoxycholate; ABCD, amphotericin B colloidal dispersion; ABLC, amphotericin B lipid complex; LAMB, liposomal amphotericin B; LNYS, liposomal nystatin; DMPC, dimiristoyl phosphatidylcholine; DMPG, dimiristoyl phosphatidylglycerol; HPC, hydrogenated phosphatidylcholine; CHOL, cholesterol; DSPG, disteaoryl phosphatidylglycerol; SUVs, small unilamellar vesicles (liposomes); MLVs, multilamellar vesicles (liposomes); C_{max}, peak plasma concentration; $AUC_{0-\infty}$, area under the concentration vs time curve from time zero to infinity; VDss, apparent volume of distribution at steady state; Cl, plasma clearance; Half-life, apparent plasma half-life during the dosing interval of 24 hours
Data represent mean values, stem from adult patients and were obtained after different rates of infusion. Concentrations of nystatin were measured in whole blood and are approximately half of those measured in serum
Modified from Groll *et al.*[62] and Cossum *et al.*[45]

Table 208.1 Amphotericin B formulations and liposomal nystatin: physicochemical properties and pharmacokinetic parameters.

The overall response rates in these trials ranged from 53 to 84% in patients with invasive candidiasis and from 34 to 5%, respectively, in patients with probable or documented invasive aspergillosis. Clinical and microbiologic responses were observed in patients with documented invasive fungal infections even when lipid formulations were used as salvage therapy after failure of conventional AmB deoxycholate. Patients with neutropenia responded to therapy with lipid formulations, but, as with other antifungal agents, recovery of neutrophil counts, remission from underlying malignancy and continued antifungal therapy were necessary for resolution of their fungal infections. Several randomized controlled trials have now been completed in which one of the new formulations has been compared with AmB deoxycholate. These studies have consistently shown at least equivalent therapeutic efficacy and reduced nephrotoxicity in comparison with AmB deoxycholate. A meta-analysis of 1149 neutropenic patients from three trials found that prophylactic or empiric use of L-AmB tended to be more effective than AmB deoxycholate in preventing breakthrough fungal infections and that it was associated with less nephrotoxicity, although it did not lead to improved survival.[35] Infusion-related side-effects of fever, chills and rigor appear to be less frequent with L-AmB and may even be increased with ABCD.[23,36,37] Several individual cases of substernal chest discomfort, respiratory distress and sharp flank pain have been noted during infusion of L-AmB,[38] and in a comparative study hypoxic episodes associated with fever and chills were more frequent in ABCD recipients than in AmB deoxycholate recipients.[39] Mild increases in serum bilirubin and alkaline phosphatase have been observed with all three formulations, Generally mild increases in serum transaminases and pancreatic enzymes with L-AmB have been observed. However, no cases of fatal liver or pancreatic diseases have been reported.

Indications and dosing

The lipid formulations are indicated for the treatment of patients with AmB-susceptible invasive mycoses that are refractory to AmB deoxycholate and for the treatment of patients who are intolerant to AmB deoxycholate; L-AmB is indicated for empiric therapy of persistently neutropenic patients. Preliminary pediatric pharmacokinetic and safety data indicate no fundamental differences in comparison with adults. The optimal dosages of each formulation for the various type and sites of invasive fungal infections remain to be defined. Based on animal data and the few randomized studies that have used AmB deoxycholate as comparator,[40,41] we and most other experts in the field consider a dose of 5mg/kg/day of ABCD, ABLC or L-AmB to be equivalent to a dosage of 1mg/kg/day of AmB deoxycholate. Accordingly, an initial dosage of 5mg/kg/day of ABCD, ABLC or L-AmB is currently recommended for treatment of suspected or documented life-threatening infections, and a dosage of 3mg/kg/day is recommended when L-AmB is selected for empiric antifungal therapy in persistently febrile, neutropenic patients. Recent data have also suggested that lipid formulation of AmB at doses of 3mg/kg can be effective in patients with histoplasmosis and in selected patients with candidiasis.[42,43] Because the favorable therapeutic index of the drug some clinicians have successfully used L-AmB at doses of 10mg/kg and 15mg/kg in patients with recalcitrant invasive fungal infections. The maximum tolerable dose appears to be at least 15mg/kg/day.

Use of lipid formulations of AmB has been limited by their high costs. Current in-vivo and clinical data indicate that L-AmB is the least toxic of the of these agents. However, as L-AmB also carries the highest drug acquisition cost, appreciation of its superior safety profile is often eclipsed by pharmacoeconomic concerns. Comprehensive economic analyses that include hospital and societal costs resulting from excess nephrotoxicity related to the use of conventional AmB deoxycholate appear to indicate that the high cost of lipid formulations of AmB may be supplanted by the even greater cost of AmB deoxycholate-induced nephrotoxicity.

Liposomal nystatin

Nystatin, the first antifungal polyene, is a tetraene–diene macrolide with a structure that is very similar to that of AmB. Like AmB, it binds to ergosterol in the cell membrane of fungi, creating a pore and leading to cell death. Although it is used widely as a topical agent, nystatin is ineffective when given orally and highly toxic when given parenterally (see Fig. 208.1). Although generally less potent on a molar basis, the spectrum of activity of this agent and its in-vitro pharmacodynamics are similar to those of AmB, and it might have activity against some amphotericin B-resistant isolates.[25,44] An intravenous multilamellar liposomal formulation of nystatin has been developed that has reached clinical trials. The plasma pharmacokinetics of multilamellar liposomal nystatin are unique among the current polyenes and are characterized by comparatively high peak plasma concentrations and rapid elimination from plasma, with a half-life of 5–7 hours.[45] Animal studies have indicated that this formulation is preferentially distributed to lung, liver and spleen, and that the kidney appears to play a major role in excretion.[46] In a phase I study, multilamellar liposomal nystatin was tolerated at multiple dosages of up to 8mg/kg.[47] The compound has demonstrated clinical efficacy in the treatment of candidemia and invasive aspergillosis and as empiric antifungal therapy for neutropenic cancer patients at dosages ranging from 2mg/kg to 4mg/kg.[48–50] Submission for approval by the US Food and Drug Administration (FDA) is expected in the near future.

FLUCYTOSINE

Flucytosine (5-fluorocytosine, 5-FC) is a low-molecular-weight, water-soluble, synthetic fluorinated analog of cytosine (Fig. 208.3). It has no antifungal activity of its own. It is taken up by the fungus-specific enzyme cytosine permease and converted in the cytoplasm by cytosine deaminase to 5-fluorouracil, which causes RNA miscoding and inhibits DNA synthesis.[51] Although it was originally synthesized as a potential antitumor agent, 5-FC is relatively nontoxic to mammalian cells because of the absence or very low level of activity of cytosine deaminase. Recently, this compound has re-emerged as an antineoplastic agent for use in tumors sensitized by the addition of fungal and bacterial cytosine deaminase genes. In the USA, 5-FC is available only as oral formulation; an intravenous formulation is available in some countries.

Antifungal activity

The antifungal spectrum of 5-FC in vitro encompasses *Candida* spp., *C. neoformans*, *Saccharomyces cerevisiae* and selected dematiaceous moulds. Flucytosine has little to no activity against *Aspergillus*

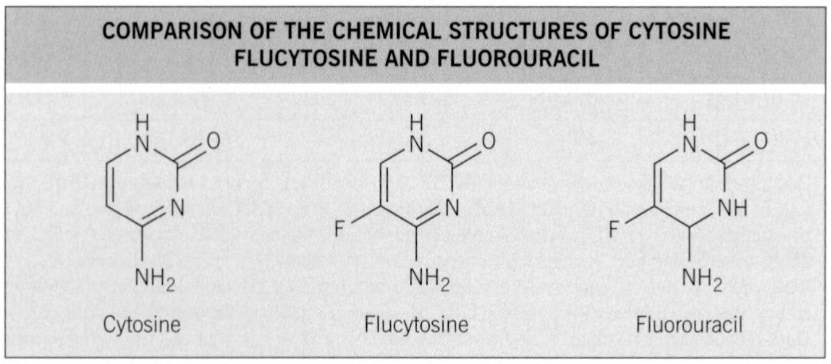

Fig. 208.3 Comparison of the chemical structures of cytosine, flucytosine and fluorouracil.

spp. and other hyaline molds.[52,53] Synergistic or additive effects in combination with AmB have been observed against *Candida* spp. and in combination with AmB, fluconazole or the investigational agent posaconazole against *C. neoformans*.[32,54] With the exception of *Candida krusei*, primary resistance to 5-FC occurs very rarely in *Candida* spp.[55] Resistance to 5-FC, defined as a MIC of 32μg/ml or greater, has been observed in 1.6–2.2% of *C. neoformans* isolates.[56] In contrast to primary resistance, secondary resistance, which occurs predominantly by selection of resistant clones, can evolve rapidly and appears to result from a single point mutation. In *C. neoformans* resistance to 5-FC has been observed in 30–40% of isolates from patients with meningitis who relapsed following monotherapy.[57] Resistance in susceptible fungi may involve either mutations in the enzymes necessary for cellular uptake, transport or metabolism, or competitive upregulation of pyrimidine synthesis.[51] As a consequence, 5-FC is rarely given alone but in combination with AmB or, more recently, fluconazole.

Pharmacodynamics

Flucytosine has demonstrated predominantly concentration-independent fungistatic (99% reduction in colony-forming units) activity against *Candida* spp. and *C. neoformans* in time-kill assays, and prolonged concentration- and exposure-dependent post-antifungal effects of up to 10 hours.[58,59] Pharmacodynamic studies in mice with experimental disseminated candidiasis have revealed that both the time above the MIC and AUC:MIC ratio were important in predicting efficacy. The C_{max}:MIC ratio was the least important parameter, and maximum efficacy was observed when levels exceeded the MIC for only 20–25% of the 24-hour dosing interval.[60] Thus, lower dosages or less frequent dosing may yield identical antifungal efficacy while further reducing potential toxicities that are mostly dose-dependent.

Pharmacokinetics

Flucytosine is readily absorbed from the gastrointestinal tract, has negligible protein binding and distributes evenly into tissues and body fluids, including the CSF, peritoneal fluid, inflamed joints and the eye. At usual dosages, the drug undergoes little hepatic metabolism and is eliminated predominantly in its active form by glomerular filtration into the urine, with a half-life in plasma of 3–6 hours. Individual dosage adjustment is necessary in patients who have impaired renal function and those undergoing hemofiltration. In patients undergoing hemodialysis, a dose of 37.5mg/kg is recommended following dialysis; in peritoneal dialysis, the compound can be administered systemically or intraperitoneally.[51] Although the data are limited, impaired liver function does not appear to alter 5-FC disposition.[61,62] The pharmacokinetics of 5-FC in pediatric patients has not been formally characterized, so that uniform dosing recommendations cannot be made.

Adverse effects

Common adverse effects of 5-FC that occur in 5–6% of patients include gastrointestinal intolerance and reversible elevations of hepatic transaminases and alkaline phosphatase. Rarer side-effects are skin rashes, ulcerative colitis and bowel perforation, blood eosinophilia and crystalluria.[62] Hematologic adverse effects have been reported in 6% of patients receiving oral 5-FC overall; these adverse effects may include neutropenia, thrombocytopenia or pancytopenia. Among 202 AIDS patients receiving combination therapy with AmB and 5-FC for cryptococcal meningitis, the drug toxicity withdrawal rate of 3% was similar to the rate in those receiving AmB monotherapy.[63] Flucytosine-associated adverse effects are usually reversible after discontinuation of the drug or dosage reduction; however, fatal outcomes have been reported.[64] Some of the adverse effects of 5-FC may be due to the conversion of the compound to 5-fluorouracil by the gastrointestinal bacterial flora and the toxic effects of endogenous metabolites.[51] In patients treated with intravenous 5-FC, in whom the drug presumably did not undergo metabolism by the human intestinal microflora, 5-fluorouracil levels were not detected, but some toxicity was still observed.[65] Hematologic adverse effects are less frequent if plasma levels of 5-FC do not exceed 100μg/ml.[66]

Drug interactions

Orally administered, nonresorbable antibiotics and aluminum hydroxide- and magnesium hydroxide-based antacids may delay absorption of 5-FC from the gastrointestinal tract.[62] Flucytosine is not known to interfere with CYP450 enzyme system. However, any drug that can cause a reduction in the glomerular filtration rate may increase 5-FC serum levels and thereby has the potential to enhance 5-FC-associated toxicity. This includes AmB as well as number of antimicrobial agents, anticancer drugs and ciclosporin.[61] Cytosine arabinoside competitively inhibits 5-FC and the two drugs should not be given concomitantly.

Indications and dosing

Owing to the propensity for secondary resistance, 5-FC is generally not administered as a single agent. An established indication for its use in combination with AmB deoxycholate is for induction therapy of cryptococcal meningitis.[63] The combination of AmB deoxycholate with 5-FC can also be recommended for the treatment of candidal infections involving deep tissues, particularly in critically ill patients and when *Candida* spp. other than *C. albicans* are involved.[64] This includes candidal meningitis, endophthalmitis, endocarditis, vasculitis and peritonitis, as well as osteoarticular, renal and chronic disseminated candidiasis.[62] Flucytosine has been reported to delay hematopoietic recovery after cytotoxic chemotherapy and can therefore not be recommended as an addition to AmB for empiric antifungal therapy of persistently febrile neutropenic patients.[67] The combination of 5-FC with fluconazole may be used for cryptococcal meningitis, when treatment with AmB is not feasible. In addition, this combination may also be useful as second-line therapy for individual patients with invasive candidal infections involving aqueous body compartments. Currently, we recommend a starting dosage for both adults and children of 100mg/kg/day in three or four divided doses.

Therapeutic monitoring

Monitoring of plasma concentrations is essential to adjust dosage to changing renal function and to avoid toxicity. Following oral administration, near-peak levels 2 hours postdosing overlap with trough levels as patients reach steady state and are thus sufficient for therapeutic monitoring.[64] Peak plasma levels between 40μg/ml and 60μg/ml correlate with antifungal efficacy and are seldom associated with adverse hematologic effects.[64,66] The need for monitoring plasma concentrations has limited the use of 5-FC because performance of this test is often restricted to referral laboratories.

ANTIFUNGAL TRIAZOLES

The antifungal azoles are a class of synthetic compounds that have one or more azole rings and a more or less complex side chain, which is attached to one of the nitrogen atoms. The imidazoles miconazole and ketoconazole were the first azoles developed for systemic treatment of human mycoses. Severe toxicities associated with the drug carrier (in the case of miconazole) and erratic absorption and significant interference with the human cytochrome P450 system (in the case of ketoconazole) have limited their clinical usefulness.[62] The subsequently developed triazoles fluconazole and itraconazole (Fig. 208.4), however, have become extremely useful

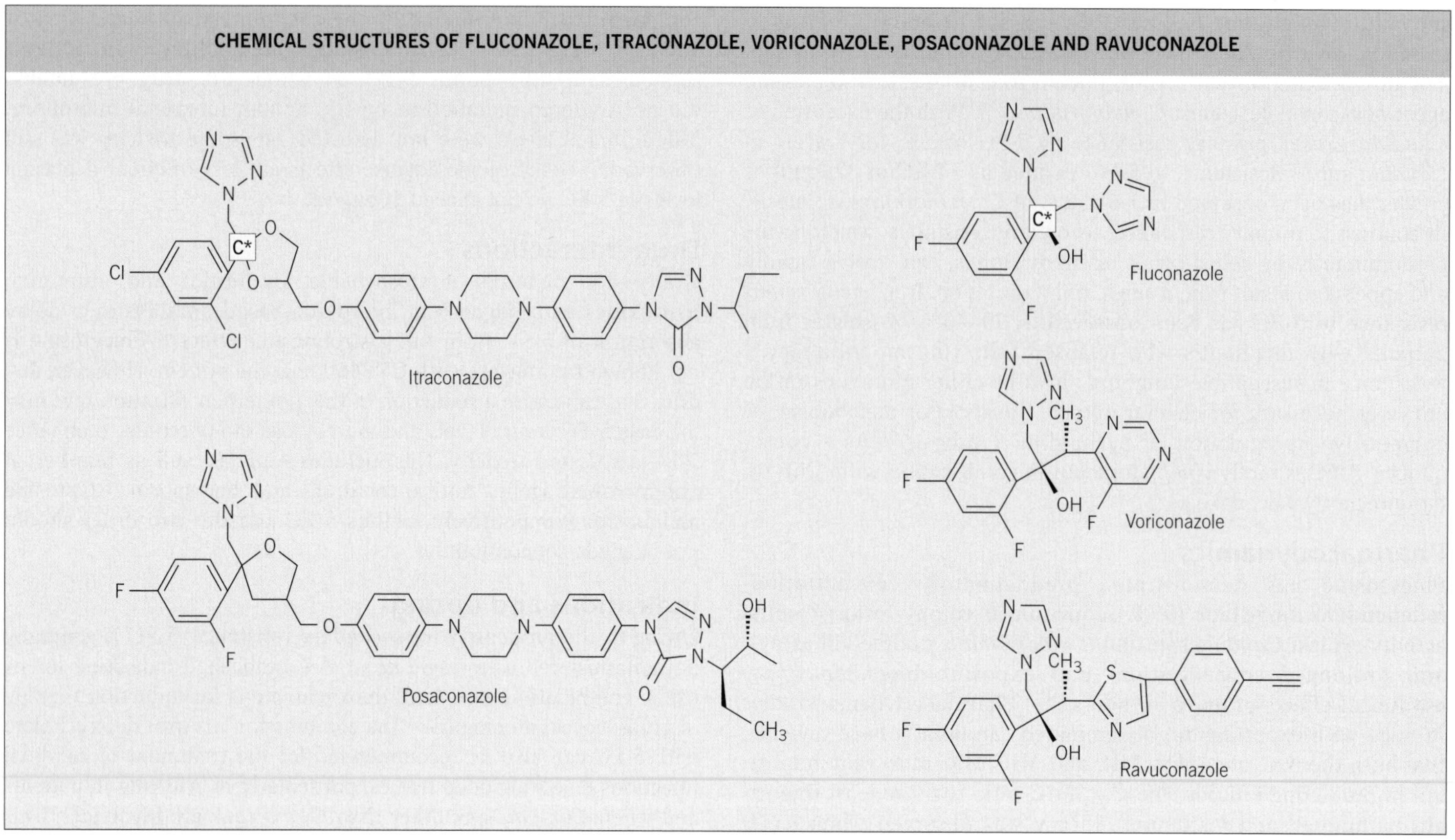

Fig. 208.4 Chemical structures of fluconazole, itraconazole, voriconazole, posaconazole and ravuconazole.

components of the antifungal armamentarium. They possess an expanded spectrum of activity and greater target specificity and are well tolerated overall.

Mechanism of action

The antifungal azoles target ergosterol biosynthesis by inhibiting the fungal cytochrome P450-dependent enzyme lanosterol 14-α-demethylase. This inhibition interrupts the conversion of lanosterol to ergosterol, which leads to accumulation of aberrant 14-α-methylsterols and depletion of ergosterol in the fungal cell membrane (see Fig. 208.2). This alters cell membrane properties and function and, depending on the organism and the compound, may lead to cell death or inhibition of cell growth and replication. In addition, the azoles also inhibit cytochrome P450-dependent enzymes of the fungal respiration chain.[62]

Antifungal activity

Fluconazole and itraconazole are principally active against dermatophytes, *Candida* spp., *C. neoformans, T. beigelii* and some other uncommon yeast-like organisms, and dimorphic fungi such as *Histoplasma capsulatum*, *Coccidioides immitis*, *Blastomyces dermatitidis*, *Paracoccidioides brasiliensis* and *Sporothrix schenckii*.[62] These azoles have less activity against *Candida glabrata* and almost none against *C. krusei*.[68] Useful activity against *Aspergillus* spp. and dematiaceous molds is restricted to itraconazole. Itraconazole and fluconazole are quite inactive against *Fusarium* spp. and the zygomycetes.[62] The second-generation triazoles, voriconazole and the investigational agents posaconazole and ravuconazole, are active against *C. albicans* and *C. krusei*, *Aspergillus* spp. and some *Fusarium* spp. Posaconazole is also active against the zygomycetes.[69]

Resistance

Selection and nosocomial spread of azole-resistant *Candida* spp. has become a matter of increasing concern. Resistance in *Candida* spp. is encountered most commonly in form of a primarily resistant species or through selection of resistant subclones during exposure to azoles. Several mechanisms of resistance have been identified, including but not limited to alterations at the target binding site, increased target expression and induction of cellular efflux pumps.[7] Before the advent of highly active antiretroviral therapy, azole-resistant oropharyngeal and esophageal candidiasis was a major clinical conundrum in HIV-infected patients.[70] In addition, emergence of *C. glabrata* and *C. krusei* infections in association with fluconazole prophylaxis has been observed in several bone marrow transplant centers, although frequency and attributable mortality of these breakthrough infections appears to be low overall.[71] Although cross-resistance of *Candida* spp. to antifungal azoles is common,[72] it is not obligate; patients with microbiologic and clinical fluconazole-resistant mucosal candidiasis may respond to itraconazole or newer triazoles. Acquired azole resistance has been documented in a few patients with *C. neoformans* meningitis receiving maintenance therapy. Very little is known, however, about frequency and mechanisms of secondary azole resistance in filamentous fungi.[62]

Fluconazole

Pharmacodynamics

Conventional time-kill assays performed over incubation periods of 24–48 hours in susceptible *Candida* spp. and *C. neoformans* show fungistatic activity of fluconazole with variable concentration-related growth effects.[73,74] However, with extended incubation of up to 14 days and under nonproliferating growth conditions, fungicidal activity has been observed against *C. albicans*.[75] In serum-free growth media, fluconazole displays no measurable post-antifungal effect against *C. albicans* and *C. neoformans*, but concentration-dependent post-antifungal effects of 1–3.6 hours were observed in the presence of fresh serum.[16] Pharmacodynamic studies in murine models of disseminated *C. albicans* infection collectively suggest that the AUC:MIC ratio is the most predictive pharmacodynamic parameter of fluconazole.[76] Overall, the dose-independent pharmacokinetics and the available experimental and clinical data are in support of once daily dosing regimens.

Pharmacokinetics

Fluconazole is available for oral and parenteral use, and it exhibits linear plasma pharmacokinetics that are independent of route and formulation.[77] Steady state is generally reached within 4–7 days with once-daily dosing, but it can be rapidly achieved by doubling the dose on the first day. Protein binding is low, and the drug distributes evenly into virtually all tissue sites and body fluids, including the CSF, brain tissue and the eye. More than 90% of a dose is excreted via the kidney, with approximately 80% recovered as unchanged, active drug and 11% recovered as inactive metabolites. In patients with a creatinine clearance of ≤50ml/minute, a 50% reduction in dosage is required, and with a creatinine clearance of 21ml/minute, a 75% reduction is needed; the initial loading dose need not be adjusted. Fluconazole is dialyzable; in patients undergoing hemodialysis, 100% of the target dose is given after each dialysis session. In continuous hemofiltration, clearance of fluconazole may be faster, requiring therapy at maximum approved dosages, and in patients with peritoneal dialysis the compound can be administered either systemically or intraperitoneally. Hepatic insufficiency per se does not require dose adjustments, but careful monitoring of additional hepatic toxicity is warranted.[62,77]

The pharmacokinetics of fluconazole in pediatric age groups reflects developmental changes characteristic for a water-soluble drug with minor metabolism and predominantly renal elimination. Except for premature neonates, in whom clearance is initially decreased, pediatric patients tend to have an increased weight-normalized clearance rate from plasma, which leads to a shorter half-life compared with adults.[78,79] Therefore, dosages at the high end of the recommended dosage range are necessary for the treatment of invasive mycoses in children.

Adverse effects

In adults, fluconazole has been safely administered over prolonged periods of time at dosages of up to 1600mg/day.[80] Compiled data from adult patients who received dosages of 100–400mg/day indicate an overall incidence of significant adverse effects or laboratory abnormalities leading to the discontinuation of the drug of 2.8%. Nausea, vomiting and other gastrointestinal symptoms are seen in <5% of adult patients, skin rashes and headaches in <2% and asymptomatic hepatic transaminase elevations (which are usually reversible) in up to 7%.[81] In pediatric patients of all age groups, fluconazole is generally well tolerated at dosages of up to 12mg/kg/day, with no differences from adults in frequency and profile of adverse events.[82] Severe side-effects, including liver failure and exfoliative dermatitis, have been reported anecdotally.[62] Alopecia can be seen with higher dose fluconazole (400mg/day) given for 2 months or longer; it is reversed by discontinuing therapy or substantially reducing the daily dose.[83]

Drug interactions

Fluconazole undergoes minimal CYP-mediated metabolism, but inhibits CYP3A4 and several other CYP isoforms in vitro and interacts with enzymes involved in glucuronidation, leading to a number of significant drug–drug interactions (Table 208.2).[81,84] On the other

Table 208.2 Drug–drug interactions of fluconazole and itraconazole.

DRUG–DRUG INTERACTIONS OF FLUCONAZOLE AND ITRACONAZOLE		
Mechanism and drug involved	**Triazole involved**	**Comment**
Decreased plasma concentration of triazole		
Decreased absorption of triazole • Antacids, H_2-antagonists • Omeprazole, sucralfate • Didanosine, grapefruit juice	Itra **	Take antacids and antifungal agent at least 2 hours apart
Increased metabolism of triazole • Isoniazid, rifampin • Rifabutin, phenytoin • Phenobarbital, carbamazepine	Itra **, flu	Potential for therapy failure; increased potential for hepatotoxicity
Increased concentration of coadministered drug through inhibition of its metabolism by triazole		
Terfenadine, astemizole, cisapride	Flu‡, Itra‡	Concom. use prohibited
Lovastatin, simvastatin,atorvastatin	Itra‡, Flu‡	Concom. use prohibited
Phenytoin	Flu*, Itra*	Monitor levels
Benzodiazepines	Flu†, Itra†	Monitor closely
Carbamazepine	Flu†	Monitor closely
Haloperidol	Itra†	Monitor closely
Rifampin, rifabutin	Flu†, Itra†	Monitor closely
Clarithromycin	Itra†	Monitor closely
Indinavir, ritonavir	Itra†	Monitor closely
Vincristine, vinblastine, vindesine	Itra*	Avoid concom. use
Busulfan	Itra†	Avoid concom. use
All-trans retinoic acid	Flu†	Monitor closely
Nifedipine, felodipine	Itra†, Flu†	Monitor closely
Ciclosporin A, tacrolimus	Flu†, Itra†	Monitor serum level
Sulfonylurea drugs; warfarin; prednisolone	Flu†, Itra†	Monitor closely
Digoxin; quinidine	Itra†	Monitor levels (digoxin)
Zidovudine; theophyllin	Flu†	Monitor closely

Flu, fluconazole; Itra, itraconazole
* Major significance; † moderate significance; ‡ contraindicated
Modified from Groll *et al.*[62]

hand, drugs notorious for hepatic enzyme induction may lead to decreased fluconazole levels and therapeutic failure as the ultimate consequence.[62] Altogether, the number of relevant drug–drug interactions appears to be lower than for ketoconazole and itraconazole.

Clinical indications and dosages

Fluconazole is highly effective for the treatment of superficial and invasive candidal infections, including infections in neutropenic patients.[85] However, in unstable patients and in those who have received antifungal azoles for prophylaxis, AmB remains the agent of choice for initial therapy. Further potential indications for fluconazole include consolidation therapy for chronic disseminated candidiasis, cryptococcal meningitis and infections with *T. beigelii.* Fluconazole is the drug of choice for treatment of coccidioidal meningitis and has effectiveness in nonmeningeal coccidioidal infections;[86,87] against paracoccidioidomycosis, blastomycosis, histoplasmosis and sporotrichosis, the compound appears comparatively less active than itraconazole.[33,88–90] In the prophylactic setting, fluconazole has proven efficacy for primary prevention of invasive candidal infections in high-risk patients with acute leukemia and in patients who have undergone bone marrow or liver transplantation, for primary prevention of cryptococcosis and histoplasmosis in HIV-infected patients with very low CD4+ cell counts, and for secondary prevention of cryptococcisis and coccidioidomycosis in HIV-infected patients.[91–93]

In adults, the recommended dosage range for treatment of invasive infections is 400–800mg; in the preventive setting 100–400mg is recommended. In pediatric patients of all age groups, the recommended dosage range of fluconazole is 6–12mg/kg/day. However, in view of the faster clearance rate, the larger volume of distribution and the safety profile of fluconazole, 12mg/kg/day may be the more appropriate dosage for treatment of serious infections in full-term neonates and in infants and children. Given the extreme variability in extravascular water content and renal function, particularly in very low birth-weight preterm infants, predictably effective and safe treatment with fluconazole may not be possible in this patient population during the first days of life.

Itraconazole

Pharmacodynamics

Itraconazole exerts species- and strain-dependent fungistatic or fungicidal pharmacodynamics in vitro. Time-kill experiments have demonstrated concentration-independent, fungistatic activity of itraconazole against *Candida* spp. and *C. neoformans.*[16] Against *Aspergillus* spp., however, itraconazole displayed time and concentration-dependent fungicidal activity with >87 to >97% killing within 24 hours of drug exposure.[94] Persistent effects have not been reported thus far, and it remains to be determined which pharmacodynamic parameter best predicts antifungal efficacy in vivo.[16]

Pharmacokinetics

Itraconazole is a high-molecular-weight, highly lipophilic bis-triazole. It is available as capsules, as oral solution in hydroxypropyl-β-cyclodextrin (HP-β-CD), and as a parenteral solution that also uses HP-β-CD as solubilizer. Absorption from the capsule form is dependent on a low intragastric pH and is compromised in the fasting state, and is thus unpredictable in granulocytopenic cancer patients and in patients with hypochlorhydria. Absorption is improved when the capsules are taken with food or an acidic cola beverage. The novel oral solution of itraconazole in HP-β-CD provides better oral bioavailability, which is further enhanced in the fasting state.[95]

Following oral administration, peak plasma concentrations occur within 1–4 hours; systemic absorption of the cyclodextrin carrier is negligible. With once-daily dosing, steady state is achieved after 7–14 days, but it can be reached more rapidly by doubling the dose over the first 2–3 days. Following administration of intravenous HP-β-CD itraconazole, drug and carrier rapidly dissociate and follow their own disposition. Peak plasma levels of itraconazole and its carrier occur immediately after completion of the 1-hour infusion. The carrier HP-β-CD is not significantly metabolized, and virtually 100% is eliminated from plasma within 24 hours in unchanged form via glomerular filtration. Itraconazole is highly protein-bound and is extensively distributed throughout the body. Whereas concentrations in nonproteinaceous body fluids are negligible, tissue concentrations in many organs, including the brain, exceed corresponding plasma levels by 2–10 times.[95,96]

Itraconazole is extensively metabolized in the liver and is excreted in metabolized form into bile and urine. The major metabolite, hydroxy-itraconazole, possesses antifungal activity similar to that of itraconazole. After oral administration, the plasma concentrations of hydroxy-itraconazole at steady state are 1.5–2 times higher than those of the parent compound, whereas they are considerably lower than those of itraconazole after intravenous dosing.[62,97] It is important to note that plasma concentrations of itraconazole measured by bioassay are different from those determined by high-performance liquid chromatography, since the latter method usually does not account for hydroxy-itraconazole. The elimination of itraconazole from plasma follows a biphasic pattern; in comparison to single dosing, the elimination half-life at steady state is about twice as long, reflecting saturable excretion mechanisms.[62]

The dosage of oral itraconazole does not need to be adjusted in patients with renal insufficiency or dialysis. However, since the elimination of HP-β-CD parallels the glomerular filtration rate, intravenous itraconazole is contraindicated in patients with a creatinine clearance of <30ml/minute; no data are available for its use in patients undergoing dialysis. In patients with severe hepatic insufficiency, the elimination half-life of itraconazole can be prolonged, and additional hepatic toxicity or possible drug interactions should be carefully monitored.[95]

Despite considerable variability between patients, the pharmacokinetics of oral HP-β-CD itraconazole in pediatric patients beyond the neonatal period appear not to be fundamentally different from those in adults.[98,99] No data are currently available in this population for the capsule form and intravenous HP-β-CD itraconazole.

Adverse effects

Itraconazole usually is well tolerated, with a similar spectrum and frequency of adverse effects to that of fluconazole. Adverse events leading to the discontinuation of itraconazole occur in approximately 4% of patients treated for systemic fungal infections at dosages of up to 400mg/day. Most observed reactions are transient, and include nausea and vomiting (in <10% of patients), hypertriglyceridemia (in 9%), hypokalemia (in 6%), elevated hepatic transaminases (in 5%), rash or pruritus (in 2%), headaches or dizziness (in <2%) and pedal edema (in 1%).[100] Gastrointestinal intolerance appears to be exceedingly frequent with oral HP-β-CD itraconazole at dosages exceeding 400mg/day. Only a few cases of more severe hepatic injury or hepatitis have been described. Itraconazole can have negative inotropic effects; because of a possible, albeit low, risk of cardiac toxicity, itraconazole should not be administered to patients with ventricular dysfunction.[101] Oral HP-β-CD itraconazole was safe and well tolerated in pharmacokinetic studies in pediatric patients.[102] Vomiting (12%), abnormal liver function tests (5%) and abdominal pain (3%) were the most common adverse effects in 103 neutropenic pediatric cancer patients who received the drug at a dosage of 5mg/kg/day or 2.5mg/kg twice daily for antifungal prophylaxis; 18% of patients withdrew from the study because of adverse events.[103]

Drug interactions

In comparison to fluconazole, both the propensity for and the extent of drug–drug interactions are greater with itraconazole (see Table 208.2). Itraconazole is a substrate of CYP3A4, but also interacts with the heme moiety of CYP3A, resulting in noncompetitive inhibition of oxidative metabolism of many CYP3A substrates and increased (and potentially toxic) concentrations of co-administered drugs. Increased metabolism of itraconazole resulting in decreased plasma levels can be induced by drugs known for their induction of hepatic metabolizing enzymes. Patients who receive itraconazole along with one of the drugs listed in Table 208.2 should be followed closely and plasma concentrations, ideally of both compounds, should be monitored carefully. Finally, the systemic availability of itraconazole depends in part on the activity of intestinal CYP3A4 and P-glycoprotein, which contributes to its variable bioavailability after oral administration.

Clinical indications and dosing

Itraconazole is a useful agent for dermatophytic infections, pityriasis versicolor and all forms of cutaneous and mucosal candidiasis; however, its clinical efficacy in invasive candidal infections has not been evaluated. The experience with itraconazole for induction therapy of cryptococcal meningitis is scant, but itraconazole has been used with success for consolidation and maintenance treatment of this condition in patients with HIV infection, although with less success than fluconazole (see Chapter 126).[104] Itraconazole is approved as a second-line agent for the treatment of invasive *Aspergillus* infections; few data exist on its use for first-line treatment in neutropenic patients.[105] Itraconazole may be useful in the management of infections by certain dematiaceous molds,[106] but it has no documented activity against zygomycosis and fusariosis. Itraconazole is the current treatment of choice for lymphocutaneous sporotrichosis and non-life-threatening, nonmeningeal paracoccidioidomycosis, blastomycosis and histoplasmosis. In progressive, nonmeningeal coccidioidomycosis, itraconazole appears at least as active as fluconazole.[86] However, AmB remains the treatment of choice for most immunocompromised patients and for those with life-threatening forms of endemic mycoses.

Itraconazole has been successfully used as antifungal prophylaxis in patients undergoing stem cell transplantation or intensive chemotherapy.[103] Hydroxypropyl-β-cyclodextrin itraconazole may reduce the incidence of proven or suspected invasive fungal infections in neutropenic patients with hematologic malignancies, but prophylactic efficacy against invasive aspergillosis has not been convincingly demonstrated thus far.[34] Itraconazole was at least as effective as conventional AmB and was superior with respect to its safety profile as empiric antifungal therapy in persistently febrile neutropenic patients,[107] which has led to the approval of this indication by the FDA.

The recommended dosage range of oral itraconazole is 100–400mg/day (capsules) and 2.5mg/kg twice daily (HP-β-CD solution). For life-threatening infections, however, more aggressive dosing may be necessary. For such conditions, we recommend a loading dose of 600–800mg/day for 3–5 days followed by a maintenance dose of 400–600mg/day, with monitoring of serum levels. The approved dosage of intravenous HP-β-CD itraconazole is 200mg twice daily for 2 days, followed by 200mg/day for a maximum of 12 days. Itraconazole is not approved for patients under 18 years of age; based on the available pharmacokinetic data, a starting dosage of 2.5mg/kg twice daily of oral HP-β-CD itraconazole can be advocated. The recommended dosage range for the capsule formulation is 5–8mg/kg/day with a loading dose of 4mg/kg three times daily for the first 3 days. Data on the use of intravenous itraconazole in pediatric patients are currently lacking.

Therapeutic monitoring

While experimental studies have provided evidence of a relationship between plasma concentrations and antifungal efficacy, the main rationale for monitoring plasma levels has been the erratic oral bioavailability of itraconazole, particularly in neutropenic patients. Historically, the target plasma level for itraconazole has been estimated at 0.25μg/ml (by high-performance liquid chromatography) at trough based on the IC_{90} of a large set of clinical isolates. However, more recent clinical data from a large cohort of patients undergoing intensive chemotherapy for acute leukemia and receiving antifungal prophylaxis with itraconazole have demonstrated a significant statistical association of trough concentrations <0.5μg/ml with the occurrence of invasive fungal infections.[108] We therefore recommend rapid achievement and maintenance of trough levels of ≥0.5μg/ml when itraconazole is given for prevention or treatment of invasive fungal infections.

Second-generation antifungal triazoles

Further improvements in the structure–activity relationship of antifungal triazoles have led to a new group of synthetic compounds that are collectively known as second-generation triazoles. The FDA has approved voriconazole, and the investigational agents posaconazole and ravuconazole are currently in advanced stages of clinical development. While ravuconazole and voriconazole are structurally related to fluconazole, the structure of posaconazole is similar to that of itraconazole.

Pharmacology

The second-generation triazoles possess enhanced target activity and specificity. They are active against a wide spectrum of clinically important fungi, including *Candida* spp., *T. beigelii, C. neoformans, Aspergillus* spp., *Fusarium* spp. and other hyaline molds, and dematiaceous as well as dimorphic moulds; they have demonstrated efficacy in various animal models of invasive fungal infections. As with itraconazole, these novel triazoles exert fungistatic activity against susceptible yeast-like organisms and strain-dependent fungicidal activity against susceptible filamentous fungi. Fundamental differences in potency, spectrum and antifungal efficacy between posaconazole, ravuconazole and voriconazole have not surfaced, but posaconazole appears to have the best activity against the zygomycetes. Against *Candida* spp. and *C. neoformans*, voriconazole exhibits nonconcentration-dependent pharmacodynamics. Near-maximal fungistatic activity is achieved at a drug concentration of approximately three times the MIC.[109] A post-antifungal effect of up to 4 hours has been observed with *C. albicans*.[110]

Voriconazole is available as a tablet and as parenteral solution that uses sulfobutyl ether-β-cyclodextrin as solubilizer. Taken in tablet form, voriconazole is rapidly absorbed from the gastrointestinal tract. Although bioavailability is near 100%, steady-state plasma concentrations are achieved more rapidly if an intravenous loading dose is given. Multiple enzymes of the cytochrome P450 system, including CYP2C19, which exhibit genetic polymorphism in certain racial groups, metabolize voriconazole. Drug levels in poor metabolizers, which may include up to 20% of Asian populations, can be significantly elevated. Following its metabolism in the liver, the drug is mostly excreted in urine. In addition to undergoing metabolism by the P450 system, voriconazole inhibits several CYP enzymes. Therefore, there is extensive potential for drug–drug interactions. While all three second-generation triazole agents display some nonlinearity in their disposition, undergo hepatic metabolism and have the potential for drug–drug interactions through their affinity to CYP450 isoenzymes, key pharmacokinetic parameters (oral bioavailability, extent of protein binding, plasma clearance and volume of distribution) vary. Whether these differences are of clinical significance, however, remains to be elucidated.

Mild and reversible visual disturbances occur in approximately 30% of patients. The mechanism is unknown, but is thought to be retinal in origin. Other common adverse reactions include rashes including phototoxicity, gastrointestinal disturbances and hepatic abnormalities.

Clinical studies

In a randomized, unblinded trial of patients with invasive aspergillosis, initial therapy with voriconazole led to better responses, improved survival and less toxicity than the standard approach of initial therapy with AmB.[111] Voriconazole has been used successfully in the treatment of invasive fungal infections, including aspergillosis in children who were refractory to or intolerant of conventional antifungal therapy.[112] Voriconazole has also been shown to be effective in the treatment of oropharyngeal and esophageal candidiasis in immunocompromised patients.[113] A large randomized multicenter trial has been completed that compared voriconazole (3mg/kg intravenously twice daily or 200mg by mouth twice daily) with liposomal AmB (3mg/kg intravenously) for empiric antifungal therapy. This study showed comparable composite success rates but less proven and probable breakthrough infections, infusion-related toxicity and nephrotoxicity in the voriconazole-treated cohort. However, patients receiving voriconazole had significantly more frequent episodes of transient visual disturbances and hallucination.[114]

For treatment of invasive fungal infections in children and adults an intravenous loading dose of 6mg/kg every 12 hours on day 1 followed by 4mg/kg every 12 hours thereafter is used. Whenever feasible the drug should be given by the oral route at 200mg twice daily (in children weighing less than 40kg, the dose is 100mg twice times daily). Because sulfobutyl ether-β-cyclodextrin clearance is related to glomerular filtration rate, oral voriconazole should be used in patients whose creatinine clearance is <50ml/min. In patients with mild to moderate hepatic cirrhosis, the standard loading dose is recommended, but the maintenance dose should be halved.

To date, preliminary data from phase II and III studies have been presented for posaconazole and voriconazole. Posaconazole (50–400mg by mouth) was well tolerated and as effective as fluconazole (100mg) in two large randomized comparative studies in HIV-infected patients with oropharyngeal candidiasis.[115] Furthermore, in a salvage study in patients with a variety of invasive fungal infections, response rates in subjects with aspergillosis, fusariosis, cryptococcosis, candidiasis and phaeohyphomycoses after 4–8 weeks of therapy with a dose of 800mg/day by mouth ranged from 44 to 80%.[116] Further clinical trials and development of an intravenous formulation are underway.

ECHINOCANDIN LIPOPEPTIDES

The echinocandins are a novel class of semisynthetic amphiphilic lipopeptides composed of a cyclic hexapeptide core linked to a variably configured lipid side chain. The echinocandins act by noncompetitive inhibition of the synthesis of 1,3-β-glucan, a polysaccharide in the cell wall of many pathogenic fungi (Fig. 208.5). Together with chitin, the rope-like glucan fibrils are responsible for the strength and shape of the cell wall. They are important in maintaining the osmotic integrity of the fungal cell and play a key role in cell division and cell growth.[117,118] Caspofungin has recently received approval by the FDA for treatment of refractory invasive aspergillosis and candidal esophagitis. Anidulafungin and micafungin are in advanced stages of clinical development. (Fig. 208.6).

Antifungal activity

The current echinocandins appear to possess very similar pharmacologic properties. All three compounds have potent and broad spectrum, fungicidal in-vitro activity against *Candida* spp. and potent inhibitory activity against *Aspergillus* spp.; their antifungal efficacy against these organisms in vivo has been demonstrated in various animal models. The current echinocandins have variable activity against dematiaceous and endemic mold and are inactive against most hyalohyphomycetes, zygomycetes, *C. neoformans* and *T. beigelii*.[119] Furthermore, all echinocandins have demonstrated preventive and therapeutic activity in animal models of *Pneumocystis carinii* pneumonitis. In-vitro resistance has been observed in fungal isolates overexpressing a gene encoding for a Golgi protein involved in the transport of cell wall components.[120] Primary resistance to echinocandins in otherwise susceptible fungal yeast species is rare, and resistance-induction studies have demonstrated a low potential for secondary resistance in *Candida* spp. The frequency of primary echinocandin resistance among clinical isolates of *Aspergillus* spp. and induction of secondary resistance in vitro have not been studied thus far.

Pharmacodynamics

The echinocandins demonstrate a species-dependent mode of antifungal activity. They have fungicidal activity against most *Candida* spp. but not against *Aspergillus* spp. In the latter, microscopic exami-

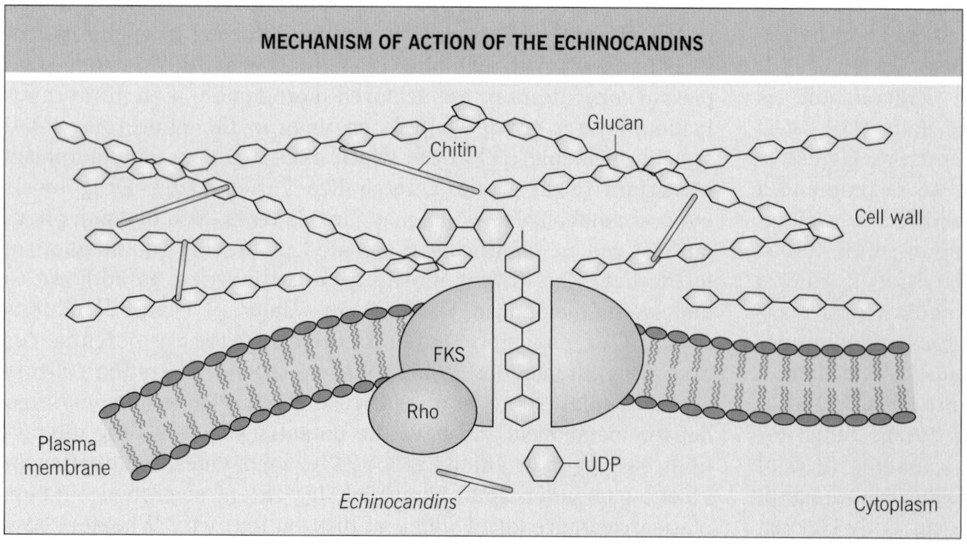

Fig. 208.5 Mechanism of action of the echinocandins.

STRUCTURES OF ECHINOCANDINS CURRENTLY IN CLINICAL PRACTICE OR IN CLINICAL TRIALS

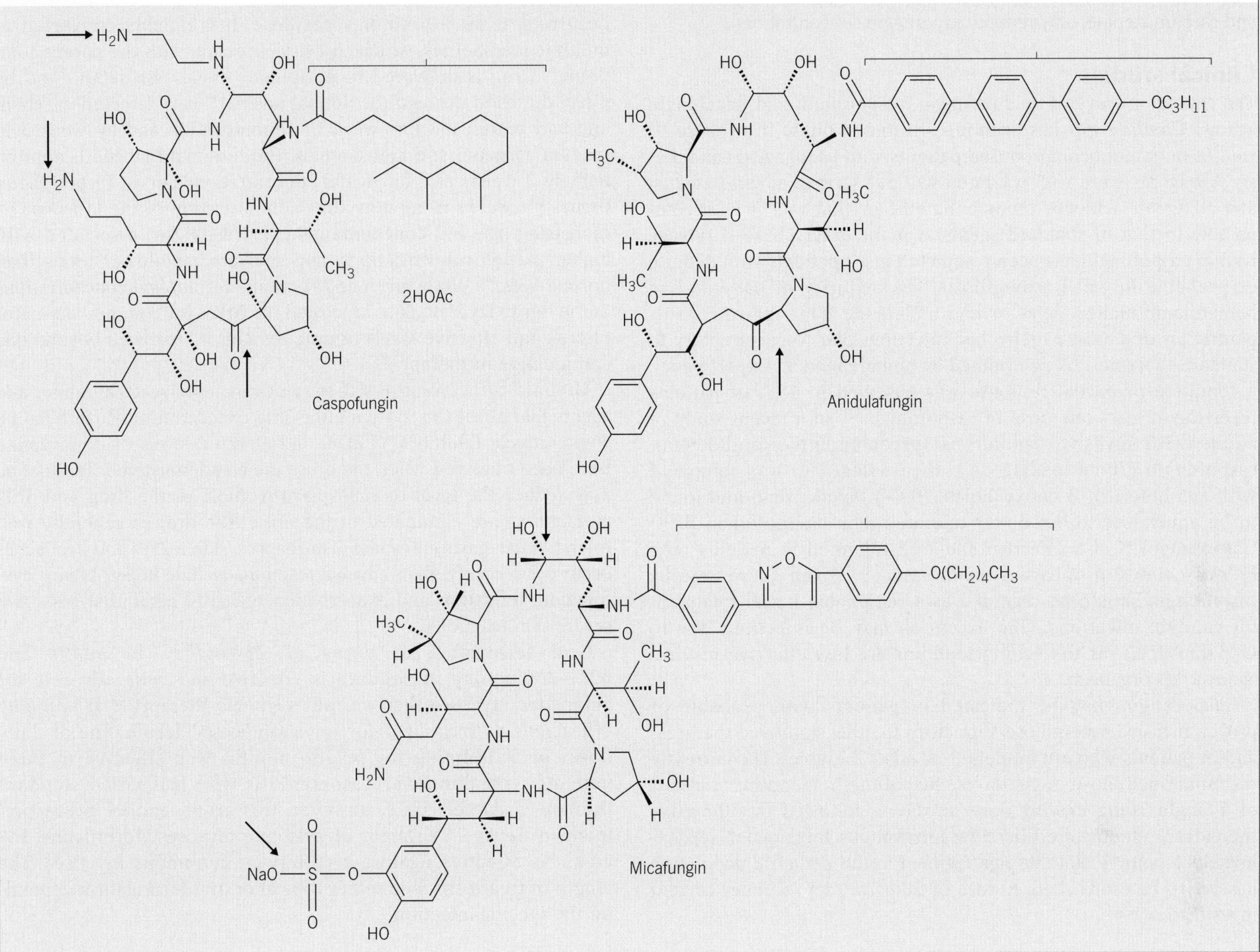

Fig. 208.6 Structures of echinocandins currently in clinical practice or in clinical trials.

nation of exposed hyphae show a dose-dependent formation of microcolonies with progressively truncated, swollen hyphal elements that appear to be cell-wall deficient but that are able to regain their cell walls upon subculture in the absence of the drug. In a process that has been likened to pruning, caspofungin preferentially kills cells at the active centers for new cell wall synthesis within *A. fumigatus* hyphae.[121] These observations indicate differences in functional target sensitivity in both species that are not fully understood. In-vitro pharmacodynamic studies in *Candida* spp. have shown predominantly concentration-dependent fungicidal activity and rate of kill (≥99.9% reduction in colony-forming units) and concentration-dependent prolonged post-antifungal effects of up to 12 hours.[15,122] In-vivo pharmacodynamic animal studies suggest similar concentration-dependent activity of the current echinocandins.

Pharmacokinetics

At present, all current echinocandins are available only for intravenous administration. They exhibit dose-proportional plasma pharmacokinetics with a β-half-life of between 10 and 15 hours, which allows for once-daily dosing. All echinocandins are highly protein bound (>95%) and distribute into all major organ sites, including the brain; however, concentrations in uninfected CSF are low. The echinocandins are metabolized by the liver and slowly excreted into urine and feces; only small fractions are excreted into urine in unchanged form.[123] The pharmacokinetic parameters are generally lower in children than in adults. Drug levels are especially low in smaller, younger children. The β-half-life in children is reduced by over one-third relative to adults.[124]

Adverse effects and drug interactions

At the currently investigated dosages, all echinocandins are generally well tolerated, and only a small fraction of patients enrolled in the various clinical trials (<5%) discontinued therapy because of drug-related adverse events. The most frequently reported adverse effects include increased liver transaminases, gastrointestinal upset and headaches. As with other basic polypeptides, the echinocandins have the potential to cause histamine release; however, histamine-mediated symptoms have been observed in isolated cases only. The current echinocandins appear to have no significant potential for drug interactions mediated by the CYP450 enzyme system. Caspofungin can reduce the AUC of tacrolimus by approximately 20% but has no effect on ciclosporin levels. However, ciclosporin increased the AUC of caspofungin by approximately 35%; because of transient elevations of hepatic transaminases in single-dose interaction studies, the concomitant use of both drugs is currently not recommended. Finally, inducers of drug clearance or mixed inducer–inhibitors, namely efavirenz, nelfinavir, nevirapine, phenytoin, rifampin, dexamethasone and carbamazepine, may reduce caspofungin concentrations.

Clinical studies

The clinical efficacy of anidulafungin, caspofungin and micafungin against *Candida* spp. has been investigated in phase II or phase III studies in immunocompromised patients with esophageal candidiasis. All agents were well tolerated without serious adverse events, and all agents achieved therapeutic efficacy that was at least comparable to that of standard agents. A multicenter phase II salvage trial of caspofungin has been completed in 90 patients with definite or probable invasive aspergillosis. The majority of patients had hematologic malignancies or had undergone bone marrow transplantation, and most patients had infections that were refractory to standard therapies. As determined by an independent expert panel, a complete or partial response was observed in 45% of patients receiving at least one dose of caspofungin.[125] In a recent study of adults with invasive candidiasis (predominantly candidemia), caspofungin (70mg loading dose then 50mg/day) was compared with amphotericin B deoxycholate (0.6–1.0mg/kg/day) and found to be equivalent to but better tolerated than amphotericin B.[125a] Caspofungin is also effective and well tolerated in patients with HIV-associated esophageal candidiasis.[126] Given these results, caspofungin should be regarded as a reasonable initial treatment for candida infections. One exception may be infections due to C. parapsilosis, as the echinocandidins are less effective in vitro against this organism.

Caspofungin may be indicated in patients with probable or proven invasive aspergillosis refractory to other approved therapies and in patients who are intolerant of other therapies. The currently recommended dose regimen of caspofungin in adults consists of a single 70mg loading dose on day 1, followed by 50mg/day thereafter, administered by slow intravenous infusion of approximately 1 hour. A daily dosage regimen in the pediatric population has yet to be established. A dose of 50mg/m^2/day is under current investigation.[124]

TERBINAFINE

Terbinafine is a highly lipophilic and keratophilic allylamine inhibitor of ergosterol biosynthesis. It is a potent noncompetitive inhibitor of fungal squalene epoxidase and prevents squalene epoxidation, an important early step in the synthesis of ergosterol. Treated fungi accumulate squalene and become deficient in ergosterol. Cell death is associated with the development of high intracellular squalene concentrations, which interfere with fungal membrane function and cell wall synthesis.[7,127] In addition to its antifungal properties terbinafine is also anti-inflammatory and can act as a free radical scavenger.

Terbinafine is active in vitro against a wide range of pathogenic fungi, including dermatophytes, molds, dimorphic fungi, *C. neoformans* and some but not all *Candida* and *Aspergillus* spp.[128] In-vitro studies with *Aspergillus* spp. have shown terbinafine and AmB to have additive, synergistic interactions depending on the isolate. In combination with itraconazole or voriconazole, terbinafine displays potent synergistic interactions against *Aspergillus* spp. Fluconazole also increases the activity of terbinafine in an additive to synergistic fashion.[129] In vitro, combinations of terbinafine with voricoazole can overcome azole resistance in *Candida* spp. Terbinafine in combination with AmB or voriconazole is synergistic against some zygomycetes isolates. Resistance to terbinafine has been observed following a single gene mutation in *Aspergillus*.[130] In *Candida*, cross-resistance following treatment with fluconazole can occur because of upregulation of target enzymes.[131] Multidrug efflux pumps may also reduce susceptibility.[132]

Oral terbinafine is rapidly absorbed, with peak concentration occurring at 60–90 minutes postdose. It is quickly converted to multiple metabolites, which co-exist in plasma with the parent compound. Drug is delivered to peripheral tissues via sebum and by direct diffusion through the dermal layers.[133] It is detected in sebum and hair within the first week of administration and by week 3 in stratum corneum and nail samples. The terminal half-life is approximately 3 weeks and fungicidal concentrations persist in peripheral tissues for weeks to months after administration of the last dose.[134] Increasing age and concomitant hypertension are associated with higher plasma concentrations, and smokers have lower levels than nonsmokers.[135] When given as 1% cream, terbinafine concentrations in the horny layer of skin far exceed the MICs for common dermatophytes, and effective levels of drug remains in skin well beyond discontinuation of therapy.[136]

Multiple cytochrome P450 enzymes metabolize terbinafine, and agents that affect this system alter drug concentration.[137] Terbinafine competitively inhibits CYP2D6, and elevated levels of desipramine have been observed when the drugs are co-administered. Terbinafine may reduce the level of ciclosporin A. Most of the drug and drug metabolites are eliminated in the urine. The drug is generally well tolerated, but gastrointestinal disturbances, skin rashes and headaches occur occasionally. Rare adverse reactions include hepatobiliary dysfunction, induction and exacerbation of lupus, agranulocytosis and severe skin reactions.

Oral terbinafine at doses of 250mg/day in adults and 62.5–250mg/day in children is effective and generally safe for cutaneous mycoses that warrant systemic therapy.[138] It is highly efficacious as treatment for onychomycosis. Terbinafine at daily doses of 5–15mg/kg for several months was effective in three patients with pulmonary aspergillosis who had failed standard therapy.[139] At this time, however, this agent, cannot be recommended for the treatment of systemic mycoses. Terbinafine 1% cream is effective against a variety of cutaneous mycoses. The length of treatment with either topical or oral formulation depends on the specific infection.

GRISEOFULVIN

Griseofulvin, a metabolic product of *Penicillium*, was the first oral agent available for treatment of dermatomycoses. This compound inhibits fungal cell mitosis and nucleic acid synthesis, and disrupts spindle and cytoplasmic microtubule function.[140] Griseofulvin is active against many dermatophytes, but not all. High-level resistance can develop following drug exposure, and a multiple-layered thick cell wall, which may limit griseofulvin entry, has been observed in resistant isolates.[141,142] Griseofulvin has extremely low water solubility and moderate lipid solubility. Absorption from the gastrointestinal tract is variable and depends on the amount of dissolved drug that reaches the intestine.[143] Absorption is enhanced by a fatty meal. The bioavailability of the ultamicrosize formulation is higher than that of the microsize formulation. Once absorbed, drug is highly protein-bound. Griseofulvin is detected in the outer layer of the stratum corneum soon after it is ingested and is diffused from the extracellular fluid and sweat. Deposition of drug in growing cells may account for entry into hair and nails.[140] Concentration in plasma peaks at 3–4 hours and in skin blister fluid at 6 hours. The terminal half-life in plasma and in skin blisters is approximately 9–10 hours. During chronic administration, plasma and skin blister levels equilibrate.[144] Griseofulvin is largely metabolized in the liver and degradation metabolites are excreted in the urine. Griseofulvin is also effective in several inflammatory skin conditions, possibly because of its anti-inflammatory properties mediated by modulation of the expression of cell adhesion molecules on leukocytes and vascular endothelial cells.[145]

Adverse effects include gastrointestinal disturbances, headaches, hepatitis and rashes. Liver and thyroid neoplasia, abnormal germ cell maturation, teratogenicity and embroyotoxicity have been observed in animal studies. The reproductive toxicity as well as the induction of chromosome aberrations in somatic cells may result from disturbance of microtubuli formation. Griseofulvin also induces accumulation of porphyrins and formation of Mallory bodies in hepatocytes. These may represent additional carcinogenic mechanisms.[146] Less common adverse events include exacerbation of lupus, porphyrias and blood dyscrasias. Drug interactions are related to induction of hepatic enzymes and include phenobarbital, oral anticoagulants and oral contraceptives.

For onychomycosis, griseofulvin has been largely supplanted by newer antifungals. Currently, its main indication is for the treatment of tinea capitis and other cutaneous mycoses. Doses of 500–1000mg/day in adults and 15–20mg/kg/day in children have been used successfully. Length of treatment depends on the site and type of infection.

AMOROLFINE

The morpholine derivative amorolfine is currently used only as a topical agent. This compound interferes with ergosterol biosynthesis and leads to the depletion of ergosterol and the subsequent accumulation of sterol precursors within the cell membrane.[147] Amorolfine also weakly inhibits the fungal enzyme squalene epoxidase. In vitro, amorolfine has a broad spectrum of activity that includes dermatophytes, dimorphic, dematiaceous and filamentous fungi, and yeasts.[148,149] In patients, amorolfine has eradicated infections caused both by *C. albicans* and by a broad range of dermatophytes.[150] In a murine model of dermatophytosis the combinations of amorolfine with griseofulvin, terbinafine, itraconazole and fluconazole were synergistic, but 5-FC appears to be antagonistic in some fungal isolates.[151]

Amorolfine has been formulated as 0.125%, 0.25% and 0.5% creams and as a 5% lacquer. Following application, the amorolfine penetrates the nails rapidly and within 24 hours of contact it exceeds the MIC of most fungi that cause onychomycosis.[152] Following topical application, active concentration of amorolfine is retained in the skin for several days. In experimental models of systemic mycosis, amorolfine shows no significant activity, which may be due to strong protein binding or to rapid metabolism (or both).[147] The bioavailabilty of topical amorolfine is 4–10% and drug is excreted in urine and feces.[153]

Treatment-related adverse events are generally limited to burning, itching, erythema, skin dryness and scaling. Topical amorolfine has been used successfully in a variety of dermatomycoses and for the treatment of onychomycosis. Combination therapy with oral itraconazole or terbinafine may be a promising option for patients with severe disease.[154,155]

CICLOPIROX

Ciclopirox is a poorly absorbable, synthetic hydroxypyridone antifungal agent. The mechanism of action is related to its affinity for trivalent cations. By chelating essential metal cofactors, ciclopirox inhibits fungal enzymes that are responsible for diverse metabolic processes and ultimately causes membrane and cytoplasmic disruption.[156] Ciclopirox at subinhibitory concentrations impairs candidal adherence to mucosal surfaces.[157] It has potent antifungal activity against a broad range of dermatophytic and nondermatophytic fungi. It is available in a variety of topical formulations, including as 0.77% gel and 8% nail lacquer. It readily penetrates the skin via the epidermis and the hair follicles and achieves the highest concentration in the horny layer.[158] When used as 8% nail lacquer, the drug achieves uniform distribution within the nail-plate after daily use for 1 week, and it reaches a maximum at 3–4 weeks with uniform distribution to all nail layers.[159] Within the nail the drug achieves concentrations in excess of inhibitory and fungicidal concentrations for most pathogens.[156] The bioavailabilty of topical ciclopirox is 2–5% and absorbed drug is mainly metabolized by glucuronidation. Excretion is predominantly renal with an elimination half-life of approximately 2 hours.[159,160]

Treatment-related adverse events are uncommon, but local reactions such as pruritus and burning sensation can occur.

Ciclopirox has been used successfully for a variety of cutaneous mycotic infections, mucosal candidiasis and seborrheic dermatitis, and as a treatment for onychomycosis.

FUTURE DIRECTIONS

The past decade has seen a considerable expansion in antifungal drug research and the clinical development of several new compounds targeted against invasive fungal infections. Major progress has been made in defining paradigms for antifungal intervention and in designing and implementing clinical trials. The field of antifungal therapy is currently undergoing accelerated changes. Combination therapy is being explored. Several novel and promising antifungal compounds are currently in the early stages of pre-clinical investigation, and the pursuit of novel biochemical and molecular targets will result in further candidate drugs. In the light of past and present epidemiologic trends, invasive fungal infections are likely to remain a common and important complication in immunocompromised patients. An expanded drug arsenal, elucidation of resistance mechanisms, integration of pharmacokinetic and pharmacodynamic relationships, and combination therapies offer hope for further substantial progress in prevention and treatment.

REFERENCES

1. Gagos M, Koper R, Gruszecki WI. Spectrophotometric analysis of organisation of dipalmitoylphosphatidylcholine bilayers containing the polyene antibiotic amphotericin B. Biochim Biophys Acta 2001;1511:90–8.
2. Milhaud J, Ponsinet V, Takashi M, Michels B. Interactions of the drug amphotericin B with phospholipid membranes containing or not ergosterol: new insight into the role of ergosterol. Biochim Biophys Acta 2002;1558:95–108.
3. Sawaya BP, Briggs JP, Schnermann J. Amphotericin B nephrotoxicity: the adverse consequences of altered membrane properties. J Am Soc Nephrol 1995;6:154–64.
4. Barwicz J, Dumont I, Ouellet C, Gruda I. Amphotericin B toxicity as related to the formation of oxidatively modified low-density lipoproteins. Biospectroscopy 1998;4:135–44.
5. Barwicz J, Gruda I, Tancrede P. A kinetic study of the oxidation effects of amphotericin B on human low-density lipoproteins. FEBS Lett 2000;465:83–6.
6. Barwicz J, Beauregard M, Tancrede P. Circular dichroism study of interactions of Fungizone or AmBisome forms of amphotericin B with human low density lipoproteins. Biopolymers 2002;67:49–55.
7. Ghannoum MA, Rice LB. Antifungal agents: mode of action, mechanisms of resistance, and correlation of these mechanisms with bacterial resistance. Clin Microbiol Rev 1999;12:501–17.
8. Sokol-Anderson ML, Brajtburg J, Medoff G. Amphotericin B-induced oxidative damage and killing of *Candida albicans*. J Infect Dis 1986;154:76–83.
9. Sokol-Anderson ML, Brajtburg J, Medoff G. Sensitivity of *Candida albicans* to amphotericin B administered as single or fractionated doses. Antimicrob Agents Chemother 1986;29:701–2.
10. Sokol-Anderson M, Sligh JE Jr, Elberg S, *et al.* Role of cell defense against oxidative damage in the resistance of *Candida albicans* to the killing effect of amphotericin B. Antimicrob Agents Chemother 1988;32:702–5.

11. Perea S, Patterson TF. Antifungal resistance in pathogenic fungi. Clin Infect Dis 2002;35:1073–80.
12. Yoon SA, Vazquez JA, Steffan PE, *et al.* High-frequency, *in vitro* reversible switching of *Candida lusitaniae* clinical isolates from amphotericin B susceptibility to resistance. Antimicrob Agents Chemother 1999;43:836–45.
13. Groll AH, Walsh TJ. Uncommon opportunistic fungi: new nosocomial threats. Clin Microbiol Infect 2001;7(Suppl.2):8–24.
14. Vanden Bossche H, Dromer F, Improvisi I, *et al.* Antifungal drug resistance in pathogenic fungi. Med Mycol 1998;36(Suppl.1):119–28.
15. Ernst EJ, Klepser ME, Pfaller MA. Postantifungal effects of echinocandin, azole, and polyene antifungal agents against *Candida albicans* and *Cryptococcus neoformans*. Antimicrob Agents Chemother 2000;44:1108–11.
16. Groll AH, Piscitelli SC, Walsh TJ. Antifungal pharmacodynamics: concentration–effect relationships *in vitro* and *in vivo*. Pharmacotherapy 2001;21:133S–148S.
17. Turnidge JD, Gudmundsson S, Vogelman B, Craig WA. The postantibiotic effect of antifungal agents against common pathogenic yeasts. J Antimicrob Chemother 1994;34:83–92.
18. Andes D, Stamsted T, Conklin R. Pharmacodynamics of amphotericin B in a neutropenic-mouse disseminated-candidiasis model. Antimicrob Agents Chemother 2001;45:922–6.
19. Bekersky I, Fielding RM, Dressler DE, *et al.* Plasma protein binding of amphotericin B and pharmacokinetics of bound versus unbound amphotericin B after administration of intravenous liposomal amphotericin B (AmBisome) and amphotericin B deoxycholate. Antimicrob Agents Chemother 2002;46:834–40.
20. Bekersky I, Fielding RM, Dressler DE, *et al.* Pharmacokinetics, excretion, and mass balance of liposomal amphotericin B (AmBisome) and amphotericin B deoxycholate in humans. Antimicrob Agents Chemother 2002;46:828–33.
21. Christiansen KJ, Bernard EM, Gold JW, Armstrong D. Distribution and activity of amphotericin B in humans. J Infect Dis 1985;152:1037–43.
22. Benson JM, Nahata MC. Pharmacokinetics of amphotericin B in children. Antimicrob Agents Chemother 1989;33:1989–93.
23. Walsh TJ, Finberg RW, Arndt C, *et al.* Liposomal amphotericin B for empirical therapy in patients with persistent fever and neutropenia. National Institute of Allergy and Infectious Diseases Mycoses Study Group. N Engl J Med 1999;340:764–71.
24. Eriksson U, Seifert B, Schaffner A. Comparison of effects of amphotericin B deoxycholate infused over 4 or 24 hours: randomised controlled trial. BMJ 2001;322:579–82.
25. Arikan S, Rex JH. Nystatin LF (Aronex/Abbott). Curr Opin Investig Drugs 2001;2:488–95.
26. Harbarth S, Pestotnik SL, Lloyd JF, *et al.* The epidemiology of nephrotoxicity associated with conventional amphotericin B therapy. Am J Med 2001;111:528–34.
27. Carnevale NT, Galgiani JN, Stevens DA, *et al.* Amphotericin B-induced myelopathy. Arch Intern Med 1980;140:1189–92.
28. Inselmann G, Volkmann A, Heidemann HT. Comparison of the effects of liposomal amphotericin B and conventional amphotericin B on propafenone metabolism and hepatic cytochrome P-450 in rats. Antimicrob Agents Chemother 2000;44:131–3.
29. Louie A, Kaw P, Banerjee P, *et al.* Impact of the order of initiation of fluconazole and amphotericin B in sequential or combination therapy on killing of *Candida albicans in vitro* and in a rabbit model of endocarditis and pyelonephritis. Antimicrob Agents Chemother 2001;45:485–94.
30. Drutz DJ, Spickard A, Rogers DE, Koenig MG. Treatment of disseminated mycotic infectioons. A new approach to amphotericin B therapy. Am J Med 1968;45:405–18.
31. Swenson CE, Perkins WR, Roberts P, *et al.* *In vitro* and *in vivo* antifungal activity of amphotericin B lipid complex: are phospholipases important? Antimicrob Agents Chemother 1998;42:767–71.
32. Ernst EJ, Yodoi K, Roling EE, Klepser ME. Rates and extents of antifungal activities of amphotericin B, flucytosine, fluconazole, and voriconazole against *Candida lusitaniae* determined by microdilution, Etest, and time-kill methods. Antimicrob Agents Chemother 2002;46:578–81.
33. Kauffman CA, Pappas PG, McKinsey DS, *et al.* Treatment of lymphocutaneous and visceral sporotrichosis with fluconazole. Clin Infect Dis 1996;22:46–50.
34. Menichetti F, Del Favero A, Martino P, *et al.* Itraconazole oral solution as prophylaxis for fungal infections in neutropenic patients with hematologic malignancies: a randomized, placebo-controlled, double-blind, multicenter trial. GIMEMA Infection Program. Gruppo Italiano Malattie Ematologiche dell' Adulto. Clin Infect Dis 1999;28:250–5.
35. Johansen HK, Gotzsche PC. Amphotericin B lipid soluble formulations vs amphotericin B in cancer patients with neutropenia. Cochrane Database Syst Rev, 2000:CD000969.
36. Wingard JR, White MH, Anaissie E, *et al.* A randomized, double-blind comparative trial evaluating the safety of liposomal amphotericin B versus amphotericin B lipid complex in the empirical treatment of febrile neutropenia. L Amph/ABLC Collaborative Study Group. Clin Infect Dis 2000;31:1155–63.
37. Bowden R, Chandrasekar P, White MH, *et al.* A double-blind, randomized, controlled trial of amphotericin B colloidal dispersion versus amphotericin B for treatment of invasive aspergillosis in immunocompromised patients. Clin Infect Dis 2002;35:359–66.
38. Johnson MD, Drew RH, Perfect JR. Chest discomfort associated with liposomal amphotericin B: report of three cases and review of the literature. Pharmacotherapy 1998;18:1053–61.
39. White MH, Bowden RA, Sandler ES, *et al.* Randomized, double-blind clinical trial of amphotericin B colloidal dispersion vs amphotericin B in the empirical treatment of fever and neutropenia. Clin Infect Dis 1998;27:296–302.
40. Leenders AC, Daenen S, Jansen RL, *et al.* Liposomal amphotericin B compared with amphotericin B deoxycholate in the treatment of documented and suspected neutropenia-associated invasive fungal infections. Br J Haematol 1998;103:205–12.
41. Anaissie E, White M, Uzun O. Amphotericin B lipid complex (ABLC) versus amphotericin B (AMB) for treatment of hematogenous and invasive candidiasis: a prospective, randomized, multicenter trial. Abstract LM 21. In: Abstracts of the 35th Interscience Conference on Antimicrobial Agents and Chemotherapy, 1995. Washington, DC: American Society for Microbiology; 1995:330.
42. Johnson PC, Wheat LJ, Cloud GA, *et al.* Safety and efficacy of liposomal amphotericin B compared with conventional amphotericin B for induction therapy of histoplasmosis in patients with AIDS. Ann Intern Med 2002;137:105–9.
43. Linden P, Lee L, Walsh TJ. Retrospective analysis of the dosage of amphotericin B lipid complex for the treatment of invasive fungal infections. Pharmacotherapy 1999;19:1261–8.
44. Arikan S, Ostrosky-Zeichner L, Lozano-Chiu M, *et al.* *In vitro* activity of nystatin compared with those of liposomal nystatin, amphotericin B, and fluconazole against clinical *Candida* isolates. J Clin Microbiol 2002;40:1406–12.
45. Cossum PA, Wyse J, Simmons Y, *et al.* Pharmacokinetics of Nyotran (liposomal nystatin) in human patients. Abstract A88. In: Program and Abstracts of the 36th Interscience Conference on Antimicrobial Agents and Chemotherapy, 1996. Washington DC: American Society for Microbiology; 1996:17.
46. Groll AH, Mickiene D, Werner K, *et al.* Compartmental pharmacokinetics and tissue distribution of multilamellar liposomal nystatin in rabbits. Antimicrob Agents Chemother 2000;44:950–7.
47. Boutati E, Maltezou HC, Lopez-Berestein G, *et al.* Phase I study of maximum tolerated dose of intravenous liposomal nystatin for the treatment of refractory febrile neutropenia in patients with hematological malignancies. Abstract LM22. In: Program and Abstracts of the 35th Interscience Conference on Antimicrobial Agents and Chemotherapy, 1995. Washington DC: American Society for Microbiology; 1995:330.
48. Williams AH, Moore JE. Multicenter study to evaluate the safety and efficacy of various doses of liposomal encapsulated nystatin in nonneutropenic patients with candidemia. Abstract 1420. In: Program and Abstracts of the 39th Interscience Conference on Antimicrobial Agents and Chemotherapy, 1999. Washington DC: American Society of Microbiology; 1999:567.
49. Offner FCJ, Herbrecht R, Engelhard D. EORTC-IFCG phase II study on liposomal nystatin in patients with invasive aspergillosis refractory or intolerant to conventional/lipid amphotericin B. Abstract 1102. In: Abstracts of the 40th Interscience Conference on Antimicrobial Agents and Chemotherapy, 2000. Washington DC: American Society for Microbiology; 2000:370.
50. Powles R, Mawhorter S, Williams AH. Liposomal nystatin (Nyotran) vs amphotericin B (Fungizone) in empiric treatment of presumed fungal infections in neutropenic patients. Abstract LB-4. In: Program and Abstracts of the 39th Interscience Conference on Antimicrobial Agents and Chemotherapy, 1999. Washington DC: American Society for Microbiology; 1999:14.
51. Vermes A, Guchelaar HJ, Dankert J. Flucytosine: a review of its pharmacology, clinical indications, pharmacokinetics, toxicity and drug interactions. J Antimicrob Chemother 2000;46:171–9.
52. Schmidt A, Schmidt DI. Establishment and evaluation of microdilution assays for the *in vitro* sensitivity testing of *Aspergillus fumigatus*. Arzneimittelforschung 2000;50:495–501.
53. Gehrt A, Peter J, Pizzo PA, Walsh TJ. Effect of increasing inoculum sizes of pathogenic filamentous fungi on MICs of antifungal agents by broth microdilution method. J Clin Microbiol 1995;33:1302–7.
54. Barchiesi F, Schimizzi AM, Najvar LK, *et al.* Interactions of posaconazole and flucytosine against *Cryptococcus neoformans*. Antimicrob Agents Chemother 2001;45:1355–9.
55. Pfaller MA, Messer SA, Boyken L, *et al.* *In vitro* activities of 5-fluorocytosine against 8,803 clinical isolates of *Candida* spp.: global assessment of primary resistance using National Committee for Clinical Laboratory Standards susceptibility testing methods. Antimicrob Agents Chemother 2002;46:3518–21.
56. Brandt ME, Pfaller MA, Hajjeh RA, *et al.* Trends in antifungal drug susceptibility of *Cryptococcus neoformans* isolates in the United States: 1992 to 1994 and 1996 to 1998. Antimicrob Agents Chemother 2001;45:3065–9.
57. Casadevall A, Perfect JR. *Cryptococcus*. Washington, DC: ASM Press; 1988:541.
58. Lewis RE, Klepser ME, Pfaller MA. *In vitro* pharmacodynamic characteristics of flucytosine

determined by time-kill methods. Diagn Microbiol Infect Dis 2000;36:101–5.
59. Scalarone GM, Mikami Y, Kurita N, *et al.* The postantifungal effect of 5-fluorocytosine on *Candida albicans*. J Antimicrob Chemother 1992;29:129–36.
60. Andes D, van Ogtrop M. *In vivo* characterization of the pharmacodynamics of flucytosine in a neutropenic murine disseminated candidiasis model. Antimicrob Agents Chemother 2000;44:938–42.
61. Daneshmend TK, Warnock DW. Clinical pharmacokinetics of systemic antifungal drugs. Clin Pharmacokinet 1983;8:17–42.
62. Groll AH, Piscitelli SC, Walsh TJ. Clinical pharmacology of systemic antifungal agents: a comprehensive review of agents in clinical use, current investigational compounds, and putative targets for antifungal drug development. Adv Pharmacol 1998;44:343–500.
63. van der Horst CM, Saag MS, Cloud GA, *et al.* Treatment of cryptococcal meningitis associated with the acquired immunodeficiency syndrome. National Institute of Allergy and Infectious Diseases Mycoses Study Group and AIDS Clinical Trials Group. N Engl J Med 1997;337:15–21.
64. Francis P, Walsh TJ. Evolving role of flucytosine in immunocompromised patients: new insights into safety, pharmacokinetics, and antifungal therapy. Clin Infect Dis 1992;15:1003–18.
65. Vermes A, Guchelaar HJ, van Kuilenburg AB, Dankert J. 5-fluorocytosine-related bone-marrow depression and conversion to fluorouracil: a pilot study. Fundam Clin Pharmacol 2002;16:39–47.
66. Vermes A, van Der Sijs H, Guchelaar HJ. Flucytosine: correlation between toxicity and pharmacokinetic parameters. Chemotherapy 2000;46:86–94.
67. Hiddemann W, Essink ME, Fegeler W, *et al.* Antifungal treatment by amphotericin B and 5-fluorocytosine delays the recovery of normal hematopoietic cells after intensive cytostatic therapy for acute myeloid leukemia. Cancer 1991;68:9–14.
68. Pfaller MA, Diekema DJ, Jones RN, *et al.* Trends in antifungal susceptibility of Candida spp. isolated from pediatric and adult patients with bloodstream infections: SENTRY Antimicrobial Surveillance Program, 1997 to 2000. J Clin Microbiol 2002;40:852–6.
69. Sun QN, Fothergill AW, McCarthy DI, *et al. In vitro* activities of posaconazole, itraconazole, voriconazole, amphotericin B, and fluconazole against 37 clinical isolates of zygomycetes. Antimicrob Agents Chemother 2002;46:1581–2.
70. Ruhnke M, Eigler A, Tennagen I, *et al.* Emergence of fluconazole-resistant strains of *Candida albicans* in patients with recurrent oropharyngeal candidosis and human immunodeficiency virus infection. J Clin Microbiol 1994;32:2092–8.
71. Marr KA, Seidel K, White TC, Bowden RA. Candidemia in allogeneic blood and marrow transplant recipients: evolution of risk factors after the adoption of prophylactic fluconazole. J Infect Dis 2000;181:309–16.
72. Muller FM, Weig M, Peter J, Walsh TJ. Azole cross-resistance to ketoconazole, fluconazole, itraconazole and voriconazole in clinical *Candida albicans* isolates from HIV-infected children with oropharyngeal candidosis. J Antimicrob Chemother 2000;46:338–40.
73. Klepser ME, Wolfe EJ, Jones RN, *et al.* Antifungal pharmacodynamic characteristics of fluconazole and amphotericin B tested against *Candida albicans*. Antimicrob Agents Chemother 1997;41:1392–5.
74. Klepser ME, Wolfe EJ, Pfaller MA. Antifungal pharmacodynamic characteristics of fluconazole and amphotericin B against *Cryptococcus neoformans*. J Antimicrob Chemother 1998;41:397–401.
75. Sohnle PG, Hahn BL, Erdmann MD. Effect of fluconazole on viability of *Candida albicans* over extended periods of time. Antimicrob Agents Chemother 1996;40:2622–5.
76. Louie A, Drusano GL, Banerjee P, *et al.* Pharmacodynamics of fluconazole in a murine model of systemic candidiasis. Antimicrob Agents Chemother 1998;42:1105–9.
77. Brammer, KW, Farrow PR, Faulkner JK. Pharmacokinetics and tissue penetration of fluconazole in humans. Rev Infect Dis 1990;12 (Suppl.3):S318–26.
78. Lee JW, Seibel NL, Amantea M, *et al.* Safety and pharmacokinetics of fluconazole in children with neoplastic diseases. J Pediatr 1992;120:987–93.
79. Saxen H, Hoppu K, Pohjavuori M. Pharmacokinetics of fluconazole in very low birth weight infants during the first two weeks of life. Clin Pharmacol Ther 1993;54:269–77.
80. Anaissie EJ, Kontoyiannis DP, Huls C, *et al.* Safety, plasma concentrations, and efficacy of high-dose fluconazole in invasive mold infections. J Infect Dis 1995;172:599–602.
81. Como JA, Dismukes WE. Oral azole drugs as systemic antifungal therapy. N Engl J Med 1994;330:263–72.
82. Novelli V, Holzel H. Safety and tolerability of fluconazole in children. Antimicrob Agents Chemother 1999;43:1955–60.
83. Pappas PG, Kauffman CA, Perfect J, *et al.* Alopecia associated with fluconazole therapy. Ann Intern Med 1995;123:354–7.
84. Gubbins P, McConnell S, Penzak S. Antifungal agents, in Interactions in Infectious Diseases, P. SC and R. KA, Editors. 2001, Humana Press: Totowa, NJ. p. 185–217.
85. Rex JH, Bennett JE, Sugar AM, *et al.* A randomized trial comparing fluconazole with amphotericin B for the treatment of candidemia in patients without neutropenia. Candidemia Study Group and the National Institute. N Engl J Med 1994;331:1325–30.
86. Galgiani JN, Catanzaro A, Cloud GA, *et al.* Comparison of oral fluconazole and itraconazole for progressive, nonmeningeal coccidioidomycosis. A randomized, double-blind trial. Mycoses Study Group. Ann Intern Med 2000;133:676–86.
87. Galgiani JN, Catanzaro A, Cloud GA, *et al.* Fluconazole therapy for coccidioidal meningitis. The NIAID-Mycoses Study Group. Ann Intern Med 1993;119:28–35.
88. Diaz M, Negroni R, Montero-Gei F, *et al.* A Pan-American 5-year study of fluconazole therapy for deep mycoses in the immunocompetent host. Pan-American Study Group. Clin Infect Dis 1992;14(Suppl.1):S68–76.
89. Pappas PG, Bradsher RW, Kauffman CA, *et al.* Treatment of blastomycosis with higher doses of fluconazole. The National Institute of Allergy and Infectious Diseases Mycoses Study Group. Clin Infect Dis 1997;25:200–5.
90. Wheat J, MaWhinney S, Hafner R, *et al.* Treatment of histoplasmosis with fluconazole in patients with acquired immunodeficiency syndrome. National Institute of Allergy and Infectious Diseases Acquired Immunodeficiency Syndrome Clinical Trials Group and Mycoses Study Group. Am J Med 1997;103:223–32.
91. Rotstein C, Bow EJ, Laverdiere M, *et al.* Randomized placebo-controlled trial of fluconazole prophylaxis for neutropenic cancer patients: benefit based on purpose and intensity of cytotoxic therapy. The Canadian Fluconazole Prophylaxis Study Group. Clin Infect Dis 1999;28:331–40.
92. Winston DJ, Pakrasi A, Busuttil RW. Prophylactic fluconazole in liver transplant recipients. A randomized, double-blind, placebo-controlled trial. Ann Intern Med 1999;131:729–37.
93. 1999 USPHS/IDSA guidelines for the prevention of opportunistic infections in persons infected with human immunodeficiency virus. Clin Infect Dis 2000;30(Suppl.1):S29–65.
94. Manavathu EK, Cutright JL, Chandrasekar PH. Organism-dependent fungicidal activities of azoles. Antimicrob Agents Chemother 1998;42:3018–21.
95. De Beule K, Van Gestel J. Pharmacology of itraconazole. Drugs 2001;61(Suppl.1):27–37.
96. Heykants J, Michiels M, Meuldermans W, *et al.* The pharmacokinetics of itraconazole in animals and man: an overview. In: Fromtling R, ed. Recent trends in the discovery, development and evaluation of antifungal agents. Barcelona: JR Prous Science Publishers; 1987:223–49.
97. Boogaerts J, Michaux JL, Bosly A, *et al.* Pharmacokinetics and safety of seven days of intravenous (IV) itraconazole followed by two weeks oral itraconazole solution in patients with haematological malignancy. Abstract A87, in Program and Abstracts of the 36th Interscience Conference on Antimicrobial Agents and Chemotherapy, 1996. Washington DC: American Society for Microbiology: 1996:17.
98. Schmitt C, Perel Y, Harousseau JL, *et al.* Pharmacokinetics of itraconazole oral solution in neutropenic children during long-term prophylaxis. Antimicrob Agents Chemother 2001;45:1561–4.
99. de Repentigny L, Ratelle J, Leclerc JM, *et al.* Repeated-dose pharmacokinetics of an oral solution of itraconazole in infants and children. Antimicrob Agents Chemother 1998;42:404–8.
100. Tucker RM, Haq Y, Denning DW, Stevens DA. Adverse events associated with itraconazole in 189 patients on chronic therapy. J Antimicrob Chemother 1990;26:561–6.
101. Ahmad SR, Singer SJ, Leissa BG. Congestive heart failure associated with itraconazole. Lancet 2001;357:1766–7.
102. Groll AH, Wood L, Roden M, *et al.* Safety, pharmacokinetics, and pharmacodynamics of cyclodextrin itraconazole in pediatric patients with oropharyngeal candidiasis. Antimicrob Agents Chemother 2002;46:2554–63.
103. Foot AB, Veys PA, Gibson BE. Itraconazole oral solution as antifungal prophylaxis in children undergoing stem cell transplantation or intensive chemotherapy for haematological disorders. Bone Marrow Transplant 1999;24:1089–93.
104. Saag MS, Cloud GA, Graybill JR, *et al.* A comparison of itraconazole versus fluconazole as maintenance therapy for AIDS-associated cryptococcal meningitis. National Institute of Allergy and Infectious Diseases Mycoses Study Group. Clin Infect Dis 1999;28:291–6.
105. Stevens DA, Lee JY. Analysis of compassionate use itraconazole therapy for invasive aspergillosis by the NIAID Mycoses Study Group criteria. Arch Intern Med 1997;157:1857–62.
106. Sharkey PK, Graybill JR, Rinaldi MG, *et al.* Itraconazole treatment of phaeohyphomycosis. J Am Acad Dermatol 1990;23:577–86.
107. Boogaerts M, Winston DJ, Bow EJ, *et al.* Intravenous and oral itraconazole versus intravenous amphotericin B deoxycholate as empirical antifungal therapy for persistent fever in neutropenic patients with cancer who are receiving broad-spectrum antibacterial therapy. A randomized, controlled trial. Ann Intern Med 2001;135:412–22.
108. Glasmacher A, Hahn C, Molitor E, *et al.* Definition of itraconazole target concentration for antifungal prophylaxis. Abstract 700. In: Abstracts of the 40th Interscience Conference on Antimicrobial Agents and Chemotherapy, 2000. Washington, DC: American Society for Microbiology; 2000:363.
109. Klepser ME, Malone D, Lewis RE, *et al.* Evaluation of voriconazole pharmacodynamics using time-kill methodology. Antimicrob Agents Chemother 2000;44:1917–20.
110. Garcia MT, Llorente MT, Lima JE, *et al.* Activity of voriconazole: post-antifungal effect, effects of low concentrations and of pretreatment on

the susceptibility of *Candida albicans* to leucocytes. Scand J Infect Dis 1999;31:501–4.
111. Herbrecht R, Denning DW, Patterson TF, *et al.* Voriconazole versus amphotericin B for primary therapy of invasive aspergillosis. N Engl J Med 2002;347:408–15.
112. Walsh TJ, Lutsar I, Driscoll T, *et al.* Voriconazole in the treatment of aspergillosis, scedosporiosis and other invasive fungal infections in children. Pediatr Infect Dis J 2002;21:240–8.
113. Ally R, Schurmann D, Kreisel W, *et al.* A randomized, double-blind, double-dummy, multicenter trial of voriconazole and fluconazole in the treatment of esophageal candidiasis in immunocompromised patients. Clin Infect Dis 2001;33:1447–54.
114. Walsh TJ, Pappas P, Winston DJ, *et al.* Voriconazole compared with liposomal amphotericin B for empirical antifungal therapy in patients with neutropenia and persistent fever. N Engl J Med 2002;346:225–34.
115. Nieto L, Northland R, Pittisuttithum P. Posaconazole equivalent to fluconazole in the treatment of oropharyngeal candidiasis. Abstract 1108, in Abstracts of the 40th Interscience Conference on Antimicrobial Agents and Chemotherapy. 2000, American Society for Microbiology,: Washington, DC. p. 372.
116. Hachem R, Raad II, Afif CM, *et al.* An open, non-comparative multicenter study to evaluate efficacy and safety of posaconazole (SCH 56592) in the treatment of invasive fungal infections refractory to or intolerant to standard therapy. Abstract 1109, in Abstracts of the 40th International Conference on Antimicrobial Agents and Chemotherapy. 2000. American Society for Microbiology: Washington, DC; 2000:372.
117. Georgopapadakou NH. Update on antifungals targeted to the cell wall: focus on beta–1,3-glucan synthase inhibitors. Expert Opin Investig Drugs 2001;10:269–80.
118. Kurtz MB, Douglas CM. Lipopeptide inhibitors of fungal glucan synthase. J Med Vet Mycol 1997;35:79–86.
119. Espinel-Ingroff A. Comparison of *In vitro* activities of the new triazole SCH56592 and the echinocandins MK-0991 (L-743,872) and LY303366 against opportunistic filamentous and dimorphic fungi and yeasts. J Clin Microbiol 1998;36:2950–6.
120. Osherov N, May GS, Albert ND, Kontoyiannis DP. Overexpression of Sbe2p, a Golgi protein, results in resistance to caspofungin in *Saccharomyces cerevisiae.* Antimicrob Agents Chemother 2002;46:2462–9.
121. Bowman JC, Hicks PS, Kurtz MB, *et al.* The antifungal echinocandin caspofungin acetate kills growing cells of *Aspergillus fumigatus in vitro.* Antimicrob Agents Chemother 2002;46:3001–12.
122. Ernst EJ, Klepser ME, Ernst ME, *et al. In vitro* pharmacodynamic properties of MK–0991 determined by time-kill methods. Diagn Microbiol Infect Dis 1999;33:75–80.
123. Balani SK, Xu X, Arison BH, *et al.* Metabolites of caspofungin acetate, a potent antifungal agent, in human plasma and urine. Drug Metab Dispos 2000;28:1274–8.
124. Walsh T, Adamson PC, Seibel NL, *et al.* Pharmacokinetics (PK) of caspofungin (CAS) in pediatric patients. Abstract M-896. In: Abstracts of the 42nd Interscience Conference on Antimicrobial Agents and Chemotherapy, 2002. Washington, DC: American Society of Microbiology; 2002:395.
125. Maertens J, Raad I, Petrikkos G, *et al.* Update of the multicenter noncomparative study of caspofungin (CAS) in Adults with invasive aspergillosis (IA) refractory or intolerant (I) to other antifungal agents: an analysis of 90 patients. Abstract M-868. In: Abstracts of the 42nd Interscience Conference on Antimicrobial Agents and Chemotherapy, 2002. Washington, DC: American Society of Microbiology; 2002:388.
125a. Mora-Duarte J, Betts R, Notstein C, *et al.* Comparison of caspofungin and amphotericin B for invasive candidiasis. N Engl J Med 2002;347:2020–9.
126. Villanueva A, Gotuzzo E, Arathoon EG, *et al.* A randomized double-blind study of caspofungin versus fluconazole for the treatment of esophageal candidiasis. Am J Med 2002;113:294–9.
127. Ryder NS. Terbinafine: mode of action and properties of the squalene epoxidase inhibition. Br J Dermatol 1992;126(Suppl.39):2–7.
128. Jessup CJ, Ryder NS, Ghannoum MA. An evaluation of the *in vitro* activity of terbinafine. Med Mycol 2000;38:155–9.
129. Ryder NS, Leitner I. Synergistic interaction of terbinafine with triazoles or amphotericin B against *Aspergillus* species. Med Mycol 2001;39:91–5.
130. Rocha EM, Almeida CB, Martinez-Rossi NM. Identification of genes involved in terbinafine resistance in *Aspergillus nidulans.* Lett Appl Microbiol 2002;35:228–32.
131. vanden Bossche H, Marichal P, Odds FC, *et al.* Characterization of an azole-resistant *Candida glabrata* isolate. Antimicrob Agents Chemother 1992;36:2602–10.
132. Smith WL, Edlind TD. Histone deacetylase inhibitors enhance *Candida albicans* sensitivity to azoles and related antifungals: correlation with reduction in CDR and ERG upregulation. Antimicrob Agents Chemother 2002;46:3532–9.
133. Faergemann J, Zehender H, Denouel J, Millerioux L. Levels of terbinafine in plasma, stratum corneum, dermis-epidermis (without stratum corneum), sebum, hair and nails during and after 250mg terbinafine orally once per day for four weeks. Acta Derm Venereol 1993;73:305–9.
134. Kovarik JM, Mueller EA, Zehender H, *et al.* Multiple-dose pharmacokinetics and distribution in tissue of terbinafine and metabolites. Antimicrob Agents Chemother 1995;39:2738–41.
135. Nedelman JR, Gibiansky E, Robbins BA, *et al.* Pharmacokinetics and pharmacodynamics of multiple-dose terbinafine. J Clin Pharmacol 1996;36:452–61.
136. Hill S, Thomas R, Smith SG, Finlay AY. An investigation of the pharmacokinetics of topical terbinafine (Lamisil) 1% cream. Br J Dermatol 1992;127:396–400.
137. Vickers AE, Sinclair JR, Zollinger M, *et al.* Multiple cytochrome P–450s involved in the metabolism of terbinafine suggest a limited potential for drug-drug interactions. Drug Metab Dispos 1999;27:1029–38.
138. McClellan KJ, Wiseman LR, Markham A. Terbinafine. An update of its use in superficial mycoses. Drugs 1999;58:179–202.
139. Schiraldi GF, Cicero SL, Colombo MD, *et al.* Refractory pulmonary aspergillosis: compassionate trial with terbinafine. Br J Dermatol 1996;134(Suppl.46):25–9; discussion 39–40.
140. Develoux M. Griseofulvinw. Ann Dermatol Venereol 2001;128:1317–25.
141. Zheng YC. Morphology of griseofulvin-resistant isolates of Mongolian variant of *Trichophyton schoenleini.* Chin Med J (Engl) 1990;103:489–92.
142. Fachin AL, Maffei CM, Martinez-Rossi NM. *In vitro* susceptibility of *Trichophyton rubrum* isolates to griseofulvin and tioconazole. Induction and isolation of a resistant mutant to both antimycotic drugs. Mutant of *Trichophyton rubrum* resistant to griseofulvin and tioconazole. Mycopathologia 1996;135:141–3.
143. Gramatte T. Griseofulvin absorption from different sites in the human small intestine. Biopharm Drug Dispos 1994;15:747–59.
144. Schafer-Korting M, Korting HC, Mutschler E. Human plasma and skin blister fluid levels of griseofulvin following a single oral dose. Eur J Clin Pharmacol, 1985. 29:109–13.
145. Asahina A, Tada Y, Nakamura K, Tamaki K. Griseofulvin has a potential to modulate the expression of cell adhesion molecules on leukocytes and vascular endothelial cells. Int Immunopharmacol 2001;1:75–83.
146. Knasmuller S, Parzefall W, Helma C, *et al.* Toxic effects of griseofulvin: disease models, mechanisms, and risk assessment. Crit Rev Toxicol 1997;27:495–537.
147. Polak A. Preclinical data and mode of action of amorolfine. Dermatology 1992;184(Suppl.1):3–7.
148. De Vroey C, Desmet P, Li ZQ, *et al.* Further studies on the *in vitro* antifungal activity of amorolfine. Mycoses 1996;39:41–4.
149. Okeke CN, Tsuboi R, Kawai M, Ogawa H. Fluorometric assessment of *In vitro* antidermatophytic activities of antimycotics based on their keratin-penetrating power. J Clin Microbiol 2000;38:489–91.
150. del Palacio A, Gip L, Bergstraesser M, Zaug M. Dose-finding study of amorolfine cream (0.125%, 0.25% and 0.5%) in the treatment of dermatomycoses. Clin Exp Dermatol 1992;17(Suppl.1):50–5.
151. Polak A. Combination of amorolfine with various antifungal drugs in dermatophytosis. Mycoses 1993;36:43–9.
152. Polak A. Kinetics of amorolfine in human nails. Mycoses 1993;36:101–3.
153. Roncari G, Ponelle C, Zumbrunnen R, *et al.* Percutaneous absorption of amorolfine following a single topical application of an amorolfine cream formulation. Clin Exp Dermatol 1992;17(Suppl.) 1:33–6.
154. Baran R. Topical amorolfine for 15 months combined with 12 weeks of oral terbinafine, a cost-effective treatment for onychomycosis. Br J Dermatol 2001;145(Suppl.60):15–9.
155. Lecha M. Amorolfine and itraconazole combination for severe toenail onychomycosis; results of an open randomized trial in Spain. Br J Dermatol 2001;145(Suppl.60):21–6.
156. Bohn M, Kraemer KT. Dermatopharmacology of ciclopirox nail lacquer topical solution 8% in the treatment of onychomycosis. J Am Acad Dermatol 2000;43(4 Suppl.):S57–69.
157. Braga PC, Piatti G, Conti E, Vignali F. Effects of subinhibitory concentrations of ciclopirox on the adherence of *Candida albicans* to human buccal and vaginal epithelial cells. Arzneimittelforschung 1992;42:1368–71.
158. Kellner HM, Arnold C, Christ OE, *et al.* Pharmacokinetics and biotransformation of the antimycotic drug ciclopiroxolamine in animals and man after topical and systemic administration. Arzneimittelforschung 1981:31(8A):1337–53.
159. Bohn M, Kraemer K. The dermatopharmacologic profile of ciclopirox 8% nail lacquer. J Am Podiatr Med Assoc 2000;90:491–4.
160. Coppi G, Silingardi S, Girardello R, *et al.* Pharmacokinetics of ciclopirox olamine after vaginal application to rabbits and patients. J Chemother 1993;5:302–6.

chapter 209

Antiparasitic Agents

Samuel L Stanley Jr

INTRODUCTION

Antiparasitic agents are used to treat infestations caused by a diverse and complex group of organisms encompassing the unicellular protozoa, which have intricate life cycles often involving more than one host, as well as the helminths, which have highly developed organ systems. Many antiparasitic agents are old drugs that have never been subjected to the rigorous testing of efficacy and safety currently required by agencies in various countries, such as the US Food and Drug Administration. For most of the drugs, information regarding use in pregnancy is totally lacking.

The treatment options by organism or disease entity, along with the recommended adult and pediatric dosages, are listed in Table 209.1. Agents that are not readily available in the USA are listed in Table 209.2. Few of the antiparasitic agents have been extensively studied in pregnancy. Table 209.3 divides the drugs into those that are probably safe on the basis of clinical experience, those that are possibly safe on the basis of anecdotal experience or are safe during certain trimesters, and those that are known to be hazardous or for which too little information is known to make a recommendation. In general, however, the decision to use of any of these agents in a pregnant patient must be made on an individual basis, weighing the severity of the illness and the benefit of treatment to the mother against the potential toxicity to the fetus.

ANTIPROTOZOAL AGENTS

AMODIAQUINE

Amodiaquine is a 4-aminoquinoline with antimalarial activity and a mechanism of action similar to that of chloroquine. It is available only as the dihydrochloride salt for oral administration and it undergoes extensive first-pass metabolism in the liver to the active compound desethylamodiaquine, which is widely distributed throughout the body and slowly eliminated. The side-effect profile is similar to that of chloroquine but agranulocytosis and severe hepatitis have been reported with long-term use (as chemoprophylaxis). The activity of amodiaquine against some chloroquine-resistant strains of *Plasmodium falciparum* has led to a modest revival in its use.[6–8] A recent randomized clinical trial comparing amodiaquine and chloroquine showed superior efficacy for amodiaquine and a similar safety profile in an area with high levels of chloroquine-resistant *P. falciparum*.[9]

AMPHOTERICIN B

Amphotericin B, a polyene antifungal agent, is the drug of choice for primary amebic meningoencephalitis caused by *Naegleria* spp. (see Chapter 244), and it is an alternative drug for leishmaniasis (see Chapter 172).[10–13] Its pharmacokinetics and side effects are detailed in Chapter 208. Lipid-associated formulations of amphotericin B have recently been shown to be effective in the treatment of visceral leishmaniasis in India in patients who failed to respond to antimony therapy, single dose therapy with liposomal amphotericin B giving cure rates of more than 92% with minimal toxicity.[12,13]

ANTIFOLATE AGENTS

Antifolate agents act at various steps in the folic acid cycle. For *Plasmodium* spp., *Toxoplasma* spp. and other sensitive parasites, reduced folic acid derivatives are essential for de-novo pyrimidine synthesis. Unlike mammalian cells, these parasites cannot use preformed pyrimidines. Antifolate agents are most commonly used in combination to block sequential steps in the folic acid metabolic pathway (see Chapter 197).

Pyrimethamine

Pyrimethamine is a diaminopyrimidine that inhibits plasmodial dihydrofolate reductase at a concentration that is 1000 times less than that required to inhibit the mammalian enzyme.[6,7,14–16] It is effective against the erythrocytic stages of all *Plasmodium* spp. that are pathogenic for humans and, in combination with sulfadiazine, clindamycin or atovaquone, it is used for the treatment of *Toxoplasma gondii*.[17,18] Pyrimethamine also has activity against *Isospora belli*.[19] The drug is available in oral form; it is slowly but completely absorbed, is 85% protein-bound and is extensively metabolized by the liver (< 3% is excreted unchanged). The half-life is 4–6 days.

Although pyrimethamine is available as 25mg tablets, it is almost exclusively used in combination with a sulfonamide (sulfadiazine, sulfadoxine) or a sulfone (dapsone; see below). The dosage for toxoplasmosis is listed in Table 209.1. Some clinicians give an initial pyrimethamine loading dose of 200mg. In patients who cannot tolerate sulfonamides, clindamycin (1.8–2.4g/day in divided doses) or atovaquone (1.5g q12h) may be substituted. Side effects of pyrimethamine include blood dyscrasias, rash and, very rarely, seizures or shock. At high doses, pyrimethamine causes bone marrow suppression, which can be prevented by concurrent administration of folinic acid.

Trimethoprim

Trimethoprim (TMP) is another diaminopyrimidine that inhibits microbial dihydrofolate reductase. It has activity against

- a variety of bacteria (see Chapter 197);
- *Pneumocystis carinii* (see Chapter 124); and
- the parasites *Isospora belli* and *Cyclospora cayetanensis* (see Chapter 243).[19,20]

Trimethoprim is readily absorbed, widely distributed and 50% protein-bound. Less than 20% is hepatically metabolized to inactive metabolites and the drug is excreted both in the urine and bile. The half-life is 9–11 hours.

For parasitic infections, TMP is used in fixed combination with sulfamethoxazole (SMX; see below). Side effects include rashes, pruritus, nausea, vomiting, glossitis, elevated liver enzymes, cytopenias, megaloblastic anemia, fever, aseptic meningitis and impaired renal function.

Infection	Drug	Adult dosage	Pediatric dosage
ANTIPARASITIC AGENTS AND DOSAGES			
Acanthamoeba (keratitis)			
Drug of choice	Polyhexamethylene biguanide 0.02% (topical) plus 0.1% propamidine isethionate (topical)		
Amebiasis (*Entamoeba histolytica*)			
Asymptomatic			
Drug of choice	Paromomycin	25–35mg/kg/day in three doses for 7 days	25–35mg/kg/day in three doses for 7 days
Alternatives	Diloxanide furoate	500mg q8h for 10 days	20mg/kg/day in three doses for 10 days
	Iodoquinol	650mg q8h for 20 days	30–40mg/kg/day (maximum 2g) in three doses for 20 days
Mild-to-moderate intestinal disease			
Drug of choice	Metronidazole	500–750mg q8h for 5–10 days	35–50mg/kg/day in three doses for 10 days
OR	Tinidazole	2g/day for 3 days	50mg/kg (maximum 2g) per day for 3 days
Severe intestinal disease and extraintestinal disease			
Drug of choice	Metronidazole	750mg q8h for 5–10 days	35–50mg/kg/day in three doses for 10 days
OR	Tinidazole	600mg q12h or 800mg q8h for 5 days	50mg/kg or 60mg/kg (maximum 2g) per day for 5 days
Amebic meningoencephalitis (primary)			
***Naegleria* spp.**			
Drug of choice	Amphotericin B	1mg/kg/day iv, uncertain duration	1mg/kg/day iv, uncertain duration
***Acanthamoeba* spp.**			
Drug of choice	Pentamidine, ketoconazole, flucytosine		
Balamuthia mandrillaris*			
Drugs of choice	Clarithromycin	500mg q8h	
	Fluconazole	400mg q24h	
	Sulfadiazine	1.5g q6h	
	Flucytosine	1.5g q6h	
***Sappinia diploides*†**			
Drugs of choice	Azithromycin	250mg q24h	
	Pentamidine	300mg iv q24h	
	Itraconazole	200mg q12h	
	Flucytosine	2.75g q6h	
***Ancylostoma caninum* (eosinophilic enterocolitis)**			
Drug of choice	Mebendazole	100mg q12h for 3 days	100mg q12h for 3 days
OR	Pyrantel pamoate	11mg/kg (maximum 1g) for 3 days	11mg/kg (maximum 1g) for 3 days
OR	Albendazole	400mg, single dose	400mg, single dose
Angiostrongyliasis			
Angiostrongylus cantonensis			
Drug of choice	Mebendazole	100mg q12h for 5 days	100mg q12h for 5 days
Angiostrongylus costaricensis			
Drug of choice	Mebendazole	200–400mg q8h for 10 days	200–400mg q8h for 10 days
Alternative	Thiabendazole	75mg/kg/day in three doses for 3 days (maximum 3g/day)	75mg/kg/day in three doses for 3 days (maximum 3g/day)
Anisakiasis (*Anisakis* spp.)			
Treatment of choice		Surgical or endoscopic removal	
Ascariasis (*Ascaris lumbricoides*, roundworm)			
Drug of choice	Mebendazole	100mg q12h for 3 days or 500mg, single dose	100mg q12h for 3 days or 500mg, single dose
OR	Pyrantel pamoate	11mg/kg, single dose (maximum 1g)	11mg/kg, single dose (maximum 1g)
OR	Albendazole	400mg, single dose	400mg, single dose
Babesiosis (*Babesia* spp.)			
Drug of choice	Clindamycin	1.2g q12h iv or 600mg q8h po for 7 days	20–40mg/kg/day po in three doses for 7 days
PLUS	Quinine	650mg q8h po for 7 days	25mg/kg/day in three doses for 7 days
OR	Atovaquone	750mg q12h for 7–10 days	20mg/kg q12h for 7–10 days
PLUS	Azithromycin	600mg po daily for 7–10 days	12mg/kg daily for 7–10 days

Table 209.1 Antiparasitic agents and dosages. Organism or disease entity is listed alphabetically. Both adult and pediatric dosages are indicated. Sb, antimony; SMX, sulfamethoxazole; TMP, trimethoprim. Data modified from Med Lett Drugs Ther 2002:(4):1[1]

ANTIPARASITIC AGENTS AND DOSAGES			
Infection	**Drug**	**Adult dosage**	**Pediatric dosage**
Balantidiasis (*Balantidium coli*)			
Drug of choice	Tetracycline	500mg q6h for 10 days	40mg/kg/day (maximum 2g) in four doses for 10 days
Alternatives	Iodoquinol	650mg q8h for 20 days	40mg/kg/day in three doses for 20 days
	Metronidazole	750mg q8h for 5 days	35–50mg/kg/day in three doses for 5 days
Baylisascariasis (*Baylisascaris procyonis*)			
Drugs of choice	Albendazole, mebendazole, thiabendazole, levamisole or ivermectin		
Blastocystis hominis			
Drug of choice	Metronidazole	750mg q8h for 10 days	
OR			
	Iodoquinol	650mg q8h for 20 days	
Capillariasis (*Capillaria philippinensis*)			
Drug of choice	Mebendazole	200mg q12h for 20 days	200mg q12h for 20 days
Alternative	Albendazole	400mg/day for 10 days	400mg/day for 10 days
Cryptosporidiosis (*Cryptosporidium parvum*)			
No agent has yet been conclusively proved to be effective in AIDS patients. Nitazoxanide, in the doses listed below, showed efficacy in clearing infection from immunocompetent individuals.			
	Nitazoxanide	500mg q12h for 3 days	age 4–11 years: 200mg q12h for 3 days age 1–3 years: 100mg q12h
Cutaneous larva migrans (creeping eruption, dog and cat hookworm)			
Drug of choice	Thiabendazole	Topical administration	Topical administration
OR			
	Ivermectin	150–200μg/kg, single dose	150–200μg/kg, single dose
OR			
	Albendazole	400mg/day for 3 days	400mg/day for 3 days
Cyclosporiasis (*Cyclospora cayetanensis*)			
Drug of choice	TMP–SMX	TMP 160mg, SMX 800mg q12h for 7–10 days	TMP 5mg/kg, SMX 25mg/kg q12h for 7–10 days
Dientamoeba fragilis			
Drug of choice	Iodoquinol	650mg q8h for 20 days	40mg/kg/day (maximum 2g) in three doses for 20 days
OR			
	Paromomycin	25–30mg/kg/day in three doses for 7 days	25–30mg/kg/day in three doses for 7 days
OR			
	Tetracycline	500mg q6h for 10 days	10mg/kg q6h (maximum 2g) for 10 days
Dracunculiasis (*Dracunculus medinensis*, guinea worm)			
Drug of choice	Metronidazole	250mg q8h for 10 days	25mg/kg/day (maximum 750mg) in three doses for 10 days
Entamoeba polecki			
Drug of choice	Metronidazole	750mg q8h for 10 days	35–50mg/kg/day in three doses for 10 days
Enterobiasis (*Enterobius vermicularis*, pinworm)			
Drug of choice	Pyrantel pamoale	11mg/kg, single dose (maximum 1g); repeat in 2 weeks	11mg/kg, single dose (maximum 1g); repeat in 2 weeks
OR			
	Mebendazole	100mg, single dose; repeat in 2 weeks	100mg, single dose; repeat in 2 weeks
OR			
	Albendazole	400mg, single dose; repeat in 2 weeks	400mg, single dose; repeat in 2 weeks
Filariasis			
Wuchereria bancrofti, Brugia malayi			
Drug of choice	Diethylcarbamazine	Day 1: 50mg after food Day 2: 50mg q8h Day 3: 100mg q8h Days 4–14: 6mg/kg/day in three doses	Day 1: 1mg/kg after food Day 2: 1mg/kg q8h Day 3: 1–2mg/kg q8h Days 4–14: 6mg/kg/day in three doses
Loa loa			
Drug of choice	Diethylcarbamazine	Day 1: 50mg after food Day 2: 50mg q8h Day 3: 100mg q8h Days 4–21: 9mg/kg/day in three doses	Day 1: 1mg/kg after food Day 2: 1mg/kg q8h Day 3: 1–2mg/kg q8h Days 4–21: 9mg/kg/day in three doses
Mansonella ozzardi			
Drug of choice	Ivermectin	6mg, single dose	
Mansonella perstans			
Drug of choice	Mebendazole	100mg q12h for 30 days	
OR			
	Albendazole	400mg q12h for 10 days	

Table 209.1—cont'd

ANTIPARASITIC AGENTS AND DOSAGES			
Infection	**Drug**	**Adult dosage**	**Pediatric dosage**
Mansonella streptocerca			
Drug of choice	Ivermectin	150µg/kg, single dose	
OR			
	Diethylcarbamazine	6mg/kg/day for 14 days	
Tropical pulmonary eosinophilia			
Drug of choice	Diethylcarbamazine	6mg/kg/day in three doses for 14 days	6mg/kg/day in three doses for 14 days
***Onchocerca volvulus* (river blindness)**			
Drug of choice	Ivermectin	150µg/kg, single dose, repeated every 6–12 months	150µg/kg, single dose, repeated every 6–12 months
Fluke (hermaphroditic) infection			
***Clonorchis sinensis* (Chinese liver fluke)**			
Drug of choice	Praziquantel	75mg/kg/day in three doses for 1 day	75mg/kg/day in three doses for 1 day
OR			
	Albendazole	10mg/kg for 7 days	
***Fasciola hepatica* (sheep liver fluke)**			
Drug of choice	Triclabendazole	10mg/kg, single dose	
Alternative	Bithionol	30–50mg/kg on alternate days for 10–15 doses	30–50mg/kg on alternate days for 10–15 doses
***Fasciotopsis buski, Heterophyes heterophyes, Metagonimus yokogawai* (intestinal flukes)**			
Drug of choice	Praziquantel	75mg/kg/day in three doses for 1 day	75mg/kg/day in three doses for 1 day
***Metorchis conjunctus* (North American liver fluke)**			
Drug of choice	Praziquantel	75mg/kg/day in three doses for 1 day	75mg/kg/day in three doses for 1 day
Nanophyetus salmincola			
Drug of choice	Praziquantel	60mg/kg/day in three doses for 1 day	60mg/kg/day in three doses for 1 day
***Opisthorchis viverrini* (South East Asian liver fluke)**			
Drug of choice	Praziquantel	75mg/kg/day in three doses for 1 day	75mg/kg/day in three doses for 1 day
***Paragonimus westermani* (lung fluke)**			
Drug of choice	Praziquantel	75mg/kg/day in three doses for 2 days	75mg/kg/day in three doses for 2 days
Alternative	Bithionol	30–50mg/kg on alternate for 10–15 doses	30–50mg/kg on alternate for 10–15 doses
Giardiasis (*Giardia lambia*)			
Drug of choice	Metronidazole	250mg q8h for 5 days	15mg/kg/day in three doses for 5 days
Alternative	Tinidazole	2g, single dose	50mg/kg, single dose (maximum 2g)
	Furazolidone	100mg q6h for 7–10 days	6mg/kg/day in four doses for 7–10 days
	Paromomycin	25–35mg/kg/day in three doses for 7 days	
	Quinacrine	100mg q8h for 5 days (max. 300mg/day)	2mg/kg q8h for 5 days (max. 300mg/day)
Gnathostomiasis (*Gnathostoma spinigerum*)			
Treatment of choice		Surgical removal	
OR			
	Ivermectin	200µg/kg/day for 2 days	200µg/kg/day for 2 days
OR			
	Albendazole	400mg q12h for 21 days	400mg q12h for 21 days
Hookworm infection (*Ancylostoma duodenale, Necator americanus*)			
Drug of choice	Mebendazole	100mg q12h for 2 days or 500mg, single dose	100mg q12h for 2 days or 500mg, single dose
OR			
	Pyrantel pamoate	11mg/kg (maximum 1g) for 3 days	11mg/kg (maximum 1g) for 3 days
OR			
	Albendazole	400mg, single dose	400mg, single dose
Isosporiasis (*Isospora belli*)			
Drug of choice	TMP–SMX	160mg TMP, 800mg SMX q6h for 10 days, then q12h for 3 weeks	
Leishmaniasis (*Leishmania mexicana, Leishmania tropica, Leishmania major, Leishmania braziliensis, Leishmania donovani* (kala-azar), *Leishmania infantum*)			
Drug of choice	Sodium stibogluconate	20mg Sb/kg/day iv or im for 20–28 days	20mg Sb/kg/day iv or im for 20–28 days
OR			
	Meglumine antimonate	20mg Sb/kg/day for 20–28 days	20mg Sb/kg/day for 20–28 days
Alternative	Amphotericin B	0.5–1 mg/kg by slow infusion daily or every 2 days for up to 8 weeks	0.5–1 mg/kg by slow infusion daily or every 2 days for up to 8 weeks
OR			
	Lipid-encapsulated amphotericin B	15–20mg/kg (total dose over 5 days or longer)	15–20mg/kg (total dose over 5 days or longer)
	Pentamidine isethionate	2–4mg/kg im daily or every 2 days for up to 15 doses	2–4mg/kg im daily or every 2 days for up to 15 doses
	Paromomycin	Topically q12h for 15 days	

Table 209.1—cont'd

ANTIPARASITIC AGENTS AND DOSAGES			
Infection	**Drug**	**Adult dosage**	**Pediatric dosage**
Malaria treatment (*Plasmodium falciparum, Plasmodium ovale, Plasmodium vivax, Plasmodium malariae*)			
Chloroquine-resistant *Plasmodium falciparum* (oral regimens)			
Drug of choice	Quinine sulfate	650mg q8h for 3–7 days	25mg/kg/day in three doses for 3–7 days
PLUS			
	Doxycycline	100mg q12h for 7 days	2mg/kg/day for 7 days
OR PLUS			
	Pyrimenthamine-sulfadoxine	3 tablets, single dose on last day of quinine treatment	Aged <1 year, 1/4 tablet; aged 1–3 years, 1/2 tablet; aged 4–8 years, 1 tablet; aged 9–14 years, 2 tablets
OR PLUS			
	Clindamycin	900mg q8h for 5 days	20–40 mg/kg/day in three doses for 5 days
OR			
	Atovaquone/proguanil	Two adults tablets q12h for 3 days	11–20kg: one adult tablet/day for 3 days 21–30kg: 2 adult tablets/day for 3 days 31–40kg: 3 adult tablets/day for 3 days >40kg: adult dose
Alternatives	Mefloquine	750mg followed by 500mg 12h later	15mg/kg, single dose (if body weight <45kg), followed by 10mg/kg 12h later
	Halofantrine	500mg q6h for three doses; repeat in 1 week	8mg/kg q6h for three doses (if body weight <40kg); repeat in 1 week
	Artesunate	4mg/kg/day for 3 days	
PLUS			
	Mefloquine	1250mg, single dose	
Chloroquine-resistant *Plasmodium vivax*			
Drug of choice	Quinine sulfate	650mg q8h for 3–7 days	25mg/kg/day in three doses for 3–7 days
PLUS			
	Doxycycline	100mg q12h for 7 days	2mg/kg/day for 7 days
OR PLUS			
	Pyrimethamine-sulfadoxine	3 tablets, single dose on last day of quinine treatment	Aged <1 year, 1/4 tablet; aged 1–3 years, 1/2 tablet; aged 4–8 years, 1 tablet; aged 9–14 years, 2 tablets
OR			
	Mefloquine	1250mg, single dose	25mg/kg, single dose (if body weight <45kg)
All *Plasmodium* spp. except chloroquine-resistant *Plasmodium falciparum* and chloroquine-resistant *Plasmodium vivax* (oral regimens)			
Drug of choice	Chloroquine phosphate	1g (600mg base), then 500mg (300mg base) 6 hours later, then 500mg (300mg base) at 24 hours and 48 hours	10mg base/kg (maximum 600mg base), then 5mg base/kg 6 hours later, then 5mg base/kg at 24 hours and 48 hours
All *Plasmodium* spp. (parenteral regimens)			
Drug of choice	Quinidine gluconate	10mg/kg loading dose (maximum 600mg) in normal saline slowly over 1–2 hours, followed by continuous infusion of 0.02mg/kg/minute until oral therapy can be started	10mg/kg loading dose (maximum 600mg) in normal saline slowly over 1–2 hours, followed by continuous infusion of 0.02mg/kg/minute until oral therapy can be started
OR			
	Quinine dihydrochloride	20mg/kg loading dose iv in 5% dextrose over 4 hours, followed by 10mg/kg over 2–4 hours q8h (maximum 1800mg/day) until oral therapy can be started	20mg/kg loading dose iv in 5% dextrose over 4 hours, followed by 10mg/kg over 2–4 hours q8h (maximum 1800mg/day) until oral therapy can be started
Alternative	Artemether	3.2mg/kg im, then 1.6mg/kg q24h	3.2mg/kg im, then 1.6mg/kg q24h
Prevention of relapses (*Plasmodium vivax* and *Plasmodium ovale* only)			
Drug of choice	Primaquine phosphate	26.3mg (15mg base) per day for 14 days or 79mg (45mg base) per week for 8 weeks	0.3mg base/kg/day for 14 days
Malaria prevention			
Chloroquine-sensitive areas			
Drug of choice	Chloroquine phosphate	500mg (300mg base), once per week	5mg/kg base once per week, up to adult dose of 300mg base
Chloroquine-resistant areas			
Drug of choice	Mefloquine	250mg once per week	Weight <5kg, no data; weight 5–9kg, 1/8 tablet; weight 10–19kg, 1/4 tablet; weight 20–30kg, 1/2 tablet; weight 31–45kg, 3/4 tablet; weight >45kg, 1 tablet
OR			
	Doxycycline	100mg/day	2mg/kg/day, up to 100mg/day

Table 209.1—cont'd

ANTIPARASITIC AGENTS AND DOSAGES			
Infection	**Drug**	**Adult dosage**	**Pediatric dosage**
Malaria prevention—cont'd			
OR			
	Atovaquone/proguanil	One adult tablet daily	11–20kg: 62.5mg/25mg 21–20kg: 125mg/50mg 31–40kg: 187.5mg/75mg >40kg: adult dose
Alternatives	Primaquine Chloroquine phosphate	0.5mg/kg base daily 500mg (300mg base) once per week	0.5mg/kg base daily 5mg/kg base once per week, up to adult dose of 300mg base
PLUS			
	Pyrimethamine-sulfadoxine for presumptive treatment	Carry a single dose (3 tablets) for self-treatment of febrile illness when medical care is not immediately available	Aged <1 year, 1/4 tablet; aged 1–3 years, 1/2 tablet; aged 4–8 years, 1 tablet; aged 9–14 years, 2 tablets
OR PLUS			
	Proguanil	200mg/day	Aged <2 years, 50mg/day; aged 2–6 years, 100mg; aged 7–10 years, 150mg; aged >10 years, 200mg
Microsporidiosis			
Ocular microsporidiosis (*Encephalitozoon hellem, Encephalitozoon cuniculi, Vittaforma corneae* (*Nosema corneum*))			
Drug of choice	Albendazole	400mg q12h	
PLUS			
	Fumagillin eyedrops		
Intestinal microsporidiosis (*Enterocylozoon bieneusi, Encephalitozoon (Septata) intestinalis*)			
Drug of choice	Albendazole	400mg q12h	
OR			
	Fumagillin	60mg/day po for 14 days	
Disseminated microsporidrosis (*Enterocytozoon hellem, Enterocytozoon cuniculi, Enterocytozoon intestinalis, Pleistophora* spp.)			
Drug of choice	Albendazole	400mg q12h	
Moniliformis moniliformis			
Drug of choice	Pyrantel pamoate	11mg/kg, single dose, repeat twice 2 weeks apart	11mg/kg, single dose, repeat twice 2 weeks apart
Oesophagostomum bifurcum			
Drug of choice	Albendazole or pyrantel pamoate		
Schislosomiasis (bilharziasis)			
Schistosoma haematobium			
Drug of choice	Praziquantel	40mg/kg/day in two doses for 1 day	40mg/kg/day in two doses for 1 day
Schistosoma japonicum			
Drug of choice	Praziquantel	60mg/kg/day in three doses for 1 day	60mg/kg/day in three doses for 1 day
Schistosoma mansoni			
Drug of choice	Praziquantel	40mg/kg/day in two doses for 1 day	40mg/kg/day in two doses for 1 day
Alternative	Oxamniquine	15mg/kg, single dose	20mg/kg/day in two doses for 1 day
Schistosoma mekongi			
Drug of choice	Praziquantel	60mg/kg/day in three doses for 1 day	60mg/kg/day in three doses for 1 day
Strongyloidiasis (*Strongyloides stercoralis*, threadworm)			
Drug of choice	Ivermectin	200μg/kg/day for 1–2 days	200μg/kg/day for 1–2 days
Alternative	Thiabendazole	50mg/kg/day in two doses (maximum 3g/day) for 2 days	50mg/kg/day in two doses (maximum 3g/day) for 2 days
Tapeworm infection (adult (intestinal stage))			
***Diphyllobothrium latum* (fish), *Taenia saginata* (beef), *Taenia solium* (pork), *Dipylidium caninum* (dog)**			
Drug of choice	Praziquantel	5–10mg/kg, single dose	5–10mg/kg, single dose
Alternative	Niclosamide	2g single dose	50mg/kg, single dose
***Hymenolepis nana* (dwarf tapeworm)**			
Drug of choice	Praziquantel	25mg/kg, single dose	25mg/kg, single dose
Tapeworm infection (larval (tissue stage))			
***Echinococcus granulosus* (hydatid cyst)**			
Drug of choice	Albendazole	400mg q12h for 28 days, repeated as necessary	15mg/kg/day for 28 days, repeated as necessary
Echinococcus multilocularis			
Treatment of choice		Surgical excision	

Table 209.1—cont'd

ANTIPARASITIC AGENTS AND DOSAGES			
Infection	**Drug**	**Adult dosage**	**Pediatric dosage**
Tapeworm infection (larval (tissue stage))—cont'd			
***Cysticercus cellulosae* (cysticercosis)**			
Drug of choice	Albendazole	400mg q12h for 8–30 days, repeated as necessary	15mg/kg/day (maximum 800mg) in two doses for 8–30 days, repeated as necessary
OR	Praziquantel	50mg/kg/day in three doses for 15 days	50mg/kg/day in three doses for 15 days
Alternative	Surgery		
Toxoplasmosis (*Toxoplasma gondii*)			
Drug of choice	Pyrimethamine	25–100mg/day for 3–4 weeks	2mg/kg/day for 3 days, then 1mg/kg/day (maximum 25mg/day) for 4 weeks
PLUS	Sulfadiazine	1–1.5g q6h for 3–4 weeks	100–200mg/kg/day for 3–4 weeks
Alternative	Spiramycin	3–4g/day	50–100mg/kg/day for 3–4 weeks
Trichinosis (*Trichinella spiralis*)			
Drug of choice	Corticosteroids for severe symptoms		
PLUS	Mebendazole	200–400mg q8h for 3 days, then 400–500mg q8h for 10 days	
Trichomoniasis (*Trichomonas vaginalis*)			
Drug of choice	Metronidazole	2g, single dose or 500mg q12h po for 7 days	15mg/kg/day po in three doses for 7 days
OR	Tinidazole	2g, single dose	50mg/kg, single dose (maximum 2g)
Trichostrongyliasis (*Trichostrongylus* spp.)			
Drug of choice	Pyrantel pamoate	11mg/kg, single dose (maximum 1g)	11mg/kg, single dose (maximum 1g)
Alternative	Mebendazole	100mg q12h for 3 days	100mg q12h for 3 days
OR	Albendazole	400mg, single dose	400mg, single dose
Trichuriasis (*Trichuris trichiura, whipworm*)			
Drug of choice	Mebendazole	100mg q12h for 3 days or 500mg, single dose	100mg q12h for 3 days or 500mg, single dose
Alternative	Albendazole	400mg, single dose	400mg, single dose
Trypanosomiasis			
***Trypanosoma cruzi* (American trypanosomiasis, Chagas' disease)**			
Drug of choice	Nifurtimox	8–10mg/kg/day in three or four doses for 90–120 days	Aged 1–10 years, 15–20mg/kg/day in four doses for 90 days; aged 11–16 years, 12.5–15mg/kg/day in four doses for 90 days
OR	Benznidazole	5–7mg/kg/day for 30–90 days	Aged ≤12 years, 10mg/kg/day in two doses for 30–90 days
***Trypanosoma brucei gambiense* (West African trypanosomiasis) – hemolymphatic stage**			
Drug of choice	Difluoromethylornithine (eflornithine)	400mg/kg/day iv in four divided doses for 14 days	
OR	Pentamidine isethionate	4mg/kg/day im for 10 days	4mg/kg/day im for 10 days
Alternative	Suramin	100–200mg (test dose) iv, then 1g iv on days 1, 3, 7, 14 and 21	20mg/kg iv on days 1, 3, 7, 14 and 21
***Trypanosoma brucei rhodesiense* (East African trypanosomiasis) – hemolymphatic stage**			
Drug of choice	Suramin	100–200mg (test dose) iv, then 1g iv on days 1, 3, 7, 14 and 21	20mg/kg iv on days 1, 3, 7, 14 and 21
Late disease with cental nervous system involvement, both *T. brucei gambiense* and *T. brucei rhodesiense*			
Drug of choice	Melarsoprol	2–3.6mg/kg/day iv for 3 days; after 1 week 3.6mg/kg/day iv for 3 days; repeat again after 10–21 days	18–25mg/kg over 1 month; initial dose of 0.36mg/kg iv, increasing gradually to max. 3.6mg/kg at intervals of 1–5 days for total of 9–10 doses
OR	Difluoromethylornithine	400mg/kg/day iv in four divided doses for 14 days	
Visceral larva migrans (toxocariasis)			
	Albendazole	400mg q12h for 3–5 days	400mg q12h for 3–5 days
OR	Mebendazole	100–200mg q12h for 5 days	100–200mg q12h for 5 days

* Based on a single case cited in Abramowicz.[1] † Based on a single case cited in Gelman *et al.*[2]

Table 209.1—cont'd

AVAILABILITY OF ANTIPARASITIC AGENTS		
Agent	**Trade name**	**Manufacturer**
Available from the drug service provided by the US Centers for Disease Control and Prevention		
Bithionol	Bitin	Tanabe (Japan)
Dehydroemetine	Dehydroemetine Dametine	Roche Merck
Melarsoprol	Arsobal	Aventis
Nifurtimox	Lampit	Bayer
Sodium stibogluconate	Pentostam	GlaxoSmithKline
Suramin	Germanin	Bayer
Available in the USA from the manufacturer		
Diethylcarbamazine	Hetrazan	Wyeth–Ayerst
Fumagillin	Fumidil B	Mid-Continent Agrimarketing
Nitazoxanide	Cryptaz	Romark Laboratories
Commercially available only outside the USA		
Amodiaquine	Camoquin Flavoquine	Parke–Davis Aventis
Artemether	Artenam	Arenco (Belgium)
Artesunate	(Generic)	Guilin No 1 Factory (China)
Benznidazole	Rochagan	Roche
Diloxanide furoate	Furamide	Boots (UK)
Difluoromethylornithine	Ornidyl	Hoechst Marion Roussel
Flubendazole	Fluvermal, Flumoxane	Janssen
Halofantrine	Halfan	GlaxoSmithKline
Meglumine antimonate	Glucantime	Aventis
Metrifonate	Bilarcil	Bayer
Niclosamide	Yomesan	Bayer
Ornidazole	Tiberal	Roche
Oxamniquine	Vansil	Pfizer
Proguanil	Paludrine	Wyeth–Ayerst, Zeneca
Pyrimethamine–dapsone	Maloprim	GlaxoSmithKline
Pyrimethamine–sulfadoxine–mefloquine	Fansimef	Roche
Quinacrine (discontinued in 1992)	Atabrine	Sanofi
Quinine dihydrochloride	(Generic)	ACF Chemiefarma NV (The Netherlands)
Spiramycin	Rovamycine	Aventis
Tinidazole	Fasigyn	Pfizer
Triclabendazole	Egaten	Novartis

Table 209.2 Availability of antiparasitic agents. It is often difficult to obtain antiparasitic agents. This is not a comprehensive list; many drugs have multiple trade names and manufacturers, only some of which are included. Agents are divided into those available from the drug service provided by the Centers for Disease Control and Prevention, those available from the manufacturer in the USA and those that are commercially available only outside the USA.

SAFETY OF ANTIPARASITIC AGENTS IN PREGNANCY	
Category 1 drugs: probably safe	**Category 3 drugs: insufficient data or established as unsafe**
Amphotericin B Azithromycin Chloroquine Clindamycin Dapsone Paromomycin Praziquantel Proguanil Spiramycin **Category 2 drugs: possibly safe or safe during certain trimesters** Diethylcarbamazine Ivermectin Mebendazole Mefloquine Metrifonate Metronidazole Pyrantel pamoate Pyrimethamine Sulfonamides Trimethoprim	Albendazole Artemisinin and derivatives Atovaquone Benznidazole Bithionol Dehydroemetine Diloxanide furoate Doxycycline Difluoromethylornithine Emetine Fumagillin Furazolidone Halofantrine Iodoquinol Melarsoprol Niclosamide Nifurtimox Oxamniquine Pentamidine isethionate Piperazine Primaquine Quinacrine Quinine Quinidine Sodium stibogluconate Suramin Tetracycline Thiabendazole

Table 209.3 Safety of antiparasitic agents in pregnancy. There are no well-controlled studies proving the safety of any of these antiparasitic agents in pregnancy. Category 1 drugs are those for which extensive clinical experience has demonstrated safety in pregnancy. Category 2 drugs are those that have been reported as safe only anecdotally or those that have been used safely in certain trimesters only. Category 3 drugs are those that should not be used because of either inadequate information or documented fetal harm. Adapted from Alecrim *et al.*,[3] Phillips-Howard *et al.*,[4] and Samuel and Barry.[5]

Sulfonamides

Sulfonamides, which are derivatives of sulfanilamide, interfere with microbial folic acid synthesis by competitively inhibiting the enzyme dihydropteroate synthase.[6,7,14,15] This enzyme is involved in the step in folic acid synthesis that precedes the step blocked by pyrimethamine and TMP. Sulfonamides are separated into four groups:

- short- and intermediate-acting agents;
- long-acting agents;
- agents that are limited to the bowel lumen; and
- topical agents.

Only agents from the first two of these categories are used to treat parasitic diseases; these are generally combined with either pyrimethamine or TMP.

Sulfamethoxazole

Sulfamethoxazole is an intermediate-acting sulfonamide. It is rapidly absorbed, widely distributed, 50–70% protein bound, hepatically metabolized and renally excreted. The half-life is 7–12 hours. It is available in a fixed combination with TMP (see below) for numerous indications.

Sulfadiazine

Sulfadiazine, another intermediate-acting sulfonamide, is also rapidly absorbed, widely distributed (including within the cerebrospinal fluid), 45–55% protein-bound, hepatically metabolized and renally excreted. The half-life is 12 hours. It is used with pyrimethamine in the treatment of toxoplasmosis, as detailed above.

Sulfadoxine

Sulfadoxine, a long-acting sulfonamide, is rapidly absorbed but slowly eliminated and has a half-life of 7–9 days. It is available in a fixed combination with pyrimethamine (Fansidar) for the prophylaxis and treatment of malaria (see below).

Side effects of sulfonamides

Side effects of sulfonamides are numerous. Nausea, vomiting and anorexia occur in 1–2% of patients. Hypersensitivity reactions include:

- drug eruptions (ranging from morbilliform rash to severe exfoliation);
- fever;
- serum sickness; and
- hepatocellular dysfunction and necrosis.

Acute hemolytic anemia, agranulocytosis and aplastic anemia are rare. Reversible bone marrow suppression is not uncommon in immunocompromised patients, particularly those who have AIDS. Crystalluria can occur with sulfadiazine and can be avoided by increasing fluid intake or alkalinizing the urine.

Fansidar

Fansidar tablets contain pyrimethamine 25mg and sulfadoxine 500mg. Fansidar is used in the treatment of chloroquine-resistant *P. falciparum* infections.[6,7,14–16] Fansidar is no longer recommended for malaria prophylaxis because of the possibility of fatal cutaneous eruptions, including erythema multiforme, toxic epidermal necrolysis and Stevens–Johnson syndrome. These reactions have been attributed to the sulfadoxine component; fatalities have occurred between 1 in 11,000 and 1 in 26,000 users, usually within 5 weeks of starting the agent. Serum sickness, bone marrow suppression, pneumonitis and hepatitis have also been documented in patients taking Fansidar for prophylaxis. There have been no fatalities described with Fansidar used for therapy. *Plasmodium falciparum* resistance to Fansidar has been described in South East Asia, eastern Africa, the Amazon basin, Bangladesh and Oceania.[16]

Fansimef

Fansimef is the combination of pyrimethamine (25mg), sulfadoxine (500mg) and mefloquine (250mg). It has been used in South East Asia and Brazil for both prophylaxis and treatment of chloroquine-resistant *P. falciparum*.

Maloprim

Maloprim tablets contain pyrimethamine 25mg and dapsone 100mg. Dapsone is a sulfone that is used in the treatment of leprosy (see Chapter 154) and *Pneumocystis carinii* pneumonia (see Chapter 124). This combination was used for malaria prophylaxis but is rarely employed today.[21] Hemolytic anemia, bone marrow suppression (including, very rarely, fatal agranulocytosis) and methemoglobinemia are occasionally seen. Dapsone is contraindicated in those who have glucose-6-phosphate dehydrogenase (G6PD) deficiency.

Trimethoprim–sulfamethoxazole

Trimethoprim–sulfamethoxazole (TMP–SMX) is a combination used to treat bacterial infections (see Chapter 197), *P. carinii* (see Chapter 124) and the parasites *I. belli* and *C. cayetanensis*.[19,20] This combination also has some efficacy against *P. falciparum* but resistance to the TMP component limits its use.[22,23] It is available as single-strength tablets (80mg TMP and 400mg SMX) and as double-strength tablets (160mg TMP and 800mg SMX). An oral suspension (40mg TMP and 200mg SMX per 5ml) and an intravenous formulation (80mg TMP and 400mg SMX per 5ml vial) are available as well.

The dose for isosporiasis is 1 double-strength tablet orally q6h for 10 days, followed by 1 double-strength tablet q12h for 3 weeks. Immunocompromised patients usually require maintenance therapy of 1 double-strength tablet daily or three times weekly. For cyclosporiasis, 1 double-strength tablet q12h for 7–10 days is generally used but some clinicians extend treatment to 14 days. Immunocompromised patients sometimes require 4 tablets per day and usually need maintenance therapy as well.

Side effects of TMP–SMX include those listed for each of the two component drugs, as detailed above. Dermatologic reactions (3–4%) and gastrointestinal disturbances (3–4%) are the most common side effects in non-immunocompromised patients. For unclear reasons, patients who have AIDS have a much higher rate of complications, ranging in different series from 45 to 90%.

Trimetrexate

Trimetrexate is a lipid-soluble dihydrofolate reductase inhibitor that was originally developed as a myelosuppressive agent but was found to have antiparasitic activity against *P. carinii* and *T. gondii*.[17] It is available for intravenous injection only. Adverse effects include rash, leukopenia, elevated liver enzymes and a reversible peripheral neuropathy. Folinic acid is administered concurrently to diminish the incidence of bone marrow suppression.

Proguanil

Proguanil is a biguanide that inhibits plasmodial dihydrofolate reductase.[6,7,14,16] Although it is seldom used for therapy because of its slow action, recent studies indicate that it is effective in combination with atovaquone in uncomplicated *P. falciparum* malaria (see below, under Atovaquone).[24] Daily proguanil (200mg) in combination with weekly chloroquine is used for prophylaxis against *P. falciparum* and *Plasmodium vivax*, mainly in sub-Saharan Africa. Prophylaxis failures have been reported in Kenya.[25]

Proguanil is slowly absorbed after oral administration, is 75% protein-bound, is metabolized to the active triazine metabolite cycloguanil, and is excreted in urine (40–60%) and feces (10%). The drug is safe and well tolerated. Pancytopenia has been rarely reported. Nausea, vomiting, abdominal pain, diarrhea and hematuria are associated with the use of high doses.

ARTEMISININ AND ITS DERIVATIVES

Artemisinin, or *qinghaosu*, is a sesquiterpene lactone derived from the leaves of the sweet wormwood *Artemisia annua*.[7,14,16,26] It has been used for centuries in traditional Chinese medicine and is now known to be active against intra-erythrocytic forms of *P. falciparum* and *P. vivax*, *Schistosoma mansoni*, *Schistosoma japonicum*, *Clonorchis sinensis* and *Naegleria fowleri*. Its main clinical use has been in the treatment of drug-resistant *P. falciparum* infections.

Artemisinin and two of its derivatives, the water-soluble hemisuccinate artesunate and the oil-soluble methyl ether artemether, are the most rapidly acting of known antimalarials and appear to be quite safe. They are undergoing active study to define their precise role in malaria therapy and are not currently widely available. These compounds can be given by several routes:

- artemisinin is available in oral and suppository forms;
- artesunate is available in oral, intravenous and intramuscular forms; and
- artemether is available in intramuscular form.

They appear to be rapidly absorbed and eliminated, with half-lives ranging from minutes (artesunate) to hours (artemether). The two derivatives are hepatically hydrolyzed to an active metabolite, dehydroartemisinin. These compounds are believed to act by disrupting parasite protein synthesis via the production of oxygen free radicals.

Artemisinin and its derivatives are usually administered in conjunction with a longer acting antimalarial (mefloquine) to decrease the emergence of resistance and enhance efficacy. Artesunate (4mg/kg orally) is usually given q24h for 3 days and is followed by a course of mefloquine. If given as monotherapy, artesunate is administered for 5–7 days to prevent recrudescence. Parenteral artesunate is administered at a dose of 2mg/kg initially, followed by 1mg/kg at 12–24 hours and then q24h after that. Artemether is given at a dose of 3.2mg/kg intramuscularly initially, followed by 1.6mg/kg q24h. Artemisinin suppositories, which are useful for those unable to take oral medications when there is no access to injectable formulations, can be given at 10mg/kg initially and 4 hours later, followed by 7mg/kg at 24, 36, 48 and 60 hours.

Adverse events include diarrhea, abdominal pain, transient first-degree heart block and reversible mild decreases in reticulocyte and neutrophil counts. Neurotoxicity has been described in animals but not with clinical use in humans. Resistance to artemisinin has occurred in murine malaria, and the resistant parasites also developed cross-resistance to chloroquine, quinine and mefloquine. Newer derivatives, including arteether (an ethyl ether) and the water-soluble artelinic acid, are being developed.

ATOVAQUONE AND ATOVAQUONE/PROGUANIL

Atovaquone, a synthetic hydroxynaphthoquinone derivative, has activity against *P. carinii* (see Chapter 124), *P. falciparum*, *T. gondii* and *Babesia microti*.[16,24,27] It interferes with pyrimidine synthesis by uncoupling mitochondrial electron transport. The drug is available only in liquid form. Because of its erratic absorption it is usually administered with a fatty meal. It is hepatically metabolized and excreted in the bile and urine. Atovaquone is an alternative oral agent for the treatment of mild to moderate *P. carinii* pneumonia in those who are intolerant of TMP–SMX, and experimental data indicate that it is synergistic with pyrimethamine or sulfadiazine for *T. gondii* infection. Atovaquone has also been used with azithromycin in the treatment of babesiosis.

The combination of atovaquone (1g q24h) and proguanil (400mg q24h) for 3 days has been used successfully to treat uncomplicated *P. falciparum* malaria in Gabon and Brazil,[24] and a combination pill containing atovaquone 250mg and proguanil 100mg has rapidly become one of the leading drugs for malaria prophylaxis in travellers.[28] A randomized controlled trial between mefloquine and atovaquone/proguanil for malaria prophylaxis in nonimmune travelers found equivalent efficacy for the two agents, with a similar number of adverse events, but fewer adverse effects of moderate or severe intensity were reported in the atovaquone/proguanil group.[29] The adult dosage for prophylaxis is 1 tablet q24h (250mg atovaquone/100mg proguanil), beginning 1–2 days prior to arrival in the malarious area and continuing for 1 week after return. Side effects include rash, nausea, vomiting, diarrhea, headache, fever, anemia, elevated liver function tests, hyponatremia and hyperglycemia.

BENZNIDAZOLE

Benznidazole is a nitroimidazole derivative that is active against *Trypanosoma cruzi* but it has not been as well studied and is relatively toxic.[6,7,30] It is the preferred agent for the treatment of Chagas' disease in central Brazil because of strain-susceptibility patterns. It is available in oral form and has a half-life of 12 hours. Side effects include malaise, nausea, photosensitivity rash, peripheral neuropathy, bone marrow suppression and psychiatric disturbances.

CHLOROQUINE

Chloroquine, a 4-aminoquinoline that was first synthesized in 1934 but did not become popular until the end of the Second World War, has been the agent most widely used for treating the erythrocytic stage of uncomplicated malaria caused by *P. vivax*, *Plasmodium ovale*, *Plasmodium malariae* and chloroquine-sensitive *P. falciparum*.[6,7,14,16] Its precise mechanism of action has not been delineated but chloroquine and its metabolites inhibit the ability of the parasite to polymerize the heme moiety of hemoglobin, resulting in toxic levels of free heme.[31] Chloroquine was occasionally used to treat extraintestinal *Entamoeba histolytica* infection but it has been supplanted by metronidazole.

Pharmacokinetics and distribution

Absorption after oral ingestion is excellent (90%), and the volume of distribution is large owing to its extensive tissue sequestration, particularly in the liver, spleen, kidneys and erythrocytes. It is approximately 50% bound to plasma protein and is eliminated slowly. Its half-life of 4–6 days permits weekly dosing for prophylaxis. Chloroquine is metabolized by the liver to the active metabolite desethylchloroquine, but 50% is cleared by the kidneys unchanged. Thus, dosing need not be altered for abnormal renal function but caution must be exercised in patients who have hepatic, gastrointestinal, neurologic or hematologic disorders.

Route of administration and dosage

The drug is formulated as a phosphate, sulfate or hydrochloride salt and is dosed by base content. It can be administered orally or rectally or by intravenous, intramuscular or subcutaneous injection. In the USA, chloroquine is marketed as Aralen phosphate in 500mg salt tablets (equal to 300mg base). The dosage for the treatment and prophylaxis of malaria is given in Table 209.1. If chloroquine hydrochloride is given intravenously, it must be administered by slow, constant infusion to avoid the respiratory depression, hypotension, heart block, cardiac arrest and seizures that may occur with transient toxic levels. A dose of 300mg base q8–12h may be given by intramuscular injection.

Adverse reactions

Reversible side effects include headache, gastrointestinal disturbances, blurred vision, dizziness, fatigue and pruritus. Rarer side effects include hair depigmentation, weight loss, myalgias, leukopenia and eczematous eruptions. Very rarely, acute psychosis may occur. Permanent retinal damage has been observed with long-term (longer than 5 years) prophylactic use. The drug is contraindicated in patients who have retinal disease, psoriasis and porphyria. An oral dose of 5g is fatal without immediate mechanical ventilation, epinephrine (adrenaline) and diazepam.

Resistance of *Plasmodium falciparum* to chloroquine

Resistance of *P. falciparum* to chloroquine is ubiquitous in regions where malarial transmission occurs (Fig. 209.1) with the exception of Central America west of the Canal Zone, Mexico, Haiti, the Dominican Republic and much of the Middle East (although there are reports of resistance from Yemen, Oman and Iran). Resistance to chloroquine among *P. vivax* isolates has been reported in Brazil, Colombia, India, Myanmar, Papua New Guinea and Indonesia.[31,33,34] A single oral dose of mefloquine (15mg base/kg) has been used successfully in such cases.

CLINDAMYCIN

Clindamycin, a lincosamide antibiotic, is active against bacteria (see Chapter 194), *P. falciparum*, *T. gondii* and *Babesia* spp.[16,35,36] It is well absorbed after oral administration and is 90% protein-bound and widely distributed. It is hepatically metabolized and excreted in the urine and bile; its half-life is 2.5–3 hours.

Dosages for malaria and babesiosis are listed in Table 209.1. For cerebral toxoplasmosis in the case of sulfonamide hypersensitivity, 1.8–2.4g divided into three daily doses is combined with a course of pyrimethamine. Clindamycin has been used in combination with

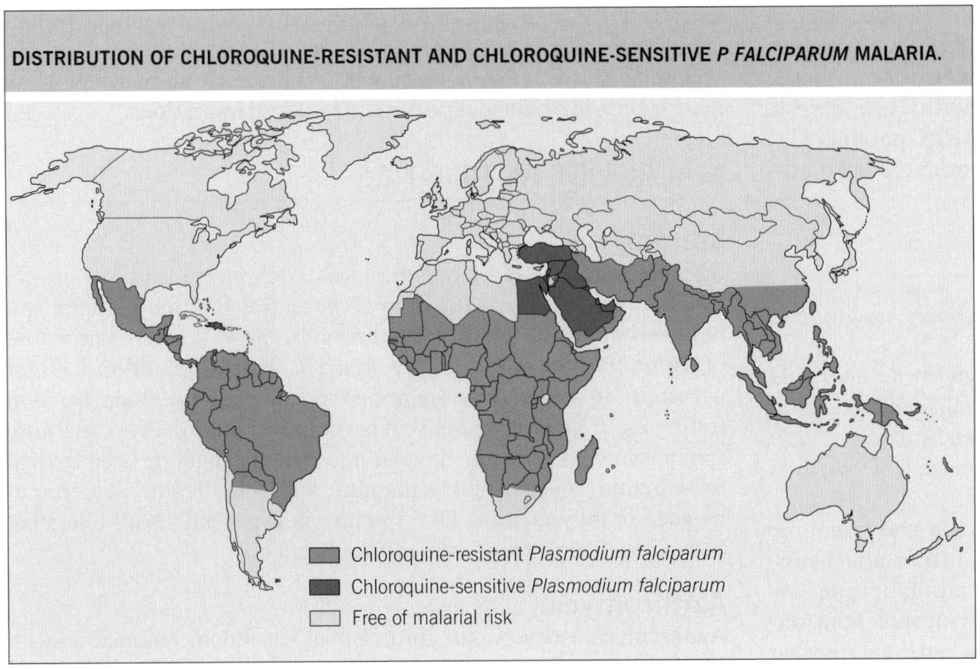

Fig. 209.1 Distribution of chloroquine-resistant and chloroquine-sensitive *P. falciparum* malaria. Adapted with permission from Lobel and Kozarsky.[32]

quinine for short-course (3-day) treatment of travelers who have *P. falciparum* malaria, with excellent results.[37] Side effects include rash, diarrhea, nausea, vomiting, abdominal pain, pseudomembranous colitis, hepatotoxicity and cytopenias.

DIFLUOROMETHYLORNITHINE

Difluoromethylornithine is an ornithine decarboxylase inhibitor that is effective in the treatment of both early and late sleeping sickness caused by *Trypanosoma brucei gambiense*.[7,38,39] It has variable efficacy against *T. brucei rhodesiense* because many strains are resistant. Difluoromethylornithine inhibits ornithine decarboxylase, an enzyme involved in the first step in polyamine synthesis. It is available as the hydrochloride salt for both oral and intravenous administration. It has a half-life of approximately 3 hours, and 80% of the drug is excreted unchanged by the kidneys.

Side effects of difluoromethylornithine include anemia, thrombocytopenia, leukopenia, abdominal pain, nausea, vomiting, weight loss, arthralgias, seizures, hearing loss and alopecia. Overall, difluoromethylornithine is less toxic than other available antitrypanosomal agents but it has not seen widespread use because of its high cost.

DILOXANIDE FUROATE

Diloxanide furoate is a dichloroacetamide derivative that is a luminally active agent used to eradicate cysts of *E. histolytica* in asymptomatic carriers and in those who have mild, noninvasive disease, as well as after treatment with metronidazole in those who have invasive amebiasis.[6,40] It is not useful in extraintestinal disease. After oral administration, diloxanide furoate is hydrolyzed by intestinal esterases, thus releasing diloxanide, the absorbable component, and the ester furoic acid, which is not well absorbed and thus attains higher intraluminal concentrations in the colon. Both compounds are amebicidal but the mechanism of action is not known. The drug has a half-life of 6 hours, is hepatically conjugated to form a glucuronide and is 60–90% excreted in the urine.

Side effects are mild; they include flatulence and, less commonly, nausea, vomiting, diarrhea, pruritus and urticaria. Because it is relatively inexpensive, diloxanide furoate is an attractive agent for use in developing countries.

EMETINE

Emetine is an alkaloid derived from ipecac, which comes from the root of *Cephaelis ipecacuanha*. This toxic tissue-active amebicide has been used since 1912, primarily for amebic colitis and amebic liver abscess. Dehydroemetine, a synthetic derivative, is less toxic but also less potent.[6,7,41] Both drugs have essentially been replaced by the safer nitroimidazoles (metronidazole, tinidazole, ornidazole) and are now used rarely. They are employed as supplemental therapy to metronidazole in individuals who are severely ill with amebic colitis or amebic liver abscess and are not responding well, or as primary therapy in the rare individual who cannot tolerate metronidazole. Because they are not active in the intestinal lumen, therapy with these agents must be followed by treatment with a luminally active drug. Dehydroemetine has also been used for infections caused by *S. mansoni*, *Schistosoma haematobium* and *Fasciola hepatica*. Emetine and dehydroemetine are both available only for intramuscular use. After deep intramuscular injection, they are well absorbed and excreted very slowly in the urine. They act by inhibiting protein synthesis.

The standard dose of dehydroemetine is 1–1.5mg/kg/day, up to a maximum of 90mg/day, for 5–10 days. Common adverse effects of emetine and dehydroemetine include local reactions at the injection site (e.g. pain, stiffness, urticaria and abscesses), nausea, vomiting and diarrhea. Cardiovascular toxicity includes precordial pain, hypotension, tachycardia, arrhythmias, electrocardiographic abnormalities, heart failure and, rarely, sudden death. Headache, myalgias, weakness and polyneuritis may also occur. Hospitalization with electrocardiographic monitoring is required while these drugs are being administered. They are relatively contraindicated in patients who have cardiac or renal disease.

FUMAGILLIN

Fumagillin, a water-insoluble antibiotic derived from *Aspergillus fumigatus*, was discovered in 1949 and originally used in humans as an amebicide. Fumagillin is an inhibitor of parasite RNA synthesis but may also act by inhibiting a key proteinase, type 2 methionine aminopeptidase.[42] A water-soluble preparation (Fumidil B) is used to control nosematosis, a disease of honey bees that results from infection with microsporidian *Nosema apis*. Topical fumagillin has been used to treat microsporidial keratoconjunctivitis caused by *Encephalitozoon hellem*, *Encephalitozoon cuniculi*, *Encephalitozoon* (*Septata*) *intestinalis* and, with less success, *Vittaforma corneae* (*Nosema corneum*) in AIDS patients.[43,44] Studies of oral fumagillin for intestinal microsporidiosis have provided promising results.[45,46]

FURAZOLIDONE

Furazolidone is a nitrofuran derivative that is commonly used to treat giardiasis in children because of its availability in a liquid form for oral use.[6,47] Furazolidone also has activity against *I. belli* and *Trichomonas vaginalis* as well as many enteropathogenic bacteria, and is increasingly being used for treatment of *Helicobacter pylori* infections. The mechanism of action involves damage to DNA. It is well absorbed and is excreted mainly in the urine.

Adverse reactions include diarrhea, fever, nausea and vomiting. Urticaria, serum sickness, hypoglycemia and orthostatic hypotension occur rarely. Furazolidone has disulfiram-like properties and patients should therefore be warned to avoid alcohol. Furazolidone has monoamine oxidase inhibitor activity, but hypertensive crises have not been reported in association with this agent. Furazolidone may cause hemolysis in patients who have G6PD deficiency.

HALOFANTRINE

Halofantrine is an oral synthetic 9-phenanthrene methanol with activity against the intraerythrocytic stages of chloroquine-sensitive and chloroquine-resistant *P. falciparum* and *P. vivax*.[6,7,14,48] It is more active and generally better tolerated than mefloquine but it is poorly absorbed. Ingestion with fatty meals increases absorption. Halofantrine is hepatically metabolized and excreted in feces, with a half-life of 1–2 days for the parent compound and 3–5 days for the active metabolite. Its mechanism of action is poorly understood.

There is some evidence of cross-resistance with mefloquine; therefore halofantrine may not be useful for those patients in areas with mefloquine resistance. Its side effects include prolongation of the PR and QT_c intervals on the electrocardiogram, diarrhea, abdominal pain, pruritus and rash. Because it prolongs the PR and QT_c intervals, halofantrine should not be given to anyone who has conduction defects or to anyone taking other drugs that affect the QT_c interval. Thus, a 28-day interval is recommended between the administration of halofantrine and mefloquine.

IODOQUINOL

Iodoquinol, a halogenated hydroxyquinoline, is a luminal amebicide used to eradicate cysts in patients who have asymptomatic *E. histolytica* infection.[6,40] It is also given after metronidazole therapy to eradicate cysts in patients who have invasive disease. Iodoquinol is the drug of choice for *Dientamoeba fragilis* infection and is an alternative for *Balantidium coli*.[49] It has been used to treat *Blastocystis hominis*, but the pathogenicity of this protozoan and its need for treatment are controversial.[50] Iodoquinol also has activity against *Giardia lamblia* and *T. vaginalis* but other agents are typically employed. The mechanism of action of iodoquinol is uncertain. It is available in oral form but it is poorly absorbed and should be given with meals. Side effects include nausea, vomiting, diarrhea, abdominal pain, headache, fever, seizures and encephalopathy.

Iodochlorhydroxyquin, a related compound, is better absorbed than iodoquinol but is rarely used because of the high incidence of subacute myelo-optic neuropathy described with its use in Japan in the early 1970s. Because iodoquinol may rarely cause this syndrome when given at high dose or for prolonged periods, treatment recommendations should not be exceeded. For this reason many clinicians, including myself, prefer alternative agents such as paromomycin, metronidazole or diloxanide furoate for these indications.

MACROLIDE ANTIBIOTICS

Spiramycin

Spiramycin is used in Europe to prevent the transmission of *T. gondii* from mother to fetus.[16] The drug is concentrated in the placenta and has been shown to reduce transmission by 60%. It is given at a dose of 1g orally q8h on an empty stomach. If fetal infection has not occurred (as assessed by amniotic fluid polymerase chain reaction testing for *T. gondii*), spiramycin is continued until delivery. Because spiramycin does not cross the placenta well, it cannot be used to treat fetal toxoplasmosis; pyrimethamine and sulfadiazine are recommended in this situation. Oral spiramycin is generally well tolerated; gastrointestinal distress is the main side effect.

Azithromycin

Azithromycin (see Chapter 194), both alone and in combination with pyrimethamine, has recently been shown to be effective in cerebral toxoplasmosis in AIDS patients.[17] It is considered relatively safe in pregnancy but has not been extensively studied in preventing the vertical transmission of *T. gondii*. Azithromycin has antimalarial activity and is effective prophylaxis against *P. vivax*. However, it offers only partial protection (70–80% efficacy) against *P. falciparum* and is therefore not recommended as a first-line agent for prevention of malaria in travelers.[51] Azithromycin has also been used with both quinine and atovaquone for babesiosis.[35] High-dose azithromycin has been used in AIDS patients who have cryptosporidiosis, with variable results.[46] Another macrolide, clarithromycin, when administered for prevention of *Mycobacterium avium* complex disease in AIDS patients, appeared to prevent cryptosporidiosis as well.[52]

MEFLOQUINE

Mefloquine is an fluorinated 4-quinoline methanol derivative of quinine. It is an oral formulation that was developed as part of a search for new antimalarials.[6,7,14,16,32,51] It is a blood schizonticide effective against all *Plasmodium* spp. that infect humans, including *P. falciparum* isolates that are resistant to chloroquine and pyrimethamine–sulfadoxine. It is ineffective against exoerythrocytic forms and gametocytes. The mechanism of action is unknown but mefloquine may interfere with the function of *Plasmodium* food vacuoles or inhibit the polymerization of heme. The drug is slowly absorbed, has a bioavailability of 85% and is almost completely protein-bound in plasma. The long elimination half-life of 2–3 weeks allows for weekly prophylaxis. Mefloquine is extensively metabolized and is excreted in bile and feces.

Common side effects at therapeutic doses include nausea, vomiting, dizziness, weakness and dysphoria.[28,51,53] Neuropsychiatric reactions, including acute psychosis, sleep disturbances and seizures, have been documented in approximately 0.5% of patients taking therapeutic doses and in less than 0.5% of those taking prophylactic doses. Thus, the drug is not recommended for those who have a history of seizures or psychiatric disorders. Judicious use is suggested for those whose occupations require spatial discrimination and fine motor coordination. Cardiac rhythm and conduction abnormalities and at least one instance of nonfatal cardiac arrest have occurred in patients on β-adrenergic blockers who took mefloquine; caution should be exercised in any patient who has cardiac disease. Mefloquine should not be co-administered with quinine, quinidine or halofantrine owing to potentially fatal prolongation of the QT_c interval. Mefloquine may also decrease the response to the live *Salmonella typhi* oral vaccine, and thus the vaccine series should be completed at least 3 days before beginning mefloquine prophylaxis.

Mefloquine resistance in *P. falciparum* isolates has been increasing along the Thailand–Myanmar and Thailand–Cambodia borders, in western Africa and in the Amazon region. In these areas, doxycycline at a dose of 100mg per day or atovaquone/proguanil may be used for prophylaxis. Treatment options include:

- quinine plus tetracycline or doxycycline for 7 days;[54]
- mefloquine plus artesunate;[55]
- mefloquine plus artemether;[56]
- doxycycline plus artesunate;[57]
- mefloquine plus doxycycline;[57] and
- quinine plus clindamycin[37].

MELARSOPROL

Melarsoprol is a trivalent arsenical compound introduced in 1949 and used for the treatment of late-stage African trypanosomiasis caused either by *T. brucei gambiense* or *T. brucei rhodesiense*.[6,7,38,39] It is also effective in treating the early or hemolymphatic stage of infection but its toxicity prohibits routine use for this stage and it should be used only in patients who have failed to respond to suramin and pentamidine.

Melarsoprol acts by interacting with protein sulfhydryl groups and subsequently inactivating enzymes, a non-specific action that is also responsible for the toxicity of the drug. Melarsoprol, formulated as a 3.6% weight per volume solution in propylene glycol, is given intravenously. A small but adequate amount of the drug penetrates the cerebrospinal fluid, where it is taken up and concentrated by susceptible trypanosomes. Resistant organisms appear to concentrate the drug poorly. Melarsoprol is rapidly excreted in the urine.

Melarsoprol is highly toxic. It is irritating to tissues and care must be taken to prevent extravasation. Fever is commonly seen. Reactive encephalopathy occurs in up to 18% of patients and may be fatal; it usually occurs during the first 3–4 days of therapy.[58] It is manifested by headache, confusion, dizziness, mental slowing and ataxia, with seizures and a progressive decline in mental status, and it is felt to be an immunologic reaction to parasite antigens released during therapy. Corticosteroids have been used to treat the encephalopathy with some success. Very rarely, a hemorrhagic encephalopathy, which is almost always fatal, may occur. Arthralgias, rash, hypertension, proteinuria and hepatic dysfunction have been seen. Abdominal pain and vomiting may be minimized by slow administration of the drug to a patient who is supine and fasting. Erythema nodosum may be precipitated in patients who have leprosy. Hemolysis may be seen in G6PD-deficient patients.

NIFURTIMOX

Nifurtimox, an oral nitrofuran, remains the drug of choice for acute Chagas' disease (American trypanosomiasis), although benznidazole is gaining favor as a first-line agent in some regions with endemic Chagas' disease (see Chapter 173).[6,7,30] Nifurtimox has also been used against resistant strains of *T. brucei gambiense*.[38] It acts by inhibiting nucleic acid synthesis by oxygen free radical formation. It is rapidly absorbed, has a half-life of approximately 3 hours, is extensively metabolized by the liver by a first-pass effect that results in low serum and tissue levels, and is excreted by the kidneys. There is considerable geographic variation in responsiveness to nifurtimox; better results are obtained in Argentina and Chile than in Brazil and other countries. Effectiveness in indeterminate-phase and chronic-phase infection is variable and organ damage is not reversible.

Gastrointestinal side effects including nausea, vomiting, anorexia and abdominal pain; weight loss may occur. Neurologic side effects include headache, restlessness, insomnia, disorientation, pares-thesias, polyneuritis, weakness and seizures. Rash, decreased sperm counts and neutropenia have also been described. Adherence to a full 4 months of therapy is often poor, and better agents are needed.

NITAZOXANIDE

Nitazoxanide is a nitrothiazole benzamide derivative with in-vitro activity against a wide variety of bacterial, protozoal and helminthic pathogens. In recent randomized double-blind placebo-controlled clinical trials it showed efficacy comparable to metronidazole in the treatment of giardiasis and amebiasis, and was very successful in eradicating helminths from individuals in Egypt and Mexico.[59] Healthy adults treated with nitazoxanide cleared cryptosporidia from their stool more rapidly than did placebo controls, but the efficacy of nitazoxanide in AIDS patients remains to be established.[59]

NITROIMIDAZOLE DERIVATIVES

Metronidazole

Metronidazole (see Chapter 201) has activity against many anaerobic parasites. It is the drug of choice for the treatment of:

- invasive enterocolitis and liver abscess caused by *E. histolytica* and the rarely reported *Entamoeba polecki*;[6,7,36,37]
- vaginitis caused by *T. vaginalis*;[60] and
- enteritis caused by *G. lamblia*.[40,47]

It has been used to treat *Blastocystis. hominis* in the stool (although its efficacy remains unproven) and is considered an alternative agent for *Balantidium. coli* infection. Metronidazole is also used in the treatment of infections with the guinea worm, *Dracunculus medinensis*; it decreases inflammation and facilitates worm removal but has no direct toxic effect on the worm itself.

Metronidazole acts as an electron sink under anaerobic or microaerophilic conditions, depriving the parasite of necessary reducing equivalents such as nicotinamide adenine dinucleotide phosphate, reduced form (NADPH). Reduced metronidazole (i.e. drug molecules that have gained electrons) causes a loss of the helical structure of DNA and strand breakage.

Metronidazole is available for oral and intravenous use. It is rapidly and almost completely absorbed orally, has limited protein binding and is widely distributed throughout the body. The half-life is 6–11 hours and metabolism is hepatic. Although excretion is mainly by the kidney, dosage adjustments are seldom needed in renal failure because the metabolites are less active compounds. However, the dosage should be modified in patients who have liver failure.

The most common side effects are headache, metallic taste, dry mouth and nausea. Less frequent are urticaria, pruritus, urethral burning, reversible neutropenia, and vaginal and oral candidiasis. Rarely, patients may experience central nervous system toxicity, including dizziness, vertigo, ataxia, encephalopathy and seizures, as well as peripheral neuropathy. Acute pancreatitis has been reported. Patients should be advised to avoid consuming alcohol because of the disulfiram-like effects of metronidazole, including headache, flushing, abdominal pain and vomiting. Some patients may experience a red–brown discoloration of the urine owing to the presence of metabolites of metronidazole.

Tinidazole and ornidazole

Tinidazole and ornidazole are two other nitroimidazole derivatives (see Chapter 201). Their antimicrobial spectrum is similar to that of metronidazole,[6,7,60] and tinidazole has been used successfully for single-dose therapy of amebic liver abscess.[61] Tinidazole has also been used to treat metronidazole-resistant *Trichomonas* spp. These compounds are well absorbed orally and are widely distributed. Tinidazole has a half-life of 14 hours and ornidazole has a half-life of 12–13 hours; both compounds are probably hepatically metabolized and are excreted primarily in the urine. Generally, these drugs are better tolerated than metronidazole; the main side effects are headache, dizziness and anorexia.

PAROMOMYCIN

Paromomycin (also known as aminosidine) is a non-absorbable aminoglycoside antibiotic (see Chapter 196) that is concentrated in the lumen of the colon. It is active against *E. histolytica*, *D. fragilis* and *G. lamblia* as well as the cestodes *Taenia saginata*, *Taenia solium*, *Diphyllobothrium latum*, *Dipylidium caninum* and *Hymenolepis nana*.[6,40,47] Although often used for the treatment of *Cryptosporidium parvum*, it was no better then placebo in double-blind clinical trials.[62,63] Paromomycin with methylbenzethonium chloride has been used topically in the treatment of cutaneous leishmaniasis and systemically for visceral leishmaniasis.[10,64] Paromomycin is available as the sulfate salt for oral administration.

The dose is 25–35mg/kg/day in three divided doses for 7 days. Side effects include cramps, nausea, vomiting, diarrhea, rash, headache and vertigo. Burning may occur with topical preparations.

PENTAMIDINE ISETHIONATE

Pentamidine isethionate, an aromatic diamidine derivative, is effective in the treatment of the early or hemolymphatic stages of sleeping sickness caused by *T. brucei gambiense*, some forms of leishmaniasis and *P. carinii* pneumonia (see Chapters 124 & 245).[6,7,10,38] It is less effective against *T. brucei rhodesiense*. It has also been used in the treatment of disseminated *Acanthamoeba* spp. infections and babesiosis.[65,66] The mechanism of action of pentamidine is unclear but it may involve the binding of DNA and the interruption of DNA replication. The drug is available for parenteral and inhalational use; the latter mode is used only in the prophylaxis and treatment of *P. carinii* pneumonia because little of the inhaled drug is absorbed systemically. Parenterally administered pentamidine isethionate penetrates extensively and is excreted slowly from tissues such as liver, spleen, kidneys and adrenal glands. Very little crosses the blood–brain barrier, accounting for the lack of utility of pentamidine in late-stage trypanosomiasis.

Route of administration and dosage

There are different recommendations for dosing pentamidine isethionate. For early *T. brucei gambiense* infection, the US Centers for Disease Control and Prevention (CDC) recommends 4mg/kg per day for 10 days. The World Health Organization (WHO) recommends 3–4mg/kg daily or every other day for 7–10 doses. Because of the rapidity with which *T. brucei rhodesiense* invades the central nervous system, this drug is generally not used for this organism. Pentamidine has also been used for prophylaxis against infection with *T. brucei gambiense* at a dose of 4mg/kg (to a maximum of 300mg) given every 3–6 months.

For leishmaniasis, the CDC recommends 2–4mg/kg/day or every other day for 12–15 doses; a second course is sometimes given after an interval of 1–2 weeks. Alternatively, the WHO recommends 4mg/kg three times a week for 5–25 weeks or longer. The dosage regimen varies slightly depending on the species of *Leishmania* and the region of the body affected.

Adverse reactions

Pentamidine isethionate may cause toxicity in 50% of patients. Precipitous hypotension with dizziness, dyspnea, tachycardia, headache, vomiting and syncope can occur with rapid intravenous infusion. Intramuscular administration may result in sterile abscesses. Hypoglycemia, which may be life-threatening, pancreatitis, hyperglycemia and diabetes mellitus probably result from a direct toxic effect of pentamidine on pancreatic β cells. Reversible renal failure occurs in up to 25% of patients. Other side effects include fever, arrhythmias (particularly *torsades de pointes*), hypocalcemia, confusion, hallucinations, leukopenia, thrombocytopenia and elevated transaminases.

PENTAVALENT ANTIMONIAL COMPOUNDS

The pentavalent antimonial compounds are a mainstay of therapy for leishmaniasis and are less toxic than the older trivalent compounds.[6,7,10,67] Sodium stibogluconate has been the most extensively studied and is the only pentavalent antimonial available in the USA. Meglumine antimoniate is used largely in French-speaking countries and parts of Latin America. These compounds appear to inhibit bioenergetic pathways such as glycolysis and fatty acid oxidation in *Leishmania* amastigotes. *Leishmania* strains resistant to pentavalent antimony compounds are becoming more common, especially in India, and this has led to treatment failures and the need for alternative agents.[68]

These compounds are available as aqueous solutions for intravenous or intramuscular use only. Each milliliter of sodium stibogluconate contains the equivalent of 100mg of pentavalent antimony, whereas each milliliter of meglumine antimonate contains 85mg. They are rapidly absorbed and are eliminated in two phases. The first has a half-life of 2 hours but the second is longer, with a half-life of between 33 hours (after intravenous administration) and 76 hours (after intramuscular administration). This slow terminal elimination may result from a conversion to trivalent antimony, which thus may be responsible for the toxicity seen with long-term therapy. Excretion is primarily renal.

Pentavalent antimonials are generally well tolerated. Malaise, nausea, vomiting, abdominal pain, headache, arthralgias, myalgias, fever, rash, elevated transaminases, nephrotoxicity and pancreatitis are seen. Dose-related electrocardiographic changes include T-wave flattening and inversion and QT_c-interval prolongation. Arrhythmias and sudden death have been described with high-dose therapy.

PRIMAQUINE

Primaquine, an 8-aminoquinoline active against hypnozoites of *P. vivax* and *P. ovale* in the liver, is the only agent with the potential for yielding complete resolution of malaria caused by these organisms.[6,7,14,16] Primaquine combined with clindamycin is also effective in the treatment of *P. carinii* pneumonia (see Chapter 124). Recently, primaquine in a dose of 30mg/day showed efficacy as prophylaxis against *P. falciparum* (88% protection) and *P. vivax* (92% protection) malaria.[69] Primaquine acts by interfering with *Plasmodium* mitochondrial function, possibly through its effects on the electron transport chain and pyrimidine biosynthesis. Primaquine phosphate, which is available only in oral form, is rapidly absorbed (bioavailability 96%), widely distributed and hepatically converted to three metabolites, yielding an elimination half-life of 6–7 hours. It is unclear whether the parent compound or the metabolites possess the antimalarial activity.

Primaquine phosphate is formulated in tablets containing 26.3mg of the salt, equivalent to 15mg of the base. Dosages are given in Table 209.1. Relapse of *P. vivax* after conventional primaquine treatment has been described in up to 30% of cases in Papua New Guinea, the Solomon Islands, Thailand and other parts of South East Asia.[70] Therefore, for cases acquired in South East Asia or Oceania, the dose should be increased to 22.5mg base per day.

The principal toxicity of primaquine is hemolysis in patients who are G6PD-deficient, and thus G6PD levels should be measured before therapy is begun. Headache, nausea, vomiting and abdominal cramps have been reported. At higher doses, mild anemia, cyanosis (due to methemoglobinemia) and leukopenia may occur. Rarely, neurotoxicity, arrhythmias, hypertension and agranulocytosis occur.

QUINACRINE

Quinacrine is an acridine dye derivative that is effective against *G. lamblia*.[6,40,47] and it has recently been used as combination therapy with metronidazole for individuals who failed therapy with metronidazole alone.[71] It also has activity against adult cestodes, but for this indication it has been supplanted by less toxic alternatives. In the Second World War, quinacrine was used for malaria prophylaxis and treatment. The mechanism of antiparasitic action is unclear, but the drug has been shown to intercalate with DNA and inhibit nucleic acid synthesis. Quinacrine is available in an oral formulation and is well absorbed and widely distributed. It has extensive tissue binding and has been detected in the urine 2 months after stopping therapy. Its metabolic fate is poorly understood.

The dosage in giardiasis is 100mg q8h for 5–7 days. A second treatment course may be given 2 weeks later. The drug has a bitter taste and may induce nausea and vomiting. Dizziness and headache are also common. Reversible yellow skin discoloration (with spared sclerae) is seen in 4–5% of those treated with quinacrine for giardiasis. Under Wood's light, a bright yellow–green fluorescence distinguishes this side effect from hyperbilirubinemia. Toxic psychosis may occur in 0.1–1.5% of patients. Other rare side effects include blood dyscrasias, ocular toxicity and urticaria. Patients who have psoriasis may experience exfoliative dermatitis. Quinacrine has a disulfiram-like effect, and thus patients should be advised to avoid alcohol consumption while taking it. It also interferes with the metabolism of primaquine, and toxic levels of the primaquine can result from co-administration of quinacrine with primaquine.

QUINIDINE

Quinidine is the dextrostereoisomer of quinine. It is a blood schizonticide and is the parenteral therapy of choice for chloroquine-resistant *P. falciparum* as a result of its wide availability as an antiarrhythmic.[6,7,14,16,72] It is supplied as the gluconate salt for intravenous use, with a half-life of 6–8 hours. It is 80–90% protein-bound, hepatically metabolized and renally excreted.

During treatment, continuous electrocardiographic and blood-pressure monitoring are recommended. Widening of the QRS complex and prolongation of the QT_c interval may be seen, and hypotension may ensue if the drug is infused rapidly. Other side effects are similar to those of quinine.

QUININE

Quinine is an alkaloid derived from the bark of the South American cinchona tree. It has been used as an antimalarial for over 350 years.[6,7,14,16] It is effective against the asexual blood stages of all four *Plasmodium* spp. that cause malaria in humans, and it is the drug of choice for chloroquine-resistant *P. falciparum* infections. Quinine is also used with clindamycin in the treatment of *Babesia. microti* infection.[31] The basis for the antimalarial activity of quinine is unclear, but three mechanisms have been proposed:

- intercalation with parasite DNA, interrupting replication and transcription;
- interaction with erythrocyte fatty acids, promoting hemolysis and preventing schizont maturation; and
- alkalinization of parasite digestive vacuoles, interfering with hemoglobin degradation.

Pharmacokinetics and distribution

Quinine is available as the sulfate, bisulfate, hydrochloride, dihydrochloride, hydrobromide and ethylcarbonate salts for oral administration and as the dihydrochloride salt for parenteral use. It is rapidly absorbed after oral administration (bioavailability 80%), extensively protein-bound (90%), hepatically metabolized (80%) and renally excreted. The therapeutic range in plasma is 8–15mg/l, which is achieved within 1–3 hours after a single oral dose. The half-life is approximately 11 hours. In cases of severe illness, the volume of distribution decreases, clearance is reduced and the half-life is prolonged. Thus, on a given dosage schedule, plasma quinine concentrations are elevated with acute illness and decrease as the patient improves. Monitoring blood levels is recommended in those who have renal or hepatic dysfunction; dosage reduction is needed with severe renal failure.

Route of administration and dosage

The oral dose of quinine sulfate (unlike other antimalarial agents, it is dosed by weight of salt) is 650mg salt q8h for 3–7 days. A longer course is preferred for those in areas where *P. falciparum* is less sensitive to quinine, including South East Asia and western Africa.[73]

Intravenous quinine dihydrochloride may be used for severe infections. A 20mg salt/kg loading dose in 5% dextrose is given over 4 hours, followed by 10mg salt/kg over 2–4 hours q8h (maximum 1800mg salt/day) until oral therapy can be given. The loading dose should be omitted in those who have received oral quinine, quinidine or mefloquine during the previous 24 hours. Intravenous quinidine gluconate has become the parenteral therapy of choice worldwide (see above).

Adverse reactions

The term cinchonism refers to a cluster of dose-related and reversible side effects of quinine, including tinnitus, decreased hearing, headache, nausea, vomiting, dysphoria and visual disturbances. Hypoglycemia can occur secondary to quinine stimulation of insulin release in conjunction with parasite consumption of glucose. Skin rashes (urticaria, flushing), pruritus, hepatitis, thrombocytopenia, agranulocytosis and massive hemolysis with hemoglobinuria (with resultant bilirubinuria termed blackwater fever) occur rarely. Quinine can cause respiratory depression in patients who have myasthenia gravis and hemolysis in those who have G6PD deficiency. Myocardial depression, vasodilation and shock may result from rapid intravenous infusion. Overdose can result in delirium, seizures, coma, respiratory depression, cortical blindness, shock and death. An oral quinine dose of 2–8g may be fatal for adults.

SURAMIN

Suramin is a sulfated naphthylamine introduced in 1920 and is used in the treatment of the early or hemolymphatic stage of African trypanosomiasis.[6,7,38] It is more effective against *T. brucei rhodesiense* than against *T. brucei gambiense*, for which pentamidine is often used for early disease. Suramin has also been used for prophylaxis in those who have intense exposure. Additionally, suramin is active against the adult forms of *Onchocerca volvulus*, but is rarely used for this infection because of its toxicity.

The mechanism of action of suramin is unclear; it is a poly-anion that inhibits many cellular enzymes. Notably, its antitrypanosomal activity correlates with inhibition of glycerol-3-phosphate oxidase and dehydrogenase, enzymes involved in energy metabolism.

Pharmacokinetics and distribution

Suramin is 99% protein-bound and persists at low levels in plasma for 3 months, which supports its use in prophylaxis. It is not metabolized and is excreted mainly by the kidneys. The large, polar, polyanionic structure affords poor cellular penetration. Very little drug penetrates into the cerebrospinal fluid, accounting for the lack of efficacy of suramin in late-stage disease.

Route of administration and dosage

Suramin is available only for intravenous use. The dosage for trypanosomiasis is given in Table 209.1 For onchocerciasis, a test dose of 100–200mg is followed by weekly infusions of 1g up to a total of 6g. Some investigators administer increasing weekly doses (200mg, then 400mg, and so on to 1g) up to a total dose of only 3–4g, with good efficacy and tolerability.

Adverse reactions

Suramin has a variety of side effects, which are generally more severe in malnourished patients. Immediate reactions include malaise, nausea, vomiting, fatigue, fever, urticaria, shock, loss of consciousness and, rarely, death. Late reactions include fever, rash, stomatitis, exfoliative dermatitis, lacrimation, photophobia, headache and hyperesthesia. Renal dysfunction (hematuria, proteinuria, casts and elevated creatinine), hepatic dysfunction (elevated transaminases and bilirubin), diarrhea, thrombocytopenia and agranulocytosis may occur. Additional side effects during treatment for onchocerciasis include pruritus, dermal edema, papular eruptions, palmoplantar paresthesias and iridocyclitis.

TETRACYCLINES

Tetracycline (see Chapter 200) is used in combination with quinine in the treatment of drug-resistant *P. falciparum* in South East Asia, where resistance to chloroquine, Fansidar and quinine is common.[6,7,16,54] Doxycycline, a longer-acting derivative, is used for malaria prophylaxis in this area, and worldwide in individuals unable to tolerate mefloquine.[32,51,74] Tetracycline is also the drug of choice for infection with the ciliate *Balantidium. coli.*

Tetracyclines are well absorbed after oral administration and are probably active against parasite protein synthesis. Side effects include gastrointestinal distress, photosensitivity and vaginal candidiasis.

TRYPARSAMIDE

Tryparsamide, a pentavalent arsenical first described in 1919, is used primarily for the treatment of advanced *T. brucei gambiense* infections resistant to other therapy.[6,7] It has poor efficacy against *T. brucei rhodesiense*. Side effects of tryparsamide include fever, rash, abdominal pain, vomiting, tinnitus, optic atrophy and blindness, and encephalopathy.

ANTHELMINTIC AGENTS

ALBENDAZOLE

Albendazole is a benzimidazole carbamate that has a broad spectrum of anthelmintic activity, including against *Ascaris lumbricoides*, *Enterobius vermicularis*, *Ancylostoma duodenale*, *Necator americanus*, *Strongyloides stercoralis*, *Echinococcus* spp. and *T. solium* cysticerci.[6,7,75–79] The drug has also been used to treat eosinophilic enterocolitis caused by *Ancylostoma caninum*, *Capillaria philippinensis*, cutaneous and visceral larva migrans, *C. sinensis*, *Gnathostoma spinigerum*, *Oesophagostomum bifurcum* and *Trichostrongylus* spp. It is also used in combination with diethylcarbamazine or ivermectin for mass treatment of lymphatic filariasis (*Brugia malayi* and *Wuchereria bancrofti*).[80] Additionally, it has variable efficacy in the treatment of microsporidiosis caused by *Encephalitozoon hellem*, *E. cuniculi*, *E. intestinalis*, *E. bieneusi*, and *Vittaforma corneae*.[81] Albendazole has some activity against *G. lamblia*.

The mechanism of action is similar to that of mebendazole with blockade of parasite microtubule assembly. Albendazole is poorly soluble in water and should be taken with a fatty meal to enhance absorption. It undergoes extensive first-pass metabolism in the liver, and albendazole sulfoxide is responsible for most of the systemic anthelmintic effects. This metabolite has a half-life of 9–15 hours and is mostly excreted renally.

Single doses of albendazole are generally well tolerated; abdominal discomfort, diarrhea, or migration of *Ascaris* into the mouth and nose occur infrequently. Prolonged, high-dose treatment can be associated with reversible aminotransferase elevations, bone marrow suppression and alopecia.

BITHIONOL

Bithionol is a chlorinated bisphenol that is used for infections with *Fasciola hepatica* but may have been supplanted by triclabendazole. Bithionol is also an alternative agent against *Paragonimus* spp.[6,7] It has activity against many other flukes but has been replaced by praziquantel. Its mechanism of action is poorly understood. Side effects include anorexia, abdominal pain, nausea, vomiting, headache, dizziness, diarrhea, urticaria and proteinuria, some of which may be allergic responses to liberated fluke antigens.

DIETHYLCARBAMAZINE

Diethylcarbamazine is a piperazine derivative used in the treatment of filariasis. It is microfilaricidal for *W. bancrofti*, *B. malayi* and *Brugia timori*.[6,7,76,82,83] It appears to be macrofilaricidal for these species as well (i.e. it kills adult worms) and is considered to be the drug of choice for these three infections. Diethylcarbamazine is a key component of mass chemotherapy approaches for the eradication of lymphatic filariasis.[80] It has been used as a sole agent for single-dose therapy, administered long-term as diethylcarbamazine-fortified dietary salt, and as a component of combination single-dose regimens with ivermectin or albendazole. Diethylcarbamazine is also the mainstay of therapy against *Loa loa* and *Mansonella streptocerca*. It has been used to treat tropical pulmonary eosinophilia, supporting the contention that the pulmonary infiltrates in this disorder are due to migrating microfilariae. It has also been used for visceral larva migrans. Diethylcarbamazine is effective in eliminating microfilariae of *O. volvulus* in the skin and eye but the resulting inflammation can cause permanent ocular damage, including uveitis, punctate keratitis and retinal pigment epithelium atrophy. Adult *Onchocerca* worms are not killed, however, and the infection may return once treatment has stopped. Ivermectin has largely replaced diethylcarbamazine for ocular onchocerciasis. Diethylcarbamazine also has activity against *A. lumbricoides*.

The mechanism of action of diethylcarbamazine involves two processes:

- first, filarial muscular activity decreases, probably secondary to hyperpolarization of membranes by the piperazine moiety of diethylcarbamazine; and
- second, diethylcarbamazine alters microfilarial surface membranes by making them more susceptible to host defenses.

Diethylcarbamazine is available as the citrate salt in 50mg tablets. It is rapidly absorbed, widely distributed in the body, hepatically metabolized and renally eliminated. It has a half-life of approximately 10 hours.

Side effects, although common, are usually mild and transient; they include headache, malaise, arthralgias, anorexia, nausea and vomiting. Toxicity can result from the destruction of organisms and release of antigens, which provokes an inflammatory response. This reaction is most severe in patients who are heavily infected with *O. volvulus*. This is termed the Mazzotti reaction and consists of severe pruritus, edema, rash, arthralgias, lymphadenopathy, fever, hypotension, increased eosinophilia, proteinuria and splenomegaly. These symptoms persist for 3–7 days. Nodular swellings along lymphatics and lymphadenitis may occur with *W. bancrofti* and *B. malayi* infections. Patients heavily infected with *L. loa* may experience encephalopathy and other neurologic complications.[84] Pretreatment with corticosteroids may lessen the severity of these inflammatory responses.

FLUBENDAZOLE

Flubendazole is a fluorine analogue of mebendazole and the two drugs have similar spectra of activity.[6,7] Flubendazole is poorly absorbed after oral administration. It has been used against many of the common intestinal helminths and, with limited success, in the treatment of neurocysticercosis.

IVERMECTIN

Ivermectin is a derivative of avermectin B1, a type of macrocyclic lactone that was discovered in the 1970s as a product of the actinomycete *Streptomyces avermitilis*.[6,7,76,77,85] Ivermectin is used as a broad-spectrum veterinary agent for infections with helminths and arthropods. Since the 1980s, it has become the drug of choice for onchocerciasis because it kills microfilariae in the skin and the eye while provoking much less inflammation than diethylcarbamazine. The response to ivermectin is rapid and can last for 6–12 months. Adult worms appear to be unaffected by ivermectin, but the drug seems to prevent developing larvae from leaving the uterus. The drug also has activity against *W. bancrofti, B. malayi, B. timori, L. loa, Mansonella ozzardi* and *Mansonella streptocerca*, and is being used as a component of mass chemotherapy for lymphatic filiriasis.[80] Ivermectin is effective against *S. stercoralis* and is active against *E. vermicularis, A. lumbricoides* and *Trichuris trichiura*. Ivermectin causes tonic paralysis of the helminth musculature but the mechanism of action is poorly understood, although it is known to include γ-aminobutyric acid (GABA) blockade.

Ivermectin is available as 6mg tablets. It is highly protein-bound, has an elimination half-life of 50–60 hours, is concentrated in liver and adipose tissue and is almost entirely excreted in the feces (only 1–2% appears in the urine). Side effects include headache, fever, pruritus, lymphadenopathy, myalgias, arthralgias and, less commonly, orthostatic hypotension.

MEBENDAZOLE

Mebendazole is a benzimidazole carbamate with a broad range of anthelmintic activity.[6,7,75–77] It is active against the larvae and adults of *E. vermicularis, A. lumbricoides, T. trichiura, N. americanus* and *A. duodenale*. It is ovicidal for *Ascaris* and *Trichuris* spp. It is less effective than thiabendazole against *S. stercoralis*. Mebendazole has been used at high doses and for long periods in the treatment of *C. philippinensis*. It can also be used for infections caused by *Angiostrongylus cantonensis, Angiostrongylus costaricensis, Toxocara canis* and *Trichostrongylus* spp. The drug has activity against adult *Trichinella spiralis*, with some activity against larval forms, and it is currently recommended in the treatment of trichinosis. Mebendazole is also effective in the treatment of certain types of filariasis; it is considered the drug of choice against *Mansonella perstans* (diethylcarbamazine is ineffective), and it has been shown to have efficacy against *L. loa, O. volvulus* and *Dracunculus medinensis* infections. The drug has activity against *T. saginata, T. solium* and *Hymenolepis nana*, although praziquantel is more effective. Although mebendazole does not eradicate echinococcal infection, the drug prevents progression of existing cysts and the development of new cysts when administered in high dose for a prolonged period. Mebendazole has largely been replaced by albendazole for echinococcosis.

Mebendazole acts by binding parasite tubulin, thus blocking microtubule assembly and interfering with glucose absorption. Susceptible helminths become paralyzed and depleted of energy stores, but death and clearance of the worms from the gastrointestinal tract can take days. Mebendazole, formulated as 100mg tablets, has low water solubility and is poorly absorbed. It is 95% protein-bound in plasma and undergoes rapid and extensive first-pass metabolism in the liver. Thus, systemic bioavailability is low, accounting not only for its poor tissue levels and relative lack of usefulness in extraintestinal infections, but also for its low rate of side effects.

Abdominal pain and diarrhea may occur after mebendazole administration. The drug also has been reported to prompt the migration of adult *Ascaris* spp. into the mouth and nose. At high doses, reversible bone marrow suppression with neutropenia, alopecia, allergic skin reactions, hepatitis, vertigo and oligospermia occur rarely.

METRIFONATE

Metrifonate is an organophosphate inhibitor of acetylcholinesterase that was originally developed as an insecticide. It has activity against *Schistosoma haematobium*.[6,7,86] It is well absorbed orally and metabolized quickly to dichlorvos, an active metabolite. The half-life is 1.5 hours. The dosage is 7.5–10mg/kg orally once every 2 weeks for three cycles. Side effects include nausea, vomiting, vertigo and lethargy. Patients receiving metrifonate should neither be exposed to other insecticides nor receive neuromuscular blocking agents in the 2 days before or after taking metrifonate.

NICLOSAMIDE

Niclosamide is a salicylamide derivative that is active against the cestodes *Diphyllobothrium latum, D. caninum, H. nana, T. saginata* and *T. solium*, as well as the trematodes *Echinostoma* spp., *Fasciolopsis buski* and *Heterophyes heterophyes*.[6] It acts by interfering with oxidative phosphorylation and production of adenosine triphosphate. Treatment failures of *Taenia* spp. with niclosamide have been reported, and praziquantel has been used successfully in these cases.[87] Niclosamide is supplied as 500mg tablets that should be chewed thoroughly because of its very poor absorption. The dosage is 2g as a single dose (or 1g and 1g, given 1 hour apart), except for *H. nana* infection, which requires 2g then 1g q24h for 6 days. Side effects include gastrointestinal distress, dizziness and rash.

OXAMNIQUINE

Oxamniquine is a tetrahydroquinoline that is effective in *S. mansoni* infections.[6,7,86] Its mechanism of action is unclear, but it causes adult worms to become paralyzed and dislodged from the veins they inhabit, resulting in subsequent killing by host defenses. The drug is available in 250mg capsules that are rapidly absorbed and extensively metabolized in the liver. The half-life is approximately 2 hours, and 70% of the drug is excreted by the kidneys. Side effects include drowsiness, dizziness, orange–red discoloration of the urine and, rarely, seizures. The drug should be given cautiously to patients who have a history of seizures.

PIPERAZINE

Piperazine has activity against *A. lumbricoides* and *E. vermicularis*.[6,7,75] In many parts of the world it has been replaced by less toxic agents such as mebendazole. However, because of its lower cost, piperazine is still frequently used. Piperazine blocks the helminth muscle response to acetylcholine by altering membrane ion permeability and causing hyperpolarization and decreased action potentials. Flaccid paralysis ensues and the worms are eliminated in the stool.

Piperazine is available as the citrate salt in 250mg tablets. There is good oral absorption and a small amount of hepatic metabolism; 60% of the drug is excreted in the urine unmodified. Different dosage schedules exist, but a single dose of 75mg/kg (maximum 4g) per day for 2 days is effective for ascariasis, and a single dose of 65mg/kg daily for 7 days is used for enterobiasis.

Side effects include gastrointestinal disturbances, headache, dizziness and urticaria. Seizures occur rarely, and piperazine is contraindicated in patients who have a history of a seizure disorder. Piperazine and pyrantel pamoate are antagonistic and should not be co-administered.

PRAZIQUANTEL

Praziquantel, a pyrazinoisoquinoline derivative developed in the early 1970s, has broad activity against trematodes and cestodes but not nematodes.[6,7,76,86] All *Schistosoma* spp. that infect humans are susceptible. The drug also has activity against the trematodes *C. sinensis*, *Dicrocoelium dendriticum*, *Echinostoma* spp., *F. buski*, *H. heterophyes*, *Metagonimus yokogawai*, *Metorchis conjunctus*, *Nanophyetus salmincola*, *Opisthorchis viverrini* and *Paragonimus westermani* and other *Paragonimus* spp. *Fasciola hepatica* does not appear to be adequately treated with praziquantel; bithionol is used instead. Praziquantel is effective in treating adult cestodes, including *D. latum* and other *Diphyllobothrium* spp., *D. caninum*, *H. nana*, *Hymenolepis diminuta*, *T. saginata* and *T. solium*. It has been used successfully to treat neurocysticercosis (larval *T. solium*), but it is not useful in echinococcosis. The drug has several actions, including promoting calcium influx and parasite muscle contraction and causing vacuolization and bleb formation in the helminth tegument, thereby activating host defenses.

Praziquantel is available as 600mg tablets that are nearly insoluble in water. There is good oral absorption, 80% protein binding and rapid first-pass metabolism. The half-life is 1.5 hours. About 80% of the drug is excreted in the urine. Side effects are common but transient and include headache, dizziness, nausea, vomiting and abdominal pain. Fever and rashes are occasionally seen.

PYRANTEL PAMOATE

Pyrantel pamoate, a tetrahydropyrimidine that was originally developed as a veterinary anthelmintic, has a broad range of activity in humans.[6,7,75,76] It is considered by many to be the treatment of choice for *E. vermicularis*. It also effective for *A. lumbricoides*, eosinophilic enterocolitis caused by *Ancylostoma caninum*, hookworm, the acanthocephalan *Moniliformis moniliformis* and *Trichostrongylus* spp. It does not have activity against *T. trichiura*. Oxantel pamoate, an *m*-oxyphenol derivative, can be given in a single dose for *Trichuris* sp. Pyrantel pamoate and its analogues act by causing depolarizing neuromuscular blockade and by blocking acetylcholinesterase, which result in spastic paralysis and muscle contracture, respectively, and allow expulsion of the worms.

Pyrantel pamoate is available as an oral suspension of 250mg of pyrantel base per 5ml. It is poorly absorbed. Less than 15% is excreted in the urine and most remains in the feces unmodified. Side effects include headache, dizziness, insomnia, nausea, vomiting, anorexia and abdominal pain. Pyrantel pamoate, which causes depolarization and increased spike frequency in worm muscle cells, should not be given with piperazine, which causes hyperpolarization and a reduction in spike frequency.

THIABENDAZOLE

Thiabendazole is a substituted benzimidazole compound that has better activity against *S. stercoralis* and *Strongyloides fuelleborni* than mebendazole.[6,7,75–77,86] It is active against *A. costaricensis*, *C. philippinensis*, *D. medinensis*, *Trichostrongylus* spp. and *T. spiralis*. In trichinosis, however, larval stages are often resistant to thiabendazole. The drug is also used in the treatment of both cutaneous and visceral larva migrans. Thiabendazole has some activity against *A. lumbricoides*, hookworm, *E. vermicularis* and *T. trichiura* but mebendazole is less toxic and is thus preferred. The drug acts by inhibiting parasite fumarate reductase, and it may bind tubulin as well.

Thiabendazole is available in tablet and liquid form and, in contrast to other benzimidazole derivatives, is rapidly absorbed. It is extensively metabolized by the liver, has a half-life of 1 hour and is mainly excreted by the kidney.

Side effects are frequent; they include nausea, vomiting, anorexia and dizziness. Pruritus, epigastric pain, headache, drowsiness, giddiness and diarrhea are less common. Rarer still are tinnitus, hallucinations, numbness, seizures, altered olfaction, altered color perception, hypotension, bradycardia, crystalluria, leukopenia, elevated liver enzymes and intrahepatic cholestasis. Allergic manifestations, including fever, angioneurotic edema, erythema multiforme and Stevens–Johnson syndrome, have been described and may result from the release of parasite antigens during treatment. Increased theophylline levels and consequent nausea and vomiting may result from the co-administration of theophylline and thiabendazole.

TRICLABENDAZOLE

Triclabendazole, a benzimidazole derivative used as a veterinary fasciolicide, has been used safely and successfully in cases of human chronic hepatic fascioliasis.[88,89] It is now considered the drug of choice for human hepatic fascioliasis, but in the USA it is available only by directly contacting Novartis Agribusiness (Basel, Switzerland).

Acknowledgment

This chapter is an update of the first edition version, written by Erik K Johnson and Rosemary Soave.

REFERENCES

1. Abramowicz M, ed. Drugs for parasitic infections. Med Lett Drugs Ther 2002;4:1.
2. Gelman BB, Rauf SJ, Nader R, *et al.* Amoebic encephalitis due to *Sappinia diploidea*. JAMA 2001;285:2450–1.
3. Alecrim WD, Espinosa FE, Alecrim MG. *Plasmodium falciparum* infection in the pregnant patient. Infect Dis Clin North Am 2000;14:83–95.
4. Phillips-Howard PA, Steffen R, Kerr L, *et al.* Safety of mefloquine and other antimalarials in the first trimester of pregnancy. J Trav Med 1998;5:121–6.
5. Samuel BU, Barry M. The pregnant traveler. Infect Dis Clin 1998;12:325–54.
6. Campbell WC, Rew RS, eds. Chemotherapy of parasitic diseases. New York: Plenum Press; 1986.
7. Frayha GJ, Smyth JD, Gobert JG, Savel J. The mechanisms of action of antiprotozoal and antihelminthic drugs in man. Gen Pharmacol 1997;28:273–99.
8. Olliaro P, Nevill C, LeBras J, *et al.* Systematic review of amodiaquine treatment in uncomplicated malaria. Lancet 1996;348:1196–201.

9. Souwunmi A, Ayede AI, Falade AG *et al.* Randomized comparison of chloroquine and amodiaquine in the treatment of acute uncomplicated *Plasmodium falciparum* malaria in children. Ann Trop Med Parasitol 2001;6:549–58.
10. Berman JD. Human leishmaniasis: clinical, diagnostic, and chemotherapeutic developments in the last 10 years. Clin Infect Dis 1997;24:684–703.
11. Brown RL. Successful treatment of primary amebic meningoencephalitis. Arch Intern Med 1991;151:1201–2.
12. Sundar S, Agrawal G, Rai M, *et al.* Treatment of Indian visceral leishmaniasis with single or daily infusions of low dose liposomal amphotericin B lipid: randomized trial. Br Med J 2001;323:419–22.
13. Yardley V, Croft SL. Activity of liposomal amphotericin B against experimental cutaneous leishmaniasis. Antimicrob Agents Chemother 1997;41:752–6.
14. White NJ. The treatment of malaria. N Engl J Med 1996;335:800–6.
15. Sibley CH, Hyde JE, Sims PF *et al.* Pyrimethamine–sulfadoxine resistance in *Plasmodium falciparum*: what next? Trends Parasitol 2001;17:582–8.
16. Winstanley P. Modern chemotherapeutic options for malaria. Lancet Infect Dis 2001;1:242–50.
17. Fung HB, Kirschenbaum HL. Treatment regimens for patients with toxoplasmic encephalitis. Clin Ther 1996;18:1037–56.
18. Chirgwin K, Hafner R, Leport C, *et al.* Randomized phase II trial of atovaquone with pyrimethamine or sulfadiazine for treatment of toxoplasmic encephalitis in patients with acquired immunodeficiency syndrome: ACTG 237/ANRS 039 Study. Clin Infect Dis 2002;34:1243–50.
19. Lindsay DS, Dubey JP, Blagburn BL. Biology of *Isospora* spp. from human, nonhuman primates, and domestic animals. Clin Microbiol Rev 1997;10:19–34.
20 Verdier RI, Fitzgerald DW, Johnson WD Jr, Pape JW. Trimethoprim–sulfamethoxazole compared with ciprofloxacin for treatment and prophylaxis of *Isospora belli* and *Cyclospora cayatanensis* infection in HIV-infected patients. A randomized, controlled trial. Ann Intern Med 2000;132:885–8.
21. Lemnge MM, Msangeni HA, Ronn AM, *et al.* Maloprim malaria prophylaxis in children living in a holoendemic village in north-eastern Tanzania. Trans R Soc Trop Med Hyg 1997;91:68–73.
22. Omar SA, Bakari A, Adagu IS, Warhurst DC. Co-trimoxazole compared with sulfadoxine-pyrimethamine in the treatment of uncomplicated malaria in Kenyan children. Trans R Soc Trop Med Hyg 2001;95:657–60.
23. Kilian AH, Jelinek T, Prislin I *et al.* Resistance in vivo of *Plasmodium falciparum* to co-trimoxazole in western Uganda. Trans R Soc Trop Med Hyg 1998;92:197–200.
24. De Alencar FEC, Cerutti C, Durlacher RR, *et al.* Atovaquone and proguanil for the treatment of malaria in Brazil. J Infect Dis 1997;175:1544–7.
25. Barnes AJ, Ong ELC, Dunbar EM, Mandal BK, Wilkins EGL. Failure of chloroquine and proguanil prophylaxis in travellers in Kenya. Lancet 1991;338:1338–9.
26. Meshnick SR, Taylor TE, Kamchonwongpaisan S. Artemisinin and the antimalarial endoperoxides: from herbal remedy to targeted chemotherapy. Microbiol Rev 1996;60:301–15.
27. Wittner M, Lederman J, Tanowitz HB, Rosenbaum GS, Weiss LM. Atovaquone in the treatment of *Babesia microti* infections in hamsters. Am J Trop Med Hyg 1996;55:219–22.
28. Hogh B, Clark PD, Camus D *et al.* Atovaquone-proguanil versus chloroquine–proguanil for malaria prophylaxis in non-immune travellers: a randomized, double-blind study. Malarone International Study Team. Lancet 2000;356:1888–94.
29. Overbosch D, Schilithuis H, Bienzle U *et al.* Atovaquone–proguanil versus mefloquine for malaria prophylaxis in non-immune travelers: results from a randomized double-blind study. Clin Infect Dis 2001;33:1015–21.
30. Kirchhoff L. Chagas disease, American trypanosomiasis. Infect Dis Clin 1993;7:487–502.
31. Tilley L, Loria P, Foley M. Chloroquine and other quinoline antimalarials. In Rosenthal PJ ed. Antimalarial chemotherapy. Totowa, NJ: Humana Press; 2001:
32. Lobel HO, Kozarsky PE. Update on prevention of malaria for travelers. JAMA 1997;278:1767–71.
33. Marlar-Than, Myat-Phone-Kyaw, Aye-Yu-Soe, Khaing-Khaing-Gyi, Ma-Sabai, Myint-Oo. Development of resistance to chloroquine by *Plasmodium vivax* in Myanmar. Trans R Soc Trop Med Hyg 1995;89:307–8.
34. Baird JK, Wiady I, Fryauff DJ, *et al.* In vivo resistance to chloroquine by *Plasmodium vivax* and *Plasmodium falciparum* at Nabire, Irian Jaya, Indonesia. Am J Trop Med Hyg 1997;56:627–31.
35. Boustani MR, Gelfand JA. Babesiosis. Clin Infect Dis 1996;22:611–5.
36. Kremsner PG, Winkler S, Brandts C, Neifer S, Bienzle U, Graninger W. Clindamycin in combination with chloroquine or quinine is effective therapy for uncomplicated *Plasmodium falciparum* malaria in children from Gabon. J Infect Dis 1994;169:467–70.
37. Parola P, Ranque S, Bandiga S *et al.* Controlled trial of 3-day quinine–clindamycin treatment versus 7-day quinine treatment for adult travelers with uncomplicated *Plasmodium falciparum* malaria imported from the tropics. Antimicrob Agents Chemother 2001;45:932–5.
38. Pepin J, Milord F. The treatment of human African trypanosomiasis. Adv Parasitol 1994;33:1–47.
39. Taelman H, Schechter PJ, Marcelis L, *et al.* Difluoromethylornithine, an effective new treatment of Gambian trypanosomiasis. Am J Med 1987;82:607–14.
40. Katz DE, Taylor DN. Parasitic diseases of the gastrointestinal tract. Gastroenterol Clin North Am 2001;30:797–815.
41. Stanley SL Jr. Extraintestinal amebiasis. In: Schlossberg D. ed. Current therapy of infectious disease, 2nd ed. St Louis, MO, Mosby; 2001:693–5.
42. Sin N, Meng L, Wang MQ, *et al.* The anti-angiogenic agent fumagillin covalently binds and inhibits the methionine aminopeptidase, MetAP-2. Proc Natl Acad Sci USA 1997;94:6099–103.
43. Diesenhouse MC, Wilson LA, Corrent GF, Visvesvara GS, Grossniklaus HE, Bryan RT. Treatment of microsporidial keratoconjunctivitis with topical fumagillin. Am J Ophthalmol 1993;115:293–8.
44. Garvey MJ, Ambrose PG, Ulmer JL. Topical fumagillin in the treatment of microsporidial keratoconjunctivitis in AIDS. Ann Pharmacother 1995;29:872–4.
45. Molina JM, Goguel J, Sarfati C, *et al.* Potential efficacy of fumagillin in intestinal microsporidiosis due to *Enterocytozoon bieneusi* in patients with HIV infection: results of a drug screening study. AIDS 1997;11:1603–10.
46. Soave R, Didier ES. Cryptosporidiosis and microsporidiosis. In: Merigan TC, Bartlett JG, Bolognesi D, eds. The textbook of AIDS medicine, 2nd ed. Baltimore: JB Lippincott: 1998:327–56.
47. Ortega YR, Adam RD. Giardia: overview and update. Clin Infect Dis 1997;25:545–50.
48. Karbwang J, Na Bangchang K. Clinical pharmacokinetics of halofantrine. Clin Pharmacokinet 1994;27:104–19.
49. Chan FTH, Guan MX, Mackenzie AMR, Diaz-Mitoma F. Susceptibility testing of *Dientamoeba fragilis* ATCC 30948 with iodoquinol, paromomycin, tetracycline, and metronidazole. Antimicrob Agents Chemother 1994;38:1157–60.
50. Markell EK. Is there any reason to continue treating blastocystis infections (Editorial)? Clin Infect Dis 1995;21:104–5.
51. Kain KC, Shanks GD, Keystone JS. Malaria chemoprophylaxis in the age of drug resistance. I. Currently recommended drug regimens. Clin Infect Dis 2001;33:226–34.
52. Holmberg SD, Moorman AC, Von Bargen JC. Possible effectiveness of clarithromycin and rifabutin for cryptosporidiosis chemoprophylaxis in HIV disease. HIV Outpatient Study (HOPS). JAMA 1998;279:384–6.
53. Croft AMJ, Clayton TC, World MJ. Side effects of mefloquine prophylaxis for malaria: an independent randomized controlled trial. Trans R Soc Trop Med Hyg 1997;91:199–203.
54. Watt G, Loesuttivibool L, Shanks GD, *et al.* Quinine with tetracycline for the treatment of drug-resistant falciparum malaria in Thailand. Am J Trop Med Hyg 1992;47:108–11.
55. Luxemburger C, ter Kuile FO, Nosten F, *et al.* Single day mefloquine-artesunate combination in the treatment of multi-drug resistant falciparum malaria. Trans R Soc Trop Med Hyg 1994;88:213–7.
56. Karbwang J, Na-Bangchang K, Thanavibul A, Ditta-in M, Harinasuta T. A comparative clinical trial of two different regimens of artemether plus mefloquine in multidrug resistant falciparum malaria. Trans R Soc Trop Med Hyg 1995;89:296–8.
57. Looareesuwan S, Viravan C, Vanijanonta S, *et al.* Randomized trial of mefloquine–doxycycline and artesunate–doxycycline for treatment of acute uncomplicated falciparum malaria. Am J Trop Med Hyg 1994;50:784–9.
58. Pepin, J, Milord F, Khonde AN, *et al.* Risk factors for encephalopathy and mortality during melarsoprol treatment of *Trypanosoma brucei gambiense* sleeping sickness. Trans R Soc Trop Med Hyg 1995;89:92–7.
59. Gilles HM, Hoffman PS. Treatment of intestinal parasitic infections: a review of nitazoxanide. Trends Parasitol 2002;18:95–97.
60. Sobel JD. Vaginitis. N Engl J Med 1997;337:1896–903.
61. Quaderi MA, Rahman MS, Rahman A, Islam N. Amoebic liver abscess and clinical experiences with tinidazole in Bangladesh. J Trop Med Hyg 1978;81:16–9.
62. White AC, Chappell CL, Hayat CS, Kimball KT, Flanigan TP, Goodgame RW. Paromomycin for cryptosporidiosis in AIDS: a prospective, double-blind trial. J Infect Dis 1994;170:419–24.
63. Hewitt RG, Yiannoutsos CT, Higgs ES, *et al.* Paromomycin: no more effective than placebo for treatment of cryptosporidiosis in patients with advanced human immunodeficiency virus infection. AIDS Clinical Trial Group. Clin Infect Dis 2000;31:1084–92.
64. Krause G, Kroeger A. Topical treatment of American cutaneous leishmaniasis with paromomycin and methylbenzethonium chloride: a clinical study under field conditions in Ecuador. Trans R Soc Trop Med Hyg 1994;88:92–4.
65. Slater CA, Sickel JZ, Visvesvara GS, Pabico RC, Gaspari AA. Brief report: successful treatment of disseminated acanthamoeba infection in an immunocompromised patient. N Engl J Med 1994;331:85–7.
66. Raoult D, Soulayrol L, Toga B, Dumon H, Casanova P. Babesiosis, pentamidine, and co-trimoxazole. Ann Intern Med 1987;107:944.
67. Herwaldt BL, Berman JD. Recommendations for treating leishmaniasis with sodium stibogluconate (Pentostam) and review of pertinent clinical studies. Am J Trop Med Hyg 1992;46:296–306.
68. Lira R, Sundar S, Makharia A *et al.* Evidence that the high incidence of treatment failures in Indian kala-azar is due to the emergence of antimony-resistant strains of *Leishmania donovani*. J Infect Dis 1999;180:564–7.

69. Baird JK, Lacy MD, Basri H *et al.* Randomized, parallel placebo-controlled trial of primaquine for malaria prophylaxis in Papua, Indonesia. Clin Infect Dis 2001;33:1990–7.
70. Luzzi GA, Warrel DA, Barnes AJ, Dunbar EM. Treatment of primaquine-resistant *Plasmodium vivax* malaria. Lancet 1992;340:310.
71. Nash TE, Ohl CA, Thomas E *et al.* Treatment of patients with refractory giardiasis. Clin Infect Dis. 2001;33:22–8.
72. Miller KD, Greenberg AE, Campbell CC. Treatment of severe malaria in the United States with a continuous infusion of quinidine gluconate and exchange transfusion. N Engl J Med 1989;321:65–70.
73. Pukrittayakamee S, Supanaranond W, Looareesuwan S, Vanijanonta S, White NJ. Quinine in severe falciparum malaria: evidence of declining efficacy in Thailand. Trans R Soc Trop Med Hyg 1994;88:324–7.
74. Ohrt C, Richie TL, Widjaja H, *et al.* Mefloquine compared with doxycycline for the prophylaxis of malaria in Indonesian soldiers: a randomized, double-blind, placebo-controlled trial. Ann Intern Med 1997;126:963–72.
75. Liu LX, Weller PF. Strongyloidiasis and other intestinal nematode infections. Infect Dis Clin 1993;7:655–82.
76. De Silva N, Guyatt H, Bundy D. Anthelmintics: a comparative review of their clinical pharmacology. Drugs 1997;53:769–88.
77. Glickman LT, Magnaval JF. Zoonotic roundworm infections. Infect Dis Clin 1993;7:717–32.
78. Horton RJ. Albendazole in the treatment of human cystic echinococcosis: 12 years of experience. Acta Trop 1997;64:79–93.
79. Garcia HH, Gilman RH, Horton J, *et al.* Albendazole therapy for neurocysticercosis: a prospective double-blind trial comparing 7 versus 14 days of treatment. Neurology 1997;48:1421–7.
80. Ottesen EA, Ismail MM, Horton J. The role of albendazole in programmes to eliminate lymphatic filariasis. Parasitol Today 1999;15:382–6.
81. Dore GJ, Marriott DJ, Hing MC, Harkness JL, Field AS. Disseminated microsporidiosis due to *Septata intestinalis* in nine patients infected with the human immunodeficiency virus: response to therapy with albendazole. Clin Infect Dis 1995;21:70–6.
82. Ottensen EA. Filarial infections. Infect Dis Clin 1993;7:619–33.
83. Noroes J, Dreyer G, Santos A, Mendes VG, Medeiros Z, Addiss D. Assessment of the efficacy of diethylcarbamazine on adult *Wuchereria bancrofti in vivo*. Trans R Soc Trop Med Hyg 1997;91:78–81.
84. Stanley SL Jr, Kehl O. Ascending paralysis associated with diethylcarbamazine treatment of a *M. loa loa* infestation – a case report and review of the literature. Trop Doctor 1982;12:16–9.
85. Alley ES, Plaisier AP, Boatin BA, *et al.* The impact of five years of annual ivermectin treatment on skin microfilarial loads in the onchocerciasis focus of Asubende, Ghana. Trans R Soc Trop Med Hyg 1994;88:581–4.
86. Ross Ag, Barley PB, Sleigh AC *et al.* Schistosomiasis. N Engl J Med 2002;346:1212–20.
87. Koul PA, Waheed A, Hayat M, Sofi BA. Praziquantel in niclosamide-resistant *Taenia saginata* infection. Scan J Inf Dis 1999;31:603–4.
88. Apt W, Aguilera X, Vega F, *et al.* Treatment of human chronic fascioliasis with triclabendazole: drug efficacy and serologic response. Am J Trop Med Hyg 1995;52:532–5.
89. Graham CS, Brodie SB, Weller PF. Imported *Fasciola hepatica* infection in the United States and treatment with triclabendazole. Clin Infect Dis 2001;33:1–6.

chapter

210 Immunomodulation

Jos WM van der Meer & Bart-Jan Kullberg

INTRODUCTION

Despite the availability of potent antimicrobial drugs, many infections are still difficult to treat. This is not only the case for infections for which suboptimal or no effective antimicrobial treatment is available, because of intrinsic or acquired resistance of the causative micro-organism, but also those due to failing host defense mechanisms. Based on data from experimental infections and from clinical studies, especially in the neutropenic patient, it is known that antibiotics alone are rarely capable of eradicting pathogenic micro-organisms; components of host defense, especially granulocytes, are required to effectively eliminate the infection, in conjunction with the antibiotics.

Another reason for failure of antibiotic treatment is that the response of the host to infection may be overwhelming. In that situation, proinflammatory cytokines, such as tumor necrosis factor-α (TNF-α), interleukin-1β (IL-1β) and IL-8, as well as secretory products of white blood cells, such as elastase, reactive oxygen metabolites and chloramines, can produce serious tissue damage.[1,2] Not only is it the proinflammatory cytokines which can be hazardous under such circumstances; the anti-inflammatory cytokines may blunt the immune response to such an extent that a state of immunodeficiency ensues. It is, however, impossible to make a simple distinction between the good and bad effects of these cytokines. Under certain circumstances a particular cytokine effect may be beneficial, whereas under other circumstances a similar effect may harm the host.

Thus, there are good reasons to try to enhance or modulate host defenses, particularly in patients with defective host defense mechanisms or when effective drug treatment is not available. If, on the other hand, the host response is overwhelming, attempts may be made to inhibit such a response.

In a general sense, treatments fall into one of the following four categories (or combinations thereof).

- The treatment stimulates the inflammatory response (e.g. by increasing the proinflammatory cytokine status or by augmenting phagocyte or T-cell function).
- The treatment inhibits the counterregulatory, anti-inflammatory response (e.g. by inhibiting anti-inflammatory cytokines such as IL-10, IL-4 or TGF-β).
- The treatment inhibits the inflammatory response (e.g. by decreasing the proinflammatory cytokine status or by inhibiting phagocyte or T-cell function).
- The treatment promotes the counterregulatory, anti-inflammatory response (e.g. by increasing the status of anti-inflammatory cytokines such as IL-10, IL-4 or TGF-β).

Stimulation of the proinflammatory cytokine response and inhibition of the anti-inflammatory response are aimed at treatment of specific, difficult-to-treat infections. Inhibition of the proinflammatory response and stimulation of the anti-inflammatory response are especially applicable during overwhelming inflammation, such as the systemic inflammatory response syndrome occurring during sepsis.

These therapeutic approaches have become a great challenge in medicine. However, such interventions may have a large impact on the delicate and complicated cytokine balance and may lead to disturbances that adversely affect the status of the host.

Immunomodulatory treatment has encountered a variety of problems.

- It has turned out to be extremely difficult to determine under which clinical circumstances a certain immunomodulatory effect may be of benefit.
- Many of the immunomodulatory agents have mainly been shown to work *in vitro* or in animal experiments. Many studies have used rather artificial models and often, the infectious challenge has been administered after the immunomodulatory treatment rather than before initiation of therapy.

STIMULATION OF THE INFLAMMATORY RESPONSE

There are, in essence, two ways to augment the inflammatory response. One is to administer an exogenous ('foreign') agent that elicits an inflammatory response, the second is to administer an endogenous substance in recombinant form. So far, the former method has met with very little human application. Among a few exceptions are the addition of an adjuvant (such as alum, monophosphoryl lipid A) to a vaccine, an interferon inducer (such as ampligen[3] and the recently developed cytokine-inducing drug imiquimod, which has been applied in dermatology for topical treatment of genital warts).[4]

An interesting approach that has been tried in humans is the administration of *Mycobacterium vaccae,* a nonvirulent mycobacterial strain, to patients with tuberculosis with the aim of inducing an enhanced type 1 cytokine response (i.e. to induce cytokines like IFN-γ). Despite application in a number of controlled trials, it is still controversial whether this approach is effective in tuberculosis.[5]

In experimental animals, a large variety of molecules have been used with the intention of augmenting the inflammatory response, such as bacterial endotoxin, muramylpeptides and glucans.[6] The antifungal drug amphotericin B does seem to have such an immunostimulatory effect[7] but it is difficult to demonstrate whether this has added value in clinical terms while treating invasive fungal infections. It is currently unclear whether the administration of nutrients, such as vitamin A and zinc, which have been shown to have a beneficial effect in the treatment of tuberculosis, should be considered as substitution therapy or immunomodulatory treatment.[8]

Colony-stimulating factors

Most clinical research has been performed with the hematopoietic growth factors granulocyte-colony stimulating factor (G-CSF), granulocyte-macrophage colony-stimulating factor (GM-CSF) and macrophage colony-stimulating factor (M-CSF).[9] In particular, G-CSF and GM-CSF have been studied extensively in patients with congenital or acquired neutropenia. In patients with severe congenital neutropenia, benefit of G-CSF has been shown in terms of prevention of infection and improved quality of life.[10,11] In cancer patients, these factors have been used both to shorten the duration of chemotherapy-induced granulocytopenia[12] and as adjunctive

IMMUNOMODULATORS FOR HUMAN USE
Stimulators of the inflammatory response • Exogenous agents ◦ adjuvants (monophosphoryl lipid A; alum) ◦ interferon inducers (ampligen) ◦ imiquimod ◦ amphotericin B ◦ *Mycobacterium vaccae* • Endogenous agents ◦ Colony-stimulating factors (G-CSF, GM-CSF, M-CSF) ◦ Cytokines (interferon-γ, IL-1, IL-2) ◦ Granulocyte transfusions (G-CSF primed)
Inhibitors of the anti-inflammatory response
Inhibitors of the inflammatory response ◦ Antiendotoxin strategies (antibodies, polymyxin B, BPI, reconstituted HDL) ◦ Anticytokine strategies – Anti-TNF strategies (infliximab, etanercept) – Anti-IL-1 strategies (IL-1ra)
Stimulators of the anti-inflammatory response ◦ Anti-inflammatory cytokines (IL-10) ◦ Glucocorticosteroids ◦ Macrolides ◦ Inhibitors of lipid mediators (PAF antagonists, cyclo-oxygenase inhibitors, n-3 fatty acids) ◦ Activated protein C ◦ Intravenous immunoglobulin preparations

Table 210.1 Immunomodulators for human use.

therapy in patients with neutropenia and fever.[13] However, in patients with acquired neutropenia, the benefits, i.e. prevention and treatment of infection and prolonged survival, have been less impressive than had been anticipated.[9]

Although most of these studies failed to show an effect of CSF therapy on recovery from infection or survival, the potential beneficial role of GM-CSF has been demonstrated in a prospective, randomized, placebo-controlled study of patients with acute myelogenous leukemia.[14] In that study, recombinant GM-CSF was associated with a higher rate of complete response than placebo, longer overall survival and a reduced fungal infection-related mortality rate which was only 2% for those randomized to receive rGM-CSF compared with 19% for those receiving placebo. G-CSF has very few side-effects and this may be due to concomitant anti-inflammatory effects (see below).

Since G-CSF not only augments the number of granulocytes but also activates their microbicidal action and inhibits their apoptotic response, the potential of G-CSF to enhance the host's inflammatory response to infection has been investigated in non-neutropenic conditions. Preclinical studies in animals have yielded favorable effects in bacterial and fungal infections and anecdotal clinical experiences also suggested positive effects.[15,16] In a small, randomized study in patients with disseminated *Candida* infection, it was suggested that recombinant G-CSF may improve resolution of infection and reduce mortality.[17] Controlled studies in patients with community-acquired pneumonia have failed to demonstrate a survival benefit.[18] It is controversial whether G-CSF may improve clinical outcome in diabetic foot infection, leading to shorter duration of illness and preventing amputation.[19–21] A multicenter study in chronic recalcitrant sinusitis did not show any clinical benefit.[22] Given the waning interest of the pharmaceutical industry in G-CSF, it is unlikely that further clinical studies with G-CSF in infectious diseases will be performed. The question therefore remains under which conditions recombinant G-CSF should be considered in the treatment of infection.

In the past, several clinical trials have investigated the potential beneficial effect of white blood cell transfusions in patients with refractory neutropenia-related bacterial infections.[23] This modality was abandoned because of the low yield of these transfusions and the toxicity in recipients including fever, chills, hypotension, pulmonary infiltrates, respiratory distress and allo-immunization. Recently, the possibility was raised that administration of rG-CSF to WBC donors would increase their neutrophil to levels that would lead to a higher yield of better quality cells. Donors achieved a 4–10-fold increase of their neutrophil count and the 24-hour post transfusion counts in recipients were favorable.[24] In a recent open study, rG-CSF-elicited WBC transfusions given to cancer patients with neutropenia and documented and refractory fungal infections have been successful.[25] This small pilot study as well as several clinical observations suggest that rG-CSF-enhanced WBC transfusions may be life saving for patients with refractory neutropenia-related fungal infections and are safe to deliver. Likewise, this approach seems to be successful in patients with chronic granulomatous disease (a phagocyte disorder characterized by defective intracellular killing; see below) and refractory pyogenic infection.[26,27]

The application of recombinant GM-CSF and M-CSF in infectious diseases has been studied less extensively and despite the expectations of many investigators, there is hardly any clinical indication for these drugs, with the possible exception of visceral leishmaniasis.[28,29]

Interferon-γ

Despite many preclinical studies demonstrating useful effects in a variety of bacterial, fungal and parasitic infections, interferon-γ (IFN-γ) has not gained much favor in clinical medicine. The only established indication for IFN-γ is the prevention of infection in chronic granulomatous disease.

Chronic granulomatous disease (CGD) is characterized by a defect in NADPH oxidase in phagocytic cells with a consecutive impairment in synthesis of reactive oxygen species, leading to recurrent pyogenic infections with catalase-positive micro-organisms.[30] Chronic treatment with IFN-γ has been shown to reduce the frequency of infections in these patients by more than 70%, without severe side effects. The mechanism of action in CGD is not clear but most likely, the effect of IFN-γ is through stimulation of the nonoxidative microbicidal effects of granulocytes and mononuclear phagocytes. Promising results have also been reported in clinical studies involving mycobacterial infections.

Recombinant IFN-γ decreases the bacterial load in patients with lepromatous leprosy.[31,32] Beneficial effects have also been observed in patients with *Mycobacterium avium* complex infection.[33,34] Recombinant IFN-γ has also been investigated as adjunctive therapy in visceral leishmaniasis. Its effect in combination with pentavalent antimony has been disappointing.[35] In a recent study, recombinant IFN-γ was suggested to reduce the incidence of opportunistic infections and resulted in a tendency towards increased survival in patients with advanced HIV disease.[36]

In animal experiments, the effects of IFN-γ on granulocytes and mononuclear phagocytes are impressive[37] and currently, several clinical trials of IFN-γ as a therapeutic agent in mycobacterial and fungal infection are ongoing. Especially now that our understanding of the mechanism of action of IFN-γ, its cellular receptor and the role of related cytokines such as IL-12, IL-18 and IL-23 has expanded, the need for such studies is compelling.

Other recombinant cytokines

So far, the use of other recombinant cytokines for therapy of infection has been limited. IL-1, which is effective in enhancing survival of mice with bacterial and fungal as well as plasmodial infection,[6] has only been used in humans as an anticancer agent.[38–40] Interestingly, IL-1 seems to be unique in that it enhances survival of lethal bacterial and fungal infections in the absence of neutrophils.[6]

IL-2 has been studied to some extent for treatment of infection. In patients with lepromatous leprosy, who exhibit impaired *Mycobacterium leprae*-specific T-cell proliferation, the administration of recombinant IL-2 may be expected to be beneficial. Indeed, in several small pilot studies, intradermal injection of IL-2 in patients with lepromatous leprosy has lead to increased infiltration of mononuclear cells and reduction of the numbers of viable acid-fast *M. leprae* in the peripheral sites.[41,42] Interestingly, recombinant IL-12 and IL-2 strongly synergize in restoring both *M. leprae*-specific T-cell proliferation and IFN-γ secretion *in vitro*.[43]

Administration of relatively high doses of recombinant IL-2 has shown an effect in HIV-infected persons by increasing their levels of circulating CD4 T cells up to normal levels.[44] Further placebo-controlled studies have confirmed a significant rise in CD4 cell count, accompanied by a reduction in plasma HIV in recipients of IL-2 relative to control patients, associated with a nonsignificant trend toward improved clinical outcome.[45] The mechanism through which IL-2 increases $CD4^+$ T cells in HIV-infected individuals is unclear. Most $CD4^+$ T cells that expand after IL-2 administration are memory cells, although increase in naïve T cells has been also reported.[46] Of interest, IL-2 administration in combination with highly active antiretroviral therapy (HAART), but not HAART alone, seems capable of reducing the pool of resting memory CD4 T cells harboring latent replication-competent HIV.[47]

Although there has been concern that the proinflammatory effects of IL-2 may be harmful in terms of transient increases in plasma viremia after each cycle of cytokine administration, the net effect of IL-2 appears to be beneficial and in several trials, no evidence of increased levels of HIV replication was found after IL-2 administration in the presence of HAART.[48] The toxicity associated with administration of relatively high doses of this cytokine to HIV-infected persons remains a major hurdle.[44] The most common toxic effect is a flu-like syndrome that manifests with fever, chills, fatigue and headache. Recent studies have suggested that low doses of intermittent sc IL-2 induced a stable increase of peripheral CD4 cells that was indistinguishable from those associated with higher, less well-tolerated doses of IL-2.[48] (see also Chapter 140).

INHIBITION OF THE ANTI-INFLAMMATORY RESPONSE

The major anti-inflammatory mediators, such as IL-4, IL-10, TGF-β, IL-1 receptor antagonist (IL-1ra) and the soluble TNF receptors, are potential targets in immunomodulatory treatment. The net effect of inhibiting these mediators is likely to be an increased proinflammatory response, enhancing the innate host defense to infection. Although such interventions have been studied in experimental infection in animals, e.g. through targeted gene disruption, such approaches have not been undertaken in humans.

IL-10 is considered a prototypic anti-inflammatory cytokine, which inhibits the production of proinflammatory cytokines *in vitro* and *in vivo*. Elevated plasma concentrations of IL-10 have been found in patients with sepsis[49] and its inhibition leads to an increased production of TNF and an enhanced mortality.[50] In contrast, the host defense against localized infection may be enhanced by treatment with anti-IL-10 antibodies. In a murine pneumonia model, antibodies against IL-10 inhibited bacterial outgrowth in lungs and improved survival.[51] There appears to be a fine balance between beneficial and deleterious effects of IL-10, since elimination of IL-10 in a model of septic peritonitis induced by cecal ligation and puncture (CLP) was associated with an increased mortality.[52,53] These findings are explained by the dual effects of the cytokine network, i.e. whereas in an infected organ a predominantly proinflammatory response contributes to the effective clearance of bacteria, at the systemic level such a response may be harmful to the host. Therefore, during septic peritonitis, endogenous IL-10 impairs bacterial clearance from the peritoneal cavity and facilitates dissemination of bacteria to distant organs, yet attenuates the systemic inflammatory reactions and multiple organ failure associated with this abdominal sepsis syndrome by a mechanism that in part involves inhibition of TNF production. There have been no human trials applying these strategies as yet.

INHIBITION OF THE PROINFLAMMATORY RESPONSE

In recent years, most of the preclinical and clinical studies on immunotherapy of infection have dealt with the inhibition of the proinflammatory response and enforcement of the anti-inflammatory response. These approaches include inhibiting the proinflammatory cytokine TNF-α as well as administration of anti-inflammatory cytokines, such as IL-10. This treatment is based on the notion that an exaggerated and harmful host response may occur during severe infection (Chapter 56), and inhibition of such a response may be beneficial. The therapeutic strategies may interfere at various steps in the inflammatory cascade (Fig. 210.1). First, interference with the infective agent that triggers the host response is a sensible approach. In this respect, prompt antibiotic treatment is a keystone in treatment. Although it has been demonstrated *in vitro* and in animal experiments that antibiotics, especially β-lactam antibiotics, may liberate endotoxin (lipopolysaccharide, LPS) and hence may be harmful,[54] it has not been convincingly shown that this phenomenon contributes to morbidity in humans.[55] In fact, in fulminant meningococcal septicemia, earlier administration of antibiotics leads to an attenuated mediator response and improved outcome.[56]

Antiendotoxin strategies

Several approaches have been undertaken to block the action of endotoxin. Despite initial optimism, polyclonal as well as monoclonal antibodies against the endotoxin molecule have not met with clinical success.[57] Likewise, an engineered form of the endotoxin-binding substance BPI has not led to a breakthrough. In a randomized study in meningococcal sepsis, this molecule led to a nonsignificant trend towards lower mortality and fewer amputations of affected limbs.[58] A major problem with this study, however, was that the time needed for enrolment of patients led to important delay and to a selection of less severe patients in the trial.[59] Further studies are needed to establish whether early administration of BPI may be beneficial. This points to a key problem with all available interventions, i.e. the timing of the intervention, given the rapidity of evolvement of sepsis.

There are three additional major problems with the antiendotoxin approach. One is that it is impossible in most cases to tell, at the bedside, whether endotoxin plays a role in the clinical illness, i.e. whether the patient has a Gram-negative infection. Fulminant meningococcal sepsis, with its characteristic clinical picture, may be an exception. The second problem is that endotoxin is not the only pathogenetic factor in Gram-negative sepsis; other components of Gram-negative bacilli are also involved. The third problem is that not all endotoxins are equal; for instance, meningococcal LPS is poorly neutralized by substances that do neutralize other endotoxin species, such as polymyxin B and reconstituted high-density lipoprotein.[60]

A subsequent target for treatment may be the site where microbial components interact with host cells. Recently, a new class of recognition molecules has been identified on cells of the host, the toll-like receptors (TLR). These TLR, of which so far at least 10 have been

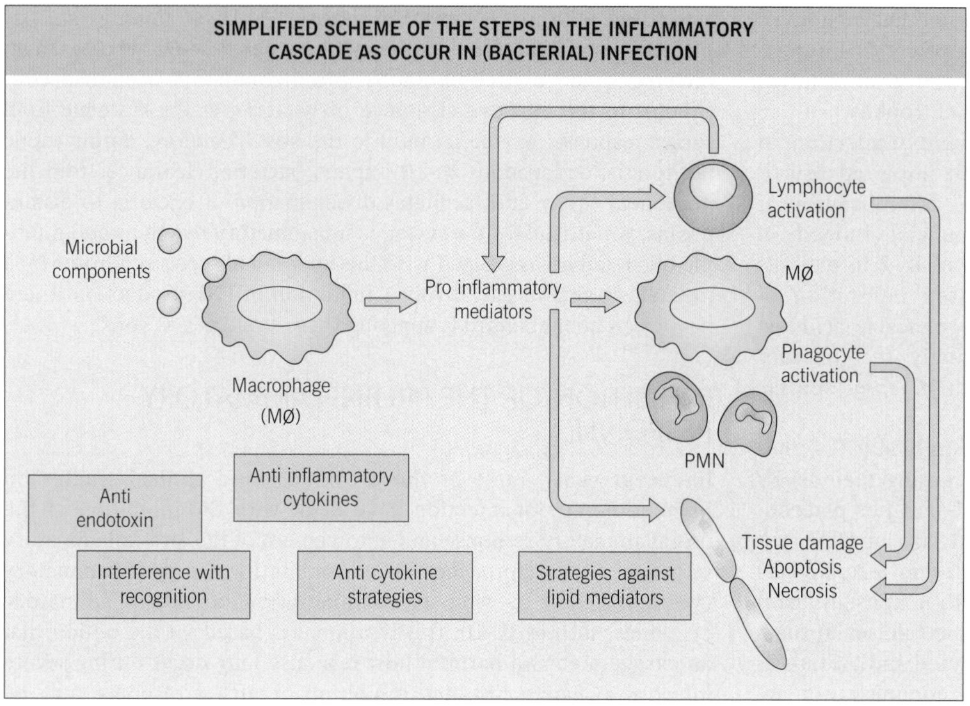

Fig. 210.1 Simplified scheme of the steps in the inflammatory cascade as occur in (bacterial) infection. The block arrows indicate sites of intervention.

identified, recognize an array of components of different micro-organisms.[61] One could envisage clinical interference at this level, but tools to do so are not yet available.

Strategies to block proinflammatory cytokines

Based on pioneering work with anti-TNF antibodies in experimental animals challenged with either high-dose bacterial endotoxin or live bacteria, in which impressive reductions of mortality were demonstrated, a series of clinical trials have been performed in sepsis. The anti-TNF strategies in these studies consisted of either murine or humanized monoclonal antibodies against TNF (which only interfere with TNF-α and not with TNF-β) or a engineered soluble TNF receptor construct (interfering with both types of TNF). None of these studies has met with consistent clinical benefit.[62] Similarly, interference with the actions of IL-1α and β in sepsis by administration of IL-1ra has been disappointing in a large placebo-controlled trial.[63] There are various explanations for the discrepancy between the results in experimental animals and those in patients. A major explanation is that many of the animal models are not realistic in terms of challenges, timing of microbial challenge and intervention, and endpoints. A second explanation is that the magnitude and the duration of the biological effects of the cytokine intervention had not been studied adequately before the large trials were started.

A third explanation is that the entry criteria in the human studies were too imprecise; based on the idea that sepsis syndrome had a homogeneous mediator response, heterogeneous patients fullfilling the broad entry criteria for sepsis syndrome were enrolled. Another issue is the required endpoint of 28-day mortality; given the complicated course of many very sick and frail patients in the intensive care unit, it is naïve to assume that a short initial intervention will still pay off 4 weeks later. Furthermore, the concept of blocking one cytokine may be too simple, in view of the redundancy within the cytokine network. It is, however, controversial whether blocking more than one cytokine at a time is beneficial.

Finally, the idea that proinflammatory cytokines are only deleterious in sepsis is also an oversimplification. In fact, in the clinical settings in which these anticytokine strategies are effective (rheumatoid arthritis and Crohn's disease), it gradually has become apparent that these treatments enhance the risk for infection. The infections that are seen are not only those caused by facultative intracellular micro-organisms (such as mycobacteria and salmonella), but also by other pathogens.[64,65] Given the capacity of the various proinflammatory cytokines to activate neutrophils for killing micro-organisms, it is likely that the host defense against common ('extracellular') bacteria (staphylococci, Gram-negative bacilli) is also hampered.

In terms of inhibiting the proinflammatory cytokine response, G-CSF is an interesting molecule. It does not only stimulate proliferation of neutrophils, activate them and inhibit their apoptotic response (as discussed above), but also downregulates the proinflammatory cytokine response. For instance, in human volunteers challenged with LPS, G-CSF pretreatment prevents neutrophil accumulation in the lung.[66] This dual action of G-CSF is not unique and other cytokines, such as IL-6, IL-10 and IFN-γ, exhibit pro- and anti-inflammatory effects and even IL-1 has been shown to inhibit TNF production and the expression of cytokine receptors *in vivo*.[67] One way to inhibit cytokine action is to limit their production. This can be done by administration of anti-inflammatory cytokines (such as IL-10, IL-4 and TGF-β) or by giving glucocorticosteroids. IL-10 has been evaluated as a new adjuvant therapy for several inflammatory diseases.[68] Treatment of Crohn's disease with IL-10 has been found to be associated with a bell-shaped dose–response curve.[69] However, although IL-10 is considered a potent anti-inflammatory cytokine, recent studies have suggested that it also possesses immunostimulatory effects.[70] At a low dose, IL-10 has induced clinical remissions but at higher dose, the beneficial effects are lost. It is hypothesized that these effects may be due to a proinflammatory effect of high-dose IL-10, and this potential IFN-γ enhancing effect may especially warrant caution for the use of recombinant IL-10 therapy for Th1-mediated illnesses such as Crohn's disease and rheumatoid arthritis.

Glucocorticosteroids

Glucocorticosteroids have several immunomodulatory effects: not only do they inhibit the production of proinflammatory cytokines, they also inhibit the function of phagocyte and T cells. Two landmark studies demonstrated the ineffectiveness of high dosages of glucocorticosteroids in sepsis.[71,72] There is, however, a renewed interest in the use of these drugs in sepsis, albeit in lower dosages, based on the concept that septic shock may be complicated by an

Table 210.2 Uses of systemic glucocorticosteroids in the treatment of infection. (Adapted from McGowan *et al*.[74])

USES OF SYSTEMIC GLUCOCORTICOSTEROIDS IN THE TREATMENT OF INFECTION		
Infection	**Strength of recommendation#**	**Evidence‡**
Gram-negative sepsis with shock	B	I
Typhoid fever (critical illness)	A	I
Tetanus	B	I
Tuberculous pericarditis	A	I
Tuberculous meningitis	B	II
EBV infection with impending airway obstruction	B	II
Bacterial meningitis (children, *Haemophilus influenzae*)	B	I
Pneumocystis carinii pneumonia with hypoxia	A	I
Acute severe laryngotracheobronchitis (requiring hospitalization)	B	I
Allergic bronchopulmonary aspergillosis	B	II
Chronic effusion after otitis media	B	I

\# A, good evidence to support the recommendation for use; B, moderate evidence to support a recommendation for use. The categories C (poor evidence for or against use), D (moderate evidence against use) and E (good evidence against use) have been excluded from the table.
‡ I, evidence from at least one properly randomized controlled trial; II, means evidence from at least one well-designed clinical trial without randomization, from cohort or case-controlled analytic studies, preferably from more than one center, from multiple time-series studies or from dramatic results in uncontrolled experiments.

occult adrenal insufficiency. In a randomized controlled trial in France, the efficacy of this approach has been demonstrated.[73] Glucocorticosteroids have a wider application as immunomodulators in infectious diseases. In Table 210.2 these applications are listed with the strength of the evidence for their use as put forward by the Infectious Diseases Society of America.[74]

The use of glucocorticosteroids has met with side effects that relate to their glucocorticoid, mineralocorticoid and anti-inflammatory effects. The latter are important within the context of this chapter. Their inhibition of influx and function of phagocytic cells (granulocytes and mononuclear phagocytes) enhances the susceptibility to bacterial and fungal infection, while the interference, T-cell distribution and function increase the risk for infection caused by facultative intracellular micro-organisms (such as mycobacteria, *Salmonella* spp. and cryptococci) and viruses (such as cytomegalovirus). Their effect on cytokine production probably impairs both phagocyte and T-cell defense. The degree to which these side-effects occur relates to dose and duration, as has become clear from a meta-analysis of controlled trials of glucocorticosteroid treatment[75] (Fig. 210.2).

Other non-specific inhibitors of inflammation

Macrolides are also able to inhibit the proinflammatory cytokine responses and probably have other anti-inflammatory actions. Although not studied in a randomized controlled fashion, their effect on survival in diffuse panbronchiolitis, a pulmonary disease that occurs in East Asia, points to a potent anti-inflammatory effect.[76] These findings are sustained by animal experiments with macrolides in which bronchial inflammation is modulated.[76]

Since many of the deleterious effects of proinflammatory cytokines are mediated by lipid mediators, such as platelet-activating factor (PAF) and prostaglandins, inhibitors for these secondary mediators have also been studied in sepsis. Controlled trials with PAF antagonists did not change overall mortality of septic shock.[77–80] Likewise, the prostaglandin inhibitor ibuprofen did not prevent the development of shock or the acute respiratory distress syndrome and did not improve survival.[81] An explanation may be that prostaglandin inhibitors tend to increase the production of the proinflammatory cytokines.[82]

Supplementation with fish oil preparations, a source of n-3 polyunsaturated fatty acids, modulates proinflammatory cytokine production and prostaglandin synthesis.[83] Although impressive effects have been found in lethally infected experimental animals, the effects in humans with infections have not been well established.[84] The effects of these supplements seem to differ in different species (humans vs mice).

INCIDENCE OF INFECTION ASSOCIATED WITH GLUCOCORTICOSTEROID USE

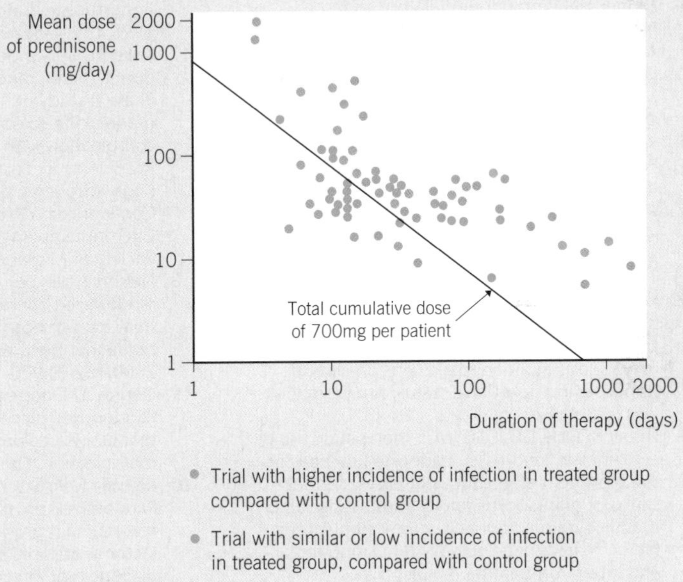

Fig. 210.2 Incidence of infection associated with glucocorticosteroid use. In this meta-analysis of 71 placebo-controlled trials of prednisone, all trials in which there was a higher incidence of infection in the treated group (compared with the controls) were located above the isodose line of 700mg. This indicates that, independent of the regimen used in the trial, patients who had a cumulative dose of less than 700mg did not have an increased risk of infectious complications. (With permission from Stuck *et al.*[75])

Intravenous immunoglobulins have been shown to possess anti-inflammatory properties. Although they induce proinflammatory cytokines shortly after infusion their major effect is a downregulation of the inflammatory response, e.g. through induction of IL-1ra and soluble cytokine receptors.[85] So far these complex effects of immunoglobulins have not been used therapeutically in the treatment of infection.

Activated recombinant protein C

Recently, activated protein C as a recombinant product has been investigated as a therapeutic agent in sepsis. Treatment with this product, which has antithrombotic, anti-inflammatory and profibrinolytic properties, was associated with an absolute reduction in the risk of death of 6% in patients with severe sepsis.[81] Further studies are needed to determine the exact indications for this expensive mode of treatment. In addition, the safety in septic patients with severe disseminated intravascular coagulation (such as occurs in fulminant meningococcal sepsis) has to be determined.

CONCLUSION

Despite elegant theoretical concepts and promising preclinical studies, the immunomodulatory adjunctive therapies in the field of infectious diseases have not come to fruition. Although a range of promising molecules is available, we have not yet been able to either discern the niche for them or apply them properly in terms of time and dosage. Another obstacle is that most of the immunomodulatory agents are expensive and hence not available for investigation in developing countries, where infections that are good candidates for immunomodulation (e.g. tuberculosis, leprosy, trypanosomiasis, leishmaniasis, typhoid fever) are prevalent.

REFERENCES

1. Hack CE, Zeerleder S. The endothelium in sepsis: source of and a target for inflammation. Crit Care Med 2001;29(suppl 7):S21–7.
2. Weiss SJ. Tissue destruction by neutrophils. N Engl J Med 1989;320(6):365–76.
3. Thompson KA, Strayer DR, Salvato PD, *et al.* Results of a double-blind placebo-controlled study of the double-stranded RNA drug polyI:polyC12U in the treatment of HIV infection. Eur J Clin Microbiol Infect Dis 1996;15(7):580–7.
4. Sauder DN. Immunomodulatory and pharmacologic properties of imiquimod. J Am Acad Dermatol 2000;43(1 Pt 2):S6–11.
5. Fourie PB, Ellner JJ, Johnson JL. Whither Mycobacterium vaccae – encore. Lancet 2002;360:1032–3.
6. van der Meer JW, Vogels MT, Netea MG, *et al.* Proinflammatory cytokines and treatment of disease. Ann N Y Acad Sci 1998;856:243–51.
7. Thomas MZ, Medoff G, Kobayashi GS. Changes in murine resistance to Listeria monocytogenes infection induced by amphotericin B. J Infect Dis 1973;127(4):373–7.
8. Karyadi E, West CE, Schultink W, *et al.* A double-blind, placebo-controlled study of vitamin A and zinc supplementation in persons with tuberculosis in Indonesia: effects on clinical response and nutritional status. Am J Clin Nutr 2002;75(4):720–7.
9. Hubel K, Dale DC, Liles WC. Therapeutic use of cytokines to modulate phagocyte function for the treatment of infectious diseases: current status of granulocyte colony-stimulating factor, granulocyte-macrophage colony-stimulating factor, macrophage colony-stimulating factor, and interferon-gamma. J Infect Dis 2002;185(10):1490–501.
10. Dale DC, Bonilla MA, Davis MW, *et al.* A randomized controlled phase III trial of recombinant human granulocyte colony-stimulating factor (filgrastim) for treatment of severe chronic neutropenia. Blood 1993;81(10):2496–502.
11. Jones EA, Bolyard A, Dale DC. Quality of life of patients with severe chronic neutropenia receiving long-term treatment with granulocyte colony-stimulating factor. JAMA 1993;270(9):1132–3.
12. Crawford J, Ozer H, Stoller R, *et al.* Reduction by granulocyte colony-stimulating factor of fever and neutropenia induced by chemotherapy in patients with small-cell lung cancer. N Engl J Med 1991;325(3):164–70.
13. Maher DW, Lieschke GJ, Green M, *et al.* Filgrastim in patients with chemotherapy-induced febrile neutropenia. A double-blind, placebo-controlled trial. Ann Intern Med 1994;121(7):492–501.
14. Rowe JM, Andersen JW, Mazza JJ, *et al.* A randomized placebo-controlled phase III study of granulocyte-macrophage colony-stimulating factor in adult patients (>55 to 70 years of age) with acute myelogenous leukemia: a study of the Eastern Cooperative Oncology Group (E1490). Blood 1995;86(2):457–62.
15. Kullberg BJ, Netea MG, Curfs JH, *et al.* Recombinant murine granulocyte colony-stimulating factor protects against acute disseminated Candida albicans infection in non-neutropenic mice. J Infect Dis 1998;177(1):175–81.
16. Kullberg BJ, Anaissie EJ. Cytokines as therapy for opportunistic fungal infections. Res Immunol 1998;149(4–5):478–88; discussion 515.
17. Kullberg BJ, Vandewoude K, Herbrecht R, *et al.* A double-blind, randomized, placebo-controlled Phase II study of filgrastim (recombinant granulocyte colony-stimulating factor) in combination with fluconazole for treatment of invasive candidiasis and candidemia in nonneutropenic patients. 38th Interscience Conference on Antimicrobial Agents and Chemotherapy. Washington DC: American Society of Microbiology; 1998.
18. Nelson S, Heyder AM, Stone J, *et al.* A randomized controlled trial of filgrastim for the treatment of hospitalized patients with multilobar pneumonia. J Infect Dis 2000;182(3):970–3.
19. Gough A, Clapperton M, Rolando N, *et al.* Randomised placebo-controlled trial of granulocyte-colony stimulating factor in diabetic foot infection. Lancet 1997;350(9081):855–9.
20. de Lalla F, Pellizzer G, Strazzabosco M, *et al.* Randomized prospective controlled trial of recombinant granulocyte colony-stimulating factor as adjunctive therapy for limb-threatening diabetic foot infection. Antimicrob Agents Chemother 2001;45(4):1094–8.
21. Yonem A, Cakir B, Guler S, *et al.* Effects of granulocyte-colony stimulating factor in the treatment of diabetic foot infection. Diabetes Obes Metab 2001;3(5):332–7.
22. van Agthoven M, Fokkens WJ, Van de Merwe JP, *et al.* Quality of life of patients with refractory chronic rhinosinusitis: effects of filgrastim treatment. Am J Rhinol 2001;15(4):231–7.
23. Freireich EJ, Levin RH, Wang J. The function and fate of transfused leukocytes from donors with chronic myelocytic leukemia in leukopenic patients. Ann NY Acad Sci 1964;113:1081–9.
24. Bensinger WI, Price TH, Dale DC, *et al.* The effects of daily recombinant human granulocyte colony-stimulating factor administration on normal granulocyte donors undergoing leukapheresis. Blood 1993;81(7):1883–8.
25. Dignani MC, Anaissie EJ, Hester JP, *et al.* Treatment of neutropenia-related fungal infections with granulocyte colony-stimulating factor-elicited white blood cell transfusions: a pilot study. Leukemia 1997;11(10):1621–30.
26. Ozsahin H, Muller I, Steinert HC, *et al.* Successful treatment of invasive aspergillosis in chronic granulomatous disease by bone marrow transplantation, granulocyte colony-stimulating factor-mobilized granulocytes, and liposomal amphotericin-B. Blood 1998; 92(8):2719–24.
27. Bielorai B, Wolach B, Mandel M, *et al.* Successful treatment of invasive aspergillosis in chronic granulomatous disease by granulocyte transfusions followed by peripheral blood stem cell transplantation. Bone Marrow Transplant 2000;26:1025–8.
28. Holland SM. Cytokine therapy of mycobacterial infections. Adv Intern Med 2000;45:431–52.
29. Badaro R, Nascimento C, Carvalho JS, *et al.* Recombinant human granulocyte-macrophage colony-stimulating factor reverses neutropenia and reduces secondary infections in visceral leishmaniasis. J Infect Dis 1994;170(2):413–8.
30. The International Chronic Granulomatous Disease Cooperative Study Group. A controlled trial of interferon gamma to prevent infection in chronic granulomatous disease. N Engl J Med 1991;324(8):509–16.
31. Nathan CF, Kaplan G, Levis WR, *et al.* Local and systemic effects of intradermal recombinant interferon-gamma in patients with lepromatous leprosy. N Engl J Med 1986;315(1):6–15.
32. Kaplan G, Mathur NK, Job CK, *et al.* Effect of multiple interferon gamma injections on the disposal of Mycobacterium leprae. Proc Natl Acad Sci USA 1989;86(20):8073–7.
33. Holland SM, Eisenstein EM, Kuhns DB, *et al.* Treatment of refractory disseminated nontuberculous mycobacterial infection with interferon gamma. A preliminary report. N Engl J Med 1994;330(19):1348–55.
34. Chatte G, Panteix G, Perrin-Fayolle M, *et al.* Aerosolized interferon gamma for Mycobacterium avium-complex lung disease. Am J Respir Crit Care Med 1995;152(3):1094–6.
35. Sundar S, Singh VP, Sharma S, *et al.* Response to interferon-gamma plus pentavalent antimony in Indian visceral leishmaniasis. J Infect Dis 1997;176(4):1117–9.
36. Riddell IA, Pinching AJ, Hill S, *et al.* A phase III study of recombinant human interferon gamma to prevent opportunistic infections in advanced HIV disease. AIDS Res Hum Retroviruses 2001;17(9):789–97.
37. Kullberg BJ, Van't Wout JW, Hoogstraten C, *et al.* Recombinant interferon-γ enhances resistance to acute disseminated Candida albicans infection in mice. J Infect Dis 1993;168(2):436–43.
38. Tewari A, Buhles Jr WC, Starnes Jr HF. Preliminary report: effects of interleukin-1 on platelet counts. Lancet 1990;336:712–14.
39. Rinehart J, Hersh E, Issell B, *et al.* Phase 1 trial of recombinant human interleukin-1 beta (rhIL-1 beta), carboplatin, and etoposide in patients with solid cancers: Southwest Oncology, Group Study 8940. Cancer Invest 1997;15(5):403–10.
40. Gershanovich ML, Filatova LV, Ketlinsky SA, *et al.* Recombinant human interleukin-1 beta: new possibilities for the prophylaxis and correction of

toxic myelodepression in patients with malignant tumors. I. Phase I-II clinical trials of recombinant human interleukin-1 beta as a leukopoiesis stimulator in cancer patients receiving combination chemotherapy. Eur Cytokine Netw 2001;12(4):664–70.

41. Kaplan G, Britton WJ, Hancock GE. The systemic influence of recombinant interleukin-2 on the manifestations of lepromatous leprosy. J Exp Med 1991;173:993–1006.
42. Villahermosa LG, Abalos RM, Walsh DS, *et al.* Recombinant interleukin-2 in lepromatous leprosy lesions: immunological and microbiological consequences. Clin Exp Dermatol 1997;22(3):134–40.
43. de Jong R, Janson AA, Faber WR, *et al.* IL-2 and IL-12 act in synergy to overcome antigen-specific T cell unresponsiveness in mycobacterial disease. J Immunol 1997;159(2):786–93.
44. Kovacs JA, Vogel S, Albert JM, *et al.* Controlled trial of interleukin-2 infusions in patients infected with the human immunodeficiency virus. N Engl J Med 1996;335(18):1350–6.
45. Emery S, Capra WB, Cooper DA, *et al.* Pooled analysis of 3 randomized, controlled trials of interleukin-2 therapy in adult human immunodeficiency virus type 1 disease. J Infect Dis 2000;182(2):428–34.
46. Connors M, Kovacs JA, Krevat S, *et al.* HIV infection induces changes in CD4+ T-cell phenotype and depletions within the CD4+ T-cell repertoire that are not immediately restored by antiviral or immune-based therapies. Nat Med 1997;3(5):533–40.
47. Chun TW, Engel D, Mizell SB, *et al.* Effect of interleukin-2 on the pool of latently infected, resting CD4+ T cells in HIV-1-infected patients receiving highly active anti-retroviral therapy. Nat Med 1999;5(6):651–5.
48. Tambussi G, Ghezzi S, Nozza S, *et al.* Efficacy of low-dose intermittent subcutaneous interleukin (IL)–2 in antiviral drug–experienced human immunodeficiency virus–infected persons with detectable virus load: a controlled study of 3 il-2 regimens with antiviral drug therapy. J Infect Dis 2001;183(10):1476–84.
49. Marchant A, Bruyns C, Vandenabeele P, *et al.* Interleukin-10 production during septicaemia. Lancet 1994;343:707–8.
50. Standiford TJ, Strieter RM, Lukacs NW, *et al.* Neutralization of IL-10 increases lethality in endotoxemia. Cooperative effects of macrophage inflammatory protein-2 and tumor necrosis factor. J Immunol 1995;155(4):2222–9.
51. Van der Poll T, Marchant A, Keogh CV, *et al.* Interleukin-10 impairs host defense in murine pneumococcal pneumonia. J Infect Dis 1996;174:994–1000.
52. van der Poll T, Marchant A, Buurman WA, *et al.* Endogenous IL-10 protects mice from death during septic peritonitis. J Immunol 1995;155(11):5397–401.
53. Sewnath ME, Olszyna DP, Birjmohun R, *et al.* IL-10-deficient mice demonstrate multiple organ failure and increased mortality during Escherichia coli peritonitis despite an accelerated bacterial clearance. J Immunol 2001;166(10):6323–31.
54. Dofferhoff AS, Esselink MT, de Vries-Hospers HG, *et al.* The release of endotoxin from antibiotic-treated Escherichia coli and the production of tumour necrosis factor by human monocytes. J Antimicrob Chemother 1993;31(3):373–84.
55. Holzheimer RG. Antibiotic induced endotoxin release and clinical sepsis: a review. J Chemother 2001;13(1):159–72.
56. van Deuren M, Brandtzaeg P, van der Meer JW. Update on meningococcal disease with emphasis on pathogenesis and clinical management. Clin Microbiol Rev 2000;13(1):144–66.
57. Bone RC. Why sepsis trials fail. JAMA 1996;276(7):565–6.
58. Levin M, Quint PA, Goldstein B, *et al.* Recombinant bactericidal/permeability-increasing protein (rBPI21) as adjunctive treatment for children with severe meningococcal sepsis: a randomised trial. rBPI21 Meningococcal Sepsis Study Group. Lancet 2000;356(9234):961–7.
59. van Deuren M, Brandtzaeg P. Parents' and GPs' key role in diagnosis of meningococcal septicaemia. Lancet 2000;356(9234):954–5.
60. Netea MG, Van Deuren M, Kullberg BJ, *et al.* Does the shape of lipid A determine the interaction of LPS with Toll-like receptors? Trends Immunol 2002;23(3):135–9.
61. Beutler B. Toll-like receptors: how they work and what they do. Curr Opin Hematol 2002;9(1):2–10.
62. Cohen J, Guyatt G, Bernard GR, *et al.* New strategies for clinical trials in patients with sepsis and septic shock. Crit Care Med 2001;29(4):880–6.
63. Opal SM, Fisher CJ Jr, Dhainaut JF, *et al.* Confirmatory interleukin-1 receptor antagonist trial in severe sepsis: a phase III, randomized, double-blind, placebo-controlled, multicenter trial. Crit Care Med 1997;25(7):1115–24.
64. Keane J, Gershon S, Wise RP, *et al.* Tuberculosis associated with infliximab, a tumor necrosis factor alpha-neutralizing agent. N Engl J Med 2001;345(15):1098–104.
65. Weisman MH. What are the risks of biologic therapy in rheumatoid arthritis? An update on safety. J Rheumatol 2002;65(suppl):33–8.
66. Pajkrt D, Manten A, van der Poll T, *et al.* Modulation of cytokine release and neutrophil function by granulocyte colony-stimulating factor during endotoxemia in humans. Blood 1997;90(4):1415–24.
67. Vogels MT, Mensink EJ, Ye K, *et al.* Differential gene expression for IL-1 receptor antagonist, IL-1, and TNF receptors and IL-1 and TNF synthesis may explain IL-1 induced resistance to infection. J Immunol 1994;153(12):5772–80.
68. van Deventer SJ, Elson CO, Fedorak RN. Multiple doses of intravenous interleukin 10 in steroid-refractory Crohn's disease. Crohn's Disease Study Group. Gastroenterology 1997;113(2):383–9.
69. Fedorak RN, Gangl A, Elson CO, *et al.* Recombinant human interleukin 10 in the treatment of patients with mild to moderately active Crohn's disease. Gastroenterology 2000;119(6):1473–82.
70. Lauw FN, Pajkrt D, Hack CE, *et al.* Proinflammatory effects of IL-10 during human endotoxemia. J Immunol 2000;165(5):2783–9.
71. Bone RC, Fisher CJ Jr, Clemmer TP, *et al.* A controlled clinical trial of high-dose methylprednisolone in the treatment of severe sepsis and septic shock. N Engl J Med 1987;317(11):653–8.
72. Veterans Administration Systemic Sepsis Cooperative Study Group, Effect of high-dose glucocorticoid therapy on mortality in patients with clinical signs of systemic sepsis. N Engl J Med 1987;317(11):659–65.
73. Annane D, Sebille V, Charpentier C, *et al.* Effect of treatment with low doses of hydrocortisone and fludrocortisone on mortality in patients with septic shock. JAMA 2002;288(7):862–71.
74. McGowan JE Jr, Chesney PJ, Crossley KB, *et al.* Guidelines for the use of systemic glucocorticosteroids in the management of selected infections. Working Group on Steroid Use, Antimicrobial Agents Committee, Infectious Diseases Society of America. J Infect Dis 1992;165(1):1–13.
75. Stuck AE, Minder CE, Frey FJ. Risk of infectious complications in patients taking glucocorticosteroids. Rev Infect Dis 1989;11(6):954–63.
76. Rubin BK, Tamaoki J. Macrolide antibiotics as biological response modifiers. Curr Opin Investig Drugs 2000;1(2):169–72.
77. Dhainaut JF, Tenaillon A, Hemmer M, *et al.* Confirmatory platelet-activating factor receptor antagonist trial in patients with severe gram-negative bacterial sepsis: a phase III, randomized, double-blind, placebo-controlled, multicenter trial. BN 52021 Sepsis Investigator Group. Crit Care Med 1998;26(12):1963–71.
78. Poeze M, Froon AH, Ramsay G, *et al.* Decreased organ failure in patients with severe SIRS and septic shock treated with the platelet-activating factor antagonist TCV-309: a prospective, multicenter, double-blind, randomized phase II trial. TCV-309 Septic Shock Study Group. Shock 2000;14(4):421–8.
79. Suputtamongko Y, Intaranongpai S, Smith MD, *et al.* A double-blind placebo-controlled study of an infusion of lexipafant (platelet-activating factor receptor antagonist) in patients with severe sepsis. Antimicrob Agents Chemother 2000;44(3):693–6.
80. Vincent JL, Spapen H, Bakker J, *et al.* Phase II multicenter clinical study of the platelet-activating factor receptor antagonist BB-882 in the treatment of sepsis. Crit Care Med 2000;28(3):638–42.
81. Bernard GR, Vincent JL, Laterre PF, *et al.* Efficacy and safety of recombinant human activated protein C for severe sepsis. N Engl J Med 2001;344(10):699–709.
82. Endres S, Cannon JG, Ghorbani R, *et al.* *In vitro* production of IL 1 beta, IL 1 alpha, TNF and IL2 in healthy subjects: distribution, effect of cyclooxygenase inhibition and evidence of independent gene regulation. Eur J Immunol 1989;19(12):2327–33.
83. Endres S, Ghorbani R, Kelley VE, *et al.* The effect of dietary supplementation with n-3 polyunsaturated fatty acids on the synthesis of interleukin-1 and tumor necrosis factor by mononuclear cells. N Engl J Med 1989;320(5):265–71.
84. Blok WL, Katan MB, van der Meer JW. Modulation of inflammation and cytokine production by dietary (n-3) fatty acids. J Nutr 1996;126(6):1515–33.
85. Aukrust P, Froland SS, Liabakk NB, *et al.* Release of cytokines, soluble cytokine receptors, and interleukin-1 receptor antagonist after intravenous immunoglobulin administration in vivo. Blood 1994;84(7):2136–43.

SECTION

8

CLINICAL MICROBIOLOGY

Timothy E Kiehn
Jan Verhoef

chapter

211 Acute Gastroenteritis Viruses

Rodolfo E Bégué & Arturo S Gastañaduy

Acute gastroenteritis constitutes a major cause of morbidity and mortality worldwide (Table 211.1). Infants and young children sustain on average 3–10 episodes per year compared with less than one episode per year for those older than 5 years. In the developing world this represents more than 1000 million cases and 3–4 million deaths every year.[3] These deaths are caused mainly by dehydration, but malnutrition also plays an important role. It has been estimated that 25% of the growth difference between children in developing countries and those in the USA is related to diarrhea. In developed countries, morbidity and mortality caused by diarrheal diseases have declined as economics and sanitation have improved, but 38 million cases still occur annually in the USA, with 2–3.7 million physician visits, 220,000 hospitalizations, 325–425 deaths and at a cost of US$23 billion.[4]

APPROACH TO MANAGEMENT

The goals of management of acute gastroenteritis are prevention and treatment of the two major complications – dehydration and malnutrition (Table 211.2). Children with no or only minimal dehydration can be managed with increased fluid intake and continuation of feeding. Those who have mild or moderate dehydration should receive an oral rehydration solution (ORS). In a few cases (<5%) oral rehydration might not be appropriate and intravenous rehydration should be used instead, for example in patients with severe dehydration, intractable vomiting, high stool output or monosaccharide malabsorption. Traditional ORSs are effective in preventing and treating dehydration, but do not reduce the stool output or duration of the diarrhea. Although cereal-based ORSs do reduce the stool output and duration of the diarrhea, these advantages become clinically insignificant when glucose-based ORSs are combined with appropriate nutritional management. Supplementing ORS with probiotics (*Lactobacillus* GG), oligoelements (zinc) or others (acetorphan) might reduce duration of diarrhea by 24–48 hours; their clinical and public health impact is uncertain at this point, though.

There is no reason not to feed children who have gastroenteritis. Full-strength feedings initiated immediately after rehydration improve the weight gain of the children and do not contribute to the severity or duration of the diarrhea compared with diluted or delayed feeding. Despite lactose malabsorption developing frequently during diarrhea, most children can still be fed their usual lactose-containing formulas in small frequent feeds. Human milk has a high lactose content; however, it reduces stool output and hence should be maintained. Milk–cereal and cereal–legume combinations are also safe and efficacious for the nutritional management of diarrhea.

APPROACH TO PREVENTION

The agents of acute gastroenteritis are transmitted by the fecal–oral route, through either direct person-to-person contact or contaminated food or water. The former is more important for the endemic pattern of disease and the latter for outbreaks. Handwashing and hygienic measures prevent person-to-person spread. However, because these measures are difficult to enforce in small children, endemic transmission of the disease continues, even in developed countries. For outbreaks, environmental control (food, water and sanitation) is important and effective. Good handwashing (especially among food handlers), furloughing of ill personnel, thorough cooking of food and disinfection of water and surfaces should prevent or control most outbreaks. For hospitalized patients, enteric precautions (i.e. contact precautions for diapered or incontinent patients, and standard precautions otherwise) must be instituted and continued for at least 48 hours after the resolution of symptoms. Breast-feeding, through a variety of mechanisms, reduces the overall incidence of diarrhea, especially in developing countries. Unfortunately, this protective effect can be overridden by exposure to a heavy inoculum. Continuation of breast-feeding through the diarrhea episode should be encouraged. Probiotics (*Lactobacillus* GG) might confer a modest protective effect.

MORBIDITY AND MORTALITY OF DIARRHEAL DISEASES IN CHILDREN

	Developing countries			USA-Canada
	Snyder *et al.* (1982)[1]	Claeson & Merson (1990)[2]	Bern *et al.* (1992)[3]	Glass *et al.* (1991)[4]
No. of studies evaluated	24	276	22	4
Episodes/child/year (median)	2.2–3.0	3.3	2.6	1.3–2.5
Diarrheal illnesses/year (millions)	1000	1500	1000	21–37
No. of diarrheal deaths/year	4.6 million	4.0 million	3.3 million	325–425

Table 211.1 Morbidity and mortality rates of diarrheal diseases in children. Estimates from longitudinal, prospective, community-based studies in developing and developed countries.

GASTROENTERITIS: MANAGEMENT GUIDELINES				
		Degree of dehydration		
		None	Mild–moderate	Severe
Assessment	Weight loss (%)	<5	5–10	>10
	Fluid deficit (ml/kg)	<50	50–100	>100
Rehydration (usually accomplished during the first 4h of therapy)	Initial fluid	ORS	ORS	iv Ringer's or 0.9% NaCl
	Amount (ml/kg)	50	50–100	20ml/kg/h
Replacement	ORS 10ml/kg or 2–4oz for each diarrheal stool			
Maintenance	Feedings should start immediately after rehydration. Human milk, lactose-containing and lactose-free formulas; milk staple and solid foods in small frequent feeds are well tolerated by most patients, foster recovery and improve nutritional outcome			

Table 211.2 Management guidelines for gastroenteritis. The essential goals of therapy are prevention and treatment of the two major complications, dehydration and malnutrition. ORS, oral rehydration solution.

APPROACH TO DIAGNOSIS

An etiologic diagnosis is not necessary for the management of most cases of gastroenteritis. It might, however, be desirable for clinical, epidemiologic or research purposes. To identify patients that might benefit from a stool culture and antibiotic treatment, it is useful to classify the diarrhea as dysenteric or watery (Table 211.3). The distinction between these two syndromes is usually evident from the patient's history and inspection of the stool. If not, simple and inexpensive tests, such as the presence of occult blood in the stool and fecal leukocytes, should assist in the differentiation. Most diarrheal diseases that need antibiotics (e.g. shigellosis) belong to the dysenteric group, whereas viral gastroenteritis always manifests with watery diarrhea. Some bacterial pathogens can also produce watery diarrhea (e.g. enterotoxigenic *Escherichia coli* and *Salmonella* spp.), but they usually resolve spontaneously.

VIRAL AGENTS OF GASTROENTERITIS

The viruses associated with acute gastroenteritis and their morphologic and clinicoepidemiologic characteristics are shown in Tables 211.4 and 211.5. Rotaviruses (RVs) and enteric adenoviruses are large (70–80nm) and have distinct appearances. Astroviruses and caliciviruses (Noroviruses and Sapoviruses) are smaller (27–40nm) and possess well-defined surface structures. They used to be collectively referred to as small round structured viruses (SRSV). Somewhat smaller (20–26nm) viruses with smooth edge and no discernible surface structure were designated 'featureless viruses' or small round viruses (SRV). These agents resemble enterovirus or parvovirus, and some may be related to them. Rotaviruses and caliciviruses are the main agents of human viral gastroenteritis.

ACUTE INFECTIOUS DIARRHEA: CLINICAL SYNDROMES		
	Watery	Dysenteric
Stools		
Appearance	Watery	Bloody
Volume	Increased: ++ / +++	Increased: + /++
Number per day	<10	>10
Reducing substances	0 to +++	0
pH	5.0–7.5	6.0–7.5
Occult blood	Negative	Positive
Fecal polymorphonuclear cells	Absent or few	Many
Mechanisms		
Toxins	Yes	No
Reduced absorption	Yes	No
Mucosal invasion	No	Yes
Complications		
Dehydration	Could be severe	Mild
Others	Acidosis, shock, electrolyte imbalance	Tenesmus, rectal prolapse, seizures
Etiology (Examples)		
	Rotaviruses Enterotoxigenic *Escherichia coli* *Vibrio cholerae*	*Shigella spp* *Campylobacter spp* *Entamoeba histolytica*
+: mild; ++: moderate; +++: marked		

Table 211.3 Acute infectious diarrhea: clinical syndromes. Separating the cases of diarrhea into dysenteric or watery is helpful when deciding on the need for laboratory evaluation.

Dehydration or vomiting, especially if it precedes the diarrhea, suggests a viral etiology. However, there is considerable overlap in the clinical manifestations of different viruses and making an etiologic diagnosis requires complex and expensive techniques, unavailable in most clinical centers. Electron microscopy (EM) was originally used to identify all gastroenteritis viruses, and still remains the preferred screening technique, especially when investigating outbreaks. If viral particles are seen by EM, depending on their morphology, more specific tests might follow. Electron microscopy requires the presence of at least one million viral particles per ml of stool; hence, the specimen must be obtained early in the illness (first 2 days). Immunoelectron microscopy (IEM) enhances the sensitivity of EM by using virus-specific antiserum that clumps the particles and makes them easier to visualize.

Immunoassays (IAs) represent simple and rapid methods to detect viruses. Unfortunately, IAs are commercially available only for the

MORPHOLOGIC CHARACTERISTICS OF GASTROENTERITIS VIRUSES					
Characteristic	**Rotavirus**	**Enteric adenovirus**	**Astrovirus**	**Norovirus**	**Sapovirus**
Family	*Reovoridae*	*Adenoviridae*	*Astroviridae*	*Caliciviridae*	*Caliciviridae*
Virion size (nm)	70–75	70–80	27–32	27–35	27–40
Genome type	dsRNA	dsDNA	ssRNA	ssRNA	ssRNA
Morphology	Triple-shelled, wheel-like capsid, segmented RNA	Icosahedral shape, similar to other adenoviruses	Round, structured, unbroken surface, with pointed star	Round, structured, ragged surface	Round, structured, surface with cup-shaped indentations

Table 211.4 Morphologic characteristics of gastroenteritis viruses. ds, double-stranded; ss, single-stranded.

EPIDEMIOLOGIC AND CLINICAL CHARACTERISTICS OF GASTROENTERITIS VIRUSES					
Characteristic	Rotavirus	Enteric adenovirus	Astrovirus	Norovirus	Sapovirus
Age group	6–24 months	<2 years	<7 years	Adults and children	Children
Mode of transmission	Person-to-person, food, water	Person-to-person	Person-to-person, water, raw shellfish	Person-to-person, water, cold foods, raw shellfish	Person-to-person, water, cold foods, raw shellfish
Disease pattern	Endemic	Endemic	Endemic, outbreaks	Outbreaks, endemic	Endemic, outbreaks
Seasonality	Winter	No	Winter	No	No
Clinical characteristics	Dehydrating diarrhea; vomiting and fever very common	Prolonged diarrhea; vomiting and fever	Watery diarrhea, usually short	Acute vomiting, diarrhea, fever, myalgia, headache, usually short	Rotavirus-like illness in children
Prodrome (days)	2	3–10	1–2	1–2	1–3
Duration of illness (days)	3–8	>7	1–4	0.5–2.5	4
Outpatient prevalence (%)	5–10	4–8	7–8	10–25 endemic, 90 outbreaks	1–10
Inpatient prevalence (%)	35–40	5–20	3–5	Rare	3–5

Table 211.5 Epidemiologic and clinical characteristics of gastroenteritis viruses.

diagnosis of RVs and enteric adenoviruses. Recent cloning and expression of the viral genomes of most gastroenteritis viruses have made reagents more available for IAs to detect the other agents.

Viral culture is tedious but still an essential technique because it allows characterization of the viruses, study of their pathogenicity and the production of diagnostic reagents. Rotaviruses, adenoviruses and astroviruses can be cultured whereas caliciviruses cannot.

Reverse transcription polymerase chain reaction (RT-PCR) detects and amplifies genetic sequences specific to each pathogen, including unculturable ones. This technique has now been successfully applied to the detection of most gastroenteritis viruses. Other diagnostic tools are polyacrylamide gel electrophoresis (PAGE) and restriction endonuclease digestion, which can be used to identify RVs or enteric adenoviruses, respectively, on the basis of their characteristic electrophoretic pattern. Finally, dot blot hybridization with complementary DNA (cDNA) has been used to identify adenoviruses and astroviruses. For diagnostic purposes, stool specimens can be stored at 39.2°F (4°C) for 1 week; for longer storage they should be frozen at –70°C. For serologic diagnosis, acute and convalescent specimens are required. An overview of the procedures can be found elsewhere.[5]

ROTAVIRUSES

Identified by Bishop *et al.* in 1973,[6] human RVs have emerged as the main agent of acute gastroenteritis in infants and young children worldwide.

NATURE

Rotaviruses belong to the family Reoviridae. Intact virions measure 70–75nm with a triple-shelled capsid composed of an outer layer (outer capsid), an intermediate layer (inner capsid) and an inner layer (core). Sixty spike-like structures (capsomers) radiating from the inner to the outer capsid, give the virus its characteristic EM appearance (Fig. 211.1) and its name ('rota' is Latin for 'wheel'). Single-shelled particles (55nm) and cores (37nm) can also be seen. Of the three forms, only intact virions are infectious. The core encloses the viral genome, which consists of 11 segments of double-stranded RNA (dsRNA). Each segment encodes for at least one protein: six structural proteins (VP1, VP2, VP3, VP4, VP6 and VP7)

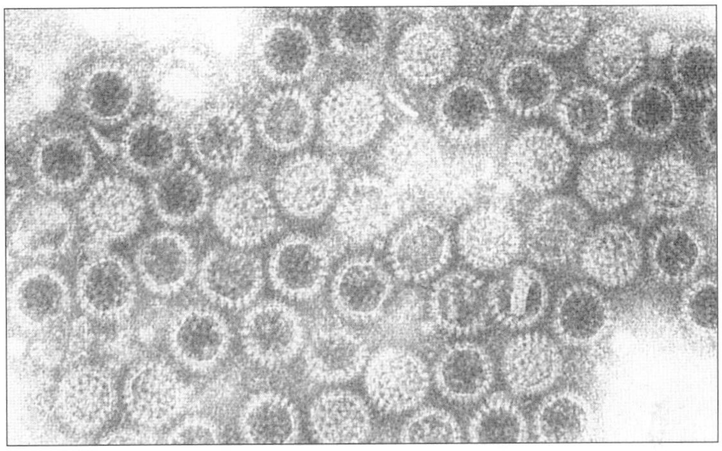

Fig. 211.1 Rotavirus. Electron micrograph. Courtesy of S Spangenberger.

which are present in the virion; and six nonstructural proteins (NSP1 through NSP6) which are identified only in the cytoplasm of infected cells (Table 211.6). The inner core is made of VP1, VP2 and VP3, with VP2 being the major constituent. VP6 is the only component of the inner capsid. The outer capsid shell is composed of two proteins: VP7 makes about 90% of the outer capsid and is perforated by 132 channels penetrating the virion and reaching the central core; VP4 forms the capsomers, which protrude from the virus surface, pass through VP7 and interact with VP6 (Fig. 211.2).

Based on antigenic specificities, RVs are classified in groups, subgroups and serotypes. Groups and subgroups are determined by VP6. To date seven groups (A–G) and two subgroups (I and II) have been described. Groups A, B and C can infect humans and animals, whereas groups D–G have been found only in animals. Most human infections are caused by group A RVs. Subgroup II is more frequent than subgroup I; however, significant geographic variations occur. The outer capsid proteins VP4 and VP7 determine the serotypes. Those defined by VP7, a glycoprotein, are called G serotypes and those defined by VP4, a protease sensitive protein, are called P serotypes. At least 14 G serotypes (G1–G14) have been described; G1–G4 produce most human infections; however, G8, G9 and G12 infections have also been recognized.[7,8] Thirteen VP4 serotypes (P1–P13)

ROTAVIRUSES' VIRAL PROTEINS			
Genome segment	**Protein product**	**Molecular weight**	**Function/property**
1	VP1	125,000	RNA polymerase
2	VP2	94,000	RNA binding
3	VP3	88,000	Guanylyltransferase, methyltransferase
4	VP4	88,000	Hemagglutinin, neutralization antigen, infectivity
	VP5* and VP8*	529 and 247	Cleavage products of VP4
5	NSP1	53,000	RNA binding
6	VP6	41,000	Subgroup antigen, protection?
7	NSP3	34,000	Binds viral mRNA, inhibits host translation
8	NSP2	35,000	RNA binding
9	VP7	38,000	Neutralization antigen, Ca^{2+} binding protection
10	NSP4	28,000	Enterotoxin, protection?
11	NSP5	26,000	RNA binding, protein kinase, interacts with NSP2 and NSP6
	NSP6	12,000	Interacts with NSP5

Table 211.6 Rotavirus genome segments and their corresponding viral proteins. VP, viral structural protein; NS, viral nonstructural protein. Modified from Estes 2001.[15]

ROTAVIRUS STRUCTURE

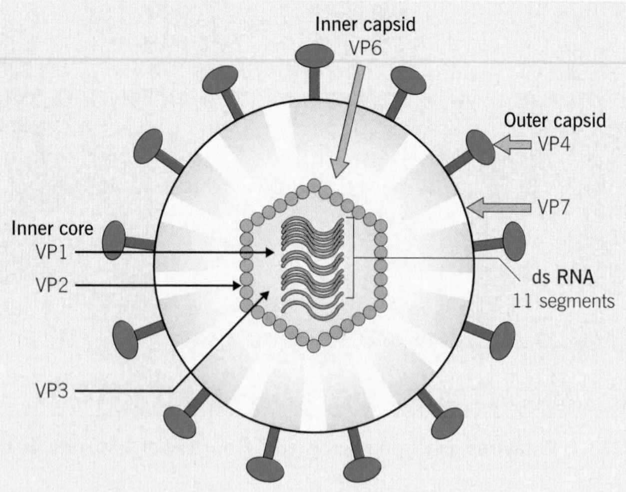

Fig. 211.2 Rotavirus structure. Inner core is made of VP1, VP2 and VP3; inner capsid is made of VP6; outer capsid is made of VP7 and VP4. Modified from Kapikian 2001.[9]

have been identified; P1, P2, and P5 include two distinct subtypes named: P1A, P1B; P2A, P2B; P5A, P5B.

Nucleic acid hybridization and sequence analysis of the VP4 and VP7 genes permit classification of RVs according to genotypes. There is full concordance between RVs VP7 serotypes and genotypes; thus, RVs classified by either method are simply designated as G1, G2, etc. On the other hand there is poor concordance between VP4 genotypes and VP4 serotypes. For example, 21 VP4 genotypes have been described, and five of them do not have a corresponding serotype; also, the assigned numbers for serotype and genotype classification are not the same. To integrate both classifications, proper designation uses the letter P followed by an open Arabic number to indicate the serotype, and a second Arabic number in brackets to indicate the genotype.[9] For example the human RV strain Wa is designated P1A[8].

EPIDEMIOLOGY

Rotaviruses are the most commonly identified viral enteropathogens among children. In the USA RVs cause 5–10% of all diarrheal episodes and 30–50% of severe diarrhea in children under 5 years of age, resulting in 3.5 million diarrhea cases, 55,000 hospitalizations, 20–40 deaths and a cost in excess of one billion dollars.[10] Worldwide estimates are 130 million episodes, 18 million moderate or severe cases and almost one million deaths annually. The proportion of diarrhea cases caused by RVs decreases from hospital to clinic to community populations, in developed and developing countries (38–89, 10–34 and 6–12%, and 20–46, 10–30 and 10–20%, respectively), reflecting the tendency of the virus to produce dehydration. Also, RVs account for a larger proportion of cases in developed countries than in developing ones (38–89 versus 20–46%, respectively) and in high-income groups than low-income ones (60 versus 4–30%, respectively).[7]

Rotavirus gastroenteritis is primarily a disease of infants and young children, with peak incidence rates at 6–24 months; it occurs at earlier ages in developing countries. Neonates and adults are affected infrequently unless they are exposed to infected children, in which case 11–70% can become infected. Outbreaks have been described in nursing homes for the elderly, hospital wards and military bases. Travelers' diarrhea is most commonly caused by enterotoxigenic *E. coli*, but RVs have been detected in as many as 20% of these cases. Asymptomatic shedding of RVs occurs in 10–15% of individuals.[7]

In temperate climates RVs appear in characteristic and predictable winter epidemics. In North America, the epidemic starts in Mexico and the southwestern USA in late fall, spreads in a northeast direction and ends in the northeastern USA and the Maritime provinces of Canada in the spring. The reasons for this spread pattern are not clear, but climate, virus characteristics or other factors may play a role.[11] In tropical climates RVs are endemic throughout the year, with some clustering in the cooler, drier months. Group A, serotype G1 strains are most commonly implicated in human disease (54%); other serotypes – G2 (18%), G3 (12%) and G4 (11%) are also seen. Circulating serotypes vary with geographic location and with time. Multiple serotypes can co-circulate during a specific year.[7] Group B RVs have been associated with epidemics of diarrhea among adults in China. Group C RVs have been identified in Central and South America, Europe, Australia and Asia.[7,12]

Pathogenicity

Person-to-person transmission through the fecal–oral route is the most likely mode of spread of RVs. Fecal excretion starts immediately before the onset of symptoms and lasts for 5–7 days. The large number of viral particles excreted in feces (approximately one trillion per ml) and the low infective dose (as few as ten RV particles in a child) favors patient-to-patient spread. Contamination of food and water has been implicated in some outbreaks, and fomites may play a role in settings such as day care centers and nurseries. Rotaviruses can survive for 60 days on environmental surfaces at different temperatures (39.2–68°F; 4–20°C) and humidities (50–90%).[13] Respiratory transmission has been suspected in two outbreaks and is supported by the way the annual RV epidemic spreads in North America. However, attempts to isolate RV from respiratory secretions have been mostly unsuccessful.

The virus preferentially infects the mature enterocytes in the villus epithelium of the small intestine. The infected cells change from columnar to cuboidal, with enlarged cisternae of the endoplasmic reticulum and fewer and shorter microvilli. The cells are eventually killed and sloughed off and, with denudation of the tip cells, the villi become shortened. Mononuclear leukocyte infiltration is minimal. These changes occur within 24 hours of infection, start proximally and progress caudally. The major mechanism of diarrhea during RV infections appears to be decreased absorption of salt and water secondary to enterocyte damage and replacement of absorptive intestinal cells by secreting cells from the crypts. Loss of disaccharidases at the damaged brush border results in carbohydrate malabsorption and osmotic diarrhea. The observation of RV diarrhea in the absence of epithelial lesions led to the discovery of a calcium-dependent signal by NSP4 that increases plasma membrane chloride permeability, leading to chloride secretion and secretory diarrhea early in the course of the illness. NSP4 is the first described viral enterotoxin. It is also postulated that RV induces intestinal fluid and electrolyte secretion by activation of the enteric nervous system.[14]

The factors that determine RV pathogenicity are not fully understood. Rotaviruses have tissue and cell-type specific tropism, suggesting the presence of receptors that mediate virus attachment or penetration. The identity of these receptors remain elusive, though. *N*-acetylneuraminic acid (sialic acid: SA) on the surface of the cells was thought to be required for virus binding; however, most RV strains are SA independent. GM1 gangliosides and cellular integrins have also been postulated as RV receptors. The VP4 spike protein mediates viral attachment to the target cells, and its cleavage into VP5* and VP8* by proteases like trypsin is essential for cell penetration. Cell penetration requires also VP7.

Two mechanisms of penetration have been proposed: direct membrane penetration and receptor-mediated endocytosis. Direct membrane penetration appears to be mediated by VP5*. Receptor-mediated endocytosis is supported by EM studies that show uptake of virus particles into coated pits, vesicles and lysosomes. Uncoating of the virus in the enterocytes is mediated by low Ca^{2+} concentrations in the cytoplasm. The next steps of RV replication have been extensively reviewed elsewhere.[15] Host factors, such as age, also influence the pathogenesis of RVs. For example symptoms are more prominent among young hosts. Although animal studies have shown that the quantity of RV-binding receptors on villus epithelial cells decreases with age, a more likely explanation for the age difference in the manifestations of the disease is the acquisition of immunity. Nutritional deficiencies, certain immunodeficiencies or co-infection with bacterial pathogens can increase the severity and duration of RV diarrhea; these situations frequently coexist in the developing world.

The mechanisms underlying immunity against RV infections and illness are not completely understood. Clinical protection may involve local (mucosal) and systemic (serum) antibodies as well as cellular immunity. Serum-neutralizing antibodies against the infecting serotype (homotypic) develop frequently and within 2 weeks of infection. Heterotypic responses (antibodies against different serotypes) also occur, but mostly among adults and vary with the infecting strain; for example G2 produces mainly homotypic antibodies, whereas G1, G3 and G4 produce homotypic and heterotypic responses. Studies have shown a correlation between the presence of homotypic neutralizing antibodies and protection. The duration of homotypic protection is probably longer than that of heterotypic; however, it is both incomplete and short-lived, as shown by the occurrence of reinfections with the same serotype. The role of serum IgM antibodies is unclear. By 3 years of age over 80% of the population has antibodies against RVs, and by 4 years of age this is practically 100%. Antibody levels are high at birth, decline by 3–6 months, rise to a peak at 2–3 years and remain elevated throughout life (probably because of repeat, mostly asymptomatic infections).[7,12] These serum antibodies do not always prevent the infection, though. Mucosal immunity appears to be more important; it develops 4 weeks after the illness and persists for several months, eventually decreasing with advancing age.[16] Passively acquired mucosal immunity by breast-feeding or orally administered immune globulins has conferred protection to high-risk individuals. Cell-mediated immunity also seems to be important. In mice, RV-specific cytotoxic T cells appear in the intestinal mucosa soon after infection, and mice with severe combined immmunodeficiency are able to clear RV infection when reconstituted with CD8 T cells, despite their lack of antibodies against the virus.[17]

PREVENTION

Breast-feeding reduces the overall incidence of diarrhea, especially in developing countries. However, its role in the prevention of RV diarrhea has been questioned. Children who have RV diarrhea are as likely to have been breast-fed as those who have non-RV diarrhea. However, the severity and duration of illness might be decreased in breast-fed children.[18]

Strict adherence to enteric precautions and careful handwashing is important to reduce transmission of the virus. Fecal contamination of surfaces and objects occurs frequently in nurseries, pediatric and geriatric wards and day care centers, and, as RVs can survive in the environment for weeks, they should be thoroughly disinfected. Effective disinfectants are 6% hydrogen peroxide, 2500ppm chlorine, 80% ethanol, ethanophenolic disinfectants, ultraviolet radiation and heat; drying and phenolic disinfectants are not effective;[13] hypochlorites are inactivated by fecal organic matter. Nondisposable containers are better cleaned by washing at 176°F (80°C) for at least 1 minute.

The search for an efficacious and safe RV vaccine started 20 years ago and still continues. Multiple vaccine candidates from animal (e.g. bovine, simian) and human (e.g. nursery strains, cold adapted) strains, as well as animal–human reassortants (rhesus–human, bovine–human) have been evaluated in both developed and developing countries with variable results (Table 211.7). The first – and so far only – licensed RV vaccine was RRV-TV. This was a rhesus-human reassortant vaccine containing a mixture of strains with specificities for the four common human RV G serotypes (i.e. G1–G4). Three doses of 4×10^5 PFU of RRV-TV given orally at 2, 4 and 6 months of age showed a protective efficacy of 49% for all RV diarrhea and 80% for severe RV diarrhea, decreasing the need for physician intervention by 73% and basically eliminating all cases of RV dehydration.[19] With these results RRV-TV was licensed for use in the USA in 1998 and was incorporated in the routine immunization schedule. Unfortunately, less than 1 year later the US Centers for Disease Control and Prevention (CDC) suspended the use of this vaccine because of its association with intussusception. Intussusception is a form of intestinal obstruction that normally occurs in 1/2000 children; the risk attributable to the vaccine was estimated as one additional

CANDIDATE ROTAVIRUS VACCINES		
Source	**Strain**	**Specificity**
Animal		
Bovine	RIT4237	G6 P6
	WC3	G6 P5
Rhesus	RRV	G3 P3
Human	M37	G1
	RV3	G3
	89–12	G1 P8
Animal–human reassortant		
Rhesus–human	RRV-TV	G1-G4 P3
Bovine–human	WC3-QV	G1-G4 P1

Table 211.7 Candidate rotavirus vaccines tested in children.

case/10,000 infants vaccinated, and was most pronounced during the week following administration of the first dose of vaccine.[20] The mechanism by which RRV-TV caused intussusception is unknown at this point. New candidate reassortant vaccines using other parent strains (e.g. bovine) are currently undergoing clinical testing. In addition, nonreplicating RV vaccines have been developed using whole virions, empty capsids, vector-expressed recombinant proteins and cell culture-derived or synthetic peptides. However, the immunogenically important antigens to be included in these products have not yet been defined. Passive immunization and inhibitors of viral replication are also under study.

DIAGNOSTIC MICROBIOLOGY

Antigen detection kits based on enzyme immunoassays (EIAs) and the latex agglutination test are commercially available. They are relatively inexpensive and permit a rapid diagnosis with high sensitivity and specificity (70–100%). Newborns and breast-feeding children might have higher false-positive rates. Samples should be obtained during the symptomatic period to optimize the performance of the test. If samples are not to be processed immediately, they can be stored at 39.2°F (4°C) or frozen. Rotavirus can also be identified by its characteristic appearance on EM; this is especially useful for strains other than group A. The technique is very specific, but it is available only in centers with substantial resources.

Characteristic migration patterns of the RV genome can be detected by PAGE, with good sensitivity (>90%) and specificity (100%). Other diagnostic methods include hybridization of radiolabeled nucleic acid probes to the viral RNA and amplification by PCR. Both are more sensitive than the antigen detection techniques and at least equally specific. Rotavirus can also be cultured in some research centers.

Clinical manifestations

The clinical spectrum of RV infections ranges from asymptomatic to severe disease with dehydration and death. The incubation period is usually less than 48 hours (range 1–7 days). The clinical picture of children attending health care facilities includes:

- vomiting (60–70%), which occurs early in the illness, often as the initial symptom;
- watery diarrhea (96%) without blood or mucus, usually 3–8 stools per day, mean duration 3–4 (up to 10) days;
- fever (60–65%) usually moderate (101.3–103.1°F; 38.5–39.5°C) but can be higher if associated with significant dehydration; and
- abdominal pain.

The disease is self-limiting; the usual total duration is 6–7 days. In severe cases death may occur through dehydration and electrolyte imbalance.[4,6,12] Repeated or sequential infections by the same or different serotypes have been documented. Chronic infection has not been described in the normal host.[7] Neonatal RV infections are infrequent, symptomatic in less than 10–20% of cases, and usually mild; severe infections may occur among premature infants and in special care units.

MANAGEMENT

In the management of RV infections, attention should be focused on the prevention or treatment of dehydration, for which ORS should suffice in most cases. A small percentage of patients will present with severe dehydration in shock or coma, and will need intravenous rehydration. Oral immune globulin and colostrum or human milk containing RV antibodies have been used in the treatment of RV diarrhea with good results. The anti-RV titer is low in human preparations, but higher in colostrum from cows immunized against RV. This form of therapy might prove useful for immunocompromised patients and for those with chronic or severe disease. Also, formulas supplemented with *Bifidobacterium bifidum* and *Streptococcus thermophilus* reduce the incidence of diarrhea and RV shedding in infected children.[21] Interference with the overgrowth of bacteria and promotion of the intestinal immune response to RV have been suggested as the possible mechanisms.

CALICIVIRUSES (NOROVIRUS AND SAPOVIRUS)

When visualized in 1972 by Kapikian *et al.*[22] in specimens from an outbreak of diarrhea that occurred in 1968 in a public elementary school in Norwalk, Ohio, USA, caliciviruses became the first viral agents implicated in human gastroenteritis. After a slow start, recent improvements in detection systems have shown that caliciviruses are the most common agents of outbreaks of gastroenteritis.

NATURE

Caliciviruses are round, approximately 27–40nm diameter viruses, with a positive-sense ssRNA. Initially designated by the location where they were first identified (e.g. Norwalk, Sapporo, Snow Mountain, Hawaii), recent cloning of the Norwalk virus (NV) and other representative strains has allowed development of sensitive molecular diagnostics and improved our understanding of this family. Caliciviruses are members of the family Caliciviridae and, based on genomic organization, the human enteric caliciviruses are now placed into two genera:

- the Norovirus with its type species NV; and
- the Sapovirus with its type species Sapporo virus (SV).[23]

Viruses previously designated SRSVs are mostly assigned to the Noroviruses, and 'classic' human calicivirus falls into both the Noroviruses and the Sapoviruses. The NLVs are furtherly divided into two genogroups (I and II).

It is now apparent that there is great genetic diversity among caliciviruses. The Noroviruses (Fig. 211.3) are 27nm in diameter with a somewhat indistinct, rough outer edge. The Sapoviruses (Fig. 211.4) are about 35nm in diameter, and their virion surface is characterized by 32 cup-shaped (chalice-like) indentations or hollows that may give the appearance of a six-pointed star ('Star of David'). Caliciviruses are unusual among human viruses in that the virions are composed of a single major capsid protein, with a molecular weight of approximately 58–62kDa. Preliminary work suggests that the capsid protein has six distinct regions, which are the determinants of structural and antigenic domains.[5]

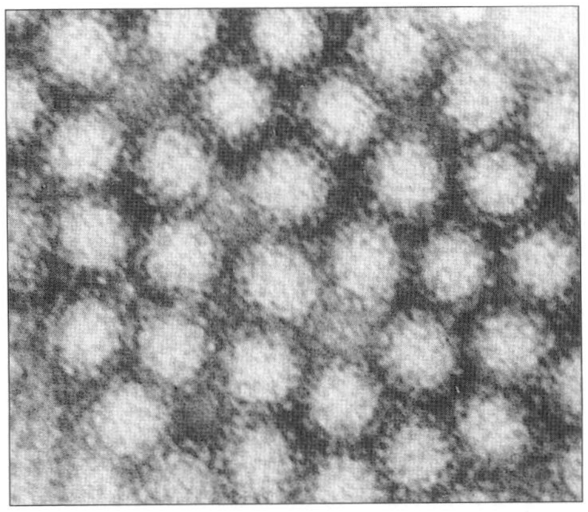

Fig. 211.3 Norovirus. Electron micrograph. Courtesy of C Humphrey, (CDC).

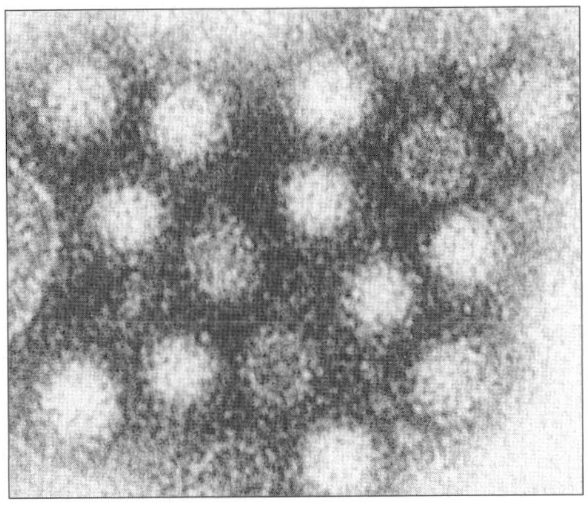

Fig. 211.4 Sapovirus. Electron micrograph. Courtesy of C Humphrey, (CDC).

EPIDEMIOLOGY

During the 1970s and 1980s limited knowledge of the epidemiology of calicivirus infection emerged when EM, IEM and first generation EIAs were applied to the study of outbreaks of gastroenteritis and experimental infection of volunteers. Nowadays this knowledge is quickly expanding with the introduction of EIAs based on recombinant virus-like particles (VLPs) and the use of RT-PCR.[24] While studies in the 1980s could identify caliciviruses in only 19% of outbreaks in the USA, more recent evaluation of cases of nonbacterial gastroenteritis occurring in the 1990s have identified Noroviruses in 86 (95%) of 90 outbreaks.[25] Caliciviruses are now considered the most common cause of nonbacterial gastroenteritis outbreaks.

The epidemiology and clinical picture of Noroviruses and Sapoviruses are different. Even though there are year-to-year and geographic variations, in general Noroviruses are more frequent than Sapoviruses. Sapporo virus was identified in Sapporo, Japan, as the cause of an outbreak of gastroenteritis in a home for infants.[26] Since, Sapoviruses have been described mainly in young children (e.g. in day care centers and pediatric hospital wards) and less often they have been found in outbreaks affecting adults. The Noroviruses on the other hand infect patients of all ages. The original Norwalk epidemic affected an elementary school with 50% of teachers and students developing gastroenteritis and a secondary attack rate of 32% among household members. Application of newer molecular diagnostics have indicated that besides adults, as previously recognized, children are also frequently affected by Noroviruses. For example, Pang *et al.*[27] found that Noroviruses were implicated in 20% of cases (second only to RV) of non-outbreak, community-acquired gastroenteritis in children in Finland (Sapoviruses were found in 9% of the specimens). Noroviruses outbreaks occur all year round, but recent data suggest a winter peak.

Early outbreaks of Norovirus gastroenteritis were traced to fecally contaminated food or water. Settings where outbreaks have occurred include nursing homes (43%), restaurants (26%), schools (11%) and vacation settings (11%). A mode of transmission was sought in 51 outbreaks, and of these, food was implicated in 37%, person-to-person contact in 20%, consumption of oysters in 10% and water in 6%.[25] Classic caliciviruses (mainly Sapoviruses) were found responsible for 3% of diarrhea episodes in a day care center. Children or the elderly are usually implicated in these outbreaks, rarely adult carers. Some outbreaks have lasted for several weeks. The attack rates during the outbreaks have ranged from 50 to 70%, with frequent asymptomatic infection. Nosocomial outbreaks have been documented in an infant–mother unit and a pediatric hospital. Travelers are at risk for acquiring caliciviruses, although this topic has been rarely evaluated. During the Gulf War, gastroenteritis was the most common illness of soldiers, and 70% of these cases were attributable to Noroviruses.[28] Both Noroviruses and Sapoviruses have worldwide distribution.

PATHOGENICITY

Caliciviruses are ubiquitous and stable in the environment, providing a persistent source of infection. The NV is stable in water chlorinated to 10mg/l (most municipal water systems contain <5mg/l chlorine) and survive freezing and heating to 140°F (60°C), permitting spread in recreational and drinking water and contaminated oysters that have been steamed. The virus is ether-stable, acid-resistant and relatively heat-stable.[22] Asymptomatic shedding of Noroviruses can persist for over 1 week. Food handlers may be an important source of infection. Air-borne transmission by droplets of vomit or through the movement of contaminated laundry has also been suspected. Caliciviruses recently identified in swine and cattle were found to be genetically related to the human caliciviruses, which raises the possibility of animal-to-human transmission.[24]

Very few viruses (<100) are needed for infection; therefore transmission by droplets, person-to-person contact or environmental contamination can occur. Secondary spread to close contacts is frequent. Individuals with O blood group might be more easily infected with NV, while those with B blood group might have decreased risk. Infection is spread by the fecal–oral route either directly or indirectly. Caliciviruses demonstrate great antigenic and genetic diversity providing little cross-protection, so people can be serially infected with various strains. Volunteer studies have established that infection with caliciviruses confers excellent short-term homologous protection. However, the existence of long-term protection is still to be elucidated. Studies of the immunity to caliciviruses is evolving. Serosurveys indicate that levels of antibodies specific for the NV are low during childhood, but rise rapidly during adolescence, reaching 50% by middle age. In developing countries, antibodies are acquired at an earlier age and peak incidence of illness may also occur among younger age groups than in developed nations.[29] Norovirus antibodies peak by the third week after infection and remain elevated until approximately the sixth week, after which they decline.

Seroprevalence studies of strains now classified as Sapoviruses indicate that antibodies are acquired during early childhood. The peak acquisition occurs between 3 months and 6 years. In London, UK a serosurvey showed that over 70% of children had evidence of infection by the age of 2 years.[30] Mothers of infected infants were rarely affected, suggesting that young adults retain immunity to classic caliciviruses, although the outbreaks among the elderly suggest that immunity may wane with age.

During gastroenteritis caused by the NV the proximal small intestine is affected preferentially, with increased epithelial cell mitoses, villus shortening, crypt hypertrophy, mucosal inflammation (mononuclear cells) and malabsorption of D-xylose, lactose and fat. Adenylate cyclase levels in jejunal mucosa are not elevated (as occurs in cholera) and fecal leukocytes are not excreted. The gastric secretion of hydrochloric acid, pepsin and intrinsic factor are unaltered, but gastric emptying is markedly delayed, which probably explains the frequent occurrence of nausea and vomiting. These findings persist for at least 4 days after clinical symptoms clear and revert to normal within 2 weeks.

PREVENTION

Handwashing, cleaning of environmental surfaces, thorough cooking of food items, boiling or disinfection of water and furlough for 2 days after resolution of symptoms of ill food handlers should prevent most calicivirus-associated outbreaks. During outbreaks, food, water (including ice) or symptomatic food handlers should be suspected as possible sources. Vigorous handwashing with soap, decontamination of surfaces, use of barriers and disposal of linen contaminated with diarrhea or vomiting should be emphasized. When a water supply is thought to be contaminated, shock chlorine concentrations (>10mg/l for 30 minutes or longer) may be helpful.[12] Vaccines against the NV using recombinant VLPs are under development.[31]

DIAGNOSTIC MICROBIOLOGY

Electron microscopy, especially IEM, were the initial means to identify caliciviruses, and they are still useful in the investigation of outbreaks. The cloning and characterization of the genome of the NV and expression of the capsid antigen in baculovirus (a virus infecting insect cells that is easier to replicate) has provided adequate and abundant reagents suitable for EIAs.[30] Since caliciviruses demonstrate great antigenic and genetic diversity, diagnostic tests need to be able to detect the range of many different virus types. EIAs are suitable for the detection of antibody in serum and antigen in stool both with good sensitivity and specificity.[32] The antibody detecting EIAs appear to be more broadly reactive; IgM and IgA detection systems are under development. As one-half of adults in the USA have pre-existing antibodies to the virus, a single specimen is insufficient to document recent infection. But, if at least one-half of affected persons in an outbreak have a fourfold rise in their antibody titers, a calicivirus can be implicated as the causative agent.[12] More recently, nucleotide primers have been developed suitable for RT-PCR to detect caliciviruses in clinical and environmental samples. Caliciviruses still can not be grown in cell culture. Despite recent advances, further work is sorely needed because current diagnostic methods are not well suited for routine clinical use.

CLINICAL MANIFESTATIONS

Norovirus gastroenteritis usually has an abrupt onset, with explosive watery diarrhea, vomiting and abdominal cramps. In the original Norwalk outbreak diarrhea occurred in 44% of cases and vomiting in 84%. These symptoms are experienced by all age groups, but diarrhea is more prevalent among adults, whereas children experience vomiting more frequently. The incubation period is 24–48 hours, and the mean duration of illness is 12–60 hours. Between 25 and 50% of affected persons also report headache, fever, chills and myalgias. Dehydration and constitutional symptoms can be seen, particularly in the elderly.[12] Of the 93 infants affected in the Sapporo outbreak, 83% had gastrointestinal symptoms, including diarrhea (95%), vomiting (44%) and fever (18%).[26] Infection with the SV is common beginning in infancy and increasing during early childhood.[33] It mimics mild rotaviral illness. The incubation period is 1–3 days, with illness lasting an average of 4 (range 1–11) days. Diarrhea (88%) and vomiting (65%) occur frequently; fever (34%) and upper respiratory symptoms (22%) are less common. In general, Sapoviruses are less common than Noroviruses, seen at younger age and cause milder symptomatology.

MANAGEMENT

No specific therapy is available for calicivirus gastroenteritis. Attention must be paid to fluid and electrolyte balance. The main focus is on the management of dehydration, which can usually be accomplished with oral rehydration.

ENTERIC ADENOVIRUSES

Described in 1975,[34] the role of enteric adenoviruses was difficult to elucidate because of the frequent and prolonged asymptomatic fecal shedding of traditional adenoviruses after respiratory infections. Current techniques distinguish the enteric adenoviruses and have identified them as important etiologic agents of viral diarrhea in both the developed and developing world in hospitalized infants and young children.

NATURE

Human adenoviruses are nonenveloped, dsDNA viruses of the family Adenoviridae (Fig. 211.5). Their size is 70–75nm, with ten structural proteins (5–120kDa). The capsid proteins are arranged as an icosahedron with 20 triangular faces and 12 vertices. Each virion contains 240 hexons and 12 pentons; each penton consists of a base and a fiber. The genus-specific antigen is located in the hexon, but because it resides in the internal part of the capsid it does not elicit protective antibodies. Type-specific antigens are located on the hexon and the fiber; being exposed on the surface of the virion, they give rise to serum-neutralizing antibodies. The fiber is a strong hemagglutinin and elicits inhibition antibodies.[35] Hemagglutination properties allow classification of adenoviruses into six subgroups: A–F. The enteric adenoviruses belong to group F and comprise mainly serotypes 40, 41 and 31. A few other serotypes (e.g. 1, 2, 3, 5, 7 and 12) have also been implicated in gastroenteritis but because they are less frequent their role is less well defined.

EPIDEMIOLOGY

Adenoviruses are identified in 4% of outpatient acute diarrheal episodes and 2–22% of those in hospitalized children.[36] Also, 1–2% of asymptomatic controls shed the virus. Outbreaks have been documented in hospitals and day care centers. In Houston, USA, adenoviruses caused ten of 131 (8%) day care center outbreaks; during the outbreaks an average of 38% of children were infected, one-half of them asymptomatically; the outbreaks lasted 7–44 (mean 24) days,[37] and secondary spread was frequent. Enteric adenovirus infections occur more frequently among children under 2 years of age (median age 12 and 19 months for type 40 and 41, respectively) but

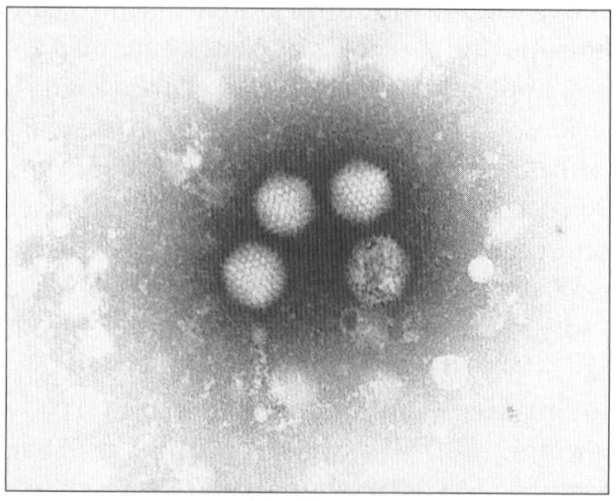

Fig. 211.5 Enteric adenovirus. Electron micrograph. Courtesy of S Spangenberger.

older children and adults may occasionally be infected. Enteric adenoviruses types 40 and 41 circulate simultaneously and all year long with no obvious seasonality; a slight increase, especially in type 41 cases, might be seen in warmer months.

PATHOGENICITY

The mode of transmission is probably fecal–oral with spread from person to person. Food and water have not been reported as vehicles. The excretion of enteric adenoviruses in stools lasts 10–14 days, on average from 2 days before to 5 days after diarrhea stops. Asymptomatic shedding occurs frequently, but infectivity parallels symptomatic disease. Infection elicits serum-neutralizing and hemagglutination-inhibiting antibodies. Long-term immunity is thought to be acquired during childhood infection.

PREVENTION

Environmental control is important for outbreak control but has little effect on endemic transmission. Enteric adenoviruses survive temporarily in porous and nonporous environmental surfaces, but less efficiently than RVs or hepatitis A virus.[13] Infectious viruses are rapidly inactivated at 132.8°F (56°C) and by exposure to ultraviolet radiation or formalin. No vaccine is under development.

DIAGNOSTIC MICROBIOLOGY

Antigen-detection techniques using adenovirus 40 and 41 type-specific or adenovirus group monoclonal antibodies are commercially available and constitute the most convenient mode of diagnosis. They are relatively inexpensive, technically simple and quick, with a sensitivity and specificity of 98% compared with EM. Some virus variants, however, might not be detected by the assay. Its use should be restricted to diarrheal illnesses of likely viral etiology in the preschool age group or younger, because it has not been validated for other groups. A latex agglutination assay is also available with improved simplicity and speed. Electron microscopy does not discriminate between enteric and respiratory serotypes. Adenoviruses can be cultured, but the enteric serotypes are fastidious and require special cell lines, such as Graham 293 transformed lung fibroblasts or Chang conjunctival cells. The characteristic cytopathic effect generally occurs within 3–7 days but might require up to 28 days. Viral culture is not well suited for routine clinical diagnosis. PCR techniques have been developed for the identification of enteric adenoviruses in stool specimens.[38]

CLINICAL MANIFESTATIONS

Gastroenteritis caused by enteric adenoviruses is similar to that caused by RVs, but less severe and of a more prolonged course. The incubation period is 3–10 days (longer than the 1–3 days seen with other viruses) and illness typically lasts 5–12 days. Diarrhea, usually watery, is the main manifestation, occurring in 97% of patients and with a mean duration of 9 (type 40) to 12 (type 41) days. Prolonged diarrhea (>14 days) occurs in one-third of children and vomiting in 79% (lasting 1–2 days); low-grade fever and respiratory symptoms are occasionally seen. Dehydration is less frequent than with RV infection. An association with intussusception has been proposed but not proved.[39]

MANAGEMENT

No specific therapy is indicated for gastroenteritis caused by adenoviruses. Dehydration is rare and usually mild, so most episodes can be managed with oral rehydration.

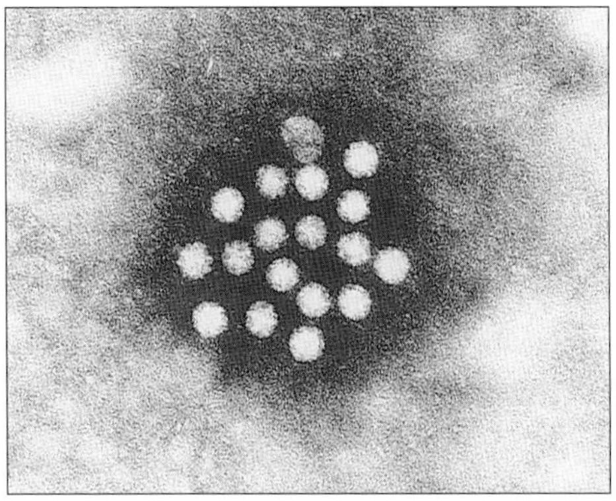

Fig. 211.6 Astrovirus. Electron micrograph. Courtesy of S Spangenberger.

ASTROVIRUSES

Although astroviruses were well known to cause diarrhea in animals, these agents were not implicated in human gastroenteritis until 1975 when small round viruses were observed by EM in stool samples of hospitalized infants.[40] Astroviruses are now recognized as an important cause of mild gastroenteritis in young children.

NATURE

Astroviruses belong to the family Astroviridae, and are 27–32nm, nonenveloped, single-stranded (ss) RNA viruses (Fig. 211.6). They have smooth edges and characteristically a five- or six-pointed star in the center. Their surface is unbroken and rounded, unlike that of the caliciviruses, which is broken by hollows. Their three structural proteins (31–34kDa, 29–31kDa and 20–24kDa) and their distinctive morphologic and immunologic features distinguish them from caliciviruses.[5,36] The complete sequence of a strain of human astrovirus serotype 1 has been described.

EPIDEMIOLOGY

Astrovirus infections occur mainly among children aged under 7 years, although adults can be infected and suffer mild disease. Community-based studies show a prevalence of 7–8%, and a 2% excretion rate in asymptomatic individuals. Among children hospitalized who have diarrhea, astroviruses account for 3–5% of cases. Outbreaks have been described in day care centers, hospitals, nursing homes and military facilities. Astroviruses were responsible for 7% of diarrhea outbreaks at a day care center, with about one-half of the infections being asymptomatic. The attack rate during outbreaks is about 50%, and secondary transmission to families occurs in one-third of the cases. Nosocomial outbreaks usually involve children aged under 2 years, with attack rates between 7 and 62%.[41,42] The largest outbreak of astrovirus infection yet recorded occurred in Japan in 1991, affecting more than 4700 students and teachers in ten primary and four junior high schools; it lasted 5 days and was linked to contaminated food.[43] Sporadic and outbreak astrovirus infections are more prevalent during late fall, winter and early spring in temperate climates; in tropical climates it might be more common during the rainy season.

PATHOGENICITY

Eight human astrovirus serotypes have been identified; serotype 1 strains are the most frequent. The characteristics of immunity to astroviruses are unknown. As reported outbreaks have involved only children and the elderly, young adults may have resistance to infection. By the age of 10 years, 75% of UK children have specific antibodies, and pooled gammaglobulin preparations in the USA, prepared from adult donors, frequently contain antibodies to astroviruses.[44] In Virginia, USA, 94 and 42% of 6–9-year-old children showed serum antibodies against astrovirus serotype 1 and 3, respectively.[45]

PREVENTION

To prevent or control outbreaks, handwashing is important, especially among food handlers and in day care centers because astroviruses may be shed asymptomatically. Adequate cooking of shellfish should prevent food-borne outbreaks; the virus is inactivated by heating to over 140°F (60°C) for at least 10 minutes. Methanol 70–90% can be used to disinfect surfaces; however, astroviruses are resistant to chloroform or alcohol.[41] No vaccine is available.

DIAGNOSTIC MICROBIOLOGY

Because astrovirus infections are usually mild and self-limiting, the diagnostic methods are not available for routine clinical diagnosis but primarily for epidemiologic studies. Electron microscopy was the only diagnostic tool until EIAs were developed using group-reactive monoclonal antibodies that detect all astroviral serotypes in stools; the sensitivity and specificity (compared with IEM) have been 91 and 96%, respectively.[42] Astroviruses can be grown in human embryonic kidney (HEK), LLC-monkey (Rhesus) kidney cells 2 (LLC-MK2) in the presence of trypsin, and other cells.[5] These systems are not well suited for routine clinical diagnosis, though. Recently, shell vial assays and latex agglutination tests have been developed, which should facilitate diagnosis. RT-PCR has been described to detect all astrovirus serotypes and seems more sensitive than EIA.[44]

CLINICAL MANIFESTATIONS

The clinical manifestations of astrovirus infection are similar to those of RV illness, but less severe. The incubation period is 3–4 days and illness lasts 1–5 days. Mild watery diarrhea is the most common symptom. Less frequent symptoms are fever (20%), vomiting (10%), dehydration (6%) and abdominal pain. Dehydration can be more prominent in children co-infected with bacterial or viral pathogens, and in immunosuppressed (including those who have HIV infection) or malnourished patients. Astroviruses have been associated with hepatitis in animals but not in humans.

MANAGEMENT

No specific therapy is indicated for gastroenteritis caused by astroviruses. Dehydration is rare and usually mild, so it can be treated with oral rehydration. In one case of protracted astrovirus diarrhea in an immunocompromised patient, the use of intravenous immune globulin was beneficial.[46]

OTHER VIRUSES

Torovirus and coronavirus are enveloped viruses, 100–150nm in diameter, with helical symmetry that belong to the family Coronaviridae. Since they do not grow reliably in cell culture, their identification is mostly limited to EM.[5] PCR techniques might hold promise.[47] Toroviruses have been associated with nosocomial outbreaks and have been implicated as the cause of acute and persistent diarrhea in children.[48,49] Pestiviruses are ssRNA viruses classified as members of the Togaviridae family. They are well-known enteric pathogens of cattle and pigs, pleomorphic and difficult to identify by EM. In a study pestivirus antigen was detected by EIA in the stools of 23% of Arizona Indian children under 2 years of age with gastroenteritis of unknown etiology, compared with 3% of controls. Illness was relatively mild, duration was 3 days and respiratory symptoms were common.[50] Other viruses collectively referred to as small round viruses (such as the Aichi strain and others),[51] parvovirus and picobirnavirus have been identified in children who have gastroenteritis but also from controls so their role as agents of gastroenteritis is not well defined.

REFERENCES

1. Snyder JD, Merson MH. The magnitude of the global problem of acute diarrhoeal disease: a review of active surveillance data. Bull WHO 1982;60:605–13.
2. Claeson M, Merson MH. Global progress in the control of diarrheal diseases. Pediatr Infect Dis J 1990;9:345–55.
3. Bern C, Martines J, de Zoysa I, Glass RI. The magnitude of the global problem of diarrhoeal disease: a ten year update. Bull WHO 1992;70:705–14.
4. Glass RI, Lew JF, Gangarosa RE, LeBaron CW, Ho MC. Estimates of morbidity and mortality rates for diarrheal diseases in American children. J Pediatr 1991;118:S27–33.
5. Petric M. Caliciviruses, Astroviruses, and other diarrheic viruses. In: Murray PR, Baron EJ, Pfaller MA, Tenover FC, Yolken RH, eds. Manual of clinical microbiology, 7th ed. Washington, DC: American Society for Microbiology; 1999:1005–13.
6. Bishop RF, Davidson GP, Holmes IH, Ruck BJ. Virus particles in epithelial cells of duodenal mucosa from children with viral gastroenteritis. Lancet 1973;ii:1281–3.
7. Haffejee IE. The epidemiology of rotavirus infections: a global perspective. J Pediatr Gastroenterol Nutr 1995;20:275–86.
8. Burke B, Desselberger U. Rotavirus pathogenicity. Virology 1996;218:299–305.
9. Kapikian AZ, Hoshino Y, Chanock RM. Rotaviruses. In: Knipe DM, Howley PM, eds. Field's virology. Philadelphia: Lippincott Williams & Wilkins; 2001:1787–1833.
10. Glass RI, Kilgore PE, Holman RC, *et al.* The epidemiology of rotavirus diarrhea in the United States: surveillance and estimates of disease burden. J Infect Dis 1996;174(Suppl.):S5.
11. LeBaron C, Lew J, Glass RI, Weber JM, Ruiz-Palacios GM. Annual rotavirus epidemic patterns in North America. Result of a 5-year retrospective survey of 88 centers in Canada, Mexico, and the United States. JAMA 1990;264:983–8.
12. Centers for Disease Control and Prevention. Surveillance summaries. Viral agents of gastroenteritis. Public health importance and outbreak management. MMWR Morb Mortal Wkly Rep 1990;39(RR-5):1–24.
13. Abad FX, Pinto RM, Bosch A. Survival of enteric viruses on environmental fomites. Appl Environ Microbiol 1994;60:3704–10.
14. Ciarlet M, Estes MK. Interactions between rotavirus and gastrointestinal cells. Curr Opin Microbiol 2001;4:435–41.
15. Estes MK. Rotaviruses and their replication. In: Knipe DM, Howley PM, eds. field's virology. Philadelphia: Lippincott Williams & Wilkins; 2001:1747–85.
16. Matson DO, O'Ryan ML, Herrera I, Pickering LK, Estes MK. Fecal antibody responses to symptomatic and asymptomatic rotavirus infections. J Infect Dis 1993;167:577–83.
17. Molyneaux PJ. Human immunity to rotavirus. J Med Microbiol 1995;43:397–404.
18. Duffy LC, Byers TE, Riepenhoff-Talty M, *et al.* The effect of infant feeding on rotavirus-induced gastroenteritis: a prospective study. Am J Publ Health 1986;76:259–63.
19. Rennels MB, Glass RI, Dennehy PH, *et al.* Safety and efficacy of high-dose Rhesus–human reassortant rotavirus vaccines. Report of the National Multicenter Trial. Pediatrics 1996;97:7–13.
20. Murphy TD, Gargiullo PM, Massoudi MS, *et al.* Intussusception among infants given rotavirus vaccine. N Engl J Med 2001;344:564–72.
21. Saavedra JM, Bauman NA, Oung I, Perman JA, Yolken RH. Feeding of *Bifidobacterium bifidum* and *Streptococcus thermophilus* to infants in hospital for prevention of diarrhoea and shedding of rotavirus. Lancet 1994;344:1046–9.
22. Kapikian AZ, Wyatt RG, Dolin R, *et al.* Visualization by immune electron microscopy of a 27nm particle associated with acute infectious non-bacterial gastroenteritis. J Virol 1972;10:1075–81.
23. Green KY, Ando T, Balayan MS, *et al.* Caliciviridae. In: Van Regenmortel MHV, Fauquet CM, Bishop DHL, *et al.* Virus taxonomy: classification and nomenclature of viruses. Seventh Report of the International Committee on Taxonomy of Viruses. San Diego: Academic Press; 2000:725–35. http:/www.ncbi.nlm.nih.gov/ICTV/.
24. Glass RI, Noel J, Ando T, *et al.* The epidemiology of enteric caliciviruses from humans: a

reassessment using new diagnostics. J Infect Dis 2000;181(Suppl.2):S254–61.
25. Frankhauser RL, Noel JS, Monroe SS, Ando TA, Glass RI. Molecular epidemiology of 'Norwalk-like viruses' in outbreaks of gastroenteritis in the United States. J Infect Dis 1998;178:1571–8.
26. Chiba S, Sakuma Y, Kogasaki R, *et al.* An outbreak of gastroenteritis associated with calicivirus in an infant home. J Med Virol 1979;4:249–54..
27. Pang XL, Honma S, Nakata S, Vesikari T. Human calciviruses in acute gastroenteritis of young children in the community. J Infect Dis 2000;181(Suppl.2):S288–94.
28. Hyams KC, Bourgeois AL, Merrell BR, *et al.* Dirrheal disease during Operation Desert Shield. N Engl J Med 1991;325:1423–8.
29. Greenberg HB, Valdesuso JR, Kapikian AZ, *et al.* Prevalence of antibody to the Norwalk virus in various countries. Infect Immun 1979;26:270–3.
30. Parker SP, Cubitt WD, Jiang X. Enzyme immunoassay using baculovirus-expressed human calicivirus (Mexico) for the measurement of IgG responses and determining seroprevalence in London, UK. J Med Virol 1995;46:194–200.
31. Estes MK, Ball JM, Guerrero RA, *et al.* Norwalk virus vaccines: challenges and progress. J Infect Dis 2000;181(Suppl.2):S367–73.
32. Jiang X, Wilton N, Zhong WM, *et al.* Diagnosis of human caliciviruses by use of enzyme immunoassay. J Infect Dis 2000;181(Suppl.2):S349–59.
33. Sakuma Y, Chiba S, Kogasaku R, *et al.* Prevalence of antibody to human calicivirus in general population of northern Japan. J Med Virol 1981;7:221–5.
34. Morris CA, Flewett TH, Bryden AS. Epidemic viral enteritis in a long-stay children's ward. Lancet 1975;i:4–5.
35. Wadell G, Allard A, Hierholzer JC. Adenoviruses. In: Murray PR, Baron EJ, Pfaller MA, Tenover FC, Yolken RH, eds. Manual of clinical microbiology, 7th ed. Washington, DC: American Society for Microbiology; 1999:970–82.
36. Blacklow NR, Greenberg HB. Viral gastroenteritis. N Engl J Med 1991;325:252–64.
37. Van R, Wun CC, O'Ryan ML, *et al.* Outbreaks of human enteric adenovirus types 40 and 41 in Houston day care centers. J Pediatr 1992;120:516–21.
38. Allard A, Kajon A, Wadell G. Simple procedure for discrimination and typing of enteric adenoviruses in stool specimens. J Med Virol 1994;44:250–7.
39. Hsu HY, Kao CL, Huang LM, *et al.* Viral etiology of intussusception in Taiwanese childhood. Pediatr Infect Dis J 1998;17:893–8.
40. Appleton H, Higgins PG. Viruses and gastroenteritis in infants. Lancet 1975;i:1297.
41. Maldonado YA. Astrovirus infections in children. Report Infect Dis 1996;6:39–40.
42. Dennehy PH, Nelson SM, Spangenberger S, Noel JS, Monroe SS, Glass RI. A prospective case–control study of the role of astrovirus in acute diarrhea among hospitalized young children. J Infect Dis 2001;184:10–15.
43. Oishi I, Yamazaki K, Kimoto T, *et al.* A large outbreak of acute gastroenteritis associated with astrovirus among students and teachers in Osaka, Japan. J Infect Dis 1994;170:439–43.
44. Jonassen TO, Monceyron C, Lee TW, Kurtz JB, Grinde B. Detection of all serotypes of human astrovirus by the polymerase chain reaction. J Virol Methods 1995;52:327–34.
45. Mitchell DK, Matson DO, Cubitt WD, *et al.* Prevalence of antibodies to astrovirus types 1 and 3 in children and adolescents in Norfolk, Virginia. Pediatr Infect Dis J 1999;18:249–54.
46. Bjorkholm M, Celsing F, Runarsson G, Waldenstrom J. Successful intravenous immunoglobulin therapy for severe and persistent astrovirus gastroenteritis after fludarabine treatment in a patient with Waldenstrom's macroglobulinemia. Int J Hematol 1995;62:117–20.
47. Duckmanton S, Luan B, Devenish J, Tellier R, Petric M. Characterization of human torovirus from faecal specimens. Virology 1997;239:158–68.
48. Jamieson F, Wang E, Bain C, Good J, Duckmanton L, Petric M. Human torovirus: a new nosocomial gastrointestinal pathogen. J Infect Dis 1998;178:1263–9.
49. Koopmans M, Goosen ESM, Lima AAM, *et al.* Association of torovirus with acute and persistent diarrhea in children. Pediatr Infect Dis J 1997;16:504–7.
50. Yolken R, Leister F, Almeido-Hill J, *et al.* Infantile gastroenteritis associated with excretion of pestivirus antigens. Lancet 1989;i:517–9.
51. Vial PA, Kotloff KL, Tall BD, Morris JG Jr, Levine MM. Detection by immune electron microscopy of 27-nm viral particles associated with community-acquired diarrhea in children. J Infect Dis 1990;161:571–3.

chapter

212 Measles, Mumps and Rubella Viruses

Peter Morgan-Capner

INTRODUCTION

The skin and mucous membranes are affected in the course of many infections, bacterial and viral. The viral exanthemata occur largely in childhood, but are not uncommon in adults. The rashes are maculopapular or vesicular, the latter being clinically characteristic of hand, foot and mouth disease and varicella; smallpox has been eradicated, although sporadic outbreaks of monkeypox still occur.[1]

The erythematous rashes present major problems of differential diagnosis.[2,3] Although there are usually associated clinical features that may be characteristic, there may be considerable overlap, such as with arthralgia in rubella and parvovirus B19, and conjunctivitis in measles and rubella. As some infections such as rubella and measles become increasingly uncommon as a result of successful immunization programs, clinicians become less familiar with their presentations and may not include them in their differential diagnosis.

Other virus infections, such as Epstein–Barr virus infection, which causes infectious mononucleosis, can give generalized rashes, as can bacterial infections such as scarlet fever associated with *Streptococcus pyogenes*, disseminated meningococcal infection and toxic shock syndrome caused by toxin-producing *Staphylococcus aureus*. In some geographic areas, a number of other viruses may present problems of differential diagnosis, such as dengue[4] and other arboviruses.

A further virus infection characteristic of childhood is mumps, although infection in young adults is not uncommon. In adolescents and adults infection may be complicated by involvement of a range of other organs such as testes, ovaries and pancreas; meningitis and encephalitis can be a complication at any age. A wide range of differential diagnoses exists, depending on the symptomatology; some of these may not be infective in origin. As for rubella and measles, infection has been well controlled in some countries by widespread use of live attenuated vaccine.

MEASLES

NATURE

Measles (rubeola) has been identified for about 2000 years, although its infectious nature was not recognized until the mid 19th century when epidemics in island communities were described. It is one of the infectious diseases targeted by the World Health Organization (WHO) for eradication because an effective and safe vaccine is available, natural infection is limited to humans, there is considerable morbidity and mortality, subclinical infection is uncommon and persistent infection is rare.

Measles virus is a member of the *Morbillivirus* genus of the Paramyxoviridae and was first isolated in cell culture in 1954; the first live attenuated vaccine became available in 1963. It is pleomorphic, with a diameter of 150nm or more. Single-stranded RNA is enclosed in a capsid of helical symmetry of 18nm. This is enclosed within an envelope, the surface of which carries the hemagglutinin and fusion proteins. Replication is mainly cytoplasmic, but there is some nuclear involvement. Although there is only one major antigenic type, there has been some genetic drift in the hemagglutinin,[5] and genome analysis can distinguish geographically distinct isolates.[6] These variations are insufficient to escape protection from immunization with current vaccines.

EPIDEMIOLOGY

Measles is endemic worldwide except in those countries in which complete control has been achieved by immunization (Fig. 212.1). Infection in childhood before the impact of immunization was almost 100%, confirming measles as the most infectious of microbial agents. Epidemics occur every 2–3 years, but are less defined in the tropics.

The epidemiology of measles has been profoundly modified by immunization strategies, which have targeted developing nations as well as the industrialized world, with worldwide eradication by 2010 being the aim of the WHO Expanded Programme on Immunization.[7] It is estimated that 1 million or so children die every year from measles, particularly in the developing world. Success has been achieved in parts of the world, however, including South America, the USA and the UK.[8]

High, but not complete, rates of measles vaccination in infancy, without achieving eradication, can lead to a change in epidemiology. Those who are not immunized or are still susceptible after immunization are not exposed to the virus during early childhood, but their continued susceptibility can lead to outbreaks in older children or young adults, as has occurred in both the USA and the UK.[8,9] These outbreaks, which occur at an age when complications are more frequent, have necessitated mass immunization campaigns and/or the introduction of a second dose of measles vaccine at an older age.

PATHOGENICITY

Infection is spread by droplet from person to person. The incubation period to onset of rash is about 14 days, with prodromal symptoms starting 1–3 days earlier. The maximum infectivity is during the prodrome, although patients are considered to be infective from 4 days before to 4 days after onset of the rash.

After infection, initial replication occurs in the respiratory epithelium with local spread by lymphatics and a primary viremia 2–3 days after infection. A secondary viremia occurs 3–4 days later and lasts for up to 7 days. The peak viremia coincides with the prodromal symptoms. The rash results from the immunologic reaction between the virus antigens and host antibody, with involvement of capillary walls. Intrauterine infection has not been convincingly reported.

PREVENTION

Live attenuated measles vaccine became available in 1963 based on the Edmonston strain, but those in current use such as Schwarz and Moraten strains are further attenuated. Measles vaccine is available in monovalent form, but also combined with mumps and rubella

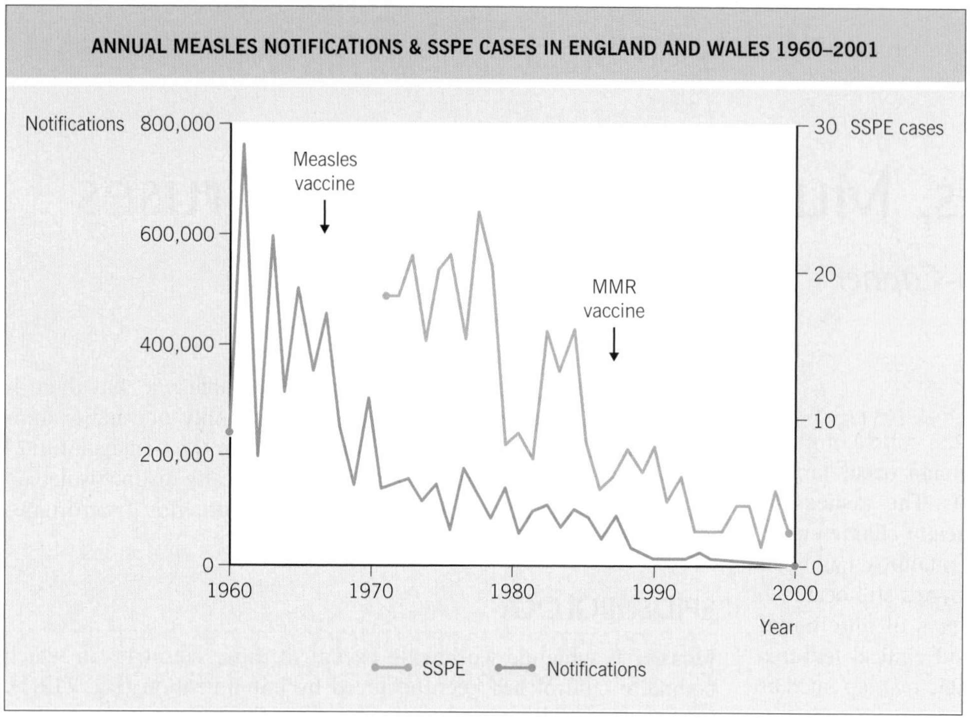

Fig. 212.1 Annual measles notifications and subacute sclerosing panencephalitis (SSPE) cases in England and Wales between 1960 and 2000. The number of cases declined from the late 1960s, and there was a further decline after the introduction of MMR vaccine in 1988. Data from the Office for National Statistics and CDSC.

vaccine (MMR). The highest efficacy rate, over 90% protection, is achieved by giving vaccine at 12–15 months of age. Earlier administration can result in lower protection because of interference by residual maternal antibody. This is especially problematic for developing countries, where many cases of measles occur in infants under 12 months of age. Attempts to improve efficacy rates at lower ages by using high titer measles vaccines have led to an unexplained and nonspecific mortality at an older age, mainly in girls, and has led to their use being discontinued.[10] Because of a small cohort who miss first immunization, and to boost protection in those with low concentrations of antibody, many countries have introduced a second dose of vaccine at age 4–5 years.

In the patient with HIV infection who is immunocompetent, serious complications from measles vaccine are rare, although seroconversion in individuals who have HIV infection is less likely.[11] Localized pain and tenderness, mild fever (about 10%) and transient rashes (about 5%) may occur, but soon resolve. Encephalitis may occur in one in a million doses, but its causal relationship with the vaccine is uncertain. Measles vaccine is contraindicated in pregnancy because of the theoretic risk from a live vaccine, but is definitely contraindicated in those with impaired cell-mediated immunity because measles-specific complications can occur. Subacute sclerosing panencephalitis (SSPE) occurs in one dose per three million or fewer. Recently, anxieties have been expressed as to whether MMR immunization may lead to inflammatory bowel disease and autism, but the evidence is inconsistent and a direct relationship seems unlikely.[12,13]

DIAGNOSTIC MICROBIOLOGY

Virus isolation may be attempted from throat swabs, conjunctival swabs, nasopharyngeal aspirates (NPAs) and sedimented cells from urine, but is technically demanding and unreliable. Cell lines susceptible to measles for primary isolation include primary human embryo and monkey kidney, but the cytopathic effect after inoculation is not immediately apparent because multinucleated giant cells can take up to 15 days to develop. Measles virus can also be detected by hemadsorption (monkey, human or guinea-pig red blood cells) and isolation can be confirmed by specific neutralization of the hemadsorption or by immunofluoresence.

Immunofluorescent antigen detection in NPA cells may be performed, and is particularly useful for diagnosing atypical cases or infection in the immunocompromised host. Measles genome may also be detected in cells obtained by throat swab or NPA, and this approach may also be used for determining the geographic origin of the infecting strain.[6]

Serologic diagnosis is dependent on demonstrating seroconversion, rising antibody titer, or detecting specific IgM. Hemagglutination inhibition and complement fixation testing (CFT) have been the established methods; the former detects both specific IgG and specific IgM, but these methods are now largely being replaced by immunoglobulin-specific enzyme immunoassays (EIAs). Measles hemagglutinating antigen and monkey red cells for hemagglutination inhibition have become difficult to obtain, and CFT can give elevated titers that do not indicate recent measles.

Serum should be obtained as soon as possible after onset of rash and, depending on results with this serum, further serum should be collected 10 days later. Specific IgM starts becoming undetectable about 4 weeks after onset. Diagnosis of recent measles can also be achieved by detecting specific IgG and IgM in saliva by antibody capture techniques.[14]

Subacute sclerosing panencephalitis may be diagnosed by detection of genome or isolation of virus by co-cultivation from brain tissue. A more usual approach, however, is the detection of elevated concentrations of measles antibody in serum and concentrations indicating intrathecal synthesis in cerebrospinal fluid (CSF) by CFT; other serologic approaches may not be reliable or have not been validated for diagnosing SSPE.

For determining past measles infection, the method of choice is plaque reduction neutralization (PRN) assay, but hemagglutination inhibition and specific IgG EIA can also be used. Using PRN, a pre-exposure titer of >120 is associated with protection against clinically apparent measles.[15]

CLINICAL MANIFESTATIONS

Toward the end of the incubation period the prodromal symptoms of fever and malaise appear and persist for up to 4 days before the rash. Pyrexia may rise to 103–104°F (39.4–40°C) and is often

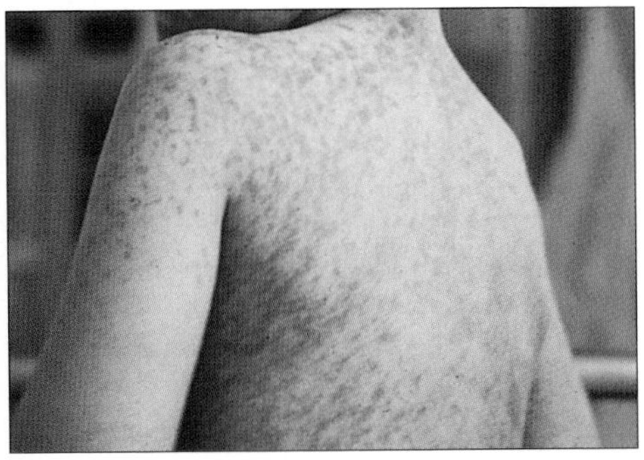

Fig. 212.2 Measles. A disseminated erythematous rash can be seen over the trunk and arms.

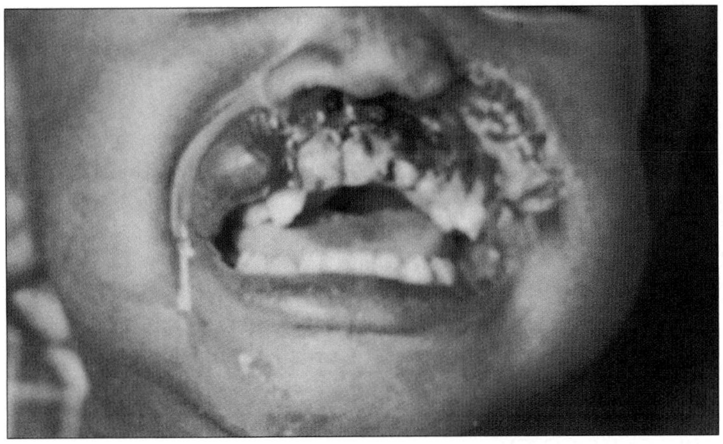

Fig. 212.3 Cancrum oris. Necrosis of the upper lip.

COMPLICATIONS OF MEASLES				
Age	USA			UK
	<5 years	5–19 years	>20 years	All ages
Otitis media	14	2	2	5
Pneumonia	9	2	7	4
Encephalitis	0.2	0.1	0.3	0.1
Death	0.3	0.2	0.3	0.25
Hospitalization	25	8	24	1

Table 212.1 Complications of measles (% of cases). USA data are broken down into three age groups, whereas UK data are not; however, UK data primarily reflect infection in early childhood.[16,17]

accompanied by conjunctivitis, cough and coryza. Koplik's spots are a pathognomonic feature of measles, and can be seen for up to 2 days before rash onset as punctate white spots on an erythematous background on the buccal mucosa.

The rash usually begins on the face and neck, and then evolves to the body and limbs (Fig. 212.2). Although lesions are usually discrete, they can coalesce, and desquamation may occur. The rash usually persists for 5–6 days. Generalized lymphadenopathy and diarrhea are common.

Complications are many, and are most common in younger and older patients (Table 212.1), and those with underlying malnutrition, as in developing countries. In industrialized countries complications are primarily respiratory or neurologic. Pneumonia, either viral or, more usually, secondary bacterial, occurs in up to 4% of patients. Neurologic complications include convulsions, in up to 1% of cases, and encephalitis, which has been reported in 1/1000 cases. Encephalitis usually starts about 1 week after onset of rash, with fever, drowsiness, convulsions, meningeal irritation, vomiting and coma: death occurs in about 15% of patients, and residual neurologic deficit occurs in a further 25%. Overall, estimates of the mortality rate for measles are 1 per 1000 patients or fewer.

Subacute sclerosing panencephalitis manifests from months to years after the initial natural measles or measles immunization; the mean interval is 7 years after natural measles and 3.3 years after immunization. The risk is less after measles immunization (1:1 million) than after natural infection (1:100,000), and is three times more common in boys than in girls. Specific risk factors for the development of SSPE have not been identified. Subacute sclerosing panencephalitis manifests as a progressive intellectual impairment, which may not be noticed for many months, although it is usually apparent in retrospect, and moves to convulsions, motor abnormalities and coma; death is inevitable after a progressive downhill course over months or years.

The immunocompromised patient with T-cell deficiencies, such as those who have leukemia or HIV, is at particular risk. A typical rash is often missing, and infection persists, manifesting as a giant cell pneumonitis or rapidly progressive encephalitis; the fatality rate is high.[18]

Measles in pregnancy seems to carry a higher risk of complications but has not been associated with congenital abnormalities, although there is an increased risk of intrauterine death or premature delivery.[19]

Measles presents special problems in developing countries, where case fatality rates of up to 25% have been described. The high mortality rate is associated with malnutrition and, in particular, vitamin A deficiency.[20] Death usually results from bacterial superinfection, such as pneumonia, or diarrheal illness, although cancrum oris, a progressive oral necrosis, is also seen (Fig. 212.3).

Measles may be attenuated by recent normal immunoglobulin, for instance given after exposure, in younger infants with residual maternal antibody, and in those who have previously received live attenuated vaccine but in whom immunity is incomplete.

Now only of historic interest is 'atypical measles', seen in those immunized in the mid 1960s with a killed measles vaccine and subsequently exposed to natural infection. Various rash appearances were seen, including allergic-type, petechial or vesicular, and these could be accompanied by pneumonia, myalgia, edema and fever.

MANAGEMENT

Postexposure prophylaxis with human normal immunoglobulin is indicated for those who are susceptible and who would be at risk from complications, in particular immunocompromised children and pregnant women. Indeed, one of the greatest benefits to be had from minimizing or eradicating measles in industrialized countries is the impact on immunocompromised children, in whom measles is a substantial risk.

In outbreak situations and in immunocompetent persons, measles vaccine prophylaxis can be considered because there is a rapid development of protection. Administration should be within 3 days of contact.

Uncomplicated measles is managed symptomatically, with vitamin A supplementation for malnourished children. Antimicrobial therapy active against *Streptococcus pneumoniae* and *Haemophilus influenzae* is indicated for presumed bacterial superinfection. In those with major complications, such as pneumonitis in the immunocompromised, specific antiviral treatment with ribavirin may be of benefit;[21] such treatment is of no value in SSPE, however.

RUBELLA

NATURE

Although rubella had been recognized since the 18th century as a distinct clinical illness, it was not until 1941 that Sir Norman

Gregg, an Australian ophthalmologist, made the association between rubella in early pregnancy and congenital abnormalities.[22] In 1962 the causative virus was isolated, leading to techniques for specific diagnosis and the development of attenuated live vaccines.

Rubella is a single-stranded RNA virus, with an icosahedral nucleocapsid surrounded by an envelope. Replication occurs in the cytoplasm of infected cells. It is the sole member of the genus *Rubivirus* within the family Togaviridae. There are three major virus polypeptides: C, E_1 and E_2. Polypeptide E_1 is present in the envelope and has hemagglutinating properties. Only one antigenic strain is recognized, and natural infection of species other than humans has not been shown.

EPIDEMIOLOGY

Rubella occurs worldwide, although its contribution to congenital disease in the developing world has not been well quantified.[23]

In countries without an effective infant vaccination policy or a policy that targets females only, rubella remains endemic, with outbreaks in spring and early summer. Epidemics occur every 7–10 years. Although not as infectious as measles, before or without immunization approximately 80–85% of young adults would have had rubella.

PATHOGENICITY

Infection is transmitted by the air-borne route, with patients being potentially infective for up to 1 week before and after onset of the rash. After replication in the upper respiratory tract and local lymph nodes a viremia infects target organs such as skin, joints and placenta. The clinical features in postnatal rubella, such as the rash and arthralgia, primarily result from the immune response to the virus, with virus being found not only in the rash lesions but in surrounding normal skin.

If the patient is pregnant, placental infection can occur; transmission to the fetus is possible but not inevitable.[24] If fetal infection occurs in the first 16 weeks of gestation, persistence of the virus is likely. Virus may still be detectable in congenitally infected infants up to a few years of age, and high concentrations may be excreted in urine or from the throat during the first year of life. The fetal damage may be a consequence of numerous mechanisms, including slowing of cell division, disordered cell differentiation, intimal damage of small blood vessels, and, at an older age, immunopathologic mechanisms.

PREVENTION

Passive prophylaxis with human normal immunoglobulin has not been proved to reduce the risk of rubella after contact or fetal infection, although it may attenuate the illness. Control of rubella has resided in using the live attenuated vaccines available since the early 1970s. The vaccine strain that has gained pre-eminence is RA27/3. It induces seroconversion in over 95% of susceptible vaccinees, and protection persists for at least 15–20 years. Vaccine virus can be isolated from the throat of vaccinees, but transmission to susceptible contacts has not been demonstrated. A mild, transient rubelliform rash illness can occur 2–3 weeks after immunization, including arthralgia, which may persist for some weeks and, rarely, some months.[25] If vaccine virus is administered to susceptible women in early pregnancy, fetal infection occurs in perhaps 1% of cases, but fetal damage has not been proved.[26] Although rubella vaccine is contraindicated in pregnancy, and conception should be avoided for 1 month after vaccine administration, if inadvertent administration in pregnancy should occur, the risk is insufficient to justify termination of pregnancy. Rubella immunization presents no significant risk to the individual who has HIV infection.

With rubella being a mild illness, control has focused on preventing infection in pregnant women. Two approaches have been used. First, as exemplified in the UK until 1988, rubella vaccine was targeted at adolescent girls and susceptible women, with rubella remaining endemic in children and men. Although cases of congenital rubella were markedly reduced, there were still 2–3% of women susceptible and at risk of rubella in pregnancy. The alternative approach, as used in the USA and in the UK from 1988, was to combine rubella vaccine with measles and mumps vaccines (MMR), and offer it to all children in the second year of life to eradicate rubella from the community. This policy was supported by identifying and immunizing susceptible women. If uptake rates of more than 90% can be obtained, control of endemic rubella is achievable (Fig. 212.4).

DIAGNOSTIC MICROBIOLOGY

With the clinical diagnosis of rubella being unreliable, laboratory confirmation is required, and is essential if a rash illness occurs in

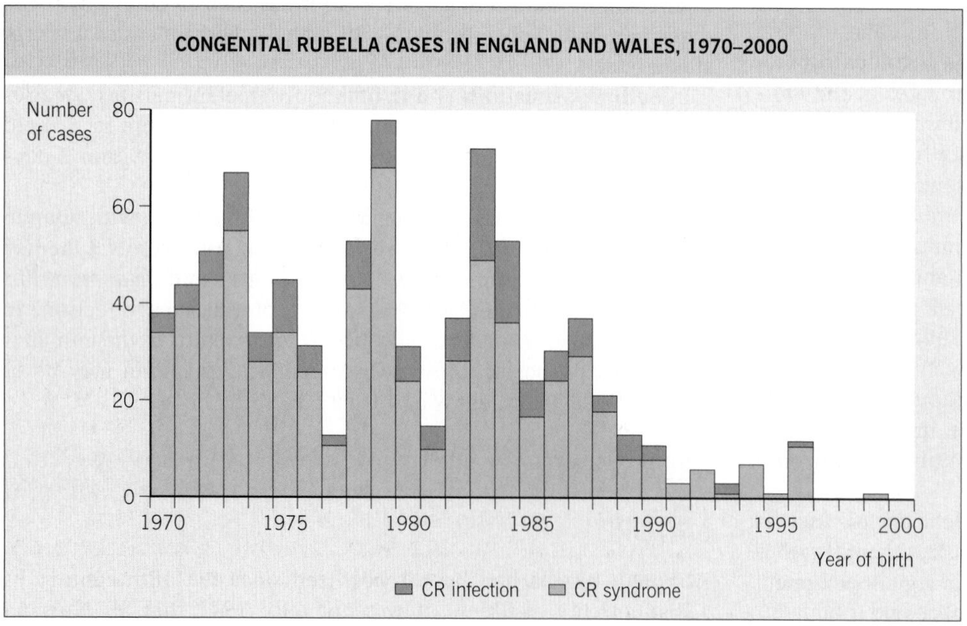

Fig. 212.4 Cases of congenital rubella (CR) syndrome and infection in the UK. The number of confirmed cases was substantially reduced by the introduction of MMR vaccine in 1988. Data from National Congenital Rubella Surveillance Programme and the PHLS Communicable Disease Surveillance Centre.

pregnancy. In addition, in pregnancy it is imperative that contact with rash illness is investigated because subclinical rubella may occur, and this has been proved to be a risk to the fetus.[27] It is debatable whether such investigation of contacts should be pursued if there is a documented history of past detection of rubella antibody or vaccine, but vaccine is not 100% effective in inducing protection and, if there has been only one previous detection of rubella antibody, there is a remote possibility that a laboratory or labeling error could have occurred.

Rubella virus isolation has no role in diagnosing postnatal rubella because it is time-consuming, unreliable and expensive; diagnosis is serologic. The serologic response is detailed in Figure 212.5; tests for total rubella antibody (such as hemagglutination inhibition) have been progressively replaced with tests specific for IgG and IgM, particularly EIAs. Serum should be obtained as soon as possible after onset of illness or after contact. Detection of rubella-specific IgG, but failure to demonstrate specific IgM, indicates past primary rubella, or that the illness being investigated is not rubella, or the existence of immunity to primary rubella if it was a contact that was being investigated. If neither rubella-specific IgG nor specific IgM are detected, a later serum is needed. The incubation period after contact may be up to 21 days, and it may take up to 10 days after onset of illness for rubella antibody to be detectable. Hence in the susceptible person it will not be until about 4 weeks after contact that a subclinical illness can be excluded.

If rubella-specific IgM is detected, this is likely to indicate recent primary rubella, but care is needed in interpretation. Rubella-specific IgM reactivity persists for about 1–3 months, but may occur in a range of other infections, including those that would be differential diagnoses of rubella such as parvovirus B19 infection and Epstein–Barr virus infection (infectious mononucleosis). Rubella-specific IgM reactivity may also be nonspecific and may occur in rubella re-infection (see below). Other serologic approaches, such as determining specific IgG avidity, are of value in confirming primary rubella,[28] with specific IgG early after infection being less tightly bound to antigen (low avidity) than the antibody found in the mature antibody response (high avidity; see Fig. 212.5).

Isolation of rubella virus in cell culture is of value in diagnosing congenital rubella because the infected infant is likely to be excreting high titers of virus in the throat and urine during the first year of life; congenitally infected infants can be highly infectious to susceptible contacts until 6 months or so of age. Rubella isolation can be performed in many cell culture lines, primary and continuous, but a cytopathic effect is only produced in a few lines, for example RK 13. Immunofluorescence is probably the best method for detecting virus growth. An alternative but less specific technique is interference, in which the cell culture is challenged with another virus such as echovirus, which will replicate with cytopathic effect in uninfected cultures but not in those in which rubella virus is growing.

The more usual approach to diagnosing congenital rubella is the detection of specific IgM; all congenitally infected infants are positive for the first 3 months of life, and most for the first 6 months.

Occasionally there may be problems with diagnosis or management of rubella in pregnancy and intrauterine diagnosis may be considered. Approaches used, but of limited availability, have included virus isolation and genome detection from amniotic fluid or trophoblast, and detection of specific IgM in fetal blood; this latter method is unreliable before 24 weeks' gestation, however, because the infected fetus may not be capable of an IgM response until that age.

In recent years assays have been developed that detect specific IgM in saliva. These assays are of limited availability, however, and although not sufficiently validated for use in pregnancy, they have been used successfully for clarifying the etiology of rashes in childhood because they are noninvasive and more acceptable for infant sampling.[14]

Irrespective of the success of population immunization and control of rubella in the community, the majority of developed countries have programs in place to identify susceptible women of child-bearing age and offer immunization. Consequently, many women are screened for rubella IgG in various health care settings such as occupational health and during antenatal care. Tests for specific IgG are many and include EIAs and latex agglutination. An area of contention is the concentration of rubella-specific IgG taken to indicate protection (or, more correctly, as not necessitating immunization), with opinions varying from any confirmed antibody [possibly as low as 3–5 international units (IU)] up to 15IU; 10IU has been recommended in the USA.[29]

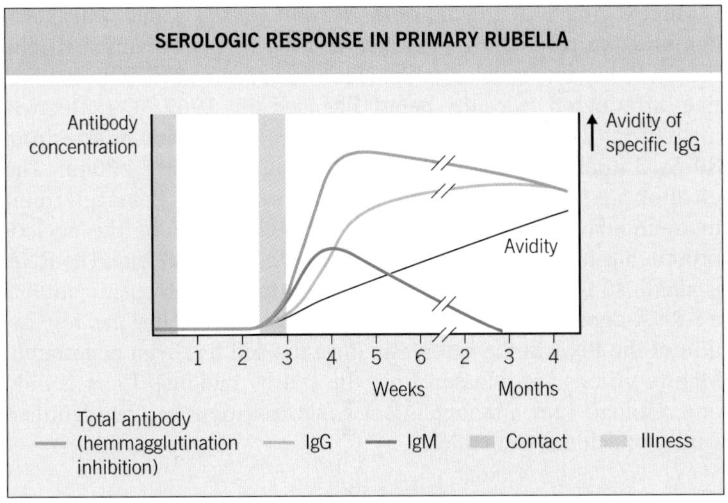

Fig. 212.5 Serologic response in primary rubella. The development of specific IgG and IgM and the increasing avidity of specific IgG are illustrated.

CLINICAL MANIFESTATIONS

In childhood, primary rubella is subclinical in perhaps 50% or more of patients, but in adolescence or older it is usually (90% or more) clinically apparent, although it may be more difficult to recognize in those with dark skin. After an incubation period of up to 21 days, usually 15–17 days, a pinkish-red maculopapular rash develops, usually starting on the face and neck but rapidly spreading over body and limbs (Fig. 212.6). Individual spots may coalesce but the rash usually clears in 3–4 days. Nonspecific symptoms, such as fever, malaise and upper respiratory tract symptoms, may precede and accompany the rash. In childhood the illness is benign and may have no systemic impact. Lymphadenopathy commonly occurs, the sub-occipital nodes being frequently involved.

In adolescence and adulthood, rubella is often far more severe, not only because of complications but also because of a more severe systemic illness. Arthralgia is a frequent complication in adults, with women (30% or more) suffering more often than men. Joints frequently involved are those of the hands and wrists; resolution usually occurs in 2–4 weeks but can persist for some months or even years. Thrombocytopenia and postinfectious encephalitis are rare complications, occurring in fewer than 1/5–10,000 patients, with fatal outcome virtually unknown. Even in patients who have HIV infection and other immunocompromised patients, rubella rarely carries any additional risk, although the serologic response may be abnormal.[30]

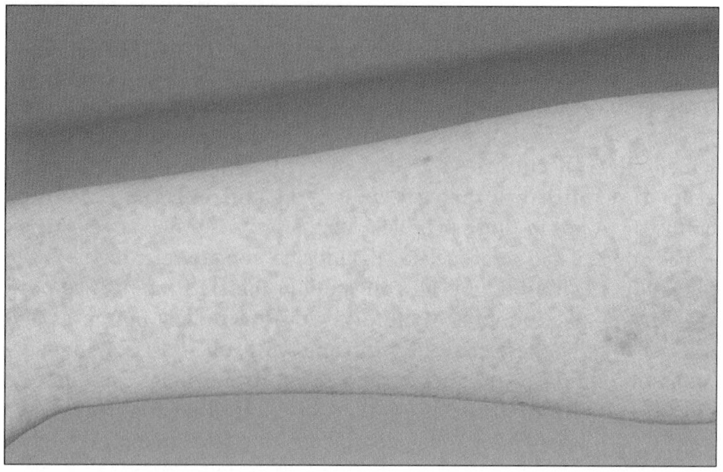

Fig. 212.6 Rubella. A pink macular rash can be seen on the forearm.

Table 212.2 Features of congenital rubella. The final four features listed become apparent in infancy or later.

FEATURES OF CONGENITAL RUBELLA
Cardiovascular defects Persistent ductus arteriosus Pulmonary artery stenosis Myocarditis
Ocular defects Cataracts (unilateral or bilateral) Pigmentary retinopathy Micro-ophthalmus Glaucoma Iris hypoplasia
Auditory defects Sensorineural deafness (unilateral or bilateral)
Central nervous system Microcephaly Psychomotor retardation Meningoencephalitis Behavioral disorders Speech disorders
Intrauterine growth retardation
Hepatitis/hepatosplenomegaly
Thrombocytopenia, with purpura
Bone 'lesions'
Pneumonitis
Diabetes mellitus
Thyroid disorders
Progressive rubella panencephalitis

Primary rubella in the first 16 weeks of pregnancy presents major risks to the fetus. Consequences for the fetus and the pregnancy include abortion, miscarriage or stillbirth. If the fetus is infected and survives to term, a wide range of abnormalities may be seen (Table 212.2), some of which may be apparent at birth, but others develop later in life as a result of persistent virus infection (e.g. progressive rubella panencephalitis, late-onset deafness) or the immune response (e.g. pneumonitis). The congenital rubella triad comprises cardiac, ophthalmic and auditory lesions, but purpura, intrauterine growth and neurologic problems are also frequent.

The gestation at which the mother suffers her rubella is critical for the outcome. Onset of rubella before conception carries little, if any, risk,[31] whereas from conception to the 12th week the risk is about 90%,[32] although figures vary in different studies. Between 12 and 16 weeks' gestation the risk falls to about 20%, with sensorineural deafness being the only consequence. Beyond 16 weeks' any risk is minimal, with only rare cases of sensorineural deafness.

It has been established for many years that re-infections can occur in those with a past history of natural rubella or successful immunization. Such re-infections are rarely clinically apparent and are usually identified by a serologic response after exposure, which is usually to a close contact such as the patient's own child. Fetal infection and damage can occur after maternal re-infection, but this is rare, with the fetal risk probably being less than 5%.[33] Because of the difference in risk to the fetus, serologically distinguishing subclinical primary rubella from re-infection is critical in early pregnancy, but may be difficult in the absence of past rubella-specific IgG test results because a specific IgM response can occur in both; IgG avidity testing will usually resolve the problem because a re-infection would be characterized by high avidity.

MANAGEMENT

Rubella is a self-limiting illness that usually runs a benign course. Supportive and symptom-relieving therapy is indicated for complications such as arthralgia, and the patient can be reassured as to the unlikelihood of symptoms persisting beyond a few months.

Management of rubella in pregnancy is first dependent on achieving a correct diagnosis, given that despite some apparently characteristic symptoms and findings, such as suboccipital lymphadenopathy and arthralgia, clinical diagnosis is notoriously unreliable. A serum sample must be taken as soon as possible after contact or onset of illness, and the testing laboratory given full details of past testing and/or vaccine, and the circumstances surrounding the investigated illness/contact. On the basis of results and the clinical details, the laboratory will advise on diagnosis and any further testing required. If primary rubella or re-infection in the first 16 weeks of pregnancy is diagnosed, further management will have to take into account social, legal and religious perspectives because in many countries the risk to the fetus is sufficient to justify consideration of termination of pregnancy.

MUMPS

NATURE

Mumps was first identified as a distinct clinical illness by Hippocrates in the 5th century BC, but has only attracted attention in the past two to three centuries, particularly because of the impact of outbreaks in the armed forces. Natural infection is limited to humans and is endemic worldwide.

Mumps virus is a member of the *Paramyxovirus* genus (which also contains the respiratory paramyxoviruses) of the Paramyxoviridae family. It was first isolated in the chick embryo in 1945, with the first live attenuated vaccine being licensed in 1967. On electron microscopy it is pleomorphic (Fig. 212.7) and varies in size from 80 to 350nm, although it is usually approximately 200nm. The envelope is studded with projections containing hemagglutinin/neuraminidase or fusion proteins. Within the envelope the nucleoprotein has helical symmetry with a diameter of 15–19nm. The RNA is single stranded and of negative sense; the nucleocapsid contains an RNA-dependent RNA polymerase. This enzyme enables replication of the RNA in the cytoplasm once the cell has been penetrated. Mature virions are released from the cell by budding. There is only one serologic type although minor strain variations can be identified with monoclonal antibodies.

EPIDEMIOLOGY

Mumps is endemic worldwide, with epidemics every 2–3 years in populations not influenced by widespread use of mumps vaccine. In

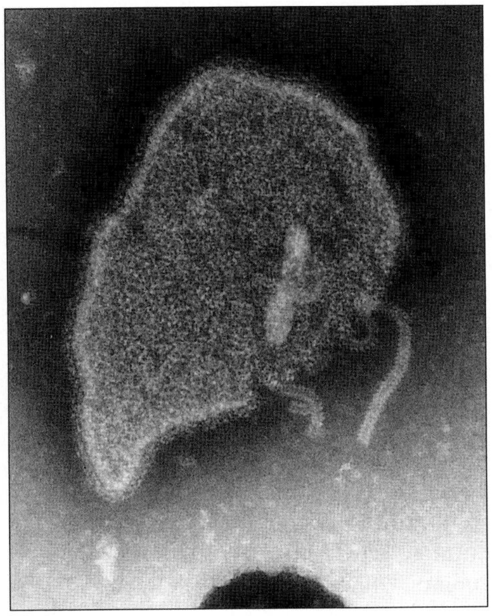

Fig. 212.7 Electron micrograph of mumps virus. Courtesy of Dr A Curry.

the UK there was a characteristic periodicity of two epidemic years followed by one low-prevalence year (Fig. 212.8).[34] Mumps primarily occurred in 5–9 year olds. When widespread population immunization is introduced, as it was in the USA in 1977 and the UK in 1988, without eradication of the disease, susceptibility in older age groups can increase,[34] leading to a resurgence. This occurred in the USA between 1986 and 1989 in 10–19 year olds,[35] although the incidence later declined.[36] This pattern of changing epidemiology necessitated the introduction of a second dose of vaccine in the preschool or early school years.

PATHOGENICITY

Infection is acquired by droplet spread or direct contact, with initial infection most likely within the upper respiratory tract. Replication in the upper respiratory epithelium is followed by spread to local lymph nodes where further replication is followed by a primary viremia, with seeding of target organs such as parotid glands, meninges and testes. A secondary viremia occurs at the onset of symptoms.

The incubation period is usually 16–18 days, with infectivity commencing 2 days or so before symptoms and persisting for 5–7 days after onset. Intrauterine infection has been reported only rarely.

PREVENTION

Two live attenuated vaccine strains have been mainly used since 1967: Jeryl Lynn and Urabe. Both are produced in chick embryo cell culture and are available in monovalent form or combined with mumps and rubella vaccine (MMR). The vaccine is usually administered as MMR at 12–15 months of age, with second doses being given later in childhood. The protective efficacy is 75–85%, with clinically apparent mumps in immunized individuals being well documented. Minor complications of mumps vaccine include mild parotitis, fever, and, very rarely, orchitis. Meningitis has been identified as a significant complication with the Urabe strain, however, and this led to its withdrawal in the UK in 1992.[34,37]

Mumps vaccine is contraindicated in those with previous anaphylaxis to egg and in pregnancy, although adverse implications for the fetus have not been reported. It should also not be given to immunocompromised patients, with the exception of children who have HIV infection, in whom no adverse consequences have been seen.

DIAGNOSTIC MICROBIOLOGY

Virus isolation may be achieved from throat swabs, saliva, CSF and possibly urine. Mumps virus is readily isolated in monkey kidney and Hep2 cells. Although cytopathic effect may sometimes be observed (multinucleated giant cells), isolation is usually confirmed by hemadsorption with chick cells. Identification is by hemadsorption inhibition with specific neutralizing serum. Direct detection of genome can be applied to CSF, and can also be used to distinguish wild-type from vaccine virus.[37] Although feasible, rapid diagnosis by antigen detection in exfoliated upper respiratory cells by immunofluorescence is little used.

Serologic diagnosis is usually achieved by CFT or EIA; neutralization and hemagglutination inhibition testing are now little used. Complement fixation testing uses both a soluble and virion antigen.

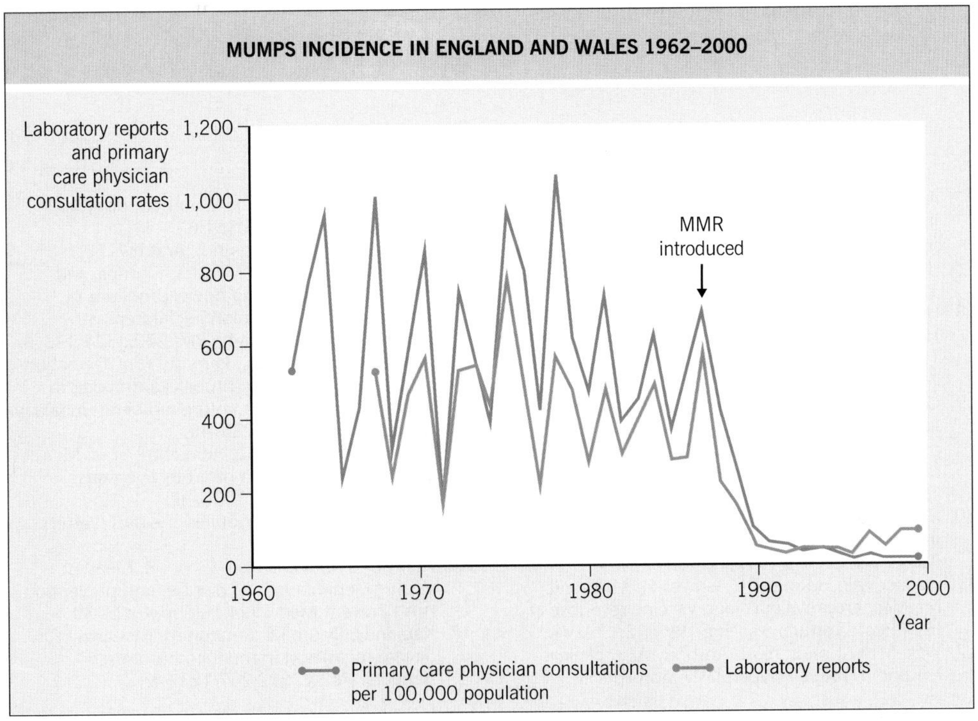

Fig. 212.8 Mumps incidence reported to primary care physicians and number of laboratory diagnosed cases in England and Wales between 1962 and 2000. The number of cases declined in response to the introduction of MMR vaccine in 1988. Data from the PHLS Communicable Disease Surveillance Centre.

Classically, antibody to soluble antigen appears before that to virion antigen, and virion antibody persists longer. This pattern may suggest that single serum diagnosis is feasible (elevated soluble antibody; low or elevated virion antibody), but this approach is highly unreliable because all patterns of antibody development can occur and persist.[38]

Enzyme immunoassay for specific IgG and IgM can be performed, and is relatively reliable, although care must be taken in the interpretation of IgM reactivity because of possible non-specificity. In addition, there is continuing uncertainty as to the possible significance of cross-reacting parainfluenza virus antibody. Saliva specimens can be used for specific IgM detection and are valuable for surveillance of mumps-like illness in the community.[34] For determining past, remote infection CFT has insufficient sensitivity and EIA for specific IgG is usually used.

CLINICAL MANIFESTATIONS

Toward the end of the incubation period of 16–18 days prodromal symptoms such as pyrexia and malaise develop, to be followed in 24–48 hours by the characteristic enlarged and tender parotid glands. There is often accompanying headache and earache. Recovery is usually complete within 4–5 days. Asymptomatic mumps is common and occurs in about one-third of infections. Parotitis is present in 95% of symptomatic infections and is unilateral in about one-quarter; other salivary glands are involved in about 10% of patients. Parotitis similar to that seen with mumps may also be found in other virus infections, such as coxsackievirus B infection, and blockage of the parotid duct may on occasion give problems with diagnosis.

Complications are common;[39] the risk is the same at all ages except for orchitis and oophoritis, which are virtually limited to post puberty. Complications may manifest 1 week before, at the same time as or 2 weeks after parotid involvement; alternatively, they may manifest with no parotid involvement. The risk of orchitis in the adolescent or adult male is about 35%, with bilateral involvement in one-third of these. There may be some persisting testicular atrophy, but sterility is remarkably uncommon, despite public perceptions. Oophoritis, in contrast, is only observed in about 5% of mumps in adult women and causes lower abdominal pain; it is uncertain whether there may be long-term consequences.

Meningeal involvement, as shown by CSF changes, occurs in about 50% of patients, with signs of meningitis or meningeal irritation in about 1–10%. In about 50% of cases of mumps meningitis there is no parotitis. Characteristic findings in the CSF are a lymphocytosis, raised protein concentrations and, occasionally, a reduced glucose concentration that may lead to a misdiagnosis of early bacterial or mycobacterial meningitis. A surprising feature of the epidemiology of mumps meningitis is that it is three times more common in males than females. In countries in which mumps vaccine has not been used for community control, mumps remains a major cause of viral meningitis; enteroviruses are the other main cause and predominate where mumps has been controlled.

Mumps virus may also cause an encephalitis, presenting as impaired consciousness, fits, aphasia, etc. Two patterns of encephalitis are seen:

- direct involvement of neural tissue; and
- a postinfection encephalitis.

The incidence is about 1/6000 patients, with a mortality rate of 1.4%. Some transient impairment of hearing as a result of a labyrinthitis is not uncommon, with persisting deafness in about 1/20,000 patients. Other complications include pancreatitis, which is usually mild, arthritis, mastitis, thyroiditis and myocarditis. Investigation of renal function will often demonstrate kidney involvement, but there are no clinical consequences.

Mumps in immunocompromised patients seems to carry no undue risk, and persistent infection has not been described. Natural infection with wild-type virus usually gives lifelong protection, although re-infection may occur in 1–2% of those re-exposed.[40]

Infection in the first trimester often leads to abortion, but infection later in pregnancy carries no undue risk, and congenital infection and damage have not been convincingly shown.

MANAGEMENT

Postexposure prophylaxis with normal immunoglobulin is of no benefit, and specific mumps immunoglobulin is no longer available, although it may have reduced the risk of orchitis in adult men. Mumps vaccine administered postexposure is of no value, nor is it of any use in the acute control of outbreaks, although it may be of some use in a continuing epidemic.

Management of infection is symptomatic, with the patient being reassured that recovery occurs in a few days, even when complications are present, although the prognosis should be guarded if encephalitis arises.

REFERENCES

1. Anonymous. Human monkeypox in Kasai Oriental, Zaire (1996–1997). Weekly Epidemiol Rec 1997;72:101–4.
2. Ferson MJ, Young LC, Robertson RW, Whybin LR. Difficulties in clinical diagnosis of measles: proposal for modified clinical case definition. Med J Aust 1995;163:364–6.
3. Anonymous. What are the causes of suspected cases of measles. Commun Dis Rep CDR Wkly 1997;7:45.
4. MacKenzie JS, LaBrooy JT, Hueston L, Cunningham AL. Dengue in Australia. J Med Microbiol 1996;45:159–61.
5. Tamin A, Rota PA, Wang Z, *et al.* Antigenic analysis of current wild type and vaccine strains of measles virus. J Infect Dis 1994;170:795–801.
6. Rota JS, Heath JL, Rota PA, *et al.* Molecular epidemiology of measles virus: identification of pathways of transmission and implications for measles elimination. J Infect Dis 1996;173:32–7.
7. Anonymous. Expanded Programme on Immunization (EPI). Meeting on advances in measles elimination: conclusions and recommendations. Weekly Epidemiol Rec 1996;71:305–9.
8. Hutchins S, Markowitz L, Atkinson W, Swint E, Hadler S. Measles outbreaks in the United States, 1987 through 1990. Pediatr Infect Dis J 1996;15:31–8.
9. Gay NJ, Hesketh LM, Morgan-Capner P, Miller E. Interpretation of serological surveillance data for measles using mathematical models: implications for vaccine strategy. Epidemiol Infect 1995;115:139–56.
10. Halsey NA. Increased mortality after high titer measles vaccines: too much of a good thing. Pediatr Infect Dis J 1993;12:462–5.
11. Wallace MR, Hooper DG, Graves SJ, Malone JL. Measles seroprevalence and vaccine response in HIV-infected adults. Vaccine 1994;12:1222–4.
12. Wakefield AJ, Murch SH, Anthony A, *et al.* Ileal-lymphoid-nodular hyperplasia, non-specific colitis, and pervasive development disorder in children. Lancet 1998;351:637–41.
13. Taylor B, Miller E, Lingam R, Andrews N, Simmons A, Stowe, J. Measles, mumps, and rubella vaccination and bowel problems or developmental regression in children with autism: population study. BMJ 2002;324:393–6.
14. Perry KR, Brown DWG, Parry JV, *et al.* Detection of measles, mumps and rubella antibodies in saliva using antibody capture radioimmunoassay. J Med Virol 1993;40:235–40.
15. Chen RT, Markowitz LE, Albrecht P, *et al.* Measles antibody: reevaluation of protective titers. J Infect Dis 1990;162:1036–42.
16. Miller CL. Severity of notified measles (Letter). BMJ 1978;i:1253.
17. Atkinson WL, Kaplan JM, Clover R. Measles: virology, epidemiology, disease, and prevention. Am J Prevent Med 1994;10(Suppl.):22–30.
18. Kaplan LJ, Daum RS, Smaron M, McCarthy CA. Severe measles in immunocompromised patients. JAMA 1992;267:1237–41.

19. Eberhart-Phillips JE, Frederick PD, Baron RC, Mascola L. Measles in pregnancy: a descriptive study of 58 cases. Obstet Gynecol 1993;82:797–801.
20. Potter ATR. Managing measles. BMJ 1997;314:316–8.
21. Forni AL, Schluger NW, Roberts RB. Severe measles pneumonitis in adults: evaluation of clinical characteristics and therapy with intravenous ribavirin. Clin Infect Dis 1994;19:454–62.
22. Gregg NM. Congenital cataract following German measles in the mother. Transact Ophthal Soc Aust 1941;3:34–45.
23. Miller CL. Rubella in the developing world. Epidemiol Infect 1991;107:63–8.
24. Alford CA, Neva FA, Weller TH. Virology and serologic studies on human products of conception after maternal rubella. N Engl J Med 1964;271:1275–81.
25. Howson CP, Katz M, Johnston RB, Fineberg HV. Chronic arthritis after rubella vaccination. Clin Infect Dis 1992;15:307–12.
26. Tookey PA, Jones G, Miller BHR, Peckham CS. Rubella vaccination in pregnancy. Commun Dis Rep CDR Rev 1991;1:R86–8.
27. Cradock-Watson JE, Ridehalgh MKS, Anderson MJ, Pattison JR. Outcome of asymptomatic infection with rubella virus during pregnancy. J Hyg 1981;87:147–54.
28. Thomas HIJ, Morgan-Capner P, Enders G, *et al.* Persistence of specific IgM and low avidity specific IgG1 following primary rubella. J Virol Methods 1992;39:149–55.
29. Skendzel LP. Rubella immunity. Defining the level of protective antibody. Am J Clin Pathol 1996;106:170–4.
30. Morris DJ, Morgan-Capner P, Wood DJ, *et al.* Laboratory diagnosis and clinical significance of rubella in children with cancer. Epidemiol Infect 1989;103:643–9.
31. Enders G, Nickerl-Pacher U, Miller E, Cradock-Watson JE. Outcome of confirmed periconceptional maternal rubella. Lancet 1988;i:1445–7.
32. Miller E, Cradock-Watson JE, Pollock TM. Consequences of confirmed maternal rubella at successive stages of pregnancy. Lancet 1982;ii:781–4.
33. Morgan-Capner P, Miller E, Vurdien JE, Ramsay MEB. Outcome of pregnancy after maternal reinfection with rubella. Commun Dis Rep CDR Rev 1991;1:R57–9.
34. Gay N, Miller E, Hesketh L, *et al.* Mumps surveillance in England and Wales supports introduction of two dose vaccination schedule. Commun Dis Rep CDR Rev 1997;7:R21–6.
35. Cochi SL, Preeblud SR, Orenstein WA. Perspectives on the relative resurgence of mumps in the United States. Am J Dis Child 1988;142:499–507.
36. Anonymous. Mumps surveillance – United States, 1988–1993. MMWR 1995;44(Suppl.S3):1–14.
37. Forsey T, Bentley ML, Minor PD, Begg N. Mumps vaccines and meningitis (Letter). Lancet 1992;340:980.
38. Freeman R, Hambling MH. Serological studies on 40 cases of mumps virus infection. J Clin Pathol 1980;33:28–32.
39. Association for the Study of Infectious Disease. A retrospective study of the complications of mumps. J Roy Coll Gen Pract 1974;24:552–6.
40. Gut J-P, Lablache C, Behr S, Kirn A. Symptomatic mumps virus reinfections. J Med Virol 1995;45:17–23.

chapter 213

Enteroviruses: Polioviruses, Coxsackie viruses, Echoviruses and Enteroviruses 68–71

Heinz Zeichhardt & Hans-Peter Grunert

NATURE

Classification and history

Human enteroviruses comprise one genus in the family Picornaviridae, which also contains the genera rhinovirus, cardiovirus, aphthovirus, hepatovirus and parechovirus.[1] The members of the enterovirus genus that infect humans include the polioviruses, the Coxsackie virus groups A and B, the echoviruses and the enteroviruses 68–71 (Table 213.1). The formerly named enterovirus type 72 has been reclassified as hepatitis A virus in its own genus hepatovirus. Echovirus types 22 and 23 have been reclassified in the new genus parechovirus. Updated information can also be found on the website of the International Committee on Taxonomy of Viruses (www.ncbi.nlm.nih.gov/ICTV/). Human enteroviruses inhabit the alimentary tract and most of them can infect the central nervous system (CNS). In addition, enteroviruses are able to induce a broad spectrum of clinical syndromes (see Table 213.3). For additional information see: Pallansch and Roos,[2] Racaniello[3] and Zeichhardt and Grunert.[4]

The crippling paralytic disease that had been recorded in ancient times was characterized as poliomyelitis with flaccid paralysis by the German orthopedist Heine and the Swedish pediatrician Medin in the 19th century, and was therefore first described as Heine–Medin disease. Evidence for a viral origin of poliomyelitis was shown in 1908 when paralytic poliomyelitis was transmitted to monkeys.[5] The animals were infected with filtered stool from a patient with paralytic disease. It took another 40 years to replace animal inoculation studies by cell culture techniques in order to propagate viruses in primate cell lines. The establishment of in-vitro cell cultures[6] was the major breakthrough for systematic diagnosis and subsequent control of poliomyelitis by vaccination.

Animal inoculation was still the basis for isolation and characterization of another enterovirus in Coxsackie, New York, in 1948. This virus was isolated in suckling mice that had been inoculated with a cell-free filtered stool from children suffering from paralysis.[7] The virus became the first member of the group A Coxsackie viruses because it could not be neutralized by antisera against any of the three poliovirus types. The first group B Coxsackie virus was isolated in 1949.[8]

Further members of the enterovirus group were isolated and characterized by using cell cultures. The first echovirus (enteric, cytopathic, human, orphan) was discovered in 1951.[9] Echoviruses were often isolated from stools of healthy children and could not, therefore, be associated with disease. This is why these enteric viruses were called ‘orphan viruses’.

Structure

Enteroviruses are small, spherical and naked RNA viruses (Fig. 213.1). Of all the enteroviruses, poliovirus is the best characterized in its structural and functional features.[3] Poliovirus has a molecular weight of 8.4×10^6 Da (156S, 1.34g/ml buoyant density in cesium chloride). An icosahedral capsid of approximately 30nm in diameter surrounds one molecule of single-stranded RNA. The capsid consists of 60 protomers, each of which contains four nonglycosylated virus proteins. The capsid proteins are virus protein (VP)1 (molecular weight 33.5kDa), VP2 (30.0kDa), VP3 (26.4kDa) and VP4 (7.4kDa).[10] Virus protein 4 is myristoylated at its *N*-terminus. Structure analysis by X-ray crystallography and biochemical accessibility studies has showed that the capsid proteins VP1, VP2 and VP3 are at the capsid surface whereas VP4 is covered inside the capsid shell and has contact to the viral RNA. Virus protein 1, VP2 and VP3 together make up a pseudoequivalent packing arrangement in the capsid, which is also typical for spherical plant viruses. Human enteroviruses therefore seem to be old viruses in evolutionary terms.

Virus protein 1 and VP3 form a depression or canyon (approximately 2.5nm deep and up to 3nm wide) that is oriented around the 5-fold symmetry axis of the capsid.[11] It is proposed that the canyon is the recognition site for the virus-specific receptor; this canyon hypothesis has also been described for the related picornavirus, human rhinovirus 14.[12] The single-stranded genomic RNA has positive-stranded sense and it codes in a single open reading frame for the four capsid proteins and additionally for functional proteins with, for example, RNA polymerase and protease activities (Fig. 213.2).

Antigenicity and neutralization

Poliovirus preparations contain two distinct antigens, the D-antigen and the C-antigen. The D-antigen is characterized by infective or ‘native’ virus whereas C-antigen comprises noninfective virus with properties of heated antigen. The C-antigens of the three poliovirus types are immunologically cross-reactive whereas the corresponding D-antigens react in a serotype-specific manner.

Four immunodominant antigenic sites at the surface of the poliovirus capsid determine the serotype specificity.[13] Exposed regions of the capsid proteins VP1, VP2 and VP3 compose neutralization antigenic sites at which neutralizing antibodies bind. The major antigenic sites for neutralization of Coxsackie virus type B3 are composed of surface structures of the capsid protein VP2.[14]

Some enteroviruses comprise antigenic relationships as determined by neutralization tests. Partial immunologic cross-reactivity has been observed for:

- poliovirus types 1 and 2;
- Coxsackie virus types A3 and A8, A11 and A15, and A13 and A18; and
- echovirus types 1 and 8, 6 and 30, and 12 and 29.

An increased cross-reactivity can be observed for several enteroviruses in the complement fixation test. This is due to the use of soluble antigen made up of common antigenic sites of the virus proteins that are located in the interior of the virus capsids. Immunoblot techniques confirm such immunologic cross-reactivity between different enteroviruses.[15]

Differences in the composition of the capsid surface define the serotypes of enteroviruses. There are three serotypes of poliovirus (see Table 213.1). Coxsackie virus group A comprises 23 serotypes

SEROTYPES OF HUMAN ENTEROVIRUSES	
Viruses	**Serotypes**
Polioviruses	1, 2, 3
Coxsackie viruses	
Group A	A1–22, A24
Group B	B1–B6
Echoviruses	1–7, 9, 11–21, 24–27, 29–33
Other enteroviruses	68–71

Table 213.1 Serotypes of human enteroviruses. Echovirus 8 has been deleted because it is identical to echovirus 1. The following viruses have been reclassified: Coxsackie virus A23 as echovirus 9; echovirus 10 as reovirus type 1; echoviruses 22 and 23 as parechoviruses 1 and 2; echovirus 28 as human rhinovirus 1A; echovirus 34 as Coxsackie virus A24; enterovirus 72 as hepatitis A virus in the new genus hepatovirus. Additional information can be found at the website of the International Committee on Taxonomy of Viruses (www.ncbi.nlm.nih.gov/ICTV/). Echo, enteric cytopathic human orphan.

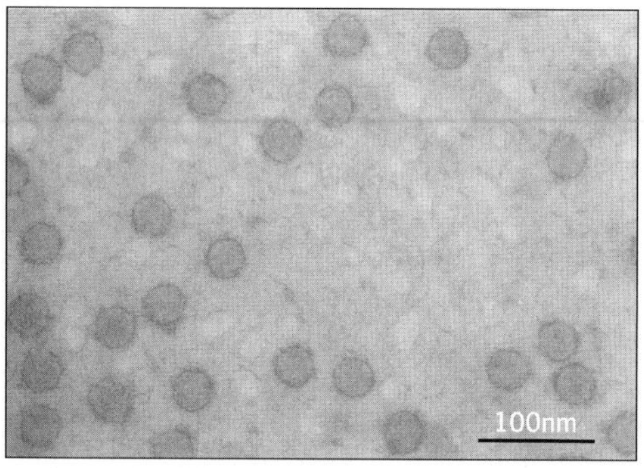

Fig. 213.1 Poliovirus type 1. The particles in this electron micrograph are negatively stained with 0.5% uranyl acetate.

ORGANIZATION OF THE POLIOVIRUS GENOME

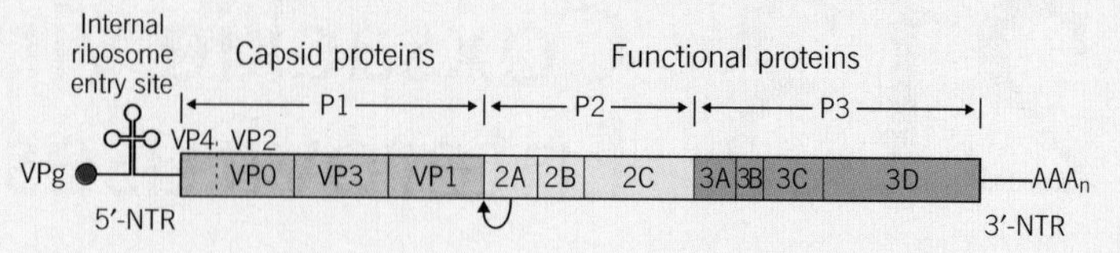

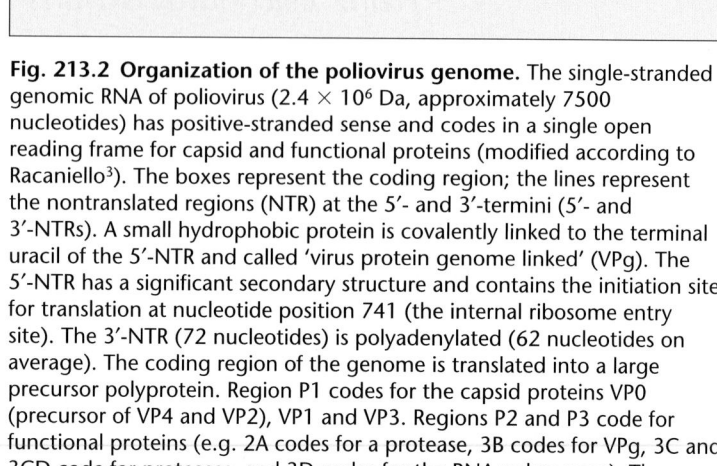

Fig. 213.2 Organization of the poliovirus genome. The single-stranded genomic RNA of poliovirus (2.4×10^6 Da, approximately 7500 nucleotides) has positive-stranded sense and codes in a single open reading frame for capsid and functional proteins (modified according to Racaniello[3]). The boxes represent the coding region; the lines represent the nontranslated regions (NTR) at the 5′- and 3′-termini (5′- and 3′-NTRs). A small hydrophobic protein is covalently linked to the terminal uracil of the 5′-NTR and called 'virus protein genome linked' (VPg). The 5′-NTR has a significant secondary structure and contains the initiation site for translation at nucleotide position 741 (the internal ribosome entry site). The 3′-NTR (72 nucleotides) is polyadenylated (62 nucleotides on average). The coding region of the genome is translated into a large precursor polyprotein. Region P1 codes for the capsid proteins VP0 (precursor of VP4 and VP2), VP1 and VP3. Regions P2 and P3 code for functional proteins (e.g. 2A codes for a protease, 3B codes for VPg, 3C and 3CD code for proteases, and 3D codes for the RNA polymerase). Three proteases mediate processing of the precursor proteins: protease 2A releases the P1 capsid precursor from the nascent polyprotein, and the proteases 3C and 3CD mediate most of the other cleavages before and during virus assembly. Virus assembly is completed when a single RNA molecule is surrounded by its capsid with 60 protomers, in which the precursor VP0 is then cleaved into mature VP4 and VP2. It is postulated that the viral RNA is involved in this final cleavage.

(A1–A22 and A24), Coxsackie virus group B has serotypes B1–B6, and the echoviruses consist of 28 serotypes (types 1–7, 9, 11–21, 24–27 and 29–33). The other human enteroviruses are the distinct serotypes 68, 69, 70 and 71.

The antigenic relationships of the enteroviruses are reflected by limited homologies among the RNA and proteins of the different viruses. Sequence identities for different enteroviruses are more than 50% over the genome as a whole. Virus strains within a species have more than 75% sequence identity over the entire genome.[1] Sequence homologies are relatively high for the functional proteins with RNA polymerase and protease activities, whereas sequence heterogeneity is observed for the sequence region coding for capsid proteins. Capsid protein homology is approximately 70% for the three poliovirus Sabin strains and approximately 50% for polioviruses and Coxsackie viruses.[3]

Reactivity to physical and chemical agents and virus stability

A prerequisite for the passage of enteroviruses through the stomach and duodenum is viral resistance to pH levels that are less than 3 as well as to several proteolytic enzymes. Because enteroviruses have no membranous envelope, they are resistant to lipid solvents (e.g. ether, chloroform and detergents). They are also resistant to several disinfectants, including 70% alcohol, 5% lysol and 1% quaternary ammonium components. Chemical inactivation can be achieved by 0.3% formic aldehyde, hydrochloric acid (0.1mol/l) and free residual chlorine (0.3–0.5 parts per million (ppm)) and other halogens (free residual bromine or iodine at a concentration of approximately 0.5ppm for 10 minutes). Because the presence of organic matter with the virus may result in protection against inactivation, the contact time may be prolonged. Enteroviruses can be inactivated by heat at 122°F (50°C) for 1 hour in the absence of magnesium chloride and calcium chloride and by light (in the presence of neutral red, acridine orange, proflavine and other vital dyes). Virus preparations may be stable at 39.2°F (4°C) for several days up to several weeks. At −4°F to −112°F (−20°C to −80°C), enteroviruses can be stored up to several years.

EPIDEMIOLOGY

Transmission

Humans are the only reservoir for human enteroviruses.[2,4] Because most enteroviruses replicate in the lower or upper alimentary tract, or both, virus spread occurs by both the fecal–oral and respiratory routes. The extensive virus reproduction that occurs in the cells of the gut epithelia leads to massive virus concentrations in the feces (10^6–10^9 infective virus particles/g feces). Viral spread in the feces can last for weeks or months. Viral spread is usually by way of fecal contamination of fingers, normal household objects (e.g. towels and toys) and food. Nosocomial transmission of enteroviruses typically takes place in newborn nurseries. Fecal–oral transmission is predominant in areas with poor sanitary conditions. Enteroviruses may be found in sewage and transmission by a fecal–water–oral route is possible. Depending on the clinical manifestations, enteroviruses can also be spread by contact infection. For example, hemorrhagic conjunctivitis caused by enterovirus 70 and a variant of Coxsackie virus A24 is effectively transmitted with conjunctival fluid. There is no evidence that enteroviruses are transmitted by sexual routes, blood transfusion or insect bites.

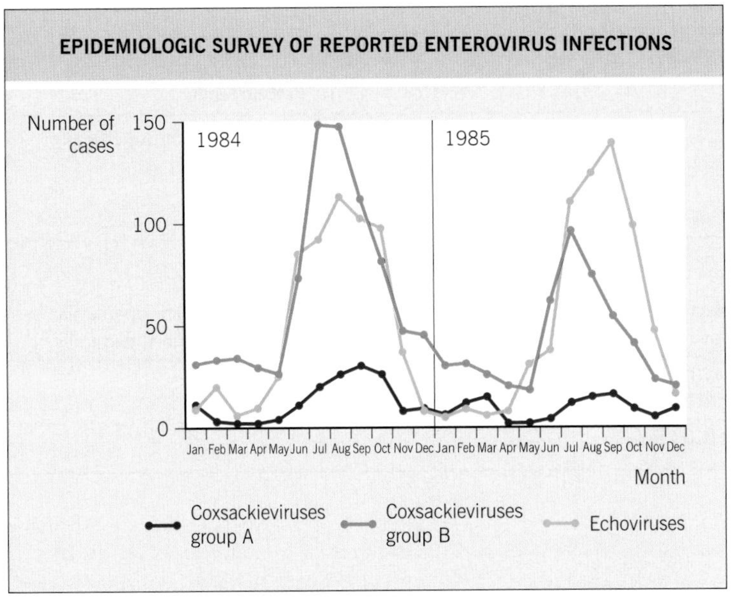

Fig. 213.3 Epidemiologic survey of reported enterovirus infections. This epidemiologic survey by the German Association for Prevention of Virus Diseases (DVV) for the years 1984 and 1985 demonstrates that most infections with coxsackieviruses groups A and B and echoviruses in Germany occur during summer and autumn. Data from Habermehl and Knocke.

Geographic, seasonal, socio-economic, sex and age factors

Enteroviruses are distributed worldwide.[2,4] In temperate zones, enterovirus infections typically occur during summer and autumn (Fig. 213.3);[16] in tropical and subtropical areas infections occur throughout the year. Enterovirus infections are most commonly infections of childhood and young children are the main transmitters. More than 90% of enterovirus infections cause no clinical symptoms or signs.

Poor hygiene and low socio-economic conditions increase the risk of enterovirus infections. Diseases caused by enteroviruses occur more frequently in males than females (male:female ratio of 1.5–2.5:1). The clinical signs of most enterovirus diseases are more severe in adults than in children, although newborn and young children may have severe clinical signs when infected with Coxsackie viruses and some echoviruses. For this reason, all efforts must be made to prevent nosocomial infections by these viruses in nurseries.

Epidemics of poliomyelitis frequently occurred before vaccination strategies were introduced with the inactivated Salk vaccine in 1954 and with the oral attenuated Sabin vaccine in 1962. In the prevaccine era, about 10 cases of paralysis per 100,000 population per year were recorded for the USA. The World Health Organization (WHO) still reported as many as 35,251 cases of poliomyelitis worldwide in 1988. (Statistics on global polio cases are available at www.polioeradication.org/.) There were 6349 cases reported for 1998 and only 494 cases for 2001. The WHO-led campaign aims to eradicate poliomyelitis worldwide by the first decade of the 21st century. As a result of vaccination programs, poliomyelitis has been eliminated in the Americas and in Europe. Isolated cases have been reported for The Netherlands, Canada and the USA before 1993 in enclaves of religious groups that are opposed to vaccination. Ten clinically apparent poliomyelitis cases (nine paralytic) occurred in Finland in 1984–85 owing to the occurrence of a genetically altered wild type of poliovirus type 3 against which the Finnish inactivated vaccine induced only partial immunity. In 1996 an outbreak of paralytic poliomyelitis in Albania, Yugoslavia and Greece resulted in 167 cases of poliomyelitis with 17 deaths.

Some Coxsackie viruses and echoviruses may lead to epidemics. One of the first epidemics observed to be caused by group B Coxsackie viruses was the Bornholm disease epidemic that occurred between 1930 and 1932. The infection caused epidemic myalgia (epidemic pleurodynia) on the island of Bornholm in the Baltic Sea. In the beginning of the 1950s, echovirus 16 was responsible for the so-called Boston exanthema disease, a febrile illness with a rash predominantly occurring in Boston, Massachusetts. Echovirus 9 was responsible for a pandemic of aseptic meningitis in 1955–60. In recent years echovirus 13 outbreaks have taken place in Germany, UK and USA. Large outbreaks of acute hemorrhagic conjunctivitis have been caused by two enteroviruses: enterovirus 70 and a variant of Coxsackie virus A24. From 1969 to 1971, enterovirus 70 spread very quickly in Africa and Asia; acute hemorrhagic conjunctivitis was first recognized in Ghana and after that in other African countries, and it finally spread to Asia. In 1981, enterovirus 70 occurred in the industrialized countries of the West. In 1970–71, acute hemorrhagic conjunctivitis was caused by a variant of Coxsackie virus A24 that originated in South East Asia and was introduced to the Western hemisphere via American Samoa in 1986.

PATHOGENICITY

Virus-specific receptors

The pathogenicity mechanism of enteroviruses is largely determined by their cell tropism. This tropism depends on the specific recognition of the virus by receptors at the surface of susceptible cells (Table 213.2). Several enterovirus receptors can be grouped into receptor families.[28,29] The receptors for the three types of poliovirus, the six types of group B Coxsackie viruses and some of the group A Coxsackie viruses are members of the immunoglobulin superfamily. The poliovirus receptor[17,18] is a glycosylated three domain membrane protein that appears in different isoforms (molecular weight 67–80kDa). The receptor for the group B Coxsackie viruses is the coxsackievirus and adenovirus receptor (CAR), a 46kDa glycoprotein that is also used as a receptor by human adenoviruses 2 and 5.[24] Coxsackie viruses A13, A18 and A21 use intercellular adhesion molecule-1 (ICAM-1, CD54) as their receptor.[23] Intercellular adhesion molecule-1 also functions as a receptor for the major group of human rhinoviruses and recognizes as its physiologic ligand an integrin, lymphocyte function-associated molecule-1 (LFA-1), at the surface of leukocytes. The superfamily of integrins contains several enterovirus receptors. Vitronectin ($\alpha_v\beta_3$) is the receptor for Coxsackie virus A9.[22] Very late-activating antigen-2 (VLA-2) serves as receptor for echoviruses 1 and 8.[25] An additional membrane protein, decay-accelerating factor (DAF, CD55), is the receptor for echoviruses 6, 7, 12 and 21[26] as well as enterovirus 70.[27]

Further membrane proteins function as specific binding proteins for enteroviruses. They are not limiting factors for virus cell tropism, however, and they might support attachment of viruses at their host cells. Examples of these poliovirus-binding proteins are the lymphocyte-homing protein CD44[19,20] and other glycosylated membrane proteins with low affinity for poliovirus.[21]

Viral reproduction cycle

The reproduction cycle of polioviruses is the best characterized of that of any of the enteroviruses. The early phase of the poliovirus reproduction cycle can be divided into adsorption, penetration and uncoating; the later phase can be divided into synthesis of virus-specific protein and RNA, virus assembly and virus release from the infected host cell.

Adsorption of poliovirus at the cell surface is regulated by the binding of the poliovirus receptor into the canyon at the capsid surface. The canyon hypothesis proposes that the *N*-terminal domain

ENTEROVIRUS-SPECIFIC RECEPTORS			
Viruses	**Serotypes**	**Receptor**	**Protein family**
Polioviruses	1, 2, 3	Poliovirus receptor[17,18] Accessory factors: CD44[19,20] 50kDa and 23–25kDa HeLa cell membrane glycoproteins[21]	Immunoglobulin superfamily
Coxsackie viruses			
Group A	A9	Vitronectin ($\alpha_v\beta_3$)[22]	Integrin
	A13, A18, A21	Intercellular adhesion molecule-1[23]	Immunoglobulin superfamily
Group B	B1–6	Coxsackie virus and adenovirus receptor (CAR)[24]	Immunoglobulin superfamily
Echoviruses	1, 8	Very late antigen-2 (α-chain)[25]	Integrin
	6, 7, 12, 21	Decay accelerating factor (CD55)[26]	
Other enteroviruses	70	Decay accelerating factor (CD55)[27]	

Table 213.2 Enterovirus-specific receptors.

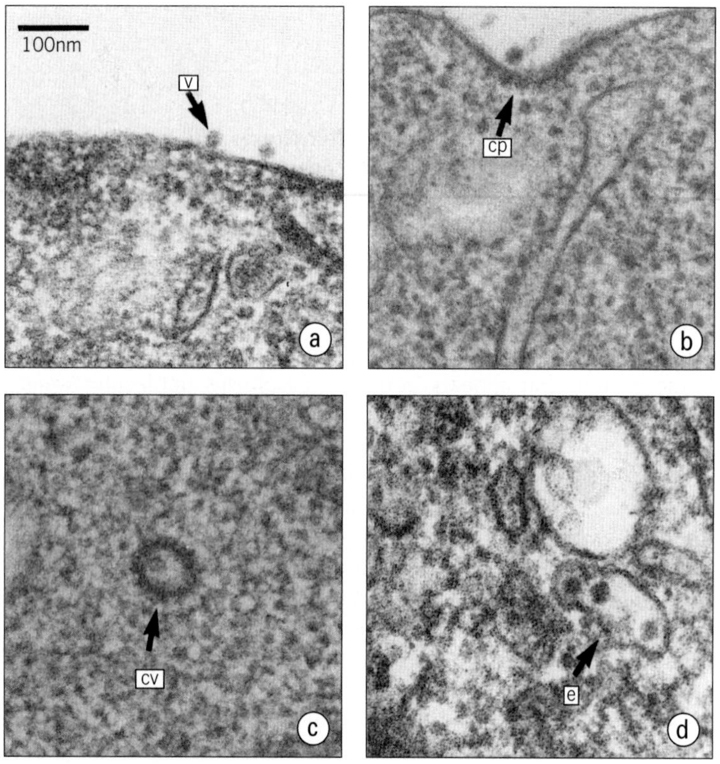

Fig. 213.4 Receptor-mediated entry of poliovirus into host cells. The entry of poliovirus into HEp-2 cells is followed by transmission electron microscopy of ultrathin sections of synchronously infected cells.[31,32] (a) Poliovirus (v) adsorbs at the cell surface immediately after infection (0 minutes after infection). (b) Beginning 1 minute after infection, poliovirus is located at areas of the cell surface that have clathrin-coated pits (cp), at which the surface membrane starts to invaginate. (c) Five minutes after infection, poliovirus is taken up by clathrin-coated vesicles (cv) into the cytoplasm. (d) Between 15 and 20 minutes after infection, poliovirus is within intracellular clathrin-free vesicles or endosomes (e), which are suggested as the sites of viral uncoating.

of the receptor interacts with the canyon, whereas other parts of the receptor are in contact with the capsid surface outside the canyon.[11,12,30]

Virus entry into the host cell (penetration) occurs by way of receptor-mediated endocytosis followed by a pH-dependent release of viral RNA from the virus capsid (uncoating; Fig. 213.4).[31,32] Poliovirus is taken up via clathrin-coated pits after adsorption at the cell surface within 1–5 minutes of infection. After 15–20 minutes, poliovirus reaches acidic compartments in the cytoplasm (endosomes) via clathrin-coated vesicles. The virus capsid undergoes conformational changes during virus entry.[3] The internal capsid protein VP4 is released from the virus and the *N*-terminus of the capsid protein VP1 becomes accessible; this alteration is characterized by antigenic changes. These altered particles have a decreased sedimentation coefficient (135S) and are known as A-particles. An alternative entry mechanism has recently been proposed for poliovirus by which low pH is not required for the release of the viral genome from the capsid.[33]

After the virus has been uncoated, synthesis of viral protein and RNA is initiated by using the viral parental positive-stranded RNA as a template (Fig. 213.5). Viral protein synthesis takes place at the rough endoplasmic reticulum after release of the 'virus protein genome-linked' (VPg) from the viral genome.[13] In contrast to cellular mRNA, enteroviral mRNA has no m^7G cap group. Initiation of viral protein synthesis takes place in the 5′-nontranslated region, which homes the internal ribosome entry site with the initiation codon AUG beginning at nucleotide position 741 (see Fig. 213.2). The polyprotein is autocatalytically processed by protease 2A via several precursor proteins into the four virus capsid proteins VP1–VP4, the virus-specific proteases 2A and 3C, and the RNA polymerases 3CD and 3D. The replication of viral RNA takes place at the smooth endoplasmic reticulum via negative-stranded RNA copies of the viral genome. During RNA synthesis, multistranded replicative intermediates occur, from which new positive-stranded RNA is released for further translation and virus assembly.

Viral transcription is regulated by interaction of the mature RNA polymerase 3D with viral and cellular factors. Secondary structural motifs in the nontranslated regions of positive- and negative-stranded RNAs are involved in the initiation of RNA transcription. The virus morphogenesis is characterized by intermediate assembly steps of the virus capsid via precursors and a procapsid. After encapsidation of one molecule of positive-stranded RNA in the provirus, a final proteolytic cleavage of the precursor protein VP0 into VP2 and VP4 finalizes the virus maturation. It is proposed that a morphopoietic factor and smooth membranes are involved in virus maturation.

One reproduction cycle of poliovirus lasts 6–8 hours, at which time up to 10,000 virus particles have been synthesized in a single cell.[2] Light microscopy shows that infected cells are rounded and contain cytoplasmic protrusions (filopodia; Fig. 213.6a,b).[34] The nucleus is pyknotic and the chromatin is condensed. Analysis by scanning electron microscopy reveals that first changes in the cell

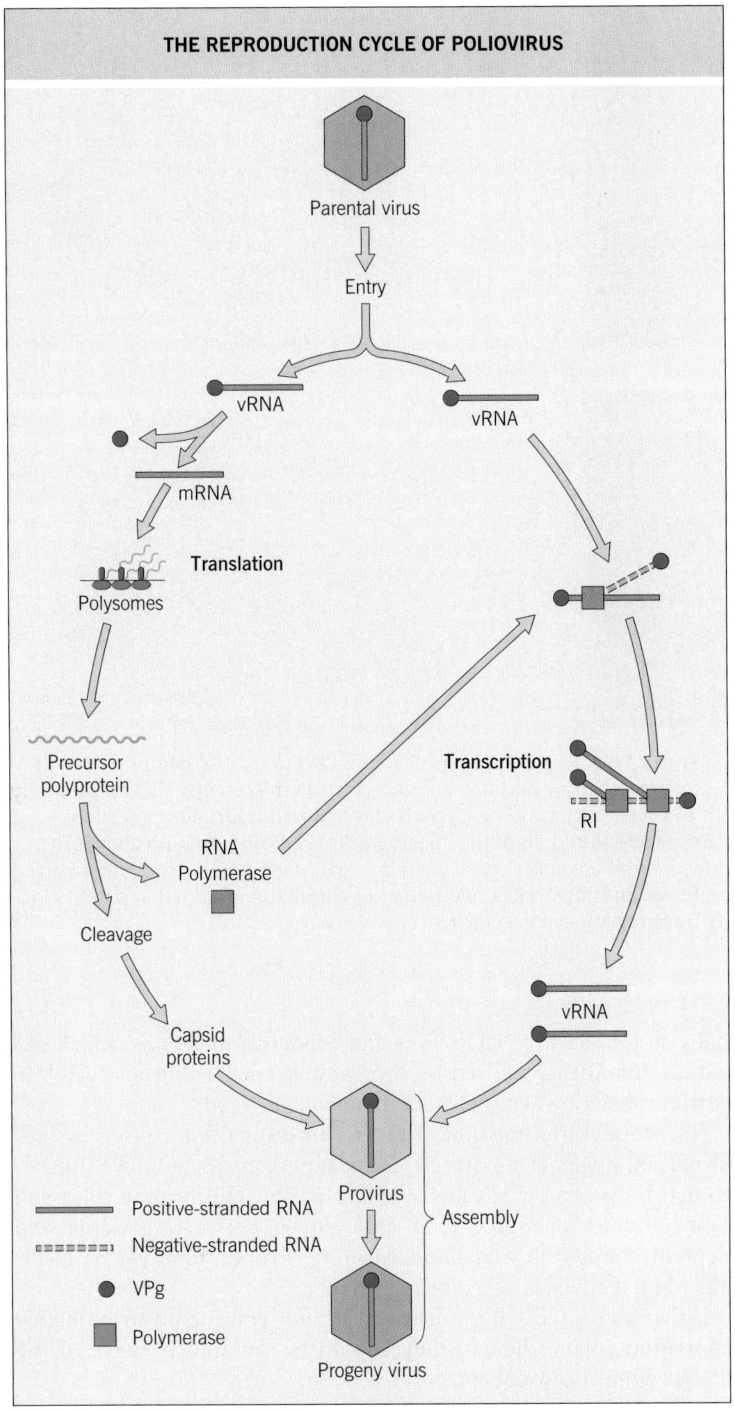

Fig. 213.5 The reproduction cycle of poliovirus. Receptor-mediated entry of poliovirus is completed by the release of the viral RNA from the virus capsid (uncoating). The syntheses of viral protein and RNA are the next reproduction steps. The viral precursor polyprotein is autocatalytically cleaved by viral proteases, resulting in the viral RNA polymerase and, via several precursor proteins, in the virus capsid proteins (see Fig. 213.2). The viral RNA polymerase mediates viral transcription (i.e. de-novo synthesis of positive-stranded RNA via negative-stranded RNA templates). Maturation of the virus is completed by encapsidation of one molecule of positive-stranded RNA into a capsid with the complete set of proteins VP1, VP2, VP3 and VP4. RI, replicative intermediate.

surface can be observed as early as 3 hours after infection. Eight hours after infection the changes (Fig. 213.6c,d) are characterized by:[35]

- condensation of collapsed microvilli;
- formation of elongated filopodia; and
- a 'rounding up' of the cell.

The nuclear and cytoplasmic alterations are characterized by lobed nuclei with irregular distribution of condensed chromatin and vesicles arranged in clusters in the cytoplasm, as shown by transmission electron microscopy (Fig. 213.6e,f).[35,36]

Characteristic mitotic changes and chromosomal alterations are induced by poliovirus. The mitosis is enhanced during the early stage of replication. In later stages of infection, the mitosis is arrested in the metaphase (a colchicine-like effect). Chromosomal damage is characterized by single chromatin breaks and pulverization.[37,38] Poliovirus induces 'shut-off' of the syntheses of cellular protein, RNA and DNA within the first 2 hours of infection. The inhibition of cellular protein synthesis is caused by a proteolytic cleavage of the cellular protein p220.[39] This protein is the initiation factor eIF-4G which, as part of the cap-binding complex eIF-4F, is involved in the initiation of cellular protein synthesis mediated by capped mRNA.

PREVENTION

Vaccination

The introduction of vaccination against the three poliovirus serotypes was a prerequisite for effective prevention of poliomyelitis.[2,4] The establishment of modern cell culture techniques[6] allowed the development of two poliovirus vaccines. Jonas Salk developed a formaldehyde-inactivated polio vaccine (IPV), which was introduced in 1954 and is administered intramuscularly. In 1962, Albert Sabin introduced an oral polio vaccine (OPV), which consists of live-attenuated viruses. Both IPV and OPV contain the three poliovirus serotypes and induce humoral immunity with circulating antibodies. In addition, OPV induces secretory IgA in the gut owing to the subclinical infection with virus multiplication that it causes in the gastrointestinal tract.

Both vaccines are administered three times several weeks apart in order to give rise to effective titers of neutralizing antibodies. Booster vaccinations are recommended every 10 years for both vaccines. In the temperate zones, it is better not to administer OPV during the summer months when there is a high frequency of other enterovirus infections. Co-infection with other enteroviruses may induce viral interference; this may also occur in the trivalent vaccine when the multiplication of one serotype of poliovirus is reduced by the other types. Such interference may be reduced by the 3-fold administration.

In very rare cases, OPV may gain neurovirulence owing to changes (often point mutations) in the genome of attenuated virus. These mutations occur not only in the genome regions that code for viral capsid proteins and the RNA polymerase but also in the 5′-nontranslated region, which is of importance for the initiation of viral protein synthesis. The Sabin type 3 polio vaccine has been observed to increase in neurovirulence because of a single base change from uracil to cytosine at position 472 in the internal ribosome entry site in the 5′-nontranslated region.[40]

The risk of developing clinical poliomyelitis, including paralysis, after live Sabin vaccination is very small; an incidence of one case of vaccine-associated paralytic poliomyelitis (VAPP) per 1.2 million doses of live vaccine administered has been reported for the USA.[2] Neurovirulent revertants occur mainly with the attenuated vaccine strains of poliovirus types 1 and 3.

All infants and young children should be vaccinated with one of the two vaccines. It is advisable that adults who have not been vaccinated as infants should be vaccinated with IPV followed by OPV. The primary IPV administration helps to prevent VAPP, which has a higher incidence in children and adults than it does in infants. Clinical personnel should be given booster vaccinations at regular intervals. In health care workers, IPV is recommended in order to prevent shedding of attenuated vaccine strains of the virus in clinical

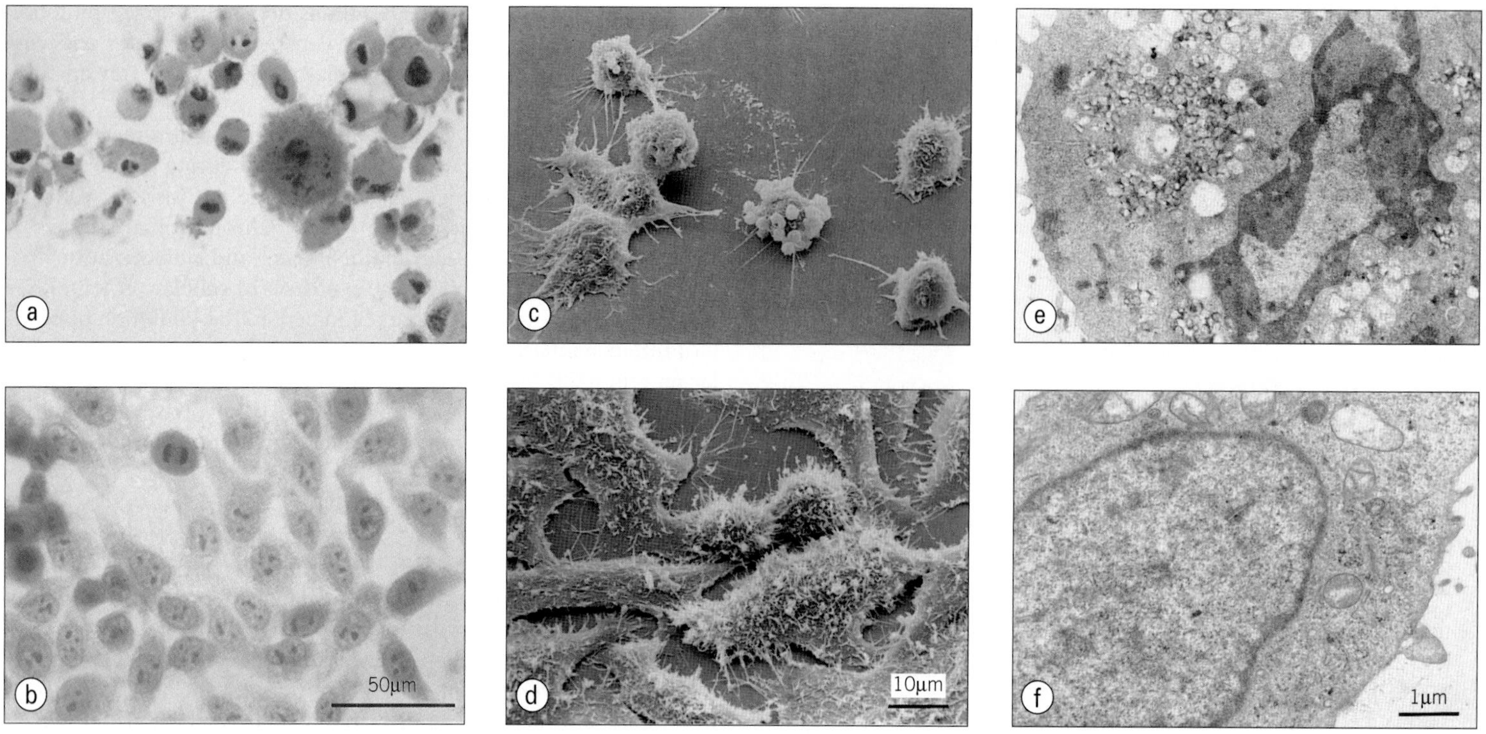

Fig. 213.6 The poliovirus-induced cytopathic effect. The cytopathic effect of poliovirus type 1 in monolayers of HEp-2 cells (a, c, e) is demonstrated in comparison to noninfected control cells (b, d, f) by light microscopy, scanning electron microscopy and transmission electron microscopy.[35] (a) Light microscopy of infected cells stained with hemalum–eosin shows rounded cells with pyknotic nuclei and condensed chromatin (8 hours after infection). (b) Light microscopy of control cells. (c) Scanning electron microscopy demonstrates severe rounding of the infected cells (12 hours after infection). The infected cells are characterized by elongated filopodia and microvilli at the cell surface; these are collapsed or even lost. (d) Scanning electron microscopy of control cells. (e) Transmission electron microscopy of ultrathin sections reveals infected pyknotic cell condensation of chromatin arranged in patches in a lobed nucleus and clusters of vesicles in the cytoplasm (8 hours after infection). (f) Transmission electron microscopy of control cells.

surroundings. National health authorities in some countries where poliomyelitis has been eliminated have recently decided to administer IPV instead of OPV because, in these countries, the risk of VAPP is now greater than the risk of infection with wild-type poliovirus.

The WHO-led campaign for eradication of poliomyelitis with the expanded programs of immunization led to a 90% decrease in poliomyelitis worldwide in the years 1988–97.[41] In 2001 only 494 confirmed cases of poliomyelitis were reported. In the Americas and in Europe poliomyelitis is eliminated. Before 1993, very rare local cases of poliomyelitis in Canada and The Netherlands were introduced in ethnic groups refusing vaccination. A prerequisite for global eradication of poliomyelitis is the maintenance of the present high levels of vaccination in developed countries and the induction of immunity in the population of developing countries. For this purpose, national immunization days are performed worldwide. In 1996 on worldwide co-ordinated national immunization days, 420 million children (approximately two-thirds of the world's children under the age of 5 years) were vaccinated against poliomyelitis. The aim is the eradication of poliomyelitis in the first decade of the 21st century.[41]

Passive immunization and hygienic prevention

In contrast to infection caused by polioviruses, infections caused by Coxsackie viruses, echoviruses and enteroviruses 68–71 presently cannot be prevented by vaccination. However, interruption of the routes of virus transmission and prophylactic passive immunization are effective in the prevention of enterovirus infections. Serum that contains antibodies against polioviruses, Coxsackie viruses and echoviruses obtained from convalescing patients can be effective in preventing infections in seronegative patients when administered within 72 hours of exposure. Immunoglobulins can prevent poliovirus infections as well as Coxsackie virus and echovirus infections, which can induce 'fulminant viral sepsis', myocarditis, encephalitis and death in newborn babies when transmitted in neonatal wards.

Nosocomial transmission of enteroviruses is often caused by lack of normal hygienic conditions. Clinical personnel can prevent nosocomial transmission of enteroviruses by obeying hygiene rules and especially by changing coat and gloves between patients and hygienic hand rub and hand washing. Proper removal of feces, including diapers, is of major importance.

Patients infected with poliovirus are not considered to be highly contagious; nevertheless, they should be isolated because of the drastic clinical consequences of infection.

Antiviral chemotherapy

Effective antiviral chemotherapy against enterovirus infections does not yet exist, with the exception of the newly developed antiviral compound pleconaril. Pleconaril shows antiviral activity against different picornaviruses and seems to be a promising new drug candidate for the therapy of enteroviral meningitis. All other antiviral compounds against enteroviruses have currently been proven to show antiviral activity only in cell culture systems. Guanidine and some benzimidazoles specifically inhibit the viral RNA polymerization. Hydrophobic compounds intercalating in the viral capsid protein VP1 stabilize the virus, resulting in inhibition of viral uncoating.[3,4,42]

DIAGNOSTIC VIROLOGY

The laboratory diagnosis of enterovirus infections is based on virus detection, including virus isolation and identification, and serologic diagnosis.[2,43]

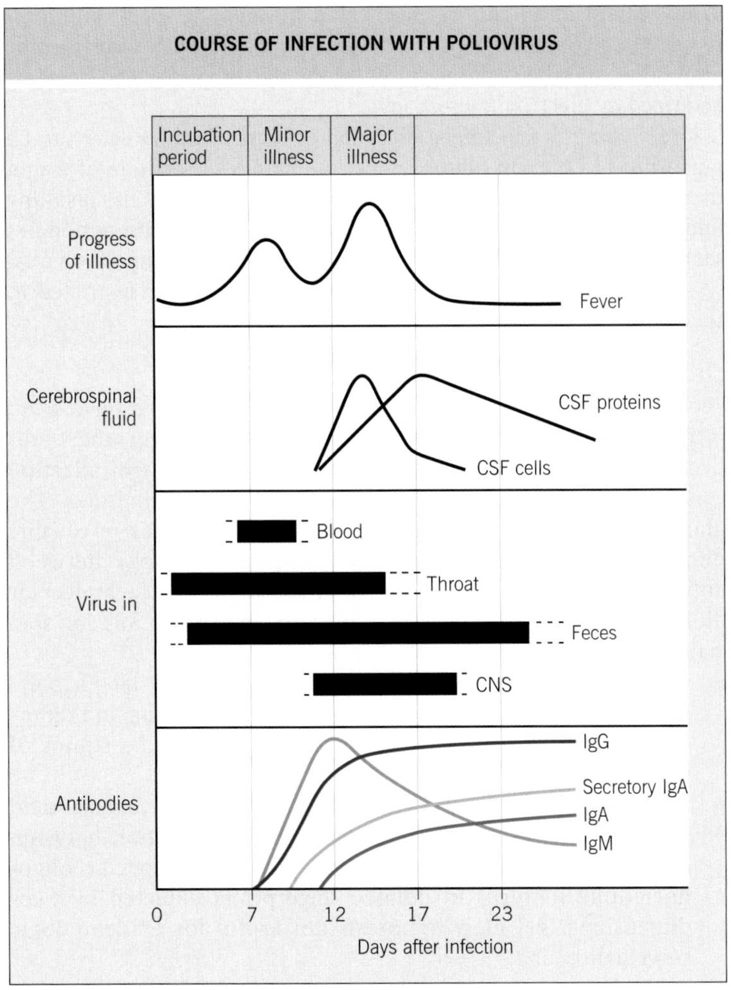

Fig. 213.7 The course of infection with poliovirus.

Collection and preparation of specimens

Specimens for virus isolation and identification

Successful virus isolation from clinical specimens depends on proper collection and is related to the time since infection (Fig. 213.7) In general, virus specimens should be collected as soon as possible after onset of clinical symptoms. The specimens should preferably be transported to the laboratory under cooled conditions. If virus isolation cannot be performed immediately after receipt the specimens should be stored at −4°F (−20°C).

Owing to the pathogenesis of enteroviruses with their enteric multiplication and clinical manifestation involving the CNS, the most useful specimens for virus isolation are stools and rectal swabs, throat swabs and washings, and cerebrospinal fluid (CSF). Most enteroviruses can be isolated most effectively from the throat up to 15 days after infection or longer, and from stools and rectal swabs up to 1 month after infection or longer. When there are symptoms involving the CNS, virus isolation is usually successful from the CSF 2–3 weeks after infection. Stools are preferred for virus isolation because virus concentrations in feces are very high (up to 10^6–10^9 virus particles/g of feces) compared with virus concentrations in other specimens.

In addition, all specimens from target organs allow virus isolation if a biopsy or autopsy specimen is taken during the clinical manifestation of disease. Viruses inducing vesicular rashes (such as Coxsackie viruses types A4, A6, A9, A10 and A16, and enterovirus type 71) can be isolated from the lesions. A Coxsackie virus A24 variant and enterovirus 70 may be responsible for hemorrhagic conjunctivitis and echovirus types 7 and 11 induce conjunctivitis; these viruses can be isolated from ocular samples, either conjunctival swabs or scrapings.

For selected diagnostic purposes, biopsy or autopsy material from the heart, muscle or brain may be successful for isolation of the virus. Autopsy specimens should be collected as soon as possible after death under sterile conditions in order to prevent virus degradation. Depending on the target organ, the order of collection should be CNS or lymph node specimens, specimens from the thorax, specimens from muscles, liver or glands, and finally specimens from peritoneum and gastrointestinal tract. For diagnosing clinical manifestation in the CNS, samples from the pons and medulla oblongata, as well as spinal cord and CSF specimens, are especially likely to yield successful isolation. A planned order of tissue collection is emphasized so that contamination from gastrointestinal contents is avoided.

Virus isolation from blood is successful only during viremia (days 6–9 after infection; see Fig. 213.7) and is therefore not generally attempted because of the short period for collection.

In rare cases, enteroviruses other than poliovirus can be isolated from urine.

Specimens for serologic diagnosis

Detection of virus-specific antibodies should be performed with at least two serum samples. The first, acute-phase serum, should be obtained as soon as possible after the onset of illness. The second, convalescent-phase serum, is usually collected 2–3 weeks later in order to monitor any increase in antibody titer. If there are CNS manifestations, antibody detection in CSF can be useful. Serum and CSF that are free of additives should be used for serologic diagnosis.

Virus isolation and identification

Virus propagation in cell cultures and animals

Virus growth in cell cultures is the preferred method for virus isolation. The human cells that are usually used for propagation of enteroviruses are primary embryonic fibroblasts of the skin and lung, permanent fibroblasts (e.g. MRC-5 cells), permanent amnion cells (e.g. FL cells), and transformed cells such as HeLa, HEp-2 and KB cells. The monkey cells that are most frequently used are primary rhesus or African green monkey kidney cells or permanent monkey kidney cells (e.g. BGM and Vero cells). These standardized cell lines for virus propagation can be obtained from national or international reference institutions (e.g. American Type Culture Collection).

Several types of group A Coxsackie viruses have exceptional growth behavior. Some of these viruses replicate only in a human rhabdomyosarcoma cell line or in newborn mice. Newborn mice are required to isolate Coxsackie virus types A1, A19 and A22.[2] Virus isolation in mice, however, is nowadays restricted to a few reference laboratories worldwide. It should be mentioned that, before the introduction of cell cultures for virus isolation, pathologic lesions in monkeys induced by polioviruses and in mice induced by Coxsackie viruses of groups A and B were the only tools for virus isolation.

Wild-type polioviruses have a tropism that is restricted to primates. Most other enteroviruses, however, also infect laboratory animals such as mice. In order to distinguish between group A and group B Coxsackie viruses before the introduction of cell culture techniques, pathologic lesions in mice were used. In newborn mice, Coxsackie group A viruses cause generalized myositis accompanied by flaccid paralysis. Group A viruses rarely induce CNS alterations. Typically, group B viruses cause focal myositis and lesions in the brain and interscapular fat pad; myocarditis, endocarditis, hepatitis and pancreatitis may also occur.

Virus neutralization with internationally standardized antiserum pools

Proof of the presence of virus in a specimen is provided by the appearance of the typical cytopathic effect in cell culture. Virus neutralization tests using virus-specific antisera are most commonly used for identification of the virus isolates. Typing of the isolates is performed with pools of internationally standardized hyperimmune equine antisera. These sera were introduced by Lim and Benyesh-Melnick[44] and can be obtained from the WHO Collaborating Center for Virus Reference and Research in Copenhagen. The Lim–Benyesh-Melnick (LBM) sera consist of eight antiserum pools (pools A–H), which can be used for the identification of 42 enterovirus serotypes.

Isolation and identification of selected enteroviruses that cannot be propagated in cell culture are restricted to a few reference laboratories that propagate viruses in animals. For virus typing in animals, additional LBM antiserum pools with neutralizing antibodies (pools J–P) are available. Virus neutralization is characterized by absence of clinical signs in inoculated animals.

Differentiation between wild-type and Sabin vaccine-like poliovirus strains

The differentiation of wild-type strains and Sabin vaccine-like strains of polioviruses is generally performed in specialized laboratories, which use the following techniques:[45]

- determination of growth markers of polioviruses represented by the viral reproductive capacity at elevated temperatures and plaquing capacities;
- intratypic serodifferentiation of virus strains using polyclonal strain-specific antibodies;[46,47]
- use of monoclonal antibodies against wild-type and vaccine-like viruses for virus neutralization;[47–49] and
- amplification of viral genome sequences by reverse transcriptase polymerase chain reaction (RT-PCR) followed by sequence analysis.[50,51]

Virus detection and identification by microscopy

Specialized laboratories perform electron microscopic techniques for direct virus visualization (see Fig. 213.1). The technique of negative staining is restricted to stool specimens, because only this material contains a sufficiently high virus concentration (see above). Direct virus identification can be performed by immune electron microscopy. Virus-containing specimens are incubated with virus-specific antibodies and the resulting virus–antibody complexes can be characterized by electron microscopy.

Virus typing in specimens obtained at biopsy and autopsy can be performed by immunofluorescence techniques. Sections of target tissues are incubated with virus-specific antibodies and the resulting immune complexes are detected in a sandwich test with antibodies that are labeled with fluorescent dye and directed against the virus-specific antibody. This laborious sandwich technique is restricted to specialized laboratories.

Detection of virus genome

Techniques for the detection of enterovirus genomes have been introduced for selected diagnostic purposes. However, the traditional immunologic techniques for virus typing by neutralization cannot yet be replaced by molecular biologic techniques. The main reason for the limited use of these techniques in routine diagnostics is the relatively high sequence homology between enteroviruses, which may result in reduced specificity. Molecular biologic techniques nevertheless are very powerful tools for specialized diagnostics:[51,52]

- the combination of PCR with restriction fragment length polymorphism analysis or sequencing allows virus typing and differentiation between wild-type and Sabin vaccine-like strains of polioviruses;
- oligonucleotide analysis ('fingerprinting') and nucleic acid sequencing is useful for detecting genome variation between different enterovirus isolates, and virus strain-specific oligonucleotide patterns in defined fingerprints detected by two-dimensional gel electrophoresis are useful for epidemiologic surveillance; and
- in-situ hybridization using labeled virus-specific gene probes is a powerful tool for enterovirus genome detection in biopsy or autopsy specimens (Fig. 213.8); the use of Coxsackie virus type B3-specific cDNA has enabled this virus to be identified as a cause of chronic dilated myocarditis,[53] which could not be proven by virus isolation in cell cultures.

The introduction of quantitative methods for nucleic acid amplification (i.e. quantitative PCR) in combination with the introduction

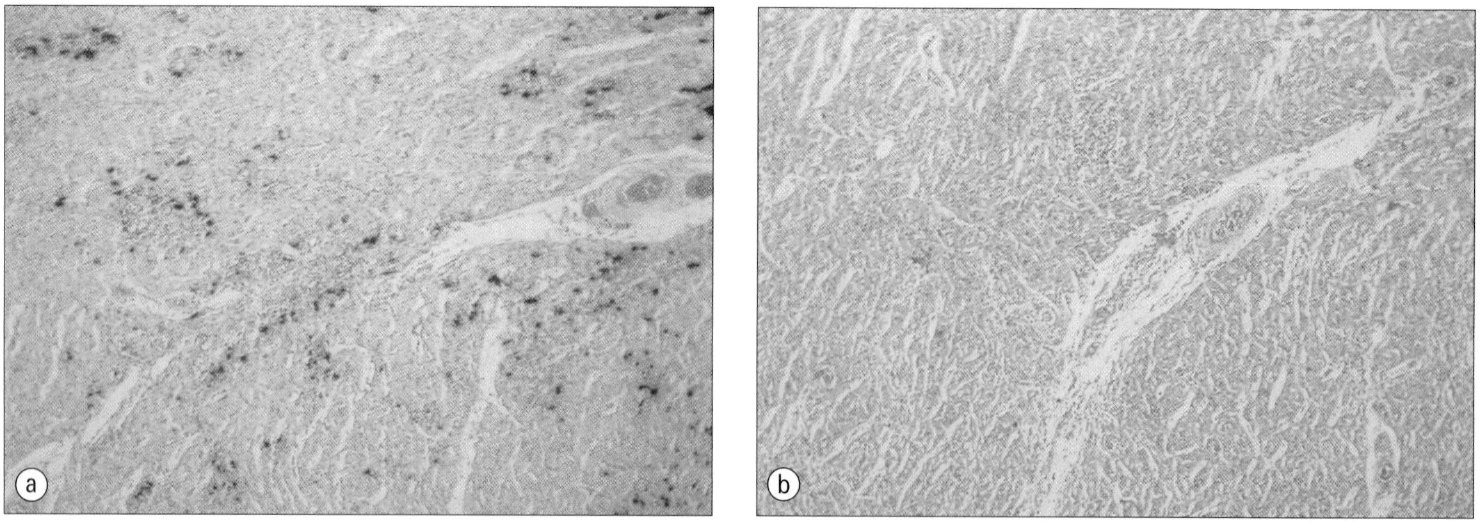

Fig. 213.8 Fulminant enterovirus-induced myocarditis. In-situ hybridization of a ^{35}S-labeled enterovirus group-specific cDNA probe to the paraffin-embedded autopsy heart tissue of an infant who died of acute enterovirus infection.[53] (a) Autoradiographic silver grains can be clearly localized to distinct infected myocytes, thereby providing the possibility of an unequivocal diagnosis of myocardial enterovirus infection. (b) Hybridization to myocardial cells was not observed when myocardial tissues were hybridized with the ^{35}S-labeled plasmid vector control probe, demonstrating the specificity of in-situ hybridization. Stained with hematoxylin and eosin. Courtesy of R Kandolf, Tübingen.

of standardized international reference material will give new possibilities for the diagnosis of enterovirus infections.

Serologic diagnosis

In order to confirm an infection with enteroviruses, a combination of serologic diagnosis with virus identification is advisable. Recent enterovirus infections can be proven by serologic means by using two kinds of documentation of a virus-specific antibody response.

Analysis of two or more sera from a patient

Ideally, the first serum of the patient should be tested at the beginning of the illness. A second serum should be collected 7–10 days later and tested in parallel with the first serum in order to detect a rise in antibody titer (see Fig. 213.7). A 4-fold or greater rise in antibody titer (i.e. at least two titer steps) proves a recent enterovirus infection.

Detection of virus-specific IgM

The detection of a single high titer of enterovirus-specific IgM proves a recent enterovirus infection. Virus-specific IgM first appears after enterovirus infection (7–10 days after infection) and persists for approximately 4 weeks in 90% of infections (see Fig. 213.7; also see below). Common procedures for isolating the IgM fraction of a patient serum from remaining serum proteins are either density gradient ultracentrifugation or column chromatography (i.e. conventional molecular sieve gel chromatography or high pressure liquid chromatography). The isolated IgM fraction is analyzed for virus specificity in neutralization tests.

This laborious and time-consuming isolation of IgM has the advantage that a single serum from a patient is sufficient for detecting 'fresh' virus-specific IgM. This depends on the precondition that this single serum was collected neither within the first 7 days of infection nor too late after infection, when the amount of virus-specific IgM has decreased below the level of detection.

Neutralization test

The virus neutralization test is still the first-choice method for detecting virus-specific antibodies. This test has a very high sensitivity and specificity and it allows the detection of serotype-specific antibodies, which is in contrast to most other serologic detection methods. The neutralization test is usually performed only in specialized laboratories with the following preconditions:

- an enterovirus infection is suspected because of a defined clinical or epidemiologic situation;
- an enterovirus has already been isolated from a defined patient's material; and
- group-specific antibodies have already been detected with another serologic technique (e.g. with the complement fixation test).

Cytopathic end-point tests that use enterovirus permissive cell cultures in a microtiter system are performed for the detection of the neutralization reaction. The patient's serum or its isolated IgM fraction is geometrically diluted (e.g. 1:10, 1:20 and so on up to 1:320) and each dilution is incubated with a constant infectious dose of a given enterovirus (100 tissue culture ID_{50} is the dose of virus that will induce a cytopathic effect in 50% of the cells). The absence of a cytopathic effect caused by virus neutralization is microscopically detected in comparison with non-neutralized control virus. The serum titer is calculated for the 50% cytopathic end point per inoculation volume against the challenge dose of non-neutralized virus.[43]

Complement fixation test

The complement fixation test is usually performed as a serologic screening method for the detection of enterovirus-specific antibodies. It only allows the detection of enterovirus group-specific antibodies. The use of denatured enterovirus antigen gives rise to immunologic cross-reaction between different enterovirus groups (see above).

Enzyme-linked immunosorbent assay (ELISA) and immunoblot

These serologic methods have not been implemented as routine tests as they have the same limited value as the complement fixation test due to the detection of enterovirus group-specific instead of serotype-specific antibodies.

CLINICAL MANIFESTATIONS

Asymptomatic infections

Most enterovirus infections are silent, mild or subclinical. Between 90% and 95% of poliovirus infections remain asymptomatic whereas only 0.1–1% of infections cause clinical signs involving the CNS, such as paralytic poliomyelitis. Enterovirus passage through the gut may be the reason for the high incidence of inapparent infections because the cells of the gut epithelia normally have a high rate of turnover. Therefore, the virus-induced lysis of the gut cells might be without clinical signs, even though more than 1000 infective virus particles can be reproduced in one infected cell.

Incubation times

The incubation times of all enteroviruses range from 2 to 35 days, with an average of 7–14 days. An exception has been reported for local infections of the eye by enterovirus type 70, which has a short incubation period of 12–30 hours.

Immune response

It is suggested that immunity to enterovirus infections is mediated mainly by humoral and secretory antibodies (see Fig. 213.7). The role of cellular immunity in enterovirus infections has not yet been well analyzed. Humoral neutralizing IgG, IgM and IgA with virus-type specificity prevent hematogenous spread of virus to the target organs. Virus-specific IgM appears first after infection (7–10 days after infection) and persists for at least 4 weeks in 90% of infections. Acquired humoral immunity is mediated by virus-specific IgG, which may persist for several years. After poliovirus infection, production of virus-specific antibodies in the CNS has been observed. Breakdown in the integrity of the meninges may enable serum antibodies to cross the blood–brain barrier and this may be the reason for their appearance in the CNS. Secretory IgA against poliovirus is located mainly in nasopharyngeal and gut tissues; it is induced 2–4 weeks after infection. Secretory IgA induced against each of the three poliovirus types after oral polio vaccination is the main barrier against subsequent wild-type infections because secretory IgA prevents or limits the spread of polioviruses in the alimentary tract.

Clinical syndromes

The lytic infection of host cells with severe cytopathic effects is the basis for the mechanism of pathogenicity of enterovirus infections (see above). Most enteroviruses induce cyclic infections in their host with a viremia and subsequent virus transport to the target organs (especially the spinal cord and brain, meninges, myocardium, skin and liver).[2,4]

Polioviruses

The mode of infection of polioviruses is the best understood of all the enteroviruses. The mouth is the portal of entry. Beginning shortly after infection, poliovirus is spread via oral and fecal routes as the virus multiplies in the mucosal tissues of the pharynx, the lymphoid tissues (tonsils and Peyer's patches) and the gut. The virus infection is clinically inapparent in 90–95% cases.

CLINICAL SYNDROMES OF ENTEROVIRUS INFECTIONS		
Viruses	**Types**	**Clinical syndromes**
Polioviruses	1–3	Abortive poliomyelitis ('minor illness', undifferentiated febrile illness) Nonparalytic poliomyelitis (aseptic meningitis) Paralytic poliomyelitis ('major illness'), encephalitis (infrequently) Postpolio syndrome
Coxsackie viruses		
Group A	2, 3, 4, 5, 6, 8, 10	Herpangina (vesicular pharyngitis)
	10	Acute lymphatic or nodular pharyngitis
	2, 4, 7, 9, 10	Aseptic meningitis
	7, 9	Paralysis (infrequently)
	4, 14, 16	Myocarditis, pericarditis
	4, 5, 6, 9, 16	Exanthema
	4, 5, 9, 10, 16	Hand, foot and mouth disease
	9, 16	Pneumonitis in children
	21, 24	Common cold
	4, 9	Hepatitis
	18, 20, 21, 22, 24	Infantile diarrhea
	24	Acute hemorrhagic conjunctivitis
	Various types	Undifferentiated febrile illness
Group B	1, 2, 3, 4, 5	Pleurodynia
	1, 2, 3, 4, 5	Bornholm disease (epidemic pleurodynia or acute epidemic myalgia)
	1, 2, 3, 4, 5, 6	Aseptic meningitis
	2, 3, 4, 5	Paralysis (infrequently)
	1, 2, 3, 4, 5	Severe systemic infection in infants, meningoencephalitis, myocarditis
	1, 2, 3, 4, 5	Myocarditis, pericarditis, chronic cardiovascular disease
	4, 5	Upper respiratory illness and pneumonia
	5	Exanthema
	2, 5	Hand, foot and mouth disease
	5	Hepatitis
	1, 2, 4	Pancreatitis
	4	Diabetes mellitus
	1, 2, 3, 4, 5, 6	Undifferentiated febrile illness
Echoviruses*	1–7, 9, 11, 13–23, 25, 27, 30, 31	Aseptic meningitis
	4, 6, 9, 11, 30; possibly 1, 7, 13, 14, 16, 18, 31	Paralysis (infrequently)
	2, 6, 9, 19; possibly 3, 4, 7, 11, 14, 18, 22	Encephalitis, ataxia, Guillain–Barré syndrome
	2, 4, 6, 9, 11, 16, 18; possibly 1, 3, 5, 7, 12, 14, 19, 20	Exanthema, Boston exanthema disease (echovirus 16)
	4, 9, 11, 20, 25; possibly 1–3, 6–8, 16, 19, 22	Respiratory illness
	7, 11	Conjunctivitis
	1, 6, 9	Epidemic myalgia (infrequently)
	1, 6, 9, 19	Myocarditis, pericarditis (infrequently)
	4, 9	Hepatitis
	Various types	Diarrhea
		Undifferentiated febrile illness
Other enteroviruses	68	Pneumonia, bronchiolitis
	70	Acute hemorrhagic conjunctivitis
	71	Aseptic meningitis
	70, 71	Paralysis
	70, 71	Meningoencephalitis
	71	Hand, foot and mouth disease

* Echoviruses 22 and 23 have been reclassified as parechoviruses 1 and 2.

Table 213.3 Clinical syndromes of enterovirus infections. Adapted from Pallansch and Roos.[2]

Abortive poliomyelitis

Poliovirus can be spread to the draining lymph nodes, most probably with the help of M cells, which are specialized microfold cells overlying Peyer's patches. This leads to a viremia at 6–9 days after infection (see Fig. 213.7). The viremia is characterized by non-specific clinical symptoms such as fever, malaise and sore throat and sometimes headache and vomiting (Table 213.3). This abortive poliomyelitis ('minor illness') occurs in about 4–8% of poliovirus infections.

Nonparalytic poliomyelitis (aseptic meningitis)

Poliovirus can cross the blood–brain barrier by as yet unknown mechanisms to infect its target cells in the CNS. The same prodromal signs as those that occur in abortive poliomyelitis are characteristic of patients who have nonparalytic poliomyelitis, which occurs in 1–2% of poliovirus infections. Between 3 and 7 days after the 'minor illness' these patients develop an illness similar to aseptic meningitis, which is accompanied by high fever, back pain and muscle spasm. The patients generally show rapid and complete recovery from the disease, which lasts 2–10 days.

Paralytic poliomyelitis

Between 0.1% and 1% of all people infected with poliovirus develop paralytic poliomyelitis, also called 'major illness'. In addition to the clinical signs of 'minor illness' and aseptic meningitis, the 'major illness' comprises flaccid paralysis (involvement of the whole muscle) or paresis (involvement of only some muscle groups) and, in rare cases, encephalitis. Spinal or bulbar damage, or both, is the consequence. The spinal form of poliomyelitis owing to an ascendent infection is more common than the bulbar form. Bulbar poliomyelitis is characterized by damage to the cerebral nerves and vegetative centers and it therefore has a poor prognosis. In spinal poliomyelitis, some recovery of motor function may occur after several months; any remaining paralysis, however, will be permanent.

The very specific extraintestinal tropism of poliovirus to target cells of the CNS is the basis for these severe clinical signs. Polioviruses especially infect the anterior horn cells of the spinal cord but also the dorsal root ganglia, certain brainstem centers, cerebellum, spinal sensory columns and, occasionally, the cerebral motor cortex. Histologic analysis reveals that vascular engorgement is first observed, accompanied by perivascular infiltration with lymphocytes and also polymorphonuclear neutrophils, plasma cells and microglia. Experimental infection of rhesus monkeys has shown that the anterior horn cells are severely damaged by a poliovirus-specific cytopathic effect. The cells are characterized by a diffuse decrease in the size of the Nissl bodies in the cytoplasm (chromatolysis) and nuclear alterations with breakage and condensation of chromatin.[54]

The severity of disease may be increased by certain factors, including male sex, very young and very old age, physical exertion, hypoxia, cold, chronic undernutrition, corticosteroid treatment, irradiation, tonsillectomy, pregnancy, adrenal-related endocrine changes and possibly hypercholesterolemia.[55]

Postpolio syndrome

A small number of infected people develop recrudescence of paralysis and muscle atrophy several decades after their experience with paralytic poliomyelitis. This postpolio syndrome owing to a progressive postpoliomyelitis muscle atrophy is not clearly understood. Postpoliomyelitis muscle atrophy cannot be assigned to persistent poliovirus infection,[2] although some reports have described poliovirus genome sequences in the CNS of these patients as detected by PCR. It is suggested, rather, that the muscle atrophy is a result of the additive effects of physiologic aging in these patients to the long-lasting loss of neuromuscular function resulting from the earlier infection.

Coxsackie viruses, echoviruses and enteroviruses 68–71

The nonpolio enteroviruses are characterized by less specific extraintestinal target organ tropism than the polioviruses and they can therefore induce a wider range of diseases (see Table 213.3). The primary multiplication of the nonpolio enteroviruses takes place in the pharynx and small intestine and viruses are shed in the feces for up to 1 month and in the respiratory secretions for several days. Owing to the broad target organ range, nonpolio enteroviruses can infect the meninges, CNS, myocardium and pericardium, striated muscles, respiratory tract, eye and skin. Enterovirus 69 is the only enterovirus that has not yet been clearly assigned to a disease.

Meningitis and central nervous system disease

Meningitis and mild paresis can be induced by most group A and group B Coxsackie viruses and by echoviruses. As with poliomyelitis 'minor illness', early symptoms are fever, malaise, headache, nausea and abdominal pain; these are followed by meningeal irritation with neck or back stiffness and vomiting before the onset of meningitis and mild paresis. Aseptic meningitis is very often accompanied by a rash. In contrast to the situation in poliovirus infection, the manifestation of the CNS disease is usually milder and patients nearly always recover from paresis. Severe CNS disease, which may be confused clinically with paralytic poliomyelitis, has been described for infections with Coxsackie viruses A7, A9 and B2–B5. Meningoencephalitis is seen (especially in children) in infections with several group B Coxsackie viruses. In 1955–60 a pandemic outbreak of aseptic meningitis was caused by echovirus 9. Encephalitis, ataxia and Guillain–Barré syndrome have been attributed to echovirus infections. In 1969–73 in California, enterovirus 71 was responsible for an epidemic outbreak of aseptic meningitis, meningoencephalitis and paralysis in parallel to hand, foot and mouth disease. In 1998 in Taiwan there was a further large outbreak of enterovirus 71 that affected young children and resulted in 78 deaths, mostly related to encephalitis.[56] A disease similar to poliomyelitis has been observed in some cases of acute hemorrhagic conjunctivitis caused by enterovirus 70.

Pleurodynia

Coxsackie viruses B1–B5 can cause pleurodynia (also known as epidemic myalgia or Bornholm disease), with abrupt onset of fever sometimes preceded by malaise, headache and anorexia. Characteristic clinical signs are severe chest pain, also called 'devil's grip', and abdominal pain, which may be intensified by movement or breathing. Children and adolescents are most often attacked by this disease, which can last from 2 days to 2 weeks and may be accompanied by generalized muscle hypotonia. An epidemic of this disease was first observed on the island of Bornholm (Denmark) in 1930–32. Epidemics predominantly occur during late summer and early autumn. Muscle pain in the lower extremities may be caused by echovirus infections. Patients may suffer from pleurodynia if this myalgia affects the intercostal muscles. Sporadic cases of pleurodynia may be caused by Coxsackie viruses A4, A6, A9 and A10 as well as echoviruses 1 and 6.

Herpangina

Herpangina is mainly caused by group A Coxsackie viruses such as A2–A6, A8 and A10. Infants are most often attacked by herpangina, with abrupt onset of fever, sore throat, vomiting and abdominal pain. Herpangina is characterized by discrete vesicles of different size, sometimes tiny, which most frequently occur on the tongue, anterior pillars of the fauces, the posterior pharynx, the palate, the uvula or the tonsils. Coxsackie virus A10 may also be responsible for lymphatic pharyngitis.

Hand, foot and mouth disease

Coxsackie virus A16 is associated with hand, foot and mouth disease, but Coxsackie viruses A4, A5, A9, A10, B2 and B5 may also cause it. The disease is characterized by vesicles on the hands and feet. The manifestation on the mucosa of the mouth leads to herpangina with generalized vesicular intraoral lesions, which may be ulcerative. Hand, foot and mouth disease caused by enterovirus 71 can be mixed with aseptic meningitis and encephalitis.[56]

Exanthemas

Rubelliform rash may be caused by several group A and B Coxsackie viruses, which most frequently attack young children. Several types of echoviruses are responsible for exanthemas, with a high incidence in infants. These exanthemas can be maculopapular and are sometimes morbilliform or rubelliform; they are accompanied by febrile illnesses or pharyngitis. Echovirus 19 was responsible for an epidemic outbreak of a maculopapular rash in Boston, Massachusetts, in the beginning of the 1950s; since then this has been known as 'Boston exanthema disease'.

Respiratory illnesses and acute febrile illnesses

Several types of echoviruses and group A and B Coxsackie viruses are responsible for infections of the upper and lower respiratory tract that cause acute febrile illnesses of short duration without distinctive features. These illnesses predominantly occur during the summer or autumn and often resemble the common cold. In some cases, infections with Coxsackie viruses may cause pneumonia in children and adults and pneumonitis of infants. Children may suffer from pneumonia and bronchiolitis when attacked by enterovirus 68. Enterovirus 71 can lead to an influenza-like illness in children.

Conjunctivitis

Enteroviral conjunctivitis is mainly caused by Coxsackie virus A24 and enterovirus 70. A variant of Coxsackie virus A24 was responsible for an epidemic outbreak of acute hemorrhagic conjunctivitis in Singapore and Hong Kong in 1970–71. This acute hemorrhagic conjunctivitis spread throughout South East Asia and first occurred outside Asia in American Samoa in 1986 (where the incidence was 47%). Acute hemorrhagic conjunctivitis caused by enterovirus 70 first occurred in Africa, South East Asia (including Singapore), Japan and India in 1969–71, with several million cases. After sporadic outbreaks in French Polynesia in 1982, enterovirus 70 was introduced to the USA. Coxsackie virus A24 and enterovirus 70 typically cause local infections of the eye; enterovirus 70, however, can also be responsible for rare manifestations in the CNS with a poliomyelitis-like paralysis. In contrast to all other enterovirus infections, the incubation time of infections with enterovirus 70 is very short (24 hours; range 12–72 hours). Conjunctivitis without hemorrhage can be caused by echoviruses 7 and 11. An epidemic outbreak of conjunctivitis caused by echovirus 7 occurred in Sweden in 1977. It must be emphasized that enterovirus-infected conjunctival fluid can be highly infectious.

Myocarditis and pericarditis

Group B Coxsackie viruses are the main cause of myocarditis, pericarditis and dilated cardiomyopathy among the enteroviruses. In addition, cases of myocarditis and pericarditis are also described for Coxsackie viruses A4, A14 and A16, and for echoviruses 1, 6, 9 and 19.

Coxsackie viruses and echoviruses may affect the myocardium, endocardium and pericardium. The infected myocardium is characterized by edema, diffuse focal necrosis and signs of acute inflammatory responses. The cardiac disease may be accompanied by meningism and convulsions. Myocarditis in newborns may be fatal (see Fig. 213.8); death occurs in 50% of cases. Young children and adolescents are more often attacked by pericarditis, which in general is less severe than neonatal myocarditis.

Chronic cardiovascular disease

Chronic cardiovascular disease with recurrent pericarditis can be caused by Coxsackie viruses (predominantly B2–B5). Virus-specific IgM may persist for years. Myocytes are persistently infected with Coxsackie viruses, which can be demonstrated by in-situ hybridization.[53] Viral RNA instead of mature virus persists in cardiac myocytes.[53,57,58] Long-lasting necrosis in the myocardium may be the consequence of this virus persistence. There are results showing that an autoimmune response is involved in Cocksackie virus-induced chronic cardiovascular disease.[59]

Gastrointestinal disease

Non-specific clinical symptoms caused by several Coxsackie viruses and echoviruses may be accompanied by diarrhea, which may be fatal in newborn babies. Generalized infections with Coxsackie viruses and echoviruses may lead to hepatitis. Pancreatitis has been associated with group B Coxsackie viruses.

Diabetes mellitus

Infections with group B Coxsackie viruses are implicated as a cause of juvenile-onset insulin-dependent diabetes mellitus. Several reports of experimental Coxsackie virus infections of animals discuss an involvement of autoimmunity in diabetes.

Neonatal disease

Nosocomial transmission of Coxsackie viruses and some echoviruses may be responsible for fatal disease in newborn babies, frequently with rapid death. Nursery outbreaks and sporadic infections, mainly with group B Coxsackie viruses and echovirus 11, cause disease within a few days of birth and may lead to an overwhelming systemic infection (viral sepsis) with acute myocarditis or pericarditis, encephalitis and hepatitis. The condition is often hemorrhagic with fatal kidney disorders. Severe diarrhea in young children may cause severe disorders of water and ion balance.

There are case reports suggesting that neonatal diseases may be acquired by intrauterine infection as a result of transplacental transmission and neonatal infection at birth by a contaminated cervix. Maternal infection in the first trimester of pregnancy with Coxsackie viruses A9, B2, B3 and B4 may be associated with fetal abnormalities of the urogenital tract, the gastrointestinal tract, the cardiovascular system and the CNS, but the risk of teratogenesis from infections with Coxsackie viruses or echoviruses cannot yet be estimated.

REFERENCES

1. King AMQ, Brown F, Christian P, *et al.* Picornaviridae. In: van Regenmortel MHV, Fauquet CM, Bishop DHL, *et al.*, eds. Virus taxonomy. Seventh report of the International Committee on Taxonomy of Viruses. New York: Academic Press; 2000:657–73.
2. Pallansch MA, Roos RP. Enteroviruses: polioviruses, coxsackieviruses, echoviruses, and newer enteroviruses. In: Knipe DM, Howley PM, eds. Field's virology, 4th ed., vol. 1. Philadelphia: Lippincott Williams & Wilkins; 2001:723–76.
3. Racaniello VR. Picornaviridae; the viruses and their replication. In: Knipe DM, Howley PM, eds. Field's virology, 4th ed., vol. 1. Philadelphia: Lippincott Williams & Wilkins; 2001:685–722.
4. Zeichhardt H, Grunert HP. Enteroviruses. In: Specter S, Hodinka RL, Young SA, eds. Clinical virology manual, 3rd ed. Washington: American Society for Microbiology, ASM Press; 2000:252–69.
5. Landsteiner K, Popper E. Übertragung der Poliomyelitis acuta auf Affen. Z Immunitätsforsch Orig 1909;2:377–90.
6. Enders JF, Weller TH, Robbins FC. Cultivation of the Lansing strain of poliomyelitis virus in cultures of various human embryonic tissue. Science 1949;109:85–7.
7. Dalldorf G, Sickles GM. An unidentified, filterable agent isolated from the feces of children with paralysis. Science 1948;108:61–3.
8. Melnick JL, Shaw EW, Curnen EC. A virus isolated from patients diagnosed as nonparalytic poliomyelitis or aseptic meningitis. Proc Soc Exp Biol Med 1949;71:344–9.
9. Robbins FC, Enders JF, Weller TH, Florentino GL. Studies on the cultivation of poliomyelitis viruses in tissue culture. V. The direct isolation and serologic identification of virus strains in tissue culture from patients with nonparalytic and paralytic poliomyelitis. Am J Hyg 1951;54:286–93.
10. Kitamura N, Semler BL, Rothberg PG, *et al.* Primary structure, gene organization and polypeptide expression of poliovirus RNA. Nature 1981;291:547–53.

11. Hogle JM, Chow M, Filman DJ. Three-dimensional structure of poliovirus at 2.9 A resolution. Science 1985;229:1358–65.
12. Rossmann MG, Arnold E, Erickson JW, *et al.* Structure of a human common cold virus and functional relationship to other picornaviruses. Nature 1985;317:145–53.
13. Mirzayan C, Wimmer E. Polioviruses: molecular biology. In: Webster RG, Granoff A, eds. Encyclopedia of virology, vol. 3. London: Academic Press; 1994:1119–32.
14. Beatrice ST, Katze MG, Zajac BA, Crowell RL. Induction of neutralizing antibodies by the coxsackievirus B3 virion polypeptide, VP2. Virology 1980;104:426–38.
15. Mertens T, Pika U, Eggers HJ. Cross antigenicity among enteroviruses as revealed by immunoblot technique. Virology 1983;129:431–42.
16. Habermehl KO. Data handling and retrieval in clinical virology by small decentralized computers. In: Habermehl KO, ed. Rapid methods and automation in microbiology and immunology. Berlin: Springer-Verlag; 1985:538–56.
17. Mendelsohn CL, Wimmer E, Racaniello VR. Cellular receptor for poliovirus: molecular cloning, nucleotide sequence, and expression of a new member of the immunoglobulin superfamily. Cell 1989;56:855–65.
18. Koike S, Horie H, Ise I, *et al.* The poliovirus receptor protein is produced both as membrane-bound and secreted forms. EMBO J 1990;9:3217–24.
19. Shepley MP, Racaniello VR. A monoclonal antibody that blocks poliovirus attachment recognizes the lymphocyte homing receptor CD44. J Virol 1994;68:1301–8.
20. Bouchard MJ, Racaniello VR. CD44 is not required for poliovirus replication. J Virol 1997;71:2793–8.
21. Barnert RH, Zeichhardt H, Habermehl KO. Identification of 50- and 23-/25-kDa HeLa cell membrane glycoproteins involved in poliovirus infection: occurrence of poliovirus specific binding sites on susceptible and nonsusceptible cells. Virology 1992;186:533–42.
22. Roivainen M, Piirainen L, Hovi T, *et al.* Entry of Coxsackie virus A9 into host cells: specific interactions with alpha v beta 3 integrin, the vitronectin receptor. Virology 1994;203:357–65.
23. Colonno RJ, Callahan PL, Long WJ. Isolation of a monoclonal antibody that blocks attachment of the major group of human rhinoviruses. J Virol 1986;57:7–12.
24. Bergelson JM, Cunningham JA, Droguett G, *et al.* Isolation of a common receptor for Coxsackie B viruses and adenoviruses 2 and 5. Science 1997;275:1320–3.
25. Bergelson JM, St John N, Kawaguchi S, *et al.* Infection by echoviruses 1 and 8 depends on the alpha 2 subunit of human VLA-2. J Virol 1993;67:6847–52.
26. Bergelson JM, Chan M, Solomon KR, *et al.* Decay-accelerating factor (CD55), a glycosylphosphatidylinositol-anchored complement regulatory protein, is a receptor for several echoviruses. Proc Natl Acad Sci USA 1994;91:6245–9.
27. Karnauchow TM, Tolson DL, Harrison BA, *et al.* The HeLa cell receptor for enterovirus 70 is decay-accelerating factor (CD55). J Virol 1996;70:5143–52.
28. Crowell RL, Tomko RP. Receptors for picomaviruses. In: Wimmer E, ed. Cellular receptors for animal viruses. Cold Spring Harbor: Cold Spring Harbor Laboratory Press; 1994:75–99.
29. Wimmer E, ed. Cellular receptors for animal viruses. Cold Spring Harbor: Cold Spring Harbor Laboratory Press; 1994.
30. Harber J, Bernhardt G, Lu HH, Sgro JY, Wimmer E. Canyon rim residues, including antigenic determinants, modulate serotype-specific binding of polioviruses to mutants of the poliovirus receptor. Virology 1995;214:559–70.
31. Zeichhardt H, Wetz K, Willingmann P, Habermehl KO. Entry of poliovirus type 1 and Mouse Elberfeld (ME) virus into HEp-2 cells: receptor-mediated endocytosis and endosomal or lysosomal uncoating. J Gen Virol 1985;66:483–92.
32. Willingmann P, Barnert H, Zeichhardt H, Habermehl KO. Recovery of structurally intact and infectious poliovirus type 1 from HeLa cells during receptor-mediated endocytosis. Virology 1989;168:417–20.
33. Tosteson MT, Chow M. Characterization of the ion channels formed by poliovirus in planar lipid membranes. J Virol 1997;71:507–11.
34. Diefenthal W, Habermehl KO. Die Bedeutung mikrokinematographischer Methoden in der Virologie. Res Film 1967;6:22–30.
35. Zeichhardt H, Schlehofer JR, Wetz K, Hampl H, Habermehl KO. Mouse Elberfeld (ME) virus determines the cell surface alterations when mixedly infecting poliovirus-infected cells. J Gen Virol 1982;58:417–28.
36. Dales S, Eggers HJ, Tamm I, Palade GE. Electron microscopic study of the formation of poliovirus. Virology 1965;26:379–89.
37. Habermehl KO, Diefenthal W. The effect of virus infections on the course of cell division. Zentralbl Bakteriol Orig 1966;199:273–314.
38. Bartsch HD, Habermehl KO, Diefenthal W. Correlation between poliomyelitis virus-reproduction-cycle, chromosomal alterations and lysosomal enzymes. Arch Gesamte Virusforsch 1969;27:115–27.
39. Lloyd RE, Etchison D, Ehrenfeld E. Poliovirus protease does not mediate cleavage of the 220,000-Da component of the cap binding protein complex. Proc Natl Acad Sci USA 1985;82:2723–7.
40. Evans DM, Dunn G, Minor PD, *et al.* Increased neurovirulence associated with a single nucleotide change in a noncoding region of the Sabin type 3 polio vaccine genome. Nature 1985;314:548–50.
41. Schlein L. Hunting down the last of the poliovirus. Science 1998;279:168.
42. Eggers HJ. Assay systems: testing of antiviral drugs in cell culture (*in vitro*). In: de Clercq E, Walker RT, eds. Antiviral drug development. New York: Plenum Press; 1988:139–48.
43. Melnick JL, Wenner HA, Phillips CA. Enteroviruses. In: Lennette EH, Schmidt NJ, eds. Diagnostic procedures for viral, rickettsial and chlamydial infections. Washington DC: American Public Health Association; 1979:471–534.
44. Lim KH, Benyesh-Melnick M. Typing of viruses by combinations of antiserum pools: application to typing of enteroviruses (Coxsackie and echo). J Immunol 1960;84:309–17.
45. World Health Organization. New approaches to poliovirus diagnosis using laboratory techniques: memorandum from a WHO meeting. Bull World Health Organ 1992;70:27–33.
46. van Wezel AL, Hazendonk AG. Intratypic serodifferentiation of poliomyelitis virus strains by strain-specific antisera. Intervirology 1979;11:2–8.
47. van Loon AM, Ras A, Poelstra P, Mulders M, van der Avoort H. Intratypic differentiation of polioviruses. In: Kurstak E, ed. Measles and poliomyelitis. New York: Springer-Verlag; 1993:359–69.
48. Osterhaus AD, van Wezel AL, Hazendonk TG, *et al.* Monoclonal antibodies to polioviruses. Comparison of intratypic strain differentiation of poliovirus type 1 using monoclonal antibodies versus cross-absorbed antisera. Intervirology 1983;20:129–36.
49. Ferguson M, Magrath DI, Minor PD, Schild GC. WHO collaborative study on the use of monoclonal antibodies for the intratypic differentiation of poliovirus strains. Bull World Health Organ 1986;64:239–46.
50. Schweiger B, Schreier E, Bothig B, Lopez Pila JM. Differentiation of vaccine and wild-type polioviruses using polymerase chain reaction and restriction enzyme analysis. Arch Virol 1994;134:39–50.
51. Mulders MN, Koopmans MPG, van der Avoort HGAM, van Loon AM. Detection and characterization of poliovirus: the molecular approach. In: Becker Y, Darai G, eds. PCR: protocols for diagnosis of human and animal virus diseases. New York: Springer-Verlag, 1995:137–56.
52. van der Avoort HG, Hull BP, Hovi T, *et al.* Comparative study of five methods for intratypic differentiation of polioviruses. J Clin Microbiol 1995;33:2562–6.
53. Kandolf R, Klingel K, Zell R, *et al.* Molecular pathogenesis of enterovirus-induced myocarditis: virus persistence and chronic inflammation. Intervirology 1993;35:140–51.
54. Bodian D. Poliomyelitis: pathogenesis and histopathology. In: Rivers TM, Horsfall FL, eds. Viral and rickettsial infections of man, 3rd ed. Philadelphia: JB Lippincott; 1959:479–518.
55. Moore M, Morens D. Enteroviruses, including polioviruses. In: Belshe RB, ed. Textbook of human virology. Littleton: PSG Publishing Company; 1984:407–83.
56. Lyn T-Y, Chang L-Y, Hsia S-H et al. The 1998 enterovirus 71 outbreak in Taiwan: pathogenesis and management. Clin Infect Dis 2002;34(suppl 2):S52–57.
57. Wessely R, Henke A, Zell R, Kandolf R, Knowlton KU. Low-level expression of a mutant coxsackieviral cDNA induces a myocytopathic effect in culture: an approach to the study of enteroviral persistence in cardiac myocytes. Circulation 1998;98:450–7.
58. Pauschinger M, Doerner A, Kuehl U, Schwimmbeck PL, Poller W, Kandolf R, Schultheiss H-P. Enteroviral RNA replication in the myocardium of patients with left vetricular dysfunction and clinically suspected myocarditis Circulation 1999;99:899–95.
59. Schwimmbeck, PL, Huber, SA and Schultheiss, H-P. Roles of T cells in coxsackievirus B-induced disease. Curr Top Microbiol Immunol 1997;233:283–303.

chapter
214 Hepatitis Viruses

Jane N Zuckerman & Arie J Zuckerman

INTRODUCTION

Viral hepatitis is a major public health problem throughout the world that affects several hundreds of millions of people. Viral hepatitis is a cause of considerable morbidity and mortality, both from acute infection and from chronic sequelae. In the case of infection with hepatitis B virus (HBV) and hepatitis C virus (HCV), these chronic sequelae include chronic active hepatitis, cirrhosis and primary liver cancer.

There is evidence that in addition to the five recognized pathogens, A–E, the so-called non-A–E hepatitis viruses exist. The evidence was based on the observation of short and long incubation periods in post-transfusion hepatitis and in experimental transmission studies; multiple bouts of hepatitis in the same patient; chronic hepatitis not due to HBV, HCV or hepatitis D virus (HDV); chloroform-resistant non-ABC virus; and cross-challenge experiments in susceptible primates.

The hepatitis viruses include a range of unrelated and often unusual human pathogens (Table 214.1).

HEPATITIS A VIRUS

Outbreaks of jaundice have been described frequently for many centuries and the term infectious hepatitis was coined in 1912 to describe the epidemic form of the disease. Hepatitis A virus (HAV) is spread by the fecal–oral route. It continues to be endemic throughout the world and hyperendemic in areas with poor standards of sanitation and hygiene.

NATURE

Classification

Electron microscopy examination of concentrates of filtered fecal extracts from patients in the early stages of infection reveals 27nm particles typical of the Picornaviridae (Fig. 214.1). Hepatitis A virus is a small, unenveloped, symmetric RNA virus and was classified in the genus enterovirus of the family Picornaviridae on the basis of its biophysical and biochemical characteristics. However, after the determination of the entire nucleotide sequence of the viral genome, comparison with other picornavirus sequences revealed limited homology to the enteroviruses and also to the rhinoviruses, although the structure and genome organization is typical of the Picornaviridae. Hepatitis A virus has now been placed as hepatovirus within the heparnavirus genus.

Organization of the Hepatitis A virus genome

The HAV genome comprises about 7500 nucleotides of positive-sense RNA. The RNA is polyadenylated at the 3′ end and has a viral polypeptide (VPg) attached to the 5′ end. A single, large open reading frame (ORF) occupies most of the genome and encodes a polyprotein with a theoretic molecular mass of M_r 252,000. An untranslated region of around 735 nucleotides precedes the ORF. Secondary structure within this region of the genome may be important for efficient translation of the RNA. There is also a short untranslated region at the 3′ end of the HAV genome.

The viral polyprotein is processed to yield the structural polypeptides (located at the amino-terminal end) and the nonstructural viral polypeptides. Many of the features of replication of the picornaviruses have been deduced from studies of prototype enteroviruses and rhinoviruses, in particular poliovirus type 1.

The three-dimensional structures of a number of picornaviruses have been resolved by high-resolution crystallography; polypeptides VP1 (1D), VP2 (1B) and VP3 (1C) are exposed on the surface of the virion, whereas VP4 (1A) is located internally. After release of the structural domain from the polyprotein, the 3C protease cleaves the 1B–1C and 1C–1D junctions to yield VP0 (VP4 plus VP2), VP3 and VP1. The three polypeptides remain associated as a protomer and five protomers assemble to form a pentamer, so that the five copies of the VP1 form the apex. Finally, 12 pentamers assemble around a molecule of viral RNA to form the icosahedral capsid. As the structure locks into place, most copies of VP0 cleave (presumably autocatalytically) to yield VP2 and VP4. However, in the case of HAV it has not been possible to demonstrate VP4, which is predicted to consist of only 23 amino acids.

The functions of some of the other products of the cleavage of the polyprotein, such as 2B, 2C and 3A, are less well understood. Product 3B corresponds to the genome-linked polypeptide VPg, which in other picornaviruses is the primer for the synthesis of both genome-sense RNA and the negative-sense RNA found in replicative intermediates. Polypeptide 3AB may be the precursor of VPg. Finally, the three-dimensional product seems to be the viral replicase and contains the Gly–Asp–Asp motif common to viral RNA-dependent RNA polymerases.

EPIDEMIOLOGY

Viral hepatitis type A (infectious or epidemic hepatitis) occurs endemically in all parts of the world, with frequent reports of minor and major outbreaks. The exact incidence is difficult to estimate because of the high proportion of subclinical infections and infections without jaundice, because of differences in surveillance and because of differing patterns of disease. The degree of under-reporting is very high.

The development of specific serologic tests for hepatitis A has made possible the study of the incidence and distribution of hepatitis A in various countries. These studies have shown that infections with HAV are widespread and endemic in all parts of the world, that chronic excretion of HAV does not occur and that the infection is rarely transmitted by blood transfusion, although transmission by blood coagulation products has been reported. There is no evidence of progression to chronic liver disease.

The seroprevalence of antibodies to HAV has declined since the Second World War in many countries, and infection results most commonly from person-to-person contact, but large epidemics do occur. For example, an outbreak of hepatitis A in Shanghai in 1988 associated with the consumption of clams resulted in almost 300,000 cases.

THE HEPATITIS VIRUSES

Virus	Description	Viral group	Mode of transmission
Hepatitis A virus	Small unenveloped symmetric RNA virus	Hepatovirus, in heparnavirus genus	Fecal–oral
Hepatitis B virus	Enveloped double-stranded DNA virus	Hepadnavirus	Blood–blood Sexual
Hepatitis C virus	Enveloped single-stranded RNA virus	Related to flavivirus	Blood–blood
Hepatitis D virus	Circular single-stranded RNA virus	Related to plant viral satellites and viroids	Blood–blood
Hepatitis E virus	Unenveloped single-stranded RNA	Related to calciviruses; closely resembles rubella virus and a plant virus (beet necrotic yellow vein virus)	Fecal contamination of water Food-borne

Table 214.1 The hepatitis viruses.

COURSE OF ACUTE HEPATITIS A

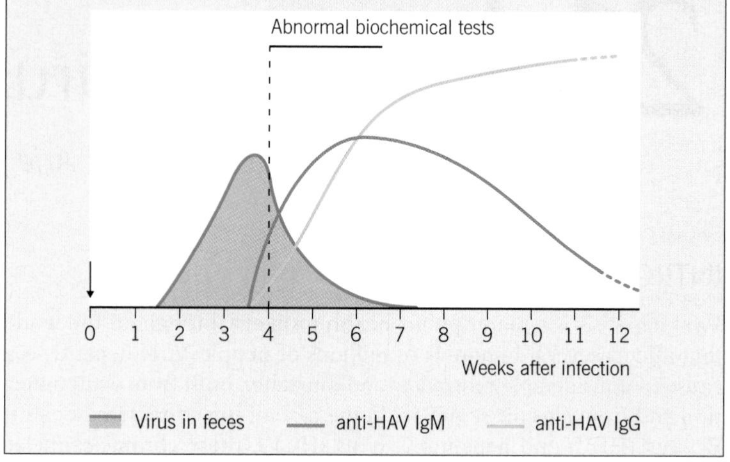

Fig. 214.2 Course of acute hepatitis A.

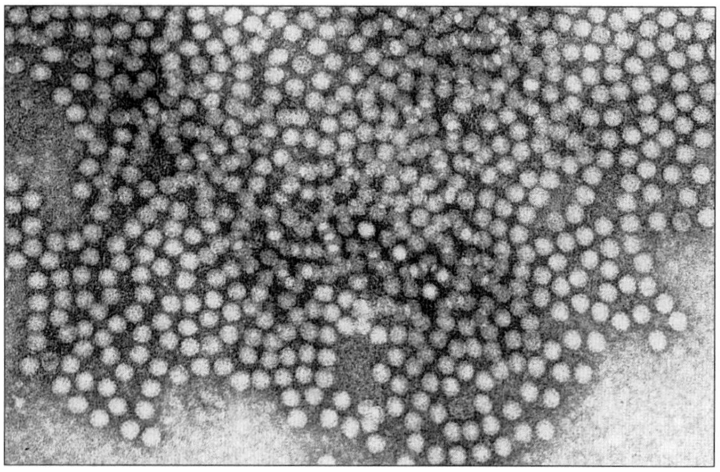

Fig. 214.1 Hepatitis A virus. Note the vast number of virus particles present in a fecal extract.

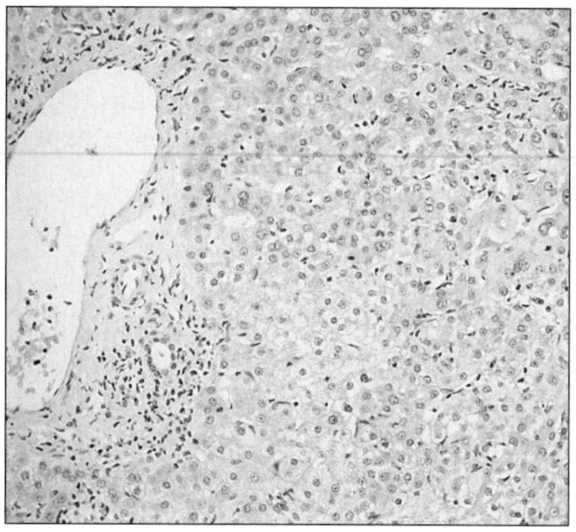

Fig. 214.3 Histologic changes in the liver of a patient with acute hepatitis A.

PATHOGENICITY

The incubation period of hepatitis A is 3–5 weeks (Fig. 214.2), with a mean of 28 days. Subclinical and anicteric cases are common and, although the disease generally has a low mortality rate, patients may be incapacitated for many weeks. There is no evidence of progression to chronic liver damage.

Hepatitis A virus is spread by the fecal–oral route, most commonly by person-to-person contact; infection occurs readily under conditions of poor sanitation and overcrowding. Common source outbreaks are initiated most frequently by fecal contamination of water and food, but water-borne transmission is not a major factor in maintaining this infection in industrialized communities. On the other hand, many outbreaks related to food have been reported. This can be attributed to the shedding of large quantities of virus in the feces by infected food handlers during the incubation period of the illness – the source of the outbreak can often be traced to uncooked food or food that has been handled after cooking. Although hepatitis A remains endemic and common in the developed countries, the infection occurs mainly in small clusters, often with only a few identified cases.

The clinical expression of infection with HAV varies considerably, ranging from subclinical, anicteric, mild illnesses in young children to the full range of symptoms with jaundice in adolescents and adults. The ratio of anicteric to icteric illnesses varies widely, both in individual cases and during outbreaks.

Hepatitis A virus enters the body by ingestion. The virus then spreads, probably by the bloodstream, to the liver, the target organ. Large numbers of virus particles are detectable in feces during the incubation period, beginning as early as 10–14 days after exposure and continuing, in general, until peak elevation of serum aminotransferases. Virus is also detected in feces early in the acute phase of illness but relatively infrequently after the onset of clinical jaundice. Immunoglobulin G antibody to HAV persists and is also detectable late in the incubation period, coinciding approximately with the onset of biochemical evidence of liver damage.

Hepatitis A viral antigen has been localized by immunofluorescence in the cytoplasm of hepatocytes after experimental transmission to chimpanzees. The antigen has not been found in any tissue other than the liver following experimental intravenous inoculation in susceptible nonhuman primates.

Pathologic changes induced by HAV appear only in the liver (Fig. 214.3). These include marked focal activation of sinusoidal lining cells; accumulation of lymphocytes and histiocytes in the parenchyma – these cells often replace hepatocytes that have been lost by cytolytic necrosis, especially in the periportal areas; occasional coagulative necrosis resulting in the formation of acidophilic bodies; and focal degeneration.

PREVENTION

In areas of high prevalence, most children are infected early in life, and such infections are generally asymptomatic. The later in life that infection occurs, the greater the clinical severity – fewer than 10% of cases of acute hepatitis A in children up to the age of 6 years are icteric, but this increases to 40–50% in the 6- to 14-year-age group, and to 70–80% in adults. Of 115,551 cases of hepatitis A in the USA between 1983 and 1987, only 9% of the cases, but more than 70% of the fatalities, were in those aged over 49 years. It is important, therefore, to protect those at risk because of personal contact with infected people or because of travel to a highly endemic area. Other groups at risk of hepatitis A infection include staff and residents of institutions for the mentally handicapped; day care centers for children; sexually active male homosexuals; intravenous drug abusers; sewage workers; certain groups of health care workers, such as medical students on elective studies in countries where hepatitis A is common; military personnel; and certain low socio-economic groups in defined community settings. Patients with hemophilia should be immunized.

Patients with chronic liver disease, especially if visiting an endemic area, should be immunized against HAV. In some developing countries, the incidence of clinical hepatitis A is increasing as improvements in socio-economic conditions result in infection later in life, and strategies for immunization are yet to be developed and agreed.

Passive immunization

Control of HAV infection is difficult. Because fecal shedding of the virus is at its highest during the late incubation period and the prodromal phase of the illness, strict isolation of cases is not a useful control measure. Spread of HAV is reduced by simple hygienic measures and the sanitary disposal of excreta.

Prevention or attenuation of a clinical illness can be achieved by the intramuscular administration of normal human immunoglobulin that contains at least 100IU/ml of hepatitis A antibody. The dosage should be at least 2IU of hepatitis A antibody per kilo of body weight but in pregnancy or in patients with liver disease this dosage may be doubled (Table 214.2). Immunoglobulin does not always prevent excretion of HAV. The efficacy of passive immunization is based on the presence of hepatitis A antibody in the normal human immunoglobulin, and the minimum titer of antibody required for protection is believed to be about 10IU/l.

Titers of HAV antibody vary among batches of pooled normal human immunoglobulin and the titers are decreasing in batches obtained from pooled plasma of donors in industrialized countries, resulting in clinical cases despite prophylaxis with immunoglobulin.[1]

PASSIVE IMMUNIZATION WITH NORMAL HUMAN IMMUNOGLOBULIN FOR TRAVELERS TO HIGHLY ENDEMIC AREAS

Body weight	Period of stay less than 3 months	Period of stay longer than 3 months
<55lb (<25kg)	50IU anti-HAV (0.5ml)	100IU anti-HAV (1.0ml)
55–66lb (25–30kg)	100IU anti-HAV (1.0ml)	250IU anti-HAV (2.5ml)
>110lb (>50kg)	200IU anti-HAV (2.0ml)	500IU anti-HAV (5.0ml)

Table 214.2 Passive immunization with normal human immunoglobulin for travelers to highly endemic areas.

Immunoglobulin is used most commonly for close personal contacts of patients with hepatitis A and for those exposed to contaminated food. Immunoglobulin has also been used effectively for controlling outbreaks in institutions such as homes for the mentally handicapped and nursery schools. Prophylaxis with immunoglobulin is recommended for people without HAV antibody who are visiting highly endemic areas. After a period of 6 months the administration of immunoglobulin for travelers needs to be repeated, unless it has been demonstrated that the recipient has developed HAV antibodies. Active immunization is recommended, particularly for travelers and for controlling outbreaks, particularly if vaccine is given to all contacts immediately.

Active immunization against hepatitis A

Killed hepatitis A vaccines

The foundations for a hepatitis A vaccine were laid in 1975 by the demonstration that formalin-inactivated virus extracted from the liver of infected marmosets induced protective antibodies in susceptible marmosets on challenge with live virus.[2] Subsequently, HAV was cultivated, after serial passage in marmosets, in a cloned line of fetal rhesus monkey kidney cells, thereby opening the way to the production of hepatitis A vaccines. Later, it was demonstrated that prior adaptation in marmosets was not a prerequisite to growth of the virus in cell cultures. Several formalin-inactivated hepatitis A vaccines are available, including combined vaccines with hepatitis B vaccine and with typhoid vaccine.

Live attenuated hepatitis A vaccines

The major advantages of live attenuated vaccines (such as the Sabin type of oral poliomyelitis vaccine) include ease of oral administration; relatively low cost, because the virus vaccine strain replicates in the gut; production of both local immunity in the gut and humoral immunity, thereby mimicking natural infection; and the longer term protection afforded.

Disadvantages include the potential of reversion toward virulence, interference with the vaccine strain by other viruses in the gut, relative instability of the vaccine, and shedding of the virus strain in the feces for prolonged periods.

The most extensively studied live attenuated hepatitis A vaccines are based on the CR 326 and HM 175 strains of the virus attenuated by prolonged passage in cell culture.

Two variants of the CR 326 strain have been investigated after passage in marmoset liver in fetal rhesus monkey kidney cells, namely MRC5 and WI-38 cells. Inoculation of susceptible marmosets demonstrated seroconversion, and protection on challenge. Biochemical evidence of liver damage did not occur in susceptible chimpanzees, although a number had histologic evidence of mild hepatitis with the F variant and the vaccine virus was shed in the feces for about 12 weeks before seroconversion. There was no evidence of reversion toward virulence. Studies in human volunteers indicated incomplete attenuation of the F variant, but better results were obtained with the F^1 variant without elevation of liver enzymes.

Studies with the HM 175 strain, which was isolated and passaged in African green monkey kidney cells, showed that this strain was not fully attenuated for marmosets, although it did not induce liver damage on challenge. Further passages and adaptation of HM 175 revealed some evidence of virus replication in the liver of chimpanzees and minimal shedding of the virus into feces. Other studies are in progress in nonhuman primates.

As with vaccine strains of polioviruses, attenuation may be associated with mutations in the 5′ noncoding region of the genome, and this affects the secondary structure of the protein compounds. There is also evidence that mutations in the region of the genome encoding the nonstructural polypeptides may be important for adaptation to cell culture and attenuation. However, markers of attenuation of HAV have not been identified, and reversion to virulence may be a problem. On the other hand, there is also concern that 'over-attenuated' viruses may not be sufficiently immunogenic.

Current candidate live attenuated hepatitis A vaccines require administration by injection. Preparations that may be suitable for oral administration are not available so far.

DIAGNOSTIC MICROBIOLOGY

Various serologic tests are available for HAV, including immune electron microscopy, complement fixation, immune adherence hemagglutination, radioimmunoassay and enzyme immunoassay. Immune adherence hemagglutination, which has been widely used, is moderately specific and sensitive. Several methods of radioimmunoassay have been described, but these have largely been replaced by sensitive enzyme immunoassay techniques.

Only one serotype of HAV has been identified in volunteers infected experimentally with the MS-1 strain of hepatitis A, in patients from different outbreaks of hepatitis in different geographic regions and in random cases of hepatitis A. Several genotypes of the virus are recognized.

Isolation of virus in tissue culture requires prolonged adaptation and it is therefore not suitable for diagnosis.

CLINICAL MANIFESTATIONS

The following description of the acute disease applies to all types of viral hepatitis. Prodromal non-specific symptoms such as fever, chills, headache, fatigue, malaise and aches and pains are followed a few days later by anorexia, nausea, vomiting and right upper quadrant abdominal pain followed by the passage of dark urine and clay-colored stools. Jaundice of the sclera and skin develops. With the appearance of jaundice, there is usually a rapid subjective improvement of symptoms. The jaundice usually deepens for a few days and persists for 1–2 weeks. The feces then darken and the jaundice diminishes over a period of about 2 weeks. Convalescence may be prolonged (see Chapter 48).

HEPATITIS E VIRUS

Retrospective testing of serum samples from patients involved in epidemics of hepatitis associated with fecal contamination of water supplies have indicated that an agent other than HAV or HBV was involved. Epidemics of enterically transmitted non-A, non-B hepatitis in the Indian subcontinent were first reported in 1980, but outbreaks involving tens of thousands of cases have also been documented in the former Soviet Union, South East Asia, northern Africa and Mexico. A huge outbreak occurred in New Delhi in 1956–7, but tests for HAV or HBV were not available then. Infection has been reported in returning travelers.

NATURE

Hepatitis E virus (HEV) is a nonenveloped single-stranded RNA virus that shares many biophysical and biochemical features with caliciviruses.

Morphologically the virus is spherical and unenveloped, measuring 32–34nm in diameter with spikes and indentations visible on the surface of the particle. Confirmation that the virus has been propagated in cell culture is awaited. The virus appears similar to the caliciviruses. However, detailed morphologic studies and the lack of similarities in genome sequence between HEV and recognized caliciviruses suggest that HEV is a single member of a novel virus genus. However, HEV resembles most closely the sequences of rubella virus and a plant virus, beet necrotic yellow vein virus. It has therefore been proposed that these three viruses should be placed in separate but related families.

Genomic organization

Hepatitis E virus was cloned in 1991 and the entire 7.5kb sequence is known. The genome is a single-stranded, positive-sense, polyadenylated RNA molecule, with three overlapping ORFs.

On the basis of the available partial sequence data, it has been suggested that HEV isolates segregate into four major groups based on full-length comparisons. However, more recent studies indicate that HEV may be distributed into at least nine different groups.

EPIDEMIOLOGY

The epidemiologic features of the infection resemble those of hepatitis A. The highest attack rates are found in young adults and high mortality rates of 20–39% have been reported in women infected during the third trimester of pregnancy.[3]

All epidemics of hepatitis E reported to date have been associated with fecal contamination of water, with the exception of a number of food-borne outbreaks in China. Sporadic hepatitis E has been associated with the consumption of uncooked shellfish and has been seen in travelers returning from endemic areas. Hepatitis E virus is an important cause of large epidemics of acute hepatitis, and these, together with a high prevalence of antibody determined by serologic tests, have occurred in the subcontinent of India, South East and central Asia, the Middle East, and northern and western Africa. There have also been outbreaks in eastern Africa and Mexico.

Unexpectedly, the highest prevalence of antibody to HEV is found in young adults and not in infants and children. In some epidemics the antibody has been found more commonly in males, although in most outbreaks the distribution between young adult males and females is equal.

Hepatitis E virus has also been isolated from patients with sporadic acute hepatitis in countries not considered to be endemic for HEV such as the USA, Italy and other European countries and in individuals who had not traveled abroad. There is now evidence that HEV may have an animal reservoir and there are HEV isolates from swine with high sequence identity to human HEV strains isolated from pigs in areas without HEV epidemics. There is recent evidence of a higher prevalence of HEV antibodies among swine farmers, particularly in those with an occupational history of cleaning barns or assisting sows at birth, and also a history of drinking raw milk.

PATHOGENICITY

Virus-like particles have been detected in the feces of infected people by immune electron microscopy using convalescent serum. However, such studies have often proved inconclusive and a large proportion of the excreted virus may be degraded during passage through the gut. Bile was shown to be a rich source. Cross reaction studies between sera and virus in feces associated with a variety of epidemics in several different countries suggest that a single serotype of virus is involved, although two distinct isolates have been recognized and designated as the Burma (B) strain and the Mexico (M) strain. Two other isolates were recently sequenced.

The average incubation period is slightly longer than for HAV, with a mean of 6 weeks.

Studies on HEV have progressed following transmission to susceptible nonhuman primates. Hepatitis E virus was first transmitted to *Cynomolgus* macaques, and a number of other species of monkeys including chimpanzees have also been infected.

PREVENTION

The provision of safe public water supplies, public sanitation and hygiene, safe disposal of feces and raw sewage, and personal hygiene are essential measures.

Passive immunization with immune globulin derived from endemic areas has not been successful. Vaccines are under development.

DIAGNOSTIC MICROBIOLOGY

Serologic tests are necessary to establish the diagnosis. The tests commercially available at present detect anti-HEV IgM in up to 90% of acute infections if serum is obtained 1–4 weeks after the onset of illness, and IgM remains detectable for about 12 weeks. Anti-HEV IgG appears early and reaches a maximum titer 4 weeks after the onset of illness, falling rapidly thereafter.

Tests for HEV RNA by the polymerase chain reaction (PCR) are available in specialized laboratories.

CLINICAL MANIFESTATIONS

Individual cases cannot be differentiated on the basis of clinical features from other cases of hepatitis. In epidemics, most clinical cases will have anorexia, jaundice and hepatomegaly. Serologic tests indicate, however, that clinically inapparent cases occur. The severity of the infection and high mortality during pregnancy have been noted above. Hepatitis E does not progress to chronicity (see Chapter 48).

HEPATITIS B VIRUS

Hepatitis B virus was originally recognized as the agent responsible for 'serum hepatitis', an important and frequent cause of acute and chronic infection of the liver.

NATURE

Hepatitis B virus is a member of the hepadnavirus group, which contains double-stranded DNA viruses that replicate by reverse transcription. Hepatitis B virus is endemic in the human population and hyperendemic in many parts of the world, The virus is transmitted essentially by blood–blood contact and by the sexual route. Mutations of the surface coat protein of the virus and of the core and other proteins have been identified in recent years.[4–10] Natural hepadnavirus infections also occur in other animals, including woodchucks, beechy ground squirrels and ducks.

Structure and organization of the virus

The hepatitis B virion is a 42nm particle comprising an electron-dense core (nucleocapsid), which is 27nm in diameter, and an outer envelope of the surface protein (hepatitis B surface antigen, HBsAg) embedded in membranous lipid derived from the host cell (Fig. 214.4). The surface antigen, originally referred to as Australia antigen, is produced in excess by the infected hepatocytes and is secreted in the form of 22nm particles and tubular structures of the same diameter.

The 22nm particles are composed of the major surface protein in both nonglycosylated (p4) and glycosylated (gp27) form in approximately equimolar amounts, together with a minority component of the so-called middle proteins (gp33 and gp36), which contain the pre-S2 domain, a glycosylated 55 amino acid amino-terminal extension. The surface of the virion has a similar composition but also contains the large surface proteins (gp39 and gp42), which include both the pre-S1 and pre-S2 regions. These large surface proteins are not found in the 22nm spherical particles (but may be present in the tubular forms in highly viremic people) and their detection in serum correlates with viremia. The domain that binds to the specific HBV receptor on the hepatocyte is believed to reside within the pre-S1 region.

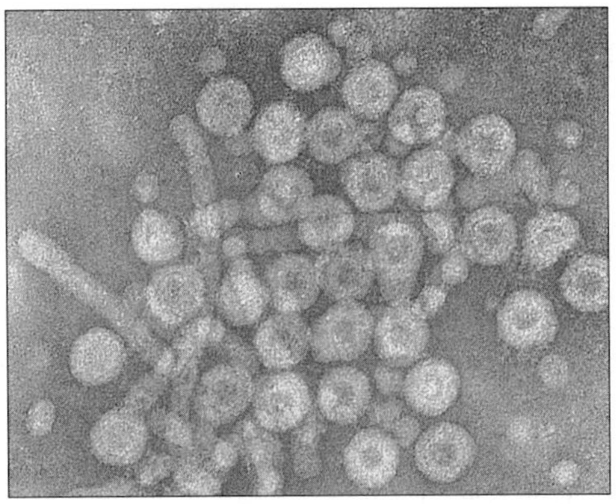

Fig. 214.4 Serum from a patient with hepatitis B. The double-shelled particle is the complete virion. Tubular structures and 22nm HBsAg particles are present in small numbers.

The nucleocapsid of the virion consists of the viral genome surrounded by the core antigen (HBcAg). The genome, which is approximately 3.2kb in length, has an unusual structure and is composed of two linear strands of DNA held in a circular configuration by base-pairing at the 5′ ends.

One of the strands is incomplete and the 3′ end is associated with a DNA polymerase molecule that is able to complete that strand in the presence of deoxynucleoside triphosphates.

The genomes of more than a dozen isolates of HBV have been cloned and the complete nucleotide sequences determined. Analysis of the coding potential of the genome reveals four ORFs, which are conserved between all of these isolates (Fig. 214.5).

The first ORF encodes the various forms of the surface protein and contains three in-frame methionine codons, which are used for initiation of translation. A second promoter is located upstream of the pre-S1 initiation codon. This directs the synthesis of a 2.1kb mRNA, which is coterminous with the other surface messages and is translated to yield the large (pre-S1) surface proteins.

The core ORF also has two in-phase initiation codons. The 'precore' region is highly conserved, has the properties of a signal sequence and is responsible for the secretion of hepatitis Be antigen (HBeAg).

The third ORF, which is the largest and overlaps the other three, encodes the viral polymerase. This protein appears to be another translation product of the 3.5kb RNA and is synthesized apparently after internal initiation of the ribosome. The amino-terminal domain is believed to be the protein primer for minus strand synthesis. There is then a spacer region followed by the (RNA- and DNA-dependent) DNA polymerase.

The fourth ORF was designated 'x' because the function of its small gene product was not known. However, 'x' has now been demonstrated to be a transcriptional transactivator.

Structure and organization of the virus

There are nine subtypes of HBV, with a common main antigenic determinant, *a*. The nine subtypes described, *ayw*1–*ayw*4, *ayr*, *adw*2, *adw*4, *adrq*⁻ and *adrq*⁺, differ in their geographic distribution. Subtyping is employed for epidemiologic studies and to trace nosocomial infection. Traditional subtyping is complemented by classification of different HBV strains into genotypes A–G.

EPIDEMIOLOGY

More than a third of the world's population has been infected with HBV, and the World Health Organization estimates that HBV results in 1,000,000–2,000,000 deaths every year.

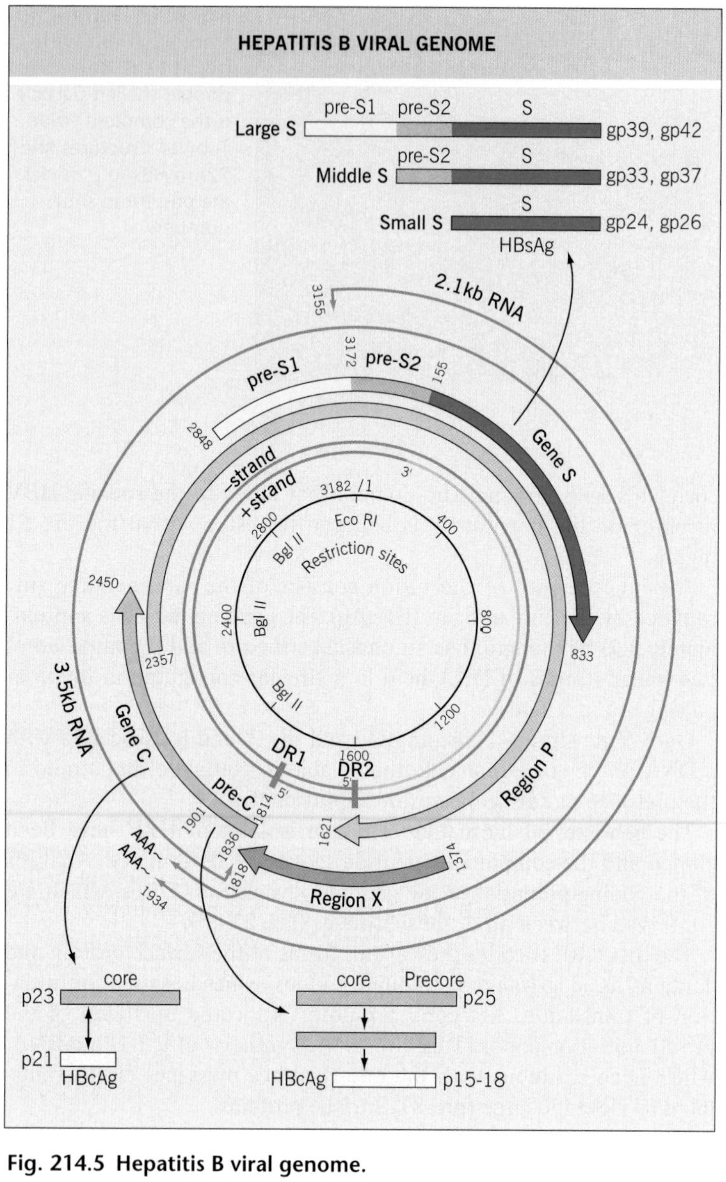

Fig. 214.5 Hepatitis B viral genome.

The virus persists in approximately 5–10% of immunocompetent adults and in as many as 90% of infants infected perinatally. Persistent carriage of HBV, defined by the presence of HBsAg in the serum for more than 6 months, has been estimated to affect about 350,000,000 people worldwide.

Although various body fluids (blood, saliva, menstrual and vaginal discharges, serous exudates, seminal fluid and breast milk) have been implicated in the spread of infection, infectivity appears to be especially related to blood and to body fluids contaminated with blood. The epidemiologic propensities of this infection are therefore wide; they include infection by inadequately sterilized syringes and instruments, and transmission by unscreened blood transfusion and blood products, by close contact and by sexual contact. Transmission of HBV from mother to child may take place – antenatal transmission is rare but perinatal transmission occurs frequently; in some parts of the world (South East Asia and Japan), perinatal transmission is very common.

PATHOGENICITY

The incubation period of hepatitis B is variable, with a range of 1–6 months.

As mentioned above, about 350 million people are carriers of HBV. The pathology is mediated by the cellular immune response of the host to the infected hepatocytes. Long-term continuing virus replication may lead to progression to chronic liver disease, cirrhosis and hepatocellular carcinoma (Fig. 214.6).

In the first phase of chronicity, virus replication continues in the liver and replicative intermediates of the viral genome may be detected in DNA extracted from liver biopsies. Markers of virus replication in serum include HBV DNA, the surface proteins (HBsAg) and a soluble antigen, HBeAg, which is secreted by infected hepatocytes. In those infected at a very young age this phase may persist for life but, more usually, virus levels decline over time. Eventually, in most infected people, there is immune clearance of infected hepatocytes associated with seroconversion from HBeAg to anti-HBe.

During the period of replication, the viral genome may integrate into the chromosomal DNA of some hepatocytes and these cells may persist and expand clonally. Rarely, seroconversion to anti-HBs follows clearance of virus replication but, more frequently, HBsAg persists during a second phase of chronicity as a result of the expression of integrated viral DNA.

Immune responses

Antibody and cell-mediated immune responses to various types of antigens are induced during the infection; however, not all of these are protective and in some instances they may cause autoimmune phenomena that contribute to disease pathogenesis. The immune response to infection with HBV is directed toward at least three antigens: HBsAg, the core antigen and the e antigen. The view that HBV exerts its damaging effect on hepatocytes by direct cytopathic changes is inconsistent with the persistence of large quantities of surface antigen in liver cells of many apparently healthy people who are carriers. Additional evidence suggests that the pathogenesis of liver damage in the course of HBV infection is related to the immune response by the host.

The surface antigen appears in the serum of most patients during the incubation period, 2–8 weeks before biochemical evidence of liver damage or onset of jaundice. The antigen persists during the acute illness and usually clears from the circulation during convalescence. Next to appear in the circulation is the virus-associated DNA polymerase activity, which correlates in time with damage to liver cells as indicated by elevated serum transaminases. The polymerase activity persists for days or weeks in acute cases and for months or years in some persistent carriers. Antibody of the IgM class to the core antigen is found in the serum 2–10 weeks after the surface antigen appears and persists during replication of the virus. Core antibody of the IgG class is detectable for many years after recovery. Finally, antibody to the surface antigen component, anti-HBs, appears.

During the incubation period and during the acute phase of the illness, surface antigen–antibody complexes may be found in the serum of some patients. Immune complexes have been found by electron microscopy in the serum of all patients with fulminant hepatitis, but are seen only infrequently in nonfulminant infection. Immune complexes are also important in the pathogenesis of other disease syndromes characterized by severe damage of blood vessels (e.g. polyarteritis nodosa, some forms of chronic glomerulonephritis and infantile papular acrodermatitis).

Immune complexes have been identified in variable proportions of patients with virtually all the recognized chronic sequelae of acute hepatitis B. Deposits of such immune complexes have also been demonstrated in the cytoplasm and plasma membrane of hepatocytes and on or in the nuclei; the reason why only a small proportion of patients with circulating complexes develop vasculitis or polyarteritis is, however, not clear. Perhaps complexes are critical pathogenic factors only if they are of a particular size and of a certain antigen–antibody ratio.

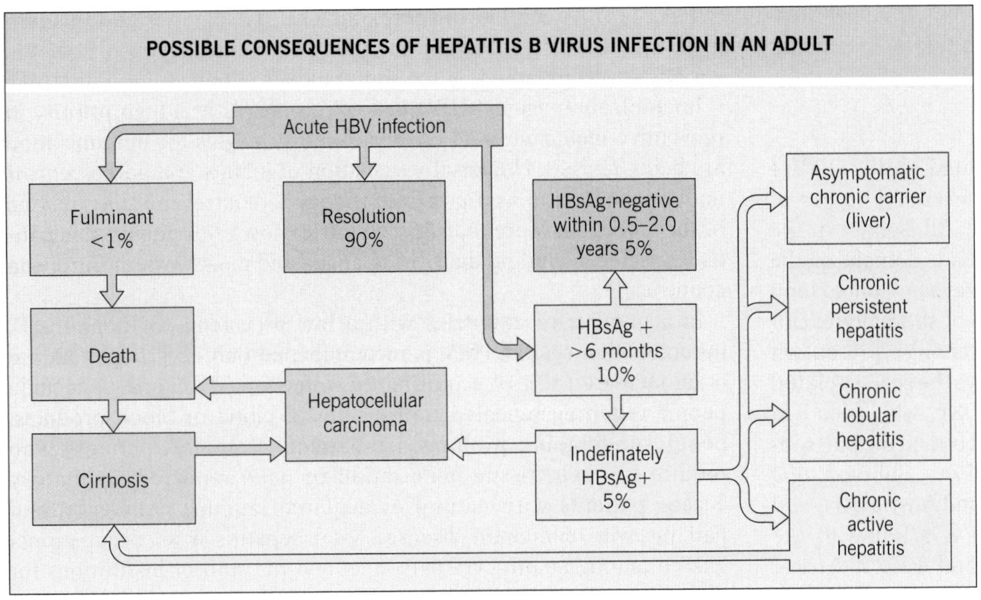

Fig. 214.6 Possible consequences of hepatitis B virus infection in an adult.

Cellular immune responses are known to be particularly important in determining the clinical features and course of viral infections. The occurrence of cell-mediated immunity to HBV antigens has been demonstrated in most patients during the acute phase of hepatitis B and in a significant proportion of patients with surface-antigen-positive chronic active hepatitis, but not in asymptomatic persistent HBV carriers. These observations suggest that cell-mediated immunity may be important in terminating the infection and, in certain circumstances, in promoting liver damage and in the genesis of autoimmunity. Evidence also suggests that progressive liver damage may result from an autoimmune reaction directed against hepatocyte membrane antigens, initiated in many cases by infection with HBV.

Hepatitis B virus and hepatocellular carcinoma

When tests for HBsAg became widely available, regions of the world where the chronic carrier state is common were found to be coincident with those where there is a high prevalence of primary liver cancer (Fig. 214.7). Furthermore, in these areas, patients with this tumor are almost invariably seropositive for HBsAg. A prospective study in Taiwan revealed that 184 cases of hepatocellular carcinoma occurred in 3454 carriers of HBsAg at the start of the study, but only 10 such tumors arose in the 19,253 control males who were HBsAg-negative.[11]

Other case–control and cohort studies and laboratory investigations indicate that there is a consistent and specific causal association between HBV and hepatocellular carcinoma and that up to 80% of such cancers are attributable to this virus. Hepatitis B is thus second only to tobacco among the known human carcinogens.[12] Primary liver cancer is the seventh most common cancer in males and the ninth most common in females. Hepatocellular carcinoma is one of the three most common causes of cancer deaths in males in east and South East Asia, the Pacific Basin and sub-Saharan Africa.

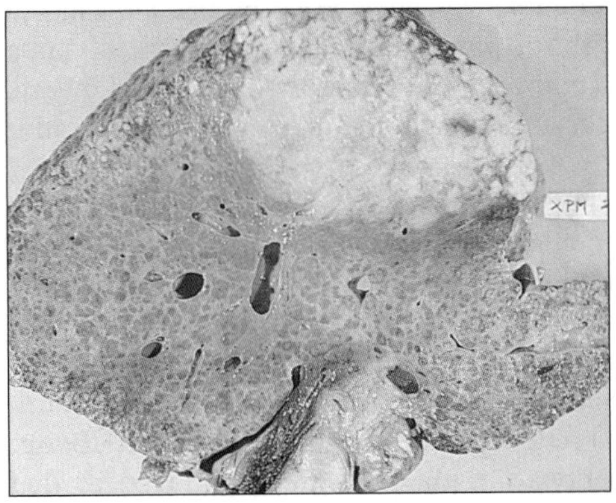

Fig. 214.7 Hepatocellular carcinoma.

Southern hybridization of tumor DNA yields evidence of chromosomal integration of viral sequences in at least 80% of hepatocellular carcinomas from HBsAg carriers. There is no similarity in the pattern of integration between different tumors, and variation is seen both in the integration sites and in the number of copies or partial copies of the viral genome. Sequence analysis of the integrants reveals that the direct repeats in the viral genome often lie close to the virus–cell junctions, suggesting that sequences around the ends of the viral genome may be involved in recombination with host DNA. Integration seems to involve microdeletion of host sequences, and rearrangements and deletions of part of the viral genome also may occur. When an intact surface gene is present, the tumor cells may produce and secrete HBsAg in the form of 22nm particles. Production of HBcAg by tumors is rare, however, and the core ORF is often incomplete, and modifications such as methylation may also modulate its expression. Cytotoxic T lymphocytes targeted against core gene products on the hepatocyte surface seem to be the major mechanism of clearance of infected cells from the liver. Thus, there may be immune selection of cells with integrated viral DNA that are incapable of expressing HBcAg.

The mechanisms of oncogenesis by HBV remain uncertain. Hepatitis B virus may act non-specifically by stimulating active regeneration and cirrhosis, which may be associated with chronicity. However, HBV-associated tumors arise occasionally in the absence of cirrhosis, and such hypotheses do not explain the frequent finding of integrated viral DNA in tumors. In rare instances, the viral genome has been found to be integrated into cellular genes such as cyclin A and a retinoic acid receptor. Translocations and other chromosomal rearrangements have also been observed. Although insertional mutagenesis of HBV remains an attractive hypothesis to explain its oncogenicity, there is insufficient supportive evidence.

Like many other cancers, the development of hepatocellular carcinoma is likely to be a multifactorial process. The clonal expansion of cells with integrated viral DNA seems to be an early stage in this process, and such clones may accumulate in the liver throughout the period of active virus replication. In areas where the prevalence of primary liver cancer is high, virus infection usually occurs at an early age and virus replication may be prolonged, although the peak incidence of tumor is many years after the initial infection.

PREVENTION

The discovery of variation in the epitopes presented on the surface of the virions and subviral particles identified several subtypes of HBV, which differ in their geographic distribution. All isolates of the virus share a common epitope – *a*. This epitope is a domain of the major surface protein, which is believed to protrude as a double loop from the surface of the particle. Two other pairs of mutually exclusive antigenic determinants – *d* or *y* and *w* or *r* – are also present on the major surface protein. These variations have been correlated with single nucleotide changes in the surface ORF, which lead to variation in single amino acids in the protein. Four principal subtypes of HBV are recognized: *adw*, *adr*, *ayw* and *ayr*. Subtype *adw* predominates in northern Europe, the Americas and Australasia, and it is also found in Africa and Asia. Subtype *ayw* is found in the Mediterranean region, eastern Europe, northern and western Africa, the Middle East and the Indian subcontinent. In the Far East, subtype *adr* predominates, but the rarer subtype *ayr* is occasionally found in Japan and Papua New Guinea.

Passive immunization

Hepatitis B immunoglobulin (HBIG) is prepared specifically from pooled plasma with high titer of hepatitis B surface antibody and may confer temporary passive immunity under certain defined conditions. The major indication for the administration of HBIG is a single acute exposure to HBV, such as occurs when blood containing surface antigen is inoculated, ingested or splashed on mucous membranes and the conjunctiva. The optimal dose has not been established but doses in the range of 250–500IU have been used effectively. It should be administered as early as possible after exposure and preferably within 48 hours. The dose is usually 3ml (200IU/ml) in adults. The first dose should not be administered after 7 days following exposure. It is generally recommended that two doses of HBIG should be given 30 days apart.

Results with the use of HBIG for prophylaxis in neonates at risk of infection with HBV are encouraging if the immunoglobulin is given as soon as possible after birth or within 12 hours of birth, and the chance of the baby developing the persistent carrier state is reduced by about 70%. More recent studies using combined passive and active immunization indicate an efficacy approaching 90%. The dose of HBIG recommended in the newborn is 1–2ml (200IU/ml).

Active immunization

The major response of recipients of hepatitis B vaccine is to the common *a* epitope with consequent protection against all subtypes of the virus. First-generation vaccines were prepared from 22nm HBsAg particles purified from plasma donations from chronic carriers. These preparations are safe and immunogenic but have been superseded in some countries by recombinant vaccines produced by the expression of HBsAg in yeast cells. The expression plasmid contains only the 3′ portion of the HBV surface ORF, and only the major surface protein, without pre-S epitopes, is produced. Vaccines containing pre-S2 and pre-S1, as well as the major surface proteins expressed by recombinant DNA technology, are undergoing clinical trials.

In many areas of the world with a high prevalence of HBsAg carriage, such as China and South East Asia, the predominant route of transmission is perinatal. Although HBV does not usually cross the placenta, the infants of viremic mothers have a very high risk of infection at the time of birth.

Administration of a course of vaccine with the first dose immediately after birth is effective in preventing transmission from an HBeAg-positive mother in approximately 70% of cases and this protective efficacy rate may be increased to greater than 90% if the vaccine is accompanied by the simultaneous administration of HBIG.

Immunization against HBV is now recognized as a high priority in preventive medicine in all countries and strategies for immunization are being revised. Universal vaccination of infants and adolescents is under examination as a possible strategy to control the transmission of this infection. More than 150 countries now offer universal hepatitis B vaccine, including the USA, Canada and most western European countries.[13]

In a number of countries with a low prevalence of hepatitis B, immunization against HBV is recommended only to groups that are at an increased risk of acquiring this infection. These groups include people requiring repeated transfusions of blood or blood products, people undergoing prolonged inpatient treatment, patients who require frequent tissue penetration or need repeated circulatory access, patients with natural or acquired immune deficiency, and patients with malignant diseases. Viral hepatitis is an occupational hazard among health care personnel and the staff of institutions for the mentally retarded and some semiclosed institutions. High rates of infection with HBV occur in narcotic drug addicts and intravenous drug abusers, sexually active male homosexuals and prostitutes. People working in highly endemic areas are at an increased risk of infection and should be immunized. Young infants, children and susceptible people (including travelers) living in certain tropical and subtropical areas where socio-economic conditions are poor and the prevalence of hepatitis B is high should also be immunized. It should be noted that, in about 30% of patients with hepatitis B, the mode of infection is not known – this is a powerful argument in favor of universal immunization.

Site of injection for vaccination and antibody response

Hepatitis B vaccination should be given in the upper arm or the anterolateral aspect of the thigh and not in the buttock. There are over 100 reports of unexpectedly low antibody seroconversion rates after hepatitis B vaccination using injection into the buttock. In one center in the USA a low antibody response was noted in 54% of healthy adult health care personnel. Many studies have since shown that the antibody response rate is significantly higher in centers using deltoid injection than centers using the buttock. On the basis of antibody tests after vaccination, the Advisory Committee on Immunization Practices of the Centers of Disease Control and Prevention in the USA recommended that the arm be used as the site for hepatitis B vaccination in adults, as has the Department of Health in the UK.

These observations have important public health implications, well illustrated by the estimate that about 20% of the 60,000 people immunized against HBV in the buttock in the USA by March 1985 had failed to attain a minimum level of antibody of 10IU/l and were therefore not protected.

Hepatitis B surface antibody titers should be measured in all people who have been immunized against HBV by injection in the buttock, and when this is not possible a complete course of three injections of vaccine should be administered into the deltoid muscle or the anterolateral aspect of the thigh, the only acceptable sites for HBV immunization.[14]

Apart from the site of injection there are several other factors that are associated with a poor antibody response or no antibody response to currently licensed vaccines. Indeed, all studies of antibody response to plasma-derived HBV vaccines and HBV vaccines prepared by recombinant DNA technology have shown that 5–10% or more of healthy immunocompetent subjects do not mount an antibody response (anti-HBs) to the surface antigen component (HBsAg) present in these preparations (i.e. they are nonresponders) or that they respond poorly (i.e. they are hyporesponders). The exact proportions of each group depends partly on the definition of nonresponsiveness and hyporesponsiveness; the usual definitions are a level of less than 10IU/l for nonresponders and 100IU/l for hyporesponders, measured against an international antibody standard.

Hepatitis B surface antibody escape mutants

Production of antibodies to the group antigenic determinant *a* mediates cross-protection against all subtypes, as has been demonstrated by challenge with a second subtype of the virus following recovery from an initial experimental infection. The epitope *a* is located in the region of amino acids 124–148 of the major surface protein and appears to have a double-loop conformation. A monoclonal antibody that recognizes a region within this *a* epitope is capable of neutralizing the infectivity of HBV for chimpanzees, and competitive inhibition assays using the same monoclonal antibody demonstrate that equivalent antibodies are present in the sera of subjects immunized with either plasma-derived or recombinant HBV vaccine.

During a study of the immunogenicity and efficacy of HBV vaccines in Italy, a number of people who had apparently mounted a successful immune response and became anti-HBs-positive, later became infected with HBV. These cases were characterized by the co-existence of noncomplexed anti-HBs and HBsAg, and in 32 of 44 vaccinated subjects there were other markers of HBV infection.

Furthermore, analysis of the antigen using monoclonal antibodies suggested that the *a* epitope was either absent or masked by antibody. Subsequent sequence analysis of the virus from one of these cases revealed a mutation in the nucleotide sequence encoding the *a* epitope, the consequence of which was a substitution of arginine for glycine at amino acid position 145.[6]

There is now considerable evidence for a wide geographic distribution of the point mutation in HBV from guanosine to adenosine at position 587, resulting in an amino acid substitution at position 145 from glycine to arginine in the highly antigenic group determinant *a* of the surface antigen. This is a stable mutation that has been found in viral isolates from children and adults. It has been described in Italy, Singapore, Japan, Brunei, Taiwan, Hong Kong, India, Germany and the USA;[7] from liver transplant recipients with hepatitis B in the USA, Germany and the UK who had been treated with specific hepatitis B immunoglobulin or humanized hepatitis B monoclonal antibody; and in patients with chronic hepatitis in Japan[8] and elsewhere.

The region in which this mutation occurs is an important virus epitope to which vaccine-induced neutralizing antibody binds, as discussed above, and the mutant virus is not neutralized by antibody to this specificity. It can replicate as a competent virus, implying that the amino acid substitution does not alter the attachment of the virus to the liver cell. Variants of HBV with altered antigenicity of the envelope protein show that HBV is not as antigenically singular as previously believed and that humoral escape mutation can occur in vivo. This finding gives rise to two causes for concern: failure to detect HBsAg may lead to transmission through donated blood or organs, and HBV may infect people who are anti-HBs-positive after immunization. Variation in the second loop of the *a* determinant seems especially important.

Hepatitis B virus precore mutants

The nucleotide sequence of the genome of a strain of HBV cloned from the serum of a naturally infected chimpanzee has been reported.[9] A surprising feature was a point mutation in the penultimate codon of the precore region, which changed the tryptophan codon (TGG) to an amber termination codon (TAG). The nucleotide sequence of the HBV precore region from a number of anti-HBe-positive Greek patients was investigated by direct sequencing PCR-amplified HBV DNA from serum.[10] An identical mutation of the penultimate codon of the precore region to a termination codon was found in 7 of 8 anti-HBe-positive patients who were positive for HBV DNA in serum by hybridization. In most cases there was an additional mutation in the proceeding codon.

Similar variants were found by amplification of HBV DNA from serum from anti-HBe-positive patients in Italy and Greece. These variants are not confined to the Mediterranean region; the same nonsense mutation (without a second mutation in the adjacent codon) has been observed in patients from Japan and elsewhere, along with rarer examples of defective precore regions caused by frameshifts or loss of the initiation codon for the precore region.

Some precore variants may be more pathogenic than the wild-type virus because in many patients with severe chronic liver disease precore variants are found.

DIAGNOSTIC MICROBIOLOGY

Direct demonstration of virus in serum samples is feasible by visualizing the virus particles by electron microscopy, by detecting virus-associated DNA polymerase, by assay of viral DNA and by amplification of viral DNA by various techniques. All these direct techniques are often impractical in the general diagnostic laboratory, and specific diagnosis must therefore rely on serologic tests (Table 214.3).

Hepatitis B surface antigen first appears during the late stages of the incubation period and is easily detectable by radioimmunoassay or enzyme immunoassay. Enzyme immunoassay is specific and highly sensitive and is used widely in preference to radioisotope methods. The antigen persists during the acute phase of the disease and sharply decreases when antibody to the surface antigen becomes detectable. Antibody of the IgM class to the core antigen is found in the serum after the onset of the clinical symptoms and slowly declines after recovery. Its persistence at high titer suggests continuation of the infection. Core antibody of the IgG class persists for many years and provides evidence of past infection.

INTERPRETATION OF RESULTS OF SEROLOGIC TESTS FOR HEPATITIS B

			Anti-HBc			
HBsAg	HBeAg	Anti-HBe	IgM	IgG	Anti-HBs	Interpretation
+	+	−	−	−	−	Incubation period
+	+	−	+	+	−	Acute hepatitis B or persistent carrier state
+	+	−	−	+	−	Persistent carrier state
+	−	+	±	+	−	Persistent carrier state
−	−	+	±	+	+	Convalescence
−	−	−	−	+	+	Recovery
−	−	−	+	−	−	Infection with HBV without detectable HBsAg
−	−	−	−	+	−	Recovery with loss of detectable anti-HBs
−	−	−	−	−	+	Immunization without or recovery from infection with loss of detectable anti-HBc

Table 214.3 Interpretation of results of serologic tests for hepatitis B virus.

CLINICAL MANIFESTATIONS

The clinical features of acute infection resemble those of the other viral hepatitides. Acute hepatitis B is frequently anicteric and asymptomatic, although a severe illness with jaundice can occur and occasionally acute liver failure may develop.

Hepatitis A and E viruses do not persist in the liver and there is no evidence of progression to chronic liver damage. Hepatitis B, with or without its satellite hepatitis D, and hepatitis C may be associated with persistent infection, a prolonged carrier state and progression to chronic liver disease, which may be severe. There is an etiologic association between hepatitis B and C viruses and hepatocellular carcinoma. GB virus C (GBV-C) tends to cause persistent infection and further studies are required (see Chapter 48).

HEPATITIS D VIRUS

This virus requires hepadnavirus helper functions for propagation in hepatocytes and is an important cause of acute and severe chronic liver damage in some regions of the world.

NATURE

Hepatitis D virus (HDV) is an unusual single-stranded circular RNA virus with a number of similarities to certain plant viral satellites and viroids.

Delta hepatitis[15] was first recognized following detection of a novel protein, δ-antigen (hepatitis D antigen, HDAg), by immunofluorescent staining in the nuclei of hepatocytes from patients with chronic active hepatitis B. Hepatitis D virus is now known to require a helper function of HBV for its transmission. The virus is coated with HBsAg, which is needed for release of the HDV from the host hepatocyte and for entry in the next round of infection.

Two forms of HDV infection are known. In the first form, a susceptible person is co-infected with HBV and HDV, often leading to a more severe form of acute hepatitis caused by HBV. In the second form, a person who is chronically infected with HBV becomes superinfected with HDV. This may cause a second episode of clinical hepatitis and accelerate the course of the chronic liver disease, or cause overt disease in asymptomatic HBsAg carriers. Hepatitis D virus itself seems to be cytopathic and HDAg may be directly cytotoxic.

The HDV particle is approximately 36nm in diameter. It is composed of an RNA genome associated with HDAg, surrounded by an envelope of HBsAg. The HDV genome is a closed circular RNA molecule of 1679 nucleotides and resembles those of the satellite viroids and virusoids of plants, and similarly seems to be replicated by the host RNA polymerase II with autocatalytic cleavage and circularization of the progeny genomes by way of *trans*-esterification reactions (ribozyme activity). Consensus sequences of viroids that are believed to be involved in these processes also are conserved in HDV.[16]

EPIDEMIOLOGY

Hepatitis D is common in some areas of the world with a high prevalence of HBV infection, particularly Italy and other countries bordering the Mediterranean; eastern Europe, particularly Romania; the Middle East; the former Soviet Union; South America, particularly the Amazon basin, Venezuela, Columbia (*hepatitis de Sierra Nevada de Santa Marta*), Brazil (labrea black fever) and Peru; and parts of Africa, particularly western Africa. Antibody to HDV has been found in most countries, commonly among intravenous drug abusers, patients with hemophilia and those requiring treatment by blood and blood products. It has been estimated that 5% of HBsAg carriers worldwide (approximately 18,000,000 people) are infected with HDV. In areas of low prevalence of HBV, those at risk of hepatitis B, particularly intravenous drug abusers, are also at risk of hepatitis D.

The ratio of clinical to subclinical cases of HDV and superinfection is not known. However, the general severity of both forms of infection suggests that most cases are clinically significant. A low persistence of infection occurs in 1–3% of acute infections and in 80% or more of cases of superinfection in chronic HBV carriers. The mortality rate is high, particularly in the case of superinfection, and ranges from 2% to 20%.

PATHOGENICITY

Hepatitis B virus provides a helper function to HDV, which is a defective virus. The histopathologic pattern in the liver is suggestive of a direct cytopathic effect.

Pathologic changes are limited to the liver and histologic changes are those of acute and chronic hepatitis with no particular distinguishing features apart from severity and, in tropical areas in particular, microvesicular steatosis.

It should be noted, however, that the virus was discovered by specific nuclear fluorescence in hepatocytes of patients with chronic hepatitis B.

The modes of transmission are similar to the parenteral transmission of HBV.

PREVENTION

Prevention and control for HDV are similar to those for HBV. Immunization against HBV protects against HDV. The difficulty is protection against superinfection of the many millions of established carriers of HBV. Studies are in progress to determine whether specific immunization against HDV based on HDAg is feasible.

DIAGNOSTIC MICROBIOLOGY

Laboratory diagnosis in acute infection is based on specific serologic tests for anti-HDV IgM or HDV-RNA or HDAg in serum. Acute infection is usually self-limiting and markers of HDV infection often disappear within a few weeks.

Superinfection with HDV in chronic hepatitis B may lead to suppression of HBV markers during the acute phase. Chronic infection with HDV (and HBV) is the usual outcome in nonfulminant disease.

CLINICAL MANIFESTATIONS

The clinical features of hepatitis D are identical to those of hepatitis A (see above). For further manifestations see Chapter 48.

HEPATITIS C VIRUS

NATURE

Hepatitis C virus (HCV) is an enveloped single-stranded RNA virus that appears to be distantly related (possibly in its evolution) to flaviviruses, although HCV is not transmitted by arthropod vectors.

Hepatitis C virus is unusual because it was identified using molecular methods rather than a conventional virologic approach. Transmission studies in chimpanzees established that the main agent of parenterally acquired non-A, non-B hepatitis was likely to be an enveloped virus some 30–60nm in diameter. Using infected chimpanzee plasma as a starting point, complementary DNA was used to create a library which was screened using serum from a patient with chronic non-A, non-B hepatitis. This approach led to the detection of a clone that was found to bind to antibodies present in the serum of several patients infected with non-A, non-B hepatitis. Eventually, clones covering the entire viral genome were assembled and the complete nucleotide sequence determined.[17]

Properties of hepatitis C virus

The genome of HCV resembles those of the pestiviruses and flaviviruses in that it comprises around 10,000 nucleotides of positive-sense RNA, lacks a 3′ poly-A tract and has a similar gene organization. It has been proposed that HCV should be the prototype of a third genus in the family Flaviviridae. All these genomes contain a single large ORF, which is translated to yield a polyprotein (of around 3000 amino acids in the case of HCV) from which the viral proteins are derived by post-translational cleavage and other modifications.

The amino acid sequence of the nucleocapsid protein seems to be highly conserved among different isolates of HCV. The next domain in the polyprotein also has a signal sequence at its carboxyl-terminus and may be processed in a similar fashion. The product is a glycoprotein that is probably found in the viral envelope and is variably termed E1/S or gp35. The third domain may be cleaved by a protease within the viral polyprotein to yield what is probably a second surface glycoprotein, E2/NS1 or gp70. These glycoproteins have not been found in vivo and the molecular sizes have been estimated from sequence data and expression studies in vitro.

Other post-translational modifications, including further proteolytic cleavages, are possible. These proteins are the focus of considerable interest because of their potential use in tests for the direct detection of viral proteins and for HCV vaccines. Nucleotide sequencing studies reveal that both domains contain hypervariable regions. It is possible that this divergence has been driven by antibody selection pressure and that these regions specify important immunogenic epitopes.

The nonstructural region of the HCV genome is divided into regions NS2 to NS5 (Fig. 214.8). In the flaviviruses, NS3 has two functional domains: a protease, which is involved in cleavage of the non-structural region of the polyprotein, and a helicase, which is presumably involved in RNA replication. Motifs within this region of the HCV genome have homology to the appropriate consensus sequences, suggesting similar functions. NS5 seems to be the replicase and contains the Gly–Asp–Asp motif common to viral RNA-dependent RNA polymerases.

Hepatitis C virus consists of a family of highly related but nevertheless distinct genotypes – presently numbering six – and various subtypes with differing geographic distribution and a complex nomenclature. The C, NS3 and NS4 domains are the most highly conserved regions of the genome and therefore these proteins are the most suitable for use as capture antigens for broadly reactive tests for antibodies to HCV. The sequence differences observed between HCV groups suggest that virus–host interactions may be different, which could result in differences in pathogenicity and in response to antiviral therapy.

It is important, therefore, to develop group-specific and virus-specific tests. The degree of divergence that is apparent within the viral envelope proteins implies the absence of a broad cross-neutralizing antibody response to infection by viruses of different groups.

In addition to the sequence diversity observed between HCV groups, there is considerable sequence heterogeneity among almost all HCV isolates in the amino-terminal region of E2–NS1, implying that this region may be under strong immune selection. Indeed, sequence changes within this region may occur during the evolution of disease in individual patients and may play an important role in progression to chronicity.

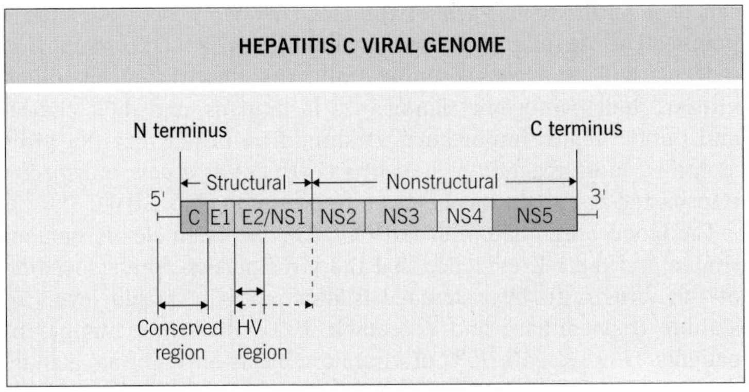

Fig. 214.8 Hepatitis C viral genome.

EPIDEMIOLOGY

Infection with HCV occurs throughout the world. Much of the seroprevalence data are based on blood donors, who represent a carefully selected population. The prevalence of antibodies to HCV in blood donors varies from 0.02% to 1.25% in different countries. Higher rates have been found in southern Italy, Spain, central Europe, Japan and parts of the Middle East, with as many as 19% in Egyptian blood donors. Until screening of blood donors was introduced, hepatitis C accounted for the vast majority of non-A, non-B post-transfusion hepatitis. However, it is clear that, although blood transfusion and the transfusion of blood products are efficient routes of transmission of HCV, these represent a small proportion of cases of acute clinical hepatitis in the USA and a number of other countries (with the exception of patients with hemophilia). Current data indicate that in some 50% of patients in industrialized countries, the source of infection cannot be identified, although 35% of patients have a history of intravenous drug use, and occupational exposure in the health care setting accounts for about 2% of cases. Household contact and sexual exposure do not appear to be major factors in the epidemiology of this common infection. Transmission of HCV from mother to infant occurs in about 10% of viremic mothers and the risk appears to be related to the level of viremia. The possibility of transmission in utero is also being investigated.

PREVENTION

Difficulties in vaccine development include the sequence diversity between viral genotypes and the substantial sequence heterogeneity among isolates in the amino-terminal region of E2–NS1. Neutralizing antibodies have not been clearly defined. The virus has not been cultivated in vitro to permit the development of inactivated or attenuated vaccines (compared with yellow fever vaccines). Much work is in progress employing recombinant DNA techniques.

DIAGNOSTIC MICROBIOLOGY

Successful cloning of portions of the viral genome have permitted the development of new diagnostic tests for infection by the virus. Because the antigen was originally detected by antibodies in the serum of an infected patient it was an obvious candidate as the basis of an enzyme-linked immunosorbent assay (ELISA) to detect anti-HCV antibodies. A larger clone, C100, was assembled from a number of overlapping clones and expressed in yeast as a fusion protein using human superoxide dismutase sequences to facilitate expression. This fusion protein formed the basis of first generation tests for HCV infection.

It is now known that antibodies to C100 are detected relatively late after acute infection. Furthermore, the first generation ELISAs were associated with a high rate of false-positive reactions when applied to low-incidence populations and there were further problems with some retrospective studies on stored sera. Second-generation tests include antigens from the nucleocapsid and nonstructural regions of the genome. The former antigen (C22) is particularly useful and antibodies to the HCV core protein appear relatively early in the course of infection.

Positive reactions by ELISA require confirmation by supplementary testing using, for example, a recombinant immunoblot assay. Nevertheless, indeterminant results obtained by ELISA represent a significant problem that need resolution. It should also be noted that the time for seroconversion is variable, and that when it can be measured more precisely (e.g. after transfusion) it is generally 7–31 weeks.

The presence of antibodies to specific antigen components is variable and may or may not reflect viremia and, in the case of interferon treatment, a correlation between response and loss of specific antibodies to the E2 component.

Detection and monitoring of viremia are important for management and treatment. Sensitive techniques are available for the measurement of HCV RNA based on reverse-transcription (RT)-PCR amplification, nested PCR, signal amplification using branched DNA analytes and others.

The identification of specific types and subtypes is becoming increasingly important, with observations suggesting that there is an association between response to interferon and particular genotypes and that different types may differ in their pathogenicity.

CLINICAL MANIFESTATIONS

Most acute infections are asymptomatic, and about 20% of acute infections cause jaundice. Fulminant hepatitis has been described. Extrahepatic manifestations include mixed cryoglobulinemia, membranous proliferative glomerulonephritis and porphyria cutanea tarda (see Chapter 48).

Current data suggest that about 80% of infections with HCV progress to chronicity. Histologic examination of liver biopsies from asymptomatic HCV carriers (among blood donors) has revealed none with normal histology; indeed up to 70% have been found to have chronic active hepatitis, cirrhosis, or both (Figs 214.9 and 214.10). Whether the virus is cytopathic or whether there is an immunopathologic element remains unclear. Infection with HCV is also associated with progression to primary liver cancer. For example, in Japan, where the incidence of hepatocellular carcinoma has been increasing despite a decrease in the prevalence of HBsAg, HCV is now believed to be a major risk factor.

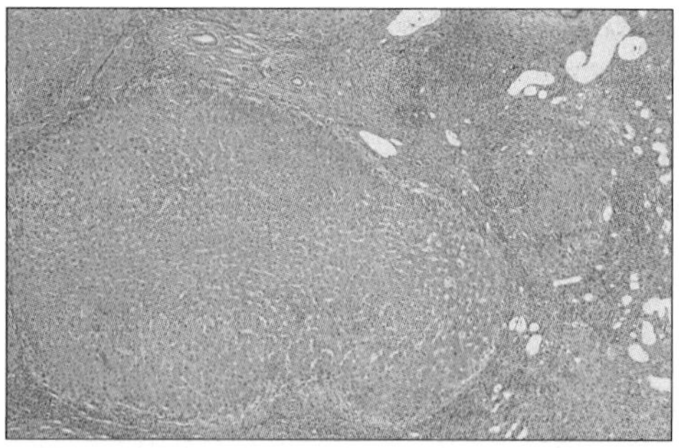

Fig. 214.9 Hepatitis C virus active cirrhosis.

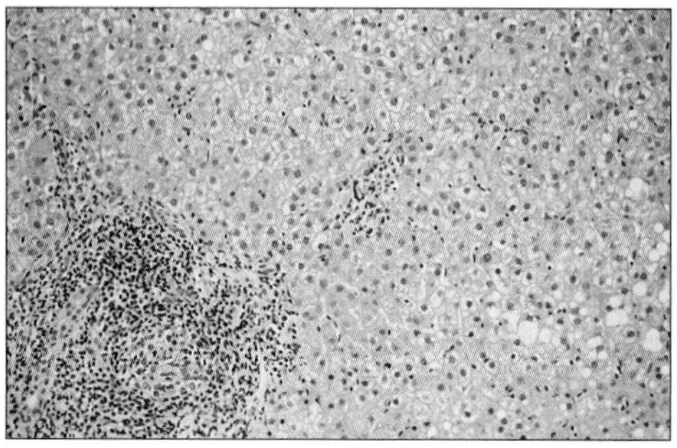

Fig. 214.10 Acute hepatitis C.

OTHER HEPATITIS VIRUSES

Virus-like particles (referred to by some as candidate hepatitis F virus) have been identified by electron microscopy in the livers and grafts in a subset of British patients with sporadic fulminant hepatitis in whom liver failure recurred about 7 days after grafting.[18] However, subsequent intensive search by advanced molecular techniques have failed to identify a candidate viral agent.

About 30 years ago, a series of transmission studies of human viral hepatitis were initiated in small South American tamarins or marmosets, which were chosen because their very limited contact with humans implied that they were unlikely to have been infected with human viruses.[19]

Serum obtained on the third day of jaundice from a young surgeon (GB) induced hepatitis in each of four inoculated marmosets and was passaged serially in these animals. These important observations remained controversial until the recent application of modern molecular virologic techniques.[20] Preliminary results indicate the identification of two independent viruses, GB virus A (GBV-A) and GB virus B (GBV-B), in the infectious plasma of tamarins inoculated with GB.[21]

GB virus A does not replicate in the liver of tamarins, whereas GBV-B causes hepatitis. Cross-challenge experiments showed that infection with the original infectious tamarin inoculum conferred protection from reinfection with GBV-B but not GBV-A. A third virus, GBV-C, was subsequently isolated from a human specimen that was immunoreactive with a GBV-B protein. GB virus C RNA was found in several patients with clinical hepatitis and was shown to have substantial sequence identity to GBV-A.

A series of studies, including phylogenetic analysis of genomic sequences, showed that GBV-A, GBV-B and GBV-C are not genotypes of HCV and that GBV-A and GBV-C are closely related. GBV-A–GBV-C, GBV-B and HCV are members of distinct viral groups. The organization of the genes of the GBV-A, GBV-B and GBV-C genomes shows that they are related to other positive-strand RNA viruses with local regions of sequence identity with various flaviviruses. The three GB viruses and HCV share only limited overall amino acid sequence identity.[22]

Serologic reagents were prepared with recombinant antigens and limited testing for antibodies and by RT-PCR for specific RNA was carried out in groups of patients, blood donors and other selected people – patients with non-A,B,C,D,E hepatitis, multitransfused patients, intravenous drug abusers and other populations with a high incidence of viral hepatitis. Preliminary studies indicated the presence of antibody to each of the GB viruses in 3–14% of these people. The development and availability of specific diagnostic reagents will establish the epidemiology of these newly identified viruses, their pathogenic significance in humans, and their clinical and public health importance. It should be noted that the virus identified more recently as hepatitis G (HGV) as a new transfusion transmitted agent[23] is now believed to be identical to GBV-C.[24]

The blood-borne nature of GBV-C/HGV has been clearly demonstrated and there is evidence that the virus persists. The association of the virus with liver damage is illustrated by raised levels of alanine transaminase and detectable HGV RNA in a number of patients. However, 40–90% of viremic subjects have normal alanine transaminase levels. In a significant proportion of patients there is co-infection with HBV, HCV, or both. The primary manifestations of

GBV-C/HGV infection may be extrahepatic or hepatic and these may be the result of co-infection with the hepatitis viruses or an (as yet unidentified) hepatotropic agent. The development of sensitive and specific serologic tests for GBV-C/HGV and the application of modern virologic techniques and histologic studies where appropriate will determine the clinical significance of this newly identified virus, which at present appears to be a virus in search of a disease.[25]

A novel human virus was isolated in Japan in 1997 from the serum of a patient with post-transfusion hepatitis and was designated TT virus (TTV) after the initials of the patient (TTV is not an acronym for transfusion-transmitted virus as has been assumed and perpetuated in numerous publications). The virus has a circular single strand DNA, non-enveloped, of negative polarity and is 3965 nucleotides in length. There is 30% diversity in the coding region accounting for numerous genotypes believed to result mainly from recombination. The virus replicates in many tissues, particularly the liver, and is shed into the blood and feces. TT virus DNA is found in saliva (78%), breast milk, semen (60%), cervical swabs and other body fluids of infected persons. The virus is ubiquitous and is found in 20% to more than 90% of the general population and healthy blood donors. There is no evidence of involvement of TTV in acute or chronic liver disease. TT virus is found in farm animals, including chickens (19%), cows (25%), pigs (20%) and sheep (30%), and in other mammals including nonhuman primates.

TTV-like mini virus (TLMV) and several related viruses such as SANBAN, YONBAN and others have been described, but without any disease association in humans. These different viruses have been divided into at least 29 genotypes with sequence divergence of more than 30% from each other and placed into four phylogenetic groups. Since 1999, much attention has been devoted to the SEN virus (again the initials of a patient infected with a virus possibly related to TTV). The SEN virus (SENV) was isolated from an immunocompromised HIV patient with post-transfusion hepatitis of unknown etiology. Eight genotypes of this virus have been described (SENV-A to SENV-H), each differing by at least 25% in nucleotide sequence. SENV-C, SENV-D and SENV-H are supposedly associated with transfusion hepatitis and, although the prevalence of these viruses is common in patients with non-A–E liver disease, a causal association has not been demonstrated and these should not be considered at present as candidate hepatitis viruses.[26]

MANAGEMENT

Although a substantial number of antiviral compounds have been evaluated for the treatment of chronic hepatitis B, interferon-α has been licensed in treatment. Under optimal conditions of careful selection of patients, 30–50% respond at least transiently and about 20% clear the virus, accompanied by improvement in liver function. Combination therapy with nucleoside analogues and other drugs have shown a variable response. Lamivudine and famciclovir are valuable for treatment of hepatitis B chronic liver disease. A comparison of prednisone withdrawal followed by treatment with interferon only did not provide evidence of added benefit for the combined regimen.

Interferon-α is also the only drug approved for the treatment of chronic hepatitis C. Again, the efficacy of interferon is limited in suitable patients, and 15–20% of patients will have a sustained virologic response. Pegylated interferon appears to be more effective, and combination therapy with ribavirin is now regarded as standard of care.

For a more detailed discussion of the management of hepatitis, see Chapters 48 and 207.

REFERENCES

1. Behrens RH, Doherty JF. Severe hepatitis A despite passive immunization. Lancet 1993;341:972.
2. Provost PJ, Hilleman MR. An inactivated hepatitis A virus vaccine prepared from infected marmoset liver. Proc Soc Exp Biol Med 1975;159:210–203.
3. Schlauder GG, Mushahwar IK. Genetic heterogeneity of hepatitis E virus. J Med Virol 2001;65:282–292.
4. Oon C-J, Lim G-K, Ye Z, *et al.* Molecular epidemiology of hepatitis B virus vaccine variants in Singapore. Vaccine 1995;13:699–702.
5. Carman WF, Thomas H, Zuckerman AJ, Harrison T. Molecular variants of hepatitis B virus. In: Zuckerman AJ, Howard HC, eds. Viral hepatitis: scientific basis and clinical management. Edinburgh: Churchill Livingstone; 1993:115–36.
6. Carman WF, Zanetti AR, Karayiannis P, *et al.* Vaccine-induced escape mutant of hepatitis B virus. Lancet 1990;336:325–9.
7. Zuckerman AJ. Effect of hepatitis B virus mutants on efficacy of vaccination. Lancet 2000;350:1382–4.
8. Kidd-Ljunggren K, Miyakawa Y, Kidd AH. Genetic variability in hepatitis B viruses. J Gen Virol 2002;83:1267–80.
9. Vaudin M, Wolstenholme AJ, Tsiquaye KN, *et al.* The complete nucleotide sequence of the genome of a hepatitis B virus isolated from a naturally infected chimpanzee. J Gen Virol 1988;69:1383–9.
10. Carman WF, Jacyna MR, Hadziyannis S, *et al.* Mutation preventing formation of hepatitis B e antigen in patients with chronic HBV infection. Lancet 1989;2:588–91.
11. Beasley RP, Hwang L-Y. Overview of the epidemiology of hepatocellular carcinoma. In: Hollinger FB, Lemon SM, Margolis HS, eds. Viral hepatitis and liver disease. Baltimore: Williams & Wilkins; 1991:532–5.
12. World Health Organization. Prevention of liver cancer. WHO Tech Rep Ser No 691. Geneva: WHO; 1983.
13. Van Damme P, Vorsters A. Hepatitis B control in Europe by universal vaccination programmes: the situation in 2001. J Med Virol 2002;67:433–439.
14. Zuckerman JN, Cockcroft A, Zuckerman AJ. Site of injection for vaccination. BMJ 1992;305:1158.
15. Gerin JL, Purcell RJ, Rizzetto M, eds. The hepatitis delta virus. New York: Wiley-Liss; 1991.
16. Lai MMC. The molecular biology of hepatitis delta virus. Annu Rev Biochem 1995;64:259–86.
17. Houghton M, Han J, Kuo G, Choo Q-L, Weiner AJ. Hepatitis C virus: structure and molecular virology. In: Zuckerman AJ, Thomas HC, eds. Viral hepatitis: scientific basis and clinical management. Edinburgh: Churchill Livingstone; 1993:229–40.
18. Fagan EA, Ellis DS, Tovey GM, *et al.* Toga-like virus as a cause of fulminant hepatitis attributed to sporadic non-A, non-B. J Med Virol 1989;28:150–5.
19. Deinhardt F, Holmes AW, Capps RB, Popper H. Studies on the transmission of human viral hepatitis to marmoset monkeys. 1. Transmission of disease, serial passages and description of liver lesions. J Exp Med 1967;125:673–88.
20. Schlauder GG, Dawson GJ, Simons JN, *et al.* Molecular and serologic analysis in the transmission of the GB hepatitis agents. J Med Virol 1995;46:81–90.
21. Simons JN, Leary TP, Dawson GJ, *et al.* Isolation of novel virus-like sequences associated with human hepatitis. Nat Med 1995;1:564–9.
22. Leary TP, Muerhoff AS, Simons JN, *et al.* Sequence and genomic organization of GBV-C. A novel member of the Flaviviridae associated with human non-A–E hepatitis. J Med Virol 1996;48:60–7.
23. Linnen J, Wages J, Zhang-Keck Z-Y, *et al.* Molecular cloning and disease association of hepatitis G virus: a new transfusion transmissible agent. Science 1996;271:505–9.
24. Zuckerman AJ. Alphabet of hepatitis viruses. Lancet 1996;347:558–9.
25. Mushahwar IK. Recently discovered blood-borne viruses: are they hepatitis viruses or merely endosymbionts? J Med Virol 2000;62:399–404.
26. Bowden S. New hepatitis viruses: contenders and pretenders. J Gastrol Hepatol 2001;16:124–31.

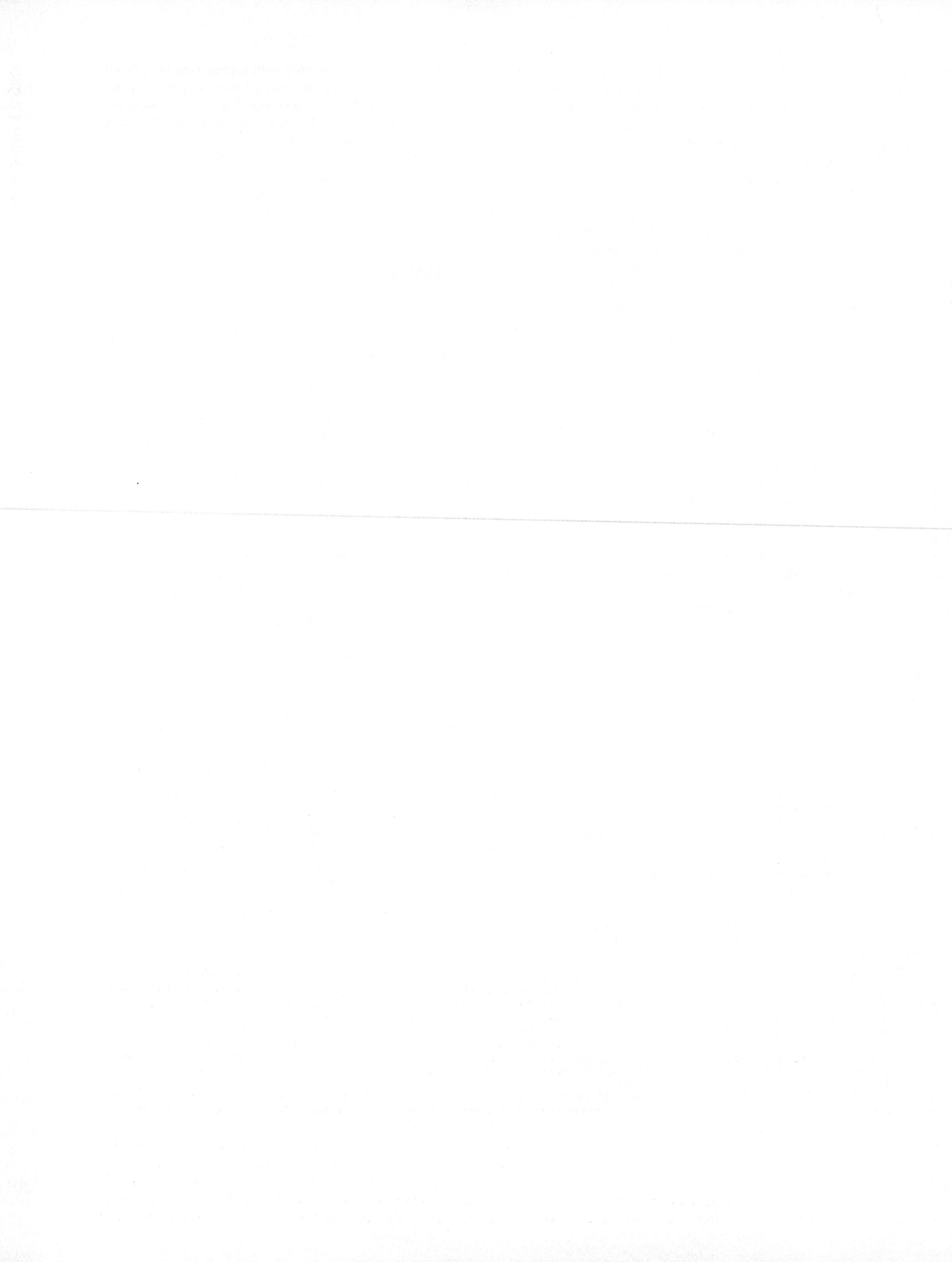

chapter

215 Herpesviruses

Anton M van Loon, Graham M Cleator & Paul E Klapper

NATURE

Taxonomy

The herpesviruses comprise a large family of DNA viruses[1] with over 150 individual members. They have been found in almost all species (both vertebrate and invertebrate) in which they have been actively sought. Their widespread occurrence suggests that they first colonized animal species at an early stage of evolution[2] and this ancient colonization has led to adaptation to their natural host so that they are generally highly host specific. This adaption is further exemplified by their high rates of infection (the prevalence of positive serology in adult populations worldwide is 80–90%), the generally mild symptoms associated with primary infection and their strategy for maintaining themselves in a population with a high level of immunity to infection by establishing a latent infection.

On the basis of their biologic properties the viruses comprising the family Herpesviridae are subdivided into three subfamilies – the Alphaherpesvirinae, the Betaherpesvirinae and the Gammaherpesvirinae (Table 215.1).[1] Each of the subfamilies is further subdivided into genera:

- the Alphaherpesvirinae has two genera – Simplexvirus and Varicellovirus;
- the Betaherpesvirinae has three genera – Cytomegalovirus, Muromegalovirus and Roseolovirus; and
- the Gammaherpesvirinae has two genera – Lymphocryptovirus and Rhadinovirus.

The current classification is somewhat subjective because it is based upon biologic properties. In the future, it is likely that a more precise system based on genetic information such as the organization and sequence of reiterated sequences within the genome of the virus (Fig. 215.1), the conservation of selected genes and gene clusters, and possibly comparisons of protein sequences will provide a more objective classification system.[3]

Under the present classification scheme[1] viruses are named according to their natural host species and numbered in accordance with the order in which they were first identified. As many viruses have acquired commonly used names – for example, human herpesvirus 1 is commonly known as herpes simplex virus (HSV) type 1 – the classification is not yet rigorously applied. However, newly discovered viruses are now named in accordance with this classification scheme, for example human herpesviruses 6, 7 and 8. At present eight herpesviruses are known to have the human species as their natural host (Table 215.2). Herpes B virus, a virus belonging to the Simplex genus of the Alphaherpesvirus subfamily and also known as cercopithecine herpesvirus 1 or herpesvirus simiae, is enzootic among old world macaques and usually causes minimal or no morbidity in its natural host. However, B virus infections in humans, mostly because of accidental exposure, may cause severe and often fatal disease.

Structure

The herpesvirus virion often has a pleomorphic appearance when seen by electron microscopy. It measures 150–300nm in diameter and is composed of an internal protein nucleocapsid enclosing the double-stranded (ds) DNA genome and an external lipid envelope. The electron microscopic appearance of a typical herpesvirus is shown in Figure 215.2.

BIOLOGIC PROPERTIES OF HERPESVIRIDAE	
Common properties	Spheric enveloped virions, 150–200nm in diameter
	Large, linear, dsDNA genome of 125–230kbp
	Synthesis of DNA and assembly of capsid within the nucleus, acquire envelope by budding through nuclear membrane
	Specify a large array of enzymes involved in nucleic acid metabolism and synthesis
	Production of progeny virus results in destruction of the host cell
	Establish latency in their natural host
Alphaherpesvirinae	Variable host range
	Short reproductive cycle
	Rapid spread in cell culture
	Efficient destruction of infected cells
	Establish latency primarily but not exclusively in sensory ganglia
Betaherpesvirinae	Restricted host range (a nonexclusive property of this subfamily)
	Long reproductive cycle
	Infection progresses slowly in culture, frequently forming enlarged (cytomegalic) cells
	Latency in secretory glands, lymphoreticular cells, kidneys and other tissues
Gammaherpesvirinae	Experimental host range limited to family or order of natural host
	In-vitro replication in lymphoblastoid cells
	In-vivo replication and latency in either T or B cells

Table 215.1 Biologic properties of the Herpesviridae.

DNA

The genetic information of the virus is encoded by a linear molecule of dsDNA and the size of this molecule varies for different herpesviruses, from approximately 80,000 to 150,000kDa (125–245kbp). The G+C composition of individual herpesvirus DNAs varies from 31 to 75%. The size of individual herpesvirus genomes varies by approximately 10kbp and this is usually attributable to the number of terminal and/or internal reiterated sequences (see Fig. 215.1). Within the virion the DNA is a linear molecule that is tightly wound in the form of a torus. The ends of this molecule appear to attach to

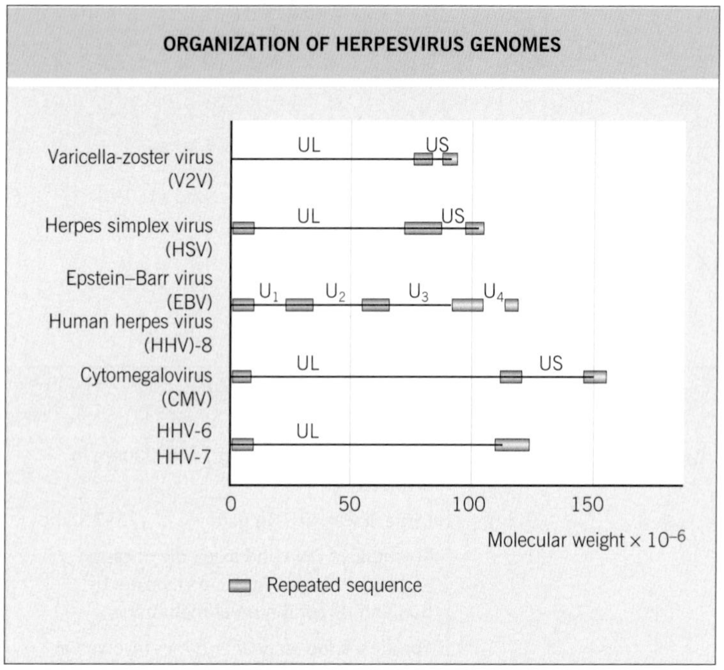

Fig. 215.1 Organization of herpesvirus genomes. Inverted repeat sequences in VZV, HSV and CMV allow the genome to recombine in 2,4, and 4 isomers, respectively. Both HSV and CMV have a UL (long unique base sequence) and a US (short unique base sequence) each terminated by two sets of inverted repeated sequences. The repeated sequences allow the UL and US to invert relative to one another, so yielding four isometric forms of DNA. As there is only one set of inverted repeats in VZV, only two isomers of DNA can be produced. Both EBV and HHV-8 have only one isomeric form with several unique regions surrounded by direct repeated sequences.

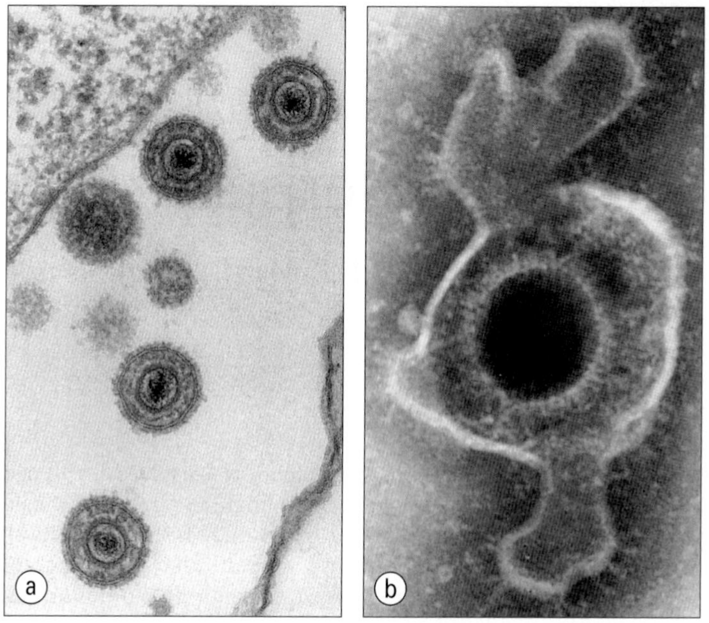

Fig. 215.2 Enveloped virus particle. (a) Thin section. (b) Negative staining. These electron microscopic views (×140,000) show HSV. The DNA is surrounded by a nucleocapsid comprised of 162 individual protein subunits (150 hexavalent capsomers and 12 pentavalent capsomers) arranged in the form of an icosahedron. The nucleocapsid is in turn enclosed by the tegument and virus envelope bearing glycoprotein spikes. Courtesy of Hans Gelderblom.

the inner surface of the nucleocapsid, which prevents the DNA from circularizing until it is released during infection.

The phylogenetic relationship, based on a neighbor-joining analysis of the glycoprotein B gene, between the human herpesviruses and herpes B virus[4] is shown in Figure 215.3.

Virion polypeptides

Herpes simplex virus type 1 virions contain about 33 virus-specific proteins, but more than double this number are found within an infected cell. The virion polypeptides (VPs) are designated by serial number. The transcription of mRNAs from the genome proceeds from both strands of the genome, in either direction, with evidence of overlapping transcription and of splicing of genes and gene products.[5] There are two sets of *cis*-acting genes embedded in the domains of viral genes. The first set enables binding of cellular transcription factors and *trans*-acting factors to initiate and enhance viral gene expression. The second set enables interaction of genes with regulatory proteins (up- or downregulation). Three rounds of transcription and translation are observed, the so-called:

- α phase (resulting in the production of 'immediate-early proteins');
- β phase (proteins responsible mainly for DNA metabolism); and
- γ phase (principally structural proteins).

Nucleocapsid

The icosahedral nucleocapsid is 100–110nm in diameter comprising 162 individual capsomers (i.e. 12 pentavalent and 150 hexavalent capsomers). Using electron cryomicroscopy and computer-aided image reconstruction the structure of herpesvirus particles has been determined at a resolution of 26Å. In HSV individual capsomers are believed to be constructed from the four major capsid proteins VP5, VP26, VP23 and VP19.[6,7] The interior and exterior of the capsid appear to be linked by transcapsomeric channels.

HUMAN HERPESVIRUSES

ICTV name	Common name	Subfamily	Genus
Human herpesvirus-1	Herpes simplex virus (HSV)-1	Alphaherpesvirinae	Simplexvirus
Human herpesvirus-2	Herpes simplex virus-2	Alphaherpesvirinae	Simplexvirus
Human herpesvirus-3	Varicella-zoster virus (VZV)	Alphaherpesvirinae	Varicellovirus
Human herpesvirus-4	Epstein–Barr virus (EBV)	Gammaherpesvirinae	Lymphocryptovirus
Human herpesvirus-5	Human cytomegalovirus (CMV)	Betaherpesvirinae	Cytomegalovirus
Human herpesvirus-6	Human herpesvirus (HHV)-6	Betaherpesvirinae	Roseolovirus
Human herpesvirus-7	Human herpesvirus (HHV)-7	Betaherpesvirinae	–
Human herpesvirus-8	Kaposi's sarcoma-associated herpesvirus (KSHV)	Gammaherpesvirinae	Rhadinovirus

Table 215.2 Human herpesviruses. Two variants, 'a' and 'b', of human herpesvirus 4 and human herpesvirus 6 are known. ICTV, International Committee on Taxonomy of Viruses.[1]

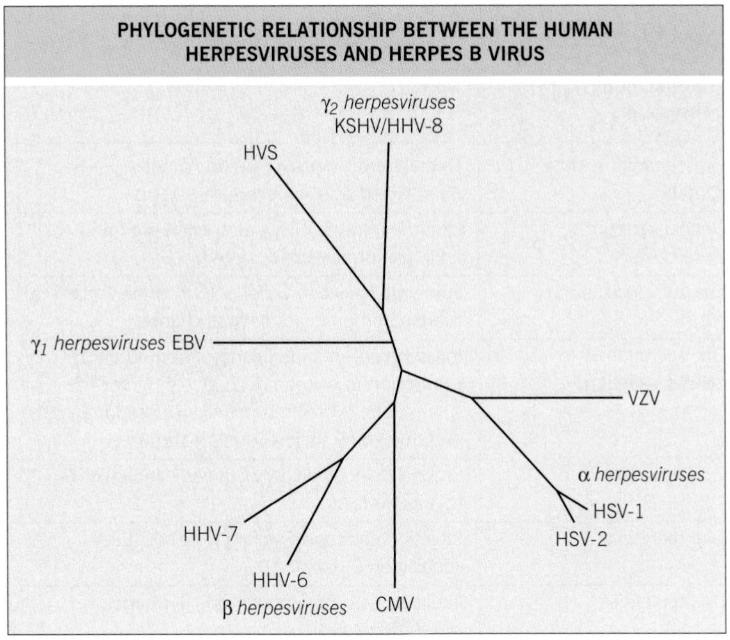

Fig. 215.3 Phylogenetic relationship between the human herpesviruses and herpes B virus. The tree was created by neighbor-joining analysis of the glycoprotein B gene sequences. HVS, herpesvirus simiae (herpes B virus). Adapted from Schultz, 2000.[5]

Tegument

The amorphous electron-dense tegument bounded by the nucleocapsid and outer envelope of the virus contains at least eight proteins. These proteins serve important functions after the virus has penetrated the host cell (see below).

Envelope

The viral envelope is an extensively modified form of the original host cell nuclear membrane and bears a series of virus-specified glycoprotein spikes 9–15nm in length (see Fig. 215.2). The glycoprotein spikes define several of the major biologic attributes of the virus. There are major antigenic differences in glycoprotein spikes between the virus species. In HSV there are at least ten glycoproteins on the viral envelope (Table 215.3).

Physical properties

Herpesviruses are thermolabile. In cell culture media the half-life at 86°F (30°C) is between 1.5 and 14 hours. Drying in air leads to desiccation of the viral envelope and loss of infectivity. Ether in water (20%) and other lipid solvents such as 70% alcohol or chloroform rapidly inactivate herpesviruses completely.

EPIDEMIOLOGY

Transmission pathways

Herpesviruses are relatively fragile in that they require a lipid envelope to achieve attachment to and penetration of the host cell. As a consequence these viruses transmit most easily on contact with warm and moist mucosal layers. Two broad groupings of virus can be distinguished:

- those where virus is transmitted most effectively by oral secretions and nongenital contact; and
- those where the virus is transmitted most effectively by genital secretions.

These modes of transmission have a profound influence upon the epidemiology of the individual viruses.

HERPES SIMPLEX VIRUS GLYCOPROTEINS

Glycoprotein	Required for replication in cell culture	Function
gB	+	Forms a dimer, essential for viral entry; induces neutralizing antibody
gC	–	Involved in cell attachment
gD	+	Required after attachment of virus to cell to allow virus entry into the cell
gE	–	In complex with gI; binds Fc portion of antibodies
gG	–	Involved in entry, egress and spread from cell to cell
gH	+	Forms complex with gL (see below); role in entry, egress and cell-to-cell spread
gI	–	gI and gE form a complex for transport to plasma membranes and gI and gE form an Fc receptor
gJ	–	Predicted from DNA sequence only
gK	+	Required for efficient egress (viral exocytosis)
gL	+	Forms complex with gH that is required for transport of gH and gL to the plasma membrane and for viral entry mediated by gH
gM	–	Not known

Table 215.3 Herpes simplex virus glycoproteins. Information relates to HSV-1; not all glycoprotein species have been identified in other herpesviruses and the size, degree of glycosylation and other post-translational modifications vary for different viruses.

Prevalence

Herpesviruses transmitted predominantly by oral secretions or nongenital contact are HSV-1, varicella-zoster virus (VZV), Epstein–Barr virus (EBV), cytomegalovirus (CMV), human herpesvirus (HHV)-6 and HHV-7. Those transmitted predominantly by the sexual route are HSV-2 and HHV-8. The peak incidence for infection transmitted nongenitally is in early childhood (Table 215.4). The peak incidence for infections acquired by genital transmission is in adolescence and early adulthood. The rates of infection by viruses transmitted by the genital route are not usually as high as those for viruses transmitted by a nongenital route. However, for both groups there is a further distinct relation between rates of acquisition, sexual preference and the socio-economic status of the study population.

Geographic aspects

Herpesviruses are distributed worldwide and no animal reservoirs of infection are known for any of the human herpesviruses. Burkitt's lymphoma, which is associated with EBV infection, is endemic only in tropical Africa.[8] Nasopharyngeal carcinoma is also associated with EBV infection and is endemic in Japan and Southern China.[9] A sporadic, non-HIV-associated Kaposi's sarcoma is found predominantly in countries bordering the Mediterranean and in Central Africa.[10]

There is evidence that in tropical areas varicella is less prevalent in childhood than in temperate climatic areas and is more common in adults.[11] Possible explanations for this include the relative isolation of clusters of population in rural areas,[12] epidemiologic 'interference' through infections caused by other viruses, especially HSV,[13] and perhaps decreased efficiency of transmission as a result of the lability of VZV in areas where there is a high ambient temperature.[11]

FEATURES OF HERPESVIRUS INFECTIONS					
Virus	Peak incidence of primary infection		Adult seroprevalence (%)	Principal route(s) of transmission	Notes
	Childhood	Adolescence			
HSV-1	+++	+	75–95+	Oral secretions, close contact	Overall seroprevalence predominantly determined by socio-economic status
HSV-2	–	+++	4–95	Genital secretions, close contact	Lifetime number of sex partners is predominant influence on rates of seropositivity
VZV	+++	+	90–95	Aerosol, close contact	Epidemic spread in childhood, in tropics relatively more common in adults than children
CMV	++	++	40–95+	Oral secretions, genital secretions	Infection common in infancy, but a significant proportion of women of childbearing age are susceptible; overall seroprevalence predominantly determined by socio-economic status
EBV	++	++	70–95	Oral secretions	Second peak of incidence in early adolescence (glandular fever)
HHV-6	+++	–	>85	Oral secretions	Infection common in infancy – peak age of acquisition 2 years
HHV-7	+++	–	>85	Oral secretions	Infection common in infancy – peak age of acquisition 3 years
HHV-8	–	+++	10–25	Oral secretions, genital secretions	Homosexual men who have AIDS have highest seroprevalence

Table 215.4 Features of herpesvirus infections. CMV, cytomegalovirus; EBV, Epstein–Barr virus; HHV, human herpesvirus; HSV, herpes simplex virus; VZV, varicella-zoster virus.

Periodicity

The human herpesviruses are endemic in human populations as a result of their strategy of establishing latent infections. In addition, because of their modes of transmission there is no seasonal variation in the efficiency of transmission. For infections for which reactivation is infrequent (e.g. VZV infection) there may be 'outbreaks' of infection (mini-epidemics) when infection spreads rapidly through a nonimmune population. Outbreaks can also occur if large numbers of susceptible individuals are brought together (e.g. infectious mononucleosis among military recruits or college students).[14]

Determinants of infection

Early acquisition of infection is common for all herpesviruses transmitted by the nongenital route. In a classic study of HSV infection Burnet and Williams[15] showed that there was a clear relationship between the age of acquisition of the virus and socio-economic status. Populations associated with a low socio-economic environment collectively showed earlier acquisition of HSV infection than more affluent populations, although in both groups, infection rates of 90–95% were observed by early adulthood. Primary HSV-1 infection was rare in those over 30 years of age. In recent years several sero-epidemiologic studies have shown a general decrease in the overall prevalence of HSV-1 antibody in developed countries. However, even within individual countries there are variations in seroprevalence, for example the seroprevalence rates are generally higher among inner city residents than among those from rural areas. Here, the major factor determining the seroprevalence is the frequency of direct person-to-person contact rather than the socio-economic status of the individual populations.

If infection does not occur in infancy, transmission routes other than direct oral contact can constitute important risk factors. An example is found in the acquisition of CMV. Although most CMV infections occur in infancy a significant proportion (40–50% in developed countries) of women of child-bearing age are still susceptible to infection and may acquire the infection during pregnancy. Sexual transmission of infection is an important mode of acquisition of infection for these women. In addition, contact with young children of less than 24 months of age is a further important risk factor.

Viruses such as HSV-2 for which the principal mode of transmission is sexual are generally not acquired until the onset of sexual activity in adolescence and early adulthood. The major influence on acquisition of infection appears to be the number of sexual partners and sexual preference of an individual (as might be expected for a sexually transmitted virus). Seroprevalence rates of up to 95% have been reported in some female commercial sex workers. Women are generally infected at an earlier age (15–20%) than men, and rates of infection in women are higher for all age groups including those of 45 or more years of age.[16] Studies among patients attending a genitourinary medicine clinic suggest that only in homosexual men are the rates of infection with HSV-2 comparable to those found in women.

Whereas the seroprevalence of HHV-8 infection is low (<2%) in general populations, except in some parts of Italy, Greece and most of Africa, it is high in groups at high risk of infection such as homosexual men with large numbers of sex partners.[17]

PATHOGENICITY

Replication

The replicative cycle of the virus is illustrated schematically in Figure 215.4. The initial attachment of a herpesvirus to a host cell is mediated by a glycoprotein or a complex of glycoproteins projecting from the virus envelope interacting with its specific receptor on the host cell.[4]

Initial contact of the herpesviruses with the cell is usually made by low-affinity binding to glycosaminoglycans, preferentially heparan sulphate, on the cell surface. In this way viruses are concentrated at the cell surface, facilitating subsequent binding to a specific receptor, for instance the complement receptor Cr2 (CD 21) in the case of EBV. The virus envelope and cell plasma membranes then fuse,

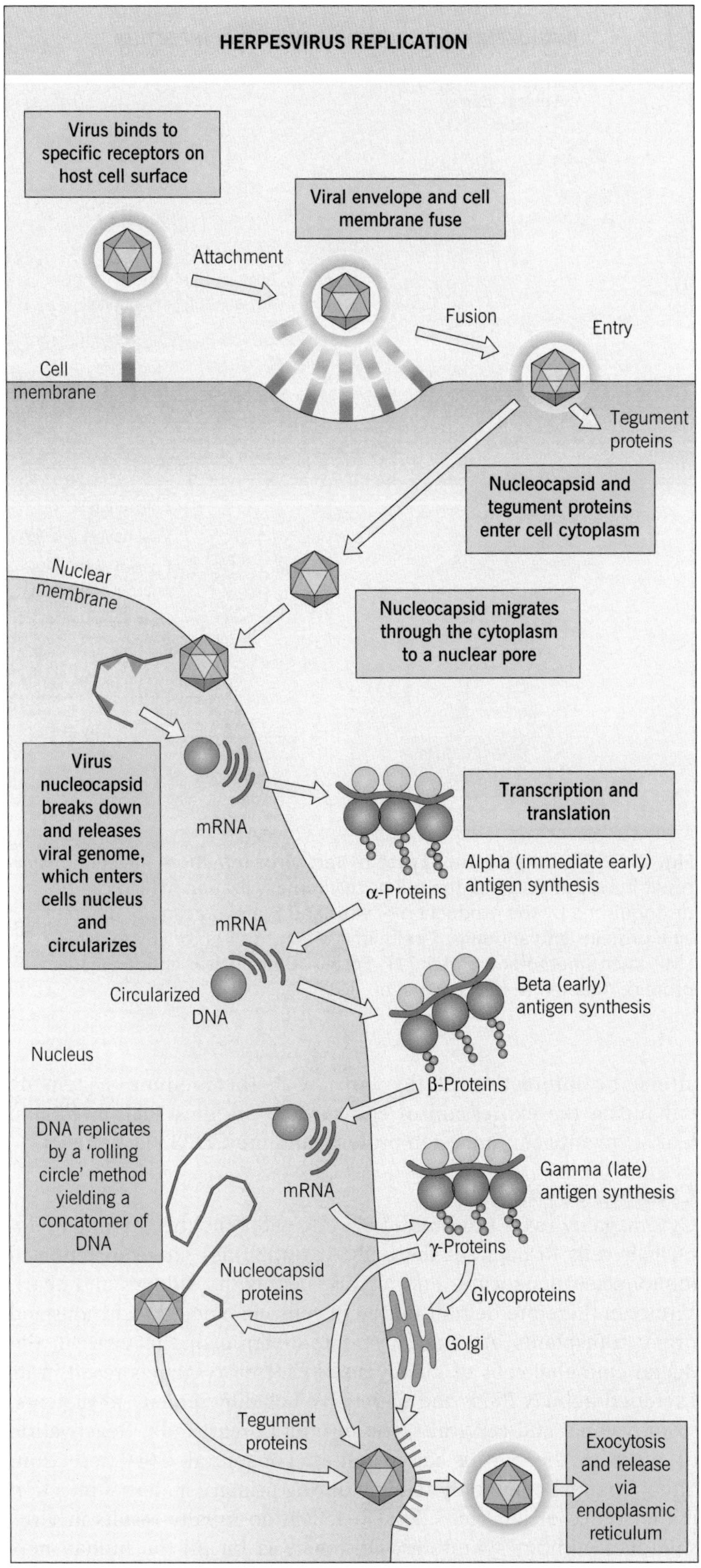

Fig. 215.4 Herpesvirus replication. The tegument proteins effect the shut-down of host cell metabolism. On entry to the nucleus the DNA circularizes and binds a tegument protein and cellular factors to initiate transcription. Transcription and translation occur in three phases: immediate-early, early and late. Capsid proteins migrate into the nucleus and the viral DNA is encapsidated. The viral glycoproteins are extensively modified post-translationally by transit through the Golgi apparatus. The glycoproteins diffuse to the nuclear envelope. The nucleocapsids bud through the modified nuclear membrane and exit the cell via the endoplasmic reticulum or are released on cell lysis.

resulting in the introduction of tegument proteins and viral nucleocapsid into the cell cytoplasm.[18] This process probably involves several, if not all, of the virion surface glycoproteins and is accomplished rapidly.

The tegument proteins serve to both 'disable' the host cell and initiate viral replication. Soon after virus entry, host cell DNA synthesis is shut off, host cell protein synthesis declines rapidly and glycosylation of host cell proteins ceases. In this way the virus ensures that the metabolic machinery of the cell is fully available for virus replication. At the same time the virion nucleocapsid is transported via the cell cytoskeleton to a nuclear pore. At the nuclear pore the viral nucleocapsid breaks down releasing its DNA into the cell nucleus where the linear DNA molecule immediately circularizes.

Transcription of viral DNA takes place within the host cell nucleus involving three classes of mRNA, α, β and γ, and including both host cell as well as viral proteins. In HSV, to initiate transcription, the circularized DNA must bind a host cell protein (OCT-1) to a *cis*-acting site and the tegument protein α *trans*-inducing factor (α-TIF) binds an additional factor designated C1 (and possibly others). This α-TIF–C1 complex then binds to the OCT-1–DNA complex.[6] α-TIF acts in *trans* to induce α (or 'immediate-early') genes – the first set of viral genes to be transcribed. Immediate-early or α proteins are control proteins that stimulate and regulate all the subsequent steps in the replicative cycle. All but one of the α proteins are regulatory proteins. Their production is essential to stimulate the production of β polypeptides, which are the enzymes and other proteins involved in viral nucleic acid reproduction (e.g. DNA-dependent DNA polymerase, which reproduces the viral genome). Products of α and β genes transactivate the translation of the γ genes, which produce the late or γ proteins, the structural proteins for the virion including the viral capsid and glycoproteins.

Productive infection is fatal for the host cell because in the process of viral DNA replication host cell chromosomes are degraded and appear as a chromatin ring around the borders of the nuclear membrane. In addition host cell metabolism is irreversible damaged.

Molecular and cellular basis of pathogenicity

The combination of virion surface glycoproteins and the distribution of cellular receptors provide a partial explanation of the cell and tissue specific tropism of members of the human herpesviruses. A common characteristic of the herpesviruses is their ability to persist in infected cells while expressing only a minimal set of genes needed for latency. After certain stimuli, or when the immune system is suppressed, the virus will be reactivated and undergo replication to produce new viral progeny. In individuals who have deficits in cell-mediated immunity (CMI), infection is more poorly controlled than in those who have intact CMI. Primary infection is in consequence more severe, and reactivation of latent infection is more likely to result in symptomatic disease.

Herpes simplex virus

In vitro, HSV can infect most types of human cells and even cells of other species, but *in vivo* it is host specific, causes lytic infection of fibroblasts and epithelial cells, and establishes latent infection in neurons. In addition, the two biotypes of HSV, HSV-1 and HSV-2, show some predilection for infecting defined anatomic sites – oropharyngeal and genital, respectively. Both viruses are capable of infecting and producing latent infection at either site, but HSV-2 reactivation 'above the waist' and HSV-1 reactivation 'below the waist' are infrequent compared with HSV-1 reactivation 'above the waist' and HSV-2 reactivation 'below the waist',[19] respectively. It is suggested that at the molecular level the site-specific reactivation phenotypes of HSV-1 and HSV-2 depend on the latency-associated transcript (LAT) regions of the viral genome.[20]

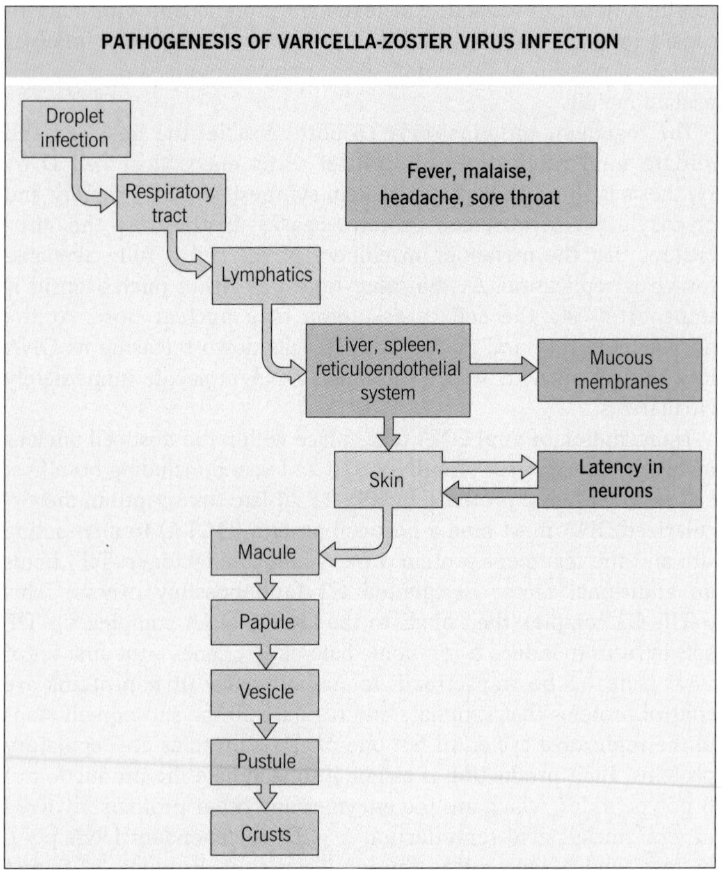

Fig. 215.5 Pathogenesis of varicella-zoster virus infection.

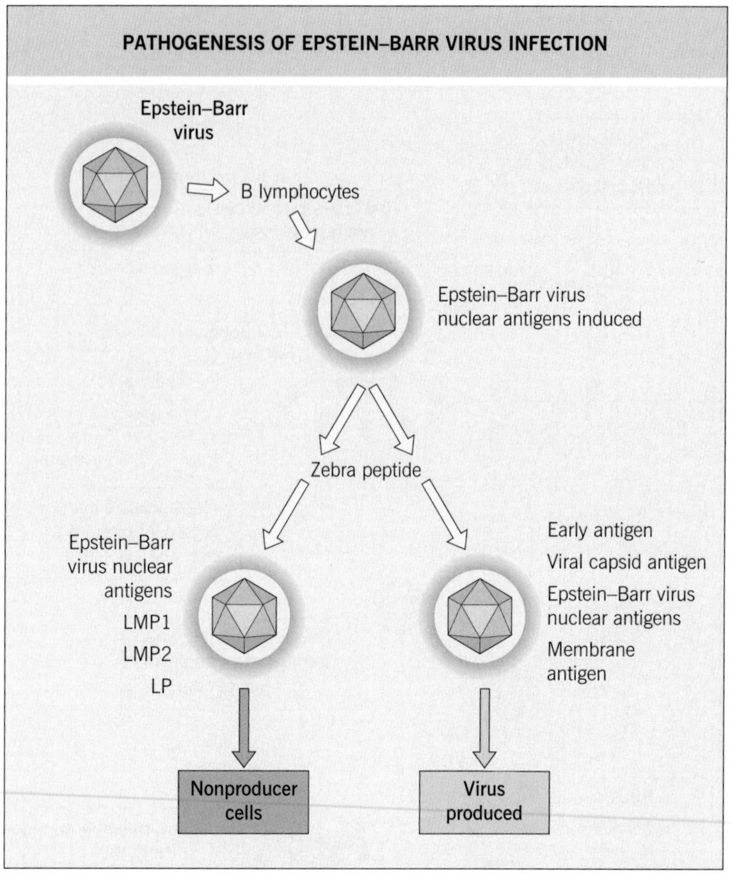

Fig. 215.6 Pathogenesis of Epstein–Barr virus infection. Infection may result in lytic infection of the cell or cell immortalization, which can be distinguished by the production of virus and the expression of different viral proteins and antigens. T cells limit the outgrowth of EBV-infected cells. LMP, latent membrane protein; LP, Epstein–Barr nuclear antigen leader protein. Adapted from Strauss *et al.*, 1993.[22]

Varicella-zoster virus

Primary VZV infection starts in the mucosa of the respiratory tract and progresses via the blood and lymphatic system to cells of the reticulo-endothelial system. A secondary viremia after 11–13 days disseminates virus to the skin where the characteristic vesicular lesions of 'chickenpox' are produced (Fig. 215.5). The virus probably establishes latent infection in the dorsal root or cranial nerves during this viremic phase. The molecular basis of latency and reactivation is poorly understood. It has been suggested that differences in the frequency and clinical expression of HSV and VZV recrudescence may be related to the type of cells that are latently infected within sensory ganglia. In one model,[21] HSV latency is restricted to neurons and virus reactivation is induced by non-specific stimuli acting upon the neuron and results in re-infection of a small area of the skin innervated by the neuron. In contrast, VZV latency is mainly established in satellite cells and reactivation requires the spread of virus to neighboring neurons within the ganglia. These neurons act as sources of virus for axonal transport and infection of a wider area of the skin. Further differences in the latency and reactivation of HSV and VZV could relate to the differing structures of the genomes of the two viruses; LATs and neurovirulence genes are encoded in the HSV genome and have no counterpart in the VZV genome.[21]

Epstein–Barr virus

During primary infection EBV establishes a productive infection in the epithelial cells of the oropharynx. Virus is shed in the saliva and gains access to B cells in lymphatic tissue and the blood.[22] A lytic infection leads to the production of EBV proteins, including the early antigens, viral capsid antigen and the glycoproteins of the membrane antigen (Fig. 215.6). Epstein–Barr virus is a B-cell mitogen, stimulating the growth and immortalization of B cells by preventing apoptosis. Epstein–Barr virus infection of B cells also alters the interaction of the virus with the immune system by enhancing the expression of cell surface proteins such as human leukocyte antigens, adhesion proteins and the CD23 blast antigen.

Cytomegalovirus

Cytomegalovirus is transmitted via infected lymphocytes and mononuclear cells throughout the body. It establishes latent infection in mononuclear leukocytes and organs such as the kidneys and heart. Virus can therefore be transmitted in cells via blood transfusions and organ transplants. Activation and replication of the virus in the ductal epithelial cells of kidney and in secretory glands result in its excretion in body fluids and secretions including semen, saliva, tears, stool, vaginal and cervical secretions, and breast milk. Reactivation of virus in the cervix can result in congenital CMV infection, although more commonly viremia during primary maternal infection is the source of fetal infection. Reactivation usually results in virus shedding without symptoms. However, as for all the human herpesvirus infections in people who have individual deficits in CMI, reactivation is often symptomatic.

Since the original sero-epidemiologic observations,[23] several studies have shown a relationship between CMV infection and atherosclerosis.[24,25] Such a correlation has also been found for other infectious agents such as *Chlamydia pneumoniae* and *Helicobacter pylori*. The evidence includes increased CMV antibody titers as well as a higher frequency of detection of CMV antigens and sequences in the wall of atherosclerotic vessels. However, results from various studies were not unambiguous, and a causal relationship between CMV and atherosclerosis has not yet been established.

Human herpesviruses 6 and 7

Human herpesvirus-6 was originally isolated from T-cell cultures derived from the blood of patients who had AIDS,[26] and HHV-7 was isolated from the CD4+ T cells of a healthy individual. Both viruses infect and kill CD4+ T cells, just like HIV, yet the outcome of infection is markedly different. In contrast to HIV infection, infection by HHV-6 or –7 is rapidly controlled by the host immune response, and the virus establishes a state of latency. HHV-6 and HHV-7 are closely related to the other member of the human Betaherpesvirinae, CMV (see Fig. 215.3). HHV-6 isolates are classified into two distinct variants, HHV-6A and HHV-6B. Although closely related, consistent differences have been observed in their biologic, immunologic, epidemiologic and molecular properties. HHV-6B is the primary etiologic agent of exanthem subitum,[27] whereas no single disease has been definitively associated with HHV-6A. In the same way, HHV-7 also remains an 'orphan' virus with no firm disease association. Infection with HHV-6 and HHV-7 occurs early in life. The viruses are present in the saliva of most adults and are readily spread by oral secretions. The cellular host range of HHV-6 appears to be extensive. Virus replication in CD4+ T cells is common and there is also limited replication in CD8+ T cells, natural killer cells, monocytes, epithelial cells and brain cells.[28]

Human herpesvirus-7, like HHV-6, grows well in CD4+ T cells, but unlike HHV-6 it uses the CD4 molecule as its receptor. Human herpesvirus-7 also downmodulates expression of CD4. The host range of HHV-7 appears to be more limited than that of HHV-6. It is less cytopathic and grows less rapidly in culture than HHV-6.[28]

Human herpesvirus-8

Using representational difference analysis[29] HHV-8 was initially identified in 90% of AIDS-related Kaposi's sarcoma (KS) lesions and in 15% of non-KS tissues from people who had HIV infection. Following these observations HHV-8 sequences were identified using polymerase chain reaction (PCR) in all forms of KS, including KS from different geographic locations in individuals who had and did not have HIV infection.[10] Human herpesvirus-8 RNA transcripts have been detected in endothelial cells lining vascular spaces, perivascular spindle cells in KS lesions and in extracts of KS tissue. Also, linear HHV-8 DNA has been noted in peripheral blood mononuclear cells from KS patients.[28] These findings suggest that certain cells in KS tumors and also mononuclear cells are able to support the replication of HHV-8.

Large numbers of HHV-8 particles can be found in phorbol ester-stimulated B lymphoma cells by electron microscopy. Nevertheless, the infectivity of the virus has proved difficult to demonstrate in the laboratory. Studies using filtered cell culture fluids from HHV-8-positive CD19+ lymphocytes, KS biopsy material co-cultured with normal CD19+ cells, and fluids from B-cell lymphoma lines activated with phorbol esters have shown the passage of the HHV-8 DNA sequences to fresh uninfected target cells, particularly CD19+ lymphocytes.[28]

Latency

The establishment of latency is central to the success of herpesviruses in maintaining themselves in human populations. During the course of a primary infection a latent infection is established; the exact site or site(s) varies for each subfamily of herpesvirus:

- Alphaherpesvirinae (HSV-1, HSV-2, VZV) favor neuronal sites of latency;
- Betaherpesvirinae (CMV, HHV-6, HHV-7) are selective for secretory glands, lymphoreticular cells, kidneys and other tissues; and
- Gammaherpesvirinae (EBV, HHV-8) remain latent in either T or B cells (Table 215.5).

Latency permits persistence of the virus in the presence of a fully developed immune response and allows lifelong infection of the host. Through periodic reactivation of latent virus and the production of recurrent infection, virus shedding occurs at intervals throughout life, allowing the virus to be spread to new susceptible hosts.

PRINCIPAL SITES OF LATENCY FOR HERPESVIRUSES

Virus	Established (most probable) site of latency	Other possible sites of latency
HSV-1	Neurons (trigeminal ganglia)	Other sensory nerve ganglia, brain, eye
HSV-2	Neurons (sacral ganglia)	Other sensory ganglia
VZV	Neurons (dorsal root ganglia, thoracic nerves, trigeminal ganglia)	Brain
EBV	B cells (epithelial cells of nasopharynx and submandibular salivary glands)	–
CMV	Monocytes, lymphocytes, epithelial cells	Salivary glands, renal tubule cells
HHV-6, HHV-7	T cells	–
HHV-8	?T and B cells, mononuclear cells	–

Table 215.5 Principal sites of latency for herpesviruses.

In order to avoid elimination by the host immune system, herpesviruses use various evasion mechanisms. Key to most mechanisms is to reduce or prevent expression of virus-specific peptide–MHC class I complexes at the cellular membrane,[30] thus preventing recognition by cytotoxic T cells that would kill the infected cell. Prevention of peptide–MHC I complexes to reach the cell surface may, for instance, be achieved through interference with the transport of these compexes to the cell surface (HSV) or by induction of degradation of MHC I molecules (CMV).

The molecular events that lead to the establishment of latency are incompletely understood. The viral genome is maintained as an episomal closed circle of DNA (analogous to a bacterial cell plasmid), but how the virus precisely switches from its replicative mode to a latency mode is unclear.

Cell transformation

Some of the human herpesviruses (HSV-1, HSV-2 and CMV) can transform cells in culture, albeit at a very low frequency, and hamster cells transformed by HSV can produce tumors when injected into hamsters. Greater oncogenic potential can be demonstrated for other herpesviruses. For example, EBV-infected human lymphocytes can be transformed into lymphoblast cell lines. All cells that carry the EBV genome express virus-specific nuclear antigens (EBNAs), regardless of whether mature virus is released. There are also clear epidemiologic links to several types of tumor. Infectious mononucleosis can progress to a fatal B-cell lymphoma in boys who are born with an X-linked immunodeficiency; EBV has also been linked to Burkitt's lymphoma and nasopharyngeal carcinoma and to the development of post-transplant lymphoproliferative disease in immunosuppressed solid-organ transplant recipients. The geographic distribution of Burkitt's lymphoma and nasopharyngeal carcinoma mentioned above suggests that factors in addition to virus infection (e.g. a genetic predisposition or an environmental cofactor) may be involved in the production of these cancers.

EBV is also known to be the etiologic agent involved in post-transplant lymphoproliferative disease (PTLD), which comprises a heterogenous group of disorders with variable clinical presentation. PTLD affects 1–5 % of transplant patients and has a very high mortality rate. EBV is also associated with a subset of cases of Hodgkin's disease as demonstrated by the presence of the viral genome and viral-coded antigens in Reed–Sternberg cells. The exact nature of the association or its relevance to the etiology of Hodgkin's disease need further elucidation.

Human herpesvirus-8 is related to EBV, but is classified in the rhadinovirus subfamily of the Gammaherpesvirinae. The prototype of this subfamily is herpesvirus saimiri, which is not pathogenic in its natural host (the owl monkey), but can induce T-cell lymphomas in other primates. Human herpesvirus-8 contains sequences resembling cyclin D, a cell cycle inducer, cytokines and other human regulatory and DNA metabolism genes. The virus also possesses a Bcl-2-like sequence that could, by preventing apoptosis, produce transformation in a similar manner to that attributed to EBV.[31]

The ubiquitous nature of herpesvirus infections and their establishment of lifelong infections make it difficult to interpret their association with tumorigenic cells. Because of the relatively low efficiencies of transformation *in vitro* it seems likely that herpesvirus infection represents only one part of a complex sequence of events that ultimately leads to neoplasia.

PREVENTION

In a well-controlled environment, such as that of a hospital, prevention of host-to-host transmission for most human herpesviruses is achieved by simple hygiene. In the home or other social situations prevention of transmission by avoiding contact with a person who has evidence of recurrent infection is only partially effective. This is because infectious virus is often excreted before the appearance of overt symptoms of recurrent infection and 'silent' recurrent infections also occur.

Herpesviruses are readily inactivated by a variety of physical and chemical agents (see Physical properties, above) and standard methods of sterilization, including autoclaving, dry heat, ultraviolet or gamma irradiation, and ethylene oxide sterilization are adequate for decontaminating medical equipment. Most common disinfectants (5% phenol, formaldehyde, glutaraldehyde, 1:10,000 quaternary ammonium compounds and 0.3ppm hypochlorites) rapidly inactivate virus. Other virucidal compounds include detergents, chlorhexidine, Merthiolate, sodium azide, β-propriolactone, ethylene oxide and some proteolytic enzymes. Ultraviolet and X-ray or gamma irradiation also inactivate herpesviruses.

Active immunization

Except for VZV infection (for which a live attenuated vaccine is available) there are currently no licensed vaccines available to prevent herpesvirus infections. Varicella-zoster virus infection causes particular problems in immunosuppressed children. Primary infection in immunosuppressed patients can result in a fulminant, generalized infection or severe respiratory disease. A live attenuated VZV vaccine has been licenced for use in Japan and the USA and is administered using the same schedule as the measles, mumps and rubella vaccine. Breakthrough infections can occur, but usually result in mild illness.[32] In the USA the vaccine is recommended for use for all children over 12 months of age and susceptible healthy adolescents and adults. In most other countries vaccination is only recommended for patients who are immunosuppressed or immunodeficient and who have never had chickenpox. Since its implementation in routine use in the USA, the vaccine has been found to be 97% effective in the prevention against moderately severe or severe disease.[33]

A number of vaccines to prevent HSV-2, CMV and EBV infections are under development or are undergoing clinical trials. The diversity of approaches used is illustrated by the vaccines under development for HSV-2 (Table 215.6).[34] For CMV a candidate vaccine was developed by Plotkin in the 1970s.[35] The vaccine was made from an isolate of a congenitally infected child (the Town strain) after frequent serial passaging in human embryonic fibroblasts. In early studies serconversion was seen in nearly 100% of volunteers, as well as a protective effect against a low-dose challenge with CMV. In addition, the vaccine appeared to provide partial protection as seen after natural infection. However, the vaccine failed to prevent infection of mothers in contact with CMV-excreting children, and therefore failed its primary objective: the prevention of primary infection in pregnancy. Later efforts have focused on the development of recombinant subunits and DNA vaccines; so far, however, with little success.

Attempts to develop an EBV vaccine include the use of purified gp340/220 virus envelope antigen, to which neutralizing antibodies are mainly directed.[36] Although vaccination of tamarins with this antigen preparation protected them against a virus challenge, further attempts to develop this into a vaccine for use in humans have not been successful.

VACCINES UNDER DEVELOPMENT TO PREVENT HSV-2 INFECTION

Vaccine type (name)	Company	HSV subunits or mechanisms	Adjuvant	Stage of research
Recombinant protein	Glaxo-SmithKline	gD2	MPL	Phase III
Recombinant protein	Chiron	gD2 and gB2	MF59	Phase III halted
Attenuated (DISC)	Cantab	Disabled virus (gH gene deleted)	None	Phase I
DNA (Genevax HSV)	Apollon	Encodes gD2	Bupivacaine (facilitator)	Phase I
Naked DNA	Pharmadigm	Encodes gD2, uses novel myoD promoter	1,25-D3, possibly DHEA	Preclinical
Naked DNA	Vical	Encodes gD2	None	Preclinical
Naked DNA	Merck	Encodes gD2	None	Preclinical
Recombinant protein (Heteroconjugate)	Cel-Sci	T-cell ligands linked with HSV-associated peptides	None	Preclinical

Table 215.6 Examples of vaccine under development for immunization to prevent herpes simplex virus-2 infection. Adapted from Hanissian, 1998.[34]

CURRENTLY USED ANTIHERPESVIRUS DRUGS			
Antiviral drug	**Chemical class**	**Mechanisms of action**	**Target virus**
Aciclovir	Guanosine analog	Virus-activated DNA polymerase inhibitor	HSV-1, HSV-2, VZV
Cidofovir	Cytidylic acid analog	DNA polymerase inhibitor	CMV, HSV-1, HSV-2
Famciclovir	Guanosine analog	Virus-activated DNA polymerase inhibitor	HSV-1, HSV-2, VZV
Foscarnet	Pyrophosphate analog	DNA polymerase inhibitor	CMV, HSV-1, HSV-2
Ganciclovir	Guanosine analog	Virus-activated DNA polymerase inhibitor	CMV (HSV-1, HSV-2)
Valaciclovir	Guanosine analog	Virus-activated DNA polymerase inhibitor	HSV-1, HSV-2, VZV

Table 215.7 Currently used antiherpesvirus drugs. CMV, cytomegalovirus; HSV, herpes simplex virus; VZV, varicella-zoster virus.

Passive Immunization

Varicella-zoster virus hyperimmune globulin (VZVIG) is an effective prophylaxis for babies born to mothers who have chickenpox 5 days before to 4 days after birth. The use of VZVIG in pregnancy, particularly during the first 20 weeks of pregnancy, is also suggested for nonimmune mothers exposed to chickenpox because pregnant women have a greater risk of developing severe pulmonary complications if they contract VZV infection. Prophylactic use of VZVIG is also appropriate to control infection in pediatric units caring for immunocompromised children (see Chapter 8).

In the future the development of human monoclonal antibody preparations may provide more reliable and consistent supplies of immunoglobulins to prevent these and other human herpesvirus infections.

Antiviral prophylaxis

A number of specific antiviral compounds are now available for the treatment of herpesvirus infection and prophylactic use of antiviral chemotherapy to control infection is now well established (Table 215.7).

DIAGNOSTIC VIROLOGY

A key feature of the herpesviruses is their close adaption to their host. In general, primary infection is often asymptomatic or is accompanied by nonspecific mild signs and symptoms. Consequently most primary infections and many recurrent infections are not recognized as herpesvirus infections. Where symptoms are observed, speed in using diagnostic procedures is important because the peak of virus replication and shedding is likely to precede the appearance of symptoms. The diagnostic method chosen (Table 215.8) varies for different herpesviruses and also depends upon the type of infection (whether primary or recurrent), duration of symptoms and clinical manifestations.

Test specimens

If there are visible lesions (HSV-1, HSV-2, VZV) the base of the lesion may be sampled with a dry cotton-tipped swab, which should be placed in virus transport medium and transported to the virus laboratory as quickly as possible. If there are vesicles, vesicle fluid can be aspirated using a fine (intradermal) needle. The fluid should

LABORATORY DIAGNOSIS OF HERPESVIRUS INFECTIONS					
Virus	**Disease manifestation**	**Virus culture**	**Serology**	**Antigen detection**	**DNA amplification**
HSV-1	Skin lesions	+++	+	+	+++
	CNS infection	–	++	–	+++
HSV-2	Genital lesions	+++	+	+	+
	CNS infection	–	+	–	+++
VZV	Skin lesions	++	++	++	+++
	CNS infection	–	+	–	+++
CMV	Mononucleosis-like illness	–	+++	–	–
	Neonatal disease	+++	++	–	+++
	Systemic infection in immunocompromised	+	+	++	+++
	CNS disease	–	+	–	+++
EBV	Mononucleosis-like illness	–	+++	–	–
	Systemic infection in immunocompromised	–	+	+	+++
	CNS disease	–	+	–	+++
HHV-6	Exanthema subitum	+	+++	–	–
	CNS disease	–	++	–	+++
HHV-8	Kaposi's sarcoma	–	+	–	+++

Table 215.8 Laboratory diagnosis of herpesvirus infections. CMV, cytomegalovirus; EBV, Epstein–Barr virus; HHV, human herpesvirus; HSV, herpes simplex virus; VZV, varicella-zoster virus.

then be transported directly to the laboratory for virus detection by electron microscopy, direct immunofluorescent antibody staining, PCR testing or culture.

Viruria and viremia are common during both primary infection and recurrent infection with CMV, EBV and HHV-6, -7 and -8. Urine collected in urine transport medium is therefore a useful specimen (only CMV). Blood collected in anticoagulant can be used to prepare buffy coat preparations that can be used for culture or direct detection techniques. In neurologic disease, cerebrospinal fluid (CSF) and a clotted peripheral blood specimen (for CSF and blood serology) are essential. Clotted blood specimens should be collected during the acute stages of illness and again after 10–14 days.

Virus culture

The fragility of the viral envelope presents a problem if virus is to be cultured. Collection of specimens into appropriate viral transport medium and rapid transportation of specimens to the diagnostic laboratory are essential for successful isolation in cell culture systems. Virus culture is only routinely attempted for HSV-1, HSV-2, VZV and CMV. For those viruses that have fastidious cell culture requirements (e.g. infection of epithelial cells and lymphocytes as for EBV and HHV-6, -7 and -8) virus propagation can be accomplished only with difficulty, and culture of these viruses is not usually attempted in routine diagnostic laboratories. Detection of virus DNA by nucleic acid amplification procedures (see below) is a more practical method for detecting these viruses.

The ability of herpesviruses to replicate in monolayer cell cultures is variable. HSV-1 and HSV-2 can be cultivated in a wide variety of cells of both human and primate origin, including primary, continuous diploid and semicontinuous heteroploid cell lines. In contrast, CMV is fastidious and in cell culture only replicates in primary or semicontinuous (fibroblast) cell cultures of human origin. VZV is intermediate in its fastidiousness. It replicates best in semicontinuous cells of human origin, but may be cultivated with less efficiency in other cells. However, with the advent of molecular diagnostic methods that are more easy to implement in daily, routine diagnostic services, many laboratories are now abandoning their herpesvirus cultures.

Shell vial culture

The efficiency of primary virus isolation and speed of diagnosis can be improved using the so-called 'shell vial' culture. In this technique specimens are inoculated onto monolayers of cells grown on coverslips. The specimen and shell vial containing the specimen are lightly centrifuged to improve the efficiency of attachment of virus to cells. After 24 or 48 hours of culture, monolayers are fixed (e.g. using cold acetone) and stained with either:

- a virus-specific antibody tagged with fluorescein isothiocyanate and examined by ultraviolet microscopy; or
- a peroxidase-labeled antibody with subsequent dye deposition within cells to identify the agent using light microscopy.

Identification of virus in cell culture

Virus growth in culture can be identified by the appearance of a cytopathogenic effect (CPE) and virus may be further characterized using specific antiserum (i.e. virus neutralization). This labor-intensive and time-consuming technique is now rapidly being replaced by more rapid methods of identification such as shell vial culture, direct immunofluorescent staining of cultures showing CPE and molecular diagnostic methods.

Electron microscopy

The limiting factor in the sensitivity of detecting virus by electron microscopy is the requirement that the sample contains at least 10^6 particles/ml. Electron microscopy is therefore useful in the examination of vesicle fluid from children who have suspected chickenpox and occasionally in the examination of atypical lesions of HSV infection as might be found in eczema herpeticum. The vesicle fluid is mixed with 3% buffered phosphotungstic acid, placed on a formvar and carbon-coated grid, blotted dry and examined in the electron microscope for the characteristic viruses (see Fig. 215.2). Although the morphology of herpesviruses is characteristic, differentiation of HSV-1, HSV-2 and VZV requires immune electron microscopy using virus-specific monoclonal antibodies.

Antigen detection

Antigen detection has a limited but important role to play in the diagnosis of most herpesvirus infections. In general, specimens may contain too little virus to allow reliable detection of antigen. Nevertheless, in a case of vesicular eruption, vesicle fluid (air dried and fixed in cold acetone) can be stained with monoclonal antibodies tagged with fluorescein isothiocyanate to provide a rapid specific diagnosis of infection.

Antigen detection also has an important role in monitoring organ transplant recipients (e.g. bone marrow transplant recipients) for the development of CMV disease. Buffy coat blood samples are examined for CMV pp65 antigen using a monoclonal antibody tagged with fluorescein. This procedure makes it possible to detect and monitor viremia and has been extremely useful to monitor and control CMV infections in various kind of transplant patients. Examination of CSF lymphocytes can provide a diagnosis of CMV infection of the central nervous system (CNS).

A variety of rapid immunoassay tests has been developed for 'within the office' testing for HSV. However, the sensitivity and specificity of these tests are too low to allow their use in diagnosis for hospitalized patients. As with virus cultures, these approaches are now being replaced by rapid molecular diagnostic techniques.

Nucleic acid amplification

The use of molecular diagnostic methods has changed the face of diagnostic virology. With increasing automation and further technical developments the very high sensitivity and the potential for early, rapid diagnosis are now outweighing the well-known disadvantages of technical complexity and lack of robustness, risk of contamination and cost. In addition to many in-house protocols used, a number of nucleic acid amplification systems[37,38] are now available commercially. They are all based upon either:

- target amplification, for example PCR, ligase chain reaction, nucleic acid sequence based amplification (NASBA) and transcription-mediated amplification (TMA); or
- signal amplification, for example branched DNA amplification (bDNA).

Of these, PCR is currently the most widely used amplification method. Many assay procedures based upon the PCR procedure have been described and the use of PCR for diagnosing neurologic disease caused by the human herpesviruses has become the gold standard.[39] Single (sPCR) and nested (nPCR) PCR procedures have been described, including procedures that detect RNA and those that detect DNA. Both qualitative and quantitative assay procedures are available. Detection of several herpesviruses within the same clinical sample is possible using multiplex PCR where primers are included in the reaction mixture for several different herpesvirus DNA targets. For all these procedures a thorough evaluation of test protocols and rigorous quality control are essential to produce reliable test results.

Many protocols have also been described for extracting DNA from clinical samples. The purpose of DNA extraction is to render the target DNA free from potential inhibitors of the DNA polymerase used in the amplification step, that could result in false-negative PCR test results. As yet, there is no 'universal' extraction procedure suitable for all procedures. To determine whether sample inhibition has occurred, PCR test reactions often include an internal control molecule. Usually this is a bacterial plasmid DNA containing regions of DNA equivalent to those in the target DNA where the primers will bind. However, between the primer-binding sequences a 'scrambled' DNA sequence is inserted so that internal control and target DNAs can be distinguished upon amplification.

Detection of amplified DNA is usually accomplished by gel electrophoresis and staining with ethidium bromide. The product can also be detected by hybridization techniques where the dsDNA product is denatured and the ssDNA is hybridized with an oligonucleotide 'probe' sequence.

Progressively this cumbersome post-amplification handling with its inherent contamination risk is being replaced by 'real-time' amplification techniques, where the generation of amplified product is measured during the amplification process itself. Furthermore, the 'real-time' methodology also makes it relatively easy to quantitate the amount of virus present in the patient's specimen. This has been a great step forward in patient management because it allows much better monitoring of the course of disease and treatment of patients by clinicians and virologists.

Nucleic acid amplification techniques are now indispensible for the diagnosis of herpesvirus infections, particularly HSV, of the CNS.[40,41] Determination of the viral load may be helpful for prognosis.[42] In transplant patients, quantitative 'real-time' assays have become of crucial importance in monitoring the development of CMV and EBV infections and a patient's response to treatment. Further rapid implementation of 'real-time' or other nucleic acid amplification techniques for the detection and quantitation of human herpesviruses is to be expected.

Genotypic analyses (restriction fragment length polymorphism)

Restriction fragment length polymorphism (RFLP) analysis is a specialist procedure of possible value in the investigation of outbreaks of infection and epidemiologic studies. Virus isolates in cell culture or PCR products are labeled with phosphorus-32 and DNA is extracted and digested using a range of restriction enzymes. On gel electrophoresis a series of fragments are segregated. Comparison of the migration of these fragments (RFLP patterns) gives information on the genetic relatedness (or unrelatedness) between strains of virus. Restriction fragment length polymorphism analysis also provides a reference procedure that allows identification and typing of isolates in one procedure.

Virus serology

Complement fixation and indirect immunofluorescence tests are still used in many viral diagnostic laboratories. However, their use is declining in favor of more reproducible and sensitive enzyme-linked immunosorbent assay (ELISA) methodologies.[39] Neutralizing antibody tests for herpesvirus antibodies are not routinely performed in diagnostic laboratories and none of these viruses has hemagglutinating capability.

Many immunoassays are available for the detection of antibodies to HHV-1 to HHV-5 and assays for antibody to HHV-6 to HHV-8 are now becoming commercially available. The antibody-capture ELISA principle is used to detect IgM antibody, but results of IgM tests must be interpreted with care:

- as IgM antibody is the first antibody to be produced in response to infection it is by nature a broadly reactive antibody, so cross-reactivity and false positivity may occur; and
- IgM antibody is produced during both acute (primary) infection and recurrent disease, although the amount produced is generally higher during primary infection.

Quantitation of virus-specific IgG antibody in serial samples (10 or more days apart) often provides a more reliable diagnostic procedure, but it takes considerably longer (up to 2 weeks) to obtain results.

Detection of IgA antibody is not generally carried out, but may have a role in the serologic diagnosis of recurrent herpesvirus infections.[43]

CLINICAL MANIFESTATIONS

With the exception of VZV, primary herpesvirus infections in the immunocompetent host are usually asymptomatic or are associated with a minor illness only, with no specific symptoms such as fever and malaise (Table 215.9). As a consequence, primary herpesvirus infections may not be recognized. When symptoms do occur, herpesvirus infections in the immunocompetent host are normally self-limiting and require only symptomatic treatment. Antiviral therapy is available for a number of herpesviruses, but is usually only indicated for those patients who have more severe disease manifestations or when it is appropriate to minimize the likelihood of complications.

Herpesvirus infections in the immunocompromised host are frequently severe and sometimes life-threatening. Antiviral drug therapy is required for these patients to control the infection (see Table 215.7).

Herpes simplex viruses

Although HSV infections can result in a wide spectrum of disease (Fig. 215.7), mucocutaneous lesions are by far the most common manifestation of primary HSV infections.[44]

Mucocutaneous manifestations

Oropharyngeal infection

Primary oropharyngeal HSV-1 infection usually occurs in childhood and is often asymptomatic. In symptomatic infections acute gingivostomatitis is seen in 10–30% of cases.[45] Lesions on the buccal and gingival mucosa evolve from vesicles to shallow ulcerations on an erythematous base. Frequently the child is unable to eat or swallow liquids because of the significant edema, ulceration of the oropharyngeal membranes and associated pain. Primary HSV gingivostomatitis is usually accompanied by fever and submandibular lymphadenopathy. The incubation period varies from 2 to 12 days (mean 4 days). The duration of clinical illness may extend from 2 to 3 weeks, with virus excretion from the oropharynx for an average of 7–10 days. In many countries the epidemiology of this infection is changing, this change being characterized by an increasing incidence of primary HSV-1 infection later in life. Primary HSV infection in an adolescent or adult is often associated with pharyngitis and a mononucleosis-like syndrome.

The severity and duration of clinical illness in recurrent infection is considerably less than in primary HSV infection. Recurrent orolabial lesions ('cold sores') are heralded by a prodrome of pain, burning, itching or tingling for several hours before the development of the characteristic vesicles. The vesicular stage persists for less than 48 hours and progresses to the ulcerative and crusting stage within 3–4 days. Pain resolves quickly during the same period, and healing is generally complete within 8–10 days. Systemic illness is usually absent in recurrent infection. Recurrence rates are highly variable and the precipitating factors involved are not well defined, but include the type of HSV (HSV-1 is more likely to recur than HSV-2), fever, stress, exposure to ultraviolet light and impaired CMI in the host.

Genital infections

Primary genital herpes usually occurs in adolescents and young adults.[16] Approximately 20–40% of first-episode genital herpes is now due to HSV-1, but the recurrence rate of genital HSV-2 infections is ten times higher than that of genital HSV-1 infections.[46,47]

CLINICAL MANIFESTATIONS OF HERPESVIRUS INFECTIONS			
Agent	**Primary infection**	**Recurrent infection**	**Complications**
HSV-1, -2	Usually asymptomatic; orofacial/genital, mucocutaneous lesions, gingivostomatitis, paronychia	Usually asymptomatic, cold sores, genital herpes, recurrent skin lesions	Meningitis, encephalitis, hepatitis, keratitis, generalized disease (neonates), eczema herpeticum
VZV	Varicella	Herpes zoster, zoster, ophthalmicus, oticus	Pneumonitis, hepatitis, encephalitis, keratitis, postherpetic neuralgia, cerebellar ataxia
CMV	Usually asymptomatic; mononucleosis-like syndrome, fever, malaise, myalgia, lymphadenopathy Neonates: growth and mental retardation, hepatosplenomegaly, microcephaly	Usually asymptomatic	Pneumonia, retinitis, esophagitis, colitis, hepatitis, enteritis
EBV	Usually asymptomatic, infectious mononucleosis	Usually asymptomatic	X-linked proliferative syndrome, persistent mononucleosis-like syndrome, Burkitt's lymphoma, nasopharyngeal carcinoma, lymphoma, encephalitis
HHV-6	Usually asymptomatic; febrile illness exanthema subitum, febrile convulsions	Usually asymptomatic	Meningoencephalitis, pneumonitis, hepatitis
HHV-7	Unknown, occasionally exanthema subitum	Unknown	Unknown
HHV-8	Unknown	Unknown	Kaposi's sarcoma, body cavity lymphoma

Table 215.9 Clinical manifestations of herpesvirus infections. CMV, cytomegalovirus; EBV, Epstein–Barr virus; HHV, human herpesvirus; HSV, herpes simplex virus; VZV, varicella-zoster virus.

The incubation period is 3–7 days. The majority of cases (50–70%) are asymptomatic or so mild that the infection is not recognized. The severity and duration of clinical symptoms depend upon both viral and host factors and include the type of virus, past exposure to HSV-1, previous episodes of genital herpes and gender.[46] (See Chapter 76.)

Primary genital herpes is characterized by the appearance of vesicular lesions – in males usually on the glans penis, on the penile shaft or in the perianal region, and in women involving the vulva, vagina, cervix and perineum. Extragenital lesions (on the buttocks and thighs) occur in 10–20% of patients. The lesions can be very painful and associated with inguinal adenopathy and dysuria. Urinary retention is observed in up to 20% of female patients. Systemic symptoms occur in 40–70% of patients who have primary genital herpes and include fever, malaise, headache and myalgia.

Patients usually present with bilateral pustular or ulcerative lesions on the external genitals that coalesce into larger areas of ulceration. The ulcerative lesions persist for 4–15 days and usually resolve without residual scarring after a phase of crusting and re-epithelialization.

The average duration of primary symptomatic genital herpes is 3 weeks. During this time the pain and irritation caused by the lesions gradually increase during the first week, reach their peak of intensity early in the second week and gradually resolve during the second and third week. Tender lymphadenopathy is usually seen in the second and third week of illness.

Complications of primary genital herpes include aseptic meningitis, which has been reported in up to 36% of women and 12% of men, and sacral radiculopathy, which may lead to urinary retention.[16,46] In homosexual men primary anal HSV-2 infection is frequently associated with proctitis.

The signs and symptoms of recurrent genital herpes are usually restricted to the genital region and are relatively mild and of shorter duration than for primary disease. Prodromal symptoms are a feature of approximately 50% of episodes. They vary from mild tingling to stabs of pain in the buttocks, legs and hips. As for primary disease, recurrent lesions in women are more often painful and of longer duration than in men (60–90 vs 30–70%, and mean 5.9 vs 3.9 days, respectively).

Other mucocutaneous manifestations

Other mucocutaneous manifestations of HSV infections include classic herpetic lesions – a close crop of vesicles on other areas of the skin, notably of the head, neck and shoulders, or the eyes, where there may be vesiculation of the eyelid and associated conjunctivitis.

Herpetic whitlow is an often painful infection of the finger that can result from auto-inoculation or direct contact with an individual who has an HSV infection. It is therefore an occupational hazard of dentists, doctors and nurses.

In patients who have atopic dermatitis, superinfection with HSV may appear as eczema herpeticum. Most cases are mild with localized lesions, but severe disseminated cases (Kaposi's varicelliform eruption, resembling severe varicella) occur, resulting in a widespread vesicular eruption and are associated with a small but significant risk of fatal disseminated infection.

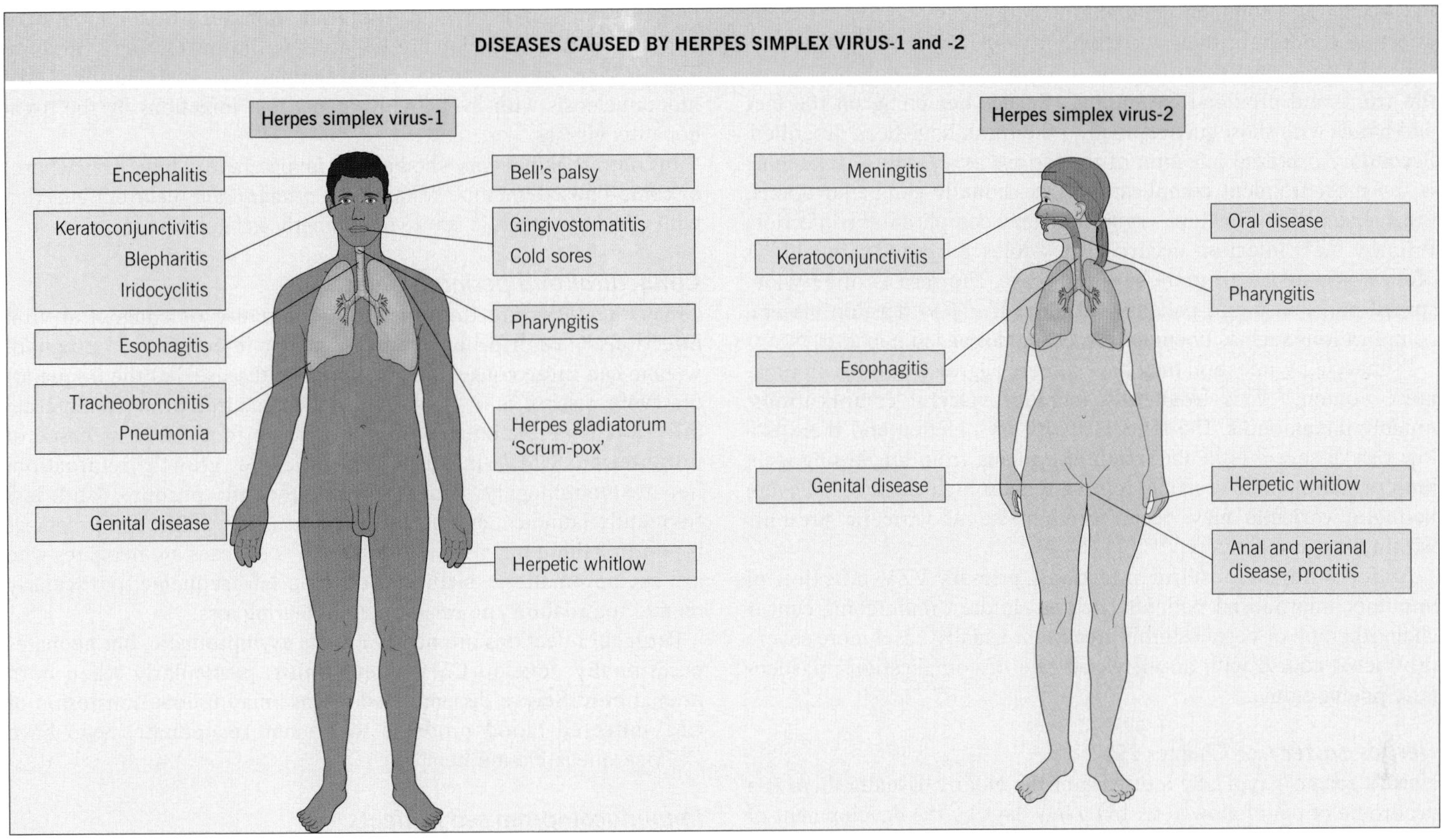

Fig. 215.7 Diseases caused by herpes simplex virus-1 and herpes simplex virus-2.

Other manifestations

Herpes simplex virus encephalitis

Herpes simplex virus encephalitis is one of the most severe manifestations of HSV infection.[48] Although rare – incidence 1/250,000 to 1/500,000 population per year – it is the most commonly diagnosed cause of sporadic fatal encephalitis. Either HSV-1 or HSV-2 can cause HSV encephalitis, but approximately 95% of cases are due to HSV-1.[49] It can occur at any time of life and there is no apparent seasonal or geographic clustering of cases. Symptoms include fever, headache, behavioral abnormalities, altered consciousness and focal or generalized seizures suggestive of focal temporal lobe disease. The amount of HSV DNA in the CSF appears to be correlated with prognosis and outcome.[42] Early antiviral treatment is imperative. If untreated, the disease is frequently fatal or results in severe persisting neurologic sequelae (see also Chapter 23).

Neonatal herpes

Neonatal infection is a rare but severe manifestation of HSV infection acquired during delivery or in the immediate postpartum period.[50] It usually occurs in neonates who do not have protective maternal HSV antibody, and HSV-2 infection is usually more severe than HSV-1 infection.

Constitutional signs and symptoms include fever, irritability, seizures, failure to feed and a characteristic vesicular exanthem. Localized neonatal infections mostly involve the skin and are characterized by clusters of discrete vesicles at multiple sites. Localized infection may also occur in the mouth and oropharynx or the eye. In disseminated disease the principal tissues involved are the liver and adrenals, but other organs such as brain, lungs, esophagus, lower gastrointestinal tract, spleen and kidneys can be affected.

If untreated the mortality rate exceeds 50% and children who have disseminated infection have the worst prognosis. Even with prompt administration of specific antiviral chemotherapy survivors often experience neurologic complications. In all cases of neonatal herpes prompt initiation of antiviral chemotherapy is mandatory to prevent the development of long-term neurologic impairment.

Herpes simplex keratoconjunctivitis

Ophthalmic infections with HSV are among the most common causes of corneal blindness.[51] Dendritic ulceration of the cornea is the most characteristic manifestation. Most frequently it is unilateral. Visual acuity is decreased in the presence of ulcers and progression of the disease can result in visual loss. Despite appropriate antiviral treatment attacks can last several weeks to months.

Immunocompromised host

Patients compromised by immunosuppressive therapy (e.g. organ transplant recipients) or patients who have immunodeficiency are at risk of developing a severe primary infection and more severe and frequent recurrent disease. Disease severity is directly related to the degree of immunosuppression or immunodeficiency. Mucocutaneous infections are usually more extensive and severe and take longer to heal, even when appropriate antiviral therapy is initiated. Progression of the infection may involve the respiratory tract, esophagus or gastrointestinal tract.

Varicella-zoster virus

Varicella (chickenpox) and herpes zoster (shingles) are due to infection with the same virus, VZV. Varicella is the usual manifestation of primary infection, herpes zoster of recurrent infection.[52]

Varicella (see Chapter 8)

After an incubation period of 14–15 days (range 10–20 days) a vesicular rash accompanied by low-grade fever and pruritus emerges in successive crops over a 3- to 6-day period. The rash is characterized by maculopapular lesions that vesiculate in about 3–4 days before crusting and scab formation. Scabs may remain in situ for up to 3 weeks.[53]

Varicella is a common childhood exanthematous disease, usually affecting children in their early school years. The exanthem is centripetal rather than centrifugal with most lesions being present on the trunk and proximal extremities. Rashes beginning on the face and hands with subsequent spread to the trunk have been described. Secondary bacterial infection of the lesions as a result of scratching is the most frequent complication. Occasionally cerebellar ataxia, transverse myelitis or Reye's syndrome may complicate the infection. Primary VZV infection occurring in adolescence and adult life is often associated with more severe disease. The rash is often widespread and dense and patients are more likely to develop visceral complications such as pneumonitis, encephalitis and hepatitis.[54]

Primary VZV infection may have a more aggressive course in pregnant women.[55] This frequently includes visceral complications, notably pneumonitis. The fetus is at risk of infection and there is a low risk of severe fetal abnormalities ranging from longlasting rash, limb or dermatomal scarring, to severe neurologic damage.[56] Severe neonatal varicella may occur when maternal varicella presents within 5 days of delivery.

As for other herpesvirus infections, primary VZV infection of immunocompromised patients such as children undergoing cancer chemotherapy or corticosteroid treatment usually has a more severe protracted course with an increased rate of complications, particularly pneumonitis.

Herpes zoster (see Chapter 29)

Herpes zoster is typically a disease of the elderly. Usually there is a prodrome of pain followed within a few days by the development of a unilateral vesicular rash within the dermatome served by the sensory nerve from the affected ganglion.[57] New lesions form over 2–5 days and the rash then pustulates and scabs over 2–3 weeks.

Persisting pain, known as postherpetic neuralgia, is the most common complication of herpes zoster. It can be severe and last for several months. The rate, severity and duration of postherpetic neuralgia are directly related to age. It is uncommon in patients under 50 years of age, but occurs in over 40% of those over 60 years of age.[58]

The sites most commonly affected by herpes zoster are the dermatomes T3 through L3, often the same as those that were most affected during chickenpox. Complications including motor weakness and visceral manifestations may occur, but are unusual. However, in up to 50% of patients where herpes zoster involves the trigeminal nerve ocular manifestations such as conjunctivitis, ulcerative keratitis, uveitis and iridocyclitis occur. Ocular complications are particularly common when the zosteriform lesions extend to the tip of the nose. Herpes zoster oticus, also called the Ramsay Hunt syndrome, consists of lesions on the ear or within the auditory canal, which are sometimes barely visible, and can result in hearing loss and facial paralysis.

Herpes zoster is frequently observed in patients who are immunocompromised, including those undergoing radiotherapy, chemotherapy and other types of immunosuppressive therapy, and those who have immunodeficiency syndromes. In such patients herpes zoster presents with larger, more extensive and hemorrhagic vesicles, which are often multidermatomal. Chronic cutaneous lesions and disseminated infections have been described, particularly in patients who have HIV infection. Meningoencephalitis, pneumonitis or hepatitis can also occur in immunocompromised patients, but are rare.

Cytomegalovirus

CMV is an uncommon cause of disease in people who are immunocompetent. Primary infection may occasionally cause a glandular fever-type illness resembling EBV mononucleosis.[59] In such patients persistent fever, myalgia and asthenia accompanied by atypical lymphocytosis and elevated liver transaminases are common signs and symptoms. Occasionally hepatitis is the presenting symptom. The presence of fever and atypical lymphocytes distinguishes CMV mononucleosis with liver involvement from infections by the usual hepatitis viruses.

In contrast, in patients who have an immature (e.g. fetus or newborn) or compromised immune system both primary and recurrent infection with CMV can result in severe and sometimes fatal disease.

Congenital and perinatal infections

CMV infections are the most common cause of congenital viral infections.[60] Both primary and recurrent infection in a pregnant woman can cause congenital and perinatal disease, but the frequency of severe disease is at least 10-fold higher after primary maternal infection. Overt clinical symptoms occur in 5–10% of cases of intrauterine CMV infection and include growth retardation, hepatosplenomegaly and thrombocytopenic purpura, and less frequently jaundice, microcephaly and chorioretinitis. The prognosis is poor for these infants. Another 10–15% of cases are neonates who are asymptomatic at birth and develop late sequelae, particularly mental retardation and sensorineural hearing loss.

Perinatal infections are nearly always asymptomatic, but neonates occasionally develop CMV pneumonitis, particularly when born prematurely. Severe disseminated disease may follow transfusion of CMV-infected blood products to premature neonates who have CMV-seronegative mothers.

Immunocompromised patients

The pathogenesis and clinical spectrum of CMV disease in patients who are immunocompromised depend upon the cause and degree of immunosuppression.[61,62] Treatment regimens must take into account the fact that the disease manifestations may have an immunopathologic or viral etiology.

Persistent intermittent fever is often the presenting symptom of CMV infection in patients who have had a transplant. The infection may progress to cause pneumonitis, gastrointestinal disease, hepatitis and retinitis. In recipients of a solid organ transplant, CMV disease most frequently occurs when the donor is CMV-seropositive and the recipient is CMV-seronegative. In bone marrow transplant patients, however, CMV disease most commonly results from reactivation of latent virus in the recipient, usually 20–90 days after the transplant. The most frequent manifestation is CMV pneumonitis. Unless treated very early, preferably before the appearance of respiratory symptoms, pneumonitis in these patients is often fatal.

Reactivation of latent CMV is usually the cause of CMV disease in patients who have HIV infection, frequently occurring in the later stages of the HIV infection when $CD4^+$ T cell counts are less than $50/mm^3$. The most frequent manifestation is CMV retinitis presenting with blurred vision and decreased acuity (see Chapter 125).[62]

Gastrointestinal disease, hepatitis, encephalitis and pneumonia also occur in patients who have HIV infection. Gastrointestinal disease includes esophagitis, gastritis, enteritis and colitis and is usually associated with fever and weight loss. Although CMV is often detected in respiratory specimens from patients with AIDS who have pneumonitis, the pulmonary process is usually caused by other pathogens, particularly *Pneumocystis carinii*.

Epstein–Barr virus

In most individuals EBV infection does not cause overt disease.[11] Primary infections in adolescents can, however, result in infectious mononucleosis. As for CMV infection, immunocompromised hosts may develop severe manifestations during both primary and recurrent EBV infection. Such severity is exemplified by the role of EBV infection in the causation of lymphoproliferative disease.[63,64]

Immunocompetent host

Infectious mononucleosis (glandular fever) usually presents as fever, fatigue and malaise accompanied by a sore throat, cervica1 lymphadenopathy, hepatomegaly and splenomegaly. A rash may develop, particularly in those treated with ampicillin. Disease manifestations, especially fatigue and malaise, can persist for several weeks. Relapses and a chronic course have been described but the relationship to EBV infection is uncertain.

The X-linked lymphoproliferative (or Duncan's) syndrome is a rare manifestation of primary EBV infection and occurs in (young) males who have an X-linked genetic defect in their immune response to EBV.[63] Most die from fulminant mononucleosis, fulminant hepatitis or aplastic anemia.

Patients who have Burkitt's lymphoma have large swollen lymph nodes, usually involving the jaw and orbital cavities.[8] The disease occurs mainly in young children. In contrast, nasopharyngeal carcinoma is usually seen in older male patients in South East Asia.[9]

EBV has been associated with Hodgkin's disease. EBV-specific sequences and EBV-induced antigens have been found in Reed–Sternberg cells.[64] The precise role of EBV in the etiology of Hodgkin's disease, however, remains to be established. Other EBV-associated lymphoepithelial tumors have been described in the parotid gland, thymus, stomach, lung and larynx.[64]

Immunocompromised host

Immunocompromised patients are at risk of developing lymphoproliferative disorders following EBV infection. The polyclonal B lymphocyte proliferation is often associated with fever, lymphadenopathy and hepatosplenomegaly,[64] and is frequently life-threatening in severely immunocompromised patients, such as bone marrow transplant patients.

Patients who have AIDS may develop oral hairy leukoplakia, which is characterized by white plaques on the lateral margin of the tongue.[65] EBV is associated with lymphocytic interstitial pneumonia (which is common in pediatric patients who have AIDS) and a rapidly progressing, diffuse encephalitis.

Human herpesviruses-6, -7 and -8

Human herpesviruses-6, -7 and -8 have only been recognized during the past 15 years.[28] Although their etiologic role in the development of a variety of disease manifestations is well documented, their full disease spectrum remains to be determined.

Human herpesvirus-6

HHV-6, variant B, is the cause of exanthema subitum (roseola infantum) in young children.[27] Symptomatic infection is characterized by fever, sometimes associated with a mild respiratory illness and lymphadenopathy, which is followed by the appearance of a fine maculopapular rash spreading from the trunk to the extremities. More recent studies have shown that the primary characteristic of HHV-6 infection in infants is a high fever for 3-4 days, often associated with inflammation of tympanic membranes. Only a small proportion of these (<10%) develops exanthema subitum.[66] Up to 20–25% of hospital admissions of children under 3 years of age with acute febrile illness is due to primary HHV-6 infection.[66,67] Primary HHV-6 infection has also been demonstrated as a frequent cause of febrile seizures in infants, and accounts for up to one-third of all febrile seizures under the age of 3 years.[67,68] Recovery is usually rapid and uneventful, although a more protracted and severe course characterized by severe meningoencephalitis, fulminant hepatitis or fatal pancytopenia has been described. In adolescents and adults primary HHV-6 infection can cause a mononucleosis-like illness.

Some recent studies have suggested a role for HHV-6 in the etiology of multiple sclerosis. This is based on the finding by PCR of HHV-6 DNA in the brain.[69] However, literature findings still remain ambiguous, and further studies are needed to define the possible role of HHV-6 in multiple sclerosis.

In severely immunocompromised patients, such as those who have AIDS or received a bone marrow transplant, reactivation of HHV-6 infection mainly has an immunosuppressive effect, subsequent to which other pathogens may cause severe disease. In bone marrow transplant patients HHV-6 reactivation is associated with bone marrow suppression, probably as the result of viral replication in particular progenitor cells.[70] HHV-6 has also been associated with interstitial pneumonia and encephalitis in these patients. Finally, mainly on the basis of *in-vitro* studies, HHV-6 has been reported as a possible cause of or cofactor for certain lymphoproliferative disorders.

Human herpesvirus-7

Although some cases of exanthema subitum appear to be due to HHV-7, a causal association between human disease and HHV-7 infection has not yet been established. HHV-7 has been associated with infant febrile illness as well as subsequent CNS complications. In renal transplant patients evidence has been obtained that HHV-7 may be a cofactor in the development of CMV disease.

Human herpesvirus-8

No association has been recognized between primary HHV-8 infection and specific clinical disease, but it is now generally accepted that HHV-8 has a causal role in KS and a rare form of abdominal B-cell lymphoma, body-cavity associated lymphoma and primary effusion lymphoma.[27,28] The virus is also found in some cases of multicentric Castleman's disease. The possible involvement of HHV-8 in the development of other endothelial cell-derived tumors requires further investigation.

Herpes B virus

Herpes virus simiae (herpes B virus) causes a benign latent infection in macaques that is analogous to HSV infection in humans.[71] The infection is infrequently transmitted to humans. After an incubation period varying from 3 days to 3 weeks there may be localized pain, redness and vesicular skin lesions near the site of the viral inoculation, followed by localized neurologic symptoms. Encephalopathy is common and fatal in up to 70% of patients. The virus is susceptible to aciclovir and early treatment can be life-saving.[72]

MANAGEMENT

As most herpesvirus infections in the immunocompetent host are self-limiting, patients usually only require supportive care. The type of supportive treatment required varies for different disease manifestations and may consist of rest, hydration, the appropriate use of antipyretics, analgesics, and treatment to soothe skin lesions and to prevent secondary bacterial infection. Effective antiviral therapy is available for more severe cases of infection caused by HSV, VZV or CMV. It is stressed, however, that although antiviral drugs can help to control a herpesvirus infection they cannot eliminate the infection.

Antiviral drugs

Most antiherpetic drugs are nucleoside analogs[73] that inhibit virus-specified DNA polymerases and terminate DNA chain elongation (see Table 215.7; see Chapter 205). The first generation of these drugs – idoxuridine, vidarabine and trifluridine – have only a limited selectivity for the viral DNA polymerase. Due to the interaction of the phosphorylated form of these drugs with cellular DNA polymerases, there are severe adverse effects.

Aciclovir is the prototype of the present generation of antiviral drugs (see Chapter 205).[74] Its high specificity and therefore safety is

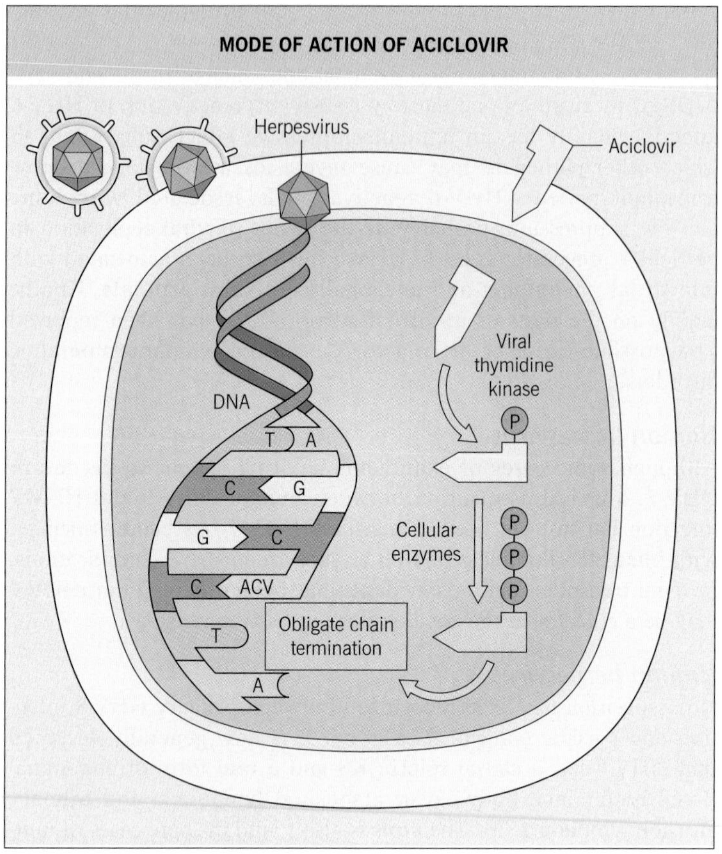

Fig. 215.8 Mode of action of aciclovir. Phosphorylation is effected by virus-specified thymidine kinase. The aciclovir monophosphate is then converted to the triphosphate form by cellular kinases. Aciclovir triphosphate binds with high affinity to the virus-specified (but not host derived) DNA polymerase, leading to inactivation of the enzyme's activity. In addition, incorporation of aciclovir in the DNA blocks further chain elongation.

based on its specific interaction with viral and not cellular enzymes (Fig. 215.8). It is an acyclic analog of guanosine that is activated by viral and not the cellular thymidine kinase to serve as substrate for the viral DNA polymerase. Aciclovir is virtually inert as administered. Approximately 90–92% is excreted unchanged by renal excretion with the majority of the remainder appearing as the metabolite 9-carboxymethoxymethylguanine. The serum half-life of the drug is about 2–3 hours. Virus-infected cells appear to be slightly more permeable to aciclovir than noninfected cells, but aciclovir is only entrapped and selectively concentrated within virus-infected cells. This is achieved by phosphorylation effected by virus-specified thymidine kinase. Host cell kinases do not appear capable of effecting this primary phosphorylation to any significant degree. Aciclovir monophosphate cannot traverse cellular membranes and is therefore selectively concentrated in virus-infected cells. The monophosphate is converted to the active antiviral aciclovir triphosphate through the action of cellular kinases. Aciclovir triphosphate is a potent and highly selective inhibitor of viral-specified DNA polymerase. A further but less significant antiviral action is the chain termination effected by the incorporation of aciclovir into the growing viral DNA chain (absence of 2' and 3' carbons of guanosine). Aciclovir is a safe, relatively nontoxic drug and is effective for therapeutic use as well as long-term suppressive treatment.

The recently approved drugs famciclovir and valaciclovir are similar to aciclovir in their mechanism of action, but have different pharmacologic properties. These drugs have improved oral bioavailability, thereby allowing less frequent administration than is required for aciclovir. As with aciclovir, famciclovir and valaciclovir have excellent safety records.

The alternate antiherpetic drugs, ganciclovir, foscarnet and cidofovir have similar mechanisms of action, (i.e. inhibition of the viral DNA polymerase), but generally have a higher toxicity profile, including neutropenia and thrombocytopenia for ganciclovir, and nephrotoxicity for foscarnet and cidofovir. The susceptibility of different herpesviruses to the various antiviral drugs is shown in Table 215.10.

Antiviral resistance has been described for all of the antiherpes compounds mentioned, particularly when antivirals are administered to immunocompromised patients over extended periods of time. Studies in these patients have shown resistance to aciclovir in 5% and to ganciclovir in 7% of patients.[75,76] Antiviral resistance is due to mutations in the viral thymidine kinase or in the DNA polymerase.[77] Resistant viruses, however, appear to be less virulent.[78] Significant circulation in the general population has not yet been found.[76] Because of their similar mechanisms of action cross-resistance frequently occurs (e.g. between aciclovir, famciclovir and valaciclovir).

Herpes simplex virus

In several placebo-controlled studies, intravenous, oral or topical administration of aciclovir, famciclovir and valaciclovir have been shown to be effective against mucocutaneous HSV infections (Table 215.11). All three drugs significantly reduce:

- duration of viral shedding;
- time to healing of lesions;
- duration of pain and itching; and
- rate of complications.

The effect is more pronounced for primary or first-episode HSV infections than for recurrent disease in the immunocompetent host. Oral or intravenous administration is generally more effective than topical treatment. Intravenous administration of aciclovir is the treatment of choice for patients who have suspected systemic or neurologic disease due to HSV (e.g. patients who have herpes encephalitis). Antiviral therapy should be initiated as soon as possi-

COMPARATIVE SUSCEPTIBILITY OF HERPESVIRUSES TO ANTIVIRAL DRUGS

Antiviral drug	Viral susceptibility				
	HSV-1	HSV-2	VZV	CMV	Main target agents
Aciclovir, valaciclovir	+++	+++	++	–	HSV-1, HSV-2, VZV
Cidofovir	+	+	++	+++	CMV, resistant HSV
Famciclovir	+++	+++	++	–	HSV-1, HSV-2, VZV
Foscarnet	++	++	+	++	CMV, resistant HSV, VZV, CMV
Ganciclovir	+	+	+	+++	CMV

Table 215.10 Comparative susceptibility of herpesviruses to antiviral drugs. CMV, cytomegalovirus; HSV, herpes simplex virus; VZV, varicella-zoster virus.

ble for these patients, even before laboratory confirmation of the clinical diagnosis.

For patients who have frequent severe episodes of genital herpes, a choice can be made between patient-initiated episodic treatment or longer-term suppressive therapy. Episodic treatment must be initiated at the first sign of prodromal symptoms to be of benefit. Long-term suppressive therapy, however, is very effective and can dramatically reduce the frequency of recurrent disease and asymptomatic shedding.[79,80] Although recurrent disease and intermittent shedding of HSV are not fully prevented,[81] suppressive therapy has been safe, effective and well tolerated in patients treated for more than 6 years. In addition, there is no evidence that it greatly enhances the emergence of antiviral resistance.[81]

Varicella-zoster virus

VZV is significantly less susceptible to aciclovir, famciclovir and valaciclovir than HSV. Therefore, higher dosage regimens are required. Intravenous therapy with aciclovir or oral administration of valaciclovir or famciclovir is indicated for children who have severe manifestations of varicella, particularly those who are immunocompromised (see Table 215.11). Therapy should also be considered for adolescent or adult patients who have varicella because of the increased risk of complications in these patients. In immunocompetent children the antiviral effect is beneficial only when therapy is started very early after the onset of disease symptoms (<48 hours).

Intravenous aciclovir therapy has become the therapy of choice for patients who have a high risk of developing severe or progressive recurrent VZV disease (herpes zoster). These include patients treated for lymphoproliferative disorders, transplant recipients, other patients who have immunodeficiency conditions and patients who have herpes zoster ophthalmicus and herpes zoster oticus.

The poor bio-availability of aciclovir after oral administration has limited its use for immunocompetent patients who have herpes zoster. Valaciclovir and famciclovir have substantially improved bio-availability, accelerate healing and reduce pain in patients who have herpes zoster,[82,83] and are now licensed for these reasons in many countries. The effect is significant only in patients who are at risk of developing severe disease (i.e. those over 50 years of age who have considerable pain at the onset of symptoms). Furthermore, treatment has to start early (within 72 hours) to be beneficial. Treatment is always indicated for patients who have herpes zoster ophthalmicus or oticus.

Cytomegalovirus

There is no generally accepted indication for using antiviral therapy for immunocompetent patients who have CMV infection. In the immunocompromised host the first line of treatment of CMV disease is, if possible, appropriate reversal of immunosuppressive therapy. Additional, antiviral therapy is often required for these patients (see Table 215.11). For this purpose three drugs are now available – ganciclovir, foscarnet and cidofovir. Because CMV disease frequently recurs after cessation of antiviral therapy in patients who are immunodeficient, lifelong maintenance treatment is often required to prevent or delay disease progression.

Of the available drugs, intravenous ganciclovir is the treatment of choice for immunocompromised patients who have an episode of CMV disease, such as pneumonia, gastrointestinal tract disease or retinitis.[84] For maintenance therapy, particularly for patients who have AIDS and retinitis, there is an approved oral preparation of ganciclovir. Oral valganciclovir (the prodrug of ganciclovir) is recommended (see Chapters 125 and 205).[85,86]

In general, foscarnet is less well tolerated than ganciclovir. Its nephrotoxicity is the most common dose-limiting adverse effect and foscarnet is mostly used for patients who have severe adverse effects to ganciclovir or who have ganciclovir-resistant CMV disease.[84]

Experience with cidofovir is limited. Its major benefit is its long half-life, permitting relatively infrequent dosing. The main application of cidofovir therapy has been for patients who have retinitis, using intravitreal administration every 6 weeks, or intravenous infusion once weekly for induction and every other week for maintenance therapy.

INDICATIONS FOR ANTIHERPESVIRUS DRUG TREATMENT

Antiviral drug	Target virus	Infections	Possible side-effects
Aciclovir, valaciclovir, famciclovir	HSV-1,2	Severe and/or frequent mucocutaneous HSV infection, including genital herpes; herpes encephalitis, herpes keratitis	Headache, nausea, diarrhea
	VZV	Severe cases of varicella, varicella in patients at risk for complications (immunocompromised, adolescents, adults) Severe cases of herpes zoster, including those at risk of developing postherpetic neuralgia, herpes zoster ophthalmicus, oticus	Headache, nausea, diarrhea
Cidofovir	CMV	CMV retinitis	Severe nephrotoxicity
Foscarnet	CMV, HSV-1, HSV-2, VZV; severe disease due to aciclovir-, valaciclovir- and famciclovir-resistant HSV or VZV strains	Severe CMV disease refractory to ganciclovir treatment	Nephrotoxicity, crystalluria
Ganciclovir	CMV	Severe CMV disease in immunocompromised host (e.g. retinitis, esophagitis, colitis, pneumonia, encephalitis)	Neutropenia, thrombocytopenia

Table 215.11 Indications for antiherpesvirus drug treatment. CMV, cytomegalovirus; HSV, herpes simplex virus; VZV, varicella-zoster virus.

Although not very effective in the treatment of CMV infection, prophylactic use of valaciclovir in renal transplant patients has been found to have a preventive effect on the development of CMV disease.[87]

Other herpesviruses

EBV and HHV-6 have shown *in-vitro* susceptibility to various antiherpesvirus drugs such as aciclovir or ganciclovir. However, apart from aciclovir treatment of oral hairy leukoplakia in patients who have AIDS, no significant clinical benefit has so far been demonstrated. As for CMV disease, antiviral drug therapy is probably only effective when the disease is due to a viral rather than an immunopathologic process.

Recent *in-vitro* studies [69b] have shown that for HHV-6, -7 and –8 the most potent, presently available drugs with the highest antiviral selectivity index were:

- for HHV-6 – foscarnet and cidofovir;
- for HHV-7 – cidofovir and foscarnet; and
- for HHV-8 – cidofovir and ganciclovir.

However, so far no data from well-designed clinical studies have been reported to show the effectiveness of these drugs in the treatment of HHV-6, -7 or –8 infections. In addition, a number of experimental compounds, particularly S2242, an acyclic guanosine analog, were also found to have a marked antiviral effect in combination with an acceptable toxicity profile.[88]

Immunotherapy

Options for immunotherapy of herpesvirus-induced disease are limited and require further development, particularly for immunopathologically mediated herpesvirus disease (e.g. as occurs in CMV and EBV infections).

A few studies have shown a beneficial effect for a combination of ganciclovir and intravenous CMV immune globulin over the use of ganciclovir alone in bone marrow transplant recipients who have CMV pneumonia.[89] More recently, promising results have been obtained in the treatment of bone marrow transplant patients with PTLD by infusing donor T cells[90] and by the use of anti-CD20 monoclonal antibodies.[91]

REFERENCES

1. Roizman B, Deroisiers RC, Fleckenstein B, *et al.* Herpesviridae. In: Murphy FA, Fauquet CM, Bishop DHL, *et al.*, eds. Sixth Report of the International Committee of Taxonomy of Viruses. Arch Virol 1995;510(Suppl.10):114–27.
2. Nahmias AJ. Herpesviruses from fish to man – a search for pathobiologic unity. Pathobiol Ann 1972;2:153–82.
3. Roizman B, Pellet PE. Herpesviridae. In: Knipe DM, Howley PM, eds. Field's virology, 4th ed. Philadelphia: Lippincott-Raven; 2001:2381–98.
4. Roizman B, Sears AE. Herpes simplex viruses and their replication. In: Knipe DM, Howley PM, eds. Field's virology, 4th ed. Philadelphia: Lippincott-Raven; 2001;2399–2464.
5. Schulz TF. Kaposi's sarcoma-associated herpesvirus (human herpesvirus 8). In: Zuckerman AJ, Banatvala JE, Pattison JR, eds. Principles and practice of clinical virology, 4th ed. Chichester, UK: John Wiley & Sons; 2000:167–86.
6. Zhou ZH, Prasad BVV, Jakana J, Rixon F, Chiu W. Protein subunit structures in the herpes simplex virus A-capsid determined from 400 kV spot-scan cryomicroscopy. J Mol Biol 1994;242:458–69.
7. Zhou ZH, He J, Jakana J, Tatman JD, Rixon FJ, Chiu W. Assembly of VP26 in herpes simplex virus-1 inferred from structures of wild-type and recombinant capsids. Nat Struct Biol 1995;2:1026–30.
8. Margrath I. The pathogenesis of Burkitt's lymphoma. Adv Cancer Res 1990;55:133–269.
9. Levine PH, Conelly PR. Epidemiology of nasopharyngeal carcinoma. In: Wittes RE, ed. Head and neck cancer. New York: John Wiley and Sons; 1995:13–34.
10. Lin JC. Pathogenesis of Kaposi's sarcoma and human herpesvirus 8. Infect Med 1998;5:264–72.
11. Evans AS, Niederman JC. Epstein–Barr virus. In: Evans AS, Kaslow RA, eds. Viral infections of humans: epidemiology and control, 4th ed. New York: Plenum Medical Book Company; 1997:253–83.
12. White E. Chickenpox in Kerala. Indian J Public Health 1978;22:141–51.
13. Sinha DP. Chickenpox – a disease predominantly affecting adults in West Bengal, India. Int J Epidemiol 1976;5:367–74.
14. Evans AS. Infectious mononucleosis in University of Wisconsin students: Report of a five-year investigation. Am J Hyg 1960;71:342–62.
15. Burnet FM, Williams SW. Herpes simplex: a new point of view. Med J Aust 1939;1:637–41.
16. Corey L, Wald A. Genital herpes. In: Holmes KK, Mardh PE, Sparling PF, *et al.*, eds. Sexually transmitted diseases, 3rd ed. New York: McGraw-Hill; 1998:285–312.
17. Martin JN, Ganem DE, Osmond DH, Page-Shafer KA, Macrae D, Kedes DH. Sexual transmission and the natural history of human herpesvirus 8 infection. N Engl J Med 1998;338:948–54.
18. Stannard LM, Fuller AO, Spear PG. Herpes simplex virus glycoproteins associated with different morphological entities projecting from the virion envelope. J Gen Virol 1987;68:715–25.
19. Reeves WC, Corey L, Adams HG, Vontver LA, Holmes KK. Risk of recurrence after first episodes of genital herpes: relation to HSV type and antibody response. N Engl J Med 1981;305:315–19.
20. Yoshikawa T, Hill JM, Stanberry LR, Bourne N, Kurawadwala JF, Krause PR. The characteristic site-specific reactivation phenotypes of HSV-1 and HSV-2 depend upon the latency-associated transcript region. J Exp Med 1996;184:659–64.
21. Hay J, Ruyechan WT. Varicella zoster virus – a different kind of herpesvirus latency? Semin Virol 1994;5:241–7.
22. Straus SE, Cohen JI, Tosato G, Meier J. Epstein–Barr virus infections: biology, pathogenesis, and management. Ann Int Med 1993;118:45–8.
23. Adam E, Melnick JL, Probstfield JL, *et al.* High levels of cytomegalovirus antibody in patients requiring vascular surgery for atherosclerosis. Lancet 1987;ii:291–3.
24. Epstein SW, Zhou YF, Zhu J. Infection and artherosclerosis. Circulation 1999;100:20–8.
25. Danesh J, Collins R, Peto R. Chronic infections and coronary heart disease: is there a link? Lancet 1997;350:430–6.
26. Salahuddin SZ, Ablashi DV, Markham PD, *et al.* Isolation of a new virus, HBLV, in patients with lymphoproliferative disorders. Science 1986;234:596–601.
27. Yamanishi K, Okuno T, Shiraki K, *et al.* Identification of human herpesvirus-6 as a causal agent for exanthem subitum. Lancet 1988;1:1065–7.
28. Levy JA. Three new human herpesviruses (HHV6, 7, and 8). Lancet 1997;349:558–63.
29. Chang Y, Cesarman E, Pessin MS, *et al.* Identification of herpesvirus-like DNA sequences in AIDS-associated Kaposi's sarcoma. Science 1994;266:1865–9.
30. Wiertz EJ, Mukherjee S, Ploegh HL. Viruses use stealth technology to escape from the human immune system. Mol Med Today 1997;3:116–23.
31. Moore PS, Boshoff C, Weiss RA, Chang Y. Molecular mimicry of human cytokine and cytokine response pathway genes by KSHV. Science 1996;274:1739–44.
32. White CJ. Varicella-zoster virus vaccine. Clin Infect Dis 1997;24:753–61.
33. Vazquez M, LaRussa PS, Gershon AA, Steinberg SP, Freudigman K, Shapiro ED. The effectiveness of the varicella vaccine in clinical practice. N Engl J Med 2001;344:955–60.
34. Hanissian J. Emerging herpes vaccines. Infect Med 1998;14:205–9.
35. Plotkin SA. Cytomegalovirus vaccines. In: Plotkin SA, Orenstein WA, eds. Vaccines, 3rd ed. Philadelphia: WB Saunders; 1999:903–8.
36. Morgan AJ, Finerty S, Lougren K, *et al.* Prevention of Epstein–Barr (EB) virus-induced lymphoma in cotton top tamarins by vaccination with the EB virus envelope glycoprotein gp 340 incorporated into immune-stimulating complexes. J Gen Virol 1988;69:2093–6.
37. Persing DH, Smith TF, Tenover FC, White TJ. Diagnostic molecular microbiology: principles and applications. Washington: American Society for Microbiology; 1993:332–56.
38. Podzoeski RP, Persing DH. Molecular detection and identification of microorganisms. In: Murray PR, Baron EJ, Pfaller MA, Tenover FC, Yolken RH, eds. Manual of clinical microbiology. Washington: American Society for Microbiology; 1995:130–57.
39. Cinque P, Cleator GM Weber T, Monteyne P, Sindic JM, van Loon AM for the EU concerted action on virus meningitis and encephalitis. The role of laboratory investigation in the diagnosis and treatment of patients with suspected herpes encephalitis: a consensus report. J Neurol Neurosurg Psych 1996;61:339–45.
40. Druce J, Catton M, Chibo D, *et al.* Utility of a multiplex PCR assay for detecting herpesvirus DNA in clinical samples. J Clin Microbiol 2002;40:1728–32.
41. Jeffery KJM, Read SJ, Peto TEA, Mayon-White RT, Bangham CRM. Diagnosis of viral infections of the central nervous system: clinical interpretation of PCR results. Lancet 1997;349:313–17.
42. Domingues RB, Lakeman FD, Mayo MS, Whitley RJ. Application of competitive PCR to cerebrospinal fluid samples from patients with herpes simplex encephalitis. J Clin Microbiol 1998;36:2229–34.

43. Doerr HW, Rentschler M, Schleifler G. Serological detection of active infections with human herpes viruses (CMV, EBV, HSV, VZV): diagnostic potential of IgA class and IgG subclass-specific antibodies. Infection 1987;15:93–8.
44. Whitley RJ. Herpes simplex viruses. In: Knipe DM, Howley PM, eds. Field's virology, 4th ed. Philadelphia: Lippincott-Raven; 2001:2461–510.
45. Mertz GJ. Herpes simplex virus infections. In: Galasso GJ, Withley RJ, Merigan TC, eds. Antiviral agents and human viral diseases, 4th ed. Philadelphia: Lippincott–Raven; 1997:305–41.
46. Corey L, Adams HG, Brown ZA, Holmes KK. Genital herpes simplex virus infections: clinical manifestations, courses and complications. Ann Intern Med 1983;98:958–72.
47. Lafferty WE, Coombs RW, Benedetti J, Critchlow C, Corey L. Recurrences after oral and genital herpes simplex virus infection. Influence of site of infection and viral type. N Engl J Med 1987;316:1444–9.
48. Whitley RJ. Viral encephalitis. N Engl J Med 1990;323:242–50.
49. Aurelius E, Johansson B, Skoldenberg B, Forsgren M. Encephalitis in immunocompetent patients due to herpes simplex virus type 1 or 2 as determined by type-specific polymerase chain reaction and antibody assays of cerebrospinal fluid. J Med Virol 1993;39:179–86.
50. Whitley R, Arvin A, Prober C, *et al.* Predictors of morbidity and mortality in neonates with herpes simplex virus infections. The National Institute of Allergy and Infectious Diseases Collaborative Antiviral Study Group. N Engl J Med 1991;324:450–4.
51. Pavan-Langston D. Ocular viral infections: herpes simplex virus, Epstein–Barr virus, adenovirus, and poxvirus. In: Galasso GJ, Withley RJ, Merigan TC, eds. Antiviral agents and human viral diseases, 4th ed. Philadelphia: Lippincott–Raven; 1997:187–227.
52. Weller TH. The propagation *in vitro* of agents producing inclusion bodies derived from varicella and herpes zoster. Proc Soc Exp Biol Med 1953;83:340–6.
53. Grose C. Varicella zoster virus infections: chicken pox, shingles and varicella vaccine. In: Glaser R, Jones JF, eds. Herpesvirus infections. New York: Marcel Dekker; 1994:117–86.
54. Guess HA, Broughton DD, Melton LJ, Kurland LT. Population-based studies of varicella complications. Pediatrics 1986;78:723–7.
55. Enders G, Miller E, Cradock Watson J, Bolley I, Ridehalgh M. Consequences of varicella and herpes zoster in pregnancy: prospective study of 1739 cases. Lancet 1994;343:1548–51.
56. Gershon AA. Chickenpox, measles, mumps. In: Remington JS, Klein JO, eds. Infectious diseases of the fetus and the newborn infant, 5th ed. Philidelphia: WB Saunders; 2001:683–732.
57. Straus SE, Ostrove JM, Inchauspe G, *et al.* NIH conference. Varicella-zoster virus infections. Biology, natural history, treatment, and prevention. Ann Intern Med 1988;108:221–37.
58. Hope-Simpson RE. The nature of herpes zoster: a long-term study and a new hypothesis. Proc R Soc Med 1965;58:9–20.
59. Naraqi S. Cytomegaloviruses. In: Belshe RB, ed. Textbook of human virology, 2nd ed. St Louis: Mosby Year–Book 1991:889–924.
60. Stagno S. Cytomegalovirus. In: Remington JS, Klein JO, eds. Infectious diseases of the fetus and newborn infant, 5th ed. Philadelphia: WB Saunders; 2001:389–424.
61. Meyers JD, Flournoy N, Thomas ED. Risk factors for cytomegalovirus infection after human marrow transplantation. J Infect Dis 1986;153:478–88.
62. Peterson PK, Balfour HH Jr, Marker SC, Fryd DS, Howard RJ, Simmons RL. Cytomegalovirus disease in renal allograft recipients: a prospective study of the clinical features, risk factors and impact on renal transplantation. Med Baltimore 1980;59:283–300.
63. Purtilo DT, DeFlorio D Jr, Hutt LM, *et al.* Variable phenotypic expression of an X-linked recessive lymphoproliferative syndrome. N Engl J Med 1977;297:1077–80.
64. Young LS, Rowe M. Epstein–Barr virus, lymphomas and Hodgkin's disease. Semin Cancer Biol 1992;3:273–84.
65. Greenspan JS, Greenspan D, Lennette ET, *et al.* Replication of Epstein–Barr virus within the epithelial cells of oral 'hairy' leukoplakia, an AIDS-associated lesion. N Engl J Med 1985;313:1564–71.
66. Pruksananonda P, Hall CB, Insel RA, *et al.* Primary human herpesvirus 6 infection in young children. N Engl J Med 1992;326:1445–50.
67. Hall CB, Long CE, Schnabel KC, *et al.* Human herpesvirus-6 infection in children. A prospective study of complications and reactivation. N Engl J Med 1994;331:432–8.
68. Kondo K, Nagafuji H, Hata A, Tomomori C, Yamanishi K. Association of human herpesvirus 6 infection of the central nervous system with recurrence of febrile convulsions. J Infect Dis 1993;167:1197–200.
69. Hay KA, Tenser RB. Leukotropic herpesviruses in multiple sclerosis. Mult Scler 2000;6:66–98.
70. Cone RW, Huang ML, Corey L, *et al.* Human herpesvirus 6 (HHV-6) infection after bone marrow transplantation: clinical and virological manifestations. J Infect Dis 1999;179:311–18.
71. Weigler BJ. Biology of B virus in macaque and human hosts: a review. Clin Infect Dis 1992;14:555–67.
72. Holmes GP, Chapman LE, Stewart JA, *et al.* Guidelines for the prevention and treatment of B-virus infections in exposed persons. Clin Infect Dis 1995;20:421–39.
73. DeClerq E. Trends in the development of new antiviral agents for the chemotherapy of infections caused by herpesviruses and retroviruses. Rev Med Virol 1995;5:149–64.
74. Whitley RJ, Gnann JW Jr. Acyclovir: a decade later. N Engl J Med 1992;327:782–9.
75. Hirsch MS, Schooley RT. Resistance to antiviral drugs: the end of innocence. N Engl J Med 1989;320:313–4.
76. Reusser P. Herpes virus resistance to antiviral drugs: a review of the mechanisms, clinical importance and therapeutic options. J Hosp Infect 1996;33:235–48.
77. Kimberlin DW, Coen DM, Biron KK, *et al.* Molecular mechanisms of antiviral resistance. Antiviral Res 1995;26:369–401.
78. Field HJ. Herpes simplex virus antiviral drug resistance – current trends and future prospects. J Clin Virol 2001;21:261–9.
79. Cassady KA, Whitley RJ. New therapeutic approaches to the alphaherpesvirus infections. J Antimicrob Chemother 1997;39:119–28.
80. Mertz GJ, Loveless MO, Levin MJ, *et al.* Oral famciclovir for suppression of recurrent genital herpes simplex virus infection in women. A multicenter, double-blind, placebo-controlled trial. Collaborative Famciclovir Genital Herpes Research Group. Arch Intern Med 1997;157:343–9.
81. Wald A, Zeh J, Barnum G, Davis LG, Corey L. Suppression of subclinical shedding of herpes simplex virus type 2 with acyclovir. Ann Intern Med 1996;124:8–15.
82. Smiley ML, Murray A, de-Miranda P. Valacyclovir HCl (Valtrex): an acyclovir prodrug with improved pharmacokinetics and better efficacy for treatment of zoster. Adv Exp Med Biol 1996;394:33–9.
83. Tyring SK. Efficacy of famciclovir in the treatment of herpes zoster. Semin Dermatol 1996;15:27–31.
84. Crumpacker CS. Ganciclovir. N Engl J Med 1996;335:721–9.
85. Cinque P, Cleator GM, Weber T, *et al.* Diagnosis and clinical management of neurological disorders caused by cytomegalovirus in AIDS patients. J Neurovirol 1998;4:120–32.
86. Emery VC. Progress in understanding cytomegalovirus drug resistance. J Clin Virol 2001;21:223–8.
87. Lowance D, Neumayer H-H, Legendre CM, *et al.* Valacyclovir for the prevention of cytomegalovirus disease after renal transplantation. International Valacyclovir Cytomegalovirus Prophylaxis Study Group. N Engl J Med 1999;340:1462–70.
88. De Clercq E, Naessens L, de Bolle L, Schols D, Zhang Y, Neyts J. Antiviral agents active against human herpesviruses HHV-6, HHV-7, and HHV-8. Rev Med Virol 2001;11:381–95.
89. Zamora MR, Fullerton DA, Campbell DN, *et al.* Use of cytomegalovirus (CMV) hyperimmune globulin for prevention of CMV disease in CMV-seropositive lung transplant recipients. Transplant Proc 1994;26:49–51.
90. Ridall SR, Greenberg PD. T cell therapy of human CMV and EBV infection in immunocompromised hosts. Rev Med Virol 1997;7:181–92
91. Kuehnle J, Huls MH, Lin Z, *et al.* CD20 monoclonal antibody (Rituximab) for therapy of Epstein–Barr virus lymphoma after hemopoetic stem-cell transplantation. Blood 2000;95:1502–5.

chapter 216

Papillomaviruses and Polyomaviruses

Keerti V Shah

Until recently, these two virus families were grouped together as subfamilies in the papovavirus family because they shared the following characteristics: small size, nonenveloped virion, icosahedral capsid made up of 72 capsomers, double-stranded, circular, supercoiled DNA genome and nuclear site of multiplication. They were separated as different families because they are unrelated genetically and immunologically and are also biologically dissimilar. Papillomaviruses grow on surface epithelia, do not have a systemic phase of infection and are etiologically linked to cancer of the uterine cervix, other lower genital tract cancers and some oropharyngeal cancers. Polyomaviruses, on the other hand, have a viremic phase during which they infect internal organs such as the kidney and the brain and human polyomavirus JC is the etiologic agent for the degenerative central nervous system (CNS) disease progressive multifocal leukoencephalopathy (PML). Polyomaviruses are not linked to naturally occurring cancers.

PAPILLOMAVIRUSES

NATURE

Papillomaviruses are widely distributed in nature; among mammals they infect humans, cattle, dogs, rabbits, monkeys and other species. Some animal papillomaviruses affect both epithelial and fibroblastic tissues and produce fibropapillomas, but human papillomaviruses (HPVs) are strictly epitheliotropic and infect the skin or the mucous membranes.

Papillomaviruses cannot be propagated in cell culture. Therefore, rapid advances in the knowledge about papillomaviruses date from the 1970s, when molecular cloning of the viral genomes allowed comparisons between viruses from different species and from different sites of the same species. The cloned genomes provided reagents for examination of affected tissues for viral sequences.

The papillomavirus particle (Fig. 216.1) is about 55nm in diameter and has a double-stranded, covalently closed, circular genome of about 8000bp. All of the genomic information is located on one strand. The genome is divided into an early region that has eight open reading frames (ORFs E1–E8), a late region that has two ORFs (L1 and L2), and a noncoding long control region (LCR), which contains regulatory elements for viral DNA replication and transcription.

The L1 ORF codes for the major L1 capsid protein, which accounts for most of the virion mass and mediates viral attachment and immune response to infection. The prophylactic HPV vaccine strategies which are being tested are based largely on the use of the L1 protein expressed by recombinant DNA technology and self-assembled as virus-like particles (VLPS). The function of the minor L2 capsid protein is unclear. The early region genes E6 and E7 of high-risk HPVs code for the transforming proteins of the virus that mediate the oncogenic properties of the virus. The E1 gene is required for viral DNA replication and the E2 gene modulates viral transcription. The E5 gene is a membrane protein that interacts with growth factor receptors; it is the main transforming gene for bovine papillomaviruses but not for HPVs. The E4 gene, although it is located in the early region, is expressed late in the virus cycle; it disrupts cytokeratins and probably facilitates virus exit from infected cells. The functions of E3 and E8 ORFs are not known.

EPIDEMIOLOGY

More than 100 individual HPV types have been described to date.[1] They naturally fall into two groups, mucosal HPVs and cutaneous HPVs.

Mucosal human papillomaviruses

The genital tract is the reservoir for mucosal HPVs, except for two HPV types (HPV-13 and HPV-32), which infect the oral cavity. About 40 HPV types infect the genital tract. Genital HPV infections are the most prevalent sexually transmitted pathogens. As many as 30–40% of sexually active young women may have a prevalent HPV infection of the genital tract, as determined by a sensitive, amplification-based DNA detection technique. A history of multiple sexual partners, and having a male sexual partner who has many sexual partners, are the main risk factors for a woman for the acquisition of HPVs. Circumcision may decrease the risk of HPV acquisition in the male.[2] The HPV prevalence reaches its peak in young adults and declines at older ages. HPV infections are largely asymptomatic and of 1–2 years' duration. Infection probably confers partial immunity to re-infection with the same type. The course of HPV infection is altered profoundly by HIV-induced immunosuppression (see Chapter 77).

HPV-6 and HPV-11 are the etiologic agents of genital warts (condylomas), which occur in sexually active individuals, and also of recurrent respiratory papillomatosis (RRP), which may have onset in childhood or in adult life. HPV-16, -18, -31, -45 and some other types account for more than 90% of cervical cancers, as described in later sections of this chapter.

HPV-13 and HPV-32 cause focal epithelial hyperplasia in the oral cavity. This condition is found frequently in indigenous populations, but rarely in other groups. How they are transmitted from person to person is unclear.

Cutaneous human papillomaviruses

Skin warts are transmitted by direct contact with an infected tissue or indirectly by contact with virus-contaminated objects. There is some specificity between HPV type, and site and morphology of the warts; plantar warts most often yield HPV-1, common warts HPV-2 and flat warts HPV-3 and HPV-10.

Epidermodysplasia verruciformis is a rare condition in which an extensive lifelong wart virus infection of the skin is never resolved.[3] The disease may be familial. The warts may be flat or they may be in the form of reddish-brown macular plaques. In about one-third of these patients, malignant transformation occurs in the reddish-brown plaques in areas exposed to sunlight. The epidermodysplasia verruciformis lesions contain a large number of HPV types. Types most commonly associated with skin cancers in epidermodysplasia verruciformis patients are HPV-5 and HPV-8.

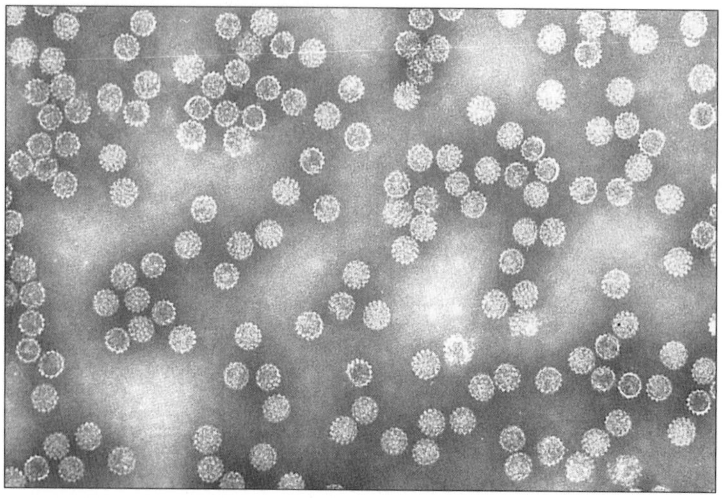

Fig. 216.1 Human papillomavirus particles. The particles are nonenveloped, have icosahedral capsids and are 55nm in diameter. Courtesy of Dr M Reissig.

Low levels of HPV DNA sequences of a number of HPV types, including several novel types, have been recovered from nonmelanoma skin cancers. HPV sequences are also found in plucked hair roots of healthy skin. It is not clear if HPVs play a role in the development of non-melanoma skin cancers.[4]

PATHOGENICITY

Infectious agent

Papillomaviruses have a high degree of species and tissue specificity. Genital HPVs are rarely detected on skin other than that of the genital tract, but they can infect other mucosal sites in the body such as the aerodigestive tract. Cutaneous HPVs are almost never encountered in the genital tract.

Papillomaviruses cannot be grown in monolayer cell cultures to yield virus particles. Full epithelial differentiation is required for the production of infectious particles.[5] Limited numbers of papillomavirus particles are produced by infection in organotypic cultures of the epithelium or by transplantation of infected human cells to certain sites in immunodeficient mice.

Pathogenesis of cervical cancer

Nearly all cervical cancers originate in the 'transformation zone', located at the lower end of the cervix, where the stratified squamous epithelium of the vagina forms a junction with the columnar cells of the endocervix. The cells in the transformation zone of the cervix must be highly susceptible to the oncogenic effects of HPVs, because cancers arise much less frequently at other sites in the genital tract (vulva, vagina, penis) that are infected with HPVs as frequently as the cervix but do not have an area similar to the transformation zone.

Invasive cervical cancer is preceded by a progressive spectrum of cytologic abnormalities, classified as atypical squamous cells of undetermined significance (ASCUS), low-grade squamous intraepithelial lesions (LSILs) and high-grade squamous intraepithelial lesions (HSILs). The progression from initial HPV infection to invasive cancer may take 15–20 years.

Although almost all squamous cell abnormalities of the cervix including cervical cancer are the result of HPV infections, the probability of any one HPV infection progressing to cervical cancer is quite small. Most HPV infections produce only transient cytologic abnormalities and are resolved completely without a trace. Cytologic abnormalities are seen in only about 10% of women who are posi-

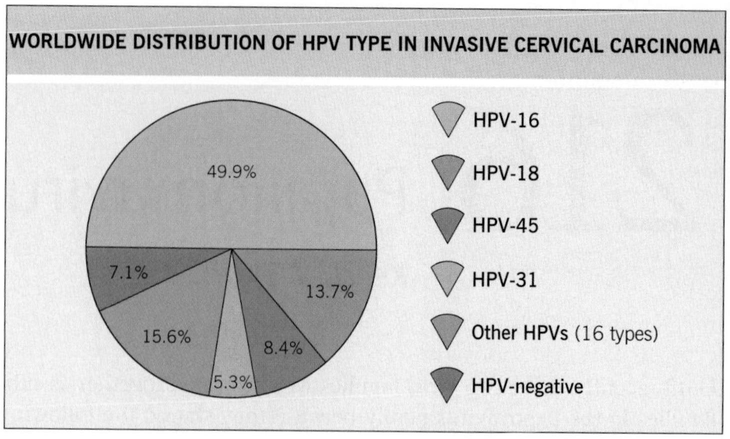

Fig. 216.2 Worldwide distribution of HPV type in invasive cervical carcinoma. The data are based on tests of over 900 cancers from different countries.[7]

tive for HPV DNA in the genital tract. A large majority of LSIL regresses completely. In the USA, annually, there are tens of millions of HPV infections but only about 15,000 cases of invasive cancer. The relatively small number of cases is partly the result of treatment of LSIL and HSIL identified from Pap smear screening programs, but it is also, in a large measure, because most HPV infections do not result in significant cervical disease. In countries that have no effective Pap smear screening programs, the number of cases of cervical cancer is still a small fraction of the number of HPV infections in women.

HPVs are found in nearly all lesions spanning the entire spectrum of cytologic abnormalities from LSIL to invasive cancer. The distribution of HPV types changes markedly with increasing severity of disease.[6] Almost all genital HPV types are represented in HPV DNA-positive cytologically normal specimens and in ASCUS and LSIL cases, but only about a dozen HPV types are found in invasive cervical cancer. Of these, four HPV types, HPV-16, -18, -45 and -31, account for nearly 80% of invasive cancers (Fig. 216.2). The genital HPV types

MAJOR CLINICAL ASSOCIATIONS OF HPV INFECTIONS		
Disease	**HPV type**	**Transmission**
Cervical cancer		
High risk	HPV-16, -18, -45, -31	
Intermediate risk	HPV-33, -35, -39, -51, -52 -56, -59, -68, -73	Sexual
Low risk	HPV-6, -11, -26, -42, -43, -44, -53, -54, -55, -62, -66	
Cancer of vulva, vagina, anal canal, penis	HPV-16 and others	Sexual
Anogenital warts	HPV-6, -11	Sexual
Juvenile-onset RRP	HPV-6, -11	Mother–child, at birth
Adult-onset RRP	HPV-6, -11	Unclear
Cutaneous warts	HPV-1, -2, -3, -4, -10 and others	Nonsexual contact
Epidermodysplasia verruciformis	HPV-5, -8 and others	Nonsexual contact
Skin cancers	EV HPVs and novel HPVs	Unclear
Focal epithelial hyperplasia of the oral cavity	HPV-13, -32	Nonsexual contact

Table 216.1 Major clinical associations of HPV infections.

have therefore been categorized as high-risk, intermediate-risk or low-risk types (Table 216.1) on the basis of their prevalence in invasive cervical cancer.[7]

The oncogenic potential of HPVs is mediated by the E6 and E7 proteins of high-risk HPVs. In laboratory studies, E6 and E7 of high-risk HPVs can each transform mouse 3T3 cells and, together, can immortalize human keratinocytes. Viral constructs containing E6 and E7 genes of high-risk HPVs produce HSIL-like lesions in organotypic cervical epithelium. The E6 and E7 genes are invariably expressed in cells of HPV-associated cervical cancers. The viral genome of HPVs remains episomal in infections that are not associated with cervical cytopathology, as well as in cases of LSIL and in most instances of HSIL. However, in most invasive cancers the viral genome is integrated into the cellular DNA. Integration requires linearization of the circular viral genome, which almost always occurs by a break in the E2 region of the genome. The E6 and E7 genes not only remain intact after integration, but they are released from the inhibitory effect of the E2 protein, and are expressed at high levels in invasive cancers. High levels of antibodies to E6 and E7 proteins are markers for invasive cancer.

The molecular mechanisms of cellular transformation by E6 and E7 genes of high-risk HPVs are well understood and are described in detail in excellent reviews.[8,9] Briefly, the E6 protein complexes with tumor suppressor protein p53 and targets it for destruction via the ubiquitin pathway. The E7 protein complexes with tumor suppressor protein Rb, thereby releasing the transcription factor E2F from its complex with Rb. The E2F activates expression of *myc* and other genes that activate the cell cycle. In the normal cell cycle, tumor suppressor proteins p53 and Rb inhibit cellular proliferation. The functional inactivation of both of these cellular tumor suppressor proteins by the HPV oncoproteins result in continued cell proliferation without time for repair of DNA damage (Fig. 216.3). This leads to genetic instability and accumulation of additional cellular mutations and chromosomal changes. Thus, infections with high-risk HPVs prepare the ground for the cellular genetic alterations that underlie cervical cancer. For example, gain of 3q chromosome was found to be consistently associated with the early stages of invasive cervical carcinoma (Fig. 216.4).[10]

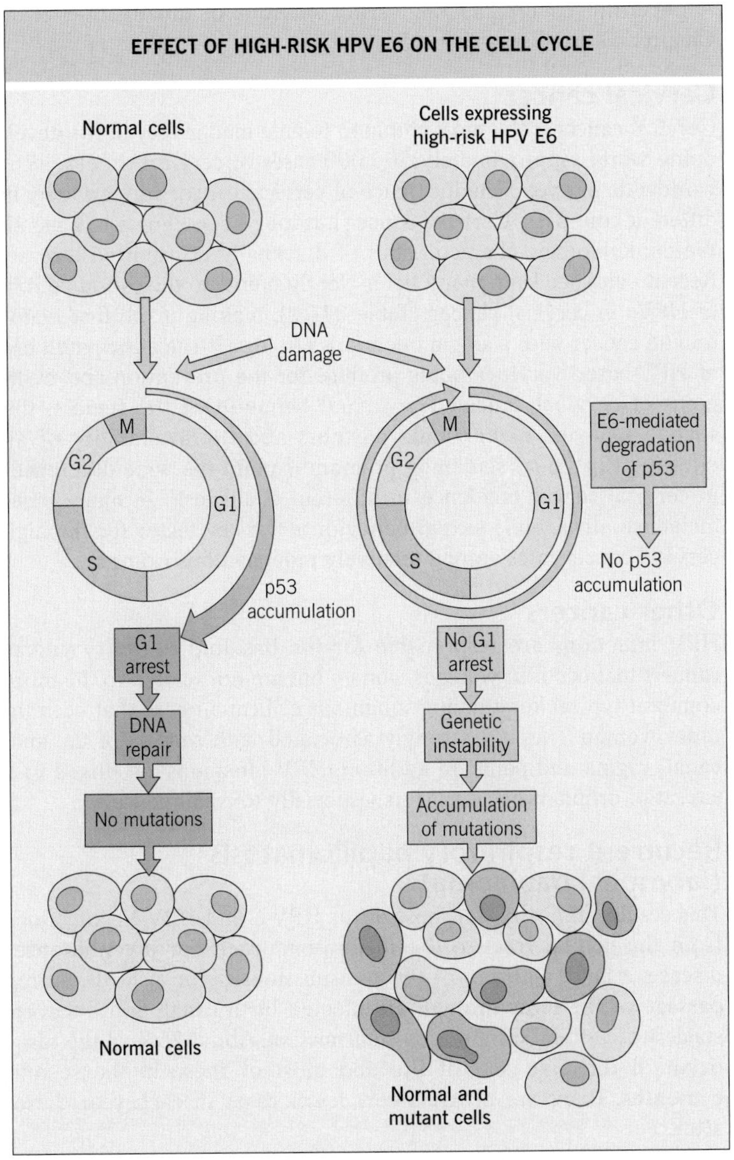

Fig. 216.3 Effect of high-risk HPV E6 on the cell cycle. In normal cells (left), DNA damage results in increased p53 production, which leads to arrest of cell cycle in G1 phase, allowing the cell time to repair DNA damage. In cells infected with high-risk HPVs (right), the HPV E6 mediates degradation of p53, so there is no accumulation of p53, no cell-cycle arrest, and continued cell multiplication. This leads to genetic instability and accumulation of cellular mutations. Courtesy of Dr TD Kessis.

PREVENTION

HPV-related diseases for which preventive strategies are being investigated are cervical and other lower genital tract cancers, genital warts and recurrent respiratory papillomatosis.

Cervical cancer

There are high hopes that HPV-based strategies will help reduce cervical cancer burden in the world. Primary cervical cancer screening by examination of cervical scrapes for DNAs of high-risk HPVs has been shown to have a sensitivity greater than that of Pap smears for the detection of HSIL and cancer.[11] Furthermore, adequate genital

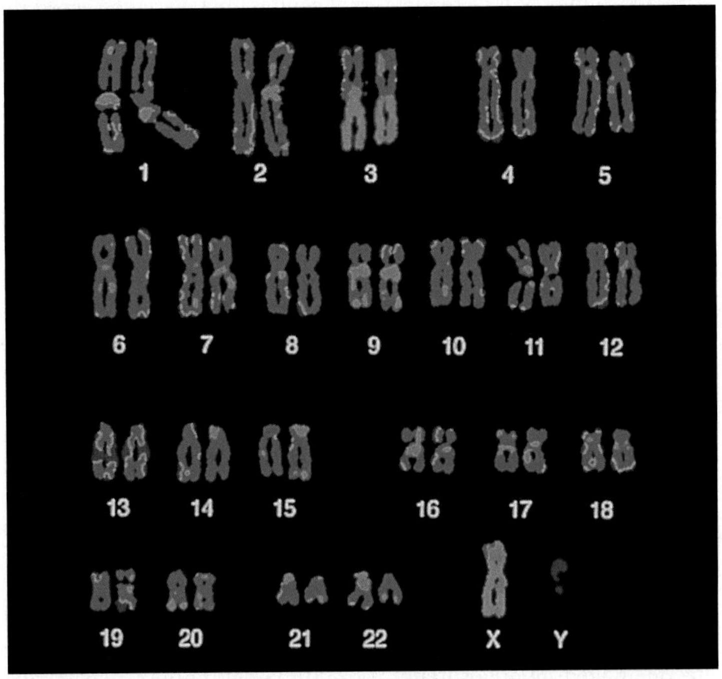

Fig. 216.4 Gain of chromosome 3q in early cervical carcinoma. The figure displays a ratio image after comparative genome hybridization, in which normal reference metaphase chromosomes are hybridized with a mixture of differentially labeled tumor DNA (green label) and normal DNA (red label). The chromosomes are ordered in a karyogram-like fashion. Chromosome 3q is gained (over-representation of green label) and chromosomal band 13q21 is lost (over-representation of red label) in this carcinoma. With permission from Heselmeyer *et al.*;[10] copyright (1996) National Academy of Sciences, USA.

tract specimens can be self-collected by the women themselves, thus making it possible to avoid a pelvic examination. Assays for genital tract HPV DNAs are useful in the clinical management of mild cervical cytological abnormalities.[12]

Virus-like particles that self-assemble from the L1 capsid protein when it is expressed by baculovirus or yeast recombinant DNA vectors have provided the immunogen for candidate prophylactic vaccines. The VLPs are free of viral DNA and possess conformational epitopes of authentic virions. Immunization with VLPs leads to very high titers of virus neutralizing antibodies and to protection against subsequent HPV infection.[13] The vaccines are expected to provide immunity only to the VLP types included in the vaccine preparation; no cross protection against other types is anticipated. Initial vaccine constructs are for HPV-16 and -18. Several strategies are also being tried for therapeutic immunization, aimed at destroying established lesions of HSIL and invasive cancer. For this purpose, the objective is to generate cytotoxic T cells directed against cells expressing the E6 and E7 proteins of high-risk HPVs.[14] Chimeric vaccines which may have both prophylactic and therapeutic properties are also under investigation.

Genital warts

Although they are benign, genital warts (condylomas) are a significant problem in sexually active populations and especially in immunocompromised individuals. Vaccine strategies, similar to those described above for cervical cancer, but using HPV-6 and HPV-11 VLPs and E6 and E7 proteins, are envisaged for the prevention and treatment of genital warts.

Recurrent respiratory papillomatosis (RRP)

Juvenile-onset RRP results from transmission of HPV-6 and HPV-11 at birth, during fetal passage through an infected birth canal. Potential ways to reduce the incidence of this disease are treatment of condylomas during pregnancy and cesarean delivery when there is an active infection of the maternal genital tract. Vaccines based on HPV-6 and HPV-11 may have a role in the prevention and treatment of juvenile-onset RRP.

DIAGNOSTIC MICROBIOLOGY

Hybridization assays

The presence of HPV in a tissue is ascertained by nucleic acid hybridization assays. The most widely used methods, especially in epidemiologic investigations, are those based on polymerase chain reaction (PCR) amplification.[15,16] Typically, consensus primers are employed to target conserved regions of the viral genome so that a large number of HPVs are amplified in a single amplification reaction. The PCR products are then screened for different HPVs by hybridization with type-specific oligonucleotide probes, and by a 'generic' probe (a mixture of probes of several HPVs) that would detect many HPVs. The methods have high analytic sensitivity and a high specificity. Recently, this assay has been modified so that the type specific hybridizations are performed in a single step as line blots against probes immobilized on a strip.[17] Hybrid Capture is a signal-amplification based hybridization assay approved by the FDA in the USA. In this assay, genital tract specimens are screened for HPVs in an enzyme-linked immunosorbent assay (ELISA)-type format with two pools of HPV probes, one pool consisting of high-risk HPVs and the other of low-risk HPVs.[18] This test has been found to be useful in 'triaging' women with abnormal Pap smears for colposcopy.[12]

Immunologic assays

Immunologic assays are rarely used for type-specific HPV diagnosis. In most HPV infections, viral particles and capsid proteins are present in very small amounts and so are difficult to detect with antiviral serum. Also, as cervical SILs progress toward higher grade disease and cervical cancer, synthesis of capsid proteins and infectious particles is completely shut down. Type-specific antiserum is not available for any HPV type.

Antibody response to HPVs may be measured using ELISA with virus-like particles.[19] Antibody response to HPV infections is low-titered and detectable in only about 40–50% of infected individuals. The proportion of infected individuals who are antibody positive increases with increased duration of infection and with greater viral load in the genital tract specimens.[20]

Antibodies to E6 and E7 proteins are markers of HPV-associated invasive cancer. These antibodies may be detected by peptide-based ELISA or by radioimmunoprecipitation assays with *in-vitro* synthesized full length E6 and E7 proteins. Elevated levels of E6 or E7 antibodies are found in about 40% of patients who have invasive cancer but in less than 1% of controls.

CLINICAL MANIFESTATIONS

The major clinical associations of HPVs are listed in Table 216.1. Aspects not covered in the earlier sections of this chapter or in Chapter 77 are discussed below.

Cervical cancer

Cervical cancer is the most common female malignancy in the developing world. Approximately 500,000 cases of cervical cancer occur worldwide per year. The incidence of cervical cancer varies widely in different countries. Cervical cancer has long been known to have all the epidemiologic characteristics of a sexually transmitted disease. Recent evidence from many fields clearly points to the causative role of HPVs in cervical cancer (Table 216.2), making it the first major human cancer with a single infectious etiology.[21] The anticipated use of HPV-based vaccines holds promise for the prevention and treatment of cervical cancer. The sexual behavior of the female, the sexual behavior of her male partners and the availability of an effective Pap smear screening program explain the wide differences in cervical cancer incidence in different countries.[22] In many high-incidence areas, male sexual behavior is the key factor for the high cervical cancer rates among relatively monogamous women.

Other cancers

HPV infections are responsible for the basaloid or warty vulvar cancers that occur in younger women but are not related to the more common typical keratinizing squamous cell carcinomas that occur in older women. They are strongly associated with cancers of the anal canal, vagina and penis. In addition, HPV infections are linked to a subset of oropharyngeal cancers, especially tonsillar cancers.

Recurrent respiratory papillomatosis (laryngeal papilloma)

This results from the transmission of HPV-6 and HPV-11 infections from the genital tract to the respiratory tract. For juvenile-onset disease, a large majority of the transmissions occur at birth, during passage of the fetus through an infected birth canal. Some reports suggest occasional intrauterine transmission. About 25% of the cases occur in the first year of life and most of these in the second 6 months. There are progressively fewer cases in each year thereafter.

The most common site of the papilloma is in the larynx on the vocal cords (Fig. 216.5). The tumors are benign but may threaten life if they grow and obstruct respiration. The tumors tend to recur after surgical removal, and in the worst cases operations may be required every few weeks. Operative procedures, especially tracheotomy, may spread the tumor by inadvertently transplanting tumor cells to other sites. Rarely, the tumor may undergo malignant transformation.

EVIDENCE LINKING HPVS WITH INVASIVE CERVICAL CANCER	
Epidemiology	• HPVs present in over 90% of cervical cancers both in low-and in high-incidence areas • HPV infections precede invasive cancer • HPV epidemiology and cervical cancer screening practices together account for differences in worldwide incidence of cervical cancer
Pathogenesis	• HPV genome present in every tumor cell and transcriptionally active • HPVs associated with the entire spectrum of cervical neoplasia, from low-grade cytologic abnormalities to invasive disease • HPV types most frequent in cancers are the most oncogenic in laboratory assays • HPV oncogenes E6 and E7 invariably expressed in cancers • Viral genome which is episomal in preinvasive disease, integrates into cellular DNA in invasive cancers
Molecular mechanisms	• Oncoproteins E6 and E7 of high-risk HPVs distort cell cycle and promote genetic instability by degradation of tumor suppressor protein p53 and inactivation of tumor suppressor protein Rb • Integration of viral genome in cellular DNA enhances E6 and E7 expression

Table 216.2 Evidence linking HPVs with invasive cervical cancer. Observations from the field, the clinic and the laboratory are mutually corroborative in building a compelling case for the HPV etiology of cervical cancer.

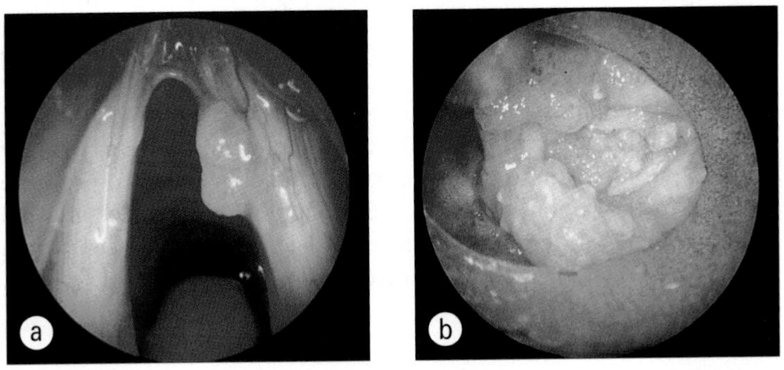

Fig. 216.5 RRP of juvenile onset. (a) A respiratory papilloma on the vocal cord of a child. (b) Papilloma obstructing the respiratory tract. Courtesy of Dr H Kashima.

MANAGEMENT

The clinical conditions associated with HPV infections are very diverse. Regular Pap smear screening and follow-up of women who have Pap smear abnormalities would greatly decrease the risk of cervical cancer. The preinvasive cervical disease is readily treated with greater than 90% cure rates. Genital and skin warts may regress spontaneously or may be treated with caustic agents (podophyllin), cryotherapy, application of an immunomodulating agent(imiquimod), or by surgical removal. Intralesional or parenteral administration of interferon has been successful in the treatment of refractory genital warts (see Chapter 77).

POLYOMAVIRUSES

NATURE

Polyomaviruses are small, nonenveloped viruses with a diameter of about 42nm. The virions have icosahedral symmetry and 72 capsomers. The viral genome is a circular, covalently closed, supercoiled, double-stranded DNA of about 5000bp. Each DNA strand carries about one-half of the genetic information. The genome is divided into an early region (2.4kb), which codes for large and small T proteins, a late region (2.3kb), which codes for viral proteins VP1, VP2 and VP3, and a non-coding regulatory region (0.4kb), which contains regulatory elements for viral DNA replication and transcription.

EPIDEMIOLOGY

BK virus (BKV) and JC virus (JCV) are two polyomaviruses that infect humans.[23] Infections with both viruses occur in childhood, but infections with BKV occur at an earlier age. In the USA, serologic studies suggest that about 50% of children are infected with BKV by the age of 3 or 4 years, and 100% by 10–11 years. JCV antibody prevalence peaks at about 75–80% by adulthood. The exact mode of transmission of these infections is not known.

Between 1955 and 1961, a large number of people in the USA and elsewhere were exposed to simian virus 40 (SV40), an infection of macaque species, because the virus was an inadvertent contaminant of inactivated poliovirus vaccines that were prepared from virus pools grown in simian kidney cultures. The contaminating SV40 virus was not fully inactivated. Although there have been occasional reports of recovery of SV40 from a number of human cancers, the significance of these observations is unclear.[24]

PATHOGENICITY

The viruses probably multiply at the site of entry (which is not known) and then reach the kidney, the main target organ, by viremia. They undergo further multiplication in the kidney and produce transient viruria. After primary infection, the viruses remain latent in the kidney for an indefinite period of time. In times of immunologic impairment, the viruses may be reactivated in the kidney and virus-infected cells are excreted in the urine. The infected urinary cells have enlarged nuclei and basophilic inclusions. The reactivated viruses may reach other organs, such as the brain. Almost all the diseases associated with BKV and JCV are a result of reactivated infections. The viruses may also persist in B cells and in the brain, after primary infection.

The pathogenesis of progressive multifocal encephalopathy (PML) is discussed below.

PREVENTION

No attempts have been made to prevent primary BKV or JCV infections, which are essentially harmless in immunocompetent individuals.

DIAGNOSTIC MICROBIOLOGY

Tests for BKV and JCV are indicated when urinary cytology reveals abnormal epithelial cells. Differential diagnosis includes urinary tract infections with other viruses, for example cytomegalovirus, and tumor cells from bladder cancer. Tests for BKV and JCV are also indicated in the investigation of cystitis, hemorrhagic cystitis and hematuria.

BKV and JCV can be readily identified by PCR assays or by Southern hybridization of DNA from infected tissue. BKV can be cultivated in several cell lines of human origin. JCV grows best in human fetal glial cell cultures, which are rich in spongioblasts. Isolation of BKV and JCV in cell cultures is rarely attempted because it is inefficient and cumbersome, and the needed cell types are not readily available.

Cells and tissues infected with BKV or JCV can be identified by immunoperoxidase and immunofluorescence tests with antiviral antiserum. Immunization of rabbits with disrupted viral capsids produces a broadly cross-reactive antiserum. The viruses in urine supernatants can be identified by ELISA. Serologic diagnosis of BKV and JCV infections can be made by hemagglutination–inhibition assays or by ELISA.

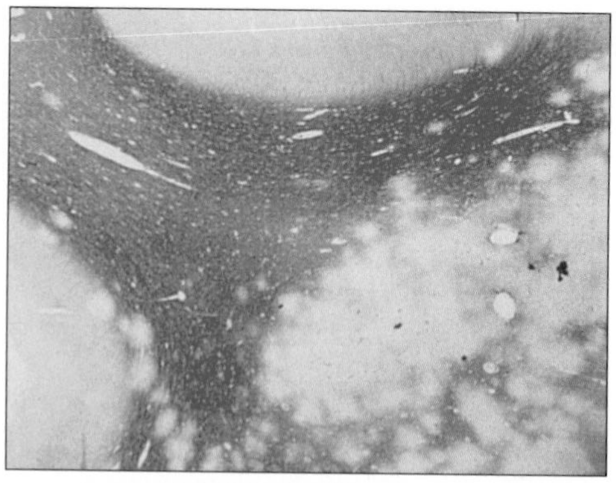

Fig. 216.6 Foci of demyelination in PML. The foci in the superior frontal gyrus are the result of PML (Luxol fast blue stain). With permission from Harrison and McArthur.[26]

CLINICAL MANIFESTATIONS

Progressive multifocal leukoencephalopathy

PML is a fatal, subacute, demyelinating disease of the CNS that occurs as a complication of conditions that impair T-cell immunity, for example HIV infection, lymphoproliferative disorders, chronic diseases and inherited immunodeficiency diseases. In addition, prolonged immunosuppressive therapy, as required for organ transplant recipients, is a risk factor for PML. Until the advent of AIDS, PML was a rare disease with onset typically in the fifth or sixth decades of life. PML cases in patients who have AIDS now outnumber PML cases in all other illnesses combined, and the age distribution of cases has shifted to lower age groups. PML was recognized as an AIDS-defining illness in 1987 and occurs in about 0.7% of patients who have AIDS.[25] Children who have inherited immunodeficiency diseases and children who have AIDS also develop PML.

PML has an insidious onset. Early signs are impairment of speech and vision and mental deterioration. Paralysis of limbs, cortical blindness and sensory impairments are common. Typically, death occurs within 3–6 months of onset. During the course of the disease, the patient is afebrile, with normal cerebrospinal fluid (CSF) and no signs of increased intracranial pressure.

The key event in the pathogenesis of PML is the infection of oligodendrocytes with JCV, which leads to the death of the infected cells. The enlarged nuclei of the oligodendrocytes are the pathognomonic lesion in PML; they contain abundant numbers of JCV viral particles. Oligodendrocytes secrete and maintain myelin; the destruction of the infected oligodendrocytes leads to the characteristic foci of demyelination of PML (Fig. 216.6).[26] The enlarged oligodendrocytes are seen at the periphery of the demyelinating lesion (Fig. 216.7). Giant bizarre astrocytes are seen within the areas of demyelination.

The multifocal nature of the PML lesions suggests that JCV reaches the CNS by the hematogenous route, probably transported by infected B cells. Alternatively, JCV seeded in the normal brain after primary infection may be reactivated by immunosuppression to cause PML. Active PML lesions contain abundant amounts of infectious JCV, JCV proteins and JCV DNA. It is likely that a rearrangement of the regulatory region of the JCV genome facilitates the growth of the virus in the CNS.[27]

Until a few years ago, diagnosis of PML required a brain biopsy but it is now possible to diagnose the disease by noninvasive techniques such as computed tomography or magnetic resonance imaging. The use of the PCR to detect JCV in CSF is still investigational.

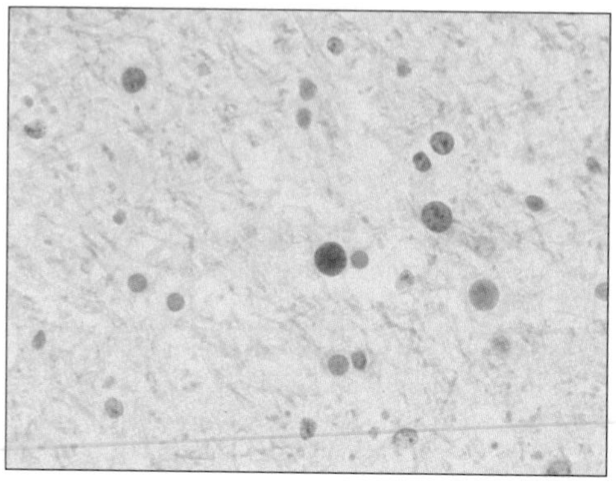

Fig. 216.7 Enlarged oligodendrocytes in PML (stained with antiviral serum). With permission from Harrison and McArthur.[26]

BKV-related diseases

BKV infection seems to be responsible for occasional cases of cystitis in healthy children and also for hemorrhagic cystitis, which is a complication of bone marrow transplantation. Atypical primary BKV infection in an immunocompromised child may cause tubulo-interstitial nephritis and irreversible renal damage.

A new syndrome, BKV nephropathy, has been recently identified in renal transplant recipients.[28,29] It may be a complication of newly introduced immunosuppressive drugs. The disease is characterized by extensive BKV multiplication in the tubular epithelium, urinary shedding of a large number of infected epithelial cells, the presence of BKV in the serum, and a loss of allograft function. An unusual tropism of BKV for endothelial cells has been described recently in a fatal case of disseminated BKV infection.[30]

MANAGEMENT

PML is almost always fatal. Nucleic acid based analogs have not been effective in the treatment of PML. For a fuller discussion on treatment options see Chapter 125. The course of disease may be slowed if it is possible to reduce iatrogenic immunosuppression (e.g. in organ transplant patients). Patients who have AIDS and PML have shown improvement with control of the HIV infection with multidrug therapy including protease inhibitors.

REFERENCES

1. deVilliers EM. Papillomavirus and HPV typing. Clin Dermatol 1997;15:199–206.
2. Castellsague X, Bosch FX, Munoz N, *et al.* Male circumcision, penile human papillomavirus infection and cervical cancer. N Engl J Med 2002;346:1105–12.
3. Jablonska S, Majewski S. Epidermodysplasia verruciformis: immunological and clinical aspects. In: zur Hausen H, ed. Human pathogenic papillomaviruses. Heidelberg: Springer Verlag; 1994:157–75.
4. Wieland U, Ritzkowsky A, Stoltidis M, *et al.* Papillomavirus DNA in basal cell carcinomas of immunocompetent patients: An accidental association? J Invest Dermatol 2000;115:124–8.
5. Meyers C, Frattini GM, Hudson JB, Laimins LA. Biosynthesis of human papillomavirus from a

continuous cell line upon epithelial differentiation. Science 1992;257:971–3.
6. Lörincz AT, Reid R, Jenson B, *et al.* Human papillomavirus infection of the cervix: relative risk associations of 15 common anogenital types. Obstet Gynecol 1992;79:328–37.
7. Bosch FX, Manos MM, Muñoz N, *et al.* Prevalence of human papillomavirus in cervical cancer: a worldwide perspective. J Natl Cancer Inst 1995;87:796–802.
8. Lowy DR, Howley PM. Papillomaviruses. In: Knipe D, Howley PM, eds. Fields virology, 4th ed., vol. 2. Philadelphia: Lippincott Williams & Wilkins, 2001:2231–64.
9. McDougal JK. Immortalization and transformation of human cells by human papillomavirus. Curr Top Microbiol Immunol 1994;186:101–19.
10. Heselmeyer K, Schröck E, du Manoir S, *et al.* Gain of chromosome 3q defines the transition from severe dysplasia to invasive carcinoma of the uterine cervix. Proc Natl Acad Sci USA 1996;93:479–84.
11. Wright TC Jr, Denny L, Kuhn L, *et al.* HPV DNA testing of self-collected vaginal samples compared with cytologic screening to detect cervical cancer. JAMA 2000;283:81–6.
12. Solomon D, Schiffman M, Tarone R, for the ALTS Group. Comparison of three management strategies for patients with atypical squamous cells of undertermined significance: baseline results from a randomized trial. J Natl Cancer Inst 2001;93:293–9.
13. Koutsky LA, Ault KA, Wheeler CM, *et al.* A controlled trial of a human papillomavirus type 16 vaccine. N Engl J Med 2002;347:1645–51.
14. Chen CH, Wang TL, Hung CF, *et al.* Enhancement of DNA vaccine potency by linkage of antigen gene to an HSP70 gene. Cancer Res 2000;60:1035–42.
15. Hildesheim A, Schiffman MH, Gravitt P, *et al.* Persistence of type-specific human papillomavirus infection among cytologically normal women in Portland, Oregon. J Infect Dis 1994;169:235–40.
16. de Roda Husman A-M, Walboomers JMM, van den Brule AJC, *et al.* The use of general primers GP5 and GP6 elongated at their 3′ ends with adjacent highly conserved sequences improves human papillomavirus detection by PCR. J Gen Virol 1994;76:1057–62.
17. Gravitt P, Peyton C, Apple R, *et al.* Genotyping of 27 human papillomavirus types using L1 consensus PCR products by a single-hybridization, reverse line blot detection method. J Clin Microbiol 1998;36:3020–7.
18. Lörincz AT. Molecular methods for the detection of human papillomavirus infection. Obstet Gynecol Clin North Am 1996;23:707–30.
19. Kirnbauer R, Hubbert NL, Wheeler CM, *et al.* A virus-like particle enzyme-linked immunosorbent assay detects serum antibodies in a majority of women infected with human papillomavirus type 16. J Natl Cancer Inst 1994;86:494–9.
20. Carter JJ, Koutsky LA, Wipf GC, *et al.* The natural history of human papillomavirus type 16 capsid antibodies among a cohort of university women. J Infect Dis 1996;174:927–36.
21. International Agency for Research on Cancer. IARC monograph on the evaluation of carcinogenic risks to humans – volume 64: Human papillomaviruses. Lyon: International Agency for Research on Cancer; 1995.
22. Skegg DCG, Corwin PA, Paul C. Importance of the male factor in cancer of the cervix. Lancet 1982;2:581–3.
23. Major EO. Human polyomavirus. In: Knipe D, Howley PM, eds. Fields virology, 4th ed., vol. 2. Philadelphia: Lippincott Williams & Wilkins, 2001:2175–96.
24. Shah KV: Does SV40 infection contribute to the development of human cancers? Rev Med Virol 2000;10:31–43.
25. Berger JR, Levy RM. The neurologic complications of human immunodeficiency virus infections. Med Clin North Am 1993;77:1–23.
26. Harrison MJG, McArthur JC. AIDS and neurology. Edinburgh: Churchill Livingstone; 1995.
27. Iida T, Kimtamura T, Guo J, *et al.* Origin of JC polyomavirus variants associated with progressive multifocal leukoencephalopathy. Proc Natl Acad Sci USA 1993;90:5062–5.
28. Nickeleit V, Hirsch HH, Zeiler M *et al.* BK-virus nephropathy in renal transplants: tubular necrosis, MHC-class II expression and rejection in a puzzling game. Nephrol Dial Transplant 2000;15:323–31.
29. Randhwa PS, Finkelstein S, Scantlebury V *et al.* Human polyoma virus-associated interstitial nephritis in the allograft kidney. Transplantation 1999;67:103–9.
30. Petrogiannis-Haliotis T, Sakoulas G, Kirby J *et al.* BK-type polyomavirus vasculopathy in a renal-transplant patient. N Engl J Med 2001;345:1250–5.

chapter

217 Parvoviruses

Stanley J Naides

NATURE

The family Parvoviridae consists of small, nonenveloped, single-stranded DNA viruses of animals. It is divided into the subfamilies Parvovirinae of vertebrates and Densovirinae of insects. Parvovirinae is further divided into three genuses: *Parvovirus*, *Erythrovirus* and *Dependovirus*. The genus *Parvovirus* consists of a number of nonhuman mammalian viruses including mice minute virus, Aleutian disease virus of mink, feline panleukopenia virus, Kilham rat virus and the bovine, porcine, canine, goose and feline parvoviruses, among others. The Erythroviruses consist of primate parvoviruses that require erythroid precursors for productive infection and notably in the case of B19, the human parvovirus, cause an erythematous rash. Dependoviruses consist of mammalian parvoviruses that require a helper virus for replication. The typical helper virus is adenovirus, hence the name adeno-associated virus (AAV). Human AAVs are candidate gene therapy vectors because they are nonpathogenic and have broad tissue tropism.

Densovirinae are viruses of insects and crustaceans; several have economic importance such as those affecting silk production.

Parvovirus B19 is the only known human pathogen. Cossart and colleagues discovered B19 serendipitously in 1974 during the development of diagnostic tests for hepatitis B virus. B19 was named after the viremic serum (number 19 in panel B) in which a new antigen was detected in Ouchterlony immunodiffusion plates.[1] In short order, the antigen was determined to be a previously unrecognized human parvovirus measuring approximately 23nm in diameter. It appeared icosahedral or spherical on electron microscopy and was non enveloped (Fig. 217.1). Molecular studies have since demonstrated that B19 has palindromic terminal repeats at both ends that are nearly identical. B19 uses a modified rolling hairpin model of replication, as do the other parvoviruses. Progeny virus is assembled in the nucleus and may be observed as intranuclear inclusions. Equal numbers of B19 positive and negative sense DNA strands are encapsidated. B19 utilizes a single strong upstream promoter from which are transcribed message for a 72 kilodalton (kDa) nonstructural protein (NS1), and 84 and 58 kDa capsid proteins (VP1 and VP2, respectively). Transcripts of the capsid proteins utilize alternate start sites, making VP1 identical to VP2 except for the addition of 227 N-terminal amino acids in VP1, often designated the unique VP1 region, uVP1. VP2 is the major capsid protein. VP1 is thought to occupy the five fold axis of symmetry of the icosahedron. Epitopes in uVP1 and adjacent regions are thought to contain the target structures for neutralizing antibodies. NS1 is a helicase and serves to reduce covalently linked monomeric (two gene copies) and dimeric (four genome copies) replicative forms to packageable progeny genome. NS1 is thought to cause transactivation of cellular genes including interleukin 6 and possibly tumor necrosis factor-α (TNF-α), virus–cell interactions that may be important in pathogenesis. Several smaller viral proteins detected during replication have unknown function. Although the B19 genome is generally highly conserved, a variant of unknown significance, designated V9, has been described.[2]

EPIDEMIOLOGY

B19 is found worldwide. It occurs as both sporadic cases and in recurrent epidemics. Transmission is via nasopharyngeal secretions, explaining the frequency of outbreaks in the late winter and spring. Occurrence in susceptible cohorts of school-aged children may also contribute to outbreaks during the school year. However, outbreaks have also been described in summer and fall. Populations of children acquire B19 antibodies in an age-dependent fashion, beginning with entry into schools. Epidemics tend to occur in 3–5-year cycles, the time required for the generation of a susceptible school cohort. Approximately 50% of adults are anti-B19 lgG seropositive, indicating past infection. Illness in susceptible individuals occurs after an incubation period of 7–18 days.[2] lgG antibody is considered protective. B19 is not removed from blood by current solvent detergent-based methods of blood decontamination and therefore pooled blood products may contain infectious B19.[3]

PATHOGENICITY

B19 is typically transmitted through nasopharyngeal secretions. Following an incubation period of 7 days in experimental infections, a brisk viremia of 10^{11} or more viral particles/ml blood occurs. Viral replication causes maturation arrest at the giant pronormoblast stage of erythroid development, likely through viral induction of apoptosis. Nonerythroid lineages may be affected as well, although they are less efficient in supporting B19 replication. In individuals with shortened erythrocyte survival, as in those with inherited or acquired hemolytic anemias, the period of areticulocytosis is associated with severe anemia. On approximately day 11 post infection, specific lgM antibody appears, followed shortly after by anti-B19 lgG.[4] Initially, lgG is directed against VP2 but after 1 week anti-VP1 lgG antibody appears. Failure to produce anti-VP1 lgG results in persistent or recurrent viremia and chronic or recurrent bone marrow suppression.[5]

Two clinical phases of illness are described in experimental infection, but these may overlap in natural infections. In the first phase, fever, malaise and myalgia may occur during the viremia. Areticulocytosis, leukopenia and thrombocytopenia may occur. In the second phase, the appearance of anti-B19 lgM is associated with rash (Fig. 217.2), arthralgia and frank arthritis.[4] In the pregnant susceptible woman, B19 may cross the placenta to cause erythroid maturation arrest, anemia and a high-output congestive heart failure characterized as hydrops fetalis. B19 viral myocarditis as a cause of fetal hydrops has been described.[2]

PREVENTION

Infection control measures include secretion precautions during periods of viremia; some institutions require respiratory precautions. Patients should be considered infectious from 7 days post exposure until either 18 days post exposure or 24 hours after onset of rash or

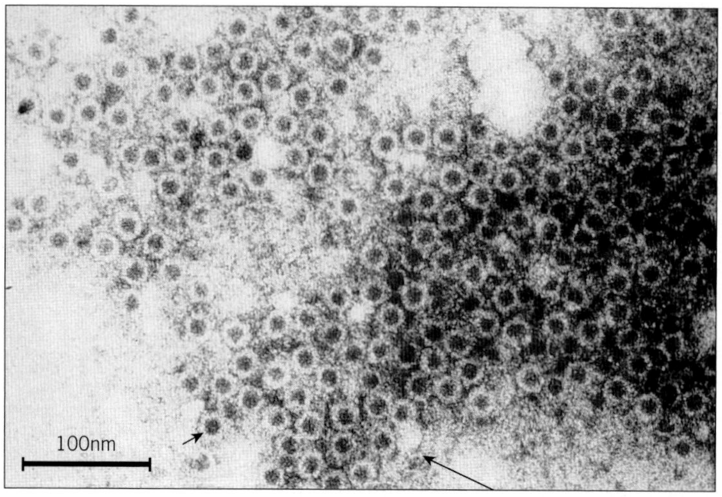

Fig. 217.1 Electron micrograph of parvovirus B19 particles showing both full particles (short arrow) and empty capsids (long arrow).

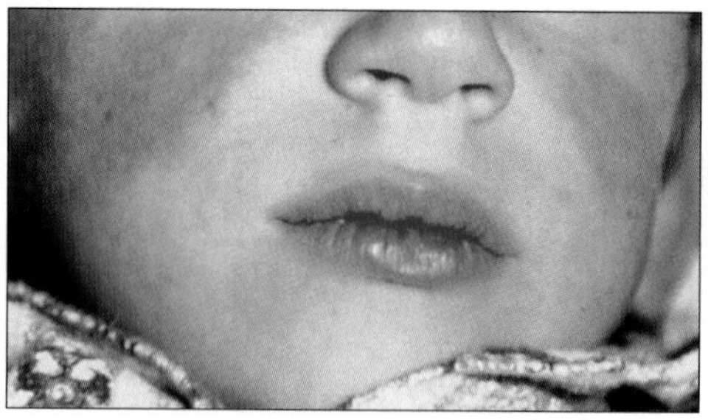

Fig. 217.3 Classic 'slapped cheeks' of a child with erythema infectiosum, or fifth disease, caused by parvovirus B19. A lacy macular erythematous eruption is also present on the trunk but not shown. Courtesy of Dr K Motton.

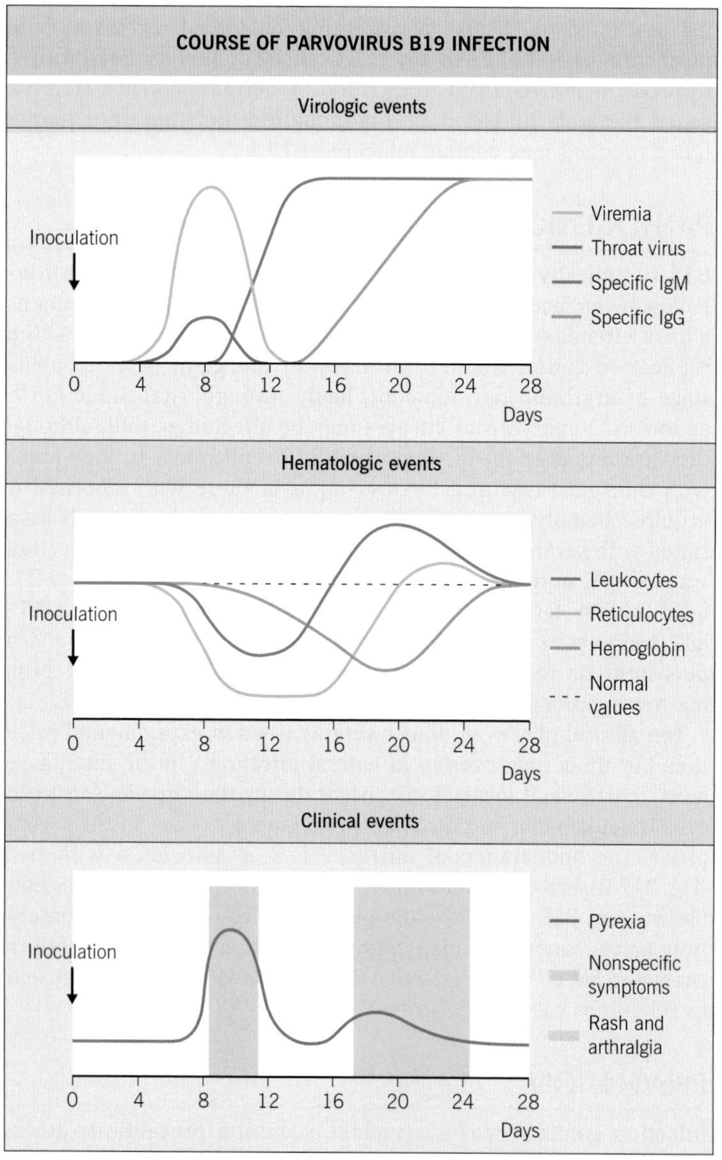

Fig. 217.2 Course of parvovirus B19 infection. Volunteers were inoculated nasally with viremic serum and virologic, hematologic and clinical events observed.

arthritis.[6] Immunocompromised individuals with chronic B19 infection tend to have low-titer viremia and are of low infection risk to others. The utility of excusing pregnant workers with frequent exposure to children from work responsibilities during an outbreak is controversial. While a susceptible teacher, for example in a class with five or more children with B19 rash, has a 50% risk of infection,[7] absence from the workplace does not prevent exposure at home or in the community. Secretion precautions and handwashing in the childcare setting remain prudent.

DIAGNOSTIC MICROBIOLOGY

Detection of viremia by immune electron microscopy, DNA hybridization or polymerase chain reaction-based methodologies is diagnostic of B19 infection. Detection of anti-B19 lgM in the setting of acute onset of consistent symptoms is likewise diagnostic (Fig. 217.3). As B19 is not readily grown in tissue culture, viremic serum or recombinant capsid proteins have been used as antigen. The presence of anti-B19 lgG is diagnostically useful only when acute and convalescent samples demonstrate seroconversion. Anti-B19 lgM is usually undetectable by 2 months after infection. Immunocompromised individuals such as those with HIV may have chronic or recurrent viremia followed by poor lgM or lgG responses.[2] Finding B19 DNA in tissues of immunocompetent patients is of questionable diagnostic significance because B19 DNA has been found in about 50% of healthy military recruits in Finland undergoing arthroscopy for joint injury.[8]

CLINICAL MANIFESTATIONS

B19 may cause asymptomatic infections. As many as 70% of childhood infections may be asymptomatic. Individuals with chronic hemolytic anemia, such as sickle cell disease or hereditary spherocytosis, develop transient aplastic crisis during the areticulocytosis phase of the infection. The most common presentation in children is the childhood exanthema erythema infectiosus, or fifth disease, characterized by bright red 'slapped cheek' macular or maculopapular rash. The eruption spreads from the trunk to the extremities in a centrifugal progression, often appearing blotchy or fishnet-like. Activity, heat or sun exposure exacerbates the rash. Headache, fever, cough, sore throat, anorexia, vomiting or diarrhea may occur but is usually mild. Rarely, children have joint symptoms.[2] Adults tend to have either no rash or a subtle one, but a sudden onset, symmetric rheumatoid-like polyarthritis may occur and may be accompanied by a more severe flu-like illness than seen in children. Joint symptoms usually improve within 2 weeks, but in some adults may persist for months to years and are associated with persistent or episodic morning stiffness and arthralgias.[9] In pregnant women the unborn child may develop hydrops fetalis. Immunocompromised individuals may develop chronic or recurrent episodes of anemia, leukopenia or thrombocytopenia. Rarely, isolated anemia, leukopenia or thrombocytopenia may occur in an immunocompetent patient. Hepatitis, acute fulminant liver failure, myocarditis, vasculitis, Henoch–Schönlein purpura, vesicular skin eruptions, 'socks and gloves' acral rash, purpura with or without thrombocytopenia, benign acute lymphadenopathy, hemophagocytic syndrome, peripheral neuropathy, sensorineural hearing loss, aseptic meningitis and rarely encephalopathy have all been described in association with B19 infection. B19 is the leading cause of pure red cell aplasia in AIDS patients.[2]

MANAGEMENT

Therapy for B19 infection is supportive in most clinical presentations. In immunocompromised patients with persistent B19 infection and chronic or recurrent bone marrow suppression because of failure to make neutralizing anti-VP1 antibody, intravenous immunoglobulin may allow clearing of apparent infection and resolution of bone marrow suppression.[5] Patients with transient aplastic crisis may require transfusion support. Likewise, fetal hydrops may require intrauterine transfusion for anemia. B19 is not considered a cause of congenital anomalies.

REFERENCES

1. Cossart YE, Field AM, Cant B, *et al.* Parvovirus-like particles in human sera. Lancet 1975;1:72–3.
2. Naides SJ. Parvoviruses. In: Specter S, Hodinka RL, Young SA, eds. Clinical virology manual. New York: Elsevier; 2000:487–500.
3. Prowse C, Ludlam CA, Yap PL. Human parvovirus B19 and blood products. Vox Sang 1997;72:1–10.
4. Anderson MJ, Higgins PG, Davis LR, *et al.* Experimental parvoviral infection in humans. J Infect Dis 1985;152:257–65.
5. Kurtzman GJ, Cohen BJ, Field AM, *et al.* Immune response to B19 parvovirus and an antibody defect in persistent viral infection. J Clin Invest 1989;84:1114–23.
6. Naides SJ. Infection control measures for human parvovirus B19 in the hospital setting. Infect Control Hosp Epidemiol 1989;10:326–9.
7. Gillespie SM, Cartter ML, Asch S, *et al.* Occupational risk of human parvovirus B19 infection for school and day-care personnel during an outbreak of erythema infectiosum. JAMA 1990;263:2061–5.
8. Soderlund-Venermo M, Hokynar K, Nieminen J, *et al.* Persistence of human parvovirus B19 in human tissues. Pathologie-Biologie (Paris) 2002;50:307–16.
9. Naides SJ, Scharosch LL, Foto F, *et al.* Rheumatologic manifestations of human parvovirus B19 infection in adults. Initial two-year clinical experience. Arthritis Rheum 1990;33:1297–309.

chapter

218 Poxviruses

R Mark L Buller

NATURE

Virion morphology, structure and biochemistry

Poxviruses are the largest of all animal viruses and can be visualized under the light microscope, although the details of the virion structure remain obscure. Using negative-staining electron microscopy and/or cryoelectron microscopy, parapoxvirus virions appear ovoid with long and short axes of approximately 260 and 160nm, respectively, whereas all other poxviruses are 'brick'-shaped, with dimensions of 350 by 250nm on average. In clinical specimens two forms of virion have been identified: the intact 'M' (mulberry; Fig. 218.1) form is found mainly in the vesicular fluid, and the 'C' (capsule) form, which appears to be a degenerative 'M' form, is associated with dried scabs.

Electron micrographs of thin sections of poxvirus-infected tissue culture cells have revealed at least three infectious forms of the virion; intracellular mature virions, extracellular enveloped virions and occluded virus in A-type inclusion body.[1]

It has been proposed that the intracellular mature virions form from the membrane structures of the intermediate compartment, and can acquire an additional two membranes from the Golgi, one of which is lost on egress at the plasma membrane. These extracellular enveloped virions are thought to be most important in cell-to-cell spread and systemic disease. In certain poxvirus species the intracellular mature virion can also occlude in a dense protein matrix within the cytoplasm to form an acidophilic inclusion body (A-type inclusion or Downie body), which is thought to protect the virion from the environment.[2] All vertebrate poxviruses have cytoplasmic basophilic (B-type) inclusion bodies, which represent areas of the infected cells that contain large amounts of virus DNA and protein.

Depending on the poxvirus, the genome can range from 130kbp for the parapoxviruses to 300kbp for the avipoxviruses, which is sufficient to encode more than 140 proteins. A schematic intracellular replication cycle based on the poxvirus vaccinia is presented in Figure 218.2 and described in more detail by Moss.[1] The poxvirus virion is notoriously stable in the environment, and this stability is increased by its association with the A-type inclusion bodies or scab material. Thus for poxviruses, fomites must be considered in disease transmission.

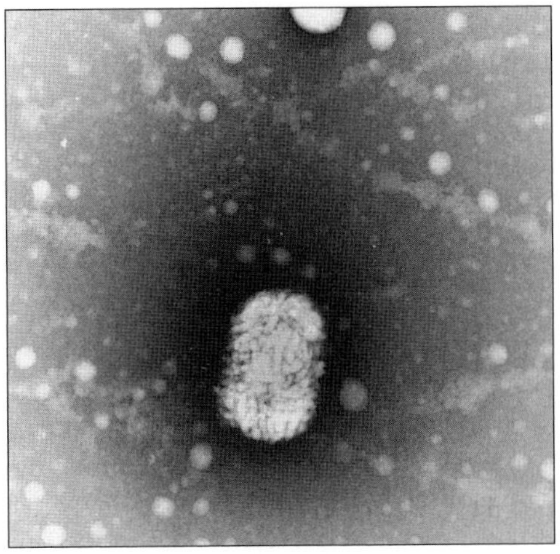

Fig. 218.1 A negative-stained M form of molluscum contagiosum virus. Molluscum contagiosum virus from lesion material.

Poxviruses pathogenic for humans

Ten poxviruses infect humans (Table 218.1).[2] Except for the 'extinct' variola virus and the increasingly important molluscum contagiosum virus, the poxvirus diseases are zoonoses. With rare exception these zoonotic poxviruses fail to establish a human chain of transmission. Most human poxvirus infections occur through minor abrasions in the skin. Orf, molluscum contagiosum, and monkeypox viruses cause the most frequent poxvirus infections worldwide; the incidence of molluscum contagiosum and monkeypox virus infections is on the rise, the former as an opportunistic infection in late-stage AIDS and the latter as a zoonotic infection in cental Africa. Individuals with atopic dermatitis may be predisposed to poxvirus infections such as molluscum contagiosum, orf or cowpox.

PREVENTION

Because most poxvirus infections are rare zoonoses or, as in molluscum contagiosum virus, cause only superficial, 'nuisance' skin lesions in immunocompetent individuals, there are no recommended prevention strategies other than education of patients and various types of workers as to how the diseases are spread.

MOLLUSCUM CONTAGIOSUM VIRUS

EPIDEMIOLOGY

Geographic range

Molluscum contagiosum virus has a worldwide distribution. Restriction endonuclease analysis of genomic DNA from molluscum contagiosum virus isolates has revealed the existence of at least four virus subtypes or strains, and one recent study suggests the distribution of subtypes can vary geographically.[3]

Prevalence and incidence

For nonsexually transmitted molluscum contagiosum, the disease is more prevalent in the tropics than in Europe. For example, molluscum contagiosum was diagnosed in 1.2% of outpatients in Aberdeen, UK between 1956 and 1963, the mean age of infection was between 10 and 12 years and spread within households and schools was infrequent. On the other hand, in Fiji in 1966, 4.5% of an entire village had the disease, mean age of infection was between 2 and 3 years and 25% of households harbored more than one case.[4,5] Prevalence of infection in New Guinea was greater than 50% in many villages. In England between 1971 and 1985 there was a 400% increase in cases of genital molluscum contagiosum; the majority of patients were aged 15–24 years, with affected women

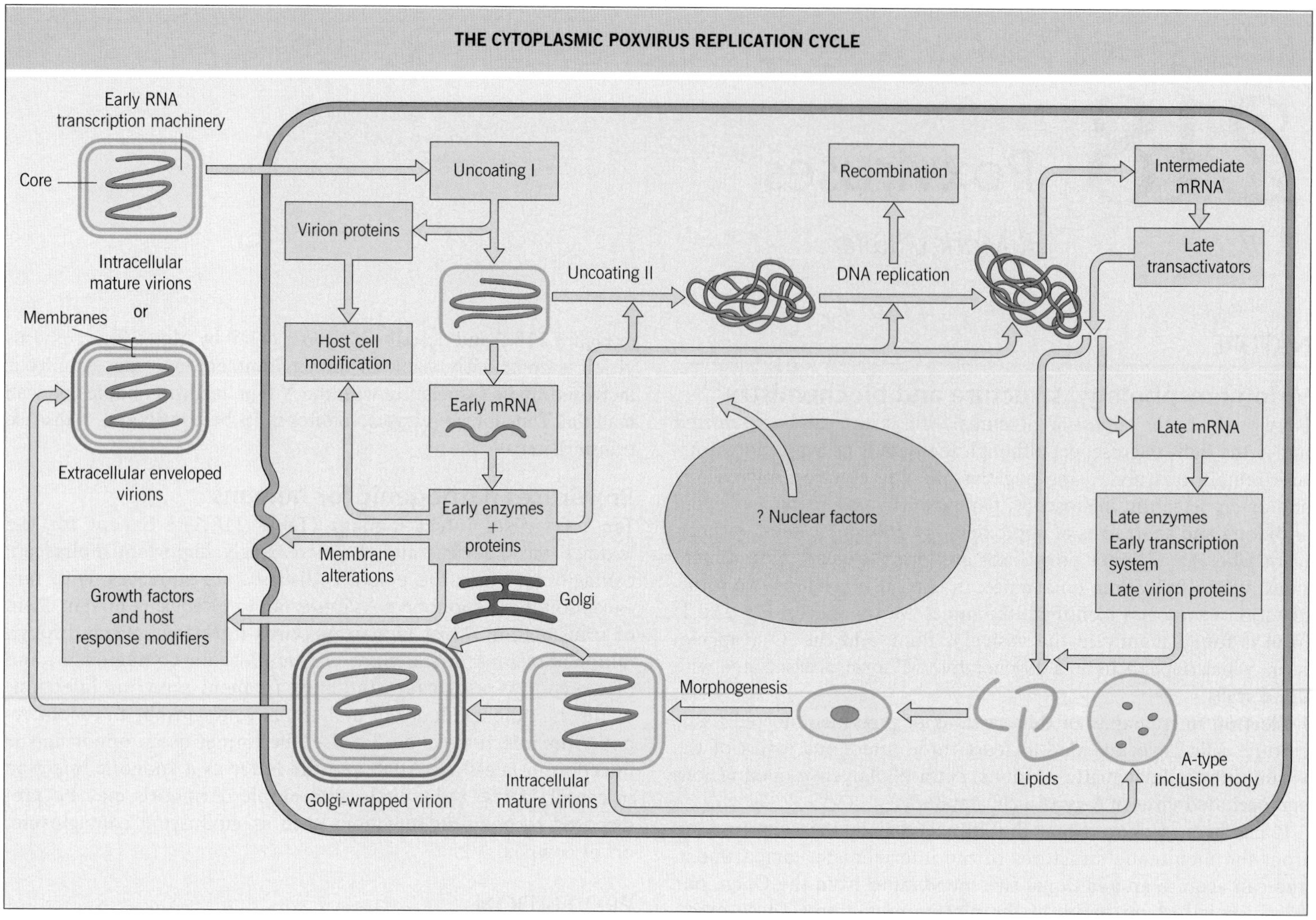

Fig. 218.2 The cytoplasmic poxvirus replication cycle. Poxvirus virions containing early RNA transcription machinery attach to, and fuse with, the plasma membrane (uncoating I). Early genes are expressed that code for a variety of functions that modify the host cell for optimal virus replication, attentuate the host response to infection and mediate virus synthetic processes. After further uncoating (II), the virus genome is replicated via concatamers, late transcription factors are expressed from intermediate genes and late gene RNA is synthesized. Late genes encode the early transcription system, enzymes and structural proteins necessary for virion assembly, which commences with the formation of membrane structures in the intermediate compartment and the packaging of resolved unit length genomic DNA. The intracellular mature virion has two membranes derived from the intermediate compartment. It may remain in the cytoplasm or (in certain virus species) become occluded in an A-type inclusion body or become wrapped by a further two membranes in the Golgi and exported from the cell with the loss of one membrane (extracellular enveloped virions). The extracellular enveloped virions are thought to be most important in cell-to-cell spread and systemic disease. This replication scheme is based on the study of the prototypic poxvirus vaccinia.[1] Other poxvirus species probably vary from this model mainly in the types of growth factors and host response modifiers encoded by the virus and the amounts of extracellular enveloped virions produced. Adapted from Moss.[1]

being younger than affected men.[5] In the USA between 1966 and 1983 there was a ten-fold increase in cases in patients aged 25–29 years.[5] Molluscum contagiosum is a common and sometimes severely disfiguring opportunistic infection of between 5 and 18% of patients with HIV infection, especially those with severely depressed $CD4^+$ T cell numbers.[6]

Pathogenicity

Transmission

Molluscum contagiosum is observed in children and adults, with spread within this latter group governed in part by sexual practices. Nonsexual transmission is a consequence of infection by direct contact or through fomites. Case histories have suggested transmission from surgeons' fingers, swimming pools, bath towels in gymnasia, contact between wrestlers and as a result of tattooing.[4] Transmission between persons in the absence of fomites requires fairly close contact. Lesions can be commonly observed on opposing surfaces and the virus can be further spread on the person by autoinoculation.

Lesion histopathology

Molluscum contagiosum virus has one of the narrowest cell tropisms of any virus, replicating only in the human keratinocyte of the epidermis.[7] As the virus-infected cell approaches the surface of the skin, the accumulation of progeny virions in a granular matrix in the cytoplasm forces the cell organelles, including the nucleus, to the periphery of the cell. Under light microscopy these cells stain as hyaline acidophilic masses, are referred to as molluscum or Henderson–Patterson bodies and are pathognomonic for disease. The higher magnification of a molluscum body reveals it to be entirely filled with virions, partial virions and debris (Fig. 218.3).

CLINICAL MANIFESTATIONS

Signs, symptoms and severity

Molluscum contagiosum manifests as small clusters of lesions in immunocompetent individuals. The lesions are generally painless; they appear on the trunk and limbs (rarely palms and soles) in the

Table 218.1 **Poxviruses pathogenic for humans.** Presented by genus in order of importance for human disease. Alternative hosts are given in parentheses. Adapted from Fenner.[2]

POXVIRUSES PATHOGENIC FOR HUMANS			
Genus/Species	**Hosts**	**Geographic distribution**	**Disease**
Molluscipoxvirus Molluscum contagiosum virus	Humans*	Worldwide	Molluscum contagiosum, single or multiple skin nodules
Parapoxvirus Orf virus (contagious pustular dermatitis virus or contagious ecthyma virus)	Sheep*, goats, dogs, bighorn sheep, thinhorn sheep, Rocky Mountain goat, chamois, reindeer, musk-ox, Himalayan tahr, Steenbok, alpaca	Worldwide	Orf, localized skin lesions
Pseudocowpox virus (milkers' nodule or paravaccinia)	European cattle*	Worldwide	Milkers' nodules, localized skin lesions
Bovine papular stomatitis virus	European cattle*	Worldwide	Localized skin lesions
Orthopoxvirus Cowpox virus	Rodents*, cats, cows, zoo animals	Europe, western Asia	Cowpox, localized pustular lesions
Monkeypox virus	Squirrels*, monkeys	Western and central Africa	Monkeypox, rash, generalized disease
Vaccinia virus	Natural host unknown (buffalo† and cattle)	Asia, India, Brazil and laboratory	Buffalopox, localized pustular lesions
Variola virus	Eradicated from humans in 1977	Was worldwide	Smallpox, rash, generalized disease
Yatapoxvirus Tanapoxvirus	Monkeys? Rodents?	Eastern and central Africa	Tanapox, localized nodular skin lesion
Yaba monkey tumor poxvirus	Monkeys?	Western Africa	Localized nodular skin lesions

* Natural reservoir. † During the smallpox eradication program, water buffalo in India and cattle in Brazil were infected with the local vaccine strain of vaccinia virus, which apparently persists in these animals and occasionally infects humans. ? Putative host.

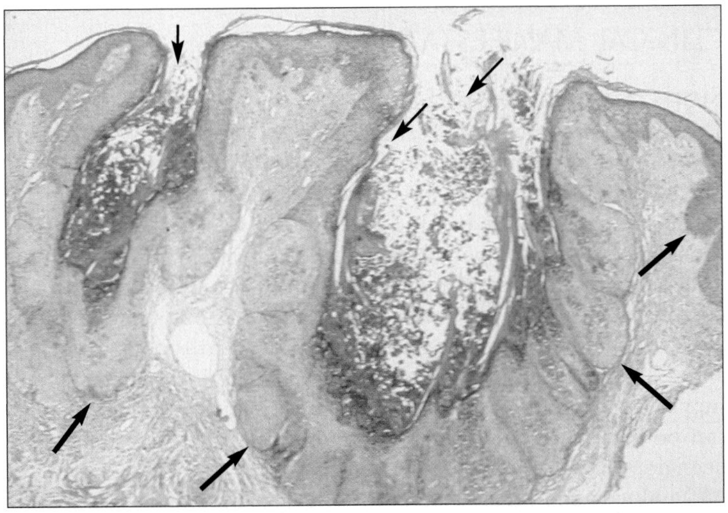

Fig. 218.3 Molluscum contagiosum lesion. In this lesion a major and minor umbilicus has formed as a result of the hypertrophy of infected cells and hyperplasia of the basal cells, which caused a severe invagination of the epidermis but no loss of integrity of the basement membrane. The molluscum bodies stain as pink to purple acidophilic hyaline masses up to 37 x 27μm in size. Small arrows: molluscum bodies. Large arrows: epidermis–dermis boundary. (H & E.)

nonsexually transmitted disease. In children, the virus can also be fairly common in the skin of the eyelids, with solitary or multiple lesions, and can be complicated by chronic follicular conjunctivitis and later by a superficial punctate keratitis.[8] There may be an associated erythema 1–11 months after the appearance of the lesion, with no correlation to a history of allergy or eczema.[9] Lesions can persist for as little as 2 weeks or as long as 2 years. Re-infections can be common. As a sexually transmitted disease in teenagers and adults, the lesions are mostly on the lower abdominal wall, pubis, inner thighs and genitalia. As yet there is no solid correlation of virion DNA type with specific pathology or location of lesions (i.e. genital versus nongenital).[10]

In immunocompromised individuals (especially those with HIV infection), the infection is not self-limiting, with more frequent and larger lesions present especially on the face, neck, scalp and upper body. Multiple adjacent lesions sometimes become confluent. Molluscum contagiosum can be considered a cutaneous marker of severe immunodeficiency.

Gross lesion pathology

In immunocompetent patients, molluscum contagiosum virus lesions are epidermal, flesh-colored, raised nodules of 2–5mm in diameter. Occasionally the gross lesions may have a hypopigmented or erythematous halo. Rarely they will present as a large lesion called giant molluscum (>5mm in diameter). Both of these types of lesions usually have an umbilicated center (Fig. 218.4). Although giant molluscum lesions have been reported frequently in severely immunodeficient individuals with HIV infection, they were observed in New Guinea before the introduction of HIV, and therefore may not be a consequence of immunodeficiency.[6,11]

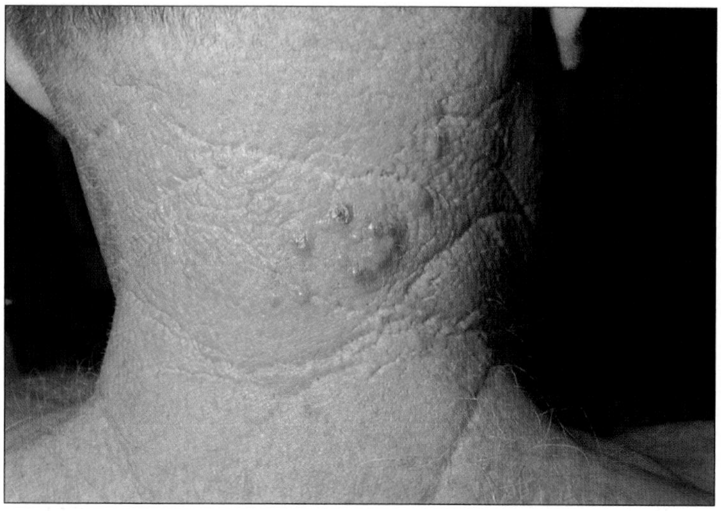

Fig. 218.4 Molluscum contagiosum lesions. These are the more typical, but still large, lesions of molluscum contagiosum. Courtesy of J Burnett.

DIAGNOSIS AND DIFFERENTIAL DIAGNOSIS

The diagnosis is usually made clinically based on the gross appearance of the lesions and their chronic nature. Confirmation is easily obtained through the detection of molluscum bodies by hematoxylin and eosin staining of a biopsy or a squash preparation of expressed material from the lesion.

Molluscum contagiosum (especially giant molluscum) can be confused with a number of other disorders such as keratoacanthoma, warty dyskeratoma, syringomas, hidrocystomas, basal cell epithelioma, trichoepithelioma, ectopic hyperplastic sebaceous glands or giant condylomata acuminata, chalazion, sebaceous cysts, verrucas, milia, lid abscess or granuloma on eyelids.[12–14] In immunodeficient patients, disseminated cutaneous cryptococcosis and cutaneous histoplasmosis can resemble typical molluscum contagiosum.[11,12] An inflamed molluscum lesion without the association of typical lesions can be mistaken for a bacterial infection.

PARAPOXVIRUSES

The parapoxviruses orf, bovine stomatitis and pseudocowpox generally cause occupational infections of humans, with orf infections being the most common. Because of the clinical similarity of the diseases caused by these agents, they have been referred to collectively as 'farmyard-pox' diseases. No human-to-human transmission of parapoxvirus infections has been reported.

EPIDEMIOLOGY

Geographic range

Orf in sheep and goat populations has been reported in Canada, the USA, Europe, Japan, New Zealand and Africa. Pseudocowpox virus and bovine papular stomatitis virus are both maintained in European-derived dairy herds in all parts of the world.

Prevalence and incidence

In a 1-year New Zealand study 500 meat workers out of a population of 20,000 at risk were infected with orf; those involved in the initial stunning, killing and hanging of the sheep had the highest risk (4%) of infection.[15] Serologic surveys of orf-infected sheep and goat herds yielded orf antibody prevalences of up to 90%. The high seroprevalence of orf antibody in herds is likely attributable to the highly stable nature of the orf virion, which contaminates the pasture.

Pseudocowpox virus and bovine papular stomatitis are probably endemic in all European-derived dairy herds.

PATHOGENICITY

Transmission

Direct transmission of orf virus has been observed as a consequence of bottle-feeding lambs, from animal bites to the hand and contact with sheep and goat products during slaughter. Fomites such as splinters, barbed wire or farmyard surfaces, including soil, feeding troughs or barn beams, have been implicated as sources of virus.

Pseudocowpox virus from lesions on teats of cows is a major source of virus for milkers' nodule of the hand.

Bovine papular stomatitis virus infection of humans occurs generally from lesions confined to the mouth, tongue, lips or nares and occasionally from the teats of infected cattle.

Lesion histopathology

Epidermis

The most striking change in the epidermis is hyperplasia in which strands of epidermal keratinocytes penetrate the dermis.[16] Generally, a mild to moderate degree of acanthosis is detected, and parakeratosis is a common feature. Cytoplasmic vacuolation, nuclear vacuolation and deeply eosinophilic, homogeneous cytoplasmic inclusion bodies often surrounded by a pale halo are also characteristic of the infection. An intense infiltrate of lymphocytes, polymorphs or eosinophils frequently involves the epidermis.

Dermis

A dense, predominantly lymphohistiocytic inflammatory cell infiltrate is present in all cases with marked edema. The most striking feature of the dermis is the massive capillary proliferation and dilatation.

CLINICAL MANIFESTATIONS

Signs, symptoms and severity

The clinical presentation of orf is usually 3–4 weeks after infection. The disease involves the appearance of single or multiple nodules (diameters of 6–27mm),[16] which are sometimes painful, usually on the hands and, less frequently, on the head or neck. Orf infection can also be associated with a low-grade fever, swelling of the lymph nodes and/or erythema multiforme bullosum. Resolution of the disease occurs over 4–6 weeks, usually without complication; however, autoinoculations of the eye can lead to serious sequelae, and enlarged lesions can arise in humans suffering from immunosuppressive conditions, burns or atopic dermatitis.[17] Lesion healing can be complicated by bullous pemphigoid.[18] Re-infections have been documented.[15]

Pseudocowpox virus lesions usually appear on the hands and are relatively painless, but may itch. The draining lymph node may be enlarged. The nodules are gradually absorbed and disappear in 4–6 weeks.[19]

In bovine papular stomatitis, lesions occur on the hands, diminish after 14 days and are no longer evident 3–4 weeks after onset.[20]

Gross lesion pathology

The orf lesion characteristically goes through a maculopapular target stage in which a red center is surrounded by a white ring of cells which is surrounded by a red halo of inflammation (approximately 1–2 weeks after infection; Fig. 218.5); however, patients usually

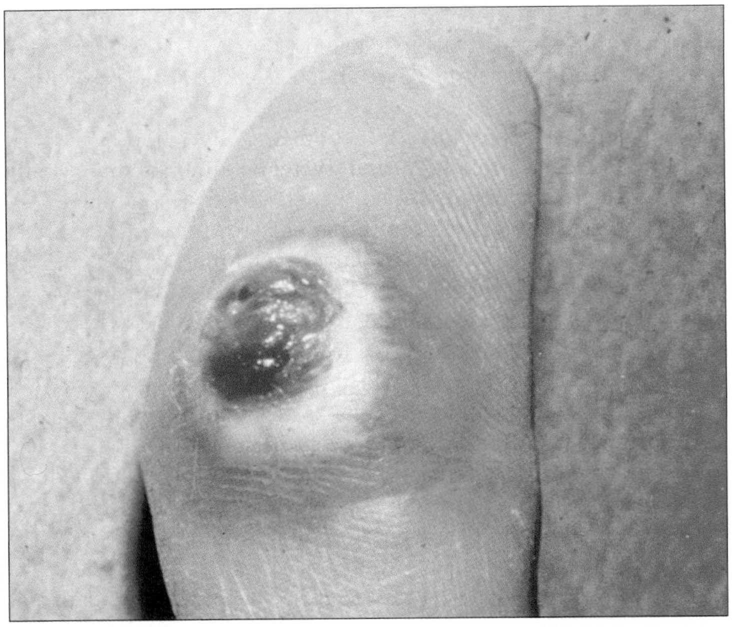

Fig. 218.5 A typical orf lesion at the target stage of development.
Courtesy of Andrew Mercer.

present later when the lesion is at the granulomatous or papillomatous stages.[17]

In pseudocowpox virus infection, milkers' nodules are first observed as round cherry-red papules; these develop into purple, smooth nodules of up to 2cm in diameter and may be umbilicated. The lesions rarely ulcerate.[19]

The lesions of bovine papular stomatitis appear as circumscribed wart-like nodules that gradually enlarge until they are 3–8mm in diameter.[20]

DIAGNOSIS AND DIFFERENTIAL DIAGNOSIS

Parapoxvirus disease diagnosis is by clinical (lesion morphology) and epidemiologic evidence (recent contact with cattle or sheep) and electron microscopy of negative-stained lesion material (presence of ovoid particles).[16]

Without knowing the animal source of the infection, orf cannot easily be differentiated from milkers' nodule on the basis of clinical finding, histology or electron microscopy (i.e. disease acquired from sheep is orf and from cattle is milkers' nodule or possibly bovine papular stomatitis).[16] Atypical giant orf lesions in patients who are immunocompromised or suffering from burns or atopic dermatitis may be confused with pyogenic granuloma.[17,21] Orf can be misdiagnosed as pyogenic granuloma or inflammatory vascular neoplasms.

ORTHOPOXVIRUSES

Although four orthopoxviruses have been shown to cause disease in humans, only two still cause significant human infections. With the global eradication of the disease smallpox in 1977, the causative agent variola virus no longer circulates in human populations, but there is concern that it may be used as a biologic weapon by terrorist groups or rogue nations (see Chapter 6).[22]

In nature, vaccinia virus infections are limited to exposure to a vaccinia-like virus infecting milking buffalos and dairy cattle in Asia and Africa (called buffalopox) and cattle in Brazil (Cantagalo virus). Vaccinia virus (smallpox vaccine) is used also in the immunization of personnel in the laboratory, but is not recommended at this time for the general population due to the occurrence of frequent and sometimes severe complications.[22] Currently only monkeypox and cowpox viruses cause significant human infections, and the incidence of human monkeypox is increasing.

EPIDEMIOLOGY

Geographic range

Monkeypox virus is found in the tropical rain forests of countries in western and central Africa, most notably Zaire. The reservoir of monkeypox virus in nature is most likely the African arboreal squirrels (*Funisciurus* and *Heliosciurus* spp.) and perhaps monkeys.[23] Cowpox virus is endemic in Europe and some western states of the former Soviet Union. Rodents (voles, wood mice and rats) have been implicated as reservoirs of cowpox virus; cows, zoo animals and cats are incidental hosts.[24]

Prevalence and incidence

Intensive surveillance between 1981 and 1986 in Zaire by the World Health Organization confirmed 338 cases of human monkeypox, with the greatest risk of infection to inhabitants of small villages within 100m of tropical rain forests.[25] In recent years there has been an increase in the frequency of human monkeypox in central Africa perhaps due in part to the cessation of vaccination for smallpox.[26]

Although humans have been infected by cows and rodents, the domestic cat is responsible for the majority of human cowpox infections. Between 1969 and 1993 there were approximately 45 human cowpox cases in the UK, three published case histories from Germany and two each from Belgium, Sweden and France.[24]

PATHOGENICITY

Transmission

The exact mode of transmission of monkeypox virus from an animal source to humans is not known but may be via the oropharynx or nasopharynx or through abrasions of the skin or oral cavity. Person-to-person transmission (like eradicated smallpox) is believed to be by the upper respiratory tract, with virus released in oropharyngeal secretions of patients who have a rash.[25] Unlike smallpox, monkeypox person-to-person transmission is very inefficient and rarely surpasses three generations.[25]

Cowpox virus is acquired usually by direct introduction of the virus from an animal source into minor abrasions in the skin; however, 30% of infections show no known risk factor.[24]

Lesion histopathology

Orthopoxvirus lesions are characterized by epidermal hyperplasia, with infected cells becoming swollen, vacuolated and undergoing 'ballooning degeneration'.[24]

CLINICAL MANIFESTATIONS

Signs, symptoms and severity

Approximately 12 days after infection with monkeypox virus, fever and headache occur. This is followed 1–3 days later by a rash and generalized lymphadenopathy. The rash (the number of lesions is variable) appears first on the face and generally has a centrifugal distribution. The illness lasts 2–4 weeks, depending on its severity. The case fatality rate is approximately 12%.[25]

With cowpox virus infection, a lesion, usually solitary, appears on the hands or face; this can be extremely painful, and the patient can present with systemic symptoms, including pyrexia, malaise, lethargy, sore throat and local lymphadenopathy. Complete recovery

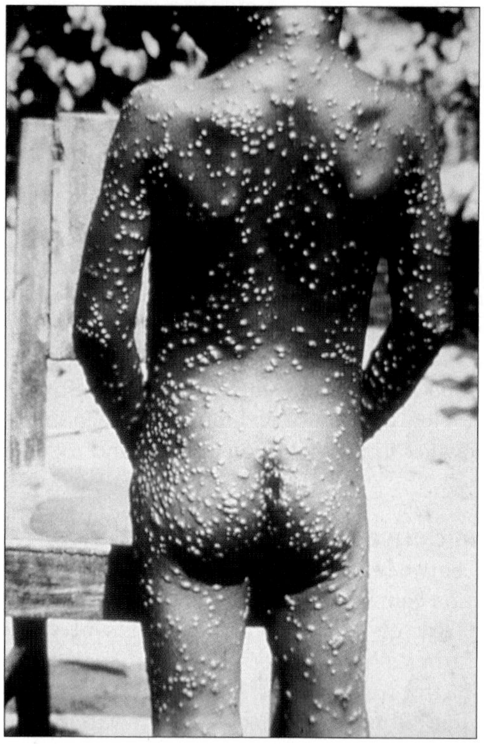

Fig. 218.6 Monkeypox rash. A 7-year-old Zairian girl, 2 days after the onset of the rash. Courtesy of M Szczeniowski.

takes between 3 and 8 weeks. Person-to-person transmission has not been reported. Complications can include ocular or generalized infections; the latter occurs in patients who have atopic dermatitis, allergic asthma or atopic eczema and in one case was associated with death.[24]

Gross lesion pathology

The monkeypox virus skin lesions begin as macules but rapidly progress to pustules. About 8 or 9 days after the onset of rash the pustules become umbilicated and dry up; by 14–16 days after the onset of the rash a crust has formed. Most skin lesions are about 0.5cm in diameter (Fig. 218.6).[25]

The cowpox lesion appears as an inflamed macule, progresses through an increasingly hemorrhagic vesicle stage to a pustule that ulcerates and crusts over by the end of the second week to become a deep-seated, hard black eschar 1–3cm in diameter (Fig. 218.7).[24]

DIAGNOSIS AND DIFFERENTIAL DIAGNOSIS

The diagnosis of monkeypox infection requires clinical (rash), epidemiologic (equatorial Africa) and laboratory (brick-shaped virion in scab material) findings. Although the rash with associated lymphadenopathy is usually pathognomonic, the sporadic nature of the disease makes it difficult to arrive at an accurate diagnosis solely on clinical grounds.[25]

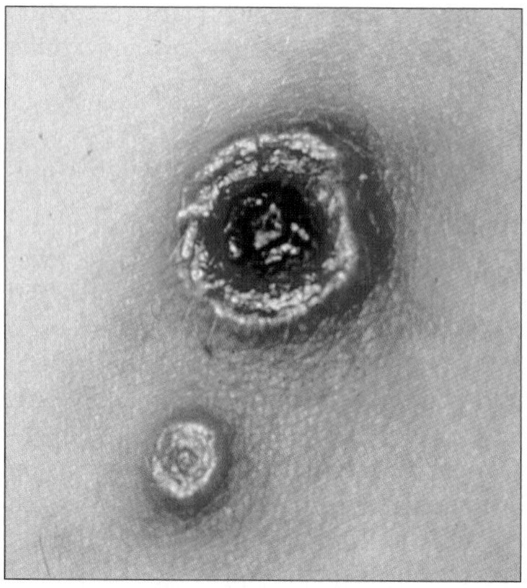

Fig. 218.7 Primary and secondary lesions of cowpox. The primary lesion is at the early eschar stage (probably 2–3 weeks after infection), whereas the secondary lesion (below) is at the early vesicular stage. With permission from Baxby *et al.*[24]

Diagnosis of cowpox virus infection is rarely made on clinical findings (lesion morphology and systemic illness) and usually requires laboratory results (brick-shaped virion in scab material). Cowpox should be considered in patients who have had contact with cats and who present in July to October with a painful hemorrhagic vesicle or black eschar, with or without erythema, accompanied by lymphadenopathy and a systemic illness.[24]

Monkeypox can be confused with a number of other conditions that result in a rash:

- chickenpox, although its varicella-zoster lesions are more superficial, appear in crops and have a centripetal distribution;
- tanapox, except the tanapox lesions evolve slowly, are nodular and large, without pustulation; and
- syphilis, although the secondary rash of syphilis does not evolve past the papular stage.[25]

Generalized cowpox can be misdiagnosed as eczema herpeticum, whereas localized cowpox is most frequently misdiagnosed as:

- orf or milkers' nodules, although the parapoxvirus lesion is clinically distinct, and there are often no systemic disease symptoms;
- herpes virus reactivation, even though herpes lesions are not usually hemorrhagic or erythematous and the scab is not so deep-seated and of lighter color; and
- anthrax, although the anthrax lesion is painless and rapidly progresses to the eschar stage (5–6 days).[24]

DIAGNOSTIC MICROBIOLOGY

The appropriate biosafety level precautions must be taken for the handling, transport and processing of infected lesion material.[26]

Molluscum contagiosum virus

For a squash preparation the keratotic dome-shaped molluscum lesion is placed on a regular slide and under a coverslip or second slide. The lesion is flattened and can be examined using light microscopy either directly or after staining with Wright's or methylene blue stains. Round to ovoid molluscum bodies up to $37 \times 27\mu m$ are diagnostic of molluscum contagiosum.[4]

For histopathologic analysis, a biopsy specimen is fixed in 10% formal saline and submitted for wax embedding, sectioning at 5μm and staining with hematoxylin and eosin. Microscopic examination should provide a field of view similar to that shown in Figure 218.3.

Parapoxvirus, orthopoxvirus and yatapoxvirus

Orthopoxvirus (brick-shaped), parapoxvirus (ovoid) and tanapox virus (enveloped brick-shaped) virions can be differentiated from one another by an experienced electron microscopist. Scab material or fluid from the vesicle should be processed by standard methods for negative-staining electron microscopy.[26]

MANAGEMENT

The management of parapoxvirus, orthopoxvirus and yatapoxvirus infections is supportive. Although at this time there are no approved systemic or topical chemotherapeutic agents commercially available for the treatment of poxvirus infections, it is anticipated that cidofovir or related compounds will be approved to treat orf virus, molluscum contagiosum virus, and orthopoxvirus infections.[27,28] Also for complications arising from the smallpox vaccine, vaccinia immune globulin may be effective. Prevention of secondary bacterial infections through the use of antibiotic ointments is an option. In the case of cowpox, corticosteroids are contraindicated and may exacerbate the illness.[24] Because of the chronic nature of molluscum contagiosum lesions, one can consider curettage and cryotherapy of lesions. Removal of giant molluscum lesions, but not regular lesions, usually results in scar formation. Molluscum lesions may remit when HIV infection is controlled with anti-HIV therapy.

Curettage with an analgesic

With children, pretreatment of molluscum lesions with lidocaine (lignocaine)–prilocaine for between 1 and 30 hours under plastic occlusion resulted in a decrease in the reported pain on lesion removal with a comedo extractor or curette.

Cryotherapy

Molluscum lesions are treated for 6–30 seconds with a cotton-tipped applicator dipped in liquid nitrogen; this is repeated at 3-week intervals as needed. Cryotherapy is relatively painless, cost-effective and yields good cosmetic results. For patients with HIV infection, this treatment has the added advantage of mitigating the risk of disease transmission to medical personnel.

REFERENCES

1. Moss B. Poxviridae: the viruses and their replication. In: Fields BN, Knipe DM, Howley PM, eds. Fields virology, 3rd ed. Philadelphia: Lippincott–Raven; 2001:2849–83.
2. Esposito JJ, Fenner F. Poxviruses. In: Fields BN, Knipe DM, Howley PM, eds. Fields virology, 3rd ed. Philadelphia: Lippincott–Raven; 2001:2885–921.
3. Nakamura J, Muraki Y, Yamada M, Hatano Y, Nii S. Analysis of molluscum contagiosum virus genomes isolated in Japan. J Med Virol 1995;46:339–48.
4. Postlethwaite R. Molluscum contagiosum [Review]. Arch Environ Health 1970;21:432–52.
5. Porter CD, Blake NW, Cream JJ, Archard LC. Molluscum contagiosum virus [Review]. Mol Cell Biol Hum Dis Ser 1992;1:233–57.
6. Schwartz JJ, Myskowski PL. Molluscum contagiosum in patients with human immunodeficiency virus infection. J Am Acad Dermatol 1992;27:583–8.
7. Buller RML, Burnett J, Chen W, Kreider J. Replication of molluscum contagiosum virus. Virology 1995;213:655–9.
8. Al-Hazzaas AF, Hidayat AA. Molluscum contagiosum of the eyelid and infraorbital margin – a clinicopathologic study with light and electron microscopic observations. J Pediatr Ophthalmol Strabismus 1993;30:58–9.
9. DeOreo GA, Johnson JHH, Binkley GW. An eczematous reaction associated with molluscum contagiosum. A M A Arch Dermatol 1955;344–8.
10. Thompson CH, De Zwart-Steffe RT, Biggs IM. Molecular epidemiology of Australian isolates of molluscum contagiosum. J Med Virol 1990;32:1–9.
11. Izu R, Manzano D, Gardeazabal J, Diaz-Perez JL. Giant molluscum contagiosum presenting as a tumor in an HIV-infected patient. Int J Dermatol 1994;33:266–7.
12. Janniger CK, Schwartz RA. Molluscum contagiosum in children. Cutis 1993; 52:194–6.
13. Itin PH, Gilli L. Molluscum contagiosum mimicking sebaceous nevus of Jadassohn, ecthyma and giant condylomata acuminata in HIV-infected patients. Dermatology (Basel) 1994;189:396–8.
14. O'Neil C. Pearly penile papules on the shaft. Arch Dermatol 1995;131:491–2.
15. Robinson AJ, Petersen GV. Orf virus infection of workers in the meat industry. NZ Med J 1983;96:81–3.
16. Groves RW, Wilson-Jones E, MacDonald DM. Human orf and milkers' nodule: a clinicopathologic study. J Am Acad Dermatol 1991;25:706–11.
17. Robinson AJ, Lyttle DJ. Parapoxviruses: their biology and potential as recombinant vaccines. In: Binns MM, Smith GL, eds. Recombinant poxviruses. Boca Raton, FL: CRC; 1992:285–327.
18. Murphy JK, Ralfs IG. Bullous pemphigoid complication human orf. Br J Dermatol 1996;134:929–30.
19. Becker FT. Milker's nodules. JAMA 1940;115:2140.
20. Carson CA, Kerr KM. Bovine papular stomatitis with apparent transmission to man. J Am Vet Med Assoc 1967;151:183–7.
21. Tan ST, Blake GB, Chambers S. Recurrent orf in an immunocompromised host. Br J Plastic Surg 1991;44:465–7.
22. Breman JG, Henderson DA. Diagnosis and management of smallpox. N Engl J Med 2002;346:1300–8.
23. Richardson M, Dumbell K. Comparisons of monkeypox viruses from animal and human infections in Zaire. Trop Geogr Med 1994;46:327–9.
24. Baxby D, Bennett M, Getty B. Human cowpox 1969–93: a review based on 54 cases. Br J Dermatol 1994;131:598–607.
25. Jezek Z, Fenner F. Human monkeypox. In: Melnick JL, ed. Monographs in virology. Basel, Switzerland: Karger; 1988:81–110.
26. Nakano JH. Poxviruses. In: Lennette EH, Schmidt NJ, eds. Diagnostic procedures for viral, rickettsial and chlamydial infections, 5th ed. Washington, DC: American Public Health Association; 1979:257–308.
27. De Clercq E. Vaccinia virus inhibitors as a paradigm for the chemotherapy of poxvirus infections. Clin Micro Rev 2001;14:382–97.
28. Toro JR, Wood LV, Patel NK, Turner ML. Topical cidofovir: a novel treatment for recalcitrant molluscum contagiosum In children infected with human immunodeficiency virus 1. Arch Dermatol 2000;136:983–5.

chapter

219 Rabies

Mary J Warrell & David A Warrell

INTRODUCTION

Rabies is a zoonosis of dogs and other mammals that is occasionally transmitted to humans, causing fatal encephalomyelitis. Rabies virus is a member of the genus *Lyssavirus*, part of the large family of Rhabdoviruses that infect animals and plants. The bullet-shaped virions contain a nonsegmented negative strand of rabies RNA encoding five proteins. A nucleoprotein is coiled with the RNA, a phosphoprotein and an RNA-dependent RNA polymerase to form a helical ribonucleoprotein complex or nucleocapsid. This is covered by a matrix protein. An outer coat is acquired by budding through a host cell membrane, which is studded with the virus-coded glycoprotein bearing club-shaped projections. Rabies virus strains from different vector species and geographic areas can now be distinguished by nucleotide sequencing and monoclonal antibody typing.

Lyssaviruses comprise seven genotypes, of which rabies is genotype 1, and six are rabies related-viruses which may also cause fatal human encephalitis (see Rabies-related viruses, below).[1,2]

EPIDEMIOLOGY

Animal rabies

Globally, the domestic dog is the most important vector of human rabies, responsible for about 97% of human deaths from this disease. In Asia, most of Africa, and a few urban areas of Latin America, the dog is the dominant vector. Separate reservoirs of enzootic infection also occur in several wild mammalian species (Table 219.1), with occasional overspill into other species. This sylvatic pattern of infection predominates in North America,[2] Europe, southern Africa[3] and parts of the Caribbean. Rabies is enzootic in most parts of the world (Fig. 219.1). The epizootiology changes constantly, and so local advice should be sought for detailed information.

Human rabies

Estimates of human rabies mortality rates are notoriously unreliable in tropical areas, where about 99% of the deaths occur. In Asia and Africa there are an estimated 40,000–70,000 cases annually. Areas of high incidence include India, Bangladesh, Pakistan and Nepal.

In the USA, 32 cases were reported in the past 11 years, of which 19% were infected abroad, and 75% were associated with indigenous insectivorous bat rabies virus, although only two of 24 had recognized a bat bite.

PATHOGENICITY

Transmission

Human infection is usually the result of a bite by a rabid dog or other mammal. Virus in saliva can penetrate broken skin or intact mucous membranes, and so scratches or licks by a rabid animal may cause infection.

On a few occasions, human rabies has possibly resulted from inhalation of virus in caves that were densely populated by insectivorous bats in the USA, or after laboratory accidents with aerosols of virus. The saliva, respiratory secretions, and tears of rabies patients contain virus,[4] which could infect another person, but the only documented instances of human-to-human transmission have been in eight recipients of corneal grafts from donors in whom rabies had not been suspected. Several women with rabies encephalitis have delivered healthy infants. Only one case of neonatal rabies has been reported, although vertical transmission is well documented in animals.

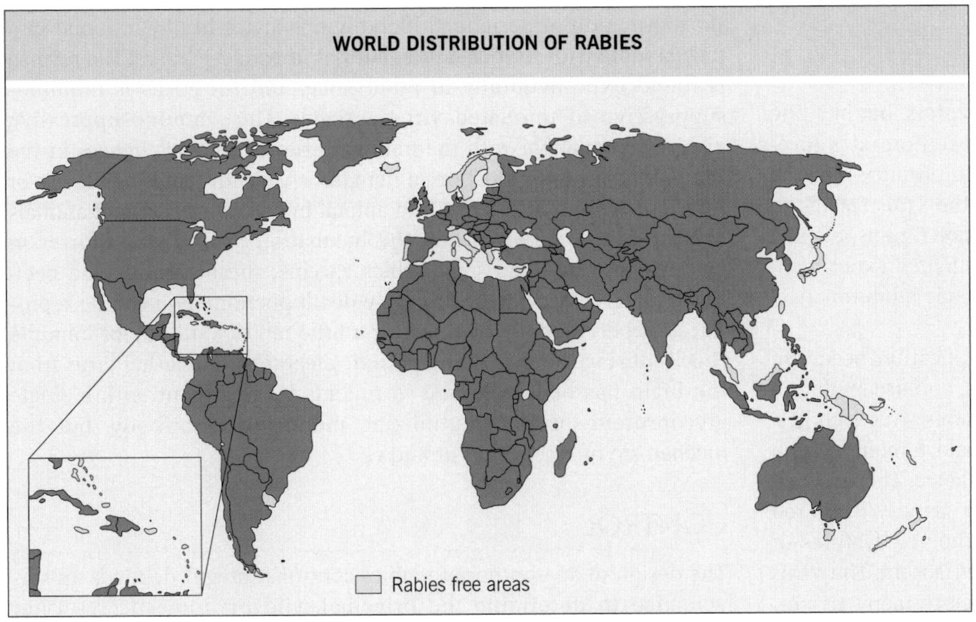

Fig. 219.1 World distribution of rabies.

IMPORTANT RABIES VECTOR SPECIES		
Africa	Domestic dog	Widespread dominant vector
	Black-backed jackals (*Canis mesomelas*)	Southern Africa
	Yellow mongoose (*Cynictis penicillata*)	
	Bat-eared fox (*Otocyon megalotis*)	
Americas	Domestic dog	Mexico, Central America, South America
	Wild canids: Arctic fox (*Alopex lagopus*), red fox (*Vulpes fulva*), gray fox (*Urocyon cinereoargenteus*), Coyote (*Canis latrans*)	Alaska, Canada, New England, Arizona, Texas
	Striped skunk (*Mephitis mephitis*)	Central Canada, central USA, California
	Racoon (*Procyon lotor*)	Mid-Atlantic, northeast, and southeast USA
	Insectivorous bats	USA, South America
	Vampire bat (Desmodontidae)	Southern Texas, Mexico, Central America, South America, Trinidad and Tobago
	Mongoose (*Herpestes* spp.)	Puerto Rico, Grenada, Cuba, Dominican Republic
Asia	Domestic dog	Widespread dominant vector
	Wolf (*Lupus lupus*)	Iran, Iraq, Afghanistan
Australia	Fruit bats (Lyssavirus genotype 7)	–
Europe	Fox (*Vulpes vulpes*)	Eastern Europe, diminishing westward
	Arctic fox (*Alopex lagopus*)	Northern Russian Federation
	Racoon dog (*Nyctereutes procyonoides*)	Poland, Baltic states, Russian Federation
	Wolf	Russian Federation
	Domestic dog	Turkey, Russian Federation
	Insectivorous bats (European bat lyssaviruses genotypes 5 and 6)	Germany, Denmark, The Netherlands, Russian Federation, Poland, Spain, France, Hungary, Switzerland, UK

Table 219.1 Important rabies vector species. All vectors carry *Lyssavirus* genotype 1 except where stated.

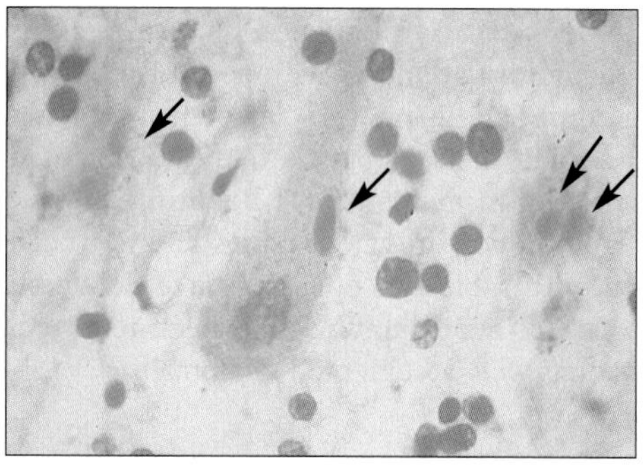

Fig. 219.2 Negri bodies in cerebellar Purkinje cells in a human victim of rabies encephalitis. The intracytoplasmic dark-staining Negri bodies are marked with arrows. Courtesy of the Armed Forces Institute, Bethesda, USA.

Pathogenesis

Rabies virus will attach to a variety of cellular receptors, but in a bite wound competitive binding to acetylcholine receptors at neuromuscular junctions is probably an important route of entry into the nervous system.[5] During the incubation period, the virus travels to the central nervous system (CNS) by retrograde axonal transport at a rate of 50–100mm/day (in vitro). Infection can be halted experimentally by sectioning the nerve or by applying metabolic inhibitors (e.g. colchicine).

When the virus reaches the brain, massive replication occurs in neurons by budding from intracellular membranes, and accumulation of viral proteins results in the formation of inclusions (Negri bodies; Fig. 219.2). The virus spreads trans-synaptically and remains within neurons where it is hidden from immune surveillance. There is evidence of neuronal dysfunction – neurotransmitter activity is altered and there are electroencephalograph changes. Pathologic features of diffuse encephalomyelitis may be minimal or even absent. The virus then progresses centrifugally via peripheral nerves to many tissues, including the salivary and lacrimal glands, where replication with production of extracellular rabies virus begins (Fig. 219.3).

Immunology

Following infection, rabies virus evades the immune system[6] and no immunologic response can be detected in unvaccinated patients before signs of encephalitis develop. Neutralizing antibody usually appears 1–2 weeks after the onset of symptoms, and a little later in the cerebrospinal fluid (CSF). Rabies-specific IgM is not detectable any earlier than IgG and it is not a sensitive means of diagnosis. The presence of antibody is diagnostic in unvaccinated patients. Specific transformation of peripheral blood lymphocytes has been found in a few patients with furious rabies, but not in paralytic cases. The reverse is found experimentally in rabid mice, and the virus is immunosuppressive to unrelated virus antigens. This immunosuppressive effect is compatible with the minimal histopathologic changes in the brain. Interferon production in humans is very low, and high levels of interferon-α and interferon-β in animal brains do not protect animals against death. Paradoxically the incubation period was shorter in patients who had had some rabies vaccine; these patients had been inadequately vaccinated. This early death phenomenon can be reproduced experimentally by injecting a little rabies antibody or immune B cells during the incubation period. Clearance of a lethal virus from the brain has been achieved in rodents by treatment with a single glycoprotein-specific neutralizing monoclonal antibody, but the mechanism of recovery is unknown.[7]

CONTROL

The design of an appropriate rabies control strategy[8] depends on surveillance to determine the principal wild or domestic reservoir

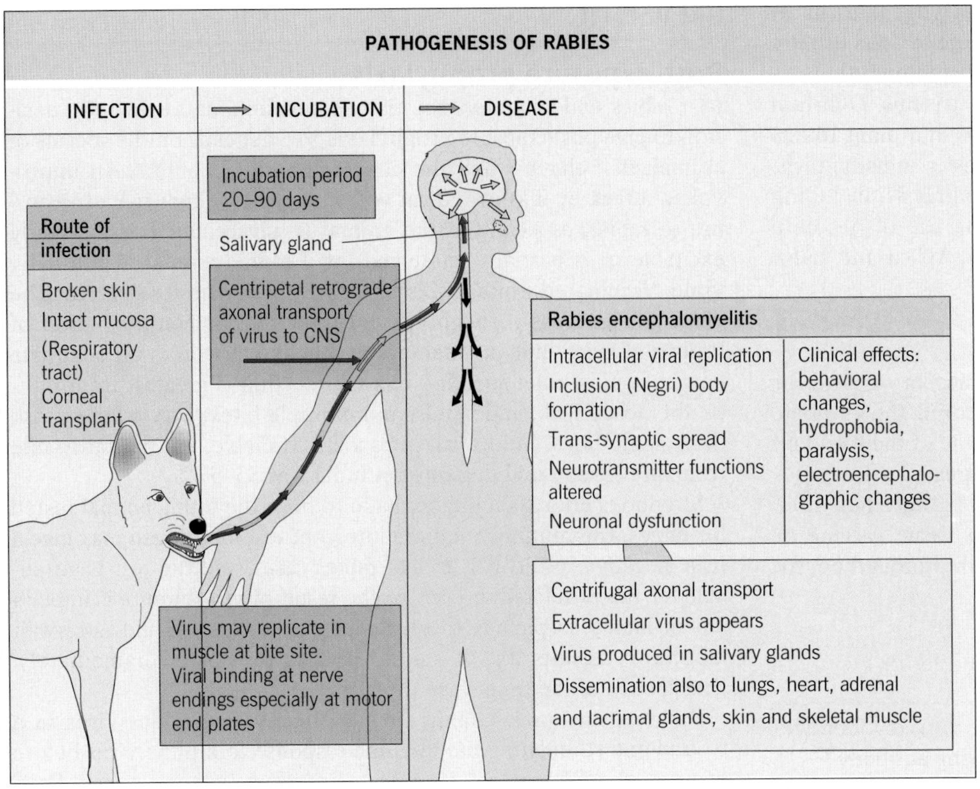

Fig. 219.3 Pathogenesis of rabies.

species, which are confirmed by laboratory diagnosis. In some places where the domestic dog was the main vector, including urban areas of Latin America, mass dog vaccination campaigns have radically reduced the incidence of rabies. In contrast, attempts at control by vaccination, poisoning or shooting have been unsuccessful in parts of Africa and Asia where stray or owned, unrestricted dogs are the greatest problem. The immunization of such dogs by distributing oral vaccine in suitable baits is now possible, but is not widely used.

Control of sylvatic rabies must be tailored to particular reservoir species. In Europe the red fox *Vulpes vulpes* is the dominant vector infecting other wild and domestic species. Repeated campaigns to distribute oral live attenuated or vaccinia-recombinant vaccine expressing rabies glycoprotein in baits has almost eradicated terrestrial rabies from western Europe. In North America racoons and coyotes have been similarly immunized, and also jackals in southern Africa. Control of vampire bat rabies, which causes many deaths in cattle in Latin America, is attempted by treating cattle with small doses of anticoagulant to poison the bats. No active measures are taken to control rabies in insectivorous bats in the Americas and Europe, but instructions are issued to encourage people to avoid direct contact with these animals.

CLINICAL MANIFESTATIONS

The incubation period (bite to first symptom) ranges from 4 days to at least 19 years, but in about 75% of cases it is between 20 and 90 days. The only prodromal symptoms that are reasonably suggestive of rabies are itching, pain, or paresthesia, either at the site of the causative bite or radiating proximally from it. After 1–7 days of generally non-specific symptoms, features of either furious or paralytic (dumb) rabies develop.

The pathognomonic symptom of furious rabies is hydrophobia[9] or aerophobia. Jerky and violent contractions of the diaphragm and accessory muscles of inspiration, are associated with an inexplicable terror. This reflex can be provoked by attempts to drink liquid or by a draught of air on the skin. The hydrophobic spasm may end with the patient in opisthotonos, having generalized convulsions and in cardiac or respiratory arrest. Other features of furious rabies are periodic excitement, sometimes with hallucinations or aggression, interspersed with lucid intervals, tachycardia and other arrhythmias, hypersalivation, lacrimation, sweating, and fluctuating temperature and blood pressure. All these features are suggestive of stimulation of the autonomic nervous system as seen in severe tetanus. Conventional neurologic examination may prove surprisingly normal but meningism, cranial nerve lesions, upper motor neuron lesions, fasciculation, and involuntary movements are sometimes detected. Without intensive care, patients usually die, often during a hydrophobic spasm, in the first few days of their encephalitic symptoms.

Paralytic or dumb rabies is probably underdiagnosed but was particularly associated with an epidemic of rabies transmitted by vampire bats in Trinidad in the 1920s and 1930s. After the prodromal symptoms described above, together with fever and headache, local paresthesia and flaccid paralysis develop, usually in the bitten limb, and ascend symmetrically or asymmetrically. There is accompanying pain and fasciculation in the affected muscles and mild objective sensory disturbances. Death follows paralysis of the muscles of deglutition and respiration; there is usually no evidence of hydrophobia or aerophobia. Some patients have survived for as long as 1 month, even without intensive care.

Patients with paralytic or dumb, or furious rabies whose lives are prolonged by intensive care may develop a variety of respiratory, cardiovascular, neurologic and gastrointestinal complications including fatal cardiac arrhythmias, pneumothorax, cerebral edema, diabetes insipidus, diffuse axonal neuropathy and hematemesis.

Differential diagnosis

Severe and unusual neurologic symptoms, whether encephalitic or paralytic, should suggest the possibility of rabies in any unimmunized person who has had contact with mammals in a rabies endemic area. Rabies patients infected by bats in the USA however, usually deny any contact with a bat.

Furious rabies can be mimicked by the pharyngeal form of cephalic tetanus ('hydrophobic tetanus'), but severe tetanus usually has a shorter incubation period than rabies. In tetanus, there is sustained muscle rigidity, often associated with trismus. Delirium tremens and the excitatory effects of some drugs and plant toxins have been confused with rabies. Paralytic rabies is indistinguishable from many other causes of an ascending paralysis, including postvaccinal encephalomyelitis complicating the use of obsolete nervous tissue rabies vaccines still used in Asia, Africa and Latin America.

Prognosis

Only five documented cases of recovery from rabies, or survival for more than eighteen months, have been reported during the virologic era.[10] No rabies virus or antigen was detected in any of them and all were diagnosed serologically. Two patients were treated after exposure with nervous tissue vaccines and recovered.[11] The other three patients, given either only pre-exposure nervous tissue vaccine or postexposure tissue culture vaccine, were left with profound neurologic deficits.

DIAGNOSIS

Rabies infection can be confirmed by isolating the virus, by identifying antigen, or, in unvaccinated patients, by detecting antibody.[12]

Viral isolation from saliva, respiratory secretions, CSF, tears, or brain biopsy[4] is the ideal method of diagnosis. Inoculation of suckling mice takes 1–3 weeks, whereas tissue culture isolation can be completed in less than 4 days. Virus identification using a panel of monoclonal antibodies or by genetic typing, will indicate the likely vector species and geographic origin of the strain. Rapid intravitam diagnosis can be made by immunofluorescent detection of rabies antigen in frozen sections of full-thickness skin biopsies from hairy areas of the nape of the neck. With controls to ensure specificity and examination of many sections, including bases of hair follicles, the sensitivity is 60–100%, the rate increasing later in the illness.[13] False-positive results have not been reported. Repeated tests should be made until the diagnosis of rabies is excluded. The corneal impression smear test is too insensitive to be useful and false-positive results have occurred. Antigen detection using polymerase chain reaction techniques has proved useful for samples of saliva and CSF.

The usual method of detecting antigen in brain samples is by the immunofluorescent antibody staining of acetone-fixed impression smears, but enzyme immunoassay can be used. Post-mortem needle necropsy of the brain can be taken without a full autopsy by inserting a Vim–Silverman needle via the medial canthus of the eye through the superior orbital fissure, or via the foramen magnum, or via the nose and ethmoid sinus into the brain.

In unvaccinated patients, diagnostic seroconversion usually occurs in the second week of illness.[14] In vaccinated patients, very high levels of antibody both in the serum and in the CSF have been used to make a diagnosis.[11]

MANAGEMENT

The life of patients with rabies encephalitis can be prolonged by intensive care. No effective antiviral or ancillary treatments have been discovered. Patients should be admitted to hospital so that their agonizing symptoms can be palliated with adequate doses of analgesic and sedative drugs. Friends, family and medical staff who have been in close contact with the patient should be given postexposure vaccination to reassure them, even though person-to-person transmission must be extremely rare.

PREVENTION

Post-exposure prophylaxis

In a rabies endemic area, the risk of infection, and hence the decision to give postexposure prophylaxis,[15,16] depends on the species of animal, its behavior and the circumstances of contact. An unprovoked attack by a known local vector suggests a high risk of exposure to rabies, especially if the animal is unvaccinated, is unusually excitable or is partially paralyzed, or if a wild animal is unusually tame. Vaccinated animals have, however, transmitted rabies. The virus gains access through any bite, scratch, or contamination of broken skin or mucous membrane, but intact skin is an adequate barrier against infection. The risk of infection is greatest from bites on the head, neck, and hands, and multiple bites carry a higher risk than single bites. Before vaccines were available, the mortality rate from all proven rabid dog bites in India was 35–57%.[17]

Strenuous efforts should be made to have the biting animal tested for rabies. The routine immunofluorescent test for antigen may give a false-negative result in 1–2% of rabies cases, and the test is unreliable for rabies-related viruses, so the result of viral culture is important in highly suspicious cases. Specific treatment should not await laboratory results and it should always be started immediately, irrespective of the time since the bite.

Postexposure prophylaxis aims at inactivating rabies virus in a wound and stimulating the immune response to kill the virus before it enters the CNS, where it is protected from immune attack. Postexposure therapy includes urgent wound treatment, and active prophylaxis with vaccine and passive immunization with rabies immune globulin (RIG). Failures of complete optimal treatment started on the day of exposure have only been reported in two patients following bites on the head.

Treatment of mammal bites, scratches or licks

The treatment can be summarized as follows:

1. Scrub vigorously with soap or detergent and water, reaching the depth of the wound, and remove foreign material.
2. Swab with a virucidal agent: povidone iodine, tincture of iodine, or 40–70% ethanol. (The virucidal effect of quaternary ammonium compounds is neutralized by soap, and so they are not recommended.) Local or even general anesthetic may be necessary to allow effective wound cleaning and debridement, especially for children.
3. Suturing of wounds should be avoided or delayed.
4. Tetanus prophylaxis (tetanus immune globulin or toxoid booster plus metronidazole) must not be forgotten. Antibiotic prophylaxis against other potential wound pathogens is recommended.
5. If there is a risk of rabies, give specific therapy immediately.

Rabies vaccines

Vaccines of nervous tissue origin

All human rabies vaccines contain killed virus. Those cultured in sheep or goat brains (Semple vaccines) and suckling mouse brain (SMB) are still used in Asia and Africa. SMB vaccine is also used in parts of South America. These are weak antigens and neurologic reactions still occur (1 in 200 Semple vaccinees).[10] Nevertheless in the absence of a modern vaccine, a nervous tissue product should be used, at least until other treatment can be procured.

Purified tissue culture vaccines

Tissue culture-grown vaccines are used exclusively in North America, most of Europe, China, Thailand, Sri Lanka and the Philippines and increasingly in other countries. The use of the original expensive human diploid cell vaccine (HDCV) is giving way to cheaper vaccines of equivalent efficacy and safety, including a

German purified chick embryo cell vaccine (PCECV) and a French purified vero cell vaccine (PVRV), which are now widely distributed in endemic areas.

Immunologic response to vaccination

The presence of serum neutralizing antibody is the best available indicator of protection against rabies, and it appears 7–14 days after starting a primary course of a modern rabies vaccine. A level of 0.5I U/ml is considered satisfactory, although the protective level cannot be ascertained in humans. Only the viral surface glycoprotein molecules induce neutralizing antibody. They also stimulate helper T-lymphocyte responses. The rabies nucleoprotein can also induce protection through the induction of non-neutralizing antibody, T-helper lymphocytes and interferon-γ. This immunity cross-reacts broadly with other strains of rabies virus and rabies-related viruses, unlike that induced by glycoprotein.

The speed and degree of the antibody response to vaccine varies, probably under genetic influence. A relatively delayed lower level of antibody is found in about 10% of people receiving vaccine; increasing age also impairs the response.

The induction of neutralizing antibody can be accelerated by increasing the amount of antigen (within limits) or by dividing the dose between multiple sites and injecting it intradermally.

Postexposure vaccine regimens

Intramuscular vaccine regimen

The standard regimen is one dose of tissue culture vaccine (1ml or 0.5ml, depending on the product) intramuscularly into the deltoid on days 0, 3, 7, 14 and 28.

Intradermal vaccine regimens

The five-dose intramuscular regimen is unaffordable by the vast majority of patients in developing countries, but economic, safe and effective regimens are now available. The World Health Organization recommends two multiple-site intradermal regimens using specified European vaccines – PVRV, PCECV and HDCV.[15] The manufacturers' instructions must be used for all other vaccines.

An eight-site regimen[18] consists of eight doses of 0.1ml intradermally on day 0 (using a whole vial) on the arms, thighs, and suprascapular and lower abdominal areas; four doses on day 7 on the arms and thighs; and one dose on days 28 and 90 also over the deltoid. Human diploid cell vaccine or PCECV can be used, when the intramuscular dose is 1ml. This has a wide margin of safety because the minimum stipulated antibody response has been achieved by only four of the initial eight intradermal doses. Only four visits are needed. Patients who are anxious about the risk of rabies do not object to the method.

A two-site regimen[15] consists of two intradermal doses (0.1 or 0.2ml depending on whether the intramuscular vaccine dose is 0.5 or 1.0ml) on days 0, 3 and 7; and one intradermal dose on days 28 and 90. The injection is over the deltoid. This has proved effective in thousands of patients who also received RIG treatment in Thailand.

The eight-site regimen induces higher levels of antibody than the two-site regimen from the earliest appearance of antibody onwards.[19] Both require a similar amount of vaccine, less than two intramuscular doses, a saving of 60%. When one ampoule is shared between several patients, a new syringe and needle must be used for each.

Postexposure treatment of previously vaccinated patients

Treatment is always urgent, but, provided that the patient has previously had a complete pre-exposure or postexposure course of tissue culture vaccine or if a neutralizing antibody level has been over 0.5I U/ml at some time, only two doses of intramuscular vaccine are needed on days 0 and 3. Rabies immune globulin treatment is unnecessary.

Side-effects of tissue culture vaccines

The incidence of minor symptoms is very variable.[10] Local pain or erythema occurs in about 15% of people vaccinated, and irritation is more common following intradermal injections. Generalized non-specific symptoms are reported by about 7% of patients, and transient maculopapular and urticarial rashes are occasionally seen. In the USA, 6% of late pre-exposure booster injections of HDCV have been accompanied by mild immune complex-like disease between three to 13 days later. All of these patients responded to symptomatic treatment. Neurologic symptoms, either Guillain–Barré-like or local limb weakness, are extremely rare, and the incidence following treatment is no greater than those following other routine vaccines. No complications have been observed in pregnancy.

Passive immunization with rabies immune globulin

Every primary postexposure vaccine course should be accompanied by RIG to cover the first 7–10 days before vaccine-induced immunity appears,[15] and it may enhance the T-cell immune response. Rabies immune globulin treatment is especially important after bites on the head, neck or hands, or multiple bites. A single dose of 20 IU/kg of human RIG or 40 IU/kg of equine RIG is given at the same time as the first dose of vaccine. As much as possible is infiltrated into and around the wound, but care is needed when injecting into fingers or other tight tissue compartments. Any remaining vaccine is injected intramuscularly away from the vaccine site. If the volume of RIG is insufficient for infiltration, it can be diluted in saline two- or threefold in order to infiltrate all wounds. Skin testing with RIG does not predict most hypersensitivity reactions, and epinephrine (adrenaline) should always be ready in case of anaphylaxis. Serum sickness occurs in 1–6% of equine RIG recipients, but has not been seen after human RIG therapy.

Pre-exposure vaccination

Pre-exposure vaccination is recommended for anyone at risk of exposure to rabies virus, including veterinary surgeons, animal handlers, zoologists, laboratory staff working with rabies, wildlife officers and people living in or traveling to rabies-endemic areas where dogs are the dominant vector species. A total of three doses of cell culture vaccine are needed on days 0 and 7 and on day 28 (or day 21). The dose can be intramuscular or intradermal. Malarial prophylaxis with choloroquine inhibits the antibody response to vaccine given intradermally, so anyone on antimalarial therapy must have intramuscular injections. A booster dose after about 1 year prolongs the antibody response, which usually lasts 5–10 years. As a prompt secondary immune response to booster doses has proved reliable, repeated booster doses are not recommended in the USA except for those at very high risk, such as laboratory staff.[16] Serologic testing is necessary only if immunosuppression is suspected or to determine the need for booster injections in those at high risk.

RABIES-RELATED VIRUSES

The *Lyssavirus* genus comprises seven genotypes: genotype 1 is classical rabies virus; genotypes 2–7 are rabies related-viruses.[1,2] Genotype 2, Lagos bat virus, unlike the others, has not been found in humans.

Africa

Genotype 3, Mokola virus, has been identified occasionally in shrews, cats, dogs and rodents in sub-Saharan Africa.[1,3,17] Isolation has been reported in two Nigerian children – from the brain of one with fatal encephalitis, without hydrophobia; and from the CSF of another with transient meningitis, but neutralizing antibody was not found in convalescent serum. Genotype 4, Duvenhage virus, is found rarely in bats in southern Africa, and has caused a rabies-like encephalitis in one patient. The true prevalence of these African infections is uncertain because the diagnosis of rabies encephalitis is normally made on clinical evidence, and the usual diagnostic rabies immunofluorescent test may give a faint result or a negative one with rabies-related viruses.

Europe

Genotype 5, European bat *Lyssavirus* type 1, is found in a variety of insectivorous bats across Europe (see Table 219.1).[1,2] Genotype 6, European bat *Lyssavirus* type 2, has rarely been isolated from *Myotis* spp. of bats in The Netherlands, Switzerland and the UK. There are four reports of fatal rabies-like encephalitis following bat bites in Europe, and European bat lyssaviruses were confirmed in three of these cases. The most recent was a European bat *Lyssavirus* type 2 infection in Scotland in 2002.

Australia

Genotype 7, Australian bat *Lyssavirus*, was identified in 1996 in flying foxes (*Pteropus*) and other bats, and has caused two fatal human infections indistinguishable from rabies encephalitis.[20] A serologic survey also indicates endemic infection in the Philippines.

REFERENCES

1. Badrane H, Bahloul C, Perrin P, Tordo N. Evidence of two Lyssavirus phylogroups with distinct pathogenicity and immunogenicity. J Virol 2001;75:3268–76.
2. Smith JS. New aspects of rabies with emphasis on epidemiology, diagnosis and prevention of the disease in the United States. Clin Microbiol Rev 1996;9:166–76.
3. King AA, Meridith CD, Thomson GR. The biology of Southern African Lyssavirus variants. In: Rupprecht CE, Dietzschold B, Koprowski H, eds. Lyssaviruses. Berlin: Springer-Verlag; 1994:267–95.
4. Helmick CG, Tauxe RV, Vernon AA. Is there a risk to contacts of patients with rabies? Rev Infect Dis 1987;9:511–8.
5 Jackson AC. Pathogenisis. In: Jackson AC, Wunner WH, eds. Rabies. San Diego: Academic Press; 2002:246–82.
6. Lafon M. Immunology. In: Jackson AC, Wunner WH, eds. Rabies. San Diego: Academic Press; 2002:351–69.
7. Dietzschold B, Morimoto K, Hooper DC. Mechanisms of virus-induced neuronal damage and the clearance of viruses from the CNS. Curr Top Microbiol Immunol 2001;253:145–55.
8. Bögel K. Control of dog rabies. In: Jackson AC, Wunner WH, eds. Rabies. San Diego: Academic Press; 2002:429–43.
9. Warrell DA, Davidson NMcD, Pope HM, *et al.* Pathophysiologic studies in human rabies. Am J Med 1976;60:180–90.
10. Warrell MJ. Rabies encephalitis and its prophylaxis. Pract Neurol 2001;1:14–29.
11. Hattwick MAW, Weis TT, Stechschulte CJ, Baer GM, Gregg MB. Recovery from rabies: a case report. Ann Intern Med 1972;76:931–42.
12. Noah DL, Drenzek CL, Smith JS, *et al.* Epidemiology of human rabies in the United States, 1980 to 1996. Ann Intern Med 1998;128:922–30.
13. Blenden DC, Creech W, Torres-Anjel MJ. Use of immunofluorescence examination to detect rabies virus antigen in the skin of humans with clinical encephalitis. J Infect Dis 1986;154:698–701.
14. Anderson LJ, Nicholson KG, Tauxe RV, Winkler WG. Human rabies in the United States, 1960 to 1979: epidemiology, diagnosis and prevention. Ann Intern Med 1984;100:728–35.
15. World Health Organisation. WHO recommendations on rabies post-exposure treatment and the correct technique of intradermal immunization against rabies. World Health Organisation; 1997: WHO/EMC/ZOO.96.6. http://www.who.int/emc-documents/rabies/docs/whoemczoo966.pdf
16. Centers for Disease Control. Human rabies prevention – United States, 1999: Recommendations of the Immunization Practices Advisory Committee (ACIP). Morbid Mortal Wkly Rep 1991;Suppl.48:RR-1.
17. Warrell MJ, Warrell DA. Rhabdovirus infections of humans. In: Porterfield JS, Tyrrell DAJ, eds. Exotic viral infections. London: Chapman and Hall Medical; 1995:343–83.
18. Warrell MJ, Nicholson KG, Warrell DA, *et al.* Economical multiple site intradermal immunisation with human diploid-cell-strain vaccine is effective for post-exposure rabies prophylaxis. Lancet 1985;i:1059–62.
19. Madhusudana SN, Anand NP, Shamsundar R. Evaluation of two intradermal vaccination regimens using purified chick embryo cell vaccine for post-exposure prophylaxis of rabies. Natl Med J India 2001;14:145–7.
20. Hooper PT, Lunt RA, Gould AR. A new lyssavirus – the first endemic rabies-related virus recognized in Australia. Bull Inst Pasteur 1997;95:209–18.

chapter
220 Respiratory Viruses

Alberto M La Rosa & Estella Whimbey

INTRODUCTION

Respiratory viral infections are among the most common diseases of humans. In the course of a lifetime, every individual will experience several episodes of respiratory viral infections. These illnesses are caused by a heterogeneous group of viruses commonly known as human respiratory viruses (HRVs) which includes adenovirus, coronavirus, reovirus, rhinovirus, respiratory syncytial virus, parainfluenza virus and influenza virus. Other viruses, such as some of the enteroviruses and some of the herpesviruses, can also cause respiratory disease but they are discussed elsewhere in this book.

Respiratory viral infections are largely benign and self-limited. Their impact is largely measured in terms of diminished sense of well-being, exacerbations of underlying chronic cardiopulmonary diseases, loss of productivity, time lost from work or school, increased visits to health care providers and unnecessary prescription of antibiotics with the entailing drug toxicities, emergence of antibiotic resistance and increase in health care cost. Among some subsets of the population such as those at the extremes of age, those with chronic cardiopulmonary diseases or those with primary or secondary immunodeficiencies, these illnesses are not infrequently associated with serious, potentially fatal complications. In recent years, significant progress has been made in our understanding of pathogenesis, natural history, epidemiology, molecular diagnosis, prevention and treatment of these organisms.

The more characteristic illnesses associated with the different respiratory viruses and the populations at higher risk are presented in Table 220.1. The most common methods for the laboratory diagnosis of viral respiratory infections are summarized in Table 220.2 and Figures 220.1–220.5

ADENOVIRUS

Nature

Adenoviruses were first isolated in the 1950s from human adenoids and later from respiratory secretions of military recruits with acute febrile respiratory illnesses. Human adenoviruses belong to the family Adenoviridae. More than 50 serotypes have been described and classified into six subgroups (A–F). Approximately one-half of these serotypes are known human pathogens. Virions are nonenveloped icosahedral particles measuring 80–100nm in diameter and containing a linear double-stranded DNA genome. The capsid consists of 252 capsomers, of which 240 are hexons and 12 are pentons (vertices). A fiber with a knob at the end projects from every penton. Virions attach to human cells via interaction of the fibers with a receptor on the cell surface and enter the cell via endocytosis. Virus uncoating occurs in the cytoplasm and the virus core is imported into the nucleus. The transcription and translation of viral DNA depend in part on host cell machinery.

Epidemiology

Although epidemiologic characteristics of the adenoviruses vary by type, the route of transmission is either via respiratory tract, fecal–oral or water-borne. Infections are most common during early childhood, but continue to occur throughout life. Nearly 100% of adults have serum antibodies against multiple serotypes. Adenoviruses have been found to account for 3–5% of acute respiratory infections in children and up to 2% in adults. Close contact in crowded institutions increases the risk for adenovirus infections and outbreaks have been described in day care centers, hospitals, shipyards and military quarters. Adenovirus infections can occur throughout the year but outbreaks of adenovirus-associated respiratory disease have been more common in the late winter, spring and early summer.

Pathogenesis

Adenoviruses causing respiratory disease can be spread via contact transmission (direct or indirect) and via droplet transmission. Direct contact transmission involves a direct body surface to body surface contact and physical transfer of micro-organisms between a susceptible host and an infected person. Indirect contact transmission involves contact of a susceptible host with a contaminated intermediate object. Adenoviruses can also be transmitted when droplets containing micro-organisms generated from the infected person are propelled a short distance (less than 3 feet) through the air and deposited on the host's conjunctivae, nasal mucosa or mouth. Droplets are particles of respiratory secretions larger than 5μm in diameter that are produced during coughing, sneezing or talking and during the performance of certain procedures such as suctioning and bronchoscopy.

The replicative cycle in the host cells may be lytic or may result in the establishment of a latent infection, primarily in lymphoid tissue. The symptoms of adenovirus disease are due to the lysis of infected epithelial cells and the resulting inflammatory response. The initial immune response is probably the recognition of infected cells by natural killer cells and monocytes, which evokes a cytokine response, followed by induction of cytotoxic T cells, as well as B cells which in turn results in the production of type-specific antibodies. Prolonged shedding of adenoviruses in stools has been recognized even in immunocompetent individuals. Some adenovirus serotypes (especially 12, 18 and 31) have been shown to induce oncogenic transformation in cultured rodent cells. In recent years, intensive research has focused on the use of adenoviruses as gene vectors.[1]

Prevention

An effective oral enteric-coated vaccine has been used to prevent adenovirus serotypes 4 and 7 infections in military recruits. This vaccine is not indicated for the general population. Contact and droplet precautions are indicated for controlling nosocomial transmission of adenovirus infection. Contact precautions include the placing of patients in private rooms, cohorting, use of gowns and globes, hand washing and the use of dedicated noncritical patient care equipment when possible. Droplet precautions include the placing of patients in private rooms, cohorting, the use of masks by the personnel caring for the patient within a distance of 3 feet and

Table 220.1 Human respiratory viruses: characteristic illnesses and populations at higher risk.

HUMAN RESPIRATORY VIRUSES: CHARACTERISTIC ILLNESSES AND POPULATIONS AT HIGHER RISK		
Virus	**Associated illnesses (most common virus subtype)**	**Patient population at higher risk**
Adenovirus	URI [1–3, 5–7]	Infants, young children
	Pharyngoconjunctival fever [3, 7, 14]	School-aged children
	URI, pneumonia [3, 4, 7, 14, 21]	Military recruits
	Pertussis-like syndrome [5]	Infants, young children
	Pneumonia [1, 2, 3, 4, 7]	Infants, young children, immunocompromised
	Hemorrhagic cystitis [11, 21]	Children, immunocompromised
	Keratoconjunctivitis [8, 11, 19, 35, 37]	All ages
	Gastroenteritis [40, 41]	Children, immunocompromised
	Hepatitis [1, 2, 5, 7, 31]	Immunocompromised
	Meningoencephalitis [7, 12, 32]	Children, immunocompromised
	Disseminated disease [1–5, 7, 11, 21, 31, 32, 34, 35, 39]	Immunocompromised
	Reye's syndrome [3, 7]	Children
Coronavirus	Common cold	All ages
	Otitis	Children
	Pneumonia	Military recruits, elderly, immunocompromised
	Exacerbation of asthma-COPD	Persons with asthma-COPD
Reovirus	Common cold (?)	All ages
	Enteritis (?)	Children
Rhinovirus	Common cold	All ages
	URI	All ages
	Exacerbation of asthma-COPD	Persons with asthma-COPD
	SARS (severe acute respiratory syndrome)	
RSV	URI	All ages
	Pneumonia	Infants, young children, elderly, immunocompromised
	Bronchiolitis	Infants, young children
	Otitis	Children
	Sudden infant death syndrome (?)	Young infants
Parainfluenza	URI	All ages
	Croup	Children
	Otitis media	Children
	Pneumonia	Children, immunocompromised
Influenza	'Flu'	All ages
	URI	All ages
	Pneumonia	Young children, elderly, persons with chronic cardiopulmonary illness, pregnant women, immunocompromised
	Croup	Children
	Otitis media	Children
	Myocarditis	Children
	Toxic shock syndrome	Children
	Reye's syndrome	Children

URI: upper respiratory tract infection

the use of a mask on the patient while being transported out of the room. Maintaining adequate levels of chlorination is necessary for preventing swimming pool-associated outbreaks of adenovirus conjunctivitis.

Diagnostic microbiology

Virus isolation, antigen detection, polymerase chain reaction assay and serology can be used to identify adenovirus infections. Adenovirus serotyping is usually accomplished by hemagglutination inhibition and/or neutralization with type-specific antisera. The isolation of adenoviruses from body secretions is not sufficient to establish a diagnosis of adenovirus disease as prolonged asymptomatic shedding of adenoviruses can occur. Examination of biopsy or autopsy materials should be pursued whenever feasible in order to identify characteristic cytopathic changes and establish a diagnosis of adenovirus disease, particularly in the setting of immunosuppression where infection with multiple organisms is frequent.

Clinical manifestations

Although adenoviruses mainly cause respiratory illness, they may also cause various other illnesses such as gastroenteritis, keratoconjunctivitis, cystitis, meningoencephalitis and hepatitis, depending on the serotype. Respiratory illnesses associated with adenovirus infections include undifferentiated upper respiratory illness, pharyngoconjunctival fever, pertussis-like syndrome and pneumonia. Adenovirus serotypes 1, 2, 3 and 5 are the most frequent among children. Adenovirus types 4 and 7 and, less often, 3, 14 and 21 are associated with outbreaks of acute respiratory disease in military recruits. Enteric adenoviruses 40 and 41 cause gastroenteritis, usually in children. Epidemic keratoconjunctivitis is associated with

HUMAN RESPIRATORY VIRUSES

Virus	Culture cell lines	Characteristic findings	Direct assay	Serology
Adenovirus	Primary human embryonic kidney (HEK) and the human lung carcinoma (A549) cell lines are sensitive for a broad range of adenoviruses. Some adenoviruses may require up to 28 days to grow. The continuous epithelial lines, such as Hep-2, HeLa and KB, are sensitive but more difficult to maintain for a long period of time as required by some serotypes	Enlarged, refractile, rounded cells forming grape-like clusters (Fig. 220.1), with some isolates forming a lattice-type arrangement of rounded cells	IF, EIA, and LA	Genus-specific EIA and CF Type-specific HI and NT
Coronavirus	Culture not performed in most laboratories. Primary isolation of human respiratory coronaviruses often requires human fetal tracheal or intestinal organ cultures	Cytocidal coronavirus infections may form multinucleated syncytia, lysis or both	EIA used in research settings	CF, HI, EIA used in research settings
Reovirus	Rarely isolated in the routine diagnostic setting. PRMK, LLC-MK2, HNK, HeLa, MDBK and H292 cell lines may support the growth of this virus	CPE is slow to develop. CPE may be non-specific with increased granularity, and progressive degeneration. HI or IFA can be used for typing	IF used in research settings	CF, NI, NT, EIA used in research settings
Rhinovirus	Human embryonic kidney and human fibroblast cell lines have been used most extensively: WI-38, HFF and MRC-5. HeLa is also sensitive	CPE is usually detected in the first week. CPE consists of rounded, highly refractile cells in loose clusters (Fig. 220.2). CPE permits a presumptive diagnosis of picornavirus infection. Demonstration of lability at pH 3 is used for differentiation from enteroviruses	EIA used in research settings	NT, CF, EIA used in research settings
RSV	Hep-2 is the preferred cell line. Alternatives include HeLa, A549, MRC-5, RhMK and Vero. Calcium and glutamine in the culture medium are important for optimal replication and cytopathic effect	CPE requires 3–7 days or more. Syncytia develops along with non-specific granular degeneration (Fig. 220.3). Confirmation by means of IF (Fig. 220.3) or EIA	IF (Fig. 220.3), EIA, IP	CF, IF, EIA, NT
Parainfluenza	Primary rhesus monkey kidney (PRMK) or MDCK are the preferred cell lines. LLC-MK2, a rhesus kidney heteroploid cell line, and NCI-H292, a human lung carcinoma line, are also sensitive	CPE is variable and non-specific. HPIV-2 and HPIV-3 may induce syncytia formation. Growth may be detected by means of Had (Fig. 220.4), with confirmation and typing by IF (Fig. 220.5), EIA, HAdI or HI	IF, EIA	HI, CF, EIA, NT
Influenza	PRMK and Madin–Darby canine kidney (MDCK) cells are preferred	CPE may be absent or minimal, with non-specific degeneration and granularity. Growth may be detected by means of HAd assay (Fig. 220.4), with confirmation and typing by IF (Fig. 220.5) or EIA	IF, EIA	Type-specific CF, EIA Subtype-specific HI, EIA

IF, immunofluorescence; EIA, enzyme immunoassay; LA, latex agglutination; HAdI, hemadsorption assay; HAd, hemadsorption inhibition; HI, hemagglutination inhibition; NT, neutralization test; IP, immunoperoxidase staining; CF, complement fixation; CPE, cytopathic effect

Table 220.2 Human respiratory viruses. Most common methods for laboratory diagnosis: culture, direct assay and serology.

adenovirus types 8, 19 and 37. Hemorrhagic cystitis is more frequent with types 11 and 21. In children, the occurrence of cerebral edema, fatty liver and liver failure characteristic of Reye's syndrome has been reported in association with adenovirus types 3 and 7. With the exception of pharyngoconjunctival fever, the respiratory symptoms are not specific. The incubation period for the endemic serotypes ranges from 5 to 10 days and the symptoms last approximately 1 week. Chronic lung damage in the form of bronchiolitis obliterans has been reported after infections with serotypes 1, 3, 4, 7 and 21.

Severe and potentially fatal disease has been observed in neonates and individuals with primary or secondary immunodeficiencies.[2] However, cases of severe adenovirus disease have also been reported in apparently normal hosts. Immunocompromised patients, particularly hematopoietic stem cell transplant (HSCT) and solid organ transplant recipients, are susceptible to severe and potentially fatal adenovirus disease,[3–5] such as protracted hemorrhagic cystitis, encephalitis, nephritis leading to renal failure, hepatitis leading to liver failure, enteritis causing gastrointestinal bleeding, pneumonia leading to respiratory failure or a combination of those illnesses (disseminated disease).

Management

Most infections are mild and require no therapy or only symptomatic treatment. Ribavirin has *in vitro* activity against several adenovirus serotypes but the clinical experience in immunocompromised individuals has produced conflicting results.[5–10] Aerosolized ribavirin is cumbersome to administer, while intravenous administration may be complicated by the development of hemolytic anemia. Cidofovir is a nucleotide analog with a broad antiviral effect *in vitro*, including against adenoviruses. The drug is administered intravenously every 2 weeks, after two initial weekly doses. Data on the efficacy of cidofovir against adenoviruses are limited to case reports and uncontrolled series.[10–12] The most significant side-effects of cidofovir include proximal renal tubular acidosis with azotemia, as well as uveitis with hypotony. Concomitant administration of probenecid and normal saline can reduce the risk of renal toxicity.

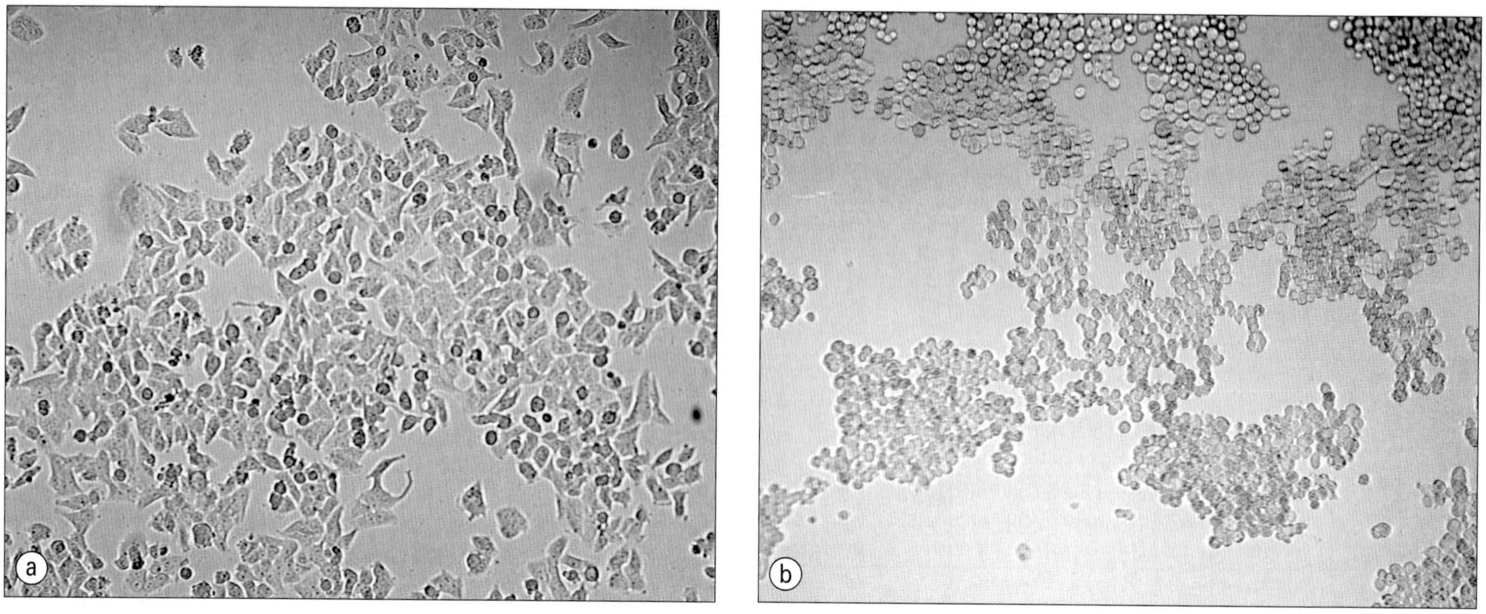

Fig. 220.1 Cytopathic effect caused by adenovirus on Hep-2 cell line culture. (a) Uninoculated cell line. (b) Enlarged, refractile, rounded cells forming grape-like clusters.

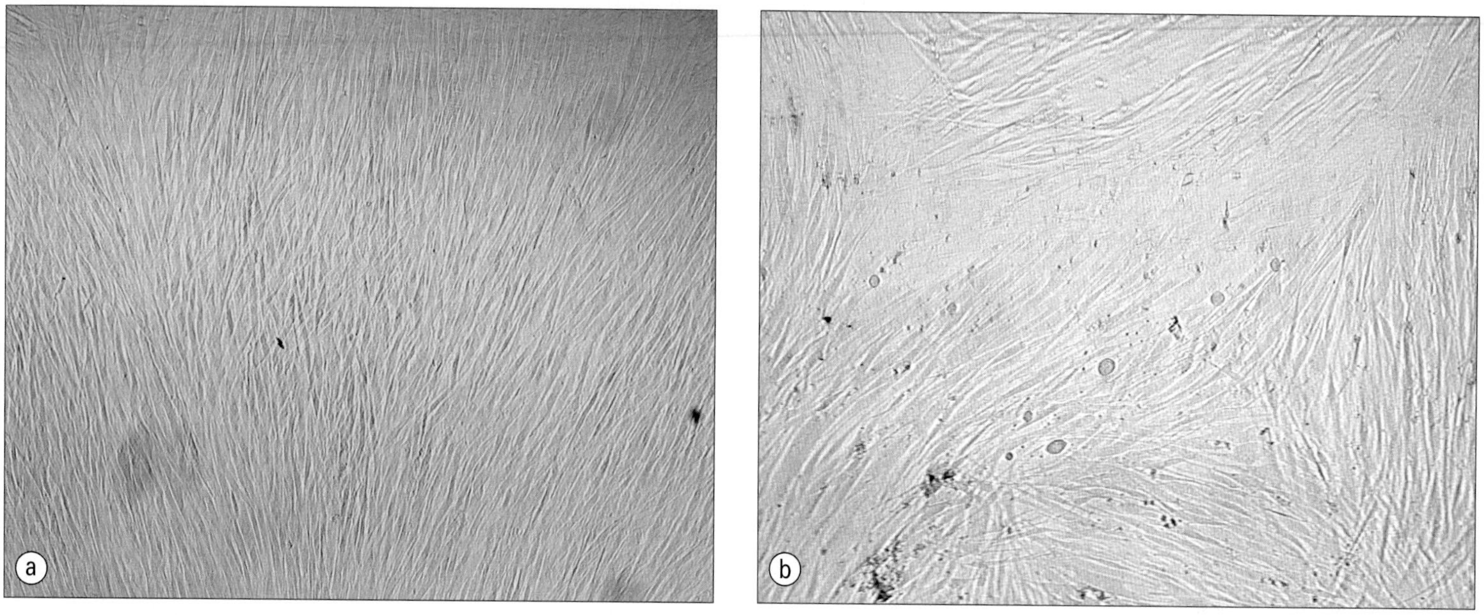

Fig. 220.2 Cytopathic effect caused by rhinovirus on human foreskin fibroblasts (HFF) cell line culture. (a) Uninoculated cell line. (b) Formation of small teardrop- to oval-shaped highly refractile cells.

CORONAVIRUS

Nature

Human coronavirus (HCoV) was first isolated in 1965 from a patient with symptoms of the common cold. Virions are pleomorphic and measure 80–200nm in diameter. The outer envelope bears distinctive 'club-shaped' peplomers that correspond to the S (long spike) glycoprotein. The resulting 'crown-like' appearance under electron microscopy gives the family its name. The S glycoprotein is involved in receptor binding and cell fusion and is a major target for neutralizing antibodies. Other structural proteins include the M (matrix) protein, the E (envelope) protein and the N (nucleocapsid) phosphoprotein. In some types, there is also a glycoprotein HE (hemagglutinin-esterase, short spike). Entry occurs via endocytosis and membrane fusion. Replication of the linear single-stranded positive-sense RNA genome takes place in the cytoplasm. HCoV-229E and HCoV-OC43 serve as the prototype human coronaviruses.

Epidemiology

HCoVs are ubiquitous. Serologic studies have suggested that these viruses are a major cause of respiratory disease and account for 10–30% of all common colds. Serologic studies have also suggested that one-half of the infections with coronaviruses are asymptomatic. The peak activity occurs between late fall and early winter. Outbreaks of HCoV-229E in a community occur at 2–4-year intervals and outbreaks of HCoV-OC43 occur in alternate years when the incidence of HCoV-229E infection is low.[13]

Pathogenesis

Intranasal inoculation of volunteers with these viruses results in common colds. Disruption of the ciliated epithelium and ciliary dyskinesia was observed in histological examinations.[14] Aminopeptidase N (APN), the receptor for HCoV-229E, is expressed on the apical surfaces of respiratory and intestinal epithelium, myelocytic cells, kidney tubular epithelium and synaptic junctions.

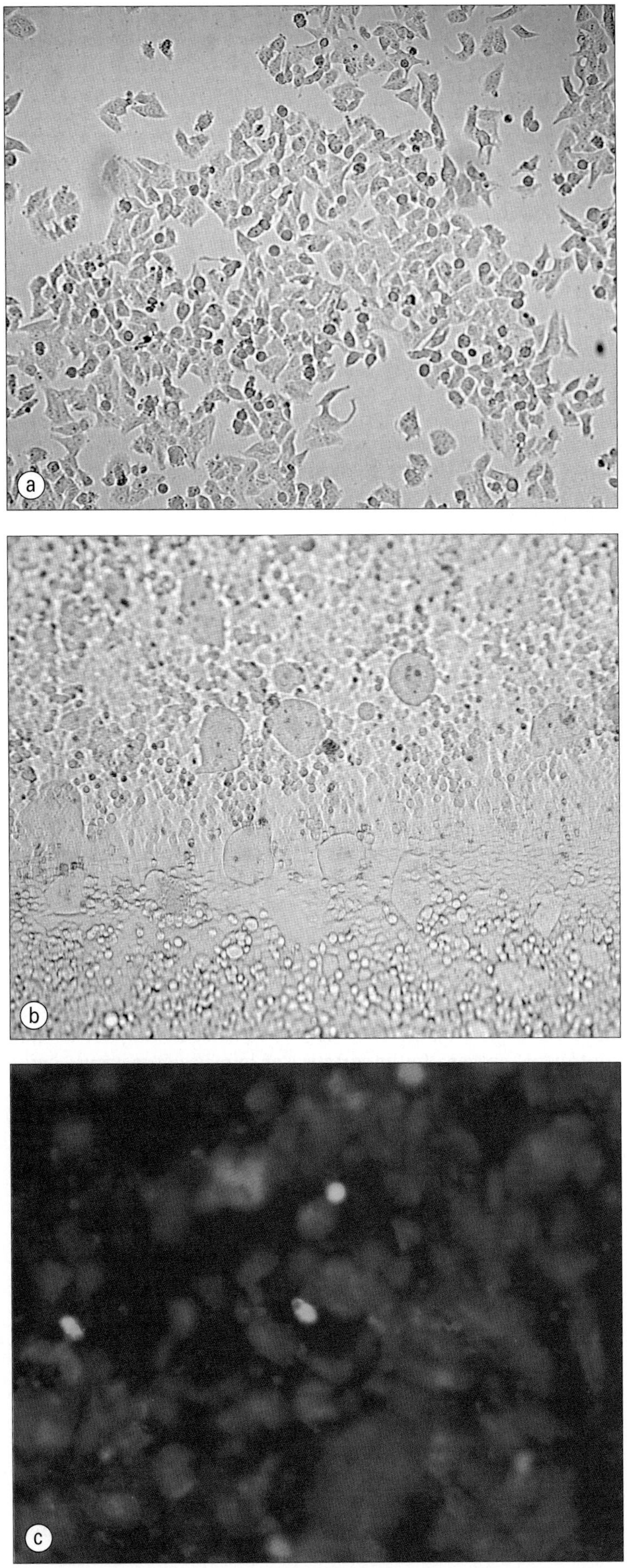

Fig. 220.3 Cytopathic effect of RSV on Hep-2 cell line culture and identification of RSV antigen by means of IFA. (a) Uninoculated cell line. (b) Syncytia formation in cell line culture. (c) Positive cells coloring green under IF microscope.

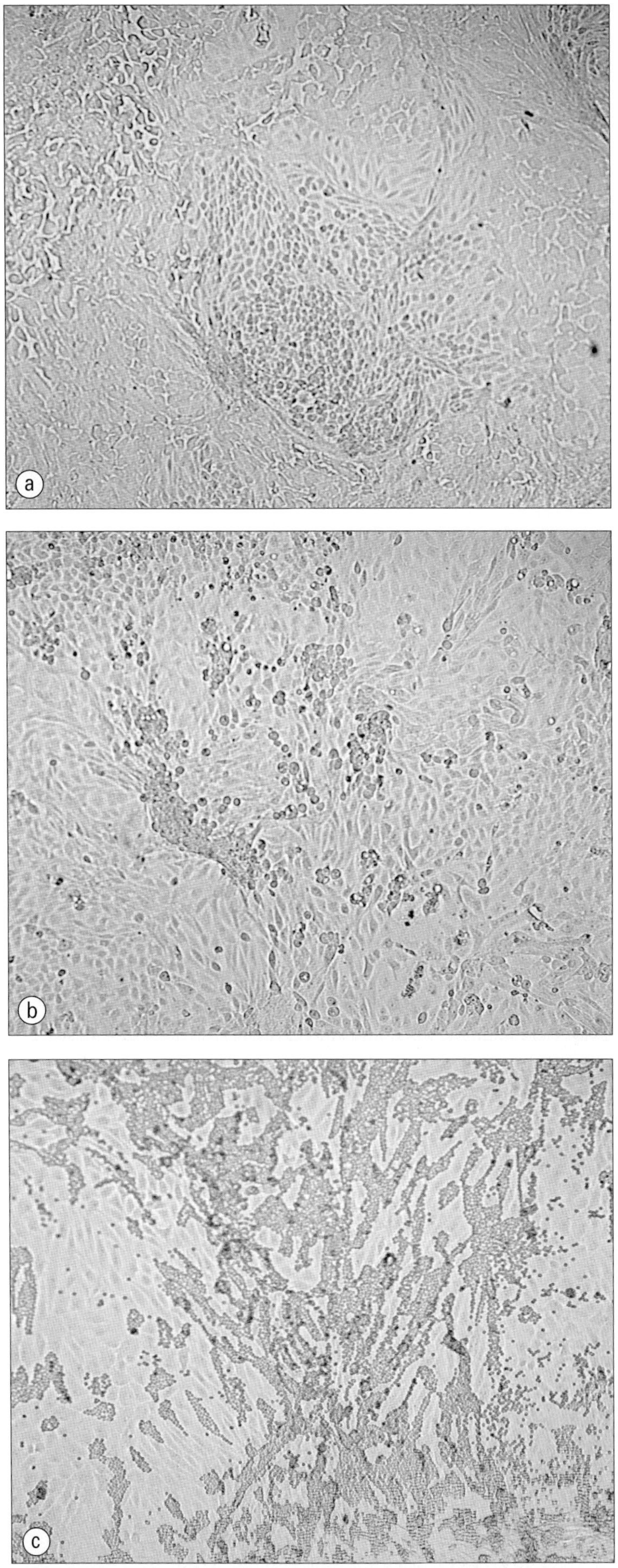

Fig. 220.4 Identification of hemadsorbing viruses. (a) Uninoculated primary rhesus monkey kidney (PRMK) cell line. (b) Non-specific rounding or clumping of PRMK cells. (c) Positive hemadsorption of guinea-pig red blood cells.

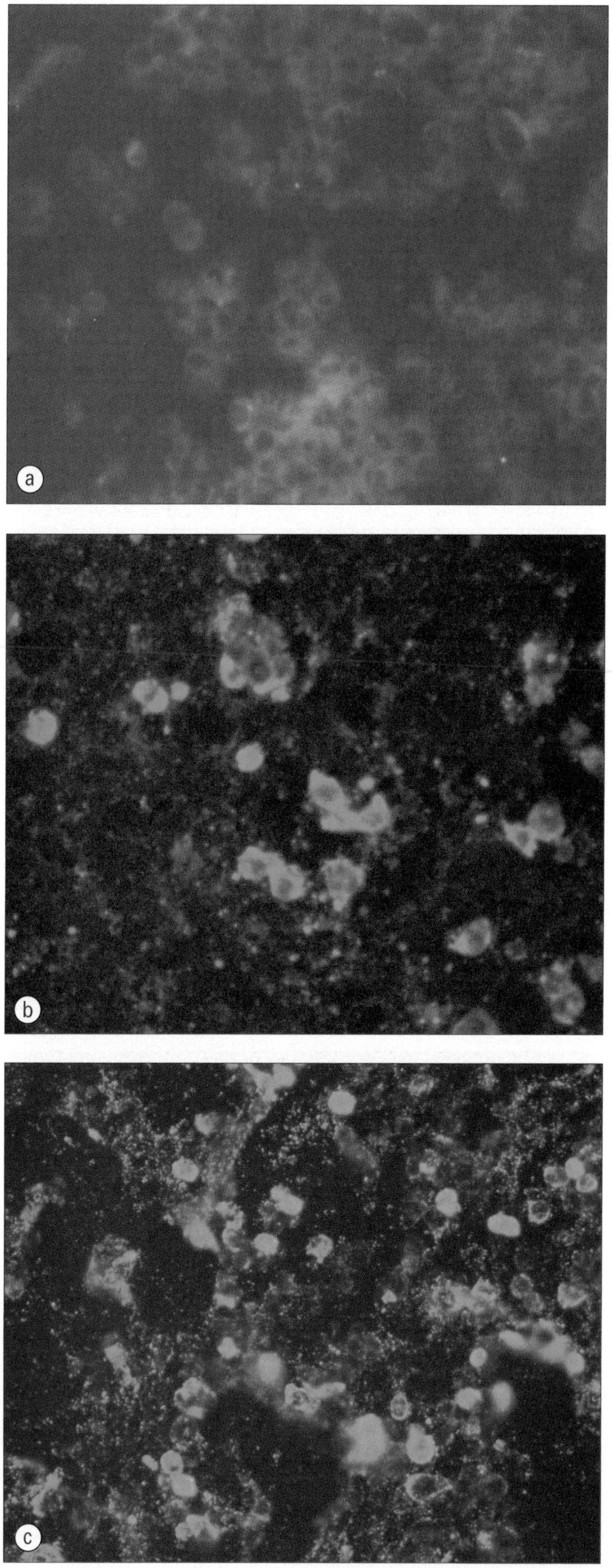

Fig. 220.5 **Differentiation of hemadsorbing viruses by means of IFA.** (a) Negative control. (b) Influenza B positive. (c) Parainfluenza-3 positive, showing a comparatively more finely granular staining.

HCoV-OC43 binds to cells by means of the HE glycoprotein or the viral S glycoprotein, which can recognize 9-*O*-acetylated sialic acid on the cell surface.

Prevention

No specific antiviral drugs or vaccines are currently available. Infection control measures aimed at reducing exposure to respiratory secretions of infected patients should reduce the transmission of these viruses.

Diagnostic microbiology

Although animal coronaviruses can be readily isolated from infected tissues and serially propagated in continuous cell lines, isolation of human coronaviruses from infected individuals is not possible with generally available culture systems. Primary isolation of HCoVs generally requires culture in human fetal tracheal or intestinal organs. The genomes of HCoV-229E and HCoV-OC43 have been sequenced and RT-PCR can be used in the research setting.[15] Most of the population studies of HCoVs have used serologic methods, including complement fixation, hemagglutination inhibition (OC43 only) and recently EIA.

Clinical manifestations

HCoVs are second only to rhinoviruses as a cause of the common cold and the symptoms are indistinguishable. In a study of adult volunteers the mean incubation period was 3.3 days, with a range of 2–4 days. The symptoms lasted for a mean of 7 days, with a range of 3–18 days.[16] HCoVs have also been associated with otitis media, exacerbation of asthma and chronic pulmonary disease and have occasionally been associated with pneumonia, particularly in immunosuppressed patients.[17,18] Early in 2003 an outbreak of severe pneumonia that originated in China, SARS (severe acute respiratory syndrome) was associated with atypical strains of coronavirus. The case fatality rate was approximately 4%.[110–112] Coronavirus particles have also been seen (via electron microscopy) in the stools of children and adults with diarrhea and gastroenteritis. The possible role of HCoVs in the genesis of multiple sclerosis (MS) is supported by the observation of coronavirus-like particles in brain tissue of patients with MS and by RT-PCR studies that have identified gene sequences of HCoV-229E and HCoV-OC43 in human brain tissue and cerebrospinal fluid with a higher frequency in MS patients than controls. However, the importance of human coronaviruses as a cause of diseases outside the respiratory tract remains to be determined.

Management

Treatment remains supportive. Potential targets for antiviral therapy are being identified, but no candidate drugs have been tested in clinical trials.

REOVIRUS

Nature

Isolation of the first reovirus was made in 1951, but it was in 1959 that Sabin coined the term reovirus to emphasize the fact that these viruses were isolated from the respiratory and enteric tracts and that they were not associated with any known human disease (Respiratory Enteric Orphan viruses). Reoviruses are nonenveloped viruses of about 65–75nm in diameter. They are composed of two concentric icosahedrically symmetric protein capsids, containing 10 discrete segments of genomic dsRNA. After attachment to cellular receptors, endocytosis of viral particles takes place. Replication occurs in the cytoplasm and results in cell death and lysis. Three distinct serotypes are identified by means of neutralization and hemagglutination inhibition tests (T1L, T2L and T3L).

Epidemiology

A study in which ELISA was used as the diagnostic method showed that the prevalence of antibodies against reovirus increased steadily throughout life from about 35% among 6-month to 1-year-old children to 60% among 11–19-year-olds and to more than 85% among those older than 60 years of age.[19] Infection can be achieved by intranasal inoculation as demonstrated in experiments with volunteers. Reoviruses have been recovered from water supplies and sewage effluents, presumably reflecting contamination of water with human and animal excreta. This could conceivably represent another source of virus for human infection.

Pathogenesis

It has been difficult to provide convincing evidence linking reovirus to specific human diseases. Cellular infection occurs by means of receptor-mediated endocytosis. Replication occurs in the cytoplasm. *In vitro* infection results in cell lysis. Interestingly, it has been observed that some reoviruses selectively replicate in and destroy cancer cells with an activated Ras signaling pathway, raising a possible role in the treatment of human neoplasms such as ovarian and colon cancer.[20]

Prevention

No specific strategies for prevention of transmission of reoviruses have been studied in clinical trials. Observance of appropriate handling of respiratory secretions from infected patients and avoidance of potentially contaminated water supplies could conceivably reduce the transmission of these viruses.

Diagnostic microbiology

The routine search for reovirus in clinical specimens in not recommended. In the research setting, a variety of techniques are available. In addition to identification of characteristic cytopathic effect (CPE) in cell line cultures, the presence of viral antigen can be confirmed using either immunofluorescence or immunocytochemistry. Immunocytochemical techniques can also be employed for the detection of reovirus antigens in tissue specimens. ELISA techniques have been widely used for detection of reovirus antibodies in serum. A variety of molecular techniques, including PCR, can be used for the detection of reovirus in tissues or body fluid samples.

Clinical manifestations

In a study of adult volunteers, intranasal inoculation of reovirus was followed by an increase in serotype-specific antibodies, recovery of the virus from anal swabs and development of respiratory illness in a third of the individuals infected with T1L.[21] The illness began 24–48 hours after the challenge and symptoms lasted for 4–7 days. The predominant symptoms included headache, pharyngitis, sneezing, rhinorrhea, cough and malaise. Because those findings have not been reproduced consistently, there is currently no definite etiological association of reovirus infection with human disease.

Management

Although ribavirin and other compounds exhibit *in vitro* activity against reoviruses, clinical trials seem unlikely to be performed for an organism that remains an 'orphan'.

RHINOVIRUS

Nature

Rhinovirus (RV) was first isolated in the 1950s from nasopharyngeal secretions of patients with the common cold. RV belongs to the Picornaviridae family, which includes the genera Enterovirus (poliovirus, coxsackieviruses groups A and B, echovirus and numbered enteroviruses) and Hepatovirus (hepatitis A virus). Rhinoviruses are small (30nm), nonenveloped particles that contain a linear single-stranded positive-sense RNA genome. The icosahedral capsid is composed of 60 subunits arranged as 12 pentameres. Each subunit is composed of one of each four structural proteins (VP1 to VP4). VP1–3 have exterior projections that are targets for neutralizing antibodies. More than 100 serotypes have been identified. The leukocyte binding protein ICAM-1 is the receptor for the majority of rhinovirus serotypes. The receptor-binding site resides in a depression of the capsid surface that is not accessible to antibodies. After endocytosis, an acid-dependent conformational change of the capsid allows the release of the RNA into the host cell cytoplasm, where viral replication and assembly take place. A polyprotein precursor is processed mainly by two viral proteases designated 2A and 3C. The 2A protease makes the first cleavage between the structural and nonstructural proteins, while the 3C protease catalyzes most of the remaining internal cleavages.

Epidemiology

Rhinoviruses are ubiquitous and infections occur in all age groups. They cause about half of all common colds and are also linked to a variety of complications such as otitis media, sinusitis, bronchitis and exacerbations of asthma and chronic obstructive pulmonary disease. RV infections result in frequent health care contacts, hospitalizations and excess of antibiotic use. These infections occur throughout the year with peaks in the fall and spring and with multiple serotypes circulating simultaneously in a given geographic location. Preschool children commonly introduce the virus to the rest of the family, with a secondary attack rate of about 50%, after an interval of 2–5 days. Extensive studies in susceptible individuals have shown that 95% of challenged subjects become infected and about 75% of them become ill. The major factor determining the risk of illness is the prechallenge level of neutralizing antibodies.

Pathogenesis

In spite of the extensive literature on the transmission of rhinovirus, controversy still exists about the predominant mode of transmission. Most data support the notion that contact transmission, primarily as hand shaking followed by inoculation of the nasal mucosa and lacrimal canals, is the most efficient mode of transmission. RV could survive from a few hours to as long as 4 days on nonporous surfaces and for at least 2 hours on human skin. Although droplet or airborne transmission of rhinovirus infection is possible, prolonged and close exposure is apparently required. There is no good clinical evidence to support the common notion that exposure to cold weather, getting wet or becoming chilled play a role in the genesis of RV illness.

Rhinoviruses attach to respiratory epithelium and spread locally. Most serotypes use ICAM-1 as a receptor for attachment and for subsequent viral uncoating during cell invasion. Some serotypes can upregulate the ICAM-1 expression on human epithelial cells, resulting in an increased susceptibility to infection. Infection is followed by activation of several inflammatory mechanisms including the release of cytokines (particularly IL-8), bradykinins, prostaglandins and histamine, as well as stimulation of parasympathetic reflexes.

The resulting process includes vasodilation of nasal blood vessels, transudation of plasma, glandular secretion and stimulation of nerve fibers, triggering sneeze and cough reflexes. Nasal mucociliary transport is reduced markedly during the illness and may be impaired for weeks. Immunity to individual rhinoviruses is type specific and not long lasting. Protection correlates more with the level of locally synthesized lgA antibodies, which decline within months of infection, rather than with lgG in serum, which may persist for a few years.

Prevention

Hand washing after shaking hands with someone who has a cold or after touching environmental objects potentially contaminated with relatively fresh secretions is strongly recommended. Alcohol-based, waterless antiseptics are also effective for this purpose. Symptomatic patients should be advised to hand wash frequently and to use disposable tissues. The CDC recommends contact precautions for the prevention of nosocomial RV infections. Some institutions also observe droplet isolation precautions.

The diversity of serotypes and the specificity of the immune response have precluded the development of an effective vaccine. A number of drugs have been studied for the prophylaxis of RV infection, including interferon α, pirodavir and recombinant soluble ICAM-1 molecule. However, the practical utility of these prophylaxis modalities remains to be demonstrated.

Diagnostic microbiology

Traditionally, RV infections have been detected by virus isolation in cell culture followed by acid lability testing. Virus isolation requires typically 2–14 days. Presumptive identification of a cell culture isolate as rhinovirus is based on a combination of enterovirus-like cytopathic effect and clinical information.

Further differentiation from enteroviruses is based on the diminished replication of rhinoviruses at 98.6°F compared to that at 91.4°F and at pH 3.0 compared with pH 7.0. ELISA has been developed for the detection of rhinovirus antigens. The use of serological assays is limited by the diversity of serotypes and the lack of a group-specific antigen. Recently developed RT-PCR assays are more rapid and sensitive than isolation techniques for detection of RV RNA in clinical specimens.

Clinical manifestations

Symptoms of the common cold include profuse watery rhinorrhea, nasal congestion, sneezing and quite often headache, sore throat and or cough. The symptoms begin within 8–10 hours of infection and peak around 1–3 days. There is little or no fever. By days 3–5 of the illness, nasal discharge may become mucopurulent from polymorphonuclear leukocytes that have migrated to the infection site in response to cytokines such as IL-8. Resolution of symptoms generally occurs within a week. Complications of RV infection include sinusitis, otitis media and exacerbation of asthma-COPD. Secondary bacterial infections may occur. Recent studies using CT of the sinuses have shown that RV infections can cause the accumulation of secretions in the sinuses, possibly from the passage of nasal secretions into the sinuses during nose blowing.[22,23] Mounting evidence suggests an association between RV infections and lower respiratory tract illness, especially in immunocompromised individuals.[24–29]

Management

Symptomatic treatment with decongestants, antihistamines and antitussives is currently the mainstay of therapy. The efficacy of zinc lozenges is controversial and their practical utility is limited because of their metallic taste. A variety of candidate drugs have been studied.[30]

Interferon-α has been found to be effective for the prevention of rhinovirus-associated colds but ineffective for the treatment of established colds. When administered through nasal spray, 80% of secondary RV cold were prevented but some patients developed blood-tinged nasal discharge and concerns about cost-effectiveness have been raised. Pirodavir (R77975) is a capsid-binding antipicornaviral agent with *in vitro* activity against most RV serotypes. Frequent intranasal sprays of pirodavir have been found to be effective in preventing experimentally induced RV illness[31] but ineffective in providing significant clinical benefit in naturally occurring rhinovirus colds.[32] Major recent therapeutic advances include the development of protease 3C inhibitors, recombinant soluble intercellular adhesion molecule (sICAM-1) and capsid-function inhibitors (pleconaril), all of which exhibit potent antirhinoviral activity *in vitro* and varying activity in clinical trials. AG7088, an irreversible inhibitor of rhinovirus 3C protease with *in vitro* activity against a broad range of RV serotypes,[33] is undergoing clinical trials. Recombinant soluble ICAM-1 molecule (Tremacamra) has been found to be effective in reducing the symptoms of experimental common colds in randomized controlled trials. This reduction in symptoms has been apparent regardless of whether the drug was given before or after the challenge with the virus.[34]

Pleconaril binds to a hydrophobic pocket in the viral capsid, inducing conformational changes that lead to altered receptor binding and viral uncoating. Pleconaril is orally bio-available and achieves serum concentrations in excess of those required to inhibit 90% of clinical rhino- and enteroviral isolates *in vitro*. In a placebo-controlled study of rhinovirus infections, pleconaril-treated patients had a 1.5-day reduction in time to resolution of symptoms, significant reduction in symptom severity within 12–24 hours after initiation of therapy and a significant reduction in median viral titers in nasal mucus.[35] The US FDA Advisory Committee has not yet recommended the approval of pleconaril for treatment of the common cold. Additional studies on safety, development of resistance and drug interactions are ongoing.

RESPIRATORY SYNCYTIAL VIRUS

Nature

Respiratory syncytial virus (RSV) belongs to the Paramyxoviridae family of viruses, which also includes parainfluenza viruses, mumps virus and measles virus. RSV was first isolated in the mid-1950s from a symptomatic laboratory chimpanzee during an outbreak of illness resembling the common cold. This virus derives its name from the characteristic formation of multinucleated giant cells in tissue culture.

RSV has a linear single-stranded, negative-sense genomic RNA. Virions are pleomorphic, with both spherical and filamentous forms seen under the electron microscope, and with an average diameter between 120 and 300nm. The envelope consists of a lipid bilayer derived from the host plasma membrane and contains three virally encoded transmembrane surface glycoproteins: the attachment protein G, the fusion protein F and the small hydrophobic SH protein. The F protein can mediate fusion with neighboring cells to form syncytia. The G glycoprotein plays a major role in the process of attachment. Two major types of RSV – A and B – are distinguished serologically based on the antigenic characteristics of the surface glycoprotein G. Other viral proteins include the matrix proteins (M and M2), the major nucleocapsid (N) protein, a phosphoprotein (P) and the major polymerase (L).

Epidemiology

RSV is the most common cause of bronchiolitis and pneumonia among infants and young children worldwide. Virtually all children are infected by the time they reach 3 years of age. Natural immunity is transient and reinfection is common. Crowding in households and day care centers increases the attack rate of RSV. In the USA, it has been estimated that 100,000 hospitalizations and 4500 deaths are related to RSV infection annually. The associated health care expenses are in excess of 300 million dollars per year. In older children and immunocompetent adults, RSV infections are seldom severe and are usually manifested as upper respiratory infection (URI) or tracheobronchitis. Individuals at high risk for severe RSV infection include premature infants (particularly those born at less than 34 weeks of gestation), young infants (particularly those with chronic lung disease, formerly designated bronchopulmonary dysplasia), elderly individuals and immunocompromised subjects.

RSV activity follows a seasonal pattern in temperate zones of the world. In urban centers, annual outbreaks occur during the fall, winter and early spring. In the northern hemisphere most outbreaks peak in February or March. In tropical or subtropical areas, epidemics peak during the rainy season.

Pathogenesis

Humans are the major reservoir. RSV is present in large numbers in the respiratory secretions of symptomatic infected persons and viral titers remain high for about 1 week after the onset of symptoms, followed by a gradual decline that may last for up to 3–4 weeks. The portal of entry is usually the conjunctiva or the nasal mucosa. Although transmission can occur via large droplets, contact transmission predominates.[36] Virus can be cultured for >5 hours on impervious surfaces such as bed rails. Thus, caregivers can contaminate their hands during routine care and transmit the virus by contact to other patients. Neutralizing antibodies to the surface glycoproteins F and G correlate with resistance to reinfection, but protection is far from complete and is of short duration.[37]

Pathologic examination of patients with bronchiolitis has revealed necrosis of ciliated bronchiolar epithelial cells, mononuclear infiltrate and edema of the peribronchial space. Bronchiolar obstruction results from the increased mucous production by goblet cells and the above-mentioned pathologic changes. Partial obstruction results in air trapping, and total obstruction results in atelectasis.

Pathologic examination of patients with pneumonia has revealed marked interstitial inflammation and edema of the lung parenchyma, along with the findings of bronchiolitis. Chronic alterations of pulmonary function tests have been described after RSV infection, but a cause–effect relationship remains to be confirmed.[38]

Prevention

In the household setting, the transmission of RSV may be decreased by means of frequent hand washing and refraining from sharing items such as cups, glasses and utensils with persons who have RSV illness. The CDC recommends contact precautions for the prevention of nosocomial RSV infections. Some institutions also observe droplet isolation precautions. Studies have shown that the implementation of multifaceted infection control strategies results in a reduction of the incidence of nosocomial RSV infection.[39]

Passive immunoprophylaxis is indicated for high-risk children. The available evidence supports the use of RSV-IVIG or palivizumab for the prophylaxis of RSV infections among infants with chronic lung disease (formerly designated bronchopulmonary dysplasia) and premature infants. Passive immunoprophylaxis is not recommended for children with cyanotic congenital heart disease.[40]

RSV intravenous immunoglobulin (RSV-IVIG, RespiGam®) is a human polyclonal immunoglobulin with high RSV microneutralization titers. In placebo-controlled studies, monthly intravenous doses of 750mg/kg during the RSV season significantly reduced the incidence of RSV hospitalizations and the severity of illness among premature infants and infants with bronchopulmonary dysplasia.[41,42] Palivizumab is a humanized monoclonal antibody that specifically inhibits an epitope at the A antigenic site of the F protein of RSV subtypes A and B. It is dosed monthly at 15mg/kg intramuscularly during RSV season. In a large multicenter placebo-controlled trial involving high-risk infants, palivizumab prophylaxis resulted in a 55% reduction in hospitalization rates and number of hospital days ascribed to RSV infection.[43] Both agents have been well tolerated, with a few adverse effects; however, their high cost necessitates strict guidelines for their use. Cost-saving benefit has not been observed uniformly,[44–48] perhaps as a result of major differences in the prevalence of RSV lower respiratory tract infections in different countries and regions, suggesting the need for locally adapted recommendations. Palivizumab is easier to administer and does not interfere with the MMR vaccine or varicella vaccine. RSV-IVIG, however, provides additional protection against other respiratory viral illnesses and may be preferred for children receiving replacement IVIG because of underlying immune deficiency.[43]

The role of passive immunoprophylaxis for the prevention of RSV infections in high-risk adults remains to be defined. Development of an RSV vaccine is ongoing but none is yet available.

Diagnostic microbiology

The gold standard diagnostic method is isolation of the virus from respiratory secretions. Appropriate samples for diagnosis include nasopharyngeal aspirate, wash or swab, tracheal aspirates, bronchioalveolar lavage and biopsy material. Given the lability of the virus, the samples should be kept cold and should be inoculated as quickly as possible. Cell line cultures show characteristics of RSV cytopathic effect after 3–7 days of incubation.

RSV was the first respiratory virus to be readily identified by means of rapid diagnostic tests based on antigen detection. Current methods for rapid detection of RSV antigen include enzyme immunoassay, immunoperoxidase staining, direct and indirect immunofluorescence tests and PCR. Serologic diagnosis requires a convalescent-phase RSV lgG antibody titer at least four times higher than the acute-phase titer.

Clinical manifestations

The incubation period ranges from 2 to 8 days. Illness begins most frequently with rhinorrhea, sneezing and cough. When fever is present it is generally low grade. Most children experience recovery from illness after 8–15 days. During their first RSV infection, 25–40% of infected infants and young children have signs or symptoms of bronchiolitis or pneumonia and 0.5–2% require hospitalization. In contrast, hospitalization will be required in up to 25% of high-risk children such as those with history of prematurity or chronic lung disease. RSV bronchiolitis or pneumonia should be suspected when an infant or young child presents with progressive cough, wheezing and dyspnea during a RSV season. Radiographic findings in patients with bronchiolitis include hyperlucency, diaphragmatic flattening and outward bowing on the intercostal spaces. Findings compatible with pneumonia include interstitial infiltrates and, less frequently, consolidation, particularly in the right upper and middle lobes.

In neonates, the clinical presentation may be atypical with lethargy, irritability or poor oral intake. RSV has been detected in lung tissue of infants with sudden death syndrome, but a cause–effect relationship has not been confirmed. Prolonged pulmonary function deficit and airway hyperreactivity have been reported following RSV infection but it remains unclear whether these abnormalities were present before the infection. Otitis media has also been associated with RSV infection.

Among immunocompetent adults, RSV infection usually manifests with rhinorrhea, pharyngitis, cough, bronchitis, headache, fatigue and fever. In older persons, particularly the institutionalized elderly and those with chronic cardiopulmonary illnesses, severe pneumonia may occur, leading to respiratory failure. Among immunocompromised individuals, RSV has been the most frequently isolated viral respiratory pathogen in surveillance studies performed at large cancer centers.[49] In this setting RSV infection typically begins as a URI and may evolve into lower respiratory tract disease in up to 50% of cases. A particularly high rate of progression to pneumonia (70–80%) has been reported among adult HSCT recipients developing RSV infection within the period prior to engraftment. In such setting the RSV pneumonia resulted in 60–80% mortality, regardless of the inclusion of antiviral drugs in the treatment strategy.

Management

For patients with mild disease, no specific treatment is necessary other than the treatment of symptoms. Children with severe disease may require hospitalization for supplemental oxygen therapy, hydration, nutrition and, sometimes, mechanical ventilation. Improvements in supportive care have made a significant impact on the mortality from RSV bronchiolitis and pneumonia. The use of bronchodilators is likely beneficial for patients with significant bronchospasm. Corticosteroids are commonly used as anti-inflammatory therapy, although there is lack of data demonstrating the benefits of such intervention. Aerosolized ribavirin (Virasole®) was approved in 1986 for the treatment of infants and children with severe RSV disease. The treatment is cumbersome to deliver and its impact on mortality remains controversial.[50,51]

A combination of passive immunoprophylaxis and ribavirin has been reported to be well tolerated and to improve the outcome of severe RSV infection among bone marrow transplant recipients.[52,53] In one open trial the mortality was only 22% among nine adults with pneumonia in whom therapy was initiated prior to the onset of profound respiratory failure.[53] Pre-emptive treatment strategies are being investigated primarily in immunocompromised individuals. Delay of immunosuppressive chemotherapy should be considered when severely immunosuppressed individuals, such as HSCT recipients, develop acute RSV infection.

PARAINFLUENZA VIRUS

Nature

Human parainfluenza viruses (HPIVs) were first described in the 1950s, originally as croup-associated viruses. The term parainfluenza was coined because of the associated influenza-like symptoms and the hemagglutinin and neuraminidase activities exhibited by HPIVs. However, HPIVs belong to the Paramyxoviridae family.

The virions are pleomorphic and range in average diameter from 150 to 200nm. They are enveloped particles with a linear single-stranded negative-sense RNA genome. The HPIVs encode two surface glycoproteins: an attachment protein called HN (hemagglutinin-neuraminidase), that binds to sialic acid-containing receptors on host cell surfaces, and a fusion protein F that is involved in the fusion of the viral membrane with the cellular plasma membrane. The HN protein is a multifunctional molecule with binding activity (binding to sialic acid containing surface glycoproteins and glycolipids), neuraminidase activity and fusion promotion activity. The attachment activity can be measured by hemagglutination assay. The neuraminidase activity prevents aggregation of virus particles by removing sialic acid from the virion glycoproteins and facilitates infection in the respiratory tract by digesting the mucin coating of epithelial cells.

These viruses also encode three nucleocapsid associated proteins, NP, P and L, and the nonglycosilated internal protein M. The four HPIVs are segregated in two genera, the Respirovirus (HPIV-1 and HPIV-3) and the Rubulavirus (HPIV-2 and HPIV-4), based on antigenic and structural characteristics, including additional accessory proteins (V,D,W,I,X,C and SH).

Epidemiology

HPIVs are distributed worldwide. Each of the four HPIVs can cause a full spectrum of acute respiratory tract illnesses. HPIV-1 and HPIV-2 are the most common pathogens associated with croup or laryngotracheobronchitis.[54] HPIVs 1, 2 and 3 are also important causes of bronchiolitis and pneumonia among infants and young children.[54,55] Less is known about HPIV-4. Most children have serologic evidence of infection by 5 years of age. Reinfection is common and occurs throughout life. Most HPIV infections are detected during seasonal epidemics. In a study on an outpatient pediatric population,[56] HPIV-1 occurred in the fall of odd-numbered years, HPIV-2 was less predictable and HPIV-3 appeared yearly with peak activity in spring or summer. In a study of data from the US National Hospital Discharge Survey obtained from 1979 through 1997,[55] 3-month periods of widespread activity for each of the HPIVs were identified: HPIV-1 from September through November of odd-numbered years; HPIV-2 from October through December each year, and HPIV-3 from April through June during 1995 and 1997 and from May through July during 1994 and 1996. The estimated number of hospitalizations associated with HPIV-1–3 infections was 7600 to 48,000 among children aged <1 year and 8100 to 42,600 among children aged 1–4 years. The estimated rates of HPIV-associated hospitalizations ranged from 1.9 to 12 per 1000 children <1 year old and from 0.5 to 2.0 per 1000 children aged 1–4 years.

Pathogenesis

Although droplet transmission can occur, contact is though to be the primary mode of transmission of HPIV infection. This can be direct person to person or indirect through intermediate objects. Inoculation is into the mouth, nasopharynx or oral mucosa. The characteristic tendency to cause laryngotracheobronchitis and croup is not completely understood. Some of the HPIVs can induce syncytia formation but the role of this phenomenon is not well understood. Immune response is complex and includes the production of serum-neutralizing antibodies directed towards epitopes of the HN and F proteins. An important role in the protection against HPIVs infections is played by the mucosal immune response, primarily through the production of IgA antibodies. In animal model studies, it has been demonstrated that the role of $CD8^+$ T cells is critical for virus clearance.

Prevention

General principles for the prevention of respiratory viral infections apply to the prevention of HPIV infections. The CDC recommends contact precautions for the prevention of nosocomial HPIV infections. Some institutions also observe droplet isolation precautions. No specific vaccine is yet available and no drugs have been tested for prophylactic use.

Diagnostic microbiology

Definite diagnosis relies on the isolation of the virus from respiratory secretions. Other diagnostic methods include detection of viral antigens or nucleic acid, and serologic analysis. Primary isolation and identification, by means of hemadsorption assay, can be followed by typing of the virus by means of immunofluorescence or hemadsorption inhibition. PCR assays can be more sensitive than isolation and antigen detection methods.[57]

Clinical manifestations

Infection in children is associated with an acute febrile illness in up to 80% of cases. Initial symptoms include coryza, sore throat, hoarseness and dry cough. In cases of croup, a brassy or barking cough may progress to stridor and some may progress to airway obstruction. The anteroposterior radiograph of the neck shows glottic and subglottic narrowing ('steeple sign') which differentiate this disease from epiglottitis. In cases of bronchiolitis and pneumonia, progressive cough is accompanied by wheezing, tachypnea and hypoxemia. Chest X-ray examination may reveal air trapping and interstitial infiltrates. Otitis media with presence of HPIVs in the middle ear fluids is common.

In older children and adults, HPIV infections tend to be milder and present as URI. However, HPIV-1 and 3 have been diagnosed by means of serologic assay in a significant number of adults admitted with acute respiratory illness.[58] A few cases of HPIV meningitis have been described.[59] Immunocompromised pediatric and adult individuals such as hematopoietic stem cell,[60–65] lung[66] and renal[67] transplant recipients may develop severe HPIV infections with a high rate of progression to pneumonia. The use of corticosteroids was linked with a higher risk of HPIV-3 pneumonia among recipients of hematopoietic stem cell transplantation.[62]

Management

Symptomatic treatment of croup usually includes humidification of air by ultrasonic nebulizer and inhalations of racemic epinephrine. Epinephrine provides rapid but transient relief of the airway obstruction. The anti-inflammatory effect of systemic corticosteroids is advocated to prevent or shorten the period of intubation in severe croup. Patients with bronchiolitis are also treated with bronchodilators. Ribavirin has exhibited *in vitro* activity against HPIVs[68] but data from controlled clinical trials are lacking.

INFLUENZA VIRUS

Nature

The existence of acute, usually self-limited, febrile respiratory illness that occurs in outbreaks of variable severity almost every winter has been known for centuries.[69–71] The term 'influenza' was derived from Italian in the mid-1300s to indicate that the disease resulted from astrological influences. The etiology of the disease and the explanation for its peculiar behavior remained elusive. It was not until the late 1920s that the etiology of influenza was better understood. Shope[72] showed that swine influenza could be transmitted with filtered mucus, suggesting that the causative agent was a virus. In the 1930s, Smith *et al* isolated the influenza virus from humans with respiratory illness.[73]

Influenza virions are enveloped particles of spherical or elongated shape, measuring 80–120nm in diameter and containing a linear segmented, single-stranded, negative-sense RNA. They belong to the Orthomyxoviridae family of RNA viruses. There are three major antigenic types – A, B and C – that also differ in genetic organization, structure, clinico-epidemiologic characteristics and host range (Table 220.3).

Influenza A virus serves as the prototype strain. The virion has two surface glycoproteins (hemagglutinin and neuraminidase) and a major nucleocapsid glycoprotein (NP) that associates with three other proteins (PA, PB1 and PB2) to form the transcription complex, two matrix proteins (M1 and M2) and two nonstructural proteins (NS1 and NS2). Influenza A virus adsorption to host cells involves the binding of hemagglutinin to sialic acid-containing cell surface glycoproteins or glycolipids. This is followed by virion entry into the cell via receptor-mediated endocytosis. The M2 protein ion channel activity leads to the acidification of the vesicle and fusion of the virus membrane to the vesicle membrane, resulting in the release of the viral nucleocapsid into the cytoplasm. Influenza RNA replication and translation depend on viral proteins and cell machinery functions. Budding from the plasma membrane completes assembly. The emerging virions are coated with sialic acid that is then cleaved by the neuraminidase, allowing the virus to be free and able to infect other cells.

Influenza A viruses are divided into subtypes. The current nomenclature system[74] includes the host of origin, geographic location of first isolation, strain number and year of isolation. The antigenic description of the hemagglutinin (HA) and neuraminidase (NA) is given within parentheses (e.g. A/Swine/lowa/15/30 (H1N1)). By convention, the host of origin of human strains is omitted (e.g. A/Puerto Rico/8/34 (H1N1)). There are 15 HA and nine NA subtypes; the subtypes differ by 30% or more in amino acid sequence homology.

Epidemiology

There is no evidence of persistent or latent infection with human influenza viruses. The virus is maintained in humans by person-to-person spread during acute infection. Influenza virus is also known to infect a variety of birds and mammals (including swine, horses, seals, whales, mink and primates). The current information supports the concept that mammalian influenza viruses are derived from avian influenza reservoirs.[75–77] Some avian species, such as ducks, are asymptomatic carriers perhaps as a result of virus adaptation over many centuries.

The influenza viruses are unique among the respiratory tract viruses in that they undergo significant antigenic variation. Antigenic drift involves minor antigenic changes in the HA and NA that occur by accumulation of point mutations, resulting in amino acid substitutions in antigenic sites. These changes render the new strain different enough to avoid the immunity induced by previous strains. Influenza epidemics have been recognized as a major cause of morbidity and increased mortality, especially in the very young, the very old, people with chronic cardiopulmonary conditions, pregnant women and immunocompromised individuals. In the USA, epidemics of influenza typically occur during the winter months and are responsible for an average of approximately 16,000 to 220,000 hospitalizations and 20,000 to 40,000 deaths per epidemic.[78] In the tropics, influenza can occur throughout the year and in the temperate regions of the southern hemisphere the majority of influenza activity occurs during the months of April to September.

Table 220.3 Comparison of influenza virus types.

COMPARISON OF INFLUENZA VIRUS TYPES			
Antigenic type	A	B	C
RNA segments	8	8	7
Surface glycoproteins	Hemagglutinin (1 to 15) Neuraminidase (1 to 9)	Hemagglutinin Neuraminidase	HEF: hemagglutinin esterase fusion protein
Genetic variability	Drifts and shifts	Drifts	Drifts
Human disease	Epidemic, pandemic, sporadic	Epidemic, sporadic	Sporadic
Known hosts	Humans, swine, horses, poultry, sea mammals several avian species	Humans	Humans, swine
Target for current antivirals	M2 protein (amantadine, rimantadine) Neuraminidase (zanamivir, oseltamivir)	Neuraminidase (zanamivir, oseltamivir)	Not available

During influenza A pandemics, the impact of influenza becomes global and results in significant morbidity and mortality for a broader range of hosts, including young healthy people.[70] The greatest influenza pandemic, so-called Spanish influenza, spread around the globe in 1918–19 after the First World War and resulted in the deaths of approximately 20–40 million persons, more than the war itself. The emergence of pandemic influenza A can be explained by antigenic shifts resulting from genetic reassortment within cells dually infected by human and animal influenza viruses.[79] The exchange of RNA segments between the two viruses occurs in a manner analogous to the exchange of parental chromosomes during meiosis. Interestingly, all major antigenic shifts have originated in China and have been confined to the H1, H2 and H3 subtypes. Avian influenza can be transmitted to humans with swine acting as an intermediary host in which reassortment takes place. However, a direct transmission of a pathogenic avian influenza to humans was observed in Hong Kong in 1997, when 18 people were infected with an avian H5N1 influenza virus and six died of its complications.[80] In addition, it has been observed that the Russian influenza (H1N1), that appeared in northern China in 1977, was identical to the virus that caused a human influenza epidemic in 1950, suggesting that certain influenza strains may remain confined in a natural reservoir for many years and re-emerge when the herd immunity has waned.

Pathogenesis

Droplet transmission is considered the primary mode of transmission of influenza. However, scarce data also support the notion that airborne transmission can occur, spread from person to person by direct inhalation of droplet nuclei or small-particle aerosols measuring less than 5μm in diameter. After evaporation, micro-organisms remain suspended in the air for long periods of time and can be dispersed by air currents. Susceptible hosts may inhale the particles within the same room or over a longer distance from the source patient. The extent to which transmission might also occur by contact with virus-contaminated hands or fomites is less well understood.

Acute diffuse mucosal inflammation and edema of the upper airway and bronchi are observed in uncomplicated influenza. The columnar ciliated cells become vacuolated and edematous. This is followed by desquamation of the ciliated and mucus-producing epithelial cells. In cases of influenza viral pneumonia, there is an interstitial pneumonitis with a predominantly mononuclear leukocyte infiltration. The alveolar walls become denuded of epithelium; hyaline membranes form, and the intra-alveolar space becomes filled with exudate and hemorrhage.[81] At a cellular level, influenza virus disrupts protein synthesis and also induces apoptosis.

The immune response against influenza is complex and involves multiple arms of the immune system. Neutralizing antibodies in respiratory secretions are primarily of the IgA isotype[82] and constitute the first line of defense. However, the major role is played by the humoral response via neutralizing antibodies. The level of serum antibody to the HA and NA correlates with resistance to illness and with restriction of the influenza virus replication in the respiratory tract of humans.[83,84] Interleukin-6 (IL-6), interferon-α and other pro-inflammatory cytokines are produced in response to influenza infection, with the peak of their production coinciding with the peak of systemic symptoms.[85] The cellular immunity also plays an important role in the immune response to influenza virus. Cytotoxic T cells participate by interacting with B cells and also by destroying cells infected with influenza.[86]

Prevention

Influenza vaccination is the primary method for preventing influenza. To be effective, the vaccine components need to match the circulating strains of the target season. Intensive surveillance of new influenza strains is maintained around the globe in order to make an informed selection of strains for the next yearly influenza vaccine and to detect early on strains that could potentially cause a new influenza pandemic. The primary target groups for annual vaccination are:

- people aged ≥65 years;
- residents of nursing homes and other chronic care facilities;
- people who have chronic disorders of the pulmonary or cardiovascular systems;
- those who have required regular medical follow-up or hospitalization during the preceding year because of chronic metabolic diseases (including diabetes mellitus), renal dysfunction, hemoglobinopathies or immunosuppression (including immunosuppression caused by medications or by human immunodeficiency virus);
- children and teenagers (aged 6 months to 18 years) who are receiving long-term aspirin therapy and therefore might be at risk for developing Reye's syndrome after influenza infection;
- and women who will be in the second or third trimester of pregnancy during the influenza season.

Vaccination of health care workers and others in close contact with persons at high risk, including household members, is recommended. When feasible, vaccination is also recommended for people aged 50–64 years, because this group has an increased prevalence of high-risk conditions, and for otherwise healthy children aged 6–23 months, because they are at increased risk for influenza-related hospitalization.[78] Depending on vaccine availability, vaccination should also be provided to any person who wishes to reduce the likelihood of becoming ill with influenza.

Vaccination results in reductions of influenza-related respiratory illness and number of physician visits among all groups of age, hospitalization and death among persons at high risk, otitis media among children and work absenteeism among adults. In the United States, the inactivated (i.e. killed virus) vaccine is recommended.[87] The vaccine contains three strains (i.e. two type A and one type B), representing the influenza viruses more likely to circulate in the upcoming winter. The vaccine is made from highly purified, inactivated virions. Subvirion and purified surface antigen preparations are also available. The effectiveness of influenza vaccine depends primarily on the age and immunocompetence of the vaccine recipient and the degree of similarity between the viruses in the vaccine and those in circulation. Local reactions to the vaccine are generally mild. Fever, malaise, myalgia and other systemic symptoms can also occur. The 1976 swine influenza vaccine was associated with an increased frequency of Guillain–Barré syndrome (<10 cases/1,000,000 persons vaccinated).

Live attenuated influenza vaccines can be administered directly to the respiratory tract, avoiding the need for injections and providing a means of inducing the production of IgA by the respiratory mucosa. Strains prepared by reassortment from cold-adapted mutants of both influenza A and B viruses have been widely shown to be well tolerated in both adults and children and to be highly efficacious.[88,89]

Antiviral chemoprophylaxis is approximately 70–90% effective in preventing illness in healthy adults. Amantadine, rimantadine and oseltamivir are approved for chemoprophylaxis of influenza A virus infections; only oseltamivir is approved for chemoprophylaxis of influenza B virus infections (Table 220.4). Chemoprophylaxis can be considered for persons at high risk who are expected to have an inadequate antibody response to influenza vaccine, and for those with a history of anaphylactic reactions to egg protein. The efficacy of chemoprophylaxis for the prevention of influenza has not been established in immunocompromised patients.

Strategies for prevention of nosocomial transmission of influenza include vaccination programs, the use of chemoprophylaxis and compliance with droplet isolation precautions. Although influenza

COMPARISON OF ANTIVIRAL DRUGS FOR PROPHYLAXIS AND TREATMENT OF INFLUENZA					
Drug	**Trade name**	**Influenza type**	**Dosing for prophylaxis**	**Dosing for treatment**	**Main side-effects**
Amantadine	Symmetrel®	A	Age 1–9 years: 5mg/k/d po div bid Age 9 and up: 100mg po bid	Age 1–9 years: 5mg/k/d po div bid Age 9 and up: 100mg po bid	Central nervous system
Rimantadine	Flumadine®	A	Age 1–10 years: 5mg/k/d po qd Age 10 and up: 100mg po bid	Adults: 100mg po bid	Central nervous system
Zanamivir	Relenza®	A and B	N/a	Age >7 years: 10mg inhaled bid	Bronchial
Oseltamivir	Tamiflu®	A and B	Age ≥13 years: 75mg po qd	Age 1–12 years: dose per weight* Age 13 and up: 75mg po bid	Gastrointestinal

* For children who weigh ″15kg the dose is 30mg bid; for those who weigh 15–23kg, 45mg bid; for those who weigh 23–40kg, 60mg bid; and for those who weigh >40kg, 75mg bid.

Table 220.4 Comparison of antiviral drugs for prophylaxis and treatment of influenza.

can be transmitted via the air-borne route, the use of negative air pressure rooms has not been assessed.

Diagnostic microbiology

Diagnostic tests available for influenza include viral culture, serology, rapid antigen testing and immunofluorescence. Viral culture remains essential for determining the influenza subtypes and strains causing illness and for surveillance of new strains that may need to be included in the influenza vaccine. Because influenza may not produce cytopathic effects in cell culture, the hemadsorption test is used to screen for evidence of viral replication. The early diagnosis of influenza can reduce the inappropriate use of antibiotics and allow the early administration of antiviral therapy. Commercially available rapid influenza diagnostic tests differ in their ability to detect and distinguish between influenza A and B virus infections, methodologies, processing time and cost. The sensitivities of the rapid tests are lower than viral culture of respiratory specimens and a negative result might not exclude influenza virus infection. Rapid influenza tests provide results within 24 hours, while viral culture takes 3–10 days. Appropriate samples for influenza testing include nasopharyngeal or throat swabs, nasal wash or nasal aspirates, depending on which type of test is used. Samples should be collected within the first 4 days of illness. Acute and convalescent serum samples can also be tested for influenza antibodies to diagnose recent infection.

Clinical manifestations

The incubation period is 1–4 days, with an average of 2 days. The typical uncomplicated influenza A syndrome has an abrupt onset with headache, high-grade fever, chills, dry cough, myalgias, malaise and anorexia. In more severe cases, prostration is observed. Respiratory symptoms such as rhinorrhea, nasal congestion and sore throat are present but are overshadowed by the systemic symptoms during the first 3 days of illness. The cough frequently changes from a dry, hacking nature to one that is productive of small amounts of sputum that are usually mucoid but can be purulent. After the fever and upper respiratory tract symptoms resolve, cough and weakness can persist for 1–2 additional weeks. Influenza B virus can cause the same spectrum of disease as that seen after influenza A virus infection, and severe illness can occur. Influenza C virus causes sporadic, usually afebrile upper respiratory tract illness and is rarely associated with severe lower respiratory tract disease.

Influenza attack rates are higher in children compared to adults. High-grade fever, cervical lymphadenopathy, nausea and vomiting are frequent manifestations of influenza in children. Croup is a less frequent manifestation of influenza, limited to children.

Pneumonia complicates influenza predominantly in the elderly, patients with chronic cardiopulmonary disease, pregnant women and immunocompromised individuals. The etiology may be viral, bacterial or mixed viral-bacterial.[90] In primary viral pneumonia, typical influenza is followed by a rapid progression of fever, cough, dyspnea and cyanosis. Physical examination and chest X-ray disclose diffuse bilateral infiltrates consistent with adult respiratory distress syndrome. A combined viral-bacterial pneumonia is more common than primary viral pneumonia. The bacteria most commonly involved are *Streptococcus pneumoniae* and *Staphylococcus aureus*. A third type of complication is a bacterial pneumonia developing after a clinical improvement from influenza. In this case, physical and chest X-ray examinations are more likely to show localized signs of consolidation. Influenza can also exacerbate chronic underlying medical conditions such as asthma, chronic obstructive pulmonary disease and congestive heart failure.

A variety of nonrespiratory complications have been described. Myositis has been reported more frequently in children with influenza B but adults may also be affected and may develop rhabdomyolysis with acute renal failure.[91] Myocarditis and rarely pericarditis[92,93] have been described in patients with influenza A and B. Reye's syndrome has been reported most frequently after influenza B[94] and has also been described after infections with other viruses such as varicella-zoster. The syndrome is characterized by a rapidly progressive noninflammatory encephalopathy and fatty infiltration of the viscera, especially the liver, resulting in severe hepatic dysfunction. The administration of therapeutic doses of salicylates appears to increase the risk for the development of Reye's syndrome. A wide spectrum of CNS involvement has been observed during influenza A and B virus infection, ranging from irritability and confusion to severe encephalopathy.[95] Toxic shock syndrome has been observed in association with influenza virus infection and is believed to be the consequence of the bacterial exotoxin (TSST-1) secreted by colonizing *Staph. aureus* strains.[96] Febrile convulsions leading to hospitalization occur in children with and without underlying CNS abnormalities.

Influenza viruses can cause severe disease in immunocompromised individuals.[97–103] Severe lymphopenia, elderly age, receipt of an allogeneic hematopoietic stem cell transplant and concurrent opportunistic infections were identified as independent risk factors for a complicated course in a study of adults with leukemia and adult recipients of hematopoietic stem cell transplant. In that study, significant morbidity and mortality were observed with both influenza A and B viruses. Prolonged shedding of influenza virus and rapid emergence of resistance to amantadine and rimantadine has been observed in immunocompromised persons.[104]

Management

Four antiviral medications – amantadine, rimantadine, oseltamivir and zanamivir – are approved for treatment of influenza A virus infections. Oseltamivir and zanamivir are also approved for treatment of influenza B virus infections. When administered within 48 hours of symptom onset, antiviral treatment of influenza can reduce the duration of illness by approximately 1 day in healthy adults.

Amantadine and rimantadine inhibit the M2 protein of influenza A virus. Their side-effects include CNS symptoms such as nervousness, anxiety, difficulty concentrating and lightheadedness. Central nervous system side-effects are more frequent with amantadine than with rimantadine.[105] Gastrointestinal side-effects include nausea and loss of appetite. Amantadine and rimantadine are the least expensive antivirals against influenza and have been in use for several years.

Zanamivir and oseltamivir are analogs of sialic acid that were designed to inhibit the neuraminidase of both influenza A and B viruses.[106] Zanamivir is inhaled and may induce bronchospasm in those with underlying lung disease such as asthma and chronic obstructive pulmonary disease. Other less frequent side-effects include diarrhea, nausea, headache and dizziness. Oseltamivir may induce gastrointestinal side-effects, including nausea and vomiting, especially if the drug is not taken with food (see Table 220.4).

Data are limited concerning the effectiveness of amantadine, rimantadine, zanamivir and oseltamivir for the treatment of influenza among persons at high risk for serious complications of influenza. A retrospective analysis of a surveillance study in immunocompromised individuals showed a decreased rate of progression to pneumonia in patients with influenza A treated with amantadine or rimantadine.[107]

HUMAN METAPNEUMOVIRUS

In June 2001, it was reported that a new respiratory virus had been isolated from nasopharyngeal aspirates of 28 young children in The Netherlands. Based on virological data, sequence homology and gene constellation, the virus was classified as a member of the Metapneumovirus genus of the Paramyxoviridae family and was named human metapneumovirus (HMPV). The clinical syndrome was similar to that caused by RSV. Serological studies showed that by the age of 5 years, virtually all children in The Netherlands have been exposed to HMPV and that the virus had been circulating in humans for at least 50 years.[108] Investigators from other countries, including Australia, Canada, the UK and Finland, have reported further evidence that HMPV is an important human respiratory pathogen. The associated clinical presentation includes flu-like illness, bronchospasm and pneumonia. The severity varies from self-limiting mild respiratory illness to respiratory failure requiring mechanical ventilation. Severe lower respiratory tract infections have been observed in very young children, the elderly and immunocompromised patients.[109] The virus shows cytopathic effect in LLC-MK2 (tertiary monkey kidney) cells and molecular methods for rapid detection and identification are being developed.

CONCLUSION

A better understanding of the profound impact that HRVs have on human morbidity and mortality has resulted in more resources being devoted to their study. More efficient diagnostic tools, new antiviral agents, the use of passive immunoprophylaxis, improvements in vaccination programs and in strategies to control the nosocomial transmission of these infections are among the most significant accomplishments.

Acknowlegment

Illustrations are contributed by Joseph Yarsa BS, MT(ASCP) and Xiang-Yang Han MD, PhD from the Microbiology Laboratory at The University of Texas MD Anderson Cancer Center, Houston, Texas, USA.

REFERENCES

1. Russell WC. Update on adenovirus and its vectors. J Gen Virol 2000;81(Pt11):2573–604.
2. Hierholzer JC. Adenoviruses in the immunocompromised host. Clin Microbiol Rev 1992;5(3):262–74.
3. Flomenberg P, Babbitt J, Drobyski WR, *et al.* Increasing incidence of adenovirus disease in bone marrow transplant recipients. J Infect Dis 1994;169(4):775–81.
4. Baldwin A, Kingman H, Darville M, *et al.* Outcome and clinical course of 100 patients with adenovirus infection following bone marrow transplantation. Bone Marrow Transplant 2000;26(12):1333–8.
5. La Rosa AM, Champlin RE, Mirza N, *et al.* Adenovirus infections in adult recipients of blood and marrow transplants. Clin Infect Dis 2001;32(6):871–6.
6. Cassano WF. Intravenous ribavirin therapy for adenovirus cystitis after allogeneic bone marrow transplantation. Bone Marrow Transplant 1991;7(3):247–8.
7. Liles WC, Cushing H, Holt S, Bryan C, Hackman RC. Severe adenoviral nephritis following bone marrow transplantation: successful treatment with intravenous ribavirin. Bone Marrow Transplant 1993;12(4):409–12.
8. Jurado Chacon M, Hernandez Mohedo F, Navarro Mari JM, Ferrer Chaves C, Escobar Vedia JL, de Pablos Gallego JM. Adenovirus pneumonitis successfully treated with intravenous ribavirin. Haematologica 1998;83(12):1128–9.
9. Miyamura K, Hamaguchi M, Taji H, *et al.* Successful ribavirin therapy for severe adenovirus hemorrhagic cystitis after allogeneic marrow transplant from close HLA donors rather than distant donors. Bone Marrow Transplant 2000;25(5):545–8.
10. Bordigoni P, Carret AS, Venard V, Witz F, Le Faou A. Treatment of adenovirus infections in patients undergoing allogeneic hematopoietic stem cell transplantation. Clin Infect Dis 2001;32(9):1290–7.
11. Legrand F, Berrebi D, Houhou N, *et al.* Early diagnosis of adenovirus infection and treatment with cidofovir after bone marrow transplantation in children. Bone Marrow Transplant 2001;27(6):621–6.
12. Hoffman JA, Shah AJ, Ross LA, Kapoor N. Adenoviral infections and a prospective trial of cidofovir in pediatric hematopoietic stem cell transplantation. Biol Blood Marrow Transplant 2001;7(7):388–94.
13. Monto AS, Lim SK. The Tecumseh study of respiratory illness. VI. Frequency of and relationship between outbreaks of coronavirus infection. J Infect Dis 1974;129:271–6.
14. Chilvers MA, McKean M, Rutman A, Myint BS, Silverman M, O'Callaghan C. The effects of coronavirus on human nasal ciliated respiratory epithelium. Eur Respir J 2001;18(6):965–70.
15. Vabret A, Mouthon F, Mourez T, Gouarin S, Petitjean J, Freymuth F. Direct diagnosis of human respiratory coronaviruses 229E and OC43 by the polymerase chain reaction. J Virol Methods 2001;97(1–2):59–66.
16. Bradburne AF, Bynoe ML, Tyrrell DA. Effects of a 'new' human respiratory virus in volunteers. BMJ 1967;3:767–9.
17. Riski H, Hovi T. Coronavirus infections of man associated with diseases other than the common cold. J Med Virol 1980;6(3):259–65.
18. Folz RJ, Elkordy MA. Coronavirus pneumonia following autologous bone marrow transplantation for breast cancer. Chest 1999;115(3):901–5.
19. Selb B, Weber B. A study of human reovirus IgG and IgA antibodies by ELISA and Western blot. J Virol Methods 1994;47:15–26.
20. Hirasawa K, Nishikawa SG, Norman KL, Alain T, Kossakowska A, Lee PW. Oncolytic reovirus against ovarian and colon cancer. Cancer Res 2002;62(6):1696–701.
21. Rosen L, Evans HE, Spickard A. Reovirus infections in human volunteers. Am J Hyg 1963;77:29–37.
22. Gwaltney JMJ, Hendley JO, Phillips CD, Bass CR, Mygind N, Winther B. Nose blowing propels nasal fluid into the paranasal sinuses. Clin Infect Dis 2000;30(2):387–91.
23. Gwaltney JMJ, Phillips CD, Miller RD, Riker DK. Computed tomographic study of the common cold. N Engl J Med 1994;330(1):25–30.
24. Ghosh S, Champlin R, Couch R, *et al.* Rhinovirus infections in myelosuppressed adult blood and marrow transplant recipients. Clin Infect Dis 1999;29(3):528–32.
25. Juven T, Mertsola J, Waris M, *et al.* Etiology of community-acquired pneumonia in 254 hospitalized children. Pediatr Infect Dis J 2000;19(4):293–8.
26. Imakita M, Shiraki K, Yutani C, Ishibashi-Ueda H. Pneumonia caused by rhinovirus. Clin Infect Dis 2000;30(3):611–2.
27. El-Sahly HM, Atmar RL, Glezen WP, Greenberg SB. Spectrum of clinical illness in hospitalized patients with 'common cold' virus infections. Clin Infect Dis 2000;31(1):96–100.

28. Malcolm E, Arruda E, Hayden FG, Kaiser L. Clinical features of patients with acute respiratory illness and rhinovirus in their bronchoalveolar lavages. J Clin Virol 2001;21(1):9–16.
29. Falsey AR, Walsh EE, Hayden FG. Rhinovirus and coronavirus infection – associated hospitalizations among older adults. J Infect Dis 2002;185(9):1338–41.
30. Jefferson TO, Tyrrell D. Antivirals for the common cold. Cochrance Database Syst Rev 2001;3(CD002743).
31. Hayden FG, Andries K, Janssen PA. Safety and efficacy of intranasal pirodavir (R77975) in experimental rhinovirus infection. Antimicrob Agents Chemother 1992;36(4):727–32.
32. Hayden FG, Hipskind GJ, Woerner DH, *et al.* Intranasal pirodavir (R77,975) treatment of rhinovirus colds. Antimicrob Agents Chemother 1995;39(2):290–4.
33. Kaiser L, Crump CE, Hayden FG. *In vitro* activity of pleconaril and AG7088 against selected serotypes and clinical isolates of human rhinoviruses. Antiviral Res 2000;47(3):215–20.
34. Turner RB, Wecker MT, Pohl G, *et al.* Efficacy of tremacamra, a soluble intercellular adhesion molecule 1, for experimental rhinovirus infection: a randomized clinical trial. JAMA 1999;281(19):1797–804.
35. Hayden FG, Kim K, Hudson S. Pleconaril treatment reduces duration and severity of viral respiratory infection (common cold) due to picornaviruses. Abstract H-659. 41st Interscience Conference on Antimicrobial Agents and Chemotherapy, 2001.
36. Hall CB, Douglas RGJ. Modes of transmission of respiratory syncytial virus. J Pediatr 1981;99(1):100–3.
37. Hall CB, Walsh EE, Long CE, Schnabel KC. Immunity to and frequency of reinfection with respiratory syncytial virus. J Infect Dis 1991;163(4):693–8.
38. McBride JT. Pulmonary function changes in children after respiratory syncytial virus infection in infancy. J Pediatr 1999;135(2 Pt 2):28–32.
39. Garcia R, Raad I, Abi-Said D, *et al.* Nosocomial respiratory syncytial virus infections: prevention and control in bone marrow transplant patients. Infect Control Hosp Epidemiol 1997;18(6):412–6.
40. Simoes EA, Sonndheimer HM, Top FHJ, *et al.* Respiratory syncytial virus immune globulin for prophylaxis against respiratory syncytial virus disease in infants and children with congenital heart disease. The Cardiac Study Group. J Pediatr 1998;133(4):492–9.
41. Anonymous. Reduction of respiratory syncytial virus hospitalization among premature infants and infants with bronchopulmonary dysplasia using respiratory syncytial virus immune globulin prophylaxis. The PREVENT Study Group. Pediatrics 1997;99(1):93–9.
42. Atkins JT, Karimi BH, McDavid G, Shim S. Prophylaxis for respiratory syncytial virus with respiratory syncytial virus-immune globulin intravenous among preterm infants of thirty-two weeks gestation and less: reduction in incidence, severity of illness and cost. Pediatr Infect Dis J 2000;19(2):138–43.
43. Anonymous. Palivizumab, a humanized respiratory syncytial virus monoclonal antibody, reduces hospitalization from respiratory syncytial virus infection in high-risk infants. The IMpact-RSV Study Group. Virus Res 1998;55(2):167–76.
44. Schrand LM, Elliott JM, Ross MB, *et al.* A cost-benefit analysis of RSV prophylaxis in high-risk infants. Ann Pharmacother 2001;35(10):1186–93.
45. O'Shea TM, Sevick MA, Givner LB. Costs and benefits of respiratory syncytial virus immunoglobulin to prevent hospitalization for lower respiratory tract illness in very low birth weight infants. Pediatr Infect Dis J 1998;17(7):587–93.
46. Joffe S, Ray GT, Escobar GJ, Black SB, Lieu TA. Cost-effectiveness of respiratory syncytial virus prophylaxis among preterm infants. Pediatrics 1999;104(3 Pt 1):419–27.
47. Thomas M, Bedford-Russell A, Sharland M. Hospitalization for RSV infection in ex-preterm infants – implications for use of RSV immune globulin. Arch Dis Child 2000;83(2):122–7.
48. Stevens TP, Sinkin RA, Hall CB, Maniscalco WM, McConnochie KM. Respiratory syncytial virus and premature infants born at 32 weeks' gestation or earlier: hospitalization and economic implications of prophylaxis. Arch Pediatr Adolesc Med 2000;154(1):55–61.
49. Whimbey E, Champlin RE, Couch RB, *et al.* Community respiratory virus infections among hospitalized adult bone marrow transplant recipients. Clin Infect Dis 1996;22(5):778–82.
50. Moler FW, Steinhart CM, Ohmit SE, Stidham GL. Effectiveness of ribavirin in otherwise well infants with respiratory syncytial virus-associated respiratory failure. Pediatric Critical Study Group. 1996;128(3):422–8.
51. Randolph AG, Wang EE. Ribavirin for respiratory syncytial virus infection of the lower respiratory tract. Cochrane Database Syst Rev 2000(2):CD000181.
52. DeVincenzo JP, Hirsch RL, Fuentes RJ, Top FHJ. Respiratory syncytial virus immune globulin treatment of lower respiratory tract infection in pediatric patients undergoing bone marrow transplantation – a compassionate use experience. Bone Marrow Transplant 2000;25(2):161–5.
53. Whimbey E, Champlin RE, Englund JA, *et al.* Combination therapy with aerosolized ribavirin and intravenous immunoglobulin for respiratory syncytial virus disease in adult bone marrow transplant recipients. Bone Marrow Transplant 1995;16(3):393–9.
54. Henrickson KJ, Kuhn SM, Savatski LL. Epidemiology and cost of infection with human parainfluenza virus types 1 and 2 in young children. Clin Infect Dis 1994;18(5):770–9.
55. Counihan ME, SHAY DK, Holman RC, *et al.* Human parainfluenza virus-associated hospitalizations among children less than five years of age in the United States. Pediatr Infect Dis J 2001;20(7):646–53.
56. Knott AM, Long CE, Hall CB. Parainfluenza viral infections in pediatric outpatients: seasonal patterns and clinical characteristics. Pediatr Infect Dis J 1994;13(4):269–73.
57. Fan J, Henrickson KJ. Rapid diagnosis of human parainfluenza virus type 1 infection by quantitative reverse transcription-PCR-enzyme hybridization assay. J Clin Microbiol 1996;34(8):1914–7.
58. Marx A, Gary HE Jr, Marston BJ, *et al.* Parainfluenza virus infection among adults hospitalized for lower respiratory tract infection. Clin Infect Dis 1999;29(1):134–40.
59. Arisoy ES, Demmler GJ, Thakar S, Doerr C. Meningitis due to parainfluenza virus type 3: report of two cases and review. Clin Infect Dis 1993;17(6):995–7.
60. Wendt CH, Weisdorf DJ, Jordan MC, Balfour HHJ, Hertz MI. Parainfluenza virus respiratory infection after bone marrow transplantation. N Engl J Med 1992;326(14):921–6.
61. Cortez KJ, Erdman DD, Peret TC, *et al.* Outbreak of human parainfluenza virus 3 infections in a hematopoietic stem cell transplant population. J Infect Dis 2001;184(9):1093–7.
62. Nichols WG, Corey L, Gooley T, Davis C, Boeckh M. Parainfluenza virus infections after hematopoietic stem cell transplantation: risk factors, response to antiviral therapy, and effect on transplant outcome. Blood 2001;98(3):573–8.
63. Hohenthal U, Nikoskelainen J, Vainionpaa R, *et al.* Parainfluenza virus type 3 infections in a hematology unit. Bone Marrow Transplant 2001;27(3):295–300.
64. Whimbey E, Vartivarian SE, Champlin RE, Elting LS, Luna M, Bodey GP. Parainfluenza virus infection in adult bone marrow transplant recipients. Eur J Clin Microbiol Infect Dis 1993;12(9):699–701.
65. Lewis VA, Champlin R, Englund J, *et al.* Respiratory disease due to parainfluenza virus in adult bone marrow transplant recipients. Clin Infect Dis 1996;23(5):1033–7.
66. Vilchez RA, McCurry K, Dauber J, *et al.* The epidemiology of parainfluenza virus infection in lung transplant recipients. Clin Infect Dis 2001;33(12):2004–8.
67. DeFabritus AM, Riggio RR, David DS, Senterfit LB, Cheigh JS, Stenzel KH. Parainfluenza type 3 in a transplant unit. JAMA 1979;241(4):384–6.
68. Browne MJ. Comparative inhibition of influenza and parainfluenza virus replication by ribavirin in MDCK cells. Antimicrob Agents Chemother 1981;19(5):712–5.
69. Patterson K. Pandemic and epidemic influenza, 1830–1848. Soc Sci Med 1985;21(5):571–80.
70. Ghendon Y. Introduction to pandemic influenza through history. Eur J Epidemiol 1994;10(4):451–3.
71. Beveridge W. The chronicle of influenza epidemics. Pubbl Stn Zool Napoli II 1991;13(2):223–34.
72. Shope RE. Swine influenza. III. Filtration experiments and etiology. J Exp Med 1931;54:373–80.
73. Smith W, Andrewes C, Laidlaw P. A virus obtained from influenza patients. Lancet 1933;2:66–8.
74. WHO. A revised system of nomenclature for influenza viruses. Bull WHO 1980;58(1):585–91.
75. Subbarao K, Katz J. Avian influenza viruses infecting humans. Cell Mol Life Sci 2000;57(12):1770–84.
76. Webster R. Influenza virus: transmission between species and relevance to emergence of the next human pandemic. Arch Virol Suppl 1997;13:105–13.
77. Zambon M. The pathogenesis of influenza in humans. Rev Med Virol 2001;11(4):227–41.
78. CDC. Prevention and control of influenza: recommendations of the Advisory Committee on Immunization Practices (ACIP). MMWR 2002;51(RR03):1–31.
79. Palese P, Young J. Variation of influenza. Science 1982;215(4539):1468–74.
80. Shortridge K. Pandemic influenza: a zoonosis? Semin Respir Infect 1992;7(1):11–25.
81. Martin CM, Kunin CM, Gottlieb LS. Asian influenza A in Boston, 1957–1958. I. Observations in thirty-two influenza-associated fatal cases. Arch Intern Med 1959;103:515–31.
82. Artenstein M, Bellanti J, Buescher E. Identification of the antiviral substances in nasal secretions. Proc Soc Exp Biol Med 1964;117:558–64.
83. Couch RB. Assessment of immunity to influenza using artificial challenge of normal volunteers with influenza virus. Dev Biol Stand 1975;28:295–306.
84. Clements M, Betts R, Tierney E, Murphy BR. Serum and nasal wash antibodies associated with resistance to experimental challenge with influenza A wild-type virus. J Clin Microbiol 1986;24:157–60.
85. Hayden F, Scott F, Lobo M, Alvord W, Strober W, Straus SE. Local and systemic cytokine responses during experimental human influenza A virus infection: relation to symptom formation and host defense. J Clin Invest 1998;101:643–9.
86. Yewdell J, Hackett C. The specificity and function of T lymphocytes induced by influenza A virus. New York: Plenum Press; 1989.
87. Couch RB, Keitel WA, Cate TR. Improvement of inactivated influenza virus vaccines. J Infect Dis 1997;176(suppl 1):S38–44.
88. Wareing M, Tannock G. Live attenuated vaccines against influenza: an historical review. Vaccine 2001;19(25–26):3320–30.
89. Beyer W, Palache A, de Jong J, Osterhaus AD. Cold-adapted live influenza vaccine versus inactivated vaccine: systemic vaccine reactions,

local and systemic antibody response, and vaccine efficacy. A meta-analysis. Vaccine 2002;20(9–10):1340–53.
90. Cate TR. Clinical manifestations and consequences of influenza. Am J Med 1987;82(6A):15–9.
91. Berry L, Braude S. Influenza A infection with rhabdomyolysis and acute renal failure – a potential fatal complication. Postgrad Med J 1991;67(786):389–90.
92. Miura M, Asaumi Y, Wada Y, *et al.* A case of influenza subtype A virus-induced fulminant myocarditis: and experience of percutaneous cardio-pulmonary support (PCPS) treatment and immunohistochemical analysis. Tohoku J Exp Med 2000;195(1):11–19.
93. Nolte K, Alakija P, Oty G, *et al.* Influenza A virus infection complicated by fatal myocarditis. Am J Forensic Med Pathol 2000;21(4):375–9.
94. Glezen WP, Couch RB, Taber LH, *et al.* Epidemiologic observations of influenza B virus infections in Houston, Texas, 1976–1977. Am J Epidemiol 1980;111(1):13–22.
95. Kimura S, Ohtuki N, Nezu A, Tanaka M, Takeshita S. Clinical and radiological variability of influenza-related encephalopathy or encephalitis. Acta Paediatr Jpn 1998;40(3):264–470.
96. Prechter G, Gerhard A. Postinfluenza toxic shock syndrome. Chest 1989;95(5):1153–4.
97. Aschan J, Ringden O, Ljungman P, Andersson J, Lewensohn-Fuchs I, Forsgren M. Influenza B in transplant patients. Scand J Infect Dis 1989;21(3):349–50.
98. Ljungman P, Gleaves C, Meyers JD. Respiratory virus infections in immunocompromised patients. Bone Marrow Transplant 1989;4(1):35–40.
99. Hirschhorn LR, McIntosh K, Anderson KG, Dermody TS. Influenzal pneumonia as a complication of autologous bone marrow transplantation [letter]. Clin Infect Dis 1992;14(3):786–7.
100. Ljungman P, Andersson J, Aschan J, *et al.* Influenza A in immunocompromised patients. Clin Infect Dis 1993;17(2):244–7.
101. Whimbey E, Elting LS, Couch RB, *et al.* Influenza A virus infections among hospitalized adult bone marrow transplant recipients. Bone Marrow Transplant 1994;13(4):437–40.
102. Garantziotis S, Howell D, McAdams H, Davis RD, Henshaw NG, Palmer SM. Influenza pneumonia in lung transplant recipients: clinical features and association with bronchiolitis obliterans syndrome. Chest 2001;119(4):1277–80.
103. Faul J, Akindipe O, Berry G, Theodore J. Influenza pneumonia in a pediatric lung transplant recipient. Transpl Int 2000;13(1):79–81.
104. Englund JA, Champlin RE, Wyde PR, *et al.* Common emergence of amantadine- and rimantadine-resistant influenza A viruses in symptomatic immunocompromised adults. Clin Infect Dis 1998;26(6):1418–24.
105. Hayden FG, Gwaltney JMJ, van de Castle RL, Adams KF, Giordani B. Comparative toxicity of amantadine hydrochloride and rimantadine hydrochloride in healthy adults. Antimicrob Agents Chemother 1981;19(2):226–33.
106. Gubareva LV, Kaiser L, Hayden FG. Influenza virus neuraminidase inhibitors. Lancet 2000;355(9206):827–35.
107. La Rosa AM, Malik S, Englund JA, *et al.* Influenza A in hospitalized adults with leukemia and hematopoietic stem cell transplant (HSCT) recipients: risk factors for progression to pneumonia. 39th Annual Meeting of the Infectious Diseases Society of America, San Francisco, California, 2001.
108. van den Hoogen BG, de Jong JC, Groen J, *et al.* A newly discovered human pneumovirus isolated from young children with respiratory tract disease. Nat Med 2001;7(6):719–24.
109. Boivin G, Abed Y, Pelletier G, *et al.* Virological features and clinical manifestations associated with human metapneumovirus: a new paramyxovirus responsible for acute respiratory-tract infections in all age groups. J Infect Dis 2002;186(9):1330–4.
110. Peiris J, Lai S, Poon L, *et al.* Coronavirus as a possible cause of severe acute respiratory syndrome. Lancet 2003;363:1319–25.
111. Ksiazek TG, Erdman D, Goldsmith CS, *et al.* A novel coronavirus associated with severe acute respiratory syndrome. N Engl J Med. 2003;348:1947–58.
112. Drosten C, Günther S, Preiser W, *et al.* Identification of a novel coronavirus in patients with severe acute respiratory syndrome. www.nejm.org. April 10, 2003.

chapter 221

Retroviruses and Retroviral Infections

Charles AB Boucher

INTRODUCTION

The Retroviridae constitute a large family of viruses that infect both humans and animals. Retroviruses predominantly infect vertebrates, although infections of insects and molluscs have also been described. Retroviral infections may cause a wide spectrum of diseases ranging from malignancies to immune deficiencies and neurologic disorders. However, most retroviral infections occur without any detectable deleterious effect to the host. In spite of the diversity of associated pathology and the broad range of hosts, all retroviruses are united by a common mode of replication and a similar virion structure and genome organization.

This chapter discusses some general features of the retroviruses, such as virion structure, genome organization and taxonomy of retroviruses. Although there have been concerns about the potential clinical significance of porcine retroviruses in the context of xenotransplantation[95], the main focus of attention is on human retroviruses. During the past decades, the AIDS pandemic has resulted in an upsurge of scientific interest in retroviral infections and related pathology in humans. Several human retroviruses have been identified, of which only HIV and the human T-lymphocyte leukemia viruses (HTLVs) are known to cause clinical manifestations. These two human retroviruses have been well characterized and are discussed in more detail.

NATURE

The electron microscopic view of retroviral particles shows spheric particles approximately 100nm in diameter with an electron-dense core (Fig. 221.1). Retroviruses are enveloped viruses. The envelope consists of a phospholipid double layer derived from the plasma membrane of the host cell. Viral encoded transmembrane glycoproteins are inserted into the envelope, enabling the virus to attach to the host cell (Fig. 221.2). The envelope surrounds the nucleocapsid core, which contains the viral genome: two identical RNA molecules, having the same polarity as mRNA, with which an RNA-dependent DNA polymerase enzyme, reverse transcriptase (RT), is closely associated. Also present in the core is the integrase enzyme.

The genome of retroviruses is approximately 10,000 base pairs (bp) in length. Each end of the genome consists of repeating nucleotide sequences of 4–6bp, called the long terminal repeats (LTRs). The LTRs flank the three genomic regions that encode for sets of structural genes:

- the group antigen (*gag*) region, which codes for the core antigens;
- the polymerase (*pol*) region, which codes for the enzymes protease, RT and integrase; and
- the envelope (*env*) region, which codes for glycoproteins of the envelope.

The structural genes always appear in the same order: *gag–pol–env* (Fig. 221.3).[1] There are several retroviruses that contain additional genes that encode for viral proteins involved in the regulation of several processes in the replication cycle of the virus, such as the rate of transcription, the splicing of mRNA, the transport of mRNA from the nucleus to the cytoplasm and the release of progeny virus. Retroviruses that contain additional genes are called complex retroviruses; examples of these are the HIVs and the HTLVs. The genomes of so-called simple retroviruses only contain a *gag*, *pol* and *env* gene.

The first step in the replication cycle of retroviruses is attachment of the virus to a host cell through interaction of the envelope glycoprotein with a receptor molecule on the host cell surface (Fig. 221.4). This interaction between virus and host cell largely determines the host range of the virus (i.e. which species or cell type the virus will infect). After attachment, fusion of the envelope membrane with the host cell membrane takes place and the nucleocapsid core is released into the cell. However, some retroviruses enter the cell by receptor-mediated endocytosis followed by fusion of the viral envelope with the endosomal membrane.[2]

Following the entry of the nucleocapsid core into the cytoplasm of the host cell, the viral RNA is transcribed into double stranded DNA (dsDNA). This process is catalyzed by the viral enzyme RT. The viral dsDNA, in association with RT and the viral enzyme integrase, is transferred to the nucleus. Subsequently the dsDNA is integrated into the chromosomal DNA of the cell by the action of the enzyme integrase. The integrated viral DNA copy is called provirus.

Using the proviral DNA as template, cellular DNA-dependent RNA polymerases synthesize viral mRNA. Some viral mRNA molecules are spliced and transported to the cytoplasm, where translation yields full-length viral precursor polyproteins. These polyproteins, combined with two copies of unspliced genomic viral RNA, are assembled into immature virus particles. By budding through the plasma membrane the immature particles acquire a bilipid layer envelope. Maturation into infectious and replication-competent virions is accomplished after release of the immature particles from the host cell; this process requires processing of the polyproteins by the viral-encoded protease. Then, a new cycle of replication may start.

As described above, during the replication cycle of retroviruses the viral DNA is integrated in the chromosomal DNA of the host cell. The result of this integration is that the retroviral DNA is now inherited into the progeny of the infected cell. When retroviruses infect germline cells (sperm or egg cells) and the viral DNA is integrated into the chromosomal DNA of these cells, the retrovirus is passed from parent to offspring of the infected host. In this case, the virus is named an endogenous retrovirus. We all carry the remnants of retroviral DNA in our chromosomes as a result of common ancestors who were infected with endogenous retroviruses.

Retroviruses that are not integrated in germline cells of their host are called exogenous retroviruses. The transmission route of exogenous retroviruses is both horizontally and vertically via blood and saliva and by sexual intercourse.

HUMAN ENDOGENOUS RETROVIRUSES

Approximately 1% of the human genome consists of sequences of human endogenous retroviruses (HERVs).[3] Full-length HERVs contain sequences that are homologous to the *gag*, *pol* and *env* genes

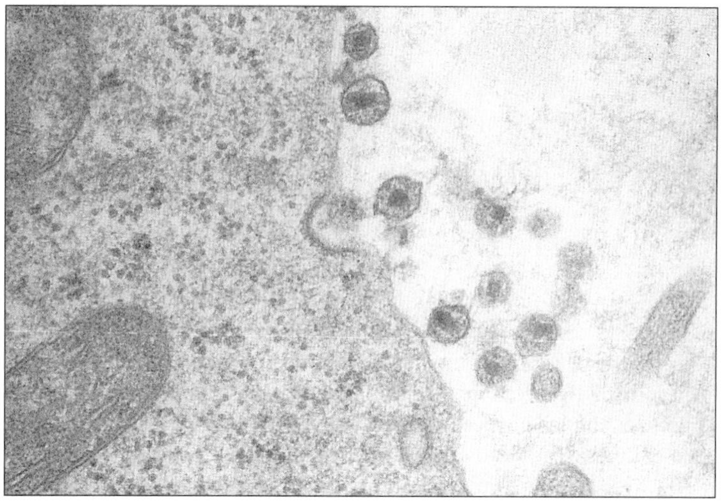

Fig. 221.1 **Typical electron microscopic view of retroviruses (HIV) showing an electron-dense core.** Courtesy of Dr Piet Joling.

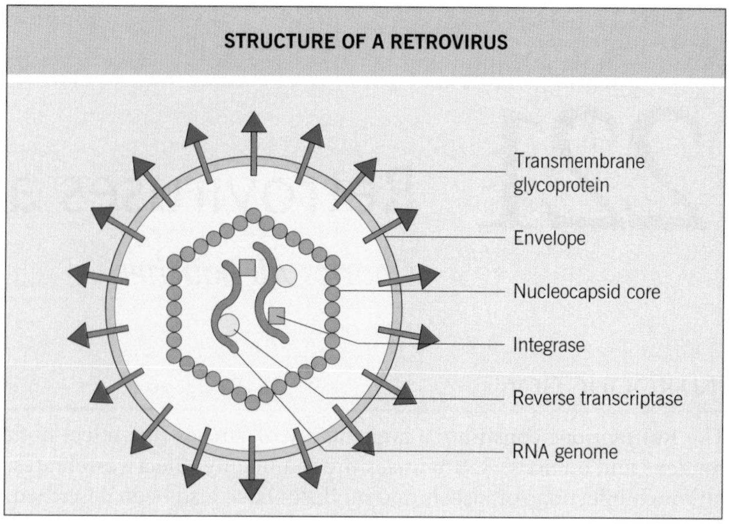

Fig. 221.2 Structure of a retrovirus.

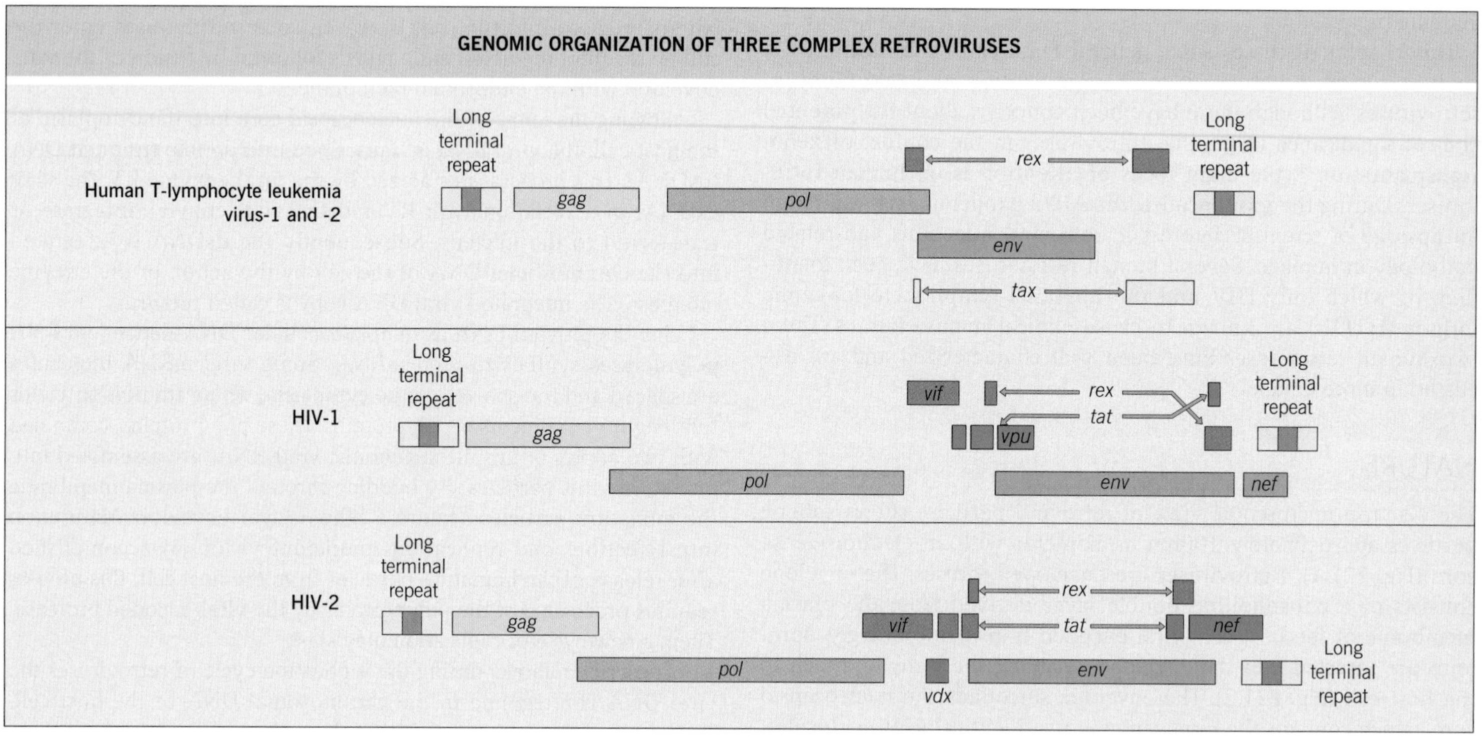

Fig. 221.3 Genomic organization of three complex retroviruses. The diagram shows HIV-1, HIV-2 and HTLV. The components of the long terminal repeats are shaded. The open reading frames that encode viral proteins are depicted by unshaded boxes. Adapted from Galasso *et al.*[1]

of infectious exogenous retroviruses. The biologic properties and functions of endogenous retroviruses are still under investigation.

In general, HERVs are highly defective proviruses.[3,4] Expression of HERV mRNA and HERV proteins has been demonstrated in several normal and pathologic tissues, and HERV retroviral particles have been detected by electron microscopy in these tissues.

Nine different HERV families have been described, some of which have as many as 50 copies in the human genome.[3] A description of the specific characteristics of the different HERV families does not fit into the scope of this chapter.

Because it was demonstrated that HERV mRNA and proteins can be expressed, it has been postulated that HERVs might be etiologically involved in human disease. In the literature, numerous pathologic conditions have been related to HERVs, such as inflammatory and degenerative diseases of the nervous system and several autoimmune diseases (systemic lupus erythematosus, rheumatoid arthritis, Sjögren's syndrome and the mixed connective tissue disease). Evidence has been found for HERV antigen expression in some of these conditions. However, no definitive proof for the putative involvement of HERVs in any of these pathologic conditions has been published. The possible role of HERVs in human disease has been reviewed,[4] but more research is required to elucidate the general role of HERVs and their specific role in human disease.

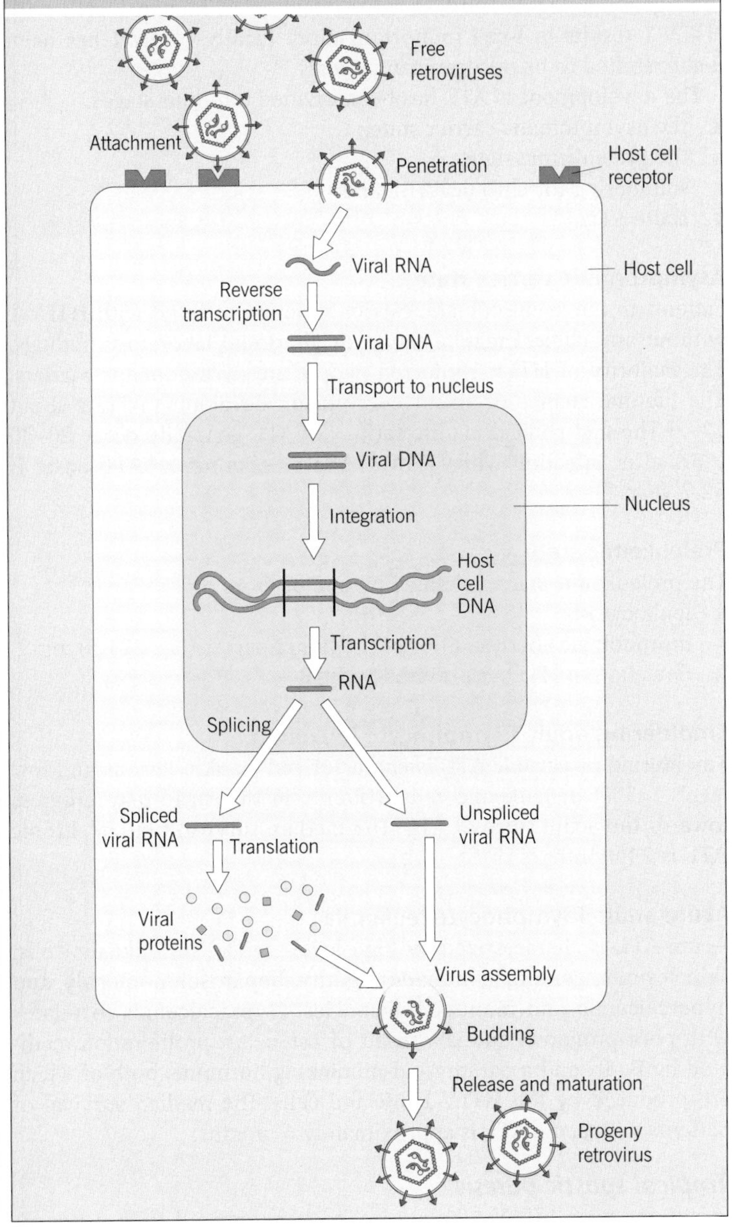

Fig. 221.4 Replication cycle of retroviruses.

HUMAN FOAMY VIRUS

In 1971, a human foamy virus (HFV) was the first human exogenous retrovirus to be successfully isolated from human tissue.[5] Human foamy virus is a member of the family of Spuma retroviruses. A clear relationship between HFV and human disease has never been established, although in several publications HFV has been associated with possible involvement in the pathogenesis of disease of the thyroid gland.

Human foamy virus can be isolated from patients who have subacute thyroiditis, also known as granulomatous thyroiditis or de Quervain's thyroiditis.[6] Furthermore, evidence for an association between Graves' disease and HFV infections has been found. The presence of HFV provirus in the peripheral blood mononuclear cells (PBMCs) of 19 out of 29 patients (66%) with Graves' disease has been demonstrated using polymerase chain reaction (PCR)-based techniques.[7] In the same study the PBMCs of 23 control patients were negative for HFV provirus. In another study, it was demonstrated that antibodies directed against the *gag* antigen of HFV reacted with the thyroid glands of all seven patients who had Graves' disease.[8]

In contrast, in two other studies, no HFV provirus was found in the PBMCs of 81 patients who had Graves' disease. In conclusion, more research is needed to establish the putative relation between diseases of the thyroid gland and human Spuma virus infections.

Human foamy virus infections have also been associated with numerous other pathologic conditions, such as the chronic fatigue syndrome, hemodialysis encephalopathy,[9] multiple sclerosis, Guillain–Barré syndrome, amyotrophic lateral sclerosis[10] and Kawasaki's disease. However, again no definitive evidence has been found to support involvement of HFV in any of these diseases.

Several epidemiologic studies using an enzyme-linked immunosorbent assay (ELISA) technique to investigate the distribution of antibodies to the human Spuma virus suggest a high prevalence of the virus in patients from the African continent and low prevalence in Europe. However, in one study HFV provirus could not be detected in the PBMCs of the patients who were serum positive in the ELISA.[11] Therefore, these epidemiologic data need confirmation in additional studies.

In conclusion, more research is needed to resolve the controversy on the epidemiology and virulence of human Spuma viruses.

HUMAN T-LYMPHOCYTE LEUKEMIA VIRUSES

NATURE

Human T-lymphocyte leukemia virus-1 and HTLV-2 are complex retroviruses. In addition to a *gag*, *pol* and *env* gene, they contain four open reading frames in the pX region; these open reading frames have regulatory and accessory functions.[12] Two of these proteins, *rex* and *tax* (see Fig. 221.3), play an important role in regulation of viral replication. The *rex* protein is involved in the stabilization of viral mRNA and the transport of viral mRNA from nucleus to cytoplasm. The *rex* protein also regulates the splicing and processing of viral mRNA. The *tax* protein is a transactivator protein and is also essential for viral replication. By acting on the LTR located 5′ to the viral *gag* gene, *tax* induces the transcription of viral mRNA. Apart from regulating viral replication, the *tax* protein is also believed to play a role in oncogenesis through transactivation of cellular proto-oncogenes (see below).

EPIDEMIOLOGY

Seroepidemiologic studies have shown that the highest incidence of anti-HTLV-1 antibodies is found in south-western Japan, ranging from 5 to 35% in endemic areas. Other areas with high incidence are the Caribbean islands, some regions of South and Central America, the south-west Pacific and Papua New Guinea.[2,11] The general incidence in the USA and Europe is low (0.05%), although an increasing incidence has been reported among homosexuals and intravenous drug users.

The epidemiology of HTLV-2 has been less well studied. It is difficult to distinguish serologically between HTLV-1 and HTLV-2 because of antigenic cross-reactivity. Therefore, HTLV-2 incidence has been studied with the help of a technique based on a PCR using primers specific for the HTLV-2 proviral genome. A high incidence of HTLV-2 has been found among native Americans in Panama and New Mexico and among intravenous drug users in the USA and Italy.[13–16]

PATHOGENESIS

It is believed that HTLV-1 is transmitted by infected lymphocytes and not as free virus in cell-free body fluids. Three transmission routes for HTLV-1 have been described.

- first, transmission of HTLV-infected lymphocytes from mother to child is a major route; it can occur via the placenta, during birth, or after birth through the mother's milk;
- second, evidence has also been found for transmission from male to female during sexual intercourse – no evidence has been found for sexual transmission of HTLV-1 in the other direction, from female to male; and
- finally, blood transfusions are an efficient transmission route of HTLV-1.[2,11]

Human T-lymphocyte leukemia virus-1 is a lymphotropic virus that preferentially infects $CD4^+$ T cells. Usually, the leukemic cells in adult T-lymphocyte leukemia (ATL) have the following phenotype: $CD2^+$, $CD3^+$, $CD5^+$, $CD7^-$, $CD4^+$ and $CD8^-$; they also express the activation surface markers CD38 (the interleukin (IL)-2 receptor), CD30 and major histocompatibility complex class II.[17,18] The cellular receptor mediating the HTLV-1 infection of lymphocytes has not been identified.

The molecular mechanisms by which HTLV-1 is able to induce cell transformation have not been unraveled. Human T-lymphocyte leukemia virus does not contain a typical oncogene. Several other hypothetic mechanisms of HTLV-induced oncogenesis have been formulated.

It has been hypothesized that in HTLV-1-infected T cells the *tax* protein may transactivate cellular growth factor genes such as the IL-2 gene or the IL-2 receptor gene, thus promoting unbridled division of T cells. Human T-lymphocyte leukemia virus-1-infected, immortalized cells have been demonstrated to express high levels of the IL-2 receptor. Normally, in an uninfected person, most of the T cells are in a quiescent state, with low levels of IL-2 production and IL-2 receptor expression, and they only become activated in cases of clone-specific stimulation caused by the presence of an antigen.

Another mechanism of cell transformation that has been postulated is transactivation of proto-oncogenes by the *tax* protein of HTLV-1, such as c-*fos* and the platelet-derived growth factor gene.

Furthermore, in patients who have ATL, several chromosomal aberrations have been described. It is not clear whether these chromosome aberrations are induced by insertion of the HTLV proviral DNA.[2,11,19]

However, these hypotheses do not explain why it takes an average incubation time of 20–30 years to develop ATL or why only a small number of HTLV-1-infected people develop clinical manifestations of ATL. More research is required to answer these questions.

DIAGNOSTIC MICROBIOLOGY

The definite diagnosis of ATL is made by demonstrating the presence of HTLV-1 proviral DNA in the DNA of tumor cells using a PCR-based technique.

CLINICAL FEATURES

Human T-lymphocyte leukemia virus-1

Adult T-lymphocyte leukemia

Human T-lymphocyte leukemia virus-1 is considered to be the etiologic agent of ATL, a disease first recognized as a nosologic entity in 1977.[20] Several pieces of evidence established the causal relationship between HTLV-1 and ATL. First, ATL has an identical geographic distribution to that of HTLV-1, having a high incidence in south-western Japan, as was shown in seroepidemiologic studies.[21] Second, all ATL tumor cells contain one or more copies of the HTLV-1 provirus in their genomic DNA. Third, in-vitro infection of human T cells with HTLV-1 results in T-cell immortalization. Finally, HTLV-1 has been demonstrated to be oncogenic in animals.[19]

The development of ATL has been divided into four stages:

- the asymptomatic carrier state,
- the preleukemic state,
- smoldering (or chronic ATL), and
- acute ATL.

Asymptomatic carrier state

Patients in the asymptomatic carrier state are infected with HTLV-1 without any clinical manifestation or abnormal laboratory findings. The majority of HTLV-1-infected people are asymptomatic carriers. The lifetime chance of an infected person developing ATL is about 1%.[22] The first clinical manifestations of ATL generally occur 20–30 years after infection with HTLV-1. The median age of ATL onset is 52.7 years.[23]

Preleukemic state

The preleukemic state is defined by one or more of:

- leukocytosis,
- morphologic abnormalities of the lymphocytes (Fig. 221.5), or
- detection of HTLV-1 provirus by PCR.

Smoldering adult T-lymphocyte leukemia

Smoldering or chronic ATL is characterized by skin lesions and low levels (<5%) of leukemic cells. Patients in this stage may progress towards the acute stage of ATL. The median survival time in chronic ATL is 24 months.

Acute adult T-lymphocyte leukemia

Acute ATL is characterized by high levels (>5%) of leukemic cells, skin lesions, general lymphadenopathy, hepatosplenomegaly and hypercalcemia and immunodeficiencies. Hypercalcemia correlates with poor prognosis and is a result of osteoclast proliferation mediated by IL-1α and a parathyroid-mimicking hormone, both of which are produced by the HTLV-1-infected cells. The median survival of patients with acute ATL is approximately 6 months.

Tropical spastic paresis

Infections with HTLV-1 have also been associated with a neurologic syndrome called tropical spastic paresis, also known as HTLV-1-associated myelopathy (HAM). This disorder is characterized by a

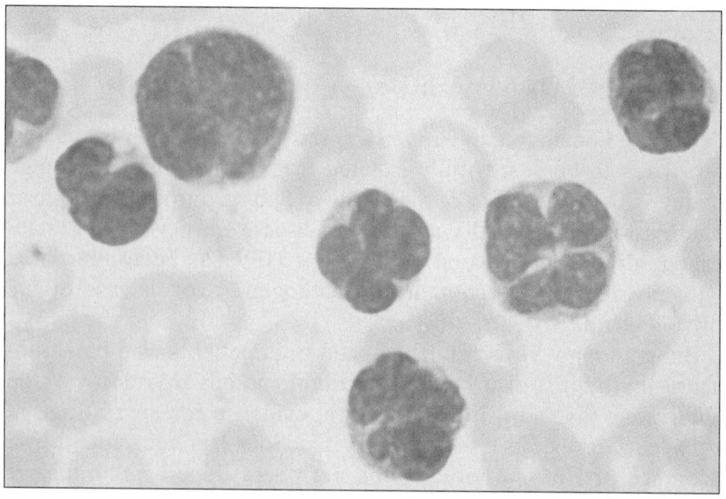

Fig. 221.5 Typical 'clover leaf' appearance of nuclei of HTLV-1 induced adult T cell leukemic cells. Courtesy of Steven M Opal.

slowly progressive symmetric myelopathy combined with high titers of antibodies to HTLV-1 in plasma and cerebrospinal fluid (CSF). The myelopathy primarily affects the pyramidal tract. The mechanisms by which HTLV-1 infection causes HAM is unclear, but patients show signs of an activated immune system with high levels of immunoglobulins and increased numbers of activated T cells in the blood and CSF, which suggests an immunologic (possibly an autoimmunologic) pathogenesis. There have been reports that patients who have HAM respond to corticosteroids but this is always short-lived and unfortunately no form of therapy has been shown to have lasting benefit.[2,11]

Ophthalmologic complications

Human T-lymphocyte leukemia virus-1 infections have also been associated with ophthalmologic complications, which are frequently observed in patients suffering from ATL or HAM. These include a wide range of neoplastic, infectious and noninfectious vascular or inflammatory lesions.[24] However, ocular lesions have also been found in patients who are positive for HTLV-1 antibodies but who have no other clinical manifestation of HTLV-1 infection. In a recent study of 93 patients who had HTLV-1 infection (23 asymptomatic and 70 patients who had HAM tropical spastic paresis), 48.4% of the patients were diagnosed with keratoconjunctivitis and 16.1% with uveitis.[25]

Arthropathy

Finally, HTLV-1 infections have been associated with chronic inflammatory arthropathy, both in the presence and in the absence of clinical ATL. Polyarthritis may be the presenting manifestation of HTLV-I-associated ATL. It has been demonstrated that the synovial fluid of patients who have HTLV-1-associated arthritis contains high titers of anti-HTLV-1 antibodies and atypical lymphocytes.[2,11]

Human T-lymphocyte leukemia virus-2

Human T-lymphocyte leukemia virus-2 infections have been associated with T-cell malignancies, predominantly hairy T-lymphocytic leukemia and chronic lymphatic leukemia. Neurologic complications similar to those seen in HAM or tropical spastic paresis have also been described.

MANAGEMENT

The therapy for ATL usually consists of combined antineoplastic chemotherapy. However, antineoplastic therapies have proved to have only a limited ability to improve the prognosis of ATL. In most patients, resistance of the leukemic cells to the drugs is believed to be the prominent reason for failure to induce a complete remission. However, two promising novel strategies to improve the prognosis of ATL are under investigation. In one study using a combination of zidovudine and interferon-α, a prolonged survival in previously untreated patients was reported.[26] The other a therapeutic approach is directed against the IL-2 receptor on the leukemic cells. Lymphocytes in ATL express high levels of the IL-2 receptor, in contrast to normal resting, non-HTLV-1-infected lymphocytes. A favorable response has been reported in patients treated with antibodies against the IL-2 receptor that are armed with toxins or emitting radionuclides.[27]

HUMAN IMMUNODEFICIENCY VIRUSES

NATURE

The human immunodeficiency viruses HIV-1 and HIV-2 are members of the family of Lentiviruses. Both HIV-1 and HIV-2 are the causative agents of AIDS. For detailed information regarding the clinical manifestations of HIV infection and AIDS (see Chapters 122, 124–133), antiretroviral therapy (see Chapters 139 and 204) and

HIV-1 VIRION

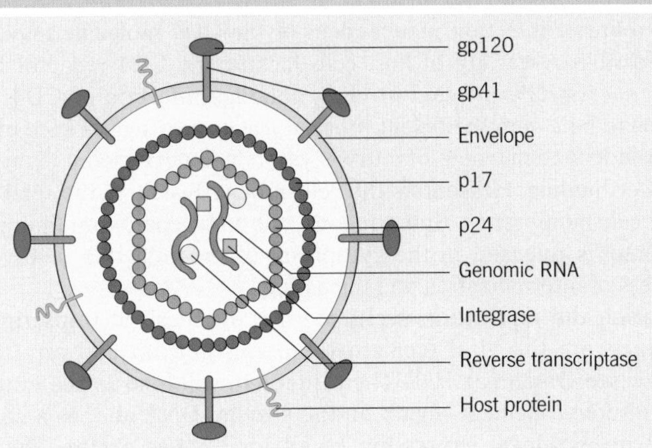

Fig. 221.6 HIV-1 virion.

therapy evaluation and vaccine strategies (see Chapter 118). This chapter describes viral structure, pathogenesis and epidemiology of HIV.

Virion structure

The electron microscopic view of human immunodeficiency retroviruses shows an electron-dense cone-shaped core. The viral p24 capsid protein functions as a shell for the condensed core, which contains the two identical genomic RNA strands in close association with RT (Fig. 221.6). The viral genome is approximately 9200 bases long and contains nine genes (see Fig. 221.3). Previously it was believed that the p6 protein was also located in the viral core, but this protein does not seem to co-purify with the core structure, suggesting another localization.[28] The viral protein Vpr (in HIV-1) and Vpx (in HIV-2) is also found in the virion and is probably located outside the core.[29] The Vif protein may also be present in the viral particle in close association with the viral core.[30] More research is required to increase our knowledge on the structure of the viral particle and to determine the exact localization of p6, Vpr/Vpx and Vif. The inner part of the viral membrane is covered with a myristylated p17 core protein, which provides the matrix for the viral structure. Glycoprotein spikes project from the virion surface and are anchored into an envelope that consists of a phospholipid bilayer derived from the host cell membrane. The spikes contain two viral glycoproteins (gp), gp120 and gp41. The gp41 acts as a transmembrane protein and its central portion binds to the external surface gp120. In addition to gp41 and gp 120, the viral envelope can contain various proteins derived from the host cell.

Replication cycle

Infection starts with the binding of gp120 glycoprotein to the cellular surface CD4 molecule, which acts as a high-affinity receptor. Recently, two secondary or co-receptors have been identified: CXCR4 (also known as fusin) and CCR5.[31] These co-receptors are members of a cellular transmembrane chemokine receptor family. All HIV strains tested to date use CXCR4 or CCR5, or both, as a co-receptor. However, several other co-receptors for HIV have also been identified, one of which is encoded by the cytomegalovirus. Co-receptor usage determines the cell tropism of the HIV strain. The CCR5 co-receptor is used by HIV strains that in vitro do not cause cell fusion (syncytia) in T-cell lines (non-syncitium-inducing (NSI) strains). Syncytium-inducing (SI) HIV variants use both co-receptors CXCR4 and CCR5. In general, NSI variants are found throughout the complete course of HIV infection, whereas SI variants emerge only in a later stage of HIV infection. The presence of SI variants in a patient is associated with a more rapid CD4 decline and faster disease progression (see below).

A route of infection independent of the CD4 molecule may also be possible. A variety of host cells lacking the CD4 receptor have been successfully infected in vitro, although infection of CD4 cells seems to be a very inefficient process. The in-vivo significance of the CD4-independent route of entry is yet to be determined.

After binding, HIV enters the cell through fusion of the viral and host cell membranes. Subsequently, the viral core, containing the genome, is released in the cytoplasm of the cell; this involves a process of internalization and uncoating.

During the replication cycle, the first synthesized transcription products are the viral regulatory proteins *nef*, *tat* and *rev* (for a review see Greene *et al.*[32]). The *tat* protein will bind to the transactive response element region on the proviral DNA and, as a consequence, high-level expression of all viral genes occurs. The *nef* protein is required for high-level viral replication in vivo (see Pathogenesis, below), and it decreases CD4 on the cell membrane. The *nef* protein may enhance the efficiency of reverse transcription, but its precise functions have not been completely elucidated.

Through the action of *rev* a switch may occur toward the synthesis of late regulatory and viral structural proteins. The *rev* protein facilitates the nuclear transport of unspliced and incompletely spliced RNA transcripts that contain the *rev*-responsive element, located in the *env* gene. In addition it promotes translation of messages containing the *rev*-responsive element. It remains unclear to what extent the relative amounts of each of these regulatory proteins and their interaction with cellular factors can determine whether the infection of a cell results in a productive cycle or merely a viral latent state.

The *gag* and the *pol* open reading frames (ORFs) overlap. The *pol* ORF is positioned in the –1 frame relative to the *gag* ORF. In the unspliced, full-length mRNA, both reading frames are present. Translation starts at the beginning of the *gag* ORF and continues in most cases until the end of the ORF, and a 55kDa *gag* precursor protein (p55), containing p17, p24, p7, p2, p1 and p6, is made. During translation of full-length mRNA, approximately 5–10% of the ribosomes slip back one nucleotide (frame shift) and gain access to the *pol* ORF, and translation continues. A partial *gag* precursor protein is fused to the *pol* polyprotein, resulting in a *gag–pol* polyprotein. The *pol* gene encodes for three proteins: protease, RT and integrase. Cleavage of the *gag–pol* protein generates protease, RT and integrase. The 99-amino acid protease is coded for at the 5′ end of the *pol* gene. HIV protease is active only as homodimer, which is generated by an autolytic process. It is possible that aggregation of two *gag–pol* proteins is required to generate the active form, thereby limiting activation to the budding site. Both *gag* and *gag–pol* polyproteins are post-translationally modified by a covalent attachment of a lipophilic myristyl group onto their aminoterminal glycine by a host cell-derived myristyl transferase. Myristylation may be required for intracellular transport to the cell membrane because, in the absence of myristylation, no infectious particles are produced.

The *gag* precursor protein is cleaved by viral protease into four structural proteins (p17, p24, p7 and p6) and two smaller proteins (p2 and p1). The protein p2 may be important for proper assembly of the virions. The *gag* precursor protein may also play a role in the packaging of viral RNA into the virus particle, specifically through the action of the nucleic acid binding protein p7. This protein binds to a sequence at the 5′ end of the viral genome, possibly through the interaction of so-called cystine–histidine motifs. The p6 protein has been shown to be rich in proline, and through binding to p6, Vpr is incorporated in the viral particle. Viruses with a mutation in p6 are not released from the cell surface.

The accessory genes *vif*, *vpr* and *vpu*/*vpx* influence the viral assembly and budding process, and alterations in these genes leads to a decrease in infectivity. These proteins may be more important for replication in macrophages and primary lymphocytes than for T-cell lines. The protein Vpr can cause cell cycle arrest in the G2 phase, and it is as yet unclear whether this phenomena plays a role in viral replication. The protein Vpu interacts with CD4 and may cause CD4 degradation.[2,11] The Vif protein is considered to enhance infectivity and the underlying mechanism is still under investigation.[32]

EPIDEMIOLOGY OF HIV AND VIRAL SUBTYPES

Twenty-six nonhuman primates in Africa have been reported to be infected with the retrovirus simian immunodeficiency virus (SIV). Two of these viruses are the cause of AIDS in humans. It has been estimated that they have been transmitted to humans on at least seven different occasions.[33]

The global HIV-1 epidemic is seen as a composite of infections from at least nine genetically distinct subtypes or clades of virus, designated A to H.[34] Together they form the M group.[35] These subtypes can be distinguished on the basis of sequence information of the *env* gene (30% difference) and *gag* gene (15% difference). Two isolates that are highly divergent from group M have been fully sequenced. The results show that viruses from the new group O are almost as close to HIV-2 as to HIV-1. The distribution of certain HIV-1 subtypes is still geographically limited, but geographic dispersion will contribute to the growing pandemic (see Chapter 115). The distribution of subtypes within countries as well as throughout the world shows that there is no evidence for host specificity for certain subtypes.[35] Dual infection with two subtypes and hybrids between two subtypes have been described in infected individuals.

Five distinct subgroups have been identified for HIV-2, and in analogy with HIV-1 these were designated A to E. The observed viral variation has clear implications for vaccine development and has also implications for development of drugs or treatment of patients. The non-nucleoside RT inhibitors (NNRTIs) inhibit RT activity through binding various amino acids of RT, the most important amino acid being the tyrosine residue at codon 181 for HIV-1 RT. Selection of drug-resistant HIV-1 isolates both in vitro and in vivo results in a substitution at codon 181 of a cysteine. The cysteine substitution gives a considerable increase in the 50% inhibitory concentration for all NNRTIs. Sequence analysis of several HIV-2 RT genes has shown that at codon 181 the cysteine is normally present. The presence of the cysteine variant makes HIV-2 viruses naturally resistant to the NNRTIs.

The *env*-based classification of widely divergent HIV-1 strains into sequence subtypes is also supported by nucleotide sequence analysis of the *gag* genes. The distinction between SI and NSI viruses, conferred by gp120 described in clade B, is also present among other HIV-1 subtypes. Detailed information is available on the prevalence of the different subtypes for certain areas in the world. Information on the prevalence of different clades in a region may give interesting information on the spread of the infection and the possible transmission routes. For instance, in Thailand it has been shown that type A is mainly spreading through sexual intercourse, whereas type B is transmitted among intravenous drug users. Monitoring the prevalence of different clades around the world and searching for possible new clades is important for the use and development of diagnostic procedures. For instance, some screening assays for HIV antibodies have been shown to be relatively insensitive for clade O viruses. The use of diagnostic PCR procedures, especially in children born to mothers who have HIV infection, may be complicated by sequence variation in the region where the primers have to anneal to their substrate. The quantitative molecular assays may also vary in their sensitivity for different clades. From the perspective of vaccine development, it will also be extremely important to continue to generate information on the worldwide prevalence and geographic distribution of the various clades (see also Chapter 115).[36]

PATHOGENICITY

Transmission

The three major routes of transmission of HIV are by sexual contact or blood or blood products or vertically through maternal–fetal transmission. The first step in infection is binding of the viral particles to submucosal dendritic cells (H). These cells which normally process antigens and present them to immune cells, express a protein termed DC–SIGN. The viral gp120 binds to DC-SIGN with high affinity; subsequently the viral particles are internalized and presented again at the cell surface after the dendritic cells have migrated to the regional lymph tissues and present viral particles to the T cells (see Chapter 120).

It is very likely that the amount of HIV in the inoculating material is the most important factor determining the risk of transmission. The amount of virus is, at least in the blood of the donor, determined by disease stage and antiretroviral therapy. In contrast, data on the relation between the amount of HIV in semen and disease stage is contradictory.[37] Modeling of the epidemic supports the notion that viral load may be the major factor for determining the rate of infection. It has been demonstrated that people who have a primary infection are an important source of transmission.[38] The amount of virus in the blood of people who have a primary infection is generally very high (see below). A prospective study showed that the transmission rate within heterosexual couples tended to increase when the index case was in a more advanced stage of disease, again pointing at an inoculum effect.[39]

Two recent studies showed that the risk of heterosexual transmission is dependent on the HIV RNA concentration in the peripheral blood of the positive partner.[40,41] In one cohort no cases of transmission were noted if the seropositive partners had HIV RNA concentrations under 1500 copies/ml. In this cohort of 415 couples there was a clear dose–response relation of increased transmission with increasing viral load.[40]

The rate of transmission may also be determined by biologic properties of the virus. Transmission of HIV-2 seems to be considerably lower than of HIV-1 in western Africa. In addition, infection with HIV-2 seems to protect against infection with HIV-1. In a prospective study among commercial female sex workers in Senegal, the HIV-1 infection rate was lower in those workers who were already infected with HIV-2.[42,43]

Other protective host factors may also play a role, such as the integrity of mucocutaneous membranes of the urogenital tract. Among heterosexual couples the risk of transmission increases when the negative partner had a genital infection.[39,40]

It has been demonstrated that protection against transmission is also offered by a 32bp deletion in the *CCR5* gene, encoding a cellular co-receptor for HIV (see Replication cycle, above). The CCR5 allele with the 32bp deletion (CCR5 32) is common in the Caucasian population with a frequency of 8080 per 100,000 individuals (13.3% heterozygous, 1.4% homozygous). The CCR5 32 is not found among Asians and Africans. In 1252 homosexual males of the Multicenter AIDS Cohort Study from Chicago none of the HIV-infected participants was homozygous for the CCR5 32 allele, whereas 3.6% of the at-risk but uninfected Caucasian participants were found to be homozygous.[44] This suggests that homozygosity for the CCR5 32 allele is an important protection factor. Heterozygosity has not been found to protect against infection, although it is associated with a delayed disease progression (see below).[44]

Finally, a study among a group of 25 seronegative subjects who had a history of multiple exposures to HIV-1 showed that the CD4+ lymphocytes in a subgroup of patients had a relative resistance to infection with clinical isolates in vitro.[45] These CD4+ lymphocytes produced more chemokines – RANTES, macrophage inflammatory protein (MIP)-1α, MIP-1β – than sensitive CD4+ lymphocytes. Addition of recombinant chemokines to sensitive CD4+ lymphocytes increased their resistance to infection. These chemokines are the natural ligands of chemokine receptors CCR5 and CXCR4, which have been identified as HIV co-receptors. It has been hypothesized that chemokines compete with HIV for the receptor binding sites, thus inhibiting the efficiency of HIV infection.

Studies addressing transmission from mother to baby have also shown that the risk of vertical transmission increases with a higher viral load in the mother at the time of delivery (as measured as by HIV p24 antigen, HIV-1 RNA, proviral DNA or PBMC viral titer) and with lower CD4+ lymphocyte counts.[46] The current opinion is that the majority of infections of the child occur late during pregnancy and most commonly during delivery, because elective cesarean section lowers the transmission rate by approximately 50%.[47] This notion is supported by the outcome of a multicenter, randomized, placebo–controlled trial of the efficacy and safety of zidovudine in reducing the risk of vertical transmission.[48] A protective effect of treatment was seen despite the fact that the treated women received the study drug only for a median of 11 weeks before giving birth. Moreover, the risk of transmission increases when the fetal membranes rupture more than 4 hours before delivery.[49,50] This also suggests that most transmissions occur late in pregnancy or during delivery (see Chapter 134).

Incubation period and viral replication

Initially, it was believed that during the asymptomatic or clinically latent phase the amount of viral replication would be very low and the amount of virus present in the body minimal. It has been shown over the past few years that this concept was seriously flawed. Prospective studies show that in most people during the asymptomatic phase of the infection a gradual decline of the CD4+ lymphocytes is paralleled by a gradual rise in viral HIV-1 RNA in the peripheral blood. Moreover, it has been shown that in the asymptomatic phase, virus replicates in the lymphoid tissue in those people who lack cell-free virus in their peripheral blood. Analysis of the viral burden in the peripheral blood compared with the burden in lymphoid tissues shows that the viral load in lymphoid tissues is 1 log higher than in blood. In-situ hybridization studies and electron microscopic analyses have shown that the lymph nodes from asymptomatic carriers can contain high quantities of HIV.[51] Viral particles covered with antibody and complement are trapped by the follicular dendritic cells in the germinal center of the lymph nodes. Thus, the incubation period is characterized by ongoing viral replication.

Viral dynamics and CD4+ lymphocyte depletion

The effects of therapy with two protease inhibitors (ritonavir (10 patients) and indinavir (8 patients)) and a NNRTI (nevirapine (4 patients)) were investigated.[52] In addition to measuring the response of HIV RNA and CD4+ lymphocytes, this study also measured the appearance of drug-resistant mutations in both plasma and PBMCs. The viral clearance rate was calculated (using three methods) and found to range between 1.8 (±0.9) days and 3.0 (±1.7) days. There were no differences observed in viral clearance rates with the three different drugs. In both studies the clearance rate constants were independent of the initial viral loads and the CD4+ lymphocyte counts, suggesting that the viral clearance rate constant is independent of the stage of HIV infection. Monitoring the appearance of drug-resistant mutations over time led to an estimated

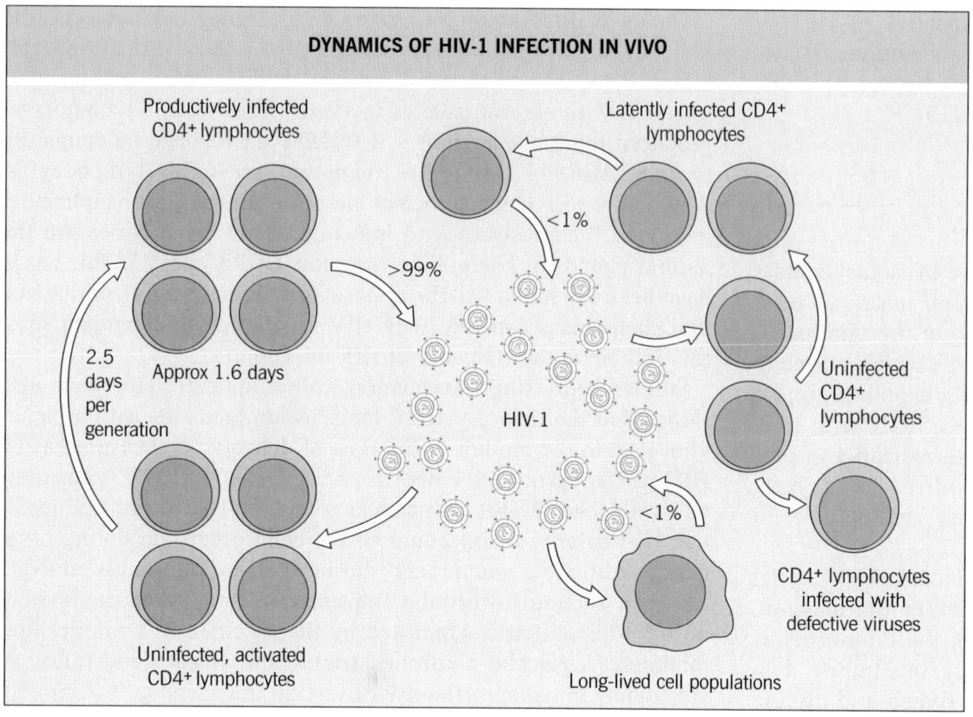

Fig. 221.7 Dynamics of HIV-1 infection in vivo. Shown in the center is the cell-free virion population that is sampled when the viral load in plasma is measured. Adapted from Perelson *et al.*[54]

doubling time of approximately 2 days, in accordance with the estimated half-life for HIV in plasma.

In agreement with previous results, an estimate of 2×10^9 $CD4^+$ lymphocytes (about 5% of the total $CD4^+$ lymphocyte population) has been calculated to be produced and destroyed daily. In other studies data have been generated with zidovudine and lamivudine that support the observations described above.[53]

All the data together show that HIV-1 infection is a highly dynamic process in which billions of viruses are being produced (Fig. 221.7). The vast majority of the high number of circulating viruses is derived from continuous rounds of new infections that take place on a daily basis.[54] The contribution of long-living, chronically virus-producing cells is very small. In a review, these insights were placed in the context of genetic variation, pathogenesis and therapy.[55] Our current understanding of the kinetics of HIV infection has changed our views on antiretroviral therapy.

Relationship of viral load and $CD4^+$ lymphocyte levels to disease progression

Several approaches have been developed to obtain information on the amount of virus present in a person with HIV infection and to relate the amount of virus to the duration of the incubation period, rate of disease progression and survival. Both the amount of provirus and the amount of virus in the peripheral blood have been evaluated using quantitative culture techniques and quantitative molecular approaches.

The first quantification of virus was carried out by determination of viral capsid antigen in serum using the HIV p24 or antigen assays. Later, quantitative virus culture assays were developed to measure the amount of culturable virus in serum or plasma.[56,57] In the first studies, the mean titers ranged from 30 tissue culture infective doses (TCID) for asymptomatic infection to 3200 TCID in patients who have AIDS, but a later study reported higher titers in a small number of patients.[58] Several cross-sectional studies showed a relationship between a more progressed disease stage, lower $CD4^+$ lymphocyte counts and higher plasma titers. Antiretroviral therapy lowers the plasma titers and cellular viral titers.[59,60] The costs and the need for fast transport of plasma to the laboratory have prevented widespread use of quantitative cultures for estimating the risk of fast disease progression as well as for therapy evaluation.[61]

The amount of provirus has been measured by two methods:

- quantification of the viral titer in patient PBMCs; and
- quantification of the amount of proviral DNA using various PCR-based techniques.

A correlation has been found between a high frequency of positive cells or an increase in the number of positive cells and disease progression in all studies that have addressed the relationship between proviral DNA levels and disease progression, either by comparing patients in different disease stages cross-sectionally[62–68] or by following patients over time who progressed clinically.[64,69–71] The increase observed over time was relatively small (range of 1–2 log). In one longitudinal study of seroconverters, a relationship was found between a high proviral load from the moment of seroconversion and a rapid progression to disease.[70] During the incubation time, the increase in proviral load was relatively small, indicating that the set point obtained around seroconversion determined the subsequent outcome. Similar observations have been made with HIV RNA levels in seroconverters.[72,73] Two studies were carried out to analyze the amount of proviral DNA in patients infected with HIV-2.[74,75] The numbers obtained were not significantly different from those in patients infected with HIV-1.

In a recent study the amount of HIV viral DNA was compared between HIV-specific memory cells and other memory cells.[76] It was shown that the HIV-specific memory $CD4^+$ cells contained significantly more HIV viral DNA at all stages of disease, indicating indeed that HIV-specific $CD4^+$ cells are preferentially infected by HIV in vivo.

Several studies have determined the amount and pattern of viral mRNA expression and have correlated these with disease progression and decline in $CD4^+$-lymphocyte counts.[77] The outcomes of all these studies are remarkably similar. In all studies, independent of the disease stage, viral transcription can be detected. Furthermore, these studies indicate that in patients who show immunologic or clinical deterioration, a shift takes place from a predominantly spliced mRNA pattern to a predominantly unspliced pattern. It has been suggested that this may be caused by post-translational replication block, a model suggesting true in-vivo latency. However, the observed differences in the relative abundance of the different mRNA species may also be caused by de-novo viral replication.[77] Until this type of study is performed on single cells, it will be difficult to find out to what extent latency in cells on the basis of post-transcriptional block is a frequent event. The authors of some of these studies advocate the use of quantitative mRNA measurements and pattern analysis as tools for clinical management. It is very unlikely, however, that this type of assay will show an advantage over the well-established methods for quantifying the amount of genomic RNA copies in serum or plasma.

The development of quantitative assays for the determination of viral RNA in serum has revolutionized the field of antiretroviral therapy and our insights into the pathogenesis of disease. The first cross-sectional studies showed that HIV-1 RNA could be detected in all stages of disease and that levels as high as 10^7 copies/ml could be measured.[78–80] In general, there is a significant correlation between HIV RNA levels and the other quantitative parameters for cell-free virus (extracellular virions), such as HIV p24 antigen, although these parameters are often undetectable.[81,82] Furthermore, a strong correlation has been found between cell-free HIV RNA levels and cellular RNA levels in PBMCs.[72] The sensitivity and dynamic range of the HIV RNA measurements is much greater, however, and therefore more information has been obtained on the significance of viral load for pathogenesis and therapy evaluation by using the HIV RNA measurements.

Currently, several longitudinal studies on the relationship between HIV RNA load patterns over time and disease progression or $CD4^+$-lymphocyte decline on four different cohorts of seroconvertors have been performed.[72,73,83–85] These studies showed that a plateau phase or set point is obtained a couple of months after acute HIV infection. This plateau phase is stable during the course of years. A clear variation (2–3 log) was observed, however, in the height of the set point, and this value, obtained some months after seroconversion, was directly related to the ultimate clinical outcome.

With the introduction of the highly active antiretroviral therapy it has become possible to inhibit viral replication completely in some treated individuals. This, however, does not lead to eradication of the infection because pretherapy infected cells not undergoing a full viral replicative cycle can persist. Currently it is not clear how long these latent reservoirs may persist, but most studies estimate that these reservoirs could persist for life.[86]

Indeed, even patients who have supressed their viral replication for as long as 5 years experience a rebound in viral replication if they interrupt their therapy.

This indicates that for eradication of HIV infection alternative strategies need to be developed. The challenge will be to find a way to eliminate the provirus from the T-memory cells, which are currently assumed to represent reservoir cells with the longest survival.

Factors that determine the duration of the incubation period

Presently, it is not clear why the incubation period can greatly differ between individuals and why the decline in $CD4^+$ lymphocyte counts is typically a gradual process (40–80 cells/mm^3/year).[87] It is likely, however, that multiple factors are involved in determining the time to disease progression. Some factors have been identified. These factors can be divided into viral and immunologic (host) factors (see also Chapter 120).

To get more insight into the factors influencing the incubation period and pathogenesis of HIV infections, studies have been performed on patients with HIV infection who have not shown clinical progression and who have moderate immunologic deterioration, or none at all during long-term follow up (generally up to 10–15 years after infection).[88,89] These so-called long-term survivors or long-term nonprogressors seem to have some characteristics in common. The viral burden and proviral burden in the peripheral blood was found to be several orders of magnitude lower than the levels normally found in subjects who have progressive disease.[88,89] The lymph nodes showed significantly less activation (germinal center formation) than the lymph nodes of control subjects with progressive disease, and furthermore the germinal centers did not show signs of involution and lymphocyte depletion.[89] Viruses could nevertheless be cultured from the mononuclear cells in the lymph nodes, indicating that HIV in these individuals was replication competent.[89]

Three viral factors have been found that seem to play a role in the duration of the incubation time. First, deletions in the *nef* regulatory gene causing a decrease in virulence have been shown to be present in a group of six long-term survivors, all of whom were intravenously infected by blood products from the same donor. However, in another study it was demonstrated that 91.1% of the *nef* genes of 10 long-term nonprogressors had no such deletions. The events described in all cases in which a *nef* deletion was observed are remarkably similar to the events described in rhesus monkeys inoculated with a derivative of the pathogenic SIV containing a 183bp deletion in *nef*. These animals became persistently infected but had low viral burden and normal $CD4^+$-lymphocyte counts and did not show any sign of disease progression.[90]

Recently, a detailed analysis of a long-term survivor was published.[91] This patient, also infected via a blood transfusion, harbored viruses with only a low frequency of defective *nef* genes, but in contrast the viral population contained inactivating mutations in several other accessory genes (*vif*, *vpr*, *vpu*, *tat* and *rev*).

Thus, some studies show that, in at least in some long-term nonprogressors, specific virologic changes in their HIV cause a decrease in virulence, which may account for their sustained incubation period.

The second viral property that contributes to the rate of disease progression comes from studies that compared the rate of disease development between patients infected with HIV-1 and those infected with HIV-2.[45,92] These studies suggest that people infected with HIV-2 have a reduced rate of developing a $CD4^+$ lymphocyte count below 400 cells/mm^3 and reduced disease progression compared with people infected with HIV-1. The limitation of this type of data is that the differences may be caused by differences in duration of infection between the HIV-1 and HIV-2 groups. The mechanism responsible for the reduced virulence of HIV-2 needs further research.

A third virologic factor that contributes to the duration of the incubation period is the capacity of HIV to induce syncytia in a MT-2 cell line ex vivo. Prospective studies in the Amsterdam cohort have shown that untreated subjects who switch in viral phenotype from NSI to SI isolates develop a more rapid decline in $CD4^+$-lymphocyte counts and show a faster progression to AIDS than those who have persisting NSI phenotypic isolates.[93] The SI isolates appeared 2 years before the progression to AIDS.

Several host factors seem to contribute to the duration of the incubation time. The immune response to HIV plays a crucial role in controlling HIV replication in long-term nonprogressors. The cytotoxic T-lymphocyte activity to HIV antigens is believed to protect against disease progression. Recently, several studies have shown that heterozygosity for a deletion of 32bp in the gene encoding the CCR5 HIV co-receptor predicts delayed disease progression. In one study it was shown that 30 months after seroconversion CCR5 32 heterozygotes had a 1.5-fold slower decline in $CD4^+$ T-cell count and a 2.6-fold lower plasma viral load than CCR5 wild-type homozygotes. The predictive value of the CCR5 genotype for disease progression was independent of high HIV RNA plasma load, low $CD4^+$ T-cell counts, low T-cell functionality and the presence of SI variants of HIV.[94]

CLINICAL FEATURES

The hallmark of HIV infection is a selective reduction in the number of $CD4^+$ T cells, resulting in a progressive loss of cellular immunity and development of AIDS, which is characterized by opportunistic infections and the development of opportunistic malignancies. In addition, several organs may be directly affected by HIV, including the gastrointestinal tract, bone marrow and the central nervous system, resulting in wasting, AIDS dementia, neuropathy and thrombocytopenia. The incubation period of primary HIV infection is approximately 4 weeks. Primary HIV infection is symptomatic in up to 70% cases and is associated with fever, arthralgia, adenopathy, myalgia, truncal (and facial) maculopapular rash and neurologic symptoms, including neuritis, myelopathy and aseptic meningoencephalitis (see Chapter 122). Primary HIV infection is followed by an asymptomatic carrier state of variable duration (median 10 years), after which most patients develop AIDS. The asymptomatic phase of HIV infection is frequently characterized by a persistent generalized lymphadenopathy. On histologic examination, lymph nodes of asymptomatic HIV carriers who have persistent generalized lymphadenopathy show follicular hyperplasia with endothelial cell proliferation, and HIV is found in large amounts on the follicular dendritic cells. Clinical progression toward AIDS is reflected by a rapid decrease in $CD4^+$ lymphocytes and deterioration of the lymph node architecture, from follicular hyperplasia to follicular involution and follicular depletion. The many symptoms and complications of AIDS are beyond the scope of this chapter. For a detailed discussion of the clinical manifestations during late-stage HIV disease, see Chapters 124–133.

MANAGEMENT

In a majority of patients with HIV infection, highly active antiretroviral therapy consisting of two RT inhibitors and one protease inhibitor results in profound and sustained suppression of HIV replication, increasing $CD4^+$ lymphocyte counts and preventing AIDS-defining illnesses and death. Reduction of plasma HIV RNA concentrations below the level of detection can be achieved for up to 2 years. For a review of the general principles and details of antiretroviral therapy, see Chapters 138, 139, and 204.

REFERENCES

1. Galasso GJ, Whitley RJ, Merigan TC, eds. Antiviral agents and human diseases, 4th ed. Philadelphia: Lippincott-Raven; 1997:610.
2. Fields BN. Virology, 3rd ed. Philadelphia: Lippincott-Raven; 1996.
3. Löwer R, Löwer J, Kurth R, *et al.* The viruses in all of us: characteristics and biological significance of human endogenous retroviruses. Proc Natl Acad Sci 1996;93:5177.
4. Urnovitz HB, Murphy WH. Human endogenous retroviruses: nature, occurrence and clinical implications in human disease. Clin Microbiol Rev 1996;9:72–99.
5. Achong BG, Mansell PW, Epstein MA, Clifford P. An unusual virus in cultures from a human nasopharyngeal carcinoma. J Natl Cancer Inst 1971;46:299.
6. Stancek D, Gressnernova M. A viral agent isolated from a patient with subacute de Quervain type thyroiditis. Acta Virol 1974;18:365.
7. Lagaye S, Vexiau P, Morozov V, *et al.* Human spuma retrovirus related sequences in the DNA of leukocytes from patients with Graves disease. PNAS 1992;89:10070–4.
8. Wick G, Grubeck-Loebenstein B, Trieb K, *et al.* Human foamy virus antigens in thyroid tissue of Grave's disease patients. Int Arch Allergy Immunol 1992;99:153–6.
9. Cameron KR, Birchall SM, Moses MA. Isolation of foamy virus from a patient with dialysis encephalopathy. Lancet 1978;2:796.
10. Westarp ME, Fuchs D, Bartmann P, *et al.* Amyotrophic lateral sclerosis an enigmatic disease with B-cellular and antiretroviral immune responses. Eur J Med 1993;2:327–32.
11. Levy JA. The retroviridae, volume 2. New York: Plenum Press; 1992.
12. Albrecht B, Lairmore MD. Critical role of human T-lymphotropic virus type 1 accessory proteins in viral replication and pathogenesis. Microbiol Mol Biol Rev 2002;66:396–406.
13. Levy JA. The retroviridae, volume 4. New York: Plenum Press; 1992:281.
14. Lee H, Swanson P, Shorty VS, *et al.* High rate of HTLV-II infection in seropositive IV drug abusers in New Orleans. Science 1989;244:471–5.
15. Zella D, Mori L, Sala M, *et al.* HTLV-II infection in Italian drug abusers. Lancet 1990;336:575–6.
16. Lairmore MD, Jacobson S, Gracia F, *et al.* Isolation of T cell lymphotropic virus type 2 from Guaymi Indians in Panama. Proc Natl Acad Sci 1990;87:8840–4.
17. Hjelle B, Scalf R, Swenson S. High frequency of human T cell leukemia virus type II infection in New Mexico blood donors: determination by sequnce-specific oligonucleotide hybridization. Blood 1990:76:450–4.
18. Hattori T, Uchiyama T, Toibana T, Takatsuki K, Uchino H. Surface phenotype of Japanese adult T cell leukemia cells characterized by monoclonal antibodies. Blood 1981;58:645–7.
19. Raphael M. T-cell leukemia-lymphoma in adults and other blood diseases in HTLV-I infection. Ann Med Interne (Paris) 1996;147:582–5.
20. Levine AJ. Viruses. New York: Scientific American Library; 1992.
21. Seno S, Takaku F, Irino S, eds. Topics in haematology. Amsterdam: Excerpta Medica; 1977.
22. Shimoyama M. Diagnostic criteria and classification of clinical subtypes of ATL lymphoma. (A report from the lymphoma study group.) Br J Haematol 1991;79:428–37.
23. Kondo T, Kono H, Nonaka H, *et al.* Risk of adult T-cell leukemia/lymphoma in HTLV-1 carriers. Lancet 1987;24:851–6.
24. Kawano F, Yamaguchi K, Nishimura H, Tsuda H, Takatsuki K. Variation in the clinical courses of adult T cell leukemia. Cancer 1985;55:851.
25. Merle H, Smadja D, Le Hoang P, *et al.* Ocular manifestations in patients with HTLV-I associated infection – a clinical study of 93 cases. Jpn J Ophthalmol 1996;40:260–70.
26. Bazarbachi A, Hermine O. Treatment with a combination of zidovudine and alpha-interferon in naive and pretreated adult T-cell leukemia/lymphoma patients. J Acquir Immune Defic Syndr Hum Retrovirol 1996;13(Suppl.1):186–90.
27. Waldmann TA, White JD, Goldman CK, *et al.* The interleukin-2 receptor: a target for monoclonal antibody treatment of human T-cell lymphotrophic virus I-induced adult T-cell leukemia. Blood 1993;82:1701–12.
28. Gelderblom HR. Assembly and morphology of HIV: potential effect of structure on viral function [Editorial]. AIDS 1991;5:617–37.
29. Lu YL, Spearman P, Ratner L. Human immunodeficiency virus type 1 viral protein R localization in infected cells and virions. J Virol 1993;67:6542–50.
30. Cullen BR. Regulation of human immunodeficiency virus replication. Annu Rev Microbiol 1991;45:219–50.
31. Lee B, Doranz BJ, Ratajczak MZ, Doms RW. An intricate web: chemokine receptors, HIV-1 and hematopoiesis. Stem Cells 1998;16:79–88.
32. Greene WC, Peterlin BM. Charting HIV's remarkable voyage through the cell: basic science as a passport to future therapy. Nat Med 2002;8:673–80.
33. Hahn BH, Shaw GM, De Cock KM, *et al.* AIDS as a zoonosis: scientific and public health implications. Science 2000;287:607–14.
34. Robertson DL, Anderson JP, Bradac JA, *et al.* HIV-1 nomenclature proposal. Science 2000;288:55–7.
35. Myers G. Tenth anniversary perspectives on AIDS. HIV: between past and future. AIDS Res Hum Retrovir 1994;10:1317–24.
36. Gaschen B, Taylor J, Yusim K, *et al.* Diversity considerations in HIV-1 vaccine selection. Science 2002;296:2354–60.
37. Vernazza PL, Eron JJ, Cohen MS, *et al.* Detection and biologic characterization of infectious HIV-1 in semen of seropositive men. AIDS 1994;8:1325–9.
38. Jacquez JA, Koopman JS, Simon CP, Longini IM Jr. Role of primary infection in epidemics of HIV infected in gay cohorts. J Acquir Immune Defic Syndr 1994;7:1169–84.
39. de Vincenzi I. A longitudinal study of human immunodeficiency virus transmission by heterosexual partners. European Study Group on Heterosexual Transmission of HIV [see comments]. N Engl J Med 1994;331:341–6.
40. Gray RH, Wawer MJ, Brookmeyer R, *et al.* Probability of HIV-1 transmission per coital act in monogamous, heterosexual, HIV-1-discordant couples in Rakai, Uganda. Lancet 2001;357:1149–53.
41. Quinn TC, Wawer MJ, Sewankambo N, *et al.* Viral load and heterosexual transmission of human immunodeficiency virus type 1. N Engl J Med 2000;342:921–9.
42. Travers K, Mboup S, Marlink R, *et al.* Natural protection against HIV-1 infection provided by HIV-2. Science 1995;268:1612–5.
43. Sotoramirez LE, Renjifo B, McLane MF, *et al.* HIV-1 Langerhans' cell tropism associated with heterosexual transmission of HIV. Science 1996;271:1291–3.
44. Huang Y, Paxton WA, Wolinsky SM, *et al.* The role of a mutant CCR5 allele in HIV-1 transmission and disease progression. Nature Med 1996;2:1240.
45. Marlink R, Kanki P, Thior I, *et al.* Reduced rate of disease development after HIV-2 infection as compared to HIV-1. Science 1994;265:1587–90.
46. Peckham C, Gibb D. Mother-to-child transmission of the human immunodeficiency virus. N Engl J Med 1995;333:298–302.
47. Anonymous. Caesarean section and risk of vertical transmission of HIV-1 infection. The European Collaborative Study. Lancet 1994;343:1464–7.

48. Connor EM, Sperling RS, Gelber R, *et al.* Reduction of maternal–infant transmission of human immunodeficiency virus type 1 with zidovudine treatment. Pediatric AIDS Clinical Trials Group Protocol 076 Study Group. N Engl J Med 1994;331:1173–80.
49. Landesman SH, Kalish LA, Burns DN, *et al.* Obstetrical factors and the transmission of human immunodeficiency virus type I from mother to child. N Engl J Med 1996;334:1617–23.
50. Biggar RJ, Miotti PG, Taha TE, *et al.* Perinatal intervention trial in Africa: effect of a birth canal cleansing intervention to prevent HIV transmission. Lancet 1996;347:1647–50.
51. Embretson J, Zupancic M, Ribas JL, *et al.* Massive covert infection of helper T lymphocytes and macrophages by HIV during the incubation period of AIDS. Nature 1993;362:359–62.
52. Wei X, Ghosh SK, Taylor ME, *et al.* Viral dynamics in human immunodeficiency virus type 1 infection. Nature 1995;373:117–22.
53. Schuurman R, Nijhuis M, van Leeuwen R, *et al.* Rapid changes in human immunodeficiency virus type 1 RNA load and appearance of drug-resistant virus populations in persons treated with lamivudine (3TC). J Infect Dis 1995;171:1411–9.
54. Perelson AS, Neuman AU, Markowitz M, Leonard JM, Ho DD. HIV-1 dynamics *in vivo*: virion clearance rate, infected cell life-span, and viral generation time. Science 1996;271:1582–6.
55. Coffin JM. HIV population dynamics *in vivo*: implications for genetic variation, pathogenesis, and therapy. Science 1995;267:483–9.
56. Ho DD, Moudgil T, Alam M, *et al.* Quantitation of human immunodeficiency virus type 1 in the blood of infected persons. N Engl J Med 1989;321:1621–5.
57. Coombs RW, Collier AC, Allain JP, *et al.* Plasma viremia in human immunodeficiency virus infection. N Engl J Med 1989;321:1626–31.
58. Saag MS, Crain MJ, Decker WD, *et al.* High-level viremia in adults and children infected with human immunodeficiency virus: relation to disease stage and $CD4^+$ lymphocyte levels. J Infect Dis 1991;164:72–80.
59. Lu W, Andrieu JM. Early identification of human immunodeficiency virus-infected asymptomatic subjects susceptible to zidovudine by quantitative viral coculture and reverse transcription-linked polymerase chain reaction. J Infect Dis 1993;167:1014–20.
60. Fiscus SA, DeGruttola V, Gupta F, *et al.* Human immunodeficiency virus type 1 quantitative cell microculture as a measure of antiviral efficacy in a multicenter clinical trial. J Infect Dis 1995;171:305–11.
61. Moudgil T, Daar ES. Infectious decay of human immunodeficiency virus type 1 in plasma. J Infect Dis 1993;167:210–2.
62. Simmonds P, Balfe P, Peutherer JF, Ludlam CA, Bishop JO, Brown AJ. Human immunodeficiency virus-infected individuals contain provirus in small numbers of peripheral mononuclear cells and at low copy numbers. J Virol 1990;64:864–72.
63. Genesca J, Wang RY-H, Alter HJ, Shih JW-K. Clinical correlation and genetic polymorphism of the human immunodeficiency virus proviral DNA obtained after polymerase chain reaction amplification. J Infect Dis 1990;162:1025–30.
64. Escaich S, Ritter J, Rougier P, *et al.* Relevance of the quantitative detection of HIV proviral sequences in PBMC of infected individuals. AIDS Res Hum Retrovir 1992;8:1833–7.
65. Yerly S, Chamot E, Hirschel B, Perrin LH. Quantitation of human immunodeficiency virus provirus and circulating virus: relationship with immunologic parameters. J Infect Dis 1992;166:269–76.
66. Hufert FT, Laer van D, Schramm C, Tarnok A, Schmitz H. Progression of HIV-1 infection. Monitoring of HIV-1 DNA in peripheral blood mononuclear cells by PCR. Arch Virol 1991;120:233–40.
67. Verhofstede C, Reniers S, Van Wanzeele F, Plum J. Evaluation of proviral copy number and plasma RNA level as early indicators of progression in HIV-1 infection: correlation with virological and immunological markers of disease. AIDS 1994;8:1421–7.
68. Lee TH, Sunzeri FJ, Tobler LH, Williams BG, Busch MP. Quantitative assessment of HIV-1 DNA load by coamplification of HIV-1 gag and HLA-DQ-alpha genes. AIDS 1991;5:683–91.
69. Schnittman SM, Greenhouse JJ, Psallidopoulos MC, *et al.* Increasing viral burden in $CD4^+$ T cells from patients with human immunodeficiency virus (HIV) infection reflects rapidly progressive immunosuppression and clinical disease. Ann Intern Med 1990;113:438–43.
70. Lee TH, Sheppard HW, Reis M, Dondero D, Osmond D, Busch MP. Circulating HIV-1-infected cell burden from seroconversion to AIDS: importance of postseroconversion viral load on disease course. J Acquir Immune Defic Syndr 1994;7:381–8.
71. Gupta P, Kingsley L, Armstrong J, Ding M, Cottrill M, Rinaldo C. Enhanced expression of human immunodeficiency virus type 1 correlates with development of AIDS. Virology 1993;196:586–95.
72. Mellors JW, Kingsley LA, Rinaldo CR Jr, *et al.* Quantitation of HIV-1 RNA in plasma predicts outcome after seroconversion. Ann Intern Med 1995;122:573–9.
73. Katzenstein TL, Pedersen C, Nielsen C, Lundgren JD, Jakobsen PH, Gerstoft J. Correlation to viral phenotype at seroconversion and clinical outcome. AIDS 1996;10:167–73.
74. Simon F, Matheron S, Tamalet C, *et al.* Cellular and plasma viral load in patients infected with HIV-2. AIDS 1993;7:1411–7.
75. Berry N, Ariyoshi K, Jobe O, *et al.* HIV type 2 proviral load measured by quantitative polymerase chain reaction correlates with $CD4^+$ lymphopenia in HIV type 2-infected individuals. AIDS Res Hum Retroviruses 1994;10:1031–7.
76. Douek DC, Brenchley JM, Betts MR, *et al.* HIV preferentially infects HIV-specific $CD4^+$ T cells. Nature 2002;417:95–8.
77. Furtado MR, Kingsley LA, Wolinsky SM. Changes in the viral mRNA expression pattern correlate with a rapid rate of $CD4^+$ T-cell number decline in human immunodeficiency virus type 1-infected individuals. J Virol 1995;69:2092–100.
78. Piatak M Jr, Saag MS, Yang LC. High levels of HIV-1 in plasma during all stages of infection determined by competitive PCR. Science 1993;259:1749–54.
79. Baumberger C, Kinloch de Loes S, Yerly S, Hirschel B, Perrin L. High levels of circulating RNA in patients with symptomatic HIV-1 infection. AIDS 1993;7(Suppl.2):59–64.
80. Winters MA, Tan LB, Katzenstein DA, Merigan TC. Biological variation and quality control of plasma human immunodeficiency virus type 1 RNA quantitation by reverse transcriptase polymerase chain reaction. J Clin Microbiol 1993;31:2960–6.
81. Piatak M Jr, Saag MS, Yang LC, *et al.* Determination of plasma viral load in HIV-1 infection by quantitative competitive polymerase chain reaction. AIDS 1993;7(Suppl.2):65–71.
82. Cao Y, Ho DD, Todd J, *et al.* Clinical evaluation of branched DNA signal amplification for quantifying HIV type 1 in human plasma. AIDS Res Hum Retroviruses 1995;11:353–61.
83. Mellors JW, Rinaldo CR, Gupta P, White RM, Todd JA, Kingsley LA. Prognosis in HIV-1 infection predicted by the quantity of virus in plasma. Science 1996;272:1167–70.
84. Henrard DR, Phillips JF, Muenz LR, *et al.* Natural history of HIV-1 cell-free viremia. JAMA 1995;274:554–8.
85. Jurriaans S, van Gemen B, Weverling GJ, *et al.* The natural history of HIV-1 infection: virus load and virus phenotype independent determinants of clinical course? Virology 1994;204:223–33.
86. Chun T, Fauci AS. Latent reservoirs of HIV: obstacles to the eradication of virus. Proc Natl Acad Sci USA 1999;96:10958–61.
87. Phillips AN, Lee CA, Elford J, *et al.* Serial CD4 lymphocyte counts and development of AIDS. Lancet 1991;337:389–92.
88. Cao Y, Qin L, Zhang L, Safrit J, Ho DD. Virologic and immunologic characterization of long-term survivors of human immunodeficiency virus type 1 infection. N Engl J Med 1995;332:201–8.
89. Pantaleo G, Menzo S, Vaccarezza M, *et al.* Studies in subjects with long-term nonprogressive human immunodeficiency virus infection. N Engl J Med 1995;332:209–16.
90. Kestler HW 3rd, Ringler DJ, Mori K, *et al.* Importance of the *nef* gene for maintenance of high virus loads and for development of AIDS. Cell 1991;65:651–62.
91. Michael NL, Chang G, d'Arcy LA, *et al.* Defective accessory genes in a human immunodeficiency virus type 1-infected long-term survivor lacking recoverable virus. J Virol 1995;69:4228–36.
92. Whittle H, Morris J, Todd J, *et al.* HIV-2-infected patients survive longer than HIV-1-infected patients. AIDS 1994;8:1617–20.
93. Koot M, Keet IP, Vos AH, *et al.* Prognostic value of HIV-1 syncytium-inducing phenotype for rate of $CD4^+$ cell depletion and progression to AIDS. Ann Intern Med 1993;118:681–8.
94. de Roda Husman AM, Koot M, Cornelissen M, *et al.* Prognostic value of CCR5 genotype in relation to virological and immunological parameters in the clinical course of HIV-1 infection. Ann Intern Med 1997;127:882–90.
95. Blusch JH, Patience C, Martin U. Pig endogenous retroviruses and xenotransplantation. Xenotranspl 2002;9:242–51.

chapter

222 Zoonotic Viruses

David Brown & Graham Lloyd

INTRODUCTION

Zoonotic infections are infections of animals that can naturally infect humans. More than 400 viruses cause clinically important zoonoses and infection is acquired by several different routes. Humans can be infected directly from the host animal species, for example following the bite of a rabies-infected animal, or through inhalation of rodent urine (hantavirus) or by direct contact with rodent urine (Lassa fever). However, the majority of zoonotic infections are spread by arthropod vectors and are classified as arboviruses.

The geographic distribution of the infections described in this chapter depends on many factors and changes over time. Recent examples include West Nile fever, which has recently spread to and become established across the USA. Nipah and hendra viruses, newly recognized causes of encephalitis in humans, have been identified in Australia, Malaysia, Singapore and India. Congo–Crimean hemorrhagic fever has re-emerged in Kosovo, following social dislocation resulting from conflict. Other important zoonotic infections include DNA viruses, such as poxviruses and herpes B virus, and RNA viruses, such as rabies. A number of rare occupational viral zoonoses have been described, including foot and mouth disease, vesicular stomatitis virus and swine vesicular disease.[1,2]

ARBOVIRUSES

Over 400 viruses that cause human disease are classified as arboviruses. These are distributed worldwide because of their close association with lower vertebrates and insects and their wide host range. Most arbovirus infections are caused by RNA viruses and include members of the togaviruses, bunyaviruses and reoviruses.

Many arboviruses that infect humans cause non-specific symptoms such as acute fever. Three broad clinical patterns are recognized with arbovirus infection:

- fever, rash and arthritis or retinitis;
- encephalitis; and
- viral hemorrhagic fevers (VHFs).

Several comprehensive reviews are available.[3,4]

The key features of the clinically important arboviruses transmitted to humans by hematophagous arthropod vectors, such as mosquitoes, ticks and *Phlebotomus* flies (sandfly), are given in Figure 222.1.

Most arboviruses are maintained in complex life cycles that involve nonhuman vertebrate hosts with or without a primary vector. Mosquitoes are the most important arbovirus vector, followed by ticks, sandflies (*Phlebotomus* spp.) and midges (*Culicoides* spp.). These arbovirus life cycles only become evident when humans are bitten directly by the natural enzootic focus, or when they are exposed to a virus that has escaped the primary cycle via a secondary vector or vertebrate host. Many arboviruses have several vertebrate hosts and many can be transmitted by a number of vectors.

Viruses such as urban dengue, urban yellow fever and occasionally urban St Louis encephalitis cause significant viremia and represent the simplest form of epidemic transmission cycle, in which the virus is transmitted directly between mosquitoes and humans (see Fig. 222.1). In some cases the introduction of a secondary vector may allow the transmission of the virus to other nonhuman vertebrate reservoirs (sylvatic cycle), many of which can be regarded as blind-end hosts (Fig. 222.2). Prime examples of sylvatic cycles with multiple hosts are the encephalitides such as Western equine encephalitis, eastern encephalitis and St Louis encephalitis. Many arboviruses are maintained in arthropods, through transovarial transmission. Amplification of the cycle occurs by spread to and from small mammals (Fig. 222.3). The flavivirus infections are discussed in Chapter 23. The key features of the clinically important arboviruses transmitted to humans by hematophagous arthropod vectors, such as mosquitoes, ticks and *Phlebotomus* flies (sandfly), are given in Table 222.1. Yellow fever is an example of a mosquito-borne zoonotic virus infection.

YELLOW FEVER

Nature

Yellow fever has historically been one of the great killers of humans. Regrettably, this mosquito-borne virus continues to exact a considerable toll on human populations living in endemic areas even today. Yellow fever is principally responsible for the failure of the French to successfully complete the Panama Canal in the 1880s as the work force was decimated by epidemics of yellow fever. Yellow fever was the first virus shown to be transmissible by a mosquito vector. Pioneering work by Carlos Finlay and Walter Reed are credited with this important discovery, which led to mosquito control efforts and dramatic reductions in the incidence of yellow fever. Yellow fever remains a considerable public health risk to travelers and inhabitants in endemic regions of South America and Africa.

Epidemiology

The World Health Organization (WHO) reported that between 1987 and 1991 there were 18,735 cases of yellow fever worldwide, with 4522 deaths.[5] This represented the greatest number of reported cases over a 5-year period since active reporting began in 1948. Yellow fever primarily occurs in jungle regions of the world and it is estimated that the incidence of yellow fever is grossly under-reported. The WHO estimates that perhaps as many as 200,000 cases of yellow fever occur annually.[6] Countries reporting active cases of yellow fever as of January of 1999 are indicated in Figure 222.4.[7] Yellow fever has caused significant outbreaks in recent years; in Guinea in 2000, Peru in 2001 and Senegal in 2002. The value of mass vaccination for controlling an outbreak was demonstrated in Guinea.[8]

There are two transmission cycles of yellow fever. The first and most common today is the jungle (or sylvatic) cycle of yellow fever. The jungle transmission cycle consists of a natural reservoir of disease in nonhuman primates with transmission by forest-dwelling mosquitoes. In South America the mosquito primarily responsible for yellow

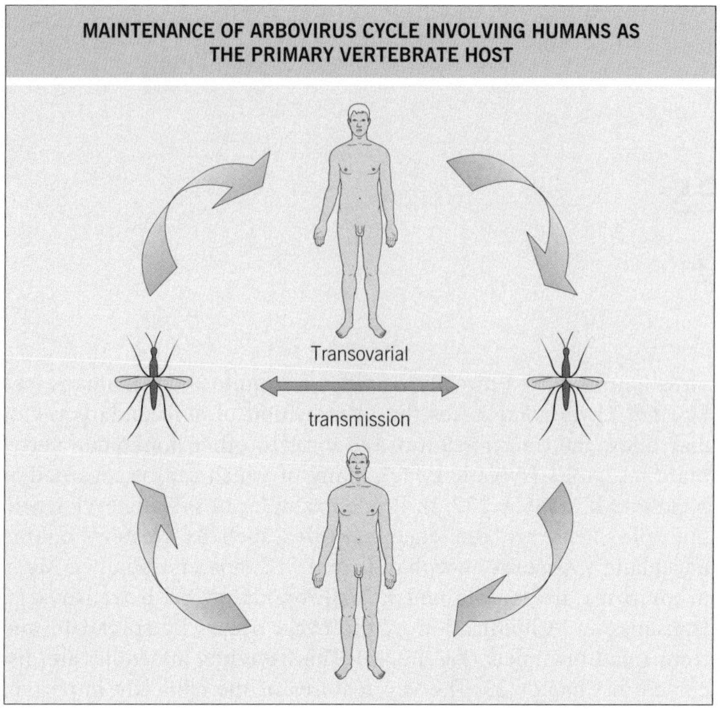

Fig. 222.1 Maintenance of arbovirus cycle involving humans as the primary vertebrate host (e.g. urban dengue and urban yellow fever).

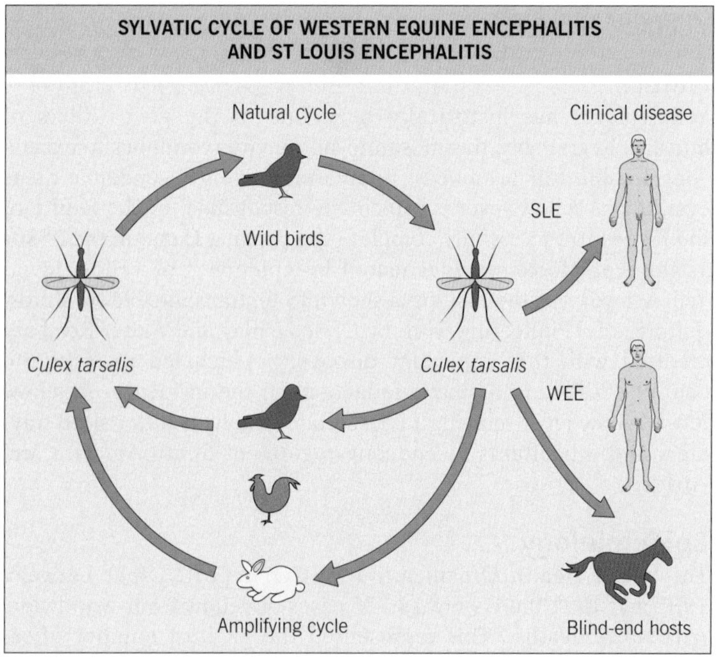

Fig. 222.2 Sylvatic cycle of Western equine encephalitis (WEE) and St Louis encephalitis (SLE).

fever transmission to humans is the *Haemagogus* sp. mosquito. In sub-Saharan Africa yellow fever is transmitted in rural areas primarily by *Aedes africanus*. The urban (or epidemic) cycle of yellow fever is related to urban outbreaks transmitted by the human-adapted mosquito *Aedes aegypti*.

All susceptible populations appear to be equally at risk for disease yet most cases occur in children or young men (particularly those involved in the logging industry or construction in heavily forested areas). The increased incidence of yellow fever recently may reflect population expansion and economic development of rainforest areas and inadequate distribution of yellow fever vaccine in regions of the world where yellow fever remains endemic. Expanding commercial trade and international travel increases the risk of yellow fever outbreaks in nonendemic regions of the world in which the mosquito vector is found. Competent vectors for yellow fever are found in southern USA where the risk for yellow fever outbreaks remains a public health concern.[9]

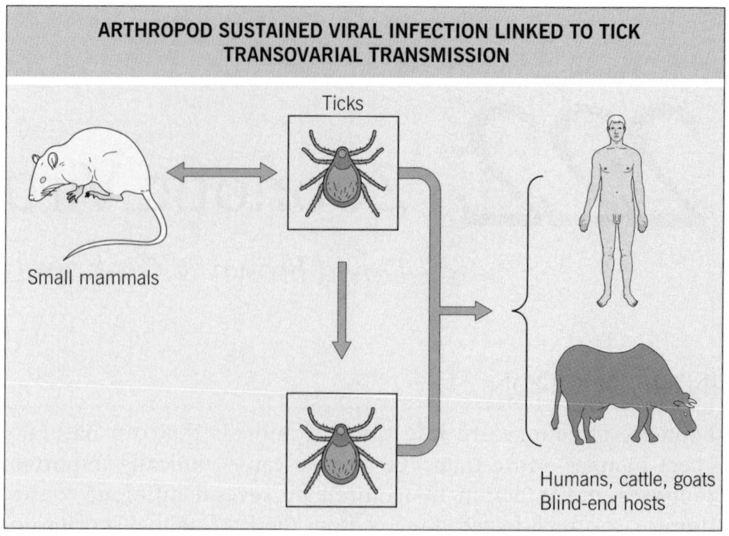

Fig. 222.3 Arthropod sustained viral infection linked to tick transovarial transmission.

Pathogenesis

Yellow fever is a prototypic mosquito-borne viral hemorrhagic fever. The virus is a 38nm ssRNA virus with a genome of approximately 4×10^6 Da. The virus is injected into humans during the course of a mosquito bite as the salivary contents of the mosquito contaminate the bite site. Local replication of the virus takes place in human skin and regional lymph nodes followed by viremia and dissemination to multiple organs of the body.

Major pathologic findings are found in the liver, kidney, heart and gastrointestinal tract. The virus infects the liver and causes massive hepatic necrosis. The characteristic pathologic finding is that of mid-zone necrosis with sparing of hepatocytes around the central vein and portal triads (Fig. 222.5). Another characteristic finding is that of Councilman bodies within degenerating hepatocytes (Fig. 222.6). Councilman bodies are acidophilic cytoplasmic deposits and not viral inclusion bodies. Diffuse areas of petechial hemorrhage are found throughout the body with the most marked changes found in the brain, kidney and gastrointestinal tract.

Prevention

The most important preventive measure is to avoid the mosquito vector within endemic regions where yellow fever exists. This can be accomplished by environmental control measures that remove mosquito habitats from areas of human habitation. There is a highly effective preventive vaccine against yellow fever. This is a live attenuated yellow fever vaccine known as vaccine strain 17-D.[10] The vaccine is highly efficacious and results in a prolonged neutralizing antibody response that will persist in the circulation for more than 10 years after immunization. Travelers to yellow fever endemic areas and residents within these areas should be vaccinated to prevent yellow fever.

Diagnostic microbiology

The virus can be isolated from a number of cell lines including Vero cells and AP-61 cells. Virus isolation represents an extreme biohazard and should only be attempted in specialized laboratory facilities.

IMPORTANT ARBOVIRUS INFECTIONS THAT CAUSE HUMAN DISEASE											
Genus	Virus	Geographic distribution								Main hosts	Clinical diseases
		Afr.	Asia	Aust.	Eur.	N. Am.	C. Am.	S. Am.	Pac.		
Mosquito vector											
Alphavirus	Western equine encephalitis	–	–	–	–	+	–	+	–	Rodents, birds, marsupials, equines	Encephalitis
	Eastern equine encephalitis	–	–	–	–	+	–	–	–	Wild birds, bats, rodents, equines, reptiles	Encephalitis
	Venezuelan equine encephalitis	–	–	–	–	–	+	+	–	Rodents, birds, marsupials, equines	Encephalitis
	Chikungunya	+	+	–	–	–	–	–	–	Primates, birds, bats, squirrels	Fever, rash, myalgia, polyarthritis
	Ross River	–	–	+	–	–	–	–	+	Large mammals, marsupials	Fever, rash, myalgia, arthralgia, hemorrhagic fever
Flavivirus	Dengue	+	+	+	–	–	+	+	+	Nonhuman primates	Encephalitis
	Japanese B encephalitis	–	+	+	–	–	–	–	–	Birds, pigs	Encephalitis
	St Louis encephalitis	–	–	–	–	+	–	+	–	Rodents mammals	Encephalitis
	Murray Valley encephalitis	–	+	+	–	–	–	–	–	Birds	Encephalitis
	West Nile fever	+	+	–	+	+	–	–	–	Birds	Fever, rash, myalgia, polyarthritis, encephalitis
	Yellow fever	+	–	–	–	–	+	+	–	Primates, marsupials	Hemorrhagic fever
Phlebovirus	Rift Valley fever	+	–	–	–	–	–	–	–	Wild mammals, domestic livestock	Hemorrhagic fever, retinitis, encephalitis
Tick vector											
Flavivirus	Central European encephalitis	–	–	–	+	–	–	–	–	Rodents	Encephalitis
	Russian spring–summer encephalitis	–	–	–	+	–	–	–	–	Rodents	Encephalitis
	Omsk hemorrhagic fever	–	+	+	–	–	–	–	–	Water voles, muskrats	Encephalitis
	Powasson	–	–	–	–	+	–	–	–	Rodents	Encephalitis
Nairovirus	Crimean–Congo hemorrhagic fever	+	+	–	+	–	–	–	–	Wild and domestic mammals	Hemorrhagic fever
Coltivirus	Colorado tick fever virus	–	–	–	–	+	–	–	–		Febrile illness
Sandfly vector											
Phlebovirus	Sandfly fever Naples	+	+	–	+	–	–	–	–	Rodent	Febrile illness, myalgia, conjunctivitis
	Sandfly fever Sicilian	+	+	–	+	–	–	–	–	Rodent	Febrile illness, myalgia, conjunctivitis
	Toscana	–	–	–	+	–	–	–	–	Rodent	Febrile illness, myalgia, conjunctivitis

Table 222.1 Important arbovirus infections that cause human disease.

Serodiagnosis is possible within 1 week of onset of infection with IgM antibodies detectable using enzyme-linked immunoabsorbent assay (ELISA), hemagglutination inhibition or plaque reduction neutralization tests. Virus detection can also be accomplished using reverse transcriptase semi-nested polymerase chain reactions (PCRs) from blood as well as tissue samples.[11]

Clinical manifestations

Human infection with yellow fever follows three discrete phases. The first phase of infection last approximately 72 hours and is initiated by headache, malaise, weakness, nausea and vomiting. The virus is replicating rapidly and high titers of infectious virus are found in the body fluids of patients at this point. This initial period of infection is followed by a brief period of remission where fever and symptoms remit. After 24–48 hours, symptoms recur and are dominated by symptoms of acute hepatic failure and renal failure. Patients develop jaundice and very high fever (hence the name yellow fever) and begin developing clinically overt signs of a hemorrhagic diathesis with petechiae, mucosal hemorrhages and gastrointestinal bleeding. A characteristic physical finding is marked bradycardia in the face of high fever (Fagetis' sign). Patients develop delirium, seizures, coma, acute renal failure and death within 7–10 days of illness. The mortality rate may be as high as 50% in some outbreaks and as low as 5% if optimal medical care is available.[12]

Management

The management of yellow fever remains primarily supportive. Intravenous fluids, blood product support and management of hepatic and renal insufficiency are the mainstays of therapy. Ribavirin does not appear to be effective and no other antiviral

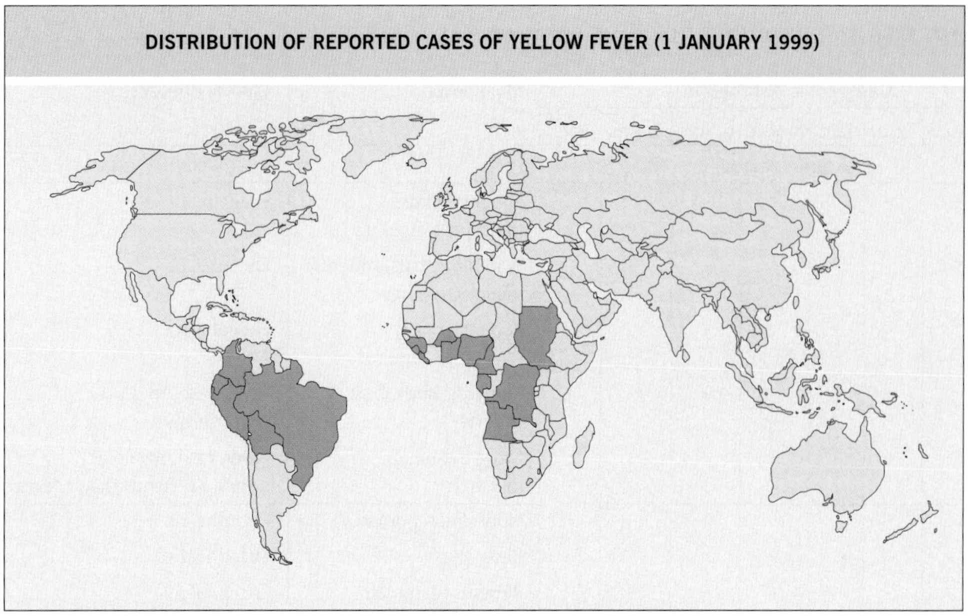

Fig. 222.4 Distribution of reported cases of yellow fever, 1 January 1999. Dark purple areas show the worldwide distribution of reported cases.

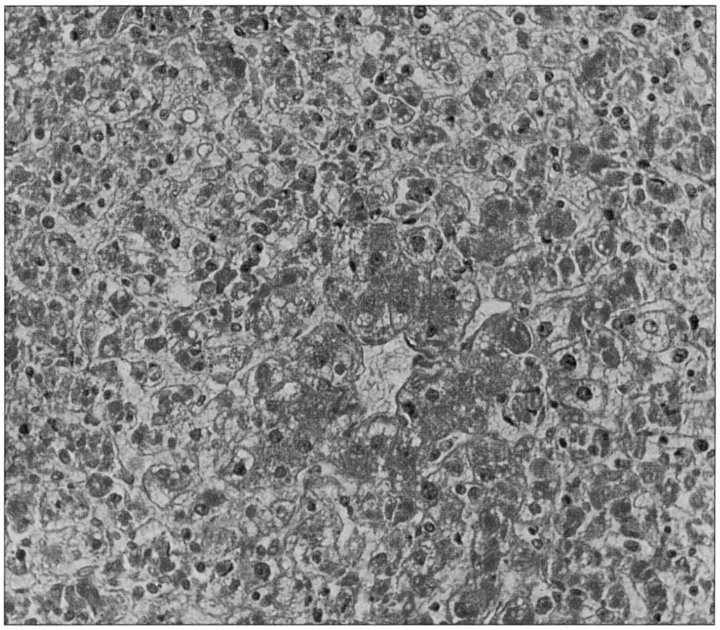

Fig. 222.5 Histopathology of yellow fever in the liver. Yellow fever virus causes mid-zone necrosis of the liver tissue with sparing of hepatocytes around the central vain and the portal triads. From Binford CH, Connor DH. Pathology of tropical and extraordinary diseases. Volume 1. Washington DC: Armed Forces Institute of Pathology; 1976.

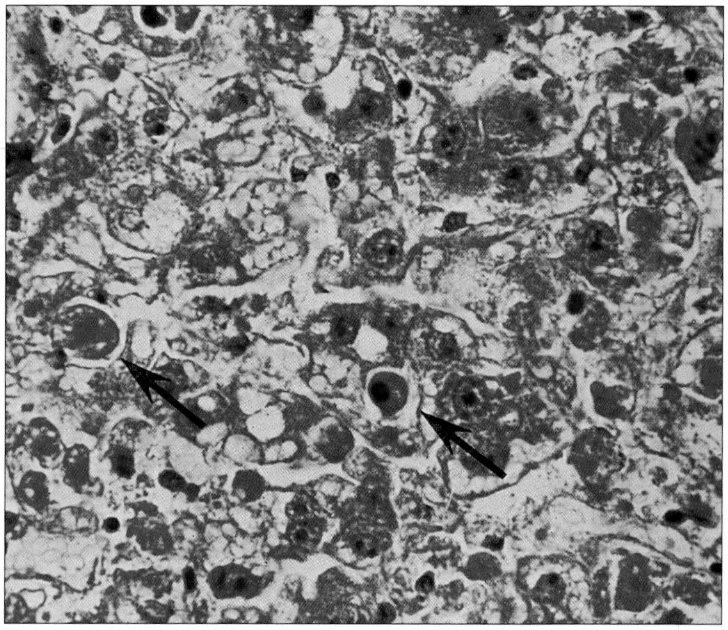

Fig. 222.6 Histology of liver tissue in a fatal case of yellow fever. Note the Councilman bodies (arrowed), which are visible within degenerating hepatocytes. From Binford CH, Connor DH. Pathology of tropical and extraordinary diseases. Volume 1. Washington DC: Armed Forces Institute of Pathology; 1976.

agent has been shown to be useful to treat yellow fever thus far. Patients should be isolated as their blood and body secretions may contain viral particles. Transmission to health care workers, particularly after needlestick injuries, has been described.

WEST NILE VIRUS

Recently human and horse West Nile virus (WNV) infection have been identified in new temperate regions of Europe and North America. Clinical presentation is variable, but severe infection is characterized by encephalitis and a significant mortality rate in humans and horses as well as certain domestic and wild birds. The virus was first isolated from the blood of a febrile women in the West Nile district of Uganda in 1937[13] and was subsequently isolated from patients, birds and mosquitoes, in Egypt in the early 1950s.[14] The WNV was first recognized as a cause of human meningoencephalitis in Israel in 1957 and as a cause of equine disease in Egypt and France in the early 1960s.

Virology

The WNV is an RNA virus belonging to the family Flaviviridae (genus flavivirus). It is a member of the Japanese encephalitis complex, which also includes Kunjin, Murray Valley encephalitis and St Louis encephalitis. The WNV virus strains can be divided genetically into two lineages. Only members of lineage 1 have been associated with clinical human encephalitis. Lineage 1 has been isolated from Africa, India, Europe, Asia and North America. Among lineage 1 WNV causing the recent human and equine outbreaks throughout Europe and Asia are closely related to the WNV (strain ROM96) first isolated in Romania and subsequently in Kenya in 1998. The virus responsible for the outbreak in the USA (NY99) is genetically distinguishable from ROM96, but it is closely related to the virus circulating in Israel form 1997 to 2000 (Isi98). Only the USA and Israel have reported illness and death in humans and animals caused by the WNV strains Isi98 and NY99. The close relations between these strains suggest that the virus causing the outbreak in the USA was imported from the Middle East.

Epidemiology

Since the original isolation of WNV, outbreaks have occurred infrequently in humans, those in Israel (1951–4 and 1957) and South Africa (1974) being the most noticeable. Since the mid-1990s there have been three distinct epidemiologic trends.

First, there has been an increase in disease frequency in humans, notably in Romania,[15] Czech Republic and Russia. Epizootics of disease in horses have occurred in Morocco where 42 of 94 affected horses died, Italy (14 cases in 1998, six died), USA (1999–2002) and the Camargue region of France.

Second, there has been a noticeable increase in severity of human disease, with large outbreaks with significant mortality rates, especially in temperate urban areas. They include Bucharest, Romania (1996, over 400 cases, 17 deaths); Volgograd, Russia (1999, over 800 human cases, 40 deaths); New York City (1999–2000, 83 human cases, nine deaths); and Israel (2000, over 300 human cases, 29 deaths).[16] Since the introduction of WNV into the USA in 1999[17] it has been responsible for the identification of an increased number of cases (1999–2001, 149 human cases, 18 deaths; during the first 9 months of 2002, 2369 human cases, 139 deaths). The WNV has now been responsible for the spread of human disease westward, found in 34 states of the USA in less than 3 years.

Finally, high avian death rates accompanying human outbreaks have been a significant feature of WNV outbreaks in the USA and Israel.

The principal vectors are mosquitoes, predominantly of the genus *Culex* (*C. pipiens* and *C. restuans*), and the principal amplifying hosts are wild birds. Humans and horses are considered 'end-hosts' or 'incidental hosts'. A striking feature of the initial human epidemic in New York City 1999 was the high number of avian deaths among American crows *(Corvi brachrhynchos)* and other corvids.

Clinical manifestations

The incubation time in humans is reported to be 3–14 days. Symptoms generally last 3–6 days. Reports from earlier outbreaks describe a mild form of WNV infection presenting as a febrile influenza-like illness with sudden onset. This is often accompanied by malaise, anorexia, nausea, vomiting, rash, myalgia, lymphadenopathy and retro-orbital pain. A small proportion of cases (<1%) develop severe illness, such as acute encephalitis, aseptic meningitis or Guillain–Barré syndrome. In the recent outbreak in the USA those patients hospitalized with severe disease reported fever, weakness, gastrointestinal symptoms and flaccid paralysis. A minority of patients with severe disease develop a maculopapular rash or morbilliform rash involving the neck, trunk, arms or legs. Neurologic presentations include ataxia and extrapyramidal signs, cranial nerve abnormalities, myelitis, optical neuritis and seizures, and are more common in those over 50 years of age and in young children.

Diagnostic microbiology

Diagnosis of patients with WNF encephalitis or meningitis is made by the detection of IgM antibody to WNV in serum or cerebrospinal fluid (CSF) collected within 8 days of illness using the IgM antibody capture ELISA (MAC-ELISA). As IgM does not cross the blood–brain barrier, IgM antibody in the CSF strongly suggests central nervous system (CNS) infection. Therefore, the laboratory diagnostic confirmation strategy involves the serologic detection of IgM or IgG ELISA in CSF and serum with subsequent plaque reduction neutralization test (PRNT) confirmation. In addition, highly sensitive reverse transcriptase (RT)-PCRs have been described. Virus isolation on acute CSF samples provides an alternative approach. Antigenic cross-reactivity with other closely related flaviviruses is a major problem in serologic testing, and this underlines the need for confirmation with PRNT. It should be noted that samples from patients recently vaccinated against or recently infected with related flaviviruses (e.g. yellow fever, Japanese encephalitis) may give positive WNV MAC-ELISA results.

Management

There is no specific therapy or vaccine available and management is supportive.

ARENAVIRIDAE

Nature

Members of the Arenaviridae have been isolated from diverse species of rodents, which are their natural hosts, in a wide range of geographic locations. Two arenavirus complexes are recognized – the complex of lymphocytic choriomeningitis virus and Lassa virus (LCMV–LASV), or old world arenaviruses, and the Tacaribe complex, or new world arenaviruses.[18] This broad antigenic classification is supported by more detailed phylogenetic comparisons. The important arenavirus infections of humans are listed in Table 222.2.

Arenavirus virions range from spheric to pleomorphic and have a mean diameter of 110–130nm. Particles are characterized by a variable number of electron-dense ribosomes (diameter 20–25nm) within the virus particles. They have a lipid membrane with glycoprotein spikes that project 8–10nm from the surface (Fig. 222.7).

ARENAVIRUSES KNOWN TO CAUSE HUMAN DISEASE

Virus	Host in nature	Geographic distribution	Main features of human disease
Lymphocytic chorio-meningitis virus (LCMV)	*Mus domesticus, Mus musculus*	Europe, Americas, perhaps elsewhere	Isolated 1933; causes lymphocytic choriomeningitis, which usually presents as an aseptic meningitis with a mortality rate <1%
Lassa fever	*Mastomys* spp.	West Africa	Isolated 1969; causes Lassa fever, a severe systemic illness; severe cases suffer shock and hemorrhages; mortality rate 16%
Junin virus	*Calomys musculinus*	Argentina	Isolated 1958; causes Argentine hemorrhagic fever (AHF), which causes a similar illness to Lassa but hemorrhage and CNS disease more frequent; mortality rate up to 30%
Machupo virus	*Calomys callosus*	Beni region of Bolivia	Isolated 1963; causes Bolivian hemorrhagic fever; similar clinical picture to AHF; mortality rate 25%
Guanarito virus	*Zygodontomys brevicauda: Sigmodon aistoni*	Venezuela	Isolated 1990, similar to AHF; mortality rate 25%
Sabia virus	Unknown	Brazil	Isolated 1990; only three human cases described, one fatal; clinical picture probably similar to AHF

Table 222.2 Arenaviruses known to cause human disease.

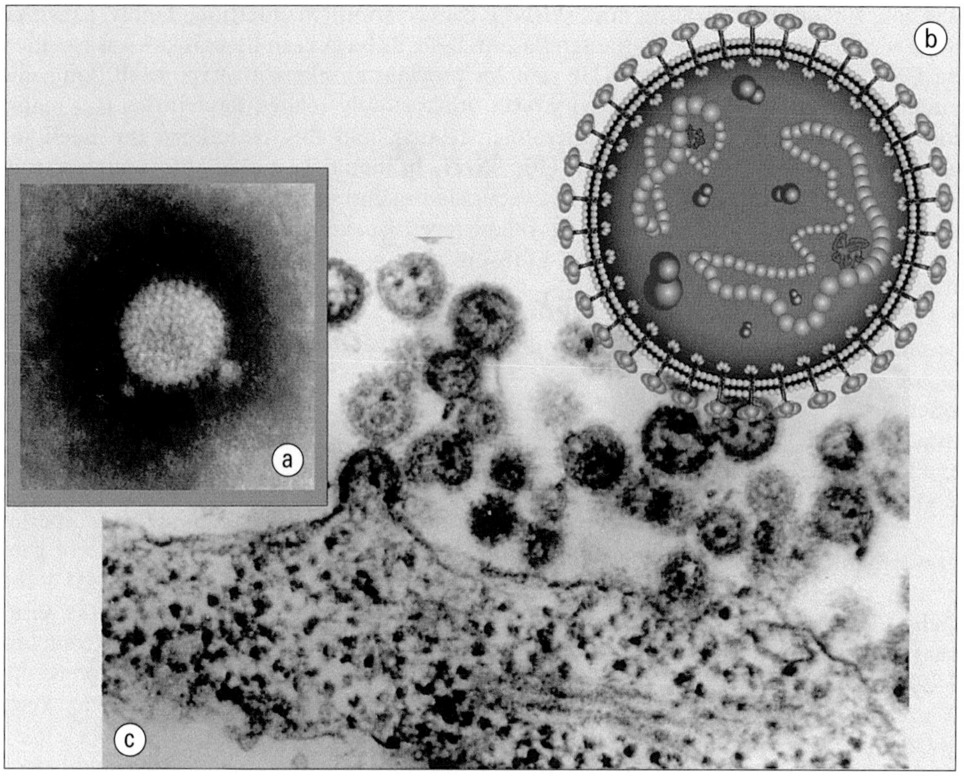

Fig. 222.7 Arenaviruses. (a) Negative contrast electron micrograph of Lassa virus. (b) Arenavirus particle showing coiled nucleocapsid ribosomes and glycoprotein spikes. (c) Thin sections of infected Vero cells, showing extracellular virus, budding particles and intracellular inclusions. Courtesy of G Lloyd, B Dowsett and ASR Featherstone.

The genome consists of two ssRNA molecules, L (large) and S (small). The L and S RNAs of arenaviruses have an ambience coding arrangement; nucleocapsid (N) is encoded in the viral-complementary sequence corresponding to the 5´ half of segment S, whereas the viral glycoprotein precursor (GPC) is encoded in the viral-sense sequence corresponding to the 3´ half of S.[18]

The N protein, which is the most abundant polypeptide, is non-glycosylated and forms a ribonucleoprotein (RNP) complex with the genomic RNA. Two glycosylated proteins, GP-1 and GP-2, are derived by post-transitional cleavage from the GPC. The L segment codes for the L protein, which is an RNA polymerase, and the Z protein, a putative zinc binding protein. α-Dystoglycan has recently been identified as a receptor for LCMV and Lassa fever virus.[19] This belongs to a highly conserved family of proteins found in epithelial, muscle and neurologic cells in humans.

Pathogenesis

In their natural rodent hosts, arenavirus infections occur in two distinct patterns: during the neonatal period, a chronic viremic infection is established; in adult rodents the infection is transient and self-limiting. This lifelong infection does not have major clinical sequelae for the infected rodent.[18]

In humans several arenavirus infections cause severe illness, including meningoencephalitis and hemorrhagic fever, with significant mortality rates. The pathogenesis is not fully understood, and microscopic changes found at autopsy are modest and do not account for the severity of illness. Petechial hemorrhages of the skin are found, and multiple hemorrhages and focal necrosis may be present in internal organs. Serous effusions and interstitial pneumonia have been described. Hemorrhages are more common with South American arenavirus infections. In contrast to these modest pathologic lesions, the physiologic changes are extensive. The state of shock characteristic of severe disease reflects an increase in vascular permeability. The mechanism involved is not fully understood, but it may be an indirect effect of immune mediators on endothelial cells produced by infected macrophages and monocytes, rather than direct viral damage.

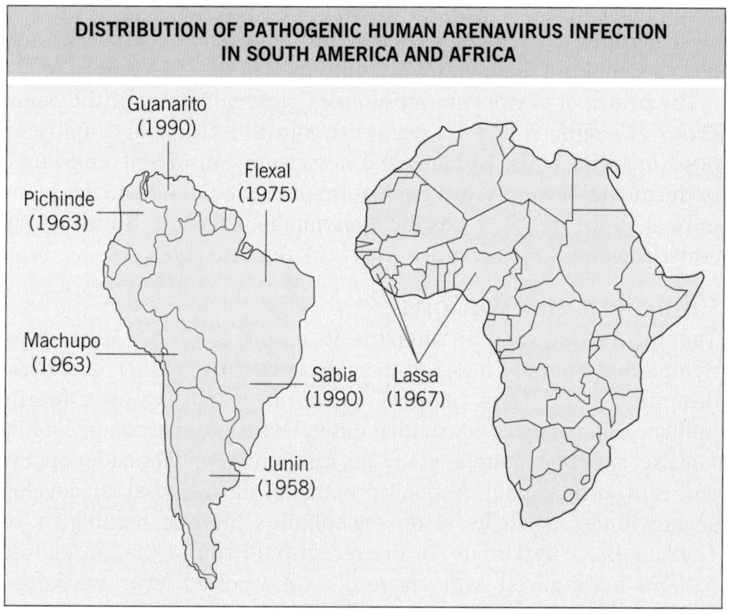

Fig. 222.8 Distribution of pathogenic human arenavirus infection in South America and Africa, and year of first isolation of each virus.

Epidemiology

The epidemiology of individual arenaviral disease in humans is dependent on the geographic distribution of infected rodents and the nature of their contacts with humans (Fig. 222.8).

Several distinct patterns are seen. In Lassa fever, which is a common human infection, the reservoir host is *Mastomys* spp., which is a peridomestic rodent found in sub-Saharan Africa. The rodents are persistently infected and contaminate the environment with the virus, which generates infectious aerosols on drying. Other routes of transmission include direct contact with rodent excretions during the capture and killing of these animals for consumption. The host of junin virus, the cause of Argentine hemorrhagic fever, is *Colomys musculinus*. The natural habitat of this rodent is the hedgerow and transmission occurs at harvest time, presumably because of aerosol transmission during mechanical harvesting.

Infection by LCMV is found worldwide, wherever its natural hosts *Mus domesticus* or *Mus musculus* are infected. The burden of disease is not well established, but LCMV infection is linked with up to 10% of CNS disease of suspected viral origin. Antibody studies show a prevalence of 5% in urban populations in the USA,[20] 9% in urban populations in Germany, and 2.2% in Argentina. An increase in the number of cases is reported in the autumn, which may result from the reservoir host moving into homes for the winter.

Lassa fever is a serious public health problem in West Africa, in two distinct hyperendemic areas – Sierra Leone, Guinea and Liberia and Nigeria. Identification of a recent case in Côte D'Ivoire indicates that infection may be distributed more widely in West Africa.[21] Infections are found throughout the year, but a peak incidence is seen in the dry season. Lassa fever is a more common infection than previously thought, with estimates of up to 400,000 human cases annually and an overall mortality rate of 2%.[22] More severe hospitalized cases have a mortality rate of 16%.[23]

Several hundred cases of Argentine hemorrhagic fever are identified each year, and are associated with the harvest. Most cases occur in adult males.

Bolivian hemorrhagic fever was first identified in 1963–4, when it caused an extensive outbreak in San Joaquin that resulted in 113 deaths.[24] This followed the rodent host entering the small town. However, the disease has since been uncommon, with occasional cases reported in rural communities in those more likely to come into contact with the infected rodent host.

Prevention

Two strategies have been proposed to prevent arenaviral disease in humans – rodent control and vaccination. Rodent control was important in controlling the Bolivian hemorrhagic fever outbreak, by the eradication of *Colomys callosus*. The house mouse, *Mus domesticus*, can be effectively eliminated from homes, thus reducing exposure to LCMV. However, its value in controlling other arenavirus infections has not been established. *Mastomys natalensis* is widespread and it has not proved practical to control rodent populations with living conditions found in West Africa. Both *C. callosus* and *C. musculinus* inhabit rural areas and control is not feasible.

A live, attenuated junin vaccine (Candid–1) has been developed and its efficacy demonstrated in a trial of 6500 volunteers.[25] It is now used for high-risk workers.

Lassa fever is the most important human arenavirus infection and vaccination seems to be the best hope for control. Killed and live vaccines have been developed and evaluated in animal models, and the most promising candidate vaccine is a vaccinia recombinant containing the Lassa virus glycoprotein gene. In challenge experiments this vaccine prevented death from Lassa challenge in guinea pigs and nonhuman primates. No human studies have been performed.[18]

Diagnostic microbiology

All arenavirus infections present similar diagnostic problems; the virus can be isolated early in the disease and this is followed by the later development of IgM and IgG antibody responses. There has been relatively little development of diagnostic assays for these agents because they are relatively rare and geographically localized.

Infection by LCMV is generally diagnosed by the detection of specific antibody. Usually immunofluorescence is used, but an ELISA test has been described. For virus isolation, blood and CSF samples are the most useful. Mice and guinea pigs are the most sensitive culture system, but isolation in Vero cells is more practical.

Lassa fever and several of the South American hemorrhagic fevers cause severe infections and can be transmitted by aerosol. Consequently, they have been classified as biohazard level 4 viruses and work on these agents is confined to the few high-containment laboratories worldwide.

The early clinical diagnosis of Lassa fever is difficult, and because ribavirin is an effective treatment if started early in the disease course, laboratory confirmation of infection is important. For rapid diagnosis either virus culture in Vero E6 cells or genome detection by RT-PCR are used on acute blood samples. Now RT–PCR is the first-line diagnostic test because it enables same-day diagnosis, and the use of guanadinium to extract RNA also inactivates viral infectivity, which makes the sample safe to work on outside the containment laboratory. In a recent study all Lassa fever patients were diagnosed by RT-PCR within 3 days of admission (Fig. 222.9).[26] Detection of Lassa-specific antibody by immunofluorescence is widely used, but antibody rises late in clinical disease and is often not detectable until the second week of illness, which is often too late to effect patient management. Baculovirus-expressed nucleoprotein (NP) has been used for serologic diagnosis and avoids the need to culture virus. Quantitative real-time PCR has now been applied to the diagnosis of Lassa fever, and the results obtained on sequential samples from a recent case are illustrated in (Fig 222.10). The ability to quantify and monitor viral load may have prognostic value and help to guide treatment, but substantive studies are required.

The South American arenaviruses can be cultured from acute blood samples in newborn mice and hamsters or Vero cells. The detection of virus-specific IgG and IgM by immunofluorescence is widely used, and more recently ELISA using baculovirus-expressed viral proteins to detect antibody and RT-PCR tests have been described.

Clinical features

Arenavirus infections are often mild or subclinical. Even in severe infections, early illness is characterized by non-specific

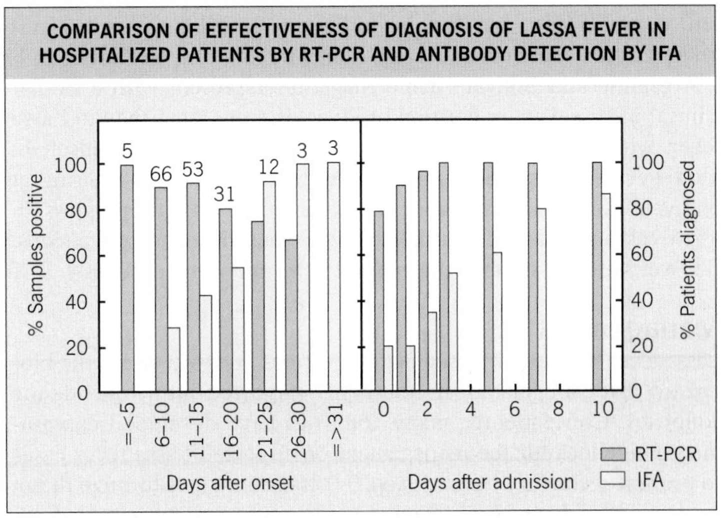

Fig. 222.9 Comparison of effectiveness of diagnosis of Lassa fever in hospitalized patients by reverse transcriptase polymerase chain reaction (RT-PCR) and antibody detection by immunofluorescent antibody (IFA). (a) Samples from all patients were stratified with respect to the time since the onset of disease. The number of serum specimens in each group is indicated. (b) Samples were analyzed on a patient-by-patient basis with respect to time since admission to the hospital. Adapted from Demby *et al.*[26]

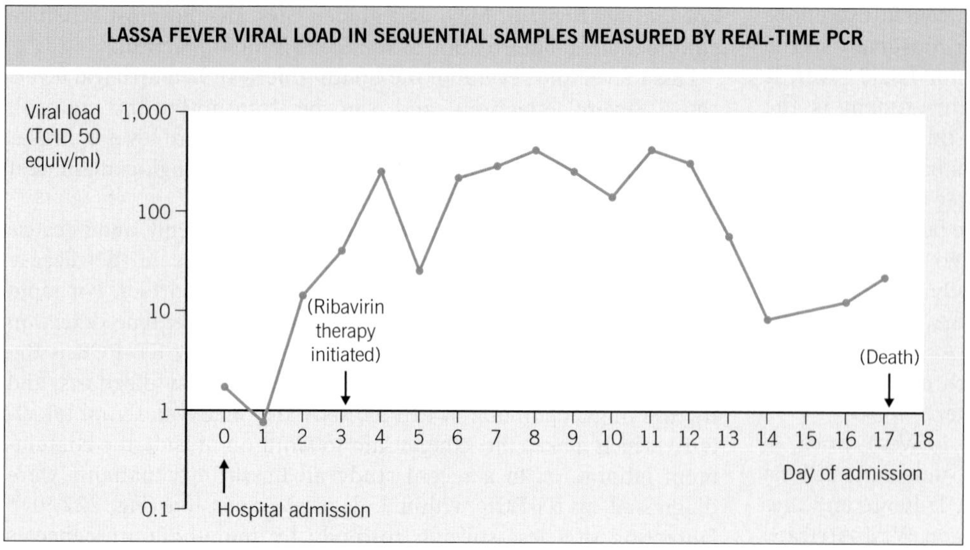

Fig. 222.10 Lassa fever viral load in sequential samples from a case measured by real-time polymerase chain reaction.

symptoms, such as fever and myalgia, before the onset of severe systemic disease.

In LCMV infection headache, nausea or vomiting accompany the febrile prodrome. In the second week of illness CNS disease develops in a minority of cases and usually presents as an aseptic meningitis. In severe cases encephalitis can develop and this accounts for a significant minority of hospitalized cases. Full recovery is the most common outcome, but occasional deaths have been reported.

The incubation period of Lassa fever is about 10 days. It generally begins with a gradual onset of fever and malaise. As the disease progresses, abdominal pain, nausea and vomiting become more pronounced and an exudative pharyngitis and conjunctivitis are common. More pathognomonic signs and symptoms develop during the second week of illness, including facial edema, pleural edema, encephalopathy and shock. In severe cases illness is progressive, with shock followed by death. In survivors, defervescence is followed by recovery after 2–3 weeks. Hemorrhagic complications are not uncommon in severe cases and generally present with epistaxis, bruising and conjunctival hemorrhage. In the convalescent period pericarditis has been described. Deafness is now recognized as a late complication.[27] It can be unilateral or bilateral and is not related to the severity of disease; it may be immune mediated.

Argentine and Bolivian hemorrhagic fever present with a similar clinical picture. The progression of illness is more rapid than in Lassa fever, with severe prostration developing 3–4 days after onset. In more severe cases mucous membrane hemorrhage and bruising at intravenous injection sites are seen, which indicate a poor progress. In a few cases substantial neurologic involvement leads to convulsions. Recovery usually starts at the end of the second week of illness.

Management

Lassa fever has caused nosocomial infections in Africa and is the biohazard level 4 agent most commonly imported into nonendemic countries. Consequently, many countries have developed containment guidelines for the management of suspected Lassa fever cases to prevent secondary transmission.[28,29] Transmission is through direct contact with infected body fluids and little evidence suggests that airborne transmission is important. The guidelines follow a similar approach based on an initial patient-risk assessment, which leads to different levels of investigation, containment and monitoring of close contacts, depending on risk (see also Chapters 183 and 186a).

Ribavirin, a guanosine analog, is effective in vitro against arenaviruses, but its mode of action is unknown. Ribavirin has been evaluated for the treatment of severe Lassa fever cases and dramatically reduces the mortality rate.[30] Its use for prophylaxis of contacts with Lassa fever cases and for the treatment of other arenavirus infections has been proposed, but no trial reports are yet published.

Treatment of Argentine hemorrhagic fever infections with convalescent human plasma is effective in reducing the mortality rate from 15–30% to <2% if given during the first 8 days of illness. Convalescent plasma could potentially play a role in Lassa fever treatment, but this has not been established in practice. Patient management of arenaviral infections requires general supportive care, with particular attention to fluid balance.

HANTAVIRIDAE

Nature

Hantavirus is the most recently described genus in the Bunyaviridae family and comprises a growing number of isolated viruses, including those that cause hemorrhagic fever with renal syndrome (HFRS) and hantavirus pulmonary syndrome (HPS).[31,32] Some recently recognized probable species that have been identified by molecular genetic analysis have not yet been isolated (Table 222.3). Hantaviruses contain a tripartite, single-stranded, negative-sense RNA genome. The three segments are designated as small (S), medium (M) and large (L), and encode for the nucleocapsid (N) protein of 50–53kDa, the two envelope proteins (G1 and G2) of 65 and 74kDa, respectively, and an associated virus of 200kDa.[33]

Epidemiology

The epidemiology of hantavirus disease in humans is dependent on the geographic distribution of persistently infected rodent hosts.[34] The hantaviruses linked with HFRS are associated with specific rodent hosts, each named for the region in which they were first isolated:

- *Apodemus agrarius* (the striped field mouse) for the hantavirus;
- *Rattus norvegicus* (the Norway rat) and *Rattus rattus* (the black rat) for the Seoul virus; and
- *Apodemus flavicollus* (the yellow neck field mouse) for the Dobrava virus.

The hantavirus from Korea, Russia and China and the Dobrava virus from the Balkan countries of Europe (Bosnia, Croatia, Yugoslavia, Albania, Greece and Bulgaria) are associated with the severe form of HFRS, with an estimated mortality rate of 5–15% (see Table 222.3).[35] A moderate form of HFRS is caused by the Seoul virus, which (along with its host) is found virtually worldwide. Serologic evidence for infection with Seoul-like hantaviruses has been found in rodents in major cities within the USA.

CHARACTERISTICS OF SOME KNOWN HANTAVIRUSES FOUND IN EUROPE, ASIA, RUSSIA AND INDIA					
Species	**Human illness**	**Pathology**	**Mortality rate (%)**	**Reservoir**	**Geographic virus distribution**
Hantaan (HTN)	Severe: HFRS, EHF, KHF	Renal	5–15	*Apodemus agrarius* (striped field mouse)	China, Russia, Korea
Dobrava/Belgrade (DOB)	Severe: HFRS	Renal	5–15	*Apodemus flavicollis* (yellow neck mouse)	Balkans
Seoul (SEO)	Moderate: HFRS	Renal	1	*Rattus norvegicus* (Norway rat)	Worldwide
Puumala (PUU)	Mild; NE	Renal	1	*Clethrionomys glareolus* (bank vole)	Europe, Russia, Scandinavia
Khabarovsk (KHB)	?	?	?	*Microtus fortis* (reed mole)	Russia
Tula (TUL)	?	?	?	*Microtus arvalis* (European common vole)	Europe
Thailand (THAI)	?	?	?	*Bandicot indica* (bandicoot rat)	Thailand
Thottapalayan (TMP)	?	?	?	*Suncus murinus* (musk shrew)	India
Topografov (TOP)*	?	?	?	*Lemmus sibircus* (Siberian lemming)	Siberia

* Virus not yet isolated/molecular analysis suggests they are probable hantavirus species
? Not yet documented

Table 222.3 Characteristics of some known hantaviruses found in Europe, Asia, Russia and India. EHF, epidemic hemorrhagic fever; HFRS, hemorrhagic fever with renal syndrome; KHF, Korean hemorrhagic fever; NE, nephropathia epidemica.

A mild form of HFRS, caused by the Puumala virus, is responsible for nephropathia epidemica (NE) in Scandinavia, the European regions of the former USSR and south of this through much of Europe to France, Spain and Portugal.

The hantavirus associated with HPS, Sin Nombre virus (SNV), has been recognized throughout the USA since its discovery in 1993.[36] Molecular biologic studies have identified similar viruses – Black Creek Canal (BCC), New York, Bayou (BAY) and Andes – that are also associated with HPS illness, that extend their geographic distribution from North America to Mexico and South America (Table 222.4). The distribution of specific host species throughout the Americas suggests a wider distribution of hantaviruses, which potentially could cause further clinical cases.

All rodent hosts are persistently infected with specific hantavirus strains that apparently cause no illness. In wild rodent populations, most infections occur through age-dependent horizontal routes, predominately in mature males. Horizontal transmission among cage mates was experimentally demonstrated via the aerosol route at median infectious doses of 1.0 plague forming units (pfu) for each virus tested. However, although rodents are susceptible to hantavirus through the aerosol route, their susceptibility is increased by inoculation (median infectious doses 0.003–0.016pfu). Vertical transmission from dam to pup has proved negligible or absent, both in wild and experimental settings.

Hantavirus disease, irrespective of strain, is a seasonal disease. This seasonality is associated with population dynamics of the rodent hosts that maintain each virus and their interaction with local human populations. Rodent population cycles vary according to climatic changes and interspecies competition. Rural-associated HFRS in Asia and Europe is linked to human rodent contact during the planting and harvesting of crops (late autumn and early winter). Similarly, in Scandinavia Puumala virus causes most cases of NE during the same period. Both Puumala outbreaks in Scandinavia and the original HPS outbreak in America were associated with increases in the natural rodent population followed by rodent migration from the fields to buildings in response to adverse weather conditions. Alternatively, in Greece, HFRS is observed predominately in the warmer months as a result of increased human outdoor activities, including camping. These cases point to higher risk being experienced by people such as forestry workers and shepherds. In China HFRS induced by Seoul virus appears to be most common in the spring.

The aerosol route of infection is regarded as the most common means of transmission among rodents and to humans. Rodent bites cannot be excluded as a way of maintaining the disease among rodents or occasionally resulting in human infection. Epidemiologic investigations link virus exposure to farming activities, sleeping on the ground and military exercises. Indoor exposure has been linked to rodent infestation of homes during cold weather or to nesting rodents in or near dwellings. Many hantavirus infections are identified among people who live in poor housing conditions or in those who pursue recreational activities such as camping and various water sports. Human-to-human transmission is rare and consequently hantaviruses do not pose a risk to hospital workers. However, recent outbreaks of HPS in South America suggested that minimal exposure to body fluids of infected patients resulted in apparent person-to-person spread.

The annual incidence of HFRS involving hospitalization throughout the world is estimated to be between 150,000 and 200,000 cases. More than half these cases predominate in the endemic center of epidemic hemorrhagic fever in the Chinese provinces of Hubei, Heilongjiang, Jiangxi, Jilin and Shanxi. Annual incidence rates here range from 0.05 to 3.0/1000. Russia and Korea also report hundreds to thousands of cases of HFRS each year. Most of the remaining cases (a few hundred) are reported from Japan, Finland, Sweden, Belgium, The Netherlands, Greece, Hungary, France and the Balkan countries formally constituting Yugoslavia. Mortality rates range from less than 0.1% for HFRS caused by Puumala to approximately 5–10% for HFRS caused by hantavirus.

Several hundred cases of HPS have been reported throughout North and South America (see Table 222.4).[37] Most of the identified cases in America and Canada were caused by SNV. Cases of HPS in south-western USA and South America are caused by molecularly identified strains that include BAY, BCC and Andes viruses.

A number of hantavirus infections have caused several laboratory-associated outbreaks of HFRS, all of which were traced to persistently infected rodents obtained from breeders, to wild-caught naturally infected rodents or to experimentally infected rodents. No illness has been associated with laboratory workers using cell-culture adapted viruses, although asymptomatic seroconversions have been documented.

Pathogenesis

The process by which hantaviruses cause multisystem organ dysfunction syndrome is unclear. Thrombocytopenia, defects in platelet function, transient disseminated intravascular coagulation (DIC) and increased vascular fragility are all thought to play a key role in the

SOME KNOWN HANTAVIRUSES FOUND IN NORTH AND SOUTH AMERICA					
Species	Human illness	Pathology	Mortality rate (%)	Reservoir	Geographic virus distribution
Sin Nombre virus (SNV)	Severe: HPS	Pulmonary	50	*Peromyscus maniculatus* (deer mouse)	USA, Canada Mexico
New York (NY)	HPS	Pulmonary	Not recorded	*Peromyscus leucopus* (white-footed mouse)	USA
Black Creek Canal (BCC)	HPS	Pulmonary	Not recorded	*Sigmodon hispidus* (cotton rat)	USA
El Monro Canyon (ELMC)	?	?	?	*Rethrodontomys megalotis* (Western harvest mouse)	USA, Mexico
Bayou (BAY)*	HPS	Pulmonary/renal	?	*Oryzomys palustris* (rice rat)	USA
Andes (AND)*	HPS	Pulmonary	50	*Oligoryzomys longicaudatus* (long tailed pygmy rice rat)	Argentina
Unnamed*	HPS	Pulmonary	?	*Colomys laucha* (vesper mouse)	Paraguay
Rio Segundo (RIOS)*	?	?	?	*Reithronontomys mexicanus* (Mexican harvest mouse)	Costa Rica
Rio Manore (RIOM)*	?	?	?	*Oligoryzomys mictrotis* (small-eared pygmy rice rat)	Bolivia
Iala Vista (ISLA)*	?	?	?	*Microtis californicus* (California vole)	USA
Bloodland Lake (BLL)*	?	?	?	*Microtis ochrogaster* (prairie vole)	USA

* Virus not yet isolated/molecular analysis suggests they are unique hantavirus strains
? Not yet documented

Table 222.4 Some known hantaviruses found in North and South America. HPS, hantavirus pulmonary syndrome.

early stages of the disease. Hantavirus disease is mainly microvascular in nature and endothelium is the predominant cell type involved. The presence of hantavirus antigen has been demonstrated by immunochemistry in vascular endothelial cells of fatal HFRS infections, experimentally infected rodents and endothelium of lung capillaries in the highly lethal form of HPS.[38] Endothelial damage or dysfunction leads to capillary engorgement, leakage of erythrocytes and increased permeability.

Recent studies implicated the disease process as being immunologically based, with lymphocytes playing a key role, especially T cells. The CD4:CD8 ratio is greatly decreased, although abundant $CD4^+$ and $CD8^+$ lymphocytes have been reported in the lung interstitium of HPS patients.[38] Lymphocyte induction of migrating macrophages and other inflammatory cells results in the production of cytokines, such as tumor necrosis factor (TNF)-α, interleukin (IL)-1 and IL-2, and interferon (IFN)-γ, which in turn increases vascular permeability.

Prevention

Prevention of hantavirus infection is dependent upon reducing contact between humans and infected rodents. However, many rodent control programs in known highly endemic areas, such as China, have been ineffective. Guidelines in the USA to control HPS infections have been aimed at reducing rodent access to homes, clean up recommendations of buildings with heavy rodent infestations, and precautions for workers exposed to rodents and for campers and hikers in infected areas.

Although a number of candidate (inactivated, recombinant) vaccines against hantaviruses are under development, none are currently available.

Both wild-caught rodents introduced into laboratories and laboratory-bred colonies have caused a number of laboratory-based infections. Current recommendations directed at the manipulation of hantaviruses call for handling at biosafety containment levels 2 and 3, dependent on the strain. Work with infected laboratory rodent colonies that may lead to the generation of infectious aerosols in urine or feces should be undertaken in facilities that have suitable room ventilation and high-efficiency particulate air (HEPA) filtration, primary containment of animals, and personal protective equipment at a minimum of biosafety containment level 3. Precautions should also ensure suitable decontamination of animal bedding, cages and animal waste.

It is prudent to introduce hantavirus screening of laboratory-bred and wild-caught rodents and cell lines that originate from rodent tissue before use. Such animals and cells should be segregated from other animals, with care being taken to prevent possible aerosolized spread of infectious virus.

Diagnostic microbiology

Diagnosis of hantavirus infection relies upon the recognition of characteristic clinical features, a history consistent with the epidemiology of the disease and serologic confirmation.[37]

Direct isolation of hantavirus from acutely ill patients is prolonged and often unsuccessful and consequently of little diagnostic value. Similarly, the success of antigen-capture ELISA or the application of RT-PCR on acute blood samples is of no practical value for the diagnosis of human infection.

Although the immunofluorescence assay is regarded as a useful diagnostic tool, the method of choice to diagnose acute hantavirus infection is an IgM antibody assay of high sensitivity and specificity.[39] Currently two alternatives are available:

- M antibody capture IgM enzyme immunoassay (EIA) based on the use of cell-culture grown hantavirus antigen; and
- M antibody capture IgM EIA based on baculovirus or *Escherichia coli* expressed full-length nucleocapsid protein.[40]

Both in humans and rodents IgG antibodies persist for life, and therefore the presence of IgG seropositivity may not reflect a recent infection. In addition, a rise in IgG has not always been observed in recent clinical cases. The IgG ELISA or immunofluorescent antibody (IFA) test is well suited for epidemiologic studies, whereas determination of the specific infecting virus is best achieved by focus reduction neutralization tests.

Other methods are also under development to investigate hantavirus:

- hantavirus recombinant immunoblot assay (RIBA), which uses recombinant and synthetic peptides; and
- application of RT-PCR and immunohistochemical staining of antigen contained in formalin-fixed autopsy tissues.[41]

MAIN CHARACTERISTICS OF THE TWO SEVERE FORMS OF HANTAVIRUS DISEASE		
Characteristics	**Hemorrhagic fever with renal syndrome (HFRS)**	**Hantavirus pulmonary syndrome (HPS)**
Primary target organ	Kidney	Lung
Acute phase	Febrile	Febrile 'prodrome'
Later phases	Shock, hemorrhage	Shock, pulmonary edema
Disease progression	Hypotensive, oliguric, diuresis, convalescence	Diuresis, convalescence
Other clinical and laboratory features	Thrombocytopenia, leukocytosis, proteinuria, hematuria, creatinine >100mmol/l, hemoconcentration, raised transaminases	Thrombocytopenia, leukocytosis, hemoconcentration, shortness of breath, abnormal respiratory rate, lung infiltrates
Mortality rate (%)	1–15	≥50

Table 222.5 Main characteristics of the two severe forms of hantavirus disease.

Clinical manifestations

Although HFRS has been clinically recognized and reported in Asia, Russia and Scandinavia for the past century, the causative agent, hantavirus, was not isolated until 1978.[42] The HFRS complex comprises three distant clinical diseases, each infection being caused by a specific hantavirus.[34,36] The spectrum of disease ranges from nonapparent infection to fulminant hemorrhagic fever with renal failure (sometimes having a fatal outcome). Depending on which hantavirus is responsible for the illness, HFRS can appear as a mild, moderate or severe disease. Fatality rates range from less than 1% for HRFS caused by Puumula virus to approximately 5–10% for HFRS caused by hantavirus (Table 222.5).

The clinical course of pathogenic hantavirus infection comprises an acute febrile illness characterized by variable degrees of hemorrhagic and renal dysfunction. More severe disease involves five overlapping stages – febrile, hypotensive, oliguric, diuretic and convalescent.

The onset of the disease is abrupt and characterized by high fever of 102.2–104°F (39–40°C), chills, intensive headache, malaise, myalgia, dizziness and anorexia. A petechial rash may also appear on the face, neck and trunk. The main laboratory findings include normal-to-elevated white blood count (WBC), decreasing platelets, rising hematocrit and rising proteinuria.

As the febrile phase ends, hypotension can abruptly develop and last for a few hours or days. Prominent features are tachycardia, falling arterial pressure and narrowing pulse pressure, and in severe cases classic shock. Laboratory findings include leukocytosis with a left shift, thrombocytopenia and prolonged bleeding times. Urinalysis shows heavy proteinuria, mild hematuria and hyposthenuria. About one-third of fatalities occur during this phase.

The oliguric phase lasts 3–7 days, during which blood pressure returns to normal or is slightly raised because of hypervolemia. Laboratory findings include normal WBC and platelet counts, initially normal and then depressed hematocrit, continual marked hematuria and elevated blood urea nitrogen and creatinine. Hyponatremia, hyperkalemia and hypocalcemia result from renal failure. Pulmonary edema may occur and fluid management should be handled with care. Almost half of the deaths occur during this phase, often from pulmonary edema or infection, electrolyte imbalance, late shock, or hemorrhage into the brain.

Clinical recovery is signaled by the diuretic phase, with improved renal function and normal clotting. Diuresis over a few hours or days is evident, with an output of 3–6 liters. Fluid management must be maintained to prevent negative fluid balance that may lead to shock. The final (convalescent) phase can last weeks to months before recovery is complete.

Seoul virus infections (mild HFRS) are less severe than those caused by hantavirus. Typically the phases are shorter and difficult to recognize or even absent. The disease is characterized by fever, anorexia, chills and nausea, and vomiting. Palatal injection is common, although other hemorrhagic signs (epistaxis, melena, hematemesis) are observed in fewer than 30% of patients. Laboratory findings include lymphocytosis, thrombocytopenia, microscopic hematuria and proteinuria, and elevation of serum transaminase. Renal involvement is less severe and fatalities are uncommon.

Puumula virus infection (NE) is characterized by a sudden onset of fever accompanied by headache. Characteristically, by the fourth day of illness nausea, vomiting, petechiae in the throat and soft palate, and facial flush and petechial rash have occurred. A mild thrombocytopenia can be observed. Hypotension may be found, but evidence of shock is rare. Onset of oliguria or recognition of renal failure around the sixth day of disease is the main cause of hospital admission. Serum creatinine levels rise and dialysis may be required in 10% of cases. As with other hantavirus infections, the onset of polyuria indicates the recovery process.

First recognized as a severe, often fatal respiratory illness in adults, HPS was characterized as a severe, systemic illness with a non-specific onset, fever, myalgia, cough or dyspnea, gastrointestinal symptoms and headache that typically lasted 3–5 days.[43] Rapid and abrupt onset of noncardiogenic edema, hypotension (systolic blood pressure ″80mmHg) then follow, resulting in shock and death in over half of the recognized cases (see Table 222.5). Laboratory findings indicate leukocytosis, an increase in polymorphonuclear leukocytes, left shift, increased hematocrit, thrombocytopenia, prolonged prothrombin and partial thromboplastin time, elevated serum lactate dehydrogenase, decreased serum protein concentrations and proteinuria. Increases in hematocrit and thromboplastin time are considered to be predictors of death. Radiographic examinations show bilateral pulmonary infiltrates and evidence of pleural effusions in the majority of hospitalized patients. Histopathologic features seen in lung tissue reveal mild-to-moderate interstitial pneumonitis with variable degrees of congestion, edema and mononuclear infiltrates. The virus has been identified extensively within endothelial cells of the pulmonary microvasculature, spleen and lymph nodes.

Current understanding of the disease indicates little evidence of renal damage as a feature of this hantavirus infection. The extensive pulmonary endothelial involvement and severe pulmonary edema make clinical management difficult.

Management

Effective management of HFRS and HPS requires early diagnosis, knowledge of disease course and prompt hospitalization. Aggressive clinical management is essential to improve survival. Care should be phase specific, with special attention given to fluid management. Ribavirin can be efficacious in the treatment of HFRS patients, but its treatment of HPS is not proved.

FILOVIRIDAE

Nature

The family Filoviridae consists of two distinctive species, Marburg and Ebola, which cause severe and often fatal hemorrhagic disease in humans and monkeys (see Chapter 183). The viruses have a distinctive filamentous morphology under the electron microscope with a genome that consists of a nonsegmented, negative stranded RNA

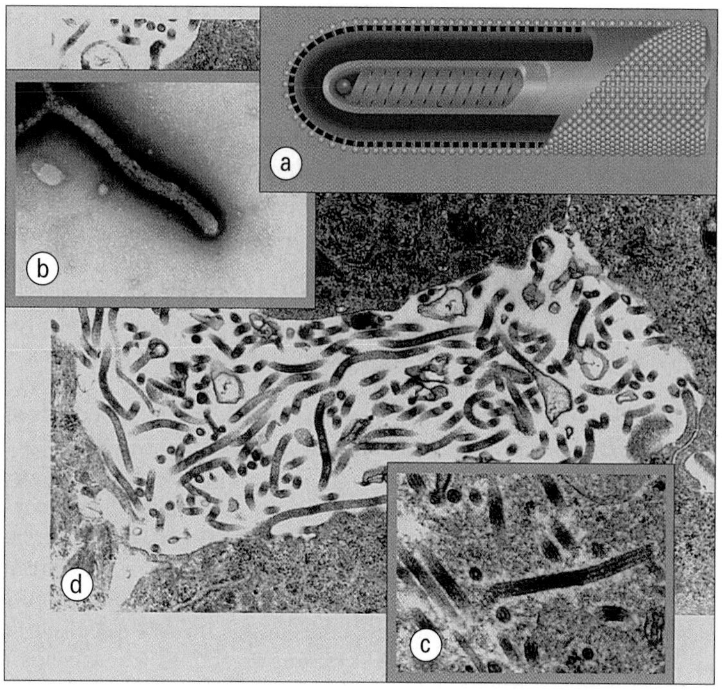

Fig. 222.11 Filoviruses. (a) Filovirus particle in cross-section (not to scale) showing glycoprotein surface projections, nucleocapsid core inside the envelope. (b) Negative contrast micrograph of Ebola (Reston). (c) Intracellular filamentous particles showing nucleocapsid core. (d) Sections of Ebola (Republic of Congo, formerly Zaire) infected Vero cells, showing extracellular virus, budding particles. Courtesy of G Lloyd, B Dowsett and ASR Featherstone.

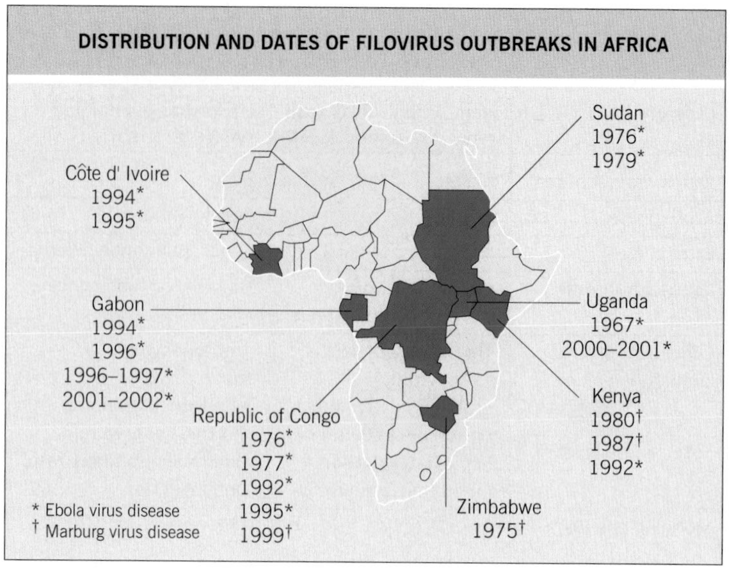

Fig. 222.12 Distribution and dates of filovirus outbreaks in Africa.

approximately 19kb in length (Fig. 222.11). Several features of their molecular organization and structure have linked these viruses to members of the Paramyxoviridae and Rhabdoviridae under the taxonomic order Mononegavirales.[41] The virions are composed of a central core formed by an RNP complex, which is surrounded by a lipid envelope derived from the host cell plasma membrane. The RNP is composed of a genomic RNA molecule bound by the NP, virion structural protein 30 (VP30), VP35 and the L protein (RNA transcriptase polymerase). The three remaining structural proteins are membrane-associated – GP, VP24 and VP40 are located on the inner side of the membrane. Among the newly isolated Ebola viruses are differences in molecular structure, pathogenicity and virulence in humans.[44]

Marburg and Ebola were first detected in 1967[45] and 1976,[46,47] respectively, although human infections since then have been rare. Fresh outbreaks of Ebola infections were identified in Côte d'Ivoire (1994, 1995), Republic of Congo, (formerly Zaire; 1995),[48] and Gabon (1996, 1997, 2001) and Uganda (2000). In addition, importation of Ebola-infected monkeys into the USA (1989–1990, 1996) and Italy (1992) attracted extensive worldwide media coverage and raised public concerns about the potential public health threat of these pathogens through international travel and commerce.[49,50]

Pathogenesis

The precise mechanisms by which filoviruses cause the most severe forms of VHF are unclear, but there is marked hepatic involvement, DIC and shock, producing extremely high fatality rates (30–90%). In the early stages of infection laboratory findings, such as high aspartate transaminase/alanine transaminase (AST/ALT) ratios, and marked lymphopenia followed by a marked neutropenia with left shift, suggest other extrahepatic targets affected by the virus. As with other VHF infections (HFRS, Lassa, dengue) fluid imbalance and platelet abnormalities indicate endothelial cell and platelet damage or dysfunction. Human monocytes and/or macrophages, fibroblasts and endothelial cells support virus replication. Infected monocyte and/or macrophages have been shown in in-vitro models to secret the cytokine TNF-α, which has the ability to increase vascular endothelial cell damage.[51] The data currently available support mediator-induced vascular damage that leads to increased permeability and shock observed in severe cases. Hemorrhage is likely to be caused by reticuloendothelial system damage that cannot be repaired because of platelet and coagulation malfunctions.

Epidemiology

The natural history and reservoirs of filoviruses remain a mystery, as does a detailed understanding of their pathogenesis. In 1967, a fulminating hemorrhagic fever, Marburg disease, occurred in Marburg and Frankfurt, Germany, and Bosnia, Croatia and Yugoslavia among laboratory workers handling blood and tissue from a shipment of African Green Monkeys (*Cercopithecus aethiops*) soon after being imported from Uganda via London. Among the 31 human cases, 25 of which were primary infections, there were seven (23%) deaths.[45] None of the secondary cases died. Since then, sporadic cases have been reported from South Africa and Kenya (Fig. 222.12).

In 1976, the first known cases of Ebola hemorrhagic fever were identified in southern Sudan (Table 222.6) and in a simultaneous outbreak in northern Republic of Congo (formerly Zaire), with fatality rates of about 60 and 90%, respectively.[46,47] A further smaller outbreak occurred in the same region of Sudan in 1979, when 22 (65%) of 34 infections proved fatal. Lack of community co-operation hampered control efforts and investigations during an outbreak of Ebola in the Republic of Congo during 2002. Recent instances of Ebola infection were the severe illness of a Swiss zoologist working with infected chimpanzees (*Pan troglodytes verus*) in the Taï National Park in Côte d'Ivoire, West Africa, in late 1994 and a major epidemic in Kikwit, Bandundu Province, Republic of Congo (formerly Zaire), in 1995. Of 315 recorded cases of Ebola hemorrhagic fever a total of 244 died (77% mortality rate).[51] In the later part of 1995 further cases were identified in the Côte d'Ivoire among refugees who originated in Liberia. Finally, three reportedly independent human outbreaks of Ebola have occurred in the forested areas found in northeastern Gabon (1994, February 1996, July 1996, December 2001). Subsequent investigations of the 2001–2 outbreak suggested that cases in villages north of Mekambo resulted from contact with a gorilla whose remains were found to be positive for Ebola virus. A severe outbreak occurred between August

CHARACTERISTICS OF SOME KNOWN FILOVIRUS INFECTIONS IN AFRICA			
Date	Filovirus Infections	Documented fatalities/total cases	Main characteristics
		Marburg	
1967	Marburg, Germany	5/23	Infected through contact with African green monkeys imported from Uganda
1967	Frankfurt, Germany	2/6	Infected through contact with African green monkeys imported from Uganda
1967	Belgrade, Yugoslavia	0/2	Infected through contact with African green monkeys imported from Uganda
1975	Zimbabwe	1/3	Contracted by travelers entering region – source unknown
1980	Mount Elgon, Kenya	1/2	Contracted by travelers entering region – source unknown
1987	Mount Elgon, Kenya	1/1	Contracted by travelers entering region – source unknown
1999	D.R. Congo	52/76 (estimates)	Gold miners near Durba
Total mortality rate		**62/113 (54.5%)**	
		Ebola (Africa)	
1976	Yambuku, D.R. Congo	280/318	Virus when introduced into hospital amplified disease
1976	Maridi, Sudan	151/284	Virus when introduced into hospital amplified disease
1976	England	0/1	Laboratory acquired
1977–8	Tandala, D.R. Congo	1/1	Child infected
1979	Nzara & Yambio, Sudan	22/34	Amplified by nosocomal transmission in hospital
1994	Taï Forest, Côte d'Ivoire	0/1	Worker infected after autopsy of chimpanzee–repatriated to Switzerland
1994	Gabon	32/44	Origin gold mining camps at Mekokou and Andcock. Primarily reported as yellow fever
1995	Kikwit, D.R. Congo	244/315	Included laboratory confirmed cases. Rapid transmission among unprotected health care workers
1995	Taï Forest, Côte d'Ivoire	0/1	Case originated in Liberia ? four additional cases in Liberia
1996 (January–March)	Mayibout, Gabon	21/37	Contact with dead chimpanzees
1996 July & January 1997	Booué & Libreville, Gabon	45/61	Index case hunter living in forest area – infected chimpanzees identified
1996	South Africa	1/1	Epidemiologically linked with outbreak in Gabon. Fatal case – nosocomial infection of nurse by patient transferred from Gabon
2000–1	Uganda	225/425	Occurred in Gulu, Misindi & Mbarara districts of Uganda. Spread associated with attending funerals, community nursing and medical care without personal protective measures
2001–2	Gabon	53/65	Community outbreak evidence suggest contact with dead nonhuman primates (gorilla)
2001–2	Republic of Congo Mboma district Kelle district	 20/32 23/25	Outbreak occurred over the border of Gabon and the Republic of the Congo
Total mortality rate		**1118/1645 (68%)**	

Table 222.6 Characteristics of some know filovirus infections in Africa.

RECORDED FILOVIRUS (EBOLA (RESTON)) INFECTIONS			
Date	Filovirus infections	Documented fatalities/total cases	Main characteristics (all isolates originated from same compound)
1989	Richmond, Virginia, USA	0/4	Reston strain isolated from monkeys imported from Philippines. Serologic evidence of asymptomatic infection among animal workers
1990	Manila, Philippines	0/12	Serologic evidence of asymptomatic infection among animal workers
1992	Siena, Italy	No cases	Reston strain isolated from monkeys imported from Philippines
1996 (April)	Alice Texas, USA	No cases	Reston strain in monkeys imported from Philippines
Total mortality rate		**0/16 (0%)**	

Table 222.7 Recorded filovirus (Ebola (Reston)) infections.

2000 and January 2001 in Uganda (Gulu and Masindi districts) that recorded 423 cases with 225 fatalities.[52] A case from the 1996 infection was treated in South Africa and the source of a fatal nosocomial transmission to a health care worker. All three outbreaks were associated with the deaths of chimpanzees, also thought to be from Ebola virus infection.

Hence, since 1994 West Africa has been considered to be part of the African filovirus map (see Fig. 222.12). Although filovirus outbreaks are rare events, the public health importance lies in their high mortality rate rather than the total number of infections in the 30 years since they were first identified (Tables 222.6 and 222.7).

Ebola virus has also appeared outside Africa, among shipments of imported cynomolgus monkeys in Reston, Philadelphia and Texas, USA, in 1989, 1990 and 1996, respectively, and Sienna, Italy, in 1992.[49] The monkeys involved in each epizootic event were imported from the Philippines and traced to the same handling facility, where the presence of the virus was also documented. The epizootics indicate that monkeys acutely infected with filoviruses present a major veterinary emergency and possibly could pose a serious hazard to other animals or humans if not recognized in the future. Although an Asian origin of these virus strains cannot be discounted, molecular biologic and serologic studies carried out to date suggest a close similarity with the original Ebola viruses isolated from the 1976 African outbreaks.

Prevention

The imposition of ecologic controls to prevent outbreaks is impossible until the natural history of the viruses has been discovered. It is important that health care workers in areas where hemorrhagic fever exists are aware of the high risk of nosocomial spread if patients are not recognized early and placed in complete isolation.[53] In nonendemic areas an awareness of the changing epidemiology associated with viral re-emergence or emergence should always be considered, bearing in mind the threat and consequences of importation.[54] High-risk patients are those who during the 3 weeks before illness had:

- traveled into areas where VHF occurred recently;
- been in contact with body fluids from a person with VHF; or
- worked in a laboratory environment handling the virus.

(See also Chapters 183 and 186a).

Importantly, filovirus illness is a rare event if patients do not meet any of these criteria.

As nonhuman primates are responsible for the introduction of Marburg into Europe, and of Ebola into the USA and Italy, the management of transportation, quarantine facilities and animal husbandry must ensure that personnel understand the hazards of handling nonhuman primates, and thus reduce the risks of future human outbreaks.[55]

Clinical manifestations

The incubation period for Ebola ranges from 4 to 10 days and for Marburg from 3 to 9 days.[45] The shorter times have been associated with exposure to contaminated needles.[56]

Filoviruses enter the host through close contact with contaminated body fluids. Epidemiologic studies in humans indicate that infection is not readily transmitted by the aerosol route. Although studies in nonhuman primates have established that the aerosol transmission can cause infection,[57] extra care must be taken with contaminated body fluid, tissue, hospital material and waste.

Both Marburg and Ebola virus infections follow a similar pattern of illness. Following exposure, initial symptoms include an abrupt onset with fever, severe frontal headache, malaise and myalgia. Such symptoms are similar to those of many viral illnesses that originate locally and in tropical areas. The initial diagnosis of a filovirus infection is very difficult. Disease progression is characterized by pharyngitis, nausea, severe vomiting of blood and production of bloody stools. Uncontrolled bleeding follows, which can be seen from under the skin, from venepuncture sites and from other orifices of the body. A characteristic maculopapular rash occurs 7–10 days (range 1–21 days) after onset of the clinical disease. If fatal, death occurs 6–9 days after onset of the clinical disease and results from severe blood loss and shock. Convalescence is slow, taking many weeks, and is marked by weight loss, prostration and amnesia of the acute phase of illness.[58]

Clinical laboratory findings in the early acute phase include lymphopenia followed by neutrophilia, marked thrombocytopenia and abnormal platelet aggregation. Serum AST and ALT are elevated and characterized by an AST/ALT ratio of between 10 and 3:1.

Diagnostic microbiology

The clinical diagnosis of Ebola or Marburg should be considered in patients who show acute, febrile illness and have traveled in known epidemic or suspected endemic areas of rural sub-Saharan Africa and Asia, particularly when hemorrhagic signs are present. As the differential diagnosis in the early acute phase of illness is difficult, other causes (malaria, typhoid) should not be excluded and treatment delayed. Laboratory diagnosis carried out on patient specimens is undertaken by more than one procedure to guard against false positives.

Care should be taken when drawing or handling blood specimens at the acute stage of illness because they contain large amounts of infectious virus – the virus is stable for long periods at room temperature at this stage.

Although their morphologic appearance is similar by electron microscopy, Marburg and Ebola are immunologically distinct. The basic diagnostic tool for filovirus infection and the only one to date that has widespread acceptance for the diagnosis of human filovirus disease is IFA, although some epidemiologic serology based on this assay has been regarded as non-specific and unreliable. A rising antibody in paired serum or a high IgG titer (>64) and the presence of IgM antibody together with clinical symptoms compatible with hemorrhagic fever are consistent with a diagnosis of filovirus infection.

Filoviruses can be readily isolated from fresh or stored (–94°F) specimens of blood or serum collected during the acute phase of illness. Vero cells (clone E6) and MA104 have proved the most sensitive for the propagation and assay of Marburg and Ebola viruses. Primary isolation using tissue culture rarely produces a specific cytopathic effect; thus, evidence of infection is confirmed by immunofluorescence staining using antivirus specific monoclonal or polyclonal antibodies. Some strains of Ebola, such as Ebola Sudan, proved difficult to grow in tissue culture and success was improved through interperitoneal inoculation of young guinea pigs. The resultant febrile response coincides with high levels of virus in the blood, which can be easily recovered by tissue culture or examined directly by electron microscopy. The isolation or propagation of filoviruses should not be attempted outside a biosafety containment level 4 laboratory.

During recent epizootic and human African outbreaks, early detection of filovirus infections was considerably improved by the development of an antigen-capture ELISA, amplification of filovirus RNA by RT-PCR, and immunohistochemistry identification of Ebola in skin biopsies. Skin biopsies fixed in formalin can be safely transported to reference facilities for confirmation without the need for low temperature preservation. Recent advances in molecular biology have expressed the NP gene of Ebola virus in a baculovirus expression system. The noninfectious N protein can replace the need for inactivation of infectious virus used in many serologic assays (IFA and ELISA). The diagnostic capabilities of such a system are currently being evaluated.

Management

No specific treatment is available. Treatment is limited to the provision of intensive nursing and effective control of blood volume and electrolyte balance. Shock, renal failure, depletion of blood clotting factors, severe bleeding and oxygen depletion must be managed. Human interferon and human convalescent plasma have been used to treat patients, but their efficacy is not proved. Ribavirin has no therapeutic value.

Patient management is further complicated by the need to isolate the patient and protect medical and nursing staff.[50,53] Use of patient isolators is a requirement in many countries, whereas strict barrier nursing techniques are acceptable in others. The latter can be supplemented using high efficiency particulate air filter respirators for protection against aerosols if considered feasible. Particular emphasis should be placed on ensuring that high-risk procedures (such as handling blood, secretions, catheters and introducing intravenous lines) are undertaken under barrier nursing conditions. It is recommended that patients who die from the disease should be buried or cremated promptly.

NIPAH AND HENDRA VIRUSES

Epidemiology

Both Hendra virus (HeV; formerly called equine morbillivirus) and Nipah virus (NiV) are newly recognized hazard group 4 zoonotic viruses.

Two outbreaks of a new zoonotic disease affecting horses and animals in Australia were reported within 1 month of each other in Brisbane (southeast Queensland) and Mackay (central Queensland) in 1994. A third event involving a single fatal equine case occurred near Cairns (North Queensland) in 1999. To date, two humans and 16 horses have died from this disease with acute respiratory failure.[59–61] Within the subfamily Paramyxovirinae, the extent of nucleotide homology in the N gene between different viruses in the same genus ranges from 56 to 78%, whereas the extent of nucleotide similarity between viruses from different genera is 39–78%. The N genes of HeV and NiV have 78% nucleotide homology, but the two viruses have no more than 49% similarity with any other members of the Paramyxovirinae.[66] Phylogenetic analysis of the N gene sequences show that HeV and NiV form a distinct cluster within the subfamily Paramyxovirinae. The cause of the infection has been identified as HeV, a new member of the family Paramyxoviridae.[62]

Another member of the Paramyxoviridae (NiV) was responsible for an outbreak of severe febrile encephalitis in humans in Malaysia in 1998–9. The outbreak was associated with respiratory illness in pigs and was initially considered to be Japanese encephalitis. Of a total of 256 cases 105 were fatal. In March 1999, a cluster of 11 cases (one fatality) was described in Singapore in abattoir workers who handled pigs imported from the outbreaks regions in Malaysia.[63] Measures to control the concurrent outbreak of respiratory disease in pigs resulted in the culling of over one million pigs (almost half the national pig herd) and had major domestic and international trade implications.

The geographic distribution of both HeV and NiV is currently undefined although Australia and South East Asia are considered to be endemic areas on the basis of the known incidents reported in the literature. Fruit bats of the genus *Pteropus* are considered to be the natural hosts of HeV and NiV[64] and are found in north, east and south-east areas of Australia, Indonesia, Malaysia, Philippines and some of the Pacific Islands. Pigs were the apparent source of infection among most human cases in the Malaysian outbreak of NiV, but other sources, such as infected dogs and cats, cannot be excluded.

Virology

Nipah and Hendra are closely lelated and difficult to distinguish serologically, although they have a diverse geographical distribution.[61,65] Both NiV and HeV share a nonsegmented, negative-stranded RNA genome and similar genome organization, replication strategy and domain structure in the polymerase proteins to members of the Filoviridae, Paramyxoviridae, Rhabdoviridae and Bornaviridae. While being related to these families they are closely related to the Paramyxoviridae and more specifically the morbilliviruses. The genome organization of NiV and HeV is the same as for the rest of the Paramyxoviridae. There are a total of six transcription units encoding six structural proteins. These are the nucleocapsid protein (N), phosphoprotein (P), matrix protein (M), fusion protein (F), glycoprotein (G) or attachment protein, and large protein (L) or RNA polymerase. They are found on the genome in the order 3′-N-P-M-F-G-L-5′. Evidence suggests that NiV and HeV forms a distinct group of viruses within the subfamily Paramyxovirinae.[65]

Clinical features

The emergence of NiV and HeV has raised clinical concerns in the management of individuals returning from Australia and South East Asia presenting with pyrexia and other non-specific signs and symptoms. The incubation period for NiV and HeV is generally from 4 to 18 days. Onset of disease is usually influenza-like with high fever and myalgia. Sore throat, dizziness, and drowsiness and disorientation have been described. The case fatality rate for clinical cases is about 50% and subclinical infections may be common.

Experimental studies have confirmed the possibility of transmission through close contact with infected body fluids and that aerosol transmission does not seem to be significant. Human-to-human transmission has not been reported and the risk of transmission from horse to human, neither of which are considered natural hosts for the viruses, is thought to be very low. The mode of transmission from animal to animal, and from animal to human is uncertain.

Laboratory diagnosis

Virus isolation has been an important primary diagnostic tool in early outbreaks.

Both NiV and HeV grow well in Vero cells. A cytopathic effect (CPE) usually develops within 3 days but two 5-day passages are recommended before virus isolation is considered to be unsuccessful. However, isolation should only be attempted in a containment level 4 laboratory.

Virus neutralization tests are considered to be the reference standard in the serologic identification of NiV and HeV infection. This procedure needs to be carried out at a containment level 4 laboratory. Sera are added into the media covering virus-inoculated Vero monolayers in a 96-well plate format. Positive results are demonstrated by the inhibition of CPE production by sera.[66]

To reduce the dependence on high containment facilities (CL4), both the indirect IgG and capture IgM ELISA NiV and HeV systems can use irradiated viral antigens purified from cell culture. The level of sample processing involved to make the antigen safe to use outside Advisory Committee on Dangerous Pathogens (ACDP) 4 containment reduces the specificity and sensitivity of the assay.

NiV-specific primers that amplify a 228bp segment of the N gene region of the virus will form the basis of the RT-PCR detection system that has proven of diagnostic value when used in conjunction with specimens (sera, tissue from humans and animals) implicated in HeV and NiV outbreaks.[67] In addition, another published primer pair that amplifies a 200bp region of the matrix (M) protein will form a proven alternative primer set for the RT-PCR detection of HeV originally designed by Halpin *et al.*[64]

Management

As there are neither vaccine nor antivirals for treatment and because the viruses are potentially able to transmit by the aerosol route, both HeV and NiV have been classified as hazard group 4 agents. Working with these agents requires the use of ACDP containment level 4 laboratories. Therefore, with the increasing movement of horses and travelers to endemic areas, both clinicians and veterinarians have increasingly expressed a need to consider these infections as part of the current differential diagnosis.

REFERENCES

1. Beran GW, ed. Handbook of zoonoses, Section B, 2nd edn. Boca Raton: CRC Press; 1994.
2. Palmer SR, Lord Soulsbury, Simpson DHI. Zoonoses, biology, clinical practice and public health control. Oxford: Oxford University Press; 1998.
3. Monath TP, ed. The arboviruses: epidemiology and ecology, vols 1–4. Boca Raton: CRC Press; 1988.
4. World Health Organization. Arthropod-borne and rodent-borne viral diseases. World Health Organization: Technical Report Series No 719. Geneva, Switzerland: WHO; 1985.
5. World Health Organization. Yellow fever in 1992 and 1993. Wkly Epidemiol Rec 1995;70:65–70.
6. Division of Epidemiological Surveillance and Health Situation and Trend Assessment. Global health situation and projections: estimates. Document WHO/HST 9221. Geneva, Switzerland: World Health Organization; 1992.
7. Centers for Disease Control. Summary of health information for international travel. US Department of Health and Human Services. Atlanta, GA: Centers for Disease Control and Prevention; 1999.
8. Nathan N, Barry M, Van Herp M, Zeller H. Shortage of vaccines during a yellow fever outbreak in Guinea. Lancet 2001;358:2129–30.
9. Robertson SE, Hull BP, Tomori O, Bele O, LeDuc JW, Esteves K. Yellow fever – a decade of re-emergence. JAMA 1996;276:1157–63.
10. Centers for Disease Control. Yellow fever vaccine. MMWR Morb Mortal Wkly Rep 1990;39:1–5.
11. Duebel V, Huerre M, Cathomas G, *et al.* Molecular detection and characterization of yellow fever virus in blood and liver specimens of a non-vaccinated fatal human case. J Med Virol 1997;53:212–7.
12. McFarland JM, Baddour LM, Nelson JE, *et al.* Imported yellow fever in a United States citizen. Clin Infect Dis 1997;95:1143–7.
13. Smithburn KC, Hughes TP, Burkw AW, Paul JH. A neurotropic virus isolated from blood of a native Ugandan. Am J Trop Med Hyg 1940;20:37–43.
14. Melnick JL, Paul JR, Riordan JT, Barnett VHH, Gildblum N, Zabin E. Isolation from human sera in Egypt of a virus apparently identical to West Nile virus. Proc Soc Exp Biol Med 1951;77:661–5.
15. Tsai TF, Popovici F, Cernescu C, Campbell GL, Nedelcu NI. West Nile encephalitis epidemic in southeastern Romania. Lancet 1998;352:767–71.
16. Nash D, Mostashari F, Fina A, *et al.* The outbreak of West Nile virus infection in the New York City area in 1999. N Engl J Med 2001;3441:1807–14.
17. Petersen LR, Roehrig JT. West Nile Virus: a reemerging global pathogen. Emerg Infect Dis 2001;7(4):611–4.
18. Salvato MS, ed. The arenaviridae. New York: Plenum; 1993.
19. Cao W, Henry MD, Borrow P, *et al.* Identification of alpha-dystroglycan as a receptor for lymphocytic choriomeningitis virus and Lassa fever virus. Science 1998;282:2079–81.
20. Childs JC, Glass GE, Korch GW, Ksiazek TG, Leduc JW. Lymphocytic choriomeningitis virus infection and house mouse (*Mus musculus*) distribution in urban Baltimore. Am J Trop Med Hyg 1992;47:27–34.
21. Gunther S, Emmerich P, Laue T, *et al.* Imported lassa fever in Germany: molecular characterization of a new lassa virus strain. Emerg Infect Dis 2000;6:466–76.
22. McCormick JB, Webb PA, Krebs JW, Johnson KM, Smith ES. A prospective study of the epidemiology and ecology of Lassa fever. J Infect Dis 1987;155:437–44.
23. McCormick JB, King IJ, Webb PA, *et al.* A case–control study of the clinical diagnosis and course of Lassa fever. J Infect Dis 1987;155:445–55.
24. Mackenzie RB. Epidemiology of Machupo virus infection. I. Pattern of human infection, San Joaquin, Bolivia, 1962–1964. Am J Trop Med Hyg 1965;14:808–13.
25. World Health Organization. Vaccination against Argentine hemorrhagic fever. Weekly Epidemiol Rec 1993;68:233–4.
26. Demby AH, Chamberlain J, Brown DWG, Clegg CS. Early diagnosis of Lassa fever by reverse transcription PCR. J Clin Microbiol 1994;32:2898–903.
27. Cummins D, McCormick JB, Bennett D, *et al.* Acute sensorineural deafness in Lassa fever. JAMA 1990;264:2093–6.
28. Centers for Disease Control. Management of patients with suspected viral hemorrhagic fever. MMWR Morb Mortal Wkly Rep 1998;37:S1–15.
29. Fisher-Hoch SP. Stringent precautions are not advisable when caring for patients with viral haemorrhagic fevers. Rev Med Virol 1993;3:7–13.
30. McCormick JB, King IJ, Webb PA, *et al.* Lassa fever, effective therapy with ribavirin. N Engl J Med 1986;314:20–6.
31. Gajdusek DC, Goldfarb LG, Goldgaber D. Bibliography of hemorrhagic fever with renal syndrome, 2nd ed, Pub No 88–3603. Bethesda MD: National Institutes of Health; 1987.
32. Schmaljohn CS, Hjelle B. Hantavirus: A global problem. Emerg Infect Dis 1997;3:95–103.
33. Schmaljohn CS. Molecular biology of hantaviruses. In: Elliot RM, ed. The Bunyaviridae. New York: Plenum Press; 1996:63–90.
34. World Health Organization. Haemorrhagic fever with renal syndrome: memorandum from a WHO meeting. Bull WHO 1983;61:269–75.
35. Clement J, Heyman P, McKenna P, *et al.* The hantaviruses of Europe: from the bedside to the bench. Emerg Infect Dis 1997;3:205–9.
36. Butler JC, Peters CJ. Hantaviruses and hantavirus pulmonary syndrome. Clin Infect Dis 1994;19:387–95.
37 Hughes JM, Peters CJ, Cohen ML, *et al.* Hantavirus pulmonary syndrome: an emerging infectious disease. Science 1993;262:850–1.
38. Zaki SR. Hantavirus pulmonary syndrome: pathogenesis of an emerging infectious disease. Am J Path 1995;146:552–79.
39. Groen J, van der Groen G, Hoofd G, *et al.* Comparison of immunofluorescence and enzyme linked immunosorbent assays for the serology of hantavirus infections. J Virol Methods 1989;23:195–203.
40. Zoller L, Yang S, Zeyer M. Rapid diagnosis of haemorrhagic fever with renal syndrome due to hantavirus. Lancet 1991;338:183.
41. Pringle CR. Order Mononegavirales. Arch Virol 1991;117:137–40.
42. Lee H, Lee P, Johnson K. Isolation of the etiologic agent of Korean haemorrhagic fever. J Infect Dis 1978;137:298–308.
43. Duchin JS, Koster FT, Peters CJ, *et al.* Hantavirus pulmonary syndrome: a clinical description of 17 patients with a newly recognized disease. N Engl J Med 1994;330:949–55.
44. Feldman H, Klenk HD, Sanchez A. Molecular biology and evolution of filoviruses. Arch Virol 1993;7(Suppl.):87–100.
45. Martini GA. Marburg virus disease, clinical syndrome. In: Martini GA, Siegert R, eds. Marburg virus disease. Berlin: Springer Verlag; 1971:1–9.
46. World Health Organization/International Commission to Sudan. Ebola hemorrhagic fever in Sudan; 1976. Bull WHO 1976;56:247–70.
47. World Health Organization/International Commission to Zaire. Ebola hemorrhagic fever in Zaire; 1976. Bull WHO 1978;56:271–93.
48. World Health Organization. Ebola hemorrhagic fever, Zaire. Weekly Epidemiol Rec 1995;70:241–2.
49. Hayes CG, Burans, JP Ksiazek TG, *et al.* Outbreak of fatal illness among captive macaques in the Philippines caused by an Ebola-related filovirus. Am J Trop Med Hyg 1992;46:664–71.
50. World Health Organization. Viral hemorrhagic fever in imported monkeys. Weekly Epidemiol Rec 1992;67:142–3.
51. Feldman H, Bugany H, Mahner F, *et al.* Filovirus-induced endothelial leakage triggered by infected monocytes/macrophages. J Virol 1996;70:2208–14.
52. Centers for Disease Control. Outbreak of Ebola hemorrhagic fever – Uganda, August 2000–January 2001. MMWR Morb Mortal Wkly Rep 2001;50:73–6.
53. World Health Organization. Viral hemorrhagic fevers – management of suspected cases. Wkly Epidemiol Rec 1995;70(35):249–52.
54. Advisory Committee on Dangerous Pathogens. Management and control of viral haemorrhagic fevers. London: The Stationery Office; 1996.
55. Center for Disease Control. Ebola related filovirus infection in non-human primates and interim guidelines for handling non-human primates during transit and quarantine. MMWR Morb Mortal Wkly Rep 1990;39:22–30.
56. Emond RTD. Isolation, monitoring and treatment of a case of Ebola infection. In: Pattyn SR, ed. Ebola virus infection. Amsterdam: Elsevier/North Holland Biomedical Press; 1978:27–32.
57. Peters CJ, Sanchez A, Feldman H, Rollin PE, Nichol S, Kscazek TG. Filoviruses as emerging pathogens. Semin Virol 1994;5:147–54.
58. Peters CJ, Sanchez A, Rollin PE, Kscazek TG, Murphy FA. Filoviridae: Marburg and Ebola viruses. In: Fields BN, Knipe DM, eds. Virology, 3rd ed. Philadelphia: Lippincott-Raven; 1996.
59. Murrey K, Selleck P, Hooper P, *et al.*A morbillivirus that caused fatal disease in horses and humans. Science 1995:268;94–7.
60. Rogers RJ, Donglas IC, Baldock FC, *et al.* Investigation of a second focus of equine morbillivirus infection in coastal Queensland. Aust Vet J 1996;74:243–4.
61. Field H, Barrat PC, Hughes RJ, Sheild J, Sullivan ND. A fatal case of Hendra virus infection in a horse in north Queensland – clinical and epidemiological features. Aust Vet J 2000;78:279–80.
62. Wang LF, Michalski WP, Yu M, *et al.* 1998). A novel P/V/C gene in a new member of the Paramyxoviridae family which causes lethal infection in humans, horses and other animals. J Virol 72, 1482–1490
63. Madeleine HL, Arguin PM, Shay DK, *et al.* Risk factors for nipah virus infection among abattoir workers in Singapore. J Infect Dis 2000;181:1760–3.
64. Halpin K, Young PL, Field HE, Mackenzie JS. Isolation of hendra virus from pteropid bats: a natural reservoir of hendra virus. J Gen Virol 2000;81;1927–32.
65. Wang LF, Harcourt BH, Yu M, *et al.* Molecular biology of hendra and nipah. Microbes Infect 2001;4:279–87.
66. Daniels P, Ksiazek T Eaton BT. Laboratory diagnosis of nipah and hendra virus infection. Microbes Infect 2001;4:289–95.
67. Chua KB, Bellini WJ, Rota PA, *et al.* Nipah virus: a recently emergent deadly paramyxovirus. Science 2000;288:1432–4.

chapter

223 Prions

Dominique Dormont

Transmissible spongiform encephalopathies (TSEs) are a group of human and animal diseases. In humans, TSEs include Creutzfeldt–Jakob disease (CJD), Gerstmann–Sträussler–Scheinker syndrome (GSS), kuru and fatal familial insomnia (FFI). In animals, scrapie in sheep and goats, feline spongiform encephalopathy, mink transmissible encephalopathy, chronic wasting disease in wild ruminants, and bovine spongiform encephalopathy (BSE), which appeared in the UK in the mid-1980s,[1] belong to the TSE group. These diseases are all transmissible among individuals of the same species and in some cases they may pass from one species to another.

Unconventional micro-organisms known as TSE agents or prions induce TSEs. These agents have biologic and physicochemical characteristics that differ significantly from those of other micro-organisms; for example, they are resistant to inactivation processes that are effective against conventional viruses. Today, the exact nature of TSE agents or prions remains unknown even though it is likely that they consist of protein only. Transmissible spongiform encephalopathies are characterized by the accumulation, within the central nervous system (CNS) of the infected individual, of an abnormal isoform of a particular protein from the host organism, namely the prion protein (PrP).[2]

A dual causality, 'infectious' and 'genetic', of these diseases can be inferred from the various current theories. Indeed, the genetic basis of the familial forms in humans has now been confirmed. Furthermore, transmissibility has been proved in natural situations such as the outbreak of CJD among patients treated with pituitary-derived hormones and the appearance in 1986 of BSE that affected UK cattle. The fact of the transmissibility of TSEs requires strict compliance with safety regulations in sterilization, in the preparation of biologic products for therapeutic use and in the prevention of risks associated with graft processes.

NATURE

The nature of TSE agents is unknown. However, because TSEs are transmissible between different species, there are several animal models. The most common are scrapie in mice and hamsters and most of the experiments have been conducted using these two models, including attempts to isolate and to characterize TSE agents or prions.

The size of TSE agents or prions has been evaluated by utrafiltration to be between 15 and 40nm.[3] These agents aggregate easily because of their hydrophobicity; this could explain the variations in size and density that have been reported in the literature.

The inactivation processes that have been demonstrated to be effective against scrapie agents are those that denature or hydrolyze protein components: treatment with high doses of proteinase K, trypsin[4] or SDS. Diethylpyrocarbonate, guanidium thiocyanate or urea alters infectivity. Conversely, procedures that interact with nucleic acids do not modify infectivity titers: nucleases, ultraviolet treatment, Zn^{2+} hydrolysis[2] and psoralens. Therefore, one may hypothesize that TSE agents either consist of protein only or harbor a small nucleic acid that is protected within a shell that may have a lipidic or lipoproteic nature.

Because numerous experimental data indicate the absence of specific nucleic acid in the infectious fractions, the theory of a self-propagating proteic agent, or 'prion' (for proteinaceous infectious particle), was proposed at the end of the 1970s.[2] Prusiner has purified a 27–30kDa protein specifically associated with infectivity, the PrP^{SC}. This protein is present in the brains of infected individuals in proportion to the level of infection. In 1985, it was demonstrated that PrP^{SC} is an abnormal isoform of a host-encoded normal component of the host,[5] PrP^{C}, that accumulates as a result of a post-translational mechanism in the brains of infected individuals. Differences between PrP^{C} (isolated from normal individuals) and PrP^{SC} (isolated from infected individuals) have been investigated. Because the amino acid sequences of the two proteins are identical, the differences between PrP-c and PrP-res are thought to be at the level of conformation. The sensitivity to proteolytic enzymes varies; PrP^{C} is totally degraded by proteinase K concentrations that only partially degrade PrP^{SC} (Fig. 223.1); and PrP^{SC} is insoluble in detergents, although PrP^{C} is soluble. It is impossible to remove PrP^{SC} from infectious fractions without rendering them noninfectious.[6] The amount of PrP^{C} is 50 times greater in brain than in other organs; this may be a critical parameter of the pathogenesis of TSEs.[5] Other investigators have identified fibrillary structures specific for spongiform subacute encephalopathies in detergent-treated brain extracts from infected individuals, namely scrapie-associated fibrils (SAFs),[7] which are polymers of PrP^{SC}. PrP^{C} is anchored at the cell membrane, in rafts, through a glycosyl phosphatidyl inositol (GPI); its half-life at the cell surface is 5 hours, after which the protein is internalized through a caveolae-dependent mechanism and degraded in the endolysosome compartment. Conversion between PrP^{C} and PrP^{SC} occurs likely during the internalization process; this explains why PrP^{SC} is only detectable in the cytoplasm.

Prion protein amino acid and gene sequences are now well known. In humans, PrP is a 253 amino acid protein. It has two hexapeptides and repeat octapeptides at the *N*-terminus, a disulfide bond and is associated at the *C*-terminus with a GPI, which enables it to anchor to the external part of the cell membrane (Fig. 223.2). The fragment of PrP that is resistant to proteinase K digestion (PrP-res) in infected individuals is between amino acid residues 90 and 233 (molecular weight 27–30kDa). PrP^{C} has two putative sites of glycosylation; thus, three glycoforms of PrP can be described. The relative proportions of these glycoforms and the size of the unglycosylated PrP-res fragment are dependent on the strain of prion.[8] Infrared spectroscopy and circular dichroism have shown that the secondary structure of PrP^{C} is mainly composed of α-helices, whereas PrP^{SC} is mainly β-sheets;[9] transconformation of α-helices into β-sheets has been proposed as the structural basis by which PrP acquires pathogenicity in TSEs. Recently, the three-dimensional structures of a normal murine, bovine and hamster PrP have been published:[10–12] the protein is made of a globular domain (amino acids 121–231), which includes three α-helices and two small antiparralel β-sheet

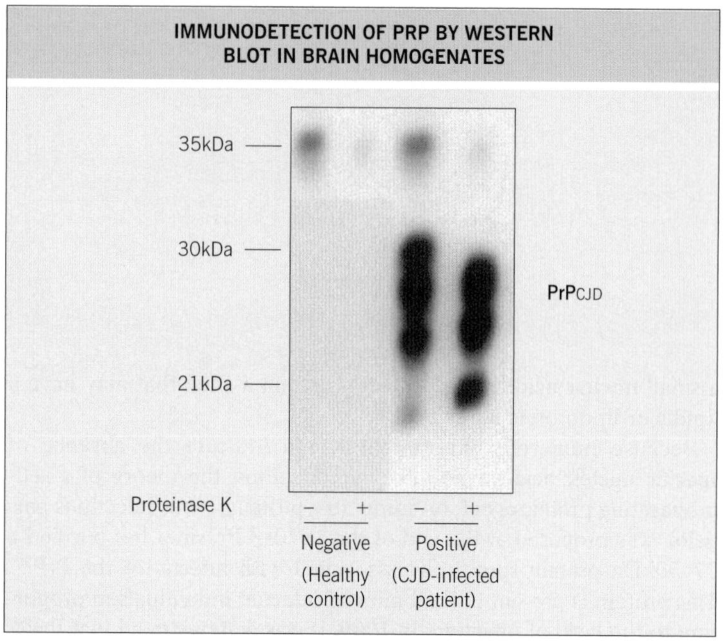

Fig. 223.1 Immunodetection of PrP by Western blot in brain homogenates.

structures, and a long flexible tail whose conformation depends on the biophysical parameters of the environment (Fig. 223.3). Crystals of the globular domain of PrP have been obtained; their analysis suggest a possible dimerization of the protein through the three-dimensional swapping of the *C*-terminal helix 3 and rearrangement of the disulfide bond.[13] In-vitro conversion of PrP^{C} into PrP^{SC} is possible in acellular experimental system, and at least one of the biochemical strain characteristics of PrP^{SC}, resistance to PK digestion, can be 'transmitted' to PrP^{C}.[14]

The PrP gene (*PRNP*) is located on the short arm of chromosome 20 in humans (Fig. 223.4). It consists of two exons and one large 10kb intron. The entire coding sequence is within the second exon. The promoter of the PrP gene resembles those of housekeeping genes. Prion protein RNA is 2.1kb in length and is detected at various levels in almost all organs: brain, lung, spleen, heart, etc. (lowest expression level in liver and testicle).[5] Gene expression level is not modulated during TSEs.

Even among the most recent hypotheses, none gives a definite and complete account of the biologic, epidemiologic and clinical observations. Several hypotheses have been advanced:

- the virino hypothesis,[15] which suggests that the agent consists of a nucleic acid, which codes only for its own replication surrounded by host-encoded PrP (thus accounting for the lack of an immune response);
- the unknown conventional virus hypothesis; current concepts of microbiology indicate that this is most unlikely; and
- the protein-only hypotheses that include the seeding model, the chaperone-disease model and the prion theory.

The protein-only hypotheses are supported by the most recent results from transgenic experiments and molecular biology. In these theories, PrP^{SC} is the agent or a major constituent of the infectious fractions.[2] The prion theory postulates that pathogenicity is enciphered into the tertiary structure of PrP^{SC}. Propagation of the abnormal conformation results from the ability of PrP^{SC} to form dimers with PrP^{C}; this heterodimerization induces a transconfor-mation of PrP^{C} into PrP^{SC} and, therefore, the propagation of this abnormal isoform of PrP (i.e. PrP^{SC}). Recently, it has been suggested that PrP^{C} transconformation into PrP^{SC} requires a host-encoded cellular factor, factor X,[16] which is thought to be a chaperone (Fig. 223.5).

Other theories involving chaperoning molecules[17] or nucleation have also been proposed;[18] in this latter hypothesis, the transformation of PrP^{C} into PrP^{SC} is reversible, PrP^{SC} being stable only when aggregated. Then, binding of PrP^{C} to PrP^{SC} aggregates results in PrP^{C} transconformation. The size of the aggregate then increases until the limit of cohesion of the aggregate, above which a dissociation occurs, giving birth to small seeds efficient for PrP^{C} transconformation. Moreover, the excess of β-sheet measured in PrP^{SC} could be the consequence of aggregation through the globular domains which could trap a part of the flexible tail inside the aggregate and therefore induce a β-sheet conformation of a part of the molecule that was not structured before. If demonstrated, this mechanism would not require any transconformation process of PrP.

There are major uncertainties that hinge on the nature of the agent and on the precise level at which the host's genetic background is implicated. The presence of sporadic diseases and familial forms suggests that several diseases probably co-exist under the same designation; some are of infectious origin, whereas others are probably of a metabolic and/or genetic origin. It might therefore be advisable to refer to Creutzfeldt–Jakob syndrome rather than disease in the strict sense of the word.

EPIDEMIOLOGY

Human TSEs are rare diseases, CJD being the most common. Creutzfeldt–Jakob disease can be sporadic (85–90% of cases), familial (10–15% of cases) or iatrogenic (<1%). Its incidence does not differ significantly in countries in which epidemiologic surveillance is performed;[19] incidence ranges between 1 and 1.7 per million inhabitants per year. To date, no link has been described with animal TSE except for the new variant of CJD (vCJD), which occurred mainly in the UK and is thought to be caused by the BSE agent.[20] Several clusters of CJD have been described in the past, especially in Slovakia and Israel. Progress in molecular genetics has demonstrated that these clusters were in fact inherited forms of CJD. It should be noted that all forms of human TSEs are transmissible, including the genetic diseases.

PATHOGENICITY

Incubation and transmission

Natural and experimental TSEs are characterized by a long incubation phase without clinical symptoms; this silent phase may last as long as 40 years in humans with kuru or infected through extracted growth hormone treatment. Once started, the clinical course of the disease evolves slowly without remission. No inflammatory process is identifiable in blood or cerebrospinal fluid (CSF); none of the usual immunologic stigma or specific signs of chronic viral infections are observed in infected individuals. No virus-like or microorganism-like structure is identifiable in the brains of infected patients, regardless of which microscopic technique is used. Transmission can be achieved by injecting ultrafiltrates of some organ extracts from infected individuals. The CNS is by far the most infectious; the spleen is also highly infectious in sheep and rodents, but at least 1000 times less so than the brain. In a given genetic background, infectivity depends on the amount injected, the strain of TSE agent and the route of infection; the intracerebral route is the most effective and the oral route the least effective (1 intracerebral route infectious unit = 125,000 oral route infectious units).[21] This has been demonstrated in experimental models, but natural disease-associated agents, especially the BSE agent, may behave differently and be more infectious by a peripheral route (including oral exposure). In-vivo, there are no alterations of the B, T and non-T non-B

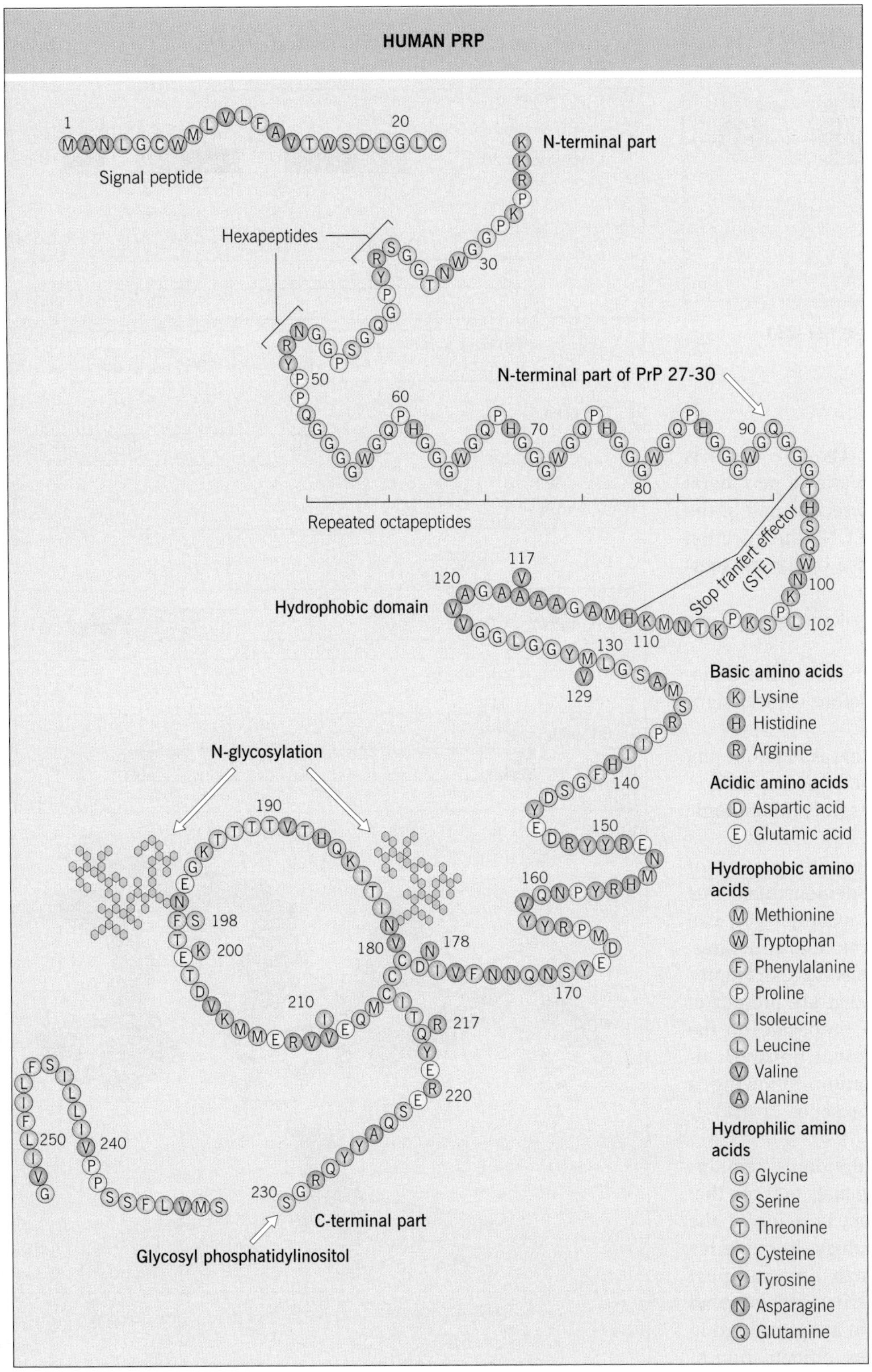

Fig. 223.2 Human PrP. Representation of the 253 amino acid primary sequence of the human prion protein. Stop tranfert effector (STE) is a sequence that facilitates integration of the protein into the cell membrane.

cells (quantitative or functional) and no antibody against PrP has been detected in natural or experimental diseases; therefore, there is no test available for screening asymptomatic infected individuals. These diseases are always fatal.

Transmissibility is easy in the same species, but is also possible between different species. The strength of the species barrier is variable; for example, BSE is not transmissible to hamsters although it can be transmitted to mice. Several species have never been infected with any TSE agent despite extensive attempts (e.g. rabbit or dog). The major molecular determinant of the species barrier is the homology between the PrP gene of the donor and the PrP gene of the recipient. Other genes play minor roles in TSE agent or prion susceptibility, for example major histocompatibility genes. In humans, the PrP gene exhibits a polymorphism at codon 129; either valine or methionine can be encoded, 50% of the general population being homozygous. Homozygosity at codon 129 has been associated with susceptibility to sporadic and iatrogenic CJD;[22] methionine/methionine homozygosity has also been reported in all the cases of vCJD so far described.

The role of the prion protein

The kinetics of PrP-res accumulation has been studied in a number of experimental animal models. Results have confirmed that

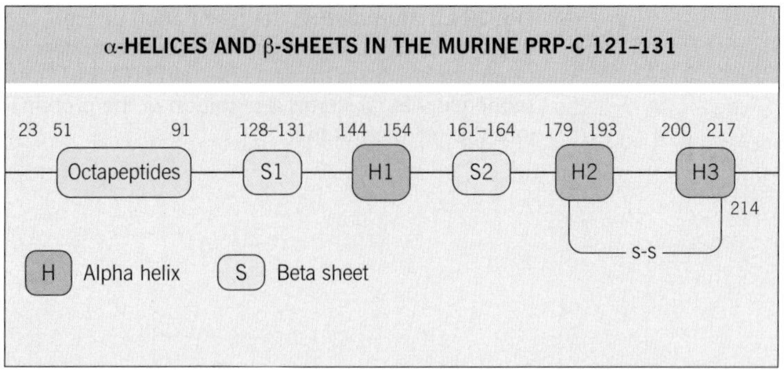

Fig. 223.3 α-Helices and β-sheets in the murine PrP-c 121–231 fragment. Adapted from Riek *et al.*[11]

accumulation follows the increase in infection. The TSE agent is detectable in the spleen of infected animals soon after a peripheral inoculation; it then appears in the CNS during the second half of the total duration of the experimental disease. In the CNS the infection develops almost exponentially until the appearance of clinical signs and death.

These facts illustrate two main characteristics of the spongiform subacute encephalopathies:

- certain organs of the infected individual, particularly the brain, spinal cord and retina, are heavily infected before clinical signs appear (Table 223.1);[23] and
- these diseases develop without interruption, that is, without any latency of the infectious agent during the asymptomatic phase.

This must be taken into consideration for the safety of biologic products and grafting processes.

The immune system plays a role during the pathogenesis of peripheral infection with TSE agents. It has been demonstrated that immune cells (most probably dendritic cells and macrophages) can be the first site of replication of these agents. In lymphoid structures, infectivity is associated with follicular dendritic cells (FDCs). Neuroinvasion then occurs through the nerve endings that are present in lymphoid organs. It is not known whether PrP^{SC} propagates in the peripheral nervous system (PNS) via a retroaxonal transport or through a propagation of abnormal conformation following a 'domino model' at the surface of the axon; the presence of PrP^{C} is required for agent propagation in the PNS.

The precise function of PrP in healthy individuals remains unknown. Several results obtained in transgenic animals indicate that PrP^{C} might play a role in long-term potentiation, in aging of the Purkinje cells of the cerebellum, in sleep physiology, in oxidative burst compensation (PrP can fix 4 Cu^{++} through its octarepeat domain), in interactions with the extracellular matrix (PrP^{C} can bind to the precursor of the laminin receptor, LRP),[24] in apoptosis and in signal transduction (co-stimulation of PrP^{C} induces a modulation of Fyn kinase phosphorylation).[25]

In TSE-affected individuals, PrP has a determinant role in the incubation time and in the species barrier[26] and its role in pathogenesis is now well established. Transgenic mice lacking *PRNP* expression (i.e. knockout mice that do not express any PrP) are not susceptible to TSE agent or prion infection, demonstrating the key role of PrP in the subacute spongiform encephalopathies.[26] Susceptibility to TSE agents or prions thus depends upon the presence of PrP^{C} on the cell membrane of the host; prions do not propagate in brains that lack PrP^{C}.[27] Moreover, in transgenic animals that express large numbers of *PRNP* copies, it has been demonstrated that incubation time is inversely correlated with PrP-c expression; that is, susceptibility to infection and prion propagation depend on the amount of PrP-c available in the host. Finally, transgenic animals with a PrP gene mutation equivalent to one described in human familial disease spontaneously exhibit a spongiform encephalopathy that is transmissible under certain conditions.[28]

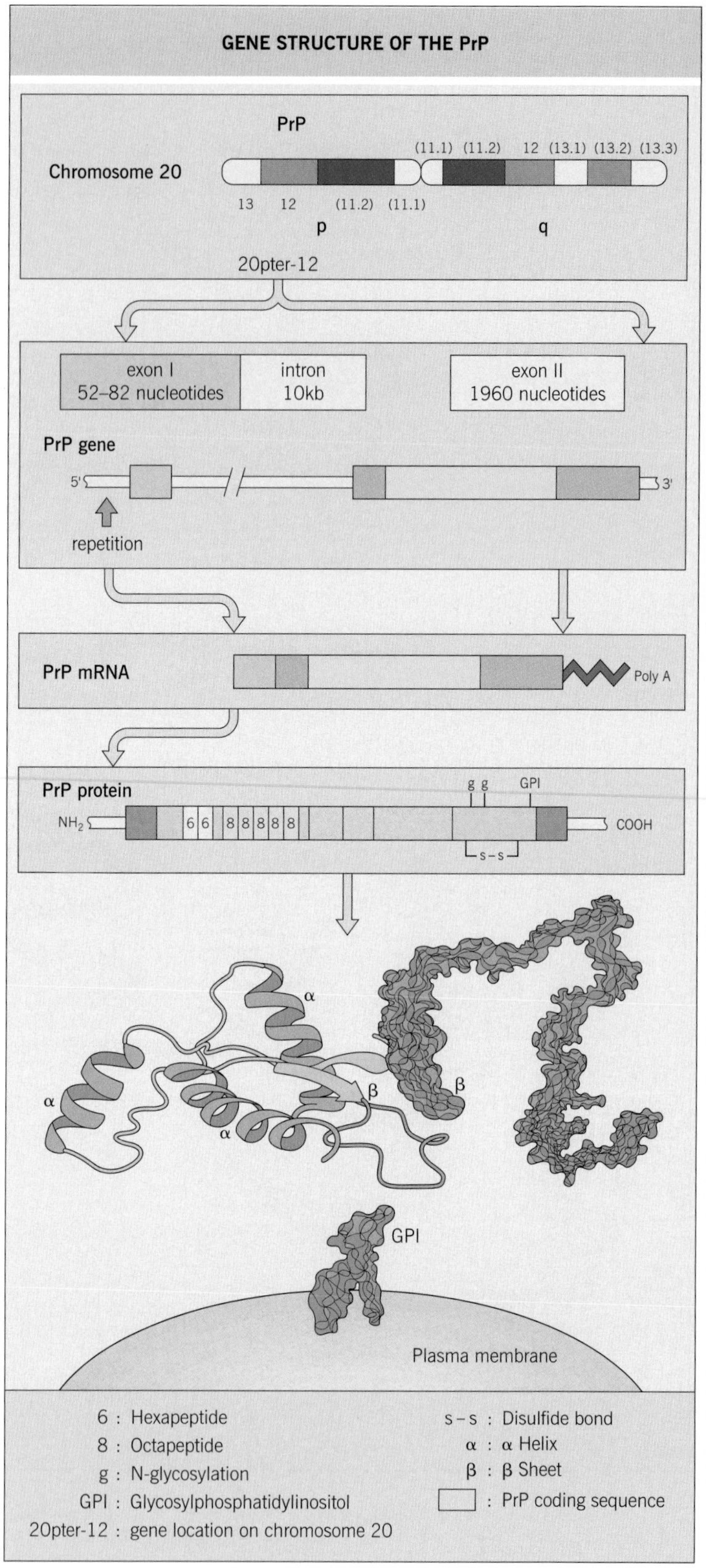

Fig. 223.4 Gene structure of the PrP.

Neuropathology

Neuropathology of TSEs consists of neuronal death, spongiosis and gliosis with hyperastrocytosis. The precise mechanisms that lead to brain cell damage are not known. Nevertheless, several experi-

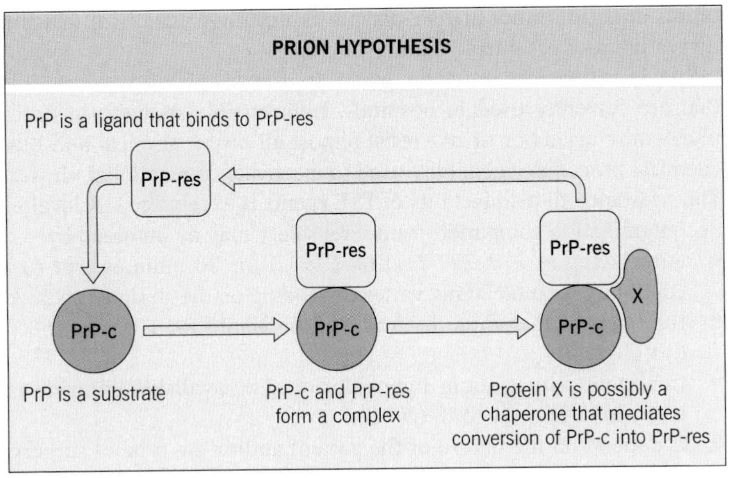
PRION HYPOTHESIS
PrP is a ligand that binds to PrP-res
PrP-res
PrP-res
PrP-res
X
PrP-c
PrP-c
PrP-c
PrP is a substrate
PrP-c and PrP-res form a complex
Protein X is possibly a chaperone that mediates conversion of PrP-c into PrP-res

Fig. 223.5 Prion hypothesis. With permission from SB Prusiner, 1996.

WORLD HEALTH ORGANIZATION CLASSIFICATION OF RISK ASSOCIATED WITH SCRAPIE

Category	Infectivity	Tissue/body fluid
I	High	CNS (brain, spinal cord)
II	Medium	Spleen, tonsil, lymph nodes, ileum, proximal colon, placenta
IIIa	Some	Sciatic nerve, pituitary, adrenal, distal colon, nasal mucosa
IIIb	Minimal	CSF, thymus, bone marrow, liver, lung, pancreas, white blood cells
IV	None detectable	Skeletal muscle, heart, mammary gland, colostrum, milk, blood clot, feces, kidney, thyroid, salivary gland, ovary, uterus, testis, seminal vesicle

Table 223.1 World Health Organization classification of risk associated with scrapie. (Blood might be in category IIb).

mental results indicate that neuronal death can occur in two ways: by accumulation of PrP^{SC} in vacuoles that fuse and induce cell death through a toxic mechanism; and by apoptosis of noninfected neurons induced by PrP. Indeed, exposure of primary neuronal cell cultures to peptides derived from the 106–126 domain of the PrP molecule induces apoptosis.[29] This apoptosis requires the presence of microglial cells and the presence of PrP^{C} at the cell surface; apoptotic pathway requires NMDA receptor activation. Microglial cells exposed to PrP 106–126 or to PrP^{SC} secrete interleukin(IL)-1β, IL-6 and other neurotoxic mediators that could participate in neuronal death observed during TSEs. On the other hand, exposure of primary astrocyte cell culture to PrP^{SC} in liposomes induces astrocyte activation and hyperexpression of the glial fibrillary acidic protein (GFAP) gene, which is a biochemical hallmark of natural and experimental TSE (unpublished data). Thus, molecular pathogenesis of brain damage can be summarized as follows (Fig. 223.6).

- PrP^{C} transconformation occurs through direct contact with PrP^{SC}.
- Because of its resistance to proteolysis, PrP^{SC} accumulates in the cytoplasm of infected cells.
- Neuronal death is induced by PrP^{SC} accumulation and PrP^{sc} is released into the extracellular compartment.
- Contact with PrP^{SC} induces either apoptosis of noninfected neurons or infection.
- Contact with PrP^{SC} induces microglial cell activation and release of neurotoxic metabolites.
- Exposure of astrocytes to PrP^{SC} induces activation and hyperexpression of GFAP characteristic of gliosis.

PREVENTION

Several iatrogenic contaminations (Table 223.2) have been reported in the literature.[30] All of them have implicated the CNS as the ‘donor tissue’ of prions. They have occurred mainly after treatment with extracted pituitary hormones (growth hormone, gonadotropins), dura mater transplantation and the use of surgical instruments contaminated with prions. In several of these cases, transmission has been precisely documented.

In medical practice TSE-associated risk may be, theoretically, at different levels:

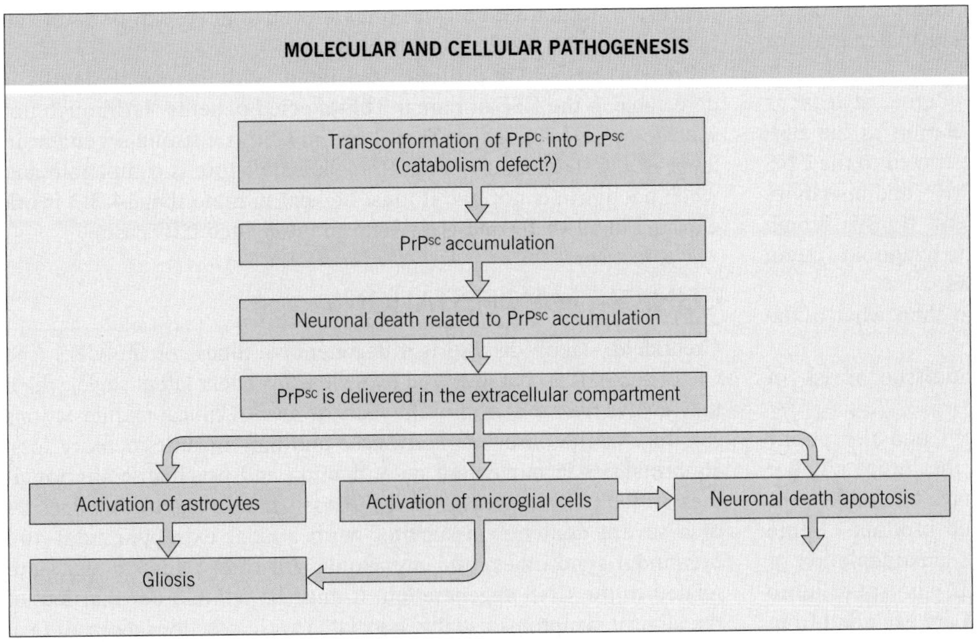
MOLECULAR AND CELLULAR PATHOGENESIS
Transconformation of PrPc into PrPsc (catabolism defect?)
PrPsc accumulation
Neuronal death related to PrPsc accumulation
PrPsc is delivered in the extracellular compartment
Activation of astrocytes
Activation of microglial cells
Neuronal death apoptosis
Gliosis

Fig. 223.6 Molecular and cellular pathogenesis.

IATROGENIC CONTAMINATIONS WITH CJD AGENT			
Mode of infection	Number of patients	Route of entry into brain	Mean incubation period
Instruments			
Neurosurgery	4	Intracerebral	20 months
Stereotactic EEG	2	Intracerebral	18 months
Tissue transfer			
Corneal transplant	2 (+1?)	Optic nerve	18 months
Dura mater implant	115	Cerebral surface	33 months
Tympanic transplant	1	Auditory nerve	48 months
Tissue extract transfer			
Growth hormone	>120	Peripheral	15 years
Gonadotropin	5	Peripheral	13 years

Table 223.2 Iatrogenic contaminations with Creutzfeldt–Jakob disease agent.

- tissue grafting, including blood transfusion;
- products used in therapy that are extracted from humans, sheep or cattle, including products derived from human blood (drugs and medical devices); and
- hospital sterilization.

The appearance of vCJD in the UK and its possible link with the BSE agent also raises the risk of human contamination by the BSE prion through food or the use of bovine-derived products that are utilized in medicine.

The existence of TSEs has a number of consequences for safety in the use of biologic products in therapy. Such products must be evaluated for the potential risk of transmission of TSE agents; safety will depend on the screening of the donor or the animal source, the purification process (which may include several steps that can inactivate or eliminate TSE agents), the dose and the administration route of the final product (the intracerebral route being the most risky), and the indication for which the product is used. The replacement of biologic products with synthetic/recombinant molecules is desirable whenever possible. For biologic and synthetic molecules a precise evaluation of the therapeutic risk/benefit ratio should be performed.

Patient who have subacute encephalopathy should not be considered as graft or blood donors. Patients belonging to families with cases of familial CJD, GSS or FFI should also be excluded. Finally, it is strongly recommended that individuals with a medical history of treatment with pituitary-derived hormones or dura mater graft be excluded from blood and organ or tissue donation.

Risk associated with vCJD must also be considered, at least in countries in which exposure of the human population to the BSE agent is highly suspected. Although infectivity is restricted to the CNS and retina in classic CJD (sporadic and familial), PrP^{SC} and infectivity can be detected in lymphoid organs of vCJD patients (tonsils, lymph nodes, appendix) in all cases. This implication of the lymphoid system raises several questions, two of which are as follows.

- Are there infectious particles in blood? If so then what is the infectious load?
- Is any surgery involving contact with lymphoid tissue 'at risk' of prion transmission?

These problems are under evaluation at present and the public health consequences of vCJD will depend upon the future number of cases. Nevertheless, precautionary measures have been taken for blood transfusion and the use of plasma-derived products. Some European countries have introduced a systematic leukodepletion of blood donations; in several countries, individuals who spent more than 6 months in the UK between 1980 and 1996 are excluded from blood donation, and British plasma is no longer used for plasma derivative product purification.

Special attention must be given to the sterilization protocols that are currently used in hospitals. Transmissible spongiform encephalopathy agents or prions resist almost all of the physical and biochemical procedures generally used to inactivate conventional viruses. The resistance to disinfectants of TSE agents is exceptional. A level of decontamination compatible with viral safety may be obtained by:

- autoclaving at 273–277°F (134–136°C) for 20 minutes, but susceptibility to autoclaving varies depending on the strain of agent;[20]
- treatment with sodium hydroxide 1 or 2mol/l for 1 hour at 68°F (20°C); and
- treatment with sodium hypochloride (2% available chlorine at least) for 1 hour at 68°F (20°C).

Risks depend on the nature of the patient and/or the type of surgery. High-risk patients include CJD patients, all neurosurgical patients, patients who have a history of treatment with pituitary-extracted hormone and patients from families with documented familial CJD. High-risk procedures include neurosurgery and ophthalmology and otorhinolaryngology surgery. In all these cases (high-risk patients and/or high-risk surgery) decontamination should include at least one of the procedures recommended by World Health Organization.[23] Several countries in Europe stipulate that two of these procedures be applied consecutively. Of course, the definition of 'high-risk patients' may evolve depending upon the spread of vCJD in the human population.

DIAGNOSTIC MICROBIOLOGY

Because the nature of the TSE agent is unknown and because of the lack of a detectable immune response to infection, there is as yet no routine test that permits the diagnosis of infection in asymptomatic individuals or in patients with subacute encephalopathies. Therefore, diagnosis of TSE is most often post mortem. Neuropathology, immunohistochemistry of PrP-res accumulation in the brain and Western blot detection of proteinase K-resistant PrP (see Fig. 223.1) are the most common diagnostic tests that can be used in medical practice. Electron microscopy detection of SAF can also be used for diagnosis. Transmissibility to primates or to rodents can be helpful, but it requires a high level of safety in animal care facilities; moreover, incubation times during primary interspecies passages are often very long.

It is worth noting that neuropathology can be very discrete and that PrP^{SC} accumulation can be undetectable in several parts of the brain; a negative result is inconclusive.

Protein 14-3-3, a protein associated with neuronal death, is detectable in the CSF of human TSE-affected patients.[31] Although not specific of CJD, a positive 14-3-3 test in CSF is a strong argument in favor of a CJD diagnosis when the clinical picture is compatible and when neopterin is normal. It must be kept in mind that 14-3-3 is not elevated in all vCJD and growth hormone-related CJD cases.

CLINICAL MANIFESTATIONS

Creutzfeldt–Jakob disease is a degenerative illness of the CNS (see Chapter 26). It is characterized by a clinically silent latent stage, which may evolve over a period of 20 years or more. Clinical manifestations can vary at the onset of the disease and may include memory loss, abnormalities in movement co-ordination and psychiatric abnormalities. At the full-blown stage of the disease, the clinical picture consists of a severe dementia associated with ataxia, extrapyramidal and pyramidal syndromes, and myoclonia. All of the clinical signs are related to the CNS degeneration. It must be pointed out that few of the clinical symptoms usually associated with infectious diseases (e.g.

fever) are observed in CJD patients. Routine serological testing and nuclear magnetic resonance imaging (except for vCJD) are of little assistance; for example, there are no abnormalities in blood or CSF chemistry or cell populations, except for the frequent detection of neuron-specific enolase and protein 14-3-3 in the CSF. Conversely, the electroencephalogram exhibits pseudoperiodic abnormalities that are constituted by 1–1.5Hz triphasic sharp waves in all derivations in 75% of patients. The evolution of the disease is subacute and always fatal; patients die after a short period of coma. Creutzfeldt–Jakob disease lasts an average of 6 months in adults, but may reach more than 1 year in infants or young adults with iatrogenic disease or with CJD.

MANAGEMENT

No curative or palliative treatment for CJD or other TSEs currently exists. Only a few drugs have proved relatively effective when administered at the time of the experimental infection; they are Congo red, dextran sulfate, polyoxometalates from the tungstoantimoniate family, and amphothericin B and its derivatives.[32,33] Polyene antibiotics seem the most promising class of drugs that may be suitable for therapy; in experimental scrapie, positive effects on survival are correlated with PrP-res accumulation delay in the brain. This underlines the key role of PrP in the pathogenesis of TSEs.

Unfortunately, none of these drugs are effective once the first clinical signs have appeared; therefore, no drug is suitable for human use.

Recently, treatment with anti-PrP antibodies has been reported as capable of curing infected cells in vitro.[34] Moreover, transgenic animals for anti-PrP antibody have been demonstrated to be less susceptible to peripheral infection than the wild-type controls.[35] This may be the proof of the principle of such a therapeutic approach and may support the possibility of a vaccine against TSEs in the future.

REFERENCES

1. Wells GAH, *et al.* A novel progressive spongiform encephalopathy in cattle. Vet Rec 1987;121:419–20.
2. Prusiner SB. Novel proteinaceous infectious particles cause scrapie. Science 1982;216:136–44.
3. Prusiner SB, *et al.* Sedimentation characteristics of the scrapie agent from murine spleen and brain. Biochemistry 1978;17:4987–92.
4. Prusiner SB, *et al.* Scrapie agent contains a hydrophobic protein. Proc Natl Acad Sci USA 1981;78:6675–9.
5. Oesch B, *et al.* A cellular gene encodes scrapie PrP 27–30 protein. Cell 1985;40:735–46.
6. Prusiner SB. Chemistry and biology of prions. Biochemistry 1992;31:12277–88.
7. Merz PA, *et al.* Abnormal fibrils from scrapie-infected brain. Acta Neuropathol 1981;54:63–74.
8. Parchi P, *et al.* Molecular basis of phenotypic variability in sporadic Creutzfeld–Jakob disease. Ann Neurol 1996;39:767–78.
9. Cohen FE, *et al.* Structural clues to prion replication. Science 1994;264(5158):530–1.
10. Riek R, *et al.* NMR structure of the mouse prion protin domain PrP (121–231). Nature 1996;382:180–2.
11. Riek R, *et al.* NMR characterization of the full-length recombinant murine prion protein mPrP(23-231). FEBS Lett 1997;413:282–88.
12. Zahn R, *et al.* NMR solution structure of the human prion protein. Proc Natl Acad Sci USA 2000;97:145–50.
13. Knaus KJ, *et al.* Crystal structure of the human prions protein reveals a mechanism for oligomerisation. Nat Struct Biol 2001;8:770–4.
14. Kocisko DA, *et al.* Species specificity in the cell-free conversion of prion protein to protease-resistant forms: a model for the scrapie species barrier. Proc Natl Acad Sci USA 1995;92:3923–7.
15. Kimberlin RH. Scrapie agent: prions or virinos? Nature 1982;297:107–8.
16. Telling GC, *et al.* Transmission of Creutzfeldt–Jakob disease from humans to transgenic mice expressing chimeric human-mouse prion protein. Proc Natl Acad Sci USA 1994;91:9936–40.
17. Liautard JP. Are prions misfolded molecular chaperones? FEBS Lett 1992;294:155–7.
18. Jarrett JT, Lansbury PT. Seeding one-dimensional crystallization of amyloid – a pathogenic mechanism in Alzheimer's disease and scrapie. Cell 1993;73:1055–8.
19. Alpérovitch A, *et al.* Incidence of Creutzfeld–Jakob disease in Europe in 1993. Lancet 1994;343:918.
20. Will RG, *et al.* A new variant of Creutzfeldt–Jakob disease in the UK. Lancet 1996;347:921–5.
21. Kimberlin RH, Walker CA. Pathogenesis of mouse scrapie: effect of route of inoculation on infectivity titres and dose-response curves. J Comp Pathol 1978;88:39–47.
22. Collinge J, *et al.* Inherited prion disease (PrP lysine-200) in Britain – two case reports. Br Med J 1993;306:301–2.
23. Report of a WHO consultation on public health issues related to animal and human spongiform encephalopathies. Geneva: WHO; 1991.
24. Gauczynski S, *et al.* The 37-kDa laminin receptor acts as the cell-surface receptor for the cellular prion protein. EMBO J 2001;20:5863–75.
25. Mouillet-Richard S, *et al.* Signal transduction through prion protein. Science 2000;289:1925–8.
26. Büeler H, *et al.* Mice devoid of PrP are resistant to scrapie. Cell 1993;73:1339–47.
27. Brandner S, *et al.* Normal host prion protein necessary for scrapie-induced neurotoxicity. Nature 1996;379:339–43.
28. Hsiao KH, *et al.* Serial transmission in rodents of neurodegeneration from transgenic mice expressiong mutant prion. Proc Natl Acad Sci USA 1994;91:9126–30.
29. Forloni G, *et al.* Neurotoxicity of a prion protein fragment. Nature 1993;362:543–6.
30. Brown P, Preece MA, Will RG. Friendly fire in medicine – hormones, homografts, and Creutzfeldt–Jakob disease. Lancet 1992;340:24–7.
31. Hsich G, *et al.* The 14-3-3 brain protein in cerebrospinal fluid as a marker for transmissible spongiform encephalopathies. N Engl J Med 1996;335:924–30.
32. Kimberlin RH, Walker CA. Suppression of scrapie infection in mice by hetero-polyanion 23, dextran sulfate, and some other polyanions. Antimicrob Agents Chemother 1986;30:409–13.
33. Demaimay R, *et al.* Pharmacological studies of a new derivative of amphotericin-B, MS-8209, in mouse and hamster scrapie. J Gen Virol 1994;75:2499–503.
34. Enari E, Flechsig E, Weissmann C. Scrapie prion protein accumulation by scrapie-infected neuroblastoma cells abrogated by exposure to a prion protein antibody. Proc Natl Acad Sci USA 2001;98:9295–9.
35. Heppner FL, *et al.* Prevention of scrapie pathogenesis by transgenic expression of anti-prion protein antibodies. Science 2001;294:178–82.

chapter

224 Staphylococci and Other Micrococcaceae

Jan Verhoef, Ad C Fluit & Franz-Josef Schmitz

NATURE

Staphylococci were first observed and cultured by Pasteur and Koch but the first thorough studies on staphylococci were made by Ogston in 1881[1] and Rosenbach in 1884.[2]

The genus *Staphylococcus* was given its name by Ogston in 1881 when he observed grape-like clusters of bacteria in pus from human abscesses.[1] Three years later, Rosenbach[2] was able to isolate and grow these micro-organisms in pure culture. He gave them the specific epithet *Staphylococcus aureus* Rosenbach because of the yellow-to-orange pigmented appearance of their colonies.[2] Rosenbach showed that *S. aureus* was responsible for wound infections and furunculosis, and that *Staphylococcus epidermidis* was a normal colonizer of the skin. Ever since Rosenbach first described the growth of this 'golden' coccus, surgeons have feared staphylococcal wound infections after surgery.[3] Staphylococci also caused life-threatening disease after trauma and fatal pneumonia during the influenza season, killing young people in the prime of their lives.[4] Therefore, in the pre-antibiotic era, *S. aureus* was known as a major life-threatening pathogen.

Because of penicillin's important contribution to the fight against *S. aureus* disease, the period between 1946 and 1950 was referred to as 'a golden age' for the treatment of staphylococcal disease. However, the rapid spread of resistant staphylococci soon led to a return of this major pathogen.

An excellent up-to-date review on staphylococci is provided by Crossley and Archer.[5]

Taxonomy

The family of Micrococcaceae consists of four genera:

- *Planococcus*;
- *Stomatococcus*;
- *Micrococcus*; and
- *Staphylococcus*.[6]

Planococci are not found in humans, whereas *Stomatococcus* and *Micrococcus* can colonize humans but rarely produce disease.

Staphylococci are Gram-positive nonmobile cocci that characteristically divide in different patterns to form irregular grape-like clusters (Fig. 224.1). They usually produce catalase. They are facultative anaerobes but grow better under aerobic than under anaerobic conditions. Traditionally, they have been divided into coagulase-positive and coagulase-negative staphylococci. The coagulase-negative staphylococci can be subdivided at present into 32 different species (Fig. 224.2). Of the large number of staphylococci, only three are commonly associated with human disease:

- *S. aureus*;
- *S. epidermidis*; and
- *Staphylococcus saprophyticus*.

In addition, *Staphylococcus lugdunensis* and *Staphylococcus schleiferi* must be mentioned since these two species are relatively aggressive and can cause a variety of infections, including foreign body infections, bacteremia, endocarditis, bone infections and abscesses in various organs.

At the genus level staphylococci are a homogenous group of bacteria. On the basis of DNA rRNA hybridization and comparative oligonucleotide analysis of 16S rRNA they appear to be related to the *Bacillus*, *Enterococcus* and *Listeria* cluster (Fig. 224.3).

The micrococci and stomatococci are more related to *Actinomycetes*, although their cytosine–guanine rates vary from 30% to 70%.

Anatomy of the staphylococcus

Capsular polysaccharides

Staphylococci are often surrounded by a loose-fitting polysaccharide capsule. This capsule can be used to identify serotypes. Serotypes 5 and 8 are the most common and many methicillin-resistant *S. aureus* (MRSA) belong to these serotypes.[7]

When isolated from infections, *S. aureus* expresses high levels of polysaccharide but rapidly loses it upon subculture in the laboratory. The function of the capsule is not clear. It may impede phagocytosis (see below) and may therefore contribute to the invasive character of *S. aureus*.

Peptidoglycan

The peptidoglycan layer is the major macromolecule present in the cell wall (Fig. 224.4). The glycan chains are built with approximately 10 alternating subunits of *N*-acetylmuramic acid and *N*-acetylglycosamine. Pentapeptide side chains are attached to the *N*-acetylmuramic acid subunits. The glycan chains are then cross-linked with peptide bridges between the side chains.

Protein A

The surface of all strains of *S. aureus* contains proteins that protrude through the peptidoglycan layer and are anchored covalently. One of these proteins, protein A (Fig. 224.5), has the capacity to bind the Fc fragment of immunoglobulin subclasses IgG1, IgG2 and IgG4.[8] Protein A is not produced by coagulase-negative staphylococci.

Teichoic acid

The teichoic acids are macromolecules of phosphate containing polysaccharides (Fig. 224.6). Teichoic acid is bound both to the peptidoglycan layer and to the cytoplasmic membrane. The polysaccharides are species specific; ribitol teichoic acids are present in *S. aureus* cell walls and glycerol teichoic acids are present in *S. epidermidis*.[9]

EPIDEMIOLOGY

Every human being is colonized with *S. epidermidis*. The normal habitats of these staphylococci are the skin and the mucous membranes. The major habitats of the most pathogenic species, *S. aureus*, are the anterior nares and perineum.

Neonates are readily colonized by *S. epidermidis* and often by *S. aureus*. Newborn infants usually acquire *S. aureus* first on the skin (umbilical area) and later in the nose.[10,11] Soon after the neonatal period some individuals become permanent carriers, often with the

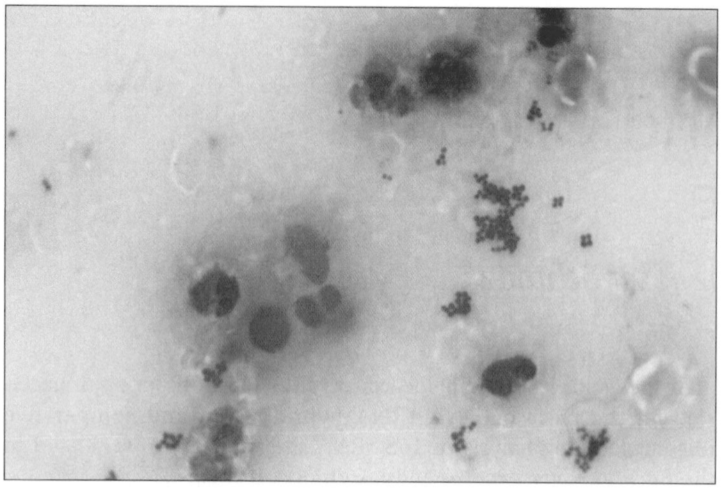

Fig. 224.1 *Staphylococcus aureus* in a Gram stain of pus.

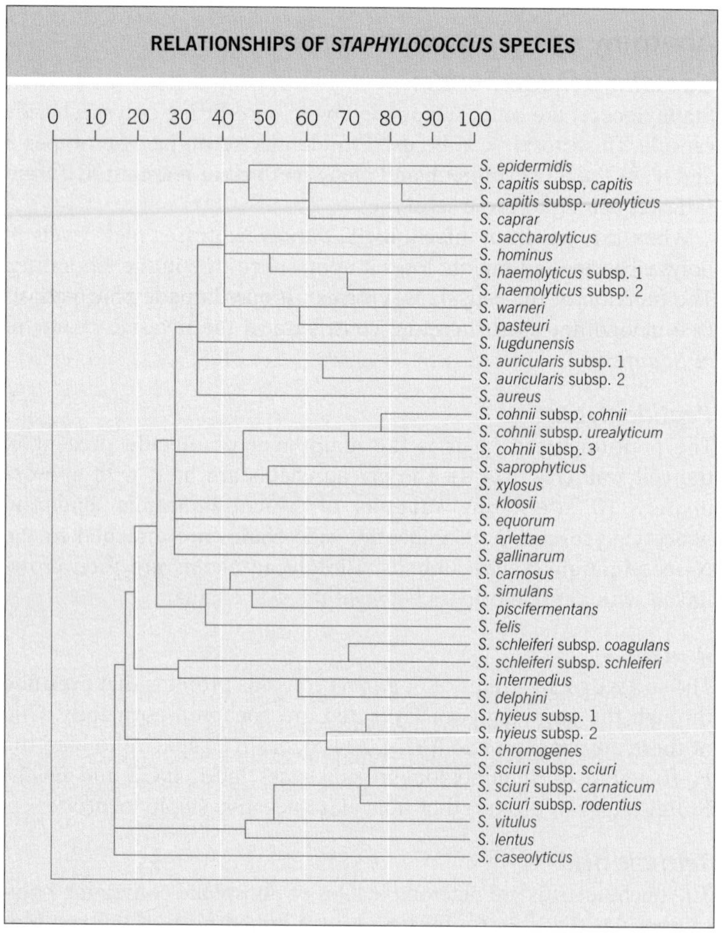

Fig. 224.2 Relationship of *Staphylococcus* species. Dendrogram of the DNA relationships of *Staphylococcus* spp. and subspecies based on the relative percentage of DNA–DNA hybridization (reassociation) at optimal conditions. Adapted with permission from Crossley and Archer.[5]

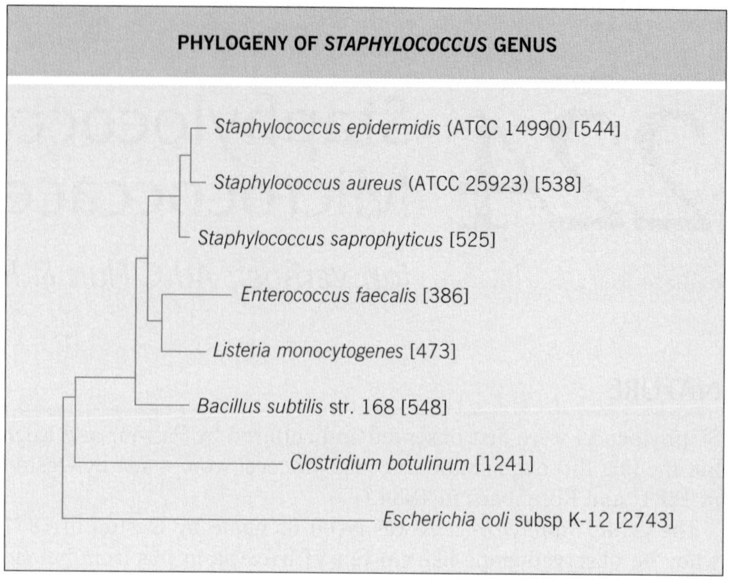

Fig. 224.3 Phylogeny of *Staphylococcus* genus based on 16S rRNA sequences. Adapted with permission from Crossley and Archer.[5]

same strain. Although some spread of *S. aureus* may occur within a family, generally the established flora of the nose prevents the acquisition of new strains.[12] However, colonization with other strains may occur when antibiotic treatment is given that leads to elimination of the susceptible carrier strain. Because this situation occurs in hospital, patients may become colonized with resistant staphylococci. Carriage rates of *S. aureus* in the nares of people outside hospital varies from 10% to 40%. Hospital patients and personnel have higher carriage rates. The carriage rates of patients may increase during their stay in hospital through colonization and nosocomial transmission. The rates are especially high in patients undergoing hemodialysis and in diabetics, drug addicts and patients who have a variety of dermatologic conditions.[13,14]

The carrier state is clinically relevant because carriers undergoing surgery have more infections than noncarriers. This has led to the application of mupirocin (a local antibiotic) to the anterior nares in some centers just before open heart surgery to lower the incidence of postoperative wound infection.[15] Dispersers among the carriers are important because dispersers transmit staphylococci not only by direct contact but also by airborne transmission. Heavy perineal carriers almost always disperse large amounts of staphylococci. Staphylococci may accumulate rapidly on the clothes and bedding of dispersers and may disseminate when these fomites are disturbed. Dust particles containing staphylococci may be carried for considerable distances.

Since 1944, an increasing proportion of hospital-acquired *S. aureus* strains have developed resistance to penicillin because of their ability to produce β-lactamase. By 1950, approximately 80% of hospital-acquired infections were caused by these penicillinase producers.[16] In the mid-1950s, penicillin-resistant *S. aureus* of a new phage type (the so-called phage type 80, see below) was first detected in Australia and then spread rapidly, causing a major pandemic of hospital-acquired infections.[17] Because of the 'resistance advantages' of the new *S. aureus* strain, referred to as 'hospital staph', there were again outbreaks on hospital wards. In 1959, the British Ministry of Health published guidelines for the prevention of further spread of the multiresistant – penicillin–streptomycin–tetracycline–erythromycin (PSTE)-resistant – *S. aureus* strains.[18]

A temporary respite in the war against resistant *S. aureus* occurred in the early 1960s, when Rolinson and Stevens discovered a β-lactamase-stable penicillin (methicillin).[19] In the following years the introduction of the semisynthetic penicillins (methicillin, oxacillin, flucloxacillin) and the application of infection control measures probably contributed to the spontaneous decrease in the epidemic spread of *S. aureus* strains. However, coinciding with the disappearance of PSTE strains was the appearance of MRSA.

Early MRSA epidemics were reported in the UK in the early 1960s.[20] Later, two surveillance studies conducted by the Cross Infection Reference Laboratory in London showed that the frequency of methicillin resistance in clinical isolates from London hospitals and

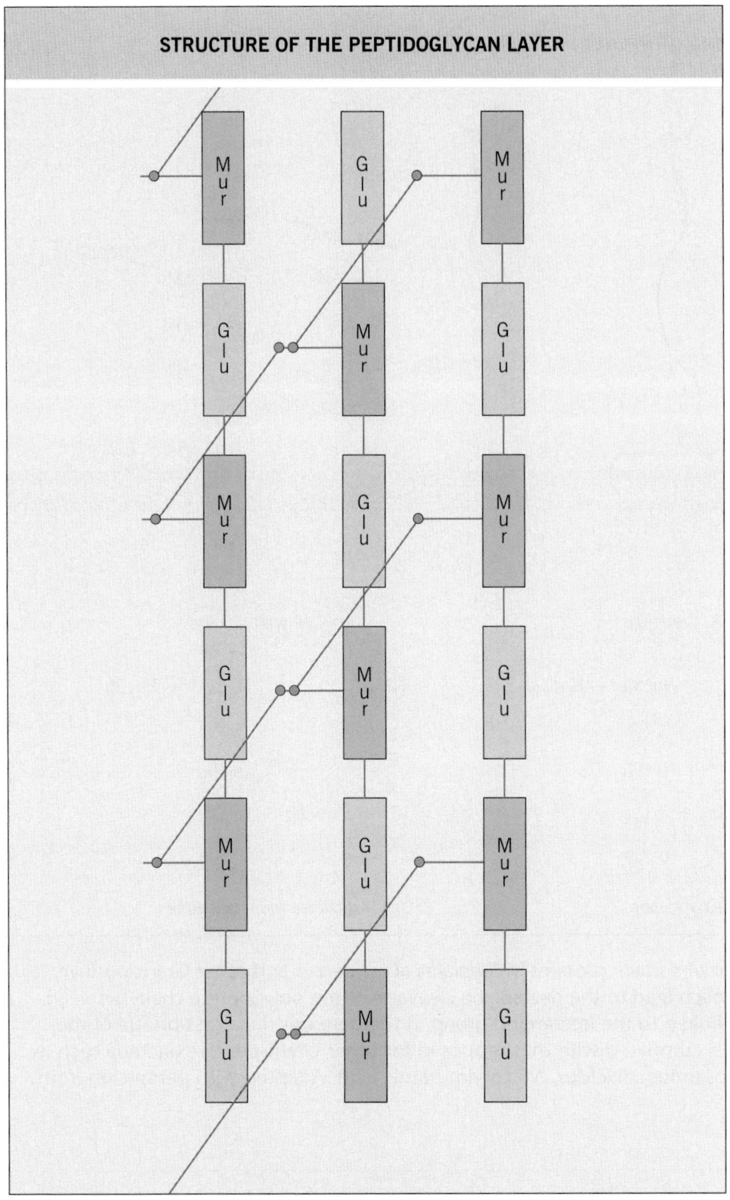

Fig. 224.4 Structure of the peptidoglycan layer. The peptidoglycan layer consists of three integral parts. The glycan chains are built with 10–12 alternating *N*-acetylglucosamine (Glu) and *N*-acetylmuramic acid (Mur) subunits jointed with β-1,4 glycosidic bonds. Vertical pentapeptide side chains are linked to the muramic acids subunits, and the side chains are in turn cross-linked with diagonal intrapeptide bridges. For example, the glycan chains in *Staphylococcus aureus* are cross-linked with pentaglycine bridges attached to L-glycine in one pentapeptide chain and D-alanine in an adjacent chain.

from hospitals in south east England increased until 1963, when it was followed by a stationary phase (below or around 1%) until 1968.[21] The rate of methicillin resistance rose sharply in the period 1968–69 (up to 5%). After another decline in major MRSA epidemics, the first serious hospital outbreaks were reported in 1970. The early MRSA epidemics could be controlled by aminoglycosides. In the late 1970s, however, resistance to gentamicin emerged in *S. aureus* and led to a new wave of hospital outbreaks.[22] Since then the MRSA strains have spread all over the world,[23] not only in hospitals but also in the community.[24] In the USA, the percentage of MRSA in all hospitals in the National Nosocomial Infection Survey system increased from 2.4% in 1975 to 29% in 1991. The incidence varied according to hospital bed capacity, with hospitals of less than 200 beds reporting 14.9% of *S. aureus* isolates as MRSA, and hospitals of 500 beds reporting a 38.3% frequency.[25] Meanwhile, the incidence has increased to nearly 40% MRSA in the USA and 6% in Canada. Within European countries a systematic survey of 27 laboratories documented a wide variation in incidence ranging from less than 1% in northern European countries to over 30–50% in Spain, France and Italy.[26]

Patients at highest risk for MRSA infection are:

- those in large tertiary-care hospitals, particularly the elderly and immunocompromised;
- those in intensive care units;
- burns patients;
- those who have surgical wounds; and
- patients who have intravenous lines.

Duration of hospitalization, previous antibiotic treatment and proximity to a patient colonized or infected with the organism also predispose to MRSA infection. In acute care and nursing facilities, colonized and infected patients are the major MRSA reservoir. Person-to-person transmission of MRSA usually occurs via the hands of health care workers.[14]

Typing of staphylococcal isolates

Nosocomial infections caused by *S. aureus*, especially by MRSA, are an increasing problem in hospitals. Quick and reliable typing methods are required to obtain information about the relatedness of individual *S. aureus* isolates in order to implement hygienic measures faster and more effectively. The epidemiologic goal of bacterial typing is to accurately identify the source, extent and mechanisms of transmission of outbreaks of infection. Investigations are typically triggered by an increase in the prevalence of *S. aureus* infection or by noting the appearance of isolates with a distinctive antibiotic susceptibility pattern. A convenient basis for classifying typing methods is to divide them into:

- phenotypic techniques – those that detect characteristics expressed by the micro-organisms, such as biotyping, antimicrobial susceptibilities, serotyping, bacteriophage typing, immunoblotting and multilocus enzyme electrophoresis; and
- genotypic techniques – those that involve direct DNA-based analyses of chromosomal or extrachromosomal genetic elements, such as plasmid restriction digests, ribotyping, Southern blot analysis, pulsed-field gel electrophoresis (PFGE) and polymerase chain reaction (PCR)-based methods.[27]

Bacteriophage typing (Fig. 224.7) has played an important role in the study of many epidemics of *S. aureus* infection.

The temperate bacteriophages of *S. aureus* have a narrow host range, lysing only some strains of the same species, and are therefore useful as typing phages. When phage typing became widespread, it became clear that some phage types were more endemic than others.[28]

Also, molecular typing methods are now being introduced into the study of *S. epidermidis* and *S. aureus*, particularly MRSA. Plasmid analysis has been used extensively with success but it has the disadvantage that plasmids can easily be lost and acquired and are therefore inherently unreliable. Methods designed to recognize restriction fragment length polymorphisms (RFLP) using a variety of gene probes, including rRNA genes (ribotyping), have had limited success in the epidemiology of MRSA. In this technique the choice of both the restriction enzyme used to cleave the genomic DNA and the probes is crucial.

Although there is no definitive typing technique for staphylococci, the preponderance of data indicate that PFGE is currently the single most useful and reliable reference method. This technique, in which genomic DNA is cut with a restriction enzyme that generates large fragments of 50–700kb,[29] is a variation of agarose gel electrophoresis because the orientation of the electric field across the gel is changed periodically. This change of orientation in the electric field enables DNA fragments as large as several megabases to be separated effectively by size. The restriction profiles often demonstrate remarkable

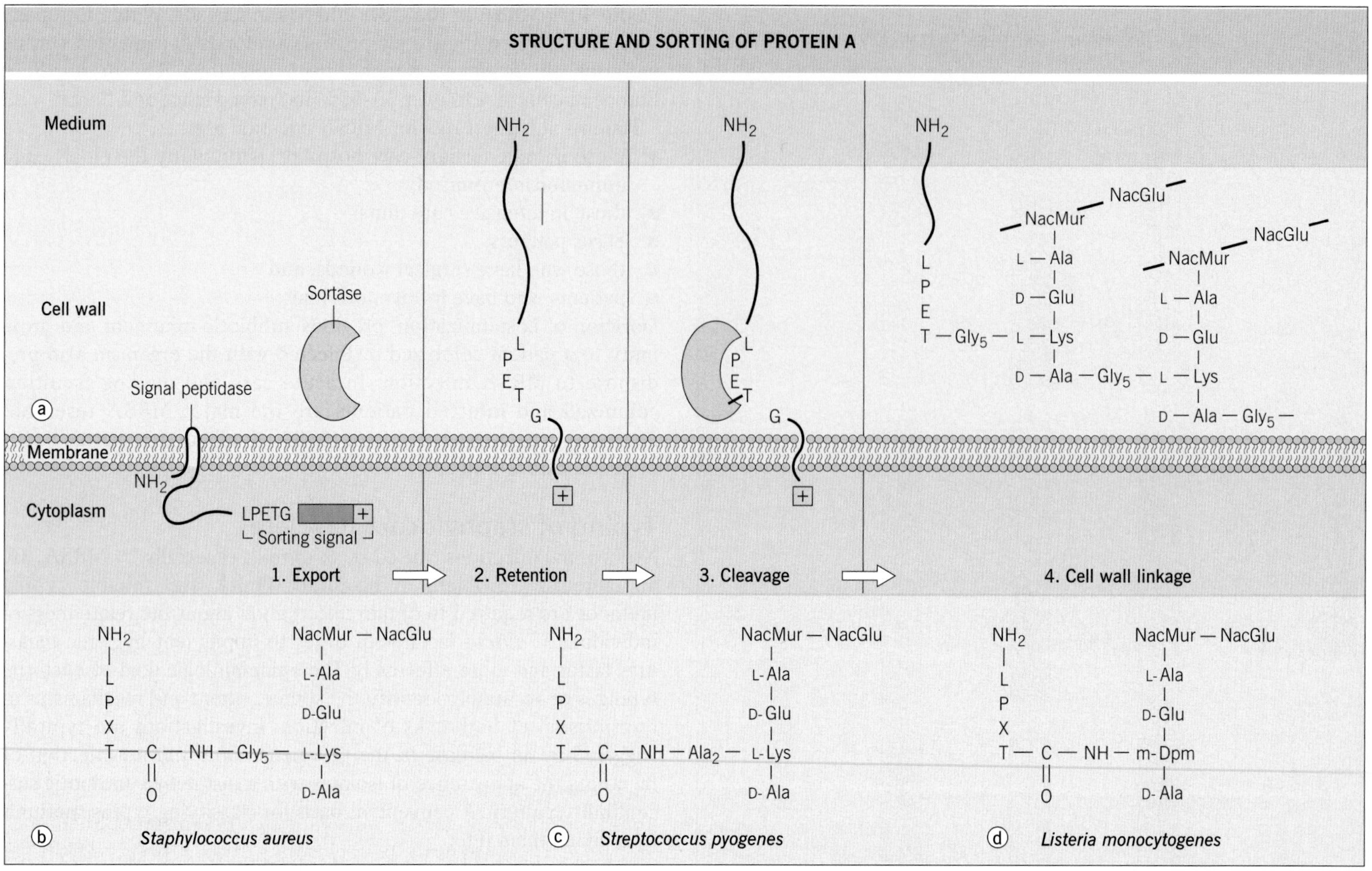

Fig. 224.5 Structure and sorting of protein A. Structure of the cell wall anchor of surface proteins in *Staphylococcus aureus* and other Gram-positive bacteria. (a) Cell wall sorting of surface proteins consists of four distinct steps, which lead to the proteolytic cleavage of the polypeptide chain between threonine (T) and glycine (G). The carboxyl of threonine is subsequently amide-linked to the free amino group in the pentaglycine cross-bridge of the staphylococcal cell wall. The cell wall linkage of surface proteins in *S. aureus* (b) is compared with that proposed for other Gram-positive bacteria such as *Streptococcus pyogenes* (c) and *Listeria monocytogenes* (d). NacGlu, *N*-acetylglucosamine; NacMur, *N*-acetylmuramic acid. Adapted with permission from Crossley and Archer.[5]

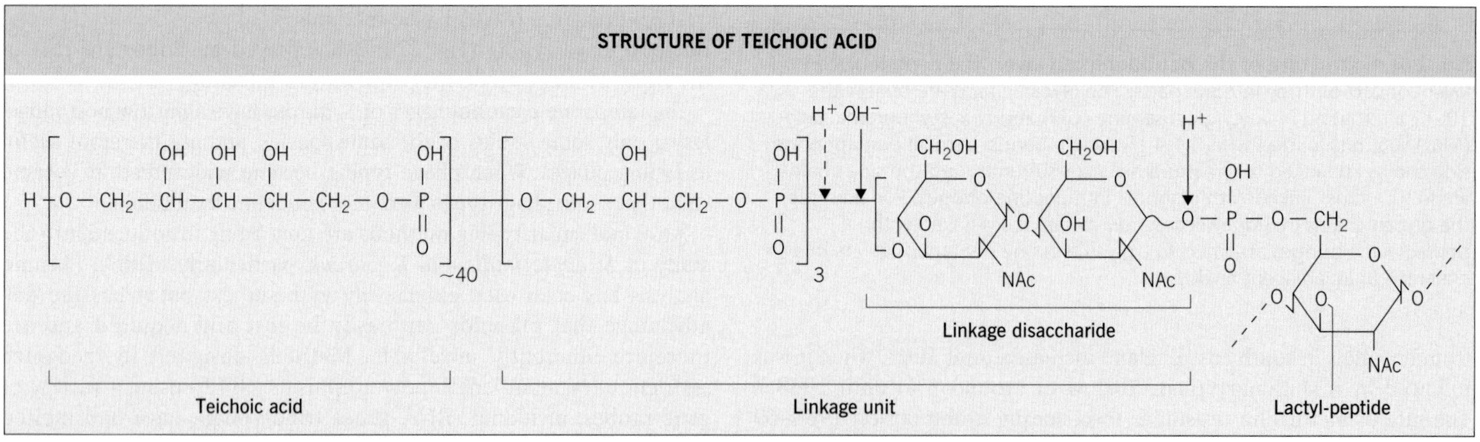

Fig. 224.6 Structure of teichoic acid and linkage unit attaching teichoic acid to peptidoglycan in *Staphylococcus aureus*. The C2 and C4 positions of the ribitol residues are substituted by D-alanyl and *N*-acetylglucosamine residues. Adapted with permission from Crossley and Archer.[5]

variation among different strains, greatly facilitating the analysis and comparison of multiple isolates.

The most obvious 'challengers' to PFGE as the current standard for typing staphylococci are systems based on the PCR. The essential feature of PCR is the ability to replicate a particular DNA sequence rapidly and exponentially. Several different approaches have been proposed (i.e. restriction digestion of PCR products, PCR based on repetitive chromosomal sequences, arbitrarily primed PCR).

The application of molecular techniques to staphylococcal typing has provided a powerful set of new tools that can facilitate both epidemiologic investigations and patient management.[27]

Coagulase-negative staphylococci

The high prevalence of coagulase-negative staphylococci on the skin and the frequent implantation of foreign devices during hospitalization provide these bacteria with an ideal opportunity to cause infec-

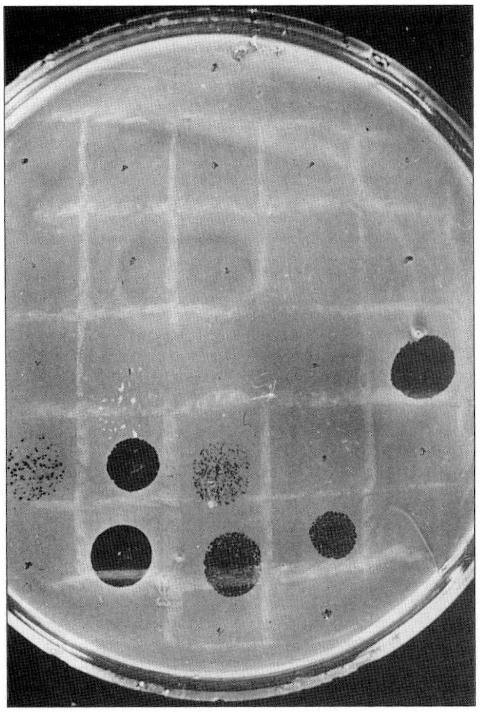

Fig. 224.7 Phage type III of *Staphylococcus aureus*.

STAPHYLOCOCCAL VIRULENCE FACTORS		
Enzymes	**Toxins**	**Other**
Coagulase Catalase Hyaluronidase Fibrinolysin Lipase Nuclease Penicillinase	Cytotoxins (α, β, δ, γ leukocidin) Exfoliative (epidermolytic) toxin Toxic shock syndrome Enterotoxin (A–F)	Slime production Capsule Cell wall

Table 224.1 Staphylococcal virulence factors. Overview of enzymatic, toxic and other staphylococcal virulence factors that may participate in the etiology of staphylococcal disease. Several enzymes and toxins are known to play a role in the pathogenesis of staphylococcal infection. Adapted from Kuroda *et al.*[33]

tions. Common characteristics of coagulase-negative staphylococci infections are as follows.

- They are usually nosocomial.
- *S. epidermidis* is the most common species involved.
- They are associated with implanted foreign devices such as intravascular catheters, prosthetic heart valves or cerebrospinal fluid shunts.

Evaluation of the hospital reservoir of coagulase-negative staphylococci remains problematic because these bacteria form part of the normal skin flora. Although several typing systems have helped to elucidate their epidemiology,[30] evaluate their transmission and define outbreaks of nosocomial infection, little is known about the hospital reservoir of coagulase-negative staphylococci, including that of methicillin-resistant strains (MR coagulase-negative staphylococci). Such strains also serve as a reservoir for antibiotic resistance genes that may be transferred to other Gram-positive organisms, including strains of *S. aureus*. The National Nosocomial Infection Survey (NNIS) of the USA found that, between 1980 and 1989, the incidence of coagulase-negative staphylococci as a cause of nosocomial bacteremias increased from 9% to 27% to become the single most common cause of these infections. Furthermore, NNIS data revealed that during this period the proportion of MR coagulase-negative staphylococci increased from 20% to 60%. Data from the worldwide SENTRY study indicated that, independent of geographic origin, 70–75% of coagulase-negative staphylococci are nowadays resistant to methicillin. Most of these strains were also resistant to multiple additional antimicrobial agents.[26] There is therefore an association between the dramatic increase of coagulase-negative staphylococci as a cause of nosocomial infections and the resistance of these pathogens to antimicrobial agents.[31]

STAPHYLOCOCCUS AUREUS

PATHOGENICITY

The pathogenesis of *S. aureus* infections is determined by the interaction of *S. aureus* surface-associated and extracellular proteins with host cell determinants. The pathogenesis of staphylococci is multifactorial[32] and therefore it is difficult to determine precisely the role of each individual staphylococcal component in the etiology of staphylococcal disease (Table 224.1).

Adherence

In order to initiate infection, the pathogen must gain access to the host and attach to host cells or tissues (adherence). The *S. aureus* cells express surface proteins that promote attachment to host proteins such as laminin, fibronectin, elastin, vitronectin, fibrinogen and many other molecules that form part of the extracellular matrix. These surface proteins of *S. aureus* are called extracellular matrix binding proteins.[34]

The extracellular matrix molecules are present on epithelial and endothelial surfaces as well as being a component of blood clots. The receptor that promotes attachment to collagen is particularly associated with strains that cause osteomyelitis and septic arthritis.

Antibodies against a fusion protein encompassing α-galactosidase and the domains of fibronectin binding protein may be protective by blocking the binding of *S. aureus* to fibronectin, suggesting a possible therapeutic approach.[35]

Role of adherence in infections associated with medical devices

Staphylococcus aureus and *S. epidermidis* can cause infections associated with indwelling medical devices ranging from simple intravenous catheters to prosthetic joints and replacement heart valves. Soon after biomaterial is implanted in the human body it becomes coated with a complex mixture of host proteins and platelets (Fig. 224.8). Extracellular matrix binding proteins also play a role in the binding of *S. aureus* and *S. epidermidis* to biomaterials. Interbacterial adherence leads to biofilm formation. Recently, a polymer from *S. epidermidis* has been characterized that is involved in the intracellular adhesion between cells, leading to the formation of large cell clusters following the attachment of cells to a plastic surface during biofilm formation. The polymer, known as polysaccharide intracellular adhesin, is a linear homopolymer of β-1,6-linked glucosamine residues, 80–85% of which are *N*-acetylated.[36]

In addition, *S. aureus* can adhere to the surface of endothelial cells and become internalized by a phagocytosis-like process. It is not clear whether attachment involves a novel receptor or a known surface protein of *S. aureus*. Some researchers think that *S. aureus* can initiate endocarditis by attaching to the undamaged endothelium. Others believe that trauma, even if very minor, is required to promote attachment of bacteria.

Invasion

As soon as microbes invade the tissues, circulating polymorphonuclear leukocytes (PMNLs) are activated. They adhere to endothelial

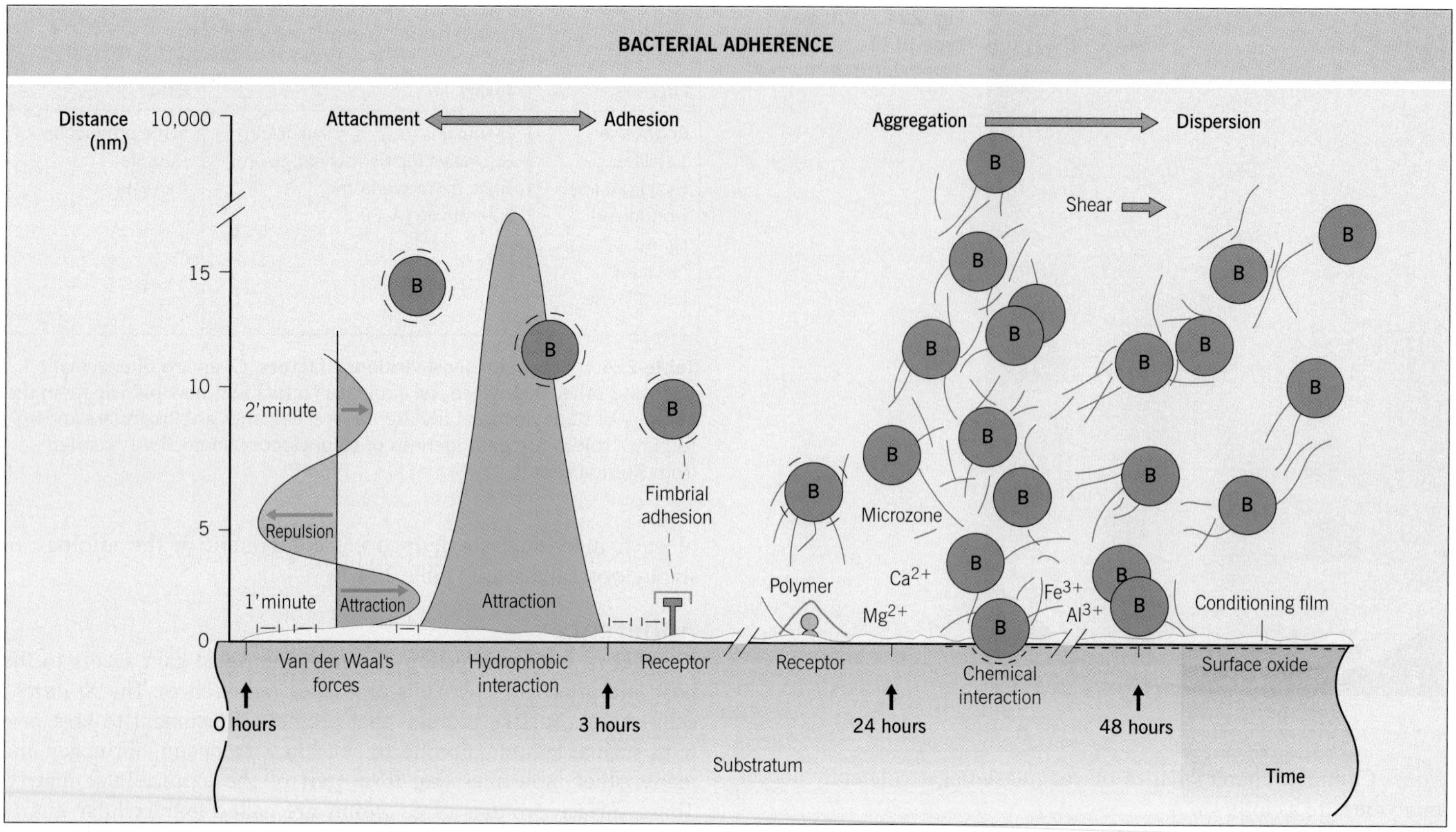

Fig. 224.8 Bacterial adherence. The figure illustrates the events associated with bacterial (B) adherence to a biomaterial in relation to time and the molecular sequence in bacterial attachment, adhesion, aggregation and dispersion at substratum surface. A number of possible interactions may occur depending on the specificities of the bacteria or substratum system, the distance from the biomaterial and the stage of adherence. The attachment stage is mediated by non-specific forces. Adhesion is driven by specific adhesin–receptor interactions. The final aggregative step results in a bacterial macrocolony on the biomaterial surface in which the bacteria are firmly adherent to the biomaterial and each other. Bacterial exopolysaccharide blankets the macrocolony and may serve to improve the nutritional microenvironment and protect the bacteria from host defenses. In the dispersion phase, bacteria disaggregate, break loose from the macrocolony and drift free into the bloodstream. Adapted with permission from Gristina AG. Biomaterial centered infection: microbial adhesion versus tissue integration. Science 1987;237:1588. © 1987 American Association for the Advancement of Science.

cells and move through the endothelial barrier (chemotaxis). While leukocyte migration occurs, the microbes are opsonized and the microbial surface is coated with antibodies and complement factors for recognition by PMNLs.[37]

Encapsulated *S. aureus* is much more difficult to opsonize than unencapsulated strains. Four mechanisms of opsonization of unencapsulated *S. aureus* strains have been described (Fig. 224.9):

- interaction of PMNLs with *S. aureus* through antibodies against peptidoglycan;
- interaction through antibodies and C3b;
- interaction through C3b generated by direct interaction of peptidoglycan with complement (classic pathway); and
- interaction through direct activation via the alternative pathway.

Opsonization of encapsulated *S. aureus* is largely mediated by antibodies against the *O*-acetyl group of the capsular polysaccharide.[38]

Antibodies bound to specific antigens on the cell wall of bacteria (mostly peptidoglycans) serve as ligands for the attachment of bacteria to PMNLs. Antibodies against peptidoglycan are opsonic.[39] Peptidoglycan is able to activate the complement system, leading to deposition of C3b on the surface of the bacteria. During *S. aureus* infection, antibodies are also produced against teichoic acid. Their role in opsonization is questionable and is probably indirect via activation of the complement cascade. Antipeptidoglycan antibodies promote phagocytosis in vitro but their opsonic capacity in vivo is unclear as most strains grown under in-vivo conditions contain a capsule (Figs 224.9–224.11).

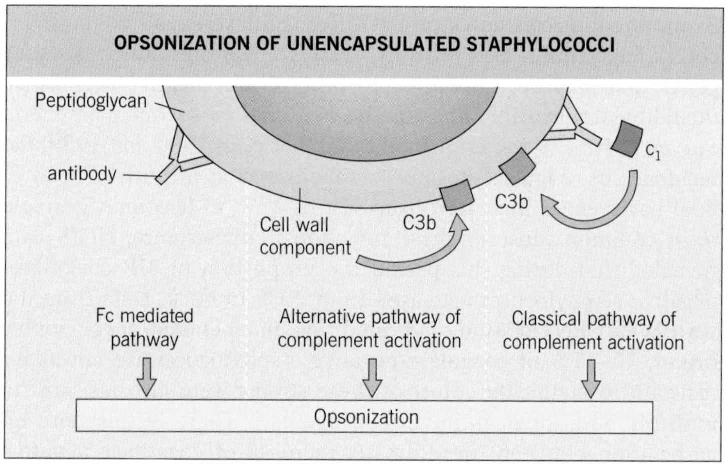

Fig. 224.9 Opsonization of unencapsulated staphylococci. Opsonization through complement activation is primarily a function of C3b and iC3b. When antibody (ab) molecules bind to antigen, the antigen–antibody complex activates the first complement component, C1. C1 is then converted into an esterase, initiating the classical pathway. Additionally, some cell-wall components can activate the alternative pathway.

Although the acidic polysaccharides are not activators of the complement pathway by themselves, in the presence of anticapsular antibody they may become activators of the classic and alternative complement pathways, and binding sites for C3b may be created

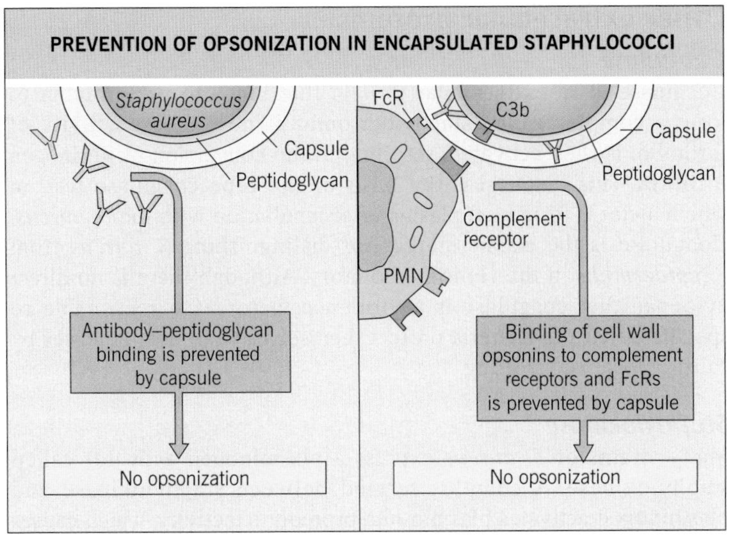

Fig. 224.10 Prevention of opsonization in encapsulated staphylococci. (Left) The capsule of *Staphylococcus aureus* prevents binding of antibodies to peptidoglycan: no opsonization. (Right) The capsule prevents binding of opsonins on the cell wall of *Staphylococcus aureus* to complement and Fc receptors on PMNLs.

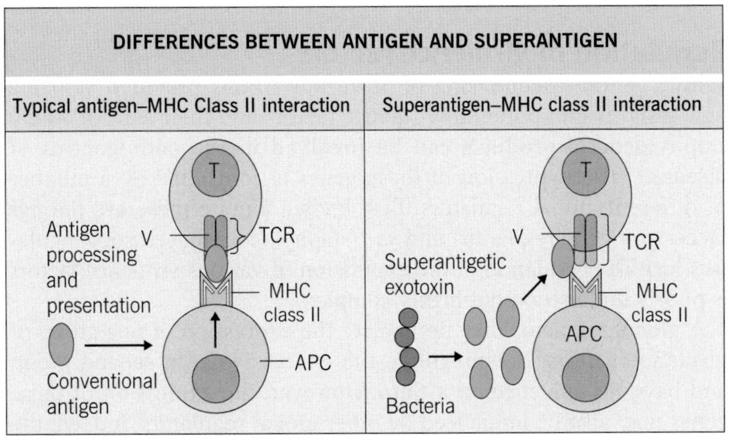

Fig. 224.11 Differences between antigen and superantigen. Staphylococcal enterotoxin and TSST-1 act as superantigens, binding directly to MHC class II and the Vβ chains of the T cell receptor (TCR) without the need for normal antigen processing.

within the capsular matrix so that these antibodies and C3b finally act as opsonins (see Fig. 224.9).[40]

Opsonization

Opsonization in the absence of antibody and complement

Some bacteria are able to adhere to PMNLs in the absence of antibodies and/or complement through the help of extracellular matrix molecules. These molecules may act as a bridge between PMNLs and bacteria, thus facilitating phagocytosis in the absence of specific opsonins. How important fibronectin is as an opsonin, for example, is not yet known. It is likely that optimal phagocytosis only occurs in the complement process.[41]

Evasion of opsonization

Many staphylococci have developed a defense against opsonophagocytosis and are therefore able to escape phagocytosis by PMNLs. The most important antiphagocytic defense of staphylococci is an enveloping capsule (see Fig. 224.10). These capsules protect the microbes against PMNLs by interfering with opsonization. Two other cell wall components that help microbes evade the phagocytic defense of the host are peptidoglycans and protein A. Indeed, two mechanisms have been described to explain why encapsulated strains resist phagocytosis in the absence of type-specific anticapsular antibodies (see Fig. 224.10). The capsule shields the peptidoglycan macromolecule from reacting with antibodies and C3b, thereby preventing opsonization. No antibody reaction with peptidoglycan occurs and no complement is activated. It is also possible that, although peptidoglycan reacts with antibodies and iC3b is generated on the peptidoglycan moiety, the capsule prevents the interaction of C3b and IgG on peptidoglycan with the receptors in the membrane of PMNLs.[37]

Protein A probably plays a triple antiphagocytic role in the bacteria–cell recognition process by its binding to the Fc portion of IgG.

- Extracellular soluble protein A can react with the Fc terminal of IgG molecules of human serum, thereby producing immune aggregates that consume complement, which leads to depletion of complement needed for phagocytosis.
- Extracellular protein A can bind to the Fc portion of specific antistaphylococcal antibodies coating the micro-organism with their Fab fragment, thereby preventing further interaction of the complex with the Fc receptor of phagocyte.
- Cell-bound protein A binds to the Fc fragment of any IgG molecule in its neighborhood, thus eliminating non-specific and specific antibodies.[42]

It has been shown that strains with high levels of protein A are less able to activate complement than strains with low levels of protein A.[43] Indeed, mutants of *S. aureus* lacking protein A are more efficiently phagocytosed in vitro, and studies with mutants in infection models suggest that protein A enhances virulence.

After opsonization, staphylococci are phagocytosed and killed. Some bacteria are usually able to escape killing and are able to survive inside PMNLs. Some strains of *S. aureus* with a special coagulase genotype may be better able to survive inside the PMNL.[33]

Toxins

Staphylococcus aureus can express several different types of protein toxin, which are probably responsible for some symptoms during infections.[44]

α-Toxin

The most potent membrane-damaging toxin of *S. aureus* is α-toxin. It is produced by a large percentage of strains and is expressed as a monomer that forms cylindric oligomeric heptamers and binds to the membrane of susceptible cells. Susceptible cells have a specific receptor for α-toxin that allows low concentrations of toxin to bind resulting in small pores through which monovalent cations can pass. At higher concentrations the toxin reacts non-specifically with membrane lipids, resulting in larger pores through which divalent cations and small molecules can pass. α-Toxin is toxic to a wide range of mammalian cells and animals and is dermonecrotic and neurotoxic.

β-Toxin

This toxin is a sphingomyelinase that damages membranes containing sphingomyelin. Lysis of sheep erythrocytes by *S. aureus* is caused by β-toxin. The majority of human isolates of *S. aureus* express β-toxin but its role in disease is poorly understood. It is produced in high concentration, especially in animal strains, suggesting that it must provide some form of selective advantage to the microbe. This is supported by the fact that β-toxin-deficient mutants are less virulent. It may play a role in the pathogenesis of bovine mastitis.

γ-Toxin and Panton–Valentine leukocidin

Staphylococcus aureus strains produce bicomponent toxins composed of two independently secreted nonassociated proteins. These toxins, γ-toxin and Panton–Valentine leukocidin (PVL), are synergistically toxic to PMNLs and monocytes and macrophages, and γ-toxin is additionally lytic for red cells from a variety of mammalian species. Recently it was shown that PVL-producing *S. aureus* strains cause rapidly progressive, hemorrhagic, necrotizing pneumonia, mainly in otherwise healthy children and young adults. This pneumonia is often preceded by influenza-like symptoms and has a high mortality rate.[45]

δ-Toxin

A variety of features have been attributed to δ-toxin.

- It can damage a variety of cell types as a result of its action on cell membranes.
- It causes dose-dependent damage to the bowls of guinea pigs, leading to speculation that it is a mediator of staphylococcal membranous enterocolitis.
- It increases vascular permeability in guinea pig skin, inhibits water absorption and activates adenylate cyclase.
- It has many other effects on various cell systems, such as activation of membrane phospholipase A_2, stimulation of prostaglandin synthesis, release of lysozyme and β-glucuronidase from PMNL granules and activation of the acetyltransferase.

Enterotoxins and toxic shock syndrome toxin-1

The enterotoxins, of which there are several serotypes (A, B, C^{1-3}, D, E, G, J, K) cause diarrhea and vomiting when ingested and are responsible for staphylococcal food poisoning. Systemically, enterotoxins can cause toxic shock syndrome (TSS). First described in 1978 in association with severe infections with *S. aureus* among children, the major symptoms of TSS are high fever, generalized exanthema, hypotension, multiorgan failure and desquamation of the skin. Menstruation-related TSS is much more common than non-menstruation-related TSS. Most *S. aureus* isolates from patients who have TSS produce toxic shock syndrome toxin (TSST)-1. Enterotoxins B and C cause 50% of nonmenstrual TSS. The TSST-1 is responsible for 75% of TSS, including all menstrual cases.

The TSS can occur as a sequela to any staphylococcal infection if an enterotoxin or TSST-1 is released systemically and the host lacks appropriate neutralizing antibodies. Tampon-associated TSS is not a true infection; rather it is caused by growth of *S. aureus* in a tampon and absorption of the toxin into the bloodstream. The incidence of TSS rose sharply with the introduction of superabsorbent tampons and, although the number of such cases has decreased dramatically, they still occur despite the withdrawal of certain types of tampon from the market.

The enterotoxins and TSST-1 are superantigens. Superantigens (see Chapter 1) stimulate T cells non-specifically without normal antigenic recognition (see Fig. 224.11). Up to one in five T cells may be activated, whereas only 1 in 10,000 are stimulated during normal antigen presentation. It has been postulated that this massive activation of lymphocytes results in cytokine release, which may contribute to some of the features of TSS.

Epidermolytic (exfoliative) toxin

The epidermolytic toxin (ET) causes scalded skin syndrome in neonates, with widespread blistering and loss of the epidermis. The two antigenically distinct forms of the toxin are ETA and ETB. These toxins have protease activity. They have a sequence similarity with the *S. aureus* serine protease, and the three most important amino acids in the active site of the protease are conserved. Changing the active site of serine to a glycine completely eliminates toxin activity. It is therefore possible that the target of the toxins is a very specific protein involved in maintaining the integrity of the epidermis. Recent data indicated that the gene coding for ET is located on a phage and that isolates displaying ET activity are often clonally related.

Other extracellular proteins

Coagulase

Coagulase is an extracellular protein that binds to prothrombin to form a complex called staphylothrombin. The protease activity of thrombin is then activated, resulting in the conversion of fibrinogen to fibrin. This reaction is the basis of the tube coagulase test, in which a clot is formed in plasma after incubation with the *S. aureus*. Coagulase is the classic marker for distinguishing *S. aureus* from *S. epidermidis* in the clinical laboratory. Although there is no direct evidence that coagulase is a virulence factor, it is reasonable to speculate that the bacteria protect themselves from host defenses by causing localized clotting.

Staphylokinase

Many strains of *S. aureus* express a plasminogen activator called staphylokinase. A complex formed between staphylokinase and plasminogen activates plasmin-like proteolytic activity, which causes dissolution of fibrin clots. The mechanism is identical to that of streptokinase, which is used to treat patients who have coronary thrombosis.

Another enzyme produced by staphylococci is catalase, which converts hydrogen peroxidase into nontoxic H_2O and O_2. Catalase may contribute to virulence because its production allows staphylococci to evade the killing mechanism of PMNLs.

Regulation of virulence factors

Whole genome sequencing of *S. aureus* strains provided valuable new insights into potential virulence factors and their control. Many staphylococcal products can be involved in the pathogenesis of disease.[33] The expression of these genes is controlled by a number of different global regulators. Best known among these are the *agr* (accessory gene regulator) and *sar* (staphylococcal accessory regulator) loci. The regulation of the expression of various virulence factors is poorly understood but highly complex.

A global regulator may upregulate the expression of one group of virulence factors, downregulate the expression of a second group and have no influence on a third. However, the expression of these genes may also be influenced by other global regulators. Indeed, the expression of one regulator may be influenced by the expression of another. In addition, this regulation network responds to stimuli from the environment (e.g. adhesion to epithelial cells, adhesion to catheter material, presence of other staphylococcal cells). Unraveling this highly complex regulation network may help to explain the different clinical manifestations seen in *S. aureus* infections.

CLINICAL MANIFESTATIONS

Staphylococcal infections are characterized by intense suppurative inflammation of local tissues with a tendency for the infected area to become encapsulated, leading to abscess formation.[46]

Furuncle

The most common staphylococcal infection is the furuncle or boil, which is a localized painful superficial skin infection that develops in a hair follicle or gland. Similar infections at the base of the eyelashes are the common styes. The most common sites for boils are the neck and the buttocks, often as a result of wearing tight clothes. The infected patient is often a carrier of the staphylococcus that causes the infection, usually in the anterior nares. A total of 65% of furuncles, especially those on the head and neck, are caused by a strain indistinguishable from that in the patient's nose, and there are indications that perineal carriage is associated with furuncles on the legs. No specific pathogenicity factors are responsible for the pathology of furuncles. Although about 50% of strains involved in carbuncles and furuncles have been found to produce PVL, only 2% of all *S. aureus* are producers. The course of infection is usually benign. No specific treatment is needed and most often the infection resolves after spontaneous drainage of the pus or surgical incision.

Chronic furunculosis

Approximately 2–3% of the population have chronic furunculosis, in which repeated attacks of boils are often caused by the same phage type of *S. aureus*. The most appropriate management of patients who have recurrent furunculosis includes a course of an oral antibiotic combined with chlorhexidine washes and the use of an antistaphylococcal intranasal ointment.

Carbuncle

Staphylococcal infection may spread from a furuncle to the deeper subcutaneous tissues, resulting in the development of one or more abscesses known as carbuncles. These abscesses occur mostly on the back of the neck, but may involve other skin sites. They may result in bloodstream invasion.

Bullous impetigo

Certain strains of *S. aureus* can cause bullous impetigo. This is characterized by small bullae, which form and burst. When this occurs in infants it may be described as pemphigus neonatorum.

Bullous impetigo is a highly contagious superficial skin infection characterized by large blisters containing many staphylococci in the superficial layers of the skin. Bullous impetigo is seen most often in infants and children under conditions where direct spread can occur (e.g. sharing of contaminated towels). Impetigo mainly occurs on the face and limbs. Extensive atypical bullous impetigo is associated with HIV infection.

The strains often produce exfoliative toxin and impetigo can therefore be considered as a localized form of scalded skin syndrome. The bullae are the result of epidermolytic toxins, which are serine proteases.

Botryomycosis

Botryomycosis is a rare chronic skin infection that resembles mycetoma or actinomycosis. The lesions may be nodular or granulomatous and may have draining sinuses.

Secondary cutaneous infection

The most common secondary infection occurs in people who have eczema, especially atopic dermatitis. Colonization of lesions in adults approaches 100%; children are colonized only slightly less often. Skin ulcers, especially those of the legs in the elderly, may also become heavily colonized by *S. aureus*. Similarly, hidradenitis suppurativa, a chronic suppurative disease of the skin that occurs in areas bearing apocrine glands, most often the axilla and groin, also yields *S. aureus*.

Paronychia

Another common *S. aureus* infection is paronychia, which involves the soft tissue around the nails.

Deep lesions

Staphylococcus aureus can cause a wide variety of deep tissue, often metastatic, infections. These infections include osteomyelitis, arthritis, endocarditis and cerebral, pulmonary and renal abscesses, and breast abscesses in nursing mothers.

Staphylococcus aureus can also cause bacterial pneumonia, which is almost always secondary (e.g. after influenza or other viral infections).

In many of these situations, diabetes mellitus, leukocyte defects or a general reduction of host defenses by alcoholism, malignancy, old age or corticosteroid or cytotoxic therapy are predisposing factors. Severe *S. aureus* infections, including endocarditis, are particularly common in intravenous drug abusers.

Wound infections

Staphylococcus aureus is a notorious cause of wound infection. Infections can be major complications following surgery. The source may be the patient's own carrier state, other carriers (e.g. doctors or nurses) or other infected patients. Whether a staphylococcal wound infection occurs following surgery depends upon a complex interaction between:

- host factors, including the status of the immune system and the presence of diseases such as diabetes mellitus;
- surgical factors, such as the disruption of tissue perfusion that accompanies the surgical procedure and whether foreign bodies are used;
- staphylococcal factors, including substances that mediate tissue adherence and invasion or that enable staphylococci to survive the host defenses and antibiotics in the tissues; and
- the use of antimicrobial prophylaxis.

Staphylococcal infections at the site of intravenous lines can result in bacteremia with metastatic infection.

Staphylococcal scalded skin syndrome

This term refers to a group of primarily cutaneous diseases (e.g. generalized scalded skin syndrome, staphylococcal scarlet fever and bullous impetigo) caused by the staphylococcal exfoliatin toxins exfoliatoxin A and exfoliatoxin B.

Toxic epidermal necrolysis (Lyell's disease) is also known as generalized scalded skin syndrome. It results from the production of exfoliatin toxin in a staphylococcal lesion, which can be quite minor. The toxin is absorbed into the bloodstream, and intraepidermal desquamation may occur at remote sites from which *S. aureus* cannot be isolated. The disease is most common in neonates and in children under 8 years of age, and epidemics may occur in nurseries. The face, axilla and groin are most often affected first but the erythema, bullous formation and subsequent desquamation of epithelial sheets can spread to all parts of the body. Generalized scalded skin syndrome is the most severe manifestation of exfoliatin-producing staphylococcal infections.

Milder versions of the same disease are staphylococcal scarlet fever, in which erythema occurs without desquamation, and bullous impetigo, in which there is only local desquamation.

Toxic shock syndrome

Toxic shock syndrome is a serious disease associated with *S. aureus*. As mentioned above it has been most commonly seen in young women during or immediately after menstruation and is associated with the use of highly absorbent intravaginal tampons. In such cases, *S. aureus* grows in large numbers in and around the tampon and liberates TSST-1. The disease is characterized by the development of high fever, vomiting, diarrhea, sore throat and muscle pain. Within 48 hours it may progress to severe shock with evidence of renal and hepatic damage. A skin rash may develop, followed by exfoliation at a deeper level than in scalded skin syndrome. Blood cultures are usually negative.

Staphylococcal food poisoning

Staphylococcal food poisoning results from the production of staphylococcal enterotoxin in food before ingestion. It is an intoxication, not an infection. Because of the heat resistance of the toxin, toxicity persists even if the food is heated to boiling. Ingestion of the food results in acute vomiting and diarrhea within 1–5 hours. There is prostration but usually no fever. Recovery is rapid, except sometimes in the elderly and in those with other diseases. The diagnosis is suspected on the basis of exposure history and of the typical symptoms (nausea, vomiting, abdominal cramping and diarrhea). Worldwide, 30% of cases of food-borne illness are caused by staphylococci.

DIAGNOSIS

Most staphylococcal lesions contain numerous PMNLs and large numbers of *S. aureus*. These findings are readily demonstrated by a direct Gram smear of pus. This method is also advised for sputum samples from cases of staphylococcal pneumonia and stool specimens from patients who have staphylococcal enterocolitis.

Staphylococci grow aerobically on blood agar and typical colonies of 2mm or more in diameter develop overnight. Rapid and accurate identification of *S. aureus* is important. Rapid methods commonly used by laboratories to differentiate *S. aureus* from other staphylococcal species are:

- the slide coagulase factor reaction; and
- latex agglutination assays.

In the latter, latex particles coated with fibrinogen and IgG are used to detect protein A and clumping factor ('bound coagulase') on the cell surface of *S. aureus*. However, decreased sensitivity has been reported for several tests, especially in identifying MRSA.[47] An additional penicillin binding protein is produced by MRSA that is absent from susceptible strains. It is termed PBP2a or PBP2' and has reduced affinity to β-lactam antibiotics. Therefore, latex agglutination assays have been developed in order to detect PBP2a. In addition, methods of DNA amplification such as the PCR are becoming increasingly useful for the specific and sensitive detection of *S. aureus* in clinical specimens. In most laboratories the presence of coagulase, coded for by the *coa* gene, is used to identify *S. aureus*. Polymerase chain reactions have been described in which staphylococcus-specific sequences have been amplified for species identification. In these studies DNA was extracted from preincubated colonies or single colonies were picked from agar plates and transferred directly to a PCR assay.[48]

Blood cultures from untreated bacteremia patients are usually positive after overnight incubation.

Deep staphylococcal infection such as osteomyelitis or endocarditis poses special diagnostic problems when the lesion cannot be aspirated. Antibodies to staphylococcal products such as hemolysin, nuclease and cell wall ribitol–teichoic acid can be detected by a variety of immunologic techniques. However, the sera of many individuals who do not have deep staphylococcal infections may also contain such antibodies and there is considerable overlap in the antibody titers of those who are and those who are not infected. Consequently, these assays have a low predictive value and are not cost-effective. These assays are ancillary at best and their results must be interpreted with caution.

MANAGEMENT

Superficial staphylococcal lesions are generally adequately treated by simple drainage of the lesion. Drainage is also important in the treatment of chronic staphylococcal infections.

Acute serious staphylococcal infections (e.g. pneumonia or bacteremia) require immediate antibiotic therapy. Antibiotic susceptibility tests should always be done because of unpredictive staphylococcal susceptibility patterns. A penicillinase-resistant penicillin or cephalosporin is normally used pending the results of a susceptibility test. Infections proved to be caused by strains susceptible to benzylpenicillin are best treated with that antibiotic. There is synergy between cell-wall-active antibiotics and the aminoglycosides when the staphylococcus is susceptible to both. Combinations of a β-lactamase-stable semisynthetic penicillin and an aminoglycoside are often used for severe systemic infections, particularly in the immunocompromised host. Other antibiotics with good antistaphylococcal activity include clindamycin, rifampin (rifampicin) and fusidic acid.

Some chronic or recurrent infections of the compromised host can be controlled by administration of an oral preparation of one of the penicillinase-resistant penicillins over months or years.

As mentioned, an additional penicillin binding protein, PBP2a, is produced by MRSA. It has reduced affinity to β-lactam antibiotics. The 2kb gene encoding PBP2a, *mec*A, is carried on a 40–60kb segment of DNA inserted into the staphylococcal chromosome. The added DNA often contains genes encoding resistance to other antimicrobials, insertion-sequence-like elements and genes regulating the expression of *mec*A. Methicillin-resistance of *S. aureus* mediates clinically inadequate susceptibility to all currently available β-lactam antibiotics, and MRSA is typically resistant to several other antimicrobial agents, including aminoglycosides, chloramphenicol, clindamycin, fluoroquinolones and macrolides. Multiple resistance varies greatly geographically, so in planning treatment it is imperative to carry out susceptibility testing.[49] So far most clinical isolates have been susceptible only to vancomycin, which consequently has become the agent of choice for MRSA infections, although recently several investigators have described clinical isolates of *S. aureus* with diminished sensitivity to vancomycin. In the laboratory, vancomycin resistance has been transferred from *Enterococcus faecalis* to *S. aureus* and is stably expressed.[50] In addition, the first vancomycin-resistant *S. aureus* isolate has been detected in the USA. Probably the *van*A gene, coding for vancomycin resistance, was transferred from enterococci to *S. aureus*.

In addition, *S. aureus* isolates with reduced vancomycin susceptibility were described worldwide (GISA isolates, isolates with reduced susceptibility to glycopeptides). As far as has been studied, all these isolates contained thickened cell walls. Furthermore, all of them, with the exception of the Illinois isolate, showed reduced cross-linking when compared to isogenic revertants. Interestingly, only some of them showed a reduction in D-glutamic acid amidation. The data described so far on GISA strains seem to indicate that, depending on the strain studied, several independent mutations have been accumulated in these strains, which in various combinations lead to the observed resistance phenotype.

Probably, the following mechanisms are associated with the appearance of GISA strain:

- accelerated cell wall synthesis, which leads to a thickened cell wall that is capable of affinity trapping large amounts of vancomycin and shielding the membrane associated lipid II target molecules; and
- most probably caused by the accelerated cell wall synthesis, modifications of the nascent wall precursors, as amidation of the D-glutamic acid cannot be ensured as completely as under non-accelerated conditions. The same may apply to the cross-linking reaction, although cross-linking will also be reduced because nonamidated precursors are poor substrates for the staphylococcal transpeptidation reaction.

Since lower nonamidation and lower cross-linking both lead to even higher consumption of vancomycin per unit of cell wall weight, they also contribute positively to the GISA resistance phenotype.

Should vancomycin resistance and reduced susceptibility to glycopeptides become widespread, alternative MRSA therapies will be urgently needed. Careless prescription of drugs active against MRSA will inevitably lead to the emergence of resistance and the permanent loss of a valuable agent. Responsible antibiotic prescription therefore mandates close and frequent consultation between the prescribing physician, the medical microbiologist and the infectious disease specialist.

Recently, new antimicrobial substances have been introduced that are valuable antistaphylococcal agents. Synercid® is a new, injectable, water-soluble semisynthetic derivative of pristinamycin. It is composed of a streptogramin B, quinupristin and a streptogramin A, dalfopristin, combined in a 30:70 ratio. Both compounds bind to the 23S RNA of the 50S ribosomal subunit. They act synergistically to inhibit protein synthesis and show good activity against MSRA. The new oxazolidinone linezolid clearly demonstrates an in-vitro activity against MRSA equal to that of vancomycin. In addition to this in-vitro potency, linezolid also possesses other promising features, most noticeably its lack of cross-resistance with any other mechanisms. Linezolid has been shown to possess a mechanism of action unique among Gram-positive organisms by inhibiting protein synthesis by binding to the 50S ribosomal subunits.

PREVENTION

For patients who have recurrent infection such as chronic furunculosis, preventive measures are aimed at controlling re-infection and, if possible, eliminating the carrier state. For adults, the use of chlorhexidine or hexachlorophene soaps in showering and washing increases the bactericidal activity of the skin. For those individuals or medical personnel found to be a source of infection to patients, anterior nasal carriage can be reduced and often eliminated. Although many different agents and drug combinations have been used for eradicating nasal carriage of *S. aureus*, there is a consensus that topical mupirocin is presently the regimen of choice.[51] The high-level mupirocin resistance rate is less than 5%. Attempts to remove nasal carriage of MRSA with local antiseptics (e.g. chlorhexidine or povidone iodine) or antibiotics (e.g. bacitracin) have frequently failed. Chemotherapeutic agents for elimination include topical antimicrobials and antiseptics applied directly to the nares or other sites of carriage, systemic agents that achieve adequate concentrations in these sites, and antiseptic soaps for bathing.

Chemoprophylaxis is usually considered mandatory for surgical procedures such as hip and cardiac valve replacements, in which infection with coagulase-positive or coagulase-negative staphylococci can have devastating consequences for the prosthesis and for the patient. Brief high-dose chemoprophylaxis is given around the time of surgery with the intention of preventing superinfections, which often complicate longer periods of antibiotic administration.

More than 30 years have passed since methicillin resistance was first detected in *S. aureus*. Now hospitals worldwide experience MRSA as a major nosocomial pathogen. Three possible strategies in the control of epidemics of staphylococci, especially those of MRSA, have been proposed.[52] They include:

- the 'search and destroy' strategy;
- the *S. aureus* limitation technique (SALT) strategy; and
- the Scutari strategy.

The 'search and destroy' strategy has become the major tactic for MRSA control in countries where the MRSA threat was recognized in the 1980s. In the UK, the Hospital Infection Society and the British Society for Antimicrobial Chemotherapy published MRSA control guidelines in 1986 that were revised in 1990.[53] Included in these guidelines is the installation in hospitals during an outbreak of a dedicated isolation unit. Patients who have MRSA should be nursed in separate rooms or wards by designated personnel using special barrier techniques: the use of gloves and handwashing with an antiseptic detergent, disposable gowns, masks and strict environmental hygiene. This last point is especially important as MRSA is extremely resistant to drying and can survive anywhere (e.g. in tourniquets, mattresses, air-conditioning systems).[54] These guidelines were followed to control the three MRSA epidemics that occurred in the Utrecht University Hospital in The Netherlands.[55]

The SALT strategy stresses the isolation of MRSA-infected patients, whereas MRSA-colonized patients are nursed with precautions for infections only. This would be a rational strategy if one could assume that MRSA carriers do not spread MRSA and that MRSA from infection sites are more virulent. However, there is no indication that MRSA strains differ in virulence. Nevertheless, the SALT strategy may be the only manner in which hospitals with high rates of MRSA can achieve some degree of control.

The Scutari strategy was named after the hospital where Florence Nightingale worked during the Crimean War (1854–1856) and is based on simple hygiene such as handwashing and barrier nursing. This strategy, however, is insufficient to combat MRSA in hospitals. Nevertheless, these general guidelines of simple hygiene can be applied in other settings, such as nursing homes.

Is it worth spending so much time and money to try to prevent the spread of MRSA, a bacterium that often colonizes patients but only causes infections in a minority of cases, most of which can be treated? In those countries where the incidence is still low the answer should be 'yes'. Several authors have proposed that the carriage of MRSA poses an increased risk of infection over the carriage of methicillin-susceptible *S. aureus* (MSSA). Among patients on continuous ambulatory peritoneal dialysis, MRSA carriers have a higher risk for MRSA infections than noncarriers. Perioperative colonization with MRSA significantly increases the risk for postoperative MRSA infection in patients on the intensive care unit. Studying the rate of bacteremia in patients admitted to the intensive care unit, patients colonized with MSSA in the nares had a significantly increased risk for the development of *S. aureus* bacteremia but patients colonized with MRSA had a much higher risk. It seems clear that MRSA carriage constitutes a greater risk for the development of *S. aureus* infection than MSSA carriage.[56] Several studies have failed to show a difference between MRSA and MSSA in terms of virulence. It is therefore most likely that the increased infection rate observed in carriers of MRSA is primarily due to the selection of a more vulnerable group of patients who become carriers of MRSA.

Furthermore, time is running out for the treatment of MRSA infections. Already, the first vancomycin-resistant MRSA has been reported. Increased use of mupirocin as a topical therapy for MRSA carriage may also result in increased mupirocin resistance.[57]

Vaccines and new approaches to combating nosocomial infections

No vaccine is currently available to combat staphylococcal infection. Hyperimmune serum from human volunteer donors or humanized monoclonal antibodies directed toward surface components (e.g. capsular polysaccharide or surface protein adhesions) could both prevent bacterial adherence and promote phagocytosis of bacterial cells. A prototype vaccine based on capsular polysaccharide from *S. aureus* has been administered to volunteers to raise hyperimmune serum, which could be given to patients in hospital before surgery. A vaccine based on fibronectin-binding protein induces protective immunity against mastitis in cattle and might also be used as a vaccine in humans.[58]

STAPHYLOCOCCUS EPIDERMIDIS

PATHOGENICITY

Coagulase-negative staphylococci are frequently isolated from various clinical specimens in the clinical microbiology laboratory. In the past, these isolates were often discarded as contaminants. This situation has radically changed during the past two decades, with coagulase-negative staphylococci now being recognized as an important cause of nosocomial infections.[59]

Intravascular catheters, cerebrospinal fluid shunts, peritoneal dialysates, prosthetic cardiac valves and blood cultures frequently yield coagulase-negative staphylococci. Every isolate from such sources must be carefully evaluated for its clinical significance, although interpretation of the culture remains a challenge to all physicians, even in combination with the clinical presentation of the patient.

In general, coagulase-negative staphylococci become potentially pathogenic as soon as the natural balance between micro-organisms and the immune system is disturbed. This is exemplified in immunocompromised patients such as oncology patients and premature neonates in whom coagulase-negative staphylococcal infections frequently occur in association with the use of intravascular devices. The increase in incidence of infections with coagulase-negative staphylococci is probably related to the increased use of intravascular devices. Furthermore, the presence of large numbers of coagulase-negative staphylococci on the skin, their ability to adhere to biomaterial surfaces and the selection of resistant strains by the use of broad-spectrum antibiotics in hospital have all been cited as possible reasons for the increased rate of infection with coagulase-negative staphylococci.

Of all coagulase-negative staphylococci, *S. epidermidis* is the most frequently isolated species associated with catheter-related infections. The main adhesins responsible for binding *S. epidermidis* to catheters are:

- a capsular polysaccharide; and
- a protease-sensitive surface constituent from the slime-producing strains of *S. epidermidis*.

In addition to promoting adherence to foreign bodies, these adhesins may also protect coagulase-negative staphylococci against phagocytosis and prevent reaction of antibodies to cell-wall components. Specific antibodies to these adhesins may neutralize this shield and are often needed for efficient opsonization of the bacteria. Monoclonal and polyclonal antibodies against *S. epidermidis* adhesins facilitate phagocytosis of homologous *S. epidermidis* strains and protect animals against endocarditis.[60] Most important in the pathogenesis of foreign-body-associated infections is the ability of these bacteria to colonize the polymer surface through the formation of a thick, multilayered biofilm. Biofilm formation takes place in two phases. The first phase involves the attachment of the bacteria to polymer surfaces, which may be either unmodified or coated with host extracellular matrix proteins. In the second phase, the bacteria proliferate and accumulate into multilayered cell clusters embedded in an extracellular material.

The major PMNL receptor for *S. epidermidis* opsonins is the FcRIII receptor.[61] For strains that have a hydrophobic surface structure, however, antibodies alone are not sufficient for opsonization. Either C3b or iC3b is also needed, but deposition or transformation of C3 into the opsonic-active C3b on the surface of *S. epidermidis* is largely facilitated by antibodies. In hypogammaglobulinemic preterm babies, C3b generation by *S. epidermidis* may therefore be impeded and the antibody deficiency state may contribute to the persistence of *S. epidermidis* bacteremia in very-low-birth-weight infants.[62]

CLINICAL MANIFESTATIONS

Catheter-related infections

Staphylococcus epidermidis is the most frequently isolated coagulase-negative staphylococcal species in catheter-related infections, especially in children.[63] These infections have been reported in association with central hyperalimentation catheters, peripheral intravenous catheters, subclavian catheters, Hickmann and Broviac central lines and Swan–Ganz catheters. As can be seen in Figure 224.12, there are different potential sources for bacterial contamination of intravascular catheters.

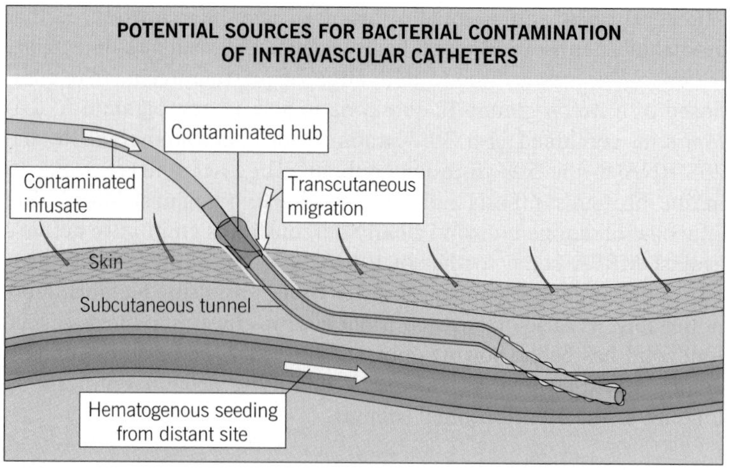

Fig. 224.12 Potential sources for bacterial contamination of intravascular catheters. Bacteria gain access to the catheter by the following routes: contamination of the catheter hub, contamination of the infusate, transcutaneous migration and hematogenous seeding.

The diagnosis of a catheter-related infection is often a physician's nightmare. Catheters may be colonized without local signs of infection (i.e. without gross evidence of purulence or erythema at the insertion site of the catheter). Furthermore, blood cultures may yield *S. epidermidis* without the patient showing major clinical symptoms.

A diagnosis of catheter-related infection is based on a proper collection of at least three blood cultures from different sites of venepuncture within 24 hours. In addition, culture of the intravascular catheter segment should be performed according to current standards. In most clinical microbiology laboratories, the intravascular segment of the catheter is cultured according to the method of Maki and colleagues.[64] Catheter segments are cultured after being 'rolled' over a blood agar plate and, after incubation for 18 hours at 98.6°F (37°C), the number of colony-forming units (cfu) are counted. Cultures yielding more than 15cfu/blood agar plate are associated with catheter-related bacteremia (see also Chapter 57).

Cerebrospinal fluid shunt infections

Both *S. epidermidis* and *S. aureus* strains are the most frequently encountered isolates in cerebrospinal fluid shunt infections. Infections usually occur within 2 weeks of implantation or manipulation of the shunt. Clinical manifestations are usually non-specific (see Chapter 28).

Peritonitis

About 40% of patients who have continuous ambulatory peritoneal dialysis develop peritonitis during the first year (overall incidence ranging from 0.6 to 6.3 episodes/patient-year). Criteria for diagnosis include a combination of:

- abdominal pain;
- cloudy fluid containing more than 100 white blood cells/mm^3 (the majority of which are PMNLs); and
- a positive dialysate culture.

Staphylococcus epidermidis is by far the most frequently isolated organism in patients who have peritonitis associated with continuous ambulatory peritoneal dialysis.

Endocarditis

Infections of native cardiac valves with coagulase-negative staphylococci are uncommon, accounting for only about 5% of all cases of infective endocarditis. However, *S. epidermidis* and *S. aureus* account for the majority of cases of nosocomial infective endocarditis. These bacteria are the single most common cause of infections of prosthetic cardiac valves, and *S. epidermidis* is the cause of approximately 40% of cases of prosthetic valve endocarditis (see Chapter 57).

In more than 80% of patients, *S. epidermidis* valve endocarditis is associated with valve dysfunction or persistent fever during therapy. The infection is most frequently located in the valve sewing ring, resulting in complications such as dehiscence, dysrhythmia and obstruction of the valve orifice. Fever usually persists during therapy because the valve ring abscess is relatively protected from antibiotics. *Staphylococcus epidermidis* prosthetic valve endocarditis shows an indolent clinical picture without the classic endocarditis findings such as peripheral emboli and multiple positive blood cultures.

Valve dysfunction and fever are the most frequent symptoms. Most patients are infected at the time of cardiac surgery but the incubation period can vary, with a latency of 2–13 months before symptoms arise.

Orthopedic implant infections

Although the incidence of infection of indwelling prostheses is only 1–5%, such infections are devastating. Usually, infected prostheses must be removed, which may result in organic defects. Fewer than 10% of prosthetic hip and knee infections have been treated successfully without removing the prosthesis. Prosthetic joints may become infected either by local introduction of organisms or by hematogenous seeding. Staphylococci are the most frequently isolated pathogens, causing more than 70% of prosthetic joint infections (see also Chapter 53).

Infections in immunocompromised patients

The coagulase-negative staphylococci have emerged as pathogens in immunocompromised hosts, notably patients on neonatal intensive care units and oncology patients. Most coagulase-negative staphylococci infections in these patients are related to the use of foreign devices, especially central intravascular catheters (see Chapter 100).

Urinary tract infection

Among the coagulase-negative staphylococci, *S. saprophyticus* can cause spontaneous acute urinary tract infection in previously healthy people. With a few exceptions these are women aged 16–25 years. The disease appears soon after the woman becomes sexually active and the symptomatology closely resembles that of urinary tract infection caused by *Escherichia coli* (see Chapter 67).

REFERENCES

1. Ogston A. Report upon microorganisms in surgical diseases. Br Med J 1881;1:369–75.
2. Rosenbach FJ. Mikro-organismen bei den Wund-Infektions-Krankheiten des Menschen. Wiesbaden: JF Bergmanns Verlag; 1884.
3. Hart D. Operation room infections. Arch Surg (Chicago) 1937;34:874–96.
4. Bennett IL, Beeson PB. Bacteremia: a consideration of some experimental and clinical aspects. Medicine 1954;26:241–62.
5. Crossley KB, Archer GL, eds. The staphylococci in human disease. New York: Churchill Livingstone; 1997.
6. Kloos W. Taxonomy and systematics of staphylococci indigenous to humans. In: Crossley KB, Archer GL, eds. The staphylococci in human disease. New York: Churchill Livingstone; 1997:113–37.
7. Fournier JM. Capsular polysaccharides of *Staphylococcus aureus*. In: Wadström T, Eliason I, Holder I, Ljungh A, eds. Pathogenesis of wound and biomaterial-associated infections. London: Springer-Verlag; 1990:533–45.
8. Karakawa WW. The role of capsular antigens in *Staphylococcus aureus* immunity. Zentralbl Bakteriol 1992;277:415.
9. Wilkinson BJ. Biology. In: Crossley KB, Archer GL, eds. The staphylococci in human disease. New York: Churchill Livingstone; 1997:1–38.
10. Mevissen-Verhage EAE, Marcelis JH, Harmsen-van Amerongen WCM, de Vos NM, Berkel J, Verhoef J. Iron affects the intestinal flora. I. Development of the neonatal gut flora during the first week of life. Eur J Clin Microbiol 1985;4:14–8.
11. Kauffman CA, Bradley SF. Epidemiology of community acquired infection. In: Crossley KB, Archer GL, eds. The staphylococci in human disease. New York: Churchill Livingstone; 1997:287–308.
12. Hollis RJ, Barr JL, Doebbeling BN, Pfaller MA, Wenzel RP. Familial carriage of methicillin-resistant *Staphylococcus aureus* and subsequent infection in a premature neonate. Clin Infect Dis 1995;21:328–32.
13. Frénay HME, Vandenbroucke-Grauls CMJE, Molkenboer MJCH, Verhoef J. Long-term carriage, and transmission of methicillin-resistant *Staphylococcus aureus* after discharge from hospital. J Hosp Infect 1992;22:207–15.
14. Boyce JM. Epidemiology and prevention of nosocomial infections. In: Crossley KB, Archer GL, eds. The staphylococci in human disease. New York: Churchill Livingstone; 1997:309–29.
15. Kluytmans JA, Mouton JW, IJzerman EP, *et al.* Nasal carriage of *Staphylococcus aureus* as a major risk factor wound infections after cardiac surgery. J Infect Dis 1995;171:216–9.
16. Barber M, Roswadowska-Dowzenko M. Infection by penicillin-resistant staphylococci. Lancet 1948;2:641–4.
17. Wilson R, Hamburger M. Fifteen years' experience with staphylococcus septicemia in a large city hospital. Am J Med 1957;22:437–57.
18. Pavillard R, Harvey K, Douglas D, *et al.* Epidemic of hospital-acquired infection due to methicillin-resistant *Staphylococcus aureus* in major Victorian hospitals. Med J Aust 1982;1:451–4.
19. Rolinson GN, Stevens S. Microbiological studies on a new broadspectrum penicillin 'Penbritin'. Br Med J 1961;2:191–6.
20. Ministry of Health. Staphylococcal infections in hospital. Report of the Subcommittee of the Central Health Services Counsel. London: HMSO; 1959.
21. Colley EW, McNicol MW, Bracken PM. Methicillin-resistant staphylococci in a general hospital. Lancet 1965;1:595–7.
22. Speller DCE, Raghunath D, Stephens M, *et al.* Epidemic infection by a gentamicin resistant *Staphylococcus aureus* in three hospitals. Lancet 1976;1:464–6.
23. Townsend DE, Ashdown N, Bolton S, *et al.* The international spread of methicillin-resistant *Staphylococcus aureus*. J Hosp Infect 1987;9:60–71.
24. Frénay HME, Van Leeuwen WJ, De Neeling AJ, *et al.* Surveillance of methicillin-resistant *Staphylococcus aureus* (1989–1992). Br Med J 1994;308:58–64.
25. Panlilio AL, Culver DH, Gaynes RP, *et al.* Methicillin-resistant *Staphylococcus aureus* in US hospitals, 1975–1991. Infect Control Hosp Epidemiol 1992;13:582–6.
26. Diekema DJ, Pfaller MA, Schmitz FJ, *et al.* Survey of infections due to *Staphylococcus* species: frequency of occurrence and antimicrobial susceptibility of isolates collected in the United States, Canada, Latin America, Europe, and the Western Pacific region for the sentry antimicrobial surveillance program, 1997–1999. Clin Infect Dis 2001;32(Suppl.2):S114–32.
27. Arbeit RD. Laboratory procedures for epidemiologic analysis. In: Crossley KB, Archer GL, eds. The staphylococci in human disease. New York: Churchill Livingstone; 1997:253–86.
28. Wenzel RP. The emergence of methicillin-resistant *Staphylococcus aureus*. Ann Intern Med 1982;97:440–2.
29. Easmon CSF, Goodfellow M. *Staphylococcus* and *Micrococcus*. In: Parker MT, Duerden BI, eds. Topley & Wilson's principles of bacteriology, virology and immunity, vol. 2. London: Edward Arnold; 1990;161–6.
30. John JF, Grieshop TJ, Atkins LM, Platt CG. Widespread colonization of personnel at a veterans affairs medical center by methicillin-resistant, coagulase-negative staphylococcus. Clin Infect Dis 1993;17:380–8.
31. Archer GL, Climo MW. Antimicrobial susceptibility of coagulase-negative staphylococci. Antimicrob Agents Chemother 1994;38:2231–7.
32. Projan SJ, Novick RP. The molecular basis of pathogenicity. In: Crossley KB, Archer GL, eds. The staphylococci in human disease. New York: Churchill Livingstone; 1997:55–81.
33. Kuroda M, Ohta T, Uchiyama I, *et al.* Whole genome sequencing of methicillin-resistant *Staphylococcus aureus*. Lancet 2001;357:1225–40.
34. Westerlund B, Korhonen K. Bacterial proteins binding to the mammalian extracellular matrix. Mol Microbiol 1993;9:687.
35. Wadström T. Molecular aspects on pathogenesis of staphylococcal wound and foreign-body infections: bacterial cell surface hydrophobicity, fibronectin, fibrinogen, collagen, binding surface proteins, determine the ability of staphylococci to colonize in damaged tissues and on prosthesis materials. In: Jeljaszewicz J, Ciborowski P, eds. The staphylococci. New York: Gustav Fischer; 1991:37–51.
36. Mack D, Fischer W, Krokotsch A, *et al.* The intracellular adhesion involved in biofilm accumulation of *Staphylococcus epidermidis* is a linear 1,6-linked glycosaminoglycan: purification and structural analysis. J Bacteriol 1996;178:175.
37. Verhoef J. Host defense against infection. In: Crossley KB, Archer GL, eds. The staphylococci in human disease. New York: Churchill Livingstone; 1997:213–33.

38. Verhoef J, Visser MR. Neutrophil phagocytosis and killing: normal function and microbial evasion. In: Abramson JS, Wheeler JG, eds. The neutrophil. Oxford: IRL Press; 1993:109–37.
39. Karakawa WW, Sutton A, Schneerson A, *et al.* Capsular antibodies induce type-specific phagocytosis of capsulated *Staphylococcus aureus* by human polymorphonuclear leukocytes. Infect Immun 1988;56:1090.
40. Verbrugh HA, Van Dijk WC, Peters R, *et al.* Opsonic recognition of staphylococci mediated by cell wall peptidoglycan: antibody dependent activation of human complement and opsonic activity of peptidoglycan antibodies. J Immunol 1980;124:1167.
41. Verbrugh HA, Peterson PK, Bach-Yen T, *et al.* Opsonization of encapsulated *Staphylococcus aureus*; the role of specific antibody and complement. J Immunol 1982;129:1681.
42. Peterson PK, Verhoef J, Sabatk LD, Quie PG. Effect of protein A on staphylococcal opsonization. Infect Immun 1977;15:760.
43. Spika JS, Verbrugh HA, Verhoef J. Protein A effect on alternative pathway complement activation and opsonization of *S. aureus*. Infect Immun 1981;34:455–60.
44. Bohach GA, Dinges MM, Mitchell DT, Ohlendorf DH, Schlievert PM. Exotoxins. In: Crossley KB, Archer GL, eds. The staphylococci in human disease. New York: Churchill Livingstone; 1997:83–112.
45. Gillet Y, Issartel B, Vanhems P, *et al.* Association between *Staphylococcus aureus* strains carrying gene for Parton-Valentine leukocidin and highly lethal necrotising pneumonia in young immunocompetent patients. Lancet 2002;359:753–9.
46. Easmon CSF. Staphylococcal diseases. In: Smith GR, Easmon CSF, eds. Topley & Wilson's principles of bacteriology, virology and immunity, vol. 3. London: Edward Arnold; 1990:215–38.
47. Wanger AR, Morris SL, Ericsson C, Singh KV, LaRocco MT. Latex agglutination negative, methicillin-resistant *Staphylococcus aureus* recovered from neonates: epidemiological features and comparison of typing methods. J Clin Microbiol 1992;30:2583–8.
48. Vannuffel P, Gigi J, Ezzedine H, *et al.* Specific detection of methicillin-resistant *Staphylococcus* species by multiplex PCR. J Clin Microbiol 1995;33:2864–7.
49. Berger-Bächi B. Resistance not mediated by β-lactamase (methicillin resistance). In: Crossley KB, Archer GL, eds. The staphylococci in human disease. New York: Churchill Livingstone; 1997:158–74.
50. Nobel WC, Virani Z, Cree RGA. Co-transfer of vancomycin and other resistance genes from *Enterococcus faecalis* NCTC 12201 to *Staphylococcus aureus*. FEMS Microbiol Lett 1992;93:195–8.
51. Kauffman CA, Terpenning MS, He X, *et al.* Attempts to eradicate methicillin-resistant *Staphylococcus aureus* from a long-term care facility with the use of mupirocin ointment. Am J Med 1993;94:371.
52. Spicer WJ. Three strategies in the control of staphylococci including methicillin-resistant *Staphylococcus aureus*. J Hosp Infect 1984;5(Suppl.A):45–9.
53. Revised guidelines for the control of epidemic methicillin-resistant *Staphylococcus aureus* (Working Party Report). Report of a combined working party of the Hospital Infection Society and the British Society for Antimicrobial Chemotherapy. J Hosp Infect 1990;16:351–77.
54. Berman DS, Schaeffer S, Simberkoff MS. Tourniquets and nosocomial methicillin-resistant *Staphylococcus aureus* infections. N Engl J Med 1986;315:514–5.
55. Vandenbroucke-Grauls CMJE, Frénay HME, Van Klingeren B, Savelkoul TJ, Verhoef J. Control of epidemic methicillin-resistant *Staphylococcus aureus* in a Dutch university hospital. Eur J Clin Microbiol Infect Dis 1991;10:6–11.
56. Pujol M, Pena C, Pallares R, *et al.* Nosocomial *Staphylococcus aureus* bacteremia among nasal carriers of methicillin-resistant and methicillin-susceptible strains. Am J Med 1996;100:509–16.
57. Cookson BD. MRSA: major problem or minor threat? (Editorial). J Med Microbiol 1993;38:309–10.
58. Mamo W, Jonsson P, Flock J-I, *et al.* Vaccination against *Staphylococcus aureus* mastitis: immunological response of mice vaccinated with fibronectin-binding protein (FnBP-A) to challenge with *S. aureus*. Vaccine 1994;12:988–92.
59. Kloos WE, Bannerman TL. Update on clinical significance of coagulase-negative staphylococci. Clin Microbiol Rev 1994;7:117–40.
60. Takeda S, Pier GB, Kojima J, *et al.* Protection against endocarditis due to *Staphylococcus epidermidis* by immunization with capsular polysaccharide/adhesin. Circulation 1991;84:2539.
61. Schutze GE, Hall MA, Baker CJ, Edward MS. Role of neutrophil receptors in opsonophagocytosis of coagulase-negative staphylococci. Infect Immun 1991;59:2573.
62. Correa AG, Baker CJ, Schutze GE, Edward MS. Immunoglobulin G enhances C3 degradation on coagulase-negative staphylococci. Infect Immun 1994;62:2362.
63. Fleer A, Senders RS, Visser MR, *et al.* Septicemia due to coagulase-negative staphylococci in a neonatal intensive care unit: clinical and bacteriological features and contaminated parenteral fluids as a source of sepsis. Pediatr Infect Dis 1984;2:426–31.
64. Maki DG, Weise CE, Sarafin HW. A semiquantative culture method for identifying intravenous-catheter- related infection. N Engl J Med 1977;296:1305–9.

chapter

225 Streptococci and Related Genera

Ellen M Mascini & Stig E Holm

INTRODUCTION

The genus *Streptococcus* consists of round or slightly oval Gram-positive cocci with a diameter of <2μm. The cocci are often in pairs or chains. The detection of cytochrome enzymes with the catalase test distinguishes members of the catalase-positive family of Micrococcaceae from the members of the family of Streptococcaceae, which are catalase negative. Most of these micro-organisms are facultative anaerobes, but some need carbon dioxide for growth and others may be strictly anaerobic. The major representatives of the genus *Streptococcus* include *Streptococcus* and *Enterococcus*.[1] The further division of streptococci has been the topic of an extensive taxonomic re-evaluation and we still lack a complete picture of the genetic relationship between different subgenera and species. Some of the older classification systems are therefore still in use despite access to more accurate genetic taxonomic methods.

The traditional division of streptococci into α-streptococci, β-streptococci and γ-streptococci on the basis of the capacity of the bacterial colony to hemolyze erythrocytes in the blood agar medium is still considered the first step in the classification of streptococci. The clear zone produced by lysis of the erythrocytes around the colony is typical of the β-hemolytic streptococci, but the zone may vary considerably in size (Fig. 225.1). Colonies of α-hemolytic streptococci are surrounded by a zone that is usually green (Fig. 225.2), whereas no color changes (and no hemolysis) are seen around the colonies of γ-streptococci on blood agar plates.

In addition, the colony size of the β-hemolytic streptococci is sometimes used as a taxonomic tool. Thus, β-hemolytic streptococci belonging to Lancefield groups A, C and G can be separated into large-colony (>0.5mm diameter) and small-colony (<0.5mm diameter) streptococci. The large-colony forms are usually designated 'pyogenic streptococci'; the small ones are representatives of the *Streptococcus milleri* group.

The further classification of streptococci involves biochemical analysis, including carbohydrate fermentation and detection of enzymatic activities. During the past 10 years genetic methods have been applied increasingly to taxonomic studies of streptococci and related organisms, for instance DNA–DNA and DNA–rRNA hybridization analysis, and small subunit (16S) rRNA sequencing. The latter technique has become the most powerful approach for delineating the phylogenetic interrelation of micro-organisms. Whereas the pyogenic streptococci (groups A, C and G) phylogenetically cluster together, the α-hemolytic streptococci fall into several different phylogenetic groups.

DIAGNOSTIC MICROBIOLOGY

Streptococci can be identified (Table 225.1) on the basis of:

- their hemolytic qualities;
- rapid antigen detection tests;
- serologic assays for detection of cell wall or capsular antigens;
- physiologic and biochemical tests; and
- molecular biologic tests.[2]

Streptococci are catalase negative and fermentation of carbohydrates is accompanied by the production of lactic acid. Streptococci are oxidase negative, a property that, together with the Gram stain, differentiates streptococci from *Neisseria* spp. Nutritional requirements are high; medium containing blood or serum is necessary for their growth (Fig. 225.3). Streptococcal colonies on blood agar can appear as mucoid mat or glistering. This appearance relates to the amount of hyaluronic acid capsule produced by the streptococci. Some of the oral streptococci may form bactericidal substances, so-called bacteriocins, which might inhibit the growth of other (β-hemolytic) streptococcal species in the surrounding area (Fig. 225.4).[3]

The surface structure of the pyogenic streptococci (groups A, C and G), together with the highly biologically active toxins and enzymes released by the cells, forms the basis of the pathogenesis of these streptococci. The cell wall is composed of a framework of peptidoglycan similar to that found in other Gram-positive bacteria. The group-specific polysaccharide is fixed to peptidoglycan through phosphate bridges, composed of one or several units of glycerol and glycerol rhamnoside.

A rapid, preliminary diagnosis of infections caused by streptococci can be achieved by Gram stain of properly obtained specimens (e.g. sputum, cerebrospinal fluid, pus). The presence of Gram-positive cocci in chains or pairs associated with leukocytes is indicative of the diagnosis of streptococcal infections (Figs 225.5 and 225.6). The skin is not normally colonized by streptococci, but streptococci are part of the commensal oropharyngeal flora; their presence in respiratory specimens collected from patients with pharyngitis has poor predictive value.

Further identification of streptococci may be achieved using extended biochemical and physiologic tests. For this purpose, diagnostic microbiologic laboratories can use standardized, commercially available laboratory kits such as API-20 Strep and Rapid Ig 32 Strep (Fig. 225.7).[4] Generally, these tests have high stability and good reproducibility between different laboratories and there is a database for interpretation of the reaction patterns.

For special epidemiologic purposes, molecular biologic typing techniques may be employed but these are not yet used in routine diagnosis.

β-Hemolytic streptococci

The β-hemolytic streptococci have long been considered the main pathogenic streptococci. Table 225.2 illustrates the characteristics of β-hemolytic streptococci in groups A, C and G, as well as those of streptococci in groups B and F, which may also produce β-hemolytic colonies on blood agar plates.[2,5]

Serologic analysis is based on differences in group-specific antigens, which are either carbohydrates or teichoic acids on the cell wall. This allows separation of streptococci into 20 different serogroups (the Lancefield grouping system).[6] Grouping involves a two-stage procedure with rapid acid or enzymatic antigen extraction, followed by immunospecific precipitation or agglutination reactions.

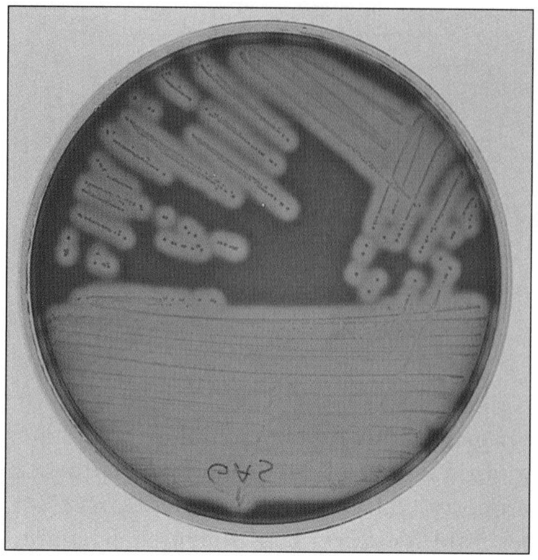

Fig. 225.1 β-Hemolytic streptococci group A on a blood agar plate. Note the clear β-hemolytic zone.

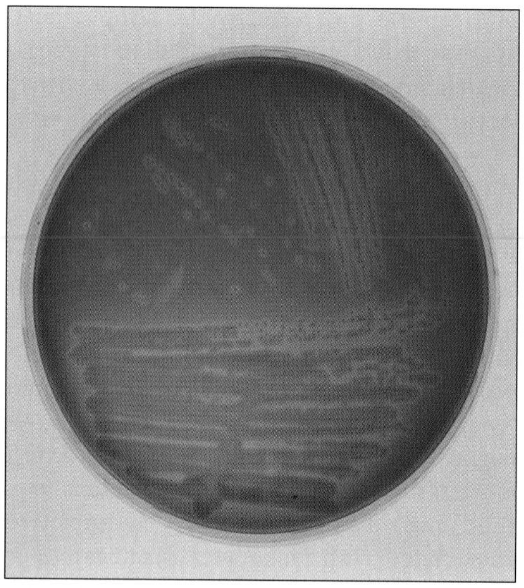

Fig. 225.2 α-Hemolytic streptococci on a blood agar plate. Note the small greenish zone surrounding the colonies, which is a characteristic of viridans streptococci.

COMMONLY USED METHODS FOR TYPING STREPTOCOCCI		
Serologic methods	M typing and T typing	
	R typing	
	OF typing (inhibition of the opacity reaction) group A streptococci	
	Polysaccharide antigen typing combined with protein antigen typing in group B streptococci	
	Latex agglutination	
Molecular methods	DNA fingerprinting	• M genotyping • pulsed-field gel electrophoresis • multilocus sequence typing • amplified fragment length polymorphism
	Ribotyping	
Other methods	Multilocus enzyme electrophoresis	
	Whole cell protein analysis	
Rarely used methods	Bacteriophage typing	
	Bacteriocin typing	

Table 225.1 Commonly used methods for typing streptococci.

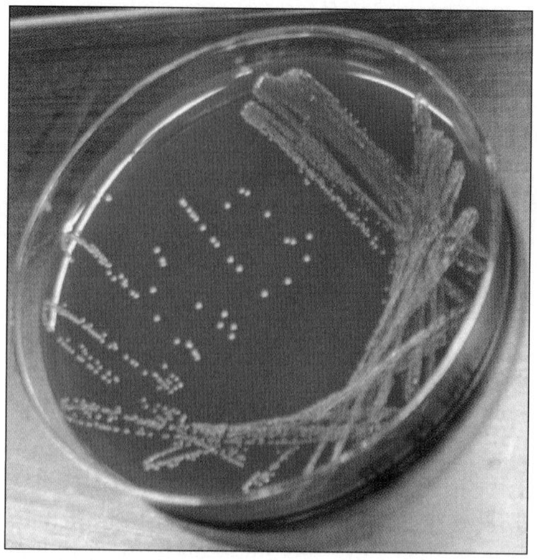

Fig. 225.3 γ-Streptococci on a blood agar plate. Note the absence of hemolysis.

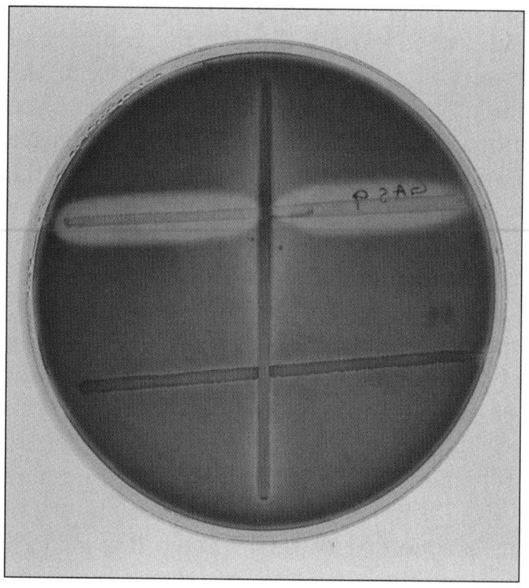

Fig. 225.4 Bacterial interference. Inhibition of growth of β-hemolytic streptococci by an α-hemolytic *Streptococcus* sp. No such inhibition is seen with other streptococci.

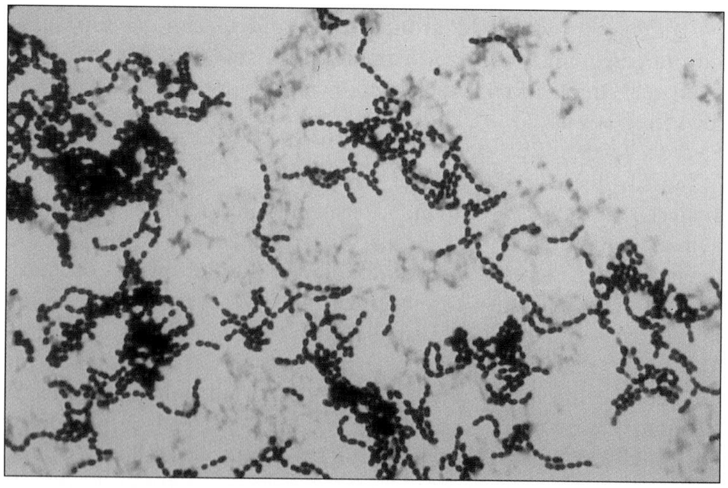

Fig. 225.5 Gram-stain of β-hemolytic streptococci group A.

Commercial kit systems in which group-specific antisera (usually containing A, B, C, D, F or G antibodies) are coupled to latex beads are now widely used for identification of β-hemolytic streptococci.[7] In a positive test the latex particles clump together; in a negative test they stay separate, giving the suspension a milky appearance (Fig. 225.8).

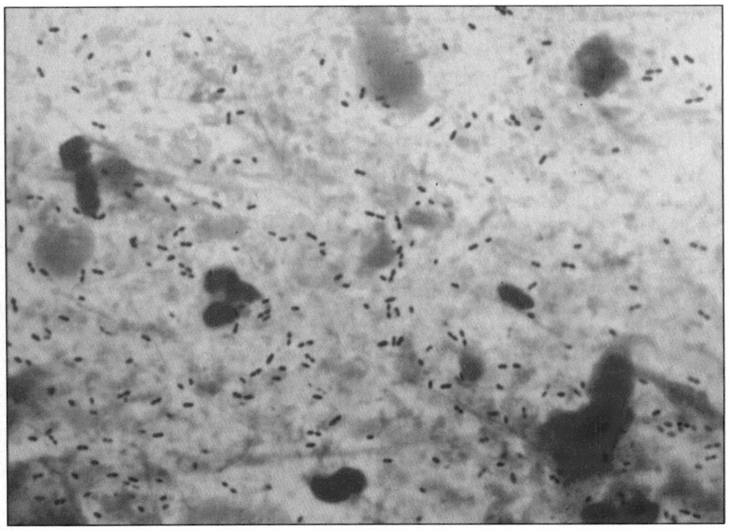

Fig. 225.6 Gram stain of a sputum sample infected with *Streptococcus pneumoniae*.

Nonhemolytic streptococci do not possess Lancefield cell wall grouping antigens, but some strains may possess similar antigens that show cross-reaction with β-hemolytic streptococcal group-specific antisera. Thus, proper assessment of hemolysis is essential for the reliability of the test because, for instance, *Streptococcus pneumoniae* may cross-react with group C latex reagent.

Group A streptococci

Cell wall antigens

From the blood agar plates, suspected hemolytic streptococcal colonies are subjected to Lancefield grouping as described above. Typing of group A streptococcal isolates is reserved mainly for laboratories specializing in streptococcal diagnostics and research. The cell wall proteins of group A streptococci that are used in strain typing include T protein and M protein. T protein is used for classification purposes, although it does not contribute to streptococcal pathogenesis. All group A streptococci carry one or more T antigens, which have a correlation with the M protein. The presence or absence of opacity factor divides the streptococci into two groups, which further facilitates a final typing by the T agglutination test. M antigen, a potent virulence factor, is the basis for the further serologic and genetic identification of more than 100 types.[8] Using specific antisera against these M proteins and sequence typing, more than 90% of fresh isolates of group A streptococcal isolates can be typed. Thus, subclones within group A streptococci carrying the same M protein have been described. However, the discriminatory power of these sera depends on the quality of the antisera and the size of the serum panel. This means that many isolates will be registered as 'nontypable'. This is also true for isolates that have lost the M protein or express only very low amounts of M protein on their surface.

Streptococcal typing by M-genotyping has been useful not only as a tool for general epidemiologic studies but also in analyses of correlation between streptococcal types and a clinical condition (see Clinical manifestations, below). Further discrimination between isolates belonging to the same M-type may be achieved by pulsed-field gel electrophoresis, multilocus sequence typing or amplified fragment length polymorphism.

Rapid antigen detection tests

Nonculture rapid antigen kits for direct detection of group A streptococci in patient samples are widely used.[9] The grouping antigen is extracted from the throat swab using nitrous acid or enzymatic treatment, followed by a procedure to detect the antigen. Most assays use latex agglutination or other immunoassays for antigen detection. It has been shown that these tests have high specificity (>95% in most kits) but variable sensitivity (50–90%) compared with culture techniques. False-negative results are common in the nonhospital setting; specimens from patients with clinical signs of pharyngitis and a negative antigen detection test should undergo routine culturing for streptococcal identification.

The use of rapid diagnostic tests eliminates the need for further epidemiologic analysis and streptococcal surveillance, but the costs of the kits and the extra clinical time spent on carrying out the tests limit their usefulness.

Serology

Determination of antistreptococcal antibodies may be helpful for diagnosing recent streptococcal infections. Streptolysin O is a strong immunogen and antibodies against this factor can be determined for demonstration of a recent infection with group A streptococci.[10] Streptolysin O binds easily to cholesterol and this binding eliminates its hemolytic and immune-stimulating activities. Therefore, in contrast to other streptococcal infections such as pharyngitis, infection in the skin often gives poor immune response to streptolysin O. Deoxyribonuclease (DNase) is produced by group A streptococci in four different antigenic variants, designated A, B, C and D. Most strains produce the B type and antibodies against this can be determined routinely to complement the antistreptolysin O determination in streptococcal infections of the skin; anti-DNase B antibodies appear after exposure to both dermal and respiratory infections. Ideally, two serum samples (acute-phase serum and convalescent serum) are tested for antistreptolysin O and anti-DNase B; a 4-fold increase in the titer is suggested as being significant. However, antibody responses may be depressed in patients receiving early antibiotic treatment for the infection.

The group A streptococci also produce other enzymes such as nicotinamide adenine dinucleotidase (NADase) and hyaluronidase. Antibodies are developed against both these enzymes and anti-hyaluronidase determination can be used in parallel with anti-streptolysin O determination to detect a previous streptococcal infection.

Biochemical and enzymatic assays

Streptolysin S, which is heat stable, is responsible for the β-hemolysis that occurs around the streptococcal colonies in blood agar. The so-called pyr test demonstrates the presence of pyrolidonylamidase, which is almost exclusively produced by β-hemolytic streptococci of group A and is often used for biochemical characterization of streptococci. It should be mentioned, however, that β-hemolytic colonies of enterococci can also produce this enzyme. The differentiation between these micro-organisms is often easily done by their differences in colony size and morphology.

The Vogues–Proskauer (VP) test for demonstration of ascetoin production helps to differentiate the small colony forming β-hemolytic streptococci belonging to the *S. milleri* group, which carry the polysaccharide antigens of Lancefield groups A, C, F and G, from the large colony forming pyogenic streptococci of these serologic groups.

Group B streptococci

Cell wall antigens

The group B streptococci can also be divided into several types based on the differences in the polysaccharide capsule of the organism. These types are designated 1a, 1b and 2–10. These capsular polysaccharides are high molecular weight polymers with straight backbone structures containing short side chains. The composition of the polysaccharide varies but contains galactose, glucose, *N*-acetylglucosamin and *N*-acetylneuraminic acid (sialic acid).[11] The

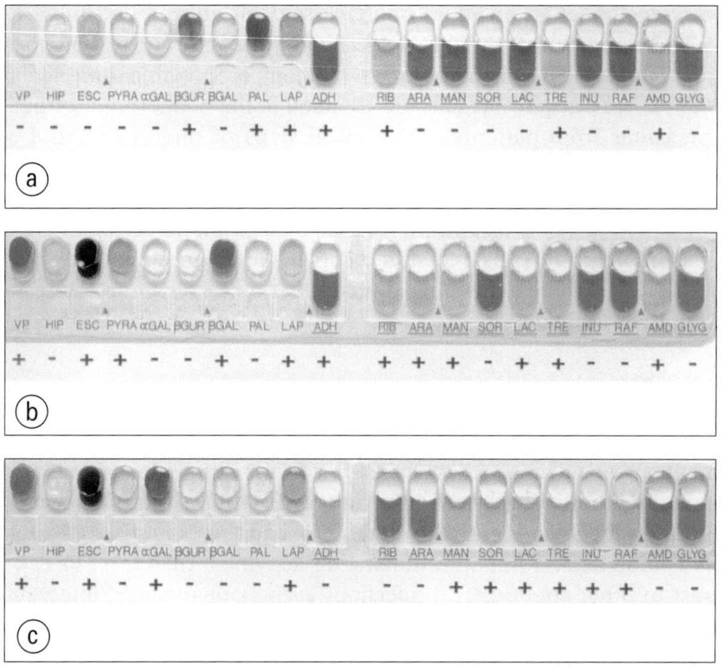

group B streptococci also have several protein antigens on the surface (designated C, R and X), which can be used to characterize the different serotypes. Their functional significance has not been defined.

Rapid antigen detection tests

Group B streptococci can be diagnosed in cerebrospinal fluid, serum and urine by agglutination assays, in which antibodies against group-specific antigens attached to latex particles recognize the group B streptococcus. These assays cannot be used to screen pregnant women for carriage of group B streptococci. Rapid tests to screen pregnant women include enzyme immunoassays, but because they are not yet sensitive and specific enough, their clinical use is limited.[12]

Biochemical and enzymatic assays

The CAMP assay is used for identification of group B streptococci. It is based on the production of an extracellular protein, the so-called CAMP (Christie, Atkins and Munck-Pedersen) factor. This factor has the capacity to lyse erythrocytes in the presence of staphylococcal β-lysin. A β-lysin-producing strain of *Staphylococcus aureus* is streaked at right angles to a streak of the suspected group B streptococci on a sheep blood agar plate. After incubation at 95°F (35°F)

API-20 STREP TESTS FOR THE IDENTIFICATION OF STREPTOCOCCI

	VP	HIP	ESC	PYRA	αGAL	βGUR	βGAL	PAL	LAP	ADH	RIB	ARA	MAN	SOR	LAC	TRE	INU	RAF	AMD	GLYG	βHEM
Streptococcus acidominimus	1	95	4	13	1	66	30	75	99	17	17	0	42	10	87	85	0	0	10	0	0
Streptococcus adjacens	0	0	10	80	0	25	0	0	99	0	0	0	0	0	0	0	0	0	0	0	0
Streptococcus agalactiae	100	99	1	1	4	79	1	96	99	99	98	0	1	1	50	87	0	1	35	4	75
Streptococcus anginosus	100	1	99	0	97	0	5	99	100	100	1	0	99	1	95	96	6	95	96	0	40
Streptococcus bovis I	97	2	100	2	71	4	14	0	97	0	2	12	93	0	100	98	63	94	100	93	0
Streptococcus bovis II 1	95	4	97	1	91	1	8	0	100	1	0	14	0	0	93	30	61	99	73	65	0
Streptococcus bovis II 2	86	4	100	13	90	94	94	0	100	13	0	1	0	0	99	99	13	72	40	13	0
Streptococcus canis	0	0	25	90	95	1	80	100	100	100	100	0	0	0	99	1	0	1	99	0	100
Streptococcus constellatus	100	1	1	0	0	0	7	99	100	96	0	0	2	1	1	85	0	1	2	0	90
Streptacoccus defectivus	25	0	15	99	100	0	100	0	97	0	0	0	0	0	99	100	5	97	100	0	0
Streptococcus dysgalactiae	0	0	1	1	1	99	0	100	99	100	99	0	1	50	92	100	0	1	99	30	0
Streptococcus equi equi	1	0	1	0	0	100	0	100	100	100	0	0	0	0	0	0	0	0	100	100	100
Streptococcus equi zooepidemicus	0	1	15	0	0	100	1	99	100	100	85	0	0	99	100	0	0	0	99	99	99
Streptococcus equinus	100	0	95	0	28	0	1	1	100	0	0	0	30	0	25	7	25	15	17	10	0
Streptococcus equisimilis	0	1	25	1	0	99	1	99	100	97	97	0	1	0	45	99	0	1	98	40	95
Streptococcus gr. L	0	75	1	0	0	100	1	100	100	100	100	0	0	0	75	100	0	0	100	98	94
Streptacoccus intermedius	100	1	97	0	3	0	5	94	100	99	1	0	2	1	94	96	8	2	75	0	50
Streptococcus mitis 1	0	0	0	0	2	0	60	50	100	25	2	0	0	0	100	0	4	0	100	2	0
Streptococcus mitis 2	0	0	15	0	0	0	0	15	100	35	10	0	0	0	90	25	0	0	20	10	0
Streptococcus mutans	99	0	99	0	64	0	1	1	100	18	0	0	99	90	90	100	81	81	1	0	1
Streptococcus oralis	0	0	10	0	75	0	75	87	100	0	5	0	0	0	100	25	0	75	99	1	0
Streptococcus pneumoniae	0	0	39	60	78	3	85	3	100	57	3	0	0	0	100	99	64	92	89	10	1
Streptococcus porcinus	100	5	99	1	19	99	1	100	100	100	98	0	95	95	83	99	0	0	50	0	100
Streptococcus pyogenes	0	1	5	98	0	15	0	100	100	99	0	0	8	1	99	98	0	1	61	22	98
Streptococcus salivarius salivarius	91	0	98	1	8	0	70	20	100	0	0	0	5	1	86	67	34	93	74	1	1
Streptococcus sanguis	0	1	74	0	41	0	13	41	99	74	2	3	5	9	79	78	35	48	58	3	2
Streptococcus suis I	0	1	82	53	80	94	76	1	100	91	0	0	7	0	94	100	75	0	100	89	0
Streptococcus suis II	0	1	81	41	91	91	52	3	100	95	0	0	3	1	99	98	63	100	100	98	1
Streptacoccus uberis	99	99	100	25	10	91	5	30	100	99	99	0	99	98	99	100	93	10	50	20	0
Enterococcus casseliflavus	96	34	100	96	83	17	100	0	96	66	100	100	100	16	100	100	70	99	89	3	0
Enterococcus durans	100	43	100	97	32	2	80	0	91	100	99	15	2	0	84	81	0	0	56	0	18
Enterococcus faecalis	99	46	99	97	0	0	20	4	99	97	98	0	98	92	94	100	0	0	96	2	0
Enterococcus faecium	94	43	99	95	42	0	94	2	97	93	85	84	83	14	90	98	20	0	73	3	0
Enterococcus gallinarum	100	99	100	100	95	80	100	0	99	100	100	100	100	1	100	100	99	100	83	20	0
Enterococcus avium	100	60	100	94	6	0	10	1	99	0	99	40	100	95	95	99	1	40	15	0	1
Aerococcus viridans I	8	50	99	54	33	16	37	1	5	1	83	33	85	79	83	99	33	41	95	33	1
Aerococcus viridans 2	15	80	50	85	10	20	20	1	1	5	25	1	35	1	70	89	1	5	20	1	5
Aerococcus viridans 3	22	88	99	40	85	48	14	14	1	1	8	2	82	5	91	99	37	99	14	1	1
Gardnerella vaginalis	0	95	0	0	0	1	53	0	99	0	46	6	1	0	1	0	0	0	73	53	0
Gemella haemolysans	25	0	0	90	0	0	1	100	25	1	1	0	20	10	5	2	0	0	10	5	1
Gemella morbillorum	3	0	0	25	0	0	10	25	99	4	5	0	0	0	1	11	1	1	14	5	0
Lactococcus lactis cremoris	100	15	41	1	13	0	41	4	89	0	27	0	17	0	96	30	0	20	25	0	0
Lactococcus lactis lactis	90	40	99	25	3	0	25	5	96	95	95	15	45	0	72	96	2	5	90	3	0
Lactococcus plantarum	100	0	100	0	0	0	0	0	100	0	0	0	100	50	0	100	0	0	0	0	0
Leuconostoc spp	95	1	47	5	61	0	75	2	67	10	37	42	29	4	42	72	0	42	5	0	0
Listeria grayi	100	0	100	0	0	0	0	0	80	0	90	0	100	10	60	100	20	30	90	0	0
Listeria spp	97	88	98	0	0	0	0	0	85	0	6	0	0	0	49	92	1	0	72	0	26

(d)

Fig. 225.7 API-20 Strep tests for the identification of streptococci. (a) *Streptococcus equisimilis* ATCC 35666. (b) *Enterococcus faecium* ATCC 35667. (c) *Streptococcus mutans* ATCC 35668. (d) Interpretation scheme.

SEROLOGIC AND BIOCHEMICAL DIFFERENTIATION OF β-HEMOLYTIC STREPTOCOCCI					
Species or group	Serologic group	Test			
		Voges–Proskauer	Pyrrolidonyl arylamidase	Trehalose	Sorbitol
Streptococcus pyogenes	A	–	+	NA	NA
Streptococcus agalactiae	B	–	–	NA	NA
Streptococcus equi	C	–	–	–	–
Streptococcus equisimilis	C	–	–	+	–
S. zooepidemicus	C	–	–	–	+
Lancefield group G	G	–	–	NA	NA
Streptococcus anginosus	A, C, F, G or none	+	–	NA	NA

Table 225.2 Serologic and biochemical differentiation of β-hemolytic streptococci. +, positive reaction; –, negative reaction; NA, not applicable. *Streptococcus anginosus* is considered a representative of *Streptococcus milleri*. Data from Facklam and Washington.[5]

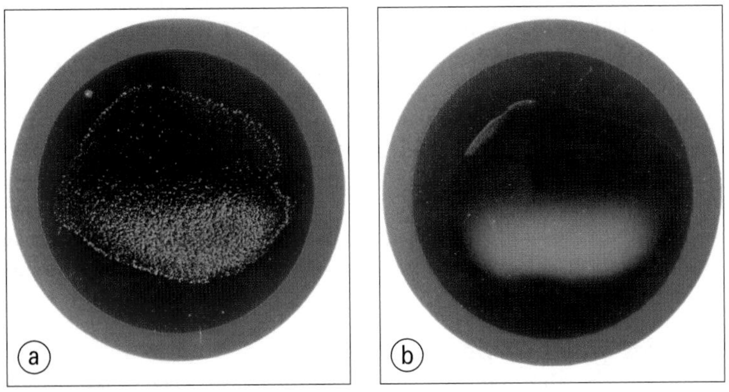

Fig. 225.8 Latex agglutination for the identification of β-hemolytic streptococci group A. (a) Positive agglutination. (b) Negative agglutination.

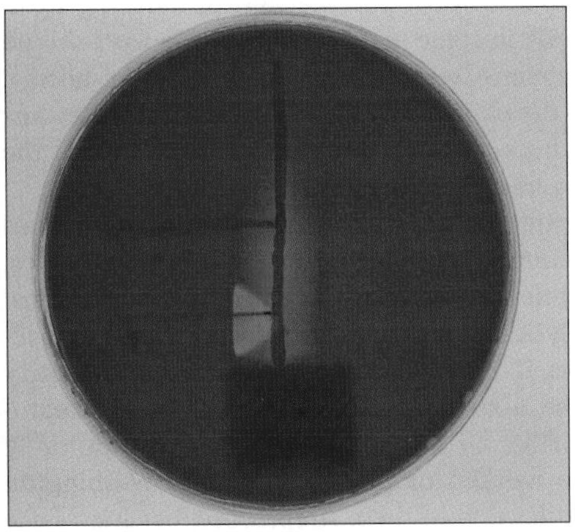

Fig. 225.9 The CAMP test. Induced hemolysis of a group B streptococcus culture in the vicinity of a streak of *Staphylococcus* spp.

overnight, an arrowhead-shaped zone of β-hemolysis will be seen in the area where staphylococcal β-lysin and CAMP factor meet (Fig. 225.9). Otherwise, group B streptococci can be distinguished by hydrolysis of hippurate or by growth on selective media (e.g. new Granada medium).[13]

Group C and G streptococci

Group C isolates can be differentiated into species on the basis of their capacity to ferment carbohydrates (see Fig. 225.4). However, genetic analysis of group C and G streptococci has shown that human isolates of the group C species *Streptococcus equisimilis* are closely related to group G large colony human isolates and may therefore be classified in the same species. Furthermore, molecular studies have indicated that *Streptococcus zooepidemicus* probably is a subspecies of *Streptococcus equi*.[14] The large colony forming β-hemolytic streptococci belonging to the Lancefield groups C and G have a disease spectrum and an epidemiology similar to those of the group A streptococci.[15–17] It should be added that these streptococci are not identified with the quick tests usually employed today to aid streptococcal diagnosis in primary health care. This means that if culture is not performed the diagnosis of throat infections caused by these micro-organisms will be missed.

Group D streptococci (enterococcal and nonenterococcal species)

It is now generally accepted that enterococci are sufficiently different from the other members of the *Streptococcus* genus to represent a separate genus, *Enterococcus*. This is based on the genetic information on *Streptococcus faecalis* and *Streptococcus faecium*, but further analysis by DNA–DNA and DNA–RNA hybridization as well as sequencing by 16S RNA indicate that at least 11 more species should be incorporated into this genus.

Biochemical and enzymatic assays

Most enterococci produce an α-hemolytic (greenish) zone on the blood agar plates but also nonhemolytic colonies as well as complete lysis of the blood around the colonies may be produced by some species (Fig. 225.10). Other characteristics of the enterococcus group, such as growth in broth containing 6.5% sodium chloride and hydrolysis of esculin in the presence of 40% bile salts (bile–esculin medium), help to distinguish between streptococci and enterococci. Furthermore, all strains produce leucinaminopeptidase. In most cases it is possible to extract a cell wall-associated glycerol-teichoic acid, which is identical to the streptococcal group D antigen. The physiologic characteristics of the enterococcus group mentioned above are not restricted to the genus *Enterococcus* and it is now accepted that a number of other micro-organisms may have several or all of these characteristics, including most species of the genus *Pediococcus* and several species of the genus *Leuconostoc* (see Fig. 225.8). *Leuconostoc* spp. can, for example, grow in a bile–esculin milieu and in high salt concentrations, and the group D antiserum test is also positive. However, they show intrinsic resistance to vancomycin, which is not usually the case with *Enterococcus* spp. Additionally, *Streptococcus*

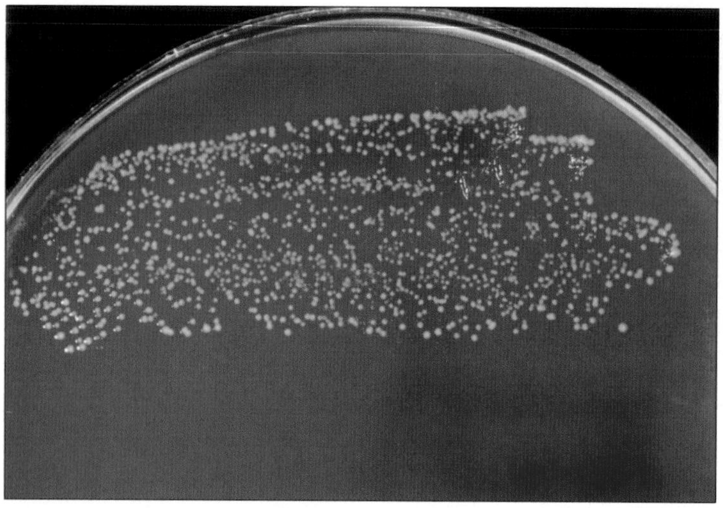

Fig. 225.10 *Enterococcus faecalis* on a blood agar plate.

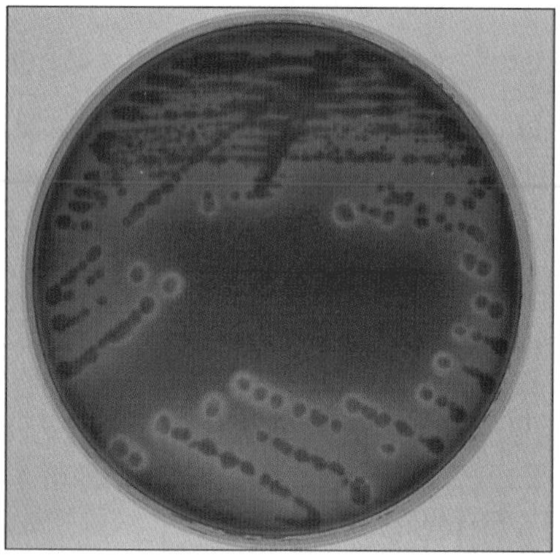

Fig. 225.11 Mucoid *Streptococcus pneumoniae* on a blood agar plate.

bovis and *Streptococcus equinus*, of which the primary hosts are animals, belong to the nonenterococcal group D streptococci. *Streptococcus bovis*, unlike the enterococci, does not grow in 6.5% sodium chloride.

α-Hemolytic streptococci

Streptococcus pneumoniae (or pneumococci) are facultative anaerobic bacteria that are usually found as lancet-shaped cells in diploid form or in short chains. In order to be reliable, sputum specimens tested for the presence of pneumococci should be devoid of saliva containing epithelial cells and viridans streptococci, the most prevalent organisms among the oral flora.

Cell wall antigens

Differences in the capsular polysaccharide structure among the isolates allow discrimination between 84 different pneumococcal serotypes. The appearance of pneumococcal colonies depends on the degree of encapsulation; heavily encapsulated strains form larger colonies and appear very mucoid (Fig. 225.11). In Gram stains the capsule is visible as a pink halo or a nonstaining zone around the bacteria. On prolonged incubation, colonies on blood agar plates typically appear as checker pieces surrounded by an intensely greenish color (the α-hemolytic zone).

Rapid antigen detection tests

Soluble pneumococcal capsular polysaccharides can be rapidly detected in infected body fluids by very sensitive immunologic assays. This is especially beneficial in patients who have pneumococcal meningitis. In about half of meningitis patients, cultures may be negative after the administration of even a single dose of antibiotics, yet the antigen detection tests will remain positive.

Biochemical and enzymatic assays

Pneumococci are fastidious and some strains also need carbon dioxide for good growth. They produce an autolytic enzyme (L-alanine-uramylamidase), which has a capacity to hydrolyze the cell wall. This enzyme is activated by detergents such as bile, which results in the lysis of the cell. Optochin (ethylhydrocupreinhydrochloride) inhibits the growth of most pneumococci, in contrast to other α-hemolytic streptococci, and is thus an easy method for distinguishing between these species.

Serology

In routine diagnosis, serologic tests for pneumococcal infections are of limited clinical value because acute and convalescent sera are usually not available and only a limited number of antigens can be used. However, using the C polysaccharide and pneumolysin as antigens, antibody tests have been developed. Unfortunately, antibodies against C polysaccharide develop poorly in children, but in adults an enzyme-linked immunosorbent assay (ELISA) technique based on the C polysaccharide has been valuable for the diagnosis of pneumococcal pneumonia. Determination of antibodies against pneumolysin by ELISA has been applied successfully to establish the pneumococcal etiology in adult patients with pneumonia.

Molecular biology

Development of rapid DNA diagnostic tests such as polymerase chain reaction (PCR) for detection of pneumococci in middle-ear fluid are in progress.[18]

Viridans group streptococci

Traditionally, the name viridans streptococci was given to α-streptococci isolated from the oral region but lacking the Lancefield grouping antigen. The term viridans is not quite correct as this group of streptococci are also nonhemolytic (not producing a green zone of hemolysis in the agar medium around the colonies).

Because viridans group streptococci are capable of inducing significant infections, especially in some high-risk patients, efforts should be made to obtain specimens free of contamination by the normal flora. Determination of the clinical significance of each isolate must be made with caution because such determinations influence the need to direct therapy against these organisms.

Because the viridans streptococci give poor and variable reactions in serologic and conventional physiologic tests and, in many cases, are of relatively low virulence, they have been studied less extensively than the β-hemolytic streptococci. In selected cases of bacteremia or endocarditis it may be clinically helpful to identify viridans streptococci. The taxonomic classification of these streptococci has caused confusion for a long time but was substantially simplified by a scheme worked out by Facklam and Washington (Table 225.3).[5] The identification of these streptococci has long since been recognized as unsatisfactory, with the result that a significant proportion of these isolates remain misidentified or unidentified.[4,19,20]

Biochemical and enzymatic assays

Although they are named viridans, these organisms do not all produce α-hemolysis; the property of green coloration on blood agar is affected by the growth medium used.[4] Commercially developed kits may be of great help in the species identification of viridans streptococci, but misidentification or lack of identification of members of the *S. milleri* group, *Streptococcus oralis*, *Streptococcus mitis*, *Leuconostoc* spp. and other *Streptococcus*-like organisms is a signi-

BIOCHEMICAL IDENTIFICATION OF VIRIDANS GROUP STREPTOCOCCI						
Species or group	Test					
	Mannitol	Sorbitol	Voges–Proskauer	Arginine	Esculin	Urease
S. mutans (includes *S. cricetus, S. downei, S. ferus, S. macace, S. rattus* (arginine positive), *S. sobrinus*)	+	+	+	−	+	−
S. salivarius (includes *S. intestinalis, S. vestibularis*)	−	−	+	−	+	±
S. sanguis (includes *S. gordonii*, groups H and W streptococci)	−	− (+)	−	+	+	−
S. mitis (includes *S. mitior, S. oralis, S. sanguis* biotype II)	−	−	−	−	−	−
S. anginosus (includes *S. intermedius, S. constellatus, S. milleri*, DNA groups I and III)	− (+)	− (+)	+ (−)	+	+	−

Table 225.3 Biochemical identification of viridans group streptococci. +, positive reaction; −, negative reaction; ±, some strains positive, other strains negative; + (−), usually positive but occasional exceptions; − (+), usually negative but occasional exceptions. Data from Facklam and Washington.[5]

THE VIRIDANS GROUP OF STREPTOCOCCI	
S. mutans group	*S. mutans, S. sobrinus, S. rattus, S. cricatus*
S. salivarius group	*S. salivarius, S. vestibularis, S. thermophilus*
S. milleri group	*S. anginosus, S. constellatus, S. intermedius*
S. sanguis group	*S. sanguis I, S. gordinii, S. parasanguis, S. crista*
S. mitis	*S. mitior, S. oralis* and the previous *S. sanguis II, S. mitis*

Table 225.4 The viridans group of streptococci. Current and previous nomenclature.[1]

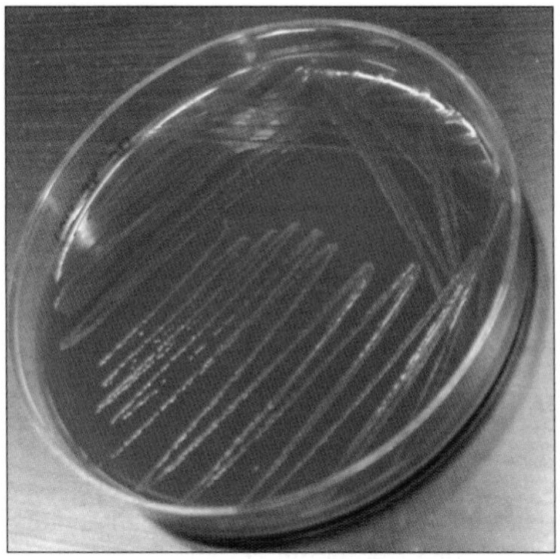

Fig. 225.12 *Leuconostoc* on a blood agar plate.

ficant problem. Five species or groups of species can be identified on the basis of various biochemical tests or fermentation capacities (Table 225.4; Fig. 225.12).[1,5,21] *Streptococcus milleri* produces small, pinpoint colonies on blood agar, among which α-hemolytic and α-hemolytic strains and nonhemolytic strains with or without identifiable Lancefield antigens (A, C, F and G) are represented. At least seven distinct species in the *Streptococcus mutans* group are recognized, including *Streptococcus sobrinus, Streptococcus rattus,* and *Streptococcus cricetus*, besides the cariogenic *S. mutans*. The sanguis group, which was formerly designated *Streptococcus sanguis* I, consists of *Streptococcus sanguis, Streptococcus gordoni, Streptococcus parasanguis* and *Streptococcus crista*.

Molecular biology

Molecular biology-based analyses, such as DNA–DNA or RNA–DNA hybridization and restriction fragment length polymorphism analysis of rRNA genes (ribotyping), have helped to clarify the taxonomy of viridans streptococci.[22] The streptococci belonging to the *S. mitis* group were earlier recognized as *Streptococcus mitior, S. sanguis II* and *Streptococcus oralis*. In the *S. milleri* group, the species *Streptococcus anginosus, Streptococcus intermedius* and *Streptococcus constellatus* are now listed, based on similarities found in genetic studies.

Nutritionally variant streptococci (Abiotrophia)

A subgroup of the viridans streptococci has been isolated from patients who have endocarditis and otitis media. These are nutritionally deficient, being dependent on pyridoxal or vitamin B6. They are also designated thiol-dependent streptococci and symbiotic streptococci.[23] These bacteria will not grow on ordinary media, which usually lack pyridoxal, but they will grow in the vicinity of other micro-organisms that produce this substance (e.g. *Staphylococcus aureus, Escherichia coli* and members of several enterobacter groups). Like other viridans streptococci they are normal inhabitants of the oral flora. Nutritionally variant streptococci should be suspected when Gram stains of specimens reveal the presence of cocci but cultures are negative.[24]

Streptococcus-like organisms

Streptococcus-like organisms can be found in the genera *Aerococcus, Facklamia, Pediococcus* and *Leuconostoc*. They have a particular resemblance to the viridans streptococci and share many characteristics with the viridans group of streptococci (Table 225.5). These micro-organisms have a low pathogenic potential but can be found in immunocompromised patients and especially in patients with endocarditis. They can be recovered from wounds, urine and saliva and should be recognized because they may be resistant to vancomycin; this is true for *Pediococcus* and *Leuconostoc* spp. The identification of *Facklamia* spp. is problematic because none of the biochemical testing systems currently include them in their databases.

EPIDEMIOLOGY

Streptococci are widely distributed in nature and can be found in animals and humans as part of the normal flora in the respiratory tract as well as the gastrointestinal and urogenital tracts. They are

CHARACTERIZATION OF VIRIDANS STREPTOCOCCUS-LIKE BACTERIA						
	Growth in 6.5% sodium chloride	Growth in bile esculin	Pyrrolidonyl arylamidase	Leucinamino-peptidase	Hippurate	Vancomycin
Aerococcus spp.	+	V	+	–	+	S
Pediococcus spp.	V	+	–	+	+	R
Leuconostoc spp.	V	V	–	–	+	R
Facklamia spp.	+	–	+	+	V	S

Table 225.5 Characterization of viridans streptococcus-like bacteria. V, variable; S, susceptible; R, resistant.

also the causative agents of various types of infections with or without late sequelae.[25–27]

β-Hemolytic streptococci of groups A, C and G

β-Hemolytic streptococci of groups A, C and G are often found in the upper respiratory tract, especially in children aged between 5 and 15 years, although people of all ages may be infected. The frequency of streptococcal-induced upper respiratory tract infections and especially pharyngitis and tonsillitis is higher during the early autumn months and the spring.[25–27] This seasonal variation is fairly constant over the years but fluctuations between years have been noted, especially before the antibiotic era when it was easy to follow the fluctuation in scarlet fever epidemics, which varied widely. Infections in the upper respiratory tract are transferred to the surroundings via droplets and also directly through physical contact; a higher number of streptococcal upper respiratory tract infections is found in highly populated areas in narrow localities. Spread among family members and in classrooms is therefore a common finding. In residential schools and detention centers pharyngeal carriage rates approach 50%. Except in epidemics, skin carriage is not common. However, in certain geographic areas where streptococcal pyoderma is common, skin colonization rates may be as high as 40%. Colonization rates are higher in patients who have skin diseases, such as eczema and psoriasis, and wounds. Children who have streptococcal pharyngitis may excrete this organism in their feces or carry it in the perianal region, which may be the cause of widespread streptococcal infections in closed facilities.

Large numbers of pyogenic streptococci are shed in the immediate environment, where the bacteria may be cultivated from clothing as well as sheets and mattresses belonging to the infected person. This is important, especially in the treatment of patients who have skin infections such as impetigo. Recurrent streptococcal throat or skin infections is a common finding within families or institutions. In the search for sources, pets as well as family members are usually incriminated. Generally, pets are not a common source of reinfection because group A streptococci are highly host specific. Otherwise, group C streptococcal infections can be acquired by close contacts with infected horses and group G streptococci can be obtained from dogs, in which group G streptococci are the dominant cause of streptococcal pharyngitis (see Chapter 91).

In a given population only a limited number of M types are prevalent and the population gradually seems to acquire immunity to these. New types seem to enter the population when the immunity against these diminishes below a certain level.

Scarlet fever used to be a frightening disease, but during the past few decades it seems to have had a mild course in the Western world. However, since the mid-1980s a worldwide increase in the incidence of severe group A streptococcal disease has been reported, including rheumatic fever, cellulitis, necrotizing fasciitis and other invasive forms. These serious infections were reported as being associated with the reappearance of M1 and M3 strains and the production of pyrogenic exotoxins A and B although subsequently other exotoxins have also been implicated.[26,28,29] Food-borne epidemics (especially carried by milk) were common before pasterurization and were usually caused by group A streptococci, but groups C and G streptococci were also implicated on occasion. Food-borne infection can cause epidemic outbreaks of streptococcal infections such as scarlet fever and pharyngitis.

Recently, *Streptococcus iniae*, a fish pathogen that produces β-hemolytic colonies on blood agar, has been reported as an additional cause of cellulitis and invasive soft tissue infections.[30]

Group B streptococci

Group B streptococci are less commonly found in the upper respiratory tract, but their presence in the vagina of women aged between 15 and 45 years is rather common. Their numbers fluctuate and are higher before the monthly menstrual period and in pregnancy.[3,31,32] Isolation frequencies as high as 30–35% have been recorded in some surveys. During delivery, vaginal colonization causes transmission to the infant in 50–75% of cases. A small number of these infants will develop symptoms of disease (see Clinical manifestations, below).

Enterococci

Enterococci are the most prevalent aerobic cocci in the bowel. Resistance against glycopeptides is emerging, especially in *E. faecium* isolated in intensive care units and nursing homes. This increase in resistance is thought to be associated with the administration of high doses of glycopeptides. In many hospitals, the increasing prevalence of methicillin-resistant *Staphylococcus aureus* (MRSA) was accompanied by a similar increase in the prescription of vancomycin. In addition, glycopeptides have been used as growth promoters in the livestock industry, thus inducing resistant enterococci in poultry products for human consumption.

Streptococcus pneumoniae

Streptococcus pneumoniae is an obligate parasite in humans, who may be colonized at a very early stage of life. The pneumococcus is a regular inhabitant of the nasopharynx in humans, especially among children, although adults are also frequently colonized. In certain populations carrier rates of 70% are found. In general, the rate of disease in a population depends on the frequency with which invasive serotypes are carried in the nasopharynx.[33] Nasopharyngeal carriage is often accompanied by the development of protection against infection by the same serotype. Carriage rates are inversely related to age and the levels of anticapsular antibody, and thus it is clear that the immune status of the host is an important determinant of the prevalence and longevity of carriage.[33] Like the β-hemolytic streptococci, pneumococci are spread from person to person by sneezing and coughing. Of the 84 capsular types in the pneumococci, some seem to be more invasive than others (e.g. type 3 is among the most invasive strain types).[34] The capsular types 6a, 6b, 14, 19a, 19f and 23f are the dominant types found in pneumococcal

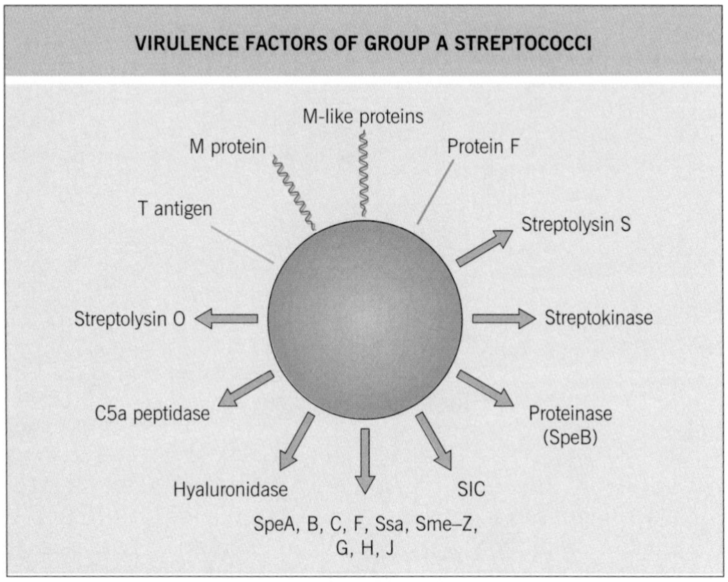

Fig. 225.13 Virulence factors of group A streptococci. Spe, streptococcal pyrogenic exotoxins; SIC, streptococcal inhibitor of complement-mediated lysis; Ssa, streptococcal superantigens.

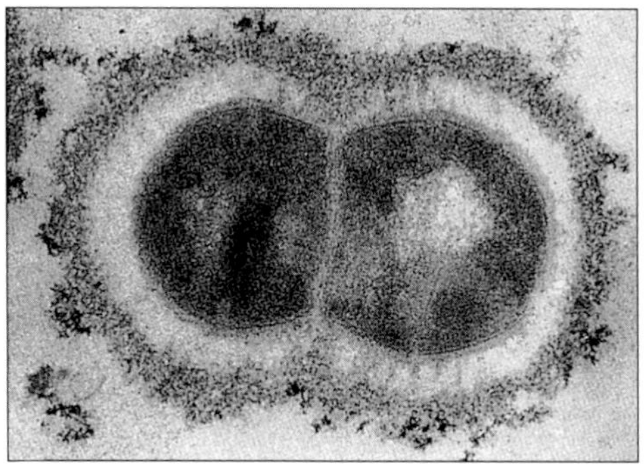

Fig. 225.14 Electron microscopy of group A streptococcus. The fuzzy M protein layer can be seen protruding from the cell wall.

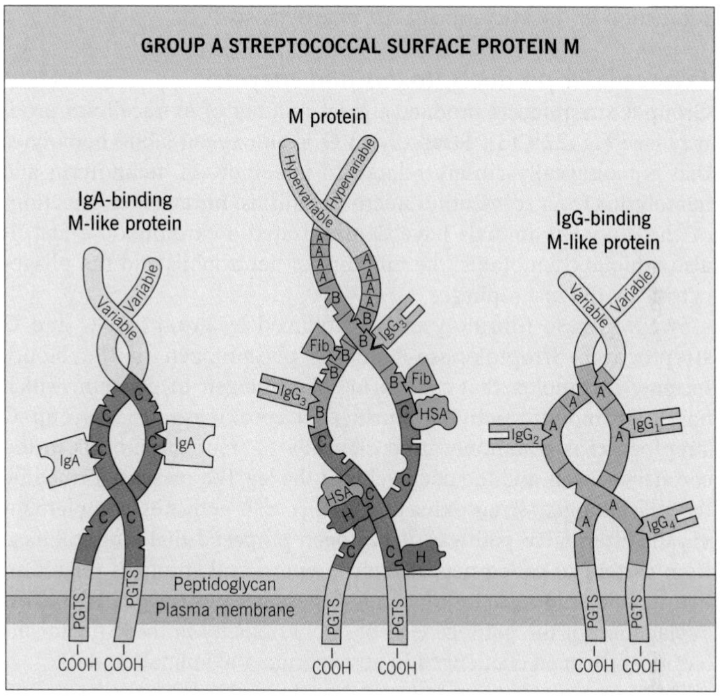

Fig. 225.15 Group A streptococcal surface protein M. A, B and C represent various regions of the M protein characterized by different degrees of variability of the protein structure. H, S, A and Fib denote human serum albumin and fibrinogen binding structures, respectively.

infection during the first 2 years of life, whereas in adults these types and the types 1, 3, 4, 7f, 8, 9, 10a, 11a, 12f, 14, 15b, 17f, 18c, 20 and 22f seem to cause the greatest number of bacteremic infections recorded in the USA.

A viral infection may predispose to a pneumococcal infection; this seems to be the case in children, who very often get pneumococcal otitis media 1–2 weeks after a virus infection. Support for this theory might be the finding in vitro that certain strains of adenovirus enhance the adherence of pneumococci to human respiratory tract epithelial cells.[31] Consequently, pneumococcal infections vary with the season in relation to the frequency and type of virus infections.

Certain penicillin-resistant pneumococcal clones may have a strong epidemic potential owing to their relative resistance to penicillin and other commonly used antibiotics, showing a facilitated spread in subpopulations regularly exposed to both the pneumococcus and to numerous antibiotics.[35]

Viridans group streptococci

Viridans group streptococci are fairly constant in the upper respiratory tract and dominate the aerobic normal flora in this region in the same way that enterococci dominate the aerobic normal flora in the gut. Viridans group streptococci are part of the normal flora of human mucous membranes in the mouth and upper respiratory tract as well as in stool samples.

PATHOGENESIS

Group A streptococci

The virulence factors of group A streptococci comprise both surface structures and proteins released from the cells during growth (Fig. 225.13).

Cell wall antigens

According to some scientists the M protein is a prerequisite for the binding of group A streptococci to epithelial cells in the skin, and F protein, another surface protein, is responsible for the binding to the epithelial cells in the airways, probably by binding to fibronectin.[32] Biochemically, M protein is an α-helicoidal structure similar to some muscle proteins such as myosin and tropomysin (Figs. 225.14 and 225.15).[36] The M protein has also been shown to cross-react immunologically with these contractile proteins.[36–38] It has been speculated whether this is of significance for the pathogenesis of rheumatic fever. A type-specific immunity is induced during the streptococcal infection and it has been shown in vaccination experiments[38] that purified M protein can be used to induce immunity. Because these antibodies cross-react with human heart muscle proteins, there has been a reluctance to proceed with these experiments in humans. Lately it has been shown that M proteins may also function as superantigens and this has further emphasized that the proteins in the M-protein family may be important virulence factors.[39]

The amount of M protein on the surface of streptococci varies within wide ranges and in some streptococci this antigen cannot be demonstrated. M-negative streptococci are phagocytosed quickly in serum milieu after being opsonized via the alternative complement pathway in the absence of antibodies against the M antigen, whereas M-positive streptococci resist phagocytosis in the absence of type-specific antibodies. The inability of M-positive streptococci to bind to phagocytosing cells efficiently indicates that C3b is not deposited on the surface of the streptococci or it is not accessible to the C3b receptor on the streptococci. The deposition of C3b is probably regulated by factor H, for which the M antigen has a high affinity.[40]

Several other M-like factors have been identified on the surface of group A streptococci. These have been shown to bind immunoglobulins such as IgG and IgA as well as several other serum proteins, including fibrinogen, plasmin, β_2 microglobulin and factor H. It has also recently been shown that some group A streptococcal strains have the ability to inhibit the activation of complement via the classic pathway by binding C4b to M-protein like structures. The way in which all these factors influence the virulence of the streptococci is not clear at present, but these factors can be seen as an expression of the complex interplay between the host and the micro-organism in group A streptococcal infections.[39,40]

Another example of this is C5a peptidase, which is a surface protein that by its specific ability to cleave C5a hinders the activation of polymorphonuclear leukocytes and thereby contributes to the protection of the bacteria against phagocytosis.[41]

Extracellular products, toxins and enzymes

Group A streptococci produce a great number of extracellular products (see Fig. 225.13). Streptolysin O is an oxygen-labile hemolysin that is biologically closely related to pneumolysin, tetanolysin and hemolysins from some other micro-organisms. Intravenous injections of this toxin in animals have demonstrated a cardiotoxic effect. It also inhibits chemotaxis, the mobility of neutrophils and the phagocytosis by the macrophages.

Streptokinase (fibrinolysin) is produced by groups A, C and G streptococci. Streptokinase binds to plasminogen in the blood, forming a complex that transforms plasminogen to plasmin, which has a fibrinolytic activity. Purified streptokinase from group C streptococci is commonly used clinically to treat thrombosis in the coronary vessels and the deep veins of the leg. The plasmin formed by the plasminogen–streptokinase complex also activates complement via the alternative pathway. It has been proposed that streptokinase from certain so-called nephrogenic streptococcal strains is related to the nephrogenic capacity of some of these isolates (Fig. 225.16). This explanation of the pathogenesis of nephrotoxicity in these organisms has recently been challenged in an experimental animal model.[42]

The pyrogenic exotoxins (scarlatina toxins) have been proposed as being responsible for the scarlatina erythema. Numerous different toxins are produced; they are designated streptococcal pyrogenic exotoxin (Spe)A, SpeC, SpeF, SpeG, SpeH, SpeJ, SmeZ, mitogenic factor (MF) and streptococcal superantigen (Ssa). (SpeB is now known to be a constitutive cysteine protease and SpeE and MF have been shown to be identical.) Most group A strains produce more than one of these toxins. Several biologic effects have been attributed to the toxins, including pyrogenicity, a decrease in the blood–brain barrier permeability, cardiotoxic effect, T-cell activation and potentiation of the effects of endotoxin. The toxins may be responsible for the development of the shock syndrome that sometimes appears after streptococcal infections.[43,44] It has been suggested that this reaction, like many of the biologic effects, is induced by the release of cytokines because these toxins function as very active superantigens and thereby stimulate a high level of proliferation of T cells (Fig. 225.17). Patients who develop the toxic shock syndrome have been shown to have very low or undetectable levels of neutralizing antibodies against one or more of these toxins.[44] Development of the streptococcal toxic shock syndrome might be hindered if toxin-neutralizing antibodies could be administered at a very early stage (see Chapter 56).

Groups C and G streptococci

The species *S. equisimilis* (a group C streptococcal species) produces streptolysin O as well as streptokinase, and *S. zooepidemicus* and *S. equi* (also group C streptococci) form hemolysins that differ from streptolysin S and O. Group C streptococci often have a very strong antiphagocytic hyaluronic capsule similar to that of group B streptococci. Group C streptococci, like group G streptococci, have not been isolated from patients who have rheumatic fever, but both can cause bacteremia and sepsis. Like the group A streptococci, they have an antiphagocytic M protein on their surface and form several enzymes. They should be regarded as pathogens.

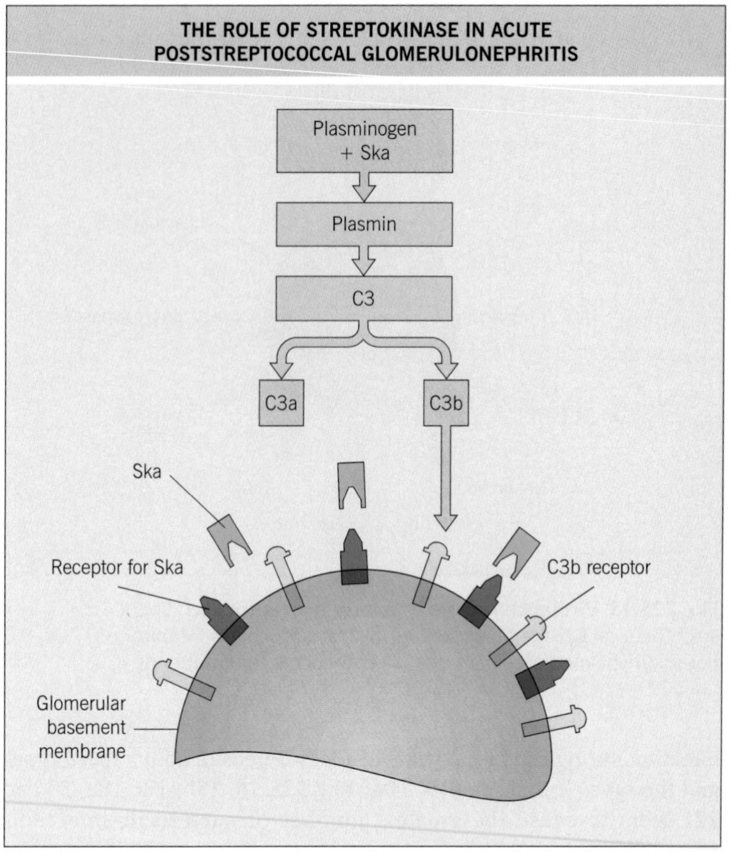

Fig. 225.16 The role of streptokinase in acute poststreptococcal glomerulonephritis. Theoretic model of the pathogenesis of acute post-streptococcal glomerulonephritis as induced by streptokinase. The affinity of the streptokinase isotypes (Ska) is probably dependent on differences in the amino acid composition. This model explains the early deposition of C3b in the glomeruli that is typical of the early phase of acute post-streptococcal glomerulonephritis. Ska, streptokinase from Group A streptococci.

Group B streptococci

Vaginal colonization with group B streptococci is common among adult women and transmission to the infant during childbirth occurs in 50–75% of cases. A small proportion of these infants will be infected (see Chapter 65). This indicates that particular strains or a defect in the immunity of the host play a role in the establishment of infection. It has long been known that antibodies against the capsular polysaccharide are a crucial factor for protection against group B streptococcal infections.[45,46] In-vitro studies indicate that phago-cytosis and killing by polymorphonuclear leukocytes require the presence of both antibodies and complement. The capsular polysaccharide types 1a, 1b, 2 and 3 are clinically the most important, as they are responsible for infections during the early weeks after birth. Nonencapsulated mutants of group B streptococci belonging to type 3 have been demonstrated to lack virulence in an experimental neonatal rat model. The significance of the capsular polysaccharide for the virulence of group B streptococci was further strengthened by the finding that transplacentally acquired maternal antibodies to the group B streptococcal polysaccharides conferred protection against infection of the baby. Consequently, human experiments have been performed with

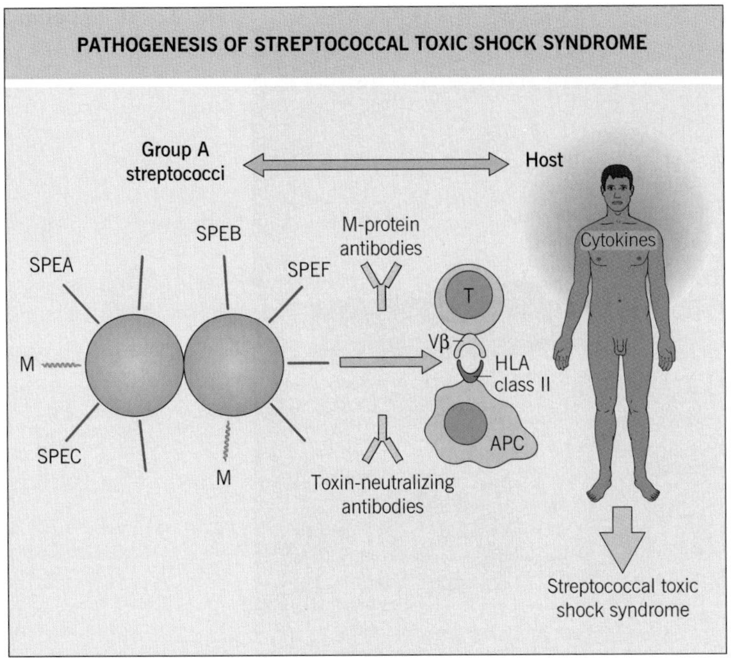

Fig. 225.17 Pathogenesis of streptococcal toxic shock syndrome. In this model, patients who have opsonizing antibodies against the M antigen are protected against infection. In the absence of these antibodies, they may develop a serious infection if they are also lacking neutralizing antibodies against the streptococcal pyrogenic exotoxins which, as superantigens, may induce a cytokine cascade. This process will be hindered by the presence of toxin-neutralizing antibodies. The affinity of the toxins to the class II major histocompatibility complex of antigen presenting cells (APC) and T-cell receptors of specific Vβ (variable region of β chain of the T cell receptor) bearing T cells determines the outcome in each individual patient.

polysaccharide–protein conjugate vaccines, which were capable of inducing opsonizing antibodies and killing group B streptococci.[47] The significance of sialic acid as part of the capsular polysaccharide in the inhibition of complement activation adds to the importance of the capsule in the pathogenesis of group B streptococcal disease.

Group B streptococci also produce other potential virulence factors, such as the CAMP factor, hemolysins and neuraminidase. Although these substances may contribute to the pathogenesis, their exact role awaits further studies.

Enterococci

Although members of the genus *Enterococcus* cause many different infections in humans, very little is known about the pathogenic mechanisms involved and the virulence factors carried by these micro-organisms are less well understood than those of many other streptococci. It is clear, however, that infections caused by enterococci are often found in patients who have various types of immunodeficiencies, in patients using mechanically compromising devices, such as intravascular lines and urinary catheters, and in seriously ill patients. The increasing importance of enterococci as nosocomial pathogens may in part be explained by their natural ability to acquire and exchange extrachromosomal elements encoding virulence traits or antibiotic resistance. Adherence to host tissue may be mediated by enterococcal aggregation substance, fibronectin-binding protein and surface carbohydrates. Extracellular toxins such as cytolysin may also contribute to the pathogenesis.[48]

Streptococcus pneumoniae

Pneumococci are a perfect example of the significance of the role that the mucous lining plays in the inhibition of potentially pathogenic micro-organisms. Thus, pneumococcal infections often occur after a respiratory tract viral infection that has damaged the epithelium, thereby helping the pneumococci to establish themselves in the mucous membranes. Factors that disrupt the normal clearing process in the airways predispose patients to pneumococcal infections in the lungs. Defects in systemic host defenses (i.e. HIV infection, asplenia, immunoglobulin deficiency) may also contribute to pneumococcal infections in the respiratory tract, sometimes causing invasive infections such as bacteremia, meningitis and endocarditis.

The virulence of *S. pneumoniae* is associated with an antiphagocytic capsular polysaccharide.[49] Thus, laboratory strains that have lost the ability to produce a capsule are nonpathogenic. The virulence capacity of pneumococci is neutralized by complement-dependent opsonizing antibodies. Protection is afforded by type-specific antibodies with opsonizing capacity.[34,49] Not all types of pneumococci are equally invasive. Thus, during the first 2 years of life about 50% of the pneumococcal infections are caused by six serotypes (6A, 6B, 19A, 19F and 23F) and in adults these six types together with 15 others are responsible for 80% of pneumococcal bacteremia in the USA.

Besides polysaccharide, the pneumococci produce a hemolysin similar to the streptolysin O of group A streptococci, as well as hyaluronidase and a neuraminidase. None of these seems to play a direct role in the disease process.[33]

Viridans group streptococci

Viridans group streptococci can be divided into those that have a tendency to induce endocarditis and those that do not. The endocarditis-related species usually produce dextrans and this is true for the species mutants, *S. sanguis* and *S. mitior*, as well as *S. bovis*. A prerequisite for the endocarditis-inducing capacity seems to be a capacity to adhere to endothelial cells in the endocardium and this is in turn related to dextran production. In contrast, *S. salivarius* produces levan as its exopolysaccharide and is usually not related to endocarditis. Dextran production is probably not the only virulence factor because these micro-organisms can cause several other types of infections (see Chapter 59).

Patients undergoing intensive cytotoxic treatment that results in neutropenia are predisposed to severe infections with viridans streptococci, the so-called viridans shock syndrome. The mechanism is not well understood (see Chapter 100).

CLINICAL MANIFESTATIONS

Groups A, C and G streptococci

Group A streptococcus, or *Streptococcus pyogenes*, is considered the most pathogenic species of β-hemolytic streptococci. Group A streptococci are involved in a wide variety of clinical syndromes, which can be roughly divided into:

- uncomplicated superficial infections,
- severe invasive infections, and
- postinfectious autoimmune sequelae.

Depending on climate and portal of entry, the infections are preferentially related to the upper airways or to the skin.

Uncomplicated superficial infections

Uncomplicated respiratory infections

Group A streptococci are the most prevalent cause of bacterial pharyngitis and tonsillitis, especially in school children aged between 5 and 15 years; however, people of all ages can be affected. Typically in streptococcal pharyngitis, after 1–5 days of incubation, the first clinical symptom is general malaise with excessive tiredness, headache and fever. The tonsils are swollen and red, showing exudates and deposits together with local petechiae. The patient may have

CLINICAL MANIFESTATIONS OF SORE THROAT

Typical streptococcal pharyngitis	Atypical streptococcal pharyngitis
Temperature >100°F (38°C) Acute throat pain Tender lymph nodes in the neck Redness in pharynx Tonsillar exudate Petechiae Sore nose Scarlatina	Cough Hoarseness Watery nose secretion Conjunctivitis

Table 225.6 Clinical manifestations of sore throat.

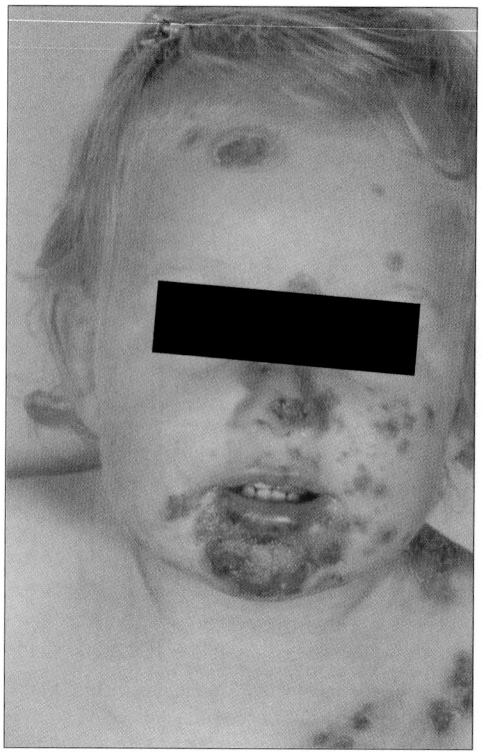

Fig. 225.18 Impetigo in a child.

difficulty in swallowing. Tenderness and enlargement of the anterior cervical lymph nodes are common findings. Based on the symptoms and signs, streptococcal pharyngitis is not easily differentiated from viral infections (Table 225.6). Cough is not a usual finding in streptococcal pharyngitis but is not uncommon in viral infections (see Chapter 31).

When the infecting strain produces one of the so-called pyrogenic (or erythrogenic) exotoxins, scarlet fever may be a complication of streptococcal pharyngitis. Although there are no scarlatinogenic streptococcal types the disease has a higher prevalence in streptococcal infections caused by M types 1, 3, 4, 6, 12, 18, 22 and 66. Group A streptococci are the main causative agents in scarlet fever, but streptococci of groups C and G are isolated from a small number of patients. As well as the signs observed in pharyngitis, scarlet fever is characterized by a diffuse erythematous rash over the trunk, the neck and face and the limbs. The area around the lips is generally free of erythema (circumoral palor). The rash is a diffuse light erythema that blanches on pressure. A white coating on the tongue develops and then resolves, leaving red swollen papillae, the so-called 'strawberry tongue'. Patients usually recover within about 5–7 days. The rash disappears within 10 days, followed by a characteristic discoloration of the skin during the following week. This desquamation is most pronounced on the palms and soles. In certain cases, progression of infection is observed locally causing sinusitis, otitis media, and retropharyngeal or peritonsillar abscesses.

The symptoms of group A streptococcal respiratory infections in young children may have a different clinical appearance. Young children under 3 years usually present with (mucopurulent) nasopharyngitis, which tends to a prolonged course and may be complicated by sinusitis and otitis media.

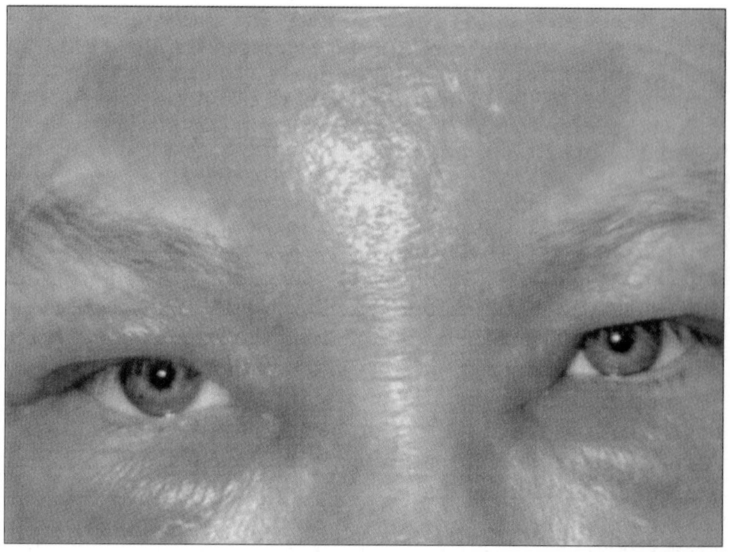

Fig. 225.19 Erysipelas. Note the sharp demarcation of the affected skin.

Uncomplicated skin infections

Streptococci can cause skin infections of various forms and the clinical features are determined by which skin layers are infected:

- infections immediately below the stratum corneum result in impetigo;
- infections in the epidermis can give rise to ecthyma; and
- infections in the dermis give rise to erysipelas and cellulitis.

Pyoderma (impetigo) is most common in young children and is associated with warm, moist climates and poor hygiene (Fig. 225.18). Colonization of the skin occurs first and this is followed by an infection in sites where the integrity of the skin is lost (e.g. in scratches, pierced ear lobes, paronychia or insect bites). Streptococcal infections in more superficial lesions usually result in an impetigenous type of infection, starting with small red papules and developing into vesicles with clear yellow contents. The vesicles change into pustules which, when broken, are covered with a honey-colored crust. Underneath the crust there is a slightly red, blistering surface. The lesions contain numerous bacteria and tend to spread over the body surface, resulting in a multitude of lesions. The name 'impetigo contagiosa' indicates the contagious tendency of this infection, which is especially apparent in closed institutions such as day care centers and in overcrowded conditions. The lesions may heal spontaneously after some weeks and they usually heal without scarring. Strict hygiene precautions are necessary to prevent further spread of the disease.

Erysipelas is an acute superficial cellulitis of the skin that most often involves the face or the limbs (Fig. 225.19). Erysipelas is sharply demarcated and the affected skin is painful and appears red and swollen, with lymphatic involvement. Erysipelas occurs mostly in young children and older adults and is often accompanied by generalized symptoms such as fever and rigors and sometimes by nausea and vomiting. This is usually a relatively mild disease with few complications, but some patients develop pronounced septic symptoms and local complications such as skin necrosis or necrotizing fasciitis (see below; also see Chapters 9 and 10).

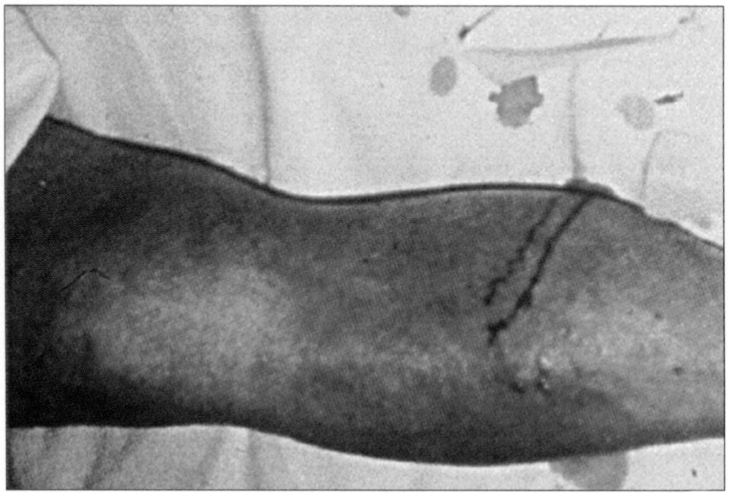

Fig. 225.20 Necrotizing fasciitis caused by group A streptococci. There is only moderate erythema but at surgery there was extensive soft tissue damage.

Invasive infections

Invasive group A streptococcal infections occasionally occur. Examples are sepsis (including puerperal sepsis), pneumonia, meningitis and lymphangitis. Puerperal sepsis usually occurs as an ascending genital infection in the postnatal period after obstetric manipulation in combination with poor hygiene. Additionally, group A streptococcus is the second most common cause of nongonococcal septic arthritis after *Staphylococcus aureus*.[29,50]

Remarkably, the most severe infections, such as necrotizing fasciitis (Fig. 225.20) with or without the toxic shock-like syndrome (analogous to the toxic shock syndrome caused by *Staphylococcus aureus*), have been increasingly seen since the mid-1980s.[26,28,29,43,44] The skin serves as the main portal of entry, followed by the mucous membranes of the throat, but in many cases the portal of entry is unknown. Early clinical features of group A streptococcal infections, before the development of toxic shock, may be flu-like in nature, with fever, sore throat, vomiting and diarrhea. Sometimes there is a history of blunt trauma. Necrotizing fasciitis is often difficult to diagnose; although redness and bullae may be visible, edema is sometimes the only superficial sign. Discrepancy between the unimpressive clinical observations and the extremely severe pain indicated by the patient is then the only clue to the correct diagnosis. Subsequent surgery may reveal massive tissue necrosis along the fascial planes. In the course of hours or days, toxic shock with hypotension and multiple organ failure may develop. A faint erythematous rash may be seen mainly on the chest. Clinically this disease resembles the staphylococcal toxic shock syndrome (Table 225.7) and it is interesting to note that streptococcal pyrogenic exotoxin A and the enterotoxin B of *Staphylococcus aureus* have a similar molecular structure. Despite adequate antibiotic treatment and intensive care, these infections are characterized by a high mortality rate of between 30% and 80% with up to 50% of the survivors having to have limbs amputated and requiring major debridement of tissue (see Chapter 10).[26,28,29]

DEFINITION FOR STREPTOCOCCAL TOXIC SHOCK-LIKE SYNDROME
I. Isolation of GAS from: A. a normally sterile site (e.g. blood, cerebrospinal, pleural or peritoneal fluid, tissue biopsy, surgical wound, etc.) B. a nonsterile site (e.g. throat, sputum, vagina, superficial skin lesion, etc.)
II. Clinical signs of severity A. Hypotension: systolic blood pressure ≤90mmHg in adults or <5th percentile for age in children *and* B. ≥2 of the following signs 1. Renal impairment: creatinine ≥177μM for adults or ≥2 × the upper limit of normal for age. In patients with pre-existing renal disease, a ≥2-fold elevation over the baseline level. 2. Coagulopathy: platelets ≤100 × 10^9/l or disseminated intravascular coagulation defined by prolonged clotting times, low fibrinogen level and the presence of fibrin degradation products. 3. Liver involvement: alanine aminotransferase, aspartate aminotransferase or total bilirubin levels ≥2 × the upper limit of normal for age. In patients with pre-existing liver disease, a ≥2-fold elevation over the baseline level. 4. Adult respiratory distress syndrome defined by acute onset of diffuse pulmonary infiltrates and hypoxemia in the absence of cardiac failure or evidence of diffuse capillary leak manifested by acute onset of generalized edema or pleural or peritoneal effusions with hypoalbuminemia. 5. A generalized erythematous macular rash that may desquamate. 6. Soft tissue necrosis, including necrotizing fasciitis or myositis or gangrene.

Table 225.7 Definition for streptococcal toxic shock-like syndrome. An illness fulfilling criteria IA and II (A and B) is defined as a *definite* case. An illness fulfilling criteria IB and II (A and B) is defined as a *probable* case if no other etiology for the disease is identified.

Autoimmune sequelae

In some cases, streptococcal disease is followed by autoimmune sequelae, either acute rheumatic fever or acute glomerulonephritis.

Rheumatic fever (see also Chapter 60)

Rheumatic fever is seen predominantly during fall and winter in children aged between 5 and 15 years, who also show the highest incidence of streptococcal pharyngitis. Clinical manifestations may vary from mild to highly aggressive. The disease is largely self-limiting. Most patients give a history of preceding pharyngitis. Acute rheumatic fever is a clinical syndrome; there is no specific diagnostic test. Guidelines for the diagnosis of initial attacks of acute rheumatic fever are described in the Jones criteria (Table 225.8). The presence either of two major criteria or of one major criterion and two minor criteria is suggestive of rheumatic fever if a case history of preceding group A streptococcal infection can be documented. Typically, patients present 10–25 days after the preceding streptococcal infection with fever, tachycardia and nonsuppurative inflammatory changes of the joints, heart, skin and subcutaneous tissue. Migratory arthritis is the most common manifestation and can be diagnosed in 70% of patients; carditis is found in about 50% of patients. There is an inverse relationship between the severity of joint involvement and the risk of developing carditis. The carditis is a pancarditis, which means that the pericardium, the myocardium and the endocardium can all be affected. Although carditis may be asymptomatic, clinical symptoms can include:

- heart murmurs,
- arrhythmias,
- cardiac enlargement,
- congestive heart failure,
- pericardial friction rubs, and
- pericardial effusion.

Repetitive group A streptococcal infections tend to cause relapses in these patients, resulting in chronic progressive damage to the cardiac valves. Carditis is the only manifestation of rheumatic fever that has the potential to cause long-term disability or death. In order to prevent valvular destruction, these patients should receive prophylactic penicillin (or alternative antibiotic) therapy.

REVISED JONES CRITERIA FOR THE DIAGNOSIS OF POSTSTREPTOCOCCAL RHEUMATIC FEVER		
Major manifestations	**Minor manifestations**	
Carditis	Clinical	Previous rheumatic fever or rheumatic heart disease
Polyarthritis		Arthralgia
Chorea		Fever
Erythema marginatum	Laboratory	Acute phase reactants
Subcutaneous nodules		Leukocytosis
Positive throat culture		Elevated erythrocyte sedimentation rate
Increased titer(s)		Elevated C-reactive protein
Recent scarlet fever		Prolonged P–R interval on electrocardiogram
	Supporting evidence of streptococcal infection	
The presence of two major criteria or of one major and two minor criteria is highly suggestive of rheumatic fever, if supported by evidence of preceding group A streptococcal infection		

Table 225.8 Revised Jones criteria for the diagnosis of poststreptococcal rheumatic fever.

Firm, painless, subcutaneous nodules may appear in association with severe carditis, usually over bony surfaces and tendons. Erythema marginatum, a nonpruritic erythematous eruption, may appear on the trunk or the proximal extremities.

In addition, the central nervous system (CNS) may be affected with emotional lability, muscular weakness and rapid, uncoordinated movements (Sydenham's chorea or St Vitus' dance). About 10% of patients develop chorea after a latent period of 3–12 months. The specificity of this disease in relation to rheumatic fever is a matter of controversy. The general distribution of the chorea is interesting. The frequency is equal between the sexes before puberty but after puberty chorea disappears in males and is not seen in military epidemics. In contrast, pregnancy aggravates and exacerbates the disease.

Strains of certain M types are strongly associated with rheumatic fever, especially strains that appear mucoid on blood agar plates. Other equally prevalent serotypes fail to initiate the disease or even to reactivate it in susceptible hosts. Rheumatic fever is associated with pharyngeal strains carrying M proteins of types 1, 3, 4, 5, 6, 12, 14, 18, 19 and 24.

In the developed world, the incidence of rheumatic fever has declined throughout the 20th century, probably owing to improved living conditions, effective antibiotic treatment of upper respiratory tract infections and good health care. However, rheumatic fever is still a problem in developing countries, where it is still the most common cause of acquired heart disease (Table 225.9).

Acute glomerulonephritis

Acute glomerulonephritis is diagnosed on the basis of the clinical presentation in combination with evidence of a recent infection (in the previous 1–3 weeks) with *S. pyogenes*. This syndrome of acute inflammation of the glomeruli comprises oliguria, hematuria, proteinuria, hypertension and edema, but the presentation may be mild. The laboratory findings include proteinuria, hematuria and reduced renal function as evidenced by renal function tests. Decreased serum complement is an important parameter to support the diagnosis.

The toxic effect of streptokinase is thought to be involved in the pathogenesis of acute glomerulonephritis. Autoimmune reactions caused by shared components between glomeruli and streptococcal membranes may also play a role. While the significance of these presumed mechanisms awaits further proof, autoantibodies to glomerular connective tissue components have been identified in patients who have streptococcal glomerulonephritis.

The prognosis in young adults is usually favorable, but sporadically acute disease is followed by chronic glomerulonephritis and subsequent renal failure. The incidence of glomerulonephritis is lower in Western Europe than in the USA, as is the incidence of pyoderma.

RHEUMATIC HEART DISEASE IN SCHOOL-AGE CHILDREN IN VARIOUS REGIONS OF THE WORLD		
Location	**Prevalence per 1000**	**Year(s) of report(s)**
USA	0.6	1965
Latin America	1.0–17.0	1968–1980
Asia	0.4–21.0	1970–1979
Africa	0.3–15.0	1970–1985
Pacific region (except Japan)	1.0–18.6	1978–1985
Japan	0.7	1979

Table 225.9 Rheumatic heart disease in school-age children in various regions of the world.

The attack rate varies within wide ranges but it seems to decrease substantially in the developed world and many cases can only be detected by slight proteinuria and confirmed by renal biopsies.

Glomerulonephritis is observed more in connection with skin isolates of M types M2, M49, M55, M57, M59, M60 and M61, and throat isolates of M1, M4, M12 and M25. Although the incidence of rheumatic fever has declined dramatically in the developed world, it is still a major concern in developing countries.

Groups C and G streptococci

Groups C and G streptococci can induce similar infections to those caused by group A streptococci, such as pharyngitis. They have been recognized as part of the normal flora of the pharynx, skin, intestinal tract and vagina.[51,52] Group C streptococci are a common cause of infection in animals, including mastitis in cows. Human infections regularly develop after contact with animals or animal products.[16,52] Groups C and G streptococci have occasionally been reported as the cause of nosocomial and opportunistic infections, including endocarditis, arthritis, puerperal sepsis and septic abortion, neonatal sepsis, pleuropulmonary infection, peritonitis, meningitis and cellulitis.[51–53] Malignancy, diabetes, cardiovascular disease and alcoholism are important host determinants of invasive streptococcal infections.[26,28,29,51–54]

Group B streptococci

Neonatal disease

Group B streptococci (*Streptococcus agalactiae*) are a leading cause of bacteremia and meningitis in neonates (see Chapter 65).[55] Most group B streptococci infections are thought to be transmitted to the infant from the maternal genital tract during delivery.[45]

Early-onset group B streptococcal infection (up to 5 days of age) is associated with a high mortality rate and occurs predominantly in immature neonates whose deliveries have been characterized by complications predisposing to infection (premature onset of labor, rupture of membranes for more than 24 hours before delivery, maternal fever or anogenital colonization of the mother).[55]

With rapid diagnosis, including screening of pregnant women, and better supportive care, mortality has decreased and is now between 15% and 40%. A substantial proportion of children with group B streptococcal sepsis develop meningitis and lumbar punctures should therefore be performed in all infants with suspected sepsis. Pulmonary involvement occurs in 40% of neonates with group B streptococcal sepsis, which cannot be distinguished from hyaline membrane disease on the basis of clinical or radiologic findings.[55]

Late-onset disease (occurring at 7 days of age or older) is infrequently associated with obstetric complications, but is acquired from exogenous sources (e.g. the mother or another infant). Typically, septic patients present with fever, poor feeding and irritability; 80% have meningitis. Death rates are much lower than in early-onset disease, but survivors of meningitis may have permanent neurologic sequelae, including central diabetes insipidus, thermal dysregulation, cortical blindness, deafness, mental retardation and generalized spasticity.[55]

As with group A streptococci, a correlation has been found between certain clinical conditions and the streptococcal type causing the infection. In early-onset neonatal infections, all four of the first serotypes are isolated at about the same frequency, whereas in the late-onset type 3 streptococci are the most prevalent.

Adult disease

In recent years, group B streptococci have been recognized with increasing frequency as a substantial cause of morbidity and mortality among adults.[56,57] Two groups of adults are at increased risk of group B streptococcal infection: pregnant women and patients with serious underlying disease (e.g. diabetes mellitus, malignancy).[55,57] The spectrum of group B streptococcal disease in adults includes:[55,57]

- bacteremia with or without sepsis,
- cellulitis and other soft tissue infections,
- pneumonia,
- arthritis,
- meningitis,
- osteomyelitis,
- pyometritis,
- endocarditis, and
- urinary tract infection.

Mortality is 30–35% and is associated with advanced age (over 60 years).[56,57]

Postpartum sepsis is generally seen as endometritis or wound infection. Because most young mothers are in good health, the prognosis is excellent when appropriate therapy is started.

Enterococci

Enterococci are the most common aerobic, Gram-positive cocci found in the bowel flora and lower female genital tract of humans and other animals. Initially thought of as merely harmless commensals because of their low intrinsic virulence compared with other organisms such as group A streptococci, enterococci have become the second most common nosocomial pathogen overall. This appears to have been caused by selection of these organisms by the widespread use of broad-spectrum antibiotics, such as the cephalosporins, which lack enterococcal activity, and acquisition of new mechanisms of antibiotic resistance.[58,59]

Enterococci are commonly associated with urinary tract infections, particularly in patients who have indwelling catheters and are recovered from abdominal and pelvic wound infections and abscesses. However, most clinical studies suggest that patients who have normal host defenses are resistant to enterococcal infections.[58] Furthermore, there is a low frequency of enterococcal bacteremia originating from an intra-abdominal source when antimicrobial agents that do not cover enterococci are used.[58] Enterococcal bacteremia in surgical patients is almost always associated with the ongoing or previous use of antimicrobial agents that are not specific for enterococci.

The most frequently seen infections are infections of the cardiovascular system, with bacteremia related to an intravascular catheter being the most common,[58,59] although endocarditis also occurs. Other types of infection caused by enterococci include:[59–61]

- intra-abdominal infections;
- soft tissue and skin infections;
- bone and joint infections, especially in prosthetic joints;
- infections of the CNS associated with shunts;
- deep surgical wound infections;
- urinary tract infections; and
- endometritis.

Classically, enterococcal endocarditis is a disease of older people, with a male predominance as a result of obstructive urinary tract disease; it can also affect those who have prosthetic valves.[59] Enterococcal meningitis is rarely seen; it is associated with underlying disease, immunosuppressive therapy and CNS trauma or surgery.[61]

It has been reported that 60% of enterococcal infections are nosocomial, with half of them occurring in intensive care units. *Enterococcus faecalis* is responsible for 80–90% of enterococcal infections and *Enterococcus faecium* for 10–20%.[58–60]

Streptococcus bovis infections are most often manifest as bacteremia or endocarditis. In addition, there is a strong association with underlying colonic malignancy (up to 50% in some series), so all patients with *S. bovis* bacteremia should undergo colonoscopy.

Streptococcus pneumoniae

Streptococcus pneumoniae is an important agent of human disease at the extremities of age and in those who have underlying disease.[62–64] Pneumococcal disease is most commonly associated with an antecedent viral respiratory infection such as influenza or with chronic conditions such as chronic obstructive pulmonary disease, diabetes mellitus, congestive heart failure, renal failure, smoking and alcoholism. Immunodeficiency such as that caused by splenic dysfunction or splenectomy is an additional risk factor for the development of severe pneumococcal disease because of decreased bacterial clearance and defective production of antibodies.

Streptococcus pneumoniae is the causative agent of the majority of cases of community-acquired pneumonia and otitis media, one of the three most common pathogens in bacterial meningitis and an important cause of sepsis and sinusitis.[33,62] Bacteremia occurs in 25–30% of patients who have pneumococcal pneumonia and in more than 80% of patients who have pneumococcal meningitis. Children with sickle cell disease and individuals with hypogammaglobulinemia or who have had a splenectomy are at greatly increased risk of fulminating pneumococcal sepsis, which has a high mortality.

Pneumococcal pneumonia

Pneumococcal pneumonia is characterized by an abrupt onset with chills and high fever. Most patients complain of a productive cough with blood-tinged sputum, and chest pain (caused by pleurisy) is common. Physical examination may reveal decreased expiratory excursion as a result of pain, and dullness to percussion. Crackles are present in nearly all cases. Infiltrations on chest radiograph vary between occupying less than a full segment to lobar consolidation. Empyema, endocarditis, pericarditis, peritonitis and brain abscess are rare complications.[62,65] Because the disease is related to aspiration, the infection is generally localized in the lower lobes of the lungs.

Recovery is usually rapid after initiation of appropriate antibiotics, with complete resolution in 2–3 weeks. Despite antibiotic therapy, the case fatality rate of pneumococcal pneumonia is about 5–7% in the developed world[33] and can be higher in disease caused by serotype 3, in elderly patients and in cases of bacteremia (see Chapter 34).

Pneumococcal meningitis

Pneumococcal meningitis may follow otitis, sinusitis or bacteremia. It is an infrequent cause of neonatal meningitis, but it is responsible for 15% of cases of meningitis in children and for 30–50% of cases in adults. Mortality and severe neurologic sequelae are more frequent with disease caused by *Strep. pneumoniae* than with the other common causes of bacterial meningitis (see Chapter 22).

Viridans group streptococci

Viridans group streptococci are usually found as normal inhabitants of the oral cavity, the upper respiratory tract and the bowel.[66] When these organisms gain access to the bloodstream, people who have damaged heart valves are at increased risk of endocarditis.[20] Infection is usually endogenous and is preceded by disease, dental extraction or trauma to a mucosal surface. It is often associated with an immunocompromised condition.[67,68] However, blood cultures that are positive for α-hemolytic streptococci or nonhemolytic streptococci have no clinical relevance in many cases.[69] If the same strain is isolated from more than one blood culture bottle or is isolated on repeated occasions, the assumption of clinical relevance is strengthened (see Chapter 59).

Viridans group streptococci are the most frequent cause of endocarditis and are generally associated with a better clinical outcome than endocarditis caused by staphylococci, enterococci or fungi.[20] A special population prone to develop infections with viridans streptococci is those with hematologic malignancies, who are treated with cytotoxic drugs with high cytotoxicity for mucosal surfaces. The course of infection in these patients may vary from mild to highly severe, with shock, adult respiratory distress syndrome and death.[67]

Streptococcus milleri is a cause of abscesses in association with previous surgery, trauma, diabetes and immunodeficiency.[24] The digestive tract has been recognized as the most likely portal of entry.[70] A notable feature is the preponderance of reported cases of infection in men.[66,71,72] *Streptococcus milleri* has been isolated in association with:[24,66,70,71]

- periodontitis,
- odontogenic abscesses,
- sinusitis,
- intracranial abscesses,
- pleuropulmonary abscesses and empyema,
- abdominal infections, including hepatic abscesses, and
- subcutaneous sepsis following human bite wounds.

These bacteria are an infrequent cause of endocarditis and pharyngitis.

Streptococcus bovis can be isolated from patients who have endocarditis and bacteremia. There is a strong association between bacteremia caused by this micro-organism and adenocarcinoma of the colon, as well as neonatal sepsis and meningitis.[73]

The nutritionally variant streptococci (pyridoxal-dependent streptococci) can also cause endocarditis. These bacteria, which are part of the normal oral flora, account for up to 5% of endocarditis cases.[23,74] These bacteria are the cause of much higher rates of treatment failure, relapse and mortality in endocarditis than other streptococci.[74]

Infections caused by *Leuconostoc* spp. are mostly nosocomial, occurring in immunocompromised patients or neonates. Previous antibiotic therapy or interrupted integrity of the skin or mucosal barriers are usually additional risk factors in patients infected with these micro-organisms.[75,76]

MANAGEMENT

Groups A, B, C and G streptococci

Penicillin is the traditional first-choice therapy for infections caused by groups A, B, C or G streptococci or pneumococci. *Streptococcus pyogenes* is still extremely sensitive to penicillin and erythromycin is a good alternative in case of penicillin allergy. However, an increase in the prevalence of erythromycin-resistant group A streptococcal strains has been reported in several areas. Resistance occurs in relation to an increased macrolide consumption and may reach 40%.[77]

Acute streptococcal pharyngitis should be treated; amoxicillin is an appropriate choice in the outpatient setting. Generally, there is no need to treat carriers. Persistent oropharyngeal carriage after a complete course of penicillin therapy can occur in up to 30% of patients. β-Lactamase production by pharyngeal flora as well as penicillin tolerance of the group A streptococci have been suggested as causes of failure of penicillin in the eradication of group A streptococci.

Septic scarlet fever should be treated in order to prevent suppurative and late complications. Again, penicillin is the first-choice therapy but a synergistic effect can be achieved by addition of an aminoglycoside. In cases of allergy, erythromycin, clindamycin and vancomycin appear to be adequate alternatives.[51]

The object of therapy in patients who have acute rheumatic fever is to reduce inflammation, to decrease fever and toxicity and to control cardiac failure. Depending on the clinical condition of the patient, treatment varies from analgesia to anti-inflammatory drugs (aspirin-like agents or, in severe cases, corticosteroids). Antibiotic treatment of streptococcal infections effectively prevents development of acute rheumatic fever and minimizes the possibility of transmission of rheumatogenic streptococcal strains. On the other hand, a favorable effect of penicillin on prevention of acute glomerulonephritis has never been demonstrated. However, in order to eradicate the nephritogenic streptococcal strain, penicillin should also be administered to these patients. Thus, it is essential to distinguish acute post-streptococcal nephritis from other forms of glomerulonephritis. In fact, no form of treatment is known that influences the generally favorable outcome of acute post-streptococcal glomerulonephritis. Therefore, therapy is symptomatic and usually confined to salt and fluid restriction to prevent circulatory overload. Sometimes, additional treatment including diuretics or antihypertensive therapy is indicated.

In life-threatening infections, such as necrotizing fasciitis and streptococcal toxic shock, a rapid diagnosis immediately followed by adequate treatment is essential. Surgery (debridement of necrotic tissue or even amputation) is the key event in the treatment of necrotizing fasciitis.[26,28,29,43] The combination of penicillin and clindamycin is the therapy of choice. Preliminary data suggest that the addition of intravenous immunoglobulin preparations may be efficacious, although convincing clinical trial data are lacking. Supportive therapy in the intensive care unit, including fluid replacement, inotropics, hemodialysis and resuscitation, is also required (see Chapter 10).

In immunocompromised patients who have serious group C and G streptococcal infections, such as endocarditis, meningitis or septic arthritis, penicillin–aminoglycoside combinations are used.[51–53]

Failure of antibiotic therapy should prompt investigation to discover underlying disease or undrained foci of infection.

Group B streptococci

Group B streptococci remain susceptible to penicillin G. However, the MIC of penicillin G for group B streptococci is considerably higher (average 0.04μg/ml) than that observed for group A streptococci.[55] Susceptibility to ampicillin and cephalosporins is also uniform, whereas resistance to erythromycin and clindamycin occurs in 1–18% of isolates and tetracycline resistance is seen in 85–92% of recent isolates.[55,56] Resistance to aminoglycosides is uniform, but the combination of penicillin and gentamicin has synergistic activity and accelerates the killing of group B streptococci *in vitro*.

Because of the inoculum-like effect and the direct relation between delayed sterilization of the CNS and the occurrence of neurologic sequelae, initial therapy of suspected group B streptococcal meningitis should include increased dosages of penicillin to ensure efficacy.

Although the duration of therapy is relatively arbitrary, most investigators recommend parenteral penicillin G for 10 days for bacteremia, 2–3 weeks for meningitis and 3–4 weeks for osteomyelitis or endocarditis.[55]

Enterococci

Antimicrobial therapy for enterococcal infections is complicated because most antibiotics are not bactericidal at clinically relevant concentrations. Combination therapy with a cell wall agent plus an aminoglycoside improves the outcome of enterococcal endocarditis and probably of enterococcal meningitis, but it may not improve the outcome in bacteremia.[59,61,78] High-level aminoglycoside resistance, β-lactamase production, vancomycin resistance and high-level ampicillin resistance are increasing in prevalence.[58,59,78]

Enterococcus faecium is typically high-level penicillin and ampicillin resistant and this type of resistance has been reported as a significant predictor of lack of cure.[58,59,78] Therapy of enterococcal infections caused by vancomycin-resistant *E. faecium* is very difficult because these organisms are usually resistant to alternative antibiotics currently available.[58,59] Several types of glycopeptide resistance phenotypes are now known.[58] The VanA phenotype is associated with acquired inducible resistance to both vancomycin and teicoplanin. VanA, which is carried on a transposon (a mobile genetic element), is transferrable to other susceptible enterococci by conjugation. The VanB phenotype, which is chromosomally mediated, inducible and transferrable by conjugation, mediates inducible resistance to vancomycin but not to teicoplanin (see Chapters 189 and 199).[58]

There has been some interest in the use of quinolones against vancomycin-resistant enterococci. Ciprofloxacin displays bacteriostatic activity against enterococci and synergistic bactericidal activity has been demonstrated in vitro when combined with ampicillin or gentamicin. However, in-vitro activity does not guarantee in-vivo success.[78] The newly developed streptogramins (quinupristin and dalfopristin) and oxazolidinones (linezolid) appeared promising against vancomycin-resistant enterococci.[79] Nitrofurantoin is active against many strains of vancomycin-resistant enterococci and should be useful for urinary tract infections.[78]

Streptococcus bovis should be differentiated from the enterococci because it is usually susceptible to penicillin alone, and both endocarditis and meningitis due to *S. bovis* have a better prognosis.[73]

Streptococcus pneumoniae

Penicillin used to be the first-choice therapy for pneumococcal disease, and in penicillin-sensitive strains it still is. For patients who have penicillin allergy, cephalosporins and erythromycin are valuable alternatives.

Resistance to penicillin is increasing in many parts of the world (Fig. 225.21) and is associated with a decreased affinity of the antibiotic for penicillin-binding proteins present in the bacterial cell wall. Penicillin resistance is thought to be due to horizontal transfer of

WORLDWIDE FREQUENCY OF ISOLATION OF PENICILLIN-RESISTANT PNEUMOCOCCI

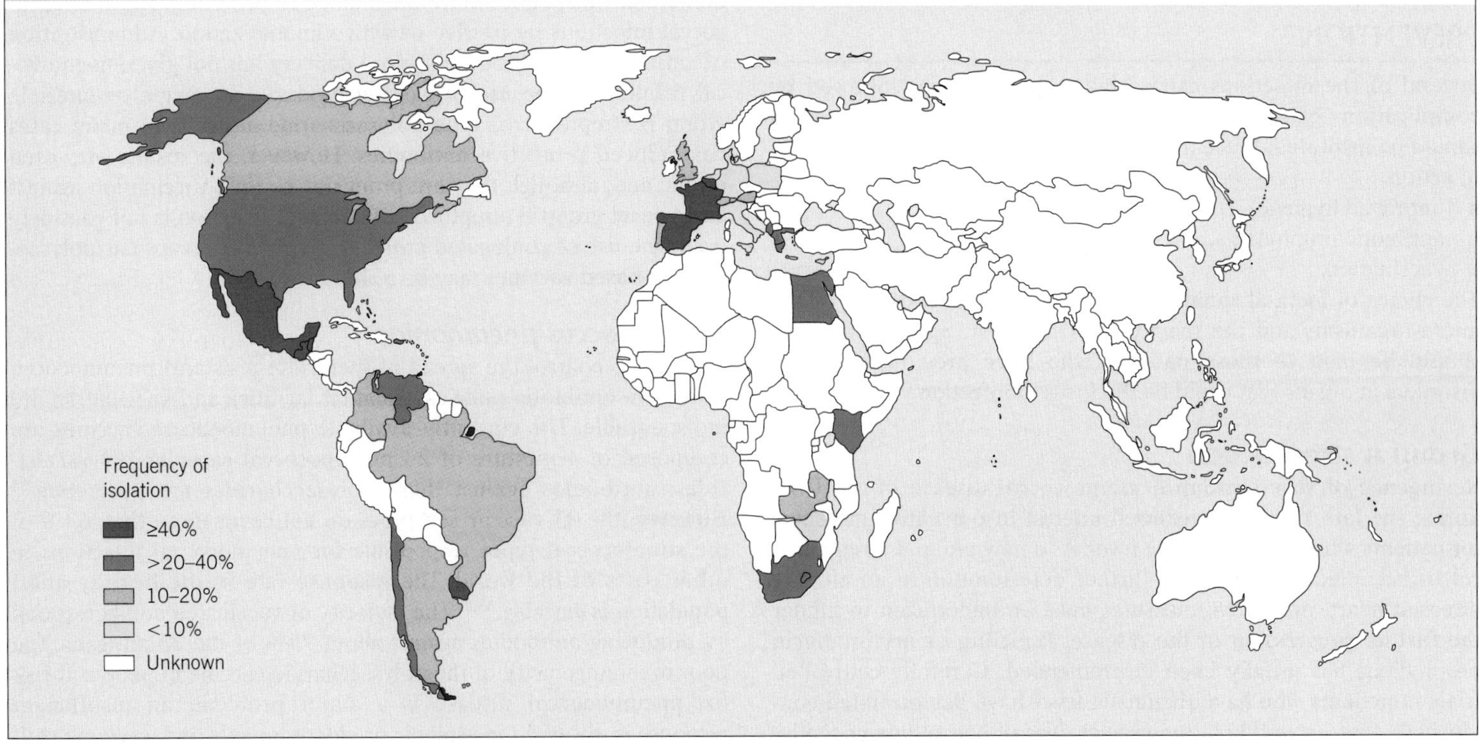

Fig. 225.21 Worldwide frequency of isolation of penicillin-resistant pneumococci. Strains with MIC 0.1–2.0μg/ml are said to be intermediate resistant and high-level penicillin-resistant strains are defined as MIC >2.0μg/ml.

genes of altered penicillin-binding proteins with lowered affinity to penicillin and other β-lactams.

At least 30% of the pneumococcal strains in the USA show intermediate resistance to penicillin (MIC 0.1–2.0μg/ml). Except for meningitis patients, these are readily treatable with increased doses of penicillin.

Of more concern is the appearance of pneumococcal isolates that are regarded as highly resistant to penicillin (MIC ≥2.0μg/ml). It is suggested that the extended consumption of oral cephalosporins contributes to pneumococcal resistance to penicillin. If these strains are circulating, it might be more reliable to treat severe pneumococcal infections with vancomycin.[65] However, the rate of resistance to other commonly used antibiotics such as erythromycin, tetracycline and trimethoprim–sulfamethoxazole is much greater in penicillin-resistant strains than in penicillin-sensitive strains (see Chapter 189).[35,62,80]

Viridans group streptococci

Viridans group streptococci have long been considered uniformly susceptible to β-lactams, macrolides, lincosamines, rifampin (rifampicin) and vancomycin.[67] Occasionally, however, mostly under the pressure of long-term penicillin therapy, serious infections due to penicillin-resistant or penicillin-tolerant strains have been reported.[68,81] In endocarditis, high-dose penicillin in combination with an aminoglycoside is recommended. If MIC values are below 0.12μg/ml, the duration of this combination therapy may be limited to 14 days, but alternatively penicillin monotherapy can be given for 4 weeks. In cases of penicillin allergy, vancomycin is a good alternative.[23,67,74,81] (See also Chapter 59).

Surgical drainage remains central to the management of abscesses (caused by *S. milleri*) and is often augmented by antibiotics.[70] The antibiotic of choice for infections caused by *S. milleri* is penicillin, to which all but a few strains are very sensitive.[66,70–72] Suitable alternatives include erythromycin, clindamycin and cephalosporins.[66,70,71]

Leuconostoc and *Pediococcus* spp. are vancomycin resistant but are generally susceptible to clindamycin, carbapenems and gentamicin, and most are susceptible to penicillin as well.[75,82]

PREVENTION

Several of the infections caused by streptococci are followed by complications of such a serious nature that preventive measures should be instituted. Preventive measures can include several modes of action:

- improved hygiene,
- antibiotic prophylaxis, and
- vaccination.

The choice of method should be based on the pathogenicity of the micro-organisms and the reactivity of the host. Special attention should be paid to those patients who have previously known disorders in organs that could be the focus of infection.

Group A streptococci

Resurgence of severe group A streptococcal disease in the USA during the late 1980s has renewed interest in preventive measures for patients who have rheumatic fever. As a new group A streptococcal throat infection can cause further deterioration in an already diseased heart, preventive measures must be undertaken to hinder the further progression of the disease. Penicillin or erythromycin prophylaxis has usually been recommended. Carefully controlled trials in patients who have rheumatic fever have demonstrated convincingly that a monthly intramuscular dose of benzathine penicillin produces a statistically significant reduction in the frequency of recurrent streptococcal infections and subsequent attacks of rheumatic fever. Where benzathine penicillin is no longer available, procaine penicillin may be a suitable alternative. The intramuscular route of penicillin injection is preferred to the oral route because of the higher compliance rates associated with it. The recommended dose is benzathine penicillin intramuscularly 1.2 million units every 4 weeks or penicillin V orally 250mg q12h. It is not clear how long prophylaxis should be continued, but presumably it should be for life.

In contrast, a favorable effect of penicillin prophylaxis in cases of glomerulonephritis has never been demonstrated, and relapses of glomerulonephritis occur at such a low frequency that prophylaxis is not warranted. In rare cases, patients who have streptococcal cellulitis or erysipelas with frequent recurrences should be considered for penicillin prophylaxis.

No vaccine is at present available for protection against group A streptococcal infections, but intensive research is ongoing.

Group B streptococci

Group B streptococci colonize the vagina, vulva and rectum of about 25% of fertile women. This micro-organism therefore represents a threat of bacterial sepsis to the newborn baby, especially in those cases where obstetric complications or prematurity are likely. Although the incidence of serious infections, such as septicemia and meningitis, is only around 1%, antibiotic prophylaxis has been recommended for patients who have obstetric complications, especially if earlier pregnancies have been complicated by group B streptococcal infections. Studies have clearly demonstrated that intrapartum administration of penicillin or ampicillin reduces the transmission of group B streptococci from the mother to the infant, and at least 80% of early-onset group B streptococcal disease can be prevented in this way.[83] Local prophylactic regimens have also been suggested, including vaginal washing with various antiseptics during the last month of pregnancy and at delivery, although the effect of this is still controversial (see Chapter 65).

Another approach is based upon the observation that antibodies toward the capsular polysaccharide of group B streptococci are protective in animal models and appear to correlate also with human immunity. Thus, efforts have been made to prevent group B streptococcal infections by passive or active immunization. Administration of antibodies to the mother before delivery has not given unequivocal results, but the use of vaccine produced by single or multiple group B streptococcal type polysaccharide antigens in many cases has induced protective antibodies. However, the results are often erratic and, although they are promising overall, vaccination against early-onset group B streptococcal neonatal infection is not routinely used. The use of conjugated group B streptococcal capsular polysaccharide-based vaccines may be a step forward.[47]

Streptococcus pneumoniae

In order to control the spread of (penicillin-resistant) pneumococci, restrictive antibiotic policies, isolation facilities and vaccination are indispensable. The currently available pneumococcal vaccines are composed of a mixture of 23 pneumococcal capsular polysaccharides; antibodies against these polysaccharides are protective.[84] However, the 23 vaccine serotypes do not cover more than 63% of the streptococcal types responsible for pneumococcal infections in other parts of the world. The response rate in the healthy adult population is variable.[33,85] The majority of vaccinated adults respond by producing antibodies against about 75% of the 23 antigens. The poor immunogenicity of the polysaccharide vaccine in people at risk for pneumococcal disease is a major problem; an insufficient response is observed in asplenic or elderly people and in young children. Antibody levels subside with time and may no longer be detectable after 5 years in older adults. Therefore, patients who are prone to develop pneumococcal disease should be vaccinated every 3–5 years.[62,63,85,86]

The pneumococcal types most commonly found in children are those that seem to be less immunogenic than other types. Furthermore, polysaccharide vaccines do not evoke an antibody response in children aged under 2 years. This problem can at least be partly overcome by preparation of conjugate vaccines, in which the polysaccharides are bound to a protein carrier such as bacterial toxoids, thereby inducing a T cell-dependent immunoreactivity. Further research along these lines is presently being performed. Pneumococcal protein antigens, such as pneumolysin and surface proteins, are currently being examined as candidates for a pneumococcal vaccine, together with the polysaccharide vaccine.

Prevention of endocarditis

There is an obvious risk of endocarditis in patients undergoing dental, surgical or interventional procedures that might induce transient bacteremia. In certain high-risk groups the bacteria can adhere to the heart valves and give rise to endocarditis. This is often the case in patients who have congenital heart failure, rheumatic heart disease, valve prostheses or earlier incidences of endocarditis. In many countries, amoxicillin as a single dose 1 hour before the intervention and ampicillin combined with an aminoglycoside in extended operative procedures are recommended. The prophylaxis is mainly directed against viridans group streptococci when the intervention is localized to the oral cavity and against enterococci if the intervention is directed to the gut or the urinary tract (see Chapter 59).

REFERENCES

1. Bruckner DA, Colonna P, Bearson BL. Nomenclature for aerobic and facultative bacteria. Clin Infect Dis 1999;29:713–23.
2. The Gram-positive cocci part II: streptococci, enterococci, and the 'streptococcus-like' bacteria. In: Koneman EW, Allen SD, Janda WM, Schreckenberger PC, Winn WC, eds. Color atlas and textbook of diagnostic microbiology, 5th ed. Philadelphia: JB Lippincott; 1997.
3. Tagg JR, Dajani AS, Wannamaker LW. Bactericins of Gram-positive bacteria. Bacterial Rev 1976;40:722–56.
4. French GL, Talsania H, Charlton JRH, Phillips I. A physiological classification of viridans streptococci by use of the API-20STREP system. J Med Microbiol 1989;28:275–86.
5. Facklam RR, Washington JA. II. Streptococcus and related catalase-negative gram positive cocci. In: Belows A, Hausler WJ Jr, Herrman KL, *et al*, eds. Manual of clinical microbiology, 5th ed. Washington DC: American Society for Microbiology; 1991:238–57.
6. Lancefield RC. A serological differentiation of human and other groups of hemolytic streptococci. J Exp Med 1933;57:571–95.
7. Daly JA, Seskin KC. Evaluation of rapid, commercial latex techniques for serogrouping beta-hemolytic streptococci. J Clin Microbiol 1988;26:2429–31.
8. Facklam RF, Martin DR, Lovgren M, *et al.* Extension of the Lancefield classification for group A streptococci by addition of 22 new M protein gene sequence types from clinical isolates: *emm103* to *emm124*. Clin Infect Dis 2002;34:28–38.
9. Roe M, Kishiyama C, Davidson K, Schaefer L, Todd J. Comparison of BioStar strepA OIA optical immune assay, Abbott testpack plus strep A, and culture with selective media for diagnosis of group A streptococcal pharyngitis. J Clin Microbiol 1995;33:1551–3.
10. Wannamaker LW. Streptococcal toxins. Rev Infect Dis 1983;5:723–32.
11. Wessels MR, Kasper DL. Group B streptococcus. In: Gorbach SL, Bartlett JG, Blacklow NR, eds. Infectious diseases. Philadelphia: WB Saunders; 1992:1421–5.
12. Hordnes K, Eide M, Ulstein M, Digranes A, Haneberg B. Evaluation of a rapid enzyme immunoassay for detection of genital colonization of group B streptococci in pregnant women: own experience and review. Aust NZ J Obstet Gynaecol 1995;35:251–3.
13. de la Rosa M, Perez M, Carazo C, Pareja L, Peis JI, Hernandez F. New Granada medium for detection and identification of group B streptococci. J Clin Microbiol 1992;30: 1019–21.
14. Farrow JAE, Collins XM. Taxonomic studies on streptococci of serological groups C, G and L and possibly related taxa. Syst Appl Microbiol 1984;5:483–93.
15. Shlaes DM. Miscellaneous streptococci. In: Gorbach SL, Bartlett JG, Blacklow NR, eds. Infectious diseases. Philadelphia: WB Saunders; 1992:1425–8.
16. Vartian C, Lerner PI, Shlaes DM, Goplakristena KV. Infections due to Lancefield group G streptococci. Medicine 1988;64:75–88.
17. Mohr DN, Feist DJ, Washington II JA, Hermans PE. Infections due to group C streptococci in man. Am J Med 1979;66:450–6.
18. Virolainen A, Salo P, Jero J, Karma P, Eskola J, Leinonen M. Comparison of PCR assay with bacterial culture for detecting *Streptococcus pneumoniae* in middle ear fluid of children with acute otitis media. J Clin Microbiol 1994;32:2667–70.
19. Facklam R, Hollis D, Collins D. Identification of Gram-positive coccal and coccobacillary vancomycin-resistant bacteria. J Clin Microbiol 1989;27:724–30.
20. Sussman JI, Baron EJ, Tenebaum MJ, *et al.* Viridans streptococcal endocarditis: clinical, microbiological, and echocardiographic correlations. J Infect Dis 1986;154:597–603.
21. Coykendall AL. Classification and identification of the viridans streptococci. Clin Microbiol Rev 1989;2:315–28.
22. Kikuchi K, Enari T, Totsuka KI, Shimizu K. Comparison of phenotypic characteristics, DNA–DNA hybridization results, and results with a commercial rapid biochemical and enzymatic reaction system for identification of viridans streptococci. J Clin Microbiol 1995;33:1215–22.
23. Ruoff KL. Nutritionally variant streptococci. Clin Microbiol Rev 1991;4:184–90.
24. Brook I, Frazier EH. Microaerophilic streptococci as a significant pathogen: a twelve-year review. J Med 1994;25:129–44.
25. Gray BM. Streptococcal infections. In: Evans AS, Brackman PS, eds. Bacterial infections in humans. Epidemiology and control, 2nd ed. New York: Plenum; 1991.
26. Bisno AL, Group A streptococcal infections and acute rheumatic fever. N Engl J Med 1991;325:783–93.
27. Stollerinan GH. *Streptococcus pyogenes* (group A streptococci). In: Gorbach SL, Bartlett JG, Blacklow NR, eds. Infectious diseases. Philadelphia: WB Saunders; 1992.
28. Stevens DL. Streptococcal toxic shock syndrome associated with necrotizing fasciitis. Ann Rev Med 2000;51:271–88.
29. Sharkawy A, Low DE, Saignor R, *et al.* Severe Group A streptococcal infections in Outario, 1992–1996. Clin Infect Dis 2002;34:454–60.
30. Weinstein MR, Litt M, Kertesz DA, *et al.* Invasive infections due to a fish pathogen, *Streptococcus iniae.* N Engl J Med 1997;337:589–94.
31. Håkansson A, Kidd A, Wadell G, Sabharwal H, Svanborg C. Adenovirus infection enhances *in vitro* adherence of *Streptococcus pneumoniae.* Infect Immun 1994;62:2707–14.
32. Okada N, Pentland AP, Falk P, Caparon MG. M protein and protein F act as important determinants of cell-specific tropism of *Streptococcus pyogenes* in skin tissue. J Clin Invest 1994;94:965–77.
33. Boulnois GJ. Pneumococcal protein and the pathogenesis of disease caused by *Streptococcus pneumoniae.* J Gen Microbiol 1992;138:249–59.
34. Austrian R. Some observations on the pneumococcus and on the current status of pneumococcal disease and its prevention. Rev Infect Dis 1981;3(Suppl.):1–17.
35. Hermans PWM, Sluijter M, Elzenaar K, *et al.* Penicillin-resistant *Streptococcus pneumoniae* in the Netherlands: results of 1-year molecular epidemiologic survey. J Infect Dis 1997;175:1413–22.
36. Fischetti VA. Streptococcus M protein: molecular design and biological behaviour. Clin Microbiol Rev 1989;2:285–314.
37. Cunningham MW, McCormack JM, Fenderson PG, Ho MK, Beachey EH, Dale JB. Human and murine antibodies crossreactive with streptococcal M protein and myosin recognize the sequence glu–lys–ser–lys–glu–M protein. J Immunol 1989;143:2677–83.
38. Bessen DE, Fischetti VA. M protein-based vaccines against mucosal colonization by Group A streptococci of a heterologous serotype. In: Orefici G, ed. New perspectives on streptococci and streptococcal infections. Stuttgart: Gustav Fischer Verlag; 1990:200–2.
39. Ohnishi R, Tomai M, Aelion J, Geller AM, Kotb M. A family of streptococcal superantigens represented by rheumatogenic serotypes of M proteins sharing specificity for human TCR-V04 elements. In: Totolian A, ed. Pathogenic streptococci: present and future. St Petersburg, Russia: Lorca; 1994:462–5.
40. Robinson JH, Kehoe MA. Group A streptococcal M proteins: virulence factors and protective antigens. Immunol Today 1992;13:362–7.
41. Kehoe MA. Cell-wall-associated proteins in Gram-positive bacteria. In: Ghuysen JM, Hakenbald R, eds. Bacterial cell wall. 1994:217–26.
42. Nordstrand A, Norgren M, Ferretti JJ, Holm SE. Streptokinase as a mediator of aute poststreptococcal glomerulonephritis in an experimental mouse model. Infect Immun 1998;66:315–21.
43. Stevens DL. Streptococcal toxic shock syndrome. Clin Microbiol Infect 2002;8:133–6.
44. Norrby-Teglund A, Kotb M. Host-microbe interactions in the pathogenesis of invasive group A streptococcal infections. J Med Microbiol 2000;49:849–52.
45. Hoogkamp-Korstanje JAA, Gerhards LJ, Cats BP. Maternal carriage and neonatal acquisation of group B streptococcal infection. J Infect Dis 198;145:800–3.
46. Baker CJ, Edwards MS. Group B streptococcal infections. In: Remington JS, Klin JO, eds. Infectious diseases of the fetus and new born infant. Philadelphia: WB Saunders; 1990:72–81.
47. Kasper DL, Paoletti LC, Wessels MR, *et al.* Immune response to type III group B

streptococcal polysaccharide – tetanus toxoid conjugate vaccine. J Clin Invest 1991;98:2308–14.
48. Jett BD, Huycke MM, Gilmore MS. Virulence of enterococci. Clin Microbiol Rev 1994;7:462–78.
49. Bruyn GAW, Zegers BJM, van Furth R. Mechanisms of host defence against infection with *Streptococcus pneumoniae*. Clin Infect Dis 1992;4:251–62.
50. Schattner A, Vosti KL. Bacterial arthritis due to beta-hemolytic streptococci of serogroups A, B, C, and G. Medicine 1998;77:122–39.
51. Vartian C, Lerner PI, Shlaes DM, Gopalakrishna KV. Infections due to Lancefield group G streptococci. Medicine 1985;64:75–88.
52. Bradley SF, Gordon JJ, Baumgartner DD, Marasco WA, Kauffman CA. Group C streptococcal bacteremia: analysis of 88 cases. Rev Infect Dis 1991;13:270–80.
53. Liu CE, Jang TN, Wang FD, Wang LS, Liu CY. Invasive group G streptococcal infections: a review of 37 cases. China Med J [Taipei] 1995;56:173–8.
54. Salata RA, Lerner PI, Shlaes DM, Gopalakrishna KV, Wolinsky E. Infections due to Lancefield group C streptococci. Medicine 1989;68:225–39.
55. Baker CJ. Group B streptococcal infections. Ann Intern Med 1980:475–5.
56. Colford JM, Mohle-Boetani J, Vosti KL. Group B streptococcal bacteremia in adults. Medicine 1995;74:176–90.
57. Schwartz B, Schuchat A, Oxtoby MJ, Cochi SL, Hightower A, Broome CV. Invasive group B streptococcal disease in adults; a population-based study in metropolitan Atlanta. JAMA 1991;266:1112–4.
58. de Vera ME, Simmons RL. Antibiotic-resistant enterococci and the changing face of surgical infections. Arch Surg 1996;131:338–42.
59. Evans Patterson J, Sweeney AH, Simms M, *et al.* An analysis of 110 serious enterococcal infections; epidemiology, antibiotic susceptibility, and outcome. Medicine 1995;74:191–200.
60. Raymond NJ, Henry J, Workowski KA. Enterococcal arthritis: case report and review. Clin Infect Dis 1995;21:516–22.
61. Stevenson KB, Murray EW, Sarubbi FA. Enterococcal meningitis: report of four cases and review. Clin Infect Dis 1994;18:233–9.
62. Musher DM. Infections caused by *Streptococcus pneumoniae*: clinical spectrum, pathogenesis, immunity, and treatment. Clin Infect Dis 1992;14:801–9.
63. Totapally BR, Walsh WT. Pneumococcal bacteremia in childhood. Chest 1998;113:1207–14.
64. Pastor P, Medley F, Murphy TV. Invasive pneumococcal disease in Dallas County: results from population-based surveillance in 1995. Clin Infect Dis 1998;26:590–5.
65. Aronin SI, Mukherjee SK, West JC, Cooney EL. Review of pneumococcal endocarditis in adults in the penicillin era. Clin Infect Dis 1998;26:165–71.
66. Whithworth JM. Lancefield group F and related streptococci. J Med Microbiol 1990;33:131–51.
67. Bochud PY, Calandra T, Francioli P. Bacteremia due to viridans streptococci in neutropenic patients: a review. Am J Med 1994;97:256–4.
68. Tunkel AR, Sepkowitz KA. Infection caused by viridans streptococci in patients with neutropenia. Clin Infect Dis 2002;34:1524–29.
69. Swenson FJ, Rubin SJ. Clinical significance of viridans streptococci isolated from blood cultures. J Clin Microbiol 1982;15:725–7.
70. Salavert M, Gómez L, Rodriguez-Carballeira M, Xercavins M, Freixas N, Garau J. Seven-year review of bacteremia caused by *Streptococcus milleri* and other viridans streptococci. Eur J Clin Microbiol Infect Dis 1996;15:365–71.
71. Shlaes DM, Lerner PI, Wolinski E, Gopalakrishna KV. Infections due to Lancefield group F and related streptococci (*S. milleri, S. anginosus*). Medicine 1981;60:197–207.
72. Gossling J. Occurrence and pathogenicity of the *Streptococcus milleri* group. Rev Infect Dis 1988;10:257–85.
73. Cohen LF, Dunbar SA, Sirbasku DM, *et al.* *Streptococcus bovis* infection of the central nervous system: report of two cases and review. Clin Infect Dis 1997;25:819–23.
74. Bouvet A. Human endocarditis due to nutritionally variant streptococci: *Streptococcus adjacens* and *Streptococcus defectivus*. Eur Heart J 1995;16(Suppl.B):24–7.
75. Dhodapkar KM, Henry NK. *Leuconostoc* bacteremia in an infant with short-gut syndrome: case report and literature review. Mayo Clin Proc 1996;71:1171–4.
76. Handwerger S, Horowitz H, Coburn K, Kolokathis A, Wormser GP. Infection due to *Leuconostoc* species: six cases and review. Rev Infect Dis 1990;12:602–10.
77. Seppälä H, Klaukka T, Vuopio-Varkila J, *et al.* The effects of changes in the consumption of macrolide antibiotics on erythromycin resistance in group A streptococci in Finland. N Engl J Med 1997;337:441–6.
78. Landman D, Quale JM. Management of infections due to resistant enterococci: a review of therapeutic options. J Antimicrob Chemother 1997;40:161–70.
79. Qadri SM, Ueno Y, Abu-Mostafa FM, Halim M. *In vitro* activity of quinupristin/dalfopristin, RP59500, against Gram-positive clinical isolates. Chemotherapy 1997;43:94–9.
80. Friedland IR, McCracken GH. Management of infections caused by antibiotic-resistant *Streptococcus pneumoniae*. N Engl J Med 1994;331:377–82.
81. Quinn JP, DiVincenzo CA, Lucks DA, Luskin RL, Shatzer KL, Lerner SA. Serious infections due to penicillin-resistant strains of viridans streptococci with altered penicillin-binding proteins. J Infect Dis 1988;157:764–9.
82. Swenson JM, Facklam RR, Thornsberry C. Antimicrobial susceptibility of vancomycin-resistant *Leuconostoc, Pediococcus*, and *Lactobacillus* species. Antimicrob Agents Chemother 1990;34:543–9.
83. Siegel JD. Prophylaxis for neonatal group B streptococcal infections. Semin Perinatol 1998;22:33–49.
84. Shapino ED, Berg AT, Austrian R, *et al.* The protective efficacy of polyvalent pneumonoccal polysaccharide vaccine. N Engl J Med 1991;325:1453–60.
85. Alonso de Velasco E, Verheul AFM, Verhoef J, Snippe H. *Streptococcus pneumoniae*: virulence factors, pathogenesis, and vaccines. Microbiol Rev 1995;59:591–603.
86. Douglas RM, Paton JC, Duncan SJ, Hansman DJ. Antibody response to pneumococcal vaccination in children younger than five years of age. J Infect Dis 1983;148:131–7.

chapter

226 Aerobic Gram-positive Bacilli

Robert Bortolussi & Timothy Mailman

INTRODUCTION

The aerobic Gram-positive bacilli are a heterogeneous group of bacteria whose members cause a wide variety of infections in both healthy and immuno-compromised individuals, and several organisms have been implicated in outbreak infections. The major pathogens are *Listeria monocytogenes*, *Bacillus anthracis*, *Corynebacterium diphtheriae*, *Erysipelothrix rhusiopathiae* and *Nocardia* spp. Other organisms discussed are *Arcanobacterium*, *Oerskovia*, *Rhodococcus*, *Rothia* and other corynebacteria.

LISTERIA MONOCYTOGENES

NATURE

Listeria monocytogenes is a short, motile, Gram-positive, non-spore-forming bacillus that is the causative agent in a spectrum of human disease ranging from gastroenteritis to invasive infections – notably in neonates, the elderly and immunocompromised patients. In addition to its importance as a human pathogen, it has a significant association with abortion and encephalitis in sheep and cattle.

The genus *Listeria* is described in *Bergey's Manual of Determinative Bacteriology* as a non-spore-forming, non-acid-fast and nonencapsulated Gram-positive regular short-rod occurring singly or in short chains.[1] *Listeria* is divided into six species based on biochemical properties and DNA relatedness. *Listeria monocytogenes* is distinguished by its ability to produce acid from the sugars L-rhamnose and α-methyl-D-mannoside, lack of acid production from D-xylose and by narrow zones of β-hemolysis on blood agar. The organism exhibits a positive Christie, Atkins and Munch–Petersen (CAMP) test using *Staphylococcus aureus* or *Rhodococcus equi* as the second indicator hemolytic strain. A positive CAMP test for *L. monocytogenes* differs from that seen for *Streptococcus agalactiae* by producing a rectangular, rather than arrow shaped, zone of accentuated hemolysis (Fig. 226.1a). Other key tests for the identification of *L. monocytogenes* include a positive catalase reaction, tumbling motility when viewed microscopically at room temperature, and an 'umbrella' pattern of motility in soft agar incubated at room temperature (Fig. 226.1b).

Growth of the organism occurs between 39°F (4°C) and 98.6°F (37°C), with fastest growth between 86°F (30°C) and 98.6°F. Cold enrichment techniques or selective agar may be used to isolate *L. monocytogenes* from contaminated specimens but are generally of limited value in the clinical laboratory.

Only *L. monocytogenes* and *Listeria ivanovii* have been associated with significant infection in humans. Six serovars of *L. monocytogenes* have been described and are distinguished on the basis of somatic O and flagellar H antigens. Serovars 1/2a, 4a and 4b are the most common isolates from animals and humans with clinical disease. In the USA, serovars 4b and 1/2a account for 95% of strains, serotype 4b being the most common overall. In Canada serovar 1/2a occurred in 42% of clinical isolates in 1988. Other serovars originate from soil or other environmental sources but are rarely seen as clinical pathogens.

EPIDEMIOLOGY

Reservoir

Listeria monocytogenes is commonly present in soil, decayed matter, wood and other material and is widespread in the natural environment.[2,3] Spoiled silage appears to be a source of infection to animals. Fecal carriage of *L. monocytogenes* in animals allows recontamination of soil, with subsequent ingestion of contaminated silage to complete the cycle in animals.

Recent evidence suggests that almost all human cases of *L. monocytogenes* are acquired through ingestion of contaminated food. In the early and mid 1980s large outbreaks of *L. monocytogenes* occurred in both pregnant women and immunocompromised hosts. The first outbreak that demonstrated indirect transmission from an animal reservoir was reported from the Atlantic maritime provinces of Canada.[4] In this outbreak, *Listeria*-contaminated sheep manure was used to fertilize cabbages that were placed in cold storage over the winter; clinical disease developed in pregnant women and immunocompromised patients who subsequently consumed the cabbages. Outbreaks of infection attributed to consumption of many foods, including inadequately pasteurized dairy products and contaminated processed meats, have been reported since.[5]

The improved ability to culture *L. monocytogenes* with selective media provides an opportunity to examine food eaten by patients who have sporadic listeriosis. Evidence that most sporadic listeriosis cases result from ingestion of contaminated food was provided by the Listeriosis Study Group at the Centers for Disease Control and Prevention (CDC).[6,7] Their studies implicated undercooked chicken and soft cheeses as significant sources of disease and are supported by subsequent sampling surveys performed by food regulatory agencies.

Fecal carriage of listeriosis is uncommon but ranges from 1% in hospitalized patients to 26% in household contacts of patients who have listeriosis. In the Canadian outbreak fecal surveys demonstrated carriage in approximately 5% of family contacts.[4] Several studies have shown that fever and gastroenteritis are clinical features of *L. monocytogenes* infection[5] after ingestion of contaminated food. *Listeria monocytogenes* may also cause a self-limited symptomatic gastrointestinal infection.

Occurrence

Active surveillance in the USA suggests an annual incidence of 0.7 cases per 100,000 population,[8] resulting in 1700 cases of listeriosis per year in the USA, with a mortality rate of 40%. Slightly lower figures have recently been reported from Europe. Risk of listeriosis varies among segments of the population. Immunocompromised patients and those at the extremes of age – neonates and the elderly – appear to be at highest risk. Immunocompromised patients comprise two-thirds of adult listeriosis cases. This parallels

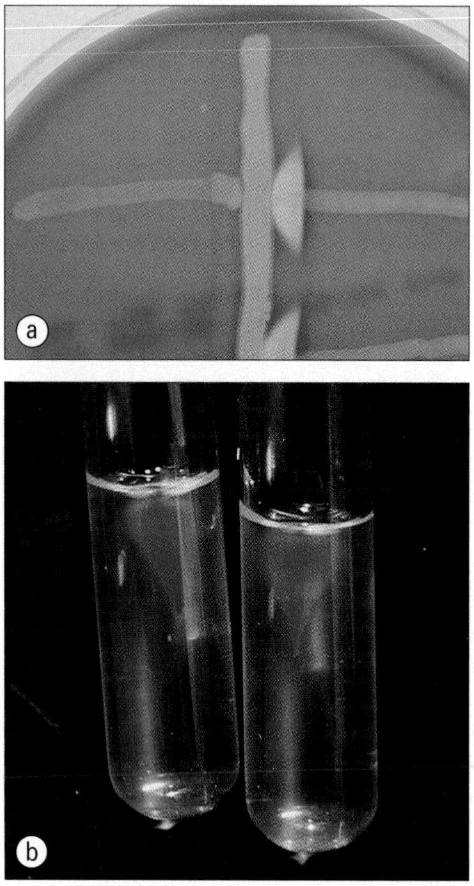

Fig. 226.1 Tests for the identification of *Listeria monocytogenes*. (a) CAMP test. Enhanced hemolysis patterns for *L. monocytogenes* (left) and *Streptococcus agalactiae* (right) colonies are shown; these are growing adjacent to a streak of *Staphylococcus aureus* colonies in the center. (b) Demonstration of motility of *L. monocytogenes* grown in semisolid agar at room temperature. Note that the migration of the organism from the central stab is more pronounced at the surface of the soft agar, forming the typical umbrella-shaped pattern in both tubes.

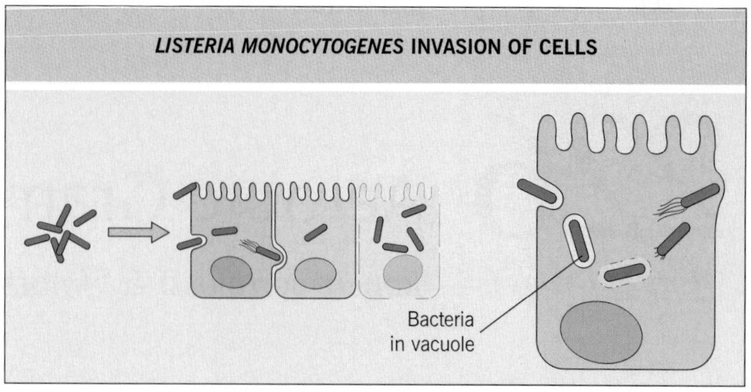

Fig. 226.2 *Listeria monocytogenes* can invade both 'professional' phagocytic cells – polymorphonuclear leukocytes and monocytes – and nonphagocytic cells. Attachment of the bacteria to the surface of nonphagocytic cells may be determined by heparin sulfate recognition proteins on the surface of the organism. Once internalized, the bacterial product listeriolysin O will lyse the phagosome, liberating the bacteria into the cytoplasm, where they proliferate. After a few hours, actin filaments polarize at one end of the bacterium, propelling it to the internal membrane surface. The organism will break through the membrane to enter the exterior of the cell or an adjacent cell.

animal models, in which risk of listeriosis is increased by administration of corticosteroids, ciclosporin A and prostaglandins. Renal transplantation appears to be a particularly significant risk factor and a nosocomial outbreak in this population has been reported. Patients who have AIDS have an estimated 1000-fold risk of acquiring invasive listeriosis. Alcoholism, diabetes, cirrhosis, hemochromatosis and decreased gastric acidity are additional risk factors. Community-acquired listeriosis, however, often occurs in patients who have no apparent predisposing conditions.

Incidence of neonatal listeriosis in the USA is approximately 13 per 100,000 live births – approximately 30% of the total number of cases of reported listeriosis. A similar incidence has been reported in studies from Europe. Epidemics of food-borne listeriosis have disproportionately involved perinatal cases. No differences in carriage rates between pregnant women and nonpregnant individuals have been found in fecal and vaginal specimens. Fecal carriage may lead to vaginal colonization and the development of 'late-onset' infection in infants born to healthy mothers.

While most large outbreaks of listeriosis have occurred in the community, case clusters of nosocomial listeriosis in both newborn infants and adults have been described. In infants, the index case typically presents with 'early-onset' infection within 1 week of birth, and subsequent cases develop 'late-onset' listeriosis after the 7th day of life. A dramatic nosocomial outbreak occurred in Costa Rica when an infant who had 'early-onset' listeriosis was bathed in mineral oil that became contaminated with the epidemic strain. A cluster of 'late-onset' disease then erupted after other infants were bathed with the same oil.[9]

PATHOGENICITY

Intracellular growth

Since the 1960s, it has been known that *L. monocytogenes* can survive within macrophages in the liver and spleen. In the late 1980s it was also appreciated that *Listeria* can infect nonphagocytic cells – epithelial, hepatocellular and fibroblast cell lines – thus providing the organism with an intracellular environment temporarily sheltered from more hostile host defense forces.[10]

Microbial attachment to host cells is the initial step in cell invasion (Fig. 226.2). Recent work has shown that interaction with a heparin sulfate peptidoglycan receptor on the surface of cells is involved in *L. monocytogenes* adhesion.[11] The stage is then set for internalization of the organism. A family of surface proteins known as internalins are secreted in large amounts by all strains of *Listeria* capable of invading host cells.[12] Although these proteins may be an important factor associated with entrance into epithelial cells and hepatocytes, they do not explain intracellular spread and multiplication. The intracellular survival of *Listeria* requires synthesis of a specific hemolysin, termed listeriolysin O. Listeriolysin enables the organism to escape from the phagosome by lysing the phagosomal membrane. Release of *L. monocytogenes* from intracellular vacuoles precipitates both intracellular growth and polymerization of actin of the host cell around *Listeria*. Actin polymerization is important in the cell-to-cell transfer of *L. monocytogenes* and is encoded by the *actA* gene. The liberated organism thrives in the cytoplasm, which provides more abundant growth conditions. Through these mechanisms *Listeria* can enter, grow and spread inside a wide variety of cells including renal epithelial cells, fibroblasts, vascular endothelium, hepatocytes and enterocytes. By producing ActA, *Listeria* causes host-cell actin to assemble into filaments at one end of the bacterium. This 'rocket tail' provides the propulsive force for the organism to move through the cytoplasm. When the bacteria reach the cell membrane, they form filopods that become ingested by adjacent cells.

Acquired immunity

Some 3–4 days after infection begins there is normally a decrease in viable bacteria in the monocyte/macrophage phagocytic system. This heralds the onset of the immune T-cell-dependent stage of antilisterial defense, termed 'acquired resistance'.

The process leading to acquired immunity to *Listeria*, cell-to-cell interaction, cytokines and cytolytic activity is now partially elucidated (Fig. 226.3 and 226.4). In adult immunocompetent animals, *Listeria* are phagocytosed by 'professional' phagocytes –

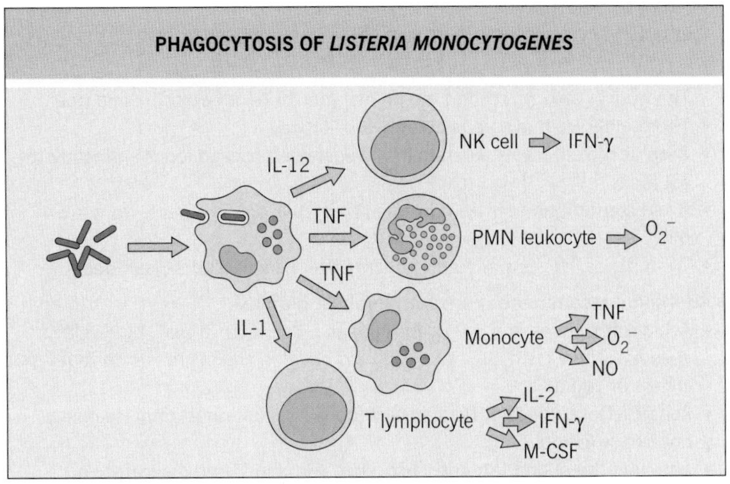

Fig. 226.3 Phagocytosis of *Listeria monocytogenes*. Opsonized *L. monocytogenes* is phagocytosed by professional phagocytic cells through a complement-receptor-mediated process. Once ingested into a phagosome of a monocyte or macrophage, most bacteria are quickly killed by oxidative radicals (O_2^-), lysozyme, nitric oxide (NO) and other products of the cell. Tissue macrophages produce a variety of protein products essential for the activation of natural killer (NK) cells (interleukin(IL)-12), T cells (IL-1) and polymorphonuclear (PMN) leukocytes and other monocyte/macrophages (tumor necrosis factor (TNF)-α). These cells in turn produce cytokines, interferons (IFN), interleukins that cause cell proliferation (IL-2; macrophage colony stimulating factor (M-CSF)) or further activation of cell populations involved in elimination of the organism and of infected nonprofessional cells.

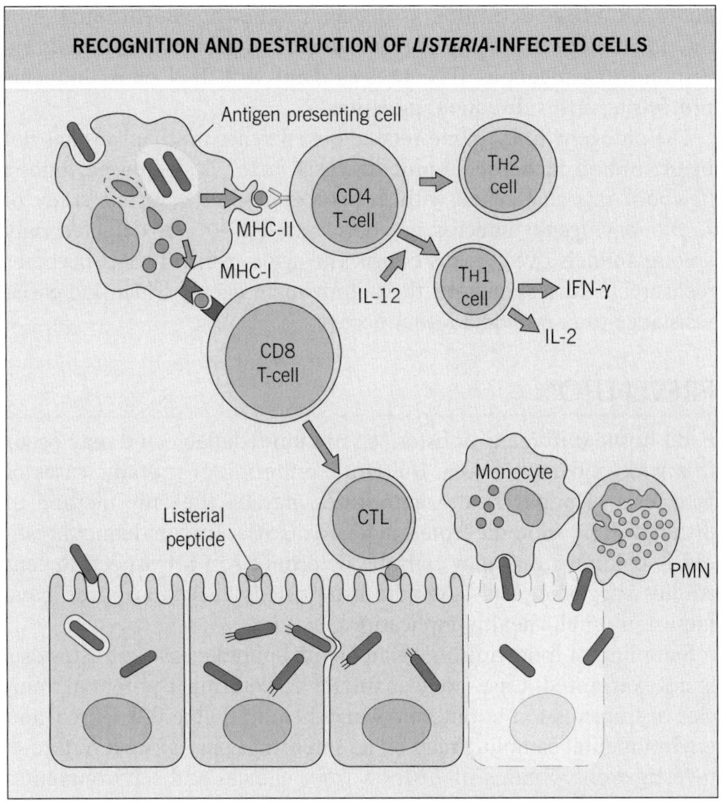

Fig. 226.4 Recognition and destruction of *Listeria*-infected cells. Cytotoxic T lymphocytes and NK lymphocytes migrate to the site of infection and recognize and destroy *Listeria*-infected cells by the presence of listerial peptides on the surface of such cells. Intracellular bacteria are then exposed to the extracellular environment. Organisms in the extracellular space are efficiently phagocytosed and killed by polymorphonuclear leukocytes (PMN) and monocytes that have been primed or activated by cytokines (TNF-α, M-CSF, IL-8) and IFN-γ.

macrophages and monocytes; and by 'nonprofessional' phagocytic cells – fibroblasts, hepatocytes, etc. Macrophages take up and process listerial proteins and produce interleukin (IL)-12 and IL-1. Peptides resulting from digestion of *Listeria* are actively processed by the macrophage in the endoplasmic reticulum, where the peptides bind to major histocompatibility complex (MHC) class I molecules.[12] The *Listeria*–peptide–MHC complex is transported to the cell surface, where it is recognized by cytotoxic T cells ($CD8^+$ phenotype) and helper T-cells (Th). In the presence of IL-12, naive Th cells differentiate into Th1 cells, which proliferate, producing IL-2, interferon (IFN)-γ and lymphotoxin.[13] Interleukin-12 also stimulates activation and proliferation of natural killer (NK) cells and γ/δ T cells. Both cell clones produce IFN-γ. Cytotoxic T cells interact with cells bearing *L. monocytogenes* antigen, causing them to lyse. Natural killer cells are further stimulated by IFN-γ, inducing an enhanced ability of these cells to lyse infected fibroblasts and hepatocytes (Fig. 226.4).

Cytokines such as macrophage colony-stimulating factor (M-CSF) and tumor necrosis factor (TNF)-α also appear during the first 5 days and have been implicated as mediators of listerial clearance. Peak immunity to *Listeria* is expressed at about the sixth day of infection, which coincides with maximal T-cell synthesis of IFN-γ. The role for endogenous IFN-γ for resolution for *L. monocytogenes* infection has been clearly shown.[14] Tumor necrosis factor-α enhances a variety of antibacterial or antiparasitic resistance mechanisms. Several cells produce TNF-α, including NK cells; however, monocytes/macrophages are probably the most abundant source. Endotoxin (lipopolysaccharide) and other agents including mitogens, viruses, protozoa and cytokines such as M-CSF, IL-1, IL-2 and IFN-γ have been identified as inducers of TNF-α. When administered before infection, TNF-α induces enhanced resistance of the host to bacterial infection. Endogenously produced TNF-α during sublethal *Listeria* infection in adult animals appears to function as an inducer of resistance,[15] suggesting that TNF-α-dependent mechanisms limits intracellular infection early in the course of infection. Down-modulation of the immune response is mediated by γ/δ T cells, an important role for such cells in controlling unregulated proinflammatory cytokines.[14]

Perinatal listeriosis

The pathogenesis of fetal listeriosis is not clear. Since the heaviest foci for neonatal infection are lung and gut, the fetus is probably infected by swallowing contaminated liquid as well as through the transplacental hematogenous route.[16] An ascending pathway from the lower genital tract may occur; however, infection via the transplacental route is favored by most authors. *Listeria monocytogenes* chorioamnionitis diagnosed by transabdominal amniocentesis (free from vaginal bacterial contamination) has been reported, supporting a maternal-to-newborn blood-borne route of infection.

Host response in the neonate

In newborn animals, susceptibility to *Listeria* is increased and is associated with delayed activation of macrophages. Studies on the afferent and efferent arms of the immune system in newborn mice have shown that macrophage–T-cell interaction is impaired and macrophage activation does not occur.[17]

Natural killer cells also contribute to the early response to *L. monocytogenes* infection. The proportion of mononuclear cells expressing NK cell phenotype and NK cell activity is decreased at birth, particularly for premature infants. Both NK cell phenotype and function increase rapidly in the weeks after birth.

In adult animals, IFN and agents that induce or augment IFN production confer protection against lethal listeriosis. Synthesis of IFN, IL-2, IL-4 and IL-12, all of which modulate the immune response and macrophage activation, is deficient in newborns. Although production of these factors may be defective, newborn animals do respond to exogenous IFN; pretreatment with IFN or its inducers protects against subsequent infection.

The ontogeny of cytokine-related host defense mechanisms has not been studied in depth. Tumor necrosis factor is decreased among newborn rats challenged with *L. monocytogenes*.[18] In this study of *L. monocytogenes* infected newborn rats, TNF-α was detected only among animals over 8 days of age. The age at which TNF-α becomes measurable corresponds to the approximate age at which increased resistance to *L. monocytogenes* occurs.

PREVENTION

Food-borne outbreaks of listeriosis are unpredictable and may occur in a wide geographic area. Therefore, reporting of sporadic cases of listeriosis to public health authorities may be the only method of distinguishing sporadic from epidemic disease. The epidemic threshold is unknown and may only be determined in retrospect. Recent studies suggesting that sporadic listeriosis is also food-borne have important public health implications.

Sampling of foodstuffs associated with sporadic cases of listeriosis is not warranted. Case–control studies to determine potential vehicles of transmission in outbreaks may help to define the source, and environmental sampling may be an important part of such outbreak investigations. Strains of *Listeria* from clinical and environmental isolates should be forwarded to a reference laboratory for appropriate epidemiologic typing. At a minimum, serotyping, phage-typing and multifocus enzyme electrophoresis typing should be performed to characterize the epidemic strain.

During an outbreak of listeriosis, high-risk groups such as pregnant women or those who have AIDS who develop a flu-like illness should be empirically treated with ampicillin and an aminoglycoside after appropriate cultures of blood, cerebrospinal fluid (CSF), sputum, rectum and vagina have been obtained. In pregnant women, amniocentesis for diagnosis of chorioamnionitis may be appropriate. If membranes have ruptured and contamination is suspected, use of selective media may enhance the isolation of *Listeria* from these patients.

Identification of early- or late-onset listeriosis in a newborn nursery should prompt appropriate epidemiologic and clinical history taking from the mother as well as postpartum cultures of rectum and vagina. Infection control precautions with gowning, gloves and careful handwashing will prevent nosocomial transmission between infected infants and is consistent with current procedures for all forms of neonatal sepsis.

The recognition that sporadic cases of listeriosis are primarily food-borne has also prompted publication of preventive guidelines by the CDC (Table 226.1).

DIETARY RECOMMENDATIONS FOR PREVENTING FOOD-BORNE LISTERIOSIS
• Thoroughly cook raw food from animal sources (e.g. beef, pork and poultry)
• Thoroughly wash raw vegetables before eating
• Keep uncooked meals separate from vegetables, cooked foods and ready-to-eat foods
• Avoid consumption of raw (unpasteurized) milk or foods made from raw milk
• Wash hands, knives and cutting boards after handling uncooked foods
Additional recommendations for people at high risk
• Avoid soft cheeses (e.g. Mexican-style, feta, Brie, Camembert, blue-veined cheeses). There is no need to avoid hard cheeses, cream cheese, cottage cheese or yogurt
• Reheat leftover foods or ready-to-eat foods (e.g. hot dogs) until steaming hot before eating
• Although the risk for listeriosis associated with foods from delicatessen counters is relatively low, pregnant women and immunosuppressed persons should avoid these foods or thoroughly reheat cold cuts before eating

Table 226.1 Dietary recommendations for preventing food-borne listeriosis. People at high risk are those who are immunocompromised as a result of illness or medications, pregnant women and the elderly. Adapted from Centers for Disease Control.[19]

DIAGNOSTIC MICROBIOLOGY

Serologic evaluation

The agglutination reaction (Widal test) demonstrates antibodies against somatic O and flagellar H antigens of the various *Listeria* serovars. Unfortunately, because of the antigen complexity of *L. monocytogenes*, no agreement has been reached as to the interpretation of agglutination reactions for diagnostic purposes.

Attempts to demonstrate complement-fixing *Listeria* antibodies date back to the 1930s. In one study, serum samples collected from 32 mothers who had perinatal *Listeria* infection were compared with 128 samples from matched controls.[20] The sensitivity and specificity of the complement fixation test were shown to be 78% and 91%, respectively; however, the positive predictive value was only 75%. Thus, the complement fixation test can be regarded as reliable only in some patients who have acute *Listeria* infection.

Detection of antibodies to listeriolysin O has been used to diagnose human listeriosis. Sensitivity and specificity of the test were over 90%. Although these results were impressive, the technique is not available commercially and results have not yet been confirmed in other centers.

Isolation of the organism

Cultivation of *L. monocytogenes* is the only reliable means of proving that the cause of an infection is due to *Listeria*. Culture of venous blood, ascitic and other fluids, cervical material, urine, amniotic fluid, lochia and meconium and tissues at biopsy or autopsy offer the best chances for identifying *Listeria* in persons who have an infection. Culture of the stool is not helpful. Feces are positive for *Listeria* in 1–5% of healthy adults.

Microscopic diagnosis may be attempted by use of Gram's stain only in specimens that normally do not contain bacteria – CSF, meconium and tissue smears. The finding of short (sometimes coccoid, and in pairs) Gram-positive rods strongly supports a suspicion of listeriosis and is indicative of this infection (Fig. 226.5). *Listeria monocytogenes* may not Gram stain as well as other Gram-positive organisms. Particularly with longstanding disease or when the patient has received antibiotics, the organisms may appear Gram-negative and be confused with *Haemophilus influenzae* when observed in the CSF. In other instances, *Listeria* has been mistaken for pneumococci or corynebacteria.

The submission of clinical specimens for culture may be facilitated by the use of transport-enrichment fluid. It is, however, advisable to submit specimens such as blood, sputum, CSF and pus without any additives. For patients who have received antibiotics, the use of a commercial antibiotic-removing device in sterile body fluid cultures is useful.

CLINICAL MANIFESTATIONS

The clinical features of listeriosis have considerable variability and may mimic other infections or other disease states. Based on the most common clinical manifestations, four or more clinical groups may be distinguished.

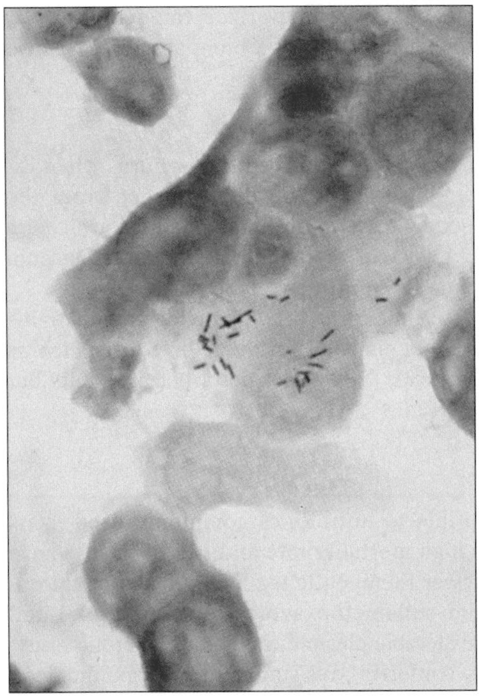

Fig. 226.5 Gram stain of clinical specimen showing intra- and extracellular Gram-positive bacilli.

CLINICAL AND LABORATORY FEATURES OF EARLY-ONSET LISTERIOSIS

Feature		Proportion of cases (%)
Male sex		64
Preterm infants (gestation age <35 weeks)		63
Mortality (of live-born infants)		15
Features in infants	Meconium stain	69
	Pneumonia	62
	Anemia	62
	Thromobocylopenia (<150 × 10^9/l)	35
	Meningitis	21
Source of isolate	Blood	73
Maternal features	Flu-like illness	45
	Blood isolate	35

Table 226.2 Clinical and laboratory features of early-onset listeriosis. Age at onset for early-onset listeriosis is under 7 days, but most cases occur at less than 2 days of age. Anemia is defined as hemoglobin less than 14g/dl and/or hematocrit less than 45. Meningitis is based on compatible clinical or autopsy findings or observation of the organism on Gram stain of the CSF. Flu-like illness is defined as the presence of respiratory symptoms, myalgia and fever occurring from 3 days to 1 month before delivery. Blood isolates are defined as of *Listeria monocytogenes* from mother's blood at any time before delivery of the infant.

Listeriosis during pregnancy

Susceptibility to *L. monocytogenes* is markedly increased in pregnant animals. The predilection of *Listeria* for the fetoplacental unit and intrauterine infection is well documented.[21,22] Maternal listeriosis can be transmitted to the fetus by an ascending or transplacental route. Early gestational listeriosis is associated with septic abortion; however, most cases of perinatal listeriosis are found after the fifth month of pregnancy, with premature delivery of a septic or stillborn infant the result.

Maternal influenza-like illness with fever and chills, fatigue, headache and muscle pains often precedes delivery by 2–14 days. Although symptoms in the mother may subside before delivery, infection and fever precipitating delivery is common. Blood cultured from such women can yield *Listeria* at the time of initial symptoms or later. Premature labour in mothers who have listeriosis is common; approximately 70% deliver newborns at less than 35 weeks of gestation. The mortality rate, including stillbirth and abortion, is 40–50%. Early treatment of *Listeria* sepsis in pregnancy, however, can prevent infection and its sequelae.

Listeriosis in the newborn infant

Neonatal listeriosis has become recognized as the most common clinical form of human listeriosis. Infection in the neonatal period is usually divided into two clinical groups defined by age: early- and late-onset infection.

Some clinical and laboratory manifestations of early-onset neonatal listeriosis are outlined in Table 226.2, which is compiled from clinical cases in which early and late forms of the disease could be differentiated. Classically (as illustrated in Table 226.2), early-onset neonatal listeriosis develops within 1–2 days of life. However, in one outbreak involving 10 infants who had nosocomially acquired listeriosis, an atypical clinical picture was described.[9] Nine of these infants were bathed shortly after birth with mineral oil contaminated with *L. monocytogenes*. Clinical features of infection developed 4–8 days later and were similar to those seen in late-onset infection, insidious onset of illness with fever and meningitis being common.

Evidence of preceding maternal illness is often described in infants who have early-onset disease. Although some symptoms in mothers are vague and non-specific – malaise, myalgia – others are sufficiently distinctive – fever, chills – to alert physicians to the risk of prenatally acquired listeriosis. Blood cultures from such mothers are often positive for *Listeria*.

Although early-onset disease may occur up to 7 days of age, most cases are clinically apparent at delivery, with meconium staining, cyanosis, apnea, respiratory distress and pneumonia. Meconium-stained liquor is a common feature in such infants and may occur at any gestational age, even less than 32 weeks. Pneumonia is also common, but radiographic features are not specific – peribronchial to widespread infiltration. In more longstanding infection, a coarse, mottled or nodular pattern has been described. Assisted ventilation is frequently necessary in such infants. Persistent hypoxia in spite of ventilatory assistance is seen in severely affected infants. Laboratory features are non-specific; a leukocytosis with presence of immature cells may be seen or, if infection is severe, neutropenia. Similarly, thrombocytopenia may also occur. Many infants are anemic, which is perhaps attributable to hemolysin produced by the organism. These laboratory and clinical features will not help to distinguish listeriosis from early-onset group B streptococcal or other bacterial infection.

In severe infection a granulomatous skin rash has been described (Fig. 226.6). Slightly elevated, pale patches measuring 1–2mm in diameter with a bright, erythematous base are seen. If such areas are biopsied, a leukocytic infiltrate with multiple bacteria is found.

Neonatal listerial infection that occurs after 7 days of life is termed late-onset infection. Although there is some overlap between early- and late-onset forms of listeriosis, the clinical pattern of the two is usually distinct. The common clinical and laboratory features of late-onset neonatal listeriosis are shown in Table 226.3. By far the most common form of *Listeria* infection over this period is meningitis, which is present in 94% of late-onset cases. In many centers, *Listeria* ranks second only to group B streptococci as a cause of bacterial meningitis in this age group, causing approximately 20% of such infections.

Clinical features do not distinguish listerial meningitis in this age group from other causes. A striking predominance of males has been noted in most series. Fever and irritability are predominant clinical

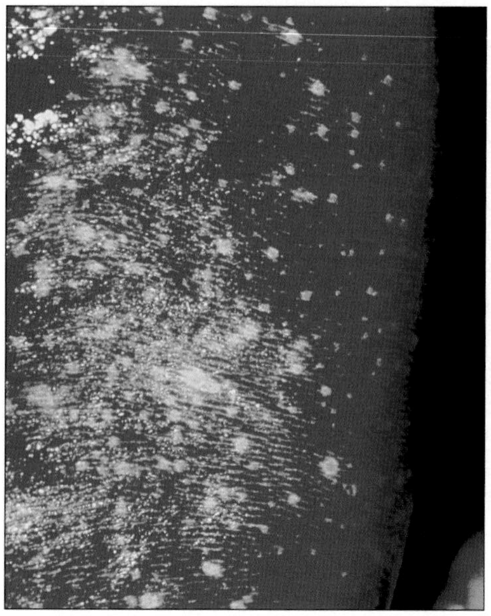

Fig. 226.6 Skin rash on premature infant who has sepsis due to *Listeria monocytogenes*. This form of infection, known as granulomatosis infantisepticum, is characterized by disseminated microabscesses on the skin, spleen and liver. The elevated pale patches (1–2mm in diameter) on the skin are clearly seen in contrast to the bright erythema of surrounding skin.

CLINICAL AND LABORATORY FEATURES OF LATE-ONSET LISTERIOSIS

Feature		Proportion of cases (%)
Male sex		67
Signs at presentation	Fever	94
	Irritability	75
	Diarrhea	Occasional
Isolates	CSF	94
	Blood	17

Table 226.3 Clinical and laboratory features of late-onset listeriosis. Mean age is 12–20 days.

features. Often, infants do not appear excessively ill and may therefore elude diagnosis for several days.

Laboratory features of late-onset infection are not specific. Cell count in the CSF is usually high, with a predominance of polymorphonuclear and band forms. Occasionally, in longstanding disease, a relatively high number of monocytes may be seen. Gram stain of CSF may not always suggest a diagnosis, both because the organism may be rare and because the morphology is atypical. Variable decolorization of Gram's crystal violet–iodine stain may result in organisms appearing as Gram-negative rods. The appearance of organisms as illustrated in Figure 226.5 is characteristic of listeriosis in the early phase of severe infection.

Mortality in late-onset newborn infection is generally low, unless diagnosis is delayed by more than 3–4 days after onset of infection. Long-term sequelae and morbidity are uncommon.

Central nervous system infection

Bacteria invade the central nervous system through a variety of mechanisms. For *L. monocytogenes*, invasion of the central nervous system may be mediated by bacterial invasion of endothelial cells at the blood–brain interface followed by cell-to-cell spread of the organism in microvascular endothelial cells. Some investigators have also speculated on a 'Trojan horse' mechanism, whereby monocytes or neutrophils infected with *L. monocytogenes* transport organisms to the central nervous system, where they are released when these cells are lysed.[23] Among adults who have central nervous system infection, a high incidence of prolonged ataxia, hydrocephalus and cerebellar atrophy visualized via computerized tomography (CT) have been reported. Rhombencephalitis and brain abscess have also been seen and appear to have a good prognosis.[22]

Other clinical forms of infection

Papular cutaneous lesions are often observed in newborns when listeriosis is disseminated. These are to be distinguished from the primary skin lesions caused by *Listeria* observed in adults, which are the result of direct contact, such as the handling of a cow's placenta after abortion by a veterinarian or farmer.

In the course of the septicemic form, accompanying conjunctivitis is sometimes observed. Other unusual forms of listeriosis such as endocarditis and septic arthritis have been described in adults but appear to be rare in infants.

THERAPY

Listeria remains susceptible to antibiotics commonly used in its treatment. However, the high mortality rate and risk of relapse have prompted a search for newer therapeutic regimens, including fluoroquinolones, trimethoprim–sulfamethoxazole (co-trimoxazole) and rifampin (rifampicin). Transferable plasmid-mediated antibiotic resistance has been reported, conferring resistance to chloramphenicol, tetracycline and erythromycin.

In-vitro studies

Conflicting reports of in-vitro activity of antibiotics against clinical isolates of *L. monocytogenes* probably reflect a variable pattern of susceptibility for strains as well as differences in laboratory technique. Two large in-vitro studies of antibiotic susceptibility of human clinical isolates of *L. monocytogenes* have been reported, using broth dilution susceptibility methods.[24,25] Both studies found that the strains represented a homogeneous population susceptible to ampicillin, penicillin, erythromycin and tetracycline. In-vitro results, however, are greatly influenced by methodology – inoculum size, media and definition of end points. As reported in these two studies, the minimal bactericidal concentration (MBC) of antibiotics is often much higher than levels attainable clinically. Thus, most antibiotics tested are bacteriostatic but not bactericidal. Although bacteriostatic antibiotics have been used in the past, bactericidal antibiotics have a potential advantage for patients who have impaired host defense mechanisms, including neonates. Results of cephalosporin antibiotic in-vitro and in-vivo studies have been consistently disappointing. The organism is uniformly highly resistant to all the cephalosporin antibiotics tested.

In-vivo studies

Several combinations of antibiotics have been compared for their bactericidal activity against *L. monocytogenes* in vivo. Animal models appear to provide the only practical method of assessing therapeutic regimens, since large clinical studies in humans are not available. Murine models employing normal adults or immunodeficient animals have been reported.[26,27] A rabbit model using animals injected intracisternally with *Listeria* has also been described. The model most analogous to neonatal disease has also been described.[28]

In the in-vivo model of neonatal listeriosis, the combination of ampicillin with gentamicin gave significantly better eradication of organisms in spleen than ampicillin alone.[28] Similarly, the combination of trimethoprim and sulfamethoxazole was superior to either drug alone. Reports of efficacy of other antibiotics in vivo are conflicting. Rifampin has been found by some authors to be highly effective in eradicating organisms, while others have found it to be ineffective. Sensitivity of individual strains to rifampin may account for the widely discrepant results. Also, rifampin resistance may develop in vivo when it is used as a single drug. The use of ciprofloxacin in animal models has not suggested any therapeutic advantage over ampicillin.

Clinical reports

There have been no prospective clinical trials reported for *L. monocytogenes* human infection. Anecdotal reports of single cases or reviews of outbreaks support the conclusions drawn from in-vivo models. In one review of clinical management of 119 cases of listeriosis from three centers in the USA, excellent therapeutic results were seen for patients treated empirically with penicillin or ampicillin; all had a reduction of fever and clinical improvement. However, patients treated initially with cephalosporins had persistent fever and infection.[2] In the largest assessment of treatment regimens during a single outbreak,[29] lower mortality was reported for children given ampicillin (16% of 57 children) compared to those treated with chloramphenicol, tetracycline or streptomycin (33% of 82 children). Nevertheless, in the absence of controlled clinical trials, a definitive recommendation for treatment cannot be made.

SUGGESTED MANAGEMENT

Listeriosis during pregnancy

If amnionitis is present, initial treatment should be given by intravenous route to assure adequate tissue levels – ampicillin 4–6g per day (divided into four equal doses) plus an aminoglycoside. If amnionitis is not present or if acute symptoms of amnionitis have subsided, then oral antibiotics are probably adequate – amoxicillin 2–3g per day (divided into four equal doses). In both situations, treatment should continue for 14 days. If the patient has a significant allergy to ampicillin, therapeutic options are limited. Erythromycin may be given. The estolate form of this drug should be avoided since there is increased liver toxicity during pregnancy. Trimethoprim–sulfamethoxazole should not be used, since premature delivery of the infant may occur as a consequence of infection, in which case the drug may cause displacement of bilirubin from protein and increase the potential for toxicity in the infant.

Neonatal listeriosis

Ampicillin in combination with an aminoglycoside is the preferred management for early-onset infection. For infants with a body weight under 2000g, administer 100mg/kg per day (divided into two equal doses) for the first week of life. For infants with a body weight over 2000g, administer 150mg/kg per day (divided into three equal doses) for the first week of life. For the second week of life the appropriate daily dosages are 150mg/kg and 200mg/kg for infants under and over 2000g body weight, respectively. Aminoglycoside doses vary with the agent chosen.

For gentamicin the suggested dosages are 5mg/kg per day (divided into two equal doses) for the first week of life and 7.5mg/kg per day (divided into three equal doses) for the second week of life. A treatment duration of 14 days is recommended for early-onset neonatal sepsis due to *L. monocytogenes*; however, a 3-week course of treatment should be given in the uncommon event of early-onset neonatal listeriosis with meningitis.

Listeriosis in infants and adults

Meningitis is commonly present in the late-onset type of neonatal listeriosis and in listeriosis in adults. Delayed eradication of the organism may be seen in such cases. Ampicillin 200–400mg/kg per day (divided into 4–6 equal doses for 3 weeks), in combination with an aminoglycoside, is recommended.[22] Lumbar punctures should be repeated daily until the organism has been cleared. In the event of delayed clearance (more than 2 days), further investigations are indicated and should include CT scan or cranial ultrasound (in infants) to assess for the presence of cerebritis, abscess, rhombencephalitis or intracranial hemorrhage. Treatment should be prolonged to 6 weeks if cerebral pathology is identified.

If the organism persists in the CSF the addition of rifampin or use of trimethoprim–sulfamethoxazole may be considered if the organism is sensitive in vitro. Experience with rifampin and trimethoprim–sulfamethoxazole in the neonatal period and with this organism is limited. Cephalosporin antibiotics have no role in treatment since the organism is uniformly resistant. Vancomycin has been used successfully in patients who are allergic to penicillin.[22]

BACILLUS ANTHRACIS

NATURE

The genus *Bacillus* comprises a variety of Gram-positive, spore-forming bacilli that are differentiated from *Clostridium* spp. by a positive catalase test and the ability to produce endospores in the presence of oxygen. *Bacillus* spp. are found worldwide as inhabitants of soil, water and airborne dust. Some species are part of the normal intestinal flora of humans and animals. Endospores resistant to extremes of heat, pH and salinity are able to survive harsh environmental conditions.

Bacillus anthracis was the first bacterium proved to cause a specific disease when, in 1877, Robert Koch induced anthrax in experimental animals by injecting them with pure cultures of the organism. Today, three well-defined cycles are recognized for the organism: spore multiplication in soil; infection of herbivorous animals; and human infection. Spore multiplication is favored in moist, alkaline soils rich in organic matter. As spore density increases, infection of grazing animals can occur. Human disease is often associated with animal outbreaks. Spores can survive in the soil for decades and contribute to persistence in a geographic area.

Bacillus anthracis can be differentiated from other *Bacillus* spp. by its lack of motility, absence of β-hemolysis on sheep blood agar and penicillin susceptibility.

EPIDEMIOLOGY

Anthrax is a zoonotic disease of herbivores endemic to many rural areas of the world. Although anthrax spores have been found in soil samples worldwide, the disease has been controlled in most developed countries through animal immunization programs. Human infection occurs incidentally by contact with infected animals or animal products such as hides, hair or wool. Most human cases are related to occupational exposure by agricultural workers, veterinarians or those in the textile industry where animal hides and hair are frequently handled. Transmission to humans usually occurs by direct inoculation of spore-containing material to skin abrasions (cutaneous anthrax) but also via spore aerosolization (inhalational anthrax or 'wool sorter's disease') and ingestion (gastrointestinal anthrax). Accidental infections have occurred in laboratory workers. Person-to-person transmission has not been documented. The incubation period is generally 1–7 days following exposure. Suggestions that delayed onset of disease may occur following exposure to aerosolized spores has led to the current recommendation for a 2-month course of antibiotic prophylaxis following inhalational exposure.[30]

Anthrax remains enzootic in parts of Africa and Asia, despite its decreasing prevalence in the developed world. Multiple epidemics of human disease have been associated with epizootics in agricultural herds. More than 10,000 human cases occurred in Zimbabwe between 1979 and 1985 following an outbreak in cattle.[31] An outbreak in Chad during 1988 resulted in 716 human cases and 88 deaths.[32] Other outbreaks have occurred in the Middle East, South East Asia and the

Indian subcontinent. While most cases have been of cutaneous disease, clusters of inhalational and gastrointestinal anthrax have been reported.[33] Anthrax is probably under-reported in developing nations because of the difficulty in diagnosing gastrointestinal disease and limited public health statistics.

In developed countries, outbreaks have mostly been associated with the handling of imported animal products. An epidemic in a textile factory in Switzerland involved 24 cutaneous cases and one case of inhalational anthrax. The infections were traced to goat hair imported from Pakistan.[34] In North America, intermittent outbreaks occur among wildlife herds but domestic human disease is rare.

The development of anthrax as a biologic warfare and bioterrorism agent has drastically heightened global awareness of the disease. Japan, the USA, the UK, Iraq and the Soviet Union are among countries known to have worked on military applications of anthrax. Its subsequent use in terrorist acts has dissolved the perception of anthrax as merely an uncommon and occupational disease. Health care workers and public health agencies have been re-educated to recognize patterns of illness suggestive of anthrax and to develop contingency plans for epidemics. The lethal inhalational dose for anthrax spores is a millionth of a gram, yielding the potential for a small amount of aerosolized spores to devastate urban populations. These concerns were foreshadowed in April 1979 when anthrax spores were accidentally released from a military microbiology facility in the central Russian city of Sverdlovsk.[35] An anthrax epidemic occurred among people who lived or worked downwind of the site. The 96 cases and 64 deaths that ensued constituted the largest documented outbreak of inhalational anthrax in history. Livestock up to 50km from the site perished from anthrax.

PATHOGENICITY

The virulence of *B. anthracis* is largely mediated by the production of anthrax toxin and encapsulation. Anthrax toxin is an exotoxin composed of three thermolabile proteins, protective antigen (PA), lethal factor (LF) and edema factor (EF), which mediate most of the pathologic findings of anthrax. A capsule containing poly-D-glutamic acid assists the organism in evading phagocytosis. Production of toxin and capsule is mediated by the plasmids pX01 and pX02, respectively.[36]

Anthrax usually begins by the introduction of spores from the organism through the skin, gastrointestinal tract or respiratory epithelium. Spores may be phagocytosed by tissue macrophages and remain at the site of inoculation or be transported to regional lymph nodes. In either case, spores germinate to vegetative bacilli, which are capable of toxin production. Local damage to tissue results from toxin-mediated edema and tissue necrosis. Toxin, organisms or both may spread via the vascular system to produce systemic disease.

When organisms release anthrax toxin, the PA component binds specific cell-surface receptors, forming a membrane channel that enables EF and LF to enter the cell.

Edema factor is an adenylate cyclase, similar to the adenylate cyclase toxin of *Bordetella pertussis*. Recent studies have demonstrated that activation of EF depends on binding to calmodulin.[37] It combines with PA to form *edema toxin*. In experimental models, cells treated with edema toxin exhibit increased intracellular cyclic adenosine monophosphate (cAMP). In monocytes and macrophages, cAMP regulates TNF-α production and as cAMP rises TNF production decreases. The ensuing cytokine dysregulation produces edema and destruction of local tissues.

Lethal factor combines with PA to form *lethal toxin*, the dominant virulence factor and major cause of death in infected animals. Following entry of lethal toxin into host cells, calcium influx occurs and cellular synthetic pathways are disrupted. Apoptosis and necrosis occur, mediated by protein phosphatases. Cell lysis follows. These tissue effects are seen clinically as the black necrotic lesions of cutaneous anthrax, the hemorrhagic mediastinitis of inhalational anthrax and the necrotic ulcers of pharyngeal or gastrointestinal disease.

Together, lethal toxin and edema toxin contribute to the inhibition of phagocytosis. If ingestion does occur, lethal toxin and edema toxin inhibit the oxidative burst of neutrophils and prevent intracellular killing of ingested bacteria (Fig. 226.7).

PREVENTION

Public health measures for preventing the spread of anthrax have focused on the identification and destruction of diseased animals and quarantine of potentially infected livestock. Repeated outbreaks in Africa have illustrated that reservoirs of disease in wildlife herds can

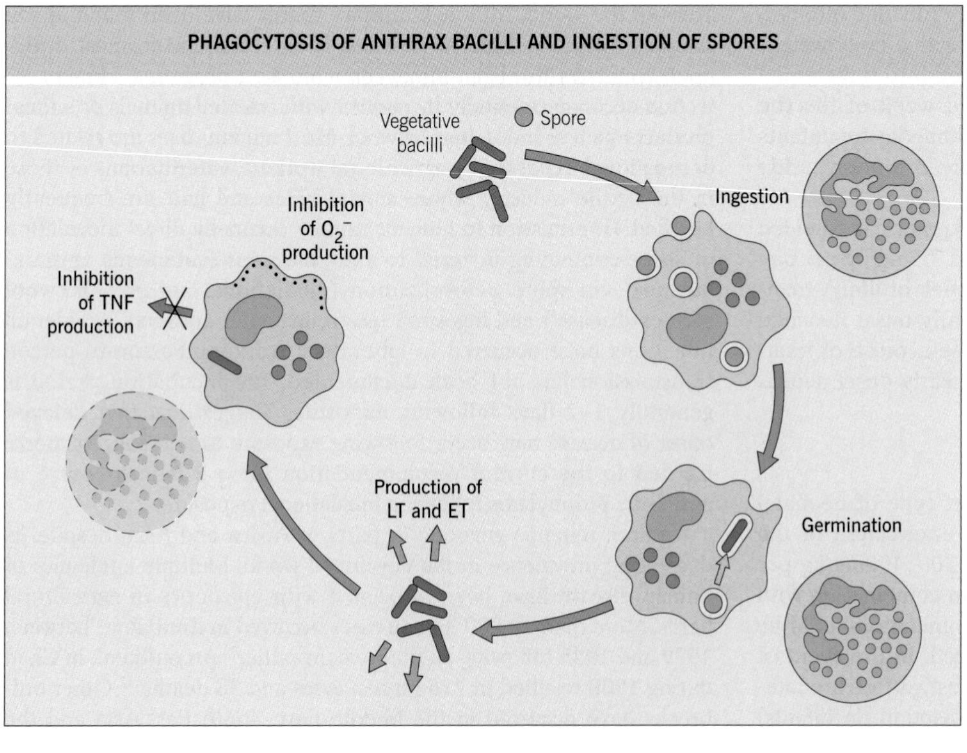

Fig. 226.7 Phagocytosis of anthrax bacilli and ingestion of spores. Vegetative bacilli are relatively resistant to phagocytosis by polymorphonuclear leukocytes and monocytes, whereas spores are readily ingested. Once ingested by polymorphonuclear leukocytes or macrophage cells, however, the spores germinate into vegetative forms, which are able to reduce the normal production of bactericidal oxidative radicals by the cell. *Bacillus anthracis* produces lethal toxin (LT) and edema toxin (ET), which are cidal to cells and inhibit TNF-α production and oxidative radical production by phagocytic cells.

be a source of re-introduction to domestic animals. Animal vaccines are available but require annual re-vaccination to maintain efficacy.

Control of anthrax in humans can be achieved by surveillance and control of industrial and agricultural sources of *B. anthracis* by public health authorities. International controls on the export of contaminated animal products has contributed to a decrease in industrial cases of anthrax. Both a live attenuated and a killed vaccine have been developed. The former vaccine has undergone large trials in the former Soviet Union, which demonstrated good protective efficacy. In North America, a cell-free vaccine, BioThrax®, is mandated for all US military personnel and is available for persons who have an occupational risk of acquiring anthrax. The vaccine contains purified protective antigen and can significantly reduce the occurrence of cutaneous anthrax in adults. Protection against aerosol challenge has not been evaluated.[38] Vaccine safety and efficacy have not been evaluated in a postexposure setting.

Postexposure prophylaxis against gastrointestinal and inhalation anthrax has been effective with several antibiotics. In one animal study, antibiotics such as penicillin, ciprofloxacin or doxycycline significantly improved survival when administered after aerosol exposure but before onset of symptoms.[39] Prophylactic antibiotics have also been effective after ingestion of contaminated food. The potential for genetically manipulated strains of military or terrorist origins to exhibit penicillin resistance has made ciprofloxacin or doxycycline the preferred prophylactic options in patients who have such inhalational exposures. The duration of prophylaxis for inhalational anthrax is 60 days.[40]

DIAGNOSTIC MICROBIOLOGY

Diagnostic specimens from patients suspected to have anthrax must be handled in biosafety cabinets to minimize the risk of transmission to laboratory workers. Laboratories should refer presumptive isolates to a reference laboratory capable of the appropriate biosafety containment level and notify public health authorities immediately.

Bacillus anthracis can be isolated from blood, sputum, CSF, vesicular fluid or eschar, gastric aspirates and stool (gastrointestinal anthrax). Blood cultures should be part of the evaluation for all forms of anthrax. Gram staining of clinical specimens may reveal Gram-positive 'boxcar-shaped' *B. anthracis* organisms. M'Fadyean's or India ink stains may be used to visualize the capsule. Direct fluorescent antibody (DFA) testing and polymerase chain reaction (PCR) have been used for rapid diagnosis in clinical specimens but are unavailable in most clinical laboratories.

Bacillus spp. can be cultured on standard media without special nutrient supplementation and typically produce flat, spreading colonies. The filamentous outgrowths from *B. anthracis* colonies are described as forming a 'Medusa-head' appearance. Colonies are gray–white and tenacious. Encapsulation is lost on standard media but may be demonstrated on nutrient agar with 0.8% sodium bicarbonate after overnight incubation in 5% CO_2. Isolation of *B. anthracis* from non-sterile sites may be achieved with selective media such as polymyxin B-lysozyme EDTA-thallous acetate (PLET) agar or spore selection techniques using heat or alcohol treatment of specimens to kill vegetative cells.

Bacillus anthracis is included with the *Bacillus cereus* group (*B. cereus*, *B. anthracis*, *Bacillus mycoides* and *Bacillus thuringiensis*), whose members are distinguished by production of egg yolk lecithinase. One potential algorithm for *B. anthracis* identification is outlined below.

Presumptive identification criteria

1. From clinical samples such as blood, CSF or skin lesion (vesicular fluid or eschar): large encapsulated Gram-positive rods lacking β-hemolysis on sheep blood agar;
2. From growth on sheep blood agar: large spore-forming Gram-positive rods;
3. Non-motile; and
4. Non-hemolytic on sheep blood agar.

Confirmatory criteria

1. Visualization of capsule; and
2. Lysis by gamma-phage; or
3. DFA assay.

While wild strains of *B. anthracis* are penicillin-susceptible, the potential for genetically altered strains to exhibit penicillin resistance makes this a less reliable trait. Commercial test strips are also available to assist in differentiating *B. anthracis* from other *Bacillus* spp.

Serology has a limited role in acute diagnosis but is useful for epidemiologic studies and as a confirmatory test when the organism has not been isolated. Both an enzyme-linked immunosorbent assay (ELISA) and an electrophoretic immunotransblot (EITB) method have been found to be reliable for detection of antibodies to the capsule and PA respectively. Demonstration of a 4-fold rise in titer between the acute and convalescent phases or a single titer greater than 1:32 is required for confirmation of infection.[38]

Since bacteriologic confirmation is achieved in less than half of anthrax cases, a skin test of cell-mediated immunity to anthrax was developed as a complementary diagnostic tool. An evaluation in the former Soviet Union found the test to have a sensitivity of 81.8% in the first 3 days of illness, 97–99% during the second and third weeks of illness and a sensitivity over 72% up to three decades following recovery – providing a useful method of retrospective diagnosis.[41]

CLINICAL MANIFESTATIONS

Three primary forms of human anthrax are recognized: cutaneous, gastrointestinal and inhalational. Cutaneous anthrax accounts for over 95% of naturally occurring anthrax cases; gastrointestinal anthrax ranks second. Inhalation anthrax is rare. Prior to the outbreak in the Soviet Union in 1979, only 30 inhalational cases had been described.[42]

Clinically, cutaneous anthrax usually begins as a small, pruritic, painless papule 1–10 days after direct contact with infected material. The papule generally develops into one or more vesicles surrounded by a ring of erythema and edema (Fig. 226.8). The vesicles may rupture, exposing an ulcer covered with a black eschar. The word 'anthrax' is derived from the Greek word for coal, in reference to the eschar's dark appearance. Regional lymphadenopathy is also evident and may be severe. Untreated cutaneous anthrax has a fatality rate of 10–20%. However, antibiotic treatment drastically reduces the mortality rate and sequelae.

Gastrointestinal anthrax is associated with ingestion of contaminated meat products that are raw or incompletely cooked. Early symptoms include nausea, vomiting and fever. Severe abdominal pain and bloody diarrhea develop within 2–3 days. Toxemia, shock

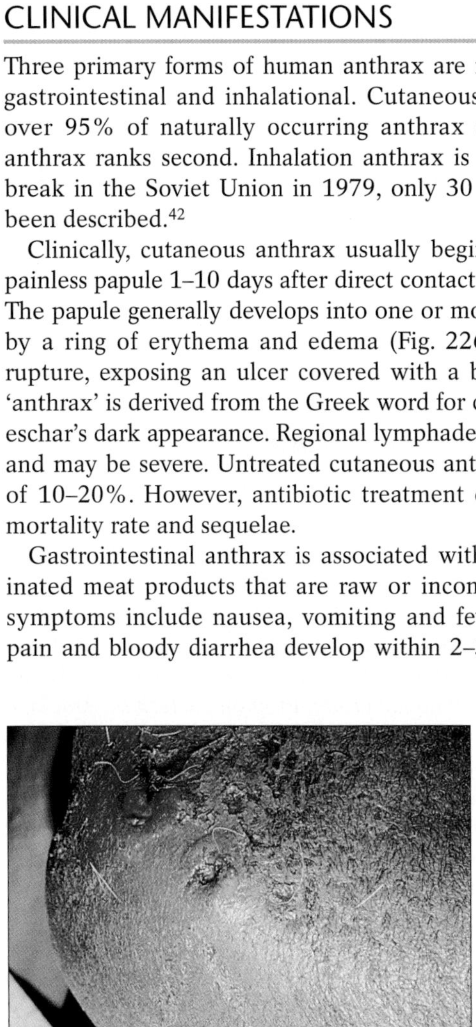

Fig. 226.8 Cutaneous anthrax, demonstrating marked erythema, edema and vesicle rupture.

and death can develop shortly after the start of severe symptoms. Lesions can be found anywhere from the oropharynx (pharyngeal anthrax) to the large bowel, with the cecum being frequently involved. Pathologically, a hemorrhagic enteritis is noted, with necrotic ulcerations of the mucosa.

Respiratory anthrax was well characterized during the 1979 outbreak at Sverdlovsk and in more recent cases in the USA.[42] Initial symptoms include sore throat, fever, myalgias and fatigue. Rapid progression to dyspnea, cough, headache, vomiting, chills, weakness, abdominal pain and chest pain is typical. Respiratory failure and shock develop in most patients. The presence of infiltrates is variable on chest radiograph but a widened mediastinum with pleural effusions is a key diagnostic finding and reflects the underlying pathology of hemorrhagic mediastinitis.

In the Sverdlovsk cases, onset of symptoms was typically 3–14 days following exposure. Hospitalized patients were treated with penicillin or other antibiotics, antianthrax globulin, steroid and artificial ventilation. The average hospital stay was 1–2 days for fatal cases and approximately 3 weeks for survivors. Historical data suggest that the mortality rate for untreated inhalational anthrax is approximately 97%. With modern antibiotic treatment and intensive care support, the fatality rate remains at least 75%.

Meningitis may develop following dissemination of cutaneous, gastrointestinal or respiratory anthrax but occurs in fewer than 5% of cases.

MANAGEMENT

Given the potential severity of disease, patients who have suspected anthrax should receive empiric therapy pending diagnostic tests. Historically, penicillin G has been the treatment of choice. Doses of two million units given intravenously every 2 hours have been used in adults. The addition of an aminoglycoside such as gentamicin may confer some improvement in response to treatment. All naturally occurring strains of *B. anthracis* have been sensitive to erythromycin, chloramphenicol, gentamicin and ciprofloxacin. As noted previously, in potential bioterrorism or biowarfare settings, penicillin susceptibility cannot be assured and doxycycline or ciprofloxacin should be used. One recent review has recommended treatment with intravenous ciprofloxacin (400mg q8–12h).[43] Supportive therapy for shock, fluid volume deficit and ventilatory assistance may also be needed (see also Chapter 185).[43]

CORYNEBACTERIUM DIPTHERIAE

NATURE

Corynebacterium diphtheriae is a member of a group of irregular non-spore-forming aerobic Gram-positive bacilli characterized by an ability to grow in the atmosphere of air, lack of endospores and an irregular shape on Gram-stained smears. This group includes human, plant and animal pathogenic species, the human pathogens including *Oerskovia*, *Rothia*, *Actinomyces*, *Arcanobacterium*, *Propionibacterium*, *Arachnia* and *Gardnerella* spp. in addition to *Corynebacterium* spp.

The genus *Corynebacterium* is characterized by pleomorphic Gram-positive bacilli that tend to stick together in parallel groupings and bend when dividing to create ‘Chinese letter’ arrangements (Fig. 226.9). They are all catalase- and cytochrome-oxidase-positive and can grow in facultative anaerobic conditions.[44]

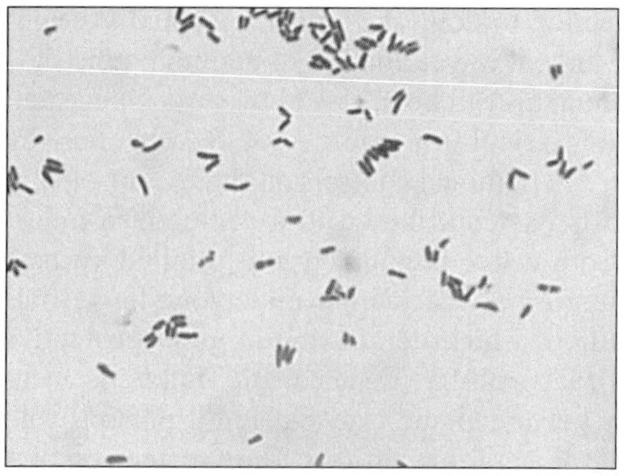

Fig. 226.9 Chinese letter and picket-fence appearance of *Corynebacterium* spp. on Gram-stained smears.

EPIDEMIOLOGY

Diphtheria, the disease caused by *C. diphtheriae*, was first described in manuscripts of the 6th century AD but was not recognized as a specific disease until Bretonneau defined it in 1826. In the 1880s the bacillus was discovered by Klebs and soon after Koch’s postulates were fulfilled. The first successful diphtheria immunization was performed in 1913 by von Behring, at a time when epidemics in Europe and the UK made diphtheria the leading cause of death in children 4–10 years of age. Mass immunization was introduced in the early 1940s, by which time the numbers of cases were already declining. The introduction of diphtheria toxoid immunization was associated with a substantial decrease in reported cases in both Europe and North America for 25 years. A study of an immunization program in Toronto, Canada from 1926–9 showed a 75% reduction in cases of diphtheria in immunized children compared with controls who were unimmunized.[45]

Outbreaks of diphtheria in recent years have been rare. In 1990 an epidemic that began in Moscow rapidly spread to the newly independent states of the former Soviet Union, first in the cities and later into rural areas. Poor immunization practices may have created a large population of susceptible hosts. Toxigenic strains that had not circulated in this part of Europe for about 25 years were finally able to colonize a pool of susceptible hosts large enough to start an epidemic.

Prior to childhood immunization programs, epidemics among European school-aged children occurred about every 25 years through the 17th, 18th and 19th centuries. Speculation that the resurgence of this infectious disease might be due to cyclic intrinsic factors of the micro-organism itself evolved from evidence that non-toxigenic oropharyngeal colonizing strains of *C. diphtheriae* can be made toxigenic by introduction of toxin genes by bacteriophages. Perhaps immunization with diphtheria toxoid does not prevent colonization with non-toxigenic strains of this organism, allowing natural cycling of more virulent strains into a population with waning immunity. The epidemic in the former USSR largely involved the adult population. Poor socio-economic conditions and mass population movements during the dissolution of the Soviet Union may have also contributed to the development of this epidemic. A total of 47,808 cases of diphtheria were reported in the former Soviet Union from 1990–5.[46] Spread of cases by travelers has occurred in western Europe. This is confirmed by the fact that isolates from Finland showed the same prevalent *C. diphtheriae* var. *gravis* strain belonging to the same G1 ribotype as in 91% of a series isolated in northern Russia during this epidemic.[47]

Transmission is generally through contact with infected respiratory droplets or skin wounds. Raw milk and milk products and clothing have been associated with diphtheria transmission. It is transmissible for 2–4 weeks in untreated individuals but with antibiotic treatment the risk of transmission is greatly reduced after the first 48 hours.

PATHOGENICITY

Corynebacterium diphtheriae is not an invasive organism but causes disease by colonizing the skin and upper respiratory epithelium, inducing a mild inflammatory reaction and releasing a potent exo-

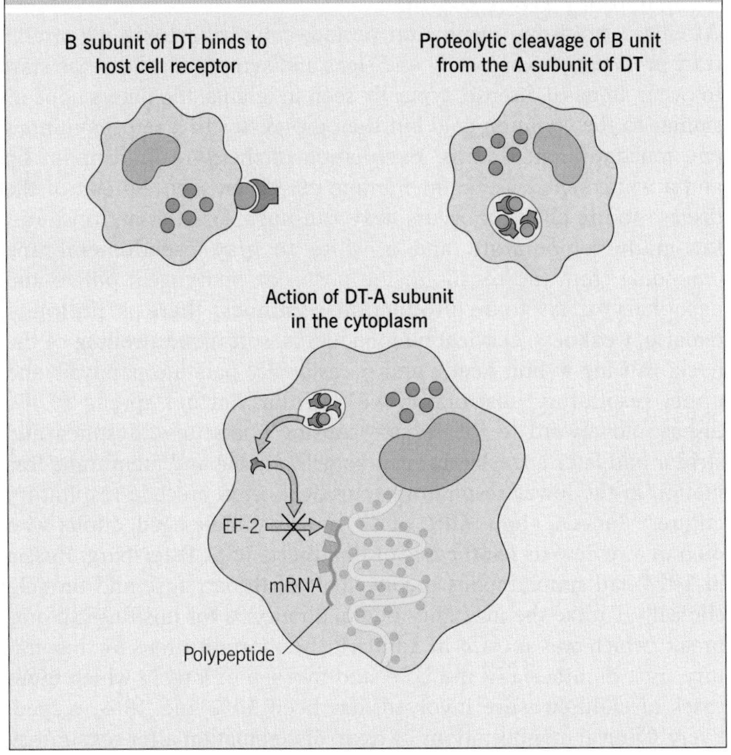
MOLECULAR ACTION OF CORYNEBACTERIUM DIPHTHERIAE
B subunit of DT binds to host cell receptor
Proteolytic cleavage of B unit from the A subunit of DT
Action of DT-A subunit in the cytoplasm
EF-2
mRNA
Polypeptide

Fig. 226.10 Molecular action of *Corynebacterium diphtheriae*. The B subunit of diphtheria toxin (DT) binds to host cell receptor. Proteolytic cleavage of the B subunit from the A subunit (the active DT) in cell endosome. The DT-A subunit escapes from the endosome into the cytoplasm, where it inhibits the transfer of triple code from mRNA to growing polypeptide at the ribosomes on the endoplasmic reticulum. It does this by modifying the enzyme elongation factor (EF)-2 that catalyzes this mRNA transfer.

toxin that, when taken up by animal cells, inhibits protein synthesis. Locally, the toxin causes tissue necrosis. If circulating toxin antibodies are not present, it will be absorbed into the circulation and transported to distant sites, causing extensive end-organ damage, especially to the kidneys, brain and heart.

On a molecular level, the diphtheria toxin (DT) is synthesized as a 62kDa polypeptide comprising a B subunit that binds to cell receptors and an A subunit that is the active moiety. The DT binds to the host animal cell receptor via its B subunit and is taken up by cellular endosomes at clathrin-coated pit sites (Fig. 226.10). Proteolytic cleavage of DT occurs releasing the A subunit (DT-A; see Fig. 226.10). The acidic condition of the cell's endosome causes conformational change in the B subunits, resulting in opening of cation channels in the endosome membrane and release of the active DT-A moieties into the cytoplasm. There, DT-A inhibits cellular protein synthesis by adenosine diphosphate (ADP)-ribosylation of diphthamide in elongation factor 2-GTP, thus inactivating it. This elongation factor 2 (EF-2) is important for catalyzing the transfer of triple code from messenger RNA to the developing amino-acid polypeptide sequence via transfer RNA at the ribosome. In this way, DT-A acts as a polypeptide chain terminator of host cell protein synthesis, causing an inability of the cell to repair its own membranes and cellular cytotoxicity (see Fig. 226.10). Toxin production by *C. diphtheriae* is induced by a lysogenic bacteriophage β that co-infects certain strains of this colonizing organism. It is also known that this toxin has DNA fragmentation capabilities and can cause cell cytotoxicity by a mechanism other than inhibition of protein synthesis.[48]

The localized tissue destruction initially forms a gray exudate of dead host cells and white blood cells, which may be removed. Later, with the addition of fibrin and red blood cells, a tough gray-brown pseudomembrane is produced that is difficult to remove and bleeds after such attempts. If the membrane is extensive, it may lead to respiratory tract obstruction. The underlying submucosa is often very edematous. Secondary invasion of bacteria, especially *S. aureus* and *Streptococcus pyogenes*, can occur. End-organ toxin-mediated damage can initiate a myocarditis with edema, mononuclear cell infiltration and fatty changes of heart myofibrils and its conducting system, neuritis and nerve demyelinization and acute tubular necrosis of the kidney.[49]

PREVENTION

The best form of prevention is an active immunization program of children and adults that covers over 90% of the population. Immunization coverage of less than this target leaves enough susceptible people to cause spread in an enclosed population. Infants should receive a primary series of diphtheria toxoid immunization with other childhood immunizations at 2, 4 and 6 months of age and booster shots at 18 months, 4 years and every 10 years thereafter through adulthood.

Because of an excess of local and systemic reactions, the adult vaccine dosage is usually decreased to 2 Lf units in those over 7 years of age. In an outbreak situation in older children and adults, if no immunization was previously administered, the primary series can be given in two doses 4 weeks apart and the third 6 months later.

Carriers or close contacts of a case of diphtheria should receive not only vaccination with diphtheria toxoid but erythromycin or penicillin prophylaxis for 7 days to prevent subsequent spread of the organism. Eradication of asymptomatic pharyngeal colonization is slow and difficult, with many people excreting organisms for more than 1 month despite antibiotic therapy.[50]

DIAGNOSTIC MICROBIOLOGY

Corynebacterium diphtheriae colonizes the respiratory tract of humans alone. Isolation of the organism requires specialized media containing potassium tellurite (Tinsdale agar) to inhibit other normal flora, including non-*diphtheriae Corynebacterium* spp. After 24–48 hours of incubation at 35°C, gray–black colonies are seen with a surrounding brown halo due to the precipitation of a tellurium sulfide secondary to cysteine breakdown utilizing the bacteria's cysteine desulfatase. Methylene-blue-stained smears will show the pleomorphic club-shaped nonsporulating rods. The organism's name is derived from the Greek word *korynee*, meaning 'club', and *diptheria,* meaning 'leather pouches', referring to the thick, leather-like pharyngeal membranes this organism produces. Other normal flora, *Neisseria* and *Staphylococcus* spp. can also occasionally appear black on this specialized media but have a different morphology on stained smear. In addition, specimens should be streaked onto a blood agar plate to detect *S. aureus* and β-hemolytic streptococci, which can co-infect tissues with this organism. If transportation to the laboratory is delayed for more than 24 hours, the specimens should be streaked onto a specialized Loeffler transport media agar slant, leaving the swab on top, for later delivery to the laboratory.[51]

Corynebacterium diphtheriae can be distinguished from other *Corynebacterium* spp. biochemically as it is catalase, cysteinase and nitrate reaction-positive; urease, esculin, pyrazinamidase and gelatin hydrolysis reaction-negative; and uses glucose and maltose but not mannitol or xylose sugars for growth requirements.[44] A modification of the normal concentrations of biochemical substrate concentrations and the use of an enriched basal media can allow for rapid 1 hour identification from a pure subculture of a 18- to 24-hour growth of the organism.[52] A commercial API-Coryne® strip of 20 biochemical substrates may identify this and other *Corynebacterium* spp.within a 24-hour period.

Subdivision of this organism into three biotypes – *gravis*, *mitis* and *intermedius* – can be done using colony size, blood agar hemolysis, morphology on stained smear and biochemical tests. It is also important to establish bacterial toxin production because biotype *mitis* is usually non-toxigenic. Treatment is generally reserved for people carrying toxigenic strains.[44] Recently, in Germany, toxin-producing *C. diphtheriae* var. *mitis* strains have been described that cause invasive disease.[53] Toxin can be demonstrated using the Elek plate, on which the organism and controls are streaked perpendicular to an antitoxin-impregnated filter paper strip embedded in the agar, causing immunoprecipitin lines to form if the organism is a toxin-producer (Fig. 226.11). The PCR technique may be more sensitive by directly detecting toxin genes.[54]

Antimicrobial susceptibility testing of isolates has shown that they are generally susceptible to penicillin, vancomycin and erythromycin but they are methicillin-resistant. Recent isolates from France and Vietnam show that multiresistant strains are becoming increasingly common. Erythromycin resistance was seen in 15% and tetracycline resistance in 20% of 88 strains from Vietnam between 1992 and 1996.[55] Isolates from France between 1987 and 1993 showed a 19% resistance to rifampin.[56]

Multilocus enzyme electrophoresis and ribotyping techniques can be used in molecular characterization of strains of these clinical bacterial isolates to determine whether an outbreak is occurring from a particular clone introduced into a population.[57] Other laboratory diagnostic tests have more limited value and include the Schick test and serology testing to the diphtheria toxin to detect previous exposure to the organism either in the form of a vaccine or infection. The Schick test is an intracutaneous inoculation of a small amount of purified diphtheria toxin. If the subject has circulating antitoxin antibodies, there will be an absence of the redness, tenderness and induration of greater than 10mm that occurs 5 days later. This test is not useful for acute diagnosis of diphtheria, and a negative result does not necessarily indicate that the antitoxin antibody levels present are protective against acquisition of this disease.[49] Indeed, serology testing for antitoxin antibody levels is problematic because protective levels have not been well defined. It is believed that antibody levels of 0.01–0.09IU/ml or more provide some protection.[58]

DETECTION OF DIPHTHERIA TOXIN PRODUCTION

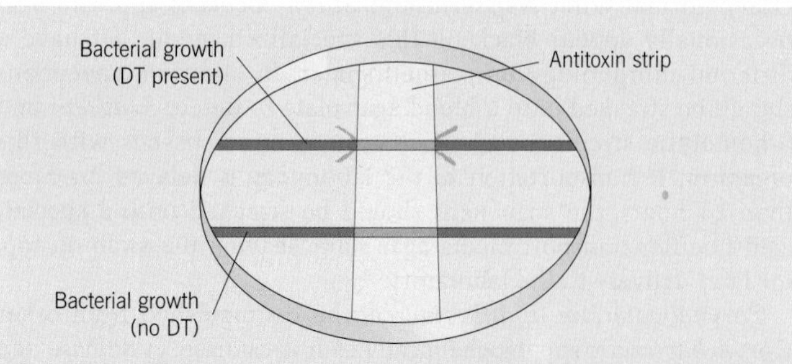

Fig. 226.11 Detection of diphtheria toxin production. The Elek test detects DT production in a bacterial clinical isolate. A paper strip soaked in diphtheria antitoxin is placed perpendicular to a horizontal streak of bacterial growth. If it produces toxin, an arrow-shaped precipitin line develops in the agarose plate.

CLINICAL MANIFESTATIONS (see also Chapter 178)

Respiratory tract disease

After a 2- to 4-day incubation period, colonizing toxigenic strains start producing toxin locally and signs and symptoms of disease start to occur. In nasal disease, typically seen in infants, the illness appears similar to the common cold but then progresses to a serosanguinous and mucopurulent rhinitis. Excoriation of the nares and upper lip and a white septal pseudomembrane may been seen. Spread of the disease to the pharynx occurs next, causing a sore throat, tonsillitis, low-grade temperature and a white to gray pseudomembrane extending from the tonsils to the posterior pharyngeal pillars and nasopharynx. As toxin production continues, there is profound malaise, weakness, cervical lymphadenitis, soft tissue swelling of the neck, causing a 'bull neck', and occasionally palatine paralysis and upper respiratory obstruction with stridor. Further spread of the disease downward to the larynx, causing hoarseness, dyspnea and stridor and later a tracheobronchitis with edema and membrane formation in the lower respiratory tract, will often precede respiratory failure.[49] Indeed, about 60% of 42, mostly middle-aged, adults who died in a review of 1860 cases of diphtheria in St Petersburg, Russia in 1994 had simultaneous involvement of throat, nose and bronchi clinically. Unlike the mortality rate of about 2% for this Russian outbreak, which was mostly in adults,[59] the mortality rate for respiratory tract diphtheria in the USA and Sweden of late, in which more cases of children were involved, has been 10% and 18%, respectively. Clinical manifestations of toxin dissemination after respiratory tract diphtheria occurs as the localized disease is waning. Cardiac toxicity is the next most prevalent cause of death after respiratory failure and neurotoxicity is generally a much later phenomenon that adds to the morbidity from this disease.

Cutaneous disease

Diphtheria involving the skin usually is more common in tropical climates and is associated with infection of pre-existing skin lesions, lower mortality, an indolent and mild course, and superinfection with *Staphylococcus aureus* and *Streptococcus pyogenes*. This disease is characterized by chronic, nonhealing, sharply bordered ulcers that have an adherent gray pseudomembrane over the top of them. Despite their mild clinical course, they produce good protective antitoxin antibodies, do not respond to antitoxin therapy and act as reservoirs for respiratory tract illness, can contaminate objects in the environment and are shed for longer periods of time than pharyngeal colonization. Cutaneous diphtheria is seen in outbreaks among the poor, homeless and alcoholics with close-confined living arrangements. This form of disease may be an important means of person-to-person transmission of diphtheria and is thought to be the means of starting outbreaks of respiratory tract diphtheria.

Myocardial toxicity

When the local disease is improving, 1–2 weeks from onset, up to two-thirds of patients have electrocardiographic evidence of myocardial toxicity, with ST wave alterations and first-degree heart block, but most of them are asymptomatic. Heart failure and arrhythmias occur in up to one-quarter of patients who have severe disease, increasing mortality by three to four times compared with those who do not have these manifestations. Such patients present with dyspnea, weakness, diminished heart sounds, a gallop rhythm, a dilated heart, low cardiac output and conductive disturbance arrhythmias.

A rather uncommon but often fatal cardiac complication of diphtheria is endocarditis. Most reported cases were in patients who had *C. diphtheriae* bacteremia. A total of 33 cases were reported between 1893 and 1993, and at least 20 of those reported since 1950 are associated with non-toxigenic strains. Non-toxigenic strains have been thought not to be associated frequently with invasive disease but this increased incidence may be due to an increasing prevalence of patients in whom intravenous drug usage is a pre-existing risk factor. Almost half of these cases were children aged 16 years and younger, and a high incidence of septic arthritis and mycotic aneurysms of the lower extremities occurred. Although most patients had a known predisposing factor for endocarditis, such as intravenous drug abuse, valvular heart disease or congenital heart disease, one-third occurred in patients who had no known predisposition. The mitral valve is the most commonly affected heart valve. The mortality rate was about 40%. Very few of these patients received surgical therapy in conjunction with antibiotic therapy and it is unclear whether early surgical intervention would have improved the prognosis of this disease.[60]

Neuronal toxicity

Up to two-thirds of severely involved cases of diphtheria show evidence of neuronal toxicity, presenting early as palatine and pharyngeal paralysis and then cranial palsies involving muscles of the eye, face, pharynx and larynx, causing dysphagia and predisposing these patients to aspiration. The ocular manifestations of diphtheria include blurred vision and failure of accommodation. Later, several weeks after the sore throat, a peripheral motor demyelinating neuritis occurs, starting in the proximal extremities and progressing distally. Generally, there is slow and total resolution of the limb weakness.

MANAGEMENT

The management of a clinical case of diphtheria is described in Figure 226.12 (see also Chapter 178).

Hyperimmune diphtheria antitoxin

This product is made from immunized horses and, because up to 10% of the population shows hypersensitivity to horse serum, this preparation must be diluted 1:1000 with saline and a test dose of 0.1ml administered intracutaneously. An area of redness at the administration site greater than 10mm requires epinephrine (adrenaline) to be given, followed by a desensitization regimen.[49] If no hypersensitivity to horse serum is found, 20,000–40,000 units for pharyngeal or laryngeal disease of less than 48 hours duration, 40,000–60,000 units for nasopharyngeal pseudomembrane formation and 80,000–100,000 units for extensive disease of 3 or more days duration or with neck swelling should be administrated intravenously (or some suggest a spit between intramuscular and intravenous administration) over 60 minutes, as recommended by the American Academy of Pediatrics Red Book Committee. Repeat administrations are of no benefit and may increase the risk of anaphylaxis to horse serum protein.[50]

Antibiotic therapy

Antibiotics do not seem to alter the course of clinical disease but are administered in an effort to terminate toxin production and extension of local disease and prevent spread of the organism to other people. Erythromycin 40mg/kg per day (maximum 2g/day) intravenously or orally in four divided doses has been shown in some studies to be more efficacious than penicillin G (procaine penicillin G 25–50,000U/kg per day intramuscularly in two divided doses for 14 days). Elimination of the organism should be documented by three negative daily cultures after antibiotic therapy before strict isolation is discontinued. Communication of the organism to others can occur up to 4 days after commencement of antibiotic therapy.[50]

Supportive therapy

Strict bed rest is usually advocated during the maximum period of myocardial toxicity, the first 2–3 weeks from onset of illness. Serial

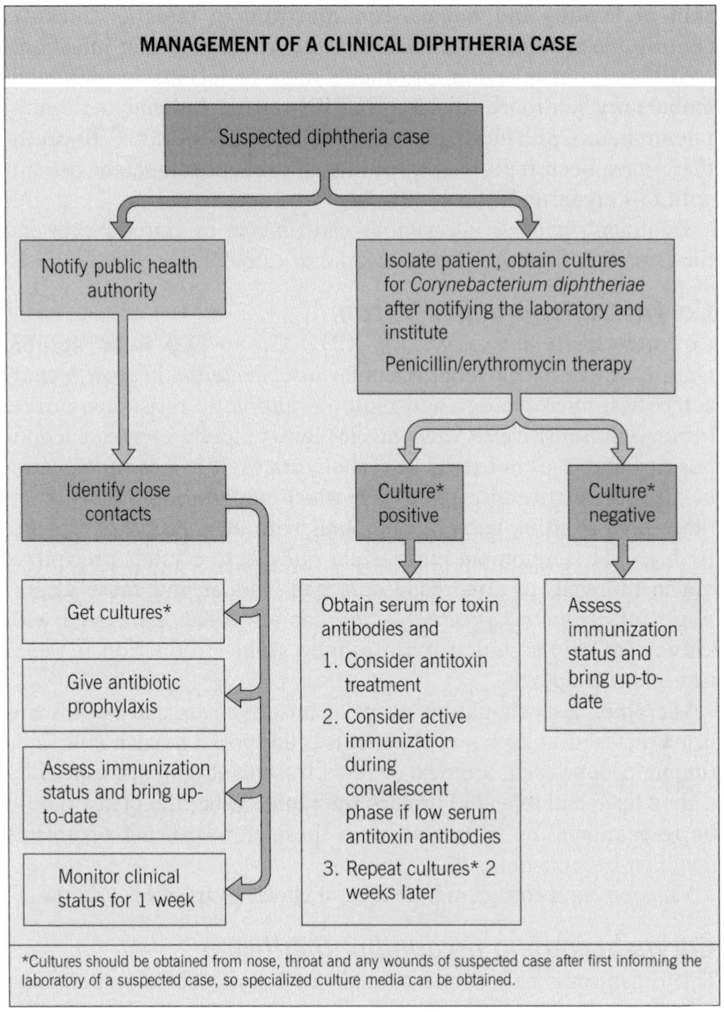

Fig. 226.12 Management of a clinical diphtheria case. Adapted from Farizo.[61]

electrocardiograms may be useful for earlier detection of this complication. Tracheostomy equipment should be placed by the bedside to be prepared for acute upper airway obstruction. Nasogastric tube feeding may be required to prevent aspiration in the patient who has palatine or pharyngeal paralysis. Long-term immunity is unusual in cases of diphtheria and adequate immunization is required to prevent recurrence of this disease. This is given in the convalescent phase.[50]

OTHER *CORYNEBACTERIUM* SPECIES

Corynebacterium jeikeium

This species is the most commonly isolated *Corynebacterium* sp. from human blood and sterile body fluids. It is a pleomorphic, nonsporulating, aerobic Gram-positive bacillus that forms nonhemolytic, small, whitish colonies on blood agar after 24 hours of incubation. It requires lipid to grow and is unable to reduce nitrate or hydrolyze urea. In addition, it is resistant to most antibiotics, with the exception of being sensitive to vancomycin.[62]

This organism has emerged as a cause of serious nosocomial infections in immunocompromised patients. Predisposing factors for this infection include neutropenia, prior multiple antibiotic usage, prolonged hospitalization and disruption of the skin by surgery or an indwelling catheter. *Corynebacterium jeikeium* heavily colonizes the skin (axillary, inguinal and rectal) of about one-third to one-half of oncology patients for weeks to months but only lightly colonizes the skin of healthy individuals. The spectrum of infection includes central-line-related septicemias, wound and soft tissue infections, prosthetic joint infection, prosthetic valve endocarditis, continuous ambulatory peritoneal dialysis (CAPD)-related catheter peritonitis, pneumonia, CSF shunt infections and liver abscesses.[63] Recently, there have been reports of infections in immunocompetent patients with this organism.[64]

Treatment involves intravenous vancomycin or ciprofloxacin and the removal of the prosthetic material or catheter.

Corynebacterium urealyticum

Corynebacterium urealyticum (CDC Group D2) is an aerobic Gram-positive bacillus that is similar to *C. jeikeium* in growth characteristics, microbiology and multiple antibiotic resistance profile (often only sensitive to vancomycin) but is rapidly urease-reaction-positive and does not ferment carbohydrates. It is a common cause of alkaline-encrusted cystitis,[65] in which ammonia produced from these urea-splitting bacteria combines with magnesium phosphate. At high pH, ammonium magnesium phosphate crystals precipitate out in the walls of an already damaged bladder and cause ulceration. *Corynebacterium urealyticum* has also been associated with kidney infections and struvite kidney stone production in renal transplant recipients.

Microbiologists should be aware of this organism and not discard urine plates after 24 hours in patients predisposed to such infections (immunosuppressed, urologic or renal transplant patients, especially if they have had repeated urinary tract infections); the plates should be re-examined at 48 hours, when these slow-growing organisms may first become noticed.

Vancomycin is considered the drug of choice to treat this infection.[63]

Corynebacterium pseudodiphtheriticum

This organism is part of the normal oropharyngeal flora, looks like *C. diphtheriae* but does not produce a toxin and, unlike *C. diphtheriae*, possesses both urease and pyrazinamidase enzymes and does not ferment carbohydrates. It has been found to cause endocarditis, necrotizing bronchitis and pneumonia in patients who have chronic disease. Rare case reports of urinary tract infection following renal transplantation, suppurative arthritis and osteomyelitis have been reported.[63]

Corynebacterium minutissimum

Corynebacterium minutissimum has been associated with erythrasma a red-brown pruritic macular skin rash usually found in the intertriginous regions of toes, fingers and axillae. Both the superficial skin lesions and the organism's minute colony growth are noted for their coral-red–orange fluorescence under ultraviolet light produced by a Wood's lamp.[51]

Corynebacterium ulcerans

This organism is morphologically similar to *C. diphtheriae* and is found in the pharynx of persons who drink unpasteurized cows milk or who have had contact with milking cows. In cattle and horses it is part of the normal flora and causes mastitis. This organism can be cultured from the throats of asymptomatic people and occasionally from patients who have an exudative pharyngitis[63] and diphtheria-like illness, in whom the bacterium has been found to produce diphtheria and dermatonecrotic toxins.[66] Both colony morphology and Gram stain of isolates growing on Tinsdale selective medium are indistinguishable from *C. diphtheriae* but the colonies, unlike *C. diphtheriae*, show a narrow zone of hemolysis on blood agar and have a positive urease reaction. The antibiotic susceptibility profile of this organism is similar to that of *C. diphtheriae* in that it is sensitive to most β-lactam antibiotics and erythromycin.[63]

ERYSIPELOTHRIX RHUSIOPATHIAE

NATURE

Erysipelothrix spp. are short, slender, non-spore-forming Gram-positive rods. While two species of the genus are recognized, *Erysipelothrix rhusiopathiae* and *Erysipelothrix tonsillarum*, only *E. rhusiopathiae* has been described as a pathogen in humans. The organism inhabits soil and water worldwide and has been found in mammals, birds, fish and shellfish, presumably following ingestion of contaminated matter. In 1886, *E. rhusiopathiae* was established as the cause of 'swine erysipelas', and the organism continues to have economic importance as a cause of septicemia in swine, calves, lambs, turkeys and other farm animals.[67] Animals may exhibit asymptomatic carriage or disease. Domestic pigs appear to be the major reservoir.

EPIDEMIOLOGY

Infection with *E. rhusiopathiae* occurs worldwide and is considered to be a zoonosis. Transmission to humans usually occurs by direct cutaneous contact with infected fish or animals and manifests as erysipeloid, a localized cellulitis that appears 2–7 days after exposure. Most human infections follow occupational exposure. While persons who handle fish or shellfish appear to be at highest risk, erysipeloid is also more common in abattoir workers, butchers, farmers and veterinarians. The frequent occurrence of erysipeloid in whalers earned it the title 'whale finger'. Systemic *E. rhusiopathiae* infection has been reported following ingestion of undercooked pork. Human-to-human transmission has not been reported.

PATHOGENICITY

Infection of laboratory animals with *E. rhusiopathiae* leads to production of specific antibodies that are protective against re-infection. The virulence of *E. rhusiopathiae* appears to be related to resistance to phagocytosis and to multiplication and survival within cells after uptake. One group described the presence of a capsule on virulent strains when the organism was viewed by electron microscopy.[68] The presence of a capsule appeared to be associated with virulence. Mutant strains lacking the capsule were less virulent than parent strains.[68] Strains with a capsule were relatively resistant to phagocytosis by polymorphonuclear leukocytes unless the organism had been opsonized with organism-specific antiserum.

Virulent *E. rhusiopathiae* can also survive, and subsequently replicate, within macrophages when ingested in the presence of nonimmune serum. Survival within the macrophage appears to be associated with the organism's ability to reduce the production of reactive oxidative products.[69]

DIAGNOSTIC MICROBIOLOGY

In patients who have erysipeloid, organisms are found only in deeper parts of the skin, requiring aspiration or biopsy specimens that include the entire dermal thickness for optimal results. Blood cultures may isolate the organism in patients who have systemic disease. *Erysipelothrix rhusiopathiae* is a short, slender, non-spore-forming Gram-positive rod that grows best on routine blood agar plates in an atmosphere of 5–10% CO_2 at 92°F (35°C). Microscopically, they appear straight or slightly curved and occasionally form long filaments over 60μm long.[70] Unlike *Listeria*, *Bacillus* and *Corynebacterium*, *Erysipelothrix* spp. are catalase-negative. Colonies are small and translucent with α or no hemolysis. Two major discriminatory tests are the production of H_2S on TSI slants (highly suggestive of *E. rhusiopathiae*) and a 'pipe cleaner' pattern of growth in gelatin stab cultures inoculated at 71.6°F

(22°C). The organism is typically vancomycin-resistant – an uncommon trait among Gram-positive rods. The ability of *E. tonsillarum* to ferment saccharose distinguishes it from *E. rhusiopathiae*.[70]

CLINICAL MANIFESTATIONS

Human infections with *E. rhusiopathiae* have three patterns of presentation: erysipeloid (a localized skin lesion), multiple skin lesions with or without systemic symptoms, or bacteremia/endocarditis.

Erysipeloid constitutes the majority of *E. rhusiopathiae* infections and presents as a subacute cellulitis. Most lesions occur on hands or other areas of the body exposed directly to infected fish or animals. The diagnosis is suggested by a nonsuppurative, insidious cellulitis with severe disproportionate pain – usually in a person who has an occupational exposure. The incubation period is typically 2–7 days. Lesions are usually well demarcated, slightly raised, erythematous and accompanied by swelling of the surrounding tissue. Regional painful lymphadenopathy or lymphangitis may occur. Low-grade fever and arthralgias are present in a minority of cases. Erysipeloid usually resolves within 3–4 weeks of onset without treatment and earlier with appropriate antibiotic treatment.

Untreated, erysipeloid occasionally spreads proximally from the initial lesion to producing multiple noncontiguous lesions. Lesions developing at sites remote from the initial inoculum have also been described, presumably via hematogenous dissemination.

Bacteremia due to *E. rhusiopathiae* is unusual; however, the organism has been identified as a cause of persistent bacteremia and endocarditis in adults.[71] The vast majority of serious infections due to *E. rhusiopathiae* have occurred in men who had a history of occupational exposure such as farming or animal handling.[72] Patients with a history of alcohol abuse or immunosuppression have occasionally been seen with only mild fever in the presence of bacteremia due to *Erysipelothrix*. The possibility of a carrier state of infection in such patients has been proposed.[71] Bacterial endocarditis, particularly involving the aortic valve, has been described. In one review, 40% of patients who have endocarditis had an antecedent erysipeloid cutaneous lesion. Overall mortality due to *E. rhusiopathiae* endocarditis is approximately 40%. The one case of neonatal septicemia that has been described was attributed to cutaneous contamination shortly after birth.[73]

MANAGEMENT AND PREVENTION

Erysipelothrix rhusiopathiae is susceptible to penicillin but resistant to vancomycin.[74] Vancomycin resistance is notable since this drug is commonly used as empiric treatment for bacteremia due to Gram-positive organisms. Therefore, a high index of suspicion for this organism should be maintained for patients who have unusual cutaneous sites of infection or animal exposure. Penicillin is the drug of choice for serious infection caused by *E. rhusiopathiae*; however, the organism is also highly susceptible in vitro to cephalosporins, clindamycin, imipenem and ciprofloxacin.[75]

Prevention is achieved mainly through the use of protective gloves in high-risk occupations.

ARCANOBACTERIUM HAEMOLYTICUM

NATURE AND DIAGNOSTIC MICROBIOLOGY

Arcanobacterium haemolyticum is often overlooked in clinical specimens, as organisms appear similar in morphology to *Corynebacterium* spp. that are resident normal flora of the skin and oropharynx. In fact, the organism was originally named *Corynebacterium haemolyticum*. The name of the genus is derived from the Greek word *arcanus*, meaning 'secretive' or 'mysterious'. Colonies are small, gray–white and take 24–48 hours to appear on sheep blood agar, displaying a narrow zone of β hemolysis that may not appreciated until a colony is picked off of the plate. A colony Gram stain shows pleomorphic short V- and club-shaped Gram-positive bacilli that, with older growth, appear beaded and streptococcus-like in appearance. The β-hemolysis and lack of catalase activity distinguish them from *Corynebacterium* spp. In addition, they ferment glucose, lactose, maltose and sucrose but do not reduce nitrate or hydrolyze urea, esculin or gelatin. They are nonmotile and produce a reverse CAMP test with inhibition of the β-hemolysin activity of *S. aureus*.[76,77]

EPIDEMIOLOGY

Humans appear to be the primary host for this organism, which causes pharyngitis in teenagers and young adults,[78] as well as cellulitis[79] and chronic skin ulcers, mostly in tropical countries.[80] Although it can be associated with symptomatic pharyngitis, this is uncommon. Pharyngitis associated with this organism is predominantly found in females aged 15–22 years. Rarely, this organism has been found as a cause of septicemia, meningitis, endocarditis, osteomyelitis, sinusitis and cavitary pneumonia in adults who have underlying chronic diseases.[81] One study showed an increase in isolation of this bacterium from throat swabs in spring and autumn.[82] Person-to-person spread by fomites is thought to be the predominant mechanism of transmission, although this has not been adequately studied.

PATHOGENICITY

Evidence that *A. haemolyticum* is a cause of pharyngitis in adolescents and young adults is derived from studies showing its presence in the throats of symptomatic but not asymptomatic subjects. However, some investigators dispute this conclusion. *Arcanobacterium haemolyticum* has been isolated singularly and in association with *S. aureus* and β-hemolytic streptococci; however, insufficient data exist to rule out concomitant infection with viruses or *Mycoplasma* spp. In a study of seven volunteers who had a pure culture of this organism applied to their pharynx, none became symptomatic in 6 weeks of follow-up despite having heavy pharyngeal colonization.[77] Indeed, several studies have shown an association of *A. haemolyticum* pharyngitis with Epstein–Barr virus infection. Preceding viral colonization may be required in the pharynx before symptomatic infection can occur.[83]

This organism produces phospholipase A and D, lipase, hemolysin and a dermotoxin when injected into the skin of a guinea pig.[77] Occasionally a serologic response has been found in patients who have either skin or pharyngeal infection. The organism can persist intracellularly.[84] Skin biopsies of two patients who had concomitant scarlatiniform-like rash, often seen with the pharyngeal infection, showed no organism or immunoglobulin deposits but a mild lymphocytic perivascular infiltration.[85] This indicates that the rash may be due to a toxin-mediated event similar to the scarlet fever rash of group A streptococci.

CLINICAL MANIFESTATIONS

The signs and symptoms of pharyngitis due to *A. haemolyticum* are listed in Table 226.4[82,83,86] and are similar to those of group A streptococcal pharyngitis with the exception of the rash and presence of more upper respiratory symptoms of dry cough and hoarseness. The rash appears 1–4 days after the onset of pharyngitis and is usually scarlatiniform, appearing first on extensor surfaces of the extremities and then spreading to trunk and chest, sparing palms and soles. It often persists for more than 2 days.[86] Unlike streptococcal scarlet

SIGNS AND SYMPTOMS OF PHARYNGEAL *A. HAEMOLYTICUM* INFECTION	
Sign or symptom	**Frequency (%)**
Sore throat	97–100
Tonsillar exudate	50–70
Fever	60–80
Dry cough/hoarseness	40–60
Cervical lymphadenopathy	40–67
Rash	50

Table 226.4 Signs and symptoms of pharyngeal *Arcanobacterium haemolyticum* infection.

fever, circumoral pallor does not occur. Less frequently, the rash is maculopapular or urticarial. Skin infections with *A. haemolyticum* were first described in US military personnel stationed in South Pacific islands and have been described as ecthyma, resembling chronic ulcers. Cellulitis and wound infections in these tropical environments often have mixed bacterial infections with this organism.

MANAGEMENT

Arcanobacterium haemolyticum isolates are highly susceptible to erythromycin with MICs of less than 0.01μg/ml. As a result, erythromycin is considered the drug of choice for pharyngitis. As a bacteriostatic compound it is generally inappropriate for therapy of bacteremia. Penicillin is bactericidal but the MICs are more variable and tolerance and antibiotic failure have been documented.[81] Clinical evidence of antibiotic efficacy is anecdotal and largely involves the use of intravenous penicillin to treat *A. haemolyticum* septicemia.

RHODOCOCCUS SPECIES

NATURE

Rhodococcus are aerobic Gram positive bacilli similar to *Nocardia* in that they produce a substrate mycelium in soil environments that fragments into bacillary and coccoid forms. Also like *Nocardia*, *Rhodococcus* is partially acid-fast using the modified Kinyoun stain, because of its mycolic-acid-containing cell wall. Unlike *Nocardia*, it does not produce aerial mycelia and its cell wall composition is different. There are 15 species in this genus and *Rhodococcus equi*, formerly *Corynebacterium equi*, is the predominant pathogen in humans.[87,88]

EPIDEMIOLOGY

Rhodococcus equi causes bronchopneumonia in foals, cattle, pigs and felines.[89,90] It is found in soil and herbivore manures[90] and is not part of the normal bacterial flora in healthy humans. Transmission occurs via the respiratory tract and appears to be through contact with soil and animals. Human disease usually occurs in patients who have disturbances of cell-mediated immunity such as AIDS, cancer, transplantation or chronic disease.[91] Human-to-human transmission has not been documented. Many investigators suggest that infection with this organism should warrant testing for concomitant HIV infection.

PATHOGENICITY

Both animals and humans acquire this infection via respiratory tract. There, organisms are taken up by alveolar macrophages, in which they grow intracellularly and cause a granulomatous inflammatory response. This progresses to caseous necrosis of lung tissue. Later there may be hematogenous dissemination from a focal lung infection to brain, liver, kidney, skin, muscle or bone.[92]

DIAGNOSTIC MICROBIOLOGY

Rhodococcus equi produces large, mucoid, salmon-pink colonies on blood agar. Initial Gram staining may reveal Gram-positive coccobacilli. As colonies age, longer Gram-positive bacilli are formed that demonstrate branching and fragmentation into both coccoid and bacillary forms. *Rhodococcus equi* are partially acid-fast, nonmotile and have positive catalase and urease reactions.[87,88]

CLINICAL MANIFESTATIONS

The overwhelming majority of *R. equi* infections involve the lung. As noted, most patients have an underlying condition such as AIDS or post-transplant immunosuppression that impairs their cell-mediated immunity. Clinical presentation may be insidious, with onset of fatigue, fever and nonproductive cough over several weeks. Chest radiographs often show nodular or cavitary lesions in the upper lung lobes that may mimic lesions due to *Mycobacterium tuberculosis* or *Nocardia* spp.[93] The underlying pathology is a necrotizing pneumonia and *R. equi* lesions have a propensity to show air–fluid levels, which are rarely seen in tuberculosis. Bacteremic pneumonia occurs more frequently in patients who have AIDS and their mortality rate is higher than that of patients who are not infected with HIV.

Fewer than 10% of patients present with extrapulmonary disease, usually abscesses in skin or soft tissues, osteomyelitis, meningitis or endophthalmitis. Recently, several cases of *Rhodococcus* infections have been found associated with medical devices such as central lines, ventriculoperitoneal shunts and chronic ambulatory peritoneal dialysis catheters.[92–94]

MANAGEMENT

As large numbers of organisms exist both intracellularly in macrophages and in abscesses in patients who have impaired cell mediated immunity, treatment of such infections may be problematic. *Rhodococcus* spp. are commonly resistant to penicillins and cephalosporins or will rapidly develop resistance during therapy. They usually are sensitive to erythromycin, clindamycin, rifampin, vancomycin, imipenem, aminoglycosides, chloramphenicol and fluoroquinolones,[84] but antibiotic therapy alone may not be successful without surgical excision and drainage. Reduction in immunosuppression where possible (i.e. reduction of corticosteroid or ciclosporin dosage).

Antibiotics with enhanced intracellular penetration and concentration abilities such as the macrolide antibiotics and rifampin appear to be the most potent and act synergistically to kill these intracellular bacteria.[95] Duration of therapy is not established but most patients require long courses of at least two antibiotics, even after surgical excision and drainage.

NOCARDIA SPECIES

NATURE

The genus *Nocardia* is a member of the order Actinomycetales, found in soil, plants and decomposing organic material. These organisms are also present in the gastrointestinal tract, oropharynx and skin of animals.

The taxonomy of Actinomycetales has been controversial. In recent editions of *Bergey's Manual of Determinative Bacteriology*, several new species have been recognized, and others reclassified.[96]

Nocardia was first described by Nocard in 1889 and is now divided into several species, only a few of which cause disease in humans – *Nocardia asteroides*, *Nocardia brasiliensis*, *Nocardia otitidiscaviarum*, *Nocardia transvalensis*, *Nocardia farcinica* and *Nocardia nova*. *Nocardia asteroides* accounts for the vast majority of clinical nocardial infection in humans.[97] Ribotyping has been proposed as a tool for taxonomic classification of this organism.[98]

EPIDEMIOLOGY

The incidence of systemic *Nocardia* infection in humans is probably underestimated since there is no comprehensive reporting system. However, based on a survey of US infectious disease physicians, the incidence in the mid-1970s was estimated at between 500 and 1,000 cases annually (2–4/10^6 people).[97] Since immunocompromised patients are profoundly susceptible to the development of nocardiasis, it is likely that the incidence of the disease in the 2000s is far greater than this estimate would suggest. Over the past 20 years there has been a marked increase in the number of immunocompromised patients due to aggressive chemotherapeutic management of cancer and to the epidemic of AIDS.[99]

Although immunosuppression is a major predisposing factor for infection, *Nocardia* spp. may occasionally cause disease in the absence of any predisposing factor. Cases may go undiagnosed because appropriate investigations are not undertaken before antimicrobial therapy is prescribed.

PATHOGENICITY

Nocardia elicits an inflammatory response in the host characterized by infiltration of polymorphonuclear leukocytes, activated lymphocytes and monocytes at the site of infection.

Although the pathogenic mechanisms contributing to elimination of *Nocardia* spp. from the body are poorly understood, a model of nocardiasis in mice shows many similarities to intracellular parasites such as *Listeria monocytogenes* and *Toxoplasma gondii*.[100] In the murine model of *Nocardia* infection, the organism persists for 3–4 weeks in high concentrations in the spleen and liver of intravenously or intraperitoneally infected animals. A large number of macrophages are seen in infected granulomas. Electron microscopic studies demonstrate that these macrophages contain organisms within the cytoplasm in various stages of degeneration. When compared with control cells, macrophages isolated from *Nocardia*-infected animals produce high amounts of TNF-α after ex-vivo stimulation with lipopolysaccharide. Since TNF-α and other cytokines upregulate the phagocytic system, this finding suggests that macrophage activation occurs during *Nocardia* infection. In support of this is the observation that animals treated with TNF-α antibodies fail to eliminate the organism from their liver when this would normally occur. Eradication of the organism from the body therefore appears to depend on TNF-α or its effects on the immune system.

DIAGNOSTIC MICROBIOLOGY

Diagnosis of invasive nocardial infection usually depends on demonstrating the organism in tissue. Specimens of sputum, bronchial wash, exudate, tissue biopsy or CSF should be collected for culture and staining in suspected cases. Gram's stain and a modified Kinyoun stain are recommended. Because the clinical picture is often unclear, clinical material should be examined for other potential pathogens including acid-fast bacilli and fungi.

Although *Nocardia* resemble fungi morphologically, producing a mycelial-like hyphae growth, they exhibit cellular characteristics of bacteria including the presence of procaryotic cellular organization. *Nocardia* spp. grow slowly on laboratory-enriched media. Specimens should be maintained for at least 2–4 weeks before being called negative. *Nocardia* grows well on enriched media such as blood or brain heart infusion agar. However, the microscopic morphology of *Nocardia* is best demonstrated by examining colonies grown on minimal medium such as tap water agar or cornmeal agar without dextrose. A period of 2–3 weeks of cultivation is needed before growth is evident on such media (Fig. 226.13). Colonies may have a smooth, chalky-white appearance; however, gross morphology is variable and may depend on the medium of cultivation and length of inoculation time. The color of *N. asteroides* colonies varies from salmon-pink to orange, while other *Nocardia* spp. vary from orange to tan colored.

The organisms are Gram-positive with short, extensively branched vegetative hyphae that break up into short rods and are less than 1μm in diameter (Fig. 226.14). Aerial hyphae may only be evident when viewed microscopically. Short chains of conidia may be found on the aerial hyphae. Most isolates of *Nocardia* in cultured material are weakly acid-fast by the modified Kinyoun stain.

Although some studies have proposed the use of a complement fixation serologic test to aid in the diagnosis, this is typically available only in research settings. The clinical value of this and other serologic or skin testing remain uncertain.

CLINICAL MANIFESTATIONS

The clinical manifestations of nocardial infection vary from localized to disseminated.

Nocardia spp. are recognized as pathogens among severely immunosuppressed patients such as those who have severe systemic lupus erythematosus,[101] transplant recipients[102] or patients who have advanced HIV infection.[99] Although nocardiasis has been described in patients who have AIDS, it remains relatively uncommon. The clinical manifestations of nocardiasis in HIV-infected patients are nonspecific, with fever, productive cough and weight loss most common. About two-thirds of patients who have systemic nocardial infection with AIDS have the lung as the primary site of infection.

Radiographic features of pulmonary nocardiosis at the time of presentation include unilateral involvement (18 of 22 AIDS patients) with an alveolar pattern (14 out of 22).[100] The upper lobe was most commonly affected. CT scans of patients who have pulmonary

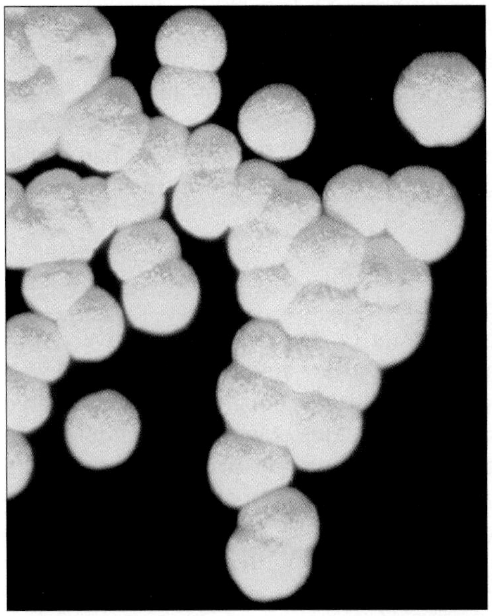

Fig. 226.13 Colonies of *Nocardia asteroides*, showing a smooth, chalky-white appearance.

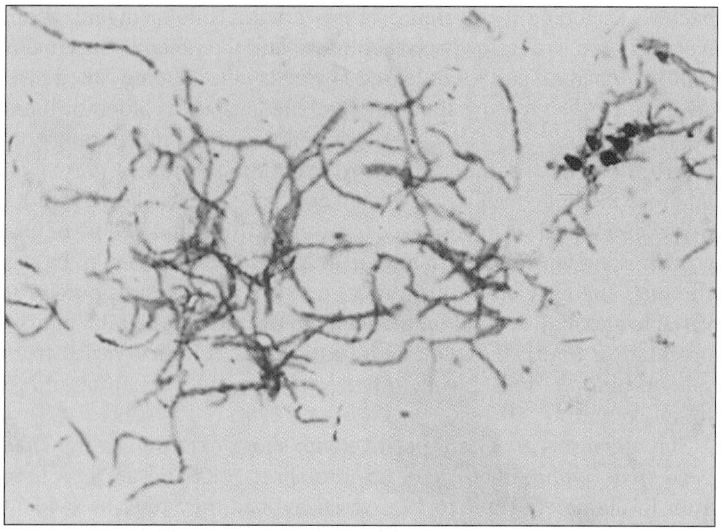

Fig. 226.14 *Nocardia asteroides* on Gram stain, showing extensively branched vegetative hyphae that break into short rods.

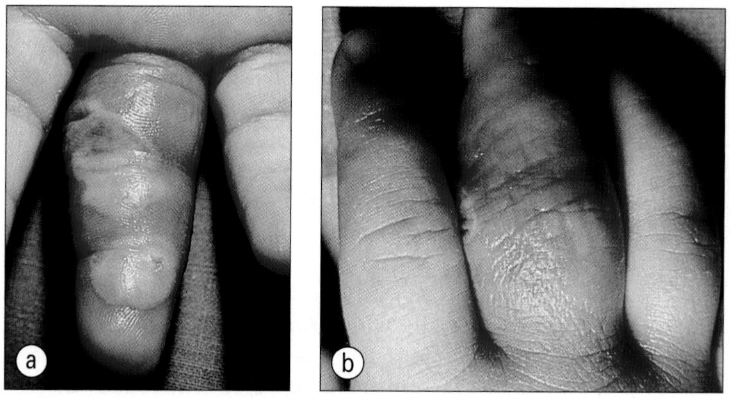

Fig. 226.15 Primary cutaneous nocardial infection is characteristically painless, localized and slowly progressive. (a) There is marked swelling and erythema in this child's finger. (b) However, because the finger was painless the child was not brought to medical attention until the infection had progressed to involve the entire finger.

infection show enlarged nodules or other masses (83%), cavitation (33%), consolidation (33%) and pleural thickening (29%).[104] Among patients who have severe immunosuppression such as AIDS, evidence of cavitation is seen more commonly.

Primary cutaneous infection may be caused by *N. asteroides*, *N. brasiliensis* or *N. otitidiscaviarum*.[104,105] In contrast to pulmonary or disseminated nocardiasis, cutaneous nocardial infection commonly occurs in immunocompetent individuals. Four clinical types of cutaneous nocardiasis have been described: mycetoma, lymphocutaneous involvement, superficial cellulitis and cutaneous involvement with disseminated disease. Primary cutaneous nocardial infection usually results from traumatic inoculation with the organism. Cutaneous lesions are characteristically painless, slowly progressive and localized (Fig. 226.15).

Rarely, localized infections may become invasive. Such infections have been described both in immunocompetent and immunocompromised subjects and may occur secondary to trauma or direct spread from adjacent anatomic sites.

A total of 131 patients who had *N. asteroides* brain abscess have been described.[106] Only about a third of these patients had a history of an underlying disease or treatment that might have affected the immunocompetence of the subjects. Co-existent *Nocardia* infection outside the central nervous system is common (71%). CT scans using contrast enhancement characteristically show single or multiple ring-enhancing brain abscesses. Most abscesses are located in the supratentorial space. Solitary brain abscess was present in 71 of 121 cases. Patients who had single abscesses had a lower mortality (32%) than those who had multiple abscesses (66%).

MANAGEMENT

In most clinical settings *Nocardia* can be managed effectively with antibiotic therapy. Recommendations for antibiotic therapy of localized or systemic nocardial infection are problematic since no large clinical trials have been undertaken. Moreover, the clinical relevance of in-vitro susceptibility testing has not yet been established. The most commonly used testing method has been the gradient strip diffusion test (E-test, AB Biodisk, Solna, Sweden). Susceptibility testing guidelines have been published by the National Committee for Clinical Laboratory Standards.[107] The most active parenteral agents for *N. asteroides* are amikacin (95% susceptible), imipenem (88%), ceftriaxone (82%) and cefotaxime (82%). The most active oral agents are sulfonamides (100%), minocycline (100%) and amoxicillin (40%). In many studies the combination of trimethoprim–sulfamethoxazole has been found to be synergistic in vitro. Since both drugs penetrate tissue, including CSF, and are usually well tolerated, the combination of trimethoprim and sulfamethoxazole is often recommended as the first line of therapy.[97] Other drug combinations, such as amikacin–imipenem and amikacin–ceftriaxone, have been proposed for severe infection requiring parenteral therapy.

Nocardial brain abscesses should be managed with a combination of medical and surgical techniques. The largest review on this subject recommended conservative medical treatment if the brain abscess is less than 2cm in diameter.[106] For patients who had larger abscesses or deteriorating conditions, stereotactic aspiration to confirm the diagnosis and decompress the lesion was advocated.

MISCELLANEOUS AEROBIC GRAM-POSITIVE BACILLI

ROTHIA DENTOCARIOSA

This pleomorphic, aerobic Gram-positive bacillus is catalase-reaction-positive, hydrolyzes esculin and forms coccoid spherules in broth culture and branching slender rods on solid agar. It is found as part of the normal flora in the oropharynx, where it has been associated with dental caries and chronic periodontal disease in the immunocompetent host and septicemia, pneumonia and infective endocarditis in the immunocompromised host. This organism remains susceptible to most β-lactam antibiotics, erythromycin and vancomycin.[108]

OERSKOVIA SPECIES

These aerobic, non-sporulating Gram-positive bacteria are found in soil. They form yellow colonies without aerial mycelia and produce a substrate mycelium that fragments into non-acid-fast, motile rods. They resemble *Nocardia* spp. in their ability to hydrolyze casein, xanthine and hypoxanthine to a varying degree. They have been associated with bacteremias, endocarditis, catheter-associated infections and infections after direct trauma involving soil contact, especially, but not exclusively, in immunocompromised hosts.[109]

REFERENCES

1. Regular non-spore forming aerobic Gram-positive bacilli. In: Holt JG, Kreig NR, Sneath PHA, eds. Bergey's manual of determinative bacteriology, 9th ed. Philadelphia: Lippincott Williams & Wilkins; 1993:542–70.
2. Cherubin CE, Appleman MD, Heseltine PNR, Khayr W, Stratton CW. Epidemiologic spectrum and current treatment of listeriosis. Rev Infect Dis 1991;13:1108.
3. Bojsen-Moller J. Human listeriosis: diagnostic, epidemiologic and clinical studies. Acta Pathol Microbiol Scand Suppl 1992;229:1–157.
4. Schlech WF III, Lavigne PM, Bortolussi R, *et al.* Epidemic listeriosis – evidence for transmission by food. N Engl J Med 1983;308:203.
5. Dalton CB, Austin CC, Sobel J, *et al.* An outbreak of gastroenteritis and fever due to *Listeria monocytogenes* in milk. N Engl J Med 1997;336:100–5.
6. Pinner RW, Schuchat A, Swaninathan B, *et al.* Role of foods in sporadic listeriosis, II: microbiologic and epidemiologic investigations. JAMA 1992;267:2046–50.
7. Schuchat A, Deaver KA, Wenger JD, *et al.* Role of foods in sporadic listeriosis. I. Case-control study of dietary risk factors. The Listeria Study Group. JAMA. 1992 Apr 15;267:2041–5.
8. Gellin BG, Broome CV, Bibb WF, *et al.* The epidemiology of listeriosis in the United States – 1986. Am J Epidemiol 1991;133:392–401.
9. Schuchat A, Lizano C, Broome CV, *et al.* Outbreak of neonatal listeriosis associated with mineral oil. Pediatr Infect Dis J 1991;10:183–9.
10. Southwick FS, Purich DL. Intracellular pathogenesis of listeriosis. N Engl J Med 1996;334:770–6.
11. Alvarez-Domingues C, Vasquez-Boland J-A, Carrasco-Marin E, Lopez-Mato P, Leyva-Cobian F. Host cell heparan sulfate proteoglycans mediate attachment and entry of *Listeria monocytogenes*, and the listerial surface protein ActA is involved in heparin sulfate receptor recognition. Infect Immun 1997;65:78–88.
12. Shen H, Miller JF, Fan X, Kolwyck D, Ahmed R, Harty JT. Compartmentalization of bacterial antigens: differential effects on priming of CD8 T cells and protective immunity. Cell 1998;92:535–45.
13. Hsieh C-S Macatonia SE, Tripp CS, *et al.* Development of TH1 $CD4^+$ T cells through IL-12 produced by *Listeria*-induced macrophages. Science 1993;260:547–9.
14. Skeen MJ, Rix EP, Freeman MM, Ziegler- HK. Exaggerated proinflammatory and Th1 responses in absence of γ/δ T cells after infection with *Listeria monocytogenes*. Infect Immun 2001;69:7213–23.
15. Topalovski M, Yang S, Boonpasat Y. Listeriosis of the placenta: clinicopathologic study of seven cases. Am J Obstet Gynecol 1993;169:616–20.
16. Wilson CB. The ontogeny of T lymphocyte maturation and function. J Pediatr 1991;118(Suppl.4):S4–9.
17. Bortolussi R, Rajaraman K, Serushago B. Role of tumor necrosis factor-alpha and interferon gamma in newborn host defense against *Listeria monocytogenes* infection. Pediatr Res 1992;32:460–4.
18. Hudak AP, Lee SH, Issekutz AC, *et al.* Comparison of three serological methods – enzyme-linked immunoabsorbent assay, complement fixation, and microagglutination – in the diagnosis of human perinatal *Listeria monocytogenes* infection. Clin Invest Med 1984;7:349–54.
19. Centers for Disease Control. Update: foodborne listeriosis – United States, 1988–1990. MMWR Morb Mortal Wkly Rep 1992;41:251.
20. Ahlfors CE, Goetzman BW, Halstad CC, *et al.* Neonatal listeriosis. Am J Dis Child 1977;131:405.
21. Lorber B. Listeriosis. Clin Infect Dis 1997;24:1–11.
22. MacGowan AP, Holt HA, Bywater MJ, Reeves DS. *In vitro* antimicrobial susceptibility of *Listeria monocytogenes* isolated in the UK and other *Listeria* species. Eur J Clin Microbiol Infect Dis 1990;9:767–70.
23. Dreuets DA, Jelinek TA, Freitag NE. *Listeria monocytogenes*-infected phagocytes can initiate central nervous system infection in mice. Infect Immun 2001;69:1344–50.
24. Wiggins GL, Albritton WL, Feeley JC. Antibiotic susceptibility of clinical isolates of *Listeria monocytogenes*. Antimicrob Agents Chemother 1978;3:854–60.
25. Hof P, Emmerling P, Seeliger HPR. Murine model for therapy of listeriosis in the compromised host. Chemotherapy 1981;27:214–9.
26. Bakker-Woudenberg IAJM, de Bos P, van Leeuwen WB, *et al.* Efficacy of ampicillin therapy in experimental listeriosis in mice with impaired T-cell-mediated immune response. Antimicrob Agents Chemother 1981;19:76–81.
27. Hawkins AE, Bortolussi R, Issekutz AC. *In vitro* and *in vivo* activity of various antibiotics against *Listeria monocytogenes* type 4b. Clin Invest Med 1984;7:335–41.
28. Weingartner L, Ortel S. Zur Behandlung der Listeriose mit Ampicillin. Dtsch Med Wochenschr 1967;92:1098–104.
29. Holt JG, Krieg NR, Sneath PHA, Stanley JT, Williams ST. Genus *Bacillus*. In: Holt JG, Krieg NR, Sneath PH, Staley JT, Williams ST, eds. Bergey's manual of determinative bacteriology, 9th ed. Baltimore: Williams & Wilkins; 1994:559–62.
30. CDC. Interim guidelines for investigation of and response to *Bacillus anthracis* exposures. MMWR Morb Mortal Wkly Rep 2001;50(RR-44):987–90.
31. Anthrax control and research, with special reference to national programme development in Africa: memorandum from a WHO meeting. Bull World Health Organ 1994;72:13–22.
32. Lamarque D, Haessler C, Champion R, *et al.* Anthrax in Chad: a zoonosis that still exists today. Med Trop (Mars) 1989;49:245–51.
33. Kunanusont C, Limpakarnjanarat K, Foy HM. Outbreak of anthrax in Thailand. Ann Trop Med Parasitol 1990;84:507–12.
34. Pfisterer RM. An anthrax epidemic in Switzerland. Clinical, diagnostic and epidemiological aspect of a mostly forgotten disease. Schweiz Med Wochenschr 1991;121:813–25.
35. Meselson M, Guillemin J, Hugh-Jones M, *et al.* The Sverdlovsk anthrax outbreak of 1979. Science 1994;266:1202–8.
36. Bhatnagar R, Batra S. Anthrax toxin. Crit Rev Microbiol 2001;27:167–200.
37. Drum CL, Yan SZ, Bard J, *et al.* Structural basis for the activation of anthrax adenyl cyclase exotoxin by calmodulin. Nature 2002;415:396–402.
38. Harrison LH, Ezzell JW, Abshire TG, Kidd S, Kaufman AF. Evaluation of serologic tests for diagnosis of anthrax after an outbreak of cutaneous anthrax in Paraguay. J Infect Dis 1989;160:706–10.
39. Stepanov AV, Marinin LI, Pomerantsev AP, Staritsin NA. Development of novel vaccines against anthrax in man. J Biotechnol 1996;44:155–60.
40. CDC. Update: investigation of bioterrorism-related anthrax and interim guidelines for clinical evaluation of persons with possible anthrax. MMWR Morb Mortal Wkly Rep 2001;50:941.
41. Shylyakhov E, Rubinsein E. Evaluation of the anthraxin skin test for diagnosis of acute and post human anthrax. Eur J Clin Microbiol Infect Dis 1996;15:242–5.
42. Meselson M, Guillemin J, Hugh-Jones M, *et al.* The Sverdlovsk anthrax outbreak of 1979. Science 1994;266:1202–8.
43. Franz DR, Jahrling PB, Friedlander AM, *et al.* Clinical recognition and management of patients exposed to biological warfare agents. JAMA 1997;278:399–411.
44. Holt JG, Krieg NR, Sneath PH, *et al.* The irregular non-spore forming aerobic Gram-positive bacilli. In: Holt JG, Krieg NR, Sneath PH, Staley JT, Williams ST, eds. Bergey's manual of determinative bacteriology, 9th ed. Baltimore: Williams & Wilkins; 1994:571–98.
45. Dixon JMS. Diphtheria in North America. J Hyg 1984;93:419–32.
46. Hard IRB, Dittmann S, Sutter RW. Current situations and control strategies for resurgence of diphtheria in newly independent states of the former Soviet Union. Lancet 1996;347:1739–44.
47. DeZoysa A, Efstratiou A, George RC, *et al.* Molecular epidemiology of *Corynebacterium diphtheriae* from northwest Russia and surrounding countries studied by using ribotyping and pulsed-field gel electrophoresis. J Clin Microbiol 1995;33:1080–3.
48. Mims CA, Dimmock NJ, Nash A, Stephen J. Mechanism of cell and tissue damage. In: Mims pathogenesis of infectious disease, 4th ed. London: Academic Press; 1995:209–13.
49. Feigin RD, Stechenberg BW, Strandgaard BH. Diphtheria. In: Feigin RD, Cherry JD, eds. Textbook of pediatric infectious diseases, 3rd ed. Philadelphia: WB Saunders; 1992:1110–6.
50. Committee on Infectious Diseases. Diphtheria. In: 1994 Red Book; report of the Committee on Infectious Diseases of the American Academy of Pediatrics, 23rd ed. Elkgrove, IL: American Academy of Pediatrics; 1994:177–81.
51. Clarridge JE, Spiegel CA. *Corynebacterium* and miscellaneous, irregular Gram-positive rods, *Erysipelothrix* and *Gardnerella*. In: Murray PR, Baron EJ, Pfaller MA, Tenover FC, Yolken RH, eds. Manual of clinical microbiology, 6th ed. Washington, DC: ASM Press; 1995:357–70.
52. Thompson SJ, Gates-Davis DR, Yong DC. Rapid microbiochemical identification of *Corynebacterium diphtheriae* and other medically important corynebacteria. J. Clin Microbiol 1983;18:926–9.
53. Barakett V, Bellaich G, Petit JC. Fatal septicemia due to a toxigenic strain of *Corynebacterium diphtheriae* subspecies *mitis*. Eur J Clin Microbiol Infect Dis 1992;11:761–2.
54. Mikhailovich VM, Melnikov VG, Mazurova IK, *et al.* Application of PCR for detection of toxigenic *Corynebacterium diphtheriae* strains isolated during the Russian diphtheria epidemic, 1990 through 1994. J Clin Microbiol 1995;33:3061–3.
55. Parry C, Hoa NTJ, Wain J, *et al.* The *in-vitro* susceptibilities of 88 toxigenic strains of *Corynebacterium diphtheriae* isolated at the Centre for Tropical Diseases between 1992 and 1996. In: Abstracts of the IDSA 35th Annual Meeting, San Francisco, CA 1997;Abst 746:210.
56. Paety O, Bimet F, Riegel P, *et al.* Clinical and molecular study of *Corynebacterium diphtheriae* systemic infections in France. J Clin Microbiol 1997;35:441–5.
57. Popovic T, Kombarova SY, Reeves MW, *et al.* Molecular epidemiology of diphtheria in Russia, 1985–1994. J Infect Dis 1996;174:1064–72.
58. Mofredj A, Guerin JM. Management of respiratory diphtheria. Clin Infect Dis 1993;17:937–8.
59. Rakhmanova G, Lumio J, Goundstroem KA, *et al.* Diphtheria outbreak in St Petersburg:

clinical characteristics of 1,860 adult patients. Scand J Infect Dis 1996;28:37–40.
60. Tiley SM, Kociuba KR, Heron LG, Munro R. Infective endocarditis due to non-toxigenic *Corynebacterium diphtheriae*: report of seven cases and review. Clin Infect Dis 1993;16:271–5.
61. Farizo KM, *et al.* Fatal respiratory disease due to *Corynebacterium diphtheriae*: case report and review of guidelines for management, investigation and control. Clin Infect Dis 1993;16:59.
62. Soriano F, Fernandez-Roblas R, Calvo R, *et al. In vitro* susceptibilities of aerobic and facultative non-spore-forming gram-positive bacilli to HMR 3647 (RU 66647) and 14 other antimicrobials. Antimicrob Agents Chemother 1998;42:1028-33.
63. Coyle MB, Lipsky BA. Coryneform bacteria in infectious diseases: clinical and laboratory aspects. Clin Microb Rev 1990;3:227–46.
64. Van Bosterhaut B, Surmont I, Vandeven J, *et al. Corynebacterium jeikeium* endocarditis: a report of five cases. Diagn Microbiol Infect Dis 1989;12:265–8.
65. Aguado JM, Ponte C, Soriano F. Bacteriuria with a multiple resistant species of *Corynebacterium* (*Corynebacterium* group D2): an unnoticed cause of urinary tract infection. J Infect Dis 1987;156:144–50.
66. Wong TP, Groman N. Production of diphtheria toxin by selective isolates of *Corynebacterium ulcerans* and *Corynebacterium pseudotuberculosis*. Infect Immun 1984;43:1114–6.
67. Wang Q, Hidalgo S, Chang BJ, Mee BJ, Riley TV. The detection and recovery of Erysipelothrix spp. in meat and abattoir samples in Western Australis. J Appl Microbiol 2002;92(5):844–50.
68. Shimoji Y, Yokomizo Y, Sekizaki T, Mori Y, Kubo M. Presence of a capsule in *Erysipelothrix rhusiopathiae* and its relationship to virulence for mice. Infect Immun 1994;62:2806–10.
69. Shimoji Y, Yokomizo Y, Mori Y. Intracellular survival of *Erysipelothrix rhusiopathiae* within murine macrophages: failure of induction of the oxidative burst of macrophages. Infect Immun 1996;64:1789–93.
70. Holt JG, Krieg NR, Sneath PHA, Staley JT, Williams ST. Genus *Erysipelothrix*. In: Holt JG, Krieg NR, Sneath PH, Staley JT, Williams ST, eds. Bergey's manual of determinative bacteriology, 9th ed. Baltimore: Williams & Wilkins; 1994:566.
71. Schuster MG, Brennan PJ, Edelstein P. Persistent bacteremia with *Erysipelothrix rhusiopathiae* in a hospitalized patient. Clin Infect Dis 1993;17:783–4.
72. Gorby GL, Peacock JE Jr. *Erysipelothrix rhusiopathiae* endocarditis: microbiologic, epidemiologic, and clinical features of an occupational disease. Rev Infect Dis 1988;10:317–25.
73. Jones N, Khoosal M. *Erysipelothrix rhusiopathiae* septicemia in a neonate. Clin Infect Dis 1997;24:511.
74. Patel R. Enterococcal-type glycopeptide resistance genes in non-enterococcal organisms. FEMS Microbiol Lett 2000 Apr 1;185(1):1–7.
75. Fidalgo SG, Longbottom CJ, Riley TV. Susceptibility of Erysipelothrix rhusiopathiae to antimicrobial agents and home disinfectants. Pathology 2002 Oct;34(5):462–5.
76. Clarridge JE. The recognition and significance of *Arcanobacterium haemolyticum*. Clin Microb Newslett 1989;11:41–5.
77. Funke G, Lucchini GM, Pfyffer GE, Marchiani M, von Graevenitz A. Characteristics of CDC group 1-like coryneform bacteria isolated from clinical specimens. J Clin Microbiol 1993 Nov;31(11):2907–12.
78. Gaston DA, Zurowsk SM. *Arcanobacterium haemolyticum* pharyngitis and exanthem. Arch Dermatol 1996;132:61–4.
79. Esteban J, Zapardiel J, Soriano F. Two cases of soft tissue infection caused by *Arcanobacterium haemolyticum*. Clin Infect Dis 1994;18:835–6.
80. Kotrajaras RP, Buddhavudhikral S, Sukroongreung S, *et al.* Endemic leg ulcers caused by *Corynebacterium pyogenes* in Thailand. Int J Dermatol 1982;21:407–9.
81. Waagner DC. *Arcanobacterium haemolyticum:* biology of the organism and diseases in man. Pediatr Infect Dis J 1991;10:933–9.
82. Carlson P, Renkonen OV, Kontiainen S. *Arcanobacterium haemolyticum* and streptococcal pharyngitis. Scand J Infect Dis 1994;26:203–7.
83. MacKenzie A, Fuite L, Chan FT, *et al.* Incidence and pathogenicity of *Arcanobacterium haemolyticum* during a 2-year study in Ottawa. Clin Infect Dis 1995;21:177–81.
84. Osterlund A. Are penicillin treatment failures in *Arcanobacterium haemolyticum* pharyngotonsillitis caused by intracellularly residing bacteria? Scand J Infect Dis 1995;27:130–4.
85. Miller RA, Brancato F, Holmes KK. *Corynebacterium haemolyticum* as a cause of pharyngitis and scarlatiniform rash in young adults. Ann Intern Med 1986;105:867–72.
86. Cherry JD. *Arcanobacterium haemolyticum*. In: Feigin RD, Cherry JD, eds. Textbook of pediatric infectious diseases, 3rd ed. Philadelphia: WB Saunders; 1992:1185–7.
87. Holt JG, Krieg NR, Sneath PH, *et al.* The irregular non-sporing Gram-positive rods. In: Holt JG, Krieg NR, Sneath PH, Staley JT, Williams ST, eds. Bergey's manual of determinative bacteriology, 9th ed. Baltimore: Williams & Wilkins; 1994:571.
88. Coyle MB, Hollis DG, Groman NB. *Corynebacterium spp.* and other coryneform organisms. In: Lennette EH, Ballows A, Hauser WJ Jr, *et al.*, eds. Manual of clinical microbiology, 4th ed. Washington, DC: ASM Press; 1985:193–204.
89. Lipsky BA, Goldberger AC, Tompkins LS, *et al.* Infections caused by non-diphtheriae corynebacteria. Rev Infect Dis 1982;4:1220–35.
90. Barton MD, Hughes KL. Ecology of *Rhodococcus equi*. Vet Microbiol 1984;9:65–76.
91. Emmons WB, Reichwein B, Winslow DL. *Rhodococcus equi* infection in the patient with AIDS: literature review and report of an unusual case. Rev Infect Dis 1991;13:91–6.
92. Jones MR, Neale TJ, Say PJ, Horne JG. *Rhodococcus equi*: an emerging opportunistic pathogen? Aust NZ J Med 1989;19:103–7.
93. Magnani G, Elia GF, McNeil MM, *et al. Rhodococcus equi* cavitary pneumonia in HIV infected patients: an unsuspected opportunistic pathogen. J Acquire Immun Defic Syndr 1992;5:1059–64.
94. Prescott JF. *Rhodococcus equi:* an animal and human pathogen. Clin Microbiol Rev 1991;4:20–34.
95. McNeil MM, Brown JM. Distribution and antimicrobial susceptibility of *Rhodococcus equi* from clinical specimens. Eur J Epidemiol 1992;8:437–43.
96. Holt JG, Krieg NR, Sneath PH, Stanley JT, Williams ST. Genus *Bacillus*. In: Holt JG, Krieg NR, Sneath PH, Staley JT, Williams ST, eds. Bergey's manual of determinative bacteriology, 9th ed. Baltimore: Williams & Wilkins; 1994:626.
97. McNeil MM, Brown JM. The medically important aerobic actinomycetes epidemiology and microbiology. Clin Microbiol Rev 1994;7:357–417.
98. Laurent F, Carlotti A, Boiron P, Villard J, Freney J. Ribotyping: a tool for taxonomy and identification of the *Nocardia asteroides* complex species. J Clin Microbiol 1996;34:1079–82.
99. Uttamchandani RB, Daikos GL, Reyes RR, *et al.* Nocardiosis in 30 patients with advanced human immunodeficiency virus infection: clinical features and outcome. Clin Infect Dis 1994;18:348–53.
100. Silva CL, Faccioli LH. Tumor necrosis factor and macrophage activation are important in clearance of *Nocardia brasiliensis* from the livers and spleens of mice. Infect Immun 1992;60:3566–70.
101. Mok CC, Yuen KY, Lau CS. Nocardiosis in systemic lupus erythematosus. Semin Arthritis Rheum 1997;26:675–83.
102. Arduino RC, Johnson PC, Miranda AG. Nocardiosis in renal transplant recipients undergoing immunosuppression with cyclosporine. Clin Infect Dis 1993;16:505–12.
103. Buckley JA, Padhani AR, Kuhlman JE. CT features of pulmonary nocardiosis. J Comput Assist Tomogr 1995;19:726–32.
104. Clark NM, Braun DK, Pasternak A, Chenoweth CE. Primary cutaneous *Nocardia otitidiscaviarum* infection: case report and review. Clin Infect Dis 1995;20:1266–70.
105. Sachs MK. Lymphocutaneous *Nocardia brasiliensis* infection acquired from a cat scratch: case report and review. Clin Infect Dis 1992;15:710–1.
106. Mamelak AN, Obana WG, Flaherty JF, Rosenblum ML. Nocardial brain abscess: treatment strategies and factors influencing outcome. Neurosurgery 1994;35:622–31.
107. National Committee for Clinical Laboratory Standards. M24-T2 susceptibility test of mycobacteria, nocardia, and other aerobic actinomycetes; tentative standard, 2nd ed. Washington, DC: National Committee for Clinical Laboratory Standards; 2000.

chapter

227 Neisseria

Jacob Dankert

INTRODUCTION

The genus *Neisseria* was named after Albert Neisser who observed diplococci in leukocytes in urethral exudates from patients who had gonorrhea in 1879.[1] Three years later Leistikow and Loeffler were able to cultivate the bacterium, termed gonococcus, in pure culture.

Although various species within the Neisseriaceae family can cause disease in humans and various animals, the two well-known pathogenic species for humans are *Neisseria gonorrhoeae*, or gonococcus, and *Neisseria meningitidis* or meningococcus.

Neisseria gonorrhoeae causes gonorrhea, a sexually transmitted disease. Gonorrhea was named by Galen in AD130 after the Greek words *gonor* (seed) and *rhoia* (flow), suggesting that the disease was related to the flow of semen. In the 13th century Maimonides recognized that the urethral discharge of male gonorrhea patients was not semen, but a sexually transmitted disease. Gonorrhea was not clearly distinguished from syphilis until the 19th century. In 1885 Bumm proved the causal relationship between the bacterium and the onset of gonorrhea by inoculating gonococci into volunteers. Although it was known that untreated infection healed spontaneously, treatment was warranted because reinfections were common. Effective therapy became available in the 1930s when sulfonamides were developed and in 1943 when penicillin was produced. Sulphonamide resistance occurred early and rapidly in gonococci. Penicillin-resistant gonococci due to penicillinase production were documented in various parts of the world in 1975 and 1976. The prevalence of strains resistant to penicillin and other antibiotics has risen steadily worldwide. Therefore, the pathogenesis of gonorrhea, the host response to infection and the molecular biology of the gonococcus have been studied intensively over the past two decades.

Neisseria meningitidis is a cause of endemic and epidemic disease in developed and developing countries. Epidemic meningococcal meningitis was first described by Vieusseaux in 1805 in Geneva.[2] Throughout the 19th century periodic epidemics occurred, involving mainly young children and military men in recruit camps. In 1887 Weichselbaum isolated the meningococcus from six of eight cases of primary sporadic community-acquired meningitis. Kiefer described the nasopharyngeal meningococcal carrier state among healthy people in 1896. Recognition of an association between increasing rates of meningococcal carriage and the onset of epidemic disease stimulated studies of the epidemiology and prevention of meningococcal infection. Serum therapy, used by Flexner and Jobling in 1908, resulted in survival from a previously fatal disease. The outcome of meningococcal disease improved drastically by treatment with sulfonamides in 1937. In addition, sulfonamides to eradicate the carrier state were used as prophylaxis to prevent epidemics. Nevertheless, an epidemic in two military bases in California in 1963 could not be aborted by sulfonamide prophylaxis because of the occurrence of sulfonamide-resistant meningococci. This led to the development of vaccines derived from selected meningococcal capsular polysaccharides. Such vaccines have been successfully used in military recruits and have also been given to civilian populations.

A successful vaccine that prevents infection caused by *N. meningitidis* serogroup B, which causes most cases of disease in temperate countries, has not, however, been developed. The absence of a group B vaccine limits the effective control of meningococcal disease. Other problems of meningococcal infection are:

- enhanced susceptibility of certain age groups;
- mechanisms involved in the upper respiratory carrier state leading to invasion of the meningococcus into the bloodstream; and
- reasons for the fulminant nature of the infection in certain patients.

NATURE

Taxonomy

In the 1984 edition of *Bergey's manual of systemic bacteriology*,[3] the family of the Neisseriaceae included the following four genera:

- *Neisseria*,
- *Moraxella*,
- *Kingella*, and
- *Acinetobacter*.

The taxonomy of the family has been extensively revised over the past decade. This has led to the renaming of certain genera and species, as well as the addition of new ones.

The genus *Neisseria* contained 11 species considered as 'true *Neisseria*' recovered from human sources and three animal species called the 'false *Neisseria*'. The genus *Moraxella* had two subgenera – the subgenus *Moraxella* with six species and the subgenus *Branhamella* with four species. The genus *Kingella* contained three species and the genus *Acinetobacter* was made up of various phenotypes.

Studies of the family Neisseriaceae making use of DNA–rRNA hybridization, DNA–DNA hybridization and 16S rRNA sequence analysis have revealed substantial differences between the genera and certain species within each of the four genera.[4,5] The family Neisseriaceae, as defined in *Bergey's manual of systematic bacteriology*, is genetically heterogeneous. Its members cluster in two separate rRNA superfamilies that exhibit no significant levels of relatedness. The true Neisseriaceae and two *Kingella* spp. belong to the β-subclass of the Proteobacteria. Because the false *Neisseria, Moraxella, Branhamella* and *Acinetobacter* genera belong to the γ-subclass of the Proteobacteria, recommendations have been made to remove them from the family Neisseriaceae. Molecular genetic techniques have demonstrated that the genera *Eikenella, Simonsiella* and *Alysiella* and four CDC groups (EF-4a and 4b, M-5 and M-6) are close genetic relatives of the true *Neisseria* and two *Kingella* spp.[5] The newly amended family Neisseriaceae, containing true *Neisseria* spp. from humans as well as false *Neisseria* spp., is shown in Table 227.1. The taxonomic status of the false *Neisseria* is debated, but they are considered as *Neisseria* spp. from animal origin.

Neisseria weaveri and *N. elongata* subspp. *nitroreducens* are the former CDC groups M-5 and M-6, respectively. The true *Neisseria* and both *Kingella* spp. form a cluster with 91% or more DNA homology,

AMENDED CLASSIFICATION OF MICRO-ORGANISMS WITHIN THE FAMILY NEISSERIACEAE

Neisseria			*Kingella*	*Eikenella*	*Simonsiella*	*Alysiella*
Habitat, humans		Habitat, various animals	Habitat, humans	Habitat, humans	Habitat, humans and animals	Habitat, humans and animals
Urogenital tract	*N. gonorrhoeae*	Oropharynx	Oropharynx and urogenital tract	Oropharynx	Oral cavity	Oral cavity
Oropharynx	*N. meningitidis, N. lactamica, N. sicca, N. subflava, N. flavescens, N. mucosa, N. cinerea, N. polysaccharea, N. elongata*	Monkeys: *N. macacae*; cats: *N. canis*; dogs; *N. weaveri*; guinea-pigs: *N. denitrificans*; iguanas: *N. igaunae*; cats/dogs: CDC, EF-4a, CDC, EF-4b; guinea-pigs: *N. caviae*; sheep/cattle: *N. ovis*; rabbits: *N. cuniculi*	*K. kingae* *K. denitrificans*	*E. corrodens*		

Table 227.1 Amended classification of micro-organisms within the family Neisseriaceae. The taxonomic status of *N. caviae, N. ovis* and *N. cuniculi* is debated.

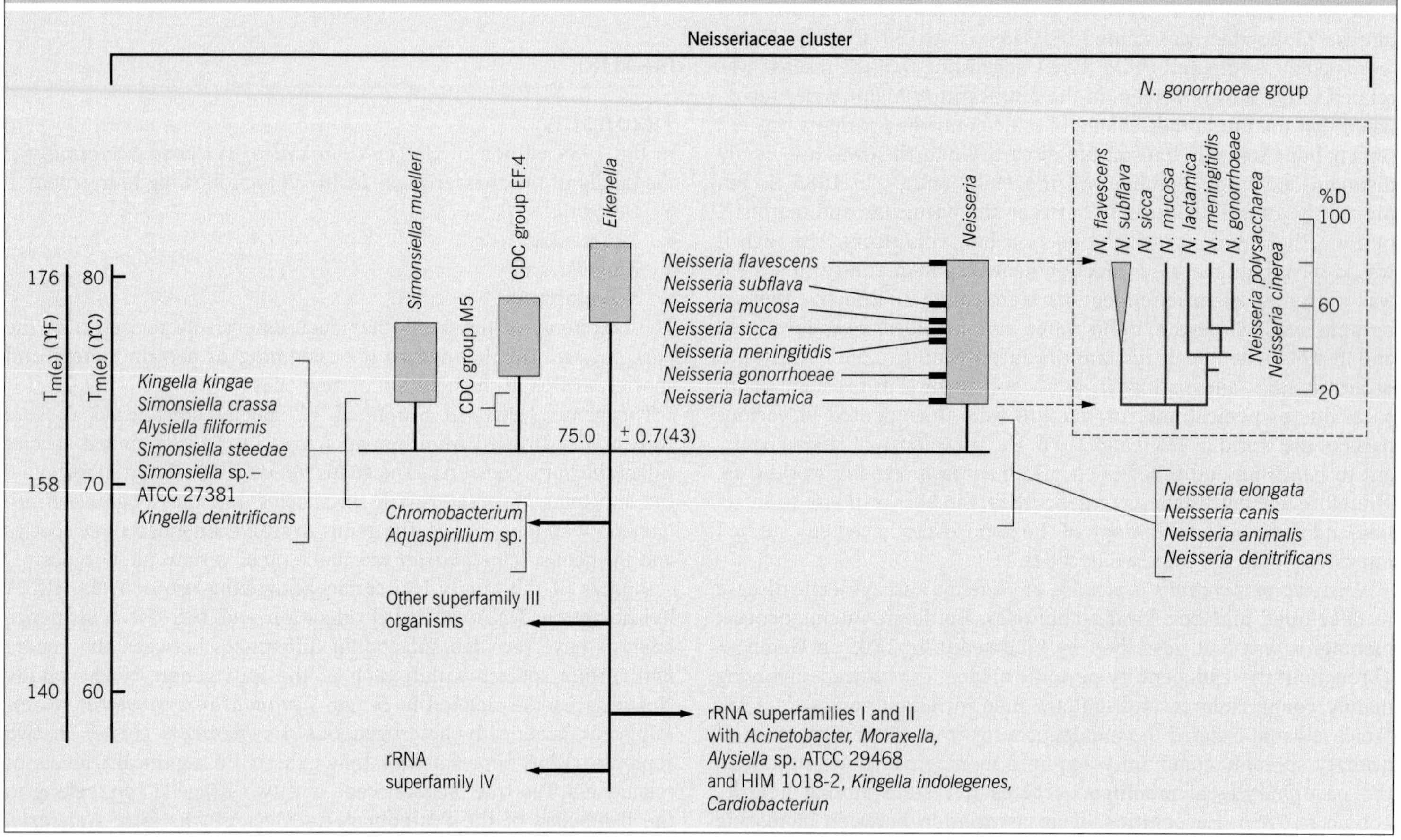

Fig. 227.1 Neisseriaceae family. $T_{m(e)}$ is the melting temperature at which 50% of a hybrid is denatured. (Adapted from Rossau *et al.*[5])

but are rather distantly related (Fig. 227.1). The relationship between *Neisseria* spp. is as follows:

- *N. gonorrhoeae* and *N. meningitidis* are very closely related;
- *N. lactamica, N. polysaccharea* and *N. cinerea* are related to *N. gonorrhoeae* and to each other more distantly;
- saccharolytic Neisseriaceae (*N. subflava, N. sicca* and *N. mucosa*) are more distantly related to the other Neisseriaceae; and
- species of animal origin are still more distantly related.

The closest neighbors of the family of Neisseriaceae are the genera *Chromobacterium* and *Aquaspirillium*.

General characteristics of the amended family of Neisseriaceae are that the micro-organisms are coccal, coccoid or rod shaped or exhibit a multicellular micromorphology (*Simonsiella* spp. and *Alysiella* spp.).[4,5] They are Gram-negative. Several species possess capsules and are fimbriated (piliated). Endospores are not found, and flagella are absent. Members of the genus *Simonsiella* and *Alysiella* show gliding motility. Some *Neisseria* spp., including *N. meningitidis*, may show surface-bound twitching motility. All species are aerobic, but *Kingella* and *Eikenella* spp. also grow under anaerobic conditions. The optimum growth temperature is 89.6–98.6°F. The guanine-plus-cytosine content of DNA ranges from 41 to 58mol %. Most species are not pathogenic and their main habitat is the mucosal surface of the nasopharynx and oropharynx of humans and various mammals.

Neisseria gonorrhoeae and *N. meningitidis* are primarily pathogens of humans. Both *Kingella* spp. and *Eikenella corrodens* are occasionally isolated from human infections, and are discussed in Chapter 229.

General characteristics

The genus *Neisseria* is composed of 10 species that may be isolated from humans and 10 species that may be cultured from various animals.[6]

The *Neisseria* spp. are the only true coccal members of the family Neisseriaceae, with the exception of *N. elongata* and *N. weaveri*, which are medium-to-large plump rods that sometimes occur in pairs or short chains. *Neisseria* spp. grow best aerobically in an atmosphere containing 5–10% carbon dioxide at a temperature of 89.6–98.6°F and pH of 7–7.5. The micro-organisms are Gram-negative cocci that typically appear in pairs (diplococci) and occasionally in tetrads or clusters. Diplococci have flattened opposing sides, imparting the characteristic kidney or coffee bean appearance seen in stained smears. Cell size ranges from 0.6 to 1.5μm depending upon the species source of the isolate and the age of the culture.

Neisseria spp. can be grown on several kinds of media, though growth may be inhibited by fatty acids in the medium. Inhibition can be eliminated by adding starch or blood. Blood agar medium or chocolate medium (blood heated at 176–194°F) are suitable media for growing *Neisseria* spp.

Colonies of *N. gonorrhoeae* vary in diameter from 0.5 to 1μm. Colonies of *N. meningitidis* are usually larger (1–2μm in diameter) and flatter than those of *N. gonorrhoeae*. Colonies of *N. flavescens* are yellow and opaque and colonies of *N. elongata* have a dry clay-like appearance. Colonies of the other nonpathogenic *Neisseria* spp. are similar in size, appearance and consistency to those of the two pathogenic *Neisseria* spp., except those of the saccharolytic *Neisseria* spp. (*N. subflava, N. sicca* and *N. mucosa*). Colonies of these species are larger (1–3μm in diameter), more convex and smooth (*N. mucosa*). Colonies of *N. subflava* and *N. sicca* are opaque and have varying consistency. *Neisseria sicca* adhere to the agar surface and become wrinkled with prolonged incubation. Some nonpathogenic *Neisseria* spp. form a yellow pigment (*N. flavescens*) or a greenish-yellow pigment (*N. mucosa, N. subflava*).

Neisseria spp. are oxidase positive and catalase positive, except *N. elongata*, which is catalase negative.

All species produce acid from a few carbohydrates by oxidation. The ability to produce polysaccharide from sucrose, to produce catalase and deoxyribonuclease, to reduce nitrate and nitrite, and to oxidize the tributyrin fatty acid are also used to identify *Neisseria* spp.

Habitat and prevalence

Neisseria spp. are normal inhabitants of the nasopharyngeal and oropharyngeal mucous membrane of humans and various mammals.[2,6] *Neisseria meningitidis* is usually carried in the nasopharynx without causing disease.[7] Colonization may persist for many months. One-third of the carriers have chronic carriage for more than 16 months. Carriage may also occur on anogenital mucosal membranes. In children under 4 years of age the carriage rate is 1% or less. Carriage rates rise progressively through the first two decades of life to peak at about 20–25% in late teenage and early adult life, and then slowly decline. During carriage the expression of capsule polysaccharide is absent or low. Therefore, nongroupable (capsular polysaccharide absent) meningococci are predominantly cultured from the nasopharynx of carriers. Meningococcal carriage may not be confined to the mucosal surface.[8] Carriage rate among patients undergoing tonsillectomy as assessed by nasopharyngeal swabbing was 10%, whereas meningococci detected by immunohistochemical methods were present within the epithelial layer and tonsillar tissues from 45% of such patients. These findings show that the conventional swabbing method to determine carriage rate is an insensitive procedure, assuming that the majority of the subepithelial meningococci are viable cells. Carriage induces bactericidal antibodies. Since the development of such antibodies increases progressively at a young age when carriage of meningococci is low, other bacteria with cross-reaction most likely induce bactericidal antibodies. *Neisseria lactamica* carriage elicits bactericidal antibodies against various meningococcal serogroups and serotypes. Carriage of *N. lactamica* is higher than that of *N. meningitidis* in infancy and in young children and is approximately 4% by 3 months of age and peaks at 21% by 18–24 months of age.[7]

STRUCTURE OF *NEISSERIA GONORRHOEAE*

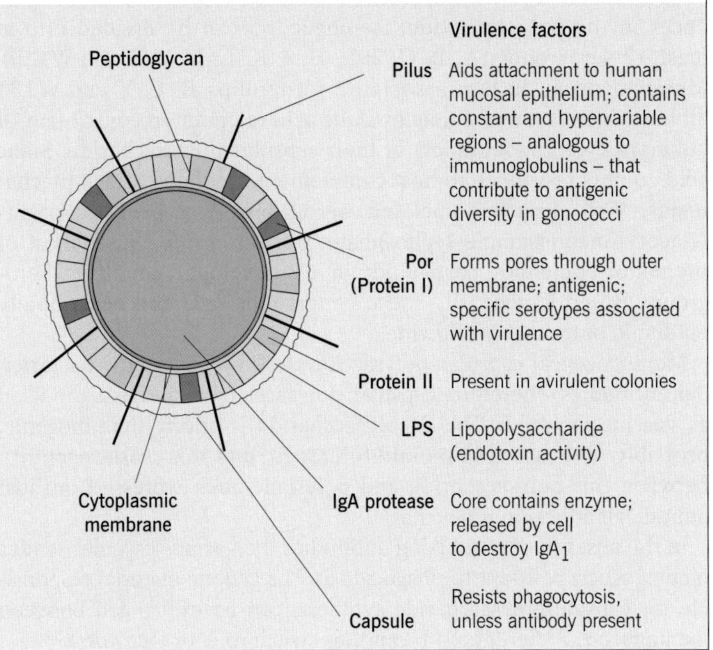
Virulence factors
Peptidoglycan
Pilus
Aids attachment to human mucosal epithelium; contains constant and hypervariable regions – analogous to immunoglobulins – that contribute to antigenic diversity in gonococci
Por (Protein I)
Forms pores through outer membrane; antigenic; specific serotypes associated with virulence
Protein II
Present in avirulent colonies
LPS
Lipopolysaccharide (endotoxin activity)
Cytoplasmic membrane
IgA protease
Core contains enzyme; released by cell to destroy IgA1
Capsule
Resists phagocytosis, unless antibody present

Fig. 227.2 Structure of *N. gonorrhoeae*. (Adapted from Mims *et al.*[9])

Both children and adults can be colonized either by strains of the sucrose-positive *Neisseria* spp. (*N. mucosa, N. perflava, N. sicca*) or by several other *Neisseria* spp. Both patterns of colonization are stable and generally persistent for many months.

Neisseria gonorrhoeae strains are always considered to be pathogenic, in contrast to *N. meningitidis*, of which only some strains can cause meningococcal disease. Gonococci infect those surfaces which are lined with columnar epithelial cells: endocervix, urethra, anogenital and oropharyngeal mucous membranes and conjunctiva.

Both *Kingella* spp. are part of the normal upper respiratory and genitourinary tract flora. *Eikenella corrodens* is a commensal of the human oropharynx and upper respiratory tract.

Structure

Neisseria spp., like other Gram-negative bacteria, possess an inner cytoplasmic membrane, a thin peptidoglycan layer and an outer membrane containing proteins, phospholipids and a lipo-oligosaccharide (LOS), as shown in Figure 227.2 for *N. gonorrhoeae*.[9]

Capsules

Neisseria gonorrhoeae is covered with a loosely adherent capsular-like structure containing high-molecular weight polyphosphate. Its function is unknown.[6]

Neisseria meningitidis also produces polyphosphate loosely adherent to the surface. In contrast to gonococci most meningococci have a polysaccharide capsule.[6] On the basis of structural differences in the polysaccharide, meningococci can be divided into at least 12 serogroups (A, B, C, 29E, H, I, K, L, X, Y, Z and W135). Meningococcal disease-associated serogroups B, C, Y and W135 all have *N*-acetylneuraminic or sialic acid (a common constituent of eukaryotic cell membranes) in their capsular polysaccharide. Sialic acid confers resistance to host complement-mediated attack mechanisms. The disease-associated serogroup A capsule contains *N*-acetyl-mannosamine-1-phosphate. This serogroup causes most of the major epidemics, particularly in less developed countries. Serogroups B and C generally cause endemic disease and occasionally epidemic outbreaks worldwide.

Meningococcal capsular polysaccharides induce specific bactericidal antibodies. Therefore, capsular polysaccharide antigens are used as vaccine materials. The B-polysaccharide is poorly immunogenic, probably because of immunotolerance due to cross-reactivity between this polysaccharide and polysialic acid expressed on host neural cell adhesion molecules.

In the absence of opsonizing antibodies the various capsules render meningococci resistant to phagocytosis. The genetic material responsible for capsule polysaccharide synthesis can be exchanged between meningococci.[10] Serogroup B can thus switch to C or vice versa.[11]

Pili

Pili are hair-like filamentous proteins consisting of repeating peptide subunits (pilin). Pathogenic *Neisseria* spp. have long pili (4300nm in length) protruding through the capsular structures (see Fig. 227.2). Nonpathogenic *Neisseria* spp. have short pili (175–210nm in length) and long pili.

Neisseria gonorrhoeae has pilin protein subunits that have an apparent molecular weight of 16.5–21.5kDa. Gonococci produce one type of pilus; the main subunit is Pil E. CD 46 has been identified as the pili receptor.[12] Pili undergo both phase variation and antigenic variation. Expression of pili is a function of the *pil* gene complex.

Gonococci contain one copy of *pil E* and multiple copies of *pil S*, which are transcriptionally silent. *pil C* encodes a protein involved in pilus assembly. Phase variation involves several mechanisms. Deletions and frame shift mutations produce truncated pilin and a stable P^--phenotype. Reversible phase variation can be due to changes in the *pil C* region.

Colonial morphology is associated with piliation: cells from small domed colonies are piliated (P^+ and P^{++} colonies) in contrast to cells from large, flat colonies (P^- colonies).

Freshly isolated gonococci from patients carry pili. Initially grown on culture media, gonococci form colony types P^+ and P^{++}. P^- colonies lacking pili predominate after 20 hours of growth. This shift between P^+ or P^{++} to P^- colony types is due to pili phase variation. *In vitro* the frequency of phase variation is high, being 10^{-2} to 10^{-4}, and usually occurs in only a fraction of the bacterial population.

Antigenic variation of pili is due to the variability of pilin sequences residing primarily in the C-terminal half of the protein. The genome of the *pil* gene complex contains many incomplete sequences, which can be recombined with expressed loci on the same chromosome. Lysing gonococci release transforming DNA, which can recombine effectively with partly homologous regions. The frequency of antigenic pili variation may be *in vitro* as high as 10^{-3} per cell in a fraction of the bacterial population.

Neisseria meningitidis expresses two different classes of pili (either class I or class II), which are antigenically and structurally distinct. During infection pili undergo rapid phase shifts and antigenic variation.[13] Unlike gonococci, piliated meningococci form colonies that are indistinguishable from their nonpiliated isogenic forms.

Pili are essential for adhesion to epithelial and endothelial cells and impart tissue tropism.[14] Piliated *Neisseria* spp. adhere to susceptible cells and can initiate infection. Pili can overcome the electrostatic repulsion between the negatively charged mucosal surfaces and also play a role in transformation (the acquisition of homologous and heterologous DNA from the environment).[15] Neisserial competence for transformation is much greater in piliated cells than in nonpiliated cells. Pil E and Pil C are required for DNA uptake.[15]

Outer membrane proteins

The outer membrane proteins of gonococci and meningococci are similar. For both species various proteins are present within or on the surface of the outer membrane.[16] The trimeric proteins provide channels or porins, allowing low-molecular nutrients to diffuse through the outer membrane.

Neisseria gonorrhoeae porin protein is termed Por (formerly protein I). There are two different antigenic forms of Por (Por A and Por B) with molecular weights of 32kDa to 36kDa. Por is LOS associated and shows stable interstrain variation. The antigenic heterogeneity is the basis for serologic typing schemes of gonococci. Strains expressing Por IA are associated with resistance to normal human serum and disseminated gonococcal infection.

Neisseria gonorrhoeae can also express a family of other membrane proteins called protein II (20–28kDa). Colonies of bacteria expressing protein II have a more opaque surface than those not expressing PII. Therefore, PII is designated as an opacity (Opa) protein.[17] Each of the 10–12 Opa proteins is produced from its own *opa* gene. Expression of Opa varies, in contrast to Por, due to high-frequency variation in the *opa* gene because of translational frame shifting. The expression of each gene can be independently switched on and off. These phase transitions occur frequently, yielding expression of up to three different Opa types at one colony (Opa^-, Opa^+, Opa^{++}). Antigenic variation among the Opa proteins of a strain also occurs.

Opa proteins have an important role in bacterial adherence. Heparin-related compounds[18] and CD 66[19] have been identified as Opa receptors. Cell tropism is determined by the variable expression of the Opa proteins.

Neisseria meningitidis is able to express two porins simultaneously: a class 1 protein, or Por A (44–47kDa), and either a class 2 (40–42kDa) or class 3 (37–39kDa) protein, Por B.[16] Por A is cation selective, whereas class 2 and 3 porins are anion selective. Class 2 and class 3 porins are the equivalent of the gonococci Por protein. The antigenic differences between class 2 and class 3 proteins of different strains are used for serotyping meningococci.

Neisseria meningitidis possesses an outer membrane protein, class 5 protein (26–30kDa), known as opacity protein. So far five variants of protein 5 are known, and from none to all five may be expressed by a single strain. There is no relationship between colonial opacity and the expressions of these proteins in contrast to *N. gonorrhoeae*. As in gonococci, the Opa proteins can undergo antigenic variation during natural infection. Two proteins, Opa and Opc, play a role in attachment of the bacteria to tissue. CD66e and heparin sulfate proteoglycan are their receptors, respectively.[20,21] The variable expression of these proteins represents an important cell tropism determinant. The outer membrane of both *Neisseria* spp. also contains a protein which increases in molecular weight upon treatment with a reducing agent. This reduction modifiable protein (Rmp) in *N. gonorrhoeae* is designated as protein III and in *N. meningitidis* as class 4 protein. The protein is immunologically conserved. Rmp antibodies interfere with the bactericidal activity of antibodies directed to other surface antigens. Therefore Rmp antibodies are so-called blocking antibodies. Both *Neisseria* spp. also have a number of environmentally regulated outer membrane proteins. These proteins may be expressed depending upon the bacterial growth conditions. The iron-regulated proteins are essential for survival of gonococci and meningococci *in vivo*. The transfer-binding proteins (Tbp-1 and Tbp-2) and the lactoferrin-binding proteins (Lbp) mediate internalization of iron into the bacterium.

Lipo-oligosaccharide

Approximately 50% of the outer membrane is LOS. Gonococcal and meningococcal LOS lack the multiple repeating sugars of enterobacterial lipopolysaccharide (LPS). Therefore the neisserial LPS has been termed LOS. Lipo-oligosaccharide is composed of lipid A and a short sugar chain of 8–12 saccharide units, the core oligosaccharide. The lipid A portion anchors LOS in the outer membrane and is the active moiety of endotoxin. The core oligosaccharide is divided into an inner and outer core region. The inner core has a common structure. Lipo-oligosaccharide outer core sugars undergo high-frequency phase and antigenic variation[22,23] during the course of infection and are used for immunotyping of meningococci.

The terminal structure of LOS is the target for sialylation by bacterial sialyltransferase. Gonococci utilize cytidine-5-monophospho-*N*-acetylneuraminic accid (CMP-NANA) present in the host tissues and add NANA to the LOS. Meningococci synthesize the CMP-NANA. Sialylation protects against the bactericidal activity of normal serum and generates a structure that mimics a structure present on host tissue cells. The neisserial outer membrane continuously sheds vesicles, which occur as blebs. These blebs contain DNA, protein and high levels of LOS, including lipid A. The latter component is implicated in the onset of shock if bacteria gain entrance into the circulation.[24]

Peptidoglycan

The peptidoglycan layer of *N. gonorrhoeae* and *N. meningitidis* may contribute to the inflammatory response, especially in gonococcal disease. In addition, peptidoglycan causes complement activation.

Typing of *N. gonorrhoeae* and *N. meningitidis*

Studies of the pathogenesis and epidemiology of gonorrhea and meningococcal meningitis have been enhanced by the availability of appropriate typing methods.

Characterization of *N. gonorrhoeae* is based on auxotyping and serotyping.[6] Gonococcal strains that have specific requirements for certain nutritional growth factors are known as auxotypes and include prototrophic (none requiring), proline-requiring and arginine-, hypoxanthine- and uracil-requiring (AHU) strains. *Neisseria gonorrhoeae* can be subdivided in 35 auxotypes. Arginine, hypoxanthine and uracil auxotypes are more likely to cause asymptomatic infection and more subtle inflammatory signs than other auxotypes.

Serotyping for *N. gonorrhoeae* is performed using a panel of monoclonal antibodies directed against epitopes on Por (protein I). Strains are divided into two major serogroups, Por IA and IB strains. Subdivision into serovars is based on patterns of reaction with specific protein IA and protein IB antibodies. In total there are at least 55 serovars. Typing systems have been used in epidemiological studies of gonorrhea in communities and in analyzing patterns of antibiotic resistance. Strain typing is also done by analysis of DNA sequence variations, by Opa typing or DNA sequencing of the *por* gene.

The phenotypic classification of *N. meningitidis* is based upon serologic methods to detect antigenic differences on four surface antigens:

- capsular polysaccharide,
- epitopes on class 2 and 3 outer membrane proteins,
- epitopes on the class 1 outer membrane, and
- LOS epitopes.

The 12 serogroups are recognized on the basis of the immune reaction of the polysaccharide capsule. Serotyping is based on the difference in the class 2 and 3 proteins (Por B). Strains are further subdivided into serosubtypes based on differences in the class 1 protein, Por A.

Lipo-oligosaccharides can also be used as typing antigens, giving rise to immunotypes L1, L2, L3, etc. Six different gonococcal LOS immunotypes and 12 different meningococcal LOS immunotypes have been recognized. Among meningococcal serogroups B and C immunotypes L1–9 are found, and in serogroup A immunotypes L10–12. Double epitopes may be recognized depending upon phase variation or the presence of incomplete epitopes on the same bacterium. Using the current typing scheme, a meningococcus is characterized as follows:

- B: serogroup, the capsular polysaccharide composition;
- 15: serotype, class 2/3 (Por B) protein antigen;
- P1.7, 16: serosubtype, class 1 (Por A) protein antigen;
- L 3,7: immunotype, LOS antigen.

Characterization of gonococcal and meningococcal immunotype is relevant for pathogenetic studies. Meningococcal serogroup, serotype and serosubtype characterization are of great value in epidemiologic surveillance.

In addition to the serologic classification of meningococci, other typing methods are used.[25] Multilocus enzyme electrophoresis gives the electrophoretic type (ET). Multilocus sequence typing has been used to show that specific complexes of related hypervirulent strains have caused epidemics.[26] DNA restriction analysis, randomly amplified polymorphic DNA (RAPD), restriction fragment length polymorphism (RFLP) and ribotyping are also used.

EPIDEMIOLOGY

Gonorrhea

Gonorrhea caused by *N. gonorrhoeae* is a common sexually transmitted disease and a worldwide public health problem. Its incidence reflects the lifestyle of the human community. The incidence in most Western European countries is lower than in the USA, with approximately 200 cases/100,000 population in 1992.[27] In the 1995 survey the incidence in the USA was 124 cases/100,000 population.[28] The highest incidence is in countries of the developing world, ranging from 4000 to 10,000/100,000 population. Commonly the highest attack rates occur in 15–25-year-old men and women.

Gonococci are obligate human pathogens. They cannot spontaneously infect animals or reside free in the environment. Gonorrhea is commonly transmitted by sexual intercourse with an infected partner. The risk of acquiring the urethral infection for men is approximately 20% after a single exposure to vaginal intercourse with an infected woman, rising to 60–80% after four or more exposures.

The transmission rate from male to female is approximately 50% per contact, rising to 90% after three exposures. Gonococci may also be transmitted by orogenital contact or rectal intercourse. Perinatal transmission may also occur.

Although gonococci can survive for brief periods outside the human reservoir, transmission is extremely rare. Transmission of purulent vulvovaginitis in prepubescent girls through a contaminated washing glove has been reported, but currently children who have gonorrhea are considered to be victims of sexual abuse by an infected adult.

The major reservoir for continued spread of gonorrhea is the asymptomatic patient. Among infected women 30–50% are asymptomatic or show no symptoms associated with a sexually transmitted disease. Among infected men only 5–10% are asymptomatic. Asymptomatic women and men remain infectious for months. In addition, people who have symptoms that they ignore may continue to spread the disease. The rate of transmission of gonococcal infection varies with the type of sexual practice.

The incubation period for gonorrhea is on average 2–7 days, but may vary between 1 and 14 days.

Meningococcal disease

Meningococcal disease is a major worldwide health problem.[29,30] Among populations of meningococci, different patterns of epidemiological behavior are recognized. These disease patterns are termed endemic, hyperendemic, epidemic and pandemic. The five serogroups A, B, C, Y and W135 account for almost all the disease-causing isolates.

In western Europe and the Americas, endemic meningococcal disease is caused mainly by serogroup B or C organisms occurring at a low level affecting 1–3/100,000 people.[30,31] Sporadic increases of disease incidence, termed hyperendemic are often localized to a small area or restricted to a particular population or community. For example, hyperendemic outbreaks due to group B have been reported in Brazil, The Netherlands and the UK.[25,32] Recently, increasing proportions of cases due to serogroup C have been reported from various European countries.[31,33] Serogroups A and C predominate in China, the Middle East and parts of Africa. In the African 'meningitis belt', disease occurs as major periodic epidemics occurring every 5–12 years and is caused by serogroup A with attack rates of 500/100,000 population or higher.[25,30] Occasionally, particularly virulent strains arise that cause pandemic outbreaks across continents.[25,29]

In the USA, Israel and Sweden, disease due to serogroup Y has increased in recent years.[30]

Serogroup B and C generally cause endemic cases and small outbreaks; in addition, distinct groups of genetically related serogroup B and C organisms have been recognized, which spread worldwide. Young adults who socialize frequently at discos and parties may particularly be at higher risk if they smoke.[34] These clusters may contain both serogroup B and C organisms, presumably because of horizontal gene transfer of capsule synthesis genes. As only a small fraction of the clones colonizing the throat of healthy individuals can cause disease, there is a difference in virulence potential of different meningococcal strains.[26]

In the mid-1970s, ET-5 complex serogroup B strains resulted in an increased incidence of meningococcal disease in north west Europe and Central and South America.[25] In other countries in Western Europe, ET-5 (serogroup B) strains were also isolated, although the increase in incidence was much lower. Strains of this cluster caused a severe epidemic in Cuba starting in the 1980s, followed by outbreaks in Florida in 1981 and 1982. The ET-5 strains were isolated only sporadically in North America in the following years, until in 1994 this complex was associated with an increased incidence in the states of Washington and Oregon. In Brazil and Chile the incidence of meningococcal disease rose due to strains of this complex in the mid-1980s and ET-5 strains were isolated in countries in Africa and Asia.[25]

Another cluster that has been identified worldwide is the lineage III. The first strain was isolated in The Netherlands.[32] Since 1980, the number of lineage III isolates has risen in The Netherlands, simultaneously with an increased incidence of disease. Most strains of this genotype are characterized by the serosubtype P1.4 (mostly B:4:P1.4), although lineage III strains with different serosubtypes and nonlineage III strains with P1.4 have been found. Since then B:4:P1.4 strains have been identified in many other European countries, resulting in an increased incidence of disease in Belgium and England and an ongoing epidemic in New Zealand.[25] Meningococci of the ET-37 complex cause much of group C cases worldwide as well as the international outbreaks of W135 disease among pilgrims returning from the Hajj and their close contacts.[35]

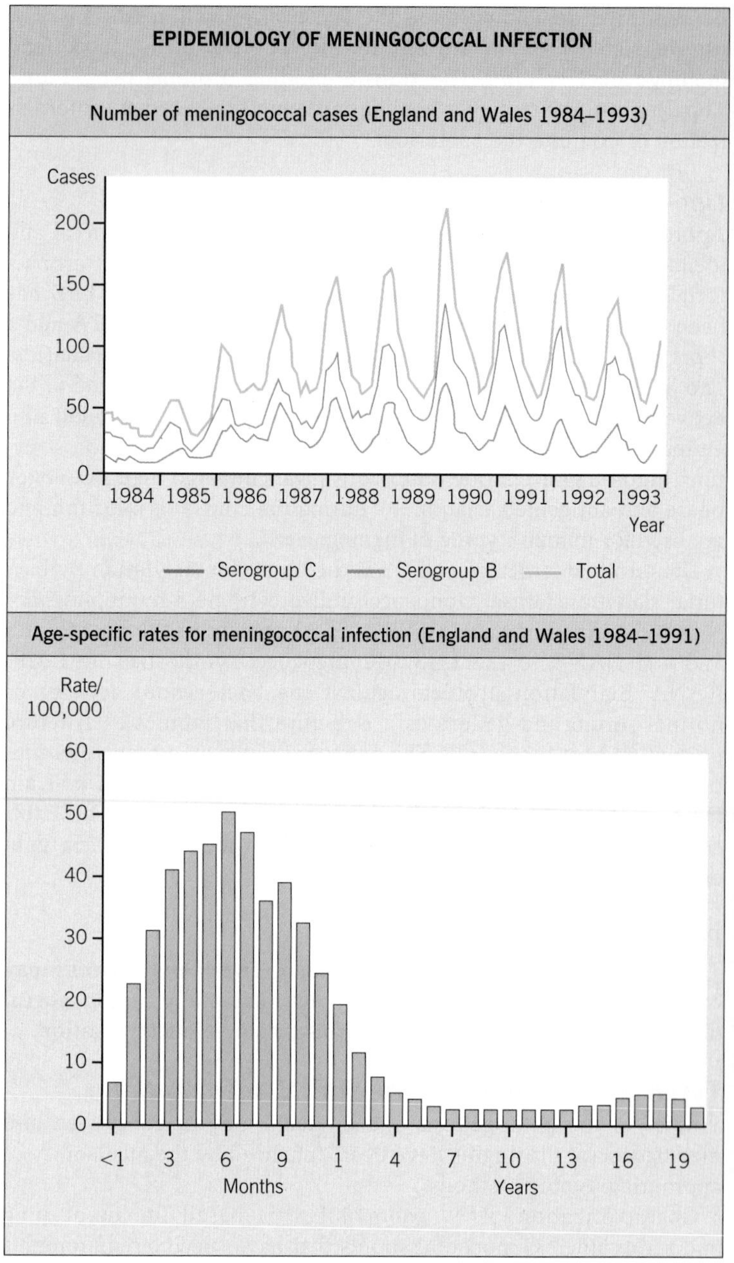

Fig. 227.3 Epidemiology of meningococcal infection. (Adapted from Jones.[36])

Meningococcal disease irrespective of the serogroup involved is often seasonal in nature. Serogroup A and C disease increases during the dry season in Africa. The number of serogroup B and C cases peaks during the winter months in the developed countries (Fig. 227.3).[36] The reasons for the different epidemiological characteristics of the different serogroups and the cyclic nature of outbreaks are poorly understood.

The incidence of meningococcal disease appears to predominate in children under school age in the Western world (see Fig. 227.3).[36] Infants and children aged between 1 and 4 years account for approximately 50% of the cases. In the meningitis belt young school-aged children represent the peak age group.

Transmission of meningococci is by respiratory droplets, requiring close contact. The attack rate among family members of a clinical case is 1000-fold higher than in the general population. *Neisseria meningitidis* has a particular preference for the nasopharyngeal mucosal membrane.[7] Humans are the only natural host, but the incidence of disease cannot be attributed simply to acquisition of any strain. Invasive disease can be produced by:

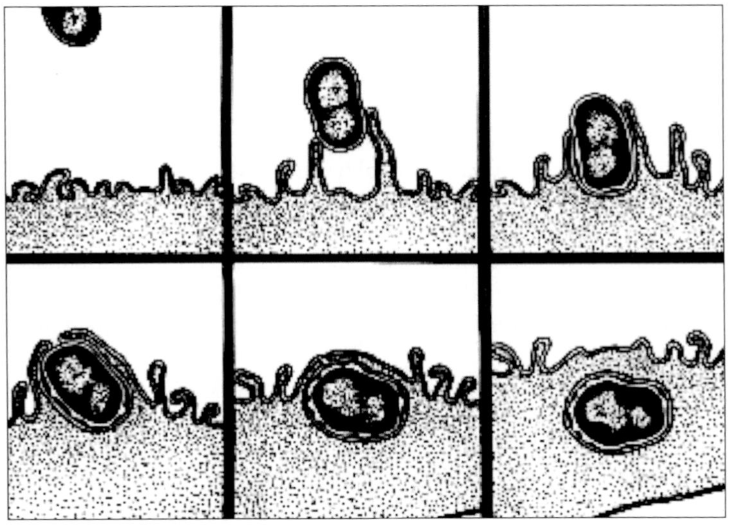

Fig. 227.4 Steps in the pathogenesis of *N. gonorrhoeae* infection. (Reproduced with permission from Weel.[40])

- a pathogenic organism;
- a susceptible host;
- the influence of a coincidental viral or mycoplasma upper respiratory tract infection; or
- most frequently, a combination of all four.

Although there can be sudden and large changes in the rates of meningococcal acquisition and carriage, there is in general much less variation in rates of carriage than in rates of disease.

PATHOGENESIS

Gonorrhea

Gonococci primarily infect columnar or cuboidal epithelium. In males the anterior urethra is the primary site of infection and in females the endocervix. Colonization may occur, often followed by infection once the mucosal membrane of the genitourinary tract, rectum, oropharynx or eyes has been reached by gonococci. In most cases infection remains restricted to the initial site of colonization, although certain gonococcal strains have the ability to spread to distant sites. The infective dose for the male urethra is over 10^3 gonococci and for the female cervix ranges from 10^2 to more than 10^7 gonococci.[27]

Histopathologic examination of infected mucosa shows gonococci attached to the epithelial cell surface and within the epithelial cells, and occasionally in the submucosal tissue. Fulminant infection is characterized by a vigorous neutrophil response, sloughing of the epithelium, development of (sub)mucosal microabscesses and exudation of pus with gonococci inside polymorphonuclear cells. Several weeks after the start of the infection gonococci can no longer be observed histologically or recovered by culture.

The first step in the pathogenesis of gonorrhea is the attachment of gonococci to mucosal surfaces and the ability of the gonococci to remain attached despite the continuous flow of body fluids (Fig. 227.4). Gonococci attach to microvilli of nonciliated columnar epithelial cells. Nearly all attached gonococci are piliated. Shortly after initial attachment gonococci become more tightly anchored to the epithelial cell surface. This second stage of binding is in part mediated by the gonococcal PII or Opa proteins to their cell receptors.[18,20] Opa also mediates the binding of gonococci to each other to form microcolonies, probably aiding the initial colonization.

After attachment there is a critical interaction between gonococci and host defenses.[37] Gonococci have multiple mechanisms by which the bacteria resist innate defense as well as the defense by antibodies elicited by a previous infection. Sialylation of LOS may limit or alter complement binding.[38] The binding of cross-reactive blocking antibodies to Rmp (protein III) hinders the binding of bacterial antibodies.[39] *Neisseria gonorrhoeae* varies its surface proteins, especially pili antigens, by phase variation and antigenic variation.[22] In the case of pili, gonococci have an antigenic repertoire that may be as large as one million different antigenic variants. The antigenic repertoire for protein II (Opa) is smaller. The LOS composition is also changed due to antigenic variation.

Gonococci secrete an IgA protease that specifically cleaves IgA_1 in the hinge region. In response to environmental conditions gonococci synthesize iron-repressed gonococcal outer membrane proteins, which bind lactoferrin and transferrin, providing iron internalization. Cell damage is caused by LOS shed from viable bacteria and peptidoglycan fragments liberated from lysed bacteria.

In vitro it has been shown that after attachment gonococci invade epithelial cells as a result of endocytosis[40] (see Fig. 227.4). Whether this process represents a normal feature of uncomplicated mucosal infection is unclear. Cellular invasion is an important factor in the pathogenesis of a complicated infection such as salpingitis or disseminated infection. Invasion of gonococci is characterized by the formation of intimate contacts between the bacteria and the cell membrane, the zipper mechanism. Por and certain Opas facilitate invasion. Por is inserted into the plasma membrane of eukaryotic cells, probably making pores. Inside the cells the porin protein binds to calmodulin. As a result of this, microfilament-dependent processes are modified.

Por IB variant strains inserting into the host cell membrane remain localized, whereas Por IA variants translocate and are associated with disseminated gonorrhea. In addition, gonococci produce Yop-like substances, that interfere with host cell signal transduction systems and affect the host cell cytoskeleton. Bacteria-mediated rearrangement of actin is associated with forced endocytosis.

Inside the cells gonococci are transported within vacuoles, which coalesce to form larger vacuoles. Por prevents phagolysome fusion. Sheltered from innate host defenses, the gonococci multiply. Vacuoles fuse with the basement membrane. Although the majority of phagocytosed gonococci die, the viable gonococci are discharged into the subepithelial connective tissue.

As gonococci do not produce exotoxins, tissue damage results from the bacterial cell wall components such as LOS and peptidoglycan. Both constituents induce the production of tumor necrosis factor (TNF)-α. The inflammatory reaction is most likely responsible for the local symptoms.

A prominent feature of gonococcal infection is the intimate association with granulocytes, intracellularly as well as extracellularly. Opa+ gonococci adhere to granulocytes, bypassing phagocytosis and killing.[37] Also pili have antiphagocytic properties and sialylation of LOS reduces the opsonization of bacteria. The gonococci are able to resist oxidative killing inside phagocytes and may survive inside the granulocytes by binding of Por to calmodulin and upregulation of catalase production.

Certain strains have the ability to spread. Strains isolated from the fallopian tube lack Opa (protein II). Gonococci from other distant sites have the Por IA type protein. Host factors also play a role in the dissemination of gonococci. People who have terminal complement deficiencies have a high risk of developing bacteremia.[41]

Meningococcal disease

Infection due to *N. meningitidis* commonly results from asymptomatic nasopharyngeal carriage.[7] At any time approximately 10–20% of the population may be carriers of meningococci. Protective antibodies are evoked within 1 week by the meningococcal carrier state. Susceptibility to infection has been shown to correlate with the absence of specific antibodies. Another important host factor playing a role in the pathogenesis of meningococcal disease is the complement system.[42]

The pathogenic effects of meningococci lie in the ability of the organism to traverse the epithelial lining of the respiratory tract, evade the host immune system and invade the bloodstream (Fig. 227.5).[43,44] Meningococci either disseminate further into the subarachnoid space or remain circulating in the bloodstream. The mechanisms by which this occurs are only partially understood. *In vitro* studies have shown that meningococci adhere to the host cell receptor CD46, a complement regulatory protein[45] of the microvilli on nonciliated epithelial cells via type IV pili and class 5 proteins.[14,20,21] Nonencapsulated strains adhere better than capsulated parent strains. Adherent meningococci cause ciliostasis at a distance, probably due to the induction of TNF-α or interleukin (IL)-1 by bacterial cell wall constituents. Meningococci produce $sIgA_1$ protease, which is though to help bacterial survival on the mucosal membranes. After mucosal adherence meningococci may initiate a bacterial-directed endocytosis.[46] Nonencapsulated meningococci traverse the cytoplasm, whereas encapsulated meningococci are transported in phagocytic vacuoles. The IgA1 protease and PorB may promote the survival of meningococci in the epithelial cell.[30]

In the migration from the mucosa to the deeper tissues the pili are downregulated. However, *in vitro* studies have shown that piliated meningococci associate with endothelial cells more readily than their nonpiliated counterparts. The presence of pili is also associated with a greater degree of cytopathic effects, including disruption of intercellular junctions and rounding up of cells.[43] It is not known why in an unknown percentage of colonized persons pathogenic meningococci are not adequately contained by the local host defenses and traverse the endothelial lining of the vascular bed, probably through widened intercellular junctions.[44] In the bloodstream meningococci may:

- be inactivated by the combined actions of antibody, complement and granulocytes; or
- reach the subarachnoid space; or
- multiply within the circulation.

Little is known of this early bacteremic phase and dissemination to the subarachnoid space. It is thought that there are at least three potential mechanisms by which bacteria may gain access to the subarachnoid space:[44]

- paracellular transport after disruption of tight junctions of the blood–brain barrier in the chord plexus;
- transport within circulating phagocytic cells, such as monocytes; and
- transcellular transport within endothelial cell vacuoles.

Systemic meningococcal infection is a bacteremic disease. The number of bacteria/ml of blood has been correlated with the severity of clinical presentation, probably due to the quantity of LOS.[24] Indeed, there is a correlation between clinical outcome and strains of meningococci that shed large amounts of LOS from surface blebs. The subsequent tissue injury is related to the host inflammatory response to LOS; circulating levels of proinflammatory mediators TNF-α, IL-1 and interferon-γ at admission are strongly correlated with outcome.

Pathophysiologic sequelae of meningitis are also due to host responses to the presence of bacteria within the subarachnoid space. Host responses are elicited by intact bacteria as well as bacterial constituents such as LOS and peptidoglycan. They include the influx of leukocytes into the subarachnoid space (Fig. 227.6) and the release of soluble inflammatory mediators such as various cytokines, prostaglandins and platelet-activating factor.

Individuals who have inherited deficiencies in the late complement components (C6–C9) have a greatly increased risk of developing meningococcal infection. Intriguingly, however, they acquire the infection at a much later age, have frequent recurrences and the fatality rate is much lower than for normocomplementemic individuals.[42]

Other genetic defects such as polymorphisms in the mannose-binding lectin[47,48] and TNF-α may also alter susceptibility to the disease.[49]

PREVENTION

Gonococcal infection

Condoms provide a high degree of protection from acquisition of gonorrhea, as well as other STDs. Other important approaches for prevention of gonorrhea are early diagnosis and treatment, partner notification and screening and case finding. A new approach is the use of topical microbicides for intravaginal or intrarectal use.

Attempts to develop a gonococcal vaccine have been hampered by the high degree of antigenic variability in pili, Opa and LOS of gonococci during the natural course of infection. Porin (protein I), antigenically stable, inducing specific antibodies, is a preferred protein to produce a vaccine.[50]

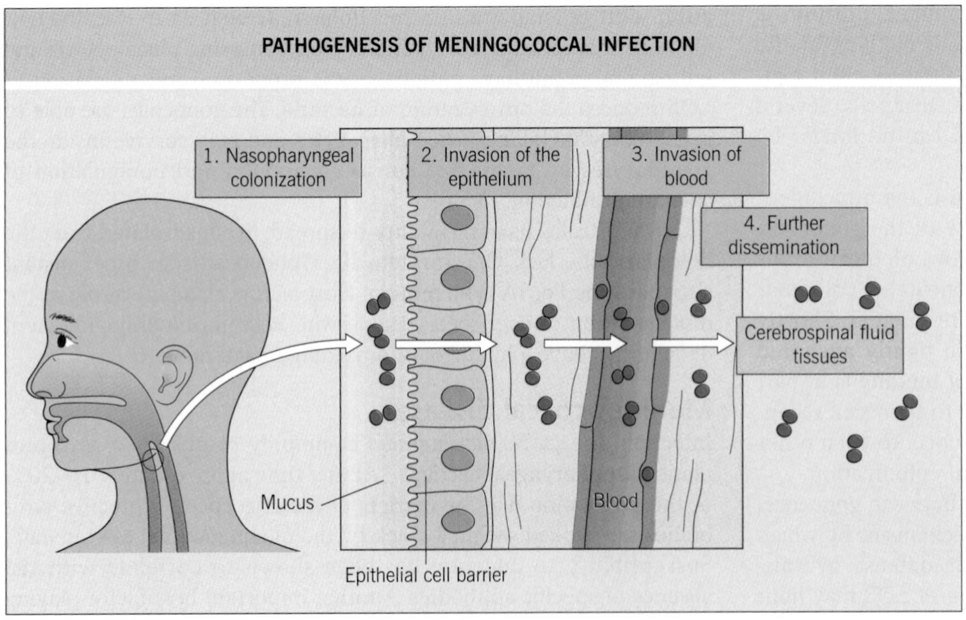

Fig. 227.5 Pathogenesis of meningococcal infection. (Adapted from Virji.[43])

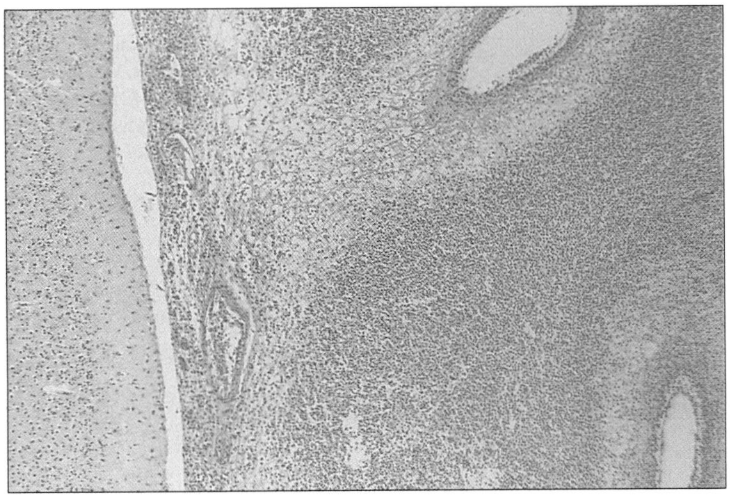

Fig. 227.6 Bacterial meningitis. Exudate of acute inflammatory cells in the subarachnoid space. Courtesy of P Garen. (Reproduced with permission from Mims *et al.*[9])

Meningococcal disease

Prevention of meningococcal disease is based on two different approaches: chemoprophylaxis and the use of vaccines.[30,51]

Chemoprophylaxis

The aim of chemoprophylaxis is to reduce secondary cases of meningococcal disease and to arrest outbreaks. The risk of a secondary case among close contacts of the index case in the household setting is 150–1000 times higher than that in the general population. Children are at greatest risk, but secondary disease can occur at all ages. Risk is maximal in the week following recognition of the index case but extends for several weeks.

Many of the antibiotics that are useful in treating infection do not effectively eradicate or prevent carriage of meningococci because of their inability to achieve adequate levels in oropharyngeal secretions. A number of agents, however, have been shown to be effective.[30,52] Minocycline, a tetracycline, can eradicate meningococcal carriage, but its use is associated with an unacceptably high incidence of side-effects, particularly vestibular problems causing vertigo. Rifampin (rifampicin) is widely used as a chemoprophylactic agent now. Carriage is eradicated in 70–95% of the contacts after a 2-day course. Failures may be due to the emergence of meningococci resistant to rifampin. Side-effects include discoloration of soft contact lenses, interference with the oral contraceptive pill and red urine and it is contraindicated during pregnancy. Two other antibiotics have also been shown to effectively eradicate meningococcal carrier status. Ceftriaxone, in a single intramuscular dose, was 97% effective in household contacts after 1–2 weeks after infection. The advantage of ceftriaxone is that it can be used in pregnancy and to small children.

Ciprofloxacin and ofloxacin as a single oral dose have an efficacy of 93–97% in eliminating carriage.[52]

Chemoprophylaxis is recommended for close household contacts of cases and other intimate contacts. In addition, patients who have meningococcal disease should receive chemoprophylaxis before discharge from the hospital, because parenteral antibiotic treatment of meningococcal disease (except ceftriaxone) is unreliable in eliminating meningococci from the nasopharynx.

Vaccines

In the past two decades, increasing effort has been put into the development of new meningococcal vaccines, in particular against serogroup B disease. Two main approaches have been taken, based on polysaccharide or outer membrane protein (OMP) components.

Polysaccharide vaccines

These vaccines have been used successfully to reduce the incidence of infection among military recruits, to reduce the progress of epidemics of group A disease and to protect individuals known to be susceptible because of various complement deficiencies.[53] The vast majority of antibodies appear to bind to epitopes that are affected when the polysaccharide is de-O-acetylated, indicating that O-acetyl groups are critical in a polysaccharide vaccine.[54] However, immunity provided by polysaccharide vaccines is short-lived in adults (as no T-helper response occurs) and no protection is achieved in young children. Polysaccharide vaccines are used by travelers visiting countries with a high incidence of meningococcal disease and in these cases the short duration of the immune response is immaterial. A drawback of polysaccharide vaccines is that there is no vaccine in use against serogroup B meningococci, which causes most cases of disease in temperate countries. Early studies with serogroup B polysaccharide vaccines failed to show evidence of antibody response in human volunteers. There was a reluctance to include the group B polysaccharide in further vaccination approaches because of the possibility of inducing an autoimmune response.[51]

Conjugate vaccines

Following the success of the conjugate vaccines to prevent *Haemophilus influenzae* type b meningitis, serogroup A, C, Y and W135 meningococcal polysaccharides have been conjugated to carrier proteins.[51] Such polysaccharide protein vaccines are immunogenic in young infants. They induce a T cell-dependent response, prime immunologic memory and result in long-term protection. Initial field trials of these vaccines yielded encouraging data. In the United Kingdom meningococcal group C conjugate vaccine was introduced in health care programs in late 1999.[33] Rates of disease caused by serogroup C meningococci fell rapidly in the vaccinated age group.[55]

Age-specific vaccine efficacy had been estimated to be 88% in young children and 95% in young adolescents. Carriage of serogroup C meningococci studied in the vaccinated young adolescents group showed a reduction by 66%.[56] Meningococci have the capacity to exchange genes that induce the enzymes involved in capsular synthesis.[10,11] It has been documented that the bacteria can switch from serogroup C to serogroup B or vice versa. Capsule switching, replacement by strains having capsular groups not contained in the vaccine providing serogroup specific protection, and replacement by non-groupable strains having the genetic material encoding the capsule but downregulating the capsule expression may occur with the widespread use of monovalent serogroup conjugate vaccines, but have not been established yet.

Bivalent A plus C polysaccharide conjugate vaccines have been assessed in clinical trials. Multivalent polysaccharide A,C,Y and W135 protein conjugate vaccines are being developed.[51]

Outer member protein vaccines

The observation that outer membrane components stimulated cross-reactive antibodies and promoted complement-mediated, bactericidal killing of capsulated strains led to alternative approaches to vaccination against serogroup B disease. The first experimental outer membrane vaccines used membrane preparations as close to the native membrane structure as possible. Detergent extraction was used to remove LOS from outer membrane vesicles obtained from a common disease-causing strain. Such vaccines were used in clinical trials and showed efficacies in the range of 50–80%. However, young children were not protected. There are a variety of novel OMP-based meningococcal vaccines currently under investigation,[51] such as construction of multivalent vaccine strains based on common variants of Por A;

OMPs complexes with group C polysaccharide; immunization with synthetic peptides; use of other organisms as vehicles for the delivery of a meningococcal OMPs; and investigation of vaccine potential of iron-regulated proteins (Tbp-1 and Tbp-2). The rational design of OMP-based vaccines must take into account the antigenic variability of circulating meningococcal strains to determine the most appropriate epitopes for inclusion in a vaccine. Therefore, new vaccine candidates on the basis of conserved antigens are being identified.

Novel vaccine candidates

The completion of the genomic sequencing of a serogroup B meningococcus made it possible to find open reading frames encoding novel surface-exposed proteins.[57] These proteins and those derived from a serogroup A meningococcus and a gonococcus (*N. gonorrhoeae*) were compared to identify similar conserved surface-exposed proteins. Such proteins were cloned, expressed in *Escherichia coli* and antisera were prepared to the recombinant proteins. Genome-derived antigens inducing antibodies which bind to the serogroup B meningococcal surface and eliciting bactericidal activity against serogroup B meningococcus may be vaccine candidates for providing broad protection.[57]

CLINICAL FEATURES

Gonococcal infection

Neisseria gonorrhoeae usually causes an infection of the urethra (urethritis) and cervix (cervicitis).[27] The bacterium may spread to the upper urogenital tract or may disseminate.

In addition, gonococci may cause localized infections at sites outside the urogenital tract.

Urogenital gonococcal infection of men

Acute anterior urethritis

This is the most common manifestation of gonorrhea (Fig. 227.7). It is characterized by a purulent urethral discharge and dysuria.

Acute epididymitis

This is the most common local complication of gonococcal infection and usually presents as gradually increasing unilateral scrotal pain.

Urogenital gonococcal infection of women

Cervicitis

The endocervix is the primary site of urogenital gonococcal infection. The infection is characterized by (muco)purulent discharge and intermenstrual bleeding, but is often asymptomatic.

Acute anterior urethritis

Urethral infection is present in 70–90% of women who have gonococcal cervicitis.

Abscess formation in glands adjacent to the vagina

About 35% of the women who have genital tract gonococcal infection have an infection of Bartholin's glands or Skene's ducts, by which abscess formation may occur.

Ascending gonococcal infection

Endometritis or acute salpingitis develops in 10–20% of women who have lower urogenital gonococcal infection. The high frequency of the asymptomatic infection of the endocervix is an important factor in the development of these complications because the initial infection is neither recognized nor treated. Symptoms of this clinical syndrome of pelvic inflammatory disease (PID) include lower abdominal pain abnormal cervical discharge and bleeding, fever and peripheral leukocytosis. The onset of salpingitis due to gonococci occurs early rather than late in infection and either during or shortly after menstruation.

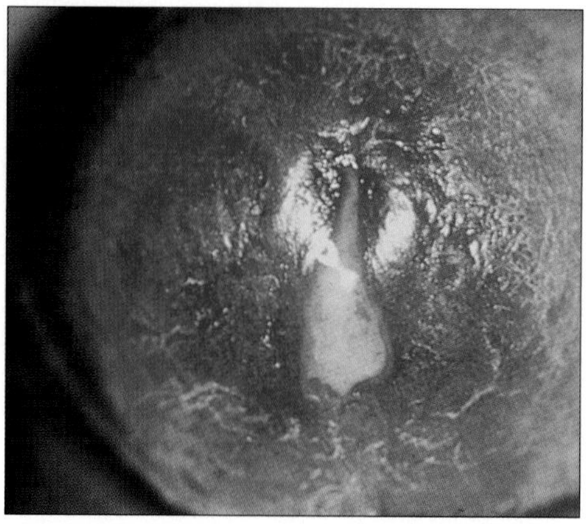

Fig. 227.7 Gonococcal urethritis. Courtesy of J Clay. (Reproduced with permission from Mims *et al.*[9])

Obstruction of the fallopian tubes leading to infertility occurs in 10–20% of patients who have PID after a single episode of gonorrhea.

Gonorrhea in pregnancy

In pregnant women gonorrhea is associated with an increased risk of spontaneous abortion, premature labor, early rupture of fetal membranes and perinatal infant mortality. Pelvic inflammatory disease is uncommon after the first trimester.

Gonorrhea in children

Historically gonococcal infection in children included only ophthalmia neonatorum (acute gonococcal conjunctivitis). Recently, studies have shown that children can acquire gonococcal infection by sexual contact with an infected person. Such infection therefore indicates sexual abuse. In girls the infection often produces a vulvovaginitis. Complications affecting the internal genital organs are rare.

Localized gonococcal infection outside the urogenital tract

Proctitis

Anorectal gonorrhea is present in up to 5% of women who have gonorrhea, although gonococci can be cultured from the anorectal region of 40% of women with gonorrhea. A similar proportion of homosexual men have positive rectal cultures for gonococci. Proctitis is manifested by anal pruritus, tenesmus, purulent discharge or rectal bleeding.

Pharyngeal gonorrhea

Pharyngeal infection occurs in 10–20% of women who have gonorrhea and in 10–25% of homosexual men who have the infection and in 3–7% of heterosexual men. The infection is due to orogenital sexual exposure. Most cases are asymptomatic and resolve spontaneously.

Acute conjunctivitis

Ocular gonococcal infection is seen in neonates. Ophthalmia neonatorum is acquired during passage through an infected birth canal. In adults ocular infection usually results from autoinoculation of the conjunctiva in a person who has the infection. Gonococcal conjunctivitis is usually severe, with an overt purulent exudate and corneal ulceration.

Disseminated gonococcal infection

In 0.5–3% of infected individuals gonococci invade the bloodstream, resulting in disseminated gonococcal infection.

Dermatitis–arthritis–tenosynovitis syndrome

This infection is characterized by fever, hemorrhagic painful skin lesions, primarily on the hands or feet, tenosynovitis, polyarthralgias and frank arthritis (Fig. 227.8).

Monoarticular septic arthritis

In 30–40% of patients who have disseminated gonococcal infection, gonococci are localized in one joint and cause a purulent arthritis.

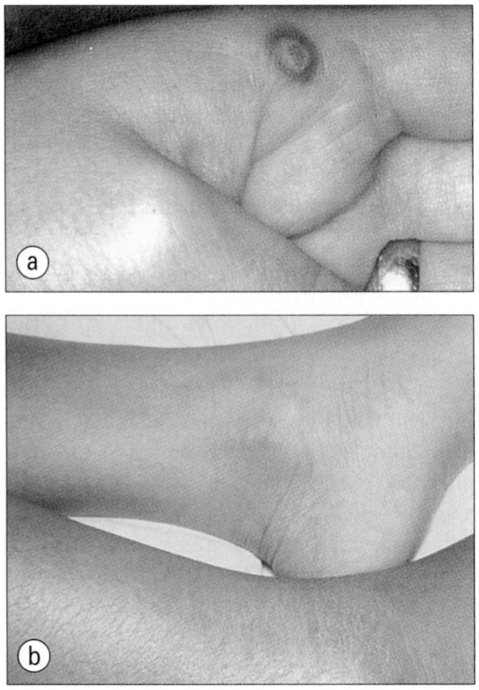

Fig. 227.8 Disseminated gonococcal infection. (a) Skin lesions. Courtesy of JS Bingham. (b) Arthritis. Courtesy of TF Sellers Jr. (Reproduced with permission from Mims *et al.*[9])

The elbows, wrists, fingers and knee or ankle joints are commonly involved.

Perihepatitis

Acute perihepatitis (Fitz-Hugh–Curtis syndrome) occurs by direct extension of gonococci from the fallopian tube, lymphangitic spread or bacteremic dissemination to the liver capsule.

Endocarditis and meningitis

These complications are reported in 1–2% of patients who have disseminated gonococcal infection.

Meningococcal infection

On presentation 60% of cases have had symptoms for less than 24 hours and 12–20% for less than 2 days. Meningococcal disease may be manifested in various forms.[24,30,58]

Meningitis

The most frequent form of meningococcal infection is acute pyogenic meningitis due to inflammation of the meninges. Meningitis may occur with or without meningococcemia. Of patients who have meningococcal disease 75% have meningitis; 40% of them also have bacteremia.

Meningococcemia

Meningococcemia may occur with or without meningitis and may be transient, occult or result in severe sepsis. Bacteremia without meningitis occurs in 7–10% of patients. A distinguishing factor of meningococcemia is the appearance of skin lesions (Fig. 227.9). Initially these lesions appear on the mucous membranes and conjunctivae. Three patterns may be seen:

- a maculopapular rash.
- petechiae, and
- ecchymotic hemorrhagic or necrotic lesions or purpura fulminans.

However, skin lesions may be atypical, evanescent or even entirely absent in patients who have blood culture-positive meningococcal sepsis. Meningococcal sepsis may progress to disseminated intravascular coagulation characterized by increasing petechiae or purpura fulminans, resulting in extensive areas of tissue destruction secondary to coagulopathy, rapid onset of hypotension and adrenal hemorrhage (Waterhouse–Friderichsen syndrome).

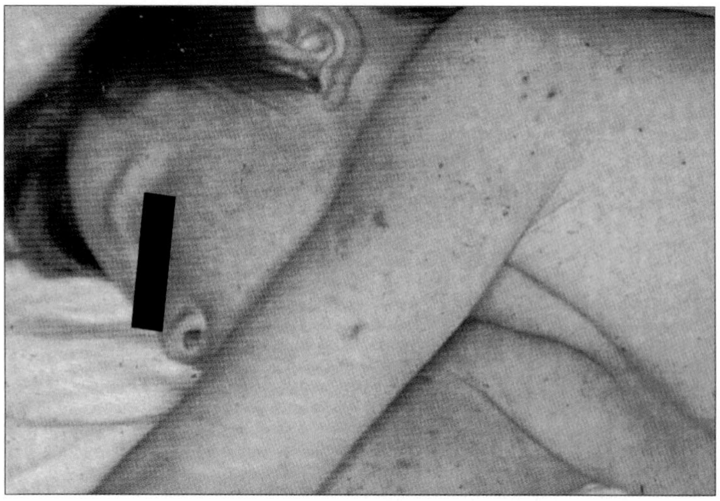

Fig. 227.9 Typical rash of meningococcal sepsis. Fine erythematous macules and petechiae are present in some areas.

Chronic meningococcemia

Persistent meningococcal bacteremia is associated with low-grade fever, rash and arthritis (arthritis–dermatitis syndrome).

Respiratory infection

Meningococci are implicated as the etiologic agent in approximately 5–14% of patients who have community-acquired pneumonia. Pharyngitis is associated with recent contact with individuals who are colonized by meningococci and is often a prior symptom and sign of serious meningococcal disease.

Other infections

Neisseria meningitidis may cause other infections as a result of hematogenous spread. Infections due to blood-borne dissemination include endocarditis, pericarditis, arthritis, endophthalmitis, osteomyelitis, conjunctivitis and peritonitis. Arthritis is particularly common with an incidence of 11% in adults and 5% in children.

LABORATORY DIAGNOSIS

Gonococcal infection

Because *N. gonorrhoeae* can cause infection at a variety of body sites, collection of appropriate specimens for diagnosis depends upon the clinical manifestations and the sites exposed. In men suspected of having gonorrhea, urethral exudate is the best specimen. In females cervix swabs are preferred over urethral or vaginal specimens. Swabs coated with charcoal to absorb toxic substance are transported to the laboratory in specific transport media (Stuart's or Amies's). Specimens from the male urethra or the female endocervix should be collected from all cases of suspected gonococcal infection. Both specimens are taken for direct examination and culture. A finding of neutrophils containing Gram-negative cocci in the Gram-stained smear is presumptive evidence of gonococcal infection (Fig. 227.10). Gram stain is highly sensitive and specific for diagnosing genital gonorrhea in men. Gram-stained smears made from endocervix specimens from symptomatic women have a sensitivity of only 40–60% relative to culture, but a high predictive value. In asymptomatic women Gram stain has a low predictive value and is not useful.

Direct nonculture tests are also used. An enzyme-linked immunosorbent assay test detects gonococcal antigen. A nucleic acid probe test is also available. The polymerase chain reaction has also been applied for direct detection of gonococci in clinical specimens. The ligase chain reaction using highly sensitive nucleic acid amplification is used on urine and urogenital specimens. It has proved to be as

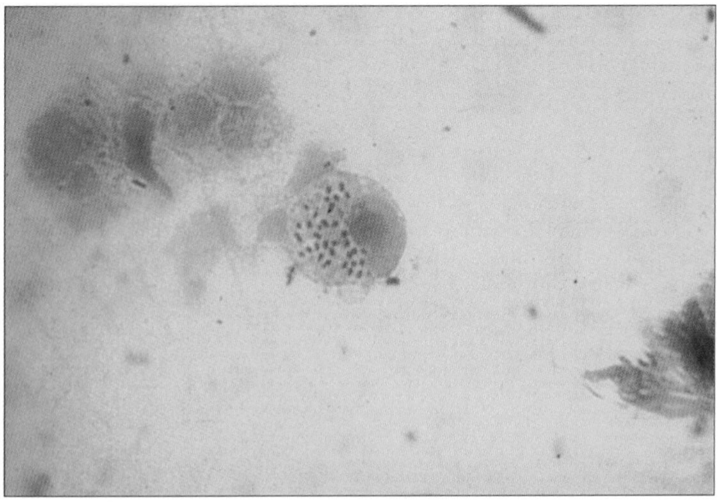

Fig. 227.10 Gram stain of a urethral discharge from a male who has gonorrhea. Note the intracellular Gram-negative diplococci with neutrophils.

sensitive and specific as culture. Ligase chain reaction has the advantage of requiring only a freshly voided urine sample, avoiding invasive sampling of the endocervix and urethra.

Culture is used for making a diagnosis of gonococcal infection of the urethra, the endocervix or an extragenital site. Depending upon sexual practices, samples are also collected from the rectum and/or pharynx. In cases of disseminated gonococcal infection blood cultures are obtained and biopsies from skin lesions and joint fluid aspirates are cultured. Maximal recovery of gonococci from infected sites is obtained when specimens for culture are plated directly onto growth medium. If this is not possible or practical, various commercial nonnutritive transport media are available.

Diagnosis of gonococcal infection is made at two levels: presumptive and confirmed. Antimicrobial treatment may be started based on the results of the presumptive tests, but additional tests have to be performed to yield a confirmatory diagnosis.

A variety of enriched selective media are available to grow gonococci. Commonly used media (Thayer–Martin medium and Martin–Lewis medium) contain lysed or heated blood (chocolate agar) supplemented with growth factors and a variety of antimicrobials to suppress the growth of other bacteria and yeast. Specimens taken from sites that are normally sterile are cultured on antibiotic-free media because occasional strains of gonococci are susceptible to the antibiotics added to the growth media. Growth media are placed in a carbon dioxide incubator or candle jar at 95–98.6°F. After incubation for 24–48 hours colonies of gonococci have a characteristic appearance. Isolates on primary culture media are predominantly of the P^+ and P^{++} (piliated) colony types, being small, glistening and raised. After subculture P^- (nonpiliated) colonies appear. They are larger and flatter than P^+ colonies and there is no glistening. Smears are prepared from suspicious colonies and examined with Gram stain and the oxidase and catalase tests. Gram-negative diplococci that give a positive oxidase and catalase test may be *N. gonorrhoeae*.

For confirmatory identification of gonococci other types of *Neisseria* spp. as well *Branhamella* and *Kingella* spp. have to be considered. Certain characteristics differentiate between species of the genera.

Confirmatory identification tests include carbohydrate utilization test, monoclonal antibody fluorescence test, coagulation test, chromogenic detection of specific enzyme activities or the DNA probe culture confirmation test. Gonococci oxidize glucose (but not maltose, sucrose and lactose). Serologic tests are not used, because none has sufficient sensitivity and specificity for clinical use.

Meningococcal infection

Cerebrospinal fluid (CSF), blood, skin biopsies and aspirates are relevant specimens for the diagnosis of meningococcal disease. Additionally, synovial fluid, sputum and conjunctival and nasopharyngeal swabs may be cultured if clinically indicated. Because meningococci, like gonococci, are susceptible to desiccation and temperature extremes, specimens should be cultured as soon as possible after collection.

For presumptive diagnosis appropriate specimens are examined by Gram stain. Gram-stained smears are made from uncentrifuged CSF if the CSF is cloudy and from centrifuged CSF if the CSF is clear. The probability of detecting Gram-negative diplococci, typically present inside as well as outside polymorphonuclear cells, depends on the number of bacteria present. The majority of the smears will be positive when the CSF bacterial count is 10^5 bacteria per ml or greater. Smears from CSF containing 10^3 bacteria per ml or less will be positive in only 25%; on average 60–90% of cases of CSF specimen will have a positive Gram stain, since the bacterial number per ml CSF ranges from 1.5×10^2 to 6×10^5 (mean 1.3×10^5). Gram-stained smears from petechial skin lesions due to meningococcemia may detect meningococci in more than 70% of cases.

Direct examination of CSF to detect meningococcal capsular polysaccharides can be done by performing direct antigen tests. Currently direct antigen tests contain a polyclonal antibody for serogroups A, C, Y and W135 and a reagent for serogroup B. Using latex agglutination and coagglutination tests, 0.02–0.05mg antigen per ml CSF from infected patients can be detected. The sensitivity of the tests is only about 50%.

The mean CSF leukocyte count is higher in patients who have meningitis than in patients who have meningococcemia. The proportion of polymorphonuclear cells in CSF from patients who have meningitis ranges from 49% to 98% with a mean of 86%. Other CSF abnormalities include low glucose concentration and an elevated protein concentration. In patients partially treated with antibiotics for meningococcal disease the CSF leukocyte count, glucose and protein concentration and the antigen tests remain abnormal for several days, whereas bacteria are not evident on smear and CSF culture is often negative. Blood cultures are positive in only 50% of the patients with meningococcal disease. In those who have received antibiotics prior to the collection of blood for culture, blood cultures are sterile. A nasopharyngeal swab from young children can provide worthwhile information in cases of suspected meningococcal disease. Meningococci are rarely recovered from healthy young children. Therefore, a well-capsulated serogroup B or C meningococcus grown from a throat swab is strong evidence that a meningococcus is the cause of disease.[58]

The aforementioned tests should be accompanied by a culture of specimens on nonselective growth media in order to isolate *N. meningitidis*. It is noteworthy that CSF cultures may be positive even when other tests are negative. Such a finding is encountered particularly in early meningococcal meningitis and in patients who have meningococcemia without clinical evidence of meningitis. Appropriate nonselective media are 5% sheep blood agar (in contrast to gonococci, meningococci grow well on this medium) and chocolate agar. Selective media used to culture nasopharyngeal specimens are the same as those mentioned for gonococci. Most blood culture media support the growth of meningococci, although liquid sodium polyanethole sulfonate (SPS)-containing media may be toxic for some meningococcal strains.

After inoculation, meningococci will grow quite rapidly on agar media in a 3–7% carbon dioxide-enriched atmosphere with rather high humidity at 95–98.6°F. After 18–24 hours of incubation flat, gray–brown, translucent, smooth, 1–3mm in diameter colonies of *N. meningitidis* are present. Mucoid colonies are often serogroup A or C strains. If sufficient growth is present a presumptive diagnosis is made with a Gram stain, an oxidase test and a catalase test. The finding of Gram-negative diplococci that are oxidase and catalase positive grown from appropriate specimens may be sufficient to initiate antibiotic treatment for meningococcal disease. For confirmatory identification other species of *Neisseria*, *Kingella* and *Branhamella* have to be taken into account. Characteristics that differentiate *N. meningitidis* from these species are the production of acid from glucose and maltose. Gonococci acidify only glucose, and *N. lactamica* produces acid from glucose, maltose and lactose, though a number of commensal *Neisseria* spp. may be misidentified as *N. meningitidis* on the basis of carbohydrate oxidation. In order to specify *N. meningitidis* enzyme substrate tests are also used. Meningococci produce γ-glutamylaminopeptidase. In addition, the polysaccharide from sucrose test differentiates between *N. polysaccharea* (polysaccharide positive) and *N. meningitidis* (polysaccharide negative).

A polymerase chain reaction test has been used for the detection of meningococci in CSF or blood. This test may be useful to confirm the diagnosis in patients who have had antibiotic treatment prior to collection of CSF and whose CSF Gram stain, antigen test and culture are negative.

MANAGEMENT

Gonorrhea

Data from the pre-antibiotic era indicate that in males the urethral infection subsides after 2–3 months. Repeated infection, if untreated, leads to stricture of the urethra. Such sequelae are now rare, because the signs of urethritis bring most men to diagnosis and treatment.

In 10–20% of women gonorrhea results in ascending genital infection and PID, manifested by endometritis, salpingitis, tubo-ovarian abscess and pelvic peritonitis. Infertility due to fallopian tube obstructions is the most serious sequela of PID and occurs in 15–20% of women after a single episode and in 50–80% of women after three or more episodes.[27] In addition, disseminated gonococcal infections may occur. In the pre-antibiotic era *N. gonorrhoeae* was a frequent cause of endocarditis and meningitis.

In 1937 sulfonamides were introduced for treatment of gonorrhea. Sulfonamide-resistant strains emerged rapidly and penicillin was traditionally used to treat gonorrhea. Before 1976 *N. gonorrhoeae* was not generally tested for its antimicrobial susceptibility, although gonococcal isolates with a decreased sensitivity for penicillin (MIC >0.1mg/1) had been recovered. This chromosomally encoded penicillin insensitivity is the result of a number of mutations at the *pen A*, *pen B env* and *mtr* genes. Mutations in the *pen* genes alter penicillin-binding proteins, reducing their affinity for penicillin. The mtr locus is an efflux pump. Mutations of *mtr* and *env* alter the permeability of the gonococcal membrane. Gonococci with this form of penicillin resistance were designated chromosomally resistant *N. gonorrhoeae* (CMRNG). These strains represent 1–6% of all gonococci in the Western world. In 1976 strains of gonococci that were totally resistant to penicillin due to β-lactamase production were recovered.[27] These isolates contain a plasmid (Pc^r) that carries the genes for a TEM-1 type β-lactamase. Although the prevalence of such penicillinase-producing *N. gonorrhoeae* (PPNG) remains stable at about 5–10% in Western Europe and the USA, it is no longer common practice to treat patients who have gonococcal infection with penicillin. One of the reasons for this is that failure to cure a case of gonorrhea has implications for the infected patient as well as for public health, because of the possibility for transmission of the disease and the resistant gonococcus. Therefore, antibiotic regimens for gonorrhea require high patient compliance and an efficacy of 100%. In addition, the antibiotic regimens for gonorrhea should have potential efficacy for a concurrent sexually transmitted disease (STD) infection, such as syphilis and STD due to *Chlamydia trachomatis*. Many studies have shown that *C. trachomatis* can be recovered from 15–30% of men who have gonococcal urethritis and from 35–50% of women who have endocervical gonorrhea.[59] In 1985 *N. gonorrhoeae* strains were isolated that showed high-level tetracycline resistance, designated TRNG, so tetracycline is also no longer recommended for the primary treatment of uncomplicated gonococcal infections. This type of tetracycline resistance is due to a conjugative plasmid into which the *tetM* transposon has been inserted. The *tetM* determinant is readily transferable to other gonococci and various other microorganisms. The prevalence of TRNG among gonococci in Western Europe and the USA is about 5–8%.

Present recommendations for treatment of uncomplicated gonorrhea are based on regimens that provide high efficacy, have potential, efficacy against concurrent sexually transmitted bacterial infections, particularly *Chlamydia trachomatis*, and that can be given as a single dose in order to obtain maximal patient compliance. Typical regimens are ceftriaxone (one intramuscular dose) or a single oral dose of cefixime, ciprofloxacin or ofloxacin.[60] Each of the therapies also includes a single oral dose of azithromycin or doxycycline for 1 week for the treatment of co-infecting *C. trachomatis*. One oral dose of azithromycin is active against both gonococci and *C. trachomatis*. Ciprofloxacin, ofloxacin and doxycycline are contraindicated during pregnancy. Pregnant women who have gonococcal infection are treated with ceftriaxone followed by 7–10 days of erythromycin. In the past decade gonococcal isolates with decreased sensitivity to ciprofloxin and ofloxacin have been isolated,[61] particularly in South East Asia and Africa. The high-level resistance (MIC >1–16mg/l) is chromosomally mediated, mainly due to mutations in *gyr A* (DNA gyrase) and *par C* (topoisomerase IV). The rapid emergence of such resistant strains most likely requires reassessment of ciprofloxacin and ofloxacin for the treatment of gonorrhea in the near future.

Treatment of PID has been performed with a large number of antibiotic combinations. The important role of both gonococci and *C. trachomatis* in producing PID has been elucidated and, although the role of various anaerobes in PID is not ascertained, many studies have shown that anaerobic cover is essential for treatment of PID patients. The recommended regimens now include intravenous cefotetan or cefoxitin plus doxycycline.[60] An alternative regimen is clindamycin or metronidazole plus gentamicin or tobramycin, followed with oral doxycycline or clindamycin to complete 14 days of treatment. The recommended regimen for treatment of outpatients is a 2-week combination of oral ofloxacin and clindamycin or metronidazole. Amoxicillin–clavulanic acid together with doxycycline will also cover the major pathogens responsible for PID.[59] Azithromycin in combination with amoxicilin-clavulanic acid may also give excellent activity against *N. gonorrhoeae*, anaerobes and *C. trachomatis*.

Complicated gonococcal infection in males (acute epididymitis) is treated with a single dose of ceftriaxone plus doxycycline for 10 days or ofloxacin.[60] Treatment of disseminated gonorrhea is always started with ceftriaxone.[60] This treatment is not changed into doxycycline or ciprofloxacin if arthritis or meningitis is present. Children who have gonococcal infection are also treated with ceftriaxone.

Meningococcal disease

The overall case fatality rate of meningococcal disease is 9–12% and has remained fairly stable over the last decades.[30] Approximately 5% of patients who have meningitis, and 25–35% of patients who have meningococcal sepsis, will die. Of the survivors, 11–19% have serious sequelae, such as loss of hearing, scars after skin necrosis and cranial nerve palsies.

After the introduction of the sulfonamides, meningococcal disease could be treated by chemotherapy. Now sulfonamides have no role in the treatment of meningococcal infection, because resistant strains appeared in 1963. The mainstay of treatment for patients who have meningococcal disease is benzylpenicillin.[52,58] For most cases of uncomplicated meningococcal meningitis a 7-day course is adequate.[58] Since the etiology is not known at admission, ceftriaxone or cefotaxime is used for the first 24–48 hours to cover the possibility of other bacterial pathogens.[58] Routine susceptibility testing is not indicated,[30] although β-lactamase producing strains have occasionally been recovered. These strains harbor the same plasmid as many PPNG. In addition, there are *N. meningitidis* strains that are not β-lactamase positive but have decreased sensitivity to penicillin. This diminished sensitivity is due to reduced affinity of penicillin to penicillin-binding proteins 2 and 3, resulting from an altered *pen A*. Although the frequency of relatively penicillin-resistant meningococci is low, continued surveillance is necessary. Cefotaxime or ceftriaxone is used when relatively penicillin-resistant strains are isolated.

A novel approach to treat children with severe meningococcal sepsis is the use of bactericidal/permeability-increasing protein (BPI). BPI is a cationic protein contained within granules of polymorphonuclear leukocytes. Since BPI binds endotoxin, a recombinant fragment of BPI ($rBPI_{21}$) was used to treat children with severe meningococcemia. The results of the first clinical trial showed a beneficial effect of $rBPI_{21}$ in decreasing complications of meningococcal disease.[62]

INFECTIONS CAUSED BY OTHER *NEISSERIACEAE*

The so-called nonpathogenic *Neisseria* spp. colonize the human nasopharynx and oropharynx. They comprise eight species (*N. lactamica, N. cinerea, N. polysaccharea, N. sicca, N. subflava, N. flavescens, N. musosa* and *N. elongata*), which do not grow on the enriched media containing antibiotics used for the isolation of gonococci and meningococci.

Strains of *N. lactamica, N. subflava, N. cinerea* and *N. polysaccharea* can be isolated from the selective media and must be differentiated from meningococci and gonococci. *Neisseria* spp. may be differentiated by their patterns of acid production. Rapid methods have been developed to detect acid production. Without additional tests including chromogenic enzyme substrate tests and serologic tests, however, the eight species may be misidentified as meningococci or gonococci.

Neisseria lactamica, which produces acid from lactose and can thus be differentiated from meningococci, has been isolated from cases of meningitis or sepsis in both adults and children.[63]

Four true *Neisseria* spp., *N. sicca, N. subflava, N. flavescens* and *N. mucosa*, have been reported most frequently with native and prosthetic endocarditis.[63] Most patients who had endocarditis had underlying heart abnormalities. In many cases the use of intravenous drugs was a risk factor: oral secretions are used as a solvent for the drug or to clean or lubricate the needle before injection, or result in infection of the valve.

Neisseria sicca is associated with cases of native and prosthetic valve endocarditis. It has also been isolated from meningitis cases. It is a rare cause of pneumonia and osteomyelitis.

Neisseria subflava has been isolated from a small number of patients who have endocarditis, meningitis and sepsis.

Neisseria flavescens, producing yellow-pigmented colonies, has been isolated once in association with an outbreak of meningitis. Occasionally this species is the cause of sepsis resembling chronic meningococcemia.

Neisseria mucosa forms large mucoid colonies adherent on the agar and is isolated as an unusual cause of endocarditis, meningitis, ocular infections, cellulitis, pneumonia and empyema.

Neisseria cinerea colonies may resemble gonococcal colonies on selective media. Occasionally this species is recovered from genital sites and may be associated with syndromes similar to those caused by gonococci, such as conjunctivitis in newborns (ophthalmia neonatorum), proctitis and lymphadenitis. Meningitis occurred in a patient who had facial trauma. Pneumonia in immunodeficient patients has also been reported.

Neisseria polysaccharea grows on the selective media and resembles *N. meningitidis* because acid is produced from glucose and maltose. Infections due to this species have not been reported.

Neisseria elongata, a rod-shaped *Neisseria* spp., has been cultured from blood specimens of patients who have endocarditis or sepsis. It has also been associated with wound infections, and osteomyelitis after oral surgery.[63]

The six false *Neisseria* spp. are common inhabitants of the oropharynx of various animals. *Neisseria canis*, first recovered from a healthy dog, is a normal commensal in the upper respiratory tract of cats and has been cultured from wounds due to cat bites.

Neisseria weaveri, a rod-shaped *Neisseria* spp., was formerly called CDC group M-5 and is part of the oropharyngeal flora of dogs. It has been isolated from human wounds due to dog bites.

N. denitrificans and *N. iguanae* are present in the oropharynx of guinea pigs and iguanas, respectively, and have not been associated with human disease.

Centers for Disease Control and Prevention groups EF-4a and 4b are normal inhabitants of the oropharynx of cats and dogs. Most human infections follow dog and cat bites.[63]

In general the commensal *Neisseria* spp. are susceptible to penicillin, ampicillin and tetracyclines. Only *N. mucosa* is penicillin resistant and sensitive to chloramphenicol. Some strains of *N. lactamica* have an altered penicillin-binding protein 2 similar to the penicillin-binding protein 2 in relatively penicillin-resistant *N. meningitidis*. Rare strains of *N. sicca, N. flavescens* and *N. subflava* are penicillin resistant because of production of β-lactamase. Such strains are a potential source of β-lactamase genes that are transferable to meningococci and gonococci.

REFERENCES

1. Morton RS. Gonorrhoea. London: WB Saunders; 1977.
2. Knapp JS. Historical perspectives and identification of Neisseria and related species. Clin Microbiol Rev 1988;1:415–31.
3. Bovre K. Family VIII. Neisseriaceae Prevot 1933, 119AL. In: Krieg NR, Holt JG, eds. Bergey's manual of systematic bacteriology. Baltimore: Williams and Wilkins; 1984:288–309.
4. Dewhirst FE, Paster BJ, Bright PL. Chromobacterium, Eikenella, Kingella, Neisseria, Simonsiella and Vitreoscilla species comprise a major branch of the beta group Proteobacteria by 16 S ribosomal nucleic acid sequence comparison: transfer of Eikenella and Simonsiella to the Family Neisseriaceae (emend.). Int J Syst Bacteriol 1989;39:258–66.
5. Rossau R, Vandenbussche G, Thielemans S, *et al.* Ribosomal ribonucleic acid cistron similarities and deoxyribonucleic acid homologies of Neisseria, Kingella, Eikenella, Simonsiella, Alysiella and Centers for Disease Control groups EF-4 and M-5 in the emended family Neisseriaceae. Int J Syst Bacteriol 1989;39:185–98.
6. Morse SA, Genco CA. Neisseria. In: Collier L, Balows A, Sussman M, eds. Topley and Wilson's microbiology and microbial infections, 9th ed. London: Arnold; 1998:877–900.
7. Cartwright K. Meningococcal carriage and disease. In: Cartwright K, ed. Meningococcal disease. Chichester: John Wiley; 1995:115–46.
8. Sim RJ, Harrison MM, Moxon ER, Tang CM. Underestimation of meningococci in tonsillar tissue by nasopharyngeal swabbing. Lancet 2000;356:1653–54.
9. Mims CA, Playfair JHL, Roitt IM, Wakelin D, Williams R. Sexually transmitted diseases. In: Mims CA, Playfair JHL, Roitt IM, Wakelin D, Williams R, eds. Medical microbiology. St. Louis: Mosby; 1993:24.1–24.22.
10. Vogel U, Claus H, Frosch M. Rapid serogroup switching in Neisseria. N Engl J Med 2000;324:219–20.

11. Swartley JS, Marfin AA, Edupuinganti S, *et al.* Capsule switching of Neisseria meningitidis. Proc Natl Acad Sci USA 1997;94:271–6.
12. Kallstrom H, Liszwski MK, Atkinson JP, Johnston AB. Membrane cofactor protein (MCP or CD46) is a cellular pilus receptor for pathogenic Neisseria. Mol Microbiol 1997;25:639–47.
13. Virji M, Saunders JR, Sims G, Makepeace K, Maskell D, Ferguson DJP. Pilus-faciliated adherence of Neisseria meningitidis to human epithelial and endothelial cells: modulation of adherence phenotype occurs concurrently with changes in primary aminoacid sequences and the glycosylation of pilin. Mol Microbiol 1993;10:1013–28.
14. Heckels JE. Structure and function of pili of pathogenic Neisseria species. Clin Microbiol Rev 1989;2(suppl):66–73.
15. Meyer TF, Pohlner J, Van Putten JPM. Biology of pathogenic Neisseria. Curr Top Microbiol Immune 1994;192:283–317.
16. Hitchcock PJ. Unified nomenclature for pathogenic Neisseria species. Clin Microbiol Rev 1989;2(suppl):64–5.
17. Swanson J. Colony, opacity and protein II compostions of gonoccci. Infect Immun 1982;37:359–68.
18. Van Putten JPM, Duensing TD, Cole RL. Entry of Opa A^+ gonococci into Hep-2 cells requires concerted action of glycosaminoglycans, fibronectin and integrin receptors. Mol Microbiol 1998;29:369–79.
19. Wang J, Gray-Owens SD, Knorre A, *et al.* Opa binding to cellular CD 66 receptors mediates the transcellular traversal of Neisseria gonorrhoeae across polarized T84 epithelial cell monolayers. Mol Microbiol 1998;30:657–71.
20. Virji M, Evans D, Hadfield S, *et al.* Critical determinants of host receptor targetting by Neisseria meningitidis and Neisseria gonorrhoeae: identification of Opa adhesitopes on the N-domain of CD 66 molecules. Mol Microbiol 1999;34:538–51.
21. De Vries FP, Cole R, Dankert J, Frosch M, Van Putten JP. Neisseria meningitidis producing Opc adhesin binds epithelial cell proteoglycan receptors. Mol Microbiol 1998;27:1203–12.
22. Swanson J, Belland RJ, Hill SA. Neisserial surface variation: how and why? Curr Opin Genet Dev 1992;2:805–11.
23. Gotschlich EC. Genetic locus for the biosynthesis of the variable portion of Neisseria gonorrhoeae lipoligosaccharide. J Exp Med 1994;180:2181–90.
24. Brandtzaeg P. Systemic meningococcal disease: clinical pictures and patho-physiological background. Rev Med Microbiol 1996;7:63–72.
25. Caugant DA. Population genetics and molecular epidemiology of Neisseria meningitidis. APMIS 1998;106:505–25.
26. Maiden MCJ, Bygraves JA, Feil F, *et al.* Multilocus sequence typing: a portable approach to the identification of clones within populations of pathogenic micro-organisms. Proc Natl Acad Sci USA 1998;95:3140–5.
27. Jephcott AE. Gonorrhoeae, chaucroid and granuloma venereum. In: Collier L, Balows A, Sussman M, eds. Topley and Wilson's microbiology and microbial infections, 9th ed. London: Arnold; 1998:623–40.
28. Division of STD/HIV Prevention. Sexually transmitted disease surveillance, 1995. US Department of Health and Human Services, Public Health Service. Atlanta: Centers for Disease Control and Prevention; 1996.
29. Achtman M. Epidemic spread and antigenic variability of Neisseria meningitidis. Trends Microbiol 1995;3:186–92.
30. Rosenstein NE, Perkins BA, Stephens DS, Popovics T, Hughes JM. Meningococcal disease. N Engl J Med 2002;344:1378–88.
31. Conolly M, Noah N. Is group meningococcal disease increasing in Europe? A report of surveillance of meningococcal infection in Europe 1993–6. Epidemiol Infect 1999;122:41–9.
32. Scholten RJP, Poolman JT, Valkenburg HA, *et al.* Phenotypic and genetic changes in a new clone-complex of Neisseria meningitidis in The Netherlands 1958–1990. J Infect Dis 1994;169:673–6.
33. Cartwright K, Noah N, Peltola H. Meningococcal disease in Europe: epidemiology, mortality and prevention with conjugate vaccines. Report of a European advisory board meeting Vienna, Austria, 6–8 October 2000. Vaccine 2001;18:4347–56.
34. Fitzpatrick PE, Salmon RL, Palmer SR, Hunter PR, Roberts RJ. Risk factors for carriage of *Neisseria meningitides* during an outbreak in Wales. Emerg Infect Dis 2000;181:65–70.
35. Taha MK, Achtman M, Alonso JM, *et al.* Serogroup W135 meningococcal disease in Haji pilgrims. Lancet 2000;356:2159.
36. Jones DM. Epidemiology of meningococcal disease in Europe and the USA. In: Cartwright K, ed. Meningococcal disease. Chichester: John Wiley; 1995:147–57.
37. Cohen MS, Sparling PF. Mucosal infection with Neisseria gonorrhoeae: bacterial adaptation and mucosal defences. J Clin Invest 1992;89:1699–705.
38. Parsons NJ, Andrade JRC, Patel PV, Cole JA, Smith H. Sialylation of lipopolysaccharide and loss of absorption of bactericidal antibody during conversion of gonococci to serum resistance by cytidine 5′-monophospho-N-acetyl neuraminic acid. Microbiol Pathol 1989;7:63–72.
39. Plummer FA, Chubb H, Simonsen JN, *et al.* Antibody to Rmp (outer membrane protein 3) increases susceptibility to gonococcal infection. J Clin Invest 1993;91:339–43.
40. Weel JFL. The pathogenesis of the gonococcal infection of epithelial cells. Thesis. University of Amsterdam: 1991.
41. Petersen BH, Lee TJ, Snyderman R, Brooks GF. Neisseria meningitidis and Neisseria gonorrhoeae bacteremia associated with C6, C7 or C8-deficiency. Ann Intern Med 1979;90:917–20.
42. Figueroa JE, Densen P. Infectious diseases associated with complement deficiencies. Clin Microbiol Rev 1991;4:359–95.
43. Virji M. Glycosylation of the Meningococcus pilus protein. Am Soc Microbiol News 1998;64:398–405.
44. Tunkel AR, Scheld WM. Pathogenesis and pathophysiology of bacterial meningitis. Ann Rev Med 1993;44:103–20.
45. Harrison OB, Robertson BD, Faust SN, *et al.* Analysis of pathogen–host cell interactions in purpura fulminans: expression of capsule, type IV pili, and Por A by *Neisseria meningitidis in vivo.* Infect Immun 2002;70:5195–201.
46. De Vries FP, Van der Ende A, Van Putten JPM, Dankert J. Invasion of primary nasopharyngeal epithelial cells by Neisseria meningitidis is controlled by phase variation of multiple surface antigens. Infect Immun 1996;64:2998–3006.
47. Hibberd ML, Sumiya M, Summerfield JA, *et al.* Association of variants of the gene for mannose-binding lectin with susceptibility to meningococcal disease. Lancet 1999;353:1049–53.
48. Jack DL, Read RC, Tenner AJ, Frosch M, Turner MW. Mannose-binding lectin regulates the inflammatory response of human professional phagocytes to *Neisseria meningitides* serogroup B. J Infect Dis 2001;184:1152–62.
49. Nadel S, Newport MJ, Booy R, Levin M. Variation in the tumor necrosis factor-alpha gene promotor region may be associated with death from meningococcal disease. J Infect Dis 1996;174:878–80.
50. Tramont RC. Gonococcal vaccines. Clin Microbiol Rev 1989;2(suppl):S74–S77.
51. Jòdar L, Feavers JM, Salisbury D, Granof DM. Development of vaccines against meningococcal disease. Lancet 2002;359:1499–508.
52. Lambert HP. Infections of the central nervous system. In: O'Grady F, Lambert HP, Finch RG, Greenwood D, eds. Antibiotics and chemotherapy, 7th ed. New York: Churchill Livingstone; 1997:742–59.
53. Fijen CA, Kuijper EJ, Drogari-Apiranthitou M, Van Leeuwen Y, Daha MR, Dankert J. Protection against meningococcal serogroup A C Y W disease in complement-deficient individuals vaccinated with the tetra valent meningococcal polysaccharide vaccine. Clin Exp Immunol 1998;114:362–9.
54. Berry DS, Lynn F, Lee C-H, Frasch CE, Bash MC. Effect of O-acetylation of *Neisseria meningitides* serogroup A capsular polysaccharide on development of functional immune responses. Infect Immun 2002;70:3707–13.
55. Ramsey ME, Andrews N, Kaczmarski EB, Miller E. Efficacy of meningococcal serogroup C conjugate vaccine in teenagers and toddlers in England. Lancet 2001;357:195–6.
56. Maiden MJC, Stuart JM, for the UK Meningococcal Carriage Group. Carriage of serogroup C meningococci 1 year after meningococcal C conjugate polysaccharide vaccination. Lancet 2002;359:1829–30.
57. Pizza M, Scarlato V, Masignani V, *et al.* Identification of vaccine candidates against serogroup B meningococcus by whole-genome sequencing. Science 2000;287:1816–20.
58. Cartwright KAV. Bacterial meningitis. In: Collier L, Balows A, Sussman M, eds. Topley and Wilson's microbiology and microbial infections, 9th ed. London: Arnold; 1998:299–318.
59. Miller ARO. Sexually transmitted infections. In: O'Grady F, Lambert HP, Finch RG, Greenwood D, eds. Antibiotics and chemotherapy, 7th ed. New York: Churchill Livingstone; 1997:815–30.
60. Centers for Disease Control and Prevention. 1998 Guidelines for treatment of sexually transmitted diseases. MMWR 1997;47(suppl RR-1):S59–S69.
61. Gransden WR, Warren C, Philips I. 4-Quinolone-resistant Neisseria gonorrhoeae in the United Kingdom. J Med Microbiol 1991;34:23–7.
62. Levin M, Quint PA, Goldstein B, *et al.* and the rBPI21 Meningococcal Sepsis Study Group. Recombinant bactericidal/permeability-increasing protein (rBPI21) as adjunctive treatment for children with severe meningococcal sepsis: a randomised trial. Lancet 2000;356:961–7.
63. Gröschel DHM. Moraxella catarrhalis and other Gram-negative cocci. In: Mandell GK, Bennett JE, Dolin R, eds. Mandell, Douglas and Bennett's principles and practice of infectious diseases, 4th ed. New York: Churchill Livingstone; 1995:1926–34.

chapter

228 Enterobacteriaceae

Maja Rozenberg-Arska & Maarten R Visser

INTRODUCTION

Enterobacteriaceae are ubiquitous organisms that are found worldwide in soil, water and vegetation, and they are part of the normal flora of the gastrointestinal tract of most animals, including humans. Some members of the family Enterobacteriaceae are more frequently associated with disease in humans (e.g. *Shigella, Salmonella, Yersinia* spp.) than others (e.g. *Escherichia coli, Klebsiella* spp., *Proteus* spp.). These others are members of the normal commensal flora, which in some situations can cause human disease ranging from mild symptoms to severe infections with fatal septicemia. Infections can be of exogenous (e.g. *Salmonella* and *Shigella* spp.) or endogenous origin (e.g. *E. coli*).

NATURE

Taxonomy and nomenclature

The nomenclature and classification of Enterobacteriaceae has always been confusing, with many changes over time. Micro-organisms previously grouped on the basis of biochemical and antigenic properties in certain families may in fact not be closely related.[1]

In recent years, however, techniques of nucleic acid hybridization and nucleic acid sequencing have provided powerful tools that can enable better definition of the evolutionary relationships of all micro-organisms[2] and the relationships of the organisms in one family. Indeed, it is the application of this technology that has led to the current nomenclature.

In addition, molecular information on the complete genome of *E. coli*[3] will provide further valuable insight into the taxonomy of bacteria and will be used to refine current classification schemes.

In 1986, Ewing proposed dividing the family of Enterobacteriaceae into eight tribes that are associated with human diseases (Escherichiae, Edwardsiellae, Citrobactereae, Salmonellae, Klebsiellae, Proteae, Yersiniae, Erwiniae and a group of miscellaneous genera).[4] This tribal concept has been used in some recent descriptions of the Enterobacteriaceae[5,6] but others have not used it because of lack of diagnostic and taxonomic significance.[2,5,7,8] The classification that is used in this chapter is based on the current bacterial names of the Enterobacteriaceae (see Tables 228.4–228.13).

Members of the family Enterobacteriaceae show many common properties. They are all Gram-negative, non-spore-forming bacilli, and they are all relatively small (2–3μm × 0.4–0.6μm). They are either motile by peritrichous flagella or nonmotile (e.g. *Shigella* and *Klebsiella* spp.). Some of them are encapsulated. Enterobacteriaceae grow rapidly on ordinary laboratory media under aerobic and anaerobic conditions. All species utilize glucose fermentatively, often with the formation of either acid or acid and gas. They are oxidase-negative and, with only a few exceptions (certain biotypes of *Pantoea agglomerans* and some *Serratia* spp.), catalase-positive. They reduce nitrates to nitrites.

Anatomy of Enterobacteriaceae

As shown in Figures 228.1 and 228.2, the major structural compounds of cell wall of Enterobacteriaceae are:

- an inner cytoplasmic membrane;
- the peptidoglycan layer; and
- an outer membrane consisting of two layers – a phospholipid protein layer and an outer lipopolysaccharide (LPS) layer.

Many organisms, such as *Klebsiella* spp. and a number of *E. coli* strains, possess an additional capsular layer (the capsule).

Some Enterobacteriaceae possess flagella, proteinaceous structures that give mobility to the bacteria. In addition, the presence of pili and fimbriae, also proteinaceous in nature, is an important factor in bacterial attachment or adherence to mucosal surfaces.

Cell wall

The cytoplasmic membrane is an important part of the cell envelope, is the boundary between the cytoplasm and environment, and is primarily responsible for regulating the flow of nutrient and metabolic products into and out of the cell. The cytoplasmic membrane is involved in almost every aspect of bacterial growth and metabolism. The chemical units of peptidoglycan, LPS and phospholipids are synthesized by enzymes within this membrane.[9]

Peptidoglycan forms a thinner layer in Gram-negative bacteria than in Gram-positive bacteria. Peptidoglycan consists of a network in which linear amino-sugar chains containing alternating *N*-acetylglucosamine and *N*-acetyl muramic acid residues are linked to tetrapeptides. The peptidoglycan layer maintains the shape of bacteria.[10]

The periplasm, or periplasmatic space, lies between the inner and the outer membranes. A number of processes that are vital for the growth and the viability of the cell occur within this compartment.

Changes in the outer membrane or in the LPS allow the release of periplasmatic enzymes and binding proteins, which play a role in protection and interaction of the bacteria and the host defenses.[11]

The outer membrane of Enterobacteriaceae forms an asymmetric bilayer of phospholipids[12] and LPS.[12,13] The hydrophobic parts of the LPS molecules face the environment and the hydrophilic part interacts with the hydrophilic part of the phospholipid. The LPS molecules generally have three regions: the O-specific polysaccharide chain, the core region and lipid-A moiety.

The O-specific polysaccharide chain is chemically unique for each type of organism and LPS, and it confers serologic specificity on an organism. The O-specific chain normally consists of 20–40 repeating units of oligosaccharides, each containing between two and eight different monosaccharides interlinked with glycosidic bonds. At least 160 different chemical arrangements of O-antigens have been identified in *E. coli* alone.[13,14] Based on the presence or absence of the O-specific chain, bacterial endotoxin can be smooth (S) or rough (R), named after the appearance of the bacterial colonies on agar plates.

There is uncertainty about the part played by the O antigen in the virulence of the Enterobacteriaceae; however, most of the isolates

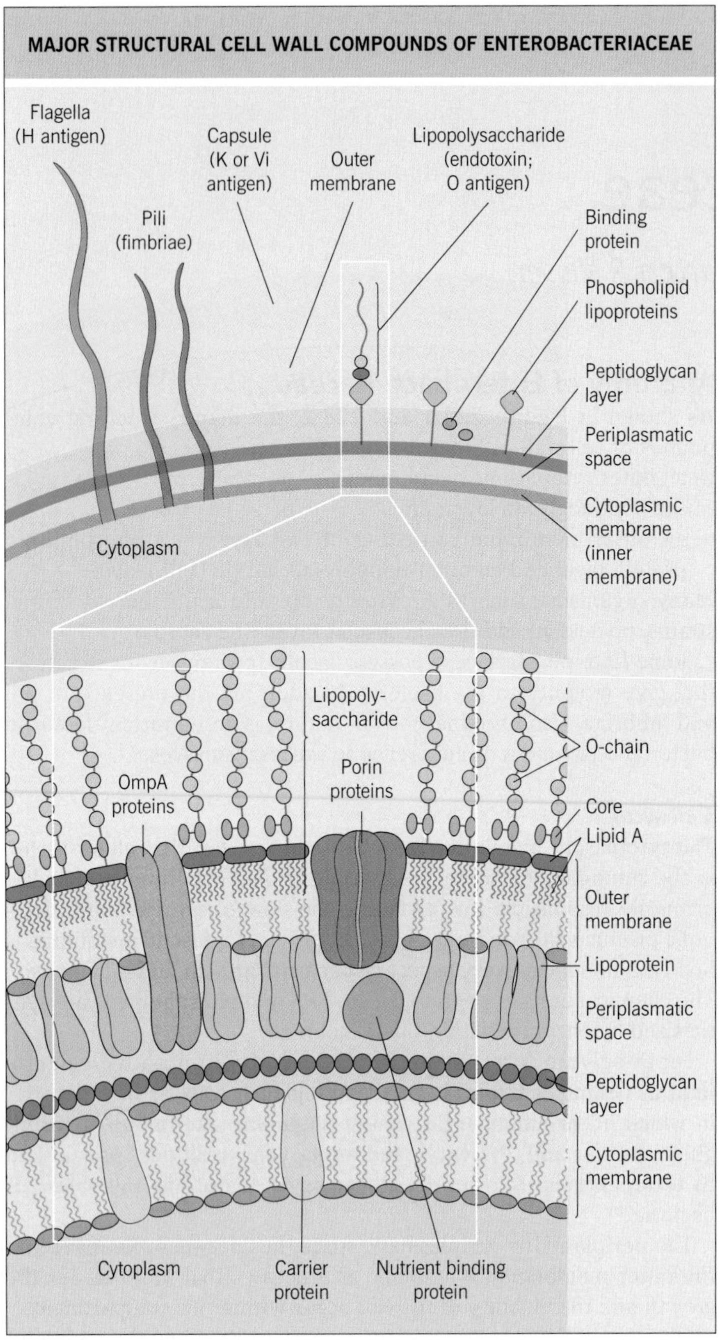

Fig. 228.1 Major structural cell wall compounds of Enterobacteriaceae. The figure also illustrates the molecular organization of the outer membrane, and the most likely positions of outer membrane constituents are indicated. Lipopolysaccharide and phospholipid molecules are the major constituents of the asymmetric bilayer. Divalent cations (not indicated) are believed to play important roles in interactions of LPS: Only three types of protein are shown: the pore proteins (LamB protein not shown), OmpA protein and lipoprotein (their interactions with peptidoglycan and lipoprotein are not shown – that such interactions occur cannot be excluded). Several O-antigen chains are much longer than shown here. Enterobacterial core antigen has been omitted for simplicity. The P pili and fimbriae are discussed and illustrated in more detail in Chapter 1.

from infected sites have smooth LPS. Epidemiologic surveys have demonstrated association between certain O types and clinical infections.[15] It is now generally felt that the O serogroup may act primarily as a marker for a specific cluster of virulence properties needed for a certain infectious process. Certain serogroups possess adhesive factors that are important specifically in urinary tract infection, whereas other serogroups possess colonization factors and toxins that are necessary for the organism to cause gastroenteritis.

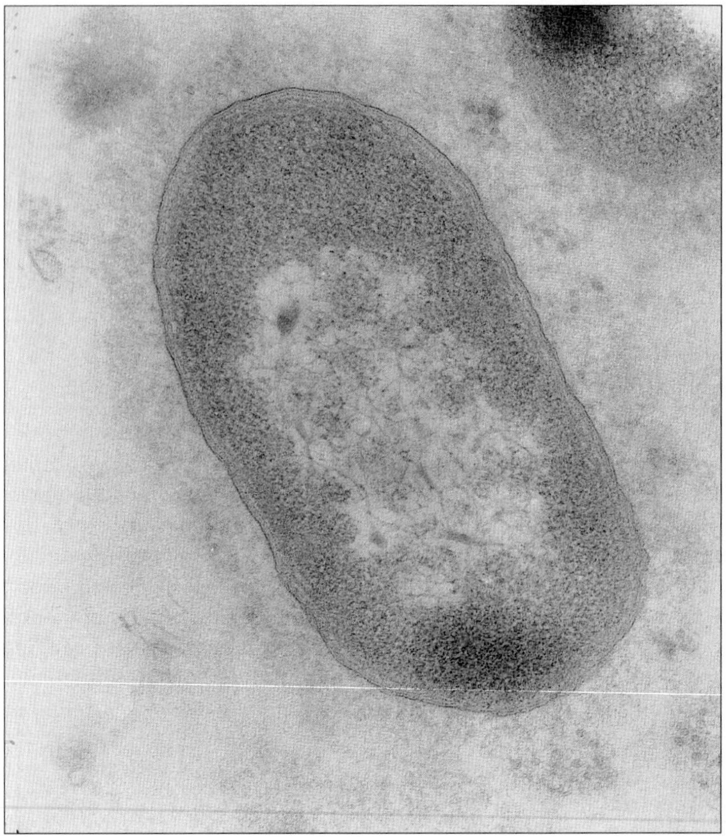

Fig. 228.2 Longitudinal section of *Escherichia coli*. The bacterial cell is surrounded by a visible cell wall (outer membrane, cytoplasmic membrane and – in between – periplasm).

The core polysaccharide region of outer membrane, which shows much less variability than the O-specific chain and is often identical in large groups of Gram-negative bacteria, contains deoxy-sugar, 2-keto-deoxyotonic acid and heptose. The core region connects the polysaccharide chain and lipid-A components.

Lipid-A is the most conserved part of LPS and the basic structure is similar in various Gram-negative bacteria. Lipid-A consist of a glucosaminyl-β-(1–6) glucosamine backbone, which is substituted with six or seven fatty acid residues, all of them saturated. Lipid-A is responsible for the biologic properties of endotoxin. However, lipid-A-associated protein and polysaccharide side chains exert modifying effects and separately may exhibit biologic activities.[16]

Capsule

Two types of capsular polysaccharides are found in Enterobacteriaceae. The M antigen (mucous antigen) or colanic acid is produced by most enteric bacteria, presumably by means of protection against desiccation. Mucous antigen is non-specific and serologically cross-reactive among different micro-organisms. In contrast, K antigen polysaccharides have structures specific to each serotype within a species and presumably help these bacteria to evade phagocytosis.[17,18]

The presence of K antigen is determined by means of the bacterial agglutination test. It can block the agglutination by specific O antisera; however, these strains become agglutinable when the cells are heated. Two important examples of K antigens are the Vi antigen of *Salmonella typhi* and the K1 antigen of *E. coli*, which is associated with neonatal meningitis and urinary tract infection.[19,20] Classification of K antigen is now based on electrophoretic mobility, reflecting differences in charge and molecular size.[17]

Flagella

Many members of the Enterobacteriaceae possess proteinaceous structures called flagella, which provide bacteria with mobility.[21]

There are some similarities between several flagellar proteins and proteins involved in either the expression of virulence genes or the export of virulent proteins, or both (e.g. in *Salmonella* spp.).[21] Flagella carry the heat-labile H antigen. The H antigen is dominant to the O antigen; therefore, O-antigen reactivity requires prior denaturation of the H antigen by heating or treatment with acid or alcohol.[17]

Fimbriae

The presence of fimbriae (pili) in bacteria is an important factor for attachment or adherence to the mucosal surfaces of the alimentary, respiratory or genitourinary tract and to red blood cells (causing hemagglutination). These adhesive properties of piliated bacteria play an important role in bacterial colonization of epithelial surfaces and are therefore referred to as colonization factors.[22]

PATHOGENICITY

Normal host defenses limit the majority of bacterial interactions. Therefore, infections caused by members of the Enterobacteriaceae are determined by several virulence factors in the pathogenic strains and the state of the host defenses. Most of the infections are preceded by: colonization of the mucosal site and adherence; evasion of host defenses; multiplication; and host damage.

Virulence factors

Adherence

In order to initiate infection, bacteria must enter the host and attach to host cells. Among Enterobacteriaceae, adhesion is mediated by both fimbrial and nonfimbrial adhesins that are encoded on plasmids and on the bacterial genome (Table 228.1).[23–26] Most Enterobacteriaceae express the common fimbriae, which can attach to a number of cells; however, the role of this molecule in disease is still unknown.

Fimbriae have been characterized in two different ways, one antigenic and the other functional. Type 1 fimbriae, together with colonization factor antigens CFA/I and CFA/II, are present in enterotoxigenic *E. coli* (ETEC) and are responsible for adherence to the small bowel mucosa[29]; bundle forming pili (Bfp) are responsible for adherence of enteropathogenic *E. coli* (EPEC) to the small intestine; GvvPG fimbriae mediate adherence of enteroaggregative *E. coli* (EAEC) to the small intestine. Intemin is an adhesin that causes the intimate association found among EPEC and enterohemorrhagic *E. coli* (EHEC). This is associated with the 'attachment and effacement' (E/A) phenomenon, which leads to destruction of the intestinal surface cells[27,28] of the small as well as the large intestine. The role of nonfimbrial adhesions, other than in uropathogenic *E. coli* (UPEC), are less defined and their role in adherence is not yet clear. The P-fimbriae adhesion factors, known for their ability to bind to P blood group antigens on urinary tract cells, are associated with *E. coli* responsible for urinary tract infections, in particular pyelonephritis and urosepsis.[23,27] The S-fimbriae, which recognize O-linked sialo-oligosaccharides of glycophorin A, are associated with sepsis and meningitis in neonates.[28]

Phase variation of all fimbrial antigens protects the bacteria from immune-mediated clearance.

The role of adhesins in the pathogenesis of infections caused by Enterobacteriaceae other than *E. coli* is not well characterized. Types 1, 3 and 6 fimbriae have been found in *Klebsiella* spp. but their function as a virulence factor remains largely unknown.[30]

Capsule

The surface of Gram-negative bacteria can play an important role in the protection of the bacterium in a hostile environment. A number of surface antigens appear to be acid polysaccharides; these include the Vi antigen, some of the K antigens of *E. coli* (Table 228.2) and the capsular polysaccharides of *Klebsiella* spp. The capsule provides bacteria with a mechanism for avoiding non-specific host defenses.[31] The K antigen polysaccharides enhance the virulence of invasive bacteria because they counteract the bactericidal action of complement by inhibiting the alternative pathway.

Because the alternative pathway accounts for much of the bactericidal activity of serum and for opsonization in the absence of specific antibodies, it has been suggested that strains with K antigen avoid host defenses more easily, particularly in the early course of infection before the antibody response is mounted. In addition, the capsule may act as a physical barrier to phagocytosis by preventing contact between the bacterium and the phagocytic cell, a result of the anionic and hydrophobic nature of its constituent polysaccharide.[31,32] Moreover, some of the K antigens are poor immunogens and activators of complement. However, the presence of K antigen alone does not appear to account fully for the virulence of an organism.

Bacterial toxins

Exotoxins

A number of enterotoxins have been identified in Enterobacteriaceae (Table 228.3). Heat-labile enterotoxin (which resembles the cholera toxin) acts by way of activation of cyclic adenosine monophosphate (cAMP), leading to increased electrolyte and fluid secretion and inhibition of resorption. This results in increased fluid in the small intestine. This toxin is produced by enterotoxigenic *E. coli* and occasionally by *Klebsiella* and *Salmonella* spp.[33,34]

Heat-stable enterotoxin acts via the activation of cGMP in the intestinal epithelium, leading to changes in ion transport, which also result in increased fluid and electrolytes in the intestinal lumen. This toxin is produced by enterotoxigenic *E. coli* and occasionally by *Yersinia enterocolitica* and *Citrobacter freundii*.[33,35]

Shiga toxin produced by *Shigella flexneri* may elicit a diarrheal prodrome that often precedes bacillary dysentery; however, its role in human disease remains to be defined.[36] Shiga toxin from *Shigella dysenteriae* type 1, a potent cytotoxin, causes capillary dysfunction and focal hemorrhage. This toxin is associated with the hemolytic–uremic syndrome (HUS).[36] Closely related to the Shiga toxin from *S. dysenteriae* type 1 are toxins expressed by enterohemorrhagic *E. coli*.[36]

Hemolysins are present in many species and can cause cell destruction that is not limited to red cells but extends to white cells and other cell types. By killing host cells, hemolysins make iron more available by releasing hemoglobin-bound iron from lysed cells. To release this iron from the host-binding proteins (transferrin and lactoferrin) *E. coli* produces siderophores. α-Hemolysin is produced by pathogenic *E. coli* belonging to a restricted set of O serogroups that are associated with extraintestinal infection.[37]

Endotoxins

As discussed above, Gram-negative bacteria express various macromolecules at their surface. Of these, LPS are of particular microbiologic, immunologic and medical significance.[12,13] Lipopolysaccharides have been implicated as major factors in the pathogenesis of serious Gram-negative infections (see Chapter 56).[38]

Lipopolysaccharides are released from the bacterial outer membrane during rapid bacterial growth and are released in large quantities on bacterial lysis and death. In animal studies and human volunteer studies,[39] intravenous administration of purified LPS can induce pathophysiologic changes similar to those associated with Gram-negative sepsis and septic shock, including hypotension, metabolic acidosis, coagulation disorders and the progressive failure of multiple organs. These pathophysiologic changes ultimately lead to death.

BACTERIAL ADHESINS PROMOTING COLONIZATION AND INFECTIONS BY ENTEROBACTERIACEAE		
Virulence factor	**Action**	**Organism, site affected and disease**
Bacterial adhesins	Adherence to mucosal surfaces	
P fimbriae		*Escherichia coli* (UPEC): urinary tract infections, pyelonephritis
Type 1 fimbriae		*E. coli*: respiratory tract infections, sepsis *E. coli* (ETEC): gastroenteritis *Klebsiella pneumoniae*: cystitis
Type 3 fimbriae		*Klebsiella* spp.: cystitis, urinary tract infections
Type 6 fimbriae		*Klebsiella* spp.: diseases uncertain
S fimbriae		*E. coli*: sepsis and meningitis in neonates
Bundle-forming pili (Bfp)		*E. coli* (EPEC): gastroenteritis, watery diarrhea
Colonization factor antigens (CFA/I, CFA/II)		*E. coli* (ETEC): gastroenteritis, watery diarrhea in infants and travelers
AAF/I and II fimbriae		*E. coli* (EAEC/some strains): persistent diarrhea in young children, traveler's diarrhea, no inflammation, no fever
Intimin		*E. coli* (EPEC): gastroenteritis, watery diarrhea (EHEC): bloody diarrhea
AFA-I; AFA-III; Dr adhesin		*E. coli* (UPEC)
Outer membrane protein		*E. coli* (EIEC)?
		E. coli (EPEC)? *Proteus mirabilis*: urinary tract infection? *E. coli* (EAEC)?
Afimbrial adhesions	Tight binding to host cells	*Klebsiella pneumoniae*: urinary tract infection, infection of cerebrospinal fluid

Table 228.1 Bacterial adhesins promoting colonization and infections by Enterobacteriaceae. EAEC, enteroaggregative *Escherichia coli*; EHEC, enterohemorrhagic *E. coli*; EIEC, enteroinvasive *E. coli*; EPEC, enteropathogenic *E. coli*; ETEC, enterotoxigenic *E. coli*; UPEC, uropathogenic *E. coli*.

BACTERIAL CAPSULES AND INFECTION BY ENTEROBACTERIACEAE		
Virulence factor	**Action**	**Organism and disease**
Bacterial capsules	Inhibition of opsonization, prevention of phagocytic uptake	
K antigen		*Escherichia coli* K1: meningitis and sepsis in neonates *Escherichia coli*: invasive extraintestinal infections in adults

Table 228.2 Bacterial capsules and infection by Enterobacteriaceae

The effects of LPS are ascribed to several inflammatory mediators that result from the interaction of LPS with components of both cellular and humoral limbs of the host defense system. Monocytes and macrophages respond to LPS by secreting cytokines, such as tumor necrosis factor and interleukins, that heighten host defense but at the same time activate inflammatory processes that lead to organ failure. Neutrophils play a role in the defense against bacteria but may contribute to the damaging effect of exposure to LPS by enhanced production of oxygen radicals, secretion of proteases and increased cellular adhesiveness.[40] It has been established that the lipid-A part of LPS is responsible for the toxicity.

PREVENTION

Enterobacteriaceae are primarily spread in the hospital from person to person via the hands of hospital personnel.

Escherichia coli diarrheal disease is best controlled by preventing fecal hand–mouth transmission, by stressing the importance of improved hygiene and by introducing appropriate infection-control procedures.

Prevention of *E. coli* infections is difficult because most of the infections (with the exception of intestinal infections) are caused by endogenous bacteria (e.g. community-acquired urinary tract infection) or bacteria acquired during the hospital stay (nosocomial infections). Use of antibacterial chemoprophylaxis in neutropenic patients has reduced the morbidity and mortality attributable to Enterobacteriaceae, especially *E. coli*.[41] For the prevention of nosocomial infections certain risk factors (e.g. the unrestricted use of antibiotics, the unnecessary use of urinary catheters) should be avoided. Unfortunately, many of these factors tend to be found in patients at greatest risk for infections (e.g. immunocompromised patients and patients in intensive care units).

DIAGNOSTIC MICROBIOLOGY

Members of most genera form 'coliform-type' colonies on simple media (i.e. the colonies are circular with a diameter of 1–3mm and have a low convex, smooth-surfaced, colorless to gray and translucent appearance).

For recovery of the Enterobacteriaceae from the specimens containing mixed flora (e.g. fecal samples) several media are used: nonselective media (e.g. blood agar; Fig. 228.3), selective or differential media (e.g. MacConkey agar, *Salmonella–Shigella* agar; Figs 228.4 and 228.5) and enrichment broth to enhance the growth of certain bacteria while inhibiting the growth of other, unwanted bacteria.

On MacConkey (lactose-containing) media (see Fig. 228.4) the colonies may be pink, indicating that the organisms ferment lactose

Table 228.3 Bacterial toxins and infections by Enterobacteriaceae

BACTERIAL TOXINS AND INFECTIONS BY ENTEROBACTERIACEAE		
Virulence factor	**Action**	**Organism and disease**
Exotoxins		
Hemolysins α, β	Cell destruction Cell lysis, often leading to cytokine release and inflammatory response	*Escherichia coli*: extraintestinal infection, urinary tract infections, pyelonephritis
Enterotoxins		
Heat-stable toxins (Sta; STb) Heat-stable toxins (LT-I; LT-II)	Hypersecretion of fluid and electrolytes	*E. coli* (ETEC): gastroenteritis (noninvasive, no inflammation, no fever) Watery diarrhea in infants and travelers
Verotoxin (VT1 and 2)	Intestinal mucosal destruction	*E. coli* (EHEC): hemorrhagic colitis, diarrhea; hemolytic–ureic syndrome
Enteroaggregative heat-stable toxin (EAST)?		*E. coli* (EAEC), diarrhea
Endotoxin		
Lipopolysaccharide	Complement activation, liberation of cytokines, leukocyte mobilization and degranulation, platelet and coagulation pathway activation	Enterobacteriaceae: fever, sepsis, shock with multiorgan failure

rapidly, or pale, indicating that the organisms either do not ferment lactose or that they cause 'late' fermentation after several days of incubation.[8] This procedure makes possible an immediate presumptive distinction between colonies (e.g. between true intestinal pathogens such as *Salmonella* or *Shigella* spp. and common intestinal commensals). These findings need to be confirmed by other tests.

Differences in biochemical activities provide the main means of differentiating the genus and species.[42] A number of identification methods are readily available from commercial sources (e.g. API-20E system – bioMérieux, 'sHertogenbosch, The Netherlands; Fig. 228.6). These methods give a range of simple biochemical tests, and the biochemical profile for a high percentage of bacterial species can be obtained within 24 hours of incubation at 98.6°F (37°C).[43] The biochemical profile is translated into a numeric code, which can be read from a profile index. Computer-based identification services for unusual organisms are available. The rapid API-20E system allows the identification of Enterobacteriaceae by detection of preformed enzymes in suspension of the test organisms. The rapid system gives a result in 4 hours. Fully automated identification systems, such as Vitek2 (bioMérieux) and Phoenix (BD Diagnostic Systems Europe, France) are also available.

With *E. coli* infections the problem is generally to characterize the pathogenic types from the commensal types. For the isolation of *E. coli* from sterile body sites where its presence indicates infection, such as blood or urine, the standard technique can be used. With the emergence of EHEC as an important pathogen, special media were developed to identify those from feces and food. Most commonly used is sorbitol MacConkey agar, on which some but not all EHEC will appear as nonfermenting colonies, while most other *E. coli* ferment sorbitol.

The diagnosis of diarrheagenic *E. coli* strains depend on identification of virulence characteristics of those strains. This may include in-vitro phenotypic assays that correlate with the presence of specific virulence traits, such as adherence, toxins or the detection of genes encoding those traits. Molecular diagnostic methods are developed to diagnose diarrheagenic *E. coli* strains. These methods allow the differentiation of diarrheagenic strains from nonpathogenic strains of the stool flora and also to make it possible to distinguish one category from another. Nucleic-acid-based probes as well as polymerase chain reaction (PCR) techniques can be applied to isolated bacteria but also directly to fecal samples.[25,44]

Molecular methods can be used for clinical purposes to detect and identify pathogenic Enterobacteriaceae in order to be able to treat patients and also to perform epidemiologic studies.

CLINICAL MANIFESTATIONS

Escherichia coli is a normal inhabitant of the human gastrointestinal tract that can cause infections under certain conditions. The development and the severity of the infection depends strongly on both the virulence of the bacteria and the state of the host's defense mechanisms. Different strains are associated with different diseases. The versatility of *E. coli* is due to the fact that different strains have acquired different sets of virulence genes. Most of the infections caused by *E. coli*, with the exception of intestinal infections, are endogenous.

Urinary tract infection (see Chapter 67)

Escherichia coli is a leading cause of urinary tract infection (UTI) in humans.[45] Infecting strains originate from the gastrointestinal tract and several virulence factors have been found to be involved in the pathogenesis of UTI. The most important of these virulence factors are the O–K serotypes, hemolysins and the presence of adhesins for uroepithelial cells.[46,47]

Urinary tract infections generally start with the colonization of the urethra by *E. coli* strains from the colon or vagina. The bacteria have the ability to adhere to uroepithelial cells. A number of adhesins of uropathogenic *E. coli* strains have been identified.

Type 1 fimbriae may mediate adherence to the bladder cells, and they contribute to virulence in the urinary tract when expressed against the background of a fully virulent uropathogen.[48] These strains do not appear to be specific for uropathogenic strains. The most important type of adhesin, particularly in strains that cause pyelonephritis, are P-fimbriae.[49] They bind specifically to the P blood group antigen, which is present not only on red cells but also on the uroepithelial cells of approximately 99% of people. Uropathogenic strains also have adhesins that are not pili. Some examples are the afimbrial adhesins (AFA I, AFA III) and hemagglutinin that bind to Dr blood group antigen.

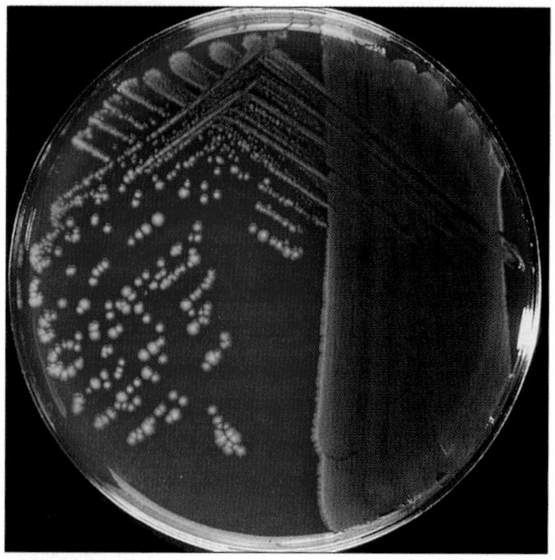

Fig. 228.3 Mixed culture of two morphotypes of Enterobacteriaceae (*Escherichia coli* and *Salmonella* spp.) on blood agar plate.

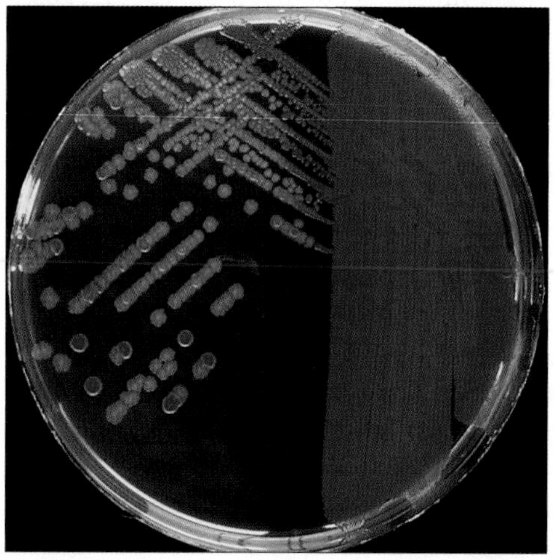

Fig. 228.4 Mixed culture of lactose-fermenting colonies (red) and non-lactose-fermenting colonies (pale) on MacConkey agar plate.

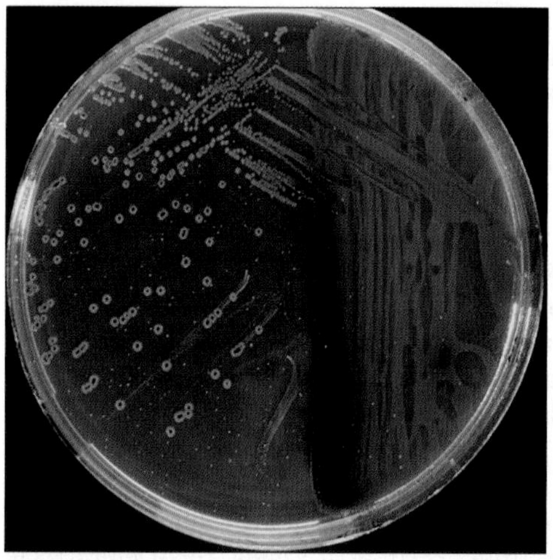

Fig. 228.5 *Salmonella–Shigella* agar plate showing growth of *Salmonella typhimurium* (pale colonies with black pigmentation indicating hydrogen sulfide production).

Some uropathogenic *E. coli* strains also produce an extracellular toxin, hemolysin.[37] Hemolysin acts generally as a membrane-damaging toxin, leading to the lysis of the cell with subsequent release of cytoplasmic components.

Another important virulence factor is the ability of *E. coli* to acquire iron for growth, and uropathogenic *E. coli* strains have multiple iron-sequestration systems, including a siderophore-based system. Many uropathogenic *E. coli* are encapsulated.[20]

Neonatal meningitis

Some strains of *E. coli* with a capsular antigen (K1) are uniquely associated with neonatal meningitis.[50] The severity of the disease is directly related to the presence, amount and persistence of K1 antigen.[51] The presence of K1 antigen interferes with phagocytosis and, in combination with certain O antigens, shows increased resistance to the bactericidal effect of serum complement.

Escherichia coli K1 antigen is composed of sialic acid residues and shows cross-reactivity with the group B meningococcal polysaccharide capsule. Although colonization of infants with *E. coli* at the time of delivery is common, disease is relatively infrequent.

Intestinal infections (see Chapter 43)

Certain *E. coli* strains are associated with intestinal infections in infants and adults. Most of these strains are the cause of 'traveler's diarrhea'. A characteristic feature of diarrheagenic *E. coli* is their ability to colonize the host's intestinal surface despite host defenses such as gastric acid, peristalsis and competition from other microbial gut flora. This is partly attributed to surface fimbriae for mucosal adherence. Diarrheagenic *E. coli* possess specific fimbrial antigens that increase their ability to colonize the intestine and adhere to the small bowel mucosa – a site that is not normally colonized[25,52] – once colonization is established. The virulence factors are distinct for each of the groups of diarrheagenic *E. coli*. The versatility of the *E. coli* genome is conferred mainly by two genetic configurations: virulence-related plasmids and chromosomal pathogenicity islands.

There are six main categories of diarrheagenic *E. coli*.[33] Although these categories are quite distinct, they have certain underlying similarities with respect to pathogenesis:

- their virulence properties are encoded on the plasmids;
- they have a characteristic interaction with the intestinal mucosa; and
- they produce enterotoxins or cytotoxins.

Within each category the strains tend to fall within certain O:H serotypes.

Before the availability of DNA techniques, knowledge of the epidemiology of enterodiarrheagenic *E. coli* was based on immunoassays and bioassays for identification of virulence factors such as toxins. These assays were cumbersome and time-consuming. Recent advances in DNA techniques have provided a new approach to

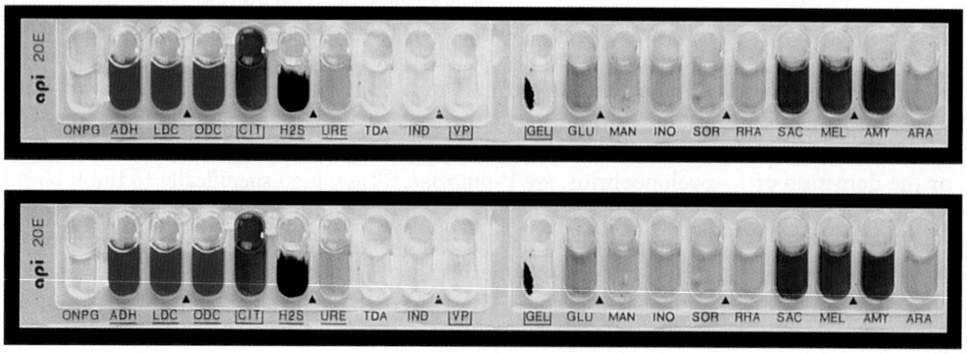

Fig. 228.6 API-20E strip after 24 hours incubation at 95°F (35°C).

screening a range of virulent genes of *E. coli*.[40] Six major categories of *E. coli* that cause diarrhea have been identified:[33]

- enterotoxigenic *E. coli* (ETEC);
- enteroinvasive *E. coli* (EIEC);
- enterohemorrhagic *E. coli* (EHEC);
- enteropathogenic *E. coli* (EPEC);
- enteroaggregative *E. coli* (EAEC, also known as EaggEC); and
- diffusely adherent *E. coli* (DAEC).

Enterotoxigenic Escherichia coli

Enterotoxigenic *E. coli* causes 'travelers' diarrhea' (in developing countries) by colonizing the small intestine and producing one or more enterotoxin, giving rise to a net secretory state.[29,53] The heat-labile enterotoxin (LT) is structurally similar to *Vibrio cholera* toxin and, by activation of adenylate cyclase, leads to hypersecretion of fluids and electrolytes into the small intestines. The heat-stable enterotoxin (ST) activates guanylate cyclase and stimulates fluid secretion.

Besides the enterotoxins, three other factors have been used to identify and characterize ETEC: O serogroup, H serogroup and CFAs.[29] The mechanism by which ETEC adheres to small bowel enterocytes is mediated by surface fimbriae (pili). The ETEC fimbriae confer the species specificity of the pathogen; human ETEC possess an array of colonization fimbriae, the CFAs (CFA/I rod-shaped fimbriae; CFA/III; a Bfp CFA/II and CFA/IV). The CFA genes are usually encoded on plasmids, which typically also encode the enterotoxins ST and/or LT.[54]

Infection by ETEC, after an incubation period of 1–2 days, is characterized by diarrhea, nausea and vomiting but usually no fever; the symptoms are usually mild and self-limiting, with a duration of 3–4 days.

Enteroinvasive Escherichia coli

Enteroinvasive *E. coli* causes a dysenteric form of diarrheal illness.[55] Strains of EIEC closely resemble *Shigella* spp. Like *Shigella* spp., they are capable of invading and proliferating within epithelial cells of the large intestine, eventually causing death of the cell. The invasive capacity is dependent on the presence of plasmid coding for the production of several outer membrane proteins involved in invasiveness.[56] Among the genes responsible for invasion are the *mxi* and *spa* loci, which encode a so-called type III secretion apparatus.[56,57] In addition, both EIEC and *Shigella* spp. elaborate one or more secretory enterotoxins, which may play a role in diarrheal pathogenesis. They do not form enterotoxins, like ETEC. Clinically, the illness is marked by watery diarrhea, often with mucus and leukocytes, a scant bloody stool, severe abdominal cramps and fever. The symptoms are usually self-limiting.

Enterohemorrhagic Escherichia coli

Enterohemorrhagic *E. coli*, also called verocytotoxin-producing *E. coli*, is associated with two syndromes: hemorrhagic colitis, with abdominal pain and bloody diarrhea; and hemolytic–uremic syndrome (HUS), characterized by hemolytic anemia, thrombocytopenia and acute renal failure.[58,59] *Escherichia coli* O157:H7 has been associated most frequently with hemorrhagic colitis and HUS; however, several other serotypes have also been associated with disease.

Both plasmid-encoded adherence factors for distinct fimbriae and cytotoxin production are important factors in the pathogenesis of disease.[60] Enterohemorrhagic *E. coli* as well as EPEC have the ability to induce a characteristic 'attacking and effacing' (A/E) histopathology on gut enterocytes characterized by localized destruction of brush border microvilli, intimate bacterial adhesion and gross cytoskeletal reorganization.[26,61] A/E lesion formation is essential for full EPEC and EHEC pathogenicity.

The genes encoding for the A/E histopathology are contained on a 35.6kb pathogenicity island called the locus of enterocute effacement (LEE). The EHEC LEE contains genes encoding intimin type III secretion pathway and some other protein O. Enterohemorrhagic *E. coli* and EPEC strains use the LEE type III secretion system – secretion of virulence factors, some of which are injected (translocated) directly from the pathogen's cytoplasm into the host cell cytosol – to secrete several LEE-encoded proteins. All contacts stimulate the expression of LEE-encoded proteins and the assembling of a protein translocation apparatus (translocon) that provides a continuous channel from the bacterial cytoplasm to the host cell cytosol. The translocon is used to translocate receptor into the host cell, where it becomes inserted into the host membrane; excreted effector proteins are now probably able to make cytoskeletal changes and as a result form A/E lesions.

There are 'typical' EHEC strains, such as O157:H7, that produce stripe-like (Stx) toxins and A/E lesions and possess the 60MDa plasmid; and 'atypical' EHEC strains that do not produce A/E lesions and/or do not possess the 60MDa EHEC plasmid.[25] The development of HUS involves direct cytotoxic action of Stx on renal endothelial cells, but cytokines are probably also indirectly involved in this process.[62]

The symptoms are usually self-limited. They vary in severity from mild symptoms of nonbloody diarrhea to severe hemorrhagic colitis, sometimes ending in death (especially in children and the elderly).

The use of antibiotics for the treatment of severe infection is controversial and a recent study[63] showed that patients treated with antibiotics are at greater risk of developing HUS. The harmful potential is explained by lysis of bacteria and an increase in release of toxins. Recent outbreaks of EHEC disease have raised public concern about the safety of the food supply.[64]

Enteropathogenic Escherichia coli

Enteropathogenic *E. coli* plays a role in infant diarrhea and can also be associated with chronic diarrhea in young children.[65] Plasmid-encoded adhesiveness is the most important factor in the pathogenesis of the disease.[66] Strains of EPEC are responsible for different clinical signs of the infection, depending on the diffuse and localized adherence to cells. The clinical signs range from mild nonbloody diarrhea to more severe diarrhea.

The hallmark of infections due to EPEC is the A/E histopathology similar to that of EHEC (see above), characterized by effacement of microvilli and intimate adherence between the bacteria and the epithelium cell membrane.[26,61]

In the first step of infection, localized adherence to epithelial cells mediated by Bfp occurs. Bfp is encoded on plasmids called EAF plasmids. In the second step adherence induces a variety of signal induction pathways. Genes responsible for this signal transduction are encoded on a 35kb pathogenicity island (LEE). Intimate adherence of EPEC to epithelial cells is mediated by a 94–97kDa outer membrane protein called intimin. At least four proteins are secreted extracellularly by EPEC and three of them are essential for A/E histopathology.

As with other diarrheal pathogens, the treatment of EPEC diarrhea is to prevent dehydration by correcting fluid and electrolyte imbalances. Antibiotic treatment had been used in many patients, with good results, but multiple antibiotic resistance is common for EPEC.[67]

Enteroaggregative Escherichia coli

Enteroaggregative *E. coli* are an increasingly important cause of diarrhea.[68] They cause nonbloody, watery diarrhea that is often persistent and can be inflammatory. Enteroaggregative *E. coli* have been implicated in sporadic diarrhea in children and adults in both developing and developed countries, and recently have been reported to cause 'traveler's diarrhea'.

Enteroaggregative *E. coli* are characterized by their ability to adhere to epithelial cells in a characteristic 'stacked-brick' pattern but are otherwise highly heterogeneous. The adherence consist of two phenotypes – diffuse and aggregative. The exact mechanism of pathogenesis is not completely known but adhesins, toxins and several other factors contribute to disease.

Adhesins (plasmid-encoded) are aggregative adherence fimbria I (AAF/I), which is shown to mediate aggregative adherence to epithelial cells and Hep-2 hemagglutination, and to be involved in formation of biofilm. The other type of fimbria, AAF/II, is more associated with diarrhea in children. Other virulence factors include invasion and plasmid-encoded toxin production, but these factors were shown to be present only in some strains. The general problem with *E. coli* infections is to distinguish the pathogenic from the commensal types.

Diffusely adherent Escherichia coli

Diffusely adherent *E. coli* are now recognized by most authors as an independent category of potentially diarrheagenic *E. coli*. In a number of studies DAEC was associated with endemic pediatric diarrhea lasting longer than 2 weeks. The diffuse adherence to Hep-2 cells is mediated by a unique fimbrial structure known as the F1845 fimbria, which can be found on either bacterial chromosome or a plasmid.

BACTEREMIA AND NOSOCOMIAL INFECTIONS

As a group, Enterobacteriaceae are the most frequent bacterial isolates recovered from both inpatient and outpatient clinical specimens. In 1990–2 Enterobacteriaceae accounted for 30% of pathogens isolated from all infection sites in the Centers for Disease Control and Prevention (CDC) and National Nosocomial Infection Surveillance system.[69]

In the past few years, with the increased use of invasive devices and broad-spectrum antibiotics, Enterobacteriaceae, specifically *E. coli*, have become somewhat less prevalent than Gram-positive cocci as a cause of nosocomial infection. Nevertheless, *E. coli* is still an important cause of hospital-acquired infections despite adequate antibiotic therapy and supportive care.

The increasing antibiotic resistance among *E. coli* resulting in nosocomial infections is a major cause of concern in hospitals. There are several factors that predispose hospitalized patients to such infections: the use of antibiotics that eradicate normal flora, impaired skin and mucous membranes, intubation, intravenous and bladder catheters and surgical procedures. These infections, including UTIs, wound infections, pneumonia, intra-abdominal abscesses and peritonitis, are often followed by bacteremia. However, bacteremia without primary focus is sometimes detected in immunocompromised patients.

Bacteremia

Escherichia coli is the most common cause of nosocomial bacteremia. In 1979 it had an incidence of 2.7 per 10,000 hospital charges.[70] The most common portal of entry of infection for both community-acquired and nosocomial *E. coli* bacteremia is the urinary tract.[71] The overall mortality rate from *E. coli* bacteremia is approximately 20%. Bacteremia that does not originate in the urinary tract tends to have a worse outcome.

Bacteremia is frequently due to pulmonary infections in intubated patients receiving ventilation therapy or to UTIs caused by indwelling urinary catheters. Patients with granulocytopenia due to leukemia, cancer or chemotherapy are at high risk of bacteremia.

Septic shock

Septic shock occurs in approximately 40% of patients with Gram-negative bacteremia. The high frequency of septic shock in bacteriemia caused by Enterobacteriaceae is attributed to the toxic effect on the circulatory system of endotoxin (LPS).[38,40] Endotoxin within the circulatory system has multiple and complex effects on neutrophils, platelets, complement, clotting factors and the inflammatory mediators in the blood. These complex effects may result in multiple organ failure and eventually in death. Mortality rates from Gram-negative shock range from 40% to 70%.

Urinary tract infections

Urinary tract infections are the most common hospital-acquired infections and *E. coli* is a leading pathogen, implicated in about 25% of all nosocomial UTIs.[69] Recognized major risk factors for hospital-acquired UTIs include urinary catheterization and obstruction to urine flow.

Other sites of hospital-acquired infection

The lungs are a common site of hospital-acquired infection, although it is often difficult to discriminate between *E. coli* colonizing the upper airways and *E. coli* causing pulmonary infection.

Approximately a quarter of surgical infections are caused by Enterobacteriaceae, among which *E. coli* accounts for about 8%.

Nosocomial central nervous system infections occur mainly in neurosurgical patients, neonates and patients undergoing procedures that penetrate the central nervous system. Of postsurgical meningitis, 69% is caused by Gram-negative bacilli, with a majority (70%) of these due to *E. coli*.

MANAGEMENT

Antibiotic therapy for infections with *E. coli* and other Enterobacteriaceae must be guided by an in-vitro susceptibility test and by clinical experience. Although most strains of *E. coli* are still susceptible to the commonly used antibiotics, resistance, especially in hospital-acquired infections, is increasing.

The treatment of infective diarrhea is oral fluid and electrolyte replacement. Antibiotics are generally not recommended and only in chronic or life-threatening infections should antibiotic treatment be considered.[72] The duration and breadth of antimicrobial treatment in other infections caused by *E. coli* or other Enterobacteriaceae depend on the site and severity of the infection. For example, uncomplicated cystitis in otherwise healthy women can be often managed with a single dose of antibiotic, whereas sepsis requires about 10 days' therapy, and prostatitis or deep-seated renal infection requires as much as 6 weeks' treatment.

Conventional approaches to control nosocomial infections caused by Enterobacteriaceae are not always successful. Therefore, antibiotic prophylaxis has been studied to prevent colonization and nosocomial pneumonia in the critically ill, and selective decontamination of the gastrointestinal tract has been investigated as a method of preventing infections by Enterobacteriaceae in ventilated patients in intensive care units.[73] A recent meta-analysis of 22 randomized trials demonstrated that selective decontamination reduced the incidence of respiratory tract infection by 63%.[74] However, in most studies, even when pneumonia rates were reduced, selective decontamination had no effect on the mortality rate or hospital stay. The development of antibiotic resistance is the most feared complication of selective decontamination.[75]

MEDICALLY IMPORTANT GENERA OF ENTEROBACTERIACEAE

Escherichia

Escherichia coli makes up the largest proportion of aerobic Gram-negative bacteria of the intestinal tract. It is a non-spore-forming rod and is often motile by means of peritrichous flagella. It can grow aerobically as well as anaerobically.

Most strains ferment lactose rapidly, and the colonies on MacConkey medium are smooth, glossy and translucent in appearance and rose pink in color. On blood agar the colonies of some strains are surrounded by zones of hemolysis. Most strains of *E. coli* attack carbohydrates fermentatively, with the production of acid and gas; a few strains will produce acid but not gas. Although most strains of *E. coli* ferment lactose rapidly, there are some strains with a slow fermentation pattern or that are non-lactose-fermenting. Furthermore, *E. coli* is characterized by the ability to reduce nitrates to nitrites. Most of the strains produce indole, give a positive methyl-red reaction and the Voges–Proskauer test is negative. *Escherichia coli* strains do not hydrolyze urea or produce hydrogen sulfide, and phenylalanine deaminase activity is absent. *Escherichia coli* cannot use citrate as the sole source of carbon and will not grow in the presence of potassium cyanide.[2,42]

Although conventional approaches to identification (e.g. sugar fermentation) are still valid and useful, there are several other methods available now. For example, there are commercially available tests that use rapid chromogenic enzyme substrates, such as the API system or automated methods.[43] Together with growth on selective or differential media, colonial characteristics and cell morphology on a Gram stain, identification can be completed.

Escherichia coli can be subdivided into serogroups, serotypes and biotypes.[1] Two *E. coli* surface compounds form the basis for the serologic classification system: heat-stable somatic O antigen of LPS, and heat-labile flagella H antigen (H stands for *hauch*, the German word for 'breath', because of the mist-like effect around the bacterium caused by the presence of flagella; O denotes *ohne*, 'without', i.e. lacking flagella). The O antigen identifies the serogroup of a strain and the H antigen identifies its serotype. The biotype is determined by the biochemical profile.

To date, 173 different serogroups have been identified, and there are at least 56 identified serotypes.[17] There is some correlation between serogroup and virulence. For example, O86 is commonly found on members of the residual colonic microflora, and members of this serogroup rarely cause disease; on the other hand, group O55 is rarely found in the residual microflora and is almost always associated with disease. If the bacteria is enveloped by a capsule, a capsular (K) antigen is also used for classification. Only a few of the 80 distinct K antigens isolated from natural populations are associated with invasive *E. coli* disease.[18] Strains classified as K1, for example, are a common cause of systemic disease in infants.[17]

Escherichia fergusonii, *Escherichia hermannii* and *Escherichia vulneris* (Table 228.4) are occasionally isolated from patients, but their clinical significance is not well defined. *Escherichia blattae* has been recovered from cockroaches but its role in human infections has not been established.[76]

Shigella

The genus *Shigella* is closely related to the genus *Escherichia*, as shown by genetic analysis. The genetic relationship is so close that it has been advocated that both genera form a single genetic species. However, the distinction between the two genera remains useful from a clinical point of view. The *Shigella* organisms differ from a typical *Escherichia coli* strain in that they are nonmotile, do not ferment lactose and do not produce gas from glucose. One member of the genus *Escherichia*, *E. coli* inactive (formally called 'Alcalescens-Dispar'), has many characteristics similar to those of *Shigella* organisms and they be considered to be a species in between Escherichiae and Shigellae.

Four species of medical importance are traditionally described within the genus *Shigella*: *S. dysenteriae*, *S. flexneri*, *Shigella boydii* and *Shigella sonnei* (see Table 228.4). Members of the species are hard to differentiate from each other by biochemical testing. Using serologic methods, *S. dysenteriae* makes up group A, *S. flexneri* group B and *S. boydii* group C. Each group can be further subdivided into different serotypes, and this is useful for epidemiologic purposes. Serologic cross-reactions with *E. coli* strains and other members of the family of Enterobacteriaceae do occur. *Shigella sonnei* (group D) can be separated from the other *Shigella* spp. by a positive ornithine reaction; this species may show lactose fermentation after incubation for more than 48 hours.

Dysentery caused by *Shigella* spp. occurs worldwide. The annual number of *Shigella* episodes is estimated to be 163.2 million in developing countries and 1.5 million in industrialized countries.[77] In industrialized countries, person-to-person transmission, perhaps via hands, is the most common form of transmission, and *S. sonnei* is now the most frequently isolated species of the Shigellae in these countries.[77] In developing countries, the predominant species is *S. flexneri* and the mode of transmission is often by contaminated water, food or perhaps flies. The low inoculum (less than 200 viable bacteria) needed for disease is often assumed to be one of the factors responsible for the high secondary attack rate during outbreaks. Long-term excretion is uncommon but does occur. Long-term excreters are probably important as a reservoir; in these people, carriage of the *Shigella* strains is often in the colon.

Salmonella

The classification of *Salmonella* organisms has been controversial over the years.[42] Biochemical and genetic studies show so much similarity between *Salmonella* and Arizona group that all strains may belong to a single species. For epidemiologic purposes, serotyping of O antigens (type A, B, C and so on) and of H (flagellate) antigens has resulted in more than 2000 distinct serotypes, which are often named as if they were species (e.g. '*Salmonella typhimurium*' rather than '*Salmonella* serotype *typhimurium*' or even '*Salmonella choleraesuis* subsp. *choleraesuis* serotype *typhimurium*').

The genus *Salmonella* can be subdivided into different groups.[2] More than 99% of clinical isolates belong to subgroup 1 (*S. choleraesuis* subsp. *choleraesuis*; Table 228.5). Other subgroups include *S. choleraesuis* subsp. *salamae* (subgroup 2), *S. choleraesuis* subsp. *arizonae* (subgroup 3a), *S. choleraesuis* subsp. *diarizonae* (subgroup 3b), *S. choleraesuis* subsp. *houtenae* (subgroup 4) and *S. bongori* (subgroup 5). Subgroup 6 has been proposed to contain the subspecies *indica*. The name *Salmonella enterica* has been used by bacteriologists and has caused confusion in the nomenclature of *Salmonella*.[78]

A presumptive identification of '*S. typhi*' can often be made biochemically because these strains are mostly citrate-negative, produce hydrogen sulfide slowly, are ornithine-decarboxylase-negative, do not produce gas from glucose and do not ferment arabinose and rhamnose, in contrast to most other strains of *Salmonella*.

Salmonella gastroenteritis and enteric fever occur worldwide. The reservoir for the serotypes *typhi* and *paratyphi* A, B and C are human, but the other Salmonellae are widely distributed among animals. Some strains are associated with particular animals (e.g. subspecies *arizonae* with reptiles), but exchange of strains between animals is frequent. Transmission is mostly by contaminated water and food, and perhaps by insects such as flies, although direct person-to-person transmission has been described.

Citrobacter

The name *Citrobacter* is derived from the ability of these strains to use citrate as a source of carbon. *Citrobacter* organisms are widely found in environmental samples. Eleven species in this genus have now been listed (Table 228.6).[7] *Citrobacter freundii* is frequently

THE GENERA *ESCHERICHIA* AND *SHIGELLA*	
Name	Synonym
Escherichia blattae	
Escherichia coli	
Escherichia fergussonii	CDC enteric group 10
Escherichia hermannii	CDC enteric group 11
Escherichia vulneris	CDC enteric group 1
Shigella boydii	*Shigella* biogroup C
Shigella dysenteriae	*Shigella* biogroup A
Shigella flexneri	*Shigella* biogroup B
Shigella sonnei	*Shigella* biogroup D

Table 228.4 The genera *Escherichia* and *Shigella*.[7]

THE GENUS *SALMONELLA*	
Name	Synonym
Salmonella bongori	*Salmonella* subgroup 5
Salmonella choleraesuis subsp. *arizonae*	*Salmonella* subgroup 3a
Salmonella choleraesius subsp. *choleraesius*	*Salmonella* subgroup 1 (includes most serotypes: *S. typhi, S. cholerasuis, S. paratyphi, S. gallinarum, S. pullorum)*
Salmonella choleraesius subsp. *diarizonae*	*Salmonella* subgroup 3b
Salmonella choleraesius subsp. *houtenae*	*Salmonella* subgroup 4
Salmonella choleraesius subsp. *salamae*	*Salmonella* subgroup 2

Table 228.5 The genus *Salmonella*.[7]

THE GENUS *CITROBACTER*	
Name	Synonym
Citrobacter amalonaticus	*Levinea amalonatica*
Citrobacter braakii	*Citrobacter freundii*
Citrobacter farmeri	*Citrobacter amalonaticus* biogroup 1
Citrobacter freundii	*Citrobacter freundii*
Citrobacter genomospecies 10	*Citrobacter freundii*
Citrobacter genomospecies 11	*Citrobacter freundii*
Citrobacter koseri	*Citrobacter diversus*
Citrobacter rodentium	*Citrobacter* genomospecies 9,
Citrobacter sedlakii	*Citrobacter freundii*
Citrobacter werkmanii	*Citrobacter freundii*
Citrobacter youngae	

Table 228.6 The genus *Citrobacter*.[7]

isolated from nosocomial infections, including hospital-acquired pneumonia, bacteremia, UTIs and wound infections. Nosocomial transmission may be related to antimicrobial resistance; many strains of *C. freundii* produce an inducible broad-spectrum β-lactamase.[79] In addition, *C. freundii* has been associated with gastroenteritis.[2,5] New species, formally within the *C. freundii* complex, include *Citrobacter braakii*, *Citrobacter rodentium*,[80] *Citrobacter sedlakii*, *Citrobacter werkmanii*, *Citrobacter youngae*, *Citrobacter gillenii* (genomospecies 10) and *Citrobacter murliniae* (genomospecies 11).[81] Identification of newly described *Citrobacter* spp. by commercial systems has been studied.[82]

Citrobacter koseri (formerly designated *C. diversus*) may be a causative agent of sepsis, meningitis and brain abscesses, especially in young children.[83] Transmission from mother to newborn has been described.[84] Many strains of *C. koseri* produce an inducible class A β-lactamase, as does *Proteus vulgaris*,[79] although other strains may produce a class C β-lactamase like *C. freundii*. *Citrobacter amalonaticus* is rarely involved in human disease. It has recently been proposed that melibiose-positive variants of *C. amalonaticus* (biotype 1) should be named *Citrobacter farmeri*.[2]

Klebsiella

The current classification of the genus *Klebsiella* recognizes five species with several subspecies (Table 228.7). All the species are nonmotile. *Klebsiella* strains can be found in the feces of healthy adults.[85] *Klebsiella pneumoniae* is well known as the cause of Friedländer's pneumonia and nosocomial infections. Strains of this species often grow as mucoid lactose-positive colonies on MacConkey agar. The subspecies *rhinoscleromatis* is Voges–Proskauer-negative and does not ferment lactose or several other sugars. It is the causative agent of rhinoscleroma, a granulomatous diseases of the nose and associated tissues.[86] *Klebsiella ozaenae* is another biochemically less active subspecies, which is associated with ozena, an atrophic condition of the nasal mucosa. *Klebsiella planticola*, *Klebsiella terrigena* and *Klebsiella ornithinolytica* are uncommon isolates in the clinical setting,[87] and the genus name *Raoultella* has been proposed for these species.[88] Indole-positive strains of *Klebsiella* are classified as *Klebsiella oxytoca*; these strains may cause infections similar to those caused by *K. pneumoniae*. Most strains of *K. pneumoniae* and *K. oxytoca* produce a chromosomal class A β-lactamase that renders them resistant to ampicillin but susceptible to β-lactamase inhibition by clavulanic acid and analogues. Since 1982, extended-spectrum β-lactamases have been described that are mutations of the TEM or SHV type of β-lactamase; these have increased hydrolytic activity against third-generation cephalosporins or are less inhibited by clavulanate.[79] Genetic information for these enzymes is carried on plasmids, often in combination with other resistance factors such as aminoglycoside-modifying enzymes, and this type of resistance may spread relatively rapidly in settings of increased antibiotic use.

Enterobacter

The species in the genus *Enterobacter* are listed in Table 228.8. *Enterobacter cloacae* is a common clinical isolate. It is a frequent cause of opportunistic infections and is often acquired in hospital. Antibiotic resistance is frequent, especially against third-generation cephalosporins, by means of an inducible chromosomal β-lactamase.[89]

Another frequently isolated species in this setting is *Enterobacter aerogenes*. Because this motile strain resembles the genus *Klebsiella* more than other *Enterobacter* organisms, it has been proposed that this species be renamed *Klebsiella mobilis*.[42] A yellow pigment is produced by *Enterobacter sakazakii*, a species that has been described as causing neonatal infections.[90] Another yellow-pigmented species, *Enterobacter agglomerans*, has recently been renamed *Pantoea agglomerans* (see below). *Enterobacter hormaechei*, *Enterobacter cancerogenus* ('*Enterobacter taylorae*'), *Enterobacter intermedium*, *Enterobacter asburiae* and *Enterobacter gergoviae* are among the less common *Enterobacter* spp. that have been isolated from blood cultures and various other specimens from patients with infections.[91–93] *Enterobacter amnigenus* has also been isolated from human tissue but it is unclear whether it causes disease.[2]

Enterobacter kobei is a recently proposed species[94] that closely resembles *E. cloacae*. Many *Enterobacter* spp. are resistant to second-generation and third-generation cephalosporins by virtue of

THE GENUS *KLEBSIELLA*	
Name	**Synonym**
Klebsiella ornithinolytica	*Klebsiella oxytoca* ornithine positive
Klebsiella oxytoca	
Klebsiella planticola	*Klebsiella travisanii*
Klebsiella pneumoniae subsp. *ozaenae*	*Klebsiella ozaenae*
Klebsiella pneumoniae subsp. *pneumoniae*	*Klebsiella pneumoniae*
Klebsiella pneumoniae subsp. *rhinoscleromatis*	*Klebsiella rhinoscleromatis*
Klebsiella terrigena	

Table 228.7 The genus *Klebsiella*.[7]

THE GENUS *ENTEROBACTER*	
Name	**Synonym**
Enterobacter aerogenes	*Aerobacter aerogenes*
Enterobacter amnigenus	
Enterobacter asburiae	CDC enteric group 17
Enterobacter cancerogenus	*Enterobacter taylorae*
Enterobacter cloacae	
Enterobacter gergoviae	
Enterobacter hormaechei	CDC enteric group 45
Enterobacter kobei	
Enterobacter sakazakii	

Table 228.8 The genus *Enterobacter*.[7]

an inducible broad-spectrum cephalosporinase encoded by genetic information on the chromosome. These strains may seem susceptible at first isolation, but subsequent isolates may show resistance to these agents.[79,89]

Serratia

The genus *Serratia* consists of nine species (Table 228.9).[7] *Serratia marcescens* is the one most commonly associated with nosocomial infections, in part because it is often resistant to commonly used β-lactam antibiotics and in part because it is not fastidious in its growth conditions. This species and other *Serratia* spp. have been implicated in ocular infections associated with soft contact lenses.[95] Red pigment is formed under suitable conditions by some strains of *S. marcescens*, as well as by *Serratia plymuthica* and *Serratia rubidaea*, two other opportunistic pathogens.[96,97] Two other species, *Serratia liquefaciens* and *Serratia odorifera*, are less frequently associated with clinical infections.[98]

Serratia grimesii, *Serratia proteamaculans* subsp. *proteamaculans* and *Serratia proteamaculans* subsp. *quinovora* are closely related to *S. liquefaciens*.[5] *Serratia ficaria* and *Serratia fonticola* are rarely involved in human disease.[99]

Proteus

The genus *Proteus* once contained many species but currently only three are listed: *Proteus mirabilis*, *Proteus penneri* and *Proteus vulgaris* (Table 228.10). Characteristics of *Proteus* spp. include their tendency to display swarming motility during growth on nonselective media and their strong urease reaction.[100] This urease activity has been associated with the formation of kidney stones, as UTIs are commonly caused by *Proteus* spp. *Proteus mirabilis* is indole-negative and often susceptible to most common antibiotics, with the exception of nitrofurantoin, whereas indole-positive *P. vulgaris* is more resistant to β-lactam antibiotics. *Proteus penneri* is closely related to *P. vulgaris* but is indole-negative and can be distinguished from *P. mirabilis* by its negative ornithine reaction. The name *Proteus hauseri* has been proposed for *P. vulgaris* biogroup 3.[101]

Morganella

Morganella morganii is currently the only species in the genus (see Table 228.10). Two subspecies (*morganii* and *sibonii*) can be distinguished by the ability to ferment trehalose.[102] Urinary tract infections and other opportunistic infections are associated with this species. *Morganella morganii* was originally part of the genus *Proteus*.

Providencia

Members of the genus *Providencia* are a diverse group of organisms (see Table 228.10). The two species *Providencia rettgeri* and *Providencia stuartii* may be urease positive (*P. rettgeri* more often than *P. stuartii*), and both are a frequent cause of UTIs and other opportunistic infections.[103] *Providencia alcalifaciens* has been implicated in gastrointestinal infections in children.[104] *Providencia rustigianii* has rarely been isolated from humans.[2]

Yersinia

The genus *Yersinia* includes three species that can cause a variety of infections in the host (Table 228.11).[105] *Yersinia pestis* is the causative agent of plague.[106,107] The plague bacillus grows slowly on conventional media. Like infections with other *Yersinia* spp., plague is a zoonosis. The natural reservoir are small animals, and transmission occurs through bites of fleas from these animals, by handling contaminated parts of the animals and by human-to-human transmission from patients with pneumonic plague. Plague has been implicated as a potential biologic weapon, and recommendations for measures to be taken by medical and public health professionals have been developed.[108] *Yersinia pseudotuberculosis* closely resembles *Y. pestis*, and it has even been suggested that the two are a single species. *Yersinia pseudotuberculosis* is associated with mesenterial lymphadenitis, which simulates appendicitis, mainly in children and adolescents. Sepsis with *Y. pseudotuberculosis* has mainly been described in patients with liver disease and other chronic illnesses. *Yersinia enterocolitica* can cause mesenterial lymphadenitis, gastroenteritis, infections in many other tissues and sepsis. Notorious sources of infections include blood transfusion products,[109] in which *Y. enterocolitica* can proliferate at storage temperatures of 39°F (4°C). Serotypes 3 and 9 are most common in Europe, whereas serotype 8 is more frequently encountered in the USA.[76] Complications of *Y. enterocolitica* infection include polyarthritis, erythema nodosum and Reiter's syndrome.

Yersinia frederiksenii, *Yersinia intermedia* and *Yersinia kristensenii* have recently been separated from *Y. enterocolitica*. As with *Yersinia bercovieri*, *Yersinia mollaretii* and *Yersinia rohdei*, their association with human disease is less clear.[110] For a fuller description of the microbiology of *Yersinia* spp. see Chapter 231.

Edwardsiella

In nature, *Edwardsiella* spp. are found in many cold-blooded animals. *Edwardsiella tarda* has been the cause of liver abscesses, bacteremia and infections in various other tissues.[111] In addition, it has been associated with gastrointestinal infections. It produces large amounts of hydrogen sulfide in culture. The association of *Edwardsiella ictaluri* and *Edwardsiella hoshinae* with human disease is less clear.

Hafnia

Hafnia alvei is presently the only species within the genus *Hafnia*. Fewer carbohydrates are fermented than in *Enterobacter* spp.

THE GENUS *SERRATIA*	
Name	**Synonym**
Serratia ficaria	
Serratia fonticola	
Serratia grimesii	*Serratia liquefaciens*
Serratia liquefaciens	*Enterobacter liquefaciens*
Serratia marcescens	
Serratia odorifera	
Serratia plymuthica	
Serratia proteamaculans subsp. *proteamaculans*	*Serratia liquefaciens*
Serratia proteamaculans subsp. *quinovora*	*Serratia liquefaciens*
Serratia rubidaea	

Table 228.9 The genus *Serratia*.[7]

THE GENERA *MORGANELLA, PROTEUS* AND *PROVIDENTIA*	
Name	**Synonym**
Morganella morganii subsp. *morganii*	*Proteus morganii*
Morganella morganii subsp. *sibonii*	*Proteus morganii*
Proteus mirabilis	
Proteus penneri	*Proteus vulgaris* indole negative
Proteus vulgaris	
Providencia alcalifaciens	*Proteus inconstans*
Providencia rettgeri	*Proteus rettgeri*
Providencia rustigianii	*Providencia alcalifaciens* biogroup 3
Providencia stuartii	*Proteus inconstans*

Table 228.10 The genera *Morganella, Proteus* and *Providentia*[7]

THE GENUS *YERSINIA*	
Name	**Synonym**
Yersinia aldovae	
Yersinia bercovieri	*Yersinia enterocolitica* biogroup 3b
Yersinia enterocolitica	*Pasteurella enterocolitica*
Yersinia frederiksenii	
Yersinia intermedia	
Yersinia kristensenii	
Yersinia mollaretii	*Yersinia enterocolitica* biogroup 3a
Yersinia pestis	*Pasteurella pestis*
Yersinia pseudotuberculosis	*Pasteurella pseudotuberculosis*
Yersinia rohdei	

Table 228.11 The genus *Yersinia*.[7]

MISCELLANEOUS ENTEROBACTERIAL GENERA	
Name	**Synonym**
Budvicia aquatica	
Buttiauxella agrestis	
Buttiauxella noackiae	CDC enteric group 59
Cedecea davisae	CDC enteric group 15
Cedecea lapagei	
Cedecea neteri	*Cedecea* sp. 4
Cedecea sp. 3	
Cedecea sp. 5	
Edwardsiella hoshinae	
Edwardsiella ictaluri	
Edwardsiella tarda	
Ewingella americana	CDC enteric group 40
Hafnia alvei	*Enterobacter hafniae*
Kluyvera ascorbata	CDC enteric group 8
Kluyvera cryocrescens	
Kluyvera georgiana	CDC enteric group 36/37 *Kluyvera* sp. group 3
Leclercia adecarboxylata	*Escherichia adecarboxylata* CDC enteric group 41
Leminorella grimontii	CDC enteric group 57
Leminorella richardii	
Moellerella wisconsensis	CDC enteric group 46
Pantoea agglomerans	*Enterobacter agglomerans*
Photorhabdus luminescens	*Xenorhabdus luminescens*
Rahnella aquatilis	
Tatumella ptyseos	CDC group EF-9
Yokenella regensburgei	*Koserella trabulsii* CDC enteric group 45

Table 228.12 Miscellaneous enterobacterial genera.[71]

THE NEWER ENTEROBACTERIACEAE GENERA AND THEIR DISTINGUISHING REACTIONS		
Newer genus	**Related genus**	**Selected differentiating reactions**
Buttiauxella	*Escherichia*	Citrate
Cedecea	*Serratia*	DNAase, gelatin, lipase
Ewingella	*Pantoea*	Xylose, arabinose
Kluyvera	*Escherichia*	Citrate
Leclercia	*Escherichia*	Adonitol, lysine, malonate
Leminorella	*Proteus*	Urease, phenylalanine, arabinose
Moellerella	*Providentia*	Lactose, phenylalanine
Rahnella	*Pantoea*	Phenylalanine
Tatumella	*Pantoea*	Mannitol, phenylalanine
Trabumella	*Salmonella*	Ortho-nitrophenyl-β-galactosidase, dulcitol
Yokenella	*Hafnia*	Voges–Proskauer

Table 228.13 The newer Enterobacteriaceae genera and their distinguishing reactions. Adapted from Koneman *et al.*[5]

The organism has been isolated from environmental samples, infected wounds and other tissues, and has been implicated in gastroenteritis.[112–115]

Pantoea

Pantoea agglomerans was until recently a member of the genus *Enterobacter*. Strains produce a yellow pigment. This species became notorious because of an outbreak of nosocomial bacteremia associated with contaminated intravenous fluids.[116]

Miscellaneous other Enterobacteriaceae

Newer members of the family Enterobacteriaceae have been described in recent years and many have been associated with human diseases.[116–122] Tables 228.12 and 228.13 list the newer genera, together with other genera that are closely related and selected reactions to distinguish these strains. In addition to the genera mentioned in these figures, other new genera include *Budvicia*, which are mainly isolated from water sources, *Erwinia*, which are mostly plant pathogens,[123] and *Photorhabdis*.[124]

REFERENCES

1. Kauffman F. The bacteriology of Enterobacteriaceae. Baltimore: Williams & Wilkins; 1966.
2. Farmer JJ III. Enterobacteriaceae: introduction and identification. In: Murray PP, ed. Manual of clinical microbiology. Washington, DC: ASM Press; 1999:442–48.
3. Blattner FR, Plunkett G, Bloch CA, *et al.* The complete genome sequence of *Escherichia coli* K-12. Science 1997;277:1453–62.
4. Ewing WH. Edward and Ewing's identification of Enterobacteriaceae. New York: Elsevier; 1986.
5. Koneman EW, Allen SD, Janda WM, *et al.* Color atlas and textbook of diagnostic microbiology. Philadelphia: JB Lippincott; 1997.
6. Mandell GL, Bennet JE, Dolin R. Principles and practice of infectious diseases. New York: Churchill Livingstone; 2000.
7. Bruckner DA, Colonna P. Nomenclature for aerobic and facultative bacteria. Clin Infect Dis 1999;29:713–23.
8. Brenner DJ. Enterobacteriaceae. In: Krieg NR, Holt JG, eds. Bergey's manual of systematic bacteriology, vol. 1. Baltimore: Williams & Wilkins; 1984:408–20.
9. Osborn MJ, Gauder JE, Parisi E, Carson J. Mechanism of assembly of the outer membrane of *Salmonella typhimurium.* Isolation and characterization of cytoplasmic and outer membrane. J Biol Chem 1972;247:3962–72.
10. Schleifer KH, Kandler O. Peptidoglycan types of bacterial cell walls and their taxonomic implications. Bacteriol Rev 1972;36:407–77.
11. Oliver DB. Periplasm. In: Neidhardt FC, Curtiss R III, Ingraham JL, *et al.*, eds. *Escherichia coli* and *Salmonella typhimurium*: cellular and molecular biology, 2nd ed. Washington, DC: ASM Press; 1996:88–103.
12. Lugtenberg B, Van Alphen L. Molecular architecture and functioning of the outer membrane of *Escherichia coli* and other gram-negative bacteria. Biochim Biophys Acta 1983;737:51–115.
13. Revees P. Biosynthesis and assembling of lipopolysaccharides. In: Ghuysen J-M, Hakenbeck R, eds. Bacterial cell wall. New comprehensive biochemistry, vol. 2. Amsterdam: Elsevier; 1994:218–317.
14. Jann K, Jann B. Structure and biosynthesis of O-antigens. In: Rietschel ET, ed. Handbook of endotoxin, vol. 1. Chemistry of endotoxin. Amsterdam: Elsevier North Holland; 1984:138–66.
15. Achtman M, Pluschke G. Clonal analysis of descent and virulence among selective *Escherichia coli.* Annu Rev Microbiol 1986;40:185–210.
16. Zähringer U, Linder B, Rietschel ET. Chemical structure of lipid A: recent advances in structural analysis of biologically active molecules. In: Brade H, *et al.*, eds. Endotoxin in health and disease. New York: Marcel Dekker; 1999:93–114.
17. Ørskov F, Ørskov I. *Escherichia coli*, serotyping and disease in man and animals. Can J Microbiol 1992;38:699–704.
18. Jann K, Jann B. The K antigen of *Escherichia coli.* Prog Allergy 1982;33:53–79.
19. Wilfert C. *E. coli* meningitis antigen and virulence. Annu Rev Med 1978;29:129–36.
20. Ørskov I, Ørskov F, Birch-Andersen A. O, K, H and fimbrial antigens in *Escherichia coli* serotypes associated with pyelonephritis and cystitis. Scand J Infect Dis 1982;33:18–26.
21. MacNab RM. Flagella and motility. In: Neidhart FC, Ingraham JL, Low KB, *et al.*, eds. *Escherichia coli* and *Salmonella typhimurium*: cellular and molecular biology. Washington, DC: ASM Press; 1996:123–45.
22. Low D, Braaten B, van der Woude M. Fimbriae. In: Neidhart FC, Ingraham JL, Low KB, *et al*, eds. *Escherichia coli* and *Salmonella typhimurium*: cellular and molecular biology. Washington DC: ASM Press; 1996:146–57.
23. Hacker J. Role of fimbrial adhesins in the pathogenesis of *Escherichia coli* infections. Can J Microbiol 1992;38:720–7.
24. Krogfelt KA. Bacterial adhesion: genetics, biogenesis and role in pathogenesis of fimbrial adhesions of *Escherichia coli.* Rev Infect Dis 1991;13:721–35.
25. Natarro JP, Kaper JB. Diarrheagenic *Escherichia coli.* Clin Microbiol Rev 1998;11:142–201.
26. Donnenberg MS, Kaper JB, Finaky BB. Interactions between enteropathogenic *Escherichia coli* and host epithelial cells. Trends Microbiol 1997;5:109–14.
27. Johnson JR, Roberts PL, Stamm WE. P-fimbriae and other virulence factors in *Escherichia coli* urosepsis: association with patients' characteristics. J Infect Dis 1987;156:225–9.
28. Saukkonen KMJ, Nowichi B, Leinonen M. Role of type 1 and S-fimbriae in the pathogenesis of *Escherichia coli* O18:K1 bacteremia and meningitis in the infant rat. Infect Immun 1988;56:892–7.
29. Wolf MK. Occurrence, distribution and association of O and H serogroups, colonization factor antigens and toxins of enterotoxigenic *Escherichia coli.* Clin Microbiol Rev 1997;10:569–84.
30. Tarkkanen AM, Allen BL, Williams PH, *et al.* Fimbriation, capsulation, and iron-scavenging systems of *Klebsiella* strains associated with urinary tract infection. Infect Immun 1992;60:1187–92.
31. Moxon ER, Kroll JS. The role of bacterial polysaccharide capsules as virulence factors. Curr Top Microbiol Immunol 1990;150:65–85.
32. Horowitz MA. Phagocytosis of microorganisms. Rev Infect Dis 1982;4:104–23.
33. Levine MM. *Escherichia coli* that cause diarrhea: enterotoxigenic, enteropathogenic, enteroinvasive, enterohemorrhagic, and enteroadherent. J Infect Dis 1987;155:377–89.
34. Holmes RK, Jobling MG, Connel TD. Cholera toxin and related enterotoxins of Gram-negative bacteria. In: Moss J, Iglewski B, Vaugh M, Tu AT, eds. Handbook of natural toxins, vol. 8. Microbial toxins. New York: Marcel Dekker; 1995:225–55.
35. Smith HW, Gyles CL. The relationship between two apparently different enterotoxins produced by enteropathogenic strains of *Escherichia coli* of porcine origin. J Med Microbiol 1970;3:387–401.
36. O'Brien AD, Holmes RK. Shiga and shiga-like toxins. Microbiol Rev 1987;51:206–20.
37. Bentin L. The different hemolysins of *Escherichia coli.* Med Microbiol Immunol 1991;180:167–82.
38. Alexander C, Rietschel E T. Bacterial lipopolysaccharides and innate immunity. J Endotox Res 2001;7:167–202.
39. Suffredini AF, Fromm RE, Parker MM, *et al.* The cardiovascular response of normal humans to the administration of endotoxin. N Engl J Med 1989;321:280–7.
40. Cohen J. The Immunopathogenesis of sepsis. Nature 2002;420:885–91.
41 Verhoef J, Rozenberg-Arska M, Dekker A. Prevention of infection in neutropenic patients. Rev Infect Dis 1989;2(Suppl.2):1545–50.
42. Barrow GJ, Feltham RKA, eds. Cowan and Steel's manual for the identification of medical bacteria. Cambridge: Cambridge University Press; 1993:128–50.
43. D'Amato RF, Bottone EJ, Amsterdam D. Substrate profile systems for the identification of bacteria and yeasts by rapid and automated approaches. In: Balows A, Hausler WJ, Herrmann KL, *et al.*, eds. Manual of clinical microbiology. Washington, DC: AMS Press; 1991:128–36.
44. Tenover FC. Diagnostic deoxyribonucleic acid probes for infectious diseases. Clin Microbiol Rev 1988;1:82–100.
45. Stamm WE, Turck M. Urinary tract infection. Adv Intern Med 1983;28:141–59.
46. Mabeck CE, Ørskov F, Ørskov J. *Escherichia coli* serotypes and renal involvement in urinary tract infection. Lancet 1971;1:1312–4.
47. Johnson J. Virulence factors in *Escherichia coli* urinary tract infection. Clin Microbiol Rev 1991;4:80–128.
48. Connel H, Agace W, Klemm P, *et al.* Type-1 fimbrial adhesion enhances *Escherichia coli* virulence for the urinary tract. Proc Natl Acad Sci USA 1996;93:9827–32.
49. Kallenius G, Molby R, Svenson S, *et al.* Occurrence of P-fimbriated *Escherichia coli* in urinary tract infections. Lancet 1981;2:1369–72.
50. Robbins JB, McCracken GH, Gotschilch EC, *et al. Escherichia coli* K1 capsular polysaccharide associated with neonatal meningitis. N Engl J Med 1974;280:1216–20.
51. McCracken GH, Sarff JD, Glode MD, *et al.* Relationship between *Escherichia coli* K1 capsular polysaccharide antigen and clinical outcome in neonatal meningitis. Lancet 1974;2:246–50.
52. Okeke IN, Nataro JP. Enteroaggregative *Escherichia coli.* Lancet Infect Dis 2001;1:304–13.
53. Steffen R, VanderLinde F, Gyr K, *et al.* Epidemiology of diarrhea in travelers. JAMA 1983;249:1176–80.
54. De Graaf FK, Gaastra J. Fimbriae of enterotoxigenic *Escherichia coli.* In: Klemm P, ed. Fimbriae: adhesion, genetics, biogenetics, and vaccines. Boca Raton, FA: CRC Press; 1994:58–83.
55. DuPont HL, Formal SB, Hornick RB, *et al.* Pathogenesis of *Escherichia coli* diarrhea. N Engl J Med 1971;285:1–9.
56. Harris JR, Wachsmuth IK, David BF, Cohen ML. High molecular weight plasmid correlates with *Escherichia coli* invasiveness. Infect Immun 1982;37:1235–8.
57. Allaoui A, Sansonetti PJ, Menard R, *et al.* MxiG, a membrane protein required for secretion of *Shigella* spp. Ipa invasins: involvement in entry into epithelial cells and in intercellular dissemination. Mol Microbiol 1995;17:461–70.
58. Riley LW. The epidemiologic, clinical and microbiologic features of hemorrhagic colitis. Annu Rev Microbiol 1987;41:383–40.
59. Karmali MA, Petric M, Lim C, *et al.* The association between idiopathic hemolytic uremic syndrome and infection by verotoxin-producing *Escherichia coli.* J Infect Dis 1985;151:775–82.
60. Karch H, Heeseman J, Laufs R, O'Brien AD, Tachet CO, Levine MM. A plasmid of enterohemorrhagic *Escherichia coli* O157:H7 is required for expression of new fimbrial antigen and for adhesion to epithelial cells. Infect Immun 1987;55:455–61.
61. Frankel G, Phillips AD, Rosenshine I, Dougan G, Kaper JB, Knutton S. Enteropathogenic and enterohaemorrhagic *Escherichia coli*: more subversive elements. Mol Microbiol 1988;30:911–21.
62. Louise CB, Obrig TG. Shiga toxin-associated hemolytic–uremic syndrome: combined cytotoxic effect of Shiga toxin, interleukin-1 beta, and tumor necrosis factor alpha on human vascular endothelial cells in vitro. Infect Immun 1991;59:4173–9.
63. Wong CS, Jelacic S, Habeeb RL, Watkins SL, Tarr PI. The risk of hemolytic–uremic syndrome after antibiotic treatment of *Escherichia coli* O157:H7 infections. N Engl J Med 2000;342:1930–6.
64. Moss PJ, McKendrick W. Bacterial gastroenteritis. Curr Opin Infect Dis 1997;10:402–7.
65. Levine MM, Bergquist EJ, Nalin DR, *et al. Escherichia coli* strains that cause diarrhea but do not produce heat-labile or heat-stable enterotoxins and are not invasive. Lancet 1978;1:1119–22.
66. Levine MM, Nataro JP, Karch H, *et al.* The diarrheal response of humans to some classic serotypes of enteropathogenic *Escherichia coli* is

dependent on a plasmid encoding and enteroadhesiveness factor. J Infect Dis 1985;152:550–9.
67. Donnenberg MS. Enteropathogenic *Escherichia coli*. In: Blaser MJ, Smith PD, Ravchin I, Greenberg HB, Guerraut RL, eds. Infections of the gastrointestinal tract. New York: Raven Press; 1995:709–26.
68. Okeke IN, Natarro JP. Enteroaggregative *Escherichia coli*. Lancet Infect Dis 2001;1:304–13.
69. Hariharan R, Weinstein RA. Enterobacteriaceae. In: Mayhall CG, ed. Hospital epidemiology and infection control. Baltimore: Williams & Wilkins; 1996:345–66.
70. Centers for Disease Control and Prevention. National nosocomial infection study report. Annual Summary 1979. MMWR Morb Mortal Wkly Rep March 1982.
71. Gransden WR, Elykyn SJ, Philips I, Rowe B. Bacteremia due to *Escherichia coli*: a study of 861 episodes. Rev Infect Dis 1990;12:1008–18.
72. Farthing MJ, Feldman R, Finch R, *et al.* The management of infective gastroenteritis in adults: a consensus statement by an expert panel convened by the British Society for the Study of Infection. J Infect 1996;33:143–52.
73. Van Saene HK, Stoutenbeek CP, Stoller JK. Selective decontamination of the digestive tract in the intensive care unit: current status an future prospects. Crit Care Med 1992;20:691–703.
74. Selective Decontamination of the Digestive Tract Trialists' Collaborative Group. Meta-analysis of randomized trials of selective decontamination of the digestive tract. Br Med J 1993;307:525–32.
75. Daschner F. Emergence of resistance during selective decontamination of the digestive tract. Eur J Clin Microbiol Infect Dis 1992;11:1–3.
76. Greenwood D, Slack RCB, Peutherer JF. Medical microbiology. New York: Churchill Livingstone; 1997.
77. Kotloff KL, Winickoff JP, Invanoff B, *et al.* Global burden of *Shigella* infections: implications for vaccine development and implementation of control strategies. Bull World Health Organ 1999;77:651–666.
78. Ezaki T, Kawamura Y, Yabuuchi E. Recognition of nomenclatural standing of *Salmonella typhi* (approved lists1980), *Salmonella enteritidis* (approved lists 1980) and *Salmonella typhimurium* (approved lists 1980), and conservation of their specific epithets *enteritidis* and *typhimurium*. Request for an opinion. Int J Syst Evol Microbiol 2000;2:945–7.
79. Livermore DM. Beta-lactamases in laboratory and clinical resistance. Clin Microbiol Rev 1995;8:557–84.
80. Schauer DB, Zabel BA, Pedraza IF, O'Hara CM, Steigerwalt AG, Brenner DJ. Genetic and biochemical characterization of *Citrobacter rodentium* sp. nov. J Clin Microbiol 1995;33:2064–8.
81. Brenner DJ, O'Hara CM, Grimont PA, *et al.* Biochemical identification of *Citrobacter* species defined by DNA hybridization and description of *Citrobacter gillenii* sp. nov. (formerly *Citrobacter* genomospecies 10) and *Citrobacter murliniae* sp. nov. (formerly *Citrobacter* genomospecies 11). J Clin Microbiol 1999;37:22619–24.
82. O'Hara CM, Roman-SB, Miller JM. Ability of commercial identification systems to identify newly recognized species of *Citrobacter*. J Clin Microbiol 1995;33:242–5.
83. Doran TI. The role of *Citrobacter* in clinical disease of children: review. Clin Infect Dis 1999;28:384–94.
84. Papasian CJ, Kinney J, Coffman S, Hollis RJ, Pfaller MA. Transmission of *Citrobacter koseri* from mother to infant documented by ribotyping and pulsed-field gel electrophoresis. Diagn Microbiol Infect Dis 1996;26:63–7.
85. Van Kregten E, Westerdaal NAC, Willer JMN. New, simple medium for selective recovery of *Klebsiella pneumoniae* and *Klebsiella oxytoca* from human feces. J Clin Microbiol 1984;20:936–41.
86. Avery RK, Salman SD, Baker AS. Rhinoscleroma treated with ciprofloxacin: a case report. Laryngoscope 1995;105:854–6.
87. Westbrook GL, O'Hara CM, Roman SB, Miller JM. Incidence and Identification of *Klebsiella planticola* in clinical isolates with emphasis on newborns. J Clin Microbiol 2000;38:1495–7.
88. Drancourt M, Bollet C, Carta A, Rousselier P. Phylogenetic analyses of *Klebsiella* species delineate *Klebsiella* and *Raoultella* gen. nov., with description of *Raoultella ornithinolytica* comb. nov., *Raoultella terrigena* comb. nov. and *Raoultella planticola* comb. nov. Int J Syst Evol Microbiol 2001;51:925–32.
89. Pitout JD, Moland ES, Sanders CC, Thomson KS, Fitzsimmons SR. Beta-lactamases and detection of beta-lactam resistance in *Enterobacter* spp. Antimicrob Agents Chemother 1997;41:35–9.
90. Lai KK. *Enterobacter sakazakii* infections among neonates, infants, children, and adults. Case reports and a review of the literature. Medicine (Baltimore) 2001;80:113–22.
91. Davin-Regli A, Bosi C, Charrel R, *et al.* A nosocomial outbreak due to *Enterobacter cloacae* strains with the *E. hormaechei* genotype in patients treated with fluoroquinolones. J Clin Microbiol 1997;35:1008–10.
92. Abbott SL, Janda JM. *Enterobacter cancerogenus* (*'Enterobacter taylorae'*) infections associated with severe trauma or crush injuries. Am J Clin Pathol 1997;107:359–61.
93. O'Hara CM, Steward CD, Wright JL, *et al.* Isolation of *Enterobacter intermedium* from the gallbladder of a patient with cholecystitis. J Clin Microbiol 1998;36:3055–6.
94. Kosako Y,Tamura K, Sakazaki R, Miki K. *Enterobacter kobei* sp. nov., a new species of the family Enterobacteriaceae resembling *Enterobacter cloacae*. Curr Microbiol 1996;33:261–5.
95. Parment PA. The role of *Serratia marcescens* in soft contact lens associated with ocular infections. A review. Acta Ophthalmol Scand 1997;75:67–71.
96. Carrero P, Garrote JA, Pacheco S, Garcia AI, Gil R, Carbajosa SG. Report of six cases of human infection by *Serratia plymuthica*. J Clin Microbiol 1995;33:275–6.
97. Ursua PR, Unzaga MJ, Melero P, *et al. Serratia rubidaea* as an invasive pathogen. J Clin Microbiol 1996;34:216–7.
98. Grohskopf LA, Roth VR, Feikin DR, *et al. Serratia liquefaciens* bloodstream infections from contamination of epoetin alfa at a hemodialysis center. N Engl J Med 2001;344:1491–7.
99. Badenoch PR, Thom AL, Coster DJ. *Serratia ficaria* endophthalmitis. J Clin Microbiol 2002;40:1563–4.
100. Rozalski A, Sidorczyk Z, Kotelko K Potential virulence factors of *Proteus* bacilli. Microbiol Mol Biol Rev 1997;61:65–89.
101. O'Hara CM, Brenner FW, Steigerwalt AG, *et al.* Classification of *Proteus vulgaris* biogroup 3 with recognition of *Proteus hauseri* sp. nov., nom. rev. and unnamed *Proteus* genomospecies 4, 5 and 6. Int J Syst Evol Microbiol 2000;50:1869–75.
102. Janda JM, Abbott SL, Khashe S, Robin T. Biochemical investigations of biogroups and subspecies of *Morganella morganii*. J Clin Microbiol 1996;34:108–13.
103. Woods TD, Watanakunakorn C. Bacteremia due to *Providencia stuartii*: review of 49 episodes. South Med J 1996;89:221–4.
104. Murata T, Iida T, Shiomi Y, *et al.* A large outbreak of foodborne infection attributed to *Providencia alcalifaciens*. J Infect Dis 2001;184:1050–5.
105. Straley SC, Perry RD. Environmental modulation of gene expression and pathogenesis in *Yersinia*. Trends Microbiol 1995;3:310–7.
106. Perry RD, Fetherston JD. *Yersinia pestis* – etiologic agent of plague. Clin Microbiol Rev 1997;10:35–66.
107. Cornelis GR. Molecular and cell biology aspects of plague. Proc Natl Acad Sci USA 2000;97:8778–883.
108. Inglesby TV, Dennis DT, Henderson DA, *et al.* Plague as a biological weapon: medical and public health management. Working Group on Civilian Biodefense. JAMA 2000;283:2281–90.
109. Beresford AM. Transfusion reaction due to *Yersinia enterocolitica* and review of other reported cases. Pathology 1995;27:133–5.
110. Sulakvelidze A. *Yersinia* other than *Y. enterocolitica*, *Y. pseudotuberculosis*, and *Y. pestis*: the ignored species. Microbes Infect 2000;2:497–513.
111. Slaven EM, Lopez FA, Hart SM, Sanders CV. Myonecrosis caused by *Edwardsiella tarda*: a case report and case series of extraintestinal *E. tarda* infections. Clin Infect Dis 2001;32:1430–3.
112. Fazal BA, Justman JE, Turett GS, Telzak EE. Community-acquired *Hafnia alvei* infection. Clin Infect Dis 1997;24:527–8.
113. Gunthard H, Pennekamp A. Clinical significance of extraintestinal *Hafnia alvei* isolates from 61 patients and review of the literature. Clin Infect Dis 1996;22:1040–5.
114. Janda JM, Abbott SL, Albert MJ. Prototypal diarrheagenic strains of *Hafnia alvei* are actually members of the genus *Escherichia*. J Clin Microbiol 1999;37:2399–401.
115. Maki DG, Rhame FS, Mackel DC, *et al.* Nationwide epidemic of septicemia caused by contaminated intravenous products: epidemiologic and clinical features. Am J Med 1976;60:471–85.
116. Aguilera A, Pascual J, Loza-E, *et al.* Bacteraemia with *Cedecea neteri* in a patient with systemic lupus erythematosus. Postgrad Med J 1995;71:179–80.
117. Sezer MT, Gultekin M, Gunseren F, Erkilic-M, Ersoy-F. A case of *Kluyvera cryocrescens* peritonitis in a CAPD patient (letter). Perit Dial Int 1996;16:326–7.
118. Matsukura H, Katayama K, Kitano N, *et al.* Infective endocarditis caused by an unusual gram-negative rod, *Rahnella aquatilis*. Pediatr Cardiol 1996;17:108–11.
119. Reina J, Lopez A. Clinical and microbiological characteristics of *Rahnella aquatilis* strains isolated from children. J Infect 1996;33:135–7.
120. De Baere Th, Wauters G, Huylenbroeck A, *et al.* Isolations of *Leclercia adecarboxylata* from a patient with a chronically inflamed gallbladder and from a patient with sepsis without focus. J Clin Microbiol 2001;39:1674–5.
121. Longhurst CA, West DC. Isolation of *Leclercia adecarboxylata* from an infant with acute lymphoblastic leukemia. Clin Infect Dis 2001;32:1659.
122. Carinder JE, Chua JD, Corales RB, *et al. Rahnella aquatilis* bacteremia in a patient with relapsed acute lymphoblastic leukemia. Scand J Infect Dis 2001;33:471–3.
123. O'Hara CM, Steigerwalt AG, Hill BC, *et al.* First report of a human isolate of *Erwinia persicinus*. J Clin Microbiol 1998;36:248–50.
124. Akhurst RJ, Mourant RG, Baud L, Boemare NE. Phenotypic and DNA relatedness between nematode symbionts and clinical strains of the genus *Photorhabdus* (Enterobacteriaceae). Int J Syst Bacteriol 1996;46:1034–41.

chapter 229

Pseudomonads and Miscellaneous Gram-negative Bacilli

Eugénie Bergogne-Bérézin

INTRODUCTION

Strictly aerobic Gram-negative bacilli have become increasingly important as human pathogens over the past 20 years.[1,2] Dominated by *Pseudomonas aeruginosa*, which is well known for its significant pathogenicity for the human host, this large group of saprophytic organisms has undergone confusing taxonomic changes for many years. New definitions of species and genera using modern genotyping analysis, together with reliable identification methods, have resulted in a better knowledge of these bacteria and a significantly increased awareness of their pathogenic role in hospitals and in rare cases of community-acquired infection. In descending order of importance the following are commonly isolated in nosocomial infections:

- *P. aeruginosa*;[1]
- *Acinetobacter baumannii*;[3]
- *Stenotrophomonas maltophilia*;[4] and
- *Burkholderia cepacia*.[5]

Species of *Flavobacterium*, *Comamonas* and *Alcaligenes* groups have only recently (late 1980s) been recognized as potential pathogens. A few other groups less frequently colonize or infect patients (as compared with *P. aeruginosa* and the other groups cited above) in intensive care units (ICUs).[6]

EPIDEMIOLOGY

Because of their ability to grow in environments providing limited nutrients, pseudomonads and other aerobic Gram-negative bacilli are saprophytic organisms and are found in water, soil and various other origins, plants, vegetables, insects and sewage. They may survive in hostile conditions, dry, cold or warm environments, and in a variety of foods such as dairy products, poultry and frozen foods. As nonfastidious organisms, most aerobic Gram-negative bacilli can use a wide variety of substrates as sole carbon and energy sources.[1–3] Their presence as saprophytes in the human environment, industrial environment (agricultural, food, cosmetic industries) and medical environment (pharmaceutical preparations, antiseptics, warm ICU humidifiers and ventilators) is unavoidable and they have been particularly successful at adapting themselves to new environments created by human activities.

PATHOGENIC ROLE

Aerobic Gram-negative bacilli can be carried as transient commensals in the human body. Although considered as low-virulence organisms, *Pseudomonas* spp. behave as opportunistic pathogens, being responsible for severe infections in hospitals, and are recognized as important human pathogens worldwide.[7]

ANTIBIOTIC THERAPY

Aerobic Gram-negative bacilli are frequently multiresistant to major antibiotics and this contributes to their prominent role in the morbidity and mortality of patients hospitalized in ICUs, oncology units, burn centers and surgery wards.[7–9] Various mechanisms of resistance have been recognized. Combination antibiotic therapy is often recommended for treatment, on the basis of careful antibiotic susceptibility testing. This chapter deals with *P. aeruginosa* and other potentially pathogenic aerobic Gram-negative bacilli. (Species that are animal or plant pathogens are not included in this review.)

PSEUDOMONAS AERUGINOSA

NATURE

Taxonomic classifications of *Pseudomonas* spp. have evolved considerably over the years. As the traditional phenotypic classifications based on morphologic, biochemical and antigenic characteristics have been replaced by the genotypic classification systems, these groups of bacteria are now much easier to understand. However, divisions and subdivisions based on genetic homologies, DNA hybridizations and rRNA sequence comparisons have undergone designation changes; new genera have been identified such as *Burkholderia* spp. (previously included in *Pseudomonas* spp.).[5] One of the most significant examples of taxonomic changes is the recent conversion of the species initially designated *Pseudomonas maltophilia* in 1961[8] and then *Xanthomonas maltophilia* in 1983[10] to *Stenotrophomonas maltophilia* (Table 229.1).

EPIDEMIOLOGY

The large majority of *Pseudomonas* spp.[7,11] are ubiquitous organisms and are widely distributed in nature. Their increasing involvement in infections in humans results from multiple factors but mainly the development of antibiotic usage and the resulting selective pressure in favor of inherently or potentially resistant Gram-negative species from the environment.[12,13] Hospitals, ICUs, immunodepressed patients, invasive procedures and antibiotic usage have provided opportunities for emergence, persistence and transfer of *P. aeruginosa* between patients or from patients to staff and to inanimate reservoirs.

Pseudomonas aeruginosa is also a saprophyte in the normal individual and is by far the predominant aerobic Gram-negative bacillus causing illness in patients who have risk factors and immunosuppressed defense mechanisms. Recent studies using molecular typing methods have shown a variety of environmental sources in hospitals and nursing homes: *P. aeruginosa* isolates from sinks, wash basins and toilets were similar (*exotoxin A* typing) to those isolated from the hands of staff and the urinary tracts of paraplegic patients, and transmission over a 6-month period in an ICU for newborns has been related to a source implicating air valves in the ventilator tubes. It is well recognized that *P. aeruginosa* can be present on surgical and medical material, in antiseptic (quaternary ammonium compounds) or contact lens cleaning solutions, and in ventilatory equipment in ICUs.[7,11] In humans, few intestinal carriers are found in the general population (about 4%) but they are much more

CURRENT NOMENCLATURE OF NON-ENTEROBACTERIACEAE, NONFERMENTATIVE GRAM-NEGATIVE BACILLI		
Main groups (genera)	**Current name**	**Previous name**
Acinetobacter	*Acinetobacter baumannii*	*Acinetobacter anitratus*
	Acinetobacter calcoaceticus	*Acinetobacter anitratus, Acinetobacter calcoaceticus subsp. calcoaceticus*
	Acinetobacter haemolyticus	*Acinetobacter anitratus*
	Acinetobacter johnsonii	
	Acinetobacter junii	
	Acinetobacter lwoffi	*Acinetobacter anitratus, Acinetobacter calcoaceticus subsp. lwoffi*
Alcaligenes	*Agrobacterium tumefaciens*	*Agrobacterium radiobacter* CDC group Vd-3
	Alcaligenes faecalis	*Alcaligenes odorans, Pseudomonas odorans*
	Alcaligenes piechaudii	
	Alcaligenes xylosoxidans subsp. *denitrificans*	*Alcaligenes denitrificans* CDC group Vc
	Alcaligenes xylosoxidans subsp. *xylosoxidans*	*Alcaligenes denitrificans* subsp. *xylosoxidans, Achromobacter xylosoxidans* CDC groups IIIa, IIIb
Burkholderia	*Burkholderia cepacia*	*Pseudomonas cepacia, Pseudomonas multivorans, Pseudomonas kingae* CDC group EO-1
	Burkholderia gladioli	*Pseudomonas gladioli, Pseudomonas marginata*
	Burkholderia mallei	*Pseudomonas mallei, Actinobacillus mallei*
	Burkholderia pickettii	*Pseudomonas pickettii* CDC groups Va-1, Va-2, *Pseudomonas thomasii*
	Burkholderia pseudomallei	*Pseudomonas pseudomallei*
Comamonas	*Comamonas acidovorans*	*Pseudomonas acidovorans*
	Comamonas testosteroni	*Pseudomonas lestosteroni* CDC group EF-19
	Comamonas terrigena	
Chryseobacterium	*Chryseomonas luteola*	*Pseudomonas luteola* CDC group Ve-1
	Chryseobacterium gleum	*Flavobacterium gleum* CDC group IIb
	Chryseobacterium indolongenes	*Flavobacterium indologenes* CDC group IIb
	Chryseobacterium meningosepticum	*Flavobacterium meningosepticum* CDC group IIa
	Chryseobacterium odoratum (Myroides odoratus)	*Flavobacterium odoratum* CDC group M-4f
Flavobacterium	*Empedobacter brevis*	*Flavobacterium breve*
	Flavimonas oryzihabitans	*Pseudomonas oryzihabitans* CDC group Ve-2
	Flavobacterium sp. group IIe	CDC group IIe
	Flavobacterium sp. group IIh	CDC group IIh
	Flavobacterium sp. group IIi	CDC group IIi
Pseudomonas	*Pseudomonas aeruginosa*	
	Pseudomonas alcaligenes	
	Pseudomonas chlororaphis	*Pseudomonas aureofaciens*
	Pseudomonas delafieldii	
	Pseudomonas fluorescens	
	Pseudomonas mendocina	CDC group Vb-2
	Pseudomonas pertucinogena	*Bordetella pertussis* rough phase IV
	Pseudomonas pseudoalcaligenes	*Pseudomonas alcaligenes* biotype B
	Pseudomonas putida	
	Pseudomonas stutzeri	CDC group Vb-1
	Pseudomonas stutzeri-like	CDC group Vb-3
	Pseudomonas sp. group 1	*Pseudomonas denitrificans*
	Pseudomonas-like group 2	CDC group IV-d
Sphingobacterium	*Sphingobacterium mizutaii*	*Flavobacterium mizutaii*
	Sphingobacterium multivorum	*Flavobacterium multivorum* CDC group IIk-2
	Sphingobacterium spiritivorum	*Flavobacterium spiritivorum, Sphingobacterium versatilis* CDC group IIk-3
	Sphingobacterium thalpophilum	*Flavobacterium thalpophilum*
	Sphingobacterium yabuuchiae	*Favobacterium yabuuchiae*
	Sphingomonas paucimobilis	*Pseudomonas paucimobilis* CDC group IIk11
	Weeksella virosa	*Flavobacterium genitale* CDC group II-f
Stenotrophomonas	*Stenotrophomonas maltophilia*	*Xanthomonas maltophilia*
		Pseudomonas maltophilia

Table 229.1 Current nomenclature of non-Enterobacteriaceae, nonfermentative Gram-negative bacilli. The list is limited to those potentially involved in infections.[1,6,7]

common among hospital patients (i.e. up to 18% on average for all hospital populations). Intestinal carriage of *P. aeruginosa* is significantly increased after gastrointestinal surgery, and can reach 73% of patients.[14] Many other carriage sites have been described in hospital patients, including the respiratory tract, genitourinary tract and skin, which can also be the source of dissemination of *Pseudomonas* strains as well as the origin of endogenous contamination (Table 229.2).

CARRIAGE IN HUMAN FLORA				
Organisms	**Respiratory tract**	**Gastrointestinal tract**	**Genitourinary tract**	**Skin, ear, eye, miscellaneous**
Pseudomonas aeruginosa	2+	1+	0	0
Other *Pseudomonas* spp.	0	1+	0	0
Acinetobacter spp.	2+	1+	1+	2+
Burkholderia cepacia	1+	0	0	1+
Alcaligenes faecalis	0	1+	0	1+
Weeksela virosa	0	0	1+	0

Table 229.2 Carriage in human flora. Incidence of carriage of aerobic Gram-negative bacilli in human flora (quantitative presence).[2,15] 2+, frequently isolated; 1+, rarely isolated; 0, not typically isolated.

PATHOGENICITY

Pseudomonas aeruginosa is responsible for a variety of infections in patients who have many risk factors such as:

- surgery;
- immunosuppression; and
- prolonged hospital stay, mainly in an ICU.

Pseudomonas aeruginosa possesses many virulence factors and various resistance mechanisms, which confer upon it a predominant role as a nosocomial pathogen. Recent surveys have shown that *P. aeruginosa* is responsible for between 10% and more than 20% of all nosocomial infections[7] and that the predominant site of infection is the respiratory tract, although there are many other infection sites (Table 229.3).[13,14]

PATHOGENESIS

Pseudomonas aeruginosa is pathogenic as a result of toxigenic and invasive properties. It produces many virulence factors that have been characterized and some of them have already been cloned (Table 229.4).[20] The pathogenic factors may act at or away from the site of infection.

At the site of infection

The adhesion factors (pili in nonmucoid strains and/or alginate in mucoid strains) and exoenzyme S play a significant role in the pathogenesis of most respiratory infections; they are particularly involved in pulmonary invasion in cystic fibrosis (CF). Nearly all strains produce pili under favorable conditions; they are uni- or bipolar in distribution and are composed of pili protein (molecular weight 18kDa).[20]

Local enzymatic activities at the site of infection are those of proteases, neuraminidase and phospholipases. They disrupt epithelial cell membranes, phospholipids and protecting cell surface proteins, resulting in tissue damage. Proteases appear to contribute to necrotic skin lesions (ecthyma gangrenosum). Elastolytic activities disrupt the elastin of blood vessels, resulting in hemorrhages. All enzymes contribute to the invasiveness of *P. aeruginosa*.[11,20,21]

PREDOMINANT SITES AND INCIDENCES OF NOSOCOMIAL INFECTIONS			
		Hospital wide (%)	**Intensive care unit (%)**
Pseudomonas aeruginosa	Sepsis	18.2*	–
	Nosocomial pneumonia	16.9†	20.8–36.4
	Urinary tract infection	12.0–18.8	11.3
	Surgical wound	8.2	9.5
	CF respiratory infection	70–90% of CF cases	
	Burns – SSTI	15.4	
Stenotrophomonas maltophilia[16] (total 3.7% of 2569 *S. maltophilia* strains)	Sepsis, endocarditis	1.4	
	Surgical wound	15.8	
	Secondary meningitis	–	
	Nosocomial pneumonia	66.4	
	Urinary infection	8.7	
	CF	About 7% of CF lung infections	
Burkholderia cepacia[17] (of 786 strains)	Blood culture	1.8	
	Respiratory infection	78.8	6–20% of CF cases
	Miscellaneous fluids and pus	7.8	
	Urine	3.7	
	Environment	7.6	
Acinetobacter baumannii[18] (of total *Acinetobacter* spp.)	Nosocomial pneumonia		25–29
	Urinary infections		21–30
	Bacteremia, endocarditis		6–9
	Burn infections, wounds		2–12
	CF respiratory infections		Rare
Chryseobacterium meningosepticum[19] (rarely pathogenic)	Neonatal meningitis, sepsis	Predominant sites in neonates	
	Surgical wound, nosocomial pneumonia	Occasional	

* % of all Gram-negative bacteremia.[7]
† % of all bacterial species including Gram-positives.[19]

Table 229.3 Predominant sites and incidences of nosocomial infections. Predominant sites of nosocomial infections due to aerobic Gram-negative bacilli and incidences (% of total organisms).[2,3,6,7] CF, cystic fibrosis; SSTI, skin and soft tissue infection.

PSEUDOMONAS AERUGINOSA VIRULENCE-ASSOCIATED FACTORS		
Nature		**Human effects**
Constitutive	Lipopolysaccharide Endotoxin	Cascade of inflammatory events Septic shock
	Mucopolysaccharide capsule in mucoid *Pseudomonas aeruginosa* (alginate: polymer of β-1, 4-D-mannuronic and L-glucuronic acid)	Bacterial adhesion to epithelial cells Barrier to antibiotics Increased viscosity of bronchial secretions (cystic fibrosis)
	Pili (fimbriae) Cytoplasmic lectins PAI, PAII	Act as adhesins PAI specific for D-galactose PAII specific for D-mannose
Exoproducts	Proteases (alkaline and neutral metalloproteinase)	Damage tissues (active on elastin, collagen, fibrin) Digestion of protecting proteins serving as host defenses
	Neuraminidase	Enhances pilin-mediated adherence
	Phenazine pigment (pyocyanin) Elastolytic activity (two enzymes Las A, Las B)	Ciliary disruption Breakdown elastin of blood vessels, hemorrhages
	2 Hemolysins: phospholipase C glycolipid-rhamnolipid (heat-stable)	Disruption of phospholipids of cell membranes, hydrolysis of lung surfactant and ciliostatic action
	Siderophores (pyochelin and pyoverdin)	Help growth in iron-limited condition Generation of toxic oxygen-free radicals
	Exotoxin A	Causes tissue damage Similar to diphtheria toxin Inhibits phagocytes Inhibits protein synthesis
	Exoenzyme S (functions as adhesin)	Binding specificity for glycolipids (glycososphingolipid)
	Cytotoxin: leucocidin	Cytopathic effects on leukocytes and alteration of phospholipids of cell membrane
	Antibiotic-inactivating enzymes	β-Lactamases Aminoglycoside-inactivating enzymes

Table 229.4 ***Pseudomonas aeruginosa*** **virulence-associated factors.**[20–22]

Away from the site of infection

The invasive properties are those of:

- lipopolysaccharide (LPS), an endotoxin responsible for septic shock;
- cytotoxins, which have cytopathic effects on leukocytes; and
- exotoxin A, produced by approximately 90% of strains, which exhibits cytotoxicity by inhibiting protein synthesis, causing intense tissue damage and inhibiting phagocytic activities.

Exotoxin A acts by a similar mechanism to that of diphtheria toxin, but has a different receptor (a 300kDa glycoprotein) on host cells. It is encoded by a single copy of a structural gene, *tox*A, regulated by two genes, *reg*A and *reg*B. It is remarkable that, whereas most Gram-negative bacilli are pathogenic via an endotoxin, *P. aeruginosa* also produces an exotoxin, which enhances the virulence of this pathogen.

Risk factors in patients

A wide variety of *P. aeruginosa* infections of varying severity have been observed. Predominant sites of infections and patient risk factors are directly related to:

- immune status;
- underlying pathologies; and
- hospitalization in an ICU.

Specific factors that determine the site and the severity of *Pseudomonas* infection include:

- extended burns;[23]
- CF in children;[24]
- prosthetic heart valves; and
- intubation or tracheostomy.[13,25]

PREVENTION

Prevention plays a major role in controlling *Pseudomonas* infections. Preventive measures are based on the identification of sources and modes of transmission of the pathogens (Table 229.5). Numerous guidelines have been established in the USA and in European countries. Isolation policies, administrative and regulatory measures and hospital epidemiology surveillance are increasingly applied to control outbreaks involving *P. aeruginosa*. Among the main guidelines, the aims of three approaches can be summarized as follows:

- elimination of endogenous nosocomial *P. aeruginosa* and reduction of oropharyngeal, intestinal and skin colonization in ICU patients;
- prevention of cross-contamination and control of various sources of *P. aeruginosa* that can be transmitted from patient to patient or from personnel to patient (i.e. proper disinfection and care of catheters, respiratory equipment, humidifiers, endotracheal tubes, dialysis systems, etc.); and
- prevention of contamination in burns patients, surgical wounds and the oropharyngeal area in ventilated patients (i.e. antibiotic prophylaxis in postoperative high-risk patients; for burns patients either systemic antibiotics or local antibiotics or disinfection could be recommended; and aerosolized polymyxin B and/or endotracheal aminoglycosides to prevent *Pseudomonas* pneumonia, which has the highest fatality rate).[13,24,25]

In addition, selective digestive decontamination[34] has been advocated in ICU patients; this should prevent colonization of the oropharynx and the gut by potentially pathogenic bacteria, as the digestive tract can be an important reservoir for multiresistant *P. aeruginosa*, and so prevent nosocomial infection. Topical chemoprophylaxis includes nonabsorbable antibiotics, generally polymyxin E, tobramycin (or norfloxacin) and amphotericin B (the latter to control fungal colonization). Most investigations have included coadministration of systemic ceftazidime but a clear consensus about the effectiveness of selective digestive decontamination has not been established, possibly because of the heterogeneous groups of patients and varying oral regimens involved and the inconsistent addition of systemic cefotaxime or ceftazidime (see Chapter 84).

DIAGNOSTIC MICROBIOLOGY

Bacteriology of *Pseudomonas aeruginosa*

Microscopy

Pseudomonas aeruginosa is a thin, motile Gram-negative bacillus that moves relatively fast considering that it has only a single polar flagellum.[1,11,15]

It grows easily on simple agar medium and produces characteristic pigments. Its phenotypic characteristics, such as motility, pigment production and positive oxidase reactions, mean that it can be

SOURCES, METHODS OF CONTAMINATION AND RISK FACTORS FOR NOSOCOMIAL INFECTIONS DUE TO AEROBIC GRAM-NEGATIVE BACILLI			
Organisms and reference	**Settings**	**Mechanism (source)**	**Risk factor/comments**
Pseudomonas aeruginosa[15,23]	SICU/MICU, HU, BU	Contaminated equipment, solutions, antiseptics; endogenous	Cross-contamination; exposure to broad-spectrum antibiotics; severely ill patients; burns outbreaks
Pseudomonas putida, *Pseudomonas fluorescens*[1,15,23]	SICU	Contaminated blood and blood byproducts, antiseptics	Few in wound infections; rare cases of opportunistic infections
Stenotrophomonas maltophilia[2,15,16,27]	Surgery, SICU	Contaminated devices, disinfectants, catheters	Dialysis fluids; exploratory procedures; neutropenia; respiratory devices (CF); tracheostomized patients; backflow from nonsterile tubes
Burkholderia cepacia[2,15,17]	ICU	Airborne transmission; contaminated skin preparations, ventilator, thermometer, antiseptic solutions	CF patients; hand carriage; calibration bath (contaminated with 10^5cfu/ml); immunodepressed patients
Chryseobacterium meningosepticum (*Flavobacterium* spp.)[19,28,29]	NICU	Contaminated water, ice, disinfectants, humidifiers	Bacteremia; neonatal meningitis; infected wounds
Alcaligenes xylosoxidans[30–32]	ICU, HDU	Contaminated chlorhexidine solution, dialysis fluid, aerosols, respirators	Aqueous source; hemodialysis; peritonitis; bacteremia; meningitis; severe underlying disease
Acinetobacter spp.[3,33]	MICU/SICU	Contaminated ventilators, moist devices, burns; endogenous	Severely ill patients; cross-contamination; outbreaks

Table 229.5 Sources, methods of contamination and risk factors for nosocomial infections due to aerobic Gram-negative bacilli. BU, burns unit; HDU, hemodialysis unit; HU, hematology unit; MICU, medical intensive care unit; NICU, neonatal intensive care unit; SICU, surgical intensive care unit.

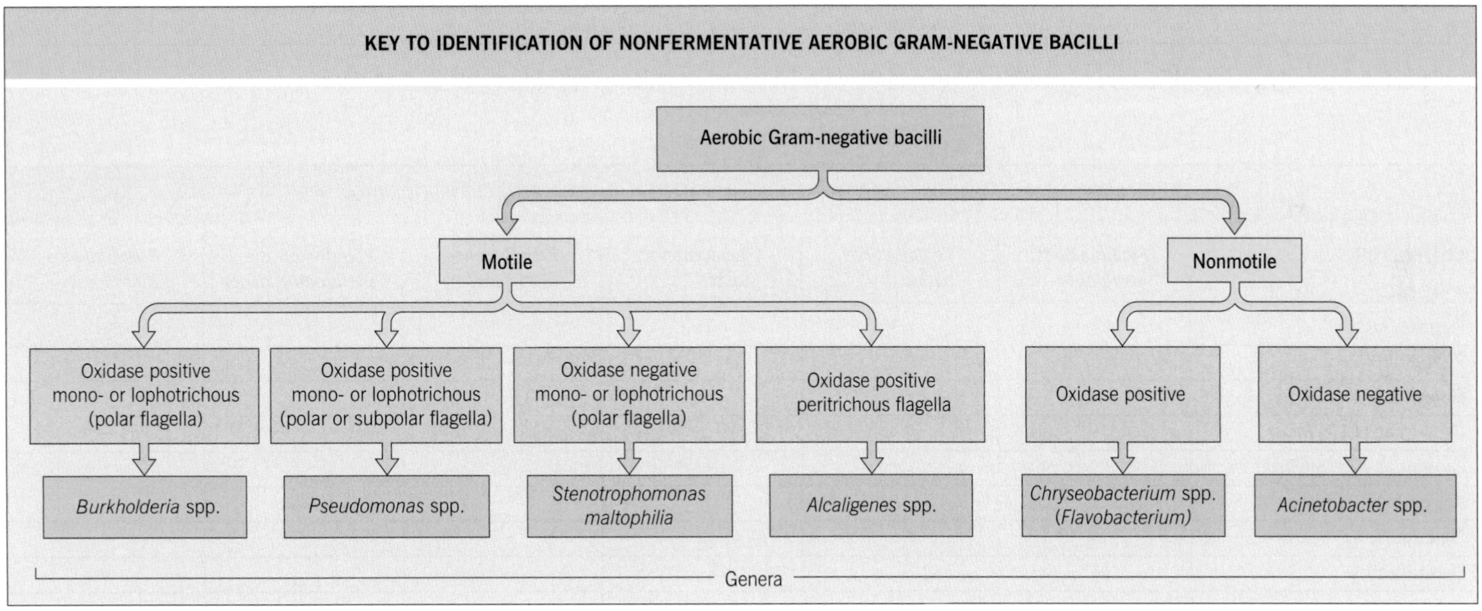

Fig. 229.1 Key to identification of nonfermentative aerobic Gram-negative bacilli. Note that *Burkholderia mallei* has no flagella and is nonmotile; *Pseudomonas aeruginosa* is monotrichous; oxidase-negative organisms use carbohydrates (activity of α-glucosidase, β-glucosidase, β-galactosidase, β-xylosidase); *Alcaligenes* spp. have degenerated peritrichous flagella, which are functional; *Chryseobacterium* spp. produce variably pigmented colonies due to yellowish-orange pigment; and *Stenotrophomonas* spp. (except nonpigmented mutants) produce yellow pigment.

rapidly identified. Details of diagnostic microbiology techniques are shown in Figure 229.1, Table 229.6 and Table 229.7.

Electron microscopy

Figure 229.2 clearly shows the very long, thin polar flagellum and the irregular surface of the bacillus.

Culture

Colonies of *Pseudomonas aeruginosa* on agar culture at 98.6°F (37°C) are smooth and flat (Fig. 229.3). The pigments (pyocyanin and fluorescein) give the characteristic blue–green pigmentation due to production of pyocyanin, which is enhanced by culture on King's A medium.

Epidemiologic markers

Reliable epidemiologic tools are needed to trace the geographic spread of strains (Table 229.8).

Conventional phenotypic methods

These are based on biochemical profiles, antibiotic susceptibility patterns, bacteriophage and bacteriocin susceptibilities; more recently developed are outer membrane protein profiles and multilocus

PHENOTYPIC IDENTIFICATION OF AEROBIC GRAM-NEGATIVE BACILLI BASED ON MICROSCOPY, PIGMENTS AND OXIDASE		
Tests	**Characteristics**	
Microscopy	**Gram-negative bacilli**	
Morphology	Thin bacilli: *Pseudomonas aeruginosa*	Coccobacilli (diplobacilli): *Acinetobacter* spp.
Motility	Motile: *P. aeruginosa* (fast motion): *Pseudomonas* spp.	Nonmotile: *Acinetobacter* spp., *Flavobacterium* spp. (*Chryseobacterium*)
Flagella*	Monotrichous, polar unique: *P. aeruginosa; Pseudomonas stutzeri; Pseudomonas pseudoalcaligenes* Lophotrichous polar: *Stenotrophomonas maltophilia; Burkholderia cepacia; Pseudomonas fluorescens: Burkholderia pseudomallei* Peritrichous, nonpolar, degenerated: *Alcaligenes faecalis*	None (gliding motility)
Pigments (on nutrient agar)	*P. aeruginosa/Pseudomonas* spp. Pyocyanin: bluish-green Phenazinic pigment: yellowish-orange (*Pseudomonas aureofaciens*) Pyoverdin: greenish-yellow (*P. aeruginosa, P. fluorescens, Pseudomonas putida*) Carotenoïd pigment (*P. stutzeri*) Light-straw yellow pigment (*S. maltophilia*) Yellow-purple (violacein) or brownish in 10% *B. cepacia*	*Flavobacterium* spp. (*Chryseobacterium*) (inconstantly produced) Light-yellow, yellowish-orange or bright yellowish-orange; nondiffusible pigment
Oxidase†	Positive: *Pseudomonas* spp. *Alcaligenes* spp. *Flavobacterium* spp. *B. cepacia* (rare strains negative)	Negative: *S. maltophilia* (or weakly and tardily positive) *Acinetobacter* spp.

* Staining of flagella: Leifson's staining (tannic acid, basic fuchsin) or Rhode's silver-plating staining method.
† Oxidase reaction: on Mueller-Hinton agar, 1% solution of N-dimethyl paraphenylene-diamine (ready-to-use discs or solution prepared in the laboratory).

Table 229.6 Phenotypic identification of aerobic Gram-negative bacilli based on microscopy, pigments and oxidase.

DIAGNOSTIC MICROBIOLOGY CHARACTERISTICS DIFFERENTIATING IMPORTANT *PSEUDOMONAS* SPP.

Characteristics	*Pseudomonas aeruginosa*	*Pseudomonas putida*	*Pseudomonas stutzeri*	*Pseudomonas alcaligenes*	*Pseudomonas pseudoalcaligenes*	*Pseudomonas fluorescens*
Flagella number	1	>1	1*	1	1	>1
Pyocyanin	+ (or v)	–	–	–	–	–
Fluorescent pigments	v	+	–	–	–	+
Growth at 105.8°F	+	–	v	+	+	–
Growth at 39.2°F	–	v	–	–	–	+
Arginine dihydrolase	+	+	–	+	v	+
Oxidase	+	+	+	+	+	+
Denitrification	+	–	+	+	v	– or +
Gelatin hydrolysis	+	–	–	v	v	+
Use of glucose	+	+	+	–	–	+
Use of 2-ketagluconate	+	+	–	–	–	+
Use of L-valine	v	+	+	–	–	NS
Use of β-alanine	+	+	–	v	v	+
Use of DL-arginine	+	+	–	+	+	+
Guanine + cytosine % content in DNA	67.2	62.5	60.6–66.3	64–68	62–64	59.4–61.3

* Lateral flagella produced under certain conditions.

Table 229.7 Diagnostic microbiology characteristics differentiating important *Pseudomonas* spp.[15] v, variable; NS, not stated.

enzyme electrophoresis. Most 'traditional' typing methods are based on unstable properties of the organisms and phenotypic characters may change during the course of an outbreak or during a prolonged period of observation of endemic cases with apparently identical pathogens. However, biotyping, resistance phenotyping and serotyping remain popular methods because they are rapid and easy to

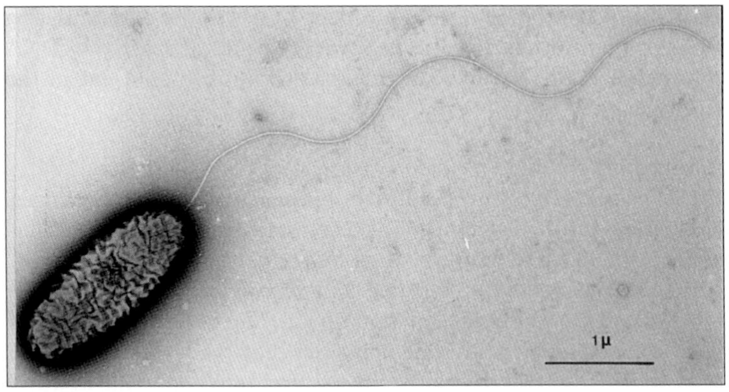

Fig. 229.2 ***Pseudomonas aeruginosa*** **monotrichous polar flagellum seen on electron microscopy.** Courtesy of Professor A Marty.

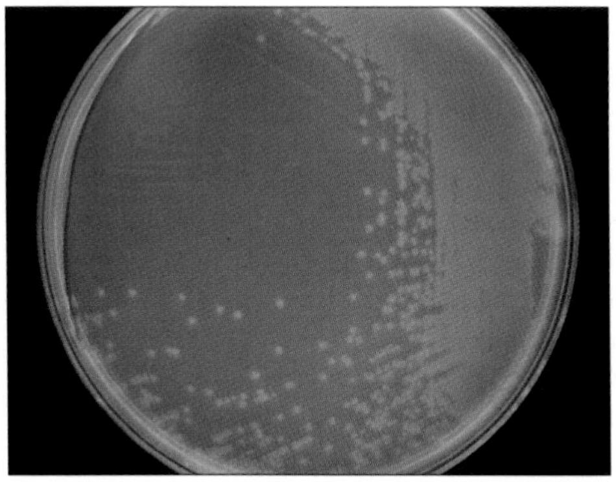

Fig. 229.3 ***Pseudomonas aeruginosa*** **colonies on agar medium.** Courtesy of Professor E Bingen.

EPIDEMIOLOGIC MARKERS FOR *PSEUDOMONAS AERUGINOSA* TYPING

Epidemiologic markers		Principles and characteristics	Advantages	Drawbacks
Phenotypic	Biotyping	Utilization of substrates, production of enzymes, biotyping schemes for identification	Rapid, easy to perform, API 20NE panel or automated (Vitek GNI), inexpensive	Unstable, variability of metabolic characters, poorly discriminating
	Resistance phenotype	Antimicrobial susceptibility pattern always carried out, multiple resistance markers	Rapid, easy to perform, standardized (National/International guidelines), early and useful during outbreak	Unstable profiles, plasmid acquisition or loss during an outbreak, derepression of inducible enzymes, mutations, poorly discriminating, unreliable
	Serotyping	Based on somatic O specific antigen (LPS), polyclonal/monoclonal antibodies, 20 serotypes, 17 antisera (IATS)	Rapid, early results, easy to perform, available reagents, inexpensive, most commonly used	50–70% of CF strains nontypable, polyagglutination of some CF strains, reproducibility of anti-LPS monoclonal antibodies is 75%
	Phage typing	Colindale set of 21 phages, cell surface receptors (OM, LPS, slime)	Limited requirements, inexpensive, available reagents	Lack of reproducibility, low discrimination, insensitivity of CF and LPS-defective strains
	Pyocin typing	R, F, S pyocins, specific lytic activity, 105 types, 26 subtypes	Limited requirements, inexpensive	Poor discrimination, complexity of the system, time-consuming technique
Genotypic	Plasmidotyping	Relatively rare plasmid in *Pseudomonas aeruginosa*, plasmids of 1.2–60MDa in 15% of strains	No advantage for *P. aeruginosa* typing	Low frequency, acquisition or loss during epidemics
	Genomic DNA, total DNA	Polymorphism of DNA, REA endonucleases (*Eco*R1, *Hin*dII, *Sma*I), conventional agarose electrophoresis	Good discriminatory power	Large number of fragments making resolution of bands difficult to interpret
	DNA RFLP	Detection of genes coding for exotoxin A (*exo*A). elastase (*las*B). alginate (*alg*D). two probes necessary	Good discriminatory power, good correlation with ribotyping	Laborious techniques, small numbers of isolates can be compared
	Ribotyping (ribosomal DNA)	Three genes coding for rRNA, probes for 16S and 23S RNA, restriction enzymes (*Eco*R1, *Cla*I, *Sal*I)	Universal, excellent reproducibility, stable ribotype patterns within outbreaks	Laborious techniques, sensitivity and specificity not established for *P. aeruginosa*
	Pulsotyping (PFGE)	DNA fingerprinting, restriction enzymes *Dra*I, *Spe*I (fragments >50kb requiring PFGE)	The most specific discriminant technique	Interpretation somewhat delicate, heavy workload

Table 229.8 Epidemiologic markers for *Pseudomonas aeruginosa* typing. O serotypes internationally recognized; types O18 to O20 not validated yet.[22,35,36] IATS, International Antigenic Typing System; OM, outer membrane; PFGE, pulse-field gel electrophoresis; REA, restriction endonuclease analysis; RFLP, restriction fragment length polymorphism.

perform, are cheap and little equipment is needed; they are useful in emergency situations and are a great help in laboratories with limited facilities.[15,22]

Serotyping

Pseudomonas aeruginosa is serologically heterogeneous because it possesses many somatic and flagellar antigens. Based upon the specificity of somatic antigen O (polysaccharide side chains of the LPS), an O antigenic scheme has been internationally recognized with agreement for 17 O serotypes in the International Antigenic Typing Scheme.

Limitations to serotyping include poor discriminating power, polyagglutination for some strains, failure of serotyping in LPS-defective strains and autoagglutination in CF strains. However, serotyping of *P. aeruginosa* remains useful and epidemiologically significant. For example, it has been shown that the most frequent serotypes involved in nosocomial infections are O6, O11, O1 and O3 and that serotype O12 is characterized by its exceptional multi-resistance pattern.[22]

Bacteriophage typing

A large number of bacteriophages active against *P. aeruginosa* attach to specific cell surface receptors: outer membrane proteins, LPS and slime polysaccharide. The Colindale set of 21 phages is the most popular and constitutes the reference system, with more than 80% of isolates sensitive to these phages. Many *P. aeruginosa* strains are lysogenic and about 10 lysogenic phages may interfere with typing procedures.[22]

Phage typing lacks reproducibility and mucoid and LPS-defective strains are insensitive to phage typing.

Bacteriocin typing

Pyocin particles, identified as R, F and S pyocins (retractile, flexuous and soluble respectively), have been used for typing, on the basis of specific lytic activity, and permit identification of 105 types plus 26 subtype patterns.[37]

Although reproducible (90% of clinical strains typable), pyocinotyping is not a widely used method because of the complexity of the system and inadequate discrimination and reproducibility requiring strict standardization of inoculum and media (reagents are not commercially available).

Multilocus enzyme electrophoresis

This is based upon the electrophoretic motilities of a large number of cellular enzymes. One strain is characterized by a combination of alloenzymes (motility variants) designated 'zymotype'. When applied to *P. aeruginosa* this method has proved complex and time-consuming and is carried out only in specialized laboratories.[35]

Genotypic markers

The many drawbacks and limitations of phenotypic markers have led investigators to develop more reliable typing procedures based upon genomic DNA, and many new epidemiologic tools have become available in clinical laboratories.

Plasmid profile

This is a rapid and simple method for species carrying many plasmids but is relatively useless for *P. aeruginosa* because only 15–20% of the strains carry plasmids; the majority of clinical isolates lack demonstrable plasmids.[36]

DNA fingerprints

DNA fingerprints, which are restriction endonuclease digestions of genomic DNA, can use total chromosomal DNA, resulting in thousands of fragments ranging in size from 2kb to 25kb. The banding patterns for a series of isolates, visualized by ethidium bromide staining in gel, are compared either visually or by scanning densitometry and digitization. Because of the large number of fragments generated, it can be difficult to resolve the bands. DNA restriction fragment length polymorphism may be used to detect specific genes; good discriminatory power, using DNA probes specific for genes coding for exotoxin A (*exo*A), alginate (*alg*D), elastase (*las*B) or pilin (*PAK*), has been observed for differentiating isolates from different patients, provided that at least two DNA probes are used (5% of *P. aeruginosa* strains are deficient in the *exo*A gene).[35,36]

Ribotyping

This is based on interspecies differences in genomic RNA sequences. Restriction fragment length polymorphisms are detected by differences in the banding pattern (three to six bands for *P. aeruginosa*). Although recognized as a stable and reproducible typing system for *Escherichia coli* and *Haemophilus influenzae,* it seems likely that its sensitivity and specificity are not well established for *P. aeruginosa*.[35] Ribotyping requires combination with another typing method, which involves a great deal of work.

Pulsotyping

Pulsed-field gel electrophoresis uses restriction endonucleases, which cut the chromosome infrequently, producing large fragments (5–800kb) resolved into 10–50 bands by field inversion gel electrophoresis or a contour-clamped homogeneous electric field. Field inversion gel electrophoresis and contour-clamped homogeneous electric field analyses are considered to be the most discriminant tools for establishing the relatedness of strains; isolates that differ by more than three bands are considered to be different, but pulsotyping requires careful interpretation and the techniques for typing require equipment, time and expense.[36]

Other typing procedures

Molecular biology techniques are evolving very rapidly and many new applications are being developed for typing. Polymerase chain reaction has been applied to comparative typing of *P. aeruginosa* – random primed or enterobacterial repetitive intergenic consensus sequences have been used. Both approaches were reproducible and discriminatory.[38] In addition, they require less work and expense than the methods discussed above, and so are becoming methods of choice for fingerprinting strains in the laboratory.

CLINICAL MANIFESTATIONS

Pseudomonas respiratory infections

Pseudomonas *pneumonia*

This generally occurs after endogenous aspiration from a colonized oropharynx, often in patients who have an underlying malignancy; these people carry *P. aeruginosa* in the oral flora more frequently (18–25%) than subjects who do not have malignancies (≤5%).

Pseudomonas pneumonia usually occurs in hospitalized patients and the clinical features do not distinguish it from other Gram-negative nosocomial pneumonias. The clinical presentation and radiographic findings (nodular infiltrates, sometimes with cavitation and lesions, predominantly in the lower lobes) are not specific; various degrees of hemorrhagic edematous lung with scattered micro-abscesses and vascular involvement (thrombosis) are often seen on anatomic pathology. The microscopic appearances are of necrosis of alveolar septa (Fig. 229.4) and arterial walls, with areas of focal hemorrhage and, in intact areas, infiltration with macrophages, mononuclear cells and polymorphonuclear leukocytes.[13,39]

Bacteremic Pseudomonas *pneumonia*

A different lung pathology has been described in bacteremic *Pseudomonas* pneumonia, which occurs in even more severely ill patients who have the risk factors listed in Table 229.9. The pneumonia is diffuse and bilateral and there is a pleural effusion. On cut section, the lesions are either nodular, hemorrhagic with necrotic foci, or umbilicated nodules surrounded by dark hemorrhage. Intra-

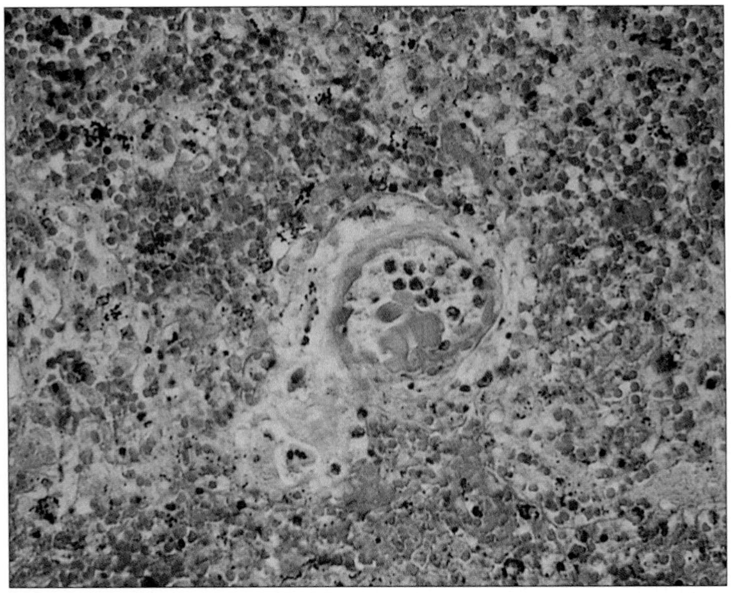

Fig. 229.4 Anatomic pathology of *Pseudomonas aeruginosa* pneumonia showing acute inflammatory exudate, necrosis of alveolar membranes and fibrinous thrombosis in a venula. Hematoxylin–eosin stain. Courtesy of Professor Groussard.

alveolar hemorrhages with patchy alveolar septal necrosis are seen on microscopy. The lesions contain many bacteria but lack a leukocytic reaction. The pneumonia is accompanied by bloodstream invasion that often spreads to metastatic sites of infection. The pneumonia rapidly progresses, resulting in pulmonary edema and necrotizing bronchopneumonia. The fatality rate is extremely high (up to 80–100% of cases).[20,21,39,40]

Strategies for the treatment of *Pseudomonas* bacteremic pneumonia have emphasized the importance of early initiation of empiric appropriate therapy because the majority of fatal cases occur within the first 48–72 hours. Combination therapy is generally recommended (antipseudomonal β-lactam and an aminoglycoside), but there is a poor correlation between clinical response and the in-vitro synergistic effects of antibiotics.[26,41,42]

Respiratory infections in cystic fibrosis patients

Pathogenesis

Cystic fibrosis is a congenital disease affecting exocrine gland secretions.[43,44] A protein, the CF transmembrane conductance regulator, which is responsible for transporting chloride across membranes, is abnormal in CF patients and this decreases the electrochemical gradient for sodium ion movement into the CF duct cell. This results in abnormal sodium absorption in airway epithelium and mucous airway secretions contain decreased water and electrolyte concentrations, with twice the normal ratio of macromolecules (mucins) to electrolytes. These glycoprotein mucins form thick tenacious secretions, which obstruct the airways and contribute to the development of progressive suppurative pneumonia (see Chapter 33).

The leading cause of morbidity and mortality in patients who have CF is progressive pulmonary deterioration with chronic necrotizing bronchopneumonia. These pulmonary infections mainly involve *P. aeruginosa*. Cystic fibrosis also causes a wide range of other major organ deficiencies (diarrhea, malabsorption, pancreatic insufficiency) (see Chapter 40g).

Mucoid *Pseudomonas aeruginosa*

In the early 1960s the importance of mucoid variants of *P. aeruginosa* was recognized. Mucoid *P. aeruginosa* are morphologic and functional variants of *P. aeruginosa* characterized by the ability to produce copious amounts of an exopolysaccharide, which is an acetylated polymer of D-mannuronic and L-glucuronic acids (alginate; see Table 229.4). Molecular weights of the polysaccharide vary from 100kDa to 480kDa. It should be distinguished from the 'slime' polysaccharide, which has different biologic properties and is found in nonmucoid *P. aeruginosa* as well as in mucoid *P. aeruginosa*. The controlling genes (*alg*) for the alginate biosynthetic pathway have

INFECTIONS DUE TO *PSEUDOMONAS AERUGINOSA* LISTED IN DESCENDING ORDER OF INCIDENCE

Infection		Associated factors
Respiratory infections	*Pseudomonas* pneumonia (30–60% mortality rate)	Mechanical ventilation Endotracheal or tracheostomy tube Neurologic disease Nasogastric tube Prolonged stay in intensive care unit Broad-spectrum antibiotics
	Bacteremic *Pseudomonas* pneumonia (80–100% mortality rate)	Neutropenia Underlying malignant neoplasm Chronic bronchiectasis (terminal state) Diabetes mellitus Severe immunodepression Cytotoxic chemotherapy Coronary artery disease Severe burns
	Respiratory tract infections in people with cystic fibrosis (ultimately fatal unless a pulmonary transplant is carried out)	Presence of the lethal genetic disease cystic fibrosis Chronic colonization with *Pseudomonas aeruginosa* Progressive lung deterioration Altered immune response to *Pseudomonas* spp.
Bacteremia	Primary	Same factors as above
	Secondary	Leukemia, lymphoma Intravenous devices Intravenous drug abuse Trauma Prematurity Ulceration of the gastrointestinal tract Solid organ or bone marrow transplant Various endoscopic instrumentation procedures
Skin and soft tissue infections (50–78% mortality rate in burn wound sepsis)		Burn wound sepsis (78% *Pseudomonas* spp.) Wound infection Ecthyma gangrenosum Dermatitis, pyoderma
Urinary tract infections		Acute Chronic (obstruction)
Endocarditis		Intravenous drug abusers Prosthetic heart valves
Miscellaneous		Meningitis (secondary) Brain abscesses Bone and joint infections (chronic *Pseudomonas* osteomyelitis) Ear infections (otitis externa, malignant external otitis) Eye infections (*Pseudomonas* keratitis, endophthalmitis, contact lens keratitis)

Table 229.9 Infections due to *Pseudomonas aeruginosa* listed in descending order of incidence.[13,20,21,26]

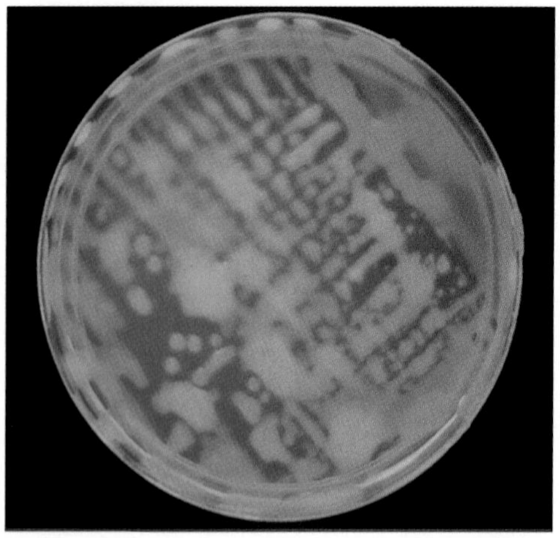

Fig. 229.5 Mucoid colonies of a strain of *Pseudomonas aeruginosa* isolated from a patient who has cystic fibrosis. Courtesy of Professor E Bingen.

ANATOMIC SITES OF PRIMARY INFECTION IN *PSEUDOMONAS* BACTEREMIA		
Infection	**Hospital acquired Gram-negative bacilli (%)**	**Community acquired (%)**
Urinary tract	18.8	5.2
Gastrointestinal tract	20.0	4.3
Skin/soft tissue infection	15.4	6.3
Respiratory tract	36.4	27.8
Other	4.8	6.7

Table 229.10 Anatomic sites of primary infection in *Pseudomonas* bacteremia. Adapted from MacCue.[40]

been partially cloned; multiple gene control of alginate production involves several enzymatically controlled steps.[43] It seems likely that most *P. aeruginosa* possess the genetic information for mucoid exopolysaccharide production. They are capable of producing mucoid exopolysaccharide when grown under appropriate environment conditions, such as those present in the CF lung. Figure 229.5 shows colonies of mucoid *P. aeruginosa*.

In vivo, in areas with impaired local defenses, such as in the airways of CF patients, the organism grows in microcolonies surrounded by the thick polysaccharide matrix. In autopsied lungs of people who had CF there are microcolonies adherent to the walls of larger airways and in the alveoli. Mucoid *P. aeruginosa* are present in abundance in foci of active inflammation in small bronchioles but not in destroyed parenchymal areas. This observation is consistent with the simultaneous role of bacterial growth in the active inflammatory process and of toxins produced by *P. aeruginosa* diffusing away from microcolonies. For instance:

- exotoxin A is one of the major factors responsible for tissue injury in the lungs of patients who have CF and they have high titers of antibodies to toxin A; and
- 86% of mucoid *P. aeruginosa* isolates produce proteases, elastase, collagenase and fibrinolysin.

In contrast it seems likely that mucoid *P. aeruginosa* LPS contributes little to the pathogenesis of lung injury but stimulates local inflammation.

Clinical features

The clinical signs, pulmonary functions and radiographic features seen in patients who have CF vary considerably according to the extent of the disease and the frequency of acute exacerbations. A chronic productive cough, wheezing, tachypnea and low-grade fever develop during acute exacerbations. As the pulmonary disease progresses, fever, chest pain and a cough producing abundant purulent viscous sputum are the predominant symptoms of infection. Lung damage results in pulmonary vascular obstruction and a deteriorating pulmonary function. Arterial hypoxemia is progressive and correlates with clinical pulmonary status. Chest radiographs show overaeration, peribronchial thickening, patchy atelectasia and pneumonia. These features are reversible during the early stages of the disease in the first year of infection.

Appropriate management of the disease and acute exacerbations with aggressive antibiotic therapy, chest physiotherapy and nutritional therapy may result in a symptomatic improvement and slow the inevitable progression of pulmonary deterioration.

Pseudomonas bacteremia

Of all nosocomial bacteremias, *P. aeruginosa* accounts for 20–35% of isolates.[13,40] *Pseudomonas aeruginosa* is particularly common in series of patients who have hematologic malignancy or high risk factors (see Table 229.9).

Primary bacteremia

Pseudomonas bacteremia may occur following instrumentation procedures using contaminated equipment or solutions. Equipment used for endoscopic retrograde cholangiopancreatography, intra-aortic balloon pump placement and many other invasive exploratory investigations have been reported as sources of *Pseudomonas* bacteremia. Many cases of bacteremia have also occurred in narcotic addicts.[13,26]

Secondary bacteremia

Pseudomonas bacteremia is most often related to focal infection (Table 229.10) and the most frequent source is the respiratory tract;[40] the skin and soft tissues, especially in burns patients, and urinary tract are also common sources. Less frequently, colonization of the gastrointestinal tract may precede infection, which develops in the presence of a variety of risk factors such as hospitalization in an ICU, the presence of neutropenia or treatment with cytotoxic chemotherapy; 50% of these patients develop intestinal carriage, which occurs in only 5–15% of the general population, and translocation of *P. aeruginosa* is the potential mechanism for blood invasion and metastatic infection, predominantly in the respiratory tract.

Endocarditis

Endocarditis due to *P. aeruginosa* occurs predominantly in intravenous drug abusers and in those who have prosthetic heart valves. The tricuspid valve is most frequently involved but the aortic or mitral valve and mural endocardium can also be affected.[26] Adherence mechanisms in *P. aeruginosa* (pili, exoenzyme S, alginate) are likely to play a role in the colonization of prosthetic valves, resulting in microcolonies embedded in polysaccharide material and therefore protected from host defenses and antibacterial agents. Similar mechanisms may occur in bacterial colonization of intravenous and intra-arterial catheters.[20,44]

Skin and soft tissue infections

Burn wound sepsis

Pseudomonas aeruginosa is the most common cause of burn wound sepsis, which is the predominant form of skin and soft tissue infection complicating severe thermal injury. The mortality rate is high (50–78%) despite improvements in management and antibiotic therapy.[26] Colonization of the burned skin surface by *P. aeruginosa* may result from the patient's own flora or from environmental sources. The bacteria penetrate into the subcutaneous tissues via hair follicles and breaks in the burned skin, and may enter with the help of proteolytic enzymes they produce. Other virulence factors (see Table 229.4) make a significant contribution to the severity of the

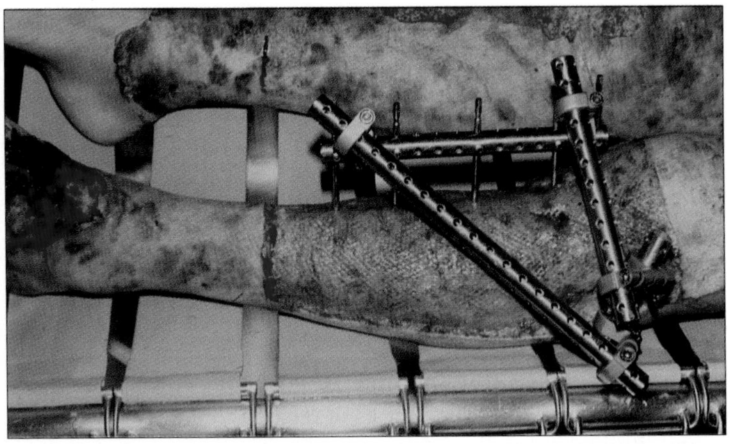

Fig. 229.6 Burned leg that has been superinfected with *Pseudomonas aeruginosa*. Courtesy of Professor H Carsin.

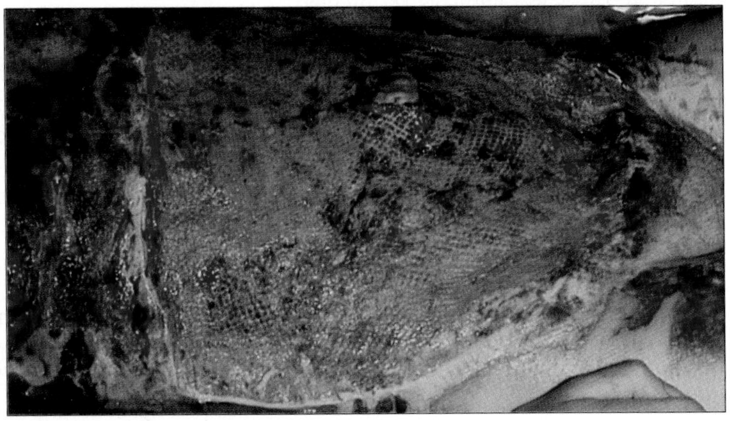

Fig. 229.7 Burned abdominal wall that has been superinfected with *Pseudomonas aeruginosa*. Courtesy of Professor H Carsin.

burn infection, which can be the source of bloodstream invasion. Sepsis, which is clinically characterized by fever or hypothermia, hypotension, oliguria and abdominal distension in addition to the extensive burn eschar, requires specific management in burns centers. Figures 229.6 and 229.7 show extensive burn lesions.

Ecthyma gangrenosum

This is a focal skin lesion that is often associated with *Pseudomonas* bacteremia. The lesion is characterized by an erythema surrounded by hemorrhage, necrosis of skin tissues and bacterial invasion. Other pseudomonal skin lesions may complicate *Pseudomonas* bacteremia, such as subcutaneous nodules, deep abscesses and cellulitis. These extensive and destructive lesions of the skin are particularly seen in neutropenic patients.

Wound superinfections with Pseudomonas aeruginosa

These occur occasionally and their characteristics were described early in the medical literature, particularly because of the blue–green exudate and the colored bandages due to the production of pyocyanin pigments.

Urinary tract infections

Most *Pseudomonas* urinary tract infections are hospital-acquired and associated with either catheterization or surgery or with any cause of obstruction or persistent site of infection (e.g. chronic prostatitis).

Pseudomonas urinary tract infections have no specific clinical presentation but tend to evolve with frequent recurrences and chronic evolution. A characteristic picture of ulcerative or necrotic lesions and multiple renal abscesses is seen in patients who have metastatic bacteremia with urinary tract invasion.[26]

Eye infections

Of all Gram-negative organisms, *P. aeruginosa* is the most common ocular pathogen, despite not forming part of the normal ocular flora. Ocular metastatic infection is rare and the most common source is exogenous. Ocular infections vary from mild (conjunctivitis) to extremely severe (orbital cellulitis).[45]

Keratitis

The most frequent manifestation is keratitis. The predominant predisposing factors of *Pseudomonas* keratitis are prosthetic devices (contact lenses), congenital abnormalities, burns or trauma, altered host defenses (people who have HIV infection) and prematurity. Viral keratitis (herpes simplex) may also be associated with a secondary bacterial infection. The corneal damage results from the exocellular products of *P. aeruginosa* and from strong adhesion to the exposed basement membrane of the epithelium; exotoxins, proteases and phospholipases degrade the corneal stroma, resulting in extensive loss of collagen fibers from the stroma.

Contact-lens associated Pseudomonas *keratitis*

This is common and is mainly observed in association with extended-wear contact lenses, inappropriate disinfecting regimens and poor hygiene. The bacteria may adhere to the lens, resulting in the development of a thick coat of mucopolysaccharide forming the same biofilm as on other prosthetic devices.

Endophthalmitis

This most often results from an endogenous origin, occurring by hematogenous spread from other infected sites. It may also occur after intraocular inoculation of *P. aeruginosa* by either trauma, burns or ocular surgery. Endophthalmitis is an acute fulminant disease, with pain and decreased acuity, which are potentially followed by panophthalmitis. The prognosis is poor without appropriate local and systemic management.[26,45]

Miscellaneous

Central nervous system infections

These include meningitis and brain abscesses, which can result from either direct inoculation (head trauma, surgery), a contiguous infection (sinus, mastoid) or bloodstream infection. Other occasional sources are spinal anesthesia, lumbar puncture and cancer (the latter being one of occasional causes of central nervous system infections).

Bone and joint infections

These may result from contiguous spread, hematogenous origin or trauma. They occur predominantly in patients who have predisposing factors such as diabetes mellitus, intravenous drug abuse and chronic debilitation. Examples are:

- *Pseudomonas* osteomyelitis, which tends to have a chronic evolution;
- pyarthrosis, which frequently involves the sternoclavicular or sternochondral joints, in drug abusers;
- vertebral osteomyelitis in elderly patients in association with genitourinary instrumentation or surgery (*P. aeruginosa* has a particular affinity for cartilaginous joints of the axial skeleton); and
- *Pseudomonas* osteochondritis of the foot, which occurs in children following puncture wounds (this infection, like other fibrocartilaginous infection sites, involves cartilage, synovium, joint space and contiguous bone).

Pain, swelling, fever and other systemic signs are variable, depending upon the underlying diseases and the immune status of the patient.[20,21,26]

The management of bone and joint *Pseudomonas* infections is dependent upon the site of the infection and the immune status of the patient (see Table 229.9).

Ear infections

Pseudomonas aeruginosa is frequently isolated from the external auditory canal, particularly in infants. The significance of the presence of this potential pathogen is not always clear. In some cases, *P. aeruginosa* is involved in a superficial self-limited external otitis, which resolves spontaneously. Occasionally, the pathogen invades the epithelium between cartilage and bone in the lateral portion of the auditory canal, penetrating soft tissue, cartilage and bone.

Malignant external otitis

Malignant external otitis is a severe invasive necrotizing ear infection, clinically characterized by otalgia, otorrhea, early facial nerve paralysis and a swollen erythematous external auditory canal. Adjacent soft tissue is often involved. There is visible extension with cellulitis and bone erosions, the tympanic membrane is generally perforated and there is a purulent discharge.[26,46]

Pseudomonas aeruginosa is isolated from the external auditory canal and from surgical specimens in all cases of malignant external otitis. Most cases occur in elderly people who have diabetes mellitus, but can occur in infants who have severe underlying diseases.

Management of this severe and extensive ear infection requires prolonged antibiotic therapy, surgical debridement and drainage.[46] The fatality rate is high (about 15–20%). Relapses are frequent and malignant external otitis requires prolonged follow-up.

MANAGEMENT

Antibiotic resistance in *Pseudomonas aeruginosa*

Paradoxically, although *P. aeruginosa* is the aerobic Gram-negative bacillus most frequently involved in nosocomial infection, it is not the most resistant organism among 'pseudomonads' and other aerobic Gram-negative bacilli. A number of β-lactams considered to be 'antipseudomonal' drugs are still active against this species (Table 229.11). These drugs include:

- semisynthetic penicillins – carboxypenicillins (ticarcillin), ureidopenicillins (piperacillin);
- third-generation cephalosporins (ceftazidime, cefpirome, cefepime). For both penicillins and cephalosporins the percentages of susceptible strains were between 55% and 75% according to recent European[49,50] and international surveys.[47]
- for carbapenems (imipenem), rates of susceptibility were about 80%; and
- for monobactams (aztreonam) – 70–80% susceptible strains.

Variations occur between countries in relation to different antibiotic usages. Besides natural resistance to many β-lactam antibiotics, high resistance rates are seen in *P. aeruginosa* with aminoglycosides and fluoroquinolones. The incidence of plasmids in *P. aeruginosa* is relatively low and the major resistance mechanisms are chromosomally mediated. These mechanisms are mainly:

- altered outer membrane permeability (altered protein porins or lack of protein porin OprD);[51]
- production of chromosomally mediated β-lactamases, inducible cephalosporinases or plasmid-mediated enzymes, including extended spectrum β-lactamases;[50–52]
- aminoglycosides inactivating enzymes;[53] and
- active efflux mechanism pumping out different antibiotic classes from the cell.[54]

Resistance during therapy may develop and multiple resistance in *P. aeruginosa* is frequent, resulting in diminished permeability to β-lactams, increased production of β-lactamases, aminoglycoside-inactivating enzymes and efflux mechanisms pumping out fluoroquinolones, ticarcillin, aztreonam, cefsulodin, chloramphenicol and tetracyclines.[48] This results in strains with multiresistance profiles that are extremely difficult to eradicate and the choice of a poten-

RESISTANCE MECHANISMS IN *PSEUDOMONAS AERUGINOSA*

Antibiotics		Percentage resistant[47]	Percentage resistant[49]	Mechanisms	Genetic bases
Penicillins	Ticarcillin	30–40	12	Altered PBPs targets	Chromosomal
	Piperacillin	15–20	22	Altered PBPs targets	Chromosomal
Cephalosporins	Cefsulodin	12–15	–	Reduced permeability	Chromosomal
	Cefoperazone	15–20	–	Reduced permeability	Chromosomal
	Ceftazidime	2–8	6	β-Lactamase inactivation (83%)	Chromosomal or plasmid mediated
	Cefpirome	5–8	–	β-Lactamase inactivation (83%)	Chromosomal or plasmid mediated
Monobactams	Aztreonam	5–10	13	β-Lactamase inactivation	
Carbapenems	Imipenem	10–15	2	Altered protein porin D2, imipenemase	Chromosomal
	Meropenem	10–15	–	Altered protein porin D2, imipenemase	Chromosomal
Aminoglycosides	Gentamicin	30–50	14	Reduced permeability, enzymatic inactivation	Chromosomal or plasmid mediated
	Tobramycin	25–35	4	Reduced permeability, enzymatic inactivation	Chromosomal or plasmid mediated
	Netilmicin	25–40	12	Reduced permeability, enzymatic inactivation	Chromosomal or plasmid mediated
	Amikacin	11–30	2	Reduced permeability, enzymatic inactivation	Chromosomal or plasmid mediated
Fluoroquinolones	Ciprofloxacin	10–50	28	Altered DNA gyrase target, efflux	Chromosomal
	Ofloxacin	10–50			
Fosfomycin		–	50–80	Altered transport system	Chromosomal mutation
Rifampin (rifampicin)		–	–	Altered DNA polymerase target	Chromosomal

Table 229.11 Resistance mechanisms in *Pseudomonas aeruginosa*. Distribution of β-lactamases in *P. aeruginosa*: plasmid mediated – PSE-1 to PSE-4 36%, OXA (1–10) 25%, TEM-1 and TEM-2 11.5%; inducible chromosomal cephalosporinase. Main modifying enzymes in *P. aeruginosa*: AAC (3)-I, AAC (3)-III; AAC (3)-IV, V; AAC (6')-I, AAC (6')-II; ANT (2''), AAC (6')-I + ANT (2''). PBP, penicillin-binding protein. Data from Chen *et al.*,[8] Wiedemann *et al.*[47] and Li *et al.*[48]

ANTIBIOTIC THERAPY FOR *PSEUDOMONAS* INFECTIONS		
Choices	**Drugs**	**Indications**
Monotherapy	Antipseudomonas penicillins: ticarcillin, piperacillin, azlocillin; Cephalosporins: ceftazidime, cefoperazone, cefpirome; Carbapenems: imipenem; Fluoroquinolones: ciprofloxacin	Limited to nongranulocytopenic patients, non-life-threatening infections, short courses, bacteriologic monitoring
Conventional combinations	Aztreonam, ticarcillin or ceftazidime plus clavulanate and/or sulbactam plus tobramycin; imipenem plus amikacin; ciprofloxacin plus ceftazidime; ciprofloxacin plus fosfomycin	Severe *Pseudomonas* infections – pneumonia, bacteremia, burns (plus topical), malignant external otitis media (plus surgery), central nervous system infection (plus local), cystic fibrosis (plus topical)
Alternatives	Antipseudomonas penicillin plus fluoroquinolone; aztreonam plus aminoglycoside; aminoglycoside plus fluoroquinolone	
Adjuvants	Burns – mafenide acetate (local), local debridement; Cystic fibrosis – mucolytics, passive immunization (anti-TNF MAb, IL-1); vaccines O-polysaccharide-based	

Table 229.12 Antibiotic therapy for *Pseudomonas* infections. Anti-TNF MAb, monoclonal antibody to tumor necrosis factor; IL-1, interleukin-1. Data from Pollack,[26] Bustamante *et al.*[41] and Figueredo and Neu.[55]

tially efficient antibiotic therapy becomes limited. Serotype O12 has been recognized as one of the most resistant *P. aeruginosa* types; during an outbreak in a burns unit,[23] a serotype O12 strain was resistant to ticarcillin, ceftazidime, aztreonam, imipenem and ciprofloxacin, being only susceptible to amikacin. Paradoxically, 96% of these multiresistant strains were susceptible to fosfomycin.

Management of *Pseudomonas aeruginosa* infection

A summary of appropriate antipseudomonal treatments in various indications is given in Table 229.12.

Conventional antibiotic therapy of Pseudomonas aeruginosa *infections*

Systemic severe infections, bacteremic pneumonia, life-threatening infections

The antibiotic therapy, either empiric or documented, is based upon an antibiotic combination, such as an aminoglycoside and a β-lactam with antipseudomonal activity. Before laboratory data and antibiogram are available, a knowledge of local epidemiology of resistance in a particular ward or ICU and antibiotic susceptibilities as established in recent publications should be a great help in choosing a suitable combination.[41,42,56] Data shown in Tables 229.11 and 229.13 indicate the current situation in terms of susceptibilities and minimum inhibitory concentrations (MICs) and should permit an empirical choice to be confirmed by the local clinical laboratory results.

Monotherapy

This has been documented using the following as monotherapy in moderately severe infections:[57]

- a third-generation cephalosporin, preferentially ceftazidime or cefpirome;
- imipenem/cilastatin; or
- a fluoroquinolone.

Agents such as ceftazidime or cefoperazone have been reported to achieve high serum bactericidal levels against bacteria isolated from patients who have *Pseudomonas* pneumonia.

Results from controlled clinical trials have shown that monotherapy is as good as combination therapy in nongranulocytopenic patients.

Antibacterial agents proposed as single-agent treatments of nosocomial pneumonia include imipenem and fluoroquinolones. Monotherapy with quinolones has narrow indications in severe *Pseudomonas* infection; short-term therapy is recommended when quinolones are used as monotherapy, and close bacteriologic monitoring is advised. Therapeutic results with quinolones against *Pseudomonas* infection were initially encouraging. Mild-to-moderate infections in CF patients have been controlled by oral ciprofloxacin when *P. aeruginosa* strains were resistant to β-lactam agents and aminoglycosides. In some cases patients probably responded to therapy as a result of high tissue concentrations and a favorable ratio of quinolone concentration in vivo to the MICs for the pathogens.[56] However, the susceptibilities of hospital pathogens have evolved, and *Pseudomonas* systemic infections should be monitored carefully for antibiotic resistance.

The major risk of using single-agent treatment for *Pseudomonas* pneumonia is the possible emergence of antibiotic-resistant bacteria during therapy with quinolones or imipenem.

Indications for antibiotic combinations

In microbiologically documented cases of *Pseudomonas* infections, β-lactam and aminoglycoside combinations offer a broad spectrum of antibacterial activity with synergistic bactericidal effect. Many reports have described in-vitro synergism, and in-vivo studies in animal models of *P. aeruginosa* pneumonia have confirmed the efficacy of such regimens.[58] However, in patients who have *Pseudomonas* nosocomial infections, there were frequent therapeutic problems due to the presence of multiresistant bacteria.[49] In a survey in our hospital, of 762 *Pseudomonas* strains:

- 39% were resistant to all β-lactams;
- 21% were imipenem resistant;
- 21% were resistant to all aminoglycosides; and
- 37.5% were resistant to all fluoroquinolones.

Among imipenem-resistant strains, however, 41% were susceptible to ticarcillin and ceftazidime. The emergence of resistance has been prevented by using ciprofloxacin with ceftazidime or imipenem in *P. aeruginosa* pneumonia, but the in-vitro effect of combinations is additive or indifferent rather than synergistic.[41] An absence of correlation between in-vitro synergism and clinical outcome with a combination of ciprofloxacin and azlocillin has been observed.[42] When quinolones are combined with β-lactam drugs (ureidopenicillins, ceftazidime or imipenem), the combination prevents or at least reduces the risk of emergence of resistance. Combinations of fluoroquinolones with fosfomycin have been found to be useful in preventing the emergence of resistant mutants[55] and to be generally synergistic.

Management of specific Pseudomonas *infections*

Central nervous system infections due to *Pseudomonas aeruginosa*

These require bactericidal antibiotics that reach high concentrations in cerebrospinal fluid (CSF) – in *Pseudomonas* meningitis a

Table 229.13 Antibiotic susceptibility of *Pseudomonas aeruginosa*.[47]

ANTIBIOTIC SUSCEPTIBILITY OF *PSEUDOMONAS AERUGINOSA*					
Antibiotics		Number of strains tested	Range (mg/l)	MIC_{50} (mg/l)	MIC_{90} (mg/l)
Beta-lactams	Apalcillin	72	0.25–256	2	256
	Aztocillin	100	0.25–512	8	512
	Aztreonam	100	0.125–128	4	16
	Carbenicillin	76	≤2 to ≥512	64	512
	Cefepime	60	0.5–16	4	16
	Cefixime	322	0.25 to ≥16	≥16	≥16
	Cefmenoxime	110	2 to ≥128	32	≥128
	Cefoperazone	100	0.5–128	4	128
	Cefoperazone and sulbactam	72	8 to ≥128	64	128
	Cefotaxime	100	0.25–512	16	64
	Cefotetan	100	32–64	64	64
	Cefpirome	60	2–32	2	16
	Cefsulodin	110	1 to ≥128	4	64
	Ceftazidime	110	1–128	4	32
	Ceftazidime	100	0.5–64	2	4
	Ceftizoxime	100	0.5–64	32	64
	Ceftriaxone	99	≤0.06 to ≥16	8	≥16
	Imipenem	322	0.25–8	1	2
	Latamoxef	100	2–128	32	128
	Meropenem	100	0.03–32	0.5	2
	Mezlocillin	76	≤2 to ≥512	25	128
	Piperacillin	100	0.5–512	8	512
	Piperacillin and tazobactam	100	0.06–256	4	128
	Temocillin	72	256	256	256
	Ticarcillin	100	0.5–512	32	512
	Ticarcillin and clavutanic acid	100	0.06–512	16	512
Aminoglycosides	Amikacin	100	0.125–2	0.5	2
	Gentamicin	100	0.06–128	0.5	8
	Isepamicin	100	0.125–2	0.5	1
	Tobramycin	100	0.03–32	0.125	4
Quinolones	Ciprofloxacin	100	0.015–2	0.06	0.25
	Enoxacin	100	0.5–4	1	4
	Fleroxacin	100	0.06–32	1	4
	Lomefloxacin	100	0.125–8	0.5	2
	Nalidixic acid	100	≥128	≥128	≥128
	Norfloxacin	100	0.25–2	1	2
	Ofloxacin	100	0.5–8	2	4
	Pefloxacin	100	2–16	8	16
Miscellaneous	Trimethoprim–sulfamethoxazole	25	4 to ≥128	128	≥128

combination of ceftazidime, which is highly concentrated in CSF when the meninges are inflamed, and an aminoglycoside (amikacin, which is the drug with the lowest resistance rates; see Table 229.11). If there is obstruction of the subarachnoid space the aminoglycoside may be instilled directly into the ventricular system. *Pseudomonas* brain abscess is treated surgically together with a similar prolonged antibiotic therapy.[26]

Malignant external otitis

Malignant external otitis, which is an extremely severe infection, must be treated with a combination of local surgical debridement and drainage together with a potent antibiotic therapy combining an aminoglycoside and antipseudomonal β-lactam.[46]

Pseudomonas burn wound sepsis

This requires a combination of antibiotics, as mentioned above, although there is frequent emergence of resistance due to high bacterial counts and limited access of antibiotic to burn sites. Local measures with topical agents and surgical debridement of necrotic tissue are always applied in addition to systemic antibiotics.[26,52]

Pseudomonas pneumonia in cystic fibrosis patients

Respiratory infections in CF are among the most serious types of infection, because they occur in children, who suffer for prolonged periods. Eradication of *Pseudomonas* spp. (or other pathogens) from the airways occurs provisionally only, whatever strategy is used. Proper management of acute exacerbations of *Pseudomonas* lung infection requires antibiotic combinations, usually aminoglycosides and β-lactams (ceftazidime or piperacillin) at larger than usual doses. Although not recommended in children, fluoroquinolones have been used successfully and a combination of ciprofloxacin with fosfomycin has demonstrated in-vitro synergy.[55] Courses of aggressive antibiotic therapy every 3 months in combination with other measures such as mucolytics, antiproteases and topical antibiotic therapy and physiotherapy increase the 5- to 20-year survival of patients who have CF.

Topical antibiotic therapy for nosocomial *Pseudomonas* pneumonia in cystic fibrosis patients

Depending upon their physicochemical characteristics, many injected antibiotics do not achieve significant concentrations in the lung. Administration of antibiotics directly into the tracheobronchial tree should therefore increase local antibiotic concentrations so that the free drug concentration exceeds the MIC of the pathogen.[59,60] A good clinical tolerance has been reported for gentamicin, tobramycin and amikacin, although some reduction of the maximum expired volume per second has occasionally been observed. Carbenicillin and ceftazidime were also administered topically but poorly tolerated. Successful inhaled tobramycin therapy has been demonstrated recently in 69 CF centers in the USA.[59]

Among the drawbacks of this route of administration are:

- a low or heterogeneous deposition of antibiotic in lung areas where there is consolidation or atelectasis; and
- resorption of aminoglycoside from the respiratory tract to the blood resulting in a low antibiotic concentration that may promote the emergence of resistant bacteria (this has been observed in *P. aeruginosa* pneumonia when continuous local polymyxin B has been used for prophylaxis).[60]

Nosocomial *Pseudomonas* pneumonia

It has been suggested that parenteral conventional therapy should be combined with direct instillation of aminoglycoside into the respiratory tract via an endotracheal or tracheostomy tube. In a double-blind randomized trial, using endotracheal tobramycin versus placebo, pathogens were eradicated in 68% versus 31% respectively.[61]

EPIDEMIOLOGY AND PATHOGENICITY OF THE NON-*AERUGINOSA PSEUDOMONAS* SPP.		
Habitat and epidemiology	**Pathogenicity**	**Species**
Environment, water, plants; hospital environment; rare opportunistic pathogens	Occasional bacteremia (contaminated blood, solutions); rare cases	*Pseudomonas alcaligenes, Pseudomonas pseudoalcaligenes*
Soil, water, plants; hospital sinks, floor; food spoilage (eggs, meat, fish, milk); opportunistic pathogens	Rarely isolated from clinical specimens; rare cases of isolation in patients with cystic fibrosis, bacteremia, urinary tract infection, wounds	*Pseudomonas putida, Pseudomonas fluorescens*
Ubiquitous, soil, water, sewage water; hospital environment, antiseptics, injectable solutions; relatively more frequent than other non-*aeruginosa Pseudomonas* spp.; opportunist; more susceptible to antibiotics than other species	Outbreaks of pseudobacteremia; frequent isolation from pus, urine, blood, cerebrospinal fluid; contamination of bone marrow transplant	*Pseudomonas stutzeri*

Table 229.14 Epidemiology and pathogenicity of the non-*aeruginosa Pseudomonas* species

OTHER *PSEUDOMONAS* SPECIES

EPIDEMIOLOGY

Among *Pseudomonas* spp. (see Table 229.1), a few may be involved in rare cases of opportunistic infection. Their common habitat is in the natural environment: water, soil and plants. Some of these species, in particular *Pseudomonas putida, Pseudomonas fluorescens* and *Pseudomonas stutzeri,* are widespread in the animal and human environment and are frequently found in the hospital environment; they occasionally contaminate antiseptic solutions, dialysis fluids, transfusion blood and blood byproducts.

DIAGNOSTIC MICROBIOLOGY

Characteristics differentiating *Pseudomonas* spp. are shown in Table 229.7. This simplified scheme for identification of these bacteria is mainly based on morphologic features (flagella), pigment production and the main metabolic characteristics. The taxonomic status of non-*aeruginosa Pseudomonas* spp. has evolved significantly (see Table 229.1). Some species, such as *P. fluorescens* and *P. putida*, are heterogeneous and several biovars are recognized: five biovars in *P. fluorescens* (I–V) and two biovars in *P. putida* (A and B), which differ in a few metabolic properties.[1,7,11]

PATHOGENICITY AND CLINICAL MANIFESTATIONS

Some of these *Pseudomonas* spp. have been isolated from human clinical specimens (blood, urine, stools) and occasional cases of opportunistic infection occur as a result of transfusion, antiseptic use, dialysis and other mechanisms of transmission. *Pseudomonas fluorescens*, a psychrophilic organism, may grow at 39°F (4°C), which favors its presence in blood products.[15] Outbreaks of bacteremia, respiratory infections in CF patients, wound infections and rare cases of community-acquired pneumonia have been reported.[7] These *Pseudomonas* spp. have been also implicated in rare cases of endophthalmitis and keratitis, particularly *P. fluorescens*, *P. stutzeri* and *Pseudomonas paucimobilis* (the last species being rarely cited). Most cases occur in severely debilitated patients, and these *Pseudomonas* spp. behave as opportunistic pathogens in immunocompromised patients (Table 229.14).[15,39,26]

MANAGEMENT

Based on their in-vitro susceptibilities,[47] these organisms can be eradicated by using carbapenems (MICs 0.5–8mg/l) in combination with fluoroquinolones (ciprofloxacin MICs 0.5–16mg/l). Aminoglycosides have poor activity and management of infections due to *P. putida* or *P. fluorescens* is difficult. *Pseudomonas stutzeri* is more susceptible to antibiotics than other species.

ACINETOBACTER SPECIES

NATURE

Acinetobacter spp. are Gram-negative bacteria that are commonly present in soil and water as free-living saprophytes and are also isolated as commensals from skin, throat and various secretions of healthy people. They have emerged as important nosocomial pathogens in outbreaks of hospital infections and rank second after *P. aeruginosa* among aerobic Gram-negative bacilli nosocomial pathogens. The increasing number of these infections and the natural resistance of the strains has led to studies of epidemiology and resistance mechanisms in *Acinetobacter* spp.[3]

EPIDEMIOLOGY

In the natural environment

Acinetobacter spp. are widely distributed in nature and can be found in virtually 100% of soil and freshwater samples when appropriate culture techniques are used.[6,62] They use a wide variety of substrates as a sole carbon source. In freshwater samples, less than 1–7.9 × 10^4cfu/100ml have been recorded, whereas in raw sewage effluents up to 10^6cfu/100ml have been found. *Acinetobacter* spp. can also be isolated from food and form part of the normal flora of fresh meats; they may contribute to the spoilage process of refrigerated meats.

In the human environment

In hospitals

Acinetobacter spp. have been found in:

- moist situations such as room cold-air humidifiers, tap water, hand washbasins, waterbaths, moist respirometers and all types of ventilatory equipment, which are capable of aerosolizing the organism;
- angiography catheters;
- blood collection tubes; and
- plastic urinals.

The presence of *Acinetobacter* spp. in mattresses in burns units has been reported,[3,62] and Acinobacter have caused considerable problems on some intensive care units.

Human carriage of Acinetobacter *species*

This has been demonstrated in normal individuals, indicating that the source of nosocomial infections might be endogenous as well as from the external environment. *Acinetobacter* spp. form part of the bacterial flora of the skin and are found in the axilla, groin and toe webs; they can colonize the oral cavity, the respiratory tract and the normal intestine (see Table 229.2).[62] However, the value of this approach has not been independently confirmed and is not widely used.

PATHOGENICITY

Pathogenesis of infections: virulence of *Acinetobacter* species

Several factors may be responsible for the virulence of *Acinetobacter* spp.:

- the presence of a polysaccharide capsule formed of L-rhamnose, L-glucose, D-glucuronic acid and D-mannose that makes the surface of strains more hydrophilic;
- the adhesiveness of *Acinetobacter* spp. to human epithelial cells in the presence of fimbriae and/or mediated by the capsular polysaccharide;
- enzymes (butyrate esterase, caprylate esterase and leucine arylamidase) potentially involved in damaging tissue lipids; and
- the LPS component of the cell wall and the presence of lipid A, which are likely to participate in the pathogenicity of *Acinetobacter* spp.[33]

Host predisposing factors

Susceptible patients include those who have severe underlying conditions such as malignancy, burns and immunosuppression or who have undergone major surgery. Age plays a role in the occurrence of nosocomial infections with *Acinetobacter* spp. in elderly patients and neonates. The settings for infection are medical or surgical ICUs, and renal and burns units. Tubes, catheters and all kinds of artificial devices act as portals of entry at the site of infection (see Table 229.5). In French hospitals, *Acinetobacter* spp. were found in 9.7% of nosocomial infections.[3]

DIAGNOSTIC MICROBIOLOGY

Acinetobacter strains are nonfermentative, nonfastidious, aerobic Gram-negative coccobacilli, usually found in diploid formation or in chains of variable length (Fig. 229.8). They are not motile (*akinetos* means 'unable to move' in Greek), but the cells display a 'twitching motility'. Strictly aerobic, they grow well on all common media at temperatures of 68–86°F (20–30°C), but for most strains the optimum is 91.4–95°F (33–35°C). A few species can grow at 105.8°F (41°C) and 111.2°F (44°C) and this is a discriminating character between species. Identification of *Acinetobacter* spp. is based upon:

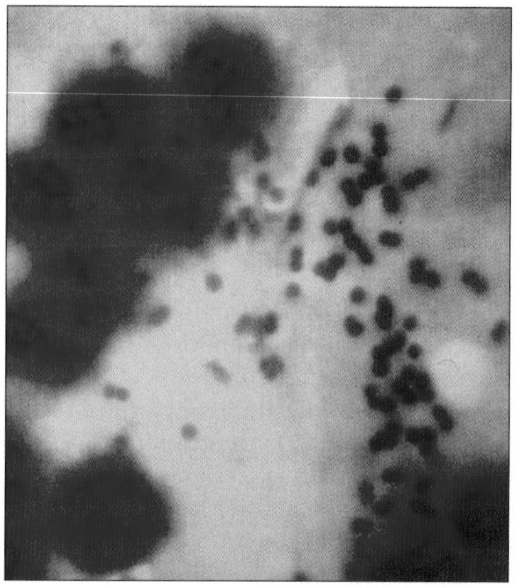

Fig. 229.8 Morphology of *Acinetobacter baumannii* on Gram stain. Preparation from a lung infection in mice. Courtesy of Dr ML Joly-Guillou.

- oxidase-negative, catalase-positive, indole-negative, nitrate-negative tests; and
- production or not of acid from D-glucose, D-ribose, D-xylose and L-arabinose (used oxidatively as carbon sources; Table 229.15).

Acinetobacter is the only genus with an oxidase-negative test among non motile aerobic Gram-negative bacilli.[3,7]

Nomenclature of *Acinetobacter* species

This has undergone considerable taxonomic changes. By using modern methods of taxonomy (genetic transformations, DNA hybridizations and rRNA sequence comparisons), the classification proposed by Bouvet and Grimont[63] identified more than 15 genomic species including *Acinetobacter baumannii* (formerly *A. calcoaceticus* var. *anitratus* and *A. glucidolytica non liquefaciens*), *Acinetobacter haemolyticus*, *Acinetobacter junii*, *Acinetobacter johnsonii* and *Acinetobacter radioresistens*.

Species of clinical importance

Most studies have supported the initial observation that *A. baumannii* is the main species associated with outbreaks of nosocomial infection. Other species, *A. haemolyticus*, *A. junii* and *Acinetobacter lwoffi*, have been associated with clinical infections; they can be natural inhabitants of human skin and repeated isolation of non-*A. baumannii* species suggests that they are potential pathogens.[3]

CLINICAL MANIFESTATIONS

The main sites of infections are the respiratory and urinary tracts. Endocarditis, burn infections, and skin and wound sepsis may also occur (see Table 229.3).

Acinetobacter pneumonia

This is common in hospitals, especially in ICUs. Large outbreaks of *Acinetobacter* pneumonia have been described. All patients had severe underlying disease, assisted ventilation and tracheostomy or were intubated. *Acinetobacter* spp. represent 15.6% of the total Gram-negative bacilli involved in nosocomial pneumonia in France.[18]

Community-acquired cases of *Acinetobacter* pneumonia have been reported in middle-aged and elderly people who have a chronic underlying disease or are alcoholic.

IDENTIFICATION OF THE MOST FREQUENTLY ISOLATED *ACINETOBACTER* SPECIES.[3,63]									
	Genospecies	Growth at	Glucose (acidified)	Hemolysis	Gelatin hydrolysin	Utilization tests*			
						β-alanine	DL-lactate assimilation	Citrate	Malonate
A. anitratus (glucose acidified)	*A. calcoaceticus* 1	–105.8°F	+	–	–	+	100% positive strains	+	+
	A. baumannii 2	+111.2°F	+		–	+	+	+	+
	Unnamed species 3	–111.2°F	+(at 41°C)	–	–	+		+	+
	A. haemolyticus 4	+98.6°F	+(52%)	+(100%)	+(96%)	–	0% positive strains	+(91%)	–
A. lwoffi (glucose negative)	*A. junii* 5	+98.6°F	–	–	–	–	+	+(82%)	–
	Unnamed species 6	+98.6°F	+(66%)	+(100%)	+(100%)	–	–	+	–
	A. johnsonii 7		–	–	–	–	+	+	–
	A. lwoffi 8/9	+98.6°F	–	–	–	–	+	–	–
	A. radioresistens 12†	+98.6°F	–	–	–	–	–	+	+

* Eleven other assimilation tests of carbon and energy sources can be used[53] data not shown for unnamed genospecies 10 and 11.
† Five other unnamed genospecies have been identified – 13, 14, 15, 16, 17 – and are being studied.

Table 229.15 Identification of the most frequently isolated *Acinetobacter* species.[3,63] Red indicates a positive result, and white a negative result. The numbered genospecies are based on DNA–DNA hybridizations. *A. alcaligenes* is hemolytic.

Urinary tract infection

Several reviews[9,18,62] have described *Acinetobacter* spp. in 2–61% of nosocomially acquired urinary tract infections. A recent investigation in France has indicated an overall incidence of 30.5% of acquired urinary tract infection.[18]

Meningitis

Nosocomial meningitis is an infrequent manifestation of *Acinetobacter* infection. The first case report was in 1908 by Von Lingelsheim and the organism was designated *Diplococcus mucosus*, later renamed *Mima* by Debord (1939) because of its resemblance to *Neisseria meningitidis*. Cases of *Acinetobacter* meningitis have been reported after neurosurgical procedures, but rare cases of primary meningitis, especially in children, have also occurred.[3]

Miscellaneous

Skin and wound infections, abscesses, sepsis, endocarditis, peritonitis and burn wound infections have been reported.[3]

MANAGEMENT

Antibiotic resistance

Since 1980 successive surveys have shown increasing resistance in clinical isolates of *Acinetobacter* spp.[3,9,18,64] High proportions of strains are resistant to most commonly used antibacterial drugs including aminopenicillins, ureidopenicillins, cephalosporins of the first generation (cephalothin) and second generation (cefamandole), cephamycins such as cefoxitin, most aminoglycosides, aminocyclitols, chloramphenicol and tetracyclines. Differences in susceptibilities of *Acinetobacter* isolates as a function of countries and areas could be attributable to environmental factors and different patterns of antibiotic usage.[3,64,65]

Management of *Acinetobacter* infections

Only a few antibiotics are active in the treatment of *Acinetobacter* spp. infections. A few β-lactams might be used after careful in-vitro susceptibility testing:

- ticarcillin combined with sulbactam (the latter being a β-lactamase inhibitor often active by itself against *Acinetobacter* spp.);[3,66]
- ceftazidime; and
- most often imipenem, which is by far the most active drug for treating *Acinetobacter* infection.

Combination therapy is always recommended, combining a β-lactam with an aminoglycoside, a fluoroquinolone or rifampin (rifampicin). The addition of β-lactamase inhibitors, clavulanic acid to ticarcillin, or sulbactam to a third-generation cephalosporin, may significantly enhance the β-lactam activity. In a recent study,[64] pneumonia and sepsis due to *A. baumannii* were treated using synergistic combinations of imipenem plus either amikacin or tobramycin (14 cases) or ampicillin–sulbactam with tobramycin and ticarcillin–clavulanate with tobramycin (four cases), underlining the importance of β-lactamase inhibitors in combination therapy in *Acinetobacter* infections.

BURKHOLDERIA SPECIES

NATURE AND EPIDEMIOLOGY

Burkholderia spp. were transferred from the genus *Pseudomonas* (see Table 229.1). Three species are recognized as opportunistic agents involved in nosocomial infections:

- *Burkholderia cepacia* (type species),
- *Burkholderia gladioli*, and
- *Burkholderia pickettii*.

Two species are responsible for specific infections in horses (glanders) – *Burkholderia mallei* and *Burkholderia pseudomallei* – and are occasionally transmitted to humans, resulting in a disease named melioidosis (the organism was identified by Whitmore in 1913).[5]

All *Burkholderia* spp. are genetically related on the basis of DNA–DNA homologies, 16S rRNA sequences and phenotypic characters. They are ubiquitous organisms, being widespread in water, soil and plants, and are present in the human environment. *Burkholderia cepacia* is an environmental organism that has no specific nutritional requirements and survives for months in water, sinks, antiseptic solutions (chlorhexidine, quaternary ammoniums, povidone–iodine), pharmaceutical products, dialysis fluid and various injectable solutions. It may even survive on environmental surfaces[11] and may be found in nebulizers, ventilatory equipment and many other medical and dental devices (see Table 229.5).

PATHOGENICITY

Although weakly virulent with a limited invasive capacity, *B. cepacia* has become an important nosocomial pathogen. Clinical manifestations are dependent upon the source of contamination. Most cases and outbreaks of *B. cepacia* infection have been bacteremias with septic shock, nosocomial urinary tract infections, peritonitis (in dialysis units), endophthalmitis and keratitis, and nosocomial pneumonias.[26,39,44,67] All infections due to *B. cepacia* have been described in immunocompromised patients, who have usually been hospitalized in ICUs. The predominant site of infection is the respiratory tract (see Table 229.3), mainly in patients who have CF.[44,68–70]

Burkholderia cepacia in severe respiratory infections in cystic fibrosis patients

The pathogenesis of *B. cepacia* in severe respiratory infections in people who have CF has not been extensively studied. Virulence factors suspected in *B. cepacia* could be mainly exoproducts (proteases, lipases, exopolysaccharides), which act in addition to the LPS forming part of O antigen, responsible for severe pneumonia and sepsis in CF patients.[44,17] Cases of fulminant and extensive necrotizing pneumonia with a rapidly fatal outcome have been observed.[71]

Other *Burkholderia* species

Burkholderia pickettii *and* Burkholderia gladioli

These are ubiquitous organisms that can be found in water and soil and may play a role as nosocomial pathogens. Rare outbreaks of infection have been described and emergence of multiresistance is a potential problem.[11,70]

Burkholderia mallei *and* Burkholderia pseudomallei

These are environmental organisms predominantly found in Asia, Africa and South America. *Burkholderia mallei* is not motile but is genetically related to *B. pseudomallei*. The latter, an animal pathogen, can be transmitted to humans; sepsis with severe pneumonia and subacute pulmonary cavitating disease are the main human forms of melioidosis (see Chapter 175). These infections are severe and have high fatality rates.[26]

DIAGNOSTIC MICROBIOLOGY

Identification tests for *Burkholderia* spp. are summarized in Table 229.16.

DIAGNOSTIC MICROBIOLOGY OF *BURKHOLDERIA* SPECIES

Characteristics	*Burkholderia cepacia*	*Burkholderia mallei*	*Burkholderia pseudomallei*
Cell length (μm)	1.6–3.2	1.4–4.0	1.5
Flagella number	>1	0	>1
Pigment (diffusible)	■		■
Oxidase	■	■	■
Poly-β-hydroxybutyrate accumulation	■	■	■
Gelatin	v	■	■
Lipase (Tween 80 hydrolysis)	■	v	■
Denitrification		■	■
Arginine dihydrolase		■	■
Growth at 105.8°F	v	■	■
Guanine + cytosine content in DNA (%)	67.4	69.0	69.5

Table 229.16 Diagnostic microbiology of *Burkholderia* species. Main characteristics differentiating species.[1,11] Red indicates a positive result, and white a negative result. v, variable.

MANAGEMENT

The susceptibility of strains to aztreonam, ceftazidime, ceftriaxone and fluoroquinolones suggests the use of combinations of drugs belonging to these classes for treating these severe infections, particularly in people who have CF. Imipenem is not the most active β-lactam (MICs 1 to ≥32mg/l) and aminoglycosides have variable efficacy (MICs 2 to >32mg/l). However, aminoglycoside plus imipenem may be a synergistic combination.[11] Highly multiresistant strains can be isolated from CF during exacerbations of pulmonary infection; consecutive sequences of antibiotic treatments[70,71] may have exerted a selective pressure leading to a therapeutic 'dead end'. In those cases, inhaled antibiotic therapy[59,60] associated with an intravenously administered antibiotic combination can control pulmonary exacerbation by *B. cepacia*.

STENOTROPHOMONAS MALTOPHILIA

NATURE AND EPIDEMIOLOGY

Stenotrophomonas maltophilia is an emerging opportunistic pathogen that belonged to the *Pseudomonas* genus, was transferred to the *Xanthomonas* group[10] and then received a new designation, *S. maltophilia*,[4] belonging in the newly defined genus *Stenotrophomonas*. Isolated from soil, plants, water and raw milk, this ubiquitous bacterium is common in the hospital environment.[27] It has often been isolated from ventilatory equipment (thermal humidifying units) and from moist respirometers, as well as from dialysis fluids and antiseptic solutions (see Table 229.5).

DIAGNOSTIC MICROBIOLOGY

These bacteria are characterized by the presence of a single or a small number of polar flagella (motile bacteria), frequently pigmented colonies (yellow or yellowish orange) and oxidase-negative reaction.[4,11,15] (Table 229.17; also see Fig. 229.1 and Table 229.6). *Stenotrophomonas maltophilia* acidifies sugars (except for rhamnose or mannitol) and is generally proteolytic. Its identification tests are shown in Table 229.17.

CLINICAL MANIFESTATIONS

Stenotrophomonas maltophilia can be isolated from patients who have respiratory tract infections, endocarditis, bacteremia, meningitis and urinary tract infections, and can also be implicated in severe cutaneous infections (ecthyma gangrenosum similar to that due to *P. aeruginosa*), cellulitis and abscesses. It produces proteolytic enzymes and other pathogenic extracellular enzymes such as DNAse, RNAse, elastase, lipase, hyaluronidase, mucinase and hemolysin, which contribute to the severity of *S. maltophilia* infection in immunodepressed patients in ICUs.[2,4,27] There is a high incidence of infection with *S. maltophilia* in patients who have cancer, leukemia or lymphoma, and *S. maltophilia* is increasingly implicated in pulmonary superinfections in patients who have CF (see Table 229.3). It can be underlined that *S. maltophilia* is a rapidly developing agent of nosocomial infection, with an increasing incidence in respiratory infections in CF patients. Another species, identified as *Stenotrophomonas africana*, is an emergent pathogen, a strictly aerobic, nonproducer of oxidase close to *S. maltophilia*. It has been isolated in east Africa from the CSF of an HIV-positive patient with meningoencephalitis. This organism is one of the most resistant bacteria, susceptible only to ciprofloxacin and colistin.[72]

TESTS FOR IDENTIFICATION OF MOTILE GRAM-NEGATIVE NONFERMENTATIVE AEROBIC (OXIDASE-POSITIVE) BACILLI.						
Features		***Stenotrophomonas maltophilia***	***Empedobacter breve***	***Chryseobacterium* (synonym *Flavobacterium*) *gleum* (group IIb)**	***Chryseobacterium meningosepticum***	***Alcaligenes xylosoxidans* subsp. *xylosoxidans***
Oxidase			100†	96	99	100
Tests	Catalase		100	99	100	98
	Citrate (Simmons)		0	3	12	95
	DNase		100	4	100	
	Esculin, hydrolyzed		0	70	99	0
	Gelatin, hydrolyzed		100	78	91	0
	Indole		100	98	100	0
	MacConkey agar, growth		100	63	92	100
	Nitrate reduced		0	22	0	100
	Nitrite reduced		0	20	37	
	Urease		0	42	8	0
	107.6°F, growth		0	42	45	84
Acidified	Ethanol		0†	16	57	100
	D-Glucose*		86	98	99	78
	Lactose		0	0	57	0
	Maltose		86	98	100	0
	Mannitol		0	10	99	0
	Sucrose		0	14	0	0
	D-Xylose		0	31	3	99

* Sugars acidified by *S. maltophilia* in 48 hours in the presence of a concentration of less than 1% of sugar.
† Percentage of strains positive.

Table 229.17 Tests for identification of motile Gram-negative nonfermentative aerobic (oxidase-positive) bacilli. Clinically important species of the genera *Stenotrophomonas, Chryseobacterium–Flavobacterium* group and *Alcaligenes* (*Stenotrophomonas maltophilia* is not in fact oxidase-positive). Genera and species of *Empedobacter breve, Chryseobacterium gleum* and *Chryseobacterium meningosepticum* are derived from the genus *Flavobacterium*. Red indicates a positive result, white a negative result and pink a variable result.[1,2,4]

Stenotrophomonas maltophilia is frequently associated with other bacterial species at sites of infection but is increasingly isolated as the sole pathogen.

MANAGEMENT

Resistance

Stenotrophomonas maltophilia is naturally resistant to most antibiotics as a result of chromosomally mediated mechanisms, poor permeability of the outer membrane and naturally produced inactivating enzymes.[6,67]

- Many β-lactamases have been described in *Stenotrophomonas maltophilia* and it is susceptible only to latamoxef and combinations of ticarcillin plus clavulanic acid or piperacillin plus tazobactam. It is naturally resistant to imipenem and meropenem as a result of carbapenemase production.
- Only a few strains are susceptible to gentamicin, neomycin and kanamycin. Resistance to aminoglycosides is probably plasmid-mediated. *Stenotrophomonas maltophilia* is poorly susceptible to quinolones.
- Resistance to quinolones is generally associated with resistance to chloramphenicol and to doxycycline in more than 50% of cases and is associated with alteration of outer membrane proteins.[16]
- An active efflux mechanism has been also demonstrated.[67]

Stenotrophomonas maltophilia is variably susceptible to minocycline, rifampin and trimethoprim–sulfamethoxazole.

Management of infections due to *Stenotrophomonas maltophilia*

Infections due to *S. maltophilia* require combination therapy including rifampin plus a fluoroquinolone or plus β-lactams (mezlocillin, ceftazidime or cefotaxime; MICs 8, 128 and 16mg/l respectively). Combinations decrease the MICs of β-lactams.[67,73]

MISCELLANEOUS AEROBIC GRAM-NEGATIVE BACILLI

Many other aerobic Gram-negative bacilli either derived from the *Pseudomonas* group or originating from dispersed groups of environmental organisms have been identified. Some are increasingly involved in human infection.[5,11,72,73] These genera and species have undergone many taxonomic changes; some have been identified recently, and the wide use of analysis of ribosomal 16S RNA gene sequences has allowed a clearer taxonomic position to be established for most aerobic Gram-negative bacilli. The following section includes a short description of the pathogenic role of those involved in human infections and of the management of these infections. For easy reading, the generic groups are described in alphabetical order (Table 229.18). Species cited in the list are those isolated from human infections (see also Table 229.1).

ACHROMOBACTER spp.

See *Ochrobacterium* spp.[74]

CURRENT AND PREVIOUS NOMENCLATURE OF MISCELLANEOUS AEROBIC GRAM-NEGATIVE BACILLI		
Main groups (genera)	**Current name**	**Previous name**
Achromobacter	*Ochrobactrum anthropi*	*Achromobacter* Vd
Aeromonas	*Aeromonas enteropilogenes* *Aeromonas ichtiosemia* *Aeromonas salmonicida* *Aeromonas caviae*	*Aeromonas trota* *Aeromonas veronii* *Haemophilus piscium* –
Agrobacterium	*Agrobacterium radiobacter* *Agrobacterium tumefaciens* *Pantoea agglomerans*	*Agrobacterium tumefaciens* *Agrobacterium gypsophilae*
Alcaligenes (see Table 229.1)	*Alcaligenes faecalis type 1*	
Alcaligenes xylosoxidans	*Alcaligenes odorans*	
Achromobacter xylosoxidans		
Bergeyella	*Bergeyella zoohelcum*	*Weeksella zoohelcum*
Burkholderia (see Table 229.1)	*Burkholderia cepacia*	
Burkholderia mallei		
Burkholderia pseudomallei	*Pseudomonas kingii*	
Pseudomonas mallei		
Pseudomonas pseudomallei		
Calymmatobacterium	*Calymmatobacterium granulomatis*	*Klebsiella granulomatis*
Capnocytophaga	*Capnocytophaga ochracea* *Capnocytophaga gingivalis* *Capnocytophaga sputigena*	*Bacteroides ochraceus* – –
Chromobacterium	*Chromohalobacter marismortui*	*Chromobacterium marismortui*
Chryseobacterium (see Table 229.1)	*Chryseobacterium meningosepticum*	*Flavobacterium meningosepticum*
Chryseomonas (formerly *Flavobacterium*)	Chryseomonas luteola	Pseudomonas luteola
Comamonas	*Comamonas terrigena* *Comamonas testosteroni* *Delftia acidovorans*	*Pseudomonas terrigena* – *Comamonas acidovorans*
Ochrobactrum	*Ochrobactrum anthropi* *Ochrobactrum intermedium*	*Achromobacter* Vd *Ochrobactrum* nov. sp.
Oligella	*Oligella urethralis*	*Moraxella urethralis*
Plesiomonas	*Proteus shigelloides*	*Plesiomonas shigelloides*
Ralstonia	*Ralstonia picketii* *Ralstonia eutropha*	*Burkholderia picketii* *Pseudomonas/Alcaligenes eutrophus*
Shewanella	*Shewanella hanedai* *Shewanella putrefaciens*	*Alteromonas hanedai* *Pseudomonas/Alteromonas putrefaciens*
Sphingobacterium (see Table 229.1)	*Sphingobacterium mizutae, S. multivorum*	*Flavobacterium* spp.
Stenotrophomonas	*Stenotrophomonas maltophilia* *Stenotrophomonas africana*	*Xanthomonas maltophilia* –
Weeksella	*Bergeyella zoohelcum*	*Weeksella zoohelcum*

Table 229.18 Current and previous nomenclature of miscellaneous aerobic Gram-negative bacilli. Only species seen as pathogenic in humans are listed. This table completes and/or modifies the taxonomic data in Table 229.1.

AEROMONAS spp.

Originally included in the Vibrionaceae group, *Aeromonas* spp.[70,76] form their own family (the Aeromonadaceae). Their natural habitat is water, fish and other aquatic animals, and the gut of pigs, dogs and cats. At least seven species have been recognized, four of which are the most pathogenic for humans (see Table 229.18).

Microbiology

These organisms are motile, Gram-negative rods (one single polar flagellum), oxidase- and catalase-positive and facultatively anaerobic. They grow easily at low temperatures (between 41°F/5°C and 72–82°F/22.2–27.8°C) on nutrient agar. Selective growth media that contain ampicillin has been formulated, as ampicillin inhibits the growth of *Aeromonas* spp. at more than 32mg/l.

Pathogenic role

Aeromonas spp. isolated from contaminated water produce enteric infections with diarrhea, abdominal pain and fever. *Aeromonas* spp. present in the hospital environment may also be responsible for systemic infections, bacteremia, meningitis, peritonitis, cholecystitis and liver infections, all of which occur generally in patients who have severe underlying disease or immunodepression.

Aeromonas hydrophila strains have been involved in nosocomial infections. They may also be transmitted by sanguivorous leeches used in plastic or graft surgery, being responsible for severe cellulitis, osteitis and pyomyositis.

Management

Aeromonas spp. are resistant to most β-lactams; they produce several β-lactamases, including a carbapenemase, which confers resistance to imipenem. Infections are treated using third-generation cephalosporins, aminoglycosides, tetracyclines, fluoroquinolones and trimethoprim–sulfamethoxazole.[72]

AGROBACTERIUM spp.

Initially included in the group of *Alcaligenes* spp. (see Table 229.1), these bacteria are considered as emerging pathogens but only one species, namely *Agrobacterium radiobacter,* has been involved in human infections.[72,73]

Microbiology

These phytopathogenic organisms, present in water, soil and environmental plants, are strictly aerobic coccobacilli, motile with peritrichous flagella (one to six). They grow easily on conventional media and produce oxydase and catalase; these bacteria are identified by using commercial identification kits.

Pathogenic role

Oncogenic in plants, *Agrobacterium* spp. have not been found to be oncogenic in humans, but they have been implicated in bacteremia, endocarditis, catheter infection, peritonitis and urinary tract infections. A limited number of cases have been cited in the literature.

Management

Agrobacterium spp. are susceptible to cephalosporins (second- and third-generation), ticarcillin, imipenem, tetracyclines, colistin, trimethoprim–sulfamethoxazole and fluoroquinolones, but outcomes of treatment depend on underlying pathologies in infected patients.

ALCALIGENES spp.

See Tables 229.1, 229.5, 229.17 and 229.18 and Figure 229.1.

Epidemiology

The natural habitat of *Alcaligenes* spp. is the same as that of *Pseudomonas* spp. In the hospital environment, *Alcaligenes faecalis* and *Alcaligenes xylosoxidans* can be isolated from various environmental sources, such as respirators, hemodialysis systems, intravenous solutions and disinfectants.[1,2,3,30,77]

Microbiology

These are short, Gram-negative rods (0.5–2.6μm), strictly aerobic and motile with one to eight peritrichous (nonpolar) flagella, usually described as degenerated (see Fig. 229.1 and Table 229.6). They are oxidase-positive and catalase-positive. *Alcaligenes faecalis, Alcaligenes piechaudii* and *A. xylosoxidans* subsp. *denitrificans* are not saccharolytic. The only saccharolytic species is *A. xylosoxidans* subsp. *xylosoxidans*. Not all *Alcaligenes* spp. possess specific physiologic or biochemical characteristics (see Table 229.17) and those most commonly involved in nosocomial infections are *A. faecalis* and *A. xylosoxidans.*

Pathogenic role

Alcaligenes spp. have been isolated from blood, feces, sputum, urine, cerebrospinal fluid, wounds, burns and swabs taken from throat, eyes and ear discharges. *Alcaligenes* spp. strains do not seem to possess any specific virulence determinants. They are infrequent causes of hospital-acquired infection in patients who have severe underlying disease. Rare cases of peritonitis, pneumonia, bacteremia, meningitis and urinary tract infections are found in the literature. In many instances the organism is considered to be a colonizer. Nosocomial outbreaks of infection are usually associated with an aqueous source of contamination.[30] Recent findings have underlined the fact that *Alcaligenes* spp. are predominantly isolated from respiratory tract specimens and that recovery of these organisms from the sputum of CF patients is associated with an exacerbation of pulmonary symptoms.[31]

Management

Alcaligenes spp. are resistant to aminoglycosides, chloramphenicol and tetracyclines; they are variably susceptible to trimethoprim–sulfamethaxazole and newer β-lactams. *Alcaligenes xylosoxidans* has been shown to be susceptible to ureidopenicillins, latamoxef, imipenem and some fluoroquinolones (ciprofloxacin, ofloxacin). There have been several reports of multiple β-lactam resistance to broad-spectrum penicillins in *A. xylosoxidans* due to constitutive β-lactamase production; three different types of cephalosporinase and the presence of other β-lactamases have been demonstrated.[32,77] Treatment of *Alcaligenes* infection requires combination therapy including expanded-spectrum β-lactams (piperacillin, imipenem) and recent fluoroquinolones (ciprofloxacin, sparfloxacin) or trimethoprim–sulfamethaxazole.

BERGEYELLA spp.

See *Weeksella* spp.

CALYMMATOBACTERIUM sp.

One known species, *Calymmatobacterium granulomatis*, an aerobic Gram-negative bacillus, remains of uncertain taxonomy. The only reservoir of the organism is humans and its main epidemiologic characteristic is its presence intracellularly in macrophages of the lesions in donovanosis (granuloma inguinale). This sexually transmitted disease is endemic in Asian countries, India, South America, Australia and Africa. *Calymmatobacterium* has not been cultured yet (only 15 successful isolations) since it does not grow on conventional media; knowledge on the microbiology of this organism is limited. The diagnosis is based on bacterial inclusions found in biopsies (Giemsa or Wright staining). Extensive granuloma inguinale is seen in pregnant women and in HIV patients. Antibiotic treatment requires lipid-soluble drugs that can penetrate intracellularly and the first-line therapy is a combination of trimethoprim–sulfamethoxazole, tetracycline or thiamphenicol. Additional options include lincomycin, chloramphenicol or gentamicin.[72,78]

CAPNOCYTOPHAGA spp.

These Gram-negative, strictly aerobic organisms are oxydase- and catalase-negative (group DF-1) or positive (group DF-2). Group DF-1 includes three species – *Capnocytophaga ochracea*, *Capnocytophaga gingivalis* and *Capnocytophaga sputigena* (see Table 229.18) – found as commensals of the human oral cavity. They can be responsible for cervicofacial infections and, in patients who have valvular lesions or prosthetic valves, endocarditis and bacteremia. *Capnocytophaga canimorsus,* a commensal of the oral cavity of dogs, has been cited as responsible for human infection after dog bites (septicemia, endocarditis).

These bacteria grow easily on blood agar and identification is based on conventional tests. Treatment of infection uses penicillins, cephalosporins, clindamycin and fluoroquinolones but *Capnocytophaga* spp. are resistant to aminoglycosides.[72]

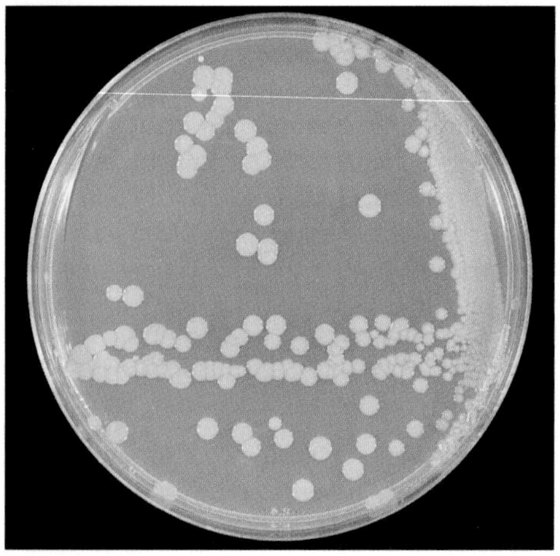

Fig. 229.9 Colonies of *Flavobacterium–Chryseobacterium* group grown on Mueller–Hinton agar. Courtesy of Professor H Monteil.

CHROMOBACTERIUM spp.

These bacteria of uncertain taxonomic position and designation have a limited pathogenic role. They are motile by one to four subpolar flagella. Grown on agar plates, colonies are violet and the bacterium has some fermentative activities on sugars and is proteolytic. Found in soil and water in tropical countries, *Chromobacterium violaceum* is occasionally pathogenic in humans, causing occasional pyogenic or septicemic infection.[2,15]

CHRYSEOBACTERIUM spp.

Chryseobacterium spp. (formerly *Flavobacterium* spp.; see Table 229.1) are ubiquitous organisms that can be found in the hospital environment. Epidemiologic studies have traced the bacterial source to contaminated water, ice machines and humidifiers. Phenotypic markers used for the delineation of outbreaks of *Chryseobacterium meningosepticum* infections were serology based on the O antigenic type; nine O serovars have been identified (A–H and K).

Microbiology

These organisms grow at between 41°F (5°C) and 86°F (30°C) and strains isolated from human specimens can grow at 98.6°F (37°C). On nutrient agar they produce colonies of 1–2mm in diameter, which are frequently pigmented light yellow or yellowish orange (nondiffusible pigment; Fig. 229.9). The metabolism is strictly aerobic and sugars are metabolized by the oxidative pathway – except for *Chryseobacterium odoratum* (*Myroides odoratus*) and *Sphingobacterium multivorum*, which do not acidify glucose. Indole-positive species (i.e. *Empedobacter breve*, *C. meningosepticum*, *Chryseobacterium gleum*) are usually strongly proteolytic; esculin, citrate and urease tests are variably positive (see Table 229.17).[15,28,29,72,73]

Clinical manifestations

Infections due to Chryseobacterium meningosepticum *and* Chryseobacterium indologenes

These have been isolated in sepsis, meningitis and endocarditis. Meningitis due to *C. meningosepticum* (still designated under its previous name, *Flavobacterium*) has been often observed in neonates but infrequently in immunocompromised patients.[28,29,19] *Chryseobacterium meningosepticum* has been isolated from adults suffering from pneumonia, postoperative bacteremia and meningitis, usually in patients who had severe underlying pathologies.[29,19] Rare cases of community-acquired *C. meningosepticum* pneumonia have been cited in the literature.[79]

Infections with *Flavimonas oryzihabitans* (an emerging Gram-negative aerobic bacillus previously designated *Pseudomonas oryzihabitans* and closely related to *Chryseobacterium* spp.; see Table 229.1) have been reported.[80] *Chryseobacterium indologenes* has been cited in association with infections due to indwelling devices.[29] *Chryseomonas luteola* (previously designated *Pseudomonas luteola*), *Comamonas testosteroni* and *Comamonas acidovorans* have been implicated in bacteremia, catheter infections, prosthetic valve endocarditis and peritonitis in patients who are being treated with continuous ambulatory peritoneal dialysis.[72]

Management

These bacteria are generally resistant to aminoglycosides (MIC >16mg/l), third-generation cephalosporins, antipseudomonal penicillins (mezlocillin, piperacillin, ticarcillin), aztreonam, imipenem, erythromycin and tetracycline. The most active antibiotics are rifampin and clindamycin (MICs 1–4mg/l). Ciprofloxacin has proven effective for treating pneumonia in pediatric patients. Cases of neonatal sepsis have been treated with clindamycin combined with piperacillin.[73,81] Susceptibility to β-lactams can be recovered by combining β-lactamase inhibitors with β-lactam antibiotics.

COMAMONAS spp.

These aerobic Gram-negative oxydase-positive bacilli are seldom implicated in human infections. Rare cases of catheter-induced bacteremia (*C. testosteroni*, *Delftia acidovorans*), conjunctivitis (*C. testosteroni*) and otitis media (*D. acidovorans*) have been cited in the literature. These straight or slightly curved rods are motile by means of tuft of polar flagella. They grow easily on standard media and are susceptible to piperacillin, cefotaxime, imipenem and ciprofloxacin.[72]

OCHROBACTRUM spp.

Derived from the genus *Achromobacter*, two species have been recognized as having a medical role, *Ochrobactrum anthropi* and *Ochrobactrum intermedium*. These environmental organisms are considered as opportunistic pathogens. A few recent publications have pointed out their role in nosocomial infections, induced by contaminated catheters.[72,82] Endocarditis, postoperative cases of endophthalmitis and necrotizing fasciitis have been cited as well. These nonfastidious bacteria are easily grown on conventional media and identified by using classical biochemical tests. The major problem regarding these organisms is their resistance to most β-lactams, since they produce β-lactamases of AmpC class 1. They are susceptible to imipenem, aminoglycosides and fluoroquinolones but strains of *O. intermedium* have been cited as resistant to tobramycin and colistin.

OLIGELLA sp.

This genus was created in 1987 and *Oligella urethralis* was derived from *Moraxella urethralis*. These small rods, often occurring in pairs, develop slowly on blood agar and exhibit a limited metabolic activity. They are oxidase- and catalase-positive. Their potential pathogenic role is limited to the genitourinary tract.[72]

PLESIOMONAS sp.

Only one species, *Plesiomonas shigelloides*, until recently designated *Proteus shigelloides*, is present in the environment (water, soil) in tropical and subtropical areas. Its pathogenic role in humans is controversial but rare cases of gastroenteritis, septicemia and neonatal meningitis have been cited in Japan and the USA. Raw oysters and contact with contaminated water or with aquatic animals have been implicated. *Plesiomonas* sp. is not a strictly aerobic organism and may grow on selective media used for isolation of Enterobacteriaceae. Its production of oxidase and other biochemical characteristics permit its identification. Antibiotic testing of *P. shigelloides* shows a general resistance to penicillins and aminoglycosides but this organism is susceptible to cephalosporins, imipenem and fluoroquinolones, the latter antibiotics being very active in treating gastrointestinal infections.[83]

RALSTONIA spp.

Ralstonia picketii was derived from *Burkholderia picketii* or *Pseudomonas picketii*, and *Ralstonia eutropha* from *Alcaligenes eutrophus* (see Table 229.18). Both are emerging pathogens isolated from infections in immunodepressed patients or from respiratory tract infections in CF patients.[72,73]

SHEWANELLA spp.

Derived from *Alteromonas* spp. or *Pseudomonas* spp., *Shewanella putrefaciens* belongs to the Vibrionaceae class but grows in media used for Enterobacteriaceae and produces SH_2, which may result in confusions with *Salmonella* spp. or *Proteus* spp. This bacterium is present in the environment and has been isolated from otitis media, intra-abdominal infections and bacteremia, most cases occurring in immunodepressed patients. Treatment of these infections is based on third-generation cephalosporins, imipenem, ciprofloxacin, aminoglycosides, trimethoprim–sulfamethoxazole and tetracyclines.[72]

SPHINGOBACTERIUM spp.

Two species (see Table 229.18) of *Sphingobacterium* are derived from *Flavobacterium* spp. (see Table 229.1). They are characterized by colonies that develop a yellow pigment after a few days at room temperature. Their presence in the hospital environment and in most aquatic sources is frequent but their clinical significance is limited to rare cases of opportunist infection.

WEEKSELLA spp.

Designated currently *Bergeyella* spp. and deriving from *Flavobacterium* spp., these organisms include *Weeksella virosa* (see Table 229.1) and *Weeksella zoohelcum*. Both grow as pigmented colonies (brown or yellow). Their pathogenic role is doubtful and is limited to local infection after animal bites or genitourinary tract infection.[73]

REFERENCES

1. Kiska DL, Gilligan PH. *Pseudomonas*. In: Murray PR, Baron EJ, Pfaller MA, Tenover FC, Yolken RH, eds. Manual of clinical microbiology, 7th ed. Washington, DC: ASM Press; 1999:517–25.
2. Bergogne-Bérézin E, Towner KJ. *Acinetobacter* spp. as nosocomial pathogens: microbiological, clinical and epidemiological features. Clin Microbiol Rev 1996;9:148–65.
3. Denton M, Kerr KG. Microbiological and clinical aspects of infection associated with *Stenotrophomonas maltophilia*. Clin Microbiol Rev 1998;11:57–80.
4. Yabuuchi E, Koosako Y, Oyaisu H, *et al.* Proposal of *Burkholderia* gen. nov. and transfer of seven species of the genus *Pseudomonas* homology group II to the new genus, with the type species *Burkholderia cepacia* (Palleroni & Holmes 1981) comb. Nov Microbiol Immunol 1992;36:1251–75.
5. Von Gravenitz A. Ecology, clinical significances and antimicrobial susceptibility of infrequently encountered glucose-nonfermenting Gram-negative rods. In: Gilardi GL, ed. Non-fermentative Gram-negative rods: laboratory identification and clinical aspects. New York: Marcel Dekker; 1985:181–232.
6. Von Graevenitz A. *Acinetobacter, Alcaligenes, Moraxella*, and other non fermentative Gram-negative bacteria. In: Murray PR, Baron EJ, Pfaller MA, Tenover FC, Yolken RH, eds. Manual of clinical microbiology, 6th ed. Washington DC: ASM Press; 1995;520–32.
7. Pitt TL, Barth AL. *Pseudomonas aeruginosa* and other medically important pseudomonads. In: Emmerson AM, Hawkey PM, Gillespie SH, eds. Principles and practice of clinical bacteriology. Chichester: John Wiley & Sons; 1997:494–517.
8. Chen HY, Yuan M, Ibrahim-Elmagboul IB, Livermore DM. National survey of susceptibility to antimicrobials amongst clinical isolates of *Pseudomonas aeruginosa*. J Antimicrob Chemother 1995;35:521–34.
9. Buisson Y, Tran Van Nhieu G, Ginot L, *et al.* Nosocomial outbreaks due to amikacin-resistant tobramycin sensitive *Acinetobacter* species: correlation with amikacin usage. J Hosp Infect 1990;15:83–93.
10. Swings J, De Vos P, Van den Mooter M, *et al.* Transfer of *Pseudomonas maltophilia* to the genus *Xanthomonas* as *Xanthomonas maltophilia* (Hugh 1981) comb. nov. Int J Syst Bacteriol 1983;33:409–13.
11. Monteil H. *Pseudomonas–Burkholderia.* In: Eyquem A, Alouf J, Montagnier L, eds. Traité de microbiologie clinique. Padua: Piccin Nuova Libraria; 2000:23–41.
12. Gould IM. Risk factors for acquisition of multiply-drug-resistant Gram-negative bacteria. Eur J Clin Microbiol Infect Dis 1994;13(Suppl.1):30–8.
13. Aksamit TR. *Pseudomonas* pneumonia and bacteremia in the immunocompromised patient. In: Fick RB, ed. *Pseudomonas aeruginosa*, the opportunist, pathogenesis and disease. Boca-Raton, FL: CRC Press; 1993:177–88.
14. Boukadida J, Montalembert M, Gaillard JL, Grimont F, *et al.* Outbreak of gut colonisation by *Pseudomonas aeruginosa* in immunocompromised children undergoing total digestive decontamination: analysis by pulse-gel electrophoresis. J Clin Microbiol 1991;29:2068–71.
15. Richard C, Kiredjian M. Laboratory methods for the identification of strictly aerobic Gram-negative bacilli, 2nd ed. Paris: Institut Pasteur; 1995.
16. Khardori N, Elting L, Wong E, Schable B, Bodey GP. Nosocomial infections due to *Xanthomonas maltophilia* (*Pseudomonas maltophilia*) in patient with cancer. Rev Infect Dis 1990;12:997–1003.
17. Segonds C, Chabanon G, Conetdic G, *et al.* Epidemiology of pulmonary colonization with *Burkholderia cepacia* in cystic fibrosis patients. Eur J Clin Microbiol Infect Dis 1996;15:841–2.
18. Joly-Guillou ML, Decré D, Wolff M, *et al.* *Acinetobacter* spp: clinical epidemiology in 89 intensive care units. A retrospective study in France during 1991. 2nd International Conference on the Prevention of Infection (CIPI), Nice, 4–5 May 1992:Abstract CJ1.
19. Brunn B, Tvenstrup Jensen JE, Lundström K, Andersen GE. *Flavobacterium meningosepticum* infection. Eur J Clin Microbiol Infect Dis 1989;8:509–14.
20. Salyers AA, Whitt DD. *Pseudomonas aeruginosa.* In: Bacterial pathogenesis. Washington, DC: ASM Press; 1994:260–70.
21. Fick RB Jr. *Pseudomonas aeruginosa.* The microbial hyena and its role in disease. In: Fick RB, ed. *Pseudomonas aeruginosa*, the opportunist, pathogenesis and disease. Boca-Raton, FL: CRC Press; 1993:1–5.
22. Pitt TL. Epidemiological typing of *Pseudomonas aeruginosa*. Eur J Clin Microbiol Infect Dis 1988;7:238–47.
23. Richard P, Le Floch R, Chamoux C, *et al.* *Pseudomonas aeruginosa* outbreak in a burn unit: role of antimicrobials in the emergence of multiply resistant strains. J Infect Dis 1994;39:53–62.
24. Munck A, Bonacorsi S, Mariani-Kurdjian P, *et al.* Genotypic characterization of *Pseudomonas aeruginosa* strains recovered from patients with cystic fibrosis after initial and subsequent colonization. Pediatr Pulmonol 2001;32:288–92.
25. Bergman DC, Bonten MJ, Stobberingh EE, *et al.* Colonization with *Pseudomonas aeruginosa* in patients developing ventilator-associated pneumonia. Infect Control Hosp Epidemiol 1998;19:853–5.
26. Pollack M. *Pseudomonas*. In: Gorbach SL, Bartlett JG, Blacklow NR, eds. Infectious diseases. Philadelphia: WB Saunders; 1992:1502–13.
27. Marshall WF, Keating MR, Anhalt JP, *et al.* *Xanthomonas maltophilia*: an emerging nosocomial pathogen. Mayo Clin Proc 1989;64:1097–104.
28. Abrahamsen TG, Finne PH, Lingaas E. *Flavobacterium meningosepticum* infections in a neonatal intensive care unit. Acta Paediatr Scand 1989;78:51–5.
29. Hsueh PR, Teng LJ, Ho SW, Hsieh WC, Luh KT. Clinical and microbiological characteristics of *Flavobacterium indologenes* infections associated with indwelling devices. J Clin Microbiol 1996;34:1908–13.
30. Mandell WF, Garvey GJ, Neu HC. *Achromobacter xylosoxidans* bacteremia. Rev Infect Dis 1987;9:1001–5.
31. Dunne WM, Maisch S. Epidemiological investigation of infection due to *Alcaligenes* species in children and patients with cystic fibrosis: use of repetitive-element-sequence polymerase chain reaction. Clin Infect Dis 1995;20:836–41.
32. Decré D, Arlet G, Danglot C, *et al.* A beta-lactamase-overproducing strain of *Alcaligenes denitrificans* subsp. *xylosoxydans* isolated from a case of meningitis. J Antimicrob Chemother 1992;30:769–79.

33. Avril JL, Mesnard R. Factors influencing the virulence of *Acinetobacter*. In: Towner KJ, Bergogne-Bérézin E, Fewson CA, eds. The biology of *Acinetobacter*. New York: Plenum Publishing; 1991:77–82.
34. Stoutenbeek CP, Van Saen HKF, Miranda DR, Zandstra DF. The effect of selective decontamination of the digestive tract on colonisation and infection rate in multiple trauma patients. Intens Care Med 1984;10:185–92.
35. Bingen EH, Denamur E, Elion J. Use of ribotyping in epidemiological surveillance of nosocomial outbreaks. Clin Microbiol Rev 1994;7:311–27.
36. Ogle JW, Vasil ML. Molecular approaches to epidemiologic typing of *Pseudomonas aeruginosa*. In: Fick RB, ed. *Pseudomonas aeruginosa*, the opportunist, pathogenesis and disease. Boca-Raton, FL: CRC Press; 1993:141–58.
37. Fyfe JAM, Harris G, Govan JRW. Revised pyocin typing method for *Pseudomonas aeruginosa*. J Clin Microbiol 1984;20:47–50.
38. Lau YJ, Liu PYF, Hu BS, *et al.* DNA fingerprinting of *Pseudomonas aeruginosa* serotype O11 by enterobacterial repetitive intergenic consensus polymerase chain reaction and pulsed-field gel electrophoresis. J Hosp Infect 1995;31:61–6.
39. Eisenstadt J, Crane LR. Gram negative bacillary pneumonias. In: Pennington JE, ed. Respiratory infections: diagnosis and management, 3rd ed. New York: Raven Press; 1994:369–406.
40. MacCue JD. Improved mortality in Gram-negative bacillary bacteremia. Arch Intern Med 1985;145:1212–6.
41. Bustamante CI, Drusano GL, Wharton RC, Wade JC. Synergism of the combinations of imipenem plus ciprofloxacin and imipenem plus amikacin against *Pseudomonas aeruginosa* and other bacterial pathogens. Antimicrob Agents Chemother 1987;31:632–4.
42. Hilf M, Yu VL, Sharp J, Zuravleff JJ, Korvick JA, Muder RR. Antibiotic therapy for *Pseudomonas aeruginosa* bacteremia: outcome correlations in a prospective study of 200 patients. Am J Med 1989;87:540–7.
43. MacCubbin M, Fick RB Jr. Pathogenesis of *Pseudomonas* lung disease in cystic fibrosis. In: Fick RB, ed. *Pseudomonas aeruginosa*, the opportunist, pathogenesis and disease. Boca-Raton, FL: CRC Press; 1993:189–211.
44. Govan JRW, Deretic V. Microbial pathogenesis in cystic fibrosis: mucoid *Pseudomonas aeruginosa* and *Burkholderia cepacia*. Microbiol Rev 1996;60:539–74.
45. Holland SP, Pulido JS, Shires TK, Costerton JW. *Pseudomonas aeruginosa* ocular infections. In: Fick RB, ed. *Pseudomonas aeruginosa*, the opportunist, pathogenesis and disease. Boca-Raton, FL: CRC Press; 1993:159–76.
46. Rubin J, Yu VL. Malignant external otitis: insights into pathogenesis, clinical manifestations, diagnosis and therapy. Am J Med 1988;85:391.
47. Wiedemann B, Grimm H. Susceptibility to antibiotics: species incidence and trends. In: Lorian V, ed. Antibiotics in laboratory medicine, 4th ed. Baltimore: Williams & Wilkins; 1996:900–1168.
48. Li XZ, Livermore MD, Nikaido H. Role of efflux pump(s) in intrinsic resistance of *Pseudomonas aeruginosa*: active efflux as contributing factor to β-lactam resistance. Antimicrob Agents Chemother 1994;38:1742–52.
49. Spencer RC. An 8 year microbe base survey of the epidemiology, frequency and antibiotic susceptibility of *Pseudomonas aeruginosa* hospital isolates in the United Kingdom. J Antimicrob Chemother 1996;37:295–301.
50. Bert F, Lambert-Zechovsky N. *Pseudomonas aeruginosa*: actualités sur la résistance aux β-lactamines et implications thérapeutiques. Antibiotiques 2000;2:195–201.
51. Livermore DM. Interplay of impermeability and chromosomal β-lactamase activity in imipenem-resistant *Pseudomonas aeruginosa*. Antimicrob Agents Chemother 1992;36:2046–8
52. Luzzaro F, Mantengoli E, Perilli M, *et al.* Dynamics of a nosocomial outbreak of multidrug-resistant *Pseudomonas aeruginosa* producing the PER-1 extended-spectrum β-lactamase. J Clin Microbiol 2001;39:1865–70.
53. Aminoglycoside Resistance Study Group. The most frequently occurring aminoglycoside resistance mechanisms: combined results of surveys in eight regions of the world. J Chemother 1995;7(Suppl.2):17–30.
54. Ramos Aires J, Köhler T, Nikaido H, *et al.* Involvement of an active efflux system in the natural resistance of *Pseudomonas aeruginosa* to aminoglycosides. Antimicrob Agents Chemother 1999;43:2624–8.
55. Figueredo VM, Neu HC. Synergy of ciprofloxacin with fosfomycin *in vitro* against *Pseudomonas* isolates from patients with cystic fibrosis. J Antimicrob Chemother 1988;22:41–50.
56. Church DA, Kanga JF, Kuhn RJ, *et al.* Sequential ciprofloxacin therapy in pediatric cystic fibrosis: comparative study vs. ceftazidime/tobramycin in the treatment of acute pulmonary exacerbations. The Cystic Fibrosis Study Group. Pediatr Infect Dis J 1997;16:97–105.
57. Guerra JG, Casalino E, Palomino JC, *et al.* Imipenem/cilastatin versus gentamicin/clindamycin for the treatment of moderate to severe infections in hospitalized patients. Rev Infect Dis 1985;7S:763–70.
58. Fantin B, Carbon C. *In vivo* antibiotic synergism: contribution of animal models. Antimicrob Agents Chemother 1992;36:907–12.
59. Moss RB. Long-term benefits of inhaled tobramycin in adolescent patients with cystic fibrosis. Chest 2002;121:55–63.
60. Thys JP, Aoun M, Klastersky J. Local antibiotic therapy for bronchopulmonary infection. In: Pennington JE, ed. Respiratory infections: diagnosis and management, 3rd ed. New York: Raven Press; 1994:741–66.
61. Brown A, Kruse JA, Counts GW, Russel JA, *et al.* Endotracheal tobramycin study group. Double-blind study of endotracheal tobramycin in the treatment of Gram-negative pneumonia. Antimicrob Agents Chemother 1990;34:269–72.
62. Bergogne-Bérézin E, Joly-Guillou ML. Hospital infection with *Acinetobacter* spp: an increasing problem. J Hosp Infect 1991;18(Suppl.A):250–5.
63. Bouvet PJM, Grimont PAD. Taxonomy of the genus *Acinetobacter* with the recognition of *Acinetobacter baumannii* sp. nov., *Acinetobacter haemolyticus* sp. nov., *Acinetobacter johnsonii* sp nov., and *Acinetobacter junii* sp. nov. and amended descriptions of *Acinetobacter calcoaceticus* and *Acinetobacter lwoffi*. Int J Syst Bacteriol 1986;36:228–40.
64. Marques MB, Brookings ES, Moser SA, *et al.* Comparative *in vitro* antimicrobial susceptibilities of nosocomial isolates of *Acinetobacter baumannii* and synergistic activities of nine antimicrobial combinations. Antimicrob Agents Chemother 1997;41:881–5.
65. Vila J, Marcos A, Marco F, *et al. In vitro* antimicrobial production of β-lactamases, aminoglycoside-modifying enzymes, and chloramphenicol acetyltransferase by and susceptibility of clinical isolates of *Acinetobacter baumannii*. Antimicrob Agents Chemother 1993;37:138–41.
66. Urban C, Go E, Mariano N, *et al.* Effect of sulbactam on infections caused by imipenem-resistant *Acinetobacter calcoaceticus* biotype *anitratus*. J Infect Dis 1993;67:448–51.
67. Alonso A, Martinez JL. Multiple antibiotic resistance in *Stenotrophomonas maltophilia*. Antimicrob Agents Chemother 1997;41:1140–2.
68. Pankhurst CL, Philpott-Howard J. The environmental risk factors associated with medical and dental equipment in the transmission of *Burkholderia* (*Pseudomonas*) *cepacia* in cystic fibrosis patients. J Hosp Infect 1996;32:249–55.
69. Ryley HC, Ojeniyi B, Hoiby N, Weeks J. Lack of evidence of nosocomial cross-infection by *Burkholderia cepacia* among Danish cystic fibrosis patients. Eur J Clin Microbiol Infect Dis 1996;15:755–8.
70. Simpson IN, Finlay J, Winstanley J, *et al.* Multiresistant isolates possessing characteristics of both *Burkholderia* (*Pseudomonas*) *cepacia* and *Burkholderia gladioli* from patients with cystic fibrosis. J Antimicrob Chemother 1994;34:353–61.
71. Tomashefski JF, Thomassen MJ, Bruce MC, *et al. Pseudomonas cepacia*-associated pneumonia in cystic fibrosis. Arch Pathol Lab Med 1988;112:166–70.
72. Raoult D, Tilton R. Dictionary of infectious diseases. Paris: Elsevier; 1999.
73. Monteil H, Harf-Monteil C. Aerobic Gram-negative bacilli: newer nosocomial pathogens. Int J Antimicrob Agents 1997;8:217–31.
74. Brisou J, Prévôt AR. Etudes de systématique bacterienne. X-revision des especes réunies dans le genre *Achromobacter*. Ann Inst Pasteur 1954;86:722.
75. Abbott SL, Seli LS, Catino MJR, Hartley MA, Janda JM. Misidentification of unusual *Aeromonas* species as members of the genus *Vibrio*: a continuing problem. J Clin Microbiol 1998;36:1103–4.
76. Janda JM. Recent advances in the study of the taxonomy, pathogenicity and infectious syndromes associated with the genus *Aeromonas*. Clin Microbiol Rev 1991;4:397–410.
77. Bizet C, Tekaïa F, Philippon A. *In vitro* susceptibility of *Alcaligenes faecalis* compared with those of other *Alcaligenes* species to antimicrobial agents including seven beta-lactams. J Antimicrob Chemother 1993;32:907–10.
78. Richens J. *Calymmatobacterium granulomatis*. In: Yu VL, Merigan TC, Barriere SL, eds. Antimicrobial therapy and vaccines. Baltimore: Williams & Wilkins; 1999:97–101.
79. Ashdown LR, Previtera S. Community acquired *Flavobacterium meningosepticum* pneumonia and septicaemia. Med J Austr 1992;156:69–70.
80. Esteban J, Valero-Moratalla ML, Alcazar R, *et al.* Infections due to *Flavimonas oryzihabitans*: case report and literature review. Eur J Clin Microbiol Infect Dis 1993;12:797–800.
81. Raimondi A, Moosdeen F, Williams JD. Antibiotic resistance pattern of *Flavobacterium meningosepticum*. Eur J Clin Microbiol 1986;5:461–3.
82. Deliere E, Vu-Thien H, Levy V, *et al.* Epidemiological investigation of *Ochrobactrum anthropi* strains isolated from a haematology unit. J Hosp Infect 2000;44:173–8.
83. Kain KC, Kelly MT. Clinical features, epidemiology and treatment of *Plesiomonas shigelloides* diarrhea. J Clin Microbiol 1989;27:990–1001.

chapter

230 Curved and Spiral Bacilli

Francis Mégraud & Steven FT Thijsen

INTRODUCTION

The curved and spiral bacilli are a heterogeneous group of bacteria that share little morphology.

Helicobacter pylori was previously called *Campylobacter pylori*[1] and in the first part of the 20th century *Campylobacter* was called *Vibrio*. *Campylobacter*, *Helicobacter* and *Vibrio* spp. all produce infections of the gastrointestinal tract. Moreover, they are all Gram-negative organisms and have a similar, curved shape. Using nucleic acid sequence determination of 16S rRNA, the genera *Campylobacter* and *Helicobacter* have been classified (together with *Arcobacter*, *Sulfurospirillum* and *Wolinella*) as members of the superfamily VI of Gram-negative bacilli (Table 230.1).[2] Only those bacteria belonging to this superfamily that are involved in human infections are discussed in this chapter.

Treponema, *Borrelia* and *Leptospira* are all members of Spirochaetales. These spirochetes are thin, helical, Gram-negative bacteria.

CAMPYLOBACTER SPP., HELICOBACTER PYLORI AND VIBRIO CHOLERAE

CAMPYLOBACTER SPP.

Nature

Campylobacter spp. are micro-aerophilic, Gram-negative, curved rods which obtain their energy by using fatty acids and amino acids rather than carbohydrates, and are adapted to life in mucus of the digestive tract. With the genera *Arcobacter* and *Sulfurospirillum*, they form the family *Campylobacteraceae*. At least 15 species and six subspecies have been differentiated. Not all, however, cause disease in humans.[3] *Campylobacter jejuni* and *Campylobacter coli* are responsible for enteric infections and are the most common Campylobacters found in humans. *Campylobacter fetus* is the third most frequently isolated, but is mostly involved in systemic diseases. The other species (*Campylobacter lari, Campylobacter upsaliensis*) occur only anecdotally. They also lead to enteric infections.

Epidemiology

Campylobacter spp. infections can be considered as zoonoses, because the primary reservoir for *Campylobacter* spp. is animals. These bacteria are essentially present in the digestive tract of animals, especially birds, where they do not cause disease. They can cause septic abortion in cattle. Humans can become infected by ingesting contaminated food or water or through contact with infected animals, including pets. The majority of *Campylobacter* spp. infections are sporadic, although outbreaks do occur. *Campylobacter* enteritis is generally more common than *Salmonella* and *Shigella* enteritis and is a major cause of travelers' diarrhea. Infections can be caused by the ingestion of undercooked, contaminated poultry or contaminated milk as well as by cross-contamination of foods which will be consumed raw. It has been estimated that there are 2.4 million cases annually in the USA.[4] Transmission of the disease from human to human has also been described but seldom occurs. In temperate countries there is a peak incidence in summer and early autumn, although infections occur throughout the year.[5] The highest incidence is found in infants and young children, with a second peak in young adulthood. The incidence in developing countries, with less hygienic living conditions, is even higher than in developed countries and direct transmission from poultry to humans seems to occur.

Pathogenesis

Campylobacter bacilli are acid sensitive. Because of the relative barrier imposed by the gastric acid environment, infection is more likely to occur when large numbers of bacteria are ingested. Histologic examination of gut biopsies obtained from patients who have *Campylobacter* enteritis reveals inflammation and edema of the mucosa, with infiltration of neutrophils in the lamina propria. Lesions are mainly restricted to the ileum and colon.

In vitro co-culture of epithelial cells with *C. jejuni* has shown that these bacteria can adhere and penetrate into the cells. Pili, flagellin (major antigen), outer membrane proteins and lipopolysaccharides (LPS) could play the role of adhesins. *C. jejuni* is also able to synthesize proteins which may play a role in internalization and cytoskeletal rearrangement. *C. jejuni* can survive in vacuoles and induce IL-8 synthesis. Its translocation may occur by transcellular as well as paracellular means.[6] In addition, *C. jejuni* produces a cytolethal distending toxin (cdt) acting on the cell cycle and leading to apoptosis. Nevertheless, the numerous pathogenicity studies performed have not determined a specific mechanism. Recent knowledge of the whole genomic sequence of *C. jejuni*[7] should bring insight to this field. The molecular mimicry of human ganglioside with the LPS molecules present in strains of *C. jejuni* expressing the O:19 antigen has been implicated in the association of *C. jejuni* infection with the Guillain–Barré syndrome.[8]

Immune persons in endemic areas, where infections are frequent, can become asymptomatic carriers. Infection can have a protracted course in the case of reduced resistance, such as in patients suffering from hypogammaglobulinemia. In HIV-infected patients, opportunistic infections with atypical *Campylobacter* spp. also suggest a role for cellular immunity.

An interesting mechanism to avoid elimination by the immune system has been discovered for *C. fetus*. Almost all *C. fetus* strains express a surface protein that abrogates complement C3b binding. This prevents opsonization, thereby conferring resistance to killing by phagocytes and adding to the pathogenicity of the species.[9]

Prevention

Preventive measures for *Campylobacter* spp. infections include adequate disinfection of drinking water supplies, adequate heating of contaminated food and reinforcement of hygiene in the kitchen in order to avoid cross-contamination. Eradication of the animal reservoir is impossible but adequate measures taken in poultry farms and abattoirs can decrease the level of contamination. Development of vaccines is an alternative. Research in this direction has been boosted

CLUSTERS OF THE rRNA VI SUPERFAMILY OF GRAM-NEGATIVE BACILLI		
rRNA group I	**rRNA group II**	**rRNA group III**
Campylobacter jejuni	*Arcobacter butzleri*	*Helicobacter pylori*
Campylobacter coli	*Arcobacter cryaerophilus*	*Helicobacter acinonyx*
Campylobacter hyointestinalis	*Arcobacter nitrofigilis*	*Helicobacter bilis*
Campylobacter fetus	*Arcobacter skirrowii*	*Helicobacter bizzozeronii*
Campylobacter upsaliensis		*Helicobacter canis*
Campylobacter concisus		*Helicobacter cinaedi*
Campylobacter curvus		*Helicobacter felis*
Campylobacter gracilis		*Helicobacter fennelliae*
Campylobacter helveticus		*Helicobacter hepaticus*
Campylobacter hyoilei		*Helicobacter muridarum*
Campylobacter lari		*Helicobacter mustelae*
Campylobacter mucosalis		*Helicobacter nemestrinae*
Campylobacter rectus		*Helicobacter pametensis*
Campylobacter showae		*Helicobacter pullorum*
Campylobacter sputorum		CLO-3
Bacteroides ureolyticus		*Gastrospillum hominis*
		Wolinella succinogenes

Table 230.1 Clusters of the rRNA VI superfamily of Gram-negative bacilli. *B. ureolyticus* is placed in this group based on 16S rRNA. CLO, *Campylobacter*-like organism. Adapted from Koneman *et al.*[105]

by the discovery of an association between *Campylobacter* enteritis and the Guillain–Barré syndrome, because the latter can cause permanent disability in a significant number of cases. Vaccines using killed whole-cell preparations have been successful in animal models and experiments with humans are under way.[10]

Diagnostic microbiology

The curved motile rods can be demonstrated in a fecal sample using Gram staining or dark-field microscopy. Culturing *Campylobacter* spp. necessitates special conditions, sometimes difficult to implement.[11] Cultures are commonly performed with an atmosphere comprising 5% oxygen, 10% carbon dioxide and 85% nitrogen. Some species, such as *Campylobacter rectus* and *Campylobacter hyointestinalis*, also require hydrogen in the atmosphere for growth. Selective culture media contain antibiotics such as cefoperazone to suppress the growth of normal intestinal bacteria and blood or charcoal to neutralize inhibiting factors such as oxygen radicals. Commonly used media are Skirrow's, Butzler's, Campy (cefoperazone–vancomycin–amphotericin) agar and cefoperazone charcoal deoxycholate agar. An important disadvantage of selective media is that bacteria such as *C. hyointestinalis, C. fetus* and *C. upsaliensis*, which are sensitive to antibiotics used in these selective media, can be missed. To circumvent this problem, membrane filtration of feces can be performed to eliminate contaminants followed by culturing on nonselective media. However, this filtration technique is less sensitive than direct plating.

Although the most important species (i.e. *C. jejuni* and *C. coli*) grow at 107.6°F, some species (i.e. *C. fetus*) grow best at 98.6°F and will be missed when cultures are only incubated at 107.6°F. Typically, colonies with a gray color and growing flat and confluently are visible after 2–3 days of culture. Definite identification of suspect colonies is performed using standard biochemical tests showing positive oxidase and catalase tests for *C. jejuni* and *C. coli*.

Campylobacter jejuni is the only *Campylobacter* spp. that is capable of hydrolyzing hippurate, which is essential for its differentiation from other Campylobacters, especially *C. coli*. Growth at 77°F is essential for diagnosing *C. fetus*. Given the high level of resistance of Campylobacters to quinolones, the nalidixic acid susceptibility test is no longer a key test in *Campylobacter* identification. Molecular identification (PCR, sequencing) is now being performed more frequently in this group of bacteria.

The presence of *Campylobacter* spp. can also be determined using PCR directly on feces. Typing of isolates is important for epidemiologic studies. More than 60 serotypes of *C. jejuni* and *C. coli* have been identified with the Penner O typing system but molecular typing methods are now commonly used, including PCR-RFLP of *fla* genes, macrorestriction of the genome and AFLP.[12] Serology can also be helpful in diagnosing a *Campylobacter* spp. infection because serum IgG and IgM levels start to rise in response to infection 5 days after infection and reach a peak 2–4 weeks later. This is the essential method to diagnose the Guillain–Barré syndrome due to *C. jejuni*. Immunoglobulin A is also produced and excreted in the gut lumen.

Clinical features

Most *Campylobacter* spp. infections manifest as acute enteritis.[13] The ensuing diarrhea can vary from modest to voluminous stools that may be watery or bloody. The infection can also run a subclinical course, especially in hyperexposed populations. Disease will develop 1–3 days after ingestion of the bacilli and symptoms usually disappear after 1 week. Stool samples typically remain positive for *Campylobacter* spp. for several weeks. In most cases, *Campylobacter* enteritis is a self-limiting disease and it tends to be more severe in patients at the extreme ends of age. Fever, malaise and abdominal pain may precede diarrhea or may be the most predominant signs. Infection with *Campylobacter* spp. gives rise to inflammation of the gut mucosa. The accompanying pain and fever may also lead to disease resembling Crohn's colitis or ulcerative colitis. When pain is the major feature of the infection, differentiation from appendicitis may be difficult. When fever is the major feature, differentiation from *Salmonella* enteritis may be difficult. *Campylobacter jejuni* can grow in bile and can occasionally cause acute cholecystitis and pancreatitis.[14]

Only a few patients who have a *C. jejuni* infection develop systemic disease. Bacteremia can occur, but this is considered rare and generally occurs in patients who have an underlying disease.[15]

As with other pathogenic bacteria, a postinfectious syndrome may occur after *C. jejuni* infection. One is an acute reactive arthritis which is very similar to the complication seen after enteritis caused by *Salmonella* spp., *Shigella* spp. or *Yersinia* spp. and is associated with the presence of the HLA-B27 antigen.

Another important complication of *Campylobacter* enteritis is the Guillain–Barré syndrome. This syndrome is an acute demyelinating disease affecting the peripheral neurons and is characterized by an ascending paralysis.[8] *Campylobacter jejuni* enteritis is the infection most frequently observed before Guillain–Barré syndrome and occurs in 20–40% of cases. The risk of developing Guillain–Barré syndrome after *Campylobacter* spp. infection is estimated at 1 per 2000 infections. Major neurological sequelae exist in 20% of the cases.

Campylobacter coli infections are very similar to infections with *C. jejuni*, but they tend to follow a less severe course.

Infections with *C. fetus* tend to disseminate from the intestine, especially in patients who have conditions that cause impaired immunity, such as chronic alcoholism, diabetes mellitus, malignancies and HIV infection, and in the elderly. Systemic *C. fetus* infections can lead to endocarditis, thrombophlebitis, meningitis and septic abortion.

Campylobacter upsaliensis, C. lari and *C. hyointestinalis* can also cause enteritis. *Campylobacter consisus, C. gracilis, C. curvus, C. mucosalis, C. rectus, C. showae, C. sputorum* and *Bacteroides ureolyticus* can be associated with periodontal infections.

Management

Disease management is primarily symptomatic. Depending on the severity of the diarrhea, fluid replacement can be performed with oral rehydration fluids or with saline infusions. Antibiotic intervention is especially effective early in the disease and is of benefit in cases of prolonged illness, recurrent disease and secondary sepsis, for example in patients who have reduced resistance. The first-choice antibiotic is erythromycin (500mg q6h orally for 2 weeks) or another macrolide, resistance being low for this class of antibiotics. Ciprofloxacin (500mg q12h orally for 2 weeks) can also be used, but a high incidence of resistance to quinolones exists (see Chapter 43). Other alternatives include tetracycline and amoxicillin-clavulanic acid. Gentamicin in association with amoxicillin-clavulanic acid is the antibiotic of choice for systemic diseases.

HELICOBACTER PYLORI

Helicobacter pylori was cultured for the first time in 1982, from the stomach which was previously thought to be sterile.[16] Currently this bacterium is considered to be the most important bacterium responsible for chronic infections. It is also the first bacterium known to be involved in a cancer in humans.

Nature

Helicobacter spp. are spiral-shaped, Gram-negative bacilli with between five and seven terminal flagella. They are micro-aerophilic and use amino acids and fatty acids rather than carbohydrates to obtain their energy. At present, about 17 species of *Helicobacter* have been identified, only eight of which cause disease in humans (Fig. 230.1). *Helicobacter pylori* is the third bacterium for which the entire genome has been sequenced[17] and the first for which the genome of two strains has been sequenced.[18]

Epidemiology

The prevalence of an *H. pylori* infection is strongly linked to the socio-economic level of the community.[19] The infection rate decreases as the socio-economic level increases. Infection usually occurs in childhood and the bacilli persist in the stomach for decades and possibly for life. The socio-economic level of the family into which a child is born and raised is a more important risk factor than his or her socio-economic status in adult life. The corresponding risk factors are poor sanitation, poor education and sharing a bed.[20] Given the substantial improvement in socio-economic conditions in developed countries during recent decades, there has been a gradual decrease in the acquisition of the infection. Because the infection is lifelong, a cohort effect is present: the oldest people in a population are infected more often than the youngest.[21]

The current prevalence of *H. pylori* infections in the 20–29 year age group in Europe shows a gradient decreasing from east to west and from south to north. The prevalence in young adults in Western countries does not exceed 20%. The incidence of *H. pylori* infection is low in adulthood (less than 0.5%), but higher in developing countries than in the West. Although the source of the infection is known (i.e. the stomach of humans), the mode of transmission remains uncertain: it may be fecal–oral or oral–oral. Vomiting may play an important role.

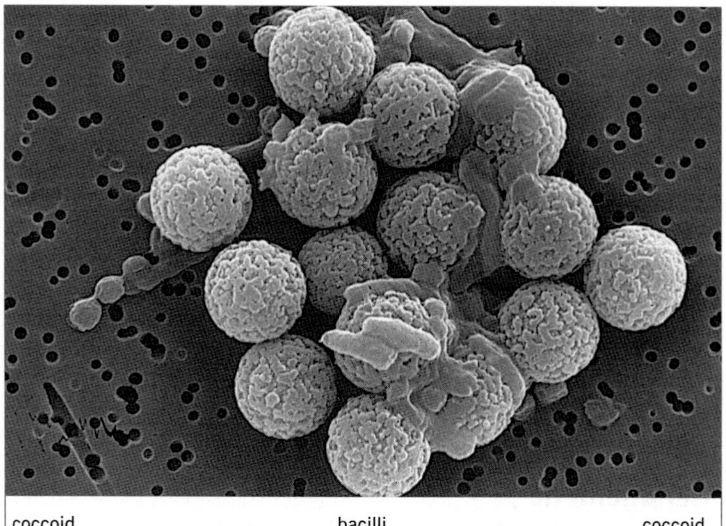

Fig. 230.1 Cultured *H. pylori* in coccoid and bacilli forms, bound to immunomagnetic beads. Adapted from Murray *et al.*[106]

Pathogenesis

Helicobacter pylori is adapted to the acid milieu of the stomach: it produces urease, which breaks down the urea diffusing from the mucosa and buffers the pH around the bacterium. *Helicobacter pylori* moves into the mucus and produces different kinds of adhesins that allow it to adhere very specifically to mucus cells. *Helicobacter pylori* appears in the duodenum when metaplasia of these mucus cells is present and disappears from the stomach when intestinal metaplasia is present.

Helicobacter pylori can persist by escaping host-defense mechanisms. For example, it synthesizes catalase and superoxide dismutase enzymes, which destroy bactericidal products from inflammatory cells. Moreover, urease increases the pH of the phagolysosomal compartment, thereby disturbing phagocyte function. It has also been proposed that the large amount of released antigens could saturate local antibodies. In addition, *H. pylori* triggers a response from T helper (TH)l lymphocytes with IgG production and inflammation, whereas a TH2 lymphocyte response would be more appropriate.[22]

Helicobacter pylori strains do not all share the same virulence factors; some produce the vacuolating cytotoxin A (VacA) and some possess a pathogenicity island. VacA may be responsible for the epithelial cell damage observed in *H. pylori* infection. The main action of VacA is on the mitochondria, vacuole formation being the consequence of the late endocytosis compartment when weak bases are present, in this case, NH_4Cl.[23] The sequence of the *vacA* gene is not homogeneous. There are two main regions of variation: the signal sequence (s) and the midregion (m). Typing has been proposed: s1–ml, s1–m2 and s2–ml, corresponding to high, low and no production of toxin, respectively. The pathogenicity island is named *cag* and has the *cagA* gene as a marker. It is a 40kB fragment containing 27–31 open reading frames. Six of them have sequence similarities to genes coding for a type IV secretion system, i.e. a complex protein structure that allows the bacterium to inject compounds into eukaryotic cells. The CagA protein is one of them which is phosphorylated and leads to a reorganization of the actin cytoskeleton. The other effect associated with the *cag* pathogenicity island is an increased production of IL-8 via an NFκB pathway.[24] Nevertheless, *cag*-negative *H. pylori* also induce inflammation, which stresses the fact that other factors present in all *H. pylori* strains may also be involved. Lipopolysaccharide moieties of the outer membrane of *H. pylori* may be identical to Lewis x and y antigens. Such antigen mimicry could confer autoimmunity and play a role in the pathogenesis of, for example, gastric atrophy.[25]

Prevention

Because the route of transmission is unclear, it is difficult to take preventive measures. The first attempts at developing a vaccine using recombinant urease as the only antigen have not been successful in humans. Other vaccine candidates antigens are under study. Mucosal administration seems to be the most popular route.

Diagnostic microbiology

Invasive methods for diagnosing *H. pylori* infection depend on endoscopy to obtain biopsies. These biopsies can then be processed for histological examination and stained with hematoxylin–eosin, Giemsa stain or silver stain. *Helicobacter pylori* is usually abundant and its typical morphology and the presence of polymorphs make diagnosis easy. The use of immunoperoxidase staining can be considered when atypical bacilli are detected. The examination of a smear is quick and can be performed in the endoscopic ward using either dark-field examination of a wet smear or Gram staining.

Because *H. pylori* is a fragile organism, transport conditions are extremely important for culture. Biopsies can be transported in saline for 3–4 hours, but (commercially) available transport medium must be used if preservation up to 24 hours is necessary. The media must be maintained at a low temperature ($<50°F$) before plating. Biopsies must be ground with a homogenizer and plated on media enriched with 5–10% blood and antibiotics to inhibit growth of nonrelevant bacteria. The plates must then be incubated for up to 10 days in a micro-aerobic atmosphere. Growth usually occurs within 3–4 days. *Helicobacter pylori* colonies are easily identified by their morphology and their urease, catalase and oxidase activities.

The urease test is specific for *H. pylori*. A color change is observed if *H. pylori* urease is present when the biopsy is introduced into a medium containing urea and a pH indicator. Tests using semisolid agars show an optimal sensitivity after 24 hours. In contrast, strip tests show a high sensitivity after just 2 hours.

Polymerase chain reaction for diagnosing *H. pylori* infection does not require specific transport conditions and can be performed with a urease test kit sent by mail. Several genes can be targeted: urease, 16S rRNA, 29kDa antigen, *cagA* gene or *vacA* gene. Recently a real-time PCR has been developed which allows detection of both *H. pylori* and its resistance to macrolides. Primers target the 23S rRNA gene and the dissociation curve of the hybrids indicates the mutation present.

Less invasive methods for obtaining material are aspiration of gastric juice or a capsulated string. Diagnosis can also be made using noninvasive tests. The urea breath test measures urease production by *H. pylori*. Samples of breath air are collected by having the patient blow into a tube before and 30 minutes after ingestion of ^{13}C-labeled urea. The tubes can be maintained for months and sent by mail to a laboratory that has a mass spectrometer in order to measure the ^{13}C:^{12}C ratio.

Antibodies are mainly detected by enzyme-linked immunosorbent assay (ELISA). There are numerous kits commercially available. Immunoblot methods can also be used.

Detection of specific antibodies has also been proposed but shows a lower sensitivity than in blood. It is also possible to detect *H. pylori* antigens in stools using ELISA. Polyclonal antibodies were first used as a reagent. A second generation of tests employs monoclonal antibodies and gives excellent results.

Since none of the tests are perfect in terms of sensitivity, a combination of tests is recommended.[26] All these tests have a comparable sensitivity except for the smear examination, the agar-based urease and rapid serology tests which are inferior. The urea breath test is ideal for follow-up after eradication therapy. Serology cannot be used for this purpose because the antibody titer may be high for months after the disappearance of *H. pylori*.

Clinical features

The presence of *H. pylori* in the stomach is always accompanied by inflammation of the mucosa. However, this infection is not always symptomatic. Duodenal ulcer, gastric ulcer, gastric carcinoma, gastric lymphoma and some nonulcer dyspepsia syndromes can develop. Symptoms of these diseases (e.g. epigastric pain and dyspepsia) are not specific.

Duodenal ulcer

Duodenal ulcer occurs in subjects who are infected by *H. pylori* and also have gastric metaplasia in the duodenal bulb, which will be colonized with *H. pylori*.[27] Hyperproduction of acid following a decrease in somatostatin, and an increase in gastrin production are observed. Antral gastritis is the usual pattern of histological lesions. Smoking and infection with *cag*-positive *H. pylori* strains are important risk factors.

Gastric ulcer

In contrast, gastric ulcer occurs in patients who have multifocal gastritis or pangastritis leading to a decreased acid production by the corpus. The lesions have been explained by a retrodiffusion of hydrogen ions in the gastric wall. A vascular factor is also probably important. Gastric ulcer in Western countries is about five times less frequent than duodenal ulcer and occurs in older people. Smoking, dietary factors (e.g. high salt intake) and infection with *cag*-positive *H. pylori* strains are important risk factors. In some instances, gastric ulcer may be a precursor of gastric carcinoma, motivating endoscopic follow-up.

Gastric carcinoma

The incidence of gastric carcinoma is currently decreasing in developed countries. This decrease has been attributed to a decrease in the rate of *H. pylori* infection. Indeed, gastric carcinoma is virtually absent when gastric mucosa is normal.[28] Most gastric carcinomas are of the intestinal type and are thought to result from chronic gastritis followed by atrophy, intestinal metaplasia and dysplasia ultimately leading to carcinoma. These events occur over several decades. They can be reproduced in an animal model, the Mongolian gerbil infected with *H. pylori*.[29] A very early acquisition of the bacterium, infection with *cag*-positive strains and dietary factors (e.g. high salt consumption and low vitamin intake) are risk factors for this evolution. The diffuse type of gastric cancer does not follow the pattern described above, but it is associated with *H. pylori* infection.

Gastric lymphoma

Gastric lymphoma involves mucosa-associated lymphoid tissue (MALT). The stomach is normally free of lymphoid follicles; they only occur when *H. pylori* is present.[30] T cells stimulated by *H. pylori* antigens trigger a monoclonal B-cell proliferation, giving rise to lymphoid follicles. *H. pylori* infection is responsible for 80% of gastric MALT lymphoma.

Nonulcer dyspepsia

Nonulcer dyspepsia occurs in dyspeptic patients in whom no organic lesion is found at endoscopy. *Helicobacter pylori* is found in about 50% of the cases in Western countries. In most of these cases, however, the presence of *H. pylori* is probably incidental, with only about 10% of cases being the consequence of *H. pylori* infection.[31]

Other diseases

Helicobacter pylori infection has been implicated in children's diseases including iron deficiency anemia, growth retardation and recurrent abdominal pain. It may also be a risk factor for myocardial infarction, possibly because of the long-lasting chronic inflammation induced.[32]

Management

Eradication of *H. pylori* in duodenal ulcer and gastric ulcer avoids relapses, increases the healing process and normalizes the mucosa and gastric physiology. In low-grade gastric MALT lymphoma, eradication leads to a disappearance of the lesions. Nevertheless, follow-up is needed for several years. Eradication of *H. pylori* at an early stage can have a positive effect in gastric carcinoma. Nevertheless, surgery and other cancer treatments remain essential.

The optimal regimen to eradicate *H. pylori* consists of two orally administered antibiotics for 7–10 days with an antisecretory drug. The combinations favored are:

- clarithromycin (500mg q12h) and amoxicillin (1g q12h), or
- clarithromycin (250mg q12h) and metronidazole (500mg q12h).

Most studies have been performed with omeprazole. However, lansoprazole and pantoprazole and rabeprazole are also effective. A double dose of proton pump inhibitors is also usually given.[33] Currently, resistance to amoxicillin is seldom found, whereas resistance to macrolides occurs in up to 20% of the strains and resistance to metronidazole in 10–80%. Follow-up is performed 4–6 weeks after treatment has been stopped.

In case of failure, the recommended second-line treatment is a quadruple therapy with metronidazole, tetracycline, bismuth salts and a proton pump inhibitor for a week, or the use of the new compound ranitidine–bismuth citrate, plus two antibiotics.[33] The use of dual therapy (e.g. a proton pump inhibitor with amoxicillin or clarithromycin) is no longer recommended. The main risk factors for treatment failure are the resistance of *H. pylori* and lack of patient compliance (see Chapter 42 for further discussion on gastritis).

VIBRIO CHOLERAE

Nature

Vibrio cholerae is a Gram-negative, comma-shaped rod belonging to the family *Vibrionaceae*. Its natural habitat consists of fresh-water and salt-water environments. Based on differences in the composition of the major cell wall antigen (O), 139 serotypes have been differentiated. *Vibrio cholerae*, which belongs to either serogroup O1 or serogroup O139, has been associated with epidemic cholera. *Vibrio cholerae* serogroup O1 can be subdivided into El Tor and classic biotypes as well as the Ogawa, Inaba and Hikojima serotypes. Other serogroups of *V. cholerae*, in addition to nontoxigenic *V. cholerae* O1 or O139, do not cause epidemic cholera; they may, however, cause individual cases of diarrhea (see Chapter 43).

Epidemiology

Cholera has raged in seven pandemics since 1817. It is possible that an eighth is superimposed on the seventh. The fifth and sixth pandemics have been explored and were caused by the classic biotype and originated in the Indian subcontinent. The seventh and current one is caused by the El Tor strain and began in 1961 in Indonesia. It has gradually affected most of Asia and Africa and is found incidentally in parts of Europe. In 1991, this pandemic reached South America and has since spread throughout Latin America (Fig. 230.2).[34] Persons who have blood group O are at higher risk of El Tor cholera than those with blood group A, B or AB.[35] This is particularly important for Latin America, where 73% of the population carries the blood type O. An episode of classic cholera protects nearly entirely against recurrent cholera of either biotype, but an episode of El Tor cholera does not protect against future attacks. In 1992, a novel *V. cholerae* variant O139 (synonym Bengal), which has the same origin as the El Tor strain, emerged in southern Asia. This 1992 epidemic was the first one caused by a serogroup other than O1, and it occurred in populations assumed to be largely immune to *V. cholerae* O1. The impact of a *V. cholerae* O139 infection on the risk of a subsequent *V. cholerae* infection, either O1 or non-O1, has not yet been determined. The Bengal strain has the potential to spread pandemically. It has now affected areas throughout the Indian subcontinent, neighboring states and other

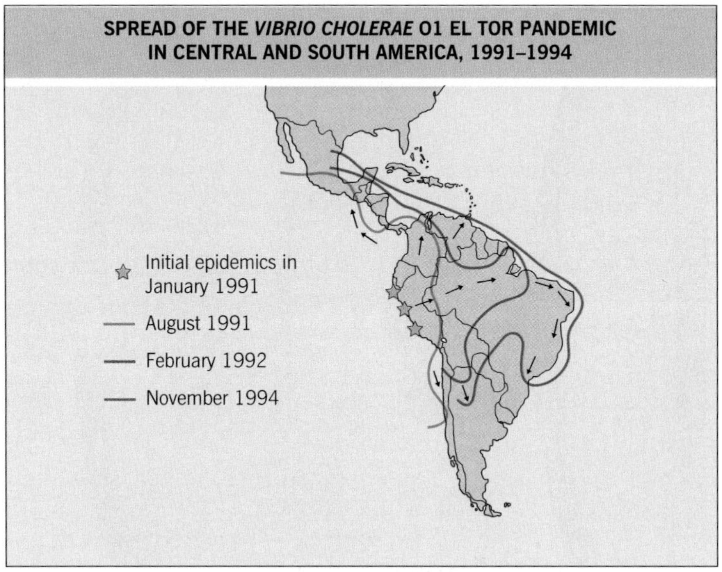

Fig. 230.2 Spread of the *Vibrio cholerae* O1 El Tor pandemic in Central and South America, 1991–94. (Adapted from Tauxe *et al.*[35])

parts of Asia. Cases occurring as far away as the USA and Western Europe have also been described.

V. cholerae, including serogroups O1 and O139, exist as natural inhabitants of aquatic ecosystems and are therefore facultative human pathogens. Within the marine environment they attach to zooplankton and are able to form biofilm, facilitating environmental persistence. It was suggested but largely debated that *V. cholerae* can switch into a viable but nonculturable state. It is likely that the aquatic environment harbors different virulence-associated genes scattered among environmental vibrios, which possess a lower virulence potential than the epidemic strains. The clustering of such genes in a proper combination could lead to the emergence of new *V. cholerae* strains with epidemic potential.[36]

Pathogenesis

Infection starts with ingestion of water or food contaminated with *V. cholerae*. The infectious dose is high due to the acid sensitivity of the bacteria. Persons who have impaired gastric acidity or who take acid-suppressing medication have an increased risk of infection. In addition, *Helicobacter pylori* gastritis is also associated with an increased risk of cholera.[37] The surviving bacteria adhere to and colonize the small intestine epithelial cells, producing the cholera toxin and causing acute watery diarrhea. In the intestine *V. cholerae* is faced with growth inhibitory substances like bile salts and defense factors like complement, defensins, against which it has developed survival strategies. The powerful enterotoxin then released is a 68kDa protein consisting of an active (A) subunit and five binding (B) subunits. These B subunits attach to the GM1 ganglioside receptor at the lining of the mucosal cells (Fig. 230.3). The A subunit triggers a cascade of reactions involving cyclic adenosine monophosphate, prostaglandins, 5-hydroxytryptamine and calmodulin.[38] This results in an increased level of intracellular cAMP leading to an increase in intestinal chloride secretion and a decrease in sodium chloride absorption. The outcome is a passive watery excretion that leads to diarrhea. The volume typically exceeds 1 liter per hour in adults and 10ml/kg/h in children. Since cholera results from a locally acting enterotoxin, it is not accompanied by systemic manifestations caused by a cytokine-induced acute-phase reaction.

Molecular knowledge of pathogenesis has recently improved. The most important colonization factor was identified as a type IV pilus named toxin-coregulated pilus (TCP). The genes required for TCP synthesis are located on a pathogenicity island (PI) named Vibrio PI.[39]

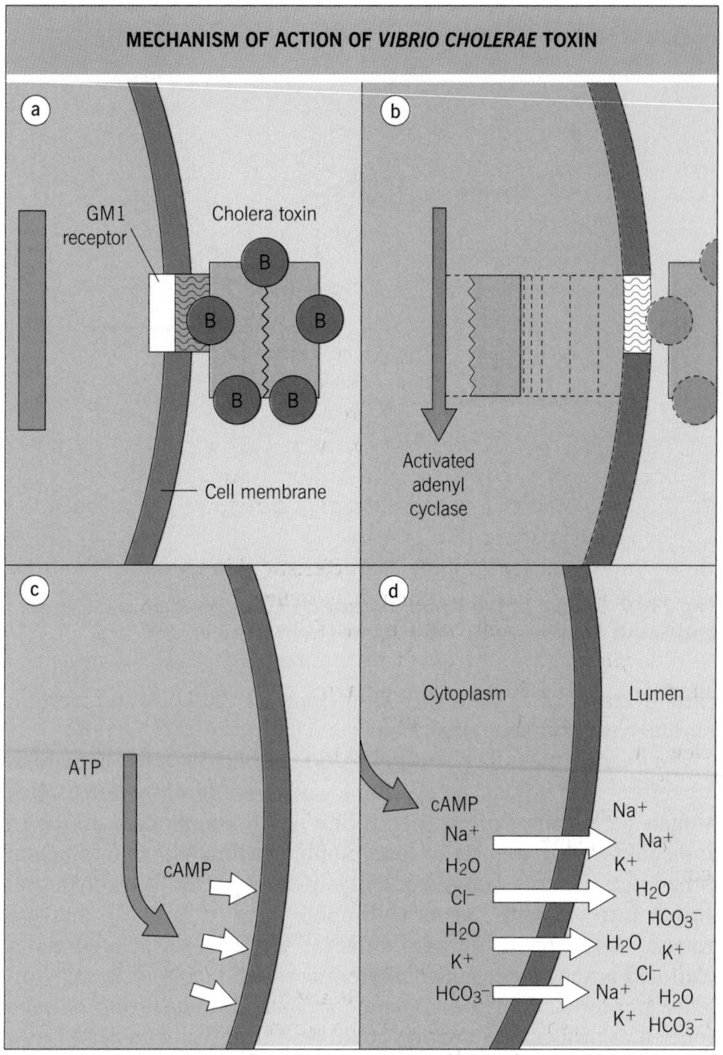

Fig. 230.3 Mechanism of action of *Vibrio cholerae* toxin. The toxin binds to the GM1 ganglioside receptor on the intestinal mucosal cell membrane via the binding (B) subunits (a). The active portion of the A subunit enters the cell and activates adenyl cyclase (b), which results in the accumulation of cyclic adenosine monophosphate (cAMP), derived from adenosine triphosphate (ATP), along the cell membrane (c). The cAMP causes active secretion of sodium (Na^+), chloride (Cl^-), potassium (K^+), bicarbonate (HCO_3^-) and water (H_2O) out of the cell into the lumen of the intestine (d). Adapted from Murray *et al.*[106]

The genes encoding the cholera toxin are enclosed by a phage named CTX integrated into the large chromosome of the two *V. cholerae* chromosomes.[40] The surface antigens (capsule, LPS, outer membrane proteins) are important virulence factors.

A unique regulatory system co-ordinates the expression of TCP and cholera toxin. Interestingly, it was recently shown that quorum sensing systems control virulence genes in *V. cholerae*.[41]

The complete genome sequence of the two chromosomes of *V. cholerae* O1 El Tor, now available,[42] will help further dissection of cholera pathogenesis.

Prevention

Cholera is difficult to eradicate from water and is likely to remain a serious threat to public health for some time. Measures to prevent cholera include separating sewage and drinking water systems, disinfection of drinking water and food, hygiene measures (e.g. handwashing with soap), active case finding and effective case management with the use of oral rehydration. Breast-feeding provides important protection to infants, not because of transmission of maternal antibodies but because of the lower exposure to contaminated food and water. During epidemics, the bodies of persons who died of cholera should be disinfected and buried rapidly and the consumption of food at gatherings, including funerals, should be discouraged. The currently licensed, parenteral, killed cholera vaccine is no longer recommended by the World Health Organization because of its limited protective efficacy. To induce mucosal immunity, oral vaccines, both inactivated (whole cell/B-subunit) and live (CVD103-HgR), have been developed; these show no side effects and a longer lasting protection than the parenteral vaccine.[43] Vaccines that include the B-subunit of the toxin provide cross-protection against heat-labile enterotoxigenic *Escherichia coli*, a result of the close relationship between the two toxins. CVD103-HgR produces higher resistance to the homologous classic strain than to the El Tor strain. Attenuation of El Tor has led to several new candidate vaccines that have proven safe and highly effective against El Tor cholera.[44] Because immunity against the O1 type is not protective against O139, *V. cholerae* O139 type vaccines are urgently needed. To date, one live, attenuated candidate vaccine, Bengal-15, has shown a protective efficacy as high as 83%.

Diagnostic microbiology

The diagnosis of cholera is confirmed when *V. cholerae* is identified in a stool culture on thiosulfate citrate bile salts sucrose agar directly or after enrichment, taking advantage of *V. cholerae*'s tolerance to alkaline conditions. For rapid diagnosis, dark-field examination of a fresh, unstained stool specimen is highly sensitive and specific: a characteristic finding is the 'shooting star' phenomenon caused by the motility of the single polar flagellum of the organism. Once identified at the species level, additional tests include serotyping for O antigens and the 3 antigen variants recognized, as well as biotyping to differentiate classic and El Tor biotypes. A rapid, colorimetric immunodiagnostic method is available for the detection of *V. cholerae* O1. The immunochromatographic strip test may be the simplest, most rapid and most sensitive and specific test for the detection of *V. cholerae*. Two rapid immunodiagnostic test kits based on the use of monoclonal antibodies have been developed for the direct detection of *V. cholerae* O139: a co-agglutination test and Bengal DFA (a direct fluorescent-antibody test). In epidemic settings in developing countries, a bacteriological diagnosis is not indicated in all suspected cases because the management of dehydrating diarrhea is guided by the extent of fluid loss rather than by the nature of the infecting organism. In contrast, the diagnosis should be confirmed in individual cases of suspected cholera in the developed world.

Clinical features

In Latin America, well-established case management has kept fatality rates low (at about 1%). In contrast, cholera in Africa has been sporadic and as a result less well recognized. The fatality rates there also tend to be higher (about 10%).[45] Children are more likely to have only subclinical infection or mild diarrhea, whereas adults tend to develop more severe disease and require hospitalization. Cholera is in principle a self-limiting disease if dehydration is sufficiently remedied. Cholera gravis is a voluminous painless watery diarrhea that can lead to dehydration and even death within a few hours. The case fatality rate for untreated cholera gravis is 50%. Symptoms include nausea, vomiting (especially early in the illness) and muscle cramps, followed by signs of hypovolemic shock.

Cholera stool is not malodorous and is often described as 'rice water' in character because it contains small flecks of mucus but little fecal matter; bloody stool is not suggestive of cholera. Because *V. cholerae* does not invade the epithelial lining of the intestine, there is little inflammatory response and hence the stool contains few if any leukocytes and patients are afebrile. The degree of dehydration is based on physical signs and measuring stool, vomit and urine output.

Complications from cholera (e.g. acute tubular necrosis) are mostly due to inadequate rehydration. Metabolic abnormalities may also occur, including hypokalemia as the result of potassium loss, acidosis from both bicarbonate loss and increased lactate production resulting from anaerobic glycolysis, and hypoglycemia due to deficient gluconeogenesis resulting in seizures and other neurologic abnormalities. Hyperventilation (Kussmaul breathing) may occur as a result of the metabolic acidosis. Shock from cholera can precipitate abortion in pregnant women, although this is less likely to occur if rehydration is prompt.

Management

The management of cholera patients consists of two components:

- rehydration, which is critical; and
- antimicrobial therapy, which is optional and intended to shorten the duration of the illness and prevent spread of the disease.

Effective fluid replacement can be expected to reduce mortality to less than 1% of the severely affected individuals. Mild and moderately dehydrated patients can be treated using oral rehydration solution (ORS), which has three basic components: sugars, salts and water. Physiologically, the sugar acts as the vehicle whereby salts can be absorbed by the mucosal cell; water follows passively.[46] Patients on ORS should remain on ORS until the diarrhea stops. Severely dehydrated patients should be treated intravenously. When intravenous solutions and equipment are not available, severely dehydrated patients may be treated through a nasogastric tube.

Antibiotic treatment serves to shorten the illness and save rehydration fluids. Incomplete courses have contributed to antibiotic resistance. Options are guided by local sensitivity patterns. These are tetracycline 250mg q12h for 7–10 days or amoxicillin 250mg q6h for 5 days. Tetracyclines and quinolones are not recommended during pregnancy. During epidemics, prophylactic antibiotics should be used for the immediate family only and should be limited to a single-dose therapy.

In conclusion, it can be said that during the last decade of cholera research two important findings have emerged: the characterization of a novel serogroup (O139) which circumvented established immunity against O1 and the discovery that cholera toxin genes were encoded on the genome of a bacteriophage. These two characteristics illustrate how bacterial pathogens can rapidly evolve through the acquisition of horizontally transferred genetic elements.[47]

Other pathogenic *Vibrio* spp.

Vibrio parahaemolyticus is a halophilic, or salt-requiring, *Vibrio* sp. that has been related to food poisoning and ingestion of raw or inadequately cooked seafood. The epidemiology results from the ubiquitous presence of the organism in coastal waters. The median incubation time is estimated at 23 hours with a range of 5–92 hours; secondary cases are rare. Preventive measures include the use of boiled water for cooking food. It is not known whether clinical disease confers immunity. There is no effective vaccine available. Stool culture on selective thiosulfate citrate bile salts sucrose agar demonstrates distinct opaque green colonies; final identification is made using standard biochemical tests. The clinical picture ranges from mild, watery diarrhea with low-grade fever to frank dysentery. Specific treatment is not required in most cases because the illness is self-limiting and no benefit has been established from antimicrobial agents.

Other less common halophilic *Vibrio* spp. include *Vibrio vulnificus*, *V. alginolyticus*, *V. fluvialis*, *V. hollisae* and *V. damsela*. Molecular methods, especially PCR, can be used for identification or detection of these species, including in the environment. In contrast to the *Vibrio* spp. discussed so far, *V. vulnificus* and *V. alginolyticus* are more associated with soft tissue wound infection and sepsis than with diarrhea.[48] *Vibrio vulnificus* may be considered an emerging pathogen and its virulence is the strongest among the noncholera *Vibrio* spp. Pathogenicity is generally reserved for the immunocompromised host and is related to disease states that exhibit high serum iron levels, including liver disease. Prevention involves avoidance of contaminated salt water. Immunocompromised patients should be warned against the ingestion of raw oysters and shellfish.[33] At higher latitudes, severe *V. vulnificus* infections have been reported in association with very hot weather conditions and seawater temperatures above 68°F. A vibrio polysaccharide conjugate vaccine may be useful in the management of *V. vulnificus* infections. Antibodies that react with the capsular polysaccharide of the organism are detectable in infected patients and in persons without known exposure to the organism, suggesting that cross-reacting antibodies are present in the general population.

Vibrio vulnificus infections present as two main clinical syndromes:

- primary sepsis secondary to ingestion of raw oysters; and
- localized infection from wound exposure to salt water in which the organism lives.

Both syndromes demonstrate characteristic skin lesions of the trunk and extremities. These present as hemorrhagic bullae and progress to necrotic ulcerations. Necrotizing fasciitis of the foot associated with *V. vulnificus* can cause death within 48 hours and has an overall mortality rate of 50%, even with appropriate antibiotic and surgical treatment.[49] Besides these two syndromes, *V. vulnificus* may also cause acute diarrhea in those on antacid therapy. Early suspicion is critical, because *V. vulnificus* is not always susceptible to aminoglycosides, and tetracycline is the first-choice treatment.

Vibrio alginolyticus may cause bacteremia and death in immunocompromised hosts. Among immunocompetent hosts, it may cause cellulitis and otitis media in swimmers and fishermen.

Vibrio mimicus, a nonhalophilic vibrio, produces a clinical spectrum that is indistinguishable from that of *V. parahaemolyticus*. The epidemiology of *V. mimicus* reflects a global distribution; outbreaks have been associated with heavy contamination of water sources. Prevention involves adequate purification of water sources and proper cooking practices. The diagnosis is confirmed by identifying the agent on thiosulfate citrate bile salts sucrose agar and subsequent specific antiserum testing. Treatment is limited to fluid and electrolyte replacement.

TREPONEMA SPP., *BORRELIA* SPP. AND *LEPTOSPIRA* SPP.

The order of the Spirochaetales is divided into the families Spirochaetaceae and Leptospiraceae. These families include, among others, the genera *Treponema, Borrelia* and *Leptospira* (Table 230.2).

TREPONEMA SPP.

Nature

The genus *Treponema* includes *Treponema carateum*, the causative agent of pinta, and *Treponema pallidum*. The latter species is subdivided into;

- *T. pallidum* subsp. *pallidum*, the causative agent of human venereal and congenital syphilis;
- *T. pallidum* subsp. *pertenue*, the cause of yaws; and
- *T. pallidum* subsp. *endemicum*, the cause of bejel.

Treponemata are motile, thin, spiralliform bacteria (Fig. 230.4).

Treponema pallidum

Epidemiology

In the majority of cases, *T. pallidum* subsp. *pallidum* is transmitted by sexual intercourse, with a moderate to high probability of transmission

ORDER SPIROCHAETALES			
Spirochaetaceae		**Etiologic agent**	**Human disease**
Family Spirochaetaceae	Genus *Cristispira*		None
	Genus *Serpulina*		None
	Genus *Spirochaeta*		None
	Genus *Treponema*	*Treponema pallidum* subsp. *pallidum* *Treponema pallidum* subsp. *endemicum* *Treponema pallidum* subsp. *pertenue* *Treponema carateum*	Syphilis Bejel Yaws Pinta
	Genus *Borrelia*	*Borrelia recurrentis* Many *Borrelia* spp. *Borrelia burgdorferi, Borrelia garinii, Borrelia afzelii*	Epidemic relapsing fever Endemic relapsing fever Lyme borreliosis
Family Leptospiraceae	Genus *Leptonema*		None
	Genus *Leptospira*	*Leptospira interrogans*	Leptospirosis

Table 230.2 Order Spirochaetales. The genera *Treponema, Borrelia* and *Leptospira* contain pathogens associated with human infections. The genera *Cristispira, Serpulina, Spirochaeta* and *Leptonema* are not known to cause disease in humans.

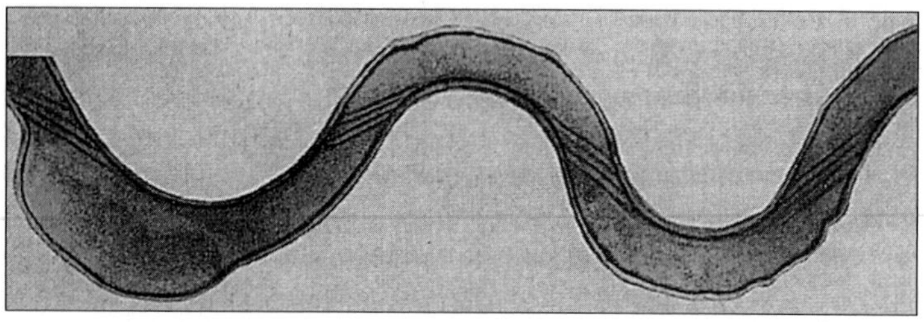

Fig. 230.4 Helical structure of *T. pallidum* with the periplasmic flagella. From Binford and Connor.[107]

during contact between susceptible and infectious sexual partners (see Chapter 75). It can also be transmitted by kissing, transfusion of fresh blood, placental passage or during birth. Patients are most contagious early during the illness when fresh lesions exist. As a sexually transmitted disease, syphilis has the highest incidence among young adults.

A high incidence was observed in homosexual men until the mid-1980s when, in response to the threat of HIV infection, changes in sexual behavior (e.g. increased condom use) led to a lower incidence. During the 1990s, a resurgence of syphilis among male homosexuals occurred because the tenets of safe sex education gave way to the reacceptance of risky behavior. This, combined with the uncertainty of immunity to reinfections, helps ensure the long-term persistence of syphilis.[50] All patients who have syphilis should be screened for other sexually transmitted pathogens because many patients carry more than one.

Pathogenesis

Treponema pallidum passes through the abraded skin or mucous membrane and spreads throughout the body. The incubation time is proportional to the size of the inoculum. The immunoevasiveness of *T. pallidum* is largely the result of its unusual molecular architecture; its outer membrane contains a paucity of poorly immunogenic proteins, the *T. pallidum* rare outer membrane proteins (TROMPS), whereas its highly immunogenic lipoproteins are anchored predominantly in the periplasmic leaflet of the cytoplasmic membrane.[51]

The presence of granulocytes and macrophages can be demonstrated in a primary chancre, and CD8+ cytotoxic lymphocytes are found in both primary and secondary lesions.[52] The pathologic hallmark of syphilis is endarteritis obliterans, which consists of concentric endothelial and fibroblastic proliferation. In late syphilis, endarteritis affects the vasa vasorum and leads to the formation of gummas with their typical necrotic, coagulated center, most notably in the ascending aorta and the meningeal arteries.

Prevention

Along with individually oriented strategies, such as case finding, partner notification and presumptive treatment, the use of epidemiologic information is recommended when designing community-oriented, population-based strategies, which should include (but not be limited to) selective mass treatment in high-prevalence populations.[53] Widespread treatment of syphilis with penicillin in the USA, beginning in the mid-1940s, led to a decline of more than 85% in its incidence. The increased incidence seen after 1955 was attributed to the relaxation of control measures and increased sexual promiscuity. Surveillance data from Switzerland suggest that the incidence of infection with *Neisseria gonorrhoeae, T. pallidum* and *Chlamydia trachomatis* has declined notably since the 1980s. This is a result of population-based strategies, which include more widespread treatment with specific antibiotics and changes in behavior education, leading to a major increase in safe sex practices, including condom use, in combination with the control of drugs and alcohol abuse. The cost effectiveness of antenatal screening for syphilis has been shown in various settings.[54] A vaccine for syphilis is not available for public health purposes.

Diagnostic microbiology

The lack of a method for *in vitro* culturing of *T. pallidum* necessitates the use of alternative methods (e.g. animal inoculation, dark-field microscopy or serology). Serologic tests, divided into two classes, do not become positive until several week after the appearance of the lesion. The nontreponemal tests detect antibodies to cardiolopin; examples include the Venereal Disease Research Laboratory (VDRL) test, the rapid plasma reagin (RPR) test, the automated reagin test (ART) and the syphilis screen. Because of their ease of use and low cost, these tests are applied for screening purposes. Reactivity in these tests generally indicates host tissue damage that may not be specific for syphilis. False-positive tests may occur in the elderly, drug addicts and patients who have chronic infections and autoimmune disease. Confirmation is required with treponemal tests such as the fluorescent treponemal antibody absorbed (FTA-ABS) test and the *T. pallidum* hemagglutination (TPHA) test. The TPHA and FTA-ABS are good markers for screening potential blood donors who have high-risk sexual behavior because they are more sensitive than the reagin tests. Syphilis Screen is claimed to be an alternative for the TPHA method.[55] After 3 months and following treatment, the non-specific cardiolipins begin to decline, whereas the FTA-ABS remains positive for life. In suspected neurosyphilis, VDRL should be performed on the cerebrospinal fluid (CSF); in unexpected cases, a positive FTA-ABS should be confirmed by a second sample. A number of direct antigen, ELISA and PCR techniques are currently being developed.[56] Recently, a specific and highly sensitive reverse transcriptase PCR was developed for detecting very low numbers of organisms. Syphilis serology findings (both RPR and TPHA) may be altered in the presence of HIV infection, although in at least one study the serologic response to therapy was similar in HIV-positive and HIV-negative patients.[57] The high prevalence of neurosyphilis in HIV-infected patients who have syphilis warrants examination of the CSF regardless of the stage of illness.

Congenital syphilis is often a presumptive diagnosis based on serology, because confirmation requires the identification of *T. pallidum* in fetal or neonatal tissue or in the placenta, by either histopathology or PCR.

Clinical features

Local symptoms develop as primary syphilis following an incubation period of 10–90 days. This involves a painless, indurated or firm, sharply demarcated chancre (ulcus), usually distinctly different from the more painful, soft and bleeding ulcers caused by *Haemophilus ducreyi* (chancroid). The most common site is the coronal sulcus or prepuce in males and the labia or cervix in females. Primary lesions may also occur on the lips, breasts, mouth and anus. These local lesions heal in 3 months. These symptoms may be followed by regional lymphadenopathy.

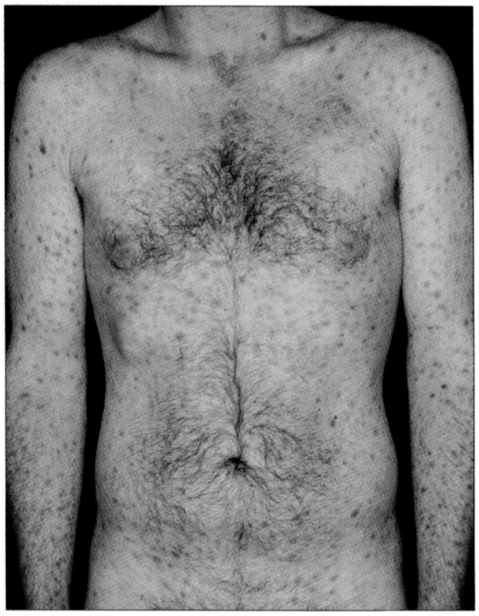

Fig. 230.5 Secondary syphilis with typical skin rash. (Reproduced with permission from Habif.[58])

If the primary infection is untreated, secondary syphilis may develop 2–8 weeks later, manifesting as a generalized, dry, nonpruritic rash that persists for 2–6 weeks. Patients are highly contagious during this stage (Fig. 230.5). The rash heals spontaneously, but it relapses in 25% of cases and may be accompanied by condylomata lata in the axillae or anogenital region and by mucous patches in the mouth, pharynx and cervix. Concurrent symptoms of secondary syphilis include generalized lymphadenopathy, low-grade fever, arthralgia, malaise, hepatitis, nephritis and pleuritis. As such, secondary syphilis may mimic other infectious diseases (e.g. brucellosis, rickettsiosis and certain viral diseases).

The rash and the other symptoms may disappear gradually in 1–3 months, marking the beginning of tertiary syphilis or the latent stage. Approximately one-third of the patients go on to develop granulomatous inflammation (gummas) in various organs, cardiovascular lesions (classically an aortic aneurysm), Charcot joints and the involvement of the central nervous system (neurosyphilis).

Management

Penicillin G is the drug of choice. A recent study showed that the addition of amoxicillin and probenecid did not improve the outcome, whether or not patients were co-infected with HIV.[59] Current recommendations for the management of early syphilis remain unchanged and a lumbar puncture is not necessary unless neurologic signs or symptoms are present. Because the effectiveness of the nonpenicillin alternative treatment regimens for syphilis (tetracycline or erythromycin) has not been well studied and because these regimens require the patient to comply with 15–30 days of oral therapy, desensitization of penicillin-allergic patients and treatment with penicillin rather than the use of oral therapy is preferred. Tetracycline-resistant bacteria have been increasingly found since the early 1950s. Treatment options are summarized in Table 230.3. *Treponema pallidum* infection in the fetus during early pregnancy can be successfully treated by maternal treatment. The same treatment recommendations apply to pregnant women with penicillin as the preferred agent.

Nonsyphilitic treponematoses

Nature and epidemiology

Treponema pallidum subsp. *pertenue, T. carateum* and *T. pallidum* subsp. *endemicum* are morphologically indistinguishable from *T. pallidum* and cause yaws, pinta and bejel, respectively. The distribution of yaws spans the warm and humid tropics; pinta is limited to equatorial America and bejel is prevalent in arid subtropical and temperate climates. The prevalence of yaws decreased from 50–100 million

TREATMENT OPTIONS FOR TREPONEMATOSIS

		Antibiotic regimen		
Bacterium	Clinical features	First choice	Second choice	Third choice
Treponema pallidum subsp. *pallidum*	Syphilis, all stages except neurosyphilis	Benzathine penicillin G 2.4MU once weekly im for 3 weeks	Doxycycline 200mg q12h po for 2–4 weeks	Erythromycin 500mg q6h po for 2–4 weeks
	Neurosyphilis	Penicillin G 2MU q4h iv for 2 weeks	Ceftriaxone 1000mg q24h iv or im for 2 weeks	Doxycycline 200mg q12h po for 2–4 weeks
Treponema pallidum subsp. *pertenue*	Yaws (frambesia)	Benzathine penicillin G 1.2MU single dose im	Doxycycline 100mg q12h po 10–14 days	
Treponema pallidum subsp. *endemicum*	Bejel	Benzathine penicillin G 1.2MU single dose im		
Treponema carateum	Pinta	Benzathine penicillin G 1.2MU single dose im	Doxycycline 100mg q12h po 10–14 days	

Table 230.3 Treatment options for treponematosis.

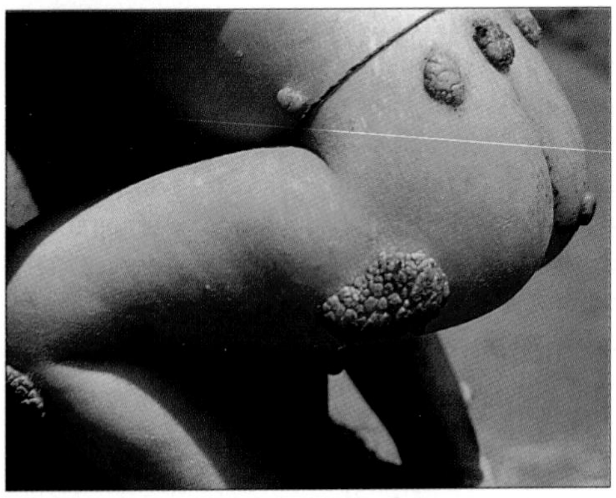

Fig. 230.6 The papillomatous skin lesions of yaws. (Reproduced with permission from Peters & Giles.[60])

infected people during the 1950s to fewer than 2 million during the 1970s because of a mass treatment campaign sponsored by the World Health Organization. Yaws has been virtually eliminated in the Americas but it has re-emerged in western Africa and areas of the western Pacific. Pinta is limited to remote areas of Colombia, Central America and Mexico. Bejel is prevalent in parts of Africa and western Asia (see Chapter 156).

Pathogenesis and prevention

The treponemata that cause these three diseases are transmitted by direct contact among children living under unhygienic circumstances. The contacts of patients may be treated with antibiotics. Vaccines for public health use are not available.

Diagnostic microbiology and clinical features

Yaws is characterized by early papillomatous skin lesions and periostitis, late destructive skin lesions (including hyperkeratosis) and bone and skin gummata (Fig. 230.6). As in syphilis, the diagnosis can be confirmed directly by dark-field microscopy or fluorescent antibody staining, or serologically by the VDRL test, the RPR test, the treponemal FTA-ABS test or the specific microhemagglutination antibody tests. The incubation period is 3–5 weeks.

Pinta is suspected in patients from endemic areas who present with papulosquamous or depigmented skin lesions. The diagnosis is confirmed by dark-field microscopy or serologic tests (VDRL, FTA-ABS) that become positive after the lesions appear. The incubation period is about 1–3 weeks.

Bejel is suspected in patients from endemic areas who present with early mucous membrane and skin lesions and late gummata of skin and bone.

Management

Long-acting penicillin G is recommended for patients and their contacts in a single dose of 1.2 million units for those over age 10 years and 600,000 units for children below 10 years of age (see Fig. 230.6).

BORRELIA SPP.

Lyme disease

Borrelia spp. have gained importance during the past 25 years. This genus has become a well-known pathogen to many medical specialists since the first description of Lyme disease and the discovery that *Borrelia* spp. are the causative agents.

Nature

All *Borrelia* spp. are loosely coiled, left-handed bacteria characterized by the presence of a protoplasmic cylinder that is surrounded by a cell membrane, a periplasmic flagellum and an outer membrane (Fig. 230.7). The genome has been sequenced and is relatively small, with 150 megabases comprising a linear chromosome and plasmids.

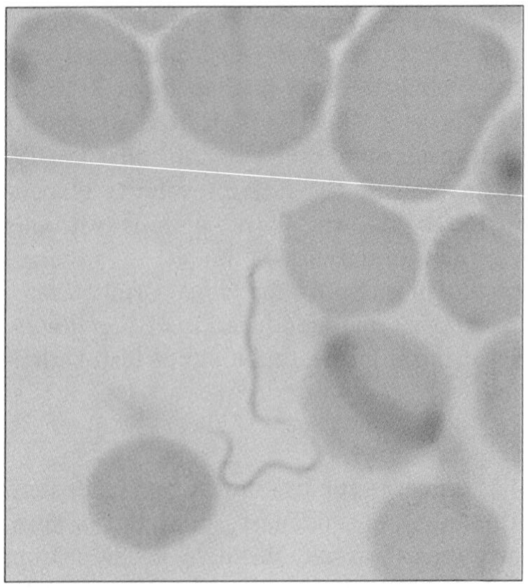

Fig. 230.7 Giemsa stain of blood with *B. burgdorferi*. Adapted from Murray *et al.*[106]

Three species have been associated with disease in humans: *B. burgdorferi sensu stricto, B. afzelii* and *B. garinii*, which together form the *Borrelia burgdorferi sensu lato* complex.[61] In Europe, *Borrelia afzelii* and *Borrelia garinii* are predominant but *B. burgdorferi sensu stricto* can also be encountered. In North America, only infections with *B. burgdorferi sensu stricto* have been observed.

Epidemiology

Lyme disease surveillance data, collected since 1982, show that it is the commonest vector-borne infection in the USA. *Borrelia burgdorferi* is transmitted by ticks of the *Ixodes ricinus* complex. The principal vector in Europe is *I. ricinus*, in north-eastern and mid-west USA *Ixodes scapularis*, in the western coastal states *Ixodes pacificus*, and in Asia *Ixodes persulcatus*. Deer serve as hosts for *I. ricinus*. Small rodents, rats and mice serve as transitional hosts for the tick in its larval and nymph stages. Humans are more or less accidental hosts. The total developmental cycle from egg to adult takes 2 years. The tick is active during the summer and early autumn. In their larval stage, 1–4% of ticks are infected; in their nymph and adult stages, up to 25% are infected. In endemic areas Lyme disease is an important health problem in school-aged children, with a reported incidence of clinical Lyme disease of 10.1 cases per 1000 person-years and a reported incidence of asymptomatic *B. burgdorferi* infection of 3.8 cases per 1000 person-years.

Pathogenesis

Most tick bites do not cause infection and if they do, serious illness is rare. Early during the illness, the distribution of the spirochete is widespread. This is facilitated by the capacity of *B. burgdorferi* to resist elimination by phagocytes, to adhere to epithelial and brain cells, to cross intracellular junctions and penetrate cytoplasm, and to induce tumor necrosis factor (TNF)-α and interleukin (IL)-1b.[62] *Borrelia burgdorferi* actively attaches to, invades and kills human B and T cells. The cellular immune response seen locally in erythema migrans is mainly composed of $CD4^+$ lymphocytes, $CD8^+$ lymphocytes and macrophages. The immune response is suppressed initially, but it is heightened 3–6 weeks later at the peak of the specific IgM response, which is usually directed toward the spirochetal 41kDa flagellar antigen. This IgM response is associated with polyclonal B-lymphocyte activation, including elevated total serum IgM levels, cryoglobulins, circulating immune complexes, rheumatoid factor and antinuclear antibodies or anticardiolipin antibodies. After a further 6–8 weeks, a specific IgG response develops to different spirochetal antigens. At this stage, affected tissues show lymphocyte and plasma cell infiltration and signs of vascular damage.

Prevention

Preventing tick-borne diseases such as Lyme disease can be accomplished by tucking trousers into socks, covering the neck and head (especially of small children) and inspection of the body for ticks after a possible exposure. The use of environmental modifications (e.g. removal of leaf litter, deer fencing or eradication, and the application of insecticides around residential areas) are all effective for various periods of time. Since no scientific evidence is present supporting antibiotic prophylaxis after exposure, adverse affects and resistance development should discourage this approach.[63] The Food and Drug Administration approved in 1998 the LYMErix (Glaxo Smith Kline) vaccine for persons 15–70 years of age. The vaccine is composed of recombinant OspA (outer surface protein A) and aims at the elimination of the spirochete in the gut of the tick before entry in the host.[64] Efficacy in preventing Lyme disease was 49% and 76% after two and three injections, respectively.[65] A theoretical concern is the induction of inflammatory arthritis by vaccination although no proven cases have been documented. All strains in the USA have been shown to express the same OspA variant; in Europe, however, a polyvalent vaccine will be obligatory.[66,67]

Diagnostic microbiology

Lyme disease is primarily a clinical diagnosis for which erythema migrans is pathognomonic (Fig. 230.8).[68] It should be suspected in young patients from endemic areas who present with facial palsy or unexplained heart block. Because of the scarcity of organisms, infection can rarely be proven from samples other than the skin on histologic staining. Culturing *B. burgdorferi* from erythema migrans lesions or infected ticks is relatively easy. *Borrelia burgdorferi* grows as fastidious microaerophilic bacteria, at 91–92% F in Barbour–Stoenner–Kelly II medium. Serologic tests serve only as an adjunct to the clinical diagnosis because false positivity may occur. Enzyme-linked immunosorbent assays are preferred to the indirect fluorescent antibody staining method because of their higher sensitivity and reproducibility.[69] False-positive results and considerable variation within and between laboratories have been reported. Despite these shortcomings, the CDC has developed criteria for a two-step approach to determine antibodies against *B. burgdorferi* using ELISA and Western blotting.[65] These criteria apply only for the situation in the USA since antibody production against *Borrelia* spp. other than *B. burgdorferi sensu stricto* is less predictable. None of the laboratory tests can be used to estimate the extent of infection, its prior duration or its prognosis. In general, antibody response is slow and may persist for many years after treatment.

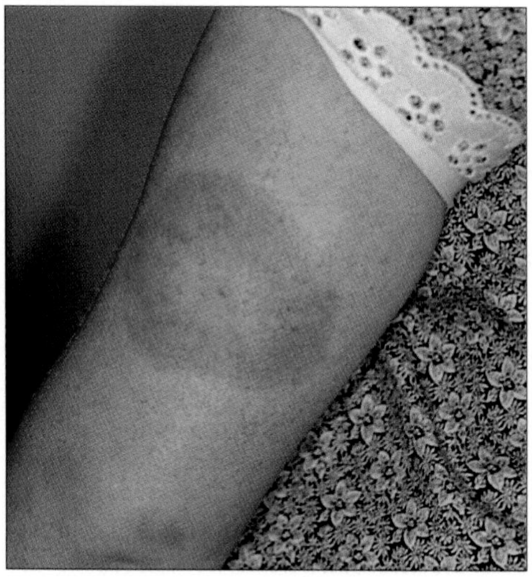

Fig. 230.8 Typical erythema migrans rash. Adapted from Murray *et al.*[106]

Borrelia burgdorferi DNA has been demonstrated with PCR in skin biopsies from patients who have erythema migrans and acrodermatitis chronica atrophicans, in CSF from patients who have neuroborreliosis and in synovial fluid and synovial tissue from patients who have Lyme arthritis.[70] Urine is an important source of *Borrelia* DNA in patients who have erythema migrans, acrodermatitis chronica atrophicans, neuroborreliosis and Lyme arthritis.[71] In general, molecular diagnostics for Lyme disease should be reserved for patients with a high clinical probability in the early phase of disease before seroconversion.[72]

Clinical features

Although erythema migrans, the major presenting feature of the illness, is similar in all parts of the world, differences in disease manifestations, disease severity and frequency occur. These differences may reflect regional variation in the prevalence of genospecies of *B. burgdorferi*. In general, a wider spectrum of disease presentations has been noted in Europe than in North America. Borreliosis may evolve in three clinical stages.[73] The clinical heterogeneity results in the tendency to overdiagnose Lyme disease. Stage 1 may remain asymptomatic, whereas stages 2 and 3 may not occur in sequence or may not develop at all. A summary of the clinical manifestations is given in Table 230.4.

Stage 1 (localized infection)

Three days to a month after the tick bite, a flu-like illness develops together with erythema migrans. Erythema migrans may also be the sole presenting feature. It begins at the site of the tick bite, expands from a macule or papule to a large circular lesion of 3–60cm diameter and fades spontaneously in the course of weeks. Most commonly, the lesions are found on the trunk or lower extremities. Differential diagnoses for erythema migrans include streptococcal and staphylococcal cellulitis, hypersensitivity reactions to arthropod bites, plant dermatitis, tinea and granuloma annulare.

Stage 2 (early dissemination)

Multiple secondary lesions may occur several days after the first lesion of erythema migrans and result from the spread of the organism. Lymphadenopathy and malaise may be evident. After an interval of weeks or months, neurologic abnormalities occur in 10–15% of cases. The cranial nerves can be affected, particularly the facial nerve, resulting in a Bell's palsy. Lymphocytic meningitis develops in 5% of cases. Even less frequent complications include meningoencephalitis, chorea, myelitis, radiculitis and peripheral neuritis. A lymphocytoma, which is sometimes painful, especially when exposed to cold, may also develop. These symptoms may disappear spontaneously or become chronic or relapsing. Transient arthritis or arthralgia may occur as well. At this stage, 10% of the patients develop myocarditis, with atrioventricular blocks of various degrees, which may resolve spontaneously or require a temporary pacemaker.

Stage 3 (persistent infection)

Months to years after the primary exposure, 50% of the patients who have not received adequate treatment develop monoarthritis or oligoarthritis, which becomes chronic in 10–20% of cases. Late complications may also include chronic encephalomyelitis, uveitis and acrodermatitis chronica atrophicans.

Management

Stage 1 and mild manifestations of stage 2 can be treated with oral doxycycline or amoxicillin for 2–3 weeks; early treatment may prevent the development of antibodies.[76] Treatment with doxycycline has the advantage that human granulocytic ehrlichiosis (HGE) is treated as well. Cefuroxime axetil can serve as an alternative for patients allergic to doxycycline or amoxicillin. Macrolides should only

CLINICAL FEATURES OF LYME BORRELIOSIS			
System	**Localized (stage 1)**	**Early infection, disseminated (stage 2)**	**Late infection, persistent (stage 3)**
Skin	Erythema migrans	Secondary erythema migrans, lymphadenosis benigna cutis	Acrodermatitis chronica atrophicans
Musculoskeletal		Migratory pain in joints, tendons, muscle, bone; brief attacks of arthritis	Prolonged attacks of arthritis, arthritis, peripheral chronic enthesopathy, joint subluxation below the lesions of acrodermatitis chronica atrophicans
Neurologic		Meningitis, cranial neuritis, Bell's palsy, motor or sensory radiculoneuritis, encephalitis	Chronic encephalomyelitis, spastic parapareses, mental disorders, dementia
Heart		Atrioventricular block, myopericarditis, pancarditis	
Lymphatic	Regional lymphadenopathy	Regional or generalized lymphadenopathy	
Eyes		Conjunctivitis, iritis	
Liver		Hepatitis	
Respiratory		Nonproductive cough	
Renal		Microscopic hematuria or proteinuria	
'Constitutional symptoms'	Minor	Fatigue, malaise	Fatigue

Table 230.4 Clinical features of Lyme borreliosis. (Adapted from Steere[74] and Blaauw.[75])

TREATMENT OPTIONS FOR BORRELIOSIS				
		Antibiotic		
Bacteria	**Clinical features**	**First choice**	**Second choice**	**Third choice**
Borrelia recurrentis	Recurrent fever	Doxycycline 100mg 1 dose po	Erythromycin 500mg 1 dose po	Tetracycline 500mg 1 dose po
Borrelia spp.		Doxycycline 100mg q12h po 5–10 days	Erythromycin 500mg q6h po 5–10 days	
B. burgdorferi	Stage 1	Doxycycline 100mg q12h 14–21 days	Amoxicillin 500mg q8h 14–21 days	Cefuroxime axetil 500mg q12h 14–21 days
	Stage 2 and 3 mild Cranial nerve palsy, 1st or 2nd degree heart block, arteritis	Doxycycline 100mg q12h 14–28 days	Amoxicillin 500mg q8h 14–28 days	Cefuroxime axetil 500mg q12h 14–28 days
	Stage 2 and 3 serious disease Meningitis, radiculopathy, 3rd degree heart block	Ceftriaxone 2g once daily 14–28 days	Cefotaxime 2g q8h 14–28 days	Penicillin G 18–24 million units iv/d given q4h 14–28 days

Table 230.5 Treatment options for borreliosis. Adapted from Speelman *et al.*[108]

be used when patients are intolerant to the aforementioned drugs. The more serious complications of stage 2 and stage 3 such as meningitis, radiculopathy and third-degree atrioventricular heart block will require parenteral antibiotics such as ceftriaxone. Intravenous penicillin G or cefotaxime can serve as an alternative. Oral doxycyline is probably equally effective for the treatment of neuroborreliosis (Table 230.5).[77] Prophylactic treatment is not recommended, especially if the tick has been attached for less than 24 hours.

Borrelia recurrentis

Nature and epidemiology

The louse-borne epidemic relapsing fever, caused by *Borrelia recurrentis*, is transmitted by the human body louse and is associated with unhygienic living circumstances. The tick-borne endemic relapsing fever is caused by different *Borrelia* spp. and is transmitted by the *Ornithodorus* tick.

Pathogenesis and prevention

When lice are crushed, *B. recurrentis* is released and penetrates the skin or mucous membranes. Organisms can be detected in the blood when the patient has a fever. They sequester in internal organs in the afebrile periods. Mutational changes in the antigenic properties of the organism and consequent antibody production account for the relapses, which end when sufficient borrelicidal antibody has been developed.

Preventive measures are similar to those recommended for Lyme disease and involve the elimination or avoidance of the spirochete vector. A vaccine is not yet available for public health purposes.

Diagnostic microbiology

Diagnosis is based on the clinical presentation and detection of the bacteria in the blood. Spirochetes are found in the majority of wet or stained blood smears. They have also been detected in the CSF of patients who have signs of central nervous system involvement. Up to 10% show positive serologic tests for syphilis.

An early clinical diagnosis of louse-borne relapsing fever is not difficult during epidemics. In contrast, the initial differential diagnosis in an isolated case includes many different diseases such as malaria, typhoid fever, leptospirosis and dengue fever.[78]

Clinical features

Epidemic louse-borne relapsing fever and endemic tick-borne relapsing fever have very similar clinical manifestations; heterogeneity reflects differences in, for example, spirochete strains and the condition of the patient. Louse-borne relapsing fever and tick-borne relapsing fever both have a very acute onset of high fever with chills and muscle and joint aches. Headache and lethargy may be accompanied by neurologic findings, including meningitis and seizures leading to coma. Photophobia and iridocyclitis may develop, causing permanent damage to the sight. Coughing may result from bronchitis or pneumonia. A 2-day truncal rash may occur at the end of the first febrile period. Abdominal tenderness with enlargement of liver and spleen may be associated with jaundice, lymphadenopathy and hemorrhagic diathesis.

The first bout of fever usually lasts 3–6 days, sometimes with fatal complications including myocarditis, cerebral hemorrhage and hepatic failure. The fever may suddenly reappear after a 7–10-day interval. Louse-borne disease typically has a longer incubation period and a more elongated cycle of febrile and afebrile periods, and it is associated with a single relapse. Tick-borne disease manifests with multiple relapses that taper off in duration and intensity.

Management

First-choice antibiotic is doxycycline 100mg q12h for 5–10 days. One 500mg dose of erythromycin is the second-choice option. Antibiotic treatment may be accompanied by a Jarisch–Herxheimer reaction that cannot be prevented by prior corticosteroid therapy.[79] and that reflects clearance of the spirochetemia. It may be advisable to give the first dose of antibiotics at a lower dose (e.g. erythromycin 250mg) to limit the severity of the Jarisch–Herxheimer reaction (see Chapter 182 for further management guidelines).

LEPTOSPIRA INTERROGANS SPP.

Nature

Leptospira interrogans spp. are thin, motile, coiled bacilli. The serotypes of the *Leptospira interrogans* sp. group include *icterohaemorrhagiae, canicola, pomona, autumnalis, grippotyphosa, hebdomadis, ballum* and *australis*.[80] Each of these has a different natural habitat. For example, *L. interrogans* serotype *icterohaemorrhagiae* is most commonly found in rats, *L. interrogans* serotype *canicola* in dogs and *L. interrogans* serotype *pomona* in pigs.

Epidemiology

Leptospirosis is a zoonosis that occurs worldwide (see Chapter 181). In the USA, rats are the most common vector for human infection, followed by dogs, livestock, rodents, wild mammals and cats. Humans are dead-end hosts because person–person transmission is very rare. The peak incidence is during the summer and early autumn; young adult men often become infected, for example, after recreational exposure to contaminated water. Leptospirosis has long been considered an occupational disease affecting farmers, veterinary surgeons and abattoir workers through indirect contact with infected animals via urine-contaminated water or soil.[81]

Pathogenesis

Leptospira spp. penetrate the intact mucous membranes or abraded skin, enter the bloodstream and spread to all parts of the body, including the CSF and eyes. Liver damage is subcellular and may lead to jaundice. Renal failure may result from a direct toxic effect of the leptospires on the tubules. Meningeal irritation may occur when the leptospires enter the CSF. They are abundant during the early stage of the meningeal disease and disappear when serum antibodies develop. A chronic or recurrent uveitis may result from leptospires persisting in the corpus vitrium of the eye. Myalgia, particularly of the calves, may be an early sign, and pathologic changes such as polymorphonuclear infiltration of the muscle occur late.[82]

Prevention

Effective control of leptospirosis is difficult because leptospires can establish a symbiotic relationship with many hosts, even if they have been vaccinated, and persist in the renal tubules (with excretion in the urine) without causing illness or pathologic changes in the kidneys. In addition, wild animals represent a reservoir from which domestic animals are continually infected. Widespread vaccination of livestock and pets in the USA has reduced the incidence of infection in some species, although adequately vaccinated dogs can still infect humans.[83] Immunization of rice fieldworkers in China with polyvalent vaccines has been practiced. In France a vaccine against serovar *icterohaemorrhagiae* is available for human use.[84] Prohibition of recreational activities in contaminated waters and measures to reduce the number of rats have been successful in reducing the incidence of disease. Prevention can be considered using 200mg doxycycline once a week for heavily exposed individuals such as soldiers who train in the jungle.[85]

Diagnostic microbiology

Isolating the organism from patient material or the detection of seroconversion confirms the clinical suspicion of leptospirosis. Leptospires can be isolated from blood or CSF during the first 10 days of illness. During the second week, they appear in the urine and can be detected in biopsies from various organs. Tween 80-albumin is viewed as the best available medium.[86] Cultures should be maintained in the dark for up to 6 weeks at 82–86°F. Leptospires grow in semisolid media in a ring 0.5–1cm below the surface, appearing 6–14 days after inoculation. They remain viable in heparinized blood for more than 1 week and can be mailed to a reference laboratory for identification.

The laboratory technique most commonly used to diagnose leptospirosis is a two-step serologic procedure, although antibiotic treatment may interfere with antibody development and account for false-negative results.

Macroscopic slide agglutination is used for screening purposes, followed by microscopic agglutination test (MAT) with live antigens for determining antibody titers and identifying serotypes. Both tests use pools of antigens representative of most serogroups. Nevertheless, cross-reactions often occur and serologic tests cannot accurately identify the serotype responsible for infection. Currently, the sensitivity and specificity necessary for reliable clinical diagnosis is best achieved using a battery of 23 antigens. The presumptive diagnosis may be based on a microscopic agglutination titer of 1:100 or greater or on a positive slide agglutination test. Agglutinins appear after 1 week of illness and decline after the third or fourth week. For areas in the world where laboratory resources are limited a dipstick assay using a broadly reactive leptospiral antigen on a solid support for the detection of IgM antibodies was demonstrated to have satisfactory specificity and sensitivity.[87]

Other techniques to identify leptospires include dark-field examination and silver staining. Polymerase chain reaction has proven valuable as a rapid, sensitive and specific means of diagnosing leptospiral infection, especially during the first 10 days of illness when the clinical expression of the disease may be confusing.[88]

Clinical manifestations

Leptospirosis may evolve subclinically or clinically. It has an incubation period of approximately 7–12 days; clinical illness typically follows a biphasic course. During the initial phase of 4–7 days, patients present with sudden onset of fever, severe general malaise, muscular pain, especially in the calves, conjunctival congestion and leptospires can be isolated from most tissues. Two days without fever follow. During the second phase of up to 30 days, leptospires are still detectable in the urine, kidney and vitreous body. Circulating antibodies emerge and meningeal inflammation, uveitis and rash develop.[89]

Icteric leptospirosis, or Weil's disease, occurs in 10% of the clinically ill patients; 90% remain anicteric. Icteric leptospirosis can be caused by any type of leptospire including *L. interrogans* subtype *icterohaemorrhagiae*. Prominent features are renal and liver malfunction, hemorrhage and impaired consciousness; the mortality rate is 5%.[90] The combination of a direct serum bilirubin level of less than 20mg/100ml (342mmol/l), a marked elevation in serum creatine phosphokinase and an elevation in transaminase (SGOT and SGPT) of less than 200 units is suggestive of the diagnosis.[91] Hepatocellular necrosis rarely occurs and no residual hepatic dysfunction ensues. Hepatomegaly is found in 25% of cases. The severity of the illness probably reflects the degree of the vasculitis.

Anicteric leptospirosis is a more common and less severe form of leptospirosis. It has a sudden onset and is accompanied by remittent fever and chills, persistent headache, severe myalgia, malaise, prostration and abdominal pain with nausea and vomiting lasting up to 7 days. During the following so-called immune stage, the fever virtually subsides. Delirium and meningism, however, may develop. Several organ systems can be affected, including the lungs, which may show pulmonary infiltrates, and the eyes.[92] A rash may develop as well. Distinct erythematous pretibial lesions can be found in the Fort Bragg fever syndrome, which is caused by *Leptospira interrogans* serotype *autumnalis*.

Management

Severely ill patients should be treated with intravenous penicillin or amoxicillin for 7 days (Table 230.6).[93] Less severely ill patients should receive oral doxycycline for 7 days.[94] Severe disease is not limited to adults but may also affect children, who benefit from antibiotics even late during the illness.[95] Careful monitoring and supportive therapy are important in order to prevent possible complications, including renal failure, hypotension and major hemorrhage.

TREATMENT OPTIONS FOR LEPTOSPIROSIS

	Antibiotic	
Bacteria	First choice	Second choice
Leptospira icterohaemorrhagiae, copenhageni (Weil's disease)	Penicillin G 1MU q4–6h iv for 7 days	Doxycycline 100mg q12h po for 7 days
Leptospira hardjo (Milker's disease)	Alternative: Amoxicillin 500mg q6h for 7 days	
Leptospira grippotyphosa		

Table 230.6 Treatment options for leptospirosis. Adapted from Speelman *et al.*[108]

SPIRILLUM MINUS

Rat-bite fever can be caused by either *Streptobacillus moniliformis* or *Spirillum minus*. The first description of the spirillum dates back to 1888 when Carter reported a spiral organism which he called *Spirillum minor* in the blood of wild rats. Later the organism was named *Spirocheta morsus muris* and in 1924 the organism was renamed *Spirillum minus*.[96]

Nature

The literature on *Spirillum minus* is very puzzling since largely conflicting properties of the organism have been reported. The basic problem lies in the fact that the description of the organism is purely morphological.[97] No biochemical properties or nucleotide sequence data are available. *Spirillum minus* is a Gram-negative spiral microorganism. It measures 0.2–0.5μm in width and 3–5μm in length. It possesses two to three windings and is actively motile by means of bipolar tufts of flagella.

Epidemiology and pathogenesis

Spirillum minus can be detected in the oropharynx of rats and small rodents. Infections occur throughout the world. Data on incidence are lacking so the widely held belief that infections with *S. minus* are more often seen in the Pacific region cannot be substantiated. Transmission from human to human has not been documented.

Prevention

No studies have been reported on the use of prophylactic antibiotics after a rat bite.

Diagnostic microbiology

The spiral bacteria can be made visible using dark-field microscopy or Giemsa staining of blood smears, smears from eschars or lymph node aspirates. *Bergey's manual of determinative microbiology* states that the organism cannot be cultured on artificial media but can be detected in the blood of mice or guinea-pigs 3 weeks after intraperitoneal injection of clinical samples.[97] A practical problem concerning this approach is the fact that these animals are the natural reservoir of these spirilla. Animal inoculation studies should include control animals and preinoculaton evaluation for spirilla.[98] Most reports in the literature do not describe if such controls were performed. Diagnosis of *S. minus* infection in the literature is based on either clinical presentation,[99] direct visualization of the organism[100] or animal inoculation.[98] These spirilla could not be cultured on artificial media. Other reports indicate an easily cultivable *S. minus* as an etiologic agent for endocarditis[101,102] and recurrent fever.[103] These spirilla could be cultured on simple media such as blood agar and an antibiogram could be established. Further characterization of the spirilla is warranted to determine if we are dealing with one or multiple species or even genera.[104] No specific serological test can be used; however, the VDRL is positive in 50% of cases.

Clinical features

Spirillum minus rat bite fever is also called sodoku: 'so' means rat and 'doku' means poison in Japanese.[96] The initial lesion of the rat bite usually heals promptly. One to 36 days after the exposure the patient becomes ill and develops fever. At the site of the bite, the wound reactivates and an eschar develops. Regional lymphadenitis is present in the majority of cases. A violaceous maculopapular rash on palms and soles, very similar to the one seen in syphilis, is a common feature. If untreated, relapsing fever will develop. As compared to the rat-bite fever caused by *Streptobacillus moniliformis*, sodoku has a longer incubation period and arthritis is not a frequent event.

Management

Penicillin is the treatment of choice although no clearcut guidelines can be presented about dose and duration. A Jarisch–Herxheimer reaction can occur after initiation of antibiotic therapy. Tetracycline can be used for patients with an allergy for penicillin.

REFERENCES

1. Goodwin CS, Armstrong JA, Chilvers T, *et al.* Transfer of *Campylobacter pylori* and *Campylobacter mustelae* to *Helicobacter pylori* gen. nov. and *Helicobacter mustelae* comb. nov. respectively. Int J Syst Bacteriol 1989;39:397.
2. Vandamme P. Taxonomy of the family *Campylobacteraceae*. In: Nachamkin I, Blaser MJ, eds. *Campylobacter*, 2nd ed. Washington DC: American Society for Microbiology; 2000:3–26.
3. Lastovica AJ, Skirrow MB. Clinical significance of Campylobacter and related species other than *Campylobacter jejuni* and *C. coli*. In: Nachamkin I, Blaser MJ, eds. *Campylobacter*, 2nd ed. Washington DC: American Society for Microbiology; 2000:89–120.
4. Freedman CR, Neimann J, Wegener HC, Tauxe RV. Epidemiology of *Campylobacter jejuni* infections in the United States and other industrialized nations. In: Nachamkin I, Blaser MJ, eds. *Campylobacter*, 2nd ed. Washington DC: American Society for Microbiology; 2000:1,21–138.
5. Nylen G, Dunstan F, Palmer SR, *et al.* The seasonal distribution of Campylobacter infection in nine European countries and New Zealand. Epidemiol Infect 2002;28:383–90.
6. Konkel ME, Joens LA, Mixter PF. Molecular characterization of *Campylobacter jejuni* virulence determinants. In: Nachamkin I, Blaser MJ, eds. *Campylobacter*, 2nd ed. Washington DC: American Society for Microbiology; 2000:217–40.
7. Parkhill J, Wren BW, Mungall K, *et al.* The genome sequence of the food-borne pathogen *Campylobacter jejuni* reveals hypervariable sequences. Nature 2000;403:665–8.
8. Yuki N. Infectious origin of, and molecular mimicry in, Guillain–Barré and Fisher syndromes. Lancet Infect Dis 2001;1:29–37.
9. Blaser MJ, Smith PF, Repine JE, *et al.* Pathogenesis of *Campylobacter fetus* infections. Failure of C3b to bind explains serum and phagocytosis resistance. J Clin Invest 1988;81:1434–44.
10. Scott DA, Tribble DR. Campylobacter infection and vaccine development. In: Nachamkin I, Blaser MJ, eds. *Campylobacter*, 2nd ed. Washington DC: American Society for Microbiology; 2000:303–19.
11. On SLW. Identification methods for campylobacters, helicobacters, and related organisms. Clin Microbiol Rev 1996;9:405–22.
12. Newell DG, Frost JA, Duim B, *et al.* New developments in the subtyping of *Campylobacter* species. In: Nachamkin I, Blaser MJ, eds. *Campylobacter*, 2nd ed. Washington DC: American Society for Microbiology; 2000:27–44.
13. Skirrow MB. *Campylobacter* enteritis: a 'new' disease. BMJ 1977;2:9–11.
14. Skirrow MB, Blaser MJ. Clinical aspects of Campylobacter infection. In: Nachamkin I, Blaser MJ, eds. *Campylobacter*, 2nd ed. Washington DC: American Society for Microbiology; 2000:69–88.
15. Pigrau C, Bartolome R, Almirante B, Planes A, Gavalda J, Pahissa A. Bacteremia due to *Campylobacter* species: clinical findings and antimicrobial susceptibility patterns. Clin Infect Dis 1997;25:1414–20.
16. Warren JR, Marshall BJ. Unidentified curved bacilli on gastric epithelium in active gastritis. Lancet 1983;1:1273–5.
17. Tomb JF, White O, Kerlavage AR, *et al.* The complete genome sequence of the gastric pathogen *Helicobacter pylori.* Nature 1997;388:539–47.
18. Alm RA, Ling L-SL, Moir DT. Genomic-sequence comparison of two unrelated isolates of the human gastric pathogen *Helicobacter pylori.* Nature 1999;397:176–80.
19. Mégraud F, Brassens-Rabbé MP, Denis F, Belbouri A, Hoa DQ. Seroepidemiology of *Campylobacter pylori* infection in various populations. J Clin Microbiol 1989;27:1870–3.
20. Webb P, Knight T, Wilson A, Newell D, Elder J, Forman D. Relation between infection with *H. pylori* and living conditions in childhood: evidence for person to person transmission in early life. BMJ 1994;308:750–3.
21. Banatvala N, Mayo K, Mégraud F, Jennings R, Deekd JJ, Feldman RA. The cohort effect and *H. pylori*. J Infect Dis 1993;168:219–21.
22. Ernst PB, Takaishi H, Crowe SE. *Helicobacter pylori* infection as a model for gastrointestinal immunity and chronic inflammatory diseases. Dig Dis 2001;19:104–11.
23. Galmiche A, Rassow J, Doye A, *et al.* The N-terminal 34kDa fragment of *Helicobacter pylori* vacuolating cytotoxin targets mitochondria and induces cyrochrome C release. Embo J 2000;19:6361–70.
24. Foryst-Ludwig A, Naumann M. PAKI activates the NIK-IKK NF-kappa-B pathway and proinflammatory cytokines in *H. pylori*-infection. J Biol Chem 2000;275:39779–885.
25. Appelmelk BJ, Negrini N, Moran AP, Kuipers EJ. Molecular mimicry between *H. pylori* and the host. Trends Microbiol 1997;5:70–3.
26. Monteiro L, de Mascarel A, Sarrasqueta AM, *et al.* Diagnosis of *Helicobacter pylori* infection: noninvasive methods compared to invasive methods and evaluation of two new tests. Am J Gastroenterol 2001;96:353–8.
27. Mégraud F, Lamouliatte F. *Helicobacter pylori* and peptic ulcer: evidence suggesting causation. Dig Dis Sci 1992;37:769–72.
28. Uemura N, Okamoto S, Yamamoto S, *et al.* *Helicobacter pylori* infection and the development of gastric cancer. N Engl J Med 2001;345:784–9.
29. Watanabe T, Tada M, Nagai H, Sasaki S, Nakao M. *Helicobacter pylori* infection induces gastric cancer in Mongolian gerbils. Gastroenterology 1998;115:642–8.
30. Wotherspoon AC, Ortiz-Hidalgo C, Falzon MR, Isaacson PG. *H. pylori* associated gastritis and primary B-cell gastric lymphoma. Lancet 1991;338:1175–6.
31. Moayyedi P, Soo S, Decks J, *et al.* Systemic review and economic evaluation of *Helicobacter pylori* eradication treatment for non-ulcer dyspepsia. BMJ 2000;321:659–64.
32. Danesh J, Youngman L, Clark S, Parish S, Peto R, Collins R. *Helicobacter pylori* infection and early onset myocardial infarction: case-control and sibling pairs study. BMJ 1999;319:1157–62.
33. Malfertheiner P, Mégraud F, O'Morain C, *et al.* and the European *Helicobacter pylori* Study Group (EHPSG). Current concepts in the management of *Helicobacter pylori* infection – the Maastricht 2–2000 Consensus Report. Aliment Pharmacol Ther 2002;16:167–80.
34. Faruque SM, Albert MJ, Mekalanos JJ. Epidemiology, genetics, and ecology of toxigenic *Vibrio cholerae.* Microbiol Mol Biol Rev 1998;62:1301–14.
35. Tauxe RV, Mintz ED, Quick RE. Epidemic cholera in the new world: translating field epidemiology into new prevention strategies. Emerg Infect Dis 1995;1:141–6.
36. Faruque SM, Nair GB. Molecular ecology of toxigenic Vibrio cholerae. Microbiol Immunol 2002;46:59–66.
37. Clemens J, Albert MJ, Rao M, *et al.* Impact of infection by *Helicobacter pylori* on the risk and severity of endemic cholera. J Infect Dis 1995;171:1653–6.
38. Beubler E, Kollar G, Saria A, *et al.* Involvement of 5-hydroxytryptamine, prostaglandin E2 and cyclic adenosine monophosphate in cholera toxin-induced fluid secretion in the small intestine of the rat *in vivo*. Gastroenterology 1989;96:368–76.
39. Karakolis DK, Johnson JA, Bailey CC, Boedeker EC, Kaper JB, Reeves PR. A *Vibrio cholerae* pathogenicity island associated with epidemic and pandemic strains. Proc Natl Acad Sci USA 1998;95:3134–9.
40. Walder KW, Mekalanos JJ. Lysogenic conversion by a filamentous phage encoding cholera toxin. Science 1996;272:1910–14.
41. Miller M, Skorupski K, Lenz D, Taylor R, Bassler B. Parallel quorum sensing systems converge to regulate virulence in *Vibrio cholerae.* Cell 2002;110:303.
42. Heidelberg JF, *et al.* DNA sequence of both chromosomes of the cholera pathogen *Vibrio cholerae.* Nature 2000;410:40.
43. Clemens JD, Van Loon FPL, Sack DA, *et al.* Biotype as a determinant of the natural immunizing effect of *V. cholerae* O1. Lancet 1991;337:883–4.
44. Coster TS, Killeen KP, Waldor MK, *et al.* Safety, immunogenicity, and efficacy of live attenuated *Vibrio cholerae* O139 vaccine prototype. Lancet 1995;345:949–52.
45. Glass RI, Claeson M, Blake PA, Waldman RJ, Pierce NF. Cholera in Africa: lessons on transmission and control for Latin America. Lancet 1991;338:791–5.
46. Hirschhorn N, Kinzie JL, Sachar SB, *et al.* Decrease in net stool output in cholera during intestinal perfusion with glucose-containing solutions. N Engl J Med 1968;4:176–81.
47. Reidl J, Klose KE. *Vibrio cholerae* and cholera: out of the water and into the host. FEMS Microbiol Rev 2002;26:125–39.
48. Ali A, Mehra MR, Stapleton DD, *et al.* *Vibrio vulnificus* sepsis in solid transplantations: a medical nemesis. J Heart Lung Transplant 1995;14:598–600.
49. Yip KM, Fung KS, Adeyemi-Doro FA. Necrotizing fasciitis of the foot caused by an unusual organism, *Vibrio vulnificus*. J Foot Ankle Surg 1996;35:222–4.
50. Garnett GP, Aral SO, Hoyle DV, Cates W, Anderson RM. The natural history of syphilis. Implications for the transmission dynamics and control of infection. Sex Transm Dis 1997;24:185–200.
51. Radolph JD, Robinson EJ, Bourell KW, *et al.* Characterization of outer membranes isolated from *Treponema pallidum*, the syphilis spirochete. Infect Immun 1995;63:4244–52.

52. Van Voorhis WC, Barrett LK, Nasio JM, Plummer FA, Lukehart SA. Lesions of primary and secondary syphilis contain cytotoxic T cells. Infect Immun 1996;64:1048–50.
53. Cates W, Rothenberg RB, Blount JH. Syphilis control. The historic context and epidemiologic basis for interrupting sexual transmission of *Treponema pallidum*. Sex Transm Dis 1996;23:68–75.
54. Abyad A. Cost-effectiveness of antenatal screening for syphilis. Health Care Women Int 1995;16:323–8.
55. De Majo E, Bianchini G, Parri F, Tocci E, Monaci M, Paoli C. Evaluation of a competitive enzyme immunoassay in screening for syphilis. New Microbiol 1996;19:31–8.
56. Larsen SA, Steiner BM, Rudolph AH. Laboratory diagnosis and interpretation of tests for syphilis. Clin Microbiol Rev 1995;8:1–21.
57. Goeman J, Kivivu M, Nzila N, *et al.* Similar serological response to conventional therapy for syphilis among HIV-positive and HIV-negative women. Genitourin Med 1995;71:275–9.
58. Habif TP. Clinical dermatology: a color guide to diagnosis and therapy. St Louis: Mosby; 1996.
59. Rolfs RT, Joesoef MR, Hendershot EF, *et al.* A randomized trial of enhanced therapy for early syphilis in patients with and without human immunodeficiency virus infection. The Syphilis and HIV Study Group. N Engl J Med 1997;337:307–14.
60. Peters W, Giles HM. A colour atlas of tropical medicine and parasitology, 4th ed. London: Wolfe; 1995.
61. Van Dam AP, Kuiper H, Vos K, *et al.* Different genospecies of *Borrelia burgdorferi* are associated with distinct clinical manifestations of Lyme borreliosis. Clin Infect Dis 1993;17:707–17.
62. Goodman JL, Bradley JF, Ross AE, *et al.* Bloodstream invasion in early Lyme disease: results from a prospective, controlled, blinded study using the polymerase chain reaction. Am J Med 1995;99:6–12.
63. Poland GA. Prevention of Lyme disease: a review of the evidence. Mayo Clin Proc 2001;76:713–24.
64. Van Solingen RM, Evans J. Lyme disease. Curr Opin Rheumatol 2001;13:293–9.
65. Steere AC. Lyme disease. N Engl J Med 2001;345:115–25.
66. Rahn DW. Lyme vaccine: issues and controversies. Infect Dis Clin North Am 2001;15:171–87.
67. Keller D, Koster FT, Marks DH, *et al.* Safety and immunogenicity of a recombinant outer surface protein A Lyme vaccine. JAMA 1994;271:1764–8.
68. Feder HM, Whitaker DL. Misdiagnosis of erythema migrans. Am J Med 1995;99:412–9.
69. Craft JE, Fisher DK, Shimamoto GT, Steere AC. Antigens of *B. burgdorferi* recognized during Lyme disease: appearances of a new immunoglobulin M response and expansion of the immunoglobulin G response late in the illness. J Clin Invest 1986;78:934–9.
70. Melchers W, Meis J, Rosa P, *et al.* Amplification of *Borrelia burgdorferi* DNA in skin biopsies from patients with Lyme disease. J Clin Microbiol 1991;29:2401–6.
71. Schmidt B, Muellegger RR, Stockenhuber C, *et al.* Detection of *Borrelia burgdorferi*-specific DNA in urine specimens from patients with erythema migrans before and after antibiotic therapy. J Clin Microbiol 1996;34:1359–63.
72. Dumler JS. Molecular diagnosis of Lyme disease: review and meta-analysis. Molec Diagnostics 2001;6:1–11.
73. Steere AC, Taylor E, McHugh GL, Logigian EL. The overdiagnosis of Lyme disease. JAMA 1993;269:1812–6.
74. Steere AC. Lyme disease. N Engl J Med 1989;321:586–96.
75. Blaauw AAM. Lyme arthritis in the Netherlands [thesis, Maastricht University], Maastricht. The Netherlands: University Press; 1993.
76. Massarotti EM, Luger SW, Rahn DW, *et al.* Treatment of early Lyme disease. Am J Med 1992;92:396–403.
77. Karlsson M, Hammers S, Nilsson-Ehle I, Malmborg AS, Wretlind B. Concentrations of doxycycline and penicillin G in sera and cerebrospinal fluid of patients treated for neuroborreliosis. Antimicrob Agents Chemother 1996;40:1104–7.
78. Johnson WD. *Borrelia* species (relapsing fever). In: Mandell GL, Bennett JE, Dolin R, eds. Mandell, Douglas and Bennett's principles and practice of infectious diseases, 4th ed. New York: Churchill Livingstone; 1995:2141–3.
79. Butler TC. Relapsing fever: new lessons about antibiotic action. Ann Intern Med 1985;102:397–9.
80. Emond R, Rowland H. Color atlas of infectious diseases, 3rd ed. London: Wolfe; 1995.
81. Faine S, ed. Guidelines for the control of leptospirosis. Geneva: World Health Organization; 1982.
82. Heath CW, Alexander AD, Galton MM. Leptospirosis in the United States. Analysis of 483 cases in man, 1949–1961. N Engl J Med 1965;273:915–22.
83. Feigin RD, Lobes LA, Anderson D, *et al.* Human leptospirosis from immunized dogs. Ann Intern Med 1973;79:777–85.
84. Levett PN Leptospirosis. Clin Microb Rev 2001;14:296–326.
85. Guidugli F, Castro AA, Atallah AN. Antibiotics for preventing leptospirosis (Cochrane Review). Cochrane Library, issue 1. Oxford: Update Software; 2002.
86. Farrar WE. *Leptospira* species (Leptospirosis). In: Mandell GL, Bennett JE, Dolin R, eds. Mandell, Douglas and Bennett's principles and practice of infectious diseases, 4th ed. New York: Churchill Livingstone; 1995:2137–41.
87. Smits HL, Ananyina YV, Chereshsky A, *et al.* International multicenter evaluation of the clinical utility of a dipstick assay for detection of Leptospira-specific immunoglobulin M antibodies in human serum specimens. J Clin Microbiol 1999;37(9):2904–9.
88. Brown PD, Gravekamp C, Carrington DG, *et al.* Evaluation of the polymerase chain reaction for early diagnosis of leptospirosis. J Med Microbiol 1995;43:110–4.
89. Kobayashi Y. Clinical observation and treatment of leptospirosis. J Infect Chemother 2001;7:59–68.
90. Arean VM. The pathologic anatomy and pathogenesis of fatal human leptospirosis (Well's disease). Am J Pathol 1962;40:393.
91. Johnson WD, Silva IC, Rocha H. Serum creatine phosphokinase in leptospirosis. JAMA 1975;233:981–2.
92. O'Neil KM, Rickman LS, Lazarus AA. Pulmonary manifestations of leptospirosis. Rev Infect Dis 1991;13:705–9.
93. Munnich D, Lakatos M. Treatment of human leptospira infections with Semicillin (ampicillin) or with Amoxil (amoxycillin). Chemotherapy 1973;20:113–9.
94. Takafuji ET, Kirkpatrick JW, Miller RN, *et al.* An efficacy trial of doxycycline chemoprophylaxis against leptospirosis. N Engl J Med 1984;310:497–500.
95. Marotto PC, Marotto MS, Santos DL, Souza TN, Seguro AC. Outcome of leptospirosis in children. Am J Trop Med Hyg 1997;56:307–10.
96. Roughgarden JW. Antimicrobial therapy for ratbite fever. Arch Intern Med 1965;116:39–54.
97. Breed RS, Murray EGD, Smith NR, *et al*, eds. Bergey's manual of determinative bacteriology, 7th ed. Baltimore: Williams and Wilkins; 1957.
98. Beeson PB. The problem of the aetiology of rat bite fever. JAMA 1943;123:332–334.
99. Frank L, Perlman H. Ratbite fever caused by Spirillum minus treated with penicillin. Arch Derm Syph 1948;57:261–3.
100. Burk SB, Hodas JH. Rat bite fever. Am J Surg 1943;60:453–4.
101. Hitzig WM, Liebesman A. Subacute endocarditis associated with a spirillum. Arch Intern Med 1994;73:415–24.
102. McIntosh CS, Vickers PJ, Isaacs AJ. Spirillum endocarditis. Postgrad Med J 1975;51:645–8.
103. Schwartzman G, Florman AL, Bass MH, Karelitz S, Richtberg D. Repeated recovery of a spirillum by blood culture from two children with prolonged and recurrent fevers. Pediatrics 1951;8:227–36.
104. Kowal J. Spirillum fever. N Engl J Med 1961;264:123–8.
105. Koneman EW, Allen SD, Janda WM, Schreckenberger PC, Winn WC, eds. In: Diagnostic microbiology, chapter 6. Curved Gram-negative bacilli and oxidase-positive fermenters: Campylobacteraceae and Vibronaceae. Lippincott-Raven, Philadelphia 1997:321–62.
106. Murray PR, Rosenthal KS, Kobayashi GS, Pfaller GS, eds. Medical microbiology, 3rd ed, chapter 31. Campylobacter and Helicobacter. Mosby, St Louis 1998:251–7.
107. Binford CH, Connor DH. Pathology of tropical and extraordinary diseases, vol 1. Washington DC: Armed Forces Institute of Pathology; 1976.
108. Speelman P, Kullberg BJ, Rietra PJGM, eds. Compendium infectieziekten. Utrecht: Bunge; 1996.

chapter

231 Gram-negative Coccobacilli

Mary PE Slack

INTRODUCTION

The Gram-negative coccobacilli that are important human pathogens include *Bordetella*, *Brucella*, *Francisella*, *Haemophilus*, *Legionella*, *Pasteurella* and *Yersinia* spp. *Actinobacillus*, *Cardiobacterium*, *Eikenella*, *Kingella* and *Moraxella* (*Branhamella*) spp. occasionally cause human disease. All of these genera except *Yersinia* are fastidious, requiring special nutrients and growth factors for isolation. *Yersinia* spp. are members of the Enterobacteriaceae and are not exacting in their growth requirements.

The genera *Brucella*, *Francisella*, *Pasteurella* and *Yersinia* cause zoonotic infections in humans. *Legionella* infections are acquired through exposure to environmental contamination. *Haemophilus* and most *Bordetella* infections arise through person-to-person transmission. Rarely *Bordetella bronchiseptica*, an animal pathogen, produces opportunistic human infections.

BORDETELLA SPECIES

NATURE

Bordetella spp. are minute Gram-negative coccobacilli. They often demonstrate bipolar staining. They may be nonmotile or motile by means of peritrichous flagella. They are strictly aerobic and the optimum temperature for growth is 95–98.6°F (35–37°C). No acid is produced from carbohydrates. There are seven species in the genus; these differ in their fastidiousness and growth requirements. *Bordetella pertussis* is the most exacting and requires special media for isolation. *Bordetella parapertussis* is slightly less exacting. *Bordetella bronchiseptica* and *Bordetella avium* will grow on ordinary laboratory media. *Bordetella pertussis* and *B. parapertussis* show homogenous clonality. *Bordetella avium* is a distinct species, the G + C content of its DNA being 62mol%, whereas the other species have a G + C content of 66–70mol%. The mol% of guanine and cytosine (G + C) bases in the DNA is the measurement of the genetic unrelatedness of bacterial species. The relatedness of the newly identified species *B. hinzii*, *B. holmesii* and *B. trematum* to *B. pertussis* has not yet been determined.

Bordetella pertussis and *B. parapertussis* are human pathogens of the respiratory tract causing pertussis or whooping cough. *B. bronchiseptica* and *B. avium* are primary respiratory tract pathogens of birds and mammals. *B. bronchiseptica*, *B. avium*, *B. hinzii*, *B. holmesii* and *B. trematum* may infrequently cause infection in humans, particularly in the immunocompromised host.

EPIDEMIOLOGY

Pertussis is highly contagious, being transmitted via aerosolized droplets of respiratory secretions, and in the prevaccine era nearly all children became infected between the ages of 1 and 5 years. Attack rates range from 50% for school contacts to 80–90% for close family contacts. Patients disseminate organisms for weeks or months and are highly infectious in the non-specific catarrhal and early paroxysmal stages of the infection. It is therefore easy for the infection to spread to susceptible individuals before the possibility of whooping cough is considered. There is little evidence of asymptomatic carriers.

Whooping cough is still a major disease worldwide and an important cause of death in malnourished children. It is estimated that there are over 51,000,000 cases each year worldwide and 600,000 deaths.[1] In most populations the disease is endemic, with epidemics occurring every 4 years in late winter and spring. There is no animal reservoir.

With the use of whole-cell pertussis vaccine the incidence of pertussis in children aged 1–5 years declines sharply but there is an increase in the incidence of the disease in children younger than 1 year. Unfortunately, these young children are those at greatest risk of morbidity and mortality from pertussis. Females are more likely to be infected than males.[2] Adults with waning vaccine-induced immunity are increasingly also suffering from pertussis, which often goes undiagnosed because the infection may be atypical. It has been suggested that up to 30% of adults with a prolonged cough may be suffering from pertussis.

There are three serotypes of *B. pertussis* pathogenic for humans, which contain agglutinins 1,2; 1,2,3; and 1,3. Strains may switch serotype both in vitro and in vivo. For this reason, a genotypic method of classification, based on techniques such as restriction fragment length polymorphism (RFLP) or pulsed-field gel electrophoresis (PFGE) is preferable.

PATHOGENICITY

Bordetella spp. possess a common cell wall somatic O antigen. There are 14 capsular polysaccharide types or factors. Factor 7 is found in all species of *Bordetella*. Factors 1–6 are specific to *B. pertussis*. Factor 1 is a lipo-oligosaccharide; it may be involved in attachment. Pertactin is an outer membrane protein that is also involved in adhesion. *Bordetella pertussis* produces a number of other factors that may play a part in pathogenesis[3,4] (Table 231.1).

Filamentous hemagglutinin is a protein that is involved in the binding of *B. pertussis* to receptors on respiratory cilia. Pertussis toxin is a four-polypeptide toxin with many biologic activities. It acts as a histamine-sensitizing factor and a lymphocytosis-promoting factor, enhances insulin secretion and is also a potent adjuvant. It is composed of two subunits, A and B. Subunit B mediates binding of the toxin and subunit A carries out the biologic activities of the toxin. Pertussis toxin acts by activating adenyl cyclase, which results in increased cyclic adenosine monophosphate (cAMP) in the host cell. The toxin is only expressed by *B. pertussis*. *Bordetella parapertussis* and *B. bronchiseptica* contain the toxin gene but it is not expressed. Adenylate cyclase toxin is an extracytoplasmic protein that can enter leukocytes. Once inside the cells, adenylate cyclase toxin is activated by calmodulin to catalyze the production of cAMP from adenosine triphosphate (ATP). The increased cAMP interferes with leukocyte function. Dermonecrotic toxin is a heat-labile toxin

VIRULENCE FACTORS OF *BORDETELLA PERTUSSIS*			
Toxin	**Synonyms**	**Composition**	**Action**
Filamentous hemagglutinin	FHA	Protein	Adhesion
Pertactin	PRN	Protein (outer membrane)	Adhesion
Pertussis toxin	PT	Protein	Activation of cAMP, HSF, LPF, IAP Impairs leukocyte function ?Adhesion
Adenylate cyclase toxin	ACT	Protein	Activation of cAMP Interference with leukocyte function Hemolytic
Dermonecrotic toxin	DNT, heat-labile toxin	Polypeptide	Vascular smooth muscle contraction Focal necrosis
Tracheal cytotoxin	TCT	Glycopeptide	Ciliostasis Inhibition of DNA synthesis Lethal to ciliated epithelial cells
Lipopolysaccharide	LPS	Lipopolysaccharide	Endotoxin
Agglutinogens	Fimbriae, FIM	Protein	Adhesion

Table 231.1 Virulence factors of *Bordetella pertussis*. With the exception of pertussis toxin, similar toxins are expressed in *B. parapertussis* and *B. bronchiseptica*. cAMP, cyclic adenosine monophosphate; HSF, histamine sensitizing factor; IAP, islet-activating protein; LPF, lymphocytosis promoting factor.

that can cause vascular smooth muscle contraction resulting in focal ischemic necrosis. Tracheal cytotoxin is a peptide derived from the bacterial peptidoglycan. It causes ciliostasis, inhibits DNA synthesis and kills ciliated epithelial cells, which are then sloughed off. The lipopolysaccharide (LPS) of *B. pertussis* probably also plays a part in pathogenicity.

Following inhalation, *B. pertussis* adheres to the ciliated epithelium of the trachea and bronchi. Adhesion is mediated by filamentous hemagglutinin, pertactin and possibly pertussis toxin. The bacilli then begin to multiply, producing pertussis toxin, which disrupts cell function; tracheal cytotoxin, which inhibits ciliary motion; and adenylate cyclase toxin, which interferes with phagocytosis. The dermonecrotic toxin causes local necrosis. The organisms remain localized on the respiratory epithelium. They do not invade.[5,6]

PREVENTION

Prevention of pertussis depends on immunization. The vaccines generally used are killed suspensions of whole bacterial cells adsorbed with aluminum hydroxide, which acts as an adjuvant and also results in fewer adverse reactions. The vaccine should be administered routinely to infants. To be effective the vaccine must contain all three agglutinogens, 1, 2 and 3. Pertussis vaccine was introduced into the UK during the 1950s and resulted in a steady decline in the size of pertussis epidemics until the mid-1970s.

Many concerns have been voiced about the safety of whole-cell vaccines and fears of possible neurologic sequelae. In the UK these fears resulted in a dramatic fall in the rate of vaccine uptake and three large epidemics of pertussis occurred in the late 1970s (Fig. 231.1). Since that time, parental confidence in the vaccine has gradually been restored and the number of cases has again declined. There is no strong evidence that whole-cell pertussis vaccine does produce long-term adverse effects but it may trigger the appearance of pre-existing neurologic problems. A severe adverse reaction to a previous dose of vaccine is a contraindication for further doses. Vaccination should be delayed in children who are unwell.

Acellular pertussis vaccines have been developed. They contain inactivated pertussis toxin and filamentous hemagglutinin. Some also contain fimbrial agglutinogen. Acellular vaccines are currently licensed and being used in the UK, USA, Japan, Germany and Italy. They appear to be safe and effective and may soon replace whole-

WHOOPING COUGH NOTIFICATIONS – CASES AND DEATHS

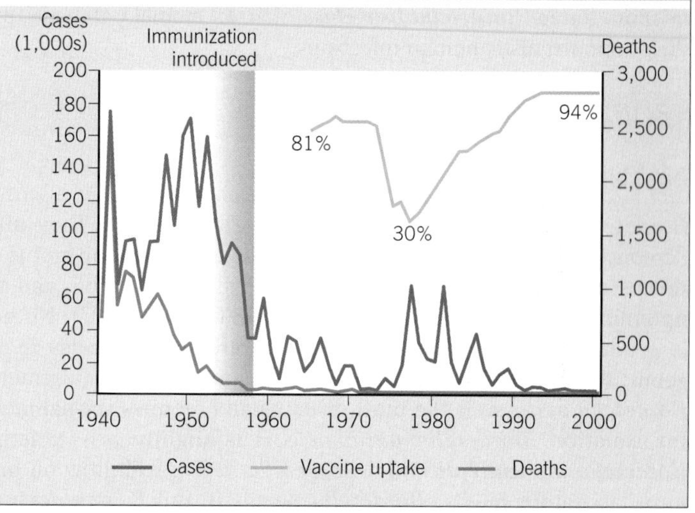

Fig. 231.1 Whooping cough notifications – cases and deaths. Figures are for England and Wales 1940–2000. Data supplied by the Public Health Laboratory Service Communicable Disease Surveillance Centre.

cell vaccines.[7,8] Because the incidence of pertussis in older children and adults is increasing there may be a case for using acellular pertussis vaccine to boost waning vaccine-induced immunity in older age groups.

DIAGNOSTIC MICROBIOLOGY

With careful sampling and culture techniques *B. pertussis* can be recovered for up to 3 months after the onset of the illness. Ideally, a flexible pernasal swab should be used to collect material. This is far superior to 'cough plates' and postnasal swabs. The material collected should be plated immediately on a suitable medium. If this is not possible it should be placed in a charcoal transport medium.[9] The traditional Bordet–Gengou agar, a potato infusion agar containing 10% glycerol and 20% sheep blood, has the disadvantage of a short shelf life. Better growth is obtained on charcoal blood agar, which can be made selective by the addition of cephalexin.

Fig. 231.2 Colonies of *Bordetella pertussis* on charcoal blood agar.

DIFFERENTIATION OF SPECIES OF *BORDETELLA* FOUND IN CLINICAL MATERIAL				
Species	**Growth on blood agar**	**Motility**	**Oxidase**	**Urease**
Bordetella pertussis	–	–	+	–
Bordetella parapertussis	+	–	–	+
Bordetella bronchiseptica	+	+	+	+

Table 231.2 Differentiation of species of *Bordetella* found in clinical material.

Cultures should be incubated in a moist aerobic atmosphere at 98.6°F (37°F) for at least 5 days. After 3–5 days of incubation, typical 'bisected pearl' colonies appear (Fig. 231.2). Suspect colonies should be checked by Gram-staining and identified using slide agglutination with type-specific antisera. *B. pertussis* and *B. parapertussis* can be differentiated by a series of simple tests (Table 231.2). *B. bronchiseptica* can be identified using a commercial galley test kit such as API 20NE.

Direct immunofluorescence can be applied to respiratory secretions to give a rapid diagnosis.[9] False-negative results may occur because of host antibody adsorbed to the organism. The sample must therefore be pretreated with enzymes. False-positive results may be obtained because of cross-reactions with other organisms such as staphylococci. A polymerase chain reaction (PCR) method may be used to improve the diagnosis of pertussis[10] and has the advantage that it can give a positive result even in the absence of viable organisms.

Immunoglobulin (Ig)M and IgG antibodies in serum or IgA in respiratory secretions can be assayed using an enzyme-linked immunosorbent assay (ELISA) technique. A diagnosis of whooping cough relies on a rising titer of IgG and IgM antibody in two samples collected at least 5 days apart, or a single raised level of IgM or IgG antibodies. However, the antibody response may be slow and weak, especially in young children. Cross-reactions with other organisms and the long-term persistence of pertussis antibodies can produce false-positive results.

CLINICAL MANIFESTATIONS

In a typical case, after an incubation period of 7–14 days, the patient develops red eyes, a runny nose, a mild cough and sneezing ('catarrhal stage'); this is a picture indistinguishable from many viral upper respiratory tract infections. After about 1 week the cough becomes more severe and the patient experiences paroxysmal bouts of a severe, hacking cough. A paroxysm consists of repeated coughing followed by an inspiratory gasp as the patient finally breathes in. This is the characteristic 'whoop'. Paroxysms may be triggered by a variety of stimuli, including cold air and loud noises. The child may become cyanosed during a paroxysm and can suffer fatal hypoxia. Often the child vomits at the end of a paroxysm and is left exhausted. The 'paroxysmal stage' may last for 1–4 weeks. This is followed by a lengthy 'convalescent stage' as the paroxysms decline and the patient slowly recovers. Many cases, but not all, develop a lymphocytosis. Pertussis is most severe in very young infants. In this age group the presentation may be atypical, with no characteristic paroxysmal whooping. Similarly, partially immunized children and adults may have an atypical form of pertussis.[11,12]

The principal complications of pertussis are secondary infections, notably pneumonia and otitis media, and mechanical damage, including subconjunctival hemorrhage and diaphragmatic herniation during paroxysms. Encephalopathy and fits may also occur.

Bordetella parapertussis is a cause of acute bronchitis or pertussis-like infections in children.[13]

Bordetella bronchiseptica may rarely cause pneumonia, meningitis or whooping cough in highly immunocompromised patients.[14]

MANAGEMENT

The most important aspect of management is supportive care, ensuring that the patient is adequately hydrated, oxygenated and fed. Erythromycin is the antibiotic of choice and appears to reduce the severity and duration of the disease. Trimethoprim–sulfamethoxazole (co-trimoxazole) is an alternative for older patients who are unable to tolerate erythromycin. Corticosteroids may be indicated in infants who have life-threatening disease. Secondary bacterial infections should be treated with appropriate antibiotics.

BRUCELLA SPECIES

NATURE

Brucella spp. are small, nonmotile, nonsporing, noncapsulated Gram-negative coccobacilli. They are aerobic, but some strains require 5–10% carbon dioxide for primary isolation. Growth on culture media is improved by the addition of serum or blood. Growth in vitro is slow and primary isolation may require up to 4 weeks incubation. *Brucella* spp. are catalase-positive but oxidase activity, urease activity and hydrogen sulfide production are variable. They are facultative intracellular parasites that infect a wide variety of domestic and wild animals. The G + C content of DNA is 58–59mol%. DNA–DNA hybridization shows more than 95% homology between all types of *Brucella*. They are to be regarded as a single species, *Brucella melitensis,* with multiple biovars. In practice it is more useful to refer to separate species, which have differing host specificities. Thus, there are six species of *Brucella*, four of which can infect humans (Table 231.3). *B. melitensis* is the most virulent and is responsible for the majority of human infections. Both *Brucella abortus* and *Brucella suis* cause considerable morbidity in countries where brucellosis persists in domestic animals.

EPIDEMIOLOGY

Brucella spp. can infect a wide variety of domestic and wild animals. Brucellosis is a true zoonosis because humans acquire the infection directly or indirectly from infected animals. About 500,000 cases of human brucellosis are reported annually worldwide but this almost certainly is a gross underestimate of the true incidence of the disease.

Brucellosis is prevalent in Mediterranean countries, the Middle East, the Gulf of Arabia, the Indian subcontinent and Central and South

SPECIES OF *BRUCELLA* PATHOGENIC TO MAN			
Species		Primary host	Humans as secondary host
Brucella abortus (biovars 1–6, 9)		Cattle	+
Brucella melitensis (biovars 1–3)		Goats, sheep, camels	+
Brucella suis	biovars 1–3	Pigs	+
	biovar 4	Reindeer	+
	biovar 5	Small rodents	+
Brucella canis		Dog, fox, coyote	+

Table 231.3 Species of *Brucella* pathogenic to humans.

America. Some countries have eradicated brucellosis, including the UK, much of northern Europe, Australia, New Zealand and Canada.

In their natural hosts, *Brucella* spp. tend to cause chronic infections that are mild or asymptomatic. The bacteria localize in the reproductive tissues of ruminants, which are rich in mesoerythritol. Erythritol stimulates the multiplication of *Brucella* spp. This accounts for the main symptoms of brucellosis in animals – sterility or abortion. Erythritol is not present in human tissue. *Brucella* spp. are shed in large numbers in the products of conception, in urine and in milk, and when the animals are slaughtered. Humans are infected either by direct contact with infected animals or animal products or indirectly by ingesting infected milk or dairy produce.

In endemic areas the majority of cases occur in dairymen, herdsmen, abattoir workers, butchers and veterinary surgeons. Children may become infected in rural areas of developing countries if they live in close proximity with domestic animals. The general public generally acquires the infection through the ingestion of unpasteurized milk and milk products such as fresh soft cheese. Case-to-case transmission in humans is very rare. Self-inoculation with live *Brucella* vaccine is a recognized risk among veterinary surgeons. Laboratory workers are at risk of acquiring brucellosis through the inhalation of aerosols.[15] This has occurred when handling as yet unidentified Gram-negative coccobacilli without adequate safety precautions.

Brucella melitensis is responsible for the majority of human infections and is primarily food-borne. The primary hosts for *B. melitensis* are sheep and goats. *Brucella abortus* and *B. suis* infections are generally sporadic and occur in people who work with cattle or pigs respectively.[16] *Brucella canis* infections are the least common in humans and are generally laboratory-acquired.

PATHOGENICITY

Brucella spp. are facultative intracellular parasites, surviving and multiplying within cells of the reticuloendothelial system. The organisms enter the body by inhalation, ingestion or after penetration of intact skin, abrasions or the conjunctival mucosa. The major virulence determinant is the LPS of smooth strains (S-LPS). Organisms possessing S-LPS are more resistant to killing by normal serum. Soon after entry into the body, the bacteria are ingested by polymorphonuclear and mononuclear phagocytes. Virulent *Brucella* spp. can survive and multiply within these cells by releasing AMP and guanine monophosphate (GMP), which inhibit the bactericidal myeloperoxidase–peroxide–halide system of the phagocytes. Other factors that contribute toward the intracellular survival of *Brucella* spp. are the production of copper–zinc superoxide dismutase, which prevents oxidative destruction, S-LPS and stress-induced proteins that promote survival within macrophages.[17,18]

After ingestion by phagocytes, the organisms proliferate in the local lymph nodes. The infection spreads hematogenously to tissues rich in elements of the reticuloendothelial system, including the liver, bone marrow, lymph nodes and spleen. Organisms may also localize in other tissues, including joints, the central nervous system, the heart and the kidneys.

In humans, *Brucella* spp. infection results in the formation of minute granulomata consisting of epithelioid cells, polymorphonuclear leukocytes, lymphocytes and some giant cells. In *B. melitensis* infections the granulomata are very small but there is often marked toxemia. *Brucella suis* is often accompanied by chronic abscess formation in joints and the spleen.

Endotoxin and hypersensitivity to *Brucella* antigens may cause some of the symptoms of brucellosis, including fever and weight loss. Antibodies against the *Brucella* LPS appear within a few days of the onset of the acute phase of the disease and are important in preventing re-infection. However, cell-mediated immunity, particularly the production of activated mononuclear phagocytes, is more important in promoting recovery.

Macrophages process *Brucella* antigens and present them to T cells, which excrete lymphokines, thus inactivating the bactericidal mechanisms of macrophages. The T-cell-derived lymphokines are also responsible for attracting cells to the foci of infection, resulting in the formation of granulomata. At the same time as the development of cell-mediated immunity, delayed-type hypersensitivity to numerous protein antigens can be demonstrated.

PREVENTION

The ideal method of prevention of human brucellosis is to eliminate the disease from domestic livestock. This has been achieved in several countries. An eradication campaign first focuses on mass vaccination of susceptible animals to reduce the incidence of brucellosis in domestic animals. *Brucella abortus* strain 19 vaccine is used for cattle and *B. melitensis* strain Rev-1 vaccine is used for sheep and goats. In the second phase of the campaign, infected animals are detected, using skin tests for sheep and serologic tests on milk or blood samples for cattle. Any infected animals must be compulsorily slaughtered, with financial compensation for their owners. The movement of animals must also be carefully controlled. All these measures require a program of effective education to ensure the co-operation of all those working with susceptible animals.

Where eradication has not been achieved, people who are occupationally exposed should minimize the risk of infection by wearing protective clothing, gloves, goggles and masks. These measures are particularly important when handling animals that have recently given birth or aborted.

In the past, live, attenuated animal vaccines have been given to workers at high risk of contracting brucellosis. However, these vaccines may produce infection in humans and therefore are far from ideal. Recent work on pure mutants of *B. melitensis* has given promising results in animals but clinical trials in humans have not been undertaken. *Brucella* spp. are killed after heating at 140°F (60°C) for 10 minutes. Boiling or pasteurizing milk will therefore eliminate the risk of transmission via dairy products.

Laboratory-acquired infections can be prevented by handling all cultures and material possibly infected with *Brucella* spp. in a containment level 3 laboratory and in a category I or III exhaust protective cabinet.

DIAGNOSTIC MICROBIOLOGY

A definitive diagnosis depends on the isolation of *Brucella* spp. from cultures of blood, bone marrow or tissue taken early in the disease. Bone marrow cultures are reported to give a slightly higher yield than peripheral blood cultures but, since modern blood culture methods can produce positive results in up to 80% of cases, bone marrow cultures are not generally required or advocated. Biphasic Castaneda bottles are traditionally recommended to reduce the risk of contamination during subculturing. Cultures should be incubated at 98.6°F (37°F) for at least 6 weeks before they are discarded. The modern semiautomated blood culture techniques (e.g. Bactec®, Bact-Alert®) are suitable for the isolation of *Brucella* spp. and are in use in many diagnostic laboratories. The lysis centrifugation method also gives good results. These commercial systems may give positive results in a matter of days rather than weeks, depending on the initial inoculum of organisms in the sample.

Positive cultures should be subcultured onto serum dextrose agar or a similar medium. Selective culture media are not necessary for human blood cultures but may be required for contaminated material. *Brucella* spp. produce small, smooth, translucent colonies after 48 hours of incubation at 98.6°F (37°C) in air plus 5–10% carbon dioxide.[19] The identity of the organisms can be confirmed by agglutination with monospecific antisera and lysis by specific Tbilisi bacteriophage.

Commercial galley-test identification systems may misidentify *Brucella* spp. as *Moraxella phenylpyruvica*,[15] and isolates should be sent to a reference laboratory for further tests to determine the biovar of the strain. This classification is based on the production of hydrogen sulfide and the tolerance of the organism to the bacteriostatic dyes basic fuchsin and thionin.

A PCR for diagnosing brucellosis has been described but awaits standardization and evaluation.[20] Antigen detection is another potential diagnostic tool.

Many serologic tests have been described for brucellosis. Interpretation of results is often difficult since both IgG and IgM antibodies can persist for a long time. A sample of serum should be collected as early as possible in the course of the disease. The serum agglutination test (SAT) using *B. abortus* strain 119 is widely used. False-negative results can occur if serum samples are not diluted beyond 1:320, owing to a prozone phenomenon. False-positive reactions have also been reported owing to cross-reactivity with strains of *Escherichia coli*, *Vibrio cholerae*, *Yersinia enterocolitica* and *Francisella tularensis*. The SAT measures both IgM and IgG. To measure the quantity of specific IgG the serum is treated with 2-mercaptoethanol to inactivate IgM. The SAT will not detect antibodies to *B. canis*. Enzyme-linked immunosorbent assay has the advantage that it can quantify IgM, IgG and IgA antibodies. Immunoglobulin G and IgA antibodies seem to be the best indicators of acute infection. A rise in antibody titer is observed in more than 97% of patients who have acute brucellosis and positive blood cultures. An initial IgM antibody response is followed after 1–2 weeks by a rise in IgG. During recovery the IgG antibody titers slowly decline over a period of months but IgM antibodies may persist at a low level in the serum for several years. Sustained IgG antibody titers or a second rise in IgG antibody levels are seen in chronic infection or relapse. Immunoblotting analysis of *Brucella* cytoplasmic antigens may be a way of differentiating active infection from past infection.[21,22]

CLINICAL MANIFESTATIONS (see also Chapter 180)

Brucellosis is a systemic infection that can affect any tissue of the body. The protean, vague clinical symptoms are generally not specific for brucellosis.[23] The possibility of brucellosis should be considered in any fever of unknown origin, especially in patients who have occupational exposure or have recently traveled in endemic areas.

In about 50% of cases, the onset is acute following an incubation period of 2–8 weeks. An acute presentation is more commonly seen with *B. melitensis* than with the other species. The patient develops 'flu-like' symptoms of headache, myalgia, anorexia, depression, sweats, weight loss and fever. The fever often shows diurnal variation

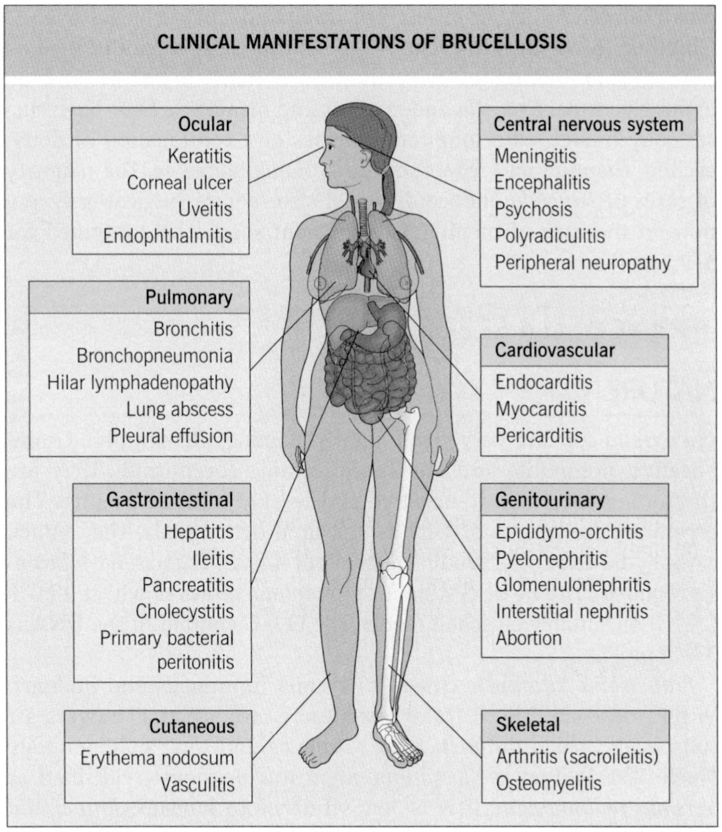

Fig. 231.3 Clinical manifestations of brucellosis.

and may come and go over a few weeks or months if the patient is untreated. This 'undulant' fever pattern is not invariably seen. On examination the patient may have hepatosplenomegaly and lymphadenopathy. The white cell count is often raised and liver function tests may be abnormal.

Some patients present with focal or localized infections (Fig. 231.3). Almost any organ of the body can be involved. Given this myriad of clinical features the only unequivocal way of diagnosing brucellosis is to isolate the organism from blood or tissue cultures (see above).

With appropriate treatment the majority of patients will recover within a few weeks or months. Relapses of infection are, however, fairly common. In some patients the symptoms persist for 12 months or more. This is called chronic brucellosis, an ill-defined condition in which a definitive diagnosis is often elusive. It is usually due to the persistence of a deep-seated focus of infection in a bone, joint, kidney, liver or spleen. Chronic brucellosis has similar features to the chronic fatigue syndrome. Typically, the patient suffers from malaise, depression and a fever, which comes and goes in 2- or 3-week cycles.

MANAGEMENT

Before the introduction of antibiotics, brucellosis was a chronic, relapsing illness. A number of antimicrobial agents are active against *Brucella* spp. in vitro but they are not always clinically effective. *Brucella* spp. tend to be sequestered intracellularly, so agents that achieve adequate intracellular concentrations should be used. It is also necessary to give a prolonged course of treatment to reduce the rate of relapsing infection (see also Chapter 180).

Treatment with doxycycline and rifampin (rifampicin) for 6 weeks is recommended for treating acute brucellosis in adults. Doxycycline plus streptomycin (or gentamicin) is an alternative and may result in fewer relapses. The combination of a quinolone, such as ofloxacin, plus rifampin looks promising but awaits adequate clinical trials.[24] Children, in whom tetracyclines are contraindicated, can be treated with a combination of trimethoprim–sulfamethoxazole and an aminoglycoside. *Brucella* endocarditis and meningitis have been successfully treated with long-term courses of a combination of doxycycline, rifampin and trimethoprim–sulfamethoxazole. The majority of cases of *Brucella* endocarditis will also require surgical intervention. In the case of meningitis, treatment should be continued for 6–9 months.

FRANCISELLA SPECIES

NATURE

Francisella spp. are very small, faintly staining, pleomorphic Gram-negative, nonmotile and non-spore-forming coccobacilli. They are strictly aerobic, oxidase-negative and weakly catalase-positive. The organisms are surrounded by a thin, lipid-rich capsule. They attack carbohydrates slowly, producing acid but no gas. *Francisella tularensis* requires cysteine or cystine for growth and grows slowly at 98.6°F (37°C) on suitably enriched media. The G + C content of the DNA is 33–36mol%.

Francisella tularensis causes tularemia in animals and humans. Within the species *F. tularensis* there are several biovars or subspecies, which differ in their virulence and their epidemiology (Table 231.4). *Francisella philomiragia* was previously classified as *Yersinia philomiragia*. It is of low virulence to humans. *Francisella tularensis* biogroup *novicida* causes infections in laboratory animals but is of low virulence for humans.

EPIDEMIOLOGY

Francisella tularensis is distributed throughout the world but the majority of human infections occur in the northern hemisphere between latitudes 30° and 71°. It is well recognized in North America, Scandinavia and Russia. It has not been described in the UK. The organism is found in many species of wild and domestic animals, birds, fish and blood-sucking arthropods.

In the USA the most important reservoirs of *F. tularensis* are rabbits, hares, muskrats and ticks. In Scandinavia and Russia, rodents (such as voles and mice) and mosquitoes are important reservoirs. The modes of transmission to humans include tick or mosquito bites, contact with infected animal tissues, inhalation of an infectious aerosol or ingestion of contaminated meat or water. There is an increased risk of tularemia in certain occupations that bring people into contact with infected material.

There are approximately 200 cases each year reported in the USA, with over 50% occurring in the southern and southern–central states of Missouri, Oklahoma, Arkansas, Texas and Kansas. Most infections occur in males. There are more cases in summer (when there is a greater risk of exposure to biting insects) and in winter when animals are hunted and trapped.[25,26]

PATHOGENICITY

The infectious dose in humans depends on the route of entry. It can be as low as 10–50 organisms when inoculated through the skin or by inhalation. The infecting dose rises to 10^8 when the organisms are ingested. In most cases infection follows an insect bite or contact with infected animal products. Laboratory workers are at high risk through handling infected laboratory animals or cultures of the organism. *Francisella tularensis* is a hazard group 3 pathogen. *Francisella tularensis* biogroup *tularensis* is more virulent to animals and humans than biogroups *palearctica* and *novicida*.

After entry into the body, the organisms spread to the regional lymph nodes, from where they may disseminate via the lymphatic system or bloodstream to involve multiple organs. There is probably a transient bacteremia at this early stage. In affected animals large numbers of bacilli are present in the cells of the liver and the spleen. Focal necrosis occurs in affected tissue and granulomata may develop. The granulomata may sometimes caseate, giving an appearance similar to tuberculosis.

Francisella tularensis is a facultative intracellular parasite and can survive for prolonged periods within macrophages, hepatocytes and endothelial cells. Intracellular survival is associated with a failure of phagosome–lysosome fusion. Recovery from tularemia depends on cell-mediated immunity, which is directed against the protein antigens of the organism. The bacilli are protected from humoral antibodies, which are directed against carbohydrate antigens.[27]

Pathogenic strains of *F. tularensis* possess an antiphagocytic capsule. Loss of the capsule results in decreased virulence. Like other Gram-negative bacilli, *F. tularensis* has endotoxin activity.

PREVENTION

Prevention of tularemia is best achieved by avoiding exposure to the organism. Gloves, masks and goggles should be worn when skinning or eviscerating animals. Animals that look sick should be left intact. Game meat should be thoroughly cooked and fresh water that is possibly contaminated should not be drunk. Ticks should be promptly removed and chemical insect repellants may be used.

A live attenuated vaccine that induces both humoral and cell-mediated immunity is available for high-risk groups such as laboratory staff working on *F. tularensis*.[28] Live attenuated vaccine must be administered by scarification and does not induce complete protection but will reduce the severity of accidental infection. New tularemia vaccines based on individual components of *F. tularensis* are currently being developed and are attracting considerable interest, since *F. tularensis* is a potential biologic weapon.[29]

DIAGNOSTIC MICROBIOLOGY

Isolation of *F. tularensis* from clinical material is potentially hazardous and it is imperative that the laboratory is notified if tularemia is suspected so that appropriate containment precautions can be

FRANCISELLA SPECIES AND BIOGROUPS					
Species	**Biogroup**	**Synonyms**	**Virulence in humans**	**Virulence in rabbits**	**Main animal hosts**
Francisella tularensis	*tularensis*	Type A neoarctica	+++	+++	Rabbits, hares, ground squirrels
F. tularensis	*palearctica*	Type B holoarctica	++	+	Rodents, beavers, muskrats
F. tularensis	*novicida*	(formerly *F. novicida*)	+	+	Rodents, rabbits
F. philomiragia		(formerly *Yersinia philomiragia*)	+	?	Muskrats

Table 231.4 *Francisella* species and biogroups. All the groups listed are found in North America; *Francisella tularensis* biogroup *palearctica* is also found in Asia and Europe.

taken. *Francisella tularensis* is a category 3 pathogen and should only be knowingly handled in a containment level 3 facility and in a class I or class III exhaust protective cabinet by trained and experienced staff.

The detection of *F. tularensis* in a Gram-stained smear of aspirates or other samples is rarely successful. Direct immunofluorescence of tissue smears is more sensitive and specific. A PCR method has been described that can be applied to blood samples. However, this does not appear to be any more sensitive than culture.

The organism requires cysteine or cystine for growth. Specialized media such as cysteine–glucose–blood agar have been devised, but *F. tularensis* will grow on some media that are routinely used for other organisms. Chocolate blood agar is often supplemented with cysteine (e.g. IsoVitaleX) and will then support the growth of *F. tularensis*. Similarly, *F. tularensis* will grow on buffered charcoal yeast extract agar (BCYE), which is normally used to isolate *Legionella* spp. Occasionally, strains of *F. tularensis* will grow on ordinary laboratory media. It is therefore imperative to warn the laboratory if tularemia is suspected to ensure that proper containment precautions are taken when processing the specimens.

Cultures should be incubated at 98.6°F (37°F) with additional carbon dioxide in the atmosphere of incubation. *Francisella tularensis* grows slowly, taking 3–5 days to produce visible colonies, and cultures should be incubated for 3 weeks before being discarded as negative. The addition of penicillin to the medium will suppress the overgrowth of contaminants.

Colonies of *F. tularensis* are blue–gray, round, smooth and somewhat mucoid. They are α-hemolytic on blood-containing media. A slide agglutination method using commercial antiserum or a fluorescent antibody technique can be used to confirm the identity of the organism. Biochemical tests are of little value. Further subspeciation should only be undertaken in a reference laboratory.

However, most cases of tularemia are diagnosed serologically. An agglutination test using killed *F. tularensis* antigen is generally used. A 4-fold rise in antibody titer or a single titer of more than 1:160 is considered diagnostic. Immunoglobulin G and IgM antibodies can persist for months or years and it may be very difficult to distinguish past from current infection. Infections with *Brucella* spp., *F. novicida* and *F. philomiragia* can give rise to antibodies that cross-react with *F. tularensis*. An ELISA test has been described.

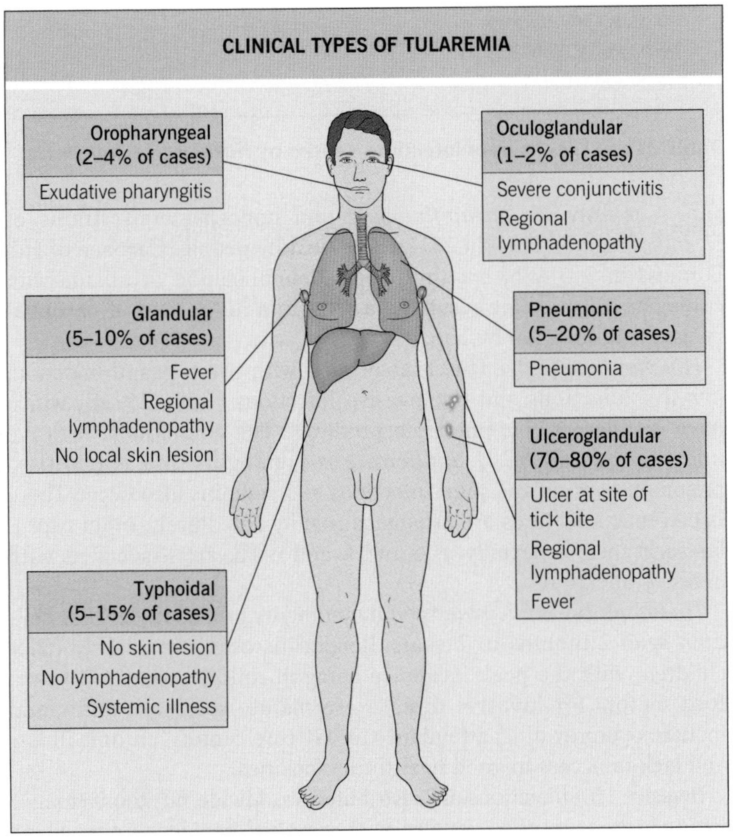

Fig. 231.4 Clinical types of tularemia.

CLINICAL MANIFESTATIONS

The clinical manifestations of *F. tularensis* infection depend on the portal of entry, the virulence of the infecting organism and the immune status of the individual host. After 3–5 days of incubation the patient develops an abrupt onset of flu-like symptoms – fever, chills, malaise, anorexia and tiredness. The cases are classified clinically into six types, based on the site of the infection and the presence of skin lesions and lymphadenopathy. This division is somewhat artificial because there is considerable overlap between the types (Fig. 231.4) (see Chapter 177).[30]

The most common presentation is ulceroglandular tularemia, which accounts for 70–85% of cases. The patient has a painful red papular skin lesion at the site of entry of the organism, which proceeds to ulcerate with regional lymphadenopathy. There is an accompanying systemic illness with fever, headache, sweating and myalgia. In oculoglandular tularemia (1–2% of cases) the organisms are inoculated via the conjunctival route, resulting in a severe conjunctivitis and regional lymphadenopathy. Oropharyngeal tularemia (2–4%) occurs when the primary invasion is via the oropharynx. There is a severe exudative pharyngitis and regional lymphadenopathy.

In some cases there is regional lymphadenopathy and no local skin lesion. This glandular form of tularemia occurs in 5–10% of cases. Other cases present with a systemic illness but no local skin lesions or lymphadenopathy. This typhoidal form of tularemia accounts for 5–15% of cases. Many of these patients have serious underlying illnesses and the infection may follow an acutely fulminating course. Pneumonic tularemia (5–20% of cases) may follow inhalation of contaminated aerosols or may occur as a complication of bacteremic dissemination of organisms in any of the other groups.

The severity of the infection is highly variable and ranges from a mild afebrile or asymptomatic self-limiting infection to fulminant sepsis. Milder cases are often associated with biogroup *palearctica* infections.

Tularemia may result in chronic debility lasting for several months, with fatigue and suppuration of infected lymph nodes. The overall mortality rate is 1–3% with antimicrobial treatment, but typhoidal tularemia and secondary pneumonic tularemia carry a higher morbidity and mortality.[31]

Francisella tularensis biogroup *novicida* infection results in a milder form of tularemia. *Francisella philomiragia* may cause pneumonia, sepsis and meningitis in patients with underlying conditions, including chronic granulomatous disease, myeloproliferative disorders or near-drowning in salt water.

MANAGEMENT

Streptomycin remains the drug of first choice for treating all forms of tularemia. Gentamicin is an acceptable alternative.[25] Tetracycline and chloramphenicol have been used to treat infections but both are bacteriostatic for *F. tularensis* and there is a high rate of relapse when these agents are used. *Francisella tularensis* produces a β-lactamase, and β-lactamase-stable β-lactams, such as cefotaxime, ceftriaxone and imipenem, may be of use, although they have not been fully evaluated. Other potentially useful but unproven agents include erythromycin and fluoroquinolones such as ciprofloxacin (see Chapter 177).[31]

SPECIES OF *HAEMOPHILUS* ASSOCIATED WITH INFECTION OF HUMANS									
Species	Requirement for			Hemolysis	Acid from				
	X factor	V factor	CO_2		Glucose	Sucrose	Lactose	Mannose	Xylose
H. influenzae	+	+	–	–	+	–	–	–	+
H. influenzae biogroup *aegyptius*	+	+	–	–	+	–	–	–	+
H. haemolyticus	+	+	–	+	+	–	–	–	±
H. parainfluenzae	–	+	–	–	+	+	–	+	–
H. parahaemolyticus	–	+	–	+	+	+	–	–	–
H. aphrophilus	h	–	+	–	+	+	+	+	–
H. paraphrophilus	–	+	+	–	+	+	+	+	–
H. segnis	–	+	–	–	w	w	–	–	–
H. ducreyi	+	–	–	–	–	–	–	–	–

Table 231.5 Species of *Haemophilus* associated with infections of humans. h, requires hemin for primary isolation; w, weak reaction.

HAEMOPHILUS SPECIES

NATURE

Haemophilus spp. are small, pleomorphic, nonmotile, nonsporing Gram-negative rods or coccobacilli. They are aerobic and facultatively anaerobic. Growth is often enhanced by the addition of 5–10% carbon dioxide to the incubation atmosphere. The oxidase and catalase reactions vary among the species. *Haemophilus* spp. require one or both of two accessory growth factors (X and V). X factor can be provided by hemin, protoporphyrin IX or other iron-containing porphyrins. X-dependent *Haemophilus* spp. cannot synthesize protoporphyrin from δ-aminolevulinic acid, a process involving several enzyme-mediated steps, some or all of which may be defective. V factor is nicotinamide adenine dinucleotide (NAD) or NAD phosphate or certain unidentified precursors of these compounds. It is essential for oxidation–reduction processes.

The differential requirements for X and V factors are important criteria for defining *Haemophilus* spp., which are obligate parasites of humans and animals. There are eight species of *Haemophilus* associated with infections in humans (Table 231.5). *Haemophilus influenzae* is the major human pathogen in the group. Some strains of *H. influenzae* have a polysaccharide capsule, of which there are six distinct antigenic types, designated a–f. The most important is type b, which has a capsule consisting of polyribosyl ribitol phosphate (PRP). *Haemophilus influenzae* type b (Hib) strains are associated with the majority of invasive infections.

Haemophilus influenzae biogroup *aegyptius* (formerly *Haemophilus aegyptius*) is a cause of epidemic conjunctivitis and Brazilian purpuric fever. *Haemophilus ducreyi* is the causative agent of chancroid. *Haemophilus aphrophilus*, *H. paraphrophilus* and *H. parainfluenzae* are occasionally implicated in infective endocarditis and in brain and liver abscesses.

The genus *Haemophilus* is a member of the family Pasteurellaceae, which also encompasses the genera *Pasteurella* and *Actinobacillus*. The G + C content of DNA in *Haemophilus* spp. is 37–44mol%.

EPIDEMIOLOGY

Haemophilus influenzae is an obligate parasite of human mucous membranes; it is not found in any other animal species. It colonizes the throat and nasopharynx, and to a lesser extent the conjunctivae and genital tract. The respiratory tract is colonized by *Haemophilus* spp. – mainly *H. parainfluenzae* and noncapsulated strains of *H. influenzae* (ncHi) – in 25–75% of healthy people. Carriage of Hib is found in 3–5% of healthy people. Immunization of infants with conjugate Hib vaccine results in a reduction in the rate of nasopharyngeal colonization by Hib.[32]

SPECTRUM OF INFECTIONS CAUSED BY *HAEMOPHILUS INFLUENZAE*		
Infections	Age group affected	Strains
1. Invasive infections: Meningitis Epiglottitis Pneumonia Septic arthritis Osteomyelitis Cellulitis Bacteremia	90% children <4 years old 10% older children and adults	90% type b 10% ncHi 1% types e, f
2. Neonatal and maternal sepsis	Neonates Parturient mothers	Over 90% ncHi
3. Noninvasive respiratory infections, otitis media, sinusitis, conjunctivitis, acute exacerbations of chronic bronchitis	Children and adults	Over 90% ncHi

Table 231.6 Spectrum of infections caused by *Haemophilus influenzae*.

Haemophilus influenzae is associated with two types of infection, invasive infections and noninvasive infections (Table 231.6), which have distinctive epidemiologic profiles.[33] The commonest invasive infection caused by *H. influenzae* is meningitis, but epiglottitis, pneumonia, bone and joint infections and cellulitis also occur. These bacteremic infections are usually caused by Hib. Rarely, other capsular serotypes, especially a, e and f, and ncHi, are associated with invasive infections.

Haemophilus influenzae type b meningitis principally affects children aged 2 months to 2 years. Epiglottitis occurs in slightly older children, with the peak incidence being in children aged 2–3 years. Risk factors for invasive disease are mainly socio-economic and include overcrowding, attendance at day care centers, chronic illness and lack of access to good health care facilities.

Invasive Hib infections are distributed worldwide but the incidence varies from country to country with very high incidence rates being found in certain racial groups, for example Apache and Navajo Native

ANNUAL INCIDENCE OF *HAEMOPHILUS INFLUENZAE* TYPE b MENINGITIS	
Country	**Incidence**
England	25
Finland	26
USA (Texas, North Carolina, Maryland, California)	19–69
Australia (New South Wales, Victoria)	20–25
Hong Kong Chinese	2.7
Gambia	60
Alaskan Inuit	282
Apache Native Americans	254
Australian Aborigines	454

Table 231.7 Annual incidence of *Haemophilus influenzae* type b meningitis. Figures for incidence per 100,000 children under the age of 5 years and are from various countries and ethnic groups prior to the introduction of routine immunization.

Americans, Alaskan Inuit and Australian Aborigines (Table 231.7).[34] In these racial groups the peak incidence of infection occurs at a younger age. By contrast, a very low incidence rate has been reported in Hong Kong Chinese. There is seasonal variation, with most cases occurring in the winter months.

The introduction of vaccines effective against Hib in infants has dramatically reduced the incidence of invasive disease in children in countries using this vaccine, and consequently the epidemiology is changing.

The noninvasive infections of the respiratory tract associated with *H. influenzae* include otitis media, sinusitis, acute exacerbations of chronic bronchitis and conjunctivitis. The majority of these infections are caused by ncHi and many occur in adults. There is often an underlying physiologic or anatomic abnormality. These infections have a worldwide distribution and all of them are more common in the winter months.

Haemophilus influenzae biogroup *aegyptius* is associated with an acute form of seasonal conjunctivitis and septicemia (Brazilian purpuric fever) in hot climates; these conditions occur in children.[35]

PATHOGENICITY

Haemophilus influenzae is transmitted by aerosols of respiratory secretions or by direct contact with contaminated material. The primary event is colonization of the nasopharynx. Prior infection with respiratory viruses (e.g. influenza) promotes colonization and subsequent infection by *Haemophilus* spp. The microbial factors that promote colonization include fimbriae, LPS, IgA1 protease and a ciliotoxin.[36] Noninvasive infections of the respiratory tract result from contiguous spread of organisms colonizing the respiratory tract. Acute sinusitis, otitis media and acute exacerbations of chronic bronchitis usually follow a viral infection. This predisposes to secondary infection with potentially pathogenic components of the local resident bacterial flora by mechanisms including obstruction to the outflow of respiratory secretions, depression of local immunity and suppression of mucociliary clearance. The majority of these infections are caused by ncHi. Possession of the outer membrane protein P2 is an important virulence factor for ncHi. Immunoglobulin A1 protease and ciliotoxin appear to be important in the pathogenesis of pneumonia.

Invasive infections, notably meningitis and epiglottitis, are mainly caused by Hib and result from invasion of the bloodstream. The pathogenesis of these infections has been elegantly elucidated using an infant rat model.[37] The capsule of type b *H. influenzae* is the single most important determinant of virulence for invasion because it protects the organism from phagocytosis and complement-mediated lysis. The rarity of infections in the first 2 months of life correlates with the presence of maternal antibodies to PRP and the occurrence of infection in early infancy with the absence of antibodies having such specificity. As the mean level of PRP antibodies in the population rises, so Hib infections become less common. It is unclear whether natural antibody production is stimulated by exposure to Hib or to some other organism (e.g. *E. coli* K100) that possesses cross-reacting antigens.

Brazilian purpuric fever is caused by a single clone of *H. influenzae* biogroup *aegyptius*.[35] The LPS phenotype is a critical determinant of virulence for *H. influenzae* biogroup *aegyptius*.

PREVENTION

Vaccination

Conjugate vaccines have now been developed in which the PRP is covalently linked to a protein carrier (Table 231.8).[38] These vaccines produce a lasting anamnestic response, which is not age-related. They can be given effectively to infants as young as 2 months of age and are also effective in high-risk groups of patients who give a poor response to polysaccharide vaccines. The Hib vaccine can be given concurrently with diphtheria–tetanus–pertussis immunization. In the UK, Hib vaccine is thus administered at 2, 3 and 4 months of age. Most countries except the UK and the Republic of Ireland give a booster dose in the second year of life. Countries where Hib vaccine is routinely offered have witnessed a dramatic decline in the occurrence of Hib infections (Fig. 231.5).[39,40]

Administration of Hib conjugate vaccine has the important additional effect of reducing nasopharyngeal colonization with Hib.[34]

Haemophilus influenzae type b vaccine is recommended after splenectomy, or for patients who have functional asplenia, together with pneumococcal vaccine and meningococcal vaccine.

There is as yet no effective vaccine for ncHi infections.

CONJUGATE *HAEMOPHILUS INFLUENZAE* TYPE B (Hib) VACCINES			
Scientific name	**Product name**	**Carbohydrate**	**Protein carrier**
PRP-T	Act Hib (Aventis Pasteur) Infanrix Hib (Glaxo SmithKline)	PRP	Tetanus toxoid
HbOC	Hib TITER (Wyeth)	Oligosaccharide	Nontoxic mutant diphtheria toxin (CRM_{197})
PRM–OMPC	Pedvax HIB (Merck)	PRP	*Neisseria meningitidis* group B outer membrane protein complex
PRP-D	ProHIBit (Connaught)	PRP	Diphtheria toxoid

Table 231.8 Conjugate *Haemophilus influenzae* type b (Hib) vaccines.

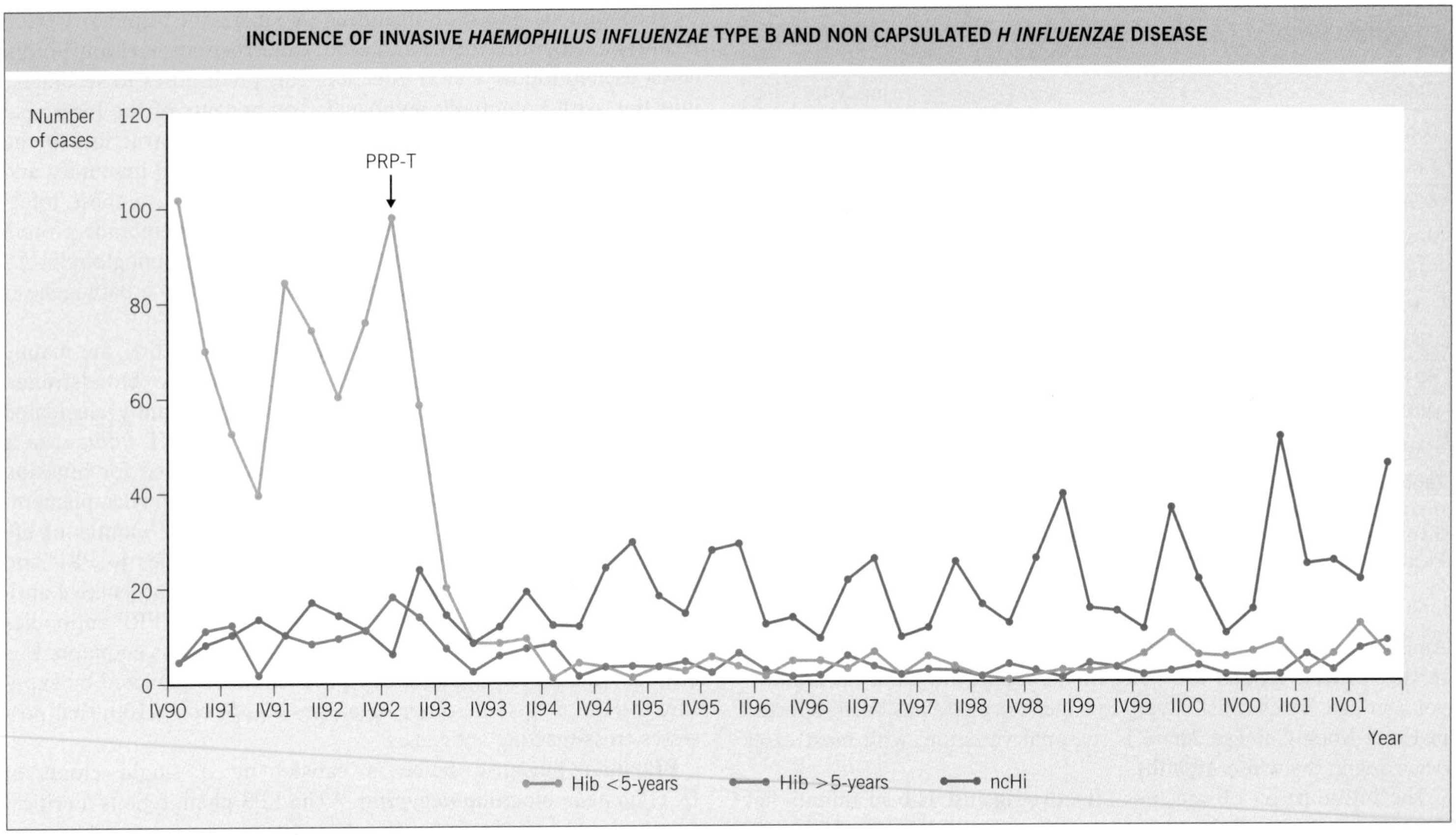

Fig. 231.5 Incidence of invasive *Haemophilus influenzae* type b and noncapsulated *H. influenzae* disease. Figures are for the period from October 1990 to June 1997 in England.

Chemoprophylaxis

Oral rifampin for 4 days is recommended for eradicating carriage of *H. influenzae* and has been used to prevent secondary infection in household and nursery contacts. Its efficacy is unproven. Unvaccinated siblings of a case who are more than 4 years old and less than 10 years old should be immunized with Hib conjugate vaccine. Unvaccinated siblings less than 4 years old should be offered both chemoprophylaxis and vaccine. Children less than 4 years of age who have invasive Hib disease should also be offered both vaccine and chemoprophylaxis in order to eliminate nasopharyngeal carriage, because disease sometimes fails to induce immunity in the very young. Widespread use of the vaccine may soon render chemoprophylaxis unnecessary.

DIAGNOSTIC MICROBIOLOGY

Gram-stained smears of cerebrospinal fluid, pus, sputum or aspirates from joints, middle ear or sinuses may provide a rapid diagnosis. *Haemophilus influenzae* tends to stain poorly and dilute carbol fuchsin is a better counterstain than neutral red or safranin.

Rapid tests for Hib capsular antigens, such as latex agglutination or a PCR-based method, can be applied to clinical material. False-positive latex agglutination results have been reported in cerebrospinal fluid samples collected from children who had recently received Hib vaccine.

Specimens should be plated on appropriate culture media as soon as possible. Chocolate agar is the most commonly used medium for culturing *Haemophilus* spp. It can be used without further supplementation for specimens from normally sterile sites. The addition of bacitracin to chocolate agar will assist the recovery of *H. influenzae* from respiratory samples because it will suppress the growth of other respiratory organisms.[41] Good growth can also be obtained on certain transparent media that contain blood extracts (e.g. Levinthal's agar or Fildes peptic digest agar).

The cultures should be incubated at 98.6°F (37°C) in an aerobic atmosphere enriched with 5–10% carbon dioxide. After 24 hours of incubation, colonies of ncHi are small, circular, smooth and pale gray. Capsulated strains produce somewhat larger, mucoid colonies, which have a characteristic seminal odor. On clear media, such as Levinthal's agar, colonies of capsulated strains exhibit iridescence when viewed obliquely with transmitted light. Type b capsulated strains can also be detected by the presence of precipitin haloes on transparent media containing hyperimmune Hib antiserum.

Confirmation of the identity of colonies depends on demonstrating a requirement for X factor, V factor, or both. This is usually performed as a disk test. The culture is plated onto a nutrient agar that is deficient in both X and V factor, and paper disks containing X factor alone, V factor alone, and both X and V factors are placed on the surface of the agar. After overnight incubation, growth is observed around the disks supplying the required growth factors (Fig. 231.6).

Haemophilus influenzae strains should be typed to determine their capsular serotype. This is normally carried out by slide agglutination using type-specific antisera. This method is prone to misinterpretation, with problems of autoagglutination, cross-reacting antisera and observer error. The definitive method of typing *H. influenzae* is capsular genotyping using a PCR-based method.

CLINICAL MANIFESTATIONS

Invasive infections

Meningitis is the commonest and most serious manifestation of systemic infection with *H. influenzae* (see Table 231.6). It is a disease of infants, principally between the ages of 2 months and 2 years.

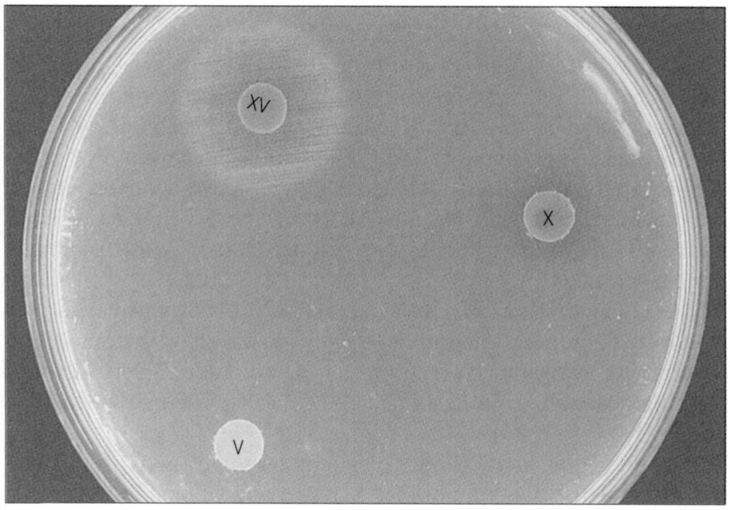

Fig. 231.6 Growth factor requirement of *Haemophilus influenzae*. Strain of *H. influenzae* sown on Columbia agar plate. Filter paper disks containing X factor, V factor, and both X and V factors have been placed on the surface of inoculated plate, but colonies of *H. influenzae* grow only around the disk with both X and V factors.

There is often a history of a preceding viral upper respiratory tract infection or otitis media. There are no clinical features that distinguish *Haemophilus* meningitis from other forms of bacterial meningitis. Up to 20% of survivors of *Haemophilus* meningitis have long-term neurologic sequelae – notably sensorineural deafness. *Haemophilus* meningitis can also occur in neonates,[42] older children and adults. In neonates the causative organism is almost invariably ncHi and the presentation can resemble group B streptococcal sepsis. In adults the infection may be secondary to head injury, neurosurgery, chronic sinusitis or mastoiditis. Both ncHi and Hib may be responsible.[43]

Epiglottitis is a life-threatening infection that is almost always caused by Hib. It occurs in slightly older children, aged 2–5 years, with a peak incidence in those aged 2–3 years. Typically there is a rapid onset of sore throat, fever and dyspnea, which may progress to airway obstruction requiring emergency tracheostomy and ventilation. Examination of the larynx is potentially hazardous because it may provoke respiratory obstruction. The diagnosis should be based on the clinical findings confirmed by blood culture results (see also Chapter 31).

Other less common manifestations of invasive *H. influenzae* disease include pneumonia, periorbital cellulitis (which is generally unilateral), septic arthritis and osteomyelitis, or a bacteremia without any obvious focus of infection. *Haemophilus* pneumonia is a major cause of mortality among young children in the developing world.

Noninvasive infections

A variety of local infections, principally in the respiratory tract, may be seen. These include otitis media, sinusitis, conjunctivitis and acute exacerbations of chronic bronchitis (see Chapter 33). Most of these infections are caused by noncapsulated strains of *H. influenzae*. *Haemophilus influenzae* is an important cause of purulent conjunctivitis. This may be sporadic but can occur in outbreaks. Severe conjunctivitis associated with severe sepsis and a high mortality was first described in 1984 in Brazilian children aged 1–4 years. The causative organism is a clone of *H. influenzae* biogroup *aegyptius*, which is indistinguishable in routine laboratory tests from ncHi.

Rarely *H. influenzae* may be associated with other infections, including urinary tract infections, cholecystitis, salpingitis and epididymo-orchitis. Many of these unusual infections are associated with pre-existing damage, including the presence of urinary stones or gallstones.

Haemophilus parainfluenzae, *H. aphrophilus* and *H. paraphrophilus* may be associated with infective endocarditis, meningitis and cerebral abscesses.[44] These species form part of the HACEK group (see below).

Haemophilus segnis is occasionally associated with acute appendicitis.

MANAGEMENT

Cefotaxime, ceftriaxone and related third-generation cephalosporins are the antibiotics of choice for treating *Haemophilus* meningitis. They are bactericidal for *H. influenzae*, achieve high concentrations in the meninges and cerebral tissues, and have proved highly effective in clinical practice.

Chloramphenicol was formerly the treatment of choice. Resistance may be encountered but in most parts of the world this remains uncommon. Ampicillin is also effective but resistance due to a β-lactamase is now encountered in an unacceptably high percentage of strains.[45] For example, 25% of Hib strains in the UK are β-lactamase-producing. In view of this, ampicillin should no longer be used as a single agent in *Haemophilus* meningitis in countries where ampicillin resistance is prevalent.

Antibiotic therapy is only one component of the clinical management of meningitis and full supportive care is required to achieve the most favorable outcome. Skilled medical and nursing care is essential in cases of epiglottitis to maintain the patient's airway.

The risk of infection is increased 500-fold for close contacts of a case of invasive Hib disease. Close contacts should be given rifampin chemoprophylaxis and, where appropriate, offered Hib vaccine (see above).

For the treatment of less serious respiratory infections, oral antibiotics including amoxicillin, amoxicillin–clavulanate, tetracycline, erythromycin or newer macrolides such as clarithromycin or azithromycin are all effective. β-Lactamase-mediated amoxicillin resistance may again be a problem. In the UK, 20% of ncHi isolates are β-lactamase producers. Occasional strains are resistant to ampicillin by an intrinsic mechanism.

HAEMOPHILUS DUCREYI

EPIDEMIOLOGY

Haemophilus ducreyi is the causative agent of the sexually transmitted disease chancroid, or soft sore.[46] Chancroid is endemic in tropical areas, particularly central and southern Africa, South East Asia, India and the Caribbean. It occurs sporadically in other parts of the world and recently there have been major outbreaks in Canada and the USA. It is more common in nonwhite, uncircumcised males and in low socio-economic groups living in poor hygienic conditions. Infection may be asymptomatic or inapparent in females. Genital ulcers, including chancroid, are associated with increased transmission of HIV.

PATHOGENICITY

Haemophilus ducreyi has not been isolated from nonhuman sources and is sexually transmitted. The organisms gain access via a break in the epithelium and establish infection in a focal area of mucosa or skin in the genital tract. The pathogenesis of chancroid is poorly understood. Potential virulence factors include fimbriae, LPS, cytotoxins and outer membrane protein (OMP).[47,48]

PREVENTION

The use of condoms dramatically reduces the transmission of *H. ducreyi*. All sexual partners should be identified by contact tracing and treated. Education is vitally important.

DIAGNOSTIC MICROBIOLOGY

Specimens should be collected from the base and margins of ulcers using a saline-moistened swab or by aspirating a bubo. On Gram-stained examination pleomorphic coccobacilli or short rods may be seen. They are more commonly extracellular but may be intracellular. Characteristically they resemble 'shoals of fish'. However, ulcer material is generally contaminated with other bacteria and direct Gram-staining identifies only about 10% of culture-positive cases.

Haemophilus ducreyi is a fastidious organism that grows slowly on chocolate agar. In general a suitable medium contains a growth supplement such as IsoVitaleX and is made selective by the addition of vancomycin.[49,50]

Cultures should be incubated for up to 5 days at 95–97°F (35–36°C) with added moisture and carbon dioxide.

The appearance of colonies of *H. ducreyi* varies with the medium used. Typically, after 24 hours incubation the colonies are pinpoint, yellow–gray and translucent or semiopaque. Cultures often appear mixed, with a variety of colonial forms. The colonies are very cohesive and can be pushed across the agar surface with an inoculating loop.

Haemophilus ducreyi requires X factor but not V factor for growth. It can be identified using a number of rapid test systems, including API-ZYM, Minitek and RapIDNH.

A variety of noncultural techniques have also been developed for *H. ducreyi* including indirect immunofluorescence, ELISA-based antigen detection and PCR-based methods.[51]

CLINICAL MANIFESTATIONS

After exposure there is an incubation period varying from 1 day to several weeks (average 5–7 days). Initially, tender papules develop on an area of genital skin or mucosa, surrounded by a zone of erythema. After 2–3 days the papules become pustular and then break down to form sharply circumscribed, painful ulcers with ragged, undermined edges. The base of the ulcer bleeds easily when it is scraped. Ulcers may be single or multiple. The ipsilateral regional inguinal lymph nodes become painful and enlarged. If left untreated, nodes may become fluctuant, forming an abscess or bubo. In some cases, buboes may spontaneously rupture, leading to chronic sinus formation (see Chapter 78).

MANAGEMENT

Most isolates of *H. ducreyi* are susceptible to erythromycin and the newer macrolides azithromycin, clarithromycin and roxithromycin. A 1-week course of oral erythromycin is well established as an effective treatment for chancroid. A single dose of azithromycin[52] or ceftriaxone appears to be effective but there have been reports of treatment failures with ceftriaxone in HIV-positive men in Kenya. Indeed, HIV-positive patients may respond poorly to any treatment for chancroid.

The susceptibility of *H. ducreyi* to antimicrobial agents varies from one geographic area to another.[53] Many strains are β-lactamase producers and resistance to tetracycline is common. Trimethoprim–sulfamethoxazole resistance is being increasingly seen, especially in the Far East.

Other agents that show excellent in-vitro activity against *H. ducreyi* include quinolones such as ciprofloxacin, rifampin, spectinomycin and amoxicillin–clavulanate.[54]

Buboes should be drained to prevent sinus formation.

HACEK GROUP

NATURE

The HACEK group of organisms includes *H. parainfluenzae*, *H. aphrophilus*, *H. paraphophilus*, *Actinobacillus actinomycetemcomitans*, *Cardiobacterium hominis*, *Eikenella corrodens* and *Kingella kingae*. They are all small, fastidious, pleomorphic Gram-negative bacilli that form part of the normal commensal flora of the oropharynx and are infrequent causes of human infections. They are slow-growing, their growth being enhanced by the use of enriched culture media and an increased carbon dioxide tension. Some biochemical properties that can be used to differentiate the individual species are listed in Table 231.9.

Cardiobacterium hominis and *E. corrodens* usually require hemin (X factor) and CO_2 on primary isolation and may be misidentified as *Haemophilus* spp.; these requirements are lost on subculture. The colonies of *E. corrodens* have a characteristic 'bleach-like' odor and often 'pit' the surface of the agar. Colonies of *K. kingae* produce slight β-hemolysis on blood agar.

CLINICAL MANIFESTATIONS

Collectively, the HACEK group of organisms causes 3% of all cases of infective endocarditis[55] and is responsible for a variety of other infections (see Chapter 59).

DIFFERENTIATION OF HACEK SPECIES

Species	Growth on blood agar	Requirement for		CO_2	Hemolysis	Oxidase	Catalase	Indole	Urease	Nitrate reductase	Acid from glucose
		X factor	V factor								
Haemophilus aphrophilus	–	+	–	+	–	–	–	–	–	+	+
Haemophilus paraphrophilus	–	–	+	+	–	+	–	–	–	+	+
Haemophilus parainfluenzae	–	–	+	–	–	+	±	V	V	+	+
Actinobacillus actinomycetemcomitans	+	–	–	+	–	+	+	–	–	+	+
Cardiobacterium hominis	+	+*	–	+*	–	+	–	+	–	–	+
Eikenella corrodens	+†	+*	–	+	–	+	–	–	–	+	–
Kingella kingae	+‡	–	–	–	(+)	+	–	–	–	–	+

* Requirements on primary isolation; usually lost on subculture. † Colonies pit the agar. ‡ Pitted colonies.

Table 231.9 Differentiation of HACEK species. V, reactions vary with the different biotypes.

Actinobacillus actinomycetemcomitans was originally thought to be a secondary pathogen in actinomycotic infections caused by *Actinomyces israelii*. It is now recognized as a cause of periodontal infections, brain and other soft tissue abscesses, osteomyelitis and infective endocarditis.[56]

Cardiobacterium hominis has been implicated in cases of natural and prosthetic valve endocarditis[57] but rarely causes other types of infection.

Eikenella corrodens tends to cause indolent infections, often in association with other organisms. Infections associated with *E. corrodens* include periodontitis, human bite wounds, sinusitis, meningitis, brain abscess, pulmonary infections, pelvic infections, endocarditis, osteomyelitis and septic arthritis.[58–60] Clenched fist injuries are the most serious human bite wounds and are sustained when the knuckles of the assailant's hand strike the teeth of the adversary.

Kingella spp. (*K. kingae* and *K. denitrificans*) are associated with endocarditis and osteoarticular infections. Since the introduction of routine Hib immunization in the USA, and consequent decline in Hib septic arthritis, *K. kingae* has emerged as a major cause of septic arthritis in children under 2 years of age.[61]

Haemophilus parainfluenzae, *H. aphrophilus* and *H. paraphophilus* may all cause endocarditis. *Haemophilus parainfluenzae* has been reported as a rare cause of the spectrum of infections associated with *H. influenzae*: meningitis, epiglottitis, septic arthritis, osteomyelitis, pneumonia and bacteremia. *Haemophilus aphrophilus* may cause brain abscesses, septic arthritis, osteomyelitis or meningitis. *Haemophilus paraphrophilus* has been implicated in cases of epiglottitis, brain abscess and osteomyelitis.

PREVENTION

Approximately 60% of cases of endocarditis caused by HACEK organisms are associated with poor oral hygiene, bad dentition or recent dental work.[55] Prevention of endocarditis should therefore be based on good dental and oral hygiene in patients at risk of endocarditis.

MANAGEMENT

The treatment of endocarditis caused by HACEK organisms should be based on antimicrobial susceptibility tests, including tests for β-lactamase activity. Since many of these organisms are slow-growing, such tests can be problematic. Currently, third-generation cephalosporins, including cefotaxime or ceftriaxone, are the drugs of choice for treating endocarditis caused by the HACEK organisms.

Eikenella corrodens is generally susceptible to penicillin, but consideration should be given to the possibility of β-lactamase-producing aerobic and anaerobic organisms when treating mixed infections, such as human bites.

LEGIONELLA SPECIES

NATURE

Legionella spp. are slender, aerobic, noncapsulated, non-spore-forming Gram-negative rods. In clinical material they often appear as coccobacilli but they tend to form elongated filamentous forms on some culture media. They are motile with polar flagella. *Legionella* spp. stain poorly with Gram stain. Basic fuchsin is a better counterstain for these organisms. They do not attack carbohydrates, and nitrate is not reduced. *Legionella* spp. are nutritionally fastidious and will not grow on ordinary culture media. A suitable medium for their isolation is buffered charcoal yeast extract (BCYE) supplemented with L-cysteine, α-ketoglutarate and ferric ions. The cell wall contains branched-chain fatty acids with high concentrations of ubiquinones, which give characteristic profiles by gas–liquid chromatographic analysis.

LEGIONELLA SPECIES ASSOCIATED WITH DISEASE IN HUMANS

Species	Number of serogroups
Legionella pneumophila	15
Legionella micdadei	1
Legionella bozemanii	2
Legionella dumoffii	1
Legionella longbeachae	2
Legionella anisa	1
Legionella birminghamensis	1
Legionella cincinnatensis	1
Legionella feeleii	2
Legionella gormanii	1
Legionella hackeliae	2
Legionella jordanis	1
Legionella lansingensis	1
Legionella maceachernii	1
Legionella oakridgensis	
Legionella parisiensis	1
Legionella sainthelensi	2
Legionella tucsonensis	
Legionella wadsworthii	1

Table 231.10 ***Legionella*** **species associated with disease in humans.**

There are more than 40 species and 64 subgroups in the genus *Legionella*. More than 15% of human infections are caused by *Legionella pneumophila* serogroup 1, but other serogroups and other species, particularly *Legionella micdadei*, have also been implicated (Table 231.10).

EPIDEMIOLOGY

Legionella spp. are distributed worldwide. They are found in natural bodies of fresh water – streams, rivers, ponds, lakes and thermal pools – in moist soil and mud. They have even been found in the canopy of the rain forest. The organisms are able to survive in moist environments for long periods of time and can withstand temperatures of 32–154°F (0–68°C) and a pH range of 5.0–8.5. They can survive chlorination and can thus enter water supply systems and proliferate in thermal habitats, including air-conditioning cooling towers, hot water systems, shower heads, taps, whirlpool spas and respiratory ventilators. The organisms are found in biofilms on the surfaces of these systems, where they are far less susceptible to the effects of biocides and chlorine. The growth of *Legionella* spp. is aided by co-existing micro-organisms, which provide nutrients, and free-living amebae, in which the *Legionella* spp. can reside and multiply.[62]

The exact incidence of *Legionella* infections is difficult to determine. There is no doubt that exposure to *Legionella* spp. is a fairly frequent event and serologic surveys suggest that asymptomatic infection and seroconversion are common. Large-scale surveys of pneumonia suggest that *Legionella* spp. cause 2–5% of community-acquired pneumonia and up to 30% of nosocomial pneumonia.

Cases may be sporadic or occur as part of an outbreak. The original description of Legionnaires' disease was of an outbreak of a febrile respiratory illness in delegates at an American Legion convention in Philadelphia in 1976. A total of 221 people developed pneumonia and 34 died.[63] Retrospective studies have revealed that the first proven case occurred in 1947 and the first known epidemic was in 1965 in Washington, DC.

Sporadic cases are reported throughout the year, but most cases of epidemic infection occur in the summer and autumn, presumably because warmer weather encourages proliferation of the bacteria in water. The disease tends to occur in the middle-aged and elderly, especially in people who have impaired respiratory and cardiac function, who are heavy smokers or who are immunocompromised. Cases have been documented in children. Person-to-person spread has not been demonstrated. Surgery is a major predisposition in nosocomial infection, with transplant patients at the greatest risk.

Legionella is a good example of an organism that has been present in the environment for a long time but has been brought into close contact with humans as a result of technical developments. Organisms are disseminated via contaminated water droplets from nebulizers and humidifiers and in aerosols from cooling towers, whirlpools and evaporative condensers. Infection arises from inhalation of contaminated aerosols, direct instillation during surgery or possibly by ingestion of contaminated water. Hospital equipment that has been rinsed in tap water prior to use may be a source of infection.

PATHOGENICITY

Legionella spp. residing in water are transmitted to humans via aerosols. Droplet nuclei of less than 5μm will reach the alveoli, where the organisms are ingested by alveolar macrophages. *Legionella* is a facultative intracellular parasite and multiplies freely within the macrophages. The bacteria bind to the alveolar macrophages via complement receptors and are engulfed in phagosomes. Phagolysosome fusion is inhibited by an unknown mechanism that prevents intracellular killing. The bacteria multiply within the phagosomes. Eventually the cell ruptures, releasing bacteria, which are then taken up by other macrophages. This process produces chemotactic substances that attract polymorphonuclear leukocytes and monocytes. The inflammatory response results in a destructive pneumonia.

The virulence factors of *L. pneumophila* have not been fully determined. A 24kDa protein, macrophage infectivity potentiator, appears to be required for virulence. The major outer membrane protein may be important in the uptake of *Legionella* spp. by macrophages. A variety of extracellular enzymes are produced by *Legionella*, including proteases, esterases and hemolysins, but these have not been shown to be important virulence factors.[64] The virulence of *L. pneumophila* may be enhanced by multiplication in amebae.

PREVENTION

Prevention of legionellosis depends upon identification of the environmental source and reduction of *Legionella* colonization. The most commonly used method of decontamination is periodic superheating and flushing of water supplies. This method is particularly useful for urgent disinfection during an outbreak. Hyperchlorination is no longer recommended because chlorine decomposes in hot water and *Legionella* spp. are relatively chlorine-tolerant. Biocides are relatively ineffective. The most effective method appears to be copper-silver ionization units, which generate metallic ions that disrupt and kill bacterial cells.[65] Despite these costly measures it is often impossible to eliminate *Legionella* spp. from water supplies.[66]

New water systems should be designed to minimize the risk of heavy colonization with *Legionella* spp., avoiding 'dead spaces', stagnation, materials that support the growth of *Legionella* spp. and the build-up of sediment. Regular monitoring for *Legionella* spp. is also advisable, particularly in high-risk areas.

Several putative vaccines have been developed that induce cell-mediated immunity in guinea pigs. These may be an option in the future for highly susceptible patients.

DIAGNOSTIC MICROBIOLOGY

Definitive diagnosis of legionellosis depends on culturing *Legionella* organisms, detecting *Legionella* antigens in body fluids or demonstrating a serologic response to the infection.[67] A PCR method is also available but does not appear to be any more sensitive than culture. A PCR test can be successfully used to identify *Legionella* in water samples.

Legionella spp. can be cultured from sputum, endotracheal aspirates, bronchoalveolar lavages, lung biopsies and pleural fluid. Sputum samples should not be diluted in saline, because this can prove inhibitory to some *Legionella* spp., but in distilled water. Gram-stained smears of the sample will reveal poorly staining Gram-negative rods, which are suggestive of legionellosis. Direct immunofluorescence of the smear using a monoclonal antibody to a major outer membrane protein common to all the serogroups of *L. pneumophila* can give a rapid provisional diagnosis but this test is not as sensitive as culture and will only detect *L. pneumophila*.

Cultures must therefore also be carried out. The sample should be cultured on a specific medium such as BCYE. *Legionella* spp. do not grow on blood agar. It is possible to render BCYE semiselective by the inclusion of antibiotics, but this may prove inhibitory to some strains of *Legionella* spp. It is therefore prudent to culture samples on both BCYE and BCYE supplemented with antibiotics. Contaminated material, such as sputum, can be heated at 122°F (50°C) for 30 minutes to suppress the growth of other less heat-stable organisms prior to inoculating the culture plates. Cultures should be incubated at 98.6°F (37°C) in 2–5% carbon dioxide for up to 14 days. *Legionella* spp. are slow growing, and on primary isolation it may take 3–5 days for colonies to appear. Colonies of *Legionella* spp. have a ground-glass appearance, which may be white, gray, pale blue, or purple-tinged (Fig. 231.7). Often the colonies will fluoresce under ultraviolet light.

Colonies that grow on BCYE but not blood agar, that are catalase-positive and have a characteristic Gram-stain morphology should be regarded as presumptive *Legionella* spp. *Legionella pneumophila* hydrolyzes hippurate, starch and gelatin but in general biochemical tests are not of great help in identifying *Legionella* spp. Serologic typing using direct or indirect fluorescent antibody tests with polyclonal or monoclonal antibodies will confirm the identity of clinical isolates.

Urine samples can be examined for *Legionella* soluble antigen using an ELISA test. This test is specific for *L. pneumophila* sero-

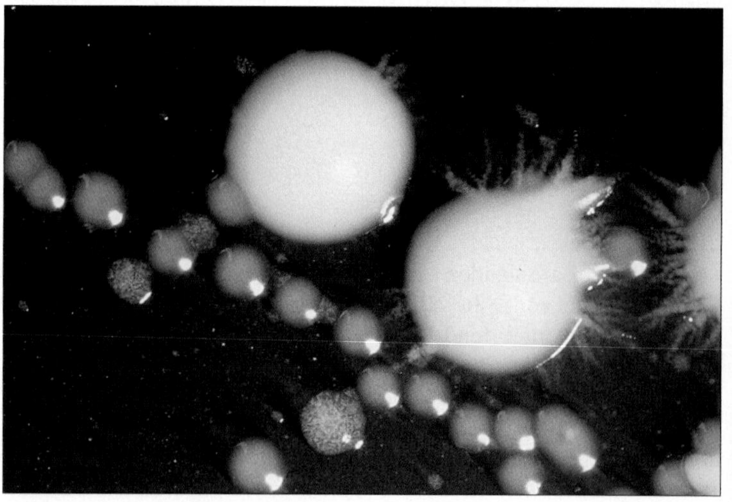

Fig. 231.7 Colonies of *Legionella pneumophila* on BCYE agar, showing the typical ground-glass appearance. With permission from Harrison TG, Taylor AG (eds). A laboratory manual for *Legionella*. Chichester: Wiley;1998.

group 1 (which causes 70–80% of human infections) and can give a rapid diagnosis. However, it will not detect infections caused by other *Legionella* spp. The antigen persists in the urine for 1–3 weeks but some patients continue to excrete antigen for months.

Serologic tests can be used to make a diagnosis of legionellosis. The most commonly used technique is an indirect fluorescent antibody test, but other techniques, such as ELISA or a rapid micro-agglutination test, are also available. A 4-fold or greater rise in antibody titer or a single titer of 256 or more indicates *Legionella* infection. It may take weeks or even months for the antibody titer to rise, and antibodies can persist for years, so serology is less useful than culture or antigen detection in the diagnosis of acute cases. Serology is much more useful in epidemiologic studies. The only validated serologic test is for *L. pneumophila* serogroup 1. Cross-reacting antibodies may be found in patients who have *Campylobacter* spp. infection.

CLINICAL MANIFESTATIONS

Asymptomatic *Legionella* infections are relatively common, as demonstrated by seroepidemiologic surveys.

Symptomatic *Legionella* infection can present in two distinct ways: a severe pneumonia – Legionnaires' disease – and an acute influenza-like illness known as Pontiac fever.[68]

Legionnaires' disease

The most common presentation is an acute pneumonia,[69] which accounts for 5% of community-acquired pneumonia and up to 30% of nosocomial pneumonia (see also Chapter 34). After an incubation period of 2–10 days there is an acute onset of fever, malaise, myalgia and headache, followed by a nonproductive cough and dyspnea. Confusion can be a prominent feature, and abdominal pain and diarrhea may also be present. The severity of the illness ranges from a mild infection not requiring hospitalization to life-threatening multilobar *Legionella* pneumonia and respiratory failure. The infection may progress to involve many organs, and renal and hepatic dysfunction are commonly seen. Many of the manifestations are not specific for Legionnaires' disease and may occur in other infective pneumonias. Characteristic features suggestive of *Legionella* spp. are hyponatremia (serum sodium less than 130mmol/ml) and a Gram-stained smear of respiratory secretions showing many polymorphs but few if any visible organisms. Legionnaires' disease should be considered in any pneumonia that has failed to respond to β-lactam antibiotics.

In previously healthy people, the mortality is approximately 10%, but the mortality rate may be 30–50% in immunocompromised patients or those in whom there is a delay in making the diagnosis.

The chest radiograph characteristically shows patchy interstitial inflammation. Initially this is unilateral and involves the lower lobe. The initial infiltrates progress to areas of consolidation over a few days. Pleural effusions are commonly seen.

Bacteremic dissemination may occur, particularly in immunocompromised patients. Cellulitis, pancreatitis, endocarditis and sinusitis have all been reported.

Cases of wound infection and prosthetic valve endocarditis due to *Legionella* infection have been described. These are generally nosocomial infections.

Pontiac fever

Pontiac fever[68] is an acute, self-limited, flu-like, febrile illness that occurs 1–2 days after exposure. It is thought to represent a hypersensitivity reaction following acute exposure. The illness lasts for 2–5 days and there is no evidence of pneumonia. The chest radiograph is clear. The condition resolves spontaneously. Pontiac fever has a high attack rate, in contrast to Legionnaires' disease, in which only a small proportion of people exposed to the organism develop the disease.

MANAGEMENT

Azithromycin, ciprofloxacin or high-dose erythromycin is the treatment of choice. In the patient who is acutely ill with Legionnaires' disease, azithromycin or a quinolone should be administered together with rifampin (rifampicin), although it should be noted that good comparative clinical trials in this area are lacking.

Cases of Pontiac fever resolve spontaneously without the need for antibiotic therapy.

MORAXELLA SPECIES

NATURE

The genus *Moraxella* is composed of two subgenera, *Moraxella* and *Branhamella*.[70] *Moraxella* (*Moraxella*) spp. are short, oxidase-positive, catalase-positive, DNA-ase-negative Gram-negative coccobacilli that often appear in pairs. They are strictly aerobic and asaccharolytic. The G + C content of DNA is 40–40mol%.

Moraxella (*Moraxella*) *lacunata* is associated with conjunctivitis. *Moraxella* (*Moraxella*) *non-liquefaciens* is a commensal in the upper respiratory tract and may be a secondary invader in respiratory infections. *Moraxella* (*Moraxella*) *osloensis* is a common commensal in the genital tract and may be misidentified as *Neisseria gonorrhoeae*. Unlike *N. gonorrhoeae*, *M. osloensis* grows well on blood agar. *M. osloensis* has been reported in cases of septic arthritis, osteomyelitis and bacteremia. These three organisms will not be further discussed.

Moraxella (*Branhamella*) spp. are Gram-negative diplococci that morphologically and phenotypically resemble *Neisseria* spp. They are aerobic, oxidase-positive, catalase-positive, DNA-ase-positive and asaccharolytic. The G + C content of DNA is 40–45mol%. *Moraxella* (*Branhamella*) *catarrhalis* is now recognized as an important cause of upper and lower respiratory tract infections in children and adults.

EPIDEMIOLOGY

Moraxella (*Branhamella*) *catarrhalis* is exclusively found in humans. The nasopharyngeal carriage rate of *M. catarrhalis* is 1–3% in healthy adults, but up to 75% of infants and young children are colonized with this organism. This remarkable disparity remains unexplained. Nasopharyngeal carriage rates are significantly higher in the autumn and winter months. It also appears that the carriage rate is higher in adults who have chronic lung disease than in healthy adults.

PATHOGENICITY

The majority of *M. catarrhalis* infections result from contiguous spread of organisms colonizing the upper respiratory tract. Little is known of the events that alter the host–pathogen relationship and cause a shift from asymptomatic colonization to infection in the upper or lower respiratory tract.

The virulence factors of *M. catarrhalis* have not been fully elucidated. The majority of strains possess pili or fimbriae, which play a role in adherence to host mucosal cells. The outer membrane lipo-oligosaccharide (LOS) is probably a virulence factor. Three serotypes of LOS have been identified. Some strains are serum-resistant, by virtue of interference with the formation of the membrane attack complex of complement. There is some evidence that *M. catarrhalis* possesses a polysaccharide capsule. *M. catarrhalis* synthesizes a significant amount of histamine, which results in decreased mucociliary clearing and increased colonization of the respiratory tract.[71]

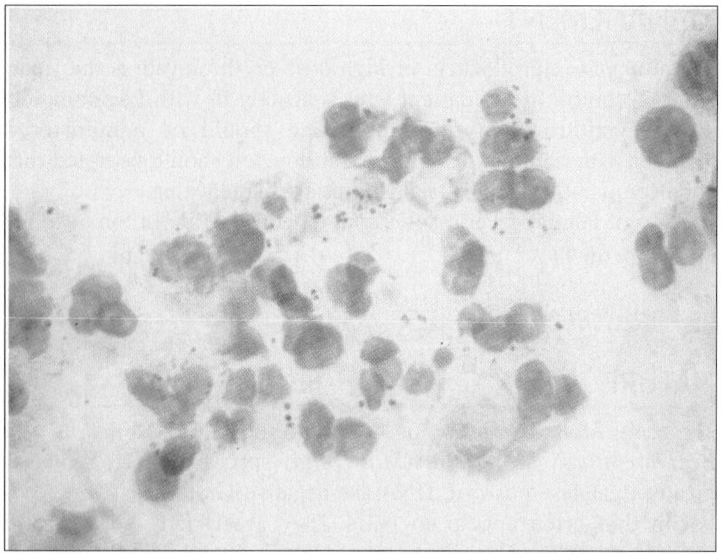

Fig. 231.8 Gram-stained smear of sputum containing *Moraxella catarrhalis*. Sample from a patient suffering an acute exacerbation of chronic bronchitis showing Gram-negative diplococci and leukocytes (*Moraxella catarrhalis*).

PREVENTION

Currently there is considerable interest in the development of a vaccine to prevent *M. catarrhalis* infections based on OMPs including UspA, CopB, OMP B1 and OMP CD.

DIAGNOSTIC MICROBIOLOGY

Moraxella catarrhalis grows well on blood agar and chocolate agar, producing small, nonhemolytic, grayish-white colonies that slide across the agar surface, like a hockey puck, when pushed with a bacteriologic loop. It may be difficult to distinguish *M. catarrhalis* from commensal *Neisseria* spp. in respiratory tract specimens, and the use of selective media may be necessary. Gram-stained films reveal Gram-negative diplococci but *M. catarrhalis* often resists destaining and thus may appear to be Gram-positive (Fig. 231.8). The bacteria are oxidase-positive. *M. catarrhalis* is DNA-ase-positive, nitrate-reductase-positive and hydrolyzes tributyrin, tests that differentiate it from the majority of *Neisseria* spp.

A PCR test has been devised that can be applied to clinical material without the need for bacterial culture. This test has been successfully used to detect *M. catarrhalis* in middle ear effusions and appears to be more sensitive than culture.

CLINICAL MANIFESTATIONS

Moraxella catarrhalis is an important cause of otitis media and sinusitis in children, being the third most common cause of these conditions after *Streptococcus pneumoniae* and *H. influenzae*.

In adults *M. catarrhalis* is associated with acute exacerbations of chronic bronchitis, being the third most common isolate after *H. influenzae* and *S. pneumoniae*. *M. catarrhalis* may cause pneumonia, especially in the elderly and is associated with a poor prognosis. Lower respiratory tract infection with *M. catarrhalis* is more common in the winter months.

There have been several reports of nosocomial outbreaks of lower respiratory tract infections due to *M. catarrhalis* in respiratory units.[69]

Moraxella catarrhalis may occasionally cause invasive infections, including bacteremia, meningitis and endocarditis.

MANAGEMENT

Before 1977 no β-lactamase-positive isolates of *M. catarrhalis* had been reported. By 1980 75% of *M. catarrhalis* isolates in the USA were β-lactamase-positive and now virtually all strains of *M. catarrhalis* are β-lactamase-positive. There are two *M. catarrhalis* β-lactamases, BRO-1 and BRO-2, which are unique to this genus. There is some evidence that, in mixed infections, *M. catarrhalis* β-lactamases can protect other respiratory pathogens such as *S. pneumoniae* and *H. influenzae* from the action of β-lactam antibiotics. The β-lactamases of *M. catarrhalis* are chromosomal and inducible; therefore ampicillin therapy should be avoided.

Many infections due to *M. catarrhalis* can be treated with oral antibiotics, including amoxicillin–clavulanate, trimethoprim, sulfamethoxazole, tetracyclines, (contraindicated in children aged under 7 years), cefaclor, clarithromycin, azithromycin and ciprofloxacin.

PASTEURELLA SPECIES

NATURE

Pasteurella spp. are very small, nonmotile, non-spore-forming Gram-negative bacteria that are coccoid, oval or rod-shaped. They often exhibit bipolar staining. They are aerobic and facultatively anaerobic. Most species are catalase-positive and slowly oxidase-positive. They attack carbohydrates readily, forming acid but no gas. Nitrates are reduced to nitrite. *Pasteurella* spp. will grow on ordinary laboratory media at 98.6°F (37°C). The G + C content of the DNA is 40–45mol%.

The family Pasteurellaceae encompasses the genera *Pasteurella*, *Actinobacillus* and *Haemophilus*. There are 11 species within the genus *Pasteurella*. The species *Pasteurella multocida* is further subdivided into subspecies on the basis of acid production from dulcitol and sorbitol. Most human infections are caused by *P. multocida*.

EPIDEMIOLOGY

Pasteurella spp. are distributed worldwide. They are commensals or parasitic organisms in the upper respiratory tract and gastrointestinal tracts of many domestic and wild animals and birds.

Pasteurella multocida is found in the oropharynx of 50–90% of domestic cats, 50–70% of dogs and 50% of pigs. It is the cause of hemorrhagic sepsis in cattle and water buffalo, pneumonia in pigs and sheep, snuffles in rabbits and fowl, and cholera in chickens, ducks and turkeys. It is generally carried asymptomatically by cats and dogs but may infect bites inflicted on these animals by feline or canine assailants. Humans become infected through contact with infected animals.

Pasteurella multocida can remain viable in soil and water for up to 4 weeks and may survive in animal carcasses for up to 3 months. Most human infections are caused by *P. multocida* subsp. *multocida* and *P. multocida* subsp. *septica*. *Pasteurella canis*, *Pasteurella dagmatis* and *Pasteurella stomatis* have also been associated with human disease (Table 231.11).

PATHOGENICITY

Pasteurella multocida is transmitted to humans by contact with infected animals. The most common source of infection is bites, scratches, or licks from cats or dogs (see Chapter 91).[72] Respiratory tract infections in those handling animals may result from airborne transmission. In a few patients it is not possible to document an animal source of the infection.

SPECIES OF *PASTEURELLA* ASSOCIATED WITH INFECTIONS IN HUMANS
Pasteurella multocida subsp. *multocida*
Pasteurella multocida subsp. *septica*
Pasteurella canis
Pasteurella dagmatis
Pasteurella stomatis

Table 231.11 Species of *Pasteurella* associated with infections in humans.

Virulence in *P. multocida* is associated with the degree of encapsulation. Strains with large capsules are more resistant to phagocytosis in vivo. There are four capsular types – A, B, D and E – and 11 somatic antigens.

PREVENTION

The only way of effectively preventing *Pasteurella* infections is to avoid contact with domestic or wild animals. Animal bites should be cleaned promptly and devitalized tissue should be debrided. Prophylactic antibiotics may be indicated after cat and dog bites, particularly if the patient is immunocompromised or diabetic or the wound affects the hands or face.

DIAGNOSTIC MICROBIOLOGY

A clinical history of animal bites will, in most instances, alert the laboratory to the possibility of *Pasteurella* spp. Samples should be cultured on blood agar plates at 98.6°F (37°C) for 24 hours. *Pasteurella multocida* grows as small, nonhemolytic colonies. Gram-stained films reveal very small Gram-negative coccobacilli. The organisms often show bipolar staining in methylene blue preparations. The identity of the organism can be confirmed by a series of biochemical and serologic tests and serology (Table 231.12).[73]

CLINICAL MANIFESTATIONS

Pasteurella infections in humans usually present as soft tissue infections. The onset is acute, several hours after being bitten or scratched by a domestic or wild animal. Open wounds may be infected by animal licks. The area is erythematous, painful and swollen. In nearly 50% of cases the infection spreads to deeper tissues, leading to tenosynovitis, abscess formation, septic arthritis or osteomyelitis. There may be an accompanying regional lymphadenopathy or lymphangitis. The severity of the infection is often greater than one would suspect on first inspection. Some *Pasteurella* infections present as respiratory infections, which may be chronic. In other cases the patient presents with a bacteremic infection, which may or may not result in a localized focus of infection (Fig. 231.9).[73,74]

CLINICAL MANIFESTATIONS OF *PASTEURELLA* INFECTIONS IN HUMANS

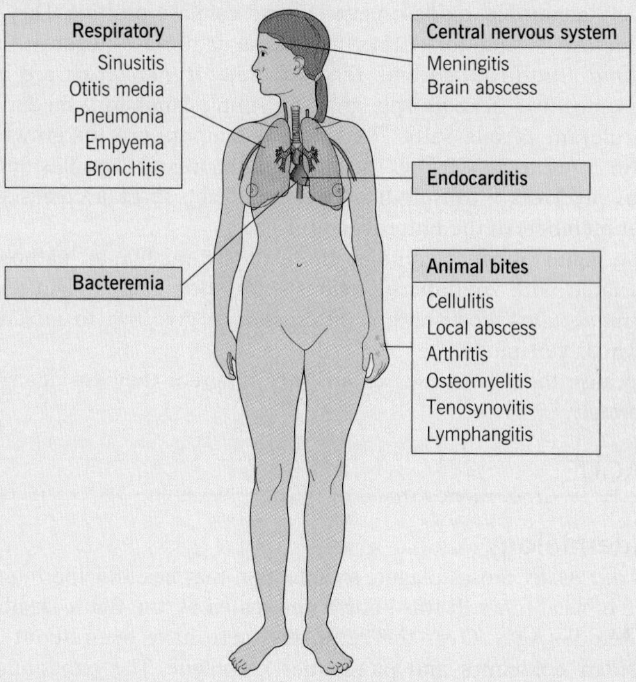

Fig. 231.9 Clinical manifestations of *Pasteurella* infection in humans.

Approximately one-third of patients who have bacteremia have underlying cirrhosis.

MANAGEMENT

Animal bites should be carefully cleaned, irrigated and debrided. Penicillin is the treatment of choice for *Pasteurella* infections. Other agents with good activity include ampicillin, amoxicillin–clavulanate, cefuroxime and ciprofloxacin. Many infected animal bites have a polymicrobial etiology and it is prudent to use a regimen that provides good cover against anaerobes and streptococci as well, such as amoxicillin–clavulanate. A strain of *P. multocida* that produced ROB-1 β-lactamase has been reported.

Prophylactic antibiotics for cat and dog bites are sometimes advocated but their value is not clearly established (see Chapter 91).

YERSINIA SPECIES

NATURE

Yersinia spp. are members of the Enterobacteriaceae. They are short, pleomorphic Gram-negative rods or coccobacilli, which often exhibit

DIFFERENTIATION OF *YERSINIA* AND *PASTEURELLA* SPECIES

Species	Growth on MacConkey agar	Oxidase	Catalase	Motility at 22°C	ONPG	Acid (no gas) production from		Indole	Urease	Ornithine decarboxylase
						Sucrose	Maltose			
Yersinia pestis	+	–	+	–	+	–	+	–	–	–
Yersinia enterocolitica	+	–	+	+	+	+	–	–	+	+
Yersinia pseudotuberculosis	+	–	+	+	+	–	+	–	+	–
Pasteurella multocida	–	±	+	–	–	+	–	+	–	+

Table 231.12 Differentiation of *Yersinia* and *Pasteurella* species.

bipolar staining. *Yersinia pestis* is nonmotile. Other species are nonmotile at 98.6°F (37°C) but motile at temperatures less than 86°F (30°C) by means of peritrichous flagella. They are aerobic and facultatively anaerobic, oxidase-negative and catalase-positive. They are nonlactose fermenters. *Yersinia pestis* is urease-negative, and *Yersinia enterocolitica* and *Yersinia pseudotuberculosis* are both urease-positive. *Yersinia* spp. grow on simple laboratory media and are tolerant of bile salts. The optimal temperature for growth is 82–86°F (27.8–30°C). They do not form spores or capsules, but *Y. pestis* produces a capsule-like envelope. They share antigens with other members of the Enterobacteriaceae.

The genus *Yersinia* contains three important human pathogens associated with zoonotic infections – *Y. pestis* causes plague, and *Y. pseudotuberculosis* and *Y. enterocolitica* give rise to infections known as yersiniosis.

Because these two diseases are very different they are described separately.

PLAGUE

Epidemiology

Yersinia pestis causes plague, an infection that has afflicted humans since biblical times. It was known and feared as 'the Black Death' in the Middle Ages. Over the centuries there have been about 150 recorded epidemics and pandemics of plague. The pandemic of plague that swept across Europe in the 14th century killed about one-third of the total population of continental Europe and England. The 'Great Plague' of 1665 killed more than 100,000 people in London. In the 20th century plague is still found in many parts of the world, including China, Mongolia, South East Asia, India, central and southern Africa, the Middle East, South America and the southwestern states of the USA. Major epidemics or pandemics no longer occur, possibly because of improved standards of hygiene, more effective rodent control and the use of insecticides. Worldwide, approximately 3000 cases of plague were reported in 1994.[75] Males and females are equally affected.

Pathogenicity

Plague is a zoonotic infection. It is transmitted between its natural hosts, wild rodents, by rodent flea bites or by the consumption of infected animal carcasses. The rodents may succumb to plague or become carriers of the organism. This carrier state ensures the endemicity of plague in some parts of the world. *Yersinia pestis* persists in many sylvatic rodent species, including ground squirrels, tree rats, voles and prairie dogs. Urban rats – *Rattus rattus* and *Rattus norvegicus* – are the most important reservoirs of plague for human infections.

Humans are accidentally infected when they are bitten by a plague-carrying rodent flea. Occasionally, humans are infected by handling infected animal tissues. Only rarely, during an epidemic, does person-to-person spread occur. The most efficient vector is the oriental rat flea, *Xenopsylla cheopsis,* but there are over 30 species of rodent fleas capable of transmitting plague. Occasionally, infection may pass from patient to patient via the human flea, *Pulex irritans.* This may have been an important vector in some of the medieval epidemics. During an epizootic there is a build-up of infections in the rodent population and many may die. It is at this time that human infections are more likely to occur, since the rodent fleas turn to humans in search of food (Fig. 231.10).

The flea vector becomes infected by feeding on the blood of a diseased rodent. It ingests *Y. pestis* with the blood meal. The organisms multiply within the stomach of the flea. At temperatures of less than 80°F (26.7°C), *Y. pestis* produces coagulase and a blood clot is formed. This fibrinous clot, which contains viable *Y. pestis*, blocks the proventriculus of the flea. When the hungry flea attempts to feed from another rodent or human, the fresh blood meal, together with thousands of *Y. pestis* bacilli, is regurgitated back into the bite wound. Thus the infection is transmitted to a new host. When the ambient temperature is over 80°F (26.7°C), *Y. pestis* does not produce coagulase and may form fibrinolysin, so a clot does not form and blockage and regurgitation do not occur. Transmission of *Y. pestis* is therefore uncommon during hot, dry seasons.

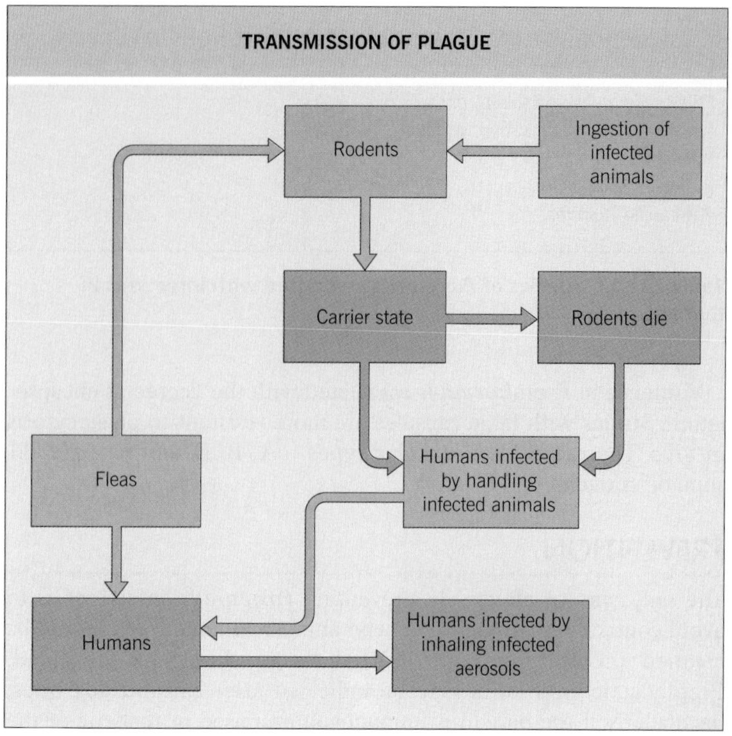

Fig. 231.10 Transmission of plague.

On entering the new host, the bacilli migrate via the lymphatics to the regional lymph nodes. In the flea, *Y. pestis* produces only a small amount of envelope antigen (F-1 antigen). The ingested organisms are readily phagocytosed by polymorphonuclear phagocytes and mononuclear phagocytes. *Yersinia pestis* is a facultative intracellular parasite and resists killing within the mononuclear phagocytes. *Y. pestis* can multiply within these cells, where it elaborates F-1 envelope antigen. If the macrophages are lysed, the re-enveloped organisms are able to resist phagocytosis and can multiply freely in the extracellular environment. The regional lymph nodes become hot, tender and inflamed and undergo hemorrhagic necrosis. This produces the black buboes characteristic of plague. The infection then spills into the bloodstream and may rapidly spread to the liver, lungs and spleen. If the lungs are affected, a severe pneumonia develops and large numbers of plague bacilli are expectorated into the air.[76]

There are a number of putative virulence factors – F-1 antigen consists of a glycoprotein (F-1A) and a carbohydrate-free protein (F-1B). It is antiphagocytic and stimulates protective immunity in mice and humans.

Other important virulence factors are V–W antigens and *Yersinia* outer membrane proteins (YOPs).[77] These protein antigens are produced at 98.6°F (37°C) in the presence of low concentrations of calcium. They appear to be important both for intracellular survival and multiplication and for extracellular survival by virtue of their antiphagocytic activity. The LPS of *Y. pestis* is in part responsible for hemorrhagic necrosis and vascular collapse, but the mechanism is again poorly understood (Table 231.13). Coagulase and fibrinolysin are produced by *Y. pestis*. They aid survival and dissemination within the invertebrate host.

VIRULENCE FACTORS OF *YERSINIA PESTIS*		
Factor	**Composition**	**Pathogenic role**
F-1 antigen 'envelope'	Glycoprotein F^1A + protein F^1B	Antiphagocytic
V antigen + W antigen	Protein Lipoprotein	Antiphagocytic (Aids intracellular survival)
YOPs	Proteins	Antiphagocytic
LPS	Lipopolysaccharide	Hemorrhagic Focal necrosis

Table 231.13 Virulence factors of *Yersinia pestis*.

Prevention

Prevention depends on effective control of the rodent and flea populations that harbor *Y. pestis*. Fleas can be controlled by the use of insecticides in domestic settings. A variety of measures have been used to control rats in urban environments (e.g. ratproofing houses) and to prevent rats migrating on ships or airplanes. It is, however, virtually impossible to eliminate sylvatic rodents, which remain a reservoir for plague.

A formalin-killed vaccine is effective against bubonic plague but not pneumonic plague. It is recommended for travelers to endemic areas, workers who handle rodents and laboratory staff working with *Y. pestis*. Protection is only short-lived and booster doses are required for those who continue to be exposed to the risk of infection. A subunit vaccine containing recombinant F1 and V antigens is under development and appears to be protective in an animal model.[78]

Diagnostic microbiology

Plague should be suspected in febrile patients exposed to flea bites or rodents in endemic parts of the world. It is important to notify the laboratory if plague is suspected so that appropriate precautions can be taken. There is a considerable risk of laboratory-acquired infection. Material suspected of containing *Y. pestis* must be handled in a containment level 3 laboratory in a category I or III exhaust protective cabinet by experienced, trained personnel. Smears taken from bubo aspirates, blood, sputum or cerebrospinal fluid should be examined using Gram's stain and methylene blue. Gram's stain will reveal Gram-negative pleomorphic coccobacilli with rounded ends. Methylene blue stain will demonstrate bipolar staining. *Yersinia pestis* appear light blue with dark blue polar bodies. Smears can also be examined by direct immunofluorescence.

Material can be cultured on blood agar or MacConkey agar or in broth cultures. Cultures should be incubated at 80°F (26.7°C). Tiny, translucent, nonhemolytic colonies appear on blood agar after 24 hours. After further incubation the colonies enlarge and become opaque. *Yersinia pestis* grows rather poorly in MacConkey agar and the colonies tend to autolyze after 2–3 days. In fluid culture *Y. pestis* tends to form chains.

The identity of presumptive colonies of *Y. pestis* can be confirmed using cultural and biochemical tests. Alternatively, definitive identification can be made by direct immunofluorescence of the organisms. A serologic diagnosis can be made using a passive hemagglutination test using tanned sheep red cells to which F-1 antigen has been adsorbed, or a complement fixation test. A 4-fold or greater rise in titer or a single titer over 1:16 in convalescent serum indicates plague infection. For large-scale seroepidemiologic surveys an ELISA test for antibodies to F-1 antigen can be used.

Strains of *Y. pestis* can be typed using bacteriophage typing.

PLAGUE SYNDROMES	
Syndrome	**Clinical features**
Bubonic plague	Fever Painful lymph node Bubo
Pneumonic plague	Primary following inhalation of *Yersinia pestis* or secondary to bubonic plague Fever Cough Dyspnea Hemoptysis ± bubo
Septicemic plague	Fever Shock Purpura Distal gangrene No bubo
Plague meningitis	Secondary to bubonic plague

Table 231.14 Plague syndromes.

Clinical manifestations

There are a number of distinct clinical presentations of plague (Table 231.14) (see also Chapter 176).

Bubonic plague

The most common presentation is bubonic plague. Following a flea bite, which is often on the lower extremities, the bacteria proliferate in the regional lymph nodes for 2–8 days. The patient then develops a fever of sudden onset and an intensely painful swelling in a group of lymph nodes. This is the bubo. The most common site for the primary bubo is the groin. From this site the bacteria disseminate throughout the body in a transient bacteremia. Some patients will develop a secondary pneumonia or sepsis. Most patients do not develop skin lesions. Untreated patients may die within 2–4 days of the onset of symptoms.

Pneumonic plague

In some patients who have bubonic plague the infection spreads to the lung via the bloodstream. The patient develops a high fever and cough, chest pain and hemoptysis. Less commonly, pulmonary plague may be the primary event following the inhalation of infected droplet nuclei from patients who have pneumonic disease. Patients who have primary pulmonary plague do not have buboes. Pneumonic plague is highly contagious because large numbers of plague bacilli are expectorated during coughing. This form of plague carries a higher mortality than bubonic plague.

Septicemic plague

In some cases a flea bite is followed by proliferation of *Y. pestis* in the circulation without any localization in lymph nodes and bubo formation. This form is more common in children and is often rapidly fatal.

Other manifestations of plague include a meningitis secondary to inadequately treated bubonic plague. Overall, the mortality of untreated plague is more than 50%.

Management

The treatment of choice remains streptomycin. It is essential to institute therapy as soon as possible because untreated plague runs a rapidly fulminating course. With prompt effective antimicrobial therapy the mortality rate is reduced from over 50% to 6%. Streptomycin resistance has been reported in some parts of the world. Oral tetracycline is an alternative but it is contraindicated in children and during pregnancy. Chloramphenicol may also be used and is the treatment of choice for plague meningitis. All cases of plague should be reported to national health authorities and to the World Health Organization (see Chapter 176).

YERSINIOSIS

Yersiniosis encompasses a wide spectrum of infections caused by *Y. enterocolitica* and *Y. pseudotuberculosis*. The clinical features range from gastroenteritis, enterocolitis, or mesenteric adenitis to sepsis.

Epidemiology

Yersinia enterocolitica is harbored in the gastrointestinal tract of a wide range of mammals, including rodents, cattle, sheep, pigs, cats and dogs. Infected animals tend to become chronic carriers and excrete large numbers of bacilli, which can contaminate water and dairy products. Humans are infected by eating inadequately cooked meat (especially pork) or other food contaminated with *Yersinia* spp. Infection may also arise following contact with an infected domestic animal. In the USA, outbreaks associated with dairy products, chocolate and milk have been reported. Rarely, water is the source of the infection. The ability of *Y. enterocolitica* to grow at 39°F (4°C) means that refrigerated meat and meat products can become a potent source of infection. Infections are more common in children than adults. Most cases occur in the autumn and winter. *Yersinia enterocolitica* sepsis has been reported following the transfusion of blood that has been stored for more than 3 weeks at 39°F.

Yersinia enterocolitica is a well-recognized cause of abdominal pain and diarrhea in Scandinavia and northern Europe. It is less commonly seen in the USA. Cases have been reported from other parts of the world. In Europe, infections are generally sporadic and the predominant serotypes are 03 and 09. In the USA, sporadic infections are less common but food-borne outbreaks caused by serotypes 03 and 09 have been described.[79]

Yersinia pseudotuberculosis infection is less commonly seen. The organism is harbored in the gastrointestinal tract of rodents, farm animals and birds. Human infections have been reported from all parts of the world but, as with *Y. enterocolitica*, it is more common in northern Europe than elsewhere. Infection is generally seen in children and affects males more frequently than females. The majority of infections occur in the winter.[80]

Pathogenicity

Yersinia enterocolitica generally gains entry to the body via the gastrointestinal tract. The infecting dose is 10^8–10^9 organisms/ml. Within the ileum the organisms adhere to the mucosa and incite an inflammatory response. They also invade mucosal cells, Peyer's patches and macrophages, where they can survive intracellularly and multiply. This results in a severe diarrhea and abdominal pain mimicking acute appendicitis. There may be necrosis of Peyer's patches, ulcerative ileitis or mesenteric adenitis.

The organisms may disseminate through the body, producing sepsis and splenic and hepatic abscesses. A reactive polyarthritis can occur, particularly in HLA-B27-positive patients.[81]

Yersinia pseudotuberculosis generally gives rise to mesenteric adenitis. Both species produce V–W and YOPs antigens, which are essential for virulence, and an outer membrane protein, invasin, which is involved in adherence to and invasion of cells.

Prevention

Prevention of yersiniosis depends on good animal husbandry and careful slaughtering techniques to minimize contamination of meat with orofecal material. Meat should not be consumed raw and should not be stored at 39°F (4°C) for prolonged periods before consumption. There is no effective vaccine.

Diagnostic microbiology

Material for culture will include stool specimens, blood, lymph nodes and food samples. Specimens should be cultured on blood agar and MacConkey agar at 80°F (26.7C) for 24 hours. Heavily contaminated samples such as feces can be subjected to a cold enrichment technique whereby the sample is inoculated into phosphate-buffered saline and incubated at 39°F (4°C) for 3 weeks or more. The broth is subcultured at weekly intervals on to MacConkey agar or a special selective medium, CIN (cefsulodin, irgasan, novobiocin) agar. *Yersinia pseudotuberculosis* is rarely isolated from feces.

Presumptive colonies of *Yersinia* spp. are identified using a range of physical and biochemical tests (see Table 231.12). The serotype can be determined using slide agglutination tests.

A serologic diagnosis depends on demonstrating a significant rise of serotype-specific antibodies.

Clinical manifestations

A variety of clinical presentations have been documented in yersiniosis (Table 231.15). The commonest form is acute gastroenteritis due to *Y. enterocolitica*.[81,82] This is often indistinguishable from *Salmonella* or *Campylobacter* gastroenteritis, and the patient complains of abdominal pain, diarrhea and vomiting. The incubation period is probably 3–7 days. The commonest presentation of *Y. pseudotuberculosis* infection is mesenteric adenitis, which can mimic acute appendicitis.

Some patients develop a reactive polyarthritis a few days after the onset of enteritis. This is associated with the presence of HLA-B27. Erythema nodosum occurs in about one-third of patients.

Sepsis is uncommon and is generally associated with a variety of underlying conditions. These include diabetes mellitus, cirrhosis, old age, malignancy, hemachromatosis, multiple blood transfusions and iron overload, particularly when treated with deferoxamine. Patients who have sepsis may develop hepatic or splenic abscesses, endocarditis or meningitis.

The mortality of *Yersinia* sepsis is 50%.

Management

Yersinia enteritis and mesenteric adenitis do not generally require antimicrobial chemotherapy. Sepsis, extraintestinal foci of infection and enteritis in immunocompromised patients should be treated with antimicrobials. *Yersinia enterocolitica* is generally resistant to penicillin, ampicillin and first-generation cephalosporins. Aminoglycosides, quinolones, tetracyclines and third-generation cephalosporins have all been used successfully to treat *Y. enterocolitica* infections. *Yersinia pseudotuberculosis* is usually sensitive to benzylpenicillin and ampicillin.

CLINICAL MANIFESTATIONS OF YERSINIOSIS

Yersinia enterocolitica	*Yersinia pseudotuberculosis*
Gastroenteritis	Mesenteric lymphadenitis
Mesenteric lymphadenitis	Ulcerative ileitis
Ulcerative ileitis	Septicemia
Septicemia	Erythema nodosum
Hepatic or splenic abscesses	
Reactive polyarthritis (HLA-B27)	
Reiter's syndrome	
Erythema nodosum	
Meningitis	
Exudative pharyngitis	

Table 231.15 Clinical manifestations of yersiniosis. Note that septicemia in *Yersinia enterocolitica* infection is associated with underlying conditions, including diabetes mellitus, cirrhosis, malignancy, hemochromatosis, old age, anemia, iron overload and deferoxamine treatment.

REFERENCES

1. Henderson RH. EPI: 'Shots' that save lives. World Health 1987;Jan–Feb:4–7.
2. Black S. Epidemiology of pertussis. Pediatr Infect Dis J 1997;16:S85–9.
3. Hewlett EL. A commentary on the pathogenesis of pertussis. Clin Infect Dis 1999;28:S94–8.
4. Kerr JR, Matthews RC. *Bordetella pertussis* infections: pathogenesis, diagnosis, management and the role of protective immunity. Eur J Clin Microbiol Infect Dis 2000;19:77–88.
5. Heininger U. Recent progress in clinical and basic pertussis research. Eur J Pediatr 2001;160:203–13.
6. Locht C, Antoine R, Jacob-Dubuisson F. *Bordetella pertussis*, molecular pathogenesis under multiple aspects. Curr Opinion Microbiol 2001;4:82–9.
7. Grant CC, Cherry JD. Keeping pace with the elusive *Bordetella pertussis*. J Infect 2002;44:7–12.
8. Campins-Martí M, Cheng HK, Forsyth K, *et al.* Recommendations are needed for adolescent and adult pertussis Immunisation: rationale and strategies for consideration. Vaccine 2002;20:641–6.
9. Müller F-MC, Hoppe JE, von König C-HW. Laboratory diagnosis of pertussis: state of the art in 1997. J Clin Microbiol 1997;35:2435–43.
10. Ewanowich CA, Chui LW-L, Paranchych MG, *et al.* Major outbreak of pertussis in Northern Alberta, Canada: analysis of discrepant direct fluorescent-antibody and culture results by using polymerase chain reaction methodology. J Clin Microbiol 1993;31:1715–25.
11. Schneider B, Gross R. *Bordetella pertussis*: increasing problems with a well-known pathogen and its relatives. In: Mühldorfer I, Schäfer KP, eds. Emerging bacterial pathogens. Contributions in Microbiology vol 8. Basel: S Karger; 2001:123–36.
12. Cherry JD. Epidemiological, clinical and laboratory aspects of pertussis in adults. Clin Infect Dis 1999;28(Suppl.2):S112–7.
13. Hoppe JE. Update on respiratory Infection caused by *Bordetella parapertussis*. Pediatr Infect Dis J 1999;18:375–81.
14. Woolfrey BF, Moody JA. Human infections associated with *Bordetella bronchiseptica*. Clin Microbiol Rev 1991;4:2243–55.
15. Young EJ. Brucellosis: current epidemiology, diagnosis, and management. Curr Top Infect Dis 1995;15:115–18.
16. Luzzi GA, Brindle R, Sockett Solera J, Klenerman P, Warrell DA. Brucellosis: imported and laboratory acquired cases and an overview of treatment trials. Trans R Soc Trop Med Hyg 1993;87:138–41.
17. Madkour MM. Brucellosis. London: Butterworths; 1989.
18. Boschiroli M-L, Foulogne V, O'Callaghan D. Brucellosis: a worldwide zoonosis. Curr Opin Microbiol 2001;4:58–64.
19. Corbel MJ. Recent advances in brucellosis. J Med Microbiol 1997;46:101–3.
20. Matar GM, Khneisser IA, Abdelnoor AM. Rapid laboratory confirmation of human brucellosis by PCR analysis of a target sequence on the 31-kilodalton *Brucella* antigen DNA. J Clin Microbiol 1996;34:477–8.
21. Ariza J, Pellicer T, Pallares R, *et al.* Specific antibody profile in human brucellosis. Clin Infect Dis 1992;14:131–40.
22. Young EJ. Serologic diagnosis of human brucellosis: analysis of 214 cases by agglutination tests and review of the literature. Rev Infect Dis 1991;13:359–72.
23. Young EJ. An overview of human brucellosis. Clin Infect Dis 1995;21:283–90.
24. Hall WH. Modern chemotherapy for brucellosis in humans. Rev Infect Dis 1990;12:1060–99.
25. Choi C. Tularemia and Q fever. Med Clin North Am 2002;86:393–416.
26. Sjöstedt A, Tärnvik A, Sandström G. *Francisella tularensis*: host–parasite interaction. FEMS Immunol Microbiol 1996;13:181–4.
27. Nierengarten MB, Lutwick LI. Developing new tularaemia vaccines. http://www.medscape.com/viewarticle/431539.
28. Robinson-Dunn B. The microbiology laboratory's role in response to bioterrorism. Arch Pathol Lab Med 2002;126:291–3.
29. Dennis DT, Inglesby TV, Henderson DA, *et al.* Tularaemia as a biological weapon: medical and public health management. JAMA 2001;285:2763–73.
30. Cross JT, Penn RL. *Francisella tularensis* (tularemia). In: Mandell GL, Benneft JE, Dolin R, eds. Principles and practice of infections disease, 5th ed. New York: Churchill Livingstone; 2000;2393–402.
31. Limaye AP, Hooper CJ. Treatment of tularaemia with fluoroquinolones: two cases and review. Clin Infect Dis 1999;29:922–4.
32. Takala AK, Santosham M, Almeido-Hill J, *et al.* Vaccination with *Haemophilus influenzae* type b meningococcal protein conjugate vaccine reduces oropharyngeal carriage of *Haemophilus influenzae* type b among American Indian children. Pediatr Infect Dis J 1993;12:593–9.
33. Turk DC, May JR. *Haemophilus influenzae*: its clinical importance. London: English Universities Press; 1967.
34. Bijlmer HA. World-wide epidemiology of *Haemophilus influenzae* meningitis: industrialized versus non-industrialised countries. Vaccine 1991;9:55–9.
35. Brenner DJ, Meyer LW, Carlone GM, *et al.* Biochemical, genetic and epidemiological characterisation of *Haemophilus influenzae* biogroup *aegyptius* (*Haemophilus aegyptius*) strains associated with Brazilian purpuric fever. J Clin Microbiol 1988;26:1524–34.
36. VanAlphen L, van Ham SM. Adherence and invasion of *Haemophilus influenzae*. Rev Med Microbiol 1994;5:245–55.
37. Moxon ER, Zwahlen A, Rubin LB. Pathogenesis of *Haemophilus influenzae* meningitis: use of a rat model for studying microbial determinants of virulence. In: Sande M, Smith A, Root R, eds. Bacterial meningitis. New York: Churchill Livingstone;1985:23–36.
38. Decker MD, Edwards KM. *Haemophilus influenzae* type b vaccines: history, choice and comparisons. Pediatr Infect Dis J 1998;17:S113–6.
39. Wenger JD. Impact of *Haemophilus influenzae* type b vaccines on the epidemiology of bacterial meningitis. Infect Agents Dis 1994;2:324–33.
40. Heath PT, McVernon J. The UK Hib vaccine experience. Arch Dis Child 2002;86:396–9.
41. Slack MPE, Jordens JZ. *Haemophilus*. In: Collier LH, Balows A, Sussman M, eds. Topley and Wilson's microbiology and microbial infections, vol 2. London: Arnold; 1998:1167–90.
42. Friesen CA, Cho CT. Characteristic features of neonatal sepsis due to *Haemophilus influenzae*. Rev Infect Dis 1986;8:777–80.
43. Murphy TF, Apicella MA. Non-typable *Haemophilus influenzae*: a review of clinical aspects, surface antigens and the human response to infection. Rev Infect Dis 1987;9:1–15.
44. Albritton WL. Infections due to *Haemophilus* species other than *H. influenzae*. Ann Rev Microbiol 1982;36:199–216.
45. Doern GV, Brueggemann AB, Pierce G, *et al.* Antibiotic resistance among clinical isolates of *Haemophilus influenzae* in the United States in 1994 and 1995 and detection of β-lactamase-positive strains resistant to amoxicillin–clavulanate: results of a national multicenter surveillance study. Antimicrob Agents Chemother 1997;41:292–7.
46. Morse SA. Chancroid and *Haemophilus ducreyi*. Clin Microbiol Rev 1989;2:137–57.
47. Al-Tawfiq JA, Spinola SM. *Haemophilus ducreyi*: clinical disease and pathogenesis. Curr Opin Infect Dis 2002;15:43–7.
48. Fletcher MA. Vaccine candidates in STD. Int J STD AIDS 2001;12:419–22.
49. Lewis DA. Diagnostic tests for chancroid. Sex Transm Infect 2000;76:137–41.
50. Tree DL, Morse SA. Chancroid and *Haemophilus ducreyi*: an update. Clin Microbiol Rev 1995;8:357–75.
51. Chui L, Albritton W, Paster B, MacLean I, Marusyk R. Development of the polymerase chain reaction for diagnosis of chancroid. J Clin Microbiol 1993;31:659–64.
52. Martin DH, Sargent SJ, Wendel GD Jr, *et al.* Comparison of azithromycin and ceftriaxone for the treatment of chancroid. Clin Infect Dis 1995;21:409–14.
53. Ison CA, Dillon J-AR, Tapsall JW. The epidemiology of global antibiotic resistance among *Neisseria gonorrhoeae* and *Haemophilus ducreyi*. Lancet 1998;351:8–11.
54. Schulte JM, Schmid GP. Recommendations for treatment of chancroid, 1993. Clin Infect Dis 1995;20(Suppl.1):39–46.
55. Brouqui P, Raoult D. Endocarditis due to rare and fastidious bacteria. Clin Microbiol Rev 2001;14:177–207.
56. Kaplan AH, Weber DJ, Oddone EZ, Perfect JR. Infection due to *Actinobacillus actinomycetemcomitans*: 15 cases and review. Rev Infect Dis 1989;11:46–63.
57. Wormser GP, Bottone EJ. *Cardiobacterium hominis*: review of microbiologic and clinical features. Rev Infect Dis 1983;5:680–691.
58. Chen CKC, Wilson ME. *Eikenella corrodens* in human oral and non-oral infections: a review. J Periodontol 1992;63:941–53.
59. Joshi N, O'Bryan T, Appelbaum PC. Pleuropulmonary Infections caused by *Eikenella corrodens*. Rev Infect Dis 1991;13:1207–12.
60. Goldstein EJC. Bite wounds and infection. Clin Infect Dis 1992;14:633–40.
61. Moylett EH, Rossmann SN, Epps HR, Demmler GJ. Importance of *Kingella kingae* as a pediatric pathogen in the United States. Pediatr Infect Dis J 2000;19:263–5.
62. Fields BS. The role of amoebae in Legionellosis. Clin Microbiol Newsl 1991;13:92–3.
63. Fraser DW, Tsai TR, Orenstein W, *et al.* Legionnaires' disease: description of an epidemic of pneumonia. N Engl J Med 1977;297:1189–97.
64. Cianciotto NP. Pathogenicity of *Legionella pneumophila*. Int J Med Microbiol 2001;291:331–43.
65. Stout JE, Lin YSE, Goetz AM, Muder RR. Controlling *Legionella* in hospital water systems: experience with the superheat-and-flush method and copper–silver ionization. Infect Control Hosp Epidemiol 1998;19:911–14.
66. Muraca PW, Yu VL, Goetz A. Disinfection of water distribution systems for *Legionella*: a review of application procedures and methodologies. Infect Control Hosp Epidemiol 1990;11:79–88.
67. Waterer GW, Baselski VS, Wunderink RG. Legionella and community-acquired pneumonia: a review of current diagnostic tests from a clinician's viewpoint. Am J Med 2001;110:41–8.
68. Glick TH, Gregg MB, Berman B, *et al.* Pontiac fever. An epidemic of unknown etiology in a health department. 1. Clinical and epidemiologic aspects. Am J Epidemiol 1978;107:149–60.
69. Stout JE, Yu VL. Current concepts: legionellosis. N Engl J Med 1997;337;12:322–8.
70. Verduin CM, Hol C, Fleer A, van Dijk H, van Belkum A. *Moraxella catarrhalis*: from emerging to established pathogen. Clin Microbiol Rev 2002:125–44.
71. Enright MC, McKenzie H. *Moraxella* (*Branhamella*) *catarrhalis* – clinical and molecular aspects of a rediscovered pathogen. J Med Microbiol 1997;46:360–71.
72. Francis DP, Holmes MA, Brandon G. *Pasteurella multocida*: infections after domestic animal bites and scratches. JAMA 1975;233:42–5.
73. Adlam C, Rutter JM. *Pasteurella* and pasteurellosis. London: Academic Press; 1989.

74. Weber DJ. *Pasteurella multocida* infections: report of 34 cases and review of the literature. Medicine (Baltimore) 1984;63:135–54.
75. Human plague in 1994. Wkly Epidemiol Rec 1996;71:165–8.
76. Butler T. Plague and other *Yersinia* infections. New York: Plenum Press; 1983.
77. Straley SC, Skrzypek E, Plano GV, Bliska JB. YOPs of *Yersinia* spp. pathogenic for humans. Infect Immun 1993;61:3105–10.
78. Williamson ED. Plague vaccine research and development. J Appl Microbiol 2001;91:606–8.
79. Anderson JK, Sørensen R, Glensbjerg M. Aspects of the epidemiology of *Yersinia enterocolitica*: a review. Int J Food Microbiol 1991;13:231–8.
80. Naktin J, Beavis KG. *Yersinia enterocolitica* and *Yersinia pseudotuberculosis*. Clin Lab Med 1999;19:523–36.
81. Bottone EJ. *Yersinunia enterocolotica*: overview and epidemologic correlates. Microbes Infect 1999;323–33.

chapter

232 Anaerobic Bacteria

Itzhak Brook

INTRODUCTION

Infections caused by anaerobic bacteria are common, and may be serious and life-threatening. Anaerobes are the predominant components of the bacterial flora of normal human skin and mucous membranes,[1] and are therefore a common cause of bacterial infections of endogenous origin. Because of their fastidious nature, these organisms are difficult to isolate from infectious sites and are often overlooked. Delay in appropriate therapy against these organisms often leads to clinical failures. Their isolation requires appropriate methods of collection, transportation and cultivation of specimens.[2–4] Treatment of anaerobic bacterial infection is complicated by the slow growth of these organisms, which makes diagnosis in the laboratory only possible after several days, by the often polymicrobial nature of the infection and by the growing resistance of anaerobic bacteria to antimicrobial agents.

NATURE

Anaerobic bacteria do not grow on solid media in the presence of room air (10% carbon dioxide and 18% oxygen), whereas facultative anaerobic bacteria grow both in the presence and in the absence of air. Microaerophilic bacteria grow poorly or not at all aerobically, but grow better under 10% carbon dioxide or anaerobically. Anaerobes can be divided into strict anaerobes that are unable to grow in the presence of more than 0.5% oxygen and moderate anaerobes that are capable of growing at between 2 and 8% oxygen.[4] Anaerobes generally do not possess catalase, but some clinical isolates produce superoxide dismutase that can protect them from oxygen.

The clinically important anaerobic bacteria are:

- six genera of Gram-negative rods (*Bacteroides, Prevotella, Porphyromonas, Fusobacterium, Bilophila* and *Sutterella* spp.);
- Gram-positive cocci (primarily *Peptostreptococcus* spp.);
- Gram-positive spore-forming (*Clostridium* spp.) and nonspore-forming bacilli (*Actinomyces, Propionibacterium, Eubacterium, Lactobacillus* and *Bifidobacterium* spp.); and
- Gram-negative cocci (mainly *Veillonella* spp.) (Table 232.1).[4–6]

The frequency of recovery of anaerobic bacterial strains differs in various infectious sites (Table 232.2). Mixed infections caused by numerous aerobic and anaerobic organisms are observed commonly in clinical situations (Fig. 232.1).[2,3]

The taxonomy of anaerobic bacteria has changed in recent years because of improved characterization methods using genetic studies.[4,6] The ability to differentiate between similar strains enables better characterization of type of infection and predicted antimicrobial susceptibility.

The species of anaerobes most frequently isolated from clinical infections are, in decreasing frequency:

- Gram-negative bacilli,
- Gram-positive cocci,
- *Clostridium* spp.,
- *Fusobacterium* spp.,
- Gram-positive bacilli (*Eubacterium, Lactobacillus, Propionibacterium, Actinomyces* and *Bifidobacterium* spp.), and
- Gram-negative cocci (*Veillonella* and *Acidaminococcus* spp.).[2–4]

Approximately 95% of the anaerobes isolated from clinical infections are members of these genera. The remaining isolates belong to species not yet described, but these usually can be assigned to the appropriate genus on the basis of morphologic characteristics and fermentation products. The frequency of recovery of anaerobic strains differs in various infectious sites.

EPIDEMIOLOGY

Most infections are caused by anaerobes that belong to the normal flora. Only when the situation is out of balance and the local defenses are decreased in capacity, anaerobic infection can then occur. Some anaerobic infections are caused by contamination of

PREDOMINANT ANAEROBIC BACTERIA	
Gram-positive cocci	*Peptostreptococcus* spp.: *P. magnus, P. asaccharolyticus, P. prevotii, P. intermedius, P. anaerobius, P. micros* Microaerophilic streptococci (not true anaerobes)
Gram-positive nonspore-forming bacilli	*Propionibacterium* spp.: *P. acnes, P. propionicum, P. granulosum* *Eubacterium tentum* *Bifidobacterium* spp.: *B. eriksonii, B. dentium* *Actinomyces* spp.: *A. israelii, A. naestundii, A. viscosus, A. odontolyticus, A. meyerii*
Gram-positive spore-forming bacilli	*Clostridium* spp.: *C. perfringens, C. ramosum, C. septicum, C. novyi, C. histolytica, C. sporogenes, C. difficile, C. bifermentans, C. butyricum, C. innocuum, C. sordellii, C. botulinum, C. tetani*
Gram-negative bacilli	*Bacteroides fragilis* group: *B. fragilis, B. thetaiotaomicron, B. distasonis, B. vulgatus, B. ovatus, B. uniformis* Other *Bacteroides* spp.: *B. gracilis, B. ureolyticus* Pigmented *Prevotella* spp.: *P. melaninogenica, P. intermedia, P. denticola, P. loescheii, P. corporis, P. nigrescens* Other *Prevotella* spp.: *P. oris, P. buccae, P. oralis* group (*P. oralis, P. buccalis, P. veroralis*), *P. bivia, P. disiens* *Porphyromonas* spp.: *P. asaccharolytica, P. gingivalis, P. endodontalis* *Fusobacterium* spp.: *F. nucleatum, F. necrophorum, F. gonidiaformans, F. naviforme, F. mortiferum, F. varium*

Table 232.1 Predominant anaerobic bacteria.

ANAEROBIC BACTERIA MOST FREQUENTLY ENCOUNTERED IN SPECIFIC INFECTION SITES		
Organism		Infection site
Gram-positive cocci	*Peptostreptococcus* spp.	Respiratory tract, intra-abdominal and soft-tissue infections
	Microaerophilic streptococci (not obligate anaerobes)	Sinusitis, brain abscesses
Gram-positive bacilli	Nonspore-forming: *Actinomyces* spp.	Intracranial abscesses, chronic mastoiditis, aspiration pneumonia, head and neck infections
	Propionibacterium acnes	Shunt infections (cardiac, intracranial), infections associated with foreign body
	Bifidobacterium spp.	Chronic otitis media, cervical lymphadenitis, abdominal infections
	Spore-forming: *Clostridium perfringens*	Soft-tissue infection, sepsis, food poisoning
	Clostridium septicum	Sepsis, neutropenic enterocolitis
	Clostridium difficile	Colitis, antibiotic-associated diarrheal disease
	Clostridium botulinum	Botulism
	Clostridium tetani	Tetanus
	Clostridium ramosum	Soft-tissue infections
Gram-negative bacilli	*Bacteroides fragilis* group	Intra-abdominal and female genital tract infections, sepsis, neonatal infections
	Pigmented *Prevotella* and *Porphyromonas* spp.	Orofacial infections, aspiration pneumonia, periodontitis
	Prevotella oralis	Orofacial infections
	Prevotella oris-buccae	Orofacial infections, intra-abdominal infections
	Prevotella bivia, Prevotella disiens	Female genital tract infections
	Fusobacterium nucleatum	Orofacial and respiratory tract infections, brain abscesses, bacteremia
	Fusobacterium necrophorum	Aspiration pneumonia, bacteremia

Table 232.2 Anaerobic bacteria most frequently encountered in specific infection sites.

wounds by soil containing anaerobes. Such is the case with some *Clostridium* infections. *Clostridium difficile* enterocolitis can lead to epidemics in the hospital. In geriatric wards and nurseries in particular, these bacteria are transmitted by hands from one patient to another. *Clostridium botulinum* causes food poisoning due to the presence of the toxin produced by *C. botulinum* in food.

Gram-positive spore-forming bacilli

Anaerobic spore-forming bacilli belong to the genus *Clostridium*. Morphologically, the clostridia are highly pleomorphic, ranging from short, thick bacilli to long filamentous forms, and are either ramrod straight or slightly curved. The clostridia found most frequently in clinical infections are *Clostridium perfringens* (Fig. 232.2), *Clostridium septicum*, *Clostridium ramosum*, *Clostridium novyi*, *Clostridium sordellii*, *Clostridium histolyticum*, *Clostridium fallax*, *Clostridium bifermentans* and *Clostridium innocuum*.

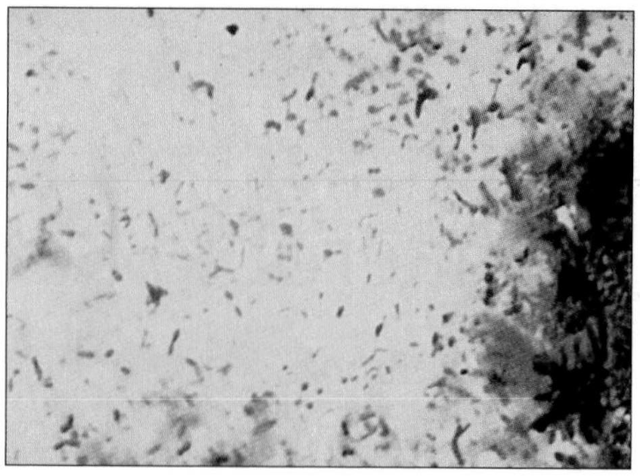

Fig. 232.1 Gram stain of a perirectal abscess caused by polymicrobial aerobic and anaerobic flora.

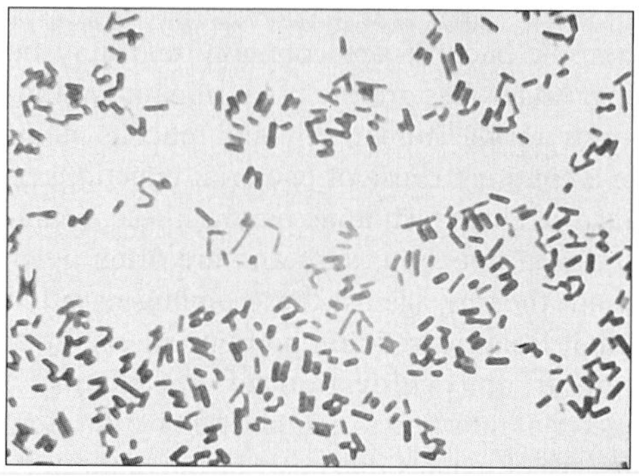

Fig. 232.2 Gram stain of *Clostridium perfringens*.

Clostridium perfringens, the most commonly recovered *Clostridium* isolate, is an inhabitant of soil and of intestines of humans and animals, and is the most frequently encountered histotoxic *Clostridium* species. This micro-organism, which elaborates a number of necrotizing extracellular toxins,[7,8] is easily isolated and identified in the clinical laboratory. It can be characterized in direct smears of a purulent exudate by the presence of stout Gram-variable rods of varying length, frequently surrounded by a capsule. *Clostridium perfringens* can cause a devastating illness with a high mortality rate. Bacteremia caused by *Clostridium* spp. is associated with extensive tissue necrosis, hemolytic anemia and renal failure.

Clostridium septicum has often been found to be associated with malignancy. The intestinal tract is thought to be the source of the organism, and most of the isolates are recovered from blood and subcutaneous tissue.

Although *C. botulinum* is usually associated with food poisoning, wound infections caused by this organism are being recognized with increasing frequency. Proteolytic strains of types A and B have been reported from food poisoning and wound infections. Infant botulism occurs with types A, B and F.[7] Disease caused by *C. botulinum* is usually an intoxication produced by ingestion of contaminated food (uncooked meat, poorly processed fish, improperly canned vegetables) containing a highly potent neurotoxin.[8] The polypeptide neurotoxin is relatively heat labile, and food containing this toxin may be rendered innocuous by exposure to 212°F (100°C) for 10 minutes. Infection of a wound with *C. botulinum* occurs rarely and can produce botulism.

Clostridium difficile has been incriminated as the causative agent of antibiotic-associated and spontaneous diarrhea and colitis.[9] *Clostridium tetani* is found in soil and is rarely isolated from human feces. Infections caused by this bacillus are a result of contamination of wounds with soil containing *C. tetani* spores.[8] The spores will germinate in devitalized tissue and produce the neurotoxin that is responsible for the clinical findings.

Gram-positive, nonspore-forming bacilli

Anaerobic, Gram-positive, nonspore-forming rods comprise part of the microflora of the gingival crevices, the gastrointestinal tract, the vagina and the skin. Several distinct genera are recognized: *Actinomyces, Arcanobacterium, Atopobium, Bifidobacterium, Eubacterium, Lactobacillus, Mobiluncus, Propionibacterium* and *Pseudoramibacter*. The most frequently recovered species are *Propionibacterium, Eubacterium, Bifidobacterium* and *Lactobacillus*.

The *Actinomyces, Arcanobacterium* and *Bifidobacterium* spp. are Gram-positive, pleomorphic, anaerobic to microaerophilic bacilli.

Actinomyces israelii, Actinomyces naeslundii and *Propionibacterium propionicum* are normal inhabitants of the human mouth and throat and are the most frequent cause of actinomycosis. The organisms have been recovered from intracranial abscesses, chronic mastoiditis, aspiration pneumonia and peritonitis.[3,5] The lesions of actinomycosis occur most commonly in the tissues of the face, neck, lungs, pleura and ileocecal regions. Bone, pericardial and anorectal lesions are less common, but virtually any tissue may be invaded; even disseminated infection with bacteremia has been described.

Most organisms of the genus *Eubacterium* and anaerobic lactobacilli seem to be nonpathogenic. They are almost invariably isolated as part of mixed flora in the oral, vaginal and gastrointestinal areas. These organisms have been recovered most commonly in infections associated with predisposing or underlying conditions that include malignancy, previous surgery, immunodeficiency, diabetes mellitus, the presence of a foreign body, dental extraction and broad-spectrum antibiotic therapy.[10]

Propionibacterium spp. ordinarily are not pathogens, but can be found in association with implanted cardiac prostheses or central nervous system (CNS) shunts or as a cause of endocarditis on previously damaged valves. They have been recovered from parotid and dental infections, brain abscesses, conjunctivitis associated with contact lens, peritonitis and pulmonary infections. The most common species, *Propionibacterium acnes*, may be isolated from blood cultures but is associated only rarely with bacteremia or endocarditis. Because these organisms are part of the normal skin flora, they are common laboratory contaminants or may grow in blood cultures from skin contamination if the skin surface has been improperly decontaminated before the blood sample is drawn. *Propionibacterium acnes* can cause bacteremia, especially in association with shunt infections,[11] and is believed to play a role in the pathogenesis of acne vulgaris.

Gram-negative bacilli

Bacteroides fragilis group are the most frequently recovered species of Bacteroidaceae in clinical specimens (Fig. 232.3). *Bacteroides fragilis* group are resistant to penicillins, mostly through the production of β-lactamase. They include ten members – the most commonly isolated are *B. fragilis* (the most commonly recovered member), *Bacteroides thetaiotaomicron, Bacteroides distasonis, Bacteroides ovatus* and *Bacteroides vulgatus*. These organisms are part of the normal gastrointestinal flora[1] and predominate in intra-abdominal infections and other infections that originate from the gut flora (i.e. perirectal abscesses, decubitus ulcers).[3,5]

Pigmented *Prevotella* spp. (*Prevotella melaninogenica* and *Prevotella intermedia*), *Porphyromonas* spp. (*Porphyromonas asaccharolytica*) and nonpigmented *Prevotella* spp. (*Prevotella oralis, Prevotella oris*) are part of the normal oral and vaginal flora and are the predominant Gram-negative anaerobic species isolated from respiratory infections and their complications, aspiration pneumonia, lung abscess, chronic otitis media, chronic sinusitis, abscesses around the oral cavity, human bites, paronychia, brain abscesses and osteomyelitis.[12] *Prevotella bivia* and *Prevotella disiens* are important isolates from obstetric and gynecologic infections.

Fusobacterium species

Fusobacterium spp. are moderately long and thin organisms with tapered ends, and have typical fusiform morphology (Fig. 232.4). The species of *Fusobacterium* seen most often in clinical infections are *Fusobacterium nucleatum, Fusobacterium necrophorum, Fusobacterium mortiferum* and *Fusobacterium varium*. *Fusobacterium nucleatum* is the predominant *Fusobacterium* sp. from clinical specimens, and is often associated with oral, pulmonary and intracranial infections.[13] *Fusobacterium* spp. are frequently isolated from abscesses, obstetric and gynecologic infections, blood and wounds.

A growing resistance of Gram-negative anaerobic bacilli to penicillins has been noticed in the past decade.[14] These include the pigmented *Prevotella* and *Porphyromonas*, *Prev. oralis, Prev. disiens, Prev. bivia* and *Fusobacterium* spp. The main mechanism of resistance is through the production of the enzyme β-lactamase. Testing for antimicrobial susceptibility and the ability to produce β-lactamase of all Gram-negative anaerobic bacilli can assist in the selection of proper antimicrobials.

The recovery rates of the different anaerobic Gram-negative bacilli in infected sites are similar to their distributions in the normal flora.[3,5] *B. fragilis* group were more often isolates in sites proximal to the gastrointestinal tract (abdomen, bile), pigmented *Prevotella* spp. were more prevalent in infections proximal to the oral cavity (bones, sinuses, chest), and *Prev. bivia* and *Prev. disiens* were more often isolates in obstetric and gynecologic infections (see Table 232.2). Knowledge of this common mode of distribution allows for logical choice of antimicrobials that are adequate for the therapy of infections in these sites.

Gram-positive cocci

The species most commonly isolated are *Peptostreptococcus magnus, Peptostreptococcus asaccharolyticus, Peptostreptococcus anaerobius, Peptostreptococcus prevotii* and *Peptostreptococcus micros*.

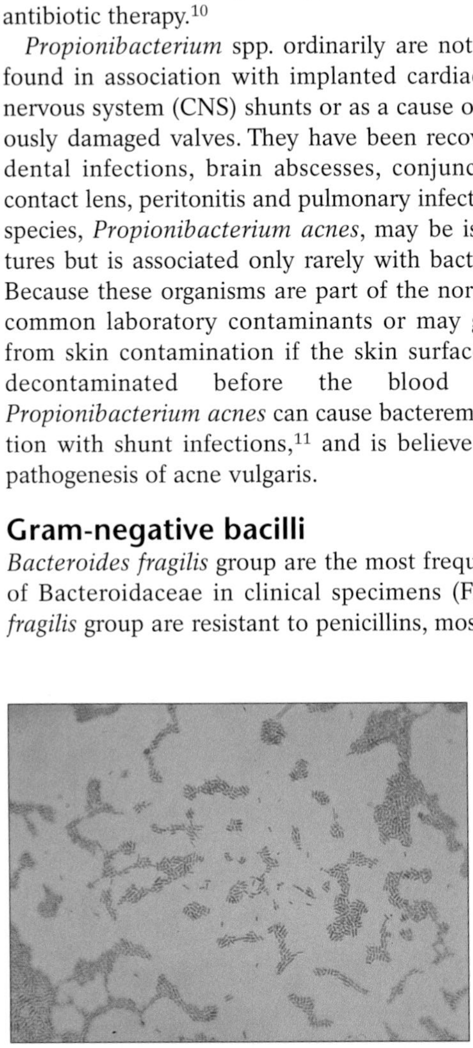

Fig. 232.3 Gram stain of *Bacteroides fragilis*. Courtesy of Mike Cox.

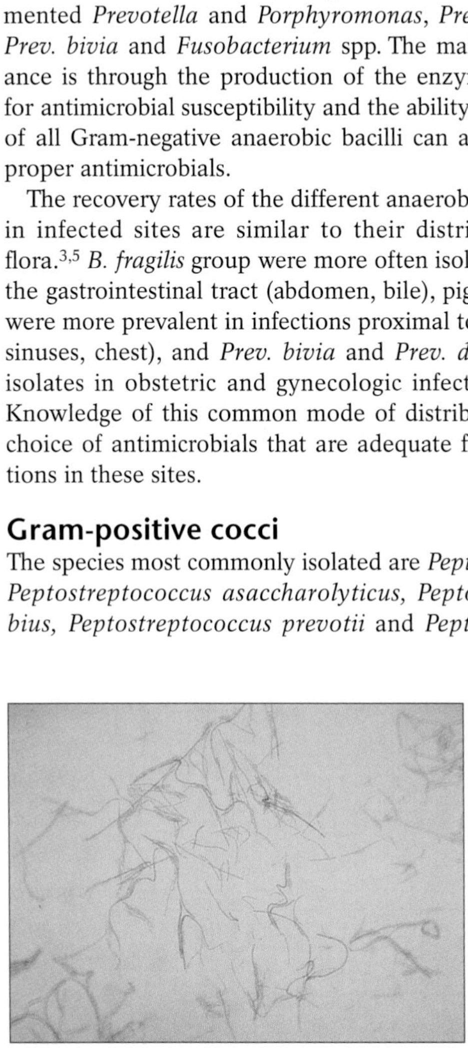

Fig. 232.4 Gram stain of *Fusobacterium nucleatum*. Courtesy of Mike Cox.

Additional anaerobic cocci include *Coprococcus, Peptococcus, Ruminococcus sarcina* and *Staphylococcus saccharolyticus*. These organisms are part of the normal flora of the mouth, upper respiratory tract, intestinal tract, vagina and skin.

These organisms can be isolated in all types of anaerobic infections. They also predominant in all types of respiratory infections (including chronic sinusitis, mastoiditis, acute and chronic otitis media, aspiration pneumonia and lung abscess), and necrotizing, subcutaneous and soft tissue infections.[15] They are generally recovered mixed with other aerobic or anaerobic organisms, but in many cases they are the only pathogens recovered. This may be of particular significance in cases of bacteremia. Microaerophilic Gram-positive cocci include *Streptococcus anginosus, Streptococcus constellatus, Streptococcus intermedius* and *Gemella morbillorum.* Microaerophilic streptococci are of particular importance in chronic sinusitis and brain abscesses. They are also recovered from obstetric and gynecologic infections and abscesses.[16]

Gram-negative cocci

There are three genera described as anaerobic Gram-negative cocci: *Veillonella*, *Acidaminococcus* and *Megasphaera* spp. There are two described species of *Veillonella* and only one each of the other two genera. *Veillonella* is the most frequently involved of the three genera and *Veillonella* spp. are part of the normal flora of the mouth, vagina and the small intestine of some persons. Although they are rarely isolated from clinical infections, these organisms have been recovered occasionally from almost every type of anaerobic infection.[17]

PATHOGENICITY

Anaerobes as part of the normal flora

The human body mucosal and epithelial surfaces are colonized with aerobic and anaerobic micro-organisms.[1] Differences in the environment, such as oxygen tension, pH and variations in the ability of bacteria to adhere to these surfaces, account for changing patterns of colonization. Microflora also vary in different sites within the body system, as in the oral cavity; for example, the micro-organisms present in the buccal folds vary in their concentration and types of strains from those isolated from the tongue or gingival sulci. However, the organisms that prevail in one body system tend to belong to certain major bacterial species, and their presence in that system is predictable. The relative and total counts of organisms can be affected by various factors, such as age, diet, anatomic variations, illness, hospitalization and antimicrobial therapy. However, these sets of bacterial flora, with predictable pattern, remain stable through life, despite their subjection to perturbing factors. Anaerobes outnumber aerobic bacteria on all mucosal surfaces, and certain organisms predominate in the different sites (see Table 232.3).

Knowledge of the composition of the flora at certain sites is useful for predicting which organisms may be involved in an infection adjacent to that site and can assist in the selection of a logical antimicrobial therapy, even before the exact microbial etiology of the infection is known. Recognition of the normal flora can also help the clinical microbiology laboratory to choose proper culture media that will be selective in inhibiting organisms that may interfere with the growth of certain anaerobic bacteria.

The anaerobic microflora of the skin is largely made up of the genus *Propionibacterium*[11] (mostly *Propionibacterium acnes*) and, to a lesser extent, *Peptostreptococcus* spp. The perineum and lower extremity may harbor members of the colonic and vaginal flora.

The microflora of the upper airways, including oral cavity, nasopharynx and oropharynx, is complex and contains many types of obligate anaerobes. The distribution of bacteria within the mouth seems to be a function of their ability to adhere to the oral surfaces. The differences in numbers of the anaerobic microflora probably occur because of considerable variations in the oxygen concentration in parts of the oral cavity. The ratio of anaerobic bacteria to aerobic bacteria in saliva is approximately 10:1. The total count of anaerobic bacteria in the saliva and elsewhere in the oral cavity reach 10^7–10^8 bacteria/ml. The predominant anaerobic bacteria in the upper airways include *Fusobacterium* spp. (especially *F. nucleatum*), pigmented *Prevotella* and *Porphyromonas* spp., *Prev. oralis* and *Peptostreptococcus* spp. These organisms also predominate in oropharyngeal, otolaryngologic and pulmonary infections.

The gastrointestinal flora varies in bacterial concentration at different levels. The stomach acidity reduces the number of organisms swallowed from the oropharynx. The stomach, duodenum, jejunum and

NORMAL FLORA			
Site	No. of organisms/g fecal material		Predominant anaerobic bacteria
	Aerobes	Anaerobes	
Skin	–	–	*Propionibacterium acnes* *Peptostreptococcus* spp.
Mouth/upper respiratory tract	10^8–10^9	10^9–10^{11}	Pigmented *Prevotella* and *Porphyromonas* spp. *Fusobacterium* spp. *Peptostreptococcus* spp. *Actinomyces* spp.
Gastrointestinal tract:			
Upper	10^2–10^5	10^3–10^7	*Bacteroides fragilis* group *Clostridium* spp.
Lower	10^5–10^9	10^{10}–10^{12}	*Peptostreptococcus* spp. *Bifidobacterium* spp. *Eubacterium* spp.
Female genital tract	10^8	10^9	*Peptostreptococcus* spp. *Prevotella bivia* *Prevotella disiens*

Table 232.3 Normal flora. For predominant anaerobic bacteria in the gastrointestinal tract, all organisms can be found both in the upper and lower gastrointestinal tracts.

proximal ileum normally contain relatively few bacteria. However, the flora becomes more complex, and the number of different bacterial species increase in the distal portion of the gastrointestinal tract. However, interruption in intestinal motility may result in an increase in the number of anaerobic and aerobic bacteria. The bacterial counts in the small intestine are relatively low, with total counts of 10^2–10^5 organisms/ml. The organisms that predominate up to the ileocecal valve are Gram-positive facultative, whereas below that structure *Bacteroides*, *Peptostreptococcus* and *Clostridium* spp., and coliform bacteria are the major isolates.[2] The mean number of bacteria in the colon exceeds 10^{11} bacteria/g fecal material. Approximately 99.9% of these bacteria are anaerobic (ratio of aerobes to anaerobes is 1:1000–10,000). In the colon 300–400 different species or types of bacteria can be found, many of whom are not yet identified.

The female genital flora is composed of mixed aerobic and anaerobic flora. However, the concentration and type of bacteria is less stable than that of the gastrointestinal flora and can be influenced by antimicrobial therapy, pregnancy and gynecologic surgery. A concentration of 10^8 organisms/ml is found during the reproductive years. Changes occur in the number of organisms at the various stages of the menstrual cycle.[18] The predominant aerobic organisms are aerobic lactobacilli, and the predominant anaerobic bacteria are anaerobic *Lactobacillus*, *Peptostreptococcus*, *Prevotella* and *Bacteroides* and *Clostridium* spp. Other anaerobic isolates include *Porphyromonas*, *Fusobacterium*, *Bilophilia*, *Bifidobacterium*, *Actinomyces*, *Eubacterium* and *Propionibacterium* spp. Enterobacteriaceae can be found in postmenopausal flora. Bacterial vaginosis is associated with an increase in the number of anaerobic flora and a decrease in the concentration of lactobacilli.[19]

Most infections caused by anaerobic bacteria originate from the endogenous mucosal membrane and skin flora. An exception is *C. difficile*, the major cause of antibiotic-associated colitis. Anaerobes belonging to the indigenous flora of the oral cavity can be recovered from various infections adjacent to that area, such as cervical lymphadenitis, subcutaneous abscesses and burns in proximity to the oral cavity, human and animal bites, paronychia, tonsillar and retropharyngeal abscesses, chronic sinusitis, chronic otitis media, periodontal abscess, thyroiditis, aspiration pneumonia and bacteremia associated with one of the above infections.[3,5] The predominant anaerobes recovered in these infections are *Prevotella*, *Porphyromonas*, *Fusobacterium* and *Peptostreptococcus* spp., which are all part of the normal flora of the mucous surfaces of the oropharynx (Fig. 232.5).

A similar correlation exists in infections associated with the gastrointestinal tract. Such infections include peritonitis after rupture of a viscus, liver and spleen abscess, abscess and wounds near the anus, intra-abdominal abscess, and bacteremia associated with any of these infections.[3,5] The anaerobes that predominate in these infections are *B. fragilis* group, *Clostridium* spp. (including *C. perfringens*) and *Peptostreptococcus* spp.

Another site where a correlation exists between the normal flora and the anaerobic bacteria recovered from infected sites is the genitourinary tract. The infections involved are amnionitis, septic abortion and other pelvic inflammations.[3,5] The anaerobes usually recovered from these sites are species of anaerobic Gram-negative bacteria and *Peptostreptococcus* spp. Organisms belonging to the vaginal–cervical flora are also important pathogens of neonatal infections. They can be acquired by the newborn before delivery in the presence of amnionitis or during passage through the birth canal.

Conditions predisposing to anaerobic infection

The clinical situations that predispose to anaerobic infections include exposure of the sterile body sites to a high inoculum of indigenous mucous membrane flora. Poor blood supply and tissue necrosis lower the oxidation and reduction potential and favor the growth of anaerobic bacteria. Any condition that lowers the blood supply to an affected area of the body can predispose to anaerobic infection. Therefore, trauma, foreign body, malignancy, surgery, edema, shock, colitis and vascular disease may predispose to anaerobic infection. Other predisposing conditions include diabetes mellitus, splenectomy, immunosuppression, hypogammaglobinemia, neutropenia, leukemia, collagen vascular disease and cytotoxic drugs. Previous infection with aerobic or facultative organisms may make the local tissue conditions more favorable for the growth of anaerobic bacteria. The human defense mechanisms may also be impaired by anaerobic conditions and anaerobic bacteria. The noted effects include impairments in phagocytosis and intracellular killing (often caused by encapsulated anaerobes[20] and by succinic acid produced by *Bacteroides* spp.), inhibition of chemotaxis (by *Fusobacterium*, *Prevotella* and *Porphyromonas* spp.), degradation of serum proteins by proteases (by *Bacteroides* spp.) and production of leukotoxins (by *Fusobacterium* spp.).[21]

Suppuration, abscess formation, thrombophlebitis and gangrenous destruction of tissue associated with gas formation are the hallmarks of anaerobic infection (Table 232.4). Anaerobes are especially common in chronic infections, and they are commonly seen after failure of therapy with antimicrobials that are effective against them, such as aminoglycosides, trimethoprim–sulfamethoxazole (co-trimoxazole) and earlier quinolones.

Certain infections are very likely to involve anaerobes as important pathogens, and their presence should always be assumed. Such infections include brain abscess, oral or dental infections, human or animal bites, aspiration pneumonia and lung abscesses, peritonitis after perforation of viscus, amnionitis, endometritis, septic abortions,

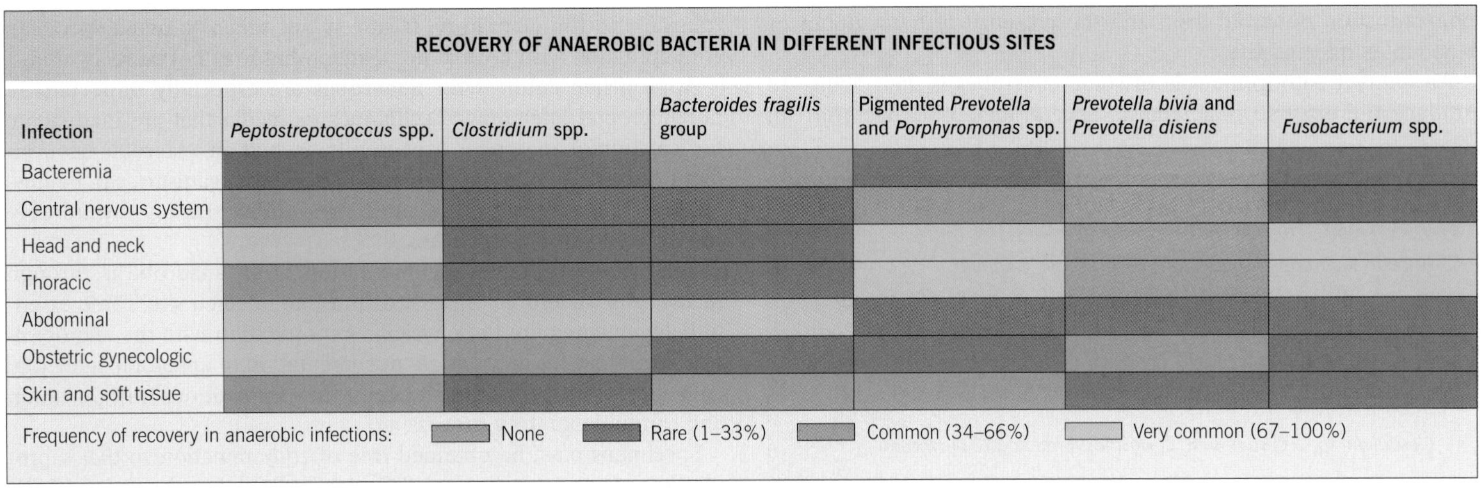

RECOVERY OF ANAEROBIC BACTERIA IN DIFFERENT INFECTIOUS SITES
Infection
Peptostreptococcus spp.
Clostridium spp.
Bacteroides fragilis group
Pigmented Prevotella and Porphyromonas spp.
Prevotella bivia and Prevotella disiens
Fusobacterium spp.
Bacteremia
Central nervous system
Head and neck
Thoracic
Abdominal
Obstetric gynecologic
Skin and soft tissue
Frequency of recovery in anaerobic infections:
None
Rare (1–33%)
Common (34–66%)
Very common (67–100%)

Fig. 232.5 Recovery of anaerobic bacteria in different infectious sites.

CLINICAL SIGNS OF ANAEROBIC INFECTION
• Infection adjacent to a mucosal surface
• Foul-smelling discharge
• Necrotic gangrenous tissue and abscess formation
• Free gas in tissue
• Bacteremia or endocarditis with no growth on aerobic blood cultures
• Infection related to the use of antibiotics effective against aerobes only
• Infection related to tumors or other destructive processes
• Infected thrombophlebitis
• Infection after bites
• Black discoloration of exudates containing *Bacteroides melaninogenicus*, which may fluoresce under ultraviolet light
• 'Sulfur granules' in discharges caused by actinomycosis
• Clinical presentation of gas gangrene
• Clinical condition predisposing to anaerobic infection (after maternal amnionitis, perforation of bowel, etc.)

Table 232.4 Clinical signs of anaerobic infection.

tubo-ovarian abscess, abscesses in and around the oral and rectal areas, pus-forming necrotizing infections of soft tissue or muscle and postsurgical infections following procedures on the oral or gastrointestinal tract or female pelvic area. Certain solid malignant tumors, such as colon, uterine and bronchogenic carcinomas, and necrotic tumors of the head and neck, have the tendency to become infected with anaerobic bacteria.[22] The anoxic conditions in the tumor and exposure to the endogenous adjacent mucous flora may predispose to these infections.

Virulence factors

Anaerobes contribute to the severity of infection through their synergy with their aerobic counterparts and with each other.[23] Anaerobic bacteria generally take longer than aerobic bacteria to become virulent. This is because some of the major virulence factors of certain anaerobic bacteria (i.e. the production of a capsule) are expressed only after the infection has become chronic.[20]

Anaerobic bacteria possess several virulence factors that assist them to adhere and invade epithelial surfaces. These factors include the presence of surface structures (such as capsule polysaccharide or lipopolysaccharide), production of superoxide dismutase and catalase, immunoglobulin proteases, coagulation promoting, spreading factors (such as hyaluronidase, collagenase and fibrinolysin), adherence factors, and the production of toxins.[21] Other factors that enhance the virulence of anaerobes include mucosal damage, oxidation–reduction potential drop and the presence of hemoglobin or blood in an infected site.

An indirect pathogenic role of some anaerobes is their ability to produce the enzyme β-lactamase. Several anaerobic bacteria can produce β-lactamase (Table 232.5). β-lactamase-producing bacteria (BLPB) can protect not only themselves but also other penicillin-susceptible organisms from the activity of penicillins. This can occur when the enzyme β-lactamase is secreted into the infected tissue or abscess fluid in sufficient quantities to degrade the β-lactam ring of penicillin before it can kill the susceptible bacteria.[24]

In-vitro and *in-vivo* studies have demonstrated protection of penicillin-susceptible bacteria from penicillin by aerobic and anaerobic BLPB (i.e. protection of group A streptococci by *Staphylococcus aureus* or *Bacteroides* spp.).[24] The predominant anaerobic BLPB are pigmented *Prevotella* and *Porphyromonas*, *Bacteroides* and *Fusobacterium* spp.

PRINCIPAL β-LACTAMASE-PRODUCING ANAEROBES
• *Fusobacterium* spp.: *F. nucleatum*, *F mortiferum*, *F. varium*
• Pigmented *Prevotella* and *Porphyromonas* spp., *Prevotella oralis* group
• Other *Prevotella* spp.: *P. oris*, *P. buccae*, *P. bivia*, *P. disiens*
• *Bacteroides fragilis* group, *Bacteroides splanchnicus*
• *Bilophila wadsworthia*
• *Clostridium* spp.: *C. ramosum*, *C. clostridioforme* and *C. butyricum*

Table 232.5 Principal β-lactamase-producing anaerobes.

PREVENTION

Proper therapy of acute infections can prevent the occurrence of chronic infections where anaerobes predominate. In settings where anaerobic infections are expected to occur, such as intra-abdominal and wound infections after surgery, proper antimicrobial prophylaxis reduces the chance of such infections.

Prevention and early therapy of conditions that may lead to anaerobic infection can reduce their rate. Preventing oral flora aspiration by improving the neurologic status of the patient, repeated suctioning of oral secretion, improving oral hygiene and maintaining lower stomach pH can reduce the risk of aspiration pneumonia and its complications. Skin and soft-tissue infections can be prevented by irrigation and debridement of wounds and necrotic tissue, drainage of pus and improvement of blood supply.

Prophylactic therapy before surgery is generally administered when the operative field is expected to be contaminated by the normal flora of the mucous membrane at the operated site. Cefazolin is effective in surgical prophylaxis in sites distant from the oral or rectal areas, when anaerobic cover is not required. Cefoxitin or cefotetan are used in procedures that involve the oral, rectal or vulvovaginal surfaces because their spectrum includes the anaerobic flora likely to be encountered.

DIAGNOSTIC MICROBIOLOGY

Collection of specimens for anaerobic bacteria

The proper management of anaerobic infection depends on appropriate documentation of the bacteria causing the infection. Without such an approach, the patient may be exposed to inappropriate, costly and undesirable antimicrobial agents with adverse side-effects. Some laboratories may fail to recover certain or all of the anaerobes present in a specimen. This situation can occur particularly when the specimen is not promptly placed under anaerobic conditions for transport to the laboratory. If care is not taken to avoid specimen contamination with normal flora, anaerobes may not be recovered.

Appropriate cultures for anaerobes are especially important in polymicrobial infections.[4] Techniques or media that are inadequate for isolation of anaerobes because of a lack of an anaerobic environment or because of an overgrowth of aerobic organisms, can be misleading. This may cause the clinician to direct therapy toward only the isolated aerobic organisms.

The most acceptable documentation of an anaerobe is through recovery of anaerobic organisms from the infected site. Three essential elements require the physician's cooperation with the microbiology laboratory for appropriate documentation of anaerobic infection: collection of appropriate specimens, their expeditious transportation and careful laboratory processing.

Specimens must be obtained free of contamination so that saprophytic organisms or normal flora are excluded and culture results can be interpreted correctly. Because indigenous anaerobes are often

METHODS FOR COLLECTION OF SPECIMENS FOR ANAEROBIC BACTERIA	
Infection site	**Methods**
Abscess or body cavity	Aspiration by syringe and needle Incised abscesses: syringe or swab (less desirable); specimen obtained during surgery after cleansing the skin
Tissue or bone	Surgical specimen using tissue biopsy or curette
Sinuses or mucus surface abscesses	Aspiration after decontamination or surgical specimen
Ear	Aspiration after decontamination of ear canal and membrane; in perforation, cleanse ear canal and aspirate through perforation
Pulmonary	Transtracheal aspiration, lung puncture, bronchoscopic aspirate (using double lumen catheter and quantitative culture)
Pleural	Thoracentesis
Urinary tract	Suprapubic bladder aspiration
Female genital tract	Culdocentesis after decontamination, surgical specimen Transabdominal needle aspirate of uterus Intrauterine brush (using double lumen catheter and quantitative culture)

Table 232.6 Methods for collection of specimens for anaerobic bacteria.

APPROPRIATE AND INAPPROPRIATE SPECIMENS FOR ANAEROBIC CULTURE	
Inappropriate	**Appropriate**
Feces or rectal swabs Throat or nasopharyngeal swabs Sputum or bronchoscopic specimens Routine or catheterized urine Vaginal or cervical swabs Material from superficial wound or abscesses not collected properly to exclude surface contaminations Material from abdominal wounds obviously contaminated with feces (e.g. an open fistula)	All normally sterile body fluids other than urine (e.g. blood, pleural and joint fluids) Urine obtained by suprapubic bladder aspiration Percutaneous transtracheal aspiration or direct lung puncture Culdocentesis fluid obtained after decontamination of the vagina Material obtained from closed abscesses Material obtained from sinus tracts or draining wounds

Table 232.7 Appropriate and inappropriate specimens for anaerobic culture.

BACTERIOLOGIC FINDINGS SUGGESTIVE OF ANAEROBIC INFECTION

- Organisms seen on Gram stain that cannot be grown in aerobic cultures
- Typical morphology for anaerobes on Gram stain
- Anaerobic growth on proper media containing antibiotic-suppressing aerobes
- Growth in anaerobic zone of fluid or agar media
- Gas, foul-smelling odor in specimen or bacterial culture
- Characteristic colonies on anaerobic plates
- Colonies of pigmented *Prevotella* or *Porphyromonus* spp. may fluoresce red under ultraviolet light, and older colonies produce a typical dark pigment

Table 232.8 Bacteriologic findings suggestive of anaerobic infection.

present on the surfaces of skin and mucous membranes in large numbers, even minimal contamination of a specimen with normal flora can give misleading results. On this basis, specimens can be designated according to their acceptability for anaerobic culture to the acceptable or the unacceptable category. Materials that are appropriate for anaerobic cultures should be obtained using a technique that bypasses the normal flora (Table 232.6). Unacceptable or inappropriate specimens can yield normal flora also and therefore have no diagnostic value.

Acceptable specimens (Table 232.7) include blood specimens, aspirates of body fluids (pleural, pericardial, cerebrospinal, peritoneal and joint fluids), urine collected by percutaneous suprapubic bladder aspiration, abscess contents, deep aspirates of wounds and specimens collected by special techniques, such as transtracheal aspirates or direct lung puncture. Specimens of the lower respiratory tract are difficult to obtain without contamination with indigenous flora. Double-lumen catheter bronchial brushing and bronchoalveolar lavage, cultured quantitatively, can be useful. Direct needle aspiration is probably the best method of obtaining a culture, and the use of swabs is much less desirable. Specimens obtained from sites that are normally sterile may be collected after thorough skin decontamination, as is the case for the collection of blood, or spinal, joint or peritoneal fluids.

Transportation of specimens

Prompt delivery of specimens to the laboratory to allow for microbiologic processing is essential. Various transport devices are available that generate an oxygen-free environment. These systems generally contain an oxygen-free environment provided by mixture of carbon dioxide, hydrogen and nitrogen, plus an indicator that illustrates aerobic conditions. The specimens should be placed into an anaerobic transporter as soon as possible after collection. Aspirates of liquid specimen or tissue are always preferred to swabs, although systems for the collection of all culture forms are commercially available.

Liquid specimens may be inoculated into a commercially available anaerobic transport vial. A plastic or glass syringe and needle may also be used for transport. After the specimen is collected and all air bubbles are expelled from the syringe and needle, the needle tip should be inserted into a sterile rubber stopper. Because air gradually diffuses into the plastic syringe, no more than 30 minutes should elapse before the specimen is processed. This inexpensive transport device for liquid specimens is especially useful in the hospital situation where it can be rapidly transported to the microbiology laboratory.

Swabs may be placed in the sterilized tubes containing carbon dioxide or prereduced, anaerobically sterile Carey and Blair semisolid media. Tissue specimens or swabs can be transported in an anaerobic jar or in a Petri dish inside a sealed plastic bag that can be rendered anaerobic by use of a catalyzer.

Laboratory diagnosis

Certain findings are suggestive of anaerobic infection (Table 232.8). However, laboratory diagnosis of anaerobic infections begins with the examination of a Gram-stained smear of the specimen (see Fig. 232.1). The appearance of the Gram-stained organisms will give important preliminary information regarding types of organisms present, suggest appropriate initial therapy and serve as a quality control on the final culture analysis. The laboratory should be able to recover all of the morphologic types in the approximate ratio in which they are seen.

The techniques for cultivation of anaerobes should provide optimal anaerobic conditions throughout processing. Detailed procedures of these methods can be found in microbiology manuals.[4]

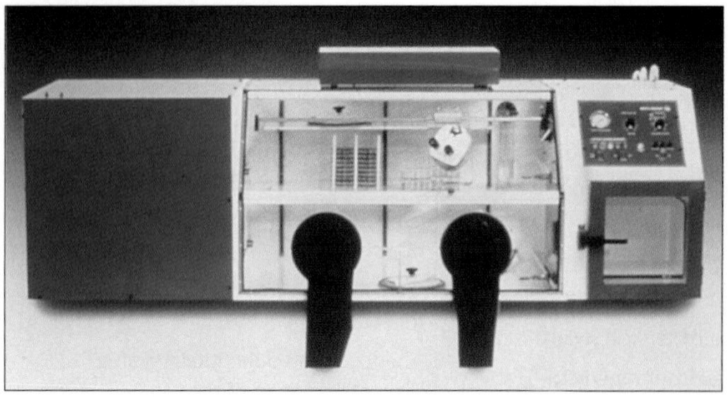

Fig. 232.6 Anaerobic glove-box used in the microbiology laboratory for processing of specimens and identifying anaerobic bacteria. Courtesy of Mike Cox.

Briefly, these methods could be the prereduced tube method, the anaerobic glove-box technique (Fig. 232.6), which provides an anaerobic environment throughout processing, or the anaerobic jar or bag systems, which are more simplified.

As a minimum requirement for the recovery of anaerobes, specimens should be inoculated onto enriched blood agar medium (containing vitamin K1 and hemin) and a selective medium (for *Bacteroides* spp.), such as laked sheep blood agar with kanamycin and vancomycin, should be used. The use of selective media along with a nonselective one increases the recovery rate and can shorten the time to identification of organisms.

Although prereduced vitamin K1 enriched thioglycolate broth is generally used as a back-up culture, this media alone should never be used as a substitute for a solid media. The major limitation of liquid media is the possibility of overgrowth of slow-growing strict anaerobes by rapid-growing aerobic and facultative organisms. Selective media can supplement nonselective media in increasing the bacterial yield and facilitating recovery.

Cultures should be placed immediately under anaerobic conditions and incubated for 48 hours or longer. Plates should then be examined for approximate number and types of colonies present. Each colony type should be isolated, tested for aerotolerance and identified.

An additional period of 36–48 hours is generally required to identify completely the anaerobic bacteria to a species or genus level using biochemical tests. Kits containing these biochemical tests are commercially available. These are good with fast growing anaerobes (i.e. *B. fragilis* and *C. perfringens*). Rapid enzymatic tests have recently been introduced. This panel test enables an identification of the anaerobes after only 4 hours of aerobic incubation and seems to be as good as the biochemical tests. Other rapid tests that have potential use and can also be used directly on clinical isolates are the direct fluorescent microscopy and direct gas liquid chromatography. Direct fluorescent microscopy can identify *Actinomyces* spp and *P. propionica*. This method is inaccurate in identification of *B. fragilis* group, pigmented *Prevotella* and *Porphyromonas* spp. Gas-liquid chromatography of metabolites can be employed to assist in the identification of anaerobes. Direct cellular fatty acid analysis using gas liquid chromatography with capillary column can also be useful. Nucleic acid probes and polymerase chain reaction methods are also being developed for rapid identification of anaerobic bacteria.

Most clinical microbiology laboratories are able to identify the major anaerobic bacteria. Peptostreptococci are generally not speciated because they are generally susceptible to commonly used antimicrobials. *Clostridium* spp. can be identified by the presence of spores and their ability to survive 30 minutes exposure to ethanol or heating to 176°F (80°C) for 10 minutes. Speciation requires biochemical testing. Nonspore-forming Gram-positive bacilli can be speciated by gas liquid chromatography and biochemical tests. *Propionibacterium* spp., which are often a contaminant, can be separated from other nonspore-forming Gram-positive bacilli by using a catalyze test and indole reaction. *Bacteroides fragilis* group organisms grow on 20% bile and are generally catalase positive. Pigmented *Prevotella* and *Porphyromonas* spp. produce black or brown pigment within a week when growing on rabbit blood agar medium. *Fusobacterium* spp. have a distinct morphology on Gram stain and, in contrast to *Bacteroides* spp., are susceptible to kanamycin.

Identification of an anaerobe to a species level is often cumbersome, expensive and time-consuming, taking up to 72 hours. Identification is most helpful in selecting an antibiotic against a species that has predictable antibiotic susceptibility. The level of speciation adequate for identifying an anaerobe is often controversial.

Occasionally, species identification of an organism will provide the diagnosis, as with *C. difficile* in patients who have colitis or *C. botulinum* in infants with botulism. However, because most anaerobes are endogenous, there are rarely epidemiologic reasons to perform complete identification. Identifying *B. fragilis* group, which often cause bacteremia and septic complications, has significant prognostic value.

Antimicrobial susceptibility testing

The antimicrobial susceptibility of anaerobes has become less predictable. Resistance to several antimicrobials, especially by anaerobic Gram-negative bacilli and *Fusobacterium* spp., has increased over the past decade.[13] It is important, therefore, to perform susceptibility testing for anaerobes recovered from sterile body sites, those with particular epidemiologic or prognostic significance (e.g. *C. difficile*), or those that are clinically important and have variable susceptibilities.

Screening of anaerobic Gram-negative bacilli isolates (particularly *Prevotella*, *Bacteroides* and *Fusobacterium* spp.) for β-lactamase activity may be helpful. This can provide information regarding their penicillin susceptibility. However, occasional bacterial strains may resist β-lactam antibiotics through other mechanisms.

Routine susceptibility testing of all anaerobic isolates is extremely time-consuming and in many cases unnecessary. Susceptibility testing should be limited to anaerobes isolated from blood cultures, bone, CNS and serious infections, as well as to those isolated in pure culture from properly collected specimens. Antibiotics tested should include penicillin, a broad-spectrum penicillin, a penicillin plus a β-lactamase inhibitor, clindamycin, chloramphenicol, a second-generation cephalosporin (e.g. cefoxitin), metronidazole and a carbapenem (e.g. imipenem).

The method recommended by the National Committee for Clinical Laboratory Standards (NCCLS) includes agar dilution testing, microbroth and macrobroth dilution.[25] Newer methods include the E-test and the spiral gradient end-point system.

CLINICAL MANIFESTATIONS

Anaerobic bacteria have been recovered in infections at all anatomic locations. However, their frequency of isolation and the type of bacterial isolates depend on the microbial flora at their source, or at the adjacent mucocutaneous sites.

Central nervous system infections

Anaerobic bacteria can cause a variety of intracranial infections. These organisms induce brain abscess, subdural empyema and infrequently cause epidural abscess and meningitis. The main source of brain abscess is an adjacent, generally chronic infection in the ears, mastoids, sinuses, oropharynx, teeth or lungs.[26] Ear or mastoid infection tend to spread to the temporal lobe or cerebellum, whereas facial sinusitis often causes abscess of the frontal lobe.

Hematogenous spread often occurs after dental, oropharyngeal or pulmonary infection. Rarely bacteremia of another origin or endocarditis can lead to such infection.

Meningitis caused by anaerobes is rare and can follow respiratory infection or develop as a complication of a cerebrospinal fluid shunt. Shunt infections are generally caused by skin flora such as *Prop. acnes*,[11] or in instances of ventriculoperitoneal shunts that perforate the gut, by anaerobes of enteric origin (i.e. *B. fragilis*).[27] *Clostridium perfringens* has been reported as a cause of brain abscesses and meningitis after head injuries or after intracranial surgery.[2]

The anaerobic bacteria generally recovered from brain abscesses that complicate respiratory and dental infections include *Prevotella*, *Porphyromonas*, *Bacteroides*, *Fusobacterium* and *Peptostreptococcus* spp. Microaerophilic and other streptococci are also often isolated. Actinomyces are less frequently encountered.

At the stage of encephalitis, antimicrobial therapy accompanied by measures to control the increase in the intracranial pressure can prevent the abscess formation. Once an abscess has formed, surgical excision or drainage may be needed, combined with a long course of antibiotics (4–8 weeks). Some neurosurgeons advocate complete evacuation of the abscess, whereas others advocate repeated aspirations.[28] In patients who have multiple abscesses or in those who have abscesses in essential brain areas, repeated aspirations are preferable. High-dose antibiotics for an extended period may represent an alternative approach in this group of patients and have often replaced surgical drainage.[28]

Because of the difficulty involved in the penetration of various antimicrobial agents through the blood–brain barrier, the choice of antibiotics is restricted. The antimicrobials advocated for these infections are metronidazole, penicillins, carbapenems and

Table 232.9 Aerobic and anaerobic bacteria isolated in head and neck and upper respiratory tract infections.

AEROBIC AND ANAEROBIC BACTERIA ISOLATED IN HEAD AND NECK AND UPPER RESPIRATORY TRACT INFECTIONS

Type of infection	Aerobic and facultative organisms	Anaerobic organism
Otitis media and mastoiditis: acute	*Streptococcus pneumoniae* *Haemophilus influenzae** *Moraxella catarrhalis**	*Peptostreptococcus* spp.
chronic	*Staphylococcus aureus** *Escherichia coli** *Klebsiella pneumoniae** *Pseudomonas aeruginosa**	Pigmented *Prevotella* and *Porphyromonas* spp.* *Bacteroides* spp.* *Fusobacterium* spp.* *Peptostreptococcus* spp.
Peritonsillar and retropharyngeal abscess	*Streptococcus pyogenes* *Staphylococcus aureus**	*Fusobacterium* spp.* Pigmented *Prevotella* and *Porphyromonas* spp.*
Recurrent tonsillitis	*Streptococcus pyogenes* *Haemophilus influenzae** *Staphylococcus aureus**	*Fusobacterium* spp.*
Suppurative thyroiditis	*Streptococcus pyogenes* *Staphylococcus aureus**	Pigmented *Prevotella* and *Porphyromonas* spp.* *Peptostreptococcus* spp.
Sinusitis: acute	*Haemophilus influenzae** *Streptococcus pneumoniae* *Moraxella catarrhalis**	*Peptostreptococcus* spp.
chronic	*Staphylococcus aureus** *Streptococcus pneumoniae* *Haemophilus influenzae**	Pigmented *Prevotella* and *Porphyromonas* spp.* *Fusobacterium* spp.* *Bacteroides fragilis* group*
Cervical lymphadenitis	*Staphylococcus aureus** *Mycobacterium* spp.	Pigmented *Prevotella* and *Porphyromonas* spp.* *Peptostreptococcus* spp.
Postoperative infection disrupting oral mucosa	*Staphylococcus* spp.* Enterobacteriaceae* *Streptococcus pyogenes*	*Fusobacterium* spp.* *Bacteroides* spp.* Pigmented *Prevotella* and *Porphyromonas* spp.* *Peptostreptococcus* spp.
Deep neck abscesses and parotitis	*Streptococcus* spp. *Staphylococcus* spp.*	*Bacteroides* spp.* *Fusobacterium* spp.* *Peptostreptococcus* spp.*
Odontogenic complications	*Streptococcus* spp. *Staphylococcus* spp.*	Pigmented *Prevotella* and *Porphyromonas* spp.* *Peptostreptococcus* spp.
Oropharyngeal: Vincent's angina and necrotizing	*Streptococcus* spp. *Staphylococcus* spp.*	*Fusobacterium necrophorum**

* Organisms that have the potential of producing β-lactamase

chloramphenicol. However, the choice may vary according to the specific isolates and their susceptibilities. A significant improvement in the mortality rate has been associated with the introduction of computed tomography (CT) and use of metronidazole therapy.

Head and neck and upper respiratory tract infections

Anaerobic bacteria can be recovered from a variety of head and neck and upper respiratory tract infections and predominate more in their chronic forms (Table 232.9). These include chronic otitis media, sinusitis and mastoiditis, tonsillar, peritonsillar and retropharyngeal abscesses, all deep neck space infections, parotitis, thyroiditis, odontogenic infections, and postsurgical and nonsurgical head and neck wounds and abscesses. The predominant organisms are of oropharyngeal flora origin and include *Prevotella*, *Porphyromonas*, *Bacteroides*, *Fusobacterium* and *Peptostreptococcus* spp.

Most dental infections involve anaerobes. These include endodontal pulpitis and periodontal (gingivitis and periodontitis) infections, periapical and dental abscesses, and perimandibular space infection.[29,30] Pulpitis may progress to an abscess and eventually involve the mandible and other neck spaces. In addition to the organisms mentioned above, microaerophilic streptococci and *Streptococcus salivarius* can also be involved.

Vincent's angina (or trench mouth) is a distinct form of ulcerative gingivitis; the causative organisms include *Fusobacterium* spp. and anaerobic spirochetes.[2]

Deep neck infections after oral, dental and pharyngeal infections are usually polymicrobial. These include mediastinitis after perforation of the esophagus, extension of retropharyngeal abscess or cellulitis, and dental abscess.[31]

Otitis media

Anaerobes were isolated in 5–15% of patients who had acute otitis media[32] and 42% of culture-positive aspirates of patients who had serous otitis media.[33] The predominant isolates in acute otitis media were *Peptostreptococcus* spp. and *Prop. acnes*. These organisms, as well as Gram-negative anaerobic bacilli, were recovered in serous otitis media.

Several studies reported the recovery of anaerobes in about 50% of the patients who have chronic suppurative otitis media.[3,5,34,35] The infection is often polymicrobial and the predominant anaerobes were Gram-negative bacilli and peptostreptococci, and the common aerobes were *Pseudomonas aeruginosa* and *S. aureus*. Many of these organisms can produce β-lactamase and might have contributed to the high failure rate of β-lactam antibiotics in the therapy of this infection. Anaerobes were isolated from 23 out of 24 (96%) specimens of chronic mastoiditis[36] and from most patients who have intracranial abscesses that complicate chronic suppurative otitis media.[3,5,26]

Anaerobes were recovered from infected cholesteatomas.[37,38] The production of organic acids by anaerobic bacteria may promote the process of bone destruction in cholesteatoma.[38] Because infected cholesteatoma contains bacteria similar to those recovered from chronically infected ears, it may serve as a nidus for chronic infection.

Sinusitis

Sinus disease may develop when allergy, viral infection, or anatomic obstruction occurs, preventing normal drainage. In the first stages of infection, the most common pathogens are similar to those recovered in acute otitis media: *Streptococcus pneumoniae*, *Haemophilus influenzae* and *Moraxella catarrhalis*. Anaerobic organisms become involved as the infection becomes chronic and the levels of tissue oxygen decline.[39] The transition in the bacterial flora from aerobic to anaerobic flora has been demonstrated.[40] An elevated serum antibody level to *Prevotella* and *Fusbacterium* spp. was demonstrated in patients with chronic sinusitis.[41] Although anaerobes are generally isolated from only about 7% of patients who have acute sinusitis (generally in maxillary sinusitis secondary to periodontal infection), they can be isolated from up to 67% of patients who have chronic infection.[3,5,42] An average of three anaerobes per aspirate were recovered in patients who had chronic sinusitis.[43]

Sinus infection may spread via anastomosing veins or contiguously to the CNS. Complications include orbital cellulitis[44] meningitis, cavernous sinus thrombosis, and epidural, subdural and brain abscesses.[3,5]

Parotitis

Viral parotitis can be caused by paramyxovirus (mumps), Epstein–Barr virus, coxsackievirus, HIV, and influenza A and parainfluenza virus. Acute suppurative parotitis is generally caused by *S. aureus*, streptococci and, rarely, aerobic Gram-negative bacteria. Anaerobes, mostly *Peptostreptococcus*, *Bacteroides*, and pigmented *Prevotella* and *Porphyromonas* spp., have also been recognized as an important cause of this infection.[45] Empiric antibiotic therapy should be directed against both aerobic and anaerobic bacteria. Surgical drainage may be indicated when pus has formed.

Cervical lymphadenitis

The anterior cervical, the submandibular or the posterior cervical nodes are the most prevalent sites of infection. The most common causes in children are viruses. The organisms causing acute unilateral infection associated with facial trauma or impetigo are *S. aureus* and *Streptococcus pyogenes*. *Bartonella henselae* and mycobacterial infections are important in chronic infections. Anaerobes (mostly *Fusobacterium* and *Peptostreptococcus* spp.) were isolated in about 25% of the infections, often in pure culture.[46] Their recovery was associated with a primary dental, periodontal, or tonsillar infection.

Thyroiditis

Anaerobic Gram-negative bacilli and peptostreptococci were identified as causative agents in thyroiditis.[3,5,47] *Eikenella corrodens* and *Actinomyces* spp. were also reported.

Infected cysts

Thyroglossal duct, branchial cleft and dermoid cysts, cystic hygromas and laryngoceles can become infected. The organisms that can cause these infections can originate from either the skin or the oropharynx. *Staphylococcus aureus* and *S. pyogenes* are the predominant aerobic isolates, whereas pigmented *Prevotella* and *Porphyromonas* spp. are the predominate anaerobes.[48]

Infection after head and neck surgery

Infections after head and neck surgery are caused by the exposure of the surgical site to the oropharyngeal flora, by the decreased blood supply and by the presence of necrotic tissues. They are common after surgery for malignant tumors. The wounds are generally infected by polymicrobial aerobic and anaerobic flora; the average number of isolates varies from one to nine (average six).[49] The most common isolates are peptostreptococci, *S. aureus,* anaerobic Gram-negative bacilli (i.e. *Bacteroides* spp.), *Fusobacterium* spp. and Enterobacteriaceae. The presence of this flora warrants the use of antimicrobial agents that are effective against these organisms in the prophylaxis and therapy of this infection.[50]

Tonsillitis

Indirect evidence is mounting that anaerobes are involved in both acute and chronic tonsillitis. The evidence is mainly derived from studies of complications of anaerobic tonsillitis (i.e. bacteremia, abscesses) where anaerobes play a major role. The organisms associated with the infection are *Fusobacterium* spp., peptostreptococci and Gram-negative anaerobic bacilli. Polymicrobial flora predominate in peritonsillar and retropharyngeal abscesses, where the number of isolates is between one and 12 (average five anaerobes and two aerobes).[3,5,51] Anaerobes have also been isolated from the cores of tonsils of children with recurrent group A β-hemolytic streptococci (GABHS) infection[24,42,52] and non-GABHS tonsillitis.[52] These organisms can be isolated from 25% of suppurative cervical lymph nodes and are mostly associated with the presence of dental or tonsillar infections.[46] Anaerobic organisms were associated with thrombophlebitis of the internal jugular veins, which often causes postanginal sepsis.[3,5]

The pathogenic role of anaerobes in the acute inflammatory process in the tonsils is also supported by several clinical observations:

- their recovery in tonsillar or retropharyngeal abscesses often without any aerobic bacteria;[51]
- their isolation from tonsils in Vincent's angina;[5]
- the recovery of encapsulated pigmented *Prevotella* and *Porphyromonas* spp. in acutely inflamed tonsils;
- the isolation of anaerobes from the core of recurrently inflamed non-GABHS tonsils;[52] and
- the response to antibiotics in patients who have non-GABHS tonsillitis.[53,54]

Furthermore, immune response against *Prev. intermedia* can be detected in patients who have non-GABHS tonsillitis;[55] and against *Prev. intermedia* and *F. nucleatum* in patients who recovered from peritonsillar cellulitis or abscesses[56] and infectious mononucleosis.[57]

Metronidazole therapy alleviated the symptoms of tonsillar hypertrophy and shortened the duration of fever in patients who had infectious mononucleosis.[53] Because metronidazole has no antiviral or aerobic antibacterial efficacy, suppression of the oral anaerobic flora may contribute to diminishing the inflammation induced by the Epstein–Barr virus. This is supported by the increased recovery of *Prev. intermedia* and *F. nucleatum* during the acute phases of mononucleosis.[58]

Recurrent pharyngotonsillitis and failure to eradicate the GABHS with penicillin can be a serious clinical problem. One explanation for penicillin failure is that repeated administrations result in selection of BLPB.[24] β-lactamase-producing strains of pigmented *Prevotella* and *Porphyromonas* spp., *B. fragilis*, *Fusobacterium* spp., *H. influenzae* and *Staph. aureus* were isolated from the tonsils of more than 75% of children with recurrent GABHS tonsillitis[24,42,59,60] and from 40% of children with non-GABHS tonsillitis.[52] Similar organisms were recovered from patients who had adenoiditis and adenoid hypertrophy.[61]

The recovery of these bacteria in more than three-quarters of the patients who had recurrent GABHS tonsillitis,[24,59,60] the ability to measure β-lactamase activity in the core of these tonsils[62] and the response of patients to antimicrobials effective against BLPB (i.e. clindamycin or amoxicillin plus clavulanic acid)[24,63,64] support the role of these aerobic as well as anaerobic organisms in the inability of penicillin to eradicate GABHS tonsillitis.

Pleuropulmonary infections

Aspiration of oropharyngeal secretions or gastric contents, and severe periodontal or gingival disease are the most prevalent risk factors for developing anaerobic pleuropulmonary secretion. The infection can progress from pneumonitis into necrotizing pneumonia and pulmonary abscess, with or without empyema.[65] The lesions tend to develop in the dependent pulmonary segments, in either of the superior segments of the lower lobes and in the posterior segments of the upper lobes. The infection is generally polymicrobial where the causative organisms of community-acquired infection (in 60–80% of cases) are aerobic and anaerobic members of oropharyngeal flora. The anaerobes isolated are *Prevotella*, *Porphyromonas*, *Fusobacterium* and *Peptostreptococcus* spp., and the aerobes are α-hemolytic streptococci and microaerophilic streptococci (Table 232.10).[66] Anaerobes can also be recovered in about one-third of patients who have nosocomial-acquired aspiration pneumonia and pneumonia associated with tracheostomy with and without mechanical ventilation,[67] where they are generally recovered mixed with Enterobacteriaceae, *Pseudomonas* spp. and *Staph. aureus*. Specimens for culture should be obtained in a manner that will avoid their contamination by the oral flora. They can be obtained using bronchoalveolar lavage, bronchoscopy via bronchial brush protected in a double-lumen plugged catheter (using quantitative cultures in the last two methods), percutaneous transtracheal aspiration, lung biopsy and thoracentesis (of empyema fluid). Management of these infections includes drainage of the pleural space, in the presence of empyema, and antimicrobials effective against the anaerobic and aerobic bacteria (see Chapter 36).

Intra-abdominal infections

Secondary peritonitis and intra-abdominal abscesses generally occur because of the entry of enteric micro-organisms into the peritoneal cavity through a defect in the wall of the intestine or other viscus as a result of obstruction, infarction or direct trauma. Perforated appendicitis, inflammatory bowel disease with perforation and gastrointestinal surgery are often associated with polymicrobial infections caused by aerobic and anaerobic bacteria, where the number of isolates can average 12 (two-thirds are generally anaerobes). Diverticulitis and its complications is also associated with such an infection.[68]

The initial infection that follows perforation is peritonitis. This is a synergistic infection in which more than one organism is involved. Characteristically, the more types of bacteria that can be isolated, the graver the morbidity. The specific micro-organisms involved in peritonitis are generally those of the gastrointestinal tract flora where anaerobes outnumber aerobes in the ratio 1:1000–10,000.[1] Of the more of the 400 bacterial species that constitute the gut flora, only the virulent ones survive in the peritoneum to cause the infection. The more distal the perforation in the gastrointestinal tract, the more numerous are the types and number of organisms that spill into the peritoneal cavity. An average of 11.6 organisms per specimen (8.5 anaerobes and 3.1 nonanaerobes) was recovered in a study of 71 patients with gangrenous and perforated appendicitis.[69] The predominant aerobic and facultatives are *Escherichia coli* and *Streptococcus* spp. (including *Enterococcus* spp.), and the most frequently encountered anaerobes are the *B. fragilis* group, and *Peptostreptococcus*, *Clostridium*, *Fusobacterium* and *Eubacterium* spp. (see Table 232.10).[3,5]

Intra-abdominal infections are characteristically biphasic: in the initial stages a generalized peritonitis occurs, which is primarily associated with *E. coli* sepsis, and in the later stages, in which the infection is contained and intra-abdominal abscesses emerge, *B. fragilis* can be recovered.

The clinical manifestations of secondary peritonitis are a reflection of the underlying disease process. Fever, diffuse abdominal pain, nausea and vomiting are characteristic. Physical examination reveals signs of peritoneal inflammation, including rebound tenderness, abdominal wall rigidity and decrease in bowel sounds. These early findings may be followed by signs and symptoms of shock.

The manifestations of shock from a ruptured viscus merge with those of peritonitis and may be followed by toxemia, restlessness and irritability, a higher temperature, an increase in pulse rate, chills and convulsions. Biliary tract infection is caused by *E. coli*,

Table 232.10 Aerobic and anaerobic bacteria isolated in various types of infections.

AEROBIC AND ANAEROBIC BACTERIA ISOLATED IN VARIOUS INFECTIONS		
Type of infection	**Aerobic and facultative organisms**	**Anaerobic organism**
Pleuropulmonary	*Staphylococcus aureus** viridans streptococci *Pseudomonas aeruginosa** Enterobacteriaceae*	Pigmented *Prevotella* spp. (*P. denticola, P. melaninogenica, P. intermedia, P. nigrescens, P. loescheii*) Nonpigmented *Prevotella* spp. (*P. oris, P. buccae, P. oralis*) *Fusobacterium nucleatum* *Peptostreptococcus* spp. (*P. micros, P. anaerobius, P. magnus*) *Bacteroides fragilis* group Nonspore-forming Gram-positive rods (*Actinomyces, Eubacterium, Lactobacillus* spp.)
Intra-abdominal	*Escherichia coli* *Enterococcus* spp. *Pseudomonas aeruginosa**	*Bacteroides fragilis* group *Bilophila wadsworthia* *Peptostreptococcus* spp. (especially *P. micros*) *Clostridium* spp.
Female genital tract	*Streptococcus* (groups A, B, others) *Escherichia coli* *Klebsiella pneumoniae* *Neisseria gonorrhoeae* (in sexually active patients) *Chlamydia* spp. (in sexually active patients) *Mycoplasma hominis* (in postpartum patients)	*Peptostreptococcus* spp. *Prevolella* spp. (especially *P. bivia, P. disiens*) *Bacteroides fragilis* group *Clostridium* spp. (especially *C. perfringens*) *Actinomyces, Eubacterium* spp. (in intrauterine contraceptive device-associated infections)
Skin and soft tissue	*Staphylococcus aureus* *Streptococcus* (*Strep. milleri* group, groups A and B, viridans group) *Enterococcus* spp.‡ Enterobacteriaceae‡ *Pseudomonas aeruginosa**	*Peptostreptococcus* spp. (*P. magnus, P. micros, P. asaccharolyticus*) Pigmented *Prevotella* spp.† *Actinomyces* spp. *Fusobacterium nucleatum*† *Bacteroides fragilis* group‡ *Clostridium* spp.‡

* Recovered in hospital-acquired infection
† After exposure to oral flora
‡ After exposure to colonic flora

Klebsiella and *Enterococcus* spp. Anaerobes (mostly *B. fragilis* group, and rarely *C. perfringens*) can be recovered in complicated infections associated with carcinoma, recurrent infection, obstruction, bile tract surgery or manipulation.[70]

Laboratory studies reveal an elevated blood leukocyte count in excess of 12,000/mm^3 with a predominance of polymorphonuclear forms. Radiographs of the abdomen may reveal free air in the peritoneal cavity, evidence of ileus or obstruction and obliteration of the psoas shadow. Diagnostic ultrasound, gallium and CT scanning[71] may be useful in detecting appendiceal or other intra-abdominal abscesses. Postoperative wound infections can occur after appendectomy.

Appropriate management of mixed aerobic and anaerobic intra-abdominal infections requires the administration of antimicrobials that are effective against both aerobic and anaerobic components of the infection[2,5] as well as surgical correction and drainage of pus.[72] Single and easily accessible abscesses can be drained percutaneously, thus avoiding a surgical procedure. The outcome of the infection depends on a variety of factors that include the general condition of the patient (as measured by the Apache score[73]), the site of perforation, the bacteriology of the infection and the antimicrobial chosen for therapy. The principle of using antimicrobial coverage effective against both the aerobic and anaerobic offenders has become the cornerstone of practice and its efficacy has been confirmed by numerous studies.[72]

The choice of therapy should cover Enterobacteriaceae and anaerobes (mainly *B. fragilis* group), and can be achieved by combination or single-agent therapy. Single-agent therapy provides the advantage of avoiding the ototoxicity and nephrotoxicity of aminoglycosides and may be less expensive. However, a single agent may not be effective against hospital-acquired resistant bacterial strains, and the use of a single agent is devoid of antibacterial synergy, which may be important in immunocompromised hosts. However, for otherwise healthy persons, when therapy is initiated without a long delay, single agents provide adequate therapy. An anti-Enterobacteriaceae agent, such as an aminoglycoside, a quinolone or a third-generation cephalosporin, plus an anti-anaerobic agent, such as clindamycin, metronidazole or cefoxitin, is used as combination therapy. Single agent therapy includes a carbapenem (i.e. imipenem, meropenem), or a penicillin plus a β-lactamase inhibitor (i.e. ticarcillin–clavulanate). The need to add therapy directed at *Enterococcus* spp. is controversial and some authorities advocate adding such a drug (i.e. amoxicillin or vancomycin). However, these organisms are isolated in only 10–20% of cases, and rarely in pure culture (see also Chapter 47).

Antimicrobial prophylaxis before colonic surgery includes either an oral preparation such as erythromycin plus neomycin, or a parenteral antimicrobial such as cefoxitin. Use of prophylaxis has reduced the rate of postsurgical wound infection (see also Chapter 190).[74]

Female genital tract infection

Female genital tract infections involving anaerobes are polymicrobial and include the following: bacterial vaginosis; soft-tissue perineal, vulvar and Bartholin gland abscesses; endometritis; pyometra; salpingitis; tubo-ovarian abscesses; adnexal abscess; pelvic inflammatory disease, which may include pelvic cellulitis and abscess; amnionitis; septic pelvic thrombophlebitis; intrauterine contraceptive device-associated infection; septic abortion; and postsurgical obstetric and gynecologic infections.[3,5] Obtaining proper cultures is often difficult, and avoiding their contamination by the normal genital flora can be achieved by use of culdocentesis, laparoscopy or quantitative endometrial cultures of transcervical samples obtained with a telescoping catheter.

The predominant anaerobes include *Prev. bivia*, *Prev. disiens*, and *Peptostreptococcus*, *Porphyromonas* and *Clostridium* spp. *Bacteroides fragilis* group is less often isolated in these infections than in intra-abdominal infection. *Actinomyces* spp. and *Eubacterium nodatum* are commonly isolated in infections associated with intrauterine devices. *Mobiluncus* spp. may be involved with bacterial vaginosis.[3,5,75] The aerobic organisms also isolated mixed with these anaerobes include Enterobacteriaceae, *Streptococcus* spp. (including groups A and B), *Neisseria gonnorhoeae* and *Chlamydia* spp. (in sexually active females) and *Mycoplasma hominis* (see Table 232.10).

Clinical findings associated with the presence of anaerobes include gas in the tissues, abscess formation and foul-smelling discharge. Management of polymicrobial pelvic infection includes the use of antimicrobials effective against all potential aerobic and anaerobic pathogens. Additionally, coverage against sexually transmissible pathogens should be provided. The therapeutic regimens include doxycycline or a macrolide in combination with cefoxitin, cefotetan, clindamycin or metronidazole.

Skin and soft-tissue infections

Skin and soft-tissue infections that generally involve anaerobes include superficial infections, such as infected cutaneous ulcers, cellulitis, pyoderma, paronychia, hidradenitis suppurativa and a variety of secondary infected sites. These include secondary infected diaper rash, gastrostomy or tracheostomy site wounds, infected subcutaneous sebaceous or inclusion cysts, eczema, scabies or kerion infections, and postsurgical wound infection.[3,5,76–78]

Subcutaneous tissue infections that may also include skin involvement include cutaneous and subcutaneous abscesses, breast abscess, decubitus ulcers, infected diabetic (vascular or trophic) ulcers (Fig. 232.7), bite wound (Fig. 232.8), anaerobic cellulitis (Fig. 232.9) and gas gangrene, bacterial synergistic gangrene, infected pilonidal cyst or sinus, Meleney's ulcer and burn wound infection.[77,78] Anaerobic soft-tissue infections that occur deeper are necrotizing fasciitis (Fig. 232.10), necrotizing synergistic cellulitis, gas gangrene and crepitus cellulitis.[79] These infections can involve the fascia and the muscle surrounded by the fascia, and can induce myositis (Fig. 232.11) and myonecrosis.

The organisms recovered from soft-tissue infections vary according to the type of infections. However, the location and the circumstances leading to the infection can influence the type of the organisms involved in the infection. Cultures from lesions involving

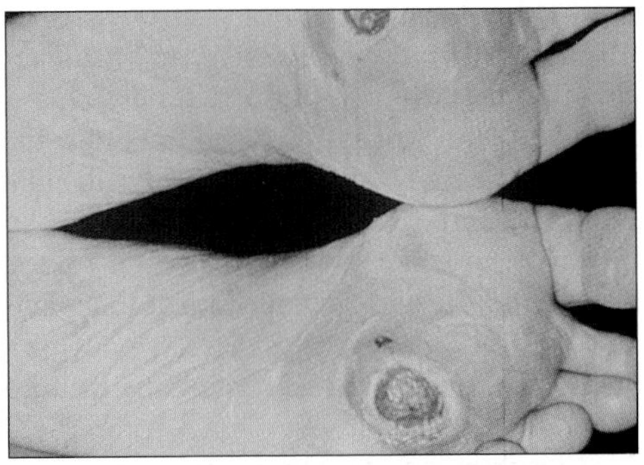

Fig. 232.7 Infected diabetic ulcer.

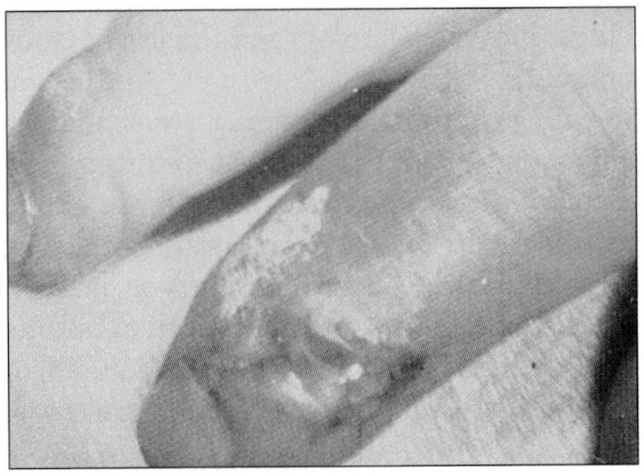

Fig. 232.8 Human bite wound.

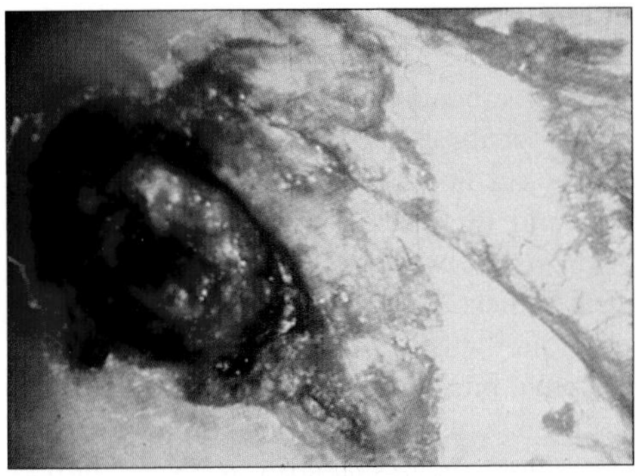

Fig. 232.9 Polymicrobial necrotizing cellulitis. The initial lesion is a reddish-brown bleb and is accompanied by local tenderness.

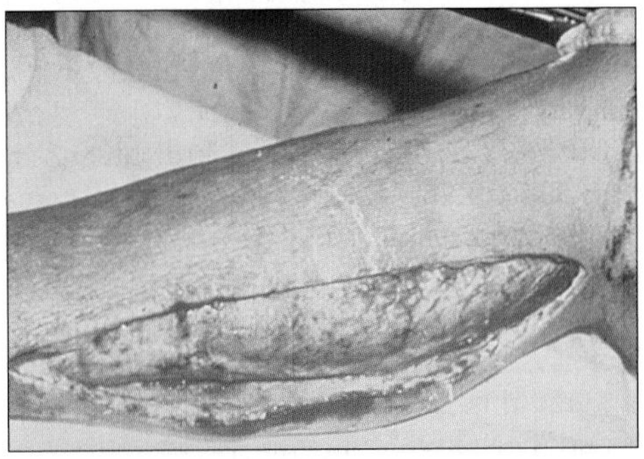

Fig. 232.10 Necrotizing fasciitis caused by multiple aerobic and anaerobic bacteria. The fascia inspected through a surgical incision is swollen and dull in appearance, with areas of necrosis. A thin, brownish discharge exudes from the wound, with no pus.

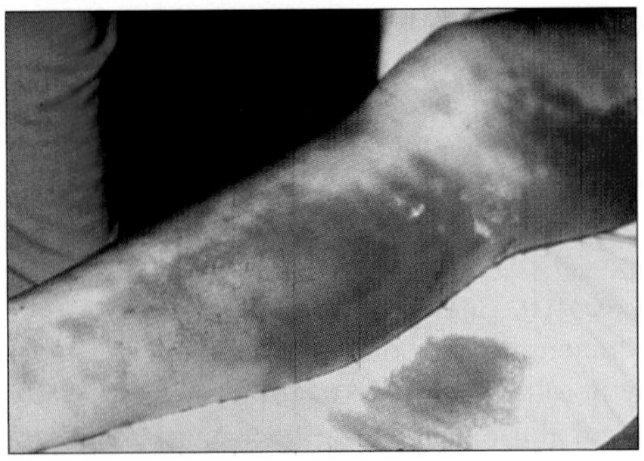

Fig. 232.11 Anaerobic streptococcal myositis involving muscle and fascial planes.

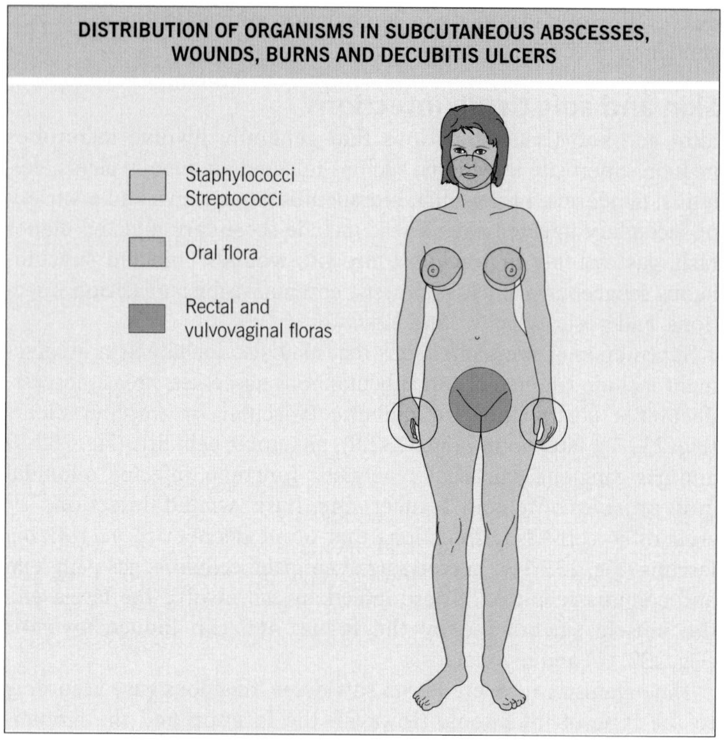

Fig. 232.12 Distribution of organisms in subcutaneous abscesses, wounds, burns and decubitus ulcers.

anaerobes frequently contain bacterial species that are members of the 'normal flora' of the region of the infection (Fig. 232.12).

Aspirates from wounds and subcutaneous tissue infections and abscesses of the rectal area (decubitus ulcer, perirectal abscess) or those that originate from the gut flora (i.e. diabetic foot infection) tend to yield organisms found in the colonic flora.[3,5,77–79] These include *B. fragilis* group, *Clostridium* spp., Enterobacteriaceae and *Enterococcus* spp. In contrast, infections in and around the oropharynx, or those that originate from that site, generally contain members of the oral flora (i.e. paronychia, bites, breast abscess). These include pigmented *Prevotella* and *Porphyromonas*, *Fusobacterium* and *Peptostreptococcus* spp. Skin flora organisms such as *Staph. aureus* and *Streptococcus* spp., or nosocomially acquired organisms can be isolated at all body sites (see Table 232.10). In addition to oral flora, human bite infections often contain *Eikenella* spp. and animal bites harbor *Pasteurella multocida*.[80]

Infections involving anaerobes are generally polymicrobial, and in some (i.e. decubitus ulcers, diabetic foot ulcer) they are often complicated by osteomyelitis or bacteremia.[81] Deep tissue infections such as necrotizing cellulitis, fasciitis and myositis often involve *Clostridium* spp., *S. pyogenes* or a polymicrobic combination of aerobic and anaerobic bacteria. They often contain gas in the tissues and putrid-like pus with a gray thin quality, and are associated with a high rate of bacteremia and mortality.[79,82]

Management of deep-seated soft-tissue infection includes surgical debridement, drainage and vigorous surgical management. Improvement of oxygenation of the involved tissues through enhancement of blood supply and administration of hyperbaric oxygen, especially in clostridial infection, may be helpful, although there is no formal evidence demonstrating the benefit of hyperbaric oxygen.

Osteomyelitis and septic arthritis

Osteomyelitis caused by anaerobic bacteria is often indistinguishable from infection caused by aerobic bacteria. Anaerobes are especially notable in oesteomyelitis of the long bones after trauma and fracture, osteomyelitis related to peripheral vascular disease, and decubitus ulcers and osteomyelitis of cranial and facial bones.[81,83] Most of these infections are polymicrobial.

Anaerobic osteomyelitis of cranial and facial bones is generally caused by spread from a contiguous soft-tissue source or from sinus, ear or dental infection. The high number of anaerobes within the oral flora accounts for their importance in cranial osteomyelitis. The predominance of intestinal anaerobes in pelvic osteomyelitis has been related to their spread from decubitus ulcers.[5] The anaerobes in osteomyelitis associated with peripheral vascular disease access the involved bone from adjacent soft-tissue ulcers. Osteomyelitis of long bones is generally caused by hematogenic spread, trauma or the presence of a prosthetic device.

Anaerobic streptococci and *Bacteroides* spp. are the most common organisms at all sites, including osteomyelitis associated with bites and cranial infection. Pigmented *Prevotella* and *Porphyromonas* spp. are especially prevalent in skull and bite infections, whereas members of the *B. fragilis* group are associated with vascular disease or neuropathy. Fusobacteria, which are members of the oral flora, are most frequently isolated from bites and from cranial and facial infections. Clostridia are most often found in long bones, especially in association with environmental wound contamination after trauma. Because clostridia colonize the lower gastrointestinal tract, they may contaminate compound fractures of the lower extremities.

Septic arthritis caused by anaerobic bacteria is uncommon, and is often associated with hematogenous and contiguous spread of infection, trauma and prosthetic joints.[81,84] Most cases of septic arthritis caused by anaerobes are monomicrobial. The predominant isolated anaerobes are peptostreptococci and *Prop. acnes* (often in prosthetic joint infection), *B. fragilis* and fusobacteria (often in infections of hematogenic origin), and clostridia (associated with trauma).

Bacteremia

The incidence of anaerobes in bacteremia is 5–15%.[82,85] The most prevalent blood culture isolates are *B. fragilis* group (over 75% of anaerobic isolates). Other common isolates include *Clostridium* spp. (10–20%), *Peptostreptococcus* spp. (10–15%), *Fusobacterium* spp. (10–15%) and *Prop. acnes* (2–5%).

The specific organisms involved in bacteremia largely depend on the portal of entry and underlying disease. Recovery of *B. fragilis* group and clostridia is mostly associated with a gastrointestinal source, pigmented *Prevotella* and *Porphyromonas* spp. and fusobacteria with oropharynx and pulmonary sources, fusobacteria with the female genital tract, *Prop. acnes* with foreign body, and peptostreptococci with all sources, but especially with oropharyngeal, pulmonary and female genital tract sources. The predominance of these isolates in conjunction with the specific sources is related to the origin of the primary infection and the endogenous flora at the infection site.

The predisposing factors to anaerobic bacterial bacteremia include malignant neoplasms; hematologic disorders; organ transplant; recent gastrointestinal, obstetric, or gynecologic surgery; intestinal obstruction; decubitus ulcers; dental extraction; the newborn; sickle cell disease; diabetes mellitus; postsplenectomy; and the use of cytotoxic agents or corticosteroids.[3,5]

The clinical presentations of anaerobic bacteremia are similar to those seen with aerobic infection, except for the signs of infection at the portal of entry of infection. It commonly includes fever, chills, hypotension, leukocytosis, shock, disseminated intravascular coagulation and anemia. Features typical of anaerobic infection include metastatic lesions, hyperbilirubinemia, and suppurative thrombophlebitis. Mortality rate varies between 15 and 30% and is improved with early and appropriate antimicrobial therapy and resolution, when present, of the primary infection.

MANAGEMENT

The recovery from an anaerobic infection depends on prompt and proper management. The principles of managing anaerobic infections include neutralizing toxins produced by anaerobes, preventing their local proliferation by changing the environment and hampering their spread into healthy tissues.

Toxin neutralization by specific antitoxins may be employed, especially in infections caused by *Clostridium* spp. (tetanus and botulism). Controlling the environment is achieved by debriding of necrotic tissue, draining the pus, improving circulation, alleviating the obstruction and increasing the tissue oxygenation. Certain types of adjunct therapy such as hyperbaric oxygen (HBO) may also be useful. The primary role of antimicrobials is in limiting the local and systemic spread of the organism.

Hyperbaric oxygen

There is controversy regarding whether HBO should be used in infection of spore-forming Gram-positive anaerobic rods. There are several uncontrolled reports that demonstrated efficacy in individual cases.[3,5,86] However, because no well-controlled studies are available, the efficacy of HBO is unproved. Using HBO in conjunction with other therapeutic measures is not contraindicated, except when it may delay the execution of other essential procedures. Topical application of oxygen-releasing compounds may be useful as an adjunct to other procedures.

Surgical therapy

In many cases surgical therapy is the most important and sometimes the only form of treatment required, whereas in others surgical therapy is an important adjunct to a pharmacologic approach. Surgery is important in draining abscesses, debriding necrotic tissues, decompressing closed space infections and relieving obstructions. When surgical drainage is not used, the infection may persist and serious complications can develop.

Antimicrobial therapy

Appropriate management of mixed aerobic and anaerobic infections requires the administration of antimicrobial drugs effective against both the aerobic and the anaerobic components. A number of factors should be considered when choosing appropriate antimicrobial agents. They should have efficacy against all target organisms, induce little or no resistance, achieve sufficient levels in the infected site, and have minimal toxicity and maximum stability.

Antimicrobials often fail to cure the infection. Among the reasons for this are the development of bacterial resistance, achievement of insufficient tissue levels, incompatible drug interaction and the development of an abscess. The environment of an abscess is detrimental to many antibiotics. The abscess capsule interferes with the penetration of drugs, and the low pH and the presence of binding proteins or inactivating enzymes (i.e. β-lactamase) may impair their activity. The low pH and the anaerobic environment within the abscess are especially unfavorable for the aminoglycosides and quinolones. However, an acidic pH, high osmolarity and an anaerobic environment can also develop in the absence of an abscess.

When choosing antimicrobials for the therapy of mixed infections, their aerobic and anaerobic antibacterial spectrum (Fig. 232.13) and their availability in oral or parenteral form should be considered (Table 232.11). Some antimicrobials have a limited range of activity. For example, metronidazole is active only against anaerobes and therefore cannot be administered as a single agent for the therapy of mixed infections. Others (i.e. carbapenems) have wide spectra of activity against Enterobacteriaceae and anaerobes.

The selection of antimicrobial agents is simplified when reliable culture results are available. However, this may be difficult to achieve in anaerobic infections because of the problems in obtaining appropriate specimens. For this reason, many patients are treated empirically on the basis of suspected, rather than established, pathogens. Fortunately, the types of organisms involved in many anaerobic infections and their antimicrobial susceptibility patterns tend to be predictable. However, the pattern of resistance to antimicrobials may vary in a particular hospital and resistance to antimicrobial agents may emerge while a patient is receiving therapy.

The susceptibility of the *B. fragilis* group to the frequently used antimicrobial drugs has been studied systemically over the past two decades. These surveys have failed to reveal strains resistant to chloramphenicol or metronidazole and minimal resistance (<1%) to imipenem or the combinations of a penicillin and β-lactamase inhibitors, but resistance to other agents varies. The rate differs among various medical centers and generally increases with extensive use of some antimicrobial agents (penicillins, cephalosporins and clindamycin).[87]

Aside from susceptibility patterns, other factors influencing the choice of antimicrobial therapy include the pharmacologic characteristics of the various drugs, their toxicity, their effect on the normal flora and bactericidal activity. Although identification of the infecting organisms and their antimicrobial susceptibility may be needed for selection of optimal therapy, the clinical setting and Gram-stain preparation of the specimen may indicate the types of anaerobes present in the infection as well as the nature of the infectious process.

SUSCEPTIBILITY OF ANAEROBIC BACTERIA TO ANTIMICROBIAL AGENTS

Bacteria	Penicillin	A penicillin and a β-lactamase inhibitor	Ureido- and carboxy-penicillin	Cefoxitin	Chloramphenicol	Clindamycin	Macrolides	Metronidazole	Carbapenems
Peptostreptococcus spp.									
Fusobacterium spp.									
Bacteroides fragilis group									
Prevotella and *Porphyromonas* spp.									
Clostridium perfringens									
Clostridium spp.									
Actinomyces spp.									

Degrees of activity: ☐ Minimal ☐ Moderate ☐ Good ☐ Excellent

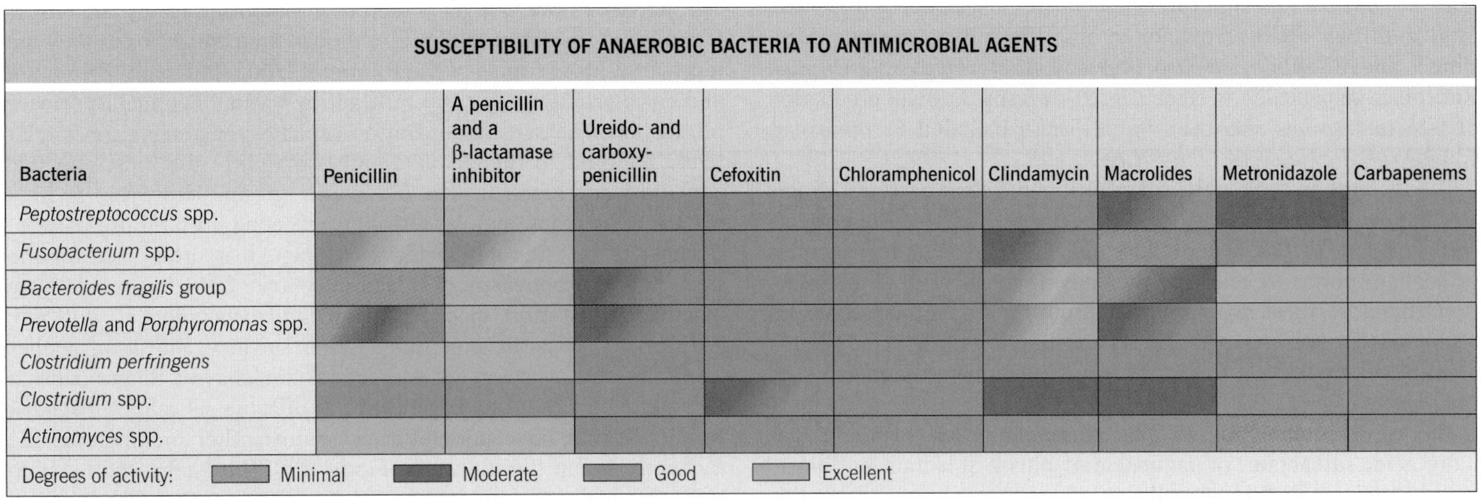

Fig. 232.13 Susceptibility of anaerobic bacteria to antimicrobial agents.

ANTIMICROBIAL DRUGS RECOMMENDED FOR THE THERAPY OF SITE-SPECIFIC ANAEROBIC INFECTIONS			
	Surgical prophylaxis	Parenteral	Oral
Intracranial	Penicillin (vancomycin)	Metronidazole† (chloramphenicol)	Metronidazole† (chloramphenicol)
Dental	Penicillin (erythromycin)	Clindamycin (metronidazole†, chloramphenicol)	Clindamycin, amoxicillin + CA (metronidazole†, chloramphenicol)
Upper respiratory tract	Cefoxitin (clindamycin)	Clindamycin (chloramphenicol, metronidazole†)	Clindamycin, amoxicillin + CA (chloramphenicol, metronidazole‡)
Pulmonary	NA	Clindamycin* (chloramphenicol, a penicillin + BLI§, a carbapenem)	Clindamycin* (chloramphenicol, metronidazole‡, amoxicillin + CA)
Abdominal	Cefoxitin (clindamycin*)	Clindamycin*, cefoxitin*, metronidazole* (a carbapenem, a penicillin + BLI)	Clindamycin*, metronidazole* (chloramphenicol, amoxicillin + CA)
Pelvic	Cefoxitin (doxycycline)	Cefoxitin§, clindamycin* (a penicillin + BLI§ metronidazole§)	Clindamycin§ (amoxicillin + CA§, metronidazole§)
Skin	Cefazolin# (vancomycin)	Clindamycin, cefoxitin (metronidazole† + methicillin)	Clindamycin, amoxicillin + CA (metronidazole‡)
Bone and joint	Cefazolin# (vancomycin)	Clindamycin, a carbapenem (chloramphenicol, metronidazole†, a penicillin + BLI)	Clindamycin (chloramphenicol, metronidazole†)
Bacteremia with BLPB	NA	A carbapenem, metronidazole (cefoxitin, a penicillin + BLI)	Clindamycin, metronidazole (chloramphenicol, amoxicillin + CA)
Bacteremia with BLPB	NA	Penicillin (clindamycin, metronidazole, cefoxitin)	Penicillin (metronidazole, chloramphenicol, clindamycin)

* Plus an anti-aerobic bacilli agent (aminoglycoside)
† Plus a penicillin
‡ Plus a macrolide (i.e. erythromycin)
§ Plus doxycycline
# In location proximal to the rectal and oral areas use cefoxitin

Table 232.11 Antimicrobial drugs recommended for the therapy of site-specific anaerobic infections. Therapies are given as drug(s) of choice (alternative drugs). BLI, β-lactamase inhibitor; BLPB, β-lactamase-producing bacteria; CA, clavulanic acid; NA, not applicable.

Antimicrobial agents

Some classes of agents have poor activity against anaerobic bacteria. These include the aminoglycosides, the monobactams and the currently available quinolones. Antimicrobial agents suitable for use in controlling aerobic infections are discussed in more detail below.[88,89]

Penicillins

Penicillin G (benzypenicillin) is still the drug of choice against most non-BLPB. These include anaerobic streptococci, *Clostridium* spp. and nonsporolating anaerobic bacilli, and most non-β-lactamase-producing Gram-negative anaerobic rods (i.e. *Bacteroides*, *Fusobacterium*, *Prevotella* and *Porphyromonas* spp.).[88] However, in addition to the *B. fragilis* group, which is known to resist the drug, many other anaerobic Gram-negative rods are showing increased resistance. These include *Fusobacterium* spp., pigmented *Prevotella* and *Porphyromonas* spp. (prevalent in orofacial infections), *Prev. bivia* and *Prev. disiens* (common in obstetric and gynecologic infections), and *Bilophila wadsworthia* and *Bacteroides splanchinus*. Resistance to penicillin of some *Clostridium* spp. through production of β-lactamase has also been noted. These included *C. ramosum*, *C. clostridioforme* and *C. butyricum*.

The increase in the number of penicillin-resistant bacterial strains has important implications for antimicrobial therapy. Many penicillin-resistant bacteria can produce enzymes that degrade penicillins or cephalosporins by releasing the enzyme in the area of the infection. Therefore, these organisms may protect not only themselves but also penicillin-sensitive pathogens. Penicillin therapy directed against a susceptible pathogen might therefore be rendered ineffective by the presence of BLPB.[24]

The use of combinations of β-lactamase inhibitors (such as clavulanic acid, sulbactam, or tazobactam) plus a β-lactam antibiotic (ampicillin, amoxicillin, ticarcillin or piperacillin) can overcome this phenomenon in organisms that produce a β-lactamase that can be bound by the inhibitor. However, if other mechanisms of resistance emerge, blockage of the enzyme β-lactamase will not prevent resistance. Other mechanisms of resistance include alteration in the porin canal through which the antimicrobial penetrates into the bacteria and changes in the penicillin-binding protein that inhibit binding of the drug into the bacterial cell wall.

The semisynthetic penicillins, carbenicillin, ticarcillin, piperacillin and mezlocillin are generally administered in large quantities to achieve high serum concentrations. These drugs have good activity against Enterobacteriaceae and most anaerobes in these concentrations. However, they are not absolutely resistant to β-lactamase produced by Gram-negative anaerobic bacilli.

Cephalosporins

The efficacy of cephalosporins varies against *Bacteroides* spp.[88,89] The activity of the first-generation cephalosporins against anaerobes is similar to that of penicillin G, although on a weight basis they are less active. Most strains of the *B. fragilis* group and many *Prevotella* and *Porphyromonas* spp. are resistant by virtue of cephalosporinase production. The second-generation cephalosporin cefoxitin is relatively resistant to this enzyme and is therefore the most effective cephalosporin against the *B. fragilis* group. However, 5–15% of *B. fragilis* group may be resistant, reflecting hospital use pattern. Because of its wide antibacterial coverage, it is often used for the therapy and prophylaxis of mixed infections. Cefoxitin is relatively inactive against most species of *Clostridium* (including *C. difficile*); *C. perfringens* is an exception. Other second-generation cephalosporins, such as cefotetan and cefmetazole, have a longer half-life than cefoxitin. These two agents are as effective as cefoxitin against *B. fragilis*, but have poor efficacy against other members of the *B. fragilis* group (i.e. *B. thetaiotaomicron*). Third-generation cephalosporins have activity against *Bacteroides* spp. that is inferior to that of second-generation cephalosporins.

Carbapenems (imipenem, meropenem, ertapenem)

The β-lactam carbapenems imipenem and meropenem have excellent activity against a broad spectrum of aerobic bacteria and anaerobic bacteria, including β-lactamase-producing *Bacteroides* spp. and Enterobacteriaceae and *Pseudomonas* spp.[89] Resistance of *B. fragilis* group is very rare (<1%). Ertapenem has similar efficacy , but is not active against *Pseudomonas* spp. and *Acinetobacter* spp.[90]

Chloramphenicol

Chloramphenicol shows excellent *in-vitro* activity against most anaerobic bacteria, and resistance is rare. The drug is also effective against many Enterobacteriaceae and Gram-positive cocci. However, the experience of using this drug in intra-abdominal sepsis was disappointing. The toxicity of chloramphenicol, the rare but fatal aplastic anemia and the dose-dependent leukopenia, limit its use, especially in neutropenic patients.

Clindamycin and lincomycin

Clindamycin and lincomycin are effective against anaerobes and have good activity against aerobic Gram-positive cocci.[88] Clindamycin has the broader coverage against anaerobes, including β-lactamase-producing *Bacteroides* spp. Resistance of *B. fragilis* group is 5–10%, and some *Clostridium* spp. other than *C. perfringens* are resistant. Antibiotic-associated colitis caused by *C. difficile* was first described after clindamycin therapy. However, colitis has been associated with many other antimicrobial agents, including penicillins and cephalosporins.

Metronidazole

Metronidazole has excellent activity against anaerobes. However, its antibacterial efficacy is limited to anaerobic bacteria. Microaerophilic streptococci, *Prop. acnes* and *Actinomyces* spp. are often resistant. Concern was raised about the carcinogenic and mutagenic effects of this drug; however, these effects were shown only in one species of mice and were never substantiated in other animals or humans.[3,5]

Macrolides (erythromycin, azithromycin, clarithromycin)

The macrolides erythromycin, azithromycin and clarithromycin have moderate-to-good *in-vitro* activity against anaerobic bacteria other than *B. fragilis* group and fusobacteria. They are active against *Prevotella* and *Porphyromonas* spp., microaerophilic and anaerobic streptococci, Gram-positive nonspore-forming anaerobic bacilli and certain clostridia. They show relatively good activity against *C. perfringens* and poor or inconsistent activity against Gram-negative anaerobic bacilli.

Glycopeptides (vancomycin, teicoplanin)

The glycopeptides are effective against all Gram-positive anaerobes (including *C. difficile*), but are inactive against Gram-negative bacilli.

Tetracyclines

Tetracycline is of limited use because of the development of resistance by all types of anaerobes, including *B. fragilis* group. The newer tetracycline analogs doxycycline and minocycline are more active than the parent compound. Because there is significant resistance to these drugs, they can be used if the organisms are susceptible or in less severe infections in which a therapeutic trial is feasible.

Quinolones

The first generation of fluoroquinolones such as ciprofloxacin and ofloxacin are inactive against most anaerobic bacteria. However, some broad-spectrum quinolones, which have recently become clinically available or are under active development, have significant anti-anaerobic activity. Quinolones with low activity against anaerobes include ciprofloxacin, ofloxacin, levofloxacin, fleroxacin, pefloxacin, enoxacin and lomefloxacin. Compounds with intermediate anti-anaerobic activity include sparfloxacin and grepafloxacin. Trovafloxacin, gatifloxacin and moxifloxacin yield low minimum inhibitory concentrations (MICs) against most groups of anaerobes. Quinolones with the greatest *in-vitro* activity against anaerobes include clinafloxacin and sitafloxacin.[91] The use of the quinolones is restricted in growing children and pregnancy because of their possible adverse effects on the cartilage.

Other agents

Bacitracin is active against pigmented *Prevotella* and *Porphyromonas* spp. but is inactive against *B. fragilis* and *Fusobacterium nucleatum*.[2] Quinupristin–dalfopristin shows antibacterial activity against anaerobic organisms tested, including *C. perfringens* and *Lactobacillus* and *Peptostreptococcus* spp.[92] Linezolid is active against *F. nucleatum*, other fusobacteria and *Porphyromonas*, *Prevotella* and *Peptostreptococcus* spp.[93] Little clinical experience has been, however, gained in the treatment of anaerobic bacteria using these agents.

Choice of antimicrobial agents

The parenteral antimicrobials that can be used in most infectious sites (Tables 232.11, 232.12) are clindamycin, metronidazole, chloramphenicol, cefoxitin, a penicillin (e.g. ticarcillin, ampicillin, piperacillin) and a β-lactamase inhibitor (e.g. clavulanic acid, sulbactam, tazobactam), and a carbapenem (e.g. imipenem, meropenem, ertapenem).

An agent effective against Gram-negative enteric bacilli (e.g. aminoglycoside) or an antipseudomonal cephalosporin (e.g. cefepime) are generally added to clindamycin, metronidazole and, occasionally, cefoxitin, when treating intra-abdominal infections to provide coverage for these bacteria. Failure of therapy in intra-abdominal infections has been noticed more often with chloramphenicol and, therefore, this drug is not recommended.

Penicillin can be added to metronidazole in the therapy of intracranial, pulmonary and dental infections to cover for microaerophilic streptococci, and *Actinomyces* spp. A macrolide (i.e. erythromycin) is added to metronidazole in upper respiratory infections to treat *Staph. aureus* and aerobic streptococci. Penicillin is added to clindamycin to supplement its coverage against *Peptostreptococcus* spp. and other Gram-positive anaerobic organisms.

ANTIMICROBIAL DRUGS OF CHOICE FOR ANAEROBIC BACTERIA

	First choice	Alternative
Peptostreptococcus spp.	Penicillin	Clindamycin, chloramphenicol, cephalosporins
Clostridium spp.	Penicillin	Metronidazole, chloramphenicol, cefoxitin, clindamycin
Clostridium difficile	Vancomycin	Metronidazole, bacitracin
Gram-negative bacilli (BL−)	Penicillin	Metronidazole, clindamycin, chloramphenicol
Gram-negative bacilli (BL+)	Metronidazole, a carbapenem, a penicillin and BL inhibitor, clindamycin	Cefoxitin, chloramphenicol, piperacillin

Table 232.12 Antimicrobial drugs of choice for anaerobic bacteria. Gram-negative bacilli include *Bacteroides fragilis* group and *Prevotella*, *Porphyromonas* and *Fusobacterium* spp. BL, β-lactamase.

Doxycycline is added to most regimens in the treatment of pelvic infections to provide therapy for chlamydia and mycoplasma. Penicillin is still the drug of choice for bacteremia caused by non-BLPB. However, other agents should be used for the therapy of bacteremia caused by BLPB.

Because the duration of therapy for anaerobic infections, which are often chronic, is generally longer than for infections caused by aerobic and facultative anaerobes, oral therapy is often substituted for parenteral therapy. The agents available for oral therapy are limited and include clindamycin, amoxicillin plus clavulanic acid, chloramphenicol and metronidazole.

Clinical judgment, personal experience, safety and patient compliance should direct the physician in the choice of the appropriate antimicrobial agents. The duration of therapy generally ranges between 2 and 4 weeks, but should be individualized depending on the response. In some cases, such as lung abscesses, treatment may be required for as long as 6–8 weeks, but can often be shortened with proper surgical drainage.

REFERENCES

1. Hentges DJ.The anaerobic microflora of the human body [Review]. Clin Infect Dis 1993;164:S175–80.
2. Finegold SM. Anaerobic infections in humans: an overview. Anaerobe 1995;1:3–9.
3. Brook I. Pediatric anaerobic infection: diagnosis and management. 3rd ed. New York: Marcel Dekker; 2002.
4. Summanen P, Baron EJ, Ciron DM, *et al.* Wadsworth anaerobic bacteriology manual, 5th ed. Belmont, CA: Star Publishing; 1993.
5. Finegold SM. Anaerobic bacteria in human disease. Orlando: Academic Press Inc; 1977.
6. Jousimies H, Summanen P. Microbiology terminology update: clinically significant anaerobic Gram-positive and Gram-negative bacteria (excluding spirochetes). Clin Infect Dis 1999;29:724–7.
7. Hurst DL, Marsh WW. Early severe infantile botulism. J Pediatr 1993;122:909–11.
8. Hatheway CL. Toxogenic clostridia. Clin Microbiol Rev 1990;3:66–98.
9. Price AB, Davies DR. Pseudomembranous colitis. J Clin Pathol 1977;30:1–12.
10. Brook I, Frazier EH. Significant recovery of nonsporulating anaerobic rods from clinical specimens. Clin Infect Dis 1993;16:476–80.
11. Brook I, Frazier EH. Infections caused by *Propionibacterium* species. Rev Infect Dis 1991;13:819–22.
12. Brook I. *Prevotella* and *Porphyromonas* infections in children. J Med Microb 1995;42:340–7.
13. Brook I. Fusobacterial infection in children. J Infect 1994;28:155–65.
14. Rosenblatt JE, Brook I. Clinical relevance of susceptibility testing of anaerobic bacteria. Clin Infect Dis 1993;16(Suppl.4):S446–8.
15. Brook I. Peptostreptococcal infection in children. Scand J Infect Dis 1994;26:503–10.
16. Brook I, Frazier EH. Microaerophilic streptococci as a significant pathogen: a twelve-year review. J Med 1994;25:129–44.
17. Brook I, Frazier EH. Infections caused by *Veillonella* species. Infect Dis Clin Pract 1992;1:377–381.
18. Bartlett JG, Polk BF. Normal vaginal flora in relation to vaginitis. Obstet Gynecol Clin N Am 1989;16:329–36.
19. Vallor AC, Antonio MA, Hawes SE, *et al.* Factors associated with acquisition of, or persistent colonization by, vaginal lactobacilli: role of hydrogen peroxide production. J Infect Dis 2001;184:1431–6.
20. Brook I, Myhal LA, Dorsey HC. Encapsulation and pilus formation of *Bacteroides* sp. J Infect 1991;25:251–7.
21. Hofstad T. Virulence determinants in non-spore-forming anaerobic bacteria. Scand J Infect Dis 1989;(Suppl.62):15–24.
22. Brook I, Frazier EH. Aerobic and anaerobic infection associated with malignancy. Support Care Cancer 1998;6:125–31.
23. Brook I. Enhancement of growth of aerobic and facultative bacteria in mixed infections with *Bacteroides* sp. Infect Immun 1985;50:929–31.
24. Brook I. The role of beta-lactamase-producing bacteria in the persistence of streptococcal tonsillar infection. Rev Infect Dis 1984;6:601–7.
25. Hecht DW. National Committee for Clinical Laboratory Standards Working Group on Susceptibility Testing of Anaerobic Bacteria. Methods for antimicrobial susceptibility testing of anaerobic bacteria, 4th ed. approved standard. Villanova, PA: NCCLS document M11-A4; 1997;13(26).
26. Chaudhry R, Dhawan B, Laxmi BV, *et al.* The microbial spectrum of brain abscess with special reference to anaerobic bacteria. Br J Neurosurg 1998;12:127–30.
27. Brook I, Johnson N, Overturf GD, Wilkins J. Mixed bacterial meningitis: a complication of ventriculo- and lumbo-peritoneal shunts. J Neurosurg 1977;47:961–4.
28. Osenbach RK, Loftus CM. Diagnosis and management of brain abscess. Neurosurg Clin North Am 1992;3:403–20.
29. Brook I, Frazier EH, Gher ME. Aerobic and anaerobic microbiology of periodontal abscess. Oral Microbiol Immunol 1991;6:123–5.
30. Schlegel-Bregenzer B, Persson RE, Lukehart S, Braham P, Oswald T, Persson GR. Clinical and microbiological findings in elderly subjects with gingivitis or periodontitis. J Clin Periodontol 1998;25:897–907.
31. Brook I, Frazier EH. Microbiology of mediastinitis. Arch Intern Med 1996;156:333–6.
32. Brook I, Anthony BV, Finegold SM. Aerobic and anaerobic bacteriology of acute otitis media in children. J Pediatr 1978;92:13–5.
33. Brook I, Yocum P, Shah K, Feldman B, Epstein S. The aerobic and anaerobic bacteriology of serous otitis media. Am J Otolaryngol 1983;4:389–92.
34. Brook I. Prevalence of beta-lactamase-producing bacteria in chronic suppurative otitis media. Am J Dis Child 1985;139:280–4.
35. Sweeney G, Picozzi GI, Browning GG. A quantitative study of aerobic and anaerobic bacteria in chronic suppurative otitis media. J Infect 1982;5:47–55.
36. Brook I. Aerobic and anaerobic bacteriology of chronic mastoiditis in children. Am J Dis Child 1981;135:478–9.
37. Brook I. Aerobic and anaerobic bacteriology of cholesteatoma. Laryngoscope 1981;91:250–5.
38. Lino Y, Hoshimi E, Tomioko S, *et al.* Organic acids and anaerobic microorganisms in the contents of the cholesteatoma sac. Ann Otol Rhinol Laryngol 1983;92:91–4.
39. Carenfelt C, Lundberg C. Purulent and non-purulent maxillary sinus secretions with respect to pO_2, pCO_2 and pH. Acta Otolaryngol 1977;84:138–43.
40. Brook I, Frazier EH, Foote PA.Microbiology of the transition from acute to chronic maxillary sinusitis. J Med Microbiol 1996;45:372–5.
41. Brook I, Yocum P. Immune response to *Fusobacterium nucleatum* and *Prevotella intermedia* in patients with chronic maxillary sinusitis. Ann Otol Rhinol Laryngol. 1999;108:293–5.
42. Nord CE. The role of anaerobic bacteria in recurrent episodes of sinusitis and tonsillitis. Clin Infect Dis 1995;20:1512–24.
43. Brook I, Thompson DH, Frazier EH. Microbiology and management of chronic maxillary sinusitis. Arch Otolaryngol Head Neck Surg 1994;120:1317–20.
44. Brook I, Friedman EM, Rodriguez WJ, Contoni G. Complications of sinusitis in children. Pediatrics 1980;66:568–72.
45. Brook I. Aerobic and anaerobic microbiology of acute suppurative parotitis. Laryngoscope 1991;101:170–2.
46. Brook I. Aerobic and anaerobic bacteriology of cervical adenitis in children. Clin Pediatr 1980;19:693–6.
47. Bussman YC, Wong ML, Bell MJ, *et al.* Suppurative thyroiditis with gas formation due to mixed anaerobic infection. J Pediatr 1977;90:321–2.
48. Brook I. Microbiology of infected epidermal cysts. Arch Dermatol 1989;125:1658–61.
49. Brook I, Hirokawa R. Post surgical wound infection after head and neck cancer surgery. Ann Otol Rhinol Laryngol 1989;98:322–5.
50. Johnson JT, Yu VL, Myers RN, Wagner RL. Assessment of the need for Gram-negative bacterial coverage on antibiotic prophylaxis for oncological head and neck surgery. J Infect Dis 1987;155:331–3.
51. Brook I, Frazier EH, Thompson DH. Aerobic and anaerobic microbiology of peritonsillar abscess. Laryngoscope 1991;101:289–92.
52. Brook I, Yocum P. Comparison of the microbiology of group A streptococcal and non-group A streptococcal tonsillitis. Ann Otol Rhinol Laryngol 1988;97:243–6.
53. Helstrom SA, Mandi PA, Ripa T. Treatment of infectious mononucleosis with metronidazole. Scand J Infect Dis 1978;10:7–9.
54. Puto A. Febrile exudative tonsillitis: viral or streptococcal. Pediatrics 1987;80:6–12.
55. Brook I, Foote PA Jr, Slots J, Jackson W. Immune response to *Prevotella intermedia* in patients with recurrent non-streptococcal tonsillitis. Ann Otol Rhinol Laryngol 1993;102:113–6.
56. Brook I, Foote PA, Slots J. Immune response to *Fusobacterium nucleatum* and *Prevotella intermedia* in patients with peritonsillar cellulitis and abscess. Clin Infect Dis 1995;20(Suppl.2):S220–1.
57. Brook I, de Leyva F. Immune response to *Fusobacterium nucleatum* and *Prevotella intermedia* in patients with infectious mononucleosis. J Med Microbiol 1996;44:131–4.
58. Brook I, de Leyva F. Microbiology of tonsillar surfaces in infectious mononucleosis. Arch Pediatr Adolesc Med 1994;148:171–3.
59. Brook I, Yocum P, Friedman EM. Aerobic and anaerobic bacteria in tonsils of children with recurrent tonsillitis. Ann Otol Rhinol Laryngol 1981;90:261–3.
60. Tuner K, Nord CE. Beta-lactamase-producing microorganisms in recurrent tonsillitis. Scand J Infect Dis 1983;(Suppl.39):83–8.
61. Brook I., Shah K, Jackson W. Microbiology of healthy and diseased adenoids. Laryngoscope. 2000;110:994–9.
62. Brook I, Yocum P. Quantitative measurement of beta-lactamase in tonsils of children with

recurrent tonsillitis. Acta Otolaryngol 1984;98:556–60.
63. Kaplan EL, Johnson OR. Eradication of group A streptococci from treatment failure of the upper respiratory tract by amoxicillin with clavulanate after oral penicillin. J Pediatr 1988;113:400–3.
64. Brook I, Hirokawa R. Treatment of patients with a history of recurrent tonsillitis due to group A beta-hemolytic streptococci. Clin Pediatr 1985;24:331–6.
65. Brook I, Frazier EH. Aerobic and anaerobic microbiology of empyema. A retrospective review in two military hospitals. Chest 1993;103:1502–7.
66. Bartlett JG, Gorbach SL, Finegold SM. The bacteriology of aspiration pneumonia. Am J Med 1974;56:202–7.
67. Brook I. Bacterial colonization tracheobronchitis and pneumonia, following tracheostomy and long-term intubation in pediatric patients. Chest 1979;70:420–4.
68. Brook I, Frazier EH. Aerobic and anaerobic microbiology in intra-abdominal infections associated with diverticulitis. J Med Microbiol. 2000;49:827–30.
69. Bennion RS, Thompson JE, Baron EJ, Finegold SM. Gangrenous and perforated appendicitis with peritonitis: treatment and bacteriology. Clin Ther 1990;12(Suppl.C):31–44.
70. Sheen-Chen S, Chen W, Eng H, *et al.* Bacteriology and antimicrobial choice in hepatolithiasis. Am J Infect Control 2000;28:298–301.
71. Mongmorey RS, Wilson SE. Intra-abdominal abscesses: image-guided diagnosis and therapy. Clin Infect Dis 1996;23:28–36.
72. Bohnen JMA, Solomkin JS, Dellinger EP, Bjornson S, Page CP. Guidelines for clinical care: anti-infective agents for intra-abdominal infection. Arch Surg 1992;127:83–9.
73. Bohnen JMA, Mustard RA, Oxholm SE, Schouten BD. APACHE II score and abdominal sepsis. Arch Surg 1988;123:225–9.
74. Gorbach SL. Antimicrobial prophylaxis for appendectomy and colorectal surgery. Rev Infect Dis 1990;13(Suppl.3):S815–20.
75. Shafer MA, Sweet RL. Pelvic inflammatory disease in adolescent females. Epidemiology, pathogenesis, diagnosis, treatment and sequelae. Pediatr Clin North Am 1989;36:513–32.
76. Brook I, Frazier EH. Clinical features and aerobic and anaerobic microbiological characteristics of cellulitis. Arch Surg 1995;130:786–92.
77. Brook I, Finegold SM. Aerobic and anaerobic microbiology of cutaneous abscesses in children. Pediatrics 1981;67:891–5.
78. Meislin HW, Lerner SA, Graves MH, *et al.* Cutaneous abscesses: anaerobic and aerobic bacteriology and outpatient management. Ann Intern Med 1977;97:145–50.
79. Brook I, Frazier EH. Clinical and microbiological features of necrotizing fasciitis. J Clin Microb 1995;33:2382–7.
80. Goldstein EJC, Citron DM, Finegold SM. Role of anaerobic bacteria in bite wound infections. Rev Infect Dis 1984;6(Suppl.3):S177–83.
81. Brook I, Frazier EH. Anaerobic osteomyelitis and arthritis in a military hospital: a 10-year experience. Am J Med 1993;94:21–8.
82. Brook I. Anaerobic bacterial bacteremia: 12 years experience in two military hospitals. J Infect Dis 1989;160:1071–4.
83. Raff MJ, Melo JC. Anaerobic osteomyelitis. Medicine 1978;57:83–103.
84. Fitzgerald RA, Rosenblatt J, Tenney JH, Bourgault AM. Anaerobic septic arthritis. Clin Orthopedics 1982;164:141–8.
85. Dorsher CW, Rosenblatt JE, Wilson WR, *et al.* Anaerobic bacteremia: decreasing rate over a 15-year period. Rev Infect Dis 1991;16:633–6.
86. Kindwall EP. Uses of hyperbaric oxygen therapy in the 1990s. Cleve Clin J Med. 1992;59:517–28.
87. Snydman DR, Jacobus NV, McDermott LA, *et al.* Multicenter study of in vitro susceptibility of the *Bacteroides fragilis* group, 1995 to 1996, with comparison of resistance trends from 1990 to 1996. Antimicrob Agents Chemother 1999;43:2417–22.
88. Sutter VL, Finegold SM. Susceptibility of anaerobic bacteria to 23 antimicrobial agents. Antimicrob Agents Chemother 1976;10:736–52.
89. Appelbaum PC, Spangler SK, Jacobs MR. Susceptibility of 394 *Bacteroides fragilis*, non-*B. fragilis* group *Bacteroides* species, and *Fusobacterium* species to newer antimicrobial agents. Antimicrob Agents Chemother 1991;35:1214–8.
90. Hoellman DB, Kelly LM, Credito K, *et al.* In vitro antianaerobic activity of ertapenem (MK-0826) compared to seven other compounds. Antimicrob Agents Chemother 2002;46:220–4.
91. Goldstein EJ. Possible role for the new fluoroquinolones (levofloxacin, grepafloxacin, trovafloxacin, clinafloxacin, sparfloxacin, and DU-6859a) in the treatment of anaerobic infections: review of current information on efficacy and safety. Clin Infect Dis 1996;23:S25–30.
92. Finch RG. Antibacterial activity of quinupristin/dalfopristin. Rationale for clinical use. Drugs 1996;51:31–7.
93. Goldstein EJ, Citron DM, Merriam CV. Linezolid activity compared to those of selected macrolides and other agents against aerobic and anaerobic pathogens isolated from soft tissue bite infections in humans. Antimicrob Agents Chemother 1999;43:1469–74.

chapter

233 Mycobacteria

Clark B Inderlied

INTRODUCTION

In his review article entitled 'The White Plague', MF Perutz recounted that Cardinal Richelieu (1585–1642), Heinrich Heine (1797–1856), Frédéric Chopin (1810–49), Anton Chekhov (1860–1904), Franz Kafka (1883–1924), George Orwell (1903–50) and Eleanor Roosevelt (1884–1962) all shared a common fate.[1] Each of these famous people died of tuberculosis. In some cases their disease was not understood or only poorly understood, while in other cases management of the disease was inadequate, often because of a lack of effective therapeutic agents. Indeed, while the virulence and transmissibility of *Mycobacterium tuberculosis* are critical factors, there are additional factors that influence the occurrence and spread of this disease.

Clearly, the presence of a concurrent disease (especially AIDS) as well as the overall state of person's health and host defense mechanisms are critical determinants of the morbidity and mortality rates of tuberculosis. However, even more complex factors strongly influence the incidence of tuberculosis including poverty, ignorance and indifference about the disease, and the lack of access to health care. Indeed, in the World Health Organization (WHO) 2002 report on global tuberculosis control, 22 countries were identified as having a 'high burden' of tuberculosis. For example, while 62% of the world's human population (estimated at 6.1 billion persons in 2000) live in these 22 countries, nearly 80% of cases of tuberculosis worldwide occur in these countries. Nevertheless, even within the 'high burden' countries the incidence of tuberculosis varies from a low of 68 cases to more than 584 cases per 100,000 population. The nearly 9-fold difference in the incidence of tuberculosis reflects the plethora and complexity of factors that influence the spread and incidence of tuberculosis.

The goals of the WHO global tuberculosis control program are to detect 70% of tuberculosis cases in the high burden countries and to successfully treat 85% of the identified cases. Although the WHO sponsored program is focused on tuberculosis, many of the principles of diagnosis, treatment and control of tuberculosis pertain to other nontuberculous infections. The laboratory diagnosis of tuberculosis and other mycobacterial diseases is an important element of the effective treatment and control of all of these diseases and is the focus of this chapter.

NATURE

Lehmann and Neumann first introduced the genus *Mycobacterium* into the scientific literature in 1896. The subsequent history of the genus in terms of our knowledge and understanding of these micro-organisms has been profoundly influenced by the fact that only one of the more than 40 currently recognized species has been a devastating cause of human disease and suffering for time immemorial: *M. tuberculosis*. Indeed, Wayne[2] noted in his discussion of mycobacterial speciation that taxonomic studies of the genus have been undoubtedly skewed because of the focus on the need for the detection and accurate identification of *M. tuberculosis*. Thus, studies of microbial physiology, structure, genetics and diagnostic tools have focused on *M. tuberculosis* and secondarily on *Mycobacterium leprae*. Nevertheless, during the past several years other species of mycobacteria, notably the rapidly growing mycobacteria and the *M. avium* complex, have been the subject of extensive investigations largely because of the increased incidence of human disease and increased awareness of disease caused by these mycobacteria.

All members of the genus *Mycobacterium* are aerobic, nonspore-forming, nonmotile single cell bacteria. In general, the size of mycobacteria are significantly smaller than other types of bacteria and cell shape varies from coccobacilli to elongated rods, but pleomorphic morphology is common. The most prominent feature of mycobacteria that is uniformly present and distinctive to the genus is the complex, lipid-rich cell envelope. Indeed, it is the complex cell envelope of mycobacteria that confers upon these bacteria the property of 'acid-fastness' (i.e. resistance to decolorization when stained with carbolfuchsin and decolorized with dilute hydrochloric acid). The mycobacterial cell envelope has been the subject of extensive investigations because of the chemical uniqueness of the structure, the importance of the envelope to the biology of the micro-organism, and the role of envelope antigens in immunobiology and diagnostics.

Mycobacteria are classified with the Gram-positive bacteria, but most mycobacteria do not stain well with Gram's stain. Mycobacteria possess a cell wall polysaccharide that resembles that of Gram-positive bacteria; however, the mycobacterial peptidoglycan contains lipids in place of proteins and polysaccharides.[3] Furthermore, the mycobacterial envelope contains a plasma membrane that is quite similar in structure and function to the plasma membrane of other bacteria except for the presence of lipoarabinomannan (LAM), lipomannan and phosphatidylinositol mannosides.[3] The cell wall component of the envelope confers size, shape, protection against osmotic pressure, and probably protects the plasma membrane from deleterious molecules in the environment of the cell. The peptidoglycan confers cell shape while the next layer of the envelope, arabinogalactan esterified to the mycolic acids (fatty acids), is largely believed to restrict permeability.

At the exterior surface of the cell envelope are the mycosides, a mixture of glycolipids. The mycosides confer the agglutination serotype of a strain and influence colony morphology and may influence virulence. The mycosides are 'in charge of public relations for mycobacteria' and in this capacity are analogous to the 'O' antigens of Gram-negative bacteria.[4] In 1947, Middlebrook first described growth of tubercule bacilli in the shape of serpentine cords ('cording'), and for many years cording was correlated with virulence and was considered to be a distinctive feature of *M. tuberculosis* (Fig. 233.1). However, it is now known that several species of mycobacteria display cording and the correlation with virulence, if any, is unclear. Cord factor appears to be a mixture of mycolate-containing molecules including the original cord factor associated with *M. tuberculosis*, trehalose 6,6′-dimycolate. Thus, the structure of the mycobacterial cell envelope (Fig. 233.2) includes a plasma membrane, a peptidoglycan layer, an arabinogalactan layer esterified to an uneven mycolate layer, and a glycolipid layer. Lipoarabinomannan and a

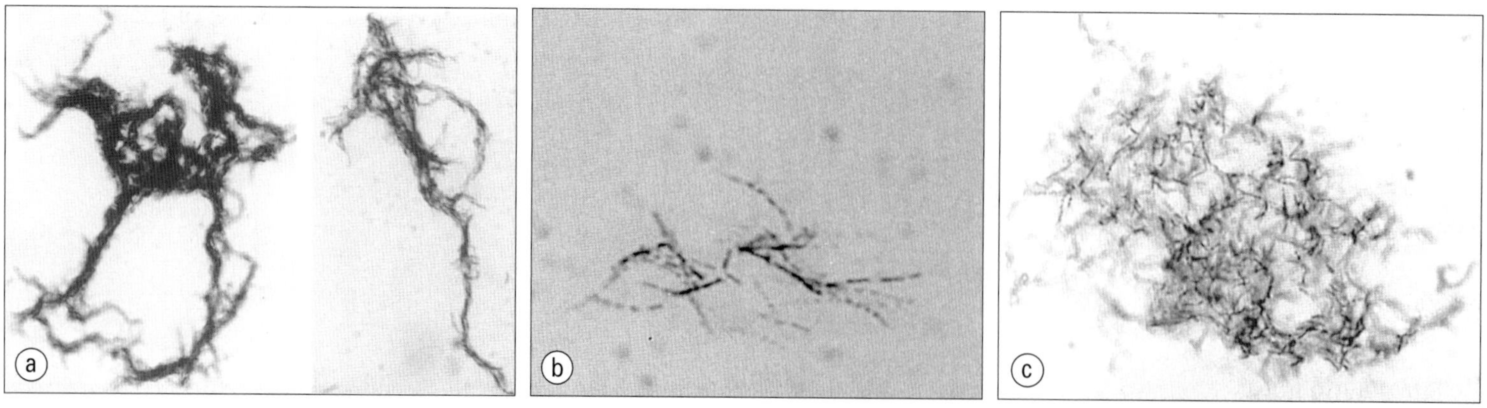

Fig. 233.1 Microscopic clusters of three different species of mycobacteria. (a) Serpentine cording of *Mycobacterium tuberculosis*. (b) Cross-banding of *Mycobacterium kansasii*. (c) Loose clusters of *Mycobacterium avium* complex. Photomicrographs taken from Attorri *et al.*[5]

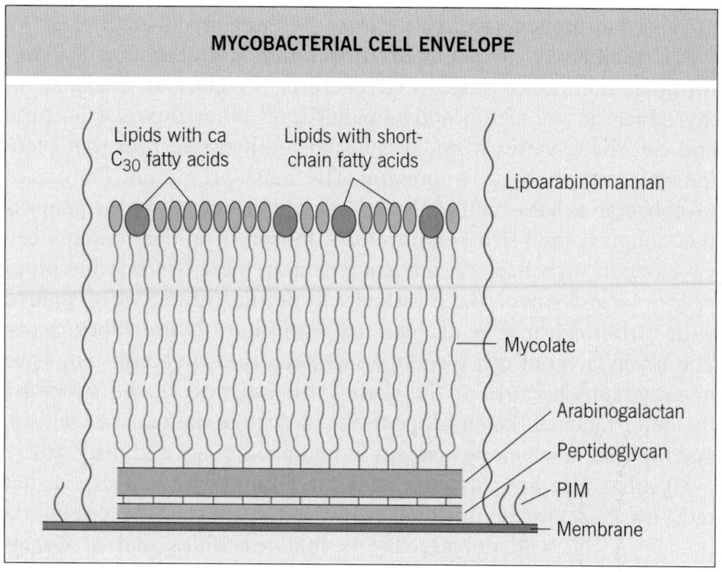

Fig. 233.2 Mycobacterial cell envelope. This model displays the asymmetric array of the structural elements extending from the plasma membrane that surrounds the cytoplasm of the mycobacterial cell. The arabinogalactan is covalently linked to the peptidoglycan, which along with the lipoarabinomannan and phosphatidylinositol mannosides (PIM) are associated with the plasma membrane. The cell wall lipids are shown in a possible arrangement with the mycolates linked to the arabinogalactan. Two classes of polar lipids with medium and short chain fatty acids complement the varying hydrocarbon chains of the mycolates to create an even cell envelope. There is evidence for a small number of porins within the hydrophobic bilayer. Adapted from Brennan and Draper.[3]

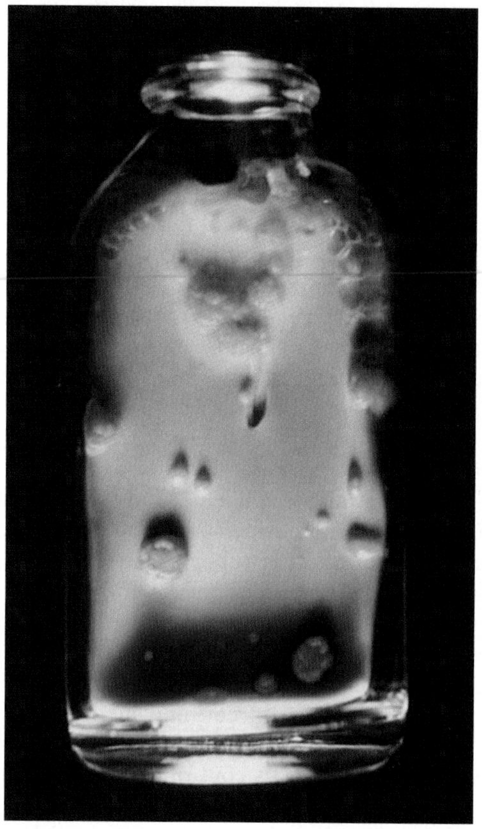

Fig. 233.3 *Mycobacterium kansasii,* a photochromogenic mycobacterium, grown on Löwenstein–Jensen medium in light. Courtesy of S Froman and A Gaytan.

small number of porins traverse the width of the mycobacterial envelope. As in other bacteria the mycobacterial porins provide a mechanism for the passage of low molecular weight molecules from the environment into the intracellular matrix.

Many species of mycobacteria are capable of producing carotenoids and this feature can be an important aid in the presumptive identification of an unknown mycobacterial isolate. The principal carotenoids produced by mycobacteria are carotenes and xanthophylls and it appears that all mycobacteria are at least capable of producing some carotenoids. However, the production of carotenoids is strongly influenced by the composition of the media and growth conditions. Light has a significant effect on pigment production for some species. Scotochromogens (e.g. *M. scrofulaceum*) produce pigment in the absence of light whereas photochromogens (e.g. *M. kansasii*) produce pigment when stimulated by light (Fig. 233.3). Nonphotochromogens (e.g. *M. avium* complex and *M. tuberculosis*) may or may not produce carotenoids, but most strains usually do not. The function of mycobacterial carotenoids is largely unknown, but some evidence suggests that carotenoids provide protection from phototoxic effects.

The genome of mycobacteria is large ($3–5.5{\times}10^9$ Da) and like other prokaryotes is arranged as a closed circle. The nucleotide base composition of mycobacterial DNA is extraordinarily rich in guanine (G) and cytosine (C; i.e. 66–71 mol% GC). Most of the environmental species of mycobacteria, in particular *M. avium* complex, *M. scrofulaceum* and the rapid growers, contain plasmids. The size and number of plasmids vary; the function(s) of the plasmids are largely unknown, but may include resistance to heavy metals. There has been some evidence and considerable speculation that plasmids in mycobacteria include DNA sequences that encode a variety of virulence factors. However, plasmids would appear to have no role in antibiotic resistance or virulence in *M. tuberculosis*, since the majority of *M. tuberculosis* strains do not contain plasmids.

A phylogenetic tree, based on 16S rRNA sequence information, of selected species of slowly growing mycobacteria is shown in Figure 233.4.[6] The lack of separation of 'species' within the *M. tuber-*

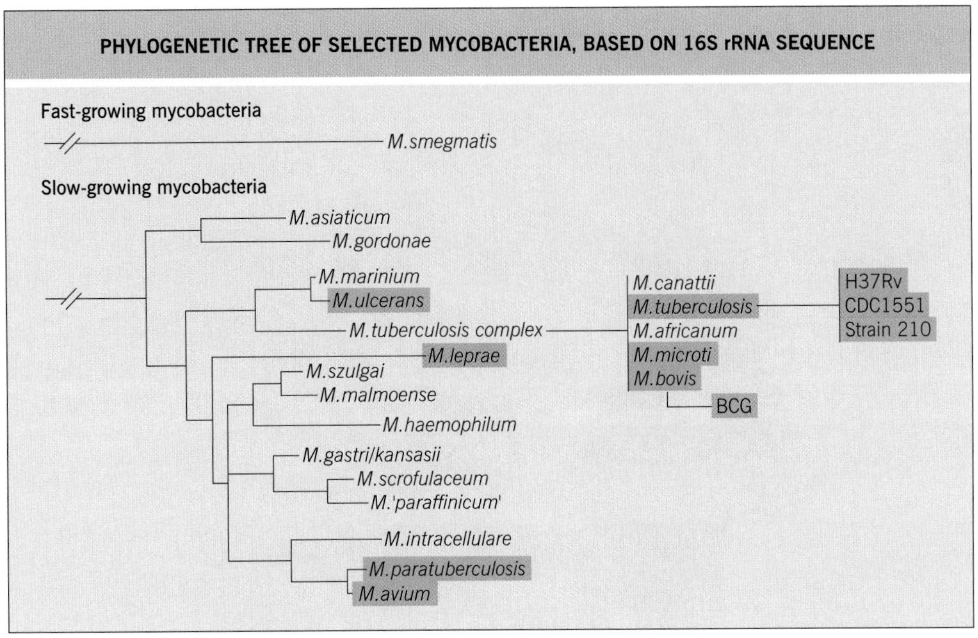

Fig. 233.4 Phylogenetic tree of selected mycobacteria, based on 16S rRNA sequence information, including species whose genome sequence is completed (red) or is in progress (green). Figure adapted from Brosch *et al.*[6]

culosis complex reflects that these mycobacteria should be viewed more as pathovars or subspecies. Overall, however, this analysis of genetic relatedness confirms the classical classification scheme based on pigmentation and growth rate. However, genome sequence information has already revealed interesting information about differences within the *M. tuberculosis* complex. For example, comparisons of *M. tuberculosis* H37Rv (a human isolate that is also virulent in mice) with bacille Calmette–Guérin (BCG) Pasteur revealed that 18 variable sequence regions are missing in BCG Pasteur. Perhaps even more intriguing is the presence of two large tandem duplications in BCG Pasteur, whereas other BCG strains lack one of these duplications and neither of the duplications are seen in H37Rv. Furthermore, the genome size of *M. bovis* is significantly smaller than that of *M. tuberculosis*, which seems at odds with the fact that *M. bovis* has a significantly wider host range than *M. tuberculosis*.[6] Indeed, sequence information has placed in doubt the longheld belief that *M. tuberculosis* evolved from an animal pathogen (i.e. *M. bovis*) and indicates that *M. tuberculosis* was always a human pathogen.[7]

EPIDEMIOLOGY

Tuberculosis

Tuberculosis is the leading cause of death worldwide that can be attributed to a single infectious disease agent.[8–10] The vast majority of tuberculosis cases are found in the developing world and disease occurs predominantly during the prime period of life from 15 to 59 years of age. The estimated incidence of tuberculosis worldwide in 2000 was 8.7 million cases, of which nearly 80% (6.9 million) were found in 22 high-burden countries (Fig. 233.5).[11] Conversely, less than 3% of the worldwide incidence of tuberculosis is found in the industrialized countries.[12] The mortality rate due to tuberculosis closely tracks the worldwide incidence with the highest mortality rate again in South East Asia and Africa. Overall, tuberculosis is estimated to cause over 25% of avoidable adult deaths in the developing world. Indeed, before the development of effective chemotherapy, the mortality rate for tuberculosis was 50–60%. However, following the discovery of isoniazid and then rifampin (rifampicin), the majority of pulmonary and extrapulmonary tuberculosis became treatable. Nevertheless, the treatment of tuberculosis remains problematic because of the lack of or intermittent access to therapy, poor adherence to therapy and the emergence of resistance.

Leprosy

Epidemiology of leprosy (Hansen's disease) is difficult to assess accurately because of the lack of a diagnostic skin test, inability to cultivate the leprosy bacillus in vitro and the nature of the geographic distribution of endemic disease. Leprosy appears to be primarily spread from human to human through nasal secretions. Skin contact is most likely an uncommon route of transmission.[13] Although there has been speculation that an insect vector may be responsible for the spread of some leprosy, this has not been demonstrated. It does appear that transmission by any route requires prolonged exposure to an infected individual. However, the transmission of leprosy is similar to tuberculosis in that, while prolonged exposure is the most common risk factor, a single exposure involving coincident but otherwise singly rare circumstances can result in the transmission of disease. Treatment appears to decrease infectiousness significantly. The global incidence of leprosy is estimated to be between 5.5 and 6.5 million patients.[4] The vast majority of patients are in the developing world, predominantly South East Asia and mostly in India. The care and treatment of leprosy have two equally difficult components. The first is treatment of active disease, especially in patients with physical deformities or at risk of developing deformities. The second is care of effectively treated patients, but with disabling or debilitating deformities due to the pathology associated with the various manifestations of this disease.

Mycobacterium avium complex

Mycobacterium avium complex (MAC) disease occurs as a disseminated disease usually, but not exclusively, in people with HIV infection. *Mycobacterium avium* complex also causes pulmonary disease in immunocompetent patients and cervical lymphadenitis in normal hosts, mostly children. It is ubiquitous in the environment, including and especially soil and water, but also in certain foods (e.g. hard cheese). Portals of infection are probably both gastrointestinal and pulmonary by ingestion of contaminated food or water and inhalation of aerosols. Disseminated MAC disease was rarely reported before the first reports of opportunistic infections and AIDS, published in the early 1980s. Based on complete follow-up information (even at the peak of the AIDS epidemic in the USA disseminated MAC was infrequently the AIDS-defining opportunistic infection) disseminated MAC disease occurs in 20–35% per year of people with HIV infection.[14] However, even this is an historic figure and MAC prophylaxis (rifabutin, azithromycin or clarithromycin) and the

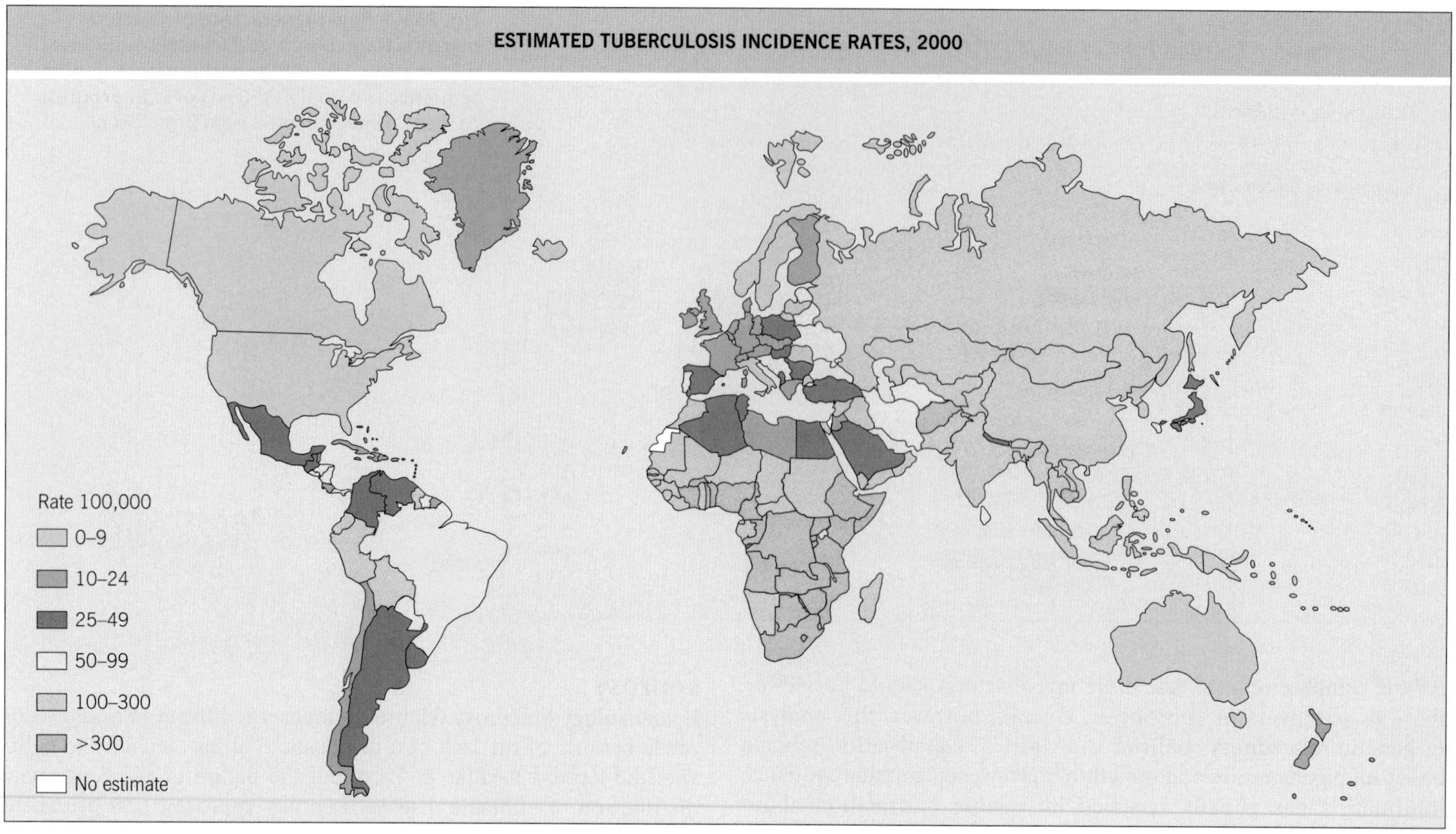

Fig. 233.5 Estimated tuberculosis incidence rates, 2000. Data and map adapted from World Health Organization. Global tuberculosis control: surveillance, planning, financing. WHO Report 2002, Switzerland, WHO/CDS/TB/2002.295.[11]

use of highly active antiretroviral therapy (HAART) has significantly decreased the incidence of MAC disease in people with HIV infection. The incidence of disseminated MAC disease in children with HIV infection is nearly the same as in adults and the manifestations of disseminated MAC disease in these patients are virtually identical to those in adults. *Mycobacterium avium* complex pulmonary disease is seen worldwide with an overall incidence of about 1/100,000 persons. The incidence of pulmonary disease appears to be increasing, but this may be due in part to increased surveillance and awareness by the medical community. Although MAC pulmonary disease has been associated with a history of chronic lung infection including cystic fibrosis, many patients have no identifiable risk factors except age. *Mycobacterium avium* complex cervical lymphadenitis is mostly a pediatric disease and primarily seen in children under 5 years of age. There are several reports of disseminated MAC disease in children who do not have HIV infection, but it seems likely that these children have a very specific immunodeficiency that causes the patient to be at risk for MAC infection.

Rapid growers

Although there are over 30 species of rapidly growing mycobacteria, the vast majority (>90%) of disease that occurs in humans is caused by three species: *Mycobacterium fortuitum*, *Mycobacterium chelonae* and *Mycobacterium abscessus*. These species are important causes of cutaneous, pulmonary and postsurgical wound infections especially following catheter placement, augmentation mammaplasty and cardiac bypass surgery. Disseminated disease is rare and almost invariably occurs in immunocompromised patients, but disease is not common in people with HIV infection.

The distribution of rapidly growing mycobacteria appears to be worldwide. The three species associated with human disease have been isolated from drinking water as well as natural waters. In addition, these mycobacteria are commonly found in animal drinking water, waste water and soil. The ubiquitous nature of these microorganisms, their resistance to disinfectants including relative resistance to chlorine, and their ability to grow on unusual substrates such as polyhalogenated phenols account for the fact that rapidly growing mycobacteria are found as contaminants of medical equipment, prosthetic valves and disinfectants.

The incidence of pulmonary disease caused by rapidly growing mycobacteria is unclear (80% by *M. abscessus*), but an increased awareness of these species as human pathogens is leading to greater insight into the true incidence of disease. Nevertheless, the isolation of rapidly growing mycobacteria from respiratory tract specimens must be interpreted with great caution because contamination and colonization are common. True infection is usually associated with chronic pulmonary disease such as cystic fibrosis, previous mycobacterial lung disease and bronchiectasis due to previous respiratory infection. Rapidly growing mycobacteria are intrinsically resistant to antituberculous agents including isoniazid, rifampin and pyrazinamide.

PATHOGENICITY

The pathogenicity of mycobacterial infections in the immunocompetent host has as much to do with the immune response of the host as with destructive virulence properties of the mycobacterial pathogen. Thus, the principal virulence factor of mycobacteria is the ability to invade and persist or replicate within macrophages. Tubercle bacilli are believed to attach to macrophages by binding to the mannose receptor on the macrophage via the mycobacterial cell envelope LAM. Alternatively tubercle bacilli can indirectly bind via CR1/CR3 complement receptors or Fc receptors.

The bacilli enter the macrophage by phagocytosis and once internalized the bacilli are surrounded by a membrane-bound vacuole to form a nascent phagosome. With the maturation of the phagolysosome, bacilli are exposed to a variety of antimicrobial factors including reactive oxygen intermediates, hydrolytic activities and a highly acidic pH. Cytokine-activated macrophages may also produce reactive nitrogen intermediates, although this has been conclusively shown only in murine macrophages. Virulent mycobacteria obstruct the maturation of phagosomes, inhibiting acidification, and can escape from the phagolysosome into the cytoplasm. Other bacilli appear able to adapt to life within the phagolysosome.

Recent evidence indicates that the maturation of the phagolysosome varies depending on the bacterial pathogen and varies even between intracellular pathogens.[15] The composition of the phagosome membrane is determined in part by the infecting mycobacteria; for example, phagosomes containing *M. avium* do not contain the vacuolar H^+-ATPase that is needed for acidification of the phagosome. Phagosomes containing either *M. tuberculosis* or *M. avium* bacilli are frequently incompetent for fusion with endocytic organelles, suggesting a mechanism for the block in phagolysosome fusion. Inhibition of acidification can occur as a consequence of the exclusion of a proton pump (as with *M. avium*) or fusion with a lysosome that does not contain a pump or perhaps by the release of an ammonia metabolizing enzyme such as glutamine synthetase. Once mycobacteria have modified or adapted to the intracellular environment the bacilli may proliferate, but the mechanism of intracellular replication of mycobacteria is poorly understood.

The immunopathogenesis of mycobacterial infections primarily involves a cell-mediated immune response. This response includes the activation of macrophages to identify and inhibit or kill mycobacteria and the detection and lysis of phagocytes in which mycobacteria are in a state of growth and replication (Fig. 233.6).

Mycobacterial antigens are presented by antigen-presenting cells (monocyte/macrophage lineage) resulting in secretion of interleukin (IL)-2 and clonal proliferation of $CD4^+$ and $CD8^+$ lymphocytes (α/β T cells). Mycobacterial antigens arising from the phagosome are presented by major histocompatibility complex (MHC) class II molecules while antigens arising from the cytoplasm are presented by MHC class I molecules.[15] This difference determines, in part, the fate of the antigen-presenting cell, stimulation or destruction, because the presentation of antigen arising from the cytoplasm indicates that the cell has failed to control the mycobacteria. The release of interferon (IFN)-γ by the clonally expanded CD4 cells, but also to a lesser extent by CD8 cells, natural killer (NK) cells and $\gamma\delta$ cells, activates macrophages. This initiates a cascade of events including the hydrolysis of vitamin D that leads to further activation of macrophages and the release of tumor necrosis factor (TNF)-α by the activated macrophages. The sequence of cellular responses at the site of mycobacterial infection appears to be polymorphonuclear granulocytes (PNGs), NK cells, $\gamma\delta$ cells and then α/β T cells; however, with time the α/β T cells become predominant in the cellular response. The sequence of recruitment is probably determined by the proximity of the cells to the site of infection; for example, $\gamma\delta$ cells are likely to be one of the first cells recruited to the site of *M. tuberculosis* infection in the lung. The PNGs produce highly proteolytic enzymes that cause tissue liquefaction while each of the T-cell types possesses cytotoxic activity. Activated macrophages have an increased capacity for seeking out, engulfing and destroying mycobacteria, but the production of TNF-α by macrophages contributes to tissue necrosis and, therefore, to the immunopathology of the disease.

The activity of macrophages to resist mycobacterium multiplication, which determines in part host susceptibility or host resistance to tuberculosis, is determined by the presence of the gene *Bcg/Ity/Lsh* in mice with its human homolog *NRAMP1* (natural resistance-associated macrophage protein 1).[17,18]

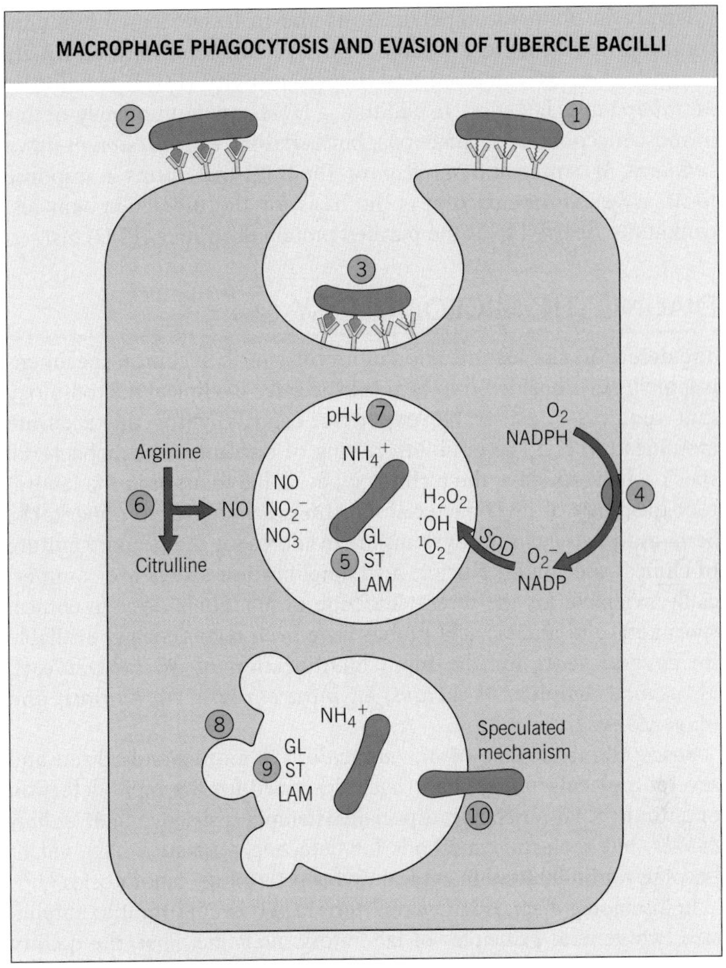

Fig. 233.6 Macrophage phagocytosis and evasion of tubercle bacilli. The tubercle bacilli bind via lipoarabinomannan (LAM) (1) or complement receptors (2); phagocytosis occurs (3) with the activation of an oxidative burst (4); glycolipids (GL), sulfatides (ST) and LAM can downregulate the oxidative burst (5); reactive nitrogen intermediates may play a role in antimycobacterial activity (6), as does the acidic pH of the phagolysosome (7). Finally, the production of ammonia by tubercle bacilli may diminish the effect of reactive nitrogen intermediates (8) and contribute to the failure to form a phagolysosome fusion (9). Tubercule bacilli may evade the antimycobacterial activities of the phagolysosome by producing a hemolysin that releases the bacilli into the cytoplasm (10). NADP, nicotinamide adenine dinucleotide phosphate; NADPH, nicotinamide adenine dinucleotide phosphate, reduced form; SOD, superoxide dismutase. Adapted from Chan and Kaufmann.[16]

On the other hand, mycobacteria are equipped to resist oxidative killing by phagocytic cells. This resistance is controlled by the *katG* promoter in the micobacterial genome. The *katG* gene encodes an enzyme with catalase, peroxidase and peroxynitritase activities.[19]

Granulomas develop as a mycobacterial infection becomes more chronic. Granulomas are aggregates of activated macrophages that take on epithelial cell-like morphology (epithelioid cells), and typically lymphocytes are found at the periphery of the granuloma. Although the formation of a granuloma effectively contains the mycobacteria where they can be killed, bacilli can persist within giant cells (fused epithelioid cells) and the granuloma may never sterilize. With time a fibrotic wall (collagen) will encapsulate the granuloma and the center of the granuloma may become necrotic with a cheese-like appearance, which is the source of the descriptive word caseation. Hippocrates termed granulomas 'tubercles' because they were similar in morphology to the tubers of plants, hence the name tuberculosis.[4]

Finally, in immunocompetent hosts and to lesser degree immunocompromised hosts (e.g. people with HIV infection may be totally anergic), there is a delayed-type hypersensitivity (DTH) reaction to *M. tuberculosis* infection. In addition, a DTH reaction probably occurs in most mycobacterial infections, but certainly with *M. avium-intracellulare*, *M. leprae* and *M. ulcerans*. The DTH that occurs in response to *M. tuberculosis* infection is the basis for the tuberculin skin test commonly referred to as the purified protein derivative (PPD) test.

DIAGNOSTIC MICROBIOLOGY

The detection and identification of mycobacteria in clinical specimens is largely still considered to be a subspecialty in clinical microbiology that requires considerable expertise, especially for the accurate identification and susceptibility testing of uncommon mycobacterial species. Nevertheless, the technology available to assist in the laboratory diagnosis of mycobacterial infections has improved remarkably. Semi-automated culture systems are available for the primary culture of clinical specimens. Nucleic acid amplification assays are commercially available for the direct detection of *M. tuberculosis* in clinical specimens and nucleic acid probes have been commercially available for several years for the rapid identification of *M. tuberculosis*, *M. avium* complex, *M. avium*, *M. intracellulare*, *M. kansasii* and *M. gordonae* from culture.

Susceptibility testing of *M. tuberculosis* is more standardized and several molecular assays have been described for the rapid detection of antimicrobial resistance, especially rifampin resistance in *M. tuberculosis*, but molecular methods for detecting resistance have yet to become routinely used in clinical mycobacteriology laboratories.[20–22]

In discussing diagnostic mycobacteriology it is important to emphasize two general principles of laboratory medicine. First, the quality of any clinical test is highly dependent on the quality of the specimen, including the time of collection in the course of the disease, the appropriateness and sufficiency of the specimen, and the prompt and proper transport of the specimen to the laboratory. Second, the intended purpose of the test, as it was designed and verified, must be understood by the physician who orders the test. Was the test designed to screen for disease, to provide a definitive diagnosis based on a clinical index of suspicion, to confirm another test, to monitor therapy (test of cure), or to provide epidemiologic information? Although any one test may have multiple purposes, most tests have been designed and evaluated for a limited purpose. Use of a test for a purpose for which it was not designed and evaluated could be misleading. For example, nucleic acid amplification assays for the direct detection of *M. tuberculosis* in clinical specimens were evaluated as diagnostic assays, not as tests of cure or for monitoring response to therapy.

Laboratory diagnosis

The laboratory diagnosis of mycobacterial infections often consists of five steps:

- first, mycobacteria can be directly detected in clinical specimens by microscopic examination and molecular assays;
- second, mycobacteria can be detected in clinical specimens by culture using a variety of liquid and solid media;
- third, the isolated mycobacteria can be identified using morphologic, biochemical and molecular tests;
- fourth, the activity of antimicrobial agents can be measured using in-vitro tests; and
- fifth, strains of mycobacteria can be characterized by molecular or other methods for epidemiologic and public health purposes.

The isolation of *M. tuberculosis* strains resistant to multiple antibiotics and the increase in the incidence of tuberculosis in the USA for a short time led to concerns about the length of time (commonly believed to be at least 4–8 weeks) necessary for a conventional laboratory diagnosis. Therefore, in providing laboratory services for the diagnosis of tuberculosis and other mycobacterial diseases, one must recognize the need for prompt as well as accurate information. Salfinger[23] led in designing and implementing 'fast-track' mycobacteriology services, initially in response to an acute need during an outbreak of multidrug resistant *M. tuberculosis* in New York City. However, even before the 'fast-track' era, it was possible to provide mycobacteriology services in a reliable and prompt manner. All that was required was the appropriate diligence and awareness of the laboratory, physicians and public health officials.

Specimen collection

The most critical step in the laboratory diagnosis of any infectious disease occurs before the specimen arrives at the laboratory. The quality, quantity, timing, transport and appropriateness of the specimen have a greater impact on the outcome of a laboratory test than almost any other factor (Table 233.1). Mycobacterial infections can be localized or disseminated, or disseminated with foci of infection that are more likely than other body sites to yield mycobacteria. Once a specimen has been collected it is important to transport the specimen in a container that is sterile, leak-proof and wax-free. The specimen must be accompanied by a request form or transmittal slip that includes the patient's name, medical record number, date and time collected, name of the laboratory, diagnosis, therapy, type of specimen, and test(s) requested. It is important that physicians notify the laboratory if they suspect an uncommon or fastidious mycobacterial infection such as *M. ulcerans*, *M. marinum* or *M. haemophilum*. These and other species of mycobacteria have growth requirements that are significantly different from the majority of other species of mycobacteria isolated from clinical specimens.

Sputum

Sputum is the best specimen for the diagnosis of pulmonary tuberculosis. Expectorated sputum specimen should be collected early in the morning on three occasions. Sputum should be collected directly into a wide-mouthed, sterile, plastic container (wax free) with a tight fitting cap. The specimen should be immediately transported to the laboratory or held at 32–39.2°F (0–4°C) until processed. Prompt processing of sputum is required because of the potential for overgrowth of normal respiratory tract microflora. Alternative respiratory tract specimens are induced sputum, endotracheal aspiration, bronchial washings or aspirates taken during bronchoscopy, laryngeal swabs (not a simple throat swab) and gastric lavage. Bronchoscopes must be carefully cleaned and decontaminated after collecting specimens from a patient with suspected tuberculosis.

Gastric lavage

Gastric lavage (for swallowed sputum) is useful for collecting specimens from patients who for a variety of reasons are unable to produce sputum by other means. Gastric lavage is frequently used to collect specimens from young children. In performing a gastric lavage it is common to suggest to patients that they sip water or swallow a small amount of ice to help pass the gastric tube into the stomach. However, *M. gordonae* is frequently found in many hospital water supplies and especially in ice machines, and use of such contaminated water during the collection of a gastric aspirate may result in a false-positive smear or culture. A gastric lavage must be promptly sent to the laboratory because it must be processed as soon as possible or neutralized with 10% sodium carbonate to avoid loss of mycobacteria due to gastric acidity. As with expectorated sputum specimens, gastric lavage specimens should be collected early in the morning, before eating, and on three separate occasions.

SPECIMEN TYPES AND REQUIREMENTS FOR DIAGNOSIS OF MYCOBACTERIAL INFECTIONS			
Specimen type	Requirements	Collection device	Note
Abscess fluid	10ml*	Syringe with cap	Dry swab unacceptable
Blood	10ml	SPS tube, Isolator, Bactec 13A	EDTA tube unacceptable, treat coagulated blood as tissue
Fluids (pleural, pericardial, peritoneal)	10–15ml*	Sterile container, syringe	
Bone	Bone chip	Sterile container, no fixative	Formalin fixed unacceptable
Bone marrow	100mg* 1–3ml aspirate	SPS tube, 1.5ml Isolator	Aspirate volumes >5ml may be primarily peripheral blood
Bronchoalveolar lavage or bronchial washing	≥5ml	Sterile container	Avoid contamination of bronchoscope with tap water – possible false positive
CSF	10ml*	Sterile tube	Smear is STAT
Gastric lavage	5–10ml	Sterile container, collect in morning before arising and before eating	Neutralize with 10% carbonate, if delayed processing
Lymph node	Whole node or part, caseous part	Sterile container	Formalin fixed unacceptable
Skin biopsy	Sterile container, aspirate in syringe	Biopsy at periphery or aspirate from under margin of lesion	Note if suspect *M. ulcerans, M. haemophilum,* or *M. marinum* – need special culture conditions or extended incubation
Sputum	5–10ml	Sterile, wax-free container	Use sterile hypertonic saline for induced sputum, avoid exposure to tap water
Stool	≥1g	Sterile, wax-free container	Do *not* freeze
Tissue bropsy	1g	Sterile container	Caseous portion, formalin fixed unacceptable
Transtracheal aspirate	10ml*	Syringe with cap	
Urine	50ml*	Sterile container, syringe with cap	24-hour urine, catheter urine are unacceptable

* As much as possible up to or in excess of the weight shown

Table 233.1 Specimen types and requirements for the diagnosis of mycobacterial infections. SPS, sodium polyanetholsulfonate.

Urine

Three early morning midstream urine specimens should be collected into a sterile plastic container (wax-free) with a leak-proof cap. Large volumes of urine can be concentrated by filtration, but 24-hour urine should not be used because of contamination and dilution of any mycobacteria present. True positive urine cultures for mycobacteria almost invariably indicate infection elsewhere in the patient.

Blood and bone marrow

Blood, bone marrow aspirates or cores are ideal specimens for the diagnosis of disseminated MAC, disseminated *M. tuberculosis*, and other disseminated mycobacterial infections. Blood should be processed using an agent that causes blood cell cytolysis and the cell-free mycobacteria collected by centrifugation using either an Isolator tube (Wampole, Cranbury, NJ) or a sodium polyanethol sulfonate (SPS) tube.[24] Blood collected in an SPS tube must be treated with a lytic agent such as desoxycholate and then concentrated by centrifugation before inoculating media. Alternatively, blood can be collected into an SPS tube and transferred directly to a Bactec460 TB 13A medium or other semi-automated systems (Table 233.2) for the detection of *M. avium* complex. Bone marrow aspirate can be collected in a pediatric Isolator tube, but bone marrow core should be processed as tissue. Bone marrow specimens should also be inoculated into a liquid medium such as Bactec460 TB 12B or Middlebrook 7H9. Blood and bone marrow for culture should not be collected in an EDTA tube; however, an albumin-citrate-dextrose (ACD) tube can be used if an SPS tube is not available.

Other fluids

Cerebrospinal fluid (CSF), pleural, pericardial, synovial and ascitic fluids as well as pus and bone marrow aspirates may be submitted for smear and culture. *Mycobacterium tuberculosis* meningitis is a medical emergency and CSF specimens should be collected, transported and processed in a manner that reflects the urgent nature of such a diagnosis. Aseptically collected sterile body site fluids should not be decontaminated, but these specimens can be concentrated. Fluids should be promptly processed and inoculated into a liquid growth medium as well as solid media.

Tissues

Tissue should be submitted for both histology and mycobacteriology. Tissue is preferred over necrotic material or pus for culture, therefore, it is important to have fresh tissue and not swabs submitted to the microbiology laboratory for smear and culture. Formalin-preserved tissue should be submitted for histologic studies. Although not suitable for culture, formalin-preserved and paraffin-embedded tissue can be submitted for polymerase chain reaction (PCR) analysis, especially if acid-fast bacilli are observed on microscopic examination of the tissue sections.[25,26]

Feces

Feces are not a particularly useful specimen for the diagnosis of tuberculosis or other mycobacterial infections, with the exception of suspected gastrointestinal tract infection with MAC in HIV-positive patients. However, the recovery of MAC from feces is poor (low sensitivity) even in HIV-positive patients. If *M. avium* is isolated from the feces the positive predictive value of the culture is high, meaning that the patient is likely to develop disseminated disease.[27] In order to avoid overgrowth of normal gastrointestinal tract microflora, feces must be rather harshly decontaminated, but this is likely to also decrease the yield of mycobacteria.[28] The use of a selective medium such as Mitchison's selective medium may assist in the recovery of mycobacteria from feces.

SEMI-AUTOMATED SYSTEMS FOR THE DETECTION OF *MYCOBACTERIUM TUBERCULOSIS* AND OTHER MYCOBACTERIA IN CLINICAL SPECIMENS			
Instrument/medium	**Manufacturer**	**Detection system**	**SIRE/PZA susceptibility testing**
Bactec 9000MB MYCO/F medium + supplements (modified 7H9 broth)	Becton Dickinson Microbiology Systems, Sparks, MD, USA	Detects changes in O_2 concentration in the growth medium using an O_2 sensor based on fluorescence quenching	No/No
Bactec MGIT 960 (modified 7H9 broth)	Becton Dickinson Microbiology Systems, Sparks, MD, USA	O_2 sensor based on fluorescence quenching	Yes/Yes
ESP Culture System II/ESP Myco (modified 7H9 broth)	TREK Diagnostic Systems, Westlake, OH, USA	Detects production and consumption of gas by measuring changes in partial pressure of gas phase of culture medium	Yes/No
MB/BacT	BioMerieux, Durham, NC, USA	Detects changes in CO_2 concentration in gas phase of the growth medium using a colorimetric sensor and reflected light	Yes/No
Bactec 460/Bactec 12B and Bactec 13A (modified 7H9 broth)	Becton Dickinson Microbiology Systems, Sparks, MD, USA	Detection of radioactively labeled CO_2 released during the catabolism of ^{14}C-labeled palmitic acid in the growth medium	Yes/Yes

Table 233.2 Semi-automated systems for the detection of *Mycobacterium tuberculosis* and other mycobacteria in clinical specimens. PZA, pyrazinamide; SIRE, streptomycin, isoniazid, rifampin and ethambutol.

Processing contaminated specimens

Most respiratory tract specimens are expected to be contaminated with normal respiratory tract microflora. In addition, the mucin matrix of these specimens makes the specimens difficult to process and mucin both protects and traps micro-organisms. Such contaminated specimens must be treated to liquify the specimen and release any micro-organisms trapped in the mucin or cells. Then, the specimen is decontaminated to reduce or eliminate other micro-organisms that would be likely to overgrow the mycobacteria that might be present in the specimen. The most common mucolytic agents used to digest sputum are *N*-acetyl-L-cysteine (NALC) and dithiothreitol (DTT or sputolysin). Both NALC and DTT are unstable in air and must be prepared fresh; sodium citrate is usually added to NALC/DTT to chelate heavy metals that may inactivate these compounds. Both NALC and DTT have sulfhydryl groups that reduce the disulfide bridges of the glycoprotein that confers upon sputum its mucilaginous property. A combination of NALC and sodium hydroxide is most commonly used for digesting and decontaminating sputum. Other agents used for digestion and decontamination are zephiran (benzalkonium chloride)-trisodium phosphate, oxalic acid, cetylpyridinium chloride (CPC)-sodium chloride, and sulfuric acid.

There is no ideal method for digesting and decontaminating sputum and other respiratory tract specimens and invariably mycobacteria are lost during decontamination. Indeed, it has been estimated that up to one-third of the mycobacteria present in a sputum specimen may be lost during decontamination. If *M. gordonae* is naturally found in the environment of the laboratory, one should expect about 5% of clinical specimens processed in the laboratory will be contaminated with this mycobacterium. If less than 5% *M. gordonae* contamination is observed, the decontamination procedure may be too harsh. Detailed descriptions of the various procedures for digesting and decontaminating sputum and other contaminated specimens have been well described elsewhere.[29,30]

Processing uncontaminated specimens

Aseptically collected tissues and fluids from normally sterile body sites usually do not require processing before inoculation of cultures. Certain fluids such as pericardial or pleural fluid may require the addition of an anticoagulant to the collection container. The primary concern about specimens from sterile body sites is the quantity of specimen submitted for smear and culture. Swabs usually contain insufficient material for culture and 1g of tissue or 10ml of fluid are ideal. To improve recovery of mycobacteria, centrifugation or filtration should be used to concentrate large volumes of fluids.

Centrifugation

Although the chemical components of the digestion and decontamination procedure are critical to specimen processing and the successful recovery of mycobacteria, the concentration of mycobacteria by centrifugation is a frequently overlooked component of the procedure that may contribute to poor recovery if not performed properly. Two aspects of the centrifugation step are important:

- the sedimenting efficiency or relative centrifugal force (RCF); and
- the heat generated during centrifugation.

The sedimenting efficiency should be 95% and the RCF should be at least 3000G for 15–20 minutes. Higher RCF values can be used; however, the type of centrifuge tube used will also determine the maximum permissible RCF. Aerosols generated during centrifugation are a high-risk factor for transmission of tuberculosis to laboratory workers. Therefore, specimens must be placed in aerosol-free canisters or in an aerosol-free centrifuge. Manipulation of the supernatant must follow appropriate biohazard protection guidelines.

Culture

A variety of solid and liquid media are available for the culture of mycobacteria from clinical specimens. It is prudent to use several media to ensure recovery and provide good growth for subsequent identification and susceptibility testing. The macroscopic and microscopic growth of mycobacteria may vary with the type of media and these differences in morphology, rate of growth and pigmentation are valuable in making a presumptive identification (see Fig. 233.1).

Several semi-automated systems are designed to detect mycobacteria in clinical specimens (Table 233.2) in addition to the radiorespirometric system developed in the late 1970s by Middlebrook and commercially developed as the Bactec460 TB 460 system in the early 1980s by Becton Dickinson Co. In the various studies that were performed to evaluate these newer systems, comparisons were usually made with conventional culture (e.g. Löwenstein–Jensen medium) and the Bactec460 TB system. Indeed, the Bactec460 TB 460 system became a 'gold standard' for the rapid detection of mycobacteria in semi-automated systems. In the Bactec460 TB 460 the growth of mycobacteria is detected by measuring the release of $^{14}CO_2$ from ^{14}C-labeled palmitate, which is the primary carbon source in the Bactec460 TB 12B culture medium. The limitations of the Bactec460 TB 460 system are that the medium includes a radioactive substrate, the media are expensive and the system is surprisingly labor intensive.

Information about the performance of the new semi-automated systems, the studies published to date indicate that these systems (Becton Dickinson's Bactec460 TB 9000MB and Bactec MGIT 960, Trek Diagnostic System's ESP II and bioMerieux's MB/BacT) perform well in comparison with conventional culture and the Bactec 460 system.[31–44] The new systems are convenient, do not require the use of radioisotope, and are truly labor-saving. In comparison with the Bactec460 TB 460 system the newer systems are 5–10% less sensitive and the time to detection is the same or 1–5 days longer. It is important to emphasize that a liquid medium, of one of the types described here, as well as a solid medium must be included in the laboratory diagnosis of mycobacterial infections to ensure maximum recovery (sensitivity).

Additional manual culture systems used for the detection of mycobacteria are the Septi-Chek acid-fast bacillus (AFB) biphasic system, the MB Redox tube system and the Mycobacteria Growth Indicator Tube (MGIT). These are manual culture systems, although the MGIT system has been recently adapted to a semi-automated detection system. The Septi-Chek AFB system is a biphasic medium consisting of 30ml of Middlebrook 7H9 broth and a triangular-shaped plastic paddle with Middlebrook 7H11 agar on one side and Middlebrook 7H11 with NAP and chocolate agar on the remaining surfaces. Comparison studies with conventional culture and the Bactec460 TB 460 system indicated that the Septi-Chek AFB system is reliable and practical.[45,46] MB Redox tubes contain 4ml of modified Kirchner medium (Kirchner base medium plus glucose, horse serum, a vitamin combination and OADC (oleic acid, albumin, dextrose and catalase)). In addition, the medium contains a mixture of antimicrobial agents (polymyxin B, amphotericin B, carbenicillin and trimethoprim) and a redox indicator (tetrazolium salt). Mycobacteria reduce the tetrazolium salt to a pink-, red- and violet-colored formazan. The accumulation of reduced dye on the surface of the bacilli results in the appearance of visible microcolonies. The MGIT culture is a highly enriched Middlebrook 7H9 broth that contains a disk of silicon rubber impregnated with ruthenium pentahydrate that acts as a fluorescence-quenching oxygen sensor. Growth is detected by exposing an inoculated MGIT tube to ultraviolet light and examining for fluorescence, which is an indication of growth and oxygen consumption. The performance of these aforementioned manual systems varies in comparison with the Bactec 460 standard, but most investigators have concluded that each of these systems, in combination with conventional solid media, are a satisfactory substitute for the Bactec.[40,47–51] Indeed, deciding factors are more likely to reflect differences in cost, convenience and safety, availability and workload.

Identification

In 1958, Ernest Runyon proposed that by dividing mycobacteria into four groups based on the rate of growth and pigmentation one could make a preliminary identification. Rapid growers were separated from slowly growing mycobacteria according to the time required to produce clearly visible colonies (≤7 days for rapid growers). Slowly growing mycobacteria were separated based on pigment production: photochromogenic, scotochromogenic (Fr. Gk *skotos*, darkness) and nonphotochromogenic. Forty years later Dr Runyon's simple scheme, now the Runyon groups, remains a valuable guide for the initial identification of mycobacteria isolated by culture, and the logic of this classification has been corroborated by 16S rRNA sequence analysis.[52] Indeed, the correlation between an initial classification into a Runyon group and the final identification ranges from 87% (nonphotochromogens) to 97% (rapid growers).[53] The first challenge for the clinical mycobacteriology laboratory is to distinguish between an isolate that is in the *M. tuberculosis* complex (Table 233.3) and an isolate that is a nontuberculous mycobacterium, a taxonomically imprecise but clinically important distinction. In many ways clinical mycobacteriology remains an arcane field and experience is a critical factor in assuring the accurate identification of mycobacteria, especially the nontuberculous mycobacteria (Table 233.4).

Nature and appearance of cultures

The growth of *M. tuberculosis* on Middlebrook 7H10 or 7H11 agar at 95°F (35°C) is usually detected in 2–3 weeks. The colonies are beige-colored, rough, dry, corded, flat and with irregular borders (Fig. 233.7). On egg media such as Löwenstein–Jensen or Ogawa media the colonies are frequently warty and granular and with time heap into a cauliflower shape (Fig. 233.8). Although the growth of

THE *MYCOBACTERIUM TUBERCULOSIS* COMPLEX

Species	Geographic distribution	Taxonomic features	Identifying features
M. tuberculosis	Widespread, humans are the definitive host		TCH-resistant, PZA-susceptible, nitrate reductase activity positive, aerobic
M. bovis	Widespread, broad host range including cattle, nonhuman primates, goats, cats, dogs, buffalo badgers, possums, deer and bison. Humans are viewed as a 'spillover' host	While probably more properly viewed as a subspecies of *M. tuberculosis*, epidemiologic and economic factors presently compel separation of species	TCH-susceptible, PZA-resistant, nitrate reductase activity negative, microaerophilic
M. bovis BCG	Nonvirulent vaccine strain	First reported in 1908 as a nonvirulent strain of *M. tuberculosis*; appears to be a regulatory mutant of *M. bovis*	TCH-susceptible, PZA-resistant, nitrate reductase activity negative, aerobic
M. africanum		Probably more properly viewed as a subspecies or biovar of *M. bovis*	TCH-susceptible, PZA-resistant, nitrate reductase activity negative, microaerophilic
M. microti	Usually considered strictly an animal pathogen (e.g. voles), severe human cases were reported in 1998*	Probably more properly viewed as a subspecies or pathovar of *M. tuberculosis*	
M. canetti	East Africa, but probably worldwide. Appears to have a very limited incidence	Taxonomic status is unclear, but PRA results suggest a distinct taxonomic cluster	Smooth colony variant of *M. tuberculosis*, PZA-resistant

Table 233.3 The *Mycobacterium tuberculosis* complex. PRA, PCR restriction analysis; PZA, pyrazinamide; TCH, thiophen-2-carboxylic acid hydrazide. Adapted from Grange[4] and Goh *et al.*[54] *From van Soolingen *et al.*[55]

NONTUBERCULOUS MYCOBACTERIA							
Clinical disease/ specimen/site	**Occurrence**	**Species**	**Growth rate**	**Recovered from environment**	**Geographic distribution**	**Risk factors**	**Microbiologic features/ diagnostic tools**
Cutaneous, wound	Common	*M. chelonae*	Rapid	Yes	Widespread		
Cutaneous, wound	Common	*M. fortuitum*	Rapid	Yes	Widespread	Central catheter postsurgical wound	Rapid growth (<7 days, especially on subculture), not pigmented, growth in salt and MacConkey agar is temp dependent
Cutaneous, wound	Common	*M. haemophilum*	Slow	Yes?	Australia, Europe, North America	AIDS, organ transplant, lymphoma, children	Growth requires hemin or ferric ammonium citrate, growth at 86–89.6°F (30–32°C), growth stimulated by CO_2, colony variants occur, may be missed
Cutaneous	Common	*M. marinum*	Rapid/ slow	Yes	Widespread	Skin abrasion or trauma	Photochromogen, slow-to-rapid growth, initial culture ≤89.6°F (32°C), colony variants occur
Cutaneous, ulcers	Common	*M. ulcerans*	Slow	Yes	Ghana, Uganda, South East Asia, Tropics, Central and South America, Australia	Normal host, third most prevalent mycobacterium isolated from human specimens and continuing to emerge	Culture – slow growth at 77 and 98.6°F (25 and 37°C), HPLC, microaerophilic, mycolic acids similar to *M. marinum*
Cutaneous, wound	Uncommon	*M. abscessus*	Rapid	Yes			
Cutaneous, wound	Uncommon	*M. avium complex*	Slow	Yes			
Cutaneous	Uncommon	*M. kansasii*	Rapid	Yes			
Cutaneous	Uncommon	*M. smegmatis*	Rapid	Yes			
Cutaneous, wound	Unknown	*M. conspicuum*	Slow	No			Culture, HPLC, 16S rRNA
Cutaneous Urine Fluids (BAL, joint) Blood	Unknown	*M. immunogenicum*	Rapid	Yes	Unknown	Respiratory pseudo-outbreaks (contaminated bronchoscopy equipment). Newly described species	Culture 77–86°F (25–30°C), 16S rRNA or DNA hybridization, *M. abscessus-chelonae*-like
Cutaneous	Unknown	*M. novocastrense*	Rapid	Yes		Potential human pathogen	Culture, pigmented (yellow), HPLC, 16S rRNA, *M. marinum*-like
Disseminated		*M. xenopi*	Slow	Yes	Worldwide	AIDS	
Disseminated	Common	*M. avium complex*	Slow	Yes	Widespread	AIDS, hairy cell leukemia, congenital immunodeficiencies	Slow growth (>7 days), nonpigmented but pigmented colonies occur, colony variants isolated from blood, bone marrow, other biopsies
Disseminated	Common	*M. chelonae*	Rapid	Yes	Widespread		
Disseminated Blood or bone marrow	Common	*M. haemophilum*	Slow	Yes?	Australia, Europe, North America	Common and continuing to emerge	Culture (requires hemin), HPLC, GLC, TLC, 16S rRNA
Disseminated	Common	*M. kansasii*	Rapid	Yes	Europe, USA		
Disseminated	Uncommon	*M. abscessus*	Rapid	Yes			
Disseminated Blood, bone marrow, liver, spleen	Uncommon	*M. genavense*	Slow	Yes	Widespread, isolated from pet birds	Disease in humans established, especially in AIDS, malnourished	
Disseminated	Uncommon	*M. malmoense*	Very slow	Yes		AIDS	

Table 233.4 Nontuberculous mycobacteria. BAL, bronchoalveolar lavage; GLC, gas liquid chromatography; PRA, PCR restriction analysis; TLC, thin layer chromatography. Information compiled and adapted from a variety of sources including Falkinham,[56] Grange,[4] Kiehn and White,[57] American Thoracic Society[58] and Brown-Elliot *et al.*[59]

NONTUBERCULOUS MYCOBACTERIA—CONT'D							
Clinical disease/ specimen/site	**Occurrence**	**Species**	**Growth rate**	**Recovered from environment**	**Geographic distribution**	**Risk factors**	**Microbiologic features/ diagnostic tools**
Disseminated	Unknown	*M. celatum*	Slow	No	Europe, USA	Disease in humans established	Culture, nonphotochromagen, HPLC, TLC, cross-reacts with GenProbe Mtb probe, 16S rRNA
Disseminated, blood	Unknown	*M. conspicuum*	Slow	No			Culture, HPLC, 16S rRNA
Disseminated Spinal osteomyelitis Lymphadenitis	Unknown	*M. lentiflavin*	Slow	No		Disease in humans established, especially HIV and AIDS	Culture, 16S rRNA
Disseminated Lymph nodes, spinal fluid, pericardial and peritoneal fluids	Unknown	*M. triplex*	Slow	No	Unknown	Disease in humans established	Culture, HPLC, 16S rRNA, *M. simiae-avium*-like
Intestinal		*M. paratuberculosis*	Slow	Yes			Cause of Johne's disease in cattle
Lymphadenitis	Common	*M. avium* complex	Slow	Yes	Widespread	Children	
Lymphadenitis	Common	*M. malmoense*	Very slow	Yes	UK, Northern Europe, Scandinavia	Childhood	Slow growth (6 weeks), subculture growth is similarly slow, easily missed
Lymphadenitis	Common	*M. scrofulaceum*	Slow	Yes	Widespread	Children	
Lymphadenitis	Uncommon	*M. abscessus*	Rapid	Yes			
Lymphadenitis	Uncommon	*M. chelonae*	Rapid	Yes			
Lymphadenitis	Uncommon	*M. fortuitum*	Rapid	Yes			
Lymphadenitis	Uncommon	*M. haemophilum*	Slow	Yes?			
Lymphadenitis Soft tissue	Unknown	*M. bohemicum*	Slow	Yes	Unknown	Potential pathogen	Culture, GLC, 16S rRNA
Lymphadenitis	Unknown	*M. heidelbergense*	Slow	No	Germany, unknown?	Potential pathogen	Growth, HPLC, PRA
Lymphadenitis Pulmonary	Unknown	*M. tusciae*	Slow	Yes	Tuscany, unknown?	Potential pathogen	Culture, HPLC, 16S rRNA
Lymphadenitis Disseminated	Unknown	*M. interjectum*	Slow/ rapid	No		Disease in humans established	HPLC, TLC, 16S rRNA
Pulmonary	Common	*M. abscessus*	Rapid	Yes	Widespread, predominantly USA		Rapid growth (<7 days), not pigmented
Pulmonary	Common	*M. avium complex*	Slow	Yes	Widespread	Chronic lung disease, cystic fibrosis	Slow growth (>7 days), usually not pigmented, colony variants
Pulmonary	Common	*M. kansasii*	Rapid	Yes	Localized USA, UK, Europe	Alcoholism, AIDS, chronic lung disease	Photochromogen, intensely pigmented, large, beaded, acid-fast, elongated bacilli
Pulmonary	Common	*M. malmoense*	Very slow	Yes	Localized UK, Northern Europe	Pneumoconiosis, silicosis, industrial dust disease. Common and continuing emerge	Slow growth (6 weeks), subculture growth is similarly slow, easily missed
Pulmonary	Common	*M. xenopi*	Slow	Yes	Localized UK, Europe, Canada	Underlying lung disease. Common and continuing to emerge	Culture, slow growth, pigmented, growth at 113°F (45°C), 'birds nest' colony
Pulmonary	Uncommon	*M. asiaticum*	Slow	Yes	Localized Australia, USA		
Pulmonary	Uncommon	*M. fortuitum*	Rapid	Yes			
Pulmonary	Uncommon	*M. gordonae*	Slow	Yes	Widespread	Chronic lung disease, but frequent contaminant and rare cause of disease	'Tap-water' scotochromogen

Table 233.4 Nontuberculous mycobacteria. BAL, bronchoalveolar lavage; GLC, gas liquid chromatography; PRA, PCR restriction analysis; TLC, thin layer chromatography. Information compiled and adapted from a variety of sources including Falkinham,[56] Grange,[4] Kiehn and White,[57] American Thoracic Society[58] and Brown-Elliot *et al.*[59]—cont'd

NONTUBERCULOUS MYCOBACTERIA—CONT'D							
Clinical disease/ specimen/site	**Occurrence**	**Species**	**Growth rate**	**Recovered from environment**	**Geographic distribution**	**Risk factors**	**Microbiologic features/ diagnostic tools**
Pulmonary	Uncommon	*M. haemophilum*	Slow	Yes?	Unknown, seems localized		
Pulmonary	Uncommon	*M. shimoidae*	Slow		Australia, Japan		
Pulmonary	Uncommon	*M. simiae*	Slow	Yes	Israel, Thailand, France, USA, Australia	Underlying lung disease, pneumonia	Photochromogen, slow but good growth at 98.6°F (37°C), produces niacin
Pulmonary	Uncommon	*M. szulgai*	Slow	Yes?	Europe, Japan, USA	Underlying disease, alcoholism	Scotochromogen, slow growth at 77–98.6°F (25–37°C), no growth at 107.6°F (42°C)
Pulmonary, sputum	Unknown	*M. alvei*	Rapid	Yes	Unknown, first isolated and described in Spain	Potential human pathogen	GLC, DNA hybridization
Pulmonary	Unknown	*M. branderi*	Slow	No	Unknown	Potential pathogen	Culture, chromatography, 16S rRNA
Pulmonary	Unknown	*M. brumae*	Rapid	Yes	Unknown	Potential human pathogen	Culture, arylsulfatase-negative
Pulmonary	Unknown	*M. celatum*	Slow	No	Europe, USA		Culture, nonphotochromagen, HPLC, TLC, cross-reacts with GenProbe Mtb probe, 16S rRNA
Pulmonary, sputum	Unknown	*M. confluentis*	Rapid	No	Unknown	Potential human pathogen	Culture, brown pigment, chromatography, 16S rRNA
Pulmonary	Unknown	*M. conspicuum*	Slow	No	Europe	Disease in humans established	
Pulmonary	Unknown	*M. heckeshornense*	Slow	No	Unknown	Potential pathogen	Culture, GLC, TLC, HPLC, *M. xenopi*-like organism
Pulmonary	Unknown	*M. interjectum*	Slow/ rapid	No		Disease in humans established	
Pulmonary	Unknown	*M. intermedium*	Slow/ rapid	No	Unknown	Disease in humans established	Culture, photochromogen, GLC, TLC
Pulmonary	Unknown	*M. kubicae*	Slow		Unknown	Potential human pathogen	Culture, HPLC, 16S rRNA
Pulmonary, sputum?	Unknown	*M. mageritense*	Rapid	No	Spain, unknown	Potential human pathogen	DNA hybridization, 16S rRNA
Pulmonary, wounds	Unknown	*M. mucogenicum*	Rapid	Yes	Unknown	Newly described, occurrence unknown	Culture, HPLC, GLC, 16S rRNA
Pulmonary	Unknown	*M. triplex*	Slow	No	Unknown	Disease in humans established	Culture, HPLC, 16S rRNA, *M. avium* complex-like
Urine	Unknown	*M. hassiacum*	Rapid	Yes	Unknown	Nonpathogen?	Culture, scotochromagen, HPLC, PRA
Wound	Unknown	*M. branderi*	Slow	No	Unknown	Disease in humans established	Culture, HPLC, GLC, TLC, 16S rRNA
Wound, soft tissue, blood	Unknown	*M. fortuitum* 3rd biovariant	Rapid	Yes		Newly described, occurrence unknown	Culture, 16S rRNA, includes *M. septicum*
Wound, pulmonary	Unknown	*M. goodii*	Rapid	No	Unknown	Newly described, occurrence unknown, nosocomial?	Culture, pigmented/HPLC, 16S rRNA, *M. smegmatis*-like
Wound, osteomyelitis	Unknown	*M. wolinskyi*	Rapid	No	Unknown	Post-traumatic and postsurgical. Newly described, occurrence unknown	Culture, HPLC, 16S rRNA, *M. smegmatis*-like

Table 233.4 Nontuberculous mycobacteria. BAL, bronchoalveolar lavage; GLC, gas liquid chromatography; PRA, PCR restriction analysis; TLC, thin layer chromatography. Information compiled and adapted from a variety of sources including Falkinham,[56] Grange,[4] Kiehn and White,[57] American Thoracic Society[58] and Brown-Elliot *et al.*[59]—cont'd

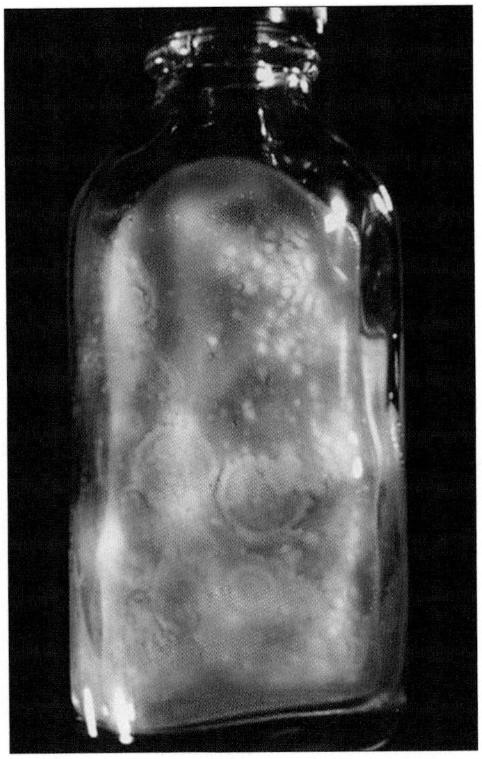

Fig. 233.7 Primary isolate of *M. tuberculosis* grown from sputum on Löwenstein–Jensen medium displaying characteristic beige, rough and dry-appearing growth. Courtesy of S Froman and A Gaytan.

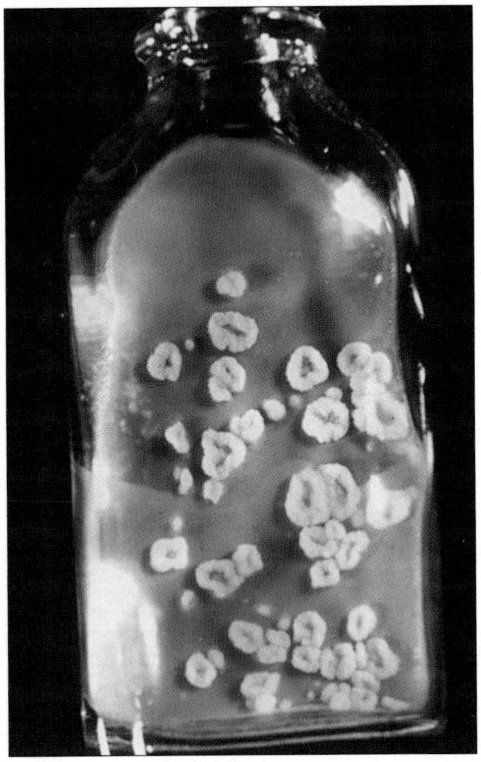

Fig. 233.8 Primary isolate of *Mycobacterium tuberculosis* grown from sputum on Löwenstein–Jensen medium displaying 'cauliflower' or verrucose colonies. These are also characteristic of other mycobacteria including MAC and rapid growers, especially as a culture ages. Courtesy of S Froman and A Gaytan.

M. tuberculosis is quite distinct and it is not unreasonable for an experienced mycobacteriologist to make a presumptive report of *M. tuberculosis* isolated based on the rate and appearance of growth, the identification must always be confirmed by biochemical, chromatographic or nucleic acid probe tests.

Three species of mycobacteria have optimal growth temperatures less than 95–98.6°F (35–37°C): *M. ulcerans*, *M. marinum* and *M. haemophilum*. If these species are suspected the cultures should be incubated at 86°F (30°C). In addition, *M. haemophilum* requires hemin for growth and, therefore, specimens suspected to harbor this species should be inoculated onto chocolate agar, Middlebrook 7H10 agar with hemolyzed blood or 7H10 agar with a hemin-containing paper strip.

The most common clinically significant mycobacterium isolated in many clinical microbiology laboratories is MAC. *Mycobacterium avium* complex isolated from blood or sputum appears as non-pigmented colonies within 10–14 days after inoculation. When grown on Middlebrook 7H10 or 7H11 agar two colony variants are commonly observed. One variant is smooth, opaque and domed while the second variant is flat and transparent. The distinction between variant types diminishes with the age of the culture and eventually the colonies become verrucose and many develop pigment. The initial distinction between colony types is important because the transparent variants tend to be more resistant to antimicrobial agents and these colonies should be picked for susceptibility testing. The colony variant types are not observed when MAC is grown on egg-based media.

Growth rate

Mycobacteria are commonly separated into rapid growers and slowly growing based on whether growth appears before or after 7 days of incubation. It is important to note that the most accurate measure of growth rate is made with subcultures. Harsh digestion–decontamination of a specimen may significantly increase the time it takes for a rapid grower to appear on primary culture.

Acid-fast stain

An acid-fast stain remains the most rapid, convenient and least expensive method for directly detecting mycobacteria in clinical specimens. Although an acid-fast stain is not specific, the presence of acid-fast bacilli in a specimen from a patient with signs and symptoms of tuberculosis or another mycobacterial infection is an important guide to effective treatment and the initiation of public health measures. Furthermore, an acid-fast stain can be used to monitor the response to therapy and quickly assess patient infectiousness, and is used to confirm that a culture is acid-fast. The sensitivity of the acid-fast stain has been estimated to be 5000–10,000 bacilli/ml of sputum while culture is estimated to be 100- to 1000-fold more sensitive[53] (i.e. the sensitivity of an AFB stain may be only 22–78% compared with culture).[51] The threshold for the detection of MAC in bone marrow by either immunoperoxidase (Fig. 233.9) or Kinyoun staining is of a similar magnitude.[60] The importance of the acid-fast stain and the need for a prompt turnaround time cannot be over-emphasized. In laboratories that do not perform cultures, an acid-fast stain can be performed using a specimen treated for a short time with 5% sodium hypochlorite. If specimens are sent to a reference laboratory, insist that acid-fast stain results are reported within 24 hours of specimen collection.[61]

Acid-fastness is a distinctive feature of mycobacteria that is shared with only a few other bacteria such as *Nocardia* spp. and *Rhodococcus* spp., and parasites such as *Cryptosporidium* spp. and *Isopora* spp. The three stains that are commonly used to detect acid-fast bacteria are Ziehl–Neelsen, Kinyoun and auramine–rhodamine fluorochrome stains. With each of these procedures, acid-fastness is defined as resistance to decolorizing with acid–alcohol (e.g. 3% hydrochloric acid in 95% ethanol). When mycobacteria are stained with Gram's crystal violet and safranin they often appear as beaded Gram-positive bacilli or fail to stain at all. It is important to note, however, that culture media, incubation conditions and the age of the culture influence the acid-fastness of mycobacteria. The critical role of the mycobacterial cell wall in acid-fastness is underscored by the observation that isoniazid causes a loss of 'acid-fastness' in susceptible strains of *M. tuberculosis*.

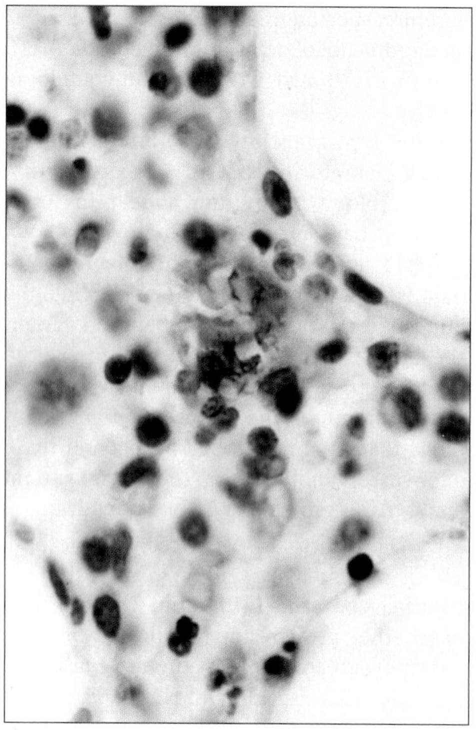

Fig. 233.9 Immunoperoxidase stain of *Mycobacterium avium* complex in the bone marrow of a patient who has HIV infection and disseminated disease. The presence of mycobacteria in the bone marrow and blood of a patient is the microbiologic hallmark of disseminated MAC disease. The presence of mycobacteria in bone marrow sections using either an immunoperoxidase stain or a conventional acid-fast stain requires the presence of approximately 1.5×10^4 bacilli/g of bone marrow.

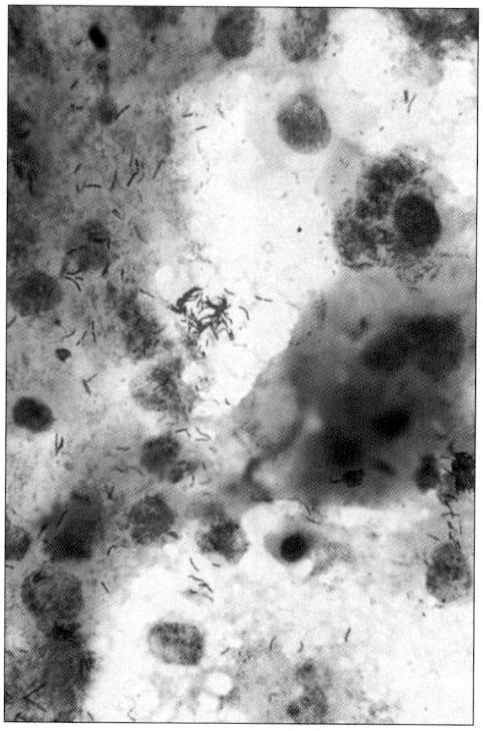

Fig. 233.10 Ziehl–Neelsen acid-fast stain of sputum containing 4+ tubercle bacilli. Courtesy of S Froman and A Gaytan.

The preparation of the smear is the critical first step in performing an acid-fast stain. Using a glass slide cleaned with ethanol, make a smear of approximately 1×2cm of a single specimen or isolate. For CSF specimens previously concentrated by centrifugation, three drops of the concentrate are placed on a clean glass slide, one drop at a time. The drop is allowed to air dry before the next drop is added. The slide is heated at 149–167°F (65–75°C) for 2–24 hours or alternatively 176°F (80°C) for 15 minutes – it is important to note that heat fixing may not kill all the mycobacteria on the slide. Mycobacteria appear brightly fluorescent against a dark background in the auramine–rhodamine stain and the increased sensitivity of the fluorescence stain compared with the other stains is used to rapidly screen slides at a lower (250–450×) magnification. However, fluorescent objects must be examined at 800–1000× to confirm morphology and positive fluorescent smears should be confirmed with the Ziehl–Neelsen or Kinyoun stains. The Ziehl–Neelsen stain requires that the carbolfuchsin stain be heated for the stain to penetrate the mycobacterial cell. In contrast, heating is unnecessary with the Kinyoun stain because the concentration of basic fuchsin and phenol have been increased to ensure that the basic fuchsin penetrates the mycobacterial cell wall. Using a 100× oil immersion lens, 100–300 fields of a properly prepared smear and stain should be examined. It should be remembered that examining even 100–300 fields, only 1–4% of a 1×2cm smear would be examined. Mycobacteria usually appear as slender rod-shaped bacilli; however, pleomorphic shapes are common and range from coccoid to long rods with curves or bends (Fig. 233.10; see Fig. 233.1).

Conventional biochemical tests

The salient biochemical features used in the conventional identification of mycobacteria are shown in Table 233.5. Although many of these tests have been supplanted by other more convenient or rapid tests, the conventional biochemical tests represent a 'gold standard'. Details about the many biochemical tests used in the conventional identification of mycobacteria are described in a variety of sources and Wayne and Sramek[62] described a strategy for the use of these tests.

Although biochemical testing is a reliable and accurate approach to the identification of mycobacteria, alternative methods have largely supplanted biochemical tests for the identification of most

BIOCHEMICAL FEATURES OF THE MOST COMMON CLINICAL ISOLATES OF *MYCOBACTERIUM* SPP.

Species	Pigment	Niacin	Nitrate reductase	154.4°F (68°C) catalase	Semi-quantitative catalase (>45mm)	Tween 80 hydrolysis	Iron uptake	Arylsulfatase	Urease
M. tuberculosis	N	+	+	–	–	–	–	–	+
M. kansasii	P	–	+	+	+	+	–	–	+
M. avium complex	N/S	–	–	+	–	–	–	–	–
M. fortuitum	N	–	+	+			+	+	
M. chelonae	N	V	–	V			–	+	
M. abscessus	N		–				–	+	

Table 233.5 Biochemical features of the most common clinical isolates of *Mycobacterium* spp. N, none; P, photochromogenic; S, scotochromogenic; V, variable.

mycobacteria commonly isolated from clinical specimens. These alternative methods include high performance liquid chromatography (HPLC), the Bactec460 TB NAP test, nucleic acid probes and nucleic acid sequencing.

Developed in the late 1960s, HPLC is used in many sections of the clinical laboratory for a variety of analytes including the detection and quantitation of antimycobacterial agents.[63] In addition, HPLC has proven to be a useful and reliable technology for the rapid identification of mycobacteria.[64] Other applications of HPLC have been developed for the direct detection of mycobacteria in smear-positive clinical specimens or positive liquid cultures.[65] For the identification of mycobacteria, HPLC is used to analyze mycolic acids extracted from an unknown organism. The mycolic acids are extracted by saponification and then derivatives are prepared with either a phenyl ester or a fluorescent compound for detection by ultraviolet absorption or fluorescence spectroscopy. The HPLC pattern of an unknown is then compared with a library of known patterns usually facilitated by a decision analysis system.[66] The equipment cost and the expertise required to perform HPLC analyses has restricted use of this technology mostly to large hospital, and reference and public health laboratories. Alternative chromatographic methods that can be used in the identification of mycobacteria include thin-layer chromatography of lipids and capillary gas chromatography of mycobacterial fatty acids. Instrumentation and software for the identification of mycobacteria as well as other micro-organisms using whole cell fatty acid analysis is commercially available (e.g. Microbial Identification Systems, Newark, DL).

Nucleic acid probes

Nucleic acid probes are commercially available (AccuProbe, Gen-Probe, San Diego, CA) for the identification of five of the most common species of mycobacteria isolated from clinical specimens: *M. tuberculosis* complex, *M. avium*, *M. intracellulare*, MAC, *M. gordonae* and *M. kansasii.* The AccuProbe culture confirmation test is based on the use of DNA probes that are complementary to species-specific rRNA. The rRNA is released from the mycobacteria using a combination of a lysing reagent, sonication and heat. The rRNA-containing lysate is reacted with a species-specific DNA probe that is labeled with an acridinium ester. If a stable RNA–DNA duplex forms, the acridinium label is protected from a selection reagent while free acridinium label is inactivated. Stable duplexes are detected by the addition of an alkaline hydrogen peroxide solution, which in combination with the bound acridinium ester generates chemiluminesence. The amount of light emitted is proportional to the amount of probe hybridized to the target rRNA. The amount of light produced is measured in a luminometer as relative light units (RLU). The AccuProbe test cannot be used for the direct detection of mycobacteria in clinical specimens; the test is for culture identification only. Ribosomal RNA from a rare number of MAC isolates (identified based on biochemical characteristics or 16S rDNA sequence analysis) will not hybridize to the MAC probe. These strains of *M. avium* may represent a third genospecies within the MAC.[67] *The M. tuberculosis* complex AccuProbe test does not differentiate between the species of the *M. tuberculosis* complex. The MAC AccuProbe test does not differentiate between *M. avium* and *M. intracellulare*. In general, the AccuProbe tests are considered to be highly reliable and simple to perform. In addition, the AccuProbe tests can be successfully combined with the semi-automated culture systems (Table 233.2).[68–71]

Molecular methods

Molecular methods have been described and in many instances are commercially available for:

- detecting and identifying mycobacteria directly in clinical specimens;
- identifying culture isolates; and
- identifying strains of a mycobacterium for epidemiologic purposes.

Molecular methods have also been developed to detect antimicrobial resistance in mycobacteria based on a knowledge of the genetic basis of resistance.

Two molecular tests are commercially available in the USA for the direct detection of *M. tuberculosis* in clinical specimens:

- the Amplicor *M. tuberculosis* Test (Roche Diagnostic Systems, Inc.); and
- the Amplified *M. tuberculosis* Direct Test (MTD; GenProbe, Inc.).

Both these tests are based on a knowledge of prokaryotic 16S rDNA sequence information. ‘Signature’ sequences (unique rDNA or rRNA sequences that serve to distinguish one organism or group of organisms from another) have been determined for a majority of clinically relevant, slowly growing mycobacteria.[72] The Amplified *Mycobacterium tuberculosis* Direct (MTD) test detects viable and nonviable tubercle bacilli in a clinical specimen. The test uses transcription-mediated amplification and a hybridization protection assay to qualitatively detect all members of the *M. tuberculosis* complex. Mycobacterial rRNA is released by sonication from bacilli present in a clinical specimen, the rRNA is denatured with heat and transcribed into cDNA with a reverse transcriptase. One part of the oligonucleotide used in the reverse transcription step includes a promoter region for a high efficiency RNA polymerase (e.g. phage T7 polymerase); the other part of the oligonucleotide includes a 16S rRNA target-specific sequence. As a result of cycles of denaturation, reverse transcription and RNA synthesis there is an amplification of the mycobacterial rRNA. The repetitive cycles of denaturation and synthesis can be performed under isothermal conditions – 107.6°F (42°C) – because the RNase H activity associated with the reverse transcriptase used in the assay destabilizes RNA–DNA duplexes. *Mycobacterium tuberculosis* complex-specific amplified sequences are detected using the GenProbe hybridization protection assay. The probe in this assay is an acridinium ester-labeled single-stranded DNA molecule that is complementary to the amplified *M. tuberculosis* complex-specific rRNA sequences. Stable RNA–DNA duplexes protect the acridinium label (using a proprietary selection agent) and hybridized label is measured as chemiluminesence in a luminometer.

When initially approved by the US Food and Drug Administration, the assay was limited to use with AFB stain-positive specimens from untreated patients suspected of having tuberculosis. Furthermore, the patients must have received less than 7 days of therapy or, if previously treated, the patient must not have had therapy in the previous 12 months. However, in September 1999, an enhanced version of the GenProbe MTD test was approved for use with respiratory specimens, regardless of the AFB stain results. In several studies the negative predictive value for the enhanced MTD test was 99% or higher. Nevertheless, the MTD test should be performed in conjunction with a routine mycobacterial culture in order to:

- identify subspecies (e.g. *M. tuberculosis* vs *M. bovis*);
- detect mycobacteria other than *M. tuberculosis*; and
- provide growth for susceptibility testing.

The presence of large numbers of nontuberculous mycobacteria in a specimen may generate a weak false-positive reaction (low relative light units) with the MTD test. The MTD test should be performed only with sediments prepared using a standard NALC/NaOH procedure for decontamination and concentration. An acid-fast stain should always be performed on the same specimen at the time the MTD test is performed.

The Amplicor *M. tuberculosis* test is a PCR assay designed for the qualitative detection of *M. tuberculosis* complex DNA in concentrated sputum specimens, bronchial specimens, bronchial alveolar aspirates or washes and endotracheal aspirates. The PCR assay targets a 584 base pair (bp) sequence within the 16S rDNA that is amplified with oligonucleotide primers conjugated to biotin. Amplified DNA is detected by capturing single-stranded forms of the PCR-amplified DNA with a species-specific probe bound to bovine serum albumin that is, in turn, bound to the wells of a microtiter plate. The DNA duplex of probe and amplified target DNA are detected with an avidin–horse radish peroxidase conjugate in a colorimetric enzyme assay. The result is measured as a 450nm optical density read in a microtiter plate spectrophotometer. The amplification reaction includes deoxyuridine in place of deoxythymidine along with the three other nucleotide triphosphates. In this manner the carryover of previously amplified target DNA can be eliminated because the PCR reaction mix includes uracil-N-glycosylase (UNG), an enzyme that degrades DNA that contains deoxyuridine. The UNG itself is denatured in the first cycle of amplification when the temperature reaches 131°F (55°C). Both the GenProbe MTD and Roche Amplicor assays perform extremely well (≥95% sensitivity and specificity) with smear-positive specimens; however, only the GenProbe test has been approved for use with AFB stain-negative specimens. An algorithm for the use of these nucleic acid amplification tests is shown in Table 233.6, which is based on the recommendations of the Centers for Disease Control and Prevention, USA. In considering the use of these tests it is important to realize that AFB-staining is itself only 40–60% sensitive and, of course, is not specific for *M. tuberculosis*. Furthermore, while culture is commonly accepted as the 'gold standard', in reality it too is an imperfect standard and is only 70–80% sensitive when compared with all other laboratory data, patient history and clinical observations.

Another important application of molecular methods has been for epidemiologic studies of *M. tuberculosis*, *M. avium* and other species of mycobacteria. Two methods were initially used:

- restriction endonuclease analysis (REA) using field inversion or pulse field electrophoresis to separate large DNA fragments generated by restriction enzymes with infrequent restriction sites; and
- fragment length polymorphism analysis of the number and pattern of certain insertion sequences (IS) or repetitive DNA elements present in a collection of potentially related strains.

REA is cumbersome because the patterns generated are complex and sometimes difficult to reproduce. IS6110 analysis for the identification of strains of *M. tuberculosis* is based on differences in the copy number of this genetic element. IS6110 is a 1355bp insertion sequence that was first identified in 1990, and was found to be widely distributed in strains of *M. tuberculosis*. There are 0–20 copies of IS6110 in most strains of *M. tuberculosis*. In strains of *M. tuberculosis* with a small number of IS6110 sequences, the elements are uniformly distributed throughout the genome. This factor can limit the epidemiologic value of IS6110 analysis involving such strains because the resulting patterns often do not discriminate between strains. However, a majority of strains of *M. tuberculosis* carry several copies of IS6110 and the distribution of these IS elements within the genome appears to be stable over several months to years. Slight variations in the distribution of IS6110 elements can usually be tolerated in focused epidemiology studies.[74] Insertion sequence analysis is conceptually straightforward, but technically subject to operator error or variations in protocol. Therefore, standard methods of analysis and interpretation have been developed to ensure comparability of results.[75] Basically, the method involves extraction of genomic DNA, restriction of the DNA with an appropriate enzyme (e.g. *Pvu*II) and electrophoretic separation of the restriction fragments (RFLP analysis). The IS6110 pattern is revealed by Southern hybridization using a labeled fragment of the IS6110 sequence. A computer-based method of analysis of the IS6110 patterns was described by Heersma *et al.*[76] A drawback to this method is the relatively large amount (about 2μg) of genomic DNA that is required for analysis. Therefore, PCR-based typing methods were developed that have comparable discrimination and reproducibility to RFLP analysis. Spoligotyping uses primers to PCR amplify the 36bp direct repeats (DR) in the genomic DR region of *M. tuberculosis* DNA.[77] The resulting PCR products are hybridized to 43 different oligonucleotides fixed to a membrane. The 43 oligonucleotides were derived from the sequences of the spacer DNA between the DRs. However, in general spoligotyping is used as a screen for IS6110 analysis. Other methods of analysis include polymorphic GC-rich sequence (PGRS) RFLP typing,[78] genome sequence-based fluorescent-amplified fragment length polymorphism analysis (FAFLP)[79,80] and PCR-based typing.[81]

ALGORITHM FOR THE USE AND INTERPRETATION OF NUCLEIC ACID AMPLIFICATION TESTS FOR TUBERCULOSIS

	Specimen	Smear	NAA	Interpretation/response
	1st	–	–	Repeat smear and culture, do not repeat NAA
↓	2nd	–	X	Repeat smear and culture, do not repeat NAA
	3rd	–	X	Presume patient to not have tuberculosis
↓	1st, 2nd or 3rd	+	+	Presume patient to have tuberculosis. Unless NTM are a consideration, the NAA test adds little diagnostic value
	1st	+	–	If inhibitors of NAA test not present, test 2nd specimen
↓	2nd	+	–	If inhibitors not present, patient presumed to have NTM
	1st	+	–	If inhibitors present, NAA test is of no diagnostic value NAA up to two additional specimens
	1st	–	MTD+	Test 2nd specimen. Note Roche Amplicor test is *not* approved for testing smear-negative specimens.
	2nd	–	MTD+	Presume patient has tuberculosis
↓	2nd	–	MTD–	Test 3rd specimen
	3rd	–	MTD+	Presume patient has tuberculosis
	3rd	–	MTD–	Rely on clinical judgment

Table 233.6 Algorithm for the use and interpretation of nucleic acid amplification tests for tuberculosis. Respiratory specimens (e.g. sputum) should be collected on three different days for AFB smear and culture. The nucleic acid amplification (NAA) test (Roche Amplicor *Mycobacterium tuberculosis* Test or GenProbe Amplified *Mycobacterium Tuberculosis* Direct Test) should be performed on the first specimen, first smear-positive specimen, or as indicated in the table. MTD, *Mycobacterium tuberculosis* direct test; X, test not performed; NTM, nontuberculous mycobacteria. Adapted from Centers for Disease Control and Prevention.[73]

ANTIMICROBIAL RESISTANCE AND SUSCEPTIBILITY TESTING

Resistance

Antimicrobial resistance in mycobacteria is fundamentally a reflection of the large populations of mycobacteria present in infected tissues and fluids and the frequencies of individual gene mutations that result in a resistant phenotype. In pulmonary tuberculosis there are 10^7–10^9 bacilli in lung cavities, but only 10^2–10^4 bacilli in hard caseous lesions. In disseminated *M. avium* disease the level of bacteremia ranges from 1 to 10^6 colony forming units (cfu) per milliliter of blood, but may be orders of magnitude higher in bone marrow and other tissues. Therefore, drug resistance is a more common occurrence in cavitary tuberculosis than noncavitary disease and resistance in disseminated *M. avium* complex infections develops rapidly when patients are given macrolide monotherapy. Antimicrobial resistance in *M. tuberculosis* is classically defined as a significant difference in the activity of an antimycobacterial between a wild-type strain and another strain. A wild-type strain is defined as a strain isolated from a patient before treatment and less than 1% of a population of that strain is resistant to any antimycobacterial agent. Resistance emerges as a consequence of individual mutations in mycobacterial genes that lead to a structural or functional change such that an antimycobacterial agent is no longer active against that strain.[16] For example, there is compelling evidence that resistance to isoniazid results from a mutation or a combination of mutations in the *katG*, *ahpC*, *inhA* or the *kasA* genes of *M. tuberculosis* (Table 233.7).[82,83]

Resistance to rifampin is a result of a mutation within an 81bp (27 amino acid) sequence of the core region of the *rpoB* gene (RNA polymerase β subunit) and streptomycin resistance has been attributed to mutations in either the *rrs* gene (16S rRNA gene) or the *rpsL* gene (ribosomal protein S12). Quinolone resistance has been ascribed to mutations in the *gyrA* genes[100] and pyrazinamide resistance to mutations in the *pncA* gene that encodes pyrazinamidase/nicotinamidase activity.[97,99] The targets for the major classes or types of antimycobacterial agents are shown in Figure 233.11. Antibiotic resistance does not appear to transfer between strains of mycobacteria by either plasmid exchange or resistance transfer factors. The *M. tuberculosis* multidrug resistance phenotype (minimally resistant to isoniazid and rifampin) appears to be entirely the result of accumulation of individual mutations. Intrinsic resistance to antimicrobial agents is also common in both slowly and rapidly growing mycobacteria. In most instances this form of resistance appears to be the result of the impermeability of the mycobacterial cell envelope. For example, most MAC isolates are resistant to rifampin despite the fact that the isolate has a wild-type *rpoB* gene. However, *M. avium* resistance to isoniazid may reflect the lack of an effective antimicrobial activity rather than or in addition to a lack of permeability.[107,108] Both *M. chelonae* and *M. abscessus* are intrinsically resistant to quinolones, while *M. fortuitum* is susceptible.

MYCOBACTERIAL GENES WITH MUTATIONS ASSOCIATED WITH ANTIMICROBIAL RESISTANCE

Antimicrobial Agent	Species	Gene	Proportion of resistance (%)	Product	References
Rifampin	*M. tuberculosis* *M. africanum* *M. leprae* *M. avium*	*rpoB*	>96	β subunit of RNA polymerase	84 85 86
Isoniazid	*M. tuberculosis*	*katG*	} (katG, inhA, ahpC, kasA collectively)	Catalase peroxidase	83 22 86
Isoniazid/ethionamide	*M. tuberculosis*	*inhA* locus		*envM* analog 3-ketoacyl-acyl carrier protein reductase analog	87
Isoniazid	*M. tuberculosis* *M. leprae*	*ahpC*		Subunit of alkyli hydroperoxide reductase	88 89 90
Isoniazid	*M. tuberculosis*	*acpM (kasA)*		β-ketoacyl ACP synthase	91
Ethambutol	*M. tuberculosis*	*embB*	47–65	Arabinosyltransferase	92
Streptomycin	*M. tuberculosis*, *M. smegmatis*	*rpsL*	70	Ribosomal protein S12	93 94 55
Streptomycin	*M. tuberculosis*	*rrs*	70	16S rRNA	94 96
Pyrazinamide	*M. tuberculosis*	*pncA*	72–97	Pyrazinamidase	97, 98 99
Fluoroquinolone	*M. tuberculosis*, *M. smeginatis*	*gyrA*	75–94	DNA gyrase A subunit	100 101
Azithromycin/clarithromycin	*M. avium*, *M. intracellulare*, *M. chelonae* *M. abscessus*	V domain 23S rRNA	95	23S rRNA	102–104

Table 233.7 Mycobacterial genes with mutations associated with antimicrobial resistance. Proportion of resistance represents the estimated percentage of resistance that can be accounted for by mutations in the respective genes; mutations in *katG*, *ahpC*, *inhA* and/or *kasA* collectively probably account for 90% of isoniazid resistance. Adapted from Musser.[22] Percentage figures taken in part from Alcaide and Telenti.[21]

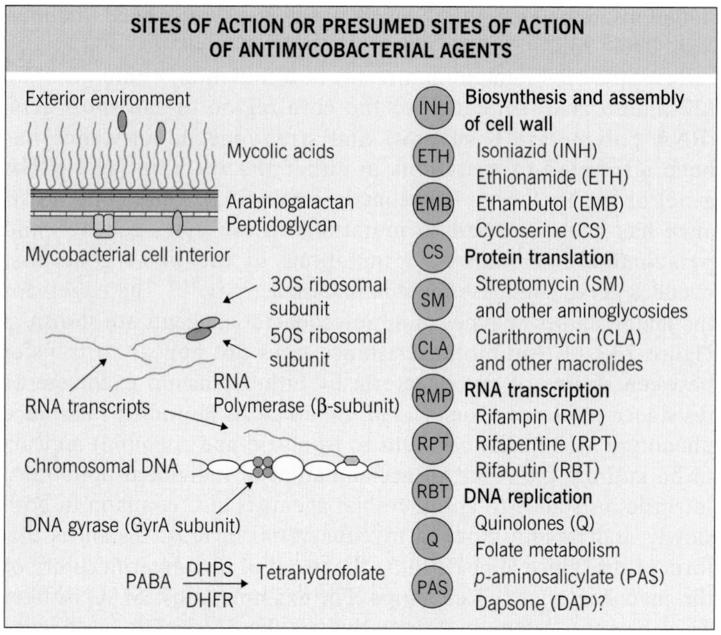

Fig. 233.11 Sites of action or presumed sites of action of antimycobacterial agents. DHFR, dihydrofolate reductase; DHPS, dihydropteroate synthase; PABA, *p*-aminobenzoic acid; PAS, *p*-aminosalicylic acid. Figure adapted from Parsons *et al.*[105] and Young.[106]

Antimicrobial agents

There are a variety of antimicrobial agents available for the treatment of mycobacterial infections; however, until recently almost all clinical studies of these agents were focused on *M. tuberculosis* and to a lesser extent *M. leprae*. The emergence of MAC as an important opportunistic infection associated with HIV infection and increased recognition that rapidly growing mycobacteria are a significant cause of human disease led to an expansion in our knowledge about the activity of certain agents against these and other mycobacteria. Infections caused by rapidly growing mycobacteria must be treated with antimicrobial agents other than the primary antituberculous agents. *Mycobacterium avium* complex is resistant to isoniazid and only variably susceptible to rifampin, but MAC infections can be successfully treated with a macrolide and at least one other agent such as ethambutol. For most other species there is often only limited information about the effectiveness and efficacy of antimycobacterial agents, perhaps with the exception of *M. kansasii* and *M. marinum*. The antimicrobial agents recommended for the treatment of various mycobacterial infections are shown in Table 233.8; however, it is not always appropriate to perform susceptibility tests on all of the agents because of a lack of standardized procedures and well-established interpretive criteria (see also Chapter 202).

ANTIMYCOBACTERIAL AGENTS RANKED BY CLINICAL USE

Species	Primary or first choice	Secondary or second choice	Notes
M. tuberculosis	INH, RMP, PZA, SM, EMB	Amikacin, ciprofloxacin, levofloxacin or sparfloxacin	Treatment plan varies depending on incidence of INH resistance in community, if MDR (INH plus RMP resistance), patient adherence (viz. DOT), other factors
M. bovis	INH, RMP, EMB		Uniformly PZA resistant, 9–12 months therapy recommended by some. Confirm identity of isolate, sometimes nontuberculous mycobacterium
M. leprae	Dapsone, RMP, clofazimine, clarithromycin	Ethionamide, prothionamide, minocycline, pefloxacin, sparfloxacin	Treatment plan varies depending on paucibacillary or multibacillary disease
M. avium *M. intracellulare*	Azithromycin or clarithromycin, ethambutol, rifabutin	Amikacin, streptomycin, moxifloxacin	Isoniazid resistance is usual. Drugs and does vary depending on immunocompetency, disseminated or pulmonary or other, and treatment vs prophylaxis
M. chelonae *M. fortuitum* *M. abscessus*	Amikacin, cefoxitin, ciprofloxacin, clarithromycin, doxycycline or minocycline, sulfonamides	Imipenem, levofloxacin, tobramycin (*M. chelonae* only)	All resistant to INH, PZA, RMP, SM, EMB and clofazimine. EMB may be useful for treating *M. smegmatis*. Contamination with these species is common, confirm clinical significance
M. kansasii	RMB, INH, EMB	Pyridoxine, clarithromycin, rifabutin, sulfamethoxazole	PZA resistance is uniform. Only test RMP; testing of INH and EMB can be misleading. Clarithromycin resistance occurs. Treatment for 12 or more months
M. scrofulaceum	Surgical excision without chemotherapy	Azithromycin, clarithromycin	INH and PZA resistant
M. ulcerans	Surgical excision, RMP, amikacin	EMB, trimethoprim–sulfamethoxazole, SM, ciprofloxacin, sparfloxacin	Chemotherapy rarely effective
M. marinum	Clarithromycin, minocycline, doxycycline, RMB, EMB, trimethoprim–sulfamethoxazole		INH and PZA resistant
M. haemophilum	Clarithromycin, rifabutin, ciprofloxacin. Surgical debridement		Limited clinical experience
M. simiae	Treat like *M. avium* complex		INH, RMP, EMB and PZA resistant
M. xenopi	Azithromycin, clarithromycin, RMP	Rifabutin, SM	
M. celatum	Clarithromycin		RMP resistant
M. genavense	EMB, RMP, rifabutin, clarithromycin	Amikacin, clofazimine	
M. gordonae	INH, RMP, EMB	Amikacin, ciprofloxacin	Common contaminate, confirm clinical significance

Table 233.8 Antimycobacterial agents ranked by clinical use. First-choice agents are expected to be active against wild-type isolates (i.e. from untreated patients); second-choice agents are less preferred, usually due to toxicity, expense or unclear efficacy. DOT, directly observed therapy; EMB, ethambutol; INH, isoniazid; MDR, multiple drug resistance; PZA, pyrazinamide; RMP, rifampin; SM streptomycin. (See also Chapter 202.)

Susceptibility testing

The susceptibility testing of mycobacteria and the definition of antimicrobial resistance have been influenced by decades of focus on *M. tuberculosis*. Thus, there is more information about antimicrobial agents and the susceptibility testing of *M. tuberculosis* than for all other species of mycobacteria. Indeed, the susceptibility testing of many nontuberculous mycobacteria has been largely extrapolated from experience with *M. tuberculosis*, including adoption of the same interpretive criteria. In some instances this extrapolation has proven to provide useful and reliable information, but in other situations this practice can be misleading. Therefore, with the exception of the routine testing of *M. tuberculosis* isolates against the first-line antimycobacterial agents (isoniazid, rifampin, ethambutol, streptomycin and pyrazinamide), susceptibility testing of mycobacteria should be performed in laboratories with extensive experience in this aspect of clinical mycobacteriology. Although the laboratory can provide valuable guidance in the interpretation of results, the application of those results to the treatment of a patient with an uncommon mycobacterial infection is likely to require the involvement of a physician with experience in the management of such infections.

Critical concentrations

The most common method of susceptibility testing *M. tuberculosis* is based on the concept of 'critical concentrations' of antituberculosis agents and the percentage of resistant tubercle bacilli within a test population. Critical concentrations for antituberculosis agents were established on an empiric clinical basis. Therapeutic success was unlikely if the proportion of drug-resistant mutants within a population of *M. tuberculosis* isolated from a patient exceeded a threshold of 1% at a concentration of the antituberculosis agent that was known to be therapeutically effective against a 'wild-type' or fully susceptible strain. The susceptibility test method used to measure the percentage of resistance is, therefore, referred to as the 'proportion method'. The critical concentration may not be the same as the peak serum concentration of a drug and only recently has there been an interest in applying the use of minimum inhibitory concentration (MIC) testing to mycobacteria.[109] However, there are no standardized methods for MIC testing of mycobacteria and the testing of *M. tuberculosis* continues to follow the conventions of critical concentrations and the 1% growth inhibition threshold.

Test methods

Four methods are used for susceptibility testing of *M. tuberculosis*:

- agar proportion method,
- radiometric (Bactec460 TB) proportion method,
- absolute concentration method, and
- resistance ratio method.

The agar proportion and radiometric proportion methods are widely performed in the USA, UK and Western Europe and the following discussion will focus on these methods.

Agar proportion method

The proportion method can be applied as either a direct or an indirect test. In the direct test, a specimen that is positive for acid-fast bacilli by stain is used as the source of inoculum for the susceptibility test. The specimen is inoculated directly onto the test agar media with and without drugs. In the indirect test, a pure culture of acid-fast bacteria is used as the inoculum source for the susceptibility test. On average, the results of the direct test are available 3–4 weeks before the results of an indirect test. The results of a direct test should be confirmed with the indirect test. Inoculating several dilutions of a standardized suspension of mycobacteria onto Middlebrook 7H10 agar plates is the basis of the agar proportion method. The number of cfu that grow on the drug-containing plates or quadrants are compared with the number of cfu on a drug-free plate or quandrant. If the number of cfu that grow on drug-containing medium exceeds 1% of the total number of cfu on the drug-free medium, then the isolate is considered 'resistant' to that drug at that concentration. Some advocate the use of Middlebrook 7H11 agar because some drug-resistant strains of *M. tuberculosis* do not grow on the 7H10 medium.

Radiometric proportion method

The radiometric proportion method is simply an adaptation of the agar proportion method to the Bactec460 TB 12B medium and radiometric measurement of growth inhibition. The test isolate is inoculated into Bactec460 TB 12B medium with or without the addition of test drug. The concentration of mycobacteria inoculated into medium without drug is 100-fold less than the concentration inoculated into Bactec460 TB media with drug. If a drug inhibits the growth of the test strain such that the growth of the control (no drug with 100-fold fewer organisms) reaches a growth threshold before growth in the drug-containing medium reaches that same threshold, then the test isolate is considered susceptible to that drug at the concentration tested. Although partial inhibition of growth occurs, more commonly an isolate of *M. tuberculosis* is either fully susceptible (no growth) or fully resistant (growth exceeds the control). Nevertheless, the growth of resistant isolates may be particularly slow and a report that an isolate is susceptible to a drug should be made only after a full period of incubation. Resistance can be reported as soon as growth in the presence of a drug is detected and exceeds the growth of the control, but the report should be preliminary until the performance of the controls can be assured.

It is prudent to consider the limitations of the Bactec460 TB method. In some clinical situations the Bactec method might be best considered as a screening test because the method does not allow an estimate of the percent of resistant bacilli and is vulnerable to major errors (false susceptibility or resistance) due to mixed populations of mycobacterial species. Indeed, when a multiple drug resistance isolate of *M. tuberculosis* is detected for the first time using the Bactec460 TB method, the identity of the isolate should be confirmed and the presence of a contaminant or mixed culture should be ruled out before proceeding with the testing of secondary agents. Although the importance of promptly reporting a multiple drug resistant isolate of *M. tuberculosis* cannot be overstated, the consequences of a false report of multiple drug resistance must be recognized as well.

Pyrazinamide testing

Pyrazinamide is only active at an acidic pH, and therefore susceptibility tests for this drug must be performed in media with a pH of 5.5–6.0. Methods have been developed for testing pyrazinamide using either Middlebrook 7H10 agar or Bactec460 TB 12B media adjusted to pH 5.5 or 6.0, respectively. The Bactec460 TB method is more convenient and the higher pH is less toxic to *M. tuberculosis* isolates.[76] It should be noted that pyrazinamide monoresistance is rare in *M. tuberculosis* and virtually all *M. bovis* isolates are intrinsically resistant to pyrazinamide. Therefore, pyrazinamide testing of *M. tuberculosis* could be restricted to isolates that are known to be resistant to isoniazid or rifampin and the occurrence of pyrazinamide monoresistance is suggestive that the isolate is *M. bovis*.

Other methods

Three semi-automated mycobacteria culture systems have procedures for testing the primary antituberculosis agents (see Table 233.2), but only the MGIT system can be used to test PZA.[77] The absolute concentration method consists of inoculating media with and without antimycobacterial agents with a carefully controlled inoculum containing 2×10^3–1×10^4 cfu of mycobacteria. Resistance is defined as growth that is greater than a certain number of cfu (usually 20) at a particular drug concentration and the drug concentrations must be precisely confirmed for each batch of media. The resistance ratio method is similar to the absolute concentration method except that a second identical series of tubes are inoculated with the standard *M. tuberculosis* H37Rv strain. The susceptibility test results are expressed in terms of the ratio of the MIC of drug necessary to inhibit the growth of the test isolate of *M. tuberculosis* to that of the standard H37Rv strain. The advantage of this method is that small batch-to-batch variations in the test media can be disregarded because the results are normalized using the H37Rv strain.

Mycobacterium avium complex, *Mycobacterium kansasii* and other slowly growing mycobacteria

In-vitro susceptibility testing of MAC and most of the other nontuberculous mycobacteria, using the methods and interpretive criteria described for *M. tuberculosis*, has little value as a guide to antimicrobial treatment. One important exception is *M. kansasii*, for which in-vitro results based on the interpretive criteria used with *M. tuberculosis* correlate with clinical efficacy. Interpretive criteria have been proposed for clarithromycin and azithromycin, macrolides with proven efficacy in the treatment of *M. avium* and other nontuberculous mycobacteria. For many uncommon nontuberculous mycobacteria (e.g. *M. simiae* and *M. szulgai*) there are few clinical cases, often initially confused with tuberculosis, to form a basis for interpretive criteria. Indeed, it is often difficult to distinguish between contamination, colonization, infection and disease with many of the nontuberculous mycobacteria, especially the rapidly growing mycobacteria.

In general, the in-vitro susceptibility testing of MAC has limited value primarily because of the lack of a correlation with clinical response and, therefore, the lack of interpretive criteria. The important exceptions are for azithromycin, clarithromycin and roxithromycin because these macrolides have proven clinical and microbiologic efficacy in the prophylaxis and treatment of MAC disease with interpretive criteria based, at least in part, on monotherapy trials in humans. Although wild-type MAC is uniformly susceptible to macrolides, macrolide resistance develops quickly with monotherapy. An analysis of these resistant isolates showed that over 95% of clinically significant macrolide resistance in MAC is a consequence of mutations in the V-domain of the 23S rRNA gene.[107,108] Therefore, clinically significant macrolide resistance can be defined as a MIC for clarithromycin and azithromycin at pH 6.8 of ≥64µg/ml and ≥512µg/ml, respectively.[110]

Mycobacterium avium complex isolates from patients with breakthrough azithromycin, roxithromycin or clarithromycin prophylaxis can be tested against one macrolide. Testing one drug is sufficient, since all evidence indicates that resistance crosses between these macrolides. If a patient has not received macrolide prophylaxis, it is unnecessary to perform a susceptibility test on initial MAC isolates from blood or tissue to guide treatment. However, establishing baseline MIC values for a MAC isolate may prove valuable in interpreting susceptibility test results for a subsequent isolate from the same patient weeks or months later. Susceptibility testing is also warranted if a patient relapses, if the infection is intractable or if the clinical situation is desperate. Testing may assist in deciding to add drugs; however, macrolide treatment should probably be continued even in the face of resistance.

The interpretation of in-vitro test results for ethambutol should not be attempted at this time. Ethambutol is commonly used as a 'second' agent in the treatment of MAC to prevent macrolide resistance,[111,112] but ethambutol has little or no therapeutic activity alone against MAC.[113] The drug does, however, increase the activity of other agents including macrolides and this may influence the mutation frequency.[114] The National Committee for Clinical Laboratory Standards (NCCLS) now recommends that MAC be tested using either a Bactec 460 or microtiter method.[115]

Mycobacterium marinum is predictably susceptible to rifampin and ethambutol; alternative agents are amikacin and kanamycin as well as tetracycline, doxycycline, minocycline, ciprofloxacin, clarithromycin and trimethoprim–sulfamethoxazole (co-trimoxazole). Routine susceptibility testing of *M. marinum* isolates using methods and interpretive criteria described for *M. tuberculosis* appears to be inappropriate and the methods and interpretive criteria for testing rapidly growing mycobacteria are more likely to provide clinically useful results. Wild-type isolates of *M. haemophilum* are susceptible to quinolones, rifamycins, clarithromycin and azithromycin, and resistant to pyrazinamide, ethambutol and are likely to be resistant to isoniazid and streptomycin.[116] *Mycobacterium simiae* is highly resistant to antimycobacterial agents; however, there are exceedingly few cases of disease to base any firm conclusions about susceptibility and clinical usefulness. Based on an animal test system, clarithromycin in combination with ethambutol and perhaps a quinolone such as ofloxacin is effective.[117] Testing *M. gordonae* isolates is usually inappropriate because actual disease is quite rare and contamination quite common. Before testing such isolates the following questions should be asked.

- Is the isolate a true *M. gordonae*?
- Is there convincing evidence that the isolate is playing a role in the disease?

Rapid growers

Although four methods have been described for measuring the in-vitro susceptibility of rapidly growing mycobacteria, the NCCLS now recommends only the broth microdilution method.[115] Broth microdilution provides a quantitative result and better supports the growth of *M. chelonae*. The broth microdilution method is essentially a modification of a standard method for nonmycobacteria that grow aerobically as described, for example, by Brown *et al.*[118] Commercially prepared broth microdilution panels can be used if the appropriate drugs are available at the necessary concentrations. Alternatively, broth microdilution panels can be prepared in house. The agents that should be tested are listed in Table 233.9. The inoculum can be either a subculture in broth or prepared directly by picking colonies from a plate. Typically the plates are incubated for 3–5 days at 86°F (30°C) and longer periods of incubation should be avoided because of potential drug instability. The MIC is defined as the lowest concentration of antimicrobial agent that completely inhibits visible growth. The testing of rapidly growing mycobacteria should be restricted to laboratories with more extensive experience testing these mycobacteria.

MANAGEMENT AND PREVENTION

In general the treatment of mycobacterial infections requires the use of multiple antimicrobial agents administered over several months (e.g. 6–9 months). Patients with an underlying immunodeficiency or other complicating medical condition may require even longer periods of treatment, or in the case of people with HIV infection, some advocate lifelong treatment. Multiple agents are used to prevent the emergence of resistance,[119] but increasingly in the hope of achieving a synergistic effect and improved outcome. Disseminated and localized MAC infections can be successfully treated with a macrolide (clarithromycin) or an azalide (azithromycin), usually in combination with at least one additional agent such as ethambutol, but also rifabutin, amikacin or a quinolone. Indeed, clarithromycin and azithromycin have emerged as valuable chemotherapeutic agents for the treatment of several nontuberculous mycobacteria, if not as first-line agents, then as second-line agents.[58] For example, clarithromycin may be useful in the treatment of infections caused by

ANTIMICROBIAL AGENTS TO TEST AGAINST SELECTED MYCOBACTERIA			
	Antimicrobial agent	Susceptible (μg/ml)	Resistant (μg/ml)
M. tuberculosis			
	Primary agents		
	INH	0.05–0.2	
	RMP	0.5	
	PZA	20	
	EMB	1–5	
	Secondary agents		
	Streptomycin	8	
	Capreomycin	1–50	
	Kanamycin	5	
	Cycloserine	5–20	
	Ethionamide	0.6–2.5	
	PAS	1	
	Alternative agents		
	Rifabutin	0.06–8	
	Rifapentine		
	Amikacin	1	
	Ciprofloxacin	0.25–3	
	Ofloxacin	0.5–2.5	
M. avium complex			
	Clarithromycin	≤16	≥64
	Azithromycin	≤128	≥512
M. kansasii and selected other slowly growing mycobacteria			
	RMP	1–2	
	Rifabutin	0.5–2	
	Ethambutol	5	
	Isoniazid	5	
	Streptomycin	10	
	Clarithromycin	32	
	Amikacin	10	
	Ciprofloxacin	2	
	Trimethoprim–sulfamethoxazole	2/38	
Rapidly growing mycobacteria			
	Amikacin	≤16	≥64
	Cefoxitin	≤16	≥128
	Ciprofloxacin	≤1	≥4
	Clarithromycin	≤2	≥8
	Doxycycline	≤1	≥16
	Imipenem	≤4	≥16
	Sulfamethoxazole	≤32	≥64
	Tobramycin	≤4	≥16

Table 233.9 Antimicrobial agents to test against selected mycobacteria as adapted from National Committee for Clinical Laboratory Standards (NCCLS).[115] Susceptible (μg/ml) for *M. tuberculosis* refers to the typical MIC for a susceptible isolate. Susceptible and resistant breakpoints for other mycobacteria refer to the NCCLS recommended breakpoints.

M. chelonae, *M. abscessus*, *M. leprae*, *M. kansasii*, *M. marinum* and *M. malmoense*. Rapidly growing mycobacteria are resistant to the conventional antimycobacterial agents, but can be effectively treated with amikacin, cefoxitin, imipenem, ciprofloxacin, augmentin, sulfonamides and doxycycline as well as clarithromycin (see Chapter 38).

Prophylaxis with isoniazid for 6–12 months is recommended for people with significant exposure to drug-susceptible tuberculosis or following conversion of their skin test (see Chapters 37 and 202). In the latter situation, isoniazid is used more as preventive therapy than prophylaxis. Prophylaxis or preventive therapy is especially important in children, who are at greater risk than adults for extrapulmonary tuberculosis including meningitis. Clarithromycin, azithromycin and rifabutin are effective prophylactic agents for disseminated MAC infection in people with HIV infection with $CD4^+$ lymphocytes counts below 100 cells/mm^3. The evidence now seems compelling that a restoration of $CD4^+$ cells to levels above this threshold, in response to treatment of HIV infection with highly active antiretroviral agents, is protective against disseminated MAC infection (see Chapter 129).[120]

CLINICAL MANIFESTATIONS

Tuberculosis in the most common form is a chronic pulmonary disease classified as either primary or post-primary disease. Post-primary disease can be a consequence of either reactivation (endogenous infection) or re-infection (exogenous infection). By far, the most common (95%) route of infection is inhalation of infectious droplet nuclei, but exposure to *M. tuberculosis* bacilli neither always lead to infection nor are all patients with disease infectious. Risk of infection is directly related to the number and distribution of tubercle bacilli in the inhaled and respired air, emphasizing the importance of infectious droplet nuclei to airborne transmission. Unless a patient receives prophylaxis, symptomatic disease eventually occurs in 5–10% of infected patients. The appearance and extent of disease varies with only one-half of infected patients developing disease within the first 2 years. Hematogenous spread of tubercle bacilli from the lung probably invariably occurs, but the bacteremia is usually occult and usually does not produce symptoms or disease. Nevertheless, hematogenous dissemination accounts for the occurrence of extrapulmonary involvement of lymph nodes, kidneys, reproductive organs, bones and gastrointestinal tract (see Chapter 37).

Leprosy is a chronic disease of the skin, nerves and mucous membranes. The immunologic response (e.g. hypersensitivity) becomes an important component of the pathogenesis of the disease. The clinical manifestations of leprosy have been separated into six categories according to the Ridley–Jopling classification scheme.[13] This classification system is both a clinical classification based on the nature and severity of symptoms and a histopathologic classification. The classification groups are:

- (1) polar tuberculoid,
- (2) borderline tuberculoid,
- (3) borderline,
- (4) borderline lepromatous,
- (5) lepromatous (subpolar), and
- (6) lepromatous polar.

Lepromatous leprosy is the most severe form of the disease with numerous skin lesions involving the face and nose. At one pole, lepromatous leprosy, acid-fast bacilli are numerous and present in immature macrophages while at the other pole, tuberculoid leprosy, macrophages have matured into epithelioid cells (see also Chapter 154).

Mycobacterium arium complex disease is frequently viewed as disease in two groups of patients, persons with and without underlying HIV infection. Although there are some similarities in the manifestation of MAC disease in both groups, the mortality rate, extent and pathologic manifestations of disease are frequently dissimilar.[121] Disseminated MAC disease in people with HIV infection is a progressive illness characterized by intermittent fever, sweats, weakness, anorexia and weight loss. Patients may have nausea, diarrhea and vomiting along with abdominal pain. The microbiologic hallmark of MAC disease is a positive blood or bone marrow culture; however, duodenal, rectal, spleen or liver biopsies may be diagnostic (Fig. 233.12). The level of the bacteremia ranges from intermittently culture positive to 10^6 cfu/ml. The level of infection of bone marrow may be orders of magnitude higher than in blood.[122]

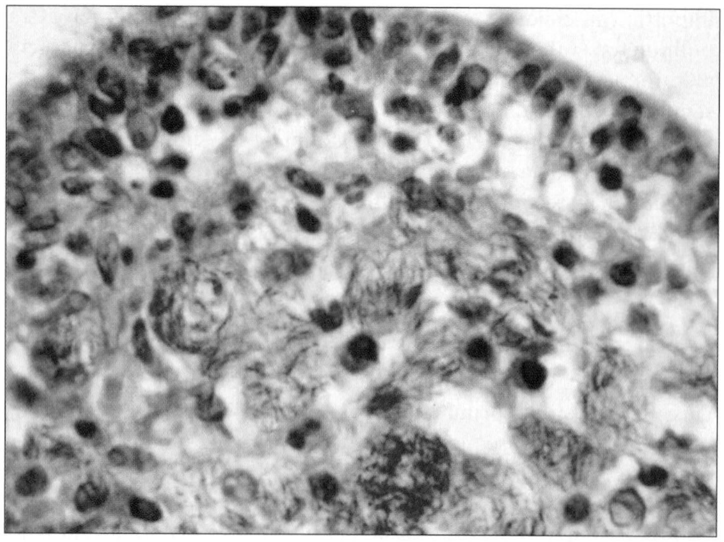

Fig. 233.12 Acid-fast stain of a section of small intestine from a patient who has HIV infection and disseminated *Mycobacterium avium* disease. The photomicrograph shows many acid-fast bacilli within a villus tip of the intestinal tract biopsy. The cuboidal cells at the periphery of the tip are in disarray and appear abnormal with cell nuclei not evenly distributed at the base of the cells. There is no evidence of granuloma, but the overwhelming number of mycobacteria may be partially obscuring the host's cellular response. The histopathology is consistent with the symptoms of patients with MAC gastrointestinal tract infections, including abdominal pain, diarrhea and wasting. Courtesy of LS Young.

Disseminated MAC infection in people with HIV infection clearly decreases survival and treatment with a macrolide and another agent improves survival and the quality of life. MAC disease in people with HIV infection may be focal including pulmonary infection, peripheral lymphadenitis and cutaneous infection (see Chapter 129). The majority (≥90%) of disseminated MAC disease is caused by *M. avium*; however, other species should be considered for symptomatic patients with negative cultures, such as *M. triplex*, *M. genavense* and *M. conspicuum* or, for patients with cutaneous infections, *M. haemophilum* (see Table 233.4). In patients without underlying HIV infection, MAC can cause pulmonary disease, usually in patients with a history of chronic pulmonary disease, including patients with chronic obstructive pulmonary disease and cystic fibrosis. Symptoms are varied and non-specific, including chronic productive cough, dyspnea, sweats, malaise and fatigue (see Chapter 38).

Distinction between infection with MAC and transient colonization may be difficult. *Mycobacterium intracellulare* is isolated about as frequently as *M. avium*, but the isolation of *M. avium* has been associated with a poorer prognosis.

Mycobacterium arium complex lymphadenitis in immunocompetent children usually presents as an insidious, painless, unilateral process involving one or more lymph nodes. Mycobacteria isolated from infected lymph nodes are mostly (60–80%) MAC with the remainder being *M. scrofulaceum* and *M. tuberculosis* (see Chapter 39). *Mycobacterium arium* complex lymph node infection of children over 12 years of age is rarely simple lymphadenitis and may indicate disseminated disease and immunodeficiency. Disseminated MAC disease in HIV-negative patients is usually associated with congenital immunodeficiency, immunosuppression, malignancy or a specific immunodeficiency such as a deficiency in IFN-γ production or IFN-γ receptors. Disseminated MAC disease with visceral involvement has been associated with a high (82%) mortality rate in children without HIV infection.

REFERENCES

1. Perutz MF. The white plague. The New York Review of Books. New York: NYREV; 1994:35–9.
2. Wayne LG. Mycobacterial speciation. In: Kubica GP, Wayne LG, eds. The mycobacteria: a sourcebook, part A. New York and Basel: Marcel Dekker, Inc.; 1984:25–65.
3. Brennan PJ, Draper P. Ultrastructure of *Mycobacterium tuberculosis*. In: Bloom BR, ed. Tuberculosis: pathogenesis, protection and control. Washington, DC: American Society for Microbiology; 1994:271–84.
4. Grange JM. Mycobacteria and human disease. London: Arnold; 1996.
5. Attorri S, Dunbar S, Clarridge III JE. Assessment of morphology for rapid presumptive identification of *Mycobacterium tuberculosis* and *Mycobacterium kansasii*. J Clin Microbiol 2000;38:1426–9.
6. Brosch R, Pym A, Gordon S, Cole S. The evolution of mycobacterial pathogenicity: clues from comparative genomics. Trends Microbiol 2001;9:452–8.
7. Brosch R, Gordon SV, Marmiesse M, *et al.* A new evolutionary scenario for the *Mycobacterium tuberculosis* complex. Proc Natl Acad Sci USA 2002;99:3684–9.
8. Snider D Jr, La Montagne JR. The neglected global tuberculosis problem: a report of the 1992 World Congress on Tuberculosis. J Infect Dis 1994;169:1189–96.
9. Raviglione MC, Snider Jr D, Kochi A. Global epidemiology of tuberculosis. Morbidity and mortality of a worldwide epidemic. JAMA 1995;273:220–6.
10. Wallis RS, Johnson JL. Adult tuberculosis in the 21st century: pathogenesis, clinical features and management. Curr Opin Pulm Med 2001;7:124–33.
11. World Health Organization. Global tuberculosis control: surveillance, planning, financing. WHO Report 2000. Geneva, Switzerland: World Health Organization; 2002.
12. Snider Jr D, La Montagne J. The neglected global tuberculosis problem: a report of the 1992 World Congress on Tuberculosis. J Infect Dis 1994;169:1189–96.
13. Godal T, Levy L. *Mycobacterium leprae*. In: Kubica GP, Wayne LG, eds. The mycobacteria: a sourcebook, part B. New York and Basel: Marcel Dekker, Inc; 1984:1083–128.
14. Horsburgh Jr C. Epidemiology of *Mycobacterium avium* complex disease. Am J Med 1997;102:11–15.
15. Garcia-del Portillo F, Finlay BB. The varied lifestyles of intracellular pathogens within eukaryotic vacuolar compartments. Trends Microbiol 1995;3:373–80.
16. Chan J, Kaufmann SHE. Immune mechanisms of protection. In: Bloom BR, ed. Tuberculosis: pathogenesis, protection and control. Washington DC: American Society for Microbiology; 1994:389–415.
17. Gros P, Skamene E, Forget A. Genetic control of natural resistance to *Mycobacterium bovis* BCG. J Immunol 1981;127:417–21.
18. Bellamy R. The natural resistance-associated macrophage protein and susceptibility to intracellular pathogens [Review]. Micobes Infect 1999;1:23–7.
19. Master S, Zahrt TC, Song J, Deretic V. Mapping of *Mycobacterium tuberculosis katG* promoters and their differential expression in infected macrophages. J Bacteriol 2001;183:4033–9.
20. Telenti A. Genetics of drug resistance in tuberculosis. Clin Chest Med 1997;18:55–64.
21. Alcaide F, Telenti A. Molecular techniques in the diagnosis of drug-resistant tuberculosis. Ann Acad Med Singapore 1997;26:647–50.
22. Musser JM. Antimicrobial agent resistance in mycobacteria: molecular genetic insights. Clin Microbiol Rev 1995;8:496–514.
23. Salfinger M, Morris AJ. The role of the microbiology laboratory in diagnosing mycobacterial diseases. Am J Clin Pathol 1994;101:S6–13.
24. Salfinger M, Stoll EW, Piot D, Heifets L. Comparison of three methods for recovery of *Mycobacterium avium* complex from blood specimens. J Clin Microbiol 1988;26:1225–6.
25. Rish JA, Eisenach KD, Cave MD, Reddy MV, Gangadharam PR, Bates JH. Polymerase chain reaction detection of *Mycobacterium tuberculosis* in formalin-fixed tissue. Am J Respir Crit Care Med 1996;153(Pt 1):1419–23.
26. Bascunana CR, Belak K. Detection and identification of mycobacteria in formalin-fixed, paraffin-embedded tissues by nested PCR and restriction enzyme analysis. J Clin Microbiol 1996;34:2351–5.
27. Chin DP, Hopewell PC, Yajko DM, *et al.* *Mycobacterium avium* complex in the respiratory or gastrointestinal tract and the risk of *M. avium* complex bacteremia in patients with human immunodeficiency virus infection. J Infect Dis 1994;169:289–95.
28. Yajko DM, Nassos PS, Sanders CA, *et al.* Comparison of four decontamination methods for recovery of *Mycobacterium avium* complex from stools. J Clin Microbiol 1993;31:302–6.
29. Gullans Sr CR. Digestion and decontamination procedures. In: Isenberg HD, ed. Clinical microbiology procedures handbook.

Washington DC: American Society for Microbiology; 1992:3.4.1–14.
30. Baron EJ, Peterson LR, Finegold SM. Bailey and Scott's diagnostic microbiology, 9th ed. Philadelphia: Mosby; 1994.
31. Alcaide F, Benitez MA, Escriba JM, Martin R. Evaluation of the BACTEC MGIT 960 and the MB/BacT systems for recovery of mycobacteria from clinical specimens and for species identification by DNA AccuProbe. J Clin Microbiol 2000;38:398–401.
32. Chien HP, Yu MC, Wu MH, Lin TP, Luh KT. Comparison of the BACTEC MGIT 960 with Löwenstein–Jensen medium for recovery of mycobacteria from clinical specimens. Int J Tuber Lung Dis 2000;4:866–70.
33. Flanagan PG, Williams R, Paull A. Comparison of two automated systems for the isolation of mycobacteria from clinical specimens. Eur J Clin Microbiol Infect Dis 1999;18:912–4.
34. Hanna BA, Ebrahimzadeh A, Elliott LB, *et al.* Multicenter evaluation of the BACTEC MGIT 960 system for recovery of mycobacteria. J Clin Microbiol 1999;37:748–52.
35. Huang TS, Chen CS, Lee SS, Huang WK, Liu YC. Comparison of the BACTEC MGIT 960 and BACTEC 460TB systems for detection of mycobacteria in clinical specimens. Ann Clin Lab Sci 2001;31:279–83.
36. Idigoras P, Beristain X, Iturzaeta A, Vicente D, Perez-Trallero E. Comparison of the automated nonradiometric Bactec MGIT 960 system with Löwenstein–Jensen, Coletsos, and Middlebrook 7H11 solid media for recovery of mycobacteria. Eur J Clin Microbiol Infect Dis 2000;19:350–4.
37. Jayakumar KV, Forster T, Kyi MS. Improved detection of *Mycobacterium* spp. using the Bactec MGIT 960 system. Br J Biomed Sci 2001;58:154–8.
38. Leitritz L, Schubert S, Bucherl B, Masch A, Heesemann J, Roggenkamp A. Evaluation of BACTEC MGIT 960 and BACTEC 460TB systems for recovery of mycobacteria from clinical specimens of a university hospital with low incidence of tuberculosis. J Clin Microbiol 2001;39:3764–7.
39. Rohner P, Ninet B, Metral C, Emler S, Auckenthaler R. Evaluation of the MB/BacT system and comparison to the BACTEC 460 system and solid media for isolation of mycobacteria from clinical specimens. J Clin Microbiol 1997;35:3127–31.
40. Sharp SE, Lemes M, Erlich SS, Poppiti R, Jr. A comparison of the Bactec 9000MB system and the Septi-Chek AFB system for the detection of mycobacteria. Diagn Microbiol Infect Dis 1997;28:69–74.
41. Tortoli E, Cichero P, Piersimoni C, Simonetti MT, Gesu G, Nista D. Use of BACTEC MGIT 960 for recovery of mycobacteria from clinical specimens: multicenter study. J Clin Microbiol 1999;37:3578–82.
42. Williams-Bouyer N, Yorke R, Lee HI, Woods GL. Comparison of the BACTEC MGIT 960 and ESP culture system II for growth and detection of mycobacteria. J Clin Microbiol 2000;38:4167–70.
43. Woods GL, Fish G, Plaunt M, Murphy T. Clinical evaluation of Difco ESP culture system II for growth and detection of mycobacteria. J Clin Microbiol 1997;35:121–4.
44. Yan JJ, Huang AH, Tsai SH, Ko WC, Jin YT, Wu JJ. Comparison of the MB/BacT and BACTEC MGIT 960 system for recovery of mycobacteria from clinical specimens. Diag Microbiol Infect Dis 2000;37:25–30.
45. Sewell DL, Rashad AL, Rourke WJ, Jr., Poor SL, McCarthy JA, Pfaller MA. Comparison of the Septi-Chek AFB and BACTEC systems and conventional culture for recovery of mycobacteria. J Clin Microbiol 1993;31:2689–91.
46. Isenberg HD, D'Amato RF, Heifets L, *et al.* Collaborative feasibility study of a biphasic system (Roche Septi-Chek AFB) for rapid detection and isolation of mycobacteria. J Clin Microbiol 1991;29:1719–22.
47. Liu YC, Huang TS, Huang WK. Comparison of a nonradiometric liquid-medium method (MB REDOX) with the BACTEC system for growth and identification of mycobacteria in clinical specimens. J Clin Microbiol 1999;37:4048–50.
48. Heifets L, Linder T, Sanchez T, Spencer D, Brennan J. Two liquid medium systems, mycobacteria growth indicator tube and MB redox tube, for *Mycobacterium tuberculosis* isolation from sputum specimens. J Clin Microbiol 2000;38:1227–30.
49. Piersimoni C, Scarparo C, Cichero P, *et al.* Multicenter evaluation of the MB-Redox medium compared with radiometric BACTEC system, mycobacteria growth indicator tube (MGIT), and Löwenstein–Jensen medium for detection and recovery of acid-fast bacilli. Diagn Microbiol Infect Dis 1999;34:293–9.
50. Somoskovi A, Magyar P. Comparison of the mycobacteria growth indicator tube with MB redox, Löwenstein–Jensen, and Middlebrook 7H11 media for recovery of mycobacteria in clinical specimens. J Clin Microbiol 1999;37:1366–9.
51. Woods GL. The mycobacteriology laboratory and new diagnostic techniques. Infect Dis Clin North Am 2002;16:127–44.
52. Stahl DA, Urbance JW. The division between fast- and slow-growing species corresponds to natural relationships among the mycobacteria. J Bacteriol 1990;172:116–24.
53. Kent PA, Kubica GP. Public health mycobacteriology – a guide for the level III laboratory. Atlanta: US Department of Health and Human Services, Public Health Service, Centers for Disease Control; 1985.
54. Goh KS, Legrand E, Sola C, Rastogi N. Rapid differentiation of *Mycobacterium canettii* from other *Mycobacterium tuberculosis* complex organisms by PCR-restriction analysis of the *hsp65* gene. J Clin Microbiol 2001;39:3705–8.
55. van Soolingen D, van der Zanden AG, de Haas PE, *et al.* Diagnosis of *Mycobacterium microti* infections among humans by using novel genetic markers. J Clin Microbiol 1998;36:1840–5.
56. Falkinham III JO. Epidemiology of infection of nontuberculous mycobacteria. Clin Microbiol Rev 1996;9:177–215.
57. Kiehn TE, White MH. The changing nature of nontuberculous mycobacteriology. In: Scheld W, Armstrong D, Hughes J, eds. Emerging infections. Washington DC: ASM Press; 1998:207–19.
58. American Thoracic Society. Diagnosis and treatment of disease caused by nontuberculous mycobacteria. This official statement of the American Thoracic Society was approved by the Board of Directors, March 1997. Medical Section of the American Lung Association. Am J Respir Crit Care Med 1997;156:S1–25.
59. Brown-Elliott B, Griffith D, Wallace Jr R. Newly described or emerging human species of nontuberculous mycobacteria. Infect Dis Clin North Am 2002;16:187–220.
60. Inderlied CB, Nash KA. Microbiology and in vitro susceptibility testing. In: Benson CA, Korvick JA, eds. *Mycobacterium avium*-complex infection: progress in research and treatment. New York: Marcel Dekker; 1995:109–40.
61. Ebersole LL. Acid-fast stain procedures. In: Isenberg HD, ed. Clinical microbiology procedures handbook. Washington DC: American Society for Microbiology; 1992:3.5.1–11.
62. Wayne LG, Sramek HA. Agents of newly recognized or infrequently encountered mycobacterial diseases. Clin Microbiol Rev 1992;5:1–25.
63. Peloquin CA. Using therapeutic drug monitoring to dose the antimycobacterial drugs. Clin Chest Med 1997;18:79–87.
64. Thibert L, Lapierre S. Routine application of high-performance liquid chromatography for identification of mycobacteria. J Clin Microbiol 1993;31:1759–63.
65. Jost K Jr, Dunbar DF, Barth SS, Headley VL, Elliott LB. Identification of *Mycobacterium tuberculosis* and *M. avium* complex directly from smear-positive sputum specimens and BACTEC 12B cultures by high-performance liquid chromatography with fluorescence detection and computer-driven pattern recognition models. J Clin Microbiol 1995;33:1270–7.
66. Glickman SE, Kilburn JO, Butler WR, Ramos LS. Rapid identification of mycolic acid patterns of mycobacteria by high-performance liquid chromatography using pattern recognition software and a mycobacterium library. J Clin Microbiol 1994;32:740–5.
67. Soini H, Eerola E, Viljanen MK. Genetic diversity among *Mycobacterium avium* complex AccuProbe-positive isolates. J Clin Microbiol 1996;34:55–7.
68. Metchock B, Diem L. Algorithm for use of nucleic acid probes for identifying *Mycobacterium tuberculosis* from BACTEC 12B bottles. J Clin Microbiol 1995;33:1934–7.
69. Reisner BS, Gatson AM, Woods GL. Use of Gen-Probe AccuProbes to identify *Mycobacterium avium* complex, *Mycobacterium tuberculosis* complex, *Mycobacterium kansasii*, and *Mycobacterium gordonae* directly from BACTEC TB broth cultures. J Clin Microbiol 1994;32:2995–8.
70. Ephraim DA, Spitzer ED. Use of acridinium-ester-labeled DNA probes for identification of mycobacteria in Bactec 13A blood cultures. Diagn Microbiol Infect Dis 1994;18:137–9.
71. Labombardi VJ, Carter L, Massarella S. Use of nucleic acid probes to identify mycobacteria directly from Difco ESP-Myco bottles. J Clin Microbiol 1997;35:1002–4.
72. Böddinghaus B, Rogall T, Flohr T, Blöcker H, Böttger EC. Detection and identification of mycobacteria by amplification of rRNA. J Clin Microbiol 1990;28:1751–9.
73. Centers for Disease Control and Prevention. Update: nucleic acid amplification tests for tuberculosis. MMWR Morb Mortal Wkly Rep 2000;49:593–4.
74. Cave MD, Eisenach KD, Templeton G, *et al.* Stability of DNA fingerprint pattern produced with IS6110 in strains of *Mycobacterium tuberculosis*. J Clin Microbiol 1994;32:262–6.
75. van Embden JDA, Cave MD, Crawford JT, *et al.* Strain identification of *Mycobacterium tuberculosis* by DNA fingerprinting: recommendations for a standardized methodology. J Clin Microbiol 1993;31:406–9.
76. Heersma HF, Kremer K, van Embden JD. Computer analysis of IS6110 RFLP patterns of *Mycobacterium tuberculosis*. Meth Mol Biol 1998;101:395–422.
77. Kamerbeek J, Schouls L, Kolk A, *et al.* Simultaneous detection and strain differentiation of *Mycobacterium tuberculosis* for diagnosis and epidemiology. J Clin Microbiol 1997;35:907–14.
78. Yang ZH, Ijaz K, Bates JH, Eisenach KD, Cave MD. Spoligotyping and polymorphic GC-rich repetitive sequence fingerprinting of *Mycobacterium tuberculosis* strains having few copies of IS6110. J Clin Microbiol 2000;38:3572–6.
79. Goulding JN, Hookey JV, Stanley J, *et al.* Fluorescent amplified-fragment length polymorphism genotyping of *Neisseria meningitidis* identifies clones associated with invasive disease. J Clin Microbiol 2000;38:4580–5.
80. Goulding JN, Stanley J, Saunders N, Arnold C. Genome-sequence-based fluorescent amplified-fragment length polymorphism analysis of *Mycobacterium tuberculosis*. J Clin Microbiol 2000;38:1121–6.
81. Yates MD, Drobniewski FA, Wilson SM. Evaluation of a rapid PCR-based epidemiological typing method for routine studies of *Mycobacterium tuberculosis*. J Clin Microbiol 2002;40:712–4.
82. Musser JM, Kapur V, Williams DL, Kreiswirth BN, van Soolingen D, van Embden JD. Characterization of the catalase-peroxidase gene

(*katG*) and *inhA* locus in isoniazid-resistant and -susceptible strains of *Mycobacterium tuberculosis* by automated DNA sequencing: restricted array of mutations associated with drug resistance. J Infect Dis 1996;173:196–202.
83. Heym B, Zhang Y, Poulet S, Young D, Cole ST. Characterization of the *katG* gene encoding a catalase-peroxidase required for isoniazid susceptibility of *Mycobacterium tuberculosis*. J Bacteriol 1993;175:4255–9.
84. Telenti A, Imboden P, Marchesi F, *et al.* Detection of rifampicin-resistance mutations in *Mycobacterium tuberculosis*. Lancet 1993;341:647–50.
85. Williams DL, Waguespack C, Eisenach K, *et al.* Characterization of rifampin-resistance in pathogenic mycobacteria. Antimicrob Agents Chemother 1994;38:2380–6.
86. Telenti A, Honore N, Bernasconi C, *et al.* Genotypic assessment of isoniazid and rifampin resistance in *Mycobacterium tuberculosis*: a blind study at reference laboratory level. J Clin Microbiol 1997;35:719–23.
87. Banerjee A, Dubnau E, Quemard A, *et al. inhA*, a gene encoding a target for isoniazid and ethionamide in *Mycobacterium tuberculosis*. Science 1994;263:227–30.
88. Dhandayuthapani S, Mudd M, Deretic V. Interactions of OxyR with the promoter region of the *oxyR* and *ahpC* genes from *Mycobacterium leprae* and *Mycobacterium tuberculosis*. J Bacteriol 1997;179:2401–9.
89. Wilson TM, Collins DM. *ahpC*, a gene involved in isoniazid resistance of the *Mycobacterium tuberculosis* complex. Mol Microbiol 1996;19:1025–34.
90. Kelley CL, Rouse DA, Morris SL. Analysis of *ahpC* gene mutations in isoniazid-resistant clinical isolates of *Mycobacterium tuberculosis*. Antimicrob Agents Chemother 1997;41:2057–8.
91. Mdluli K, Slayden R, Zhu Y, *et al.* Inhibition of a *Mycobacterium tuberculosis* -ketoacyl ACP synthase by isoniazid. Science 1998;280:1607–10.
92. Sreevatsan S, Stockbauer KE, Pan X, *et al.* Ethambutol resistance in *Mycobacterium tuberculosis*: critical role of *embB* mutations. Antimicrob Agents Chemother 1997;41:1677–81.
93. Nair J, Rouse DA, Bai GH, Morris SL. The *rpsL* gene and streptomycin resistance in single and multiple drug-resistant strains of *Mycobacterium tuberculosis*. Mol Microbiol 1993;10:521–7.
94. Finken M, Kirschner P, Meier A, Wrede A, Böttger EC. Molecular basis of streptomycin resistance in *Mycobacterium tuberculosis*: alterations of the ribosomal protein S12 gene and point mutations within a functional 16S ribosomal RNA pseudoknot. Mol Microbiol 1993;9:1239–46.
95. Kenney TJ, Churchward G. Cloning and sequence analysis of the *rpsL* and *rpsG* genes of *Mycobacterium smegmatis* and characterization of mutations causing resistance to streptomycin. J Bacteriol 1994;176:6153–6.
96. Douglass J, Steyn LM. A ribosomal gene mutation in streptomycin-resistant *Mycobacterium tuberculosis* isolates [Letter]. J Infect Dis 1993;167:1505–6.
97. Scorpio A, Zhang Y. Mutations in *pncA*, a gene encoding pyrazinamidase/ nicotinamidase, cause resistance to the antituberculous drug pyrazinamide in tubercle bacillus [see comments]. Nat Med 1996;2:662–7.
98. Scorpio A, Lindholm Levy P, Heifets L, *et al.* Characterization of *pncA* mutations in pyrazinamide-resistant *Mycobacterium tuberculosis*. Antimicrob Agents Chemother 1997;41:540–3.
99. Sreevatsan S, Pan X, Zhang Y, Kreiswirth BN, Musser JM. Mutations associated with pyrazinamide resistance in *pncA* of *Mycobacterium tuberculosis* complex organisms. Antimicrob Agents Chemother 1997;41:636–40.
100. Takiff HE, Salazar L, Guerrero C, *et al.* Cloning and nucleotide sequence of *Mycobacterium tuberculosis gyrA* and *gyrB* genes and detection of quinolone resistance mutations. Antimicrob Agents Chemother 1994;38:773–80.
101. Revel Viravau V, Truong QC, Moreau N, Jarlier V, Sougakoff W. Sequence analysis, purification, and study of inhibition by 4-quinolones of the DNA gyrase from *Mycobacterium smegmatis*. Antimicrob Agents Chemother 1996;40:2054–61.
102. Nash KA, Inderlied CB. Genetic basis of macrolide resistance in *Mycobacterium avium* isolated from patients with disseminated disease. Antimicrob Agents Chemother 1995;39:2625–30.
103. Meier A, Kirschner P, Springer B, *et al.* Identification of mutations in 23S rRNA gene of clarithromycin-resistant *Mycobacterium intracellulare*. Antimicrob Agents Chemother 1994;38:381–4.
104. Wallace R Jr, Meier A, Brown BA, *et al.* Genetic basis for clarithromycin resistance among isolates of *Mycobacterium chelonae* and *Mycobacterium abscessus*. Antimicrob Agents Chemother 1996;40:1676–81.
105. Parsons LM, Driscoll JR, Taber HW, Salfinger M. Drug resistance in tuberculosis. In: Tenover FC, McGowan JE Jr, eds. Infectious disease clinics of North America: antimicrobial resistance. Philadelphia: WB Saunders; 1997:905–28.
106. Young DB. Strategies for new drug development. In: Bloom BR, ed. Tuberculosis: pathogenesis, protection and control. Washington DC: American Society for Microbiology; 1994:559–67.
107. Barry III C, Mdluli K. Drug sensitivity and environmental adaptation of mycobacterial cell wall components. Trends Microbiol 1996;4:275–81.
108. Mdluli K, Swanson J, Fischer E, Lee R, Barry C III. Mechanisms involved in the intrinsic isoniazid resistance of *Mycobacterium avium*. Mol Microbiol 1998;27:1223–33.
109. Heifets LB. Drug susceptibility tests in the management of chemotherapy of tuberculosis. In: Heifets LB, ed. Drug susceptibility in the chemotherapy of mycobacterial infections. Boca Raton: CRC Press; 1991:89–121.
110. Inderlied CB, Pfyffer GE. Susceptibility test methods: mycobacteria. Manual of clinical microbiology, (Vol. 1), 8th edition. Washington DC: American Society for Microbiology; 2003:1149–77.
111. Benson C. Disseminated *Mycobacterium avium* complex disease in patients with AIDS. AIDS Res Hum Retroviruses 1994;10:913–6.
112. Benson CA. Treatment of disseminated *Mycobacterium avium* complex disease: a clinician's perspective. Res Microbiol 1996;147:16–24.
113. Kemper CA, Havlir D, Haghighat D, *et al.* The individual microbiologic effect of three antimycobacterial agents, clofazimine, ethambutol, and rifampin, on *Mycobacterium avium* complex bacteremia in patients with AIDS. J Infect Dis 1994;170:157–64.
114. Rastogi N, Goh KS, Bryskier A. Activities of roxithromycin used alone and in combination with ethambutol, rifampin, amikacin, ofloxacin, and clofazimine against *Mycobacterium avium* complex. Antimicrob Agents Chemother 1994;38:1433–8.
115. National Committee on Clinical Laboratory Standards. Susceptibility testing of mycobacteria, nocardia and other aerobic actinomycetes; tentative standard M24-T2. Villanova, PA: National Committee on Clinical Laboratory Standards; 2000.
116. Straus WL, Ostroff SM, Jernigan DB, *et al.* Clinical and epidemiologic characteristics of *Mycobacterium haemophilum*, an emerging pathogen in immunocompromised patients. Ann Intern Med 1994;120:118–25.
117. Valero G, Moreno F, Graybill JR. Activities of clarithromycin, ofloxacin, and clarithromycin plus ethambutol against *Mycobacterium simiae* in murine model of disseminated infection. Antimicrob Agents Chemother 1994;38:2676–7.
118. Brown B, Swenson J, Wallace R Jr. Broth microdilution test for rapidly growing mycobacteria. In: Isenberg HD, ed. Clinical microbiology procedures handbook. Washington DC: American Society for Microbiology; 1992:5.11.1–10.
119. Espinal MA, Laszlo A, Simonsen L, Boulahbal F, Sang J-K, Reneiro A, *et al.*, for the WHO-International Union Against Tuberculosis and Lung Disease Working Group on Anti-Tuberculosis Drug Resistance Surveillance. Global trends in resistance to antituberculosis. N Engl J Med 2001;344:1294–303.
120. Currier JS, Williams PL, Koletar SL, *et al.* Discontinuation of *Mycobacterium avium* complex prophylaxis in patients with antiretroviral therapy-induced increases in CD4+ cell count. A randomized, double-blind, placebo-controlled trial. AIDS Clinical Trials Group 362 Study Team. Ann Intern Med 2000;133:493–503.
121. Inderlied CB, Kemper CA, Bermudez LEM. The *Mycobacterium avium* complex. Clin Microbiol Rev 1993;6:266–310.
122. Inderlied CB. Microbiology and minimum inhibitory concentration testing for *Mycobacterium avium* complex prophylaxis. Am J Med 1997;102:2–10.

chapter
234 Mycoplasma and Ureaplasma

Per-Anders Mårdh

INTRODUCTION

The first mycoplasma strain was isolated in 1936 from a female genital tract specimen and was most likely a strain of *Mycoplasma hominis*.[1] Since then a number of other *Mycoplasma* spp. have been recovered from the human genital tract and from other organ systems. They have been found in otherwise sterile samples such as blood, cerebrospinal fluid (CSF) and synovial fluid, as well as in pus from abscesses in a variety of organs.[2,3]

The mycoplasmas and ureaplasmas taxonomically belong to the order Mycoplasmatales in class Mollicutes together with organisms of the families Acholeplasmataceae and Spiroplasmataceae. Apart from being human pathogens, some organisms of the order Mollicutes are economically important plant and animal pathogens.

The initial division of mycoplasmas into different species was based on inhibition of growth of the organisms on agar media by homologous antibodies. In later studies, sequencing of the genome of mycoplasmas has confirmed the relevance of the initial classification method.

The role of *Mycoplasma pneumoniae* in primary atypical pneumonia became established in the 1940s; earlier it was believed that the condition was caused by a virus, known as the 'Eaton agent'. Chanock and Hayflick succeeded in 1961 in isolating the organism on an agar medium.[4]

First recovered by Tully and Taylor-Robinson in 1981,[5] *Mycoplasma genitalium* is the most recently recognized human mycoplasma pathogen. It has been regarded as a urogenital pathogen, for example causing nongonococcal urethritis (NGU).[6,7]

Ureaplasma urealyticum was first discovered in 1954 by Shepard.[8] It was isolated from the urethra of men who had signs of urethritis.[2,3] Its role in NGU has, however, remained controversial and some studies indicate that *M. genitalium* may instead be the responsible agent in such cases.[6] *Ureaplasma urealyticum* is an otherwise common inhabitant of the genital tract of healthy people. Ureaplasmas have been associated with low-birth-weight infants and can cause neonatal meningoencephalitis.[9]

Apart from the species mentioned above, several other species of *Mycoplasma* occur in the human indigenous flora of the mouth and the genital tract (e.g. *Mycoplasma buccale*, *M. faucium*, *M. lipophilum*, *M. orale* and *M. salivarium*).

NATURE

Mycoplasma and ureaplasma measuring 400–500nm are the smallest organisms so far identified as being capable of reproducing in broth and on agar media; on the latter they form colonies barely visible to the naked eye.[10] They also have the smallest known genome of any 'free-living' organisms (i.e. 4.5×10^8 Da). The genome has been completely sequenced for some species.[11] The guanine and cytosine (GC) content is low (i.e. approximately 25% as compared with the approximately 80% found in eubacteria).

The organisms are regarded as so unique that they form their own taxonomic class (i.e. Mollicutes), which refers to their 'soft skin' (they lack the rigid cell wall found in eubacteria) and to their pleomorphic shape (Figs 234.1 and 234.2). Thus, they differ from eubacteria by lacking peptidoglycan, which gives the latter a rigid shape and a strong osmotic stability. The mycoplasmas are surrounded by a 8–10nm thick protoplasma membrane. The absence of peptidoglycan and β-lactam receptors (i.e. for penicillins and cephalosporins) explains their resistance to these antimicrobial agents interfering with cell wall integrity.

Interestingly, two of the human pathogens, namely *M. genitalium* and *M. pneumoniae*, have an adherence organ in contrast to the rest of the species of the family Mycoplasmataceae.[5]

Ureaplasma urealyticum derives its name from the fact that it processes the enzyme urease. Previously, the organism was called T-strain mycoplasma as it produced tiny (T) colonies in comparison to those of mycoplasmas. *Ureaplasma urealyticum* has remained the single species in the genus *Ureaplasma*, although there have been several proposals for a differentiation based, for example, on biochemical and serologic characteristics. Fourteen different serotypes of *U. urealyticum* have been described. One biovar of human ureaplasmas (biovar no. 1) has been called *Ureaplasma parvum*.[12]

EPIDEMIOLOGY

Mycoplasma hominis

This organism has been isolated from the fallopian tubes of women with laparoscopic signs of acute salpingitis (i.e. pelvic inflammatory disease (PID)), and in whom an antibody response to the organism could be demonstrated.[13,14] The organism seems to be able to spread through the cervical canal via the uterine cavity as well as by the lymphatic vessels of the parametrium to the tubes (Fig. 234.3). The relative role of *M. hominis* and *M. genitalium* in endometritis and salpingitis is currently under investigation.

Mycoplasma hominis is a common finding in women who lack a lactobacilli-dominated vaginal flora and who present with a mixture of bacterial species in the vagina. Many of these species are strictly anaerobic, most of which normally occur in the intestinal flora. Up to 75% of all women with a flora change, such as that seen in bacterial vaginosis (BV), are carriers of *M. hominis*.[15] A role for *M. hominis* in both BV and non-specific vaginitis has been considered, but has been difficult to prove. One of the reasons is that *M. hominis* can also occur in the vagina of women with vaginal flora changes who do not fulfill the criteria for BV.[16] The recovery rates of *M. hominis* (and of *Mobiluncus* spp.) in women with BV, trichomoniasis, vulvovaginal candidosis and in a group of healthy women are shown in Table 234.1.

Salpingitis can occur as secondary infections of the fallopian tubes in women in whom the tubes have been primarily damaged by sexually transmitted disease agents, such as *Chlamydia trachomatis* and *Neisseria gonorrhoeae*.[17] *Mycoplasma hominis* may increase the risk for tubal occlusion and infertility, if infection has already damaged the tubes.

Mycoplasma hominis has been recovered from blood of women who have had a septic (febrile) abortion.[18] A significant change in

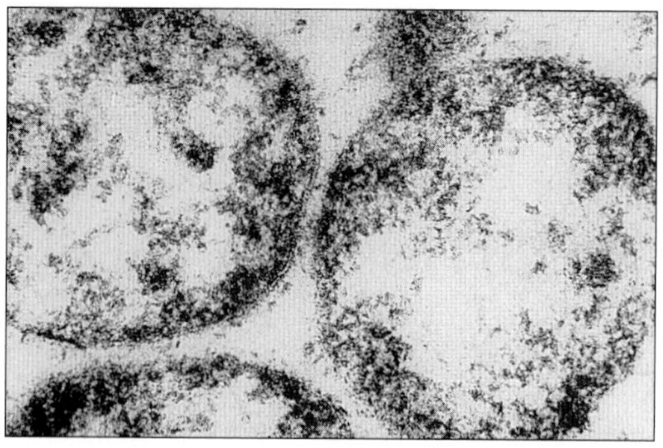

Fig. 234.1 Electron micrograph of a mycoplasma organism. It has a diameter of approximately 300nm and lacks a rigid cell wall containing peptidoglycan.

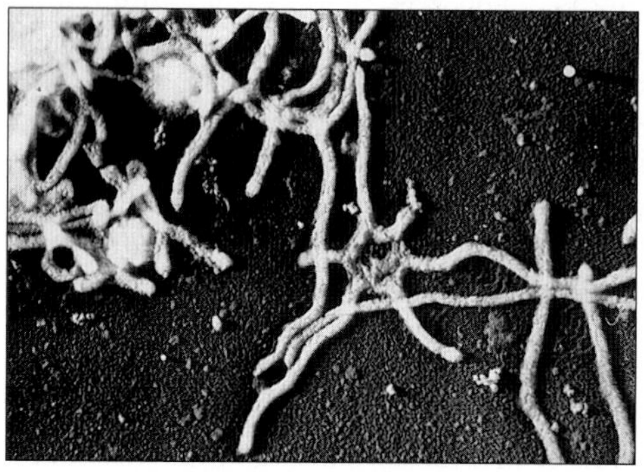

Fig. 234.2 Electron micrograph of a mycoplasma organism producing filamentous structures in a broth culture. This gives the organism the appearance of a fungal mycelium. ('Myco' in mycoplasma refers to this feature.)

MODES OF SPREAD OF *M. HOMINIS* IN UPPER GENITAL TRACT

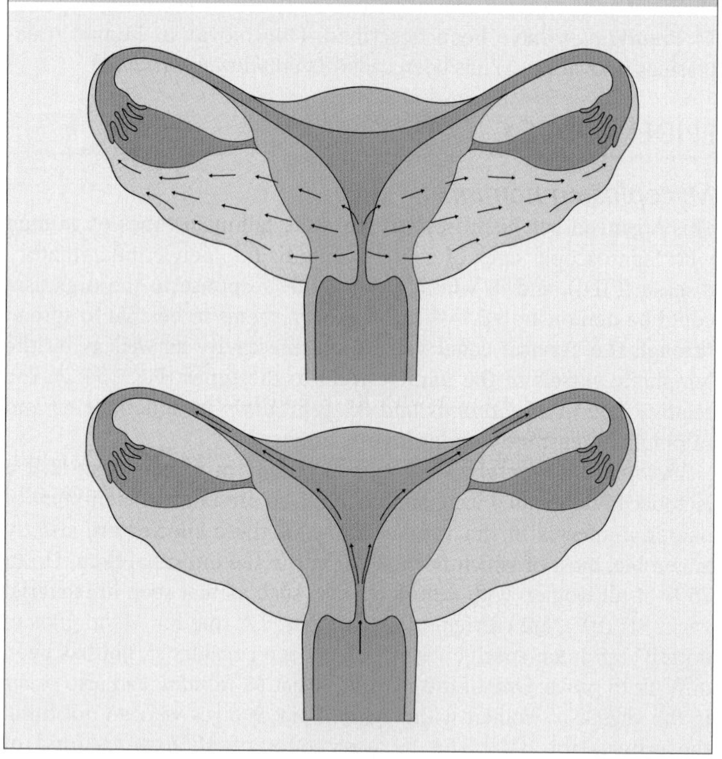

Fig. 234.3 Modes of spread of *Mycoplasma hominis* to the upper genital tract. The canalicular spread to the tubes is indicated in the lower panel of the figure and the lymphatic spread to the parametria in the upper one.

the antibody titer to the organism has been found in such patients. *Mycoplasma hominis* has also been recovered from blood cultures of women with postpartum fever. These findings have been associated with a specific antibody response and a positive culture from the amniotic surface of placentas of such cases. A pure culture of

RECOVERY OF *MYCOPLASMA HOMINIS, MOBILUNCUS MULIERIS* AND *MOBILUNCUS CURTISII*

Study group	No. tested	No. of persons positive for		
		M. hominis	*M. mulieris*	*M. curtisii*
Bacterial vaginosis	62	31	51	47
Trichomoniasis	13	3	0	0
Candidiasis	37	1	0	6
Healthy women	25	5	2	6
Partners to BV cases	47	8	1	5

Table 234.1 Recovery of *Mycoplasma hominis, Mobiluncus mulieris* and *Mobiluncus curtisii.* Samples taken from women with bacterial vaginosis (BV), vulvovaginal candidiasis and trichomoniasis, and from healthy females and male partners of women with BV.

M. hominis has been obtained from synovial fluid of a woman post-partum who had septic arthritis.

Mycoplasma hominis has also been recovered from the blood and CSF of newborns with signs of sepsis and meningoencephalitis.[15,19,20] There is a series of case reports in the literature of infants infected by *M. hominis* with malformation of the central nervous system, such as spina bifida, but also in cases without any malformation.[15] A significant antibody response to *M. hominis* has been detected in infants who have signs of pneumonia and from whom *M. hominis* has been isolated from the upper respiratory tract. In stillbirth, the organism has been recovered from lung and liver tissue.

There is no evidence that either *M. hominis* or *U. urealyticum* is the cause of bartholinitis as earlier believed.

Mycoplasma genitalium

Mycoplasma genitalium has been claimed to play an etiologic role in acute and possibly also in chronic cases of NGU.[6] Further studies have supported an independent role of *M. genitalium* and *Chlamydia trachomatis* in NGU in men.[7] Likewise, *M. genitalium* has been recovered from the urethra of HIV-infected men.[21] It can be found in urethral cultures from men with and without urethral discharge. There is no evidence of a role for the organism in chronic prostatitis.

In a recent study of women in the second and third trimesters of pregnancy, *M. genitalium* was recovered from vaginal lavage samples in 1.6% of the 500 women who had reached the second trimester. This percentage had increased in those who returned for repeated examination in the third trimester. The corresponding percentages for *M. hominis* were 10.8 and 22.3, respectively.[22]

Mycoplasma genitalium is likely a cause of cervicitis and endometritis[23] which may induce pre-term birth. Carriage of *M. genitalium* was associated with mucopurulent discharge, smoking, frequent vaginal douching and a history of miscarriage.[24] On the other hand, there seems to be no evidence of an association with bacterial vaginosis.

Mycoplasma genitalium antibodies were detected in 40% of women with PID, in whom microimmunofluorescence tests indicated a 4-fold or greater titer change within 1 month of clinical onset of upper genital tract infection.[25] Such antibodies were detected by immunoblotting in approximately half of the women with proven tubal factor infertility, and there was a correlation between the occurrence of specific anti-mycoplasma antibodies and tubal scarring.

Mycoplasma genitalium has also been associated with pneumonia and arthritic conditions.[26]

Mycoplasma pneumoniae

Mycoplasma pneumoniae infection is one of the most frequent causes of atypical pneumonia.[26–29] Endemic infections occur on a regular basis in between epidemic outbreaks which, at least for some decades, occurred in many countries every 3–5 years. However, this sequence pattern has become less distinct in many countries during recent decades.

Young adults are particularly affected by *M. pneumoniae*. The incubation period, as indicated by case-to-case transmission studies, is estimated at a mean of 20 days (range 11–25 days). The reported attack rates in closed communities, such as in families, have been 17–66%.[26,30]

Ureaplasma urealyticum

The prevalence of *U. urealyticum* in the genital tract is associated with sexual experience.[2] Disappearance of the organism from the genital tract after long-term sexual abstinence has been documented.

There have been a large number of studies on the possible role of *U. urealyticum* in NGU, since it was first recovered from the urethra of US military men by Shepard.[8] One major problem in evaluating its possible role in nongonococcal, nonchlamydial urethritis has been to find suitable comparison groups as the organism is a very common member of the indigenous microbial flora of the male urethra. A quantitative approach in culture studies of *U. urealyticum* in NGU cases has been undertaken. If the organism establishes itself as a pathogen, it is likely to increase in number. However, such studies have not been consistent and are therefore difficult to interpret. Furthermore, an extensive etiologic investigation is required to prove a role of *U. urealyticum* in NGU, including highly sensitive diagnostic tests for *Chlamydia trachomatis* and *M. genitalium*.[7] However, these organisms were not known at the time when many of the NGU studies were performed. Phenotyping and serotyping of ureaplasma isolates and antibody tests have not confirmed a pathogenic role for *U. urealyticum* in NGU. The difference in susceptibility of *U. urealyticum* and other possible causative agents of urethritis has been utilized in attempts to establish the role, if any, of *U. urealyticum* in NGU.[2,3] However, none of the studies have yielded conclusive results.

Ureaplasma urealyticum often recolonizes the genital tract of individuals after attempts to eradicate it by antibiotic therapy. This may be seen as a criterion for the organism belonging to the indigenous human microbial flora, meaning that it does not represent an exogenous pathogen.

Like most organisms found in the urogenital tract of men, *U. urealyticum* has also been proposed to be a causative agent of nonbacterial prostatitis. Cultures of urethral secretion, voided urine as well as expressed prostatic fluid do not prove an etiologic role of ureaplasmas in prostatitis because of the risk of contamination of the samples from nonprostatic sites. Likewise, antibiotic therapeutic trials cannot easily prove such a role of the agent in nonbacterial prostatitis.

Ureaplasma urealyticum is found in the lower genital tract in up to 75% of all women of reproductive age. It may ascend to the fallopian tubes.[13] Treatment of infertile couples with tetracyclines has provided inconclusive support for a role for *U. urealyticum* as a cause of infertility.

The higher recovery rate of *U. urealyticum* from babies with low birth weight than from infants of normal weight has remained a puzzling observation. There is also a statistical correlation of carriage of *U. urealyticum* with pre-term birth. Several studies have shown that *U. urealyticum* is a comparatively common isolate, not only from the urethra[31] but also from amniotic fluid in women with adverse pregnancy outcome, such as premature birth.[24] The organism may be recovered from the respiratory tract of newborns. Respiratory distress syndrome, the need for assisted ventilation, severe respiratory insufficiency and death of newborns have been found to be more common in those colonized than not colonized by *U. urealyticum* in the nasopharynx or elsewhere in the upper respiratory tract. Studies have not proved an etiologic role of *U. urealyticum* in chronic lung disease in persons born pre-term.

It is an important observation that *U. urealyticum*, like *M. hominis*, can cause meningoencephalitis in newborns. Such infections should be considered as a differential diagnosis in any investigation of meningitis in newborns, particularly when the CSF glucose level is normal.[15,20]

PATHOGENICITY

Pathogenetic mechanisms are not known for the vast majority of *Mycoplasma* spp. One obvious exception is *M. neurolyticum*, which produces a neurotoxin, explaining the course of infections by this animal pathogen.

Mycoplasmas are generally epiparasites, attaching to eukaryotic cell surfaces. However, the fact that *M. genitalium, M. fermentans* and *M. penetrans* can grow intracellularly means that the organisms can be protected from many host defense mechanism. For example, in experimentally infected vero cell cultures *M. genitalium* penetrated the cells. This capability may give the organism the ability to persist in AIDS patients, from whom the organisms have been recovered (see below).[21,32–38]

Both *Mycoplasma pneumoniae* and *M. genitalium* have a flask-like appearance under the electron microscope.[5] They both have an adherence organ. These structures probably represent a pathogenic mechanism. The adherence structure has a 170kDa epitope, which is shared by *M. pneumoniae* and *M. genitalium*. A distinct binding site for *M. pneumoniae* on mononuclear cells has also been identified. *Mycoplasma pneumoniae* is motile and produces hydrogen oxide, which may contribute to its pathogenicity.

Both *M. hominis* and *M. genitalium* are able to cause salpingitis experimental infections in subhuman primates.[39,40] Oviduct inoculation of *M. genitalium* in grivet monkeys and marmosets resulted in a moderate-to-severe endosalpingitis with consequent adhesions between the mucosal folds. The changes were similar to those found in experimental infections by *M. hominis* and *C. trachomatis* as well as being consistent with alterations seen in women naturally infected with these agents who had developed PID.

In tissue cell cultures of human fallopian tubes infected by *M. hominis*, a pathologic swelling or so-called 'ballooning' of the cilia has been seen (Fig. 234.4). Whether a similar phenomenon occurs in vivo in women who have contracted the organism is, however, not known.

In mice, estradiol predisposes animals to infection by *M. hominis*. Progesterone induces susceptibility to *M. genitalium* in the murine genital tract when the organism has been installed intravaginally. However, this does not account for experimental infection with *M. hominis* in this animal model.

Fig. 234.4 Swelling ('ballooning') of cilia in tissue cell cultures experimentally infected by *Mycoplasma hominis*.

Mycoplasma pneumoniae causes a polyclonal stimulation of both B and T lymphocytes and results in cytokine production. A marked increase in the total serum IgM is often seen in people infected by *M. pneumoniae*, often by as much as 100% or more.[30,41]

Antibodies directed against the blood group antigen (i.e. cold agglutinins) may occur in *M. pneumoniae* infection and may, although very seldom, cause hemolytic anemia and intravascular coagulation, which may be fatal.[26,27]

The development of antibodies to a number of tissue antigens (e.g. to brain[42] and kidney tissue epitopes) occurs as a transient autoimmune phenomenon in persons infected by *M. pneumoniae*, often without any obvious pathologic effects.

Ureaplasma urealyticum has the ability to split urea, which has been considered to be a mechanism by which the organism could cause stone formation in the urinary tract, including calculi formation in the kidney pelvices. Calculi formation has been seen in female rats experimentally infected by *U. urealyticum* after bladder installation of the organism. It is not clear, however, whether colonization by ureaplasmas occurs more easily in persons who have already developed stones in the urinary tract.

Ureaplasma urealyticum also expresses a specific immunoglobulin A1 protease that cleaves human immunoglobulin into Fab and Fc fragments, the clinical relevance of which is unknown.

Colonization with *U. urealyticum* in experimentally infected female mice is enhanced by estradiol therapy.

There have been several observations of a correlation between low birth weight and culture positivity for genital mycoplasmas and/or ureaplasmas from the nose and throat in newborns.[2,3] The influence on pregnancy outcome has remained difficult to explain. Therapeutic trials in which the organisms have been eradicated from the lower genital tract of pregnant women resulting in an increased birth weight of their offspring is an even more puzzling observation. Confounding, unrecognized factors might have played a role.

Mycoplasmas and AIDS

It has been claimed that *M. fermentans* might play a role in AIDS.[33,34,36] When first recovered from AIDS patients, the isolates of *M. fermentans* were named *M. incognitus*. The organism has been detected in urine samples and antigen of the organism has been detected in blood samples of HIV-infected persons.

Mycoplasma genitalium has been recovered from genital samples of AIDS patients.[21] In contrast to many of the infections observed in untreated AIDS patients, no relation between *M. genitalium* positivity on one hand and $CD4^+$ lymphocyte count, HIV p24 antigenemia and any opportunistic infections on the other has been demonstrated, and it is no longer believed that mycoplasma have any causative role.

PREVENTION

Prevention of mycoplasmal genital infections should follow the principles of any sexually transmitted infection, including partner notification and treatment of infected partners at the same time as the index case to prevent 'ping-pong' infections. However, there are no data proving the positive effect of such interventions.

As there is a markedly increased risk of tubal occlusion with each new episode of salpingitis and thereby a risk of infertility, eradication of *M. hominis* may be indicated in females who are vaginal carriers of the organism and who have a history of PID.

Treatment of pregnant women who are carriers of *M. hominis* and *U. urealyticum* to prevent obstetric and perinatal infections has been recommended, but there is no hard evidence for such a recommendation. It is unclear whether *M. genitalium* should be screened for and whether therapy should be given both to carriers and their sexual partners.

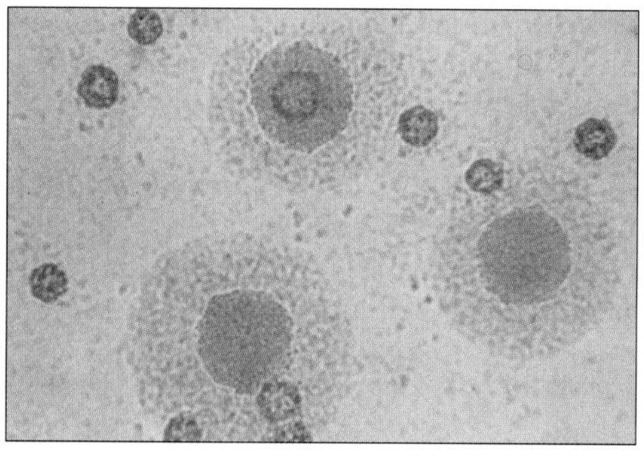

Fig. 234.5 Colonies of *Mycoplasma hominis* on PPLO agar with 'fried egg' appearance.

Prevention of mycoplasmal (i.e. *M. pneumoniae*) respiratory tract infections is generally not feasible.

DIAGNOSTIC MICROBIOLOGY

Mycoplasmas can be recovered on special pleuropneumonia-like organism (PPLO) agar media, where they produce colonies with a characteristic 'fried egg' morphology (Fig. 234.5). Growth inhibition on agar media by species-specific antibodies (lysis of organisms) has been used for speciation of mycoplasmas. Growth inhibition in broth cultures by specific antisera (e.g. in tests for interference with arginine metabolism by growing mycoplasmas) has also been used for this purpose. The latter test, however, requires reading the result at an unpredictable time after initiating the test, making it impractical to use.[10]

The suitability of each batch of mycoplasma medium should be checked before use (e.g. serum components may be toxic to the mycoplasma organisms). A number of commercial media are available. Solid media should be incubated at 36°C or 96.8°F in an atmosphere of 5% carbon dioxide (for ureaplasmas the concentration may be as high as 15%) and 95% nitrogen.[10]

Polymerase chain reaction (PCR) has become more frequently used for diagnosing mycoplasma infections.[31,43] Specific primers that assess not only the occurrence of the organism but also its species can be obtained. Anti-*M. pneumoniae* IgM antibodies are often not detected in pneumonia caused by the agent.[44] Also, secretory IgA antibodies to *M. pneumoniae* occur in cases with other types of respiratory tract infections and in healthy controls. Culture facilities are generally not available and, even if they are, cultures are often negative in cases where serologic tests indicate a current infection by the agent.

Mycoplasma pneumoniae

Attempts to diagnose *M. pneumoniae* infections by culture usually fail. If successful, it takes weeks before colonies (Fig. 234.6) can be detected when inspected under a microscope. *Mycoplasma pneumoniae* can be distinguished from other human *Mycoplasma* spp. by its

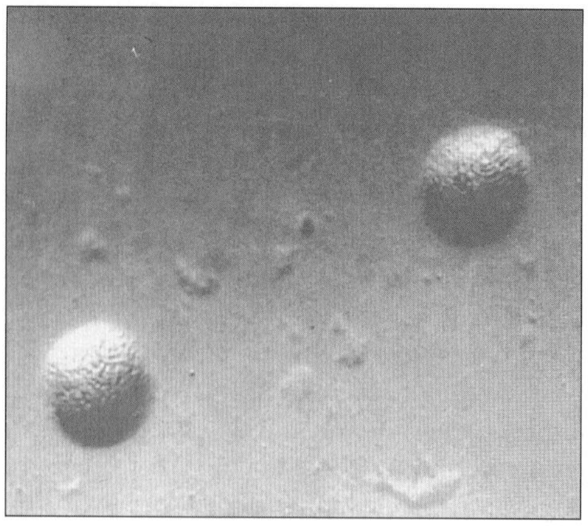

Fig. 234.6 Colonies of *Mycoplasma pneumoniae* on PPLO agar with 'golf ball' appearance.

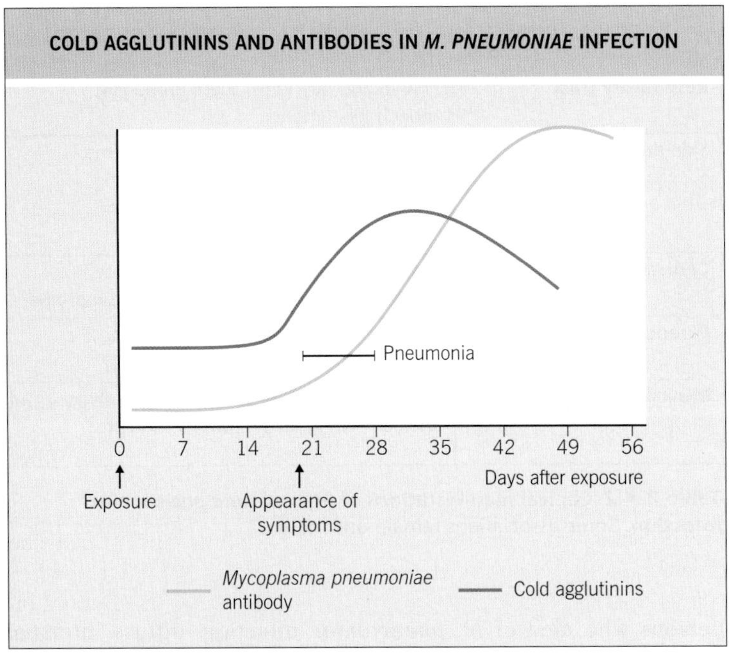

Fig. 234.7 Kinetics of appearance of cold agglutinins and specific antibodies to *Mycoplasma pneumoniae* related to time after being taken ill with *M. pneumoniae* pneumonia.

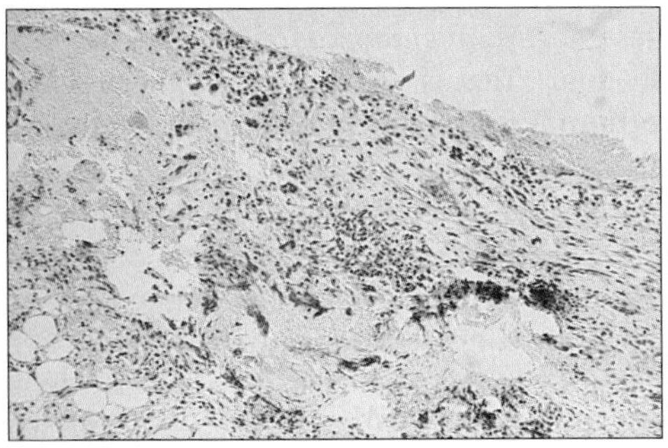

Fig. 234.8 Section of parametrium from which *Mycoplasma hominis* was recovered. The patient had parametritis and developed an antibody response to the organism.

ability to adsorb red blood cells, resulting in a mulberry-like appearance of the colonies.

Serology and detection of cold agglutinins have played a more important role in diagnosis of *M. pneumoniae* than culture studies (Fig. 234.7).[26] Detection of IgM antibodies to *M. pneumoniae* has a limited diagnostic value for detecting current infection. Cold agglutinins occur before specific antibodies to *M. pneumoniae* appear (see Fig. 234.7). However, detection of cold agglutinins alone has low sensitivity and specificity in patients with community-acquired pneumonia. The possibility of diagnosing *M. pneumoniae* pneumonia by one seropositive sample plus a positive cold agglutinin test has been stressed.[27] At admission, an IgM antibody response to *M. pneumoniae* has been shown in 86% of patients with *M. pneumoniae* pneumonia. However, some have questioned the diagnostic value of such antibody tests in routine practice. Approximately 20% of patients with such pneumonia have not developed a specific antibody response to *M. pneumoniae* at their first visit. Antibodies to a number of tissue antigens develop during the course of a *M. pneumoniae* infection,[42] the clinical significance of which has remained unestablished.

Progress in the diagnosis of infections by *M. pneumoniae* has been achieved by the use of nucleic acid-based techniques[43,45] (e.g. ^{125}I-labeled DNA probe), directed against sequences specific for *M. pneumoniae* rRNA (GenProbe) or probes. The test has the disadvantage of requiring metabolically active organisms but it has been claimed to be more sensitive than enzyme immunoassays. PCR tests can detect only 10^2–10^3 organisms/ml, but adequate internal controls are necessary to avoid false-negative results. The usefulness of PCR tests is limited in the post-therapy situation, as dead *M. pneumoniae* organisms may be detected. Such organisms are shed for up to 1 month after finishing antibiotic therapy. A comparison of the outcome of cultures, PCR tests and serology in suspected *M. pneumoniae* cases showed that, in 21 cases in which cultures were performed, 19 were found to harbor the organism and 14 of the same 21 cases were seropositive for the organism. Only two of another 62 culture- and serology-negative cases were positive for *M. pneumoniae* in a study using a PCR assay. Both sputum and pharyngeal swabs may be tested by PCR to prove a mycoplasma etiology in pneumonia cases.

Mycoplasma pneumoniae DNA has also been detected in intestinal biopsy samples of persons with inflammatory bowel disease (e.g. in cases of Crohn's disease and in those with ulcerative colitis as well as in healthy controls).[46]

Thus, there are obvious difficulties in diagnosing *M. pneumoniae* infections, even when laboratory support makes use of PCR assays. The use of more than one diagnostic test may be helpful. The clinical picture may also be misleading. For example, there may be difficulties in distinguishing between mycoplasmal and chlamydial infections.[47] The diagnostic difficulties have been stressed by the US Practice Guidelines for the Management of Community-acquired Pneumonia, which state that it is not possible to diagnose *M. pneumoniae* infection with any degree of accuracy in a routine health care situation.[28]

Mycoplasma hominis

Mycoplasma hominis is easy to isolate on agar media.[10] Isolates can be typed by homologous antisera, causing growth inhibition. The capacity of *M. hominis* to metabolize arginine can be tested by the production of ammonia as an end-product, the presence of which results in a pH increase that can be visualized by an indicator strip. Colonies of *M. hominis* produce pinpoint nonhemolytic colonies on blood agar plates. Polymerase chain reaction tests may also be used.[32]

Mycoplasma genitalium

Mycoplasma genitalium is difficult to grow on artificial media, which is why the introduction of PCR-based methods for its detection has been important. The organism is susceptible to thallium acetate. This may explain why it has been detected only recently, as thallium acetate has often been added to mycoplasma media to reduce any overgrowth of eubacteria and fungi.[7]

Ureaplasma urealyticum

Growth in a broth medium containing urea and an indicator causing a color change has been used to diagnose ureaplasmas.[10] This test is useful for detection of ureaplasmas in genital samples. Tests for the urea-splitting capability of ureaplasmas can also be carried out on agar media, where the color of colonies of *U. urealyticum* turns dark brown after adding the test substrate. Ureaplasmas do not grow in the presence of thallium acetate, which is often used in mycoplasma media to avoid overgrowth of other microbes. Using 16S rRNA gene-based PCR tests, *U. urealyticum* is more often detected in the lower female genital tract than by culture.[32]

CLINICAL MANIFESTATIONS

Women with *M. hominis* salpingitis may be afebrile and present with a malodorous vaginal discharge that is often characterized as 'having a smell of rotten fish'. They may have palpatory pain over the adnexa and pain at movement of the cervix during vaginal examination. However, as in PID of any etiology, mycoplasmal PID may be more or less asymptomatic.[13] *M. hominis* may cause parametritis (Fig. 234.8).

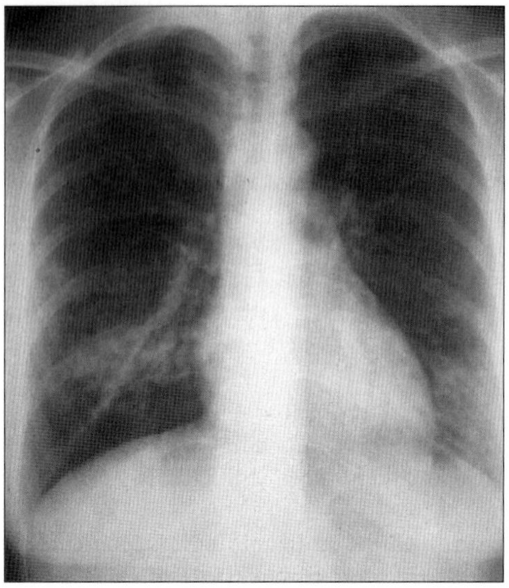

Fig. 234.9 *Mycoplasma pneumoniae* pneumonia. There were few signs on auscultation.

CLINICAL MANIFESTATIONS OF *MYCOPLASMA PNEUMONIAE* INFECTION	
Respiratory tract	Pharyngitis, laryngitis, acute bronchitis, bronchopneumonia
Skin and mucosa	Maculopapular and vesicular exanthema, urticaria, purpura, erythema nodosum, erythema multiforme, Stevens–Johnson syndrome
Central nervous system	Meningitis, meningoencephalitis, acute psychosis, cerebellitis, Guillian–Barré syndrome?
Parenchymatous organs	Pancreatitis, diabetes mellitus, non-specific reactive hepatitis, subacute thyroiditis?
Miscellaneous	Hemorrhagic bullous myringitis, hemolytic anemia, pericarditis, thromboembolism?

Table 234.2 Clinical manifestations of *Mycoplasma pneumoniae* infection. Some associations remain uncertain.

Mycoplasma hominis sepsis may be suspected in women who have aborted and who develop fever, particularly in cases in which bacterial blood cultures are negative for bacterial pathogens.

Symptoms of *M. pneumoniae* infections are initially malaise, muscle pain, headache, fever, throat pain, chills and nonproductive cough. The latter occurs in up to 90% of cases.[26,28,29,41,48] The symptoms and signs of mycoplasma pneumonia are more like those of a viral than a bacterial pneumonia. However, cough and headache do occur more often, and rhinitis less often, in mycoplasmal than viral pneumonia cases. Later, often after 1–2 weeks, cough may become productive and, although less commonly, hemorrhagic. The expectorate is often sparse. Cough may continue during the convalescent period. Tracheitis, bronchitis and tracheobronchitis may occur, but less often than pneumonia. Severe deterioration of the general condition may occur with high body temperature, due to the development of generalized aveolitis.

Findings on auscultation are often sparse or even normal, even when there are obvious radiographic changes. The alterations are usually unilateral and found in a lower lobe (Fig. 234.9). Chest radiography usually shows multiple interstitial or alveolar consolidation in one of the lower lobes, often radiating from the hilum. A solid lobular consolidation may be seen and there may be pleuritis. The chest radiographic findings may be mistaken for a viral pneumonia. Symptoms of fatigue may last for many months, and in children this may result in poor performance at school.[49] (see Chapter 34)

In children, the clinical course of a *M. pneumoniae* infection usually runs a milder course than in adults.[28] The infection in children may even pass as a clinically silent or relatively asymptomatic upper respiratory infection that ones pay no attention to. In elderly persons, the infection may manifest itself as pharyngitis, laryngitis or bronchitis rather than pneumonia.

Truly asymptomatic *M. pneumoniae* infections are uncommon. Only a small percentage of such infections run a clinically silent course as evidenced from serologic findings. Transient carriage of *M. pneumoniae* may occur after repeated exposure in those who have developed a cellular immunity to *M. pneumoniae*.

Mycoplasma pneumoniae infection has been associated with a large number of other conditions (Table 234.2) although in many cases evidence to support an etiologic role for *Mycoplasma* is uncertain.[30,41,48,50–53]

Death in infections with *M. pneumoniae* is very unusual. In such cases, either intravascular coagulation or complications from the central nervous system have been diagnosed. At autopsies of persons who died of *M. pneumoniae* infection, diffuse interstial pneumonia has been demonstrated. Other autopsy findings have included bronchial edema. Histology has revealed macrophage, lymphocyte and plasma cell infiltrates in bronchial tissue.

The broad spectrum of complications described in *M. pneumoniae* infections must be considered in the light of recent studies that have found that nucleic acid tests for *M. pneumoniae* may often be positive even in healthy individuals. That is, without serologic evidence of an ongoing acute infection, it is difficult to confirm any etiologic relationship to various conditions.

MANAGEMENT

Mycoplasmas are resistant to β-lactam antibiotics as they lack a cell wall and penicillin-binding proteins. They are generally susceptible to tetracyclines. Tetracycline resistance in *M. hominis* is, however, common in certain areas[54] and is often due to decreased intracellular uptake of the drug.[55]

Children should not be given tetracylines. Erythromycin is the drug of choice for children, except for infections by *M. hominis*, which has natural resistance to this antibiotic. The reason for this diversity from all other species of *Mycoplasma* is unknown. Clindamycin is a suitable alternative for *M. hominis* infections in newborns.

Azithromycin and clarithromycin are alternative drugs for the treatment of *M. pneumoniae* infections in adults. Intravenous treatment of *M. pneumoniae* pneumonia has not proved to be superior to oral therapy (see Chapter 34).

Mycoplasma genitalium has an antibiotic susceptibility pattern similar to that of *M. pneumoniae* (i.e. being susceptible to macrolides and tetracyclines).[56,57] Azithromycin has been recommended for therapy of *M. genitalium* infections.

Aminoglycosides and chloramphenicol are second- and third-line therapy alternatives. Chloramphenicol has, however, been used successfully to treat meningoencephalitis in newborns infected by tetracycline-resistant strains of *M. hominis*.

A number of antibiotics are less active against mycoplasmas than macrolides and tetracyclines (e.g. quinolones, such as cinoxacin, ciprofloxacin and norfloxacin). Sparfloxacin is the most active quinolone against *M. genitalium*.[57] Mycoplasmas, like ureaplasmas, are resistant to sulphonamides and trimethoprim–sulfamethoxazole.

Ureaplasmas are known to have a similar susceptibility pattern to mycoplasmas. However, they are usually susceptible to erythromycin, in contrast to *M. hominis*.

Mycoplasma pneumoniae pneumonia in adults can be treated with a macrolide or tetracycline.

For younger patients, apart from those infected by *M. hominis*, erythromycin can be given for 10–14 days with a dose adjusted to the weight of the infant or child under treatment.[28]

REFERENCES

1. Dienes L, Edsall F. Observation on the L-organism of Klieneberger. Proc Soc Exp Biol Med 1937;36:740–4.
2. Taylor-Robinson D, McCormack WM. The genital mycoplasmas. N Engl J Med 1980;302:1003–8.
3. McCormack M, Taylor-Robinson D. The genital mycoplasmas. In: Holmes KK, Mårdh PA, Sparling PF, *et al.*, eds. Sexually transmitted diseases. New York: McGraw-Hill; 1984:408–20.
4. Chanock RM, Hayflick L, Barile MF. Growth on artificial medium of an agent associated with atypical pneumoniae and its identification as a PPLO. Proc Nat Acad Sci (Wash) 1962;48:41–9.
5. Tully JG, Taylor-Robinson D, Rose DL, Cole RM, Bovo JM. *Mycoplasma genitalium*, a new species from the urogenital tract. Int J Syst Bact 1983;3:387–96.
6. Horner PJ, Gilroy CB, Thomas BJ, Naidoo ROM, Taylor-Robinson D. Association of *Mycoplasma genitalium* with acute non-gonococcal urethritis. Lancet 1983;342:582–5.
7. Taylor-Robinson D. *Mycoplasma genitalium* – an update. Int J STD AIDS 2002;13:145–51.
8. Shepard MC. The recovery of pleuro-pneumonia-like organisms from negro men with and without non-gonococcal urethritis. Am J Syph Gonor Vener Dis 1954;38:113–24.
9. Waites KB, Rudd PT, Crouse DT, *et al.* Chronic *Ureaplasma urealyticum* and *Mycoplasma hominis* infections of central nervous system in pre-term infants. Lancet 1988;1:17–21.
10. Mårdh P-A. Laboratory diagnosis of sexually transmitted diseases. Bacteria, chlamydiae and mycoplasmas. In: Holmes KK, Mårdh PA, Sparling PF, *et al.*, eds. Sexually transmitted diseases. New York: McGraw-Hill; 1984:829–55.
11. Glass JI, Lefkowitz EJ, Glass JS, *et al.* The complete sequence of the mucosal pathogen *Ureaplasma urealyticum.* Nature 2000;12:757–62.
12. Heggie AD, Bar-Shain D, Boxerbaum B, *et al.* Identification and quantification of ureaplasmas colonizing the respiratory tract and assessment of their role in the development of chronic lung disease in pre-term infants. Pediatr Infect Dis 2001;20:854–9.
13. Mårdh P-A, Weström L. Tubal and cervical cultures in acute salpingitis with special reference to *Mycoplasma hominis* and T-strain mycoplasmas. Br J Vener Dis 1970;46:179–86.
14. Mårdh P-A, Weström L. Antibodies to *Mycoplasma hominis* in patients with genital infections and in healthy controls. Br J Vener Dis 1970;46:390–7.
15. Hjelm E, Jonsell G, Linglöf T, Mårdh P-A, Möller BR, Sedin G. Meningitis in a newborn infant caused by *Mycoplasma hominis.* Acta Paediatr Scand 1980;69:415–8.
16. Mårdh P-A, Elshibly S, Kallings I, Hellberg D. Vaginal flora changes associated with *Mycoplasma hominis.* Am J Obstet Gynecol 1996;176:173–8.
17. Möller BR, Mårdh P-A, Ahrons S, Nüssler E. Infection with *Chlamydia trachomatis, Mycoplasma hominis* and *Neisseria gonorrhoeae* in patients with acute pelvic inflammatory disease. Sex Transm Dis 1981;8:198–202.
18. Donders GG, van Bulck B, Caudron J, *et al.* Relationship of bacterial vaginosis and mycoplasmas to the risk of spontaneous abortion. Am J Obstet Gynecol 2000;183:431–7.
19. Rudd PT, Brown MB, Cassell GH. A prospective study of mycoplasma infection in the pre-term infant. Isr J Med Sci 1984;20:899–901.
20. Mårdh P-A. *Mycoplasma hominis* infection of the central nervous system in newborn infants. Sex Transm Dis 1983;10:331–4.
21. Savio ML, Caruso A, Allegri R, *et al.* Detection of *Mycoplasma genitalium* from urethral swabs of human immunodeficiency virus-infected patients. Microbiologica 1996;19:203–10.
22. Mårdh P-A, Novikova N, Herbst A, Christiansen G. Prevalence of *M. hominis, M. genitalium* and *U. urealyticum* in 2nd and 3rd trimester pregnancy. 14th IOM Congress, Vienna, 7–12 July 2002. Abstract 366.
23. Manhart L, Holmes K, Dutro I. *Mycoplasma genitalium* is associated with mucopurulent cervicitis. 2002 National STD Prevention Conference, San Diego, March 4–7. Abstract.
24. Lu GC, Schewbke Jr, Duffy LB, *et al.* Midtrimester vaginal *Mycoplasma genitalium* in women with subsequent spontaneous pre-term birth. Am J Obstet Gynecol 2001;185:163–5.
25. Clausen HF, Fedder J, Drasbek M, *et al.* Serological investigation of *Mycoplasma genitalium* in infertile women. Hum Reprod 2001;16:1866–74.
26. Foy H, Grayston J, Kenny G, Alexander E, McMahan R. Epidemiology of *Mycoplasma pneumoniae* infection in families. JAMA 1966;197:859–66.
27. Lind K, Bentzon MW. Epidemiology of *Mycoplasma pneumoniae* in Denmark from 1958 to 1974. Infect J Epidemiol 1976;5:267–7.
28. Hammerschlag MR. *Mycoplasma pneumoniae* infection. Curr Opin Infect Dis 2001;14:181–6.
29. Ito I, Ishida T, Osawa M, *et al.* Culturally verified *Mycoplasma pneumoniae* pneumonia in Japan: a long-term observation from 1979–99. Epidemiol Infect 2001;127:365–7.
30. Biberfeld G. A study of *Mycoplasma pneumoniae* infections in families. Scand J Infect Dis 1969;1:39–46.
31. Aaltone R, Jalava J, Laurinkainen E, *et al.* Cervical *Ureaplasma urealyticum* colonization; comparison of PCR and culture for its detection and association with pre-term birth. Scand J Infect Dis 2002;34:35–40.
32. Horowitz S, Mazor M, Romero R, *et al.* Infection of the amniotic cavity with *Ureaplasma urealyticum* in the midtrimester of pregnancy. J Reprod Med 1995;40:375–9.
33. Blanchard A, Montagnier L. AIDS-associated mycoplasmas. Ann Rev Microbiol 1994;48:687–712.
34. Bebear C, de Barbeyrac B, Clerc M-T, Renaudin H, Fleury HJA. Mycoplasmas in HIV-1 seropositive patients. Lancet 1993;341:758–9.
35. Hawkins RE, Rickman LS, Vermund SH, Mitchell C. Association of mycoplasma and human immunodeficiency virus infection: detection of amplified *Mycoplasma fermentans* DNA in blood. J Infect Dis 1992;165:581–5.
36. Katseni VL, Gilroy CB, Ryait BK, *et al.* *Mycoplasma fermentans* in individuals seropositive and seronegative for HIV-1, Lancet 1993;341:271–3.
37. Behbahani N, Blanchard A, Cassell GII, Montagnier L. Phylogenetic analysis of *Mycoplasma penetrans*, isolated from HIV-infected patients. FEMS Microbiol Lett 1993;109:63–6.
38. Wang RY-H, Shih JW-K, Weiss SH, *et al.* *Mycoplasma penetrans* infection in male homosexuals with AIDS: high seroprevalence and association with Kaposi's sarcoma. Clin Infect Dis 1993;17:724–9.
39. Möller BR, Freundt EA. Monkey animal model for study of mycoplasmas infections of the urogenital tract. Sex Trans Dis 1983;10(Suppl.4):359–62.
40. Taylor-Robinson D, Furr PM, Tully JG, *et al.* Animal models of *Mycoplasma genitalium* urogenital infection. Isr J Med Sci 1987;23:561–4.
41. Ali N, Sillis M, Andrews BE, *et al.* The clinical spectrum and diagnosis of *Mycoplasma pneumoniae* infection. Q J Med 1986;38:241–51.
42. Biberfeld G. Antibodies to brain and other tissues in cases of *M. pneumoniae* infection. Clin Exp Immunol 1971;8:319–33.
43. Luneberg E, Jensen J, Forsch M. Detection of *Mycoplasma pneumoniae* by polymerase chain reaction and nonradioactive hybridization in microtiter plates. J Clin Microbiol 1993;31:1088–94.
44. Sillis M. The limitations of IgM assays in the serological diagnosis of *Mycoplasma pneumoniae* infections. J Med Microbiol 1990;33:253–8.
45. de Barbeyrac B, Bernet-Poggi C, Febrer F, *et al.* Detection of *Mycoplasma pneumoniae* and *Mycoplasma genitalium* in clinical samples by polymerase chain reaction. Clin Infect Dis 1993;17(Suppl.1):S83–9.
46. Chen W, Li D, Paulus B, *et al.* High prevalence of *Mycoplasma pneumoniae* in intestinal mucosal biopsies from patients with inflammatory bowel disease and controls. Dig Dis Sci 2001;46:2529–35.
47. Wadowsky RM, Castilla EA, Laus S, *et al.* Evaluation of *Chlamydia pneumoniae* and *Mycoplasma pneumoniae* as etiological agents of persistent cough in adolescents and adults. J Clin Microbiol 2000;40:637–40.
48. Murray HW, Masur H, Seenterfit LB, *et al.* The protean manifestations of *Mycoplasma pneumoniae* infections in adults. Am J Med 1975;58:229–42.
49. Kjellman, B. Pulmonary function in children with *Mycoplasma pneumoniae* pneumonia. Infection 1976;4(Suppl.1):71–4.
50. Sands MJ Jr, Satz JE, Turner WE, Soloff LA. Pericarditis and perimyocarditis associated with active *Mycoplasma pneumoniae* infection. Ann Intern Med 1977;86:544–8.
51. Mårdh P-A, Ursing B. The occurrence of acute pancreatitis in *Mycoplasma pneumoniae* infection. Scand J Infect Dis 1974;6:167–71.
52. Sterner G, Biberfeld G. Central nervous system complications of *Mycoplasma pneumoniae* infection. Scand J Infect Dis 1969;1:203–8.
53. Lambert HP. Syndrome with joint manifestations in association with *Mycoplasma pneumoniae* infection. Br Med J 1968;3:156–7.
54. Koutsky LA, Stamm WE, Brunham RC, *et al.* Persistance of *Mycoplasma hominis* after therapy: importance of tetracycline resistance and of coexisting vaginal flora. Sex Transm Dis 1983;10(Suppl.4):374–81.
55. Christiansson A, Mårdh P-A. Tetracycline resistance in *Mycoplasma hominis* due to decreased uptake over the cell membrane. Sex Transm Dis 1983;10(Suppl.4):371–3.
56. Bygdeman S, Mårdh P-A. Antibiotic susceptibility and susceptibility testing of *Mycoplasma hominis.* Sex Trans Dis 1983;10(Suppl.4):366–70.
57. Renaudin H, Tully JG, Bebear C. *In vitro* susceptibility of *Mycoplasma genitalium* to antibiotics. Antimicrob Agents Chemother 1992;36:870–2.

chapter

235 Rickettsia and Rickettsia-like Organisms

Peter R Mason & Patrick J Kelly

INTRODUCTION

The family Rickettsiaceae was established to accommodate fastidious, obligate intracellular, pleomorphic coccobacilli that could not survive for long outside the host cell and were transmitted to vertebrate hosts by arthropods. Members of the family usually stained weakly with Gram's stain but stained well with Giemsa or Gimenez stains. Cross-reactivity with antisera indicated that they shared common antigens, although this did not always lead to cross-protection against infection. Two organisms, *Rochalimaea* (now *Bartonella*), which was capable of growth in cell-free media, and *Coxiella*, which was able to survive outside a host cell for long periods of time, were regarded as rickettsias because of their morphologic similarity to other members of the family and because of their association with arthropod vectors. The family was further divided into three tribes, Rickettsiae, Ehrlichiae and Wolbachiae on the basis of pathogenicity for humans, pathogenicity for other vertebrate animals or exclusive association with insects, respectively. All human pathogens then known were classified in the tribe Rickettsiae.

Molecular techniques are now used to classify bacteria. Phylogenetic trees, constructed from 16S rRNA gene sequences, show three major groups of rickettsias, each belonging to a different subdivision of the Proteobacteria. The genera *Rickettsia*, *Ehrlichia* and *Anaplasma* belong to the α_1 subdivision, the genus *Bartonella* is found in the α_2 subdivision, and these two groups are themselves only distantly related to *Coxiella*, which belongs to the γ subdivision (Fig. 235.1).

Within the genus *Rickettsia*, three groups were originally recognized: the typhus group, the spotted fever group and the scrub typhus group. Molecular techniques show close affinity between the typhus and spotted fever groups, confirming their status as members of the same genus. On the basis of differences in ultrastructure and DNA composition the causative organism of scrub typhus, *Rickettsia tsutsugamushi*, has been reclassified into a new genus, *Orientia*. Some members of the genus *Ehrlichia* are now known to infect humans and cause diseases that were previously unrecognized. Finally, an increasing number of members of the genus *Bartonella* are being recognized as human pathogens and the cause of an expanding array of diseases. The field of rickettsiology is thus undergoing rapid change and expansion, with recognition of new organisms, of new relationships between rickettsias and other bacteria, and of new diseases.

The rickettsias are found on all continents, occupying many different ecologic niches and are associated with a variety of arthropod and vertebrate hosts. Human rickettsioses may be subclinical, may cause mild, self-limiting disease or may cause severe, life-threatening disease. In general, early treatment greatly decreases the severity of infection, with consequent reduction in the risk of mortality. Unfortunately, early diagnosis is seldom easy. Tick bites are often painless and go unnoticed. Rickettsioses are clinically non-specific, and isolation of organisms requires specialized techniques and carries a risk to laboratory staff. Serodiagnosis is simpler and safer, but the commonly used Weil–Felix agglutination test has low sensitivity and specificity. Even with more reliable serologic tests, false-negative results are common early in infection. A high index of suspicion is therefore critical in detecting rickettsioses. Fortunately, most infections respond rapidly to therapy with widely available antibiotics.

SPOTTED FEVER GROUP RICKETTSIAS

NATURE

The spotted fever group (SFG) rickettsias are intracellular coccobacilli, of 1μm × 0.3μm, that are found within the cytoplasm, and sometimes the nucleus, of the host eukaryotic cell. Ultrastructural studies show that the cell membrane has an inner leaflet that is thicker than the outer leaflet, a characteristic that distinguishes *Rickettsia* from related genera. The cell wall has a high content of lipopolysaccharides (LPS), which are highly immunogenic and are responsible for the serologic cross-reactivity of different SFG rickettsias. The LPS also confers cross-reactivity with *Proteus* and *Legionella*. High-molecular-weight proteins can be recognized in cell-wall preparations using sodium dodecyl sulfate polyacrylamide gel electrophoresis (SDS-PAGE), and specific antigenic characteristics have been demonstrated by Western blot.[1]

The SFG rickettsias do not grow on cell-free media but will grow in animals, including guinea pigs and embryonated chicken eggs, and in tissue cultures. Members of the group are often distinguished using reactivity with homologous and heterologous murine antisera in the micro-immunofluorescence (MIF) test. The reliability of this is

PHYLOGENETIC RELATIONSHIPS BETWEEN RICKETTSI BASED ON 16S rRNA GENE SEQUENCES

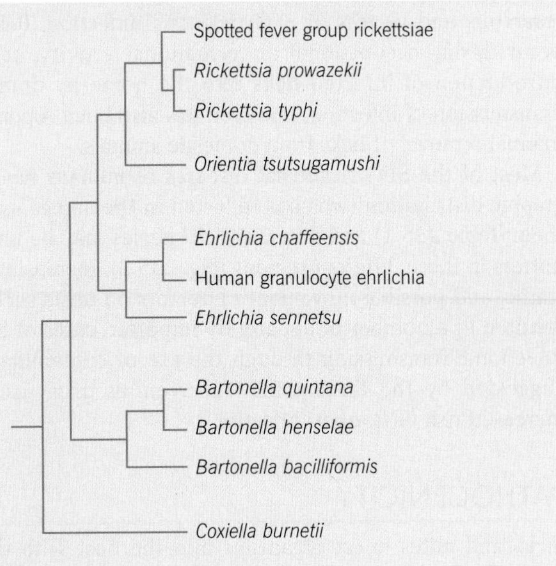

Fig. 235.1 Phylogenetic relationships between rickettsias based on 16S rRNA gene sequences.

unclear, however. If molecular criteria were strictly applied, many of the currently recognized 'species' would have to be considered serotypic variants of *Rickettsia rickettsii*, despite the differences in epidemiologic, antigenic and pathogenic characteristics.

Before 1984, only six SFG rickettsioses were recognized: Rocky Mountain spotted fever, Mediterranean spotted fever, Siberian tick typhus, Queensland tick typhus, rickettsialpox and Israeli spotted fever. Another eight new tick-borne rickettsioses have been described in recent years: Japanese spotted fever, Chinese spotted fever, Flinders Island spotted fever, Astrakhan fever, African tick bite fever and three so far unnamed spotted fevers (caused by *Rickettsia mongolotimonae*, *Rickettsia helvetica* and *Rickettsia slovaca*). In addition, the ELB agent, transmitted by cat fleas, is now recognized as *Rickettsia felis*, and is the causative agent of flea typhus in southern USA and parts of Mexico.[2] The list will undoubtedly continue to enlarge as more investigations are completed.

Sequence analysis of genes coding for outer membrane proteins indicate that there are three main complexes within the SFG:[3]

- cluster I: *Rickettsia conorii* complex, including Malish, M1, Moroccan and Indian tick typhus strains as well agents of Astrakhan fever and Israeli tick typhus;
- cluster II: *Rickettsia africae*, *Rickettsia parkeri*, *Rickettsia sibirica* and *R. mongolotimonae*; and
- cluster III: *Rickettsia aeschlimannii*, *Rickettsia rhipicephali*, *Rickettsia japonica*, *Rickettsia massiliae* and *Rickettsia montanensis*.

Other rickettsias, including *Rickettsia rickettsiae*, *R. japonica*, *R. slovaca* and Thai tick typhus rickettsias, show greater divergence in gene sequences and do not fit within these groups.

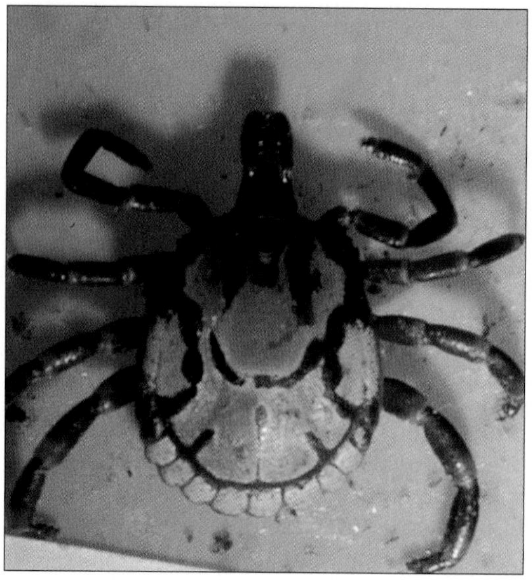

Fig. 235.2 ***Amblyomma hebraeum*, a typical tick vector of spotted fever group rickettsial infection.**

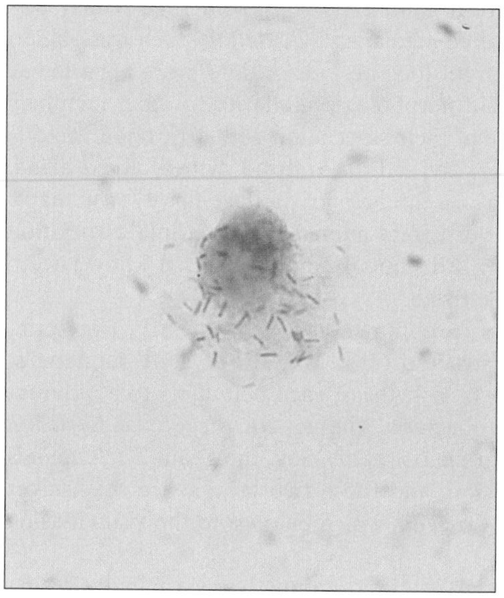

Fig. 235.3 Gimenez stain of tissue culture cells infected with spotted fever group rickettsias.

EPIDEMIOLOGY

With the exception of *Rickettsia akari* (transmitted by mites) and *R. felis* (transmitted by fleas), ticks are the vectors of most SFG rickettsias. The prevalence of infected ticks may be high.[4] Ticks probably become infected when they feed on rickettsemic wild or domestic animals and the rickettsias then multiply rapidly in many organs of this host. Infection of the ovaries and oocytes of a female tick leads to transovarial transmission, with at least some eggs becoming infected. Thereafter infections are transmitted trans-stadially, probably to all stages of the tick, and each time the larvae, nymphs or adults feed they may transmit the infection to the vertebrate host. Because all of the stages may be infected with rickettsias, ticks are regarded as both reservoirs and vectors of SFG rickettsial infection. Tick bites usually occur during occupational or recreational activity, or following the introduction of infected ticks into the home by domestic animals. Transmission of infection, however, has also been reported during the manual removal of ticks from domestic animals.

Most of the SFG rickettsial diseases of humans have limited geographic distribution (which is reflected in the names used to describe them; Table 235.1) and different tick species may be important transmitters in these different regions (Fig. 235.2). Increasing international traffic, and possibly movement of vectors on hosts such as birds, has resulted in a number of apparently imported cases of SFG rickettsial infection.[5] Transmission through the use of contaminated needles is suggested by the finding that intravenous drug users may be at increased risk of *R. akari* infection.[6]

PATHOGENICITY

Ticks and mites inject organisms into the host with their saliva. At the site of the bite the rickettsias localize in contiguous endothelial cells. Entry into the cells appears to be by receptor-mediated attachment and phagocytosis. Organisms move out of the phagolysosome, probably by means of a phospholipase, into the cytoplasm and start to divide by binary fission (Fig. 235.3). Dilation of rough endoplasmic reticulum can be observed after about 48 hours. The bacteria can move between adjacent cells via cytoplasmic extrusions, and movement is associated with polymerization of actin molecules. The resulting vascular damage results in moderate to severe lymphohistiocytic vasculitis, increased vascular permeability leading to edema, and cutaneous necrosis. As an eschar forms at the bite site and organisms escape from infected cells and spread via lymphatics to endothelial cells in blood vessels throughout the body. The resulting widespread cell death, vasculitis and increased vascular permeability result in the typical 'spotted fever' and 'tick typhus' diseases.

PREVENTION

Preventive measures include tick control programs for domestic and wild animals and the use of tick repellents on clothing and skin. Vaccines are effective in laboratory animals but have not been developed for use in humans. Antibiotic prophylaxis for people exposed to tick bites is not recommended as tetracyclines may be bacteriostatic and so only delay the onset of disease rather than prevent it.

GLOBAL DISTRIBUTION OF SPOTTED FEVER GROUP RICKETTSIAS

Geographic distribution	Human disease	Organism	Principal vector(s)
Africa			
Mediterranean	'Mediterranean spotted fever' 'Boutonneuse fever'	*Rickettsia conorii*	*Rhipicephalus sanguineus*
Sub-Saharan Africa	'Kenyan tick typhus', 'South African tick-bite fever'	*Rickettsia conorii*	*Rhipicephalus simus* *Haemaphysalis leachii* *Rhipicephalus mushamae*
	'African tick bite fever'	*Rickettsia africae*	*Amblyomma hebraeum* *Amblyomma variegatum*
Morocco	None known	*Rickettsia aeschlimannii*	*Hyalomma marginatum*
Central African Republic	None known	*Rickettsia rhipicephali*	*Rhipicephalus* spp.
	None known	*Rickettsia massiliae*	*Rhipicephalus lunulatus* *Rhipicephalus sulcatus* *Rhipicephalus mushamae*
America			
USA	'Rocky Mountain spotted fever'	*Rickettsia rickettsii*	*Dermacentor andersoni* *Dermacentor variabilis*
	None known	*Rickettsia belli*	*Dermacentor variabilis*
	None known	*Rickettsia montanensis*	*Dermacentor andersoni* *Dermacentor variabilis*
	None known	*Rickettsia parkeri*	*Amblyomma maculatum*
	None known	*Rickettsia rhipicephali*	*Dermacentor* spp.
	None known	*Rickettsia peacocki*	*Dermacentor andersoni*
	'Rickettsial pox'	*Rickettsia akari*	*Allodermanyssus sanguineus*
	'Rocky Mountain spotted fever'	*Rickettsia amblyommii*	*Amblyomma americanum*
Mexico, southern USA	Flea typhus	*Rickettsia felis*	*Ctenocephalides felis*
Brazil	'Brazilian spotted fever'	*Rickettsia rickettsii* (*R. sibirica*?)	*Amblyomma cajennense*
Guadeloupe	'Tick-borne fever'	*Rickettsia africae*	*Amblyomma variegatum*
Australasia			
Australia	'Queensland tick typhus'	*Rickettsia australis*	*Ixodes holocyclus*
Tasmania	'Flinders Island spotted fever'	*Rickettsia honei*	*Ixodes tasmani*
Asia			
Former Soviet Asia	'Siberian tick typhus'	*Rickettsia sibirica*	*Dermacentor nuttali* *Dermacentor marginatus* *Dermacentor silvarum* *Dermacentor sinicus* *Haemaphysalis concinna*
Japan	'Japanese spotted fever'	*Rickettsia japonica*	*Dermacentor taiwanensis?*
Thailand	'Thai tick typhus'	'TTT rickettsia'	*Rhipicephalus sanguineus* *Ixodes* spp.
China	'Chinese spotted fever'	*Rickettsia heilongjiangjii*	*Dermacentor silvarum*
		Rickettsia hulinii	*Haemaphysalis concinna*
		Rickettsia mongolotimonae	*Hyalomma asiaticum*
India	'Indian tick typhus'	*Rickettsia conorii*	*Rhipicephalus sanguineus*
Astrakhan	'Astrakhan spotted fever'	'Astrakhan SFG rickettsia'	*Rhipicephalus sanguineus* *Rhipicephalus pumulio*
Israel	'Israeli spotted fever'	'ISF rickettsia'	*Rhipicephalus sanguineus*
Europe			
Mediterranean coast	'Mediterranean spotted fever' 'Boutonneuse fever'	*Rickettsia conorii*	*Rhipicephalus sanguineus*
European Russia	'Siberian tick typhus'	*Rickettsia sibirica*	*Dermacentor nuttali* *Dermacentor marginatus* *Dermacentor silvarum* *Haemaphysalis concinna*
Germany	Flea typhus	*Rickettsia felis*	Not known
Slovakia, Switzerland, France, Portugal	Febrile illness, meningoencephalitis	*Rickettsia slovaca*	*Dermacentor marginatus*
Switzerland, France, Sweden	Fever, myocarditis	*Rickettsia helvetica*	*Ixodes ricinus*
France	Fever, eschar, lymphangitis	*Rickettsia mongolotimonae*	Not known
	None known	*Rickettsia rhipicephali*	*Rhipicephalus sanguineus*
France, Greece, Portugal	None known *Rhipicephalus turanicus*	*Rickettsia massiliae*	*Rhipicephalus sanguineus*
Russia	Rickettsialpox	*Rickettsia akari*	*Allodermanyssus sanguineus*

Table 235.1 Global distribution of spotted fever group rickettsias.

DIAGNOSTIC MICROBIOLOGY

Early diagnosis is necessary for prompt and appropriate therapy, a factor that significantly reduces morbidity and mortality. A history of tick-bite, the presence of an eschar at the bite site, fever, headache and rash are the classic features of SFG rickettsioses, but these may occur together in only 50–75% of patients. Tick bites are usually painless and may go unnoticed, particularly if they occur in the anogenital region or among the hairs on the scalp. The lesion at the bite site may be confused with traumatic, parasitic, bacterial or viral skin lesions. Fever, headache and rash may be due to a variety of causes. There are, therefore, no clinical or epidemiologic findings that are reliable in diagnosis.

Spotted fever group rickettsias can be isolated from blood or from biopsies of the eschar, using rodents or embryonated chick eggs. Organisms may not, however, be detected for a week or more after inoculation, and special laboratory facilities are needed. Close attention to safety is required in order to prevent transmission to laboratory workers. The centrifugation-shell vial technique, where samples are centrifuged on to a cell monolayer, may reduce the time for detection to 3–4 days.

Rickettsial antigens can be detected in endothelial cells in dermal blood vessels by direct immunofluorescence staining of frozen skin sections from the eschar or sites affected by rash. Direct immunofluorescence may also be used to detect antigens in circulating endothelial cells isolated from whole blood. Even greater sensitivity may be achieved with polymerase chain reaction (PCR) assays, using various primers.[7] These technologies are, however, only rarely available in diagnostic laboratories.

The classic serologic test for rickettsial infection is the Weil–Felix test, which relies on the antigenic cross-reactivity between epitopes in the LPS of *Rickettsia* spp. and in particular strains of *Proteus* spp. Although very simple, and widely available, the test has low specificity and sensitivity and is regarded as unacceptable for accurate diagnosis. There are a number of other tests such as latex agglutination, hemagglutination, indirect fluorescent antibody (IFA) and the enzyme-linked immunosorbent assay (ELISA).[7] The latter two show high sensitivity and can be adapted to detect different antibody isotypes, which may be useful in acute infections. There is extensive cross-reactivity of sera with the different species of SFG rickettsias, and so IFA or ELISA cannot be reliably used to make a specific diagnosis. Recently, dried blood spots have been shown to be effective for serologic testing.[8]

Demonstration of rising titers in paired sera is more reliable than examination of a single specimen, although this is seldom of benefit since treatment must be initiated as early as possible. Western blotting may detect significant antibody titers one day earlier than IFA or ELISA, but patients who present soon after the onset of symptoms may have antibody titers below the threshold of detection by any test (Fig. 235.4). Kinetic studies show that IgM and IgG antibodies appear 3–10 days after the appearance of symptoms, and peak titers are reached after 3–4 weeks. Titers then decline slowly, and IgM and IgG are still detectable after 1 and 4 years, respectively. Administration of therapy within 2 days of the onset of symptoms may abrogate antibody production.

WESTERN BLOT TECHNIQUE IN SPOTTED FEVER GROUP INFECTION

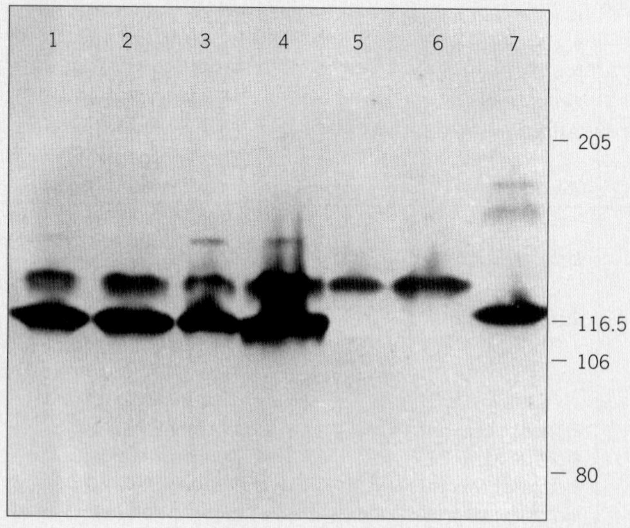

Fig. 235.4 Western blot technique in spotted fever group infection. Western blot of pooled mouse antisera to *Rickettsia africae* – human isolate (lane 1), *Rickettsia africae* – tick isolate (lanes 2–4), *Rickettsia conorii* – Kenyan strain (lane 5), *Rickettsia conorii* – Moroccan strain (lane 6) and Israeli SFG rickettsia (lane 7). Molecular masses (in thousands) are shown.

CLINICAL MANIFESTATIONS

The SFG rickettsioses are usually named after the geographic region in which they are detected (e.g. 'Rocky Mountain spotted fever', 'Mediterranean spotted fever', 'African tick bite fever', 'Indian tick typhus', etc.). After an incubation period of 4–10 days, common clinical features in Rocky Mountain spotted fever include:[9]

- an eschar or '*tache noire*' at the site of tick attachment;
- regional lymphadenopathy;
- fever (100.4–104°F (38–40°C));
- severe headache;
- chills;
- joint and muscle pain;
- malaise; and
- general weakness.

Within 3–4 days of the onset of fever, a maculopapular rash may develop on the trunk and extremities, frequently but not consistently including the soles and the palms. If untreated, the fever persists for 6–12 days and the rash may still be visible for up to 3 weeks. In African tick bite fever, and other SFG infections, pyrexia, headache and lymphadenopathy may be common but a rash is seen infrequently.[10]

Many organs may become involved, with hepatomegaly and splenomegaly and gastrointestinal symptoms such as vomiting, diarrhea and abdominal discomfort. Nephritis and renal failure may occur, and cardiac and circulatory abnormalities such as dysrhythmia, myocarditis, pericarditis, heart failure, deep venous thrombosis and embolism have been described. Pulmonary disorders such as pneumonitis and pleuritis and neurologic signs including impaired consciousness, seizures and vertigo may occur.[11]

Hematologic abnormalities include anemia and thrombocytopenia, with neutropenia in the acute phase of the disease and leukocytosis in the later stages. Biochemical changes include decreased levels of protein, particularly albumin, sodium, potassium and chloride during the first 10 days of the disease. Alkaline phosphatase, alanine aminotransferase and aspartate aminotransferase are usually elevated. Creatinine phosphokinase and lactic dehydrogenase are also often raised in acute infection. Cytokine abnormalities may also be seen, with raised levels of macrophage colony stimulating factor, interleukin (IL)-1β, IL-10, interferon-γ and tumor necrosis factor-α.

Predisposing factors for the development of severe infections include initiation of treatment after the seventh day of illness, old age, diabetes, cardiac insufficiency, heavy smoking, alcoholism, chronic liver disease and glucose-6-phosphate dehydrogenase deficiency.

MANAGEMENT

Based on in-vitro susceptibility testing and in-vivo experience, doxycycline is the currently recommended drug of choice for the treatment of the SFG rickettsioses.[12,13] The most commonly used regimen is 200mg daily for 2–5 days or until 24 hours after defervescence. Two single 200mg doses of doxycycline are also effective. Ciprofloxacin has been shown to be at least as effective as doxycycline. Treatment for 5 days with the macrolide josamycin has been successful in children and pregnant women in whom quinolones are not considered safe. Other macrolides, such as clarithromycin, have been shown to have in-vitro activity against a number of rickettsias[14] and may be useful in treatment. Treatment failure has been reported with chloramphenicol. The aminoglycosides, β lactams, erythromycin and trimethoprim–sulfamethoxazole are ineffective, and the latter is in fact contraindicated as it may stimulate bacterial growth and increase the severity of disease. Studies indicate there may be considerable heterogeneity in susceptibility to rifampin (rifampicin), and this may explain discrepancies in the outcome of treatment with this antibiotic.[12]

TYPHUS GROUP RICKETTSIAS

NATURE

Rickettsia typhi is the etiologic agent of endemic or murine typhus and *Rickettsia prowazekii* is the agent of epidemic typhus. They are both small, Gram-negative coccobacilli and, as with other members of the genus *Rickettsia*, their outer walls have an inner leaflet that is thicker than the outer. A polysaccharide slime layer may cover the outer leaflet, although its function is unknown and it is not associated with virulence.

There is considerable sharing of antigens by these two rickettsias and, while this gives cross-immunity, it creates problems in serologic surveys. The surface antigens include both high-molecular-weight proteins and low-molecular-weight LPS. The latter do not react with monoclonal antibodies to LPS of SFG rickettsia, suggesting structural differences. Combinations of immunofluorescence tests and Western blots can help to distinguish epidemic and endemic typhus in most cases.[15] Species specific epitopes occur on a 120kDa major surface protein, and monoclonal antibodies to these can distinguish *R. typhi* from *R. prowazekii.*

The complete genome sequence of *R. prowazekii* has been published, although less is known about *R. typhi.*[16]

EPIDEMIOLOGY

Endemic typhus, caused by *R. typhi*, is transmitted by the rat flea *Xenopsylla cheopsis* and is distributed throughout the world, but particularly in developing countries where there is close contact between humans and rodents. *Rickettsia prowazekii*, causing epidemic typhus, is transmitted in the feces of infected body lice, *Pediculus humanus* var. *corporis*, and occurs in epidemic foci where conditions are disrupted by poverty, famine, wars or natural disasters (Table 235.2). The historic association between epidemic typhus and war has been noted by many authors but, in recent years, the disease has been described mainly from disaster areas in Africa, such as Burundi,[17] and from outbreaks in Central and South America. Epidemic typhus occurs occasionally in developed countries and, while many such infections are probably imported, some appear to be locally acquired.[18] Older people, who may have had contact with epidemic typhus years before, may serve as a source of epidemics in areas in, for instance, eastern Europe, where conflict and political turmoil have disrupted normal living conditions.

COMPARISON OF FEATURES OF ENDEMIC AND EPIDEMIC TYPHUS		
	Endemic typhus	**Epidemic typhus**
Causative agent	*Rickettsia typhi*	*Rickettsia prowazekii*
Vector	Rat flea	Human louse
Occurrence	Worldwide	Outbreaks associated with war, famine
Onset	Slow	Sudden
Eschar	Rare	Rare
Lymphadenopathy	Rare	Rare
Rash	Mascular, becoming papular	Macular, becoming petechial or necrotic
CNS symptoms	Rare, mild	Common, sereve
Duration	1–2 weeks	3–4 weeks
Mortality	<5%	Up to 60%
Recrudescence	Does not occur	Brill–Zinsser disease may occur
Diagnosis	Weil–Felix (OX 19), immunofluorescent assay, extensive cross-reactivity	

Table 235.2 Comparison of features of endemic and epidemic typhus.

PATHOGENICITY

After multiplication at the injection site, there is hematogenous spread to endothelial cells of capillaries and small veins throughout the body. The rickettsias invade the cytoplasm of host cells but not the nucleus. Unlike SFG rickettsias, *R. prowazekii* grows to large numbers without causing significant injury until cell lysis. Polymerization of actin filaments is not a characteristic of typhus group infection, suggesting that these rickettsias do not migrate through the cytoplasm or move directly from one cell to another. Fibrin and platelet deposition in infected blood vessels leads to perivascular infiltration, and this may lead to local thrombosis, which affects many organs but particularly the heart, kidney and liver.

PREVENTION

Vector control with insecticides such as permethrin powder (1%) at doses of 30–50g for an adult and 15–25g for a child is the mainstay of protection. Insecticide should also be applied at 125–250mg/m^2 to kill lice in clothes and bedding. For endemic typhus both the normal murine host of the vector and the vector itself are the target of control measures. Insecticides can be used in buildings where rodents abound, and when the flea population has been reduced traps are used to limit the rodent population. Insecticide applied around the traps ensures control of fleas leaving the dead host. A recombinant 120kDa protein has been shown to confer protection against *R. prowazekii* in laboratory animals but there is little information on safety and efficacy in humans. Older vaccines, produced in yolk sacs, are protective but may induce non-specific reactions in recipients.

DIAGNOSTIC MICROBIOLOGY

A history of exposure to the vector is a crucial aid in the diagnosis of typhus. Isolated cases of epidemic typhus occur rarely,[19,20] and usually there is a focus associated with war, famine or other disaster.[17] Organisms can be recovered from blood, using cell or animal cultures, and shell-vial assays using human embryonic lung fibroblasts may be useful. Organisms are highly infectious and safety facilities are essential.

Antibodies to typhus group rickettsias develop within 1–2 weeks of illness in the majority of patients. In the Weil–Felix test there is a rise in the agglutination titer with OX19 *Proteus vulgaris* antigen, but the low specificity of this test makes it unreliable. More sensitive and specific tests, such as IFA and ELISA, are available. There is extensive cross-reactivity between *R. typhi* and *R. prowazekii*, and infections can be distinguished by serology sometimes only with difficulty.[15] Cross-reactivity with some SFG rickettsial antigens may also occur, adding further to the difficulties of accurate serologic diagnosis. Detection of DNA sequences by PCR has been described[18] and has been used to detect *R. prowazekii* in cerebrospinal fluid.[19]

CLINICAL MANIFESTATIONS

The clinical features of endemic and epidemic typhus are similar, although the former is a milder disease. After an incubation period of 7–14 days, there is a high fever (>102°F (>39°C)), with headache, backache, chills, malaise and generalized pain. In epidemic typhus the onset is sudden but in endemic typhus signs of the infection develop over several days. Eschars, lymphadenopathy and splenomegaly are unusual features. A macular rash develops between day 5 and day 7 of the illness but it may be absent in 50% of endemic typhus cases, especially in children. Unlike SFG rickettsial infections, the rash is more prominent on the trunk than on the limbs and rarely involves the face, palms or soles. In epidemic typhus, a pink macular rash usually spreads from axillary regions to the trunk and limbs.[20] The rash may become petechial or necrotic.

Invasion into the central nervous system is characteristic and confusion, coma, meningitis, delirium or manic symptoms develop toward the end of the first week, especially, although not exclusively, in epidemic typhus. Other features of infection include pulmonary (pneumonitis, bronchitis, bronchiolitis), cardiovascular (myocarditis, hypotension, tachycardia) and renal (oliguria) dysfunction. Similar but milder symptoms occur in endemic typhus.

If untreated, symptoms persist for 1–2 weeks (endemic typhus) or 3–4 weeks (epidemic typhus). In epidemic typhus the mortality can be over 40% but in endemic typhus mortality is low and is usually restricted to the elderly or immunocompromised. Recovery in epidemic typhus is slow, with convalescence lasting several months, while in endemic typhus defervescence and recovery occurs within 2–3 days of commencing therapy.

Recrudescent typhus (Brill–Zinsser disease) can occur years after patients show clinical recovery from epidemic typhus, usually at a time of immunodepression. Relapses present as a mild febrile illness, often without a rash, and diagnosis requires a history of previous rickettsial disease. The site and mechanism of survival of rickettsias within the body is not known, but they remain virulent and are transmissible to lice. Testing, contact tracing and the implementation of delousing programs may be needed to prevent outbreaks arising from recrudescent epidemic typhus.

MANAGEMENT

In-vitro antibiotic tests show both *R. typhi* and *R. prowazekii* are susceptible to tetracyclines, chloramphenicol and erythromycin. Resistance to erythromycin may emerge rapidly in vivo, and treatment failure has been reported in Brill–Zinsser disease with azithromycin. As with other rickettsial diseases, doxycycline is the recommended therapy in typhus infections, and quinolones may be suitable alternatives. Patients become afebrile within 3 days of starting treatment, but treatment should continue for 2–3 days longer to prevent relapse.

SCRUB TYPHUS

NATURE

Unlike true *Rickettsia* spp., the outer leaflet of the cell membrane of the agent of scrub typhus is thicker than the inner leaflet. This and other structural, immunologic and genotypic characteristics led to the reclassification of this agent as *Orientia tsutsugamushi*.[21]

Orientia tsutsugamushi is a weakly Gram-negative, obligate intracellular coccobacillus that can be cultured in fertilized eggs or in cell monolayers, where it forms plaques. In human cells, the bacteria are 1.2–1.6μm by 0.5–0.6μm, but in insect cells they may grow considerably longer (up to 4μm). Escape from the intracellular environment is via projections on the cell surface and is not necessarily related to cell damage.

Different strains can be recognized on the basis of serologic reactivities but they are not associated with a specific vector, geographic area or host species. Indeed, different serotypes of *O. tsutsugamushi* have been detected in the same host at the same time. An immunodominant 56kDa major outer membrane protein is found in all isolates, although there may be variation in amino acid sequences in this protein.

EPIDEMIOLOGY

Scrub typhus is a disease that occurs most frequently in South East Asia, but it has been reported from the Indian subcontinent, Australia and from Astrakhan in central Asia. Infections may be endemic or seasonal, depending to a large extent on the numbers of the vector, namely mites of the genus *Leptotrombidium*. These mites feed on vertebrates only in their larval stage, the nymphs and adults feeding on organic matter in the soil. The larva or 'chigger' takes only a single meal, and so can infect only one host. In the mite, rickettsias multiply in many organs, and are transmitted transovarially to the offspring. They do not, however, infect spermatogonal cells and so are not transmitted from male to female. Sex ratio distortions occur in some infected mite populations, with the almost complete absence of males. The mechanism for this is not known, but other related bacteria are associated with parthenogenesis and male-killing in insects.

In areas where ideal climatic conditions, vegetation and hosts are present, hyperendemic 'mite islands' may occur. In these areas transmission of scrub typhus is rapid and frequent.[22]

The usual vertebrate hosts for the mites are rats, mice and voles. In naturally infected rodents, rickettsemia may last several months. The significance of rickettsemia is unknown, however, since chiggers feed on tissue juices rather than blood, and the majority of mite infections are maintained by transovarian transmission rather than by infection from vertebrate reservoirs.

The recovery of viable *O. tsutsugamushi* from packed red cells has raised the possibility of transmission via blood transfusion from asymptomatic donors[23] and cell filtration or the use of psoralen photochemistry have been suggested as ways of preventing this.

PATHOGENESIS

Organisms are introduced into the skin by the bite of the mite, and adherence to cell surfaces is mediated by specific polypeptides of about 54–56kDa. Monoclonal antibodies directed against these can differentiate serotypes that may show differing degrees of virulence. *Orientia* induce host cell phagocytosis in order to enter cells and then escape to the cytoplasm, through which they migrate using microtubules.[24] Endothelial cells are the main targets of *O. tsutsugamushi*, and cell culture studies indicate that they induce apoptosis.[25]

Multiplication occurs in the endothelial cells of many organs, and organisms have been recovered from the heart, lung, brain, kidney, pancreas and skin. Spread is via the lymphatics and blood stream and, while initially regional, lymphadenopathy quickly becomes generalized. Proinflammatory cytokines such as IL-6 and IL-8 may be stimulated during infection.

PREVENTION

No vaccines are available for scrub typhus, and prevention is by use of insect repellents such as DEET (diethyl toluamide) or DEPA (diethyl phenyl acetamide) to reduce the risk of being bitten, and both of these compounds can be used on clothing. Rapid removal of mites is recommended since they do not feed until several hours after attachment.

DIAGNOSTIC MICROBIOLOGY

Scrub typhus should be suspected in patients from endemic areas who present with high fever and lymphadenopathy. Hematologic signs – a neutropenia and/or mononucleosis – are not specific, and most infections are diagnosed by serology. The Weil–Felix test detects cross-reacting antibodies that agglutinate the OXK strain of *Proteus*, probably through common epitopes on membrane LPS molecules. The test is rapid and simple but unreliable, with a sensitivity of less than 50%. The IFA is more specific but requires at least four antigenically distinct strains of *O. tsutsugamushi*, because responses may be serotype-specific.[26] Hemagglutination using recombinant 56kDa protein has been found to be sensitive and specific, and rapid testing for IgM and IgG antibodies by an immunochromatography flow assay has been described.[27] A PCR assay uses primers derived from the gene coding for the 56kDa protein, and can be used to detect bacteria in blood with high sensitivity.[23,28]

CLINICAL MANIFESTATIONS

The presentation of scrub typhus depends on features of both host and pathogen and can vary from a mild, inapparent infection to a fulminant, rapidly fatal disease. After the bite of an infected mite, incubation takes 1–3 weeks. A vesicular lesion forms at the site of the bite in about 75% cases, particularly in visitors to infective areas, and develops into a necrotic eschar. Systemic disease is indicated by a sudden onset high fever (>102°F (>39°C)), with headache, myalgia and regional and generalized lymphadenopathy, the latter particularly in patients who do not develop an eschar. A maculopapular rash appears about 5–6 days after onset in up to 80% cases in some studies.[29] Purpuric or hemorrhagic lesions are rare and transient. In the absence of treatment, defervescence starts by the end of week 3.

Neurologic signs such as lethargy, asthenia, confusion and delirium may occur. Respiratory symptoms are reported frequently, and radiologic abnormalities may be common.[29] Retinal vein occlusion with retinal hemorrhage, gastrointestinal vasculitis, pericarditis, myocarditis, acute renal failure and encephalomyelitis have all been reported as serious complications of scrub typhus.

Recently it was shown that there was a significant reduction in HIV-1 viral load during acute *Orientia* infection.[30] Moreover, sera from HIV-1 negative patients who had scrub typhus had potent HIV-1 suppressive effects in vitro, indicating the release of HIV-1 suppressive agents during scrub typhus infection. These findings are under further investigation.

MANAGEMENT

As with other rickettsial infections, tetracycline antibiotics are the drugs of choice in treatment. With doxycycline defervescence usually occurs within 24 hours. Resistance may occur in some areas, such as northern Thailand. Rifampin or azithromycin may be useful alternatives, and chloramphenicol may be effective.

HUMAN EHRLICHIOSIS

NATURE

The tribe Ehrlichiae was originally established to include veterinary pathogens such as *Anaplasma marginale*, *Cowdria ruminantium*, *Ehrlichia canis* and *Ehrlichia phagocytophila*. The first human infection with an *Ehrlichia* species, thought to be *E. canis*, was described in 1987 and, shortly after this, retrospective examination of sera from patients who had suspected SFG rickettsioses demonstrated many who had antibodies reactive with *E. canis* antigen. Prospective studies showed that human ehrlichiosis occurred frequently in some parts of the USA.[31] The application of tissue culture techniques led to the isolation of an *Ehrlichia* species from the blood of a febrile soldier at Fort Chaffee, Arkansas and its description as a new species, *Ehrlichia chaffeensis*.[32] The two species, *E. canis* and *E. chaffeensis*, share a number of antigens, and it is likely that at least some reports of *E. canis* infection in humans may be serologic cross-reactivity.

Sequence analysis of ehrlichial 16S rRNA and other genes suggests that there are three related genogroups: the *Ehrlichia*, the *Anaplasma* and the *Neorickettsia* (Table 235.3). Changes in nomenclature have been proposed to unify members of each of the genogroups into a single genus.[33] The agent of human granulocytic ehrlichiosis (HGE) is so similar to *E. phagocytophila* and *Ehrlichia equi* that all three are included in a single species, *Anaplasma phagocytophila*. It remains to be seen if this proposed classification becomes widely accepted.

It is now recognized that there are two etiologically and epidemiologically distinct forms of disease: human monocytic ehrlichiosis (HME) and HGE. *Ehrlichia chaffeensis* is the main agent of HME. While the other species that invade monocytes, such as *E. canis*, may be human pathogens, their role in HME is at best a minor one. The agent of HGE is a member of the *E. phagocytophila* group, and both this agent and *Ehrlichia ewingii* invade granulocytes.[34] Serologic evidence from Japan suggests that *Ehrlichia muris* may also occasionally infect humans, but no isolates have been made.

The characteristic structures of ehrlichias, visible by light microscopy, are the morulas that lie within vacuoles in host cells (Fig. 235.5). Electron microscopy has shown the morulas to be aggregates of bacteria with two distinct morphologic forms. Larger (1μm in diameter) reticulate forms have evenly dispersed nucleoid filaments and ribosomes, while smaller forms (0.6μm in diameter) have filaments and ribosomes that are condensed in a central mass. These small forms are often actively dividing by binary fission. The cell wall of members of the genus *Ehrlichia* has outer and inner leaflets of equal thickness.

EPIDEMIOLOGY

Both HME and HGE have been detected in clinical samples from the USA and Europe. While there is serologic evidence of these infections in Africa, South America and Israel, the organisms are closely related and cross-reactions occur within and between groups. Isolation of organisms and/or molecular identification of pathogens will be needed to confirm the distribution of these two infections. It is probable that many infections go unrecognized because of the lack of specific clinical features and the difficulty of diagnosis. A prospective surveillance study of hospitalized febrile patients in Georgia showed that the incidence of human ehrlichiosis was six times that of Rocky Mountain spotted fever.[31]

Table 235.3 Genogroups of ehrlichias.

GENOGROUPS OF EHRLICHIAS				
	Human infection	Animal infection	Vector	Host cell
Group I: *Ehrlichia* group				
Ehrlichia chaffeensis	Yes	Deer	*Amblyomma*	Monocyte/macrophage
Ehrlichia canis	Possibly	Dogs	*Rhipicephalus*	Monocyte/macrophage
Ehrlichia ewingii	Yes	Dogs	*Amblyomma*	Neutrophil
Ehrlichia muris	Possibly	Vole	?	Monocyte/macrophage
Ehrlichia ruminantium	No	Cattle, sheep, goats	*Amblyomma*	Endothelium
Group II: *Anaplasma* group				
Anaplasma bovis	No	Cattle	*Boophilus*	Erythrocyte
Anaplasma platys	No	Dogs	*Rhipicephalus*	Neutrophil
Anaplasma phagocytophila (incl. *Ehrlichia phagocytophila*, *E. equi* and 'HGE' agent)	Yes	Horses, cattle, sheep, deer	*Ixodes*	Neutrophil
Group III: *Neorickettsia* group				
Neorickettsia helminthoeca	No	Dogs	Fish	Macrophage
Neorickettsia sennetsu	Yes	No	Possibly fish	Monocyte/macrophage
Neorickettsia risticii	No	Horses	Trematode larvae	Monocyte/enterocyte

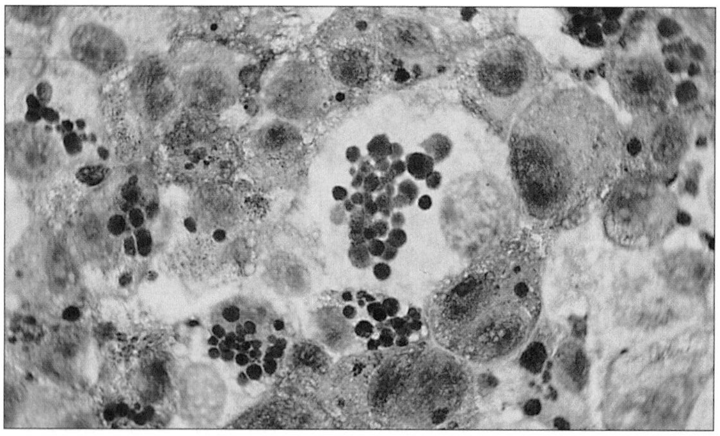

Fig. 235.5 Multiple morulas of *Ehrlichia canis* in culture DH82 cells.

Surveys of tick populations using monoclonal antibodies or PCR have shown *Amblyomma americanum*, the 'lone star tick', to be the main vector of *E. chaffeensis* in the USA. The vectors of HGE are *Ixodes* ticks in both the USA and Europe. In some areas, both HGE and *Borrelia burgdorferi* may be found in the same tick at the same time.[35] Reservoirs of infection are found in many vertebrates, including deer, dogs and rodents. Ticks probably become infected in their larval and nymph stages, and the infection can be transmitted transstadially, so that both nymphs and adults can transmit the infection. There is no evidence for transovarian transmission of ehrlichias.

PATHOGENICITY

Both *E. chaffeensis* and the HGE agent are introduced into the skin by the bite of a tick. From there the organisms spread hematogenously to their respective target cells. *Ehrlichia chaffeensis* is taken into the phagosomes of macrophages and monocytes in the liver, spleen and lymph glands. Human granulocytic ehrlichiosis organisms are thought to primarily infect granulocyte precursor cells in the bone marrow rather than to invade mature peripheral neutrophils. The agent of HGE does, however, stimulate IL-8 production, inducing neutrophil migration to sites of infection.

Animal studies show that ehrlichiosis has an impact on immune function, with macrophage necrosis, inhibition of phagocytosis and killing, downregulation of immunoglobulin production, and decreased lymphocytic responses to mitogens.[36] An immunopathologic basis for HGE has also been suggested in mouse models of infection.[37] Patients who are infected with *E. chaffeensis* show a lymphocytopenia with an abnormal predominance of $\gamma\delta$ T cells in the peripheral circulation[38] and neutrophils infected with HGE show inhibited superoxide anion generation.[39] The mechanisms of these immunologic abnormalities and their clinical significance is not well understood, but autopsy studies of patients who had HGE have shown that many patients had opportunistic lung infections, suggesting that impaired host defenses are a primary feature of human ehrlichiosis.

PREVENTION

There are no vaccines for ehrlichiosis and prevention is based on avoiding areas where ticks are common or the use of tick repellents. Tick control programs in wild and domestic animals may be beneficial in reducing the risk of exposure. Daily removal of ticks may not be effective in preventing infection as transmission may occur within 24 hours of tick attachment.[40]

DIAGNOSTIC MICROBIOLOGY

Ehrlichiosis should be included in the differential diagnosis of patients who have acute febrile illness where there has been a history of exposure to ticks. Hematologic abnormalities, particularly a leukopenia and thrombocytopenia, would be consistent with this diagnosis but there are no pathognomonic signs. The presence of arthralgias and/or an elevated C-reactive protein may help differentiate ehrlichiosis from other infections such as tick-borne encephalitis. Careful examination of peripheral blood or buffy coat smears may show morulas in macrophages or neutrophils but in most cases such examinations are fruitless. The majority of cases of human ehrlichiosis have been diagnosed on the basis of serology, using IFA or ELISA, or detection of specific DNA sequences. Using IFA with *E. chaffeensis* antigen, antibody titers rise during the third week of illness, peak and then decline rapidly about a year later. Serology has been negative, however, in a number of patients confirmed to have ehrlichiosis using PCR, and the sensitivity of IFA may be low. Cell-free recombinant antigens of *E. canis* have been described, and may become useful in serologic tests for HME.[41] Serologic tests for HGE using *E. equi* infected horse neutrophils or cultured human isolates also detect antibodies within 2 weeks after onset of symptoms, and peak titers are reached during the first month. Antibodies may still be detected in about 50% of patients after 1 year.[42] The *E. phagocytophila* group is, however, characterized by antigenic diversity, and this may lead to interlaboratory differences in interpretation of serology assays. Recombinant antigens, derived from *E. phagocytophila* or HGE isolates, have been used to develop rapid serologic assays, and these may give more consistent results.[43] Specific sequences for PCR, using primers from the 16S rRNA gene sequences, have been described for both *E. chaffeensis* and HGE, but diagnostic procedures continue to be revised.[44]

CLINICAL MANIFESTATIONS

Studies of seroconverters suggest that two-thirds of human ehrlichial infections are asymptomatic. In symptomatic cases, there is a moderate to severe illness, with the majority requiring hospitalization. There are no clinically distinct diagnostic features but fever, headache, myalgia, anorexia, vomiting and nausea are common. Skin rash, cough, pharyngitis, diarrhea, abdominal pain and confusion are reported from less than 25% of patients. Involvement of the central nervous system may lead to seizures and coma, and myocardial damage has been recorded. The symptoms are similar in both human monocytic and granulocytic ehrlichiosis, although rash is very rare in the latter. The mortality is probably less than 5% in HME, but may be higher in HGE.[45] In untreated patients, symptoms persist for 3–11 weeks before resolving, leaving a long lasting immunity to further infection.

Both leukopenia and thrombocytopenia are laboratory common findings, with an increase in band neutrophil counts in early infection. A reduced lymphocyte count may be the most significant hematologic finding in HGE culture positive cases.[46] A mildly elevated hepatic transaminase activity may occur.

MANAGEMENT

In-vitro studies have shown that *E. chaffeensis* is susceptible to doxycycline and rifampin but is resistant to quinolones, aminoglycosides, erythromycin and trimethoprim–sulfamethoxazole. Studies with *E. phagocytophila* show a similar picture, except that the organisms are susceptible to quinolones.[47] Administration of doxycycline leads to defervescence in 2–3 days in over 90% of patients and so this is the antibiotic of choice. With other antibiotics, the fever may persist for up to 7 days. Persistence of viable ehrlichias after treatment is known to occur in animal infections, even after 6 weeks of treatment, and has been reported from at least one human case. The significance of persistent ehrlichiosis in humans is not known. Rifampin has been successfully used to treat HGE in a pregnant woman.

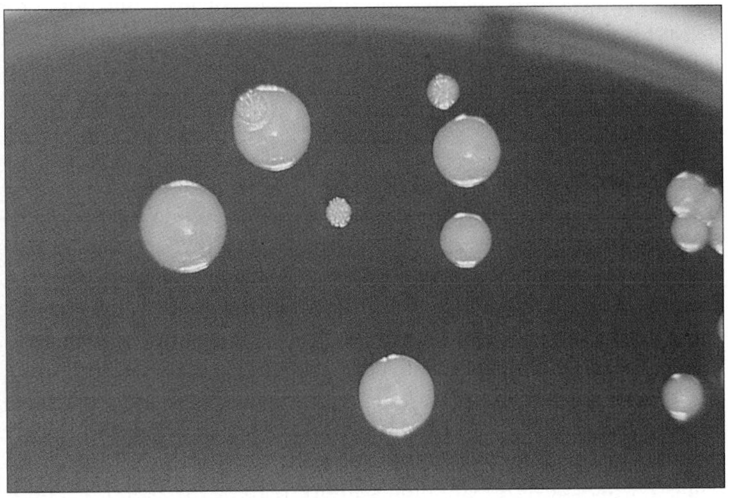

Fig. 235.6 Colonies of *Bartonella henselae* on blood agar. Courtesy of R. Birtles.

BARTONELLOSIS

NATURE

The *Bartonella* are Gram-negative rods that belong in the α_2 subgroup of the class Proteobacteria.[48] They can be grown in tissue culture and also on cell-free media containing blood. Identification of *Bartonella* is based on genomic analysis, as the organisms are biochemically inert.

There are now 19 species in the genus, each with a mammalian reservoir host and each probably transmitted by an arthropod vector.[49] The principal human pathogens are *Bartonella quintana*, *Bartonella henselae* (Fig. 235.6) and *Bartonella bacilliformis*. Six other species have been implicated in human disease: *Bartonella elizabethae* and *Bartonella vinsonii* subsp. *berkhoffii* have been found to cause endocarditis, *B. vinsonii* subsp. *arupensis* was isolated from a febrile patient who had heart valve disease, *Bartonella grahamii* has been implicated in cases of neuroretinitis, *Bartonella clarridgeiae* has been implicated in cat scratch disease and *B. washoensis* has been identified as a cause of myocarditis (Table 235.4).

EPIDEMIOLOGY

Infections with *B. bacilliformis* have been reported only from valleys in the Andean regions of Peru and Ecuador, where sandfly vectors of the genus *Lutzomyia* occur. Infections with *B. quintana* and *B. henselae* have been reported from North America, Europe, the Middle East, Africa and Asia, and so are presumed to occur worldwide. Both the body louse *P. humanus* var. *corporis* and the head louse *P. humanus* var. *capitis* are experimentally capable of transmitting *B. quintana*, but epidemiologic evidence is that natural transmission is effected only by the body louse. In the louse, the organism is extracellular in the gut lumen and causes no pathology. They are, however, excreted in large numbers in louse feces. Humans are the only known natural animal host of *B. quintana*, and even under experimental conditions primates are the only susceptible animals. This contrasts with *B. henselae*, which has frequently been isolated from domestic cats. Cats can transmit the infection to humans in bites and scratches, and the presence of *B. henselae* in cat fleas indicates that these may also be a source of human infection. *Ixodes* ticks infected with *Bartonella* closely related to human pathogens have been described, and some infections may be transmitted this way.[50]

PATHOGENICITY

Microscopic examination of tissue infected with *Bartonella* frequently shows tumor-like capillary lobules indicating neovascular proliferation, and these lesions regress during antibiotic therapy. Experimental studies show that contact with a number of *Bartonella* species enhances proliferation of endothelial cell lines.[51] These observations suggest that *Bartonella* directly stimulates angiogenesis, possibly through secretion of one or more angiogenic factors, and there is some evidence that production of these is mediated through extrachromosomal elements.[52]

Table 235.4 *Bartonella* spp. associated with human disease.

BARTONELLA SPP. ASSOCIATED WITH HUMAN DISEASE			
***Bartonella* sp.**	**Disease**	**Vector**	**Reservoir**
B. bacilliformis	Oroya fever Verruga peruana	*Lutzomyia*	Human
B. quintana	Trench fever Bacteremia Endocarditis Bacillary angiomatosis	*Pediculus humanus*	Human
B. henselae	Cat scratch disease Endocarditis Bacteremia Bacillary angiomatosis Juvenile arthritis	Cat flea	Cats
B. vinsonii subsp. *berkhoffii*	Endocarditis	Fleas and ticks	Dogs
B. vinsonii subsp. *arupensis*	Endocarditis	Not known	Rodents
B. elizabethae	Endocarditis	Fleas	Rodents
B. clarridgeiae	Cat scratch disease	Cat flea	Cats
B. grahamii	Neuroretinitis	Not known	Rodents
B. washoensis	Myocarditis	Not known	Rodents
Other species (e.g. *B. vinsonii* subsp. *vinsonii*, *B. tribocorum*, *B. weissii*, *B. alsatica*, *B. taylorii*, *B. doshiae*, *B. schoenbuchii*, *B. capreoli* and *B. koehlerae*) may be found in rodents, rabbits and ruminants but have not so far been associated with human infections.			

PREVENTION

Control of the arthropod vectors and avoidance of close contact with cats and cat fleas are the only preventive measures available.

DIAGNOSTIC MICROBIOLOGY

Recovery of *Bartonella* from blood requires prolonged incubation using highly enriched media and/or cultivation in endothelial cell lines. The timing of blood sampling may be important since the numbers of bacteria in the blood stream varies. Primary isolation may require a month or more of culture in a humid (80%), CO_2-enriched (5%) atmosphere using media containing horse or rabbit blood. The addition of fetal calf serum and maintenance of hemin concentration within the range 50–250μg/ml improves growth. For *B. bacilliformis* an incubation temperature of 82.4°F (28°C) is preferred.

Primary isolates produce rough colonies deeply embedded in the agar. On subculture, growth is more rapid, with smooth, shiny colonies developing in 5 days or less. Organisms will also grow in liquid media, and acridine orange staining of culture samples is useful because of the slow growth and because little or no CO_2 is produced. Suspect isolates can be presumptively identified on the basis of slow growth, Gram stain appearance and lack of biochemical activity. Specific identification of isolates is usually based on molecular analysis[52,53] or serologic typing.[54]

Serologic diagnosis can be made using hemagglutination, IFA and ELISA. There is little cross-reactivity with other rickettsias, but cross-reactions with *Coxiella* and *Chlamydia* spp. have been described. Removing LPS from antigen preparations improves the specificity. Serology is particularly useful in endocarditis, where culture may take several weeks.[55] Cross-reacting protein antigens are common to different species of *Bartonella*, and serologic tests cannot reliably distinguish between *B. quintana* and *B. henselae* infections. Polyvalent murine antisera and monoclonal antibodies can, however, be used to differentiate *Bartonella* species isolated in the laboratory.[56]

Polymerase chain reaction assays, based on primers for the 16S rRNA gene, can be used to detect *Bartonella* in clinical specimens.

CLINICAL MANIFESTATIONS

A number of different clinical conditions have been associated with *Bartonella* infections.

Trench fever

A relapsing fever accompanied by severe pain in the legs became prominent as a disease among troops serving in the trenches during the First World War and the etiologic agent is now named *B. quintana*. Infection occurs by penetration of organisms in excreta of body lice into skin broken from scratching as a result of intense pruritus. The incubation period is usually 2–3 weeks, and infection leads to sudden onset of fever, retro-orbital headache, weakness, pain in the legs, shivering, intestinal disturbance and insomnia. The severity of symptoms increases over the first 2–3 days. There may be neck stiffness and the disease may resemble meningitis. Intense pain in the tibia is characteristic, and is exacerbated by cold and damp conditions. Pyrexia is often periodic, recurring about every 5 days (hence the name *quintana*), with each attack being less severe than the previous one. Laboratory findings are non-specific, with a polymorphonuclear leukocytosis, anemia and disturbance of liver function. The disease is usually not fatal, although it may persist for 4–6 weeks and is very debilitating. More recently, trench fever has been described in refugees in Burundi,[17] and also as so-called 'urban trench fever' among louse-infested homeless persons.[57]

Bacteremia and endocarditis

In a study of homeless, chronic alcoholics, bacteremia with *B. quintana* persisted for more than 10 days in 4/10 patients, and untreated bacteremia persisted for over 8 weeks.[58] Prolonged bacteremia with *B. henselae* is also common and, in HIV-infected patients, this may be asymptomatic or be associated with an insidiously developing, prolonged symptom complex of malaise, fatigue, weight loss and recurring fevers. Both *B. henselae* and, more frequently, *B. quintana* have been associated with endocarditis,[59] with extensive damage to heart valves, fibrosis and calcification suggestive of prolonged infection. Failure to detect more common pathogens from the blood of endocarditis patients should alert the physician to the possibility of *Bartonella*-induced endocarditis.

Cat scratch disease

Cat scratch disease, caused by *B. henselae* and perhaps other *Bartonella* spp., is now considered to be the most common cause of chronic, benign lymphadenopathy in children and young adults. Epidemiologic evidence suggests that transmission is through cat scratches, bites or contact with cat fleas and studies in the USA have shown that up to 40% of domestic cats have an asymptomatic *B. henselae* bacteremia, which may persist for more than 1 year. In humans the initial lesion develops as a nonpruritic vesicle, papule or pustule, usually on the head, neck or arms, 3–10 days after a scratch or bite. The lesion heals without scar formation within a week. Regional lymphadenopathy may persist for 2–4 months before resolving spontaneously. Transient mild systemic symptoms include fever, malaise, fatigue, headache, anorexia and weight loss. Atypical manifestations include conjunctivitis with pre-auricular lymphadenopathy, hemolytic anemia, hepatosplenomegaly, glomerulonephritis, pleural effusion and neurologic abnormalities and severe chest and pulmonary diseases have been reported.[60]

Arteriolar proliferation and widening of the arteriolar walls, reticulum cell hyperplasia, multiple microabscesses, frank abscess formation and tubercle-like granulomas may be seen on histology of affected lymph nodes. Organisms can be seen using Warthin–Starry stain in clumps or as filaments in the walls of vessels and epithelial cells and free in necrotic debris. Dissemination of organisms can result in the formation of granulomas, identical to those described in lymph nodes, in bone, liver, mesenteric lymph nodes and/or spleen.

Bacillary angiomatosis

Bacillary angiomatosis and epithelioid angiomatosis are vascular proliferative diseases that usually, but not exclusively, involve the skin and are associated with immunodeficiency (Fig. 235.7). Both *B. quintana* and *B. henselae* have been detected in patients in Europe and North America. A similar condition, verruga peruana, is caused by *B. bacilliformis*, but has a limited geographic distribution. Cutaneous lesions may be single or multiple red or purple papules that increase in size and become nodular and bleed profusely when punctured. They may be superficial, dermal or subcutaneous and sometimes involve the oral, anal, conjunctival or intestinal mucosa. While they may resemble lesions of Kaposi's sarcoma, there is no evidence that herpesvirus is involved in the vascular proliferation.[61] Other organs that may be affected include bone marrow, spleen, liver and lymph nodes. Severely immunocompromised patients, particularly those who have HIV, may develop peliosis hepatitis, characterized by cystic, blood-filled spaces in the hepatic parenchyma. Histology shows masses of bacteria in dense clumps of granular material.

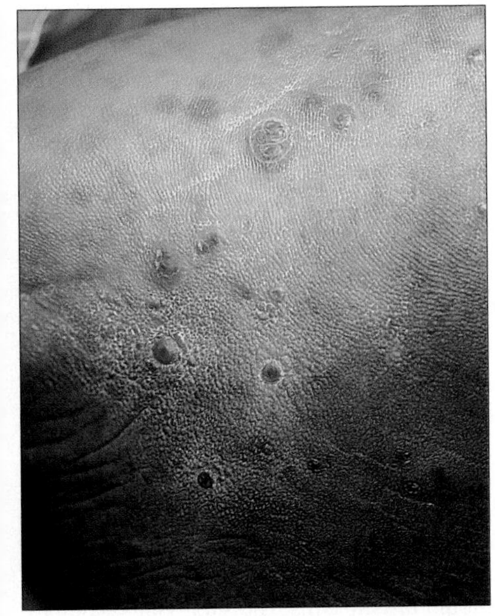

Fig. 235.7 Skin lesions of bacillary angiomatosis. Courtesy of P. Kelly.

Concurrent lymphadenopathy is more frequent in *B. henselae* infected patients, while concurrent central nervous system disorders are more frequent in *B. quintana* infected patients.[62,63] The main risk factor in *B. henselae* bacillary angiomatosis patients is contact with cats and fleas, while homelessness, poor socio-economic status and contact with lice are the main risk factors in *B. quintana* patients.

Carrion's disease

Carrion's disease, caused by the intra-erythrocytic organism *B. bacilliformis*, was first described in 1907. The disease is restricted geographically to the Andean regions of Peru and Ecuador, and occurs in two forms: a febrile anemia ('Oroya fever') and an angioprolific cutaneous disease ('verruga peruana') that resembles bacillary angiomatosis.

MANAGEMENT

Most *Bartonella* isolates are susceptible in vitro to β-lactams (except oxacillin and cephalothin), rifampin, chloramphenicol, macrolides and tetracyclines but susceptibility to clindamycin, quinolones and trimethoprim–sulfamethoxazole is more variable. Clinical trial data are scarce, but most report a poor relationship between in-vitro susceptibility and in-vivo efficacy. Recommendations on treatment depend to a larger extent on clinical presentation rather than on etiology. In immunocompetent patients who have cat scratch disease there is no evidence that antibiotic therapy reduces the duration of symptoms. The use of antibiotics in immunosuppressed patients, however, is associated with rapid clinical improvement. *Bartonella quintana* bacteremia has been reported to respond well to doxycycline, ceftriaxone and macrolides.[57] The majority of patients who have bacillary angiomatosis respond initially to amoxicillin, aminoglycosides or trimethoprim–sulfamethoxazole but relapses occur frequently. The efficacy of tetracyclines and erythromycin appears to depend on the duration of therapy, with fewer relapses occurring in patients treated for more than 1 month. There are few data on treatment of *Bartonella* endocarditis but complex regimens using combinations of β-lactams, aminoglycosides and rifampin have been used.[57] Valve replacement is almost always essential because of the extent of damage to the valves by the time a diagnosis is made.

Q FEVER

NATURE

'Query' or Q fever was first recognized as a disease of humans in abattoir workers in Queensland, Australia in the 1930s and it is now known to occur worldwide. The causative agent, *Coxiella burnetii*, is an obligate intracellular organism that requires the acidic environment within the phagolysosome of eukaryotic cells for its metabolism. While originally included within the Rickettsiaceae, *C. burnetii* has always been regarded as an unusual member of this family because of unique features of its life cycle and epidemiology. It is more closely related to organisms such as *Legionella* and *Francisella* than to *Rickettsia* spp.

Morphologically, *C. burnetii* is a Gram-negative, intracellular, pleomorphic coccobacillus 0.2–1.0μm in diameter. The organism may occur as a small-cell variant (SCV) or large-cell variant (LCV). The SCV is a compact, small rod with a very electron-dense center of condensed nucleoid filaments. The LCV is larger and less electron-dense, and has a clear, periplasmic space between the outer and cytoplasmic membranes. A dense, endospore-like body 130–170nm in diameter might be found at one pole of some LCV. The SCV are

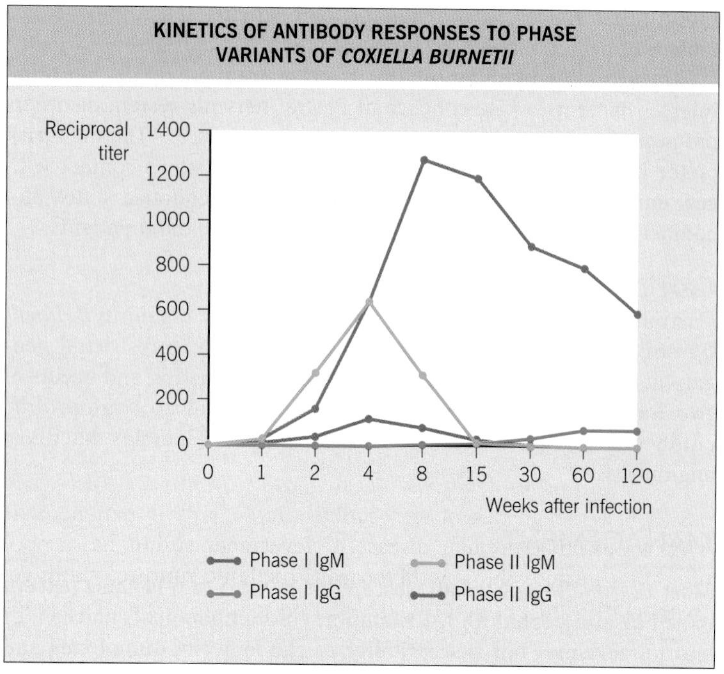

Fig. 235.8 Kinetics of antibody responses to phase variants of *Coxiella burnetii*.

metabolically inactive and are the extracellular form of the organism. Once within a phagolysosome, the SCV is activated by the acidic environment and forms an LCV. The LCV is the metabolically active intracellular form of the bacterium, and undergoes sporogenic differentiation to produce resistant, spore-like forms of the bacterium. These develop to SCVs, which are released when the cells lyse.

In addition to this morphologic change, there is also phase variation, which is associated with changes in the LPS of the outer membrane. Phase I organisms can be readily isolated from acutely infected animals, and remain virulent, while phase II organisms, obtained after serial passage in eggs or tissue culture, are of low virulence. Phase II organisms revert to phase I following passage in a vertebrate host. There are no distinct morphologic changes associated with this phase variation, and SDS-PAGE studies show only minor changes in immunogenic protein profiles (Fig. 235.8).

EPIDEMIOLOGY

With the notable exception of New Zealand, *C. burnetii* infections occur worldwide. The ability of *C. burnetii* to survive extreme environmental conditions for many years, and the low infective dose, results in ready transmission of infection, probably in most cases by inhalation of infectious aerosol particles. While cattle, sheep and goats are the most important animal reservoirs, *C. burnetii* has also been detected in fish, birds, rodents, marsupials, snakes, tortoises and many domestic animals, and has been recovered from ticks and other arthropods. Naturally infected cattle, sheep or goats carry large numbers of bacteria in blood and tissues, and they excrete viable organisms in milk. In most cases these animal infections are asymptomatic. While abortion occurs only rarely, the placenta of an infected animal frequently contains large numbers of organisms. It is contamination of the environment from these sources that usually precedes transmission to humans.

Because the minimum infective dose is a single viable organism,[64] exposure need only be minimal. Most human cases of Q fever occur sporadically but outbreaks occur with high-risk occupations (farmers, hunters, workers in meat or milk processing plants, slaughterhouses, veterinary schools, etc.). Outbreaks have also been reported in such disparate groups such as inhabitants of a village through which infected sheep were herded, golf players on a course previously used as a sheep pasture, military personnel coming into contact with infected hay and poker players exposed to a parturient cat. Extracellular *C. burnetii* are extremely resistant to desiccation, low or high pH, disinfectants and ultraviolet light, and may remain infective in aerosols for up to 2 weeks and in the soil for as long as 5 months. Amebae may also be infected with *C. burnetii* and may be another reservoir for contamination of the environment.[65] Ticks are probably important only in maintaining infections in small rodents and lagomorphs. There is little evidence for direct tick transmission to humans, but organisms may be excreted in large numbers in tick feces, leading to environmental contamination.

In addition to inhalation of viable *C. burnetii* in aerosols, infection may also occur through ingestion of infected milk and meat products. Most such infections result in seroconversion without symptoms, however. *Coxiella burnetii* has been isolated from the human placenta and breast milk, and transmission may also be from mother to child. Sexual transmission of Q fever has recently been reported.[66]

PATHOGENICITY

Monocytes and macrophages are target cells for *C. burnetii*, and alveolar macrophages are the usual primary target. Attachment to the host cell is followed by passive entry into the phagolysosome, where production of a potent acid phosphatase protects the organism from enzyme attack.[67] Disturbance of cytokine regulatory processes, allowing survival and replication of *C. burnetii* within host cells, is also important in establishing infection.[68]

In animals, the great majority of infections produce no obvious pathology, apart from inflammation in the uterus and placenta, where there may be massive replication of *C. burnetii* during the final stages of pregnancy.

Monoclonal antibodies react specifically with epitopes on isolates associated with acute (Nine Mile strain) and chronic (Priscilla strain) infections. Plasmids that code for surface proteins may also be associated with virulence. For example the plasmid QpHI is found in isolates from acute infection, while the plasmid QpRS is found in isolates from patients who have endocarditis. Other studies suggest, however, that differences in host response are more important that genomic variation in determining the clinical outcome of infection.

PREVENTION

The extent to which Q fever organisms contaminate the environment, the ability of these organisms to survive harsh conditions and the low infective dose means that prevention through the use of environmental measures is difficult. Some measures, such as the avoidance of unpasteurized dairy products, may prevent some forms of transmission. Q fever can be prevented in animals using vaccines prepared from extracted subunits of phase I cells, and vaccines may also be useful for people at high risk when they can be identified.[69] Vaccines prepared from phase II organisms have been shown to prevent abortion in animals, but vaccinated animals may still transmit infection to humans.

DIAGNOSTIC MICROBIOLOGY

The suspicion of acute Q fever is not dependent on a specific history of exposure to animals, since organisms persist in the environment for many years. Symptoms are not pathognomonic and may readily be confused with influenza or with other rickettsial diseases. Because organisms are highly infectious, all specimens from patients who have suspected Q fever should be handled with extreme care. *Coxiella* can be recovered from blood, urine and other body fluids during acute infection, using mice or vero cell lines, although only laboratories with adequate safety facilities should attempt this. The shell vial assay may improve recovery of organisms from patients who have endocarditis. A PCR assay, using primers derived from the *htpAB*-associated sequence, has been used to detect organisms in a variety of specimens, including heart valves and milk.[70] *Coxiella burnetii* plasmid DNA has also been identified in human serum specimens by PCR.[71]

Serologic diagnosis is more usual, and is especially useful in areas of high endemicity. While complement fixation and IFA have been used, ELISA is useful for epidemiologic screening and as a diagnostic test. The stage of the infection may be distinguished by using isotype-specific tests, and phase specific antigens. Immunoglobulin M antibodies reactive with phase II *C. burnetii* appear rapidly, reach high titers within 14 days and persist for 10–12 weeks. Immunoglobulin M antibodies reactive with phase I antigens are usually at a much lower titer during acute infection. Immunoglobulibn G antibodies reactive with phase II antigens reach peak titers about 8 weeks after the onset of symptoms, while those reactive with phase I antigens develop only very slowly and remain at lower titers than antibodies to phase II antigens, even after a year. In chronic Q fever, where there is persistence of organisms, the IgG titers to phase I and phase II antigens may both be high, and the presence of IgA antibody to phase I antigen is usually, although not exclusively, associated with chronic infection. Thus elevated levels of IgG (>1/200) and IgM (>1/25) to phase II but not phase I antigens indicates acute infection, while high titers of IgG (1/800) and IgA (>1/50) to phase I antigen is more predictive of chronic infection. An analysis of three isotype-specific assays (IgG, IgM and IgA) is therefore more useful than total antibody assays in laboratory investigations of suspected Q fever.[72] Moreover, patients who have increased levels of IgA2, rather than IgA1, to phase II antigens appear to be at high risk of developing endocarditis.[73]

CLINICAL MANIFESTATIONS

The incubation period depends on the route of exposure, the inoculum dose and the age of the patient, but is usually about 3–4 weeks. A variety of clinical manifestations may be recognized. The most frequent of these are mild fever (>99.5°F (>37.5°C)), headache, chills, sweating, cough, nausea and bradycardia relative to body temperature[69]. A maculopapular rash develops in about 20% of acute infections. The fever usually subsides gradually during week 1, with recovery by week 3 of the illness. There is an inverse relationship between severity of disease and age, and infections in children may go unnoticed. Other frequently occurring presentations include pneumonia and hepatitis, and the prevalence of these may vary geographically. Possible reasons for this geographical variation include strain characteristics, the source, the route and the dose of infection and a variety of host factors.

Clinical recovery usually occurs by the third week but *C. burnetii* organisms may persist in the tissues much longer, and can be recovered from tissues years or even decades after primary infection. A post-Q-fever fatigue syndrome, associated with cytokine dysregulation and presenting with fatigue, myalgia, arthralgia, night sweats, mood change and sleep disturbance, may occur in up to 20% of patients. Chronic Q fever may result in osteomyelitis or encephalitis but there is a high risk of endocarditis, particularly in patients who have pre-existing valvular disease. Q fever endocarditis has a poor prognosis despite therapy. Myocarditis, splenic rupture, meningoencephalitis and pericarditis are all rare manifestation of acute Q fever.[74]

Management

In-vitro studies have shown that rifampin, doxycycline and oxytetracycline and quinolones inhibit the growth of *C. burnetii*, although within the acidic environment of the phagolysosome other agents such as ceftriaxone and fusidic acid may be more effective. Prompt treatment of acute Q fever with doxycycline or tetracycline reduces the duration of fever, but it is not known whether this correlates with elimination of organisms. Combinations of doxycycline with either hydroxychloroquine, or ofloxacin taken daily for 18–36 months has been recommended for chronic infections and may prevent development of endocarditis.[75] The treatment of Q fever endocarditis is problematic. Prolonged regimens that include doxycycline and either rifampicin, trimethoprim–sulfamethoxazole or lincomycin have been reported to be effective but organisms can still be demonstrated in tissues months or even years later.

REFERENCES

1. Beatti L, Kelly PJ, Mason PR, Raoult D. Species specific Balb/c mouse antibodies to rickettsiae studied by Western blotting. FEMS Microbiol Lett 1994;119:339–44.
2. Bouyer DH, Stenos J, Crocquet-Valdes P, *et al.* *Rickettsia felis*: molecular characterization of a new member of the spotted fever group. Int J Syst Evol Microbiol 2001;51:339–47.
3. Fournier PE, Roux V, Raoult D. Phylogenetic analysis of spotted fever group rickettsiae by study of the outer surface protein rOmpA. Int J Syst Bacteriol 1998;48:839–49.
4. Stromdahl EY, Evans SR, O'Brien JJ, Guiterrez AG. Prevalence of infection in ticks submitted to the human tick test kit program of the US Army Center for Health Promotion and Preventive Medicine. J Med Entomol 2001;38:67–74.
5. Raoult D, Fournier PE, Fenollar F, *et al.* *Rickettsia africae*, a tick-borne pathogen in travelers to sub-Saharan Africa. N Engl J Med 2001;344:1504–10.
6. Comer JA, Tzianabos T, Flynn C, Vlahov D, Childs JE. Serologic evidence of rickettsialpox (*Rickettsia akari*) infection among intravenous drug users in inner-city Baltimore, Maryland. Am J Trop Med Hyg 1999;60:894–8.
7. La Scola B, Raoult D. Laboratory diagnosis of rickettsioses: current approaches to diagnosis of old and new rickettsial diseases. J Clin Microbiol 1997;35:2715–27.
8. Fenollar F, Raoult D. Diagnosis of rickettsial diseases using samples dried on blotting paper. Clin Diag Lab Immunol 1999;6:483–8.
9. Walker DH, Lane TW. Rocky Mountain spotted fever: clinical signs, symptoms and pathophysiology. In: Walker DH, ed. Biology of rickettsial diseases, vol 1. Boca Raton: CRC Press; 1998:63–78.
10. Fournier PE, Roux V, Caumes E, Donzel M, Raoult D. Outbreak of *Rickettsia africae* infections in participants of an adventure race in South Africa. Clin Infect Dis 1998;27:316–23
11. Drancourt M, Raoult D, Harl JR, *et al.* Biological variations in 412 patients with Mediterranean spotted fever. Ann NY Acad Sci 1990;590:39–50.
12. Rolain JM, Maurin M, Vestris G, Raoult D. *In-vitro* susceptibilities of 27 rickettsiae to 13 antimicrobials. Antimicrob Agents Chemother 1998;42:1537–41.
13. Raoult D, Drancourt M. Antimicrobial therapy of rickettsial diseases. Antimicrob Agents Chemother 1991;35:2457–62.
14. Ives TJ, Marston EL, Regnery RL, Butts JD, Majerus TC. *In-vitro* susceptibilities of *Rickettsia* and *Bartonella* spp. to 14-hydroxy-clarithromycin as determined by immunofluorescent antibody analysis of infected vero cell monolayers. J Antimicrob Chemother 2000;45:305–10.
15. La Scola B, Rydkina L, Ndihokubwayo JB, Vene S, Raoult D. Serologic differentiation of murine typhus and epidemic typhus using cross-adsorption and Western blotting. Clin Diag Lab Immunol 2000;7:612–6.
16. Andersson JO, Andersson SG. A century of typhus, lice and *Rickettsia*. Res Microbiol 2000;151:143–50.
17. Raoult D, Ndihokubwayo JB, Tissot-Dupont H, *et al.* Outbreak of epidemic typhus associated with trench fever in Burundi. Lancet 1998;352:353–8.
18. Carl M, Tibbs CW, Dobson ME, *et al.* Diagnosis of acute typhus infection using the polymerase chain reaction. J Infect Dis 1990;161:791–3.
19. Massung RF, Davis LE, Slater K, McKechnie DB, Perzer M. Epidemic typhus meningitis in the southwestern United States. Clin Infect Dis 2001;32:979–82.
20. Niang M, Brouqui P, Raoult D. Epidemic typhus imported from Algeria. Emerg Infect Dis 1999;5:716–8.
21. Tamura A, Ohashi N, Urakami H, Myamura S. Classification of *Rickettsia tsutsugamushi* in the new genus, *Orientia* gen nov., as *Orientia tsutsugamushi* comb. nov. Int J Syst Bacteriol 1995;45:589–91.
22. Currie B, O'Conor L, Dwyer B. A new focus of scrub typhus in tropical Australia. Am J Trop Med Hyg 1993;49:425–9.

23. Castleton BG, Salata K, Dasch GA, Strickman D, Kelly DJ. Recovery and viability of *Orientia tsutsugamushi* from packed red cells and the danger of acquiring scrub typhus from blood transfusion. Transfusion 1998;38:680–9.
24. Kim SW, Ihn KS, Han SH, Seong SY, Kim IS, Choi MS. Microtubule- and dynein-mediated movement of *Orientia tsutsugamushi* to the microtubule organizing center. Infect Immun 2001;69:494–500.
25. Kim MK, Kee SH, Cho KA *et al.* Apoptosis of endothelial cell line ECV304 persistently infected with *Orientia tsutsugamushi.* Microbiol Immunol 1999;43:751–7.
26. Chang WH, Kang JS, Lee WK, Choi MS, Lee JH. Serological classification by monoclonal antibodies of *Rickettsia tsutsugamushi* isolated in Korea. J Clin Microbiol 1990;28:656–8.
27. Ching WM, Rowland D, Zhang Z, *et al.* Early diagnosis of scrub typhus with a rapid flow assay using recombinant major outer membrane protein (r56) of *Orientia tsutsugamushi.* Clin Diag Lab Immunol 2001;8:409–14.
28. Sugita Y, Yamakawa Y, Takahashi K, Nagatani T, Okuda K, Nakajima H. A polymerase chain reaction system for rapid diagnosis of scrub typhus within six hours. Am J Trop Med Hyg 1993;49:636–40.
29. Choi YH, Kim SJ, Lee JY, Pai HJ, Lee KY, Lee YS. Scrub typhus: radiologic and clinical findings. Clin Radiol 2000;55:140–4.
30. Watt G, Kantipong P, de Souza M, *et al.* HIV-1 suppression during acute scrub typhus infection. Lancet 2000;356:475–9.
31. Fishbein DB, Kemp A, Dawson JE, Greene NR, Redus MA, Fields DH. Human ehrlichiosis: prospective active surveillance in febrile hospitalized patients. J Infect Dis 1989;160:803–9.
32. Anderson BE, Dawson JE, Jones DC, Wilson KH. *Ehrlichia chaffeensis*, a new species associated with human ehrlichiosis. J Clin Microbiol 1991;29:2838–42.
33. Dumler JS, Barbet AF, Bekker CP, *et al.* Reorganization of the genera in the families Rickettsiaceae and Anaplasmataceae in the order Rickettsiales: unification of some species of *Ehrlichia* with *Anaplasma*, *Cowdria* with *Ehrlichia* and *Ehrlichia* with *Neorickettsia*, description of six new species combinations and designation of *Ehrlichia equi* and the 'HGE agent' as subjective synonyms of *Ehrlichia phagocytophila.* Int J Syst Evol Microbiol 2001;51:2145–65.
34. Buller RS, Arens M, Hmiel SP, *et al. Ehrlichia ewingii*, a newly recognized agent of human ehrlichiosis. N Engl J Med 1999;341:148–55.
35. Alekseev AN, Dubinina HV, Van De Pol I, Schouls LM. Identification of *Ehrlichia* spp. and *Borrelia burgdorferi* in *Ixodes* ticks in the Baltic regions of Russia. J Clin Microbiol 2001;39:2237–42.
36. Larsen HJS, Overness G, Waldeland H, Johansen GM. Immunosuppression in sheep experimentally infected with *Ehrlichia phagocytophila.* Res Vet Sci 1994;56:216–24.
37. Martin ME, Caspersen K, Dumler JS. Immunopathology and ehrlichial propagation are regulated by interferon γ and interleukin 10 in a murine model of human granulocytic ehrlichiosis. Am J Pathol 2001;158:1881–8.
38. Caldwell CW, Everett ED, McDonald G, Yesus YW, Roland WE. Lymphocytosis of γδ T cells in human ehrlichiosis. Am J Clin Pathol 1995;103:761–6.
39. Mott J, Rikihisa Y. Human granulocyte ehrlichiosis agent inhibits superoxide anion generation by human neutrophils. Infect Immun 2000;68:6697–703.
40. Des Vignes F, Piesman J, Heffernan R, Schulze TL, Stafford KC, Fish D. Effect of tick removal on transmission of *Borrelia burgdorferi* and *Ehrlichia phagocytophila* by *Ixodes scapularis* nymphs. J Infect Dis 2001;183:773–8.
41. Alleman AR, McSherry LJ, Barbet AF, *et al.* Recombinant major antigenic protein 2 of *Ehrlichia canis*: a potential diagnostic tool. J Clin Microbiol 2001;39:2494–9.
42. Aguero-Rosenfeld ME, Kalantarpour F, Baluch M, *et al.* Serology of culture-confirmed cases of human granulocytic ehrlichiosis. J Clin Microbiol 2000;38:635–8.
43. Lodes MJ, Mohamath R, Reynolds LD *et al.* Serodiagnosis of human granulocytic ehrlichiosis by using novel combinations of immunoreactive recombinant peptides. J Clin Microbiol 2001;39:2466–76.
44. Weinberg GA. Laboratory diagnosis of ehrlichiosis and babesiosis. Pediatr Inf Dis J 2001;20:435–7.
45. McQuiston JH, Paddock CD, Holman RC, Childs JE. The human ehrlichioses in the United States. Emerg Infect Dis 1999;5:635–42.
46. Bakken JS, Dumler JS. Human granulocyte ehrlichiosis. Clin Infect Dis 2000;31:554–60.
47. Horowitz HW, Hsieh TC, Aguero-Resenfeld ME, *et al.* Antimicrobial susceptibility of *Ehrlichia phagocytophila.* Antimicrob Agents Chemother 2001;45:786–8.
48. Houpikian P, Raoult D. Molecular phylogeny of the genus *Bartonella*: what is the current knowledge? FEMS Microbiol Lett 2001;200:1–7.
49. Jacomo, V, Kelly PJ, Raoult D. Natural history of *Bartonella* infections (an exception to Koch's postulates). Clin Diag Lab Immunol 2002;9:8–18.
50. Chang CC, Chomel BB, Kasten RW, Romano V, Tietze N. Molecular evidence of *Bartonella* spp. in questing adult *Ixodes pacificus* ticks in California. J Clin Microbiol 2001;39:1221–6.
51. Anderson B. The interactions of *Bartonella* with endothelial cells and erythrocytes. Trends Microbiol 2001;9:530–2.
52. Maurin M, Raoult D. *Bartonella* (*Rochalimaea*) *quintana* infections. Clin Microbiol Rev 1996;9:273–92.
53. Handley SA, Regnery RL. Differentiation of pathogenic *Bartonella* by infrequent restriction site PCR. J Clin Microbiol 2000;38:3010–5.
54. Liang Z, Raoult D. Differentiation of *Bartonella* species by microimmunofluorescence assay, sodium dodecyl sulfate-polyacrylamide gel electrophoresis, and Western immunoblotting. Clin Diag Lab Immunol 2000;7:617–24.
55. Fournier PE, Mainardi JL, Raoult D. Value of microimmunofluorescence for diagnosis and follow-up of *Bartonella* endocarditis. Clin Diagn Lab Immunol 2002;9:795–801.
56. Liang Z, La Scola B, Lepidi H, Raoult D. Production of *Bartonella* genus-specific monoclonal antibodies. Clin Diagn Lab Immunol 2001;8:847–9.
57. Ohl ME, Spach DH. *Bartonella quintana* and urban trench fever. Clin Infect Dis 2000;31:131–5.
58. Spach DH, Kanter AS, Dougherty MJ, *et al. Bartonella* (*Rochalimaea*) *quintana* bacteremia in inner city patients with chronic alcoholism. N Engl J Med 1995;332:424–8.
59. Fournier PE, Lelievre H, Eykyn SJ, *et al.* Epidemiologic and clinical characteristics of *Bartonella quintana* and *Bartonella henselae* endocarditis: a study of 48 patients. Medicine 2001;80:245–51.
60. Margileth AM, Baehren DF. Chest-wall abscess due to cat-scratch disease (CSD) in an adult with antibodies to *Bartonella claridgeiae*: case report and review of the thoracopulmonary manifestations of CSD. Clin Infect Dis 1998;27:353–7.
61. Relman DA, Fredricks DN, Yoder KE, Mirowski G, Berger T, Koehler JE. Absence of Kaposi's sarcoma-associated herpesvirus DNA in bacillary angiomatosis-peliosis lesions. J Infect Dis 1999;180:1386–9.
62. Koehler JE, Sanchez MA, Garrido CS, *et al.* Molecular epidemiology of *Bartonella* infections in patients with bacillary angiomatosis-peliosis. N Engl J Med 1997;337:1876–83.
63. Gasquet S, Maurin M, Brouqui P, Lepidi H, Raoult D Bacillary angiomatosis in immunocompromised patients. AIDS 1998;12:1793–803.
64. Ormsbee R, Peacock M, Gerloff R, Tallent G, Wilke D. Limits of rickettsial infectivity. Infect Immun 1978;19:239–45.
65. La Scola B, Raoult D. Survival of *Coxiella burnetii* within free-living amoeba *Acanthamoeba castellani.* Clin Microbiol Infect 2001;7:75–9.
66. Milazzo A, Hall R, Storm PA, Harris RJ, Winslow W, Marmion BP. Sexually transmitted Q fever. Clin Infect Dis 2001;33:399–402.
67. Baca OG, Roman MJ, Glew RH, Christner RF, Buhler JE, Aragon AS. Acid phosphatase activity in *Coxiella burnetii*: a possible virulence factor. Infect Immun 1993;61:4232–9.
68. Ghigo E, Capo C, Raoult D, Mege JL. Interleukin-10 stimulates *Coxiella burnetii* replication in human monocytes through tumor necrosis factor down-regulation: role in microbicidal defect of Q fever. Infect Immun 2001;69:2345–52.
69. Maurin M, Raoult D. Q fever. Clin Microbiol Rev 1999;12:518–53.
70. Stein A, Raoult D. Detection of *Coxiella burnetii* by DNA amplification using polymerase chain reaction. J Clin Microbiol 1992;30:2462–6.
71. Fournier PE, Raoult D. Predominant immunoglobulin A response to phase II antigen of *Coxiella burnetii* in acute Q fever. Clin Diag Lab Immunol 1999;6:173–7.
72. Camacho MT, Outschoorn I, Echevarria C, *et al.* Distribution of IgA subclass response to *Coxiella burnetii* in patients with acute and chronic Q fever. Clin Immunol Immunopathol 1998;88:80–3.
73. Harris RJ, Storm PA, Lloyd A, Arens M, Marmion BP. Long term persistence of *Coxiella burnetii* in the host after primary Q fever. Epidemiol Infect 2000;124:543–9.
74. Raoult D, Tissot-Dupont H, Foucault C, *et al.* Q fever 1985–1998. Clinical and epidemiological features of 383 infections. Medicine 2000;79:109–23.
75. Fenollar F, Fournier PE, Carrieri MP, Habib G, Messana T, Raoult D. Risk factors and prevention of Q fever endocarditis. Clin Infect Dis 2001;33:312–6.

chapter

236 Chlamydia

Pekka AI Saikku

INTRODUCTION

The disease of trachoma was described for the first time some 3000 years ago. Chlamydial inclusions were first observed in patients with trachoma in 1908 by Halberstaedter and Prowazek[1] but the causative agent was isolated in chicken egg yolk sacs only in 1957.[2] Although the association was found before the First World War, it was not until the 1970s that the prominent role of the trachoma agent in sexually transmitted disease (STD) was realized and soon its importance in pelvic inflammatory disease (PID) was revealed.[3,4]

The causative agent of psittacosis ('parrot fever'), transmitted by caged birds, was discovered in the 1930s. In several animal diseases, similar small bacteria that multiply in inclusions were found, and later it was realized that they were related to lymphogranuloma venereum and the trachoma agent. In the 1960s, these agents were finally classified on the basis of their multiplication cycle and the common group antigen as belonging to the genus *Chlamydia*, which was further divided, on the basis of glycogen content of inclusions, into two species: *C. trachomatis* (trachoma and human STD strains) and *C. psittaci* (which included all the other strains).[3]

Once serologic diagnosis of psittacosis was available, it became apparent that 'bird-transmitted pneumonia' could be transmitted without any apparent contact with birds. A chlamydial strain that had been isolated in 1965 as a result of trachoma studies in Taiwan was found to be responsible for the majority of chlamydial respiratory infections in humans. It represented a new chlamydial species, *C. pneumoniae*, and is in fact the most common chlamydial species infecting humans.[5]

The diseases seldom occur abruptly and they are not easily recognized; rather, chlamydial infections may run an insidious, chronic course, causing severe damage only after years of infection. Moreover, their obligatory intracellular growth makes normal bacteriologic analysis difficult.[6] The sequencing of whole genomes of several chlamydial species[7] has provided new possibilities for studying these organisms and our concepts of the nature of chlamydiae are changing accordingly.

NATURE

Current classification of chlamydial species is rapidly evolving and there are proposals to name new species and even new genera.[8] The genus *Chlamydia* includes *C. trachomatis* as a human pathogen with relatives found in the mouse (*C. muridarum*) and pig (*C. suis*). The genus *Chlamydophila* includes *C. pneumoniae* as a human pathogen with relatives reported in the horse and koala. *Chlamydophila psittaci* is a pathogen of birds, *C. abortus* and *C. pecorum* are pathogens of ruminants, *C. felis* is a pathogen of cats and *C. caviae* is found in guinea pigs. All except the last species also cause diseases in humans.

Two new families are proposed, Parachlamydiaceae and Simkaniaceae. Both currently contain a single species and *S. negevensis* seems to be common in humans. Its possible association to human diseases is still poorly understood.[9] The closest relatives of *Chlamydia* spp. are small aquatic bacteria that, like *Chlamydia* spp., do not use peptidoglycan as the structural component of the infective particle (Table 236.1).

Chlamydiae are small, Gram-negative bacteria that are obligatory intracellular parasites. They are not cultivable on synthetic media. They exist in nature in two forms: a non-replicating, infectious dense particle called the elementary body (EB); and a loose, larger, intracellular form, the reticulate body (RB), which is able to multiply by binary fission but is noninfectious (Fig. 236.1).[10] The EB is a spherical particle about 300nm in diameter; it can be stored at −94°F (–70°C) in sucrose-containing buffers and cultured in cell cultures.

Chlamydiae have a double layer membrane of Gram-negative bacteria with a periplasmic space. They are usually devoid of peptidoglycan, but seem to use it when dividing.[11] The circular genomes of *C. pneumoniae* and *C. trachomatis* contain 1,230,000 and 1,039,000 base pairs, respectively, with just over 1000 potential genes.[7] Species-specific plasmid is present in 10 copies in *C. trachomatis*,[12] but is not found in the human type of *C. pneumoniae*. The major outer membrane protein (MOMP) forms the outer membrane of the particle with some minor proteins, of which two are rich in cysteine. *Chlamydia trachomatis* has nine and *C. pneumoniae* 21 genes for putative membrane proteins (PMPs). Cysteine-rich proteins apparently have replaced the peptidoglycan with their S–S bridges in maintaining the rigidity of the chlamydial membrane. On electron microscopy, the surface can be seen to consist of a hexagonal pattern with substructures made up of a few rosettes with short spikes (Fig. 236.2).[13]

The MOMP of *C. trachomatis* contains four variable regions, which divide it into about 20 immunotypes denoted alphabetically.[14] The MOMP of *C. pneumoniae* is more homogeneous and the surface structure differs from that of *C. trachomatis*. Chlamydial lipopolysaccharide (LPS) is of rough type, weakly endotoxic and situated in the outer membrane.

The multiplication cycle is best known in the case of *C. trachomatis*. The EBs attach to the surface of susceptible cells and are passively engulfed by activity of the cell. *Chlamydia trachomatis* lymphogranuloma venereum biotype is wrapped by heparan sulfate that is taken from the cell by the chlamydial organism, which can then use heparin receptors on the cell surfaces;[15] *C. pneumoniae* and *C. psittaci* may also use heparin in the attachment. An oligosaccharide containing mannose residues that are covalently bound to MOMP may also participate in the attachment process.[16]

Chlamydiae can prevent the fusion of the endocytic vacuole with lysosomes and travels on microtubules joining to the exocytic pathway. The EB envelope changes, transforming the metabolically inactive inert EB into the metabolically active RB, which is 0.8–1μm in diameter. In the process, the disulfide bridges are reduced and MOMP acts as a porin. DNA, RNA and proteins are synthesized within the RB, which divides successively by binary fission. The endosomal walls intercept nearby trans-Golgi vesicles that incorporate sphingomyelin and glycerophospholipids into the swelling chlamydial inclusion (Figs 236.3 and 236.4) Metabolically active RBs acquire

GENERAL PROPERTIES OF *CHLAMYDIA*
• Obligatory intracellular Gram-negative parasites
• Elementary body–reticulate body cycle
• Lack of peptidoglycan
• Common group antigen (lipopolysaccharide)
• Tendency to persistent infections
• Immune defense participates in the development of lesions

Table 236.1 General properties of *Chlamydia*.

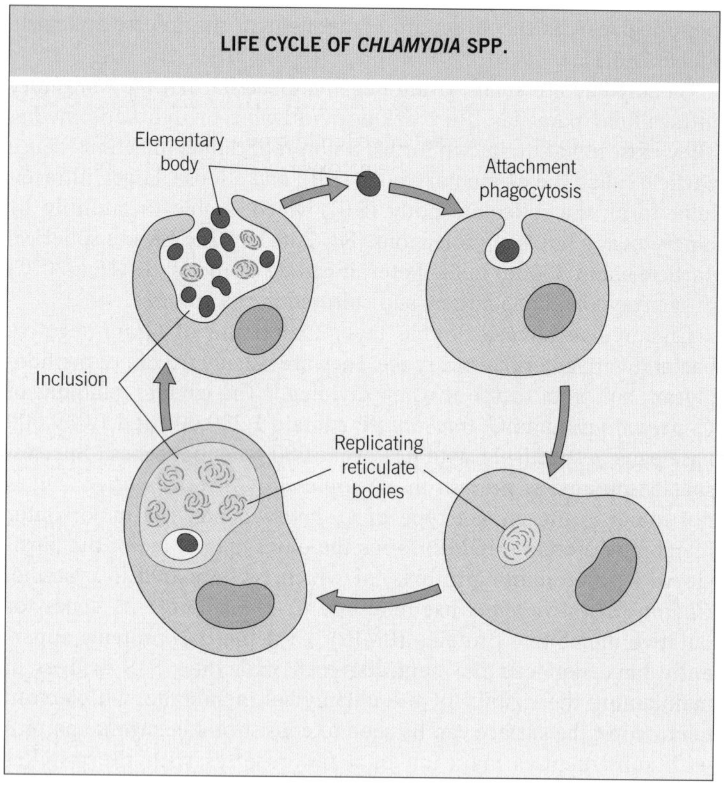

Fig. 236.1 Life cycle of *Chlamydia* spp.

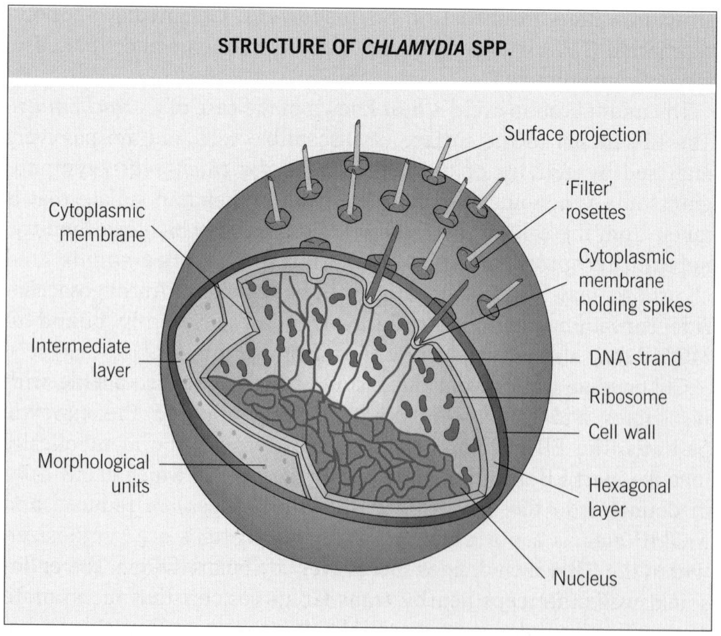

Fig. 236.2 Structure of *Chlamydia* spp. Courtesy of Dr A Matsumoto.

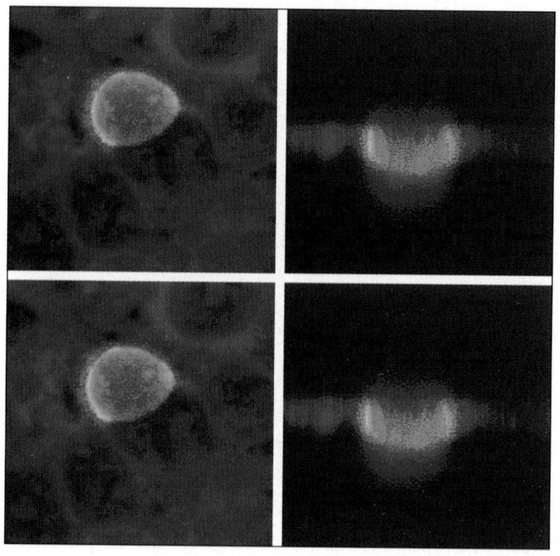

Fig. 236.3 Chlamydial inclusion in confocal stereomicroscopy. *Chlamydia pneumoniae* cultured in human line (HL) cells are shown. Fluorescein isothiocyanate (FITC)-labeled anti-LPS monoclonal antibody stain. Courtesy of Dr A Laurila.

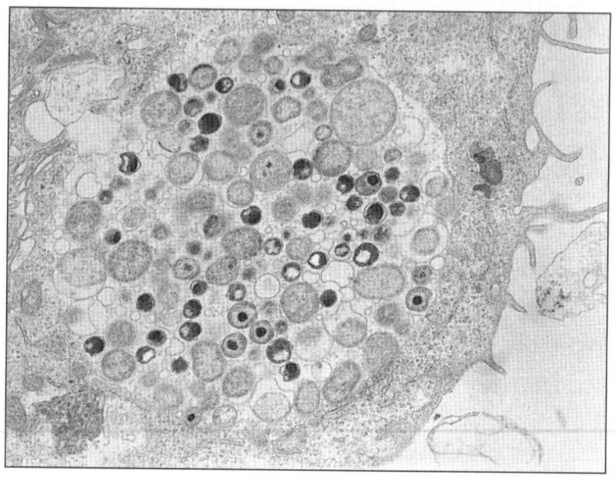

Fig. 236.4 Electron microscopy of chlamydial inclusion. Reticulate bodies and transition stages to dense elementary bodies are shown. *Chlamydia pneumoniae* cultured in HL cells. Courtesy of Dr CH von Bonsdorff.

nutrients and metabolic building blocks, including nucleotides and ATP ('energy' parasites) from host cells.[17] Chlamydial LPS is present in RBs and seems to attach to host cell membranes.

Chlamydiae use their type III secretion system to gain control over the host cell. Apoptosis is prevented during the growth period but induced in nearby inflammatory cells.[18] Eventually, the inclusion body may contain several thousand chlamydial RBs. At the end of the replication cycle, chlamydiae start to condense into EBs and apoptosis and proteolysis are promoted in order to liberate the new infectious particles. Recently, the presence of a chlamydial cytotoxin has been demonstrated.[19] Sometimes the mature inclusion is expelled intact but usually the inclusion bursts open, releasing infective chlamydial particles and the cell dies. The whole cycle takes 2–3 days. Depletion of tryptophan or iron or the presence of penicillin or interferon-γ in subinhibitory concentrations induces an aberrant, slowly metabolizing form of RB, which can persist for long periods. In chronic infections this may be the dominant form of chlamydia.[20] The microscopic appearance of chlamydial inclusion varies with different strains, and the inclusions of *C. trachomatis* contain glycogen.

EPIDEMIOLOGY

Chlamydia trachomatis is transmitted by direct contact and via vectors such as flies and contaminated towels in poor sanitary conditions in trachoma-endemic areas. Newborn infants contract the infection from their mother, sometimes before birth, and can infect their siblings via excretions. In industrialized countries, *C. trachomatis* is by far the most common bacterial STD. The incidence is greatest in young sexually active people and varies widely among different areas, from very low levels in Scandinavian countries to 15–20% in some urban areas of other developed countries (see Chapter 74).

Chlamydia pneumoniae is a common respiratory pathogen worldwide. In tropical countries, infections are common during the first years of life, especially in urban slums. In industrialized countries, children begin to seroconvert at school age at the rate of 10% each year.[21] The rate seems to depend on population density, but at the age of 15 years 25–50% of populations have demonstrable antibodies against the agent. The antibody prevalence continues to rise; nearly all elderly people have measurable antibodies. Because antibodies are lost by a few years after an acute infection, this steady increase points to repeated infections during life and to possible chronic infections. Spread via droplets has been proposed. Asymptomatic carriers are found but their number is disputed and there is a possibility that only some people are effective transmitters of the agent. In sparsely inhabited areas in high latitudes, *C. pneumoniae* causes epidemics at intervals of 5–7 years. In lower latitudes, the interval between epidemics is shorter and an endemic situation can be found near the equator. In military garrisons with susceptible recruits, the epidemics are prolonged and can last 6 months.[22]

Avian *C. psittaci* is contagious in dried droppings of diseased birds for several days and is typically transmitted by the inhalation of dust. Patients are usually turkey or duck farmers, plant processors or persons who have contact with diseased caged or wild birds. Person-to-person transmission occasionally occurs. Infections caused by *C. psittaci* strains from mammals are less well known. Ovine abortion strains are known to cause septic abortions in pregnant women who are in contact with affected farm cattle.[23] Pet cats can be a source of *C. felis* infections. *C. psittaci* strains are well known for their capacity to cause severe laboratory infections.

C. pneumoniae, like *Legionella*, is able to multiply in amebae[24] but the significance of this property in epidemiology is so far not known.

PATHOGENICITY

Owing to their unique life cycle, in which they parasitize only living, metabolically active cells, chlamydiae are not harmless commensals.[3,25] It is not known whether the pathogen stays dormant inside cells, protected from antibodies, for prolonged periods, only to be activated later by some signal, or whether there is a special form of chronically infecting *Chlamydia* spp.[26] In chronic persistent infections in vitro, it is possible that chlamydiae respond with morphologically abnormal forms,[27] in which internal proteins such as heat shock proteins (hsps) are produced and antigens of mature EBs are diminished.[20]

Chlamydiae are potent inducers of cytokines, such as interferon-γ and interleukin-1, which prevent the multiplication of the agent in vitro.[17] In chronic infections such as trachoma, there are findings that point to diminished cell-mediated immunity and increased humoral immunity.[28] Chlamydial immunity is relatively short-lived and immunotype specific and reinfections are common. In repeated chlamydial infections,[29] there is a hypersensitivity component, apparently caused by common internal cross-reactive proteins. Chlamydial hsp60, a protein produced in chronic infections, has been blamed for the hypersensitivity reactions seen.[30] Moreover, it is related to the host's hsp60 and may initiate autoimmune reactions.[31]

In chronic chlamydial infections, chlamydia can persist in noncultivable form and damage results partly from persistent inflammation.[25] Blinding trachoma[32] was thus named after *C. trachomatis* and long-term sequelae of lymphogranuloma venereum (rectal strictures, elephantiasis and esthiomena) have been known for some time,[33] but infertility and ectopic pregnancies caused by tubal occlusion have only recently been associated with chronic *C. trachomatis* infection.[4] *Chlamydia pneumoniae* (Fig. 236.5) is able to disseminate inside white blood cells in the circulation[34,35] and multiply in vascular tissue.[36] Human hsp60 and chlamydial hsp60 co-localize in atherosclerotic plaques.[37] Chlamydial LPS induces cytokine and adhesin responses and formation of foam cells in macrophages.[38]

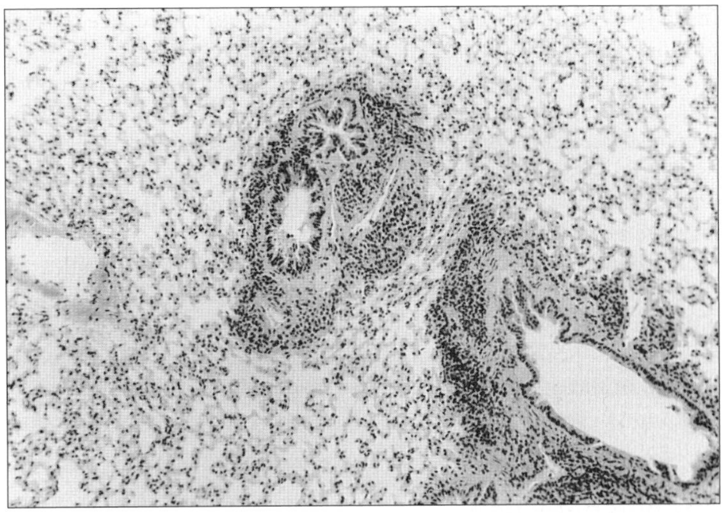

Fig. 236.5 Chronic chlamydial infection in mouse lung. Note the infiltration of mononuclear cells. Hematoxylin and eosin stain. Courtesy of Dr A Laurila.

PREVENTION

Vaccines against *Chlamydia* spp. have been under development for 40 years without evident success. *Chlamydia trachomatis* has several immunotypes, making development of a vaccine complicated, and the protective antigens of *C. pneumoniae* are not known. Knowledge of the complete genome and progress in immunology may alter this situation in the future.[39]

Mass medication campaigns have been used against trachoma in Africa and there are local projects to eradicate the agent with generalized antibiotic courses for the whole population.[40] However, improvement in living standards would be a better long-term preventive measure. Washing the face every second day with clear water and wiping it with a towel that is not shared with other people is effective.[41] Dirty water and shared towels are effective disseminators of the infection from eye to eye. Latrine hygiene is effective in controlling flies that spread trachoma. Using an undamaged condom protects against genital chlamydial infection.

Active tracing and treatment have been effective against sexually transmitted *C. trachomatis*. The new nucleic acid-based tests have raised the question of general screening in order to eradicate *C. trachomatis* from populations. In the USA screening of sexually active women under 25 years of age is recommended (see Chapter 73).[42]

DIAGNOSTIC MICROBIOLOGY

The clinical features of chlamydial infections, such as their slow onset, the low numbers of infectious agents present and the cross-reactions seen in serology, make usual diagnostic methods difficult.[43,44]

Culture

Culture was originally the gold standard in *C. trachomatis* diagnosis but it is an unsatisfactory standard for *C. trachomatis* and even more so for *C. pneumoniae*. Moreover, culture of *C. psittaci* is a well-known cause of laboratory infections.

Samples for culture should contain live cells from the diseased area and this can be problematic if the pathogen has invaded to deeper tissues. The sample is collected in a medium that contains sucrose, aminoglycosides, vancomycin and antifungal agents. McCoy cell lines and green monkey kidney cell lines are commonly used for *C. trachomatis* and Hep2 and HL cells are commonly used for *C. pneumoniae*. Centrifugation onto cells and the addition of cytostat (usually cycloheximide) into the growth medium are needed for optimal growth. Multiwell plates are suitable for mass isolation attempts, but vials are better protected from cross-contamination. *Chlamydia trachomatis* can be stained by Lugol's iodine stain. Immunofluorescence staining gives a more clear-cut result and, when using LPS-specific monoclonal antibody, stains all *Chlamydia* spp. The culture result is available in 2–3 days, but blind passage can improve sensitivity.

Chlamydia trachomatis can be present in clinical samples in sufficient amounts to be toxic for cell cultures. The situation is quite different with *C. pneumoniae*, because as a rule only a few inclusions are found in primary isolations, pointing to the paucity of *C. pneumoniae* in throat epithelium collected by swabbing. Nasopharyngeal swabs for *C. pneumoniae* rather than throat swabs have been recommended in some studies.

Antigen detection

All enzyme immunoassay (EIA) kits for the diagnosis of *C. trachomatis* measure the common LPS group antigen that is present in all chlamydiae and produced in large amounts during the growth cycle. Several commercial kits, some fully automated, are available and widely used. Because massive microbial contamination can cause false-positive reactions, positive results should be confirmed. Confirmatory EIA tests are available, but in the case of *C. trachomatis*, EBs can be concentrated from the positive sample and visualized with direct fluorescent antibody (DFA) staining. Lipopolysaccharide-EIA kits can probably also be used for the detection of *C. pneumoniae* LPS from respiratory tract samples, but they have not been systematically tested.

Direct fluorescent antibody staining has been successfully used in *C. trachomatis* diagnosis. This test seems to be marginally more sensitive than EIA; moreover, the quality of the sample can be controlled in the stained smear. However, the interpretation demands expertise and is tiring to the reader, and therefore the test is often used only in the confirmation of EIA tests. In this circumstance, samples that are weakly positive (under the cut-off range) should be tested with DFA staining, which will reveal the true positives among the weakly positive samples. The test is insensitive in the demonstration of *C. pneumoniae* in throat swabs. The pharyngeal microbial flora is quite variable, and the search for very small numbers of EBs is difficult. *Chlamydophila psittaci* can also be seen in smears. The lack of species-specific monoclonal antibodies for *C. psittaci* necessitates the use of anti-LPS antibody, and the results can then be difficult to interpret, especially if the number of EBs is small.

Serology

In individual *C. trachomatis* infections, serologic tests are often of questionable value, although serology has been important in epidemiologic and disease association studies. The infection is often superficial without detectable seroconversion. Proper antibiotic therapy can also prevent antibody formation. Serology has been the method most commonly used for *C. psittaci* and *C. pneumoniae*. The need for paired samples considerably lessens the value of serology in acute situations.

The time-honored complement fixation (CF) test has traditionally been used for the diagnosis of chlamydial respiratory tract infections. The CF test is sensitive in psittacosis, but in *C. pneumoniae* infections it is sensitive only in primary infections of young adults.[22] The use of the CF test in *C. trachomatis* infections is limited to lymphogranuloma venereum.

Enzyme immunoassay tests based on chlamydial EBs or chlamydial LPS (group antigen) are commercially available but have not gained wide popularity. In acute infections, in most cases they demonstrate seroconversions satisfactorily. Synthetic peptides should enable EIA to be made species-specific in the future.

Microimmunofluorescence (MIF) testing, if properly done, can differentiate between species and even immunotypes. It is, however, demanding and can be performed in relatively few laboratories. Chlamydial antibodies are rare in young children, but at school age antibodies against *C. pneumoniae* begin to rise rapidly. *Chlamydia trachomatis* antibodies start to appear at the sexually active age and peak at about 30 years of age. They are more often found in females than in males; the opposite is seen with *C. pneumoniae* antibodies, where males predominate. Microimmunofluorescence testing seems, for the moment, to be the most convenient test for the serologic diagnosis of an acute *C. pneumoniae* infection.[44] In primary infections the diagnosis can be obtained from the first sample that contains IgM antibodies specific for *C. pneumoniae*. The possibility of a false-positive reaction due to IgM rheumatoid factor should always be kept in mind, especially in elderly patients. In elderly patients undergoing reinfections, the rapid response can be missed if the first serum sample is not collected early enough after the onset of disease. Apart from the situation in which strong group reaction interferes with the result, an experienced reader can interpret the reaction to differentiate not only the species but also the immunotype. In MIF testing, strains of *C. pneumoniae* react much more uniformly than do those of *C. trachomatis*. In *C. trachomatis* infections, MIF testing is usable in lymphogranuloma venereum, perihepatitis and infant pneumonitis, and it can give a clue to the triggering agent in reactive arthritis.

Detection of nucleic acids

The use of nuclei acid-based detection systems has altered the former concept of culture as the 'gold standard' of *C. trachomatis* diagnosis[42] and is replacing other diagnostic methods. Three methods have already appeared on the market, based on polymerase chain reactions (PCR), ligase chain reaction or transcription-mediated amplification. A great advantage is the possibility of using mailed morning void urine, tampons and self-collected samples for detection.

In the case of *C. pneumoniae* commercial PCR kits are not currently available and in-house PCR kits vary widely in their sensitivity.[43] In acute infections, they seem to be more sensitive than isolation. Upper respiratory tract samples can be negative and sputum is preferred.[44]

Diagnosis of chronic chlamydial infections

Diagnosing chronic chlamydial infections is problematic. The number of infective organisms can be small and the site of infection can be difficult to reach. Culture often remains negative, especially if the sample is from a peripheral site. Antibody responses can be quite variable or even lacking. Persistently elevated titers, especially of IgA, have been suggested as a marker, but their value in individual diagnosis is doubtful. Enzyme immunoassay tests have been inferior when compared to the MIF test. Antigen detection by immunohistochemistry is more sensitive and diagnostic but, like nucleic acid-based methods (e.g. amplification, in-situ hybridization), they are currently used in research laboratories only.[44] The value of demonstrating circulating immune complexes that contain chlamydial antigens in blood samples is under evaluation, as is the value of detecting nucleic acid in circulating white blood cells. Both markers, however, can also be found in healthy persons and are affected by age and season.[34,45]

CLINICAL MANIFESTATIONS

The diseases associated with chlamydial infection are listed in Table 236.2.

DISEASES ASSOCIATED WITH *CHLAMYDIA* SPP., OR IN WHICH A POSSIBLE ASSOCIATION HAS BEEN PROPOSED				
Species	**Infection**	**Distribution**	**Disease**	**Incidence**
Chlamydia trachomatis	Acute infections	Females	Cervicitis Endometritis PID Perihepatitis, splenitis, appendicitis Bartholinitis	About 30% Common 10–70% Isolated case reports Rare
		Males	Urethritis Epididymitis	10–30% In young males
		Both sexes	Conjunctivitis Reactive arthritis	Isolated case reports Common cause
		Neonates	Conjunctivitis Infant pneumonitis	<10% By definition
	Chronic infections		Trachoma Chronic PID	By definition Common
Chlamydia pneumoniae	Acute infections		Pneumonia Endemic Pneumonia Epidemic Acute bronchitis Sinusitis Otitis media Upper respiratory tract infection	10% up to 50% 5% <5% Isolated case reports ~10% of school children annually
			Carditis Vasculitis (erythema nodosum) Reactive arthritis	Isolated case reports Isolated case reports Isolated case reports
	Chronic infections		Chronic obstructive lung disease Asthma Sarcoidosis Atherosclerosis	10–50% ? ? up to 50%
Chlamydia psittaci			Psittacosis–ornithosis Infectious abortion	By definition Rare

Table 236.2 Diseases associated with *Chlamydia spp.*, or in which a possible association has been proposed.

Chlamydia trachomatis infections

Genital infections in females (see Chapter 74)

Chlamydia trachomatis is the most important cause of bacterial genital infections in women. Infected women often remain asymptomatic carriers and can thus transmit the disease. The prevalence of carriers varies widely depending on the population (2–20%). Immunotypes E–K and B are usually found in genital infections.

Vaginitis due to *C. trachomatis* is seen only in childhood and after the menopause. Women aged 15–25 years are particularly susceptible to *C. trachomatis* cervicitis, both for anatomic reasons and because of the slow development of immunity. It cannot be differentiated clinically from cervicitis caused by other agents, although mucopurulent discharge and hypertrophic follicular formations in an edematous and friable epithelium ('genital trachoma') are typical of the disease (Fig. 236.6).[46] One of the causes of 'aseptic', culture-negative cystitis in women is *C. trachomatis*.[47] *Chlamydia trachomatis* has been isolated as pure culture in cases of bartholinitis. It is much more common in patients with endometritis.[48] Plasma cell infiltration is the typical microscopic hallmark in the chronic form of this disease.

Pelvic inflammatory disease is the most important complication of female genital infection with *C. trachomatis*, and in areas where the prevalence of gonorrhea has decreased *C. trachomatis* is the most common cause of PID. Clinically, chlamydial PID cannot be differentiated from gonococcal PID, but in chlamydial PID the patients tend to be younger and the onset of the disease is slower with a less marked fever. Markers of acute infection, such as erythrocyte sedimentation rate (ESR) and C-reactive protein, are clearly elevated. Infection can proceed to the abdominal cavity and cause 'sterile' peritonitis with ascites.

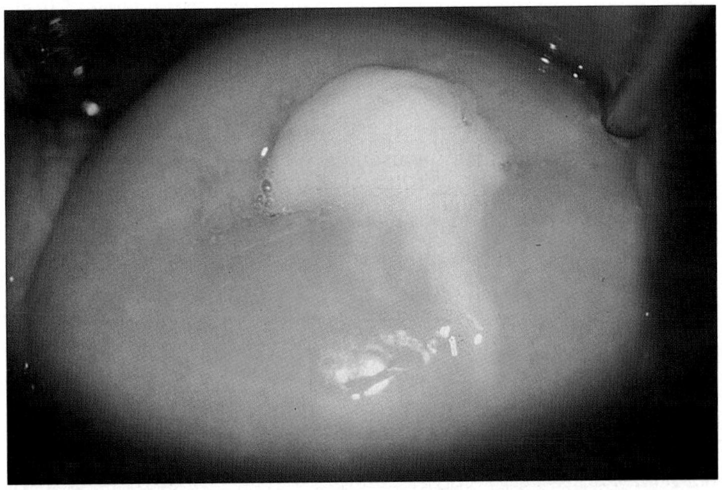

Fig. 236.6 Mucopurulent cervicitis caused by *Chlamydia trachomatis*. Courtesy of Dr J Paavonen.

Typically, however, the symptoms come from more localized areas of infection. Acute perihepatitis (Fitz-Hugh–Curtis syndrome) is commonly caused by *C. trachomatis* and this should be kept in mind when young female patients complain of right upper quadrant abdominal pain. In perihepatitis, the capsule of the liver, not the liver tissue itself, is inflamed, typically leading to 'violin-string' adhesions. Periappendicitis and perisplenitis have also been reported.

Chlamydial PID often goes unrecognized. As a result, the patient is not treated, infection becomes chronic and over years can severely damage the fallopian tubes. Almost 50% of patients with tubal occlusions and elevated chlamydial antibody titers deny any episode of PID. Ectopic pregnancies and infertility problems are the most important complications of genital chlamydial infections in women.[49] Chronic chlamydial infection has been associated with fetal death, pre-term labor and late-onset puerperal fever.[50]

Genital infections in males

One-third of cases of nongonococcal urethritis are caused by *C. trachomatis*. The incubation period is 6–12 days, which is longer than for gonorrhea, and the course is milder than in gonorrhea. Asymptomatic carriers of *C. trachomatis* are also more common (up to 10% in some areas) than asymptomatic *N. gonorrhoea* carriers. Treatment aimed at gonococci does not affect *Chlamydia* spp. and the majority of postgonococcal urethritis cases are due to simultaneously acquired *C. trachomatis* infection.

The role of *Chlamydia* spp. in prostatitis is unclear. Cultures are negative but chlamydial nucleic acids and antigens have been demonstrated in prostatic tissue. It has not been proven that chlamydiae are a cause of azoospermia or infertility in men. However, epididymitis in young males is most commonly caused by *C. trachomatis*, and if the infection is bilateral this can cause infertility.

Infections in newborns

Chlamydial infection can be transmitted in utero and cause serious disease in the pre-term infant. Half the children born to a chronically infected mother are infected during birth. Topical prophylaxis is not effective and mothers should be treated before birth. Inclusion conjunctivitis of the newborn (ophthalmia neonatorum; Fig. 236.7) develops in 50% of the infants, usually after they have been discharged from hospital. The disease is milder than gonococcal ophthalmia neonatorum and there is no danger of perforation; only minute scarring can be seen. The disease is usually unilateral, but edema of both eyelids can be marked. *Chlamydia* spp. can also infect the nasopharynx, middle ears, lungs, intestine and vagina of the newborn.

Infant pneumonitis is a well-characterized complication.[51] The disease starts at 3–12 weeks of age with a stuffy nose, difficulty in breathing and a gradually worsening staccato cough. The infant is usually afebrile, but chest radiographs may show marked hyperexpansion and prominent striations in the lungs. Specific IgM levels are elevated, as may those of eosinophils. Although the radiograph findings are often marked, the short-term prognosis is good and only rarely does the patient require intensive therapy. In the long term, however, the lungs seem to be damaged and these children are sensitive to repeated respiratory tract infections and often go on to develop asthma.[52] *Chlamydia trachomatis* is a rare cause of respiratory tract infections after 6 months of age. There are reports in the literature of pharyngeal carriage of *C. trachomatis* in adults, but the agent has not been clearly associated with pharyngitis.

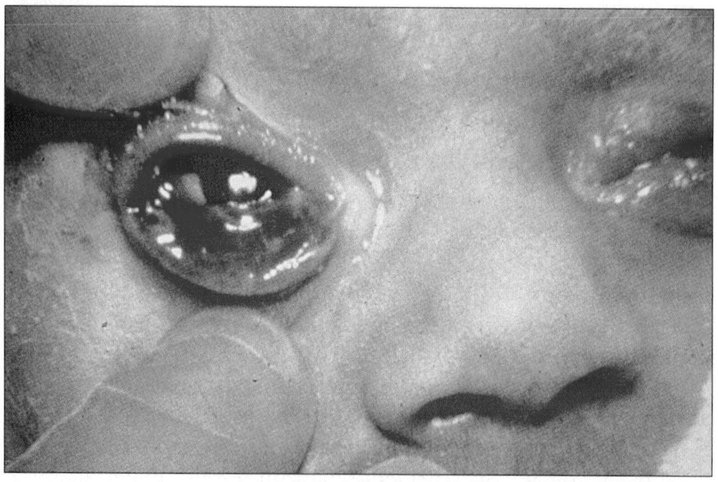

Fig. 236.7 Ophthalmia neonatorum. Courtesy of Dr M Puolakkainen.

Eye infections

Trachoma, which is due to *C. trachomatis*, is still a great scourge in developing countries, where it is the most common preventable cause of blindness.[32] About 500 million people are victims of this disease and 7 million are blind as a result of the chronic follicular conjunctivitis it causes. Although the pathogenesis of trachoma has been intensively studied, it is not known why only some of the children exposed to repeated inoculations by chlamydial agents (immunotypes A–C) develop chronic disease. The clinical features of the chronic disease include a pannus over the cornea and scarring of the lids by entrichiasis (eyelashes turn inwards and scrape the cornea). Trachoma occurs in poorly developed areas with a low standard of sanitation and lack of washing facilities.

Occasionally, genital *C. trachomatis* infection can lead to 'inclusion conjunctivitis', because of self-inoculation or oral sex with an infected partner. Follicular formation is seen, but corneal lesions are rare. Infection is usually unilateral and associated with palpebral edema. The disease is typically diagnosed only after topical treatments have failed. Although the first *C. pneumoniae* strains to be isolated were from eyes, conjunctivitis is rarely seen in *C. pneumoniae* infections.

Lymphogranuloma venereum

Chlamydia trachomatis immunotypes L_1, L_2 and L_3 differ from other *C. trachomatis* strains in their invasive nature and in belonging to the lymphogranuloma venereum biovar. Instead of multiplying in epithelial cells, they multiply in the reticuloendothelial system. Inguinal lymph nodes are the target organs, but the agent spreads systemically and can affect various organs. Sequelae include strictures in pelvic lymphatic vessels, which may lead to elephantiasis, and rectal strictures. The disease is not common in industrialized countries, but it is important in some tropical areas (see Chapter 78).[33]

Chlamydophila pneumoniae and *Chlamydophila psittaci* infections

Chlamydophila pneumoniae and *C. psittaci* multiply in similar target cells. The patterns of disease they cause are identical except that the ovine abortion agent of *C. psittaci* can cause infectious abortion in pregnant women and acute infections due to *C. psittaci* tend to be more severe than those caused by *C. pneumoniae*.

Respiratory infections

In children the typical disease picture is a mild upper respiratory tract infection, but pneumonia has been reported, even in infants. This pneumonia should not be confused with *C. trachomatis* infant pneumonitis, in which the parents must be treated for their STD. Chlamydial pneumonias typically have an insidious onset, fulminant psittacosis being an exception. Epithelial cells and mononuclear phagocytes are target cells and the result is pneumonitis without purulent sputum. If the sputum turns purulent, there is likely to be an accompanying bacterial infection. Except for true psittacosis and in elderly patients with underlying predisposing disease, the prognosis is good, but convalescence can be prolonged by persisting fatigue. There is a tendency for relapses.[53]

C. pneumoniae can cause sinusitis and otitis, but dry cough with mild pharyngitis is often the most common manifestation.[22]

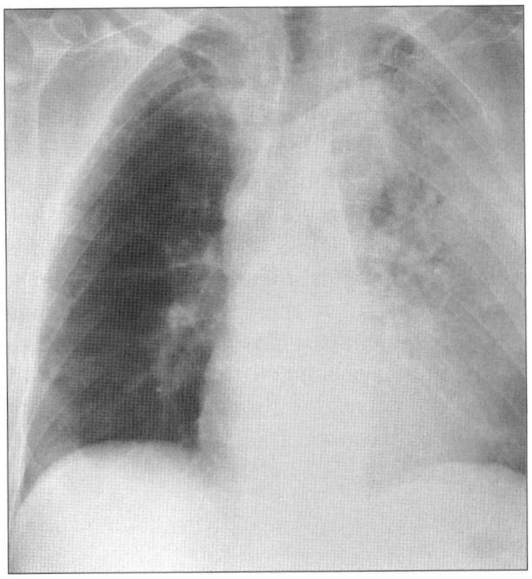

Fig. 236.8 *Chlamydia pneumoniae* reinfection pneumonia in a 63-year-old male.

C. pneumoniae is the cause of acute bronchitis in 5% of cases.[5] Infection can be asymptomatic, especially in children, but the number of carriers is unknown.

In young adults, 10% of cases of *C. pneumoniae* infections are pneumonias, which often have an insidious-onset pharyngitis followed by a mild pneumonia. The throat is hoarse and there is a persistent dry cough and usually a low-grade fever. Erythrocyte sedimentation rate and C-reactive protein are elevated, but the white cell count is usually normal or only mildly elevated. Differential diagnosis from other causes of pneumonia is impossible on clinical grounds. Chlamydial pneumonia cannot be reliably differentiated from pneumococcal pneumonia on chest radiograph, because chlamydial pneumonia can have a lobar pattern as well as its more usual pattern of 'atypical' pneumonia (Fig. 236.8) (see Chapter 34).

Generalized Chlamydophila pneumoniae *and* Chlamydophila psittaci *infections*

Chlamydophila pneumoniae and *C. psittaci* are able to multiply in mononuclear phagocytes and this enables dissemination into the circulation. Headache and confusion are common in severe infections, and meningoencephalitis and Guillain–Barré syndrome have been described. In some patients liver enzymes are elevated and proteinuria is present. Endocarditis, myocarditis and pericarditis have been found.[54] All of these symptoms have been described in the absence of any preceding overt respiratory infection.

C. pneumoniae infection has a tendency to remain persistent and low levels of the agent have been demonstrated in the lungs of healthy young adults by immunohistochemistry.[55] *Chlamydophila*-specific IgA levels are elevated in serum and especially in the local secretions of patients with chronic obstructive lung disease.[56] Exacerbations associated with acute *C. pneumoniae* infections have been reported[57] but more often there seems to be chronic carriage without seroconversion; the agent is detected in pulmonary secretions by using PCR and is shown to be abundant in histologic samples by immunohistochemistry and electron microscopy.[55,58] The extent to which this carriage participates in the inflammatory process is not known.

Recent studies have also suggested an association between *C. pneumoniae* and asthma, in both adults and children.[59] Favorable outcomes in therapeutic trials with antibiotics effective against *C. pneumoniae* have been claimed in adult-onset asthma,[60] where the presence of specific IgA antibodies again seems to be a better marker of chronic infection than IgG. The role of the agent in childhood asthma is uncertain, but carriage demonstrated by both culture and PCR has been reported, as has *C. pneumoniae*-specific IgE and local IgA antibodies. The first large intervention trial against *C. pneumoniae*-associated asthma in adults with antibiotics left the question open.[61]

One of the most unexpected findings in *Chlamydia* research has been the association of *C. pneumoniae* with atherosclerosis.[62] If proven, it will be of enormous significance.

Over 50 seroepidemiologic surveys have repeatedly demonstrated that the presence of elevated antibodies against *C. pneumoniae* is associated with an increased risk of having a cardiac event.[63,64] The magnitude of the increased risk is dependent partly on the prevalence of antibodies in control population; it is greatest in young populations during periods between epidemics. The risk increases usually about 2-fold but higher risks have been reported. The antibody findings are further supported by the presence of circulating immune complexes containing *C. pneumoniae* antibodies and antigens, pointing to an access of chlamydial components into the circulation.[45] Final demonstration of the common presence of the agent in the atherosclerotic lesion has been obtained by electron microscopy, immunohistochemistry, nucleic acid demonstration by PCR, in-situ hybridization[65] and even isolation of the agent from lesions.[35,66,67]

The important question is does this presence have an effect on the atherosclerotic process? There is a possibility that *C. pneumoniae* is simply an innocent bystander in atherosclerotic lesions. However, it is a nonmotile intracellular pathogen, able to multiply in macrophages, endothelial cells and smooth muscle cells.[36] This multiplication is accompanied by induction of cytokines, adhesion molecules, proteases and oxidative substances as the host defense mechanisms against chlamydial infection. Infected macrophages tend to become foam cells, the characteristic pathologic feature of the atherosclerotic plaque.[38] Several well-known risk factors for coronary heart disease are also associated with a chronic *C. pneumoniae* infection, such as smoking, elevated cholesterol levels, lowered levels of high-density cholesterol[64] and elevated blood pressure.[68] Continuous induction of cytokines may be responsible for this association. Recent animal experiments point to the possibility that it could even initiate the process[69] and that this could be prevented with antibiotics. Recent preliminary human intervention trials with macrolides[70–75] or doxycycline[76] have given partly contradictory results.

If chlamydial infection is a significant factor in the development of atherosclerosis, it would open new perspectives in the battle against this disease and even the prospect of the development of an 'anti-atherosclerosis vaccine' is possible.

Chlamydia*-associated arthritis*

Chlamydiae have long been known to trigger reactive arthritis which is typically seen after an episode of urethritis in males (Reiter's syndrome – a similar association is elusive in females) and in cases of *C. pneumoniae* and *C. psittaci* after a respiratory tract infection. Patients usually have HLA-B27 antigen and a complete Reiter's triad of urethritis, conjunctivitis and arthritis can occasionally be seen. Although chlamydial cultures are usually negative, recent studies have demonstrated chlamydial particles in synovial fluid and metabolically active chlamydia in synovial tissue, which is not the original concept of reactive arthritis. This could also explain why prolonged antibiotic treatment is effective in chlamydial arthritis[77] but not in enterobacterial reactive arthritis. *Chlamydia trachomatis* seems to be the most common cause of chlamydial arthritis. Whether this is a reflection of differing tissue tropism of the different *Chlamydia* spp. is not known.

Chlamydiae in cancer and chronic neurologic processes

By the 1930s, *C. trachomatis* lymphogranuloma venereum biovars had been associated with anorectal cancers and subsequently they were associated with cervical dysplasia and cancer. Recently, these observations have been repeated and there seems to be an association between *C. trachomatis* infection and invasive squamous cell cervical carcinoma.[78] In smokers, *C. pneumoniae* has been associated with squamous cell carcinoma and small cell carcinoma in lungs.[79] The situation is analogous to the association between *Helicobacter pylori* and gastric cancer and it deserves further study. There are some claims that *C. pneumoniae* is associated with chronic neurologic processes such as multiple sclerosis and Alzheimer's disease, but this has remained unproven.[80]

MANAGEMENT (see Chapters 18, 34 and 74)

Chlamydiae are sensitive to tetracyclines, macrolides, azalides and newer fluoroquinolones. An antimicrobial effect is also seen with rifampin (rifampicin), clindamycin and chloramphenicol. Chlamydiae are resistant to aminoglycosides, vancomycin and cephalosporins.

Chlamydiae contain penicillin-binding proteins and amoxicillin has been recommended for *C. trachomatis* cervicitis or carriage during pregnancy.[81] However, there is a danger of infection becoming chronic. Single-dose 1g azithromycin is replacing the traditional 7–10 days' tetracycline or macrolide treatment in uncomplicated genital chlamydial infections.[82] In complications such as PID, longer treatment periods of 2 weeks are recommended, and a possible polymicrobial origin must be considered. In *C. trachomatis* conjunctivitis, whether neonatal or adult, topical treatment is not sufficient. *C. pneumoniae* can be very resistant to therapy and in pneumonia 3-week macrolide or doxycycline courses have been recommended. In chronic chlamydial infections, prolonged treatment courses of 1–3 months have been used. Persistent forms seem to be very resistant to treatment and in intervention trials even 1-year courses have been tried.

REFERENCES

1. Halberstaedter L, Prowazek S von. Über Zelleinschlüsse parasitärer Natur beim Trachom. Arb Gesundheitsa 1907;26:44–7.
2. Tang FF, Chang HL, Huang YT, Wang KC. Trachoma virus in chick embryo [in Chinese]. Natl Med J China 1957;43:81–6.
3. Schachter J. Chlamydial infections. N Engl J Med 1978;298:428–35;490–5;540–9.
4. Mårdh PA, Paavonen J, Puolakkainen M. *Chlamydia*. New York: Plenum Press; 1988.
5. Kuo CC, Jackson LA, Campbell LA, Grayston JT. *Chlamydia pneumoniae* (TWAR). Clin Microbiol Rev 1995;8:451–61.
6. Stephens RS. Introduction. In: Stephens RS, ed. Chlamydia: intracellular biology, pathogenesis, and immunity. Washington DC: American Society for Microbiology; 1999:xi–xxiii.
7. Rockey DD, Lenart J, Stephens RS. Genome sequencing and our understanding of chlamydiae. Infect Immun 2000;68:5473–9.
8. Everett KD, Bush RM, Andersen AA. Emended description of the order Chlamydiales, proposal of *Parachlamydiaceae* fam. nov. and *Simkaniaceae* fam. nov., each containing one monotypic genus, revised taxonomy of the family *Chlamydiaceae*, including a new genus and five new species, and standards for the identification of organisms. Int J Syst Bacteriol 1999;49:415–40.
9. Kahane S, Greenberg D, Friedman MG, *et al.* High prevalence of 'Simkania Z,' a novel Chlamydia-like bacterium, in infants with acute bronchiolitis. J Infect Dis 1998;177:1425–9.
10. Hatch TP. Developmental biology. In: Stephens RS, ed. Chlamydia: intracellular biology, pathogenesis and immunity. Washington DC: American Society for Microbiology; 1999:29–67.
11. Brown WJ, Rockey DD. Identification of an antigen localized to an apparent septum within dividing chlamydiae. Infect immun 2000;68:708–15.
12. Palmer L, Falkow S. A common plasmid of *Chlamydia trachomatis*. Plasmid 1986;16:52–62.
13. Matsumoto A. Structural characteristics of chlamydial bodies. In: Baron AL, ed. Microbiology of *Chlamydia*. Boca Raton: CRC Press; 1988;21–46.
14. Stephens RS, Wagar EA, Schoolnik G. High resolution mapping of serovar-specific and common antigenic determinants of the major outer membrane protein for *Chlamydia trachomatis*. J Exp Med 1988;167:817–31.
15. Zhang JP, Stephens RS. Mechanism of attachment of *Chlamydia trachomatis* to eukaryotic host cells. Cell 1992;69:861–9.
16. Kuo CC, Takahashi N, Swanson AF, *et al.* An N-linked high-mannose type oligosaccharide, expressed at the major outer membrane protein of *Chlamydia trachomatis*, mediates attachment and infectivity of the microorganism to HeLa cells. J Clin Invest 1996;98:2813–8.
17. Hackstadt T. Cell biology. In: Stephens RS, ed. Chlamydia: intracellular biology, pathogenesis and immunity. Washington DC: American Society for Microbiology; 1999:101–38.
18. Jendro MC, Deutsch T, Korber B, *et al.* Infection of human monocyte-derived macrophages with *Chlamydia trachomatis* induces apoptosis of T cells: a potential mechanism for persistent infection. Infect Immun 2000;68:6704–11.
19. Belland RJ, Scidmore MA, Crane DD, *et al.* *Chlamydia trachomatis* cytotoxicity associated with complete and partial cytotoxin genes. Proc Natl Acad Sci USA 2001;98:13984–9.
20. Beatty WL, Morrison RP, Byrne GI. Persistent *Chlamydiae*: from cell cultures to a paradigm for chlamydial pathogenesis. Microbiol Rev 1994;58:686–99.
21. Aldous MB, Grayston JT, Wang SP, Foy HM. Seroepidemiology of *Chlamydia pneumoniae* TWAR infection in Seattle families, 1966–1979. J Infect Dis 1992;166:646–9.
22. Ekman MR, Grayston JT, Visakorpi R, *et al.* An epidemic of infections due to *Chlamydia pneumoniae* in military conscripts. Clin Infect Dis 1993;17:420–5.
23. Hyde SR, Benirschke K. Gestational psittacosis: case report and literature review. Mod Pathol 1997;10:602–7.
24. Essig A, Heinemann M, Simnacher U, Marre R. Infection of *Acanthamoeba castellanii* by *Chlamydia pneumoniae*. Appl Environ Microbiol 1997;63:1396–9.
25. Ward MJ. Mechanisms of Chlamydia-induced disease. In: Stephens RS, ed. Chlamydia: intracellular biology, pathogenesis and immunity. Washington DC: American Society for Microbiology; 1999:171–210.
26. Moulder JW, Levy NJ, Schulman RP. Persistent infection of mouse fibroblast (L cells) with *Chlamydia psittaci*: evidence for a cryptic chlamydial form. Infect Immun 1980;30:874–83.
27. Kutlin A, Flegg C, Stenzel D, *et al.* Ultrastructural study of *Chlamydia pneumoniae* in a continuous-infection model. J Clin Microbiol 2001;39:3721–3.
28. Holland MJ, Bailey RL, Hayes LJ, *et al.* Conjunctival scarring in trachoma is associated with depressed cell-mediated immune responses to chlamydial antigens. J Infect Dis 1993;168:1528–31.
29. Grayston JT, Wang SP, Yeh LJ, Kuo CC. Importance of reinfection in the pathogenesis of trachoma. Rev Infect Dis 1985;7:717–25.
30. Morrison RP, Belland RJ, Lyng K, Caldwell HD. Chlamydial disease pathogenesis: the 57-kD chlamydial hypersensitivity antigen is a stress response protein. J Exp Med 1989;170:1271–83.
31. Yuan Y, Lyng K, Zhang Y-X, *et al.* Monoclonal antibodies defining genus-specific, species-specific and cross-reactive epitopes of the chlamydial 60 kilodalton heat shock protein (hsp60): specific immunodetection and purification of chlamydial hsp60. Infect Immun 1992;60:2288–96.
32. Schacter J, Dawson CR. The epidemiology of trachoma predicts more blindness in the future. Scand J Infect Dis 1990;20(Suppl.69):55–62.
33. Burgoyne RA. Lymphogranuloma venereum. Prim Care 1990;17:153–7.
34. Boman J, Söderberg S, Forsberg J, *et al.* High prevalence of *Chlamydia pneumoniae* DNA in peripheral blood mononuclear cells in patients with cardiovascular disease and in middle-aged blood donors. J Infect Dis 1998;178:274–7.
35. Maass M, Bartels C, Engel PM, *et al.* Endovascular presence of viable *Chlamydia pneumoniae* is a common phenomenon in coronary artery disease. J Am Coll Cardiol 1998;31:827–32.
36. Godzik KL, O'Brien ER, Wang SK, Kuo CC. *In vitro* susceptibility of human vascular wall cells to infection with *Chlamydia pneumoniae*. J Clin Microbiol 1995;33:2411–4.
37. Kol A, Sukhova GK, Lichtman AH, Libby P. Chlamydial heat shock protein 60 localizes in human atheroma and regulates macrophage tumor necrosis factor-α and matrix metalloproteinase expression. Circulation 1998;98:300–7.
38. Kalayoglu MV, Byrne GI. Induction of macrophage foam cell formation by *Chlamydia pneumoniae*. J Infect Dis 1998;177:725–9.
39. Whittum-Hudson JA, An LL, Saltzman M, *et al.* Oral immunization with an anti-idiotypic antibody to the exoglycolipid antigen protects against experimental *Chlamydia trachomatis* infection. Nature Med 1996;2:1116–21.
40. Schachter J, West SK, Mabey D, *et al.* Azithromycin in control of trachoma. Lancet 1999;354:630–5.
41. West S, Munoz B, Lynch M, *et al.* Impact of face-washing on trachoma in Kongwa, Tanzania. Lancet 1995;345:155–8.
42. US Preventive Services Task Force. Screening for chlamydial infection: recommendations and rationale. Am J Prev Med 2001;20(3 Suppl.):90–4.
43. Black CM. Current methods of laboratory diagnosis of *Chlamydia trachomatis* infections. Clin Microbiol Rev 1997;10:160–84.

44. Dowell SF, Peeling RW, Boman J, *et al.* Standardizing *Chlamydia pneumoniae* assays: recommendations from the Centers for Disease Control and Prevention (USA) and the Laboratory Centre for Disease Control (Canada). Clin Infect Dis 2001;33:492–503.
45. Saikku P, Leinonen M, Tenkanen L, *et al.* Chronic *Chlamydia pneumoniae* infection as a risk factor for coronary heart disease in the Helsinki Heart Study. Ann Intern Med 1992;116:273–78.
46. Brunham R, Paavonen J, Stevens CE, *et al.* Mucopurulent cervicitis – the ignored counterpart in women of urethritis in men. N Engl J Med 1984;311:1–6.
47. Stamm WE, Wagner KF, Amsel R, *et al.* Causes of the acute urethral syndrome in women. N Engl J Med 1980;303:409–15.
48. Eckert LO, Hawes SE, Wolner-Hanssen PK, *et al.* Endometritis: the clinical-pathologic syndrome. Am J Obstet Gynecol 2002;186:690–5.
49. Cates W, Wasserheit JN. Genital chlamydial infections. Epidemiology and reproductive sequelae. Am J Obstet Gynecol 1991;164:1771–81.
50. Sorensen JL, Thranov I, Hoff G, Dirach J. Early- and late-onset pelvic inflammatory disease among women with cervical *Chlamydia trachomatis* infection at the time of induced abortion – a follow-up study. Infection 1994;22:242–6.
51. Beem MO, Saxon EM. Respiratory tract colonization and a distinctive pneumonia in infants infected with *Chlamydia trachomatis*. N Engl J Med 1977;296:306–10.
52. Weiss SG, Newcomb RW, Beem MO. Pulmonary assessment of children after chlamydial pneumonia of infancy. J Pediatr 1986;108:659–64.
53. Kauppinen M, Saikku P. Pneumonia due to *Chlamydia pneumoniae*: prevalence, clinical features, diagnosis and treatment. Clin Infect Dis 1995;21(Suppl.):244–52.
54. Odeh M, Oliven A. Chlamydial infections of the heart. Eur J Clin Microbiol Infect Dis 1992;11:885–93.
55. Wu L, Skinner SJ, Lambie N, *et al.* Immunohistochemical staining for *Chlamydia pneumoniae* is increased in lung tissue from subjects with chronic obstructive pulmonary disease. Am J Respir Crit Care Med 2000;162:1148–51.
56. Hertzen L von, Leinonen M, Surcel HM, *et al.* Measurement of sputum antibodies in the diagnosis of acute and chronic respiratory infections associated with *Chlamydia pneumoniae*. Clin Diagn Lab Immunol 1995;2:454–7.
57. Blasi F, Legnani D, Lombardo VM, *et al.* *Chlamydia pneumoniae* infection in acute exacerbations of COPD. Eur Respir J 1993;6:19–22.
58. Theegarten D, Mogilevski G, Anhenn O, *et al.* The role of chlamydia in the pathogenesis of pulmonary emphysema. Electron microscopy and immunofluorescence reveal corresponding findings as in atherosclerosis. Virchows Arch 2000;437:190–3.
59. Hahn DL. *Chlamydia pneumoniae*, asthma, and COPD: what is the evidence? Ann Allergy Asthma Immunol 1999;83:271–88.
60. Hahn DL. Treatment of *Chlamydia pneumoniae* infection in adult asthma: a before–after trial. J Fam Pract 1995;41:345–51.
61. Black PN, Blasi F, Jenkins CR, *et al.* Trial of roxithromycin in subjects with asthma and serological evidence of infection with *Chlamydia pneumoniae*. Am J Respir Crit Care Med 2001;164:536–41.
62. Saikku P, Leinonen M, Mattila K, *et al.* Serologic evidence of an association of a novel *Chlamydia*, TWAR, with chronic coronary heart disease and acute myocardial infarction. Lancet 1988;ii:983–6.
63. Danesh J, Collins R, Peto R. Chronic infections and coronary heart disease: is there a link? Lancet 1997;350:430–6.
64. Leinonen M, Saikku P. Evidence for infectious agents in cardiovascular diseases and atherosclerosis. Lancet Infect Dis 2002;2:11–17.
65. Kuo CC, Shor A, Campbell LA, *et al.* Demonstration of *Chlamydia pneumoniae* in atherosclerotic lesions of coronary arteries. J Infect Dis 1993;167:841–9.
66. Ramirez JA, for the *Chlamydia pneumoniae* Atherosclerosis Study Group. Isolation of *Chlamydia pneumoniae* from the coronary artery of a patient with coronary atherosclerosis. Ann Intern Med 1996;125:979–82.
67. Taylor-Robinson D, Thomas BJ. *Chlamydia pneumoniae* in arteries: the facts, their interpretation, and future studies. J Clin Pathol 1998;51:793–7.
68. Cook PJ, Lip GYH, Davies P, *et al.* *Chlamydia pneumoniae* antibodies in severe essential hypertension. Hypertension 1998;31:589–94.
69. Fong IW. Antibiotics effects in a rabbit model of *Chlamydia pneumoniae*-induced atherosclerosis. J Infect Dis 2000;181(Suppl.3):S514–8.
70. Gupta S, Leatham EW, Carrington D, *et al.* Elevated *Chlamydia pneumoniae* antibodies, cardiovascular events, and azithromycin in male survivors of myocardial infarction. Circulation 1997;96:404–7.
71. Gurfinkel E, Bozovich G, Beck E, *et al.* Treatment with the antibiotic roxithromycin in patients with acute non-Q-wave coronary syndromes. The final report of the ROXIS Study. Eur Heart J 1999;20:121–7.
72. Anderson JL, Muhlestein JB, Carlquist J, *et al.* Randomized secondary prevention trial of azithromycin in patients with coronary artery disease and serological evidence for Chlamydia pneumoniae infection. The Azithromycin in Coronary Artery Disease: Elimination of Myocardial Infection with Chlamydia (ACADEMIC) study. Circulation 1999;99:1540–7.
73. Neumann F, Kastrati A, Miethke T, *et al.* Treatment of *Chlamydia pneumoniae* infection with roxithromycin and effect on neointima proliferation after coronary stent placement (ISAR-3): a randomised, double-blind, placebo-controlled trial. Lancet 2001;357:2085–9.
74. Sinisalo J, Mattila K, Valtonen V, *et al.* Effect of 3 months of antimicrobial treatment with clarithromycin in acute non-q-wave coronary syndrome. Circulation 2002;105:1555–60.
75. Wiesli P, Czerwenka W, Meniconi A, *et al.* Roxithromycin treatment prevents progression of peripheral arterial occlusive disease in *Chlamydia pneumoniae* seropositive men. A randomized, double-blind, placebo-controlled trial. Circulation 2002;105:2646–52.
76. Mosorin M, Juvonen J, Biancari F, *et al.* Use of doxycycline to decrease the growth rate of abdominal aortic aneurysms: a randomized, double-blind, placebo-controlled pilot study. J Vasc Surg 2001;34:606–10.
77. Lauhio A, Leirisalo-Repo M, Lähdevirta J, *et al.* Double-blind, placebo-controlled study of three-month lymecycline course in reactive arthritis with special reference to *Chlamydia* arthritis. Arthritis Rheum 1991;34:6–14.
78. Anttila T, Saikku P, Koskela P, *et al.* Serotypes of Chlamydia trachomatis and risk for development of cervical squamous cell carcinoma. JAMA 2001;285:47–51.
79. Laurila A, Anttila T, Läärä E, *et al.* Serological evidence of an association between *Chlamydia pneumoniae* infection and lung cancer. Int J Cancer 1997;71:31–4.
80. Yucesan C, Sriram S. *Chlamydia pneumoniae* infection of the central nervous system. Curr Opin Neurol 2001;14:355–9.
81. Alary M, Joly JR, Moutquin JM, *et al.* Randomised comparison of amoxycillin and erythromycin in treatment of genital chlamydial infection in pregnancy. Lancet 1994;344:1461–5.
82. Clinical Effectiveness Group (Association of Genitourinary Medicine and the Medical Society for the Study of Venereal Diseases). National guideline for the management of *Chlamydia trachomatis* genital tract infection. Sex Transm Infect 1999;75(Suppl.1):S4–8.

chapter

237 Opportunistic Fungi

Andy IM Hoepelman

INTRODUCTION

Fungal infections have become increasingly important clinically because of the rising incidence of immunocompromised patients as a result of infection, malignancy (especially leukemia), chemotherapy and immunosuppressive therapy, especially in transplantation medicine and in critical care. Moreover, the use of current antimicrobial prophylactic strategies has likely contributed to the changing epidemiology of invasive mycoses. Table 237.1 gives a list of medically important fungi that can cause disseminated infection in humans. Table 237.2 shows the variables that likely account for the current trends in the epidemiology of opportunistic fungal infections.

CANDIDIASIS

NATURE

Candida spp. are yeast-like fungi that can form true hyphae as well as pseudohyphae. They are ubiquitous in soil and food and can be found as normal commensals on skin and mucosal membranes of the human gastrointestinal, genitourethral and respiratory tracts.

Candida spp. that under certain conditions are clinically important are *C. albicans, C. guilliermondii, C. krusei, C. parapsilosis, C. tropicalis, C. kefyr, C. lusitaniae, C. rugosa, C. dubliniensis* and *C. glabrata* (also called *Torulopsis glabrata*).

The fungal origin of these lesions was first proposed in 1839.[1]

EPIDEMIOLOGY

Since the introduction of antibiotics in the 1940s, there has been a sharp increase in the incidence of candidal infections. In a survey of 180 hospitals from 1980 to 1990, *Candida* spp. were the sixth most commonly isolated nosocomial pathogens, most frequently cultured from the urinary tract (46%).[2] *Candida* spp. were the fourth most common cause of bloodstream infection (BSI; 8%), and were associated with a mortality of 29% (compared with 17% for BSIs caused by nonfungal pathogens).[2,3]

In addition, there is an increasing shift toward non-*albicans* spp. in candidemia. A surveillance program of BSIs in the USA, Canada, Latin America and Europe from 1997 through 1999 detected 1184 episodes of candidemia in 71 medical centers (32 in the USA, 23 in Europe, nine in Latin America and seven in Canada). Overall, 55% of the yeast BSIs were due to *C. albicans*, followed by *C. glabrata* (20%) and *C. parapsilosis* (15%), *C. tropicalis* (9%) and miscellaneous *Candida* spp. (6%).[4]

Changes in the frequency of invasive candidiasis are most notable in the following subgroups of patients: those hospitalized in critical care units, patients with hematologic malignancies, hematopoietic stem cell transplant recipients and organ transplant recipients.[5] In a recent review of 74 published studies,[6,7] the most important risk factors for nosocomial colonization and infection with *Candida* spp. were as follows: underlying diseases (hematologic cancer (OR 1.7–45), renal failure (OR 1.4–22), hepatic failure (OR 7–42)); invasive procedures or devices (central venous or arterial catheter (OR 5.8–26), urinary catheter (OR 13)); interhospital transfer of a patient (OR 21); and prolonged use of antibiotics (OR 1.7–25), especially vancomycin (OR 275). In mice and humans, vancomycin has indeed been shown to enhance gastrointestinal colonization with *C. albicans*.[2]

Among hematopoietic stem cell transplant recipients, an overall decrease has been documented in the frequency of candidal infections, as well as a shift toward isolation of non-*albicans* species of *Candida*.[8,9] It has been proposed that use of fluconazole as antifungal prophylaxis largely accounts for these trends.[8] Antifungal prophylaxis with fluconazole during neutropenia and acute graft-versus-host disease (until day 75 after transplantation) was associated with a significant reduction in the incidence of invasive candidiasis and improved survival rates.[9] However, although *C. albicans* was the most common colonizing isolate before transplantation, resistant species such as *C. krusei* and *C. glabrata* were isolated after transplantation and exposure to fluconazole.[9] In another study, fluconazole prophylaxis was the most important determinant for the relative increase in isolation of *C. krusei* (OR 27.07) and *C. glabrata* (OR 5).[8] A meta-analysis of 16 randomized controlled trials, however, showed that fluconazole prophylaxis in neutropenic non-bone marrow transplant patients did not decrease fungus-related mortality or systemic fungal infections.[10]

Among organ transplant recipients, invasive candidal infections are most relevant for liver and pancreas transplant recipients. An overall decline in the incidence of invasive candidiasis has been noted in liver transplant recipients, even in the absence of systemic antifungal prophylaxis; many centers now report incidences of under 10%.

Molecular typing has shown that, in the majority of cases, candidemia arises from an endogenous origin after previous colonization. This holds true for *C. albicans* and most non-*albicans* spp. except for infections with *C. parapsilosis*, which are thought to arise mainly from infected biomaterials, intravenous fluids or the hands of health care workers.[3] Also, human-to-human transmission (patient-to-patient, nurse-to-patient and between sexual partners) has become increasingly important.

Recurrence of oropharyngeal candidiasis in patients who have AIDS has been shown to be mostly due to recurrence of the same strain (relapse), although infection with a new strain also occurs.[3]

PATHOGENICITY

Intact barrier function is an essential feature of host defense against candidiasis. The virulence of the *Candida* spp. has been shown to correlate with their ability to adhere to epithelial cells (especially *C. albicans*) or plastic polymers such as intravascular or urethral catheters (*C. tropicalis*). The fungus is capable of secreting proteinases and lipases that can assist invasion, although the clinical importance of these enzymes is not clear.[11]

After candidal invasion of the dermis or bloodstream, neutrophils constitute the first line of defense, followed by monocytes and eosinophils, which can kill *Candida* spp. via oxidative and nonoxidative

FUNGI CAUSING DISSEMINATED INFECTION IN HUMANS	
Fungi	**Medically important species**
Penicillium	*Penicillium marneffei*
Candida	*C. albicans, C. guilliermondii, C. krusei, C. lusitaniae, C. parapsilosis, C. pseudotropicalis, C. rugosa, C. stellatoidea, C. tropicalis, Torulopsis (or Candida) glabrata*
Cryptococcus	*C. neoformans var. neoformans, C. neoformans var gattii*
Aspergillus	*A. fumigatus, A. flavus, A. niger, A. terreus, A. nidulans*
Mucorates	*Rhizopus oryzae, R. arrhizus, R. rhizopodiformis, Rhizomucor pusillus, Absidia oryzae, A. corymbifera, A. ramosa, Mucor circinelloides*
Histoplasma	*H. capsulatum*
Coccidioides	*C. immitis*
Blastomyces	*B. dermatitidis*
Sporothrix	*S. schenckii*
Fusarium	*F. solani, F. oxysporum, F. moniliforme, F. dimerum, F. chlamydosporum, F. anthophilum*
Trichosporon	*T. beigelii, T. capitatum*
Geotrichum	*G. candidum*
Rhodotorula	*R. rubra*
Dermatiaceous molds (phaeohyphomycetes)	*Pseudallescheria boydii* (scedosporium apiospermum), *Bipolaris, Alternaria,* Scedosporium prolificans

Table 237.1 Fungi causing disseminated infection in humans.

VARIABLES THAT LIKELY ACCOUNT FOR THE CURRENT TRENDS IN THE EPIDEMIOLOGY OF OPPORTUNISTIC FUNGAL INFECTIONS
Increasing number of susceptible hosts
Greater laboratory expertise in the detection and identification of fungi
Use of new transplantation modalities for hematopoietic stem cell transplantation (e.g. $CD34^+$ selected autografts and peripheral blood stem cell transplantation)
Evolution in organ transplantation practices
Advances in surgical technology
Use of corticosteroid-sparing regimens and an overall conservative approach to immunosuppression
Use of novel immunosuppressive agents
Use of antimicrobial prophylactic practices, e.g. use of fluconazole for antifungal prophylaxis, ganciclovir for cytomegalovirus prophylaxis, quinolones for Gram-negative bacterial prophylaxis

Table 237.2 Variables that likely account for the current trends in the epidemiology of opportunistic fungal infections.[5]

pathways. Patients who have neutropenia are particularly at risk of developing candidiasis, which underscores the importance of neutrophils in host defense against this fungus. The clinical outcome of infection is primarily determined by the host defense status. Clinical and experimental data suggest that:

- an impairment of acquired cellular immunity (e.g. in HIV infection) predisposes mainly to mucocutaneous candidiasis (gastrointestinal and vaginal); and
- impaired innate immunity, especially neutrophil function, with or without impaired T-cell function, is the major risk factor for the development of systemic candidiasis.

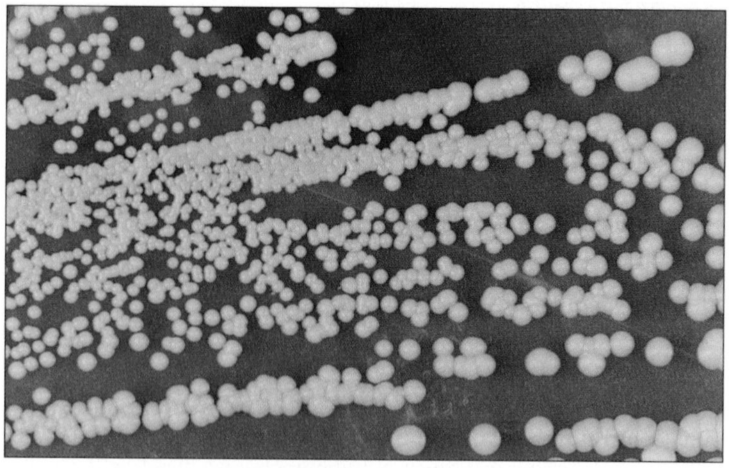

Fig. 237.1 Colonies of *Candida albicans* on culture plate.

In the rare chronic mucocutaneous candidiasis syndrome, various combinations of defect in T cell response to *Candida* spp. have been described[12] (see Chapter 98).

The role of humoral acquired immunity in the body's defense against candidal infection remains to be determined.[11]

DIAGNOSTIC MICROBIOLOGY

In general, a diagnosis of candidiasis faces the dual problem of:

- differentiating between colonization and infection, and
- under-detection of deep-seated infection.

In culture, *Candida* spp. grow rapidly at 77–98.6°F (25–37°C) on simple media. On special culture media, hyphae or elongating pseudohyphae are formed.

Candida spp. grow in routine ventilated blood culture flasks and on agar plates as smooth creamy white colonies (Fig. 237.1). A differential culture medium (CHROMagar Candida) can distinguish between *C. albicans* and certain non-*C. albicans* spp.

The yield from blood cultures in disseminated disease using conventional methods is low (15–30%), but improved culture techniques such as biphasic cultures and lysis–centrifugation have greatly improved the diagnostic capacity.[13,14] Recently developed new methods to detect fungi more rapidly in blood cultures are BACTEC and BacT/Alert (Table 237.3). Therefore, appropriate communication about any clinical suspicion of candidemia to the diagnostic laboratory is of paramount importance.

Specimens for microscopic evaluation give a better diagnostic yield after treatment with 10% potassium hydroxide, which lyses epithelial cells. The demonstration of blastoconidia (budding yeast), hyphae and pseudohyphae is highly suggestive but not diagnostic for tissue invasion.[13] Staining with calcofluor white (the preferred method) is a sensitive method for the detection of fungi, but requires a fluorescent microscope. Alternatives to the calcofluor white stain are Gram stain (fungal elements stain Gram positive) and the germ tube test, which enables identification of *C. albicans* (but not most non-*albicans* spp.) by showing the formation of hyphal elements within 90 minutes.[13]

Nonculture methods being developed and evaluated for mycotic infections include polymerase chain reaction (PCR), galactomannan (GM) antigenemia, Western blot (WB) to detect antibodies, and detection of the fungal metabolites D-arabinitol and (1,3)-β-D-glucan. Sample preparation for PCR from blood specimens depends on fractionation of peripheral blood, its pre-incubation in blood culture broth or a total DNA method, which does not rely on fractionation or pre-incubation. Targets for PCR of fungi in the 18S or ITS2 subunits of the ribosomal RNA genes facilitated the design of *Aspergillus* and *Candida* genus and species probes.

DETECTION OF FUNGAL INFECTIONS			
Diagnostic technique	**Major features**	**Useful**	**Not useful**
Microscopy/ histopathology	Rapid Relies on distinctive appearance of organism	Histopathologic identification of: *Cryptococcus* *Blastomyces* *Histoplasma* *Coccidioides*	Cannot give a specific species classification for: *Aspergillus* *Candida*
Culture-based methods			
• Traditional culture	Inexpensive	*Cryptococcus* grows rapidly *Aspergillus* – tissue sample	Slow growth for most endemics Poor sensitivity for *Candida* and *Aspergillus* blood samples
• Automated blood culture methods	Early detection of growth Capital expense	*Candida* and BSIs *Cryptococcus* and *Histoplasma*	No value for *Aspergillus*
Nonculture methods			
• Antigen	Sensitive and specific	*Cryptococcus* and *Histoplasma* *Aspergillus*–galactomannan may be useful	No reliable tests for other mycoses
• Antibody	Moderately sensitive and specific	Endemic mycoses	No reliable tests for opportunisitic fungi
• PCR	Still experimental	Potential use for *Candida* and *Aspergillus*	

Table 237.3 Detection of fungal infections.

GENERAL PATTERNS OF SUSCEPTIBILITY OF *CANDIDA* SPECIES						
Candida species	Fluconazole	Itraconazole	Flucytosine	Amphotericin B	Caspofungin	Voriconazole
C. albicans	S	S	S	S	S	S
C. tropicalis	S	S	S	S	S	S-I
C. parapsilosis	S	S	S	S	S-R	S
C. glabrata	S-DD to R	S-DD to R	S	S-I	S	S
C. krusei	R	S-DD to R	I-R	S-I	S	S
C. lusitaniae	S	S	S	S to R	S	S

Table 237.4 General patterns of susceptibility of *Candida* species (Adapted from Rex *et al.*[27])

The measurement of anticandidal antibodies in the serum of patients does not allow a distinction between colonization and local infection from disseminated disease.[14] The diagnostic sensitivity and specificity reported in the literature of various enzyme immunoassays for cell wall mannan tested on a mixed patient population ranged from 53% to 100% and from 89% to 100%, respectively.[14–16] The diagnostic yield increases significantly with repeated sampling.

The performance of a rapid test based on the ratio of D/L-arabinitol in urine has been disappointing. Many patients were positive, positivity was shown late in infections and many infections due to *C. krusei* remained undetected due to nonproduction of arabinitol.

Molecular diagnosis by PCR appears very promising since fungal DNA can be detected in the blood of infected patients before conventional methods. Furthermore, a broad range of yeasts and molds can be identified to species level. Automation of sample preparation and use of real-time PCR systems will help standardize the procedure and reduce false-positive results due to contamination.[16] Candidal strain typing is mainly used in hospital infection control and for epidemiologic investigation.

Susceptibility testing and drug dosing

Intensive efforts to develop standardized, reproducible and clinically relevant susceptibility testing methods for the fungi have resulted in the development of the NCCLS M27-A methodology for susceptibility testing of yeasts.[17] Data-driven interpretive breakpoints using this method are available for testing the susceptibility of *Candida* spp. to the most important antifungals (Table 237.4). Several features of these breakpoints are important. First, these interpretive breakpoints should not be used with other methods without extensive testing. Second, these breakpoints place a strong emphasis on interpretation in the context of the delivered dose of the azole antifungal agent. The novel category S-DD (susceptible-dose/delivery dependent) indicates that optimizing dosage and bioavailability is critical to successful therapy. In the case of fluconazole, both human and animal data suggest that S-DD isolates may be treated successfully with 12mg/kg/day. In the case of itraconazole, oral absorption is somewhat unpredictable and achievement of blood levels of 0.5g/ml (as determined by high-performance liquid chromatography) appears important to successful therapy. Finally, these breakpoints have been developed on the basis of data from two groups of infected patients: patients with oropharyngeal and esophageal candidiasis and patients with invasive candidiasis (mostly non-neutropenic patients with candidemia).

Reliable and convincing interpretive breakpoints are not yet available for amphotericin B. The NCCLS M27-A methodology does not reliably identify amphotericin B-resistant isolates. Although these methods are as yet insufficiently standardized to permit routine use, several generalizations are becoming apparent. First, amphotericin B resistance appears uncommon among isolates of *C. albicans, C. tropicalis* and *C. parapsilosis*. Second, isolates of *C. lusitaniae* most often demonstrate readily detectable and clinically apparent amphotericin B resistance. However, the exact frequency of this event is uncertain and not all isolates are resistant. Third, a growing body of data suggests that a significant proportion of the isolates of *C. glabrata* and *C. krusei* may be resistant to amphotericin B. Importantly, delivery of additional amphotericin B by use of a lipid-based preparation may not always be adequate to overcome this resistance.

CLINICAL MANIFESTATIONS

Clinical manifestations of candidal infections are also discussed in Chapter 111.

The clinical manifestations of candidal infection can be divided into mucocutaneous infections and deep-seated infections. Mucocutaneous infections include thrush, candidal esophagitis, nonesophageal gastrointestinal candidiasis, candidal vaginitis and cutaneous candidiasis syndromes. Deep-seated infections include chronic disseminated candidiasis (hepatosplenic candidiasis), candidemia and candidiasis of various organ systems.

Mucocutaneous candidiasis

The most common clinical manifestation of candidal infection is oral thrush (acute pseudomembranous candidiasis), which presents as curd-like plaques on examination. It is diagnosed by the demonstration of yeast hyphae and pseudohyphae in a Gram-stained direct smear, 10% potassium hydroxide preparation, calcofluor preparation or culture of scrapings. Oral thrush should alert the physician to the possibility of an underlying disease.

Candidal esophagitis (Fig. 237.2) is frequently associated with AIDS, lymphoma or leukemia, although it can occur in people who are not immunocompromised. In up to 30% of cases of esophagitis there are no oral lesions on examination.

Of women with vulvovaginal candidiasis 75% have no risk factors. Diagnosis is made on the basis of the combination of clinical symptoms, microscopy with 10% potassium hydroxide (include a wet preparation as well to exclude *Trichomonas vaginalis* and clue cells) and/or culture. The vaginal pH in candidiasis should be in the normal range (4.0–4.5); a pH higher than 4.7 indicates bacterial vaginosis, trichomoniasis or a mixed infection.

Chronic mucocutaneous candidiasis is a relatively rare disease characterized by protracted and persistent infections with *Candida* spp. of skin, mucosal membranes, hair and nails, and it is frequently associated with endocrinopathies or autoimmune disorders. Severe disease may prove fatal, usually due to bacterial sepsis. Disseminated candidiasis is a rare complication.[12]

Deep organ infection

Disseminated candidiasis and candidemia constitute major clinical and diagnostic problems. Overall, in more than 50% of cases, fungal blood cultures remain negative,[13] although increased blood volume, ventilation of culture flasks and Isolator lysis–centrifugation cultivation have improved the diagnostic yield to 82%.[14] The value of surveillance cultures is controversial, although absence of *C. albicans* in surveillance cultures has a high predictive value for the absence of disseminated candidiasis in patients who have leukemia or lymphoma or in bone marrow transplantation patients.[2,14] However, isolation of *C. tropicalis* in surveillance cultures is highly suggestive of disseminated infection because more than 50% of these patients will develop candidemia. Skin and eye lesions (Fig. 237.3) are present in only 10% of cases of disseminated candidiasis. In general, only 15–40% of cases are diagnosed early enough to initiate therapy.

For a detailed clinical discussion of disseminated candidiasis, candidemia and chronic disseminated or hepatosplenic candidiasis (Fig. 237.4), see Chapter 111.

Virtually every organ can be infected by *Candida* spp.

Candidal meningitis and encephalitis usually occur as a complication of disseminated candidiasis. In disseminated candidiasis, 62% of cases developed candidal myocarditis,[13] with electrocardiographic changes mimicking infarction and supraventricular tachycardias.

Candida spp. are the major cause of fungal endocarditis, with up to 41% of cases caused by non-*albicans* spp. Blood cultures are positive in 54% of patients; additional means of diagnosis are culture of the cardiac vegetation (73% sensitivity) and histologic examinations.[18a]

Candidal pneumonia (Fig. 237.5) is usually associated with disseminated candidiasis. Primary candidal pneumonia is rare. Diagnosis is based on transbronchial biopsy.

In abdominal surgery, heavy growth of *Candida* spp. in the first culture (intraoperative or from abdominal drain) or an increasing

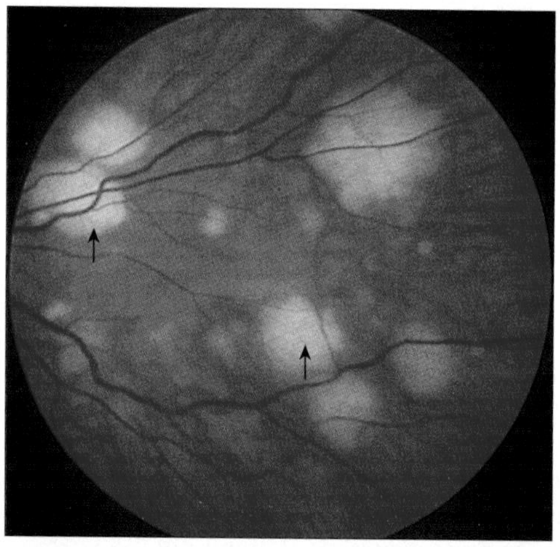

Fig. 237.3 Retina of a patient who has lesions (arrows) due to disseminated candidiasis.

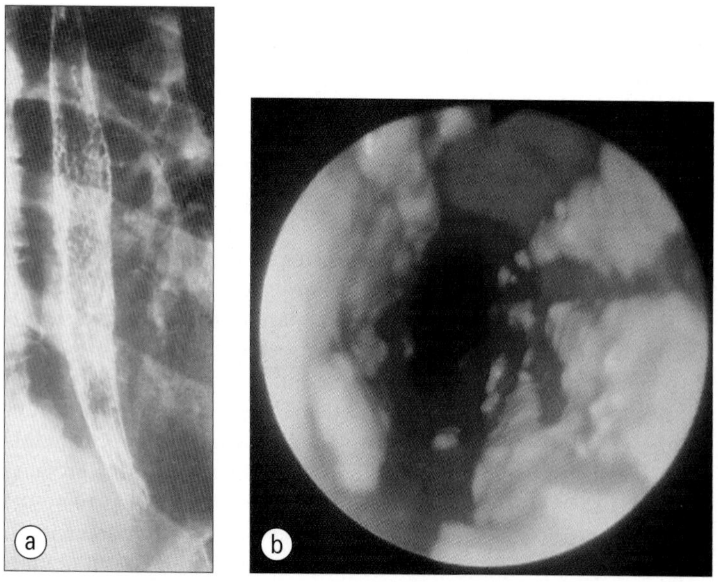

Fig. 237.2 Candidal esophagitis. (a) Double-contrast radiography in candidal esophagitis. (b) Endoscopy of same patient.

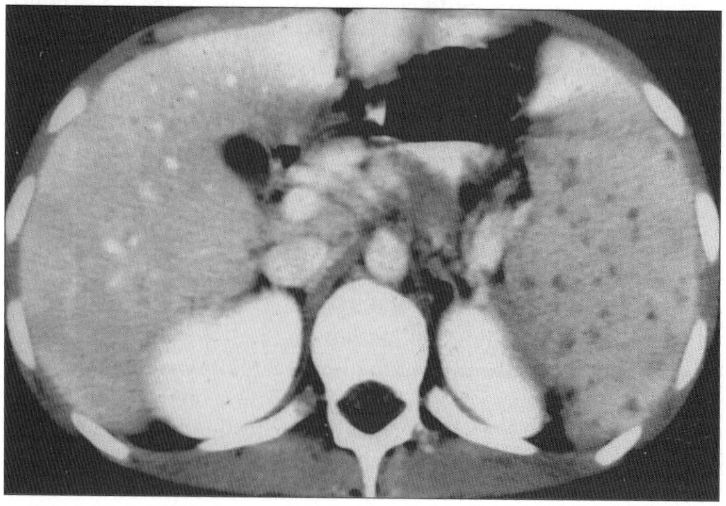

Fig. 237.4 Hepatosplenic candidiasis. Multiple abscesses can be seen.

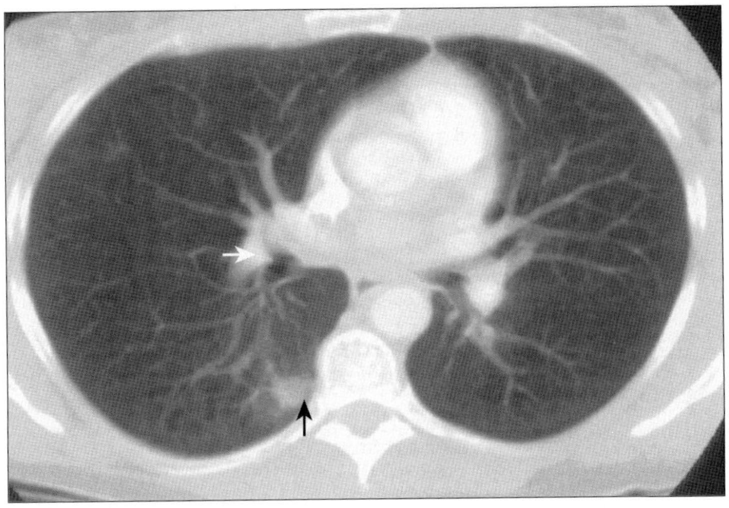

Fig. 237.5 CT scan showing enlarged right hilar lymph node (top arrow) and a posterior infiltrate (bottom arrow) due to *Candida albicans.*

fungal load in serial cultures has been shown to be highly predictive of the development of candidiasis.

Infection of the urinary tract with *Candida* spp. is difficult to discriminate from colonization or from disseminated candidiasis. Microscopic urine analysis does not discriminate, unless renal casts containing yeasts are found, and quantitation of candiduria (such as is used for bacterial urinary infections) is not a reliable indicator of deep infection. Any patient who has persistent candiduria without a recent history of urinary tract instrumentation should be evaluated for diabetes mellitus, renal insufficiency or genitourinary tract abnormalities.[18]

'*Candida* hypersensitivity syndrome'

For many years, *C. albicans* has been mentioned as the cause of a chronic syndrome called *Candida* hypersensitivity syndrome, also known as chronic candidiasis, *Candida*-related complex and 'the yeast connection'.[19] Symptoms include general malaise, fatigue and non-specific gastrointestinal, genitourinary and neuropsychiatric complaints. The syndrome is said to be caused by intestinal and vaginal fungal overgrowth, inflammation, production of fungal toxins and invasion of mucous membranes. Therapy usually consists of a rigorous 'yeast elimination' diet and long-term antifungal treatment.

In an effort to characterize the disease, 100 individuals who had chronic fatigue syndrome were evaluated, including eight who had been given a diagnosis of 'yeast connection'. No differences in laboratory or physical findings, including candidal skin testing, could be detected between patients and control subjects.[20] A prospective randomized clinical trial comparing nystatin treatment with placebo failed to show an improvement in the systemic complaints[21] and analysis of the diet demonstrated nutritional imbalances that could lead to the development of nutritional deficiencies if the diet were followed over a prolonged period of time. The American Academy of Allergy and Immunology reviewed the literature and concluded that the *Candida* hypersensitivity syndrome is 'speculative and unproven'.[22]

MANAGEMENT

Recently the mycoses study group of the Infectious Diseases Society of America (IDSA) published practice guidelines for the treatment of fungal infections.[17,23] These will be followed throughout this part of the chapter. The current drugs approved for treatment of systemic fungal diseases in the USA are listed in Table 237.5. Their mechanism of action is shown in Fig. 237.6.

Mucocutaneous candidiasis

Oropharyngeal candidiasis

Initial episodes can be treated with clotrimazole troches (one 10mg troche 5 times daily) or nystatin (available as a suspension of 100,000 U/ml (46ml 4 times daily) or as flavored 200,000 U pastilles (one or two 4–5 times daily) for 7–14 days). Oral fluconazole (100mg/day for 7–14 days orally) is as effective as and in some studies superior to topical therapy. Itraconazole solution (200mg/day for 7–14 days orally) is as efficacious as fluconazole.[24] Ketoconazole and itraconazole capsules are less effective than fluconazole because of variable absorption. Suppressive therapy is effective for the prevention of recurrent infections, but to reduce the likelihood of development of antifungal resistance it should be used only if the recurrences are frequent or disabling. Fluconazole-refractory oropharyngeal candidiasis will respond to itraconazole (200mg/day orally, preferably as the solution) approximately two-thirds of the time. Amphotericin B oral suspension (1ml 4 times daily of the 100mg/ml suspension) is sometimes effective in patients who do not respond to itraconazole. Intravenous amphotericin B (0.3mg/kg/day) is usually effective and may be used as a last resort in patients with refractory disease. Denture-related disease may require thorough disinfection of the denture for definitive cure.

DRUGS APPROVED FOR TREATMENT OF SYSTEMIC FUNGAL DISEASES

Class	Generic name	Brand name	Available formulation(s)	Year initially approved
Polyene	Amphotericin B	Fungizone (Apothecon Products, Princeton, NJ)	Intravenous, oral solution	1958
Polyene	Amphotericin B lipid complex	Abelcet (Liposome, Princeton, NJ)	Intravenous	1995
Polyene	Amphotericin B cholesteryl sulfate	Amphotec (SEQUUS Pharmaceuticals, Menlo Park, CA)	Intravenous	1996
Polyene	Amphotericin B liposomal	AmBisome (Fujisawa Healthcare, Deerfield, IL)	Intravenous	1997
Pyrimidine	Flucytosine	Ancoban (ICN Pharmaceuticals, Costa Mesa, CA)	Oral tablet, intravenous	1972
Azole	Ketoconazole	Nizoral (Janssen Pharmaceutica, Titusville, NJ)	Oral tablet	1981
Azole	Fluconazole	Diflucan (Pfizer, New York, NY)	Intravenous, oral tablet, oral suspension	1990
Azole	Itraconazole	Sporanox (Janssen Pharmaceutica, Titusvilie, NJ)	Intravenous, oral capsule, oral solution	1992
Azole	Voriconazole	Vfend (Pfizer, New York, NY)	Intravenous, oral tablet	2002
Echinocandin	Caspofungin	Cancidas (MSD, Whitehouse Station, NJ)	Intravenous	2001

Table 237.5 Drugs approved for treatment of systemic fungal diseases.

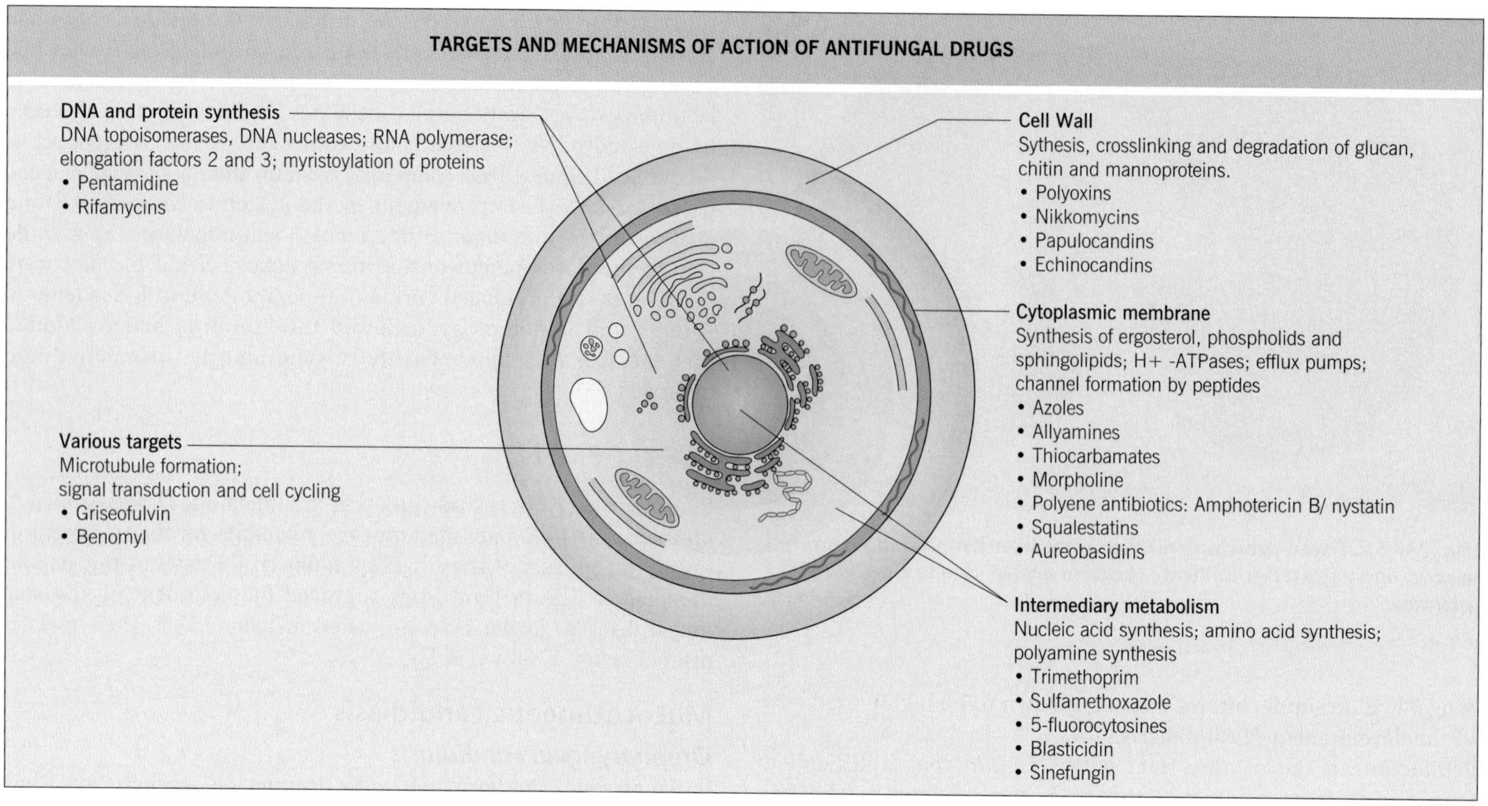

Fig. 237.6 Targets and mechanisms of action of antifungal drugs.

Esophageal candidiasis

Systemic therapy is required for effective treatment of esophageal candidiasis. Although symptoms of esophageal candidiasis may be mimicked by other pathogens, a diagnostic trial of antifungal therapy is often appropriate before endoscopy to search for other causes of esophagitis. A 14- to 21-day course of either fluconazole (100mg/day orally) or itraconazole solution (200mg/day orally) is highly effective. Suppressive therapy should be used occasionally in patients with disabling recurrent infections. Fluconazole-refractory esophageal candidiasis should be treated with itraconazole solution (200mg/day orally). Intravenous amphotericin B (0.3–0.7mg/kg/day as needed to produce a response) may be used in patients with otherwise refractory disease.

In mainly HIV-positive patients with esophageal and oropharyngeal candidiasis, the new antifungal agent caspofungin in a dosage of 35 or 50mg/day showed superior efficacy compared with low-dose amphotericin B (0.5mg/kg/day). This compound, representing the first clinically studied agent from a new class of antifungals inhibiting the synthesis of β-(1,3)-D-glucan in the fungal cell wall, was extremely well tolerated.[25]

For *Candida*-associated denture stomatitis, the treatment of choice is fluconazole (50mg daily for 2 weeks) combined with chlorhexidine.[26]

Candidal vulvovaginitis

This may be classified into complicated (severe, resistant species, impaired host defenses) and uncomplicated forms. Uncomplicated vaginitis is seen in 90% of patients and responds readily to short-course oral or topical treatment with any of the therapies listed above, including the single-dose regimens. In contrast, the complicated vaginitis seen in 10% of patients requires antimycotic therapy for 7 days. Azole therapy is unreliable for non-*albicans* spp. of *Candida*. *Candida glabrata* and the other non-*albicans* infections frequently respond to topical boric acid 600mg/day for 14 days or topical flucytosine. Azole-resistant *C. albicans* infections are extremely rare.

Recurrent vaginitis is usually due to azole-susceptible *C. albicans*. After control of causal factors (e.g. uncontrolled diabetes), induction therapy with 2 weeks of a topical or oral azole should be followed by a maintenance regimen for 6 months. Suitable maintenance regimens include fluconazole (150mg orally every week), ketoconazole (100mg/day), itraconazole (100mg every other day) or daily therapy with any topical azole.

The persistent immunologic defect of chronic mucocutaneous candidiasis requires a long-term approach.[12] Systemic therapy is needed and all of the azole antifungal agents have been used successfully. The dosages required are similar to those used for other forms of mucocutaneous candidiasis. As with HIV-infected patients, development of resistance to these agents has also been described.

Systemic candidiasis

Candidemia and intravenous catheter-related candidal infections

Candida BSIs are frequently associated with clinical evidence of the sepsis syndrome and high associated attributable mortality. In addition, hematogenous seeding may compromise the function of one or more organs.

In the past, there was controversy regarding whether every candidemia should be treated. Currently, the consensus is that all patients with a positive blood culture should be treated, even if the sample is drawn from a catheter.[17] Additionally, indwelling intravascular catheters should be removed or changed, preferably without using a wire for replacement. The evidence for this recommendation is strongest in the non-neutropenic patient population. In neutropenic patients, the role of the gut as a source for disseminated candidiasis is evident from autopsy studies, but in an individual patient it is difficult to determine the relative contribution of gut versus catheter as the primary source of fungemia. An exception is made for fungemia due to *C. parapsilosis*, which is very frequently associated with catheters.

The standard treatment for candidemia was amphotericin B (0.7–1.5mg/kg/day) with or without 5-FC, but recent clinical trials have shown that for stable non-neutropenic and stable neutropenic patients who have not previously been exposed to azoles, fluconazole (at 400mg/day, not to exceed 6mg/kg intravenously for the first week) can be as effective as amphotericin B and is less toxic.[27] For neutropenic patients who have evidence of deep organ infection or for unstable patients, amphotericin B with or without 5-FC is advised. If fluconazole is used in these groups, a higher dose up to 800mg/day (12mg/kg) is preferable. Three lipid formulations of amphotericin B have been developed and approved for use in humans: amphotericin B lipid complex (ABLC), amphotericin B colloidal dispersion (ABCD) and liposomal amphotericin B (Ambisome). Only ABLC and liposomal amphotericin B have been approved for use in proven candidiasis. These approvals are for second-line therapy of patients who are intolerant of or refractory to therapy with conventional amphotericin B (defined in one study using ABLC as: failure of 500mg amphotericin B, initial renal insufficiency, creatinine clearance <25ml/min), a significant rise in creatinine (to 2.5mg/dl for adults or 1.5mg/dl for children) or severe acute administration-related toxicity. Open-label therapy of candidemia with ABCD at 26mg/kg/day has been successful. In a randomized trial, ABLC at 5mg/kg/day was found to be equivalent to 0.6–1.0mg/kg/day amphotericin B as therapy for nosocomial candidiasis (mostly candidemia). Trials with caspofungin and voriconazole in candidiasis are underway. A recent study showed that caspofungin is at least as effective as amphotericin B for the treatment of invasive candidiasis.[27a]

Antifungal treatment should be continued for at least 2 weeks after the last positive blood culture or after the clinical symptoms have subsided, and patients should be followed for 3–6 months to detect long-term sequelae due to hematogenous seeding.

An increased incidence of the less fluconazole-sensitive *C. krusei* and *C. glabrata* in neutropenic patients has been associated with frequent use of fluconazole as prophylaxis.[8,9] This warrants caution in treating candidemia in immunocompromised patients with fluconazole before the *Candida* sp. has been identified (germ tube test), especially if there has been previous fluconazole exposure.

Data on the use of itraconazole in candidemia are limited. Unlike fluconazole, itraconazole also acts against *Aspergillus* spp., which is a theoretic advantage over fluconazole in neutropenic patients.

If 5-FC is added to amphotericin B, the dose (on average 100mg/kg/day) should be regularly adjusted according to peripheral blood cell counts, nomograms for renal functions or serum 5-FC levels (under 50–100μg/ml) to prevent bone marrow toxicity. Because of the rapid development of resistance, 5-FC should not be given as monotherapy.

Recommended treatment of candidal meningitis or encephalitis has been high-dose (0.7–1mg/kg) amphotericin B combined with flucytosine. The flucytosine dose should be adjusted to produce serum levels of 40–60μg/ml. The role of fluconazole remains to be determined. Data on the use of intrathecal amphotericin B or fluconazole are sporadic and this treatment should be reserved for severe therapy-refractory cases. Intracranial shunts should be removed. The occurrence of a brain abscess worsens the prognosis considerably. The indication for surgery remains to be determined but surgical drainage, if feasible, is probably advisable.[17]

Candidal endocarditis should be treated with combined antifungal treatment (amphotericin B plus 5-FC) and early valve replacement. Without surgical intervention, the mortality is high (90%); with combined surgical and medical treatment, the mortality has dropped to 45%.[17] Because of the high relapse rate of candidal endocarditis, continuation of amphotericin B plus 5-FC for at least 6–10 weeks (but possibly much longer) after surgery has been recommended. Because recurrences have occurred years later patients should be followed up for at least 2 years. Primary therapy with fluconazole has been successfully used on occasion, but fluconazole is more often employed as part of a long-term suppressive regimen.

In urinary candidiasis, the clinical circumstances dictate the management because candiduria can represent colonization, cystitis, pyelonephritis, disseminated candidemia or a fungus ball. If the candiduria is not catheter related and diabetes mellitus, neutropenia, urinary tract obstruction and urinary tract abnormalities have been ruled out and the patient is otherwise in good physical condition, observation is justified. Postcatheter candiduria in the stable patient usually resolves without treatment as well. In contrast, most patients who are neutropenic or who have had a recent renal transplant or have ureteric stents need systemic treatment with either amphotericin B or fluconazole (provided that *C. krusei* and *C. glabrata* have been ruled out). Treatment is not invariably indicated for catheter-related asymptomatic candiduria (eradication of candiduria in almost 40% of patients). Catheter-related candidal cystitis, where the catheter cannot be removed, can be treated with fluconazole 50–200mg/day for 2–3 days or a single intravenous dose of amphotericin B (0.3mg/kg). A recently completed placebo-controlled trial found that fluconazole at 200mg/day for 14 days hastened the time to a negative urine culture, but that 2 weeks after the end of therapy the frequency of a negative urine culture was the same in both treatment groups (60% for catheterized patients and 73% for non-catheterized patients).

Bladder irrigation with amphotericin B (50g/ml in sterile water or 5% glucose administered continuously over a three-way Foley catheter for 5–7 days) has been shown to clear the infection temporarily in over 80% and can be used as a diagnostic 'wash-out' test for systemic or renal candidiasis but is not recommended as definitive treatment. If there is a fungus ball in the urinary tract, then the treatment is surgical.

There are two major syndromes of peritoneal candidiasis. In disease related to peritoneal dialysis catheters, catheter removal is usually required for successful therapy. Both amphotericin B and fluconazole have been used successfully. Intraperitoneal amphotericin B has been associated with painful chemical peritonitis and should in general be avoided.

Candida peritonitis may also develop in association with surgical or traumatic injury to the gut wall. In this setting, *Candida* is usually part of a polymicrobial infection and case series suggest that therapy directed toward *Candida* is indicated, particularly when it is isolated as part of a complex infection or in an immunocompromised patient (as opposed to isolation in association with promptly repaired acute traumatic injury). The required duration of therapy for all forms of *Candida* peritonitis is not well defined and should be guided by the patient's response. In general, 2–3 weeks of therapy seems to be required. Surgical patients with recurrent gastrointestinal perforation are at increased risk for *Candida* peritonitis and may benefit from prophylactic antifungal therapy.

Chronic disseminated candidiasis (hepatosplenic candidiasis) is difficult to treat; this syndrome is not acutely life-threatening but does require prolonged therapy to produce a cure. Fluconazole at 6mg/kg/day is generally preferred in stable patients. Amphotericin B at 0.6–0.7mg/kg/day may be used in acutely ill patients or patients with refractory disease. Some but not all experts recommend an initial 1–2 week course of amphotericin B for all patients, followed by a prolonged course of fluconazole. Therapy should be continued until calcification or resolution of lesions, particularly in patients receiving continued chemotherapy or immunosuppression. Premature discontinuation of antifungal therapy may lead to recurrent infection.

Prophylaxis

Antifungal prophylaxis is highly controversial because the relationship between candidal colonization and dissemination is often not clear and azole prophylaxis may select for *Candida* spp. that are resistant to azoles.

Randomized, prospective, placebo-controlled trials have shown that systemically active antifungal agents can reduce the rate of development of invasive *Candida* infections in high-risk patients. The best data have compared fluconazole at 400mg/day with placebo in bone marrow transplant recipients.[9]

No consensus exists over the prophylactic use of azoles in other neutropenic patients.[17] Also, prophylaxis for high-risk (≥2 risk factors such as retransplantation, creatinine >2mg/dl, choledochojejunostomy, intraoperative use of ≥40 units of blood products, fungal colonization within the first 3 days after transplantation) liver transplant recipients is advised.[17] The risk for candidiasis following pancreatic transplantation may be comparable to that following liver transplantation. The risk of invasive candidiasis following transplantation of other solid organs appears to be too low to warrant systemic prophylaxis.

Apart from pharmacologic prophylaxis, simple measures such as handwashing by medical personnel are of paramount importance, especially in preventing the spread of *C. parapsilosis*.[3]

ASPERGILLOSIS

NATURE

Aspergillus spp. can cause disease in humans by:

- colonization and subsequently allergic reactions,
- colonization of pre-existing cavities (fungus ball or aspergilloma), or
- tissue invasion.

Aspergilli are found ubiquitously in organic debris such as hay, decaying vegetation (compost piles), soil, potted plants, in pepper and spices and in construction sites. The genus *Aspergillus* contains over 250 species, although only a few are associated with disease.

EPIDEMIOLOGY

Worldwide, aspergillosis is the most common invasive mold infection.[28]

In a 10-year autopsy survey,[29] the overall incidence of invasive aspergillosis was 1.4%. In the subgroup of immunocompromised patients, however, the incidence was found to be 10.7% and was highest in liver transplant recipients and patients who have hematologic malignancies. Mini-outbreaks of aspergillosis in immunocompromised patients have been reported in association with local construction work.[30] The most common sites of infection are the lungs and the brain. In patients who have AIDS, invasive aspergillosis is often diagnosed at autopsy. Surveys of clinically diagnosed disease report an incidence of 0.9–8.6%,[31] all before the highly active antiretroviral therapy (HAART) era.

The reported prevalence of allergic bronchopulmonary aspergillosis (ABPA) in patients who have asthma varies from 6% to 28%. In cystic fibrosis, 6–25% of patients are reported to have ABPA.[32]

PATHOGENICITY

The main route of infection in aspergillosis is airborne, via inhalation of the 2.5–3.0μm conidia (spores), which settle in lungs, nose or paranasal sinuses. However, most studies suffer from a lack of correlation between air spore counts and the rate of infection. Very recently, the hospital water supply has been recognized as a source of infection.[33] Other routes of infection are traumatized skin, especially due to burns, insertion openings of indwelling intravenous catheters and intravenous drug use. No patient-to-patient spread has been described.

The main risk factors for invasive aspergillosis include prolonged profound granulocytopenia ($<0.5 \times 10^9$/l), especially in bone marrow transplant recipients, high-dose corticosteroid therapy, broad-spectrum antibiotic therapy, chronic granulomatous disease, AIDS with a $CD4^+$ lymphocyte count below 50/l, and treatment with cytotoxic drugs such as ciclosporin. Less commonly encountered risk factors are diabetes mellitus, alcohol excess, influenza, prematurity and exposure to aspergilli in large quantities.[34]

In chronic granulomatous disease, phagocytes are unable to generate the respiratory burst to kill micro-organisms. The fact that these patients and patients who have neutropenia are at risk of developing aspergillosis underscores the importance of phagocytes in host defense. The role of T-cell-mediated immunity in aspergillosis is not clear. In the past, HIV infection was not considered to be an independent risk factor for aspergillosis, but this view has recently been challenged, even though patients who have late-stage HIV infection ($CD4^+$ lymphocyte count <50/l) frequently have other risk factors as well, such as neutropenia or treatment with glucocorticosteroids or broad-spectrum antibiotics.[34]

Alveolar macrophages and neutrophils play a major role in the defense against aspergilli.[35] Alveolar macrophages form the first line of defense by ingesting and killing conidia, even in the absence of opsonins. When conidia escape and germinate to form hyphae, granulocytes will adhere to and kill the fungus. The conidia that have not been cleared may germinate in the alveolar spaces and hyphal forms invade the pulmonary tissue and vasculature, leading to hematogenous dissemination to other organs (brain). However, blood cultures are rarely positive. Conidia that stay in the dormant state can survive for many days in the reticuloendothelial system. Killing of aspergilli by phagocytes is impaired by corticosteroids.

The role of humoral immunity is double-edged. In ABPA, aspergilli elicit an anti-aspergillus IgE antibody response, which evokes a type I immediate hypersensitivity reaction. Anti-aspergillus IgG antibodies have been demonstrated in ABPA, aspergilloma and in the convalescence phase of invasive aspergillosis. These antibodies do not seem to play a significant role in host defense.

The fungus secretes various metabolic products (gliotoxin) and enzymes, such as phospholipases, hemolysin and elastase, which may play a role in virulence.[34] However, the biologic significance of these agents is not clear, since molecular studies in which gene-deletion mutants have been constructed do not show diminished virulence.

DIAGNOSTIC MICROBIOLOGY

Aspergillus is a mold that grows with dichotomously branching septate hyphae (Fig. 237.7). Only pathogenic *Aspergillus* spp. are able to grow in temperatures between 95°F (35°C) and 98.6°F (38°C) and *A. fumigatus* can even grow at 127.4°F (53°C). *Aspergillus fumigatus* (80–90%) and *A. flavus* (5–10%) account for the majority of all *Aspergillus* infections. Other infections are caused by *A. niger* (1–2%), *A. terreus* (2–5%) and *A. nidulans* (<1%).

Aspergilli can be isolated from the sputum of 1–6% of healthy individuals. Also, *Aspergillus* colonization is found in patients who have chronic lung disease, cigarette smokers and those who have HIV infection. However, in immunocompromised patients who do not have AIDS, positive sputum cultures have a high positive predictive value for invasive aspergillosis, even without chest radiograph abnormalities. The positive predictive value may be as high as 80–90% in patients with leukemia or bone marrow transplants.

The negative predictive value of sputum cultures in these patients is low. Growth of aspergilli in cultures from nasal swabs of leukemic patients who have neutropenia has been shown to be predictive of invasive pulmonary aspergillosis.

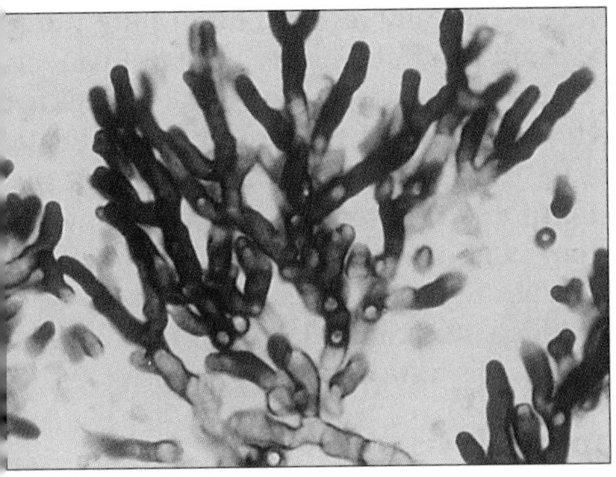

Fig. 237.7 *Aspergillus* hyphae.

In invasive aspergillosis, positive blood cultures for aspergilli are rare. In neutropenia, *Aspergillus* spp. are responsible for 8% of all fungemias and there is an overall mortality of 56%. Patients who undergo cardiac surgery have a risk of developing fungemia and *Aspergillus* endocarditis, probably due to contamination of the operating room air.[34]

Even though *Aspergillus* spp. can grow on standard bacteriologic media, mycologic media will give a higher yield and are therefore recommended. A potential diagnostic and management problem is pseudofungemia (i.e. contamination of blood specimens of uninfected patients in the laboratory). For patients at risk, however, culture results have to be taken seriously until proven otherwise.[34]

Because of the ubiquitous nature of the organism, establishing a definitive diagnosis of disease caused by *Aspergillus* is difficult. The use of antibodies against *Aspergillus* to diagnose invasive aspergillosis has produced conflicting results. Patients in high-risk groups are too frequently falsely seronegative. With antibody or antigen testing, serial assays appear more valuable than isolated tests, but specific recommendations about frequency of testing have not been established. Several promising assays have been developed to detect *Aspergillus* galactomannan in urine, sera, cerebrospinal fluid and bronchoalveolar lavage specimens by EIA, ELISA and immunoblot. These appear more sensitive and reproducible than earlier latex agglutination methodology. Studies with an EIA system commercially available in Europe for detection of *Aspergillus* galactomannan reported positive predictive values of 54% and negative predictive values of 95%, largely among bone marrow transplant recipients in France.[36,37] A problem in some studies with antigen testing was that case detection occurred too late to be useful, although early detection has been noted in some studies with ELISA methodology. In some studies, true positives were more frequent among the high titer results and false positives more common in children.

In addition, assays that use PCR have been reported to detect fragments within the 18S rRNA of *Aspergillus* spp., the 135-bp fragment in the mDNA of *Aspergillus* spp. and a 401-bp fragment in the rDNA complex of *A. fumigatus*, and PCR assays may prove more sensitive than antigen detection.[16] However, few of these PCR assays have been tested with body fluids in prospective trials of invasive aspergillosis, and reproducibility must be verified.

Therefore, a diagnosis of invasive aspergillosis is ideally based on a combination of culture results and histologic proof of tissue invasion.

CLINICAL MANIFESTATIONS

Clinical manifestations of aspergillus infections are also discussed in Chapter 111.

Aspergillosis can manifest as either fungal colonization, which can cause allergic disease and saprophytic disease (aspergilloma), or invasive disease.

The spectrum of disease caused by *Aspergillus* spp. includes:

- noninvasive aspergillosis – sinotracheobronchial colonization, allergic (bronchopulmonary) aspergillosis, aspergilloma (i.e. secondary saprophytic colonization of pre-existing cavities) and obstructing bronchial aspergillosis (mainly in patients who have AIDS); and
- invasive aspergillosis with pulmonary involvement such as acute bronchopneumonia, cavitation or slowly progressive bronchopneumonia, or extrapulmonary involvement of paranasal sinuses, central nervous system (CNS), skin, bone and heart.

Allergic bronchopulmonary aspergillosis

Allergic aspergillosis can either manifest as an extrinsic allergic alveolitis, causing a hypersensitivity pneumonitis in nonatopic patients, or it can cause ABPA in atopic individuals.

For a diagnosis of ABPA, Rosenberg and Wang established seven criteria:[32]

- episodic bronchial obstruction (asthma),
- immediate cutaneous reactivity to *A. fumigatus*,
- elevated total serum IgE (>150IU/ml),
- precipitating antibodies to *Aspergillus* antigen,
- proximal bronchiectases,
- history of infiltrates on chest radiography, and
- peripheral blood eosinophilia at the same time as infiltrates on chest radiography.

The diagnosis of ABPA was felt likely if the first six diagnostic criteria were present, and the presence of all seven made the diagnosis certain. The presence of central bronchiectases in ABPA signifies more permanent lung damage.[32]

Aspergilloma

Aspergillomas are fungus balls that colonize pre-existing cavities in the lungs, and occasionally in the sinuses and the nose. They can cause massive hemoptysis, which is fatal in 10% of cases.[34] Other symptoms can include fever, malaise and weight loss. A pulmonary computerized tomography (CT) scan may show a cavitary mass surrounded by air. Microscopic and cultural identification of *Aspergillus* spp. in a sputum smear and high antibody titers to *Aspergillus* support the diagnosis. Over 95% of patients have detectable IgG antibodies to *Aspergillus*, and antibody levels usually decrease after successful surgical removal of the aspergilloma.

Invasive aspergillosis

Invasive aspergillosis is a life-threatening aggressive disease that affects immunocompromised patients and is described in detail in Chapter 111.

If a pulmonary infiltrate (Fig. 237.8) occurs during granulocytopenia, it is more likely to be due to invasive aspergillosis than if an infiltrate develops during recovery from neutropenia, which is more

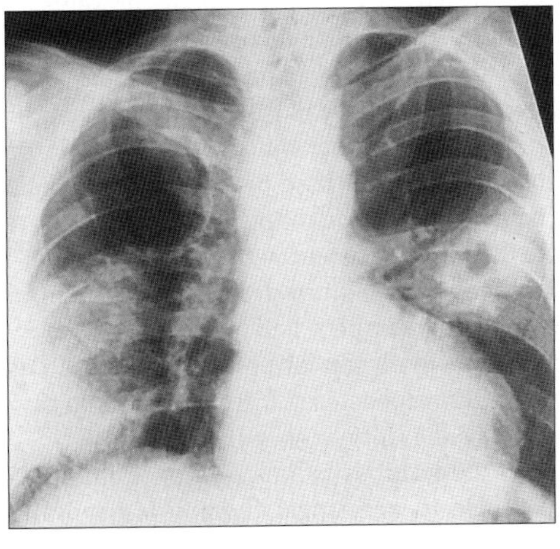

Fig. 237.8 *Aspergillus* pneumonia.

likely to represent a resolving bacterial pneumonia.[38] If invasive pulmonary aspergillosis is suspected in an immunocompromised patient, then a chest CT scan or magnetic resonance imaging (MRI) should be performed, even if the chest radiograph shows no abnormalities. Typical abnormalities on CT scan in aspergillosis are a halo sign (low radiographic density around an area of infiltration), air crescent lesions or a cavitary lesion or consolidation combined with pneumothorax, although *Mucorales* can cause similar lesions.

A retrospective study of 300 immunocompromised patients, evaluating the diagnostic value of cytology from bronchoalveolar lavage (BAL) fluid for the diagnosis of invasive pulmonary aspergillosis, reported a sensitivity of 64%, a specificity of 99%, a positive predictive value of 84.2% and a negative predictive value of 97%. Compared with cytology, the positive and negative predictive values for culture from BAL fluid were slightly less favorable.[37] Colonization with aspergilli occurs, but an immunocompromised patient who has *Aspergillus* spp. in sputum or BAL fluid and fever or radiographic infiltrates that are not responding to antibiotic treatment warrants antifungal treatment.[37,38]

For definite proof of invasive aspergillosis, additional biopsy results are important. Transbronchial biopsies are often negative in invasive aspergillosis due to sampling error, and so percutaneous or open lung biopsies may be required.

Recent studies published in abstract only show that a combination of HRCD scan of the thorax in combination with galactomannan detection in BAL has a high positive predictive value.

Chronic invasive (necrotizing) aspergillosis

Chronic invasive aspergillosis is a more indolent form of pulmonary aspergillosis. This syndrome may be seen with aspergillomas, at the interface of the fungus ball and normal lung. Presumably, the slowly progressive nature of this infection is a function of the host immune response, which is enough to barely hold the organism in check, but not to completely kill it. CIA is usually seen in middle-aged and elderly patients with documented or suspected underlying lung diseases like COPD, inactive tuberculosis, previous lung resection, radiation therapy, pneumoconiosis, cystic fibrosis, lung infarction, or, rarely, sarcoidosis. It also has been described in patients with mild immunosuppression, including those with diabetes mellitus, those with poor nutrition, those undergoing low-dose corticosteroid therapy, and those with connective tissue diseases such as rheumatoid arthritis and ankylosing spondylitis Cough, hemoptysis, weight loss of 1 to 6 months' duration and low grade fever may be seen. The chest x-ray shows an infiltrative process in the upper lobes or the superior segments of the lower lobes. A fungal ball may be seen in nearly one half of the cases. Adjacent pleural thickening is a characteristic finding and may be an early indication of a locally invasive process. However, interpretation of radiologic studies may be complicated by the presence of concomitant lung disease, since this is the setting in which chronic invasive aspergillosis usually presents.

The diagnosis is confirmed by a histologic demonstration of tissue invasion by the fungus and the growth of Aspergillus species on a culture. However, the yield of transbronchial biopsy specimens or percutaneous aspirates is relatively poor, and a thoracoscopic or open-lung biopsy is rarely performed in these patients. So, a clinical diagnosis of CNA could be made using the following criteria:

- Clinical and radiologic features consistent with the diagnosis;
- Isolation of Aspergillus species by culture from sputum or from bronchoscopic or percutaneous samples; and
- Exclusion of other conditions with similar presentations, such as active tuberculosis, atypical mycobacterial infection, chronic cavitary histoplasmosis, or coccidioidomycosis.

Treatment with antifungal medications is indicated once the diagnosis is made.[38a] The response to antifungal therapy is generally favorable. Surgical resection is generally reserved for healthy young patients with focal disease and good pulmonary reserves, patients not tolerating antifungal therapy, and patients with residual localized but active disease despite adequate antifungal treatment. In the initial series by Binder et al,[38b] 90% of patients who underwent surgical resections had good responses. However, there were significant postoperative complications, and one patient died. The long-term prognosis for patients with CNA is not well-documented. In the original series, 73% of the patients were alive 1 to 2 years following therapy, and the majority of deaths were due to other causes.

Extrapulmonary aspergillosis

Extrapulmonary dissemination of pulmonary aspergillosis, especially to the brain, is common in the immunocompromised host. Meningitis due to *Aspergillus* spp. can occur, but it is rare. A multivariate discriminant analysis of autopsy-proven fungal infections of the CNS demonstrated that a combination of pulmonary infiltrates and focal neurologic disease in an immunocompromised patient is more likely to be caused by *Aspergillus* spp. than by either *Candida* spp. or *Cryptococcus neoformans*. Definite diagnosis is made by biopsy.[38]

Virtually any organ can be infected by *Aspergillus* spp. The fungus may cause local infection in the ear or eye (endophthalmitis, keratomycosis). Direct bony invasion can occur or hematogenous spread causing osteomyelitis. In the gastrointestinal tract, aspergillosis can lead to fatal perforation. Black necrotizing skin lesions can be a sign of disseminated aspergillosis.

As in candidiasis, aspergilli can form fungal balls in the urinary tract, which present as renal colic.

Fungal sinusitis

Fungal sinusitis (Fig. 237.9) should be considered in all patients who have chronic sinusitis.[39] Clinical features and predisposing conditions are listed in Table 237.6. It is important to distinguish between noninvasive and invasive sinusitis because the latter can progress through invasion into soft tissue, cartilage and bone into the palate and nose or it can invade cerebral blood vessels, resulting in ischemic infarction and direct infection of the brain.

Chronic indolent invasive sinonasal infections occur in immunocompetent hosts in regions with high levels of environmental spores, such as the Sudan, Saudi Arabia, and other tropical or desert areas, and occasionally in patients with diabetes in other locales. *Aspergillus flavus* is the most common causative agent of these infections, in contrast to the frequent isolation of *A. fumigatus* from sites of infection in immunocompromised hosts. These infections have a progressive clinical course over months to years, with invasion of the surrounding tissues: the ethmoid sinuses, orbit and subsequent cranial bone osteomyelitis and intracranial extension.

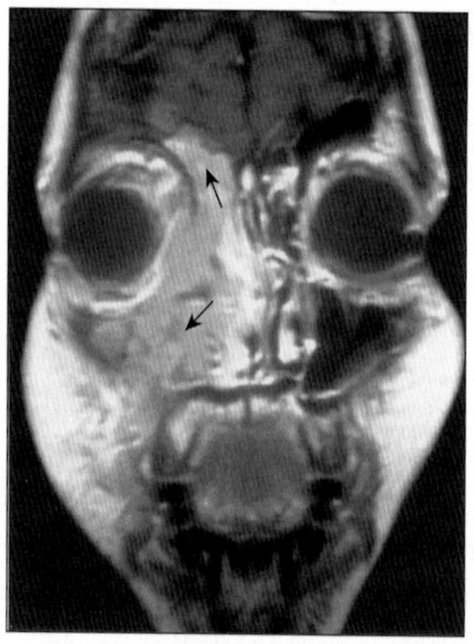

Fig. 237.9 *Aspergillus* sinusitis. Involvement of right maxillary sinus with extension to adjacent structures and the brain (arrows). Coronal section.

KEY CLINICAL POINTS IN THE DIAGNOSIS AND TREATMENT OF FUNGAL SINUSITIS				
Type	Clinical clues	Most common causes	Diagnosis	Initial management
Noninvasive fungal sinusitis	Immunocompetent patient: intractable symptoms despite adequate treatment for bacterial sinusitis; allergic rhinitis, asthma, nasal polyps. Calcifications in sinus on CT; proptosis in children	Hyaline molds; *Aspergillus* spp.; *Fusarium* spp.; dematiaceous molds; *Bipolaris* spp.; *Curvularia lunata*; *Pseudallescheria boydii*	Aspiration of sinus contents should be followed by silver impregnation staining and culture of aspirate; sinus contents often have the consistency of peanut butter or cottage cheese; in patients who have diabetes mellitus or other conditions involving immunocompromise, biopsy of healthy and diseased mucosa and bone should be considered to rule out tissue invasion	Surgery is necessary to establish drainage and to remove impacted mucus, polyps or fungus ball
Invasive fungal sinusitis	Fever, headache, epistaxis and cough in an immunocompromised patient; diabetes mellitus; hemochromatosis; protein-calorie malnutrition; leukemia; neutropenia. Nasal mucosal ulcer or eschar; calcifications in sinus on CT; orbital apex syndrome; proptosis in adults	Hyaline molds, zygomycetes; *Rhizopus oryzae*; *Cunninghamella bertholetiae*; *Aspergillus* spp.; *Fusarium* spp.; dematiaceous molds; *P. boydii*	Early endoscopic evaluation should be followed by biopsy of healthy and diseased mucosa and bone; sinus contents should be cultured; aspiration of sinus contents should be followed by silver impregnation staining and culture of aspirate; if the results of endoscopic evaluation are negative, open biopsy should be performed immediately	Emergency surgery is necessary to remove necrotic and devitalized tissue; treatment with amphotericin B should be initiated on demonstration of tissue invasion and before culture results become available; immunosuppression should be reversed, including discontinuation of corticosteroids and treatment of iatrogenic neutropenia

Table 237.6 Key clinical points in the diagnosis and treatment of fungal sinusitis. Adapted from DeShazo *et al.*[39]

Radiologic findings associated with fungal sinusitis are calcifications and loss of bony sinus margins, as well as features that are common in bacterial sinusitis, such as air–fluid levels of more than 8mm of mucoperiosteal thickening.

To distinguish between invasive and noninvasive fungal sinusitis, adequate tissue biopsies as described in Table 237.6 are necessary. The presence of hyphae excludes chronic bacterial sinusitis. In superficial fungal disease, hyphae are found only in mucopurulent material within the sinus. In invasive fungal infection, hyphae penetrate into the sinus submucosa, blood vessels or bone.

The main differential diagnosis is zygomycosis.

Aspergillosis and AIDS

Aspergillosis and AIDS is discussed in Chapter 126.

MANAGEMENT

In ABPA, the treatment of choice is systemic corticosteroids. Generally, prednisone is advised, 0.5mg/kg for 2 weeks followed by gradual tapering, although no randomized studies have been performed. Parameters for monitoring the treatment response are pulmonary function, chest radiograph and serum IgE concentration.

Another approach to the treatment of ABPA is to eradicate *Aspergillus* spp. from the airways. A recently completed double-blind, randomized, placebo-controlled trial[40] for ABPA showed that itraconazole 200mg twice daily for 16 weeks resulted in statistically significant differences in ability to ameliorate disease, as assessed by the reduction in corticosteroid dose and IgE and the improvement in exercise tolerance and in pulmonary function. Itraconazole may be useful as a corticosteroid-sparing agent. Detailed therapeutic guidelines are provided by Stevens *et al.*[41]

For aspergillomas, the natural history is variable, and therapy must be individualized. A conservative approach is prudent. Surgical resection (or where available, selective radiologic embolization of the feeding vessels) is indicated for hemoptysis. Spontaneous resolution of pulmonary aspergillomas has been reported.

The medical treatment options for invasive pulmonary aspergillosis are listed in Table 237.7. For neutropenic patients, the isolation of *Aspergillus* spp. from any site warrants immediate antifungal treatment. The same is true for any sudden intracranial event in this group, especially in the presence of pulmonary infiltrates, with or without fever.[38]

The largest therapeutic experience is with amphotericin B deoxycholate, which should be given at maximum tolerated doses (e.g. 1–1.5mg/kg/day) and should be continued, despite modest increases in serum creatinine levels. Lipid formulations of amphotericin are indicated for the patient who has impaired renal function or who develops nephrotoxicity while receiving deoxycholate amphotericin.

Itraconazole, the only triazole presently licensed for the treatment of aspergillosis, has recently become available for intravenous administration. In neutropenic patients with hematologic malignancies and refractory fever, intravenous itraconazole has shown at least equivalent efficacy (47% vs 38%) to D-AmB.[42] Not surprisingly, it was better tolerated (withdrawal due to toxicity 19% vs 38%) and showed less nephrotoxicity than D-AmB. Beyond that, about one-third of patients given intravenous itraconazole could be switched to the oral formulation after a median of 9 days of treatment.

Caspofungin has also shown significant efficacy as a salvage antifungal in 63 patients with documented invasive aspergillosis refractory or intolerant to conventional antifungals.[43] Based upon the clearly documented response to caspofungin in 41% of these patients, the drug was approved in early 2001 by the Food and Drug Administration (FDA) for the treatment of patients with aspergillosis refractory or intolerant to other licensed antifungals.

The US Mycoses Study Group and the Invasive Fungal Infections Co-operative Group of the European Organization for Research and Treatment of Cancer recently reported that in patients with proven or probable invasive aspergillosis, voriconazole is significantly superior to AmB with respect to response rates (53% vs 31%) and survival (71% vs 58%).[44] Walsh *et al.*[45] were able to show that voriconazole was as effective as L-AmB for empiric therapy in neutropenic patients with fever refractory to broad-spectrum antibiotics. The rate of breakthrough fungal infections was significantly lower in patients treated with voriconazole compared even with those receiving L-AmB (1.9% vs 5%). However, the response rates (defined as defervescence during neutropenia and absence of breakthrough

FIRST- AND SECOND-LINE THERAPY FOR INVASIVE ASPERGILLOSIS		
Generic (trade) name	**Dosage**	**Comments**
Amphotericin B deoxycholate	0.8–1.25mg/kg/day iv	High doses in neutropenia; significant interaction with ciclosporin
Itraconazole	Intravenous form, recently available 200mg iv qd; 200mg q8h for 4 days, then 200mg q12h po (for cerebral disease 400mg q12h)	If patient can eat and does not take hepatic cytochrome P450-inducing co-medication; significant interaction with ciclosporin; measure itraconazole serum levels; new itraconazole cyclodextrin oral solution has better bioavailability; limited data on iv use >14 days
Voriconazole	Loading 6mg/kg twice daily, thereafter 3mg/kg twice daily or 200mg orally twice daily	At least as effective as liposomal amphotericin B for emperical antifungal therapy in febrile neutropenia[45] More effective than D-AmB for invasive aspergillosis[45]
Caspofungin	70mg iv on day 1 50mg iv thereafter	FDA approved for refractory aspergillosis
Lipid-formulations of amphotericin (all iv)		
Liposomal amphotericin (AmBisome)	1–5mg/kg/day	Less toxic than amphotericin B deoxycholate, but higher dosage needed to be equally effective
Amphotericin B colloidal dispersion (ABCD, Amphotec)	4–6mg/kg/day	Less toxic than amphotericin B deoxycholate, but higher dosage needed to be equally effective; expensive
Amphotericin B lipid complex (ABLC, Abelcet)	5mg/kg/day	Less toxic than amphotericin B but higher dosage needed to be equally effective; expensive

Table 237.7 First- and second-line therapy for invasive aspergillosis. Adapted from Denning.[28]

fungal infections and no withdrawal due to adverse events and survival) were disappointing in both groups (26% vs 31%). Two issues with voriconazole must be taken into account: the occurrence of transient visual disturbances in about 30% of patients, and the considerable number of drugs showing important interactions with voriconazole.[45]

The optimal duration of therapy is unknown and dependent on the extent of invasive aspergillosis, the response to therapy and the patient's underlying disease(s) or immune status. A reasonable course would be to continue therapy to treat microfoci, after clinical and radiographic abnormalities are resolving, cultures (if they can be readily obtained) are negative, and reversible underlying predispositions have abated. Duration of therapy should be guided by clinical response rather than any arbitrary total dose. Continuation of antifungal therapy through reinduction cancer chemotherapy, or resumption of antifungal therapy in patients with apparently resolved fungal infection who are about to receive reinduction chemotherapy, is worthy of consideration. The ultimate response of these patients to antifungal therapy is largely related to host factors, such as the resolution of neutropenia and the return of neutrophil function, lessening immunosuppression and the return of graft function from a bone marrow or organ transplant, as well as the extent of aspergillosis when diagnosed.

PREVENTION

If untreated, the mortality of invasive aspergillosis reaches 100%.[28]

Patients who have cancer and who develop invasive aspergillosis during cytotoxic chemotherapy have been shown to have a 50% risk of recurrence during subsequent cytotoxic chemotherapy cycles. Therefore, empiric administration of amphotericin B or voriconazole at the onset of granulocytopenia with fever or even before the development of neutropenia has been advocated if the patient has a positive history of invasive aspergillosis or residual cavitary disease.

Preventive measures include reduction of environmental exposure of patients from sources of infection and antifungal prophylaxis. Specialized air-handling systems capable of excluding *Aspergillus* spores, such as high-efficiency particulate air (HEPA) filtration with or without laminar air flow ventilation, have proven to be very efficacious. Given recent data, the water systems should be evaluated in facilities with high-risk patients. Targeted antifungal prophylaxis for hematologic patients who are at high risk for developing invasive fungal infections is not currently recommended.

CRYPTOCOCCOSIS

NATURE

Cryptococcosis is a systemic infection caused by the encapsulated yeast-like fungus *Cryptococcus neoformans*. As early as 1894, Otto Busse described 'corpuscular' tumor-like lesions caused by 'coccidia species'. Since then *C. neoformans* has been known by a variety of names, including *Saccharomyces neoformans* and *Torula histolytica*. Of the existing cryptococcal species, only *neoformans* is known to be pathogenic.

According to the chemical structure of the cryptococcal polysaccharide capsule, four serotypes can be distinguished in three varieties:

- serotype A: *C. neoformans* var. *grubii*;
- serotype D: *C. neoformans* var. *neoformans*; and
- serotypes B and C: *C. neoformans* var. *gattii*.

The sexual form of *C. neoformans* is classified as *Filobasidiella neoformans*, and has two mating phenotypes: α- and *a*-mating type. In clinical isolates, the α-mating type is always predominant.[46]

Cryptococcus neoformans var. *neoformans* and *grubii* are ubiquitous. They are found year round, especially in aged pigeon droppings, and affect mainly the immunocompromised host.

Cryptococcus neoformans var. *gattii* has a tropical and subtropical distribution and is found mainly in Australia, South America, parts of Africa, South East Asia, southern Europe and southern California, where it is associated with the river red gum tree (*Eucalyptus camaldulensis*) and the forest red gum tree (*Eucalyptus tereticornis*). Recently, a Vancouver Island outbreak was detected. *Cryptococcus neoformans* var. *gattii* infects mainly healthy individuals. The peak incidence of disease coincides with the flowering season of the eucalyptus tree, namely November through February.

EPIDEMIOLOGY

Cryptococcal meningitis is the most common life-threatening fungal infection in people who have HIV infection.

The incidence of cryptococcosis in patients who have AIDS in the USA, western Europe and Australia has been estimated to be 6–10%, but a recent analysis of survival data of patients who have AIDS in the USA before the introduction of HAART demonstrated a decrease in the cryptococcosis-associated death rate from 7.7% in 1987 to 5% in 1992,[47] probably due to the widespread use of azoles for candidiasis. Since the introduction of HAART, a further decline in incidence of cryptococcosis has been seen.[48]

In sub-Saharan Africa, the estimated incidence of cryptococcosis in AIDS patients is 15–30%. In Zimbabwe, cryptococcosis constitutes the AIDS-defining illness in 88% of HIV-infected patients, where it currently represents the most important cause of meningitis in adults.[49] In people who have AIDS, almost 100% of cases are caused by *C. neoformans* var. *grubii*, even in areas where *C. neoformans* var. *gattii* is endemic.[50] In France, 21% of *C. neoformans* infections are caused by serotype D, which is associated with a higher incidence of skin lesions and a lower incidence of meningitis than serotype A.[51] In the immunocompetent host, 70–80% of cryptococcal infections are caused by *C. neoformans* var. *gattii*.[52]

For unknown reasons, the incidence of cryptococcal meningitis in children is much lower than statistically expected.[50]

Use of novel immunosuppressive agents may also have a role in the changing frequency, spectrum and clinical presentation of opportunistic mycoses. With the declining incidence of *C. neoformans* infection in HIV-infected patients treated with HAART, organ transplant recipients have re-emerged as one of the leading groups of immunocompromised patients at risk for cryptococcal infections.[3]

PATHOGENICITY

Cryptococcus neoformans is a facultative intracellular organism. Its pathogenicity depends upon the immune status of the host, virulence factors of the *C. neoformans* strain and the size of the inoculum.

Risk factors for cryptococcosis include (in decreasing order of frequency):

- HIV infection (especially with a low $CD4^+$ lymphocyte count),
- corticosteroid treatment,
- organ transplantation,
- chronic leukemia,
- lymphoma, and
- sarcoid, even without corticosteroid treatment.

The main fungal virulence factors consist of its:

- polysaccharide capsule,
- production of melanin and mannitol,
- alpha mating type, and
- mannoprotein-4.[53]

The polysaccharide capsule is known to interfere with phagocytosis, antigen presentation and leukocyte migration, and it can activate immunosuppressive T cells.[46] Most clinical cryptococcal strains develop large capsules during infection.[46] The cryptococcal metabolic products melanin and mannitol can function as antioxidants that can protect the yeast against oxidative attacks of phagocytes. It is not known why the alpha mating type of *C. neoformans* is correlated with enhanced virulence.[50] An interesting and still incompletely explained observation is that more than 95% of in vivo and in vitro isolates are of the alpha mating type. Moreover, studies in mice showed that this mating type was also more virulent.[50]

No direct animal-to-human cryptococcal transmission is known. Human-to-human transmission has only been described through infected corneal transplants. Laboratory technicians working with *C. neoformans* and pigeon breeders have a high incidence of positive skin tests, but active cryptococcal disease in these groups is extremely rare, except for a local cryptococcoma after accidental direct inoculation with yeasts. Infection with *C. neoformans* is thought to occur through inhalation of poorly encapsulated or acapsular organisms. Once the yeast is inhaled, it starts to regenerate its capsule. The first line of defense consists of alveolar macrophages, followed by infiltration of neutrophils and later T cells, natural killer cells and monocytes. Neutrophils can kill opsonized cryptococci in vitro. There is evidence that the capsular polysaccharide of *C. neoformans* plays an active role in interfering with neutrophil migration into the subarachnoid space during inflammation,[54,55] despite the presence of the neutrophil attractant interleukin (IL)-8 in the cerebrospinal fluid (CSF).[56] Recently, we have identified mannoprotein-4 as a novel capsular antigen prematurely activating neutrophils and desensitizing them toward a chemoattractant challenge.[53]

However, the role of neutrophils in the host defense against *C. neoformans* is not clear because patients who have severe neutropenia are not at risk of developing cryptococcosis. Experimental data have shown that functional T cells are essential in restricting cryptococcal spread. With intact T-cell function, confinement of yeasts and granuloma formation has been observed. Occasionally, *C. neoformans* can be found in granulomatous pulmonary lesions and reactivates upon decreasing host resistance and appears analogous to the primary complex in tuberculosis.[57]

The role of antibodies in the defense against *C. neoformans* is not clear, but passive immunization with anticapsular antibodies has been shown to prolong survival in mice infected with *C. neoformans*. Antibodies do play a role in opsonization and antibody-dependent cellular cytotoxicity, as well as clearance of deleterious levels of capsular polysaccharide.

A case-controlled study of the human antibody response to *C. neoformans*, comparing the serum antibody profiles of HIV-infected persons who did (HIV+/CM+) or did not (HIV-infected controls) develop cryptococcal meningitis (CM) and HIV-uninfected persons with samples obtained from the Multicenter AIDS Cohort Study, was performed. Compared with the HIV+/CM+ group, the HIV-infected control group had significantly lower levels of total IgM, IgA and antibodies expressing a certain VH3 determinant. The HIV-infected control group manifested an increase in immunoglobulin levels with a decrease in CD4 lymphocytes. The findings suggest a possible association between reduced expression of certain immunoglobulin subsets and HIV-associated CM.[58]

DIAGNOSTIC MICROBIOLOGY

Cryptococcus neoformans grows on routine laboratory media such as Sabouraud agar, producing white-to-cream colored mucoid colonies, which develop within 36–72 hours (Fig. 237.10). Unlike

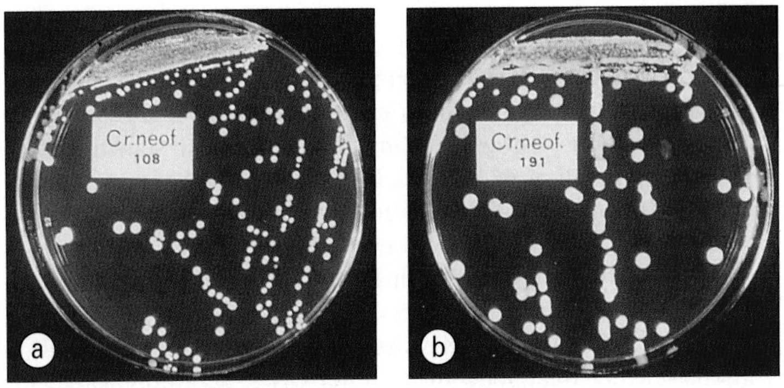

Fig. 237.10 ***Cryptococcus neoformans.*** (a) Thinly encapsuiated. (b) With a thick capsule.

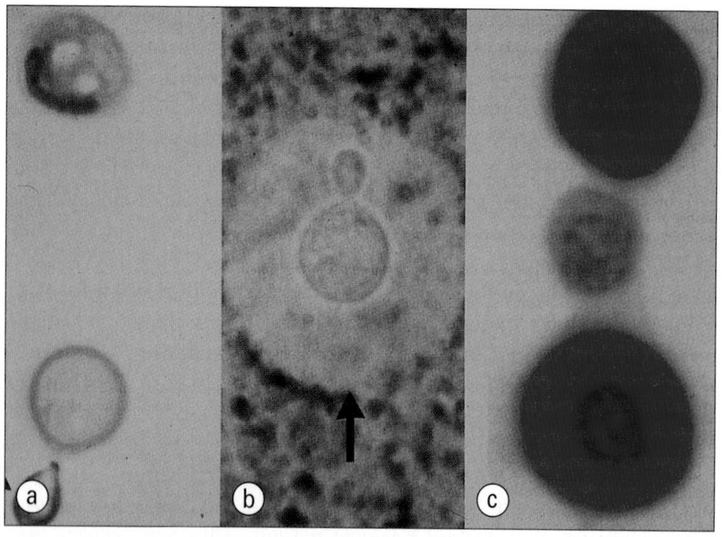

Fig. 237.11 ***Cryptococcus neoformans.*** (a) Cytologic preparation of CSF, (b) India ink preparation, (c) Mayer's mucicarmine stain. With permission from Jaster and Malecha. Copyright 1996 Massachusetts Medical Society.

nonpathogenic cryptococci, *C. neoformans* replicates at 98.6°F (37°C). For blood cultures, the lysis–centrifugation (Isolator) method has been recommended. Because *C. neoformans* is susceptible to cycloheximide, media containing cycloheximide should not be used. A rapid test to identify *C. neoformans* is the urease test because cryptococci produce large amounts of urease in the presence of urea (as do all basidiomycetous yeasts). To distinguish *C. gattii* from *C. neoformans* var. *neoformans*, glycine-L-canavanine-bromothymol blue agar can be used.

Microscopically, *C. neoformans* can be distinguished from other yeasts by its capsule, which is visualized by an India ink preparation (Fig. 237.11). The preparation is made by mixing equal volumes of sample fluid and ink, and ideally one should be barely able to read a newspaper through the preparation. The preparation typically shows budding yeast with a double refractive wall, distinctly outlined capsule and refractive inclusions in the cytoplasm. Occasionally, short hyphal yeast forms can be seen.

The laboratory diagnosis of cryptococcosis is rather straightforward compared with that of other fungal infections (see Table 237.3).

Latex agglutination tests (or ELISA) for cryptococcal antigen in body fluids are sensitive and specific and detect all serotypes. Due to differences between various commercial kits, absolute titer values are not interchangeable. In general, however, a positive test at a dilution of greater than 1:4 is highly suggestive of cryptococcal infection. False-positive results can be caused by rheumatoid factor or (rarely) through cross-reaction with other micro-organisms such as *Trichosporon beigelii* and the bacterium *Capnocytophaga canimorsus* or contamination of the specimen with agar or agarose in the laboratory. In CSF, false-negative results can be caused by either low or high antigen titers (prozone effect, especially in patients who have AIDS) or because of immune complex formation. Pronase pretreatment of the sample reduces both prozone reactions and rheumatoid factor interactions. Antigen testing in CSF is more sensitive than India ink preparation or culture. In patients who have pulmonary cryptococcosis without dissemination, serum samples may test negative for cryptococcal antigen. However, in these cases, *C. neoformans* antigen is likely to be positive in BAL fluid. Cryptococci are occasionally isolated from the sputum. In patients who are not immunocompromised it is safe to keep the patient under close observation without starting treatment. In all other cases, a careful search for infection of other sites should be made (including CSF examination), and there should be a low threshold for initiating therapy.

Antibodies to *C. neoformans* have no diagnostic value and are found in healthy people as well as in those with cryptococcosis. Presumably, antibodies have a favorable prognostic value when they become positive during convalescence in patients who do not have AIDS. In pulmonary cryptococcosis, antibodies may interfere with antigen testing due to the formation of complexes, necessitating pronase pretreatment of the samples.

For epidemiologic purposes, individual cryptococcal strains can be biotyped (e.g. AFLP or RAPD) or fingerprinted by restriction analysis or enzymatic methods.

CLINICAL MANIFESTATIONS

Clinical manifestations of cryptococcosis are also discussed in Chapters 111 and 126.

Although *C. neoformans* usually enters the body through the lungs, the main site of infection is the CNS. However, any other organ can be involved, mainly skin, bone, prostate and eye.

The clinical picture of cryptococcosis in patients who have AIDS resembles that in severely immunocompromised patients who do not have HIV infection. In patients who have AIDS, the fungal burden is usually higher and they have a higher frequency of positive blood and urine cultures, more extraneural sites of infection and a higher relapse rate, and fewer CSF inflammatory cells.[56] In the rare cases where patients who have AIDS are infected with *C. neoformans* var. *gattii*, the clinical picture resembles that of *C. neoformans* var. *neoformans* or *grubii*.

In the immunocompetent host, disease is usually more focal, with cryptococcoma formation (especially with *C. neoformans* var. *gattii*) and disease is more often confined to the lungs.[52] Although survival is higher for infection with *C. neoformans* var. *gattii*, it causes more neurologic complications, residual disease and relapses than *C. neoformans* var. *neoformans* and *grubii*.[51,52]

Pulmonary involvement

The clinical picture of pulmonary cryptococcosis depends upon the immune status of the host. In the immunocompetent host, one-third of patients are asymptomatic, and in some cases isolation of *C. neoformans* may represent colonization. The majority of patients present with pulmonary symptoms such as cough (54%), chest pain (46%) and sputum production (32%). If the cryptococcosis is confined to the lungs, cultures and antigen titers in CSF, blood and urine can be negative.

Compared with the immunocompetent host, cryptococcosis in the immunocompromised patient who does not have HIV infection has a more rapid course with early dissemination. In an analysis of 41 cases, 83% of patients presented with constitutional symptoms such as fever and malaise, and 44% presented with chest pain.[59]

Patients who have HIV infection and pulmonary cryptococcosis are almost invariably symptomatic, presenting with fever (84%), cough (63%), dyspnea (50%), weight loss (47%) and headache (41%). They have disseminated disease, as shown by positive cultures and antigen testing in CSF, blood and urine. Most patients have low $CD4^+$ lymphocyte counts, often less than 100,000/ml.

Pulmonary cryptococcosis is diagnosed through antigen detection or culture of expectorated sputum, BAL, transbronchial lung biopsy (Fig. 237.12) or needle aspiration. In all cases, serum and CSF analysis for antigen and cryptococcal culture should be performed to assess dissemination.

Central nervous system involvement

If the CNS is involved in cryptococcosis, both the brain and the meninges are usually diffusely affected. In the immunocompromised patient, cryptococcomas and focal signs of disease are rare. Approximately 70–90% of patients present with signs of subacute meningi-

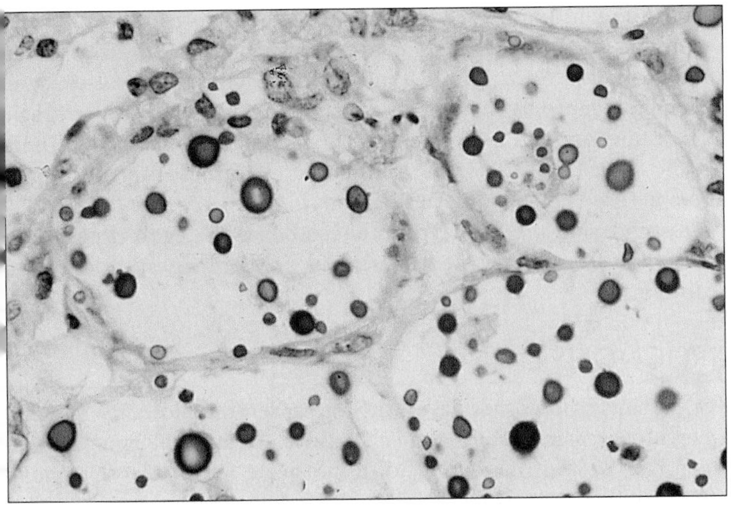

Fig. 237.12 Histology of pulmonary cryptococcosis.

tis or meningoencephalitis: headache, fever, irritability, dizziness, memory loss, personality change, somnolence, confusion or obtundation. Classic signs of meningitis such as nuchal rigidity are often absent. Papilledema is seen in one-third and cranial nerve palsies in one-fifth of cases. Symptoms may wax and wane over weeks to months and are often non-specific.

Cryptococcal meningoencephalitis in immunocompromised patients who do not have HIV infection resembles the clinical picture in patients who do have HIV infection, with three exceptions:

- the duration of symptoms is usually shorter in patients who have AIDS, due to paucity of the inflammatory response and high fungal burden;
- patients who have AIDS present more often earlier in the disease with a second site of infection such as lungs, skin or blood; and
- concomitant illness such as infections (e.g. due to *Toxoplasma gondii*) or neoplasms is more likely.

Because focal neurologic symptoms due to cryptococcosis occur in only 10% of patients who have HIV infection, these symptoms should alert the physician to concomitant pathology. Patients who are successfully treated for cryptococcosis but who present with insidious mental impairment, ataxia or other neurologic signs should be evaluated for hydrocephalus by CT. Shunting is indicated for hydrocephalus.

Analysis of CSF in cryptococcal meningitis will typically yield the following findings:

- high opening pressure (reflecting raised intracranial pressure),
- CSF glucose level that may be either low or normal, and
- elevated or normal protein levels.

Usually, the CSF contains remarkably few cells with mononuclear predominance, especially in patients who have AIDS.[56] Cryptococci can be cultured or identified directly through staining with India ink (see above, under Diagnostic microbiology); cryptococcal antigen levels in CSF and serum are almost always positive.

Cerebral CT findings can be normal in 50% of patients who have cryptococcal meningitis, regardless of whether they have HIV infection. In patients who do not have AIDS, the CT may reveal hydrocephalus, gyral enhancement and/or multiple focal nodules with or without contrast enhancement. In patients who have AIDS, diffuse cortical atrophy is more common. Cerebral MRI appears to be more sensitive than CT in cryptococcal meningoencephalitis. The finding of pseudocysts and choroidal ependymal granulomas (cryptococcomas) is thought to be relatively specific for cryptococcosis. Lesions due to *C. neoformans* var. *gattii* tend to be fewer in number, bigger in size and surrounded by edema as compared with those caused by *C. neoformans* var. *neoformans* and *grubii*.

Other sites of infection

About 10–15% of patients will develop skin manifestations, which can present in many forms. For unknown reasons, serotype D (var. *neoformans*) is relatively more often associated with skin lesions than serotype A.[51] In patients who do not have AIDS, skin lesions can be the sole site of infection; however, in patients who have AIDS, cryptococcal skin lesions are almost always a sign of disseminated disease. A diagnosis of cryptococcal skin disease is confirmed by biopsy.

The eye is a frequent site of infection and any part of the eye may be involved. Visual loss is a distinct threat, especially in cases of endophthalmitis, although some patients have visual loss without signs of endophthalmitis, possibly due to optic neuritis or elevated intracranial pressure. Early diagnosis and rapid treatment are essential to preserve sight.[50]

From 5% to 10% of patients have bone lesions, which are mostly osteolytic and must be distinguished from cold abscesses (e.g. due to tuberculosis) or neoplasms.

Many other body sites can be affected by *C. neoformans*. In men, the prostate gland is thought to serve as an extraneural reservoir and source of relapse.

Interestingly, solid organ transplant recipients receiving tacrolimus were significantly less likely to have CNS involvement than were those receiving a different agent (ciclosporin or azathioprine), on the basis of immunosuppression (78% vs 11%, respectively). On the contrary, skin, soft tissue and/or osteoarticular involvement was significantly more likely in patients receiving tacrolimus (66%) than in patients receiving a different agent.[3]

MANAGEMENT

In isolated pulmonary cryptococcosis and other non-CNS disease in patients who do not have HIV infection, patients can be treated according to their risk and disease severity. In the immunocompetent asymptomatic patient who has minor lesions on the chest radiograph and no extrapulmonary dissemination, careful observation or fluconazole monotherapy (200–400mg/day for 3–6 months) is justified because many undergo spontaneous regression. Every patient who has symptomatic or disseminated disease or a compromised immune system should be treated with antifungal medication. In all cases, lumbar puncture should be performed to exclude meningeal involvement.

There is no consensus about the treatment schedule for pulmonary cryptococcosis and other non-CNS disease. For patients who have extensive lobar consolidation or mass lesions (more frequent with *C. neoformans* var. *gattii*), surgical resection of the lesions can be warranted.

All patients who have cryptococcal meningitis should be treated, regardless of their immune status, because 10–20% will either die or develop serious neurologic sequelae.

For patients who have cryptococcal meningitis and AIDS, the antifungal regimen of choice is high-dose amphotericin B (0.7mg/kg/day) plus 5-FC (100mg/kg/day) for 2 weeks, followed by consolidation therapy with fluconazole 400mg/day for 8–10 weeks, and subsequent lifelong maintenance therapy at 200mg/day. This regimen has been shown to reduce the mortality from about 15% to 6% in the first 2 weeks in a recently published double-blind randomized multicenter trial.[60] Combination therapy of amphotericin B and flucytosine will sterilize CSF within 2 weeks of treatment in 60–90% of patients.

The addition of flucytosine to amphotericin B was independently associated with earlier CSF sterilization, and 5-FC is thought to be important in preventing early relapse. Response rates are lower if CSF cultures at 2 weeks are still positive and these patients may require longer courses of induction therapy. For consolidation therapy, itraconazole (400mg/day) compared only slightly less

PREFERRED TREATMENT OPTIONS FOR CRYPTOCOCCAL DISEASE IN HIV-NEGATIVE PATIENTS
Pulmonary and other non-CNS disease
Mild-to-moderate symptoms or culture-positive specimen from this site
Fluconazole, 200–400mg/day for 6–12months
Itraconazole, 200–400mg/day for 6–12months
Amphotericin B, 0.5–1mg/kg/day (total 1000–2000mg)
Severe symptoms and immunocompromised hosts
Treat like CNS disease
CNS
Induction/consolidation: amphotericin B 0.7–1mg/kg/day plus flucytosine 100mg/kg/day for 2 wk, then fluconazole 400mg/day for minimum 10 wk
Amphotericin B 0.7–1 mg/kg/day plus flucytosine 100mg/kg/day for 6–10 wk
Amphotericin B 0.7–1mg/kg/day for 6–10 wk
Lipid formulation of amphotericin B 3–6mg/kg/day for 6–10 wk
The clinician must determine whether to follow lung therapeutic regimen or CNS (disseminated) regimen for treatment of infection in other body sites (e.g. skin). When other disseminated sites of infection are noted or the patient is at risk for disseminated infection. It is important to rule out CNS disease. Duration of therapy is based on resolution of disease.

Table 237.8 Preferred treatment options for cryptococcal disease in HIV-negative patients. Adapted from Saag *et al.*[59]

favorably to fluconazole, which makes it a reasonable alternative to fluconazole for maintenance therapy (at 10 weeks after diagnosis, fluconazole maintenance therapy resulted in 72% negative CSF cultures vs 60% with itraconazole[59]). Weekly intravenous amphotericin B has been shown to be inferior to fluconazole in preventing relapse of cryptococcal disease in patients who have AIDS.

It has been shown that maintenance therapy can be safely discontinued if the CD4 cell count is >200 for 3 months.[61]

For patients who have cryptococcal meningitis (Table 237.8), but who do not have AIDS, the regimen of choice is less well defined. Treatment with low-dose amphotericin B plus 5-FC has proved to be as effective and less toxic than amphotericin B alone in this group and it is likely that the above-mentioned regimen of 2 weeks of amphotericin with 5-FC intravenously followed by high doses of fluconazole for 8 weeks will also be effective in patients who do not have HIV infection. A total treatment duration of 4–6 weeks has been successful, but the relapse rate may be lower with longer treatment courses or azole consolidation therapy.

It is advisable to follow patients closely over the first 6–12 months because most relapses occur in the first year after treatment. In male patients who do not have AIDS, positive urine culture after prostatic massage can predict a high risk for recurrence and prolonged oral treatment is advisable in these cases.

For those who have pre-existing neutropenia, amphotericin B (0.7–1.0mg/kg/day) monotherapy can be given to avoid additional bone marrow toxicity. Fluconazole as monotherapy is associated with a higher mortality in the first 2 weeks, with a slower CSF clearing rate than with amphotericin B.

For patients with elevated baseline opening pressure, lumbar drainage should remove enough CSF to reduce the opening pressure by 50%. Patients should initially undergo daily lumbar punctures to maintain CSF opening pressure in the normal range. When the CSF pressure is normal for several days, the procedure can be suspended. Occasionally, patients who present with extremely high opening pressures (>400mmH_2O) may require a lumbar drain, especially when frequent lumbar punctures are required to or fail to control symptoms of elevated intracranial pressure. In cases where repeated lumbar punctures or use of a lumbar drain fail to control elevated pressure symptoms, or when persistent or progressive neurologic deficits are present, a ventriculoperitoneal shunt is indicated. There are no data to support the routine use of direct intraventricular therapy (e.g. via an Ommaya reservoir).

Despite wide use of triazole (and other antifungal) drugs, drug resistance has not yet been a serious concern in cryptococcocal infections.

PROGNOSIS

For patients who do not have AIDS or cancer, the mortality rate due to cryptococcal infections is about 25–30%. After initial curative treatment, 20–25% of patients who do not have AIDS relapse. Among cured patients 40% have significant neurologic deficits such as visual loss, cranial nerve palsy, motor dysfunction, personality change and decreased mental function due to chronic increased intracranial pressure or hydrocephalus. Mortality in patients after solid organ transplantation is, given the current antifungal regimens, still high at 40%.[5]

For patients who have AIDS, the mortality rate during initial therapy has been 10–25%, and 30–60% of patients die within 12 months. The relapse rate without maintenance treatment is 50–60%. Currently, the prognosis is mainly determined by the response to HAART. The prognosis for patients who have a malignancy is worse than for patients who have AIDS, but this probably reflects the course of the underlying disease rather than the cryptococcosis.[50]

The most important prognostic predictor of early mortality in cryptococcal meningitis is the mental status of the patient at presentation.[62] Also, the prognosis is adversely affected by a high fungal burden and a poor inflammatory response.

Adverse prognostic clinical features in patients who do not have HIV infection are listed in Table 237.9.[63] Other adverse clinical prognostic signs include altered mental status and blood pressure changes.

PREVENTION

Prospective controlled trials indicate that fluconazole and itraconazole can reduce the frequency of cryptococcal disease among

ADVERSE PROGNOSTIC CLINICAL FEATURES IN CRYPTOCOCCAL MENINGITIS
• Initial positive India ink examination of CSF • High CSF opening pressure • Low CSF glucose • Low CSF leukocyte count (<20/μl) • Cryptococci isolated from extraneural sites • Initial CSF (or serum) antigen titer >32 • Corticosteroid treatment or lymphoreticular malignancy
Recurrent cryptococcal disease • Abnormal CSF glucose concentration after ≥4 weeks of therapy • Absence of anticryptococcal antibodies • Post-treatment CSF (or serum) cryptococcal antigen titer of ≥8 • No decrease in antigen titers during therapy • Daily corticosteroid treatment ≥20mg prednisone after completion of antifungal therapy

Table 237.9 Adverse prognostic clinical features in cryptococcal meningitis in patients who do not have HIV infection. A retrospective study of patients who had AIDS demonstrated only a prognostic value of antigen levels in the CSF, not in serum. There is substantial variability in titers with the different antigen detection kits used.

patients who have advanced HIV disease. However, the majority of HIV specialists recommend that antifungal prophylaxis not be used routinely to prevent cryptococcosis because of the relative infrequency, the lack of survival benefits associated with prophylaxis, possibility of drug interactions, potential antifungal drug resistance and cost.[59]

MUCORMYCOSIS AND INFECTIONS BY OTHER ZYGOMYCETES

NATURE

Mucormycosis refers to disease caused by fungi belonging to the order Mucorales. Other names for the disease include phycomycosis and zygomycosis, the latter including diseases caused by Entomophthorales. Both Mucorales and Entomophthorales belong to the class Zygomycetes.

The major forms of zygomycosis include rhinocerebral, pulmonary, cutaneous, gastrointestinal and disseminated diseases. *Rhizopus, Mucor, Rhizomucor* and *Absidia* are the most common organisms that cause zygomycosis in humans.

EPIDEMIOLOGY

Although these organisms are ubiquitous and grow in decaying organic material, mucormycosis is a rare disease and occurs almost exclusively in patients who have an underlying disease, with the exception of *Apophysomyces elegans*, a newly described species, that has been reported as a causative agent of zygomycosis, especially in immunocompetent patients.

Risk factors for mucormycosis are listed in Table 237.10. Diabetes mellitus and neutropenia are the most commonly encountered risk factors.

PATHOGENICITY

Infection with Mucorales usually occurs through inhalation of spores or deposition of spores in the nasal turbinates. In cutaneous mucormycosis, direct inoculation of abraded skin can result in disease with invasion of subcutaneous tissue.[64]

After pulmonary infection, the first line of defense is provided by alveolar macrophages. In animal studies, alveolar macrophages from healthy mice have been shown to inhibit germination of *Rhizopus oryzae* spores. In contrast, alveolar macrophages from corticosteroid-treated mice or diabetic mice fail to inhibit spore germination and the mice are rapidly killed by pulmonary and disseminated disease.

Neutrophils play an important role in the second line of host defense. It is not known how diabetes mellitus or corticosteroids interfere with elimination of the fungi. Normal human serum can inhibit the growth of *Rhizopus* spp., unlike serum from patients who have diabetic ketoacidosis, which enhances fungal growth. The precise mechanism is unknown, although alteration in the availability of iron due to the decreased pH has been suggested.[66] Iron or iron bound to circulating deferoxamine (desferrioxamine) is used by Mucorales for replication. This is underscored by the clinical observation that patients who receive deferoxamine (e.g. in renal failure with hemodialysis or patients who have iron overload) are at risk of developing mucormycosis.[66]

As in aspergillosis, a hallmark of mucormycosis is angio-invasion, resulting in thrombosis and tissue necrosis. The fungus has a predilection for veins over arteries.[66]

RISK FACTORS FOR MUCORMYCOSIS
• Diabetes mellitus, especially with ketoacidosis
• Immunosuppression, especially corticosteroid treatment
• Iron overload with or without deferoxamine treatment (e.g. hemodialysis, hemochromatosis)
• Hematologic disease, especially neutropenia
• Intravenous drug use (CNS mucomycosis)
• Sustained skin trauma (cutaneous mucormycosis)
• Kwashiorkor (gastrointestinal mucormycosis)

Table 237.10 Risk factors for mucormycosis. From Sugar[64] and Yohai *et al.*[66]

DIAGNOSTIC MICROBIOLOGY

Mucorales grow at temperatures of 77–131°F (35–55°C) with an optimal temperature of 82.4–86°F (30°C). Clinical isolates will grow at 98.6°F in the laboratory 2–5 days after incubation under aerobic conditions.[64] Cycloheximide inhibits their growth, and so culture media containing cycloheximide should not be used.

On light microscopy (Fig. 237.13), Mucorales have irregularly shaped, nonseptate, broad (10–20mm in diameter) hyphae with right-angle branching, visualized with hematoxylin and eosin staining, periodic acid–Schiff reaction or Grocott–Gomori methenamine-silver nitrate stains. In tissue samples, Mucorales are often found near blood vessels and surrounded by a neutrophilic infiltrate.

CLINICAL MANIFESTATIONS

A detailed description is provided in Chapter 111.

The clinical manifestations of mucormycosis can be divided into seven syndromes:

- rhinocerebral,
- pulmonary,
- cutaneous,
- gastrointestinal,
- CNS,
- disseminated, and
- miscellaneous (e.g. bones, kidney, heart or mediastinum).

The clinical manifestations depend upon the underlying disease. In patients who have diabetic ketoacidosis, rhinocerebral disease is the most common manifestation. Leukemic patients who have neutropenia are susceptible to rhinocerebral, pulmonary and disseminated disease. Children who have kwashiorkor (protein–calorie malnutrition) are especially at risk of developing gastrointestinal mucormycosis. Patients treated with deferoxamine because

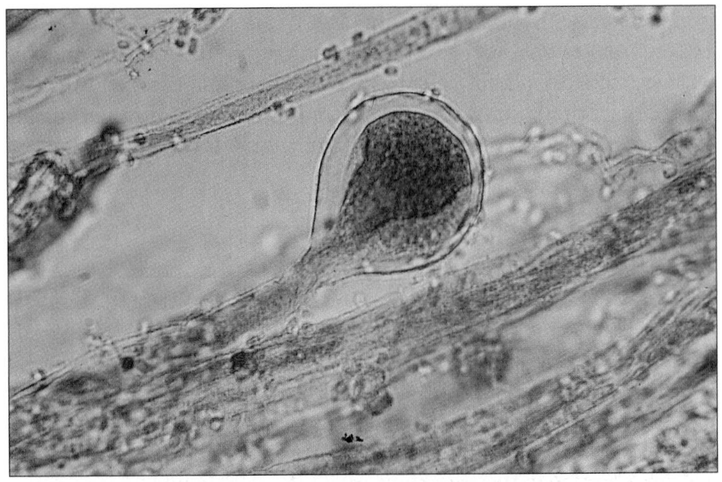

Fig. 237.13 Lactophenol cotton blue preparation of *Absidia corymbifera*.

of iron or aluminum overload mainly present with disseminated mucormycosis.

In general, clues to the diagnosis of mucormycosis are signs of vasculitis with tissue necrosis, such as a black discharge or eschar on the skin, palate or nasal mucosa. Also, any radiographic imaging that reveals a lesion that surrounds vessels without a mass effect in an immunocompromised patient is suggestive of mucormycosis.

A biopsy with culture and microscopic evaluation is needed in order to discriminate between mucormycosis, aspergillosis and infection caused by Gram-negative bacteria such as *Pseudomonas* spp. The angio-invasion of the fungus causes an unusually low tendency to bleed during diagnostic surgery, which should alert surgeons to the diagnosis.[66]

If the organism is isolated by culture only, the clinician should differentiate between colonization, contamination and infection.

About 60% of rhinocerebral mucormycosis cases occur in diabetic patients and it is a rapidly fulminant disease, presenting with fever, nasal mucosal ulceration or necrosis, sinusitis (in 26% as an early sign), headache and facial pain or orbital involvement. Typically, when a ketoacidotic diabetic patient who has decreased consciousness does not wake up within 24–48 hours after correction of serum glucose and electrolytes, (rhino)cerebral mucormycosis should be considered and the palate should be inspected for a black necrotic eschar resulting from extension of the disease towards the oropharynx.

In rare cases, rhinocerebral disease may follow a chronic course.[66]

The pulmonary form of mucormycosis is the third most commonly occurring pulmonary opportunistic mycosis, especially in severely neutropenic hematologic patients or those who have diabetes mellitus. It presents with cough, fever, chest pain and dyspnea and progresses rapidly. In diabetics, a less fulminant form of pulmonary mucormycosis may occur.

A diagnosis of pulmonary mucormycosis is often made by bronchoscopy. Chest radiographs will underestimate the actual amount of tissue damage. The appearance of an air crescent sign on chest radiography or CT may herald a potentially fatal hemoptysis and warrants surgical and medical intervention.[67]

Cutaneous mucormycosis usually occurs in people who have sustained trauma (including indwelling postoperative catheters) or who have an underlying illness such as diabetes mellitus. Occasionally, cutaneous mucormycosis is a manifestation of systemic disease.

Gastrointestinal mucormycosis is primarily found in patients who have extreme malnutrition. All segments of the gastrointestinal tract can be involved. The clinical symptomatology mimics an intra-abdominal abscess.

Central nervous system mucormycosis is rare and occurs most frequently as a direct extension from the nose or paranasal sinuses, or is associated with intravenous drug use.

Cerebral lesions appear on CT scanning as low-density masses with variable peripheral enhancement. Gadolinium-contrast MRI can suggest cavernous sinus thrombosis and thrombosis of other vessels as indirect signs of infection, or ocular muscle involvement may be demonstrated.

MANAGEMENT

Mucormycosis is a rapidly progressive disease that warrants immediate aggressive combined surgical and medical treatment. All devitalized tissue should be removed, if necessary repeatedly, followed by reconstructive surgery in a later phase. Optimal treatment of the underlying disease is vital, including rapid correction of diabetic ketoacidosis. Intravenous amphotericin B in high (initial) doses of 1–1.5mg/kg/day is the treatment of choice, with a total dose around 2.5–3g. Several case histories report positive results with lipid formulations of amphotericin B.[68] A case report describes successful treatment of disseminated mucormycosis in a neutropenic patient with a combination of surgery, ABLC and G-CSF.[69]

Other less common treatment modalities reported in the literature with presumed but unproven effect include local irrigation with amphotericin B, addition of rifampin (rifampicin) or tetracycline to amphotericin treatment and hyperbaric oxygen. Despite occasional successful case reports, the currently registered azoles have no significant in-vitro activity against mucormycosis.

PROGNOSIS

The prognosis of mucormycosis depends largely upon the underlying disease, and in general the prognosis is better for those who have diabetes mellitus. The overall mortality has been over 50%, but with early aggressive surgery combined with medical treatment, this mortality has been reduced to less than 20%. Adverse prognostic factors in rhinocerebral disease include hemiparesis or hemiplegia, bilateral infections, nondiabetic co-morbidity and extensive facial necrosis (Fig. 237.14).[66] An overall mortality of 80% has been reported in pulmonary mucormycosis, but varies widely according to the underlying disease and extension of the infection.[70]

Gastrointestinal mucormycosis has a high mortality and is usually diagnosed at autopsy.

PENICILLIOSIS

NATURE

Penicilliosis is caused by the fungus *Penicillium marneffei*, a dimorphic mold with yeast-like growth in tissue.

The fungus is endemic in South East Asia and was originally isolated from the bamboo rat *Rhizomys sinensis*. It causes deep-seated infections in humans and rodents.

EPIDEMIOLOGY

Before the AIDS era, most patients in endemic regions (northern Thailand and rural south eastern China) affected with penicilliosis had no known underlying disease. Now, the infection mainly affects patients who have HIV infection and is recognized as an AIDS-defining opportunistic infection. In Thailand's Chiang Mai province it is the third most common HIV-related opportunistic infection (after tuberculosis and cryptococcosis).[71]

PATHOGENICITY

Penicillium marneffei is a facultative intracellular organism that can survive and replicate in macrophages. The route of infection is not known but it is assumed to be airborne or through ingestion, and

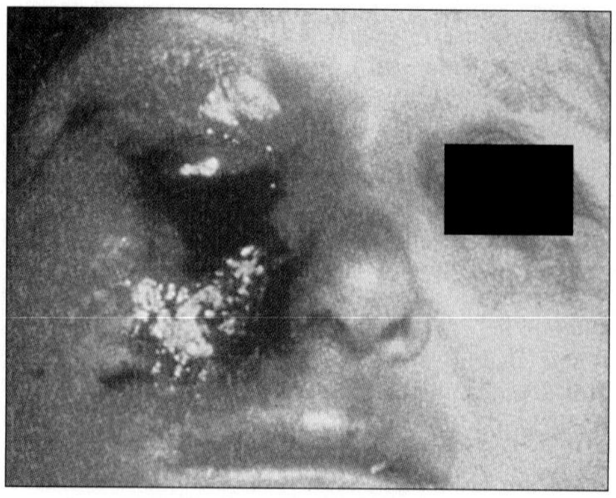

Fig. 237.14 Patient with mucormycosis. Ocular invasion by Mucor in a patient with diabetes mellitus and ketoacidosis.

occasionally infection occurs through local inoculation. *Penicillium marneffei* evokes three patterns of tissue response:

- in the immunocompetent host, granuloma formation with central necrosis;
- suppurative abscesses are found in various organs; and
- in the immunocompromised host, an anergic necrotizing reaction in lung, liver and skin is seen, with diffuse infiltration of macrophages in tissues with proliferating yeast.

Antibody-mediated immunity does not seem to play a major role in host defense.[72]

Penicilliosis affects all ages and both sexes, although 90% of the cases reported in the English literature are male.[72] Although the fungus has been repeatedly isolated from the bamboo rat, human contact with or consumption of the rat does not appear to be a risk factor. In contrast, a recent history of exposure to soil is significantly associated with the acquisition of human penicilliosis, so a common reservoir of infection for rats and humans has been suggested.[73]

DIAGNOSTIC MICROBIOLOGY

In culture, *P. marneffei* is the only thermally dimorphic *Penicillium* spp. The fungus grows as a mold at 77°F (25°C) and looks grayish and downy. It produces a distinctive red diffusible pigment, which is visible on agar media. At 98.6°F (37°C) it grows as a yeast on Sabouraud glucose agar with cerebriform colonies that do not produce the red pigment.

On microscopic examination (Fig. 237.15), *Penicillium* spp. appear as short, septate, branching hyphae as well as sausage-shaped cells that divide by fission instead of budding, and may show a central septum, which distinguishes it from *Histoplasma capsulatum*. *Penicillium* spp. can be identified both inside macrophages and extracellularly when tissue preparations are stained with periodic acid–Schiff, Wright's or Giemsa stain. Recently, a monoclonal antibody has been developed that enables immunohistochemical identification of the fungus.[72]

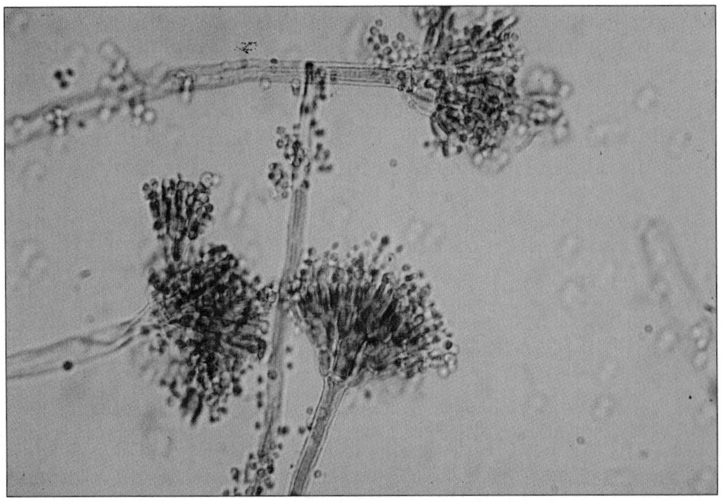

Fig. 237.15 Lactophenol cotton blue preparation of *Penicillium brevi compactum*.

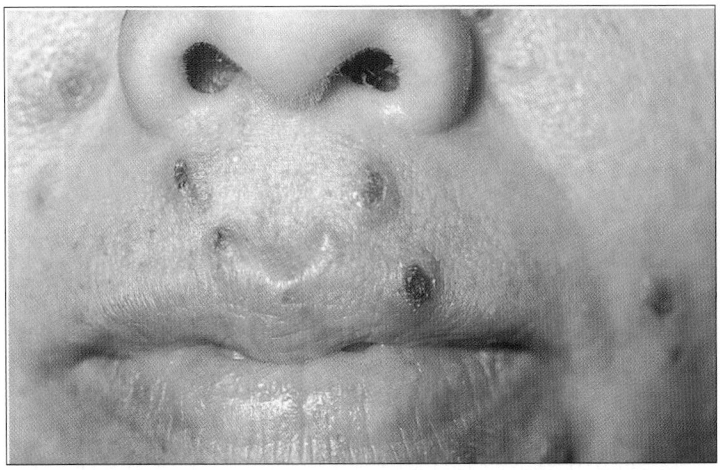

Fig. 237.16 HIV-infected patient with *Penicillium marneffei* infection with molluscum contagiosum-like lesions.

CLINICAL MANIFESTATIONS

Clinical manifestations of penicilliosis are also discussed in Chapter 126.

In patients who are not immunocompromised, the clinical picture may strongly resemble that of tuberculosis or histoplasmosis (e.g. suppurative lymphadenitis, fever, weight loss, anemia and a nonproductive cough). In patients who have HIV infection, the disease is usually disseminated, affecting skin, reticuloendothelial system, lung and gut. Other tissues that may be involved are liver and spleen, kidney, bone, joints and pericardium. In contrast to histoplasmosis and tuberculosis, adrenal involvement and CNS infections are rare. The molluscum contagiosum-like lesions of skin and mucosa indicate disseminated disease (Fig. 237.16).[72]

Chest radiographs show patchy infiltration and sometimes abscess formation. Abdominal CT scanning often demonstrates hepatomegaly or hepatosplenomegaly, but the diffuse microabscesses that cause the hepatomegaly are usually indistinguishable.

The diagnosis is made by culturing *P. marneffei* from blood, bone marrow, skin scrapings or liver biopsy specimen or by identifying the organism microscopically in a touch smear of a skin biopsy or bone marrow aspirate.

MANAGEMENT

The treatment of penicilliosis is amphotericin B (0.5–1.0mg/kg/day for 2 weeks), followed by itraconazole 200–400mg/day for 6 weeks for people who do not have HIV infection, and indefinitely for patients who have HIV infection.[69,71] In in-vitro studies, fluconazole appears to be less active. If treated appropriately, the reported response rate ranges between 59%[68] and 75%.[69]

Prevention with itraconazole in advanced HIV disease is successful, but does not provide survival benefit.

FUSARIOSIS

Fusarium spp. are found in soil with a worldwide distribution. Infections with *Fusarium* spp. (*Fusarium verticillioides* is, after *Fusarium solani*, the most common species) are rare and can lead to localized or disseminated disease. Examples of localized disease include keratomycosis, endophthalmitis, peritonitis due to implanted catheters for chronic ambulatory peritoneal dialysis, paronychia, invasive nasal infection and post-traumatic lesions of the bone, joint or skin.[73] Disseminated fusariosis has been described in a study of 97 patients.[74] These infections are supposedly airborne or inoculated through breakdown of the skin barrier. Most patients have prolonged and severe (<100 neutrophils/ml) neutropenia. The disease mimics aspergillosis and presents with an abrupt onset of fever, often combined with sinusitis, painful ecthyma gangrenosum-like skin lesions, pulmonary involvement and myalgia.

Histopathologic tissue examination with PAS or Gomori methenamine-silver staining reveals vascular invasion by hyphae with infarction and necrosis. Contrary to aspergillosis, 50–70% of cases with disseminated fusariosis have positive blood cultures.[74] *Fusarium* spp. grow rapidly on agar media but growth is inhibited by cycloheximide. The response of *Fusarium* spp. to amphotericin B and itraconazole is limited. Newer treatment modalities such as lipid formulations of amphotericin B, voriconazole and the adjuvant use of growth factors (G-CSF and GM-CSF) may be promising.[74] Localized infection usually responds to treatment, but disseminated infection has a high mortality, especially if the underlying myelosuppression is not reversed. Moreover, successfully treated disseminated fusariosis tends to recur with repeated bone marrow suppression.

REFERENCES

1. Langenbeck B. Auffingung von Pilzen aus der Schleimhaut der Speiserohre einer Typhus-Leiche. Neue Not Geb Natur Heilk (Froriep) 1839;12:145–7.
2. Jarvis WR. Epidemiology of nosocomial fungal infections, with emphasis on *Candida* species. Clin Infect Dis 1995;20:1526–30.
3. Pfaller MA. Epidemiology of candidiasis. J Hosp Infect 1995;30(Suppl.):329–38.
4. Pfaller MA. International surveillance of bloodstream infections due to *Candida* species: frequency of occurrence and *in vitro* susceptibilities to fluconazole, ravuconazole, and voriconazole of isolates collected from 1997 through 1999 in the SENTRY antimicrobial surveillance program. J Clin Microbiol 2001;39:3254–9.
5. Singh N. Trends in the epidemiology of opportunistic fungal infections: predisposing factors and the impact of antimicrobial use practices. Clin Infect Dis 2001;33:1692–6.
6. Safdar N, Maki DG. The commonality of risk factors for nosocomial colonization and infection with antimicrobial-resistant *Staphylococcus aureus, Enterococcus*, gram-negative bacilli, *Clostridium difficile*, and *Candida*. Ann Intern Med 2002;136:834–44.
7. Rocco TR, Reinert SE, Simms H. Effect of fluconazole administration in critically ill patients. Arch Surg 2000;135:160–5.
8. Abi-Said D, Anaissie E, Uzun O, Raad I, Pinzcowski H, Vartivarian S. The epidemiology of hematogenous candidiasis caused by different *Candida* species. Clin Infect Dis 1997;24:1122–8.
9. Marr KA, Seidel K, Slavin MA, *et al.* Prolonged fluconazole prophylaxis is associated with persistent protection against candidiasis-related death in allogenic marrow transplant recipients: long-term follow-up of a randomized, placebo-controlled trial. Blood 2000;96:2055–61.
10. Kanda Y, Yamamoto R, Chizuka A, *et al.* Prophylactic action of oral fluconazole against fungal infection in neutropenic patients. Cancer 2000;89:1611–25.
11. Matthews RC. Pathogenicity determinants of *Candida albicans*: potential targets for immunotherapy? Microbiology 1994;140:1505–11.
12. Kirkpatrick CH. Chronic mucocutaneous candidiasis. In: Bodey GP, ed. Candidiasis. Pathogenesis, diagnosis and treatment, 2nd ed. New York: Raven Press; 1993:167–84.
13. Walsh TJ, Pizzo PA. Caudidiasis. In: Bodey GP, ed. Candidiasis. Pathogenesis, diagnosis and treatment, 2nd ed. New York: Raven Press; 1993:109–58.
14. Pfaller MA. Laboratory aids in the diagnosis of invasive candidiasis. Mycopathologia 1992;120:65–72.
15. Mitsutake K, Miyazaki T, Tashiro T, *et al.* Enolase antigen, mannan antigen, C and-Tec antigen and beta-glucan in patients with candidemia. J Clin Microbiol 1996;34:1918–21.
16. Erjavec Z, Verweij PE. Recent progress in the diagnosis of fungal infections in the immunocompromised host. Drug Resist Updat 2002;5:3–10.
16a. Eisen DP, Bartley PB, Hope W, *et al.* Urine D-arabinitol/L-arabinitol ratio in diagnosing Candida infection in patients with haematological malignancy and HIV infection. Diagn Microbiol Infect Dis 2002;42:39–42.
17. Rex JH, Walsh TJ, Sobel JD, *et al.* Practice guidelines for the treatment of candidiasis. Clin Infect Dis 2000;30:662–78.
18. Fisher JF, Newman CL, Sobel JD. Yeast in the urine. Solutions for a budding problem? Clin Infect Dis 1995;20:183–9.
19. Crook WG. The yeast connection, a medical breakthrough, 2nd ed. New York: Vintage Books; 1984.
20. Renfro L, Feder HM, Lane TJ, Manu P, Matthews DA. Yeast connection among 100 patients with chronic fatigue. Am J Med 1989;86:165–8.
21. Dismukes WE, Wade JS, Lee JY, Dockery BK, Hain JD. A randomized, double blind trial of nystatin therapy for the candidiasis hypersensitivity syndrome. N Engl J Med 1990;323:1717–23.
22. Executive Committee of American Academy of Allergy and Immunology. Candidiasis hypersensitivity syndrome. J Allergy Clin Immunol 1986;78:271–3.
23. Dismukes WE. Introduction to antifungal drugs. Clin Infect Dis 2000;30:653–7.
24. Phillips P, de Beule K, Hoepelman IM, *et al.* A double-blind comparison of itraconazole oral solution and fluconazole capsules for the treatment of oropharyngeal candidiasis in patients with AIDS. Clin Infect Dis 1998;26:1368–73.
25. Villanueva A, Arathoon E, Gotuzzo E, Berman RS, DiNubile MJ, Sable CA. A randomized double-blind study of caspofungin versus amphotericin for the treatment of candidal esophagitis. Clin Infect Dis 2001;33:1529–35.
26. Kulak Y, Arikan A, Delibalta N. Comparison of three different treatment methods for generalized denture stomatitis. J Prosthet Dent 1994;72:283–8.
27. Rex JH, Walsh TJ, Sobel JD, *et al.* Practice guidelines for the treatment of candidiasis. Clin Infect Dis 2000;30:662–78.
27a. Mora-Duarte J, Betts R, Rotstein C, *et al.* Comparison of caspofungin and amphotericin B for invasive candidiasis. N Engl J Med 2002;347:2020–9
28. Denning DW. Invasive aspergillosis. Clin Infect Dis 1998;26:781–805.
29. Boon AP, O'Brien D, Adams DH. Ten year review of invasive aspergillosis detected at necropsy. J Clin Pathol 1991;44:452–4.
30. Walsh TJ, Dixon DM. Nosocomial aspergillosis: environmental microbiology, hospital epidemiology, diagnosis and treatment. Eur J Epidemiol 1989;5:131–42.
31. Khoo SH, Denning DW. Invasive aspergillosis in patients with AIDS. Clin Infect Dis 1994;19(Suppl.1):S41–8.
32. Vaughan LM. Therapy review. Allergic bronchopulmonary aspergillosis. Clin Pharmacol 1993;12:24–33.
33. Kullberg BJ, Oude Lashof AM. Epidemiology of opportunistic invasive mycoses. Eur J Med Res 2002;7:183–91.
34. Denning DW. Aspergillosis: diagnosis and treatment. Int J Antimicrob Agents 1996;6:161–8.
35. Levitz SM. Overview of host defenses in fungal infection. Clin Infect Dis 1992;14(Suppl.14):S37–42.
36. Sulahian A, Tabouret M, Ribaud P, *et al.* Comparison of an enzyme immunoassay and latex agglutination test for detection of galactomannan in the diagnosis of aspergillosis. Eur J Clin Microbiol Infect Dis 1996;15:139–45.
37. Levy H, Horak DA, Tegtmeier BR, Yokota SB, Forman SJ. The value of bronchoalveolar lavage and bronchial washings in the diagnosis of invasive pulmonary aspergillosis. Respir Med 1992;86:243–8.
38. Walsh TJ. Invasive pulmonary aspergillosis in patients with neoplastic disease. Semin Respir Infect 1990;5:111–22.
38a. Saraceno JL, Phelps DT, Ferro TJ, *et al.* Chronic necrotizing aspergillosis: approach to management. Chest 1997;112:541–4.
38b. Binder RE, Faling LJ, Pugatch RD, *et al.* Chronic necrotizing pulmonary aspergillosis: A discrete clinical entity. Medicine 1982; 61:109.
39. DeShazo RD, Chapin K, Swain RE. Fungal sinusitis. N Engl J Med 1997;337:254–9.
40. Stevens DA, Schwartz HJ, Lee JY, *et al.* A randomized trial of itraconazole in allergic bronchopulmonary aspergillosis. N Engl J Med 2000;342:756–62.
41. Stevens DA, Kan VL, Judson MA, *et al.* Practice guidelines for disease caused by *Aspergillus*. Clin Infect Dis 2000;30:696–709.
42. Boogaerts M, Winston DJ, Bow EJ, *et al.* Intravenous and oral itraconazole versus intravenous amphotericin B deoxycholate as empirical antifungal therapy for persistent fever in neutropenic patients with cancer who are receiving broad-spectrum antibacterial therapy. A randomized, controlled trial. Itraconazole Neutropenia Study Group. Ann Intern Med 2001;135,412–22.
43. Maertens J, Raad I, Sable CA, *et al.* Multicenter, noncomparative study to evaluate safety and efficacy of caspofungin in adults with invasive aspergillosis refractory or intolerant to amphotericin B, AMB lipid formulations, or azoles. In: Program and Abstracts of the 40th Interscience Conference on Antimicrobial Agents and Chemotherapy, Toronto, Canada, 2000. Abstract 1103, p. 371. Washington DC: American Society for Microbiology.
44. Herbrecht R, Denning DW, Patterson TF, *et al.* Open, randomised comparison of voriconazole and amphotericin B followed by other licensed antifungal therapy for primary therapy of invasive aspergillosis. In: Program and Abstracts of the 41st Interscience Conference on Antimicrobial Agents and Chemotherapy, Chicago, IL, 2001. Abstract 680, p. 378. Washington DC: American Society for Microbiology.
45. Walsh TJ, Pappas P, Winston DJ, *et al.* Voriconazole compared with liposomal amphotericin B for empirical antifungal therapy in patients with neutropenia and persistent fever. N Engl J Med 2002;346:225–34.
46. Kwon-Chung KJ, Bennet JE. Cryptococcis. In: Medical mycology. Philadelphia: Lea & Febiger; 1992:397–446.

47. Selik RM, Chu SY, Ward JW. Trends in infectious diseases and cancers among persons dying of HIV infection in the United States from 1987 to 1992. Ann Intern Med 1995;123:933–6.
48. van Elden LJR, Walenkamp AME, Hoepelman AIM. Declining number of patients with cryptococcosis in the Netherlands in the era of highly active antiretroviral therapy. AIDS 2000;14:2787–800.
49. Heyderman RS, Gangaidzo IT, Hakim JG, *et al.* Cryptococcal meningitis in human immunodeficiency virus-infected patients in Harare, Zimbabwe. Clin Infect Dis 1998;26:284–9.
50. Kwon-Chung KJ, Edman JC, Wickes BL. General association of mating types and virulence in CN. Infect Immun 1992;60:602–5.
51. Dromer F, Mathoulin S, Dupont B, Letenneur L, Ronin O. French Cryptococcosis Study Group. Individual and environmental factors associated with infection due to *Cryptococcus neoformans* serotype D. Clin Infect Dis 1996;23:91–6.
52. Speed BR, Dunt D. Clinical and host differences between infections with the two varieties of *Cryptococcus neoformans*. Clin Infect Dis 1995;21:28–34.
53. Coenjaerts FEJ, Walenkamp AME, Hoepelman AIM. Potent inhibition of neutrophil migration by cryptococcal mannoprotein-4-induced desensitization. J Immunology 2001;167:3988–95.
54. Lipovsky MM, Gekker G, Hu S, Ehrlich LC, Hoepelman AI, Peterson PK. Cryptococcal glucuronoxylomannan induces IL-8 production by human microglia but inhibits neutrophil migration towards IL-8. J Infect Dis 1998;177:260–3.
55. Lipovsky MM, van Elden LJ, Walenkamp AM, Dankert J, Hoepelman AI. Does the capsule component of the *Cryptococcus neoformans* glucuronoxylomannan impair transendothelial migration of leukocytes in patients with cryptococcal meningitis? J Infect Dis 1998;178:1231–2.
56. Chaka WS, Heyderman R, Hoepelman IM. Cytokine profiles in CSF and plasma of HIV-infected patients with cryptococcal meningitis: no leukocytosis despite high IL-8 levels. J Infect Dis 1997;176:1633–6.
57. Barker RD. The primary pulmonary lymph node complex of cryptococcosis. Am J Clin Pathol 1976;65:83–92.
58. Fleuridor R, Lyles RH, Pirofski L. Quantitative and qualitative differences in the serum antibody profiles of human immunodeficiency virus-infected persons with and without *Cryptococcus neoformans* meningitis. J Infect Dis 1999;180:1526–35.
59. Saag MS, Graybill RJ, Larsen RA, *et al.* Practice guidelines for the management of cryptococcal disease. Clin Infect Dis 2000;30:710–8.
60. van der Horst CM, Saag MS, Cloud GA, *et al.* Treatment of cryptococcal meningitis associated with the acquired immunodeficiency syndrome. N Engl J Med 1997;337:15–21.
61. Emilie D, Burgard M, Lascoux-Combe C, *et al.* Cessation of secondary prophylaxis in patients with cryptococcosis. AIDS 2001;15:1437–8.
62. Powderly WG. Cryptococcal meningitis and AIDS. Clin Infect Dis 1993;17:837–42.
63. Diamond RE, Bennett JE. Prognostic factors in cryptococcal meningitis. A study in 111 cases. Ann Intern Med 1974;80:176–81.
64. Sugar AM. Mucormycosis. Clin Infect Dis 1992;14(Suppl.1):126–9.
65. Artis WM, Fountain JA, Delcher HK, Jones HE. A mechanism of susceptibility to mucormycosis in diabetic ketoacidosis: transferrin and iron availability. Diabetes 1982;31:1109–14.
66. Yohai RA, Bullock JD, Aziz AA, Markert RJ. Survival factors in rhino-orbital-cerebral mucormycosis. Surv Ophthalmol 1994;39:3–22.
67. Dykhuizen RS, Kerr KN, Soutar RL. Air crescent sign and fatal haemoptysis in pulmonary mucormycosis. Scand J Infect Dis 1994;26:498–501.
68. Strasser MD, Kennedy RJ, Adam RD. Rhinocerebral mucormycosis. Therapy with amphotericin B lipid complex. Arch Intern Med 1996;156:337–9.
69. Heath TCB, Patel A, Fisher D, Bowden FJ, Currie B. Disseminated *Penicillium marneffei*: presenting illness of advanced HIV infection; a clinicopathological review, illustrated by a case report. Pathology 1995;27:101–5.
70. Tedder M, Spratt JA, Anstadt MP, Hegde SS, Tedder SD, Lowe JE. Pulmonary mucormycosis: results of medical and surgical therapy. Ann Thorac Surg 1994;57:1044–50.
71. Chariyalertsak S, Sirisanthana T, Supparatpinyo K, Praparattanapan J, Nelson KE. Case–control study of risk factors for *Penicillium marneffei* infection in human immunodeficiency virus-infected patients in northern Thailand. Clin Infect Dis 1997;24:1080–6.
72. Duong TA. Infection due to *Penicillium marneffei*, an emerging pathogen: review of 155 reported cases. Clin Infect Dis 1996;23:125–30.
73. Kwon-Chung KJ, Bennett JE. Infections due to miscellaneous fungi. In: Medical mycology. Philadelphia: Lea & Febiger; 1992:745–7.
74. Boutati EI, Anaissie EJ. *Fusarium*, a significant emerging pathogen in patients with hematologic malignancy: ten years' experience at a cancer center and implications for management. Blood 1997;90:999–1008.

chapter

238 Systemic Fungi

Thomas G Mitchell

INTRODUCTION

Systemic mycoses are customarily acquired by inhaling exogenous fungi that may disseminate to other internal organs, as well as the skin. The etiological agents tend to be restricted to rather circumscribed geographical areas. Consequently, the prevalence and geographic distribution of these mycoses are highly delimited. The term systemic mycoses is not exclusive, as many opportunistic (Chapter 237) and subcutaneous (Chapter 239) mycoses may also exhibit systemic clinical manifestations. Although systemic mycoses may be caused by a number of exogenously acquired fungi, this chapter will focus on the four most common primary systemic mycoses: blastomycosis, coccidioidomycosis, histoplasmosis and paracoccidioidomycosis. All are caused by thermally dimorphic fungi. The fungi that cause coccidioidomycosis and histoplasmosis exist in nature, where they are associated with dry soil or soil mixed with guano. The agents of blastomycosis and paracoccidioidomycosis are presumed to exist in nature, but their habitats have not been clearly defined. Inhalation of any one of these fungi can lead to pulmonary infection, which may or may not be symptomatic. Dissemination may occur to other parts of the body. Except for a few extremely rare cases, there is no evidence of transmission among humans or animals. Table 238.1 compares some of the epidemiological features of these systemic mycoses.

Although most symptomatic cases of blastomycosis, coccidioidomycosis, histoplasmosis and paracoccidioidomycosis occur in patients without significant pre-existing and predisposing disease, individuals with defects of cell-mediated immunity have long been recognized to be at risk for these mycoses if they are exposed by residence or travel in the appropriate endemic areas. In recent years, the incidence of each of these mycoses as opportunistic mycoses in AIDS patients has sharply increased. Indeed, the AIDS pandemic has revealed a new endemic and systemic, dimorphic, opportunistic pathogen, *Penicillium marneffei*; both the agent and the disease are confined to Asia (see Chapter 126).

Blastomycosis, coccidioidomycosis, histoplasmosis and paracoccidioidomycosis are caused respectively by the following dimorphic fungi: *Blastomyces dermatitidis*, *Coccidioides immitis* (or *Coccidioides posadasii*), *Histoplasma capsulatum* and *Paracoccidioides brasiliensis*. Each species grows as a mold in nature or the laboratory at temperatures below 98.6°F (37°C). On routine fungal culture media at 77–86°F (25–30°C), they produce mycelial colonies that vary in texture, pigment and growth rate, but may be indistinguishable from each other or many saprophytic molds. The ecology and geographic distribution of these fungi are summarized in Table 238.2. Microscopically, the hyphae are uniform in width, hyaline (not pigmented), branched, septate and similar in appearance except for the production of asexual spores or conidia, which are helpful aids to their identification. In the host or under the appropriate growth conditions *in vitro*, they convert to a distinctive form of growth that is found in tissue: *B. dermatitidis, H. capsulatum* and *P. brasiliensis* produce characteristic budding yeast cells and *C. immitis* and *C. posadasii* produce spherules.

BLASTOMYCOSIS

Blastomycosis is a chronic infection characterized by granulomatous and suppurative lesions but the clinical manifestations may be protean. The disease is undoubtedly initiated by inhalation of airborne conidia of the etiologic agent, *Blastomyces dermatitidis*. From the lung, dissemination may occur to any organ, but preferentially to the skin and bones. The disease has been called North American blastomycosis because many early cases were confined to the United States, Canada and Central America. Although the prevalence continues to be highest on the North American continent, autochthonous cases of blastomycosis have been documented in Africa, South America and Asia. In some parts of the United States it is even endemic for humans and dogs.

Blastomycosis was first described in its chronic cutaneous form in the 1890s by Gilchrist.[1] Many early case descriptions were undoubtedly confused with coccidioidomycosis, cryptococcosis (European blastomycosis) and paracoccidioidomycosis (South American blastomycosis) until Benham established the etiology of blastomycosis in 1934.[2] Eventually, Schwarz & Baum gathered histopathologic evidence to confirm that both cutaneous and systemic manifestations originate in the lung.[3] Primary cutaneous infection has been demonstrated only rarely. Thus, blastomycosis is primarily a pulmonary infection characterized by secondary spread to the skin and other parts of the body. However, the respiratory episode may be completely asymptomatic.

NATURE

Cultural characteristics

Blastomycosis is caused by a single dimorphic species, *B. dermatitidis*. The sexual or teleomorphic form is *Ajellomyces dermatitidis*. At temperatures below 95°F (35°C), *B. dermatitidis* grows as a mold, producing a colony of uniform, hyaline, septate hyphae and conidia. On Sabouraud's glucose agar at 77°F (25°C), different isolates of *B. dermatitidis* vary in their rate of growth, colony appearance and degree and type of conidiation. Colonies usually require at least 2 weeks to reach full development. Many strains produce a white, cottony mycelium that becomes tan to brown with age (Table 238.2). On enriched media at 98.6°F (37°C), *B. dermatitidis* converts to growth in the yeast form and produces colonies that are folded, pasty and moist.

Microscopic appearance

The mycelial form produces abundant conidia from short lateral conidiophores on the aerial hyphae (Fig. 238.1). The conidia are spherical, ovoid or pyriform in shape, smooth walled and up to 10μm in diameter. Thick-walled chlamydospores, 7–18μm in diameter, may also be observed. Because the colony and conidia of *B. dermatitidis* may be confused with many other fungi, identification must be confirmed by conversion to the characteristic yeast form. This conversion can be accomplished by *in vitro* cultivation on rich

EPIDEMIOLOGICAL FEATURES OF FUNGAL INFECTIONS				
Feature	**Blastomycosis**	**Coccidioidomycosis**	**Histoplasmosis**	**Paracoccidioidomycosis**
Geographic areas of high endemicity	Yes	Yes	Yes	Yes
Saprophytic form (<95°F): hyaline, septate hyphae	Yes	Yes	Yes	Yes
Predominant tissue forms	Yeasts	Spherules	Yeasts	Yeasts
High infection rate in endemic areas	?	Yes	Yes	Yes
At least 90% of infections are initiated by inhalation	Yes	Yes	Yes	Yes
Approximate percentage of infections that are asymptomatic	?	≥60	>95	>95
At least 90% of infections are self-limited	?	Yes	Yes	Yes
Approximate percentage of immunocompetent patients	>90	>90	>90	>90
Approximate percentage of males among patients with disease	50–90	75–90	80–90	95
Relative frequency of disease among AIDS patients in the endemic areas	Rare	Common	Common	Infrequent

Table 238.1 Epidemiological features of fungal infections.[25]

SUMMARY OF SYSTEMIC MYCOSES					
Mycosis	**Etiology**	**Ecology**	**Geographic distribution**	**Mycelial form***	**Tissue form**
Blastomycosis	*Blastomyces dermatitidis*	Unknown (riverbanks?)	Endemic along Mississippi, Ohio & St Lawrence River valleys & south-eastern USA	Slow to moderate growth rate. Colonies are white to tan, flat, velvety or cottony. Hyaline septate hyphae and short conidiophores bearing single globose to pyriform conidia, 2–10μm	Thick-walled yeasts with broad-based, usually single, buds, 8–15μm
Coccidioidomycosis	*Coccidioides immitis* and *C. posadasii*	Soil	Semiarid regions of south-western USA, Mexico, Central & South America	Moderate to rapid growth rate. Colonies are white to brown, flat to wooly. Hyaline s eptate hyphae and arthroconidia, 3 × 6μm.	Spherules, 10–80μm or larger, containing endospores, 2–4μm
Histoplasmosis	*Histoplasma capsulatum* var. *capsulatum* and *H. capsulatum* var. *duboisii*	Bat & avian habitats (guano); alkaline soil	Global; endemic in Ohio, Missouri & Mississippi River valleys; central Africa (var. *duboisii*)	Slow growth rate. Colonies are white to brown, powdery to wooly. Hyaline septate hyphae, tuberculate macroconidia, 8–16μm, and small oval microconidia, 3–5μm	Oval yeasts, 2 × 4μm, intracellular in macrophages
Paracoccidioidomycosis	*Paracoccidioides brasiliensis*	Unknown (soil?)	Central & South America	Slow growth rate. Colonies are flat to velvety, white to brown. Hyaline, septate hyphae and rare globose conidia and chlamydospores	Large, multiple budding yeasts, 15–30μm or larger

* Colony descriptions are for typical isolates grown at 77°F on Sabouraud's glucose agar.

Table 238.2 Summary of systemic mycoses.

medium (e.g. brain-heart infusion, chocolate agar or Kelly's medium) at 98.6°F (37°C) or by animal inoculation. Under these conditions, *B. dermatitidis* grows as a thick-walled spherical yeast that usually produces single buds (Fig. 238.2). The bud and parent yeast have a characteristically wide base of attachment and the bud often enlarges to a size equal to that of the parent cell before it separates. Yeast cells are multinucleated and normally range in size from 8 to 15μm, although some cells reach a diameter of 30μm.

Sexual reproduction

The teleomorphic state (i.e. the sexual or perfect form) of *B. dermatitidis* was discovered by McDonough and Lewis.[4] Based on its sexual apparatus and resultant ascospores, *B. dermatitidis* was renamed *Ajellomyces dermatitidis*; it has been placed in the same genus as the teleomorph of *H. capsulatum*. Both species, as well as the sexual forms of the dermatophytes, are closely related and classified in the ascomycetous family Gymnoascaceae. *Ajellomyces dermatitidis* is heterothallic and requires two compatible (opposite) mating types for sexual reproduction. Although the two mating types possess different antigens, they are similar in many other respects, including pathogenicity. Mating compatibility has been used to confirm that a single species is responsible for blastomycosis among dogs and humans and probably also for cases in North America and Africa.

EPIDEMIOLOGY

Ecology

The natural habitat of *B. dermatitidis* has not been resolved. Assuming that most cases of blastomycosis are acquired by inhalation of exogenous, infectious particles, *B. dermatitidis* must reproduce in nature and generate air-borne cells. However, there have been too few isolations of *B. dermatitidis* from the environment to establish its ecological niche. Over the years, *B. dermatitidis* has been isolated, but never repeatedly, from soil samples collected in rural environments, including a chicken house, a cattle crossing and

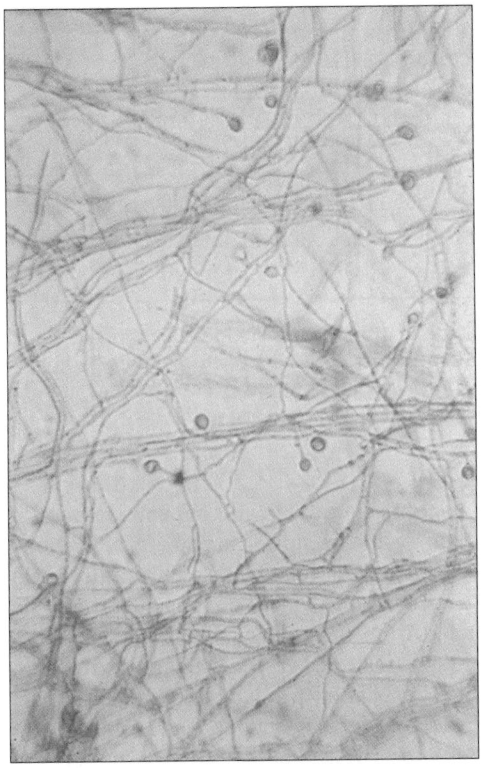

Fig. 238.1 *Blastomyces dermatitidis*, mycelial form in culture at 86°F. This shows hyaline, septate, branching hyphae and short conidiophores bearing solitary oval-to-piriform conidia.

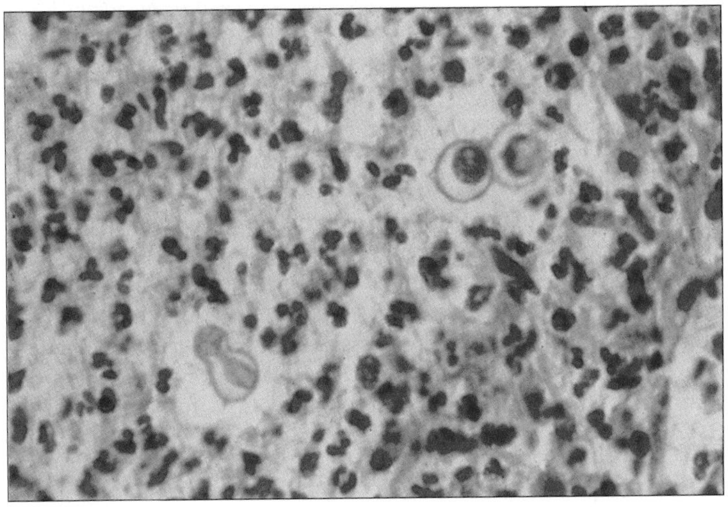

Fig. 238.2 *Blastomyces dermatitidis*, yeast form in hematoxylin and eosin-stained section of microabscess from a cutaneous lesion. This shows large spherical yeasts characterized by thick, highly refractile cell walls, single budding and a broad attachment between the parent yeast cell and bud.

several river banks. Positive samples were collected in Wisconsin from a beaver dam associated with a large outbreak of blastomycosis and at another outbreak from a fishing site. Several clusters of cases, with or without recovery of *B. dermatitidis* from environmental samples, have been associated with river banks, which suggests an association with fresh water and soil.[5–8] However, a recent study showed that the genotypes of environmental isolates proximal to outbreaks were not prevalent among the case isolates.[9]

Dogs are commonly infected and numerous reports have documented isolated cases in other animal species, but there is no evidence that an animal reservoir exists to perpetuate *B. dermatitidis*. It probably resides in nature in a protected and dormant condition during most of the year, until it is stimulated by a suitable climatic or other specific but transient event to propagate and produce conidia that become air borne and infectious.

Geographic distribution

Because *B. dermatitidis* is not readily recoverable from nature and an adequate skin test antigen is not available for conducting population surveys of exposure, the geographic distribution of blastomycosis has been estimated from reports of human and canine cases. The endemic area extends broadly eastward from states that border the Mississippi River. Blastomycosis is endemic in southern Canada east of Manitoba and, in the United States, in Illinois, Wisconsin, Minnesota, Ohio, the Atlantic coastal states and the south-eastern states, with the exception of Florida. Blastomycosis is rare in the New England and western states. The highest incidence occurs in Arkansas, Kentucky, Illinois, Louisiana, Mississippi, North Carolina, Tennessee and Wisconsin. Within these areas, local pockets of high endemicity have been identified. Canine cases exhibit the same endemic pattern as those of humans. Indeed, blastomycosis may occur more frequently in dogs than in humans.[5,10]

Clinical reports have also documented autochthonous cases in both northern and southern Africa, as well as India, Israel, Mexico and Venezuela. Reports of the infection occurring elsewhere are dubious because the diagnosis was questionable or the patients had a history of travel to an endemic area.

At least 11 outbreaks of blastomycosis have been documented.[5–8,11,12] Each outbreak consisted of a cluster of cases that occurred at approximately the same place and time. All but one area was rural. Seven outbreaks occurred during the fall and winter, and four in the summer. These outbreaks have provided helpful insights regarding the ecology of *B. dermatitidis* and natural history of blastomycosis.

Incidence

The data from large, clinical reviews indicate that blastomycosis occurs more frequently during middle age and in males. Although the disease can occur at any age, 60% of patients were between the ages of 30 and 60 years. Among the hundreds of cases compiled in several reviews, less than 4% of the patients were under 20 years of age and blastomycosis was rarely reported in children. However, in more recent studies, especially involving outbreaks, blastomycosis occurred equally in both sexes, and two-thirds of the patients associated with outbreaks have been children (<16 years old).

The male-to-female ratios reported in several surveys involving hundreds of patients vary from 6:1 to 15:1, but lower ratios have been reported in smaller studies and the overall sex ratio of outbreak cases is approximately 1. Perhaps both sexes are equally susceptible to acute blastomycosis, but males are more inclined to develop chronic or disseminated disease. The other systemic mycoses caused by exogenous fungi also occur more often in males (Table 238.1) and male animals are more susceptible (or less resistant) than females to challenge with *B. dermatitidis*. Blastomycosis may be similar to histoplasmosis in that children are equally susceptible to infection and disease, but the sex-related differences are manifested after puberty.

Genetic or racial differences in attack rates have not been confirmed. Socio-economic and occupational data have associated blastomycosis with poverty, malnutrition, manual labor, agriculture, construction work and exposure to dust and wood. The incidence of blastomycosis among immunocompromised patients, including patients with AIDS, is relatively low but apparently rising.[13,14]

PATHOGENICITY

Strains of *B. dermatitidis* vary in their virulence for experimental animals, but the explanation for these differences has not been resolved.[15] Among cell wall components, evidence has linked experimental virulence of strains of *B. dermatitidis* with the amount of α-1,3-glucan in the cell walls. This polysaccharide has been shown to vary in strains of *H. capsulatum* and *P. brasiliensis* that differ in virulence.[16]

The best characterized virulence factor is the WI-1 (also called BAD1) cell wall adhesin and immunodominant antigen. This protein contains multiple copies of a 25-amino acid tandem repeat, which binds to CR3 complement receptors and elicits both antibodies and cell-mediated immune responses.[17–19] Compared with less virulent mutants, the wild type contains less surface-bound WI-1. Although the mechanisms whereby WI-1, as well as α-1,3-glucan, contribute to virulence have not been fully elucidated, Klein and associates have postulated that shedding of WI-1 by virulent strains may neutralize macrophage defenses by occupying receptors, diminishing their ability to bind yeast cells.[17,18,20] Many strains of *B. dermatitidis* from Africa lack WI-1 and are less virulent than New World isolates.[19]

Pathogenesis

Almost all cases of blastomycosis originate in the lung. In the alveoli, *B. dermatitidis* induces an inflammatory response characterized by the infiltration of both macrophages and neutrophils and leading to the subsequent formation of granulomata. Both conidia and yeast cells are susceptible to the killing mechanisms of neutrophils and macrophages.[21] The accumulation of neutrophils presents a suppurative component that is uncharacteristic of most mycoses and other chronic diseases. Neutrophils and cell-mediated immunity combine to marshal effective resistance to blastomycosis. Unlike coccidioidomycosis and histoplasmosis, blastomycosis is relatively rare in patients with cellular immunodeficiencies.

If the pathogenesis of blastomycosis resembles that of histoplasmosis and coccidioidomycosis, most infections may be subclinical and resolve spontaneously. However, because specific and sensitive skin test antigens are lacking, the extent of exposure to *B. dermatitidis* in the general population has not been determined. In addition, calcification is uncommon and there is little radiologic or histopathologic evidence of residual blastomycotic lesions. The best evidence for the existence of subclinical blastomycosis derives from the reported outbreaks, where specific serological and skin test reactions documented exposure to *B. dermatitidis* in the absence of symptoms.[22]

Alternatively, based on the apparent scarcity of *B. dermatitidis* in nature and the limited evidence for subclinical infections, blastomycosis may be a rare and usually serious disease.[23] This hypothesis is supported by some of the studies of experimental canine blastomycosis. In humans, the primary pulmonary lesion may be inapparent to severe. If inapparent, dissemination to the skin and bones may follow. If the pulmonary episode is severe, the generalized systemic disease may develop, with the potential involvement of multiple organs.

PREVENTION

There are no clear guidelines for the prevention of blastomycosis. However, the WI-1 antigen may be an excellent vaccine candidate for future study.

DIAGNOSTIC MICROBIOLOGY

Blastomycosis is best diagnosed by direct examination or positive culture of sputa, skin lesions or other specimens. On most routine culture media, *B. dermatitidis* produces a mold with variable macroscopic features and conidia. Its identification is confirmed by growth on a rich medium at 98.6°F (37°C) and conversion to the characteristic yeast form. Alternatively, the identity of a culture may be established by an immunodiffusion test to detect a *B. dermatitidis*-specific antigen (antigen A) in a concentrated overnight, aqueous extract of the colony on solid medium or in the supernatant fluid of a short-term broth culture of the isolate. The formation of a precipitin line of identity with reference antisera and control antigen identifies the specific exoantigen extracted from the isolate. This method is rapid and applicable to nonsporulating cultures. As indicated in Table 238.3, the technique has also been expanded to identify other dimorphic pathogens. In addition, a DNA probe is commercially available to identify cultures of *B. dermatitidis*, as well as other agents of systemic mycoses.[24]

SPECIES-SPECIFIC EXOANTIGENS FOR THE IDENTIFICATION OF SYSTEMIC DIMORPHIC FUNGAL PATHOGENS

Fungus	Exoantigens
Coccidioides immitis	HS, F, HL
Histoplasma capsulatum	h, m
Blastomyces dermatitidis	A
Paracoccidioides brasiliensis	1, 2, 3

Table 238.3 Species-specific exoantigens for the identification of systemic dimorphic fungal pathogens.[1,21] Exoantigens are detected by precipitin lines of identity in immunodiffusion tests of concentrated culture supernatant fluids versus reference antigens and antisera.[25,120]

In culture at 98.6°F (37°C) or in tissue, *B. dermatitidis* forms large single-budding yeast cells with highly refractory cell walls and a broad attachment between the bud and parent yeast cell. As noted below, in fresh specimens or histopathological sections, the yeasts can be readily observed and identified.

Since the tests for complement fixing antibodies and delayed-type skin reactivity lack specificity and sensitivity, they are not helpful unless the patient is negative to heterologous fungal antigens; even then, positive, monospecific serological tests to *B. dermatitidis* may not indicate active infection. Serological tests for antibodies to the specific antigen A, which can be detected by the immunodiffusion test or an enzyme immunoassay, are more suggestive of infection, but negative tests do not exclude blastomycosis. Table 238.4 summarizes the conventional serological tests for antibodies to *B. dermatitidis* and other systemic fungi.

Microscopic examination

In calcofluor white or KOH preparations of pus, exudate, sputum, bronchial lavage fluid or other specimens, a diagnosis can be established by detecting the characteristic yeast cells of *B. dermatitidis*. The yeasts are large (8–15μm in diameter) and typically thick walled. The cell wall is highly refractile and often resembles a double wall. Budding usually occurs singly. The bud is attached to the parent cell by a broad base and enlarges to the size of the parent yeast before it is detached. These features, as depicted in Figures 238.1 and 238.2, are pathognomonic for blastomycosis. Unsuspected cases of blastomycosis are occasionally diagnosed from respiratory specimens submitted for routine cytology. In tissue stained with hematoxylin and eosin, the yeast cytoplasm stains darkly and the cell wall appears colorless. The yeasts are multinucleated. They are often abundant in cutaneous lesions and these specimens are usually positive on direct examination. If the yeasts are sparse, fungal cell wall stains, such as periodic acid–Schiff or methenamine silver, are helpful.

Rarely, small forms are seen in tissue. These cells are typical of *B. dermatitidis* in shape and budding but only 2–5μm in diameter. Their multinucleation may help to differentiate them from *Cryptococcus neoformans* and *H. capsulatum* var. *duboisii*.

SUMMARY OF SEROLOGIC TESTS FOR ANTIBODIES TO SYSTEMIC DIMORPHIC FUNGAL PATHOGENS IN PATIENTS WITHOUT AIDS					
Mycosis	Test	Antigen	Sensitivity and value		Limitation/specificity
			Diagnosis	Prognosis	
Blastomycosis	CF	By	Less than 50% of cases positive; reaction to homologous antigen only is diagnostic	Fourfold change in titer	Highly cross-reactive
	ID	Bcf	Up to 80% of cases positive, i.e. A band	Loss of A band	More specific than CF test
	EIA	A	Up to 90% of cases positive (titer ≥1:16)	Change in titer	92% specificity
Coccidioidomycosis	TP	C	Early primary infection; 90% cases positive	None	None
	CF	C	Titer ≥1:32 = secondary disease	Titer reflects severity (except in meningeal disease)	Rarely cross-reactive with H
	ID	C	More than 90% cases positive, i.e. F and/or HL band		More specific than CF test
Histoplasmosis	CF	H	Up to 83% of cases positive (titer ≥1:8)	Fourfold change in titer	Cross-reactions in patients with blastomycosis, coccidioidomycosis, cryptococcosis, aspergillosis; titer may be boosted by skin test with H
		Y	Up to 94% of cases positive (titer ≥1:8)	Fourfold change in titer	Less cross-reactivity than with H
	ID	H(10X)	Up to 85% of cases positive, i.e. m or m and h bands	Loss of h	Skin test with H may boost m band; more specific than CF test
Paracoccidioidomycosis	CF	P	80–95% of cases positive (titer ≥1:8)	Fourfold change in titer	Some cross-reactions at low titer with aspergillosis and candidiasis sera
	ID	P	98% of cases positive (bands 1, 2 and/or 3)	Loss of bands	Band 3 and band m (to H) are identical

Table 238.4 Summary of serologic tests for antibodies to systemic dimorphic fungal pathogens in patients without AIDS. A, antigen A of *B. dermatitidis*; Bcf, culture filtrate of *B. dermatitidis* yeast phase; By, yeast phase of *B. dermatitidis*; C, coccidioidin; CF, complement fixation; EIA, enzyme immunoassay; H, histoplasmin; ID, immunodiffusion; P, culture filtrate of *P. brasiliensis* yeast phase; TP, tube precipitin; Y, yeast phase of *H. capsulatum*.[27,102,103]

Culture

Clinical specimens are cultured on any of several fungal media. Sabouraud's agar, the standard medium used for morphologic descriptions of pathogenic fungi, is composed of 4% glucose, 1% neopeptone and agar. A modified Sabouraud's agar, containing 2% glucose, is a more effective isolation medium. Inhibitory mold agar is a complex medium designed for optimal recovery of pathogenic fungi. For the culture of nonsterile specimens, such as sputum, skin or urine, antibiotics are included in the media, usually cycloheximide and chloramphenicol or gentamicin, to inhibit saprophytic fungi and bacterial contaminants. Inhibitory mold agar contains all three additives. Cultures should be incubated at 86°F (30°C) or room temperature for at least 4 weeks. Primary colonies are white to brown, variably textured molds, and they produce potentially infectious conidia. The identification of *B. dermatitidis* is confirmed by detecting the A exoantigen (Table 238.3), by subculturing on an enriched medium, such as brain-heart infusion blood agar or Kelly's medium at 98.6°F (37°C), for subsequent conversion to the yeast form (Fig. 238.2) or by hybridization with a specific DNA probe.[25]

Some laboratories employ direct animal inoculation as a method of rapidly isolating and identifying *B. dermatitidis*. Mice are injected intraperitoneally with the clinical specimen and their peritoneums are examined for typical yeast cells 1–2 weeks later.

Skin test

Delayed-type hypersensitivity to *B. dermatitidis* has been detected by skin tests with both whole cell and culture filtrate antigens (blastomycin). However, the commercial blastomycin was abandoned because it lacked specificity and sensitivity. More promising antigen preparations have been developed, but they are not available for routine human skin testing.

Serology

The most useful serologic procedure is an enzyme immunoassay (EIA) for antibodies to antigen A. With titers >1:16, the sensitivity and specificity of this test were shown to be >77% and >92%, respectively,[26,27] and EIA titers reflected the severity of disease (Table 238.4). More recent evaluation of a commercial EIA reported sensitivity of 83% and false-positive results with sera from patients with histoplasmosis, but only rarely with sera from patients with other mycoses.[28] In this study, the EIA was much more sensitive than the immunodiffusion test. Using reference reagents, precipitins to antigen A can also be detected by an immunodiffusion (ID) test, as indicated in Table 238.4. Measurement of CF antibodies to various antigen preparations of *B. dermatitidis* has not proved reliable.

CLINICAL MANIFESTATIONS

Two classic forms of blastomycosis are recognized: pulmonary, often with dissemination, and chronic cutaneous blastomycosis. A wide variety of symptoms, pathology and radiographic appearances may be observed in blastomycosis. The most common symptoms include cough, weight loss, chest pain, skin lesions, fever, hemoptysis and localized swelling. After the lung, the most frequently involved organs are the skin, bones and genitourinary tract, followed by the central nervous system, liver or spleen. Less often, the lymph nodes, thyroid, heart, adrenal, omentum, gastrointestinal tract, muscles and pancreas may become infected.[14,29–33]

Pulmonary blastomycosis

Primary pulmonary blastomycosis may be asymptomatic or present as acute or subacute pneumonia, ranging from mild to severe. Cases associated with outbreaks have confirmed that spontaneous recovery can follow primary blastomycosis.[32,34] However, the possibility of subsequent reactivation cannot be excluded. Even if nonapparent, dissemination may spread to the skin, bones or other sites. If the pulmonary episode is severe, the generalized systemic disease may develop and may involve multiple organs. Cases associated with outbreaks have indicated that the incubation period is 3–12 weeks and that spontaneous recovery can follow primary blastomycosis. Overall, most cases occur in adults and in males, but in pediatric blastomycosis, children of both sexes are equally susceptible. Most pediatric cases are recognized as acute pulmonary blastomycosis.[5,30]

Patients with symptomatic, primary pulmonary infection may present with symptoms of mild respiratory infection, including cough, chest pain and high fever, as well as numerous other complaints. The primary pulmonary infection may persist locally, spread to other organ(s), or both. Alternatively, the pulmonary lesion may heal by fibrosis and absorption, leaving no residual evidence of infection. In patients whose pulmonary lesions have resolved, dissemination, generally to the skin, may already have occurred. If the pulmonary focus becomes more severe, an acute to chronic lung infection may develop. Patients with chronic pulmonary blastomycosis usually present with cough, low-grade fever, loss of weight, night sweats and other problems. The most common forms of pulmonary involvement are infiltration, cavitation, pneumonia or nodules.[22,35] A variety of pulmonary manifestations may be observed and none of the radiographic presentations are consistent enough to be diagnostic of blastomycosis.

Chronic cutaneous blastomycosis

In chronic cutaneous blastomycosis, the initial skin lesion presents as one or more subcutaneous nodules that eventually ulcerate. Lesions are most common on exposed skin surfaces, such as the face, hands, wrist and lower leg. Spread may occur by extension to the trunk or other areas and may require weeks or months for the ulcerative process to evolve. If untreated, elevated, granulomatous lesions with advancing borders will develop in time. The yeast cells can be found in microabscesses near the dermis. Extensive, often verrucous, epithelial hyperplasia overlying the abscesses may develop and resemble carcinoma. These extensive cutaneous lesions are characteristically discolored and crusty and they tend to heal and scar in the central, older areas. The active microabscesses found at the leading edge of the lesion can be aspirated or biopsied and the typical yeast cells of *B. dermatitidis* can be observed on direct microscopic examination (Fig. 238.3).

Disseminated blastomycosis

Dissemination may be widespread in blastomycosis. The most frequently involved extrapulmonary sites are the skin, bones, genitourinary tract, central nervous system and spleen. Less frequently, the liver, lymph nodes, heart and other viscera are infected. The progressive systemic form of blastomycosis develops in patients with unresolving pulmonary infection, but the degree of pulmonary involvement is not related to the extent of dissemination. This infection may be chronic, with few organisms present, or multiple pulmonary foci may be demonstrable at the time generalized systemic disease develops.

From the lungs, the yeasts disseminate with a characteristic predilection for the skin and bones. Skin lesions may be more severe than those in chronic cutaneous blastomycosis and are seen in about 75% of the cases. Overall, skeletal involvement is observed in approximately a third of patients. Osteomyelitis and, in some cases, draining sinuses to the skin develop and should be examined for the presence of characteristic yeast cells. Because of the frequency of bone involvement and because almost any bone can be affected, whenever blastomycosis is diagnosed, a complete radiographic examination is advisable. Arthritis may develop by extension from infected bone or by direct dissemination from the lung without bone infection. In up to 22% of patients, the urogenital tract is involved, especially the prostate, male genitalia, kidney and adrenals. Metastasis to the central nervous system, resulting in meningitis or brain abscess, occurs in up to 10% of patients.

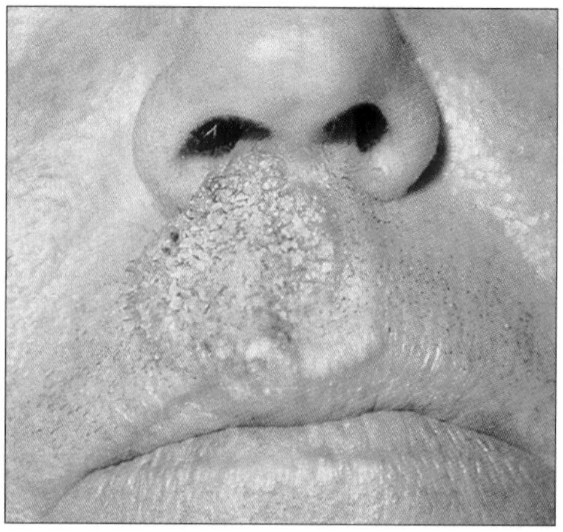

Fig. 238.3 Initial cutaneous lesion of blastomycosis.

Primary cutaneous blastomycosis

This form of blastomycosis is initiated by traumatic autoinoculation or contamination of an open wound with the infectious material. The pathogenesis differs considerably from the other forms of blastomycosis. The lymphatics and regional lymph nodes are involved, but the infection remains localized and often resolves without treatment. Several cases of accidental cutaneous inoculation have occurred in veterinarians who were examining or performing autopsies on diseased dogs. Traumatic inoculation leading to primary, subcutaneous disease can occur, albeit rarely, with any of the systemic fungi discussed in this chapter. The natural history and pathology are similar to subcutaneous mycoses (see Chapter 239) and systemic dissemination is rare in the immunocompetent host.

Blastomycosis and AIDS

Despite the consistent prevalence of blastomycosis in its endemic area, patients with HIV infection are not commonly infected. Because of the presumed rural reservoir of *B. dermatitidis* or its low census in nature, patients with AIDS may be exposed less often than similar patients in the endemic areas for coccidioidomycosis or histoplasmosis. Alternatively, the host defenses against *B. dermatitidis* may be less dependent upon cell-mediated immunity. The cases of blastomycosis and AIDS that have been reported include the presentation of acute miliary disease in the lungs and a relatively higher frequency of CNS disease.[36,37] Blastomycosis in compromised patients is being seen more frequently and has a much poorer prognosis.[13,37]

MANAGEMENT

As demonstrated by several outbreak cases, primary blastomycosis in immunocompetent individuals may not require therapy. Nevertheless, such patients with a confirmed diagnosis of primary pulmonary infection that is mild and resolves spontaneously without treatment must be closely observed for at least 2 years following the primary infection because of the possibility of reactivation blastomycosis. Patients with protracted, severe or progressive primary infection, chronic pulmonary or disseminated blastomycosis require treatment.[30,38] Depending upon the manifestations of disease and the integrity of the underlying host defenses, chemotherapeutic success rates with amphotericin B, ketoconazole or itraconazole currently vary between 70% and 95%. Survival in patients with AIDS and other immunocompromising conditions is about half this figure.[37,39] Recent guidelines recommend itraconazole for mild to moderate blastomycosis and amphotericin B for life-threatening disease and/or patients with AIDS.[39]

Ketoconazole

Ketoconazole was the first azole recommended for immunocompetent patients with mild to moderately severe disease (e.g. blastomycosis that is neither life threatening nor involving the central nervous system). An oral dose of 400–800mg per day for at least 6 months is effective in most adult patients, but patients must be closely followed because relapses have occurred on ketoconazole.[39] Successful treatment of blastomycosis has been achieved in 80–90% of adult patients. The adverse effects of ketoconazole include liver toxicity and reversible hormonal imbalances (e.g. gynecomastia), as well as nausea, pruritus, dizziness or headache. Itraconazole has supplanted ketoconazole because it offers improved absorption. tolerance and efficacy.[39]

Itraconazole

Recent trials have confirmed the efficacy of itraconazole for the treatment of mild to moderate, nonmeningeal, nonlife-threatening blastomycosis. When such adult patients were given oral dosages of 200–400mg/day for at least 6 months, the rate of cure or improvement was 95%. Itraconazole should be taken with meals and patients are treated for approximately 6 months with follow-up for 1 year or longer. Toxicity from itraconazole occurs in less than one-third of patients, is usually mild and rarely necessitates cessation of therapy. The most common side-effects are gastrointestinal symptoms, usually nausea, vomiting or diarrhea. Minor reactions include weakness, dizziness, headache, chills, fever, tinnitus, skin rash, pruritus, paresthesia and, rarely, transient, modest elevation of transaminase. Any relapse may be amenable to a second course of itraconazole.

Compared with ketoconazole, itraconazole is equally or more effective and better tolerated. For example, gastrointestinal symptoms were more than twice as frequent among patients receiving ketoconazole than itraconazole, although these symptoms occur more often in association with higher doses. Several treatment failures with ketoconazole have been successfully managed with itraconazole. The recommended pediatric regimen of itraconazole is 5–7mg/kg/day.[30,39]

Fluconazole

Fluconazole, at 400 or 800mg/day for at least 6 months, is an effective alternative for the treatment of nonlife-threatening cases of blastomycosis, especially in patients who may not have responded to another drug.[40] Its only advantage over itraconazole may be in patients with involvement of the CNS, which is penetrated well by fluconazole.

Amphotericin B

Blastomyces dermatitidis is quite susceptible to amphotericin B (AMB), which is the recommended treatment for patients with life-threatening or severe disease (e.g. involvement of multiple organs), those with meningitis, or blastomycosis in immunocompromised patients, as well as patients who do not respond to an azole.[39] A total dose of 2–2.5g is required to eradicate all the organisms, as the relapse rate is significant if <1.5g is administered. The protocol for administration of AMB and monitoring renal function are the same as its application for other mycoses (see Chapter 208). An initial test dose of 1 or 5mg in adults is administered intravenously in a solution of 5% glucose, deoxycholate and buffer. The dose is gradually increased by 5–10mg/day to a maximal daily administration of 0.5–1.5mg/kg body weight.

Most patients experience adverse side effects, including renal dysfunction, fever, anorexia, phlebitis, hypokalemia, nausea, chills, headache and anemia. Administration is interrupted when blood levels of urea nitrogen reach 40–50mg/dl or 3.0–3.5mg/dl of creatinine.

Lipid emulsions of AMB have the advantage of delivering higher doses with diminished toxicity. Adult respiratory distress syndrome due to overwhelming pulmonary blastomycosis requires aggressive treatment with AMB. Blastomycosis in patients with AIDS may require suppressive therapy, following the initial course of treatment with AMB, similar to the management of cryptococcosis and histoplasmosis in patients with AIDS. Suppressive treatment in AIDS patients would be 200–400mg/day itraconazole, or possibly 800mg/day fluconazole for CNS disease.[39]

For children, the test dose of 0.1mg/kg (maximum dose 1mg) should be followed by 0.25mg/kg at 4 hours later and 0.5mg/kg after 24 hours. Beyond 48 hours, 1mg/kg/day is administered to reach a total dose of >30mg/kg. Pediatric, as adult patients, must be closely monitored for adverse reactions.

Blastomycosis has been reported in pregnant women, and the infection may or may not be transmitted to the infant. Pregnant patients have been treated with AMB without congenital or toxic effects in the fetus. Systemic treatment with azoles must be avoided in pregnant women because of their teratogenic potential. In the endemic area, blastomycosis should be considered in any neonate with a reticulonodular lesion on chest film or whose mother has evidence of blastomycosis.

Surgery

Corrective surgery may be necessary as an adjunct to antibiotic treatment. Because of the occurrence of relapse or reactivation blastomycosis, patients should be observed for years after treatment and resolution of disease.

COCCIDIOIDOMYCOSIS

Coccidioidomycosis is caused by either of two indistinguishable species, *Coccidioides immitis* or *Coccidioides posadasii*, dimorphic fungi that normally live in well-defined geographic areas. Both the agents and coccidioidomycosis are almost entirely limited to these endemic regions. *Coccidioides immitis* was first described in 1892 by an Argentinian pathologist. Alejandro Posadas, who examined tissue from a fatal case and named the orgnaism *Coccidioides*, meaning '*Coccidia*-like', because of the spherules found in tissue.[41,42] The species name, 'immitis,' means not mild. Indeed, most early cases were diagnosed at autopsy and until 1930, the disease was erroneously thought to be invariably severe and disseminated.

It was recognized quite early that coccidioidomycosis is confined to the south-western United States, contiguous regions of northern Mexico and specific areas of Central and South America. The natural reservoir was established by isolating *C. immitis* from soil samples collected throughout the endemic areas, and the environmental conditions under which the fungus was propagated were described. From mycelial culture filtrates, the skin test antigen coccidioidin was developed and used to detect exposure to *C. immitis* or *C. posadasii* and to conduct population surveys of skin reactivity. The more common primary form is a mild, respiratory ailment, also called valley fever or San Joaquin Valley fever.

NATURE

Etiology and dimorphism

The new species, *C. posadasii*, was recently recognized by Fisher *et al.*[43] They compared the genotypes of isolates of *C. immitis* from different geographical regions and, based on their phylogenetic analyses of these populations, determined that the majority of isolates outside California belong to a different species, which they named *C. posadasii* to honor Dr Posadas. Since *C. posadasii* has a broader geographical distribution, it is the more likely cause of the majority of cases of coccidioidomycosis. Although these species differ in their geographical distribution and genotype, any differences in their phenotypes or pathogenicity have yet to be delineated. Because the two species cannot be distinguished by simple laboratory tests, the more familiar name, *C. immitis*, will continue to be used.

The life cycle of *C. immitis* (or *C. posadasii*) encompasses at least four distinct morphologic structures that are produced under different conditions. In nature and in the laboratory, either species grows as a mold, producing hyaline, branching, septate hyphae. As the culture ages, characteristic arthroconidia are formed, usually, but not invariably, in alternate hyphal cells (Fig. 238.4). With time, the arthroconidial chains fragment to release the unicellular, barrel-shaped arthroconidia, the ends of which often retain remnants of cell wall material from the disintegrated adjacent cells. Arthroconidia are approximately 3 × 6μm in size, easily air borne and small enough to be inhaled into the alveoli. They are highly resistant to desiccation, temperature extremes and deprivation of nutrients and may remain viable for years. Under appropriate growth conditions, the arthroconidia will germinate to recycle the saprophytic mycelial form (Fig. 238.4).

Following their inhalation, the arthroconidia become spherical. In the infected host, *C. immitis* exists as spherules – spherical thick-walled structures, 15–80μm in diameter that are filled with a few to several hundred endospores (Fig. 238.5). As a spherule enlarges, the nuclei undergo mitosis, the cytoplasm condenses around these nuclei and a cell wall forms around each developing endospore. At maturation, the spherule ruptures to release its endospores. The endospores are 2–5μm in size and may, in turn, enlarge to form mature spherules. Hyphae as well as spherules may form in the tissues and appear in sputum of patients with coccidioidal cavities of the lungs.

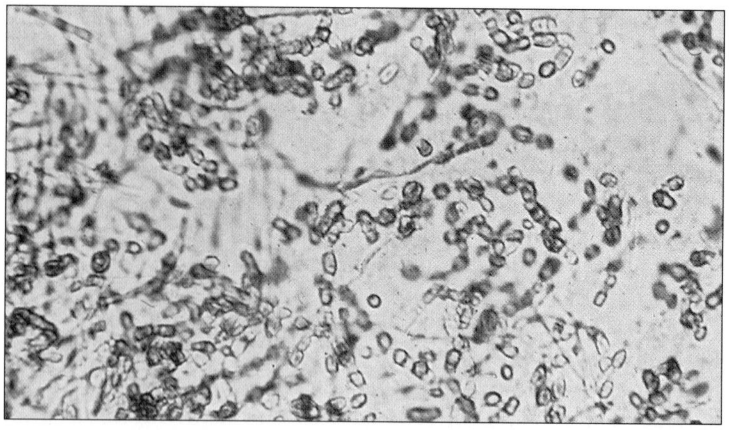

Fig. 238.4 ***Coccidioides immitis*, mycelial form in culture at 86°F.** This shows hyaline, septate, branching hyphae and chains of arthroconidia, often in alternating cells.

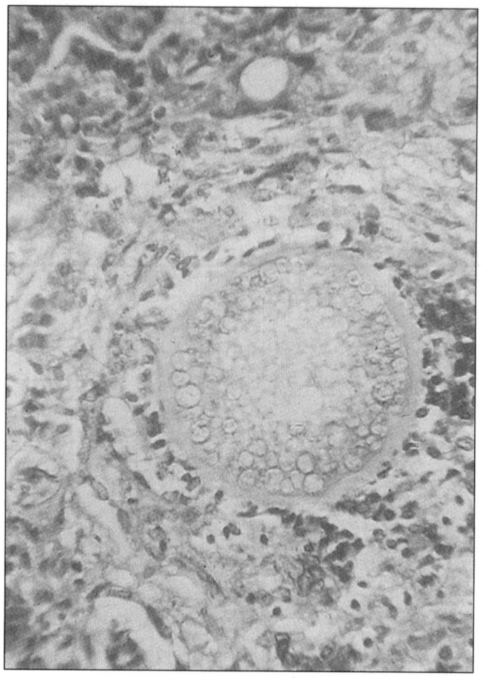

Fig. 238.5 ***Coccidioides immitis*, spherule in hematoxylin- and eosin-stained section of lung lesion.** This shows refractile cell wall and internal endospores.

Cultural characteristics

On routine mycological media, such as inhibitory mold or Sabouraud's agar, at the usual incubation temperature of 77–86°F (25–30°C), different isolates of *C. immitis* produce a wide variety of colony types. Colonies may be white, gray or brownish in color, with a powdery, wooly or cottony texture. Because numerous infectious arthroconidia are produced in culture and can be readily aerosolized in the dry state, cultures of *C. immitis* must be handled with extreme caution to prevent accidental exposure. Tubes or plates should be opened only under a safety cabinet that protects both the laboratory worker and the environment.

Spherules can be produced in the laboratory on a complex medium at 104°F (40°C) under 20% CO_2. However, *in vitro* growth of the tissue phase even under optimal conditions is seldom extensive.

EPIDEMIOLOGY

In the USA, the geographic areas endemic for coccidioidomycosis and from which *C. immitis* can be isolated from the soil correspond to the Lower Sonoran life zone. These areas are characterized by a semi-arid climate, alkaline soil and characteristic indigenous desert plants and rodents. The endemic foci in Mexico, Argentina and other scattered areas of Central and South America are associated with ecologically similar environments. Although *C. immitis* grows in the laboratory over a wide range of temperature, pH and salt concentration and requires only glucose and ammonium salts to grow, it has never become established in soils outside the endemic area, despite being transmitted to other locations by infected animals and fomites. Although *C. immitis* is inhibited by other micro-organisms, cultivated soil or treatment with various chemicals, none of these factors fully explains its restricted habitation. The mycelia, which can be found several inches beneath the soil surface, are recovered at the surface after the spring rains. As the weather becomes hot and dry, the mycelia convert to infectious arthroconidia and this accounts for the peak infection rate during the summer. In the endemic area, natural infections also occur among indigenous fauna, such as desert rodents, dogs and cattle.

Inhalation of the arthroconidia of *C. immitis* leads to infection and acquisition of a positive delayed-type hypersensitivity response to coccidioidin. More than half of these infections are benign and most of the others are symptomatic but self-limited (see Table 238.1). Approximately 1% of these cases will develop progressive pulmonary disease, dissemination or both. Some individuals have an increased risk of developing disseminated disease following primary infection (Table 238.5). These include persons in certain ethnic groups: Filipinos, African Americans, Latin Americans, and Native Americans. This ethnic predilection for severe disease clearly indicates the importance of the genetic background of the host in mounting an effective immune response to infection.[44] In addition to ethnicity, males, women in the third trimester of pregnancy, persons with a cellular immunodeficiency (including AIDS), and individuals at the age extremes are more susceptible to severe disease (see Table 238.5).

The areas of endemicity defined by case reports and by isolation of *C. immitis* from soil have been confirmed by skin test surveys with coccidioidin. Within the endemic areas, which include portions of the south-western USA (California, Arizona, New Mexico, Nevada, Utah and Texas) and north-western Mexico, the percent reactivity varies; some of the highest rates are found in Phoenix and Tucson, Arizona, and Kern County, California. Isolated cases of coccidioidomycosis occurring outside the established areas of endemicity have been attributed to fomite transmission of the arthroconidia or to patient travel through the endemic area.

Numerous outbreaks of primary infection have been reported among individuals simultaneously exposed to a heavy aerosol of arthroconidia. Coccidioidomycosis is therefore considered an occupational hazard for construction workers, archeology students and others who work the soil in the endemic areas. In a similar manner, many cases of acute disease developed subsequent to a severe wind storm in California in 1977, when contaminated soil was blown from the San Joaquin Valley far north and west, exposing large populations of unsensitized individuals. A similar epidemic of coccidioidomycosis produced a marked increase in Kern County in 1991–92.[45] The explanation for this increase has baffled investigators, but it may have been caused by concurrent earthquakes and high winds. Risks for severe pulmonary disease include diabetes, cigarette smoking, low income and old age.[46] Recently an outbreak was described among Navy SEALs who trained for 6 weeks in Coalinga, California. Forty-five percent (10 out of 22) had serologic and radiographic evidence of acute coccidiodomycosis, and all were symptomatic.[121]

PATHOGENICITY

Using reverse genetics, Cole and his colleagues have identified antigens and potential virulence factors that are elaborated by *C. immitis*. The cell wall of the infectious particle, the arthroconidium, has three distinct layers.[47] *In vivo*, potent cell wall antigens are released when the arthroconidia develop into spherules.[48] Although arthroconidia and endospores are readily engulfed by alveolar macrophages, killing is enhanced by activation of macrophages with the appropriate T cells or cytokines.[49] When stimulated by spherules, leukocytes from both patients and skin test-positive subjects secrete potentially protective cytokines, such as interferon-γ and IL-12.[50,51]

Investigators have identified several potential virulence factors. For example, *C. immitis* produces a serine proteinase with broad specificity for host substrates, such as elastin, collagen, IgG and IgA.[52,53] Other proteinases have also been detected.[16,54] These proteinases are thought to contribute to the development of spherules and release of endospores.

Many of the patients who develop disseminated coccidioidomycosis have depressed cell-mediated immunity. There is a marked inverse relationship between the antibody titer (see below) and specific cell-mediated immunity, as measured by skin test and, *in vitro*, by the numbers of $CD4^+$ and $CD8^+$ T cells, the responsiveness of T cells to mitogens or antigens, and the production of cytokines. In severe coccidioidomycosis, patients have elevated antibody titers and circulating immune complexes and depressed cellular immunity. This condition has been related to increased antigen burden, populations of suppressor cells, immune complexes and impaired lymphocyte circulation.[55] Immune complexes are detected in serum of patients with coccidioidomycosis and correlate with the severity of disease.[56] In the mouse model of experimental coccidioidomycosis, specific anergy is correlated with the amount of coccidioidal antigen present.[57] Recovery often leads to restoration of immune functions. However, the impaired cellular immune responses are likely governed by whether Th1 or Th2 responses predominate early in infection.[55,58,59] In strains of mice that differ in susceptibility to *C. immitis*, protective responses are correlated with the secretion of interferon-γ, which is a Th1-associated cytokine and potent activator of macrophages.[60] Conversely, much of the immunopathology may be attributable to excess production of TNF-α. Perhaps the ethnic predisposition to disseminated coccidioidomycosis (Table 238.5) is related to genetic control of the T cell response to *C. immitis*.

PREVENTION

Coccidioides immitis cannot be eliminated from the soil, but public health efforts to reduce the dust associated with dispersion of the arthroconidia are helpful in areas of high endemicity.[61] Another approach has focused on the development of a vaccine for persons at risk. In mice and humans, cell-mediated immunity to *C. immitis* confers excellent protection against disease. Spherule-derived vaccines in the past were not successful, but several new approaches to identify specific candidate epitopes are currently under investigation.[58,62]

DIAGNOSTIC MICROBIOLOGY

Direct examination

A definitive diagnosis of coccidioidomycosis requires the finding of spherules of *C. immitis* in sputum, draining sinuses or tissue specimens (Fig. 238.5). Clinical exudates should be examined directly in 10% or 20% potassium hydroxide, with or without calcofluor white, and tissue obtained from biopsy can be stained with hematoxylin and eosin or special fungal stains, such as Gomori methenamine silver or the periodic acid–Schiff stain, which stain fungal cell walls black or reddish, respectively. Direct microscopic examination of cutaneous or deep tissue specimens, either in calcofluor/KOH preparations or histologic sections, yields positive results in approximately 85% of proven cases. However, sputum specimens are positive by direct examination or culture in less than half of the cases.

RISK FACTORS FOR DISSEMINATED COCCIDIOIDOMYCOSIS	
Age	Infants and elderly
Sex	Male
Genetics	Filipino > African-American > Native American > Hispanic > Asian
Serum CF antibody titer	>1:32
Pregnancy	Late pregnancy and postpartum
Delayed-type hypersensitivity skin test	Negative
Depressed cell-mediated immunity	Malignancy, chemotherapy, steroid treatment, HIV infection

Table 238.5 Risk factors for disseminated coccidioidomycosis.

Culture

Clinical specimens are cultured on inhibitory mold, Sabouraud's agar or other routine fungal medium, as described above under Blastomycosis. Colonies of *C. immitis* develop within 1 or 2 weeks and are examined microscopically for the production of characteristic arthroconidia. Microscopic preparations of mycelia should always be prepared under a biosafety hood. The identification of *C. immitis* may be confirmed by the production of spherules *in vitro* by incubation in a complex medium at 104°F (40°C) with 20% CO_2 or by animal inoculation (e.g. intraperitoneal injection or mice or intratesticular inoculation of guinea-pigs). An easier method of confirmation involves the exoantigen test described in the discussion of Blastomycosis. Production of exoantigen F confirms the identity as *C. immitis* (see Table 238.3). This rapid method can be used with young, nonsporulating cultures.[25,63,64] Alternatively, DNA-based identification is available with a commercial system.[24,63]

With the exception of tissue scrapings, biopsies and surgical specimens, cultures are more often positive than microscopic examinations of clinical material. However, use of both procedures will optimize the opportunity to establish a diagnosis. Between 25% and 50% of sputa, bronchial washes, spinal fluids and urine specimens yield positive cultures. Positive blood cultures are infrequent but significantly associated with acute, disseminated coccidioidomycosis and high mortality.

Skin tests

As noted above, coccidioidin, which is a crude but standardized toluene extract of a mycelial culture filtrate, is used for skin testing. A delayed-type hypersensitivity reaction is elicited, and a positive test is defined as induration exceeding 5mm in diameter. Another *C. immitis* antigen, prepared from cultured spherules and termed spherulin, is more sensitive but less specific than coccidioidin. Skin testing with either antigen does not induce or boost an immune response. The skin test becomes positive within 2 weeks after the onset of symptoms and before the appearance of antibodies and often remains positive indefinitely. A positive reaction has no diagnostic significance without a history of conversion, but a negative test can be used to exclude coccidioidomycosis, except in patients with severe disseminated coccidioidomycosis who may have become anergic. Indeed, a negative skin test in confirmed cases is associated with a grave prognosis. Conversely, a positive skin test in healthy subjects implies immunity to symptomatic reinfection.

Serologic tests

As indicated in Table 238.3, tube precipitins or latex agglutinins measure specific IgM antibodies. They are produced early and assist in the diagnosis of primary infections. They are detected by a sensitive tube test that becomes positive in 90% of patients within 2 weeks after the appearance of symptoms and disappears in most cases by 4 months. Therefore, a positive tube precipitin (TP) test indicates active primary (or reactivation) coccidioidomycosis. Results obtained with the original TP method correlate quite well with those obtained with the more rapid and convenient latex particle agglutination test; the latter procedure is more sensitive but less specific than the TP test. The TP antigen, a component of coccidioidin, is heat stable at 140°F (60°C), whereas the antigen detected in the complement fixation (CF) test is heat labile.

The CF test, which measures IgG antibodies to coccidioidin, is a powerful diagnostic and prognostic tool. Because the CF test becomes positive more slowly and persists longer, the presence of CF antibodies may reflect either active infection or the recovery stage. The CF titer correlates with the severity of disease. Most patients with secondary coccidioidomycosis develop a titer of 1:16 or higher, whereas in nondisseminated cases, the titer is almost invariably lower. Therefore, a critical titer of 1:32 or higher reflects active, disseminated disease. However, a lower titer does not exclude disseminated disease because many patients, such as those with single extrapulmonary lesions, notably coccidioidal meningitis, do not develop high titers.

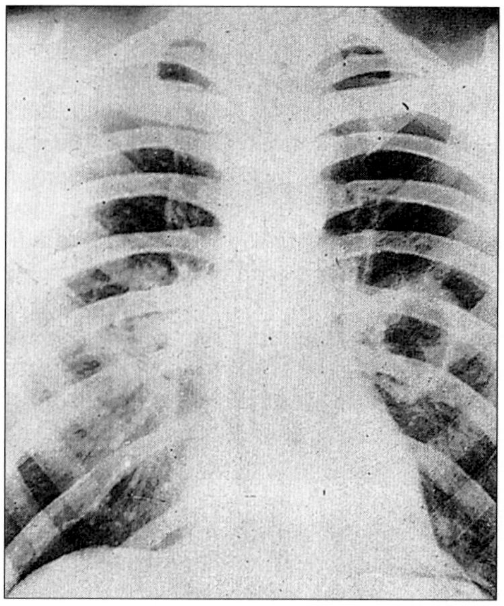

Fig. 238.6 Coccidioidomycosis, showing hilar lymphadenopathy and a cavity in the left lung.

Multiple serum specimens are most helpful because a change in the CF titer reflects the prognosis: the CF titer declines with recovery and eventually disappears. A rising titer indicates active, uncontrolled infection and a poor prognosis. A stable or fluctuating titer often indicates the presence of a recalcitrant or stabilized lesion. An exceptional situation is coccidioidal meningitis, in which only half of the patients have a titer of 1:32 or higher. However, most of these patients will have a positive CF test in their spinal fluid, which is equally valuable.

The immunodiffusion (ID) method can be used to detect both TP and CF antibodies by using reference antisera and heated (TP only) and unheated antigen. Antibodies to two specific heat-labile antigens, termed F (or CF) and HL, may be detected. The CF antigen has been determined to be a chitinase.[65]

CLINICAL MANIFESTATIONS

Primary coccidioidomycosis

Following inhalation of arthroconidia, the primary infection in most individuals is asymptomatic. Others may develop flu-like symptoms: fever, chest pain, cough or weight loss. Radiographic examination often reveals discrete nodules in the lower lobes. Primary pulmonary coccidioidomycosis has an incubation period of 10–16 days and usually resolves without complication in 3 weeks to 3 months. A small percentage of patients retain cavities (Fig. 238.6), nodules or calcifications, but endogenous reactivation of residual pulmonary lesions is rare in immunocompetent individuals.

Up to 20% of patients with primary coccidioidomycosis manifest allergic reactions, usually erythema nodosum (Fig. 238.7) or erythema multiforme, which appear with the primary symptoms, are very painful and persist for approximately 1 week. These allergic manifestations are associated with strong immunity and a good prognosis.

Secondary coccidioidomycosis

Disseminated or secondary coccidioidomycosis usually develops within a few months as a complication of the primary form. The numerous manifestations of secondary coccidioidomycosis include chronic and

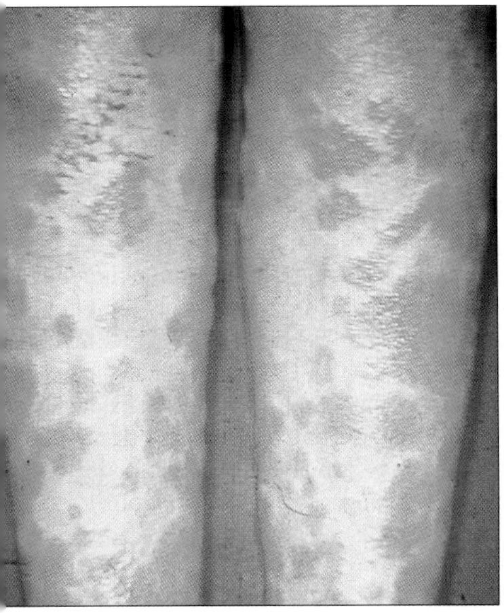

Fig. 238.7 Allergic manifestations of infection with *Coccidioides immitis*. Erythema nodosum on the lower legs.

progressive pulmonary disease, single or multiple extrapulmonary dissemination or generalized systemic infection. Chronic pulmonary coccidioidomycosis usually involves a single, thin-walled cavity, but patients may develop enlarging or multiplying nodules or cavities.

Dissemination may be fulminant or chronic, with periods of remission and exacerbation. Extrapulmonary lesions most frequently involve the meninges, skin or bone. Chronic cutaneous coccidioidomycosis develops from initial lesions that usually appear on the face or neck and that, over a period of years, evolve into thick, raised, verrucous lesions with extensive epithelial hyperplasia.[66] Bone involvement may accompany generalized systemic disease. Both osteomyelitis of long bones, vertebrae and other bones and arthritis may develop.[67] Draining sinus tracts may evolve from subcutaneous and osseous lesions.

Coccidioidomycosis and AIDS

Coccidioidomycosis is the AIDS-defining illness for many patients, who commonly present with fever and chills, weight loss and night sweats.[68,69] After pulmonary disease, coccidioidal meningitis is a frequent complication. Serologies are often negative in AIDS patients and the mortality rate is high. Diffuse pulmonary disease and low $CD4^+$ lymphocyte count (<50/μl) carry a poor prognosis.[68]

MANAGEMENT

Symptomatic treatment is usually adequate for the patient with primary coccidioidomycosis, although ketoconazole may reduce the symptoms. However, if the primary infection is persistent or severe, or if there is evidence of dissemination, ketoconazole or itraconazole should be administered at 400mg/day for 2–6 months.

The chronicity of the disseminated disease usually requires prolonged therapy, which may increase the chances of undesirable side effects. Successful treatment with ketoconazole may require continuous administration for more than a year. Chronic coccidioidal meningitis is often treated with fluconazole, which has excellent penetration across the blood–brain barrier. Some cases may require the intrathecal administration of chemotherapy. Grave disease is treated with amphotericin B in the usual formulation or as a lipid preparation to provide a higher dosage with reduced toxicity. For patients with AIDS, the total dose of amphotericin B (1.0–1.5mg/kg/day) should be at least 1.0g, after which a maintenance regimen of itraconazole or fluconazole may be started. Patients treated with amphotericin B or azoles are more likely to relapse if the delayed skin test becomes negative and the CF antibody titers equal or exceed 1:256.[70]

HISTOPLASMOSIS

Histoplasmosis, the most prevalent cause of pulmonary fungal disease in humans and animals, is caused by the thermally dimorphic fungus, *Histoplasma capsulatum*. The infection occurs worldwide and is initiated by inhalation of *H. capsulatum*. The incidence varies considerably, being negligible in many parts of the world but pronounced in local regions wherein most of the native population have been infected. Ninety-five percent of the infections are inapparent and are detected only by the manifestation of residual lung calcification(s), delayed hypersensitivity to *H. capsulatum*, or both. As one of the more common primary mycoses, throughout history, its existence has been inferred on the basis of descriptions of the pathogenesis and natural history of disease.

Around the turn of the last century, when histoplasmosis was discovered, the appearance of the organism within macrophages in histopathologic sections of infected tissue resembled encapsulated protozoa, hence the name, *Histoplasma capsulatum*.[71] The fungal etiology of histoplasmosis was subsequently confirmed and even though *H. capsulatum* is neither a parasite nor encapsulated, the name, by precedence and taxonomic custom, remains. With the discovery of a sexual reproduction cycle in *H. capsulatum*, it was transferred to the family Gymnoascaceae within the subdivision Ascomycotina. Because of the similarity between the sexual reproductive structures of the teleomorphs of *H. capsulatum* and *Blastomyces dermatitidis*, whose teleomorph, *Ajellomyces dermatitidis*, had been discovered earlier, *H. capsulatum* was transferred to that genus as *Ajellomyces capsulatus*.[72,73] The name *H. capsulatum* is retained by common usage and remains appropriate as the fungus is clinically isolated in its asexual or anamorphic state. The close relationship between *H. capsulatum* and *B. dermatitidis* has been confirmed by molecular evolutionary studies comparing ribosomal DNA sequences.[74] Of three closely related varieties of *H. capsulatum*, most human cases are caused by *H. capsulatum* var. *capsulatum*, while *H. capsulatum* var. *duboisii* is found in Africa (see below), and *H. capsulatum* var. *farciminosum* causes infection in horses.

The extent of unapparent infection was not appreciated until the 1940s. During extensive skin test surveys for tuberculosis in student nurses from various parts of the country, radiologists observed small calcifications in the lungs of many apparently healthy individuals who were nonreactive to old tuberculin.[75,76] Subsequent skin testing with histoplasmin, an antigen from *H. capsulatum* analogous to old tuberculin, revealed a high correlation between delayed skin test reactivity and pulmonary calcifications in tuberculin-negative individuals. The availability of skin test antigens for histoplasmosis has provided a very useful epidemiologic tool.

NATURE

Histoplasma capsulatum is a thermally dimorphic fungus. At temperatures below 95°F (35°C), it grows as a mold, often white or brown in color, and at 98.6°F (37°C), it grows as a yeast with small, heaped and pasty colonies. *Histoplasma capsulatum* characteristically grows slowly. Under optimal conditions, the mold colony develops after 1 or 2 weeks and conidia are produced shortly thereafter. However, cultures of clinical specimens sometimes require incubation periods of 8–12 weeks before there is detectable growth. Primary isolates are often brown and become white with prolonged cultivation.[25]

Both microconidia and macroconidia are produced at temperatures below 95°F (35°C). The microconidia are borne singly on short conidiophores, globose and 1–5μm in diameter. Upon dehydration, the conidia are easily dislodged by air currents and aerosolized. Their small size enables the microconidia to transmit the infection. The macroconidia, or tuberculate chlamydospores, are very distinctive. Mature forms are large, 8–16μm in diameter, spherical thick-walled structures with projections radiating from the cell wall (Fig. 238.8). Young macroconidia are smooth walled and the echinulations develop as the conidia mature.

At 98.6°F (37°C), the mold converts to growth as a small, budding yeast. Conversion is often difficult to effect *in vitro* but is enhanced by a rich, complex medium, such as brain-heart infusion agar. Hyphal cells may form buds directly or develop enlarged, transitional cells, which subsequently produce buds. Microconidia may also convert to budding yeast cells. The yeast cells are small, ellipsoidal, approximately 1–3μm by 3–5μm in size, and virtually identical to the yeasts observed *in vivo* within phagocytes (Fig. 238.9).

Biochemical studies of the yeast and mycelial forms of *H. capsulatum* have detected significant differences in the relative amounts of chitin, α-glucan and β-glucan of the cell walls. The three RNA polymerases in each growth form are also different. Morphogenesis in *H. capsulatum* involves a protein, histin, isolated from the cytoplasm of mycelial form. Histin inhibits RNA polymerase and may help to regulate the temperature-dependent control of transcription. An inhibitor, such as histin, may be operative in the mycelia, because protein synthesis is considerably reduced during mycelial growth.

In *in vitro* studies of the crucial mycelium-to-yeast conversion at 98.6°F (37°C), Maresca *et al.* confirmed the importance of cysteine.[77,78] This conversion proceeds in three stages:

1. during the first 40 hours at 98.6°F (37°C), respiration gradually decreases and the intracellular amino acid pools become almost depleted;
2. the cells remain dormant for 4–6 days;
3. then concentrations of intracellular cysteine and other amino acids increase and respiration is restored.

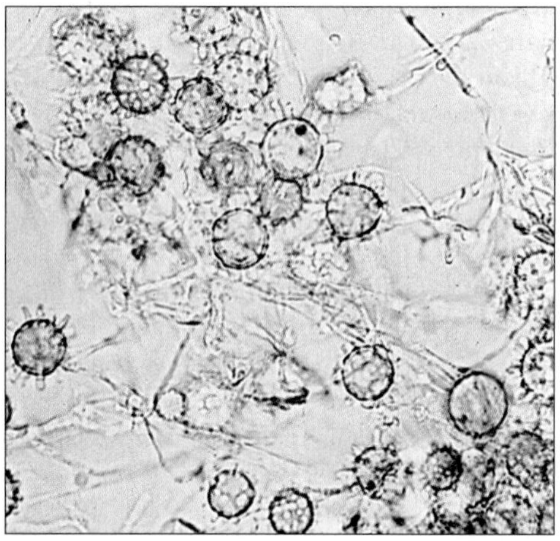

Fig. 238.8 ***Histoplasma capsulatum*****, mycelial form in culture at 86°F.** This shows hyaline septate branching hyphae, microconidia and large spherical macroconidia, with projections from the cell walls.

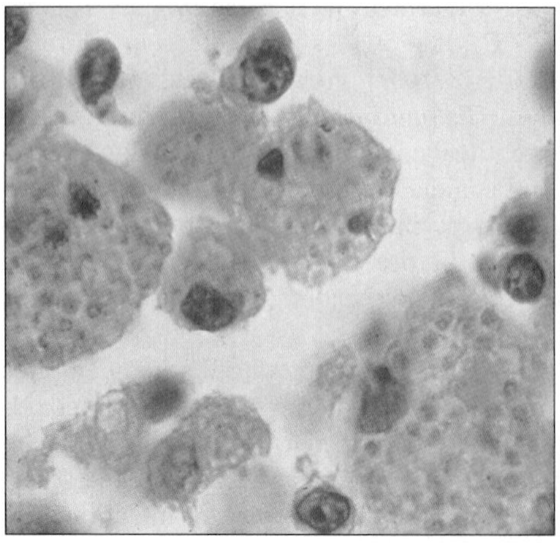

Fig. 238.9 ***Histoplasma capsulatum*****.** Small yeast cells packed inside macrophages in a Giemsa-stained smear of bone marrow aspirate.

Cysteine and cystine are essential for the transition to yeast cells. These compounds and other reducing agents appear to stimulate the mitochondrial electron transport chain, probably via a unique cysteine oxidase. This mycelium-to-yeast conversion is inhibited by elevated cyclic AMP, which may also be regulated intracellularly by the action of sulfhydryl agents.[77] Recent research from several laboratories has identified yeast form-specific genes that may be involved in the regulation of dimorphism and consequently virulence.[79–83]

In studies of virulent strains, the sulfhydryl blocking agent, *p*-chloromercuriphenylsulfonic acid (PCMS), irreversibly inhibited the conversion of mycelium to yeast at 98.6°F (37°C), but mycelial growth continued at 98.6°F (37°C).[84] PCMS-treated mycelia also failed to infect mice. Therefore, mycelium-to-yeast transformation appeared necessary for pathogenicity but not for growth at 98.6°F (37°C). PCMS-treated mycelia may provide a vaccine for histoplasmosis and indicate the essential changes for transformation.[84]

Sexual reproduction

As noted above, discovery of its sexual reproductive cycle led to reclassification of the teleomorph *A. capsulatus*, which closely resembles the teleomorph of *B. dermatitidis*.[72] Being heterothallic, *A. capsulatus* requires strains of two opposite (compatible) mating types for sexual reproduction. Although the mating types, designated '+' and '−', are equally prevalent among soil isolates, many more infections are caused by the '−' type, which suggests a linkage of this allele with pathogenicity.[85]

Biotypes

Biotyping may facilitate epidemiological studies and several DNA-based methods have been developed to identify and compare strains of *H. capsulatum* from different sources and with different phenotypes. Isolates that differ in virulence for animals have been compared with strains from the environment and with isolates from patients with and without AIDS.[86–88] In addition, phylogenetic analyses have identified major subpopulations of *H. capsulatum* that correspond with geographic groups.[89]

EPIDEMIOLOGY

Ecology

In nature, *H. capsulatum* lives in soil with a high nitrogen content and is associated with bat and avian habitats. *H. capsulatum* has been isolated many times from bird roosts, chicken houses, bat caves and similar environments. Conidia, when dry, are easily air borne and spread by wind currents, as well as by birds and bats. *H. capsulatum* is most prevalent in the environment where the infection is most endemic, namely in the Ohio–Mississippi Valley – in Missouri, Kentucky, Tennessee, Indiana, Ohio and southern Illinois. This region also has the highest population of starlings, which tend to congregate in large numbers. The excrement from these birds provides an ideal medium for the enrichment of *H. capsulatum*. In South America, the chief reservoir appears to be chicken coops and bat caves.

In cases of histoplasmosis from Africa, both *H. capsulatum* and a stable variant, *H. capsulatum* var. *duboisii*, have been isolated. Infections elsewhere are due to the global variety, *H. capsulatum* var. *capsulatum*, *H. capsulatum* var. *duboisii* causes African histoplasmosis, which is distinguished from the usual infection by:

- a greater frequency of skin and bone lesions;
- diminished pulmonary involvement;
- pronounced giant cell formation; and
- larger, thick-walled yeast cells in tissue.

Although these clinical features are characteristic and reproducible, *H. capsulatum* var. *duboisii* cannot be reliably differentiated *in vitro* from the type species on the basis of morphology, physiology and antigenic composition. Indeed, both forms of histoplasmosis are the same species, as *H. capsulatum* var. *duboisii* mates with *H. capsulatum* var. *capsulatum*, and its sexual form is identical to *A. capsulatus*.

Another variety, *H. capsulatum* var. *farciminosum*, is associated with cutaneous, subcutaneous and lymphangitic lesions in horses.[90]

Histoplasmin skin test

The antigen, histoplasmin, is produced by growing the mycelial phase of *H. capsulatum* in a specialized broth medium. The filtrate from the culture is dialyzed, the concentration is standardized and 0.1ml of the appropriate dilution is injected intradermally. A positive reaction is indicated by induration of >5mm diameter after 48 hours.

A positive test, if specific, denotes previous sensitization to *H. capsulatum*. Without a history of prior negativity, the positive test has no diagnostic significance. Histoplasmin is a crude, polyvalent mixture of antigens, only some of which are specific for *H. capsulatum*. Because some antigenic determinants are shared by other pathogenic fungi, cross-reactions can occur. For example, some individuals sensitive to *B. dermatitidis* or *C. immitis* will give a false-positive reaction to histoplasmin. Therefore, along with histoplasmin, it is routine to administer coccidioidin in the USA or coccidioidin and paracoccidioidin in South America. A reaction to a single antigen is generally considered specific. Reactions to two antigens may be caused by sensitization to one or both, although the larger reaction is often considered more specific.

Incidence

Much of the knowledge concerning the prevalence of histoplasmosis has been derived from extensive skin test surveys conducted since the 1950s all over the world. The region with the highest level of reactivity is the central USA, along the river valleys of the Ohio, Mississippi, St Lawrence and Rio Grande rivers, where in some locales 80–90% of the population may be skin test positive by the age of 20 years. Foci of high reactivity exist elsewhere in the world, such as southern Mexico, Indonesia, the Philippines and Turkey. In the USA alone, projections based on skin test surveys have led to estimations that more than 40 million people have been exposed with 500,000 new infections every year. Of these, perhaps 55,000 to 200,000 cases will be symptomatic, 1500–4000 will require hospitalization annually and 25–100 deaths will occur. These projections were made prior to 1980 and do not reflect the increasing incidence of opportunistic histoplasmosis in patients with AIDS.

Outbreaks

Outbreaks or epidemics of acute respiratory histoplasmosis result from the simultaneous exposure of a large number of people. These epidemics are not caused by direct spread among humans or animals. The experience of youths on Earth Day, 1970, in Delaware, Ohio, is more ironic than most, but otherwise typical of these epidemic outbreaks.[122] The young people gathered to reclaim an abandoned park and, in so doing, overturned several truckloads of soil, which was enriched with starling feces and contaminated with an enormous quantity of *H. capsulatum* conidia. Several cases of acute respiratory histoplasmosis followed inhalation of this heavy inocula of aerosolized microconidia. Many similar episodes have been documented: the sudden release leads to multiple exposure of a heavy inoculum that has accumulated in a dormant environment. Silos, air-conditioning units contaminated with bird droppings and accumulations of guano in caves, attics or parks have all been implicated as reservoirs for *H. capsulatum* in outbreaks of this type. Perhaps the largest outbreak occurred in Indianapolis between the fall of 1978 and 1979.[91] It is estimated that more than 100,000 persons were infected during this time, resulting in over 300 hospitalized cases and at least 15 deaths. The incidence of disseminated histoplasmosis and the fatality rate were unusually high. The environmental source of the fungus was not determined. Indeed, *H. capsulatum* was not recovered from any of the soil samples collected at the most likely site, where an abandoned amusement park had been recently dismantled.

Males develop symptomatic histoplasmosis more often than females, and approximately 75% of cases occur in males. Before puberty, the attack rate for males and females is identical and the percentage of positive skin test reactors is the same for both sexes at all ages. These epidemiologic data suggest that either adult males are inherently more susceptible to the disease or females are more resistant. Severity of disease and mortality are greater at the age extremes, in infancy and after the age of 50.

In addition to humans, many wild and domestic animals are susceptible to histoplasmosis. Some animals, including the bat, may act as vectors to disseminate the organism in nature.

PATHOGENICITY

All clinical forms are believed to evolve from the same natural history. Microconidia are inhaled from an exogenous source and penetrate to the alveoli, where they convert to small, budding yeast cells. This temperature-dependent morphogenesis is related to the virulence of strains of *H. capsulatum*.[92,93] The yeasts are readily phagocytized by alveolar macrophages. At this stage, the yeast-laden macrophages may be cleared through the upper respiratory tract. They may disseminate through the circulation, spreading the yeasts to other reticuloendothelial organs, and/or they may invoke a tissue response *in situ*. The tissue reaction may involve an early influx of neutrophils and lymphocytes, but the pyogenic inflammatory response gives way to epithelioid cell tubercle formation. In the course of these various possible reactions, the intracellular yeasts may or may not be inactivated by the phagocytes (see below).

The conversion of *H. capsulatum* to the yeast form at 98.6°F (37°C) appears to be essential for pathogenicity. As noted above, treatment of the mycelial form with PCMS blocks morphogenesis and reduces virulence, but does not inhibit survival at 98.6°F (37°C).[84] The expression of yeast-specific genes has been correlated with virulence and thermal tolerance.[80,83,92,94]

Pathogenesis

After being phagocytized, the yeast cells of *H. capsulatum* survive intracellularly by a calcium-dependent process, block acidification within the phagolysosome and multiply within macrophages.[83,95] However, macrophages from immunized animals, as well as normal macrophages activated by immune lymphocytes or cytokines, restrict the growth of intracellular yeasts.[96,97] In experimental, self-limited murine histoplasmosis, various parameters of cell-mediated immunity are depressed during the height of antigen (yeast) burden, suppressor T cells and macrophage-like suppressor cells are detected and production of IL-1 and IL-2 is impaired.[98,99] Concomitant with resolution of the infection, the number of suppressor cells in the spleen diminishes and T helper cells increases. These correlations of competent cell-mediated immune responses with resistance to infection are supported by the clinical data. Similar to coccidioidomycosis, there is an inverse relationship between the magnitude of the cell-mediated immune response, as measured by delayed-type hypersensitivity or *in vitro* lymphoblastogenesis, and high levels of specific antibody, which correlate with the severity of the disease. Additional evidence suggests that TNF-α may be crucial in the induction of protective T-cell responses.[55,100]

DIAGNOSTIC MICROBIOLOGY

Microscopic examination

Histoplasmosis can be diagnosed on finding the yeast cells in clinical material. Suitable specimens include sputa, tissue from biopsy or surgical specimens, spinal fluid and blood. The buffy coat of a blood specimen may reveal yeast-filled macrophages. Bone marrow obtained when patients are febrile may contain yeast cells. Smears of infected sputum, blood, marrow or tissue that have been fixed with methanol and stained with the Wright or Giemsa stain will reveal the characteristically small, ellipsoidal yeast cells (approximately $2 \times 4\mu m$) inside macrophages. With either stain, the larger end of the yeast cell contains an eccentric, red-staining mass (see Fig. 238.9).

Culture

Sputum specimens should be collected early in the morning and purulent or sanguineous portions should be selected for culture. A bronchial wash is even more likely to be positive. Nonsterile specimens (e.g. sputum, skin or urine) should be cultured on a blood-enriched medium and inhibitory mold or Sabouraud's agar with antibiotics (cycloheximide and chloramphenicol or gentamicin) and incubated for at least 4 weeks at 77°F (25°C) or 86°F (30°C). Because *H. capsulatum* may grow very slowly, cultures should be incubated for up to 12 weeks, if possible, before discarding as negative. If a sporulating mold develops, *H. capsulatum* can be identified by the presence of its characteristic macroconidia (see Fig. 238.8) and by conversion to the yeast from by growth on an enriched medium at 98.6°F (37°C). Alternatively, conversion to the yeast may be effected by growth in tissue cultures, such as HeLa cells, or by animal inoculation, such as the intraperitoneal injection into mice. Occasional isolates of *H. capsulatum* will not produce conidia, but it should be possible to identify these variants by conversion to the yeast form, by the detection of *H. capsulatum*-specific exoantigens (see Table 238.3) or by using a specific DNA probe.[24]

In endemic areas or in cases where histoplasmosis is suspected, specimens should be inoculated on multiple media, such as Sabouraud's agar without antibiotics at 77–86°F (25–30°C), Sabouraud's agar with antibiotics (cycloheximide and chloramphenicol, gentamicin or penicillin and streptomycin) at 77–86°F (25–30°C), brain-heart infusion agar with 5% sheep blood and antibiotics at 77–86°F (25–30°C), and brain-heart infusion agar with 5% sheep blood without cycloheximide at 98.6°F (37°C). The pH of these media should be near neutrality, since *H. capsulatum* is inhibited below pH 6.

In disseminated cases, the lysis-centrifugation method is recommended for culturing blood, although transient fungemia may be observed in patients with acute pulmonary histoplasmosis. Blood volumes of 10ml are added to a tube containing a mixture of anticoagulants and reagents to lyse the blood cells; the tubes are then centrifuged and the pellet, which contains any yeast cells in the blood, is inoculated onto plates of inhibitory mold agar and other media. Lysis-centrifugation is the most sensitive and rapid method to recover fungi from blood, especially *H. capsulatum*.[101]

Skin test

The skin test antigen, histoplasmin, is a valuable epidemiologic tool. Within weeks after infection, most persons develop a positive skin test and this reactivity usually persists for many years. The diagnostic value of the skin test is minimal. With most patients, only a history of conversion from negative to positive is diagnostic. A negative reaction can be used to rule out active histoplasmosis in the immunocompetent subject, but patients with anergy may be falsely negative. Without a prior history of a negative skin test, a positive reaction is meaningless except in infants, in whom a positive test can be presumed to result from recent or current infection. Because of its limited diagnostic value and the possibility that the skin test may confound the antibody titration (see below), skin testing with histoplasmin should be avoided in most patients.

Serology

Specific antibodies to *H. capsulatum* antigens can be detected during infection. Two serologic tests are now widely accepted because of their convenience, availability and utility: the measurement antibodies by complement fixation (CF) and the immunodiffusion (ID) test for precipitins. Both tests may be helpful in the diagnosis and prognosis of histoplasmosis, provided the results are properly interpreted (see Table 238.4).

The CF test is routinely performed under standard conditions for measuring fixation of complement by the classic pathway.[102,103] CF tests are performed to detect antibodies to two antigens of *H. capsulatum*: histoplasmin and a standardized suspension of killed yeast cells. Because of the possibility of cross-reactivity, patient sera are tested concomitantly against other fungal antigens, such as coccidioidin, spherulin, *B. dermatitidis* or *Paracoccidioides brasiliensis*. Serum antibodies specific for *H. capsulatum* antigens can be detected by the CF test 2–4 weeks following exposure. Most laboratories perform the CF test on twofold dilutions of patient serum, beginning with a dilution of 1:8. With resolution of the infection, the antibody titer gradually declines and disappears (i.e. titer <1:8), in most cases by 9 months. The CF test with either *H. capsulatum* yeast or mycelial (histoplasmin) antigen is very sensitive and 90% of patients are positive (i.e. titer >1:8).[91] A titer of 1:32 that persists or rises over the course of several weeks indicates active disease in patients with an established diagnosis of histoplasmosis. Unfortunately, in sensitive patients, the skin test antigen may boost the CF antibody titer to histoplasmin and the elevated titer may remain for as long as 3 months. Therefore, the CF test, which can deliver results as rapidly as the skin test, is preferable for diagnostic purposes. However, a positive CF test, even in high titer, is not by itself diagnostic, as the results can be caused by cross-reacting antibodies. If a patient's serum is reactive to more than one fungous antigen or if it is anticomplementary, the ID test should be conducted.

Precipitins can be detected by immunodiffusion (ID) of serum and antigen in agarose. The antigen is histoplasmin in 10-fold the concentration used for the CF test. The ID test becomes positive in up to 80% of patients with histoplasmosis by the third or fourth week of infection. This test, while less sensitive and requiring a longer time to become positive, is more specific than the CF test. Precipitin lines or bands specific for *H. capsulatum* are detected by the formation of lines of identity with reference serum. There are two specific precipitin bands, m and h. The m line, which is observed more frequently, appears soon after infection and may persist in the serum for up to 3 years following recovery. The h band, which forms closer to the serum wells, is more transient. Because it disappears soon after the disease, the presence of serum antibodies to the h antigen is better correlated with active infection. As with the CF titer, the m band may be boosted by the administration of the histoplasmin skin test, and the boosting effect may last up to 3 months.

An excellent radioimmunoassay (RIA) test for antigenemia and antigenuria has been developed by Wheat and colleagues.[104,105] Tests for polysaccharide antigen in the serum have been detected in 79% of patients with disseminated histoplasmosis and 97% had a positive test for antigen in the urine. After treatment with AMB, serum titers dropped in all the patients and urine titers dropped in 91% of patients. Testing either serum and urine had prognostic value, detecting relapses in AIDS patients.[104] This RIA is commercially available from the Histoplasmosis Reference Laboratory (Indianapolis, IN 46202). The antigen can also be measured in CSF or bronchoalveolar lavage fluid specimens. However, the test lacks optimal specificity because patients with other systemic mycoses have been shown to yield positive tests for the antigen in urine.[106]

CLINICAL MANIFESTATIONS

The manifestations of infection with *H. capsulatum* are numerous. The initial pulmonary episode may be acute or chronic or dissemination may occur by hematogenous or lymphatic spread from the lungs to other organs. Several clinical classifications have been devised, but none is completely satisfactory. Most normal individuals are able to contain the infection. The granulomata that form may undergo fibrosis, and residual scars may remain in the lungs or spleen. Resolution appears to confer some immunity to reinfection. This process occurs without symptoms in 95% of all persons with acute, primary histoplasmosis, whether disseminated or confined to the lung.

Acute pulmonary histoplasmosis

Patients with acute pulmonary histoplasmosis manifest symptoms ranging from a mild influenza-like illness that clears spontaneously to a moderate or severe disease. In healthy hosts, the degree of involvement and symptomatology seems to correlate with the size of the inoculum inhaled. In the previously sensitized individual, such reinfection exposure results in a shorter and milder infection with minimal histopathology. The incubation period varies from one to several weeks. A moderate disease is characterized by cough, chest pain, dyspnea and hoarseness. In more severe cases, patients have fever, night sweats and weight loss. Occasionally, yeast cells may be observed in the sputum. Radiologic examination may reveal multiple lesions scattered throughout the lungs and in patients with active disease, hilar lymphadenopathy is usually present (Fig. 238.10). Pulmonary lesions due to *H. capsulatum* resolve slowly. Healing may be complete or with fibrosis but, typically, calcification occurs.

The differential diagnosis includes other systemic mycoses, tuberculosis, bacterial bronchiectasis and lymphoblastoma. An experienced radiologist can differentiate between the calcifications of histoplasmosis and tuberculosis. Calcifications produced by *H. capsulatum* are more regular, with halos, and may be found in the liver and spleen as well as in the lungs. Miliary calcifications may also occur. Calcifications are produced more rapidly in children than adults. Single, solitary, uncalcified coin lesions are also produced and are similar to those seen in tuberculosis. These resemble neoplastic lesions and are often removed surgically. Another tuberculosis-like pulmonary manifestation usually found in the adult lung is a histoplasmoma, which may be 2–3cm in diameter and contains a central necrotic area encased in a fibrotic capsule. Calcification begins in the center of the lesion and is followed by the development of concentric rings of fibrosis and calcification.

Chronic pulmonary histoplasmosis

This form is seen most often in adult males. It is considered to be an opportunistic complication of underlying chronic obstructive lung disease with emphysema and abnormal pulmonary spaces. With small emphysematous air spaces, transient pneumonitis develops and infection of large bullous spaces may result in cavitary histoplasmosis. Symptoms of the latter may be indistinguishable from those of chronic cavitary tuberculosis. The chronic form is secondary to the underlying pulmonary disease. It may develop immediately after primary inhalation or after years of apparent quiescence. Pathologic and immunologic evidence suggests that the late onset results from reactivation of an old lesion rather than exogenous reinfection. Chronic pulmonary histoplasmosis is usually apical. Patients experience a low-grade fever, productive cough, progressive weakness and fatigue. Chest films show centrilobular or bullous emphysema. Prognosis depends upon control of the underlying disease as much as on treatment for histoplasmosis.

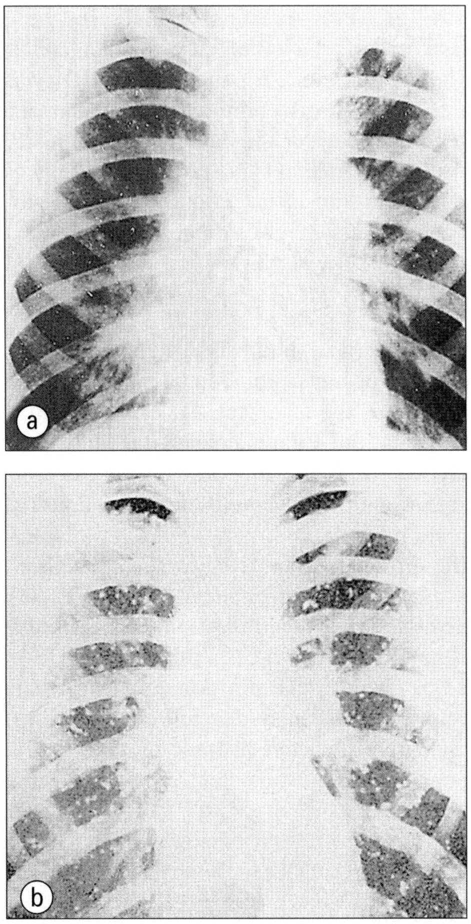

Fig. 238.10 Histoplasmosis. (a) Acute pulmonary histoplasmosis showing hilar lymphadenopathy and diffuse infiltrates. (b) Hilar lymphadenopathy and miliary calcifications throughout both lungs.

Disseminated histoplasmosis

The gamut of clinical forms and pathology observed in pulmonary histoplasmosis can also occur in any other part of the body. The yeast cells are probably disseminated throughout the body while inside macrophages. The most common sites of involvement, after the lung, are the reticuloendothelial tissues of the spleen, liver, lymph nodes and bone marrow. However, lesions have been documented in almost every organ. Dissemination may be completely benign and unapparent except for the presence of calcified lesions, usually in organs of the reticuloendothelial system.

Alternatively, disseminated histoplasmosis may be acute and progressive. In such cases, the pulmonary symptoms are insignificant and patients may have splenomegaly and hepatomegaly, weight loss, anemia and leukopenia. Granulomatous lesions and macrophages packed with yeast cells can be observed throughout the liver, spleen, marrow and, quite often, the adrenals. Acute progressive histoplasmosis is often fulminant and rapidly fatal – ultimately every organ can become diseased. This form of histoplasmosis is an opportunistic disease associated with compromised cell-mediated immunity, such as in patients with AIDS or those receiving immunosuppressive drugs and those with underlying lymphomatous neoplasia. In most cases, the compromising condition serves to reactivate a quiescent lesion that was originally acquired years earlier. Within the endemic area, infants with histiocytosis may develop disseminated histoplasmosis that is characteristically fulminant. Chronic disseminated histoplasmosis may evolve from protraction of the acute disease. This form is progressive, with eventual involvement of every organ, especially the mucocutaneous areas around the eye, tongue and anus.

Histoplasmosis and AIDS

In a recent prospective study in the endemic area, the annual incidence of subclinical and asymptomatic histoplasmosis among patients with AIDS was 4.7%. Three-quarters of the cases were symptomatic and histoplasmosis was the initial AIDS-defining condition in most of them.[107] The survival time for patients with AIDS was significantly shorter for those with disseminated histoplasmosis. Significant risk factors were identified for the development of histoplasmosis in AIDS patients: environmental exposure to likely sources of *H. capsulatum* (chicken coops), positive CF antibodies to histoplasmin, chronic medical condition(s), herpes simplex infection and a $CD4^+$ lymphocyte count of <150,000/ml.[107,108]

Other forms

Very rarely, chronic disseminated histoplasmosis develops following primary inoculation of the skin or mucocutaneous tissue. The lungs are not involved in these cases, as the organisms are typically introduced following the contamination of a traumatic wound. Such infections may be anatomically localized, as with some ocular cases, or they may chronically progress with involvement along the draining lymphatics.

Another clinical condition, probably unrelated to *H. capsulatum*, is 'presumed ocular histoplasmosis syndrome' or POHS. Patients with POHS exhibit characteristic choroidal lesions, macular subretinal membranes and peripapillary atrophy.[109] Although POHS is usually associated with a positive histoplasmin skin test, its cause is unknown. Patients with histoplasmosis may develop ocular lesions, but POHS is not seen in patients with active histoplasmosis.

MANAGEMENT

Most primary pulmonary infections with *H. capsulatum* go undetected and require no treatment. Symptomatic cases in immunocompetent persons are alleviated with itraconazole or ketoconazole. With progressive pulmonary or disseminated disease, the treatment of choice for mild to moderate or stable disease is itraconazole.[110] Severe cases of any form are treated initially with AMB followed by itraconazole. The regimen of AMB is similar to that applied to other systemic mycoses and a total dose of 1.5g AMB is recommended. Recovery following treatment with AMB is generally faster and fewer relapses occur than are experienced with blastomycosis and coccidioidomycosis. Arrested pulmonary lesions are often removed surgically. Less severe cases in nonimmunocompromised patients may be treated with itraconazole. AIDS patients with histoplasmosis may be placed on maintenance therapy with itraconazole at 200mg twice per day.[110,111] Cases of meningitis due to *H. capsulatum* are treated with amphotericin B followed by fluconazole.

PARACOCCIDIOIDOMYCOSIS

Paracoccidioidomycosis (South American blastomycosis) is an infection caused by the thermally dimorphic fungus, *Paracoccidioides brasiliensis*. The infection is restricted to endemic areas of Central and South America. It is a chronic, granulomatous disease that begins with a primary, pulmonary, usually unapparent infection that disseminates to produce ulcerative granulomata in the mucosal surfaces of the nose, mouth and gastrointestinal tract. In addition to the skin and lymph nodes, the infection may spread to the internal organs.

NATURE

Colonies of *P. brasiliensis* grow very slowly, requiring 2 or 3 weeks of incubation to reach a diameter of 1–2cm. The macroscopic features of the mold colony are variable and nonspecific. Various asexual reproductive structures are produced by *P. brasiliensis*, including chlamydospores, arthroconidia and singly borne conidia. In the absence of conidia, which may not be produced for 10 weeks

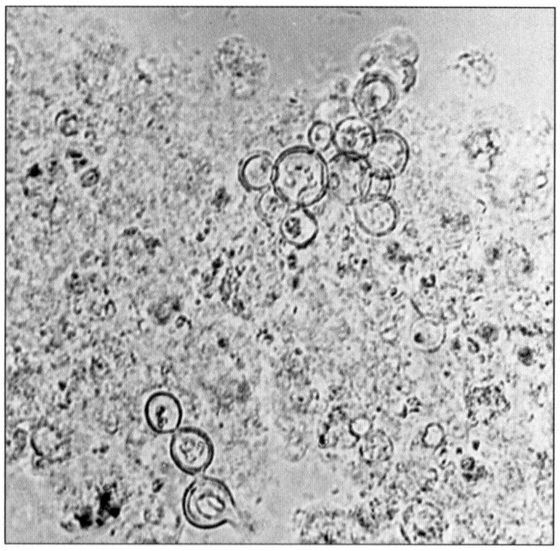

Fig. 238.11 ***Paracoccidioides brasiliensis*****.** Large multiply budding yeast cells in a potassium hydroxide preparation of a scraping of cutaneous paracoccidioidomycosis.

in culture, the mycelia and colony may be indistinguishable from *B. dermatitidis* or many saprophytes.

The yeast form can be induced by cultivation on a rich medium at 95–98.6°F (35–37°C). The yeasts are readily identified by their unique appearance. As shown in Figure 238.11, the yeasts produce multiple buds and each is attached to the parent yeast by a narrow base. The yeast cells are large, up to 30μm in diameter, and have thinner walls than the yeasts of *B. dermatitidis*. These forms have been described as 'pilot wheels'.

EPIDEMIOLOGY

The natural habitat of *P. brasiliensis* has not been proven, but is presumed to be soil. The organism has been recovered only sporadically and not repeatedly from soil in Venezuela and Argentina. Like *B. dermatitidis*, its natural existence and life cycle in nature are unknown. There is no evidence of an animal vector or transmission of the infection. Natural disease does not occur in either wild or domestic animals, although experimental infections can be established in mice and bats after inhalation of an infectious inoculum. Human infections are presumed to follow exposure to the organisms from an exogenous source. Most patients are males (>90%), agricultural workers, often malnourished, and usually 30–60 years of age.

Thousands of cases of paracoccidioidomycosis have been reported from Brazil, Venezuela, Colombia and lesser numbers from Argentina, Ecuador and other South and Central American countries, with the exception of Chile and the Caribbean nations.[112] Discrete endemic foci exist within this broad area of geographic distribution. However, all cases are isolated and outbreaks have not been observed. The endemic zones are associated with moderate temperatures 57–86°F (14–30°C) and rainfall, elevation of 500 to 6500 feet, subtropical forests and river valleys, but not all areas fitting this description have paracoccidioidomycosis.

Skin test surveys have been conducted with various antigens derived from *P. brasiliensis*. These paracoccidioidins exhibit cross-reactivity with histoplasmin and it is difficult to interpret double reactions of equal size in the same individual. As with the skin test antigens of the other dimorphic, systemic pathogens, paracoccidioidin elicits a delayed, indurative reaction that indicates previous exposure. The percentage of reactivity in the endemic areas varies up to 75% and occurs equally in both men and women. Significant risk factors for infection (i.e. positive skin test) include agricultural occupations, association with certain aquatic environments and contact with bats.[113]

Many patients with paracoccidioidomycosis are malnourished and exhibit depressed cell-mediated immune responses.

PATHOGENICITY

P. brasiliensis, like the other systemic fungi, causes disease in males more frequently than females (Table 238.1), although skin test surveys have revealed comparable reactivity between the sexes, implying equal exposure. Sex-linked differences may be associated with the generally more potent cellular immunity of females. Limited studies indicate that physiological concentrations of sex hormones do not directly inhibit these fungi. However, a protein from the mycelial cytosol of *P. brasiliensis* has been shown to bind estrogen but not testosterone or other hormones. Binding blocks conversion of the mycelium to yeast at 98.6°F (37°C) and may explain the resistance of females to paracoccidioidomycosis.[114]

Once yeast cells of *P. brasiliensis* have developed in the lung, yeast cell wall polysaccharides, such as α-glucan, are associated with virulence and the ability to stimulate granulomata.

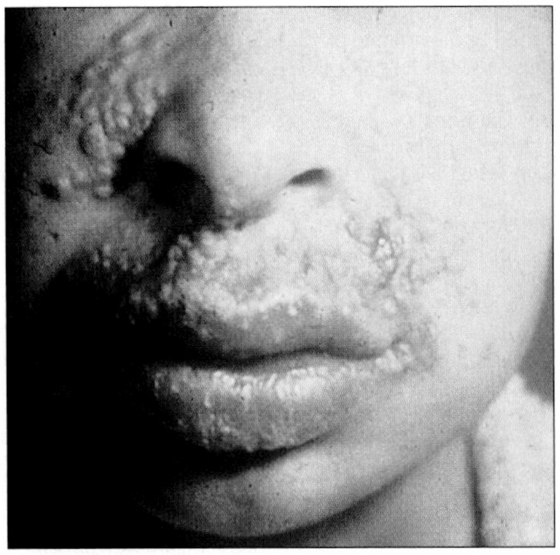

Fig. 238.12 Cutaneous and mucocutaneous paracoccidioidomycosis.

DIAGNOSTIC MICROBIOLOGY

Microscopic examination and culture

Sputum, tissue or scrapings of mucocutaneous lesions may reveal the multiply budding yeast cells that are pathognomonic for *P. brasiliensis* (Fig. 238.11). Specimens should be cultured at 77–86°F (25–30°C) on inhibitory mold agar, Sabouraud's agar with antibiotics, Sabouraud's agar without cycloheximide and on brain-heart infusion blood agar at 95–98.6°F (35–37°C). The yeast form often grows better at 95°F (35°C) or 96.8°F (36°C) than 98.6°F (37°C).

Serologic tests

A number of antigens and serological procedures have been evaluated.[115] The ID test is extremely useful. As indicated in Table 238.4, nearly 100% of patients have at least one of three specific precipitin lines (designated 1, 2 and 3) detected by identity with reference serum. The ID test also has prognostic value, as the bands disappear with clearing of the infection and the number of bands is somewhat correlated with the severity of the disease.[116] The CF test is quantitative and useful for assessing prognosis, but cross-reactions occur with other fungi.

CLINICAL MANIFESTATIONS

The initial contact with *P. brasiliensis* occurs by inhalation. This episode is unapparent and the organism becomes quiescent for an indefinite period, which may be several decades in some individuals, or the lesion may resolve, perhaps with scarring. This asymptomatic infection results in the acquisition of a positive delayed skin test reaction to paracoccidioidin. The eventual development of symptomatic disease depends upon the host–fungal interaction, namely, the integrity of the cell-mediated immunity of the individual, environmental conditions (e.g. temperature, nutrients), host conditions (e.g. age, sex, state of nutrition), and the virulence of the strain of *P. brasiliensis*.

Acute or subacute disease

Patients under 30 years of age may develop an acute, progressive infection characterized by lymphonodular lesions in the lung.[117] This juvenile form is rare. The yeasts may disseminate to the reticuloendothelial tissue, lymph nodes, liver, spleen, skin, bone, joints or other organs. The severity and duration of the illness depend upon the extent of organ involvement, but it may be fatal within a period of several weeks or months.

Chronic disease

More than 90% of cases are of this 'adult' type and develop from the latent form, usually after several years. Lesions may be localized in the lung or metastasis may occur from the lung to other organs, particularly the skin and mucocutaneous tissue, lymph nodes, spleen, liver, adrenals and combinations thereof. Mucocutaneous, often petechial, lesions frequently develop on the corners of the mouth, lips, gingiva or tongue (Fig. 238.12). Pulmonary lesions are granulomatous nodules that may cavitate but rarely calcify.[118]

MANAGEMENT

Patients should be assessed for malnourishment, alcoholism and extensive tobacco use, all of which exacerbate the disease. Since many of the antifungal drugs are effective against *P. brasiliensis*, the initial treatment choice may reflect the expense and local availability of antifungal agents.[119] Sulfonamide derivatives are among the earliest but less effective drugs. Trimethoprim-sulfamethoxazole (TMP-SMX) is the currently recommended formulation of this type. The azoles are much more effective. Some of the initial clinical trials with ketoconazole demonstrated its efficacy against paracoccidioidomycosis. Itraconazole is currently the drug of choice; a clinical cure rate approaching 100% is achievable with a daily dose of 100mg for 6 months. Relapses are rare. Fluconazole has also been shown to be effective, producing cures in about 90% of patients who received 200–400mg/day for 6 months. Although AMB is highly effective against paracoccidioidomycosis, it should be reserved for patients who fail to respond or cannot tolerate one of the azoles. The total dose usually required is 2g or less. After initiating therapy, serologies are checked every few months to monitor the effectiveness of treatment. Some clinicians recommend a maintenance regimen of sulfadoxin, TMP-SMX or ketoconazole (200mg/day) for up to 1 year after serological tests become negative.[119]

REFERENCES

1. Gilchrist TC, Stokes WR. A case of pseudo-lupus vulgaris caused by a Blastomyces. J Exp Med 1898;3:53–78.
2. Benham RW. Fungi of blastomycosis and coccidioidal granuloma. Arch Dermatol 1934;30:385–400.
3. Schwarz J, Baum GL. Blastomycosis. Am J Clin Pathol 1951;21:999–1029.
4. McDonough ES, Lewis AL. *Blastomyces dermatitidis*: production of the sexual stage. Science 1967;156:528–9.
5. DiSalvo AF. The epidemiology of blastoymcosis. In: Al-Doory Y, DiSalvo AF, eds. Blastomycosis. New York: Plenum; 1992:75–104.
6. Mitchell TG. Systemic mycoses. In: Joklik WK, Willett HP, Amos DB, Wilfert CM, eds. Zinsser microbiology. Norwalk: Appleton and Lange; 1992:1091–112.
7. Klein BS, Vergeront JM, Weeks RJ, *et al.* Isolation of *Blastomyces dermatitidis* in soil associated with a large outbreak of blastomycosis in Wisconsin. N Engl J Med 1986;314:529–34.
8. Klein BS, Vergeront JM, DiSalvo AF, Kaufman L, Davis JP. Two outbreaks of blastomycosis along

rivers in Wisconsin. Isolation of *Blastomyces dermatitidis* from riverbank soil and evidence of its transmission along waterways. Am Rev Respir Dis 1987;136:1333–8.
9. McCullough MJ, DiSalvo AF, Clemons KV, Park P, Stevens DA. Molecular epidemiology of *Blastomyces dermatitidis*. Clin Infect Dis 2000;30:328–35.
10. Rudmann DG, Coolman BR, Perez CM, Glickman LT. Evaluation of risk factors for blastomycosis in dogs: 857 cases (1980–1990). J Am Vet Med Assoc 1992;201:1754–9.
11. Cockerill FR, III, Roberts GD, Rosenblatt JE, Utz JP, Utz DC. Epidemic of pulmonary blastomycosis (Namekagon fever) in Wisconsin canoeists. Chest 1984;86:688–92.
12. Tosh FE, Hammerman KJ, Weeks RJ, Sarosi GA. A common source epidemic of North American blastomycosis. Am Rev Respir Dis 1974;109:525–9.
13. Pappas PG. Blastomycosis in the immunocompromised patient. Semin Resp Infect 1997;12:243–51.
14. Davies SF, Sarosi GA. Epidemiological and clinical features of pulmonary blastomycosis. Semin Resp Infect 1997;12:206–18.
15. Stevens DA, Brummer E, DiSalvo AF, Ganer A. Virulent isolates and mutants of *Blastomyces* in mice: a legacy for studies of pathogenesis. Semin Resp Infect 1997;12:189–95.
16. Hogan LH, Klein BS, Levitz SM. Virulence factors of medically important fungi. Clin Microbiol Rev 1996;9:469–88.
17. Klein BS, Newman SL. Role of cell-surface molecules of *Blastomyces dermatitidis* in host–pathogen interactions. Trends Microbiol 1996;4:246–51.
18. Hogan LH, Josvai S, Klein BS. Genomic cloning, characterization, and functional analysis of the major surface adhesin WI-1 on *Blastomyces dermatitidis* yeasts. J Biol Chem 1995;270:30725–32.
19. Klein BS, Chang W-L. Pathogenic properties of *Blastomyces dermatitidis*. In: Calderone RA, Cihlar RL, eds. Fungal pathogenesis: principles and clinical applications. New York: Marcel Dekker; 2002:183–204.
20. Newman SL, Chaturvedi S, Klein BS. The WI-1 antigen of *Blastomyces dermatitidis* yeasts mediates binding to human macrophage CD11b/CD18 (CR3) and CD14. J Immunol 1995;154:753–61.
21. Klein BS. Immunology of blastomycosis. In: Al-Doory Y, DiSalvo AF, eds. Blastomycosis. New York: Plenum; 1992:133–63.
22. Bradsher RW Jr. Blastomycosis. Clin Infect Dis 1992;14(suppl 1):S82–S90.
23. Furcolow ML, Smith CD, Turner C. Supportive evidence by field testing and laboratory experiment for a new hypothesis of the ecology and pathogenicity of canine blastomycosis. Sabouraudia 1974;12:22–32.
24. Stockman L, Clark KA, Hunt JM, Roberts GD. Evaluation of commercially available acridinium esterlabeled chemiluminescent DNA probes for culture identification of *Blastomyces dermatitidis, Coccidioides immitis, Cryptococcus neoformans*, and *Histoplasma capsulatum*. J Clin Microbiol 1993;31:845–50.
25. Larone DH, Mitchell TG, Walsh TJ. *Histoplasma, Blastomyces, Coccidioides* and other dimorphic fungi causing systemic mycoses. In: Murray PR, Baron EJ, Pfaller MA, Tenover FC, Yolken RH, eds. Manual of clinical microbiology. Washington DC: American Society for Microbiology; 1999:1259–74.
26. Klein BS, Vergeront JM, Kaufman L, *et al.* Serological tests for blastomycosis: assessments during a large point-source outbreak in Wisconsin. J Infect Dis 1987;155:262–8.
27. Kaufman L. Immunodiagnosis of blastomycosis. In: Al-Doory Y, DiSalvo AF, eds. Blastomycosis. New York: Plenum; 1992:123–32.
28. Bradsher RW Jr, Pappas PG. Detection of specific antibodies in human blastomycosis by enzyme immunoassay. Southern Med J 1995;88:1256–9.
29. Bradsher RW Jr. Clinical features of blastomycosis. Semin Resp Infect 1997;12:229–34.
30. Mitchell TG. Blastomycosis. In: Burg FD, Ingelfinger JR, Wald ER, Polin RA, eds. Gellis and Kagan's current pediatric therapy. Philadelphia: WB Saunders; 1996:666–7.
31. Bradsher RW Jr. A clinician's view of blastomycosis. Curr Top Med Mycol 1993;5:181–200.
32. Sarosi GA, Davies SF, Phillips JR. Self-limited blastomycosis: a report of 39 cases. Semin Resp Infect 1986;1:40–4.
33. Dwight PJ, Naus M, Sarsfield P, Limerick B. An outbreak of human blastomycosis: the epidemiology of blastomycosis in the Kenora catchment region of Ontario, Canada. Can Commun Dis Rep 2000;26:82–91.
34. Recht LD, Philips JR, Eckman MR, Sarosi GA. Self-limited blastomycosis: a report of thirteen cases. Am Rev Respir Dis 1979;120:1109–12.
35. Sheflin JR, Campbell JA, Thompson GP. Pulmonary blastomycosis: findings on chest radiographs in 63 patients. Am J Roentgenol 1990;154:1177–80.
36. Witzig RS, Hoadley DJ, Greer DL, Abriola KP, Hernandez RL. Blastomycosis and human immunodeficiency virus: three new cases and review. Southern Med J 1994;87:715–9.
37. Pappas PG, Pottage JC Jr, Powderly WG, *et al.* Blastomycosis in patients with the acquired immunodeficiency syndrome. Ann Intern Med 1992;116:847–53.
38. Bradsher RW Jr. Therapy of blastomycosis. Semin Resp Infect 1997;12:263–7.
39. Chapman SW, Bradsher RW Jr, Campbell GD Jr, Pappas PG, Kauffman CA. Practice guidelines for the management of patients with blastomycosis. Clin Infect Dis 2000;30:679–83.
40. Pappas PG, Bradsher RW Jr, Kauffman CA, *et al.* Treatment of blastomycosis with higher doses of fluconazole. The National Institute of Allergy and Infectious Diseases Mycoses Study Group. Clin Infect Dis 1997;25:200–5.
41. Rixford E, Gilchrist TC. Two cases of protozoan (coccidioidal) infection of the skin and other organs. Johns Hopkins Hosp Rep 1896;1:209–69.
42. Posadas A. Un neuvo caso de micosis fungiodea con psorospermias. An Cir Med Argent 1892;15:585–97.
43. Fisher MC, Koenig G, White TJ, Taylor JW. Molecular and phenotypic description of *Coccidioides posadasii* sp. nov., previously recognized as the non-California population of *Coccidioides immitis*. Mycologia 2002;94:73–84.
44. Louie L, Ng S, Hajjeh R, *et al.* Influence of host genetics on the severity of coccidioidomycosis. Emerg Infect Dis 1999;5:672–80.
45. Einstein HE, Johnson RH. Coccidioidomycosis: new aspects of epidemiology and therapy. Clin Infect Dis 1993;16:349–56.
46. Rosenstein NE, Emery KW, Werner SB, *et al.* Risk factors for severe pulmonary and disseminated coccidioidomycosis: Kern county, California, 1995–1996. Clin Infect Dis 2001;32:708–15.
47. Cole GT, Pope LM, Huppert M, Sun SH, Starr P. Ultrastructure and composition of conidial wall fractions of *Coccidioides immitis*. Exp Mycol 1983;7:297–318.
48. Kirkland TN, Zhu S, Kruse D, Hsu L, Seshan KR, Cole GT. *Coccidioides immitis* fractions which are antigenic for immune T lymphocytes. Infect Immun 1991;59:3952–61.
49. Beaman L. Effects of recombinant gamma interferon and tumor necrosis factor on *in vitro* interactions of human mononuclear phagocytes with *Coccidioides immitis*. Infect Immun 1991;59:4227–9.
50. Dooley DP, Cox RA, Hestilow KL, Dolan MJ, Magee DM. Cytokine induction in human coccidioidomycosis. Infect Immun 1994;62:3980–3.
51. Waite RT, Woods GL. Evaluation of BACTEC MYCO/F lytic medium for recovery of mycobacteria and fungi from blood. J Clin Microbiol 1998;36:1176–9.
52. Yuan L, Cole GT. Isolation and characterization of an extracellular proteinase of *Coccidioides immitis*. Infect Immun 1987;55:1970–8.
53. Pan SC, Cole GT. Molecular and biochemical characterization of a *Coccidioides immitis*-specific antigen. Infect Immun 1995;63:3994–4002.
54. Resnick S, Pappagianis D, McKerrow JH. Proteinase production by the parasitic cycle of the pathogenic fungus *Coccidioides immitis*. Infect Immun 1987;55:2807–15.
55. Murphy JW. Cell-mediated immunity. In: Howard DH, Miller JD, eds. VI. Human and animal relationships. Berlin: Springer-Verlag; 1996:67–97.
56. Yoshinoya S, Cox RA, Pope RM. Circulating immune complexes in coccidioidomycosis. Detection and characterization. J Clin Invest 1980;66:655–63.
57. Cox RA. Immunosuppression by cell wall antigens of *Coccidioides immitis*. Rev Infect Dis 1988;10:5415–8.
58. Kirkland TN, Cole GT. Coccidioidomycosis: pathogenesis, immune response, and vaccine development. In: Calderon RA, Cihlar RL, eds. Fungal pathogenesis; principles and clinical applications. New York: Marcel Dekker; 2002:365–99.
59. Ampel NM, Bejarano GC, Salas SD, Galgiani JN. *In vitro* assessment of cellular immunity in human coccidioidomycosis: relationship between dermal hypersensitivity, lymphocyte transformation, and lymphokine production by peripheral blood mononuclear cells from healthy adults. J Infect Dis 1992;165:710–15.
60. Magee DM, Cox RA. Roles of gamma interferon and interleukin-4 in genetically determined resistance to *Coccidioides immitis*. Infect Immun 1995;63:3514–9.
61. Smith CE, Beard RR, Rosenberger HG, Whiting EG. Effect of season and dust control on coccidioidomycosis. JAMA 1946;132:833–8.
62. Kirkland TN, Fierer J. Coccidioidomycosis: a reemerging infectious disease. Emerg Infect Dis 1996;2:192–9.
63. Padhye AA, Smith G, Standard PG, McLaughlin DW, Kaufman L. Comparative evaluation of chemiluminescent DNA probe assays and exoantigen tests for rapid identification of *Blastomyces dermatitidis* and *Coccidioides immitis*. J Clin Microbiol 1994;32:867–70.
64. Kaufman L. Laboratory methods for the diagnosis and confirmation of systemic mycoses. Clin Infect Dis 1992;14(suppl 1):S23–S29.
65. Johnson SM, Pappagianis D. The coccidioidal complement fixation and immunodiffusion-complement fixation antigen is a chitinase. Infect Immun 1992;60:2588–92.
66. Quimby SR, Connolly SM, Winkelmann RK, Smilack JD. Clinicopathologic spectrum of specific cutaneous lesions of disseminated coccidioidomycosis. J Am Acad Dermatol 1992;26:79–85.
67. Wrobel CJ, Chappell ET, Taylor W. Clinical presentation, radiological findings, and treatment results of coccidioidomycosis involving the spine: report on 23 cases. J Neurosurg 2001;95:33–9.
68. Singh VR, Smith DK, Lawerence J, *et al.* Coccidioidomycosis in patients infected with human immunodeficiency virus: review of 91 cases at a single institution. Clin Infect Dis 1996;23:563–8.
69. Jones JL, Fleming PL, Ciesielski CA, Hu DJ, Kaplan JE, Ward JW. Coccidioidomycosis among persons with AIDS in the United States. J Infect Dis 1995;171:961–6.
70. Oldfield EC III, Bone WD, Martin CR, Gray GC, Olson P, Schillaci RF. Prediction of relapse after treatment of coccidioidomycosis. Clin Infect Dis 1997;25:1205–10.
71. Darling STA. A protozoan general infection producing pseudotubercules in the lungs and focal necrosis in the liver, spleen, and lymph nodes. JAMA 1906;46:1283–5.
72. Kwon-Chung KJ. Sexual stage of *Histoplasma capsulatum*. Science 1972;175:326.

73. McGinnis MR, Katz B. *Ajellomyces* and its synonym *Emmonsiella*. Mycotaxon 1979;8:157–64.
74. Leclerc MC, Philippe H, Guého E. Phylogeny of dermatophytes and dimorphic fungi based on large subunit ribosomal RNA sequence comparisons. J Med Vet Mycol 1994;32:331–41.
75. Christie A, Peterson JC. Pulmonary calcification in negative reactors to tuberculin. Am J Pub Health 1945;35:1131–47.
76. Palmer CE. Nontuberculous pulmonary calcification and sensitivity to histoplasmin. Pub Health Rep 1945;60:513–20.
77. Maresca B, Kobayashi GS. Dimorphism in *Histoplasma capsulatum*: a model for the study of cell differentiation in pathogenic fungi. Microbiol Rev 1989;53:186–209.
78. Maresca B, Lambowitz AM, Kumar VB, Grant GA, Kobayashi GS, Medoff G. Role of cysteine in regulating morphogenesis and mitochondrial activity in the dimorphic fungus *Histoplasma capsulatum*. Proc Natl Acad Sci USA 1981;78:4596–600.
79. Patel JB, Batanghari JW, Goldman WE. Probing the yeast phase-specific expression of the *CBP1* gene in *Histoplasma capsulatum*. J Bacteriol 1998;180:1786–92.
80. Woods JP. *Histoplasma capsulatum*: molecular genetics, pathogenesis, and responsiveness to its environment. Fungal Genet Biol 2002;35:81–97.
81. Gargano S, Di Lallo G, Kobayashi GS, Maresca B. A temperature-sensitive strain of *Histoplasma capsulatum* has an altered delta 9-fatty acid desaturase gene. Lipids 1995;30:899–906.
82. Magrini V, Goldman WE. Molecular mycology: a genetic toolbox for *Histoplasma capsulatum*. Trends Microbiol 2001;9:541–6.
83. Kugler S, Sebghati TS, Eissenberg LG, Goldman WE. Phenotypic variation and intracellular parasitism by *Histoplasma capsulatum*. Proc Natl Acad Sci USA 2000;97:8794–8.
84. Medoff G, Sacco M, Maresca B, *et al.* Irreversible block of the mycelial-to-yeast phase transition of *Histoplasma capsulatum*. Science 1986;231:476–9.
85. Kwon-Chung KJ, Bartlett MS, Wheat LJ. Distribution of the two mating types among *Histoplasma capsulatum* isolates obtained from an urban histoplasmosis outbreak. Sabouraudia 1984;22:155–7.
86. Keath EJ, Kobayashi GS, Medoff G. Typing of *Histoplasma capsulatum* by restriction fragment length polymorphisms in a nuclear gene. J Clin Microbiol 1992;30:2104–7.
87. Kersulyte D, Woods JP, Keath EJ, Goldman WE, Berg DE. Diversity among clinical isolates of *Histoplasma capsulatum* detected by polymerase chain reaction with arbitrary primers. J Bacteriol 1992;174:7075–9.
88. Spitzer ED, Lasker BA, Travis SJ, Kobayashi GS, Medoff G. Use of mitochondrial and ribosomal DNA polymorphisms to classify clinical and soil isolates of *Histoplasma capsulatum*. Infect Immun 1989;57:1409–12.
89. Kasuga T, Taylor JW, White TJ. Phylogenetic relationships of varieties and geographical groups of the human pathogenic fungus *Histoplasma capsulatum* Darling. J Clin Microbiol 1999;37:653–63.
90. Weeks RJ, Padhye AA, Ajello L. *Histoplasma capsulatum* var. *farcinimosum*: a new combination for *Histoplasma farcinimosum*. Mycologia 1985;77:964–70.
91. Wheat LJ, French MLV, Kohler RB, *et al.* The diagnostic laboratory tests for histoplasmosis. Analysis of experience in a large urban outbreak. Ann Intern Med 1982;97:680.
92. Keath EJ, Painter AA, Kobayashi GS, Medoff G. Variable expression of a yeast-phase-specific gene in *Histoplasma capsulatum* strains differing in thermotolerance and virulence. Infect Immun 1989;57:1384–90.
93. Medoff G, Maresca B, Lambowitz AM, *et al.* Correlation between pathogenicity and temperature sensitivity in different strains of *Histoplasma capsulatum*. J Clin Invest 1986;78:1638–47.
94. Keath EJ, Abidi FE. Molecular cloning and sequence analysis of *yps-3*, a yeast-phase-specific gene in the dimorphic fungal pathogen *Histoplasma capsulatum*. J Gen Microbiol 1994;140:759–67.
95. Sebghati TS, Engle JT, Goldman WE. Intracellular parasitism by *Histoplasma capsulatum*: fungal virulence and calcium dependence. Science 2000;290:1368–72.
96. Newman SL, Gootee L, Bucher C, Bullock WE. Inhibition of intracellular growth of *Histoplasma capsulatum* yeast cells by cytokine-activated human monocytes and macrophages. Infect Immun 1991;59:737–41.
97. Brummer E, Stevens DA. Antifungal mechanisms of activated murine bronchoalveolar or peritoneal macrophages for *Histoplasma capsulatum*. Clin Exp Immunol 1995;102:65–70.
98. Deepe GS Jr, Kravitz GR, Bullock WE. Pharmacological modulation of suppressor cell activity in mice with disseminated histoplasmosis. Infect Immun 1983;41:114–20.
99. Watson SR, Schmitt SK, Hendricks DE, Bullock WE. Immunoregulation in disseminated murine histoplasmsosis: disturbances in the production of interleukins 1 and 2. J Immunol 1985;135:3487–9.
100. Zhou P, Miller G, Seder RA. Factors involved in regulating primary and secondary immunity to infection with *Histoplasma capsulatum*: TNF-alpha plays a critical role in maintaining secondary immunity in the absence of IFN-gamma. J Immunol 1998;160:1359–68.
101. Murray PR. Comparison of the lysis-centrifugation and agitated biphasic blood culture systems for detection of fungemia. J Clin Microbiol 1991;29:96–8.
102. Kaufman L, Reiss E. Serodiagnosis of fungal diseases. In: Rose NR, Conway de Macario E, Fahey JL, Friedman H, Penn GM, eds. Manual of clinical laboratory immunology. Washington DC: American Society for Microbiology; 1992:506–28.
103. Mitchell TG. Serodiagnosis of mycotic infections. In: Wentworth BB, ed. Diagnostic procedures for mycotic and parasitic infections. Washington DC: American Public Health Association; 1988:303–23.
104. Wheat LJ, Connolly-Stringfield PA, Kohler RB, Frame PT, Gupta MR. *Histoplasma capsulatum* polysaccharide antigen detection in diagnosis and management of disseminated histoplasmosis in patients with acquired immunodeficiency syndrome. Am J Med 1989;87:396–400.
105. Wheat LJ, Garringer T, Brizendine E, Connolly P. Diagnosis of histoplasmosis by antigen detection based upon experience at the Histoplasmosis Reference Laboratory. Diagn Microbiol Infect Dis 2002;43:29–37.
106. Wheat LJ, Wheat H, Connolly P, *et al.* Cross-reactivity in *Histoplasma capsulatum* variety *capsulatum* antigen assays of urine samples from patients with endemic mycoses. Clin Infect Dis 1997;24:1169–71.
107. McKinsey DS, Spiegel RA, Hutwagner L, *et al.* Prospective study of histoplasmosis in patients infected with human immunodeficiency virus: incidence, risk factors, and pathophysiology. Clin Infect Dis 1997;24:1195–203.
108. Hajjeh RA, Pappas PG, Henderson H, *et al.* Multicenter case-control study of risk factors for histoplasmosis in human immunodeficiency virus-infected persons. Clin Infect Dis 2001;32:1215–20.
109. Saxe SJ, Grossniklaus HE, Lopez PF, Lambert HM, Sternberg P Jr, L'Hernault N. Ultrastructural features of surgically excised subretinal neovascular membranes in the ocular histoplasmosis syndrome. Arch Ophthalmol 1993;111:88–95.
110. Wheat LJ, Sarosi GA, McKinsey DS, *et al.* Practice guidelines for the management of patients with histoplasmosis. Clin Infect Dis 2000;30:688–95.
111. Resende C, Parham SN, Tinsley C, Ferreira P, Duarte JA, Tuite MF. The *Candida albicans* Sup35p protein (CaSup35p): function, prion-like behaviour and an associated polyglutamine length polymorphism. Microbiol 2002;148:1049–60.
112. Wanke B, Londero AT. Epidemiology and paracoccidioidomycosis infection. In: Franco MF, Lacaz CS, Restrepo A, Del Negro GMB, eds. Paracoccidioidomycosis. Boca Raton: CRC Press; 1994:109–20.
113. Restrepo A. Ecology of *Paracoccidioides brasiliensis*. In: Franco MF, Lacaz CS, Restrepo A, Del Negro GMB, eds. Paracoccidioidomycosis. Boca Raton: CRC Press; 1994:121–30.
114. Salazar ME, Restrepo A, Stevens DA. Inhibition by estrogens of conidium-to-yeast conversion in the fungus *Paracoccidioides brasiliensis*. Infect Immun 1988;56:711–3.
115. de Camargo ZP, de Franco MF. Current knowledge on pathogenesis and immunodiagnosis of paracoccidioidomycosis. Rev Iberoam Micol 2000;17:41–8.
116. Restrepo A, Moncada LH. Characterization of the precipitin bands detected in the immunodiffusion test for paracoccidioidomycosis. Appl Microbiol 1974;28:138–44.
117. Del Negro G, Lacaz CS, Zamith VA, Siqueira AM. General clinical aspects: polar forms of paracoccidioidomycosis. In: Franco M, Lacaz CS, Restrepo A, Del Negro G, eds. Paracoccidioidomycosis. Boca Raton: CRC Press; 1994:225–32.
118. Mendes RP. The gamut of clinical manifestations. In: Franco MF, Lacaz CS, Restrepo A, Del Negro GMB, eds. Paracoccidioidomycosis. Boca Raton: CRC Press; 1994:233–58.
119. Mendes RP, Negroni R, Arechavala A. Treatment and control of cure. In: Franco MF, Lacaz CS, Restrepo A, Del Negro GMB, eds. Paracoccidioidomycosis. Boca Raton: CRC Press; 1994:373–92.
120. Kaufman L, Standard PG. Specific and rapid identification of medically important fungi by exoantigen detection. Annu Rev Microbiol 1987;41:209–25.
121. Crum N, Lamb C, Utz G, Amundson D, Wallace M. Coccidioidomycosis outbreak among United States Navy SEALs training in a *Coccidioides immitis*-endemic area: Coalinga, California. J Infect Dis 2002;186:865–8.
122. Brodsky AL, Gregg MB, Lowenstein MS, *et al.* Outbreak of histoplasmosis associated with the 1970 Earth Day activities. Am J Med 1973;54:333–42.

chapter 239

Subcutaneous Mycoses

Malcolm D Richardson

Although subcutaneous fungal infections exhibit extraordinary heterogeneity, they have certain features in common – infection is usually acquired from nature and not from infected humans or animals, and the endemic areas are delineated by an ecosystem that consists of altitude, temperature, rainfall, type of soil and type of vegetation. Most patients belong to low socioeconomic groups or live in rural areas. Subcutaneous mycoses arise from inoculation of soil or vegetation into the skin by minor trauma, and most patients have an occupation connected either with agriculture or an outdoor activity and do not use appropriate footwear.

The group of fungi that cause the majority of subcutaneous infections in humans are termed black molds.[1] Black molds are a heterogeneous group of darkly pigmented (dematiaceous) fungi, widely distributed in the environment, that occasionally cause infection in humans. The taxonomy and terminology of dematiaceous fungal infections is baffling. The term chromoblastomycosis was introduced in 1922 and was later modified in 1935 to a broader term 'chromomycosis'. More recently, the term 'phaeohyphomycosis' was proposed to cover 'all infections of cutaneous, subcutaneous and systemic nature caused by hyphomycetous fungi that develop in the host tissues in the form of dark walled dematiaceous septate mycelial elements'. In 1981, the term was further expanded to include deuteromycota and ascomycota whose tissue forms are filamentous and dematiaceous. This certainly excludes infections by fungi that produce thick-walled 'sclerotic bodies' in the tissues and are classically labeled as chromoblastomycosis. The line of demarcation is, however, only histopathologic and very thin because some of the fungi (e.g. *Exophiala dermatidis*), in addition to mycelial forms, produce rounded structures closely resembling sclerotic bodies. Thus, there has been plenty of overlap in the nomenclature of these cases, especially during the 1970s and 1980s.

The clinical spectrum of infection includes mycetomas, chromoblastomycosis, sinusitis and superficial, cutaneous, subcutaneous and systemic phaeohyphomycosis. During the past few years, there have been reports of infections caused by black molds in previously healthy individuals and in immunocompromised patients. Molecular studies have contributed to our understanding of the epidemiology of these infections. In addition, data on antifungal susceptibility tests have become available. Surgical excision and antifungal therapy (usually itraconazole) remain the standard treatment for these infections.

Many standard texts contain excellent reviews of all the infections described here.[1–11] Specific references and reviews are cited here where new information, particularly concerning diagnosis and therapy, supercedes that found in the general texts.

NATURE

Chromoblastomycosis

Chromoblastomycosis (or chromomycosis) is a chronic localized infection of the skin and subcutaneous tissue, most often involving the limbs. It is characterized by raised crusted lesions. It may be caused by a number of brown-pigmented (dematiaceous) fungi.

Entomophthoramycosis

Rhinofacial conidiobolomycosis is a chronic mycosis affecting the subcutaneous tissues. It originates in the nasal sinuses and spreads to the adjacent subcutaneous tissue of the face, causing disfigurement. Basidiobolomycosis is a chronic subcutaneous infection of the trunk and limbs. For an exhaustive review of entomophthoramycosis refer to Ribes *et al.*[12]

Lobomycosis

Lobomycosis is characterized by slowly developing variably sized cutaneous nodules after a traumatic event. The dermal nodules manifest as either smooth, verrucose, or ulcerated surfaces that can attain the size of a small cauliflower-like keloid. The onset of the disease is generally insidious. The increase in size or number of lesions is a slow process, progressing over a period of 40–50 years. The lesions are composed of granulomatous inflammatory tissue containing numerous globose or subglobose to lemon-shaped, yeast-like fungal cells singly or in simple and branched chains.

Mycetoma

Mycetoma is a chronic suppurative infection of the skin, subcutaneous tissue and bone. It usually affects the hand or foot and may be caused by various fungi (eumycetoma) or actinomycetes (actinomycetoma). The micro-organisms are inoculated into subcutaneous tissue by minor trauma. A characteristic feature of mycetoma is the production of grains in the infected tissue; these grains are compact masses of fungal or actinomycete elements, and they discharge to the outside through sinus tracts.

Phaeohyphomycosis

Phaeohyphomycosis is a rare infection caused by dematiaceous fungi, involving the skin and subcutis, paranasal sinuses or central nervous system (CNS). Phaeohyphomycosis refers to subcutaneous and deep-seated infections caused by brown-pigmented (dematiaceous) molds that adopt a septate mycelial form in tissue. This term was also created to separate various clinical infections caused by dematiaceous molds from the distinct subcutaneous infection known as chromoblastomycosis. Unlike mycetoma and chromoblastomycosis, phaeohyphomycosis is not limited to the skin or subcutaneous tissues, and elicits a wider variety of inflammatory responses.

Phaeohyphomycosis is characterized by a nodule, cyst, or pyogranuloma. Histopathologically, the lesions show brown-walled hyphae in the dermis, subcutis, or sometimes in the epidermis.

Rhinosporidiosis

Rhinosporidiosis is a chronic granulomatous infection of the mucous membranes, especially the nasal mucosa, caused by *Rhinosporidium seeberi.*

Sporotrichosis

Sporotrichosis is a subacute or chronic infection caused by the dimorphic fungus *Sporothrix schenckii.*[13–16] After implantation, this organism can cause cutaneous or subcutaneous infection, which commonly shows lymphatic spread. Occasionally, widespread disseminated infection also occurs.

EPIDEMIOLOGY

Chromoblastomycosis

Chromoblastomycosis is encountered mainly in arid parts of tropical and subtropical regions. Most cases occur in Central and South America, but chromoblastomycosis has also been reported in South Africa, Asia and Australia. Another major focus appears to be Madagascar.[17]

Chromoblastomycosis is caused by various dematiaceous fungi, to which a number of names have been given. There is therefore a great deal of confusion in the nomenclature used by various authors. The most frequently involved etiologic agents, beginning with the most common, are *Phialophora verrucosa*, *Fonsecaea pedrosoi*, *Fonsecaea compacta*, *Cladosporium carrionii* and *Rhinocladiella aquaspersa* (*Ramichloridium cerophilum*). Sporadic cases of chromoblastomycosis can also be caused by other dematiaceous molds. These organisms form characteristic thick-walled, dark brown muriform sclerotic cells in tissue.

The etiologic agents of chromoblastomycosis are widespread in the environment, being found in soil, wood and decomposing plant matter. Human infection usually follows the traumatic inoculation of the fungus into the skin. Minor trauma, such as cuts or wounds due to thorns or wood splinters, is often sufficient. The disease is most prevalent in rural parts of warmer climates where people go barefoot. There is no human-to-human transmission.

Chromoblastomycosis is unusual in children and adolescents. Except in Japan, men contract the disease much more frequently than women, reflecting the importance of occupational exposure. Men have a greater opportunity for soil contact and predisposition to injury while working in the fields. The majority are aged 30–50 years. The rarity of the disease in children exposed to the same environmental conditions as adults suggests a long period of latency.

A number of collections of case reports have been published.[18–20] An illustrative example is a study of 51 cases of chromoblastomycosis detected in a 17-year period, all of which were clinically and mycologically proven by direct examinations, cultures and biopsies. Most cases were males (36 of 51; 70%), the mean age was 35 years and farmers predominated (74%); the most frequent lesions were in the lower limbs (54%). Major clinical presentations were nodular (41%) and verrucous (26%). The principal etiologic agent isolated was *F. pedrosoi* (90%). Overall results of the various treatments were as follows: 31% were cured, 57% improved and 12% failed. The best results were obtained with cryosurgery for small lesions, with itraconazole for large ones, and in some cases the combination of both treatments.

Another case series reviews the clinical features and response to therapy in patients with chromoblastomycosis in the state of Rio Grande do Sul, Brazil.[19] Case records of 100 patients with skin lesions caused by chromoblastomycosis, who were treated between 1963 and 1998, were reviewed. The cases were confirmed by histopathology and culture. There was a predominance of male patients (4:1) and of white farmers whose ages ranged from 50 to 59 years, with lesions on their lower limbs. Most of them were from the northern regions of the state. The average time between the appearance of the disease and medical diagnosis was 14 years. The verrucous type proved to be the most frequently reported lesion (53%). Thorn wounds were associated with the disease in 16% of the cases. Lesions uncommon to some parts of the body were also reported. In two of the cases, cutaneous lesions caused by paracoccidioidomycosis and chromoblastomycosis were found in the same patient. Epidermoid carcinoma was found in the same parts of the body affected by chromoblastomycosis. Eumycotic mycetoma and chromoblastomycosis were associated. *Fonsecaea pedrosoi* was found in 96% of the cases and *P. verrucosa* in 4% of the cases. Severe cases of chromoblastomycosis with intense skin involvement (e.g. lesions with carcinoma) were observed. Statistical analysis showed recrudescence of the disease in 43% of cases despite the treatment used.

Entomophthoramycosis

Entomophthoramycosis occurs mainly in the tropical rain forests of East and West Africa, South and Central America, and South East Asia.

Conidiobolus coronatus (*Entomophthora coronata*), the causative organism of rhinofacial conidiobolomycosis, lives as a saprophyte in soil and on decomposing plant matter in moist, warm climates. It can also parasitize certain insects.

The most widely held view is that *Basidiobolus ranarum* is the sole agent causing basidiobolomycosis, and that *B. meristosporus* and *B. haptosporus* are synonyms of the former; not all authors are of this opinion, however. *Basidiobolus ranarum* has been recovered from soil and decaying vegetation; it has also been isolated from the gut of frogs, toads and lizards that had apparently swallowed infected insects. It is still uncertain how the disease is acquired and what is the length of incubation. Inoculation through a thorn prick or an insect bite has been suggested, as has contamination of a wound or other abrasion. The infection is most common in children. More detailed aspects of entomophthoramycosis caused by *B. ranarum* can be found in the review by Gugnani.[21]

For an exhaustive review of the epidemiology of entophthoramycosis refer to Ribes *et al.*[12]

Lobomycosis

In lobomycosis, the onset of the disease is generally insidious and difficult to document. The increase in size and number of lesions is a slow process; it can take 40–50 years. This latency period often makes it important to note the patient's history of travel or stay in areas of endemicity to arrive at a proper diagnosis. The history often reveals the cause being a trauma, for example an arthropod sting, a snake bite, a cut from an instrument, or a wound acquired while cutting vegetation. The causal agent of lobomycosis appears to be saprobic in aquatic environments, which probably plays an extremely significant part in its life cycle.

The human disease is endemic in the tropical zone of the New World and has been reported in central and western Brazil, Bolivia, Colombia, Costa Rica, Ecuador, Guyana, French Guiana, Mexico, Panama, Peru, Surinam and Venezuela. There have been isolated cases reported in Holland and a doubtful case in Bangladesh. Identification of the disease in dolphins widened the geographic distribution of the disease. Seven cases of lobomycosis involving two species of dolphins, namely marine dolphins (*Tursiops truncatus*) and marine freshwater dolphins (*Sotalia fluviatilis*), have been reported in Florida, the Texas coast, the Spanish-French coast, the South Brazilian coast and the Surinam River estuary. Although lobomycosis in dolphins has been reported in the USA, only one human case has been reported from the USA.[22]

All attempts to isolate the fungus from lesions of infected people have failed. In the dermis it appears as spheric or elliptic budding cells. Although it is accepted that the infection is exogenous in origin, the natural habitat of the causal fungus remains unknown.

The organism gains entry through the skin; it develops in situ for an unspecified period (several years) and then reaches the subcutaneous tissue. The disease is most prevalent in men aged 30–40 years; it is much less common in women and children.

Mycetoma

Mycetomas are most common in arid tropical and subtropical regions of Africa and Central America, particularly those areas bordering the great deserts. However, sporadic cases have been reported from many parts of the world. The countries surrounding the Saharan and Arabian deserts form the most important endemic area, not only because of the number of new cases occurring each year, but also because of the diversity of causal organisms. Mycetoma is also endemic in certain regions of India and in Central and South America.

Mycetomas are caused by various actinomycetes and fungi that occur as saprophytes in the soil or on vegetation. Individual species of fungi or actinomycetes are often associated with particular geographic areas. About six species of fungi are common causes of eumycetoma and five aerobic actinomycetes are common etiologic agents of actinomycetoma. The geographic distribution of these environmental organisms is influenced by climate.

In the arid regions of the tropics and subtropics, the most frequent etiologic agents are *Madurella mycetomatis*, *Actinomadura madurae*, *Actinomadura pelletieri* and *Streptomyces somaliensis*. These organisms are encountered in the great deserts of Africa and Asia and on their fringes, as well as in south-eastern Europe. In the relatively humid mountain regions of Latin America, *Nocardia brasiliensis* is the predominant organism while *Madurella grisea* is a less prominent cause of infection.

In the occasional cases of mycetoma that occur in temperate regions, the principal isolates have been *Pseudallescheria boydii*, *A. madurae* and *M. mycetomatis*. Other organisms that have occasionally been implicated as causes of mycetoma include *Leptosphaeria senegalensis*, *Neotestudina rosatii*, *Pyrenochaeta romeroi*, *Exophiala jeanselmei*, *Acremonium* spp., *Aspergillus nidulans*, *Nocardia asteroides* and *Nocardia caviae*.

Mycetomas occur more frequently in men than in women. Adults aged between 20 and 50 years are the most commonly affected, although cases in children have also been reported. Most patients come from rural districts in the tropics and subtropics, but cases often occur in some countries with a temperate climate, such as Romania.

Trauma is a critical factor in acquisition of the infection. The organisms may be implanted at the time of injury, or later as a result of secondary contamination of the wound. Traumas are often due to vegetable matter (grasses, wisps of straw, hay). In the tropics and subtropics thorny trees such as the acacia are abundant and are often used for fuel. Wounds caused by the thorns may facilitate the entry of soil organisms, or the causative agents may grow on the thorns and be implanted directly into the subcutaneous tissue. It is not surprising, therefore, that mycetomas affect mainly the feet of country-dwellers who walk barefoot.

The vast majority of organisms causing mycetomas are saprophytes of the external environment; *Nocardia* spp. exist in the soil; other species are encountered not only in the soil, but also on living and dead plants. However, little is known about their behavior outside the human host. A recent study of 264 cases of mycetoma in West Bengal illustrates the epidemiology of the causative organisms.[23] Between 1981 and 2000, 264 cases of mycetoma were diagnosed clinically and microbiologically at the Calcutta School of Tropical Medicine. Retrospective analysis of the records revealed that the ratio of actinomycetomas and eumycetomas was 197:67; the male to female ratio was 183:81. Ninety-four cases occurred in the 1980s and 170 in 1990s, with significantly more infections of *Actinomadura* spp. and fewer with *N. caviae* during the last decade. Pricking was the most common injury associated with eumycetomas. A total of 196 infections were in exposed body parts and 68 in covered areas. The localization of mycetomas differed significantly according to sex, incidence of actinomycetomas or eumycetomas, and obvious history of trauma. Exposed area cases were more common among agricultural workers, while covered area mycetomas were almost always actinomycetomas with a remarkably lower incidence of *N. caviae*, *A. madurae* and *M. grisea* infections. The peak age of onset was between 16 and 25 years. The delay of diagnosis for the 80th percentile of cases was around 6 years for cases caused by *N. brasiliensis* and *Streptomyces* spp.; 8 years for *N. caviae* and *N. asteroides*; and 10 years for *M. grisea* and *Actinomadura* spp. From the history of trauma in 130 patients, the 80th percentile incubation period was calculated for *N. brasiliensis, N. caviae* and *N. asteroides* as 3 years; for *Actinomadura* spp. 7 years; and for *M. grisea* 9 years. The minimum incubation period for all organisms was around 3 months.

Phaeohyphomycosis

Black molds are widely encountered in soil and wood. In addition, some organisms can produce yeast-like synanamorphs that adapt to aqueous environments. Typically, the infection is acquired by the inoculation of the fungus through a penetrating injury. In addition, other possible portals of entry have been suggested, including the inhalation of spores with lung or sinus invasion, the ingestion of contaminated food or water with subsequent penetration through the gastrointestinal tract, contamination of the skin at the insertion of a vascular catheter, and contamination of the catheter itself. Some cases of systemic infection have no apparent portal of entry.

Phaeohyphomycosis has a worldwide distribution, but subcutaneous infection is most often seen in the rural population of tropical parts of Central and South America. Most cases of cerebral or paranasal sinus infection have been reported from USA. There is little information on the incidence of phaeohyphomycosis. In a population-based surveillance conducted over 2 years in the San Francisco Bay area, the incidence of infection due to black molds was one case per million per year.[24]

The number of organisms implicated as etiologic agents of phaeohyphomycosis is increasing. More than 80 different molds, classified in 40 different genera, have been incriminated. These fungi have often been given different names at different times, and there is therefore a great deal of confusion in the nomenclature used in different reports.

Among the more important etiologic agents, *Alternaria*, *Bipolaris*, *Curvularia*, *Exophiala*, *Exserohilum* and *Phialophora* spp. and *Xylohypha bantiana* can be included. Many of these organisms are found in soil or decomposing plant debris; others are plant pathogens. The most important predisposing factor for cutaneous and subcutaneous infection is exposure to contaminated material present in the environment (decaying wood, plants).

Human infection follows inhalation or traumatic implantation of the fungus. In addition to these agents of phaeohyphomycosis, others are being reported. For example, *Colletotrichum* spp., which are common plant pathogens, have been reported as a cause of subcutaneous phaeohyphomycosis in patients undergoing chemotherapy for hematologic malignancies and may cause life-threatening phaeohyphomycosis in immunosuppressed patients.[25]

Rhinosporidiosis

Rhinosporidiosis is endemic in India[26] and Sri Lanka, as well as in South America and Africa. Occasional cases have been reported from the USA, South East Asia and other parts of the world. The etiologic agent is an endosporulating organism, *Rhinosporidium seeberi*. So far, all attempts to isolate this fungus from lesions have failed. In tissue, large, thick-walled sporangia (spherules) are formed. Large numbers of spores are produced within the sporangia and, when the spores are mature, they are released through a pore in the wall. Each spore may develop to form a new sporangium. Little is known about the natural habitat of *R. seeberi*, but it is believed that stagnant pools of water may be the source of human infection.

The disease is most prevalent in rural districts, particularly among people working or bathing in stagnant water (such as rice fields). Men are more commonly affected than women.

Sporotrichosis

Sporotrichosis is worldwide in distribution, but occurs most frequently in temperate humid climatic regions. At present, the largest number of reported cases comes from the North American continent.[27] Other regions where the infection is endemic include South America,[28] South Africa and South East Asia.

The causative agent is a dimorphic fungus, *Sporothrix schenckii*, which is found in the soil and on plants and sphagnum moss. It grows in nature as a mycelium, but in tissue it forms small, budding cells.

Infection usually follows the traumatic introduction of the fungus into the skin. Minor trauma, such as abrasions or wounds from thorns or wood splinters, may be sufficient. In occasional cases, infection follows spore inhalation.

It is not clear whether the infection is more common among men than women. Incidence in the different age groups is also variously assessed, but children are less often affected than adults.

Sporotrichosis is most prevalent among people who handle soil or plant materials, such as gardeners, florists, mineworkers and carpenters. For this reason sporotrichosis has been regarded as an occupational disease. Sporotrichosis is not transferred from human to human, and the multiple cases that sometimes occur in families or closed communities are usually due to common exposure to the same exogenous source of contamination.

PATHOGENICITY

Chromoblastomycosis

The causative fungi require implantation through the skin into subcutaneous tissue. The lesion appears at the site of skin trauma or puncture wound. However, the inoculation may have occurred so long before that no history of injury can be elicited. In general, the disease remains localized to the area surrounding the initial infection. In rare cases, hematogenous spread to the brain, lymph nodes, liver, lungs and other organs is observed.[9]

Entomophthoramycosis

Pathogenicity of the causal organisms is a reflection of inoculum size and frequency of exposure in endemic areas. For an exhaustive review of the pathogenicity of the agents causing entomophthoramycosis refer to Ribes *et al.*[12]

Lobomycosis

Lobomycosis develops following trauma to the skin, but in most clinical histories the event is so minimal that it is not remembered. The disease runs an extremely slow course and years may elapse before the patient seeks medical advice.

Mycetoma and phaeohyphomycosis

The organisms causing these conditions are not regarded as being pathogenic. Typically, the infection is acquired by the inoculation of the fungus through a penetrating injury

Rhinosporidiosis

Studies on the virulence of *R. seeberi* have not been carried out. Nothing is known about the mode of infection. It is most likely that trauma is an essential factor in the initiation of disease. Spores of *R. seeberi* are not able to penetrate intact epithelium. Because the nose and eyes are the most common sites of the disease it is suggested that the organisms are transmitted in dust and water.

Sporotrichosis

Sporothrix schenckii usually enters the body through traumatic implantation, but occasionally the fungus is introduced through inhalation of the conidia. Because the infection can also be hematogenously disseminated, it may be that the yeast cells are able to resist phagocytosis and intracellular killing by host effector cells, although in-vitro data suggest that the yeast cells are readily killed in the presence of human serum. Host defense mechanisms in response to *S. schenckii* have not been extensively studied.

PREVENTION

Avoidance of skin penetration is the best means of preventing chromoblastomycosis, entomophthoramycosis and phaeohyphomycosis. Suitable footwear will help to prevent chromoblastomycosis.

Very little is known about the ecology of *Loboa loboi* so it is difficult to recommend specific methods of contact and prevention for lobomycosis.

The causative agents of mycetoma normally live as saprophytes in the soil. Because the most common site for mycetoma is the foot it is reasonable to assume that the wearing of appropriate footwear would prevent infection. Avoidance of trauma to the hands and other areas is difficult to encourage because most infections seem to be related to outdoor activities.

Rhinosporidiosis can be prevented by avoiding eye and nose contact with contaminated dust and water.

Occupations that predispose persons to sporotrichosis include gardening, farming, masonry, floral work, outdoor labor and other activities involving exposure to contaminated soil or vegetation such as sphagnum moss or roses. Wearing gloves and protective clothing while carrying out these activities may therefore prevent traumatic implantation of the fungus through the skin.

DIAGNOSTIC MICROBIOLOGY

Chromoblastomycosis

Microscopic examination of wet preparations of pus, scrapings, or crusts from lesions can permit the diagnosis of chromoblastomycosis if clusters of the characteristic small, round, thick-walled, brown-pigmented sclerotic cells are seen (Fig. 239.1). These cells are often divided by longitudinal and transverse septa.[6]

The definitive diagnosis of chromoblastomycosis depends on the isolation of the etiologic agent in culture. Identifiable olive-green or brownish-black mycelial colonies can be obtained after incubation at

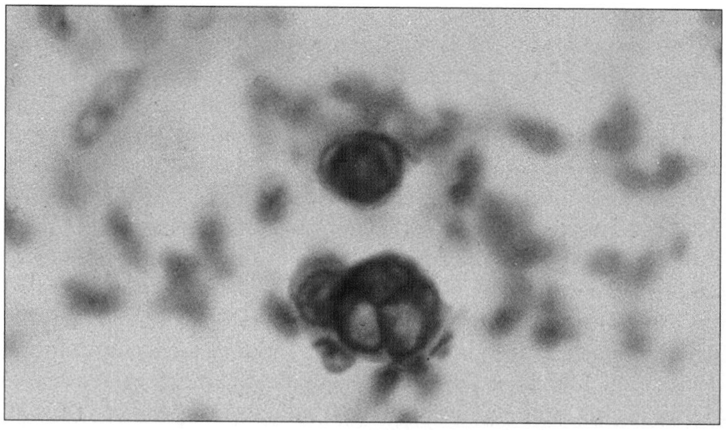

Fig. 239.1 Chromoblastomycosis. Thick-walled, septate, dematiaceous muriform cells. With permission from Richardson MD, *et al.* Slide atlas of fungal infection: subcutaneous and unusual fungal infections, Oxford: Blackwell, 1995.

77–86°F (25–30°C) for 1–2 weeks, but cultures should be retained for 4 weeks before being discarded. Identification of the individual etiologic agents is difficult. Serologic techniques have been shown to detect cases of chromoblastomycosis caused by *C. carrionii*.[29]

Entomophthoramycosis

Microscopic examination of smears or tissue from the nasal mucosa will reveal broad, nonseptate, thin-walled mycelial filaments.

The culture of causal organisms of entomophthoramycosis is difficult. To optimize the recovery of fungus from clinical material, specimens must be inoculated on the largest possible number of media; they should be incubated at 77–95°F (25–35°C).

For an exhaustive review of the diagnosis of entomophthoramycosis refer to Ribes *et al.*[12]

Lobomycosis

The etiologic agent of lobomycosis is an obligate pathogen of humans and lower mammals that has yet to be isolated and grown in vitro; therefore, nothing is known of its basic cultural characteristics and growth. Diagnosis is based on demonstrating the presence of globose, thick-walled, yeast-like cells ranging from 5 to 12μm in diameter in lesion exudate or tissue sections. The organism multiplies by budding, and thus mother cells with single buds are often observed. However, characteristic sequential budding leads to the production of chains of cells that are linked to each other by a tubular connection, or isthmus. Budding may occur at more than one point on a cell, giving rise to branched or radiating chains of cells. These thick-walled, hyaline, spherical cells with chains of cells interconnected by tubular connections are the basis on which a diagnosis of lobomycosis rests. The thick-walled, budding hyaline cells with catenate chains of conidia can be readily observed in tissue smears or exudates mounted in 10% potassium hydroxide or in Calcofluor white preparations.

Microscopic examination of specimens of pathologic material will reveal numerous hyaline, round or ovoid cells with an average diameter of 9μm (Fig. 239.2). These cells closely resemble the yeast forms of *Paracoccidioides brasiliensis* or *Histoplasma duboisii*. The cells are enclosed in a double-contoured membrane and are capable of budding. They often form chains and appear to be joined together by bridge-like structures within the chain. If the individual elements show multiple budding, the chains are divided into branches.

The epidermis is irregular in thickness, with parakeratotic zones and sometimes ulcerations and crusts. The dermis underlying it shows hypertrophic and partly hyalinized bundles of connective tissue. Between these bundles are granulomatous infiltrates that contain numerous yeasts, which are either located extracellularly or phagocytosed by mononuclear and polynuclear cells. Intracytoplasmic asteroid bodies have been observed in some giant cells. Their nature is unknown and they have been confused with the asteroid bodies seen in sporotrichosis. They are, however, different and unrelated structures.[30]

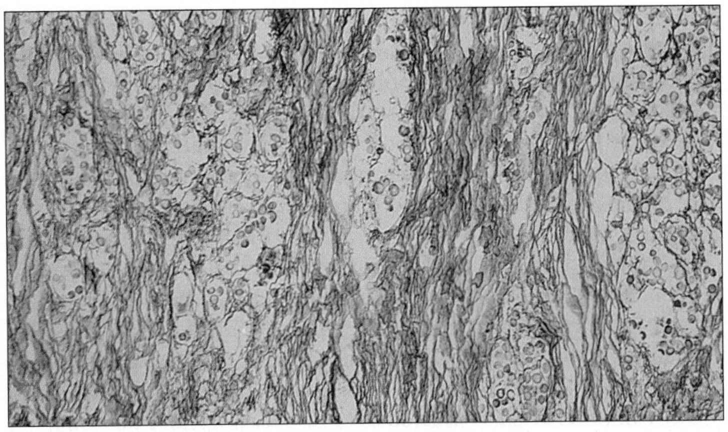

Fig. 239.2 Lobomycosis. Yeast cells are attached to each other in short chains. Nonbudding and single-budding cells are also present.

A case report describing the first case of lobomycosis diagnosed in the USA illustrates further the histopathologic features of this disease.[22] The patient had traveled to the Angel Falls in Venezuela 7 years earlier where he had been exposed to the high pressures of the falls. This resulted in a pustule and surrounding erythema on the skin of his right chest wall. The lesion gradually increased in size and had the appearance of a keloid. After an uncomplicated excision the patient recovered completely. Examination of the tissue sections showed a nodular inflammatory infiltrate of foamy histiocytes, multinucleated giant cells and scattered lymphocytes. Throughout the infiltrate were numerous globose or subglobose, lemon-shaped cells that measured 5.0–11.0μm in diameter. Many cells showed thick refractile walls and reproduced by single and multiple budding. The buds were attached to the mother cell by narrow tubular connections, giving a beaded appearance. There were many chains of cells showing narrow tubular connections characteristic of *L. loboi*.

Loboa loboi has never been successfully cultured. This distinguishes it from *P. brasiliensis*, which it closely resembles morphologically. The globose and subglobose budding cells of *L. loboi* resemble budding cells of *P. brasiliensis* in tissue. However, the central mother cells of *P. brasiliensis* become large and thick-walled compared to the daughter cells, which remain smaller. In contrast, yeast cells of *L. loboi* remain consistent in diameter, giving rise to branching chains of blastoconidia. In addition, the cell wall of *L. loboi* contains constitutive melanin,[31] which can be detected by the use of the Fontana–Masson histologic stain. The walls of cells of *P. brasiliensis* are not known to contain melanin. *Loboa loboi* has never been cultured in vitro. On the other hand, *P. brasiliensis* can be grown in artificial culture and is known to be a dimorphic pathogen.

Molecular methods have been used in an attempt to characterize the causative agent of lobomycosis.[32] Fungal-specific primers targeted for highly conserved genomic nucleic acid sequences were used in a polymerase chain reaction (PCR) to amplify DNA from lobomycosis lesions in a bottlenose dolphin. Sequence alignments of this DNA possessed high homology to fungal ribosomal DNA sequences found in the genus *Cladosporium*. When used for in-situ hybridization, the riboprobe transcribed from a cloned PCR-generated fragment bound to *L. loboi* cells. These results support the hypothesis that *L. loboi* in dolphin tissue is a fungus.

A new monotypic genus, *Lacazia*, with *Lacazia loboi* as the type species, was recently proposed by Taborda *et al.*,[31] to accommodate the obligate etiologic agent of lobomycosis in mammals. The continued placement of *L. loboi* in the genus *Paracoccidioides* as *Paracoccidioides loboi* O.M. Fonseca et Lacaz was found to be taxonomically inappropriate. The older name *Loboa loboi* Ciferri *et al.* was considered to be a synonym of *P. brasiliensis*.

Mycetoma

The diagnosis of mycetoma depends on the identification of grains. These should, if possible, be obtained by puncture from a softened, but not ulcerated, nodule with a syringe. Failing this, grains can be obtained with a dissecting needle or by aspiration from the secretion flowing from a sinus.[33] If there is no pus flowing from the lesion, small fragments of tissue should be removed. If possible, between 20 and 30 grains should be obtained; these should be rinsed in sterile saline before being cultured.

Gross examination of the grains may give a clue to the etiologic diagnosis. Black grains suggest a fungal infection; minute white

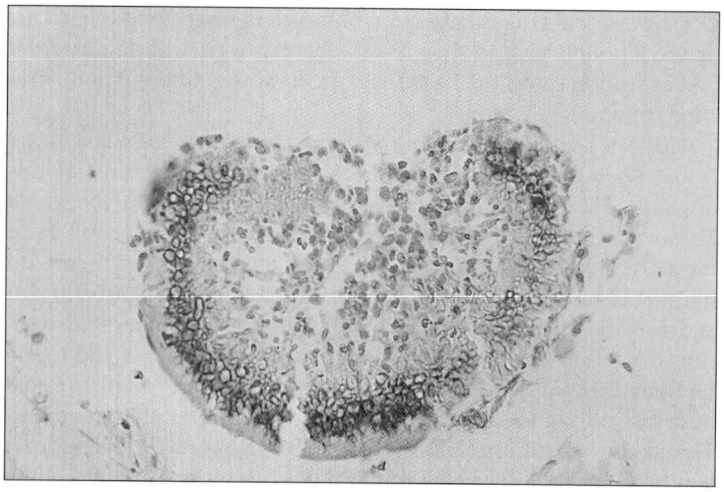

Fig. 239.3 Granule of *Madurella mycetomatis*. The granules have a deeply pigmented periphery of compact hyphae. Randomly oriented, poorly pigmented fungal elements in the interior of the granule are less compact.

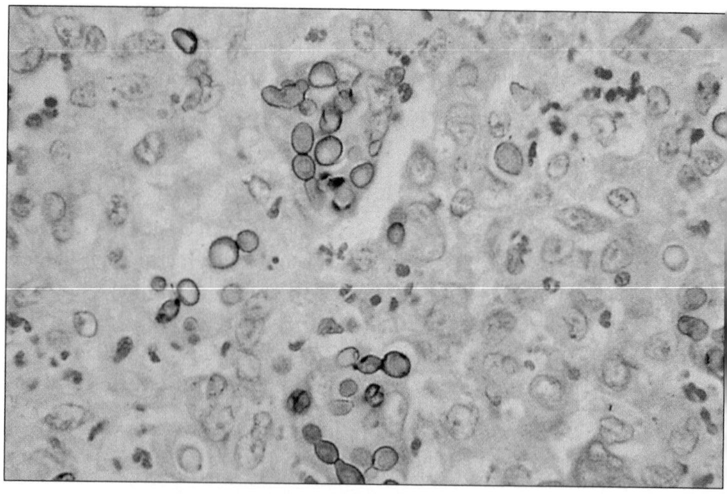

Fig. 239.4 Subcutaneous phaeohyphomycosis caused by *Bipolaris spicifera*. The fungal elements are stained with Fontana–Masson, which accentuates and confirms the presence of melanin or melanin-like pigment in the fungal cell walls.

grains often indicate a *Nocardia* infection; and larger white grains the size of a pinhead may be of either fungal or actinomycotic origin. Small, red grains are specific to *A. pelletieri*, but yellowish-white grains may be actinomycotic or fungal in origin. Their shape, consistency and structure must be carefully determined.

Direct microscopic examination will confirm the diagnosis of mycetoma, and will also reveal whether the causative organism is a fungus or an actinomycete.[33] Actinomycotic grains contain very fine filaments (<1μm diameter), whereas fungal grains contain short hyphae (2–4μm diameter), which are sometimes swollen. This can be seen by direct microscopic examination of crushed grains in potassium hydroxide, but it is much more readily observed in stained histologic sections (Fig. 239.3).

Although the identification of the causal agents of mycetoma can often be deduced from the morphologic characteristics of the grains, it is also important to isolate the organism in culture. Agar plates should be inoculated with several grains (or with secretion or tissue fragments) and incubated at 77–86°F (25–30°C) and at 98.6°F (37°C). The most commonly used agar medium is Sabouraud's agar, without antibiotics but with cycloheximide for isolation of actinomycetes, and with antibiotics but without cycloheximide for fungal agents. Alternative media for isolation of actinomycetes include brain–heart infusion or blood agar.

Cultures should be retained for up to 6 weeks before being discarded. The actinomycetes grow much more slowly than the fungi.

Madurella mycetomatis is the commonest cause of eumycetoma in Sudan and other countries in tropical Africa. Currently, the early diagnosis of mycetoma is difficult. In attempting to improve the identification of *M. mycetomatis* and, consequently, the diagnosis of mycetoma, a specific oligonucleotide primer based on the sequence of the internal transcribed spacer (ITS) regions spacing the genes encoding the fungal ribosomal RNAs has been described.[34] The ITS regions were amplified with universal primers and sequenced, and then two sets of species-specific primers were designed that specifically amplify parts of the ITS and the 5.8S ribosomal DNA gene. The new primers were tested for specificity with DNA isolated from human mycetoma lesions and DNA extracted from cultures of *M. mycetomatis* reference strains and related fungi as well as human DNA. To study the genetic variability of the ITS regions of *M. mycetomatis*, ITS amplicons were obtained from 25 different clinical isolates and subjected to restriction fragment length polymorphism (RFLP) analysis with *Cfo*I, *Hae*III, *Msp*I, *Sau*3AI, *Rsa*I and *Spe*I restriction enzymes. Restriction fragment length polymorphism analysis of the ITS region did not reveal even a single difference, indicating the homogeneity of the isolates analyzed during the study.

Phaeohyphomycosis

One common factor among these fungi is their melanin formation in the cell wall in culture and, in most cases, in human tissue. Microscopic examination of stained histopathologic sections or wet preparations of clinical material, such as pus or skin scrapings, can permit the diagnosis of phaeohyphomycosis if brown-pigmented septate mycelium with occasional branching is seen (Fig. 239.4).

Identification of the etiologic agent is essential for correct management, and this depends on its isolation in culture. Identifiable mycelial colonies can be obtained after incubation at 86°F (30°C) for 1–3 weeks. No serologic tests are available.

Rhinosporidiosis

Microscopy of clinical material reveals round or ovoid organisms that, depending on age, vary in diameter with a prominent wall.[35–37] These mature forms are known as sporangia. Sporangia measure up to 350μm in diameter and have a cell wall measuring about 5μm. The sporangia may be filled with endospores (Fig. 239.5). The immature forms of the organism are known as trophocytes; they are smaller than sporangia, have a relatively thinner wall and do not contain endospores. Trophocytes mature into sporangia. Endospores develop within sporangia. Endospores are released upon maturity and thereafter develop into trophocytes.

Rhinosporidium seeberi has traditionally been classified as a fungus on the basis of morphologic and histochemical characterisitics. Recent molecular studies have generated conflicting results. The organism may be either a cyanobacterium or a protist. Using consensus PCR, a portion of the *R. seeberi* 18S rRNA gene directly from infected tissue has been amplified.[38] Analysis of the aligned sequence and inference of phylogenetic relationships showed that *R. seeberi* is a protist from a novel clade of parasites that infect fish and amphibians. Fluorescence in-situ hybridization and *R. seeberi*-specific PCR showed that this unique 18S rRNA sequence is also present in other tissues infected with *R. seeberi*. These data support the *R. seeberi* phylogeny recently suggested by others. *Rhinosporidium seeberi* is not a classic fungus, but rather the first known

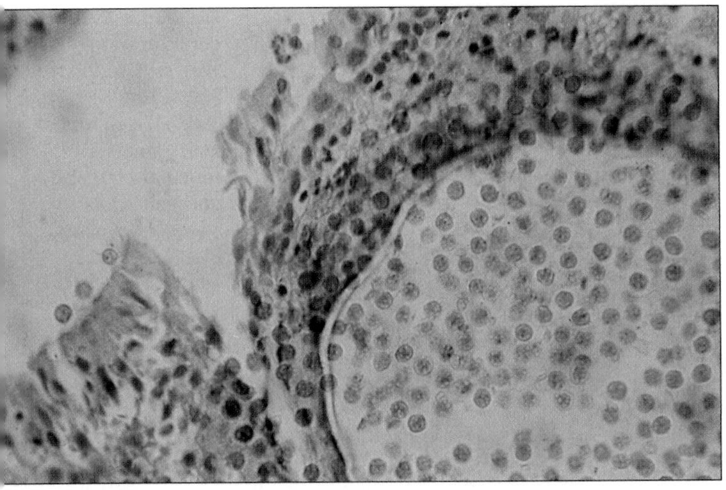

Fig. 239.5 Rhinosporidiosis.

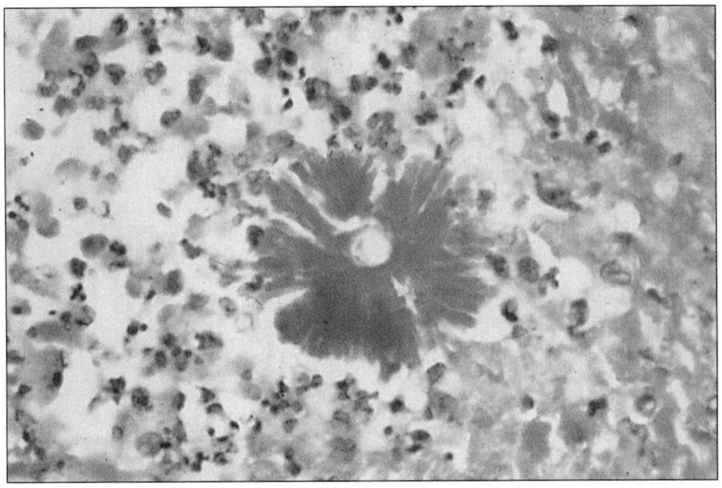

Fig. 239.6 Asteroid body in cutaneous sporotrichosis. A yeast-like cell of *Sporothrix schenckii* with faintly basophilic, retracted cytoplasm is intimately surrounded by elongated spicules of Splendore–Hoeppli material.

human pathogen on the basis of a previously aligned dataset of the DRIPs clade (named after the organisms *Dermocystidium*, the rosette agent, *Ichthyophonus* and *Psorospermium*), a novel clade of aquatic protistan parasites (*Ichthyosporea*).

Immunologic methods have been used to identify the causal agent of rhinosporidiosis in situ where the immunolocalization of *R. seeberi* antigens using sera from individuals infected with *R. seeberi* and tissue from Sri Lankan patients with rhinosporidiosis was investigated.[39] The tissues were fixed and evaluated by transmission electron microscopy for the presence of *R. seeberi* sporangia. The tissue samples were reacted with the patients's sera and then labeled with protein A colloidal gold (PACG) for immunolocalization. It was found that the PACG had fixed to antibodies that specifically recognized an internal electron lucent layer situated immediately under the mature sporangium's wall. The endospores and the juvenile and intermediate sporangia did not undergo PACG labeling. This study found that the expression of this antigen occurs only in the final developmental stages of *R. seeberi* mature sporangia. The data may explain why circulating antibodies to *R. seeberi* were not detected before in studies that used endospores as antigen in immunoassays. This appears to be the first report in which an antigenic material with a potential role in the immunology of rhinosporidiosis has been described.

Sporotrichosis

Direct examination of clinical material, such as pus or tissue, is often disappointing because the organism is seldom abundant. However, it can be of value if conducted with painstaking care. The detection of typical ovoid or cigar-shaped cells or asteroid bodies of *S. schenckii* will confirm the diagnosis (Fig. 239.6).

The definitive diagnosis of sporotrichosis depends on the isolation of the etiologic agent in culture. Clinical material should be inoculated onto several media, including Sabouraud's agar, and incubated at 72–77°F (22–25°C). Identifiable mycelial colonies will appear in 2–5 days. The color usually changes from cream or light brown to dark brown or black with age. Confirmation of the identification depends on the morphologic characteristics of the mycelial form and its conversion to the yeast form on blood agar at 98.6°F (37°C).

At present, serologic tests do not have a significant role in the diagnosis of sporotrichosis. Tube agglutination and latex particle agglutination tests can be used to detect antibodies to *S. schenckii*, but are more helpful in diagnosing the unusual extracutaneous forms of sporotrichosis than in detecting cutaneous infection.

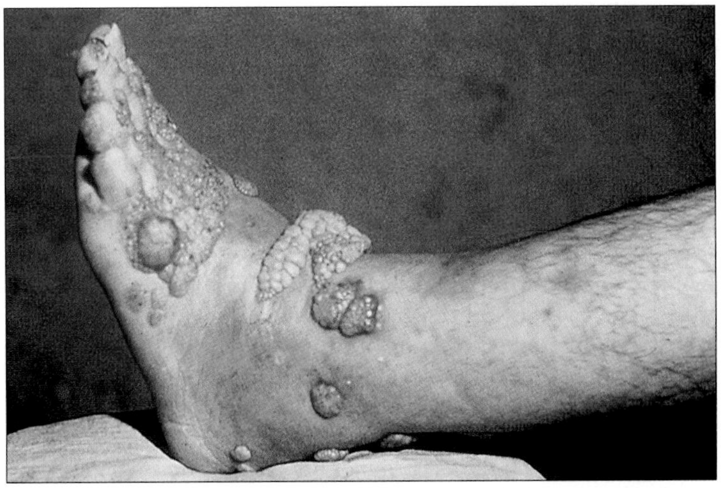

Fig. 239.7 Chromoblastomycosis lesions on the foot and ankle. The typical raised, crusted, verrucous lesions seen on the foot and ankle.

CLINICAL MANIFESTATIONS

Chromoblastomycosis

The lesions of chromoblastomycosis are usually unilateral and occur mainly on the exposed parts of the body, particularly the feet and lower legs (Fig. 239.7).[20] Other less common sites include the hands, arms, shoulders and neck (Fig. 239.8). The initial lesion is a painless papule or nodule on an erythematous and occasionally verrucous base. The condition may also present as an abscess surrounded by infiltration or as a psoriasiform lesion with erythema and scaling. As the disease develops, the affected limb becomes enlarged. Small satellite nodules may occur at the edge of the original lesion. Itching often occurs and it may be severe.

The primary lesion develops very slowly, its diameter increasing by only 1–2mm per year. It is firm and elastic in consistency and colored red or violet verging on gray. There is a warty, papillomatous margin surrounding a center that may be flat, smooth, or scaly, with areas of scarring.

Later in the disease, the lesion may become pedunculated or ulcerated (if bacterial superinfection occurs). However, the lesions usually retain a warty, dry character.

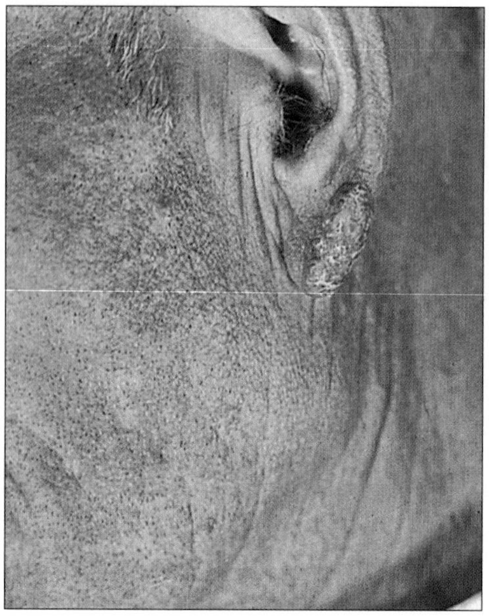

Fig. 239.8 Chromoblastomycosis lesions on the ear. A crusty lesion on the lower part of the external ear.

Secondary lesions may appear, especially along the lymphatics draining the site of infection; here again, development is slow and symptoms are few. The lymph nodes are only involved if there is superimposed bacterial infection.

In some cases the skin lesions may spread and involve an entire limb. In other cases there is spontaneous resolution, leaving behind scars that are atrophic and abnormally pigmented or, by contrast, hypertrophic and contracting.

Cutaneous dissemination is rare, but may follow autoinoculation from scratching. Lymphatic or hematogenous spread may also occur. In elderly patients the lesions may spread to involve the skin of the trunk, whereas the scalp is rarely involved. The nails may also be damaged as a result of infection of the matrix and nailbed.

Rare complications of chromoblastomycosis include carcinomatous transformation. Metastatic lesions may occur in the oral mucosa, lymph nodes, bones and other tissues.

Usually lesions on the upper limbs are erythematosquamous, psoriasiform and of low relief, whereas those on the lower limbs are more exuberant. The latter may be associated with sclerosing inflammation of the subcutaneous tissue and result in elephantiasis.

In endemic areas the unilateral development of vegetative, atrophic and scarred lesions on a lower limb is suggestive of chromoblastomycosis. The condition must be distinguished from a number of other fungal infections including blastomycosis, lobomycosis, paracoccidioidomycosis, phaeohyphomycosis, rhinosporidiosis and sporotrichosis. It must also be differentiated from protothecosis, leishmaniasis, verrucous tuberculosis, certain leprous lesions and syphilis. On the upper limbs the erythematosquamous lesions can be confused with psoriasis or subacute or discoid lupus erythematosus. Mycologic and histologic investigations are indispensable for confirmation of the diagnosis.

Entomophthoramycosis

Entomophthoramycosis is a chronic subcutaneous infection of the trunk and limbs. The subcutaneous swelling that characterizes this disease is usually localized to the buttock and thighs, but may also be found on the arm, leg or shoulder.

The initial swelling may be rapid or slow in onset and is hard and painless. The spread is slow but relentless, and a large mass is formed that is attached to the skin but not to the underlying tissue (unlike *Conidiobolus* infection). This is a disfiguring infection, but the skin covering the lesions does not ulcerate. Lymphatic obstruction may occur and can result in massive lymphedema. There is no functional impairment as long as the joints are not blocked by the volume of the swellings. The underlying bone and joints are not affected by the disease.

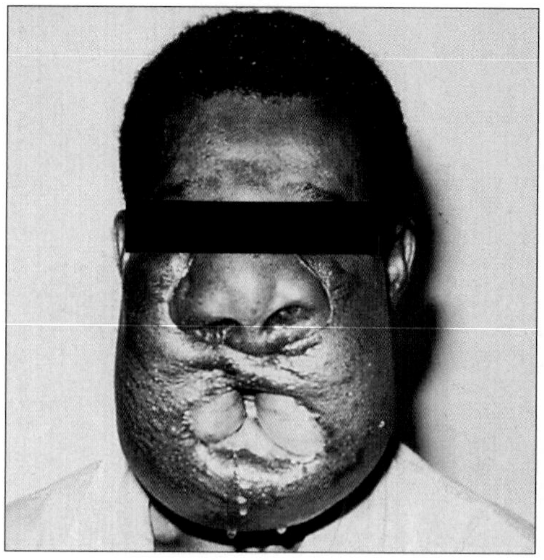

Fig. 239.9 Rhinofacial conidiobolomycosis. With permission from Richardson MD, *et al.* Slide atlas of fungal infection: subcutaneous and unusual fungal infections, Oxford: Blackwell, 1995.

The disease is most common among adult males, particularly those living or working in tropical rain forests. Infection is acquired through inhalation of spores, or their introduction into the nasal cavities by soiled hands.

Very rarely, *B. ranarum* can cause gastrointestinal basidiobolomycosis.[40]

Conidiobolus infection generally begins with unilateral involvement of the nasal mucosa. The most common nasal symptom is obstruction, but frequent nose bleeding can occur and is evidence of the development of a nasal polyp in the anterior region of the inferior turbinate. Subcutaneous nodules then develop in the nasal and perinasal regions and may be associated with epidermal lesions.

The spread of the infection is slow but relentless. It is usually confined to the face, and the development of gross facial swelling involving the forehead, periorbital region and upper lip is very distinctive (Fig. 239.9). As a rule, the lesions are firmly attached to the underlying tissue, although the bone is spared. The skin remains intact. Spread to the lymph nodes has been reported. Even if, in advanced cases, the diagnosis is obvious from the appearance, mycologic and histologic examinations are essential for its confirmation.

The disease can be diagnosed with confidence on the basis of appearance and the results of the mycologic and (in particular) the histologic examination. Specimens must be taken from the subcutaneous tissue where the infection develops.

For an exhaustive review of the clinical manifestations of entomophthoramycosis refer to Ribes *et al.*[12]

Lobomycosis

Lobomycosis is an indolent infection that first manifests as a papule or small nodule of normal pink skin color or with a grayish tinge. The nodule then proliferates and, by partial or total coalescence, may form extensive multilobar lesions. The disease spreads by peripheral extension or autoinoculation from scratching, or it may follow the draining lymphatics, especially in elderly people.

The lesions are located in the dermis and subcutis and may form massive tumors, which are firm and resistant to pressure at the outset, but which later become hard and fibrous and resemble a keloid. If there is ulceration, depressed scars may remain; their surface is smooth and shiny in places, owing to atrophy of the underlying epidermis, and wrinkled and fissured elsewhere.

The disease may be symptomless or cause itching and burning, and trauma to the affected area may be especially painful. The most common sites of infection are the coolest parts of the body – the limbs, face, ears and buttocks. The lesions may cover a whole limb. If the head is involved, the patient may be so grossly disfigured as to be completely excluded from social life. With a few exceptions there are no adenopathies.

Lesions may be keloid scars or irregular fibrous changes of the skin without secretion. Leprosy, leishmaniasis and chromoblastomycosis can produce similar lesions. Mycologic and histologic examination will confirm the diagnosis.

Mycetoma

Mycetoma is a chronic, suppurative infection of the subcutaneous tissue and contiguous bones. The lesion appears to begin at a site of minor trauma and continues to spread locally over the ensuing months and years.

The clinical features of the disease are fairly uniform, regardless of the type of organism causing it. Eumycetoma follows a slower and generally less destructive course than actinomycetoma. Spread to the internal organs and involvement of the regional lymph nodes is rare, occurring in no more than 2–5% of cases.

The feet are by far the most common site of involvement and account for two-thirds or more of cases (Fig. 239.10). Other sites include the lower legs, hands, head, neck, chest, shoulder, arms and abdomen.

In most cases, the first sign of the disease is a small, hard, usually painless, subcutaneous nodule that is not attached to the underlying tissue. It is covered by taut thinned skin, which is reddish-violet in color. A number of small nodules may coalesce to form a larger and frequently multilobar nodule.

Over the ensuing months the nodule begins to soften on the surface, caves in, ulcerates and partly empties, discharging a viscous, purulent fluid containing grains. If there is little fluid, the grains may not escape. The lesion then broadens out at the surface and also spreads inward to infect muscles and bones. The lesions, which are covered with depigmented and scarred skin, present as swellings, which are often covered with a crust. Later, the lesions develop sinus tracts that discharge pus and blood containing the characteristic grains.

The infection slowly spreads to adjacent tissue, including bone; this often causes considerable deformity. Mycetomas of the feet make the arches convex, thus preventing the toes from touching the ground. However, the general health of the patient is not affected. Pain, burning and pruritus may occur but are usually mild. Depending on the location and size of the lesion, and also on whether there is any bone involvement, limb function may be impaired.

Radiologic examination is useful in determining the extent of bone destruction. Abnormalities include periosteal reactions, sclerosis, endosteal reactions, cortical erosions and joint destruction. Computerized tomography scanning is also helpful in delineating the extent of lesions.

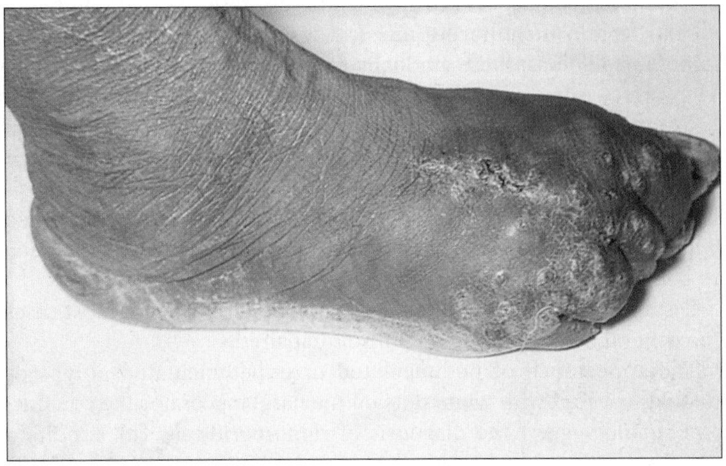

Fig. 239.10 Mycetoma of the foot.

Bacterial superinfection is not uncommon and is largely responsible for adenopathies and impairment of the general health. Visceral and especially cerebral metastases are the most serious complications; they cause cachexia and are often fatal. Fortunately, they are rare.

In most cases, the diagnosis of mycetoma of the feet presents no problems, but it may be difficult if other body sites are involved, particularly in regions where the disease is not endemic and if no grains have been discharged at the time of examination.

The characteristic feature of mycetoma is the presence in a fistulated swelling of grains that are found to contain actinomycotic or fungal filaments. This finding distinguishes mycetoma from chromoblastomycosis, cutaneous tuberculosis, certain syphilitic or leprous lesions, botryomycosis and other conditions.

Phaeohyphomycosis

Phaeohyphomycosis can be divided into a number of distinct clinical forms, including subcutaneous infection, paranasal sinus infection, cerebral infection and invasive and systemic disease.[1,41] The disease spectrum of noncutaneous phaeohyphomycosis includes sinusitis, pulmonary disease, CNS infection, ocular disease, arthritis, osteomyelitis, fungemia, endocarditis, peritonitis and gastrointestinal disease.

Subcutaneous phaeohyphomycosis

Subcutaneous phaeohyphomycosis usually follows the traumatic implantation of the fungus into the subcutaneous tissue. Minor trauma, such as cuts or wounds from thorns or wood splinters, is often sufficient. The principal etiologic agents include *E. jeanselmei*, *Exophiala spinifera*, *Exophiala dermatitidis* (*Wangiella dermatitidis*), *Phialophora richardsiae* and *Phialophora parasitica*.

The lesions occur mainly on the arms and legs. Other less common sites include the buttocks, neck and face. The initial lesion is a firm, sometimes tender, subcutaneous nodule that may enlarge slowly to form a painless cystic abscess. Lesions are attached to the skin but not to the underlying tissue or bone. Unless the cyst ruptures, the overlying skin remains unaffected. In immunosuppressed patients with subcutaneous phaeohyphomycosis, the lesions are more likely to drain through sinuses.

Phaeohyphomycosis in transplant recipients

Infection of subcutaneous tissue by black fungi has only been reported in six transplant patients, all of whom were solid organ recipients.[42] These patients presented with indolent, localized infections at least 1 year after transplant, while on maintenance immunosuppressive regimens. They were cured by surgical resection, either alone or in conjunction with antifungal agents. A further case report illustrates the features of subcutaneous phaeohyphomycosis, occurring in a bone marrow transplant recipient receiving high doses of immunosuppressive agents, in whom widespread subcutaneous infection due to *E. jeanselmei* was not eradicated by repeated resections and therapy with amphotericin B and flucytosine.[42] The infection was eventually cured after addition of itraconazole to the therapeutic regimen. Results of in-vitro testing of the isolate for susceptibility to a combination of amphotericin B, flucytosine and itraconazole confirmed the potential role of combination antifungal therapy in the setting of refractory infection.

Local recurrence of subcutaneous phaeohyphomycosis in transplant recipients after medication or surgical treatment is also seen. An illustrative case is a 42-year-old woman who had undergone a bilateral lung transplant who developed pheohyphomycotic cysts with local recurrence and then was successfully treated by local excision with pre- and postsurgery oral itraconazole treatment.[43] Simple excision or excision with postsurgery oral itraconazole resulted in local recurrence in this patient. Local excision with pre- and postsurgery oral itraconazole was effective in preventing the local recurrence. The authors conclude that local excision with pre- and postsurgery oral itraconazole can be used to treat these patients with recurrent phaeohyphomycosis.

Paranasal sinus infection

This form of phaeohyphomycosis is becoming more common. The principal etiologic agents include *Alternaria* spp., *Bipolaris spicifera*, *Bipolaris hawaiiensis*, *Curvularia lunata* and *Exserohilum rostratum*.

It is a slowly progressive condition that may remain confined to the sinuses or spread to contiguous structures. Affected people usually complain of longstanding symptoms of allergic rhinitis, nasal polyps or intermittent sinus pain. Patients present with nasal obstruction and facial pain, with or without proptosis. The sinuses are filled with a thick, dark, tenacious, inspissated mucus.

Computerized tomography scanning is the best method for evaluating the extent of the infection. The typical finding is a large mass filling one or more of the sinuses.

Alternaria and *Curvularia* spp. occasionally cause necrotic lesions of the nasal septum in patients with leukemia or AIDS.

Cerebral phaeohyphomycosis

This form of phaeohyphomycosis may follow hematogenous dissemination of infection from the lungs, or it may result from direct spread from the nasal sinuses. Involvement of the CNS carries a poor prognosis. The routes of infection have not been clearly established, but the most likely port of entry seems to be the respiratory tract, although direct inoculation into the brain and extension from the sinuses, ear and pulmonary infections have also been reported. Most cases are due to *X. bantiana* (*Cladosporium trichoides*). Other etiologic agents include *Bipolaris* spp. and *E. dermatitidis*. Many cases of cerebral infection with *X. bantiana* have occurred in people with no obvious predisposing factors.

The symptoms of cerebral phaeohyphomycosis are gradual in onset. Persistent headache is the most common presenting symptom. The most frequent clinical findings include focal neurologic signs, hemiparesis and fits. Fever is minimal or absent. Chest radiographs are normal.

Computerized tomography scans of the head will often reveal a unilateral, well-circumscribed lesion, with the frontal lobes of the brain being the most common location. Cerebrospinal fluid (CSF) findings are varied. The opening pressure may be raised, the protein concentration may be increased, the glucose concentration may be reduced, and pleocytosis may be present. It is most unusual to recover the fungus from the CSF. The diagnosis is seldom established until neurologic resection is performed.

Cutaneous infection

Alternaria spp. have been seen in and isolated from crusted, ulcerated or scaling skin lesions. Many of these infections have followed traumatic implantation and a substantial proportion have occurred in leukemic patients or transplant recipients. The arms and legs are the more common sites of infection.

Other forms of phaeohyphomycosis

Dematiaceous molds have caused endocarditis after valve insertion or replacement, and peritonitis in patients on continuous peritoneal dialysis.[40] Post-traumatic osteomyelitis and arthritis have also been reported. Fungemia due to black fungi is unusual.[40] Fever without a clear source of infection is the most frequent presentation. In a series of 23 cases occurring in a tertiary hospital, fever was the most frequent clinical manifestation, and only one patient developed signs of deep-seated infection, with a clinical picture of necrotizing pneumonia similar to that caused by *Aspergillus* spp.[40]

The lesions of subcutaneous phaeohyphomycosis can be confused with the small initial lesions of chromoblastomycosis, sporotrichosis, blastomycosis, coccidioidomycosis and paracoccidioidomycosis, as well as with cutaneous leishmaniasis. Lymphangitic spread of sporotrichosis and the development of verrucous lesions in the other conditions makes the distinction easier.

In people who are not immunosuppressed, the clinical presentation of phaeohyphomycosis of the paranasal sinuses cannot be distinguished from that of *Aspergillus* infection. In immunosuppressed patients, *Aspergillus* sinusitis is a fulminant and often lethal condition, unlike pheohyphomycotic sinusitis. However, both groups of organisms can cause black necrotic lesions of the nasal septum.

Bacterial brain abscess is the most common initial diagnosis in patients with cerebral phaeohyphomycosis. In occasional patients, the diagnosis of cryptococcosis, histoplasmosis, coccidioidomycosis or sporotrichosis must be excluded.

Rhinosporidiosis

Rhinosporidium seeberi causes the production of large polyps or wart-like lesions that occur predominantly on the mucous membranes. The nasal mucosa is affected in more than 70% of cases. The onset of the disease in the nose is insidious and the patient remains unaware of its presence until symptoms of obstruction develop. In some cases, the patient complains of itching and unilateral coryza. Rhinoscopic examination will reveal papular or nodular smooth-surfaced lesions that gradually become pedunculated and acquire a papillomatous or proliferative appearance. They are pink, red, or violet in color. The polyps may obstruct the nasal passages, particularly in the event of even slight trauma. If located low in the nostril, they may protrude and hang onto the upper lips. If they are sited in the posterior part of the fossa, they may partially obstruct the pharynx or larynx and cause dysphagia or dysphonia and dyspnea.

In some cases the eyes are affected, the lesions being located on the conjunctiva. Initially these are small, flat granulations that may grow to form multilobed polyps of a pale pink color. At the same time there is diffuse vascular dilatation, photophobia and lacrimation, which is often due to involvement of the lacrimal sac and duct.

The ears may also become involved; depending on their size and location, these polyps may impair hearing.

Lesions may also develop on the male genital organs (the penis and, in exceptional cases, the urethra) and on the vulva and vagina in women. They may resemble flat or acuminate condylomas; lesions in the anus present as polyps and may sometimes be mistaken for hemorrhoids.

Cutaneous rhinosporidiosis, which is very rare, is generally due to spread from a neighboring mucosal lesion. It presents initially as minute papillomas; these gradually become larger and pedunculated. The surface is irregular, verrucous and polypous.

Cutaneous lesions are usually asymptomatic, but depending on their location (especially if they are on the sole of the foot) or their size they may cause pain. The surface of ulcerated rhinosporidiosis lesions is dotted with white spots, which are more readily discerned when depressed with a glass spatula; on microscopy these are seen to be sporangia.

Dissemination to the internal organs or bones is rare. In most cases the general health of the patient is unimpaired.

The appearance of pedunculated or unpedunculated polyps or nodules covered with white dots on the nasal mucosa or the conjunctiva should suggest the diagnosis of rhinosporidiosis. The condition must be distinguished from cryptococcosis, cutaneous tuberculosis, leprous lesions, leishmaniasis and treponematoses.

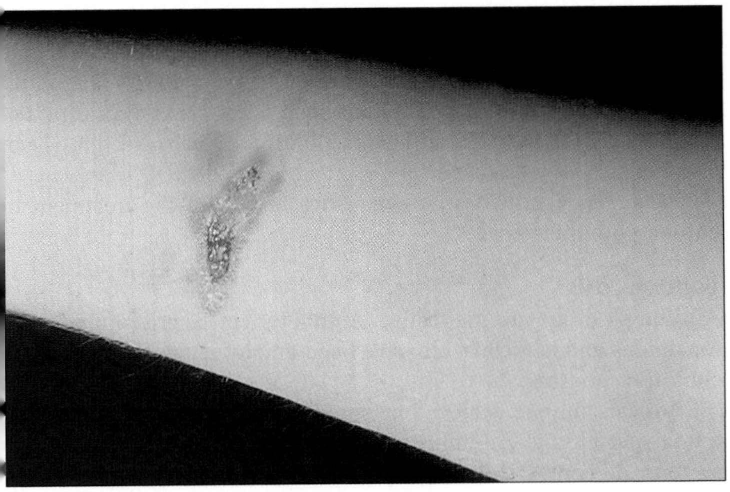

Fig. 239.11 Localized lesion in sporotrichosis. The most common clinical presentation is a localized cutaneous or subcutaneous lesion, which develops at the site of implantation of the etiologic agent, *Sporothrix schenckii.*

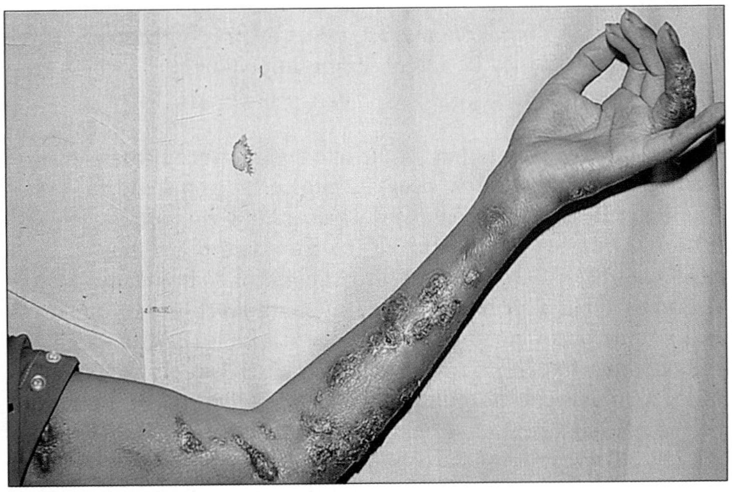

Fig. 239.12 Lymphagitic spread of sporotrichosis. The spread is from a primary digital lesion up the dorsal surface of the forearm.

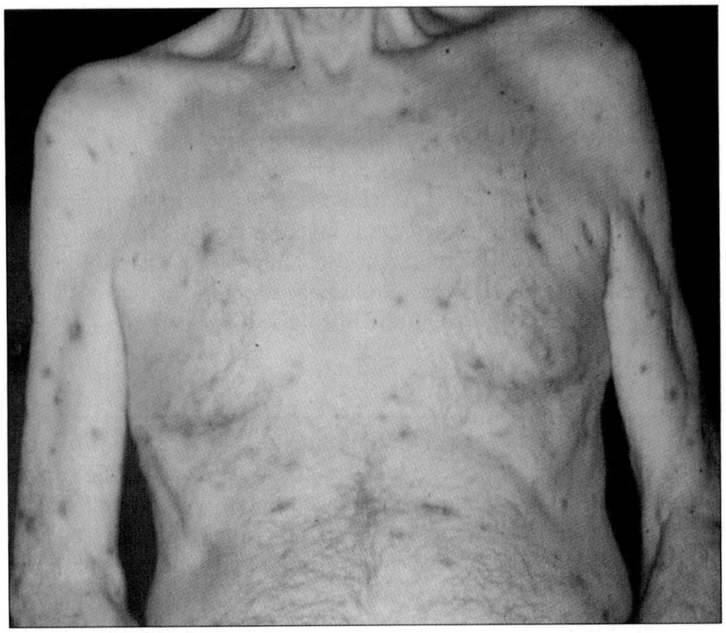

Fig. 239.13 Multiple lesions in sporotrichosis. These skin lesions are a result of hematogenous spread.

Sporotrichosis

The clinical manifestations of sporotrichosis are rather variable, which helps to explain the large number of different classification schemes that have been proposed.[14,16] The most common clinical presentation is a localized cutaneous or subcutaneous lesion (Fig. 239.11). Lymphatic spread may then lead to the development of further cutaneous lesions (Fig. 239.12). Much less commonly, the fungus may cause infection of the lungs, joints, bones, eyes and meninges. Widespread disseminated infection has been reported in patients with diabetes, alcoholics, drug abusers and patients with AIDS (Fig. 239.13).

Cutaneous sporotrichosis

Cutaneous sporotrichosis tends to affect exposed sites, mainly the limbs and especially the hands and fingers. The right hand is affected more frequently than the left. The initial lesion develops at the site of implantation of the fungus. It is a painless nodule that is movable at first but that later becomes attached to the neighboring tissue. The skin turns red then violaceous, and the nodule breaks down to form an ulcer, which discharges a serous or purulent fluid. The edge of the ulcer is often irregular and it may become edematous, vegetative and crusted.

After a period of a few days to several weeks, the primary lesion may become surrounded by satellite lesions, or further nodules along the course of the draining lymphatics may develop. These soon become palpable and ulcerate through to the skin. In most cases, however, the lymphangitis heals or remains static for a long time without ulcers forming. In most cases the regional lymph nodes are not involved. However, this is not an invariable rule. Any involvement of these lymph nodes is evidence of a superimposed bacterial infection and they may ulcerate in turn.

Apart from these very typical lesions, sporotrichosis may present a different clinical picture. Extension over large areas of skin, often described as the disseminated cutaneous form, may occur. Flat, infiltrated or papulopustular or nodulopustular lesions may develop. Whether oozing, proliferative, papillomatous or verrucous, the lesions of sporotrichosis are generally painless but often pruritic. Several ulcers may be interconnected by subcutaneous fistular passages. Confluent lesions may form a purulent and warty plaque with a continually expanding margin, whereas the center becomes atrophied, smooth and shiny.

Primary cutaneous lesions may heal spontaneously, leaving behind unsightly and even disfiguring scars, which may be a functional impediment. However, secondary lesions may persist for several years.

Extracutaneous sporotrichosis

Pulmonary sporotrichosis is a rare but well-recognized condition. It may be primary, following the inhalation of spores, and may be accompanied by enlargement of the hilar or tracheobronchial lymph nodes. It may, however, also be of a secondary character, caused by hematogenous dissemination. The symptoms are non-specific and include a productive cough, fever and weight loss. Hemoptysis may occur and can be massive and fatal. The course may be chronic. The typical radiologic finding is a single, nodular upper lobe lesion, which may or may not cavitate. The natural course of the lung lesion is gradual progression to death.

Most patients with osteoarticular sporotrichosis also have preceding cutaneous lesions. This condition presents as stiffness and pain in a large joint. The onset is indolent. In almost all cases of arthritis, the knee, elbow, ankle or wrist is involved. Osteomyelitis seldom occurs without arthritis; the lesions are usually confined to the long bones nearby affected joints.

Endophthalmitis, although very rare, may result in blindness; chorioretinitis has also been reported. Cases of meningitis have also been seen.

The development of a cutaneous lesion on the limbs following trauma is suggestive of sporotrichosis, particularly if the patient is resident in an endemic region. The development of multiple ulcers along lymphatics is also suspicious. At a later stage of development sporotrichosis must be distinguished from mycoses such as blastomycosis, chromoblastomycosis and paracoccidioidomycosis, and from leishmaniasis, verrucous tuberculosis and tertiary syphilis. The diagnosis ultimately depends on mycologic and histologic examination.

MANAGEMENT

There are no trials comparing different strategies for the treatment of infection caused by black fungi. Treatment depends on the clinical form of the disease and is reviewed by Silveira and Nucci.[1] Cutaneous and subcutaneous phaeohyphomycosis are usually treated with complete surgical excision of the lesion, resulting in complete cure in the majority of cases. In addition, various antifungal agents have been used. Itraconazole is considered the drug of choice, and the dose has ranged from 200 to 600mg daily. The duration of treatment is not established. Although unusual, progression or recurrence of disease, even with adequate itraconazole serum levels, has been observed Whenever possible, surgical resection is also recommended for lesions in other organs, in association with an antifungal agent.

A number of reviews expanding many of the guidelines given here have been published.[1,44,45]

Chromoblastomycosis

Chromoblastomycosis is a difficult condition to treat.[46] Surgical excision should be reserved for small lesions;[47] it carries a high risk of local dissemination and should only be attempted in conjunction with antifungal treatment.

There is no ideal antifungal treatment for chromoblastomycosis. The most commonly used drug is flucytosine (150–200mg/kg per day given as four divided doses), but resistance is a frequent problem during long-term treatment. Amphotericin B is not effective as monotherapy but appears to be effective in combination with 5-fluorocytosine (5FC). Ketoconazole is effective in combination with 5FC. Fluconazole is reported to be successful.[48–50]

Much better results have been obtained when 5FC (4g/day given as four divided doses) is combined with oral thiabendazole (1g/day given as two divided doses). Treatment should be continued for at least 1 month after clinical cure is obtained. Itraconazole (400mg/day) has given promising results in a few patients. Itraconazole is particularly effective when combined with liquid nitrogen cryotherapy.[51,52] Recent trials have shown terbinafine (50mg/day) to be effective, even in chronic cases.[17] The local application of heat to the lesions may be beneficial.

Entomophthoramycosis

Rhinofacial conidiobolomycosis

Treatment has so far been disappointing. Surgical resection of infected tissue is seldom successful and it may hasten the spread of infection. The condition can be treated with saturated potassium iodide solution (up to 10ml q8h as tolerated) or amphotericin B. Long-term results are poor.

Patients with rhinofacial conidiobolomycosis treated with fluconazole (200mg/day for 4 months) have been completely cured or have exhibited considerable improvement. Some patients have responded to combination treatment with amphotericin B and terbinafine,[53] or a combination of itraconazole and fluconazole.[54]

Basidiobolomycosis

The therapy of choice still appears to be saturated potassium iodide solution (30mg/kg per day) which should be given for 6–12 months. Oral ketoconazole (400mg/day) has sometimes been successful, but amphotericin B has seldom been helpful. Surgical resection is not curative.

Ribes *et al.*[12] provides an exhaustive review of the treatment of entomophthoramycosis.

Lobomycosis

Antifungal drugs are ineffective. Amphotericin B, griseofulvin, sulfonamides and ketoconazole have been employed without adequate clinical responses.

Cure can only be achieved by surgical excision, the extent of the lesions permitting. Care must be taken during surgery of lobomycosis to avoid contaminating healthy tissue. Cryosurgery has also been used. Unfortunately, however, recurrence after excision is common. In advanced cases, the extensive excision required to remove the lesion may not be justified if the infection is not life-threatening. In cases involving larger areas of infection, treatment with clofazimine is recommended. At present, the disease does not have a satisfactory medical treatment. The course of the disease is slow and chronic and the prognosis is poor. Lobomycosis never heals spontaneously and is never fatal, but it may be a very serious impediment.

Mycetoma

Early actinomycetomas (and some late and advanced cases) respond well to treatment.[47] The drug of choice is streptomycin sulfate (1000mg/day intramuscularly). This should be combined with trimethoprim–sulfamethoxazole (co-trimoxazole) 960mg q12h in cases caused by *S. somaliensis*, *A. pelletieri* or *N. brasiliensis*. Other regimens include trimethoprim–sulfamethoxazole and amikacin, and streptomycin combined with either dapsone or trimethoprim–sulfamethoxazole. If no response is seen after 3 weeks of treatment, other regimens can be substituted. These include streptomycin and rifampin (rifampicin), or streptomycin and sulfadoxine plus pyrimethamine. Therapy must be continued for months or even years. In favorable cases, edema and tenderness regress, discharge of secretion and grains diminishes, and sinuses dry up and close.

Even after symptoms and clinical signs have disappeared, the disease has become clinically silent and laboratory tests have become normal, it is recommended that treatment be continued for the same period of time as was required to achieve these results.

The response of eumycetoma to antifungal treatment is disappointing. *Madurella mycetomatis* and *P. boydii* infections have been known to respond to ketoconazole (400mg/day), but it is essential to test liver function before starting and during treatment with this drug. Long-term treatment with itraconazole has resulted in improvement in *M. grisea* mycetoma. The fungal agents causing mycetoma are resistant to amphotericin B and 5FC. Terbinafine has been successful in the treatment of maduromycetoma.

Mycetoma due to *Acremonium* spp. and *P. boydii* appear to respond to fluconazole (200mg daily for 10–12 weeks).

Surgical excision is the method of choice if the eumycotic lesions are small enough for total removal to be possible. Amputation is often required in advanced cases with bone involvement, particularly when there is no response to drug treatment. Prostheses and rehabilitation are indispensable in every case of mutilating surgery.

Phaeohyphomycosis

Subcutaneous phaeohyphomycosis

Incision and drainage of subcutaneous lesions is seldom successful. Surgical resection is required. Treatment with amphotericin B has cured or improved unresectable lesions, but later relapse has been common. Itraconazole and terbinafine have been successful in the treatment of phaeohyphomycosis.

Paranasal sinus infection

Complete surgical debridement combined with amphotericin B treatment is essential to halt the progression of this form of phaeohyphomycosis. Even so, it is not uncommon for the condition to recur. The need for repeated debridement is most evident in patients with disabling symptoms or erosion of the bone separating the paranasal sinus from the brain.

Oral treatment with itraconazole (100–400mg/day) appears promising, although the optimum dosage and duration of treatment has not been defined.

Necrotic nasal septum lesions due to *Alternaria* spp. or *Curvularia* spp. have been cured after surgical excision.

Cerebral phaeohyphomycosis

In no case has a patient survived without surgical resection of the lesion. Treatment with amphotericin B on its own is ineffective. Lesions that have not been completely removed have usually proved fatal. A single case of cerebral phaeohyphomycosis due to *Cladosporium* spp. responded partially to fluconazole (300mg daily for 5 weeks).

Cutaneous infection

Surgical debridement of cutaneous lesions combined with parenteral amphotericin B is the most effective method of treatment. Topical antifungal treatment is seldom helpful.

Other forms of phaeohyphomycosis

Too few patients have been treated for firm recommendations to be possible. However, the response to amphotericin B has been partial at best. Surgical resection of lesions or oral treatment with itraconazole should be considered.

In in-vitro tests the new azole antifungals, including voriconazole, appear to be as active as itraconazole against a number of agents of phaeohyphomycosis.

Rhinosporidiosis

The treatment of choice is surgical excision. No drug treatment has proved effective. If left untreated, the polyps will continue to enlarge slowly. In very rare cases, widely disseminated or deep-seated visceral lesions may develop. Spontaneous remission is unusual.

Sporotrichosis

Saturated potassium iodide solution remains the treatment of choice for patients in developing countries who contract cutaneous sporotrichosis, owing to its ease of administration and low cost.[55,56] The starting dose is 1ml q8h, and this is increased to 4–6ml q8h. Treatment should be continued for at least 1 month after clinical cure is obtained, which may take 2–4 months. Intolerance (iodism) is frequent and consequently therapy is often stopped.

If the patient cannot tolerate potassium iodide, oral itraconazole (100–200mg/day) can be used.[57,58] Treatment should be continued for up to 6 months. The most appropriate therapeutic regimen appears to be 200mg/day during the entire treatment period, or 200mg/day at the beginning of treatment, reduced to 100mg/day after improvement. Many cases treated in this way are cured relatively quickly. Cutaneous sporotrichosis has also been successfully treated with terbinafine (125mg/day).[59] Oral ketoconazole has given poor results.

Local heat, on its own or in combination with drug treatment, has been shown to improve cutaneous lesions. Besides thermotherapy, the simple warming of diseased limbs in winter months has proved helpful.

Amphotericin B has cured some patients with extracutaneous forms of sporotrichosis, but failures are common. In cases of arthritis or osteomyelitis, better results have been obtained when the drug has been combined with surgical debridement.

Itraconazole (400mg/day) has given good results in patients with extracutaneous infection, especially in those who have not responded to fluconazole.[60] The Mycoses Study Group of the Infectious Diseases Society of America has recently reviewed the treatment options for sporotrichosis and published detailed practice guidelines.[61] Their recommendations were derived primarily from multicenter, nonrandomized treatment trials, small retrospective series and case reports. The treatment of choice for fixed cutaneous or lymphocutaneous sporotrichosis is itraconazole 100–200mg/day for 3–6 months.

REFERENCES

1. Silveira F, Nucci M. Emergence of black moulds in fungal disease: epidemiology and therapy. Curr Opin Infect Dis 2001;14:679–84.
2. Elewski BE, ed. Cutaneous fungal infections. New York: Igaku-Shoin; 1992.
3. Hay R, ed. Bailliere's clinical tropical medicine and communicable diseases, vol. 4, no. 1: Tropical fungal infections. London: Balliere Tindall; 1989.
4. Kwon-Chung KJ, Bennett JE. Medical mycology. Philadelphia: Lea and Febiger; 1992.
5. Restrepo A. Treatment of tropical mycoses. J Am Acad Dermatol 1994;31(Suppl.3):91–102
6. Rhandhawa HS, Budimulja U, Bazazmalik G, *et al.* Recent developments in the diagnosis and treatment of subcutaneous mycoses. J Med Vet Mycol 1994;32(Suppl.S1):299–307.
7. Richardson MD, Warnock DW, eds. Fungal infection: diagnosis and management, 3rd edition. Oxford: Blackwell Science; 2003.
8. Rios-Fabra A, Restrepo Moreno A, Isturiz RE. Fungal infection in Latin American countries. Infect Dis Clin N Am 1994;8:129–54.
9. Elgart GW. Chromoblastomycosis. Dermatol Clin 1996;14:77.
10. Rivitti E, Aoki V. Deep fungal infections in tropical countries. Clin Dermatol 1999;17:171–90.
11. Anaissie EJ, McGinnis MR, Pfaller MA, eds. Clinical mycology. New York: Churchill Livingstone; 2002.
12. Ribes JA, Vanover-Sams CL, Baker DJ. Zygomycetes in human disease. Clin Microbiol Rev 2000;13:236–301.
13. Davis BA. Sporotrichosis. Dermatol Clin 1996;14:69.
14. Bustamante B, Campos PE. Endemic sporotrichosis. Curr Opin Infect Dis 2001;14:145–9.
15. De Araujo T, Marques AC, Kerdel F. Sporotrichosis. Int J Dermatol 2001;40:737–42.
16. Morris-Jones R. Sporotrichosis. Clin Exp Dermatol 2002;27:427–31.
17. Esterre P, Inzan CK, Ramarcel ER, *et al.* Treatment of chromomycosis with terbinafine – preliminary results of an open pilot-study. Br J Dermatol 1996;134:33–6.
18. Bonifaz A, Carrasco-Gerard E, Saul A. Chromoblastomycosis: clinical and mycologic experience of 51 cases. Mycoses 2001;44:1–7.
19. Minotto R, Bernardi CD, Mallmann LF, *et al.* Chromoblastomycosis: review of 100 cases in the state of Rio Grande do Sul, Brazil. J Am Acad Dermatol 2001;44:585–92.
20. Silva JP, de Souza W, Rozental S. Chromoblastomycosis: a retrospective study of 325 cases on Amazonic region. Mycopathologia 1998–1999;143:171–5.
21. Gugnani HC. A review of zygomycosis due to *Basidiobolus ranarum.* Eur J Epidemiol 1999;15:923–9.
22. Burns RA, Roy JS, Woods C, *et al.* Report of the first human case of lobomycosis in the United States. J Clin Microbiol 2000;38:1283–5.
23. Maiti PK, Ray A, Bandyopadhyay S. Epidemiological aspects of mycetoma from a retrospective series of cases in West Bengal. Trop Med Int Health 2002;7:788–92.
24. Rees JR, Pinner RW, Hajjeh RA, *et al.* The epidemiological features of invasive mycotic infections in the San Francisco Bay area, 1992–1993: results of a population-based laboratory active surveillance. Clin Infect Dis 1998;27:1138–47.
25. O'Quinn RP, Hoffman JL, Boyd AS. *Colletotrichum* species as emerging opportunistic fungal pathogens: report of three cases of

phaeohyphomycosis and review. J Am Acad Dermatol 2001;45:56–61.
26. Mohan H, Chander J, Dhir R, *et al.* Rhinosporidiosis in India – a case report and review of literature. Mycoses 1995;38:223–5.
27. Carr MM, Fielding JC, Sibbald G, *et al.* Sporotrichosis of the hand – an urban experience. J Hand Surg [Am] 1995;20A:66–70.
28. Costa EO, Diniz LSM, Netto CF, *et al.* Epidemiologic study of sporotrichosis and histoplasmosis in captive Latin-American wild mammals, São Paulo, Brazil. Mycopathologia 1994;125:19–22.
29. Romero H, Guedez E, Magaldi S. Evaluation of immunoprecipitation techniques in chromoblastomycosis. J Mycol Med 1996;6:83–7.
30. Rodriguez G, Barrera GP. The asteroid body of lobomycosis. Mycopathologia 1996;136:71–4.
31. Taborda PR, Taborda VA, McGinnis MR. *Lacazia loboi* gen. Nov., comb. Nov., the etiologic agent of lobomycosis. J Clin Microbiol 1999;37:2031–3.
32. Haubold EM, Aronson JF, Cowan DF, McGinnis MR, Cooper CR Jr. Isolation of fungal rDNA from bottlenose dolphin skin infected with *Loboa loboi.* Med Mycol 2000;38:9–14.
33. Hag IAEL, Fahal AH, Gasim ELTA. Fine-needle aspiration cytology of mycetoma. Acta Cytologica 1996;40:461–4.
34. Ahmed AO, Mukhtar MM, Kools-Sijmons M, *et al.* Developemnt of a species-specific PCR-restriction fragment length polymorphism analysis procedure for identification of *Madurella mycetomatis.* J Clin Microbiol 1999;37:3175–8.
35. Gori S, Scasso A. Cytologic and differential diagnosis of rhinosporidiosis. Acta Cytol 1994;38:361–6.
36. Azadeh B, Baghoumian N, Elbakri OT. Rhinosporidiosis – immunohistochemical and electron microscopy studies. J Laryngol Otol 1994;108:1048–54.
37. Kamal MM, Luley AS, Mundhada SG, *et al.* Rhinosporidiosis – diagnosis by scrape cytology. Acta Cytol 1995;39:931–5.
38. Fredricks DN, Jolley JA, Lepp PW, *et al.* *Rhinosporidium seeberi*: a human pathogen from a novel group of aquatic protistan parasites. Emerging Infect Dis 2000;6:273–82.
39. Herr RA, Mendoza L, Arseculeratne SN, *et al.* Immunolocalization of an endogenous antigenic material of *Rhinosporidium seeberi* expressed only during mature sporangial development. FEMS Immunol Med Microbiol 1999;23:205–12.
40. Lyon GM, Smilack JD, Komatsu KK, *et al.* Gastrointestinal basidiobolomycosis in Arizona: clinical and epidemiological characteristics and review of the literature. Clin Infect Dis 2001;32:1448–55.
41. Revankar SG, Patterson JE, Sutton DA, *et al.* Disseminated phaeohyphomycosis: review of an emerging mycosis. Clin Infect Dis 2002;34:467–76.
42. Clancy CJ, Wingard JR, Hong Nguyen M. Subcutaneous phaeohyphomycosis in transplant recipients: review of the literature and demonstration of in vitro synergy between antifungal agents. Med Mycol 2000;38:169–75.
43. Xu X, Low DW, Palevsky HI, *et al.* Subcutaneous phaeohyphomycotic cysts caused by *Exophiala jeanselmei* in a lung transplant patient. Dermatol Surg 2001;27:343–6.
44. Hossain MA, Ghannoum MA. New developments in chemotherapy for non-invasive fungal infections. Expert Opin Investig Drugs 2001;10:1501–11.
45. De Hoog GS, Queiroz-Telles F, Haase G, *et al.* Black fungi: clinical and pathogenic approaches. Med Mycol 2000;38(Suppl.1):243–50.
46. Gross ML, Millikan LE. Deep fungal infections in the tropics. Dermatol Clin 1994;12:695.
47. Gold WL, Vellend H, Salit IE, *et al.* Successful treatment of systemic and local infections due to *Exophiala* species. Clin Infect Dis 1994;19:339–41.
48. Iwasawa U, Nishiyama C, Iida T, *et al.* Successful treatment of chromoblastomycosis with oral fluconazole. Eur J Dermatol 1994;4:374–5.
49. Yu RY, Gao L. Chromoblastomycosis successfully treated with fluconazole. Int J Dermatol 1994;33:716–9.
50. Wu SX, Guo NG, Liao WQ, *et al.* Multicenter noncomparative study of fluconazole in the treatment of systemic fungal infections. J Dermatol Treat 1995;6:171–2.
51. Kullavanijaya P, Rojanavanich V. Successful treatment of chromoblastomycosis due to *Fonsecaea pedrosoi* by the combination of itraconazole and cryotherapy. Int J Dermatol 1995;34:804–7.
52. Bonifaz A, Martinez-Soto E, Carrasco-Gerard E, *et al.* Treatment of chromoblastomycosis with itraconazole, cryosurgery, and a combination of both. Int J Dermatol 1997;36:542–7.
53. Foss NT, Rocha MRO, Lima VTA, *et al.* Entomophthoromycosis – therapeutic success by using amphotericin B and terbinafine. Dermatologica 1996;193:258–60.
54. Valle AC, Wanke B, Lazera MS, *et al.* Entomophthoramycosis by *Conidiobolus coronatus.* Report of a case successfully treated with the combination of itraconazole and fluconazole. Rev Inst Med Trop Sao Paulo 2001;43:233–6.
55. Kauffman CA. Old and new therapies for sporotrichosis. Clin Infect Dis 1995;21:981–5.
56. Cabezas C, Bustamante B, Holgado W, *et al.* Treatment of cutaneous sporotrichosis with one daily dose of potassium iodide. Pediatr Infect Dis J 1996;15:352–4.
57. Kauffman CA. Newer developments in therapy for endemic mycoses. Clin Infect Dis 1994;19(Suppl.S1):28–32.
58. Bolao F, Podzamczer D, Ventin M, *et al.* Efficacy of acute-phase and maintenance therapy with itraconazole in AIDS patients with sporotrichosis. Eur J Clin Microbiol Infect Dis 1994;13:609–12.
59. Kudoh K, Kamei E, Terunuma A, *et al.* Successful treatment of cutaneous sporotrichosis with terbinafine. J Dermatol Treat 1996;7:33–5.
60. Kauffman CA, Pappas PG, McKinsey DS, *et al.* Treatment of lymphocutaneous and visceral sporotrichosis with fluconazole. Clin Infect Dis 1996;22:46–50.
61. Kauffman CA, Hajjeh R, Chapman SW. Practice guidelines for the management of patients with sporotrichosis. For Mycoses Study Group, Infectious Diseases Society of America. Clin Infect Dis 2000;30:684–7.

chapter

240 Superficial Fungal Pathogens

Richard C Summerbell & Aditya K Gupta

The majority of superficial fungal infections are caused by three groups of fungi: dermatophytes, *Candida albicans* and *Malassezia* spp.[1] Dermatophytes, the agents of dermatophytosis (ringworm, athlete's foot) are members of the phylum Ascomycota. Within that phylum, they are related to the order Onygenales, along with systemic pathogens such as *Histoplasma* and *Coccidioides*. In conventional biologic classification they are related to the genus *Arthroderma*; in the unique dual nomenclature of fungal anamorphs (asexual states), they are members of the genera *Trichophyton*, *Microsporum* and *Epidermophyton* (Fig. 240.1).

NATURE

Candida albicans, the principal agent of candidiasis, is an anamorphic (asexual) yeast also related to the Ascomycota. It and some related *Candida* spp. are mammalian commensals (normally harmless colonizers) related to the class Endomycetes, which also contains the bread yeast *Saccharomyces*.

Malassezia spp. are yeast anamorphs related to the phylum Basidiomycota, but not closely related to other human pathogens in this phylum such as *Cryptococcus* and *Trichosporon* spp. They are lipophilic (lipid-requiring) body surface commensals and agents of the skin disease tinea versicolor (pityriasis versicolor). In addition, they may be causal in the allergically mediated condition seborrheic dermatitis.

Other fungi cause less common types of superficial disease. Yeasts in the genus *Trichosporon* may cause white piedra, superficial colonizations of the scalp, and axillary and pubic hair shafts. The melanized yeast-like organism *Hortaea werneckii* (also known by several older names all ending in '*werneckii*') causes the dark skin lesions of tinea nigra. The rare hair shaft colonization black piedra is caused by the ascomycete *Piedraia hortae*. Finally, approximately 35 nondermatophytic filamentous fungi and a few yeasts have been authenticated as causing onychomycosis (i.e. fungal nail disease). Most prominent among these are members of the genera *Scytalidium*, *Aspergillus*, *Scopulariopsis*, *Fusarium* and *Onychocola*.

EPIDEMIOLOGY

Dermatophytosis is among the most common of all communicable diseases. Because many cases are never brought to medical attention, fully reliable incidence figures do not exist. Onychomycosis, in which the great majority of cases are dermatophytic,[2] may account for 10–30% of all superficial mycoses.[3,4] In the USA Medicare insurance for seniors (≥65 years old) in 1 year paid for consultations involving 662,000 patients, or 2.7% of the senior population, at a cost of over US$43,000,000. Less than 10% of those aged under 30 years and more than 20% of those aged over 75 years had tinea unguium (dermatophytic onychomycosis; Table 240.1) in population studies.[5] Tinea capitis in children is common in some areas. In an urban center in the USA up to 4% of children presenting with nondermatologic complaints at a clinic were infected by *Trichophyton tonsurans*, whereas up to 30% of asymptomatic adults accompanying infected children were carriers.[6] A study of 224 children in a Philadelphia school reported 3% symptomatic and 14% asymptomatic, infected children.[7] Tinea pedis has been found to affect 1.5% of pediatric patients, 5.9% of 11–15 year olds[6] and up to 45% of adult marathon runners.[8] There is a significant age-dependent association between sporting activities and pedal dermatophytosis.[9] Many of the most prevalent dermatophytes are cosmopolitan, but certain species, especially agents of tinea capitis, have defined endemic regions (see Table 240.1).

Cutaneous candidiasis is particularly common in infants, at least 10% of whom have candidal skin colonizations. Fifty per cent of this colonized group go on to become symptomatic, usually with candidal diaper dermatitis.[6] Many adults harbor an indigenous strain of *C. albicans*; up to 30% of healthy women, for example, are culture positive for this species in vaginal swab samples, at least when pregnant or taking oral contraceptives.[1] The lower gut may serve as a reservoir when other body sites are free of *C. albicans*. Normal skin only rarely yields *C. albicans* but the yeast may rapidly colonize chronically moist or damaged skin, including moist dermatophyte lesions.

Malassezia spp. have been found as skin commensals in over 90% of humans surveyed.[1] In the temperate zone they only occasionally proliferate to the point of causing the finely scaly maculae of tinea versicolor, but in the tropics the prevalence may reach 50% of the population.[1] *Malassezia* spp. in patients who have HIV and other immunocompromised patients may cause pustular hair follicle inflammations referred to as *Malassezia* folliculitis, and may be associated with an increased prevalence of seborrheic dermatitis.[10] In atopic individuals, *Malassezia* spp. growing commensally on skin may serve as a triggering allergen in atopic dermatitis.[11] A possible association between *Malassezia* and neonatal acne or cephalic pustulosis is under investigation.

White piedra is found worldwide, but is now uncommon because of modern hygiene. Black piedra is native to South East Asia, the Pacific and South America, and affects other primates in addition to humans. It is uncommon when discouraged but is cultivated in some cultures.[1] Tinea nigra is of tropical or subtropical origin; about 150 indigenous US cases were reported between 1950 and 1988, in addition to many more cases acquired by travelers, mostly in the Caribbean.[1] *Scytalidium* infections of nails, soles or palms are usually acquired in the tropics. *Scytalidium dimidiatum*, the most common infectious species, has rapidly growing pantropical forms as well as a distinctive slow-growing Indian subcontinent form that may be transmitted among family members in the Indian Diaspora. Most other agents of nondermatophytic onychomycosis are cosmopolitan saprobic molds and, despite their opportunistic potential, are more frequently seen as insignificant contaminants of body surfaces than as etiologic agents.[12]

PATHOGENICITY

Dermatophytes normally infect only the keratinized stratum corneum of the epithelial skin layers. They degrade keratin and other skin

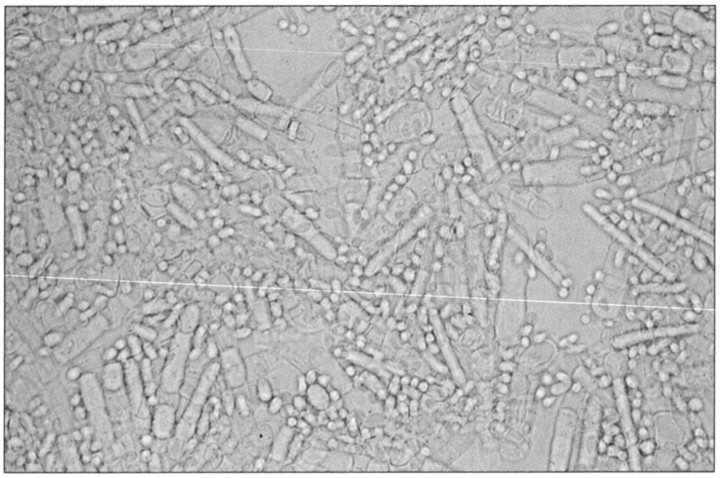

Fig. 240.1 *Trichophyton rubrum* (heavily conidial Afro-Asiatic variant). Typical micromorphology of a dermatophyte in pure culture, showing micro- and macroaleurioconidia.

proteins.[13] They are restricted to the stratum corneum by cellular immune components, and by the iron limitation and other effects mediated by transferrin.[14] A 2-fold higher prevalence in males than females may reflect inhibition by progesterone. Development of one type of dermatophytosis, tinea imbricata, requires homozygosity for an otherwise uncharacterized recessive allele;[1] involvement of an autosomal dominant susceptibility allele has been proposed in the common chronic form of *Trichophyton rubrum* infection.[15] An indication of the relative importance of lymphocytes in host defense is seen in HIV infection, in which helper T-cell counts below 100 cells/ml correlate with a marked increase in onychomycosis,[16] including the unusual 'proximal white' form. Chronic dermatophytosis in normal patients may be mediated by locally immunosuppressive fungal carbohydrates as well as incapacitation of local cellular immunity by an immediate hypersensitivity response[17] and activation of a Th2 pattern of immune response.[18]

Dermatophytes differ in their host interactions. Anthropophilic dermatophytes (Table 240.2), specific to human disease, are distinguished from zoophilic dermatophytes, which have specific animal associations but may be transmitted to humans, and from geophilic dermatophytes, which are occasionally pathogenic to humans or animals but primarily grow on decaying keratinous material. The *Trichophyton mentagrophytes* complex (Fig. 240.2), containing four sibling-species distinguishable by molecular study, has both anthropophilic and zoophilic variants. Infection of humans by zoophilic dermatophytes usually elicits a pronounced inflammatory response.[14] Such inflamed lesions may resolve spontaneously, unlike the often chronic lesions of anthropophilic dermatophytoses.

The common anthropophilic dermatophytes include lower body dermatophytes associated with sites other than the scalp, and der-

Table 240.1 Definition and distribution of dermatophytoses.

DEFINITION AND DISTRIBUTION OF DERMATOPHYTOSES

Area of infection	Disease name	Prevalent agents	Geographic area
Scalp	Tinea capitis	*Trichophyton tonsurans*	Cosmopolitan, especially urban Americas, Latin America
		Microsporum canis	Cosmopolitan; predominant dermatophyte in parts of south and east Europe
		Trichophyton violaceum	Endemic to Middle East, North Africa
		Trichophyton soudanense	Endemic to sub-Saharan Africa
Beard area	Tinea barbae	*Trichophyton rubrum*, *Trichophyton verrucosum*	Cosmopolitan
Glabrous skin (trunk, limbs, face)	Tinea corporis	*Trichophyton rubrum*, *Trichophyton tonsurans*, *Trichophyton mentagrophytes* complex, *Microsporum canis*, *Epidermophyton floccosum*	Cosmopolitan
		Trichophyton megninii	Endemic to Portugal, Sardinia
Scalp, glabrous skin	Favus	*Trichophyton schoenleinii*	Relict in rural Africa, central Asia; formerly widespread
Palms	Tinea manuum	*Trichophyton rubrum*, *Trichophyton mentagrophytes* complex	Cosmopolitan
Groin	Tinea cruris	*Trichophyton rubrum*, *Trichophyton mentagrophytes* complex, *Epidermophyton floccosum*	Cosmopolitan
Soles, toe webs	Tinea pedis	*Trichophyton rubrum*, *Trichophyton mentagrophytes* complex, *Epidermophyton floccosum*	Cosmopolitan
Nails	Tinea unguium (dermatophytic onychomycosis)	*Trichophyton rubrum*, *Trichophyton mentagrophytes* complex	Cosmopolitan

COMMON AND FORMERLY COMMON DERMATOPHYTES AND THEIR INFECTIVITY		
Anthropophiles (type of scalp infection if characteristic)	**Zoophiles (type of human scalp infection) [principal hosts]**	**Geophiles (type of human scalp infection)**
Epidermophyton floccosum	*Microsporum canis* (ectothrix) [cat, dog]	*Microsporum gypseum* (ectothrix)
Microsporum audouinii (ectothrix)	*Microsporum gallinae* [fowl]	*Microsporum praecox*
Microsporum ferrugineum (ectothrix)	*Microsporum nanum* [swine]	*Microsporum racemosum*
Trichophyton concentricum	*Microsporum persicolor* [vole]	*Microsporum vanbreuseghemii*
Trichophyton megninii (ectothrix)	*Trichophyton equinum* [horse]	The listing of geophiles does not include species that have not been well substantiated to cause human disease. These species are not properly considered dermatophytes according to Ajello[19]
Trichophyton mentagrophytes complex (phylogenetic species *Trichophyton interdigitale*)	*Trichophyton mentagrophytes* complex (phylogenetic species *Trichophyton interdigitale, Trichophyton mentagrophytes, Trichophyton erinacei*) [rodents, rabbits, hedgehogs]	
Trichophyton rubrum	*Trichophyton simii* [monkey]	
Trichophyton schoenleinii (favus)	*Trichophyton verrucosum* [cattle]	
Trichophyton soudanense (endothrix)		
Trichophyton tonsurans (endothrix)		
Trichophyton violaceum (endothrix)		

Table 240.2 Common and formerly common dermatophytes and their infectivity.

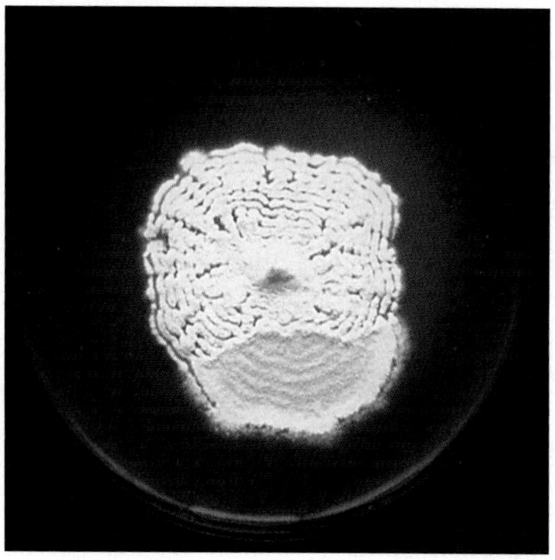

Fig. 240.2 *Trichophyton mentagrophytes* complex: a zoophilic (animal-associated) isolate showing the 'granular' colonial morphology typical of such isolates. The strain depicted has been shown through mating to belong to the phylogenetic species *Trichophyton interdigitale* (sexual state called *Arthroderma vanbreuseghemii*), one of several genetic sibling species now known to make up the *T. mentagrophytes* complex.

matophytes strongly adapted for tinea capitis, less commonly causing other tineas. *Trichophyton rubrum*, *T. mentagrophytes* complex and *Epidermophyton floccosum* are the common lower body species. Tinea capitis dermatophytes consist of two major groups distinguished by their colonization of hair (see Table 240.2). In the 'ectothrix' group, hair shafts are externally ensheathed with masses of arthroconidia (spores). In the 'endothrix' group, the hair shafts are heavily invested internally by arthroconidia. An anomalous scalp infection, favus, caused by the now rare *Trichophyton schoenleinii*, is distinguished by the presence of follicles transformed into scutula, that is, pits lined with fungal mycelium.

Tinea capitis agents primarily cause new infections in children, and may cause dramatic outbreaks. *Microsporum audouinii* infections spontaneously resolve at 15–19 years of age, but most endothrix agents cause lifelong asymptomatic infections in some adult carriers[7] and occasionally cause new tinea corporis or other infections in adults. New anthropophilic tinea capitis infections are usually acquired via shared headgear, bedding or grooming and haircutting instruments. Adults who acquire new infections caused by endothrix species usually have intimate contact with infected children. Anthropophilic lower body dermatophytoses are often acquired via the feet, either from family members or in communal aquatic or exercise facilities. After infecting the feet, these fungi may go on to infect other body sites.

Zoophilic dermatophytes (see Table 240.2) usually cause tinea corporis or tinea capitis in humans. They may be transmitted directly from infected animals or from fomites, such as fence posts in cattle yards. *Microsporum canis* may cause limited outbreaks among humans before virulence is attenuated.[20]

Candida albicans is often acquired in the birth canal or in infancy from care givers. Generally, an individual harbors only one or two strains. Cutaneous candidiasis is predisposed to by warm, moist conditions with abrasion, especially in the diaper rash of infancy but also in adult occupations that involve wet hands. In the latter cases, paronychia or interdigital erosion frequently results. Intertriginous candidiasis occurs in moist body folds and is exacerbated by diabetes mellitus or obesity. Chronic mucocutaneous candidiasis (CMCC), in which skin and mucosa are extensively colonized by *C. albicans*, results from inherited defects in cellular immunity.[21] Particular associated conditions include congenital thymus dysplasias, polyendocrine deficiencies and leukocyte dysfunctions such as chronic granulomatous disease.[1] In this latter disease, the impaired production of toxic oxygen species prevents killing of *Candida* spp. within phagocytes.

Malassezia spp. are also generally acquired as commensal surface flora in early infancy. They primarily use fatty acids secreted by the skin. Corticosteroid use, Cushing's disease, malnutrition and immunosuppression may contribute to an increased frequency of tinea versicolor; HIV infection and miscellaneous immunosuppressions predispose to folliculitis.

Nondermatophytic onychomycosis caused by genera other than *Scytalidium* is strongly predisposed to by advanced age.[22]

PREVENTION

Prevention of infections caused by anthropophilic dermatophytes adapted for tinea capitis can be achieved by a combination of sanitation and detection of asymptomatic carriers. In *Microsporum* spp. outbreaks, a Wood's light can be used to screen potentially infected individuals rapidly; lesions usually fluoresce yellow–green. The same technique can also be used to detect animal carriers when the zoophilic *M. canis* is involved. Subclinical cases are more difficult to detect in nonfluorescent *Trichophyton* outbreaks; conventional microscopy and culture analysis of slightly scaly areas in individuals likely to be infected are required. In all cases in which tinea capitis fungi are involved, infected individuals must be treated promptly and their contacts must be educated not to share materials that contact the scalp. Fomites may endure on surfaces in contaminated rooms for months and belatedly cause new infections unless adequate disinfection is performed. Strategies for dealing with institutional outbreaks have been summarized.[14]

Lower body anthropophilic dermatophytosis, for example *T. mentagrophytes* complex tinea pedis, may be prevented to some extent by minimizing barefoot walking in public showers, swimming pool and hot tub peripheries, gymnasia, barracks and similar localities. However, familial genetic susceptibility and organism carriage may outweigh exposure in public places as a risk factor in the most common lower body dermatophytoses, *T. rubrum* tinea pedis and onychomycosis.[15]

Occupational animal handlers may reduce the risk of zoophilic dermatophytosis by wearing protective gloves.

Prevention of the more severe forms of epidermal candidiasis is linked to prevention of immunodepression and will not be dealt with here. Persons whose occupations involve frequent wetting of hands should wear protective gloves. Good hygiene and prompt change of diapers may aid in preventing candidal diaper rash.

Good hygiene is instrumental in the prevention of white piedra and may also help to prevent tinea versicolor.

DIAGNOSTIC MICROBIOLOGY

Superficial mycotic infections are best tested by the combination of direct microscopy for fungal elements in hydroxide (KOH, NaOH) slides, and fungal culture. Direct microscopy may be facilitated by the use of fluorescent fungal cell wall dyes such as calcofluor or Congo red. Histopathology performed with fungal stains has been suggested as an alternative to 'KOH and culture' for onychomycosis, but the ability of this technique to distinguish dermatophyte from nondermatophyte infections has received only preliminary investigation.

Dermatophytes in direct microscopy show cylindrical fungal filaments that may include chains of rounded arthroconidia. At times filaments may be converted entirely into arthroconidia, such as within or around hair shafts in tinea capitis. In superficial white onychomycosis caused by *T. mentagrophytes* complex members, microscopy may may show 'frondose branching', an appressed, palmate spreading of fungal hyphae between keratin lamellae. In nails, soles and palms, all morphologies of dermatophyte filaments overlap with those of other potentially infectious fungi, especially *Scytalidium* spp.

Generally, dermatophyte filaments from the growing fronts of infection, such as the peripheral 'ring' in classic ringworm and adjacent to the nailbed in tinea unguium, will be alive and will stain with vital stains such as neutral red.[23] Those from prior growth fronts, such as centers of ringworm lesions or extruded, distal nail, tend to be senescent and will not yield a culture. For this reason, sampling tinea at its extending margin, and subungual onychomycosis at the juncture of nail and nailbed, is recommended. Tinea corporis is sampled by using a scalpel to remove skin scale from the advancing lesion margin after light disinfection with an ethanol swab. In subungual onychomycosis, heavily contaminated debris is scraped from the undersurface of the nail and discarded; then, after swabbing with ethanol, friable material is scraped from the nail undersurface as close as possible to the nailbed. Clippings may also be taken. In superficial white onychomycosis, white, opaque areas on the upper nail surface are scraped. As with subungual onychomycosis, superficial debris is scraped and discarded before sample collection. In tinea pedis of the sole and tinea manuum, in which growth fronts may not be apparent, the affected area should be scraped broadly so that the whole is represented in the sample.

Even with expert sampling approximately 10–25% of nail samples positive for fungal filaments in direct microscopy fail to yield a culture.[23] That such a finding accurately reflects the active infection can be cofirmed by vital staining,[20] and should not be mistaken for a technical 'false-negative' culture result. Also, approximately 45–50% of toenails and 60% of fingernails clinically suggestive of onychomycosis fail to yield any evidence of fungal infection.[24] Dermatophyte colonization in very degraded nails may be partially supplanted by secondary invaders such as *Pseudomonas* bacteria and *Scopulariopsis* mold (the latter may also appear as a sole agent of onychomycosis or as a contaminant), and the original etiologic agent may be difficult to trace.

Hair from tinea capitis or barbae is plucked so that the hair root, the best source of inoculum, is included. In 'black dot' tinea capitis, in which hairs are fragile, a few hair roots may be extracted with the tip of a scalpel and included along with surface scrapings of the lesion. *Microsporum* scalp lesions typically show strong yellow–green fluorescence under a Wood's light and can be presumptively diagnosed in this manner. In zoophilic tinea corporis and other lesions with vesicles or bullae, the apices of these may be clipped and included in the sample. Moist, suppurating lesions may be sampled with a swab. Swab samples may make direct microscopy difficult and are best evaluated by culturing.

For culture, scrapings or fragments from clippings are usually planted on Sabouraud agar supplemented with antibacterials and the selective antifungal cycloheximide. Common commercial equivalents include Mycosel, Dermasel and Mycobiotic. Dermatophytes and *C. albicans* are among the small minority of fungi able to grow well on these media. Potato glucose or potato flake agar with cycloheximide is preferred by some laboratories because the distinctive pigmentation of some species is enhanced. A cycloheximide-free medium is generally used for nails, and also recommended for soles and palms because nondermatophytic etiologic agents such as *Scytalidium* and *Fusarium* spp. must also be isolated from at least some of these sites. The most common of such media are plain Sabouraud agar supplemented with antibacterials only, and two restrictive media: Littman oxgall agar and inhibitory mold agar. These media, unlike plain Sabouraud agar, inhibit fast-growing contaminant molds from overgrowing the slower growing etiologic agents.

The characteristics and criteria used in identifying dermatophytes have been summarized.[25–27] Since most dermatophyte species are susceptible to similar therapies (duration of therapy may vary, e.g. between *Microsporum* spp. and the more rapidly inhibited endothrix

Trichophyton spp. in tinea capitis), species identification is salient primarily to recognize situations in which animal hosts or familial or institutional carriers constitute potential sources of re-infection and continuation of outbreaks. Zoophilic dermatophyte species and the endothrix tinea capitis agents are most notorious in these situations, but unusual outbreaks of anthropophilic lower body dermatophytoses may also be detected and controlled through species identification.

Candidiasis in skin and nails is recognized in direct microscopy by the presence of budding yeast cells and candidal-type filaments; the yeast cells bud through a narrow constriction, unlike *Malassezia* yeasts, and the filaments give rise to budding cells on side branches, unlike dermatophyte filaments. Although filaments indicate an invasive condition in cutaneous candidiasis, and are usually found in any genuine case of infection, masses of budding cells alone may be seen in some nail specimens. In fingernails, this often indicates nearby paronychia that was not sampled directly. In some cases, however, especially with toenails, yeast cells merely indicate harmless growth of *Candida* spp. (other than *C. albicans*) of the normal skin flora in crevices in onychomycotic or traumatized nails. *Candida albicans* should normally be identified when isolated from skin; there are a number of inexpensive, specific, rapid tests for this species such as rice-tween, cornmeal-tween or oxgall medium tests for formation of chlamydospores under a cover slip. *Candida* spp. other than *C. albicans* need not be identified to species level from superficial sites except in rare cases in which they are isolated from material with conclusive evidence of invasive yeast infection (e.g. formation of filaments with lateral budding cells) in direct microscopy. Because *C. albicans* commonly contaminates moist dermatophyte lesions without significantly exacerbating symptoms, and because normal flora yeasts may proliferate harmlessly in nail crevices, the laboratory gold standard for any diagnosis of cutaneous yeast infection is the specific presence of yeast-type filamentous elements within cutaneous tissue in direct microscopy.

Tinea versicolor is recognized in direct microscopy by the rounded yeast cells and short hyphal fragments ('spaghetti and meat balls') of *Malassezia* spp. Culture is normally unnecessary and may be problematic when attempted. Although there is considerable research interest in quantitative cultural analysis of *Malassezia* spp. in seborrheic dermatitis, clinical diagnosis based on symptoms remains the gold standard.

Other purely microscopic diagnoses not requiring culture include black and white piedra. Tinea nigra evinces distinctive dark filaments in direct microscopy (Fig. 240.3), but is also readily cultured to yield the etiologic agent, *H. werneckii*. No other organism shows melanized, two-celled yeasts budding from annellidic apertures heavily fringed with collarette remnants. Mycology laboratories must also recognize the microscopically distinctive corynebacterial and actinomycetous elements found in erythrasma, trichomycosis axillaris and pitted keratolysis.[1] All intertriginous skin samples should be stained with methylene blue preparations to detect erythrasma. In specimens from this infection, methylene blue deeply stains delicate branching filaments less than 1μm in diameter, often seen breaking up into smaller bacillary or coccoid forms. The poorly understood '*Dermatophilus*-like' agent of pitted keratolysis[1] also stains in methylene blue, and shows a mixture of coccoid cells and short filaments, at least some of which appear tapered and, in broader regions, subdivide to give rise to a second or third longitudinal series of cells. In trichomycosis axillaris, hair is heavily ensheathed in corynebacterial cells (Gram-positive rod and coccus forms less than 1μm in diameter). These may be readily distinguished in crushed preparation in hydroxide from the over 2μm in diameter arthroconidia and yeast cells seen in the macroscopically similar white piedra.

The correct diagnosis of onychomycosis caused by nondermatophyte molds can be especially challenging. These nondermatophyte filamentous fungi can easily be ascertained as causing onychomycosis if distinctive morphologic elements such as conidiophores are seen in addition to filaments in direct microscopy of nail specimen, or if a fungus from warm latitudes, such as a *Scytalidium*, is isolated in an area in which only such fungi occur in infected patients. Most cases are more ambiguous. A fungal species such as *Aspergillus sydowii* may be isolated either as a contaminant or as an etiologic agent, and filaments seen in direct microscopy may be either nonviable dermatophyte elements or genuine nondermatophyte elements. Therefore, even exclusive and heavy isolation of such a nondermatophyte from a specimen positive for fungal filaments does not guarantee that the nail is infected by the same nondermatophyte.[12] The current gold standard, which may not be easy to attain in practice, is:

- first to demonstrate fungal elements in direct microscopy compatible with the suspected agent; and
- second, in culture, to show, through correlating the results of two nail samples collected at least 1 week apart, that the nondermatophyte in question consistently grows from the diseased nail.

True mixed infection by a dermatophyte and a nondermatophyte may occur, but again can only be demonstrated scientifically by showing a consistent presence of the latter in more than one serial sample.

CLINICAL MANIFESTATIONS

Tinea capitis

The organisms that cause the 'noninflammatory type' of tinea capitis (Fig. 240.4) include *T. tonsurans, M. canis, M. audouinii* and

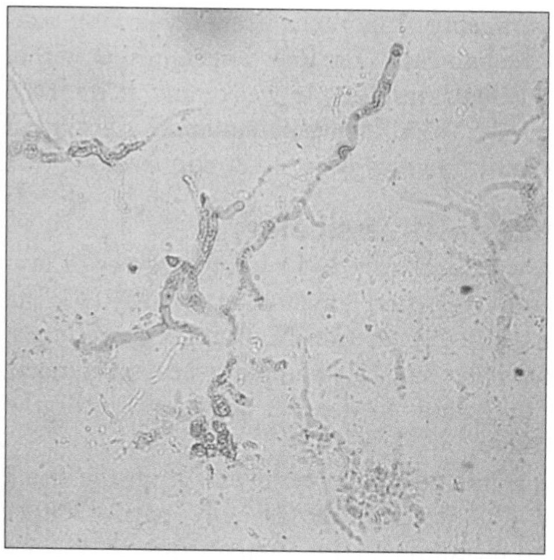

Fig. 240.3 Direct microscopy (NaOH slide) of palm skin showing distinctive dark fungal filaments of *Hortaea werneckii*, causal agent of tinea nigra.

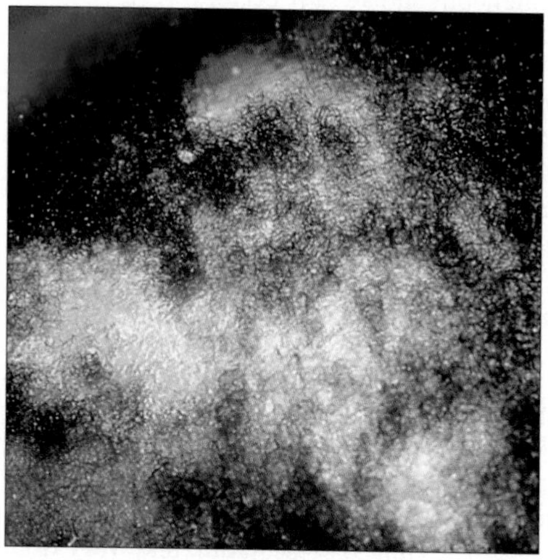

Fig. 240.4 Tinea capitis, noninflammatory type. Courtesy of Dr Natalie Roholt.

Microsporum ferrugineum. There may be variable erythema with scaling that may be minimal or clinically significant, such that scale is consistently present. One or more well-demarcated patches may be present.

The inflammatory type of tinea capitis is often caused by zoophilic or geophilic species (see Table 240.2). The inflammatory changes range from a pustular folliculitis to multiple follicular abscesses, or even a kerion. A kerion may be fluctuant with a boggy feel to it. Pus may discharge from one or more points. Within the kerion there may be patchy or complete hair loss. In some instances the kerion resolves with scarring alopecia. A patient who has a kerion may have a tender, full neck as a result of cervical lymphadenopathy. Other symptoms and signs may include fever, neck ache and pruritus of the scalp.

Tinea capitis may also manifest as 'black dot' disease, which is usually caused by endothrix organisms, such as *T. tonsurans* and *Trichophyton violaceum*. The hair is brittle and breaks off at the scalp surface with the free end of the in-situ portion of the hair manifesting as a 'black dot'. There may be a variable amount of inflammation and scale present.

The favus type of tinea capitis is caused by *T. schoenleinii*; less commonly *T. violaceum* or *Microsporum gypseum* may cause a similar presentation. Within the scalp there are typically yellow crusts and scale, known as scutula. The condition may progress to involve large portions of the scalp, with yellow, adherent scale and crusting, and cicatricial alopecia.

Tinea barbae

Three types of tinea barbae exist: inflammatory, superficial and circinate. In the inflammatory type the lesions may be pustular, boggy or nodular, with alopecia. The superficial type can manifest as a folliculitis with papules and pustules. In the circinate variety there may be an active border with vesicles and pustules, and central scaling.

Tinea faciei (tinea corporis of the face)

Typically there is an annular lesion with erythema and scaling, with central clearing. The lesion may be pruritic and the patient may give a history of the lesion worsening after exposure to the sun.

Tinea corporis

Generally the lesions are annular with central clearing. The margin is typically erythematous with scaling, and sometimes with papules, pustules or vesicles. Pigmentary change may be seen with hypopigmentation or hyperpigmentation of the lesion. The inflammatory change may be more pronounced when the infecting organism is zoophilic. Sometimes the dermatophytes infect the hair follicle, with the formation of inflammatory perifollicular nodules or pustules, also known as Majocchi's granuloma. Infrequently, nodular granulomatous changes or subcutaneous spread may occur.

Tinea cruris

The eruption can be symmetric or asymmetric, unilateral or bilateral. The patient may complain of pruritus. The lesion may demonstrate an active border with erythema, scaling, papules and vesicles. When the causal organism is *T. rubrum* there may be a reservoir of infection, such as the nails or soles of feet. With *E. floccosum* infection there is no reservoir. When infection is caused by *Candida* spp. satellite pustules are less likely to be present in adults than in children.

Tinea pedis

The three major clinical presentations are the interdigital, the 'moccasin' or chronic hyperkeratotic, and the vesiculobullous (Fig. 240.5). Interdigital tinea pedis is the most common presentation, usually with involvement of the web space between the fourth and fifth toes or the third and fourth toes. The clinical presentation may vary from

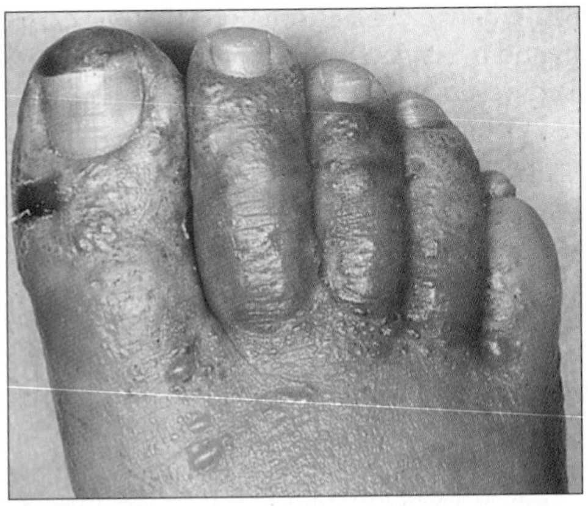

Fig. 240.5 Tinea pedis, vesiculobullous variety. Courtesy of Dr Natalie Roholt.

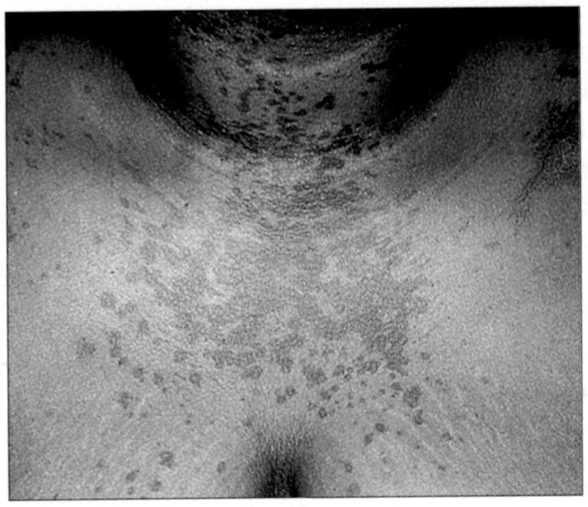

Fig. 240.6 Tinea versicolor. Courtesy of Dr Natalie Roholt.

relatively asymptomatic mild scaling to maceration, erythema and exudative changes. In the plantar, moccasin-type tinea pedis there may be scaling, hyperkeratosis and a variable degree of erythema. Sometimes the fungal infection manifests as vesicles or bullae that may be seen on the instep of the foot or the mid-anterior plantar surface.

Tinea nigra

This superficial fungal infection caused by *H. werneckii* may appear as a scaly, asymptomatic, brown–black hyperpigmentation of the palms or soles of the feet. The palm and sole or both soles may be involved. The main differential diagnosis is benign and malignant melanocytic lesions.

Piedra

In black piedra, hard black nodules of varying sizes firmly adhere to hair. Generally scalp hair is involved, although hair at any site may be affected. In white piedra, soft white nodules are of varying sizes and are less adherent to the hair shaft. The infection is present within and on the exterior of the shaft, resulting in weakening of the hair. There is no fluorescence under Wood's light. In immunocompromised individuals disseminated infection may occur with skin lesions.

Tinea versicolor (pityriasis versicolor)

The lesions are macular, with fine scale and varying degrees of erythema. There may be hypo- or hyperpigmentation (Fig. 240.6). The usual site of involvement is the upper trunk and upper extremities. The eruption may occur at other sites, including the face, scalp, neck, palms and in areas of occlusion. In inverse tinea versicolor the flexural area may be involved.

Lesions of *Malassezia* folliculitis are generally seen on the trunk and upper extremities. The lesions are typically perifollicular, inflammatory papules and pustules that are often pruritic.

Candidiasis

The cutaneous and mucosal manifestations of candidiasis are varied and include oral candidiasis, balanitis and vulvovaginal candidiasis. Cutaneous candidiasis may colonize occluded areas or folds of the skin producing infection in flexural sites (*Candida* intertrigo), diaper dermatitis, inframammary dermatitis and infection in fingerweb areas (erosio interdigitalis blastomycetica). Clinical manifestations include erythema, scaling, maceration, and satellite vesicles and pustules. Candida miliaria may occur on the trunk of febrile patients after sweating.[28] Pustules or vesicles develop from which the organism may be recovered. A folliculitis may also occur, for example, in the perioral area.

Candida spp., particularly *C. albicans*, may be associated with nail infection. *Candida* paronychia is more common when there is frequent contact with water. Typically there is erythema, swelling and tenderness of the paronychial area. The cuticle may be separated from the surface of the nailplate. Application of gentle pressure on the paronychial surface can result in the expression of pus from underneath the proximal nailfold. Concomitant bacterial infection may be present. For example, with *Pseudomonas aeruginosa* infection a greenish discoloration of the nail can be expected. Uncommonly, distal and lateral subungual onychomycosis may be caused by *Candida* spp., particularly involving the fingernails. Congenital CMCC tends to feature both severe cutaneous candidiasis, including paronychia, and oral candidiasis, with manifestations usually seen in infancy or early childhood. *Candida* granulomas may be present. The nails may be thickened and dystrophic, with the entire nailplate being involved.

Onychomycosis

Onychomycosis is a fungal infection of the nailbed with secondary involvement of the nailplate. The five main types of onychomycosis are:

- distal and lateral subungual onychomycosis (DLSO; Fig. 240.7),
- superficial white onychomycosis (SWO),
- proximal subungual onychomycosis (PSO),
- endonyx onychomycosis (EO), and
- *Candida* onychomycosis (CO).

In DLSO the distal portion of the nail is infected initially with subungual hyperkeratosis and onychomycosis. In lateral onychomycosis the infection initially involves the lateral portion of the nailbed and nailplate. In DLSO the most common causative organism is *T. rubrum*. As DLSO has a similar clinical presentation whether caused by dermatophytes or nondermatophytes it is important to obtain a nail sample for mycologic examination so that the causative organism can be identified. In SWO the infection involves the superficial portion of the nailplate, the most common organisms being members of the *T. mentagrophytes* complex and *Aspergillus*, *Fusarium* and *Acremonium* spp. In PSO the infection initially involves the proximal nailbed and nailplate, with *T. rubrum* being the most common causative organism. Endonix onychomycosis, involving the nailplate but not the nailbed, is mainly caused by *Trichophyton soudanense*.[29] It gives affected nails a milky appearance without hyperkeratosis. Proximal white superficial onychomycosis is characteristically seen in patients who are immunocompromised, for example, those who have AIDS. *Candida* onychomycosis is typically found in patients who have CMCC. It may also occur in individuals who spend time with their hands in water, for example, bar-tenders or home-makers.

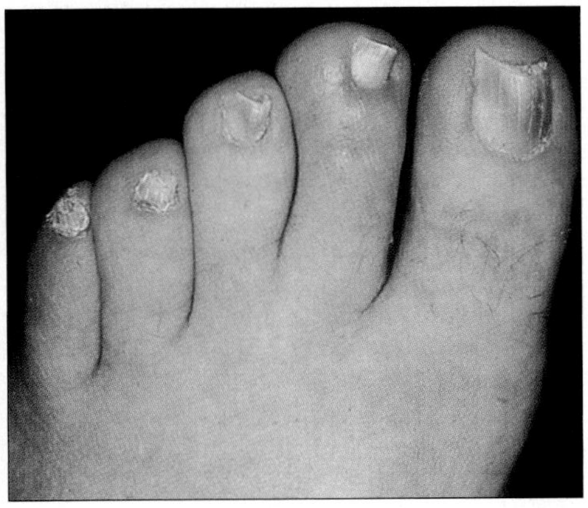

Fig. 240.7 Onychomycosis (tinea unguium), distal and lateral subungual type. Courtesy of Dr Natalie Roholt.

MANAGEMENT

In tinea capitis the causative organism should be identified whenever possible. If it is a zoophilic organism then the animal source should be treated. When the organism is anthropophilic, close contacts should be examined. Griseofulvin has been widely used to treat tinea capitis. The dose is 15–20mg/kg/day given for 6–8 weeks. In some countries a liquid formulation is available. Ketoconazole may have an efficacy similar to that of griseofulvin and has been used in patients who have responded poorly to griseofulvin. More recently terbinafine and itraconazole have been reported to be effective and safe. It may be possible to shorten the duration of therapy with the newer antifungal agents. Adjunctive measures may include cutting scalp hair short and using a shampoo such as ketoconazole or 2.5% selenium sulfide. If possible, old items of headgear should be discarded, the practice of sharing items such as caps and helmets discouraged and old combs thrown away or boiled in water, as appropriate.

With tinea barbae, tinea faciei, tinea corporis, tinea cruris and tinea pedis the source of infection should be identified and treated, whenever possible. In many instances the use of a topical antifungal agent such as an imidazole or an allylamine may suffice. Possible choices include ketoconazole, ciclopirox olamine or terbinafine creams. Some of the topical antifungal agents also have antibacterial and anti-inflammatory properties. Other topical antifungal agents, for example, tolnaftate and haloprogin, have a limited spectrum of activity. Generally, the topical antifungal agent should be applied over a small area beyond the active infection.

In instances in which the eruption involves a large area, when there is poor response (and the diagnosis has been confirmed to be a fungal infection), or if the infection involves the hair follicles and deeper cutaneous structures, then an oral agent should be considered. The traditional antifungal agent has been griseofulvin. In adults, ultramicrosize griseofulvin 330mg/day may be given for 2–4 weeks to treat tinea corporis and for 4–8 weeks in tinea pedis. In tinea pedis the dose may have to be increased to 330mg q12h. The newer antifungal agents itraconazole, terbinafine and fluconazole have also been reported to be effective. Itraconazole is a triazole that may be used as pulse therapy, 200mg/day for 1 week, to treat tinea corporis and tinea cruris. For tinea pedis the dosage of itraconazole pulse therapy is 200mg q12h for 1 week. Itraconazole may also be given as continuous therapy, 200mg/day for 2 weeks to treat tinea corporis and tinea cruris and for 4 weeks to treat tinea pedis. Terbinafine is an allylamine that is also effective in the treatment of tinea infections. The dosage regimen is 250mg/day given for 2–4 weeks to treat tinea corporis and tinea cruris and for 2–6 weeks when tinea pedis is present. In some instances a shorter duration of therapy may suffice. Reports of fluconazole used for the treatment of tinea infection suggest that a dose of 150mg once a week for 2–4 weeks may be beneficial.

For the management of onychomycosis, any co-existing tinea pedis should be identified and treated. The patient should be asked to cut the diseased nail as far back as possible, keep feet dry and clean, and wear socks made of absorbent material and, when possible, wear footwear that allows the feet to 'breathe'. The patient should use foot powders judiciously and be encouraged to use appropriate footwear when walking on communal areas that may harbor a high density of fungal inoculum, for example swimming pools, gymnasium floors or health spas. Griseofulvin is a narrow-spectrum agent that is ineffective against *Candida* spp. and nondermatophyte molds. When griseofulvin is used to treat dermatophytes, cure rates have been low (3–30%) and relapse rates high (40–60%). Therapy for fingernail and toenail onychomycosis lasts for 6–9 months and 9–18 months, respectively. With the newer antifungal agents terbinafine, itraconazole and fluconazole the response rates are higher and treatment is given for a shorter duration. These agents have a favorable adverse effects profile. The recommended dosage for terbinafine is 250mg/day given for 6 and 12 weeks for fingernail and toenail onychomycoses, respectively. With itraconazole the dosage schedule is 200mg/day given as continuous dosing for 6 and 12 weeks for fingernail and toenail onychomycoses, respectively. When itraconazole is given as pulse dosing the treatment regimen is 200mg q12h for 1 week per month given for two and three pulses for fingernail and toenail onychomycoses, respectively. Fluconazole has been given as 150mg once a week for 7–12 months to treat toenail onychomycosis. Topical agents have recently received renewed attention as alternatives in the treatment of minimal-to-moderate onychomycosis. Traditional topical therapies produced less than desirable results in onychomycosis treatment; this may, in part, have been due to the method of application because creams, gels, powders and water- or oil-based lotions can easily be wiped, rubbed and washed off. Recently, with the development of nail lacquers such as amorolfine and ciclopirox, topical agents have shown increased efficacy rates and patient compliance. Amorolfine is available in many countries for the treatment of onychomycosis, but is not approved in the USA. Ciclopirox nail lacquer 8% is approved in the USA for the treatment of mild-to-moderate onychomycosis without lunula involvement. Surgical interventions such as nail avulsion may be considered as part of a combination therapy with antifungal drugs when a single nail is diseased; however, such procedures are used infrequently, particularly with the advent of the newer, more effective oral antifungal agents.

In tinea nigra, therapy includes topical azoles. Griseofulvin is ineffective. The management of piedra includes shaving the infected hair. Spontaneous remission may occur. Topical antifungal agents have been reported to be beneficial. The management of tinea versicolor includes topical products such as 2.5% selenium sulfide shampoo, ketoconazole shampoo, other topical azoles or terbinafine, and keratolytic agents. Griseofulvin and oral terbinafine are ineffective. Short-term therapies with ketoconazole and itraconazole may be effective. The management of candidiasis depends upon the particular clinical form and is covered in detail elsewhere (see Chapters 62, 111 and 126).[30]

REFERENCES

1. Rippon JW. Medical mycology. The pathogenic fungi and the pathogenic Actinomycetes, 3rd edition. Philadelphia: WB Saunders; 1988.
2. Summerbell RC, Kane J, Krajden S. Onychomycosis, tinea pedis and tinea manuum caused by non-dermatophytic filamentous fungi. Mycoses 1989;32:609–19.
3. Scher RK. Onychomycosis is more than a cosmetic problem. Br J Dermatol 1994;130(Suppl.43):15.
4. Langer H. Epidemiologische und klinische Untersuchungen bei Onychomykosen. Arch Klin Exp Dermatol 1957;204:624–36.
5. Heikkilä H, Stubb S. The prevalence of onychomycosis in Finland. Br J Dermatol 1995;133:699–703.
6. Silverman RA. Pediatric mycoses. In: Elewski BE, ed. Cutaneous fungal infections. Tokyo: Igaku-Shoin; 1992:212–28.
7. Williams JV, Honig PJ, McGinley KJ, Leyden JJ. Semiquantitative study of tinea capitis and the asymptomatic carrier state in inner-city school children. Pediatrics 1995;96:265–7.
8. Lacroix C, Baspeyras M, de la Salmoniere P, *et al.* Tinea pedis in European marathon runners. J Eur Acad Dermatol Venereol 2002;16:139–42.
9. Caputo R, De Boulle K, Del Rosso J, Nowicki R. Prevalence of superficial fungal infections among sports-active individuals: results from the Achilles survey, a review of the literature. J Eur Acad Dermatol Venereol 2001;15:312–6.
10. Hay RJ. Clinical aspects of dermatomycoses in AIDS patients. In: Vanden Bossche H, Mackenzie DWR, Cauwenbergh G, Van Cutsem J, Drouhet E, Dupont B, eds. Mycoses in AIDS patients. New York: Plenum Press;1990:141–6.
11. Johansson C, Eshaghi H, Linder MT, Jakobson E, Scheynius A. Positive atopy patch test reaction to *Malassezia furfur* in atopic dermatitis correlates with a T helper 2-like peripheral blood mononuclear cells response. J Invest Dermatol 2002;118:1044–51.
12. Gupta AK, Cooper EA, MacDonald P, Summerbell RC. Utility of inoculum counting (Walshe and English criteria) in clinical diagnosis of onychomycosis caused by nondermatophytic filamentous fungi. J Clin Microbiol 2001;39:2115–21.
13. Apodaca G, McKerrow JH. Regulation of *Trichophyton rubrum* proteolytic activity. Infect Immunol 1989;57:3081–90.
14. Weitzman I, Summerbell RC. The dermatophytes. Clin Microbiol Rev 1995;8:240–59.
15. Zaias N, Tosti A, Rebell G, Morelli R, *et al.* Autosomal dominant pattern of distal subungual onychomycosis caused by *Trichophyton rubrum.* J Am Acad Dermatol 1996;34:302–4.
16. Daniel CR III, Norton LA, Scher RK. The spectrum of nail disease in patients with human immunodeficiency virus infection. J Am Acad Dermatol 1992;27:93–7.
17. Wagner DK, Sohnle PG. Cutaneous defenses against dermatophytes and yeasts. Clin Microbiol Rev 1995;8:317–35.
18. Leibovici V, Evron R, Axelrod O, *et al.* Imbalance of immune responses in patients with chronic and widespread fungal skin infection. Clin Exp Dermatol 1995;20:390–4.
19. Ajello L. Natural history of the dermatophytes and related fungi. Mycopathol Mycol Appl 1974;53:93–110.
20. Shah, PC, Krajden S, Kane J, Summerbell RC. Tinea corporis caused by *Microsporum canis*: report of a nosocomial outbreak. Eur J Epidemiol 1988;4:33–8.
21. Lilic D. New perspectives on the immunology of chronic mucocutaneous candidiasis. Curr Opin Infect Dis 2002;15:143–7.
22. English MP, Atkinson R. Onychomycosis in elderly chiropody patients. Br J Dermatol 1974;91:67–72.
23. Naka W, Hanyaku H, Tajima S, Harada T, Nishikawa T. Application of neutral red staining for evaluation of the viability of dermatophytes and *Candida* in human skin scales. J Med Vet Mycol 1994;32:31–5.
24. Clayton YM. Clinical and mycological diagnostic aspects of onychomycoses and dermatomycoses. Clin Exp Dermatol 1992;17(Suppl.1):37–40.
25. Kane J, Summerbell RC. *Trichophyton, Microsporum, Epidermophyton* and agents of superficial mycoses. In: Murray PR, Baron EJ, Pfaller MA, Tenover FC, Yolken RH, eds. Manual of clinical microbiology, 7th edition. Washington DC: ASM Press; 1999:1275–94.
26. Rebell G, Taplin D. Dermatophytes, their recognition and identification, 2nd edition. Coral Gables, Florida: University of Miami Press; 1970.
27. Kane J, Summerbell RC, Sigler L, Krajden S, Land G. Laboratory handbook of dermatophytes. A clinical guide and laboratory manual of dermatophytes and other filamentous fungi from skin, hair and nails. Belmont, CA: Star Publishers; 1997.
28. Martin AG, Kobayashi GS. Yeast infections: candidiasis, pityriasis (tinea) versicolor. Chapter 27. In: Freedberg, IM, Eisen AZ, Wolff K, Goldsmith, LA, Austen KF, Fitzpatrick TB, eds, Fitzpatrick's dermatology in general medicine, 5th edition, vol. 2. New York: McGraw-Hill; 1999:2358–71.
29. Tosti A, Baran R, Piraccini BM, Fanti PA. 'Endonyx' onychomycosis: a new modality of nail invasion by dermatophytes. Acta Derm Venereol 1999;79:52–3.
30. Hay RJ, Moore M. Mycology. In: Champion RH, Burton JL, Burn DA, Breathnach SM, eds. Rook/Wilkinson/Ebling Textbook of dermatology, 6th edition. Oxford, England: Blackwell Science Publications; 1998:1277–376.

chapter

241 Pneumocystis

Gunnar I Andriesse & Dana Milatovic

NATURE

Pneumocystis carinii was first described by Chagas, who misidentified the organism as the sexual state of *Trypanosoma cruzi*.[1] For years it was classified as a protozoon. However, detailed ultrastructural analysis and molecular analysis of 16S-like rRNA[2] and mitochondrial DNA from the organism revealed that it is phylogenetically closely related to the Ascomycetes and Basidiomycetes and thus is now classified as a fungus.

However, *Pneumocystis carinii* has features that are atypical for a fungus. It has the morphologic appearance of a protozoon: thick-walled cysts and amoeboid trophozoites. Furthermore, it contains only two copies of the rRNA gene, whereas most fungi contain hundreds of copies. It is resistant to antifungal agents affecting the outer sterol membranes of fungi (e.g. amphotericin or azole drugs) because it lacks ergosterol and contains cholesterol instead. Nevertheless, its similarity to fungi may ultimately prove therapeutically exploitable. In fact, the echinocandins that inhibit β-glucan synthase of fungi are very effective in a rat model of *Pneumocystis* pneumonia.

It has become apparent that there is considerable genotypic and antigenic variation among *P. carinii* isolated from different host species and among *P. carinii* found in the same host species.[3] However, controversy remains as to whether these differences establish that multiple species of *P. carinii* exist. At present, the different variants of *P. carinii* are referred to as 'special forms'. Using a trinomial nomenclature system, human *P. carinii* is now known as *P. carinii* special form *hominis* (*P. carinii* sp. f. *hominis*). Until now, molecular epidemiologic studies have identified more than 50 genotypes of human-derived *P. carinii*.

The lack of an effective culture system for *P. carinii* has hampered efforts to study the antigenic composition of the organism. However, two antigen complexes have been identified that appear to be important in pathogenesis. The highly immunogenic major surface glycoprotein (MSG, also known as glycoprotein A or gp120) is encoded by a multicopy gene family. Expression of the MSG genes is regulated by a single expression site: the upstream conserved sequence (UCS). As a result the MSG shows considerable antigenic variation. This may be the mechanism enabling the organism to evade the host immune system. In fact, analysis of pulmonary samples of patients who had *Pneumocystis carinii* pneumonia (PCP) demonstrated that multiple MSG genes were expressed in a given host and that different patterns of MSG expression were seen among different patients.[4] Another glycoprotein that migrates in a 35–45kDa band appears to be important in eliciting humoral response to *P. carinii* in humans.[5]

EPIDEMIOLOGY

Serologic studies have shown that nearly 85% of all children undergo a *P. carinii* infection early in life, often being accompanied by mild respiratory symptoms.[6,7] Up to now no environmental reservoir has been identified. Therefore it seems that humans are the only reservoir for *P. carinii* sp. f. *hominis*. As a result, for years the most accepted hypothesis for pathogenesis has been that the organisms remain latent within the lung until the host becomes severely immunocompromised and reactivation of *P. carinii* occurs. However, recent epidemiologic studies suggest that re-infection with *P. carinii* may also play a role.

The 'latency theory' is supported by several observations:

- *P. carinii* is carried in apparently healthy immunocompetent animals;
- refractoriness to grow in culture media suggests that it cannot grow outside of the mammalian host;
- host specificity implies co-evolution during long-term carriage; and
- *P. carinii* continuously changes its antigenic composition, which is consistent with the capacity for long-term carriage in an immunocompetent host.[3]

Although several studies using polymerase chain reaction (PCR) have demonstrated asymptomatic carriage of *P. carinii* in non-immunocompromised individuals,[7,8] this does not necessarily prove long-term colonization.[9] Other data suggest that exposure to *P. carinii* can result either in direct clearance of the micro-organism from the airways, temporary latency or, depending on the immune status, in PCP. In the laboratory, immunosuppressed rodents acquire infection shortly after inhalation of *P. carinii*. Electrophoretic karyotyping identifies *P. carinii* in the lungs of naive animals as the same as those in chronically infected animals, from which infections are acquired.[10] When immunosuppression is withdrawn, these rats appear capable of clearing the organism completely from their lungs. Analysis of internal transcribed spacer (ITS) and mitochondrial large-subunit genes of *P. carinii* isolates in bronchoalveolar lavage (BAL) fluid from HIV patients during several episodes of pneumonia revealed that recurrence could also be attributed to de-novo infections.[11,12] In approximately 50% of patients who had recurrent episodes of PCP, the sequence types observed at the second episode were different from those of the first, suggesting the occurrence of both reactivation of a previously acquired infection and re-infection from an exogenous source.[13,14]

A finding complicating epidemiologic studies is that latency and infection are not monoclonal. Analysis using PCR of BAL specimens from 212 patients who had PCP revealed that 23% were infected with a single *P. carinii* genotype, 50% with two and 27% with more types.[15,16] Moreover, the number of genotypes found in respiratory samples does not represent the number of genotypes found in autopsy lungs. These results suggest that there is heterogeneity and compartmentalization of *P. carinii* genotypes within the lungs.[17,18]

The organism is probably not acquired from zoonotic sources because of host restriction based on distinct (anti)genetic subgroups.[19] Although *P. carinii* DNA has been found in samples of outdoor air, no environmental reservoir for *P. carinii* has been identified. Geographic studies of HIV-associated PCP cases have shown residential areas with significantly lower risks of PCP versus clustering of cases, suggesting an environmental factor.[20]

Studies using molecular techniques support person-to-person spread, which was suggested by earlier reports on clusters and outbreaks of PCP among oncology and transplant patients.[21] *Pneumocystis carinii* DNA was detected in respiratory samples of health care workers and those with the closest occupational contact with patients who had PCP were more likely to have detectable *P. carinii* DNA.[22] Furthermore, analysis of air filters in hospitals suggests that transmission is airborne; corresponding genotypes were found in BAL specimens from PCP patients and air filters from their rooms.[23,24] Currently available information justifies the isolation of patients who have PCP from individuals who are at increased risk of acquiring the infection.

PATHOGENICITY

In-vivo studies indicate that *P. carinii* is acquired by the airborne route. Once inhaled, the organism adheres to the type I alveolar cell of the lung and interacts with alveolar macrophages through the extracellular proteins fibronectin, vitronectin and surfactant protein D, which bind the MSG of *P. carinii* (Fig. 241.1). After several weeks of cortisone treatment, small clusters of *P. carinii* can be detected in alveolar spaces throughout the lungs of previously uninfected rats. Later, the alveoli become completely filled with organisms, suggesting that replication is slow but proliferation in the lung is extensive.

Two distinct morphologic forms of the organism are detected during infection. One is a small pleomorphic trophozoite that constitutes the majority of micro-organisms in the lung and the other is a more mature, larger, thick-walled cyst that contains up to eight intracystic bodies. Examination of infected lung by light microscopy typically shows foamy alveolar exudate consisting of degenerative cell membranes, surfactant and host proteins (Fig. 241.2). A modest number of alveolar macrophages are present. As infection progresses, septal hypertrophy occurs and there is an accumulation of interstitial edema and mononuclear cell infiltration.[25] Pathophysiologic features have also been detected by electron microscopy and include subepithelial bleb formation resulting from increased alveolar-capillary permeability, degenerative changes in type-I alveolar cells and effacement of the basement membrane. Consequently, serum, fibrin and other proteins diffuse into the alveoli.[26]

Surfactant plays a major role in the pathogenesis of PCP; intratracheal instillation of surfactant improves oxygenation and pulmonary architecture in immunosuppressed laboratory animals with PCP. Furthermore, during experimental infection, there are alterations in phospholipid content of the surfactant (diminished phosphatidylcholine and increased sphingomyelin). This can be explained by the observation that the organism has uptake and catabolism of lipids[27] and that the surfactant protein A level, which regulates secretion and absorption of surfactant phospholipids, is increased. The exact relation of these changes to lung injury is unknown, although deficiency of surfactant phospholipids likely results in abnormalities in alveolar surface tension, lung distensibility and ventilation-perfusion matching. Surfactant protein A plays another role; it binds to the

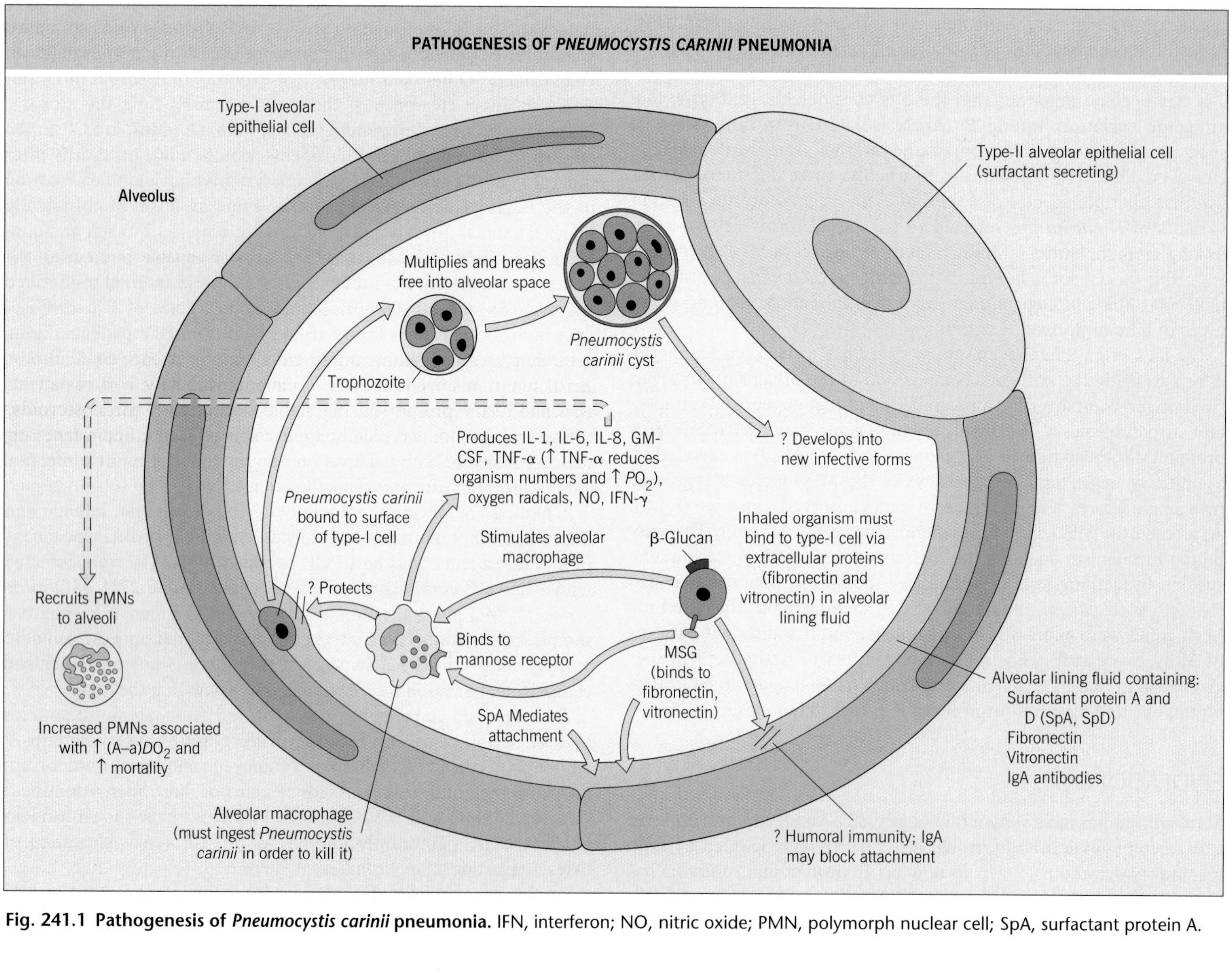

Fig. 241.1 Pathogenesis of *Pneumocystis carinii* pneumonia. IFN, interferon; NO, nitric oxide; PMN, polymorph nuclear cell; SpA, surfactant protein A.

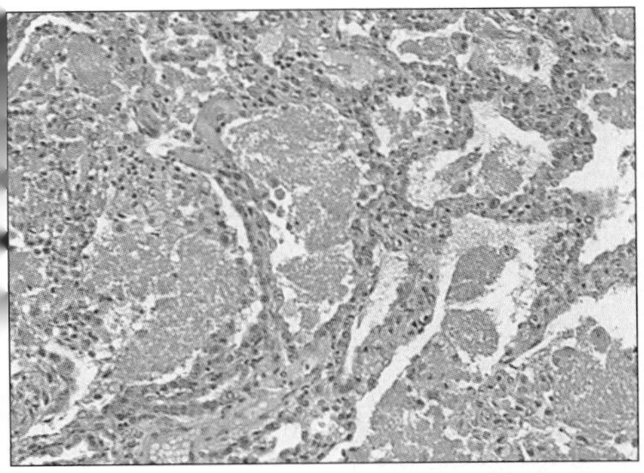

Fig. 241.2 Hematoxylin and eosin stained section of lung tissue. Characteristic intra-alveolar foamy exudates can be seen in this patient, who has *P. carinii* pneumonia. Courtesy of Michael Koss.

mannose residue the MSG[28] and thereby enhances attachment of the organism to type I pneumocytes, interfering with the phagocytosis of *P. carinii* by alveolar macrophages.[29]

The physiologic consequences of these pathologic abnormalities include the early impairment of gas exchange because of increased alveolar–capillary permeability, which is measured by decreased membrane diffusing capacity of carbon monoxide and ultimately decreased compliance, total lung capacity and vital capacity. Lung function may be further impaired by the host inflammatory response. In severe combined immunodeficiency (SCID) mice with PCP, reconstitution of the immune system by bone marrow transplantation or infusion of CD4+ lymphocytes resulted in clearance of *P. carinii* from the lungs[30] but also in early deaths from a hyperinflammatory local response. That the inflammatory response can be deleterious is also found in humans; a decrease in oxygenation occurs often soon after initiation of specific anti-*P. carinii* therapy that is blunted by adjunctive corticosteroids. Similarly, an increased number of neutrophils in BAL in patients is associated with a poor outcome.

Multiple studies have supported an important role for inflammatory mediators in the pathogenesis of PCP.[31–33] Production of interleukin (IL)-1, IL-6, IL-8, granulocyte–macrophage colony-stimulating factor (GM-CSF), tumor necrosis factor (TNF)-α, leukotriene B_4 and phospholipase A_2 are all increased in AIDS patients who have PCP. In individuals who have PCP, IL-8 is elevated in BAL fluid and correlates with BAL fluid neutrophilia, $P(\text{A–a})O_2$ and severity of illness; therapy with corticosteroids resulted in a reduction in IL-8 levels.[34] Conversely, although TNF-α expression by alveolar macrophages is also decreased by corticosteroid administration, TNF-α appears to be essential in the host defense against *P. carinii*.[35]

Macrophages play an important role in clearing *P. carinii* from the lungs and preventing the development of PCP. *Pneumocystis carinii* is phagocytosed by the alveolar macrophages either after it is opsonized by specific antibodies (Fc-receptor mediated) or after binding by the mannose receptor (MR) to the MSG of *P. carinii*. Recent studies have demonstrated[36,37] that alveolar macrophage MR activity is downregulated in HIV patients and that functional MR is shed from the macrophage cell surface. This soluble MR was detected in cell-free alveolar fluid from patients who had PCP, but not in alveolar fluid from healthy controls. When purified *P. carinii* organisms were incubated with soluble MR-containing supernatants, they were phagocytosed less readily by alveolar macrophages than were control organisms.[38] This suggests that *P. carinii* enhances the shedding of MR from the macrophage cell surface and binds to the 'free' MR, resulting in inhibition of phagocytosis.

In nude mice, SCID mice and medically immunosuppressed rodents, the common immunologic deficit predisposing these animals to PCP is severe depletion in T-cell function. Adoptive transfer of spleen T cells from phenotypically normal mice into *P. carinii* infected nude mice reduced lung cysts and resolved PCP.[39] Other adoptive transfer experiments established that helper L3T4 lymphocytes (equivalent to human CD4+ lymphocytes) were necessary to reconstitute delayed-type hypersensitivity for *P. carinii* but suppressor lymphocytes were necessary for complete expression of resistance to the organism. Administration of monoclonal antibody to CD4+ lymphocytes to conventional BALB/c mice and reconstituted SCID mice inoculated with *P. carinii* resulted in PCP and inability to eradicate the infection, respectively. These experiments all provide inferential evidence that depletion of CD4+ lymphocytes is necessary for the development of PCP.

In humans who do not have HIV infection, PCP frequently occurs in association with lymphoreticular malignancies, certain congenital disorders and chemotherapy with ciclosporin or corticosteroids that have in common variable defects in T-cell function. By contrast, adults who have pure agammaglobulinemia rarely develop PCP. Most AIDS patients have CD4+ lymphocyte counts in the range of 50–75/mm^3 at the time of their first episode of PCP, and more than 90% of episodes occur when counts are below 200/mm^3. If patients who have less than 200 CD4+ lymphocytes/mm^3 are not given prophylaxis, the risk of developing PCP is 8.4% at 6 months, 18.4% at 12 months and 33.3% at 36 months. Thus, diminished T cell function and/or numbers is most likely the critical immune deficit necessary for this opportunistic infection to occur.

Recent studies suggest that antibodies may also be important components of host defense to *P. carinii*.[40] In adoptive transfer of T cells and spleen cells from immunocompetent donors into SCID mice, B cells were necessary, in addition to T cells, for recipient mice to resolve pre-existing PCP. Both in mice and humans, intense reactivity of monoclonal antibodies from tracheobronchial lymph node B-cells[41] and a serum antibody response were found[5] following recovery from PCP. In HIV-infected patients both local antibodies (IgA) and the serum antibody levels were lower and the ability to mount an antibody response to the *P. carinii* infection was impaired, suggesting that the poor antibody response may contribute to the tendency of HIV-infected patients to have PCP.[42,43] Thus, although T-cell-mediated immunity may be the central component of the host response to *P. carinii*, humoral immunity may also have an important role in certain aspects of protection against infection.

CLINICAL MANIFESTATIONS

The clinical manifestations of PCP in patients who do not have AIDS are similar to those in AIDS patients (covered in detail in Chapter 124). Although there can be great variability, non-AIDS patients typically present more acutely, often within days of their initial symptoms.[44] Up to 20% of patients who have corticosteroid-associated PCP present during stable dosing with corticosteroids, but severe symptoms typically appear abruptly upon rapid tapering of corticosteroid therapy. These events probably represent activation of immune mechanisms that had been inhibited by the high doses of corticosteroids.

The cardinal symptoms are fever, cough and shortness of breath.[44,45] Early in the course of the disease, dyspnea may occur only on exertion and careful questioning is required to elicit a recent decrease in exercise tolerance. Cough is typically nonproductive, but small amounts of clear sputum are common, whereas purulent sputum and hemoptysis are rare in the absence of concurrent infection. Chest tightness and a dull retrosternal ache that is worse with inspiration may also occur.

Physical examination may be completely normal, particularly in individuals who have mild disease. Tachypnea, tachycardia and respiratory distress tend to signify advanced disease and a poorer prognosis.

Chest radiographs typically demonstrate fine, bilateral interstitial infiltrates extending from the hilum, but this appearance may be seen with many other pneumonias. Normal or minimally abnormal radiographs may occur early in disease or in lung transplant recipients.[46] Atypical radiographic abnormalities have been frequently reported in

AIDS patients but also occur in non-AIDS patients and include localized or unilateral infiltrates, cavitary, cystic or honeycomb lesions, hilar enlargement with lymphadenopathy, spontaneous pneumothorax, predominant upper lobe disease, solitary nodules, small pleural effusions and linear opacities.[47] Dissemination to brain, kidney, adrenal and thyroid glands, liver, intestines, spleen and eye have been reported and require biopsy for definitive diagnosis. A high index of suspicion and appropriate stains of any involved organ will yield the diagnosis.

No single routine laboratory test either excludes or is pathognomonic for PCP. Elevated serum lactic dehydrogenase (LDH) and eosinophilia[48] are frequently found, particularly during severe episodes, but these tests are non-specific and there are multiple other causes for eosinophilia or raised LDH levels in immunocompromised individuals. Impaired oxygenation is frequently present and, when arterial blood gases are normal, diffusing capacity for carbon monoxide, arterial oxygen saturation during exercise and gallium scintigraphy are potentially helpful tests but are non-specific. The diagnosis ultimately depends on demonstration of the organism in respiratory secretions or lung tissue (see Diagnostic microbiology, below). Patients who have very low $CD4^+$ counts (<100 cells/mm^3) and/or BAL neutrophilia have a poorer prognosis. The overall mortality of PCP in both HIV and non-HIV patients is approximately 40%.[49]

DIAGNOSTIC MICROBIOLOGY

Bronchoscopy with BAL is the diagnostic procedure for obtaining pulmonary secretions with which all other tests are compared. Bronchoalveolar lavage involves wedging the bronchoscope into a peripheral nondependent airway (usually the right middle lobe), instilling 100–250ml non-bacteriostatic saline as 20–30ml aliquots and aspirating fluid after each aliquot is instilled. When approximately 50ml of fluid has been recovered, the specimen is centrifuged and the pellet is stained for *P. carinii*. In 86–97% of patients, *P. carinii* organisms are detected by this procedure.

Several approaches may improve yield. Bilateral BAL resulted in a diagnosis in 31 (94%) out of 33 patients compared with 51 (84%) out of 61 historical control patients undergoing BAL only on one side.[50] Similarly, the combination of multiple-lobe, site-directed BAL plus monoclonal antibody staining increased diagnostic yield from 80% to 98%.[51] In patients who had focal infiltrates, the combination of site-directed BAL and transbronchial biopsy led to a diagnosis in 90% of patients who had a prior nondiagnostic BAL.[52]

In contrast to BAL, induced sputum specimens are easily obtained by ultrasonic nebulization of hypertonic saline, although care must be taken because many patients experience arterial oxygen desaturation during the procedure. When the sediment is appropriately stained and slides are reviewed by experts, the procedure has a sensitivity of 15–94% with corresponding negative predictive values that have also varied widely (39–96%). The procedure is laborious for respiratory therapists, but positive results usually obviate the need for bronchoscopy. Fluorescent staining with monoclonal antibodies for *P. carinii* (Fig. 241.3) may increase the yield to over 90%.[53] With the use of PCR techniques, the sensitivity of induced sputum examination may approach that of BAL (see below).

As for BAL, the yield of induced sputum may be lower for patients receiving aerosol pentamidine because the numbers of organisms may be reduced. In one study of 54 patients, the diagnosis was confirmed by induced sputum in 64% of those receiving aerosol pentamidine compared with 92% of those not receiving the aerosol (p <0.02).[54] By contrast, the respective yields were 63% compared with 64% in another trial.[55]

When transbronchial biopsies are obtained without crush artefact and contain at least 25 alveoli, the diagnostic yield is similar to that

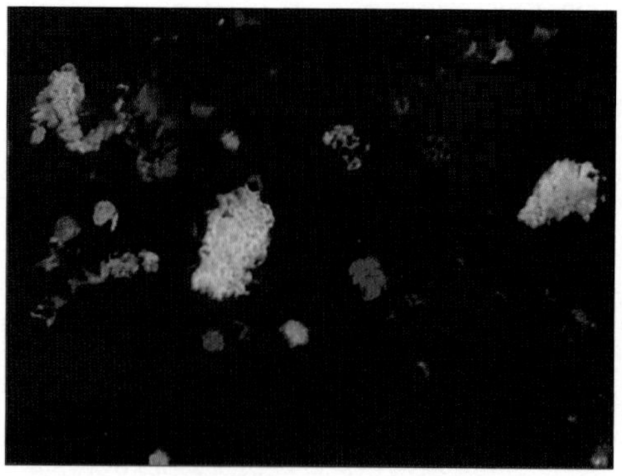

Fig. 241.3 Monoclonal immunofluorescent stain. Monoclonal immunofluorescent stain of a BAL specimen (Merifluor stain) demonstrating *P. carinii* cysts that stain with a characteristic apple-green fluorescence. With permission from Meridian Diagnostics.

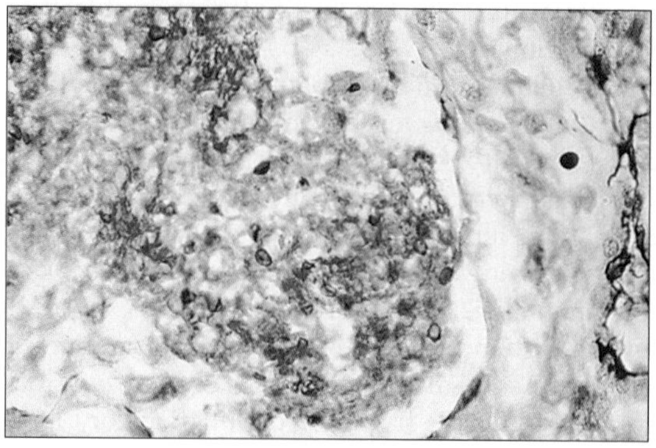

Fig. 241.4 Gomori's methenamine silver stain of lung tissue. Gomori-stained section of lung tissue showing characteristic *P. carinii* cysts.

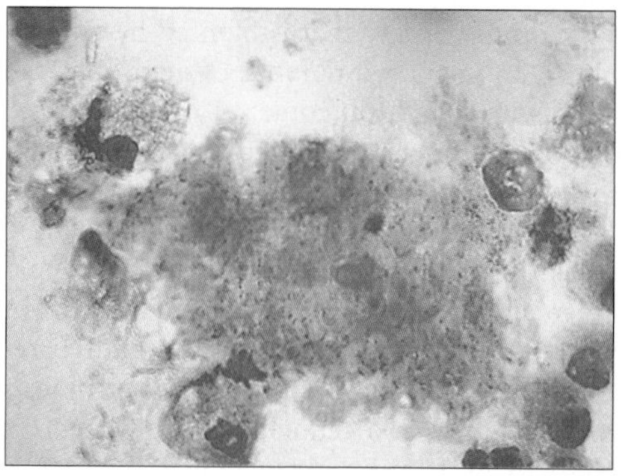

Fig. 241.5 Wright–Giemsa stain of sputum. Wright–Giemsa stained specimen of an induced sputum specimen showing clusters of *P. carinii* organisms. Courtesy of Maria Appleman.

of BAL. If both BAL and transbronchial biopsies are obtained, the diagnostic sensitivity is additive and approaches 100%. However, pneumothoraces or bleeding may occur in up to 10% of patients undergoing bronchoscopic biopsy. Thus, many pulmonologists prefer to perform only BAL with the initial bronchoscopy. If the first procedure is nondiagnostic, BAL is repeated and transbronchial biopsies are obtained if coagulation indices permit. However, one study using monoclonal antibody staining suggests that biopsy does not increase the yield of BAL and may only increase the chance of complications.[50]

Open lung biopsy can also lead to the diagnosis of PCP but is rarely needed because of the high yield with sputum induction and BAL. It is usually reserved for patients in whom bronchoscopy has been nondiagnostic because of technical problems with the procedure or where transbronchial biopsies are contraindicated because of bleeding disorders or concurrent management with mechanical ventilation.

Traditionally Gomori's methenamine silver stain is used to identify *P. carinii* cysts in patient samples (Fig. 241.4). Its diagnostic sensitivity and specificity both generally exceed 95%. However, up to 10% false negatives may occur. The procedure requires 4–6 hours but modifications have reduced processing time to 1–2 hours. The cyst wall can also be stained by toluidine blue, with the advantage that it is more rapid than standard silver stains.

Wright–Giemsa (Fig. 241.5) and Diff-Quik stains have been used to stain trophozoites, nuclei of cysts and intermediate forms and can be completed within 30 minutes. However, organisms will be missed in 10–15% of cases. The methodology also allows polymorphonuclear neutrophils to be identified in BAL fluid, a finding associated with more severe impairment in pulmonary physiology and lower survival.

Direct and indirect immunofluorescent staining using monoclonal antibodies (Fig. 241.3) are highly sensitive, with yields in excess of 90% for BAL specimens,[51,53] and are more sensitive for sputum samples than silver or Wright–Giemsa stains. Although false positives occasionally occur, this has become the diagnostic procedure of choice in many clinical laboratories.

The development of the PCR has increased the sensitivity of detection of *P. carinii* in patient samples substantially. Consequently, the PCR can also yield a positive result in asymptomatic individuals who are colonized by *P. carinii*. In several studies analysis of respiratory samples by PCR (single and nested) revealed higher numbers of false-positive results and lower positive-predictive values than microscopy for non-HIV immunocompromised and immunocompetent patients. Even with HIV patients, in whom the differences between the diagnostic results of microscopy and single and nested PCRs were quite marginal, microscopy and single PCR performed better than nested PCR with regard to specificity and positive predictive value.[56–59] Although the PCR technique has no additional value in analysis of BAL fluid, it can improve diagnostic sensitivity of induced sputum and oral washes up to the same level as that of BAL specimens.[60–62] At present, it appears reasonable to reserve PCR for epidemiologic research and diagnosis in induced sputum and oral wash specimens that prove negative by immunofluorescence.

PREVENTION

The indications for primary and secondary chemoprophylaxis of PCP in HIV-infected patients are well known and are covered in Chapters 123 and 124. In HIV-negative immunocompromised patients no general guidelines for PCP prophylaxis exist and the decision to administer prophylaxis depends on the degree and duration of the immunosuppression and on local institutional trends in PCP incidence. Patients at risk for PCP for whom chemoprophylaxis should be considered include:

- those who have primary immunodeficiency;
- those who have severe malnutrition;
- after organ transplantation;
- those who have persistent $CD4^+$ counts of below 200/mm^3; and
- in cytotoxic or immunosuppressive treatment of cancer, connective tissue disorders and other diseases.[63,64]

The incidence of PCP is highest during the first year after solid organ transplantation, except for patients who have lung transplants, who continue to have higher risks more than a year after transplantation.[65] The risk of PCP in transplant patients is also increased in cases of invasive cytomegalovirus disease, during intensive immunosuppression for allograft rejection (corticosteroids) and during periods of neutropenia.[66,67] Prophylaxis should also be considered for more than 1 year after bone marrow transplantation for patients receiving corticosteroids as well as in those who have hematologic relapse or extensive chronic graft-versus-host disease.[68] Corticosteroids are recognized as an independent risk factor if given for longer than 4 weeks at a level equivalent to 20mg of prednisone (prednisolone) daily.[69] In non-HIV patients, determination of $CD4^+$ lymphocyte counts can help to identify patients who are at risk for PCP; 91% of patients have fewer than 300 $CD4^+$ lymphocytes/mm^3 at the time of diagnosis of PCP.[70,71]

First choice of prophylaxis consists of one double-strength (960mg) tablet of trimethoprim–sulphamethoxazole (TMP–SMX) per day.[72,73] One single-strength tablet (480mg) daily or one double-strength tablet three times per week is also effective. For pediatric patients who have acute lymphoblastic leukemia, TMP–SMX (150mg/m^2 TMP plus 750mg/m^2 SMX, to a maximum of 160mg TMP and 800mg SMX) given q12h for three consecutive days per week has similar efficacy to daily administration.[74] Regimens of TMP–SMX would also be expected to provide some protection against toxoplasmosis, *Nocardia asteroides*, *Listeria monocytogenes*, bacterial pneumonia and urinary tract infections. Some patients have to discontinue TMP–SMX prophylaxis because of adverse reactions (mostly gastrointestinal symptoms and skin rashes). For these individuals dapsone (100mg/day) alone, or dapsone (50mg/day) in combination with pyrimethamine (50mg/week) and leucovorin (25mg/week) could be an alternative.[75,76] Aerosolized pentamidine (300mg once per month) may also be effective, but is more expensive.[72,72,77] Atovaquone suspension (1500mg or 750mg daily) has also proven effective after bone marrow and liver transplantation respectively.[78,79] Other drug regimens have been considered but there is insufficient evidence to recommend their use.

Furthermore, judging from the current state of knowledge about the epidemiology and transmission of *P. carinii*, direct contact of PCP patients with other immunocompromised patients should be avoided.

MANAGEMENT

The management of patients who have AIDS-associated PCP is covered in detail in Chapter 124. In HIV-negative patients, management should consist of TMP–SMX in a dosage of 15–20mg/kg/day TMP and 75–100mg/kg/day SMX in three or four divided doses (orally or intravenously). Initially, therapy should be given intravenously until clinical improvement ensues and the patient is able to tolerate oral intake well. Therapy should be continued for 21 days; shorter courses of therapy (i.e. 14–17 days) should be reserved for patients who have mild disease or who respond rapidly. Adverse events are considerably less common in non-AIDS patients[44] and include rash, fever, nausea and vomiting, leukopenia and hepatitis.

Sulfamethoxazole inhibits dihydropteroate synthase (DHPS) in the folic acid synthesis pathway. Although mutations in the DHPS genes are found more in patients who are taking sulfa or sulfone prophylaxis,[80–82] they are not invariably associated with failure of treatment or prophylaxis. Likewise, the majority of patients who have mutations respond well to sulfa or sulfone therapy.[82,83]

Intravenous pentamidine is the primary alternative agent for non-AIDS patients who are intolerant of TMP–SMX. The standard dosage is 4mg/kg q24h. Because of problems with pain and sterile abscesses, the intramuscular route should not be used. Adverse events are common and occasionally life-threatening. They include hypotension, nausea and vomiting, ventricular dysrhythmias, renal failure, pancreatitis, hypoglycemia, hyperglycemia/diabetes mellitus (which can be permanent and require chronic insulin therapy), leukopenia, thrombocytopenia and hypocalcemia.

Trimethoprim–dapsone, clindamycin–primaquine, atovaquone and trimetrexate are proven alternatives for the treatment of PCP in AIDS patients but have not been studied in non-AIDS patients. Similarly, the role of adjunctive corticosteroids for non-AIDS PCP has not undergone controlled prospective investigation. As the pathogenic mechanisms are likely to be similar for HIV and non-HIV patients, it would be reasonable to consider use of prednisone (40mg q12h for 5 days, 40mg q24h for 5 days, then 20mg q24h for the remainder of the duration of PCP therapy) for any severely ill patient (PO_2 <70mmHg or (P(A–a)DO_2 >35mmHg).[84] For indivi-duals who develop symptomatic PCP upon tapering of ongoing corticosteroid therapy, a resumption of the previous dose of corticosteroids should be considered during their initial antimicrobial therapy, with subsequent tapering after clinical improvement occurs.

Development of future treatments may include artificial surfactant, deferoxamine or echinocandins.

REFERENCES

1. Chagas C. Nova tripanozomiaze humana. Instit Oswlado Cruz 1909;1:159–218.
2. Edman JC, Kovacs JA, Masur H, *et al.* Ribosomal RNA sequence shows *Pneumocystis carinii* to be a member of the fungi. Nature 1988;334:519–22.
3. Stringer JR, Walzer PD. Molecular biology and epidemiology of *Pneumocystis carinii* infection in AIDS. AIDS 1996;10:561–71.
4. Kutty G, Ma L, Kovacs JA. Characterization of the expression site of the major surface glycoprotein of human-derived *Pneumocystis carinii*. Mol Microbiol 2001;42:183–93.
5. Peglow SL, Smulian AG, Linke JM, *et al.* Serologic responses to *Pneumocystis carinii* antigens in health and disease. J Infect Dis 1990;161:296–306.
6. Meuwissen JH, Tauber I, Leeuwenber ADEM, Beckers PJA, Sieben M. Parasitologic and serologic observations of infection with *Pneumocystis* in humans. J Infect Dis 1977;136:43–9.
7. Vargas SL, Hughes WT, Santolaya ME, *et al.* Search for primary infection by *Pneumocystis carinii* in a cohort of normal, healthy infants. Clin Infect Dis 2001;32:855–61.
8. Sing A, Roggenkamp A, Autenrieth IB, Heesemann J. *Pneumocystis carinii* carriage in immunocompetent patients with primary pulmonary disorders as detected by single or nested PCR. J Clin Microbiol 1999;37:3409–10.
9. Sing A, Geiger AM, Hogardt M, Heesemann J. *Pneumocystis carinii* carriage among cystic fibrosis patients, as detected by nested PCR. J Clin Microbiol 2001;39:2717–8.
10. Cushion MT, Stringer JR, Walzer PD. Cellular and molecular biology of *Pneumocystis carinii*. Int Rev Cytol 1991;131:59–107.
11. Latouche S, Poirot JL, Bernard C, Roux P. Study of internal transcribed spacer and mitochondrial large-subunit genes of *Pneumocystis carinii* hominis isolated by repeated bronchoalveolar lavage from human immunodeficiency virus-infected patients during one or several episodes of pneumonia. J Clin Microbiol 1997;35:1687–90.
12. Keely SP, Baughman RP, Smulian AG, Dohn MN, Stringer JR. Source of *Pneumocystis carinii* in recurrent episodes of pneumonia in AIDS patients. AIDS 1996;10:881–8.
13. Tsolaki AG, Miller RF, Underwood AP, Banerji S, Wakefield AE. Genetic diversity at the internal transcribed spacer regions of the rRNA operon among isolates of *Pneumocystis carinii* from AIDS patients with recurrent pneumonia. J Infect Dis 1996;174:141–56.
14. Keely SP, Stringer JR. Sequences of *Pneumocystis carinii* f. sp. *hominis* strains associated with recurrent pneumonia vary at multiple loci. J Clin Microbiol 1997;35:2745–7.
15. Hauser PM, Blanc DS, Sudre P, *et al.* Genetic diversity of *Pneumocystis carinii* in HIV-positive and -negative patients as revealed by PCR-SSCP typing. AIDS 2001;15:461–6.
16. Volpe G, Sbaiz L, Avanzini C, Caramello P, Savoia D. Genetic diversity of *Pneumocystis carinii* isolated from human immunodeficiency virus-positive patients in Turin, Italy. J Clin Microbiol 2001;39:2995–8.
17. Helweg-Larsen J, Lundgren B, Lundgren JD. Heterogeneity and compartmentalization of *Pneumocystis carinii* f. sp. *hominis* genotypes in autopsy lungs. J Clin Microbiol 2001;39:3789–92.
18. Ambrose HE, Ponce CA, Wakefield AE, Miller RF, Vargas SL. Distribution of *Pneumocystis carinii* f. sp. *hominis* types in the lung of a child dying of *Pneumocystis* pneumonia. Clin Infect Dis 2001;33:e100–2.
19. Gigliotti F, Harmsen AG, Haidaris CG, Haidaris PJ. *Pneumocystis carinii* is not universally transmissible between mammalian species. Infect Immun 1993;61:2886–90.
20. Morris AM, Swanson M, Ha H, Huang L. Geographic distribution of human immunodeficiency virus-associated *Pneumocystis carinii* pneumonia in San Francisco. Am J Respir Crit Care Med 2000;162:1622–6.
21. Morris A, Beard CB, Huang L. Update on the epidemiology and transmission of *Pneumocystis carinii*. Microbes Infect 2002;4:95–103.
22. Miller RF, Ambrose HE, Wakefield AE. *Pneumocystis carinii* f. sp. *hominis* DNA in immunocompetent health care workers in contact with patients with *P. carinii* pneumonia. J Clin Microbiol 2001;39:3877–82.
23. Olsson M, Lidman C, Latouche S, *et al.* Identification of *Pneumocystis carinii* f. sp. hominis gene sequences in filtered air in hospital environments. J Clin Microbiol 1998;36:1737–40.
24. Bartlett MS, Vermund SH, Jacobs R, *et al.* Detection of *Pneumocystis carinii* DNA in air samples: likely environmental risk to susceptible persons. J Clin Microbiol 1997;35:2511–3.
25. Benfield TL, Prento P, Junge J, Vestbo J, Lundgren JD. Alveolar damage in AIDS-related *Pneumocystis carinii* pneumonia. Chest 1997;111:1193–9.
26. Yoneda K, Walzer PD. Mechanism of alveolar injury in experimental *Pneumocystis carinii* pneumonia in the rat. Br J Exp Pathol 1981;62:339–46.
27. Kaneshiro ES. The lipids of *Pneumocystis carinii*. Clin Microbiol Rev 1998;11:27–41.
28. Zimmersman PE, Voelker R, McCormack FX, Paulsrud JR, Martin WJ. 120-kD surface glycoprotein of *Pneumocystis carinii* is a ligand for surfactant protein A. J Clin Invest 1992;89:143–9.
29. Koziel H, Phelps DS, Fishman JA, Armstrong MY, Richards FF, Rose RM. Surfactant protein-A reduces binding and phagocytosis of *Pneumocystis carinii* by human alveolar macrophages in vitro. Am J Respir Cell Mol Biol 1998;18:834–43.
30. Roths JB, Sidman CL. Both immunity and hyper-responsiveness to *Pneumocystis carinii* result from transfer of $CD4^+$ but not $CD8^+$ T cells into severe combined immunodeficiency mice. J Clin Invest 1992;90:673–8.
31. Krishnan VL, Meager A, Mitchell DM, Pinching AJ. Alveolar macrophages in AIDS patients: increased spontaneous tumour necrosis factor-alpha production in *Pneumocystis carinii* pneumonia. Clin Exp Immunol 1990;80:156–60.
32. Rayment N, Miller RF, Ali N, Binks MH, Katz DR. Synthesis of tumor necrosis factor-alpha mRNA in bronchoalveolar lavage cells from human immunodeficiency virus-infected persons with *Pneumocystis carinii* pneumonia. J Infect Dis 1996;174:654–9.
33. Benfield TL, Lundgren B, Levine SJ, Kronborg G, Shelhamer JH, Lundgren JD. The major surface glycoprotein of *Pneumocystis carinii* induces release and gene expression of interleukin-8 and tumor necrosis factor alpha in monocytes. Infect Immun 1997;65:4790–4.
34. Benfield TL, Steenwuk RV, Nielsen TL, *et al.* Interleukin-8 and eicosanoid production in the lung during moderate to severe *Pneumocystis carinii* pneumonia in AIDS: a role of interleukin-8 in the pathogenesis of *P. carinii* pneumonia. Respir Med 1995;89:285–90.
35. Chen W, Havell EA, Harmsen AG. Importance of endogenous tumor necrosis factor alpha and gamma interferon in host resistance against *Pneumocystis carinii* infection. Infect Immun 1992;60:1279–84.
36. Koziel H, Eichbaum Q, Kruskal BA, MY *et al.* Reduced binding and phagocytosis of *Pneumocystis carinii* by alveolar macrophages from persons infected with HIV-1 correlates with mannose receptor downregulation. J Clin Invest 1998;102:1332–44.
37. Stehle SE, Rogers RA, Harmsen AG, Ezekowitz RA. A soluble mannose receptor immunoadhesin enhances phagocytosis of *Pneumocystis carinii* by human polymorphonuclear leukocytes in vitro. Scand J Immunol 2000;52:131–7.
38. Fraser IP, Takahashi K, Koziel H, Fardin B, Harmsen A, Ezekowitz RA. *Pneumocystis carinii* enhances soluble mannose receptor production by macrophages. Microbes Infect 2000;2:1305–10.
39. Furuta T, Ueda K, Kyuwa S, Fujiwara K. Effect of T-cell transfer on *Pneumocystis carinii* infection in nude mice. Jpn J Exp Med 1984;54:57–64.
40. Graves DC, Smulian G, Walzer PD. *Pneumocystis carinii* pneumonia. In: Walzer PD, ed. Humoral and cellular immunity. New York: Marcel Dekker, 1994:267–87.
41. Gigliotti F, Garvy BA, Haidaris CG, Harmsen AG. Recognition of *Pneumocystis carinii* antigens by local antibody-secreting cells following resolution of *P. carinii* pneumonia in mice. J Infect Dis 1998;178:235–42.
42. Jalil A, Moja P, Lambert C, *et al.* Decreased production of local immunoglobulin A to *Pneumocystis carinii* in bronchoalveolar lavage fluid from human immunodeficiency virus-positive patients. Infect Immun 2000;68:1054–60.
43. Laursen AL, Andersen PL. Low levels of IgG antibodies against *Pneumocystis carinii* among HIV-infected patients. Scand J Infect Dis 1998;30:495–9.
44. Kovacs JA, Hiemenz JW, Macher AM, *et al.* *Pneumocystis carinii* pneumonia: a comparison between patients with the acquired immunodeficiency syndrome and patients with other immunodeficiencies. Ann Intern Med 1984;100:663–71.
45. Metersky ML, Aslenzadeh J, Stelmach P. A comparison of induced and expectorated sputum for the diagnosis of *Pneumocystis carinii* pneumonia. Chest 1998;113:1555–9.
46. Gryzan S, Paradis IL, Zeevi A, *et al.* Unexpectedly high incidence of *Pneumocystis carinii* infection after lung–heart transplantation. Am Rev Respir Dis 1988;137:1268–74.
47. Fishman JA. Radiological approaches to the diagnosis of *Pneumocystis carinii* pneumonia. In: Walzer PD, ed. *Pneumocystis carinii* pneumonia. New York: Marcel Dekker; 1994:415–36.
48. Dickenmann MJ, Tamm M, Tsinalis D, Binet I, Thiel G, Steiger J. Blood eosinophilia in tacrolimus-treated patients: an indicator of *Pneumocystis carinii* pneumonia. Transplantation 1999;68:1606–8.
49. Mansharamani NG, Garland R, Delaney D, Koziel H. Management and outcome patterns for adult *Pneumocystis carinii* pneumonia, 1985 to 1995: comparison of HIV-associated cases to other immunocompromised states. Chest 2000;118:704–11.
50. Meduri GU, Stover DE, Greeno RA, Nash T, Zaman MB. Bilateral bronchoalveolar lavage in the diagnosis of opportunistic pulmonary infections. Chest 1991;100:1272–6.
51. Levine SJ, Kennedy D, Shelhamer JH, *et al.* Diagnosis of *Pneumocystis carinii* pneumonia by multiple lobe, site-directed bronchoalveolar lavage with immunofluorescent monoclonal antibody staining in human immunodeficiency virus-infected patients receiving aerosolized pentamidine prophylaxis. Am Rev Respir Dis 1992;146:838–43.
52. Cadranel J, Gillet-Juvin K, Antoine M, *et al.* Site-directed bronchoalveolar lavage and transbronchial biopsy in HIV-infected patients with pneumonia. Am J Respir Crit Care Med 1995;152:1103–6.
53. Willocks L, Burns S, Cossar R, Brettle R. Diagnosis of *Pneumocystis carinii* in a population of HIV-positive drug users, with particular reference to sputum induction and fluorescent antibody techniques. J Infect 1993;26:257–64.
54. Miller RF, Kocjan G, Buckland J, *et al.* Sputum induction for the diagnosis of pulmonary disease in HIV positive patients. J Infect 1991;23:5–15.
55. Carmichael A, Bateman N, Nayagam M. Examination of induced sputum in the diagnosis of *Pneumocystis carinii* pneumonia. Cytopathology 1991;2:61–6.

56. Sing A, Trebesius K, Roggenkamp A, *et al.* Evaluation of diagnostic value and epidemiological implications of PCR for *Pneumocystis carinii* in different immunosuppressed and immunocompetent patient groups. J Clin Microbiol 2000;38:1461–7.
57. Olsson M, Stralin K, Holmberg H. Clinical significance of nested polymerase chain reaction and immunofluorescence for detection of *Pneumocystis carinii* pneumonia. Clin Microbiol Infect 2001;7:492–7.
58. Torres J, Goldman M, Wheat LJ, *et al.* Diagnosis of *Pneumocystis carinii* pneumonia in human immunodeficiency virus-infected patients with polymerase chain reaction: a blinded comparison to standard methods. Clin Infect Dis 2000;30:141–5.
59. Khan MA, Farrag N, Butcher P. Diagnosis of *Pneumocystis carinii* pneumonia: immunofluorescence staining, simple PCR or nPCR. J Infect 1999;39:77–80.
60. Lipshick GY, Gill VJ, Lundgren JD, *et al.* Improved diagnosis of *Pneumocystis carinii* infection by polymerase chain reaction on induced sputum and blood. Lancet 1991;340:203–6.
61. Fischer S, Gill VJ, Kovacs J, *et al.* The use of oral washes to diagnose *Pneumocystis carinii* pneumonia: a blinded prospective study using a polymerase chain reaction-based detection system. J Infect Dis 2001;184:1485–8.
62. Chouaid C, Roux P, Lavard I, Poirot JL, Housset B. Use of the polymerase chain reaction technique on induced-sputum samples for the diagnosis of *Pneumocystis carinii* pneumonia in HIV-infected patients. A clinical and cost-analysis study. Am J Clin Pathol 1995;104:72–5.
63. Ward MM, Donald F. *Pneumocystis carinii* pneumonia in patients with connective tissue diseases: the role of hospital experience in diagnosis and mortality. Arthritis Rheum 1999;42:780–9.
64. Lufft V, Kliem V, Behrend M, Pichlmayr R, Koch KM, Brunkhorst R. Incidence of *Pneumocystis carinii* pneumonia after renal transplantation. Impact of immunosuppression. Transplantation 1996;62:421–3.
65. Gordon SM, LaRosa SP, Kalmadi S, *et al.* Should prophylaxis for *Pneumocystis carinii* pneumonia in solid organ transplant recipients ever be discontinued? Clin Infect Dis 1999;28:240–6.
66. Fishman JA. Prevention of infection caused by *Pneumocystis carinii* in transplant recipients. Clin Infect Dis 2001;33:1397–405.
67. Arend SM, Westendorp RG, Kroon FP, *et al.* Rejection treatment and cytomegalovirus infection as risk factors for *Pneumocystis carinii* pneumonia in renal transplant recipients. Clin Infect Dis 1996;22:920–5.
68. Lyytikainen O, Ruutu T, Volin L, *et al.* Late onset *Pneumocystis carinii* pneumonia following allogeneic bone marrow transplantation. Bone Marrow Transplant 1996;17:1057–9.
69. Sepkowitz K, Brown A, Armstrong D. *Pneumocystis carinii* pneumonia without acquired immunodeficiency syndrome. Arch Intern Med 1995;155:1125–8.
70. Mansharamani NG, Balachandran D, Vernovsky I, Garland R, Koziel H. Peripheral blood $CD4^+$ T-lymphocyte counts during *Pneumocystis carinii* pneumonia in immunocompromised patients without HIV infection. Chest 2000;118:712–20.
71. Gluck T, Geerdes-Fenge HF, Straub RH, *et al.* *Pneumocystis carinii* pneumonia as a complication of immunosuppressive therapy. Infection 2000;28:227–30.
72. Chung JB, Armstrong K, Schwartz JS, Albert D. Cost-effectiveness of prophylaxis against *Pneumocystis carinii* pneumonia in patients with Wegner's granulomatosis undergoing immunosuppressive therapy. Arthritis Rheum 2000;43:1841–8.
73. Munoz P, Munoz RM, Palomo J, Rodriguez-Creixems M, Munoz R, Bouza E. *Pneumocystis carinii* infection in heart transplant recipients. Efficacy of a weekend prophylaxis schedule. Medicine (Baltimore) 1997;76:415–22.
74. Hughes WT, Kuhn S, Chearskul S, *et al.* Successful intermittent chemoprophylaxis for *Pneumocystis carinii* pneumonitis. N Engl J Med 1987;316:1627–32.
75. Maltezou HC, Petropoulos D, Choroszy M, *et al.* Dapsone for *Pneumocystis carinii* prophylaxis in children undergoing bone marrow transplantation. Bone Marrow Transplant 1997;20:879–81.
76. Souza JP, Boeckh M, Gooley TA, Flowers ME, Crawford SW. High rates of *Pneumocystis carinii* pneumonia in allogeneic blood and marrow transplant recipients receiving dapsone prophylaxis. Clin Infect Dis 1999;29:1467–71.
77. Saukkonen K, Garland R, Koziel H. Aerosolized pentamidine as alternative primary prophylaxis against *Pneumocystis carinii* pneumonia in adult hepatic and renal transplant recipients. Chest 1996;109:1250–5.
78. Colby C, McAfee S, Sackstein R, Finkelstein D, Fishman J, Spitzer T. A prospective randomized trial comparing the toxicity and safety of atovaquone with trimethoprim/sulfamethoxazole as *Pneumocystis carinii* pneumonia prophylaxis following autologous peripheral blood stem cell transplantation. Bone Marrow Transplant 1999;24:897–902.
79. Meyers B, Borrego F, Papanicolaou G. *Pneumocystis carinii* pneumonia prophylaxis with atovaquone in trimethoprim-sulfamethoxazole-intolerant orthotopic liver transplant patients: a preliminary study. Liver Transpl 2001;7:750–1.
80. Ma L, Borio L, Masur H, Kovacs JA. *Pneumocystis carinii* dihydropteroate synthase but not dihydrofolate reductase gene mutations correlate with prior trimethoprim-sulfamethoxazole or dapsone use. J Infect Dis 1999;180:1969–78.
81. Helweg-Larsen J, Benfield TL, Eugen-Olsen J, Lundgren JD, Lundgren B. Effects of mutations in *Pneumocystis carinii* dihydropteroate synthase gene on outcome of AIDS-associated *P. carinii* pneumonia. Lancet 1999;354:1347–51.
82. Kazanjian P, Armstrong W, Hossler PA, *et al.* *Pneumocystis carinii* mutations are associated with duration of sulfa or sulfone prophylaxis exposure in AIDS patients. J Infect Dis 2000;182:551–7.
83. Navin TR, Beard CB, Huang L, *et al.* Effect of mutations in *Pneumocystis carinii* dihydropteroate synthase gene on outcome of *P. carinii* pneumonia in patients with HIV-1: a prospective study. Lancet 2001;358:545–9.
84. National Institutes of Health–University of California Expert Panel for Corticosteroids as Adjunctive Therapy for Pneumocystis Pneumonia. Consensus statement on the use of corticosteroids as adjunctive therapy for *Pneumocystis* pneumonia in the acquired immunodeficiency syndrome. N Engl J Med 1990;323:1500–4.

chapter
242 Protozoa: Intestinal and Urogenital Amebae, Flagellates and Ciliates

Lynne S Garcia

This chapter discusses the amebae, flagellates and ciliates that parasitize the intestinal and urogenital systems of humans (Table 242.1). With the exception of *Trichomonas vaginalis*, all of the organisms live in the intestinal tract. Intestinal protozoa vary in pathogenicity and prevalence but, with rare exceptions, all have a worldwide distribution.

NATURE

Amebae, flagellates and ciliates are single-celled eukaryotic organisms belonging to the subkingdom or phylum Protozoa. In general, the organisms related to human infection change their form and function from the active, feeding trophozoites to the resting cyst form. All protozoa contain a nucleus, often with a karyosome near its center. The cytoplasm is composed of the endoplasm, which immediately surrounds the nucleus, and the ectoplasm, which functions as the locomotion apparatus. Reproduction is relatively simple and is accomplished through repeated asexual multiplication by binary fission. Currently, it is not completely clear whether *Blastocystis hominis* should be classified with the protozoa or is actually a fungus-like organism within the stramenopile group; however, it will be discussed in this chapter.[1]

EPIDEMIOLOGY

Intestinal amebae, flagellates and ciliates are transmitted through fecally contaminated food, water or other materials. Prevalence is correlated with socio-economic conditions and higher infection rates occur in people who have poor personal hygiene or who live in areas with poor sanitation. Contaminated water supplies are a particular problem because the usual levels of chlorination may not kill cysts. Filtration is required. Endemic and epidemic disease has been traced to water supplies that use surface water which either is not filtered or has improperly functioning filters.

These organisms generally have a cystic stage that develops when conditions in the environment are unfavorable for continued multiplication. The cyst wall is thicker than the trophozoite membrane and thus provides protection. Once these cysts have been transferred to a new host, usually by fecal–oral contamination from person to person, the organisms excyst. Excystation factors include osmotic changes in the environment, enzymatic action of the enclosed organism on the inner surface of the cyst wall and, among the parasitic protozoa, favorable pH and enzymatic action of the host tissues. Transmission of those protozoa with no identified cyst stage has not been totally explained.

Entamoeba histolytica

Infections with *E. histolytica* are seen worldwide and are more prevalent in the tropics. In 1997, over 500 million people were estimated to be infected with *E. histolytica*, 50 million had extensive symptoms, including colitis or extraintestinal abscesses, and there were 100,000 deaths.[2] For every case of invasive disease diagnosed, there are at least 10–20 asymptomatic individuals excreting infective cysts. Population groups with a higher incidence of amebiasis include people from the developing world or recent immigrants from there to the developed nations.

Social changes seen in the late 1960s – open expression of homosexuality, increased sexual contacts, increased frequency of sexual activities and anonymity of sexual partners – contributed to dramatic increases in sexually transmitted organisms, including *E. histolytica*. A number of clinical syndromes have been recognized and referred to as 'the gay bowel syndrome'. Published reports confirm that *E. histolytica* is one of the major pathogens in the gay bowel syndrome. However, some feel that this term 'gay bowel syndrome' is neither gay specific, confined to the bowel, nor a syndrome.[3] Clinical presentations within the homosexual community often differ from those seen in the heterosexual population and almost 50% of all homosexual men found to be infected with *E. histolytica* are asymptomatic. Studies have confirmed the lack of correlation between symptoms and the presence of *E. histolytica* in this risk group.[4] However, it is an accepted fact that the ameba morphologically identified as *E. histolytica* is actually two separate and distinct species. *E. histolytica* is the pathogenic species and is considered the etiologic agent of amebic colitis and extraintestinal amebiasis, while *E. dispar* is the nonpathogenic species and does not invade tissue or cause intestinal symptoms. This may explain the lack of correlation between symptoms and the presence of the morphological identification of *E. histolytica* in the group of homosexual men studied. Therefore, in epidemiologic studies prior to the development of specific reagents for the identification of true *E. histolytica*, those organisms identified as *E. histolytica* were actually *E. histolytica/E. dispar*.

Epidemiologic evidence of sexual transmission of *E. histolytica* has grown significantly since the early 1970s, particularly in New York City and San Francisco. In San Francisco, the incidence of reported symptomatic intestinal amebiasis increased by over 1000% from 1978 to 1988 among homosexual men between 20 and 39 years of age.[4] It appears that approximately 30% of urban homosexual men may be infected with *E. histolytica* (*E. histolytica/E. dispar*), a sharp increase over the estimated rate of less than 5% seen in the general population within the USA. Direct oral–anal contact (anilingus) leads to fecal exposure and oral contact with a variety of intestinal pathogens. Although anilingus has been listed as a key risk factor in potential exposure, transmission can also occur during oral–genital sex after anal intercourse has occurred. Active heterosexuals can acquire infection with *E. histolytica* through sexual activities that provide an opportunity for fecal–oral contamination. The key factor is not necessarily homosexuality, but the frequency of sexual activity and potential for fecal–oral contact. In a more recent study from Japan, symptomatic amebiasis in the east-south east area of Tokyo is a disease that predominantly afflicts males and the high rates of patients who engaged in male homosexual or bisexual practices suggest that amebiasis is likely to be a sexually transmitted disease in homosexual or bisexual men. These infections were confirmed to be true *E. histolytica*, primarily zymodeme II.[5]

AMEBAE, FLAGELLATES AND CILIATE THAT PARASITIZE THE INTESTINAL AND UROGENITAL SYSTEMS OF HUMANS		
Type	Species	Pathogenicity*
Amebae	*Entamoeba histolytica*	+
	Entamoeba dispar	–
	Entamoeba hartmanni	–
	Entamoeba coli	–
	Entamoeba polecki	–
	Entamoeba gingivalis†	–
	Endolimax nana	–
	Iodamoeba bütschlii	–
	Blastocystis hominis	±
Flagellates	*Dientamoeba fragilis*	+
	Giardia lamblia	+
	Trichomonas vaginalis‡	+
	Pentatrichomonas (Trichomonas) hominis	–
	Trichomonas tenax†	–
	Chilomastix mesnili	–
	Enteromonas hominis	–
	Retortamonas intestinalis	–
Ciliate	*Balantidium coli*	+

* Pathogenic = +; nonpathogenic = –; ± = pathogenicity controversial
† Body site: mouth
‡ Body site: urogenital system

Table 242.1 Amebae, flagellates and ciliate that parasitize the intestinal and urogenital systems of humans.

With the advent of AIDS and the subsequent modifications in sexual practices within homosexual communities, the incidence of *E. histolytica* infection has decreased. In recent years, the increased incidence of disease caused by coccidian parasites, *Isospora belli* and *Cryptosporidium parvum* and the microsporidia, *Enterocytozoon bieneusi* and *Encephalitozoon intestinalis* has become much more of a problem in patients who have AIDS.

In certain urban areas (Mexico City, Mexico; Medellin, Colombia; and Durban, South Africa), the incidence of invasive disease is considerably higher than in the rest of the world. Contributing factors may include poor nutrition, tropical climate, decreased immunologic competence of the host, stress, altered bacterial flora in the colon, traumatic injuries to the colonic mucosa, alcoholism and genetic factors.

The human is the reservoir host for *E. histolytica/E. dispar* and can transmit the infection to other humans, primates, dogs, cats and possibly pigs. The cyst stages are very resistant to environmental conditions and remain viable in the soil for days. The asymptomatic cyst passer who is a food handler is thought to play the most important role in transmission.

It has been postulated that a colonization-blocking vaccine could eliminate *E. histolytica* as a cause of human disease, particularly as humans serve as the only significant reservoir host, and a number of potential protective antigens are being investigated.[6–8]

Blastocystis hominis

Blastocystis hominis is probably transmitted via the fecal–oral route through contaminated food or water; the cysts survive in water for up to 19 days at normal temperatures.[9,10] Although other modes of transmission are not defined, the incidence and apparent worldwide distribution suggest the traditional route of infection. Prevention would involve improved personal hygiene and sanitary conditions.

Giardia lamblia (intestinalis)

Although some authorities have changed or are considering a species name change to *G. intestinalis*, we have decided to maintain *G. lamblia* for this chapter. Transmission is by ingestion of viable cysts, and contaminated food and drink are the usual sources. This infection is found most frequently in children or in groups that live in close quarters.[11,12] Also there may be outbreaks caused by poor sanitation facilities or breakdowns; travelers and campers often experience such outbreaks.[13,14] There is also an increase in the prevalence of giardiasis in the male homosexual population, probably as a result of anal and/or oral sexual practices.[15]

Decreased gastric acid production may predispose people to infection with *G. lamblia*. Normal gastric acidity may act as a barrier to infection; patients who have had a gastrectomy are prone to infection with *G. lamblia*. Reduction in gastric acid also occurs as a result of malnutrition and both factors may, as a group, increase susceptibility to infection with this organism. Impairment of the host's immune system may also play a role.

Lower incidence of giardiasis in infants up to 6 months of age may be associated with breast-feeding and some protection against infection via secretary IgA; however, lower incidence may also be related to a decreased exposure to *G. lamblia* in breast-fed infants.

Giardiasis is one of the common causes of travelers' diarrhea and is worldwide in distribution. Visitors in areas endemic for *Giardia* spp. are more likely to become symptomatic than the inhabitants of that area; this is probably because the latter have developed immunity from previous, and possibly continued, exposure to the organism. A number of outbreaks in the USA have been attributed to resort or municipal water supplies, such as Oregon, Colorado, Utah, Washington, New Hampshire and New York.[16–18] High infection rates were also reported from hikers and campers who drank stream water. Because some of these areas were remote from human habitation, infected wild animals, especially the beaver, were suspected of being the source.[13,17,19–21] Surveys show human infection rates of 2–15% in various parts of the world.

Because of potential wild animal reservoirs and possible domestic animal reservoir hosts, measures in addition to personal hygiene and improved sanitation have to be considered.[22,23] Iodine is recommended as an effective disinfectant for drinking water, but it must be used according to directions.[24,25] Filtration systems have also been recommended, although they have certain drawbacks, such as clogging.

Isoenzyme studies, used for parasite identification and classification, have provided information related to organism pathogenicity, possible implication in water-borne outbreaks and the potential cause of human disease. The examination of isoenzyme patterns of *G. duodenalis* (*G. lamblia*) obtained from humans and animals showed no obvious correlation between clinical symptoms and isoenzyme patterns. These studies also demonstrated significant differences between isolates from within a single region and those from other distant geographic locations.[26,27]

Dientamoeba fragilis

Dientamoeba fragilis infection is commonly associated with enterobiasis and it has been suggested that *D. fragilis* may infect *Enterobius* spp. eggs and thus bypass gastric acidity. Although clinical infections with *D. fragilis* occur, they are not often reported. This is probably because the infection is self-limiting, stool examination is not requested and laboratory identification is difficult. The incubation period for clinical disease is not clearly defined.

Trichomonas vaginalis

Infection with *T. vaginalis* is acquired primarily through sexual intercourse; asymptomatic men therefore need to be diagnosed and treated. The organism can survive for some time in a moist environment such as damp towels and underclothes; however, this mode of transmission is thought to be very rare.

Balantidium coli

Domestic pigs are probably the most important reservoir host for human infection with *B. coli*. In areas in which pigs are the main domestic animal, the incidence of human infection can be quite high (e.g. New Guinea). Human infection is fairly rare in temperate areas, although once the infection is established, it can develop into an epidemic, particularly when environmental sanitation and personal hygiene are poor. This situation has been seen in mental hospitals in the USA. Preventive measures involve increased attention to personal hygiene and sanitation, as the mode of transmission is ingestion of infective cysts through contaminated food or water.

PREVENTION

Transmission of the majority of the intestinal protozoa occurs through ingestion of infective cysts, which can be acquired from food, water and person to person by the fecal–oral route. These infections tend to be found more frequently in groups that live in close quarters or in certain population groups. There may be outbreaks due to poor sanitation facilities or breakdowns as evidenced by infections in travelers and campers; certainly this has been found for giardiasis. Although amebiasis is usually associated with poor sanitation and underdeveloped areas of the world, sexual transmission has also been documented, mainly among urban homosexual men. Prevention in this group is directly related to limiting sexual practices that provide an opportunity for fecal–oral contamination. The single most effective practice that prevents the spread of infections with intestinal protozoa, particularly in the childcare setting, is thorough handwashing by the children, staff and visitors. In the case of *D. fragilis*, it has been suggested that the trophozoites may infect *Enterobius* spp. eggs, thus allowing protection from gastric acidity; however, under most circumstances, total prevention of enterobiasis and/or infection with *D. fragilis* is neither realistic nor possible. *T. vaginalis* is acquired primarily though sexual intercourse, hence the need to diagnose and treat asymptomatic males. The organism can also survive for some time in a moist environment such as damp towels and underclothes; however, this manner of transmission is considered rare.

Although incomplete epidemiologic investigation and reporting make it difficult to determine the significance of the water-borne transmission of giardiasis accurately, the water-borne route seems to be more important for this protozoan than for other more commonly recognized water-borne pathogens, with the possible exception of *Cryptosporidium parvum*. Iodine has been recommended as an effective disinfectant for drinking water, but it must be used according to directions. Because of the potential for wild animal and possibly domestic animal reservoir hosts related to *Giardia* spp., measures in addition to personal hygiene and improved sanitary measures have to be considered and implemented. If appropriate procedures are followed, conventional water filtration should trap most protozoan parasites, including *Giardia*. One should avoid swallowing water when in lakes, rivers, pools or hot tubs; also do not drink directly from lakes, rivers, streams or springs. Filtration devices for hikers and campers are also available; however, one should look for 'reverse osmosis', 'absolute 1 micron', 'Standard 53', and the words 'cyst reduction' or 'cyst removal'. Boiling water, at a rolling boil, for 1 minute is sufficient to kill organisms, including *Giardia* spp. and *Cryptosporidium* spp. It is also important to thoroughly wash all fruits and vegetables if eating uncooked, use safe water for washing food, peel fruit and avoid unpasteurized milk or dairy products.

PATHOGENICITY

Some of the intestinal protozoa are nonpathogenic and produce no disease; however, microscopists must be able to distinguish pathogenic from nonpathogenic species. The presence of nonpathogenic species indicates that the person has been exposed to fecal contamination. Several species can cause mild to severe gastrointestinal symptoms, and *E. histolytica* may produce extraintestinal lesions. However, pathogenic or potentially pathogenic protozoa do not always produce symptoms or they may remain after symptoms have resolved. Asymptomatic individuals may serve as reservoirs for the infection. Detection of a potentially pathogenic protozoan does not necessarily prove that the organism is causing the illness. Patients may have diarrhea caused by other organisms such as *Salmonella* spp., *Shigella* spp., *Escherichia coli* or rotavirus. The pathogenicity of some species (e.g. *B. hominis*) has been questioned and *E. histolytica* is now considered to be two separate organisms, one pathogenic (*E. histolytica*) and one nonpathogenic (*E. dispar*). *Trichomonas vaginalis*, a urogenital flagellate, is also considered pathogenic and may cause mild to severe vaginitis and other urogenital problems.

Entamoeba histolytica

Although many people worldwide are infected with *E. histolytica*, only a small percentage develops clinical symptoms. Morbidity and mortality caused by *E. histolytica* vary, depending on geographic area, organism species (*E. histolytica* vs *E. dispar*) and the immune status of the patient.

In 1961, with the development of successful axenic culture methods requiring no bacterial co-culture, sufficient numbers of organisms could be obtained for additional studies. Approximately 15 years later, reports indicated that *E. histolytica* clinical isolates could be classified into groups using starch gel electrophoresis and review of banding patterns related to specific isoenzymes.[28] The four isoenzymes are glucophosphate isomerase (GPI), phosphoglucomutases (PGM), malate dehydrogenase (ME) and hexokinase (HK), indicating that there are pathogenic and nonpathogenic strains (zymodemes) of *E. histolytica*. On the basis of analysis of thousands of clinical isolates, the zymodeme patterns were thought to be genetic rather than phenotypic.

During the 1980s and 1990s several publications reviewed the issues regarding pathogenic *E. histolytica* versus nonpathogenic *E. dispar*. On the basis of current knowledge, pathogenic *E. histolytica* is considered to be the etiologic agent of amebic colitis and extraintestinal disease, whereas nonpathogenic *E. dispar* produces no intestinal symptoms and is not invasive in humans.[29–31] Diamond & Clark[32] redescribed the two species as *E. histolytica* (Schaudinn 1903), which is the invasive human pathogen, and *E. dispar* (Brumpt 1925), which is noninvasive and does not cause disease.

Blastocystis hominis

In spite of the published literature, the true role of this organism in terms of colonization or disease and the relevance of organism numbers are still somewhat controversial. In one recent study of patients with irritable bowel syndrome, there was a set of patients in whom the presence of *B. hominis* did not appear to be incidental.[33] The first report of a possible relationship between intestinal obstruction and a concomitant *B. hominis* infection has also been published recently.[34] In patients with other underlying conditions, the symptoms may be more pronounced.[35] There is evidence to indicate there are several ribodeme types and there may be a relationship between ribodeme type and pathogenicity, only some of which will be responsible for increased intestinal permeability and symptoms.[36,37]

Giardia lamblia (intestinalis)

The majority of individuals infected with *G. lamblia* are asymptomatic. Preliminary studies indicate that there may be two different strains of *G. lamblia*, group A and group B, associated with different degrees of virulence. Group A appears to be more pathogenic and is associated with symptomatic infection. Isoenzyme and molecular studies also support the differences between these two groups.[38–40]

Dientamoeba fragilis

Although its pathogenic status is still not well defined, *D. fragilis* has been associated with a wide range of symptoms. This uncertainty could be due in part to the existence of pathogenic and nonpathogenic variants. Evidence for two genetically distinct forms has been obtained using PCR-restriction fragment length polymorphism analysis of ribosomal genes.[41,42]

Trichomonas vaginalis

T. vaginalis is site specific and usually cannot survive outside the urogenital system. After introduction, proliferation begins, with resulting inflammation and large numbers of trophozoites in the tissues and the secretions. Nutrient acquisition and cytoadherence, immune system evasion and regulation of virulence genes are virulence factors associated with pathogenesis.[43] It appears that interference with trichomonads, mucin receptors and proteinases may form a strategy to prevent colonization with this pathogenic flagellate.[44]

DIAGNOSTIC MICROBIOLOGY

Because intestinal symptoms are non-specific, diagnosis requires laboratory identification of the organisms present. Immunodiagnostic methods for antibody detection are useful for the diagnosis of extra-intestinal amebiasis, but their utility is limited for intestinal disease.

Organism morphology varies and species characteristics often overlap. For reliable identification, microscopists must be able to differentiate all species regardless of their potential for causing disease. Special attention will be given to the clinically significant intestinal pathogens, especially *E. histolytica, B. hominis, G. lamblia, D. fragilis* and *B. coli.*

Identification of amebae in fecal specimens

Trophozoites and cysts are diagnostic stages of the amebae and either or both stages can be detected in feces. Microscopists must be able to distinguish trophozoites and cysts from epithelial cells, polymorphonuclear leukocytes and macrophages, as well as from pus cells, yeasts, pollen, moulds, and vegetable and crystalline artefacts.

Trophozoite motility in physiologic saline mounts of fresh material and cytoplasmic inclusions, such as erythrocytes in trophozoites and chromatoid bodies in cysts, can be observed. Iodine solutions are used for temporary cyst stains of fresh or fixed specimens. Cyst characteristics are less variable than those of trophozoites and species of cysts can often be identified in iodine-stained wet mounts. However, examination of permanent stained smears using oil immersion (×1000) is recommended for definitive identification of trophozoites and cysts. Size is not a reliable feature for species differentiation of either trophozoites or cysts except when separating *E. histolytica/ E. dispar* from *E. hartmanni.*

The microscopist must observe the cytoplasmic and the nuclear characteristics of several organisms before making a final identification. Although cysts are more easily identified than trophozoites, several cysts (particularly if they are immature) should be observed to ensure that the identification is reliable. If two species are identified, there should be distinct populations of each.

Sometimes, although amebic organisms are seen, species cannot be identified. In these instances, the laboratory should report 'unidentified ameba trophozoites (or cysts)'. If the genus can be determined but the species cannot, 'unidentified *Entamoeba* trophozoites or cysts' should be reported and another specimen should be requested.

Entamoeba histolytica

Intestinal infection is usually diagnosed by the microscopic identification of organisms in feces or in sigmoidoscopic material from ulcerations (Fig. 241.1). Nonpathogenic amebae can be confused with pathogens (Figs 242.2–242.5). Only trophozoites are found in tissue lesions, but both trophozoites and cysts may be found in the intes-

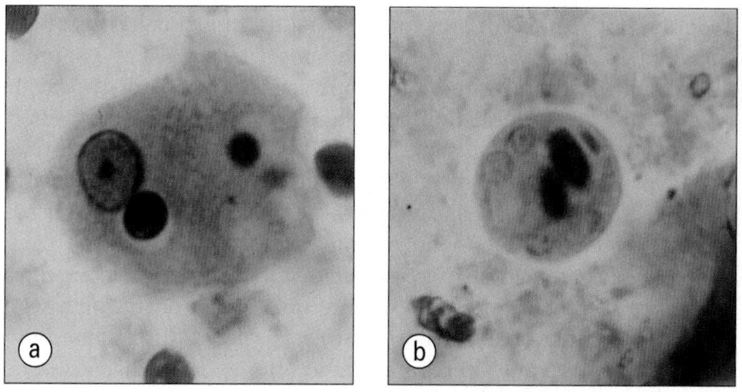

Fig. 242.1 ***Entamoeba histolytica.*** (a) Trophozoite containing ingested red blood cells (the presence of red blood cells confirms the organism is the true pathogen, *E. histolytica*). (b) ***Entamoeba histolytica/E. dispar***, cyst containing four nuclei and chromatoidal bars with smooth, rounded edges (trichrome stain). Note: from the cyst morphology, it is not possible to differentiate pathogenic *E. histolytica* from nonpathogenic *E. dispar.*

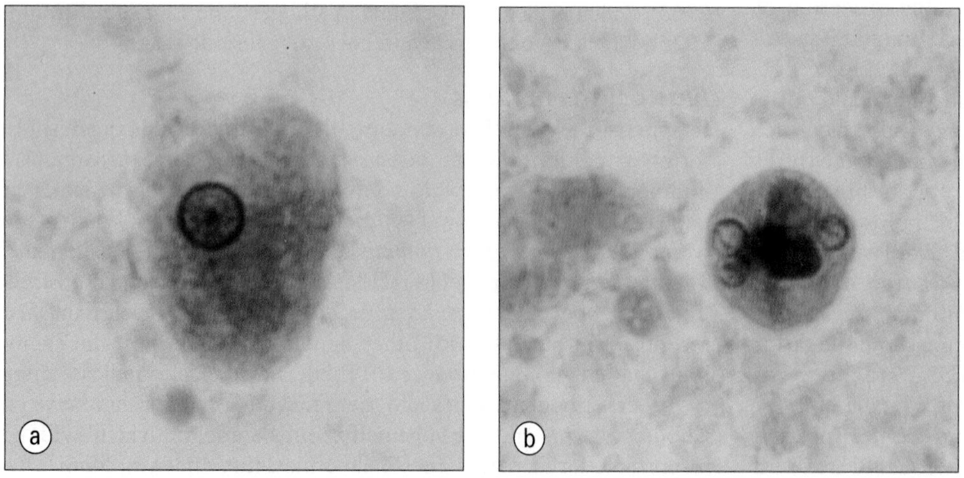

Fig. 242.2 ***Entamoeba hartmanni.*** (a) Trophozoite. (b) Cyst containing up to four nuclei and chromatoidal bars with smooth, rounded edges (trichrome stain). Note: *E. hartmanni* measures less than *E. histolytica/ E. dispar*, the trophozoite is <12μm and the cyst is <10μm.

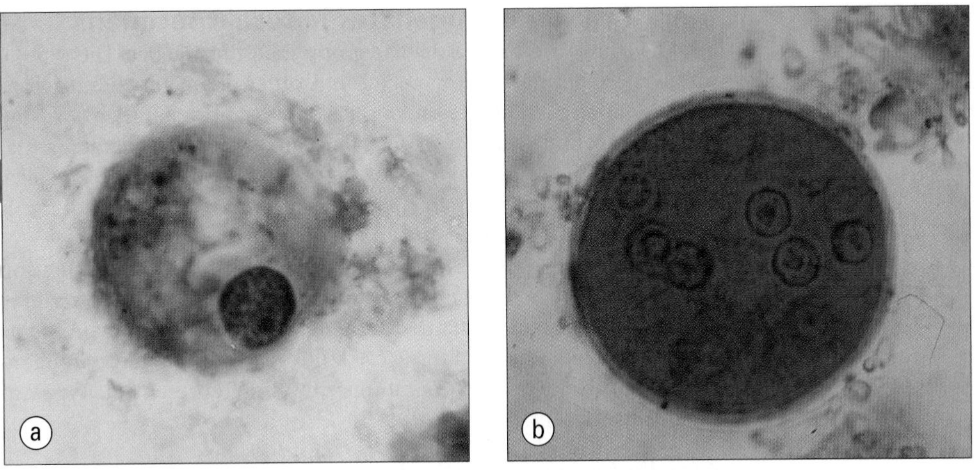

Fig. 242.3 ***Entamoeba coli.*** (a) Trophozoite containing a single nucleus in which the karyosome is eccentric (tends to be centrally located in *E. histolytica/E. dispar*). (b) Cyst contains more than five nuclei (d'Antoni's iodine).

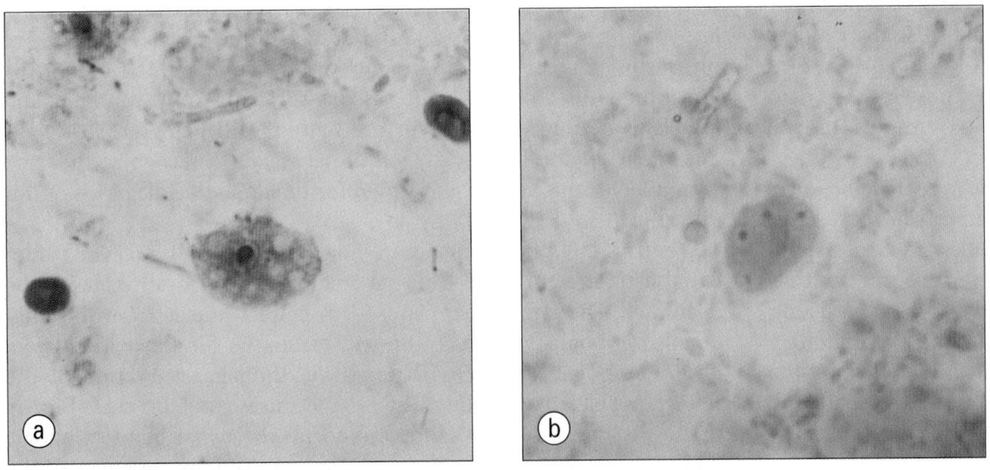

Fig. 242.4 ***Endolimax nana.*** (a) Trophozoite containing a single nucleus with no peripheral chromatin (large karyosome only) and vacuolated cytoplasm. (b) Cyst containing four nuclei (three easily visible) (trichrome stain).

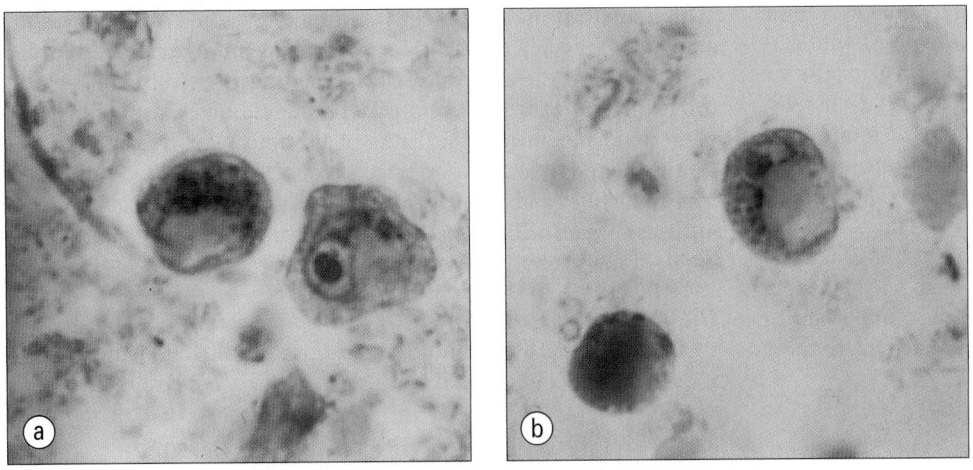

Fig. 242.5 ***Iodamoeba bütschlii.*** (a) Trophozoite containing a single nucleus with a large karyosome and cyst containing a single nucleus and a large glycogen vacuole. (b) Cyst containing a single nucleus and a large glycogen vacuole – note the size of the karyosome (trichome stain). There is also a *Blastocystis hominis* central body form present at the lower left of the image.

tinal lumen. Some patients who have invasive disease may have only trophozoites in fecal specimens and examination of permanent stained smears may be required to establish the diagnosis.

Suspected amebic abscesses are often diagnosed by positive serologic tests. Aspirates of abscesses or intestinal lesions may contain amebic trophozoites, sometimes with ingested erythrocytes seen in direct wet mounts or in permanent stains such as trichrome or iron-hematoxylin stains.[45,46] Other species of intestinal amebae are not pathogenic but must be differentiated from *E. histolytica*. *Entamoeba polecki* is seen occasionally in refugees from South East Asia and may be confused with *E. histolytica*.[45] *Entamoeba gingivalis* is a common inhabitant of the oral cavity, particularly in patients who have poor oral hygiene. It resembles *E. histolytica* but has no known cyst stage. As a result, trophozoites of *E. gingivalis* may lead to the misdiagnosis of amebic lung abscess by morphologic examination of pulmonary material, especially sputum.

Currently, there are several immunoassays that can be used to identify organisms in the genus *Entamoeba* (*E. histolytica/ E. dispar* group) and other reagents that can differentiate pathogenic *E. histolytica* from nonpathogenic *E. dispar*. The antigen detection enzyme-linked immunosorbent assay (ELISA) kits are based on specific amebic adhesin molecules found in the feces of people infected by either *E. histolytica* or *E. dispar*. The second ELISA reagent is able to detect the adhesin produced by *E. histolytica* in feces. Another immunoassay product is available for the detection of *E. histolytica* and *E. dispar* in fecal specimens; however, this kit does not differentiate between the two organisms, but is specific for the *E. histolytica/E. dispar* group.[47] These procedures are simple, sensitive and specific. It is important to remember that these kits require fresh stool specimens; specimens preserved in any of the routine stool collection fixatives are not acceptable. Polymerase chain reaction methods are also being developed for the differentiation of *E. histolytica* from *E. dispar*.[48]

Serologic testing for intestinal disease is not recommended unless the patient has true dysentery; even in these patients, the titer (e.g. indirect hemagglutination) may be low and difficult to interpret. The definitive diagnosis of intestinal amebiasis should not be made without demonstrating the organisms. When extraintestinal disease is suspected, serologic tests are much more relevant. Indirect hemagglutination and indirect fluorescent antibody tests (FAs) have been reported positive with titers of ≥1:256 and ≥1:200, respectively, in almost 100% of cases of amebic liver abscess.[49] Positive serologic results, in addition to clinical findings, make the diagnosis highly probable. In the absence of rapid serologic tests for amebiasis (tests with very rapid turnaround times for results), the decision as to causative agent often must be made on clinical grounds and on results of other diagnostic tests such as scans.

Histologic diagnosis of amebiasis can be made when trophozoites within the tissue are identified and differentiated from host cells, particularly histiocytes and ganglion cells. Periodic acid–Schiff staining is often used; the organisms will appear bright pink with a green-blue background (depending on the counterstain used). Hematoxylin and eosin staining will also allow typical morphology to be seen. As a result of sectioning, some organisms will exhibit the evenly arranged nuclear chromatin with the central karyosome and some will no longer contain the nucleus.

Blastocystis hominis

The characteristic form of *B. hominis* that is usually seen in human fecal specimens varies in size from 6 to 40μm and contains a large central body resembling a vacuole, which may be involved with carbohydrate and lipid storage. The amebic form can occasionally be seen in diarrheal fluid but may be difficult to recognize. Generally, *B. hominis* will be identified on the basis of the typical round form containing the central body.[45] Routine stool examinations are very effective in recovering and identifying *B. hominis* (Fig. 242.6), although the permanent stained smear is the procedure of choice because the examination of wet preparations may not easily reveal the organism. The organisms should be quantitated on the report form, that is, as rare, few, moderate or many. It is also important to remember that other possible pathogens should be adequately ruled out before a patient is treated for *B. hominis*.

Identification of flagellates in fecal specimens

The flagellates are a more diverse group than the amebae. The type of motility, shape, number of nuclei and other characteristics, such as an undulating membrane, sucking disk, cytostome, spiral groove, and the number and location of flagellae, are important characteristics used to identify flagellate trophozoites. The organism shape and size, number and position of nuclei, and absence or arrangement of fibrils are used to identify flagellate cysts.

In some cases, species can be determined by the examination of either direct or concentrated wet mounts. Species of cysts may be identified in iodine-stained mounts. However, permanent stains are always recommended for every stool specimen submitted; organisms identified in wet preparations may not represent all types of organisms present.

Giardia lamblia (intestinalis)

Diagnosis is usually established by the demonstration of cysts or, occasionally, trophozoites in feces (Fig. 242.7). Nonpathogenic flagellates can be seen in Figure 242.8. Because of the variable shedding of organisms, several stool specimens should be examined before the infection is ruled out. In some cases, a series of stools can be examined and be negative and yet the patient still has giardiasis. It is important for the laboratory and the clinician to recognize this fact. Permanent stains are recommended for the definitive diagnosis of this infection.

When *G. lamblia* organisms are not found in stool specimens, duodenal aspirates, string test mucus or biopsied mucosal tissue can be examined. The string test[45] is used to collect mucus from the duodenal area and its use may be less traumatic for the patient than other methods. Materials obtained by drainage, aspiration or the string test can be examined by simple, direct wet mounts. Biopsy tissue may be processed and stained by the usual histopathologic methods; however, before preservation, a fresh imprint smear of the mucosal surface on a slide can be made and stained with trichrome or Giemsa stain.

Immunoassay methods (enzyme immunoassay, FA, immunochromatographic assay) are available and may be appropriate in test ordering situations.[49a,49b] Education of the medical staff will be mandatory to ensure that tests are appropriately ordered and that there is complete understanding of the limits of the information generated (test results limited to absence or presence of *G. lamblia*). Recently, industrial companies and municipalities have shown a great deal of interest in these reagents. This is particularly relevant when the water sources are used for drinking and/or recreational purposes.[45]

Dientamoeba fragilis

Permanent stains are required to diagnose this infection and multiple specimens may be required because shedding varies from day to day.

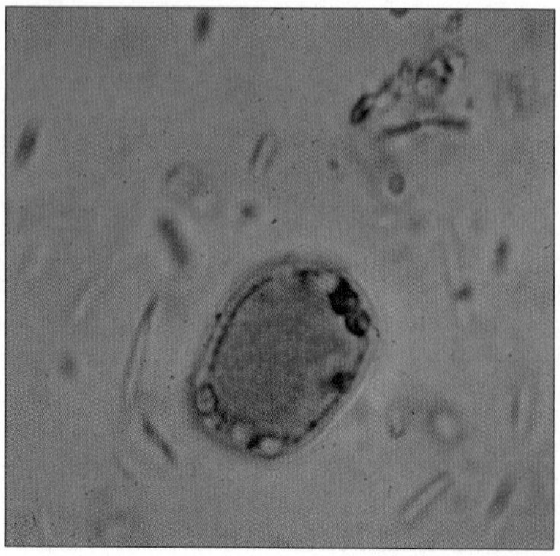

Fig. 242.6 ***Blastocystis hominis.*** (a) Central body form with large 'empty' area (appears like a vacuole) with multiple nuclei around the edges (d'Antoni's iodine). (b) Three central body forms with the large empty area surrounded by nuclei (trichrome stain).

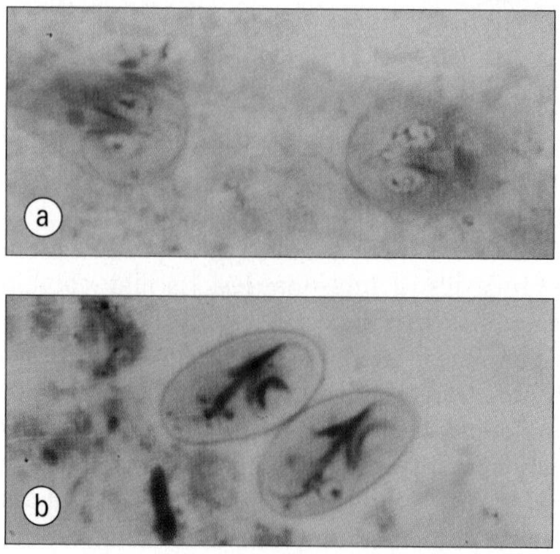

Fig. 242.7 ***Giardia lamblia.*** (a) Trophozoites in mucus – note the sucking disk area, linear axonemes, curved median bodies and two nuclei (trichrome stain). (b) Cysts containing multiple nuclei, linear axonemes and curved median bodies (iron-hematoxylin stain).

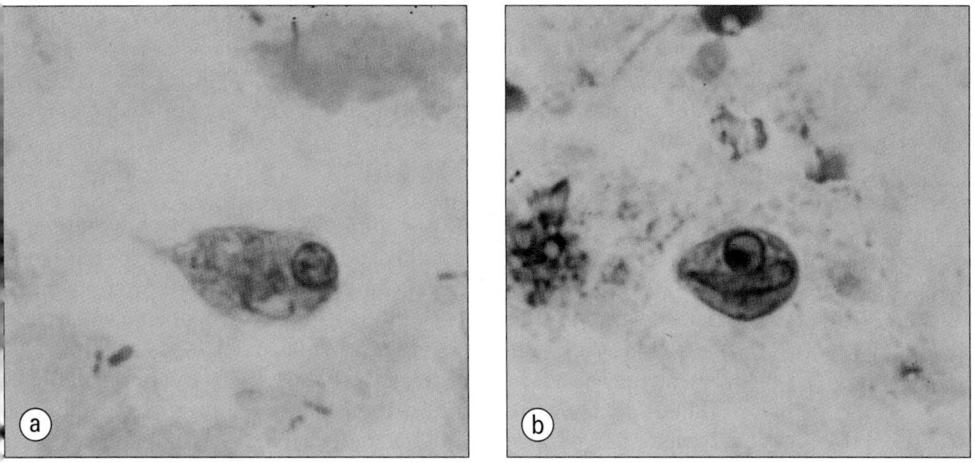

Fig. 242.8 ***Chilomastix mesnili.*** (a) Trophozoite with single nucleus and clear feeding groove/cytostome. (b) Cyst containing single nucleus and curved fibril called the 'shepherd's crook' (trichrome stain).

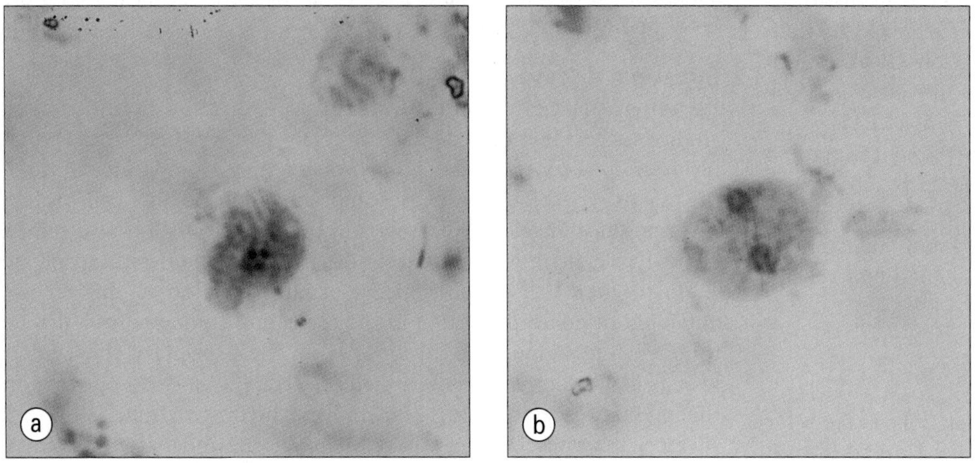

Fig. 242.9 ***Dientamoeba fragilis.*** (a) Trophozoite with single nucleus fragmented into a 'tetrad' configuration. (b) Trophozoite containing two nuclei, each showing fragmented chromatin (trichrome stain). There is no known cyst form for this organism.

The delicately staining trophozoites are usually binucleate, although the nuclei may be in different planes of focus (Fig. 242.9). The nuclei tend to be fragmented and can often be seen in a 'tetrad' formation. They must be differentiated from the trophozoites of *Endolimax nana, Iodamoeba bütschlii* and *Entamoeba hartmanni*. Nuclear characteristics, the presence of binucleate forms, tremendous size variation, and the absence of cysts aid in identification of this organism.

A permanent stained smear should be examined for every stool specimen submitted to the laboratory for an ova and parasite examination.[45,46] If this approach is not used, then many infections with this organism can be missed. If a laboratory periodically finds and identifies *G. lamblia* but never sees *D. fragilis*, then collection and diagnostic methods should be reviewed.

Identification of flagellates in urogenital specimens

Trichomonas vaginalis

Infections with *T. vaginalis* are usually detected by finding the motile trophozoites in wet mounts of vaginal fluid, prostatic fluid or sediments of freshly passed urine. In wet mounts, the trophozoites move with a jerky motion and possess an undulating membrane, which extends only one-half the length of the organism (Fig. 242.10). In old urine specimens, the organisms may be dead or badly distorted and thus cannot be identified or may be confused with host cells.

Specimens include vaginal fluid, scrapings or washings. They may be examined in a saline wet mount or as a stained smear, or the material can be cultured. Although some consider that wet mount examinations are as efficient as cultures in revealing infections, current evidence suggests that cultivation methods are superior.[50,51] Immunofluorescent and ELISA methods have also been described.

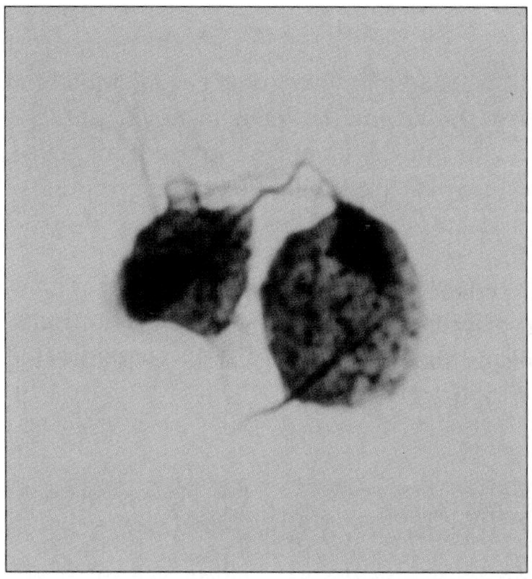

Fig. 242.10 ***Trichomonas vaginalis.*** Trophozoites showing axostyle, flagella and part of the undulating membrane (smaller organism) (Giemsa stain). There is no known cyst form for this organism.

Organisms may be difficult to recognize in permanent stains; however, if a dry smear is submitted to the laboratory, Giemsa or Papanicolaou stain can be used. Chronic *T. vaginalis* infections may cause atypical cellular changes that can be misinterpreted, particularly on the Papanicolaou smear. Organisms are routinely missed on Gram stains. The number of false-positive and false-negative results reported on the basis of stained smears strongly suggests that identification should be confirmed by observation of motile organisms, either from the direct wet mount or from appropriate culture media.

For culture, it is mandatory that the specimen be collected correctly, immediately inoculated into the proper medium and properly incubated. Excellent methods are available using plastic envelopes containing appropriate media. This envelope approach allows both immediate examination and culture in one self-contained envelope. These systems are commercially available and serve as the specimen transport container, the growth chamber during incubation and the 'slide' during microscopy.[45,50–52]

Monoclonal antibodies and DNA probe procedures for the detection of *T. vaginalis* have been reported as being very effective.[53,54] An enzyme immunoassay has been developed for the detection of the *T. vaginalis* antigen from vaginal swabs.[55,56] The predictive value of a positive test was 82% and that of a negative test was 99.3%. Commercial products based on these methodologies should be very helpful in diagnosing this infection. Serologic tests have been tried; however, none are commercially available.

Identification of ciliates in fecal specimens

Balantidium coli

In human feces, *B. coli* trophozoites are readily recognized by their large size, their shape and their rapid, rotating motion. Cysts are less easily identified, but they usually cause few diagnostic problems. The morphology of trophozoites and cysts is seen in Figure 242.11.

Examination of direct saline mounts is the most practical method of detecting these protozoa. Cysts can be recovered by concentration, but in human infections trophozoites are usually more numerous than cysts. Iodine-stained mounts and permanent stains are of little value because the organisms tend to overstain and may resemble helminth eggs and/or debris.

CLINICAL MANIFESTATIONS (see Chapter 46)

In the descriptions of diseases, the clinical manifestations noted refer to findings in patients who have symptomatic disease and do not necessarily refer to findings in every person infected with the parasite species.

Amebae

Eight species of intestinal amebae may live in the cecum and colon of humans: *E. histolytica, E. dispar, E. hartmanni, E. polecki, E. coli, E. nana, I. bütschlii* and *B. hominis*. However, of these, only *E. histolytica* and *B. hominis* are thought to cause symptoms.

Entamoeba histolytica

Infections with the true pathogen, *E. histolytica*, are classified as amebiasis irrespective of whether the person exhibits symptoms. Outbreaks have occurred in the USA, usually from contaminated food or water. *Entamoeba* spp. isolated from patients who have clinical disease have been shown by isoenzyme analysis to differ from nonpathogenic organisms and *E. histolytica* will be used to designate pathogens, whereas *E. dispar* will designate those that are nonpathogenic. The incubation is variable, from days to weeks or even months.

Asymptomatic infection

Individuals harboring *E. histolytica/E. dispar* may have either a negative or weak antibody titer and negative stools for occult blood and may be passing cysts that can be detected if a routine ova and parasite examination is performed. Although trophozoites may also be found, they will not contain any phagocytized red blood cells. Isoenzyme analyses of organisms isolated from asymptomatic individuals generally indicate that the isolates belong to nonpathogenic zymodemes (*E. dispar*).[28] Generally, asymptomatic patients never become symptomatic and may excrete cysts for a short period. This same pattern is found for patients who have either nonpathogenic or pathogenic zymodemes.

Intestinal disease

Although the exact mode of mucosal penetration is not known, studies suggest that amebae have enzymes that lyse host tissue, possibly from lysosomes on the surface of the amebae or from ruptured organisms. Cysteine proteinases and activation of host cell protein tyrosine phosphatases (PTPases) and dephosphorylation also play a critical role in the pathogenesis of invasive amebiasis caused by *E. histolytica*.[57–59] Amebic ulcers usually develop in the cecum, appendix or adjacent portion of the ascending colon and can also be found in the sigmoidorectal area. From these primary sites, other lesions may occur. Ulcers are usually raised, with a small opening on the mucosal surface and a larger area of destruction below the surface, thus described as 'flask shaped'. The mucosal lining may appear normal between ulcers. The incubation period may vary from 1 to 4 months and in an endemic area it is impossible to determine exactly when the exposure took place. Symptoms may range from none to those mimicking ulcerative colitis. Patients who have colicky abdominal pain, frequent bowel movements and tenesmus may present with a gradual onset of disease. With the onset of dysentery, bowel movements characterized by blood-tinged mucus are frequent (up to 10/day). Although dysentery may last for months, it usually varies from severe to mild over that time and may lead to weight loss and prostration. In severe cases, symptoms may begin very suddenly and include profuse diarrhea (over 10 stools/day), fever, dehydration and electrolyte imbalances. Acute illness may mimic appendicitis, cholecystitis, intestinal obstruction or diverticulitis. In some people, an increased frequency of bowel movements with or

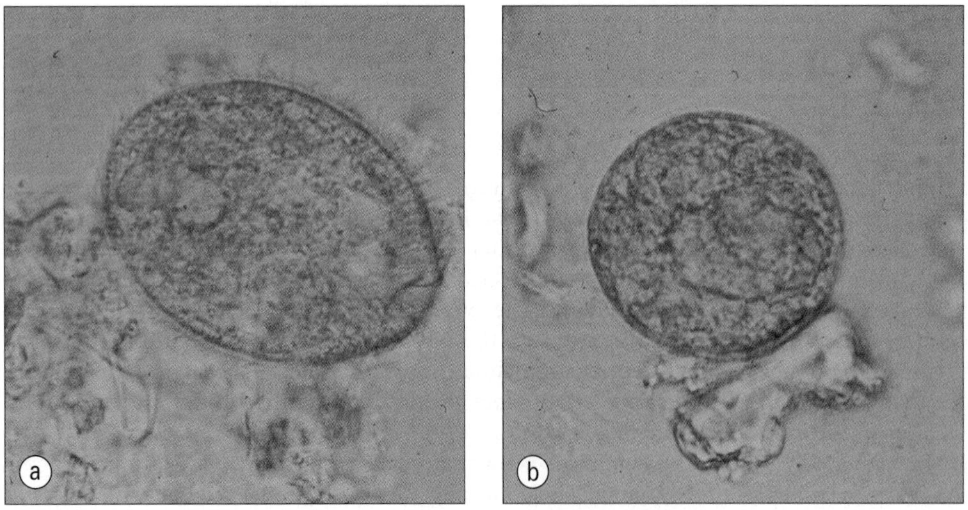

Fig. 242.11 ***Balantidium coli.*** (a) Trophozoite – note the cilia around the edges ('fuzzy football'). (b) Cyst – note the cilia are difficult to see within the cyst wall (d'Antoni's iodine – light preparation, pale color).

without blood and mucus may occur. A chronic form, amebic colitis, produces symptoms similar to those of ulcerative colitis or other forms of inflammatory bowel disease, with diarrhea, sometimes bloody, occurring over months to years, sometimes alternating with periods of constipation or normal bowel function. Some patients who have amebiasis have been misdiagnosed as having ulcerative colitis. Another, less common form of intestinal disease, ameboma, is produced by the growth of granulomatous tissue in response to the infecting amebae, resulting in a large local lesion of the bowel that radiologically resembles a carcinoma.

Other than trophozoites containing ingested red blood cells, we have no way of differentiating pathogenic *E. histolytica* from nonpathogenic *E. dispar* based on morphologic differences, so our approach to reporting and therapy may not change in the near future. Any *E. histolytica* organisms should be reported to the physician and, providing the trophozoites do not contain ingested red blood cells, should be reported as *E. histolytica/E. dispar*. There are molecular-based diagnostic reagents that can confirm the group *E. histolytica/E. dispar* and other reagents that can indicate the species identification (*E. histolytica* or *E. dispar*). Although these reagents are relatively expensive, they may become more widely used in the next few years.[60]

Hepatic disease

Infections with *E. histolytica*, with or without a history of gastrointestinal symptoms, may result in hematogenous spread of the organisms from the submucosa to the liver via the portal system, resulting in amebic abscesses of the liver. This occurs in up to 5% of patients who have symptomatic intestinal amebiasis. Approximately 40% of patients who have amebic liver abscess do not have a history of prior bowel symptoms and in some patients *E. histolytica* may not be present in stool at the time liver disease becomes manifest. Onset of symptoms may be gradual or sudden; upper right abdominal pain with fever from 100° to 102°F (38–39°C) is the most consistent finding. Weakness, weight loss, cough and sweating are less common. There is hepatomegaly with tenderness; however, liver function tests may be normal or slightly abnormal, with jaundice being very rare. There may be changes at the base of the right lung caused by the elevated diaphragm. The abscess can be visualized radiologically, sonically or by radionuclear scan and the majority of patients have a single abscess in the right lobe of the liver. The most common complication is rupture of the abscess into the pleural space. An abscess can also extend into the peritoneum and through the skin. Hematogenous spread to the brain, as well as to lung, pericardium and other sites, is possible.

Entamoeba histolytica cysts and trophozoites are found in the stools of only a few patients who have liver abscess. Usually 60% of these patients have no intestinal symptoms or any previous history of dysentery.

Blastocystis hominis

When *B. hominis* is present in large numbers in the absence of other parasites, bacteria or viruses, it may be the cause of diarrhea, cramps, nausea, fever, vomiting and abdominal pain and may require therapy. In patients who have other underlying conditions, the symptoms may be more pronounced. Incidence of this organism is found in a higher percentage of stools submitted for parasite examination than expected, especially when compared with percent positive stools for other intestinal protozoa. In symptomatic patients in whom no other etiologic agent has been identified, *B. hominis* should be considered a possible pathogen. When organisms number more than five per high-power field (×400), they should be quantitated and reported.[61] However, in one study, there did not appear to be any specific symptoms associated with *B. hominis* infection and the presence of larger numbers in the stool was not associated with more severe symptoms.[62] Other studies suggest that when a symptomatic *B. hominis* infection responds to therapy, the improvement probably represents elimination of some other undetected pathogenic organism (*E. histolytica, G. lamblia, D. fragilis*).[63] Data from other geographic areas indicate that although it is commonly seen in stool samples, *B. hominis* is thought to be nonpathogenic.[62] *Blastocystis hominis* inhabits the large intestine and organisms are passed in feces. Three morphologic forms have been described: amebic, granular and vacuolated.[64] The vacuolated ('central body') form is most commonly seen in fecal specimens.

Although *B. hominis* may be found in up to 25% of stool specimens examined, only occasional patients have clinical symptoms and the issue of pathogenicity may be explained by the confirmation of various ribodeme types. Different patient presentations can thus be explained, based on the evidence that there are several ribodeme types, only some of which will be responsible for increased intestinal permeability and symptoms.[36,37] *Blastocystis hominis* may be suspected as the etiologic agent when the complete battery of parasitologic, bacterial and viral tests on stools has failed to disclose any agent other than *B. hominis*. Although most of these patients have numerous *B. hominis* organisms in the stool, organism numbers are not always elevated in symptomatic patients. The predominant and virtually only symptom has been persistent, mild diarrhea.

Infection is diagnosed by finding the familiar spherical or ovoid form with a large central vacuole with nuclei and various other organelles arranged around the periphery (see Fig. 242.6). *Blastocystis hominis* organisms can be demonstrated by any of the methods used for the diagnosis of intestinal parasite infections; however, the permanent stained smear is recommended.

Although we normally do not quantitate protozoa on the report form, this organism should be reported and semiquantitated (rare, few, moderate or many) from the examination of the permanent stained smear. As the published literature is somewhat controversial on the relationship between organism numbers and patient symptoms, quantitation may be helpful for the clinician. The percentage of people who harbor this parasite can range from about 10% to over 50% in some areas of the world.

Flagellates

Two species, *G. lamblia* and *D. fragilis*, cause clinically significant intestinal disease, and *T. vaginalis* is a frequent cause of vaginitis.

Giardia lamblia (intestinalis)

Because the acute stage usually lasts only a few days, giardiasis may not be recognized as the cause and the condition may mimic acute viral enteritis, bacillary dysentery, bacterial or other food poisonings, acute intestinal amebiasis or travelers' diarrhea (toxigenic *E. coli*). However, the type of diarrhea plus the lack of blood, mucus and cellular exudate is consistent with giardiasis.

Although organism numbers in the crypts of the duodenal mucosa may reach very high densities, they may not cause any pathology. Organisms have been seen in biopsy material inside the intestinal mucosa, whereas others have been seen only attached to the epithelium. In symptomatic cases, there may be irritation of the mucosal lining, increased mucus secretion and dehydration.

In the compromised patient, conditions and genetic factors associated with *G. lamblia* infection may include hypogammaglobulinemia, protein or caloric malnutrition, previous gastrectomy, histocompatibility antigen HLA-B12, gastric achlorhydria, blood group A, differences in mucolytic proteins, immunoglobulin deficiencies and reduced secretory IgA levels in the gut. Trophozoites infect the upper small intestine but do not invade the tissues to produce ulcers. Infection may elicit a variety of symptoms or may be asymptomatic. The incubation period is variable, ranging from a few days to several weeks, with an average of about 9 days. In acute giardiasis, symptoms include nausea, upper intestinal cramping or pain, and malaise. There is often explosive, watery diarrhea, characterized by foul-smelling stools. These symptoms are accompanied by flatulence and abdominal distention. The acute stage of clinical giardiasis may be followed by a chronic stage or the chronic type of infection may be the first indication of infection. In such infections there is flatulence and abdominal distention. Patients may also exhibit belching, nausea, anorexia, vomiting and symptoms of heartburn. Fever and chills may be present, but to a lesser degree. Chronic disease must be differentiated from amebiasis and other intestinal parasite infections with *D. fragilis*, *C. parvum*, *Cyclospora cayetanensis*, *I. belli*, the microsporidia and *Strongyloides stercoralis* and from inflammatory bowel disease and irritable colon. On the basis of symptoms such as upper intestinal discomfort, heartburn and belching, giardiasis must also be differentiated from duodenal ulcer, hiatal hernia and gallbladder and pancreatic disease.

In some patients, the cysts may be excreted in stools in a variable pattern, although the reasons for this are not clear. This variable shedding of cysts may occur even when there are classic symptoms of disease and numerous trophozoites in the upper small intestine.

Dientamoeba fragilis

Symptoms have been reported more frequently in children than in adults and are predominantly diarrhea and abdominal distention. Outbreaks in daycare centers have been described. Nausea, vomiting and weight loss have been recorded in from one-third to one-fifth of the cases reported in the literature.[65]

Trichomonas vaginalis

The infection in men is generally asymptomatic, but 25–50% of infected women exhibit symptoms, which include dysuria, vaginal itching and burning and, in severe infections, a foamy, yellowish-green discharge with a foul odor. In many women the infection becomes symptomatic and chronic, with periods of relief in response to therapy. Recurrences of infection and disease may be caused by reinfection from an asymptomatic sexual partner or by failure of the drug metronidazole to eliminate the parasite completely. Symptomatic infections in men are rarely reported but include prostatitis, urethritis, epididymitis and urethral stricture. Rarely, *T. vaginalis* infections occur in ectopic sites and parasites may be recovered from areas of the body other than the urogenital system. *Trichomonas* spp. have been reported in pulmonary infections, presumably from oral trichomonads.

Ciliate

Balantidium coli

The symptoms of infection with *B. coli* are similar to those of amebiasis: lower abdominal pain, nausea, vomiting and tenesmus. Chronic infections may manifest with cramps, frequent episodes of watery, mucoid diarrhea and rarely with bloody diarrhea. Chronic infections have been known to last for several months. In tropical areas in which the parasite is endemic, the infection often is severe in patients who may also have other parasitic, bacterial or viral infections or who are undernourished. *Balantidium coli* causes colonic ulcers similar to those caused by *E. histolytica*, but it does not spread to other organs.

MANAGEMENT

Entamoeba histolytica

Although carriers usually harbor amebae with nonpathogenic isoenzyme patterns (*E. dispar*), pathogenic patterns also may be found in these individuals. At present, test methodologies that differentiate between *E. histolytica* and *E. dispar* are not used routinely by all diagnostic laboratories. The diagnosis of *E. histolytica/E. dispar* infection is most often based on organism morphology. For this reason, in general, patients in the USA who harbor this organism are treated, regardless of the presence or absence of symptoms.

There are two classes of drugs used in the treatment of amebic infections: luminal amebicides, such as iodoquinol, paromomycin or diloxanide furoate, and tissue amebicides, such as metronidazole, chloroquine or dehydroemetine. Because there are differences in each drug's efficacy, it is important that the laboratory report for the physician indicates whether cysts, trophozoites or both are present in the stool specimen.

Asymptomatic patients

Patients found to have confirmed *E. histolytica* in the intestinal tract, even if they are asymptomatic, should be treated to eliminate the organisms. Both diloxanide furoate and iodoquinol (650 mg 3 times a day for 20 days; pediatric dose, 30–40 mg/kg/day (max 2g) in 3 doses for 20 days) or paromomycin (25–35 mg/kg/day in 3 doses for 7 days; pediatric dose, 25–35 mg/kg/day in 3 doses for 7 days) are available for treatment of patients who have cysts in the lumen of the gut. A study involving 14 years' experience in the USA using diloxanide furoate for treating asymptomatic cyst passers indicated that the drug is safe and effective and may be particularly well tolerated in children.[66] However, diloxanide furoate is generally not available commercially, but can be compounded by several pharmacies (500mg 3 times a day for 10 days; pediatric dose, 20mg/kg/day in 3 doses for 10 days).[67] In general, these treatments are ineffective against extra-intestinal disease. If the patient is passing trophozoites and cysts, the recommended treatment is metronidazole (500–750mg 3 times a day for 7–10 days; pediatric dose, 35–50mg/kg/day in 3 doses for 7–10 days) or tinidazole (not marketed in the USA; 2g per day in 3 divided doses per day for 3 days; pediatric dose, 50mg/kg (max 2g) per day for 3 days).[67,68]

Mild to moderate disease

In mild to moderate disease, metronidazole (Flagyl) should be given as indicated above when tissue invasion occurs, regardless of the tissue involved. Drugs directed against the lumen organisms should also be used in these cases (as indicated for iodoquinol or paromomycin above).

Severe intestinal disease

Metronidazole (750mg 3 times a day for 7–10 days; pediatric dose, 35–50 mg/kg per day in 3 doses for 7–10 days) or tinidazole (not marketed in the USA; 800mg 3 times a day for 5 days; pediatric dose, 60mg/kg per day (max 2g) for 5 days) should be used for therapy.[67] Some also recommend the use of a luminal drug (see iodoquinol or paromomycin above).

Hepatic disease

Metronidazole plus one of the luminal drugs should be used to treat hepatic disease. There are also other combinations that can be used; some physicians use emetine, in which case the patient must be monitored very carefully for possible cardiotoxicity. The importance of using both luminal and tissue amebicides was emphasized in a study that reviewed the enteric phase of 50 patients who had amebic liver abscess.[66] The prevalence of asymptomatic colonization was 72% (36 out of 50); however, isoenzyme analysis indicated that all of these isolates were pathogenic. In patients treated with metronidazole (tissue amebicide), the clinical response of the hepatic lesions was 100%; failure to eliminate the organism from the bowel in 20 out of 36 patients led to second bouts, with invasive disease and intestinal colonization. Also, these carriers constituted a public health hazard.[67]

Blastocystis hominis

Although there is not a great deal of clinical evidence, there have been studies on the *in vitro* susceptibility of *B. hominis* to numerous drugs.[64] At present, metronidazole appears to be the most appropriate drug. Di-iodohydroxyquin (Yodoxin) has also been effective, and dosage schedules for these two drugs are as recommended for other intestinal protozoa. Another option would be trimethoprim-sulfamethoxazole. The development of a new drug sensitivity assay may improve our ability to evaluate the activities of various drugs against this organism scientifically.[68]

Giardia lamblia (intestinalis)

If giardiasis is diagnosed, the patient should be treated. In the majority of patients, metronidazole is the drug of choice. Metronidazole is not recommended for pregnant women; although not absorbed and not highly effective, paromomycin may be used to treat giardiasis in pregnancy. Tinidazole has proved more effective than metronidazole as a single dose.[69] Furazolidone is another option, but has been reported to be mutagenic and carcinogenic.

Dientamoeba fragilis

Clinical improvement has been observed in adults receiving tetracycline; symptomatic relief was reported in children receiving di-iodohydroxyquin, metronidazole or tetracycline. Current recommendations include iodoquinol, paromomycin or tetracycline. As symptomatic relief has been observed to follow appropriate therapy, *D. fragilis* is probably pathogenic in infected individuals who are symptomatic.

Trichomonas vaginalis

Metronidazole is recommended for urogenital trichomoniasis, although resistance to this and to other 5-nitroimidazoles has been reported.[70] Sexual partners should be treated to avoid immediate reinfection.

Balantidium coli

Tetracycline is the drug of choice, although it is considered investigational. Iodoquinol or metronidazole may be used as alternatives.

REFERENCES

1. Arisue N, Hashimoto T, Yoshikawa H, *et al.* Phylogenetic position of *Blastocystis hominis* and of stramenopiles inferred from multiple molecular sequence data. J Eukaryot Microbiol 2002;49:42–53.
2. World Health Organization. Amoebiasis. WHO Weekly Epidemiol Rec 1997;72:97–100.
3. Scarce M. Harbinger of plague: a bad case of gay bowel syndrome. J Homosex 1997;34:1–35.
4. Druckman DA, Quinn TC. *Entamoeba histolytica* infections in homosexual men. In: Ravdin J, ed. Amebiasis: human infection by *Entamoeba histolytica*. New York: Wiley; 1988:93–105.
5. Ohnishi K, Murata M. Present characteristics of symptomatic amebiasis due to *Entamoeba histolytica* in the east-southeast area of Tokyo. Epidemiol Infect 1997;119:363–7.
6. Petri WA. *Entamoeba histolytica*: clinical update and vaccine prospects. Curr Infect Dis Rep 2002;4:124–9.
7. Stanley SL Jr. Protective immunity to amebiasis: new insights and new challenges. J Infect Dis 2001;184:504–6.
8. Haque R, Ali IM, Sack RB, *et al.* Amebiasis and mucosal IgA antibody against the *Entamoeba histolytica* adherence lectin in Bangladeshi children. J Infect Dis 2001;183:1787–93.
9. Moe KT, Singh M, Howe J, *et al.* Observations on the ultrastructure and viability of the cystic stage of *Blastocystis hominis* from human feces. Parasitol Res 1996;82:439–44.
10. Doyle PW, Helgason MM, Mathias RG, Proctor IM. Epidemiology and pathogenicity of *Blastocystis hominis*. J Clin Microbiol 1990;28:116–21.
11. Keystone JS, Karjden S, Warren MR. Person-to-person transmission of *Giardia lamblia* in day-care nurseries. Can Med Assoc J 1978;119:242–4.
12. Sealy DP, Schuman SH. Endemic giardiasis and day care. Pediatrics 1983;72:154–8.
13. Moore, GT, Gross WW, McQuire D, *et al.* Epidemic giardiasis at a ski resort. N Engl J Med 1969;281:402–7.
14. Wallis PM, Matson D, Jones M, Jamieson J. Application of monitoring data for *Giardia* and *Cryptosporidium* to boil water advisories. Risk Anal 2001;21:1077–85.
15. Smith PD, Lane HC, Gill VJ, *et al.* Intestinal infections in patients with the acquired immunodeficiency syndrome (AIDS). Ann Intern Med 1988;108:328–33.
16. Shaw PK, Brodsky RE, Lyman DD, *et al.* A community wide outbreak of giardiasis with evidence of transmission by a municipal water supply. Ann Intern Med 1977;87:426–32.
17. Kirner JC. Water borne outbreak of giardiasis in Camas, Washington. J Am Waterworks Assoc 1978;January:35–40.
18. Craun GF. Waterborne giardiasis in the United States: a review. Am J Public Health 1979;69:817–9.
19. Addis DG, Davis JP, Roberts JM, Mast EE. Epidemiology of giardiasis in Wisconsin: increasing incidence of reported cases and unexplained seasonal trends. Am J Trop Med Hyg 1992;47:13–9.
20. Brightman AH Jr, Slonka GF. A review of five clinical cases of giardiasis in cats. J Am Anim Hosp Assoc 1979;12:492–7.
21. Dykes AC, Juranek DD, Lorenz RA, *et al.* Municipal waterborne giardiasis. An epidemiologic investigation. Ann Intern Med 1980;93:165–70.
22. Hewlett EL, Andrews JS, Ruffier J, Shaeffer FM. Experimental infection in mongrel dogs with *Giardia lamblia* cysts and cultured trophozoites. J Infect Dis 1982;145:89–93.
23. Slifko TR, Smith HV, Rose JB. Emerging parasite zoonoses associated with water and food. Int J Parasitol 2000;30:1379–93.
24. Jarroll EL Jr, Bingham AK, Meyer EA. *Giardia* cyst destruction: effectiveness of six small-quantity water disinfection methods. Am J Trop Med Hyg 1980;29:8–11.
25. Jarroll EL Jr, Bingham AK, Meyer EA. Effect of chlorine on *Giardia lamblia* cyst viability. Appl Environ Microbiol 1981;41:483–7.
26. Isaac-Renton JL, Byrne SK, Prameya R. Isoelectric focusing of ten strains of *Giardia duodenalis*. J Parasitol 1988;74:1054–6.
27. Proctor, EM, Isaac-Renton JL, Boyd J, Wong Q, Bowie WR. Isoenzyme analysis of human and animal isolates of *Giardia duodenalis* from British Columbia. Am J Trop Med Hyg 1989;41:411–5.
28. Sargeaunt PG, Williams JE. Electrophoretic isoenzyme patterns of the pathogenic and nonpathogenic intestinal amoebae of man. Trans Roy Soc Trop Med Hyg 1979;73:225–7.
29. Reed SL. New concepts regarding the pathogenesis of amebiasis. Clin Infect Dis 1995;21:S182–5.
30. Ortner S, Clark CG, Binder M, *et al.* Molecular biology of the hexokinase isoenzyme pattern that distinguishes pathogenic *Entamoeba histolytica* from nonpathogenic *Entamoeba dispar*. Mol Biochem Parasitol 1997;86:85–94.
31. Zaki M, Meelu P, Sun W, Clark CG. Simultaneous differentiation and typing of *Entamoeba histolytica* and *Entamoeba dispar*. J Clin Microbiol 2002;40:1271–6.
32. Diamond LS, Clark CG. A redescription of *Entamoeba histolytica* Schaudinn, 1903 (amended Walker, 1911) separating it from *Entamoeba dispar* Brumpt, 1925. J Euk Microbiol 1993;40:340–4.
33. Giacometti A, Cirioni O, Fiorentini A, *et al.* Irritable bowel syndrome in patients with *Blastocystis hominis* infection. Eur J Clin Microbiol Infect Dis 1999;18:436–9.
34. Horiki N, Kaneda Y, Maruyama M, *et al.* Intestinal blockage by carcinoma and *Blastocystis hominis* infection. Am J Trop Med Hyg 1999;60:400–2.
35. Cirioni O, Giacometti A, Drenaggi D, *et al.* Prevalence and clinical relevance of *Blastocystis hominis* in diverse patient cohorts. Eur J Epidemiol 1999;15:389–93.
36. Dagci H, Ustun S, Taner MS, *et al.* Protozoon infections and intestinal permeability. Acta Trop 2002;81:1–5.
37. Kaneda Y, Horiki N, Cheng XJ, *et al.* Ribodemes of *Blastocystis hominis* isolated in Japan. Am J Trop Med Hyg 2001;65:393–6.
38. Monis PT, Andrews RH, Mayrhofer G, Ey PL. Molecular systematics of the parasitic protozoan *Giardia intestinalis*. Mol Biol Evol 1999;16:1135–44.
39. Paintlia AS, Desoteaux S, Spencer A, *et al.* *Giardia lamblia* groups A and B among young adults in India. Clin Infect Dis 1998;26:190–1.
40. Paintlia AS, Paintlia MD, Mahajan RC, *et al.* A DNA-based probe for differentiation of *Giardia lamblia* group A and B isolates from northern India. Clin Infect Dis 1999;28:1178–80.
41. Johnson JA, Clark CG. Cryptic genetic diversity in *Dientamoeba fragilis*. J Clin Microbiol 2000;38:4653–4.
42. Dickinson EC, Cohen MA, Schlenker MK. *Dientamoeba fragilis*: a significant pathogen. Am J Emerg Med 2002;20:62–3.
43. Alderete JF. *Trichomonas vaginalis*, a model mucosal parasite. Rev Med Microbiol 1999;10:165–73.
44. Lehker MW, Sweeney D. Trichomonad invasion of the mucous layer requires adhesins, mucinases, and motility. Sex Transm Infect 1999;75:231–8.
45. Garcia LS. Diagnostic medical parasitology, 4th ed. Washington DC: ASM Press; 2001.

46. National Committee for Clinical Laboratory Standards. Procedures for the recovery and identification of parasites from the intestinal tract. Approved Guideline, M28-A. Villanova, PA: NCCLS; 1997.
47. Garcia LS, Shimizu RY, Bernard CN. Detection of *Giardia lamblia, Entamoeba histolytica/Entamoeba dispar*, and *Cryptosporidium parvum* antigens in human fecal specimens using the Triage Parasite Panel enzyme immunoassay. J Clin Microbiol 2000;38:3337–40.
48. Brittin D, Wilson SM, McNerney R, *et al.* An improved colorimetric PCR-based method for detection and differentiation of *Entamoeba histolytica* and *Entamoeba dispar* in feces. J Clin Microbiol 1997;35:1108–11.
49. Wilson, M, Schantz P, Pieniazek N. Diagnosis of parasitic infections: immunologic and molecular methods. In: Murray PR, Baron EJ, Pfaller MA, Tenover FC, Yolken RH, eds. Manual of clinical microbiology, 6th ed. Washington DC: American Society for Microbiology; 1995.
49a. Garcia LS, Shimizu RY. Detection of *Giardia lamblia* and *Cryptosporidium parvum* antigens in human fecal specimens using the ColorPAC combination rapid solid-phase qualitative immunochromatographic assay. J Clin Microbiol 2000;38:1267–8.
49b. Garcia LS, Shimizu RY, Novak S, Carroll M, Chan F. Commercial assay for detection of *Giardia lamblia* and *Cryptosporidium parvum* antigens in human fecal specimens by rapid solid-phase qualitative immunochromatography. J Clin Microbiol 2003;41:209–12.
50. Beal C, Goldsmith R, Kotby M, *et al.* The plastic envelope method, a simplified technique for culture diagnosis of trichomoniasis. J Clin Microbiol 1992;30:2265–8.
51. Borchardt KA, Smith RF. An evaluation of an InPouch™ TV culture method for diagnosing *Trichomonas vaginalis* infection. Genitourin Med 1991;67:149–52.
52. Barenfanger J, Drake C, Hanson C. Timing of inoculation of the pouch makes no difference in increased detection of *Trichomonas vaginalis* by the InPouch TV method. J Clin Microbiol 2002;40:1387–9.
53. Chang TH, Tsing SY, Tzeng S. Monoclonal antibodies against *Trichomonas vaginalis*. Hybridoma 1986;5:43–51.
54. Muresu R, Rubino S, Rissu R, *et al.* A new method for identification of *Trichomonas vaginalis* by fluorescent DNA in situ hybridization. J Clin Microbiol 1994;32:1018–22.
55. Yule AM, Gellan CA, Oriel JD, Packers J. Detection of *Trichomonas vaginalis* antigen in women by enzyme immunoassay. J Clin Pathol 1987;40:566–8.
56. Kaydos SC, Swygard H, Wise SL, *et al.* Development and validation of a PCR-based enzyme-linked immunosorbent assay with urine for use in clinical research settings to detect *Trichomonas vaginalis* in women. J Clin Microbiol 2002;40:89–95.
57. Que X, Brinen LS, Perkins P, *et al.* Cysteine proteinases from distinct cellular compartments are recruited to phagocytic vesicles by *Entamoeba histolytica.* Mol Biochem Parasitol 2002;119:23–32.
58. Hellberg A, Nowak N, Leippe M, *et al.* Recombinant expression and purification of an enzymatically active cysteine proteinase of the protozoan parasite *Entamoeba histolytica.* Protein Expr Purif 2002;24:131–7.
59. Teixeira JE, Mann BJ. *Entamoeba histolytica*-induced dephosphorylation in host cells. Infect Immunol 2002;70:1816–23.
60. Gatti S, Petithory JC, Ardoin F, *et al.* Asymptomatic amoebic infection: *Entamoeba histolytica* or *Entamoeba dispar*? That is the question. Bull Soc Pathol Exot 2001;94:304–7.
61. Nimri L, Batchoun R. Intestinal colonization of symptomatic and asymptomatic schoolchildren with *Blastocystis hominis.* J Clin Microbiol 1994;32:2865–6.
62. Shlim DR, Hoge CW, Rajah R, Rabold JG, Echeverria P. Is *Blastocystis hominis* a cause of diarrhea in travelers? A prospective controlled study in Nepal. Clin Infect Dis 1995;21:97–101.
63. Markell EK, Udkow MP. *Blastocystis hominis*: pathogen or fellow traveler? Am J Trop Med Hyg 1986;35:1023–6.
64. Zierdt CH. *Blastocystis hominis*, an intestinal protozoan parasite of man. Public Health Lab 1978;36:147–61.
65. Ayadi A, Bahri I. *Dientamoeba fragilis*: pathogenic flagellate? Bull Soc Pathol Exot 1999;92:299–301.
66. Irusen EM, Jackson TFHG, Simjee AE. Asymptomatic intestinal colonization by pathogenic *Entamoeba histolytica* in amebic liver abscess: prevalence, response to therapy, and pathogenic potential. Clin Infect Dis 1992;14:889–93.
67. Asrani CH, Damie SS, Ghotge W, *et al.* Efficacy and safety of metronidazole versus a combination of metronidazole and diiodohydroxyquinoline for the treatment of patients with intestinal amebiasis: a primary care physician research group study. Curr Ther Res Clin Exp 1995;56:678–83.
68. Dunn LA, Boreham PFL. The *in-vitro* activity of drugs against *Blastocystis hominis.* J Antimicrob Chemother 1991;27:507–16.
69. Jokipii L, Jokipii AMM. Single-dose metronidazole and Tinidazole as therapy for giardiasis: success rates, side effects, and drug absorption and elimination. J Infect Dis 1979;140:984–8.
70. Abramowicz M, ed. Drugs for parasitic infections. Med Lett Drugs Ther 1998;40:1–12.

chapter 243

Protozoa: Intestinal Coccidia and Microsporidia

Rainer Weber

Intestinal coccidia and microsporidia have increasingly gained attention as etiologic agents of HIV-associated diarrhea. These organisms, however, are not only opportunistic pathogens, but are also the cause of common, worldwide intestinal infections in immunocompetent children and adults. Also, newly described microsporidia are recognized as causing disseminated infections in immunocompromised patients.

NATURE

Intestinal coccidia

The intestinal coccidia are obligate intracellular protozoal parasites that belong to the phylum Apicomplexa, suphylum Sporozoa, and infect small intestinal enterocytes. Species of four genera (*Cryptosporidium, Cyclospora, Isospora, Sarcocystis*) are pathogenic in humans.[1-3]

The most frequent agents of human cryptosporidiosis are the human and the bovine genotype of *Cryptosporidium parvum,* although *C. meleagridis, C. felis,* and the canine genotype of *C. parvum* have also been identified in stools of patients with HIV infection and in HIV-seronegative Peruvian children.[1,4] *Isospora belli* has been identified as the only accepted cause of human isosporiasis.[3] Intestinal organisms that were previously termed blue green algae, cyanobacterium-like bodies, or coccidia-like bodies were recently characterized as belonging to the coccidians, and are now named *Cyclospora cayetanensis.*[2]

Microsporidia

The term 'microsporidia' is a nontaxonomic designation commonly used to describe a group of obligate intracellular protozoa belonging to the phylum Microsporidia. More than 140 microsporidial genera and almost 1200 species have been identified that are parasitic in every major animal group. To date, seven genera (*Enterocytozoon, Encephalitozoon, Nosema, Pleistophora, Vittaforma, Trachipleistophora* and *Brachiola)* and unclassified microsporidia (referred to collectively as *Microsporidium*) have been implicated in human infections.[5-8]

EPIDEMIOLOGY

Cryptosporidium species

Cryptosporidial infections have been detected on all continents. Cumulative prevalence rates are between 1 and 3% in industrialized nations and between 5 and 10% in developing countries.[9,10] Children, particularly those less than 2 years of age, have a higher prevalence of infection than adults. Seroepidemiologic studies indicate that cryptosporidiosis may be more common than is estimated based upon surveys of fecal oocyst shedding. Seroprevalence rates in developed countries range between 25 and 35%, and in developing countries they are up to 65%. In severely immunodeficient patients with HIV infection, cryptosporidiosis is among the most important causes of chronic diarrhea, accounting for 10–20% of diarrheal episodes.[11]

Cryptosporidial oocysts are transmitted by the fecal–oral route and infection may be acquired from contaminated surfaces, ground and recreational water, pets and farm animals (particularly cattle and sheep), contaminated foods and person-to-person contact, including transmission between household members, sexual partners, children in day care centers and nosocomial infections involving both medical care staff and patients. An increasing number of outbreaks of cryptosporidial infections attributed to drinking water have been reported, including an outbreak in Milwaukee, USA in 1993 that affected over 400,000 persons. Ingestion of as few as ten oocysts may cause diarrhea.[12]

Cyclospora species

Cyclospora spp. have been identified worldwide in stool specimens of immunocompetent and immunocompromised patients, but appears to be most common in tropical and subtropical areas. The parasite is transmitted by the fecal–oral route and infection is most probably acquired from contaminated water or food.[13] It is not known whether animals can be infected and serve as sources for human infection. Direct person-to-person transmission is unlikely because excreted oocysts require days to weeks to become infectious. Warm temperatures and high humidity facilitate sporulation.

Isospora species

Isospora belli is endemic in many parts of Africa, Asia and South America, and is particularly common in patients from developing countries who have AIDS and chronic diarrhea; for example, it occurs in 10–20% of such patients in Haiti or Africa. Modes of transmission are not known but it is assumed that they comprise water and/or food that contains oocysts.

Microsporidia

Reported human infections are globally dispersed. Although microsporidiosis appears to occur most frequently in persons infected with HIV, it is emerging as an infection in otherwise immunocompromised hosts and in immunocompetent individuals.[5]

The sources of microsporidia infecting humans and modes of transmission are uncertain. Because microsporidial spores are released into the environment via stool, urine and respiratory secretions, possible sources of infection may be persons or animals infected with microsporidia. Ingestion of microsporidial spores is the most probable mode of transmission. Transmission by the aerosol route has also been considered because spores have been found in respiratory specimens of patients who have *Encephalitozoon* spp. infection.[14] Epidemiologic and experimental studies in mammals suggest that *Encephalitozoon* spp. can be transmitted transplacentally from mother to offspring, but no congenitally acquired human infections have been reported.

PATHOGENICITY

Cryptosporidium species

Cryptosporidium spp. develop intracellularly at the microvillous border of enterocytes (Fig. 243.1). Infected cells lack microvilli at

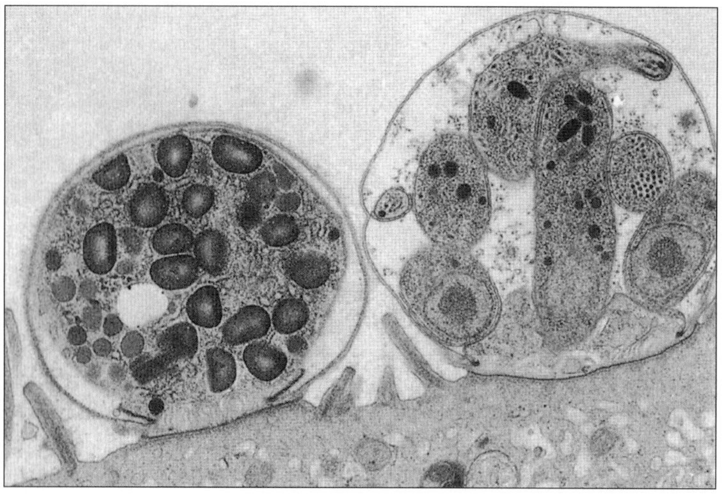

Fig. 243.1 Intestinal cryptosporidial infection. Transmission electron micrograph of duodenal tissue of a patient with HIV infection showing two different developmental stages of *Cryptosporidium* spp. on the brush border of the mucosal surface: mature schizont with merozoites (right), undifferentiated zygote (left). *Cryptosporidium* spp. develop intracellularly just under the plasma membrane of the host cell. Courtesy of MA Spycher.

the site of parasite attachment and the mucosal surface appears disrupted. In immunocompetent individuals, infection is usually limited to the intestine. In immunocompromised patients, organisms are found throughout the entire gastrointestinal tract and within epithelial cells of the biliary tree, the pancreatic ducts and the airways. In the intestines, cryptosporidial infection induces atrophy, blunting or loss of villi, crypt hyperplasia, and infiltration of lymphocytes, neutrophils, plasma cells, and macrophages into the lamina propria. Cryptosporidial infection has been associated with marked reduction in the brush border enzyme activities, including sucrase, lactase, and maltase deficiency, with impaired absorption of vitamin B12 and D-xylose, and with increased permeability of the intestinal epithelium to organic molecules. Malabsorption and intestinal injury appear to correlate with the number of organisms infecting the intestine.[15] No specific virulence determinants of the parasite have been clearly linked to direct or indirect damage of intestinal host tissues. Putative virulence factors include molecules that are involved in parasite attachment to host cells and host cell membrane disruption.[16]

The immune responses to cryptosporidial infection are poorly understood, but probably include humoral and cellular processes. Persistent cryptosporidiosis has been observed in patients who have hypo- or agammaglobulinemias and those with T-cell deficiencies. Animal studies and epidemiologic data strongly indicate the importance of the systemic cellular immunity, particularly $CD4^+$ lymphocytes, in modulating cryptosporidial infection.[1]

Isospora species

Isospora belli develops within parasitophorous vacuoles deep in the cytoplasm of the enterocyte. Histologic abnormalities associated with isosporiasis range from minimal changes of the small intestinal architecture to marked villous atrophy, crypt hyperplasia, and inflammatory infiltrates in the lamina propria consisting of eosinophils, neutrophils, lymphocytes and plasma cells. The mechanisms by which these changes occur are unknown. As a result of the intestinal injury, malabsorption and steatorrhea have been documented.[3]

Cyclospora species

Cyclosporiasis is associated with villous atrophy, crypt hyperplasia, and inflammatory infiltrates. The mechanisms that lead to the clinical features are unknown.

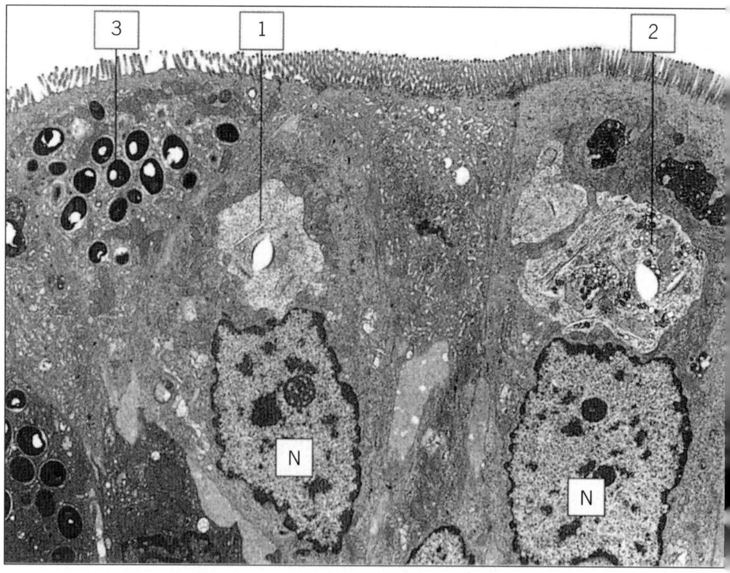

Fig. 243.2 Intestinal *Enterocytozoon bieneusi* infection. Transmission electron micrograph showing duodenal epithelium of a patient with HIV infection who has *Enterocytozoon bieneusi* infection. The different developmental stages between the enterocyte nuclei (N) and the microvillous border include: (1) a proliferative plasmodium; (2) late sporogonial plasmodia; and (3) mature spores. Courtesy of MA Spycher.

Microsporidia

Microsporidiosis has been associated with abnormalities in structure and function of infected organs but how the different microsporidial species cause disease is not sufficiently understood.[5]

Enterocytozoon bieneusi

Enterocytozoon bieneusi infection generally appears to be limited to intestinal enterocytes (Fig. 243.2) and biliary epithelium. Patients who have severe cellular immunodeficiency appear at highest risk of developing microsporidial disease but little is known about immunity to *E. bieneusi* infection. It is not understood whether microsporidial infection in these patients is primarily a reactivation of latent infection acquired before the state of suppressed immunity or whether microsporidial disease is caused by recently acquired infection.

Encephalitozoon species

Encephalitozoon cuniculi and *E. hellem* infect a variety of cells including epithelial and endothelial cells, fibroblasts, kidney tubule cells, macrophages and possibly other cell types in numerous mammalian hosts, for example rabbits, rodents, carnivores, monkeys and humans.[17] In mammals, they usually cause latent asymptomatic or chronic mildly symptomatic infection, but interstitial nephritis and severe neurologic disease caused by central nervous system vasculitis and granulomatous encephalitis may occur. The parasites are able to persist in their animal hosts despite an active immune response. Microsporidial infection activates antibody production, although antibodies alone do not appear to yield protection. The role of a competent cellular immune response in suppressing microsporidial multiplication has been established experimentally. The pathogenesis of human *Encephalitozoon* infection has yet to be defined. Rare histologic and clinical investigations in immunodeficient patients have indicated that *E. cuniculi* and *E. hellem* usually cause disseminated infection in this patient group.[14,17]

PREVENTION

Cryptosporidiosis

Cryptosporidial oocysts are remarkably resistant to many common disinfectants, including chlorine-based compounds. Adequate filter systems are required to guarantee the complete removal of cryptosporidia from water supplies. A water disinfection device delivering germicidal ultraviolet (UV) light for *Cryptosporidium* oocyst inactivation yielded promising results.[18]

Cyclosporiasis, isosporiasis

Avoiding food or water that may be contaminated with feces may prevent cyclosporiasis and isosporiasis, but details of the sources of infection and the modes of transmission are unknown.

Microsporidiosis

Laboratory experiments indicate that the thick-walled spores may survive in the environment for months or years depending on the temperature and humidity. Exposure to recommended working concentrations of most disinfectants, boiling and autoclaving seems to kill *Encephalitozoon* spp. spores but no data are available for *Enterocytozoon* spp.

DIAGNOSTIC MICROBIOLOGY

Stool examination by light microscopy is the most important test to diagnose intestinal coccidia and intestinal microsporidia. In many laboratories, tests for *Cryptosporidium* spp., *Isospora* spp., *Cyclospora* spp. and microsporidia must be specifically requested because the general request of 'stool for O & P' (ova and parasites) often does not mean that the specific methods to detect these organisms are applied. Microsporidial species that cause systemic infection are best detected in urine sediments.

Cryptosporidium species

Examination of stool specimens by light microscopy

To visualize the *Cryptosporidium* spp. oocysts in fecal smears, acid-fast staining (e.g. modified cold Kinyoun technique; Fig. 243.3) and the immunofluorescence (IF) technique are among the most sensitive, specific and widely used methods. The IF detection procedure is more sensitive than the acid-fast staining but the difference in sensitivity may not be of clinical relevance when watery stools of patients with HIV infection are examined. These patients usually excrete an amount of oocysts that can easily be detected using acid-fast staining. The oocysts should be measured in order to distinguish *Cryptosporidium* spp. (4–6μm in diameter) from *Cyclospora* spp. (8–10μm). Enhanced sensitivity of stool examination can be obtained by concentrating oocysts, preferably with the formalin-ethyl acetate (FEA) technique.

The exact sensitivity of the coprodiagnostic techniques is not known but some data raise questions about the widely held belief that these techniques are sufficient to meet the needs of clinicians and epidemiologists.[19] The minimum number of oocysts in human stool specimens that can be detected by the FEA stool concentration technique and the IF staining procedure was found to be unexpectedly high: 5000–10,000 oocysts per gram of stool in watery stool specimens and 10,000–50,000 oocysts per gram of stool in formed stool. Examination of multiple specimens may be necessary, because clinical studies have shown that examination of single stool specimens may have an insufficient diagnostic yield. Furthermore, in a prospective analyses of jejunal biopsies in patients who have AIDS, *Cryptosporidium* spp. were present in more than 10% of patients whose stool examinations were negative. These results, however, were in contrast to another study that only identified organisms on biopsy in one-third of patients shedding *Cryptosporidium* spp. in their feces.

Stool antigen detection techniques have been developed but the sensitivity of currently available tests is not better than microscopic techniques. Molecular diagnostic methods have improved diagnostic yields but currently are not ready to use in routine laboratories.[20,21]

Cytologic diagnosis

Aspiration of duodenal fluid or small intestinal brushing can be used for diagnosis when upper endoscopy is performed. Examination of centrifuged duodenal aspirates under the microscope may be the most sensitive diagnostic procedure.

Histologic examinations

Cryptosporidium spp. appear basophilic by examination under the light microscope of small intestinal tissue sections stained with hematoxylin and eosin. The intracellular organisms seem to project into the intestinal lumen because of their apical extracytoplasmic localization. Under electron microscopy the unique ultrastructural features of different developmental stages of the parasite can be seen (see Fig. 243.1), but this is rarely necessary for diagnostic purposes.

Serology

Specific IgM or IgG antibodies to *Cryptosporidium* spp. can be detected within 2 weeks of onset of symptoms in most patients. In the majority of patients IgG titers may persist for long periods. Serologic testing is mainly used as an epidemiologic tool and has no diagnostic application, particularly because antibody persistence limits its use in the diagnosis of acute infection.

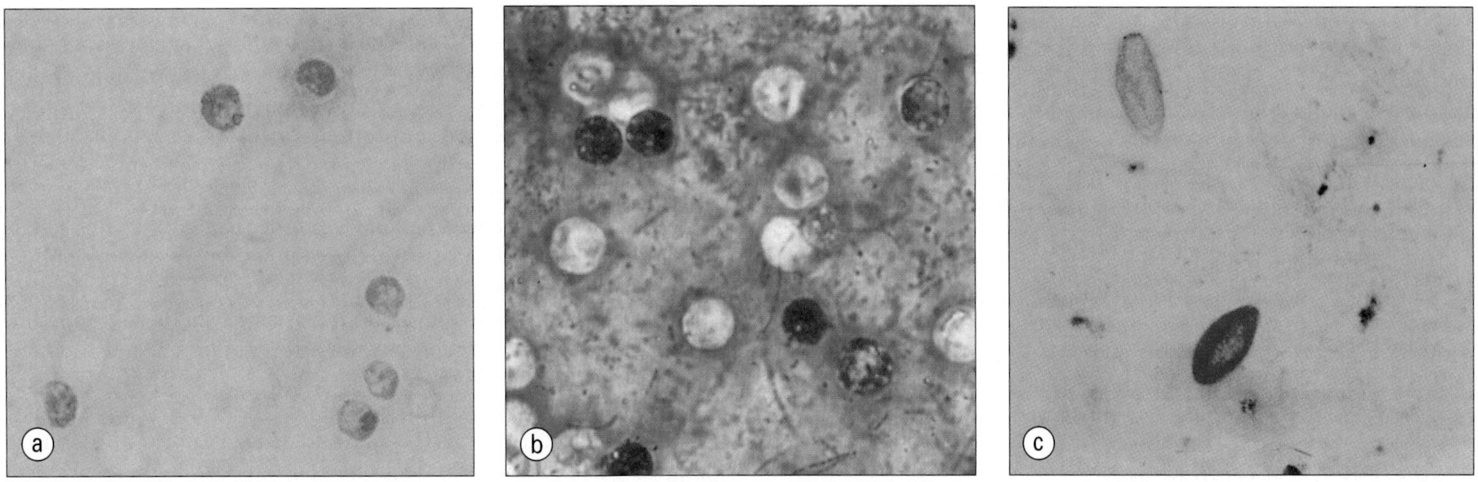

Fig. 243.3 Acid-fast stained smears of fecal specimens showing intestinal coccidia. (a) *Cryptosporidium* spp., round, 4–6μm diameter. (b) *Cyclospora* spp., round, 8–10μm diameter. Courtesy of EG Long. (c) *Isospora belli*, elliptical, 23–33μm long and 10–19μm wide. Modified Kinyoun stain.

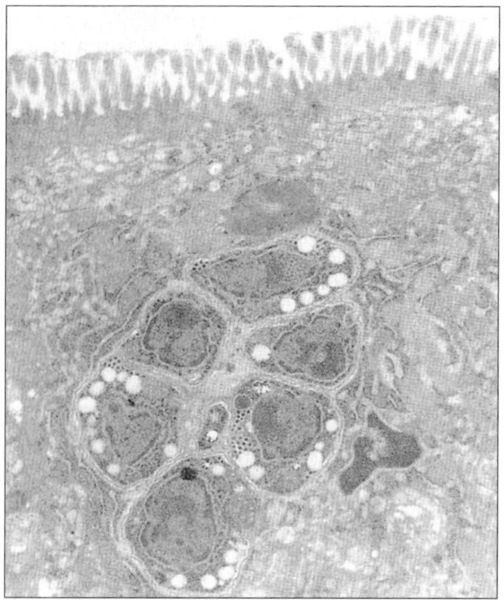

Fig. 243.4 Intestinal *Cyclospora* infection. Transmission electron micrograph of duodenal epithelium obtained from a patient with HIV infection who has *Cyclospora cayetanensis* infection. A mature schizont filled with numerous merozoites is shown. Courtesy of AM Deloul and FP Chatelet.

Fig. 243.5 Detection of microsporidia in stool samples. Smear of a formalin-fixed, unconcentrated stool specimen of a patient who has AIDS and chronic diarrhea, showing pinkish-red-stained spores of *Enterocytozoon bieneusi.* Chromotrope staining (oil immersion).

Cyclospora species

Diagnosis of *Cyclospora* spp. is dependent on detection by light microscopy of the refractile oocysts, 8–10μm in diameter, in wet mounts of fresh stool specimens or in acid-fast stained smears prepared from stool concentrated by the FEA sedimentation.[22] Acid-fast stained oocysts vary in appearance from faint pink to deep red, and with many organisms remain as unstained spheres (see Fig. 243.3). The sensitivity of the coprodiagnostic techniques is unknown. In many patients' specimens, however, the number of oocysts detected per slide is low, indicating that not all symptomatic patients excrete a large enough number of oocysts for laboratory detection to be assured. Examination of small intestinal tissue of patients who have *Cyclospora* infection often did not reveal any parasites. The presence of intracellular parasites has rarely been documented in aspirated duodenal or jejunal fluid and on duodenal and jejunal biopsy (Fig. 243.4).

Isospora species

Diagnosis of *I. belli* is usually achieved by detection under the light microscope of the parasite oocysts in wet preparations or acid-fast stained smears of concentrated stool specimens (see Fig. 243.3). Repetitive stool examinations may be necessary because the parasite may be excreted intermittently or in low numbers. Histologic examination of small intestinal tissue sections may reveal the parasite within enterocytes.

Microsporidia

Diagnosis of microsporidial infection is dependent on morphologic demonstration of the organisms themselves. This can be difficult because of the organisms' small size and staining properties hamper visualization of the spores and developing stages using routine staining techniques. The spores, the stages by which microsporidia are usually identified, are small, ranging in size from 1 to 3.5μm in diameter.

Evaluation of patients who have suspected microsporidiosis should begin with examination of body fluids by light microscopy using special staining techniques. Definitive species identification of microsporidia is made using electron microscopy, antigenic analysis, and molecular analysis. Collection of fresh material (without fixative) may be useful for cell culture and for future molecular analysis.[5,23]

Examination of stool specimens

In patients who have suspected enteric microsporidiosis, examination of stool specimens by light microscopy is the first step. It is at least as sensitive as examination of biopsy specimens. Detection of microsporidial spores requires adequate illumination and magnification [i.e. ×630 or ×1000 magnification (oil immersion)], and special staining methods. The two most commonly used stains are the chromotrope stain, which appears to be the most specific (Fig. 243.5),[24] and chemofluorescent agents, which might be more sensitive but may produce false-positive results.[25] An epidemiologic comparison of these techniques resulted in the recommendation to screen specimens with chemofluorescent agents and to confirm the results with the chromotrope stain.

The differences in spore size between *Enterocytozoon* (1–1.5μm in diameter) and *Encephalitozoon* spp. (2–3μm in diameter) often permit a tentative diagnosis of the genus from examination of stool under the light microscope. The microsporidian should be identified to the level of genus by electron microscopy or molecular analysis because *Encephalitozoon* spp. have a propensity for dissemination, and have a different drug sensitivity pattern compared with *Enterocytozoon bieneusi.*

Immunofluorescent procedures for diagnosis of *Encephalitozoon*-like microsporidial spores are promising but not widely available. Diagnostic application of polyclonal antibodies in fecal samples has been hampered by background staining, cross-reactions with yeast and bacteria, and low sensitivity. A few monoclonal antibodies against *Encephalitozoon* spp.[26] and one against spores of *Enterocytozoon bieneusi* have been generated.[27]

Histologic examination

Among patients with HIV infection who suffered from chronic diarrhea, stool examinations proved as sensitive as endoscopic evaluation for all pathogens except cytomegalovirus and *Leishmania*.[11] Examination of duodenal and terminal ileal tissue has resulted in detection of microsporidia but the parasites are rarely found in colonic tissue sections.

Only highly experienced pathologists have reliably and consistently identified microsporidia in tissue sections using routine techniques such as hematoxylin and eosin stain. Ultra-thin plastic sections stained with methylene blue-azure II–basic fuchsin or with toluidine blue may facilitate detection but these techniques are not routinely used. In our experience, tissue Gram stains such as Brown–Brenn or Brown–Hopps have proved to be the most useful for the rapid and reliable identification of HIV-associated microsporidia in routine paraffin-embedded tissue sections (Fig. 243.6). Others prefer a silver stain (Warthin–Starry stain) or the chromotrope-based staining technique.

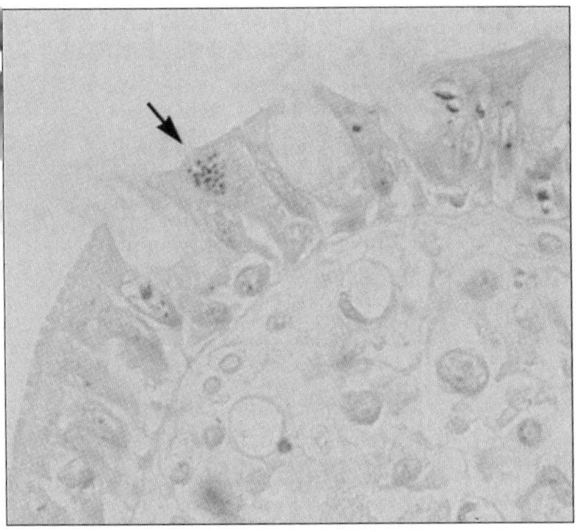

Fig. 243.6 Intestinal *Enterocytozoon bieneusi* infection. Terminal ileal tissue obtained by ileocolonoscopy in a patient who has AIDS and chronic diarrhea caused by *Enterocytozoon bieneusi* infection. Gram-positive or Gram-labile microsporidial spores (arrow) are found in supranuclear location within small intestinal enterocytes. Brown–Brenn stain.

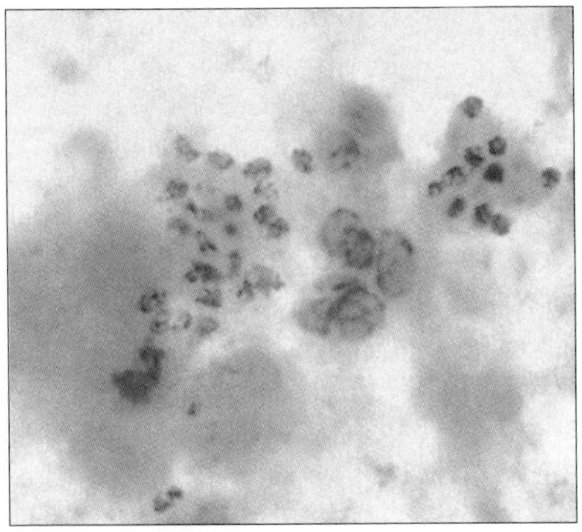

Fig. 243.7 Detection of microsporidia in urine sediment. Urine sediment from a patient who has AIDS and disseminated *Encephalitozoon hellem* infection, showing Gram-labile intracellular and extracellular microsporidial spores. Gram stain (oil immersion).

Cytologic diagnosis

Microsporidial spores have been detected in sediments of duodenal aspirate, bile or biliary aspirates, urine (Fig. 243.7), bronchoalveolar lavage fluid, cerebrospinal fluid (CSF) and in smears of conjunctival swabs, sputum and nasal discharge.[5] Microscopic examination of centrifuged duodenal aspirate obtained during endoscopy appears to be the most sensitive technique for diagnosis of intestinal microsporidiosis. Because microsporidial infection often involves multiple organs, detection of microsporidia in virtually any tissue or bodily fluid should prompt a thorough search of other sites. In particular, urine specimens of patients suspected of having disseminated microsporidiosis should be examined.

Electron microscopy

Microsporidial ultrastructure is unique and pathognomonic for the phylum and, with rare exceptions, ultrastructural features can distinguish between most genera of microsporidia (Fig. 243.8; see Fig. 243.2).

Serology

Serologic assays (including carbon immunoassay, indirect IF test, enzyme-linked immunosorbent assay and Western blot immunodetection) have been useful in detecting antibodies to *E. cuniculi* in several species of animals, but reliable serologic tests for diagnosis of human microsporidiosis are lacking. This lack of availability is partly because *Enterocytozoon* spp. have not been continuously propagated in cell culture or laboratory animals.

Cell culture

Encephalitozoon spp., *Nosema* spp., *Trachipleistophora hominis*, *Vittaforma corneae* and *Brachiola algerae* have been isolated using cell culture systems, but these tests are fastidious and costly, and the most common human species, *E. bieneusi*, has not been continuously propagated.

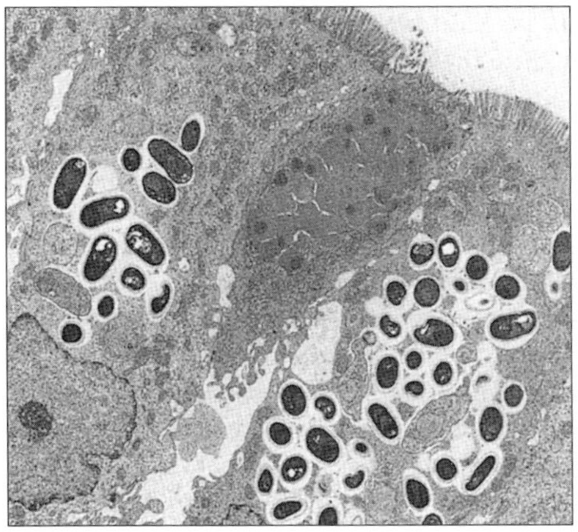

Fig. 243.8 *Encephalitozoon intestinalis* (formerly *Septata intestinalis*): developing spores within enterocytes separated by a fibrillar matrix. *Encephalitozoon intestinalis* develop within parasitophorous vacuoles, unlike *E. bieneusi*, which develops in direct contact with enterocyte cytoplasm. Courtesy of MA Spycher.

Molecular techniques

Universal panmicrosporidian and species-specific primer pairs that amplify the short regions of the small subunit rRNA gene have been developed,[17,28] but, at present, these techniques are confined to research laboratories. Diagnosis and identification of *Enterocytozoon bieneusi* and the different *Encephalitozoon* spp. have been successfully performed with fresh stool specimens, formalin-fixed stool specimens, intestinal tissue obtained by endoscopic biopsy, urine specimens and other body fluids.[17,29] *In-situ* hybridization to visualize *E. bieneusi* in tissue sections has been developed.

CLINICAL MANIFESTATIONS

Cryptosporidiosis

For cryptosporidiosis the mean incubation period between infection and onset of symptoms is approximately 7–14 days (range 5–28 days). The severity and duration of illness varies depending on the immune status of the hosts. Children, the elderly and individuals with nutritional deficiencies may suffer from a more severe and prolonged disease, as is observed in immunodeficient patients. Whether cryptosporidiosis in immunocompromised patients is mainly a reactivation of latent infection or whether clinical illness is caused by recently acquired infection is not known.

Immunocompetent patients

In immunocompetent patients, cryptosporidia cause a self-limiting, usually watery, diarrhea lasting 10–14 days (range 2–28 days), but the clinical presentation varies from asymptomatic shedding of oocysts to severe disease that may last up to 3 months.[12] Patients often complain of abdominal pain, flatulence, loss of appetite, nausea and vomiting, and may suffer from low-grade fever, anorexia, malaise, weakness, fatigue, myalgias and headaches. The diarrhea and abdominal pain are often made worse by eating. Cough appears significantly more frequent in children with cryptosporidiosis than in children with diarrhea of another etiology, but the parasite has rarely been documented in the airways of immunocompetent individuals. Single case reports of pancreatitis associated with cryptosporidiosis and reactive arthritis have been described. Poorly understood lasting adverse effects of infection in children in developing children may include deficits of linear growth, even if cryptosporidial infections is otherwise symptomless.[30]

Immunocompromised patients (see Chapter 127)

In immunocompromised patients, particularly individuals with HIV infection, cryptosporidiosis is a more severe, often chronic and incurable illness that can be life-threatening. The main clinical presentation is watery diarrhea that can lead to severe dehydration, electrolyte depletion, malnutrition and weight loss. In addition, infection of the biliary tract and the gallbladder, resulting in acalculous cholecystitis, sclerosing cholangitis ('AIDS cholangiopathy') and stenosis of the papilla of Vater, frequently occurs. Infection of the epithelial cells of the respiratory tract, including sinuses, is increasingly described, but it is not clear whether this finding is of clinical relevance because most of these patients have a concomitant respiratory infection. Systemic cryptosporidiosis has not been described.

The clinical course of HIV-associated cryptosporidiosis is highly variable. Four clinical patterns of disease have been identified:

- asymptomatic shedding of oocysts;
- transient diarrhea with transient or chronic shedding of oocysts;
- chronic diarrhea; and
- fulminant disease that leads to cachexia and death within months.

Most patients who have severe illness have $CD4^+$ lymphocyte counts below 50 cells/mm^3. Spontaneous clinical recovery may occur and is mainly correlated with higher $CD4^+$ lymphocyte counts, but a benign course of the diarrhea may also occur in severely immunodeficient patient. Clinical observations suggest that cryptosporidial disease is more severe if co-infections caused by other enteropathogens are present. Concurrent dual or multiple intestinal infection is found in up to 50% of patients who have HIV-associated cryptosporidiosis.

Cyclosporiasis

The spectrum of *Cyclospora*-associated illness is not yet fully defined but it may range from asymptomatic carriage of the organism to severe and prolonged diarrhea in immunocompetent and immunocompromised patients. Patients who have AIDS tend to have a more prolonged and severe illness, and *Cyclospora*-associated cholangiopathy has been described in this group.

The incubation period between infection and onset of symptoms ranges between 2 and 11 days and is usually about 7 days. In symptomatic infections the main clinical manifestation is mild to severe watery diarrhea, accompanied by abdominal cramps, bloating, increased flatus, nausea, anorexia, substantial weight loss and fatigue. Vomiting is less common and about 25% of the patients report fever and myalgias.

If not treated, diarrhea is self-limiting but may last for 1 month or longer (range 2–107 days), and remissions and relapses may occur during gradual resolution of the illness. *Cyclospora* infection does not appear to provide lasting immunity.

Isosporiasis

In immunocompetent persons, *I. belli* infection causes self-limited watery diarrhea accompanied by malaise, anorexia, cramping abdominal pain, weight loss and, less frequently, low-grade fever. In immunocompromised patients, the illness is more severe and prolonged, or chronic if untreated. Also, acalculous cholecystitis and two single cases of disseminated extraintestinal isosporiasis in patients with AIDS have been reported.

MICROSPORIDIAL SPECIES PATHOGENIC IN HUMANS, AND CLINICAL MANIFESTATIONS

Microsporidial species	Clinical manifestations
Enterocytozoon bieneusi	Diarrhea, wasting syndrome Cholangiopathy, cholangitis, acalculous cholecystitis Sinusitis, bronchitis, pneumonitis
Encephalitozoon intestinalis (formerly *Septata intestinalis*)	Diarrhea Cholangiopathy, cholangitis, acalculous cholecystitis Sinusitis, bronchitis, pneumonitis Urinary tract infection, nephritis Bone lesions; nodular cutaneous lesions
Encephalitozoon cuniculi	Disseminated infection Keratoconjunctivitis Sinusitis, pneumonitis Urinary tract infection, nephritis Hepatitis Peritonitis Symptomatic and asymptomatic intestinal infections Seizures, encephalitis
Encephalitozoon hellem	Disseminated infection Keratoconjunctivitis Sinusitis, bronchitis, pneumonia Nephritis, ureteritis, cystitis, prostatitis, urethritis
Pleistophora spp.	Myositis
Trachipleistophora hominis	Myositis, keratoconjunctivitis, sinusitis
Trachipleistophora anthropophthera	Disseminated infection including brain, heart, kidneys
Brachiola connori (formerly *Nosema connori*)	Disseminated infection
Brachiola vesicularum	Myositis
Brachiola algerae (formerly *Nosema algerae*)	Keratitis
Vittaforma corneae (formerly: *Nosema corneum*)	Keratitis Disseminated infection
Nosema ocularum	Keratitis
Microsporidium ceylonensis	Corneal ulcer
Microsporidium africanum	Corneal ulcer

Table 243.1 Microsporidial species pathogenic in humans, and clinical manifestations.

Microsporidiosis in immunocompromised patients

The spectrum of clinically manifest microsporidial infection is diverse and includes intestinal, ocular, muscular, cerebral, respiratory and urinary tract disease (Table 243.1).[5] The most prevalent microsporidial disease is HIV-associated chronic diarrhea.[11] Disseminated microsporidial infections are being increasingly recognized in patients who have AIDS.

Diarrhea, cholangitis, acalculous cholecystitis

Two microsporidial species – *Enterocytozoon bieneusi* and *Encephalitozoon intestinalis* – cause chronic diarrhea and wasting, cholangiopathy and acalculous cholecystitis in patients who have HIV infection or who are otherwise immunodeficient, particularly when $CD4^+$ lymphocyte counts drop below 50–100/μl.

Enterocytozoon bieneusi is estimated to be one of the most important HIV-associated intestinal pathogens, present in 5–30% of those with otherwise unexplained diarrhea. The main symptoms are chronic nonbloody diarrhea, anorexia, weight loss and bloating. Some patients experience intermittent diarrhea and a few excrete microsporidial spores without having diarrhea. The stool is watery or soft, and diarrhea seems to be worsened by most foods. Some of the patients report abdominal pain or nausea and vomiting. Laboratory evidence for intestinal malabsorption is common. *E. bieneusi* itself is not immediately life-threatening, but diarrhea is debilitating, and weight loss may lead to cachexia, which is a significant cause or cofactor in the deaths of many patients. Up to one-third of patients who have intestinal microsporidiosis have dual or multiple co-infection with other intestinal pathogens. The parasite has also been detected in the biliary tree and/or gallbladder of patients who have cholangitis and acalculous cholecystitis. Imaging procedures often reveal dilatation of both intrahepatic and common bile ducts, irregularities of the bile duct wall and gallbladder abnormalities such as wall thickening, distention or the presence of sludge.[5,11]

Encephalitozoon intestinalis primarily causes diarrhea, and the parasite may also spread into the biliary tract and gallbladder, causing cholangitis and cholecystitis. In contrast to *Enterocytozoon bieneusi*, systemic dissemination to kidneys and other sites may occur.[31]

Systemic microsporidiosis

There are three microsporidial genera, *Encephalitozoon* spp., *Trachipleistophora* spp. and *Vittaforma corneae*, which have been found to disseminate in severely immunodeficient patients who have HIV infection.[6,17,32,33] Disseminated infection caused by *Brachiola connori* (formerly *Nosema connori*) was found at autopsy in a 4-month-old athymic boy reported in 1973.

Encephalitozoon spp. was initially identified in patients who had AIDS and keratoconjunctivitis.[34] Subsequently the spectrum of recognized *Encephalitozoon*-associated disease has expanded to include keratoconjunctivitis, bronchiolitis, sinusitis, pneumonitis, nephritis, ureteritis, cystitis, prostatitis, hepatitis, peritonitis, diarrhea and encephalitis.[14,17] Clinical manifestations may vary substantially, ranging from an asymptomatic carrier state to organ failure.

Trachipleistophora anthropophthera was identified at autopsy in cerebral, cardiac, renal, pancreatic, thyroid, hepatic, splenic, lymphoid and bone marrow tissue of two patients who had AIDS and initially presented with seizures.[32]

Urinary tract infection

Predominant genitourinary signs and symptoms caused by *Encephalitozoon* infections have been observed. Clinical manifestations included asymptomatic microhematuria, urethritis, prostatitis, acute cystitis and interstitial nephritis associated with dysuria, gross hematuria and progressive renal insufficiency.[14]

Respiratory tract infection

In most patients who have respiratory tract microsporidial infection, including bronchiolitis, pneumonia and progressive respiratory failure, intestinal or systemic microsporidiosis was also present. Single cases of patients have been reported in whom sinusitis causing nasal obstruction and persistent mucopurulent nasal discharge caused by *E. bieneusi* or *Encephalitozoon* spp. was a predominant manifestation of systemic microsporidiosis.

Keratoconjunctivitis

HIV-associated ocular microsporidiosis caused by *Encephalitozoon* spp. is restricted to the superficial epithelium of the cornea and conjunctiva. Most patients exhibit bilateral coarse punctate epithelial keratopathy (Fig. 243.9), conjunctival inflammation resulting in redness and foreign body sensation, decreased visual acuity and photophobia. In patients who initially present with symptomatic keratoconjunctival microsporidiosis, dissemination of the parasite may be common, but clinical manifestations other than keratoconjunctivitis may be mild or absent.[35]

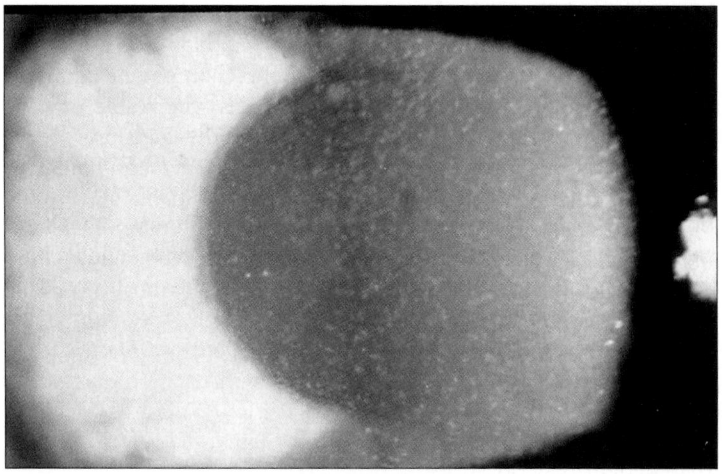

Fig. 243.9 Keratopathy caused by *Encephalitozoon hellem*. Slit-lamp demonstration of punctate epithelial keratopathy in a patient who has AIDS and keratoconjunctivitis caused by *Encephalitozoon hellem*. Ocular microsporidiosis can often be diagnosed by examination under the light microscope of a smear obtained by a nontraumatic conjunctival swab. Courtesy of M Diesenhouse and DA Schwartz.

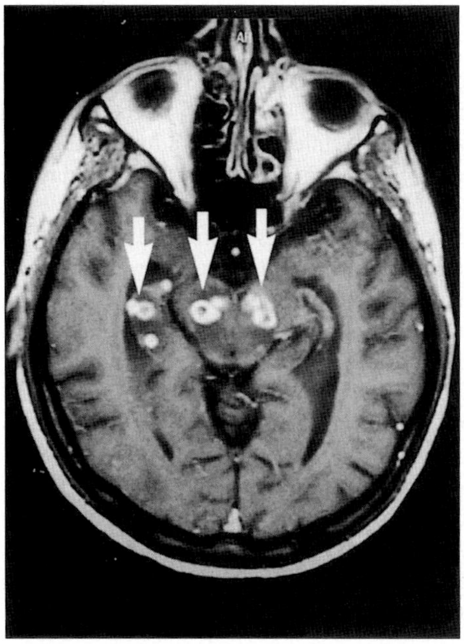

Fig. 243.10 Cerebral microsporidiosis caused by *Encephalitozoon cuniculi* in a patient with HIV infection. The MRI shows multiple small contrast-enhancing, mostly ring-like, partly micronodular, lesions in hippocampal, mesencephal and intracortical regions (arrows), partly accompanied by slight edema, and congestion of the right ethmoid sinus. *Encephalitozoon cuniculi* was isolated from CSF. From Weber *et al.*,[36] with permission from Massachusetts Medical Society.

Cerebral microsporidiosis

Microsporidia was first accepted as the etiologic agent of a neurologic disorder in two children, reported in 1959 and 1984. Both presented with seizures and might have had impaired immune responses. *Encephalitozoon cuniculi* and *Trachipleistophora anthropophthera* were detected in CSF or brain tissue of patients with HIV infection who presented with fever and somnolence or seizures and mental decline. Magnetic resonance imaging disclosed multiple small, contrast-enhancing, mostly ring-like lesions localized to the hippocampus, mesencephalon and cerebral cortex (Fig. 243.10).[32,36]

Myositis

Myositis caused by *Pleistophora* spp. has been described in an HIV-seronegative patient and in a patient with HIV infection, both of whom had severe cellular immunodeficiency. Newly characterized microsporidia, *Trachipleistophora hominis* and *Brachiola vesicularum*, were detected in muscle biopsies of patients who had AIDS and presented with myositis.[6,8]

Microsporidiosis in immunocompetent persons

Enterocytozoon bieneusi and *Encephalitozoon* spp. are associated with self-limiting watery diarrhea in immunocompetent adults as well as in children, particularly among persons who reside or have traveled in tropical countries.[37] An unexpectedly high prevalence (17%) of intestinal microsporidiosis due to *Enterocytozoon bieneusi* was found in HIV-seronegative elderly patients in Spain.[38]

Deep stromal infections of the cornea caused by different microsporidial species have been described in otherwise seemingly healthy persons who presented with severe keratitis or a corneal ulcer (see Table 243.1).

MANAGEMENT

Cryptosporidiosis

Among immunocompetent patients, cryptosporidiosis is usually self-limiting. In patients who have AIDS, case series and a randomized, controlled trial indicate that treatment with oral paromomycin (500mg q6h for at least 4 weeks) may result in decreased oocyst shedding and improved intestinal function and morphology,[39] but other investigators have not found any clinical benefit.[40] Case observations in patients who have AIDS suggest that maintenance therapy with paromomycin (1000–2000mg/day) may prevent relapses or improve the clinical course but controlled data are not available.

Randomized, double-blind trials found beneficial effects of nitazoxanide: At doses of 1–2g daily for 2 weeks, parasitologic cure was reported in 65% of Mexican patients who had AIDS.[41] Age-dependent doses of 100–500mg twice daily reduced the duration of diarrhea and oocyst shedding in HIV-seronegative children and in adults in Egypt.[42] *In-vitro* studies have indicated that nitazoxanide activity may be enhanced by the co-administration of azithromycin or rifabutin,[43] but clinical experience of such combinations is lacking. Hyperimmune bovine colostrum has been found in *in-vitro* experiments, in animal studies and in single patients to reduce or eradicate cryptosporidia, but these results could not be reproduced in larger human studies. Symptomatic treatment of diarrhea may include drugs that affect gut motility such as loperamide, diphenoxylate, opiates, somatostatin and octreotide. Immune reconstitution following initiation of potent antiretroviral therapy of patients who have HIV infection results in cessation of oocyst shedding and diarrhea, but cryptosporidial infection is controlled rather than cured because failure of antiretroviral therapy often results in relapse of cryptosporidiosis.[44]

Cyclosporiasis

A placebo-controlled trial showed that trimethoprim–sulfamethoxazole [TMP–SMX (co-trimoxazole); double-strength TMP 160/SMX 800mg q12h for 7 days] was clinically successful and shortened oocyst shedding in immunocompetent patients who have cyclosporiasis.[45] In this study, 3 days of treatment with TMP–SMX was not sufficient to eradicate cyclospora. Trimethoprim 160/SMX 800mg q6h for 10 days cured HIV-associated cyclosporiasis but the relapse rate was high (43%). Maintenance therapy with double-strength TMP–SMX three times per week did prevent relapses in these patients. There are no known alternatives to TMP–SMX.

Isosporiasis

Immunocompetent and immunocompromised patients respond promptly to therapy with TMP–SMX (double-strength TMP 160/SMX 800mg q6h for 10 days).[46] Alternatively, pyrimethamine 75mg/day plus folinic acid 10mg/day may be successful. To prevent the high rate of relapses in patients who have AIDS, maintenance therapy with double-strength TMP–SMX, three times per week, or pyrimethamine 25mg/day plus folinic acid 5mg/day, is recommended.

Microsporidiosis

Albendazole, fumagillin, its analog TNP-470, and nikkomycin Z have been found to inhibit completely or partially the replication or spore germination of *Encephalitozoon* spp. and *Vittaforma corneae* propagated in cell cultures, but did not destroy mature microsporidial spores, so that these may sustain infection.[47–49] Numerous other antiprotozoal drugs and antibiotics have been tested *in vitro*, with negative findings. *In-vitro* systems to investigate *Enterocytozoon bieneusi* are not available.

Little information on clinical experience in the therapy of human microsporidiosis is available, and only two controlled treatment trials have been conducted,[49,50] confirming previous case observations which indicated that albendazole can result in clinical cure of HIV-associated encephalitozoonosis in parallel with the cessation of spore excretion. In contrast, albendazole is not effective for the treatment of *Enterocytozoon bieneusi* infection and does not reduce the parasite load although previous observations had suggested that clinical improvement may occur in some patients. Oral purified fumagillin was recently used in a pilot study and subsequently in a small randomized trial to treat HIV-associated diarrhea due to *E. bieneusi.* Fumagillin appeared to eradicate the parasite transiently in many patients but serious adverse events and parasitic relapse were observed.[49,51] Recent experience with the antitumor necrosis factor-α agent thalidomide or potent antiretroviral treatment strategies in persons with HIV infection indicate that a modulation or improvement of the local or systemic immune function may lead to parasite clearance in this patient group.[44]

REFERENCES

1. Kosek M, Alcantara C, Lima AA, Guerrant RL. Cryptosporidiosis: an update. Lancet Infect Dis 2001;1:262–9.
2. Ortega YR, Sterling CR, Gilman RH, Cama VA, Diaz F. *Cyclospora* species – a new protozoan pathogen of humans. N Engl J Med 1993;328:1308–12.
3. Lindsay DS, Dubey JP, Blagburn BL. Biology of *Isospora* spp. from humans, nonhuman primates, and domestic animals. Clin Microbiol Rev 1997;10:19–34.
4. Morgan U, Weber R, Xiao L, *et al.* Molecular characterization of *Cryptosporidium* isolates obtained from human immunodeficiency virus-infected individuals living in Switzerland, Kenya, and the United States. J Clin Microbiol 2000;38:1180–3.
5. Weber R, Bryan RT, Schwartz DA, Owen RL. Human microsporidial infections. Clin Microbiol Rev 1994;7:426–61.
6. Hollister WS, Canning EU, Weidner E, Field AS, Kench J. Development and ultrastructure of *Trachipleistophora hominis* n.g., n.sp. after *in vitro* isolation from an AIDS patient and inoculation into athymic mice. Parasitology 1996;112:143–54.
7. Mathis A. Microsporidia: emerging advances in understanding the basic biology of these unique organisms. Int J Parasitol 2000;30(7):795–804.
8. Cali A, Takvorian PM, Lewin S, *et al. Brachiola vesicularum*, n. g., n. sp., a new microsporidium associated with AIDS and myositis. J Eukaryot Microbiol 1998;45:240–51.
9. Benoit Barbeau. Evaluating the risk of infection from the presence of *Giardia* and *Crytosporidium* in drinking water. Quant Microbiol 2000;2:37–54.
10. Thompson RCA, Chalmers RM. Cryptosporidium: from molecules to disease. Trends Parasitol 2002;18(3):98–100.
11. Weber R, Ledergerber B, Zbinden R, *et al.* Enteric infections and diarrhea in human immunodeficiency virus-infected persons: prospective community-based cohort study. Swiss HIV Cohort Study. Arch Intern Med 1999;159:1473–80.
12. MacKenzie WR, Hoxie NJ, Proctor ME, *et al.* A massive outbreak in Milwaukee of *Cryptosporidium* infection transmitted through the public water supply. N Engl J Med 1994;331:161–7.
13. Herwaldt BL. *Cyclospora cayetanensis*: a review, focusing on the outbreaks of cyclosporiasis in the 1990s. Clin Infect Dis 2000;31:1040–57.
14. Schwartz DA, Bryan RT, Hewan-Lowe KO, *et al.* Disseminated microsporidiosis (*Encephalitozoon hellem*) and acquired immunodeficiency syndrome. Autopsy evidence for respiratory acquisition. Arch Pathol Lab Med 1992;116:660–8.

15. Goodgame R, Stager C, Marcantel B, Alcocer E, Segura AM. Intensity of infection in AIDS-related intestinal microsporidiosis. J Infect Dis 1999;180:929–32.
16. Okhutsen PC, Chappell CL. Cryptosporidium virulence determinants – are we there yet? Int J Parasitol 2002;32(5):517–25.
17. Deplazes P, Mathis A, Baumgartner R, Tanner I, Weber R. Immunologic and molecular characterization of *Encephalitozoon*-like microsporidia isolated from humans and rabbits indicate that *Encephalitozoon cuniculi* is a zoonotic parasite. Clin Infect Dis 1996;22:557–9.
18. Drescher AC, Greene DM, Gadgil AJ. *Cryptosporidium* inactivation by low-pressure UV in a water disinfection device. J Environ Health 2001;64:31–5.
19. Weber R, Bryan RT, Bishop HS, *et al.* Threshold of detection of *Cryptosporidium* oocysts in human stool specimens: evidence for low sensitivity of current diagnostic methods. J Clin Microbiol 1991;29:1323–7.
20. Patel S, Pedraza-Diaz S, McLauchlin J. The identification of *Cryptosporidium* species and *Cryptosporidium parvum* directly from whole faeces by analysis of a multiplex PCR of the 18S rRNA gene and by PCR/RFLP of the *Cryptosporidium* outer wall protein (COWP) gene. Int J Parasitol 1999;29(8):1241–7.
21. Gobet P, Toze S. Sensitive genotyping of *Cryptosporidium parvum* by PCR-RFLP analysis of the 70-kilodalton heat shock protein (HSP70) gene. FEMS Microbiol Lett 2001;200(1):37–41.
22. Long EG, Ebrahimzadeh A, White EH, Swisher B, Callaway CS. Alga associated with diarrhea in patients with acquired immunodeficiency syndrome and in travelers. J Clin Microbiol 1990;28:1101–4.
23. Weber R, Schwartz DA, Deplazes P. Laboratory diagnosis of microsporidiosis. In: Wittner M, ed. The microsporidia and microsporidiosis. Washington: ASM Press; 1999:315–61.
24. Weber R, Bryan RT, Owen RL, *et al.* Improved light-microscopical detection of *Microsporidia* spores in stool and duodenal aspirates. N Engl J Med 1992;326:161–6.
25. Van Gool T, Snijders F, Reiss P, *et al.* Diagnosis of intestinal and disseminated microsporidial infections in patients with HIV by a new rapid fluorescence technique. J Clin Pathol 1993;46:694–9.
26. Enriquez FJ, Ditrich O, Palting JD, Smith K. Simple diagnosis of *Encephalitozoon* sp. microsporidial infections by using a panspecific antiexospore monoclonal antibody. J Clin Microbiol 1997;35:724–9.
27. Accoceberry I, Thellier M, Desportes-Livage I, *et al.* Production of monoclonal antibodies directed against the microsporidium *Enterocytozoon bieneusi.* J Clin Microbiol 1999;37:4107–12.
28. Da Silva AJ, Schwartz DA, Visvesvara GS, *et al.* Sensitive PCR diagnosis of infections by *Enterocytozoon bieneusi* (microsporidia) using primers based on the region coding for small-subunit rRNA. J Clin Microbiol 1996;34:986–7.
29. Weiss LM, Vossbrinck C. Molecular biology, molecular phylogeny, and molecular diagnostic approaches to the microsporidia. In Wittner M, ed. The microsporidia and microsporidiosis. Washington: ASM Press; 1999:129–71.
30. Checkley W, Epstein LD, Gilman RH, *et al.* Effects of *Cryptosporidium parvum* infection in Peruvian children: growth faltering and subsequent catch-up growth. Am J Epidemiol 1998;148:497–506.
31. Cali A, Kotler DP, Orenstein JM. *Septata intestinalis* N. G., N. Sp., an intestinal microsporidian associated with chronic diarrhea and dissemination in AIDS patients. J Eukaryot Microbiol 1993;40:101–12.
32. Yachnis AT, Berg J, Martinez-Salazar A, *et al.* Disseminated microsporidiosis especially infecting the brain, heart, and kidneys. Report of a newly recognized pansporoblastic species in two symptomatic AIDS patients. Am J Clin Pathol 1996;106:535–43.
33. Deplazes P, Mathis A, van Saanen M, *et al.* Dual microsporidial infection due to *Vittaforma corneae* and *Encephalitozoon hellem* in a patient with AIDS. Clin Infect Dis 1998;27:1521–4.
34. Didier ES, Didier PJ, Friedberg DN, *et al.* Isolation and characterization of a new human microsporidian, *Encephalitozoon hellem* (n. sp.), from three AIDS patients with keratoconjunctivitis. J Infect Dis 1991;163:617–21.
35. Schwartz DA, Visvesvara GS, Diesenhouse MC, *et al.* Pathologic features and immunofluorescent antibody demonstration of ocular microsporidiosis (*Encephalitozoon hellem*) in seven patients with acquired immunodeficiency syndrome. Am J Ophthalmol 1993;115:285–92.
36. Weber R, Deplazes P, Flepp M, *et al.* Cerebral microsporidiosis due to *Encephalitozoon cuniculi* in a patient with human immunodeficiency virus infection. N Engl J Med 1997;336:474–8.
37. Enriquez FJ, Taren D, Cruz-Lopez A, *et al.* Prevalence of intestinal encephalitozoonosis in Mexico. Clin Infect Dis 1998;26:1227–9.
38. Lores B, Lopez-Miragaya I, Arias C, *et al.* Intestinal microsporidiosis due to *Enterocytozoon bieneusi* in elderly human immunodeficiency virus-negative patients from Vigo, Spain. Clin Infect Dis 2002;34:918–21.
39. White AC Jr, Chappell CL, Hayat CS, *et al.* Paromomycin for cryptosporidiosis in AIDS: a prospective, double-blind trial. J Infect Dis 1994;170:419–24.
40. Hewitt RG, Yiannoutsos CT, Higgs ES, *et al.* Paromomycin: no more effective than placebo for treatment of cryptosporidiosis in patients with advanced human immunodeficiency virus infection. AIDS Clinical Trial Group. Clin Infect Dis 2000;31:1084–92.
41. Rossignol JF, Hidalgo H, Feregrino M, *et al.* A double-'blind' placebo-controlled study of nitazoxanide in the treatment of cryptosporidial diarrhoea in AIDS patients in Mexico. Trans R Soc Trop Med Hyg 1998;92:663–6.
42. Rossignol JF, Ayoub A, Ayers MS. Treatment of diarrhea caused by *Cryptosporidium parvum*: a prospective randomized, double-blind, placebo-controlled study of nitazoxanide. J Infect Dis 2001;184:103–6.
43. Giacometti A, Cirioni O, Barchiesi F, Ancarani F, Scalise G. Activity of nitazoxanide alone and in combination with azithromycin and rifabutin against *Cryptosporidium parvum* in cell culture. J Antimicrob Chemother 2000;45:453–6.
44. Carr A, Marriott D, Field A, Vasak E, Cooper DA. Treatment of HIV-1-associated microsporidiosis and cryptosporidiosis with combination antiretroviral therapy. Lancet 1998;351:256–61.
45. Hoge CW, Shlim DR, Ghimire M, *et al.* Placebo-controlled trial of co-trimoxazole for *Cyclospora* infections among travellers and foreign residents in Nepal. Lancet 1995;345:691–3.
46. Pape JW, Verdier RI, Johnson WD Jr. Treatment and prophylaxis of *Isospora belli* infection in patients with the acquired immunodeficiency syndrome. N Engl J Med 1989;320:1044–7.
47. Didier ES. Effects of albendazole, fumagillin, and TNP-470 on microsporidial replication *in vitro.* Antimicrob Agents Chemother 1997;41:1541–6.
48. Bigliardi E, Bernuzzi AM, Corona S, *et al. In vitro* efficacy of nikkomycin Z against the human isolate of the microsporidian species *Encephalitozoon hellem.* Antimicrob Agents Chemother 2000;44:3012–6.
49. Molina JM, Tourneur M, Sarfati C *et al.* Fumagillin treatment of intestinal microsporidosis. N Engl J Med 2002;346:1963–9.
50. Molina JM, Chastang C, Goguel J, *et al.* Albendazole for treatment and prophylaxis of microsporidiosis due to *Encephalitozoon intestinalis* in patients with AIDS: a randomized double- blind controlled trial. J Infect Dis 1998;177:1373–7.
51. Molina JM, Goguel J, Sarfati C, *et al.* Trial of oral fumagillin for the treatment of intestinal microsporidiosis in patients with HIV infection. ANRS 054 Study Group. Agence Nationale de Recherche sur le SIDA. AIDS 2000;14:1341–8.

chapter

244 Protozoa: Free-living Amebae

Govinda S Visvesvara & Augusto Julio Martinez

NATURE

The concept that small free-living amebae, particularly *Acanthamoeba* spp. have the potential to cause disease in humans was developed by CG Culbertson of the Indiana University School of Medicine and the Eli Lilly Laboratories in 1958. The basis of this observation was a chance discovery of an ameba growing in a batch of monkey kidney cell cultures that were to be used for growing polio virus for the development of polio vaccine. This ameba, described as *Acanthamoeba* sp. (Lilly A-1), was found to produce, on intracerebral, intraspinal and intranasal inoculations, meningoencephalitis in cortisone-treated monkeys and mice.[1–3] This isolate is now called *Acanthamoeba culbertsoni.*

The first case of amebic meningoencephalitis in humans, attributed initially to *Acanthamoeba* although later the causative organism was identified as a species of *Naegleria*, was described in Australia in 1962. It is now known that besides *Acanthamoeba* spp., two other free-living amebae, *Naegleria fowleri* and *Balamuthia mandrillaris*, also cause central nervous system (CNS) disease in humans and other animals.[1–4] Recently, however, *Sappinia diploidea*, a saprophytic ameba that has been previously isolated from the fecal specimens of lizards, elks and bisons, was identified in a brain biopsy specimen of a previously healthy 38-year-old man who developed visual disturbances, headache and a seizure.[5] This suggests that there are cases of human infections caused by free-living amebae other than *Acanthamoeba*, *Balamuthia* and *Naegleria* spp. that may have been either misdiagnosed or unrecognized.

Taxonomy

The free-living amebae are classified under the subphylum Sarcodina and superclass Rhizopodea.[2] The sarcodinian rhizopods are a heterogeneous group of amebae that include the free-living *Acanthamoeba, Naegleria, Balamuthia, Hartmannella* and *Vahlkampfia* spp. and others such as the parasitic amebae (e.g. *Entamoeba histolytica*) that move by producing cytoplasmic bulges, the lobopodia, from the surface of the body. In contrast to *E. histolytica*, which is a mitochondria-lacking ameba that causes gastrointestinal disease, *Naegleria, Acanthamoeba* and *Balamuthia* are mitochondria-bearing amebae that cause diseases of the CNS of humans and animals, which almost always lead to death. The term amphizoic amebae indicates the ability of these amebae to exist as free-living in nature and as parasites within host tissue; this differentiates them from the truly parasitic *E. histolytica*.[6]

Although several species of *Naegleria* have been described, so far only one species, *N. fowleri* (*Naegleria aerobia* and *Naegleria invadens* are non-valid synonyms), is known to infect the human CNS. Several of the more than 20 species of *Acanthamoeba* that have been described so far cause not only a chronic granulomatous CNS disease in humans and other animals, but also infect the cornea (*Acanthamoeba* keratitis), the skin, the nasal sinuses and pulmonary tissues. The disease caused by *Acanthamoeba* spp. has been described as granulomatous amebic encephalitis (GAE). *Balamuthia mandrillaris*, the only known species of *Balamuthia*, causes GAE and skin infections in humans and other animals.[1–4,7]

Naegleria fowleri

Naegleria fowleri is also described as an ameboflagellate because it has a transient flagellate stage in its life cycle in addition to a feeding and dividing form, the trophozoite, and a resistant cyst stage (Fig. 244.1). The trophozoite, measuring 10–25μm, normally feeds on bacteria and multiplies by binary fission. However, it is able to differentiate into a pear-shaped biflagellate stage in response to sudden changes in the ionic concentration of its environment. When the conditions become unfavorable the trophozoite differentiates into a resistant cyst stage. The trophozoite is usually uninucleate; the nucleus is spherical and contains a large, centrally placed, dense nucleolus. Additionally, numerous dumbbell-shaped mitochondria, vacuoles, lysosomes and ribosomes are present within the cytoplasm. Cysts are round and contain a single nucleus with a central dense nucleolus; the dense cyst walls are plugged with one or more flat pores. The cysts are 7–14μm in diameter, with a mean of 10μm.[2,6]

Acanthamoeba spp.

In 1930 Aldo Castellani isolated an ameba from a yeast culture; it was later named as *Acanthamoeba castellanii*.[1] Currently more than 20 species of *Acanthamoeba* have been described.[8] The acanthamebae are also called opportunistic amebae because they produce disease principally in immunodeficient individuals.

The life cycle of *Acanthamoeba* spp. consists of two stages: a feeding and reproducing trophozoite stage and a resistant cyst stage (Fig. 244.2). The trophozoites feed on bacteria and detritus present in the milieu and multiply by binary fission. They are uninucleate and are 15–45μm in size. The nucleus has a centrally placed, large, densely staining nucleolus. The cytoplasm is finely granular and contains numerous mitochondria, ribosomes and lysosomes. Cysts are 10–25μm in size and are double walled. The outer wall or the ectocyst is wrinkled and contains protein and the inner wall, the endocyst, is usually stellate, polygonal, oval or spherical and contains cellulose. Pores covered by opercula are present at the point of contact between the ectocyst and the endocyst. Cysts are uninucleate and possess a centrally placed dense nucleolus.[6,8]

Balamuthia mandrillaris

Balamuthia mandrillaris, previously called leptomyxid ameba, has two stages in its life cycle (Fig. 244.3). The trophozoite is irregular in shape and measures from 12 to 60μm with a mean size of about 30μm. It is usually uninucleate, but binucleate forms are occasionally seen. The nucleus contains a large centrally placed nucleolus. Occasionally, in infected human tissues, trophic stages containing a large nucleus with two or three nucleolar bodies have been observed. Cysts are also uninucleate, more or less spherical, and range in size from 12 to 30μm with a mean of 15μm. Cysts appear to be double walled with a wavy ectocyst and a spherical endocyst when viewed under the light microscope. However, ultrastructurally

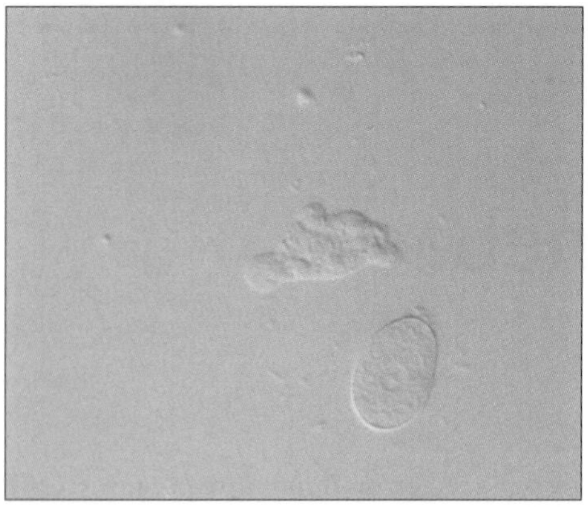

Fig. 244.1 ***Naegleria fowleri.*** The trophozoite can be differentiated from the cyst by its characteristic lobopodial locomotion; both are taken from culture. Differential interference contrast.

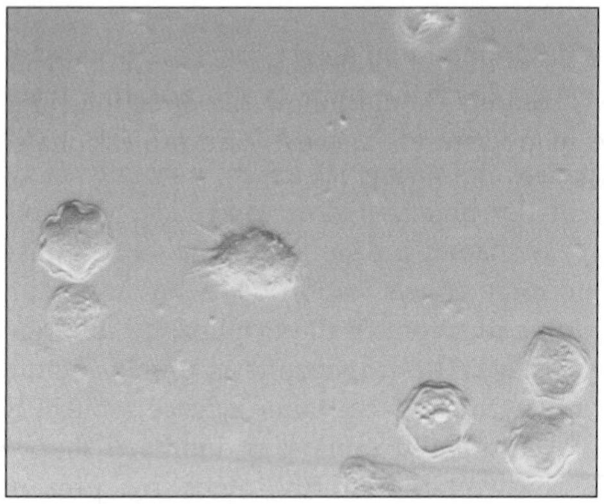

Fig. 244.2 ***Acanthamoeba castellanii.*** The trophozoite has spiny acanthopodia whereas the cyst has an outer wrinkled ectocyst and a stellate endocyst; both are taken from culture. Differential interference contrast.

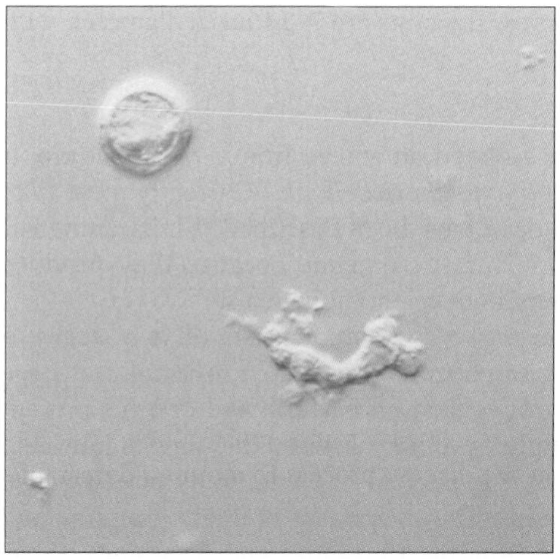

Fig. 244.3 ***Balamuthia mandrillaris.*** The trophozoite is irregularly shaped whereas the cyst is spherical; both are taken from culture. Differential interference contrast.

the cysts are tripartite with an outer thin and irregular ectocyst, an inner thick endocyst and a middle amorphous fibrillar mesocyst.[4,7]

Cultivation

Acanthamoeba spp. and *N. fowleri*, but not *B. mandrillaris*, can be cultivated on non-nutrient agar plates coated with a suitable Gram-negative bacteria such as *Escherichia coli* or *Enterobacter aerogenes*. The amebae will feed on the bacteria, multiply and differentiate into cysts within a few days. They can be easily subcultured by transplanting a small piece of agar containing trophozoites and/or cysts onto a fresh agar plate coated with bacteria as before. *Naegleria fowleri* and *Acanthamoeba* spp. can also be grown successfully on mammalian cell cultures. *Balamuthia mandrillaris* will not grow on bacteria-coated agar plates. However, it can be isolated from infected human or animal tissue by inoculating monkey kidney or human lung fibroblasts with the triturated tissue and from which a continuous culture can be established by periodic transfers.

Naegleria fowleri and *Acanthamoeba* spp. can be grown axenically (bacteria free) in a complex chemical medium. Although several different formulations are available, in our laboratory we use a modified version of Nelson's medium that contains a 0.5% solution of liver digest, 0.5% glucose and a low osmolarity buffered salt solution supplemented with 3–5% fetal bovine serum. *Acanthamoeba* spp. can also be easily grown in a medium composed of 2% proteose peptone, 0.5% yeast extract and 0.1% glucose made up in a low osmotic buffered salt solution with or without serum. Additionally, *N. fowleri* and several species of *Acanthamoeba* have also been grown in a chemically defined medium consisting of several different amino acids, vitamins, hemin and salts.[1,2] *Balamuthia mandrillaris* has also been grown in an axenic medium, and this has facilitated the screening of various pharmaceutical agents.[9]

EPIDEMIOLOGY

Naegleria fowleri is widely distributed throughout the world and has been isolated from fresh water, thermal discharges of power plants, heated swimming pools, hot springs, aquariums, soil, dust in air, sewage and even from nasal passages of children. *Naegleria fowleri* is thermophilic and grows well, even at temperatures of up to 113°F (45°C). It is therefore not surprising that primary amebic meningoencephalitis (PAM) cases have occurred in the hot summer months when many people engage in aquatic activities in lakes, ponds and swimming pools that may harbor these amebae in large numbers. In colder climates these amebae will probably encyst and remain dormant in the sediments of fresh water lakes, ponds, rivers and swimming pools.[1–3,10]

Acanthamoeba spp. have been isolated from soil, sewage, fresh, brackish and sea water, bottled mineral water, cooling towers of electric and nuclear power plants, physiotherapy pools, jacuzzis, heating and ventilating and air conditioning units, eye wash stations, dialysis machines, dust in the air, bacterial, fungal and mammalian cell cultures, contact lens paraphernalia, the nose and throat of patients who have respiratory complaints and healthy individuals, and biopsy or autopsy specimens of cornea, lungs, nasal sinus, skin and CNS tissue of humans and animals. *Acanthamoeba* spp. have been known to be hosts for *Legionella* spp., *Mycobacteria* spp. and echoviruses, which signifies the importance of these amebae to public health.[1–3]

Cases of GAE may occur at any time of the year and therefore transmission has no relation to climatologic changes.

Balamuthia mandrillaris has not as yet been isolated from the environment; it is, however, believed to have the same habitat as *Acanthamoeba* spp. and *N. fowleri*. *Balamuthia mandrillaris* has been isolated from biopsy and autopsy specimens of humans and other animals.[4,7]

PATHOGENICITY

Naegleria fowleri

Primary amebic meningoencephalitis occurs in active healthy children and young adults with no known history of immune disorder. Most patients who have PAM have a history of swimming, diving or playing under water; the ameba enters through the nasal passages and the nasal mucosa is the initial site of the primary lesions. The route of invasion into the brain is through the fila olfactoria of the olfactory nerves. The trophozoites cross the cribriform plate and reach the subarachnoid space, which is richly vascularized and bathed in the cerebrospinal fluid (CSF), thus constituting an ideal medium for their proliferation and subsequent dissemination into the brain parenchyma and other areas of the brain.[1–3,11]

Naegleria fowleri is a highly pathogenic and virulent ameba. However, the minimum number of amebae required to cause infection and death in humans is not known. Experiments with infection have shown that mice, when just a few amebae are instilled intranasally, die of PAM in a similar fashion to humans. However, different isolates of *N. fowleri* vary in their degree of virulence: some are highly virulent whereas other isolates are only moderately virulent. Furthermore, any isolate can become avirulent on prolonged cultivation in an axenic medium. It is believed that the probability of infection in nature may depend upon the number and virulence of the amebae, the temperature and the type and source of the nutrient available to the amebae in the environment.[2]

The trophozoite of *N. fowleri* is highly phagocytic and induces necrosis of the CNS tissue. It is believed to ingest human tissue directly by producing a food cup or amebostome and by producing lysosomal hydrolases and phospholipases that degrade myelin. It has also been shown experimentally that the amebae exert a contact-dependent cytolysis mediated possibly by a multicomponent system that consists of a heat-stable hemolytic protein, heat-labile cytolysin and/or phospholipase A enzyme.[1,2,12]

The incubation period of PAM varies from 2 to 15 days depending on the size of the inoculum and the virulence of the amebae. In experimental infections with a mildly virulent *N. fowleri*, the incubation period has been as long as 3–4 weeks.[2]

Acanthamoeba spp.

Granulomatous amebic encephalitis, whether caused by *Acanthamoeba* spp. or *B. mandrillaris*, usually occurs in chronically ill, debilitated individuals, in immunosuppressed patients, those who have received broad-spectrum antibiotics or chemotherapeutic medications and those who have AIDS.[1,11,13] The pathogenesis of GAE is complex and poorly understood. It is believed that the immunity is predominantly T-cell mediated and therefore depletion of $CD4^+$ and T-helper lymphocytes permits the growth and development of the amebae. The incubation period is unknown and several weeks or months may elapse before the disease becomes apparent. The respiratory tract or the skin may act as the portal of entry. One hypothesis is that ulceration of the skin may enable the amebae to enter.[1] The route of invasion to the brain must be via the bloodstream because there are no lymphatic channels within the brain.[1,13] Furthermore, trophozoites and cysts are often seen around blood vessels and within necrotic CNS tissue. The acanthamoebae are known to secrete enzymes such as lysosomal hydrolases, aminopeptidases and phospholipases, which may contribute to CNS damage.[1,2]

Acanthamoeba *keratitis*

Acanthamoeba keratitis (AK) is the inflammation of the cornea caused by ocular trauma or by contact lens wear and the use of non-sterile homemade saline solution that has been contaminated with bacteria and fungi, which support the growth and multiplication of *Acanthamoeba* spp. The latter may secrete proteolytic and collagenolytic enzymes that may damage the corneal epithelium and thus contribute to the pathogenesis of AK. If proper treatment is not provided, AK may lead to a vascularized scar within a thin cornea, causing impaired vision or perforation of the cornea and loss of the eye.[14,15]

PREVENTION

Primary amebic meningoencephalitis

The trophic and the cyst forms of *N. fowleri* are susceptible to chlorine and are killed at 1mg/l, provided the water temperature is 78.8°F (26°C) or below. If, however, the water temperature is above 78.8°F the chlorine concentration may need to be increased to 2mg/l. It is therefore important for swimming pools to be maintained properly with adequate chlorination at all times. As it is not possible to disinfect natural bodies of waters such as lakes and ponds in which *N. fowleri* may be found, appropriate warnings should be posted, particularly during the hot summer months.[1,2]

Granulomatous amebic encephalitis

New and creative preventive measures need to be formulated because GAE produced by *Acanthamoeba* spp. and *B. mandrillaris* occurs principally in immunocompromised individuals. As *Acanthamoeba* spp. can grow and colonize hot water tanks, jacuzzis, filters used in heating, ventilating and air conditioning units, and in-line filters used for purifying portable water supplies and eye wash stations, periodic inspection of these systems is recommended.[1–3]

Acanthamoeba keratitis

It is recommended that eye care professionals educate patients about the proper care and use of contact lenses. Contact lenses and contact lens paraphernalia, particularly the solutions, should be kept meticulously clean. Contact lens wearers should follow the directions and recommendations of the manufacturers and eye care professionals. Additionally, contact lenses should not be used during swimming or other water sports.[14]

DIAGNOSTIC MICROBIOLOGY

Primary amebic meningoencephalitis

In individuals who have PAM, the CSF is characterized by pleocytosis, with a predominance of polymorphonuclear leukocytes but without bacteria. The CSF pressure is elevated (100–600mmHg). Glucose concentration may be slightly reduced or normal, but the protein content is elevated, ranging from 100mg/100ml to 1000mg/100ml. Computed tomography scans show obliteration of the cisterns around the midbrain and the subarachnoid space over the cerebral hemispheres. Differential diagnosis of PAM from acute pyogenic or bacterial meningoencephalitis is dependent upon the detection of the ameba in the CSF *in situ* under a microscope. Smears of CSF should also be stained with Giemsa or trichrome stains for the delineation of the characteristic nuclear morphology. Gram stain is not useful. Care must be taken to differentiate amebic trophozoites from macrophages. Many cases have been diagnosed retrospectively based on examination of hematoxylin and eosin-stained sections or immunofluorescent tests.[1–3,11] Serologic tests are of no value in the diagnosis of PAM because most patients die too early (within 5–7 days) in the disease process to mount a detectable immune response.

Granulomatous amebic encephalitis

Examination of the CSF in patients who have GAE reveals lymphocytic pleocytosis with mild elevation of proteins and normal levels of glucose. Visual detection of *Acanthamoeba* spp. trophozoites in the CSF has rarely been reported. However, *Acanthamoeba* spp. have been identified in brain biopsies from several patients. Computed tomography scans and magnetic resonance imaging are nonspecific and of limited value in the diagnosis. Single or multiple heterogeneous, hypodense, non-enhancing, space-occupying lesions that involve the basal ganglia, cerebral cortex, subcortical white matter, cerebellum and pons may be encountered, suggesting a brain abscess, brain tumor or intracerebral hematoma. Brain and skin biopsies are important diagnostic procedures. *Acanthamoeba* spp. can be easily cultured from the brain, skin, lung and corneal tissue by placing a portion of the tissue that has been minced on non-nutrient agar plates coated with a layer of Gram-negative bacteria. Specimens for culture should be processed as quickly as possible. The incubation temperature depends upon the source of the samples. The agar plate should be incubated at 86°F (30°C), if the specimens originate from cornea or skin, but at 98.6°F (37°C) if the specimens are from the brain, the lung or any other internal organ. Amebae, if present in the samples, will feed on bacteria and multiply by binary fission. If the plates are examined under the light microscope, distinctive track marks with an ameba at the end of each track may be seen. The amebae will differentiate into cysts after a few days of incubation. Amebae can be identified to the level of genus on the basis of the characteristic morphology of trophozoites and cysts. Additionally, *Naegleria* spp. can be identified if flagellates appear within 2–4 hours of a loopful of amebae from the agar plate being suspended in distilled water. Identification to the species level, however, is difficult on the basis of morphology alone; non-morphologic methods such as serology, isoenzyme analysis or DNA profiles therefore need to be used.[2,6,16,17,18]

Balamuthia mandrillaris will not grow on bacterized agar plates. However, *B. mandrillaris* can be isolated from the CNS by inoculating monkey kidney cell culture with brain extract[4,7] and subsequently growing the amebae in an axenic medium.[9]

Acanthamoeba keratitis

For the diagnosis of AK, deep corneal scraping and biopsy is recommended. Unfixed specimens should be processed for culture. Smears should also be prepared and fixed with methanol, Schaudinn's fixative or a spray-on fixative, and stained with Giemsa–Wright or Hemacolor, or with Wheatly's or Masson's trichrome stain. Hemacolor staining is quick and stains the distinctive cyst wall pinkish-red. The trichrome stains the nucleolus of the trophozoite reddish-pink and the cytoplasm greenish-purple and is therefore useful in differentiating trophozoites of *Acanthamoeba* spp. from the host cells.[11] Confocal microscopy has also been used recently to diagnose AK.[19]

CLINICAL MANIFESTATIONS

Primary amebic meningoencephalitis

The first case of PAM was reported in 1965.[1–3] Although at that time the case was thought to be caused by *Acanthamoeba* sp., it is now considered to be caused by *N. fowleri*. It is believed that more than 200 cases of PAM have occurred worldwide as of March 2002. Further, as many as 100 cases have been reported in the USA alone. Primary amebic meningoencephalitis has also been described in a South American tapir and cattle.[1]

Primary amebic meningoencephalitis is an acute, fulminating and usually fatal CNS disease that occurs mainly in healthy young adults and children with a recent history of watersport activities. Primary amebic meningoencephalitis has a rapid onset and a short incubation period that lasts from 3 to 7 days. It is characterized by the sudden onset of bifrontal or bitemporal headaches, fever, nausea, vomiting and stiff neck. Nuchal rigidity usually occurs with positive Kernig's and Brudzinski's signs. Abnormalities in taste or smell and cerebellar ataxia may be seen early but photophobia occurs late in the clinical course. An increase in intracranial pressure has been reported in most patients. Generalized seizures leading to lethargy, confusion, coma and death within 48–72 hours have been reported in a number of patients.[1,11] Focal myocardial necrosis has also been reported.

Pathologic features

At autopsy the cerebral hemispheres are swollen and edematous. The olfactory bulbs and the orbitofrontal cortices are necrotic and hemorrhagic. Because of increased intracranial pressure, uncal and cerebellar tonsillar herniations are usually seen. The arachnoid membrane is severely congested with scant purulent exudate. Amebic trophozoites are usually seen within the Virchow–Robin spaces with minimal or no inflammatory reaction (Fig. 244.4). Cysts are not seen within the CNS lesions. Necrotizing angiitis may occasionally be seen.[1,2,11]

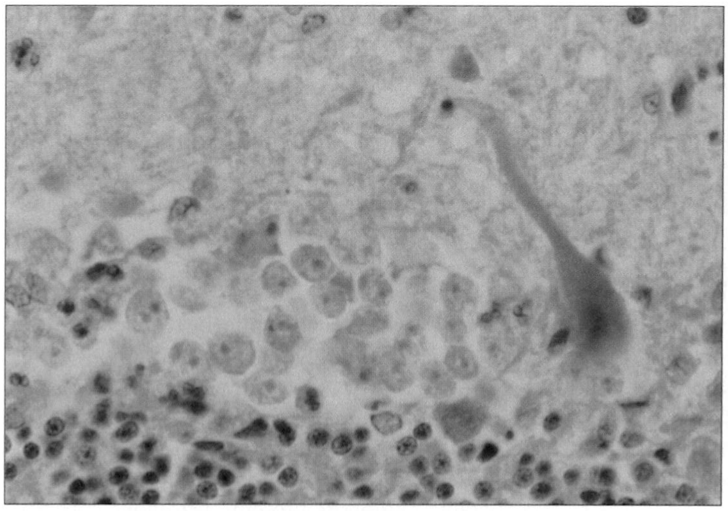

Fig. 244.4 CNS section demonstrating numerous trophozoites of *Naegleria fowleri*. Note the absence of cysts. (H & E.)

Granulomatous amebic encephalitis produced by *Acanthamoeba* spp. and *Balamuthia mandrillaris*

Granulomatous amebic encephalitis caused by *Acanthamoeba* spp. occurs principally in individuals who are immunosuppressed (either iatrogenically or because of AIDS) and GAE caused by *B. mandrillaris* occurs in either the very young or very old and in individuals who have AIDS. As of 1 April 2002, more than 200 cases (114 caused by *Acanthamoeba* spp. and 93 caused by *B. mandrillaris*) of GAE had occurred worldwide. In the USA as many as 82 cases attributable to *Acanthamoeba* spp. (60 in people with AIDS) and 44 attributable to *B. mandrillaris* had occurred. Additionally, several cases of GAE caused by *Acanthamoeba* spp. and *B. mandrillaris* have been described in gorillas, a baboon, monkeys, dogs, sheep and cows.[1,3,20]

The clinical manifestations and pathologic features of GAE are similar regardless of which of these two organisms is the cause. It is an insidious disease and has a long and protracted clinical course. Clinical signs include personality changes, headache, low-grade fever, nausea, vomiting, lethargy, hemiparesis, seizures, depressed levels of consciousness and coma. Third and sixth cranial nerve palsies may be seen in some patients. Clinically, GAE may mimic bacterial leptomeningitis, tuberculous or viral meningitis, or single or multiple space-occupying lesions. Cerebellar ataxia and diplopia have been described in some patients. Pneumonitis with the presence of trophozoites and cysts within pulmonary alveoli has also been described.[1,11] In most cases of GAE, however, final diagnosis is made at autopsy.

Pathologic features

The cerebral hemispheres are edematous. Encephalomalacia with multifocal areas of cortical softening and hemorrhagic necrosis may be seen. Multifocal necrotic lesions may also be seen in the posterior fossa structures, midbrain, thalamus, brainstem and cerebellum. Trophozoites and cysts of the infecting organisms are seen, most often in the necrotic lesions in basal ganglia, midbrain, brainstem and cerebral hemispheres (Fig. 244.5). Microglial nodules may be seen within the necrotic tissues. Occasionally, angiitis may be seen with perivascular cuffing by inflammatory cells, chiefly lymphocytes, a few plasma cells and macrophages. In patients who have advanced AIDS there is very little inflammation. Trophozoites and cysts can easily be identified by light microscopic examination of the tissue

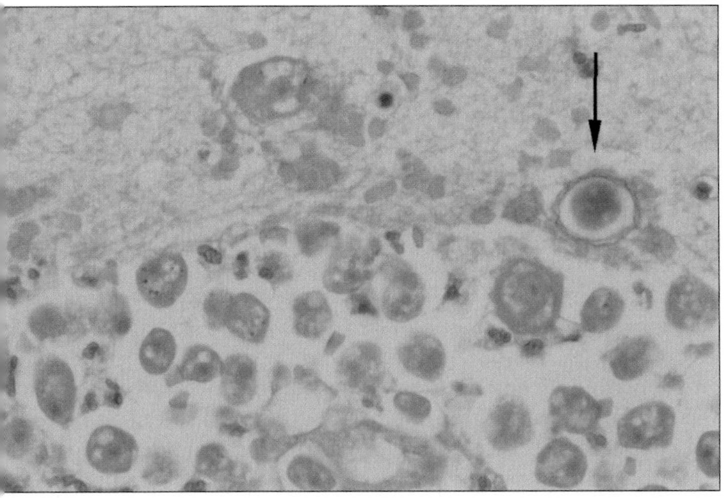

Fig. 244.5 Brain section showing numerous trophozoites and a cyst (arrow) with typical features of *Acanthamoeba culbertsoni.* (Masson's trichrome.)

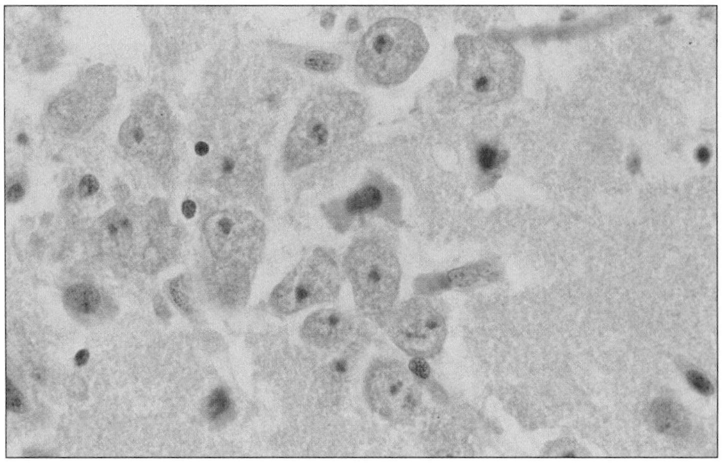

Fig. 244.7 CNS section showing many trophozoites of *Balamuthia mandrillaris.* More than one nucleoli can be seen within the nuclei of the trophozoite.

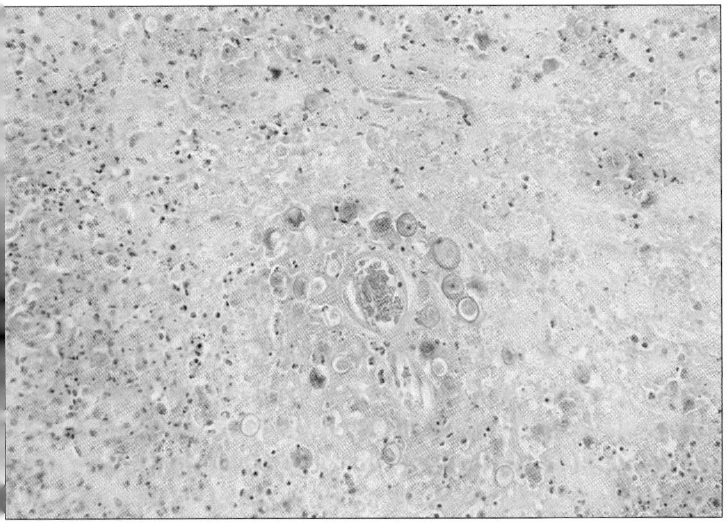

Fig. 244.6 Trophozoites and cysts of *Acanthamoeba* sp. surrounding a blood vessel in a skin biopsy of a patient who has AIDS. A diffuse but modest inflammatory reaction is seen.

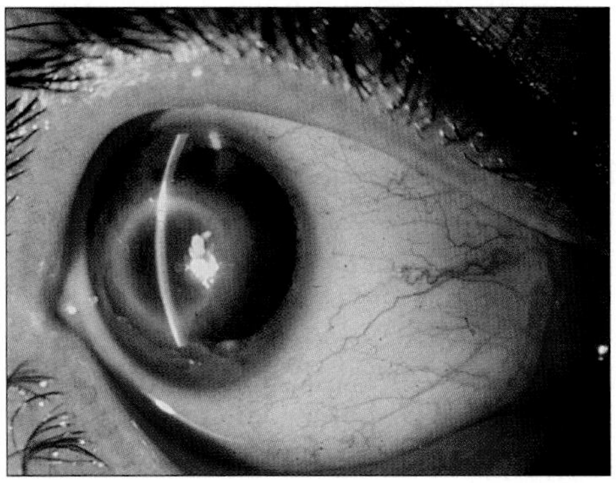

Fig. 244.8 *Acanthamoeba* keratitis. Note the typical central or paracentral ring infiltrate. Courtesy of Dr Theodore.

sections. Also in patients who have AIDS, multiple ulcerations of the skin with acute and chronic inflammation may be seen and the ulcers may contain trophozoites and cysts of the infecting ameba (Fig. 244.6). The kidneys, prostate gland, adrenal glands, lungs and liver may also be involved, suggesting hematogenous dissemination. The ulcerated skin may serve as a portal of entry for the amebae in some patients. Several cases of skin infection without dissemination into the CNS have also been reported.[1,21,22]

In general, the trophic and cyst stages of *Acanthamoeba* spp. and *B. mandrillaris* look similar in formalin-fixed and hematoxylin and eosin stained sections under the light microscope. In some patients, however, differential identification of *B. mandrillaris* can be made if the nuclei of the amebae in the sections possess two or three nucleolar elements because these are not seen in *Acanthamoeba* spp. (Fig. 244.7). A definitive identification may be arrived at by carrying out immunofluorescence analysis of the tissue sections using rabbit anti-*Acanthamoeba* spp. or anti-*B. mandrillaris* sera. The cyst wall of *B. mandrillaris* is characteristically tripartite and hence can be identified definitively by electron microscopy analysis of brain sections.[1,4,7]

Acanthamoeba keratitis

Acanthamoeba keratitis is a sight-threatening chronic inflammation of the cornea. It is associated with contact lens wear and the use of homemade nonsterile saline solution, corneal abrasion or trauma. Although the first case of AK in the USA was reported in a farmer from south Texas with ocular trauma of the right eye,[3,14] wearing contact lenses and using nonsterile homemade saline was found to be a risk factor for AK in 1985 because most of the 24 patients reported in the previous 2 years were contact lens wearers.[3,14] By December 1996, more than 700 cases of AK were estimated to have occurred worldwide.

The hallmark of AK is severe ocular pain, photophobia, a central or paracentral 360° stromal ring infiltrate (Fig. 244.8), recurrent breakdown of corneal epithelium with a waxing and waning clinical course and a corneal lesion refractory to the usual antibacterial, antiviral and antimycotic medications.[14,15]

When examined under the light microscope, corneal scrapings and/or sections of biopsied corneal tissue reveal trophozoites and cysts of *Acanthamoeba* spp. infiltrated between the lamellae of the cornea (Fig. 244.9). Polymorphonuclear leukocytes, eosinophils, lymphocytes, macrophages and plasma cells, have also been seen occasionally. Ulceration, descemetocele formation and perforation are often seen in the later stages of AK.[11,14,15]

MANAGEMENT

Primary amebic meningoencephalitis

Primary amebic meningoencephalitis has almost always resulted in death. A few patients, however, have survived, probably because of

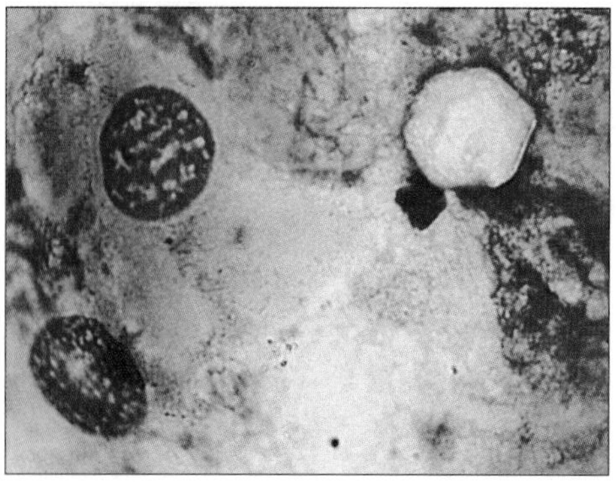

Fig. 244.9 Characteristic star-shaped morphology of the cyst of *Acanthamoeba* sp. demonstrated by a corneal scraping stained with Hemacolor. Courtesy of Dr Theodore.

early diagnosis and aggressive treatment with amphotericin B, miconazole and rifampin (rifampicin).[23] Amphotericin B and miconazole can be administered intrathecally or intravenously, alone or in combination, and rifampin can be given orally. A 9-year-old girl from California, one of the patients who survived this disease in the USA, was treated as follows: intravenous amphotericin B 1.5mg/kg body weight per day in two divided doses for 3 days and then 1mg/kg for 3 days; intrathecal amphotericin B 1.5mg/day for 2 days followed by 1mg/day for 8 days; intravenous miconazole 350mg/m^2 body surface area per day in three divided doses for 9 days; intrathecal miconazole 10mg/day for 1 day followed by 10mg every other day for 8 days; and oral rifampin 10mg/kg per day in three divided doses for 9 days. The patient was also given sulfisoxazole (sulphafurazole) q6h for 3 days, but this was discontinued once *N. fowleri* was identified as the cause of the disease. Dexamethasone and phenytoin were given to lower the intracranial pressure and seizure activity, respectively. Amebae disappeared from the CSF after 3 days of treatment. Although cell counts and biochemistry of the CSF were abnormal for several months afterwards, the patient recovered completely without any neurologic sequelae.[23] It has also been reported that a boy from Texas, USA, recovered from PAM after intravenous amphotericin B and treatment in a hyperbaric chamber.[24]

Granulomatous amebic encephalitis

There is as yet no effective treatment for GAE and therefore the prognosis is poor.[1,3,25–27] The disease has been identified in only a very few patients before death. Three such patients who were diagnosed, however, have reportedly recovered from this disease. *Acanthamoeba rhysodes* was isolated from the CSF of a Nigerian patient with neurologic disease who showed clinical improvement after treatment with sulfamethazine. He was discharged from the hospital but was lost to follow-up.[2,3]

Acanthamoeba culbertsoni was isolated from the CSF of an Indian patient with CNS impairment who recovered after treatment with chloramphenicol.[2,3]

A 7-year-old girl from Barbados with a 'brain tumor' recovered without any neurologic sequelae after surgical excision. *Acanthamoeba healyi* was isolated from the 'tumor' and also demonstrated in the hematoxylin and eosin-stained, formalin-fixed sections. The patient also received oral ketoconazole treatment for 8 months postoperatively.[28,29] It is known from *in-vitro* experiments that several drugs, including pentamidine, propamidine, dibromopropamidine, miconazole, paromomycin, neomycin, ketoconazole and 5-fluorocytosine, have inhibitory effects on several isolates of *Acanthamoeba*.[3,30] According to one study a combination of pentamidine and azithromycin may be effective in treating GAE.[9] Prognosis of patients who have disseminated skin infections without CNS involvement is, however, good. In an immunocompromised (without HIV/AIDS) patient with *A. rhysodes* skin infection, skin ulcers healed after the following treatment regimen: cleansing of skin ulcers twice daily with chlorhexidine gluconate solution followed by the application of 2% ketoconazole cream. The patient was also given 4mg/kg intravenous pentamidine isethionate for 1 day. Because of pentamidine toxicity the dosage was cut to 2700mg and given over a 4-week period. Thereafter, he was given itraconazole orally at a dose of 200mg daily for 8 months, resulting in the total healing of the skin lesions.[21]

Acanthamoeba keratitis

Treatment of AK with topical application of polyhexamethylene biguanide or chlorhexidine gluconate in combination with propamidine isethionate appears to be the treatment of choice, as several patients have been treated successfully in this way.[31,32] Many patients have also been treated with topical application of propamidine isethionate 0.1% and dibromopropamidine, in conjunction with neosporin. Ketoconazole and clotrimazole appears to be effective *in vitro* and *in vivo*. Other reports of successful treatment with 0.1% hexamidine di-isethionate eye drops have been reported. Some patients have also been treated successfully with combinations of topical propamidine and miconazole and systemic ketoconazole, or topical clotrimazole or oral itraconazole with topical miconazole.[33,34] Debridement of the cornea, penetrating keratoplasty and corneal grafting have also been performed with good results in some patients. Recurrence of AK has been reported after corneal transplantation, probably caused by cysts of *Acanthamoeba* spp. still present in the corneal stroma.

REFERENCES

1. Martinez AJ, Visvesvara GS. Free-living, amphizoic and opportunistic amebas. Brain Pathol 1997;7:583–98.
2. John DT. Opportunistically pathogenic free-living amebae. In: Kreier JP, Baker JR, eds. Parasitic protozoa. vol III, 2nd ed. San Diego: Academic Press;1993:143–246.
3. Visvesvara GS, Stehr-Green JK. Epidemiology of free-living ameba infections. J Protozool 1990;37:25S–33S.
4. Visvesvara GS, Schuster FL, Martinez AJ. *Balamuthia mandrillaris*, N.G., N. Sp., agent of amebic meningo-encephalitis in humans and other animals. J Eukaryotic Microbiol 1993;40:504–14.
5. Gelman BB, Rauf SJ, Nader R, *et al.* Amoebic encephalitis due to *Sappinia diploidea*. JAMA 285:2450–1.
6. Page FC. A new key to fresh water and soil gymnamoebae with instructions for culture. Ambleside, UK: Fresh Water Biological Association; 1988.
7. Visvesvara GS, Martinez AJ, Schuster FL, *et al.* Leptomyxid ameba, new agent of amebic meningoencephalitis in human and animals. J Clin Microbiol 1990;28:2750–6.
8. Visvesvara GS. Classification of *Acanthamoeba*. Rev Infect Dis 1991;13(Suppl.5):S369–72.
9. Schuster FL, Visvesvara GS. Axenic growth and drug sensitivity studies of *Balamuthia mandrillaris*, an agent of amebic meningoencephalitis in humans and other animals. J Clin Microbiol 1996;34:385–8.
10. Cabanes PA, Wallet F, Pringuez E, Pernin P. Assessing the risk of primary amoebic meningoencephalitis from swimming in the presence of environmental *Naegleria fowleri*. Appl Environ Microbiol 2001;67(7):2927–31.
11. Ma P, Visvesvara GS, Martinez AJ, *et al.* *Naegleria* and *Acanthamoeba* infections: review. Rev Infect Dis 1990;12:490–513.
12. Khan NA. Pathogenicity, morphology, and differentiation of *Acanthamoeba*. Curr Microbiol. 2001;43(6):391–5.
13. Martinez AJ. Acanthamoebiasis and immunosuppression: case report. J Neuropathol Exp Neurol 1982;41:548–57.
14. Stehr-Green JK, Bailey TM, Visvesvara GS. The epidemiology of *Acanthamoeba* keratitis in the United States. Am J Ophthalmol 1989;107:331–6.
15. Auran JD, Starr MB, Jakobiec FA. *Acanthamoeba* keratitis: a review of the literature. Cornea 1987;6:2–26.

16. Khan NA, Paget T. Molecular tools for speciation and epidemiological studies of *Acanthamoeba*. Curr Microbiol 2002;44(6):444–9.
17. Khan NA, Jarroll EL, Paget TA. *Acanthamoeba* can be differentiated by the polymerase chain reaction and simple plating assays. Curr Microbiol 2001;43(3):204–8.
18. Walochnik J, Obwaller A, Haller-Schober EM. Anti-*Acanthamoeba* IgG, IgM, and IgA immunoreactivities in correlation to strain pathogenicity. Parasitol Res 2001;87(8):651–6.
19. Pfister DR, Cameron JD, Krachmer JH, Holland EJ. Confocal microscopy findings of *Acanthamoeba* Keratitis. Am J Ophthalmol 1996;121:119–28.
20. Rideout BA, Gardiner CH, Stalis IH, *et al.* Fatal infections with *Balamuthia mandrillaris* (a free-living amoeba) in gorillas and other old world primates. Vet Pathol 1997;34:15–22.
21. Slater CA, Sickel JZ, Visvesvara GS, Pabico RC, Gaspari AA. Successful treatment of disseminated *Acanthamoeba* infection in an immunocomprised patient. N Engl J Med 1994;331:85–7.
22. Murakawa GJ, McCalmont T, Altman J, *et al.* Disseminated acanthamebiasis in patients with AIDS. A report of five cases and a review of the literature. Arch Dermatol 1995;131:1291–6.
23. Seidel JS, Harmatz P, Visvesvara GS, *et al.* Successful treatment of primary amebic meningoencephalitis. N Engl J Med 1982;306:346–8.
24. Ledbetter BR, Corson KP, Mader JT. Amoebic meningoencephalitis [Abstract]. J Undersea Hyperbaric Med Soc 1995;22:118.
25. Rowen JL, Doerr CA, Vogel H, Baker CJ. *Balamuthia mandrillaris*: a newly recognized agent for amebic meningoencephalitis. Pediatr Infect Dis J 1995;14:705–10.
26. Gordon SM, Steinberg JP, DuPuis M, *et al.* Culture isolation of *Acanthamoeba* species and leptomyxid ameba from patients with amebic meningoencephalitis, including two patients with AIDS. Clin Infect Dis 1992;15:1024–30.
27. Griesemer DA, Barton LL, Reese CM, *et al.* Amebic meningoencephalitis caused by *Balamuthia mandrillaris*. Pediatr Neurol 1994;10:249–54.
28. Ofori-Kwakye SK, Sidebottom DG, Herbert J, Fischer E, Visvesvara GS. Granulomatous brain tumor caused by *Acanthamoeba*. Case report. J Neurosurg 1986;64:505–9.
29. Moura H, Wallace S, Visvesvara GS. *Acanthamoeba healyi* n. sp. and the isoenzyme and immunoblot profiles of *Acanthamoeba* spp. groups 1 and 3. J Protozool 1992;39:573–83.
30. Driebe WT Jr, Stern GA, Epstein RJ, *et al.* *Acanthamoeba* keratitis, potential role for topical clotrimazole in combination therapy. Arch Ophthalmol 1988;106:1196–201.
31. Larkin DFP, Kilvington S, Dart JKG. Treatment of *Acanthamoeba* keratitis with polyhexamethylene biguanide. Ophthalmology 1992;99:185–91.
32. Kosrirukvongs P, Wanachiwanawin D, Visvesvara GS. Treatment of *Acanthamoeba* keratitis with chlorhexidine. Ophthalmology 1999;106:798–802.
33. Brasseur G, Favennec L, Perrine D, Chenu JP, Brasseur P. Successful treatment of *Acanthamoeba* keratitis by hexamidine. Cornea 1994;13:459–62.
34. Illingworth CD, Cook SD, Karabatsos CH, Easty DL. *Acanthamoeba* keratitis: risk factor and outcome. Br J Ophthalmol 1995;79:1078–82.

chapter

245 Blood and Tissue Protozoa

Pablo Martín-Rabadán & Emilio Bouza

Organisms of the genera *Plasmodium*, *Babesia*, *Toxoplasma*, *Leishmania* and *Trypanosoma* are the most prevalent protozoa able to invade blood and human tissues. They cause diseases of immense socioeconomic impact, most of them having a limited (although extensive) geographic distribution.[1]

MALARIA

Malaria means bad air in Italian, reflecting its association with marshy areas. It is caused by intraerythrocytic parasites first recognized by Laveran in 1880.

NATURE

Human malaria is caused by four species of *Plasmodium* parasites: *Plasmodium falciparum*, *Plasmodium vivax*, *Plasmodium ovale* and *Plasmodium malariae*.

The life cycle of *Plasmodium* spp. in humans is shown in Figure 245.1. The sporozoite form of the parasite is cleared from the circulation in less than 1 hour and infects hepatocytes (intrahepatic cycle). Because the number of infected liver cells is low, there are no symptoms or signs of disease at this stage. The parasite cells multiply in the infected hepatocytes (liver schizonts), and after an average incubation period of 5–20 days the liver schizonts rupture. The young parasite cells liberated into the circulation invade red cells where they grow (trophozoites) and divide (schizonts). Parasites of the species *P. vivax* and *P. ovale* may persist for months or even a few years as intrahepatocytic schizonts in a 'dormant' state (hypnozoites) before a new intraerythrocytic cycle begins. The earliest parasitic stage in the erythrocyte is the trophozoite (*trophos*, nourishment), a growing ring of cytoplasm with a nucleus on one side. As the parasite grows, a brownish-green pigment (hemozoin) accumulates in the red cell. In the schizont stage (*schizo*, to split), the nucleus of the plasmodium cell divides repeatedly giving rise to 8–24 daughter cells called merozoites (*mero*, separated part). The red cell disintegrates, releasing the merozoites into plasma where they invade new erythrocytes, to repeat the intraerythrocytic asexual cycle. After a few intraerythrocytic cycles, some trophozoites, instead of becoming schizonts, undergo sexual differentiation and develop into large uninucleate female gametocytes (macrogametocytes) and male gametocytes (microgametocytes). The gametocytes undergo no further development in humans, and eventually degenerate or are destroyed unless a susceptible mosquito feeds on them. Sexual reproduction takes place in the stomach of the mosquito (sporogonic cycle), and as a result infective sporozoites accumulate in the salivary gland of the mosquito from where they are injected into humans in the next blood meal.

EPIDEMIOLOGY

Malaria incidence is estimated to be 500 million cases/year and malaria causes at least 2 million deaths (4% of all deaths). Children account for more than 1 million of these deaths, and malaria causes 15–25% of all deaths in children under 5 years of age. About 80% of cases occur in sub-Saharan Africa, and up to 30,000 travelers from Europe and North America contract the disease each year.

Malaria transmission occurs when an infected *Anopheles* mosquito bites a susceptible individual. Infections are more likely to be acquired during the wet season in the tropics or spring and autumn in temperate climates. Figure 245.2 shows the geographic distribution of the disease.

In highly endemic areas, the disease is acquired in early childhood and the whole population is re-infected periodically throughout life.

PATHOGENICITY

The production of disease by *Plasmodium* spp. is complex and not fully understood, but essentially consists of hemolytic anemia and an impaired microcirculation (see also Chapter 166).

The anemia in malaria is due to the rupture of parasitized erythrocytes, removal of parasitized and unparasitized erythrocytes by the spleen, capillary sequestration and bone marrow dyserythropoiesis. Bleeding and, in some cases, disseminated intravascular coagulation (DIC) may contribute to the pathogenesis.

The pathogenesis of microvascular flow impairment is controversial. It is characterized by the 'packing' of red blood cells containing mature forms of the parasite in the capillaries and venules. Hemozoin or, more recently, phospholipids have been proposed as the 'toxins' that trigger the interleukin (IL) cascade and subsequent febrile reaction. Antibodies to these phospholipids and tumor necrosis factor (TNF)-α levels are elevated in malaria and correlate with the prognosis in *P. falciparum* malaria.

Several genetic and immunologic factors offer protection against malaria or against the more severe forms of the disease. The absence of Duffy antigen in red blood cells, a trait that predominates in West Africans and derived populations, prevents *P. vivax* malaria.

In patients with hereditary elliptocytosis, in those with glycophorin C deficiency (Leach phenotype) as well as in those who are heterozygous for sickle cell disease, it has been observed that the incidence of malaria is lower than expected for the general population of a given area. Other hemoglobinopathies such as thalassaemias or glucose-6-phosphate dehydrogenase (G6PD) deficiency may offer a less clinically evident level of protection.

Untreated infected patients eventually develop curative immunity against the parasitizing strain. As several strains usually circulate in any given area, re-infection is extremely common. When the patient has successive infections from a number of strains, a certain degree of immunity to the infection develops. This partial immunity prevents severe disease, conferring tolerance to high parasitemias. The immune protection reached after repeated infections eventually disappears if re-infections do not occur for years. Iron deficiency, which is very common in holoendemic areas, seems to protect against severe disease.

PREVENTION

The prevention of disease can be approached individually or as a wider disease control program. Complete eradication of the disease

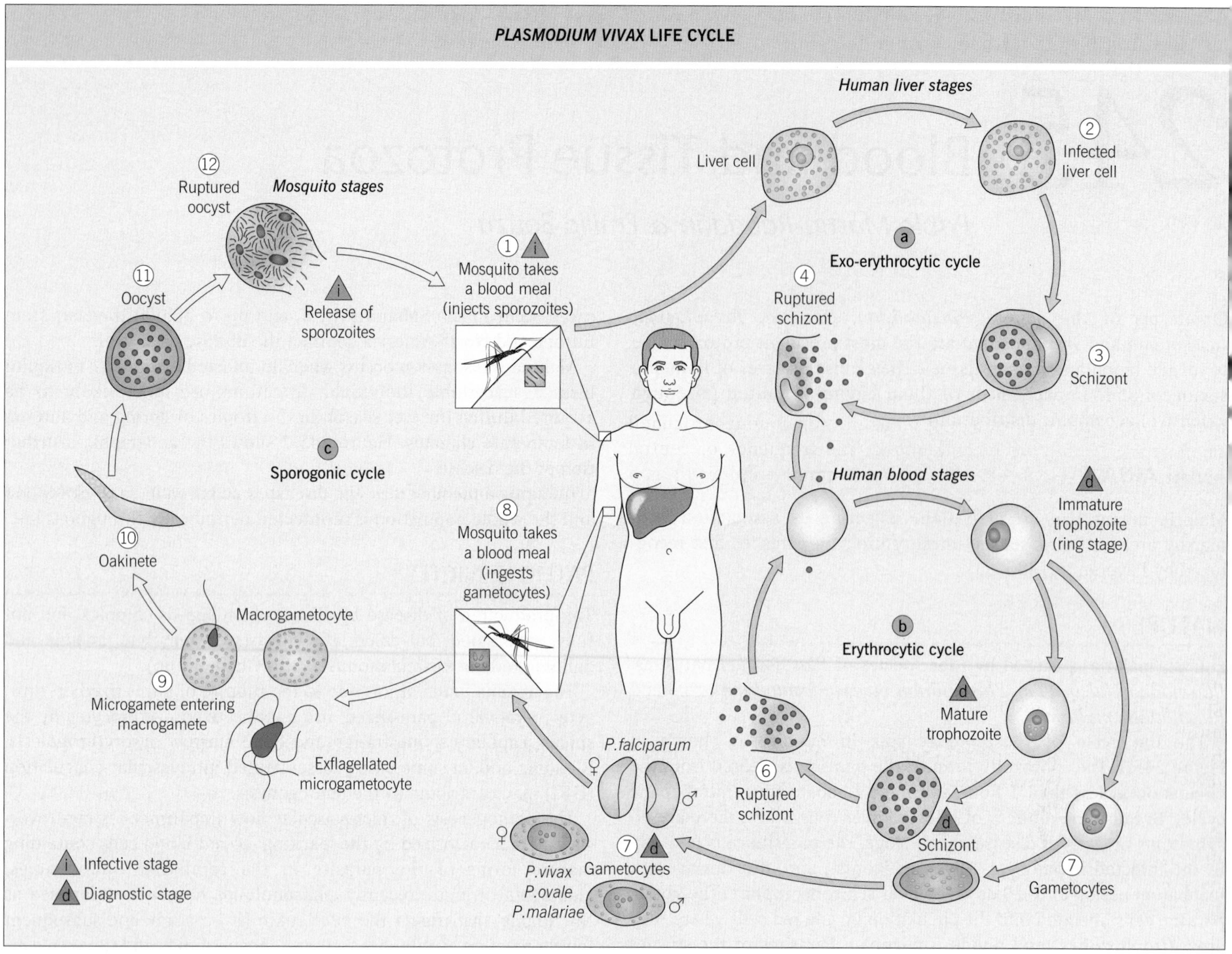

Fig. 245.1 ***Plasmodium vivax* life cycle.** The life cycle starts when an infected mosquito feeds, inoculating the sporozoite form of the parasite, which infects the hepatocytes. The parasite cells then multiply (liver schizonts) and are liberated into the circulation to invade red cells where they grow (trophozoites) and divide (schizonts). Some trophozoites differentiate into gametocytes infective for mosquitoes.

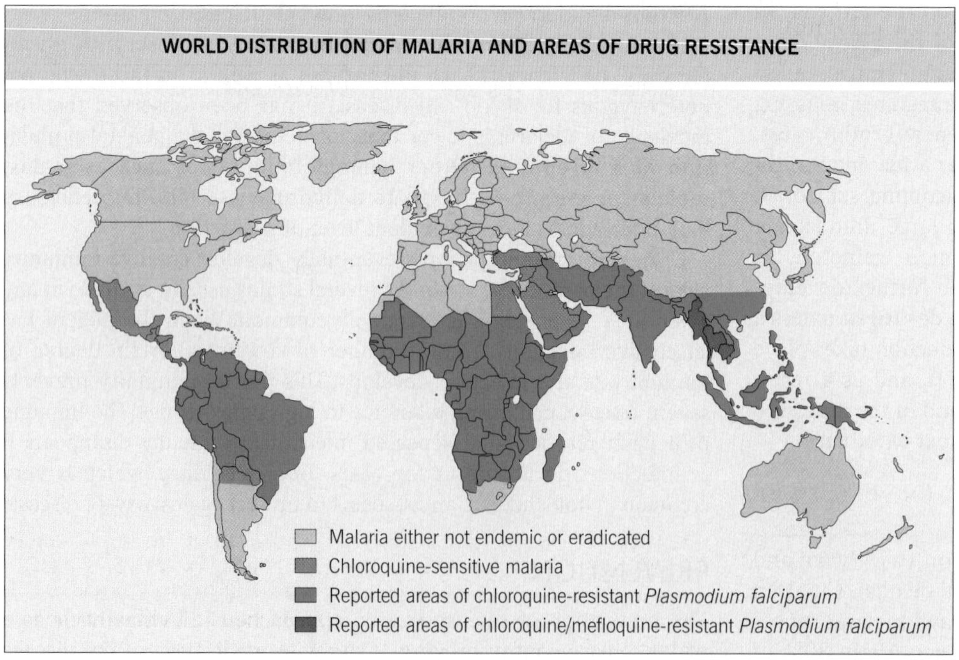

Fig. 245.2 World distribution of malaria and areas of drug resistance, 2001.

is now considered to be unfeasible. The development of a vaccine has been attempted for decades with little success.

Personal preventive measures depend upon the estimated risk of infection based on itinerary, duration of stay, type of activities, accessibility to medical facilities, age and health. Counseling may then include protection from mosquito bites and appropriate chemoprophylaxis. The traveler must understand the importance of adherence to preventive methods, but be aware that no method provides absolute protection and that symptoms may appear weeks or months after leaving the endemic area. Individuals at risk of developing severe disease such as infants, pregnant women or patients who have serious diseases should be discouraged from going to endemic areas. Appropriate protection against biting insects is strongly recommended.

In the few remaining areas of chloroquine-sensitive malaria, chloroquine prophylaxis is recommended. In chloroquine-resistant areas mefloquine, chloroquine–proguanil, atovaquone–proguanil or doxycycline may be recommended. The frequency of central nervous system (CNS) events with mefloquine prophylaxis is a matter of concern. Mefloquine prophylaxis usually should be taken for 1 week before entering a malarious area, while in the malarious area and for 4 weeks after leaving the area. Long-term (several months or years) prophylaxis is considered safe for chloroquine and mefloquine, and probably for doxycycline.[2] In areas of chloroquine resistance, strict personal antimosquito measures and chloroquine with proguanil is usually recommended to pregnant women. Mefloquine prophylaxis, which provides better protection, can be given after week 20 of pregnancy and is well tolerated.[3] Pregnancy must be avoided while on doxycycline prophylaxis. In areas of mefloquine resistance (parts of Thailand, Cambodia and Myanmar) doxycycline can be recommended for prophylaxis (Table 245.1).

Standby treatment is an alternative for selected patients. The standby treatment of choice for most areas would be atovaquone–proguanil. After leaving the endemic area, primaquine (15mg of base/day for 14 days) can be administered to eliminate any potential hypnozoites if exposure to *P. vivax* or to *P. ovale* infection has been intense.

Updated information on malaria risks and prophylaxis can be obtained from the US Centers for Disease Control and Prevention (CDC)[4] on a 24-hour toll-free telephone service (tel: (1) 877 FYI TRIP; fax: (1) 88 232 3299), or UK Travel Clinic, Hospital for Tropical Disease (tel: +44 171 388 9600), or through the internet (http://www.cdc.gov/travel/). The World Health Organization (WHO) also provides useful on-line information (http://www.who.int/ith).

MALARIA CHEMOPROPHYLACTIC DRUG DOSAGE

Drug	Adults	Pediatric
Chloroquine phosphate	300mg base weekly (=500mg product)	5mg/kg base weekly
Mefloquine	250mg salt weekly	5mg/kg salt weekly
Doxycycline	100mg/day	2mg/kg/day Not for those under 8 years old
Proguanil	200mg daily	4mg/kg daily
Atovaquone ± proguanil	Atovaquone 250mg and proguanil 100mg daily	Atovaquone 62.5mg and proguanil 25mg. 11–20kg: 1 pediatric tablet daily (one extra tablet for each extra 10kg increase). Not for those under 11kg body weight

Table 245.1 Malaria chemoprophylactic drug dosage. The maximum pediatric dosage is the adult recommended dose.

DIAGNOSTIC MICROBIOLOGY

Laboratory confirmation of malaria is still based on microscopic examination of Giemsa-stained blood smears (see Chapter 166). The detection limit is around 50–500 parasites/μl of blood depending on the skill of the microscopist. Alternatively, visualization of plasmodia can be accomplished by fluorescent microscopy of capillary-tube centrifuged blood stained with acridine orange – quantitative buffy coat (QBC) – a slightly more sensitive method than thick films.[5]

If malaria is suspected and the first smear is negative, examinations should be repeated three times at 12-hour intervals, because in synchronous falciparum malaria the mature forms are sequestered from the circulation.

Parasitologic differential diagnosis should be made between the four *Plasmodium* spp. and *Babesia* spp. If a *Plasmodium* parasite cannot be identified to species level, it should be treated immediately as *P. falciparum*. The slides should then be sent to a reference laboratory and G6PD testing should be requested. The decision on treatment of possible intrahepatic hypnozoites using primaquine can be delayed until those results arrive.

Polymerase chain reaction (PCR) is highly specific and sensitive, detecting up to 0.3 parasites/μl of blood.[6] It has been found clinically useful in the detection of low parasitemia (as in the malarial hyper-reactive syndrome) and multiple-species infections.[7]

Antibody detection may be useful in the diagnosis of hyper-reactive malarial syndrome and for retrospective diagnosis. Recently developed immunochromatographic dipstick assays permit a rapid nonmicroscopic diagnosis of most cases of malaria. Their performance varies depending on the detected antigen, the level of parasitemia and the infecting *Plasmodium* spp. Compared with PCR tests devices that detect *P. falciparum* histidine-rich protein-2 have a sensitivity of 88% and a specificity of 97%. The test may persist positive weeks after successful therapy. The detection of aldolase or parasite lactate dehydrogenase permit the detection of high parasitemias of nonfalciparum malaria. In this device mixed infections would key out as *P. falciparum*.[8]

Serial parasite counts are recommended to monitor therapy;[9] 48 hours after the initiation of treatment, parasite counts are expected to be lower than 25% of initial counts. Quinine-related

FEATURES ASSOCIATED WITH POOR PROGNOSIS IN *FALCIPARUM* MALARIA

Clinical	Serum biochemistry	Hematology
Agitation	↓ Glucose	Leukocytosis
Hyperventilation	↓ Bicarbonate	Severe anemia (PCV <15%)
Sustained body temperature >102.2°F(39°C)	↑ Lactate	Platelets $<50 \times 10^6$/ml
	↑ Creatinine	Fibrinogen <200mg/dl
Hypothermia	↑ Total billrubin	Prothrombin time >3 seconds
Bleeding	↑ AST 3×	Partial thromboplastin time ↑
Coma	↑ ALT 3×	Parasitemia $>10^5$/ml
Convulsions	↑ 5-nucleotidase	Pigment-containing parasites >20%
Anuria	↑ CPK	Pigment-containing neutrophils >5%
Jaundice	↑ Myoglobin	
Shock	↑ Urate	

Table 245.2 Features associated with a poor prognosis in *falciparum* malaria. In patients who have premunition the parasitemia level has less prognostic value. CPK, creatine phosphokinase; PCV, packed cell volume; sAST, serum aspartate aminotransferase; sALT, serum alanine aminotransferase; 3×, three times normal. Adapted from White.[11]

antimalarials do not kill gametocytes and so their presence in blood does not mean treatment failure. Recently, it has been shown that parasite lactate dehydrogenase is useful for monitoring patient progress.[10] Common laboratory findings are progressive anemia, moderate-to-severe thrombocytopenia and a normal white blood cell count. Metabolic lactic or ketotic acidosis and other biochemical findings can be observed in severe disease (Table 245.2). Reaginic tests for syphilis may become positive.

CLINICAL MANIFESTATIONS

Malaria must be suspected in any febrile patient who has been in an endemic area in the previous 3 years. Occasionally, autochthonous cases are produced in nonendemic areas through transfusion of blood or blood products, sharing needles, maternal–fetal transmission or infection from an aircraft-transported infective *Anopheles* mosquito.

Before the onset of fever, non-specific symptoms such as malaise, headache, myalgia, fatigue, abdominal discomfort, dry cough, nausea, vomiting and diarrhea can occur, misleading the diagnosis.

Fever, the hallmark of malaria, usually develops 2 weeks after the infective bite, and in 95% of cases within the first 6 weeks and occasionally may follow the classic paroxysmal patterns:

- quartan pattern (peaks on days 1, 4, 7, etc.) – characteristic of *P. malariae;* or
- the tertian pattern of fever (peaks on day 1, 3, 5, etc.) – characteristic of all other species.

The absence of a typical fever pattern should not be a reason for disregarding malaria.

Physical examination may reveal tachycardia, splenomegaly, liver enlargement and jaundice. Malaria does not cause lymph node enlargement. In uncomplicated malaria, discrete hemolytic anemia, leukopenia and thrombocytopenia and other minor abnormalities of routine laboratory tests are usual.[11]

COMPLICATIONS

Patients infected with *Plasmodium* spp. other than *P. falciparum* rarely die of the infection in the developed world. The fatalities caused by 'benign' malaria are usually related to severe chronic anemia or rupture of an enlarged spleen. Patients infected with *P. malariae* may develop nephrotic syndrome.

On the other hand, *P. falciparum* infection must always be considered a life-threatening condition. The definition of severe malaria and complicated malaria is, however, controversial. On practical grounds, in developed countries where malaria is not endemic it is our practice to treat every patient who has *P. falciparum* malaria as an inpatient. Intravenous treatment is prescribed if the patient is seriously ill, regardless of strict fulfillment of the WHO definition of severe malaria.[12]

The most important complication of acute falciparum malaria is CNS involvement. Cerebral malaria is defined strictly as unrousable coma. Less severe neurologic manifestations are common, and high fever alone can cause confusion and delirium and, in children, seizures. In cerebral malaria, focal signs are uncommon and physical examination shows symmetric encephalopathy. Cerebrospinal fluid (CSF) is usually unrevealing. Untreated cerebral malaria is uniformly fatal. If adequately treated, the mortality ranges from 15 to 25%. There are persistent neurologic sequelae in 10% of children and 3% of adults.[13] A rare complication called postmalaria neurologic syndrome has been defined in patients recently recovered from *Plasmodium falciparum* malaria who have negative blood films at the time of onset of neurological or neuropsychiatric symptoms. Clinical manifestations emerge a few days or weeks after recovery from malaria and can be confused with mefloquine neurotoxicity.

Non-neurologic complications of malaria include renal failure, heart failure, acute pulmonary edema, adult respiratory distress syndrome, shock, coagulation disorders, severe anemia, hypoglycemia, metabolic acidosis, drug-related toxicity, malaria relapses and malarial hyper-reactive syndrome.

Relapse is defined as the reappearance of malaria originating from dormant liver schizonts, whereas recrudescence is the reappearance of disease after a partially effective treatment. Relapses can be expected in 50% of patients who have *P. vivax* or *P. ovale* infection who do not receive primaquine.

A condition called tropical splenomegaly or hyper-reactive malarial syndrome is occasionally seen in countries where malaria is endemic. It is defined as the presence of an enlarged spleen (often massive), raised IgM levels and high levels of antiplasmodium antibodies in patients who have negative smears for *Plasmodium* spp. and for whom no other cause of splenomegaly can be elicited.[14]

MANAGEMENT

Antimalarial therapy must be started in most cases without delay. The selection of treatment depends upon the parasite species and the expected resistance for that area. Details of drug regimens can be found in Chapter 166.

Oral chloroquine is the treatment of choice for uncomplicated *P. falciparum* infections from chloroquine-sensitive areas, and for most *P. malariae*, *P. vivax* and *P. ovale* infections. Malaria due to the latter two species should also be treated with primaquine to eliminate hypnozoites. If the patient is pregnant or has G6PD deficiency, primaquine should not be used and any eventual relapses should be treated with chloroquine.

Occasionally, infections due to *P. vivax* are not cured by standard treatment. Chloroquine-resistant *P. vivax* and primaquine failure have been reported in areas of Asia and in Colombia.[15] It should be suspected if adequately treated *P. vivax* infection reappears within 1 month of treatment. In such a case mefloquine should be administered. If parasitemia reappears more than 1 month after the initial treatment, then primaquine failure should be suspected and more primaquine (22.5mg/day to a total cumulative dose of 6mg/kg) should be administered after chloroquine retreatment.

Uncomplicated *P. falciparum* infection from chloroquine-resistant areas can be treated with mefloquine taken with abundant water. The main side-effects are neuropsychiatric and cardiac. Intravenous physostigmine may reverse the severe neuropsychiatric side-effects of mefloquine.[16] Vomiting and diarrhea are associated with treatment failure. An acceptable alternative is 1 week of treatment with oral quinine, but lack of compliance may be a problem. When quinine is given combined with doxycycline, 3 days of treatment are equally effective. Pyrimethamine–sulfadoxine is a simple well-tolerated alternative, but parasite resistance has been reported from most endemic regions. Chloroquine plus clindamycin is also effective. Halofantrine is similar to mefloquine, but its cardiac toxicity is considered unacceptable if other alternatives are available. Atovaquone plus proguanil has proved efficacious for the treatment of uncomplicated, multidrug-resistant falciparum malaria.[17]

In some areas of Thailand, Myanmar and Cambodia, *P. falciparum* strains that have a higher level of resistance are common. Chloroquine or mefloquine does not prevent infections by these strains and their response to quinine, mefloquine and halofantrine is poor, unless these drugs are combined with other drugs. In these areas artemisin derivatives, such as artesunate, artemether or arteether, have been used extensively with remarkable success. Artesunate followed by mefloquine is the recommended treatment for malaria acquired in these areas. An alternative therapy is quinine plus doxycycline (clindamycin may be substituted for doxycycline in children nder 8 years of age and in pregnant women). In severe malaria, ıtramuscular artemether is as effective as quinine and less toxic.[18,19]

n severe *P. falciparum* infections, antimalarial treatment should be tarted parenterally because shock, vomiting and impaired swallowing may interfere with absorption. Therapy can be switched to oral dministration after initial recovery,

Hyper-reactive malaria syndrome is treated with standard doses of ntimalarials expected to be effective for the area of acquisition, folowed by chemoprophylaxis while in the endemic area. Splenectomy s indicated if severe hypersplenism persists after months of continuus prophylaxis.

Supportive treatment is an essential part of the management of evere malaria. Seizures must be promptly treated or prevented in hildren and in adults with severe disease. Corticosteroids are not ecommended for cerebral malaria.[20]

BABESIOSIS

Human babesiosis is an uncommon tick-borne parasitic zoonotic lisease that was first described by Babes in Rumanian cattle in 1888. t was not reported as a human disease until 1957.

NATURE

The genus *Babesia* belongs to the family Piroplasmida and comprises over 70 species that parasitize mammals and birds. Infection n cattle is widespread and it is an economically important disease. Four species are the main potential human parasites:

- *Babesia bovis* and *Babesia divergens* in Europe;
- *Babesia microti* in the USA; and
- a *Babesia*-like piroplasm, designated WA1, that has been recently described in a patient from Washington State and might be the cause of the cases acquired on the west coast of the USA.[21]

EPIDEMIOLOGY AND PATHOGENICITY

Babesiosis in humans occurs predominantly in the USA, although a few cases have occurred in Europe and in other areas. It is highly endemic in the coastal areas of Massachusetts, Connecticut and New York State, where seroprevalence rates reach 4–6%, indicating that subclinical infections are common. In these areas rodents are the main reservoir and humans are usually infected by the bite of an infected nymph or *Ixodes dammini* tick. Transfusions of blood or blood products have caused a few cases. In Europe recent data indicate that most infections are not detected.[22]

PREVENTION

General recommendations include avoidance of known endemic areas, especially in the warm months of the year. Clothes should be sprayed with tick repellents before going on outdoor activities and on return the skin should be thoroughly examined for the presence of ticks.

DIAGNOSTIC MICROBIOLOGY

Babesia spp. are intraerythrocytic parasites that may resemble plasmodium trophozoites, but the hemozoin pigment is never present in babesiosis. Schizonts and gametocytes are not formed. Multiple erythrocyte parasitization is common and organisms are occasionally arranged in a characteristic Maltese cross shape (Fig. 245.3).

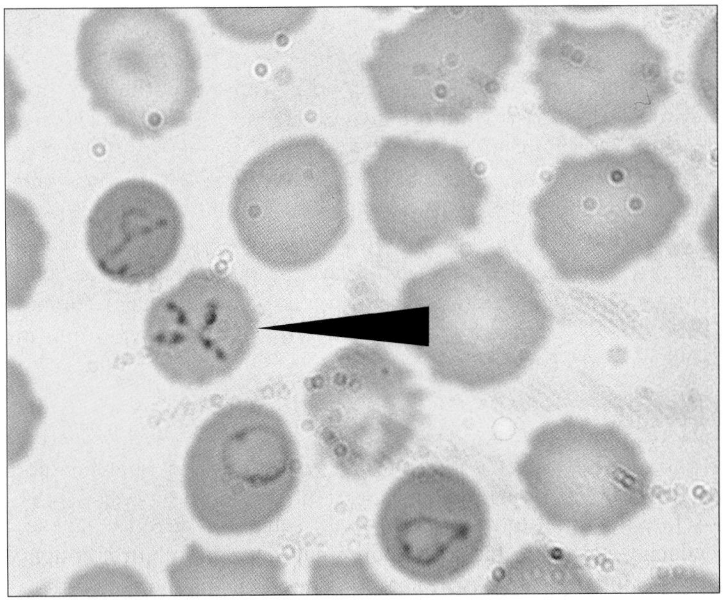

Fig. 245.3 *Babesia* spp. Single and multiple intraerythrocytic parasites can be seen. The arrow marks a typical Maltese cross.

Parasitemia usually persists, demonstrable by light microscopy, for 3–12 weeks.

Serologic diagnosis can be made using indirect immunofluorescent antibody (IFA) assay. A serum titer of at least 1/256 is diagnostic of recent *B. microti* infection. Within a few weeks, most patients who have active infection have serum titers equal to or higher than 1/1024, falling over a few months to levels under 1/256.[23] Due to the lack of cross-reactivity, individuals exposed to the infection on the West coast of the USA should be tested also for antibodies to the *Babesia WA1* species.

PCR tests are more sensitive than microscopy but are not commonly available.

CLINICAL MANIFESTATIONS

The clinical forms of babesiosis vary widely depending upon the immune status of the host and the species of *Babesia* involved.

In the American Northeast, the symptoms of *B. microti* infection (Nantucket fever) range from a non-specific flu-like self-limited febrile illness to severe hemolytic anemia. It is most severe in those who are older or asplenic. The usual incubation period is 1–3 weeks. The onset is gradual with non-specific symptoms such as malaise, fatigue, anorexia, headache, emotional lability, myalgias and arthralgias. Blood leukocytes are not elevated and platelets are usually decreased. There may be a hemolytic anemia. The mortality rate is less than 10% of symptomatic cases.

The European cases typically occur in asplenic patients who present with a high fever and severe hemolytic anemia, and the infection is usually fatal.[24]

MANAGEMENT

Early treatment is recommended for all diagnosed cases to prevent long-term sequelae and potential transmission through blood donation.

The standard treatment is clindamycin, 600mg q8h plus 650mg of quinine q8h; both drugs are given for 7–10 days. Combination of atovaquone (750mg q12h) and azithromycin (500mg on day 1 and 250mg/day thereafter) for 7 days is also effective and is associated with fewer adverse reactions.[25] Chloroquine is not recommended. Blood transfusion and general supportive treatment may be needed for severe disease. Exchange transfusion has been used in an attempt to decrease parasite load, but its usefulness has not been demonstrated. It is recommended that co-infection by other tick-transmitted micro-organisms be ruled out.

TOXOPLASMOSIS

Toxoplasmosis is a widespread zoonosis, caused by the coccidian parasite *Toxoplasma gondii*, first recognized in 1908. *Toxoplasma* (from the Greek, meaning 'shaped as a bow') is a one-species genus.

Humans are usually infected orally, developing few, if any, symptoms of infection. The infection persists for life without signs of disease. However, during immunosuppression, quiescent parasites multiply, resulting in neurologic disease or, more rarely, other organ manifestations. Congenital transmission is a cause of major concern because it is frequently associated with severe disease in the newborn (see Chapter 65).

NATURE

Toxoplasma gondii is a parasite of many species of mammals and birds. The main forms of the parasite life cycle are oocysts, tachyzoites and bradyzoites.

The oocysts result from the sexual multiplication that takes place exclusively in the intestinal epithelium of cats and other felines. They are present in feline feces, and after maturing in the environment become the source of infection for noncarnivorous animals.

In the secondary host (all hosts but felines) *T. gondii* cells have two forms:

- rapidly multiplying tachyzoites (*tachy*, rapid), and
- 'dormant' bradyzoites (*brady*, slow).

When the host is infected by oocysts, tachyzoites or bradyzoites, a disseminated infection by tachyzoite forms takes place. Tachyzoites multiply inside the host cells, which rupture when 8–32 tachyzoites are produced. The tachyzoites released infect new cells. When the immune response controls the infection, some surviving parasites persist for many years in tissue cysts, which are sacs containing hundreds or thousands of *T. gondii* bradyzoites. They represent the parasite reservoir present in secondary hosts. Tissue cysts can be found in any tissue, but are most common in muscle and brain.

Cats become infected from eating birds, small rodents or other sources of raw meat. Humans and other animals become infected from either oocysts in soil and contaminated food or tissue cysts in raw meat. When acute infection occurs during pregnancy, tachyzoites are able to infect the placenta and, in a second step, the fetus.

EPIDEMIOLOGY

Toxoplasma gondii cysts are present in 5–92% of lamb meat and in a lower percentage of beef and pork meat. The prevalence of oocyst-shedding cats has been estimated at 1%. Infection rates in humans are very variable and depend upon eating habits and environmental factors. The prevalence increases progressively with age. In the 1990s the seroprevalence in women of child-bearing age with no obstetric history ranged between 37 and 58% in central Europe, Northern Africa and Australia, while in America and sub-Saharan Africa the range was 51–77%, and in India, South East Asia and China it was 4–39%.[26]

Human disease caused by *T. gondii* is much more restricted than the infection itself, and is generally a consequence of either intrauterine acquisition or immunocompromise.

PATHOGENICITY AND IMMUNITY

Toxoplasma gondii tachyzoites invade cells from nearly every organ, where they survive inside parasitophorous vacuoles. Resistance to the infection has been found to be enhanced by interferon (IFN)-γ and diminished by IL-6. Extracellular tachyzoites are lysed by complement combined to specific antibody, and $CD4^+$ and $CD8^+$ T cells, lymphokine-activated killer and natural killer cells play a major role in infection control.

PREVENTION

Toxoplasmosis can be prevented at three different levels:

- prevention of primary infection;
- prevention of vertical transmission and congenital disease; and
- prevention of disease in infected immunocompromised individuals

To prevent primary infection, the exposure to parasite can be reduced by health education (Table 245.3). No vaccine is presently available. Maternal immunity due to toxoplasmosis passed before conception protects the fetus from the infection. Immunodeficient patients receiving trimethoprim–sulfamethoxazole (co-trimoxazole

RECOMMENDATIONS TO PREVENT TOXOPLASMOSIS
Do not eat raw or undercooked meat or eggs
Cured or smoked meat and sausages are considered safe. Freeze at −4°F (−20°C) for 1 or more days as an additional precaution
While handling raw meat, avoid touching the mouth or contaminating other food; normal hygienic washing of hands and utensils will suffice
Consume only pasteurized or ultra-heat-treated sterilized milk and dairy products
Wash or peel fruits and vegetables to be eaten uncooked
Control insect pests and their access to foodstuffs
Use gloves for gardening or handling sand where cats usually defecate
Avoid living with cats; if unfeasible, clean cat litter trays with nearly boiling water daily
Infection in cats can be reduced if they do not use raw meat, birds and rodents as a source of food

Table 245.3 Recommendations to prevent toxoplasmosis.

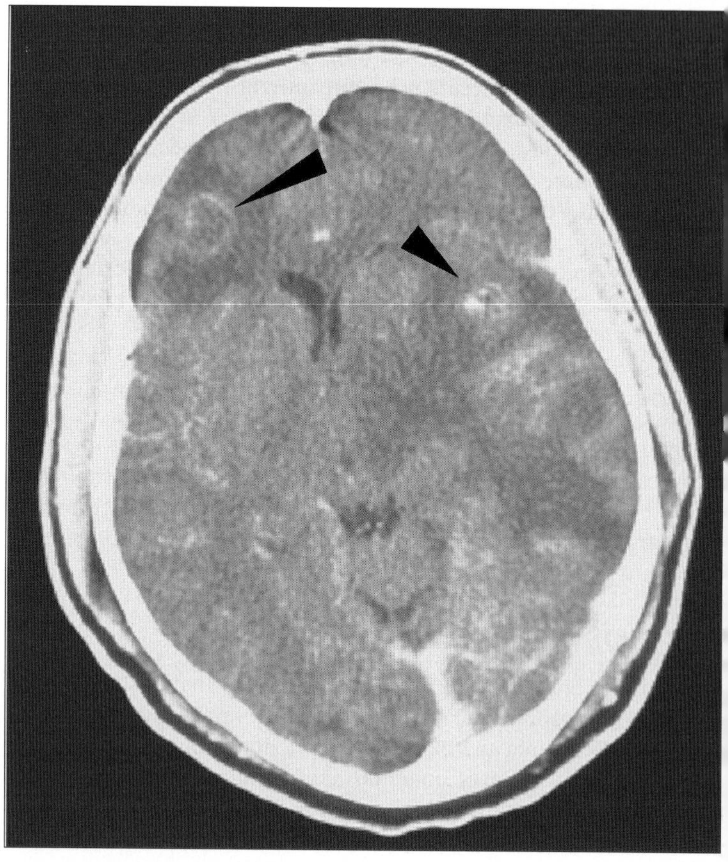

Fig. 245.4 Toxoplasmic encephalitis in person who has AIDS. A cranial CT scan shows bilateral contrast-enhanced ring lesions with peripheral edema and mass effect.

as prophylaxis for *Pneumocystis* infection are substantially protected from toxoplasmosis.

Toxoplasma gondii IgG serology should be included in the initial work-up of pre-transplant patients, and transplantation of a solid organ from a seropositive donor to a seronegative recipient should be avoided if possible. If such a transplant is performed, then the recipient should have anti-*T. gondii* treatment for at least 2 months.

Individuals who have HIV infection and are seronegative for *T. gondii* should avoid being exposed to the parasite (Fig. 245.4), and should be periodically screened for seroconversion. For those patients who have HIV infection and are seropositive for *T. gondii*, further serologic tests do not provide useful information.

Maternal screening is controversial.[27,28] Serologic screening is aimed at detecting acute maternal infection. It is, however, sometimes difficult to establish an early and reliable diagnosis of acute maternal or fetal infection. When acute infection is diagnosed in a pregnant woman, anti-*T. gondii* treatment, further assessment of fetal infection and abortion are offered.

DIAGNOSTIC MICROBIOLOGY

The diagnosis of *T. gondii* infection is usually made by serologic methods alone. The parasite can also be demonstrated by PCR, examination of stained tissue or fluid smears, cultivation in tissue cultures[29] and experimental animal inoculation.

Immunoglobulin G serology is widely used to screen for past infection. Immunoglobulin M appears earlier than IgG, declines faster and is a marker of relatively recent infection. In cases of toxoplasmic lymphadenopathy, 90% were IgM positive when tested within the first 4 months after the onset of lymphadenopathy and 22% remained positive when tested more than 12 months after the onset. In some cases, reactive IgM was undetectable.[30,31] As the functional affinity of specific IgG antibodies is initially low and increases during subsequent weeks, the measurement of high-avidity antibodies helps to discriminate between recent (less than 3 months) and past infection. To diagnose a suspected case of acute toxoplasmosis IgG and IgM serology should be ordered in paired serum samples 3–4 weeks apart. If no antibodies are detected or if there is no seroconversion, acute toxoplasmosis can reasonably be ruled out. Avidity tests should be ordered if results are equivocal or IgM is positive.

CLINICAL MANIFESTATIONS

There are three different forms of toxoplasmosis: congenital infection, acute extrauterine infection and toxoplasmosis of the immunocompromised host.

Congenital toxoplasmosis

Toxoplasmosis acquired in utero can be asymptomatic or may produce signs of disease that can be present at birth.

The risk of congenital toxoplasmosis depends upon the time of acquisition of acute maternal infection.[32] Vertical transmission of *T. gondii* increases with gestation age (15–25% in the first trimester of pregnancy, 30–54% in the second and 60–65% in the third). Conversely, the severity of congenital disease is increased when infection occurs in early pregnancy. Signs of infection at delivery are present in 21–28% of those infected in the second trimester and up to 11% of those infected in the third trimester. Overall, 10% are born with severe disease.

Clinical manifestations of congenital toxoplasmosis include strabismus, chorioretinitis, encephalitis, microcephaly, hydrocephalus, psychomotor retardation and convulsions, as well as non-specific manifestations such as anemia, jaundice, hypothermia, thrombocytopenia, diarrhea and pneumonitis. The characteristic triad of hydrocephalus, cerebral calcifications and chorioretinitis resulting in mental retardation, epilepsy and impaired vision is the most severe and extreme form of the disease. Cerebral lesions may calcify, providing retrospective evidence of congenital toxoplasmosis.

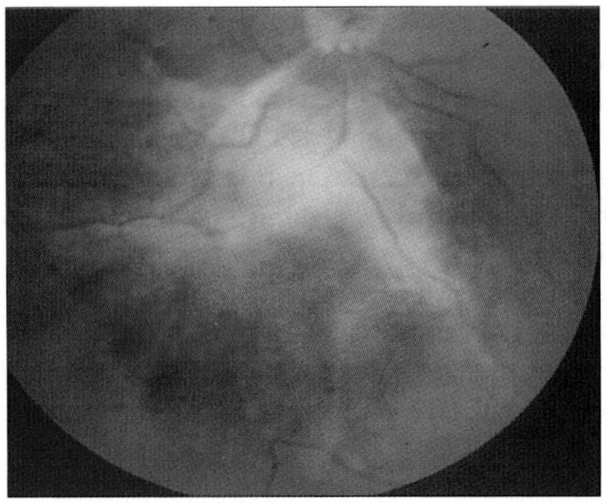

Fig. 245.5 Fundoscopic image of toxoplasmic chorioretinitis. Most cases presenting in adults represent a late manifestation of a congenitally acquired toxoplasmosis.

Toxoplasma gondii chorioretinitis in immunocompetent patients is frequently secondary to congenitally acquired infection. The proportion of congenitally infected asymptomatic individuals who develop chorioretinitis later in life (usually in the first four decades) is unknown, but may well be over two-thirds (Fig. 245.5). Up to 30% of patients relapse after treatment.

Acquired toxoplasmosis

In 90% of cases, no clinical symptoms are apparent during acute infection. Most symptomatic patients present with enlarged lymph nodes that are located mainly in the head or neck area. Malaise and low-grade fever are present in less than 50% of symptomatic cases. Although *T. gondii* organisms are not usually seen, the histologic picture of acute *T. gondii* lymphadenopathy is usually diagnostic (Piringer–Kuchinka lymphadenitis). Occasionally, the lymph node histopathology can be mistaken for that of cat-scratch disease, other infections and lymphoma.[33]

Rare manifestations of acute infection include chorioretinitis, myositis and heart, lung, liver or CNS symptomatic involvement.

Toxoplasmosis in the immunocompromised host

Toxoplasmosis is a serious disease in patients who have profound immunosuppression such as those who have received a transplant or who have AIDS (see Chapter 127).

In transplant patients, the incidence and severity of the disease depends upon previous exposure to the parasite of donor and recipient, the type of organ transplanted and the degree of immunosuppression induced. The disease can be due to reactivation of a chronic silent infection or an acute primary infection acquired from the transplanted organ. The risk of developing toxoplasmosis for seronegative recipients of an organ from a seropositive donor is 57% for heart, 20% for kidney and minimal for liver transplants, reflecting the organ tropism of tissue cysts.[34] The disease manifests as a systemic disease with diverse degrees of multiorgan involvement including pneumonitis, carditis, hepatitis, myositis and encephalitis. In cardiac transplant recipients signs of myocarditis and pericarditis predominate.[35]

In patients who have AIDS, the clinical manifestations are usually related to CNS dysfunction or ocular lesions. Myocarditis is frequently found at autopsy, but is rarely clinically apparent. Infections of lung and other organs have also been reported.

Patients who become infected with *T. gondii* risk developing toxoplasmosis when their $CD4^+$ T cell count is less than 100 cells/mm^3. The onset of *T. gondii* encephalitis is usually subacute. Fever and malaise usually precede the first neurologic symptoms. Headache, confusion, neuropsychiatric manifestations, seizures or other focal signs strongly suggest the diagnosis. Diagnosis is based upon clinical data, neuro-radiology – magnetic resonance imaging (MRI) is the procedure of choice – and response to therapy. PCR testing of cerebrospinal fluid may be diagnostic too. *Toxoplasma gondii* encephalitis in patients who have AIDS usually presents as multiple abscesses in the basal ganglia or the gray–white matter junction with a contrast-enhanced ring (see Fig. 245.4). Diffuse *T. gondii* encephalitis is an uncommon rapidly fatal form.

In people who have HIV infection there is no good serologic marker of active toxoplasmosis. The presence of anti-*T. gondii* antibody means previous exposure and therefore present infection, but not necessarily disease. The absence of specific antibodies makes toxoplasmosis unlikely.

MANAGEMENT

Congenital toxoplasmosis

In gestational toxoplasmosis, the drug therapy may be intended to treat the mother, the fetus or the newborn (Fig. 245.6).[36] Spiramycin (not available in the UK) is a macrolide antibiotic that concentrates in the placenta, reducing placental infection by 60%.[37] It does not pass consistently through the placental barrier and it is used to decrease vertical transmission. Spiramycin 3g/day q8h should be given to pregnant women who have an acute infection from diagnosis to delivery unless fetal infection is proved. In such a case, the maternal regimen must be switched to sulfadiazine 4g plus pyrimethamine 25mg and folinic acid 15mg a day until delivery.[38] The risk of serious disease in early infections outweighs any consideration of potential teratogenic effects of antifolates used in the first trimester of pregnancy. All infected newborns should have anti-*T. gondii* treatment (sulfadiazine 50mg/kg q12h plus pyrimethamine 1mg/kg/day and folinic acid 5mg/kg/day for at least 6 months). No treatment regimen seems to decrease the rate of chorioretinitis

To confirm fetal infection, ultrasound fetal examination and sampling the amniotic fluid for *T. gondii* PCR and culture are recommended.[39] Fetal blood sampling obtained by cordocentesis has been commonly used to detect fetal antibodies and for *T. gondii* culture. Cordocentesis had an inherent risk of fetal loss of 2–3% and has been replaced by PCR testing of amniotic fluid.

Termination of pregnancy is commonly offered to women who seroconvert in the first 8 weeks of pregnancy and to those infected in the first 22 weeks of pregnancy when fetal infection is confirmed. A more conservative approach recommends abortion only if there is ultrasonographic evidence of hydrocephalus, although a small percentage of cases with neurologic disease will then be born.[36,40]

Toxoplasmosis complicating a previous pregnancy is not an indication for prophylaxis during a subsequent pregnancy. Women may be reassured that they are not at greater risk of toxoplasmosis affecting the new pregnancy.

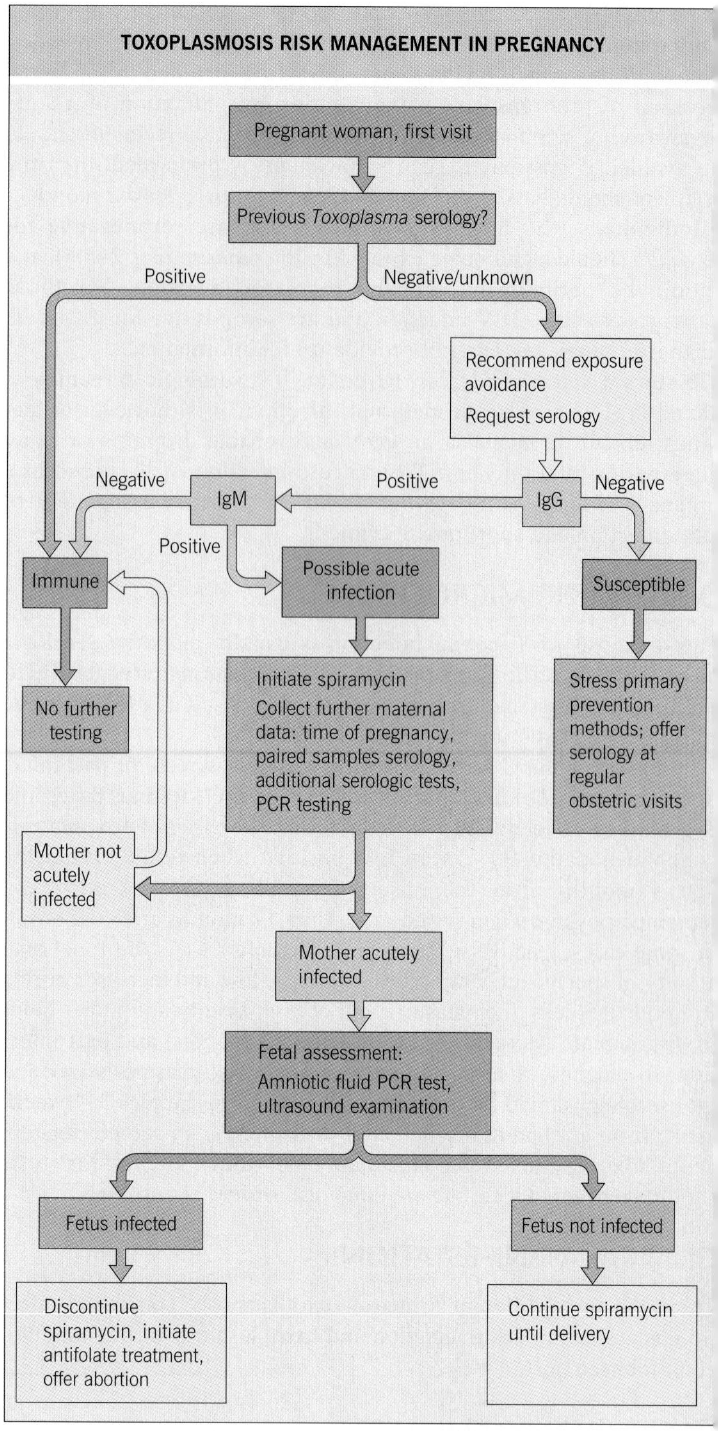

Fig. 245.6 Toxoplasmosis risk management in pregnancy.

Acquired toxoplasmosis

Symptomatic *T. gondii* infection in nonpregnant immunocompetent individuals does not need to be treated unless there is visceral involvement or the patient has been infected in a laboratory accident.

Toxoplasmosis in the immunocompromised host

Standard anti-*T. gondii* treatment is sulfadiazine 4g/day q6h plus pyrimethamine as a first 100mg loading dose followed by 50mg/day and folinic acid 15mg/day for 6–8 weeks. If brain edema is of relevance corticosteroids should be given, but the clinical response to anti-*T. gondii* therapy would be masked by the unspecific improvement due to the reduction of edema. If the patient has not improved in the first 2 weeks of therapy a control computerized tomography (CT) or MRI scan should be repeated to review the empiric diagnosis. A repeat scan should be carried out after completing treatment. With this regimen 80% of patients survive, although 50% of the survivors will have neurologic sequelae. Serious adverse effects to the medication can be expected in 40% of patients. In cases of intolerance to sulfadiazine, 75–100mg/day of pyrimethamine alone or with clindamycin has been used (see also Chapter 113 and 127).

Secondary prevention

Approximately 80% of AIDS patients relapse after an initial episode of toxoplasmosis. Daily treatment with pyrimethamine 50mg plus sulfadiazine 1g and folinic acid 10–15mg should be given to reduce the relapse rate to 5–10%. Current US Public Health Service (USPHS)/Infectious Diseases Society of America (IDSA) guidelines (http://www.hivatis.org) recommend that secondary prophylaxis may be discontinued in patients with sustained (>6 month) increase in CD4 T cells (>200 cells/mm^3) (see Chapter 123 and 127).

LEISHMANIASIS

Leishmaniasis is the term used to describe a group of chronic parasitic diseases caused by a number of species of the genus *Leishmania*. The infection can be localized in the skin or mucous membranes or disseminated in the reticuloendothelial system. It is usually a zoonosis transmitted by Phlebotominae sandflies, which are endemic in areas of Southern Europe, Asia, Africa and the Americas.

NATURE

The genus *Leishmania*, along with the genus *Trypanosoma*, belongs to the order Kinetoplastida, which comprises flagellated protozoa that possess a characteristic extranuclear DNA mass called the kinetoplast.

Leishmania parasites are classified into two broad groups:

- New World *Leishmania* spp.; and
- Old World *Leishmania* spp.

Closely related species are grouped into complexes (Table 245.4). Members of *Leishmania braziliensis* complex have been renamed *Leishmania* subgenus *viannia*.

Sandflies are small (3–4mm), hairy mosquito-like insects, and transmit the disease. Old World sandflies belong to the genus *Phlebotomus*; New World species belong to the genera *Lutzomyia* and *Psychodopygus*.[41]

Sandflies become infected when taking a blood meal containing infected macrophages, which are present in blood or skin. Leishmania live in the digestive tract of the insect as flagellated parasites (the promastigote form). The parasites divide in the midgut of the insect except for the *viannia* group, which multiply in the hindgut. The highly motile promastigotes migrate to the buccal cavity of the insect, which regurgitates them on biting, thereby infecting a vertebrate host. Promastigotes rapidly penetrate macrophages and transform into an aflagellated oval body measuring 2–3.5mm across and called an amastigote (literally, without whip). Amastigotes live as obligate intracellular parasites inside the macrophages, where they multiply and are phagocytosed by other mononuclear cells when the host cell ruptures. The infection may disseminate to internal organs, spread locally to mucous membranes or persist as a chronic skin lesion.

EPIDEMIOLOGY

Leishmaniasis is endemic in 88 countries (Fig. 245.7). The world prevalence and annual incidence have been estimated to be 12 and 2 million people, respectively. The incidence of all forms of the disease is steadily increasing.

The vast majority of patients are infected by sandflies, but rare cases in which infection is transmitted by blood transfusion have been reported. Transmission by sharing needles among intravenous drug abusers has been proposed.[42]

PATHOGENICITY

The internalization of leishmania in the macrophage results from the interaction of complement CR3 and fucose–mannose receptors with the parasite major surface protein (Gp63) cysteine proteinases, and membrane lipophosphoglycan. Parasite survival inside the parasitophorous vacuole is facilitated by iron superoxide dismutase and acidic phosphatase secreted by the parasite. In vitro the parasite inhibits inducible nitric oxide synthase activity and nitric oxide production by macrophages. In animal models, susceptibility to infection is mediated by two subsets of $CD4^+$ T cells, named T-helper (Th)1 and Th2:

- Th1 lymphocytes produce IFN-γ, which activates macrophage destruction of parasites; and
- Th2 lymphocytes produce lymphokines, which inhibit Th1 activity and activate an ineffective humoral response.

The $CD8^+$ T cells also play a major protective role. The host's immune system, parasite species and strain-dependent factors interact to create the full spectrum of clinical disease (see Chapter 172).

EPIDEMIOLOGY OF LEISHMANIASIS

Complex	Main species	Reservoir	Geographic distribution	Clinical disease
Leishmania donovani	*L. donovani*	Humans	India, Bangladesh, Burma, Sudan, Kenya, Somalia	VL, PKDL, CL
	L. infantum	Dogs	A belt from Portugal to China	VL, CL
	L. chagasi (infantum)	Foxes, dogs, opossums	South of Mexico to northern South America	VL, CL
Not included in a complex	*L. major*	Rodents	Arid areas north of the Sahara, Arabia and Central Asia, sub-Saharan savanna	CL, LR
	L. tropica	Humans	Towns in East Mediterranean countries, Middle East and central Asia	CL, LR
	L. aethiopica	Hyraxes	Highlands of Ethiopia and Kenya	CL, DCL, MCL
Leishmania mexicana	*L. mexicana*	Forest rodents	Tropical forests of Southern Mexico, Belize and Guatemala	CL (chiclero ulcer)
	L. amazonensis	Forest rodents	Tropical forests of South America	CL, DCL
	L. venezuelensis, L. garnhami, L. pifanoi	Unknown	Venezuela	CL
Leishmania braziliensis	*L. braziliensis*	Forest rodents, domestic animals	Tropical forests of South and Central America	CL, MCL, VL
	L. guyanensis	Sloths, arboreal ant-eaters	Guyana, Surinam, areas of Brazil	CL (forest pian), MCL
	L. panamensis	Sloths	Panama, Costa Rica, Colombia	CL (bejuco ulcer), MCL
	L. peruviana	Dogs	Areas of Peru and Argentina	CL (uta)

Table 245.4 Summary of the epidemiology of leishmaniasis. CL, cutaneous leishmaniasis; DCL, diffuse cutaneous leishmaniasis; LR, leishmaniasis recidivans; MCL, mucocutaneous leishmaniasis; PKDL, post-kala-azar dermal leishmaniasis; VL, visceral leishmaniasis. Common names are in parentheses. Currently, there is no firm concensus on the species classification.

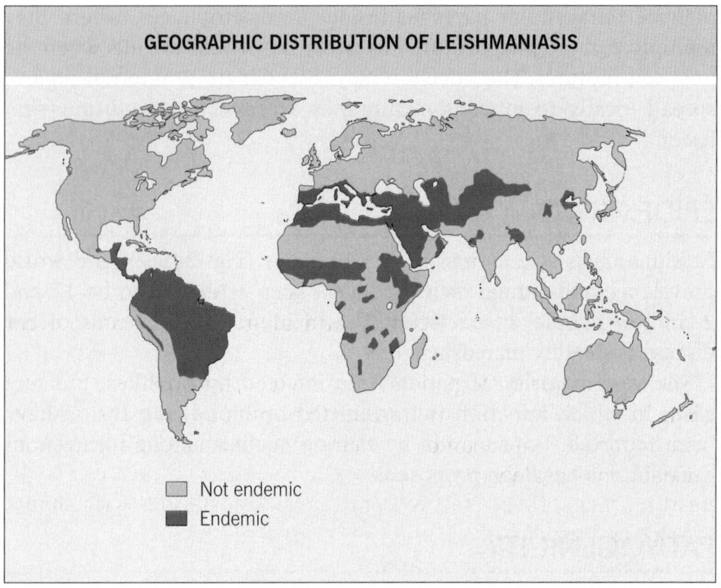

Fig. 245.7 Geographic distribution of leishmaniasis. Visceral leishmaniasis (VL): 90% of cases occur in India, Bangladesh, Sudan and Brazil. Mucocutaneous leishmaniasis (MCL): 90% of cases occur in Bolivia, Brazil and Peru. Cutaneous leishmaniasis (CL): 90% of cases occur in Afghanistan, Brazil, Iran, Peru, Saudi Arabia and Syria.

DIAGNOSTIC MICROBIOLOGY

The laboratory diagnosis can be made by demonstrating *Leishmania* by microscopy or culture, detecting parasite DNA by PCR techniques or demonstrating immune response by serology or leishmanin cutaneous tests.

To study skin lesions, smears can be prepared from the tissue juice of the raised edge of an ulcer. The sample can be aspirated with a needle or scraped with a blade. Parasites can be detected by microscopy or culture in only 30% of cases of leishmaniasis recidivans, 50% of cases of mucocutaneous leishmaniasis (MCL) and 70% of cases of cutaneous leishmaniasis (CL).

In cases of visceral leishmaniasis (VL) sternal bone marrow aspirate is the sample of choice for parasitologic diagnosis (62–100% sensitivity). Splenic fluid aspirate has a higher diagnostic rate (95–100%), but splenic rupture may complicate the procedure. Other samples such as blood, lymph nodes or liver tissue may be of value. To increase positive yield, samples should be routinely cultivated in special media. Species and strain identification can be accomplished by monoclonal antibody staining, PCR and isoenzyme typing.[43]

Serologic testing is useful in the diagnosis of VL and can be of value in cutaneous forms of leishmaniasis. The indirect fluorescent antibody test (IFAT) is sensitive and group specific and its sensitivity is 80–100% in VL patients who do not have HIV infection and 77–89% in MCL. In CL, low titers can occasionally be found. Latex and direct agglutination tests are useful for low-technical testing on field working conditions. Serologic cross-reactivity has been found in the sera of patients who have leprosy, tuberculosis, Chagas' disease, African trypanosomiasis, malaria and schistosomiasis. Refined enzyme-linked immunosorbent assay (ELISA) tests have shown promising results in VL and CL.[44] A proportion of individuals who have HIV infection and VL have persistently negative serology. The IFAT is positive in 22–57% of cases, whereas ELISA combined with IFAT is positive in 55–71% and the Western blot *Leishmania* test is positive in 83% of cases.[45] Polymerase chain reaction testing is superior to bone marrow culture and microscopy.[46] The detection of parasite antigens, that do not depend on serologic response, may eventually prove very useful.

Leishmanin tests (Montenegro reaction) assess cutaneous reactivity against a phenolized promastigote suspension. It is a useful epidemiologic marker of past infection. The test is almost invariably negative in patients who have VL, and in 80% becomes positive 6 months after successful treatment.[47] In localized cutaneous forms the test becomes positive within 3 months of appearance of the lesion and remains positive for life. In diffuse cutaneous leishmaniasis (DCL), this test is universally negative.

CLINICAL MANIFESTATIONS

Most cases of leishmanial infection are probably subclinical. The disease produced can be classified in two groups: VL (also called kala-azar) and CL. Cutaneous disease can be divided into Old World CL, New World CL and MCL. Less frequent forms include DCL, cutaneous recidivans leishmaniasis and post-kala-azar dermal leishmaniasis (PKDL) (see also Chapter 172).

Visceral leishmaniasis

The population at risk includes children under 5 years of age, immunocompromised patients and those who are malnourished. The incubation period is usually 2–8 months. Most patients do not recall having a suggestive skin lesion during the previous months. The onset is usually as an insidious febrile illness, but can be sudden with a high fever and chills. An enlarged spleen and moderately enlarged liver and lymph nodes can be detected on physical examination. As the disease progresses, signs of anemia, ecchymoses and abdominal discomfort become apparent. Anemia is due to splenic sequestration, hemodilution, bone marrow infiltration, hemolysis and bleeding. Thrombocytopenia and leukopenia are also common. In advanced disease, massive spleen enlargement, emaciation, ascites, subcutaneous edema, diarrhea, bleeding and severe anemia develop.

The mortality rate of untreated disease is 85–95%. Intercurrent infections are the cause of death in most cases.

Visceral leishmaniasis in immunocompromised patients

Patients who have HIV infection and immunosuppressed transplant recipients have an increased risk of developing leishmaniasis. In Southern Europe, the prevalence of leishmaniasis among AIDS patients is 2–9%. This represents 10,000 times the rate in the general population.[48] Several years may elapse from exposure to development of the disease. Immunodepressed patients may develop VL when infected with strains that in immunocompetent individuals cause only CL. Atypical manifestations of VL encountered in these patients include localized lesions on bony prominences (Fig. 245.8), tongue, larynx, intestinal tract and lung, and Kaposi's sarcoma. Most of these atypical manifestations have also been recognized in non-AIDS patients who have advanced disease. In immunocompromised patients the disease almost invariably relapses after treatment.[49]

Old World cutaneous leishmaniasis

There are four forms of CL with distinctive clinical and immunologic features.

Oriental sore or localized CL appears on the site of the sandfly bite after approximately 2–4 weeks. The lesion begins as an asymptomatic papule, which enlarges and forms a well-circumscribed ulcer with a raised violaceous border. The lesion spontaneously resolves over a period of months, leaving a depressed scar. Three species produce most cases: *Leishmania tropica*, *Leishmania major* and *Leishmania aethiopica*.

Leishmaniasis recidivans presents as a chronic skin lesion that appears on the skin areas where an oriental sore has been. It has also been called 'chronic relapsing CL' and 'chronic lupoid leishmaniasis' because it closely resembles lupus vulgaris both clinically and histologically.[50]

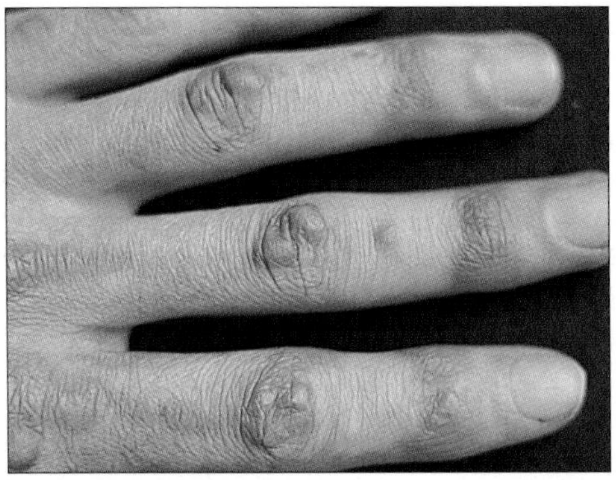

Fig, 245.8 Cutaneous manifestation of kala-azar in AIDS.

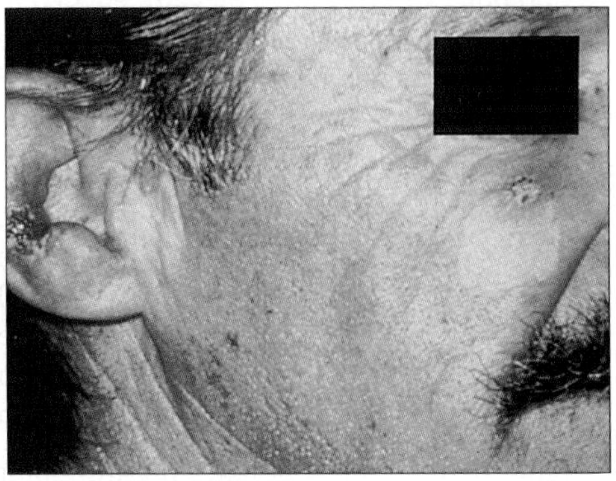

Fig. 245.9 New World cutaneous leishmaniasis.

Diffuse cutaneous leishmaniasis is a rare form of diffuse skin infection characterized by heavy parasitization of skin macrophages and absence of an effective cellular response. The lesions do not ulcerate.

Post-kala-azar dermal leishmaniasis consists of symmetric macules or nodules on the face and sometimes on the trunk and extremities of patients who have had VL.

New World cutaneous leishmaniasis

Cutaneous leishmaniasis and MCL in the Americas take several clinical forms. The most notorious are chiclero ulcer, uta, cutaneous diseases caused by *Leishmania (Viannia) braziliensis* and MCL.

Chiclero ulcer caused by *Leishmania mexicana* was originally seen in latex (chicle) collectors who entered the forest. The lesion appears as a destructive ulcer of the pinna of the ear or the face and progresses over months (Fig. 245.9).

In uta, a disease of young children caused by *Leishmania peruviana*, the skin ulcer heals in 3–6 months leaving a disfiguring scar, usually on the face.

The cutaneous diseases caused by *Leishmania (viannia) braziliensis* complex consists usually of multiple shallow ulcers that have a tendency to metastasize along the lymphatic vessels. They evolve to mucocutaneous disease in 5% of cases. Untreated, such diseases persist for years. Relapses after treatment are common.

Mucocutaneous leishmaniasis, a markedly disfiguring, life-threatening disease, is typically caused by *L. braziliensis* and appears during the first 10 years after resolution of cutaneous disease. It consists of a pseudotumoral destructive lesion. It usually starts in the nasal mucosa and spreads to oronasopharyngeal mucosa, larynx and skin of the lips and nose. Death may be due to pneumonia, laryngeal obstruction, secondary sepsis or starvation. Spontaneous cure is rare and response to therapy is poor. Differential diagnoses include carcinoma, syphilis, yaws, rhinoscleroma and rhinosporidiasis.

MANAGEMENT

Treatment schemes can be divided in two groups – those applied to localized CL and those for extensive disease (VL, MCL and DCL).

Most cutaneous sores will slowly resolve spontaneously providing lifelong immunity. Indications for treatment are infection by *L. braziliensis* complex and sores in potentially disabling sites. Surgical excision and cryotherapy are suitable for small lesions. Heating at 131°F (55°C) for 5 minutes using infrared radiation cured 90% of cases of oriental sores.[51] Infiltration of the sore with antimonials is also effective: 0.5–1.5ml of parenteral solution is carefully injected into the edges and base of the ulcer and three doses are given 3 days apart. Systemic treatment is recommended for all forms of *L. v. braziliensis* complex infections (see Chapter 172).

Alternative treatments include topical aminosidine (paromomycin) ointment (once daily for 1 month), ketoconazole (600mg/day for 4 weeks), dapsone (200mg/day for 4 weeks) and oral allopurinol (5mg/kg q6h) plus probenecid (500mg q6h) for 1 month. Some immune enhancing methods have also been found to be effective.[52]

For VL pentavalent antimonials have been the first choice of treatment for years. There are two commercial preparations with similar efficacy and toxicity:

- meglumine antimoniate, and
- stibogluconate sodium.

The recommended dosage of antimony is 20mg/kg/day. The duration of treatment is 1 month for VL and 2–3 months for DCL and PKDL. If the patient is not thrombocytopenic, intramuscular administration is recommended. Intravenous drug should be infused over 2 hours to prevent cardiac arrhythmia. If higher doses are used, cardiac monitoring is needed. Serum amylase concentration should be periodically measured because pancreatitis is frequently seen in patients who have HIV infection. Other common side-effects are arthralgia, myalgia, an exfoliative rash and abdominal cramps. In Bihar state (India) antimonial resistance is now widespread. The membrane of leishmania amastigotes contains ergosterol. For this reason, antifungals that interfere with the ergosterol pathway can be used in leishmaniasis. Amphotericin B deoxycholate, and meglumine have similar rates of initial cure, and relapse-free intervals differing in the type of toxicity.[53]

New lipid-associated amphotericin compounds are theoretically targeted against leishmania because the amphotericin B-lipid complexes are cleared from blood by the monocellular/macrophagic system where the parasite persists. None of these preparations has been tested against conventional amphotericin B, but as the treatment is of shorter duration and toxicity is diminished, it will probably be preferred where costs are not a major factor.[54,55] Present recommended cumulated dosage of liposomal amphotericin B is at least 18mg/kg (3mg/kg per day for 5 days, followed by 3mg/kg on day 10).[56]

Parenteral administration of aminosidine, a toxic aminoglycoside with parasiticidal activity has been used combined with antimonials for antimonial-resistant strains after amphotericin failure. Miltephosin (an alkyl phospholipid derivative developed as a treatment for breast cancer) is a new promising oral treatment.[57]

Continuous suppressive treatment with one dose of antimonials every 2–4 weeks is indicated for patients who have HIV infection and leishmaniasis after a full course of treatment.[58] Amphotericin every 2–4 weeks has also been used. Pentamidine might prevent relapses when used as prophylaxis against *Pneumocystis carinii* infection. When suppressive therapy was discontinued after successful antiretroviral therapy relapses were observed only in patients with CD4 counts under 350 cells/mm^3.[59]

TRYPANOSOMIASIS

Trypanosomes produce two clinically and epidemiologically different diseases that are presented separately:

- American trypanosomiasis or Chagas' disease, and
- African trypanosomiasis or sleeping sickness.

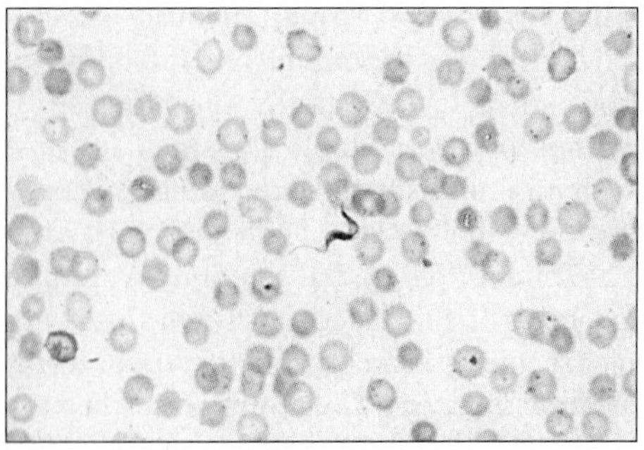

Fig. 245.10 ***Trypanosoma brucei.*** Note the central nucleon, an undulating membrane and a clump of mitochondrial DNA called kinetoplast.

FEATURES OF HUMAN TRYPANOSOMIASIS			
	Trypanosoma brucei gambiense, Trypanosoma brucei rhodesiense	*Trypanosoma cruzi*	*Trypanosoma rangeli*
Geographic distribution	Africa	Central and South America	
Name of disease produced	Sleeping sickness	Chagas' disease	Nonpathogenic
Main affected organ	Brain	Heart, colon, esophagus	None
Vector (common name)	*Glossina* spp. (tsetse fly)	Reduviidae (kissing bugs)	
Mode of transmission	Bite (insect saliva)	Insect feces	Bite (insect saliva)
Multiplying form in humans	Trypomastigote	Amastigote	Trypomastigote

Table 245.5 Features of different types of human trypanosomiasis.

When a human host is infected the organisms multiply in the inoculation area, then pass into the blood, and in a third phase they localize in some internal organs causing chronic disease.

Trypanosomes pass through the morphologic stages of amastigote and trypomastigote (Fig. 245.10). The differences between the species that can be found in humans are summarized in Table 245.5.

CHAGAS' DISEASE (AMERICAN TRYPANOSOMIASIS)

Chagas' disease is named after Carlos Chagas, who discovered *Trypanosoma cruzi* and described its life cycle and the clinical features of the disease.

The disease starts as an acute febrile illness followed by a long asymptomatic period and a chronic symptomatic stage characterized by distention and abnormal function of the heart and gastrointestinal tract.

Epidemiology

Chagas' disease is endemic in most Latin American countries. Low-income families of rural areas are most frequently affected and up to 20% of the population have the infection in the most affected regions. The WHO estimates that there are 16–18 million people who currently have the infection and that 2–3 million of them have chronic disease. It causes more than 45,000 deaths/year (see Chapter 173).

Pathogenicity

Hemipterous insects of the Reduviidae family (kissing bugs) are responsible for transmission. The parasite has a sylvatic cycle maintained by reduviids that feed on opossums and other wild animals, and which occasionally bite humans. It may also persist in a domestic cycle maintained by reduviids that live in the cracks of mud huts, feeding on humans, house rodents and domestic animals. In some areas, these two cycles overlap. As asymptomatic individuals may harbor a low number of parasites in their blood for many years, transmission by blood product transfusion is a major cause for concern. Oral transmission through breast milk or contaminated food and transplacental transmission are less common routes of infection.

Triatomid bugs infect when taking a blood meal from a host infected by *T. cruzi*. The parasite develops in the gut of the insect and infective trypomastigotes are released with insect feces. *Triatoma* spp. bugs bite humans at night and defecate soon after they are engorged, contaminating the skin with trypomastigotes that penetrate through skin erosions or mucosal surfaces (typically the conjunctiva). The parasite multiplies inside cells as amastigotes. Some amastigotes differentiate into trypomastigotes, which disseminate through the circulation and may eventually be eaten by a reduviid bug.

Although the histopathology of Chagas' disease is characteristic, the pathophysiologic mechanism that leads to these changes is not clearly understood. As a result of an inflammatory process (and perhaps a neurotoxin) the conducting system of the heart and the myenteric plexus are damaged. The mononuclear cell response gradually controls the infection, but does not usually eradicate it. In the late stages of the disease, only small numbers of parasites are found in cardiac muscle and the gastrointestinal tract, and autoimmune phenomena are probably responsible for the continuous progression of heart muscle damage. Neuronal depletion of the myenteric plexus leads to asynchronous peristaltic movement and, in the most severe cases, the esophagus, colon and other internal ducts dilate to enormous size.

Prevention

General improvement in housing standards or at least the use of noncracking plaster and the regular use of residual insecticides is recommended to eliminate domestic vectors. In endemic countries, blood donations should be serologically screened for trypanosome infection. Where this is not feasible, the addition of gentian violet to a bag of blood will 'trypanosome-sterilize' it.[60]

Diagnostic microbiology

Direct parasitologic diagnosis can be obtained by visualizing the parasite in blood or tissue, demonstrating it in culture or by xenodiagnosis. Conventional serology and PCR are especially useful for patients who have undetectable parasitemia.

Parasitemia is usually detectable in the acute phase of disease by staining the buffy coat. Needle aspiration or slit-skin smear of cutaneous inoculation lesions may be positive. The parasite can also be grown in leishmanial culture media.

Xenodiagnosis is the most sensitive method of parasite demonstration.[61] Fasted, laboratory-reared, triatomid bugs are placed in a box with a gauze on one side. The box is briefly applied to the forearm of the subject to let the bugs feed. After 10–30 days, the parasite can be found in the intestinal contents of the bugs. In acute disease xenodiagnosis is nearly always positive, but in the chronic stage of disease it is positive in only half of the patients tested.

Serology is a reliable and sensitive method of diagnosis. It usually becomes positive 1 month after infection and remains positive for life.[62] The presence of antibodies that bind to the epitopes of living trypomastigotes (called lytic antibodies) is indicative of persisting infection. Cross-reactivity exists with leishmaniasis, malaria, toxoplasmosis, pemphigus foliaceus, infectious mononucleosis and *Trypanosoma rangeli* and mycobacterial infections.

Newly developed PCR techniques may be especially useful in defining parasitologic cure, diagnosing indeterminate-stage patients and assessing suspected cross-reacting serology or combined infections.[63]

Clinical manifestations

The disease evolves through three different clinical stages: acute infection, asymptomatic period and chronic disease (see Chapter 173).

Acute infection is symptomatic in only one-third of those infected. The severity and intensity of signs are greatest in younger patients, but the prevalence of infection increases with age. Symptomatic patients may develop an inflammatory nodule at the site of inoculation and an enlarged satellite lymph node. A characteristic feature is the presence of periocular edema due to conjunctival inoculation of *T. cruzi* (Romaña's sign). Manifestations of acute disease are fever, generalized lymphadenopathy, moderate hepatosplenomegaly, erythematous rash and myocarditis. Most patients survive the acute stage and gradually become asymptomatic within a few months. Congenitally infected newborns present with myocarditis or meningoencephalitis and usually die within days.

The indeterminate form is the asymptomatic period during which the infection can only be detected by serologic methods, although some degree of esophageal dysfunction or cardiac disease may be found when appropriate diagnostic methods are used.

The chronic symptomatic stage is characterized by the chagasic megasyndromes that develop in one-third of those infected, usually 5–15 years after infection (Figs 245.11 and 245.12). Chronic cardiomyopathy is eventually present in 27%, digestive manifestations in 6% and neurologic disorders in 3% of infected individuals.

Congestive heart failure, arrhythmias and embolic disease characterize chagasic cardiomyopathy,[64] which is the most common cause of death in Chagas' disease. The presence of any of these conditions with suggestive epidemiologic data strongly suggest *T. cruzi* infection.

Esophageal disorders include achalasia, cardiospasm and enlargement. Megacolon results in constipation and abdominal pain. Associated complications include esophagitis, esophageal hemorrhage, esophageal cancer, volvulus and obstructive intestinal disease.

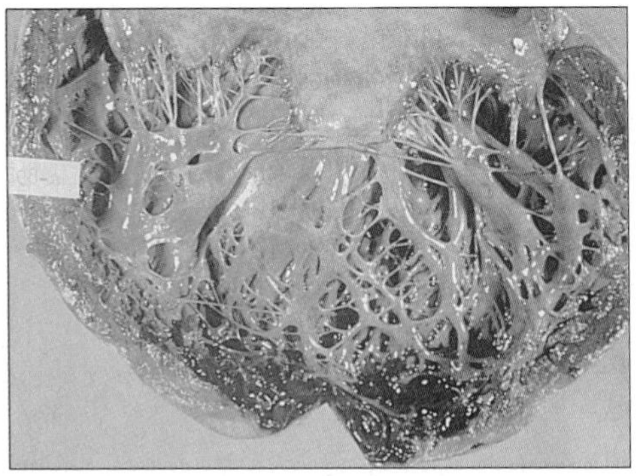

Fig. 245.11 A dilated heart from a fatal case of chagasic cardiomyopathy. Chronic heart disease is the commonest cause of death in Chagas' disease. Courtesy of Dr J Cohen, Cordoba, Argentina.

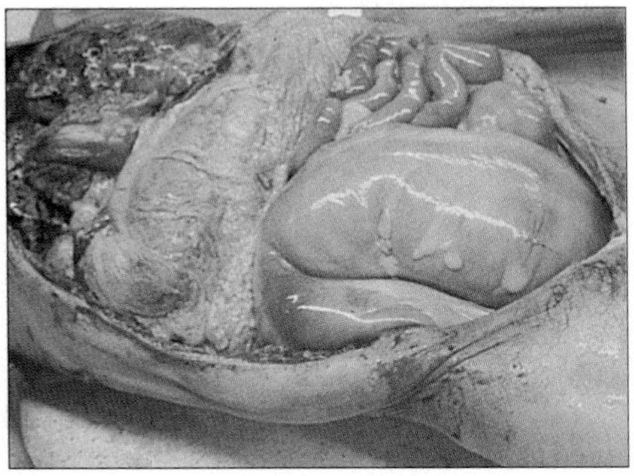

Fig. 245.12 Chagasic megacolon at autopsy. Grossly enlarged colon as shown here or other duct dilatation is characteristic of chronic Chagas' disease. Courtesy of Dr J Cohen, Cordoba, Argentina.

Latent disease reactivates in immunocompromised patients. In one series of AIDS patients who had Chagas' disease, 87% developed encephalitis and 21% acute myocarditis.[65]

Management

Antiparasitic therapy is clearly recommended only for the acute forms and parasitemic immunocompromised patients. Nifurtimox and benznidazole are the only two parasiticidal drugs used against *T. cruzi* (see Chapter 173).

Nifurtimox is seldom available. Benznidazole dosage is 7.5mg/kg up to 5g/day q12–24h given for 2 months. Some preliminary data suggest that the use of benznidazole in the early chronic stages and the use of allopurinol (600–900mg/day for 2 months) in chagasic heat disease may be beneficial.[66] Chagas' disease has traditionally been considered to be a contraindication for heart transplantation, but with the use of a low ciclosporin dosage, 80% survival at 24 months has been achieved.[67] Esophageal disease is treated with cardiac dilatation in early cases. Surgery is reserved for severe esophageal or colonic dilatation.

INFECTION BY *TRYPANOSOMA RANGELI*

Trypanosoma rangeli is an American parasite transmitted by triatomids. In some areas of Central America, human parasitization by *T. rangeli* is six times more frequent than that by *T. cruzi*. Although regarded as nonpathogenic to humans, it is medically important as a source of misdiagnosis of Chagas' disease.

AFRICAN TRYPANOSOMIASIS

Two African trypanosomes of the *T. brucei* complex infect humans:

- *Trypanosoma brucei gambiense,* which usually produces chronic infections; and
- *Trypanosoma brucei rhodesiense,* which tends to produce a more acute disease.

After an initial stage of parasitization restricted to the bloodstream, some individuals develop encephalitis. One of its most striking symptoms is a somnolence/insomnia disorder after which the disease was named 'sleeping sickness' (see Chapter 157).

Epidemiology

The vector of *T. brucei* subspecies is a fly of the genus *Glossina* (tsetse fly), which is geographically confined to tropical Africa. The incidence of the disease is unknown, but may be around 200,000 cases/year.

Several *Trypanosoma* spp. infect wild and domestic animals and the infection is an important economic problem.

Trypanosoma b. rhodesiense is transmitted by *Glossina morsitans*. This fly lives in the dry savannas of East Africa, feeding mainly on the wild ungulates, which represent the main reservoir. *Trypanosoma b. gambiense* is endemic in West Africa. Humans are considered to be the main reservoir. Transmission usually occurs in the shaded riverine areas where *Glossina palpalis* and *Glossina tachinoides* live and breed.

Trypanosoma brucei brucei is an animal pathogen that is unable to infect humans.

Nature

The vector fly is infected when taking a blood meal containing trypanosomes. The ingested parasites transform and multiply in the insect midgut and migrate to the salivary glands from where new hosts are infected by biting. In the human host the parasite multiplies asexually in the interstitial space and spreads through the lymphatic vessels to the lymph nodes and blood.

On human blood smears, two different morphologies can be observed:

- a short, stumpy form that is infective for *Glossina* spp; and
- a slender, actively multiplying, flagellated form.

Amastigote forms are not usually seen.

Pathogenicity

The parasite can produce hundreds of antigenically different surface glycoproteins serially. This process enables it to elude the host immune response, resulting in a characteristic fluctuating parasitemia pattern throughout the course of infection. After a variable period, the parasite reaches the CNS, causing meningitis and choroid plexus breakdown. Large amounts of IgM are produced in the serum and CSF. Characteristic plasmacytic morular cells can be seen in tissues, blood, bone marrow and CSF. Autoimmune phenomena, circulating immune complex deposition and increased vessel permeability play an important role in pathogenesis (see Chapter 157).

Prevention

Massive clearance of *Glossina* spp. habitats, insecticide spraying, destruction of wild game, periodic mass treatment and enforced relocation of entire populations were successfully used in the past. A more recent development for control is the use of *Glossina* spp.-attracting traps. Active surveillance is recommended periodically in areas of *T. b. gambiense* and during epidemics in *T. b. rhodesiense* areas. Travelers visiting endemic areas should be warned of the type of activities that may increase the chances of being bitten by tsetse flies and report any possible exposure. Mosquito repellents may be useful.

Diagnostic microbiology

The diagnosis of the disease essentially depends upon the careful microscopic examination of blood or CSF samples. Given the fluctuating nature of parasitemia, daily samples should be taken for 2 weeks to rule out parasitemia. Lymph node and bone marrow aspiration may be positive in cases with a low parasitemia. In-vitro culture and miniature anion exchange column test are also feasible. Serologic tests to detect antibodies against invariant surface antigens or against the most prevalent variant surface glycoproteins and PCR testing are available in some reference laboratories.

Clinical manifestations

In African trypanosomiasis, the disease develops in two stages:

- a hemolymphatic stage that spares the nervous system; and
- a second stage defined by CNS involvement.

The disease produced by *T. b. gambiense* usually develops chronically whereas in *T. b. rhodesiense* infection the disease tend to be more acute, without a clear distinction between stages.

An infective bite by a *Glossina* spp. fly may produce an inoculation chancre. Within days or weeks, the parasite disseminates to the blood. In the Gambian form of the disease, an enlarged neck lymph node may be present (Winterbottom's sign) and the patient may remain asymptomatic for years. In the hemolymphatic stage, the symptoms may be few and non-specific: undulant fever, headache, malaise, weight loss, anemia, edema, arthralgia, diarrhea and pruritus.

On physical examination there may be erythematous circinate papules on the trunk, disproportionate pain to soft tissue pressure (Kerandel's sign) and discrete enlargement of lymph nodes, liver and spleen. Pancarditis is common in the more acute forms, when it constitutes a major cause of death. Some degree of anemia, thrombocytopenia, leukocytosis, hypogonadism, renal disease and thymus atrophy may be seen.

The CNS manifestation that gave the disease its name is the disappearance of the circadian distribution of sleep and wakefulness, which are therefore fragmented throughout the day and night.[68] Other CNS manifestations include altered reflexes, paresthesiae, pareses, dyskinesia, choreoathetosis, epilepsy, slurred speech, mood changes, lethargy, delirium and psychosis. Without treatment, nearly all patients will develop neural involvement and die (see also Chapter 157).

Management

The choice of antiparasitic drug will depend upon whether the CNS is infected. Pentamidine or suramin can be used when the CNS is spared from infection. Melarsoprol and eflornithine are effective for both hemolymphatic and neural stages. Suramin dosage is 20mg/kg/day (maximum 1500mg), one intravenous injection every 5 days for 25 days. *Onchocerca volvulus* co-infection should be ruled out or treated before treatment of trypanosomiasis. Pentamidine dosage is 4mg/kg/day, one dose every second day for 20 days. *Trypanosoma b. rhodesiense* and some strains of *T. b. gambiense* do not respond to pentamidine.

Melarsoprol, a toxic trivalent arsenical derivative, has been the treatment of choice for patients who have CNS involvement for five decades. A number of empiric, dosing schemes have been used.[69] Relapse after treatment occurs in up to 6% of cases. Arsenic-related encephalopathy occurs in 10% of cases and prednisone treatment may reduce its incidence. The mortality rate of this side-effect largely depends upon the supportive treatment available, but is generally above 50%.[70]

Eflornithine (α-difluoromethylornithine) is an inhibitor of polyamine biosynthesis. Adult dosage is 400mg/kg/day in four divided doses for 1–4 weeks. Although it is less toxic than melarsoprol, drug shortages, high costs and the lack of comparative studies have relegated its use to a second-choice therapy.

General supportive treatment, anticonvulsant preventive therapy, and early recognition and treatment of associated parasitic and bacterial infections are essential.

With adequate treatment, most extraneural disease is cured. In the presence of CNS infection, cure rates are above 80%. All treated patients should be carefully followed up twice yearly for at least 3 years.

REFERENCES

1. Wilson ME. A world guide to infections, diseases, distributions, diagnoses. Oxford: Oxford University Press; 1991.
2. Lobel HO, Miani M, Eng T, Bernard KW, Hightower AW, Campbell CC. Long-term malaria prophylaxis with weekly mefloquine. Lancet 1993;341:848–51.
3. Nosten F, Kuile F, Maelankiri L, *et al.* Mefloquine prophylaxis prevents malaria during pregnancy: a double blind placebo-controlled study. J Infect Dis 1994;169:595–603.
4. Centers for Disease Control and Prevention. Health information for international travel 2001–2002. US Department of Health and Human Services. Washington DC: US Printing Office; 2001.
5. Wongsrichanalai C, Pornsilapatip J, Namsiripongpun V, *et al.* Acridine orange fluorescent microscopy and the detection of malaria populations with low-density parasitemia. Am J Trop Med Hyg 1991;44:17–20.
6. Abdullah NR, Furuta T, Taib R, Kita K, Kojima S, Wah MJ. Short report: development of a new diagnostic method for *Plasmodium falciparum* infection using a reverse transcriptase-polymerase chain reaction. Am J Trop Med Hyg 1996;54:162–3.
7. Schindler HC, Montenegro L, Montenegro R, Carvalho AB, Abath FG, Jaureguiberry G. Development and optimization of polymerase chain reaction-based malaria diagnostic methods and their comparison with quantitative

buffy coat assay. Am J Trop Med Hyg 2001;65:355–61.
8. Moody A. Rapid diagnostic tests for malaria parasites. Clin Microbiol Rev 2002;15:66–78.
9. Watt G, Loesuttiviboon L, Long GW. Prospective comparison of methods for the early prediction of treatment failure in patients with falciparum malaria. Clin Infect Dis 1995;21:1026–8.
10. Moody A, Hunt-Cooke A, Gabbett E, Chiodini P. Performance of the OptiMAL® malaria antigen capture dipstick for malaria diagnosis and treatment monitoring at the Hospital for Tropical Diseases, London. Br J Haematol 2000;109:891–4.
11. White NJ. Malaria. In: Cook GC, ed. Manson's tropical diseases. London: WB Saunders; 1996:1087.
12. World Health Organization. Division Control of Tropical Diseases: severe and complicated malaria. Trans R Soc Trop Med Hyg 1990;84(Suppl.2):1–65.
13. Brewester D, Kwiatosky D, White NJ. Neurological sequelae of cerebral malaria in childhood. Lancet 1990;336:1039–43.
14. Fakunle YM, Crane GG. Tropical splenomegaly. Clin Haematol 1981;10:963–82.
15. Soto J, Toledo J, Gutiérrez P, *et al. Plasmodium vivax* clinically resistant to chloroquine in Colombia. Am J Trop Med Hyg 2001;65:90–3.
16. Speich R, Haller A. Central anticholinergic syndrome with the antimalarial drug mefloquine. N Engl J Med 1994;331:57–8
17. de Alencar FE, Cerutti C Jr, Durlacher RR, *et al.* Atovaquone and proguanil for the treatment of malaria in Brazil. J Infect Dis 1997;175:1544–7.
18. Hensbroeck MB, Onyiorah E, Jaffar S, *et al.* A trial of artemether or quinine in children with cerebral malaria. N Engl J Med 1996;335:69–75.
19. Tran TH, Day NPJ, Nguyen HP, *et al.* A controlled trial of artemether or quinine in Vietnamese adults with severe falciparum malaria. N Engl J Med 1996;335:76–83.
20. Warrell DA, Looareesuwan S, Warrel MJ, *et al.* Dexamethasone proves deleterious in cerebral malaria: a double blind trial in 100 comatose patients. N Engl J Med 1982;306:313–9.
21. Persing DH, Herwalt BL, Glaser C, *et al.* Infection with a *Babesia*-like organism in northern California. N Engl J Med 1995;332:298–303.
22. Hunfeld KP, Lambert A, Kampen H, *et al.* Seroprevalence of *Babesia* infections in humans exposed to ticks in midwestern Germany. J Clin Microbiol 2002;40:2431–6.
23. Krause PJ, Telford S RI , Ryan R, *et al.* Diagnosis of babesiosis: evaluation of a serologic test for the detection of *Babesia microti* antibody. J Infect Dis 1994;169:923–6.
24. Homer MJ, Aguilar-Delfin I, Telford SR 3rd, Krause PJ, Persing DH. Babesiosis. Clin Microbiol Rev 2000;13:451–69.
25. Krause PJ, Lepore T, Sikand VK, *et al.* Atovaquone and azithromycin for the treatment of babesiosis. N Engl J Med 2000;343:1454–8.
26. Trenter A, Heckeroth AR, Weiss LM. *Toxoplasma gondii*: from animals to humans. Int J Parasitol. 2000;30:1217–58.
27. McCabe R, Remington JS. Toxoplasmosis: the time has come. N Engl J Med 1988;318:313–5.
28. Jeannel D, Costagliola, Niel G, Hubert B, Danis M. What is known about the prevention of congenital toxoplasmosis? Lancet 1990;336:359–61.
29. Derouin F, Mazeron MC, Garin YKF. Comparative study of tissue culture and mouse inoculation methods for demonstration of *Toxoplasma gondii*. J Clin Microbiol 1987;25:1597–600.
30. Brooks RG, McCabe RE, Remington JS. Role of serology in the diagnosis of toxoplasmic lymphadenopathy. Rev Infect Dis 1987;9:775–82.
31. Welch PC, Masur H, Jones TC, *et al.* Serologic diagnosis of acute lymphadenopathic toxoplasmosis. J Infect Dis 1980;142:256–64.
32. Desmonts G, Couvreur J. Toxoplasmosis in pregnancy and its transmission to the foetus. Bull NY Acad Med 1974;50:146–59.
33. McCabe RE, Brooks R, Dorfman RF, Remington JS. Clinical spectrum in 107 cases of toxoplasmic lymphadenopathy. Rev Infect Dis 1987;9:754–74.
34. Speirs GE, Hakim TG, Calne RY, *et al.* Relative risk of donor acquired *Toxoplasma gondii* in heart, liver and kidney transplant recipients. Clin Transplant 1988;2:257–60.
35. Wreigt TG, Harkiin M, Gray JJ, *et al.* Toxoplasmosis in heart lung transplant recipients. J Clin Pathol 1989;42:194–9.
36. Daffos F, Forestier F, Capella-Paulousky M, *et al.* Prenatal management of 746 pregnancies at risk for congenital toxoplasmosis. N Engl J Med 1988;318:271–5.
37. Couvreur J, Desmonts G, Thulliez P. Prophylaxis of congenital toxoplasmosis. Effects of spiramycin on placental infection J Antimicrob Chemother 1988;22:193–200.
38. McAuley J, Boyer K, Patel D, *et al.* Early and longitudinal evaluations of treated infants and children and untreated historical patients with congenital toxoplasmosis: the Chicago collaborative treatment trial. Clin infect Dis 1994;18:38–72.
39. Hohlfield P, Daffos F, Costa JM, Thuliez P, Forestier F, Vidaud M. Prenatal diagnosis of congenital toxoplasmosis with a polymerase chain-reaction test on amniotic fluid. N Engl J Med 1994;331:695–9.
40. Berrebi A, Kobuch WE, Bessieres MH. Termination of pregnancy for maternal toxoplasmosis. Lancet 1994;344:36–9.
41. Lane RP. Sandflies (Phlebotominae). In: Lane RP, Crosskey RW, eds. Medical insects and arachnids. London: Chapman and Hall; 1993:78–119.
42. Cruz I, Morales MA, Noguer I, Rodriguez A, Alvar J. Leishmania in discarded syringes from intravenous drug users. Lancet 2002;359:1124–5.
43. Rodriguez N, Guzman B, Rodas A, Takiff H, Bloom BR, Convit J. Diagnosis of cutaneous leishmaniasis and species discrimination of parasites by PCR and hybridization. J Clin Microbiol 1994;32:2246–52.
44. Ryan JR, Smithyman AM, Rajasekariah GH, *et al.* Enzyme-linked immunosorbent assay based on soluble promastigote antigen detects immunoglobulin M (IgM) and IgG antibodies in sera from cases of visceral and cutaneous leishmaniasis. J Clin Microbiol 2002;40:1037–43.
45. Gary-Toussaint M, Leliévre A, Marty P, Le Fichoux Y. Contribution of serological tests to the diagnosis of visceral leishmaniasis in patients infected with the human immunodeficiency virus. Trans R Soc Trop Med Hyg 1994;88:301–2.
46. Piarroux R, Gambarelli F, Dumon H, *et al.* Comparison of PCR with direct examination of bone marrow aspiration, myeloculture, and serology for diagnosis of visceral leishmaniasis in immunocompromised patients. J Clin Microbiol 1994;32:746–9.
47. Zijlstra EE, El Hasan AM. Leishmanin and tuberculin sensitivity in Sudan with especial reference to kala azar. Trans R Soc Trop Med Hyg 1993;87:425–7.
48. Alvar J. Leishmaniasis and AIDS coinfection: the Spanish example. Parasitol Today 1994;10:160–3.
49. Pintado V, Martin-Rabadan P, Rivera ML, *et al.* Visceral leishmaniasis in human immunodeficiency virus (HIV)-infected and non-HIV-infected patients. A comparative study. Medicine (Baltimore) 2001;80:54–73.
50. Momeni AZ, Yotsumoto S, Mehran DR, *et al.* Chronic lupoid leishmaniasis. Evaluation by polymerase chain reaction. Arch Dermatol 1996:132:198–202.
51. Junaid AJN. Treatment of cutaneous leishmaniasis with infrared heat. Int J Dermatol 1986;25:470–2.
52. Convit J, Castellanos PL, Rondon A, *et al.* Immunotherapy versus chemotherapy in localized cutaneous leishmaniasis. Lancet 1987;8530:401–5.
53. Laguna F, Lopez-Velez R, Pulido F, *et al.* Treatment of visceral leishmaniasis in HIV-infected patients: a randomized trial comparing meglumine antimoniate with amphotericin B. Spanish HIV–Leishmania Study Group. AIDS 1999;13:1063–9.
54. Sundar S, Agrawal NK, Sinha PR, Horwith GS, Murray HW. Short-course, low-dose amphotericin B lipid complex therapy for visceral leishmaniasis unresponsive to antimony. Ann Intern Med 1997;127:133–7.
55. Dietze R, Fagundes SM, Brito EF, *et al.* Treatment of kala-azar in Brazil with Amphocil (amphotericin B cholesterol dispersion) for five days. Trans R Soc Trop Med Hyg 1995;89:309–11.
56. di Martino L, Davidson RN, Giacchino R, *et al.* Treatment of visceral leishmaniasis in children with liposomal amphotericin Br J Pediatr 1997;131:271–7.
57. Sundar S, Makharia A, More DK, *et al.* Short-course of oral miltefosine for treatment of visceral leishmaniasis. Clin Infect Dis. 2000;31:1110–3.
58. Ribera E, Ocaña I, de Otero J, *et al.* Prophylaxis of visceral leishmaniasis in human immunodeficiency virus-infected patients. Am J Med 1996;100:496–501.
59. Berenguer J, Cosin J, Miralles P, Lopez JC, Padilla B. Discontinuation of secondary anti-leishmania prophylaxis in HIV-infected patients who have responded to highly active antiretroviral therapy. AIDS 2000;14:2946–8.
60. Ramirez LE, Lages-Silva E, Pianetti GM, Rabelo RM, Bordin JO, Moares-Souza H. Prevention of transfusion-associated Chagas' disease by sterilization of *Trypanosoma cruzi*-infected blood with gentian violet, ascorbic acid and light. Transfusion 1995;35:226–30.
61. Marsden PD. *Dipetalogaster maxima* or *D. maximus* as a xenodiagnostic agent. Rev Soc Bras Med Trop 1986;19:205–7.
62. García E, Ramirez LE, Monteón V, Sotelo J. Diagnosis of American trypanosomiasis (Chagas' disease) by the new complement fixation test. J Clin Microbiol 1995;33:1034–5.
63. Britto C, Cardoso A, Vanni CM, *et al.* Polymerase chain reaction detection of *Trypanosoma cruzi* in human blood samples as a tool for diagnosis and treatment evaluation. Parasitology 1995;110:241–7.
64. Nogueira N, Rodrigues J. American trypanosomiasis (Chagas' disease). In: Warren KS, Mahmoud AAF, eds. Tropical and geographical medicine. New York: McGraw-Hill; 1990:281–96.
65. Rocha A, Meneses AC, da Silva AM, *et al.* Pathology of patients with Chagas' disease and acquired immunodeficiency syndrome. Am J Trop Med Hyg 1994;50:261–8.
66. Rodriques Coura J, de Castro SL. A critical review on Chagas disease chemotherapy. Mem Inst Oswaldo Cruz 2002;97:3–24.
67. Bocchi EA, Bellotti G, Mocelin AO, *et al.* Heart transplantation for chronic Chagas' heart disease. Ann Thorac Surg 1996;61:1727–33.
68. Buget A, Bert J, Tapie P, *et al.* Distribution du sommeil et de la veille dans la trypanosomiasi humaine africaine. Bull Soc Pathol Exot 1994;85:362–7.
69. Blum J, Burri C. Treatment of late stage sleeping sickness caused by *T.b. gambiense*: a new approach to the use of an old drug. Swiss Med Wkly 2002;132:51–6.
70. Pépin J, Milord F, Guern C, Mpia B, Ethier L, Mansinsa D. Trial of prednisolone for prevention of melarsoprol induced-encephalopathy in gambiense sleeping sickness. Lancet 1989;8649:1246–9.

chapter

246 Helminths

John H Cross

Helminths are the most common parasites infecting humans. The world population is over six billion and there are probably a similar number of helminthic infections occurring in humans. They are transmitted to humans by food, water, soil and arthropod and molluscan vectors. Once established, they can be found in all organs, particularly intestines but also in liver, lungs, blood and occasionally in brain and other organs. This chapter describes some of these worms, their biology, epidemiology, pathogenicity, clinical aspects, diagnosis, management and prevention.

NATURE

The word helminth comes from the Greek meaning worm and refers to all types of worms, both free-living and parasitic. The major parasitic worms are found primarily in two major phyla:

- the Nematoda or roundworms; and
- the Platyhelminthes or flatworms, which are divided into the Trematoda or flukes and the Cestoda or tapeworms (Table 246.1).

Structurally the helminths have an outer covering called a cuticle or tegument. It may be tough or delicate and essentially protects the organism, especially from digestion, while in the host intestinal tract. This structure may also possess spines, hooks, cutting plates and stylets used for attachment or to aid in penetration. There are also suckers or acetabula used by the flatworms for attachment. Some species have lytic glands near the mouth and the secretions digest host tissue for food or lyse tissues during migration.

The helminths have digestive systems of various types, excretory systems and massive reproductive systems. Most of the trematodes are hermaphroditic, one worm possessing both male and female reproductive organs; the schistosomes, on the other hand, have separate sexes. Each segment of a tapeworm has both male and female sex organs, whereas the nematodes have separate sexes. Some worms produce larvae, but most produce eggs, which pass in the host's excrement. Worms in the circulatory system produce larvae, which are carried in the blood, are ingested by blood-sucking arthropods and are then transmitted to the next host via the bite. The life cycles of the parasites are highly variable, from simple direct egg transmission to complex cycles involving one or more intermediate hosts (Figs 246.1–246.4). The classification of the worms is based upon internal and external structures, and reproductive stages of eggs, larvae and adults.

EPIDEMIOLOGY

Helminthic infections are the most common parasites of humans. The highest prevalence occur in tropical countries with poor or inadequate food supplies, and where insect, molluscan and other invertebrate vectors abound and sanitary conditions are poor.

Nematodes

Intestinal nematodes

Over one billion people, primarily children, are infected with *Ascaris lumbricoides*. In some areas of Indonesia infection rates are as high as 90%.[1] Nearly one billion people are infected with hookworm, *Necator americanus, Ancylostoma duodenale* or both. The former has a worldwide distribution, whereas the latter is found in certain parts of Africa, China, India and Japan. Hookworm prevalences are highly variable, being 35% in the Philippines and 90% in Indonesia, with infection rates highest in adult males.[1] Up to 800 million people are infected with *Trichuris trichiura*; both sexes and all age groups are infected and in the Cameroons 3.1–97.3% of 22,000 children were found to be infected.[2]

Strongyloides stercoralis, like other soil-transmitted helminths, is endemic in areas with high humidity, warm temperatures and poor sanitation. The prevalence of this parasite varies from 10% to 20% in areas of Africa, South America and Asia. In surveys conducted in Indonesia and the Philippines using the Harada–Mori filter paper test-tube technique on single-stool specimens the prevalence rates were usually less than 1%.[1,3] There are reports, however, of rates as high as 25% in areas with concomitant high prevalence of human T-lymphocyte leukemia/lymphoma virus-1 virus infections.[4]

Pinworm or *Enterobius vermicularis* is a common nematode in temperate regions with an estimated 200 million infections worldwide. It is a parasite that most individuals acquire in childhood, but it is not uncommon in adults in a family with infected children. It is a common nematode infection in the USA. A high prevalence of pinworm is also reported in male homosexuals.[5]

Tissue nematodes

Larva migrans is a syndrome caused primarily by larvae of nematode parasites of lower animals. Larvae of dog hookworms such as *Ancylostoma braziliensis* and *A. caninum* penetrate human skin and migrate through this tissue causing a creeping eruption or cutaneous larva migrans. This occurs worldwide, but mostly in areas with warm, moist climates. *Ancylostoma caninum* can also cause an enteritis in humans, especially in Australia.[6] The larvae of dog and cat ascarids or *Toxocara* spp. cause visceral larva migrans in children when embryonated eggs are ingested. The larvae provoke granuloma formation, often in the central nervous system (CNS) and eye. Seroprevalence rates for *Toxocara* antibodies are high in England and France.

Although there are now seven recognized species of *Trichinella*, the only species that is important to humans is *T. spiralis*. This species has a worldwide distribution in the temperate regions,[7] whereas the other species are reported from animals in Africa (*T. nelsoni*), Arctic regions (*T. nativa*) and Palearctic and Nearctic regions (*T. pseudospiralis, T. britovi, T. murrelli*) and the Australian region (*T. papuae*). *Trichinella* spp. are ubiquitous and found in a wide variety of animal life. Transmission occurs among animals by the ingestion of *Trichinella*-infected meat. All types of carnivous mammals and birds are susceptible to infections. Most human infections are obtained by eating infected pigs, boars and other wild animals. Reports of trichinosis are sporadic, usually among groups who have participated in a communal meal. An epidemic in France reported several thousand with some deaths after the consumption of 'steak tartare' prepared from imported horse meat.[8]

THE MAJOR PARASITIC WORMS				
Nematodes (roundworms)	Intestinal			
	Ascaris lumbricoides	*Necator americanus*	*Trichuris trichiura*
	Enterobius vermicularis	*Strongyloides stercoralis*	*Capillaria philippinensis*
	Ancylostoma duodenale	*Trichostrongylus* spp.	
	Tissue		
	Trichinella spiralis	*Angiostrongylus cantonensis*	*Phocanema* spp. (larvae from saltwater fish)
	Visceral larva migrans (*Toxocara canis or Toxocara cati*)	*Angiostrongylus costaricensis*	*Contracaecum* spp. (larvae from saltwater fish)
	Ocular larva migrans (*Toxocara canis or Toxocara cati*)	*Gnathostoma spinigerum*	*Capillaria hepatica*
	Cutaneous larva migrans (*Ancylostoma braziliensis or Ancylostoma caninum*)	*Anisakis* spp. (larvae from saltwater fish)	*Thelazia* spp.
	Dracunculus medinensis		
	Blood and tissues (filarial worms)		
	Wuchereria bancrofti	*Onchocerca volvulus*	*Dirofilaria immitis* (usually lung lesion; in dogs, heartworm)
	Brugia malayi	*Mansonella ozzardi*	
	Brugia timori	*Mansonella streptocerca*	*Dirofilaria* spp. (may be found in subcutaneous nodules)
	Loa loa	*Mansonella perstans*	
Platyhelminthes (flatworms) Cestodes (tapeworms)	Intestinal		
	Diphyllobothrium latum	*Hymenolepis nana*	*Taenia solium*
	Dipylidium caninum	*Hymenolepis diminuta*	*Taenia saginata*
	Tissue (larval forms)		
	Taenia solium	*Echinococcus multilocularis*	*Spirometra mansonoides*
	Echinococcus granulosus	*Multiceps multiceps*	*Diphyllobothrium* spp.
Trematodes (flukes)	Intestinal		
	Fasciolopsis buski	*Heterophyes heterophyes*	
	Echinostoma ilocanum	*Metagonimus yokogawai*	
	Liver/lung		
	Clonorchis (opisthorchis) sinensis	*Paragonimus westermani*	*Paragonimus skrjabini*
	Opisthorchis viverrini	*Paragonimus mexicanus*	*Paragonimus* spp.
	Fasciola hepatica	*Paragonimus heterotremus*	
	Blood		
	Schistosoma mansoni	*Schistosoma japonicum*	*Schistosoma mekongi*
	Schistosoma haematobium	*Schistosoma intercalatum*	

Table 246.1 The major parasitic worms. Adapted from Garcia LS. Classification of human parasites. Clin Infect Dis 1997;25:21–3.

The 'firey serpent of Medina' or *Dracunculus medinensis* (also known as the guinea worm) is reported from 17 African countries, Yemen, Saudi Arabia, India and Pakistan. Ten million people may be infected, and in some areas 50% of a population may have the infection every year. Sex prevalences are variable, but most infection occurs in those aged 15–40 years. Transmission is seasonal and closely related to rainfall, when the population of the major copepod vectors (*Cyclops* spp.) are abundant.

Angiostrongyliasis, or parastrongyliasis, is caused by the molluscanborne nematodes *Angiostrongylus cantonensis* and *A. costaricensis*. The former is endemic in Asia, the Pacific Islands, Australia, India, Africa, the Caribbean and Louisiana in the USA. *Angiostrongylus costaricensis* is reported in Latin America and Texas, but most human infections are reported from Costa Rica. Human infection with *A. cantonensis* is reported primarily from Taiwan and Thailand with infection acquired from eating the snails *Achatina fulica* in Taiwan and *Pila ampullacae* in Thailand. In Taiwan most infections are in children of both sexes while in Thailand the parasitosis is seen mostly in adult males.[9] One human infection has been reported in a young boy in Louisiana.[10] *Angiostrongylus costaricensis* is usually seen in children who accidently ingest the slug *Vaginulus plebeius* on vegetation. Rats (*Rattus* spp.), cotton rats (*Sigmodon* spp.) and rice rats (*Oryzomys* spp.) are natural hosts for *A. costaricensis*.

Anisakiasis is caused by third-stage larvae of *Anisakis simplex* and *Pseudoterranova decipiens*, which are acquired by eating species of raw marine fish and squid. The adult worms, related to *Ascaris*, are found in marine mammals worldwide, but most infections in humans have occurred in Japan and other countries where people eat uncooked marine fish and squid.

Several *Gnathostoma* spp. larvae can invade human tissue and most infections are reported from Thailand and Japan, and occasionally Mexico. *Gnathostoma spinigerum* is the most common species in Thailand. *Gnathostoma hispidium* has also been found in humans, although there are fewer infections. Dogs and cats are the natural hosts for adult worms. Copepods serve as the first intermediate host, and fish, frogs, snakes and chicken are the second intermediate hosts. Infections are more common in adults of both sexes.

Blood and tissue nematodes

The filarids are a group of nematodes located in the lymphatics, subcutaneous and cutaneous tissues. There are eight major filarids of humans transmitted by arthropods in tropical and subtropical parts of the world.

Wuchereria bancrofti is the most widespread, being endemic in Asia, Africa, Central and South America and the Pacific Islands. Prevalence rates are highly variable depending upon the vector mosquito population, temperature, humidity, a susceptible human population and environmental sanitation. An estimated 115 million people may be infected worldwide, with 50 million in Africa, 62 million in Asia, 2 million in the Pacific Islands and less than 1 million in Latin

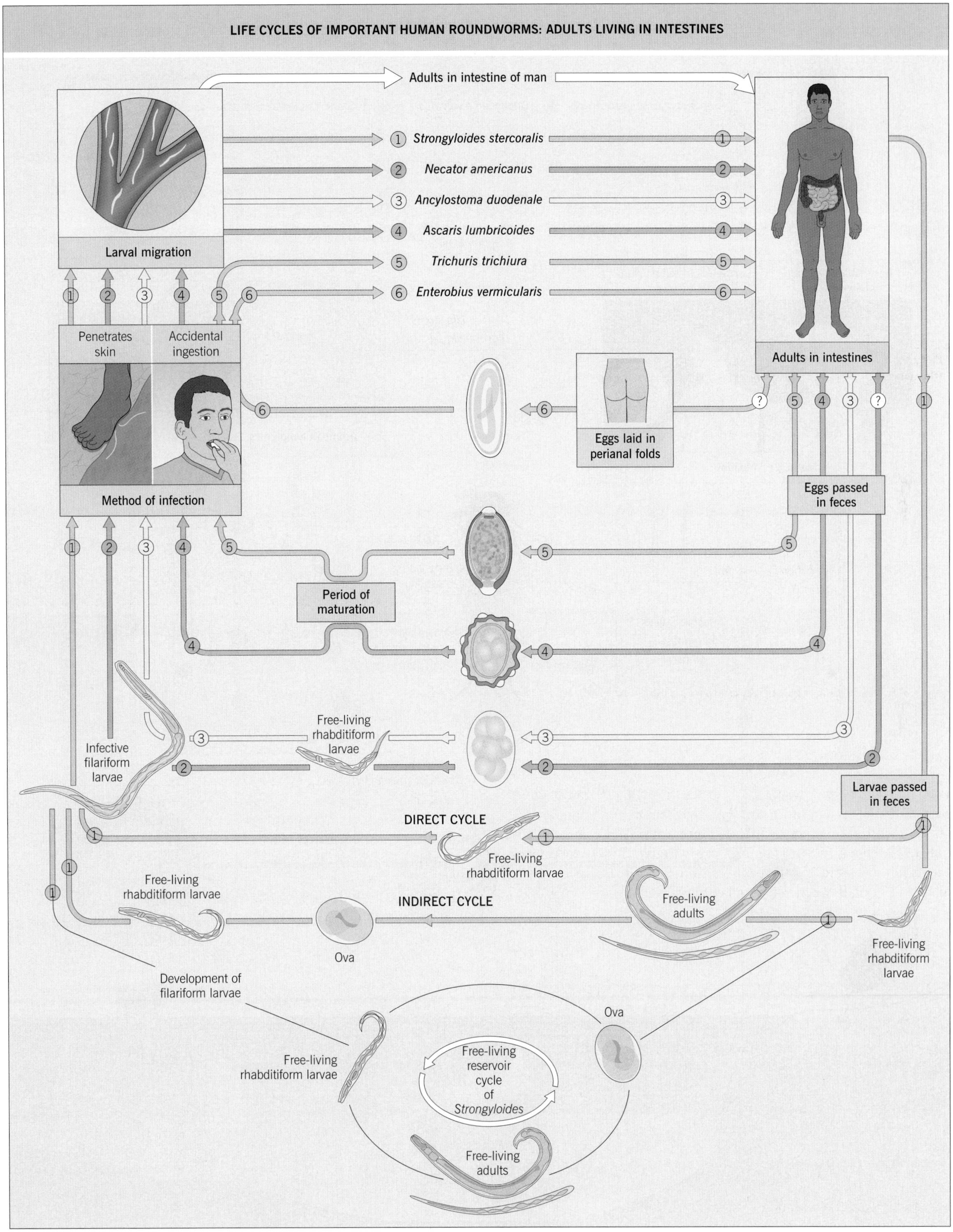

Fig. 246.1 Life cycles of important human roundworms: adults living in the intestines.

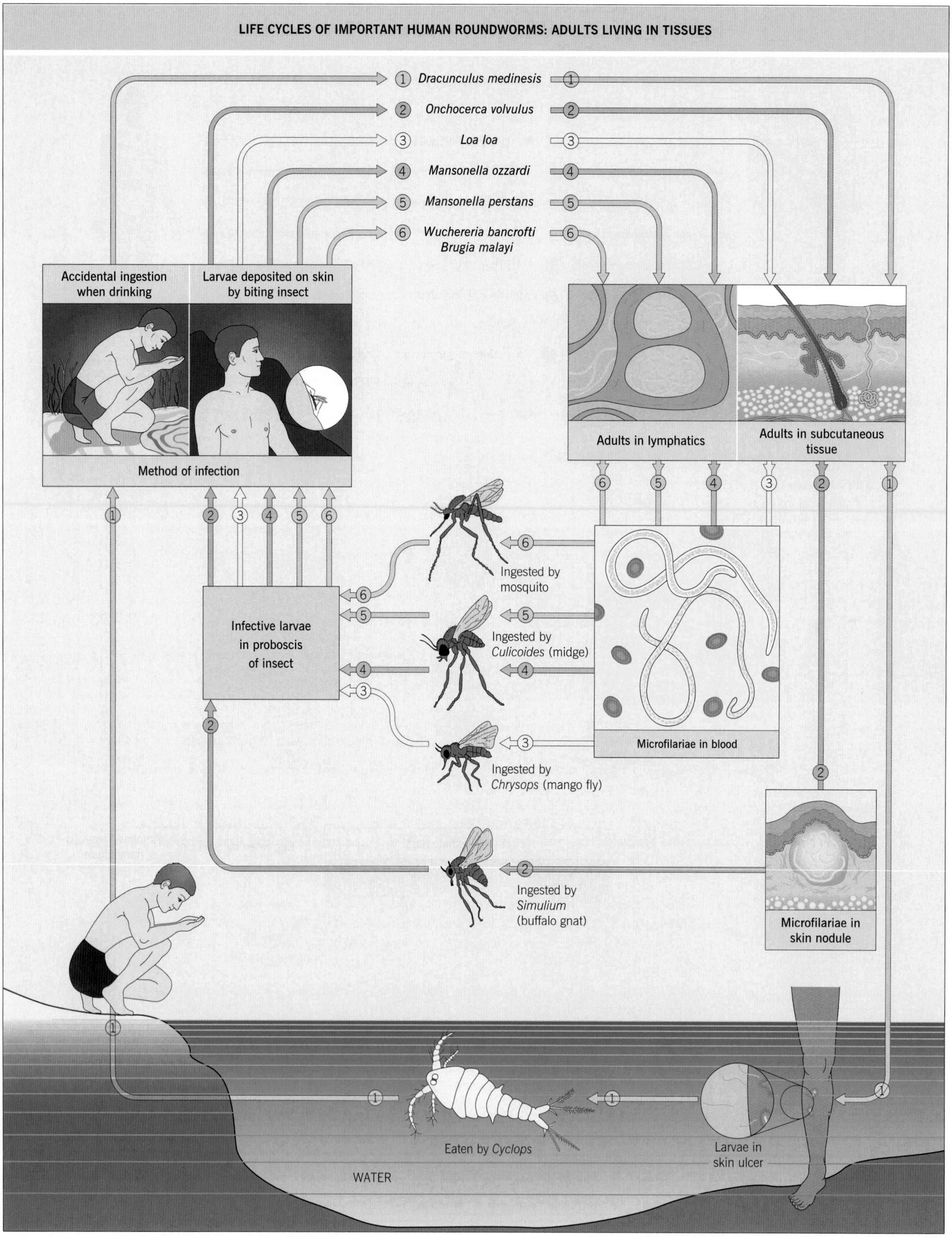

Fig. 246.2 Life cycles of important human roundworms: adults living in tissues.

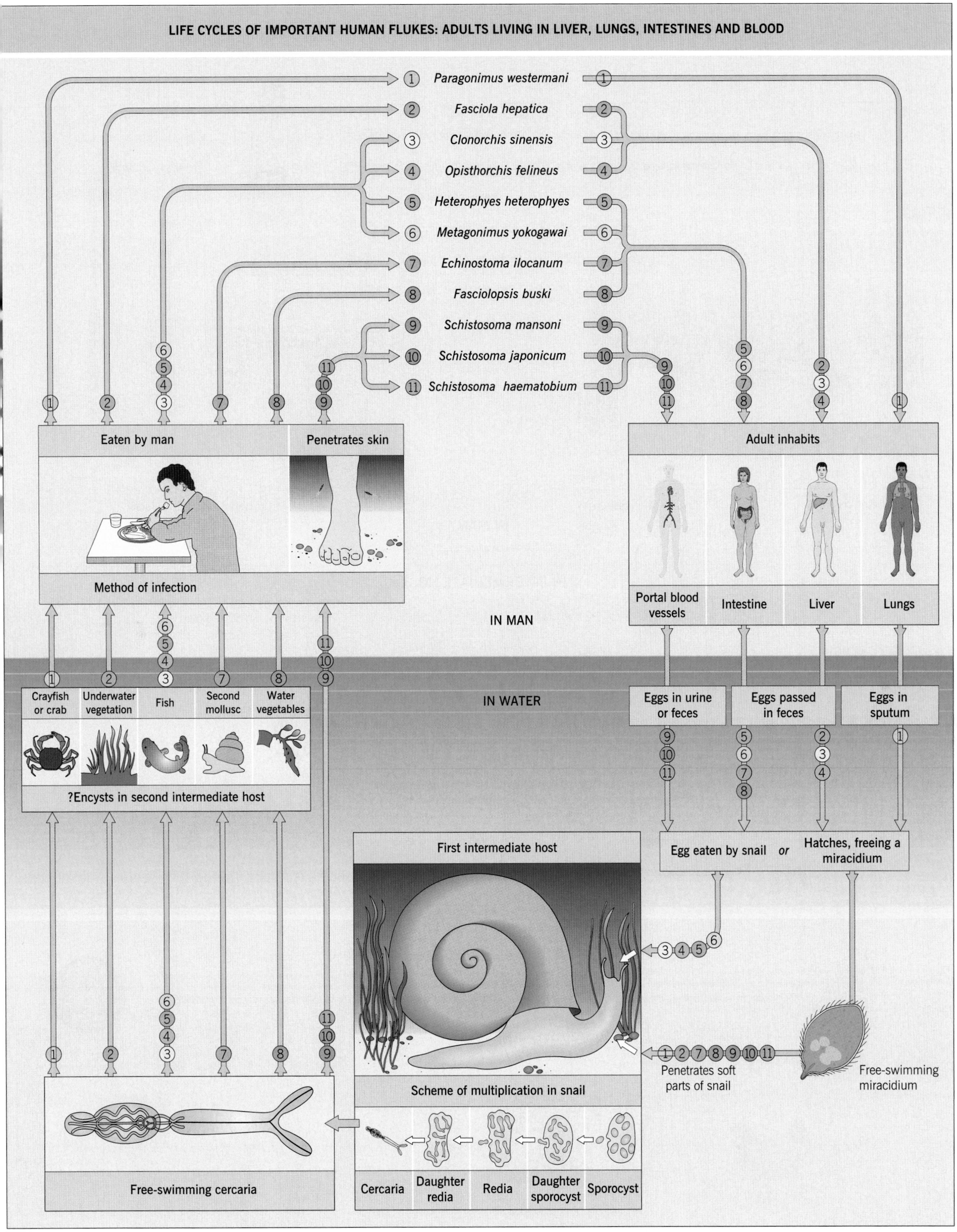

Fig. 246.3 Life cycles of important human flukes: adults living in the liver, lungs, intestines and blood.

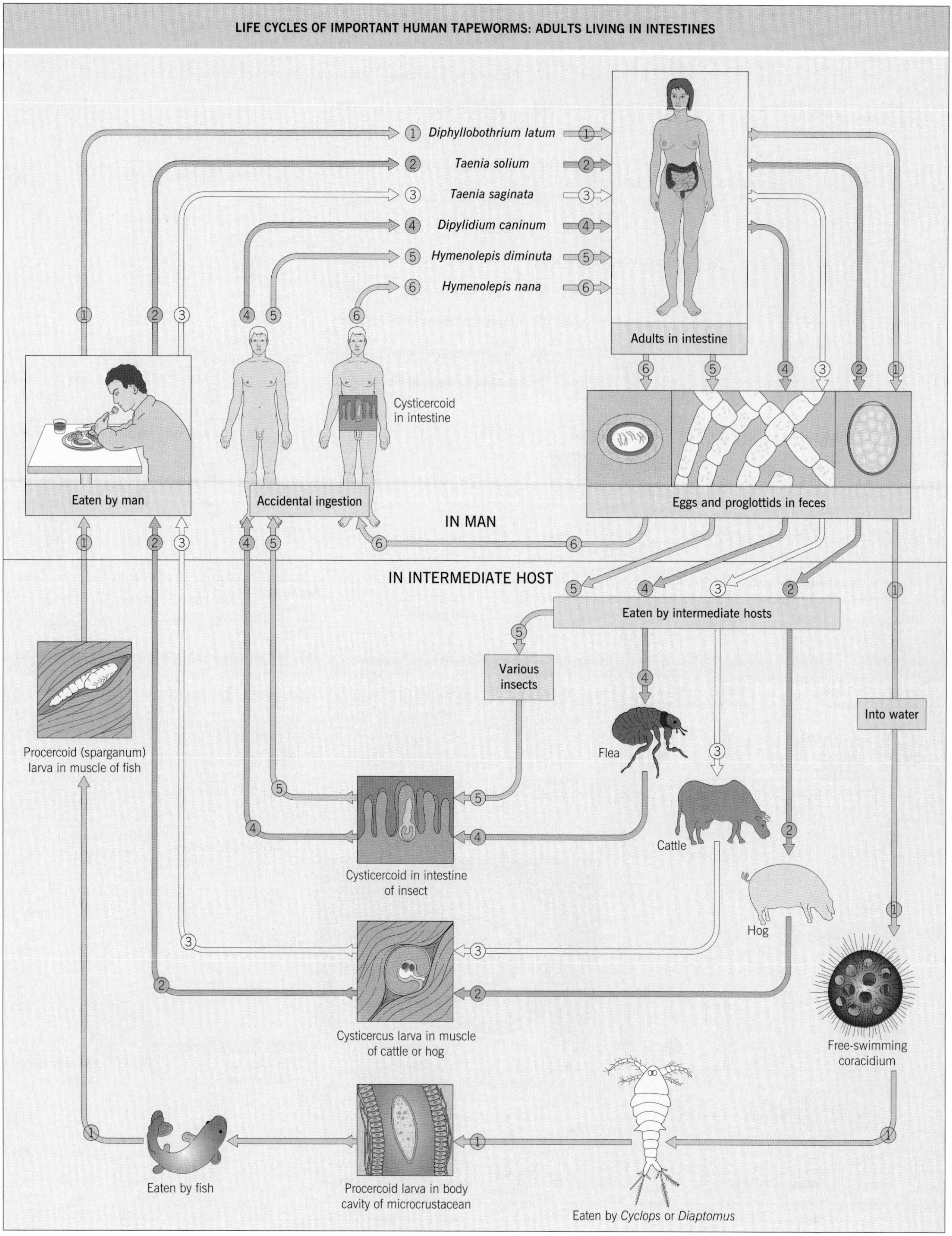

Fig. 246.4 Life cycles of important human tapeworms: adults living in the intestines.

America.[11] There are different vectors in different endemic areas; the most extensive is *Culex quinquefasciatus*, whereas *Aedes polynesiensis* is the important vector in the Pacific Islands. There is a nocturnal periodicity associated with the feeding habits of the mosquitoes, except in the Pacific where there is a diurnal periodicity and the mosquito vector feeds in the daytime. Although a limited number of monkeys have been experimentally infected with *W. bancrofti*[12] no naturally infected animal reservoirs have been documented.

Brugia malayi is found only in rural Asia and infects approximately 13 million[11] people. Many of the islands of Indonesia are endemic, with prevalence rates from less than 1% to over 30%.[13] The major mosquito vectors are *Mansonia, Anopheles* and *Aedes* spp. and cats and *Macaca* and *Presbytis* monkeys are known reservoir hosts. Most strains of brugian filariasis are periodic, but some microfilariae exhibit subperiodic periodicity.

Brugia timori is found only in the Lesser Sunda Islands of Indonesia. A prevalence rate of 25% was reported in a population on the island of Flores.[14] *Anopheles barbirostris* is a major mosquito vector and, although no naturally infected reservoirs have been found, cats and Mongolian gerbils have been experimentally infected.[15]

Onchocerca volvulus is endemic in 26 countries in Africa and six in Central and South America. Approximately 18 million people are infected and as a result 270,000 are blind and 500,000 severely disabled.[19] Infections are more common in males than females, reflecting male occupations and their higher exposure to vector flies. Prevalences are also higher in areas close to running water where the blackfly *Simulium damnosum* and related species breed. In the Americas infections are more common in the highlands 1000–4000 feet above sea level, whereas in Africa infection is common below 1000 feet. Infections decrease with distance from the rivers and streams. There are no animal reservoirs and there is no microfilarial periodicity.

Loa loa, the African eye worm, is endemic in West and Central Africa where *Chrysops* spp. are present. Prevalence rates vary from 8% to 40%, with infections increasing with age; 20–30 million people live in endemic areas. Transmission by the day-biting female deerflies is highest during wet seasons. Monkeys serve as reservoir hosts. The microfilariae are diurnal.

Three *Mansonella* spp. are found in humans:

- *M. streptocerca* is found in Africa;
- *M. perstans* in West Africa and parts of South America; and
- *M. ozzardi* in Latin America.

Culicoides spp. serve as vectors for all three species and *Simulium* spp. also transmit *M. ozzardi*. Monkeys in Africa serve as reservoir hosts. Infections are highest in adult males and some areas report prevalence rates as high as 80%. There is no microfilarial periodicity.

Trematodes (see Chapter 168)

Over 40 million people worldwide are infected with food-borne trematodes; the most important occur in the liver, lungs, blood and intestines.

Liver/lung trematodes

The opisthorchid liver flukes are reported from Asia and Europe. The Chinese liver fluke, *Clonorchis sinensis*, is reported from China, Japan, Korea, Taiwan and Vietnam. Infections are highest in older males and females and there is a tendency toward familial aggregations. An estimated 7 million people are infected, with prevalence rates in China of 15–24.6%, in Korea 11.7–30.8% and in Japan 2.9%. Infections are highest in the snail and fish intermediate hosts in the warmer months. Snails in the families Hydrobiida, Melaniidae, Assimineidae and Thiaridae are first intermediate hosts, and fish, primarily of the family Cyprinidae, are second intermediate hosts. *Opisthorchis viverrini* is endemic in Thailand, Laos and Vietnam.

The infection is found in an estimated 10 million people in all age groups increasing from childhood to adulthood, and in both sexes. Prevalences vary from 7.3% to 53.2% in Thailand. *Bithynia* spp. are important snail hosts and *Cyclocheilichthys* spp. of freshwater fish are important second intermediate hosts. Dogs, cats and other fish-eating mammals are reservoir hosts.[17]

Fasciola hepatica, the sheep liver fluke, is endemic in most sheep-raising areas of the world. Human infections are increasing and are most common in parts of Europe, South America and the Middle East. Approximately 2.4 million people are infected. Sheep, goats and cattle are the natural hosts, with infection rates varying from 25% to 92% in countries such as Bolivia. The prevalence in humans reaches 65% in Bolivia, 24–53% in Ecuador, 10% in Peru and 2–17% in Egypt.[20] Infections are more common in adults who usually acquire infection from eating watercress in salads.

Although over 40 species of *Paragonimus* are described, only a few infect humans and only one, the Oriental lung fluke, *Paragonimus westermani*, is responsible for the most serious disease. It is reported from China, Taiwan, Japan, Korea, the Philippines and Thailand. Other species occur in China, Thailand, Mexico, Ecuador, Peru and parts of Africa. The parasitosis is acquired by eating metacercariae-laden crustaceans: crabs and crayfish. In some areas the juice from crabs is used for seasoning and traditional medicine. The juice may contain metacercariae. There are 20 million suspected infections in the Chinese, and over 600,000 elsewhere.[20] There are many snail hosts, with *Semisulcospira* spp. being major vectors in China and Korea. The crabs *Eriocheir* and *Potamon* spp. and the crayfish *Cambaroides* spp. are important second intermediate hosts. Dogs, cats and other carnivorous mammals are reservoir hosts. Children often obtain the infection by eating crabs on the way home from school.

Intestinal trematodes

There is a very large number (about 70) of intestinal flukes and they are reported mostly in Asians who acquire infections because of eating raw food. *Fasciolopsis buski*, the giant intestinal fluke, is reported from China, Taiwan, Thailand, Indonesia, Bangladesh and India and occasionally from Indonesia. Over 200,000 infections have been reported in China and 10,000 in Thailand.[20] Pigs are the reservoir host, and snails such as *Segmentina*, *Hippeutis* and *Gyraulus* spp. are important vectors. Cercariae from snails encyst on water plants such as water caltrop, watercress, water bamboo and water chestnut. These are eaten uncooked and infections occur most often in children.

Other important intestinal flukes include *Echinostoma, Heterophyes* and *Metagonimus* spp. There are an estimated 150,000 cases of echinostomiasis, 240,000 cases of heterophyiasis and 650,000 cases of metagonimiasis, most in China, Korea and Japan. Echinostome metacercariae are acquired from snails, fish and other aquatic animals, whereas *Heterophyes* and *Metagonimus* infective stages occur in fish. All ages and both sexes are infected as a result of eating the second intermediate hosts uncooked.

Blood trematodes

Schistosomiasis is endemic to many tropical areas of the world:

- *Schistosoma japonicum* is found in Asia;
- *S. haematobium* and *S. mansoni* in Africa and the Middle East; and
- *S. mansoni* in South America and some islands in the Caribbean (see Chapter 167).

Other species of less importance are *S. mekongi* and *S. intercalatum*, which are focally located in South East Asia and Africa, respectively.

It is estimated that there are over 200 million infections, with the prevalence and intensity of infections being highest in children aged 5–15 years. Infection rates depend upon water contact in endemic areas. Despite the widespread distribution of snails and frequent opportunities for water contact, high transmission only occurs at a few sites. It is important to identify these sites.[21] Snail vectors are members of the genera *Bulinus* spp. for *S. haematobium*, *Biomphalaria* spp. for *S. mansoni* and *Oncomelania* spp. for *S. japonicum*. *Bulinus* and *Biomphalaria* spp. are strictly aquatic whereas the *Oncomelania* are amphibious snails. There are some animal hosts for *S. mansoni*, but humans are the most important source of infection. Humans are also the most important host for *S. haematobium*, whereas many domestic and wild animals are a reservoir host for *S. japonicum*. Although *S. japonicum* is endemic on Taiwan, the strain of parasite on the island will not infect humans. It is considered to be a zoophilic strain.[22]

Cestodes

Cestode or tapeworm infections are acquired by ingestion of intermediate hosts containing the infective larval stages:

- the beef tapeworm *Taenia saginata* and pork tapeworm *T. solium* are acquired by ingesting the cysticercus stage in beef or pork;
- the fish tapeworm *Diphyllobothrium latum* is acquired by eating raw fish infected with the plerocercoid or sparganum stage; and
- *Hymenolepis nana* and *H. diminuta* are rodent tapeworms that use fleas and beetles as intermediate hosts (see Chapter 168).

Taenia saginata is reported worldwide, with high infection rates in Africa and Asia. Most infections occur in adults. The cysticercus is found only in bovids; however, in parts of Asia, especially in Taiwan, pigs are a recognized source of infection for a strain of the parasite, namely *T. saginata (asiatica)*.[23]

Taenia solium is found sporadically in pigs worldwide, with many human cases reported from Mexico and Central and South America, South West Asia and Africa. Human cysticercosis is also present in these areas. Certain areas of Irian Jaya in Indonesia report many cases of cysticercosis because of the habit of eating uncooked pork.

Hymenolepis nana is the most common tapeworm in North America and is particularly reported in children worldwide. *Hymenolepis diminuta* is not common but reported occasionally in South East Asia.

There is a high prevalence of *D. latum* in humans in Scandinavia, Finland, Alaska, Canada and Northern USA. Other species of *Diphyllobothrium* are reported from Japan and South America.

Sparganosis or infections with the larval stage of *Spirometra* spp. is reported occasionally from many parts of the world. Infection is acquired by ingesting copepods or second intermediate host (frogs, toads or other aquatic animals). Infections in southern Asia are attributed to the use of fresh animal tissues as poultices.

Echinococcus granulosus and *E. multilocularis* are associated with human hydatid disease, whereas *E. vogeli* and *E. oligarthrus* rarely cause disease in humans. *Echinococcus granulosus* is the most important and found primarily in sheep-raising areas. Strains of the parasite are also found in goats, swine, cattle, horses and camels.

The parasitoses are found worldwide, with canines serving as the definitive host and animals such as sheep as intermediate hosts. Humans acquire infection by ingesting eggs from dogs, whereas dogs acquire the infection by eating sheep liver and other organs containing cysts with large numbers of scolices. Infections usually occur in the young and the cysts develop over a period of years.

Echinococcus multilocularis has a limited distribution in dogs, foxes, wolves and cats as the reservoir hosts and larval stages in wild rodents, especially voles. The parasite, however, is reported to be moving southward in the USA. Rare human infections are acquired by the ingestion of eggs passed by the canines. Infection with any of the *Echinococcus* spp., however, is related to poor sanitary conditions in populations with a low level of education and in people closely associated with canine reservoir hosts.

PATHOGENICITY

Helminths seem to live in peaceful coexistence with their hosts and usually cause few problems. However, if there are many worms, there may be severe disease and symptoms. The parasites, especially in the intestines, can cause obstruction and possibly perforation. The worms also secrete or excrete toxic substances, which affect the tissues. Lytic substances, such as those secreted by hookworms to obtain blood, can induce inflammation and there may be changes due to malabsorption and competition for nutrients. Larval stages may be more pathogenic, secreting antigenic substances that cause hypersensitivity, while the antigens promote antibody production and cellular immune responses. The most serious aspect of helminthic infection is that the worms end up in ectopic locations. Worms in the wrong place can be highly pathogenic.

Helminths have intricate life cycles and disease is usually associated with the larval migratory pathways and the final habitat of adult worms in the host. The amount of pathology and disease varies with the parasitosis.

Nematodes living in the intestine

Enterobius vermicularis

The life cycle of *Enterobius vermicularis* is presented in Figure 246.1. Pinworm resides in the large bowel, where mating occurs. Gravid females migrate out of the anus and deposit eggs on the perianal skin. The adult males die after copulation and the females usually after depositing eggs. The perianal region becomes itchy and scratching can lead to excoriation and weeping. Eggs under the fingernails in children lead to reinfection when the fingers are placed in the mouth. Eggs can be released onto the bedsheets and become disseminated throughout the household when the sheets are shaken. The eggs will survive for 2 weeks in a humid and cool environment. When eggs are ingested they hatch in the intestine and the larvae migrate to the large intestine to mature in 6 weeks. Adults may migrate into the vagina, cervix, uterus and fallopian tubes and peritoneal cavity. Granulomas caused by the adult worms are reported in the abdominal cavity. Young girls may experience urinary tract infection and vulvovaginitis caused by wandering female worms or the presence of eggs on the vulva.

Ascaris lumbricoides

Infection with *Ascaris lumbricoides* can occasionally be highly pathogenic. The life cycle is presented in Figure 246.1. The adult male worm may measure 15–31cm by 2–4mm and the female 20–35cm by 3–6mm. The female can live for a year or more and produce 240,000 eggs/day. The eggs pass in the feces and embryonate in the soil in 10–14 days. Upon ingestion the egg hatches in the intestine and the liberated larva penetrates the mucosa and passes to the liver via the portal vessels and then to the lungs. After a few weeks the larva penetrates the alveolar air sac, passes up the pulmonary tree, is coughed up and swallowed. The worms become sexually mature in the small intestines and produce eggs in 60–75 days.

Migrating larvae in a previously infected sensitized person can cause inflammatory lesions in the liver. Large numbers of larvae can cause an intense tissue reaction, including inflammation and the development of granulomatous lesions involving eosinophils, epithelioid cells and macrophages. This is referred to as *Ascaris* pneumonitis.

Adult worms in the intestines cause little disease unless in large numbers or if the worms become erratic and migrate into vital organs or exit from one of the orifices. Heavy infections can also cause intestinal obstruction, intussusception, volvulus, blockage of the bile ducts and cholangitis and intestinal perforation.

Trichuris trichiuria

Trichuris trichiuria has a direct life cycle (see Fig. 246.1). Adult females in the large intestine deposit eggs in the fecal stream and after a few weeks in the soil they become embryonated. When eggs are swallowed they hatch in the intestine and the larva moves down the bowel to the colon. The worms bury their narrow anterior end into the mucosa with the wider posterior end extended freely into the lumen of the colon. The females lay eggs after 3 months and produce 3000–10,000/day. The worm's longer, thinner, anterior end contains rows of cells (stichocytes) surrounding the esophogeal tube. The females measure 35–55mm and the males 30–45mm. The males have a curved tail with copulatory spicules.

Heavy infections can cause local irritation, diarrhea, cramps, edema and blood loss; the worms suck blood and there is seepage at the attachment sites. A prolapsed rectum is not uncommon, especially in children. There may be eosinophilia along with nutritional and weight loss.

Hookworms

A number of hookworm species can enter the human body, but most are natural parasites of animals other than humans (i.e. zoonotic parasites). The species from lower animals usually cause a creeping eruption or cutaneous larva migrans. Only two hookworms are considered to be important human species:

- *Necator americanus*; and
- *Ancylostoma duodenale*.

Both species measure about 10–13mm for females and 6–11mm for males and can be 0.4–0.6mm in width. The anterior mouths have cutting plates or teeth and the males have bell-shaped bursal rays at the posterior end that are used for holding females during copulation. The vulva is mid-central and eggs pass from the females into the fecal stream and out with host feces onto the soil. Female worms pass 5000–10,000 (*N. americanus*) and 10,000–20,000 (*A. duodenale*) eggs/day. In warm, moist climates the eggs embryonate in the soil and rhabditform larvae are released. Within a few days the larvae molt and develop into filariform larvae or the infective stage. The larvae climb to the top of the soil or grass, cling together and wait for a human host to come by. They usually penetrate the skin between the toes or other body surfaces. Some *A. duodenale* larvae may be ingested in water and enter the oral mucosa. The larvae are carried by the blood to the heart and then the lungs where they remain for a period, break out into the alveoli, pass up the pulmonary tree and are swallowed. The parasite matures in the small intestine, copulates and produces eggs in about 5 weeks (see Fig. 246.1).

The infections can remain active for as long as 13 years. Penetration of larvae into the skin causes ground itch and at times a secondary, bacterial infection may develop. Ground itch is caused when hookworm or other larvae enter the skin by contact with the ground, which results in irritation, erythema, edema and papulovascular eruption. Larvae in the lungs also produce minute focal hemorrhage and pneumonitis. The attachment of adult worms can cause small erosive lesions, hemorrhage, tissue cytolysis and neutrophilic infiltration. The worms change attachment sites regularly, leaving old sites oozing blood and plasma. Iron deficiency anemia and blood loss result from long-term infection with a large number of worms.

Pathologic changes occur in the bone marrow due to blood loss. Liver function may change as a result of anemia, as well as reduced capacity for albumen synthesis. Fatty deterioration of heart, liver and kidney may also occur. Hookworm disease with iron deficiency anemia, hypoproteinemia and hepatosplenomegaly may contribute to thousands of deaths each year.

Strongyloides stercoralis

Strongyloides stercoralis is a unique nematode having a parasitic life cycle as well as a free-living cycle, with males and females present in the free-living cycle (see Fig. 246.1). Only females are present in the parasitic life cycle, however. The parasitic females measure 1.5–2.5mm, and have a long cylindric esophagus. The vulva is in the posterior third of the body and the paired uteri contain thin-shelled eggs.

The eggs are deposited in the small intestinal epithelium and hatch soon after release. The first-stage or rhabditiform larva passes in the feces and develops into a second-stage and then a third or infective-stage filariform larva after a few days. The third-stage larvae penetrate the skin and migrate through the body and via the blood to the lungs; after several days they migrate up the respiratory tree and are swallowed. The larvae enter the intestinal mucosa and mature, and the female worms produce eggs parthenogenetically. Some larvae transform into infective forms in the bowel, penetrate the mucosa, migrate and develop into adults. This is internal autoinfection and can lead to hyperinfection in the immunocompromised host. Some rhabditiform larvae transform into rhabditoid free-living male and female adults in the soil and reproduce. The eggs hatch, releasing rhabditiform larvae, which develop into filariform larvae that can enter the skin of a host.

Cellular immunity is responsible for keeping infections under control, but when immunity is affected by disease or immunosuppression, the parasite multiplies unabated and this leads to hyperinfection and dissemination. Larvae entering the skin can cause inflammation with lymphocytic and eosinophilic infiltration. Larvae in the lungs cause eosinophilic infiltration and hypersensitivity reactions.

Pneumonia and hemorrhage result from hyperinfection. The intestinal mucosa is edematous and covered with mucus in cases of chronic strongyloidiasis. A cellular infiltration with eosinophils and monocytes and reactions around the worms may be seen in the lamina propria. Mucosal atrophy and flattening of villi as well as fibrotic changes with ulcerative enteritis may result from long-term infections. In disseminated infections the parasite is found in many organs, with secondary bacterial infection when bacteria are carried by the larvae from the intestines.

Capillaria philippinensis

Intestinal capillariasis is a disease in which the parasite can multiply in the digestive tract. *Capillaria philippinensis* is a tiny worm; females measure 2.5–5.3mm and males 1.3–3.9mm. The anterior body is narrow and consists of an esophagus surrounded by rows of cells or stichocytes forming the stichosome. The posterior is slightly wider and contains reproductive organs and digestive tract. The females deposit eggs, which must reach water where they embryonate. When these are eaten by small freshwater fish the eggs hatch and the larvae develop into infective stages in 3 weeks. When humans eat the fish the larvae mature in 2 weeks. After mating the females first produce larvae that will mature in the gut, whereas the second-generation worms produce thick-shelled eggs, which pass out in the feces. The parasites can multiply rapidly, producing thousands of progeny.[24] If the patient is not treated the disease is usually fatal. Over 200,000 worms were recovered from 1 liter of bowel fluid at one autopsy. The worms enter the crypts and cause atrophy, the villi are flattened and denuded, the mucosal glands are denuded and the lamina propria is infiltrated with inflammatory cells. Other organs are also affected by malnutrition and hypokalemia. Most of the pathology is in the jejunum.[25]

Nematodes living in tissues

Trichinella spiralis

Trichinella spiralis is the only species in the genus of any importance; the other six species are parasites of lower animals and rarely infect humans. The parasites are related to other trichiurids in having a slender anterior and a wider posterior end. Stichocytes line the stichosome in the anterior end. Female worms measure 2–4mm and males 1–1.5mm. Infections are acquired by eating uncooked muscle containing encysted larvae from infected animals, usually pigs.

The larvae are digested from the cyst, pass to the small intestines and burrow beneath the epithelium where they develop into adults, re-enter the gut lumen and reproduce. The larvae produced enter the gut wall, are picked up by the blood and carried throughout the body to striated muscle where they become encysted. The adult worms cause a transitory enteritis and malabsorption, eosinophilia and excessive secretion of mucin. The larvae entering the muscle cell cause alterations in morphology, which results in the characteristic 'nurse cell'. Morphologic and molecular changes occur in the cell until it eventually becomes calcified. The larvae can remain alive for many years in the cell. Chronic inflammatory cells may surround the parasitized muscle cell. Vasculitis may cause periorbital edema and neurologic manifestations and there may be a trichinal myocarditis.

Filarial nematodes

The filarial nematodes are long and slender and are found in the lymphatics, tissues and body cavities. The life cycles of some of the filarids are presented in Figure 246.2. Microfilariae are produced by female worms and arthropods are the vectors (see Chapter 170).

Wuchereria bancrofti, Brugia malayi and *Brugia timori*

The lymphatic filarids *W. bancrofti, B. malayi* and *B. timori* produce microfilariae that usually appear in the blood between 2200 and 0200 hours (nocturnal periodicity). *Wuchereria bancrofti*, found in some of the Pacific Islands, produces microfilariae that appear in the blood in the daytime (diurnal periodicity). Mosquitoes obtain blood at night and the larvae develop into the infective stage in 10–14 days. At the next feeding the infective larvae migrate from the thoracic muscles of the mosquito to the proboscis and crawl into the hole made by the bite. The larvae migrate in the host until they reach the definitive habitat and develop into adults. The worms copulate and the females produce microfilariae; the life cycle of *W. bancrofti* is a few months longer than that of *B. malayi*. Infections may persist for several years.

The pathogenesis of lymphatic filariasis has been a matter of debate and a model integrating various aspects of the parasitosis has been proposed.[16] It has also been suggested that *Wobachia*, an endosymbiont of filarids, may be associated with the pathogenesis. On the other hand, the pathology of lymphatic filariasis may be associated with immunologic responsiveness.[17] Some people who have the infection are microfilaremic but without antibodies or disease, whereas other are amicrofilaremic and have antibodies. There is an inflammatory stage with lymph channel irritation. Adult worms can be found in the lymph vessels, primarily the axillary, epitrochlear, inguinal and pelvic nodes as well as those in the testis, epididymis and spermatic cord. Attacks of lymphangitis and lymphadenitis may develop, followed by orchitis, funiculitis and epididymitis, especially in bancroftian infections. Blockage of the lymph flow by the inflammatory reaction and granuloma formation leads to lymphatic varicoses and lymphedema. Hyperplasia of the connective tissue and cellular infiltration and induration of the tissue may take place, with thickening and verrucous changes in the skin leading to elephantiasis.

Tropical pulmonary eosinophilia, 'Weingarten's syndrome', occurs in some endemic areas and is caused by granulomas containing degenerating microfilariae in the lung, spleen and lymph nodes. Patients have a cough, asthma, pulmonary infiltration, elevated eosinophils and antifilarial antibodies, but no microfilariae.

Onchocerca volvulus

Onchocerca volvulus adults are coiled in fibrous tissue nodules in the subcutaneous tissue. The females may reach 50cm in length and 0.5mm in diameter and the microfilariae produced are released into the interstitium of the skin. Males are smaller, being 5cm in length. Microfilariae are picked up by biting flies or black flies of the genus *Simulium* and after developing to the infective stage the larvae are introduced into a host at the next feeding. The larvae migrate through the tissue and after many months settle down, usually in pairs, and become encapsulated (see Fig. 246.2).

The microfilariae leave the nodule and migrate through the dermis, provoking a dermatitis; microfilariae in the eye chamber may lead to blindness. There may be a loss of skin elasticity in the pelvic region leading to hanging groin. Eye lesions begin with punctate keratitis and small opacities in the cornea caused by degenerating microfilariae, which evoke an eosinophilia. Sclerokeratitis follows. The endosymbiotic *Wobachia* bacteria in the worm may be associated with the pathogenesis of river blindness.[18] In Africa and Venezuela the nodules are located on the trunk and limbs, whereas in Mexico and Guatemala the nodules are usually on the head.

Loa loa

The African eye worm *Loa loa* actually moves through subcutaneous tissue and often traverses the conjunctiva. The males are 3–4cm and the females 4–7cm in length and 3–5mm wide. Microfilariae have a diurnal periodicity and are ingested by species of *Chrysops* at the time of a blood meal. The larvae develop to the infective stage in 10–13 days and enter the host through the hole made by the bite at the next feeding (see Fig. 246.2). The adult worms cause little damage as they migrate quickly through the tissue. Transient swellings (Calabar swellings), a subcutaneous edema caused by an allergic reaction to metabolic products of the worms or dead worms, may occur. Eosinophilic hypersensitivity reactions develop to the worms and microfilariae along with lymphadenitis.

Mansonella ozzardi, Mansonella perstans and *Mansonella streptocerca*

These are tissue parasites found in the mesenteries, visceral fat, skin and deep connective tissue. Microfilariae are found in the blood and skin and deep connective tissue. The vectors are species of *Culicoides* and *Simulium* (see Fig. 246.2). Most infections provoke little pathology except for articular pain, inguinal adenopathy, skin rash and dermatitis.

Dracunculus medinensis

Dracunculus medinensis is similar to the filarids. The females measure up to 120cm long and 2mm wide and the males 2cm. The worms mature in the connective tissue; gravid females then migrate to the subcutaneous tissue where they cause ulcers through which larvae are released when the lesion is immersed in water. The larvae are ingested by copepods and develop into infective larvae in 2 weeks. When the copepods are ingested in drinking water the larvae are liberated, penetrate the digestive tract and develop into adults in the connective tissue in a year (see Fig. 246.2). A painful localized reaction develops around the ulcer and multiple blisters and tracts may also develop. The tracts may become secondarily infected with bacteria. Once the uterus is emptied the worms may withdraw and die in the tissue. On the other hand, degeneration of the worm may lead to subcutaneous abscess and eventual calcification.

Angiostrongylus cantonensis

Angiostrongylus cantonensis is found naturally in the lungs of rats. The larvae produced by the females move up the pulmonary tree, are swallowed and pass out in the rat feces. Molluscs (snails and slugs) serve as intermediate hosts and, when eaten by rats, the larvae are digested out of the snail tissue, migrate from the gut to the brain, and after 3 weeks migrate to the lungs. Larvae are produced by adult females a few weeks later. Humans who ingest snails or slugs acquire the infective larvae, which migrate to the central nervous system (CNS) and cause eosinophilic meningitis. The females reach 2–3cm and the males 1–2cm in length and 0.2–0.3mm in width. In most human infections the larvae die in the brain and cord and elicit an inflammatory reaction in the meninges. Eosinophils, monocytes and foreign body giant cells infiltrate around the dead worms. Tissue necrosis is also evident. Larvae are reported in the eye, and are often recovered from cerebrospinal fluid (CSF). Adult worms have been found on a few occasions in the pulmonary artery.[9]

Anisakis simplex *and* Pseudoterronova decipiens

Anisakis simplex larvae measure 2–3cm by 0.3–0.6mm and *Pseudoterranova decipiens* 2–3cm by 0.3–1.2mm. They are found in the muscle and body cavity of marine fish and squid. When eaten by marine mammals (e.g. whales, seals, porpoises) the worms mature in the stomach and the females deposit eggs in the feces. In the ocean, a larva hatches from the egg and is eaten by a small marine crustacean. When the crustacean with a third-stage larva is eaten by fish the freed larva migrates to the abdominal cavity. When infected fish are eaten raw by humans the liberated larvae penetrate the stomach or small intestine and provoke a foreign body reaction around the worm. The submucosa becomes edematous with massive cellular infiltration. An abscess develops, characterized by necrosis and hemorrhagic and eosinophilic infiltration.

Gnathostoma spinigerum

Gnathostoma spinigerum is a robust nematode with a large globose head surrounded by rows of spines. The females measure 1–1.5cm by 1–2.5mm and the males 1–2.5cm by 1–2mm. The adults are coiled in the wall of the digestive tract of dogs and cats. Eggs pass in the feces, embryonate in fresh water and are ingested by copepods. The larvae hatch and develop into the second larval stage. When the copepod is eaten by a second intermediate host, the third-stage larva develops, and when this is eaten by a dog or cat the worm penetrates the gut wall and matures. Humans who eat infected fish, frogs or other aquatic food, raw or fermented, acquire the infection and the larvae migrate through the tissue. In the skin there are patches of edema, which last a few days and reappear elsewhere. The areas may be large and itchy with a rash and pain, producing lesions similar to those of cutaneous larva migrans. There is peripheral eosinophilia. The CNS may be invaded, resulting in an eosinophilic myeloencephalitis with eosinophilic pleocytosis and bloody and xanthochromic CSF. The eye may also be invaded, causing palpebral edema, exophthalmos and subconjunctival hemorrhage.

Larva migrans

Cutaneous larva migrans is caused by dog or cat hookworm larvae that enter the skin and are unable to complete the life cycle. They either migrate through subcutaneous tissue or encyst in the tissue and the larvae may cause serpiginous erythematous tracts. The tracts eventually become dry and encrusted.

Visceral larva migrans is caused by the dog and cat ascarid larvae (*Toxocara* spp.) that escape from eggs that are accidentally swallowed. The larvae migrate through the tissue and encyst as second-stage larvae. The migrating larvae produce tracts with hemorrhagic necrosis and eosinophilic and lymphocytic infiltration. Migration into the liver causes enlargement and it becomes studded with nodules containing eosinophils and plasma and giant cells. There may be interstitial eosinophilia in the lungs. Focal lung granulomas may develop around disintegrating larvae. Larvae may also enter the eye and cause endophthalmitis and retinal detachment and some larvae may enter the CNS and heart (see Chapter 174).

Trematodes living in liver, lungs, intestines and blood

Although many trematodes infect humans, only a few are considered to be important pathogens. These flat worms are found in all organs, especially the intestines, and a few are found in the liver, lungs and blood. They are hermaphoditic except for the schistosomes. The life cycles of the important trematodes are presented in Figure 246.3.

The opisthorchid liver flukes

Clonorchis sinensis, Opisthorchis viverrini and *Opisthorchis felineus* are found in the bile ducts. The worms are flat or leaf-like and about 1.5cm long and tapered at both ends. There are two branched testes at the posterior end. The eggs produced pass down the bile ducts to the intestine and out with the feces. In water, snails of a number of species (*Parafossarulus, Thiara* and *Bithynia*) serve as the first intermediate host; they ingest the egg and the miracidium is released from the egg. After reproducing by polyembryony, cercariae are produced that leave the snail and encyst as metacecariae in freshwater fish (cyprinids or carp). When the fish is eaten raw or improperly cooked the metacercariae are digested out of the fish and migrate down the bowel and then into the bile passages. There may be mechanical irritation, inflammation of the bile ducts with metaplasia and proliferation of the epithelium and periductal fibrosis. Pancreatic ducts may show epithelial metaplasia and partial obstruction. There is often biliary stone formation and bacterial superinfection. Cholangiocarcinoma is a possible complication and DNA carcinogens may be associated with such tumor formation. There may also be an association with nitrosamines, which are commonly found in Asian foods.[26]

Fasciolopsis buski

Fasciolopsis buski is the largest intestinal trematode of humans, measuring 5–7cm by 8–20mm by 1–3mm. It has an oral and ventral sucker, two large ceca, two branched testes and a central and coiled uterus. Eggs pass in the feces into water and the hatched miracidium enters a specific planorbid snail. Cercariae released from the snail attach to aquatic vegetation and form into metacercariae. When eaten the metacercariae excyst and attach to the mucosa of the small intestine. Large numbers of worms cause bleeding at attachment sites, excess mucus secretion and obstruction. Toxic secretions and excretions may be absorbed, causing generalized edema and cachexia. Death can result from massive infection.

Fasciolia hepatica

Fasciolia hepatica is acquired by eating aquatic vegetation on which the metacercariae are attached. Upon ingestion the metacercariae are released and penetrate the gut wall, traverse the peritoneal cavity, pass through the liver capsule into the liver parenchyma and into the bile duct. The migratory stages are characterized by hepatomegaly and hemorrhagic necrotic worm tracts. Eosinophils and other inflammatory cells are present. In chronic infections there may be mechanical irritation, because of the large size of the fluke and toxic metabolites, and hyperplasia of the biliary epithelium resulting in obstruction in some cases. Worms may also re-enter the liver parenchyma. The worms are large, 4cm in length and 1.5cm wide, with a large cephalic cone at the anterior end. The egg passes down the bile duct to the intestines and out with the feces. It hatches in the water and the miracidium enters into snails of the genus *Lymnea*. Cercariae are released and encyst on all varieties of aquatic vegetations.

Paragonimus westermani

Paragonimus westermani usually resides in pairs in the lung. They are reddish brown, plump bodied and shaped like coffee beans, and measure about 1.2cm long, 0.6cm wide and 0.4cm thick. They have two large branching testes in the posterior half of the body. Eggs enter the alveoli, are coughed up and swallowed, and pass out in the feces or in sputum. The egg hatches in water, enters a specific snail and multiplies, and released cercariae enter crabs and crayfish where the metacercariae encyst. When the infected crustacean is eaten the metacercariae are released from the cyst, penetrate the gut wall and enter into the peritoneum, diaphragm and lung.

Young migrating worms produce local hemorrhage and cellular infiltration. These worms may settle in ectopic locations and evoke a pronounced tissue reaction. In the lung and other locations a leukocytic infiltration develops around the worm and fibrous tissue infiltrates to form a cyst wall. Eggs may migrate into pulmonary tissue and other locations and evoke granulomatous reactions. Cerebral paragonimiasis often develops, with hemorrhage, eosinophils, a yellowish exudate and Charcot–Leyden crystals. Some lesions may eventually calcify.

Other species of *Paragonimus* can also infect humans and invade subcutaneous tissue and the abdominal cavity.

Other intestinal fluke infections

Most intestinal fluke infections are innocuous unless there is a large number of worms. Bleeding and ulceration, inflammation and excess mucus secretion may result from *Echinostoma* spp. and heterophyid infections. The eggs of the heterophyids are tiny and may be carried by the lymphatics and venules to ectopic locations such as the heart and evoke granulomas. Eggs of the intestinal flukes pass in the feces and hatch in water and the miracidia enter snails. Cercariae emerging from the snails enter fish and other aquatic animal life and when these animals are eaten the metacercariae excyst and develop into adults in the small intestine.

Human schistosomes

Human schistosomes are found in the venous bloodstream. Eggs are passed into water and the miracidia released search out specific snails in which to continue the life cycle. Cercariae released from the snails penetrate the skin and the larval schistosomulae migrate to the lungs and then to the mesenteric and vesical veins. Eggs carried back through the mesenteric veins to the liver are responsible for granuloma formation. The liver becomes enlarged, especially the left lobe. The spleen may become enlarged and portal hypertension develops and leads to obstructive liver disease, esophageal varices and ascites. Egg granulomas also form, especially in the large intestine.

Gastrointestinal symptoms such as diarrhea with blood, mucoid stools and a protein-losing enteropathy are not uncommon. In urinary schistosomiasis hematobia egg granulomas develop in the bladder, possibly leading to cancer. Inflammation and fibrosis of the urethral wall lead to stenosis, irregular dilatations and hydronephroses. Secondary bacterial infections are common and can lead to renal failure and death. *Schistosoma haematobium* eggs may reach the lung and cause fibrosis and lead to cor pulmonale. *Schistosoma japonicum* is responsible for cerebral schistosomiasis, and spinal cord involvement is reported in *S. mansoni* infections.

The schistosomes are the only trematodes with separate sexes. They have oral and ventral suckers. The females are 1.5–2.5cm in length and 0.2–0.3mm in diameter. The male is 0.5–2.0cm and, although flat, usually curls up to form the gynecophoral canal in which the female lies. The female leaves the male, crawls to the small venules close to the lumen of the gut or urinary bladder and deposits eggs. The miracidium releases enzymes to work with the spines on the *S. mansoni* and *S. haematobium* eggs to digest the tissue and enter the lumen of the intestine and bladder. Some eggs are carried back via the venules and veins to the liver. The life cycles of the human schistosomes are presented in Figure 246.3.

Cestodes living in the intestines and tissues

Adult tapeworms residing in the intestines do not cause serious disease, but larval stages of two species are highly pathogenic. The adults in the intestines pass eggs, which are taken up by an intermediate host (Fig. 246.4).

Eggs of *T. saginata* and *T. solium* are ingested by bovids and swine and the larval or cysticercus stages develop in muscles. When the meat is eaten insufficiently cooked the cysticerci are released and develop into adults in the small intestine.

The life cycles of the fish tapeworm *D. latum* and related species involves two intermediate hosts: a copepod and a fish. The egg hatches in water and the corricidium is taken in by a copepod and develops into a procercoid larva. When eaten by a fish the larva develops into a pleroceroid larva and when the fish is eaten the larva becomes an adult in the intestine.

Hymenolepid cestodes often require an insect (beetles and fleas) as an intermediate host. *Hymenolepis nana* can also be acquired by ingestion of the egg. Some strains of *H. nana* are also capable of internal autoinfection of humans.

Morphologically, all tapeworms have a scolex and neck, and immature, mature and gravid proglottids. The scolex of *D. latum* has a sucking groove as a hold-fast organ, whereas the other tapeworms have a scolex with four suckers, and *T. solium* and *H. nana* have a rostellum on the scolex with rows of hooklets. Each mature proglottid is hermaphroditic with both male and female sex organs. The lengths and width of each species varies with the longest being *D. latum* (2–15m), followed by the taeniids (1–4m), *H. nana* (1.5–4cm) and *H. diminuta* (1–6cm).

Usually, only one *Taenia* spp. in the intestines causes little disease. There may be some irritation at the site of attachment. Infection with more than one worm may cause intestinal and appendiceal blockage. At times the worms or proglottids block the pancreatic or bile ducts. Toxic substances from the worms may be responsible for systemic manifestations. The fish tapeworm causes decreased vitamin B12 absorption and eventual macrocytic and megaloblastic anemia.

Larval stages of tapeworms also infect humans (Fig. 246.5). Infection with the plerocercoid larva of diphyllobothriid species such as *Spirometra* is the cause of sparganosis. The larvae acquired from eating aquatic animals or drinking copepods in water penetrate the gut wall and migrate through the tissue. Animal poultices used in Asia are another source of infection. The larvae cause painful inflammatory swellings or transient lesions. The parasite may invade the eye causing periorbital edema.

Humans who become infected with the eggs of *T. solium* may develop cysticercosis. The larvae invade the muscles, brain, eye and skin. Although the cyst may remain intact and dormant for years, it may eventually break and the released fluids cause granulomas and calcification. Subcutaneous nodules are palpable and their presence usually indicates CNS involvement. Neurocysticercosis is responsible for arachnoiditis with pleocytosis and increased protein in the CSF. Intense inflammation may develop around dead or dying parasites.

Echinococcosis or hyatid disease develops in humans who accidentally ingest the eggs of the dog tapeworms *E. granulosus* or *E. multilocularis*. The egg hatches in the duodenum and the onco-

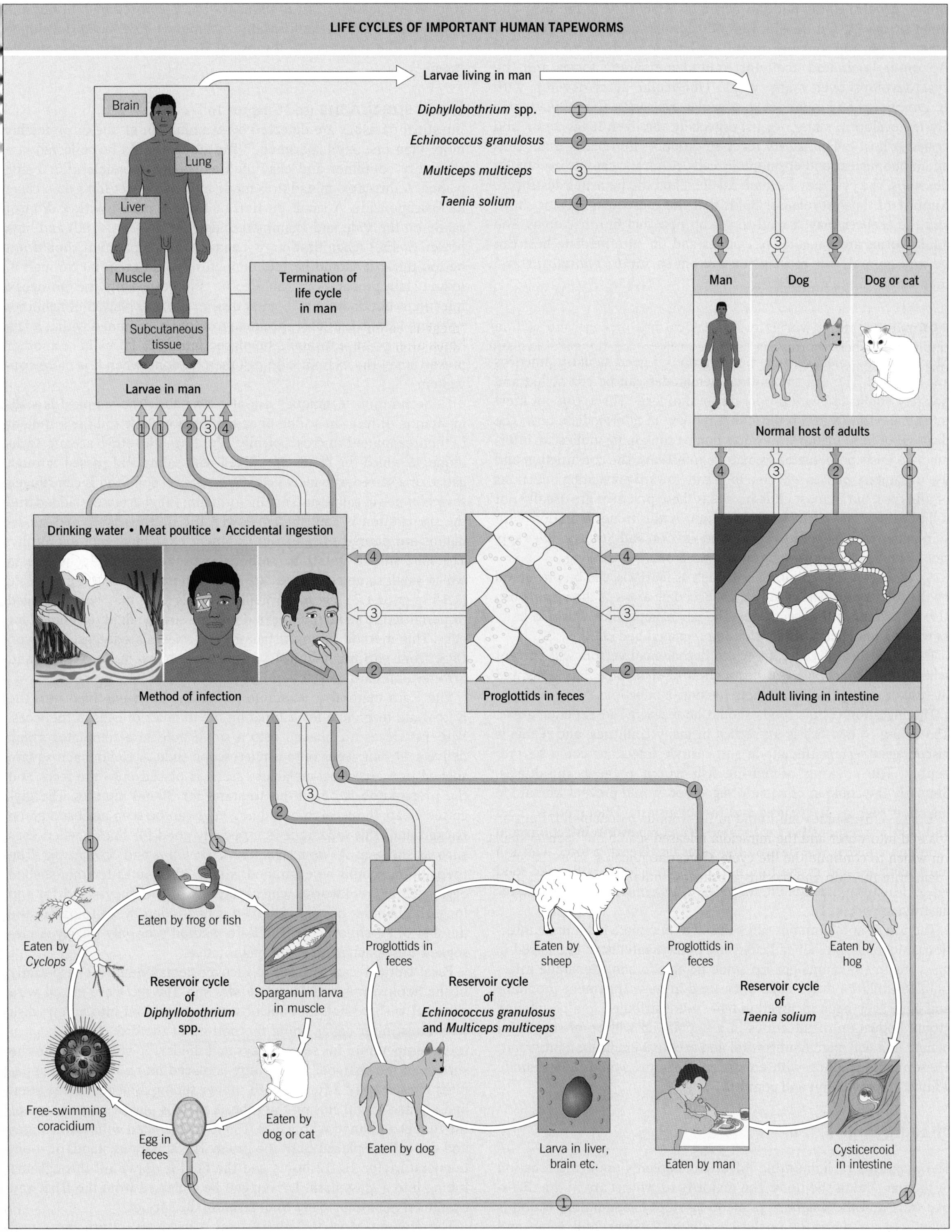

Fig. 246.5 Life cycles of important human tapeworms; adults living in tissues and intestines and blood: humans are accidental hosts.

sphere penetrates the gut and becomes established in the liver and other organs. A cyst develops brood capsules and protoscolices proliferate from the inner germinal epithelium of the brood capsule. An outer laminated acellular limited membrane forms and the cyst develops over many years. Unilocular cysts develop with *E. granulosus* and multilocular alveolar cysts with *E. multilocularis*. Cysts develop in many organs, especially the liver, lungs, brain and bones. A host inflammatory reaction produces fibroblasts, giant cells and mononuclear and eosinophilic cells. A fibrotic capsule eventually develops. The cyst may become calcified and the parasites destroyed. Rupture of the cyst releases fluids that can cause anaphylactic shock and the scolices may spread to set up new foci in other areas. The adult worms are parasites of canines and the intermediate host can be any animal, but most often are sheep for *E. granulosus* and rodents for *E. multilocularis*.

PREVENTION

Most parasitic infections can be prevented if good sanitary practices are followed. The soil-transmitted nematodes can be controlled and possibly eradicated with proper disposal of feces. This is true for most intestinal parasites, even those that require an intermediate host. The disposal of fecal matter into water bodies containing molluscan intermediate hosts perpetuates trematode infections. The construction and use of sanitary privies will go a long way toward preventing infections of all types, but in most endemic areas these practices are usually not followed and indiscriminate defecation is the trend. Infection with skin-penetrating helminths such as hookworm and *Strongyloides* spp. can be prevented by wearing shoes and protective clothing.

Arthropod-borne helminthiasis, such as filariasis, can be prevented by the use of insecticides in houses. Breeding areas of the vectors can also be treated with insecticides. The use of repellents will also help, as will sleeping under insecticide-impregnated bed nets.

The avoidance of water known to harbor snail vectors will prevent schistosome infections. The destruction of snail breeding areas and the use of molluscicides will help to control infections.

The ingestion of raw foods should be restricted in endemic areas. The eating of raw fish is a practice in many countries, and if this is discouraged certain trematode and cestode infections could be prevented. The cooking of marine fish would prevent anisakiasis. Similarly the cooking of aquatic vegetation would prevent trematode infection such as fascioliasis and fasciolopsiasis. Undercooked beef and pork are responsible for trichinosis and tapeworm infections and thorough cooking will destroy the parasites. Freezing foods will kill most parasites and in the future irradiation of foods will make food safe.[27] Microwave treatment, however, is not considered adequate for destroying parasites.

The use of anthelmintics can be used to eliminate helminthic infections. Mebendazole, albendazole and praziquantel have been used in mass treatment campaigns for some nematode and trematode infections. Antifilarial drugs have been used in mass treatment programs and have even been included in table salt distributed to a population group. Reduction of infections in a population will be of significant benefit and will augument control and eventual eradication programs. These methods along with education programs would be a definite adjunct to prevention and control.

DIAGNOSIS

The diagnosis of helminthic infections depends upon the location of the parasite in the body. The majority of worms are in the digestive tract and the diagnosis is made by stool examination. Blood is examined for parasites in the circulatory system, and urine and sputum are examined for worms in the genitourinary systems and respiratory passages. Tissue parasites are diagnosed by biopsies and by immunologic methods. Many techniques have been developed to aid in the diagnosis and most of these have been presented in detail.[28]

Stool specimens (see Chapter 165)

Intestinal parasites are detected by examination of one or preferably more than one stool specimen.[29] The stools should be collected in a clean dry container and examined as soon as possible after being passed. A direct examination is made by making wet films on a clean microscope slide. A small portion of feces is mixed with a drop of saline on the slide and examined under low power (×100) and high power (×450) magnification, if needed. The preparation should not be too thick; it should be thin enough to read newsprint through it. Iodine stain preparations can also be used, especially for protozoan infections, but do not add a great deal to the observation of helminth eggs and larvae. If a stool specimen cannot be examined within a few hours after passage it should be placed into 10% formalin or another preservative. The examination can then be done when it is more convenient.

Concentration techniques are also available. The simplest is sedimentation of feces in a tube or sedimentation flask and the sediment is then examined microscopically. The formalin–ethyl acetate technique, in which the stools are mixed with saline and passed through gauze or a screen, is widely used. The material collected is centrifuged several times in saline and finally formalin. Ethyl acetate is added and the preparation is centrifuged slowly. The detritus layer and supernatant are poured off and the sediment examined microscopically. The zinc sulfate flotation method is another simple technique in which small samples of feces are mixed thoroughly with zinc sulfate (1.18 sp gr or 1.2 sp gr for formalized stools). This may be centrifuged or permitted to stand for a period and the surface fluids examined for eggs. This method is unsatisfactory for operculated eggs, however. Eggs from various helminths as well as larvae of hookworm and *Strongyloides* are depicted in Figures 246.6 and 246.7.

The Kato method to examine stools has been modified into the Kato–Katz technique for estimating the number of eggs in the feces. Screened feces are placed into a small hole in a template, which delivers 41.7mg feces onto a microscope slide. A Cellophane square soaked in a glycerine–malachite green is placed onto the feces and the preparation is permitted to stand for 30–60 minutes. The glycerine clears the fecal material and eggs can be seen against a green background. This technique is especially good for thick-shelled eggs such as those of *A. lumbricoides, T. trichiura* and *S. mansoni*. The preparation should be examined within 30 minutes for thin-shelled eggs such as hookworm, which may dissolve if they stand for too long. The number of eggs observed is multiplied by 24 to obtain the number of eggs/g of feces. The Kato method uses only the glycerine-soaked Cellophane and is not quantitative.

Fecal cultures can be used to recover nematode larvae, especially of the hookworms and *Strongyloides* spp. The feces are mixed with charcoal with a small amount of water and placed into a Petri dish with moist filter paper lining the bottom of the dish. This is kept at room temperature for several days and the larvae will migrate to the surface of the charcoal. The culture is placed into a Baermann apparatus consisting of a funnel with rubber tubing attached to the stem and a pinch-clamp closing the tube. A sieve is placed into the top of the funnel and lined with gauze. The funnel is filled with warm water and the culture placed onto the gauze. The apparatus stands at room temperature for 10–12 hours and the fluid is drawn off through the tubing into a glass flask. Larvae can be collected from the flask and examined microscopically to determine the species.

The Harada–Mori technique is also used to culture feces and recover larvae. Filter paper strips are coated on one side with feces

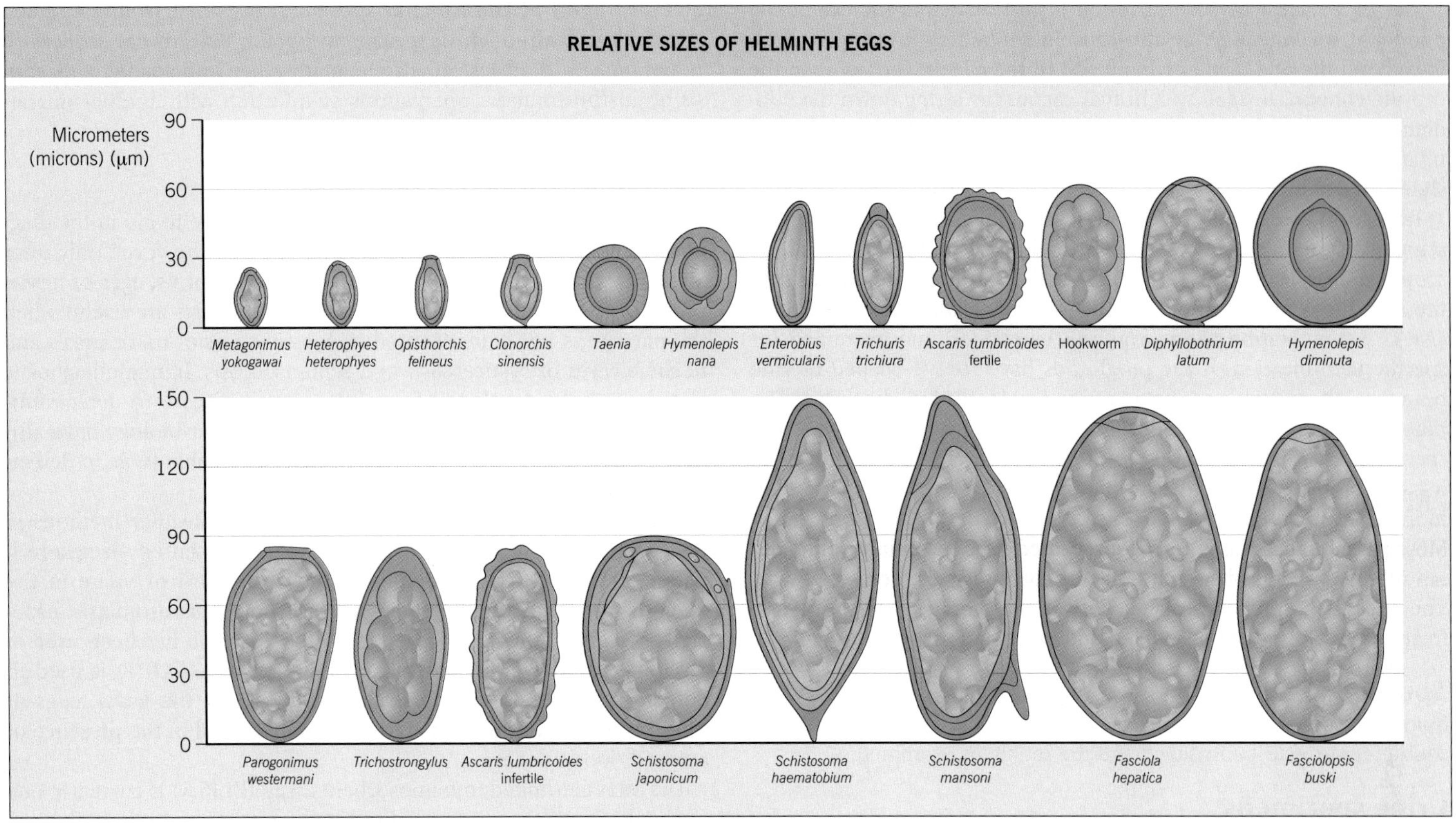

Fig. 246.6 Relative size of helminth eggs. HHS Publication No. (CDC 89–8116)

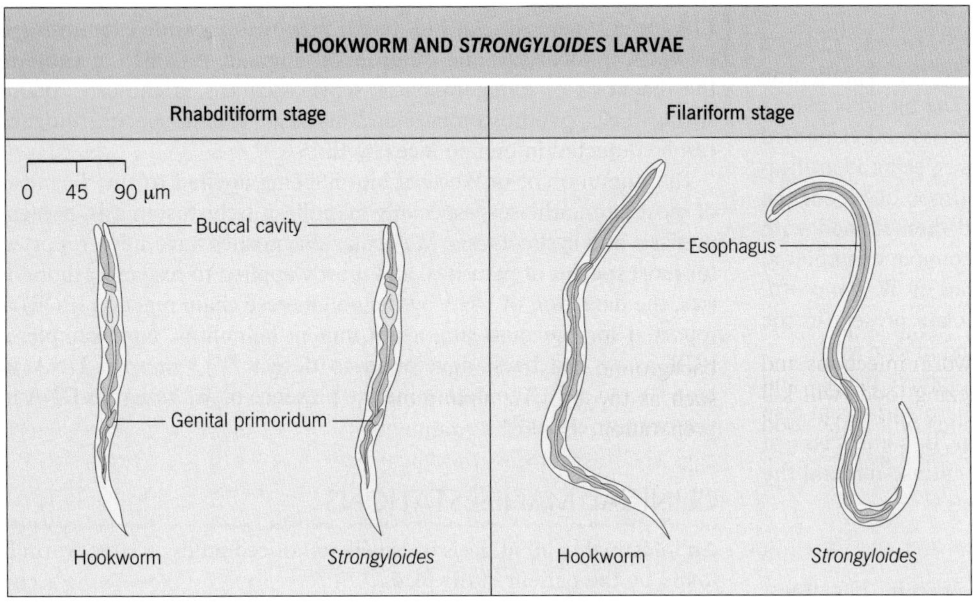

Fig. 246.7 Hookworm and *Strongyloides* larvae. HHS Publication No. (CDC 89–8116)

and placed into a tube containing a small amount of water. The tube is kept upright so that the filter paper is kept moist by capillary action. After 4–10 days the filter paper is removed and the water examined for larvae.

An agar plate culture for *Strongyloides* spp. has been developed.[30] A few grams of feces are placed into the center of the agar and the plate is incubated at room temperature for 48 hours. Tracks are made by the parasite in the agar and the larvae can be recovered by a Pasteur pipette and placed onto a microscope slide for identification.

Eggs of some parasites can be picked up on perianal swabs. Swabs such as scotch tape or paddle swabs are placed on the perianal area and then placed under a microscope for examination. Pinworm, tapeworm and *A. lumbricoides* eggs can be recovered.

Eggs of *Schistosoma* spp. can be found in feces using some of the above-mentioned examinations. An egg hatching technique can also be used in which feces are placed into a sidearm flask and water added until it reaches a level just below the sidearm. When the suspension settles more water is added until the level is above the sidearm. A dark cloth or bag is placed over the flask without covering the sidearm. The sidearm is then placed into the light and hatching miracidia from the schistosome eggs will be attracted to the light. They can be examined microscopically.

Specimens can be collected directly from the duodenum and examined for helminthic infections. Material collected by duodenal aspiration can be examined microscopically for *Strongyloides* and *Ascaris* spp. and flukes.

The Entero-Test or string capsule is also available for examining duodenal specimens. A gelatin capsule containing a string is swallowed and the end of the string taped to the cheek. The string in the capsule contains a small weight that carries the string down the duodenum after the capsule dissolves. After 4 hours the string is pulled up and the mucus adhering to the string is placed onto a microscope slide and examined.

Tapeworm proglottids are at times found in stool specimens. These segments should be washed in water and placed between two microscope slides. The slides are than tied together with string and the specimens placed into a fixative – alcohol, formalin, acetic acid (AFA). After fixation the worms can be stained and examined for specific identification. If the proglottids have rosette-shaped uterine branches the worm can be identified as a diphyllabothriid. The number of uterine branches of *Taenia* spp. can be counted and the specimen identified as *T. solium* (6–11) or *T. saginata* (15–20). India ink can be injected into the uterine pore and the branches are then more easily counted.

Adult trematodes found in feces should be washed and placed between two microscope slides that are then tied together with string. The specimens are than placed into a fixative such as AFA. After fixation the worms can be stained and examined for speciation.

Sputum specimens

Sputum to be examined for eggs or larvae should be mixed with 3% sodium hydroxide, centrifuged and the sediment examined.

Urine specimens

Urine specimens will sometimes help in the diagnosis of *S. haematobium* eggs or microfilariae of *W. bancrofti* and *O. volvulus*. The urine specimen is centrifuged and the sediment examined.

Blood samples

Several of the filarial infections can be diagnosed by the examination of drops of blood from finger or ear lobe pricks. The blood is placed onto a microscope slide and covered with a coverglass and examined under low power for thrashing microfilariae. For specific identification thick blood smears are made with several drops of blood, the smear is permitted to dry for several hours and then stained with Giemsa stain. Identifications are based upon for example microfilarial sizes, cephalic space and tail nuclei. Microfilariae of *W. bancrofti*, *B. malayi*, *B. timori*, *L. loa* and *Mansonella* spp. are present in the blood. *Onchocerca volvulus* microfilariae are found in skin snips.

Blood should be obtained at night for most lymphatic filariae and in the daytime for *L. loa* and *Mansonella* spp. Microfilariae can also be recovered from blood by membrane filtration. In some cases of lymphatic filariasis adult worms may be seen by ultrasound and the worms can be seen 'dancing' in the lymph channels.[31]

Cerebrospinal fluid

Cerebrospinal fluid is examined for evidence of helminthic infections. Eosinophilic pleocytosis is suggestive of angiostrongyliasis, paragonimiasis, cysticercosis, gnathostomiasis and schistosomiasis. Larvae of *A. cantonensis* are reported in CSF, especially in children, and *T. spiralis* larvae can be found in the CSF in very heavy infections. The CSF is centrifuged and the sediment examined for evidence of a helminth infection.

Tissue specimens

Tissue specimens may be taken and examined for helminthic infections. Muscle biopsies can be sectioned, stained and examined microscopically for *T. spiralis*, or the muscle can be pressed between two glass slides and examined for trichina larvae.

Rectal and bladder biopsy specimens can be examined for schistosome eggs. Skin biopsies may reveal the presence of microfilariae of *O. volvulus* or *Mansonella* spp. Fluid obtained from suspected hydatid cysts, although dangerous to obtain, may reveal scolices of *E. granulosus*. Biopsies can also be made when anticipating a diagnosis of gnathostomiasis, sparganosis or infection with another migrating helminth.

Immunodiagnostic tests

There are myriad immunodiagnostic tests available to aid in the diagnosis of helminthic infections. Immunologic tests, however, only offer a presumptive diagnosis, and the finding of the worms, eggs or larvae provides the definitive diagnosis. Immunologic tests are useful when the parasite is not demonstrated such as in cases of toxocariasis and in some cases of cysticercosis and echinococcosis. Immunodiagnostic tests have been developed for most parasitic disease to detect antibodies as well as antigens. Techniques in molecular biology have also been emerging and may eventually become valuable tools in detecting helminthic infections.[32]

Detailed information on immunologic and molecular methods in the diagnosis of parasitic diseases has been presented elsewhere.[33] Older tests such as complement fixation are still of value in the diagnosis of cysticercosis, paragonimiasis and schistosomiasis, especially for indicating active infections. Gel diffusion has been used in fascioliasis and the circumoval precipitation test (COPT) is used to detect antibodies in cases of schistosomiasis. In the latter, eggs of schistosomes develop precipitates around the shell in the presence of antibody-positive sera.

The enzyme-linked immunosorbent assay (ELISA) is currently one of the most widely used tests for many parasitoses. Indirect fluorescent antibody is also used, especially on tissue and parasite sections, to detect antigenic material. The indirect hemagglutination test along with EIA (enzyme immunoassay) is used for hydatid disease and EIA for cysticercosis. An EIA test is now recommended for strongyloidiasis, toxocariasis and other larval migrans. It is also of value in the diagnosis of paragonimiasis, schistosomiasis, trichinosis, angiostrongyliasis, gnathostomiasis and filariasis. *Taenia*-specific antigens can be detected in human feces by ELISA.[34]

The immunoblot or Western blot is being applied to the diagnosis of most helminthiases, especially fascioliasis, schistosomiasis, paragonimiasis and cysticercosis. Molecular diagnostics have been reported for most species of parasites, and mostly applied to research laboratories; the detection of DNA by the polymerase chain reaction (PCR) is reported for the most important human helminths. For example, a PCR assay has been developed to detect *W. bancrofti* DNA in blood[35] and a PCR to determine the presence of *W. bancrofti* DNA in vector mosquitoes.[36]

CLINICAL MANIFESTATIONS

An intestinal helminthiasis is usually unnoticed unless a large worm is found by the patient in the feces.

Pinworms

Pinworms generally cause little disease, but in children infections lead to perianal itching, eczema, nose-picking, pica and loss of sleep. Worms may migrate into the vagina, uterus and fallopian tubes and peritoneal cavity. Pinworms can be responsible for recurrent urinary tract infections in young girls.

Ascariasis

Ascariasis is innocuous unless the worms become erratic and migrate into vital organs or pass out of one of the orifices – nose, mouth or anus. Erratic ascariasis may be caused by anesthesia, trauma or some medications, such as tetrachloroethylene. A bolus of a large number of worms can cause volvulus or intussusception, abdominal distress, pneumonitis and cough, and disease is often associated with malnutrition and decreased growth.

Trichuriasis

Severe trichuriasis can lead to abdominal discomfort, dysentery, colitis, anemia and bloody stools. There may be nutritional loss, weight loss and malnutrition. Rectal prolapse occurs with some infections.

Hookworm

Hookworm larvae entering the skin may provoke a ground itch and secondary bacterial infections. Migrating larvae can cause pneumonitis and eosinophilia, and worms in the intestine can cause abdominal pain, nausea, vomiting and diarrhea. Large numbers of worms sucking blood cause iron deficiency anemia, hypoproteinemia and hepatosplenomegaly, and children will have impaired mental, physical and sexual development. Blood loss can be as high as 0.3ml/day/adult *Ancyclostoma duodenale*. Severe malnutrition develops, especially with concomitant infections with *A. lumbricoides* and *T. trichura*

Toxocariasis (see Chapter 174)

Toxocariasis (visceral larva migrans) causes hypereosinophilia, hepatomegaly and symptoms of chronic pulmonary inflammation with cough. There may also be visual difficulties due to retinochoroiditis or peripheral retinitis. Dog hookworm larvae in the skin cause cutaneous larva migrans and serpingous tunnels may present with intense pruritus. The lesion becomes erythematous and sometimes vesicular. *Ancylostroma caninum* may cause eosinophilic lesions in the intestines leading to abdominal pain.[6]

Strongyloides stercoralis

Early infections with *S. stercoralis* are similar to hookworm infections, causing ground itch and pneumonitis. Worms in the intestines cause inflammation, irritation, diarrhea, intestinal bleeding and melena. Sprue-like symptoms may also develop, along with malabsorption, weight loss and eosinophilia. Dermal lesions may occur at irregular intervals with urticarial eruptions on the buttocks, termed larval currens. Immunocompromised people, especially those with HTLV-1 associated lymphoma, are at risk of developing disseminated strongyloidiasis and present with severe enteritis, a protein-losing enteropathy, bronchitis, pneumonia, pleural effusion, cough and a blood-tinged sputum with rhabditiform larvae. Eosinophilia is usually absent in these cases. Death may result. Disseminated strongyloidiasis may also present as Gram negative pneumonia or meningitis, or as a polymicrobial bacteremia, with bacteria being spread by worms migrating from the bowel.

Capillariasis philippinensis

Capillariasis philippinensis leads to a protein-losing enteropathy, malabsorption, electrolyte imbalance, weight loss, wasting and death. Patients initially present with abdominal pain, borborygmi and diarrhea. Untreated infections usually lead to death.[24]

Trichinosis

Trichinosis is asymptomatic except when a large number of trichina larvae are ingested. After the worms become adults in the small intestines, symptoms of gastroenteritis develop, with nausea, abdominal pain, anorexia, diarrhea, fever and weight loss. Larvae are produced after copulation and these are able to enter the blood and are carried to striated muscles. During the migratory phase, muscle and joint pain develop, followed by periorbital edema and eosinophilia. Larvae passing through the heart can cause cell destruction, acute inflammatory changes and interstitial myocarditis. The infection can also cause neurologic and pulmonary complications. Dead larvae in the muscle eventually become calcified.

Lymphatic filariasis (see Chapter 170)

Symptoms associated with lymphatic filariasis are associated with the host's immune status; little immunity is associated with more severe disease. Early symptoms are fever, lymphangitis, lymphedema and lymphadenitis, which may be transitory and occur periodically. Scrotal involvement leads to orchitis, hydrocele and chyluria. Worms may block the lymph flow by an inflammatory reaction and the development of granulomas around the worms and these lead to lymphatic varicoses and eventual skin fibrosis, thickening and elephantiasis. Renal lesions may also occur, with microfilariae in the urine and chyluria. There may be enlargement of the legs, arms, scrotum, mammary glands and vulva. Tropical pulmonary eosinophilia with fever, splenomegaly, pulmonary infiltrates and hypereosinophilia is associated with *W. bancrofti* and *B. malayi* infections. Microfilariae are absent and are probably destroyed by host immune mechanisms in chronic infections.

Subcutaneous migration of *L. loa* may cause transient swelling known as Calabar swellings, which are a local reaction to the worm and its products. It is characterized by fever, eosinopilia and the urticarial swellings, which are more common in Caucasians. Migrating adult worms may pass over the bridge of the nose or through the conjunctiva across the eyeball. Migration of the worms in abnormal locations can cause symptoms in the scrotum, bowel, kidney and heart, but not usually in natives living in the African endemic areas. Visitors suffer more than indigenous populations.

Oncocercomas due to *O. volvulus* develop over bony prominences. Some nodules develop in deeper tissue and are unnoticeable. Dermatitis and blindness are caused by the microfilariae. Recent investigations suggest that the inflammatory response in the eye is induced by the endosymbiontic *Wobachia* bacteria released by dead microfilariae.[18] Lymph nodes in the groin may show lymphocyte depletion and fibrosis, followed by 'hanging groin,' especially in Africans. In the Americas nodules commonly develop on the upper part of the body, whereas in Africa the nodules develop on lower parts of the body.

Mansonellosis may cause:

- dermatitis (*M. streptocerca*);
- swellings on the hands and face, joint pains and itching (*M. perstans*); and
- allergic manifestations, articular pain, itching, headache, lymphadenopathy and eosinophilia (*M. ozzardi* in the Americas).

Guinea worm

Guinea worm in the subcutaneous tissue elicits allergic manifestations such as itching. When the female worms get close to the skin there is a localized erythema followed by pruritus, nausea, vomiting, diarrhea or asthmatic symptoms. The worm will secrete a toxic substance that causes a blister, which breaks when the area comes in contact with water, and the female releases larvae when the lesion opens up. The area becomes painful. The worm will eventually die and is resorbed or becomes calcified.

Angiostrongylus cantonensis and *Angiostrongylus costaricensis*

Migrating third-stage larvae of *A. cantonensis* may cause vague symptoms of gastroenteritis, vomiting, headache and fever. Once the worms reach the CNS they cause headache, nausea, vomiting, stiff neck, myalgia, pain and paresthesia. Coma may be a feature of heavy infections. Worms have been seen in the eyes of some patients. There may be paralysis of eye muscles. Frequent signs are abnormal tendon reflexes including abnormal Achilles' reflex, a positive Kernig's sign and impaired sensorium and vision. Infections with a large number of worms may be fatal.[9]

Abdominal angiostrongyliasis due to *A. costaricensis* resembles acute appendicitis. A tumor-like mass is palpable in the right lower quadrant. There may be fever, diarrhea or vomiting, along with eosinophilia.[37]

Gnathastome and anisakid larvae

Shortly after ingestion of gnathostome larvae there are symptoms of nausea, vomiting, pruritus and urticaria, and at times upper abdominal pain. Larval invasion into the liver will cause right upper quadrant tenderness and changes in liver function. In the lung there is a pulmonary infiltration and pneumothorax in patients with pleural infusion. Larvae migrating through the subcutaneous tissue and skin cause a rash along with red pruritic painless swellings. Invasion of the CNS often leads to death.

Anisakid larvae in the throat may lead to a 'tickle-throat', causing cough, but when they invade the mucosa of the intestinal tract they provoke eosinophilic granuloma formation, severe abdominal pain, nausea, vomiting and diarrhea. Usually, only a single worm is involved and the symptoms disappear when it is removed.

Trematodes

The trematodes, like the nematodes, cause little disease unless a large number of worms are involved. The liver flukes (*C. sinensis, O. viverrini, O. felineus*) in the bile ducts may cause symptoms early in the infection such as hepatomegaly, jaundice, diarrhea, anorexia, epigastric pain and fever. Repeated infection over a period of years may lead to ductal fibrosis, obstruction, cholangitis, cholecystitis and cirrhosis, and in some patients cholangiocarcinoma.

The sheep liver fluke *F. hepatica*, because of its large size, may block the bile ducts and cause cholangitis. Toxic secretions cause fever, chills, jaundice, an enlarged tender liver, cough, vomiting, abdominal symptoms and eosinophilia. Young worms may attack the pharyngeal mucosa, causing bleeding and edema. This occurs after eating raw sheep liver containing the parasite. The condition has been called halzoun.

The large intestinal fluke *F. buski* may cause intestinal blockage and toxemia when there is a large number of worms. Eosinophilia is common and ulcers may develop, which often hemorrhage. It causes abdominal distension, hunger pains and increased appetite, diarrhea and a foul-smelling yellowish stool. Allergic manifestations, nausea, vomiting, ascites and cachexia develop as a result of toxins secreted by the worms. Other intestinal flukes cause little disease, but tiny eggs of the heterophyids may enter the mucosa and are carried to ectopic locations such as the brain and heart, provoking granuloma formation. Echinostomes may produce inflammation and ulceration with diarrhea and abdominal pain.

The young lung fluke of *P. westermani* produces little disease during migration, but once established in the lung may cause fever, dyspnea, cough, chest pain and the production of a rusty sputum. At first the disease is often thought to be tuberculosis. The worms may enter the cranial cavity and invade the brain causing fever, headache, nausea, vomiting and visual disturbances, convulsions and meningeal signs.

Schistosome infections (see Chapter 167)

There may be petechial hemorrhages at the site of penetration where schistosome cercariae enter the skin. There will be localized edema and pruritus. After a few weeks there are toxic or allergic reactions and symptoms include fever, nausea, abdominal pain, rigor, urticarial rashes and eosinophilia. This acute stage is known as Katayama syndrome. In the chronic stage granulomas have formed around the eggs in tissue and hepatomegaly develops and the spleen becomes enlarged. This is followed by esophageal varices and finally ascites. Intestinal disease, usually with *S. mansoni* and *S. japonicum*, may involve the entire intestine or more often the large bowel. There may be abdominal cramps, tenderness and bloody mucoid stools. A protein-losing enteropathy, weight loss and anemia may also develop.

Features of *S. haematobium* infection are dysuria, urinary frequency and hematuria. Eosinophils in the urine are not uncommon. Heavy infections, with the deposition of many eggs in the bladder tissue, can lead to squamous cell carcinoma.

Pulmonary involvement can be a feature of all schistosome infections, and causes cor pulmonale with dyspnea, cough and hemoptysis.

Cerebral manifestations are common in oriental schistosomiasis, with symptoms of lethargy and confusion followed by speech difficulties and optical field defects. *Schistosoma mansoni* occasionally causes the spinal cord symptoms of a transverse myelitis, usually in the lumbar region. Flaccid paralysis of the lower limbs is also reported.

Tapeworm (see Chapter 168)

Tapeworm, even the larger ones, in the small intestines provoke few symptoms. Patients usually become aware of being infected only when worm segments are passed in the feces. If *D. latum* attaches to the proximal portion of the jejunum vitamin B12 deficiency results, with the development of pernicious anemia. This was seen in Finland but is now very rare. Sparganosis associated with other diphyllobothriid species causes painful inflammatory swellings, which may be transient. Spargana in the eyes cause intense reactions and periorbital edema.

Taenia spp. in the intestine are asymptomatic in most patients, but some have hunger pains, abdominal discomfort and indigestion. Patients usually become symptomatic when proglottids are found in the feces or passing from the anus. Eosinophilia is not uncommon. Cysticercosis or infection with larvae of *T. solium* is a serious disease, especially if there are cysticerci in the CNS. Cysticerci in the muscle are asymptomatic, but can give rise to myositis, fever and eosinophilia. The cysticerci usually die and become calcified. Cysticerci in the eye cause visual symptoms such as a decrease in visual acuity, retinal edema and hemorrhage. Neurocysticercosis results in arachnoiditis with CSF pleocytosis and an increase in CSF pressure. Obstructive hydrocephalus, cerebral infarction, epilepsy, papilledema, vomiting, headache, a toxic gait and intellectual deterioration may also develop. Dead or dying parasites may exacerbate symptoms, and location of the parasite in the CNS is responsible for a variety of CNS symptoms.

Hyperinfections with *H. nana* may cause diarrhea, loss of appetite, abdominal pain, headache, weakness, and at times epileptoid convulsion, dizziness and eosinophilia. *Hymenolepis diminuta* may cause diarrhea.

Hydatid disease (see Chapter 169)

There are usually no symptoms with hydatid disease until the cysts arelarge and in vital organs. Many years are usually required for a cyst to reach a significant size. Cysts in the liver may put pressure on the bile ducts and blood vessels. Large cysts in the lung can cause cough, shortness of breath and chest pains. Involvement of the CNS results in different symptoms depending upon the location of the cyst. Leaks of hydatid fluid sensitize the patient and can cause anaphylactic shock. A cyst in the eye causes proptosis.

MANAGEMENT (see Chapter 209)

Management of helminthic infection is variable and depends upon:

- the specific parasite;
- its location in the host; and
- the number of worms involved.

Usually anthelmintics are effective, but in some cases surgical or other intervention may be necessary. Follow-up examination and anthelmintic treatment may be required. The currently used anthelmintics are discussed in the *The Medical Letter*:[38]

- the soil-transmitted helminths *A. lumbricoides, T. trichiuria* and hookworm, found in the intestines, respond to mebendazole 100mg q12h for 3 days, pyrantal pamoate 11mg/kg once or albendazole 400mg once;
- *Strongyloides* spp. infections will respond to thiabendazole 50mg in two doses for 2 days or ivermectin 200mg/kg/day for 1–2 days; albendazole 400mg/day for 3 days may also be effective; the hyperinfection syndrome requires prolonged treatment;
- children with a history of erratic ascariasis should be treated with pyrantal pamoate first because some anthelmintics cause erratic ascariasis;
- pinworm infections are easily treated with mebendazole 100mg once followed by another dosage of 100mg in 2 weeks; pyrantal pamoate 11mg/kg or albendazole 400mg repeated 2 weeks later are also effective;
- mebendazole 200mg q12h for 20 days or albendazole 200mg q12h for 10 days along with fluid and electrolyte replacement are recommended for intestinal capillariasis; treatment is repeated in the case of relapses by giving mebendazole for 30 days or albendazole for 20 days;[24] and
- the use of anthelmintics in trichinosis is debatable; symptomatic treatment with corticosteroids is recommended and mebendazole at dosages of 200–400mg q8h for 3 days then 400–500mg q8h for 10 days, or albendazole 400–800mg may provide some benefit.

Hookworm disease with anemia may require blood transfusion and long-term treatment with ferrous sulfate until hemoglobin levels become normal.

The two anthelmintics used to treat lymphatic filariasis are:

- diethylcarbamazine (DEC); and
- ivermectin (see Chapter 170).

Diethylcarbamazine can be given in dosages of 6mg/kg for 10–12 days. Filarial lymphangitis and side-effects can be managed with antihistamines and antipyretics. Tropical pulmonary eosinophilia is treated with DEC, 6mg/kg in three doses for 21 days from diagnosis. Single-dose treatment with DEC or ivermectin, or both, repeated at 6-month intervals for a few years shows promise for both the treatment and control of lymphatic filariasis.[39] Treatment of filariasis with an antibiotic may affect the endosymbiontic *Wobachia*, which may have an affect on the fertility of the parasite.[17]

In the past DEC has been used to treat onchocerciasis, but has been replaced with ivermectin because of severe side-effects. The recommended dose of ivermectin is 150mg/kg once, repeated at 3- to 12-month intervals for a few years.

Loiasis can be treated by surgical removal of the worm as it passes over the nose or the eye. Diethylcarbamazine is effective, first in low dosages of:

- 50mg on day 1;
- 50mg q8h on day 2;
- 100mg q8h on day 3; and
- 6mg/kg/day in three doses on days 4–21.

Antihistamines and corticosteroids are used in case of side-effects. Ivermectin in a single dose of 200mg/kg caused a decrease in microfilariae. Mebendazole may also be useful. Diethylcarbamazine can be used as prophylaxis.[40]

Mansonella spp. infections do not usually require treatment, but DEC or mebendazole and possibly ivermectin can be used. Ivermectin is reported to be effective against *M. streptocerca*.[41]

Angiostrongyliasis caused by *A. cantonensis* is usually self-limiting in light infections. Some investigators recommend symptomatic treatment and not an anthelmintic because drugs can kill the worms too quickly and cause more pathology. However, albendazole and mebendazole have been reported to be effective for pediatric cases in Taiwan.[42]

Angiostrongylus costaricensis infection is treated surgically. Similarly gnathostome infections are treated surgically, but the use of albendazole shows promise.[43] Anisakiasis is also treated surgically or by removal of the worms from the stomach by gastroscopy. No specific anthelmintic treatment is needed for transient anisakiasis.

Visceral larva migrans due to *T. canis* is usually self-limiting and symptomatic treatment and corticosteroids are beneficial. However, DEC 6mg/kg/day for 7–10 days, albendazole 400mg q12h for 3–5 days or mebendazole 100–200mg q12h for 5 days have been reported to be of some value. Cutaneous larval migrans can be treated with thiabendazole either topically or as 50mg/kg/day in two doses. Ivermectin 150–200mg/kg once or albendazole 200mg q12h for 3 days have also been used (see Chapter 174).

Fluke infections

Nearly all fluke infections are treated with praziquantel, 75mg/kg/day for 1–2 days. The Chinese liver fluke *C. sinensis* responds to praziquantel. *Opisthorchis viverrini* and *O. felineus* are also treated with the drug.

Albendazole 10mg/kg/week is also effective against *C. sinensis* and may also be useful for the other opisthorchiids.

The intestinal flukes *F. buski, H. heterophyes, M. yokogawai* and the echinostomes can be treated with praziquantel 75mg/kg/day in three doses for 1 day. Tetrachlorethylene 0.1ml/kg is also effective.

Praziquantel is ineffective in treating the sheep liver fluke, *F. hepatica*. Bithional 30–50mg/kg on alternate days for 10–15 doses was used in the past, but is no longer being manufactured in Japan. Triclabendazole 10mg/kg once has been shown to be effective[44] and is the drug of choice. Dehydroemetine 1mg/kg/day for 10 days has been used, but is more toxic than other drugs.

Praziquantel is effective against *Paragonimus* spp. in dosages of 75mg/kg/day in three doses for 2 days. Biothional had also been used.

The three major schistosomes, *S. mansoni, S. japonicum and S. haematobium*, respond to praziquantel (see Chapter 167). The dosage for *S. mansoni* and *S. haematobium* is 40mg/kg in two doses for 1 day, and for *S. japonicum* 60mg/kg/day in three doses for 1 day. Oxamniquine 15mg/kg once is effective against *S. mansoni* and metrifonate 10mg/kg once every other week for a total of three doses is effective against *S. haematobium*. The latter regimen may be effective against *S. mansoni* located in the perivesical plexis. Surgery is often required for esophageal varices; splenectomy and splenorenal shunting will relieve portal pressure. Concomitant bacterial infection associated with schistosomiasis should be treated with antibiotics following antischistosome therapy. Schistosome dermatitis should be treated palliatively with antipruritics and antihistamines.

Cestode infections (see Chapter 168)

Praziquantel is effective for treating cestode infections. Adult *T. saginata, T. solium* and *D. latum* can be treated with praziquantel 10mg/kg once. An alternative drug for *T. saginata* and *D. latum* is niclosomide 2g in four chewable tablets. However, this drug causes side-effects, the proglottids disintegrate and the scolex is not easily found. Treatment may have to be repeated a few months later. Paramomycin 1g q4h for 4 days may be used, but there may be gastrointestinal disturbances. Atebrine, 0.8g divided in half and given in half-hour intervals, will often provide the whole worm intact. It is given on an empty stomach and a saline purge is given 2 hours after treatment.

The recommended treatment for *T. solium* is praziquantel; other drugs may be deleterious to the proglottids, releasing eggs, which may lead to cysticercosis.

The recommended treatment for cysticercosis is albendazole, 15mg/kg in 2–3 doses over 8–28 days, repeated as necessary. Praziquantel is also used in a dosage of 50mg/kg/day in three doses for 15 days. The cyst may also be surgically removed. Surgery (and not chemotherapy) is recommended for intraocular cysticercosis.

Sparganosis is also treated surgically or with praziquantel with a total dose of 120–150mg/kg over 2 days.[45] *Hymenolepis nana* is treated with praziquantel 25mg/kg once and *H. diminuta* with 10mg/kg once or niclosamide 2g in a single dose.

Surgery was the recommended treatment for hydatid cysts until albendazole was found to be effective at a dosage of 400mg q12h for 28 days, repeated if necessary after 14 days for up to 12 cycles. Percutaneous drainage with ultrasound guidance in addition to albendazole has been found to be valuable in the treatment of hepatic hydatid cysts. *Echinococcus multilocularis* is more difficult to treat, but albendazole should be effective (see Chapter 169).

REFERENCES

1. Cross JH, Basaca-Sevilla V. Intestinal parasitic infections. Southeast Asian J Trop Med Pub Hlth 1981;12:262–74.
2. Ratard RC, Kouemeni LE, Bessala MM, *et al.* Ascariasis and trichuriasis in Cameroon. Trans Roy Soc Trop Med Hyg 1991;85:84–8.
3. Cross JH, Basaca-Sevilla V. Biomedical surveys in the Philippines. Naval Med Research Unit No.2-Sp-47 1984:1–174.
4. Nakada K, Kohakura M, Komoda H, Hinuma Y. High incidence of HTLV antibody in carriers of *Strongyloides stercoralis* (letter). Lancet 1984;17:633.
5. Cook GC. Parasitic diseases in clinical practice. London: Springer-Verlag; 1990:114–6.
6. Prociv P, Croese J. Human eosinophilic enteritis caused by dog hookworm *Ancylostoma caninum.* Lancet 1990;335:1299–302.
7. Bailey TM, Schantz PM. Trends in the incidence and transmission patterns of trichinoses in humans in the United States: comparison of the periods 1975–1981 and 1982–1986. Rev Infect Dis 1990;12:5–11.
8. Ancelle T, Dupouy-Camet J, Bougnoux ME, *et al.* Two outbreaks of trichinosis caused by horsemeat in France. Am J Epidemiol 1988;127:1302–11.
9. Cross JH. Angiostrongyliasis. In: Connor DH, *et al.* eds. Pathology of infectious diseases. Stamford, CT: Appleton and Lange; 1997:1307–14.
10. New D, Little MD, Cross JH. *Angiostrongylus cantonensis* infection from eating raw snails. N Engl J Med 1995;333:882.
11. Michael E. The population dynamics and epidemiology of lymphatic filariasis. In: Hutman TB, ed. Lymphatic filariasis. London: Imperial College Press; 2000:41–81.
12. Cross J, Partono F, Hsu MYK, Ash LR, Oemijati S. Experimental transmission of *Wuchereria bancrofti* to monkeys. Am J Trop Med Hyg 1979;28:56–66.
13. Joesoef A, Cross JH. Human filariae in Indonesia. Southeast Asian J Trop Med Hyg 1978;9:15–9.
14. Dennis DT, Partono F, Atmosoedjono S, Soroso JS. Timor filariasis; epidemiologic and clinical features in a defined community. Am J Trop Med Hyg 1976;25:797–802.
15. Partono F, Oemijati S, Dennis, DT, Purnomo, Atmosoedjono S, Cross JH. The Timor filaria on Flores and experimental transmission of the parasite. Trans Roy Soc Trop Med Hyg 1976;70:354–5.
16. Dreyer G, Noroes J, Figueredo-Silva J, *et al.* Pathogenesis of lymphatic disease in Bancroftian filariasis. A clinical perspective. Parasitol Today 2000;16:544–8.
17. Taylor MJ. Elimination of lymphatic filariasis as a public health problem: *Wobachia* bacteria of filarial nematodes in the pathogenesis of disease and as a target for control. Trans Roy Soc Trop Med Hyg 2000;94:596–8.
18. Andre A, Blackwell N, Hall L, *et al.* The role of endosymbiontic bacteria in the pathogenesis of river blindess. Science 2002;295:1892–5.
19. World Health Organization. Onchocerciasis and its control. WHO Tech Rpt Ser 1995;852:103.
20. World Health Organization. Control of foodborne trematode infections. WHO Tech Rep Ser 1995;849:1–157.
21. World Health Organization. The control of schistosomiasis. WHO Tech Rep Ser 1993;830:1–86.
22. Cross JH. Schistosomiasis in China: a brief review. Southeast Asian J Trop Med Pub Hlth 1976;7:167–70.
23. Fan PC. Asian *Taenia saginata*: species or strain. Southeast Asian J Trop Med Pub Hlth 1991;22(Suppl.):245–50.
24. Cross JH. Intestinal capillariasis. Clin Microbiol Rev 1992;5:120–9.
25. Cross JH. Intestinal capillarisis. In: Connor DH, Chandler FW, Schwartz DA, *et al.* eds. Pathology of infectious diseases. Stamford. CT: Appleton and Lange; 1997:1345–50.
26. Sun T. Clonazchiasis and opisthorchiasis. In: Connor DH, Chandler, FW, Schwartz DA, *et al.* eds. Pathology of infectious diseases. Stamford, CT: Appleton and Lange; 1997;1351–60.
27. Laoharanu P, Murrell KD. A role for irradiation in the control of foodborne parasites. Trends Food Sci Tech 1994;5:190–5.
28. Ash LR, Orihel TC. Parasites: a guide to laboratory procedures and identification. Chicago: American Society of Clinical Pathology Press; 1987.
29. Chung PR, Cross JH. Prevalance of intestinal parasites in children on a Taiwan offshore island determined by the use of several diagnostic methods. J Formosan Med Assoc 1975;74:411–8.
30. Arakai TI, Masaki K, Fukunori S, *et al.* Efficacy of agar plate culture in detection of *Strongyloides stercoralis* infection. J Parasitol 1990;76:425–8.
31. Noroes J, Addis D, Amaral F, *et al.* Occurrence of living adult *Wuchereria bancrofti* in the scrotal area of men with microfilaremia. Trans Roy Soc Trop Med Hyg 1996;90:55–6.
32. Walker JC. Parasitology: diagnostic techniques in the laboratory. Med J Aust 1993;158:824–9.
33. Wilson M, Schantz P, Pieniazek N. Diagnosis of parasitic infections; immunological and molecular methods. In: Murray PR, *et al.* eds. Manual of clinical microbiology. Washington DC: American Society for Microbiology; 1995:1159–70.
34. Allan JC, Velasquez-Tohom M, Torres-Alverez R, Yurrita P, Garcia-Noval J. Field trial of coproantigen-based diagnosis of *Taenia solium* taeniasis by enzyme-linked immunosorbent assay. Am J Trop Med Hyg 1996;54:352–6.
35. Zhong M, McCarthy J, Bierwert L, *et al.* A polymerase chain reaction assay for detection of the parasite *Wuchereria bancrofit* in human blood samples. Am J Trop Med Hyg 1996;54:357–63.
36. Nicolas L, Luquiaud P, Lardeux F, Mercer DR. A polymerase chain reaction assay to determine infection of *Aedes polynesiensis* by *Wuchereria bancrofti.* Trans Roy Soc Trop Med Hyg 1996;90:136–9.
37. Baird JK. Abdominal panstrongyliasis. In: Connor DH, Chandler FW, Schwartz DA, *et al*, eds. Pathology of infectious diseases. Stamford, CT: Appleton and Lange; 1977:1531–5.
38. Abramowicz M, ed., Drugs for parasitic infections. Med Lett 2000:1–12.
39. Nicolas L, Plichart C, Nguyen LN, Moulia-Pelat JP. Reduction of *Wuchereria bancrofti* adult worm circulating antigen after annual treatment with diethylcarbamazine combined with ivermectin in French Polynesia. J Infect Dis 1997;175:489–92.
40. Nutman TB, Miller K, Mulligan M, *et al.* Diethylcarbamazine prophylaxis for human loiasis. Results of a double-blind study. N Engl J Med 1988;319:752–6.
41. Fischer P, Bamubiiga J, Buttner DW. Treatment of human *Mansonella streptocerca* infection with ivermectin. Trop Med Int Hlth 1997;2:191–9.
42. Hwang KP, Chen ER. Clinical studies on angiostrongyliasis cantonensis among children in Taiwan. Southeast Asian J Trop Med Pub Hlth 1991;22(Suppl.):194–9.
43. Kraivichian P, Kulkomthorn M, Yingyoard P, Akarabovorn P, Paireepai C. Albendazole for the treatment of human gnathostomiasis. Trans Roy Soc Trop Med Hyg 1992;86:418–21.
44. Apt W, Aguilera X, Vega F, *et al.* Treatment of human chronic fascioliasis with triclabendazole; drug efficacy and serologic response. Am J Trop Med Hyg 1995;56:532–5.
45. Fu S, Xiao SH, Catto BA. Clinical use of praziquantel in China. Parasitol Today 1988;11:312–5.

chapter

247 Arthropods

Thomas R Fritsche

NATURE

The phylum Arthropoda is the largest and most varied of the animal phyla, consisting of more than one million described species among a total of 30 million or more. An exceedingly small number of this total directly or indirectly affect human health, but those that do are responsible for significant morbidity and mortality. Species responsible for human disease include representatives of all major arthropod classes (Table 247.1).

PATHOGENICITY

Direct tissue invasion

Arthropods responsible for superficial tissue invasion (referred to as infestation) include chigoe fleas and scabies mites, whereas invasion of deeper body tissues and cavities (referred to as infection) may be produced by dipteran larvae (maggots) and pentastomids. Tissue invasion of any sort by maggots is referred to as myiasis, and may occur either in living or devitalized tissues, depending upon the species.[1–3]

Envenomation and hypersensitivity reactions

Humans are continually subjected to the stings and bites of many different arthropods. Reaction to these attacks varies greatly and depends upon:

- the species involved;
- the type of saliva or venom being introduced into the wound;
- the location of the wound; and
- an individual's physiologic response, which may vary depending upon previous sensitization.

Arthropod stings and bites cause only local tissue reactions in most people, but some people have serious systemic reactions, including anaphylaxis.[4–6]

Vesication

Some of the larger tropical species of millipedes are capable of spraying an irritating and vesicating (blister-causing) chemical, which is used for defensive purposes, from glands located on each body segment.[7] Blister beetles are so named because of the presence of the vesicating compound cantharidin in their body fluids. Upon handling these attractive beetles, cantharidin may be released, resulting in the appearance of fluid-filled skin blisters several hours following exposure.[1,8,9]

Transmission of infectious agents

During the act of feeding, many species of arthropods are capable of either mechanically or biologically transmitting agents responsible for serious infectious disease (Table 247.2). Filth flies, which include the common house fly *Musca domestica,* and cockroaches have been incriminated in the mechanical transmission of the agents of bacillary dysentery, cholera, typhoid, viral diarrhea, amebic dysentery and giardiasis, pinworms and tapeworms. Arthropod vectors responsible for the biologic transmission of infectious agents may serve either:

- as simple amplification vehicles for the organism; or
- in a more complex role involving changing life cycle stages of certain parasites.[1,3,9,10]

PREVENTION

Principles of prevention are directed at limiting skin and mucous membane exposure to crawling and flying arthropods and their emanations. This may be accomplished by avoiding locations serving as a habitat for those arthropods posing the greatest threat to an individual such as:

- gardens, fields, orchards or unclean picnic areas that attract bees, wasps and yellowjackets;
- crawl spaces, wood sheds or outdoor privies, which may harbor venomous spiders or scorpions;
- domiciles conducive to cockroach, bedbug or kissing bug habitation; and
- outdoor environments known to be a source of ticks and biting diptera.

Remaining indoors during evening hours lessens the risks associated with exposure to mosquitoes. The wearing of light-colored clothing, especially long pants, long-sleeved shirts and closed-toed shoes when working outdoors or pursuing outdoor recreation is less attractive than dark clothing, short pants, short-sleeved shirts and opened-toed shoes to flying insects and allows the wearer to more readily recognize the presence of ticks and other crawling arthropods. Gloves also provide additional protection when gardening, but the use of scented lotions, perfumes or soaps should be discouraged.[8,11]

In addition to these simple measures, the use of insect repellents is an important preventative when the threat of exposure to noxious or serious pests cannot otherwise be easily mitigated. A variety of chemical repellents are available on the market. Those containing the compound *N,N*-diethyl-*M*-toluamide are among the most widely used and come in a variety of preparations for use on clothing and skin in concentrations varying from about 10 to 100%. The use of high-concentration products on children is not advised because there are reports of associated seizures.[8,12]

Use of mosquito nets during night-time hours and headnets at other times is mandatory in areas where mosquitoes are plentiful, especially in the tropics and subtropics, where they serve as vectors for malaria, filariae, viruses and other infectious agents. Impregnation of nets with insecticides has proved to be especially effective in decreasing the transmission rates of malaria in highly endemic areas.[13]

Desensitization regimens are highly effective in preventing anaphylaxis in individuals who have become sensitized to bee and wasp venoms. Venom immunotherapy is usually indicated for those who have a history of moderate-to-severe anaphylaxis, positive venom skin tests and are at risk of subsequent stings. It is not indicated for those who experience transient pain and local swelling.[5] Despite the use of desensitization, up to 15% of individuals whose initial anaphylactic reaction is judged to be severe continue to be at risk for anaphylaxis if re-stung.[14] Immunotherapy reagents are also available and may prove useful for individuals with intractable allergies to, for example, cockroaches and dust mites.[8]

ARTHROPODS OF MEDICAL IMPORTANCE AND THE THREATS THEY POSE TO HUMAN HEALTH			
Class	**Subclass**	**Order**	**Pathogenic potential**
Insecta (insects)		Anoplura (sucking lice)	Biting pests, local hypersensitivity, biologic vectors
		Siphonaptera (fleas)	Biting pests, local hypersensitivity, biologic vectors, superficial tissue invasion (*Tunga penetrans*)
		Dictyoptera (cockroaches)	Mechanical vectors, allergies
		Hemiptera (bedbugs, kissing bugs)	Biting pests, local and rarely systemic hypersensitivity, biologic vector (kissing bugs)
		Hymenoptera (bees, wasps, ants)	Envenomation, local and systemic hypersensitivity including anaphylaxis, biting pests (ants)
		Coleoptera (beetles)	Mechanical and biologic vectors, urticating hairs (larvae), vesicating fluids (adults)
		Lepidoptera (moths, butterflies, caterpillars)	Urticating hairs and venomous spines (larvae), urticating hairs and scales (adults)
		Diptera (flies, mosquitoes, biting midges)	Biting pests, local hypersensitivity, mechanical and biologic vectors, tissue invasion (myiasis)
Arachnida (arachnids)	Scorpiones (scorpions)		Envenomation with neurotoxins
	Araneae (spiders)		Envenomation with neurotoxins and necrotoxins
	Acari (ticks, mites, chiggers)		Biting pests, local hypersensitivity, allergies (mites), biologic vectors, superficial tissue invasion (*Sarcoptes scabiei*), neurotoxins (ticks)
Diplopoda (millipedes)			Vesicating fluid
Chilopoda (centipedes)			Envenomation, local and rarely systemic hypersensitivity
Crustacea (crustaceans)		Copepoda (copepods, water fleas)	Biologic vectors
		Decapoda (crabs, crayfish)	Biologic vectors
Pentastomida			Tissue and body cavity infection

Table 247.1 Arthropods of medical importance and the threats they pose to human health.

CLINICAL MANIFESTATIONS, EPIDEMIOLOGY AND DIAGNOSTIC MICROBIOLOGY

Specimens recovered by physicians or submitted by patients may take the form of intact organisms or parts of organisms, skin scrapings, tissues, sputum, urine, stool, articles of clothing, bedding, carpeting and foodstuffs. It is not uncommon for patients to submit arthropods recovered from the toilet bowl following a bowel movement or urination, raising concern that they may have an intestinal or bladder infection. Such an occurrence is usually coincidental and not related to infection. Although the more common forms of medically important arthropods, especially ectoparasites (fleas, lice, mites and ticks) may be readily identifiable, detailed identification of other arthropods, especially larval forms, may require consultation with a specialist in entomology. Repeated examinations fail to reveal the presence of arthropods or parasites in cases of delusional parasitosis; it is imperative that the affected individual's domicile is thoroughly examined to rule out the possibility of unrecognized mite infestations following abandonment of an attached rodent or bird's nest.[10,15]

Insects

Insects comprise more than 90% of all described arthropod species and include many of the vectors responsible for the transmission of serious infectious diseases.

Sucking lice, order Anoplura

Sucking lice are dorsoventrally flattened, wingless insects that have characteristic claws on the ends of each leg, which allow attachment to body hairs or clothing. All species suck blood and may cause unexplained dermatitis as a result of their repetitive feeding activities and chronic exposure of the skin to louse saliva and feces. Although named for their primary site of attachment, they do not always remain confined to that location.

The head louse, *Pediculus capitis*, and the body louse, *P. humanus*, are indistinguishable to the non-specialist. They are longer than they are wide and grow to about 3mm in length (Fig. 247.1). Biologic differences are apparent; only *P. humanus* transmits the agents of epidemic typhus, trench fever and relapsing fever (see Table 247.2).[3] Infestations with both species occur among people living in crowded conditions who have little opportunity for bathing and laundering. Children of school-age are at particular risk for acquiring head lice through the sharing of caps, clothing and combs.[2,16] Lice eggs (known as nits) are typically 1mm long and when unhatched have an intact operculum (Fig. 247.2). Head louse nits are deposited primarily on hair shafts close to the scalp, especially along the nape of the neck, whereas nits of body lice are deposited primarily upon clothing. Because such objects as hair casts, dander, hair spray and fungal hair infections may mimic nits, differentiation is important. Transmission of body lice occurs primarily through the sharing of infested clothing and bedding because they tend to deposit their eggs in clusters, especially along seams or waistbands.

The pubic louse, *Phthirus pubis*, is distinctly different from the others; it is rounder, measuring up to 2mm in diameter, the abdomen is more crab-like, and their first pair of legs is significantly smaller and more slender than the other pairs (Fig. 247.3). Pubic lice and their nits are found primarily on pubic hairs, but may extend to the chest, armpit and facial hair. Transmission occurs primarily

Class	Subclass/order	Genus	Etiologic agent	Disease
SUMMARY OF THE MAJOR ARTHROPOD GENERA INVOLVED IN THE BIOLOGIC TRANSMISSION OF INFECTIOUS DISEASES				
Insecta	Anoplura	*Pediculus*	*Rickettsia prowazekii* *Bartonella quintana* *Borrelia recurrentis*	Epidemic typhus Trench fever Epidemic relapsing fever
	Siphonaptera	*Xenopsylla*	*Yersinia pestis* *Rickettsia typhi*	Plague Murine typhus
		Nosopsyllus	*Rickettsia typhi*	Murine typhus
		Ctenocephalides	*Dipylidium caninum*	Dog tapeworm disease
	Hemiptera	*Panstrongylus, Rhodnius, Triatoma*	*Trypanosoma cruzi*	Chagas' disease
	Coleoptera	*Dermestes, Tribolium, Tenebrio*	*Hymenolepis nana, H. diminuta*	Hymenolepiasis
	Diptera	*Aedes*	Flaviviruses Other arboviruses	Dengue, yellow fever Febrile illness, encephalitis
		Anopheles	*Plasmodium* spp. *Brugia malayi* Arboviruses	Malaria Filariasis Febrile illness, encephalitis
		Culex	*Wuchereria, Brugia* Arboviruses	Filariasis Febrile illness, encephalitis
		Culicoides	*Mansonella* spp.	Filariasis
		Glossina	*Trypanosoma brucei*	African sleeping sickness
		Chrysops	*Loa loa* *Francisella tularensis*	Loiasis Tularemia
		Simulium	*Onchocerca volvulus* *Mansonella ozzardi*	Onchocerciasis Filariasis
		Phlebotomus, Lutzomyia	*Leishmania* spp. *Bartonella bacilliformis* *Phlebovirus*	Leishmaniasis Bartonellosis Sandfly fever
Arachnida	Acari (ticks)	*Ixodes*	*Borrelia burgdorferi* *Ehrlichia* spp. *Babesia* spp. Arboviruses	Lyme disease Human granulocytic ehrlichiosis Babesiosis Encephalitis
		Dermacentor	*Rickettsia rickettsii* *Rickettsia siberica* *Francisella tularensis* *Coltivirus* Other arboviruses	Rocky Mountain spotted fever Siberian tick typhus Tularemia Colorado tick fever Encephalitis
		Amblyomma	*Rickettsia rickettsii* *Rickettsia conorii* *Ehrlichia chaffeensis* *Francisella tularensis*	Rocky Mountain spotted fever Boutonneuse fever Human monocytic ehrlichiosis Tularemia
		Rhipicephalus	*Rickettsia rickettsii* *Rickettsia conorii*	Rocky Mountain spotted fever Boutonneuse fever
		Haemaphysalis	*Rickettsia siberica* *Rickettsia conorii* Arboviruses	Siberian tick typhus Boutonneuse fever Encephalitis, Kyasanur Forest disease
		Hyalomma	*Rickettsia siberica* Arbovirus	Siberian tick typhus Crimean–Congo hemorrhagic fever
		Ornithodoros	*Borrelia* spp.	Relapsing fever
	Acari (mites)	*Leptotrombidium*	*Rickettsia tsutsugamushi*	Scrub typhus
		Liponyssoides	*Rickettsia akari*	Rickettsialpox
Crustacea		Decapods	*Paragonimus* spp.	Paragonimiasis
		Copepods	*Diphyllobothrium* spp. *Dracunculus medinensis* *Gnathostoma spinigerum*	Diphyllobothriasis Guinea worm disease Gnathostomiasis

Table 247.2 Summary of the major arthropod genera involved in the biologic transmission of infectious diseases. Adapted from Fritsche, 1999.[10]

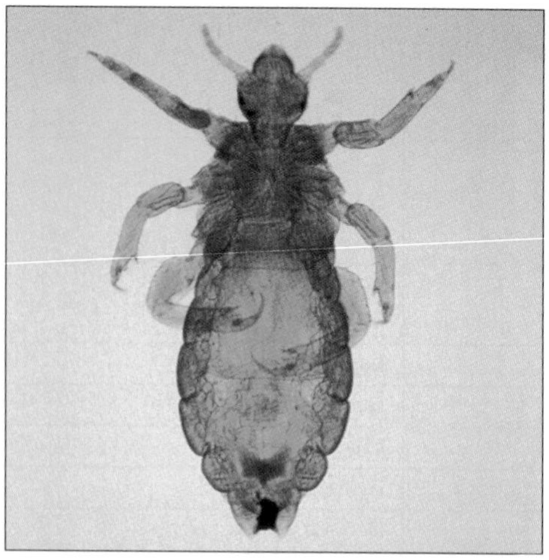

Fig. 247.1 Adult *Pediculus capitis*, the human head louse. Note the prominent claws for grasping hair.

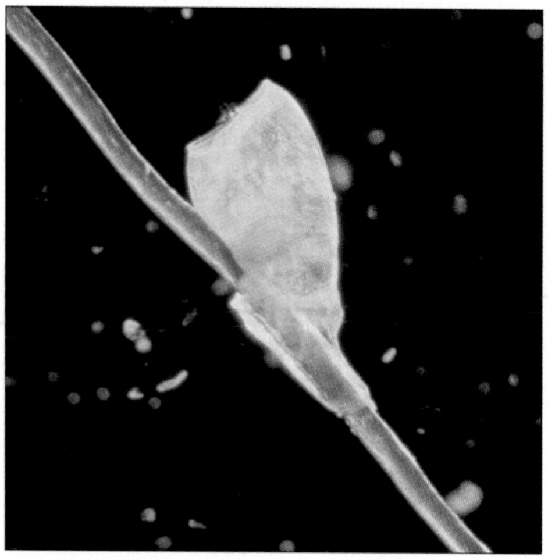

Fig. 247.2 Egg or nit of human head louse attached to a hair shaft. Note that the operculum is missing indicating previous emergence of the larval louse.

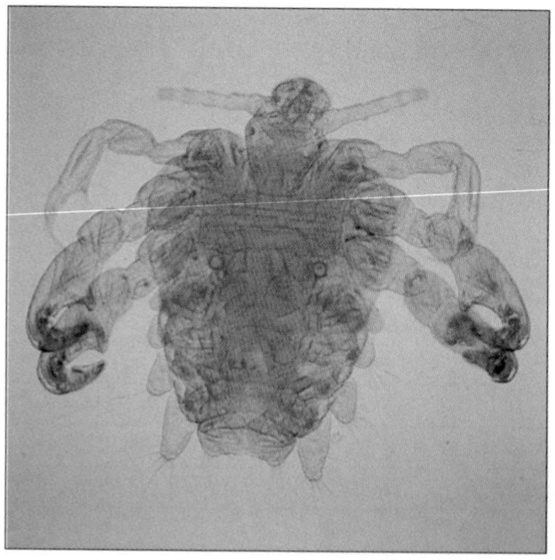

Fig. 247.3 Adult *Phthirus pubis*, the human crab louse. The bodies of these lice are rounder and more crab-like than those of head or body lice. With permission from ASM Press.

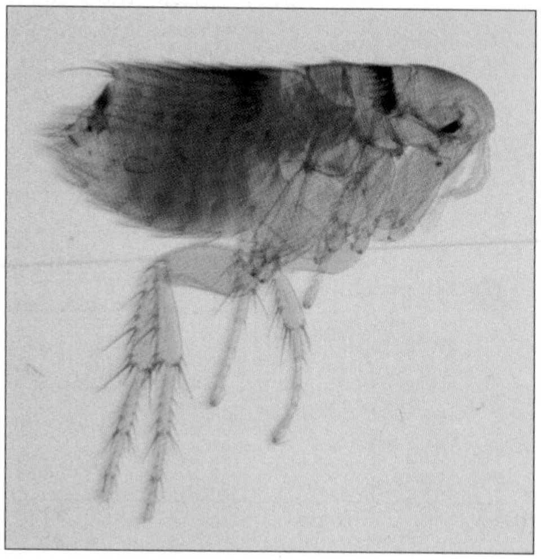

Fig. 247.4 Adult *Ctenocephalides canis*, the dog flea. Note the strong muscular hind legs.

during sexual intercourse. The life cycle for all human lice averages 3–4 weeks.[2,9]

Fleas, order Siphonaptera

Fleas are small (1–2mm), laterally compressed, wingless ectoparasites with long muscular legs adapted for jumping great distances (Fig. 247.4). Fleas that attack humans include both blood-sucking pests (many species) and tissue-penetrating jiggers or chigoes. Infestations commonly occur with exposure to domestic animals and pets; the most pestiferous species are the dog flea (*Ctenocephalides canis*), the cat flea (*C. felis*) and the human flea (*Pulex irritans*). Some individuals become highly sensitized to flea bites, whereas others are unaffected. Fleas probe their hosts repeatedly, often leaving clustered bite sites, which may produce intense itching with papule formation in sensitized individuals. Cat and dog fleas are also the usual intermediate hosts for the tapeworm *Dipylidium caninum* and less frequently for *Hymenolepis diminuta* and *H. nana*. Because larvae of these species often develop in an animal's bedding or in carpets and furniture, eradication may require fumigation and cleaning of these articles. The Oriental rat flea, *Xenopsylla cheopis*, is an extremely important species because it transmits the plague bacillus *Yersinia pestis* and the agent of murine typhus, *Rickettsia typhi* (see Table 247.2). Although normally parasitizing several species of rats, this flea readily attacks humans should the rodent host die.[1,3,8]

Tunga penetrans, the jigger or chigoe flea, is found in both Central and South America and regions of tropical Africa. The female flea attaches to and embeds itself in the skin, especially between the toes and under the toenails, where it grows to the size of a small pea.

After the eggs are discharged, the flea dies, prompting an inflammatory response and possible secondary bacterial infection. Tungiasis is diagnosed by identifying the dark portion of the flea's abdomen (displaying the respiratory spiracles) protruding from the skin surface of an enlarging lesion.[1,8,9]

Cockroaches, order Dictyoptera

Cockroaches are nuisance pests that have closely adapted themselves to human habitation, sharing our food, shelter and warmth. In addition to mechanically transmitting pathogenic bacteria, they may also spread hepatitis virus and polioviruses, intestinal protozoa and enteric nematodes. Allergies and asthma may develop in some individuals following exposure to their excreta, cast skins or body parts.[8]

Cosmopolitan species include *Blattela germanica* (the German cockroach), *Blatta orientalis* (the Oriental cockroach) and *Periplaneta americana* (the American cockroach).

Control programs include limiting entry to buildings, denying access to food, and the use of pesticides.[9,17]

Bedbugs and kissing bugs, order Hemiptera

Bedbugs (family Cimicidae) and kissing bugs (family Reduviidae) are blood-sucking insects that have a long narrow proboscis, which is folded underneath the body when not in use. Bedbugs (*Cimex lectularius* and *C. hemipterus*) are reddish-brown, dorsoventrally flattened, wingless insects that are approximately 5mm in length (Fig. 247.5). They are cosmopolitan in distribution and will attack almost any mammal, feeding primarily at night. During daylight hours they hide under mattresses, loose wallpaper and floorboards. Although not known to transmit disease, bedbug bites may cause painful wheals or bullae, depending upon an individual's sensitivity to their saliva.[1,3,18]

Kissing bugs (genera *Triatoma, Rhodnius, Panstrongylus*) have a cone-shaped head on a narrow neck and an abdomen that is widened in the middle. These insects are black or brown and some have orange and black markings on the abdomen. They average 1–3cm in length and unlike bedbugs have well-developed wings for flight. Like bedbugs, kissing bugs are relatively painless feeders on vertebrates and produce similar skin reactions. In Mexico and Central and South America they transmit the agent of Chagas' disease, *Trypanosoma cruzi*, in the feces, which is secondarily inoculated into the skin by the human host while scratching.[1,9]

Assassin bugs are closely related to kissing bugs and are also able to transmit *T. cruzi*. Unlike kissing bugs, assassin bugs have less conspicuous body markings and produce a painful bite.

Bees, wasps and ants, order Hymenoptera

Hymenopterans are social insects that readily defend their nests when disturbed. In nonreproductive females the ovipositor is modified as a stinger capable of injecting venom for use in the capture of prey or for defense. The venom of bees (genera *Apis, Bombus*), paper wasps (genus *Polistes*), hornets (genus *Vespa*) and yellowjackets (genera *Vespula, Paravespula* and *Dolichovespula*) causes only transient swelling and discomfort in most individuals, but may be responsible for systemic reactions, including anaphylaxis, in others who have been previously sensitized. The africanized honey bee was introduced into Brazil in 1956 and has since spread throughout parts of South, Central and North America. These bees, which are more easily provoked than other honey bees, exhibit massive stinging behavior, although their venom is no more toxic than that of the European honey bee.[5,8]

Many species of ants are problematic for humans because of their abilities to bite, and some groups, such as harvestor ants (genus *Pogonomyrmex*) in North America, fire ants (genus *Solenopsis*) in North and South America, bull ants (genus *Myrmecia*) in Australia and *Myrmica* ants elsewhere are capable of giving painful stings, to which some individuals may develop serious allergic reactions.[19] Fire ants in particular are easily disturbed and will attack in large numbers.[8]

Beetles, order Coleoptera

Although beetles are perhaps best known as pests of agricultural crops, some species can give a painful bite, and others, especially the blister beetles, can exude vesicating fluids, including cantharidin, that cause dermatitis or blister formation. Cantharidin is the chief component of the aphrodisiac known as 'Spanish Fly'. The larvae of certain larder beetles have barbed urticating hairs, which may be responsible for dermatitis or, if ingested, irritation of the gastrointestinal tract. Larval and adult larder and grain beetles can also serve as intermediate hosts for the rodent and human tapeworms *H. diminuta* and *H. nana*.[1,3,8]

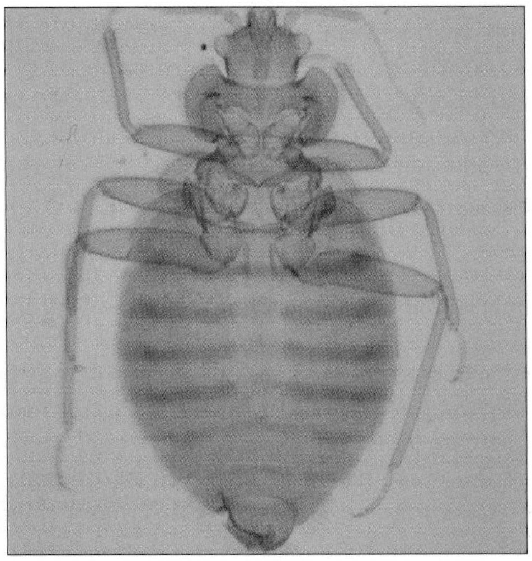

Fig. 247.5 Adult bedbug *Cimex lectularius*. With permission from ASM Press.

Moths and butterflies, order Lepidoptera

Certain larvae (caterpillars) of lepidoptera possess urticating hairs or spines capable of injecting venom when handled. Although most effects of these toxins remain localized to the skin and can produce a severe local burning sensation, systemic effects, including shock and paralysis, have been reported.[8] Adult tussock and gypsy moths are known to have urticating scales and hairs that can cause dermatitis, eye irritation and respiratory tract irritation, especially among forestry workers.[20]

Flies, mosquitoes and midges, order Diptera

Diptera are characterized by the presence of a single pair of membranous wings. Among all arthropods, they are responsible for the greatest share of human disease through their blood-sucking activities, direct tissue invasion by larval forms (myiasis) and mechanical or biologic transmission of infectious agents (see Table 247.2). Bites from a variety of flies, mosquitoes and biting midges often cause local irritation from sensitivity to the saliva and, in some individuals, systemic reactions. In addition to blood-sucking activities, the repeated attacks themselves can be physically and psychologically damaging.

Myiasis may occur in an accidental, facultative or obligatory fashion and involve cutaneous, auricular, ocular, nasopharyngeal, gastrointestinal or genitourinary sites. Pseudomyiases occur occasionally and can cause significant psychologic distress, but usually result from the contamination of sputum, urine or stool samples with fly eggs following improper collection or storage.[8,10]

Accidental and facultative myiasis

The house fly, *Musca domestica*, has no requirement for developing in mammalian tissue, yet is occasionally found in dead tissue or under plaster casts. This type of accidental myiasis is not uncommon, but is rarely clinically significant. Facultative myiasis is most often caused by blowflies and flesh flies, which ordinarily feed on dead tissues, but may move into adjacent viable tissues or infest exposed ulcers or traumatic wounds.

Obligatory myiasis

Obligatory myiasis is caused by certain species that develop only in living tissues. Those species that infect humans are all of zoonotic origin. The human botfly, *Dermatobia hominis*, develops in boil-like subcutaneous lesions with the posterior end of the maggot appearing at the skin surface (Fig. 247.6). This species is most commonly found in individuals who have spent time in Central or South America or, less frequently, Africa. Other botflies that occasionally infest humans are those parasitic on domestic and wild animals, including the horse botfly *Gasterophilus intestinalis*, cattle botfly *Hypoderma bovis*,

Fig. 247.6 Larva of *Dermatobia hominis*, the human botfly, following recovery from a furuncular skin lesion. With permission from J Brad Thomas, David L Bergeron and James J Plorde.

the sheep botfly *Oestrus ovis* and rodent botflies of the genus *Cuterebra*.[21]

The tumbu fly (*Cordylobia anthropophaga*), found in sub-Saharan Africa, also causes a furuncular-type of myiasis. Eggs of this species are usually laid on the ground or on hanging laundry and larvae rapidly penetrate the skin upon contact.

The most serious obligatory myiasis is caused by the Old World screw-worm, *Chrysomya bezziana,* and the New World screw-worm, *Cochliomyia hominivorax*. These species lay their eggs directly on their cattle hosts, usually on wounds or near the nostrils. The larvae actively feed and move through living tissues. Human infections can be particularly destructive if the larvae invade the eye, nose or mouth. A variety of other species are also known to be responsible for traumatic obligatory myiasis in humans.[3,8,9,22]

Arachnids

Medically important arachnids include the scorpions, spiders, ticks and mites. Scorpions and spiders are best known for their abilities to inject poisonous venoms, whereas ticks and mites are best known as vectors for viral, bacterial and protozoal pathogens.[1,11,18]

Scorpions, subclass Scorpiones

Scorpions are predatory in nature and paralyze their intended victim with a neurotoxic venom from the sting, which may also be used for defensive purposes. Toxicity to humans varies depending upon the species. Many elicit no more reaction than that of a bee sting, but some species are deadly, causing over 1000 deaths annually, especially among children. Poisonous species occur in the western hemisphere, Europe, Africa and the Middle East.[1,3,4,8]

Spiders, subclass Araneae

Spiders lack a tail with attached stinger, but instead have fang-like chelicerae among their mouthparts, through which venom can be expressed. Although the majority of spiders are venomous, few have chelicerae capable of penetrating human skin; among those that can most envenomations produce no more than transient local effects with pain, numbness, erythema and swelling (e.g. wolf spiders in the genus *Lycosa* and tarantulas, among many others). More serious disease results from those species capable of producing local or systemic arachnidism with potent dermonecrotic enzymes or neurotoxins, respectively.[8]

Necrotic arachnidism occurs worldwide and is produced most commonly by a number of species in the genus *Loxosceles*, especially the cosmopolitan *L. reclusa* (brown recluse), whereas in South America *L. laeta* is well known for producing severe dermonecrosis. Variously named violin, fiddleback or recluse spiders, they measure 1–2cm long, are tan to dark brown in color and have a darkened violin-shaped marking oriented base forward on the dorsum of the cephalothorax. When present in homes they are reclusive in their habits, preferring undisturbed areas. Their bite is painless and often goes unrecognized until several hours later when the area becomes red, swollen and painful. The venom contains multiple enzymes including sphingomyelinase D and is both dermonecrotic and hemolytic, producing variable degrees of cutaneous necrosis and sloughing of the involved skin over several days. The resulting lesion may be difficult to heal and subject to secondary infection. Systemic reactions such as hemolysis and acute renal failure occur rarely.[1,3,8] Other spider genera implicated in producing necrotic arachnidism include the hobo spider *Tegenaria agrestis* in Europe and the Pacific Northwest of North America, crab spiders (genus *Sicarius*) in Africa and sac spiders (genus *Chiracanthium*), which are found worldwide.[4,23]

Widow spiders (genus *Latrodectus*) are found worldwide and are responsible for systemic arachnidism through the action of a potent neurotoxin capable of producing weakness, myalgia, paralysis and convulsions, and occasionally death. Latrodectism is one of the leading causes of death from arthropod envenomations worldwide, with published mortality rates varying from <1 to 6%.[4] *Latrodectus mactans,* the black widow, and *L. geometricus*, the brown widow, are among the most widespread species. Female widow spiders vary in appearance by species, being glossy black to brown with a characteristic red or orange hourglass-shaped marking on the underside of the abdomen, and displaying a leg span of 3–4cm (Fig. 247.7). They live in protected locations such as woodsheds, basements and outdoor privies.[3,8] Other spiders producing dangerous neurotoxins include the funnel web spiders (genus *Atrax*) in Australia and armed spiders (genus *Phoneutria*) in South America.

Fig. 247.7 Female *Lactrodectus mactans*, the black widow spider. Note the characteristic red hourglass marking on the underside of the abdomen. With permission from New England Journal of Medicine 1994;331:777.

Ticks, subclass Acari

Unlike spiders and scorpions, ticks have a fused cephalothorax and abdomen and a characteristic toothed hypostome for feeding. Tick development progresses through four stages – egg, larva, nymph and adult – with a blood meal required for progression. Humans usually acquire ticks in grassy or brushy areas in close proximity to the usual animal hosts. All species are obligate blood-sucking ectoparasites and are important vectors of viral, bacterial and protozoal pathogens to humans and domestic animals (see Table 247.2). Their feeding activities may also produce local tissue damage and blood loss, especially in livestock and wildlife, or tick paralysis, a syndrome caused by a neurotoxin secreted by a tick's salivary glands that produces ascending flaccid paralysis and toxemia. The symptoms may closely mimic those of Guillain–Barré syndrome, poliomyelitis or botulism. Removal of the attached tick, often found in an unnoticed location such as above the hair line on the nape of the neck, usually results in resolution of the symptoms within hours to days.[24,25]

Species affecting humans include members of the family Ixodidae (hard ticks) and Argasidae (soft ticks):

- hard ticks have anteriorly directed mouthparts and a sclerotized plate or scutum, on the dorsum, with the scutum covering the entire dorsum of the male, but only the anterior portion in the female, allowing the body to swell when engorged (Fig. 247.8); and
- argasid ticks have a soft leathery body lacking a scutum and ventrally directed mouthparts that are not visible when viewed from above (Fig. 247.9).

Unengorged ticks are generally 2–5mm long, but may enlarge to several times this size following engorgement. Engorged hard ticks may mimic soft ticks, so care must be exercised in their identification.[24] Most ticks found crawling on or embedded in human skin are hard ticks. Soft ticks tend to feed only briefly and then often at night.

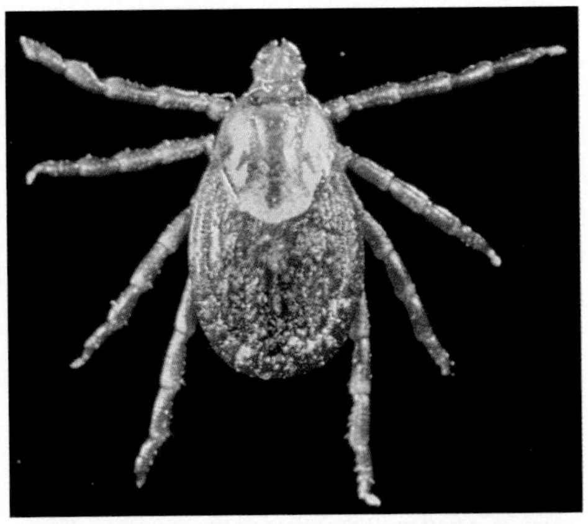

Fig. 247.8 Non-engorged adult female *Dermacentor variabilis*, the common dog tick, of the family Ixodidae (hard ticks). With permission from Northwest Infectious Disease Consultants.

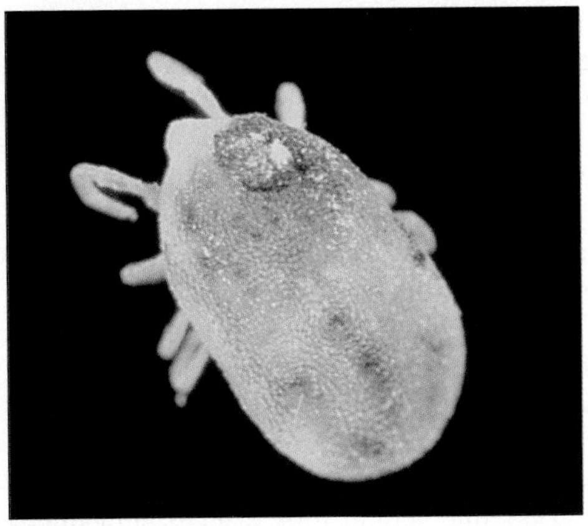

Fig. 247.9 Non-engorged adult *Ornithodoros hermsi*, of the family Argasidae (soft ticks). With permission from Northwest Infectious Disease Consultants.

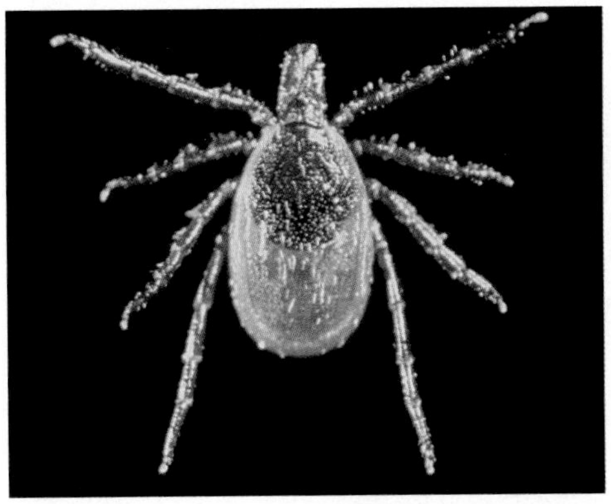

Fig. 247.10 Non-engorged adult female *Ixodes scapularis*, the black-legged tick or deer tick, of the family Ixodidae (hard ticks). With permission from Northwest Infectious Disease Consultants.

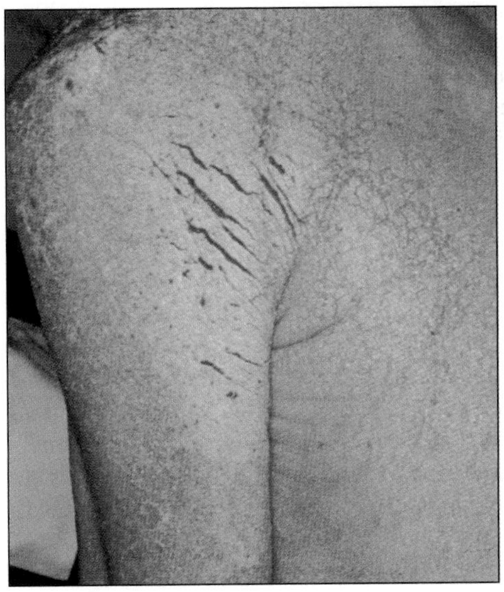

Fig. 247.11 Crusted Norwegian scabies in a patient who has AIDS. With permission from New England Journal of Medicine 1994;331:777.

Disease transmission is produced most commonly by hard ticks in six genera (see Table 247.2). *Ixodes* spp., primarily *I. scapularis* and *I. pacificus* in North America and *I. ricinus* and *I. persulcatus* in Europe and parts of Asia, are responsible for transmitting the agents of Lyme disease, babesiosis and human granulocytic ehrlichiosis (Fig. 247.10). The latter is an emerging rickettsial-like disease that produces an influenza-like illness that varies from being subclinical to fatal. Old World *Ixodes* spp. are also capable of transmitting encephalitis-producing arboviruses. *Dermacentor variabilis* and *D. andersoni* are vectors for the agents of Rocky Mountain spotted fever, tularemia and Colorado tick fever in the New World, whereas *D. marginatus*, *D. silvarum* and *D. nuttalli* are capable of transmitting Siberian tick typhus and encephalitis-producing arboviruses in Europe and Asia.[3,8,11,26]

Ticks in the genera *Amblyomma* and *Rhipicephalus* are found worldwide and are capable of transmitting Rocky Mountain spotted fever in the New World. *Rhipicephalus* ticks also transmit boutonneuse fever in southern Europe and Africa, whereas *Amblyomma* ticks have recently been implicated as vectors of *Ehrlichia chaffeensis*, the agent of human monocytic ehrlichiosis. Infection with this organism produces an illness similar to that of human granulocytic ehrlichiosis and the disease has been documented widely in the USA as well as in Europe and Africa.[8,26]

Haemaphysalis ticks transmit Siberian tick typhus in parts of Eurasia, boutonneuse fever in Africa, and arboviruses responsible for encephalitis in parts of Eurasia and Kyasanur Forest disease in India.

Hyalomma ticks are widespread in parts of Europe, Africa and Central Asia and transmit both Siberian tick typhus and the viral agent of Crimean–Congo hemorrhagic fever.[3,8]

Soft ticks of the genus *Ornithodoros* occur in many parts of the New and Old worlds and are important vectors of the relapsing fever spirochetes (*Borrelia recurrentis* and related forms; see Table 247.2).[11]

Mites, subclass Acari

Mites are microscopic (usually <1mm) arachnids that are widely distributed in the environment. Medically important species may:

- attack humans directly;
- serve as vectors for infectious diseases; and
- cause dust allergies.

Most humans are naturally infested with both *Demodex folliculorum* and *D. brevis*, the follicle mites. Follicle mites are minute (0.1–0.4mm) elongated parasites with stubby legs that can be recovered from hair follicles and sebaceous glands. They are common incidental findings on histologic skin preparations. Although their presence has been associated with various skin conditions, they are commonly found in healthy individuals as well, which makes their significance hard to assess.[27]

Sarcoptes scabiei, the itch or mange mite, is of greater medical importance because of its ability to create serpiginous tunnels through the upper layers of the epidermis. Transmitted through personal contact, these mites are found primarily in the interdigital spaces and the flexor surfaces of the wrists and forearms, and less commonly in other areas, including the breasts, buttocks and external genitalia. Inflammation and intense itching results from the tunneling activity and from the deposition of eggs and excreta. Clinical manifestations vary depending upon the degree of sensitization to the parasites and their products. Lesions often become secondarily infected. A generalized dermatitis occurring in the presence of thousands of mites, typically in elderly or immunocompromised individuals, is known as crusted or Norwegian scabies (Fig. 247.11). Diagnosis is made by placing skin scrapings collected from tunneled areas in 20% potassium hydroxide or mineral oil for clearing and

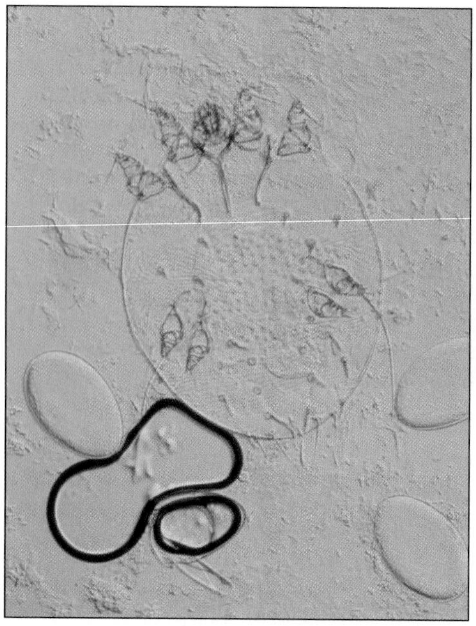

Fig. 247.12 Adult *Sarcoptes scabiei*, the human itch or mange mite, seen in skin scrapings. With permission from New England Journal of Medicine 1994;331:777.

examining under the microscope. Detection of eggs, six-legged larvae and eight-legged nymphs or adults is diagnostic, but may be difficult to demonstrate (Fig. 247.12).

A number of animal mite species can attack humans for a blood meal, either as larval forms or as adults, when the normal mammalian or bird hosts are not available.[15,28,29] Larval chigger mites (family Trombiculidae) are problematic in many parts of the world because their saliva can produce large wheal-and-flare reactions with intense itching. Often red in color, these tiny six-legged larvae commonly attach to the skin in areas where clothing is restrictive such as ankles, waistline, armpits and wrists. In parts of Asia and Australia trombiculid mites are vectors for transmitting the agent of scrub typhus (see Table 247.2).[3,9]

Classes of lesser medical importance

Millipedes and centipedes

Millipedes are worm-like arthropods with numerous apparent body segments, each with two pairs of legs, that are commonly found in and under decaying vegetation.

Many species produce vesicating secretions composed of quinonoids and parabenzoquinones from glands located on each body segment. Larger tropical forms (up to 25cm) can squirt these secretions over several centimeters when handled roughly. Exposure of the skin or mucous membranes to these fluids may produce a burning sensation and blister formation. Exposure of the eye may result in periorbital 'burns', conjunctivitis and keratitis, which may progress to corneal perforation and blindness.[7,8]

Centipedes are flatter than millipedes, have only one pair of legs per body segment and display long antennae. They are fast moving and can inflict a painful sting from a pair of forward-directed pincers that are modified from the first pair of legs. The larger species (26–45cm) found in subtropical and tropical regions are able to penetrate human skin when handled, giving a painful burning sting with a local tissue reaction. Although systemic reactions can occur in individuals who have been previously sensitized, fatalities are rare.[3,8]

Crustaceans

Crustaceans, most notably crabs, crayfish and microscopic copepods are of medical importance by serving as hosts and vectors for larval stages of several different helminths (see Table 247.2).[1,18]

Pentastomes

Pentastomes or tongue worms are arthropods of uncertain affinities that possess few distinctive morphologic characteristics. Larval stages resemble mites and have occasionally been reported producing liver and lung infections in humans in Asia and Africa. Adult stages are wormlike organisms that live in the nasal passages of certain predatory reptiles, birds and mammals; they have been recovered from the nasopharynx of individuals from the Middle East and Africa where they are responsible for an obstructive condition known as halzoun.[1,18]

MANAGEMENT

Medical management of most exposures to arthropods involves:

- removal of the offending organism if attached or embedded;
- palliative treatment for most bites and stings;
- use of antihistamines for local and systemic allergic phenomena and epinephrine (adrenaline) for serious systemic reactions; and
- administration of appropriate antivenoms for exposure to certain spider bites and scorpion stings.

Most embedded chigoe fleas and maggots can be removed as a minor surgical procedure either with a sterile needle, curettage or excision; use of mineral oil alone to occlude the spiracles (breathing tubes) of maggots at the skin surface may result in their spontaneous emergence. Care must be taken to ensure complete removal or serious secondary infection may result. Similarly, removal of the mouthparts of attached ticks is important as transmission of infectious agents may continue for a period of time should they remain embedded. Tweezers may be used to grasp the tick as close as possible to the skin surface followed by the use of steady pressure in a direction perpendicular to the skin.[8,11]

Physiologic responses to the large variety of arthropod bites and stings varies significantly between individuals. Exposure to the excreta, molted skins and body parts of cockroaches, lice, fleas, bedbugs, scabies mites and dust mites may produce sensitization. Treatment is usually directed at counteracting the effects of histamine and other vasoactive compounds, released either by mast cells as a consequence of previous sensitization or introduced as a component of hymenopteran venom. Administration of oral, and occasionally parenteral, antihistamines may be indicated, depending upon the severity of symptoms. The development of systemic allergic reactions, most commonly associated with bee and wasp stings, may result in anaphylaxis and irreversible shock. Angioedema of the upper airway may produce occlusion, whereas pulmonary edema and bronchial constriction may result in respiratory failure, requiring the immediate administration of epinephrine and/or bronchodilators.[3,4,8]

Treatment for the effects of biting arthropods and exposure to the spines and urticating hairs of lepidoptera and coleoptera includes palliative remedies such as antipruritic lotions, creams and ointments, and, if more severe, a short course of systemic corticosteroids. Respiratory allergies, usually developing following sensitization to dust mites or cockroaches, are treated using inhaled corticosteroids or cromolyn sodium (sodium cromoglicate), although removal or control of the offending allergen should be attempted.

Bites or stings that involve neurotoxic or necrotic venoms are managed by counteracting the effects of the venom and providing supportive treatment. Antivenoms for widow spider bites are commercially available. Antivenoms for bites by South American *Loxosceles* spiders and stings by scorpions are available locally in endemic areas.[3,4]

Eradication of body lice, head lice, pubic lice and scabies mites often becomes a challenge for both patient and physician and reports of insecticide-resistant strains have made the task more complex. Mechanisms of resistance are unclear and the possibility of reinfestation or noncompliance with treatment regimens must be taken into account. Generally:

- body lice are treated with a combination of pyrethrins with piperonyl butoxide;
- head lice and pubic lice are treated using 1% permethrin lotion or lindane (1% gamma benzene hexachloride lotion or shampoo); and
- scabies infestations are usually treated with 5% permethrin cream, 10% crotamiton lotion or cream or 1% lindane lotion or cream.

With any of these compounds there is a possibility of allergic skin reactions; in addition lindane has the potential for central nervous system toxicity, especially in children and the elderly.[3,8]

Management of delusional parasitoses are invariably difficult and time-consuming, requiring a team approach involving the family practitioner, dermatologist and psychiatrist. Treatment may include the use of psychoactive drugs such as pimozide or risperidone.[30]

REFERENCES

1. Beaver P C, Jung RC, Cupp EW. Clinical parasitology, 9th ed. Philadelphia: Lea & Febiger; 1984.
2. Orkin M, Maibach HI. Cutaneous infestations and insect bites. New York: Marcel Dekker; 1985.
3. Strickland GT, ed. Hunter's tropical medicine, 8th ed. Philadelphia: WB Saunders; 2000.
4. Binder LS. Acute arthropod envenomation. Incidence, clinical features and management. Med Toxicol Adverse Drug Exp 1989;4:163–73.
5. Reisman RE. Insect stings. N Engl J Med. 1994;331:523–7.
6. Frazier CA, Brown PA. Insects and allergy and what to do about them. Norman: University of Oklahoma Press; 1980.
7. Hudson BJ, Parsons GA. Giant millipede 'burns' and the eye. Trans Roy Soc Trop Med Hyg 1997;91:183–5.
8. Goddard J. Physician's guide to arthropods of medical importance, 2nd ed. Boca Raton: CRC Press; 1996.
9. Lane RP, Crosskey RW. Medical insects and arthropods. London: Chapman & Hall; 1993.
10. Fritsche TR. Arthropods of medical importance. In: Murray PR, Baron EJ, Jorgensen JH, Pfaller MA, Yolken RH, eds. Manual of clinical microbiology, 7th ed. Washington, DC: ASM Press; 1999:1449–66.
11. Spach DH, Liles WC, Campbell GL, *et al.* Tick-borne diseases in the United States. N Engl J Med 1993;329:936–47.
12. Centers for Disease Control and Prevention. Seizures temporarily associated with use of DEET insect repellent – New York and Connecticut. MMWR Morb Mortal Wkly Rep 1989;38:39.
13. Luxemburger C, Perea WA, Delmas GA, *et al.* Permethrin-impregnated bed nets for the prevention of malaria in schoolchildren on the Thai–Burmese border. Trans Roy Soc Trop Med Hyg 1994;88:155–9.
14. Reisman DE. Duration of venom immunotherapy: relationship to the severity of symptoms of initial insect sting anaphylaxis. J Allergy Clin Immunol 1993;92:831–6.
15. Chung SL, Hwang SB, Kwon SB, Kim DW, Jun JB, Cho BK. Outbreak of rat mite dermatitis in medical students. Int J Dermatol 1998;37:591–94.
16. Juranek DD. *Pediculus capitis* in school children: epidemiologic trends, risk factors, and recommendations for control. In: Orkin M, Maibach HI, eds. Cutaneous infestations and insect bites. New York: Marcel Dekker; 1985:199–211.
17. National Communicable Disease Center. Pictorial keys: arthropods, reptiles, birds, and mammals of public health significance. Atlanta: Communicable Disease Center; 1969.
18. Garcia LS. Diagnostic medical parasitology, 4th ed. Washington, DC: ASM; 2001.
19. Kemp SF, deShazo RD, Moffitt JE, Williams DF, Buhner WA. Expanding habitat of the imported fire ant (*Solenopsis invicta*): a public health concern. J Allergy Clin Immunol 2000;105:683–91.
20. Shama SK, Etkind PH, Odell TM, *et al.* Gypsy moth caterpillar dermatitis. N Engl J Med 1982;306:1300–1.
21. MacDonald PJ, Chan C, Dickson J, Jean-Louis F, Heath A. Ophthalmomyiasis and nasal myiasis in New Zealand: a case series. NZ Med J 1999;112:445–7.
22. James MT. The flies that cause myiasis in man. USDA Misc Publ No 631. Washington DC: US Department of Agriculture; 1947.
23. Fisher RG. Necrotic arachnidism. West J Med 1994;160:570–2.
24. Sonenshine DE. Biology of ticks, Vol. 1. New York: Oxford University Press; 1991.
25. Dworkin MS, Shoemaker PC, Anderson DE. Tick paralysis: 33 cases in Washington State, 1946–1996. Clin Infect Dis 1999;29:1435–9.
26. Walker DH, Dumler JS. Emergence of the ehrlichioses as human health problems. Emerg Infect Dis 1996;2:18–29.
27. Burns DA. Follicle mites and their role in disease. Clin Exp Dermatol 1992;17:152–5.
28. Millikan LE. Mite infestations other than scabies. Semin Dermatol 1993;12:48–52.
29. Parish LC, Schwartzman RM. Zoonoses of dermatological interest. Semin Dermatol 1993;12:57–64.
30. Elmer KB, George RM, Peterson K. Therapeutic update: use of risperidone for the treatment of monosymptomatic hypochondriacal psychosis. J Am Acad Dermatol 2000;43:683-86.

NDEX

ɔtes:

ge numbers in **bold** refer to major discussions in the text; page numbers suffixed by (i) and (t) refer to pages in which illustrations and tables appear, respectively; page numbers ffixed by (PP) refer to Practice Points.

oss-references from individual drugs back to the drug group have not been made, but are assumed; cross-references in *italics* are either general cross-references, or refer to bentries within the same main entry .

denotes differential diagnosis.

dex abbreviations:

- BCG (Bacille Calmette-Guérin)
- BSE (bovine spongiform encephalopathy)
- CJD (Creutzfeldt-Jakob disease)
- CMV (cytomegalovirus)
- COPD (chronic obstructive pulmonary disease)
- CSF (cerebrospinal fluid)
- CT (computed tomography)
- EBV (Epstein-Barr virus)
- ELISA (enzyme-linked immunosorbent assay)
- FDA (Food and Drug Administration)
- HAART (highly active antiretroviral therapy)
- HBV (hepatitis B virus)
- HCV (hepatitis C virus)
- HHV (human herpesvirus)
- HIV (human immunodeficiency virus)
- HPV (human papillomavirus)
- HSV (herpes simplex virus)
- HTLV (human T leukemia virus)
- NNRTI (non-nucleoside reverse transcriptase inhibitor)
- NRTI (nucleoside reverse transcriptase inhibitor)
- PCR (polymerase chain reaction)
- RSV (respiratory syncytial virus)
- STD (sexually transmitted disease)
- TNF (tumor necrosis factor)
- VZV (varicella-zoster virus)

A

C

D

E

G

H

I

L

M

P

Q

R

T

U

V

W

X

Y

Z

LSEVIER SCIENCE CD-ROM LICENSE AGREEMENT

.EASE READ THE FOLLOWING AGREEMENT CAREFULLY BEFORE USING THIS
)-ROM PRODUCT. THIS CD-ROM PRODUCT IS LICENSED UNDER THE TERMS
ONTAINED IN THIS CD-ROM LICENSE AGREEMENT ("Agreement"). BY USING
HIS CD-ROM PRODUCT, YOU, AN INDIVIDUAL OR ENTITY INCLUDING
APLOYEES, AGENTS AND REPRESENTATIVES ("You" or "Your"), ACKNOWLEDGE
HAT YOU HAVE READ THIS AGREEMENT, THAT YOU UNDERSTAND IT, AND THAT
OU AGREE TO BE BOUND BY THE TERMS AND CONDITIONS OF THIS
GREEMENT. ELSEVIER INC. ("Elsevier") EXPRESSLY DOES NOT AGREE TO LICENSE
HIS CD-ROM PRODUCT TO YOU UNLESS YOU ASSENT TO THIS AGREEMENT. IF
OU DO NOT AGREE WITH ANY OF THE FOLLOWING TERMS, YOU MAY, WITHIN
HIRTY (30) DAYS AFTER YOUR RECEIPT OF THIS CD-ROM PRODUCT RETURN THE
NUSED, PIN NUMBER PROTECTED, CD-ROM PRODUCT, ALL ACCOMPANYING
OCUMENTATION TO ELSEVIER FOR A FULL REFUND.

EFINITIONS

s used in this Agreement, these terms shall have the following meanings:

Proprietary Material" means the valuable and proprietary information content f this CD-ROM Product including all indexes and graphic materials and oftware used to access, index, search and retrieve the information content om this CD-ROM Product developed or licensed by Elsevier and/or its ffiliates, suppliers and licensors.

CD-ROM Product" means the copy of the Proprietary Material and any ther material delivered on CD-ROM and any other human-readable or achine-readable materials enclosed with this Agreement, including without mitation documentation relating to the same.

WNERSHIP

his CD-ROM Product has been supplied by and is proprietary to Elsevier nd/or its affiliates, suppliers and licensors. The copyright in the CD-ROM roduct belongs to Elsevier and/or its affiliates, suppliers and licensors and is rotected by the national and state copyright, trademark, trade secret and ther intellectual property laws of the United States and international treaty rovisions, including without limitation the Universal Copyright Convention nd the Berne Copyright Convention. You have no ownership rights in this D-ROM Product. Except as expressly set forth herein, no part of this D-ROM Product, including without limitation the Proprietary Material, may e modified, copied or distributed in hardcopy or machine-readable form vithout prior written consent from Elsevier. All rights not expressly granted to ou herein are expressly reserved. Any other use of this CD-ROM Product by ny person or entity is strictly prohibited and a violation of this Agreement.

COPE OF RIGHTS LICENSED (PERMITTED USES)

sevier is granting to You a limited, non-exclusive, non-transferable license to se this CD-ROM Product in accordance with the terms of this Agreement. ou may use or provide access to this CD-ROM Product on a single computer r terminal physically located at Your premises and in a secure network or nove this CD-ROM Product to and use it on another single computer or erminal at the same location for personal use only, but under no ircumstances may You use or provide access to any part or parts of this D-ROM Product on more than one computer or terminal simultaneously.

ou shall not (a) copy, download, or otherwise reproduce the CD-ROM roduct in any medium, including, without limitation, online transmissions, ocal area networks, wide area networks, intranets, extranets and the Internet, r in any way, in whole or in part, except for printing out or downloading onsubstantial portions of the text and images in the CD-ROM Product for our own personal use; (b) alter, modify, or adapt the CD-ROM Product, ncluding but not limited to decompiling, disassembling, reverse engineering, r creating derivative works, without the prior written approval of Elsevier; c) sell, license or otherwise distribute to third parties the CD-ROM Product or ny part or parts thereof; or (d) alter, remove, obscure or obstruct the display f any copyright, trademark or other proprietary notice on or in the CD-ROM roduct or on any printout or download of portions of the Proprietary Aaterials.

ESTRICTIONS ON TRANSFER

his License is personal to You, and neither Your rights hereunder nor the angible embodiments of this CD-ROM Product, including without limitation he Proprietary Material, may be sold, assigned, transferred or sublicensed to ny other person, including without limitation by operation of law, without he prior written consent of Elsevier. Any purported sale, assignment, transfer r sublicense without the prior written consent of Elsevier will be void and will utomatically terminate the License granted hereunder.

ERM

his Agreement will remain in effect until terminated pursuant to the terms of his Agreement. You may terminate this Agreement at any time by removing rom Your system and destroying the CD-ROM Product. Unauthorized opying of the CD-ROM Product, including without limitation, the Proprietary Aaterial and documentation, or otherwise failing to comply with the terms nd conditions of this Agreement shall result in automatic termination of this icense and will make available to Elsevier legal remedies. Upon termination of his Agreement, the license granted herein will terminate and You must mmediately destroy the CD-ROM Product and accompanying documentation. All provisions relating to proprietary rights shall survive termination of this Agreement.

LIMITED WARRANTY AND LIMITATION OF LIABILITY

NEITHER ELSEVIER NOR ITS LICENSORS REPRESENT OR WARRANT THAT THE CD-ROM PRODUCT WILL MEET YOUR REQUIREMENTS OR THAT ITS OPERATION WILL BE UNINTERRUPTED OR ERROR-FREE. WE EXCLUDE AND EXPRESSLY DISCLAIM ALL EXPRESS AND IMPLIED WARRANTIES NOT STATED HEREIN, INCLUDING THE IMPLIED WARRANTIES OF MERCHANTABILITY AND FITNESS FOR A PARTICULAR PURPOSE. IN ADDITION, NEITHER ELSEVIER NOR ITS LICENSORS MAKE ANY REPRESENTATIONS OR WARRANTIES, EITHER EXPRESS OR IMPLIED, REGARDING THE PERFORMANCE OF YOUR NETWORK OR COMPUTER SYSTEM WHEN USED IN CONJUNCTION WITH THE CD-ROM PRODUCT. WE SHALL NOT BE LIABLE FOR ANY DAMAGE OR LOSS OF ANY KIND ARISING OUT OF OR RESULTING FROM YOUR POSSESSION OR USE OF THE SOFTWARE PRODUCT CAUSED BY ERRORS OR OMISSIONS, DATA LOSS OR CORRUPTION, ERRORS OR OMISSIONS IN THE PROPRIETARY MATERIAL, REGARDLESS OF WHETHER SUCH LIABILITY IS BASED IN TORT, CONTRACT OR OTHERWISE AND INCLUDING, BUT NOT LIMITED TO, ACTUAL, SPECIAL, INDIRECT, INCIDENTAL OR CONSEQUENTIAL DAMAGES. IF THE FOREGOING LIMITATION IS HELD TO BE UNENFORCEABLE, OUR MAXIMUM LIABILITY TO YOU SHALL NOT EXCEED THE AMOUNT OF THE LICENSE FEE PAID BY YOU FOR THE SOFTWARE PRODUCT. THE REMEDIES AVAILABLE TO YOU AGAINST US AND THE LICENSORS OF MATERIALS INCLUDED IN THE SOFTWARE PRODUCT ARE EXCLUSIVE.

If this CD-ROM Product is defective, Elsevier will replace it at no charge if the defective CD-ROM Product is returned to Elsevier within sixty (60) days (or the greatest period allowable by applicable law) from the date of shipment.

Elsevier warrants that the software embodied in this CD-ROM Product will perform in substantial compliance with the documentation supplied in this CD-ROM Product. If You report a significant defect in performance in writing to Elsevier, and Elsevier is not able to correct same within sixty (60) days after its receipt of Your notification, You may return this CD-ROM Product, including all copies and documentation, to Elsevier and Elsevier will refund Your money.

YOU UNDERSTAND THAT, EXCEPT FOR THE 60-DAY LIMITED WARRANTY RECITED ABOVE, ELSEVIER , ITS AFFILIATES, LICENSORS, SUPPLIERS AND AGENTS, MAKE NO WARRANTIES, EXPRESSED OR IMPLIED, WITH RESPECT TO THE CD-ROM PRODUCT, INCLUDING, WITHOUT LIMITATION THE PROPRIETARY MATERIAL, AND SPECIFICALLY DISCLAIM ANY WARRANTY OF MERCHANTABILITY OR FITNESS FOR A PARTICULAR PURPOSE.

If the information provided on this CD-ROM contains medical or health sciences information, it is intended for professional use within the medical field. Information about medical treatment or drug dosages is intended strictly for professional use, and because of rapid advances in the medical sciences, independent verification of diagnosis and drug dosages should be made.

IN NO EVENT WILL ELSEVIER, ITS AFFILIATES, LICENSORS, SUPPLIERS OR AGENTS, BE LIABLE TO YOU FOR ANY DAMAGES, INCLUDING, WITHOUT LIMITATION, ANY LOST PROFITS, LOST SAVINGS OR OTHER INCIDENTAL OR CONSEQUENTIAL DAMAGES, ARISING OUT OF YOUR USE OR INABILITY TO USE THE CD-ROM PRODUCT REGARDLESS OF WHETHER SUCH DAMAGES ARE FORESEEABLE OR WHETHER SUCH DAMAGES ARE DEEMED TO RESULT FROM THE FAILURE OR INADEQUACY OF ANY EXCLUSIVE OR OTHER REMEDY.

U.S. GOVERNMENT RESTRICTED RIGHTS

The CD-ROM Product and documentation are provided with restricted rights. Use, duplication or disclosure by the U.S. Government is subject to restrictions as set forth in subparagraphs (a) through (d) of the Commercial Computer Restricted Rights clause at FAR 52.22719 or in subparagraph (c)(1)(ii) of the Rights in Technical Data and Computer Software clause at DFARS 252.2277013, or at 252.2117015, as applicable. Contractor/Manufacturer is Elsevier Inc., 360 Park Avenue South, New York, NY 10010 USA.

GOVERNING LAW

This Agreement shall be governed by the laws of the State of New York, USA. In any dispute arising out of this Agreement, You and Elsevier each consent to the exclusive personal jurisdiction and venue in the state and federal courts within New York County, New York, USA.